Joah Bonilla

French , Polk State College

The Oxford–Hachette Concise French Dictionary
Le Dictionnaire Hachette–Oxford Compact

Le Dictionnaire Hachette-Oxford Compact

français–anglais · anglais–français

Sous la direction éditoriale de

Marie-Hélène Corréard · Valerie Grundy

Oxford   New York   Toronto

OXFORD UNIVERSITY PRESS

1995

The Oxford-Hachette
Concise French
Dictionary

French–English · English–French

Edited by

Marie-Hélène Corréard · Valerie Grundy

HACHETTE
Livre

Oxford   New York   Toronto

OXFORD UNIVERSITY PRESS

1995

Oxford University Press, Walton Street, Oxford OX2 6DP

Oxford New York Toronto
Delhi Bombay Calcutta Madras Karachi
Petaling Jaya Singapore Hong Kong Tokyo
Nairobi Dar es Salaam Cape Town
Melbourne Auckland

and associated companies in
Berlin Ibadan

Oxford is a trade mark of Oxford University Press

Published in the United States
by Oxford University Press, New York

British Library Cataloguing in Publication Data

Data available

Library of Congress Cataloging in Publication Data

Data available

ISBN 0–19–864329–2

10 9 8 7 6 5 4 3 2 1

Typeset in Monotype Nimrod
by Oxford University Press and Barbers Ltd.
Printed in Great Britain
by Clays Ltd., St Ives PLC
Bungay, Suffolk

Preface
Préface

Based on the *Oxford–Hachette French Dictionary*, this new concise edition is the result of the continued collaboration between two of the world's foremost reference book publishers. Like the parent volume, it revolutionizes bilingual dictionary-making in its use of electronic corpora of current language.

The compilation of the dictionary was carried out by a team of English and French native-speakers who worked together in continuous consultation during the writing of entries. Editors drew on two databases of electronic texts, one of French and one of English, each containing over 10 million words of language in use. Access to these databases has made possible a study of real language as it is actually used in a wide range of contexts, both written and spoken.

The *Concise Oxford–Hachette French Dictionary* is the first dictionary of its size to offer extended notes within the text on points of usage and grammar, and to devote a separate section to letter-writing and other documents. This unparalleled level of guidance, and the authority of the translations provided, make this dictionary an indispensable tool for communication in French and English today.

The Publishers

Oxford University Press

Project Director   Timothy Benbow
Commissioning Editor   Susie Dent

Le *Dictionnaire Hachette–Oxford Compact* a été conçu et rédigé à partir du grand *Dictionnaire Hachette–Oxford*. Comme lui, il innove et révolutionne la lexicographie bilingue.

Les rédacteurs anglophones et francophones ont travaillé ensemble en équipes. Des corpus électroniques leur ont permis un repérage précis et authentique des mots et expressions, des contextes d'utilisation et ont pu garantir la pertinence des traductions.

La rigueur de cette méthode scientifique assure aux utilisateurs de tous niveaux une langue actuelle et vraie, des traductions justes, c'est-à-dire celles qui correspondent à chacune des situations que l'on rencontre, tant à l'écrit qu'à l'oral.

Le *Dictionnaire Hachette–Oxford Compact* n'est pas seulement un ouvrage essentiel, il est indispensable, car il est le premier à offrir, au fil du texte, des notes d'usage (lexicales et grammaticales), et en annexes, des modèles de lettres, des documents types, des organigrammes.

Toutes ces informations linguistiques et culturelles font du *Dictionnaire Hachette–Oxford Compact* le meilleur outil pour communiquer aujourd'hui en anglais et en français.

Les éditeurs

Dictionnaires Hachette

Direction   Mireille Maurin
Responsable d'édition   Héloïse Neefs

The Oxford–Hachette Concise French Dictionary
Le Dictionnaire Hachette–Oxford Compact

Chief Editors/Direction éditoriale
Marie-Hélène Corréard · Valerie Grundy

Editors/Rédacteurs

Nicola Addyman	Laurence Delacroix	Mary O'Neill	Catherine Roux
Jennifer Barnes	Frances Illingworth	Françoise de Peretti	Susan Steinberg
Marianne Chalmers	Gérard G. Kahn	Martine Pierquin	
Glynnis Chantrell	Pascal Lecler	Georges Pilard	
Gearóid Cronin	Jacques Lesca	Natalie Pomier	

Lexicographical adviser/
Conseiller en lexicographie
Beryl T. Atkins

Lexical usage notes and correspondence/
Notes d'usage lexicales et correspondance
Henri Béjoint
Richard Wakely

Assisted by/Assistés de
Ghislaine Ansieau
Lucy Atkins
Agnès Sauzet

Specialist terminology consultants/
Consultants en terminologie
Centre de Recherche en Traduction et Terminologie
Université Lumière-Lyon II
Philippe Thoiron
Malcolm Harvey

University of Brighton
Tony Hartley

Malcolm Slater
Dimity Castellano

North American English/Anglo-américain
Charles Lynn Clark
Kristin Clayton

French outside France/Français d'ailleurs
Liliam Hurst
Dominique Péladeau

Phonetics/Phonétique
Jane Stuart-Smith
Isabelle Vodoz

Administration/Administration
Isabelle Lemoine

Data-capture/Saisie des données
Senior keyboarder/Responsable de la saisie
Philip Gerrish

Alison Curr
Diane Diffley
Božidar Novaković

Proofreaders/Correcteurs
Genevieve Hawkins
Isabelle Lemoine

Design/Maquette
Fran Holdsworth (*text/texte*)
Information Design Unit
(*diagrams/organigrammes*)
Raynor Design (*letters/correspondance*)

Contents
Table des matières

Acknowledgements
Remerciements

The editors would like to extend their warmest thanks to a certain number of people and organizations not mentioned in the list of contributors, particularly Beth Levin of Northwestern University, who allowed us to make use of her work on English verb classification.

We are also indebted to all those who made it possible for us to build the corpus of contemporary French, which, with the Oxford Corpus of Modern English, has been the cornerstone of this dictionary. We thank too all the people who contributed to the unabridged *Oxford–Hachette French Dictionary* on which the present volume is based.

Finally we would like to thank all those people, too numerous to mention here, who have contributed their support and the benefit of their knowledge to the writing of this dictionary.

Nous tenons à remercier ici un certain nombre de personnes et d'organismes qui n'ont pas été mentionnés dans la liste des collaborateurs du projet, en particulier Beth Levin, de Northwestern University, qui nous a permis d'utiliser son travail sur la classification des verbes anglais.

Nous remercions également tous ceux qui nous ont aidés à constituer le corpus de français contemporain qui, avec le corpus d'anglais moderne d'Oxford, a joué un rôle linguistique important dans l'élaboration de ce dictionnaire. Nous remercions également tous ceux qui ont collaboré au grand *Dictionnaire Hachette–Oxford* et dont le travail a rendu possible le présent ouvrage.

Nous adressons nos remerciements à tous ceux qui nous ont apporté leur aide et fait bénéficier de leur savoir tout au long de notre entreprise.

This dictionary is based on the *Oxford–Hachette French Dictionary*. The editorial principles are similar to those applied in the larger dictionary and we have taken an equal degree of care to safeguard the interests of the various types of user. The entries have been simplified in order to make the dictionary more accessible to less experienced language learners. Whilst providing a thorough treatment of the basic vocabulary of both languages, we have also found space to offer the wide coverage of idiomatic expression and new words necessary for understanding the foreign language.

Particular care has been taken in the selection of the translations. As a general rule, only one translation will be given for each sense of the headword. Each translation has been checked using our electronic corpora (see p. xi), which give us a wealth of examples of words in use in real, everyday circumstances. Where appropriate, other translations, which have been found to work in more restricted contexts, will be shown in examples. The grammatical information necessary for using a translation is given wherever necessary.

Where nuances of meaning within a sense of the headword are translated in different ways, these nuances are pinpointed by semantic indicators and/or typical collocates. For a step-by-step guide to using this information to arrive at the most suitable translation, see the section *Using this Dictionary* on pp. xv–xx.

Headwords, compounds, and phrasal verbs stand out clearly on the page. For easy reference, English compounds and French hyphenated compounds are to be found in their proper place within the overall alphabetical order of headwords. Phrasal verbs are given full and explicit presentation, which avoids ambiguous metalanguage and, for the French user, shows clearly the position of the noun object.

The dictionary has a wide coverage of North American as well as British English, and exclusively British or North American usage is marked. The French headword list includes vocabulary of French outside France.

For users working in a language not their own, access to the language is not confined to the individual dictionary entry. Leafing through the dictionary, they will find lexical usage notes, notes on function words, model letters, documents, advertisements, verb tables, and organizational diagrams.

Lexical usage notes

These are boxed notes which appear within the dictionary text. They give the user facts about certain types of word that behave alike, for example, names of countries, languages, colour terms, and days of the week and provide ways of discussing topics such as age, dates, time and measurement. Many of them represent a functional approach to language learning and as such may serve both as accessible points of reference for students and valuable vocabulary-teaching tools for teachers. Cross-references to the notes are given at all the relevant entries.

Notes on function words

The notes within or near function word entries are again intended for use by people seeking to work in a foreign language. They provide basic translation information on such grammatical words as pronouns, prepositions, and modal verbs.

The function word notes are readily identifiable in the dictionary. In cases where the information can be presented fairly briefly, the note will be found at the top of the entry, immediately under the headword. In cases where the necessary information is more lengthy and complex, the notes are boxed and clearly visible, appearing as close as possible to the headword concerned.

Letters and documents

A rich and comprehensive set of model letters and documents, designed to help users to express themselves in a foreign language, is to be found in a special section in the centre of the dictionary. A list of the types of letters and documents is given on p. 643.

Advertisements

Unlike the material described above, these are aids to comprehension. They allow the user to make use of small ads in a foreign newspaper, which are often made incomprehensible by their extensive use of abbreviations. The sample advertisements, with accompanying guides to understanding them, are to be found on pp. 691–6 in the centre of the dictionary.

Introduction

Le *Dictionnaire Hachette–Oxford Compact* a été rédigé à partir du grand *Dictionnaire Hachette–Oxford*. Nous en avons repris les principes et les avons adaptés pour des utilisateurs moins expérimentés ou plus jeunes. Nous présentons le vocabulaire de base, les mots nouveaux et les expressions idiomatiques indispensables à la compréhension de l'anglais et du français.

Le choix des traductions a fait l'objet d'un soin particulier. En règle générale, à chaque acception d'un mot correspond une seule traduction. Cette traduction a été vérifiée dans les très nombreux exemples de langue réelle tirés de nos corpus électroniques (voir p. xiii). On ne trouvera deux ou plusieurs traductions équivalentes que dans les rares cas où elles sont vraiment interchangeables. Les mots sont accompagnés de leurs structures grammaticales usuelles et de la traduction de ces structures.

Divers éléments (indicateurs de contexte et/ou indicateurs de collocations, décrits en détail dans *Comment se servir du dictionnaire?*, p. xxi) distinguent une acception et ses différentes nuances. Il est ainsi facile de choisir la traduction la plus appropriée.

Pour faciliter l'accès à l'information, les mots composés anglais et les mots composés français avec trait d'union figurent à leur place, dans l'ordre alphabétique.

La présentation des verbes à particule anglais met en évidence la position du complément.

La nomenclature anglaise accorde une large place à l'anglo-américain et les usages purement britanniques ou anglo-américains sont spécifiés comme tels. La nomenclature française prend en compte le français des pays francophones autres que la France. Dans la partie français–anglais, nous offrons en traduction les variantes graphiques ou lexicales de l'anglo-américain chaque fois que cela s'impose.

Pour répondre plus complètement aux besoins de l'utilisateur, nous lui proposons, pour aborder la langue qu'il apprend, des outils supplémentaires sous forme de notes d'usage sur le lexique et sur les mots grammaticaux, des modèles de correspondance, des tableaux de conjugaison, des organigrammes, etc.

On trouvera au fil du dictionnaire ces notes d'usage dont l'objectif est d'aider l'utilisateur qui apprend une langue étrangère. Elles présentent les particularités d'expression de l'une et l'autre langue. Elles sont rédigées en français dans la partie français–anglais et en anglais dans la partie anglais–français pour permettre à l'utilisateur de s'exprimer dans une langue qui n'est pas la sienne.

Notes d'usage lexicales

Elles apparaissent en encadré dans le corps du dictionnaire. Elles donnent sous une entrée générique (pays, langue, couleur, jour de la semaine, âge, date, etc.), l'essentiel des exemples de constructions qu'on ne peut, faute de place, faire figurer sous chacun des mots spécifiques qui constituent cet ensemble générique. Points de repère pratiques pour tout utilisateur, elles offrent aussi à l'enseignant un matériau pédagogique appréciable. La liste de ces notes lexicales se trouve p. 1420.

Notes d'usage grammaticales

Elles mettent en évidence la façon dont les mots lexicaux s'articulent autour des mots grammaticaux pour donner un sens aux phrases. Elles rassemblent des éléments essentiels d'usage et de structure. Les notes courtes figurent au début de l'article, les plus longues apparaissent en encadré à proximité de celui-ci.

Correspondance et documentation

Dans la partie centrale du dictionnaire, l'utilisateur trouvera un ensemble de lettres et de documents qui lui permettront, dans diverses situations, de s'exprimer dans l'autre langue. On en trouvera la liste détaillée p. 667.

Petites annonces

Sous cette rubrique, dans la partie centrale du dictionnaire, se trouve un choix d'annonces classées. Un guide explicatif des abréviations qui les constituent permettra à l'utilisateur de les lire et de les comprendre.

Notre objectif est d'offrir aux utilisateurs un dictionnaire fiable pour apprendre, traduire et rédiger.

A corpus-based dictionary

The dictionary was written using two electronic databases or 'corpora', one French and one English.

A corpus is a database containing extracts from the text of books, newspapers, magazine articles, etc as well as transcripts of a variety of recordings of spoken language. In a matter of seconds, the computer finds and displays all the occurrences of a particular word in the corpus. The corpus contains some 1,500 concordance lines for the word *measure*, two samples of which are given below. The computer displays the various forms of a word along with those which come before and after it in the sentence. Fig. 1 shows the lines ordered alphabetically according to the words after *measure* and Fig. 3 according to those that come immediately before it. Displaying the word in context like this allows us to focus on important constructions and their relative frequency.

For an English–French entry, the English-speaking editor scanned the corpus for an overview of the various meanings of the word, for constructions that had to be included, for examples of usage, and for common collocations that should not be missed. The French-speaking editor also studied the English corpus in order to get a clear idea of the scope and range of meaning of the word. The French corpus offered the chance of checking exactly how a French word or phrase was used and comparing this with the way the headword was used in the English corpus. Was it safe to give a particular French word as a translation of the English headword, or to translate an English phrase or idiom in a particular way? Were the English word and its French equivalent used in the same type of contexts? Did one have informal or technical overtones that the other did not have? We shall look at some real examples of what the corpus

measure /'meʒə(r)/ ▶ **1045**], **1309**], **789**], **1381**], **1392**], **1260**] **I** *n* **1** (unit) unité *f* de mesure; **weights and ~s** les poids *mpl* et mesures *fpl*; **liquid ~** mesure *f* de capacité pour les liquides; **it's made to ~** (garment) c'est fait sur mesure, c'est du sur mesure; **2** (of alcohol) mesure *f*; **he gave me short ~** il a triché sur la quantité; **3** (device for measuring) instrument *m* de mesure; **4** (qualified amount, extent) **a ~ of success** un certain succès; **a small ~ of support** un soutien limité; **a good** ou **wide ~ of autonomy** une grande autonomie; **in large ~** dans une large mesure; **in full ~** [*feel, possess, contribute*] pleinement; **5** (way of estimating) (of price rises) mesure *f*; (of success, anger) mesure *f*, indication *f*; (of efficiency, performance) critère *m*; **to be the ~ of** donner la mesure de; **to give some ~ of** donner une idée de [*delight, talent*]; **to use sth as a ~ of** utiliser qch pour mesurer [*effects, impact*]; **this is a ~ of how dangerous it is** ceci montre à quel point c'est dangereux; **beyond ~** [*change*] énormément; [*beautiful*] extrêmement; **it has improved beyond ~** il y a eu d'énormes progrès; **to take the ~ of sb** jauger qn; **I have the ~ of them** je sais ce qu'ils valent; **6** (action, step) mesure *f*; **to take ~s** prendre des mesures; **safety ~** mesure de sécurité; **as a precautionary ~** par mesure de précaution; **as a preventive ~** à titre préventif; **as a temporary ~** provisoirement.

II *vtr* **1** (assess size) mesurer [*length, rate, person*]; **to ~ sth in** mesurer qch en [*metres*]; **to get oneself ~d for** faire prendre ses mesures pour; **2** (have measurement of) mesurer; **to ~ four by five metres** mesurer quatre mètres sur cinq; **a tremor measuring 5.2 on the Richter scale** une secousse de 5,2 sur l'échelle de Richter; **3** (assess) mesurer [*performance, ability*] (**against** à); **4** (compare) **to ~ sth against** comparer qch à [*achievement*].

IDIOMS **for good ~** pour faire bonne mesure; **to do things by half-~s** se contenter de demi-mesures.

■ **measure off**: **~ off** [sth] mesurer [*fabric*].

■ **measure out**: **~ out** [sth] mesurer [*land, flour, liquid*]; doser [*medicine*]; compter [*drops*].

■ **measure up**: ¶ **~ up** [*person*] avoir les qualités requises; **to ~ up to** être à la hauteur de [*expectations*]; soutenir la comparaison avec [*achievement*]; ¶ **~ up** [sth] mesurer [*room etc*].

Fig. 2

```
077989   takeovers between 1922 and 1988 . .PP The study 's main measure of an acquisition 's success
166340 ians from the land of Prester John . But the price was a measure of autonomy granted to what w
288665 r drink ? I 'm starving ! " .PP As Taff poured me a good measure of cider and handed me a boil
052886 e South-east , the CSO said they should not be used as a measure of comparative living standar
211311 cution of many millions of calculations . .PP The common measure of computer performance , MIP
052886 that Matthaus can be both stagehand and leading man is a measure of his impact . Schillaci 's
402323   gendarmes have been introduced to an Oxford school is a measure of how seriously schools in O
177775 would make the APR more than 5,000 per cent _ at least a measure of how very little use follow
244999 enses all practically at the last . I think Gode has the measure of most men or women , at lea
009912 s , but mainly will just to allow the two men to get the measure of one another . <sect> Forei
220797 aluminium company whose arrival in Banbury had brought a measure of prosperity to the town in
037783 sks . ` For me at any rate , ` I reply . There will be a measure of relief even in Anna 's sor
009912 e Lambeth , they do not see a low registration rate as a measure of success . .PP Lambeth 's f
052886 at kind of cash . " Money was important to him only as a measure of success , ` to prove that
287166 wn . The oil companies , whose business depends in large measure on those cars , spend similar
052886 continuing refusal by BR to set targets against which to measure performance . A 24 per cent i
224156 ox have chosen . This move has been promoted as a safety measure , permitting slip when the to
009912 ast take advantage of its new opportunities and the West measure up to its new responsibilitie
009912 r of clubs in the Football League whose press facilities measure up to UEFA 's minimum standar
104055 ive , rather than an intellectual knowing . It cannot be measured by scientific instruments _
```

Fig. 1

```
000790 jan in the Toscanini/Koussevitsky tradition , adding for good measure the name of Charles Mue
200317 ut . But he 'd done neither ! She silently swore and for good measure swore again . Then she
227590 r in the cream and stir well . Give one last beating for good measure . .PP Turn your mixture
155798 New Europe , with a sprinking of gardening thrown in for good measure , is Weidenfeld and Nic
320079 tic red , white , and blue bands with grey thrown in for good measure . The PTEs sport their
111836 ith Harold Lloyd and Fatty Arbuckle trivia thrown in for good measure ) , revealing that Keat
212161 ps Durham , Bristol , Edinburgh and Exeter thrown in for good measure . .PP A third explanati
009912 nd the soaps , are figuratively thrown into the ring for good measure . There is the daunting
006992 k to find some greenery and space for Flush and then for good measure he took a pencil and dr
```

Fig. 3

contributed to the dictionary in the case of the word *measure*.

A study of the corpus throws up many instances of *as a* [ADJECTIVE] *measure*—a construction so common that many users will be looking for it in the dictionary. Sense 6 (Fig. 2) therefore offers several examples of it, all of them taken directly from the corpus.

Ordering the concordance lines according to the word before the headword ('sorting on left context') highlighted other phrases and idioms, enabling the editors to see, for example, that the phrase *for good measure* was extremely common (Fig. 3 shows some of the 22 examples). The French editor's instinct was to translate it simply by *pour faire bonne mesure*, but even in such apparently straightforward cases the editors carry out routine checks. The translation offered must be adequate for all the contexts in which the English phrase is found and the editors must satisfy themselves that the French equivalent phrase appears in very similar contexts, i.e. that it does not have a much wider scope, or a much narrower one, than the phrase it is being used to translate. Here again, the French corpus was consulted: there were many examples of *pour faire bonne mesure*. In every case, the match between the two phrases was perfect, and the simple equivalence was recorded in the IDIOMS section of the dictionary entry.

The corpus formed the dictionary entries, shaping them to meet the needs of today's users, highlighting important constructions, exemplifying difficult meanings, focusing attention on common usages, leading the editors to subtle variations of meaning in English and French parallel constructions, helping them to pick out the best and safest translations for the headwords in all their many and varied uses.   *B. T. S. Atkins*

Un dictionnaire à partir de corpus

Le dictionnaire a été rédigé à partir de deux corpus électroniques, l'un français, l'autre anglais.

Un corpus est une base de données réunissant des textes imprimés et des transcriptions d'enregistrements d'origine et de nature très diverses. En quelques secondes l'ordinateur recense et affiche toutes les occurrences dans le corpus d'un mot donné. Le corpus contient quelque 1500 lignes de concordance du mot *measure* dont deux échantillons figurent ci-dessous. Les exemples sont présentés soit par ordre alphabétique des formes du mot recherché et des mots qui suivent (fig. 1), soit par ordre alphabétique des mots qui précèdent (fig. 3). Cette présentation du mot en contexte permet de repérer les constructions importantes et leur fréquence.

Pour chaque entrée de la partie anglais–français, le rédacteur anglophone a parcouru le corpus anglais pour avoir une vue d'ensemble des sens d'un mot, relever les constructions à inclure, trouver des exemples d'emplois particuliers et des collocations courantes à ne pas manquer. Le rédacteur francophone a également étudié le corpus anglais pour se faire une idée claire du domaine et des sens couverts par le mot en question. Ensuite, il a vérifié dans le corpus français l'emploi exact des mots ou expressions français afin de pouvoir établir une comparaison avec l'emploi de l'entrée dans le corpus anglais. Est-il bien prudent de donner tel mot français comme traduction de l'entrée anglaise, ou de traduire une expression de telle ou telle manière? Les termes anglais et français sont-ils utilisés dans le même genre de contextes? L'un d'eux a-t-il des nuances familières ou techniques que ne possède pas l'autre? Voyons, à partir d'exemples précis, en quoi, pour l'entrée *measure*, le corpus a contribué au dictionnaire.

measure /'meʒə(r)/ ▶1045 , 1309 , 789 , 1381 , 1392 , 1260 I *n* **1** (unit) unité *f* de mesure; **weights and ~s** les poids *mpl* et mesures *fpl*; **liquid ~** mesure *f* de capacité pour les liquides; **it's made to ~** (garment) c'est fait sur mesure, c'est du sur mesure; **2** (of alcohol) mesure *f*; **he gave me short ~** il a triché sur la quantité; **3** (device for measuring) instrument *m* de mesure; **4** (qualified amount, extent) **a ~ of success** un certain succès; **a small ~ of support** un soutien limité; **a good** ou **wide ~ of autonomy** une grande autonomie; **in large ~** dans une large mesure; **in full ~** [*feel, possess, contribute*] pleinement; **5** (way of estimating) (of price rises) mesure *f*; (of success, anger) mesure *f*, indication *f*; (of efficiency, performance) critère *m*; **to be the ~ of** donner la mesure de; **to give some ~ of** donner une idée de [*delight, talent*]; **to use sth as a ~ of** utiliser qch pour mesurer [*effects, impact*]; **this is a ~ of how dangerous it is** ceci montre à quel point c'est dangereux; **beyond ~** [*change*] énormément; [*beautiful*] extrêmement; **it has improved beyond ~** il y a eu d'énormes progrès; **to take the ~ of sb** jauger qn; **I have the ~ of them** je sais ce qu'ils valent; **6** (action, step) mesure *f*; **to take ~s** prendre des mesures; **safety ~** mesure de sécurité; **as a precautionary ~** par mesure de précaution; **as a preventive ~** à titre préventif; **as a temporary ~** provisoirement.
II *vtr* **1** (assess size) mesurer [*length, rate, person*]; **to ~ sth in** mesurer qch en [*metres*]; **to get oneself ~d for** faire prendre ses mesures pour; **2** (have measurement of) mesurer; **to ~ four by five metres** mesurer quatre mètres sur cinq; **a tremor measuring 5.2 on the Richter scale** une secousse de 5,2 sur l'échelle de Richter; **3** (assess) mesurer [*performance, ability*] (**against** à); **4** (compare) **to ~ sth against** comparer qch à [*achievement*].
IDIOMS **for good ~** pour faire bonne mesure; **to do things by half-~s** se contenter de demi-mesures.
■ **measure off**: **~ off** [sth] mesurer [*fabric*].
■ **measure out**: **~ out** [sth] mesurer [*land, flour, liquid*]; doser [*medicine*]; compter [*drops*].
■ **measure up**: ¶ **~ up** [*person*] avoir les qualités requises; **to ~ up to** être à la hauteur de [*expectations*]; soutenir la comparaison avec [*achievement*]; ¶ **~ up** [sth] mesurer [*room etc*].

Fig. 2

```
077989   takeovers between 1922 and 1988 . .PP The study 's main measure of an acquisition 's success
166340   ians from the land of Prester John . But the price was a measure of autonomy granted to what w
288665   r drink ? I 'm starving ! " .PP As Taff poured me a good measure of cider and handed me a boil
052886   e South-east , the CSO said they should not be used as a measure of comparative living standar
211231   cution of many millions of calculations . .PP The common measure of computer performance , MIP
052886   that Matthaus can be both stagehand and leading man is a measure of his impact . Schillaci '
402323   gendarmes have been introduced to an Oxford school is a measure of how seriously schools in O
177775   would make the APR more than 5,000 per cent _ at least a measure of how very little use follow
244999   enses all practically at the last . I think Gode has the measure of most men or women , at lea
009912   s , but mainly will just to allow the two men to get the measure of one another . <sect> Forei
220797   aluminium company whose arrival in Banbury had brought a measure of prosperity to the town in
037783   sks . ` For me at any rate , ` I reply . There will be a measure of relief even in Anna 's sor
009912   e Lambeth , they do not see a low registration rate as a measure of success . .PP Lambeth 's f
052886   at kind of cash . " Money was important to him only as a measure of success , ` to prove that
287166   wn . The oil companies , whose business depends in large measure on those cars , spend similar
052886   continuing refusal by BR to set targets against which to measure performance . A 24 per cent i
224156   ox have chosen . This move has been promoted as a safety measure , permitting a slip when the to
009912   ast take advantage of its new opportunities and the West measure up to its new responsibilitie
009912   r of clubs in the Football League whose press facilities measure up to UEFA 's minimum standar
104055   ive , rather than an intellectual knowing . It cannot be measured by scientific instruments _
```

Fig. 1

```
000790 jan in the Toscanini/Koussevitsky tradition , adding for good measure the name of Charles Mue
200317 ut . But he 'd done neither ! She silently swore and for good measure swore again . Then she
227590 r in the cream and stir well . Give one last beating for good measure . .PP Turn your mixture
155798 New Europe , with a sprinking of gardening thrown in for good measure , is Weidenfeld and Nic
320079 tic red , white , and blue bands with grey thrown in for good measure . The PTEs sport their
111836 ith Harold Lloyd and Fatty Arbuckle trivia thrown in for good measure ) , revealing that Keat
212161 ps Durham , Bristol , Edinburgh and Exeter thrown in for good measure . .PP A third explanati
009912 nd the soaps , are figuratively thrown into the ring for good measure . There is the daunting
006992 k to find some greenery and space for Flush and then for good measure he took a pencil and dr
```

Fig. 3

L'étude du corpus fait ressortir plusieurs fois la structure *as a* [ADJECTIF] *measure*, dont la fréquence suggère que de nombreux lecteurs la chercheront dans le dictionnaire. La catégorie 6 (fig. 2) en donne donc plusieurs exemples, tous extraits du corpus.

En classant les lignes de concordance selon l'ordre alphabétique des mots qui se trouvent avant le terme choisi (classement dit 'selon le contexte gauche'), les rédacteurs se sont rendu compte que la locution *for good measure* était fréquemment employée (extraits tirés de 22 exemples en fig. 3). La première réaction du rédacteur français a été de la traduire par *pour faire bonne mesure*; mais même dans des cas apparemment aussi simples, les rédacteurs ont procédé aux vérifications d'usage. Une traduction donnée doit en effet s'adapter à tous les contextes où apparaît la locution anglaise, et les rédacteurs doivent s'assurer que l'équivalent français apparaît dans des contextes très semblables,

c'est-à-dire, qu'il n'a pas une portée plus large ni plus limitée que celle de l'expression qu'il traduit. Là encore, le corpus français a été consulté, et a offert de nombreux exemples de *pour faire bonne mesure*. Les deux versions étant parfaitement adaptées dans chaque cas, cette simple équivalence a été retenue dans la section IDIOMS de l'article.

Le corpus a servi à mettre en forme les articles de façon à ce qu'ils répondent aux besoins des utilisateurs d'aujourd'hui, en faisant ressortir les constructions importantes, en illustrant les acceptions difficiles, en attirant l'attention sur les emplois les plus fréquents, en amenant les rédacteurs à établir de subtiles nuances entre des constructions anglaises et françaises apparemment parallèles et en les aidant à choisir les traductions les mieux adaptées et les plus sûres pour les diverses acceptions de chaque entrée.

B. T. S. Atkins

Using this dictionary

Each entry in the dictionary is organized hierarchically, by grammatical category, then sense category. Grammatical categories are always in the same order. In the English–French part of the dictionary, the rule is that if the word has a use as an irregular inflected form, like the entry *left* for example, this will come first. Next will come the noun category, if there is one, then the adjective, then the adverb. Verbs, idioms, and phrasal verbs come last, in that order. The way the entry *kindly* is constructed is shown in the diagram below. To translate *he thought kindly of her*, you would go through the steps shown on the right. The section that follows gives other examples of how to get the best out of the dictionary for various kinds of translation task.

As a general rule, all meanings of a word are to be found in one single entry, provided they are pronounced in the same way, exclusive of stress shifts. English compounds have their own place in the alphabetical order of the dictionary, either as separate entries or, where several fall together in the alphabet, grouped together under the first element.

❶ kindly /ˈkaɪndlɪ/ **I** *adj* [*person, nature*] gentil/-ille; **❷**/*smile, interest*/**❸** bienveillant; [*face*] sympathique. **II** *adv* **❹ 1** (in a kind way) avec gentillesse; **to speak ~ of sb** avoir un mot gentil pour qn; **2** (obligingly) gentiment; **would you ~ do/refrain from doing** auriez-vous l'amabilité de faire/de ne pas faire; **3** (favourably) **to look ~ on** approuver [*activity*]; **to think ~ of** avoir une bonne opinion de; **to take ~ to** apprécier.

The French–English entries follow a similar sequence, but adjectives precede nouns and non-hyphenated compounds appear together in a separate category at the end of the entry. French hyphenated compounds are given separate-entry status. On both sides of the dictionary, the order of sense categories reflects frequency of use, the most commonly used coming first. Within sense categories, distinctions between alternative translations are shown by means of sense indicators in round brackets and/or collocates giving typical context, which appear in square brackets.

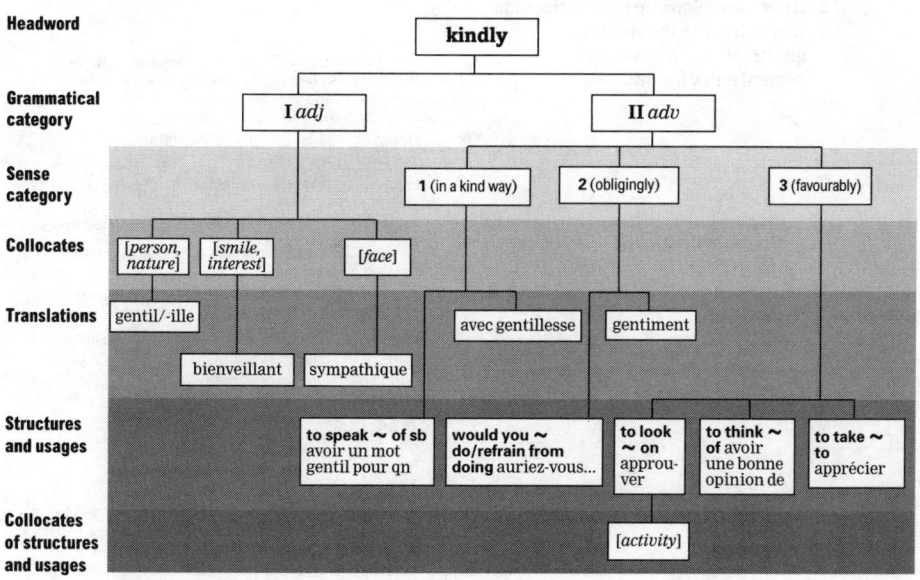

| Goal 1 | Translate | **he treated her kindly** |

Process **1** Identify the problem word or phrase.

kindly

2 Look up *kindly* and choose the appropriate grammatical category.

II *adv*

kindly /ˈkaɪndlɪ/ **I** *adj* [*person, nature*] gentil/-ille; [*smile, interest*] bienveillant; [*face*] sympathique. **II** *adv* **1** (in a kind way) avec gentillesse: **to speak ~ of sb** avoir un mot gentil pour qn; **2** (obligingly) gentiment; **would you ~ do/refrain from doing** auriez-vous l'amabilité de faire/de ne pas faire; **3** (favourably) **to look ~ on** approuver [*activity*]; **to think ~ of** avoir une bonne opinion de; **to take ~ to** apprécier.

3 Choose the appropriate sense category.

1 (in a kind way)

kindly /ˈkaɪndlɪ/ **I** *adj* [*person, nature*] gentil/-ille; [*smile, interest*] bienveillant; [*face*] sympathique. **II** *adv* **1** (in a kind way) avec gentillesse: **to speak ~ of sb** avoir un mot gentil pour qn; **2** (obligingly) gentiment; **would you ~ do/refrain from doing** auriez-vous l'amabilité de faire/de ne pas faire; **3** (favourably) **to look ~ on** approuver [*activity*]; **to think ~ of** avoir une bonne opinion de; **to take ~ to** apprécier.

4 Note the translation.

avec gentillesse

kindly /ˈkaɪndlɪ/ **I** *adj* [*person, nature*] gentil/-ille; [*smile, interest*] bienveillant; [*face*] sympathique. **II** *adv* **1** (in a kind way) avec gentillesse; **to speak ~ of sb** avoir un mot gentil pour qn; **2** (obligingly) gentiment; **would you ~ do/refrain from doing** auriez-vous l'amabilité de faire/de ne pas faire; **3** (favourably) **to look ~ on** approuver [*activity*]; **to think ~ of** avoir une bonne opinion de; **to take ~ to** apprécier.

5 If necessary look up *treat* in the same way and *her* in the special grammatical note box, near the normal entry for *her*.

her

When used as a direct object pronoun, *her* is translated by *la* (*l'* before a vowel). Note that the object pronoun normally comes before the verb in French and that in compound tenses like perfect and past perfect the past participle agrees with the pronoun:

| *I know her* | = je la connais |
| *I've already seen her* | = je l'ai déjà vue |

In imperatives, the direct object pronoun is translated by *la* and comes after the verb:

| *catch her!* | = attrape-la! (*note the hyphen*) |

When used as an indirect object pronoun, *her* is translated by *lui*:

| *I've given her the book* | = je lui ai donné le livre |
| *I've given it to her* | = je le lui ai donné |

In imperatives, the indirect object pronoun is translated by *lui* and comes after the verb:

| *phone her* | = téléphone-lui |
| *give them to her* | = donne-les-lui (*note the hyphens*) |

After prepositions and after the verb *to be* the translation is *elle*:

| *he did it for her* | = il l'a fait pour elle |
| *it's her* | = c'est elle |

When translating *her* as a determiner (*her house* etc.) remember that in French possessive adjectives, like most other adjectives, agree in gender and number with the noun they qualify; *her* is translated by *son* + masculine singular noun (*son chien*), *sa* + feminine singular noun (*sa maison*) BUT *son* + feminine noun beginning with a vowel or mute 'h' (*son assiette*), and *ses* + plural noun (*ses enfants*).

For *her* used with parts of the body ▶ 765 |.

Note the information on agreement.

| **Result** | The translation | **il l'a traitée avec gentillesse** |

| **Goal 2** | Translate *a sophisticated nightclub* in the phrase | **they spent the rest of the evening in a sophisticated nightclub in Mayfair** |

| **Process** | **1** Look up *nightclub*. English compounds appear in alphabetical order in the wordlist. | **nightcap** /'naɪtkæp/ *n* **1** (hat) bonnet *m* de nuit; **2** (drink) **to have a ~** boire quelque chose (avant d'aller se coucher). |

~ club

nightclub *n* boîte *f* de nuit.
nightclubbing *n* **to go ~** aller en boîte◦.
nightdress *n* chemise *f* de nuit.
nightie◦ /'naɪtɪ/ *n* chemise *f* de nuit.
nightingale /'naɪtɪŋgeɪl, US -tn̩g-/ *n* rossignol *m*.
night: **~life** /'naɪtlaɪf/ *n* vie *f* nocturne; **~-light** *n* veilleuse *f*.
nightly /'naɪtlɪ/ *adj* GEN de tous les soirs; [*revels, visitor, disturbance*] LITTER nocturne.

---

2 Note the translation.

boîte *f* de nuit

Note the usage information in italics. '*f*' indicates feminine gender.

nightclub *n* boîte *f* de nuit.

---

3 Look up *sophisticated* and select the most appropriate numbered sense category.

1 (smart)

sophisticated /sə'fɪstɪkeɪtɪd/ *adj* **1** (smart) [*person*] (cultured) raffiné, sophistiqué PEJ; (elegant) chic *inv*; [*clothes, fashion*] recherché; [*restaurant, resort*] chic *inv*; [*magazine*] sophistiqué; **2** (discriminating) [*mind, taste*] raffiné; [*audience, public*] averti; [*civilization*] évolué; **3** (elaborate, complex) [*equipment, technology*] sophistiqué; [*argument, joke*] subtil; [*style*] recherché.

---

4 Look for the noun collocate, in square brackets, which is closest to your context.

restaurant

sophisticated /sə'fɪstɪkeɪtɪd/ *adj* **1** (smart) [*person*] (cultured) raffiné, sophistiqué PEJ; (elegant) chic *inv*; [*clothes, fashion*] recherché; [***restaurant***, *resort*] chic

---

5 Note the translation.

chic

sophisticated /sə'fɪstɪkeɪtɪd/ *adj* **1** (smart) [*person*] (cultured) raffiné, sophistiqué PEJ; (elegant) chic *inv*; [*clothes, fashion*] recherché; [*restaurant, resort*] **chic** *inv*; [*magazine*] sophistiqué; **2** (discriminating) [*mind,*

---

6 Note the usage information in italics.

inv

This means that the form of adjective *chic* does not change in the feminine or the plural.

sophisticated /sə'fɪstɪkeɪtɪd/ *adj* **1** (smart) [*person*] (cultured) raffiné, sophistiqué PEJ; (elegant) chic *inv*; [*clothes, fashion*] recherché; [*restaurant, resort*] chic ***inv***; [*magazine*] sophistiqué; **2** (discriminating) [*mind, taste*] raffiné; [*audience, public*] averti; [*civilization*] évolué; **3** (elaborate, complex) [*equipment, technology*] sophistiqué; [*argument, joke*] subtil; [*style*] recherché.

| **Result** | The translation of the whole sentence | **ils ont fini la soirée dans une boîte de nuit chic de Mayfair** |

Goal 3	Translate	I've forgotten to bring my umbrella

Process	**1** Look up *forget* and choose the appropriate grammatical category. **I** *vtr*	**forget** /fə'get/ (*p prés* **-tt-**; *prét* **-got**; *pp* **-gotten**) **I** *vtr* **1** (not remember) oublier (**that** que; **to do** de faire; **how** comment); **~ it!** (no way) n'y compte pas!; (drop the subject) laisse tomber!; (think nothing of it) ce n'est rien!; **2** (put aside) oublier; **she'll** never let me **~** it elle n'est pas près de me le faire oublier; **3** LIT, FIG (leave behind) oublier. **II** *vi* oublier. ■ **forget about**: **~** **about** [sth/sb] (overlook) oublier.
	2 Choose the most appropriate numbered sense category. **1** (not remember)	**forget** /fə'get/ (*p prés* **-tt-**; *prét* **-got**; *pp* **-gotten**) **I** *vtr* **1** (not remember) oublier (**that** que; **to do** de faire; **how** comment); **~ it!** (no way) n'y compte pas!; (drop the subject) laisse tomber!; (think nothing of it) ce n'est rien!; **2** (put aside) oublier; **she'll** never let me **~** it elle n'est pas près de me le faire oublier; **3** LIT, FIG (leave behind) oublier. **II** *vi* oublier. ■ **forget about**: **~** **about** [sth/sb] (overlook) oublier.
	3 Note the translation. oublier	**forget** /fə'get/ (*p prés* **-tt-**; *prét* **-got**; *pp* **-gotten**) **I** *vtr* **1** (not remember) **oublier** (**that** que; **to do** de faire; **how** comment); **~ it!** (no way) n'y compte pas!; (drop the subject) laisse tomber!; (think nothing of it) ce n'est rien!; **2** (put aside) oublier; **she'll** never let me **~** it elle n'est pas près de me le faire oublier; **3** LIT, FIG (leave behind) oublier. **II** *vi* oublier. ■ **forget about**: **~** **about** [sth/sb] (overlook) oublier.
	4 Look for the basic structure you need. **to do**	**forget** /fə'get/ (*p prés* **-tt-**; *prét* **-got**; *pp* **-gotten**) **I** *vtr* **1** (not remember) oublier (**that** que; **to do** de faire; **how** comment); **~ it!** (no way) n'y compte pas!; (drop the subject) laisse tomber!; (think nothing of it) ce n'est rien!; **2** (put aside) oublier; **she'll** never let me **~** it elle n'est pas près de me le faire oublier; **3** LIT, FIG (leave behind) oublier. **II** *vi* oublier. ■ **forget about**: **~** **about** [sth/sb] (overlook) oublier.
	5 Note the translation. *de faire*	**forget** /fə'get/ (*p prés* **-tt-**; *prét* **-got**; *pp* **-gotten**) **I** *vtr* **1** (not remember) oublier (**that** que; **to do de faire**; **how** comment); **~ it!** (no way) n'y compte pas!; (drop the subject) laisse tomber!; (think nothing of it) ce n'est rien!; **2** (put aside) oublier; **she'll** never let me **~** it elle n'est pas près de me le faire oublier; **3** LIT, FIG (leave behind) oublier. **II** *vi* oublier. ■ **forget about**: **~** **about** [sth/sb] (overlook) oublier.
	6 Use the translation of the basic structure to translate your sentence looking up at the appropriate place in the dictionary any other words you don't know how to translate.	

| Result | The translation | **j'ai oublié d'apporter mon parapluie** |

Goal 4	Translate	**the police have sealed off the street**

Process	**1** *Seal off* is a phrasal verb, so go to the end of the entry *seal* where you will find the phrasal verbs listed in alphabetical order, each verb clearly signalled by a square bullet. ■ **seal off**	**seal** /siːl/ **I** *n* **1** ZOOL phoque *m*; **2** JUR, GEN (insignia) sceau *m*; **to set one's ~ on** LIT apposer son cachet sur; FIG conclure; **to set the ~ on** sceller [*friendship*]; confirmer [*trend, regime*]; **to give sth one's ~ of approval** approuver qch; **look for our ~ of quality** exigez le label de qualité; **3** (to keep intact) (on container) plomb *m*; (on package, letter) cachet *m*; (on door) scellés *mpl*; **4** (closure) fermeture *f*. **II** *vtr* **1** cacheter [*letter*]; **2** (close) sceller [*oil well, pipe*]; boucher [*gap*]; **3** (make airtight, watertight) fermer [qch] hermétiquement [*jar, tin*]; **4** FIG sceller [*alliance*] (**with** par); conclure [*deal*] (**with** par); **to ~ sb's fate** décider du sort de qn. **III sealed** *pp adj* [*envelope*] cacheté; [*door*] scellé; [*orders*] sous pli cacheté; [*jar*] fermé hermétiquement. ■ **seal in** conserver [*flavour*]. ■ **seal off**: **~** [**sth**] **off**, **~ off** [**sth**] **1** (isolate) isoler; **2** (cordon off) GEN boucler; barrer [*street*]. ■ **seal up**: **~** [**sth**] **up**, **~ up** [**sth**] fermer [qch] hermétiquement [*jar*]; boucher [*gap*].

---

	2 Look for the appropriate phrasal verb pattern. **~ [sth] off, ~ off [sth]**	■ **seal off**: **~** [**sth**] **off**, **~ off** [**sth**] **1** (isolate) isoler; **2** (cordon off) GEN boucler; barrer [*street*].

---

	3 Select the appropriate sense category of the phrasal verb pattern. **2 (cordon off)**	■ **seal off**: **~** [**sth**] **off**, **~ off** [**sth**] **1** (isolate) isoler; **2** (cordon off) GEN boucler; barrer [*street*].

---

	4 Select the appropriate collocate showing context for the translation, in this case typical objects of the verb translations. *street*	■ **seal off**: **~** [**sth**] **off**, **~ off** [**sth**] **1** (isolate) isoler; **2** (cordon off) GEN boucler; barrer [*street*].

---

	5 Identify the appropriate translation. barrer	■ **seal off**: **~** [**sth**] **off**, **~ off** [**sth**] **1** (isolate) isoler; **2** (cordon off) GEN boucler; **barrer** [*street*].

---

	6 Now construct the translation of the sentence, putting the verb in the correct tense and person.	

Result	The translation	**la police a barré la rue**

Goal 5	Translate	**chat échaudé craint l'eau froide**

Process	**1** Look up all the words you do not know and find a literal translation. If this does not make sense in your context, ask yourself whether the phrase could be an idiom, saying, or proverb. The answer is yes, because you can see immediately that cats and cold water have no relation to the wider context.	
	2 Select the word or words that you are least familiar with. échaudé	
	3 Will this word appear in this form in the dictionary? No, *échaudé* is part of a verb. Look up the infinitive form. **échauder**	**échauder** /eʃode/ [1] *vtr* **1** (décourager) to put [sb] off; **2** (ébouillanter) to scald. IDIOMS **chat échaudé craint l'eau froide** PROV once bitten, twice shy PROV.
	4 Look for the phrase in the IDIOMS category. IDIOMES **chat échaudé craint l'eau froide**	**échauder** /eʃode/ [1] *vtr* **1** (décourager) to put [sb] off; **2** (ébouillanter) to scald. IDIOMS **chat échaudé craint l'eau froide** PROV once bitten, twice shy PROV.
	5 Note the information PROV which tells you that the expression is a proverb in French as its translation is in English. PROV	**échauder** /eʃode/ [1] *vtr* **1** (décourager) to put [sb] off; **2** (ébouillanter) to scald. IDIOMS **chat échaudé craint l'eau froide** PROV once bitten, twice shy PROV.

Result	The translation	**once bitten, twice shy**

Goal 6	Understand the meaning of the acronym *SMIC* in the phrase	**ils sont payés au SMIC**

Process	**1** Look up *SMIC* and follow the indication provided by the arrowed cross-reference.	**SMIC** /smik/ *nm: abbr* ▶ **salaire**.
	2 Look up *salaire*.	
	3 Scan the entry for *SMIC*. Abbreviations and acronyms will always be in the compound block at the end of the entry. **SMIC**	**salaire** /salɛʀ/ *nm* **1** (paie) salary; (à la journée, à l'heure, à la semaine) (taux) wage; (somme) wages (*pl*); ~ **annuel/mensuel** annual/monthly salary; ~ **brut/net** gross/take-home pay; ~ **de misère** or **famine** starvation wage; **2** FIG (récompense) reward (**de** for); (châtiment) punishment (**de** for). ■ ~ **de base** basic salary GB, base pay US; ~ **d'embauche** starting salary; ~ **minimum interprofessionnel de croissance**, **SMIC** guaranteed minimum wage; ~ **unique** single income.
	4 Note the full form of the acronym. salaire minimum interprofessionnel de croissance	■ ~ **de base** basic salary GB, base pay US; ~ **d'embauche** starting salary; ~ **minimum interprofessionnel de croissance**, SMIC guaranteed minimum wage; ~ **unique** single income.

Result	The explanation or, as in this case, the equivalent	**guaranteed minimum wage**

Comment se servir du dictionnaire?

Les articles du dictionnaire ont une structure hiérarchisée; ils sont subdivisés en catégories grammaticales (introduites par des chiffres romains et présentées dans un ordre fixe) qui sont elles-mêmes subdivisées en catégories sémantiques (introduites par des chiffres arabes). Les catégories sémantiques et les nuances de sens sont différenciées par des indicateurs sémantiques et/ou des indicateurs de collocations et apparaissent selon un ordre qui donne la priorité aux sens les plus fréquents. Pour traduire *tiède* dans la phrase *boire tiède* la démarche à suivre est indiquée par les numéros dans la figure ci-contre. La structure hiérarchisée est illustrée ci-dessous avec l'arborescence de l'entrée *tiède*.

En règle générale, les homographes homophones ont été regroupés sous la même entrée sans tenir compte de l'étymologie; dans les autres cas, l'entrée est répétée et on lui a attribué un numéro d'homographe. Locutions idiomatiques et proverbes sont regroupés en fin d'article.

❶ tiède /tjɛd/ **I** *adj* **1** LIT (désagréablement) [*café, soupe*] lukewarm; [*bain*] tepid; (agréablement) [*eau, air, nuit*] warm; [*saison, température*] mild; **2** FIG (sans enthousiasme) lukewarm.
❷ II *nmf* (membre d'un parti, groupe) PEJ lukewarm ou half-hearted supporter; (adepte) **❸** PEJ half-hearted believer.
III *adv* **servez ~** serve slightly warm; **dépêche-toi ou tu vas manger ~** hurry up or your food will get cold; **il fait ~** (dehors) it's mild; (dedans) it's nice and warm.

Certaines caractéristiques liées à la structure de la langue sont particulières à un côté du dictionnaire. Ainsi dans la partie français–anglais, les mots composés sans trait d'union sont regroupés alphabétiquement en fin d'article.

Dans la partie anglais–français les verbes à particule apparaissent toujours en fin d'article, dans l'ordre alphabétique. Les mots composés sont à leur place dans la nomenclature. On trouvera dans les pages suivantes quelques exemples d'utilisation du dictionnaire tant pour la compréhension que pour la traduction en anglais.

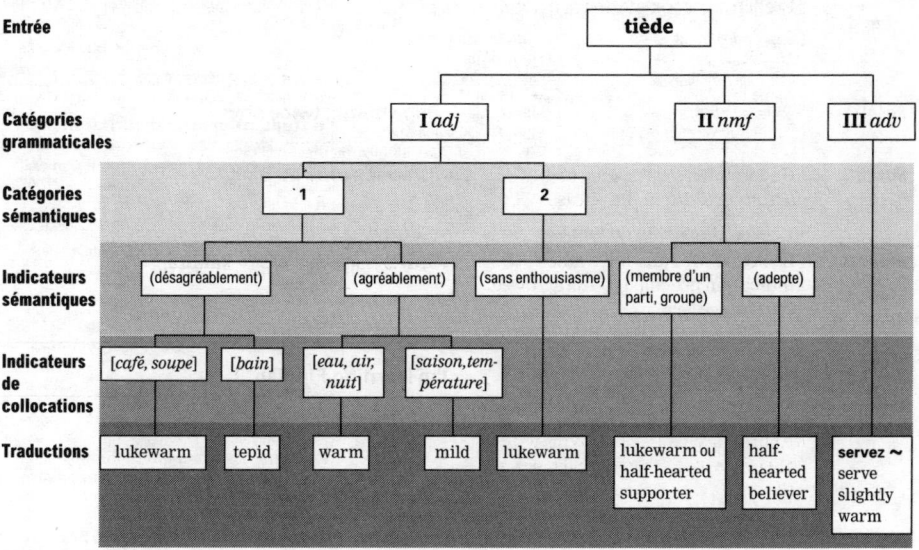

Objectif 1   Traduire   **j'apprends le finnois**

Méthode   **1** Rechercher les mots inconnus en anglais. La traduction du substantif est

finnois, ~e /finwa. az/ ▶ 338│ I *adj* Finnish.
II *nm* LING Finnish.

Finnish

2 Noter le renvoi à une note d'usage lexicale, ici la note sur les langues.

finnois, ~e /finwa. az/ ▶ 338│ I *adj* Finnish.
II *nm* LING Finnish.

▶ 338│

3 Toutes les informations nécessaires à la traduction sont fournies dans le premier exemple, il est inutile de faire d'autres recherches.

Penser à utiliser la forme progressive pour rendre l'idée de processus (être en train de).

Les langues

Les adjectifs comme anglais peuvent qualifier des personnes: un touriste anglais (▶ 394│) et des choses: la cuisine anglaise (▶ 232│). Dans les expressions suivantes, English est pris comme exemple; les autres noms de langues s'utilisent de la même façon.

Les noms de langues

L'anglais n'utilise pas l'article défini devant les noms de langues.
Noter aussi l'emploi de la majuscule, obligatoire en anglais.

apprendre l'anglais	= to learn English
étudier l'anglais	= to study English
l'anglais est facile	= English is easy
j'aime l'anglais	= I like English
parler anglais	= to speak English
parler couramment l'anglais	= to speak good English
	ou to speak English fluently
je ne parle pas très bien l'anglais	= I don't speak very good English *ou* my English isn't very good

***En* avec les noms de langues**

Avec un verbe, en anglais se traduit par in English:
dis-le en anglais   = say it in English

Mais attention:
traduire en anglais   = to translate in

***De* avec les noms de langues**

Les expressions françaises avec de se général en utilisant l'adjectif.

un cours d'anglais	= an English cl
un dictionnaire d'anglais	= an English d
une leçon d'anglais	= an English
un manuel d'anglais	= an Engli
un professeur d'anglais	= an Engli

Noter que ceci peut signifier aussi un p
Pour éviter l'ambiguïté, on peut dire a te

La traduction de l'adjectif français

l'accent anglais	= an English acc
une expression anglaise	= an English ex
la langue anglaise	= the English l
un mot anglais	= an English
un proverbe anglais	= an English

L'anglais a peu d'équivalents simples des noms français en -phone.
...phone

Résultat   Traduction   **I'm learning Finnish**

Objectif 2   Traduire   **il neigeait à notre départ de Moscou**

Méthode **1**   Rechercher l'entrée *neiger* dans la nomenclature. L'exemple et sa traduction sont au présent et la phrase à traduire est à l'imparfait, il suffit de changer le temps.

> it was snowing

neiger /nɛʒe/ [13] *v impers* to snow: **il neige** it's snowing.

      2   Rechercher l'entrée *départ* dans la nomenclature et choisir la catégorie sémantique adéquate. La première convient exactement. Une traduction générale est fournie.

> departure

départ /depaʀ/ *nm* **1** (d'un lieu) departure; **~ des grandes lignes/des lignes de banlieue** RAIL (platforms for) main line/suburban departures; **téléphone avant ton ~** phone before you leave; **se donner rendez-vous au ~ du car** (au lieu) to arrange to meet at the bus; **vols quotidiens au ~ de Nice** daily

      3   Mais un des exemples donnés plus bas a des points communs avec la phrase à traduire.

> **téléphone avant ton ~**
> phone before you leave

Le groupe nominal *ton départ* est traduit par la tournure verbale *you leave*.

départ /depaʀ/ *nm* **1** (d'un lieu) departure; **~ des grandes lignes/des lignes de banlieue** RAIL (platforms for) main line/suburban departures; **téléphone avant ton ~** phone before you leave; se donner rendez-vous au ~ du car (au lieu) to arrange to meet at the bus; **vols quotidiens au ~ de Nice** daily flights from Nice; **le train a pris du retard au ~ de Lyon** the train was late leaving Lyons; **être sur le ~** to be about to leave; **il n'y a qu'un ~ du courrier par jour** the post GB ou mail US only goes once a day; **2** (exode) exodus (**vers** to); **3** (d'une fonction, organisation) departure; (démission) resignation; **le ~ en retraite** retirement; **4** SPORT start; **~ arrêté/décalé/lancé** standing/staggered/flying start; **prendre le ~** (d'une course) to be among the starters; **prendre un nouveau ~** FIG to make a fresh start; **5** (début) start; **au ~** (d'abord) at first; (au début) at the outset; **langue de ~** source language; **salaire de ~** starting salary; **capital de ~** start-up capital.

      4   Pour trouver la construction qui nous intéresse il faut consulter l'entrée *leave* toujours en employant la même méthode: rechercher dans la nomenclature, choisir la catégorie grammaticale qui convient et la parcourir en détail.

Un exemple peut servir utilement de modèle car il contient la tournure verbale *he left* suivie de l'indication du lieu *home*.

leave /liːv/ **I** *n* **1** (also **~ of absence**) (time off) GEN congé *m*; MIL permission *f*; **to take three days' ~** prendre trois jours de congé; **2** (permission) autorisa-

II *vtr* (*prét*, *pp* **left**) **1** (depart from) GEN partir de [*house, station etc*]; (more permanently) quitter [*country, city etc*]; (by going out) sortir de [*room, building*]; **he left home early** il est parti tôt de chez lui; **to ~ school** (permanently) quitter l'école; **to ~ the road/table** quitter la route/table; **to ~ the track** [*train*] dérailler; **to ~ the ground** [*plane*] décoller; **to ~ one's seat** se lever; **I left him cleaning his car** quand je suis parti. il nettoyait sa voiture; **the smile left her**

      5   Il ne reste plus qu'à trouver la traduction de *Moscou*.

Moscou /mɔsku/ ▶ 628 | *npr* Moscow.

Résultat   La traduction n'est pas strictement parallèle au texte français mais elle est exacte et naturelle en anglais.

it was snowing when we left Moscow

Objectif 3 Traduire *to advertise* dans la phrase **there's no need to advertise our weak points**

Méthode 1 Rechercher *advertise* et choisir la catégorie grammaticale pertinente.

I *vtr*

advertise /ˈædvətaɪz/ **I** *vtr* **1** (for publicity) faire de la publicité pour [*product, service*]; annoncer [*price, rate*]; **2** (for sale) mettre or passer une annonce pour [*car, house*]; **3** mettre or passer une annonce pour [*job, vacancy*]; **4** (make known) signaler [*presence*]; afficher [*weakness*]; **I wouldn't ~ the fact** à votre place, je n'en ferais pas état.
II *vi* **1** (for sales, publicity) faire de la publicité; **2** (for staff) passer une annonce.

2 Passer en revue toutes les traductions principales données dans cette catégorie grammaticale et choisir celle qui se rapproche du contexte.

afficher [*weakness*]

advertise /ˈædvətaɪz/ **I** *vtr* **1** (for publicity) faire de la publicité pour [*product, service*]; annoncer [*price, rate*]; **2** (for sale) mettre or passer une annonce pour [*car, house*]; **3** mettre or passer une annonce pour [*job, vacancy*]; **4** (make known) signaler [*presence*]; **afficher [*weakness*]**; **I wouldn't ~ the fact** à votre place, je n'en ferais pas état.
II *vi* **1** (for sales, publicity) faire de la publicité; **2** (for staff) passer une annonce.

Résultat Traduction **il est inutile d'afficher nos points faibles**

Objectif 4 Traduire *make out* dans la phrase **I couldn't make out what he was saying**

Méthode 1 Rechercher l'entrée *make*. Rechercher les verbes à particule clairement signalés à la fin de l'article.

■ **make for:** ¶ ~ **for** [sth] **1** (head for) se diriger vers; **2** (help create) permettre, assurer; ¶ ~ **for** [sb] **1** (attack) se jeter sur; **2** (approach) se diriger vers.
■ **make good:** ¶ ~ **good** réussir; ¶ ~ **good** [sth] **1** réparer [*damage, omission*]; rattraper [*lost time*]; combler [*deficit*]; **2** tenir [*promise*].
■ **make off** filer°; **to ~ off with** se tirer° avec.
■ **make out:** ¶ ~ **out 1** (manage) s'en tirer°; **2**° us

2 Rechercher *make out* dans les verbes à particule présentés alphabétiquement.

3 Rechercher la structure qui se rapproche le plus de celle à traduire c'est-à-dire la forme transitive présentée de la façon suivante.

¶ ~ **out [sth], ~ [sth] out**

■ **make out:** ¶ ~ **out 1** (manage) s'en tirer°; **2**° us (grope) se peloter°; **3** (claim) affirmer (**that** que); ¶ ~ **out [sth], ~ [sth] out 1** (see, distinguish) distinguer; **2** (claim) **to ~ sth out to be** prétendre que qch est; **3** (understand, work out) comprendre (**if** si); **I can't ~ him out** je n'arrive pas à le comprendre; **4** (write out) faire, rédiger; **to ~ out a cheque to sb** faire un chèque à qn; **it is made out to X** il est à l'ordre de X; **5** (expound) **to ~ out a case for** argumenter en faveur de; ¶ ~ **oneself out to be** prétendre être [*rich, brilliant*]; faire semblant d'être [*stupid, incompetent*].

4 Examiner les traductions fournies.

Choisir celle qui convient au contexte.

comprendre

■ **make out:** ¶ ~ **out 1** (manage) s'en tirer°; **2**° us (grope) se peloter°; **3** (claim) affirmer (**that** que); ¶ ~ **out [sth], ~ [sth] out 1** (see, distinguish) distinguer; **2** (claim) **to ~ sth out to be** prétendre que qch est; **3** (understand, work out) **comprendre** (**if** si); **I can't ~ him out** je n'arrive pas à le comprendre; **4** (write out) faire, rédiger; **to ~ out a cheque to sb** faire un chèque à qn; **it is made out to X** il est à l'ordre de X; **5** (expound) **to ~ out a case for** argumenter en faveur de; ¶ ~ **oneself out to be** prétendre être [*rich, brilliant*]; faire semblant d'être [*stupid, incompetent*].

Résultat Traduction **je n'arrivais pas à comprendre ce qu'il disait**

Objectif 5	Comprendre *AGM* dans la phrase	**the Chamber of Commerce is holding its AGM on Wednesday**

Méthode	**1** Rechercher l'entrée dans la nomenclature. *AGM* est une abréviation dont la traduction est fournie à la forme développée comme l'indique un renvoi. ▶ **Annual General Meeting**	**AGM** *n*: *abrév* ▶ **Annual General Meeting**.
	2 L'entrée *Annual General Meeting* se trouve dans la nomenclature et elle est suivie de l'abréviation qui est répétée. **AGM** Noter que l'emploi des majuscules diffère entre les deux langues.	**Annual General Meeting, AGM** *n* assemblée *f* générale annuelle.
Résultat	Glose explicative ou, dans le cas présent, traduction de *AGM*.	**assemblée générale annuelle**

Objectif 6	Traduire	**green about the gills**

Méthode	**1** Le mot qui pose un problème de compréhension est *gills*. En supposant qu'il s'agit d'un substantif au pluriel, l'entrée recherchée sera *gill*.	
	2 Le mot figure sous deux entrées repérées par un numéro d'homographe en raison d'une différence de prononciation. Pour chaque entrée une traduction est fournie mais l'expression *green about the gills* reste difficile à comprendre.	**gill**[1] /gɪl/ *n* (of fish) branchie *f*. IDIOMS **green about the ~s** blanc/blanche comme un linge. **gill**[2] /dʒɪl/ ▶ 789 *n* (measure) quart *m* de pinte.
	3 S'agit-il d'une locution figée? Si oui, elle figurera en fin d'article sous la rubrique IDIOMS. IDIOMS L'article *gill*[1] comporte une telle rubrique et l'expression recherchée y figure.	**gill**[1] /gɪl/ *n* (of fish) branchie *f*. IDIOMS **green about the ~s** blanc/blanche comme un linge.
Résultat	La traduction rend le sens de l'expression, pas celui des mots qui la composent.	**blanc comme un linge**

The structure of French–English entries

headword — **bagage** /bagaʒ/ **I** *nm* **1** (effets) luggage; (de soldat) kit; — IPA pronunciation
2 (sac, valise) piece of luggage; **3** FIG (connaissances)
knowledge; (diplômes) qualifications (*pl*); (expérience)
credentials (*pl*).

part of speech plus gender — **II bagages** *nmpl* luggage ¢; **faire/défaire ses ~s**
to pack/unpack (one's suitcases).

compounds in block at end — ■ **~ à main** hand luggage, carry-on baggage US.
of entry

IDIOMES **plier ~**○ to pack up and go; **partir avec** — idioms in block at end of
armes et ~s to up sticks and leave; **passer à l'enne-** entry
mi avec armes et ~s to defect.

bagarre /bagaʀ/ *nf* **1** (empoignade) fight (**entre**
between); **~s avec la police** clashes with the police; — examples
~ générale free-for-all; **2** FIG (lutte) fight, struggle; — figurative use
(dispute) clash, confrontation; **entrer dans la ~** to
join the fray.

register symbol — **bagarrer**○: **se bagarrer** /bagaʀe/ [1] *vpr* to fight — number of verb group,
informal ○ (**pour** for). referring to the French verb
very informal ◑ tables at the end of the
vulgar or taboo ● dictionary

feminine form of headword — **bagarreur**○, **-euse** /bagaʀœʀ, øz/ **I** *adj* (agressif)
aggressive; (combatif) **être ~** to like to pick a fight.
II *nm,f* bruiser○, fighter.

plural form — **boyau**, *pl* **~x** /bwajo/ **I** *nm* **1** (intestin) gut; **2** (pour — roman grammatical
raquette, violon) catgut; **3** (pour saucisse) casing; **4** (pneu) category number
tubeless tyre GB ou tire US; **5** (passage) back alley; — Arabic sense number
6 (tuyau flexible) hose.
II○ **boyaux** *nmpl* (intestins) insides○.

abbreviation — **BP** *written abbr* ▶ **boîte**. — cross-reference

The structure of English–French entries

headword — **mash** /mæʃ/ **I** n **1** AGRIC pâtée f; **2** (in brewing) trempe — roman grammatical
f; **3**° GB CULIN purée f (de pommes de terre). — category number
II vtr **1** (also ~ **up**) écraser [fruit]; **to ~ potatoes** — Arabic sense numbers
faire de la purée; **2** (in brewing) brasser.

acronym — **MASH** /mæʃ/ n US (abrév = **mobile army surgical** — part of speech
hospital) unité f médicale de campagne. — translation

IPA pronunciation showing — **mask** /mɑːsk, US mæsk/ **I** n GEN masque m; (for eyes
North American variation only) loup m.
II vtr masquer [face]; dissimuler [truth, emotions]; — typical object collocates
masquer [taste].

compounds in alphabetical — **mask:** ~**ed ball** n bal m masqué; ~**ing tape** n
order ruban m adhésif.

mason /ˈmeɪsn/ ▶**1251**┃ n **1** CONSTR maçon m; **2** — page number cross-
Mason (also **Free**~) franc-maçon m. — reference to a lexical usage
note

abbreviation — **ME** n **1** MED abrév ▶**myalgic encephalomyelitis**; — cross-reference to full form
North American usage — **2** US POST abrév écrite = **Maine**; **3** LING abrév
▶**Middle English**; **4** US MED abrév ▶**medical**
examiner.

meadow /ˈmedəʊ/ n **1** (field) pré m; **2** ¢ (also — sense indicator
~**land**) prés mpl, prairies fpl; **3** (also **water** ~)
prairie f inondable.

translation — **meadowsweet** n reine-des-prés f. — gender of translation

North American variant — **meagre** GB, **meager** US /ˈmiːgə(r)/ adj [income, sum,
spelling meal] maigre (before n); [living] chiche; [response,
returns] piètre (before n).

meal /miːl/ n **1** (food) repas m; **to enjoy one's ~** — example
bien manger; **to go out for a ~** aller (manger) au — swung dash as substitute
restaurant; **2** (from grain) farine f. — for headword in examples
idioms in block at end of — **IDIOMS don't make a ~ of it**°! n'en fais pas tout un — register symbol
entry plat°! — ○ informal
— ◑ very informal
— ● vulgar or taboo

separate entry for complex — **meal ticket** n **1** (voucher) ticket-repas m; **2**° FIG (qual-
compound ity, qualification) gagne-pain m inv; (person) **I'm just a ~**
for you! pour toi je ne suis qu'un portefeuille!

Structure du texte français–anglais

entrée — **paillette** /pajɛt/ *nf* **1** (disque brillant) sequin, spangle US; **robe à ~s** a sequined ou spangled US dress; **2** (poudre brillante) glitter ¢; **3** (de roche) splinter; **savon en ~s** soap flakes (*pl*).
— information grammaticale sur la langue cible (mot non dénombrable)

transcription phonétique — **panier** /panje/ *nm* **1** (en osier, rotin, etc) basket; (corbeille à papier) wastepaper basket; (dans un lave-vaisselle) rack; **mettre** or **jeter au ~** LIT to throw [sth] out; FIG to get rid of; **2** SPORT (au basket-ball) basket; **marquer un ~** to score a basket; **3** (de jupe, robe) pannier; **robe à ~s** dress with panniers.
■ **~ à salade** (ustensile) salad shaker; (fourgon de police)◇ Black Maria GB, paddy wagon US.
IDIOMES **être un ~ percé**◇ to spend money like water; **ils sont tous à mettre dans le même ~**◇ they are all much of a muchness GB, they are all about the same; **mettre tous ses œufs dans le même ~**◇ to put all one's eggs in one basket; **le haut** or **dessus du ~**◇ the pick of the bunch.
— exemple
— idiomes regroupés en fin d'article

sigle/acronyme — **PAO** /peao/ *nf* **1** *abbr* ▶ **production**; **2** *abbr* ▶ **publication**.
— renvoi à une entrée

forme du féminin — **parcheminé, ~e** /parʃəmine/ *adj* **1** [papier] with a parchment finish (*épith*); **2** [peau] papery; **3** [visage, main] shrivelled^{GB}.

information sur l'existence d'une variante orthographique nord-américaine (donnée sous l'entrée du côté anglais/français) — **pare-brise** /parbriz/ *nm inv* windscreen GB, windshield US.
— partie du discours

pare-chocs /parʃɔk/ *nm inv* bumper.
— mot composé avec trait d'union ayant valeur d'entrée à part entière

traduction avec sa variante nord-américaine — **parking** /parkiŋ/ *nm* **1** (parc de stationnement) car park GB, parking lot US; (place de stationnement) parking space; **2** (stationnement) CONTROV parking; **~ interdit** no parking.

forme du pluriel — **passereau**, *pl* **~x** /pasro/ *nm* **1** GEN passerine; **2**† (moineau) sparrow.

numéro de catégorie grammaticale en chiffres romains — **patron, -onne** /patrɔ̃, ɔn/ **I** *nm,f* (directeur, gérant) manager, boss◇; (propriétaire) owner, boss◇; **être son propre ~** to be one's own boss◇.
II *nm* **1** (en couture) pattern; **2** (taille) large; **grand ~** extra-large.
— indicateurs de niveau de langue

mots composés sans trait d'union regroupés alphabétiquement — ■ **~ d'industrie** captain of industry; **~ de pêche** skipper, master.

peste /pɛst/ *nf* **1** ▶ **196** MÉD plague; **2**◇ (personne insupportable) pest◇.
IDIOMES **je me méfie de lui comme de la ~**◇ I don't trust him an inch.
— renvoi à une note d'usage lexicale

domaines — **poulet** /pulɛ/ *nm* **1** ZOOL, CULIN chicken; **2**◇ (terme d'affection) **mon ~** my pet◇, honey US.
■ **~ d'élevage ~** battery chicken; **~ fermier ~** free-range chicken.
— symbole indiquant un équivalent dans la langue cible

numéros de catégorie sémantique en chiffres arabes — **preuve** /prœv/ *nf* **1** (argument) proof ¢; **une ~** a piece of evidence; **donner la ~ que** to prove that; **faire ses ~s** [personne] to prove oneself; [chose] to prove itself; **jusqu'à ~ du contraire** until proved otherwise; **il doit être malade, la ~, c'est qu'il n'a pas mangé** he must be ill, the fact that he has not eaten proves it; **2** (expression) demonstration; **~ d'amour** demonstration of love; **faire ~ de** to show; **~ de bonne volonté** (de la part de) goodwill gesture (from).
— indicateurs de collocation

numéro de conjugaison — **proscrire** /prɔskrir/ [67] *vtr* (interdire) to ban; (bannir) to banish.
— indicateurs sémantiques

xxix

Structure du texte anglais–français

entrée — **mail** /meɪl/ **I** *n* **1** (postal service) poste *f*; **by ~** par la poste; **2** (**correspondence**) courrier *m*; **3** MIL HIST **a** — indicateur sémantique
coat of ~ une cotte de mailles.
II *vtr* envoyer, expédier [*letter, parcel*] (**to** à).

mot composé ayant valeur d'entrée à part entière — **main line I** /ˌmeɪn ˈlaɪn/ *n* RAIL grande ligne *f*.
II /ˈmeɪnˌlaɪn/ *noun modifier* [*station, terminus, train*] de grande ligne.

indicateur de niveau de langue — **III°** **mainline** /ˈmeɪnlaɪn/ *vi* ARGOT DES DROGUÉS se piquer.

transcription phonétique — **mainly** /ˈmeɪnlɪ/ *adv* surtout, essentiellement.

groupe de mots composés — **main**: **~ man**° *n* US copain *m*, pote° *m*; **~mast** *n* grand mât *m*; **~ memory** *n* COMPUT mémoire *f* centrale; **~ office** *n* (of company, organization, newspaper) siège *m* (social); **~ road** *n* (country) route *f* principale; (in town) grande rue *f*; **~sail** *n* grand-voile *f*.

partie du discours — **map** /mæp/ **I** *n* (of region) carte *f* (**of** de); (of town, underground) plan *m* (**of** de); **weather ~** carte météo(rologique); **street ~** plan des rues; **the political ~ of** — tiret ondulé remplaçant **Europe** FIG le paysage politique de l'Europe. l'entrée dans les exemples
II *vtr* **1** faire la carte de [*region, planet*]; faire le plan de [*town*]; **2** COMPUT faire une projection de.
IDIOMS **to put sb/sth on the ~** mettre qn/qch en vedette.

verbe à particule — ■ **map out**: **~ out** [sth], **~** [sth] **out** élaborer, — construction d'un verbe à mettre [qch] au point [*plans, strategy*]; planifier particule [*schedule*]; tracer [*sb's future*].

numéro de catégorie grammaticale en chiffres romains — **material** /məˈtɪərɪəl/ **I** *n* **1** (data) documentation *f*, documents *mpl*; **teaching ~** matériel *m* pédagogique; **reference ~** ouvrages *mpl* de référence; **2** (subject — numéro de catégorie matter) contenu *m*; **3** THEAT, TV (script) texte *m*; (show) sémantique en chiffres spectacle *m*; **she writes all her own ~** elle écrit ses arabes textes elle-même; MUS elle est auteur-compositeur; **4** (substance) GEN matière *f*, substance *f*; CONSTR, TECH — domaines matériau *m*; **packing ~** matériaux *mpl* d'emballage; **waste ~** déchets *mpl*; **5** (fabric) tissu *m*, étoffe *f*; **6** (personal potential) étoffe *f*; **she is star ~** elle a l'étoffe d'une vedette; **to be university ~** être capable d'entreprendre des études universitaires.
II materials *npl* (equipment) matériel *m*; **art ~s**, **art-ist's ~s** fournitures *fpl* de dessin; **cleaning ~s** — exemple produits *mpl* d'entretien.
III *adj* **1** (significant, relevant) [*assistance, benefit, change, damage, evidence*] matériel/-ielle; [*question*] important; [*fact*] pertinent; **to be ~ to sth** se rapporter à qch; **2** (concrete) [*comfort, gains, possessions, success*] matériel/-ielle; **in ~ terms** sur le plan matériel; **to do sth for ~ gain** faire qch par intérêt. — traduction

glose explicative — **matron** /ˈmeɪtrən/ *n* **1** GB (nurse) (in hospital) infirmière *f* en chef; (in school) infirmière *f* (*chargée également de l'intendance*); **2** (of nursing home) directrice *f*; **3** US (warder) gardienne *f*; **4** (woman) PEJ matrone *f* PEJ.

matronly /ˈmeɪtrənlɪ/ *adj* [*duties, manner*] de mère de — indicateurs de collocation famille, de matrone; [*figure*] fort, corpulent.

transcription phonétique de la prononciation nord-américaine — **minute²** /maɪˈnjuːt, US -ˈnuːt/ *adj* [*particle*] minuscule; [*quantity*] infime; [*risk, variation*] minime.

variante orthographique nord-américaine — **mouldy** GB, **moldy** US /ˈməʊldɪ/ *adj* moisi; **to go ~** moisir.

mown /məʊn/ *pp* ▶ **mow**. — renvoi à une entrée

sigles/acronymes — **MP** *n* **1** GB (*abrév* = **Member of Parliament**) député *m*; **2** *abrév* ▶ **military policeman**.
mpg *n* (*abrév* = **miles per gallon**) miles *mpl* au gallon.

The pronunciation of French

The symbols used in this dictionary for the pronunciation of French are those of the IPA (International Phonetic Alphabet). Certain differences in pronunciation are shown in the phonetic transcription, although many speakers do not observe them—e.g. the long 'a' /ɑ/ in *pâte* and the short 'a' /a/ in *patte*, or the difference between the nasal vowels 'un' /œ̃/ as in *brun* and 'in' /ɛ̃/ as in *brin*.

Transcription
Each entry is followed by its phonetic transcription between slashes, with the following exceptions:
- written abbreviations (*bd, ha,* etc.)
- cross-references from an inflected to a base form (*yeux, fol*)
- cross-references from a variant spelling to the preferred form (*clef/clé, peinard/pénard*).

Alternative pronunciations
Where the speaker has a choice of pronunciations, these are shown in one of the following two ways:
- by the use of brackets e.g. *syllabe* /sil(l)ab/, *déficit* /defisi(t)/
- in full, separated by a comma e.g. *revenir* /ʀəvniʀ, ʀvəniʀ/.

Morphological variations
The phonetic transcription of the plural and feminine forms of certain nouns and adjectives does not repeat the root, but shows only the change in ending. Therefore, in certain cases, the presentation of the entry does not correspond to that of the phonetic transcription e.g. *électricien, -ienne* /elɛktʀisjɛ̃, ɛn/.

Phrases
Full phonetic transcription is given for adverbial or prepositional phrases which are shown in alphabetical order within the main headword e.g. *emblée, d'emblée* /dɑ̃ble/, *plain-pied, de plain-pied* /d(ə)plɛ̃pje/.

Consonants
Aspiration of 'h'
Where it is impossible to make a liaison this is indicated by /'/ immediately after the slash e.g. *haine* /'ɛn/.

Assimilation
A voiced consonant can become unvoiced when it is followed by an unvoiced consonant within a word e.g. *absorber* /apsɔʀbe/.

Vowels
Open 'e' and closed 'e'
A clear distinction is made at the end of a word between a closed 'e' and an open 'e' e.g. *pré* /pʀe/ and *près* /pʀɛ/, *complet* /kɔ̃plɛ/ and *combler* /kɔ̃ble/.
Within a word the following rules apply:
- 'e' is always open in a syllable followed by a syllable containing a mute 'e' e.g. *règle* /ʀɛgl/, *réglementaire* /ʀɛgləmɑ̃tɛʀ/
- in careful speech 'e' is pronounced as a closed 'e' when it is followed by a syllable containing a closed vowel (*y, i, e*) e.g. *pressé* /pʀese/
- 'e' is pronounced as an open 'e' when it is followed by a syllable containing an open vowel e.g. *pressant* /pʀesɑ̃/.

Mute 'e'
The pronunciation of mute 'e' varies considerably depending on the level of language used and on the region from which the speaker originates. As a general rule it is only pronounced at the end of a word in the South of France or in poetry and it is, therefore, not shown. In an isolated word the mute 'e' preceded by a single consonant is dropped e.g. *parfaitement* /paʀfɛtmɑ̃/, but *probablement* /pʀɔbabləmɑ̃/.
In many cases the pronunciation of the mute 'e' depends on the surrounding context. Thus one would say *une reconnaissance de dette* /ynʀəkɔnɛsɑ̃sdədɛt/, but, *ma reconnaissance est éternelle* /maʀkɔnɛsɑ̃sɛtetɛʀnɛl/. The mute 'e' is shown in brackets in order to account for this phenomenon.

Open 'o' and closed 'o'
The difference between open 'o' and closed 'o' is not clear and speakers may hesitate, particularly in the pronunciation of compound words whose first element ends in 'o' e.g. *socioprofessionnel* etc. It is not possible to opt for one or the other to apply to all cases. Where the word seems to function more like a single word the 'o' tends to be pronounced as an open 'o'. Where the two elements of the compound retain a degree of autonomy, as is often the case when they are hyphenated, the 'o' tends to be pronounced as a closed 'o' e.g. *psychothérapie* /psikoteʀapi/, but, *psychologie* /psikɔlɔʒi /.

Stress
There is no real stress as such in French. In normal unemphasized speech a slight stress falls on the final syllable of a word or group of words, providing that it does not contain a mute 'e'. This is not shown in the phonetic transcription of individual entries.

I.V.

Vowels

a	*as in* patte	/pat/
ɑ	pâte	/pɑt/
ɑ̃	clan	/klɑ̃/
e	dé	/de/
ɛ	belle	/bɛl/
ɛ̃	lin	/lɛ̃/
ə	demain	/dəmɛ̃/
i	gris	/gʀi/
o	gros	/gʀo/
ɔ	corps	/kɔʀ/
ɔ̃	long	/lɔ̃/

œ	*as in* leur	/lœʀ/
œ̃	brun	/bʀœ̃/
ø	deux	/dø/
u	fou	/fu/
y	pur	/pyʀ/

Semi-vowels

j	*as in* fille	/fij/
ɥ	huit	/ɥit/
w	oui	/wi/

Consonants

b	*as in* bal	/bal/
d	dent	/dɑ̃/
f	foire	/fwaʀ/
g	gomme	/gɔm/
k	clé	/kle/
l	lien	/ljɛ̃/
m	mer	/mɛʀ/
n	nage	/naʒ/
ɲ	gnon	/ɲɔ̃/

ŋ	*as in* dancing	/dɑ̃siŋ/
p	porte	/pɔʀt/
ʀ	rire	/ʀiʀ/
s	sang	/sɑ̃/
ʃ	chien	/ʃjɛ̃/
t	train	/tʀɛ̃/
v	voile	/vwal/
z	zèbre	/zɛbʀ/
ʒ	jeune	/ʒœn/

Prononciation de l'anglais

Les sons et leur transcription

Alphabet phonétique

La prononciation de chaque entrée est donnée en notation phonétique entre des barres obliques / /. On trouvera le tableau des signes utilisés à la page xxxiv. A la différence de l'écriture orthographique de l'anglais dans laquelle la même lettre peut prendre des valeurs différentes, par exemple le *c* dans *cat* (/kæt/) et *city* (/'sɪtɪ/), dans l'alphabet phonétique, chaque signe représente un seul son.

Anglais britannique

La prononciation standard de l'anglais britannique suit immédiatement le mot-vedette. Cette prononciation correspond à la Received Pronunciation (RP) qui est la forme d'anglais britannique la plus répandue.

Prononciation du /r/

En anglais britannique, le *r* ou *re* à la fin d'un mot ne se prononce que si le mot qui suit commence par une voyelle. C'est pourquoi, dans la transcription phonétique, ces sons sont indiqués entre parenthèses, par exemple *hair* /heə(r)/, *hire* /haɪ(r)/.

L'accent

Accent d'intensité

Les mots anglais polysyllabiques comportent une syllabe plus fortement accentuée que les autres. L'accent d'intensité est indiqué au moyen du signe /'/ placé devant la syllabe qu'il affecte, par exemple *city* /'sɪtɪ/. Certains mots longs ont deux accents d'intensité, l'un plus fort, appelé accent primaire et également noté /'/, l'autre plus faible, appelé accent secondaire et noté /ˌ/: *pronunciation* /prəˌnʌnsɪ'eɪʃn/.

Déplacement de l'accent d'intensité

En général on évite d'avoir à prononcer deux accents d'intensité dans des syllabes adjacentes. Ainsi dans la phrase *Lisa is thirteen*, on prononcera /ˌθɜːˈtiːn/, mais dans *Lisa has thirteen bicycles*, on dira /ˌθɜːtiːn ˈbaɪsɪkls/. On notera que le déplacement de l'accent d'intensité est valable pour toutes les catégories de mots et que tout mot ayant un accent secondaire suivi d'un accent primaire peut perdre ce dernier lorsqu'il est suivi par un mot dont la première syllabe porte l'accent d'intensité primaire.

Variantes dans la prononciation

Variantes britanniques

Il arrive pour de nombreux mots que plusieurs prononciations soient acceptées. Dans ce cas les variantes sont données, la prononciation la plus courante étant placée en premier, par exemple *economic* /ˌiːkə'nɒmɪk, ˌekə'nɒmɪk/.

Formes fortes et formes faibles

Certains mots courants tels que *a, the, and, but, for, me, them, can, have*, etc. peuvent se prononcer de deux (ou plus) façons différentes: une forme forte et une (ou plus) forme faible. Des deux, la forme faible est la plus fréquente: c'est celle qui se rencontre dans la chaîne parlée.

La forme forte s'utilise pour un mot isolé, ou encore pour souligner le mot dans une phrase. On trouvera la prononciation des deux formes dans le dictionnaire, la forme forte étant donnée la première, par exemple *and* /ænd, ənd/.

Dans la chaîne parlée, les formes faibles de *be* et *have* suivent souvent un pronom personnel. On notera que pronom et verbe sont généralement combinés en une forme contractée qui est une forme faible, par exemple *you're* /jɔː(r)/, *I'm* /aɪm/.

Contractions

Dans la langue écrite, les contractions se font par omission d'une ou deux lettres auxquelles on substitue une apostrophe ('), par exemple *can't*. Dans la langue parlée, il y a contraction quand une syllabe disparaît et que la syllabe restante comporte une voyelle autre que /ə/. La contraction est très fréquente pour certains verbes auxiliaires suivis de *not*, par exemple *don't* /dəʊnt/. (Ces formes ne sont pas des formes faibles et peuvent être accentuées.)

Mots étrangers

L'anglais possède un certain nombre de mots et expressions d'origine étrangère qui se sont intégrés à la langue et ont acquis une prononciation anglaise, par exemple *coffee* /'kɒfiː/, *bungalow* /'bʌngələʊ/.

D'autres, bien que d'emploi courant, continuent à être perçus comme étrangers, d'où de grandes variations dans la manière dont ils sont prononcés. Beaucoup de ces mots sont français et de ce fait contiennent des voyelles nasales qui n'existent pas en anglais, par exemple *salon, en route*. La prononciation de ces sons est complexe pour les locuteurs de l'anglais et l'on peut entendre des sons totalement transformés aussi bien qu'une prononciation française correcte. La prononciation adoptée dans ce dictionnaire est la forme anglicisée des mots étrangers et l'on trouvera /'sælɒn/, /ˌɒn 'ruːt/.

Prononciation de l'anglais d'Amérique du Nord

Celle-ci est indiquée après la prononciation RP

chaque fois qu'il y a une différence marquée entre les deux, ainsi pour le mot *graph* /grɑːf, US græf/.

La prononciation de l'anglais d'Amérique du Nord donnée ici est celle du General American.

Bien que les symboles utilisés soient les mêmes que pour la RP, on notera que certains sons, en particulier les voyelles, ont une valeur différente. On notera également que /r/ se prononce toujours en anglais d'Amérique du Nord, ce qui n'est pas le cas en anglais britannique : *car*, *start*. Dans la transcription phonétique, la prononciation donnée sera celle de l'anglais britannique /kɑː(r)/, /stɑːt/.

Dérivés et composés

Dérivés

Les dérivés apparaissant généralement comme des entrées à part entière dans le dictionnaire, leur prononciation sera indiquée systématiquement.

Mots composés

En anglais, les mots composés s'écrivent soit en un seul mot ('closed compounds'), soit en deux mots parfois reliés par un trait d'union. Pour économiser de la place, la prononciation n'est pas toujours donnée, mais il suffira de consulter la prononciation des deux éléments du mot.

Au cours de l'articulation d'un mot composé il se produit souvent des changements phonétiques. Sous l'influence du phonème qui le suit, un son peut changer de valeur, comme dans *boatman* où le *t* devient un *p* /ˈbəʊpmən/, ou disparaître complètement, comme dans *windscreen* qui se prononce /ˈwɪnskriːn/. Ce phénomène d'assimilation, plus ou moins marqué selon la rapidité d'élocution, se rencontre constamment dans la chaîne parlée. Toutefois, c'est toujours la forme complète qui est donnée dans le dictionnaire.   *J.S.-S.*

Voyelles et diphtongues

iː	*de* see	/siː/	ɜː	*de* fur	/fɜː(r)/
ɪ	sit	/sɪt/	ə	ago	/əˈgəʊ/
e	ten	/ten/	eɪ	page	/peɪdʒ/
æ	hat	/hæt/	əʊ	home	/həʊm/
ɑː	arm	/ɑːm/	aɪ	five	/faɪv/
ɒ	got	/gɒt/	aʊ	now	/naʊ/
ɔː	saw	/sɔː/	ɔɪ	join	/dʒɔɪn/
ʊ	put	/pʊt/	ɪə	near	/nɪə(r)/
uː	too	/tuː/	eə	hair	/heə(r)/
ʌ	cup	/kʌp/	ʊə	pure	/pjʊə(r)/

Consonnes

p	*de* pen	/pen/	s	*de* so	/səʊ/
b	bad	/bæd/	z	zoo	/zuː/
t	tea	/tiː/	ʃ	she	/ʃiː/
d	did	/dɪd/	ʒ	vision	/ˈvɪʒn/
k	cat	/kæt/	h	how	/haʊ/
g	got	/gɒt/	m	man	/mæn/
tʃ	chin	/tʃɪn/	n	no	/nəʊ/
dʒ	June	/dʒuːn/	ŋ	sing	/sɪŋ/
f	fall	/fɔːl/	l	leg	/leg/
v	voice	/vɔɪs/	r	red	/red/
θ	thin	/θɪn/	j	yes	/jes/
ð	then	/ðen/	w	wet	/wet/

Abbreviations and symbols
Abréviations et symboles

abbreviation	**abbr, abrév**	abréviation
adjective	**adj**	adjectif
demonstrative adjective	**adj dém**	adjectif démonstratif
exclamatory adjective	**adj excl**	adjectif exclamatif
indefinite adjective	**adj indéf**	adjectif indéfini
interrogative adjective	**adj inter**	adjectif interrogatif
adjectival phrase	**adj phr**	locution adjective
possessive adjective	**adj poss**	adjectif possessif
relative adjective	**adj rel**	adjectif relatif
administration	**Admin**	administration
adverb	**adv**	adverbe
adverbial phrase	**adv phr**	locution adverbiale
aerospace	**Aerosp**	astronautique
agriculture	**Agric**	agriculture
anatomy	**Anat**	anatomie
architecture	**Archit**	architecture
definite article	**art déf**	article défini
indefinite article	**art indéf**	article indéfini
aerospace	**Astronaut**	astronautique
Australian	**Austral**	anglais d'Australie
automobile	**Aut**	automobile
auxiliary	**aux**	auxiliaire
aviation	**Aviat**	aviation
Belgian French	**B**	belgicisme
biology	**Biol**	biologie
botany	**Bot**	botanique
Canadian French	**C**	canadianisme
chemistry	**Chem**	chimie
cinema	**Cin**	cinéma
commerce	**Comm**	commerce
computing	**Comput**	informatique
conjunction	**conj**	conjonction
conjunctional phrase	**conj phr**	locution conjonctive
construction	**Constr**	construction, bâtiment
controversial	**controv**	usage critiqué
culinary	**Culin**	culinaire
demonstrative	**dém**	démonstratif
demonstrative determiner	**dét dém**	déterminant démonstratif
determiner	**det, dét**	déterminant
indefinite determiner	**dét indéf**	déterminant indéfini
interrogative determiner	**dét inter**	déterminant interrogatif
dialect	**dial**	dialecte
ecology	**Ecol, Écol**	écologie
economy	**Econ, Écon**	économie
electricity	**Elec, Électrotech**	électrotechnique
attributive	**épith**	épithète
euphemistic	**euph**	euphémique
exclamation	**excl**	exclamation
feminine	**f**	féminin
figurative	**fig**	figuré

finance	**Fin**	finance
formal	**fml**	soutenu
British English	**GB**	anglais britannique
generally	**gen, gén**	généralement
geography	**Geog, Géog**	géographie
Swiss French	**H**	helvétisme
history	**Hist**	histoire
humorous	**hum**	humoristique
industry	**Ind**	industrie
indicative	**indic**	indicatif
offensive	**injur**	injurieux
invariable	**inv**	invariable
ironic	**iron**	ironique
journalism	**Journ**	presse
law	**Jur**	droit
baby talk	**lang enfantin**	langage enfantin
linguistics	**Ling**	linguistique
literal	**lit**	littéral
literary	**liter, littér**	littéraire
literature	**Literat, Littérat**	littérature
phrase	**loc**	locution
adjectival phrase	**loc adj**	locution adjective
adverbial phrase	**loc adv**	locution adverbiale
conjunctional phrase	**loc conj**	locution conjonctive
exclamatory phrase	**loc excl**	locution exclamative
noun phrase	**loc nom**	locution nominale
prepositional phrase	**loc prép**	locution prépositive
masculine	**m**	masculin
mathematics	**Math**	mathématique
medicine	**Med, Méd**	médecine
meteorology	**Meteorol, Météo**	météorologie
military	**Mil**	armée
music	**Mus**	musique
mythology	**Mythol**	mythologie
noun	**n**	nom
nautical	**Naut**	nautisme
negative	**nég**	négatif
feminine noun	**nf**	nom féminin
masculine noun	**nm**	nom masculin
masculine and feminine noun	**nm,f**	nom masculin et féminin
masculine and feminine noun	**nmf**	nom masculin et féminin
plural noun	**npl**	nom pluriel
proper noun	**npr**	nom propre
onomatopoeia	**onomat**	onomatopée
computing	**Ordinat**	informatique
pejorative	**pej, péj**	péjoratif
philosophy	**Philos**	philosophie
photography	**Phot**	photographie
physics	**Phys**	physique
plural	**pl**	pluriel
politics	**Pol**	politique
postal services	**Post**	postes
past participle	**pp**	participe passé
past participle adjective	**pp adj**	participe passé adjectif

present participle	**p prés**	participe présent
proper noun	**pr n**	nom propre
prefix	**préf**	préfixe
prepositional phrase	**prep phr**	locution prépositive
preposition	**prep, prép**	préposition
present participle adjective	**pres p adj**	participe présent adjectif
present	**pres, prés**	présent
preterit	**prét**	prétérit
pronoun	**pron**	pronom
demonstrative pronoun	**pron dém**	pronom démonstratif
indefinite pronoun	**pron indéf**	pronom indéfini
interrogative pronoun	**pron inter**	pronom interrogatif
personal pronoun	**pron pers**	pronom personnel
pronominal phrase	**pron phr**	locution pronominale
possessive pronoun	**pron poss**	pronom possessif
relative pronoun	**pron rel**	pronom relatif
proverb	**Prov**	proverbe
psychology	**Psych**	psychologie
something	**qch**	quelque chose
somebody	**qn**	quelqu'un
quantifier	**quantif**	quantificateur
religion	**Relig**	religion
somebody	**sb**	quelqu'un
school	**Sch, Scol**	école
Scottish	**Scot**	anglais d'Écosse
singular	**sg**	singulier
sociology	**Sociol**	sociologie
formal	**sout**	soutenu
specialist	**spec, spéc**	spécialiste
something	**sth**	quelque chose
subjunctive	**subj**	subjonctif
technology	**Tech**	technologie
telecommunications	**Telecom, Télécom**	télécommunications
theatre	**Theat, Théât**	théâtre
always	**tjrs**	toujours
television	**TV**	télévision
university	**Univ**	université
American	**US**	anglais américain
verb	**v**	verbe
auxiliary verb	**v aux**	verbe auxiliaire
impersonal verb	**v impers**	verbe impersonnel
reflexive verb	**v refl**	verbe pronominal
intransitive verb	**vi**	verbe intransitif
reflexive verb	**vpr**	verbe pronominal
transitive verb	**vtr**	verbe transitif
indirect transitive verb	**vtr ind**	verbe transitif indirect
zoology	**Zool**	zoologie
dated	†	vieilli
archaic	‡	archaïque
trade mark	®	marque déposée ou nom déposé
informal	○	familier
very informal	◑	populaire
vulgar or taboo	●	vulgaire ou tabou
countable	C	dénombrable
uncountable	₵	non dénombrable
swung dash used as substitute for headword	~	tiret ondulé de substitution

British spelling only: US spelling varies	GB	graphie britannique: il existe une graphie nord-américaine
indicates an approximate translation equivalent	≈	pour signaler un équivalent approximatif
cross-reference	▶	renvoi

Note on proprietary status This dictionary includes some words which have, or are asserted to have, proprietary status as trade marks or otherwise. Their inclusion does not imply that they have acquired for legal purposes a non-proprietary or general significance, nor any other judgement concerning their legal status. In cases where the editorial staff have some evidence that a word has proprietary status this is indicated in the entry for that word by the symbol ®, but no judgement concerning the legal status of such words is made or implied thereby.

Les marques déposées Les mots qui, à notre connaissance, sont considérés comme des marques ou des noms déposés sont signalés dans cet ouvrage par ®. La présence ou l'absence de cette mention ne peut pas être considérée comme ayant valeur juridique.

French–English dictionary
Dictionnaire français–anglais

a, A /a, ɑ/ **I** *nm inv* (lettre) a, A; **vitamine A** vitamin A; **de A à Z** from A to Z; **le bricolage de A à Z** the A to Z of DIY; **démontrer qch à qn par A plus B** to demonstrate sth conclusively to sb.
II A *nf* (*abbr* = **autoroute**) motorway GB, freeway US.

à /a/ *prép*

■ **Note** La préposition *à* se traduit de multiples façons. Les expressions courantes du genre *machine à écrire, difficile à faire* etc sont traitées respectivement sous *machine*, *difficile* etc.
– Les emplois de *à* avec les verbes *avoir, être, aller, penser* etc sont traités sous les verbes.
– Pour trouver la traduction correcte de *à* on aura intérêt à se reporter aux mots qui précèdent la préposition ainsi qu'aux notes d'usage répertoriées ▶ 1420].
– On trouvera ci-dessous quelques exemples typiques de traductions de *à*.

1 (avec un verbe de mouvement) **se rendre au travail** to go to work; **aller de Paris ~ Nevers** to go from Paris to Nevers; **2** (pour indiquer le lieu où l'on se trouve) **~ la maison** at home; **~ Paris** in Paris; **3** (dans le temps) **~ 10 ans** at the age of 10; **au printemps** in (the) spring; **4** (dans une description) with; **le garçon aux cheveux bruns** the boy with dark hair; **5** (employé avec le verbe être) **il est ~ plaindre** he's to be pitied; **je suis ~ vous tout de suite** I'll be with you in a minute; **c'est ~ qui de jouer?** whose turn is it?; **c'est ~ toi** it's your turn; (**c'est**) **~ lui de décider** it's up to him to decide; **6** (marquant l'appartenance) **~ qui est cette montre?** whose is this watch?; **elle est ~ elle's hers**; **c'est ~ vous cette voiture?** is this your car?; **une amie ~ moi** a friend of mine; **encore une idée ~ elle** another of her ideas; **7** (employé avec un nombre) **nous avons fait le travail ~ deux** two of us did the work; (**en s'y mettant**) **~ dix on devrait y arriver** ten of us should be able to manage; **~ nous tous on devrait y arriver** between all of us we should be able to manage; **~ trois on est serrés** with three people it's crowded; **mener 3 ~ 2** to lead 3 (to) 2; **~ 100 kilomètres-heure** at 100 kilometres^GB per ou an hour; **au 74 de la rue Bossuet** at 74 rue Bossuet; **~ quatre kilomètres d'ici** four kilometres^GB from here; **~ 10 francs le kilo** at 10 francs a kilo; **un timbre ~ trois francs** a three-franc stamp; (**de**) **huit ~ dix heures par jour** between eight and ten hours a day; **8** (marquant une hypothèse) **~ ce qu'il paraît**, **~ ce que l'on dit** apparently; **~ ce qu'il me semble** as far as I can see; **~ vous entendre** to hear you talk; **9** (dans phrases exclamatives) **~ nous!** (en levant son verre) (here's) to us!; **~ ta santé**, **~ la tienne!** cheers!; **~ tes souhaits** bless you!; **~ vous l'honneur!** (de couper le gâteau) you do the honours!; (après vous) after you!; **~ nous (deux)!** (avant un règlement de compte) let's sort this out between us; **~ demain** see you tomorrow; **~ la prochaine** see you next time!; **10** (dans une dédicace) **'~ ma mère'** (dans un livre) 'to my mother'; (sur une tombe) 'in memory of my mother'.

abaissement /abɛsmɑ̃/ *nm* **1** (diminution) (de prix, taux) cut (**de** in); (de seuil, niveau) lowering; **2** (avilissement) (de soi-même) self-abasement; (d'autrui) debasement.

abaisser /abese/ [1] **I** *vtr* **1** (en valeur) to reduce [*prix*] (**à** to; **de** by); to lower [*niveau*] (**à** to; **de** by); **2** (en hauteur) to lower [*mur*] (**de** by); **3** (faire descendre) to pull down [*manette*].
II s'abaisser *vpr* **1** (descendre) [*rideau de scène*] to

fall; **2** (s'avilir) to demean oneself; **s'~ à faire qch** to stoop to doing sth.

abandon /abɑ̃dɔ̃/ *nm* **1** (état) state of neglect; **état d'~** neglected state; **être à l'~** [*maison, domaine*] to be abandoned; [*enfant*] to be running wild; [*jardin*] to be neglected; **laisser à l'~** to allow [sth] to fall into decay [*maison*]; to allow [sth] to become overgrown [*terres*]; **2** (de projet, méthode) abandonment; (de droit, privilège) relinquishment; **3** (de cours, d'épreuve) withdrawal (**de** from); (de fonctions) giving up (**de** of); **contraint à l'~** forced to withdraw; **vainqueur par ~** winner by default; **4** (attitude détendue) relaxed attitude.
■ **~ du domicile conjugal** desertion of the marital home; **~ d'enfant** abandonment of a child; **~ de poste** desertion (of one's post).

abandonné, ~e /abɑ̃dɔne/ **I** *pp* ▶ **abandonner**.
II *pp adj* **1** (délaissé) [*épouse, ami, cause*] deserted; [*véhicule, maison, nation*] abandoned; **2** (désaffecté) [*chemin, usine*] disused; **3** (qui n'a plus cours) [*méthode*] discarded; [*modèle*] discontinued.

abandonner /abɑ̃dɔne/ [1] **I** *vtr* **1** (renoncer à) GÉN to give up; (à l'école) to drop [*matière*]; **~ les recherches** to give up the search; **je peignais, mais j'ai abandonné** I used to paint, but I gave it up; **~ la partie** ou **lutte** LIT, FIG to throw in the towel; **2** (céder) to give [*bien*] (**à qn** to sb); to hand [sth] over [*gestion*] (**à qn** to sb); **3** (se retirer de) to give up [*fonction, études*]; SPORT (avant l'épreuve) to withdraw; (pendant l'épreuve) to retire; **~ la course** to withdraw from the race; **4** (quitter) to leave [*personne, lieu*]; to abandon [*véhicule, objet, navire*]; **~ Paris pour Nice** to leave Paris for Nice; **5** (délaisser) to abandon [*enfant, famille, animal*]; to desert [*foyer, épouse, poste, cause*]; **6** (livrer) **~ qch à** to leave ou abandon sth to; **~ qn à son sort** to leave ou abandon sb to his/her fate; **7** (faire défaut) [*courage, chance*] to desert [*personne*]; **mes forces m'abandonnent** my strength is failing me; **8** (lâcher) to let go of [*outil, rênes*]; **9** ORDINAT to abort.
II s'abandonner *vpr* **1** (se confier) to let oneself go; **2** (se détendre) to let oneself go; **s'~ dans les bras de qn** to sink into sb's arms; **3** (se laisser aller) **s'~ au désespoir** to give in to despair.

abasourdir /abazuʀdiʀ/ [3] *vtr* (stupéfier) to stun.

abat-jour /abaʒuʀ/ *nm inv* lampshade.

abats /aba/ *nmpl* (bœuf, porc, mouton) offal ¢; (de volaille) giblets.

abattage /abataʒ/ *nm* **1** (d'arbre) felling ¢; **2** (d'animal de boucherie) slaughter ¢.

abattant /abatɑ̃/ *nm* (de bureau) (drop) leaf; (de WC) lid.

abattement /abatmɑ̃/ *nm* **1** (dépressif) despondency; **2** (réduction) GÉN reduction; (pour impôt) allowance.
■ **~ fiscal** tax allowance GB ou deduction US.

abattis /abati/ *nmpl* CULIN giblets.

abattoir /abatwaʀ/ *nm* slaughterhouse.

abattre /abatʀ/ [61] **I** *vtr* **1** (tuer) to slaughter [*animal de boucherie*]; to destroy [*animal dangereux*]; (avec une arme à feu) to shoot [sb] down [*personne*]; to shoot [*animal*]; **l'homme à ~** the prime target; FIG the one to beat; **2** (faire tomber) to pull down [*bâtiment*]; to knock down [*mur*]; to bring down [*statue*]; to shoot down [*avion*]; [*personne*] to fell [*arbre*]; [*tempête*] to bring down [*arbre, pylône*]; **3** (découvrir) to show [*carte, jeu*]; **~ ses cartes** ou **son jeu** LIT, FIG to put one's cards on the table; **4** (accabler) (physiquement) to wear

[sb] out; (moralement) to demoralize; **on ne va pas se laisser ~!** we're not going to let things get us down!; **5** (accomplir) to get through [*travail*].

II s'abattre *vpr* **s'~ sur** [*orage*] to beat down on; [*oiseau*] to swoop down on; [*malheur*] to descend upon.

abbatiale /abasjal/ *nf* abbey church.

abbaye /abei/ *nf* abbey.

abbé /abe/ *nm* **1** (supérieur d'une abbaye) abbot; **2** (prêtre) priest; **monsieur l'~** Father; **l'~ Pop** Father Pop.

abbesse /abɛs/ *nf* abbess.

abc /abese/ *nm* ABC, rudiments.

abcès /apsɛ/ *nm inv* abscess; **~ dentaire** (dental) abscess; **crever** or **vider l'~** FIG to resolve a crisis.

abdication /abdikasjɔ̃/ *nf* LIT, FIG abdication.

abdiquer /abdike/ [1] *vi* [*souverain*] to abdicate (**en faveur de** in favour^{GB} of); (renoncer) to surrender (**devant qn/qch** to sb/sth).

abdomen /abdɔmɛn/ *nm* abdomen, stomach.

abdominal, **~e**, *mpl* **-aux** /abdɔminal, o/ **I** *adj* abdominal.

II abdominaux *nmpl* **1** ANAT abdominal muscles; **2** SPORT stomach exercises.

abeille /abɛj/ *nf* bee.

aberrant, **~e** /abɛʀɑ̃, ɑ̃t/ *adj* (absurde) absurd; (anormal) aberrant.

aberration /abɛʀasjɔ̃/ *nf* aberration.

abêtir /abetiʀ/ [3] **I** *vtr* to turn [sb] into a moron$^\circ$.

II s'abêtir *vpr* to become stupid.

abêtissant, **~e** /abetisɑ̃, ɑ̃t/ *adj* mindless.

abîme /abim/ *nm* **1** (précipice) abyss; **2** (écart) gulf (**entre** between); **un ~ nous sépare** there is a gulf between us; **3** (ruine) ruin; **toucher le fond de l'~** GÉN to hit rock bottom; (moralement) to be at one's lowest ebb.

abîmer /abime/ [1] **I** *vtr* to damage; **très abîmé** badly damaged; **il a eu le nez abîmé dans la bagarre** his nose was injured in the fight.

II s'abîmer *vpr* (se détériorer) [*objet*] to get damaged; [*fruit*] to spoil; **s'~ la vue** to ruin one's eyesight.

abject, **~e** /abʒɛkt/ *adj* despicable, abject; **de façon ~e** despicably.

abjection /abʒɛksjɔ̃/ *nf* abjectness.

abjurer /abʒyʀe/ [1] **I** *vtr* to abjure SOUT [*religion*].

II *vi* RELIG to recant.

ablatif /ablatif/ *nm* LING ablative.

ablation /ablasjɔ̃/ *nf* excision, removal; **subir une ~ de la rate** to have one's spleen removed.

abnégation /abnegasjɔ̃/ *nf* self-sacrifice; **faire preuve d'~** to act selflessly.

aboiement /abwamɑ̃/ *nm* (de chien) barking ¢.

abois /abwa/ *nmpl* **aux ~** LIT at bay; FIG in desperate straits.

abolir /abɔliʀ/ [3] *vtr* to abolish.

abolition /abɔlisjɔ̃/ *nf* abolition.

abominable /abɔminabl/ *adj* abominable.

abomination /abɔminasjɔ̃/ *nf* abomination.

abondamment /abɔ̃damɑ̃/ *adv* [*boire, illustrer*] copiously; [*pleuvoir*] heavily; [*évoquer, souligner*] at length; **l'événement fut ~ commenté** the event was commented on at considerable length; **~ documenté** [*livre*] extremely well-researched; **rincer ~ à l'eau** rinse thoroughly with water.

abondance /abɔ̃dɑ̃s/ *nf* **1** (de produits, renseignements) wealth; (de récolte, ressources) abundance; (de main-d'œuvre) abundant supply; **en ~** in abundance; **il y a ~ de** there's plenty of; **2** (aisance) affluence; **vivre dans l'~** to live in affluence.

IDIOMES **~ de biens ne nuit pas** PROV wealth does no harm.

abondant, **~e** /abɔ̃dɑ̃, ɑ̃t/ *adj* **1** (en quantité) [*nourriture, récolte*] plentiful; [*source*] LIT, FIG abundant; [*remarques, illustrations*] numerous; **une main-d'œuvre ~e** an abundant supply of labour; **un courrier ~** a large number of letters; **2** (riche) FML [*style*] rich; **être**

~ en to be rich in [*découvertes, surprises*]; **3** (fourni) [*chevelure*] thick; [*végétation*] lush.

abonder /abɔ̃de/ [1] *vi* **1** (être en quantité) [*fruits, produits, exemples*] to abound; [*gibier, poisson*] to be plentiful; **2** (avoir en quantité) **~ en** to be full of.

IDIOMES **~ dans le sens de qn** to agree wholeheartedly with sb.

abonné, **~e** /abɔne/ *nm,f* (lecteur, téléspectateur) subscriber; (voyageur, spectateur) season ticket holder; **~ au gaz** gas consumer.

abonnement /abɔnmɑ̃/ *nm* **1** (de périodique, télévision) subscription (**à** to); **souscrire un ~** to take out a subscription (**à** to); **2** (de transport, théâtre) (**carte d'**)**~** season ticket (**à** for); **3** (au téléphone) rental system charge; (au gaz, à l'électricité) standing charge.

abonner /abɔne/ [1] **I** *vtr* **~ qn à qch** (à un périodique) to take out a subscription to sth for sb; (au théâtre, concert) to buy sb a season ticket for sth.

II s'abonner *vpr* (à un périodique, la télévision) to subscribe (**à** to); (à un moyen de transport, au théâtre) to buy a season ticket (**à** for).

abord /abɔʀ/ **I** *nm* **1** (comportement) manner; **être d'un ~ aimable** to have a pleasant manner; **sous des ~s grincheux c'est un tendre** his gruff exterior hides a kind heart; **2** (approche) access; **être d'un ~ aisé** to be accessible; **à l'~ de** on approaching; **3** (contact) **au premier ~** at first sight.

II d'abord *loc adv* **1** (avant autre chose) first; **va d'~ te laver les mains** go and wash your hands first; **2** (contrairement à la suite) at first; **j'ai d'~ cru à une mauvaise plaisanterie** at first I thought it was a bad joke; **3** (primo) firstly, first; **4** (en priorité) first (of all); **les femmes et les enfants d'~** women and children first; **tout d'~** first of all; **5** (avant tout) for a start; **d'~ je refuse de lui parler** for a start I refuse to speak to him.

III abords *nmpl* area (*sg*) around; **aux ~s de qch** in the area around sth.

abordable /abɔʀdabl/ *adj* **1** [*produit, prix*] affordable; **à des prix très ~s** very reasonably priced; **2** [*texte*] accessible; **3** [*personne*] approachable.

abordage /abɔʀdaʒ/ *nm* (collision) collision; (attaque) boarding; **à l'~!** stand by to board!

aborder /abɔʀde/ [1] **I** *vtr* **1** (commencer à traiter) to tackle [*problème, sujet*]; **vous n'abordez pas le problème comme il faut** you're not going about the problem the right way; **2** (approcher) to approach [*personne, obstacle*]; **avant d'~ le virage** on the approach to the bend; **3** (entamer) to enter; **4** [*voyageur, navire*] to reach [*lieu, rive*].

II *vi* [*voyageur, navire*] to land.

aborigène /abɔʀiʒɛn/ **I** *adj* (d'Australie) Aboriginal.

II *nmf* (d'Australie) Aborigine.

abortif, -ive /abɔʀtif, iv/ *adj* abortifacient.

aboutir /abutiʀ/ [3] **I aboutir à** *vtr ind* **1** LIT **~ à** [*rue, escalier*] to lead to; [*personne*] to end up in [*village, place, rue*]; to end up at [*fontaine, église*]; **2** FIG **~ à** to lead to [*accord, résultat, rupture*].

II *vi* [*négociations, projet*] to succeed; **ne pas ~** not to come off.

aboutissants /abutisɑ̃/ *nmpl* **les tenants et les ~ de qch** the ins and outs of sth.

aboutissement /abutismɑ̃/ *nm* (de carrière, rêve, d'évolution, effort) culmination; (de conférence, parcours) outcome.

aboyer /abwaje/ [23] **I** $\circ$ *vtr* [*personne*] to bark [*ordres*] (**à** at); to shout [*injures*] (**à** at).

II *vi* [*chien*] to bark (**après, contre** at); [*personne*] to shout (**après, contre** at).

abracadabrant, **~e** /abʀakadabʀɑ̃, ɑ̃t/ *adj* bizarre.

abrasif, -ive /abʀazif, iv/ **I** *adj* abrasive.

II abrasive.

abrégé /abʀeʒe/ *nm* **1** (de texte) summary; **faire l'~ de** to summarize; **en ~** [*mot, expression*] in abbreviated form; [*texte, discours*] in summarized form; **2** (ouvrage) concise handbook.

abréger /abʀeʒe/ [15] *vtr* **1** (rendre court) to shorten [*mot, expression*]; to summarize [*texte, discours*]; ~ **'télévision' en 'télé'** to shorten 'television' to 'TV'; **version abrégée de qch** abridged version of sth; **2** (rendre bref) to cut short [*visite, carrière*]; **abrège**○**!** keep it short!; ~ **les souffrances de qn** to put an end to sb's suffering; **disons, pour ~, qu'ils se séparent** to cut GB ou make US a long story short, let's just say they are separating.

abreuver /abʀœve/ [1] **I** *vtr* to water [*animal*]; ~ **qn d'injures** to heap abuse on sb.
II s'abreuver *vpr* LITER [*animal*] to drink.

abreuvoir /abʀœvwaʀ/ *nm* (lieu) watering place.

abréviation /abʀevjɑsjɔ̃/ *nf* abbreviation.

abri /abʀi/ *nm* GÉN shelter; (pour voiture) carport; (cabane) shed; **se servir de qch comme ~** (en se mettant derrière) to shelter behind; (en se mettant dessous) to shelter under sth; **trouver un ~ provisoire sous/dans** to take shelter temporarily under/in; **à l'~** (à couvert) under cover; (en lieu sûr) safe; **être à l'~** to be sheltered; **être à l'~ de** (d'un mur) to be sheltered by; (du vent) to be sheltered from; **courir se mettre à l'~** to run for shelter; **personne n'est à l'~ d'un accident** accidents can happen to anybody; **personne n'est à l'~ d'une erreur** everybody makes mistakes; **à l'~ de l'humidité** in a dry place.
■ ~ **antiaérien** air raid shelter; ~ **antiatomique** nuclear shelter; ~ **souterrain** underground shelter ou bunker.

abricot /abʀiko/ ▶ **141** **I** *adj inv* (couleur) apricot.
II *nm* **1** (fruit) apricot; **confiture d'~s** apricot jam; **à l'~** [*yaourt, tarte*] apricot (*épith*); **2** (couleur) apricot.

abricotier /abʀikɔtje/ *nm* apricot tree.

abriter /abʀite/ [1] **I** *vtr* **1** [*bâtiment*] to shelter [*personnes, animaux*]; to house [*organisation, objets*]; to host [*activité, réunion*]; **2** [*pays*] to provide a base for [*activité*]; to provide a home for [*personnes*].
II s'abriter *vpr* (des intempéries) to take shelter (**de** from); (des balles, du feu) to take cover (**de** from); **s'~ derrière le secret professionnel** to shelter ou hide behind professional confidentiality.

abrogation /abʀɔgɑsjɔ̃/ *nf* repeal.

abroger /abʀɔʒe/ [13] *vtr* to repeal.

abrupt, ~e /abʀypt/ *adj* **1** [*colline, chemin*] steep; [*paroi*] sheer; **2** [*personne, ton*] abrupt.

abruptement /abʀyptəmɑ̃/ *adv* (en pente) steeply; (soudainement) suddenly; (de manière brusque) abruptly.

abruti, ~e /abʀyti/ **I** *adj* (idiot) stupid.
II *nm,f* OFFENSIVE moron○.

abrutir /abʀytiʀ/ [3] **I** *vtr* **1** (rendre passif) [*bruit*] to deafen; [*chaleur*] to wear [sb] out; [*alcool, médicament, fatigue*] to have a numbing effect on; [*coup*] to stun; **abruti par les médicaments** dopey with medicine; **2** (rendre idiot) [*alcool, tâche*] to stultify; **3** (accabler) ~ **qn de travail** to overwhelm sb with work.
II s'abrutir *vpr* **1** (devenir stupide) to become dull-witted; **2** (s'accabler) **s'~ de travail** to wear oneself out with work.

abrutissant, ~e /abʀytisɑ̃, ɑ̃t/ *adj* [*vacarme*] deafening; [*chaleur*] exhausting; [*tâche*] mind-numbing.

abscons, ~e /apskɔ̃, ɔ̃s/ *adj* FML abstruse.

absence /apsɑ̃s/ *nf* **1** (disparition temporaire, inexistence) absence; **'en cas d'~ adressez-vous à côté'** 'if out please enquire next door'; **on a téléphoné pendant votre ~** somebody phoned while you were out; **nous avons regretté votre ~ à la réunion** we were sorry (that) you didn't attend the meeting; **briller par son ~** HUM to be conspicuous by ou in US one's absence HUM; **2** (défaut) lack; **l'~ de pluie** the lack of rain; **3** (perte de mémoire) **il a des ~s** ou **des moments d'~** at times his mind goes blank.

absent, ~e /apsɑ̃, ɑ̃t/ *adj* **1** (éloigné longtemps) away (*jamais épith*) (**de** from); (éloigné brièvement) out (*jamais épith*) (**de** of); **2** (qui ne s'est pas présenté, ne participe pas) [*élève, employé*] absent (**de** from); **3** (inexistant) absent (**de** from); **4** (absorbé) absent-minded; **d'une voix ~e** absent-mindedly.

II *nm,f* absentee; **'~s excusés...'** 'apologies for absence...'; **Leconte était le grand ~ du tournoi** Leconte was notably absent from the tournament.
IDIOMES **les ~s ont toujours tort** PROV those who are absent always get the blame.

absentéisme /apsɑ̃teism/ *nm* absenteeism.

absenter: **s'absenter** /apsɑ̃te/ [1] *vpr* (longtemps) to go away; (brièvement) to go out; **ne vous absentez pas trop longtemps** don't be gone for long; **s'~ de** to go out of, to leave.

abside /apsid/ *nf* apse.

absolu, ~e /apsɔly/ **I** *adj* GÉN absolute; [*règle*] hard and fast; [*tempérament*] uncompromising; **sauf en cas d'~e nécessité** only if absolutely necessary; **défense ~e d'ouvrir cette porte** it is absolutely forbidden to open this door; **le secret le plus ~ sur** the utmost secrecy about; **un repos ~** complete rest.
II *nm* absolute.

absolument /apsɔlymɑ̃/ *adv* absolutely; **'êtes-vous d'accord?'—'~ pas!'** 'do you agree?'—'absolutely not!'; **tenir ~ à faire qch** to insist (up)on doing sth; **il veut ~ réussir** he's determined to succeed; **il faut ~ que tu ailles à Rome** you really must go to Rome.

absolution /apsɔlysjɔ̃/ *nf* RELIG absolution.

absolutisme /apsɔlytism/ *nm* absolutism.

absorbant, ~e /apsɔʀbɑ̃, ɑ̃t/ *adj* **1** [*substance*] absorbent; **à grand pouvoir ~** highly absorbent; **2** [*travail*] absorbing.

absorber /apsɔʀbe/ [1] *vtr* **1** (s'imbiber) [*matériau*] to absorb; **2** (consommer) to take [*nourriture, médicament*]; **3** (retenir) [*organisme, plante*] to absorb; **4** (nécessiter) to absorb [*argent*]; to occupy [*esprit*]; **absorbé par qch** absorbed in sth; **absorbé dans ses pensées** lost in one's thoughts; **5** (intégrer) [*entreprise*] to take over; [*parti, région, secteur*] to absorb.

absorption /apsɔʀpsjɔ̃/ *nf* **1** (de nourriture, médicament) taking; **l'~ de ce médicament est déconseillée aux femmes enceintes** pregnant women are advised not to take this medicine; **2** (de liquide, soleil, choc, d'oxygène) absorption; **3** (d'entreprise) takeover.

absoudre /apsudʀ/ [75] *vtr* RELIG to absolve.

abstenir: **s'abstenir** /apstəniʀ/ [36] *vpr* **1** (ne pas voter) to abstain; **2** (éviter) **s'~ de qch/de faire** to refrain from sth/from doing; **s'~ de tout commentaire** to refrain from any comment; **abstenez-vous de café** keep off coffee; **'pas sérieux s'~'** 'no time-wasters'.
IDIOMES **dans le doute, abstiens-toi** PROV when in doubt, do nowt PROV.

abstention /apstɑ̃sjɔ̃/ *nf* abstention; **il y a eu 10% d'~** 10% abstained.

abstinence /apstinɑ̃s/ *nf* abstinence.

abstraction /apstʀaksjɔ̃/ *nf* abstraction; **faire ~ de** to forget [*douleur, goût, différence*].

abstrait, ~e /apstʀɛ, ɛt/ *adj* abstract.
II *nm* **1** (opposé à concret) abstract; **dans l'~** in the abstract; **2** (art) abstract art.

absurde /apsyʀd/ **I** *adj* absurd.
II *nm* absurd; **démontrer qch par l'~** to prove sth by contradiction.

absurdité /apsyʀdite/ *nf* **1** (caractère) absurdity; **l'~ de ses déclarations** the absurdity of his/her statements; **2** (acte, parole) nonsense ¢; **tu dis des ~s** you're talking nonsense.

abus /aby/ *nm inv* abuse; **l'~ d'alcool** alcohol abuse; **'~ dangereux'** 'can seriously damage your health'; **il y a de l'~**○**!** that's a bit much○!
■ ~ **de confiance** breach of trust; ~ **de langage** misuse of language; ~ **de pouvoir** abuse of power.

abuser /abyze/ [1] **I** *vtr* LITER to fool; **se laisser ~** to be taken in.
II abuser de *vtr ind* **1** (faire un usage excessif de) ~ **de l'alcool** to drink to excess; ~ **des sucreries** to overindulge in sweet things; **2** (profiter de) ~ **de la situation** to exploit the situation; ~ **de la patience de qn** to take advantage of sb's patience; **je ne**

voudrais pas ~ (de votre gentillesse) I don't want to impose (on your kindness); ~ de sa force to abuse one's strength; 3 (violenter) ~ de qn to sexually abuse sb. **III** *vi* (exagérer) to go too far; **je suis patient mais il ne faut pas** ~ I may be patient but don't push me too far. IDIOMES **si je ne m'abuse** if I'm not mistaken.

abusif, -ive /abyzif, iv/ *adj* **1** (exagéré) excessive; **faire un usage** ~ **de qch** to use sth excessively; **2** (injuste) GÉN unfair; [*détention*] wrongful; **3** (impropre) improper; **emploi** ~ **d'un terme** improper use of a term; **donner une interprétation abusive de qch** to misrepresent sth; **4** (possessif) [*mère*] over-possessive.

abusivement /abyzivmɑ̃/ *adv* **1** (exagérément) excessively; **2** (injustement) wrongly; **3** (improprement) misguidedly; **terme employé** ~ term improperly used.

abyme /abim/ *nm* **structure** or **composition en** ~ (de pièce) play-within-a-play; (de tableau) image repeated to infinity; (de roman) 'Chinese boxes' structure.

acabit /akabi/ *nm* PEJ **de cet** or **du même** ~ of that sort; **les gens de ton** ~ people like you.

acacia /akasja/ *nm* **1** (d'Europe) **(faux)** ~ locust tree, false acacia; **miel d'**~ acacia honey; **2** (de régions chaudes) acacia.

académicien, -ienne /akademisjɛ̃, ɛn/ *nm,f* GÉN academician; (de l'Académie française) *member of the Académie française.*

académie /akademi/ *nf* **1** (école) school; ~ **de peinture** or **de dessin** art academy; **2** SCOL, UNIV ≈ local education authority GB, school district US.

académique /akademik/ *adj* **1** GÉN academic; (de l'Académie française) of the Académie française; **2** SCOL, UNIV ≈ of the local education authority GB ou school district US; **3** (en art) academic.

académisme /akademism/ *nm* academicism.

acajou /akaʒu/ **I** *adj inv* **1** ▶ 141 (couleur) mahogany; **2** (qui imite) **table** ~ imitation mahogany table. **II** *nm* (arbre) mahogany tree; (bois) mahogany; **table en** ~ mahogany table.

acariâtre /akaRjɑtR/ *adj* GÉN cantankerous.

acarien /akaRjɛ̃/ *nm* dust mite.

accablant, ~e /akablɑ̃, ɑ̃t/ *adj* [*chaleur, silence*] oppressive; [*tristesse*] overwhelming; [*fait*] damning.

accablement /akabləmɑ̃/ *nm* depression.

accabler /akable/ [1] *vtr* **1** (écraser) [*chaleur, mauvaise nouvelle*] to devastate; **être accablé de soucis** to be overwhelmed with worries; ~ **qn de** to overburden sb with [*impôts*]; ~ **qn d'injures** to heap insults on sb; **2** (condamner) [*témoignage, enquête, personne*] to condemn.

accalmie /akalmi/ *nf* (de temps) lull; FIG (de lutte, crise) lull; (d'activité) slack period.

accaparant, ~e /akapaRɑ̃, ɑ̃t/ *adj* very demanding.

accaparer /akapaRe/ [1] *vtr* to hoard [*marchandises*]; to corner [*marché*]; to monopolize [*personne, pouvoir*]; to preoccupy [*esprit*].

accédant, ~e /aksedɑ̃, ɑ̃t/ *nm,f* ~ **à la propriété** home-buyer.

accéder /aksede/ [14] *vtr ind* **1** (atteindre) ~ **à** to reach [*lieu*]; **2** (obtenir) ~ **à** to achieve [*gloire*] to obtain [*poste*]; to reach [*fonctions*]; ~ **à la propriété** to become a home-owner; ~ **au pouvoir** to come to power; **3** FML (satisfaire à) ~ **à** to grant [*prière*].

accélérateur, -trice /akseleRatœR, tRis/ *nm* AUT accelerator; **appuyer sur l'**~ to step on the accelerator; **donner un coup d'**~ **à qch** FIG to give sth a boost. ■ ~ **de particules** particle accelerator.

accélération /akseleRasjɔ̃/ *nf* (de vitesse) acceleration (de of); (de consommation) sharp increase (de in).

accéléré, ~e /akseleRe/ *adj* accelerated; **à un rythme** ~ at an increasingly fast rate; **stage de formation** ~**e** intensive course.

accélérer /akseleRe/ [14] **I** *vtr* (hâter) to speed up [*rythme, mouvement*]; to accelerate [*processus, réaction*]; ~ **le pas** to quicken one's step.

II *vi* **1** [*conducteur*] to accelerate; **accélère!** speed up!; **2** (se dépêcher)○ FIG to get a move on○.

III s'accélérer *vpr* **1** (aller plus vite) [*pouls, mouvement*] to quicken; **les événements s'accélèrent** the pace of events is quickening; **2** (s'intensifier) [*phénomène, tendance*] to accelerate.

accent /aksɑ̃/ *nm* **1** (façon de parler) accent; **avoir l'**~ **bordelais** to have a Bordeaux accent; **2** (sur une lettre) accent; **prendre un** ~ [*mot, lettre*] to have an accent; **3** (sur une syllabe) ~ **tonique** stress; ~ **de hauteur** pitch; **mettre l'**~ **sur qch** FIG to put the emphasis on sth; **4** (nuance, note) overtone; ~ **de sincérité** hint of sincerity; ~ **de vérité** ring of truth.

accentuation /aksɑ̃tɥasjɔ̃/ *nf* **1** (de crise) escalation; (d'inégalités) heightening; (de phénomène) worsening; (de tendance) increase; **2** (de syllabe) stress; (en poésie) accentuation; **3** (de lettres) accents (*pl*).

accentuer /aksɑ̃tɥe/ [1] **I** *vtr* **1** (rendre plus évident) [*situation*] to accentuate [*inégalités*]; to heighten [*tensions*]; to increase [*tendance*]; **2** (tenter de faire ressortir) [*personne*] to highlight [*trait de caractère*]; to emphasize [*aspect*]; **3** (rendre tonique) to stress; (en poésie) to accentuate [*syllabe*]; **4** (écrire) to put an accent on [*lettre*]; **lettre accentuée** accented letter. **II s'accentuer** *vpr* to become more marked.

acceptable /akseptabl/ *adj* **1** (tolérable) [*seuil, norme, condition*] acceptable; **rendre qch** ~ to make sth acceptable (**à** to); **2** (passable) [*travail, qualité*] passable; [*résultat*] satisfactory.

acceptation /akseptasjɔ̃/ *nf* acceptance; **sous réserve d'**~ subject to acceptance.

accepter /aksepte/ [1] *vtr* to accept [*invitation, personne, défi, excuse*]; to agree to [*condition, contrat*]; ~ **qch de qn** to accept sth from sb; ~ **de faire qch** to agree to do sth; **s'il te plaît, accepte!** please say yes!; **faire** ~ **qch** to get sth accepted.

acception /aksepsjɔ̃/ *nf* sense; **dans toute l'**~ **du terme** or **mot** in every sense of the word.

accès /akse/ *nm inv* **1** (moyen, possibilité d'atteindre) access; **moyens d'**~ means of access; **d'un** ~ **facile** easy to get to; [*personne*] approachable/unapproachable; **l'**~ **au village** (possibilité d'atteindre) access to the village; (moyen d'atteindre) the way into the village; **cela donne** ~ **à** (mener) it leads to; **toutes les voies d'**~ **sont barrées** (routes) all approach roads are closed off; '~ **aux quais**' 'to the trains'; **2** (moyen d'entrer) **l'**~ **à** access to; **les** ~ **du bâtiment** the entrances to the building; **les** ~ **de la ville** the approach roads to the town; **3** (droit d'entrée) **ne pas avoir** ~ **à** not to be admitted to; **interdire l'**~ **aux enfants** not to admit children; '~ **interdit**' 'no entry'; '~ **interdit aux chiens**' 'no dogs (allowed)'; **4** (possibilité d'obtenir, utiliser) access; **avoir** ~ **à** to have access to; **5** (possibilité de participer à) **l'**~ **à** access to [*profession, cours*]; admission to [*club, école*]; **6** (possibilité de comprendre) **d'un** ~ **facile** accessible; **d'un** ~ **difficile** not very accessible; **7** (crise) ~ **de colère** fit of anger; ~ **de fièvre** bout of fever; **par** ~ by fits and starts; **8** ORDINAT access.

accessible /aksesibl/ *adj* **1** [*lieu, ouvrage*] accessible (**à** to); **langage** ~ **à tous** a language which can be understood by everyone; **2** [*emploi*] ~ **à** open to; **3** [*prix, tarif*] affordable (**à qn** to sb); **4** (qu'on peut approcher) [*personne*] approachable.

accession /aksesjɔ̃/ *nf* ~ **à** accession to [*trône, pouvoir*]; attainment of [*indépendance*]; ~ **à la propriété** home-buying.

accessit /aksesit/ *nm* honourable GB mention.

accessoire /akseswaR/ **I** *adj* [*problème*] incidental. **II** *nm* **1** (d'auto, de vêtement) accessory; (d'appareil) attachment; ~**s de salle de bains** bathroom accessories; ~**s de toilette** toilet requisites; **2** CIN, THÉÂT ~**s** props. IDIOMES **ranger au magasin des** ~**s** to shelve.

accessoirement /akseswaRmɑ̃/ *adv* (en plus) incidentally, as it happens; (le cas échéant) if desired.

accessoiriste /akseswaRist/ ▶ 374 *nmf* props man/woman.

accident /aksidɑ̃/ *nm* **1** (dommage) accident; ~ **grave** serious accident; **l'~ a fait deux morts** two died as a result of the accident; **un ~ est si vite arrivé!** accidents can easily happen!; **il y a 10 000 morts par ~ chaque année** 10,000 people die in accidents every year; **2** (problème) hitch; (événement inhabituel) one off○; HUM accident; ~ **de parcours**○ hitch; HUM accident; **une découverte faite par ~** (par hasard) a chance discovery; **3** MÉD accident; ~ **cardiaque** cardiac event; **4** (inégalité) ~ **de terrain** irregularity in the landscape, accident SPÉC.
■ ~ **d'avion** plane crash; ~ **corporel** accident involving injury; ~ **ferroviaire** rail accident; ~ **de montagne** climbing accident; ~ **de la route** road accident; ~ **du travail** industrial accident.

accidenté, ~**e** /aksidɑ̃te/ **I** *adj* **1** [*personne*] injured; [*véhicule*] involved in an accident (*après n*); **2** [*chemin, terrain*] uneven.
II *nm,f* accident victim; **les ~s de la route** road accident victims; **les ~s du travail** people injured at work.

accidentel, -elle /aksidɑ̃tɛl/ *adj* accidental.

accidentellement /aksidɑ̃tɛlmɑ̃/ *adv* **1** (dans un accident) accidentally; **2** (par hasard) by accident.

accidenter /aksidɑ̃te/ [1] *vtr* to bump [*véhicule*].

acclamation /aklamasjɔ̃/ *nf* cheering ¢; **sous les ~s de** to the cheering of.

acclamer /aklame/ [1] *vtr* to cheer, to acclaim.

acclimater /aklimate/ [1] **I** *vtr* to acclimatize.
II s'acclimater *vpr* [*plante, animal*] to become acclimatized; [*personne*] to adapt.

accointances /akwɛ̃tɑ̃s/ *nfpl* contacts.

accolade /akɔlad/ *nf* **1** (embrassade) embrace; **donner l'~ à qn** to embrace sb; **2** (signe) brace.

accoler /akɔle/ [1] *vtr* ~ **une étiquette à** to attach a label to.

accommodant, ~**e** /akɔmɔdɑ̃, ɑ̃t/ *adj* [*personne*] accommodating.

accommoder /akɔmɔde/ [1] **I** *vtr* **1** to prepare [*aliment, plat*]; **l'art d'~ les restes** the art of using up leftovers; **2** (adapter) to adapt.
II *vi* [*œil*] to focus.
III s'accommoder *vpr* **s'~ de qch** (positif) to make the best of sth; (plus résigné) to put up with sth; **s'~ à** to adapt to.

accompagnateur, -trice /akɔ̃paɲatœʀ, tʀis/ ▶ 374] *nm,f* **1** MUS accompanist; **2** (d'enfants) accompanying adult; (de groupe touristique) courier; **vingt athlètes et ~s** twenty athletes and accompanying personnel.

accompagnement /akɔ̃paɲmɑ̃/ *nm* **1** MUS accompaniment; **sans ~** unaccompanied; ~ **musical** musical arrangement; **2** CULIN accompaniment; **3** (de malade) caring (**de** for); (de touristes) accompanying; **mesures d'~** attendant measures.

accompagner /akɔ̃paɲe/ [1] **I** *vtr* **1** (se déplacer avec) to accompany; (conduire) to take (**à** to); **tu m'accompagnes à la gare?** will you come to the station with me?; **je vais vous (y) ~** (en voiture) I'll take you (there); (à pied) I'll come with you; ~ **un enfant à l'école** to take a child to school; **20% de réduction à la personne qui vous accompagne** 20 % reduction for any person travelling^GB with you; **ces personnes vous accompagnent?** are these people with you?; **accompagné/non accompagné** [*bagage, enfant*] accompanied/unaccompanied; **2** (aller de pair avec) to accompany; **une cassette accompagne le livre** there's a cassette with the book; **CV accompagné de deux photos** CV ou resumé US together with two photographs; **l'inflation et les problèmes qui l'accompagnent** inflation and its attendant problems; **3** (soutenir) to back; **4** MUS to accompany (**à** on); **5** (être servi avec) **vin pour ~ un plat** wine to accompany a dish.
II s'accompagner *vpr* MUS to accompany oneself (**à** on); (s'associer à) to be accompanied (**de** by).

accomplir /akɔ̃pliʀ/ [3] **I** *vtr* (s'acquitter de) to accomplish [*tâche, mission*]; to fulfil^GB [*obligation*]; to do

[*service militaire*]; to serve [*peine de prison*]; ~ **de grandes choses** to achieve great things.
II s'accomplir *vpr* [*vœu, prévisions*] to be fulfilled^GB.

accomplissement /akɔ̃plismɑ̃/ *nm* (d'activité, de mission) accomplishment; (réalisation) achievement.

accord /akɔʀ/ *nm* **1** (consentement) agreement (**à** to); **donner son ~ à qch** to agree to sth; **donner son ~ à qn pour faire** to authorize sb to do; **d'un commun ~** by mutual agreement; **2** (pacte) agreement (**portant sur** on); (non formel) understanding; ~ **de cessez-le-feu** ceasefire agreement; **conclure un ~** to enter into an agreement; ~**s de commerce** trade agreements; **3** (avis partagé, entente) agreement (**sur** on); **en** or **d'~ avec qn** in agreement with sb; **être d'~ (que)** to agree (that); **je ne suis pas d'~ avec toi là-dessus** I disagree with you on this; **Pierre est d'~ pour faire** Pierre has agreed to do; **je suis/je ne suis pas d'~ pour payer** I am/I am not willing to pay; **je ne suis pas d'~ pour que nous fassions** I am not in favour^GB of our doing; **se mettre** or **tomber d'~** to come to an agreement; **mettre tout le monde d'~** (du même avis) to bring everybody round^GB to the same way of thinking; (mettre fin aux querelles) to put an end to the argument; **tu es d'~ pour la plage?** are you on for the beach○?; **'on signe?'—'d'~'**○ 'shall we sign?'—'OK○, all right'; **4** (entre personnes, couleurs, styles) harmony; **être en ~ avec** (avec écrit, tradition, promesse) to be in keeping ou consistent with; **agir en ~ avec le règlement** to act in accordance with the rules; **5** LING agreement; **6** MUS (notes) chord.
■ ~ **à l'amiable** informal agreement; ~ **de gré à gré** mutual agreement; ~ **de principe** agreement in principle; ~ **salarial** wage settlement.

accordéon /akɔʀdeɔ̃/ ▶ 392] *nm* accordion; **en** ~ FIG [*chaussettes*] wrinkled; [*voiture*] wrecked; **plier qch en** ~ to fold sth into pleats; **plié en** ~ folded into a concertina.
II (-)accordéon (*in compounds*) **porte** ~ folding door.

accordéoniste /akɔʀdeɔnist/ ▶ 374], 392] *nmf* accordion-player.

accorder /akɔʀde/ [1] **I** *vtr* **1** (octroyer) ~ **qch à qn** to grant sth to sb, to grant sb sth [*faveur, prêt, entretien, permission, droit*]; to give ou award sth to sb, to give ou award sth [*indemnité, bourse*]; to give sth to sb, to give sb sth [*réduction, chance, interview*]; ~ **une aide financière à qn** to give sb financial assistance; **peux-tu m'~ quelques instants?** can you spare me a few moments?; ~ **sa confiance à qn** to put one's trust in sb; **2** (prêter) to attach [*importance, valeur*] (**à** to); to pay [*attention*]; **3** (concéder) ~ **à qn que** to admit to sb that; **il n'a pas entièrement tort, je te l'accorde** he's not entirely wrong, I'll give you that; **4** (harmoniser) to match [*coloris*] (**avec** with); **5** MUS to tune [*instrument*]; **6** LING to make [sth] agree [*mot*] (**avec** with).
II s'accorder *vpr* **1** (s'octroyer) to give oneself [*repos, congé*]; (être ou se mettre d'accord) to agree (**sur** about, on); **ils s'accordent à dire** (tous les deux) they both say; (eux tous) they all say; **3** (s'entendre) [*personnes*] to get on together; **4** (s'harmoniser) [*couleurs*] to go (together) well; **leurs caractères s'accordent** they are well matched; **5** [*adjectif, verbe*] to agree (**avec** with); **6** MUS to tune up.

accordeur /akɔʀdœʀ/ ▶ 374] *nm* tuner.

accostage /akɔstaʒ/ *nm* docking.

accoster /akɔste/ [1] **I** *vtr* **1** NAUT to come alongside [*quai, navire*]; **2** (aborder) to accost [*personne*].
II *vi* NAUT to dock.

accotement /akɔtmɑ̃/ *nm* verge; ~ **meuble** or **non stabilisé** soft verge GB, soft shoulder.

accouchement /akuʃmɑ̃/ *nm* delivery; ~ **à terme/ avant terme** or **prématuré** full-term/premature birth; **préparation à l'~** preparation for birth.
■ ~ **provoqué** induced delivery; ~ **sans douleur** natural childbirth; ~ **par le siège** breech birth.

accoucher /akuʃe/ [1] **I** *vtr* to deliver.

II accoucher de *vtr ind* ~ **de** to give birth to [*enfant*]; (produire)○ ~ **de** to produce [*œuvre, idée*].
III *vi* to give birth.

accoucheur /akuʃœʀ/ ▶374 *nm* **médecin** ~ obstetrician.

accoucheuse /akuʃøz/ ▶374 *nf* midwife.

accouder: s'accouder /akude/ [1] *vpr* to lean on one's elbows (**à, sur** on).

accoudoir /akudwaʀ/ *nm* arm-rest.

accouplement /akupləmã/ *nm* **1** (pour reproduction) mating; **2** TECH coupling.

accoupler /akuple/ [1] **I** *vtr* **1** (pour reproduction) to mate (**à** with); **2** TECH to couple.
II s'accoupler *vpr* to mate.

accourir /akuʀiʀ/ [26] *vi* to run up; ~ **au secours de qn/pour faire** to rush to sb's aid/to do; **les candidats sont accourus de toute la région** candidates came running from all over the area.

accoutrement /akutʀəmã/ *nm* PEJ get-up○.

accoutrer /akutʀe/ [1] **I** *vtr* PEJ ~ **qn de qch** to rig sb out in sth.
II s'accoutrer *vpr* to get oneself up (**de** in); **il s'accoutre vraiment n'importe comment!** he dresses any old how!

accoutumance /akutymãs/ *nf* **1** GÉN familiarization; **une période d'**~ an acclimatization period; **2** (à un médicament) addiction (**à** to).

accoutumé, ~**e** /akutyme/ **I** *adj* (habituel) customary.
II comme à l'accoutumée *loc adv* as usual.

accoutumer /akutyme/ [1] **I** *vtr* FML to accustom.
II s'accoutumer *vpr* **s'**~ **à** (**faire**) **qch** to grow accustomed to (doing) sth; **être accoutumé à** (**faire**) **qch** to be used ou accustomed to (doing) sth.

accrédité, ~**e** /akʀedite/ *adj* [*représentant*] accredited (**auprès de** to); [*fournisseur*] authorized.

accréditer /akʀedite/ [1] *vtr* **1** (rendre crédible) to give credence to [*opinion, rumeur*]; to lend weight to [*idée, théorie*]; **2** (faire reconnaître) to accredit [*ambassade*].

accroc /akʀo/ *nm* (déchirure) tear (**à** in); **faire un** ~ **à qch** to tear sth; **sans** ~(**s**) FIG without a hitch.

accrochage /akʀoʃaʒ/ *nm* (affrontement) clash (**entre** between); (légère collision) bump (**avec** with).

accroche-cœur, *pl* ~**s** /akʀoʃkœʀ/ *nm* kiss curl.

accrocher /akʀoʃe/ [1] **I** *vtr* **1** (suspendre) to hang (**à** from); **2** (attacher) to hook [sth] on (**à** to); **la chaîne était mal accrochée** the chain wasn't hooked on properly; **3** (faire un accroc à) to catch [*bas, pull*] (**à** on); **4** (heurter) to bump into; **5** (attirer) to catch [*regard, attention*].
II *vi* **1** (coincer) [*fermeture*] to stick; **2** (attirer) [*titre, image, publicité*] to catch on.
III s'accrocher *vpr* **1** (se suspendre) LIT (à une corniche) to hang on; (à un poteau) to cling (on) (**à** to); **accroche-toi à la branche** hang on to the branch; **2** (s'attacher) LIT, FIG [*personne*] to cling (**à** to); **s'**~ **au bras de qn** to cling to sb's arm; **l'hameçon s'est accroché à ma veste** the hook got caught on my jacket; **3**○ (tenir bon) **s'**~ **pour faire** to try hard to do; **accroche-toi!** (sur une moto) hang on to your hat!; (avant histoire, film) brace yourself!; **4** (se disputer) **s'**~ **avec qn** to have a brush with sb.
IDIOMES **avoir le cœur** or **l'estomac bien accroché** to have a strong stomach.

accrocheur, -**euse** /akʀoʃœʀ, øz/ *adj* (attrayant) [*chanson, air*] catchy; [*image, titre*] eye-catching.

accroissement /akʀwasmã/ *nm* growth, increase.

accroître /akʀwatʀ/ [72] *vtr*, **s'accroître** *vpr* to increase.

accroupi, ~**e** /akʀupi/ *adj* GÉN squatting (down); (pour se cacher) crouching.

accroupir: s'accroupir /akʀupiʀ/ [3] *vpr* GÉN to squat (down); (pour se cacher) to crouch (down).

accru, ~**e** /akʀy/ *pp* ▶ **accroître**.

accueil /akœj/ *nm* (manière) welcome, reception; ~

froid cool reception; **il a reçu le meilleur** ~ he received the warmest of welcomes; (service) reception.

accueillant, ~**e** /akœjã, ãt/ *adj* **1** [*personne*] hospitable ou welcoming (**à l'égard de** to); **2** [*maison*] homely GB, homey US; [*ville, campagne*] friendly, welcoming; [*appartement, chambre*] inviting.

accueillir /akœjiʀ/ [27] *vtr* **1** (souhaiter la bienvenue) to welcome; **2** (recevoir) to receive [*personne, livre, décision*]; **bien/mal** ~ **qn/qch** to give sb/sth a good/bad reception; **j'ai été bien accueilli** (à l'arrivée) I was given a warm welcome; (pendant le séjour) I was made to feel very welcome; **ils ont été accueillis par des acclamations** they were greeted with cheers; **3** (contenir) to accommodate [*personnes*]; **4** (prendre en charge) [*organisme, hôpital*] to cater for.

acculer /akyle/ [1] *vtr* (dans une situation) ~ **qn à** (**faire**) **qch** to force sb into (doing) sth; ~ **qn à la ruine/au désespoir** to drive sb to ruin/to despair.

accumulateur /akymylatœʀ/ *nm* accumulator GB, storage battery; ~ **de chaleur** storage heater; ~ **de froid** freeze pack.

accumulation /akymylasjõ/ *nf* **1** (action, résultat) accumulation; **une** ~ **de preuves** a mass of evidence; **2** (emmagasinage) storage; **radiateur à** ~ storage heater.

accumuler /akymyle/ [1] **I** *vtr* (entasser) store (up) [*objets*]; (amasser) to accumulate [*biens, capital*]; (répéter) to make a succession of [*erreurs*]; to have a string of [*succès*]; (emmagasiner) to store (up) [*énergie, chaleur*].
II s'accumuler *vpr* (s'entasser) [*neige, commandes*] to pile up; (s'accroître) [*stocks, dettes*] to accrue.

accusateur, -**trice** /akyzatœʀ, tʀis/ **I** *adj* [*silence, doigt*] accusing (*épith*); [*présence, discours*] accusatory.
II *nm,f* accuser; ~ **public** HIST public prosecutor.

accusatif /akyzatif/ *nm* LING accusative.

accusation /akyzasjõ/ *nf* **1** (reproche grave) accusation; JUR (formulation) charge; **mettre qn en** ~ JUR to indict sb; **2** (ministère public) **l'**~ the prosecution.

accusé, ~**e** /akyze/ **I** *adj* (accentué) [*traits*] strong; [*ride*] deep; [*relief*] marked.
II *nm,f* defendant; **les** ~**s** the accused.
■ ~ **de réception** acknowledgment of receipt.

accuser /akyze/ [1] **I** *vtr* **1** [*plaignant*] to accuse (**de** of); [*juge*] to charge (**de** with); **accusé du meurtre de sa femme** (par le plaignant, un témoin) accused of murdering his wife; (à l'issue du procès) charged with murdering his wife; **2** (rendre coupable) [*personne*] to accuse [*personne*] (**de** (faire) of (doing)); to blame [*sort*]; [*fait*] to point to [*personne*]; **accusé d'espionnage** accused of spying; **les photos qui l'accusent** the incriminating photos; ~ **qn/qch de tous les maux** to put all the blame on sb/sth; **3** (rendre évident) to show [*baisse, déficit*]; ~ **une hausse** to show an increase; **4** (confirmer) ~ **réception** to acknowledge receipt (**de** of).
II s'accuser *vpr* **1** (soi-même) to take the blame (**de qch** for sth; **d'avoir fait** for doing); **2** (l'un l'autre) to accuse each other (**de** (faire) of (doing)); **3** (s'aggraver) to become more marked.
IDIOMES ~ **le coup** to be visibly shaken.

acerbe /asɛʀb/ *adj* acerbic.

acéré, ~**e** /aseʀe/ *adj* LIT [*objet*] sharp.

acétique /asetik/ *adj* acetic.

achalandé, ~**e** /aʃalãde/ *adj* CONTROV (approvisionné) **bien/mal** ~ well-/poorly-stocked.

acharné, ~**e** /aʃaʀne/ **I** *pp* ▶ **acharner**.
II *pp adj* [*partisan*] passionate; [*fumeur, séducteur*] incorrigible; [*travail*] unremitting; [*lutte, discussion*] fierce; **c'est un travailleur** ~ he works relentlessly.

acharnement /aʃaʀnəmã/ *nm* (énergie) furious energy; **l'**~ **de qn à faire** sb's determination to do; **son** ~ **au travail** the fact that he/she works so relentlessly; **lutter avec** ~ to fight tooth and nail.

acharner: s'acharner /aʃaʀne/ [1] *vpr* **1** (s'obstiner) to persevere; **s'**~ **à faire** to try desperately to do; **à force de s'**~ by persevering; **s'**~ **contre** to fight against [*projet*]; **2** (continuer des violences) **s'**~ **sur** [*personne, animal*] to keep going at [*victime, proie*]; FIG [*personne*] to hound [*enfant, collaborateur*]; **la fatalité s'acharne sur eux** they're dogged by bad luck.

achat /aʃa/ *nm* **1** (action) **l'~ de qch** buying sth, the purchase of sth; **un ~** a purchase; **c'est plus cher à l'~** it's more expensive to buy; **25% à l'~** 25% of the total at the time of purchase; **l'~ sur catalogue** buying by mail order; **faire des ~s** to do some shopping; **l'~ par téléphone** telephone shopping; **2** (objet acheté) purchase.

acheminement /aʃ(ə)minmɑ̃/ *nm* **1** (de personnes, vivres) transportation (**vers** to); **des retards dans l'~ du courrier** postal delays; **2** FIG **l'~ du pays vers la ruine** the country's march toward(s) ruin.

acheminer /aʃ(ə)mine/ [1] **I** *vtr* (transporter) to transport [*personne, vivres*] (**vers** to); **~ le courrier** to handle the mail.
II s'acheminer *vpr* **1** [*personne, troupe*] to make one's way (**vers** to ou toward(s)); **2** FIG **s'~ vers** [*négociations*] to move toward(s); [*pays, économie*] (aboutissement fâcheux) to head for ou toward(s); (aboutissement positif) to move toward(s).

acheter /aʃte/ [18] **I** *vtr* **1** to buy; **~ qch sur catalogue** to buy sth from a catalogueᴳᴮ; **~ qch à qn** (pour lui) to buy sth for sb; (chez lui) to buy sth from sb; **~ pour 20 francs de qch** to buy 20 francs worth of sth; **~ qch 20 francs** to buy sth for 20 francs; **~ français** to buy French products; **2** (soudoyer) to buy.
II s'acheter *vpr* **1** (pour soi) **s'~ qch** to buy oneself sth; **2** (être disponible à l'achat) **cela s'achète où?** where can you get it?

acheteur, -euse /aʃtœʀ, øz/ **I** *adj* [*pays*] importing.
II *nm,f* **1** (client) buyer, purchaser; **je vends ma voiture, es-tu ~?** I'm selling my car, would you like to buy it?; **à ce prix-là je ne suis pas ~** at that price, I'm not interested; **2 ▶374** (professionnel) buyer.

achevé, -e /aʃve/ *adj* LITER [*œuvre, technique*] accomplished; [*exemple, forme, modèle*] perfect.

achèvement /aʃɛvmɑ̃/ *nm* (de travaux, projet, roman) completion; (de discussions) conclusion.

achever /aʃve/ [16] **I** *vtr* **1** (terminer) to finish [*travail*]; to conclude [*discussions*]; to complete [*projet, visite, enquête, service militaire*]; to end [*vie*]; **~ de faire** to finish doing; **2** (réussir) **ta démonstration a achevé de me convaincre** the proof you gave me finally convinced me; **3** (tuer) to destroy [*animal*]; to finish off [*personne*]; **4** (épuiser) [*personne, effort*] to wear [sb] out, to finishᴼ; **5**ᴼ (terrasser) [*scandale, ruine*] to finish [sb] off.
II s'achever *vpr* to end (**par** with; **sur** on); **le jour s'achève** the day is drawing to a close.

achoppement /aʃɔpmɑ̃/ *nm* **pierre d'~** stumbling block.

acide /asid/ **I** *adj* **1** (pas assez sucré) [*goût*] acid, sour; (agréablement) [*goût*] sharp; (comme propriété naturelle) [*aliment*] acidic; **2** [*odeur*] acrid; **3** CHIMIE acid, acidic.
II *nm* **1** CHIMIE acid; **~ gras** fatty acid; **2**ᴼ (drogue) acidᴼ.
■ **~ aminé** amino acid.

acidité /asidite/ *nf* (désagréable) GÉN acidity; (agréable) tartness, sharpness; CHIMIE acidity.

acidulé, -e /asidyle/ *adj* **1** [*goût*] slightly acid; **2** [*parfum*] tangy; [*jaune, vert*] acid.

acier /asje/ **I ▶141** *adj inv* steel(y).
II *nm* **1** (alliage) steel; **d'~** [*cuve*] steel (*épith*); [*muscle, nerf*] of steel; **avoir un moral d'~** to be made of stern stuff; **2** (industrie) steel industry.

aciérie /asjeʀi/ *nf* steelworks (+ *v sg* ou *pl*).

acné /akne/ *nf* acne; **~ juvénile** teenage acne.

acolyte /akɔlit/ *nmf* (complice) PEJ henchman, acolyte.

acompte /akɔ̃t/ *nm* (premier versement) down payment; (arrhes) deposit; (versement partiel) part payment; **~ sur salaire** advance on salary.
■ **~ provisionnel** (pour impôt) ≈ first instalmentᴳᴮ.

acoquiner: **s'acoquiner** /akɔkine/ [1] *vpr* **s'~ avec qn** to get thickᴼ with sb.

Açores /asɔʀ/ **▶305** *nprfpl* **les ~** the Azores.

à-côté , *pl* **~s** /akote/ *nm* **1** (avantages) perk; (gains) **se**

faire de petits ~s to make a bit on the sideᴼ; **2** (dépenses) extra.

à-coup , *pl* **~s** /aku/ *nm* (secousse) jolt; **les ~s du moteur** the coughs and splutters of the engine; **par ~s** LIT, FIG by ou in fits and starts.

acoustique /akustik/ **I** *adj* acoustic.
II *nf* PHYS acoustics (+ *v sg*); (d'un lieu) acoustics (*pl*).

acquéreur /akeʀœʀ/ *nm* buyer, purchaser; **elle est ~** she's interested; **se porter ~** to state one's intention to buy; **se rendre ~ de** to purchase.

acquérir /akeʀiʀ/ [35] **I** *vtr* **1** (devenir propriétaire de) to acquire; (en achetant) to purchase; **2** (arriver à avoir) to acquire; **~ une formation** to undergo training; **~ la certitude que** to become convinced that; **~ de la valeur** to gain in value; **il est acquis à notre cause** we have his support; **il est acquis que** it is accepted that.
II s'acquérir *vpr* **1** (s'obtenir) **s'~ facilement** to be easy to acquire; **2** (s'apprendre) **quelque chose qui s'acquiert** something you acquire; **l'expérience s'acquiert avec l'âge** experience comes with age.

acquiescement /akjɛsmɑ̃/ FML *nm* **donner son ~ à** to acquiesce to.

acquiescer /akjese/ [12] *vi* to acquiesce; **~ d'un signe de tête** to nod in agreement; **et sa fille d'~** and the daughter agrees.

acquis, ~e /aki, iz/ **I** *pp* ▶ **acquérir**.
II *pp adj* **1** (obtenu, en psychologie) acquired; **2** (reconnu) [*principe, droit*] accepted, established; **les avantages ~** the gains; **tenir qch pour ~** to take sth for granted.
III *nm inv* **1** (connaissances) knowledge; **2** (avantage obtenu) **~ syndicaux** union gains; **~ sociaux** social benefits; **c'est un ~** that is one thing gained; **3** (en psychologie) **l'~** acquired knowledge.
IDIOMES **bien mal ~ ne profite jamais** PROV ill-gotten gains never prosper.

acquisition /akizisjɔ̃/ *nf* **1** (achat) purchase; **prix d'~** purchase price; **2** ORDINAT data capture; **3** (de musée, bibliothèque) acquisition; **4** (processus) acquisition.

acquit /aki/ *nm* COMM receipt; **pour ~** received.
IDIOMES **par ~ de conscience** to put one's mind at rest.

acquittement /akitmɑ̃/ *nm* JUR acquittal.

acquitter /akite/ [1] **I** *vtr* **1** JUR to acquit [*personne*]; **faire ~ qn** to get sb acquitted; **2** (payer) to pay.
II s'acquitter *vpr* **s'~ de son devoir** to discharge one's duty; **s'~ d'une dette** LIT to pay off a debt; FIG to repay a debt of gratitude.

âcre /akʀ/ *adj* [*goût, fruit*] sharp; [*fumée, odeur*] acrid.

acrimonie /akʀimɔni/ *nf* LITER acrimony LITTÉR.

acrobate /akʀɔbat/ **▶374** *nmf* LIT, FIG acrobat.

acrobatie /akʀɔbasi/ *nf* **1** (mouvement) **faire des ~s** SPORT to do ou perform acrobatics; FIG to jump through all sorts of hoops. **2** (activité) **l'~** acrobatics (+ *v sg*); **~ aérienne** aerobatics (+ *v sg*).

acronyme /akʀɔnim/ *nm* acronym.

acrylique /akʀilik/ *adj, nm* acrylic.

acte /akt/ **I** *nm* **1** (action) act; **mes/tes ~s** my/your actions; **être libre de ses ~s** to do as one wishes; **faire ~ de candidature** to put oneself forward as a candidate; **faire ~ de présence** to put in an appearance; **2** JUR deed; **j'en prends ~** I'll bear it in mind; **3** THÉÂT act; **4** PHILOS actual.
II actes *nmpl* (de congrès, réunion) proceedings; RELIG acts.
■ **~ d'accusation** bill of indictment; **~ de décès** death certificate; **~ de foi** act of faith; **~ gratuit** gratuitous act; **~ manqué** Freudian slip; **~ de mariage** marriage certificate; **~ de naissance** birth certificate; **~ sexuel** sexual act; **~ de vente** bill of sale; **l'Acte unique européen** Single European Act.

acteur, -trice /aktœʀ, tʀis/ *nm,f* **1** **▶374** CIN, THÉÂT actor/actress; **~ de cinéma/théâtre** film/stage actor; **2** (participant) **~s de la scène politique** actors on the political stage; **les ~s d'un drame** the protagonists of a tragedy; **3** (agent) agent (**de** of).

actif, -ive /aktif, iv/ I *adj* **1** (occupé) active; **les femmes actives** working women; **la vie active** working life; **2** (pas passif) [*participation*] active; **un rôle ~ dans qch** an active part in sth; **une part active à qch** an active part in sth; **3** (plein d'énergie) GÉN active; [*marché, secteur*] buoyant; **4** (agissant) [*substance, principe*] active; **5** LING [*forme, voix*] active. II *nm* **1** FIN **l'~** the assets (*pl*); **à mettre à l'~ de qn** FIG a point in sb 's favour^GB; **2** LING active (voice). III **actifs** *nmpl* ÉCON working population (*sg*).

action /aksjɔ̃/ *nf* **1** (fait d'agir) action; **il serait temps de passer à l'~** GÉN it's time to act; (combattre) it's time for action; **entrer en ~** MIL to go into action; **un homme d'~** a man of action; **en ~** [*personne*] in action; [*mécanisme*] in operation; **mettre qch en ~** to put sth into operation; **2** (façon d'agir) action; **programme d'~** plan of action; **moyens d'~** courses of action; **3** (effet) effect; **l'~ du temps** the effects of time; **sous l'~ de qch** under the effect of sth; **l'~ de qn sur qch/qn** sb's influence on sth/sb; **4** (acte) action, act; **une ~ stupide** a stupid act; **des ~s criminelles** criminal acts; **bonne/mauvaise ~** good/bad deed; **5** (initiative) initiative; MIL, JUR action; **tenter une ~ en justice à qn** to take legal action against sb; **6** (histoire) action; **l'~ se situe à Venise** the action takes place in Venice; **un film d'~** an action film; **un roman d'~** an adventure novel; **7** (en finance) share; **~s et obligations** securities; **une société par ~s** a joint stock company; **~ nominative** registered share.

actionnaire /aksjɔnɛʀ/ *nmf* shareholder, stockholder US; **~ majoritaire** majority shareholder.

actionner /aksjɔne/ [1] *vtr* (mettre en marche) to activate [*sirène, mécanisme*]; (faire fonctionner) to operate.

activement /aktivmɑ̃/ *adv* actively; **participer ~ à** to take an active part in.

activer /aktive/ [1] I *vtr* **1** (hâter) to speed up [*travail, préparatifs*]; to stimulate [*digestion*]; **2** (intensifier) [*vent*] to stir up [*flamme*]; [*personne*] to stoke [*feu*]; **3** CHIMIE to activate. II **s'activer** *vpr* (s'affairer) to be very busy (**pour faire** doing); (se dépêcher)° to hurry up.

activiste /aktivist/ *adj, nmf* activist.

activité /aktivite/ *nf* **1** (occupation) activity; **~ professionnelle** occupation; **c'est une ~ manuelle** it's manual work; **exercer une ~ rémunérée** to be gainfully employed; **cesser ses ~s** [*entreprise, commerçant*] to stop trading; [*avocat, médecin*] to stop working; **reprendre ses ~s** [*entreprise, commerçant*] to start trading again; [*malade, vacancier*] to go back to work; **2** (fonctionnement) activity; **l'~ de la rue** the bustle of the street; **être en pleine ~** [*atelier*] to be in full production; [*rue*] to be bustling with activity; [*personne*] to be very busy; **en ~** [*volcan*] active; [*usine*] in operation; [*travailleur*] working; [*militaire*] in active service GB ou on active duty US; **3** (énergie) (de personne) energy; **d'une ~ débordante** brimming with energy.

actrice *nf* ▶ **acteur**.

actualisation /aktɥalizasjɔ̃/ *nf* (mise à jour) (processus) updating ¢; (résultat) update.

actualiser /aktɥalize/ [1] *vtr* (mettre à jour) to update, to bring [sth] up to date.

actualité /aktɥalite/ I *nf* **1** (événements) current affairs (*pl*); **l'~ culturelle** cultural events (*pl*); **être à la une de l'~** to be in the headlines; **2** (d'idées, de débat, livre) topicality; (de réflexion) relevance; **sujets d'une brûlante ~** burning issues; **d'~** [*thème, question*] topical; **toujours d'~** still relevant today (*jamais épith*); **plus d'~** no longer at issue. II **actualités** *nfpl* (à la télévision, radio) news; (au cinéma) newsreel (*sg*).

actuel, -elle /aktɥɛl/ *adj* **1** (présent) present, current; **en l'état ~ de l'enquête** at the current stage of the enquiry^GB; **en l'état ~ des connaissances** in the present state of our knowledge; **à l'époque actuelle** in

the present day; **dans le monde ~** in today's world; **l'~ territoire de la Pologne** the territory of present-day Poland; **2** (d'actualité) [*œuvre, débat*] topical.

actuellement /aktɥɛlmɑ̃/ *adv* (en ce moment précis) at the moment, at present; (à notre époque) currently.

acuité /akɥite/ *nf* (d'intelligence, de perception) acuteness; (de son) shrillness; (de douleur) intensity.

acupuncteur, -trice /akypɔ̃ktœr, tʀis/ ▶ 374 *nm,f* acupuncturist.

acupuncture /akypɔ̃ktyʀ/ *nf* acupuncture.

adage /adaʒ/ *nm* saying, adage.

adaptable /adaptabl/ *adj* **1** (souple) adaptable (**à** to); **2** (réglable) adjustable; **~ à toutes les circonstances** or **tous les besoins** all-purpose (*épith*).

adaptateur, -trice /adaptatœr, tʀis/ I ▶ 374 *nm,f* CIN, THÉÂT adapter. II *nm* TECH adapter.

adaptation /adaptasjɔ̃/ *nf* **1** (réajustement) adaptation; **faculté d'~** capacity for adaptation; **~ à** adjustment to; **problèmes d'~** difficulty in adapting; **2** CIN, MUS, THÉÂT adaptation; **~ libre** loose adaptation.

adapté, ~e /adapte/ *adj* **1** (approprié) suitable (**à** for); **~ à la situation** suited to the circumstances; **2** (inséré) [*personne*] adjusted (**à** to); **3** CIN, THÉÂT adapted (**à, pour** for; **de** from).

adapter /adapte/ [1] I *vtr* **1** (poser) to fit (**à** to); **2** (modifier) to adapt [*équipement*]; **3** (rendre conforme) to adapt [*loi, formation*] (**à** to); **4** CIN, THÉÂT [*personne*] to adapt [*roman*] (**à, pour** for). II **s'adapter** *vpr* **1** TECH (s'insérer) [*outil, pièce*] to fit (**dans** into); **2** (s'habituer) [*personne*] to adapt (**à** to).

additif, -ive /aditif, iv/ I *adj* MATH additive. II *nm* (substance) additive; (article, clause) rider (**à** to).

addition /adisjɔ̃/ *nf* **1** MATH addition ¢; **il sait déjà faire les ~s** he can already do addition; **faire une erreur d'~** to make a mistake in the addition; **vérifier des ~s** to check sums; **ton ~ est fausse** your sum is wrong; **l'~ des voix** the counting of the votes; **2** (ajout de produit) addition; **3** (dans un restaurant) bill, check US; **payer l'~** LIT to foot the bill; FIG to pay for it.

additionner /adisjɔne/ [1] I *vtr* to add. II **s'additionner** *vpr* (s'accumuler) to add up.

adduction /adyksjɔ̃/ *nf* adduction; **~ d'eau** water conveyance.

adepte /adɛpt/ *nmf* (de secte) follower; (de doctrine) supporter; (de personne) disciple; (d'activité) enthusiast.

adéquat, ~e /adekwa, at/ *adj* **1** (approprié) [*réponse, environnement, choix*] appropriate; [*outil*] suitable; **2** (suffisant) [*niveau, formation, soins*] adequate.

adéquation /adekwasjɔ̃/ *nf* **1** (conformité) appropriateness (**à, avec** to); **2** (de modèle) adequacy (**à** to).

adhérence /adeʀɑ̃s/ *nf* (de colle, papier) adhesion (**à** to); (de pneu, semelle) grip; MÉD adhesion.

adhérent, ~e /adeʀɑ̃, ɑ̃t/ I *adj* [*matière*] which adheres (**à** to) (*après n*). II *nm,f* (membre) member.

adhérer /adeʀe/ [14] *vtr ind* **1** (coller) **~ à** GÉN to stick to; **le pneu adhère à la route** the tyre GB ou tire US grips the road; **2** (s'inscrire) **~ à** to join [*parti, association*]; to become a member of [*organisme*]; (être membre) to be a member of; **3** (se rallier) **~ à** to subscribe to [*doctrine, politique*].

adhésif, -ive /adezif, iv/ I *adj* adhesive. II *nm* adhesive.

adhésion /adezjɔ̃/ *nf* **1** (appartenance) membership (**à** of GB, in US); **2** (inscription) **l'~ est gratuite** membership is free; **l'~ d'un pays à l'UE** the entry of a country into the EU; **le club vient d'enregistrer dix nouvelles ~s** the club has just enrolled ten new members; **3** (soutien) support (**à** for).

adieu, *pl* **~x** /adjø/ *nm* goodbye, farewell SOUT; **se dire ~** to say goodbye (to each other); **dire ~ à qn**, **faire ses ~x à qn** to say goodbye to sb; **un discours d'~** a farewell speech; **~ le ski** it's goodbye to skiing.

adipeux, -euse /adipø, øz/ *adj* [*tissu, cellule*] fatty; [*visage*] podgy.

adjacent, ~e /adʒasɑ̃, ɑ̃t/ *adj* adjacent (à to).

adjectif, -ive /adʒɛktif, iv/ I *adj* adjectival.
II *nm* adjective; **~ déterminatif** determiner.

adjoindre /adʒwɛ̃dʀ/ [56] I *vtr* **on m'a adjoint un assistant** I've been assigned an assistant; **~ une pièce au dossier** to attach a document to the file.
II **s'adjoindre** *vpr* to take on [*collaborateur, équipe*].

adjoint, ~e /adʒwɛ̃, ɛ̃t/ *nm,f* assistant.
■ **~ au maire** deputy mayor.

adjonction /adʒɔ̃ksjɔ̃/ *nf* addition (à to).

adjudant /adʒydɑ̃/ ▶ 284┃ *nm* MIL (terre) **~** warrant officer class I GB, **~** warrant officer US; (air) *intermediate rank between flight sergeant and warrant officer* GB, **~** warrant officer US; **oui, mon ~** LIT yes, sir; FIG, HUM yes, sergeant.

adjudant-chef, *pl* **adjudants-chefs** /adʒydɑ̃ʃɛf/ ▶ 284┃ *nm* **~** warrant officer class I GB, **~** chief warrant officer US.

adjudication /adʒydikasjɔ̃/ *nf* (de biens) auction; **~ judiciaire** sale by order of the court.

adjuger /adʒyʒe/ [13] I *vtr* (vendre aux enchères) to auction; **adjugé 1000 francs** auctioned for 1,000 francs; **une fois, deux fois, adjugé!** going, going, gone!
II **s'adjuger** *vpr* to grant oneself [*part*]; to take [*coupe, titre*].

adjuration /adʒyʀasjɔ̃/ *nf* plea.

adjurer /adʒyʀe/ [1] *vtr* to implore (**de faire** to do).

adjuvant /adʒyvɑ̃/ *nm* CHIMIE additive.

admettre /admɛtʀ/ [60] *vtr* **1** (reconnaître) to accept, to admit [*fait, hypothèse*]; to admit [*tort, échec, erreur*]; **il faut (bien) ~ que la situation est difficile** it has to be admitted that the situation is difficult; **tout en admettant qu'ils ne l'aient pas fait exprès** whilst accepting that they didn't do it deliberately; **2** (accepter) to admit [*personne*] (**dans** to); **elle n'a pas réussi à se faire ~ comme déléguée** she didn't get accepted as a delegate; **je n'admets pas que l'on soit en retard** I won't tolerate people being late; **nous n'admettrons aucune exception** no exceptions will be made; **je n'admets pas qu'on me traite de cette façon** I won't be treated in this way; **3** (supposer) **~ que** to suppose (that); **'suppose que je gagne!'—'bon, admettons'** 'suppose I win!'—'all right then, suppose you do'; **4** SCOL, UNIV (accepter) to admit (**en** to); **il n'a pas été admis à se présenter à l'examen** he wasn't allowed to take the exam; **les enfants admis à l'école** children admitted to school; **être admis à l'oral** to get through to the oral; **elle a été admise au concours** she passed the exam; **5** (recevoir) to admit (**à** to); **nos salles de classe ne peuvent ~ que 20 élèves** our classrooms can only hold 20 pupils; **être admis à l'hôpital** to be admitted to hospital.

administrateur, -trice /administʀatœʀ, tʀis/ ▶ 374┃ *nm,f* **1** (de bibliothèque, théâtre) administrator; **~ général** general administrator; **2** (membre du conseil d'administration) director; **3** (de fondation, succession) trustee; **4** (gestionnaire) administrator.
■ **~ de biens** property manager.

administratif, -ive /administʀatif, iv/ *adj* **1** (relatif à l'administration) [*bâtiment, personnel, réforme*] administrative; **2** (émis par l'administration) [*rapport*] official.

administration /administʀasjɔ̃/ *nf* **1** ADMIN, POL (appareil) administration; **~ centrale** central administration; **2** (fonction publique) civil service; **entrer dans l'~** to go into the civil service; **3** (contrôle) administration; **~ d'une ville** administration of a city; **sous ~ militaire** under military rule; **4** (gestion) management; **~ des entreprises** business management; **5** (de médicament, sacrement) administration.
■ **~ douanière** customs service; **~ fiscale** Inland Revenue GB, Internal Revenue US; **~ judiciaire** JUR receivership; **~ pénitentiaire** prison service.

administré, ~e /administʀe/ *nm,f* constituent.

administrer /administʀe/ [1] *vtr* **1** (gérer) to administer [*projet, fonds*]; to run [*économie, pays, compagnie*]; **2** (donner) to administer [*médicament, sacrement*] (**à** to); to produce [*preuve*]; to give [*correction, gifle*] (**à** to).

admirable /admiʀabl/ *adj* admirable; **être ~ de dévouement** to show admirable devotion.

admirablement /admiʀabləmɑ̃/ *adv* [*faire*] admirably; [*fait*] superbly.

admirateur, -trice /admiʀatœʀ, tʀis/ *nm,f* admirer.

admiratif, -ive /admiʀatif, iv/ *adj* admiring (*épith*).

admiration /admiʀasjɔ̃/ *nf* admiration (**pour** for); **avec ~** in admiration; **être ~ devant qn/qch** to be lost in admiration for sb/sth; **avoir de l'~ pour qn** to admire sb; **digne d'~** admirable.

admirer /admiʀe/ [1] *vtr* to admire; **très admiré** much admired; **~ qn de faire** to admire sb for doing.

admis, ~e /admi, iz/ I *pp* ▶ **admettre**.
II *pp adj* (reconnu) [*opinion, pratique, théorie*] accepted.
III *nm,f* SCOL, UNIV successful candidate.

admissibilité /admisibilite/ *nf* **1** (d'étudiant) eligibility (*to take oral after written examination*); **2** (de preuve, témoignage) admissibility; **3** (d'hypothèse) acceptability.

admissible /admisibl/ *adj* **1** [*dose, seuil, comportement, argument*] acceptable; [*preuve, témoignage*] admissible; **2** [*étudiant*] eligible (*to take oral after written examination*).

admission /admisjɔ̃/ *nf* **1** (accueil) admission (**à, en** to); **~ en maison de retraite** admission to a retirement home; **faire une demande d'~** to fill in an application form; **bureau** or **service des ~s** reception; **2** (droit) **~ à** eligibility for; **3** (reconnaissance) admission (**de la part de** by; **que** that); **4** TECH intake.

admonester /admɔnɛste/ [1] *vtr* to admonish.

ADN /adeɛn/ *nm* (*abbr* = **acide désoxyribonucléique**) DNA.

ado○ /ado/ *nmf* teenager.

adolescence /adɔlesɑ̃s/ *nf* adolescence.

adolescent, ~e /adɔlesɑ̃, ɑ̃t/ I *adj* adolescent, teenage (*épith*).
II *nm,f* teenager, adolescent.

adonner: s'adonner /adɔne/ [1] *vpr* **s'~ à** to devote oneself to [*travail, sport, art*]; **s'~ au plaisir** to live a debauched life; **il s'adonne à la boisson** he drinks too much.

adopter /adɔpte/ [1] *vtr* GÉN to adopt; to pass [*loi*].

adoptif, -ive /adɔptif, iv/ *adj* [*enfant, pays*] adopted; [*parent*] adoptive.

adoption /adɔpsjɔ̃/ *nf* GÉN, JUR adoption; (de loi) passing; **pays d'~** adopted country; **Anglais d'~** English by adoption.

adorable /adɔʀabl/ *adj* adorable.

adorablement /adɔʀabləmɑ̃/ *adv* [*vêtu*] delightfully; [*naïf*] charmingly.

adorateur, -trice /adɔʀatœʀ, tʀis/ *nm,f* worshipper GB.

adoration /adɔʀasjɔ̃/ *nf* worship, adoration; **être en ~ devant qn/qch** to worship sb/sth.

adorer /adɔʀe/ [1] *vtr* to adore.
IDIOMES **brûler ce qu'on a adoré** to turn against what one used to hold dear.

adosser /adose/ [1] I *vtr* **1** (appuyer) to lean (**à** on; **contre** against); **~ un meuble contre un mur** (verticalement) to stand a piece of furniture against a wall; (un peu incliné) to lean a piece of furniture against a wall; **être adossé à qch** [*personne*] to be leaning against sth; **2** (placer à côté) **~ une maison contre qch** to build a house backing on to sth.
II **s'adosser** *vpr* **1** [*personne*] **s'~ à/contre qch** to lean back on/against sth; **2** [*maison, village*] **s'~ à qch** to back onto sth.

adoucir /adusiʀ/ [3] I *vtr* to soften [*peau, eau, éclairage, expression*]; to soothe [*gorge*]; to moderate [*son, voix*]; to sweeten [*boisson, mets*]; to alleviate [*misère*]; to ease [*sort, chagrin*]; to mitigate [*rigueur, régime*].
II **s'adoucir** *vpr* [*température*] to become milder; [*lumière, voix*] to become softer; [*pente*] to become more

gentle; [*chagrin*] to be soothed; [*conditions*] to be alleviated.

adoucissant, **~e** /adusisã, ãt/ I *adj* [*lotion*] soothing.

II *nm* (pour la lessive) softener.

adoucissement /adusismã/ *nm* (de température) improvement (**de** in); (de conditions) alleviation; (de voix) softening.

adrénaline /adʀenalin/ *nf* adrenalin.

adresse /adʀɛs/ *nf* **1** (domicile) address; **c'est une bonne ~** it's a good place; **se tromper d'~** FIG (de personne) to pick the wrong person; (de lieu) to pick the wrong place; **remarque lancée à l'~ de qn** remark directed at sb; **à l'~ des participants** for the benefit of the participants; **2** (habileté physique) dexterity; **3** (habileté intellectuelle) skill; **avec ~** skilfully^GB; **4** (allocution) address; **5** (en lexicographie) headword; (en sociolinguistique) **forme** or **formule d'~** form of address; **6** ORDINAT address.

adresser /adʀese/ [1] I *vtr* **1** (destiner) to direct [*critique, menace*] (**à** at); to put [*demande, question*] (**à** to); to make [*déclaration*]; to deliver [*ultimatum, message*] (**à** to); to present [*recommandation, pétition*] (**à** to); to put out [*appel*] (**à** to); to aim [*coup*] (**à** at); **~ la parole à qn** to speak to sb; **~ un sourire à qn** to smile at sb; **~ des éloges à qn** to praise sb; **2** (expédier) to send [*lettre*]; **3** (écrire l'adresse) to address [*lettre*]; **4** (diriger) to refer [*personne*] (**à qn** to sb).

II **s'adresser** *vpr* **1** (parler) **s'~ à qn** to speak to sb; **2** (contacter) **s'~ à** to contact [*ministère, ambassade*]; **s'~ à une firme japonaise** to go to a Japanese firm; **adresse-toi à ton père** ask your father; **pour les visas, adressez-vous au consulat** apply to the consulate for visas; **3** (être destiné) **s'~ à** [*mesure, invention*] to be aimed at; (toucher) **s'~ à** to appeal to [*instinct, conscience*]; **4** (échanger) to exchange [*salut, lettres*]; **s'~ la parole** to speak to each other.

adroit, **~e** /adʀwa, at/ *adj* [*personne*] skilful^GB; [*réponse, discours*] clever; **geste ~** deft move; **être ~ de ses mains** to be good with one's hands.

adroitement /adʀwatmã/ *adv* skilfully^GB.

aduler /adyle/ [1] *vtr* to worship, to adulate.

adulte /adylt/ I *adj* [*personne, relation*] adult, grown-up; [*nation*] mature; [*animal, plante*] full-grown.

II *nmf* adult, grown-up.

adultère /adyltɛʀ/ I *adj* adulterous.

II *nm* adultery.

adultérin, **~e** /adylteʀɛ̃, in/ *adj* **enfant ~** child born of adultery.

advenir /advəniʀ/ [36] *v impers* FML (survenir) to happen; **advienne que pourra** come what may; (devenir) **~ de** to become of.

adverbe /advɛʀb/ *nm* adverb.

adversaire /advɛʀsɛʀ/ *nmf* GÉN opponent; MIL adversary.

adverse /advɛʀs/ *adj* [*équipe*] opposing; [*thèse*] opposite; [*attaque, manœuvre*] from the opposite camp; **partie** or **camp ~** opposite camp.

adversité /advɛʀsite/ *nf* adversity.

aération /aeʀasjɔ̃/ *nf* (en ouvrant une fenêtre) airing; (avec un appareil) ventilation; **conduit d'~** airduct.

aérer /aeʀe/ [14] I *vtr* **1** to air [*pièce, draps*]; **pièce aérée** airy ou well-ventilated room; **2** to space out [*texte*].

II **s'aérer** *vpr* [*personne*] to get some fresh air; **s'~ l'esprit** to think about something different for a change.

aérien, **-ienne** /aeʀjɛ̃, ɛn/ *adj* **1** AVIAT [*transport, désastre, base, attaque, carte*] air (*épith*); [*photographie*] aerial; **2** MÉTÉO [*courant, phénomène*] air (*épith*); **3** (en l'air) [*câble, circuit*] overhead; [*racine, plante*] aerial; **métro ~** elevated section of the underground GB ou subway US; **4** (léger) [*démarche*] floating; [*grâce*] exquisite; [*musique*] ethereal.

aéro-club, *pl* **~s** /aeʀoklœb/ *nm* flying club.

aérodrome /aeʀodʀom/ *nm* (small) airfield.

aérodynamique /aeʀodinamik/ I *adj* aerodynamic.

II *nf* aerodynamics (+ *v sg*).

aérodynamisme /aeʀodinamism/ *nm* aerodynamic properties.

aérofrein /aeʀofʀɛ̃/ *nm* air brake.

aérogare /aeʀogaʀ/ *nf* (air) terminal.

aéroglisseur /aeʀoglisœʀ/ *nm* hovercraft.

aérogramme /aeʀogʀam/ *nm* aerogram, air letter.

aéronautique /aeʀonotik/ I *adj* [*industrie*] aeronautics; [*ingénieur*] aeronautical.

II *nf* aeronautics (+ *v sg*).

aéronaval, **~e**[1], *mpl* **~s** /aeʀonaval/ *adj* air and sea.

aéronavale[2] /aeʀɔnaval/ *nf* Fleet Air Arm GB, Naval Aviation US.

aérophagie /aeʀɔfaʒi/ ▶ 196 *nf* wind, aerophagia.

aéroport /aeʀɔpɔʀ/ *nm* airport.

aéroporté, **~e** /aeʀɔpɔʀte/ *adj* [*troupes*] airborne; [*matériel*] transported by air.

aéroportuaire /aeʀɔpɔʀtɥeʀ/ *adj* airport (*épith*).

aérosol /aeʀɔsɔl/ *nm* aerosol.

aérospatial, **~e**[1], *mpl* **-iaux** /aeʀɔspasjal, o/ *adj* [*industrie*] aerospace (*épith*); [*véhicule, lanceur*] space.

aérospatiale[2] /aeʀɔspasjal/ *nf* aerospace industry.

aérostatique /aeʀɔstatik/ I *adj* aerostatic.

II *nf* aerostatics (+ *v sg*).

affable /afabl/ *adj* affable.

affabulation /afabylasjɔ̃/ *nf* (invention) fabrication ₵; **c'est de l'~** that's pure fabrication.

affabuler /afabyle/ [1] *vi* to tell tall stories.

affadir /afadiʀ/ [3] I *vtr* LIT to make [sth] tasteless [*sauce*], FIG to make [sth] dull [*texte, personnage*].

II **s'affadir** *vpr* **1** LIT [*plat*] to lose its flavour^GB; **2** FIG [*intérêt*] to fade; [*argument*] to lose impact.

affaiblir /afɛbliʀ/ [3] I *vtr* to weaken.

II **s'affaiblir** *vpr* [*autorité, gouvernement, économie*] to be weakened; [*personne, voix, vue, détermination, volonté*] to get weaker; [*santé, mémoire*] to deteriorate; [*bruit*] to grow fainter; [*monnaie*] to be weakening (**face à** against); **le sens du mot s'est affaibli** the meaning of the word has weakened; **sortir affaibli d'une maladie** to be drained by an illness.

affaiblissement /afɛblismã/ *nm* **1** (de personne, pays, monnaie, sens) (processus) weakening; (état) weakened state; **2** (de bruit, vue, santé) fading; **3** (de volonté, courage, détermination) diminishing; **4** (de volume, quantité) reduction (**de** in).

affaire /afɛʀ/ I *nf* **1** (ensemble de faits) GÉN affair; (à caractère politique, militaire) crisis, affair; (à caractère délictueux, scandaleux) (d'ordre général) scandal; (de cas unique) affair; (soumis à la justice) case; **l'~ de Suez** the Suez crisis; **une ~ de corruption** a corruption scandal; **condamné pour une ~ de drogue** convicted in a drug case; **2** (histoire, aventure) affair; **une ~ délicate** a delicate matter; **j'ignore tout de cette ~** I don't know anything about the matter; **une sale ~** a nasty business; **quelle ~!** what a business!; **c'est une ~ d'argent** there's money involved; **et voilà toute l'~** and that's that; **3** (occupation, chose à faire) matter, business; **il est parti pour une ~ urgente** he's gone off on some urgent business; **c'est toute une ~** it's quite a business; **c'est une (tout) autre ~** that's another matter (entirely); **ce n'est pas une petite ~** it's no small matter; **c'est mon ~, pas la vôtre** that's my business, not yours; **ça ne change rien à l'~** that doesn't change a thing; **l'~ se présente bien** things are looking good; **j'en fais mon ~** I'll deal with it; **4** (spécialité) **il connaît bien son ~** he knows his job; **c'est une ~ de femmes** it's women's business; **la mécanique, c'est leur ~** mechanics is their thing; **c'est une ~ de spécialistes** it's a case for the specialists; **5** (transaction) deal; **une bonne/mauvaise ~** a good/bad deal; **faire ~ avec qn** to do a deal with sb; **la belle ~!**○ big deal!○; **6** (achat avantageux) bargain; **j'ai fait une ~** I got a bargain; **7** (entreprise) business, concern; **~ industrielle** industrial concern; **c'est elle qui fait marcher l'~** LIT she runs the whole business; FIG she runs the whole show; **8** (question, problème) **c'est une ~ de temps/goût** it's a matter of time/taste; **c'est l'~ de quelques jours** it'll only take a few days; **en faire toute une ~**○ to make a big deal○ of it; **on ne va pas en faire une ~ d 'État!** let's not make a big issue out of it!; **c'est une ~ de famille** it's a family affair; **9** (difficulté, péril) **être hors** or **tiré d'~** [*malade*] to be in the clear; **se tirer d'~** to get out of trouble; **on n'est pas encore sortis** or **tirés d'~** we're not out of the woods yet; **10** (relation) **avoir ~ à** to be dealing with; **tu auras ~ à moi!** you'll have me to contend with!

II affaires *nfpl* **1** (activités lucratives) GÉN business **₵**; (d'une seule personne) business affairs; **être dans les ~s** to be in business; **faire des ~s avec** to do business with; **il gère les ~s de son oncle** he runs his uncle's business affairs; **voir qn pour ~s** to see sb on business; **le monde des ~s** the business world; **2** (problèmes personnels) business **₵**; **ça, c'est mes ~s**○! that's my business!; **occupe-toi de tes ~s**○! mind your own business!; **mettre de l'ordre dans ses ~s** to put one's affairs in order; **parler de ses ~s à tout le monde** to tell everybody one's business; **3** (effets personnels) things, belongings; **mes ~s de sport** my sports things; **4** ADMIN, POL affairs; **~s publiques** public affairs.

■ **les ~s courantes** daily business (*sg*).

IDIOMES **être à son ~** to be in one's element; **il/ça fera l'~** he/that'll do; **ça a très bien fait l'~** it was just the job; **elle fait** or **fera notre ~** she's just the person we need; **ça fera leur ~** (convenir) that's just what they need; (être avantageux) it'll suit them.

affairer: s'affairer /afeʀe/ [1] *vpr* to bustle about (**à faire** doing); **s'~ auprès de qn** to fuss over sb.

affairisme /afeʀism/ *nm* PÉJ wheeling and dealing○.

affairiste /afeʀist/ *nmf* PÉJ wheeler-dealer○.

affaisser: s'affaisser /afese/ [1] *vpr* **1** [*route, terrain*] to subside; [*visage, épaules, pont*] to sag; **toit affaissé** sagging roof; **2** (s'effondrer) [*personne*] to collapse (**sur** on; **dans** into); [*tête*] to droop; **3** (se tasser) **un vieillard qui s'affaisse avec l'âge** an old man who is shrinking with age; **4** [*ventes, bénéfices*] to decline.

affaler: s'affaler /afale/ [1] *vpr* (tomber) (de fatigue) to collapse; (par accident) to fall; **affalé sur le lit** slumped on the bed.

affamé, ~e /afame/ I *pp* ▶ **affamer**.
II *pp adj* **1** LIT starving; **2** FIG **~ de** hungry for.
III *nm,f* LIT **les ~s** the starving.
IDIOMES **ventre ~ n'a pas d'oreilles** PROV ~ a hungry man is an angry man.

affamer /afame/ [1] *vtr* to starve [*personne, pays*].

affectation /afɛktasjɔ̃/ *nf* **1** (de bâtiment, d'argent) allocation (**à** to); **2** (nomination) (à un emploi, une fonction) appointment (**à** to); (dans un lieu) posting (**à** to); **3** (comportement) affectation; **avec ~** in an affected way.

affecter /afɛkte/ [1] *vtr* **1** (feindre) to feign, to affect [*sentiment, émotion*]; to affect [*genre, comportement*]; to take on [*forme*]; **gaieté affectée** feigned cheerfulness; **~ d'être** to pretend to be; **il affecte la gaieté** he's putting on a show of cheerfulness; **~ de grands airs** to put on airs; **2** (allouer) to allocate [*matériel, lieu, argent*] (**à** to); **3** (nommer) (à une activité, un poste) to appoint (**à** to); (dans un lieu, un pays) to post (**à, en** to); **4** (toucher, affliger) to affect [*pays, marché, autorité, personne*]; **affecté d'une légère surdité** slightly deaf.

affectif, -ive /afɛktif, iv/ *adj* GÉN emotional; PSYCH affective.

affection /afɛksjɔ̃/ *nf* **1** (tendresse) affection (**pour** for); **prendre qn en ~** to become fond of sb; **2** MÉD complaint.

affectionner /afɛksjɔne/ [1] *vtr* to be particularly fond of [*chose, activité*]; to be very fond of [*personne*].

affectivité /afɛktivite/ *nf* feelings (*pl*), affectivity.

affectueusement /afɛktɥøzmɑ̃/ *adv* affectionately.

affectueux, -euse /afɛktɥø, øz/ *adj* affectionate.

affermir /afɛʀmiʀ/ [3] I *vtr* **1** (consolider) to strengthen [*autorité, conviction, volonté, voix*]; to consolidate

[*pouvoir, position*]; to firm up [*muscle, chair*]; **2** (rendre plus défini) to sharpen up [*style, écriture*].
II **s'affermir** *vpr* **1** [*autorité, pouvoir, croissance*] to be consolidated; [*voix*] to become stronger; [*muscle, chair*] to firm up; [*terrain*] to become firmer; [*santé*] to become better; **2** [*style, écriture*] to become sharper.

affermissement /afɛʀmismɑ̃/ *nm* (de pouvoir, reprise) consolidation; (de volonté, muscles, voix) strengthening; (d'économie) improvement (**de** in).

affichage /afiʃaʒ/ *nm* **1** (publicitaire, électoral) billsticking, billposting; **communiqué par voie d'~** [*résultat*] posted (up); **campagne d'~** poster campaign; **à ~ numérique** [*réveil*] with digital display; **2** ORDINAT display; **3** (de connaissances, savoir) display.
■ **~ à cristaux liquides** liquid crystal display, LCD.

affiche /afiʃ/ *nf* (publicitaire, électorale) poster; (administrative, judiciaire) notice; **à l'~** CIN now showing; THÉÂT on; **tenir l'~** **pendant deux ans** [*pièce*] to run for two years; **quitter l'~** to come off.

affiché, ~e /afiʃe/ I *pp* ▶ **afficher**.
II *pp adj* **1** (coller, résultat) published; [*bénéfice*] declared; **2** FIG [*optimisme, volonté, dédain, objectif, opinion*] declared; **3** ORDINAT [*donnée, texte*] displayed.

afficher /afiʃe/ [1] I *vtr* **1** (coller) to put up [*affiche*]; **'défense d'~'** 'no fly-posting'; (faire connaître par voie d'affiche) to display [*prix*]; to post (up) [*décret, résultat*]; **~ complet** CIN, THÉÂT to be sold out; [*hôtel*] to be fully booked; [*parking*] to be full; **3** COMM, FIN [*Bourse, marché, entreprise*] to show [*hausse, résultat*]; **4** FIG (montrer) to show [*admiration, confiance, détermination*]; to declare [*ambitions*]; to display [*mépris, autorité*]; to flaunt PÉJ [*opinions, liaison, vie privée*]; **~ le sourire** LIT to have a big smile; (feindre) to put on a big smile; **5** ORDINAT to display.
II **s'afficher** *vpr* [*personne*] to flaunt oneself; [*sourire, joie*] to appear (**sur** on).

afficheur /afiʃœʀ/ *nm* (employé) poster GB ou billboard US sticker.

affichiste /afiʃist/ ▶ **374** | *nmf* poster artist.

affilé, ~e¹ /afile/ *adj* [*lame*] sharpened.

affilée²: d'affilée /dafile/ *loc adv* in a row; **pendant deux semaines d'~** for two weeks in a row; **parler trois heures d'~** [*amis*] to talk nonstop for three hours; [*politiciens, directeur*] to talk for three hours without a break.

affiler /afile/ [1] *vtr* to sharpen.

affilier /afilje/ [2] I *vtr* to affiliate (**à** to).
II **s'affilier** *vpr* to become affiliated (**à** to).

affiner /afine/ [1] I *vtr* to refine [*métal*]; to fine [*verre*]; to refine [*stratégie, style, jugement*]; to have a slimming effect on [*taille, silhouette*].
II **s'affiner** *vpr* [*jugement*] to become keener; [*style, goût*] to become (more) refined; [*taille*] to slim down.

affinité /afinite/ *nf* affinity.

affirmatif, -ive¹ /afiʀmatif, iv/ I *adj* [*réponse, signe*] affirmative; [*personne, ton*] assertive; **faire un signe de tête ~** to nod agreement.
II *nm* LING affirmative; **à l'~** in the affirmative.

affirmation /afiʀmasjɔ̃/ *nf* **1** GÉN assertion; (de sentiment, religion) affirmation; **l'~ de soi** assertiveness; **2** LING assertion.

affirmative² /afiʀmativ/ I *adj* ▶ **affirmatif**.
II *nf* affirmative; **répondre par l'~** to reply in the affirmative; **dans l'~** if the answer is yes.

affirmer /afiʀme/ [1] I *vtr* **1** (soutenir) to maintain [*vérité, contraire*]; **'je n'ai pas l'intention de démissionner', affirma-t-il** 'I have no intention of resigning,' he declared; **~ faire** to claim to do; **~ que** to maintain ou claim (that); **pouvez-vous l'~?** can you be sure about it?; **la police ne peut encore rien ~** the police are not yet able to make any positive statement; **je vous l'affirme** I can assure you (of it); **2** (prouver) to assert [*talent, personnalité, autorité*]; **3** (proclamer) to declare, to affirm [*volonté, désir*] (**à** to).
II **s'affirmer** *vpr* [*progrès, tendance*] to become

apparent; [*personnalité, style*] to assert itself ; **s'~ comme** to establish oneself/itself etc as.

affleurer /aflœʀe/ [1] *vi* **1** LIT [*récif*] to show on the surface; **~ au niveau du sol** [*eau, pétrole*] to come up to ground level; [*roche, minerai*] to come through the soil; **2** FIG [*thème, sentiment*] to surface, to crop up.

affliction /afliksjɔ̃/ *nf* FML affliction; **jeter** or **plonger qn dans l'~** to afflict sb deeply; **être dans l'~** to be in a state of distress.

affligeant, **~e** /afliʒɑ̃, ɑ̃t/ *adj* **1** (attristant) distressing; **2** (consternant) pathetic, depressing.

affliger /afliʒe/ [13] **I** *vtr* **1** (frapper) [*destin*] to afflict (**de** with); **2** (peiner) to distress.
II s'affliger *vpr* to be distressed (**de qch** about sth).

affluence /aflɥɑ̃s/ *nf* (de personnes) crowd(s); (d'objets) abundance.

affluent /aflɥɑ̃/ *nm* GÉOG tributary.

affluer /aflɥe/ [1] *vi* [*personnes*] to flock (**à, vers** to); [*eau, air, sang*] to rush (**à, vers** to); [*argent*] to flow (**à, vers** to); [*plaintes, lettres*] to pour in.

afflux /afly/ *nm inv* (de sang) rush; (de personnes) flood; (de capitaux, produits) influx.

affolant, **~e** /afɔlɑ̃, ɑ̃t/ *adj* (effrayant) frightening, disturbing; **il fume trois paquets par jour, c'est ~!** he smokes three packets a day, it's awful!

affolement /afɔlmɑ̃/ *nm* panic; **être en proie à l'~** to be in a state of panic; **pas d'~!** don't panic!

affoler /afɔle/ [1] **I** *vtr* to terrify, to throw [sb] into a panic [*personne*]; **être affolé** to be panic-stricken.
II s'affoler *vpr* [*personne, animal*] to panic; [*aiguille de boussole*] to spin.

affranchi, **~e** /afrɑ̃ʃi/ *nm,f* emancipated slave.

affranchir /afrɑ̃ʃiʀ/ [3] **I** *vtr* **1** (en collant des timbres) to stamp [*lettre*]; (avec une machine) to frank; **2** (libérer) LIT, FIG to free (**de** from).
II s'affranchir *vpr* to free oneself (**de** from).

affranchissement /afrɑ̃ʃismɑ̃/ *nm* **1** (de lettre) (avec des timbres) stamping; (avec une machine) franking; (coût) postage; **2** (libération) (de peuple, pays) liberation; (de serf, d'esclave) freeing; (de minorité) emancipation.

affres /afʀ/ *nfpl* LITTÉR agony (*sg*); (de douleur) agony (*sg*); (de faim) pangs; (de jalousie) throes; **les ~ de la mort** death throes.

affréter /afʀete/ [14] *vtr* to charter [*avion, bateau*].

affréteur /afʀetœʀ/ *nm* charter company.

affreusement /afʀøzmɑ̃/ *adv* [*se conduire, parler*] abominably; [*laid, blessé*] horribly; [*malade*] terribly; **parler ~ mal** to speak appallingly badly.

affreux, **-euse** /afʀø, øz/ *adj* (laid) hideous; (abominable) dreadful; (désagréable) [*temps, route, vacances*] awful; **c'est ~ le monde qu'il y a** it really is terribly busy.

affriolant, **~e** /afʀiɔlɑ̃, ɑ̃t/ *adj* [*femme*] alluring; [*vêtement*] titillating; [*idée*] tempting.

affront /afʀɔ̃/ *nm* affront (**à** to); **il m'a fait l'~ de refuser** he insulted me by refusing.

affrontement /afʀɔ̃tmɑ̃/ *nm* confrontation, clash (**avec** with; **entre** between).

affronter /afʀɔ̃te/ [1] **I** *vtr* to face, to confront [*adversaire, situation*]; to brave [*montagne, froid*].
II s'affronter *vpr* [*adversaires*] to confront one another; [*idées*] to clash.

affublement /afybləmɑ̃/ *nm* attire†.

affubler /afyble/ [1] **I** *vtr* PEJ **~ qn de** to deck sb out in [*vêtement, ornement*]; to saddle sb with [*prénom*].
II s'affubler *vpr* **s'~ de** to deck oneself out in [*vêtement, ornement*]; to take on [*nom*].

affût /afy/ *nm* **1** MIL **~ (de canon)** (gun) carriage; **2** (à la chasse) hide GB, blind US; **chasser à l'~** to hunt game from a hide GB ou blind US; **se tenir à l'~** LIT to lie in wait; FIG to be on the lookout (**de** for).

affûter /afyte/ [1] *vtr* to sharpen; (avec une meule) to grind.

afghan, **~e** /afgɑ̃, an/ ▶ **394**, **338** **I** *adj* Afghan.
II *nm* LING Afghan.

afin /afɛ̃/ **I** **afin de** *loc prép* **~ de faire** in order to do, so as to do; **~ de ne pas faire** so as not to do.
II afin que *loc conj* so that; **~ que les jeunes trouvent du travail** so that young people might find work; **~ qu'il ne se sente pas abandonné** so that he won't feel neglected.

AFNOR /afnɔʀ/ *nf* (*abbr* = **Association française de normalisation**) AFNOR (*French standards authority*).

AFP /aɛfpe/ *nf* (*abbr* = **Agence France-Presse**) AFP (*French news agency*).

africain, **~e** /afʀikɛ̃, ɛn/ *adj* African.

Afrique /afʀik/ ▶ **232** *nprf* Africa; **République d'~ du Sud** Republic of South Africa.

Afrique-Équatoriale /afʀikekwatɔʀjal/ *nprf* HIST française French Equatorial Africa.

Afrique-Occidentale /afʀikɔksidɑ̃tal/ *nprf* HIST française French West Africa.

afro- /afʀo/ *préf* **~-brésilien** Afro-Brazilian; **~centrisme** afrocentrism; **~-jazz** African Jazz.

AG /aʒe/ *nf*: *abbr* ▶ **assemblée**.

agaçant, **~e** /agasɑ̃, ɑ̃t/ *adj* annoying, irritating.

agacement /agasmɑ̃/ *nm* irritation.

agacer /agase/ [12] *vtr* **1** (excéder) to annoy, to irritate; **tu commences à m'~ avec tes cris** your shouting is starting to annoy me; **2** (lanciner) to set [sth] on edge [*dent*]; to grate on [*nerf*].

agapes /agap/ *nfpl* feast (*sg*), banquet (*sg*).

agate /agat/ *nf* **1** (minéral) agate; **d'~** (couleur) agate-coloured^{GB}; **2** (bille) marble.

âge /aʒ/ *nm* **1** (nombre d'années) age; **ils sont du même ~** they are the same age; **faire son ~** to look one's age; **paraître plus/moins que son ~** to look older/ younger than one's years; **bien porter son ~** to be good for one's age; **sans ~** ageless; **un homme d'un certain ~** a middle-aged man; **une personne d'un ~ avancé** an elderly person; **~ avancé, grand ~** great age; **avoir l'~** or **être en ~ de faire** to be old enough to do; **il est mort à 95 ans, c'est un bel ~** he died at 95, a fine old age; **30 ans, c'est le bel ~** 30 is a good age; **2** (vieillesse) (old) age; **s'assagir avec l'~** to calm down as one gets older; **vieux avant l'~** to be old before one's time; **prendre de l'~** to grow old; **3** (période de la vie) age; **à tout ~**, **à tous les ~s** at any age; **être entre deux ~s** to be middle-aged; **avoir passé l'~ de faire** to be past the age when one does; **être encore/ne plus être en ~ de faire** to be still young enough/to be too old to do; **va t'amuser, c'est de ton ~!** go and have fun, you're young!; **4** (époque) age; **à travers les ~s** through the ages.
■ **l'~ adulte** adulthood; **~ du bronze** Bronze age; **~ du fer** Iron age; **l'~ d'homme** manhood; **l'~ ingrat** the awkward ou difficult age; **d'~ mûr** mature; **l'~ mûr** maturity; **~ d'or** golden age; **~ de la pierre** Stone age; **l'~ de la retraite** retirement age; **l'~ scolaire** school age; **l'~ tendre** youth.

âgé, **~e** /aʒe/ *adj* [*personne*] old, elderly; **~ de 12 ans** 12 years old; **les personnes ~es de 15 à 35 ans** people aged between 15 and 35.

agence /aʒɑ̃s/ *nf* **1** COMM agency; **2** ADMIN agency, bureau; **3** (de banque) branch.
■ **~ immobilière** estate agents (*pl*) GB, real-estate agency US; **~ matrimoniale** marriage bureau; **~ de placement** employment agency; **~ de presse** news agency; **~ publicitaire** advertising agency; **~ de voyage** travel agency, travel agents (*pl*) GB; **Agence nationale pour l'emploi, ANPE** *French national employment agency*.

agencement /aʒɑ̃smɑ̃/ *nm* (de pièces) layout; (de mots, phrases) arrangement; (de couleurs, motifs) setting out.

agencer /aʒɑ̃se/ [12] *vtr* **1** (disposer) to lay out [*pièce*]; to put together [*éléments, couleurs*]; **2** (structurer) to construct [*intrigue, scénario*].

agenda /aʒɛ̃da/ *nm* **1** (carnet prédaté) diary; **2** (programme) agenda.

L'âge

Quel âge avez-vous?

L'anglais n'emploie pas le verbe to have *(avoir) pour exprimer l'âge, mais le verbe* to be *(être).*

quel âge a-t-il? = how old is he?
　　　　　　　　ou what age is he?

Les deux mots years old *peuvent être omis pour les personnes, mais pas pour les choses.*

elle a trente ans	= she is thirty years old
	ou she is thirty
il a quatre-vingts ans	= he is eighty
	ou he is eighty years old
la maison a cent ans	= the house is a hundred years old
atteindre soixante ans	= to reach sixty
Nick est plus âgé qu'Isabelle	= Nick is older than Isabelle
Isabelle est plus jeune que Nick	= Isabelle is younger than Nick
Nick a deux ans de plus qu'Isabelle	= Nick is two years older than Isabelle
Isabelle a deux ans de moins que Nick	= Isabelle is two years younger than Nick
Louis a le même âge que Mary	= Louis is the same age as Mary
Louis et Mary ont le même âge	= Louis and Mary are the same age
on te donnerait seize ans	= you look sixteen
j'ai l'impression d'avoir seize ans	= I feel sixteen
on lui donnerait dix ans de moins	= he looks ten years younger

Âgé de

il est âgé de quarante ans	= he is forty years of age
un homme de soixante ans	= a man of sixty
un enfant de huit ans et demi	= a child of eight and a half
une femme âgée de quarante ans	= a woman aged forty
M. Stein, âgé de quarante ans	= Mr Stein, aged forty
à l'âge de cinquante ans	= at fifty *ou* at the age of fifty (*GB*), at age fifty (*US*)
il est mort à vingt-sept ans	= he died at twenty-seven *ou* at the age of twenty-seven

un homme âgé de soixante ans = a sixty-year-old man

Noter l'utilisation du trait d'union. Noter aussi que year, *qui fait partie de l'adjectif, ne prend pas la marque du pluriel.*

Lorsque l'on parle d'êtres humains ou d'animaux, le mot qui suit old *peut être sous-entendu. Ainsi,* a three-year-old *peut être un enfant ou un animal (souvent* un cheval*).*

un enfant de cinq ans et demi	= a five-and-a-half-year-old
une course pour les trois ans	= a race for three-year-olds

Mais:

un vin de soixante ans d'âge = a sixty-year-old wine

L'âge approximatif

L'anglais emploie indifféremment about *et* around *dans ce cas.*

elle a dans les trente ans	= she's about thirty *ou* around thirty
elle a une cinquantaine d'années	= she's about fifty *ou* around fifty
il n'a pas encore dix-huit ans	= he's not yet eighteen
il vient d'avoir quarante ans	= he's just over forty *ou* (*plus familier*) he's just turned forty
il aura bientôt cinquante ans	= he's just under fifty
elle a entre trente et quarante ans	= she's in her thirties
elle a dans les quarante-cinq ans	= she's in her mid-forties
elle va sur ses soixante-dix ans	= she's in her late sixties *ou* she's nearly seventy
elle va avoir vingt ans	= she's in her late teens *ou* she's almost twenty
il a tout juste dix ans	= he's just ten
il a à peine douze ans	= he's barely twelve

Les personnes âgées de X ans

les plus de quatre-vingts ans	= the over eighties
les moins de dix-huit ans	= the under eighteens

Les mots anglais en -arian *sont des noms:*

ce sont des septuagénaires	= they're septuagenarians
elle est octogénaire	= she's an octogenarian

---

agenouiller: **s'agenouiller** /aʒnuje/ [1] *vpr* **1** LIT to kneel (down); **être agenouillé** to be kneeling; **2** FIG **s'~ devant** to bow to [*pouvoir*]; to kowtow to [*personne*].

agent /aʒɑ̃/ ▶ **374** *nm* **1** (de l'État) ADMIN officer, official; POL agent; **~ du gouvernement** government official; **~ secret/double** secret/double agent; **2** COMM agent; **3** (employé) employee; **~s contractuels** contract staff; **4** CHIMIE, LING agent.
■ **~ artistique** THÉÂT theatrical agent; **~ d'assurances** insurance broker; (vendeur) insurance salesman; **~ de change** stockbroker; **~ de la circulation** traffic policeman; **~ commercial** sales representative; **~ comptable** accountant; **~ hospitalier** nursing auxiliary GB, nurse's aide US; **~ de liaison** liaison officer; **~ maritime** shipping agent; **~ de police** policeman; **~ provocateur** agent provocateur; **~ technique** technician.

agglomération /aglɔmerasjɔ̃/ *nf* **1** (ville) town; (village) village; **l'~ lyonnaise** Lyons and its suburbs; **vitesse maximum en ~** AUT maximum speed in built-up areas; **2** TECH agglomeration (**de** of).

aggloméré /aglɔmere/ *nm* chipboard.

agglomérer /aglɔmere/ [14] **I** *vtr* to agglomerate.
II s'agglomérer *vpr* [*personnes*] to gather together; [*habitations*] to be grouped together.

agglutiner: **s'agglutiner** /aglytine/ [1] *vpr* [*badauds*] to crowd together (**à** at); [*mouches*] to cluster together; **s'~ autour de** [*curieux*] to crowd around; [*maisons*] to be clustered around.

aggravant, **~e** /agravɑ̃, ɑ̃t/ *adj* JUR aggravating.

aggravation /agravasjɔ̃/ *nf* (de situation, maladie) worsening; (de chômage, dette, déficit) increase (**de** in).
■ **~ de peine** JUR increase in sentence.

aggraver /agrave/ [1] **I** *vtr* **1** (rendre pire) to aggravate, to make [sth] worse; **~ son cas** to make things worse; **vol aggravé** aggravated robbery; **2** (accroître) to increase.
II s'aggraver *vpr* (devenir pire) to get worse, to deteriorate; (en augmentant) to increase.

agile /aʒil/ *adj* [*personne, animal*] agile; [*doigts, pas, esprit*] nimble.

agilement /aʒilmɑ̃/ *adv* nimbly, with agility.

agilité /aʒilite/ *nf* agility.

agios /aʒjo/ *nmpl* bank charges.

agir /aʒiʀ/ [3] **I** *vi* **1** (accomplir une action) to act; **il a agi sous le coup de la colère** he acted in anger; **il parle beaucoup mais agit peu** he's all talk and no action; **~ avec prudence** to proceed with caution; **2** (se comporter) to behave, to act; **bien/mal ~** to behave well/badly (**envers, avec** toward(s)); **~ en lâche** to act like a coward; **3** (avoir un effet) [*substance, médicament*] to take effect, to work; **~ sur qch/qn** to have an effect on sth/sb; **~ sur le marché** FIN to influence the market; **4** (intervenir) **~ auprès de qn** to approach sb.
II s'agir de *vpr impers* **1** **de quoi s'agit-il?** (question) what is it about?; (problème) what's the matter?; **mais il ne s'agit pas de ça!** but that's not the point!; **il s'agit de ta santé!** it's your health that's at stake (here)!; **il s'agit de votre mari** it's about your husband, it's to do with your husband; **on connaît maintenant les gagnants: il s'agit de messieurs X et Y** we now

know who the winners are: they're Mr X and Mr Y; **d'après les experts il s'agirait d'un attentat** according to the experts, it would appear to be an act of terrorism; **quand il s'agit d'argent/de faire le ménage** when it comes to money/ to doing the housework; **s'agissant de qch/qn** as regards sth/sb; **il s'agit bien de partir en vacances maintenant que je suis au chômage!** IRON now that I'm unemployed it's hardly the (right) time to talk about going on vacation!; **2** (il est nécessaire de) **il s'agit de faire vite** we/ you etc must act quickly; **il s'agit de savoir ce que tu veux!** make up your mind!; **il s'agit pour le gouvernement de relancer l'économie** what the government must do now is boost the economy; **il s'agirait de se mettre d'accord** we'd better get it straight.

agissements /aʒismɑ̃/ *nmpl* PEJ activities, doings.

agitateur, -trice /aʒitatœʀ, tʀis/ I *nm,f* POL agitator.
II *nm* (dispositif) agitator; (baguette) stirring rod.

agitation /aʒitasjɔ̃/ *nf* **1** (de mer) choppiness; (d'air) turbulence; (de branche) swaying; (de malade, d'impatient) restlessness; **2** (de maison, rue) bustle (**de** in); (de marché) activity; **3** (nervosité) agitation; **4** (malaise social) unrest.

agité, ~e /aʒite/ I *adj* [*mer*] rough; (moins fort) choppy; [*malade*] agitated; [*rue*] bustling; [*vie*] hectic; [*esprit, sommeil*] troubled; [*période*] turbulent; [*nuit*] restless.
II *nm,f* **1** MÉD **les ~s** the mentally disturbed; **2** (indiscipliné) troublemaker, disruptive element.

agiter /aʒite/ [1] I *vtr* **1** (remuer) to wave [*main, mouchoir*]; to shake [*boîte*]; to shake up [*liquide*]; to wag [*queue*]; to flap [*aile*]; **le vent agite les feuilles** the wind is rustling the leaves; **voile agitée par le vent** sail flapping in the wind; **barque agitée par les vagues** boat tossed by the waves; **un tremblement agitait mon corps** my whole body was shaking; **2** (brandir) to raise [*menace, spectre*]; **3** (troubler) to trouble; **4** (débattre) to debate, to discuss [*problème*].
II **s'agiter** *vpr* **1** (remuer) [*personne*] GÉN to fidget; (au lit) to toss and turn; [*branche*] to sway (in the wind); **2** (s'affairer) to bustle about; **3** (perdre son calme) [*esprit, peuple*] to become agitated ou restless.

agneau, *pl* **~x** /aɲo/ *nm* **1** ZOOL, CULIN lamb; **2** (cuir) lambskin.

agnelle /aɲɛl/ *nf* ewe lamb.

agonie /agɔni/ *nf* death throes (*pl*); **être à l'~** [*personne*] to be dying; [*régime*] to be in its death throes; **son ~ a été longue** he had a slow death.

agonir /agɔniʀ/ [3] *vtr* **~ qn d'injures** to hurl insults at sb; **en rentrant, il s'est fait ~** when he got home he was told off soundly.

agonisant, ~e /agɔnizɑ̃, ɑ̃t/ *adj* dying.

agoniser /agɔnize/ [1] *vi* LIT, FIG to be dying.

agrafe /agʀaf/ *nf* **1** (pour vêtements) hook; **2** (pour papiers) staple; **3** MÉD skin clip.

agrafer /agʀafe/ [1] *vtr* to fasten [*vêtement*]; to staple (together) [*papiers*].

agrafeuse /agʀaføz/ *nf* stapler.

agraire /agʀɛʀ/ *adj* [*société*] agrarian; [*réforme*] land (*épith*).

agrandir /agʀɑ̃diʀ/ [3] I *vtr* **1** (en dimensions) to enlarge [*ville, photo, trou*]; to extend [*pièce, maison*]; to widen [*tunnel, marge*]; **les yeux agrandis par la peur** his/their etc eyes wide with fear; **la peinture blanche agrandit la pièce** white paint makes the room look bigger ou larger; **2** (en importance) to extend [*famille*]; to expand [*entreprise, parti*].
II **s'agrandir** *vpr* [*trou*] to get bigger; [*ville, famille, entreprise*] to expand; [*marge, yeux*] to widen.

agrandissement /agʀɑ̃dismɑ̃/ *nm* **1** PHOT enlargement; **2** (de maison, pièce) extension; (d'ouverture) enlargement; (d'entreprise) expansion; **faire des travaux d'~** (dans une maison) to build an extension.

agrandisseur /agʀɑ̃disœʀ/ *nm* enlarger.

agréable /agʀeabl/ *adj* nice, pleasant; **avoir un physique ~** to be good-looking; **~ à l'œil/au**

toucher pleasing to the eye/to the touch; **~. à vivre** [*personne*] pleasant to be with; ▶ **utile**.

agréer /agʀee/ [11] *vtr* **1** (accepter) to agree to [*demande*]; **veuillez ~ mes salutations distinguées** (personne non nommée) yours faithfully; (personne nommée) yours sincerely; **2** (reconnaître officiellement) to recognize [sb] officially [*diplomate*]; to authorize [*concessionnaire*]; to register [*taxi, nourrice, médecin*]; to approve [*matériel, association, établissement*]; **agent agréé** COMM authorized dealer.

agrégat /agʀega/ *nm* **1** BIOL, CONSTR, ÉCON aggregate; **2** FIG jumble (**de** of).

agrégation /agʀegasjɔ̃/ *nf* **1** UNIV high-level competitive examination for recruitment of teachers; **2** (de particules) aggregation.

agrégé, ~e /agʀeʒe/ *nm,f*: holder of the *agrégation*.

agréger: **s'agréger** /agʀeʒe/ [15] *vpr* **1** (se coller) [*particules*] to aggregate; **2** (se joindre) **s'~ à** [*personne, groupe*] to join.

agrément /agʀemɑ̃/ *nm* **1** (validation officielle) approval; **retirer son ~ à une école** to withdraw a school's accreditation; **2** (accord) agreement; **3** (charme) (d'activité) pleasure; (de personne, lieu, chose) charm; **plein d'~** [*séjour*] very pleasant; [*lieu*] full of charm (*après n*); **sans ~** [*existence*] dull; [*visage, maison*] unattractive; [*décor, pièce*] cheerless; **voyage d'~** pleasure trip.

agrémenter /agʀemɑ̃te/ [1] *vtr* to liven up [*texte, histoire*] (**de** with); to cheer up [*réunion*] (**de** with); to brighten up [*jardin, existence*] (**de** with); to supplement [*repas, plat*] (**de** with); **un ensemble immobilier agrémenté de nombreux services** a property development offering many facilities.

agrès /agʀɛ/ *nmpl* **1** SPORT apparatus ¢; **2** NAUT tackle.

agresser /agʀese/ [1] *vtr* **1** (physiquement) to attack [*personne, pays*]; (pour voler) to mug [*personne*]; (moralement) [*personne*] to be aggressive with [*personne*]; **se sentir agressé** to feel threatened (**par** by); **les images télévisées nous agressent** we are bombarded by pictures on television; **3** (être trop fort) [*shampooing*] to be too harsh; [*fumée*] to attack.

agresseur /agʀesœʀ/ *nm* (individu) attacker; (groupe, peuple) aggressor.

agressif, -ive /agʀesif, iv/ *adj* **1** [*personne, animal*] aggressive (**avec qn** with sb; **envers qn** toward(s) sb); [*tempérament, ton, environnement, publicité*] aggressive; **d'un ton ~** aggressively; **2** [*couleur*] violent; [*son*] ear-splitting; [*images*] threatening.

agression /agʀesjɔ̃/ *nf* **1** (par une personne) attack; (pour voler) mugging; (par un pays) act of aggression; **~ à main armée** armed assault; **les ~s de la vie urbaine** the stresses and strains of city life; **2** PSYCH aggression.

agressivité /agʀesivite/ *nf* aggressiveness.

agricole /agʀikɔl/ *adj* [*produit, ouvrier*] farm; [*coopérative*] farming; [*problème*] agricultural; [*syndicat*] farm workers'.

agriculteur, -trice /agʀikyltœʀ, tʀis/ ▶ **374** *nm,f* farmer; **une famille d'~s** a farming family.

agriculture /agʀikyltyʀ/ *nf* farming, agriculture SPÉC. ■ **~ biologique** organic farming.

agripper /agʀipe/ [1] I *vtr* to grab.
II **s'agripper** *vpr* **s'~ à** to cling to.

agro-alimentaire, *pl* **~s** /agʀoalimɑ̃tɛʀ/ I *adj* [*industrie, filière*] food processing; **la recherche ~** food research.
II *nm* food processing industry; **un géant de l'~** a food giant.

agrochimie /agʀoʃimi/ *nf* agro-chemistry.

agronome /agʀɔnɔm/ ▶ **374** *nmf* (ingénieur) **~** agronomist.

agronomie /agʀɔnɔmi/ *nf* agronomy.

agrume /agʀym/ *nm* citrus fruit.

aguerrir /ageʀiʀ/ [3] I *vtr* [*expérience*] to harden [*personne*] (**à qch** to sth); **~ des troupes au combat** to toughen soldiers for battle; **soldats aguerris** (au combat) seasoned soldiers.

II s'aguerrir *vpr* to become hardened ou inured SOUT (à, contre to).

aguets: **aux aguets** /ozagɛ/ *loc adv* **être aux ~** (à l'affût) to lie in wait; (se méfier) to be on one's guard; (surveiller de près) to be watching like a hawk.

aguicher /agiʃe/ [1] *vtr* (sexuellement) to lead [sb] on; (pour vendre) to attract [*client*].

aguicheur, -euse[1] /agiʃœʀ, øz/ *adj* alluring.

aguicheuse[2] /agiʃøz/ *nf* PEJ tease PÉJ.

ah /a/ **I** *nm inv* (d'étonnement, admiration) gasp; (de soulagement, satisfaction) sigh.
II *excl* oh!; **~ non alors!** certainly not!; **~, tu vois!** see!; **~ bon?** really?; **~ ~ ~!** (rire) ha ha ha!

ahaner /aane/ [1] *vi* (grogner) to grunt with effort; (peiner) to strain.

ahuri, ~e /ayʀi/ **I** *adj* (hébété) dazed; (étonné) stunned.
II *nm,f* PEJ halfwit PÉJ.

ahurir /ayʀiʀ/ [3] *vtr* to stun.

ahurissant, ~e /ayʀisɑ̃, ɑ̃t/ *adj* [*nouvelle, bruit*] incredible; [*personne, force*] incredible; [*chiffre*] staggering; **c'est ~!** it's absolutely incredible!

ahurissement /ayʀismɑ̃/ *nm* amazement.

aide[1] /ɛd/ ▶ 374⌋ **I** *nmf* (dans un travail) assistant.
II **aide-** (*in compounds*) **~-bibliothécaire/-cuisinier** assistant librarian/cook; **~-électricien/-mécanicien** electrician's/mechanic's mate GB ou helper US; **~-soignant** nursing auxiliary GB, nurse's aide US.
■ **~ de camp** aide-de-camp.

aide[2] /ɛd/ *nf* **1** (secours) (d'individu, de groupe) help, assistance; (d'État, organisme) assistance; **appeler à l'~** to call for help; **à l'~ de** with the help ou aid of; **apporter son ~ à qn** to help sb; **venir à l'~ de qn** to come to sb's aid ou assistance; **2** (en argent) aid ¢; **recevoir des ~s de** to receive financial aid from.
■ **~ au développement** foreign aid; **~ à domicile** home help GB, home helper US; **~ familiale** mother's help GB, mother's helper US; **~ judiciaire** legal aid; **~ sociale** social security benefits GB, welfare benefits US.

aide-mémoire /ɛdmemwaʀ/ *nm inv* aide-mémoire SOUT; **c'est mon ~** I use it to jog my memory.

aider /ede/ [1] **I** *vtr* **1** (prêter son concours à) to help (à faire to do); **en quoi puis-je vous ~?** how can I help you?; **se faire ~ par qn** to get help from sb; **~ qn de ses conseils** to give sb helpful advice; **le vin aidant** wine playing its part; **2** (subventionner) to aid [*industrie, déshérités*]; to give aid to [*pays pauvre*].
II aider à *vtr ind* **~ à** to help toward(s) [*compréhension, financement*]; **~ à faire** to help in doing.
III s'aider *vpr* **1** (soi-même) **s'~ de** to use [*dictionnaire, outil*]; **en s'aidant de** with the help of; **2** (les uns les autres) to help each other.

aïe /aj/ *excl* (de douleur) ouch!; (d'inquiétude) **~** (~ **~**), **que se passe-t-il?** oh dear, what's going on?; (d'anticipation) **~ ~ ~!**... oh NO!...

aïeul, ~e /ajœl/ *nm,f* grandfather/grandmother.

aïeux /ajø/ *nmpl* LITER ancestors.

aigle /ɛgl/ *nm* ZOOL eagle.

aiglefin /ɛgləfɛ̃/ *nm* haddock.

aiglon /ɛglɔ̃/ *nm* eaglet.

aigre /ɛgʀ/ *adj* **1** LIT (au goût, à l'odorat) [*odeur*] sour; **2** FIG [*paroles*] sharp; [*caractère*] sour; **d'un ton ~** sharply; **tourner** or **virer à l'~** [*plaisanterie*] to turn sour.

aigre-doux, -douce, *pl* **aigres-doux, aigres-douces** /ɛgʀədu, dus/ *adj* **1** CULIN [*fruit, goût*] bitter-sweet; [*cuisine, sauce*] sweet and sour; **2** FIG [*propos, communiqué*] barbed.

aigrefin /ɛgʀəfɛ̃/ *nm* swindler.

aigrelet, -ette /ɛgʀəlɛ, ɛt/ *adj* [*goût, fruit*] rather sour; [*voix*] shrill; **un petit vin ~** a sharpish wine.

aigrette /ɛgʀɛt/ *nf* ZOOL (oiseau) egret; (plumes) crest.

aigreur /ɛgʀœʀ/ *nf* **1** GÉN (de lait, fruit) sourness; (de vin) sharpness; **2** MÉD **des ~s d'estomac** heartburn ¢; **3** FIG bitterness.

aigrir /egʀiʀ/ [3] **I** *vtr* to embitter [*personne*].
II s'aigrir *vpr* **1** [*personne*] to become embittered; **2** [*vin, aliment*] to turn sour.

aigu, -uë /egy/ **I** *adj* **1** [*son, voix, note*] high-pitched; **2** [*douleur, symptôme, problème*] acute; [*phase*] critical; **3** [*perception, sens*] keen.
II *nm* (de chaîne stéréo) treble; (de voix) high notes (*pl*).

aigue-marine, *pl* **aigues-marines** /ɛgmaʀin/ *nf* aquamarine.

aiguillage /egɥijaʒ/ *nm* (appareil) points (*pl*) GB, switch US; (manœuvre) switching to another line; **une erreur d'~** a signalling[GB] error; FIG a mix-up.

aiguille /egɥij/ *nf* **1** (en couture, médecine, botanique, génie nucléaire) needle; **~ à coudre/à tricoter** sewing/knitting needle; **2** (de montre, chronomètre) hand; (de jauge, d'altimètre) needle; (de balance) pointer; **dans le sens/le sens inverse des ~s d'une montre** clockwise/anticlockwise; **3** GÉOG peak; **4** ZOOL garfish.

aiguiller /egɥije/ [1] *vtr* **1** (vers un endroit) to direct [*personne*] (**vers** toward(s)); to send [*courrier, dossier*] (**vers** to); to steer [*conversation*] (**sur** toward(s)); **c'est ce qui nous a aiguillés dans nos recherches** that's what put us on the right track in our research; **2** RAIL **~ un train** to switch a train to a new line.

aiguilleur /egɥijœʀ/ ▶ 374⌋ *nm* RAIL pointsman GB, switchman US.
■ **~ du ciel** air traffic controller.

aiguillon /egɥijɔ̃/ *nm* **1** ZOOL sting; **2** (stimulant) incentive; **3** (bâton) goad; **4** BOT thorn.

aiguillonner /egɥijɔne/ [1] *vtr* **1** (stimuler) to spur [*personne*]; to stimulate [*ambition*]; **la faim m'aiguillonnant**... driven by hunger...; **2** LIT to goad [*bœuf*].

aiguiser /egize/ [1] *vtr* **1** LIT to sharpen [*lame, griffes, crocs*]; **2** FIG to whet [*appétit*]; to arouse [*curiosité*]; to heighten [*sentiment*]; to stimulate [*concurrence*]; to sharpen [*intelligence*]; to hone [*style*].

aiguiseur /egizœʀ/ ▶ 374⌋ *nm* knife grinder.

ail, *pl* **~s** or **aulx** /aj, o/ *nm* garlic.

aile /ɛl/ *nf* GÉN wing; (de moulin) sail; (de voiture) wing GB, fender US; (d'armée) flank.
■ **~ de corbeau** (noir) raven black; **~ delta** AVIAT delta wing; SPORT hang-glider; **~ du nez** ANAT wing of the nose.
IDIOMES **battre de l'~, ne battre que d'une ~** [*croissance*] to have fallen off; [*économie, entreprise*] to be struggling; **se sentir pousser des ~s** to feel exhilarated; **rogner les ~s de qn** to clip sb's wings; **prendre un coup dans l'~** to suffer a setback; **avoir un coup dans l'~**○ to be the worse for drink; **voler de ses propres ~s** to stand on one's own two feet.

ailé, ~e /ele/ *adj* winged.

aileron /ɛlʀɔ̃/ *nm* **1** (d'oiseau) wing tip; (de requin) fin; **2** (d'avion) aileron; **3** (de coque) fin; **4** (de planche de surf) skeg; **5** (de voiture de course) aerofoil GB, airfoil US.

ailier /elje/ *nm* **1** (au football) winger; **~ gauche** left winger GB ou wing US; **2** (au rugby) wing three-quarter.

ailleurs /ajœʀ/ **I** *adv* elsewhere; **ici comme ~** here as elsewhere; **des artistes venus d'~** artists from other places; **nulle part ~** nowhere else; **partout ~** everywhere else; **ici ou ~, ça m'est égal** here or somewhere else, it's all the same to me.
II d'ailleurs *loc adv* besides, moreover, what's more; **d'~, je n'étais pas là** besides, I wasn't there; **il a fait des tentatives, d'~ fort timides** he made some rather feeble attempts; **l'excuse de mon mal de tête, d'~ bien réel,...** the excuse of having a headache, which I might add was true,...
III par ailleurs *loc adv* **par ~, l'inflation a atteint un taux record** in addition, inflation has reached a record level; **par ~, je n'ai pas encore reçu les marchandises** may I also add that I have not yet received the goods; **des efforts pour comprendre un problème par ~ complexe** efforts to understand a problem which is in some respects complex.
IDIOMES **être ~, avoir l'esprit ~** to be miles away.

aimable /ɛmabl/ *adj* **1** (gentil) [*personne*] pleasant;

[*mot*] kind; **c'est très ~ à vous** it's very kind of you; **nous informons notre ~ clientèle que** we wish to inform our customers that; **2** (poli) [*propos, façon*] polite.

IDIOMES **être ~ comme une porte de prison** to be a miserable so-and-so.

aimablement /ɛmabləmɑ̃/ adv (avec politesse) politely; (avec gentillesse) kindly.

aimant, **~e** /ɛmɑ̃, ɑ̃t/ **I** adj affectionate, loving. **II** nm magnet; **~ naturel** magnetite.

aimanter /ɛmɑ̃te/ [1] vtr to magnetize.

aimer /eme/ [1] **I** vtr **1** (d'amour) to love [*personne*]; **~ qn à la folie** to adore sb; **2** (apprécier) to like, to be fond of [*personne, chose*]; **il t'aime bien/beaucoup** he's fond/very fond of you; **j'aime bien l'opéra** I like opera; **~ la chasse** to like hunting; **~ faire**, **~ à faire** LITER to like doing; **j'aime à croire que** I like to think that; **cette plante aime l'ombre** this plant likes shade; **je n'aime pas qu'on me dise ce que j'ai à faire** I don't like being told what to do; **j'aimerais autant rester à la maison ce soir** I'd rather stay at home tonight; **j'aime autant te dire qu'il n'était pas content!** I may as well tell you that he wasn't very pleased!; **j'aime mieux nager que courir** I prefer swimming to running; **j'aimerais mieux que tu ne le leur dises pas** I'd rather you didn't tell them; **il n'a rien de cassé? j'aime mieux ça!** nothing's broken? thank goodness!; **vous acceptez de me rembourser? j'aime mieux ça!** (ton menaçant) you agree to pay me back? that's more like it!

II s'aimer vpr **1** (d'amour) to love each other; **aimez-vous les uns les autres** love one another; **2** (s'apprécier) **elles s'aiment bien** they like each other.

aine /ɛn/ nf groin.

aîné, **~e** /ene/ **I** adj (de deux) elder; (de plus de deux) eldest.

II nm,f **1** (enfant) (premier de deux) elder son/daughter, elder child; (premier de plus de deux) eldest son/daughter, eldest child; **2** (frère, sœur) elder ou older brother/sister; **3** (personne plus âgée) elder; (personne la plus âgée) oldest; **c'est mon ~** he's older than me; **il est de vingt ans mon ~** he's twenty years older than me; **les ~s de la tribu** the elders of the tribe.

aînesse /enɛs/ nf **droit d'~** law of primogeniture.

ainsi /ɛ̃si/ **I** adv **1** (de cette manière) **c'est ~ que l'on faisait le beurre** that's how ou the way they used to make butter; **le mélange ~ obtenu** the mixture obtained in this way; **je t'imaginais ~** that's how I imagined you; **le monde est ~ fait que** the world is made in such a way that; **elle est ~** that's how ou the way she is; **~ va la vie** such is life, that's the way it goes; **c'est ~ qu'on m'appelait** that's what they used to call me; **~ parlait le prophète** thus spoke the prophet; **le jury se compose ~** the panel is made up as follows; **~ fut fait** that's what was done; **~ soit-il** RELIG amen; **2** (introduisant une conclusion) thus LITER, so; **~, depuis 1989...** thus, since 1989...; **~ tu nous quittes?** so you're leaving us then?

II ainsi que loc conj **1** (de même que) as well as; **les employés ~ que leurs conjoints sont invités** employees together with their partners are invited; **l'Italie ~ que quatre autres pays d'Europe** Italy, along with four other European countries; **2** (comme) as; **~ que nous en avions convenu** as we had agreed; **~ qu'un automate** like a robot.

aïoli /ajɔli/ nm: provençal garlic mayonnaise.

air /ɛʀ/ **I** nm **1** (que l'on respire) air; **le bon ~** clean air; **renouveler l'~ d'une pièce** to let some air circulate in a room; **à l'~ libre** outside, outdoors; **concert en plein ~** open-air concert; **activités de plein ~** outdoor activities; **la vie au grand ~** outdoor life; **on manque d'~ ici** it's stuffy in here; **de l'~○!** (va-t'en) get lost○!; **aller prendre l'~** to go out and get some fresh air; **2** (brise, vent) **il n'y a pas d'~** there's no wind; **un déplacement d'~** a rush of air; **un courant d'~** a draught GB ou draft US; **ça fait de l'~** there's a draught GB ou draft US; **3** (autour de la terre) air; **jeter qch en l'~** to throw sth into the air; **les bras en l'~** one's arms (up) in the air; **planer dans les ~s** to glide into the air; **par ~** by air; **regarder en l'~** to look up; **avoir le nez en l'~** to daydream; **dans l'~** FIG [*réforme, idée*] in the air; **il y a un virus dans l'~** there's a virus going around; **en l'~** [*menace, paroles*] empty; [*projet, idée*] vague; **parler en l'~** to speculate; **envoyer** or **flanquer qch en l'~** to send sth flying; **tout mettre en l'~○** (mettre en désordre) to make a dreadful mess; (faire échouer) to ruin everything; **4** (manière d'être) manner; (expression) expression; **avec un ~ résolu** in a resolute manner; **avoir un drôle d'~** to look odd ou funny; **avoir un** or **l'~ distingué** to look distinguished; **d'un ~ triste** with a sad expression; **d'un ~ fâché/désolé** angrily/helplessly; **il y a un ~ de famille entre vous deux** you two share a family likeness; **elle a eu l'~ fin(e)○!** she looked a fool!; **la maison a l'~ d'un taudis** the house looks like a slum; **cela m'en a tout l'~** it seems ou looks like it to me; **j'aurais l'~ de quoi?** I'd look a right idiot!; **cela a l'~ de rien mais** it may not look it, but; **il n'a pas l'~ de comprendre** he doesn't seem to understand; **cela a l'~ d'être solide** it looks strong; **cela a l'~ d'être une usine** it looks like a factory; **il a l'~ de vouloir faire beau** it looks as if it's going to be fine; **5** (ambiance) **un ~ d'abandon** an air of neglect; **un ~ de fête** a carnival atmosphere; **6** (mélodie) tune; **un ~ d'opéra** an aria; **jouer toujours le même ~** LIT to play the same tune over and over again; **~** FIG to come out with the same old story.

II air- (in compounds) **~-mer** air-to-sea.

■ **~ conditionné** (système) air-conditioning; (que l'on respire) conditioned air.

IDIOMES **il ne manque pas d'~○!** he's got a nerve!; **brasser** or **remuer de l'~○** to give the impression of being busy; **prendre** or **se donner de grands ~s** to put on airs; **j'ai besoin de changer d'~** (d'environnement) I need a change of scene; (par agacement) I need to go and do something else.

airain† /ɛʀɛ̃/ nm bronze.

aire /ɛʀ/ nf **1** (domaine) sphere; **~ d'activité** sphere of activity; **2** (surface) area; **3** (nid) eyrie.

■ **~ d'atterrissage** (pour avion) landing strip; (pour hélicoptère) landing pad; **~ de chargement** loading bay; **~ de jeu** playground; **~ de lancement** launching pad; **~ de loisirs** recreation area; **~ de repos** rest area; **~ de services** services (pl) GB, motorway GB ou freeway US service station; **~ de stationnement** parking area.

airelle /ɛʀɛl/ nf (myrtille) bilberry, (baie rouge) cranberry.

aisance /ɛzɑ̃s/ nf **1** (facilité) ease; **l'~ de ta démarche** the ease with which you walk; **l'~ de ton style** your flowing style; **avec ~** with ease; **2** (opulence) comfort, affluence; **vivre dans l'~** to live comfortably.

aise /ɛz/ **I** adj LITER pleased; **j'en suis fort ~** HUM I'm very pleased about it.

II nf LITER (contentement) pleasure; **d'~** [*sourire, ronronner*] with pleasure.

III aises nfpl **tenir à** or **aimer ses ~s** to like one's creature comforts; **il prenait ses ~s sur le canapé** he was stretched out on the sofa.

IV à l'aise loc **être à l'~** or **à son ~** (physiquement) to be comfortable; (financièrement) to be comfortably off; (psychologiquement) to be at ease, to feel comfortable (**avec qn** with sb); **mettre qn à l'~** to put sb at his/her ease; **mettre qn mal à l'~** to make sb feel ill at ease ou uncomfortable; **mets-toi à l'~** make yourself comfortable; **en prendre à son ~ avec qch/qn** to make free with sth/sb; **à votre ~!** as you wish ou like!

aisé, **~e** /eze/ adj **1** (simple) easy; **2** (cossu) wealthy; **être ~** to be well-off; **les classes ~es** the well-off; **3** (sans contrainte) [*manières*] easy; [*style*] flowing.

aisément /ezemɑ̃/ adv easily.

aisselle /ɛsɛl/ nf armpit.

Aix-la-Chapelle /ɛkslaʃapɛl/ **▶ 628** npr Aachen.

ajonc /aʒɔ̃/ *nm* gorse bush.

ajouré, **~e** /aʒuʀe/ *adj* **1** [*napperon*] (entièrement) openwork (*épith*); (bord) hemstitched; **2** [*clocher, balcon*] with ornamental apertures.

ajournement /aʒuʀnəmɑ̃/ *nm* (de voyage, décision) postponement; (de débat, procès) adjournment; **~ de peine** JUR *non-imposition of a sentence*.

ajourner /aʒuʀne/ [1] *vtr* to postpone, to put off [*voyage, projet, décision*]; to adjourn [*débat, procès*].

ajout /aʒu/ *nm* addition; **faire des ~s** to make additions (**à** to).

ajouter /aʒute/ [1] **I** *vtr* to add (**à** to); **~/ne pas ~ foi à qch** FML to put faith/no faith in sth; **la chaleur ajoutée à la pollution fait que...** the heat on top of all the pollution means that...

II ajouter à *vtr ind* **~ à** to add to [*confusion, chagrin*].

III s'ajouter *vpr* **s'~ à** to be added to; **à cela s'ajoute...** to that may be added...; **les désordres sociaux viennent s'~ aux difficultés économiques** on top of the economic difficulties there is also social unrest.

ajustage /aʒystaʒ/ *nm* fitting.

ajustement /aʒystəmɑ̃/ *nm* **1** TECH fit; **2** (adaptation) adjustment; **~ des prix** price adjustment.

ajuster /aʒyste/ [1] *vtr* **1** (régler) to adjust [*bretelle, prix, horaire*]; to alter [*robe, chemise*] (**à** to); to calibrate [*balance*ⓙ]; to shorten [*rênes*]; **~ qch à** or **sur qch** LIT to make sth fit sth; **corsage ajusté** close-fitting bodice; **2** (arranger) to arrange [*coiffure*]; **3** (viser) to take aim at [*lapin*]; **~ son tir** or **coup** LIT to adjust one's aim; FIG to fix a more precise target.

ajusteur /aʒystœʀ/ ▶ 374 *nm* fitter.

alacrité /alakʀite/ *nf* alacrity LITTÉR.

alaise = **alèse**.

alambic /alɑ̃bik/ *nm* CHIMIE still.

alambiqué, **~e** /alɑ̃bike/ *adj* [*expression, style*] convoluted; [*explication*] tortuous.

alanguir /alɑ̃giʀ/ FML [3] *vtr* [*amour, musique*] to make [sb] languid; [*chaleur*] to make [sb] listless; **geste alangui** languid gesture.

alarmant, **~e** /alaʀmɑ̃, ɑ̃t/ *adj* alarming.

alarme /alaʀm/ *nf* alarm; **donner l'~** to raise the alarm; **c'est ce qui a donné l'~** that was what made us/them realize something was wrong.

alarmer /alaʀme/ [1] **I** *vtr* to alarm.

II s'alarmer *vpr* to become alarmed (**de qch** about sth); **vous n'avez aucune raison de vous ~** there's no cause for alarm.

alarmisme /alaʀmism/ *nm* alarmism.

albanais, **~e** /albanɛ, ɛz/ **I** ▶ 394 *adj* Albanian.

II ▶ 338 *nm* LING Albanian.

albâtre /albɑtʀ/ *nm* alabaster.

albatros /albatʀos/ *nm inv* albatross.

albigeois, **~e** /albiʒwa, az/ *adj* Albigensian.

albinos /albinos/ *adj inv, nmf inv* albino.

album /albɔm/ *nm* **1** (livre illustré) illustrated book; **~ de bandes dessinées** comic strip book; **2** (pour timbres, cartes etc) album; **3** (disque) album.

■ **~ à colorier** colouringᴳᴮ book.

albumine /albymin/ *nf* albumin.

alcali /alkali/ *nm* alkali.

alcalin, **~e** /alkalɛ̃, in/ *adj* alkaline.

alchimie /alʃimi/ *nf* alchemy.

alcool /alkɔl/ *nm* **1** (boisson) alcohol; **vous prendrez bien un petit ~?** will you have a little drop of something?; **~ de poire** pear brandy; **sans ~** [*cocktail*] non-alcoholic; [*bière*] alcohol-free; **il ne boit que des ~ s forts** he only drinks spirits; **2** (alcoolisme) **s'adonner à** or **sombrer dans l'~** to take to drink; **3** (substance) alcohol; **boire de l'~** to drink alcohol; **forte teneur en ~** high alcohol content.

■ **~ à brûler** methylated spirits, methsᴼ GB; **~ à 90°** ~ surgical spirit GB, rubbing alcohol US; **~ de menthe** mentholated alcohol.

alcoolique /alkɔlik/ *adj, nmf* alcoholic.

alcoolisé, **~e** /alkɔlize/ *adj* alcoholic; **une boisson peu/non ~e** a low-alcohol/non-alcoholic drink.

alcoolisme /alkɔlism/ *nm* alcoholism.

alcootest /alkɔtɛst/ *nm* **1** (appareil) Breathalyzer®; **2** (contrôle) breath test.

alcôve /alkov/ *nf* alcove; **d'~** [*histoires, secrets*] of the boudoir.

aléa /alea/ *nm* (de temps, nature, marché) vagary; (économique, financier) hazard; **les ~s du métier** occupational hazards.

aléatoire /aleatwaʀ/ *adj* **1** [*événements, succès, résultat*] unpredictable; [*profession*] insecure, risky; **le caractère ~ de** the unpredictability of [*résultat*]; the unstable nature of [*emploi*]; **2** MATH, ORDINAT random; **3** JUR [*acte*] aleatory.

alémanique /alemanik/ ▶ 338 *adj, nm* Alemannic.

alène /alɛn/ *nf* awl.

alentour /alɑ̃tuʀ/ **I** *adv* surrounding; **visite de la ville et de la région** ~ visit of the town and surrounding area; **les maisons d'~** the surrounding houses.

II alentours *nmpl* (environs) surrounding area (*sg*); **les ~s de la ferme** the area around the farm.

III aux alentours de *loc prép* (de lieu) around; (de chiffre, date) about, around.

alerte /alɛʀt/ **I** *adj* **1** [*personne, esprit*] alert; [*démarche*] brisk; [*style, jeu, interprétation*] lively.

II *nf* alert; **être en état d'~** LIT to be in a state of alert; FIG to be on the alert; **donner l'~** to raise the alarm; **donner l'~ à qn** to alert sb; **~ générale** full alert.

■ **~ aérienne** air raid warning; **~ à la bombe** bomb scare.

alerter /alɛʀte/ [1] *vtr* **1** (donner l'alerte) to alert; **2** (informer) to alert (**sur qch** to sth).

alèse /alɛz/ *nf* undersheet, mattress protector.

alevin /alvɛ̃/ *nm* young fish.

alexandrin /alɛksɑ̃dʀɛ̃/ *adj m, nm* alexandrine.

alezan, **~e** /alzɑ̃, an/ *adj* [*cheval*] chestnut.

alfa /alfa/ *nm* (herbe) esparto grass; (fibre) esparto; (papier) esparto paper, alfa paper.

algèbre /alʒɛbʀ/ *nf* algebra.

algébrique /alʒebʀik/ *adj* algebraic.

Alger /alʒe/ ▶ 628 *npr* Algiers.

Algérie /alʒeʀi/ ▶ 232 *nprf* Algeria.

algérien, **-ienne** /alʒeʀjɛ̃, ɛn/ ▶ 394 *adj* Algerian.

algérois, **~e** /alʒeʀwa, az/ ▶ 628 *adj* of Algiers.

algie /alʒi/ *nf* pain; **~ dentaire** toothache.

algue /alg/ *nf* (d'eau douce) alga; (marine) seaweed ℂ; **des ~s** (d'eau douce) algae; (marines) seaweed.

Ali Baba /alibaba/ *npr* **~ et les quarante voleurs** Ali Baba and the forty thieves; **une vraie caverne d'~** a real Aladdin's cave.

alibi /alibi/ *nm* **1** JUR alibi; **fournir un ~ très solide** to give a watertight alibi; **2** (prétexte) excuse; **il a invoqué l'~ d'une importante réunion de travail** he gave an important business meeting as his excuse.

aliénation /aljenasjɔ̃/ *nf* GÉN alienation; **MÉD ~ (mentale)†** insanity.

aliéné, **~e** /aljene/ *nm,f* MÉD insane person.

aliéner /aljene/ [14] **I** *vtr* **1** (détourner) **~ qn à qn** to alienate sb from sb; **ces mesures lui ont aliéné une partie du vote socialiste** these measures have lost him/her a section of the socialist vote; **2** PHILOS, SOCIOL to alienate [*personne*].

II s'aliéner *vpr* (détourner) to alienate [*confrères, électorat, opinion publique*]; **tu t'es aliéné leur estime** you have lost their esteem.

aligné, **~e** /aliɲe/ *adj* POL [*pays*] aligned; **non ~** nonaligned.

alignement /aliɲ(ə)mɑ̃/ *nm* **1** (rang) row, line; **2** (mise côte à côte) alignment; **3** (pour la conformité) alignment; **~ de qch sur qch** alignment of sth with sth; **l'~ de sa conduite sur celle de qn d'autre** bringing one's behaviourᴳᴮ into line with sb else's; **4** (de voie publique) alignment.

aligner /aliɲe/ [1] **I** *vtr* **1** (mettre côte à côte) to put [sth] in a line, to line [sth] up; (mettre en ligne droite) to line [sth] up, to align [*objets, points*]; **2** (rendre conforme à) **~ qch sur qch** to bring sth into line with sth; **3** (énumérer) to give a list of [*arguments, chiffres*]; (accumuler) to line up [*somme*]; to notch up⚬ [*kilomètres, bons résultats*]; **~ les fautes** to make one mistake after another ou the other; **4** (présenter) to line up [*équipe*]. **II s'aligner** *vpr* **1** (être côte à côte) to be in a line; **2** (se mettre en file) to line up; (en formation militaire) to fall into line; **3 s'~ sur** to align oneself with [*pays, parti*]; **s'~ sur le règlement** to conform with the rules.

aliment /alimɑ̃/ *nm* **1** (pour êtres humains, animaux) food; (pour animaux d'élevage) feed; (pour plantes) nutrient; **2** FIG **donner ~ à qch** to feed sth.

alimentaire /alimɑ̃tɛʀ/ *adj* LIT [*besoins, comportement*] dietary; [*ration, industrie, pénurie*] food; **produits** or **denrées ~s** foodstuffs; **régime ~** diet; **trouble du comportement ~** eating disorder.

alimentation /alimɑ̃tasjɔ̃/ *nf* **1** (manière de se nourrir) diet; **~ saine** healthy diet; **une ~ riche en** a diet rich in; **2** (action de se nourrir) feeding; **3** COMM (produits alimentaires) food; (industrie) food industry; (commerce) food retailing; **magasin d'~** food shop, grocery store; **4** (approvisionnement) (en papier, oxygène) feeding (**de** of); **l'~ en eau** the water supply; **l'~ d'une arme à feu** loading a firearm.

alimenter /alimɑ̃te/ [1] **I** *vtr* **1** to feed [*personne, animal*]; **2** (approvisionner) [*torrent, eau*] to feed [*lac, turbine*]; [*tuyau, système*] to feed [*chaudière*]; **~ qch en** to feed sth with [*papier, données*]; **la centrale alimente toute la ville** the power station supplies the whole town with electricity; **~ un budget** to fund a budget; **3** FIG to fuel [*conversation, feu*]. **II s'alimenter** *vpr* **1** [*personne*] to eat; [*animal*] to feed; **s'~ de** [*personne*] to live on; [*animal*] to feed on; **2** (en eau, gaz, électricité) [*ville*] **s'~ en** to be supplied with; **3** [*conversation, haine*] **s'~ de** to thrive on.

alinéa /alinea/ *nm* (rentré) indentation; (ligne rentrée) indented line; (paragraphe) paragraph.

alitement /alitmɑ̃/ *nm* bed rest.

aliter: **s'aliter** /alite/ [1] *vpr* to take to one's bed; **être/rester alité** to be/to remain confined to bed.

alizé /alize/ *adj m*, *nm* (vent) ~ trade wind.

allaitement /alɛtmɑ̃/ *nm* (humain) feeding ₵; (animal) suckling ₵.

allaiter /alɛte/ [1] *vtr* [*femme*] to breast-feed; [*animal*] to suckle; **~ au biberon** to bottle-feed.

allant, ~e /alɑ̃, ɑ̃t/ **I** *adj* active, lively. **II** *nm* drive, bounce; **avoir de l'~, être plein d'~** to have plenty of drive, to be full of bounce; **perdre son ~** to run out of steam.

allécher /aleʃe/ [14] *vtr* to tempt (**avec** with); **~ qn avec des promesses** to tempt sb with promises.

allée /ale/ **I** *nf* **1** (chemin) (de jardin, bois) path; (de parc) GÉN path; (plus large) avenue; (de château, maison) (carrossable) drive; (de ville) avenue; **une ~ de peupliers** an avenue of poplars; **les ~s du pouvoir** FIG the corridors of power; **2** (entre des rangées de sièges) aisle. **II allées** *nfpl* **~s et venues** comings and goings; **surveiller les ~s et venues de qn** to watch sb's movements; **faire des ~s et venues entre les bureaux** to go back and forth between offices. ■ **~ cavalière** bridleway, bridle path; **~ forestière** forest trail.

allégation /alegasjɔ̃/ *nf* allegation; **~s mensongères** false allegations.

allégé, ~e /aleʒe/ **I** *pp* ▶ **alléger**. **II** *pp adj* [*aliment*] (en graisses) low-fat; (en sucre) diet (*épith*).

allégeance /aleʒɑ̃s/ *nf* allegiance.

allégement /aleʒmɑ̃/ *nm* **1** (en poids) lightening; **2** (réduction) (de charges) reduction; (de contrôles) relaxing; (de structures) simplification; **~ fiscal** tax relief; **3** (de conditions de détention) improvement.

alléger /aleʒe/ [15] **I** *vtr* **1** (rendre moins lourd) to lighten; **2** (rendre moins important) to reduce [*dette*] (**de** by); to cut [*impôt*]; to simplify [*dispositif, procédure*]; to relax [*contrôle*]; **~ les horaires scolaires** to reduce the school day; **3** (rendre moins pénible) to improve [*conditions de détention*]; to alleviate [*souffrances*]. **II s'alléger** *vpr* **1** (devenir moins lourd) to get lighter; **2** (devenir moins important) [*dette, impôt*] to be reduced; [*dispositif, procédure*] to be simplified; [*embargo*] to be relaxed; **3** (devenir moins pénible) to be improved.

allégorie /alegoʀi/ *nf* allegory.

allègre /alɛgʀ/ *adj* [*texte, style*] light; [*récit, ton*] lighthearted; [*pas, humeur*] buoyant.

allégrement /alegʀəmɑ̃/ *adv* **1** (avec allégresse) joyfully; **2** (sans souci) IRON blithely; **mettre ~ qn en prison** to throw sb in jail without a second thought.

allégresse /alegʀɛs/ *nf* joy; **dans l'~** in joyful mood; **participer à l'~ générale** to share in the general rejoicing.

alléguer /alege/ [14] *vtr* (invoquer) to invoke; (prétexter) to allege.

Allemagne /alman/ ▶ **232** *nprf* Germany; **la République fédérale d'~** the Federal Republic of Germany; **l'~ unie** unified Germany.

allemand, ~e /almɑ̃, ɑ̃d/ **I** ▶ **394** *adj* German. **II** ▶ **338** *nm* LING German.

aller¹ /ale/ [9] **I** *v aux* **1** (marque le futur) **je vais rentrer chez moi** I'm going home; **j'allais partir** I was just leaving; **j'allais partir quand il est arrivé** I was about to leave when he arrived; **l'homme qui allait inventer la bombe atomique** the man who was to invent the atomic bomb; **il va le regretter** he'll regret it; **ça va ~ mal**⚬ there'll be trouble; **tu vas me laisser tranquille?** will you please leave me alone!; **2** (marque le futur programmé) **je vais leur dire ce que je pense** I'm going to tell them what I think; **3** (marque le mouvement) **~ rouler de l'autre côté de la rue** to go rolling across the street; **~ atterrir⚬ sur mon bureau** to end up on my desk; **4** (marque l'inclination) **va savoir!** who knows?; **qu'es-tu allé te mettre en tête?** where did you pick up that idea?; **qui irait le soupçonner?** who would suspect him?; **pourquoi es-tu allé faire ça?** why did you have to go and do that?; **allez-y comprendre quelque chose!** just try and work that out!; **5** (marque l'évolution) **la situation va (en) se compliquant** the situation is getting more and more complicated; **~ (en) s'améliorant** to be improving; **la tristesse ira (en) s'atténuant** the grief will diminish.

II *vi* **1** (se porter, se dérouler, fonctionner) **comment vas-tu, comment ça va?** how are you?; **ça va (bien)** I'm fine; **les enfants vont bien?** are the children all right?; **comment va la santé?** how are you keeping?; **~ beaucoup mieux** to be much better; **bois ça, ça ira mieux** drink this, you'll feel better; **tout va bien?** is everything going all right?; **vous êtes sûr que ça va?** are you sure you're all right?; **les affaires vont bien** business is good; **ça va l'école?** how are things at school?; **ça ne va pas très fort** (ma santé) I'm not feeling very well; (la vie) things aren't too good; (le moral) I'm feeling a bit low; **ça va mal entre eux** things aren't too good between them; **qu'est-ce qui ne va pas?** what's the matter?; **la voiture a quelque chose qui ne va pas** there's something wrong with the car; **tout est allé si vite!** it all happened so quickly!; **ne pas ~ sans peine** or **mal** not to be easy; **ça va de soi** or **sans dire** it goes without saying; **l'amour ne va jamais de soi** love is never straightforward; **ça va tout seul** (c'est facile) it's a doddle⚬ GB, it's easy as pie; **les choses vont très vite** things are moving fast; **on fait ~s**⚬ struggling on⚬; **ça peut ~**⚬, **ça ira**⚬ could be worse⚬; **ça va pas, non?** or **ça va pas la tête**⚬? are you mad⚬ GB or crazy⚬?; **2** (se déplacer) to go; **allez tout droit** go straight ahead; **~ et venir** (dans une pièce) to pace up and down; (d'un lieu à l'autre) to run in and out; **la liberté d'~ et venir** the freedom to come and go at will; **les nouvelles vont vite**

news travels fast; **où vas-tu?** where are you going?, where are you off○ to?; **~ en Pologne/au marché** to go to Poland/to the market; **je suis allé de Bruxelles à Anvers** I went from Brussels to Antwerp; **allons-y!** let's go!; **je l'ai rencontré en allant au marché** I met him on the way to the market; **~ sur** or **vers Paris** to head for Paris; **~ vers le nord** to head north; **va-t-on vers une nouvelle guerre?** are we heading for another war?; **j'y vais** (je m'en occupe) I'll get it; (je pars)○ I'm going, I'm off○; **où va-t-il?** where is he off to○?; **où va-t-on**○**?**, **où allons-nous**○**?** FIG what are things coming to?, what's the world coming to?; **3** (pour se livrer à une activité) **~ au travail** to go to work; **~ à la chasse** to go hunting; **~ au pain**○ to go and get the bread; **~ aux courses**○ or **commissions**○ to go shopping; **~ aux nouvelles** to go and see if there's any news; **4** (s'étendre dans l'espace) **la route va au village** the road leads to the village; **la rue va de la gare à l'église** the street goes from the station to the church; **5** (convenir) **ma robe, ça va?** is my dress all right?; **ça va, ça peut aller**○ (en quantité) that'll do; (en qualité) it'll do; **ça va comme ça** it's all right as it is; **ça ne va pas du tout** that's no good at all; **la traduction n'allait pas** the translation was no good; **une soupe, ça (te) va?** how about some soup?; **va pour une soupe**○ soup is okay○; **ça va si je porte un jean?** can I wear jeans?; **si le contrat ne te va pas, ne le signe pas** don't sign the contract if you're not happy with it; **si ça va pour toi, ça va pour moi**○ if it's okay by you, it's okay by me○; **ma scie ne va pas pour le métal** my saw is no good for metal; **ça te va bien de faire la morale**○ IRON you're hardly the person to preach; **6** (être de la bonne taille, de la bonne forme) **~ à qn** to fit sb; **7** (flatter, mettre en valeur) **~ à qn** to suit sb; **ta cravate ne va pas avec ta chemise** your tie doesn't go with your shirt; **les meubles vont bien ensemble** the furniture all matches; **je trouve que ta sœur et son petit ami vont très bien ensemble** I think your sister and her boyfriend are ideally suited; **8** (se ranger) to go; **les assiettes vont dans le placard** the plates go in the cupboard; **9** (faculté) **pouvoir ~ dans l'eau** to be waterproof; **le plat ne va pas au four** the dish is not ovenproof; **10** (dans une évaluation) **la voiture peut ~ jusqu'à 200 km/h** the car can do up to 200 kph; **certains modèles peuvent ~ jusqu'à 1 000 francs** some models can cost up to 1,000 francs; **11** (en arriver à) **~ jusqu'au président** to take it right up to the president; **~ jusqu'à tuer** to go as far as to kill; **leur amour est allé jusqu'à la folie** their love bordered on madness; **12** (dans le temps) **~ jusqu'en 1914** to go up to 1914; **la période qui va de 1918 à 1939** the period between 1918 and 1939; **le contrat allait jusqu'en 1997** the contract ran until 1997; **~ sur ses 17 ans** to be going on 17; **13** (agir, raisonner) **vas-y doucement, le tissu est fragile** careful, the fabric is delicate; **tu vas trop vite** you're going too fast; **vas-y, demande-leur!** (incitation) go on, ask them!; **vas-y, dis-le!** (provocation) come on, out with it!; **allons, allez!** (pour encourager, inciter) come on!; **si tu vas par là, rien n'est entièrement vrai** if you take that line, nothing is entirely true; **14** (contribuer) **y ~ de sa petite larme** to shed a little tear; **y ~ de son petit discours** to do one's party piece; **y ~ de ses économies** to dip into one's savings; **y ~ de sa personne** to pitch in; **15**○ (se succéder) **ça y va la vodka avec lui** he certainly gets through the vodka; **ça y allait les coups** the fur was flying○; **16** (servir) **l'argent ira à la réparation de l'église** the money will go toward(s) repairing the church; **l'argent est allé dans leurs poches** they pocketed the money; **17** (enfreindre) **~ contre la loi** [*personne*] to break the law; [*acte*] to be against the law; **je ne peux pas ~ contre ce qu'il a décidé** I can't go against his decision.

III s'en aller *vpr* **1** (partir, se rendre) **il faut que je m'en aille** I must go ou leave; **va-t'en!** go away!; **s'en ~ au travail** to go off to work; **2** (disparaître) **les nuages vont s'en ~** the clouds will clear away; **la tache ne s'en va pas** the stain won't come out; **avec le temps, tout s'en va** everything fades with time; **3** FML (mourir) to pass away; **4** (avoir l'intention de, essayer)

aller¹

Lorsque *aller* fait partie d'une expression figée comme *aller dans le sens de*, *aller de pair avec* etc., l'expression est traitée sous l'entrée *sens*, *pair* etc.

On notera les différentes traductions de *aller* verbe de mouvement indiquant:
un déplacement unique dans le temps:

> *je vais au théâtre ce soir* = I'm going to the theatre this evening

ou une habitude:

> *je vais au théâtre tous les lundis* = I go to the theatre every Monday

aller + infinitif

La traduction dépend du temps:

> *je vais apprendre l'italien* = I'm going to learn Italian
> *il est allé voir l'exposition* = he went to see the exhibition
> *j'allais me marier quand la guerre a éclaté* = I was going to get married when the war broke out
> *va voir* = go and see
> *va leur parler* = go and speak to them
> *j'irai voir l'exposition demain* = I'll go and see the exhibition tomorrow
> *je vais souvent m'asseoir au bord de la rivière* = I often go and sit by the river
> *il ne va jamais voir une exposition* = he never goes to see exhibitions

On notera que pour les activités sportives on peut avoir:

> *aller nager* = to go swimming ou to go for a swim
> *aller faire du vélo* = to go cycling ou to go on a bike ride

On trouvera ci-dessous des exemples et des exceptions illustrant *aller* dans ses différentes fonctions verbales.

je m'en vais leur dire ce que je pense I'm going to tell them what I think; **va-t'en savoir!** who knows? **IV** *v impers* **1** (être en jeu) **il y va de ta santé** your health is at stake; **2** (se passer) **il en va souvent ainsi** that's often what happens; **il en va de même pour toi** that goes for you too; **il en va autrement en Corée** things are different in Korea; **3** MATH **40 divisé par 12 il y va 3 fois et il reste 4** 12 into 40 goes 3 times with 4 left over.

aller² /ale/ *nm* **1** (trajet) **j'ai fait une escale à l'~** I made a stopover on the way out; **j'ai pris le bus à l'~** (en allant là) I took the bus there; (en venant ici) I took the bus here; **l'~ a pris trois heures** the journey there took three hours; **il n'arrête pas de faire des ~s et retours entre chez lui et son bureau** he keeps running to and fro from his house to the office; **billet ~** GÉN single ticket GB, one-way ticket US; (d'avion) one-way ticket; **billet ~ (et) retour** return ticket GB, round trip (ticket) US; **match ~** first leg; **2** (ticket) **~ (simple)** single (ticket) GB, one-way ticket (**pour** to); **~ (et) retour** return ticket.

allergie /alɛrʒi/ *nf* MÉD allergy; **avoir une ~ à** MÉD to have an allergy to; FIG to be allergic to.

allergique /alɛrʒik/ *adj* MÉD, FIG allergic (**à** to).

allergisant, ~e /alɛrʒizɑ̃, ɑ̃t/ *adj* MÉD [*produit*] allergenic; **un produit qui a une action ~e** a product which causes allergic reactions.

allergologue /alɛrɡɔlɔɡ/ **▶ 374** *nmf* allergist.

alliage /aljaʒ/ *nm* **1** (produit) alloy; **en ~** (épith); **2** (association) combination.

alliance /aljɑ̃s/ *nf* **1** (bague) wedding ring; **2** (entente) alliance; **faire ~ avec** to form an alliance with; **3** RELIG Covenant; **4** (mariage) FML union SOUT, marriage; **5** (combinaison) FML combination.
■ **l'~ atlantique** the Atlantic Alliance.

allié, ~e /alje/ **I** *pp* ▶ **allier**
II *pp adj* (uni) (par un mariage) related by marriage (**à qn** to sb); (par un traité) [*nation*] allied; **le débarquement ~** the Allied landings.
III *nm,f* (proche) ally; (parent) relative; **les ~s** MIL HIST the Allies.

allier /alje/ [2] **I** vtr **1** TECH to alloy [*métaux*] (**à, avec** with); **2** (combiner) to combine (**et, à** with); **3** (par un mariage) to unite [sth] by marriage [*familles*].
II s'allier vpr **1** POL, MIL (s'unir) to form an alliance (**avec, à** with); **2** (s'harmoniser) [*sons, couleurs*] to go (well) together.

alligator /aligatɔʀ/ nm alligator.

allitération /al(l)iteʀasjɔ̃/ nf alliteration 𝒞.

allô /alo/ excl hello!, hallo!

allocation /al(l)ɔkasjɔ̃/ nf **1** (action) granting; **2** (somme) benefit, benefits (pl) US; **une ~ de 50 000 francs** 50,000 francs in benefit ou benefits US.
■ **~ chômage** unemployment benefit ou benefits US; **~ logement** housing benefit ou benefits US; **~ vieillesse** discretionary retirement pension; **~s familiales** family allowance (sg).

allocution /al(l)ɔkysjɔ̃/ nf address.

allonge /alɔ̃ʒ/ nf **1** (de table) leaf; **2** (de boxeur) reach.

allongé, ~e /alɔ̃ʒe/ adj **1** (longiforme) elongated; **2** [*trot, galop*] extended.

allongement /alɔ̃ʒmɑ̃/ nm **1** (de liste, procédure, délais) lengthening; (de vacances) extension; **2** (de voyelle) lengthening; **3** (de ressort) extension.

allonger /alɔ̃ʒe/ [13] **I** vtr **1** (coucher) to lay [sb] down; **2** (agrandir) to lengthen [*robe, rideau*] (**de** by); to extend [*liste, vacances*] (**de** by); to prolong [*espérance de vie*] (**de** by); **~ le visage de qn** to make sb's face look longer; **~ le pas** to quicken one's step; **3** (étirer) to stretch [sth] out [*bras*]; **4** (diluer) to water [sth] down [*café, vin*]; **allongé d'eau** watered down; **5**○ (dans un combat) to floor○ [*adversaire*].
II vi [*jours*] to lengthen.
III s'allonger vpr **1** (pour se reposer) to lie down; (s'étirer) to stretch out; **allongé sur le dos** lying on his back; **2** (s'agrandir) to get longer; **ta silhouette s'allonge** you look slimmer.

allouer /alwe/ [1] vtr **1** (donner) to allocate [*somme*] (**à qn** to sb; **à qch** for sth); **2** (accorder) to grant [*prêt, indemnité*] (**à qn** to sb; **à qch** for sth); to allot, to allow [*temps*] (**à qn** to sb; **à qch** for sth).

allumage /alymaʒ/ nm **1** AUT ignition; **2** (de lampe, chauffage) switching on; **l'~ est automatique** it switches on automatically.

allumé○, ~e /alyme/ **I** adj **1** (fou) mad○; **2** (ivre) tipsy○; **être bien ~** to be well oiled○.
II nm,f (fou) **c'est un ~** he's mad○.

allume-cigare(s) /alymsigaʀ/ nm inv cigar lighter.

allume-gaz /alymgaz/ nm inv gas lighter.

allumer /alyme/ [1] **I** vtr **1** (par la flamme) to light [*bougie, gaz*]; to strike [*allumette*]; to start [*incendie*]; **le feu ne va pas rester allumé** the fire is not going to stay alight GB, lighted US; **2** (électriquement) to switch [sth] on, to turn [sth] on; **le couloir est allumé** the light is on in the corridor; **laisser ses phares allumés** to leave one's headlights on; **allume!** switch on the light!; **3** (exciter) to stir [*imagination*]; to arouse [*désir*]; to turn [sb] on○ [*personne*].
II s'allumer vpr **1** (électriquement) [*lampe, radio, chauffage*] to switch on; **2** FIG [*regard*] to light up.

allumette /alymɛt/ nf match.

allumeur, -euse /alymœʀ, øz/ ▶374 **I** nm,f **1** **~ de réverbères** lamplighter; **2**○ (qui séduit) tease.
II nm AUT distributor.

allure /alyʀ/ nf **1** (de marcheur) pace; (de véhicule) speed; **à vive ~** at high speed; **modérer** ou **ralentir son ~** to slow down; **à toute ~** [*conduire*] at top speed; [*marcher, réciter, manger*] really fast; **à cette ~** at this rate; **2** (apparence) (de personne) appearance; (de vêtement) look; (d'événement) aspect; **avoir des ~s de** to look like; **il a une drôle d'~** he's a funny-looking chap; **prendre l'~** or **des ~s de** [*changement, révolte*] to begin to look like; **3** (distinction) style; **elle a beaucoup d'~** she's got a lot of style; **avoir fière ~** to cut a fine figure.

allusif, -ive /alyzif, iv/ adj **1** (qui contient une allusion) allusive; **2** (qui parle par allusions) indirect; **elle est restée très allusive** she spoke very indirectly.

allusion /alyzjɔ̃/ nf (sous-entendu) allusion (**à** to); **faire ~ à** to allude to; **~ perfide** innuendo.

alluvial, ~e, mpl -iaux /alyvjal, o/ adj alluvial.

alluvion /alyvjɔ̃/ nf alluvium; **des ~s** alluvia.

almanach /almana(k)/ nm almanac.

aloès /alɔɛs/ nm inv aloe.

aloi /alwa/ nm **un succès de bon ~** a well-deserved success; **une plaisanterie de mauvais ~** a tasteless joke; **une gaieté de bon ~** a simple cheerfulness.

alors /alɔʀ/ **I** adv **1** (à ce moment-là) then; **c'est ~ qu'il prit la parole** it was then that he started to speak; **il avait ~ 18 ans** he was 18 at the time; **~ seulement** only then; **le pays, ~ sorti de la crise, pourra** the country which by then will be out of recession, will be able to; **la mode d'~** the fashion in those days; **le premier ministre britannique d'~** the British Prime Minister at the time; **mes romans d'~** my novels of the time; **jusqu'~** until then; **2** (dans ce cas-là) then; **~ je m'en vais** I'm going then; **(mais) ~ cela change tout!** but that changes everything!; **et ~?** so what?; **~? que faisons-nous?** so? what shall we do?; **3** (de ce fait) so; **il était tard, ~ j'ai pris un taxi** it was late so I took a taxi; **4** (pour résumer) then; **on se voit demain ~?** we'll see each other tomorrow then?; **5** (ou bien) **ou ~** or else; **je serai dans la cuisine ou ~ dans le jardin** I'll be in the kitchen or in the garden; **6**○ (dans un récit) so; **~ il me dit... so he said to me...; 7** (pour renforcer une exclamation) **non mais ~!** honestly!; **ça ~!** (étonnement) good grief!; **~ ça!** (indignation) that's not on!
II alors que loc conj **1** (pendant que) while; **2** (tandis que) when; **tu lui souris ~ que tu le détestes** you smile at him while (in fact) you hate him.
III alors même que loc conj even though.

alouette /alwɛt/ nf lark.

alourdir /aluʀdiʀ/ [3] **I** vtr [*fardeau*] to weigh [sb] down [*personne*]; [*problème*] to make [sth] tense [*atmosphère*]; **le subjonctif alourdit la phrase** the subjunctive weighs the sentence down; **manteau alourdi par la pluie** coat heavy with rain; **le dernier témoignage a alourdi les accusations** the statement by the last witness weighed heavily against the accused.
II s'alourdir vpr [*paupières*] to grow heavy; [*air*] to get heavy; [*dépenses*] to increase; **le bilan de victimes s'est alourdi** the death toll has risen.

alourdissement /aluʀdismɑ̃/ nm (de l'impôt, de prélèvement) increase (**de** in).

alpaga /alpaga/ nm (animal, laine) alpaca.

alpage /alpaʒ/ nm mountain pasture.

alpestre /alpɛstʀ/ adj alpine.

alphabet /alfabɛ/ nm **1** (signes) alphabet; **2** (manuel) ABC (book).

alphabétique /alfabetik/ adj alphabetical.

alphabétisation /alfabetizasjɔ̃/ nf (enseignement de l'écriture) literacy tuition.

alphabétiser /alfabetize/ [1] vtr (enseigner) to teach [sb] to read and write [*personne*]; to promote literacy in [*pays*].

alphanumérique /alfanymeʀik/ adj alphanumeric.

alpin, ~e /alpɛ̃, in/ adj alpine.

alpinisme /alpinism/ ▶329 nm mountaineering.

alpiniste /alpinist/ nmf mountaineer, climber.

alsacien, -ienne /alzasjɛ̃, ɛn/ ▶509 **I** adj [*personne*] from Alsace; [*cuisine, population*] of Alsace.
II ▶338 nm LING Alsatian.

altération /alteʀasjɔ̃/ nf (détérioration) (de facultés) impairment (**de** of); (de denrée) spoiling (**de** of); (d'environnement) deterioration (**de** in); (de sentiment, couleur) change (**de** in).

altercation /altɛʀkasjɔ̃/ nf altercation.

altérer /alteʀe/ [14] **I** vtr **1** (détériorer) to affect [*saveur, relation, santé*]; to spoil [*denrée*]; to mar [*joie*]; to alter [*sentiment*]; to change [*expression*]; to fade [*couleur*]; **2** (falsifier) to distort [*fait*]; to adulterate [*substance*]; **3 être altéré de sang/de pouvoir** to thirst for blood/power.

II s'altérer *vpr* [*santé, saveur*] to become impaired; [*denrée*] to spoil; [*voix*] to falter; [*sentiment*] to change.

alternance /altɛʀnɑ̃s/ *nf* **1** GÉN alternation; **en ~ avec** alternately with; **'l'Avare' se joue en ~** 'l'Avare' is on every other night; **2** POL **choisir l'~** [*électorat, pays*] to opt for a change in power.

alternateur /altɛʀnatœʀ/ *nm* alternator.

alternatif, -ive[1] /altɛʀnatif, iv/ *adj* **1** GÉN alternate; **2** ÉLECTROTECH alternating; **3** SOCIOL alternative.

alternative[2] /altɛʀnativ/ *nf* alternative.

alternativement /altɛʀnativmɑ̃/ *adv* alternately.

alterné, ~e /altɛʀne/ *adj* alternating.

alterner /altɛʀne/ [1] **I** *vtr* GÉN to alternate; **~ les cultures** to rotate crops.
II *vi* **1** (se succéder) to alternate (**avec** with); **2** (se relayer) **~ avec qn pour faire qch** to take turns with sb (at) doing sth.

altesse /altɛs/ *nf* **1** (titre) **son Altesse royale** His/Her Royal Highness; **2** (personne) prince/princess.

altier, -ière /altje, ɛʀ/ *adj* haughty.

altimètre /altimɛtʀ/ *nm* altimeter.

altitude /altityd/ *nf* **1** (hauteur) altitude; **prendre de l'~** [*avion, ballon*] to gain altitude ou height; **à basse/haute ~** [*neiger, voler*] at low/high altitude; **quelle est l'~ du mont Blanc?** how high is Mont Blanc?; **des sommets de plus de 6 000 mètres d'~** peaks more than 6,000 metres[GB] high; **avoir une faible ~** to be close to sea-level; **2** (haute montagne) **en ~** [*pousser, neiger*] high up (in the mountains); **station d'~** mountain resort.

alto /alto/ **I** *adj* [*saxophone, clarinette*] alto.
II *nm* **1** ▶392 (instrument) viola; **2** ▶374 (musicien) viola player GB, violin US; **3** (voix) alto.

altruiste /altʀɥist/ **I** *adj* altruistic.
II *nmf* altruist.

aluminium /alyminjɔm/ *nm* aluminium GB, aluminum US; **en ~ aluminium** (*épith*) GB, aluminum (*épith*) US.

alvéole /alveɔl/ *nf* **1** (de ruche) alveolus; **2** (de poumon) alveolus; (de dent) tooth socket; **3** (de roche) cavity.

alvéolé, ~e /alveɔle/ *adj* honeycombed.

amabilité /amabilite/ **I** *nf* **1** (gentillesse) kindness; **avec ~** kindly; **quelle ~!** IRON charming!; **2** (politesse) courtesy; **avec ~** politely.
II amabilités *nfpl* (prévenances) **faire des ~s à qn** to be polite to sb; **se dire des ~s** LIT to exchange pleasantries; IRON to exchange insults.

amadouer /amadwe/ [1] **I** *vtr* to coax, to cajole [*personne, animal*]; **~ qn pour qu'il fasse qch** to cajole sb into doing sth.
II s'amadouer *vpr* [*personne*] to soften.

amaigrir /amegʀiʀ/ [3] *vtr* [*maladie, régime*] to make [sb] thinner [*personne*]; **je l'ai trouvée très amaigrie** I found her much thinner; **un visage amaigri par la maladie** a face made thin by illness.

amaigrissant, ~e /amegʀisɑ̃, ɑ̃t/ *adj* slimming.

amaigrissement /amegʀismɑ̃/ *nm* weight loss, loss of weight.

amalgame /amalgam/ *nm* **1** GÉN mixture; (d'idées) PEJ hotchpotch GB, hodgepodge US; **2** (pour les dents, en chimie) amalgam.

amalgamer /amalgame/ [1] *vtr* **1** (associer) PEJ to lump together [*problèmes*]; **2** (mélanger) to blend, to amalgamate [*ingrédients*].

amande /amɑ̃d/ *nf* BOT **1** (fruit) almond; **yeux en ~** almond(-shaped) eyes; **2** (dans un noyau) kernel.

amandier /amɑ̃dje/ *nm* almond tree.

amanite /amanit/ *nf* amanita; **~ phalloïde** death cap.

amant /amɑ̃/ *nm* lover.

amarante /amaʀɑ̃t/ **I** ▶141 *adj inv* amaranthine.
II *nf* (plante, colorant) amaranth.

amarrage /amaʀaʒ/ *nm* **1** (de bateau) mooring; **2** (fixation) tying, fastening; **3** ASTRONAUT docking.

amarre /amaʀ/ *nf* (cordage) rope; **les ~s** moorings;

rompre les ~s to break its moorings; **larguer les ~s** LIT to cast off; FIG to set off.

amarrer /amaʀe/ [1] *vtr* **1** NAUT to moor; **~ à** to moor alongside [*quai*]; to moor to [*anneau, piquet*]; **2** (attacher) to tie (**à, sur** to).

amas /ama/ *nm inv* **1** (d'objets, de sable, neige) pile; (de tôle, ruines) heap; MÉD (de sang, graisse) accumulation; **2** (en astronomie) cluster; **3** (en géologie) mass.

amasser /amase/ [1] **I** *vtr* to amass, to accumulate [*fortune, livres, papiers*]; to lay in [*provisions*]; to acquire [*connaissances*]; to amass [*preuves*]; to collect [*témoignages*].
II s'amasser *vpr* [*objets, neige*] to pile up; [*preuves*] to build up.

amateur /amatœʀ/ **I** *adj inv* amateur; **radio ~** radio ham○.
II *nm* **1** (connaisseur) (en sport, photographie) enthusiast; (en vin) connoisseur; **~ de jazz** jazz lover; **c'est un grand ~ de cigares** he's a great lover of cigars; **pour les ~s de sensations fortes** for thrill-seekers; **~ de catch** wrestling fan; **2** (collectionneur) **~ d'antiquités** antiques collector; **3** (non-professionnel) amateur.

amazone /amazon/ *nf* (cavalière) horsewoman; **monter en ~** to ride sidesaddle.

Amazone /amazon/ **I** *nf* MYTHOL Amazon.
II ▶260 *nprm* GÉOG **l'~** the Amazon (river).

Amazonie /amazoni/ ▶509 *nprf* Amazon.

ambages: sans ambages /sɑ̃zɑ̃baʒ/ *loc adv* without beating around the bush.

ambassade /ɑ̃basad/ *nf* **1** (lieu, service) embassy; **2** (employés) embassy staff; (diplomates) embassy officials.

ambassadeur, -drice /ɑ̃basadœʀ, dʀis/ *nm* ambassador; **l'~ de France au Chili** the French ambassador to Chile.

ambassadrice /ɑ̃basadʀis/ *nf* (épouse d'ambassadeur) ambassador's wife.

ambiance /ɑ̃bjɑ̃s/ *nf* **1** (atmosphère) atmosphere, ambiance; **2** (gaieté) lively atmosphere; **tu peux compter sur lui pour mettre de l'~** you can count on him to liven things up; **ça manque d'~ ici**○ it's not exactly lively here.

ambiant, ~e /ɑ̃bjɑ̃, ɑ̃t/ *adj* **1** [*air*] surrounding; **à température ~e** at room temperature; **2** FIG [*pessimisme*] pervading; [*état d'esprit*] prevailing.

ambigu, -uë /ɑ̃bigy/ *adj* [*réponse, mot, situation*] ambiguous; [*personnage*] multifaceted; [*sentiment, attitude*] ambivalent.

ambiguïté /ɑ̃bigyite/ *nf* **1** (de mot, situation) ambiguity; **sans ~** [*question*] unambiguous; [*situation*] clear-cut; [*définir, dire*] unambiguously; **2** (de personnage) enigmatic nature; (de sentiment) ambivalence.

ambitieux, -ieuse /ɑ̃bisjø, øz/ **I** *adj* ambitious.
II *nmf* ambitious person; **les ~** ambitious people.

ambition /ɑ̃bisjɔ̃/ *nf* ambition; **avoir de l'~** to be ambitious; **un homme sans ~** a man with no ambition; **avoir l'~ de faire qch** to have an ambition to do sth; **je n'ai pas l'~ de réformer le système en un mois** I don't aim to change the system in a month.

ambitionner /ɑ̃bisjɔne/ [1] *vtr* to aspire to [*poste, place*]; to aim for [*médaille, titre sportif*]; **~ de faire** to aim to do.

ambivalence /ɑ̃bivalɑ̃s/ *nf* ambivalence.

ambre /ɑ̃bʀ/ *nm* (résine) **~ (jaune)** amber; **couleur d'~** amber; **collier d'~** amber necklace.

ambré, ~e /ɑ̃bʀe/ *adj* **1** ▶141 (couleur d'ambre) amber; **2** (à senteur d'ambre) perfumed with ambergris.

ambroisie /ɑ̃bʀwazi/ *nf* MYTHOL ambrosia.

ambulance /ɑ̃bylɑ̃s/ *nf* ambulance.

ambulancier, -ière /ɑ̃bylɑ̃sje, ɛʀ/ ▶374 *nm,f* ambulance driver.

ambulant, ~e /ɑ̃bylɑ̃, ɑ̃t/ *adj* [*artiste*] itinerant; [*marchand*] mobile; [*cirque*] travelling[GB]; **théâtre ~** itinerant players (*pl*); **service de restauration ~e** train buffet trolley; **vendeur ~** (dans une gare) snack trolley man; **c'est un cadavre ~**○ he's/she's a walking skeleton○.

âme /ɑm/ *nf* **1** PHILOS, RELIG soul; **(que) Dieu ait son ~** (may) God rest his/her soul; **2** (nature profonde) soul, spirit; **avoir une ~ de poète** to have the soul of a poet ou a poetic soul; **avoir l'~ d'un chef** to have the spirit of a leader; **3** (siège de la pensée et des émotions) soul; **avoir l'~ sensible** to be a sensitive soul; **interprétation sans ~** soulless interpretation; **socialiste dans l'~** a socialist to the core; **4** (conscience morale) soul; **paix de l'~** spiritual peace; **en mon ~ et conscience** in all honesty; **5** (personne, habitant) soul; **c'est une ~ généreuse** he/she has great generosity of spirit; **pas ~ qui vive** not a (living ou single) soul; **6** (de nation, parti) soul (**de** of); (de complot) moving spirit (**de** in).
■ **~ damnée** partner in crime; **~ en peine** soul in torment; **errer comme une ~ en peine** to wander around like a lost soul; **~ sœur** soul mate.

amélioration /ameljɔʀasjɔ̃/ *nf* improvement.

améliorer /ameljɔʀe/ [1] **I** *vtr* to improve [*résultat*]; to increase [*production*]; **un pique-nique amélioré** HUM a superior picnic.
II s'améliorer *vpr* to improve; **ça ne va pas en s'améliorant**○ things aren't getting any better.

amen /amɛn/ *nm inv* RELIG amen; **dire ~ à tout** FIG to agree to everything.

aménagé, **~e** /amenaʒe/ *adj* **1** (transformé) converted; **2** (équipé) equipped; **l'appartement est mal ~** the apartment is not very well appointed.

aménagement /amenaʒmɑ̃/ *nm* **1** (de région, ville) development; **l'~ du territoire** ≈ town and country planning; **2** (de port de plaisance, routes) construction; (d'espaces verts) creation; (de parc, terrain de sport) laying out; **3** (de fermette, grenier) (en transformant) conversion; (en améliorant) improvement; **4** (en équipant) (de cuisine) equipping; (de magasin) fitting; **5** (de maison, bateau) fitting; **6** (par rapport à un règlement, une loi) adjustment; **l'~ du temps de travail** flexible working hours (*pl*).

aménager /amenaʒe/ [13] *vtr* **1** (en transformant) to convert; (en améliorant) to do up; **2** (en équipant) to equip [*cuisine*]; to develop [*région*]; to fit out [*magasin*]; **3** (créer) to create [*espaces verts*]; to build [*route*]; to make [*coin-repas*]; to lay out [*jardin*]; **4** (en adaptant) to arrange [*emploi du temps*]; to adjust [*règlement*].

amende /amɑ̃d/ *nf* fine; **être condamné à une ~** to be fined; **'défense d'afficher sous peine d'~'** 'bill-stickers will be prosecuted'.
IDIOMES **faire ~ honorable** to make amends.

amendement /amɑ̃dmɑ̃/ *nm* **1** JUR amendment (**à** to; **sur** on); **2** AGRIC (opération) enrichment.

amender /amɑ̃de/ [1] **I** *vtr* **1** JUR to amend [*loi*]; **2** AGRIC to enrich [*sol*].
II s'amender *vpr* to mend one's ways; **un criminel amendé** a reformed criminal.

amène /amɛn/ *adj* LITER affable.

amener /amne/ [16] **I** *vtr* **1** (mener) **~ qn quelque part** [*personne, train*] to take sb somewhere; **2** (venir avec) **~ qn** (**quelque part**) to bring sb (somewhere); **quel bon vent vous amène?** what brings you here?; **3** (apporter) CONTROV **~ qch** (**à qn**) to bring (sb) sth; **4** (convoyer) [*personne, organisme*] to bring [*eau, marchandises*]; **5** (provoquer) to cause [*problèmes, maladie*]; to bring [*pluie, gloire*]; to bring about [*renouveau*]; **6** (aborder) to bring up, to introduce [*sujet, question*]; **~ qch sur le tapis**○ to bring sth up; **être bien amené** [*conclusion*] to be well-presented; [*phrase, remarque*] to be well-timed; **7** (conduire) FIG **~ qn à** to lead sb to [*conclusion*]; to bring sb to [*question*]; **~ qn à faire** to lead sb to do; **nous serons amenés à nous revoir** we shall doubtless meet again; **~ un liquide à la bonne température** to bring a liquid to the right temperature; **8** (tirer vers soi) [*pêcheur*] to pull in [*filet*]; [*navigateur*] to strike [*voile*].
II s'amener *vpr* (venir) to come; (arriver) to turn up○ (**avec** with); **amène-toi!** come here!

amenuiser /amənɥize/ [1] **I** *vtr* **1** GÉN to reduce [*chance, risque*]; **2** TECH to plane down [*planche*].
II s'amenuiser *vpr* [*réserves, espoir, chance, clientèle*] to dwindle; [*risque*] to lessen; [*temps*] to slip by.

amer, -ère /amɛʀ/ *adj* LIT, FIG bitter.

américain, **~e** /ameʀikɛ̃, ɛn/ **I** ▶394| *adj* American.
II *nm* LING American English.

américaniser /ameʀikanize/ [1] **I** *vtr* to Americanize.
II s'américaniser *vpr* to become Americanized.

amérindien, -ienne /ameʀɛ̃djɛ̃, ɛn/ *adj* Amerindian.

Amérindien, -ienne /ameʀɛ̃djɛ̃, ɛn/ ▶394| *nm,f* Amerindian, American Indian.

Amérique /ameʀik/ ▶232| *nprf* America; **~ centrale/latine** Central/Latin America; **~ du Nord/du Sud** North/South America.

amerrir /ameʀiʀ/ [3] *vi* [*hydravion*] to land (on water); [*vaisseau spatial*] to splash down.

amertume /amɛʀtym/ *nf* LIT, FIG bitterness.

ameublement /amœblmɑ̃/ *nm* (meubles) furniture; (secteur d'activité) furniture trade ou business.

ameublir /amœbliʀ/ [3] *vtr* to break up [*sol*].

ameuter /amøte/ [1] *vtr* **1** (alerter) [*personne, bruit*] to bring [sb] out; **2** (attrouper à des fins hostiles) to stir [sb] up (**contre** against); **3** (pour la chasse) to whip [sth] in [*chiens*].
II s'ameuter *vpr* [*foule, passants*] to mass, to gather.

ami, ~e /ami/ **I** *adj* **nous sommes très ~s** we are very good friends.
II *nm,f* friend; **se faire des ~s** to make friends; **je m'en suis fait une ~e** I made a friend of her; **un ~ de toujours** a life-long friend; **'un ~ qui vous veut du bien'** 'a well-wisher'; **en ~** as a friend; **un ~ des bêtes** an animal lover; **l'association des ~s de Pouchkine** the friends of Pushkin; ▶ **faux¹**.
IDIOMES **les bons comptes font les bons ~s** PROV a debt paid is a friend kept; **c'est dans le besoin ou malheur qu'on connaît ses ~s** PROV a friend in need is a friend indeed.

amiable: **à l'amiable** /alamjabl/ *loc* [*se séparer*] on friendly terms; [*séparation*] amicable; [*adoption*] by private agreement; [*divorce*] by mutual consent; **s'arranger à l'~** to come to an amicable agreement.

amiante /amjɑ̃t/ *nm* asbestos.

amibe /amib/ *nf* ZOOL, MÉD amoeba.

amical, ~e¹, pl -aux /amikal, o/ *adj* friendly.

amicale² /amikal/ *nf* association.

amicalement /amikalmɑ̃/ *adv* **1** (gentiment) [*aider*] kindly; [*accueillir*] warmly; [*concourir*] in a friendly way; **bavarder ~** to chat (away) happily; **2** (en fin de lettre) (**bien**) **~** best wishes.

amidon /amidɔ̃/ *nm* starch.

amidonner /amidɔne/ [1] *vtr* to starch [*linge*].

amincir /amɛ̃siʀ/ [3] **I** *vtr* **1** (faire paraître mince) [*vêtement*] to make [sb] look slimmer; **2** (avec un outil) to plane down [*planche*].
II s'amincir *vpr* **1** [*personne, visage*] to get slimmer; **2** [*planche, couche*] to get thinner.

amincissement /amɛ̃sismɑ̃/ *nm* **1** (de personne) slimming; **2** (de couche de glace) thinning (down).

aminé, ~e /amine/ *adj* **acide ~** amino acid.

amiral, ~e, mpl -aux /amiʀal, o/ **I** *adj* **vaisseau ~** flagship.
II ▶284| *nm* admiral.

amirauté /amiʀote/ *nf* **1** (grade) admiralship; **2** (corps des amiraux) admiralty; (résidence) Admiralty House.

amitié /amitje/ **I** *nf* friendship (**pour** for); **par ~** out of friendship; **entretenir l'~** to keep friendship alive; **en toute ~** as a friend; **éprouver de l'~ pour qn** to have friendly feelings toward(s) sb; **se prendre d'~ pour qn** to take a liking to sb; **faire à qn l'~ de faire** to be kind enough to do; **se lier d'~ avec qn** to strike up a friendship with sb; **être fidèle en ~** to be a faithful friend.
II amitiés *nfpl* (en fin de lettre) kindest regards.

ammoniac /amɔnjak/ *nm* (gaz) ammonia.

ammoniaque /amɔnjak/ *nf* ammonia.

amnésie /amnezi/ *nf* amnesia.

amnésique /amnezik/ **I** *adj* amnesic.

II *nmf* amnesiac.

amniotique /amnjɔtik/ *adj* amniotic.

amnistie /amnisti/ *nf* amnesty (**en faveur de** for).

amnistier /amnistje/ [2] *vtr* to grant an amnesty to [*délinquent*]; to grant an amnesty for [*délit*].

amocher° /amɔʃe/ [1] **I** *vtr* to bash° [sb/sth] up [*personne, voiture*].
II s'amocher *vpr* to bash oneself up°; **s'~ le nez** to bash up° one's nose.

amoindrir /amwɛ̃dRiR/ [3] **I** *vtr* to reduce [*résistance*]; to weaken [*autorité, personne*]; **il est sorti très amoindri de cette épreuve** he came out of that ordeal a lesser man.
II s'amoindrir *vpr* [*forces*] to diminish; [*différences*] to grow less.

amoindrissement /amwɛ̃dRismɑ̃/ *nm* (de pouvoir, forces, facultés) weakening; (de ressources) reduction.

amollir: s'amollir /amɔliR/ [3] *vpr* **1** (devenir mou) to soften, to become soft; **2** (s'affaiblir) to grow weak.

amonceler /amɔ̃sle/ [19] **I** *vtr* to pile up.
II s'amonceler *vpr* [*nuages, sable, neige*] to build up; [*preuves, soucis, ennuis*] to pile up, to accumulate.

amoncellement /amɔ̃sɛlmɑ̃/ *nm* (processus) (de sable, terre) piling up; (résultat) (de sable, terre) pile; (de richesses) mass.

amont /amɔ̃/ **I** *adj inv* [*ski*] uphill.
II *nm* GÉOG (de cours d'eau) upper reaches (*pl*); **en ~** LIT upstream (**de** from); FIG upstream (**de** of); **naviguer d'~ en aval** to sail downstream.

amoral, ~e, *mpl* **-aux** /amɔRal, o/ *adj* amoral.

amorçage /amɔRsaʒ/ *nm* (d'obus, de pompe) priming; (de discussions, négociations) initiating; **l'~ de la reprise économique paraît difficile** getting economic recovery underway seems difficult.

amorce /amɔRs/ *nf* **1** (de processus, discussion) initiation; (de route, voie ferrée) initial section; (de pellicule) leader, tongue; **l'~ d'un sourire** the hint of a smile; **2** (pour la pêche) bait; **3** (détonateur) (d'arme) cap, primer; (de pétard) cap; **pistolet à ~s** cap gun.

amorcer /amɔRse/ [12] **I** *vtr* **1** (commencer) to begin; [*véhicule*] to go into [*virage*]; **il amorça un geste pour ouvrir la fenêtre** he made as if to open the window; **2** (appâter) to bait; **3** TECH (mettre en route) to prime [*pompe*]; to arm, to activate [*arme à feu*].
II s'amorcer *vpr* to begin, to get under way.

amorphe /amɔRf/ *adj* **1** (apathique) apathetic; **2** CHIMIE amorphous.

amortir /amɔRtiR/ [3] *vtr* **1** (atténuer) to deaden [*bruit*]; to absorb [*choc*]; to break [*chute*]; **2** (rentabiliser) **j'ai amorti mon ordinateur en quelques mois** my computer paid for itself in a few months; **3** SPORT (au tennis) to kill [*balle*]; (au football) to trap [*ballon*].

amortissement /amɔRtismɑ̃/ *nm* **1** (de bruit) deadening; (de choc) absorption; (de chute) cushioning; **2** (de dette) redemption; (d'emprunt) paying off; **3** (en comptabilité) depreciation.

amortisseur /amɔRtisœR/ *nm* TECH shock absorber; PHYS damper.

amour /amuR/ **I** *nm* **1** (affection) love; **l'~ filial** filial love; **c'est le grand ~ entre eux** they are passionately in love; **lettre d'~** love letter; **par ~ pour qn/qch** out of love for sb/sth, for the love of sb/sth; **mourir d'~** to die of a broken heart; **l'~ de la liberté** the love of liberty; **pour l'~ de l'art** for the sake of art; **pour l'~ de Dieu** LIT for the love of God; FIG for heaven's sake; **2** (personne aimée) GÉN love; (forme d'adresse) darling; **c'était un ~ de jeunesse** it was a youthful romance; **3**° (relations sexuelles) love; **faire l'~ avec** to make love with; **les plaisirs de l'~** the pleasures of lovemaking; **4**° (charmant) **~ de** adorable.
II amours *nmpl* ou *nfpl* **1** ZOOL **saison des ~s** mating season; **2** (aventures) love affairs; **les ~s de** the amorous adventures of; **à tes ~s!** (quand on éternue) bless you!

■ **~ courtois** HIST courtly love; **~ d'enfance** childhood sweetheart.

IDIOMES **vivre d'~ et d'eau fraîche** to live on love alone; **revenir à ses premières ~s** to return to one's first love.

amouracher: s'amouracher /amuRaʃe/ [1] *vpr* **s'~ de** to become infatuated with.

amourette /amuRɛt/ *nf* passing infatuation.

amoureux, -euse /amuRø, øz/ **I** *adj* **1** (de quelqu'un) **être/tomber ~** to be/to fall in love (**de** with); **2** (passionné) **être ~ de peinture** to be a lover of painting; **3** (qui dénote de l'amour) [*relation, regard*] loving; [*élan, comportement*] of love; **vie amoureuse** love life.
II *nm,f* lover; **un ~ de musique** a music-lover.

amour-propre /amuRpRɔpR/ *nm* self-esteem; **il est blessé dans son ~** his pride is hurt.

amovible /amɔvibl/ *adj* [*capuchon, housse, doublure*] detachable; [*étagère, siège, cloison*] removable.

ampère /ɑ̃pɛR/ *nm* PHYS amp, ampère.

amphibie /ɑ̃fibi/ *adj* ZOOL, AUT amphibious.

amphithéâtre /ɑ̃fiteatR/ *nm* **1** (naturel, antique) amphitheatre[GB]; **2** UNIV lecture theatre[GB] ou hall.

amphore /ɑ̃fɔR/ *nf* amphora.

ample /ɑ̃pl/ *adj* **1** (large) [*manteau, robe*] loose-fitting; [*jupe, manche*] full; [*geste*] sweeping; **2** (abondant) [*quantité*] ample; [*récolte*] abundant; [*détails*] full; **je me tiens à votre disposition pour de plus ~s renseignements** I would be pleased to provide you with any further information; **3** (puissant) [*style, phrase*] rich; [*voix*] sonorous.

amplement /ɑ̃pləmɑ̃/ *adv* fully; **c'est ~ suffisant** that's more than enough.

ampleur /ɑ̃plœR/ *nf* (de problème) size, extent; (de projet, sujet, d'étude) scope; (d'événement, de catastrophe, tâche) scale; (de dégâts, réactions) extent; **prendre de l'~** [*épidémie, rumeur*] to spread; [*manifestations, parti*] to grow in size; **le mouvement prend de plus en plus d'~** the movement is becoming more and more extensive; **de (très) grande ~** on a large ou vast scale.

amplificateur, -trice /ɑ̃plifikatœR, tRis/ **I** *adj* [*effet, force*] magnifying.
II *nm* amplifier.

amplification /ɑ̃plifikasjɔ̃/ *nf* **1** PHYS amplification; **2** (extension) (de relations, d'échanges) development; (de grève, revendications) escalation; (de débat) expansion.

amplifier /ɑ̃plifje/ [2] **I** *vtr* to amplify [*son, courant*]; to magnify [*geste, rumeur*]; to expand [*grève, échanges*].
II s'amplifier *vpr* [*son*] to grow; [*échanges*] to grow; [*grève*] to intensify; [*tendance*] to gain momentum.

amplitude /ɑ̃plityd/ *nf* amplitude.

ampoule /ɑ̃pul/ *nf* **1** ÉLECTROTECH **~ (électrique)** (light) bulb; **une ~ de 100 watts** a 100-watt bulb; **2** (de médicament) (buvable) phial; (injectable) ampoule; **3** (sur la peau) blister.
■ **~ de flash** flash bulb.

ampoulé, ~e /ɑ̃pule/ *adj* PEJ bombastic.

amputation /ɑ̃pytasjɔ̃/ *nf* amputation; FIG drastic cut (**de** in).

amputer /ɑ̃pyte/ [1] *vtr* **1** MÉD to amputate [*membre*]; to perform an amputation on [*personne*]; **il a été amputé du bras droit** he had his right arm amputated; **2** (réduire) to cut [sth] drastically [*texte, crédits, discours*]; **~ qch de qch** to cut sth from sth.

amulette /amylɛt/ *nf* amulet.

amusant, ~e /amyzɑ̃, ɑ̃t/ *adj* **1** (distrayant) entertaining; **trouver ~ de faire** to find it entertaining to do; **2** (drôle) funny, amusing; **le plus ~ c'est que** the funniest thing is that; **3** (surprenant) funny.

amusé, ~e /amyze/ *adj* [*sourire, regard, air*] amused, of amusement (*après n*); **elle a eu un sourire ~** she smiled in amusement.

amuse-gueule /amyzgœl/ *nm inv* (chose à grignoter) cocktail snack GB, munchies (*pl*) US.

amusement /amyzmɑ̃/ *nm* entertainment; **regarder qn avec ~** to enjoy watching sb.

amuser /amyze/ [1] **I** *vtr* (divertir) to entertain; (plaire) to amuse [*personne*]; **laisse-le, si ça l'amuse!** let him

be, if that's what makes him happy; **ce qui m'amuse c'est que** what I find amusing is that; **ça les amuse de faire** they enjoy doing.
II s'amuser *vpr* **1** (jouer) [*enfant, animal*] to play (**avec** with); **pour s'~** for fun; **dépêche-toi, je n'ai pas le temps de m'~** hurry up, I haven't got time to mess about○; **ne t'amuse pas à ce petit jeu avec moi** don't play that little game with me; **2** (passer du bon temps) [*enfant, adulte*] to have a good time; **s'~ comme des fous**○ to have a great time ou a ball○; **amuse-toi bien!** enjoy yourself!; **3** (s 'aviser de) **ne t'amuse pas à faire cela** don't go doing that; **4** (se moquer) LITER **s'~ de qch/qn** to make fun of sth/sb.
amuseur, -euse /amyzœʀ, øz/ *nm,f* entertainer.
amygdale /ami(g)dal/ *nf* tonsil; **se faire opérer des ~s** to have one's tonsils taken out.
an /ɑ̃/ **▶ 13|, 156|, 588|** *nm* **1** (durée) year; **une fois par ~** once a year; **2** (de date) year; **en l'~ deux mille** in the year two thousand; **en l'~ de grâce 1616** in the year of Our Lord 1616; **l'~ 55 avant J.-C./après J.-C.** 55 BC/AD; **3** (pour exprimer l'âge) **avoir huit ~s** to be eight (years old); **les moins de dix-huit ~s** the under-eighteens; **il est mort à 25 ~s** he died at the age of 25; **une fille de 7 ~s** a 7-year-old girl; **whisky de douze ~s d'âge** twelve-year-old whisky.
IDIOMES **bon ~, mal ~** year in, year out.
anabolisant, ~e /anaboliza̰, ɑ̃t/ **I** *adj* anabolic.
II *nm* anabolic steroid.
anachronique /anakʀɔnik/ *adj* anachronistic.
anachronisme /anakʀɔnism/ *nm* anachronism.
anagramme /anagram/ *nf* anagram.
anal, ~e, *mpl* **-aux** /anal, o/ *adj* anal.
analgésie /analʒezi/ *nf* analgesia.
analogie /analɔʒi/ *nf* analogy.
analogique /analɔʒik/ *adj* analogical.
analogue /analɔg/ *adj* similar (**à** to), analogous SOUT (**à** to).
analphabète /analfabɛt/ *adj, nmf* illiterate.
analphabétisme /analfabetism/ *nm* illiteracy.
analyse /analiz/ *nf* **1** GÉN (examen) analysis; **faire l'~ de qch** to analyse GB sth; **en dernière ~** in the final analysis; **avoir l'esprit d'~** to have an analytical mind; **2** MÉD test; **3** MATH (discipline) calculus; **4** PSYCH psychoanalysis; **faire une ~, être en ~** [*patient*] to be in analysis.
■ **~ grammaticale** parsing; **faire l'~ grammaticale d'une phrase** to parse a sentence; **~ logique** clause analysis; **~ de sang** blood test; **~ d'urine** urine test.
analyser /analize/ [1] *vtr* **1** GÉN to analyse GB [*problème, substance, texte*]; **2** MÉD to test [*sang, urine*]; **3** PSYCH to psychoanalyse GB; **se faire ~** to be in analysis.
analyste /analist/ **▶ 374|** *nmf* analyst.
analyste-programmeur, -euse, *mpl* **analystes-programmeurs** /analistpʀɔgʀamœʀ/ **▶ 374|** *nm,f* analyst-programmer.
analytique /analitik/ *adj* **1** GÉN, PHILOS analytical; **2** PSYCH analytic.
ananas /anana(s)/ *nm inv* pineapple.
anarchie /anaʀʃi/ *nf* LIT, FIG anarchy.
anarchique /anaʀʃik/ *adj* LIT, FIG anarchic.
anarchisme /anaʀʃism/ *nm* anarchism.
anarchiste /anaʀʃist/ **I** *adj* anarchistic.
II *nmf* anarchist.
anathème /anatɛm/ *nm* anathema.
anatomie /anatɔmi/ *nf* **1** (science, structure) anatomy; **2**○ (silhouette) figure; **elle a une belle ~** she's got a good figure; **3** (analyse) analysis.
■ **~ artistique** (spécialité) life drawing; (œuvre) life study.
anatomique /anatɔmik/ *adj* [*étude, planche, dessin*] anatomical; [*forme, objet*] anatomically designed.
ancestral, ~e, *mpl* **-aux** /ɑ̃sɛstral, o/ *adj* ancestral.
ancêtre /ɑ̃sɛtʀ/ *nmf* **1** (aïeul) ancestor; **2**○ (personne âgée) old man/woman; **3** (forme ancienne) ancestor; (précurseur) father, forerunner.

anche /ɑ̃ʃ/ *nf* MUS reed.
anchois /ɑ̃ʃwa/ *nm inv* anchovy.
ancien, -ienne[1] /ɑ̃sjɛ̃, ɛn/ **I** *adj* **1** (d'autrefois) former; **mon ancienne école** my old school; **2** (vieux) old; **dans l'~ temps** in the old days; **3** [*histoire, langue*] ancient; **la Grèce ancienne** ancient Greece; **l'~ français** Old French; **4** ART, COMM [*style, monnaie, tableau*] old; [*voiture*] vintage; [*meuble*] antique; [*livre*] old, antiquarian; **5** (dans une profession) senior.
II *nm* **1** (vétéran) (de congrégation, tribu) elder; (d'entreprise) senior member; **les ~s du village** the village elders; **les ~s** (les personnes âgées) the older people; **2** (qui a été membre) (d'entreprise) old member; (de grande école) graduate; **3** (immobilier) **l'~** older property; **4** COMM (vieilles choses) antiques (*pl*); **5** (pour distinguer des générations) elder; **Caton l'~** Cato the Elder.
III anciens *nmpl* ancients.
■ **~ combattant** veteran; **~ élève** SCOL old boy; UNIV graduate; **l'Ancien Régime** the Ancien Régime; **l'Ancien Testament** the Old Testament.
ancienne[2]: **à l'ancienne** /alɑ̃sjɛn/ *loc* [*confiture, meuble*] traditional; [*fabriqué*] in the traditional way.
anciennement /ɑ̃sjɛnmɑ̃/ *adv* formerly.
ancienneté /ɑ̃sjɛnte/ *nf* **1** (de personne) seniority (**dans** in); **promotion à l'~** promotion based on seniority; **trois mois/ans d'~** three months'/years' service; **2** (de tradition, relique) antiquity; **3** (âge) age.
ancrage /ɑ̃kʀaʒ/ *nm* NAUT (action d'ancrer) anchoring; (mouillage) anchorage.
ancre /ɑ̃kʀ/ *nf* NAUT anchor; **jeter l'~** LIT to cast anchor; FIG to settle down; **lever l'~** LIT to weigh anchor; FIG○ to get a move on○.
ancrer /ɑ̃kʀe/ [1] **I** *vtr* **1** NAUT to anchor [*navire*]; **2** (fixer) to fix [*idée*]; to establish [*parti, coutume*]; **~ qch dans la réalité** to anchor sth to reality.
II s'ancrer *vpr* **1** NAUT to anchor, to cast anchor; **2** FIG [*idée*] to become fixed (**dans** in); [*parti, coutume*] to become established; **société trop ancrée dans ses habitudes** society which is too set in its ways.
andouille /ɑ̃duj/ *nf* **1** CULIN andouille; **2**○ fool.
androgyne /ɑ̃dʀɔʒin/ **I** *adj* androgynous.
II *nm* androgyne.
androïde /ɑ̃dʀɔid/ *nm* android.
andropause /ɑ̃dʀɔpoz/ *nf* male menopause.
âne /an/ *nm* **1** ZOOL donkey, ass; **2**○ (personne stupide) dimwit○; SCOL dunce.
anéantir /aneɑ̃tiʀ/ [3] **I** *vtr* **1** (détruire) to ruin [*récoltes*]; to lay waste to [*ville*]; to wipe out [*peuple*]; to shatter [*espoir*]; **2** (abattre) [*nouvelle*] to crush; [*fatigue*] to exhaust; [*chaleur*] to overwhelm.
II s'anéantir *vpr* [*espoir, rêve*] to be shattered.
anéantissement /aneɑ̃tismɑ̃/ *nm* **1** (de ville) destruction; (de peuple) annihilation; (de récolte) devastation; **2** (d'espoir) shattering; (d'une personne) total collapse.
anecdote /anɛkdɔt/ *nf* anecdote; **un auteur qui se perd dans l'~** an author who digresses on trivial topics; **pour l'~** as a matter of interest.
anecdotique /anɛgdɔtik, anɛkdɔtik/ *adj* anecdotal.
anémie /anemi/ *nf* **1 ▶ 196|** MÉD anaemia; **2** FIG weakness.
anémier /anemje/ [2] **I** *vtr* **1** MÉD to make [sb] anaemic [*personne*]; **2** FIG to weaken.
II s'anémier *vpr* **1** MÉD to become anaemic; **2** FIG to grow feeble.
anémique /anemik/ *adj* **1** MÉD anaemic; **2** FIG weak, anaemic.
anémone /anemɔn/ *nf* anemone.
ânerie /anʀi/ *nf* (parole) silly remark; (action) silly blunder; **dire des ~s** to talk rubbish○ ou nonsense; **faire des ~s** to do silly things.
ânesse /anɛs/ *nf* she-ass, female donkey; **lait d'~** asses' milk.
anesthésie /anɛstezi/ *nf* MÉD anaesthesia; **faire une ~ locale** to give sb a local anaesthetic; **sous ~ générale** under general anaesthetic; **2** FIG (de l'opinion publique) anaesthetizing.

anesthésier /anɛstezje/ [2] *vtr* to anaesthetize.

anesthésique /anɛstezik/ *adj, nm* anaesthetic.

anesthésiste /anɛstezist/ ▶ 374 *nmf* anaesthetist GB, anesthesiologist US.

aneth /anɛt/ *nm* dill.

anévrisme /anevʀism/ *nm* aneurysm.

anfractuosité /ɑ̃fʀaktɥozite/ *nf* crevice.

ange /ɑ̃ʒ/ *nm* **1** RELIG angel; **être un ~ de patience** to be patience itself; **2** (terme d'affection) angel, darling.
■ **~ déchu** fallen angel; **~ exterminateur** avenging angel; **~ gardien** guardian angel.
IDIOMES **être aux ~s** to be in seventh heaven, to be walking on air; **'un ~ passe!'** 'somebody's walked over my grave!'; **un ~ passa** there was a lull in the conversation; **discuter du sexe des ~s** to count how many angels can dance on the head of a pin.

angélique /ɑ̃ʒelik/ I *adj* angelic.
II *nf* BOT, CULIN angelica.

angelot /ɑ̃ʒlo/ *nm* cherub.

angélus /ɑ̃ʒelys/ *nm inv* RELIG angelus.

angevin, ~e /ɑ̃ʒvɛ̃, in/ ▶ 628 *adj* Angevin (*épith*), of Anjou (*après n*).

angine /ɑ̃ʒin/ ▶ 196 *nf* MÉD throat infection.
■ **~ diphtérique** angina diphtherica; **~ de poitrine** angina pectoris; **~ rouge** tonsillitis.

angiome /ɑ̃ʒjom/ ▶ 196 *nm* angioma.

anglais, ~e¹ /ɑ̃glɛ, ɛz/ I *adj* English.
II ▶ 338 *nm* LING English.
IDIOMES **filer à l'~e** to take French leave.

Anglais, ~e /ɑ̃glɛ, ɛz/ *nm,f* Englishman/Englishwoman; **les ~** the English.

anglaise² /ɑ̃glɛz/ I *adj* ▶ **anglais**.
II *nf* **1** (boucle) ringlet; **2** (écriture) slanted script.

angle /ɑ̃gl/ *nm* **1** MATH angle; **2** (coin) corner; **être à** or **faire l'~ de deux rues** to be at the corner of two streets; **le bâtiment qui fait l'~** the building on the corner; **bibliothèque d'~** corner bookcase; **faire un ~** [*rue*] to bend; **3** (point de vue) angle; **vu sous cet ~** viewed from this angle.
■ **~ droit** MATH right angle; **faire un ~ droit avec qch** to make a right angle with sth; **se couper à ~ droit** to intersect at right angles; **~ mort** AUT, AVIAT blind spot; MIL dead angle.

Angleterre /ɑ̃glətɛʀ/ ▶ 509 *nprf* GÉOG England.

anglican, ~e /ɑ̃glikɑ̃, an/ *adj, nm,f* Anglican.

angliciser /ɑ̃glisize/ [1] I *vtr* to anglicize.
II **s'angliciser** *vpr* to become anglicized.

angliciste /ɑ̃glisist/ *nmf* (spécialiste) Anglicist; (étudiant) student of English.

anglo-américain, ~e, *mpl* **~s** /ɑ̃gloameʀikɛ̃, ɛn/ I *adj* GÉN Anglo-American; LING American English (*épith*).
II ▶ 338 *nm* LING American English.

Anglo-Normande /ɑ̃glonɔʀmɑ̃d/ ▶ 305 *adj f* **les îles ~s** the Channel Islands.

anglophone /ɑ̃glɔfɔn/ I *adj* English-speaking; **littérature ~** literature of the English-speaking countries; **civilisations ~s** the English-speaking world.
II *nmf* GÉN English speaker; (au Canada) Anglophone.

anglo-saxon, -onne, *mpl* **~s** /ɑ̃glosaksɔ̃, ɔn/ *adj* **1** HIST, LING Anglo-Saxon; **2** (d'Angleterre et des États-Unis) Anglo-Saxon, British and American.

angoissant, ~e /ɑ̃gwasɑ̃, ɑ̃t/ *adj* (alarmant) alarming; (effrayant) frightening.

angoisse /ɑ̃gwas/ *nf* **1** GÉN, PSYCH anxiety (**devant, de** about); **dans l'~ de faire** for fear of doing; **2** (crise d'anxiété) anxiety; **3** PHILOS anguish, angst.

angoissé, ~e /ɑ̃gwase/ *adj* [*voix, visage, personne*] anxious.

angoisser /ɑ̃gwase/ [1] I *vtr* to worry [*personne*].
II ⃝ *vi* to be anxious ou nervous.

angolais, ~e /ɑ̃gɔlɛ, ɛz/ ▶ 394 *adj* Angolan.

angora /ɑ̃gɔʀa/ *adj, nm* angora.

anguille /ɑ̃gij/ *nf* ZOOL, CULIN eel.

IDIOMES **il y a ~ sous roche** there's something going on.

angulaire /ɑ̃gylɛʀ/ *adj* MATH, PHYS angular.

anguleux, -euse /ɑ̃gylø, øz/ *adj* [*visage, traits*] bony; [*aspect, contours*] jagged; [*personne*] prickly.

anicroche /anikʀɔʃ/ *nf* hitch; **sans ~(s)** without a hitch.

animal, ~e, *mpl* **-aux** /animal, o/ I *adj* **1** BIOL animal (*épith*); **2** (digne de l'animal) [*foule*] savage; [*comportement*] brutish.
II *nm* animal.
■ **~ de compagnie** pet; **~ domestique** domestic animal; **~ nuisible** pest; **~ sauvage** wild animal.

animalerie /animalʀi/ *nf* **1** (dans un laboratoire) animal house; **2** ▶ 374 (magasin) pet shop GB, pet store US.

animalier, -ière /animalje, ɛʀ/ I *adj* wildlife (*épith*).
II *nm,f* ▶ 374 (dans un laboratoire) animal keeper.
III *nm* ▶ 374 ART wildlife artist.

animateur, -trice /animatœʀ, tʀis/ ▶ 374 *nm,f* **1** (de club) coordinator; (de groupe d'études, d'association) leader; (de projet, congrès, festival) organizer; **2** (présentateur) presenter; **3** CIN (technicien) animator.

animation /animasjɔ̃/ *nf* **1** (de groupe, d'émission, exposition) organization; (de ventes, service commercial) coordination; (de festival, cérémonie) orchestration; **elle a été chargée de l'~ du stand** she's in charge of running the stand; **~ culturelle** promotion of cultural activities; **2** (entrain) life, vitality; **mettre de l'~ dans une réception** to liven up a reception; **ville qui manque d'~** town that lacks vitality; **une soirée sans ~** a lacklustre GB party; **3** (de rue, marché, lieu de travail) hustle and bustle; (de personnes) excitement; **4** (activité dirigée) organized activity; **5** CIN animation.

animé, ~e /anime/ *adj* **1** (vivant) [*débat, soirée, orateur, période*] lively; [*rue*] bustling; FIN [*marché*] brisk; **2** (inspiré) **~ de bonnes intentions** spurred on by good intentions; **3** LING, PHILOS animate.

animer /anime/ [1] I *vtr* **1** (diriger) to lead [*débat, groupe*]; to run [*stage, revue*]; to present [*émission, spectacle*]; **animé par** [*groupe, spectacle*] organized by; [*mouvement*] led by; [*émission*] presented by; **2** (rendre vivant) to liven up [*ville, récit, réunion*]; **3** (inspirer) [*sentiment*] to drive (on) [*personne*]; **4** (rendre brillant) to put a sparkle into [*regard*]; **une lueur d'intérêt anima son visage** his/her face brightened with interest; **5** (insuffler la vie) LIT [*âme, vie*] to animate [*corps, matière*]; FIG [*artiste, lumière*] to bring [sth] to life [*œuvre*].
II **s'animer** *vpr* **1** (devenir vif) [*conversation, débat*] to become lively; [*réunion, jeu*] to liven up; [*visage, expression*] to light up; [*orateur, participant*] to become animated; **2** (s'agiter) [*lieu public, auditoire*] to come to life; **3** (prendre vie) to come to life.

animosité /animozite/ *nf* animosity (**envers** toward(s); **entre** between).

anis /ani/ *nm inv* **1** BOT (plante) anise; (graine) aniseed; **à l'~** [*biscuit, bonbon*] aniseed (*épith*); [*boisson*] aniseed-flavoured GB; (*bonbon*) aniseed drop.

ankyloser: s'ankyloser /ɑ̃kiloze/ [1] *vpr* [*personne, jambes, bras*] to get stiff; **j'ai les jambes ankylosées** my legs are stiff.

annales /anal/ *nfpl* **1** (de pays, période) annals; **ça restera** or **c'est à inscrire dans les ~** FIG that will go down in history; **2** (d'un examen) book of past papers.

anneau, *pl* **~x** /ano/ I *nm* **1** (bague, attache) ring; **2** (de planète, ver de terre) ring; **3** (de champignon) annulus.
II **anneaux** *nmpl* SPORT rings.

année /ane/ ▶ 588 *nf* year; **l'~ en cours** this year; **en quelle ~ le disque est-il sorti?** what year was the album released? **avec les ~s** over the years; **d'~ en ~** year by year; **d'une ~ à l'autre** from one year to the next; **l'~ 1962** the year 1962; **l'~ Mozart** the Mozart year; **ces dix dernières ~s** over the last ten years; **il a fait une ~ de droit** he has done one year of law; **souhaiter la bonne ~ à qn** to wish sb a happy new year; **tout le long de l'~** throughout the year; **en quelques ~s** within the space of a few years; **dans quelques ~s** in a few years; **en début/fin d'~** early/late in the year; **(dans) les ~s 80** (in) the eighties; **location à l'~** annual rent.

■ **~ bissextile** leap year; **~ civile** calendar year; **~ fiscale** tax year; **~ de référence** base year; **~ sabbatique** sabbatical year; **~ universitaire** academic year; **les Années folles** the Roaring Twenties.

année-lumière, *pl* **années-lumière** /anelymjɛR/ *nf* light-year.

annelé, **~e** /anle/ *adj* **1** ZOOL ringed; **2** ARCHIT annulated.

annexe /anɛks/ **I** *adj* **1** (contigu) [*local, salle*] adjoining; **2** (complémentaire) [*questions*] additional; [*dossier*] attached.
II *nf* **1** (bâtiment) annexe GB, annex US; **2** (document complémentaire) appendix.

annexer /anɛkse/ **I** *vtr* **1** POL [*État, pays*] to annex [*territoire, pays*]; **2** (joindre) to append (**à** to).
II s'annexer *vpr* (s'approprier) to appropriate.

annexion /anɛksjɔ̃/ *nf* POL annexation (**par** by).

annihilation /aniilasjɔ̃/ *nf* **1** GÉN (d'espoirs) death; (d'efforts) destruction; **2** (destruction) annihilation.

annihiler /aniile/ [1] *vtr* to destroy [*efforts, espoirs*]; to cancel out [*effet, résultats*].

anniversaire /anivɛRsɛR/ **I** *adj* **date** or **jour ~ de** anniversary of.
II *nm* **1** (de personne, d'entreprise) birthday; **bon ~ !** happy birthday!; **2** (d'événement) anniversary.

annonce /anɔ̃s/ *nf* **1** (action) announcement; **à l'~ du déficit** when the deficit was announced; **2** (message) advertisement, advert° GB, ad°; **~ publicitaire** advert°; **faire passer une ~** to place an advertisement (**dans** in); ▶**petit**; **3** JEUX declaration; **faire une ~** (au bridge) to bid; **4** (indice) sign.
■ **~ immobilière** property ad°.

annoncer /anɔ̃se/ [12] **I** *vtr* **1** (faire savoir) to announce [*nouvelle, décision*] (**à** to); **elle nous a annoncé son départ** she informed us that she was leaving; **ils nous ont annoncé la nouvelle** GÉN they told us the news; **(mauvaise nouvelle) they broke the news to us; 2** (signaler l'arrivée de) to announce; **qui dois-je ~?** what name shall I give?; **3** (prédire) to forecast [*phénomène, événement*]; **4** (être l'indice de) [*événement, signal*] to herald [*événement*]; **n'~ rien de bon** to be a bad sign; **5** (au bridge) to bid; **~ la couleur** (aux cartes) to call trumps; FIG to lay one's cards on the table.
II s'annoncer *vpr* **1** (se manifester) [*crise, tempête*] to be brewing; **2** (se présenter) **la saison s'annonce bien** the season is off to a good start; **l'été s'annonce chaud** the summer looks like being a hot one; **la récolte 92 s'annonce excellente** the '92 harvest promises to be very good; **la semaine s'annonce difficile** it looks as if this week is going to be difficult; **3** (prévenir de sa venue) **Oncle Paul s'est annoncé** Uncle Paul said he was coming.

annonciateur, **-trice** /anɔ̃sjatœR, tRis/ *adj* [*ange*] herald (*épith*); [*signe, signal*] warning (*épith*) (**de** of).

Annonciation /anɔ̃sjasjɔ̃/ *nf* Annunciation.

annotation /anɔtasjɔ̃/ *nf* annotation.

annoter /anɔte/ [1] *vtr* to annotate [*ouvrage*]; to write notes on [*copie, devoir*].

annuaire /anɥɛR/ *nm* **1** (d'adresses, du téléphone) directory; **ne pas être dans l'~** not to be in the phone book GB, to have an unlisted number; **2** (recueil) yearbook.
■ **~ électronique** electronic directory; **~ téléphonique** telephone directory, phone book GB.

annuel, **-elle** /anɥɛl/ *adj* **1** (de chaque année) annual, yearly; **2** (qui dure un an) [*abonnement*] annual, one-year (*épith*); [*contrat*] one-year (*épith*).

annulaire /anɥlɛR/ *nm* ANAT ring finger.

annulation /anylasjɔ̃/ *nf* **1** GÉN (de mesure) abolition; (de sanction, loi) repeal; (d'événement) cancellation^GB; **proposer l'~ de la dette du tiers monde** to suggest writing off Third World debts; **2** JUR (de procédure)

quashing; (d'élection) cancellation^GB; (de traité) revocation; (de mariage) annulment.

annuler /anyle/ [1] **I** *vtr* **1** (supprimer) to cancel [*rendez-vous, voyage*]; to write off [*dette*]; to discount [*résultat sportif*]; **2** JUR to declare [sth] void [*élection*]; to revoke [*testament*]; to quash [*procédure*]; to repeal [*loi*]; **~ le permis de conduire de qn** to remove sb's driving licence^GB.
II s'annuler *vpr* to cancel each other out.

anoblir /anɔbliR/ [3] *vtr* to ennoble.

anodin, **~e** /anɔdɛ̃, in/ *adj* (insignifiant) [*personne*] insignificant; (sans risques) [*substance*] harmless; [*remède*] mild; [*sujet*] safe, neutral; [*question*] innocent.

anomalie /anɔmali/ *nf* GÉN anomaly; BIOL abnormality; TECH fault.

ânon /anɔ̃/ *nm* **1** (petit de l'âne) donkey foal; **2** (petit âne) little donkey.

ânonner /anɔne/ [1] *vtr* **1** (en hésitant) to stumble through [*texte, leçon*]; **2** (sans expression) (lire) to read [sth] in a drone; (réciter) to recite [sth] in a drone.

anonymat /anɔnima/ *nm* GÉN anonymity; (discrétion) confidentiality; **sortir de l'~** (dire son nom) to reveal one's identity; (devenir célèbre) to emerge from obscurity.

anonyme /anɔnim/ **I** *adj* **1** (sans nom) [*auteur, lettre, don*] anonymous; **2** (neutre) [*décor, style*] impersonal.
II *nmf* unknown man/woman; **les ~s** anonymous people.

anorak /anɔRak/ *nm* anorak.

anorexie /anɔRɛksi/ *nf* anorexia.

anormal, **~e**, *mpl* **-aux** /anɔRmal, o/ *adj* **1** (inhabituel) [*taux*] abnormal; [*événement*] unusual; **2** (injuste) unfair; **3°** (déficient) [*enfant*] abnormal.

anormalité /anɔRmalite/ *nf* abnormality.

ANPE /aɛnpeœ/ *nf* (*abbr* = **Agence nationale pour l'emploi**) French national employment agency.

anse /ɑ̃s/ *nf* **1** (de tasse, panier) handle; **2** GÉOG cove.

antagonisme /ɑ̃tagɔnism/ *nm* antagonism.

antagoniste /ɑ̃tagɔnist/ **I** *adj* **1** [*groupes, forces*] opposing; [*méthodes, intérêts*] conflicting; **2** ANAT [*muscles*] antagonist.
II *nmf* antagonist.

antan: **d'antan** /dɑ̃tɑ̃/ *loc adj* LITER [*guerres, fêtes*] of old (*après n*); [*prestige*] former; **les métiers d'~** the old trades; **le Lyon d'~** the Lyons of yesteryear LITTÉR.

antarctique /ɑ̃taRktik/ *adj* Antarctic.

Antarctique /ɑ̃taRktik/ *nprm* **1** ▶**232** (continent et eaux) Antarctic; (continent seul) Antarctica; **2** ▶**407** (océan) **océan ~** Antarctic Ocean.

antécédent, **~e** /ɑ̃tesedɑ̃, ɑ̃t/ *nm* **1** (fait du passé) past history; **un ~ judiciaire** a criminal record; **2** MÉD medical history; **y a-t-il des ~s d'allergie dans votre famille?** do you have a family history of allergy?; **3** LING, MATH antecedent.

antéchrist /ɑ̃tekRist/ *nm* Antichrist.

antédiluvien, **-ienne** /ɑ̃tedilyvjɛ̃, ɛn/ *adj* antediluvian.

antenne /ɑ̃tɛn/ *nf* **1** (de radio, télévision) aerial; (de radar, satellite) antenna; **~ parabolique** satellite dish; **~ télescopique** telescopic aerial; **2** (liaison) **être sur** or **à l'~** to be on the air; **passer à l'~** to go on the air; **l'~ est à vous** over to you; **3** (poste détaché) branch; **~s commerciales** commercial outlets; **~ médicale** medical unit; **4** (d'insecte, de crustacé) antenna; **avoir des ~s** FIG to have a sixth sense.

antérieur, **~e** /ɑ̃teRjœR/ *adj* **1** (précédent) [*salaire, situation, œuvre*] previous; **le texte est ~ à 1986** the text was written prior to 1986; **2** (placé devant) [*partie, face*] front; [*membre, ligament*] anterior; **3** [*voyelle*] front (*épith*).

antérieurement /ɑ̃teRjœRmɑ̃/ *adv* previously; **~ à** prior to.

antériorité /ɑ̃teRjɔRite/ *nf* anteriority.

anthologie /ɑ̃tɔlɔʒi/ *nf* anthology.

anthracite /ɑ̃tʀasit/ I ▶ 141⏌ adj inv (couleur) charcoal grey GB ou gray US.
II nm anthracite.

anthrax /ɑ̃tʀaks/ nm inv MÉD carbuncle.

anthropologie /ɑ̃tʀɔpɔlɔʒi/ nf anthropology.

anthropologiste /ɑ̃tʀɔpɔlɔʒist/, **anthropologue** /ɑ̃tʀɔpɔlɔg/ ▶ 374⏌ nmf anthropologist.

anthropophage /ɑ̃tʀɔpɔfaʒ/ I adj cannibalistic.
II nmf cannibal.

anthropophagie /ɑ̃tʀɔpɔfaʒi/ nf cannibalism.

antiadhésif, -ive /ɑ̃tiadezif, iv/ adj nonstick.

antiaérien, -ienne /ɑ̃tiaeʀjɛ̃, ɛn/ adj antiaircraft (épith).

antialcoolique /ɑ̃tialkɔlik/ adj mesure/campagne ~ anti-alcohol measure/campaign; centre de cure ~ detoxification centreGB.

antiatomique /ɑ̃tiatɔmik/ adj [vêtement] (anti-)radiation (épith); abri ~ nuclear shelter.

antibiotique /ɑ̃tibjɔtik/ adj, nm antibiotic; aux ~s with antibiotics; sous ~s on antibiotics.

antiblocage /ɑ̃tiblɔkaʒ/ adj inv système ~ des roues anti-lock braking system, ABS.

antibrouillard /ɑ̃tibʀujaʀ/ adj inv AUT phare ~ fog light.

antibruit /ɑ̃tibʀɥi/ adj inv soundproof.

antibuée /ɑ̃tibye/ adj inv dispositif ~ demister.

anticalcaire /ɑ̃tikalkɛʀ/ adj agent or produit ~ water softener.

anticancéreux, -euse /ɑ̃tikɑ̃seʀø, øz/ adj [traitement] cancer (épith); [médicament] anti-cancer (épith).

antichambre /ɑ̃tiʃɑ̃bʀ/ nf LIT, FIG anteroom; l'~ de la gloire FIG the way to stardom.

antichar /ɑ̃tiʃaʀ/ adj inv antitank (épith).

antichoc /ɑ̃tiʃɔk/ adj inv 1 (protecteur) casque ~ crash helmet; 2 (incassable) [montre] shockproof.

anticipation /ɑ̃tisipasjɔ̃/ nf (prévision) anticipation; film/roman d'~ science fiction film/novel.

anticipé, -e /ɑ̃tisipe/ adj [départ, élection, libération] early; avec mes remerciements ~s thanking you in advance.

anticiper /ɑ̃tisipe/ [1] I vtr 1 (prévoir) to anticipate [réaction, coup, changement]; to foresee [invention]; ~ qch de trois mois to anticipate sth by three months; n'anticipons pas! let's not get ahead of ourselves!; 2 (effectuer à l'avance) to bring [sth] forward [paiement].
II anticiper sur vtr ind to anticipate [événements].
III vi (au tennis, aux échecs) to think ahead.

anticonceptionnel, -elle /ɑ̃tikɔ̃sɛpsjɔnɛl/ adj contraceptive.

anticonformiste /ɑ̃tikɔ̃fɔʀmist/ adj, nmf nonconformist.

anticonstitutionnel, -elle /ɑ̃tikɔ̃stitysjɔnɛl/ adj unconstitutional.

anticorps /ɑ̃tikɔʀ/ nm inv antibody.

anticorrosion /ɑ̃tikɔʀɔʒjɔ̃/ adj inv rustproof.

anti-crevaison /ɑ̃tikʀəvɛzɔ̃/ adj inv bombe ~ AUT puncture sealant spray.

antidater /ɑ̃tidate/ [1] vtr to antedate.

antidémocratique /ɑ̃tidemɔkʀatik/ adj undemocratic.

antidépresseur /ɑ̃tidepʀɛsœʀ/ nm antidepressant.

antidérapant, -e /ɑ̃tideʀapɑ̃, ɑ̃t/ adj [pneu, chaussée] nonskid; [semelle] nonslip.

antidopage /ɑ̃tidɔpaʒ/ adj inv [contrôle, test] dope; [mesure, lutte] against doping (après n); subir un contrôle ~ to be dope-tested.

antidote /ɑ̃tidɔt/ nm LIT, FIG antidote (contre against; à, de for).

antiémeute /ɑ̃tiemøt/ adj inv police/véhicule ~ riot police/vehicle.

antifasciste /ɑ̃tifaʃist/ adj, nmf antifascist.

antifatigue /ɑ̃tifatig/ adj inv [bas, collant] support (épith).

antigang /ɑ̃tigɑ̃g/ adj inv brigade ~ crime squad.

antigel /ɑ̃tiʒɛl/ adj inv, nm antifreeze.

antigouvernemental, ~e, mpl -aux /ɑ̃tiguvɛʀnmɑtal, o/ adj anti-government.

antihéros /ɑ̃tieʀo/ nm inv anti-hero.

anti-inflammatoire, pl ~s /ɑ̃tiɛ̃flamatwaʀ/ adj, nm anti-inflammatory.

anti-inflation /ɑ̃tiɛ̃flasjɔ̃/ adj inv anti-inflation.

antillais, ~e /ɑ̃tijɛ, ɛz/ adj West Indian.

Antilles /ɑ̃tij/ ▶ 509⏌ nprfpl les ~ the West Indies; les ~ françaises the French West Indies; les Petites/Grandes ~ the Lesser/Greater Antilles.
■ ~ néerlandaises Netherlands Antilles.

antilope /ɑ̃tilɔp/ nf antelope.

antimilitarisme /ɑ̃timilitaʀism/ nm antimilitarism.

antimite /ɑ̃timit/ adj, nm moth-repellent.

antinomie /ɑ̃tinɔmi/ nf antinomy.

antinomique /ɑ̃tinɔmik/ adj [lois, éléments] antinomic; [idées, concepts] paradoxical.

antiparasite /ɑ̃tipaʀazit/ adj inv dispositif ~ suppressor.

antipathie /ɑ̃tipati/ nf antipathy (pour toward(s), to; entre between); j'éprouve de l'~ pour eux I dislike them.

antipathique /ɑ̃tipatik/ adj [personne, défaut] unpleasant; il m'est ~ I dislike him.

antipelliculaire /ɑ̃tipɛlikylɛʀ/ adj [shampooing] anti-dandruff (épith).

antiphrase /ɑ̃tifʀɑz/ nf antiphrasis; par ~ ironically.

antipode /ɑ̃tipɔd/ I nm GÉOG antipodes (pl); être l'~ de to be the antipodes of; être aux ~s de LIT to be the antipodes of; FIG to be the exact opposite of.
II antipodes nmpl (pays lointain) les ~s the other side of the world.

antipoison /ɑ̃tipwazɔ̃/ adj inv centre ~ poisons unit.

antipollution /ɑ̃tipɔlysjɔ̃/ adj inv la lutte ~ the fight against pollution; barrage ~ oil-trapping boom; impôt ~ pollution tax.

antiquaire /ɑ̃tikɛʀ/ nmf ▶ 374⏌ antique dealer.

antique /ɑ̃tik/ adj 1 (de l'Antiquité) [cité, théâtre, période] ancient; la Rome/la Grèce ~ ancient Rome/Greece; 2 (ancien) [croyance, demeure] age-old (épith); 3 (démodé) [véhicule] antiquated; [costume] old-fashioned.

antiquité /ɑ̃tikite/ nf 1 (objet) antique; un magasin d'~s an antique shop; les ~s antiques; 2 (de coutume) ancientness.
II antiquités nfpl ART antiquities.

Antiquité /ɑ̃tikite/ nf antiquity; dans l'~ in antiquity.

antireflet /ɑ̃tiʀəflɛ/ adj inv [surface, verre] nonreflective; PHOT antiglare.

antirides /ɑ̃tiʀid/ adj inv anti-wrinkle (épith).

antirouille /ɑ̃tiʀuj/ I adj inv (pour protéger) rust-proofing (épith); (pour enlever) rust-removing (épith).
II nm (pour protéger) rust inhibitor; (pour enlever) rust remover.

antiroulis /ɑ̃tiʀuli/ adj inv [dispositif] roll-damping.

antisèche○ /ɑ̃tisɛʃ/ nf students' slang crib○.

antisémite /ɑ̃tisemit/ I adj anti-Semitic.
II nmf anti-Semite.

antisémitisme /ɑ̃tisemitism/ nm anti-Semitism.

antiseptique /ɑ̃tisɛptik/ adj, nm antiseptic.

antisocial, ~e, mpl -iaux /ɑ̃tisɔsjal, o/ adj antisocial.

antistatique /ɑ̃tistatik/ adj inv antistatic.

antitabac /ɑ̃titaba/ adj inv antismoking.

antitache /ɑ̃titaʃ/ adj inv traité ~ stain-resistant.

antiterroriste /ɑ̃titɛʀɔʀist/ adj inv lutte ~ fight against terrorism.

antithèse /ɑ̃titɛz/ nf antithesis; elle est l'~ de son frère FIG she's the exact opposite of her brother.

antituberculeux, -euse /ɑ̃titybɛʀkylø, øz/ adj [vaccin] tuberculosis (épith).

antivenimeux, -euse /ɑ̃tivənimø, øz/ *adj* **produit/sérum ~** antivenin product/serum.

antivol /ɑ̃tivɔl/ **I** *adj inv* **dispositif ~** antitheft device.
II *nm* (de vélo, moto) lock; (de voiture) steering lock, antitheft device.

antonyme /ɑ̃tɔnim/ *nm* antonym.

antre /ɑ̃tʀ/ *nm* **1** (d'animal) den; **2** FIG den.

anus /anys/ ▶137 | *nm inv* anus.

Anvers /ɑ̃vɛʀ/ ▶628 |, 509 | *npr* Antwerp.

anxiété /ɑ̃ksjete/ *nf* anxiety; **état d'~** anxiety state; **crise d'~** panic attack; **avec ~** anxiously.

anxieusement /ɑ̃ksjøzmɑ̃/ *adv* anxiously.

anxieux, -ieuse /ɑ̃ksjø, øz/ **I** *adj* [*personne, voix, attente*] anxious; [*attitude*] concerned; **~ de savoir** anxious to know.
II *nm,f* worrier.

aorte /aɔʀt/ *nf* aorta.

août /u(t)/ ▶382 | *nm* August.

apaisant, ~e /apɛzɑ̃, ɑ̃t/ *adj* [*paroles, voix, personne, lotion, crème*] soothing; [*influence*] calming; [*déclaration*] conciliatory.

apaisement /apɛzmɑ̃/ *nm* **geste/mesure d'~** calming gesture/measure; **politique d'~** policy of appeasement; **tentative d'~** attempt to appease.

apaiser /apeze/ [1] **I** *vtr* (calmer) to pacify [*personne*]; to ease [*conflit*]; to calm [*colère, inquiétude*]; to satisfy [*faim, soif, désir*]; to soothe [*brûlure, douleur*]; **~ les esprits** to ease people's minds; **il est revenu, l'esprit apaisé** he came back, his mind at rest.
II **s'apaiser** *vpr* [*vent, colère*] to die down; [*débat*] to calm down; [*curiosité, faim, douleur*] to subside.

apanage /apanaʒ/ *nm* **être l'~ de qch/qn** to be the prerogative of sth/sb.

aparté /apaʀte/ *nm* **en ~** GÉN in private; THÉÂT in an aside.

apathie /apati/ *nf* (personnelle, politique) apathy; (économique) stagnation.

apathique /apatik/ *adj* apathetic.

apatride /apatʀid/ **I** *adj* stateless.
II *nmf* stateless person; **les ~s** stateless people.

apercevoir /apɛʀsəvwaʀ/ [5] **I** *vtr* **1** (voir avec peine) to make out; **2** (voir brièvement) to catch sight of; **3** (prévoir) to see [*difficultés, possibilités*].
II **s'apercevoir** *vpr* **1** (se rendre compte) **s'~ que** to notice that, to realize that; **s'~ de** to notice [*erreur, supercherie*]; **sans s'en ~** without realizing; **2** (se voir) (sans se parler) to catch sight of each other; (en se parlant) to meet briefly.

aperçu /apɛʀsy/ *nm* **1** (échantillon) (de talent, caractère) glimpse (**de** of); (de politique, situation) outline (**de** of); **2** (point de vue) insight (**sur** into).

apéritif /apeʀitif/ *nm* aperitif GB, drink.

apesanteur /apəzɑ̃tœʀ/ *nf* weightlessness.

à-peu-près /apøpʀɛ/ *nm inv* vague approximation, (rough) guess.

apeuré, ~e /apœʀe/ *adj* (effrayé) frightened; (craintif) timid.

aphasie /afazi/ *nf* aphasia.

aphone /afɔn/ *adj* **être ~** to have lost one's voice.

aphorisme /afɔʀism/ *nm* aphorism.

aphrodisiaque /afʀɔdizjak/ *adj, nm* aphrodisiac.

aphte /aft/ *nm* mouth ulcer.

aphteuse /aftøz/ ▶196 | *adj f* **fièvre ~** foot-and-mouth disease.

api: d'api /dapi/ *loc adj* **pomme d'~** small apple.

à-pic /apik/ *nm inv* sheer drop.

apiculteur, -trice /apikyltœʀ, tʀis/ ▶374 | *nm,f* beekeeper.

apiculture /apikyltyʀ/ *nf* beekeeping.

apitoiement /apitwamɑ̃/ *nm* pity (**sur** for).

apitoyer /apitwaje/ [23] **I** *vtr* to move [sb] to pity [*personne*]; **n'essaie pas de m'~** don't try to get my sympathy.

II **s'apitoyer** *vpr* **s'~ sur (le sort de) qn** to feel sorry for sb.

aplanir /aplaniʀ/ [3] **I** *vtr* to level [*terrain, chemin*]; to iron out [*difficultés, problèmes*]; to ease [*tensions*].
II **s'aplanir** *vpr* [*difficultés*] to be ironed out; [*tensions*] to ease.

aplati, ~e /aplati/ *adj* [*sphère, forme*] oblate; [*fruit, tuyau*] flattened; [*nez*] flat.

aplatir /aplatiʀ/ [3] **I** *vtr* to flatten [*carton, tôle*]; to smooth out [*coussin, oreiller*]; to smooth down [*cheveux*]; to press [*coutures, plis*]; **mon chapeau est tout aplati!** my hat is all squashed!
II **s'aplatir**° *vpr* (être servile) **s'~ devant qn** to grovel in front of sb.

aplomb /aplɔ̃/ **I** *nm* **1** (confiance en soi) confidence; (équilibre) balance; **manquer d'~** to lack confidence; **avoir de l'~** to be confident; **avec ~** confidently, with aplomb; **vous ne manquez pas d'~!** you've got a nerve!; **2** (direction) **à l'~ de** directly below.
II **d'aplomb** *loc adv* **1** (en équilibre) [*étagère, armoire*] straight; [*personne*] steady; **2**° (en bonne santé) **tu te sens d'~?** do you feel well?; **ça va te remettre d'~** it will put you back on your feet.

apnée /apne/ *nf* apn(o)ea; **plonger en ~** to dive without an aqualung.

apocalypse /apɔkalips/ *nf* apocalypse; **vision/paysage d'~** apocalyptic vision/landscape.

apocalyptique /apɔkaliptik/ *adj* apocalyptic.

apocryphe /apɔkʀif/ **I** *adj* apocryphal.
II *nm* **les ~s** the Apocrypha.

apogée /apɔʒe/ *nm* **1** (paroxysme) peak (**de** of); **atteindre** or **connaître son ~** to peak; **2** (d'une période, orbite) apogee.

apolitique /apɔlitik/ *adj* apolitical.

apologétique /apɔlɔʒetik/ *adj* **1** (qui loue) laudatory; (qui justifie) justificatory; **2** RELIG apologetic.

apologie /apɔlɔʒi/ *nf* (pour louer) panegyric (**de** of); (pour justifier) apologia (**de** for); **faire l'~ de qch** (justifier) to justify sth; (louer) to applaud sth; **faire l'~ de qn** (louer) to praise sb.

apoplexie /apɔpleksi/ *nf* apoplexy; **crise d'~** LIT, FIG apoplectic fit; **elle était au bord de l'~** FIG she was on the verge of having an apoplectic fit.

a posteriori /apɔsteʀjɔʀi/ **I** *loc adj inv* [*connaissances*] inductive.
II *loc adv* [*se justifier, décider*] after the event; **~, il semblerait que** with hindsight, it would appear that.

apostolat /apɔstɔla/ *nm* **1** RELIG apostolate; **2** (activité désintéressée) apostolic mission.

apostrophe /apɔstʀɔf/ *nf* **1** ling apostrophe; **2** (remarque) remark.

apostropher /apɔstʀɔfe/ [1] *vtr* to heckle.

apothéose /apɔteoz/ *nf* (moment fort) (de spectacle) high point; (d'événement) grand finale; (d'œuvre) supreme achievement; (de carrière) culmination; **finir** or **s'achever en ~** [*spectacle*] to end in a blaze of glory; **l'arrivée de ma belle-mère a été l'~!** IRON my mother-in-law's arrival was the last straw!

apothicaire /apɔtikɛʀ/ *nm* **comptes d'~** complicated calculations.

apôtre /apotʀ/ *nm* LIT, FIG apostle.

apparaître /apaʀɛtʀ/ [73] **I** *vi* **1** (devenir visible) [*personne, spectre, bouton, problèmes, produit*] to appear; [*lune, soleil*] to come out; **~ à la télévision/en public** to appear on television/in public; **laisser ~** to reveal; **2** (se révéler) to become apparent; **laisser ~** [*analyse, rapport*] to show; **faire ~** (montrer) to show; (révéler) to reveal; **~ comme une victime** to be seen as a victim; **3** (sembler) to appear (to be); **~ à qn** to appear to sb to be; **~ (à qn) comme** to appear (to sb) to be; **~ comme un gâchis** to seem a waste.
II *v impers* **il apparaît que** it appears that.

apparat /apaʀa/ *nm* (faste) grandeur; **d'~** ceremonial; **en grand ~** [*fêter*] with pomp and ceremony; [*être habillé*] in ceremonial regalia.

appareil /apaʀɛj/ *nm* **1** (machine, instrument) device;

(pour la maison) appliance; ~ **de mesure** measuring device; ~ **de contrôle** control; ~ **de radio/télévision** radio/television set; ~ **de projection** projector; ~ **photographique** or **photo camera**; ~ **électroménager** household appliance; ~ **(dentaire)** (dentier) dentures (pl); (tige métallique) brace GB, braces (pl) US; ~ **auditif** hearing aid; ~ **orthopédique** orthopaedic appliance; **2** (téléphone) telephone; **qui est à l'~?** who's calling please?; **on te demande à l'~** you're wanted on the phone; **passe-moi l'~** give me the phone; **Vladimir à l'~** (this is) Vladimir speaking; **3** (avion) plane; **4** ANAT system; **l'~ digestif** the digestive system; **5** (système) apparatus; **l'~ d'État/du parti** the state/party apparatus; **6** (ensemble de notes) ~ **critique** critical apparatus.
IDIOMES **être dans le plus simple ~** to be in one's birthday suit.

appareillage /apaʀεjaʒ/ nm **1** NAUT (départ) **prêt pour l'~!** ready to cast off!; **2** (appareils) equipment.

appareiller /apaʀeje/ [1] vi [bateau] to cast off.

apparemment /apaʀamɑ̃/ adv **1** (selon toute apparence) apparently; ~ **pas!** apparently not!; **2** (en apparence seulement) seemingly.

apparence /apaʀɑ̃s/ nf appearance; **ne jugez pas sur les ~s** don't judge by appearances; **ne vous fiez pas aux ~s** appearances are deceptive; **pour sauver les ~s** to keep up appearances; **contre toute ~** despite every indication to the contrary; **il est jeune d'~** he looks young; **homme d'~ jeune** young-looking man; **elle n'est calme qu'en ~** she only seems calm; **en ~** seemingly; **sous l'~ de la bonté** under the guise of kindness; **'ils sont d'accord?'—'selon toute ~'** 'they agree?'—'it would seem so'; **'ils sont d'accord'—'en ~ (seulement)'** 'they agree'—'only on the surface'; **des personnes en ~ si différentes** people outwardly so different.

apparent, ~**e** /apaʀɑ̃, ɑ̃t/ adj **1** (visible) [signe, partie, bouton, couture] visible; [trouble, fragilité] apparent; **sans raison** ~**e** for no apparent reason; **2** (trompeur) [facilité, indulgence] seeming.

apparenté, ~**e** /apaʀɑ̃te/ adj [personne, famille] related (à to); [entreprise] allied; ~ **socialiste** allied to the socialist party.

apparenter: **s'apparenter** /apaʀɑ̃te/ [1] vpr **s'~ à** to resemble.

appariteur /apaʀitœʀ/ nm **1** UNIV (gardien) ~ porter GB, college staff member who handles mail and reception duties; (surveillant d'examen) invigilator GB, proctor US; **2** (de laboratoire) laboratory technician.

apparition /apaʀisjɔ̃/ nf (de personne, bouton, problème, planète, produit) appearance; (de spectre) apparition (à qn to sb); (de mouvement, science) emergence; (d'invention) advent; **refaire son ~** to reappear.

appartement /apaʀtəmɑ̃/ nm flat GB, apartment; **plante d'~** houseplant; **se retirer dans ses ~s** retire to one's chamber LITER.
■ ~ **témoin** show flat GB, show apartment US.

appartenance /apaʀtənɑ̃s/ nf affiliation; **il ne dissimule pas son ~ au mouvement** he is openly affiliated to the movement; **condamné pour ~ à un groupe terroriste** condemned for being a member of a terrorist organization.

appartenir /apaʀtəniʀ/ [36] **I appartenir à** vtr ind **1** (être la propriété) ~ **à** [objet, propriété, capital] to belong to; **2** (revenir) ~ **à** [victoire] to belong to; **la décision t'appartient** the decision is yours; **3** (faire partie) ~ **à** [personne] to be a member of; ~ **à un club** to be a member of a club.
II v impers (être du ressort de) **il appartient à qn de faire** it is up to sb to do.

appât /apɑ/ nm bait ȼ; **attirer avec un ~** to lure with bait; **mettre un ~ à l'hameçon** to bait the hook; **l'~ du gain** the lure of profit.

appâter /apɑte/ [1] vtr to lure [poisson, gibier]; to bait [hameçon, piège]; to lure [personne] (**par, avec** with).

appauvrir /apovʀiʀ/ [3] **I** vtr LIT, FIG to impoverish.
II s'appauvrir vpr to become impoverished.

appauvrissement /apovʀismɑ̃/ nm impoverishment.

appeau, pl ~**x** /apo/ nm decoy.

appel /apεl/ nm **1** (invitation pressante) call; **'dernier ~ pour Tokyo'** 'last call for Tokyo'; ~ **au secours** LIT call for help; FIG cry for help; **à l'~ de leur mère** when they heard their mother calling; **2** (supplique) appeal; **lancer un ~** to make an appeal; **lancer un ~ à la radio** to put out an appeal on the radio; **3** (incitation) ~ **à** call for [solidarité]; appeal for [calme]; call to [armes]; plea for [clémence]; ~ **à la grève** strike call; **lancer un ~ à** to call for [solidarité, grève]; to appeal for [calme]; ~ **au meurtre** death threat; **lancer un ~ au meurtre contre qn** to call for sb's assassination; **4** TÉLÉCOM call; ~ **tél éphonique/radio** phone/radio call; **5** (recours) ~ **à** appeal to [personne, bon sens]; **faire** ~ **à** [personne] to call [pompiers, police, spécialiste]; to bring in [artiste]; to call up [capitaux]; [gouvernement] to call in [armée, police, puissance étrangère]; [tâche] to call for [connaissances]; **faire** ~ **à la justice** to go to court; **6** (vérification) GÉN roll call; SCOL registration; **faire l'~** GÉN to take the roll call; SCOL to take the register; **manquer à l'~** GÉN to be absent at the roll call; SCOL to be absent at registration; **7** MIL (convocation) call up GB, draft US; **8** (attirance) **l'~ de** the call of [large, forêt]; **9** JUR appeal; **faire** ~ to appeal; **faire** ~ **d'un jugement** to appeal against a decision; **perdre en** ~ to lose an appeal; **juger en** ~ to hear an appeal; **sans** ~ LIT without further right of appeal; **une décision sans** ~ FIG a final decision; **condamner sans** ~ FIG to condemn out of hand; **10** SPORT take off; **prendre son** ~ to take off; **11** JEUX (aux cartes) signal; **faire un** ~ to signal for a card; **12** ORDINAT call; **d'~** [programme, station, séquence] calling (épith); [demande, indicatif, mot] call (épith).
■ **l'~ du 18 juin** HIST General de Gaulle's appeal of 18 June 1940; ~ **d'air** draught GB ou draft US; ~ **d'offres** invitation to tender; ~ **de phares** flash of headlights GB ou high beams US; ~ **du pied**○ veiled invitation, discreet appeal.

appelé, ~**e** /aple/ nm MIL conscript, draftee US; **les ~s du contingent** the conscripts.

appeler /aple/ [19] **I** vtr **1** (dénommer) to call [personne, chose]; **comment ont-ils appelé leur fille?** what did they call their daughter?; **comme appelles-tu cet arbre?** what's this tree called?; **j'appelle ça du vol** I call that robbery; **il se fait ~ Robert** (pour son plaisir) he likes to be called Robert; (par sécurité) he goes by the name of Robert; **2** (téléphoner) to phone GB, to call; **je t'appelle demain** I'll phone you tomorrow; ~ **qn par l'interphone** to call sb on the intercom; **3** (faire venir) to call [docteur, ambulance, pompier, taxi, ascenseur]; to send for [employé, élève]; **le devoir m'appelle** duty calls; ~ **qn sous les drapeaux** to call sb up; ~ **qn en justice** to summon sb to appear in court; **4** (inciter) ~ **qn à** to incite sb to [révolte]; ~ **qn à faire** to call on sb to do; **5** (destiner) ~ **qn à** to assign sb to [charge, fonction]; to appoint sb to [poste]; **il a été appelé à de hautes fonctions** he was called to high office; **mon travail m'appelle à beaucoup voyager** my work involves a lot of travel; **6** (exiger, entraîner) [crime, comportement] to call for [sanction]; ~ **l'attention de qn sur qch** to draw sb's attention to sth; **la violence appelle la violence** violence begets violence.
II en appeler à vtr ind to appeal to [générosité, bon sens, population].
III vi (crier) [personne] to call; **en cas de besoin, appelez** if you need anything, just call; ~ **à l'aide** to call for help; ~ **à la grève** to call for strike action.
IV s'appeler vpr **comment s'appelle cette fleur en latin?** what is this flower called in Latin?; **comment t'appelles-tu?** what's your name?; **je m'appelle Paul** my name's Paul; **voilà ce qui s'appelle une belle voiture!** now, that's what you call a nice car!; **nous nous appelons par nos prénoms** we call each other by our first names; **on s'appelle!** we'll be in touch!
IDIOMES **ça s'appelle reviens**○! don't forget to give it

back!; **~ les choses par leur nom** or **un chat un chat** to call a spade a spade.
appellation /apɛlɑsjɔ̃/ *nf* name, appellation SOUT.
appendice /apɛ̃dis/ *nm* appendix.
appendicite /apɛ̃disit/ ▶ 196] *nf* appendicitis.
appentis /apɑ̃ti/ *nm inv* (bâtiment) (adossé) lean-to; (non adossé) shed.
appesantir /apəzɑ̃tiʀ/ [3] I *vtr* [*âge, froid*] to slow down [*démarche*]; [*inactivité*] to dull [*esprit*].
II **s'appesantir** *vpr* (insister) **s'~ sur** to dwell on.
appétissant, ~e /apetisɑ̃, ɑ̃t/ *adj* **1** [*mets*] appetizing; **peu ~** unappetizing; **2**° [*personne*] appealing.
appétit /apeti/ *nm* **1** (de mangeur) appetite; **le bon air donne de l'~** fresh air gives you an appetite; **perdre l'~** to lose one's appetite; **mettre qn en ~** LIT, FIG to whet sb's appetite; **couper l'~ de qn** to take sb's appetite away; **avoir un ~ d'oiseau** to eat like a bird; **manger avec ~** to eat heartily; **bon ~!** enjoy your meal!; **2** (de plaisirs, culture) appetite (**de** for); (de gloire, pouvoir) hunger (**de** for); **les ~s de conquête du pays** the country's expansionist ambitions.
applaudir /aplodiʀ/ [3] I *vtr* LIT, FIG to applaud; **ils ont été très applaudis par le public** they got a big round of applause from the audience.
II *vi* **1** LIT [*personne, foule*] to applaud, to clap; **2** FIG (approuver) to approve; **~ des deux mains** to applaud ou approve heartily.
applaudissement /aplodismɑ̃/ *nm* **1** LIT applause ¢; **elle a quitté la salle sous un tonnerre d'~s** she left the room to thunderous applause; **2** FIG (approbation) acclaim ¢; **le livre a reçu l'~ de la critique** the book has met with critical acclaim.
applicable /aplikabl/ *adj* [*loi, sanction*] applicable (**à** to); **facilement ~** [*idée, mesure*] easy to implement.
applicateur /aplikatœʀ/ *nm* applicator.
application /aplikasjɔ̃/ *nf* **1** (soin) care; **écrire avec ~** to write with care; **2** (de loi, règlement, d'accord) (respect) application; (mise en œuvre) implementation; (de peine) administration; **étendre le champ d'~** to extend the application; **mettre en ~** to apply [*théorie*]; to implement [*loi, règlement*]; **entrer en ~** to come into force; **en ~ de l'article 5** in accordance with article 5; **3** IND, MÉD, TECH application; **4** ORDINAT (programme) application program.
applique /aplik/ *nf* (lampe) wall light.
appliqué, ~e /aplike/ *adj* **1** [*élève*] hardworking; [*travail, écriture*] careful; **2** [*science*] applied.
appliquer /aplike/ [1] I *vtr* **1** (mettre) to apply [*vernis, fond de teint, compresse*] (**sur** to); to put [*cachet*] (**sur** on); **2**° (donner) to give [*baiser, sobriquet*] (**à qn** to); **3** (mettre en œuvre) to implement; [*politique, ordres*]; to apply [*loi*]; **~ une peine à qn** to administer a sentence on sb; **4** (respecter) to abide by [*règlement*]; to follow [*quotas*]; **5** (utiliser) to apply [*technique*] (**à** to).
II **s'appliquer** *vpr* **1** (avec soin) to take great care (**à faire** to do); **elle ne s'applique pas** she doesn't take much care; **s'~ à écrire lisiblement** to take care to write legibly; **2** (concerner) **s'~ à qch/qn** to apply to sth/sb.
appoint /apwɛ̃/ *nm* **1** (somme d'argent) exact change; **faire l'~** to tender GB ou provide US the exact change; **2** (complément) **rôle d'~** supporting role; **salaire d'~** supplementary income; **chauffage d'~** additional heating GB, space heater US.
appointements /apwɛ̃tmɑ̃/ *nmpl* FML salary (*sg*).
appontement /apɔ̃tmɑ̃/ *nm* landing stage.
apport /apɔʀ/ *nm* **l'~ de** the provision of [*aide financière, solution, modifications*]; the bringing-in of [*idées nouvelles*]; **grâce à l'~ d'eau** thanks to the provision of water; **~ de capitaux** capital contribution; **les ~s de l'Asie à l'art européen** Asia's contribution to European art; **~ calorique** caloric intake.
■ **~ quotidien recommandé** recommended daily amount, RDA.
apporter /apɔʀte/ [1] *vtr* **1** (transporter) (en venant) to bring; (en allant) to take; **~ qch à qn** (en venant) to bring sb sth; (en allant) to take sb sth; **2** (fournir) to give

[*soutien, explication, sensation*]; to bring [*savoir-faire, amélioration, nouvelle, gloire, liberté, maladie*]; to bring in [*fonds, revenus*]; to bring about [*changement, révolution*]; **~ de l'aide à qn** to help sb; **~ son concours à qch** to help with sth; **~ sa contribution à qch** to contribute to sth; **~ beaucoup de soin à son travail** to do one's work with great care; **~ la preuve de qch** to bring proof of sth; **~ des modifications à qch** to modify sth; **les modifications apportées** the modifications made; **ce stage ne m'a rien apporté** I didn't get anything out of this course; **cet homme ne peut rien t'~** this man has nothing to offer you.
apposer /apoze/ [1] *vtr* FML to affix [*affiche, signature*] (sur on); **~ un visa** to stamp a visa.
apposition /apozisjɔ̃/ *nf* LING apposition.
appréciable /apʀesjabl/ *adj* substantial; **il y avait un nombre ~ de spectateurs** there were a good many spectators; **un grand jardin en ville, c'est ~** it's nice to have a big garden in the centre GB of town.
appréciatif, -ive /apʀesjatif, iv/ *adj* (approbateur) [*jugement, regard*] appreciative.
appréciation /apʀesjasjɔ̃/ *nf* **1** (de distance, résultat, proposition) estimate; (financière) evaluation; **faire une erreur d'~** to make a misjudgment; **2** (jugement) assessment; **c'est une question d'~** it's a question of taste; **être laissé à l'~ de qn** to be left to sb's discretion; **3** (de monnaie) appreciation.
apprécier /apʀesje/ [2] I *vtr* **1** (juger favorablement) to appreciate [*art, vin, qualité*]; to like [*personne*]; **elle n'a pas apprécié** IRON she wasn't exactly pleased; **un chercheur des plus appréciés** a highly valued researcher; **ce que j'apprécie chez elle** what I like about her; **2** (évaluer) to value [*objet*]; to estimate [*distance, vitesse*]; to assess [*conséquences, résultat*].
II **s'apprécier** *vpr* **1** (s'aimer) [*personnes*] to like one another; **2** (augmenter de valeur) [*monnaie*] to appreciate.
appréhender /apʀeɑ̃de/ [1] *vtr* **1** (arrêter) [*police*] to arrest, to apprehend SOUT; **2** (redouter) to dread (**de faire** doing); **j'appréhende toujours un peu les examens** I'm always a bit apprehensive before exams; **3** (concevoir) FML to comprehend [*phénomène*].
appréhension /apʀeɑ̃sjɔ̃/ *nf* **1** (crainte) apprehension; **avec ~** apprehensively; **2** (conception) apprehension.
apprendre /apʀɑ̃dʀ/ [52] I *vtr* **1** (étudier) to learn (**à faire** to do); **~ qch par cœur** to learn sth by heart, to learn sth off by heart GB; **le bonheur d'~** the joy of learning; **~ l'italien** to learn Italian; **2** (être informé de) to learn [*vérité*] (**par qn** from sb; **sur qch/qn** about sth/sb); to hear [*information*] (**par qn** from sb; **sur qch/qn** about sth/sb); to learn of [*événement, décision*] (**par qn** through sb); **~ qch par la presse** to see sth in the papers; **3** (enseigner) to teach; **~ qch à qn** to teach sb sth; **~ à conduire à qn** to teach sb (how) to drive; **cela t'apprendra!** that'll teach you!; **ce n'est pas à toi que je l'apprendrai** you don't need me to tell you; **4** (faire savoir) [*personne, journal*] to tell; **tu ne m'apprends rien** you're not telling me anything new.
II **s'apprendre** *vpr* **s'~ facilement/difficilement** to be easy/difficult to learn; **la patience, cela s'apprend** patience is something you can learn.
apprenti, ~e /apʀɑ̃ti/ I *nm,f* GÉN trainee; (d'artisan) apprentice; **être ~ chez qn** GÉN to train with sb; (avec un artisan) to serve an apprenticeship with sb; **entrer comme ~ chez qn** to be apprenticed to sb.
II **apprenti(-), apprentie(-)** (*in compounds*) **1** GÉN trainee; (de métier artisanal) apprentice; **~ boulanger** baker's apprentice; **~ serveur** trainee waiter; **2** (sans expérience) **~-ministre** novice minister.
■ **~ sorcier** sorcerer's apprentice; **jouer les ~s sorciers** to open a Pandora's box.
apprentissage /apʀɑ̃tisaʒ/ *nm* **1** GÉN training; (de métier artisanal) apprenticeship; (chez un artisan) **faire son ~ de boulanger** to train as a baker; **être en ~** GÉN to be a trainee; (chez un artisan) to be an apprentice; **2** (étude) learning; **l'~ d'une langue/de la lecture** learning a language/to read; **faire l'~ de la démocratie** to take the first steps toward(s) democracy; **faire l'~ de la vie** to learn about life.

apprêt /apRɛ/ *nm* **1** (sur mur, plafond) size; (sur bois) primer; **2** (affectation) affectation; **sans ~** unaffected.

apprêté, ~e /apRɛte/ *adj* [*style*] affected; [*coiffure*] fussy.

apprêter /apRɛte/ [1] **I** *vtr* to finish [*étoffe*]; to size [*mur, plafond*]; to prime [*bois*].
II s'apprêter *vpr* **s'~ à faire** to be about to do.

apprivoiser /apRivwaze/ [1] *vtr* to tame [*animal*]; to win [sb] over [*personne*]; **animal apprivoisé** tame animal.

approbateur, -trice /apRɔbatœR, tRis/ *adj* **sourire/ hochement ~** smile/nod of approval.

approbation /apRɔbasjɔ̃/ *nf* approval (**de** of).

approchable /apRɔʃabl/ *adj* **il n'est guère ~** (distant) he's rather unapproachable; (occupé) one never gets to see him.

approchant, ~e /apRɔʃɑ̃, ɑ̃t/ *adj* [*valeur*] approximate; **quelque chose d'~** something similar.

approche /apRɔʃ/ **I** *nf* **1** (arrivée) approach (**de** of); **il s'est enfui à mon ~** he ran off as I approached; **2** (imminence, proximité) approach (**de** of); **à l'~** or **aux ~s de l'hiver** as winter approaches; **à l'~ de la nuit** at dusk; **à l'~** or **aux ~s de la trentaine il décida que...** as he neared thirty, he decided that...; **3** (manière d'aborder) approach (**de** to); **d'~ difficile/ aisée** [*œuvre, auteur*] hard/easy to get to grips with; **personne d'~ difficile** unapproachable person; **personne d'~ aisée** friendly person.
II approches *nfpl* **aux ~s de la ville** on the outskirts of town; **aux ~s de la côte** near the coast.

approcher /apRɔʃe/ [1] **I** *vtr* **1** (déplacer) **approche ta chaise** pull up your chair; **~ le verre de ses lèvres** to raise the glass to one's lips; **2** (contacter) to approach [*personne*]; **ne m'approche pas** don't come near me; **on ne peut pas les ~** (occupés) you can never get to see them; (trop distants) they're unapproachable.
II approcher de *vtr ind* **~ de** to be (getting) close to; **nous approchons du but** we're nearly there.
III *vi* to approach; **sentir la mort ~** to feel death drawing near; **l'heure du départ approchait** it was nearly time to leave; **approche** come here; **la nuit approche** it's getting dark; **les examens approchent** the exams are coming up.
IV s'approcher *vpr* **s'~ de qn/qch** (aller) to go near sb/sth; (venir) to come near sb/sth.

approfondi, ~e /apRɔfɔ̃di/ *adj* detailed, in-depth (*épith*); **étudier de façon ~e** to study in detail.

approfondir /apRɔfɔ̃diR/ [3] **I** *vtr* **1** FIG to go into [sth] in depth [*sujet*]; **vous auriez pu ~** you could have gone into the subject in greater depth; **inutile d'~** don't go into detail; **~ ses connaissances** to improve one's knowledge; **2** LIT to deepen [*canal, trou*].
II s'approfondir *vpr* [*crevasse, trou*] to deepen.

approfondissement /apRɔfɔ̃dismɑ̃/ *nm* (de connaissances) improvement; (de débat) development; (de relations) consolidation; (de crise) deepening.

approprié, ~e /apRɔpRije/ *adj* [*moyens, technique, régime*] appropriate.

approprier: s'approprier /apRɔpRije/ [2] *vpr* to take, to appropriate SOUT [*chose, idée*]; to seize [*pouvoir*].

approuver /apRuve/ [1] *vtr* **1** GÉN to approve of [*action, décision, projet*]; **je t'approuve totalement** (sur une idée) I quite agree with you; **je t'approuve d'avoir accepté** I think you were right to accept; **2** POL [*commission, ministres*] to approve [*texte, projet, budget*]; [*parlement*] to pass [*projet de loi, décret*].

approvisionnement /apRɔvizjɔnmɑ̃/ *nm* supply (**en** of); **l'~ de la ville en eau** supplying the town with water.

approvisionner /apRɔvizjɔne/ [1] **I** *vtr* to supply [*ville, marché*] (**en** with); to load [*arme automatique*]; to pay money into [*compte en banque*]; **une boutique mal approvisionnée** a badly stocked shop; **votre compte n'est plus approvisionné depuis trois mois** your account has not been in credit for three months.
II s'approvisionner *vpr* **1** (faire des provisions) to

stock up (**en** on, with); **2** (acheter) **la compagnie s'approvisionne en papier auprès de l'usine** the company gets its supplies of paper from the factory.

approximatif, -ive /apRɔksimatif, iv/ *adj* [*devis, coût, croquis, chiffre*] rough; [*traduction*] approximate; **dans un anglais ~** in broken English.

approximation /apRɔksimasjɔ̃/ *nf* **1** (chiffre) rough estimate; (traduction, concept) approximation; **2** MATH approximation.

approximativement /apRɔksimativmɑ̃/ *adv* approximately.

appui /apɥi/ *nm* **1** (soutien) LIT, FIG support; **~ matériel/moral** material/moral support; **à l'~ de cette thèse** in support of this theory; **prendre ~ sur** to lean on; **point d'~** PHYS fulcrum; **2** CONSTR **~ (de fenêtre)** window sill; **3** MIL support; **~ aérien** air support; **4** MUS (de voix) placing.

appui-tête, *pl* **appuis-tête** /apɥitɛt/ *nm* headrest.

appuyé, ~e /apɥije/ *adj* [*regard*] intent; [*plaisanterie*] heavy.

appuyer /apɥije/ [22] **I** *vtr* **1** (poser) to rest [*tête*] (**sur** on; **contre** against); to put [*main, pied*] (**sur** on; **contre** against); to lean [*coude, objet*] (**sur** on; **contre** against); **2** (presser) to press (**sur** on; **contre** against); **~ son doigt** to press one's finger; **3** (baser) to support, to back up [*raisonnement*] (**sur** with); **4** (soutenir) to back [*personne, candidat*]; to support [*action, projet*]; [*blindés*] to support [*offensive*].
II *vi* **1** (presser) **~ sur** (avec le doigt) to press; (avec le pied) to put one's foot on; **appuie sur l'accélérateur!** put your foot down!; **~ sur la détente** to pull ou press the trigger; **2** (insister) **~ sur** to stress [*syllabe, mot*]; to emphasize [*aspect, argument*].
III s'appuyer *vpr* **1** (prendre appui) to lean (**sur** on; **contre** against); **2** (se fonder) **s'~ sur** [*personne*] to rely on [*personne, théorie, auteur*]; to draw on [*loi, rapport*]; [*étude*] to be based on [*connaissance, concept*].

âpre /apR/ *adj* **1** (désagréable) [*goût*] bitter; [*voix*] harsh; [*froid, vent*] bitter; **2** (acharné) [*lutte*] fierce; [*discussion*] bitter; **~ au gain** grasping.

après /apRɛ/ **I** *adv* **1** (dans le temps) (ensuite) afterwards; (plus tard) later; **tu finiras ~** you can finish afterwards; **aussitôt** or **tout de suite ~** straight after that ou afterwards; **longtemps ~** a long time after ou afterwards; **et ~ que s'est-il passé?** and then what happened?, and what happened next?; **peu/bien ~** shortly/long after(wards); **l'année d'~** the year after; **pas la semaine prochaine celle d'~** not next week, the week after next; **la fois d'~** the next time; **le train d'~** the next train; **l'instant d'~** a moment later; **2** (dans l'espace) **tu vois le croisement, j'habite (juste) ~ à droite** can you see the crossroads? I live (just) past ou beyond it on the right; **peu ~ il y a un lac** a bit further on there's a lake; **la page/le chapitre d'~** the next page/chapter; **3** (dans

---

après adverbe se traduit généralement par *afterwards* et *après* préposition par *after*.

Les expressions telles que *courir après qn/qch, crier après qn* etc. sont traitées respectivement sous *courir, crier* etc.

après entre dans la composition de nombreux mots qui s'écrivent avec un trait d'union (*après-demain, après-guerre, après-midi* etc.). Ces mots sont des entrées à part entière et on les trouvera dans la nomenclature du dictionnaire. Utilisé avec un nom, propre ou commun, pour désigner la période suivant un événement ou la disparition d'une personne il se traduit par *post* et forme alors un groupe adjectival que l'on fait suivre du nom approprié:

  l'après-Gorbatchev = the post-Gorbachev period
  l'après-crise = the post-recession period
  l'après-1789 = the post-1789 period

On notera:

  l'après-8 mai = the period following 8 May
  la France de l'après-de Gaulle = post-de Gaulle France

une hiérarchie) **les loisirs d'abord, le travail passe ~** leisure first, work comes after; **4** (marquant l'agacement) **et ~?** so what○?

II *prép* **1** (dans le temps) after; **passer ~ qn** to go after sb; **peu ~ minuit** shortly after midnight; **~ mon départ** after I left; **~ quelques années** a few years later; **~ impôt** after tax; **~ tout** after all; **~ quoi** after which; **~ coup** after the event, afterwards; **jour ~ jour** day after day, day in day out; **~ tout ce qu'il a fait** after all (that) he's done; **j'irai ~ avoir fait la sieste** I'll go after I've had a nap; **2** (dans l'espace) after; **~ l'église/la sortie de la ville** after the church/you come out of the town; **~ toi sur la liste** after you on the list; **~ vous!** (par politesse) after you!; **il est toujours ~ son fils**○ he's always on at his son; **3** (dans une hiérarchie) after; **faire passer qn / qch ~ qn/qch** to put sb/sth after sb/sth.

III d'après *loc prép* **1** (selon) **d'~ moi** in my opinion; **d'~ lui** according to him ou in his opinion; **d'~ la loi** under the law; **d'~ mes calculs/ma montre** by my calculations/my watch; **d'~ ce qu'elle a dit** from what she said; **2** (en imitant) from; **d'~ un dessin de Gauguin** from a drawing by Gauguin; **3** (adapté de) based on; **un film d' ~ un roman** a film based on a novel.

IV après que *loc conj* after; **~ que je leur ai annoncé la nouvelle** after I told them the news.

après-demain /apʀɛdmɛ̃/ *adv* the day after tomorrow.

après-guerre, *pl* **~s** /apʀɛgɛʀ/ *nm* ou *f* postwar years (*pl*); **la génération d'~** the postwar generation.

après-midi /apʀɛmidi/ *nm* ou *f inv* afternoon; **en début/fin d'~** early/late in the afternoon; **j'y vais le samedi ~** I go there on Saturday afternoons; **2 heures de l'~** 2 in the afternoon, 2 pm.

après-rasage, *pl* **~s** /apʀɛʀazaʒ/ *adj inv, nm* aftershave.

après-ski /apʀɛski/ *nm inv* (chaussure) snowboot.

après-vente /apʀɛvɑ̃t/ *adj inv* **service ~** (département) after-sales service department; (activité) after-sales service.

âpreté /ɑpʀəte/ *nf* **1** (de lutte) fierceness; (de discussion) bitterness; **~ au gain** greed for gain; **2** (de fruit) bitterness.

a priori /apʀijɔʀi/ **I** *loc adj inv* [*jugement*] a priori.

II *loc adv* **1** GÉN **~, ça ne devrait pas poser de problèmes** on the face of it there shouldn't be any problems; **~ je ne connais personne qui puisse** offhand I can't think of anybody who could; **~ je ne peux rien décider** right now I can't make a decision; **rejeter ~ une proposition** to reject a proposal out of hand; **2** PHILOS a priori.

III *nm inv* a priori assumption.

à-propos /apʀopo/ *nm inv* **interrompre avec ~** to make an apposite interruption; **cette déclaration manque d'~** this declaration is inapposite; **agir avec ~** to do the right thing.

apte /apt/ *adj* **1** (compétent) **~ à** good at; **c'est l'homme le plus ~ à décider** he is the best man to decide; **2** (en état) fit; **~ à l'enseignement/au travail** fit to teach/for work.

aptitude /aptityd/ *nf* **1** (compétence) aptitude (à for; à faire for doing); **2 ~ à l'enseignement/au travail/ au service** fitness to teach/for work/for active duty.

aquarelle /akwaʀɛl/ *nf* **1** (procédé) watercolours GB (*pl*); **2** (œuvre) watercolour GB.

aquarium /akwaʀjɔm/ *nm* aquarium, fish tank.

aquatique /akwatik/ *adj* **1** [*flore, faune*] aquatic; **2** [*jardin, sport*] water (*épith*).

aqueduc /akdyk/ *nm* CONSTR aqueduct.

aqueux, ~euse /akø, øz/ *adj* aqueous.

aquifère /akɥifɛʀ/ *adj* water-bearing, aquiferous SPÉC.

aquilin /akilɛ̃/ *adj m* [*nez, profil*] aquiline.

aquilon /akilɔ̃/ *nm* LITER north wind.

aquitain, ~e /akitɛ̃, ɛn/ ▶ **509** *adj* of Aquitaine; **le bassin ~** the Aquitaine Basin.

arabe /aʀab/ **I** *adj* [*architecture, civilisation*] Arab; [*chiffre, dialecte, écriture*] Arabic.

II ▶ **338** *nm* LING Arabic; **~ classique** classical Arabic.

Arabe /aʀab/ *nmf* Arab.

arabesque /aʀabɛsk/ *nf* arabesque.

Arabie /aʀabi/ ▶ **232**, **509** *nprf* Arabia; **désert d'~** Arabian desert.

■ **~ Saoudite** Saudi Arabia.

arabique /aʀabik/ *adj* (d'Arabie) Arabian.

arable /aʀabl/ *adj* arable.

arachide /aʀaʃid/ *nf* peanut, groundnut GB; **huile d'~** peanut oil.

arachnéen, -éenne /aʀaknẽ, ɛn/ *adj* **1** LIT arachnidan; **2** FIG, LITER gossamer (*épith*).

araignée /aʀɛɲe/ *nf* ZOOL spider.

■ **~ de mer** spider crab.

IDIOMES **avoir une ~ au plafond**○ to have a screw loose○.

araméen /aʀameẽ/ *nm* LING Aramaic.

araser /aʀaze/ [1] *vtr* to level off [*mur*]; (en menuiserie) to plane down.

aratoire /aʀatwaʀ/ *adj* ploughing GB, plowing US.

arbalète /aʀbalɛt/ *nf* crossbow.

arbitrage /aʀbitʀaʒ/ *nm* **1** SPORT (en boxe, football, rugby) refereeing; (en base-ball, cricket, tennis) umpiring; **2** (de différend) arbitration.

arbitraire /aʀbitʀɛʀ/ *adj* arbitrary.

arbitrairement /aʀbitʀɛʀmɑ̃/ *adv* arbitrarily.

arbitre /aʀbitʀ/ *nm* **1** ▶ **374** SPORT (en boxe, football, rugby) referee; (en base-ball, cricket, tennis) umpire; **2** FIG **être l'~ d'une consultation électorale** to hold the balance of power in an election; **3** JUR (de différend) arbitrator.

arbitrer /aʀbitʀe/ [1] **I** *vtr* **1** SPORT to referee [*match de boxe, football, rugby*]; to umpire [*match de base-ball, cricket, tennis*]; **2** (régler) to arbitrate in [*différend*].

II *vi* to arbitrate (**entre** between).

arboré, ~e /aʀbɔʀe/ *adj* [*terrain*] planted with trees (*après n*).

arborer /aʀbɔʀe/ [1] *vtr* **1** (porter avec ostentation) [*personne*] to sport [*objet*]; **2** (montrer) to wear [*sourire, air*]; to parade [*attitude, idée*]; **3** (porter normalement) [*personne, groupe*] to bear [*enseigne, couleur*]; [*navire, avion, bâtiment*] to fly [*pavillon, drapeau*].

arborescent, ~e /aʀbɔʀesɑ̃, ɑ̃t/ *adj* BOT, ORDINAT tree (*épith*).

arboriculture /aʀbɔʀikyltyʀ/ *nf* arboriculture.

arbouse /aʀbuz/ *nf* arbutus berry.

arbre /aʀbʀ/ *nm* **1** (végétal) tree; **2** (diagramme) tree (diagram); **3** TECH shaft; **~ de transmission** transmission shaft.

■ **~ à cames** AUT camshaft; **~ généalogique** family tree; **~ de Judée** Judas tree; **~ de Noël** Christmas tree.

arbrisseau, *pl* **~x** /aʀbʀiso/ *nm* small tree.

arbuste /aʀbyst/ *nm* shrub.

arc /aʀk/ *nm* **1** SPORT bow; **tendre** or **bander un ~** to bend a bow back; **2** (courbe) curve; **en (forme d') ~** arched; **3** ARCHIT arch.

■ **~ brisé** lancet arch; **~ de cercle** arc of a circle; **~ électrique** electric arc; **~ plein cintre** round arch; **~ de triomphe** triumphal arch.

arcade /aʀkad/ *nf* ARCHIT arcade; **~s** (ensemble) archways.

■ **~ sourcilière** arch of the eyebrow.

arcanes /aʀkan/ *nmpl* LITER mysteries.

arc-bouter: s'arc-bouter /aʀkbute/ [1] *vpr* to brace oneself (**contre** against).

arceau, *pl* **~x** /aʀso/ *nm* **1** (de voûte) arch; **2** (de tonnelle, croquet) hoop; **3** AUT (de voiture) roll bar; **4** (de lit) cradle.

arc-en-ciel, *pl* **arcs-en-ciel** /aʀkɑ̃sjɛl/ *nm* rainbow.

archaïque /aʀkaik/ *adj* archaic.

archaïsme /aʀkaism/ *nm* archaism.

L'argent et les monnaies

Pour la prononciation des nombres en anglais ▶ 399 |.

L'argent en Grande-Bretagne

écrire	dire
1p	one p ([pi:]) *ou* one penny *ou* a penny
2p	two p *ou* two pence
5p	five p *ou* five pence
20p	twenty p *ou* twenty pence
£1*	one pound *ou* a pound
£1.03	one pound three pence†
	ou one pound three p‡
£1.20	one pound twenty
	ou one pound twenty pence
	ou one pound twenty p
£1.99	one pound ninety-nine
£10	ten pounds
£200	two hundred pounds
£1,000§	one thousand pounds
	ou a thousand pounds
£1,000,000	one million pounds *ou* a million pounds

L'argent aux États-Unis

1c	one cent *ou* a cent
2c	two cents
5c	five cents
10c	ten cents
25c	twenty-five cents
$1*	one dollar *ou* a dollar
$1.99	one dollar ninety-nine
$10	ten dollars
$200	two hundred dollars
$1,000	one thousand dollars
	ou a thousand dollars
$1,000,000	one million dollars
	ou a million dollars

L'argent en France

0,25 F	twenty-five centimes
1 F	one franc
1,50 F	one franc fifty centimes
	ou one franc fifty
2 F	two francs
2,75 F	two francs seventy-five centimes
	ou two francs seventy-five†
20 F	twenty francs
100 F	one hundred francs *ou* a hundred francs
200 F	two hundred francs
1 000 F	one thousand francs
	ou a thousand francs
2 000 F	two thousand francs
1 000 000 F	one million francs *ou* a million francs
2 000 000 F	two million francs

* *L'anglais place les abréviations* £ *et* $ *avant le chiffre, jamais après.*

† *On ne dit jamais* point *pour les sommes d'argent.*

‡ *Si le chiffre des* pence *est inférieur ou égal à 19, on n'omet pas* pence *ou* p: one pound nineteen pence, *mais* one pound twenty.

§ *Noter que l'anglais utilise une virgule là où le français a un espace.*

¶ *Les numéraux français* millier *ou* million, *qui sont des noms, se traduisent en anglais par des adjectifs:* deux millions de francs = two million francs. *Pour plus de détails,* ▶ 399 |.

il y a 100 pennies dans une livre = there are 100 pence in a pound

il y a 100 cents dans un dollar = there are 100 cents in a dollar

il y a 100 centimes dans un franc = there are 100 centimes in a franc

Les pièces et les billets

Attention: billet *se dit* note *en anglais britannique, et* bill *en anglais américain.*

Noter l'ordre des mots dans les adjectifs composés anglais, et l'utilisation du trait d'union. Noter aussi que pound, dollar *etc. qui font partie de l'adjectif composé, ne prennent pas la marque du pluriel:*

un billet de 10 livres = a ten-pound note (*GB*)

un billet de 50 dollars = a fifty-dollar bill (*US*)

un billet de 100 F = a hundred-franc note (*GB*)
= *ou* a hundred-franc bill (*US*)

une pièce de 20 pennies = a 20p piece
(*dire* [ə twɛntɪ pi: 'pi:s])

une pièce de 50 pennies = a 50p piece

une pièce d'une livre = a pound coin

Noter que pièce *se traduit par* coin *pour l'unité monétaire et au-delà, et par* piece *pour toute fraction de l'unité monétaire.*

une pièce de 50 centimes = a 50-centime piece

une pièce de 1 F = a one-franc coin

une pièce de 10 F = a ten-franc coin

Mais aux États-Unis:

une pièce de 5 cents = a nickel

une pièce de 10 cents = a dime

une pièce de 25 cents = a quarter

Les prix

combien ça coûte? = how much does it cost?
= *ou* how much is it?

ça coûte 200 livres = it costs £200 *ou* it is £200

le prix de l'appareil est de 200 livres* = the price of the camera is £200

à peu près 200 livres = about £200

presque 200 livres = almost £200

jusqu'à 20 dollars = up to $20

100 francs le mètre = a hundred francs a metre

* *Noter l'absence d'équivalent anglais de la préposition française* de *avant le chiffre dans les expressions de ce genre.*

plus de 200 livres = over £200 *ou* more than £200

moins de 300 livres = less than £300

un peu moins de 250 livres = just under £250

Noter l'ordre des mots dans les adjectifs composés anglais et l'utilisation du trait d'union. Noter aussi que franc, cent *etc. qui font partie de l'adjectif composé, ne prennent pas la marque du pluriel:*

un timbre à 10 F = a ten-franc stamp

un timbre à 75 cents = a seventy-five-cent stamp

un billet de théâtre à 10 livres = a £10 theatre ticket (*dire* a ten-pound theatre ticket)

une bourse de deux mille livres = a £2,000 grant (*dire* a two-thousand-pound grant)

une voiture à 50 000 dollars = a $50,000 car (*dire* a fifty-thousand-dollar car)

L'anglais considère parfois une somme d'argent comme une unité indissociable, et donc comme un singulier:

ça coûte dix livres de plus = it is an extra ten pounds

encore dix livres = another ten pounds

dix livres, ça fait beaucoup d'argent = ten pounds is a lot of money

prends tes 100 F, ils sont sur la table = take your hundred francs, it's on the table

Le maniement de l'argent

payer en livres = to pay in pounds

50 livres en liquide = £50 in cash

un chèque de 500 livres = a £500 cheque

un chèque de voyage en dollars = a dollar traveller's cheque (*GB*) *ou* a dollar traveler's check (*US*)

changer des livres en francs = to change pounds into francs

le dollar vaut six francs = there are six francs to the dollar

faire la monnaie d'un billet de 100 dollars = to change a 100-dollar bill

Le système *lsd*

Le système non-décimal utilisé en Grande-Bretagne jusqu'en 1971 reposait sur la livre, *le* shilling *et le* penny. *Le* penny (*pluriel* pence) *était abrégé en* d., *à cause du latin* denarius. *Il y avait douze* pence *dans un* shilling *et vingt* shillings *dans une* livre.

archange /aʀkɑ̃ʒ/ *nm* archangel.

arche /aʀʃ/ *nf* ARCHIT arch.
■ ~ **d'alliance** Ark of the Covenant; ~ **de Noé** Noah's Ark.

archéologie /aʀkeɔlɔʒi/ *nf* archaeology.

archéologique /aʀkeɔlɔʒik/ *adj* archaeological.

archéologue /aʀkeɔlɔg/ ▶ 374 *nmf* archaeologist.

archer /aʀʃe/ *nm* archer.

archet /aʀʃɛ/ *nm* MUS bow.

archétype /aʀketip/ *nm* archetype; **l'~ du héros** the archetypal hero.

archevêché /aʀʃəveʃe/ *nm* **1** (domaine) archdiocese; **2** (siège) archbishop's palace.

archevêque /aʀʃəvɛk/ ▶ 596 *nm* archbishop.

archi° /aʀʃi/ *préf* ~**comble**, ~**plein** chock-a-block; ~**connu** really well-known; ~**millionnaire** millionaire several times over.

archiduc /aʀʃidyk/ ▶ 596 *nm* archduke.

archiduchesse /aʀʃidyʃɛs/ ▶ 596 *nf* archduchess.

archipel /aʀʃipɛl/ *nm* archipelago.

architecte /aʀʃitɛkt/ ▶ 374 *nmf* LIT, FIG architect.

architectural, ~**e**, *mpl* -**aux** /aʀʃitɛktyʀal, o/ *adj* architectural.

architecture /aʀʃitɛktyʀ/ *nf* **1** LIT, ORDINAT architecture; **2** FIG structure.

archiver /aʀʃive/ [1] *vtr* to archive.

archives /aʀʃiv/ *nfpl* archives, records; **je vais fouiller dans mes** ~ HUM I'll go through my (old) papers.

archiviste /aʀʃivist/ ▶ 374 *nmf* archivist.

arçon /aʀsɔ̃/ *nm* (en équitation) tree; **cheval d'~s** pommel horse.

arctique /aʀktik/ *adj* arctic.

Arctique /aʀktik/ *nprm* **1** ▶ 509 (région) Arctic; **2** ▶ 407 (océan) **l'océan** ~ the Arctic Ocean.

ardemment /aʀdamɑ̃/ *adv* passionately; **être** ~ **républicain** to be an ardent republican.

ardent, ~**e** /aʀdɑ̃, ɑ̃t/ *adj* [braise] glowing; [flamme, soleil] blazing; [regard, foi, désir] burning; [souhait, piété] fervent; [lutte] fierce; [zèle, discours] impassioned; [partisan] passionate; [patriote] fervent; [jeunesse] hot-blooded; **être** ~ **au combat** to fight fiercely; **être** ~ **au travail** to be an enthusiastic worker.

ardeur /aʀdœʀ/ *nf* (de personne) ardour^GB; (de foi, patriotisme) fervour^GB; (de néophyte) keenness GB, enthusiasm; **modérer** or **calmer les** ~**s de qn** to cool sb's ardour^GB; ~ **révolutionnaire** revolutionary zeal; ~ **au travail** enthusiasm for work; **travailler avec** ~ to work hard; **redoubler d'**~ to try twice as hard.

ardoise /aʀdwaz/ **I** ▶ 141 *adj inv* slate-grey GB, slate-gray US.
II *nf* **1** (roche) slate; **2** (tuile) slate; **toit d'**~(**s**) slate roof; **3** (d'écolier) slate; **4**° (dette) debt; **avoir une** ~ **chez un commerçant** to owe a shopkeeper money.

ardu, ~**e** /aʀdy/ *adj* (difficile) [travail] arduous; [négociations, problème] taxing.

are /aʀ/ ▶ 575 *nf* one hundred square metres^GB, are.

arène /aʀɛn/ *nf* **1** (dans un amphithéâtre) arena; (au cirque) ring; (pour corridas) bullring; FIG arena; **2** (amphithéâtre) ~**s** amphitheatre^GB (sg).
IDIOMES **descendre dans l'**~ to enter the ring.

arête /aʀɛt/ *nf* **1** ZOOL fishbone; **retirer les** ~**s d'un poisson** to bone a fish; **sans** ~**s** boned; **2** (de toit, montagne) ridge; (de voûte) groin; (de prisme, roche) edge; (de nez) bridge.

argent /aʀʒɑ̃/ ▶ 33 *nm* **1** (monnaie) money; **dépenser son** ~ **sans compter** to spend one's money like water°; **pour de l'**~ for money; **en avoir pour son** ~ to get one's money's worth; **2** (métal) silver; **en** ~, **d'**~ silver (épith).
■ ~ **liquide** cash; ~ **de poche** pocket money.
IDIOMES **le temps c'est de l'**~ time is money; **prendre pour** ~ **comptant** to take [sth] at face value.

argenté, ~**e** /aʀʒɑ̃te/ **I** *pp* ▶ **argenter**.

II *pp adj* (plaqué d'argent) silver-plated; **un bougeoir en métal** ~ a silver-plated candlestick.
III *adj* **1** (couleur) silvery; **2**° (fortuné) loaded°; **n'être pas très** ~ to be hard up°.

argenter /aʀʒɑ̃te/ [1] *vtr* LIT, FIG to silver.

argenterie /aʀʒɑ̃tʀi/ *nf* silverware, silver.

argentier /aʀʒɑ̃tje/ *nm* HIST treasurer.

argentin, ~**e** /aʀʒɑ̃tɛ̃, in/ *adj* **1** [son] silvery; **2** ▶ 394 (d'Argentine) Argentinian; **la République** ~**e** the Argentine Republic.

Argentine /aʀʒɑ̃tin/ ▶ 232 *nprf* Argentina.

argile /aʀʒil/ *nf* clay.

argileux, -**euse** /aʀʒilø, øz/ *adj* clayey.

argot /aʀgo/ *nm* slang; **un mot d'**~ a slang word.

argotique /aʀgɔtik/ *adj* (propre à l'argot) slang (épith); (peu raffiné) slangy.

arguer /aʀge/ [1] **I** *vtr* ~ **que** to claim that.
II arguer de *vtr ind* (prétexter) ~ **de** to give [sth] as a reason (**pour faire** for doing); **arguant du fait que** pointing to the fact that.

argument /aʀgymɑ̃/ *nm* (raison) argument (**en faveur de** for; **contre** against); ~ **choc** or **massue** decisive argument; ~ **décisif** deciding factor; **trouver de bons** ~**s en faveur de/contre qch** to make a good case for/against sth.

argumentation /aʀgymɑ̃tasjɔ̃/ *nf* line of argument.

argumenter /aʀgymɑ̃te/ [1] *vi* to argue (**sur** about; **contre** against); **défense solidement argumentée** soundly argued defence^GB.

argus /aʀgys/ *nm inv* AUT used car prices guide.

argutie /aʀgysi/ *nf* LITER quibble.

aride /aʀid/ *adj* **1** [terre, climat] arid; **2** [sujet] dry.

aridité /aʀidite/ *nf* **1** (de terre, climat) aridity; **2** (de lecture) dryness.

aristocrate /aʀistɔkʀat/ *nmf* aristocrat.

aristocratie /aʀistɔkʀasi/ *nf* aristocracy.

aristocratique /aʀistɔkʀatik/ *adj* aristocratic.

arithmétique /aʀitmetik/ **I** *adj* arithmetical.
II *nf* arithmetic.

arlequin /aʀləkɛ̃/ *nm* harlequin.

armada /aʀmada/ *nf* **1** (armée) HUM army; **l'invincible Armada** HIST the Spanish Armada; **2**° (grand nombre) (de personnes) avalanche; (de camions) huge fleet.

armateur /aʀmatœʀ/ *nm* (propriétaire) shipowner.

armature /aʀmatyʀ/ *nf* **1** (de tente, store, d'abat-jour) frame; (de soutien-gorge) underwiring ¢; (de voûte) arch reinforcement; (de béton armé) reinforcing steel rods (pl); **à** ~ [soutien-gorge] underwired; **sans** ~ [soutien-gorge] light control (épith); **2** (de région, parti, d'entreprise) infrastructure; **3** (de roman) structure.

arme /aʀm/ **I** *nf* **1** (objet) weapon; **l'~ du crime** the murder weapon; **charger une** ~ to load a gun; **2** FIG (moyen) weapon; **une** ~ **à double tranchant** a double-edged sword; **3** MIL (corps d'armée) branch of the armed services.
II armes *nfpl* **1** MIL arms (pl); **aux** ~**s!** to arms!; **reposez** ~**s!** order arms!; **prendre les** ~**s** (guerre) to take up arms; (insurrection) to rise up in arms; **par la force des** ~**s** by force of arms; **jeter** or **rendre les** ~**s** FIG to surrender; **en** ~**s** [peuple, soldats, insurgés] armed; **mourir les** ~**s à la main** to die fighting; **passer qn par les** ~**s** to execute sb by firing squad; **à** ~**s égales** LIT, FIG on equal terms; **donner** or **fournir des** ~**s contre soi** FIG to provide ammunition against oneself; **faire ses premières** ~**s** FIG to start out; **2** (armoiries) coat (sg) of arms.
■ ~ **blanche** weapon with a blade; ~ **à feu** firearm; ~ **de poing** handgun; ~ **de service** standard issue weapon.

armé, ~**e**[1] /aʀme/ **I** *pp* ▶ **armer**.
II *pp adj* **1** LIT (muni d'armes) armed (**de** with); ~ **jusqu'aux dents** armed to the teeth; **vol à main** ~ armed robbery; **2** FIG (pourvu) equipped (**de** with; **contre** against); ~ **pour faire** [personne] equipped ou in a position to do; **il est bien** ~ **pour réussir** he's well equipped to succeed.

armée² /aʀme/ nf **1** GÉN armed forces (pl); (de terre) army; **être dans l'~** to be in the army; **être à l'~** to be doing one's military service; **2** (grand nombre) army, bunch PÉJ.
■ **~ d'active** regular army; **~ de l'air** air force; **l'~ de réserve** the reserves (pl); **l'~ de terre** the army.

armement /aʀməmɑ̃/ nm **1** (moyens armés) GÉN armament; (de personne, troupe) weapons (pl); (d'unité mobile) weaponry; **~ léger/lourd** light/heavy armament; **2** (ensemble d'armes) arms (pl); **ventes d'~** arms sales; **3** (mise en état de marche) (d'arme) arming; (d'appareil photo) winding on; **4** (de navire) fitting out.

arménien, -ienne /aʀmenjɛ̃, ɛn/ I ▶394| adj Armenian.
II ▶338| nm LING Armenian.

armer /aʀme/ [1] I vtr **1** (munir d'armes) to arm (**de** with); **2** (renforcer) to reinforce [béton] (**de** with); **3** (prémunir) to arm (**contre** against); **4** (équiper) to fit out [navire]; **5** (mettre en ordre de marche) to arm [arme]; to wind on [appareil photo]; **~ un fusil** to cock a rifle.
II s'armer vpr to arm oneself (**de** with); **s'~ de patience** to summon up one's patience.

armistice /aʀmistis/ nm armistice.

armoire /aʀmwaʀ/ nf GÉN cupboard; (pour vêtements) wardrobe; **~ vitrée** glass-fronted cupboard.
■ **~ chauffante** hot cupboard; **~ électrique** switchgear cubicle; **~ frigorifique** cold store; **~ à glace** LIT wardrobe with a full length mirror; **c'est une ~ à glace**○ FIG he/she is built like a tank○; **~ à linge** linen cupboard, linen closet US; **~ métallique** metal locker; **~ normande** large wardrobe (in traditional Norman style); **~ à pharmacie** medicine cabinet; **~ de toilette** bathroom cabinet.

armoiries /aʀmwaʀi/ nfpl arms.

armure /aʀmyʀ/ nf HIST MIL armourᴳᴮ; FIG form of protection.

armurerie /aʀmyʀʀi/ nf **1** ▶374| (magasin, atelier) gunsmith's; **2** MIL gun room.

armurier /aʀmyʀje/ ▶374| nm **1** (qui vend, répare) gunsmith; **2** (dans l'armée) armourerᴳᴮ.

ARN /aɛʀɛn/ nm (abbr = **acide ribonucléique**) RNA.

aromates /aʀɔmat/ nmpl herbs and spices.

aromatique /aʀɔmatik/ adj aromatic.

aromatiser /aʀɔmatize/ [1] vtr to flavourᴳᴮ; **aromatisé au citron** lemon-flavouredᴳᴮ.

arôme /aʀom/ nm **1** (odeur) aroma; **2** (additif alimentaire) flavouringᴳᴮ; **à l'~ de fruit** fruit-flavouredᴳᴮ.

arpège /aʀpɛʒ/ nm arpeggio.

arpent /aʀpɑ̃/ nm HIST arpent; **quelques ~s** FIG a few acres.

arpenter /aʀpɑ̃te/ [1] vtr to stride along [rues]; to pace up and down [couloirs].

arpenteur /aʀpɑ̃tœʀ/ ▶374| nm (land) surveyor.

arqué, ~e /aʀke/ adj [sourcils] arched; [nez] hooked; **avoir les jambes ~es** to have bandy ou bow legs.

arquebuse /aʀkəbyz/ nf arquebus.

arquer /aʀke/ [1] I vtr to bend [barre]; **~ le dos** to arch one's back.
II s'arquer vpr [poutrelle, barre] to become bowed.

arrachage /aʀaʃaʒ/ nm (de récolte) picking; (de dent, poteau) pulling out; (de broussailles, souche) digging out; **~ des mauvaises herbes** weeding.

arraché /aʀaʃe/ nm SPORT snatch; **obtenir qch à l'~** FIG to snatch sth; **vol à l'~** bag snatching.

arrache-clou, pl **~s** /aʀaʃklu/ nm claw hammer.

arrache-pied: d'arrache-pied /daʀaʃpje/ loc adv **travailler d'~** to work flat out.

arracher /aʀaʃe/ [1] I vtr **1** (déraciner) [personne] to dig up [légumes]; to dig out [broussailles, souche, poteau]; to uproot [arbre]; [ouragan] to uproot [arbre, poteau]; **~ les mauvaises herbes** to weed; **2** (détacher vivement) [personne] to pull [sth] out [poil, dent, ongle, clou] (**de** from); to tear [sth] down [affiche]; to

rip [sth] out [page]; to tear [sth] off [masque] (**de** from); [vent] to blow [sth] off [feuilles]; to rip [sth] off [toit] (**de** from); **l'obus lui a arraché le bras** the shell blew his/her arm off; **3** (ôter de force) to snatch [personne, objet] (**de** , **à** from); **~ qch des mains de qn** to snatch sth out of sb's hands; **elle s'est fait ~ son sac** she had her bag snatched; **~ qn à la mort** to snatch sb from the jaws of death; **~ qn à la misère** to rescue sb from poverty; **~ qn à sa famille** to tear sb from the bosom of his/her family; **4** (tirer brutalement) **~ qn à** to rouse sb from [rêve, torpeur, pensées]; to drag sb away from [travail]; **5** (soutirer) to force [augmentation, compromis] (**à qn** out of sb); to extract [secret, précision, consentement] (**de, à qn** from sb); to get [mot, sourire] (**de, à qn** from sb); **ils leur ont arraché la victoire** they snatched victory from them; **~ un nul** SPORT to manage to draw GB ou tie; **la douleur lui a arraché un cri** he/she cried out in pain.
II s'arracher vpr **1** (s'ôter) **s'~ les cheveux blancs** to pull out one's grey GB ou gray US hairs; **s'~ les poils du nez** to pluck the hairs from one's nose; **2** (se disputer pour) to fight over [personne, produit]; **3** (se séparer) **s'~ à** to rouse oneself from [pensées, rêverie]; to tear oneself away from [travail, étreinte].
IDIOMES **~ les yeux à** or **de qn** to scratch sb's eyes out; **c'est à s'~ les cheveux**○! (difficile) it's enough to make you tear your hair out!; **s'~ les yeux** to fight like cat and dog.

arracheur /aʀaʃœʀ/ nm **~ de dents** quack.
IDIOMES **mentir comme un ~ de dents** to be a born liar.

arraisonner /aʀɛzɔne/ [1] vtr to board and inspect [navire, avion].

arrangeant, ~e /aʀɑ̃ʒɑ̃, ɑ̃t/ adj obliging.

arrangement /aʀɑ̃ʒmɑ̃/ nm **1** (accord) agreement; **2** (disposition) arrangement; **3** MATH permutation; **4** MUS arrangement.

arranger /aʀɑ̃ʒe/ [13] I vtr **1** (organiser) to arrange [voyage, réunion]; to organize [vie]; **2** (régler) to settle [conflit]; to sort out [malentendu, affaires]; **cela ne va pas ~ les choses** that won't help matters; **pour ne rien ~, pour tout ~** IRON to make matters worse; **le temps arrangera peut-être les choses** perhaps things will improve with time; **3** (disposer) to arrange [objets, fleurs, pièce]; **4** (remettre en ordre) to tidy [cheveux]; to straighten [châle, gilet]; **ton coiffeur t'a bien arrangé!** IRON your hairdresser has made a right mess of your hair○!; **5** (modifier) to rearrange [texte]; to arrange [morceau de musique]; IRON to doctor [faits]; **6** (réparer) to fix; **7** (convenir) **tu dis ça parce que ça t'arrange** you say that because it suits you.
II s'arranger vpr **1** (s'améliorer) to improve; **tout finira par s'~** things will sort themselves out in the end; **2** (se mettre d'accord) **s'~ avec qn** to arrange it with sb; **s'~ à l'amiable** to come to a friendly agreement; **3** (prendre des dispositions) **arrange-toi pour être à l'heure** make sure you're on time; **s'~** (se débrouiller) **il n'y a que trois lits mais on s'arrangera** there are only three beds but we'll sort something out; **arrange-toi avec ça** try and make do with that; **5**○ (s'habiller) **elle ne sait pas s'~** she doesn't know how to do herself up nicely.

arrangeur, -euse /aʀɑ̃ʒœʀ, øz/ nm,f MUS arranger.

arrérages /aʀeʀaʒ/ nmpl arrears.

arrestation /aʀɛstasjɔ̃/ nf arrest; **être en état d'~** to be under arrest; **procéder à l'~ de** to arrest.

arrêt /aʀɛ/ nm **1** (de véhicule) stopping; (de combats) cessation; (de livraison, transaction) cancellation; (de production, distribution) halt; (de croissance économique) cessation; (halte) stop; **attendez l'~ complet du train/de l'avion** wait until the train/plane has come to a complete stop; **faire un ~ de deux heures** to stop for two hours; **l'~ des hostilités/essais nucléaires** an end to hostilities/nuclear testing; **décider l'~ de la production** to decide to halt the production; **sans ~** (sans interruption) nonstop, without stopping; (à tout moment) constantly; **ce train est sans ~ jusqu'à Toulouse** this train goes nonstop to Toulouse; **il faut sans ~ répéter la même chose** the same thing has

to be repeated over and over again; **à l'~** [*voiture, camion, train*] stationary; [*machine*] (prête à fonctionner) idle; (hors tension) off; **marquer un temps d'~** to pause; **un coup d'~** a halt; **donner un coup d'~ à** to stop ou halt; **être en ~** [*chien*] to point; **être aux ~s** MIL to be under arrest; **2** (lieu) stop; **un ~ de bus** a bus stop; **3** C (sur un panneau) stop; **4** JUR ruling.
■ **~ du cœur** heart failure; **~ sur image** freeze-frame, still; **faire un ~ sur image** to freeze a frame; **~ de jeu** SPORT stoppage time; **jouer les ~s de jeu** to play injury time; **~ de mort** death sentence; **~ de travail** (pour grève) stoppage of work; (pour maladie) (événement) sick leave ¢; (document) sick note; **être en ~ de travail** to be on sick leave.

arrêté, ~e /aʀete/ I *pp* ▶ **arrêter**.
II *pp adj* **1** (convenu) settled; **2** (inébranlable) [*idée, principe*] fixed.
III *nm* ADMIN order, decree; **~ ministériel** ministerial decree; **~ d'expulsion** (contre un étranger) expulsion order, deportation order; (contre un locataire) eviction notice ou order; **~ municipal** bylaw; **~ préfectoral** bylaw (*issued by a prefecture*).

arrêter /aʀete/ [1] I *vtr* **1** (stopper) GÉN to stop; to switch off [*machine, moteur, appareil*]; to halt [*production*]; to give up [*études, alcool*]; **~ qn** (dans une conversation) to stop sb; **rien ne les arrête** FIG (pour faire un voyage, pour s'amuser) there's no stopping them; (pour gagner de l'argent) they'd stop at nothing; **qu'est-ce qui t'arrête?** what's stopping you?; **~ de faire** to stop doing; (renoncer) to give up doing; **arrête de mentir** stop lying; **~ de fumer** to give up smoking; **~ de travailler** (définitivement) to stop work; **le trafic est arrêté sur la ligne B** service has been suspended on the B line; **arrête tes bêtises!** (tais-toi) stop talking nonsense!; (cesse de faire des bêtises) stop fooling around!; **je n'arrête pas en ce moment!** I'm always on the go° these days!; **'tu n'as qu'à travailler!'—'mais je n'arrête pas!** 'you should work!'—'but that's what I'm doing!'; **être arrêté pour trois semaines** to be given a sick note for three weeks; **2** (appréhender) [*police*] to arrest; **arrêtez-la!** stop her!; **3** (déterminer) to fix [*lieu, date*]; to make [*décision*]; to decide on [*plan, principe, mesure*].
II *vi* (cesser) [*bruit, cri*] to stop; **le téléphone n'arrête pas** the phone rings all the time; **arrête!** (tu m'ennuies) stop it!; (je ne te crois pas) I don't believe you!
III **s'arrêter** *vpr* **1** (faire un arrêt) [*personne, train*] to stop; **arrête-toi ici** stop here; **sans s'~** without stopping; **s'~ pour se reposer** to stop for a rest; **s'~ à Grenoble** [*personne*] to stop off in Grenoble; [*train, car*] to stop in Grenoble; **2** (cesser de fonctionner) to stop; **3** (cesser) [*hémorragie, pluie, musique*] to stop; **s'~ de faire** to stop doing; **ils ne vont pas s'~ là** FIG they won't stop there; **4** (renoncer à) to give up (de faire doing); **s'~ de fumer** to give up smoking; **5** (se terminer) [*enquête, histoire, chemin, jardin*] to end; **l'affaire aurait pu s'~ là** that could have been the end of the matter; **6** (fixer son attention sur) **s'~ sur** to dwell on [*point*]; **s'~ à** to focus on [*détails, essentiel*] ; **ce dernier point mérite qu'on s'y arrête** this last point merits some attention.

arrhes /aʀ/ *nfpl* deposit (sg); **verser des ~** to pay a deposit.

arrière /aʀjɛʀ/ I *adj inv* [*poche*] back; MIL [*base*] rearguard; AUT [*vitre, roue, feux*] rear; [*banquette*] back; **siège ~** (de voiture) back seat; (de moto) pillion; **la partie ~ du bâtiment** the rear of the building.
II *nm* **1** (partie) (de voiture, bâtiment) back, rear; (de train, d'avion) rear; (de navire) stern; **à l'~** (dans une voiture) in the back; (dans un train, bus) at the back ou rear; (au rugby, football) at the back; **le moteur est à l'~** the engine is at the back; **une voiture avec le moteur à l'~** a rear-engine car; **en ~** (direction) GÉN backward(s); **pencher la tête en ~** to tilt one's head back; **rester en ~** (parmi les spectateurs) to stand back; (après le départ des autres) to stay behind; (par sécurité, crainte) to keep back; (traîner) to lag behind; **regarder en ~** LIT, FIG to look back; **remonter de deux ans en ~** to go back two years; **revenir en ~** LIT to turn

back; FIG to take a backward step; (sur un enregistrement) to rewind; **se coiffer en ~** to wear one's hair off the face; **en ~ de** (derrière) behind; **vers l'~** backwards; **2** SPORT (au rugby, hockey) fullback; (au football) defender; (au basket) guard; (au volley) back-line player; **les ~s** (au rugby) the backs; (au football) the defenceGB; **3** MIL (territoire) civilian zone; (population) civilian population.
III **arrières** *nmpl* rear (*sg*); **surveiller ses ~s** LIT, FIG to watch one's rear; **assurer ses ~s** FIG to cover one's back.

arriéré, ~e /aʀjeʀe/ I *adj* **1** [*idées, pratique*] outdated; [*pays, société*] backward; [*personne*] behind the times (*jamais épith*); **2** PSYCH retarded.
II *nm* arrears (*pl*).

arrière-boutique, *pl* **~s** /aʀjɛʀbutik/ *nf* back of the shop.

arrière-cour, *pl* **~s** /aʀjɛʀkuʀ/ *nf* backyard.

arrière-garde, *pl* **~s** /aʀjɛʀgaʀd/ *nf* rearguard.

arrière-goût, *pl* **~s** /aʀjɛʀgu/ *nm* aftertaste.

arrière-grand-mère, *pl* **arrière-grands-mères** /aʀjɛʀgʀɑ̃mɛʀ/ *nf* great-grandmother.

arrière-grand-oncle, *pl* **arrière-grands-oncles** /aʀjɛʀgʀɑ̃tɔ̃kl/, *pl* gʀɑ̃zɔ̃kl/ *nm* great-great-uncle.

arrière-grand-père, *pl* **arrière-grands-pères** /aʀjɛʀgʀɑ̃pɛʀ/ *nm* great-grandfather.

arrière-grands-parents /aʀjɛʀgʀɑ̃paʀɑ̃/ *nmpl* great-grandparents.

arrière-grand-tante, *pl* **arrière-grands-tantes** /aʀjɛʀgʀɑ̃tɑ̃t/ *nf* great-great-aunt.

arrière-neveu, *pl* **~x** /aʀjɛʀnəvø/ *nm* great-nephew.

arrière-nièce, *pl* **~s** /aʀjɛʀnjɛs/ *nf* great-niece.

arrière-pays /aʀjɛʀpei/ *nm inv* back country.

arrière-pensée, *pl* **~s** /aʀjɛʀpɑ̃se/ *nf* ulterior motive; **sans ~** without reservation.

arrière-petite-fille, *pl* **arrière-petites-filles** /aʀjɛʀpətitfij/ *nf* great-granddaughter.

arrière-petite-nièce, *pl* **arrière-petites-nièces** /aʀjɛʀpətitnjɛs/ *nf* great-great-niece.

arrière-petit-fils, *pl* **arrière-petits-fils** /aʀjɛʀpətifis/ *nm* great-grandson.

arrière-petit-neveu, *pl* **arrière-petits-neveux** /aʀjɛʀpətinəvø/ *nm* great-great-nephew.

arrière-petits-enfants /aʀjɛʀpətizɑ̃fɑ̃/ *nmpl* great-grandchildren.

arrière-plan, *pl* **~s** /aʀjɛʀplɑ̃/ *nm* background.

arrière-saison, *pl* **~s** /aʀjɛʀsɛzɔ̃/ | ▶542| *nf* late autumn GB, late fall US.

arrière-train, *pl* **~s** /aʀjɛʀtʀɛ̃/ *nm* **1** (d'animal) hindquarters (*pl*); **2°** (d'humain) behind.

arrimage /aʀimaʒ/ *nm* **1** NAUT stowing; **2** ASTRONAUT docking.

arrimer /aʀime/ [1] *vtr* **1** GÉN to stow [sth] away; **~ qch à** or **sur qch** to fasten sth to sth; **2** ASTRONAUT to dock (à with).

arrivage /aʀivaʒ/ *nm* COMM delivery.

arrivant, ~e /aʀivɑ̃, ɑ̃t/ *nm,f* **les premiers ~s** the first to arrive; **nouvel ~** newcomer.

arrivé, ~e[1] /aʀive/ I *pp* ▶ **arriver**.
II *pp adj* **1** (au but) **le dernier ~** the last person to arrive; **2** (socialement) **être ~** to have made it.

arrivée[2] /aʀive/ *nf* **1** (moment) arrival; **après mon ~** after I arrived; **~ au pouvoir** accession to power; **depuis son ~ au pouvoir** since he/she came to power; **guetter l'~ du courrier** to watch out for the post; **trains à l'~** arrivals; **je t'attendrai à l'~** (du train) I'll meet you off GB ou at US your train; **2** (de course) finish; **à l'~** at the finish; **3** TECH inlet; **~ d'air** air inlet.

arriver /aʀive/ [1] I *vi* **1** (parvenir) [*personne, avion, lettre*] to arrive; (s'acheminer) [*personne, pluie*] to come; **je suis arrivée avant toi** I got here before you; **l'eau arrive par ce tuyau** the water comes in through this pipe; **j'arrive!** I'm coming!; **j'arrive de Londres** I've just come from London; **~ en courant** to come running up; **~ en tête** to come first; **~ dans les premiers** (en compétition) to be among the first to finish; (à une soirée) to be among the first to arrive; **2** (atteindre) **~ à** to reach [*niveau, âge, accord*]; to find [*solution*]; to achieve [*but, résultat*]; **~ aux chevilles** [*eau*] to come up to one's ankles; [*jupe*] to come down to one's ankles; **~ (jusqu')à** qn [*nouvelle, odeur*] to reach sb; **'qu'en est-il du chômage?'—'j'y arrive'** 'what about unemployment?'—'I'm coming to that'; **3** (réussir) (socialement) to succeed; GÉN **~ à faire** to manage to do; **je n'arrive pas à faire** I can't do; **je n'arrive à rien** I'm getting nowhere; **~ à ses fins** to achieve one's ends; **4** (aboutir) **en ~ à** to come to; **on en arrive à des absurdités** you end up with nonsense; **j'en arrive à croire que...** I'm beginning to think that...; **5** (survenir) [*accident, catastrophe*] to happen; **ce sont des choses qui arrivent** these things happen, it's just one of those things.

II *v impers* **qu'est-il arrivé?** what happened? (à to); **que t'arrive-t-il?** what's wrong with you?; **il arrive un moment où** there comes a time when; **il arrive que qn fasse** sometimes sb does; **est-ce qu'il t'arrive d'y penser?** do you ever think about it?

arriviste /aʀivist/ **I** *adj* ruthlessly ambitious.
II *nmf* upstart, arriviste GB.

arrogance /aʀɔgɑ̃s/ *nf* arrogance.

arrogant, **~e** /aʀɔgɑ̃, ɑ̃t/ **I** *adj* arrogant.
II *nm,f* arrogant person.

arroger: s'arroger /aʀɔʒe/ [13] *vpr* to appropriate [*titre, prérogatives*]; to assume [*droit, pouvoir, fonction*]; **s'~ le monopole de** to claim a monopoly on.

arrondi, **~e** /aʀɔ̃di/ **I** *adj* **1** [*objet*] rounded; [*visage, encolure*] round; **femme aux formes ~es** shapely woman; **2** [*voyelle*] rounded.
II *nm* (d'objet, de visage) roundness; (d'épaule) curve; (de jupe, robe) hemline; **l'~ du col** the shape of the neck.

arrondir /aʀɔ̃diʀ/ [3] **I** *vtr* **1** (rendre rond) to round [sth] off [*objet*]; to round off [*bord*]; to open [sth] wide [*yeux*]; **~ une jupe** to make the hem of a skirt even; **coiffure qui arrondit le visage** hairstyle that makes one's face look round; **2** (adoucir) to make [sth] softer [*mouvement*]; to polish [*phrase*]; **3** (dans un calcul) to round off [*chiffre*]; **~ au franc supérieur/inférieur** to round up/down to the nearest franc; **en arrondissant** in round figures; **4** (augmenter) to increase [*fortune, patrimoine*].
II **s'arrondir** *vpr* **1** (devenir rond) [*objet*] to become round(ed); [*personne, visage, ventre*] to fill out; [*yeux*] to widen; **2** (augmenter) [*fortune*] to be growing.
IDIOMES **~ les angles** to smooth the rough edges.

arrondissement /aʀɔ̃dismɑ̃/ *nm* **1** (de ville) arrondissement; **2** (petite région) *administrative division in France, larger than a canton but smaller than a department*.

arrosage /aʀozaʒ/ *nm* **1** (de plante, champ) watering; (de sol) spraying; **2** MIL (bombardement) bombardment.

arroser /aʀoze/ [1] **I** *vtr* **1** [*personne*] (avec un arrosoir, un tuyau) to water [*plante, champ*]; (avec un arroseur) to sprinkle [*plante, champ*]; [*personne, arroseuse*] to spray [*rue, trottoir*]; [*pluie, rivière*] to water; **région bien arrosée** region with a lot of rainfall; **~ qch d'essence** to douse sth with petrol GB ou gasoline US; **un orage arrive, on va se faire ~°!** there's a storm coming on, we're going to get soaked!; **2** CULIN to baste [*rôti*]; to sprinkle [*gâteau*] (**de** with); to lace [*cocktail, café*] (**de** with); **3** (autour d'une boisson) to drink to [*promotion, victoire*]; **~ un repas à la bière** to wash a meal down with beer; **4** (avec des balles) to spray; (avec des obus) to bombard; **5°** (corrompre) **~ qn** to grease sb's palm°.
II **s'arroser°** *vpr* (se fêter) **ça s'arrose** that calls for a drink.

arroseur /aʀozœʀ/ *nm* (appareil) sprinkler.

arrosoir /aʀozwaʀ/ *nm* watering can.

arsenal, *pl* **-aux** /aʀsənal, o/ *nm* **1** NAUT naval shipyard; **2** MIL arsenal; **3°** (matériel) gear ₵; **tout un ~ de** a whole battery of.

arsenic /aʀsənik/ *nm* arsenic.

art /aʀ/ **I** *nm* **1** (création, œuvres) art; **l'~ pour l'~** art for art's sake; **2** (savoir-faire) art; (habileté) skill; **c'est tout un ~ de créer un parfum** creating a perfume is an art in itself; **c'est du grand ~** it's a real art; **avoir l'~ et la manière** to have the skill and the style (**de faire** to do); **avec ~** (artistement) artistically; (habilement) skilfully^GB; **3** (don) knack (**de faire** of doing); **il a l'~ de parler pour ne rien dire** he's very good at talking without saying anything.
II **arts** *nmpl* arts.
■ **~ déco** art deco; **~ dramatique** drama; **~ floral** flower arranging ; **~ de la guerre** art of war; **~ lyrique** opera; **~ nouveau** art nouveau; **~ oratoire** public speaking; **~ de la table** art of entertaining; **~ de vivre** art of living; **~s appliqués** applied arts; **~s décoratifs** decorative arts; **~s ménagers** home economics; **~s plastiques** plastic arts.

Artaban /aʀtabɑ̃/ *npr* **fier comme ~** proud as a peacock.

artère /aʀtɛʀ/ *nf* **1** ANAT artery; **2** (voie) artery; **grande ~, ~ principale** (rue) main thoroughfare ou street; (route) arterial road.

artériel, **-ielle** /aʀteʀjɛl/ *adj* arterial.

arthrite /aʀtʀit/ **▶ 196** *nf* arthritis.

arthrose /aʀtʀoz/ **▶ 196** *nf* osteoarthritis.

artichaut /aʀtiʃo/ *nm* (globe) artichoke.
IDIOMES **avoir un cœur d'~** to be fickle (*in love*).

article /aʀtikl/ **I** *nm* **1** (de journal) article (**sur** about, on); **2** LING article; **3** (de dictionnaire) entry; **4** COMM item; **~s de consommation courante** basic consumer items; **faire l'~ à qn** (pour vendre) to give sb the sales pitch; FIG to try to win sb over; **5** JUR (de loi, traité, convention) article; (de contrat) clause.
II **articles** *nmpl* COMM goods (*pl*); **~s de sport** sports equipment; **~s de toilette** toiletries.
■ **~ de fond** feature article; **~ de synthèse** synthesis; **~ de tête** editorial.
IDIOMES **être à l'~ de la mort** to be at death's door.

articulation /aʀtikylasjɔ̃/ *nf* **1** ANAT (jointure) joint; (mouvement) articulation; **2** (d'appareil) mobile joint; **3** (de son) articulation; **4** (de phrase) linking sentence; (de paragraphe) linking paragraph; **5** (d'argumentation) (logical) connection; (de dissertation, discours) structure.

articulé, **~e** /aʀtikyle/ *adj* [*autobus, membre*] articulated; [*glace*] adjustable.

articuler /aʀtikyle/ [1] **I** *vtr* **1** (prononcer) to articulate [*mot, son*]; to utter [*phrase*]; **articule quand tu parles!** speak clearly!; **2** (assembler) to connect [*pièce*] (**sur** to); **3** (structurer) to structure [*idées, discours*].
II **s'articuler** *vpr* **1** ANAT **s'~ à** ou **avec** to articulate with; **2** (en mécanique) **s'~ à** ou **sur** to connect to; **3** FIG **s'~ autour de** to be based on.

artifice /aʀtifis/ *nm* **1** (ruse) GÉN trick; (de séducteur) ploy; **2** (moyen) device; **les ~s du style** stylistic devices; **3** (résultat) effect; **~s scéniques** stage effects; **4** (attitude) artifice; **sans ~** [*être*] unpretentious; [*agir*] unpretentiously.

artificiel, **-ielle** /aʀtifisjɛl/ *adj* **1** (fabriqué) GÉN artificial; [*port, lac, colline*] man-made; **2** (faux) PEJ [*besoins*] artificial; [*vie, plaisirs*] superficial; [*gaieté, rire*] forced; [*enthousiasme*] false; **3** (arbitraire) GÉN arbitrary; [*argumentation*] contrived.

artificiellement /aʀtifisjɛlmɑ̃/ *adv* **1** [*produire*] by artificial means, artificially; **2** [*différencier*] arbitrarily.

artificier /aʀtifisje/ **▶ 374** *nm* **1** (de feux d'artifice) fireworks manufacturer; (d'explosifs) explosives manufacturer; **2** (qui désamorce) bomb disposal expert.

artillerie /aʀtijʀi/ *nf* MIL (matériel, corps) artillery; **~ antiaérienne** anti-aircraft guns (*pl*).

artilleur /aʀtijœʀ/ *nm* MIL artilleryman, gunner.

artisan /aʀtizɑ̃/ **▶ 374** *nm* **1** (travailleur) artisan, (self-employed) craftsman; **2** (auteur) architect.

artisanal, **~e**, *mpl* **-aux** /aʀtizanal, o/ *adj* [*activité, foire*] craft (*épith*); [*méthode*] traditional; **les petites**

entreprises ~**es** cottage industries; **de fabrication** ~**e** [objet] hand-crafted; [aliments, bombe] home-made.

artisanalement /aʀtizanalmɑ̃/ adv **fabriqué** ~ [objet] hand-crafted; [aliments] home-made.

artisanat /aʀtizana/ nm **1** (activité) craft industry, cottage industry; **2** (groupe social) artisans (pl).
■ ~ **d'art** arts and crafts.

artiste /aʀtist/ ▶374 I adj (créatif) artistic.
II nmf **1** (créateur) artist; **2** (chanteur, danseur, musicien) artist performer; (de music-hall) artiste; ~ **de cinéma** film actor; ~ **lyrique** opera singer.
■ ~ **peintre** painter.

artistement /aʀtistəmɑ̃/ adv artistically.

artistique /aʀtistik/ adj artistic.

artistiquement /aʀtistikmɑ̃/ adv artistically.

as /as/ nm inv **1** (aux cartes) ace; (au tiercé) l'~ number one; **2**○ (champion) ace○; ~ **du volant** ace○ ou crack driver; ~ **du ciel** flying ace; **être un** ~ **en cuisine** to be a brilliant○ cook; **3** SPORT (au tennis) ace.
■ ~ **de pique** LIT ace of spades; FIG○ [croupion] parson's nose; **être ficelé** or **fagoté comme l'**~ **de pique**○ to look a mess.
IDIOMES **être plein a** ~○ to be loaded○, to be stinking rich○; **passer** ○ [somme d'argent] to be ou to go down the drain. ..et, augmentation] to go by the board; [consommⴰ ̄s] GÉN to be overlooked; (sur une facture) to be left off the bill.

AS /aɛs/ nf **1** (abbr = **Armée secrète**) Secret Army; **2** abbr ▶ **association**.

ascendance /asɑ̃dɑ̃s/ nf **1** (ligne généalogique) descent; **2** (ancêtres) ancestry.

ascendant, ~**e** /asɑ̃dɑ̃, ɑ̃t/ I adj [courbe, trait] rising; [mouvement] upward; [astre] ascending.
II nm **1** (ancêtre) ancestor; (parent) ascendant; **2** (pouvoir) influence (sur over); **3** (en astrologie) ascendant.

ascenseur /asɑ̃sœʀ/ nm lift GB, elevator US.
IDIOMES **renvoyer l'**~ to return the favour○GB.

ascension /asɑ̃sjɔ̃/ nf **1** (en montagne) ascent; **faire l'**~ **de** to climb; **2** (d'avion) ascent; **3** FIG rise.

Ascension /asɑ̃sjɔ̃/ I nf Ascension.
II ▶305 nprf GÉOG **île de l'**~ Ascension Island.

ascensionnel, -**elle** /asɑ̃sjɔnɛl/ adj [mouvement] upward; [vitesse] climbing.

ascète /asɛt/ nmf ascetic.

ascétisme /asetism/ nm asceticism.

aseptique /aseptik/ adj aseptic.

aseptisation /aseptizasjɔ̃/ nf (de pièce) disinfection; (d'instrument) sterilization.

aseptisé, ~**e** /aseptize/ adj [musique, art] sanitized; [vie, monde] sterile; [décor, ambiance] impersonal.

aseptiser /aseptize/ [1] vtr to disinfect [plaie, pièce]; to sterilize [instrument].

asexué, ~**e** /asɛksɥe/ adj BIOL asexual.

asiatique /azjatik/ adj Asian.

Asie /azi/ ▶232 nprf Asia; ~ **Mineure** Asia Minor.

asile /azil/ nm **1** GÉN refuge; RELIG sanctuary; **demander l'**~ **politique** to seek political asylum; **2** (établissement) ~ **de vieillards** old people's home; ~ **d'aliénés** lunatic asylum; ~ **de nuit** night shelter; **il est bon pour l'**~○ he should be locked up○.

asocial, ~**e**, pl -**iaux** /asɔsjal, o/ I adj antisocial.
II nm,f social misfit.

asparagus /aspaʀagys/ nm asparagus fern.

aspect /aspɛ/ nm **1** (perspective) side; **voir qch sous son** ~ **positif** to see the good side of sth; **examiner qch sous tous ses** ~**s** to examine sth from every angle; **je n'avais pas vu la situation sous cet** ~ I hadn't seen the situation in that light; **2** (facettes) aspect; **par bien des** ~**s** in many respects; **3** (apparence) appearance; **changer d'**~ to change in appearance; **reprendre son** ~ **normal** to look normal again; **d'**~ **redoutable** formidable-looking; **d'**~ **engageant** pleasant-looking; **avoir l'**~ **du cuir** to look like leather; **garder l'**~ **du neuf** to stay looking new; **4** LING aspect.

asperge /aspɛʀʒ/ nf **1** (légume) asparagus; **2**○ (personne) PEJ beanpole○, string bean US.

asperger /aspɛʀʒe/ [13] I vtr (avec un jet) to spray (**de** with); (accidentellement) to splash (**de** with); (pour humecter) to sprinkle (**de** with).
II **s'asperger** vpr to splash oneself (**de** with); **il s'est aspergé de champagne** he sprayed champagne all over himself.

aspérité /asperite/ nf **1** (de sol, planche) bump (**de** in); (de paroi rocheuse) protrusion SOUT (**de** on); **2** (de voix, caractère) harshness.

aspersion /aspɛʀsjɔ̃/ nf **1** (avec un produit) spraying; **2** RELIG (avant la messe) asperges (+ v sg); (au baptême) aspersion.

asphalte /asfalt/ nm asphalt.

asphyxiant, ~**e** /asfiksjɑ̃, ɑ̃t/ adj asphyxiating.

asphyxie /asfiksi/ nf **1** MÉD death by suffocation, asphyxia; **2** FIG [de réseau, d'entreprise] paralysis.

asphyxier /asfiksje/ [2] I vtr **1** MÉD to asphyxiate; **mourir asphyxié** to die of suffocation; **2** FIG to paralyze.
II **s'asphyxier** vpr **1** MÉD to suffocate to death; (avec un gaz) to asphyxiate; **2** FIG [pays, économie] to become paralyzed.

aspic /aspik/ nm **1** ZOOL asp; **2** CULIN aspic; ~ **de légumes** vegetables in aspic.

aspirant, ~**e** /aspiʀɑ̃, ɑ̃t/ I adj [pompe] suction; [ventilateur] extractor.
II ▶284 nm MIL (armée de terre, de l'air) ~ senior officer cadet; (marine) ~ midshipman cadet.

aspirateur /aspiʀatœʀ/ nm **1** (appareil ménager) vacuum cleaner, hoover® GB; **2** MÉD aspirator.

aspiration /aspiʀasjɔ̃/ nf **1** (désir) aspiration (**à** for); **2** (de poussière) sucking up; (de liquide) drawing up; (d'air) drawing in; **3** (en respirant) inhalation; **pendant l'**~ when inhaling, when breathing in.

aspirer /aspiʀe/ [1] I vtr **1** (inhaler) to breathe in [air]; to inhale [fumée]; **2** (avec une paille, un tuyau) to suck up; (avec un aspirateur) to suck up [poussière]; to vacuum [tapis, pièce]; (avec une pompe) (pour extraire) to pump [sth] up [liquide]; (pour vider) to pump [sth] out; **3** LING **consonne aspirée** aspirated consonant.
II **aspirer à** vtr ind to yearn for [calme, liberté]; to aspire to [gloire, fonction]; ~ **à faire** to desire to do.

aspirine® /aspiʀin/ nf aspirin.
IDIOMES **être blanc comme un cachet d'**~ to be lily white.

assagir /asaʒiʀ/ [3] I vtr to quieten GB ou quiet US [sb] down.
II **s'assagir** vpr (devenir sage) to quieten down GB, to quiet down US; (se ranger) to settle down.

assaillant, ~**e** /asajɑ̃, ɑ̃t/ nm,f attacker, assailant; **les** ~**s** MIL the attacking forces.

assaillir /asajiʀ/ [28] vtr **1** (attaquer) [ennemi] to attack; [pluie] to buffet; **2** (envahir) [doute] to plague; **3** (se précipiter sur) [mendiant] to assail; [journaliste] to set upon; ~ **de questions** to bombard with questions.

assainir /aseniʀ/ [3] I vtr to clean up [maison, rivière, atmosphère, organisation]; to stabilize [économie]; to streamline [entreprise, gestion]; ~ **les finances** to make the finances healthier.
II **s'assainir** vpr [atmosphère, environnement] to become healthier; [marché, situation] to stabilize.

assainissement /asenismɑ̃/ nm **1** LIT (de logement, rivière, région, d'atmosphère) cleaning up; **2** FIG (de situation) stabilization; (d'entreprise) streamlining.

assaisonnement /asɛzɔnmɑ̃/ nm (vinaigrette) dressing; (sel, poivre, épices) seasoning.

assaisonner /asɛzɔne/ [1] vtr (avec du sel, du poivre, des épices) to season (**de** with); (avec de la vinaigrette) to dress (**de** with).

assassin, ~**e** /asasɛ̃, in/ I adj [main, regard] murderous; [campagne] vicious; **remarque** ~**e** poisoned arrow; **faire** or **lancer une remarque** ~**e à qn** to make a scathing remark to sb.
II nm GÉN murderer; (par idéologie) assassin; **'à l'**~**!'** 'murder!'

assassinat /asasina/ *nm* GÉN murder; (idéologique, politique) assassination.

assassiner /asasine/ [1] *vtr* **1** (tuer) GÉN to murder; (par idéologie) to assassinate; **2** (détruire) to destroy; **3**○ (critiquer) to slate○.

assaut /aso/ *nm* GÉN attack (**de** on); (de place forte) assault (**de** on); **donner l'~, monter à l'~** to attack; **se lancer** or **monter à l'~ de** to launch an attack on; **prendre d'~** to storm; **le buffet a été pris d'~** the buffet was besieged; **à l'~!** attack!; **les ~s du froid** the onslaught of cold weather.

assèchement /asɛʃmɑ̃/ *nm* LIT (en drainant) draining; (en vidant) emptying; (dû au climat) drying up ou out.

assécher /aseʃe/ [14] **I** *vtr* LIT (drainer) to drain; (vider) to empty; (dessécher) to dry up.
II s'assécher *vpr* [*étang, puits*] to dry up; [*marais, sol*] to dry out.

ASSEDIC /asedik/ *nf* (*abbr* = **Association pour l'emploi dans l'industrie et le commerce**) *organization managing unemployment contributions and payments.*

assemblage /asɑ̃blaʒ/ *nm* **1** (de moteur, meuble) assembly (**de** of); (de feuillets) gathering; (de vêtement) sewing together; **l'~ des pièces par soudure** the welding together of parts; **2** (en menuiserie) joint; **3** (d'objets, idées, de données) collection, assemblage; (de couleurs, sons) combination; **4** ORDINAT assembly.

assemblée /asɑ̃ble/ *nf* **1** (foule) gathering; RELIG ~ (de fidèles) congregation; **2** (réunion convoquée) meeting; **3** POL (groupe élu) assembly.
■ **~ générale**, **AG** general meeting; **l'Assemblée nationale** the French National Assembly.

assembler /asɑ̃ble/ [1] **I** *vtr* **1** (monter) to assemble, to put [sth] together [*pièces, moteur*]; to make up, to sew [sth] together [*vêtement, pull*]; **~ des pièces par collage** to glue pieces together; **2** (disposer ensemble) to combine [*mots*]; [*sons*]; **3** ORDINAT to assemble.
II s'assembler *vpr* [*foule*] to gather; [*conseillers, députés*] to assemble.
IDIOMES **qui se ressemble s'assemble** PROV birds of a feather stick together PROV.

asséner /asene/ [14] *vtr* **1** (donner) **~ un coup à qn/qch** LIT, FIG to deal sb/sth a blow; **2** FIG (lancer) to hurl [*questions, injures*] (à at); to fling [*remarque*]; to fling back [*réplique*]; **une réplique bien assénée** a well-aimed retort.

assentiment /asɑ̃timɑ̃/ *nm* assent, consent.

asseoir /aswar/ [41] **I** *vtr* **1** to sit [*personne debout*]; to sit [sb] up [*personne allongée*]; **faire ~ qn** (contraindre) to make sb sit down; (convier) to offer a seat to sb; **2** CONSTR to seat, to bed [*fondations*]; **3** to establish [*autorité, réputation*]; to set up [*argument*]; **4** to base [*cotisation, impôt*]; **5**○ to stagger○, to astound.
II s'asseoir *vpr* **1** [*personne debout*] to sit (down); [*personne allongée*] to sit up; **s'~ à une** or **autour d'une table** LIT to sit down at a table; FIG to sit down at the negotiating table; **2**○ (mépriser) **s'~ sur** not to give a damn about○.

assermenté, ~e /asɛrmɑ̃te/ *adj* [*témoin, expert*] sworn (*épith*), on oath (*jamais épith*).

assertion /asɛrsjɔ̃/ *nf* assertion.

asservir /asɛrvir/ [3] *vtr* to enslave [*peuple, personne*]; to subjugate [*pays*] (à to); to control [*presse*]; **être asservi à** to be a slave to.

asservissement /asɛrvismɑ̃/ *nm* FML **1** (de pays) subjugation; (de peuple) enslavement; (de presse) control; **2** (état) subjection (à to); **maintenir un pays dans l'~** to keep a country enslaved; **3** FIG (de personne) subservience (à to); **4** TECH (système) servomechanism.

assesseur /asesœr/ *nm* JUR magistrate's assistant.

assez /ase/ [▶486] *adv*

■ **Note** Lorsqu'il signifie 'suffisamment', *assez* se traduit par *enough*: *les pommes ne sont pas assez mûres* = the apples are not ripe enough; *tu ne manges pas assez* = you don't eat enough.

– On notera la place de *enough* avec un adjectif: *assez grand* (*pour faire*) = tall enough (to do). ▶ 1 ci-dessous.
– Lorsqu'il est utilisé pour atténuer un jugement *assez* se traduit par *quite*: *il est assez grand* = he's quite tall. ▶ 2 ci-dessous.

1 (évaluation) enough; **~ de temps** enough time; **serons-nous ~?** will there be enough of us?; **il ne travaille pas ~** he doesn't work hard enough; **j'en aurai ~ de quatre** four will be quite enough (for me); **en avoir ~**○ to be fed up○ (**de** with); **avez-vous ~ mangé?** have you had enough to eat?; **2** (jugement) quite; **~ jeune** quite young; **~ souvent** quite often, fairly often; **je suis ~ pressé** I'm in rather a hurry; **je suis ~ d'accord** I tend to agree; **je les trouve ~ ennuyeux** I find them rather boring.

assidu, ~e /asidy/ *adj* [*travail*] diligent; [*soins*] constant; [*visites*] regular; [*élève*] diligent, assiduous; [*employé, chercheur*] hard-working; [*amateur de théâtre, lecteur*] devoted, assiduous; [*amoureux*] devoted.

assiduité /asidɥite/ *nf* **1** (application) diligence; **avec ~** [*travailler*] diligently; [*s'entraîner*] assiduously; [*lire, regarder*] regularly; [*courtiser*] assiduously; **2** (fréquentation régulière) regular attendance.
II assiduités *nfpl* assiduities.

assidûment /asidymɑ̃/ *adv* [*travailler*] diligently; [*fréquenter, s'entraîner*] assiduously.

assiégeant, ~e /asjeʒɑ̃, ɑ̃t/ *nm,f* besieger.

assiéger /asjeʒe/ [15] *vtr* MIL, FIG to besiege.

assiette /asjɛt/ *nf* **1** (vaisselle, contenu) plate; **finis ton ~** finish what's on your plate; **il n'a pas touché à son ~** he hasn't touched his food; **2** (à cheval) seat; **perdre son ~** to become unseated; **3** (d'imposition) **~ (fiscale)** tax base; **détermination de l'~ fiscale** tax assessment.
■ **~ anglaise** CULIN assorted cold meats (*pl*); **~ creuse** soup plate; **~ à dessert** dessert plate; **~ plate** dinner plate; **~ à soupe** = **~ creuse**.
IDIOMES **ne pas être dans son ~** to be out of sorts.

assiettée /asjɛte/ *nf* plateful.

assignation /asiɲasjɔ̃/ *nf* **1** (attribution de crédits) allocation; **2** JUR **~ (à comparaître)** (de défendeur) summons (*sg*); (de témoin) subpoena.
■ **~ en justice** summons to appear before the court; **~ en référé** urgent summons (*to appear before the court within three days*); **~ à résidence** house arrest.

assigner /asiɲe/ [1] **I** *vtr* **1** to assign [*tâche, rôle*] (à to); to allocate [*crédits*] (à to); to fix [*date, limite*] (à to); to ascribe [*valeur*] (à to); **3** JUR **~ à comparaître** to summons [*défendeur*]; to subpoena [*témoin*]; **~ qn à résidence** to put sb under house arrest.
II s'assigner *vpr* **~ un but** to set oneself a goal.

assimilable /asimilabl/ *adj* **1** (comparable) **~ à** comparable to; **2** JUR (équivalent) **~ à** [*personne*] deemed; [*avantage, pratique*] deemed equivalent to; **3** (par l'esprit) **des notions ~s dès l'âge de cinq ans** ideas which can be assimilated from the age of five; **4** [*population, substance*] easily assimilated (**par** by).

assimilation /asimilasjɔ̃/ *nf* **1** (comparaison) comparison (**de qch à qch** between sth and sth); **2** (de connaissances, population, substance) assimilation.

assimilé, ~e /asimile/ *nm* **cadres et ~s** management and those in the same category.

assimiler /asimile/ [1] **I** *vtr* **1** (considérer équivalent) **~ leur silence à un refus** to consider their silence tantamount to a refusal; **~ les travailleurs à des machines** to treat workers as machines; **2** JUR **~ une prime à un salaire** to consider a bonus equivalent to a salary; **être assimilé cadre** to have executive status; **3** (absorber) to assimilate [*population, leçon, substance*]; to learn [*métier*].
II s'assimiler *vpr* **1** [*style, méthode*] to be comparable (à to); **2** [*population*] to become assimilated; [*substances*] to be assimilated.

assis, ~e¹ /asi, iz/ **I** *pp* ▶ **asseoir**.
II *pp adj* **1** (position) **être ~** (et non debout) to be sitting down; (et non allongé) to be sitting up; (installé sur

un siège) to be sitting down ou seated; **j'étais ~ à mon bureau** I was sitting at my desk; **rester ~ des heures à attendre** to sit about waiting for hours; **reste ~** (ne te lève pas) don't get up; (ne bouge pas) sit still; **~!** (à un chien) sit!; **on est mal ~ dans cette voiture** the seats in this car are uncomfortable; **2** [*réputation*] well-established (*épith*); **3**○ staggered.
III *adj* [*personne, position*] seated.

assise² /asiz/ **I** *nf* (fondement) basis, foundation.
II assises *nfpl* GÉN meeting; POL conference; JUR assizes.

assistanat /asistana/ *nm* **1** UNIV assistantship; **2** (aide de l'État) PÉJ charity.

assistance /asistɑ̃s/ *nf* **1** (secours) GÉN assistance; (à l'étranger) aid; **demander l'~ d'un avocat** to ask for legal representation; **~ médicale** medical care; **~ judiciaire** legal aid; **porter** or **prêter ~ à qn** to assist sb; **2** (auditoire) audience; **3** (présence) attendance (**à** at).
■ **~ respiratoire** artificial respiration; **Assistance publique ~** welfare services.

assistant, **~e** /asistɑ̃, ɑ̃t/ **[▶ 374]** *nm,f* GÉN assistant; SCOL (language) assistant; MÉD assistant doctor.
■ **~ de production** CIN, TV production assistant; **~ réalisateur** CIN, TV assistant director; **~e sociale** social worker.

assisté, **~e** /asiste/ **I** *adj* **1** [*personne*] GÉN assisted (**de** by); (par l'État) receiving benefit GB, on welfare US; **2** ORDINAT **~ par ordinateur** computer-aided (*épith*); **3** AUT [*freins, direction*] power (*épith*).
II *nm,f* person receiving benefit GB ou welfare US; **avoir une mentalité d'~** PÉJ to think one can live on government handouts PÉJ.

assister /asiste/ **[1] I** *vtr* **1** (aider) to assist (**de, par** by; **dans** with); **2** (secourir) to aid [*réfugiés, pays*].
II assister à *vtr ind* **1** (être présent) **~ à** to be at [*mariage, spectacle*]; to be present at [*couronnement*]; to attend [*réunion, cours*]; **2** (observer) **~ à** to witness.

associatif, -ive /asɔsjatif, iv/ *adj* **1** LING, MATH, PSYCH [*rapport, loi, lien*] associative; **2** JUR, SOCIOL [*personne*] belonging to an association; [*réseau, tissu*] of associations; **les milieux ~s** associations; **mouvement ~** (ensemble) association; (tendance) trend toward(s) the forming of associations; **vie associative** community life.

association /asɔsjasjɔ̃/ *nf* **1** GÉN association; **en ~ avec** in association with; **2** (de couleurs, styles, substances) combination.
■ **~ à but non lucratif** non-profitmaking organization GB, non-profit organization US; **~ de malfaiteurs** JUR criminal conspiracy; **~ sportive**, **AS** sports association.

associé, **~e** /asɔsje/ **I** *adj* (*after n*) [*membre, directeur, professeur*] associate (*épith*); [*entreprises, organismes*] associated (*épith*).
II *nm,f* associate, partner.

associer /asɔsje/ **[2] I** *vtr* **1** (réunir) to bring together [*personnes*]; **2** (faire partager) **~ qn/qch à** to include sb/sth in; **3** (combiner) to combine [*objets*] (**à** or **et** with); **4** (rapprocher) to associate (**à** with).
II s'associer *vpr* **1** (s'unir) [*personnes, sociétés*] to go into partnership, to link up (**avec** with); **s'~ pour faire** to join forces to do; **2** (se rallier) **s'~ à** to join [*mouvement*]; to join in [*décision, opération*]; **3** (partager) **s'~ à la peine de qn** to share in sb's sorrow; **4** (se combiner) (matériellement) to combine, to be combined (**à** with; **pour faire** in order to do); (abstraitement) to be associated (**à** with; **pour faire** to do).

assoiffé, **~e** /aswafe/ *adj* **1** LIT thirsty; **2** FIG **~ de** thirsting ou hungry for [*pouvoir, liberté*]; **~ de sang** bloodthirsty.

assombrir /asɔ̃bRiR/ **[3] I** *vtr* **1** LIT [*arbres, couleur*] to make [sth] dark [*lieu*]; [*nuages*] to darken [*ciel*]; **2** FIG [*nouvelle, événement*] to cast a shadow over [*période, soirée*]; [*tristesse*] to cloud [*visage*].
II s'assombrir *vpr* **1** LIT [*ciel*] to darken; **2** FIG [*visage, perspectives*] to become gloomy.

assommant○, **~e** /asɔmɑ̃, ɑ̃t/ *adj* **1** (ennuyeux)

deadly boring○; **2** (agaçant) **tu es ~ avec tes questions** you're a real pain○ with your questions.

assommer /asɔme/ **[1]** *vtr* **1** (étourdir) to knock [sb] senseless; **~ qn à coups de massue** to club sb senseless; **2**○ (ennuyer) to bore [sb] to tears○; **3**○ (agacer) **~ qn** to get on sb's nerves; **4**○ (accabler) [*nouvelle*] to stagger; [*chaleur*] to overcome.

Assomption /asɔ̃psjɔ̃/ *nf* Assumption.

assorti, **~e** /asɔRti/ *adj* **1** [*couleurs, linge*] matching; **bien/mal ~** well-/ill-matched; **un abat-jour ~ aux rideaux** a lampshade that matches the curtains; **2** (varié) [*pâtisseries, bonbons*] assorted.

assortiment /asɔRtimɑ̃/ *nm* **1** (d'outils, de pinceaux) set; (de fromages, charcuterie, légumes) assortment; (de produits de beauté) selection; (de tons, couleurs) match; **3** COMM stock.

assortir /asɔRtiR/ **[3] I** *vtr* **1** (harmoniser) to match [*couleurs, vêtements*] (**à** to; **avec** with); to match [*convives*]; **2** (compléter) **~ qch de qch** to add sth to sth; **3** COMM (approvisionner) to stock [*magasin*].
II s'assortir *vpr* **1** [*couleurs, objets, vêtements*] to match; **s'~ à** or **avec qch** to match sth; **2** (être complété) **s'~ de qch** to come with.

assoupir /asupiR/ **[3] I** *vtr* **1** (endormir) to make [sb] drowsy [*personne*]; **2** (atténuer) to dull [*sens*].
II s'assoupir *vpr* **1** LIT [*personne*] to doze off; **2** FIG [*enthousiasme, passion*] to wane; [*haine*] to abate; [*querelle*] to die down; [*activité économique*] to be in a lull.

assoupissement /asupismɑ̃/ *nm* (somnolence) drowsiness; (sommeil) doze.

assouplir /asupliR/ **[3] I** *vtr* **1** (rendre moins rigide) to make [sth] supple [*cuir*]; to soften [sth] up [*chaussures*]; to soften [*linge, lainage*]; to make [sth] more supple [*corps, membres*]; to loosen [*muscles*]; **2** (rendre moins strict) to relax [*règlement, politique, sanctions*]; to make [sth] more flexible [*méthode, système*]; to make [sth] less strict [*régime*].
II s'assouplir *vpr* **1** (devenir moins rigide) [*chaussures, linge, lainage*] to get softer; [*corps, membres, cuir*] to become more supple; FIG [*caractère, personne*] to become more accommodating; **2** (devenir moins strict) [*règlement, politique*] to become more relaxed; [*position, attitude, système*] to become more flexible.

assouplissant /asuplisɑ̃/ *nm* fabric softener.

assouplissement /asuplismɑ̃/ *nm* **1** (de cuir, lainage) softening; (de linge) conditioning; **2** SPORT **faire des ~s** or **des exercices d'~** to limber up; **3** (de règlement, politique, d'attitude) relaxing.

assouplisseur /asuplisœR/ *nm* fabric conditioner.

assourdir /asuRdiR/ **[3] I** *vtr* **1** (rendre sourd) to deafen [*personne*]; **2** (atténuer) to muffle [*bruit*].
II s'assourdir *vpr* **1** [*bruit*] to become muffled; **2** [*phonème*] to become voiceless.

assourdissant, **~e** /asuRdisɑ̃, ɑ̃t/ *adj* deafening.

assourdissement /asuRdismɑ̃/ *nm* **1** (de personne) (action) deafening; (état) temporary deafness; **2** (de bruit) muffling; **3** (de phonème) devoicing.

assouvir /asuviR/ **[3]** *vtr* to satisfy [*faim, désir, curiosité*]; to assuage [*colère, passion*].

assouvissement /asuvismɑ̃/ *nm* **1** (action) (de faim, désir, curiosité) satisfying; (de colère) assuaging; **2** (résultat) satisfaction.

assujetti, **~e** /asyʒeti/ **I** *adj* **~ à** liable for [*impôt*]; **~ à la sécurité sociale** obliged to participate in the French national health and pensions system.
II *nm,f* (à un impôt) person liable for tax; (à une cotisation) contributor.

assujettir /asyʒetiR/ **[3] I** *vtr* **1** (astreindre) to subject (**à** to); **2** (soumettre) to subjugate, to subdue [*pays, peuple*]; **3** (fixer) to secure.
II s'assujettir *vpr* [*personne*] to submit (**à** to).

assujettissement /asyʒetismɑ̃/ *nm* subjection (**à** to); **~ à l'impôt** liability to tax.

assumer /asyme/ **[1]** *vtr* **1** to take [*responsabilité*]; to hold [*fonctions*]; to meet [*coûts*]; **2** to come to terms with [*condition, identité, passé*]; to accept [*conséquences*].

II s'assumer *vpr* **1** to come to terms with oneself; **2** to take responsibility for oneself.

assurance /asyʀɑ̃s/ *nf* **1** (aisance, aplomb) (self-)confidence; (maîtrise) assurance; **montrer de l'~** to be self-confident; **prendre de l'~** to gain confidence; **regard plein d'~** confident look; **avec ~** confidently; **2** (promesse) assurance; (certitude) certainty; **obtenir** or **recevoir l'~ que** to be assured that; **donner à qn l'~ que** to assure sb that; **3** (garantie) insurance (**contre** against); (contrat) insurance (policy); (compagnie) insurance company; (prime) insurance (premium); (secteur) **l'~, les ~s** insurance; **~ sur la vie** life insurance; **souscrire une ~ contre l'incendie** to insure against fire; **avoir une bonne ~** to be well insured; **4** (prestations) benefit ¢ GB, benefits (*pl*) US; **5** (en alpinisme) belaying.

■ **~ automobile** car insurance; **~ chômage** (système) unemployment insurance; (prestations) unemployment benefit GB ou benefits (*pl*) US; **~ incendie** fire insurance; **~ individuelle accident** personal accident insurance; **~ maladie** (système) health insurance; (prestations) sickness benefit GB ou benefits (*pl*) US; **~ maternité** maternity benefit GB ou benefits (*pl*) US; **~ mixte** endowment policy ou insurance; **~ multirisque** comprehensive insurance; **~ multirisque habitation** comprehensive household insurance; **~ mutuelle** (association) mutual insurance company; **~ responsabilité civile** third-party insurance; **~ scolaire** pupil's personal accident insurance; **~s sociales** social insurance ¢; **~ au tiers** third-party insurance; **~ tous risques** comprehensive insurance; **~ vieillesse** state pension; **~ voyage** travel insurance.

assurance-crédit, *pl* **assurances-crédit** /asyʀɑ̃skʀedi/ *nf* credit insurance.

assurance-vie, *pl* **assurances-vie** /asyʀɑ̃svi/ *nf* life insurance.

assuré, **~e** /asyʀe/ I *pp* ▶ **assurer**.
II *pp adj* **1** (sûr) sure, certain (**de faire** of doing); **75% des voix leur sont ~es** they are sure of 75% of the vote; **soyez ~ de ma reconnaissance** I am very grateful to you; (protégé) insured; **la personne ~e** the insured party; **non ~** uninsured.
III *adj* **1** [*démarche, air*] confident; [*main*] steady; **dit-il d'une voix ~e** or **d'un ton ~** he said confidently; **mal ~** [*pas, main*] unsteady; [*geste, ton*] nervous; [*voix*] unsteady, trembling; **2** [*échec, réussite*] certain; [*situation, succès*] assured; **opération dont la réussite est ~e** operation which is sure to succeed.
IV *nm,f* insured party.
■ **~ social** social insurance contributor.

assurément /asyʀemɑ̃/ *adv* GÉN definitely; (pour autoriser) most certainly; **~ pas** GÉN definitely not; (pour refuser) certainly not.

assurer /asyʀe/ [1] I *vtr* **1** (affirmer) **~ à qn que** to assure sb that; **ce n'est pas drôle, je t'assure** believe me, it's no joke; **qu'est-ce que tu es maladroit, je t'assure**○! you really are clumsy!; **2** (faire part à) **~ qn de** to assure sb of [*affection, soutien*]; **3** (protéger) to insure [*biens*] (**contre** against); **4** (effectuer) to carry out [*maintenance, tâche*]; to provide [*service*]; (prendre en charge) to see to [*livraison*]; **le service ne sera pas assuré demain** there will be no service tomorrow; **~ la liaison entre** [*train, car*] to run between; [*ferry*] to sail between; [*compagnie*] to operate between; **~ la gestion de** to manage; **~ sa propre défense** JUR to conduct one's own defence^{GB}; **~ les fonctions de directeur** to be director; **5** (garantir) to ensure [*bonheur, gloire*]; to ensure, to secure [*victoire, paix, promotion*]; to give [*monopole, revenu*]; (par des efforts, une intervention) to secure [*droit, poste*] (**à qn** for sb); to assure [*position, avenir*]; to protect [*frontière*]; **il veut leur ~ une vieillesse paisible** he wants to give them a peaceful old age; **l'exposition devrait ~ 800 emplois** the exhibition ought to create 800 jobs; **~ ses vieux jours** to provide for one's old age; **6** (rendre stable) to steady [*escabeau*]; (fixer) to secure [*corde*]; to fasten [*volet*]; **7** (ne pas risquer) **~ une balle** to play a safe ball; **8** (en alpinisme) to belay [*grimpeur*].

II *vi* **1**○ (être à la hauteur) to be up to the mark○; **~ en chimie** to be good at chemistry; **~ avec les filles** to have a way with the girls; **2** SPORT to play it safe.
III s'assurer *vpr* **1** (vérifier) **s'~ de qch** to make sure of sth, to check on sth; **s'~ que** to make sure that, to check that; **2** (se procurer) to secure [*avantage, aide*]; **s'~ une bonne retraite** to arrange to get a good pension; **s'~ une position de repli** to make sure one has a fall-back position; **3** (prendre une assurance) to take out insurance; **s'~ contre l'incendie/ sur la vie** to take out fire/life insurance; **4** (se prémunir) **s'~ contre** to insure against [*éventualité, risque*]; **5** (en alpinisme) to belay oneself.

assureur /asyʀœʀ/ ▶ **374**| *nm* (contractant) underwriter; (intermédiaire) insurance agent; (compagnie) insurance company.
■ **~ conseil** insurance adviser ou consultant.

astérisque /asteʀisk/ *nm* asterisk.

astéroïde /asteʀɔid/ *nm* asteroid.

asthmatique /asmatik/ *adj*, *nmf* asthmatic.

asthme /asm/ ▶ **196**| *nm* asthma.

asticot /astiko/ *nm* maggot.

asticoter○ /astikɔte/ [1] *vtr* to needle○.

astigmate /astigmat/ *adj* astigmatic.

astiquer /astike/ [1] *vtr* to polish.

astral, **~e**, *mpl* **-aux** /astʀal, o/ *adj* astral.

astre /astʀ/ *nm* star; **l'~ du jour** LITER the sun; **l'~ de la nuit** LITER the moon.

astreignant, **~e** /astʀɛɲɑ̃, ɑ̃t/ *adj* [*tâche, horaires*] demanding; [*discipline, mesures*] strict.

astreindre /astʀɛ̃dʀ/ [55] I *vtr* **~ qn à qch** [*personne*] to force sth upon sb; [*réglementation*] to bind sb to sth; **~ qn à faire** to compel sb to do.
II s'astreindre *vpr* **s'~ à qch** to subject oneself to sth; **s'~ à faire** to force oneself to do.

astreinte /astʀɛ̃t/ *nf* **1** JUR periodic penalty payment; **2** (contrainte) LITER constraint.

astringent, **~e** /astʀɛ̃ʒɑ̃, ɑ̃t/ *adj* astringent.

astrologie /astʀɔlɔʒi/ *nf* astrology.

astrologique /astʀɔlɔʒik/ *adj* astrological.

astrologue /astʀɔlɔg/ ▶ **374**| *nmf* astrologer.

astronaute /astʀɔnot/ ▶ **374**| *nmf* astronaut.

astronautique /astʀɔnotik/ *nf* astronautics (+ *v sg*).

astronome /astʀɔnɔm/ ▶ **374**| *nmf* astronomer.

astronomie /astʀɔnɔmi/ *nf* astronomy.

astronomique /astʀɔnɔmik/ *adj* astronomical.

astrophysicien, **-ienne** /astʀɔfizisjɛ̃, ɛn/ ▶ **374**| *nm,f* astrophysicist.

astrophysique /astʀɔfizik/ *nf* astrophysics (+ *v sg*).

astuce /astys/ *nf* **1** (ingéniosité) GÉN cleverness; (sagacité) shrewdness, astuteness; **être plein d'~** [*enfant*] to be very clever; [*adulte*] to be extremely shrewd; **2** (truc) trick; **toute l'~ consiste à faire** the trick's in doing; **une ~ juridique** a crafty legal manoeuvre^{GB}; **3** (jeu de mots) pun; (plaisanterie) joke.

astucieux, **-ieuse** /astysjø, øz/ *adj* (ingénieux) clever; (sagace) sharp, shrewd.

asymétrie /asimetʀi/ *nf* asymmetry.

asymétrique /asimetʀik/ *adj* asymmetrical.

atchoum /atʃum/ *nm* (*also onomat*) atishoo.

atelier /atəlje/ *nm* **1** (d'artisan, de bricoleur) workshop; (d'artiste) studio; (de couturier) design studio; **2** (dans une usine) shop, workshop; **3** (groupe de travail) working group; (séance de travail) workshop.

atermoiement /atɛʀmwamɑ̃/ *nm* procrastination ¢.

atermoyer /atɛʀmwaje/ [23] *vi* to procrastinate.

athée /ate/ I *adj* atheistic.
II *nmf* atheist.

athéisme /ateism/ *nm* atheism.

athlète /atlɛt/ *nmf* athlete; **carrure d'~** athletic build.

athlétique /atletik/ *adj* athletic.

athlétisme /atletism/ ▶ **329**| *nm* athletics (+ *v sg*) GB, track and field events; **faire de l'~** to do athletics.

Atlantique /atlɑ̃tik/ **▶407|** *nprm* **l'(océan)** ~ the Atlantic (Ocean).

atlas /atlas/ *nm inv* **1** (livre) atlas; **2** (vertèbre) atlas.

atmosphère /atmɔsfɛʀ/ *nf* LIT, FIG atmosphere; **j'ai besoin de changer d'**~ I need a change of air.

atmosphérique /atmɔsfeʀik/ *adj* atmospheric.

atoll /atɔl/ *nm* atoll.

atome /atom/ *nm* atom.

IDIOMES **ne pas avoir un ~ de courage** not to have an ounce of courage; **avoir des ~s crochus**○ **avec qn** to hit it off with sb○.

atomique /atɔmik/ *adj* [*énergie, centrale, arme*] nuclear; [*bombe, nombre, structure*] atomic.

atomisation /atɔmizasjɔ̃/ *nf* (de pouvoir, parti, société) fragmentation, atomization.

atomiser /atɔmize/ [1] *vtr* to fragment [*secteur, parti*].

atomiseur /atɔmizœʀ/ *nm* spray, atomizer.

atomiste /atɔmist/ **I** *adj* **1** [*savant, chercheur*] nuclear; [*structure, théorie*] atomic; **2** PHILOS atomist.
II *nmf* **1** **▶374|** nuclear scientist; **2** PHILOS atomist.

atone /atɔn/ *adj* **1** [*vie, groupe*] apathetic; [*personne*] lifeless; **2** [*mot, syllabe*] unstressed, unaccented.

atonie /atɔni/ *nf* (de personne, pouvoir, marché) sluggishness, apathy; (de regard, voix) lifelessness.

atonique /atɔnik/ *adj* atonic.

atours† /atuʀ/ *nmpl* finery *₵*; **mettre ses plus beaux ~** to deck oneself out in all one's finery.

atout /atu/ *nm* **1** JEUX (carte) trump; (couleur) trumps (*pl*); **c'est ~ cœur** hearts are trumps; **2** FIG (avantage) asset; (avantage sur les autres) trump card; **jouer son dernier ~** to play one's last card; **~ supplémentaire** additional advantage; **avoir tous les ~s en main** to hold all the aces; **mettre tous les ~s dans son jeu** to leave nothing to chance.

âtre /ɑtʀ/ *nm* hearth.

atroce /atʀɔs/ *adj* **1** [*blessure, sentiment, nouvelle*] dreadful; [*souffrance, douleur*] atrocious; [*peur*] terrible; [*supplice*] horrific; [*crime, mort*] horrible; [*acte, spectacle*] horrifying; **2**○ [*nourriture, temps, accent*] atrocious, appalling; **tu es ~!** you are dreadful!

atrocement /atʀɔsmɑ̃/ *adv* **1** [*mutiler*] dreadfully; [*souffrir*] horribly, terribly; **j'ai ~ mal** I'm in agony; **2**○ [*ennuyeux, bête*] dreadfully; [*laid*] atrociously.

atrocité /atʀɔsite/ *nf* **1** (caractère) atrocity; **2** (crime) atrocity; **3** (calomnie) **dire des ~s sur** to say dreadful things about; **4**○ (chose laide) hideous monstrosity; **5** (laideur) **c'est d'une ~!** it's absolutely hideous!

atrophie /atʀɔfi/ *nf* MÉD, FIG atrophy.

atrophier: s'atrophier /atʀɔfje/ [2] *vpr* **1** MÉD to atrophy; **bras atrophié** wasted arm; **2** FIG [*facultés*] to atrophy; [*économie, marché*] to decline.

attabler: s'attabler /atable/ [1] *vpr* to sit down at (the) table.

attachant, **~e** /ataʃɑ̃, ɑ̃t/ *adj* [*personne*] charming, engaging; [*caractère*] charming; [*animal*] sweet.

attache /ataʃ/ *nf* **1** GÉN tie; (ficelle) string; (corde) rope; (courroie) strap; **2** ANAT (articulation) joint; (de muscle) point of attachment; **avoir des ~s fines** to have delicate ankles and wrists; **3** FIG (lien) tie.

attaché, **~e** /ataʃe/ **▶374|** *nm,f* attaché.
■ **~ d'administration** administrative assistant.

attachement /ataʃmɑ̃/ *nm* **1** (sentimental) attachment (à to); **2** (de principe) commitment (à to).

attacher /ataʃe/ [1] **I** *vtr* **1** (lier) GÉN to tie [*personne, animal, mains*] (à to); to tether, to fasten [*laisse, corde*] (à to); (avec une chaîne) to chain [*chien*] (à to); to lock [*bicyclette*] (à to); (en entourant) to tie up [*personne, paquet*]; **~ qn à un poteau** to tie sb to a stake; **~ ses lacets** to tie (up) one's laces; **~ ses chaussures** to do up one's shoes; **2** (fermer) to fasten [*ceinture, collier, vêtement*]; **3** (accorder) to attach [*importance, valeur*]; **4** (employer) **~ qn à son service** to take sb into one's service, to employ sb; **5** (associer) **les privilèges attachés à un poste** the privileges attached to a post; **~ son nom à une découverte** to link one's name to a discovery.

II *vi* (coller) to stick (à to).

III s'attacher *vpr* **1** (se fixer) to fasten, to do up (**par derrière** at the back); **le lierre s'attache aux pierres** ivy clings to stones; **2** (s'efforcer) **s'~ à démontrer** to set out to demonstrate; **3** (se lier affectivement) **s'~ à qn/qch** to become attached to sb/sth, to grow fond of sb/sth.

attaquable /atakabl/ *adj* **1** [*lieu, place*] **facilement ~** easy to attack; **2** [*théorie, position*] shaky; **3** [*testament*] contestable.

attaquant, **~e** /atakɑ̃, ɑ̃t/ *nm,f* **1** MIL attacker; **2** SPORT GÉN attacker; (au football) striker.

attaque /atak/ *nf* **1** MIL attack; **passer à l'~** to move onto the attack; **à l'~!** charge!; **2** (de banque, magasin) raid; (de personne) attack; **~ à main armée** armed raid; **3** FIG (critique) attack; **~ en règle** full-scale attack; **pas d'~s personnelles!** no personal comments!; **4** MÉD (d'apoplexie) stroke; (cardiaque) attack; **5** SPORT (au football, rugby) break; (en course) break; (au tennis, golf) drive; (en alpinisme) attempt; (à la rame) beginning of a stroke; **6** MUS striking up.

IDIOMES **être** ou **se sentir d'~** to feel on GB ou in US form; **être** (**assez**) **d'~ pour faire qch** to feel up to doing sth; **je ne me sens pas très d'~**○ **le matin** I don't feel too lively in the morning.

attaquer /atake/ [1] **I** *vtr* **1** MIL to attack [*troupe, pays*]; **~ sur tous les fronts** to attack on all sides; **2** (agresser) to attack [*personne*]; to raid [*banque, magasin, train*]; **3** (critiquer) to attack; **4** JUR to contest [*contrat, testament*]; **~ qn en justice** to bring an action against sb GB, to lawsuit sb US; **5** [*acide*] to attack; **6** (commencer) to launch into [*discours*]; to make a start on [*lecture, rédaction*]; to get going on [*tâche*]; to attack [*plat*]; to attempt [*escalade*]; **7** to tackle [*problème*]; **8** MUS to strike up [*air*]; to attack [*note*].

II *vi* **1** (au football, rugby) to break; (au tennis) to drive; **2** (commencer à parler) to begin (brusquely).

III s'attaquer *vpr* **s'~ à** to attack [*personne, œuvre, politique*]; to make a start on [*tâche*]; to tackle [*problème*]; **tu t'attaques à plus fort que toi** you're taking on somebody who is more than a match for you.

attardé, **~e** /ataʀde/ **I** *adj* **1** (en retard) late; **quelques passants ~s** some people out late; **2** (démodé) PEJ old-fashioned; **3** (mentalement) PEJ retarded.
II *nm,f* (handicapé mental) PEJ mentally retarded person.

attarder: s'attarder /ataʀde/ [1] *vpr* **1** LIT (rester) to stay; (traîner) to linger; **2** FIG (s'arrêter) to take one's time; **s'~ sur** to dwell on [*point, aspect*].

atteindre /atɛ̃dʀ/ [55] **I** *vtr* **1** (arriver à) to reach [*lieu, niveau*]; [*personne, réforme*] to achieve [*but*]; [*projectile*] to reach [*cible*]; **arbre qui peut ~ 40 mètres** tree which can grow up to 40 metres GB high; **2** (frapper) [*projectile, tireur*] to hit; **3** (affecter) [*maladie, malheur*] (de façon durable) to affect; (brusquement) to hit; [*parole blessante*] to affect; **~ qn dans son honneur** to cast a slur on sb's honour GB; **4** (toucher) to reach [*public*].
II atteindre à FML *vtr ind* to achieve [*connaissance*].

atteint, **~e**[1] /atɛ̃, ɛt/ *adj* **1** (affecté) affected (**de, par** by); **très ~** badly affected; **être ~ de** (de façon durable) to be suffering from [*maladie*]; **2** (frappé) (**de, par** by); **3**○ (timbré) **être ~** to be touched○.

atteinte[2] /atɛt/ *nf* **~** a attack on; **hors d'~** [*personne, paix, poste*] beyond reach; [*cible*] out of range; [*rester, sembler*] out of reach; **porter ~ à** to undermine [*crédit, prestige*]; to damage [*honneur*]; to endanger [*sécurité*]; to infringe [*droit*]; to threaten [*environnement*]; **~ aux droits de l'Homme** infringement of human rights; **~ à l'ordre public** JUR public order offence GB; **~ à la sécurité** or **sûreté de l'État** breach of national security; **~ à la vie privée** breach of the right to privacy.

attelage /atlaʒ/ *nm* **1** (système) (de cheval) harness; (de bœuf) yoke; (de wagon) coupling; (de remorque) towing attachment; (de fusée) docking ou coupling device; **2** (animaux) GÉN team; (de deux bœufs) yoke; **3** (équipage) horse-drawn carriage; **4** (sport) (carriage) driving;

5 (processus) (de cheval) harnessing; (de bœuf) yoking; (de remorque) hitching up; (de wagon) coupling.

atteler /atle/ [19] **I** *vtr* (attacher) to harness [*cheval*] (à to); to yoke [*bœuf*]; to hitch up [*remorque*] (à to); to couple [*wagon*] (à to).

II s'atteler *vpr* **s'~ à une tâche/à faire** to get down to a job/to doing.

attelle /atɛl/ *nf* MÉD splint.

attenant, **~e** /atnɑ̃, ɑ̃t/ *adj* **1** (accolé) [*pièce*] adjacent (à to); **2** (associé) [*problème*] related (à to).

attendre /atɑ̃dʀ/ [6] **I** *vtr* **1** GÉN to wait for [*personne, événement*]; to wait until ou till [*date*] (**pour faire** to do); **j'attends qu'il finisse** or **ait fini** I'm waiting for him to finish; **il attend impatiemment Noël** he can't wait for Christmas; **aller ~ qn à la gare** to (go and) meet sb at the station; **qu'attends-tu pour répondre?** why don't you answer?; **j'attends de voir pour y croire** I'll believe it when I see it; **se faire ~** to keep people waiting; **le serveur se fait ~** the waiter is taking a long time; **la réaction ne se fit pas ~** the reaction was instantaneous; **~ son jour** or **heure** to bide one's time; **reste ici en attendant que la pluie cesse** stay here until the rain stops; **en attendant mieux** until something better turns up; **où étais-tu, on ne t'attendait plus!** where were you? we'd given up on you!; ▶ **ferme**[1]; **2** (être prêt, préparé) [*voiture, taxi*] to be waiting for; [*chambre, appartement*] to be ready for; **un délicieux repas m'attendait** a delicious meal awaited me; **3** (être prévu, prévisible) [*succès, aventure*] to await, to be in store for [*personne*]; **quel avenir nous attend?** what does the future hold (in store) for us?; **les élections sont attendues comme un test** the elections are being viewed as a test; **4** (compter sur) **je les attends pour 5 heures** I'm expecting them at five; **elle attend un bébé** or **un enfant** she's expecting a baby; **~ de qn qu'il fasse** to expect sb to do; **j'attendais mieux de ce roman** I found the novel rather disappointing.

II *vi* to wait; (au téléphone) to hold; **attends un peu!** wait a moment; (menace) just (you) wait!; **faire ~ qn** to keep sb waiting; **sans plus ~** without further delay; **en attendant** (pendant ce temps) in the meantime; (néanmoins) all the same, nonetheless; **tu ne perds rien pour ~**○! I'll get you○, just you wait!

III s'attendre *vpr* **s'~ à qch/à faire** to expect sth/ to do; **s'~ à ce que qn fasse/qch se produise** to expect sb to do/sth to happen; **il fallait s'y ~** it was to be expected; **avec lui, il faut s'~ à tout** with him, anything can happen.

IDIOMES **tout vient à point pour qui sait ~** PROV everything comes to him who waits PROV.

attendrir /atɑ̃dʀiʀ/ [3] **I** *vtr* **1** (émouvoir) to touch, to move [*personne*]; to touch [*cœur*]; **se laisser ~** to soften; **tu ne vas pas te laisser ~ par lui!** you're not going to let him soften you up!; **sourire attendri** tender smile; **2** CULIN to tenderize [*viande*].

II s'attendrir *vpr* (s'émouvoir) [*personne*] to feel moved; **son regard s'attendrit** his/her eyes softened; **s'~ sur qn/soi-même** to feel sorry for sb/oneself; **s'~ sur ses malheurs** to lament one's misfortunes.

attendrissant, **~e** /atɑ̃ʀisɑ̃, ɑ̃t/ *adj* [*spectacle, mots*] touching, moving; [*candeur*] endearing; **être ~ de naïveté** to be endearingly naïve.

attendrissement /atɑ̃dʀismɑ̃/ *nm* (affectueux) tenderness; (ému) emotion; **avec ~** tenderly.

attendrisseur /atɑ̃dʀisœʀ/ *nm* tenderizer.

attendu[1] /atɑ̃dy/ **I** *prép* given, considering.

II attendu que *loc conj* given ou considering that; JUR whereas.

attendu[2], **~e** /atɑ̃dy/ **I** *adj* **1** (prévu) expected; **2** (souhaité) **le jour (tant) ~** the long-awaited day.

II *nm* JUR **~s d'un jugement** grounds for a decision.

attentat /atɑ̃ta/ *nm* (contre un individu) assassination attempt (**contre** on); (contre un groupe, bâtiment) attack (**contre** on); **~ à la bombe** bomb attack.

■ **~ à la pudeur** indecent assault.

attente /atɑ̃t/ *nf* **1** (processus) waiting ¢; (période) wait; **l'~ du verdict** waiting for the verdict; **deux heures**

d'~ a two-hour wait; **mon ~ a été vaine** I waited for nothing; **dans l'~ de vous lire** looking forward to hearing from you; **en ~** [*passager*] waiting; [*dossier, affaire*] pending (*jamais épith*); TÉLÉCOM [*appel, demandeur*] on hold (*épith, après n*); **commandes en ~** COMM back orders; **2** (espoir) expectations (*pl*); **répondre à l'~ de qn** to come up to sb's expectations.

attenter /atɑ̃te/ [1] *vtr ind* **~ à ses jours** to attempt suicide; **~ à la vie de qn** to make an attempt on sb's life.

attentif, **-ive** /atɑ̃tif, iv/ *adj* **1** [*personne*] attentive; **être ~ à** to pay attention to [*propos, détail, évolution*]; to be mindful of [*convenances*]; **sous le regard ~ de leur mère** under the watchful eye of their mother; **prêter une oreille attentive à qn** to listen carefully to sb; **2** [*lecture, travail, description*] careful; [*examen*] close; [*soin*] special; **3** [*soins*] special; **être ~ aux besoins de qn** to be attentive to sb's needs.

attention /atɑ̃sjɔ̃/ **I** *nf* **1** (vigilance) attention; **porter son ~ sur qch/qn** to turn one's attention to sth/sb; **à l'~ de F. Pons** for the attention of F. Pons; **faire ~ à qch** to mind [*voitures, piège, marche*]; to watch out for [*faux billets, verglas*]; to be careful of [*soleil*]; to consider [*conséquences*]; to take care of [*vêtements*]; to watch [*alimentation, santé*]; to pay attention to [*mode, détails*]; **ne faites pas ~ à ce qu'elle dit** don't take any notice of what she says; **fais ~ à ce que tu fais** be careful what you do; **faire ~ à qn** (écouter) to pay attention to sb; (surveiller) to keep an eye on sb; (remarquer) to take notice of sb; **fais ~ aux voleurs!** beware of thieves!; **fais ~ à toi** take care of yourself ; **avec ~** carefully; **fais ~, c'est très dangereux** be careful, it's very dangerous; **2** (marque de gentillesse) **j'ai été touché par toutes ces ~s** I was touched by all these kind gestures; **être plein d'~s pour qn** to be very attentive to sb; **il a eu la délicate ~ de faire** he was thoughtful enough to do.

II *adv* (cri) look out!, watch out!; (écrit) GÉN attention!; (en cas de danger) warning!; (panneau routier) caution!; **~ à la marche** mind the step; **~, les dossiers d'inscription doivent être retirés avant lundi** please note that application forms must be collected by Monday; **mais ~, il faut réserver à l'avance** however, you must book GB ou reserve in advance; **~, je ne veux pas dire...** don't get me wrong, I don't mean...

attentionné, **~e** /atɑ̃sjɔne/ *adj* [*personne*] attentive, considerate (**pour, envers** toward(s), to); [*soins*] special.

attentisme /atɑ̃tism/ *nm* wait-and-see attitude.

attentivement /atɑ̃tivmɑ̃/ *adv* [*écouter, suivre*] attentively; [*examiner, regarder*] carefully.

atténuantes /atenɥɑ̃t/ *adj fpl* **circonstances ~** JUR mitigating ou extenuating circumstances.

atténuation /atenɥasjɔ̃/ *nf* (de douleur, tension) alleviation, relief; (de nuisance) reduction; (d'effet) mitigation; (de rigueur) relaxation.

atténuer /atenɥe/ [1] **I** *vtr* to ease [*douleur, tension, chagrin*]; to lessen [*désespoir*]; to weaken [*impression, effet*]; to soften [*choc*]; to reduce [*inégalités, gravité*]; to tone down [*reproche*]; to relax [*sévérité*]; to dim [*lumière*]; to tone down [*couleur, éclat*]; to make [sth] less strong [*odeur, goût*]; to mitigate [*faute*].

II s'atténuer *vpr* [*douleur*] to ease; [*colère, chagrin*] to subside; [*corruption*] to lessen; [*tendance*] to become less pronounced; [*inégalités*] to be reduced; [*ride, couleur*] to fade; [*tempête, bruit*] to die down.

atterrant, **~e** /atɛʀɑ̃, ɑ̃t/ *adj* (consternant) [*bêtise*] appalling; [*image, nouvelle*] shattering.

atterré, **~e** /atere/ *adj* **1** (consterné) appalled; **d'un air ~** aghast; **2** (en état de choc) shattered.

atterrer /atere/ [1] *vtr* to leave [sb] aghast.

atterrir /ateʀiʀ/ [3] *vi* **1** AVIAT to land; **~ en catastrophe/sur le ventre** to make a crash landing/a belly landing; **2**○ [*dossier, personne*] to land up○.

atterrissage /ateʀisaʒ/ *nm* landing; **~ en catastrophe** crash landing.

attestation /atɛstasjɔ̃/ *nf* (déclaration) attestation; (sous serment) affidavit; (certificat) certificate.

attester /atɛste/ [1] *vtr* **1** (certifier) to vouch for; (témoigner) to testify to; **~ que** to vouch for the fact that; (témoigner) to testify that; **forme attestée/non attestée** LING attested/unattested form; **2** (être preuve de) to prove, to attest to.

attifer° /atife/ [1] **I** *vtr* to rig [sb] out° (**de, avec** in).
II s'attifer *vpr* to rig oneself out° (**de, avec** in).

attique /atik/ **I** *adj* Attic.
II ▶ 338 | *nm* LING Attic dialect.

attirail /atiʀaj/ *nm* gear; **~ de pêche** fishing tackle; **l'~ du parfait bricoleur** the well-equipped DIY enthusiast's tool kit.

attirance /atiʀɑ̃s/ *nf* attraction (**pour** to); **éprouver** or **avoir de l'~ pour** to feel drawn toward(s), to be attracted to; **l'~ du vide** the fascination of the abyss.

attirant, ~e /atiʀɑ̃, ɑ̃t/ *adj* attractive.

attirer /atiʀe/ [1] **I** *vtr* **1** (faire venir) GÉN, PHYS to attract [*foudre, personne, animal, capitaux, convoitises*]; **~ l'attention de qn sur qch** to draw sb's attention to sth; **~ qn à soi** to draw sb to oneself; **le bruit l'attira dans le jardin** the noise drew him to the garden GB ou yard US; **~ qn dans un coin** to take sb into a corner; **~ qn dans un piège** to lure sb into a trap; **~ qn par des promesses** to entice sb with promises; **2** (séduire) [*personne, pays*] to attract; [*études, métier*] to appeal to; **les brunes l'attirent** he goes for brunettes; **3** (susciter) to bring [*honte , critique*] (**à, sur** on); **~ des ennuis à qn** to cause sb problems.
II s'attirer *vpr* **s'~ le soutien de qn** to win sb's support; **s'~ la colère de qn** to incur sb's anger; **des nombreuses critiques** to attract criticism; **s'~ des ennuis** to get into trouble.

attiser /atize/ [1] *vtr* to kindle [*sentiment, convoitises*]; to fuel [*discorde*]; to stir up [*haine*]; to fan [*feu*].

attitré, ~e /atitʀe/ *adj* **1** (officiel) official; **chauffeur ~** official driver; **représentant ~** accredited representative; **2** (habituel) regular; **client ~** regular customer.

attitude /atityd/ *nf* **1** (maintien) bearing; (position) attitude, posture; (pose) pose; **~ de soumission** submissive attitude; **2** (conduite) attitude (**envers** to).

attouchement /atuʃmɑ̃/ *nm* **1** (sexuel) (sans consentement) (sexual) interfering *ȼ*, molesting *ȼ*; (avec consentement) fondling *ȼ*; **2** (de guérisseur) laying on *ȼ* of hands.

attraction /atʀaksjɔ̃/ *nf* GÉN, LING, PHYS attraction; **~ touristique** tourist attraction.
■ **~ terrestre** Earth's attraction; **~ universelle** gravitation.

attrait /atʀɛ/ *nm* **1** (attirance) appeal, attraction; (de l'interdit) lure; **plein d'~** very attractive; **sans ~** unattractive; **avoir de l'~ pour qn** to appeal to sb; **2** (goût) liking (**pour** for).

attrape-mouches /atʀapmuʃ/ *nm inv* **1** (plante) flytrap; **2** (piège) GÉN flytrap; (papier collant) flypaper.

attrape-nigaud, *pl* **~s** /atʀapnigo/ *nm* con°; **tomber dans un ~** to fall for a con.

attraper /atʀape/ [1] **I** *vtr* **1** (saisir en mouvement) to catch [*personne, animal, ballon*]; **tiens, attrape!** here, catch!; **2** (capturer) to catch [*malfaiteur, animal*]; **se faire ~** to get caught; **attrapez-le!** stop him!; **3** (prendre) to catch hold of [*corde, jambe*]; **~ une bouteille par le goulot** to pick up a bottle by the neck; **tu peux ~ le livre sur l'étagère?** can you reach and get the book from the shelf?; **4**° (contracter) [*personne*] to catch [*froid, maladie*]; to get [*coup de soleil, mal de tête*]; to pick up [*manie, accent*]; **tu vas ~ du mal!** you'll catch something!; **5**° (surprendre) to catch [sb] out; **il a été bien attrapé d'apprendre que** he was really caught out by the news that; **~ qn en train de faire** FIG to catch sb doing; **6**° (réprimander) to tell [sb] off; **se faire ~** to get told off; **7**° (recevoir) to get [*coup, punition*].
II s'attraper *vpr* [*maladie*] to be caught.

attrayant, ~e /atʀɛjɑ̃, ɑ̃t/ *adj* GÉN attractive;

[*lecture*] pleasant; **peu ~** GÉN unattractive; [*tâche, lecture*] unappealing.

attribuable /atʀibɥabl/ *adj* attributable (**à** to).

attribuer /atʀibɥe/ [1] **I** *vtr* **1** (donner) to allocate [*numéro, logement, tâche*]; to grant [*droit*]; to award [*prix, bourse*]; to lend [*importance, sens*]; FIN to allot [*actions*]; **~ qch à la fatigue** to put sth down to tiredness; **~ la responsabilité de qch à qn/qch** to hold sb/sth responsible for sth; **2** (reconnaître) **~ à qn** to credit sb with [*invention, qualité*]; to ascribe to sb [*œuvre*]; **on attribue ce tableau à Poussin** this painting is attributed to Poussin.
II s'attribuer *vpr* **s'~ la meilleure part** to give oneself the largest share; **s'~ tout le mérite** to take all the credit for oneself.

attribut /atʀiby/ *nm* **1** (propriété) attribute; (symbole) symbol; **2** LING **adjectif ~** predicative adjective.

attribution /atʀibysjɔ̃/ **I** *nf* GÉN allocation (**à** to); (d'avantage) awarding (**à** to); (d'actions) allotment (**à** to); (de nationalité) granting (**à** to); (d'œuvre) attribution (**à** to).
II attributions *nfpl* (de personne) remit (*sg*); (de tribunal) competence; **ça n'entre pas dans mes ~s** it doesn't come within my remit.

attristant, ~e /atʀistɑ̃, ɑ̃t/ *adj* **1** (peinant) distressing, upsetting; **2** (consternant) depressing; **d'une bêtise ~e** depressingly stupid.

attrister /atʀiste/ [1] **I** *vtr* (peiner) to sadden; **j'ai été attristé d'apprendre** I was sorry to hear.
II s'attrister *vpr* **1** (exprimer sa tristesse) to lament (**de** about); **2** (être peiné) to be saddened (**de** by).

attroupement /atʀupmɑ̃/ *nm* gathering; **~ de manifestants** crowd of demonstrators; **causer un ~** to cause a crowd to gather.

attrouper: s'attrouper /atʀupe/ [1] *vpr* to gather (**devant** in front of; **autour de** around).

au /o/ *prép* (= **à le**) ▶ **à**.

aubade /obad/ *nf* dawn serenade.

aubaine /obɛn/ *nf* **1** (chance) godsend; **2** (bonne affaire) bargain.

aube /ob/ *nf* **1** (point du jour) dawn; **à l'~** at dawn; **2** (début) dawn; **à l'~ de** at the dawn of; **à l'~ des années 20** in the early twenties; **3** TECH (en bois) paddle; (en métal) blade; **roue à ~s** paddle wheel; **4** RELIG (de prêtre) alb; (d'enfant de chœur) cassock; (pour la communion solennelle) alb.

aubépine /obepin/ *nf* hawthorn.

auberge /obɛʀʒ/ *nf* inn.
■ **~ de jeunesse** youth hostel.
IDIOMES **tu n'es pas sorti de l'~**°! you're not out of the woods yet!

aubergine /obɛʀʒin/ **▶ 141 | I** *adj inv* aubergine.
II *nf* BOT, CULIN aubergine, eggplant US.

aubergiste /obɛʀʒist/ **▶ 374 |** *nmf* innkeeper.

aubier /obje/ *nm* sapwood.

aucun, ~e /okœ̃, yn/ **I** *adj* **1** (dans une phrase négative) no, not any; **il n'y a plus ~ espoir** there's no hope left; **elle l'a fait sans ~e hésitation** or **sans hésitation ~e** she did it without any hesitation; **en ~e façon** in no way; **2** (quelque) LITER any; **je l'aime plus qu'~e autre** I love her more than anybody.
II *pron* **1** (dans une phrase négative) **je n'ai lu ~ de vos livres** I haven't read any of your books; **~ de ses arguments n'est convaincant** none of his arguments are convincing; **'tu as reçu beaucoup de lettres?'—'~e!'** 'did you receive many letters?'—'not one!'; **2** (quiconque) LITER **je doute qu'~ d'entre eux réussisse** I doubt that any of them will succeed; **d'~s** some.

aucunement /okynmɑ̃/ *adv* in no way; **je n'avais ~ l'intention de faire** in no way did I mean to; **je ne suis ~ surpris** I'm not surprised in the least, I'm not at all surprised; **il n'a ~ l'intention de l'épouser** he hasn't got the slightest intention of marrying her.

audace /odas/ *nf* **1** (hardiesse) boldness; **il manque d'~** he's not very daring; **2** (effronterie) audacity, nerve°; (de geste, propos) impudence; **avoir l'~ de**

faire qch to have the audacity ou nerve$^\circ$ to do sth; **il ne manque pas d'~** he's got a nerve$^\circ$; **3** (innovation) **les ~s des architectes** the daring creations of architects; **~s stylistiques** stylistic daring (*sg*).

audacieux, -ieuse /odasjø, øz/ **I** *adj* (hardi) audacious, daring; (effronté) bold.
II *nm,f* daring ou bold person.
IDIOMES **la fortune sourit aux ~** PROV fortune favours^{GB} the brave PROV.

au-dedans /odədɑ̃/ *adv* inside.

au-dehors /odəɔʀ/ *adv* **1** LIT outside; **'ne pas se pencher ~'** 'do not lean out of the window'; **2** FIG outwardly.

au-delà /od(ə)la/ **I** *nm* RELIG beyond, hereafter.
II *adv* beyond; **je veux bien aller jusqu'à 1000 francs mais pas ~** I'm quite prepared to go up to 1,000 francs but no more.
III au-delà de *loc prép* beyond; **~ des frontières** beyond the borders; **~ de 20%** over 20%.

au-dessous /odəsu/ **I** *adv* **1** (plus bas) below; **l'étagère ~** the shelf below; **tu vois le dictionnaire, mon livre est ~** you see the dictionary, my book is underneath; **2** (marquant une infériorité) under; **les enfants de 10 ans et ~** children of 10 years and under.
II au-dessous de *loc prép* **1** (plus bas que) below; **~ du genou** below the knee; **2** (inférieur à) **~ de zéro** below zero; **les enfants ~ de 13 ans** children under 13, the under-thirteens; **les chèques ~ de 100 francs** cheques GB ou checks US for under 100 francs; **être ~ de tout**$^\circ$ (ne pas être à la hauteur) to be absolutely useless; (moralement) to be despicable.

au-dessus /odəsy/ **I** *adv* **1** (plus haut) above; **l'étagère ~** the shelf above; **il habite l'étage ~** he lives on the next floor up ou on the floor above; **2** (marquant une supériorité) above; **les enfants de 10 ans et ~** children of 10 and over, the over-tens; **la taille ~** the next size up.
II au-dessus de *loc prép* **1** (plus haut que) above; **~ des nuages** (up) above the clouds; **deux étages ~ de chez moi** two floors up from me; **un pont ~ de la rivière** a bridge over the river; **se pencher ~ de la table** to lean across the table; **2** (supérieur à) above; **~ de zéro/de la moyenne** above zero/average; **les enfants ~ de 3 ans** children over 3 years old; **les chèques ~ de 1000 francs** cheques GB ou checks US for over 1,000 francs.

au-devant: au-devant de /odəvɑ̃də/ *loc prép* (à la rencontre) **aller ~ de qn** LIT to go to meet sb; **aller ~ des clients** FIG to go out looking for custom; **aller ~ des désirs de qn** to anticipate sb's wishes; **aller ~ des ennuis** to let oneself in for trouble.

audible /odibl/ *adj* audible.

audience /odjɑ̃s/ *nf* **1** JUR hearing; **lever l'~** to close the hearing; **salle d'~** courtroom; **2** (entretien) audience SOUT; **3** (succès, attention) success; **jouir d'une grande ~ auprès des jeunes** to have a lot of success with young people; **4** TV, RADIO (personnes) audience; (chiffres) audience ratings (*pl*).

audimat® /odimat/ *nm* audience ratings (*pl*).

audio /odjo/ *adj inv* audio.

audionumérique /odjonymeʀik/ *adj* **disque ~** digital audio disc.

audiovisuel, -elle /odjovizɥɛl/ **I** *adj* **1** RADIO, TV broadcasting; **techniques audiovisuelles** broadcasting technology; **2** LING, VIDÉO audiovisual.
II *nm* **1** RADIO, TV broadcasting; **2** (équipement) audiovisual equipment; **3** (méthodes) audiovisual methods.

audit /odit/ *nm* audit.

auditeur, -trice /oditœʀ, tʀis/ *nm,f* **1** GÉN, RADIO listener; **2** FIN auditor; **3** LING hearer.
■ **~ libre** UNIV *person following a university course with no obligation to take the exam.*

auditif, -ive /oditif, iv/ *adj* [*nerf, conduit*] auditory; [*troubles, appareil*] hearing (*épith*); [*mémoire*] aural.

audition /odisjɔ̃/ *nf* **1** (perception, écoute) hearing; **2** CIN, MUS, THÉÂT (essai) audition; **passer une ~** to be

auditioned, to go for an audition; **faire passer une ~ à qn** to audition sb; **3** JUR hearing, examination.

auditionner /odisjɔne/ [1] *vtr, vi* to audition.

auditoire /oditwaʀ/ *nm* audience.

auditorium /oditɔʀjɔm/ *nm* auditorium.

auge /oʒ/ *nf* **1** (d'animal) trough; **2** (de maçon) mortar trough; **3** GÉOG U-shaped valley; **~ glaciaire** glacial valley.

augmentation /ogmɑ̃tasjɔ̃/ *nf* **1** (accroissement) increase; **~ de 3%** 3% increase; **2** (majoration) increase; **une ~ (de salaire)** a pay rise GB ou raise US.

augmenter /ogmɑ̃te/ [1] **I** *vtr* to raise, to increase [*nombre, salaire, charge, volume*] (**de** by); to increase [*valeur, production*] (**de** by); to extend [*durée*] (**de** by); to increase [*risque*]; **~ le loyer de qn** to put sb's rent up; **~ ses revenus** to supplement one's income (**en faisant** by doing); **~ qn de 1000 francs** to give sb a rise GB ou raise US of 1,000 francs.
II *vi* (devenir plus élevé) [*prix, revenus, loyer*] to increase (**de** by); [*température*] to rise (**de** by); to go up (**de** by); [*surface, capacité*] to increase (**de** by); **les timbres ont augmenté** stamps have gone up.

augure /ogyʀ/ *nm* **1** (devin) (dans l'Antiquité) augur; FIG, HUM soothsayer, oracle; **2** (signe) omen; (dans l'Antiquité) augury; **être de bon/mauvais ~ pour qch/qn** to be a good/bad omen for sth/sb.

augurer /ogyʀe/ [1] *vtr* **1** (attendre) **que peut-on ~ de cette attitude?** what should we expect from this attitude?; **je n'augure rien de bon de cette rencontre** I can't see any good coming of this meeting; **cela augure mal de l'avenir** it doesn't bode well for the future; **cela laisse ~ une difficulté** this suggests we can anticipate a difficulty; **me laissant ~ que** giving me to understand that; **2** (annoncer) to herald.

auguste /ogyst/ **I** *adj* [*personne*] august; [*geste*] noble.
II *nm* (clown) circus clown.

aujourd'hui /oʒuʀdɥi/ *adv* **1** (ce jour) today; **~ en huit** a week (from) today; **2** (de nos jours) today, nowadays; **la jeunesse d'~** the youth of today; **la France d'~** present-day France.

aulne /on/ *nm* alder.

aumône /omon/ *nf* hand-out, alms† (*pl*); **faire l'~ à** to give alms to; **demander l'~** to ask for charity.

aumônerie /omonʀi/ *nf* chaplaincy.

aumônier /omonje/ **▶374|** *nm* chaplain.

auquel ▶ lequel.

aura /oʀa/ *nf* aura.

auréole /oʀeɔl/ *nf* **1** (tache) ring; **2** (couronne) halo; **3** (prestige) glory.

auréoler: s'auréoler /oʀeɔle/ [1] *vpr* **s'~ de** to take on an aura of; **auréolé de** basking in the glow of.

auriculaire /oʀikylɛʀ/ **I** *adj* auricular.
II *nm* little finger, pinkie.

aurifère /oʀifɛʀ/ *adj* **1** [*minerai*] auriferous; **2** FIN **valeurs ~s** gold stocks.

aurore /oʀɔʀ/ *nf* LIT, FIG dawn **℃**; **se lever aux ~s** to get up with the lark.

■ ~ **australe** aurora australis; ~ **boréale** Northern Lights (pl), aurora borealis.

auscultation /ɔskyltasjɔ̃/ nf MÉD examination.

ausculter /ɔskylte/ [1] vtr MÉD to examine.

auspices /ospis/ nmpl auspices; **sous les ~ de** under the auspices of.

aussi /osi/ **I** adv **1** (également) too, as well, also; **moi ~, j'ai du travail** I have work too; **il sera absent et moi ~** he'll be away and so will I; **2** (dans une comparaison) ~ **âgé que** as old as; ~ **riche soit-elle** (as) rich as she may be; **cette émission concerne les femmes ~ bien que les hommes** this programmeGB concerns women as well as men; ~ **longtemps que** as long as; **c'est ~ bien** it's just as well; **3** (si, tellement) so; **je ne savais pas qu'il était ~ vieux** I didn't know he was so old; **dans une ~ belle maison** in such a nice house.

II conj **1** (en conséquence) so, consequently; **je m'en doutais, ~ ne suis-je guère surprise** I suspected it, so I'm not entirely surprised; **2**° (d'ailleurs) **'on lui a volé son sac'**—**'quelle idée ~ de le laisser traîner!'** 'her bag was stolen'—'well, it was stupid to leave it lying about!'; **mais ~, pourquoi est-ce que tu y es allée?** why on earth did you go there?

aussitôt /osito/ **I** adv **1** (immédiatement) immediately, straight away; ~ **après ton départ** straight after you left; **2** (juste après) ~ **arrivé** as soon as ou the moment he arrived; **elle n'avait pas ~ quitté la pièce qu'il entra** no sooner had she left the room than he came in; ~ **dit ~ fait** no sooner said than done.

II aussitôt que loc conj as soon as.

austère /ostɛʀ, ostɛʀ/ adj [personne, éducation, allure, vie, économie] austere; [expression, visage] stern; [vêtement] severe; [monument, lieu] forbidding; [livre] dry.

austérité /osteʀite/ nf **1** (d'allure, économie, éducation, de lieu, personnne, vie) austerity; **2** (de vêtement, visage) severity; **3** (d'œuvre) dryness.

austral, -e, mpl ~**s** /ostʀal/ adj **1** (du sud) austral; **vents ~s** austral winds; **2** (de l'hémisphère Sud) southern; **été ~** southern summer.

Australie /ostʀali/ ▶ 232 nprf Australia.

Australie-Méridionale /ostʀalimeʀidjɔnal/ ▶ 509 nprf Southern Australia.

australien, -ienne /ostʀaljɛ̃, ɛn/ ▶ 394 adj Australian.

Australie-Occidentale /ostʀaliɔksidɑtal/ ▶ 509 nprf Western Australia.

austro-hongrois, ~e, mpl ~ /ostʀoɔ̃gʀwa, az/ adj Austro-Hungarian.

autant /otɑ̃/ **I** adv **il n'a jamais ~ neigé/plu** it has never snowed/rained so much; **je t'aime toujours ~** I still love you as much; **essaie** ou **tâche d'en faire ~** try and do the same; **triste ~ que désagréable** as sad as it is unpleasant; ~ **je comprends leur chagrin,** ~ **je déteste leur façon de l'étaler** as much as I understand their grief, I hate the way they parade it; **cela m'agace ~ que toi** it annoys me as much as it does you; **je les hais tous ~ qu'ils sont** I hate every single one of them; **je me moque de ce que vous pensez tous ~ que vous êtes** I don't care what any of you think; **j'aime ~ partir tout de suite** I'd rather leave straight away; **j'aime ~ te dire qu'il n'était pas content** believe me, he wasn't pleased; ~ **dire que la réunion est annulée** in other words the meeting is cancelledGB; ~ **parler à un mur** you might as well be talking to the wall; ~ **que faire se peut** as far as possible; ~ **que je sache** as far as I know; ~ **que tu peux** (comme tu peux) as much as you can; (aussi longtemps que tu peux) as long as you can.

II autant de dét indéf **1** (avec un nom dénombrable) ~ **de cadeaux/de gens** so many presents/people; **leurs promesses sont ~ de mensonges** their promises are just so many lies; ~ **de femmes que d'hommes** as many women as men; **2** (avec un nom non dénombrable) ~ **d'énergie/d'argent** so much energy/ money; ~ **de gentillesse** such kindness; **ce sera toujours ~ de fait** that'll be done at least; **je n'ai**

pas eu ~ de chance que lui I haven't had as much luck as he has; **je n'avais jamais vu ~ de monde** I'd never seen so many people.

III d'autant loc adv **cela va permettre de réduire d'~ les coûts de production** this will allow an equivalent reduction in production costs; **les salaires ont augmenté de 3% mais les prix ont augmenté d'~** salaries have increased by 3% but prices have increased by just as much; **d'~ plus!** all the more reason!; **d'~ moins** even less, all the less; **d'~ moins contrôlable** even less easy to control; **je le comprends d'~ moins** I find it even harder to understand; **d'~ que** all the more so as; **d'~ plus heureux/grand que** all the happier/bigger as

IV pour autant loc adv GÉN for all that; **je ne vais pas abandonner pour ~** I'm not going to give up for all that; **sans pour ~ tout modifier** without necessarily changing everything.

V pour autant que loc conj **pour ~ que** as far as; **pour ~ qu'ils se mettent d'accord** if they agree; **pour ~ que je sache** as far I know.

autarcie /otaʀsi/ nf autarky; **vivre en ~** to be self-sufficient.

autel /otɛl/ nm altar.

auteur /otœʀ/ nm **1** (qui a écrit) author; **2** (créateur) (de chanson) composer; (d'œuvre artistique) artist; **film d'~** art film; **3** (de réforme, loi) author; (de découverte) inventor; (de crime) perpetrator; (de coup d'État) leader; **l'~ du canular** the hoaxer; **l'~ de mes jours** HUM (mère) my revered mother; (père) my revered father.

■ ~ **dramatique** playwright.

auteur-compositeur, pl **auteurs-compositeurs** /otœʀkɔ̃pozitœʀ/ nm songwriter.

authenticité /otɑ̃tisite/ nf (de document, fait) authenticity; (de sentiment) genuineness.

authentifier /otɑ̃tifje/ [2] vtr to authenticate.

authentique /otɑ̃tik/ adj (vrai) [fait, récit] true; [tableau, document] authentic; [sentiment] genuine.

autisme /otism/ nm autism.

autiste /otist/ **I** adj autistic.

II nmf autistic person.

auto /oto/ **I** adj inv **assurance ~ car** ou motor insurance GB, automobile insurance US.

II nf car, automobile US.

■ ~ **tamponneuse** bumper car, dodgem.

autobiographie /otobjɔgʀafi/ nf autobiography.

autobiographique /otobjɔgʀafik/ adj autobiographical.

autobus /otobys/ nm inv bus.

autocar /otokaʀ/ nm coach GB, bus US.

autocensurer: s'autocensurer /otosɑ̃syʀe/ [1] vpr to practiseGB self-censorship.

autochtone /otɔkton/ **I** adj **1** (aborigène) native, autochthonous SPÉC; **2** [terrain] autochthonous.

II nmf native, autochthon SPÉC.

autocollant, ~e /otokɔlɑ̃, ɑ̃t/ **I** adj self-adhesive.

II nm sticker.

autocrate /otokʀat/ **I** adj autocratic.

II nmf autocrat.

autocratie /otokʀasi/ nf autocracy.

autocritique /otokʀitik/ nf self-criticism ¢; **faire son ~** to go through a process of self-criticism.

autocuiseur /otokɥizœʀ/ nm pressure cooker.

autodafé /otodafe/ nm **1** HIST RELIG (cérémonie) auto-dafé; **2** (destruction par le feu) book-burning; **faire un ~ de qch** FIG to throw sth on the bonfire.

autodéfense /otodefɑ̃s/ nf GÉN self-defence; MÉD auto-immunity.

autodestructeur, -trice /otodɛstʀyktœʀ, tʀis/ adj self-destructive.

autodestruction /otodɛstʀyksjɔ̃/ nf self-destruction.

autodétermination /otodeteʀminasjɔ̃/ nf self-determination.

autodétruire: s'autodétruire /otodetʀɥiʀ/ [69] vpr [person] to destroy oneself; [cassette] to self-destruct; [missile] to autodestruct.

autodidacte /otodidakt/ **I** adj GÉN self-educated; (dans un domaine) self-taught.
II nmf self-educated person, autodidact SOUT.

autodiscipline /otodisiplin/ nf self-discipline.

autodrome /otodʀom/ nm racetrack.

auto-école, pl ~s /otoekɔl/ nf driving school.

autofinancement /otofinãsmã/ nm self-financing.

autofocus /otofɔkys/ **I** adj inv autofocus.
II nm inv (appareil) autofocus camera.

autogérer: s'autogérer /otoʒeʀe/ [14] vpr [entreprise] to be run on a cooperative basis.

autogestion /otoʒɛstjɔ̃/ nf (d'entreprise) worker management, cooperative management; (de collectivité) collective management.

autographe /otogʀaf/ adj, nm autograph.

auto-immunisation, pl ~s /otoimynizasjɔ̃/ nf autoimmunity.

automate /otomat/ nm LIT, FIG robot, automaton; **gestes d'~** robotic ou robot-like movements; **comme un ~** like a robot.

automation /otomasjɔ̃/ nf CONTROV automation.

automatique /otomatik/ **I** adj automatic.
II nm **1** TÉLÉCOM l'~ STD, subscriber trunk dialling^GB; **2** (revolver) automatic (revolver); **3** PHOT automatic camera.

automatiquement /otomatikmã/ adv **1** (de façon automatique) automatically; **2°** (inévitablement) inevitably.

automatisation /otomatizasjɔ̃/ nf automation.

automatiser /otomatize/ [1] vtr to automate.

automatisme /otomatism/ nm (de personne, fonction) automatism; (de machine) automatic functioning; **acquérir des ~s** to acquire automatic reflexes.

automitrailleuse /otomitʀajøz/ nf armoured^GB car.

automne /otɔn/ ▶542| nm autumn GB, fall US; **en ~** in autumn GB, in the fall US.

automobile /otomɔbil/ **I** adj **1** [industrie, assurance, accessoire, constructeur] car (épith); **2** SPORT [course] motor (épith); [circuit] motor racing (épith).
II nf **1** (voiture) (motor) car, automobile US; **2** (industrie) l'~ the car industry GB, the automobile industry US.

automobiliste /otomɔbilist/ nmf motorist.

autonome /otonɔm/ adj **1** POL [région, république] autonomous; **2** (autogéré) [filiale, gestion] independent, autonomous; [syndicat] nonaffiliated, independent; [personne] self-sufficient; **3** ORDINAT [unité] stand-alone; [système, équipement] off-line.

autonomie /otonɔmi/ nf **1** (indépendance) autonomy; **2** (distance) range; **~ de vol** flight range.

autonomiste /otonɔmist/ adj, nmf separatist.

autoportrait /otopɔʀtʀɛ/ nm self-portrait.

autopsie /otɔpsi/ nf postmortem (examination), autopsy.

autopsier /otɔpsje/ [2] vtr to carry out a postmortem (examination) on, to perform an autopsy on [cadavre].

autoradio /otoʀadjo/ nm car radio.

autorail /otoʀaj/ nm rail car.

autorisation /otoʀizasjɔ̃/ nf **1** (accord) GÉN permission (de faire to do); (officielle) authorization (de faire to do); **2** (document) permit.

autorisé, **~e** /otoʀize/ adj **1** (approuvé) [biographie, édition, agent] authorized; [parti] legal; [représentant] COMM accredited; **non ~** unauthorized; **2** (officiel) [personne] authorized; **milieux ~s** official circles; **3** (toléré) [tension, pression] permitted; **poids maximum en charge ~** maximum permitted load.

autoriser /otoʀize/ [1] **I** vtr **1** (donner une permission) [personne] to allow [visite]; [autorités] to authorize [paiement, visite]; **~ qn à faire** to give sb permission to do, to authorize sb to do; **2** (donner un droit) [événement, loi] **~ qn à faire** to entitle sb to do; **ce qui autorise à penser que** which makes it reasonable ou legitimate to think that; **rien ne vous autorise à agir ainsi** you have no right to behave like that; **3** (rendre possible) [situation, conditions] to make [sth] possible

[réalisation, innovation]; **la situation n'autorise aucune baisse des prix** the situation doesn't allow of any price reductions; **rien n'autorise ce pessimisme** there are no grounds for such pessimism.
II s'autoriser vpr s'~ **de qch** to use sth as an excuse (**pour faire** to do).

autoritaire /otoʀitɛʀ/ adj, nmf authoritarian.

autoritarisme /otoʀitaʀism/ nm authoritarianism.

autorité /otoʀite/ nf **1** (domination) authority (**sur** over); **faire qch d'~** (de façon impérieuse) to do sth decisively; (sans consulter) to take it upon oneself to do sth; **2** (ascendant) authority; **il n'a aucune ~ sur ses enfants** he has no control over his children; **faire ~** [personne] to be an authority (**en**, **en matière de** on); [ouvrage] to be authoritative; **3** (spécialiste) authority, expert; **4** ADMIN (pouvoir établi) authority; (personnel) **les ~s** the authorities.

autoroute /otoʀut/ nf motorway GB, freeway US.

autoroutier, **-ière** /otoʀutje, ɛʀ/ adj motorway (épith) GB, freeway (épith) US.

auto-stop /otostɔp/ nm hitchhiking; **faire de l'~** to hitchhike.

auto-stoppeur, **-euse**, mpl ~s /otostɔpœʀ, øz/ nm,f hitchhiker.

autour /otuʀ/ **I** adv un parterre de fleurs avec des pierres ~ a flowerbed with stones around it; **tout ~** all around.
II autour de loc prép **1** (marquant le lieu) around, round GB; **~ de la table/du soleil** around the table/the sun; **2** (marquant une approximation) around, round GB; **~ de 10 h/200 francs** around 10 o'clock/200 francs; **3** (au sujet de) **un débat/une conférence ~ du thème du pouvoir** a debate/a conference on the theme of power; **un débat ~ de cinq thèmes** a debate centred^GB around five themes; **la publicité organisée ~ de cet événement** FIG publicity organized around this event.

autre /otʀ/

■ **Note** Lorsqu'il est adjectif indéfini et employé avec un article défini autre se traduit par other: l'autre rue = the other street.
– On notera que un autre se traduit par another en un seul mot.
– Les autres emplois de l'adjectif ainsi que le pronom indéfini sont traités ci-dessous.
– Les expressions comme nul autre, comme dirait l'autre, en voir d'autres, avoir d'autres chats à fouetter etc se trouvent respectivement sous nul, dire, voir, fouetter etc.
– En revanche l'un... l'autre et ses dérivés sont traités ci-dessous.

I adj indéf **1** (indiquant la différence) other; **l'~ jour** the other day; **une ~ idée** another idea; **un ~ jour** some other day; **pas d'~ solution** no other solution; **l'effet obtenu est tout ~** the effect produced is completely different; **quelque chose/rien d'~** something/nothing else; **quoi d'~?** what else?; **l'actrice principale n'est ~ que la fille du metteur en scène** the leading actress is no other than the director's daughter; **2** (supplémentaire) **tu veux un ~ bonbon?** do you want another sweet GB ou candy US?; **ils ne veulent pas d'~s enfants** they don't want any more children; **donnez-moi dix ~s timbres** give me another ten stamps; **3°** (après un pronom personnel) **nous ~s/vous ~s** we/you.
II pron indéf **1** (indiquant la différence) **où sont les ~s?** (choses) where are the other ones?; (personnes) where are the others?; **je t'ai pris pour un ~** I mistook you for someone else; **certains estiment que c'est juste, d'~s non** some (people) think it's fair, others don't; **elle est pourrie cette pomme, prends-en une ~** this apple is rotten, have another one; **tu n'en as pas d'~s?** haven't you got any others?; **ce que pensent les ~s** what other people think; **l'un est souriant l'~ est grognon** one is smiling the other one is grumpy; **aussi têtus l'un que l'~** as stubborn as each other, both equally stubborn; **des récits plus vivants les uns que les ~s** stories each more lively than the one before; **ils se respectent les uns les**

~s they respect each other; **'aimez-vous les uns les ~s'** 'love one another'; **l'un après l'~, les uns après les ~s** one after the other; **chez lui c'est tout l'un ou tout l'~** with him it's all or nothing; **à d'~s**⊙! pull the other one (it's got bells on⊙)!, go and tell it to the marines⊙! us; **2** (indiquant un supplément) **prends-en un ~ si tu aimes ça** have another one if you like them; **si je peux je t'en apporterai d'~s** if I can I'll bring you some more; **ils ont deux enfants et n'en veulent pas d'~s** they have two children and don't want any more.
III autre part loc adv somewhere else.

autrefois /otRəfwa/ adv GÉN in the past; (précédemment) before, formerly SOUT; (en un temps révolu) in the old days, in days gone by LITTÉR; **c'est là que je travaillais ~** that's where I worked before ou I used to work; **~, quand Paris s'appelait Lutèce** long ago, when Paris was called Lutetia; **mes habitudes/ma vie d'~** my former habits/life; **les coutumes/légendes d'~** old customs/legends.

autrement /otRəmɑ̃/ adv **1** (de façon autre) [faire, voir, agir] differently, in a different way; [décider, conclure] otherwise; [nommé, appelé] otherwise; **le sort en a voulu ~** fate decided otherwise; **ça ne s'explique pas ~** there's no other explanation for it; **un escroc n'aurait pas agi ~** it's the sort of thing you would expect from a crook; **parlez-moi ~, je vous prie** don't talk to me like that, please; **il n'en est pas ~ des films** it's no different for films; **il ne peut (pas) en être ~** that's the way it has to be; **c'est comme ça, et pas ~** that's just the way it is; **on ne peut pas faire ~** there's no other way; **comment aurait-elle pu faire ~?** what else could she have done?; **je n'ai pas pu faire ~ que de les inviter** I had no alternative but to invite them; **on ne peut y accéder ~ que par bateau** you can only get there by boat; **je ne l'ai jamais vue ~ qu'en jean** I've never seen her in anything but jeans; **ça s'est passé ~ que prévu** it did not turn out as expected; **~ dit** in other words; **2** (sans quoi) otherwise; **~ ne compte pas sur moi** otherwise don't count on me; **3**⊙ (à part cela) otherwise, apart from that; **4**⊙ (beaucoup plus) **~ grave** (much) more serious; **~ aimable** (much) nicer; **c'est ~ plus petit qu'ici** it's much smaller than here; **5**⊙ (spécialement) **il n'était pas ~ impressionné** he wasn't particularly ou unduly impressed.

Autriche /otRiʃ/ ▶232⌋ nprf Austria.

Autriche-Hongrie /otRiʃɔ̃gRi/ nprf HIST Austro-Hungary.

autrichien, -ienne /otRiʃjɛ̃, ɛn/ ▶394⌋ adj Austrian.

autruche /otRyʃ/ nf ostrich.
IDIOMES **pratiquer la politique de l'~** to bury one's head in the sand.

autrui /otRɥi/ pron indéf others (pl), other people (pl).

auvent /ovɑ̃/ nm (de maison) canopy; (de tente, caravane) awning.

aux /o/ prép (= **à les**) ▶ **à**.

auxiliaire /oksiljɛR/ I adj **1** LING auxiliary; **2** (accessoire) [machine] auxiliary; [motor] back-up (épith); [service] supplementary; [moyen] additional; ORDINAT [mémoire] additional; **3** ▶374⌋ (non titulaire) **maître ~** assistant teacher; **infirmier ~** nursing auxiliary GB, nurse's aide US.
II nmf assistant, helper.
III nm LING auxiliary (verb).
■ **~ médical** medical auxiliary GB ou aide US.

auxquels, auxquelles ▶ **lequel**.

avachi, ~e /avaʃi/ adj [valise, chaussure] which has lost its shape (épith, après n); [fauteuil] shapeless.

avachir: s'avachir /avaʃiR/ [3] vpr [fauteuil] to sag; [personne] to let oneself go; **avachi devant la télévision** slumped in front of the television.

aval /aval/ nm **1** GÉOG (de cours d'eau) downstream part; **en ~** downstream (de from); **2** GÉOG (de pente) lower slopes (pl); **en ~** lower down (de from); **3** (de processus) **en ~** downstream (de from); **4** FIN (engagement de payer) guarantee; **donner son ~ à** to endorse;

5 (approbation) **vous avez mon ~** I'm behind you; **donner son ~ à qn** to give sb one's approval.

avalanche /avalɑ̃ʃ/ nf **1** (de neige) avalanche; **2** (de critiques, coups) avalanche; (de compliments) shower.

avaler /avale/ [1] vtr **1** (ingurgiter) to swallow [aliment, sirop, carte de crédit]; FIG [entreprise] to swallow up [entreprise]; **'ne pas ~'** MÉD 'not to be taken internally'; **j'ai avalé de travers** it went down the wrong way; **~ ses mots** to swallow one's words; **2** (inhaler) to inhale [fumée, vapeur]; **3**⊙ (admettre) to swallow [mensonge]; **c'est dur à ~** it's difficult to swallow.

avaleur /avalœR/ ▶374⌋ nm **~ de sabres** sword swallower.

à-valoir /avalwaR/ nm inv FIN instalment^GB.

avance /avɑ̃s/ I nf **1** (progression) advance; **2** (avantage) lead; **conserver son ~** to keep one's lead; **avoir/prendre de l'~ sur** to be/to pull ahead of; **3** FIN (acompte) advance.
II à l'avance loc adv in advance.
III d'avance loc adv **il a perdu d'~** he has already lost; **payer d'~** to pay in advance; **d'~ je vous remercie** I thank you in advance; **avoir cinq minutes d'~** to be five minutes early.
IV en avance loc adv **1** (sur l'heure) early; **arriver en ~** to arrive early; **2** (sur les autres) **le Japon est en ~ sur l'Europe** Japan is ahead of Europe; **il est en ~ pour son âge** he's advanced for his age.
V avances nfpl advances; **faire des ~s à qn** to make advances to sb, to come on to sb⊙ us.

avancé, ~e[1] /avɑ̃se/ adj **1** (précoce) [enfant, élève] advanced; **2** (évolué) [technique, niveau de vie] advanced; [opinion, idée] progressive; **3** (décomposé) **le poisson a l'air un peu ~** the fish looks as if it's going off GB ou bad; **4** (loin du début) advanced; **dans un état de décomposition ~e** in an advanced state of decomposition; **être bien ~** [travail, recherche] to be well advanced; **la saison est bien ~e** it's late in the season; **je ne suis pas plus ~** I'm none the wiser; **te voilà bien ~!** IRON that's done you a lot of good! IRON; **5** MIL [poste] advanced.

avancée[2] /avɑ̃se/ nf **1** (de toit, rocher) overhang; **le belvédère forme une ~ sur le ravin** the belvedere projects over the ravine; **2** (progression) advance (**sur** over); **les sondages confirment l'~ du candidat** the opinion polls confirm the candidate's progress; **l'~ des connaissances en ce domaine** advances made in this field of knowledge.

avancement /avɑ̃smɑ̃/ nm **1** (dans une carrière) promotion; **2** (dans des travaux, des connaissances) progress; **3** (d'une limite) **~ de l'âge de la retraite** lowering of the retirement age.

avancer /avɑ̃se/ [12] I vtr **1** (dans l'espace) to move [sth] forward [objet]; **~ une main timide** to hold one's hand out shyly; **~ un siège à qn** to pull ou draw up a seat for sb; **la voiture de Monsieur est avancée** your car awaits, sir; **2** (dans le temps) to bring forward [départ, voyage, réunion]; **3** (faire progresser) to get ahead with [travail]; **classe les fiches, ça m'avancera** sort out the cards, it'll help me get on more quickly; **cela ne nous avance à rien** that doesn't get us anywhere; **4** (prêter) **~ de l'argent** [banque] to advance money; [parent, ami] to lend money; **5** (changer l'heure) **~ sa montre de cinq minutes** to put one's watch forward (by) five minutes; **6** (affirmer) to put forward [accusation, théorie]; to propose [chiffre]; **~ que** to suggest that.
II vi **1** (progresser dans l'espace) [personne, véhicule] to move (forward); [armée] to advance; **~ d'un mètre** to move forward (by) one metre; **elle poussait mon frère pour le faire ~** she was pushing my brother forward; **elle avança vers le guichet** (elle alla) she went up to the ticket office; (elle vint) she came up to the ticket office; **2** (progresser) [personne] to make progress; [travail] to progress; **le travail avance vite** the work is making good progress; **j'ai bien avancé dans mon travail** I've made good progress with my work; **et votre projet? ça avance**⊙? and your project? how is it coming along?; **faire ~ la science** to

further science; **3** (par rapport à l'heure réelle) **~ de dix minutes** to be ten minutes fast; **4** (faire saillie) [*menton, dents*] to stick out, to protrude; [*cap, presqu'île*] to jut out (**dans** into); [*balcon, plongeoir*] to jut out, to project (**au-dessus de** over).
III s'avancer *vpr* **1** (physiquement) **s'~ vers qch** to move toward(s) sth; **s'~ vers qn** (aller) to go toward(s) sb; (venir) to come up to sb; **ne t'avance pas près du bord** don't go near the edge; **2** (dans une tâche) to get ahead; **3** (faire saillie) to jut out, to protrude (**dans** into; **sur, au-dessus de** over); **4** (se hasarder) **je me suis un peu avancé en lui promettant le dossier pour demain** I shouldn't have committed myself by promising him I'd have the file ready for tomorrow.

avanie /avani/ *nf* LITER humiliation ¢.

avant[1] /avɑ̃/ **I** *adv* **1** (dans le temps) GÉN before, beforehand; (d'abord) first; **que faisait-il ~?** what was he doing before?; **bien ~** long before; **la séance d'~** the previous performance; **pas ce lundi mais celui d'~** not this Monday but the previous one; **la fois d'~ nous nous étions déjà perdus** we got lost the last time as well; **2** (dans l'espace) before; **tu vois l'église, j'habite (juste) ~** can you see the church? I live (just) before it; **il l'a mentionné ~ dans l'introduction** he mentioned it earlier in the introduction; **je crois que la dame était ~** I think this lady was first; **il est inutile de creuser plus ~** there's no point in digging any further; **refuser de s'engager plus ~** LIT to refuse to go any further; FIG to refuse to get any more involved; **3** (dans une hiérarchie) before; **le T vient ~ T** comes before; **mon travail passe ~** my work comes first.
II *prép* **1** (dans le temps) before; **~ mon départ/retour** before I leave/come back; **~ la fin** before the end; **peu ~ minuit** shortly before midnight; **~ le 1er juillet** by 1 July; **j'aurai fini ~ une semaine** I'll have finished within a week; **~ peu** shortly; **2** (dans l'espace) before; **~ la poste** before the post office; **3** (dans une hiérarchie) before; **faire passer qn/qch ~ qn/qch** to put sb/sth before sb/sth; **~ tout, ~ toute chose** (surtout) above all; (d'abord) first and foremost.
III avant de *loc prép* **~ de faire** before doing.
IV avant que *loc conj* **~ qu'il (ne) fasse** before he does.
V en avant *loc adv* forward(s); **se pencher/faire un pas en ~** to lean/to take a step forward(s); **en ~,
marche!** MIL forward march!; **en ~ toute!** NAUT, FIG full steam ahead!; **en ~ la musique°!** off we go!; **mettre qn/qch en ~** to put sb/sth forward; **mettre en ~ le fait que** to point out the fact that.
VI en avant de *loc prép* ahead of [*groupe*].

avant[2] /avɑ̃/ **I** *adj inv* [*roue, siège, patte*] front.
II *nm* **1** (partie antérieure) **l'~** the front; **aller de l'~** to forge ahead; **d'~ en arrière** backwards and forwards; **2** SPORT forward.

avantage /avɑ̃taʒ/ *nm* **1** (point positif, supériorité) advantage (**sur** over); **reprendre l'~** to regain the advantage (**sur** over); **être à l'~ de qn** [*situation, transaction*] to be to sb's advantage; **paraître à son ~** to look one's best; **2** (profit) advantage; **tirer ~ de qch** to take advantage of sth; **retirer un ~ de qch** to profit from sth; **avoir ~ à faire** to be better off doing; **3** SPORT (au tennis) advantage; **4** (mesure favorable) benefit; **~s sociaux** benefits package (*sg*); **~ fiscaux** tax benefits.

avantager /avɑ̃taʒe/ [13] *vtr* **1** (favoriser) [*personne*] to favour[GB]; [*situation*] to be to the advantage of; **~ Pierre par rapport à Paul** to favour[GB] Pierre over Paul; **être avantagé par rapport à qn** to be at an advantage compared with sb; **être avantagé dès le départ** [*personne, entreprise*] to have a head start; **2** (mettre en valeur) to show [sb/sth] off to advantage.

avantageusement /avɑ̃taʒøzmɑ̃/ *adv* **1** (sous un jour favorable) [*dépeindre*] favourably[GB]; **2** (honorablement) **tirer ~ parti de qch** to use sth to one's advantage; **ce système remplace ~ le précédent** this system is an improvement on the previous one.

avant[1]
Lorsque *avant* est adverbe il se traduit par *before* sauf lorsqu'il signifie 'en premier lieu, d'abord'; il se traduit alors par *first*:
> si tu prends la route, mange quelque chose avant
> = if you're going to drive, have something to eat first

Lorsque *avant* est préposition il se traduit par *before* sauf dans le cas où une limite de temps est précisée; il se traduit alors par *by*:
> à retourner avant le 30 mars = to be returned by
>   30 March

avant entre dans la composition de nombreux mots qui s'écrivent avec un trait d'union (*avant-hier, avant-guerre, avant-coureur* etc.). Ces mots sont des entrées à part entière et on les trouvera dans la nomenclature du dictionnaire. Utilisé avant un nom pour désigner une période précédant un événement ou l'avènement d'une personne il se traduit par *pre-* et forme alors un groupe adjectival que l'on fait suivre du nom approprié:
> l'avant-1945 = the pre-1945 period
> l'avant-Thatcher = the pre-Thatcher era
> l'avant-sommet = the pre-summit discussions

avantageux, -euse /avɑ̃taʒø, øz/ *adj* **1** (intéressant) [*condition, offre, solution, marché*] favourable[GB], advantageous (**pour qn** to sb); [*taux, prix, placement*] attractive; [*produit*] good value (*jamais épith*); **tirer un parti ~ de qch** to use sth to one's advantage; **2** (flatteur) [*opinion, aspect*] favourable[GB]; [*description, termes, vêtement*] flattering; [*physique*] superior; **sous un jour ~** in a favourable[GB] light; **en termes très ~** in very flattering terms.

avant-bras /avɑ̃bʀa/ *nm inv* forearm.

avant-centre, *pl* **avants-centres** /avɑ̃sɑ̃tʀ/ *nm* centre[GB] forward; **jouer ~** to play centre[GB] forward.

avant-coureur, *pl* **~s** /avɑ̃kuʀœʀ/ *adj m* **signes ~s** early warning signs.

avant-dernier, -ière, *pl* **~s** /avɑ̃dɛʀnje, ɛʀ/ **I** *adj* **l'~ jour** the last day but one.
II *nm,f* the last but one; **l'~ d'une famille de cinq enfants** the second youngest of five children.

avant-garde, *pl* **~s** /avɑ̃gaʀd/ *nf* **1** (mouvement) ART, LITTÉRAT avant-garde; **cinéma d'~** avant-garde cinema; **2** (pointe) **à l'~** in the vanguard; **à l'~ de la recherche** in the vanguard of research; **3** MIL vanguard.

avant-gardiste, *pl* **~s** /avɑ̃gaʀdist/ *adj* avant-garde.

avant-goût, *pl* **~s** /avɑ̃gu/ *nm* foretaste.

avant-guerre, *pl* **~s** /avɑ̃gɛʀ/ *nm* ou *f* **l'~** the prewar period; **l'Espagne d'~** prewar Spain.

avant-hier /avɑ̃tjɛʀ/ *adv* the day before yesterday.

avant-midi /avɑ̃midi/ *nm inv* C (matin) morning.

avant-poste, *pl* **~s** /avɑ̃pɔst/ *nm* **1** MIL outpost; **2** FIG **être aux ~s** to be in the vanguard.

avant-première, *pl* **~s** /avɑ̃pʀəmjɛʀ/ *nf* preview.

avant-propos /avɑ̃pʀɔpo/ *nm inv* foreword.

avant-scène, *pl* **~s** /avɑ̃sɛn/ *nf* **1** (partie de scène) forestage; **2** (loge) box.

avant-veille, *pl* **~s** /avɑ̃vɛj/ *nf* **l'~** two days before.

avare /avaʀ/ **I** *adj* miserly; **~ de qch** sparing with; **être ~ de paroles** to use words sparingly; **il n'est pas ~ de compliments** he's generous with his compliments.
II *nmf* miser.

avarice /avaʀis/ *nf* meanness GB, miserliness.

avarie /avaʀi/ *nf* **1** NAUT problem; **2** COMM, JUR (dommage matériel) damage ¢; (dommage de transport maritime) average ¢.

avarié, -e /avaʀje/ **I** *pp* ▸ **avarier**.
II *pp adj* (gâté) [*viande, poisson*] rotten.

avarier: s'avarier /avaʀje/ [2] *vpr* [*viande, poisson*] to go rotten.

---

avec

La préposition *avec* se traduit presque toujours par *with* quand elle marque:

l'accompagnement:
danser avec qn	= to dance with sb
du vin blanc avec du cassis	= white wine with blackcurrant

la possession:
la dame avec le chapeau noir	= the lady with the black hat
une chemise avec un grand col	= a shirt with a large collar

la relation:
être d'accord avec qn	= to agree with sb
avec lui c'est toujours pareil	= it's always the same with him

la simultanéité:
se lever avec le soleil	= to get up with the sun

l'opposition:
se battre avec qn	= to fight with sb
être en concurrence avec qn	= to be in competition with sb

l'identité de vue:
je suis avec toi	= I'm with you

le moyen:
avec une fourchette	= with a fork
avec une canne	= with a stick
avec de l'argent	= with money

Quand elle désigne la manière elle se traduit souvent par un adverbe formé à partir du nom qui la suit:
avec attention	= carefully
avec passion	= passionately

On trouvera ces expressions sous **attention**, **passion** etc.

On notera toutefois que *avec beaucoup d'attention*, *avec une grande passion* se traduisent: with great care, with a lot of passion. Les expressions telles que *avec l'âge/les années* etc. sont traitées respectivement sous **âge**, **année** etc.

On trouvera ci-dessous des exceptions et des exemples supplémentaires.

---

avatar /avataʀ/ *nm* **1** (mésaventure) CONTROV mishap; **2** (changement) change; **connaître des ~s** to undergo changes; **3** RELIG (réincarnation) reincarnation.

avec /avɛk/ **I**° *adv* **mon chapeau lui a plu, elle est partie ~** she liked my hat and went off with it.
II *prép* with; **viens ~ tes amis** bring your friends with you; **une maison ~ piscine** a house with a swimming pool; **se marier ~ qn** to marry sb, to get married to sb; **et ~ cela, que désirez-vous?** what else would you like?; **je fais tout son travail et ~ ça il n'est pas content!** I do all his work and he's still not happy!

avenant, **~e** /avnɑ̃, ɑ̃t/ **I** *adj* [*personne*] pleasant.
II à l'avenant *loc adv* **être à l'~** to be in keeping.

avènement /avɛnmɑ̃/ *nm* **1** (de souverain) accession; (d'homme politique, ère) advent; **~ au trône** accession to the throne; **2** RELIG Advent.

avenir /avniʀ/ *nm* future; **à l'~** in future GB, in the future US; **dans un ~ proche/immédiat** in the near/immediate future; **avoir de l'~** to have a future; **d'~** [*métier*] with a future; [*technique*] of the future.
IDIOMES **l'~ appartient à ceux qui se lèvent tôt** PROV the early bird catches the worm PROV.

aventure /avɑ̃tyʀ/ **I** *nf* **1** (épopée) adventure; **partir à l'~** to set off in search of adventure; **2** (péripétie) adventure; **3** (entreprise risquée) venture; **4** (intrigue amoureuse) affair.
II d'aventure *loc adv* by chance; **si d'~ il venait...** if by chance he should come...
IDIOMES **dire la bonne ~ à qn** to tell sb's fortune.

aventurer: s'aventurer /avɑ̃tyʀe/ [1] *vpr* LIT, FIG to venture (**dans** in; **sur** onto; **jusqu'à** to).

aventureux, **-euse** /avɑ̃tyʀø, øz/ *adj* adventurous.

aventurier, **-ière** /avɑ̃tyʀje, ɛʀ/ *nm,f* GÉN, PÉJ adventurer/adventuress.

avenu, **~e**[1] /avny/ *adj* **nul et non ~** null and void.

avenue[2] /avny/ *nf* LIT, FIG avenue.

avéré, **~e** /aveʀe/ *adj* [*fait, goût*] recognized; [*maladie*] confirmed; **il est ~ que** it is proven that.

avérer: s'avérer /aveʀe/ [14] *vpr* **le téléphone s'avère (être) un outil indispensable** the telephone is proving (to be) an indispensable tool; **il s'avère que** it transpires that, it turns out that.

averse /avɛʀs/ *nf* LIT, FIG shower.

aversion /avɛʀsjɔ̃/ *nf* aversion (**pour qn/qch** to sb/sth); **avoir qn/qch en ~** to have a loathing for sb/sth; **prendre qn/qch en ~** to develop a loathing for sb/sth.

averti, **~e** /avɛʀti/ *adj* **1** (avisé) [*lecteur, visiteur*] informed; **2** (expérimenté) [*professionnel*] experienced.

avertir /avɛʀtiʀ/ [3] *vtr* **1** (informer) to inform; **2** (lancer une menace à) to warn.

avertissement /avɛʀtismɑ̃/ *nm* **1** GÉN, JUR, SCOL warning; **2** SPORT caution; **3** (dans un livre) foreword.

avertisseur /avɛʀtisœʀ/ **I** *adj m* [*panneau*] warning.
II *nm* GÉN alarm; AUT horn.

aveu, *pl* **~x** /avø/ *nm* **1** (de méfait) confession; **faire des ~x** to make a confession; **2** (de défaut) admission; **de son propre ~** on his/her own admission.

aveuglant, **~e** /avœglɑ̃, ɑ̃t/ *adj* [*clarté*] blinding.

aveugle /avœgl/ **I** *adj* **1** (sans vue) blind; **devenir ~** to go blind; **2** (sans lucidité) [*confiance, passion*] blind; (sans discernement) [*violence, tir*] indiscriminate; **la passion le rend ~** he's blinded by passion.
II *nmf* blind person; **les ~s** the blind.

aveuglement /avœgləmɑ̃/ *nm* (égarement) LITER blindness; **faire preuve d'un ~ coupable** to be shamefully unaware.

aveuglément /avœglemɑ̃/ *adv* blindly.

aveugler /avœgle/ [1] **I** *vtr* (rendre aveugle) LIT, FIG to blind; (éblouir) LIT, FIG to dazzle, to blind.
II s'aveugler *vpr* to hide the truth from oneself.

aveuglette: à l'aveuglette /alavœglɛt/ *loc adv* **1** (à tâtons) **avancer à l'~** to grope one's way along; **2** (au hasard) [*décider, agir*] in an inconsidered way.

aviateur, **-trice** /avjatœʀ, tʀis/ ▶374| *nm,f* airman/ woman pilot.

aviation /avjasjɔ̃/ *nf* **1** (civile) (secteur) aviation; (industrie) aircraft industry; **2** MIL **l'~** the air force; **3** (activité) **l'~** flying; **faire de l'~** to fly.

aviatrice *nf* ▶ **aviateur**.

aviculteur, **-trice** /avikyltœʀ, tʀis/ ▶374| *nm,f* **1** (de volailles) poultry farmer; **2** (d'oiseaux) aviculturist.

aviculture /avikyltyʀ/ *nf* **1** (de volailles) poultry farming; **2** (d'oiseaux) aviculture.

avide /avid/ *adj* (vorace) [*yeux*] greedy; [*lecteur*] avid; (cupide) greedy; **~ de** avid for [*pouvoir*]; eager for [*affection, honneurs*]; **~ de sang** bloodthirsty.

avidement /avidmɑ̃/ *adv* **1** (voracement) [*manger*] greedily; [*lire*] avidly; **2** (avec ardeur) [*chercher*] eagerly.

avidité /avidite/ *nf* **1** (cupidité) greed (**de** for); **avec ~** [*manger*] greedily; **2** (vif désir) eagerness (**de** for); **avec ~** eagerly.

avilir /aviliʀ/ [3] **I** *vtr* to demean [*personne*].
II s'avilir *vpr* [*personne*] to demean oneself.

avilissant, **~e** /avilisɑ̃, ɑ̃t/ *adj* demeaning.

avilissement /avilismɑ̃/ *nm* degradation.

aviné, **~e** /avine/ *adj* LITER [*personne*] inebriated LITTÉR; [*regard, visage*] drunken.

avion /avjɔ̃/ *nm* **1** (appareil) (aero)plane GB, airplane US, aircraft (*inv*); **dans l'~** on the plane; **aller à Rome en ~** to go to Rome by air, to fly to Rome; **envoyer qch par ~** to send sth air mail; **2** (vol) flight; **3** (activité) **l'~** flying; **je déteste (prendre) l'~** I hate

avoir¹ (1)

Généralités

Dans la plupart des situations exprimant la possession, la disponibilité *avoir* se traduit par *to have* ou *to have got*:

j'ai des livres	= I have (got) books
j'ai des enfants	= I have (got) children
j'ai des employés	= I have (got) employees
je n'ai pas assez de place	= I don't have (*ou* I haven't got) enough room
je n'ai pas assez de temps	= I don't have (*ou* I haven't got) enough time
la maison a l'électricité	= the house has electricity
la maison a cinq pièces	= the house has five rooms
j'aurai mon visa demain	= I'll have my visa tomorrow
ils vont/elle va avoir un bébé en mai	= they're/she's having a baby in May

Les autres sens de *avoir*, verbe transitif simple (obtenir, porter, triompher de etc.), sont traités dans l'entrée plus bas.

On notera qu'en règle générale les expressions figées du type *avoir raison*, *avoir beau*, *il y a belle lurette*, *il y a de quoi* etc. sont traitées respectivement sous **raison**, **beau**, **lurette**, **quoi** etc.

On pourra également consulter les diverses notes d'usage répertoriées ▶ **1420 |**, notamment celles consacrées à l'expression de *l'âge*, aux **douleurs et maladies**, à l'expression de *l'heure* etc.

On trouvera ci-dessous les divers emplois de *avoir* pour lesquels une explication est nécessaire.

avoir = verbe auxiliaire

avoir verbe auxiliaire se traduit toujours par *to have* sauf dans le cas du passé composé:

ils avaient révisé les épreuves quand je suis parti	= they had revised the proofs when I left
quand ils eurent (ou ont eu) révisé les épreuves, ils sont partis	= when they had revised the proofs, they left
ils auront fini demain	= they will have finished tomorrow
il aurait (ou eût) aimé parler	= he would have liked to speak

Lorsqu'on a un passé composé en français, il se traduit soit par le prétérit:

ils ont révisé les épreuves en juin	= they revised the proofs in June
ils ont révisé les épreuves avant ma démission	= they revised the proofs before I resigned
je suis sûr qu'il l'a laissé là en partant	= I'm sure he left it here when he left

soit par le 'present perfect':

ils ont révisé les épreuves plusieurs fois	= they have revised the proofs several times

avoir = verbe semi-auxiliaire

De même, *avoir* semi-auxiliaire dans les tournures attributives du type *avoir le cœur malade/les genoux cagneux*, se traduit de façon variable (*to be* ou *to have*) selon la structure adoptée par l'anglais pour rendre ces tournures; voir, en l'occurrence, les entrées **cœur** et **cagneux**; mais c'est en général sous l'adjectif que ce problème est traité.

Emplois avec à

avoir à + *infinitif*

Exprimant l'obligation ou la convenance, cette locution verbale se rend généralement par *to have to* suivi de l'infinitif:

j'aurais à ajouter que …	= I would have to add that …
tu auras à rendre compte de tes actes	= you'll have to account for your actions
je n'ai pas à vous raconter ma vie	= I don't have to tell you my life-story
vous n'aviez pas à le critiquer	= you didn't have to criticize him
il n'a pas à te parler sur ce ton	= he shouldn't speak to you in that tone of voice
j'ai beaucoup à faire	= I have a lot to do *ou* I've got a lot to do
tu n'as rien à faire?	= don't you have anything to do? *ou* haven't you got anything to do?
j'ai à faire un rapport ou j'ai un rapport à faire	= I have to write a report *ou* I have a report to write

n'avoir qu'à

Quand cette locution équivaut à *suffire*, plusieurs possibilités de traduction se présentent:

tu n'as qu'à leur écrire	= you only have to write to them, *ou* you've only got to write to them, *ou* all you have to do is write to them
tu n'auras que cinq minutes à attendre	= you'll only have to wait five minutes
tu n'avais qu'à	= *tu aurais dû*

se rend par *you should have* suivi du participe passé.

tu n'avais qu'à faire attention	= you should have paid attention
tu n'avais qu'à me le dire	= you should have told me
tu n'avais qu'à partir plus tôt	= you should have left earlier

Emplois avec en

On trouvera sous **assez**, **marre** etc. les expressions figées *en avoir assez*, *en avoir marre* etc. Voir aussi les emplois avec *il y a* plus bas.

Expression du temps: en avoir pour

L'anglais distingue généralement entre une tâche précise (*to take*) et une activité ou absence indéterminée (*to be*):

vous en avez (ou aurez) pour combien de temps?	
(à faire ce travail)	= how long will it take you?
(à me faire attendre)	= how long are you going to be?
j'en ai pour cinq minutes	
(je reviens)	= I'll be five minutes
je n'en ai pas pour longtemps	= I won't be long
j'en ai eu pour deux heures	= it took me two hours

Expression du coût: en avoir pour

Se traduit par *to cost* suivi du pronom personnel complément correspondant au pronom sujet français (voir aussi **argent**):

j'en ai eu pour 500 francs	= it cost me 500 francs
nous en aurons pour combien?	= how much will it cost us?

☛ Voir page suivante

---

flying; **il n'a jamais pris l'~** he's never been on a plane, he's never flown. ■ **~ de chasse** fighter (plane); **~ de ligne** civil aircraft, liner; **~ en papier** paper aeroplane GB ou airplane US; **~ à réaction** jet (plane); **~ de tourisme** light passenger aircraft.

avion-taxi, *pl* **avions-taxis** /avjɔ̃taksi/ *nm* air taxi.

aviron /aviʀɔ̃/ *nm* **1** ▶ **329 |** SPORT rowing; **faire de l'~** to row; **2** (rame) oar.

avis /avi/ *nm inv* **1** (opinion) opinion (**sur** on, about); **à**

mon **~** in my opinion; **les ~ sont partagés** opinions differ; **je suis de ton ~** I agree with you; **être d'~ que** to be of the opinion that; **de l'~ général** in most people's opinion; **changer d'~** to change one's mind; **2** (conseil) advice (**sur** on, about); **sans ~ médical** without consulting your doctor; **sauf ~ contraire** unless otherwise informed SOUT; **3** (de jury, commission) recommendation; **~ favorable/défavorable** favourable^GB/unfavourable^GB recommendation; **4** (annonce) notice; **~ à la population** (affiche) public notice; (cri) public announcement; **lancer un ~ de**

avoir¹ (2)

Expression de l'existence

il y a du lait dans le réfrigérateur
= there's some milk in the fridge
il y a des souris au grenier
= there are mice in the attic
il n'y a pas de riz = there's no rice
ou there isn't any rice
il n'y a plus de riz = there's no more rice
ou there isn't any more rice
il doit y avoir des souris dans le grenier
ou *il y aura des souris dans le grenier*
= there must be mice in the attic
il n'y a pas eu moins de 50 concurrents
= there were no fewer than
50 competitors
il y a chapeau et chapeau
= there are hats and hats
il y aura Paul, Marie, …
= there will be Paul, Marie, …
et il y aura Paul et Marie!
= and Paul and Marie will be there!
il n'y a pas de raison de faire
= there's no reason to do
il n'y a pas de raison que tu fasses
= there's no reason for you to do
il a dû y avoir quelque chose de grave
= something serious must have
happened
qu'est-ce qu'il y a?
(qui ne va pas) = what's wrong?
(qui se passe) = what's going on?
il y a qu'elle m'énerve
= she's getting on my nerves, that's
what's wrong
il y a que l'ordinateur est en panne
= the computer has broken down

Attention, un mot singulier en français peut être traduit par un mot fonctionnant comme un pluriel en anglais:

il y a beaucoup de monde = there are a lot of people
y avait-il du monde? = were there many people?

Expression du temps

il est venu il y a longtemps = he came a long time ago
il est venu il y a cinq ans = he came five years ago
il y a cinq ans que j'habite ici
= I have been living here for five years
il y aura cinq ans demain que j'ai pris ma retraite
= it will be five years tomorrow since
I retired
il y aura deux mois mardi que je travaille ici
= I will have been working here for two
months on Tuesday
il n'y a que deux mois que je suis ici
= I have only been here for two
months
il n'y a que deux mois que je travaille ici
= I have only been working here for
two months
il n'y a pas cinq minutes qu'il est parti
= he left less than five minutes ago
il n'y a pas 200 ans que l'espèce est éteinte
= the species has been extinct for no
more than 200 years
il y a combien de temps que tu habites ici?
= how long have you lived here?
il y a combien d'années que tu habites ici?
= how many years have you lived
here?
il y a combien de temps qu'on s'est vus?
= how long is it since we last met?
il y a combien d'années qu'on ne s'est vus?
= how many years has it been since
we last met?

Expression de la distance

Elle se fait généralement à l'aide du verbe *to be*:

combien y a-t-il jusqu'à la gare?
= how far is it to the station?

combien y a-t-il d'ici à la gare?
= how far is it to the station from here?
combien y a-t-il encore jusqu'à la gare?
= how much further is it to the station?
il y a 15 kilomètres jusqu'à la gare
= the station is 15 kilometres away
il y a 15 kilomètres d'ici à la gare
= the station is 15 kilometres away
from here
il y a au moins 15 kilomètres
= it's at least 15 kilometres away
il y a encore 15 kilomètres
= it's another 15 kilometres
il n'y a pas 200 mètres d'ici à la gare
= it's less than 200 metres from here
to the station
il n'y a que 200 mètres d'ici à la gare
= it's only 200 metres from here to the
station

il y a à + infinitif

il y a à manger pour quatre
= there's enough food for four
il y a (beaucoup) à faire
= there's a lot to be done (ceci traduit
également *il y a de quoi faire*)
souligner le danger qu'il y a à faire
= to stress how dangerous it is to do
souligner l'avantage qu'il y a à faire
= to stress how advantageous it is to do
les risques qu'il y avait/aurait à faire
= how risky it was/would be to do
il n'y a pas à hésiter = there's no need to hesitate
il n'y a pas à s'inquiéter = there's no need to worry
il n'y a pas à discuter! = no arguments!
'il n'y a qu'à le repeindre!' = 'all you have to do is
repaint it!' *ou* 'just repaint it!'
'y a qu'à, c'est facile à dire!' = 'easier said than done!'

il y en a qui, il y en a pour

L'existence se rend par *there is/are*, le temps par *to take*, et le coût par *to cost ou to come to*:

il y en a qui n'ont pas peur du ridicule!
= there are some people who
aren't afraid of being laughed at!
il y en a toujours pour se plaindre
(ou *qui se plaignent*) = there's always someone who
complains
il y en a (ou aura) pour deux heures
= it'll take two hours
il y en a eu pour deux heures
= it took two hours
il y en aurait eu pour deux heures
= it would have taken two hours
il n'y en a plus que pour deux heures
= it'll only take another two hours
il y en a encore pour combien de temps?
= how much longer will it take?
il y en a (ou aura) pour 200 francs
= it'll cost (ou come to) 200 francs
il y en a eu pour 200 francs
= it cost (ou came to) 200 francs

Noter aussi:

il n'y en a que pour leur chien
= they only think of their dog
ou their dog comes first

Remarque: certaines formes personnelles du verbe *avoir* sont équivalentes au présentatif *il y a*. En corrélation avec le relatif *qui*, elles ne se traduisent pas; directement suivies de l'objet présenté, elles se traitent comme *il y a*:

j'ai mon stylo qui fuit = my pen is leaking
elle avait les larmes aux yeux
= there were tears in her eyes
j'ai ma cicatrice qui me fait souffrir
= my scar is hurting
à droite, vous avez une tapisserie d'Aubusson
= on your right, there's an
Aubusson tapestry

recherche (pour un disparu) to issue a description of a missing person; (pour un malfaiteur) to issue a description of a wanted person.
■ ~ **de coup de vent** gale warning; ~ **au lecteur** foreword; ~ **de passage** calling card (*left by meter reader, postman etc*).
IDIOMES **deux** ~ **valent mieux qu'un** PROV two heads are better than one.

avisé, ~**e** /avize/ *adj* [*personne, conseil*] sensible; **être bien/mal** ~ to be well-/ill-advised.

aviser /avize/ [1] I *vtr* **1** (prévenir) to notify; **2**† (apercevoir) to catch sight of.
II *vi* **nous aviserons plus tard** we'll decide later; '**et s'il n'est pas là?'—'j'aviserai'** 'and if he's not there?'—'I'll see'.
III **s'aviser** *vpr* **1** (se rendre compte) **s'~ que** to realize that; **s'~ de qch** to notice sth; **2** (oser) **ne t'avise pas de recommencer** don't do that again.

aviver /avive/ [1] I *vtr* **1** (exciter) to intensify [*chagrin, désir, colère*]; to increase [*intérêt*]; to stir up [*querelle*]; to make [sth] more acute [*douleur physique*]; **2** (rehausser) to liven up [*couleur*]; to brighten up [*teint*]; **3** (attiser) to kindle [*feu*]; **un vent violent avivait l'incendie** a strong wind fanned the flames.
II **s'aviver** *vpr* FIG [*chagrin, intérêt*] to grow stronger; [*douleur*] to become more acute.

avocat /avɔka/ ▶ 374 *nm* **1** JUR GÉN lawyer, solicitor GB, attorney (at law) US; (au barreau) barrister GB, (trial) lawyer US; ~ **de la défense** counsel for the defence; ~ **de l'accusation** counsel for the prosecution; **2** FIG (d'une idée) advocate (**de** of); (d'une cause, personne) champion (**de** of); **se faire l'~ de** to champion; **3** BOT, CULIN avocado (pear).
■ **l'~ du diable** the devil's advocate; **se faire l'~ du diable** to play devil's advocate; ~ **général** Advocate-General.

avocate /avɔkat/ *nf* female lawyer.

avoine /avwan/ *nf* oats (*pl*).

avoir[1] /avwaʀ/ *vtr* **1** (obtenir) to get [*objet, rendez-vous*]; to catch [*train, avion*]; **j'ai pu vous** ~ **votre visa** I managed to get your visa for you; **je n'ai pas eu mon train** I didn't catch my train; **2** (au téléphone) **j'ai réussi à l'~** I managed to get through to him/her; **3** (porter) to wear, to have [sth] on; **elle avait une robe bleue à son mariage** she wore a blue dress at her wedding; **4**○ (triompher) to beat, to get○, to have; **cette fois-ci, on les aura** this time, we'll get ou have them; **5** (duper) to have○; (par malveillance) to con○; **elle s'est fait ou laissée** ~ she's been had○; **6** (éprouver moralement) to feel; ~ **du chagrin/de la haine** to feel sorrow/hate; **qu'est-ce que tu as?** what's wrong ou the matter with you?; **qu'est-ce qu'il a à conduire comme ça?** why is he driving like that?; **7** (servant à exprimer l'âge, des sensations physiques) **j'ai 20 ans/faim/froid** I am 20 years old/hungry/cold; **la salle a 20 mètres de long** the room is 20 metres GB long.

avoir[2] /avwaʀ/ *nm* **1** COMM (somme) credit; (attestation) credit note; **2** (possessions) assets (*pl*), holdings (*pl*).
■ ~ **fiscal** tax credit.

avoisinant, ~**e** /avwazinɑ̃, ɑ̃t/ *adj* neighbouring GB.

avoisiner /avwazine/ [1] *vtr* **1** [*somme*] to be close to, to be about; ~ (**les**) **200 francs** to be close to 200 francs; **2** [*ferme, village*] to be near [*forêt, route*].

avortement /avɔʀtəmɑ̃/ *nm* **1** MÉD abortion; **2** (échec) collapse (**de** of).

avorter /avɔʀte/ [1] *vi* **1** MÉD (par intervention) to have an abortion; (spontanément) to abort, to miscarry; **se faire** ~ to have an abortion; **faire** ~ **qn** [*personne*] to carry out an abortion on sb; [*pilule*] to induce abortion in sb; **2** [*projet*] to be aborted.

avorton /avɔʀtɔ̃/ *nm* (personne, animal, plante) PEJ runt.

avouable /avwabl/ *adj* [*sentiment*] worthy; [*motif*] respectable; **méthode peu** ~ rather dubious method.

avoué, ~**e** /avwe/ I *adj* [*ennemi, revenu*] declared; [*intention*] avowed; [*terroriste*] self-confessed; **le mobile** ~ **du crime** the motive given for the crime.
II ▶ 374 *nm* JUR ~ solicitor GB, attorney(-at-law) US.

avouer /avwe/ [1] I *vtr* to confess [*amour, haine*]; to confess (to) [*crime*]; to admit, to confess [*ignorance, dépit, peur*]; ~ **un penchant pour qch** to admit (to) a weakness for sth; **avoue** ou **tu avoueras que c'est ridicule** you must admit, it's ridiculous.
II *vi* [*suspect*] to confess; [*fautif*] to own up.
III **s'avouer** *vpr* (se déclarer) **s'~ rassuré** to say one feels reassured; **s'~ battu** to admit defeat.

avril /avʀil/ ▶ 382 *nm* April.

axe /aks/ *nm* **1** GÉN axis; TECH axle; **2** (route) major road; **l'~ Paris–Metz** the main Paris–Metz road; **3** (prolongement) **dans l'~ du bâtiment** straight along the road from the building; **la cible est dans l'~ du viseur** the target is lined up in the sights; **4** HIST **l'Axe** the Axis.

axer /akse/ [1] *vtr* **1** LIT to centre GB [*vis*]; to line up [*pièce*]; **2** FIG (baser) to base (**sur** on); (concentrer) to centre GB (**sur** on); ~ **ses recherches sur un thème** to focus one's research on a theme.

axiome /aksjom/ *nm* axiom.

ayant droit, *pl* **ayants droit** /ɛjɑ̃dʀwa/ *nm* **1** (à une prestation, une allocation) legal claimant, beneficiary; **2** (ayant cause) assign.

ayatollah /ajatɔla/ ▶ 596 *nm* ayatollah.

azalée /azale/ *nf* azalea.

azimut /azimyt/ *nm* **1** (en astronomie) azimuth; **2** FIG défense **tous** ~**s** MIL total defence GB; **négociations/débat tous** ~**s** wide-ranging negotiations/debate; **arrestations tous** ~**s** extensive ou wholesale arrests; **dans tous les** ~**s** everywhere, all over the place.

azimuté○, ~**e** /azimyte/ *adj* crazy○.

azote /azɔt/ *nm* nitrogen.

aztèque /astɛk/ *adj* Aztec.

azur /azyʀ/ *nm* **1** ▶ 141 (couleur) azure; **2** (ciel) LITER azure, skies (*pl*).

azyme /azim/ *adj* unleavened.

Bb

b, B /be/ *nm inv* b, B; **le b a ba** the rudiments.

BA /bea/ *nf* (*abbr* = **bonne action**) good deed.

baba /baba/ I° *adj inv* **en être** *or* **rester** ~ to be flabbergasted°.
II *nm* **1** CULIN ~ **(au rhum)** (rum) baba; **2**° (personne) ~ **(cool)** hippie.

babil /babil/ *nm* twittering, chattering, babbling.

babiller /babije/ [1] *vi* to babble, to chatter.

babines /babin/ *nfpl* ZOOL chops.

babiole /babjɔl/ *nf* (objet) trinket; (affaire) trifle.

bâbord /babɔʀ/ *nm* port (side); **terre à** ~! land to port!

babouche /babuʃ/ *nf* oriental slipper.

babouin /babwɛ̃/ *nm* baboon.

baby-foot /babifut/ ▶ 329 *nm inv* table football.

bac /bak/ *nm* **1**° SCOL (*abbr* = **baccalauréat**) baccalaureate; **2** (bateau) ferry; **3** (cuve) GÉN tub; IND vat; PHOT tray; **évier à deux** ~**s** double sink.
■ ~ **blanc** SCOL mock baccalaureate; ~ **à fleurs** plant tub; ~ **à glace** ice tray; ~ **à légumes** vegetable compartment (in fridge), crisper US; ~ **professionnel** SCOL ≈ GNVQ (*secondary school vocational diploma*); ~ **à sable** sandpit GB, sandbox US.

baccalauréat /bakalɔʀea/ *nm* SCOL baccalaureate (*school leaving certificate taken at 17–18*).

bâche /baʃ/ *nf* tarpaulin; **toile de** ~ canvas sheet.

bachelier, -ière /baʃəlje, ɛʀ/ *nm,f*: holder of the (*French*) baccalaureate.

bâcher /baʃe/ [1] *vtr* to cover [sth] with tarpaulin [*véhicule*]; **un camion bâché** a covered truck.

bachotage° /baʃɔtaʒ/ *nm* SCOL cramming.

bacille /basil/ *nm* bacillus; ~ **de Koch** Koch bacillus.

bâcler /bakle/ [1] *vtr* to dash [sth] off [*devoirs, travail*]; to rush through [*cérémonie*]; **c'est du travail bâclé** it's a slapdash job.

bacon /bekɔn/ *nm* smoked back bacon.

bactéricide /bakteʀisid/ I *adj* bactericidal.
II *nm* bactericide.

bactérie /bakteʀi/ *nf* bacterium; **des** ~**s** bacteria.

bactérien, -ienne /bakteʀjɛ̃, ɛn/ *adj* bacterial.

badaud, ~e /bado, od/ *nm,f* (curieux) onlooker.

badge /badʒ/ *nm* **1** (insigne) badge; **2** (identité) badge, name tag; (avec piste magnétique) swipe card.

badgeuse /badʒøz/ *nf* time clock.

badiane /badjan/ *nf* star anise.

badigeonner /badiʒɔne/ [1] *vtr* **1** (à la chaux) to whitewash; (en couleur) to paint; **2** (barbouiller) to daub (**de** with); **3** MÉD to paint [*blessure, gorge*] (**de** with); **4** CULIN to brush (**de** with).

badin, ~e[1] /badɛ̃, in/ *adj* [*ton*] bantering; [*humeur*] playful.

badinage /badinaʒ/ *nm* **1** (attitude) bantering; **2** (propos) banter.

badine[2] /badin/ I *adj* ▶ **badin**.
II *nf* **1** (baguette) switch; **2** (canne) cane.

badiner /badine/ [1] *vi* to banter, to jest; **il ne badine pas avec le règlement** he doesn't mess about when it comes to rules.

baffe° /baf/ *nf* clout, slap.

baffle /bafl/ *nm* (enceinte) speaker; (écran acoustique) baffle.

bafouer /bafwe/ [1] *vtr* to scorn.

bafouille° /bafuj/ *nf* letter.

bafouiller /bafuje/ [1] I *vtr* to mumble [*excuse*].
II *vi* [*personne*] to mumble; [*moteur*] to splutter.

bagage /bagaʒ/ I *nm* **1** (effets) luggage; (de soldat) kit; **2** (sac, valise) piece of luggage; **3** FIG (connaissances) knowledge; (diplômes) qualifications (*pl*); (expérience) credentials (*pl*).
II **bagages** *nmpl* luggage ¢; **faire/défaire ses** ~**s** to pack/unpack (one's suitcases).
■ ~ **à main** hand luggage, carry-on baggage US.
IDIOMES **plier** ~° to pack up and go; **partir avec armes et** ~**s** to up sticks and leave; **passer à l'ennemi avec armes et** ~**s** to defect.

bagagiste /bagaʒist/ ▶ 374 *nm* baggage handler.

bagarre /bagaʀ/ *nf* **1** (empoignade) fight (**entre** between); ~**s avec la police** clashes with the police; ~ **générale** free-for-all; **2** FIG (lutte) fight, struggle; (dispute) clash, confrontation; **entrer dans la** ~ to join the fray.

bagarrer°: **se bagarrer** /bagaʀe/ [1] *vpr* to fight (**pour** for).

bagarreur°, **-euse** /bagaʀœʀ, øz/ I *adj* (agressif) aggressive; (combatif) **être** ~ to like to pick a fight.
II *nm,f* bruiser°, fighter.

bagatelle /bagatɛl/ *nf* **1** (affaire) triviality; **2** (objet) **je lui ai acheté une** ~ I bought him/her a little something; **3** (somme) trifle; ~ **de** IRON trifling sum of.

bagnard /baɲaʀ/ *nm* convict.

bagne /baɲ/ *nm* **1** (prison) penal colony; **2** (peine) penal servitude.

bagnole° /baɲɔl/ *nf* car.

bagou(t)° /bagu/ *nm* volubility, glibness PÉJ; **avoir du** ~ to have the gift of the gab.

bague /bag/ *nf* (anneau) ring; (de cigare) band; (de tuyau) collar.
IDIOMES **avoir la** ~ **au doigt** to be married; **elle lui a passé la** ~ **au doigt** she got him to the altar.

baguer /bage/ [1] *vtr* to ring [*oiseau, arbre*]; TECH to collar [*tuyau*]; **doigts bagués** be-ringed fingers.

baguette /bagɛt/ *nf* **1** (pain) baguette, French stick; **2** (bâton) GÉN stick; (de tambour) drumstick; (pour manger) chopstick; ~ **d'encens** incense stick; ~ **de chef d'orchestre** conductor's baton; **mener qn à la** ~ FIG to rule sb with a rod of iron; **3** (moulure) beading; (pour cacher) casing; **4** (de bas, chaussettes) clock.
■ ~ **de fusil** ramrod; ~ **magique** magic wand; ~ **de sourcier** water-divining rod.

bahut /bay/ *nm* **1** (buffet) sideboard; **2**° (lycée) students' slang school; **3**° (camion) truck; **4** (malle) chest.

bai, ~e[1] /bɛ/ ▶ 141 *adj* bay.

baie[2] /bɛ/ *nf* **1** GÉOG bay; **2** BOT berry; **3** ~ (vitrée) picture window.

baignade /bɛɲad/ *nf* **1** (activité) swimming; '~ **interdite**' 'no swimming'; **2** (lieu) bathing spot.

baigner /beɲe/ [1] I *vtr* **1** (donner un bain à) to bath GB, to bathe US, to give [sb] a bath [*enfant, malade*]; **2** (pour soulager) to bathe [*œil, blessure*] (**dans** with); **3** (inonder) **il avait le visage baigné de larmes** his face was bathed with tears.
II *vi* ~ **dans l'huile** [*saucisses*] to be swimming in grease; ~ **dans son sang** to be lying in a pool of one's own blood; **ça baigne**° things are going fine.
III **se baigner** *vpr* **1** (dans la mer, une piscine) to have a swim; **2** (dans une baignoire) to have GB *ou* take US a bath.

baigneur, -euse /bɛɲœʀ, øz/ **I** *nm,f* (personne) swimmer, bather†.

II *nm* (poupée) baby doll.

baignoire /bɛɲwaʀ/ *nf* **1** (pour se laver) bath GB, bathtub; **2** THÉÂT ground-floor box.

bail, *pl* **baux** /baj, bo/ *nm* GÉN lease; (de trois ans ou moins) tenancy agreement; **donner à ~** to lease out; **prendre à ~** to lease; **ça fait un ~ qu'on ne s'est pas vus**○! we haven't seen each other for ages○!

bâillement /bɑjmɑ̃/ *nm* yawn; **retenir un ~** to stifle a yawn.

bâiller /bɑje/ [1] *vi* **1** [*personne, animal*] to yawn (**de** from, out of); **2** [*col, chaussure*] to gape (open); [*porte*] to be ajar.

bailleur, bailleresse /bajœʀ, bajʀɛs/ *nm,f* lessor.
■ **~ de fonds** COMM backer, silent partner.

bâillon /bɑjɔ̃/ *nm* gag; **mettre un ~ à** to gag.

bâillonner /bɑjɔne/ [1] *vtr* to gag [*presse*].

bain /bɛ̃/ *nm* **1** (liquide) bath; **prendre un ~** to have GB ou take a bath; **être dans son ~** to be in the bath GB ou bathtub; **2** (baignade) swim; **après le ~** after a swim; **3** (bassin) **grand ~** deep end; **petit ~** children's GB ou baby pool.
■ **~ de bouche** (produit) mouthwash; **faire des ~s de bouche** to rinse one's mouth (out); **~ de boue** mudbath; **~ bouillonnant** whirlpool bath; **~ fixateur** fixing bath; **~ de foule** walkabout; **prendre un ~ de foule** [*personnalité*] to go (on a) walkabout GB, to mingle with the crowd US; **~ de friture** cooking oil; **~ de jouvence** rejuvenating experience; **~ de minuit** midnight swim; **faire des ~s de pieds** to soak one's feet; **~ à remous** Jacuzzi®; **~ révélateur** developing bath; **~ de sang** bloodbath; **~ de siège** MÉD sitz bath; **~ de soleil** (corsage) suntop; **prendre un ~ de soleil** to sunbathe; **~ de teinture** (produit) dye; (bac) vat of dye; **~ turc** Turkish bath; **~ d'yeux** (produit) eyewash; **~s de mer** sea bathing ¢.
IDIOMES **se remettre dans le ~** to get back into the swing of things; **mettre qn dans le ~** to implicate sb.

bain-douche, *pl* **bains-douches** /bɛ̃duʃ/ *nm* public baths.

bain-marie /bɛ̃maʀi/ *nm* **au ~** GÉN in a bain-marie; (crèmes, sauces) in a double boiler.

baïonnette /bajɔnɛt/ *nf* MIL bayonet; ÉLECTROTECH bayonet fitting.

baisemain /bɛzmɛ̃/ *nm* hand-kissing ¢; **faire le ~ à qn** to kiss sb's hand.

baiser /beze/ *nm* kiss; **bons ~s** love (and kisses).

baisse /bɛs/ *nf* **1** GÉN (de température, pression) fall, drop; (de lumière) fading, dimming; (d'influence, de qualité) decline; **une ~ de 10°/de pression** a fall ou drop of 10°/in pressure; **2** ÉCON (décidée) cut; (constatée) fall, drop, decrease; **la ~ du dollar** the fall in the value of the dollar; **une ~ des loyers de 2%** a 2% drop in rents; **être en ~** [*taux, actions, valeurs*] to be going down; [*résultats*] to be decreasing; **le marché est à la ~** (en Bourse) the market is bearish; **revoir des prévisions à la ~** to revise estimates downward(s); **spéculations à la ~** bear speculations.

baisser /bese/ [1] **I** *vtr* **1** (abaisser) to lower [*volet, store*]; to wind [sth] down [*vitre*]; to pull down [*pantalon, visière*]; to turn down [*col*]; **~ la tête** (par précaution) to lower one's head; (vivement) to duck one's head; (par soumission, de honte) to bow; **~ les yeux (de honte)** to look down (in shame); **~ les bras** LIT to lower one's arms; FIG to give up; **~ le nez** FIG to hang one's head; **2** (réduire) to turn down [*son, volume*]; to dim [*lumière*]; [*autorité*] to cut [*prix, taux*]; [*circonstances*] to bring down [*prix, taux*].
II *vi* **1** (diminuer de niveau) GÉN to go down (**à** to; **de** by); (brusquement) to fall, to drop; [*lumière*] to fade; [*eaux*] to subside; [*qualité, criminalité*] to decline; **~ dans l'estime de qn** to go down in sb's esteem; **~ d'un ton**○ [*personne*] FIG to calm down; **2** (diminuer de valeur) [*prix, résultat, taux, production*] to fall; [*salaires, actions*] to go down; [*pouvoir d'achat, chômage,*

emplois] to decrease; [*productivité, marché*] to decline; [*budget*] to be cut; [*monnaie*] to slide; **3** (diminuer de qualité) [*vue*] to fail; [*ouïe, facultés*] to deteriorate.
III se baisser *vpr* [*personne*] (pour passer, saisir) to bend down; (pour éviter) to duck; [*levier*] to go down.

baissier, -ière /besje, ɛʀ/ **I** *adj* bearish.
II *nm* (en Bourse) bear.

bajoue /baʒu/ *nf* **1** CULIN (de porc, veau) cheek; **2**○ (joue humaine) jowl, chop.

bal /bal/ *nm* (cérémonieux) ball; (simple) dance.
■ **~ champêtre** village dance; **~ costumé** fancy-dress ball, costume ball US; **~ masqué** masked ball; **~ musette** dance with accordion music.

balade /balad/ *nf* (à pied) walk; (à moto, vélo) ride.

balader○ /balade/ [1] **I** *vtr* **1** (à pied) to take [sb] for a walk; (en voiture) to take [sb] for a drive; **2** (emporter avec soi) to carry [sth] around.
II se balader *vpr* **1** (faire une balade) (à pied) to go for a walk; (à moto, vélo) to go for a ride; (en voiture) to go for a drive; **2** (voyager) to travel.
IDIOMES **envoyer qn ~**○ to send sb packing○.

baladeur, -euse[1] /baladœʀ, øz/ **I** *adj* [*lampe*] portable.
II *nm* walkman®, personal stereo.

baladeuse[2] /baladøz/ *nf* portable lamp.

baladin /baladɛ̃/ *nm* strolling player.

balafre /balafʀ/ *nf* (marque) scar; (entaille) slash, gash.

balai /balɛ/ *nm* **1** (pour le sol) broom; **passer le ~** to sweep the floor; **du ~**○! go away!; **2** (d'essuie-glace) blade; **3** ÉLECTROTECH brush; **4**○ (an) **avoir 50 ~s** to be fifty.

balai-brosse, *pl* **balais-brosses** /balɛbʀɔs/ *nm* stiff broom.

balai-éponge, *pl* **balais-éponges** /balɛepɔ̃ʒ/ *nm* squeeze mop.

balaise○ = **balèze**.

balance /balɑ̃s/ *nf* **1** (pour peser) scales (*pl*); **faire pencher la ~** FIG to tip the scales; **2** (de comptes) balance; **3** (équilibre) balance; **4** AUDIO balance.
■ **~ commerciale** balance of trade; **~ des comptes** balance of payments; **~ de cuisine** kitchen scales; **~ des paiements** balance of payments; **~ à plateaux** balance; **~ de précision** precision balance; **~ romaine** steelyard.

Balance /balɑ̃s/ **▶ 641|** *nprf* Libra.

balancé, ~e /balɑ̃se/ *adj* **bien ~** [*phrase*] well-balanced; [*personne*]○ well-built.

balancelle /balɑ̃sɛl/ *nf* swing seat, garden hammock.

balancement /balɑ̃smɑ̃/ *nm* (de branches, corps) swaying ¢; (de bras, jambes, hanches, corde) swinging ¢; (de tête) lolling ¢.

balancer /balɑ̃se/ [12] **I** *vtr* **1** (faire osciller) [*vent*] to sway [*branches*]; to swing [*cordage*]; **~ les bras** to swing one's arms; **2** (jeter) to throw [*projectile, ordures*] (**sur** at); to chuck out○; to throw out [*vieux habits, objets inutiles*]; **~ une gifle à qn** to whack sb○; **3**○ (dire) (brutalement) to toss off [*phrases, réponse*]; (pêle-mêle) to bandy [sth] about [*chiffres*]; **~ des statistiques à la figure de qn** to fling statistics at sb; **4**○ (dénoncer) **~ qn** to squeal on sb○; **5** to balance [*compte*].
II *vi* **1** (osciller) [*branches*] to sway; [*corde, trapèze*] to swing; [*bateau*] to rock; **2** (hésiter) **~ entre deux personnes** to hesitate ou be torn between two people.
III se balancer *vpr* **1** (se mouvoir) [*personne, animal*] to sway; [*bateau*] to rock; **se ~ d'un pied sur l'autre** to shift from one foot to the other; **se ~ sur sa chaise** to rock on one's chair; **2**○ (se jeter) **se ~ du sixième étage** to fling oneself off the sixth GB ou seventh US floor.

balancier /balɑ̃sje/ *nm* **1** GÉN (d'horloge, de métronome) pendulum; **politique de ~** FIG seesaw politics○; **2** (pour funambule) balancing pole; **3** ZOOL haltere.

balançoire /balɑ̃swaʀ/ *nf* (suspendue) swing; (qui bascule) seesaw.

balayage /balɛjaʒ/ *nm* **1** (avec un balai) sweeping; **2** (en coiffure) **se faire faire un ~** to have highlights put in; **3** (en électronique) scanning.

balayer /baleje/ [21] *vtr* **1** (avec un balai) to sweep (up); **2** (frôler) **~ le sol** [*cape, manteau*] to brush the ground; **3** [*vent*] to sweep across [*plaine*]; to sweep [sth] away [*nuages, feuilles*]; [*faisceau, regard*] to sweep; [*mitrailleuse*] to rake; **4** (faire disparaître) to brush [sth] aside [*objections, rumeurs*]; to sweep [sth] aside [*craintes*]; **5** (en électronique) to scan.
IDIOMES **~ devant sa porte** to put one's own house in order before criticizing other people.

balayette /balɛjɛt/ *nf* (short-handled) brush.

balayeur -euse[1] /balɛjœʀ, øz/ ▶374 *nm,f* (personne) road sweeper.

balayeuse[2] /balɛjøz/ *nf* (machine) mechanical road-sweeper GB, mechanical street-sweeper US.

balbutiant, ~e /balbysjɑ̃, ɑ̃t/ *adj* (qui bredouille) stammering; (qui débute) in its infancy.

balbutiement /balbysimɑ̃/ *nm* LIT stammering ¢; FIG (début) first step.

balbutier /balbysje/ [2] **I** *vtr* to stammer.
II *vi* (bredouiller) to stammer; (débuter) to be in its infancy.

balbuzard /balbyzaʀ/ *nm* osprey.

balcon /balkɔ̃/ *nm* **1** CONSTR balcony; **2** THÉÂT balcony, circle; **3** NAUT (rambarde) bow pulpit, stern pulpit; (galerie) HIST stern gallery.

baldaquin /baldakɛ̃/ *nm* canopy.

Bâle /bal/ *npr* **1** ▶628 (ville) Basel; **2** ▶509 (région) **le canton de ~** the canton of Basel.

Baléares /baleaʀ/ ▶305 *nprfpl* **les** (**îles**) **~** the Balearic Islands.

baleine /balɛn/ *nf* **1** ZOOL whale; **2** (de corset) whalebone, stay US; (de col) stiffener, stay US.
■ **~ de parapluie** umbrella rib.
IDIOMES **rire** or **se tordre comme une ~**° to laugh one's head off°.

baleinier, -ière[1] /balɛnje, ɛʀ/ **I** *adj* [*bateau, industrie*] whaling.
II ▶374 *nm* (pêcheur) whaler.

baleinière[2] /balɛnjɛʀ/ *nf* (bateau) whaleboat.

balèze° /balɛz/ *adj* **1** (grand et fort) hefty°; **2** FIG [*intellectuel*] fantastic°, brilliant GB; [*sportif*] fantastic°.

balisage /balizaʒ/ *nm* (de port, chenal) beaconing; (de piste d'aviation) runway lighting; (de route) signposting; (de sentier) marking; (de texte) tagging.

balise /baliz/ *nf* **1** AVIAT, NAUT beacon; **2** (sur route) signpost; **3** RAIL signal; **4** (de sentier, piste de ski) marker; **5** ORDINAT tag.

baliser /balize/ [1] *vtr* **1** AVIAT, NAUT to mark [sth] out with beacons; **2** (travaux publics) to signpost [*route*]; **3** RAIL to mark [sth] out with signals [*voie ferrée*]; **4** NAUT to mark out [*sentier*]; **5** ORDINAT to tag [*texte*].

balistique /balistik/ **I** *adj* [*missile*] ballistic.
II *nf* ballistics (+ *v sg*).

baliverne /balivɛʀn/ *nf* nonsense ¢.

balkanique /balkanik/ *adj* Balkan (*épith*).

balkanisation /balkanizasjɔ̃/ *nf* (de territoire) Balkanization; (d'institution) break-up.

ballade /balad/ *nf* **1** MUS (instrumentale) ballade; (chanson) ballad; **2** LITTÉRAT (forme fixe) ballade; (forme libre) ballad.

ballant, ~e /balɑ̃, ɑ̃t/ **I** *adj* [*bras*] dangling; [*tête*] lolling; [*câble, cordage*] slack.
II *nm* **avoir du ~** [*véhicule*] to sway around; [*cordage*] to be slack.

ballast /balast/ *nm* NAUT, RAIL ballast.

balle /bal/ *nf* **1** (objet) ball; **renvoyer la ~** (**à qn**) LIT to throw the ball back (to sb); FIG to retort (to sb); **se renvoyer la ~** (discuter) to keep a lively argument going; (se rejeter la responsabilité) to keep passing the buck; ▶**bond**; **2** (échange, envoi) shot; **~ coupée** sliced shot; **~ de jeu** game point; **3** (d'arme à feu) bullet; **4**° (franc) franc; **5** (de café, foin) bale; (de papier) ream; **6** BOT husk.
■ **~ à blanc** blank (bullet).

ballerine /balʀin/ *nf* **1** ▶374 (danseuse) ballerina, ballet dancer; **2** (chaussures) (de danse) ballet pump; (de ville) ballerina-style shoe.

ballet /balɛ/ *nm* **1** (danse, musique) ballet; **2** (va et vient) **~ diplomatique** diplomatic comings and goings (*pl*).
■ **~ aquatique** SPORT synchronized swimming.

ballon /balɔ̃/ *nm* **1** SPORT ball; AVIAT, MÉTÉO balloon; (jouet) balloon; **2** (verre) (**verre**) **~** wine glass; **3** AUT **~** (**alcootest**) Breathalyzer®; **4** GÉOG round-topped mountain.
■ **~ captif** tethered ou captive balloon; **~ dirigeable** airship GB, blimp US; **~ d'eau chaude** hot water tank; **~ d'essai** LIT pilot balloon, trial balloon; **~ ovale** (jeu) rugby; (objet) rugby ball; **~ d'oxygène** LIT oxygen bottle; FIG life-saver; **~ prisonnier** *team game where players hit by the ball become the prisoners of the opposite team*; **~ rond** (jeu) soccer; (objet) football GB, soccer ball.

ballonnement /balɔnmɑ̃/ *nm* bloating.

ballonner /balɔne/ [1] *vtr* **~ le ventre** to make one's stomach bloated.

ballon-sonde, *pl* **ballons-sondes** /balɔ̃sɔ̃d/ *nm* sounding balloon.

ballot /balo/ *nm* **1** (paquet) bundle; **2**° (sot) nerd°, fool.

ballotin /balɔtɛ̃/ *nm* **~ de chocolats** small box of chocolates.

ballottage /balɔtaʒ/ *nm* POL *absence of an absolute majority in the first round of an election*; **il y a ~** there has to be a runoff (ballot); **être mis en ~** to face a runoff.

ballottement /balɔtmɑ̃/ *nm* tossing, jolting.

ballotter /balɔte/ [1] **I** *vtr* **1** [*mer*] to toss [sb/sth] around [*embarcation*]; [*cahot*] to jolt [*personne, véhicule*]; **2** FIG **être ballotté entre sa famille et son travail** to be torn between one's family and one's job.
II *vi* [*bateau*] to be buffeted; [*voiture, objet, tête*] to jolt.

ball-trap, *pl* **~s** /baltʀap/ *nm* (appareil) trap (for clay pigeon shooting); (sport) clay pigeon shooting.

balluchon = **baluchon**.

balnéaire /balneɛʀ/ *adj* [*station*] seaside (*épith*).

balourd, ~e /baluʀ, uʀd/ **I** *adj* uncouth.
II *nm,f* (personne) oaf.

balourdise /baluʀdiz/ *nf* **1** (gaucherie) clumsiness; **2** (acte) blunder, faux-pas; (parole) gaffe, faux-pas.

balte /balt/ ▶509 *adj* Baltic.

baluchon /balyʃɔ̃/ *nm* bundle.
IDIOMES **faire son ~** to pack one's bags (and leave).

balustrade /balystʀad/ *nf* (en ciment, pierre) parapet; (en métal) railing; (avec colonnettes) balustrade.

balustre /balystʀ/ *nm* baluster.

bambin, ~e /bɑ̃bɛ̃, in/ *nm,f* kid°, child.

bambou /bɑ̃bu/ *nm* **1** LIT bamboo; **2** FIG **coup de ~** (facture) steep ou hefty bill; **avoir le coup de ~** (être fatigué) to be knackered⁰ GB ou bushed° US.

bamboula /bɑ̃bula/ *nf* **1**° (fête) bash°; **2** (danse, musique) assemble.

ban /bɑ̃/ **I** *nm* (applaudissements) round of applause (**pour** for); (roulements de tambour) drum roll; (sonnerie) bugle call; **ouvrir le ~** (de réunion) to start the proceedings.
II bans *nmpl* banns.
IDIOMES **mettre qn au ~ de la société** to ostracize sb from society.

banal, ~e /banal, o/ *adj* **1** (*mpl* **~s**) commonplace, unremarkable, banal; **peu** or **pas ~** rather unusual; **2** (*mpl* **-aux**) HIST communal.

banalisation /banalizasjɔ̃/ *nf* **la ~ de l'informatique** the way in which computing has become part of everyday life.

banaliser /banalize/ [1] *vtr* **1** (généraliser) to make [sth] commonplace; **2** (rendre ordinaire) **voiture banalisée** unmarked car.

banalité /banalite/ *nf* **1** (d'histoire, de vie) commonplace nature; (de remarque, d'idée) triteness; **2** (propos, écrit, manque d'originalité) banality.

banane /banan/ *nf* **1** BOT banana; **2** (coiffure) quiff, French pleat; **3** (sac) bumbag GB, fanny pack US.

bananier, -ière /bananje, εR/ **I** *adj* banana (*épith*).
II *nm* **1** BOT banana tree; **2** (bateau) banana boat.

banc /bã/ *nm* **1** (siège) bench; **~ public** bench; **sur les ~s de l'école** at school; **2** POL (au Parlement) bench GB, seats (*pl*) US; **3** (de poissons) shoal; (d'huîtres) bed; **4** (de terrain) layer, bed; **5** TECH bench.
■ **~ des accusés** dock; **au ~ des avocats** at the bar; **~ de brume** patch of mist; **~ de coraux** coral reef; **~ d'église** pew; **~ d'essai** LIT test bench; FIG testing ground; **au ~ de l'infamie** in the dock; **~ de nage** thwart; **~ de sable** sandbank; **au ~ des témoins** in the witness box GB, on the witness stand US.

bancaire /bãkεR/ *adj* **1** [*activité, secteur, service*] banking; **2** [*carte, compte, chèque, prêt*] bank (*épith*).

bancal, ~e /bãkal/ *adj* [*chaise, table*] rickety; [*solution, raisonnement*] shaky; **la dernière phrase est ~e** the last sentence does not really stand up.

banco /bãko/ *nm* (au baccara) banco; **faire ~** to go banco; **gagner le ~** FIG to make a packet○.

bandage /bãdaʒ/ *nm* (de blessure) bandage; (de roue) tyre.

bande /bãd/ *nf* **1** (de malfaiteurs) gang; **2** (de touristes, d'amis) group, crowd; **~ de crétins!** you bunch of idiots!; **ils font ~ à part** they don't join in; **3** (d'animaux sauvages) pack; **4** (de tissu, papier, cuir) GÉN strip; (plus large) band; (pour blessure) bandage; **5** (forme allongée) GÉN strip; (qui orne) (rayure) large stripe; (en bordure) band; **~ de terre** strip of land; **6** (support d'enregistrement) tape; CIN film; **7** (au billard) cushion; **8** NAUT **donner de la ~** to list.
■ **~ d'arrêt d'urgence**, hard shoulder; **~ banalisée** = **~ publique**; **~ dessinée, BD**○ (dans les journaux) comic strip; (livre) comic book; (genre) comic strips (*pl*); **~ d'essai** PHOT test strip; **~ de fréquences** waveband; **~ originale** CIN original soundtrack; **~ publique** Citizens' band, CB; **~ de roulement** AUT tread; **~ rugueuse** AUT rumble strip; **~ sonore** CIN soundtrack; (d'autoroute) rumble strip; **~ Velpeau**® crepe bandage GB, Ace bandage® US.
IDIOMES **apprendre qch par la ~**○ to hear sth on the grapevine.

bande-annonce, *pl* **bandes-annonces** /bãda nõs/ *nf* trailer.

bandeau, *pl* **~x** /bãdo/ *nm* **1** (pour ne pas voir) blindfold; (d'œil malade) eye patch; **avoir un ~ sur les yeux** FIG to be blind; **2** (de coiffure) headband.

bandelette /bãdlεt/ *nf* **1** (pour blessure, momie) bandage; **2** (de soie, papier etc) small strip.

bander /bãde/ [1] *vtr* **1** (panser) to bandage; **2** (avec un bandeau) **~ les yeux à qn** to blindfold sb; **3** (tendre) to bend [*arc*]; to stretch [*ressort*]; to tense [*muscles*].

banderole /bãdRɔl/ *nf* banner.

bande-son, *pl* **bandes-son** /bãdsõ/ *nm* soundtrack.

bandit /bãdi/ *nm* **1** (malfaiteur) bandit; **2** (homme sans scrupules) crook; **3** (enfant) rascal.
■ **~ de grand chemin** highwayman.

banditisme /bãditism/ *nm* **le ~** crime; **le grand/ petit ~** organized/petty crime.

bandoulière /bãduljεR/ *nf* shoulder strap.

bang /bãg/ *nm* (supersonique) sonic boom.

banlieue /bãljø/ *nf* **1** (périphérie) suburbs (*pl*); **de ~** [*ville, hôpital*] suburban; **2** (quartier) suburb.

banlieusard, ~e /bãljøzaR, aRd/ *nm,f* person from the suburbs, suburbanite.

banni, ~e /bani/ *nm,f* exile.

bannière /banjεR/ *nf* (tous contextes) banner.
■ **la ~ étoilée** the star-spangled banner, the Stars and Stripes.
IDIOMES **c'est la croix et la ~** it's hell.

bannir /baniR/ [3] *vtr* **1** (chasser) to banish [*personne*] (**de** from); **2** (exclure) to ban [*coutume, sujet*].

bannissement /banismã/ *nm* banishment (**de** from).

banque /bãk/ *nf* **1** (établissement) bank; **mettre un chèque à la ~** to pay in ou deposit a cheque GB ou check US; **2** (activité) banking; **3** (de jeu) bank.
■ **~ d'affaires** merchant bank; **~ de dépôt** deposit bank; **~ de données** ORDINAT data bank; **~ d'émission** issuing bank; **~ d'organes** MÉD organ bank; **~ du sang** MÉD blood bank; **Banque mondiale** World Bank.

banqueroute /bãkRut/ *nf* **1** FIN bankruptcy; **2** FIG (échec) complete failure.

banquet /bãkε/ *nm* (cérémonie) banquet; (repas) feast.

banqueter /bãkte/ [23] *vi* to banquet; (faire bonne chère) to feast.

banquette /bãkεt/ *nf* (de restaurant) wall seat, banquette US; (de train) seat; (de fenêtre) window seat.

banquier /bãkje/ ▶ **374** *nm* banker.

banquise /bãkiz/ *nf* ice floe.

bantou, ~e /bãtu/ ▶ **338** **I** *adj* GÉOG Bantu.
II *nm* LING Bantu.

bantoustan /bãtustã/ *nm* homeland.

baptême /batεm/ *nm* **1** RELIG baptism; **donner le ~ à** to baptize; **2** (de bateau) naming GB, christening; (de cloche) blessing; **3** (initiation) baptism.
■ **~ de l'air** first flight.

baptiser /batize/ [1] *vtr* **1** RELIG to baptize; **se faire ~** to be baptized; **2** (nommer) to call; (surnommer) to nickname; **3** (inaugurer) to name GB, to christen [*navire*]; to bless [*cloche*].

baptismal, ~e, *mpl* **-aux** /batismal, o/ *adj* [*eau*] baptismal.

baptisme /batism/ *nm* Baptist doctrine.

baptistère /batistεR/ *nm* baptistry.

baquet /bakε/ *nm* **1** (récipient) tub; **2** (siège) bucketseat.

bar /baR/ *nm* **1** (lieu, comptoir, meuble) bar; **2** (poisson) sea bass; **3** PHYS bar.

baragouiner /baRagwine/ [1] **I** *vtr* to gabble [*propos, phrase*]; to speak [sth] badly [*langue*].
II *vi* to witter○ GB, to gibber.

baraka /baRaka/ *nf* luck; **avoir la ~** to be lucky.

baraque /baRak/ *nf* **1** (construction légère) shack; **2**○ (maison) pad○, house; (en mauvais état) dump○.
■ **~ foraine** fairground stall ou stand US.
IDIOMES **casser la ~**○ to be a resounding success; **casser la ~**○ **à de qn** to mess things up for sb○.

baraqué○, **~e** /baRake/ *adj* hefty, husky US.

baraquement /baRakmã/ *nm* **1** (ensemble) group of huts; **2** MIL army camp.

baratin○ /baRatε̃/ *nm* (pour vendre) spiel○, sales pitch; (pour séduire) sweet-talk; (pour convaincre) smooth talk○.

baratiner○ /baRatine/ [1] **I** *vtr* (pour vendre) to give [sb] the spiel; (pour séduire) to chat [sb] up; (pour convaincre) to try to talk [sb] round GB, to try to persuade.
II *vi* to jabber (on).

baratineur○, **-euse** /baRatinœR, øz/ *nm,f* (beau parleur) smooth talker○; (menteur) liar.

baratte /baRat/ *nf* churn.

barbant○, **~e** /baRbã, ãt/ *adj* boring.

barbare /baRbaR/ **I** *adj* **1** (féroce, choquant) barbaric; **2** HIST barbarian.
II *nmf* barbarian.

barbarie /baRbaRi/ *nf* barbarity, barbarism.

barbe[1] /baRb/ *nm* (cheval) barb.

barbe[2] /baRb/ **I** *nf* **1** (d'homme) beard; **~ naissante** stubble; **une vieille ~** PEJ an old fogey○GB; **parler dans sa ~** FIG to mutter into one's beard; **rire dans sa ~** FIG to laugh up one's sleeve; **2** ZOOL (de bouc, chien) beard; (de plume) barb; (de poisson) barbel; **3** BOT (d'épi, de céréale) awn; **4** TECH (de papier) rough edge; (de pièce métallique) burr; **5**○ (chose ennuyeuse) **quelle ~!**, **c'est la ~!** what a drag○!
II○ *excl* **la ~!** I've had enough!; **la ~ avec leurs consignes!** to hell with their orders○!
■ **~ de capucin** BOT wild chicory; **~ à papa** CULIN candyfloss GB, cotton candy US.

IDIOMES **à la ~ de qn** under sb's nose; **avoir de la ~ au menton** to be an adult.

barbelé, **~e** /baʀbəle/ I *adj* [*fil*] barbed.
 II *nm* barbed wire ¢.

barber° /baʀbe/ [1] I *vtr* to bore [sb] stiff°.
 II **se barber** *vpr* to be bored stiff°.

Barberousse /baʀbəʀus/ *npr* Barbarossa.

barbiche /baʀbiʃ/ *nf* (d'homme) goatee (beard); (de chèvre) (small) beard.

barbichette /baʀbiʃɛt/ *nf* (small) goatee (beard).

barbichu, **~e** /baʀbiʃy/ *adj* with a goatee (beard) (*épith, après n*).

barbier /baʀbje/ ▶374 *nm* barber.

barbillon /baʀbijɔ̃/ *nm* **1** (petit barbeau) small barbel, small goatfish US; **2** (de poisson) barbel; (de volaille) wattle; (de bétail) barb.

barbiturique /baʀbityʀik/ I *adj* barbituric.
 II *nm* barbiturate.

barboter /baʀbɔte/ [1] I° *vtr* (voler) to nick° GB, to filch° (**à** from).
 II *vi* [*canard*] to dabble; [*enfant*] to paddle; **faire ~ un gaz** to bubble a gas through a liquid.

barboteuse /baʀbɔtøz/ *nf* romper-suit.

barbouiller /baʀbuje/ [1] I *vtr* **1** (salir) to smear (**de** with); **il est tout barbouillé** his face is all dirty; **2** (couvrir) to daub (**de** with); **3** PEJ (peindre) **~ des natures mortes** to do daubs of still lives PEJ; **~ du papier** to write drivel PEJ; **4** (rendre malade) **être** or **se sentir barbouillé** to feel queasy.
 II **se barbouiller** *vpr* (se salir) **se ~ le visage de qch** to get one's face all covered in sth.

barbu, **~e**[1] /baʀby/ I *adj* bearded.
 II *nm* bearded man.

barbue[2] /baʀby/ *nf* ZOOL brill.

barda° /baʀda/ *nm* baggage, gear°; MIL kit.

barde[1] /baʀd/ *nm* (chantre) bard.

barde[2] /baʀd/ *nf* (de lard) bard.

bardé, **~e** /baʀde/ I *pp* ▶ **barder**.
 II *pp adj* FIG (couvert) covered (**de** in).

barder /baʀde/ [1] I *vtr* CULIN to bard [*rôti, volaille*].
 II° *vi* **ça barde chez les voisins!** sparks are flying next door!

barème /baʀɛm/ *nm* (recueil de tableaux) (set of) tables; (méthode de calcul) scale; **~ d'imposition** tax schedule OU scale; **~ de correction** marking-scheme; **~ des prix** price list.

barge /baʀʒ/ *nf* (embarcation) barge.

baril /baʀil/ *nm* **1** (récipient) barrel, cask; (pour vin) cask; (pour poudre) keg; **2** (unité de capacité) barrel.

barillet /baʀijɛ/ *nm* **1** TECH (de pistolet, serrure) cylinder; (d'horloge) barrel; **2** ANAT middle ear.

bariolé, **~e** /baʀjɔle/ *adj* **1** (multicolore) [*habits, tissus*] multicoloured GB; PEJ gaudy; **2** (mélangé) [*foule*] motley.

barjaquer /baʀʒake/ [1] *vi* H (bavarder) to chatter.

baromètre /baʀɔmɛtʀ/ *nm* barometer.

barométrique /baʀɔmetʀik/ *adj* barometric.

baron /baʀɔ̃/ *nm* **1** ▶596 (personne) baron; **2** CULIN **d'agneau** saddle and hind legs of lamb.

baronne /baʀɔn/ ▶596 *nf* baroness.

baroque /baʀɔk/ I *adj* **1** ART baroque; **2** (bizarre) bizarre.
 II *nm* **le ~** the baroque.

baroud° /baʀud/ *nm* **~ d'honneur** last-ditch stand.

baroudeur /baʀudœʀ/ *nm* **1** (soldat) fighter, warrior; **2** (aventurier) adventurer.

barouf° /baʀuf/ *nm* row, racket, fuss.

barque /baʀk/ *nf* (small) boat.
 IDIOMES **mener la ~** to be in charge; **bien/mal mener sa ~** to manage things well/badly.

barquette /baʀkɛt/ *nf* (tartelette) (small) tart; (récipient) (pour fruits) punnet GB, basket US; (de margarine) tub; (pour plat cuisiné) container.

police) roadblock; (de manifestants) barricade; **faire ~ à qn/qch** FIG to block sb/sth.

barre /baʀ/ *nf* **1** (pièce de métal, bois etc) bar, rod; **2** (petite tablette) bar; **~ de chocolat** chocolate bar GB, candy bar US; **3** NAUT tiller, helm; **être à** or **tenir la ~** LIT, FIG to be at the helm; **4** (bande) band; **5** (trait écrit) stroke; **la ~ du t** the cross on the t; **6** SPORT (en football) crossbar; (en saut) bar; **7** (pour la danse) barre; **8** JUR (des avocats) bar; (des témoins) ~ witness box GB, witness stand US; **9** (seuil) mark; **tu places la ~ trop haut** you're expecting too much; **10** (dans un estuaire) sandbar; (hautes vagues) tidal wave; **11** (en géologie) ridge; **12** MUS **~ de mesure** bar (line).
 ■ **~ d'appui** safety rail; **~ d'espacement** space bar; **~ fixe** horizontal bar; **~ à mine** jumper; **~ oblique** slash, stroke; **~ de remorquage** tow bar.
 IDIOMES **avoir un coup de ~**° to feel drained all of a sudden; **c'est le coup de ~ dans ce restaurant**° that restaurant is a rip-off°; **c'est de l'or en ~** it's a golden opportunity.

barreau, *pl* **~x** /baʀo/ *nm* **1** (de cage, fenêtre, prison) bar; **2** (d'échelle) rung; **3** JUR (dans prétoire) bar; **le ~** (avocats) the Bar.
 ■ **~ de chaise** LIT rung of a chair; (cigare)° fat cigar.

barrer /baʀe/ [1] *vtr* **1** (obstruer) to block [*voie, accès*] (**avec** with); **~ le passage à qn** LIT, FIG to stand in sb's way; **'route barrée'** 'road closed'; **2** (rayer) to cross out [*mot, mention, paragraphe*]; **~ un chèque** to cross a cheque; **3** (traverser) **une cicatrice lui barrait le front** he/she had a scar across his/her forehead; **4** NAUT (prendre la barre) to take the helm of; (être à la barre) to be at the helm of; (en aviron) to cox.

barrette /baʀɛt/ *nf* **1** (pour les cheveux) (hair) slide GB, barrette US; **2** (bijou) bar brooch; **3** RELIG red biretta; **recevoir la ~** to become a cardinal; **4** (insigne de décoration) ribbon.

barreur, **-euse** /baʀœʀ, øz/ *nm,f* GÉN helmsman; (en aviron) cox; **avec ~** coxed; **sans ~** coxless.

barricade /baʀikad/ *nf* barricade.

barricader /baʀikade/ [1] *vtr* to barricade [*rue*].

barrière /baʀjɛʀ/ *nf* **1** (clôture) fence; (porte) gate; (de passage à niveau) level crossing gate GB, grade crossing gate US; **2** (obstacle) LIT, FIG barrier.
 ■ **~ automatique** RAIL automatic barrier; **~ corallienne** coral reef; **~ métallique** crowd barrier; **~s douanières** tariff barriers.

barrique /baʀik/ *nf* (tonneau) barrel.

barrir /baʀiʀ/ [3] *vi* [*éléphant*] to trumpet; [*rhinocéros*] to bellow.

bar-tabac, *pl* **bars-tabac** /baʀtaba/ *nm* café (*where stamps and cigarettes can be purchased*).

baryton /baʀitɔ̃/ ▶98 *adj, nm* MUS baritone.

bas, **basse**[1] /ba, bas/ I *adj* **1** [*maison, table, mur*] low; [*salle*] low-ceilinged (*épith*); **2** [*nuage*] low; [*côte, terre, vallée*] low-lying (*épith*); **le ciel est ~** the sky is overcast; **3** [*fréquence, pression, température, prix, salaire, latitude*] low; MUS [*note*] low; [*instrument*] bass; **vendre qch à ~ prix** to sell sth cheap; **un enfant en ~ âge** a very young child; **de ~ niveau** [*produit*] low-grade; [*élève, classe*] at a low level (*après n*); [*style, texte*] low-brow; **les cours sont au plus ~** (en Bourse) prices have reached rock bottom; **4** (origine, condition) low, lowly; **les postes les plus ~** the lowest-grade jobs; **5** (époque, période) late; **6** (esprit, vengeance, complaisance) base; **de ~ étage** [*individu*] common; [*plaisanterie*] coarse, vulgar.
 II *adv* **1** (à faible hauteur) low; **comment peut-on tomber si ~!** (dans l'abjection) how can one sink to such a low level!; **loger un étage plus ~** to live one floor below; **plus ~ dans la rue** further down the street; **2** (dans un texte) **voir plus ~** see below; **3** (doucement) [*parler*] quietly; **tout ~** [*parler*] in a whisper; [*chanter*] softly; **mettre ~** (abattre) to bring [sb/sth] down [*dictateur, régime*]; **mettre ~ les armes** LIT (se rendre) to lay down one's arms; FIG (renoncer) to give up the fight; ▶ **mettre II**; **4** (mal) **être au plus ~** (physiquement) to be extremely weak; (moralement) to be at one's lowest.

III *nm inv* **1** (partie inférieure) bottom; **le ~ du visage** the lower part of the face; **les pièces du ~** the downstairs rooms; **vers le ~** [*incliner*] downward(s); **2** (vêtement) stocking; **3** MUS ¢ **chanter dans le ~** to sing bass notes (*pl*).
IV en bas *loc* (au rez-de-chaussée) downstairs; (en dessous) down below; (sur panneau, page) at the bottom; **en ~ de** at the bottom of [*falaise, page*]; **il habite en ~ de chez moi** he lives below me; **l'odeur vient d'en ~** the smell is coming from below.
■ **~ de casse** (en imprimerie) lower case; **le ~ clergé** RELIG the lower clergy; **~ de gamme** IND, COMM *adj* low-quality (*épith*); *nm* lower end of the market; **~ de laine** FIG nest egg, savings (*pl*); **~ morceaux** CULIN cheap cuts; **~ sur pattes** short-legged (*épith*); **le ~ peuple** the lower classes; **les ~ quartiers** the seedy ou poor districts (of a town); **basse saison** TOURISME low season; **basses eaux** (de mer) low tide ¢; (de rivière) low water ¢.
IDIOMES **avoir des hauts et des ~** to have one's ups and downs; **à ~ les tyrans!** down with tyrants!
basalte /bazalt/ *nm* basalt.
basané, ~e /bazane/ *adj* (hâlé) sunburned^GB, (sun-)tanned.
bas-bleu, *pl* **~s** /bablø/ *nm* bluestocking.
bas-côté, *pl* **~s** /bakote/ *nm* **1** (de route) verge GB, shoulder US; **2** (d'église) (side) aisle.
basculant, ~e /baskylã, ãt/ *adj* **pont ~** bascule bridge; **camion à benne ~e** tipper lorry GB, dump truck.
bascule /baskyl/ *nf* **1** TECH rocker; **fauteuil/cheval à ~** rocking chair/horse; **2** (balançoire) seesaw; **3** (pour peser) weighing machine.
basculement /baskylmã/ *nm* **1** FIG (renversement) swing; **2** (sur route) lane deviation.
basculer /baskyle/ [1] **I** *vtr* TÉLÉCOM to transfer [*appel*].
II *vi* **1** (tomber) [*objet, personne*] to topple over; [*benne*] to tip up; **faire ~** to tip up [*benne*]; to tip out [*chargement*]; to knock [sb] off balance [*personne*]; **2** FIG [*match, vie*] to change radically; **~ à droite** POL to swing over to the right; **~ dans la guerre** to be plunged into war; **faire ~** to turn [*match, opinion*].
base /baz/ *nf* **1** (partie inférieure) base (de of); **2** FIG (assise de système, théorie) basis (de of); (point de départ) basis (de for); **sur la ~ de** on the basis of; **servir de ~** à to serve as a basis for; **à la ~ de qch** at the root ou heart of sth; **avoir des ~s en chimie** to have a basic grounding in chemistry; **salaire/formation de ~** basic salary/training; **données de ~** source data; **repartir sur de nouvelles ~s** FIG to make a fresh start; **3** (ingrédient essentiel) base (de of); **poison à ~ d'arsenic** arsenic-based poison; **le riz forme la ~ de leur alimentation** rice is their staple diet; **4** CHIMIE base; **5** MATH base; **6** LING (radical) root; **7** (cosmétique) make-up base, foundation; **8** MIL base; **9** (de parti) **la ~** the rank and file.
■ **~ de données** ORDINAT data base; **~ d'imposition** tax base; **~ de lancement** launching site.
Bas-Empire /bazãpiʀ/ *nprm* HIST **le ~** the Later Roman Empire.
baser /baze/ [1] **I** *vtr* **1** (fonder) to base [*théorie, stratégie, économie*] (**sur** on); **2** (installer) GÉN, MIL to base [*unité, missile, société*] (**à, en** in).
II se baser *vpr* **se ~ sur qch** to go by sth [*chiffres, étude*].
bas-fond, *pl* **~s** /baf5/ **I** *nm* (haut-fond) shoal; (dépression) dip.
II bas-fonds *nmpl* (de société) dregs (of society); (de ville) seedy parts.
basilic /bazilik/ *nm* **1** (plante) basil; **2** (animal) basilisk.
basilique /bazilik/ *nf* basilica.
basique /bazik/ *adj* GÉN, CHIMIE basic; (en géologie) basal.
basket /baskɛt/ ▶329] *nm* **1** (sport) basketball; **2** (chaussure) trainer.
IDIOMES **lâcher les ~s à qn**° to give sb a break°.
basketteur, -euse /baskɛtœʀ, øz/ *nm,f* basketball player.

basque /bask/ ▶338] **I** *adj* Basque.
II *nm* LING Basque.
basques /bask/ *nfpl* basques.
IDIOMES **être pendu aux ~ de qn**° to be always hanging on sb's coat-tails.
basse² /bas/ **I** *adj* ▶**bas I**.
II ▶98], 392] *nf* MUS (partie, chanteur, instrument) bass; (voix) bass (voice); **~ continue** (bass) continuo.
■ **~ de viole** MUS viola da gamba.
basse-cour, *pl* **basses-cours** /baskuʀ/ *nf* (poulailler) poultry-yard; (volailles) poultry.
basse-fosse, *pl* **basses-fosses** /basfos/ *nf* dungeon.
bassement /basmã/ *adv* despicably, basely.
bassesse /basɛs/ *nf* **1** (caractère vil) baseness, lowness; **avec ~** [*se comporter, agir*] basely; **2** (acte vil) base ou despicable act; **prêt à toutes les ~s** prepared to stoop to anything.
bassin /basɛ̃/ *nm* **1** (de parc) ornamental lake; (plus petit) pond; (fontaine) fountain; (de piscine) pool; **2** (plat creux) bowl; **3** GÉOG basin; **4** ANAT pelvis; **5** MÉD bedpan; **6** ÉCON area.
■ **~ d'effondrement** fault-basin, rift; **~ d'emploi** labour^GB pool; **~ hydrographique** drainage basin; **~ minier** mineral field ou basin.
bassine /basin/ *nf* (récipient) bowl; (contenu) bowlful.
■ **~ à confitures** preserving pan.
bassinet /basinɛ/ *nm* (petite bassine) small bowl.
IDIOMES **cracher au ~** to cough up°.
bassiste /basist/ ▶392], 374] *nm,f* bass player.
basson /bas5/ ▶392] *nm* **1** (instrument) bassoon; **2** (instrumentiste) bassoonist.
bastide /bastid/ *nf* **1** (ville fortifiée) (medieval) fortified town; **2** (maison) country house (*in Provence*).
bastingage /bastɛ̃gaʒ/ *nm* (garde-corps) ship's rail.
bastonnade /bastɔnad/ *nf* beating.
bas-ventre, *pl* **~s** /bavãtʀ/ ▶137] *nm* lower abdomen; **recevoir un coup dans le ~** LIT, FIG to be hit below the belt.
bât /ba/ *nm* pack-saddle.
IDIOMES **c'est là que le ~ blesse** that's where the shoe pinches.
bataille /bataj/ **I** *nf* **1** MIL battle; **livrer ~ à qn** to give battle to sb; **2** (lutte morale) battle, war; **~ du pouvoir** battle for power; **mener la ~ contre qn/qch** to wage war against sb/sth; **3** (lutte physique) fight; **4** (aux cartes) ≈ beggar-my-neighbour^GB.
II en bataille *loc adj* [*cheveux*] dishevelled^GB; [*sourcils*] bushy; [*stationnement*] perpendicular.
batailler /bataje/ [1] *vi* (lutter) FIG to battle, to battle.
batailleur, -euse /batajœʀ, øz/ **I** *adj* [*enfant*] aggressive; [*tempérament*] belligerent.
II *nm,f* fighter.
bataillon /bataj5/ *nm* LIT, FIG battalion; **Dupont? inconnu au ~** HUM Dupont? never heard of him.
bâtard, ~e /bataʀ, aʀd/ **I** *adj* **1** FIG [*solution, œuvre, style*] hybrid; [*statut*] ill-defined; [*couleur*] indefinite; **2** [*chien*] crossbred; **3** OFFENSIVE [*enfant*] bastard INJUR.
II *nm,f* **1** (chien) mongrel; **2** (enfant) OFFENSIVE bastard INJUR.
III *nm* (pain) small loaf of bread.
bateau, *pl* **~x** /bato/ **I** *adj inv* [*sujet, question*] hackneyed.
II *nm* **1** (embarcation) boat; **aller en** or **par ~** to go by boat; **faire du ~** GÉN to go boating; (voile) to go sailing; **2** (forme) **encolure ~** boat neck; **3**° (plaisanterie) joke; **mener qn en ~** to take sb in; **4** (sur un trottoir) dropped kerb GB ou curb US.
■ **~ amiral** flagship; **~ de commerce** cargo boat, merchant ship; **~ de guerre** warship; **~ de plaisance** pleasure boat; **~ pneumatique** rubber dinghy; **~ de sauvetage** lifeboat.
bateau-école, *pl* **bateaux-écoles** /batoekɔl/ *nm* training ship.
bateau-mouche, *pl* **bateaux-mouches** /bato muʃ/ *nm*: *large river boat for sightseeing.*

bateleur, -euse /batlœʀ, øz/ *nm* LIT tumbler, juggler.

batelier, -ière /batəlje, ɛʀ/ ▶ 374 *nm,f* boatman/boat-woman.

batellerie /batɛlʀi/ *nf* inland water shipping.

bâti, ~e /bati/ I *pp* ▶ **bâtir**.
II *adj* 1 [*maison*] built; **terrain ~** developed site; 2 [*histoire*] constructed.
III *nm* 1 (terrain) developed site; 2 (de fenêtre, porte, machine) frame; 3 (en couture) tacking.

batifoler /batifɔle/ [1] *vi* (jouer) to romp about; (flirter) to flirt.

bâtiment /batimɑ̃/ *nm* 1 (construction) building; 2 (métier) building trade; 3 (navire) ship.
■ **~ de guerre** battleship.

bâtir /batiʀ/ [3] I *vtr* 1 to build [*édifice*]; 2 to build [*fortune, réputation, avenir*]; to base [*argumentation, rapport*] (**sur** on); 3 to tack [*ourlet*].
II **se bâtir** *vpr* [*personne*] to build oneself [*maison*]; to build up [*fortune*]; [*maison, fortune*] to be built.

bâtisse /batis/ *nf* (maison) house; (bâtiment) building.

bâtisseur, -euse /batisœʀ, øz/ *nm* 1 HIST CONSTR (maçon) master-builder; 2 FIG (créateur) builder.

bâton /batɔ̃/ *nm* 1 (bout de bois) stick; **retour de ~** backlash; 2 (objet allongé) stick; **un ~ de cire** a stick of wax; 3 (trait vertical) vertical stroke; (pour compter) bar; 4° (dix mille francs) ten thousand francs.
■ **~ blanc** baton (*used for directing traffic*); **~ de maréchal** LIT marshal's baton; FIG pinnacle of one's career; **~ de rouge (à lèvres)** lipstick.
IDIOMES être le **~ de vieillesse de qn** to be sb's support in their old age; **discuter à ~s rompus** to talk about this and that; **mettre des ~s dans les roues de qn** to put a spoke in sb's wheel.

bâtonnet /batɔnɛ/ *nm* 1 (petit bâton) stick; 2 (de rétine) (retinal) rod.
■ **~ ouaté** cotton bud GB, cotton swab US; **~ de poisson** fish finger GB, fish stick US.

bâtonnier /batɔnje/ ▶ 596 *nm* ~ president of the Bar.

batracien /batʀasjɛ̃/ *nm* batrachian.

battage /bataʒ/ *nm* 1° publicity, hype°; **faire du ~ autour de qch** to hype sth°, to give sth the hard sell; 2 (d'or) beating; (de blé) threshing; (de beurre) churning.

battant, ~e /batɑ̃, ɑ̃t/ I *adj* **~ neuf** brand new; **à deux heures ~es** on the stroke of two; **le cœur ~** with a beating heart.
II *nm,f* fighter.
III *nm* 1 (de porte, fenêtre) hinged section; (de table, comptoir) leaf; **porte à deux ~s** double door; 2 (de cloche) clapper; 3 (de drapeau) fly.

batte /bat/ *nf* SPORT bat GB, paddle US.

battement /batmɑ̃/ *nm* 1 (de cœur, pouls) beating ¢, beat; 2 (de pluie, tambour) beating ¢; 3 MUS, PHYS beat; 4 (d'ailes) flutter; (de cils) fluttering ¢; (de paupières) blinking ¢; (de danseur) battement; (de nageur) (en crawl) flutter kick ¢; (en brasse) frog kick ¢; 5 (entre deux activités) break; (attente) wait; (période creuse) gap.

batterie /batʀi/ *nf* 1 (de grand orchestre) percussion section; (de jazz, rock) drum kit; 2 (artillerie, régiment) battery; **dévoiler ses ~s** FIG to show one's hand; 3 AUT, ÉLECTROTECH battery; 4 (série) (de caméras, missiles, tests) battery; (de projecteurs) bank; (de satellite) array; (d'avocats, experts) battery.
■ **~ de cuisine** CULIN pots and pans (*pl*).

batteur /batœʀ/ ▶ 374 *nm* 1 (de grand orchestre) percussionist; (de jazz, rock) drummer; 2 (au cricket) batsman; (au baseball) batter; 3 CULIN whisk.
■ **~ électrique** hand mixer.

batteuse /batøz/ *nf* (de céréales) threshing machine.

battoir /batwaʀ/ *nm* 1 (instrument) beater; 2° (main) paw°, hand.

battre /batʀ/ [61] I *vtr* 1 (l'emporter) to beat, to defeat [*adversaire*]; to break [*record*]; **~ qn au tennis/aux élections** to beat sb at tennis/in the elections; **se faire ~ par 6 à 2** to lose 6–2; 2 (frapper) to beat [*personne, animal*]; **~ qn à coups de pied/poing** to kick/punch sb repeatedly; 3 (taper sur) to beat [*matelas , tapis*]; to beat [*métal*]; to thresh [*blé*]; **~ l'air/l'eau de ses**

bras to thrash the air/the water with one's arms; **~ monnaie** to mint coins; 4 (heurter) [*pluie*] to beat ou lash against [*vitre*]; [*mer*] to pound ou beat against [*rocher*]; [*artillerie*] to pound [*position*]; 5 CULIN to whisk [*œuf*]; 6 JEUX to shuffle [*cartes*]; 7 MUS **~ la mesure** to beat time; 8 (parcourir) to scour [*pays, forêt*].
II **battre de** *vtr ind* 1 (agiter) **~ des ailes** to flap its wings; **~ des cils** to flutter one's eyelashes; **~ des mains** to clap (one's hands); **~ des paupières** to blink; 2 (jouer) **~ du tambour** to beat the drum.
III *vi* 1 [*cœur, pouls*] to beat; **le sang me battait aux tempes** I could feel my temples throbbing; 2 [*porte, volet*] to bang.
IV **se battre** *vpr* 1 (lutter) to fight (**contre** against; **avec** with); **se ~ pour obtenir qch** FIG to fight for sth; **se ~ avec une serrure** HUM to struggle with a lock; 2 (échanger des coups) to fight; 3 (se frapper) **se ~ la poitrine** to beat one's breast.
IDIOMES **~ en retraite devant qch/qn** to retreat before sth/sb; **~ son plein** to be in full swing; **je m'en bats l'œil**° I don't give a damn°.

battu, ~e¹ /baty/ I *pp* ▶ **battre**.
II *pp adj* [*enfant, femme*] battered; FIG [*mine, air*] tired.

battue² /baty/ *nf* (à la chasse) beat.

baudet° /bodɛ/ *nm* (âne) donkey, ass.
IDIOMES **être chargé comme un ~** to be loaded down like a mule.

baudrier /bodʀije/ *nm* 1 (d'uniforme) shoulder strap; 2 (d'alpinisme) harness.

baudroie /bodʀwa/ *nf* angler fish, monkfish.

baudruche /bodʀyʃ/ *nf* 1 (matière) rubber skin; (ballon) balloon; 2 FIG, PEJ wimp° PÉJ.
IDIOMES **se dégonfler comme une ~** to lose one's nerve.

bauge /boʒ/ *nf* 1 (de sanglier) wallow; 2 (lieu sale) pigsty; 3 (torchis) cob, clay and straw mortar.

baume /bom/ *nm* balm, balsam.
IDIOMES **mettre du ~ au cœur de qn** to be a solace to sb.

baux /bo/ *nmpl* ▶ **bail**.

bavard, ~e /bavaʀ, aʀd/ I *adj* 1 (loquace) talkative; 2 (indiscret) **il est trop ~** he talks too much; 3 PEJ (prolixe) [*roman, film, critique*] long-winded PÉJ.
II *nm,f* 1 (personne loquace) chatterbox; 2 (personne indiscrète) indiscreet person, bigmouth°.

bavardage /bavaʀdaʒ/ *nm* 1 (action) chattering; 2 (indiscrétions) gossip ¢; 3 (propos) idle chatter.

bavarder /bavaʀde/ [1] *vi* 1 (parler) to talk, to chatter; 2 (s'entretenir) to chat (**avec** with); 3 (médire) to gossip (**sur** about).

bavarois, ~e /bavaʀwa, az/ I *adj* Bavarian.
II *nm* CULIN Bavarian cream, bavarois.

bave /bav/ *nf* (de personne) dribble; (de crapaud) spittle; (d'animal) slaver; (d'escargot, de limace) slime.

baver /bave/ [1] *vi* 1 [*personne*] to dribble; [*animal*] to slaver; 2 (couler) [*stylo*] to leak; [*pinceau*] to dribble; [*encre, peinture*] to run.
IDIOMES **en ~** to have a hard time.

bavette /bavɛt/ *nf* 1 (pour bébé) bib; 2 CULIN flank; 3 AUT mudflap.
IDIOMES **tailler une ~° avec qn** to have a good chat with sb.

baveux, -euse /bavø, øz/ *adj* 1 [*enfant, bouche*] dribbling; 2 [*omelette*] runny.

bavoir /bavwaʀ/ *nm* bib.

bavure /bavyʀ/ *nf* 1 (tache) smudge; 2 (erreur) blunder.

bayer /baje/ [21] *vi* **~ aux corneilles** to gape.

bazar /bazaʀ/ *nm* 1 (magasin) general store, bazaar; 2° (désordre) mess; 3° (affaires) clutter.

bazarder° /bazaʀde/ [1] *vi* 1 (jeter) to throw out; (vendre) to sell off.

bazarette /bazaʀɛt/ *nf* convenience store.

BCBG° /besebeʒe/ *adj* (*abbr* = **bon chic bon genre**) IRON chic and conservative.

BCG /beseʒe/ *nm* (*abbr* = **bacille bilié de Calmette et Guérin**) MÉD BCG.

bd *written abbr* = **boulevard** 1.

BD○ /bede/ *nf*: *abbr* ▶ **bande**.

béant, **~e** /beɑ̃, ɑ̃t/ *adj* [*plaie, trou, sac*] gaping.

béarnaise /beaʀnɛz/ *nf* Béarnaise sauce.

béat, **~e** /bea, at/ *adj* [*personne*] blissfully happy; [*sourire, air, expression*] blissful, beatific HUM; **rester ~ devant qch** to gaze enraptured at sth; **~ d'admiration devant** wide-eyed with admiration for.

béatement /beatmɑ̃/ *adv* blissfully, rapturously.

beau (**bel** *before vowel or mute h*), **belle**[1], *mpl* **~x** /bo, bɛl/ **I** *adj* **1** (esthétiquement) [*enfant, femme, visage, yeux, cheveux*] beautiful; [*homme, garçon*] handsome; [*jambes*] nice; [*corps, silhouette*] good; [*couleur, son, jardin, objet*] beautiful; **se faire ~** to do oneself up; **faire qn ~** to smarten sb up; **ce n'est pas (bien) à voir**○! it's not a pretty sight!; **2** (qualitativement) [*vêtements, machine, spectacle*] good; [*collection, spécimen*] fine; [*travail, cadeau*] nice; [*temps, jour*] fine, nice; [*journée, promenade*] lovely; [*discours, projet*] fine; [*effort, victoire*] nice; [*geste, sentiment*] noble; [*carrière*] successful; [*succès, avenir, optimisme*] great; **fais de ~x rêves!** sweet dreams!; **il fait ~** the weather is fine; **il n'est pas ~ de faire** it's not nice to do; **un ~ jour** one fine day; **au ~ milieu de** right in the middle of; **c'est bien ~ tout ça, mais**○ that's all very fine, but; **trop ~ pour être vrai** too good to be true; **ça serait trop ~**○! one should be so lucky○!; **ce ne sont que de belles paroles** it's all talk; **3** (quantitativement) [*somme, héritage*] tidy; [*salaire*] very nice; [*appétit*] big; **belle pagaille** absolute mess; **bel égoïste** awful egoist.

II *nm* **1** (choses intéressantes) **qu'est-ce que tu as fait de ~?** done anything interesting?; **2** PHILOS (beauté) **le ~** beauty; **3** MÉTÉO **le temps est/se met au ~** the weather is/is turning fine.

III avoir beau *loc verbale* **j'ai ~ essayer, je n'y arrive pas** it's no good my trying, I can't do it; **l'économie a ~ se développer, le chômage progresse** even if the economy does develop, unemployment is still growing; **on a ~ dire, ce n'est pas si simple** no matter what people say, it's not that easy.

IV bel et bien *loc adv* **1** (irréversiblement) well and truly; **bel et bien fini** well and truly over; **2** (indiscutablement) definitely.

■ **~ fixe** MÉTÉO fine weather; **être au ~ fixe** [*temps, baromètre*] to be set fair; [*affaire, relation*] to be going well; **avoir le moral au ~ fixe**○ to be on a high○; **~ gosse** good-looking guy○; **~ parleur** smooth talker; **~ parti** (homme) eligible bachelor; (femme) good match; **épouser un ~ parti** to marry money; **~ sexe** fair sex; **~x jours** (beau temps) fine weather ¢; (belle époque) good days; **bel esprit** bel esprit; **belle page** (en imprimerie) right-hand page; **belle plante**○ gorgeous specimen○; **belles années** happy years.

IDIOMES **faire le ~** [*chien*] to sit up and beg; [*personne*] to show off; **c'est du ~**○! IRON lovely! IRON; **tout ~ (tout ~)!** (pour calmer) easy(, easy)!.

beaucoup /boku/ ▶ **486** | **I** *adv* **1** (modifiant un verbe) a lot; (dans les phrases interrogatives et négatives) much; **aimer ~ qn/qch** to like sb/sth a lot ou a great deal; **la fin du roman surprend ~** the ending of the novel is very surprising; **s'intéresser ~ à qch** to be very interested in sth; **je n'ai pas ~ aimé le concert** I didn't enjoy the concert very much; **il n'écrit plus ~** he doesn't write much any more; **~ à boire** a lot to drink; **c'est ~ dire** that's going a bit far; **c'est déjà ~ qu'elle soit venue** it's already quite something that she came; **2** (modifiant un adverbe) much, far; **elle va ~ mieux** she's much ou a lot better; **~ moins/plus d'argent** far ou much less/more money; **~ moins de livres** far fewer books; **~ plus vite** much faster; **~ trop** far too much, much too much; **~ trop grand** far ou much too big; **3** (un grand nombre) **~ de** a lot of [*objets, idées*]; (dans les phrases interrogatives et négatives) much, many; (une grande quantité) **~ de** a lot of, a great deal of [*argent, eau, bruit*]; **il ne reste**

plus **~ de pain** there isn't much bread left; **il n'y a pas ~ de monde** there aren't many ou a lot of people; **4** (avec valeur pronominale) many; **~ sont retraités** many are pensioners.

II de beaucoup *loc adv* by far.

III pour beaucoup *loc adv* **ta réussite est due pour ~ à** your success is largely due to; **être pour ~ dans** to have a lot to do with.

beauf○ /bof/ *nm* **1** (*abbr* = **beau-frère**) brother-in-law; **2** (rustre) PEJ boor○.

beau-fils, *pl* **beaux-fils** /bofis/ *nm* **1** (gendre) son-in-law; **2** (fils du conjoint) stepson.

beau-frère, *pl* **beaux-frères** /bofʀɛʀ/ *nm* brother-in-law.

beau-papa, *pl* **beaux-papas** /bopapa/ *nm* father-in-law.

beau-père, *pl* **beaux-pères** /bopɛʀ/ *nm* **1** (de conjoint) father-in-law; **2** (d'enfant) stepfather.

beaupré /bopʀe/ *nm* (mât de) **~** bowsprit.

beauté /bote/ *nf* beauty; **la ~ idéale** ideal beauty; **la ~ d'un paysage** the beauty of a landscape; **d'une grande ~** very beautiful; **de toute ~** exquisite; **être en ~** to look really good; **avoir la ~ du diable** to be in the bloom of youth; **se faire une ~** to do oneself up; **faire qch pour la ~ du geste** to do sth because it is a nice thing to do; **commencer/finir en ~** to start/to end with a flourish; **elle se prend pour une ~** she thinks she's a great beauty.

beaux-arts /bozaʀ/ *nmpl* fine arts and architecture.

beaux-parents /bopaʀɑ̃/ *nmpl* parents-in-law.

bébé /bebe/ *nm* baby; **des cheveux de ~** baby hair; **aliments pour ~s** baby food; **~ phoque** baby seal; **attendre un ~** to be expecting a baby.

bec /bɛk/ *nm* **1** (d'oiseau) beak, bill; (de tortue, poisson) beak; (de dauphin) snout; **donner des coups de ~** to peck (**dans** at); (**nez en**) **~ d'aigle** hooked nose; **2** (de pichet, casserole) lip; (de théière) spout; (d'instrument à vent) mouthpiece; (de stylo) nib; **3** C, H (baiser) kiss.

■ **~ Bunsen** Bunsen burner; **~ de gaz** gas streetlamp; **~ verseur** pourer(-spout).

IDIOMES **clouer le ~ à qn**○ to shut sb up○; **se retrouver le ~ dans l'eau**○ to be stuck, to be left high and dry; **tomber sur un ~**○ to come across a snag.

bécane○ /bekan/ *nf* (deux-roues) bike○.

bécarre /bekaʀ/ *nm* natural; **ré ~** D natural.

bécasse /bekas/ *nf* **1** (oiseau) woodcock; **2** (sotte) featherbrain○.

bécasseau, *pl* **~x** /bekaso/ *nm* **1** (oiseau de rivage) sandpiper; **2** (jeune bécasse) young woodcock.

bécassine /bekasin/ *nf* **1** (oiseau) snipe; **2** (sotte) silly goose○.

bec-de-cane, *pl* **becs-de-cane** /bɛkdəkan/ *nm* (serrure) spring lock; (poignée) door handle.

bec-de-lièvre, *pl* **becs-de-lièvre** /bɛkdəljɛvʀ/ *nm* harelip.

bêche /bɛʃ/ *nf* (à lame pleine) spade; (à dents) garden fork.

bêcher /beʃe/ [1] *vtr* to dig [sth] (with a spade) [*jardin*].

bêcheur, **-euse** /bɛʃœʀ, øz/ *nm,f* stuck-up person.

becquée /beke/ *nf* beakful; **donner la ~ à** to feed [*oisillon*].

bedaine○ /bədɛn/ *nf* paunch.

bedeau, *pl* **~x** /bədo/ *nm* verger.

bedonnant○, **~e** /bədɔnɑ̃, ɑ̃t/ *adj* [*personne*] paunchy.

bée /be/ *adj f* **être bouche ~** to gape (**devant** at); **être bouche ~ de surprise** to be open-mouthed in surprise.

beffroi /befʀwa/ *nm* ARCHIT belfry.

bégaiement /begɛmɑ̃/ *nm* (trouble) stammer, stutter.

bégayer /begeje/ [21] *vtr, vi* to stammer.

bègue /bɛg/ **I** *adj* **être ~** to stammer.

II *nmf* **c'est un/une ~** he/she has a stammer.

bégueule /begœl/ *adj* prudish.

béguin○ /begɛ̃/ *nm* **avoir le ~ pour qn** to have a crush on sb.

beige /bɛʒ/ ▶ 141 | *adj, nm* beige.

beignet /bɛɲɛ/ *nm* GÉN fritter; (à la pâte levée) doughnut, donut○ US; **~ au sucre** doughnut.
■ **~s de crevettes** prawn crackers.

bel *adj m* ▶ **beau** I, IV.

bêler /bele/ [1] *vi* to bleat.

belette /bəlɛt/ *nf* weasel.

belge /bɛlʒ/ ▶ 394 | *adj* Belgian.

belgicisme /bɛlʒisism/ *nm* Belgian French expression.

Belgique /bɛlʒik/ ▶ 232 | *nprf* Belgium.

bélier /belje/ *nm* **1** ZOOL ram; **2** HIST, MIL battering ram.

Bélier /belje/ ▶ 641 | *nprm* Aries.

bellâtre /bɛlɑtʀ/ *nm* handsome hunk.

belle² /bɛl/ **I** *adj f* ▶ **beau** I.
II *nf* **1** (femme) **courtiser les ~s** to go courting the ladies; **ma ~** darling, love○ GB, doll○ US; **2** (maîtresse) lady friend; **3** (partie) decider.
III de plus belle *loc adv* with renewed vigour^GB; **crier de plus ~** to shout louder than ever.
IV belles○ *nfpl* (paroles) stories.
■ **la Belle au Bois dormant** Sleeping Beauty.
IDIOMES **(se) faire la ~**○ (s'évader) to do a bunk○ GB, to take a powder○ US; **en faire voir de ~s**○ **à qn** to give sb a hard time.

belle-famille, *pl* **belles-familles** /bɛlfamij/ *nf* in-laws (*pl*).

belle-fille, *pl* **belles-filles** /bɛlfij/ *nf* **1** (bru) daughter-in-law; **2** (fille du conjoint) stepdaughter.

belle-mère, *pl* **belles-mères** /bɛlmɛʀ/ *nf* **1** (de conjoint) mother-in-law; **2** (d'enfant) stepmother.

belles-lettres /bɛlɛtʀ/ *nfpl* literature **C**, belles lettres **C**.

belle-sœur, *pl* **belles-sœurs** /bɛlsœʀ/ *nf* sister-in-law.

belliciste /belisist/ *adj* [*politicien, discours, opinion*] warmongering (*épith*); [*gouvernement, parti*] hawkish.

belligérant, **~e** /beliʒeʀɑ̃, ɑ̃t/ **I** *adj* [*partie, pays*] warring; [*troupes*] combatant; **États non ~s** nonbelligerent states.
II *nm* **1** (pays) belligerent, warring party; **2** (combattant) combatant.

belliqueux, **-euse** /belikø, øz/ *adj* (agressif) aggressive.

belote /bəlɔt/ ▶ 329 | *nf* belote (*card game*).

belvédère /bɛlvedɛʀ/ *nm* (pavillon) belvedere, gazebo.

bémol /bemɔl/ *nm* **1** MUS flat; **mi ~** E flat; **2** (atténuation) damper.

bénédictin, **~e** /benediktɛ̃, in/ *adj, nm,f* Benedictine; **travail de ~** FIG painstaking task.

bénédiction /benediksjɔ̃/ *nf* blessing; **cet emploi est une ~ du ciel** that job is a godsend; **c'est une ~!** it's a miracle!

bénéfice /benefis/ *nm* **1** (gain financier) profit; **~ brut/net** gross/net profit; **faire des ~s** to make a profit (**sur** on); **2** (action bénéfique) benefit; **3** (avantage) advantage; **le ~ de l'âge** the prerogative of age; **tirer ~ de qch** to gain advantage from sth; **il n'en tire aucun ~** he doesn't get anything out of it; **au ~ d'une œuvre caritative** in aid of a charity; **~ du doute** benefit of the doubt.

bénéficiaire /benefisjɛʀ/ **I** *adj* [*affaire*] profitable.
II *nmf* beneficiary.

bénéficier /benefisje/ [2] *vtr ind* **~ de** to receive [*aide financière, formation, appui*]; to enjoy [*immunité, soutien populaire, avantages*]; to benefit from [*conjoncture favorable*]; to get [*privilège, publicité*]; **faire ~ qn de** to give sb [*tarif réduit, bourse*].

bénéfique /benefik/ *adj* beneficial; **avoir un effet ~** to be beneficial; **être ~ à qn** to do sb good.

Bénélux /benelyks/ *nprm* Benelux.

benêt /bənɛ/ **I** *adj m* simple.
II *nm* half-wit.

bénévolat /benevɔla/ *nm* voluntary work.

bénévole /benevɔl/ **I** *adj* voluntary.
II *nmf* voluntary ou volunteer worker, volunteer.

bénévolement /benevɔlmɑ̃/ *adv* on a voluntary basis.

bénigne *adj f* ▶ **bénin**.

bénignité /beninite/ *nf* **1** MÉD (de maladie) mildness; (de tumeur) nonmalignancy; **2** (de faute) harmlessness; (de critique) mildness.

bénin, **-igne** /benɛ̃, iɲ/ *adj* [*maladie, blessure*] minor; [*tumeur*] benign; [*faute, erreur*] minor.

béni-oui-oui○ /beniwiwi/ *nm inv* yes-man.

bénir /beniʀ/ [3] *vtr* to bless; **Dieu vous** ou **te bénisse** God bless you; **béni soit le ciel!** thank God!

bénit, **~e** /beni, it/ *adj* [*cierge*] blessed; [*water*] holy.

bénitier /benitje/ *nm* holy water font.

benjamin, **~e** /bɛ̃ʒamɛ̃, in/ *nm,f* **1** (dans une famille) youngest son/daughter; (dans un groupe) youngest member; **2** SPORT ~ junior (*aged 10–11*).

benne /bɛn/ *nf* (de chantier, camion) skip GB, dumpster® US; (de mine) (colliery) wagon; (contenu) wagon(ful); (de téléphérique) car.
■ **~ à béton** concrete mixer; **~ à ordures** (camion) waste disposal GB ou garbage US truck; (conteneur) skip GB, dumpster® US.

béotien, **-ienne** /beɔsjɛ̃, ɛn/ **I** *adj* GÉOG Boeotian.
II *nm,f* (ignorant) ignoramus.

BEPC /beapese, bɛps/ *nm* (*abbr* = **Brevet d'études du premier cycle**) *former examination at the end of the first stage of secondary education.*

béquille /bekij/ *nf* **1** MÉD crutch; **marcher avec des ~s** to be on crutches; **2** TECH (de bicyclette, moto) kickstand.

bercail /bɛʀkaj/ *nm* **1** RELIG fold; **2**○ (foyer) home.

berçante /bɛʀsɑ̃t/ *nf* C rocking chair.

berceau, *pl* **~x** /bɛʀso/ *nm* **1** (de bébé) cradle; **dès** ou **depuis le ~** from the cradle; **2** (lieu d'origine) (de personne, famille) birthplace; (de religion, peuple) cradle.

bercer /bɛʀse/ [12] **I** *vtr* to rock [*enfant*]; **~ un enfant pour l'endormir** to rock ou lull a baby to sleep; **~ qn de promesses** to string sb along with promises.
II se bercer *vpr* **se ~ d'illusions** ou **de vains espoirs** to delude oneself.

berceuse /bɛʀsøz/ *nf* **1** (chanson) lullaby; **2** (siège) rocking chair.

béret /beʀɛ/ *nm* beret; **~ basque** Basque beret.

bergamote /bɛʀgamɔt/ *nf* **1** (poire) bergamot (pear); **2** (agrume) bergamot (orange); **thé à la ~** earl grey tea.

berge /bɛʀʒ/ *nf* (de rivière, canal) bank; **la ~ du canal** the canal bank; **voie sur ~** quayside road.

berger, **-ère**¹ /bɛʀʒe, ɛʀ/ ▶ 374 | *nm,f* shepherd/shepherdess.
■ **~ allemand** German shepherd (dog), Alsatian GB; **~ des Pyrénées** Pyrenean mountain dog.

bergère² /bɛʀʒɛʀ/ *nf* (fauteuil) wing chair.

bergerie /bɛʀʒəʀi/ *nf* (abri) sheep barn.
IDIOMES **faire entrer le loup dans la ~** to set the fox to mind the geese.

bergeronnette /bɛʀʒɔʀɔnɛt/ *nf* wagtail.

berk /bɛʀk/ *excl* yuk○!

Berlin /bɛʀlɛ̃/ ▶ 628 | *npr* Berlin.

berline /bɛʀlin/ *nf* **1** (automobile) four-door saloon GB, sedan US; **2** (attelage) berlin.

berlingot /bɛʀlɛ̃go/ *nm* (bonbon) *twisted hard candy.*

berlinois, **~e** /bɛʀlinwa, az/ ▶ 628 | *adj* Berlin (*épith*).

Berlinois, **~e** /bɛʀlinwa, az/ ▶ 628 | *nm,f* Berliner.

berlue /bɛʀly/ *nf* **avoir la ~** to be seeing things.

bermuda /bɛʀmyda/ *nm* bermudas (*pl*).

Bermudes /bɛʀmyd/ ▶ 305 | *nprfpl* **les ~s** Bermuda (*sg*).

berne /bɛʀn/ *nf* **en ~** [*drapeau*] at half-mast.

berner /bɛʀne/ [1] *vtr* to fool, to deceive.

besace /bəzas/ *nf* (sac) pouch.

besogne /bəzɔɲ/ *nf* job; **une basse ~** a menial chore; **abattre de la ~** to get through a lot of work; **tu vas vite en ~, toi!** you don't waste any time, do you!

besogneux, -euse /bəzɔɲø, øz/ *nm,f* **1** (tâcheron) drudge; **2†** (pauvre) needy person.

besoin /bəzwɛ̃/ **I** *nm* need (**de** for; **de faire** to do); **répondre à un ~** to meet a need; **si ~ est, en cas de ~** if need be; **avoir ~ de qch/qn** to need sth/sb; **j'ai bien ~ de ça**○! IRON that's all I need! IRON; **avoir ~ de faire** to need to do; **j'ai ~ de changer d'air** I need a change of scene; **tu as ~ qu'on s'occupe de toi** you need somebody to take care of you; **il n'est pas ~ de faire** there is no need to do; **est-il ~ que je vienne?** is it necessary for me to come?; **est-il ~ de le dire?** need I remind you?; **éprouver le ~ de faire** to feel a need to do; **pour les ~s de la cause** for the good of the cause; **être dans le ~** to be in need; **être à l'abri du ~** to be free from want.
II besoins *nmpl* needs; **~s actuels** today's needs; **subvenir aux ~s de qn** to provide for sb; **~s en eau/personnel** water/staff requirements.
IDIOMES **faire ses ~s**○ [*personne*] to relieve oneself; [*animal*] to do its business.

bestial, ~e, *mpl* **-iaux** /bɛstjal, o/ *adj* brutish.

bestialité /bɛstjalite/ *nf* (caractère bestial) brutality.

bestiaux /bɛstjo/ *nmpl* GÉN livestock ¢; (bovins) cattle (+ *v pl*).

bestiole○ /bɛstjɔl/ *nf* (insecte) bug; (animal) animal.

bétail /betaj/ *nm* GÉN livestock ¢; (bovins) cattle (+ *v pl*); **aliments pour le ~** cattle feed.

bête /bɛt/ **I** *adj* [*personne, air, idée, question*] stupid; [*problème*] simple; [*accident*] silly; **tu es bien ~ d'avoir accepté** it was stupid of you to accept; **il n'est pas ~** he's no fool; **ce n'est pas ~ ça!** that's not a bad idea!; **suis-je ~!** how stupid of me!; **~ à pleurer** too stupid for words; **je suis restée toute ~** I was dumbfounded; **~ et méchant** nasty; **il est ~ et discipliné** he just does as he's told; **c'est tout ~** it's quite simple; **c'est (trop) ~ d'en arriver là** it's (such) a shame that things should come to this; **c'est ~, je ne peux pas venir** it's a shame I can't come.
II *nf* GÉN creature; (quadrupède) animal; **nos amis les ~s** our four-legged friends; **il a une cinquantaine de ~s** he has around 50 head of cattle.
■ **~ à bon Dieu** ZOOL ladybird GB, ladybug US; **~ à concours** exam fiend○; **~ à cornes** ZOOL horned animal; **~ curieuse** freak; **~ féroce** ZOOL ferocious animal; **~ noire** bête noire GB, pet hate; **~ sauvage** ZOOL wild animal; **~ de somme** ZOOL beast of burden; **~ de travail** workaholic.
IDIOMES **il est ~ comme ses pieds**○ **à manger du foin**○ he's (as) thick as two short planks○ GB, he's as dumb as can be; **chercher la petite ~**○ to nitpick○; **reprendre du poil de la ~**○ to perk up; **travailler comme une ~**○ to work like crazy○.

bêtement /bɛtmɑ̃/ *adv* stupidly; **il suffit (tout) ~ de faire** you simply need to do.

bêtifiant, ~e /betifjɑ̃, ɑ̃t/ *adj* [*ouvrage, paroles, émission*] idiotic.

bêtise /betiz/ *nf* **la ~** stupidity; **il est d'une ~ incroyable** he's incredibly stupid; **c'est de la ~** it's stupid; **faire une ~** to do something stupid ou a stupid thing; **dire des ~s** to talk nonsense; **j'ai fait une ~ en acceptant** I was stupid to accept; **surtout pas de ~s!** be good now!; **se fâcher pour une ~** to get angry over nothing.
■ **~ de Cambrai** CULIN mint.

bêtisier /betizje/ *nm* collection of howlers○.

béton /betɔ̃/ *nm* concrete; **de** or **en ~** LIT concrete (*épith*), FIG watertight.
■ **~ armé** reinforced concrete.

bétonnière /betɔnjɛʀ/ *nf* concrete mixer.

bette /bɛt/ *nf* Swiss chard.

betterave /bɛtʀav/ *nf* beet; **~ rouge** beetroot.

beuglement /bøɡləmɑ̃/ *nm* **1** (de vache) mooing; (de taureau) bellowing; **2**○ (de personne) bawling, yelling.

beugler /bøɡle/ [1] **I** *vtr* to bellow (out) [*chanson, ordre, injures*].
II *vi* **1** [*vache*] to moo; [*bœuf, taureau*] to bellow; **2**○ (hurler) [*personne*] to yell; [*télévision*] to blare out.

beur○ /bœʀ/ *nmf* second-generation North African (*living in France*).

beurre /bœʀ/ *nm* butter; **~ doux** unsalted butter; **~ d'anchois/de saumon** anchovy/salmon paste.
■ **~ blanc** sauce made of butter, vinegar and shallots; **~ d'escargot** garlic and parsley butter; **~ noir** CULIN black butter; **œil au ~ noir**○ black eye.
IDIOMES **faire son ~**○ to make a packet○; **compter pour du ~**○ to count for nothing; **vouloir le ~ et l'argent du ~**○ to want to have one's cake and eat it.

beurré○, **~e** /bœʀe/ *adj* (soûl) plastered○.

beurrer /bœʀe/ [1] *vtr* to butter [*pain, tartine*]; to grease [sth] with butter [*moule à gâteau*]; **une tartine de pain beurré** bread and butter.

beurrier /bœʀje/ *nm* butter dish.

beuverie /bœvʀi/ *nf* drinking session.

bévue /bevy/ *nf* blunder.

Beyrouth /beʀut/ **▶ 628** *nprm* Beirut.

biais /bjɛ/ **I** *nm inv* (moyen) way; **par le ~ de qn** through sb; **par le ~ de qch** by means of sth.
II de biais, en biais *loc adv* **couper une étoffe en ~** to cut material on the cross; **jeter des regards en ~ à qn** to cast sidelong glances at sb.

biaiser /bjɛze/ [1] *vi* to hedge.

bibelot /biblo/ *nm* ornament.

biberon /bibʀɔ̃/ *nm* (baby's) bottle GB, (nursing) bottle US; **nourrir au ~** to bottle-feed; **c'est l'heure du ~** it's time for his/her feed.

biberonner○ /bibʀɔne/ [1] *vi* to booze○, to drink.

bibine○ /bibin/ *nf* PEJ cheap wine, plonk○ GB.

bible /bibl/ *nf* bible; **la Bible** the Bible.

bibliographie /biblijɔɡʀafi/ *nf* bibliography.

bibliographique /biblijɔɡʀafik/ *adj* bibliographical.

bibliothécaire /biblijɔtekɛʀ/ **▶ 374** *nmf* librarian.

bibliothèque /biblijɔtɛk/ *nf* **1** (endroit, collection) library; **2** (meuble) bookcase.

biblique /biblik/ *adj* biblical.

bic® /bik/ *nm* biro®.

bicarbonate /bikaʀbɔnat/ *nm* CHIMIE bicarbonate.
■ **~ de soude** sodium bicarbonate.

bicentenaire /bisɑ̃tnɛʀ/ **I** *adj* two-hundred-year-old (*épith*); **être ~** to be two hundred years old.
II *nm* bicentenary GB, bicentennial US.

biceps /bisɛps/ *nm inv* biceps; **avoir des ~** to have muscular arms; **jouer des ~**○ to flex one's muscles.

biche /biʃ/ *nf* ZOOL doe; **ma ~**○ my pet GB, honey US.

bichlorure /biklɔʀyʀ/ *nm* dichloride.

bichonner○ /biʃɔne/ [1] *vtr* (dorloter) to pamper.

bicolore /bikɔlɔʀ/ *adj* [*drapeau*] two-coloured GB (*épith*); [*étoffe*] two-tone.

bicoque /bikɔk/ *nf* little house, dump○ PÉJ.

bicorne /bikɔʀn/ *nm* (chapeau) cocked hat.

bi-cross /bikʀɔs/ **▶ 329** *nm inv* (discipline, vélo) BMX.

bicyclette /bisiklɛt/ *nf* **1** (objet) bicycle, bike○; **à ~** [*aller, parcourir*] by bike; **un tour à ~** a bike ride; **aller au travail à ~** to cycle to work; **faire de la ~** to cycle; **2** (activité) cycling.

bidasse○ /bidas/ *nm* soldier.

bide○ /bid/ *nm* (échec) flop; **faire un ~** to be a flop.

bidet /bidɛ/ *nm* **1** (de salle de bains) bidet; **2**○ (cheval) nag.

bidon /bidɔ̃/ **I**○ *adj inv* [*compagnie, numéro*] bogus; [*excuse, histoire*] phoney; **chèque ~** dud cheque.
II *nm* **1** (récipient) (portatif) can; (baril) drum; (gourde) flask; **~ d'essence** (contenant) petrol can GB, gas can US; (contenu) can of petrol GB ou gas US; **~ de peinture** tin GB ou can of paint; **2**○ (ventre) stomach; **3**○ (bluff) **c'est du ~** it is a load of hogwash○.

bidonner○: **se bidonner** /bidɔne/ [1] *vpr* to laugh, to fall about○.

bidonville /bidɔ̃vil/ *nm* shanty town.

bidule○ /bidyl/ *nm* (objet) thingy○ GB, thingamajig○.

bief /bjɛf/ *nm* reach.

bielle /bjɛl/ *nf* connecting rod; **couler une ~** to run a big end; **j'ai coulé une ~** the big end has gone.

biélorusse /bjelorys/ ▶ 394⌋ *adj* Byelorussian.

Biélorussie /bjelorysi/ ▶ 232⌋ *nprf* Byelorussia.

bien /bjɛ̃/ **I** *adj inv* **1** (convenable) **être ~ dans un rôle** to be good in a part; **être ~ de sa personne** to be good-looking; **il n'y a rien de ~ ici** there's nothing of interest here; **voilà qui est ~** that's good; **ce n'est pas ~ de mentir** it's not nice to lie; **ce serait ~** it would be nice; **ça fait ~ d'aller à l'opéra**○ it's the done thing to go to the opera; **les roses font ~** the roses look nice; **2** (en bonne santé) well; **ne pas se sentir ~** not to feel well; **t'es pas ~**○! you're out of your mind○!; **3** (à l'aise) **je suis ~ dans ces bottes** these boots are comfortable; **on est ~ au soleil!** isn't it nice in the sun!; **je me trouve ~ ici** I like it here; **nous voilà ~!** IRON we' are in a fine mess!; **4**○ (de qualité) **un quartier ~** a nice district; **des gens ~** respectable people; **un type ~** a gentleman.

II *adv* **1** (correctement) GÉN well; [*fonctionner*] properly; [*interpréter*] correctly; **~ payé** well paid; **~ joué!** FIG well done!; **aller ~** [*personne*] to be well; [*affaires*] to go well; **ça s'est ~ passé** it went well; **la voiture ne marche pas ~** the car isn't running properly; **ni ~ ni mal** SO-SO; **parler (très) ~ le chinois** to speak (very) good Chinese; **il travaille ~** (élève) his work is good; (artisan) he does a good job; **il est ~ remis** (malade) he's made a good recovery ; **~ se tenir à table** to have good table manners; **~ employer son temps** to make good use of one's time; **j'ai cru ~ faire** I thought I was doing the right thing; **il fait ~ de partir** he's right to leave; **c'est ~ fait pour elle!** it serves her right!; **tu ferais ~ d'y aller** it would be a good idea for you to go there; **~ m'en a pris de refuser** it's a good thing I refused; **2** (complètement) [*arroser, décongeler, laver, mélanger, propre, cuit*] thoroughly; [*remplir, sécher, sec, fondu*] completely; [*lire, écouter, regarder*] carefully; **~ à droite** well over to the right; **~ devant** right at the front; **~ profiter d'une situation** to exploit a situation to the full; **3** (agréablement) [*présenté, situé*] well; [*s'habiller*] well, smartly; [*décoré, meublé*] tastefully; [*logé, installé, vivre*] comfortably; **femme ~ faite** shapely woman; **aller ~ à qn** [*couleur, style*] to suit sb; **se mettre ~ avec qn** to get on good terms with sb; **~ prendre une remarque** to take a remark in good part; **4** (hautement) [*aimable, triste*] very; [*apprécier, craindre*] very much; [*simple, vrai, certain, évident*] quite; **il s'est ~ mal comporté** he behaved really badly; **il y a ~ longtemps** a very long time ago; **merci ~** thank you very much; **tu as ~ raison** you're quite right; **c'est ~ dommage** it's a real pity; **~ rire** to have a good laugh; **c'est ~ promis?** is that a promise?; **c'est ~ compris?** is that clear?; **~ au contraire** on the contrary; **c'est ~ joli tout ça, mais** that's all very well, but; **~ mieux/moins/pire** much ou far better/less/worse; **~ trop laid/tard** much too ugly/late; **~ plus riche/cher** much ou far richer/more expensive; **~ plus, il la vole!** not only that, he also takes her money; **~ sûr** of course; **~ entendu** or **évidemment** naturally; **~ souvent** quite often; **5** (volontiers) **j'irais ~ à Bali** I wouldn't mind going to Bali; **je veux ~ t'aider** I don't mind helping you; **j'aimerais ~ essayer** I would love to try; **je le vois ~ habiter à Paris** I can just imagine him living in Paris; **6** (malgré tout) **il faut ~ le faire** it has to be done; **il faudra ~ s'y habituer** we'll just have to get used to it; **il finira ~ par se calmer** he'll calm down eventually; **7** (pour souligner) **ça prouve/montre ~ que** it just goes to prove/show that; **j'espère ~ que** I do hope that; **je sais/crois ~ que** I know/think that; **insiste ~** make sure you insist; **on verra ~** we'll see; **sache ~ que je n'accepterai jamais** let me tell you that I will never accept; **je m'en doutais ~!** I thought as much!; **je t'avais ~ dit de ne pas le manger!** I told you not to eat it!; **il le fait ~ lui,**

pourquoi pas moi? if he can do it, why can't I?; **veux-tu ~ faire ce que je te dis!** will you do as I tell you!; **tu peux très ~ le faire toi-même** you can easily do it yourself; **il se pourrait ~ qu'il pleuve** it might well rain; **que peut-il ~ faire à Paris?** what on earth can he be doing in Paris?; **8** (réellement) definitely; **c'est ~ lui/mon sac** it's definitely him/my bag, it's him/my bag all right○; **c'est ~ ce qu'il a dit** that's exactly what he said; **il ne s'agit pas d'une erreur, mais ~ de fraude** it's not a mistake, it's fraud; **c'est ~ ici qu'on vend les billets?** this is where you get tickets, isn't it?; **tu as ~ pris les clés?** are you sure you've got the keys?; **est-ce ~ nécessaire?** is it really necessary?; **c'est ~ lui!** it's just like him!; **voilà ~ la politique!** that's politics for you!; **c'est ~ le moment!** IRON great timing!; **c'est ~ le moment de partir!** IRON what a time to leave!; **9** (au moins) at least; **elle a ~ 40 ans** she's at least 40, she's a good 40 years old; **10** (beaucoup) **il y a ~ des années** a good many years ago; **~ des fois** often, many a time; **~ des gens** lots of people; **il s'est donné ~ du mal** he's gone to a lot or a great deal of trouble; **mon fils me donne ~ du souci** my son is a great worry to me; **avoir ~ de la chance** to be very lucky; **je te souhaite ~ du plaisir !** IRON I wish you joy!

III *nm* **1** (avantage) good; **pour le ~ du pays** for the good of the country; **pour le ~ de tous** for the general good; **pour ton ~** for your own good; **ce serait un ~ s'il** it would be a good thing; **sacrifier son propre ~ à celui d'autrui** to put others first; **le ~ et le mal** good and evil; **faire le ~** to do good; **ça fait du ~ aux enfants** it's good for the children; **ça leur fait du ~** it does them good; **mon repos m'a fait le plus grand ~** my rest did me a world of good; **grand ~ vous fasse!** IRON much good may it do you!; **vouloir le ~ de qn** to have sb's best interests at heart; **vouloir du ~ à qn** to wish sb well; **dire du ~ de qn** to speak well of sb; **on dit le plus grand ~ du musée** people speak very highly of the museum; **on a dit le plus grand ~ de toi** a lot of nice things were said about you; **parler en ~ de qn** to speak favourably GB of sb; **2** (possession) possession; **perdre tous ses ~s dans un incendie** to lose all one's possessions in a fire; **les ~s de ce monde** material possessions; **hériter des ~s paternels** to inherit one's father's estate; **dilapider son ~** to squander one's fortune; **des ~s considérables** substantial assets; **la santé est le plus précieux des ~s** you can't put a price on good health.

IV *excl* **~!** good!

V bien que *loc conj* although; **~ qu'il le sache** although he knows.

■ **~s de consommation** consumer goods; **~s d'équipement** capital goods; **~s d'équipement ménager** household goods; **~s fonciers** land ₵; **~s immobiliers** real estate ₵; **~s mobiliers** personal property ₵; **~s personnels** private property ₵; **~s publics** public property ₵.

IDIOMES **tout est ~ qui finit ~** PROV all's well that ends well PROV.

bien-être /bjɛ̃nɛtʀ/ *nm* **1** (sensation agréable) well-being; **2** (protection sociale) welfare; **3** (situation matérielle satisfaisante) comforts (*pl*).

bienfaisance /bjɛ̃fəzɑ̃s/ *nf* charity; **société de ~** charity; **soirée de ~** charity gala.

bienfaisant, ~e /bjɛ̃fəzɑ̃, ɑ̃t/ *adj* [*influence*] beneficial; [*personne*] beneficent.

bienfait /bjɛ̃fɛ/ *nm* **1** (acte généreux) kind deed; **c'est un ~ du ciel** it's a godsend; **2** (effet bénéfique) beneficial effect.

bienfaiteur, -trice /bjɛ̃fɛtœʀ, tʀis/ *nm,f* benefactor/benefactress.

bien-fondé /bjɛ̃fɔ̃de/ *nm* (d'idée) validity; (de demande) legitimacy.

bienheureux, -euse /bjɛ̃nœʀø, øz/ **I** *adj* blessed. **II** *nm,f* **les ~** the blessed.

bien-pensant, ~e, *mpl* ~s /bjɛ̃pɑ̃sɑ̃, ɑ̃t/ *adj* [*personne*] right-thinking; PÉJ self-righteous.

bienséance /bjɛ̃seɑ̃s/ *nf* propriety; **les règles de la ~** the rules of polite society.

bientôt /bjɛ̃to/ *adv* soon; **je reviens ~** I'll be back soon; **à ~** see you soon; **à ~ le plaisir de vous lire** I look forward to hearing from you soon; **on est ~ arrivés?** are we nearly there?

bienveillance /bjɛ̃vɛjɑ̃s/ *nf* benevolence (**envers** to); **avec ~** [*regarder, parler, sourire*] benevolently; **par ~ out of kindness; étudier une requête avec ~** to look at a request favourably^{GB}; **je sollicite de votre haute ~** FML may I respectfully request.

bienveillant, ~e /bjɛ̃vɛjɑ̃, ɑ̃t/ *adj* benevolent.

bienvenu, ~e¹ /bjɛ̃vəny/ **I** *adj* welcome.
II *nm,f* être le **~** to be welcome; **soyez la ~e** welcome!

bienvenue² /bjɛ̃vəny/ *nf* welcome (**à, dans** to); **~ dans notre pays** welcome to our country; **souhaiter la ~ à qn** to welcome sb; **en signe de ~** in welcome.

bière /bjɛʀ/ *nf* **1** (boisson) beer; **de la ~** beer; **deux ~s** two beers; **~ (à la) pression** or **en fût** C draught GB ou draft US beer; **2** (cercueil) coffin, casket US; **mettre qn en ~** to lay sb in a coffin.
■ **~ blonde** lager; **~ brune** ~ stout; **~ rousse** brown ale.

biffer /bife/ [1] *vtr* to cross out.

biffure /bifyʀ/ *nf* crossing-out GB, erasure US.

bifteck /biftɛk/ *nm* steak; **~ haché** extra lean minced beef GB, chopped meat US.
IDIOMES **gagner son ~**[○] to earn a living ou crust GB; **défendre son ~**[○] to look out for number one[○].

bifurcation /bifyʀkasjɔ̃/ *nf* (de voie) fork.

bifurquer /bifyʀke/ [1] *vi* **1** [*route, voie ferrée*] to fork; **2** [*automobiliste*] to turn off; **3** (dans ses études, sa carrière) to change tack.

bigame /bigam/ **I** *adj* bigamous.
II *nmf* bigamist.

bigamie /bigami/ *nf* bigamy.

bigarré, ~e /bigaʀe/ *adj* [*tissu*] multicoloured^{GB}; [*foule, société*] colourful^{GB}.

bigleux[○], **-euse** /biglø, øz/ *adj* PEJ poor-sighted; **complètement ~** as blind as a bat[○].

bigorneau, *pl* **~x** /bigoʀno/ *nm* winkle.

bigot, ~e /bigo, ɔt/ *nm,f* religious zealot.

bigoudi /bigudi/ *nm* roller.

bigrement^{○†} /bigʀəmɑ̃/ *adv* jolly[○] GB, extremely.

bijou, *pl* **~x** /biʒu/ *nm* piece of jewellery GB ou jewelry US; (de très grande valeur) jewel; **~x en or** gold jewellery GB ou jewelry US; **leur maison est un vrai ~** their house is an absolute gem; **un petit ~ mécanique** a marvel of engineering.

bijouterie /biʒutʀi/ ▶374│ *nf* **1** (magasin) jeweller's GB, jewellery shop GB, jewelry store US; **2** (art) jewellery GB, jewelry US; **3** (commerce) jewellery GB ou jewelry US trade.

bijoutier, -ière /biʒutje, ɛʀ/ ▶374│ *nm,f* jeweller^{GB}.

bilan /bilɑ̃/ *nm* **1** (financier) balance sheet; **établir un ~** to draw up a balance sheet; **déposer son ~** to file a petition in bankruptcy; **2** (aboutissement) outcome; **3** (de catastrophe, d'accident) toll; '**accident de voiture, ~: deux morts**' 'two killed in a car accident'; **4** (évaluation) assessment; **faire** or **dresser le ~ de qch** to assess sth; **quel est le ~ de l'année?** how did the year turn out?; **~ de santé** check-up; **5** (compte rendu) report.

bilatéral, ~e, *mpl* **-aux** /bilateʀal, o/ *adj* [*négociations, contrat*] bilateral; **stationnement ~** parking on both sides of the street.

bilboquet /bilbɔkɛ/ ▶329│ *nm* cup-and-ball.

bile /bil/ *nf* bile.
IDIOMES **se faire de la ~**[○] to worry (**pour qch** about sth); **déverser sa ~**[○] to vent one's spleen.

biler: se biler[○] /bile/ [1] *vpr* to worry (**pour qch** about sth).

bilieux, -ieuse /biljø, øz/ *nm,f* (personne colérique) irritable person.

bilingue /bilɛ̃g/ *adj* bilingual.

bilinguisme /bilɛ̃gɥism/ *nm* bilingualism.

billard /bijaʀ/ ▶329│ *nm* (jeu) billiards (+ *v sg*); (table) billiard table.
■ **~ américain** pool; **~ anglais** snooker.
IDIOMES **passer sur le ~**[○] to have an operation.

bille /bij/ *nf* **1** ▶329│ (d'enfant) marble; (au billard) ball; **2** TECH ball; **déodorant à ~** roll-on deodorant.
IDIOMES **reprendre** or **retirer ses ~s**[○] to pull out; **placer ses ~s**[○] to stake out one's position; **foncer ~ en tête**[○] to go blindly ahead.

billet /bijɛ/ *nm* **1** (argent) (bank)note, bill US; **~ de 100 francs** 100-franc note; **faux ~** forged bill; **2** (de transport, d'admission) ticket.
■ **~ de banque** banknote, bank bill US; **~ doux** love letter; **~ vert**[○] dollar, greenback[○] US.
IDIOMES **je te fiche mon ~ que**[○] I bet you anything that.

billetterie /bijɛtʀi/ *nf* (de billets de banque) cash dispenser.

billettiste /bijɛtist/ ▶374│ *nmf* **1** PRESSE writer of short articles; **2** (employé) ticket clerk.

billevesées /bilvəze, bijvəze/ *nfpl* nonsense ¢.

billion /biljɔ̃/ ▶399│ *nm* (mille milliards) billion GB, trillion US.

billot /bijo/ *nm* block.

bimbeloterie /bɛ̃blɔtʀi/ *nf* (objets) knick-knacks (*pl*).

bimensuel /bimɑ̃sɥɛl/ *nm* (journal) fortnightly magazine GB, semimonthly US.

bimoteur /bimɔtœʀ/ *nm* (avion) twin-engined plane.

binaire /binɛʀ/ *adj* binary.

biner /bine/ [1] *vtr* to hoe.

binette /binɛt/ *nf* (outil) hoe.

binoclard[○], **~e** /binɔklaʀ, aʀd/ *nm,f* PEJ four-eyes[○].

binocle /binɔkl/ **I** *nm* pince-nez.
II binocles[○] *nfpl* specs[○], glasses.

binôme /binom/ *nm* MATH binomial.

bio¹ /bjo/ *préf* bio; **~ luminescence** bioluminescence.

bio² /bjo/ **I** *adj inv* (naturel) **aliments ~** health foods; **produits ~** organic produce ¢; **avoir des goûts ~** to be a health food freak; **yaourt ~** bio yoghurt.
II *nf* (biographie) biography.

biochimie /bjoʃimi/ *nf* biochemistry.

biochimique /bjoʃimik/ *adj* biochemical.

biochimiste /bjoʃimist/ ▶374│ *nmf* biochemist.

biodégradable /bjodegʀadabl/ *adj* biodegradable.

bioénergie /bjoenɛʀʒi/ *nf* bioenergetics (+ *v sg*).

biographe /bjɔgʀaf/ *nmf* biographer.

biographie /bjɔgʀafi/ *nf* biography.

biographique /bjɔgʀafik/ *adj* biographical.

biologie /bjɔlɔʒi/ *nf* biology.

biologique /bjɔlɔʒik/ *adj* **1** BIOL biological; **2** [*ferme, produit*] organic.

biologiste /bjɔlɔʒist/ ▶374│ *nmf* biologist.

bionique /bjɔnik/ *nf* bionics (+ *v sg*).

biophysique /bjofisik/ *nf* biophysics (+ *v sg*).

bip /bip/ *nm* (son) beep; **~ sonore** tone.

bipartisme /bipaʀtism/ *nm* two-party system.

bipède /bipɛd/ *nm* biped.

biphasé, ~e /bifaze/ *adj* two-phase.

biplace /biplas/ *adj, nm* two-seater.

biplan /biplɑ̃/ *nm* (avion) biplane.

bique[○] /bik/ *nf* **1** (chèvre) nanny goat; **2** (femme) PEJ **une vieille ~** an old bag[○].

biquet[○] /bikɛ/ *nm* (chevreau) kid; **mon ~** sweetheart[○].

biquette[○] /bikɛt/ *nf* (jeune chèvre) young female goat; **ma ~** sweetheart[○].

biréacteur /biʀeaktœʀ/ *nm* twin-engined jet.

birman, ~e /biʀmɑ̃, an/ ▶338│, **394**│ **I** *adj* Burmese.
II *nm* LING Burmese.

Birmanie /biʀmani/ ▶232│ *nprf* Burma.

bis¹ /bis/ **I** *adv* **1** (dans une adresse) **15** ~ 15 bis; **2** MUS (indication) bis.

II *nm inv* **l'orchestre a joué trois** ~ the orchestra did three encores.

bis², **~e¹** /bi, biz/ ▶141| *adj* [*couleur*] greyish GB ou grayish US brown.

bisaïeul, **~e** /bizajœl/ *nm,f* great-grandfather/ -grandmother.

bisannuel, **-elle** /bizanɥɛl/ *adj* biennial.

biscornu, **~e** /biskɔRny/ *adj* quirky.

biscotte /biskɔt/ *nf* continental toast.

biscuit /biskɥi/ *nm* (gâteau sec) biscuit GB, cookie US. ■ ~ **à la cuillère** sponge GB ou lady US finger; ~ **salé** cracker; ~ **de Savoie** sponge cake.

bise² /biz/ **I** *adj f* ▶ **bis²**.

II *nf* **1**° (baiser) kiss; **faire la** ~ **à qn** to kiss sb on the cheeks; **2** (vent) North wind.

biseau, *pl* **~x** /bizo/ *nm* **1** (bord) bevel (edge); **tailler en** ~ to bevel; **glace en** ~ bevelled GB mirror; **2** (outil) bevel; **tailler au** ~ to bevel.

biseauter /bizote/ [1] *vtr* to bevel; **cartes biseautées** marked cards.

bisexuel, **-elle** /bisɛksɥɛl/ *adj*, *nm,f* bisexual.

bison /bizɔ̃/ *nm* (d'Europe) bison; (d'Amérique) buffalo.

bisou° /bizu/ *nm* kiss.

bisquer° /biske/ [1] *vi* to be furious.

bissectrice /bisɛktRis/ *nf* bisector.

bissextile /bisɛkstil/ *adj* **année** ~ leap year.

bistouri /bisturi/ *nm* bistoury.

bistre /bistR/ ▶141| *adj* [*couleur*] yellowish brown; [*peau*] swarthy.

bistro(t)° /bistRo/ *nm* bistro, café.

bit /bit/ *nm* bit.

BIT /beite/ *nm* (*abbr* = **Bureau international du travail**) ILO.

bitoniau° /bitonjo/ *nm* whatsit°.

bitume /bitym/ *nm* **1** CHIMIE bitumen; **2** (de route) asphalt.

bitumer /bityme/ [1] *vtr* to asphalt [*route*].

biunivoque /biynivɔk/ *adj* MATH one-to-one.

bivouaquer /bivwake/ [1] *vi* to bivouac.

bizarre /bizaR/ *adj* [*objet*, *parole*, *acte*] odd; **comme c'est** ~ how odd!; [*personne*] strange.

bizarrement /bizaRmɑ̃/ *adv* strangely.

bizarrerie /bizaRRi/ *nf* **1** (caractère étrange) strangeness (**de** of); **2** (chose étrange) quirk; **une** ~ **de l'Histoire** a strange turn of history; **une** ~ **de la langue** a peculiarity of the language.

bizut(h) /bizy/ *nm* students' slang **1** (étudiant) fresher° GB, freshman US; **2** (novice) newcomer, rookie°.

bizuter /bizyte/ [1] *vtr* students' slang to rag°, to haze° US [*étudiant*]; (brimer) to bully [*nouveau*].

blabla° /blabla/ *nm inv* waffle° GB, hogwash° US.

blafard, **~e** /blafaR, aRd/ *adj* pale.

blague /blag/ *nf* **1**° (plaisanterie, histoire) joke; (mensonge) fib°; **c'est pas des** ~s I'm not kidding°; **ne me raconte pas de** ~s tell me the truth; **sans** ~! no kidding°!; ~ **à part** seriously, joking apart; **2**° (farce) trick; **faire une** ~ **à qn** to play a trick on sb; **3** (tabatière) ~ (**à tabac**) tobacco pouch.

blaguer° /blage/ [1] *vi* (plaisanter) to joke; **il dit ça pour** ~ he's kidding°.

blagueur°, **-euse** /blagœR, øz/ *nm,f* joker.

blaireau, *pl* **~x** /blɛRo/ *nm* **1** (animal) badger; **2** (pour rasage) shaving brush.

blâme /blɑm/ *nm* **1** (désapprobation) criticism; **2** (sanction) official warning.

blâmer /blɑme/ [1] *vtr* (désapprouver) to criticize; **on ne peut pas le** ~ you can't blame him.

blanc, **blanche¹** /blɑ̃, blɑ̃ʃ/ ▶141| **I** *adj* **1** (couleur) white; ~ **cassé** off-white; ~ **crémeux** cream; ~ **laiteux** milk white; ~ **de peur** white with fear; **2** (occidental) white; **homme/quartier** ~ white man/district; **3** (innocent) **il n'est pas** ~ **dans l'histoire** he was certainly mixed up in it; **ne pas être** ~ to have

a less than spotless reputation; **4** (vierge) blank; **page/feuille blanche** blank page/sheet.

II *adv* **il gèle** ~ there's a hoarfrost.

III *nm* **1** (couleur) white; **2** (peinture) white paint; **peindre en** ~ to paint [sth] white [*mur*, *meuble*]; **3** (linge) household linen; **4** (vêtements) white; **être habillé en** ~ to be dressed in white; **5** CULIN (de volaille) white meat; (de poireau) white part; (d'œuf) white; **un** ~ **de poulet** a chicken breast; **6** (vin) white wine; (verre de vin) glass of white wine; **7** (espace entre des mots) (volontaire) blank; (involontaire) gap; **laisser en** ~ to leave [sth] blank [*nom*, *adresse*]; **8**° (liquide correcteur) correction fluid; **9** (temps mort) lull; **10** (dans la tête) **j'ai eu un** ~ my mind went blank; **11** (en cosmétique) (poudre) white powder; **12** BOT (moisissure) powdery mildew; **13** MIL **coup à** ~ blank shot; **charger à** ~ to load [sth] with blanks.

IV blancs *nmpl* (aux échecs, aux dames) white (*sg*); **je prends les** ~**s** I'll be white.

■ ~ **de chaux** whitewash; ~ **de l'œil** white of the eye; ~ **d'œuf** egg white.

IDIOMES **c'est écrit noir sur** ~ it's there in black and white; **quand l'un dit** ~, **l'autre dit noir** they can never agree on anything; **avec lui/elle, c'est (toujours) tout** ~ **ou tout noir** he/she sees everything in black-and-white terms; **se regarder dans le** ~ **des yeux** to gaze into each other's eyes.

Blanc, **Blanche** /blɑ̃, blɑ̃ʃ/ *nm,f* white man/woman.

blanc-bec, *pl* **blancs-becs** /blɑ̃bɛk/ *nm* PEJ greenhorn.

blanchâtre /blɑ̃ʃɑtR/ ▶141| *adj* whitish.

blanche² /blɑ̃ʃ/ **I** *adj f* ▶ **blanc I**.

II *nf* MUS minim GB, half note US.

Blanche-Neige /blɑ̃ʃnɛʒ/ *npr* LITTÉRAT Snow White.

blancheur /blɑ̃ʃœR/ *nf* (couleur) whiteness.

blanchiment /blɑ̃ʃimɑ̃/ *nm* **1** (d'argent) laundering; **2** (de tissu, pâte à papier) bleaching.

blanchir /blɑ̃ʃiR/ [3] **I** *vtr* **1** (rendre blanc) to whiten [*chaussures*, *surface*]; to light up [*ciel*, *route*]; to bleach [*textile*, *pâte à papier*, *farine*]; to refine [*sucre*]; to blanch [*légumes*, *viande*, *amandes*]; ~ (**à la chaux**) to whitewash [*mur*, *plafond*]; **donner son linge à** ~ to send one's linen to the laundry; **2** (disculper) to clear [*accusé*, *nom*] (**de** of); **3** to launder [*argent sale*].

II *vi* [*cheveux*] to turn grey GB ou gray US; [*ciel*] to grow light; ~ **de rage** to go white with rage; **faire** ~ CULIN to blanch [*légumes*, *viande*, *amandes*].

III se blanchir *vpr* (se disculper) to clear oneself (**de** of; **auprès de** in the eyes of).

blanchissage /blɑ̃ʃisaʒ/ *nm* **service de** ~ laundry service.

blanchissant, **~e** /blɑ̃ʃisɑ̃, ɑ̃t/ *adj* bleaching.

blanchisserie /blɑ̃ʃisRi/ ▶374| *nf* laundry.

blanchisseur /blɑ̃ʃisœR/ ▶374|, 374| *nm* (personne) laundry worker; (magasin) laundry.

blanchisseuse /blɑ̃ʃisøz/ *nf* laundress.

blanc-seing, *pl* **blancs-seings** /blɑ̃sɛ̃/ *nm* **donner un** ~ **à qn** to give sb carte blanche.

blanquette /blɑ̃kɛt/ *nf* ~ **de veau** blanquette of veal.

blasé, **~e** /blaze/ **I** *adj* blasé; **être** ~ **de qch** to be blasé about sth.

II *nm,f* blasé person; **jouer les** ~**s**, **faire le** ~ to affect a blasé attitude.

blason /blazɔ̃/ *nm* (armoiries) coat of arms, blazon SPÉC. IDIOMES **redorer son** ~ to restore one's reputation.

blasphémateur, **-trice** /blasfematœR, tRis/ *nm,f* blasphemer.

blasphématoire /blasfematwaR/ *adj* blasphemous.

blasphème /blasfɛm/ *nm* blasphemy ₵.

blasphémer /blasfeme/ [1] *vi* to blaspheme.

blatte /blat/ *nf* cockroach.

blé /ble/ *nm* (céréale) wheat; ~ **en herbe** wheat in the blade.

■ ~ **noir** buckwheat.

bled° /blɛd/ *nm* village.

blême /blɛm/ *adj* pale.

blêmir /blemiʀ/ [3] *vi* [*personne, visage*] to pale; **~ de peur/rage** to go white with fear/rage.

blennorragie /blenɔʀaʒi/ ► 196 | *nf* gonorrhea.

blessant, ~e /blesã, ãt/ *adj* [*propos*] cutting.

blessé, ~e /blese/ *nm,f* (par accident) injured man/woman; (par arme) wounded man/woman; **les ~s** GÉN the injured; MIL the wounded; **l'explosion a fait 20 ~s** 20 people were injured in the explosion; **il n'y a pas de ~s** nobody has been hurt; MIL there are no casualties.
■ **~ de guerre** person wounded in the war; **les ~s de guerre** the war wounded; **~ de la route** road accident victim.

blesser /blese/ [1] I *vtr* 1 (par accident) to hurt; (dans un conflit armé) to wound; **il a été blessé à la tête** he sustained head injuries; **~ qn d'un coup de couteau** to stab sb; **~ qn d'un coup de revolver** to shoot sb (with a gun); **il a été blessé par balle** he received a bullet wound; **2** (offenser) to hurt [*personne, amour-propre*]; **il s'est senti blessé** he felt hurt; **~ qn au vif** to cut sb to the quick.
II **se blesser** *vpr* **je me suis blessé au bras en tombant** I fell and hurt my arm.

blessure /blesyʀ/ *nf* (lésion) injury; (plaie) wound; **~ légère/grave** minor/serious injury ou wound.

blet, blette[1] /blɛ, blɛt/ *adj* overripe.

blette[2] /blɛt/ *nf* Swiss chard.

bleu, ~e /blø/ I *adj* 1 ► 141 | (couleur) blue; **des yeux ~s** blue eyes; **~ vert** blue-green; **~ ardoise** slate blue; **~ canard** peacock blue; **~ marine** navy blue; **~ noir** blue-black; **~ nuit** midnight blue; **~ outremer** ultramarine; **~ pétrole** petrol-blue; **~ roi** royal blue; **~ turquoise** turquoise blue; **~ de peur** white with fear; **2** [*entrecôte, viande*] very rare.
II *nm* 1 ► 141 | (couleur) blue; **2** (ecchymose) bruise; **se faire un ~** to bruise oneself; **3** (vêtement) **~ (de travail)** (combinaison) overalls (*pl*); (veste et pantalon) workman's blue cotton jacket and trousers; **4** (fromage) blue cheese; **5**° (nouvelle recrue) soldiers' slang rookie°; (débutant) beginner.
IDIOMES **avoir une peur ~e de qch** to be scared stiff° of sth.

bleuâtre /bløatʀ/ ► 141 | *adj* bluish.

bleuet /bløɛ/ *nm* 1 BOT cornflower; 2 C (myrtille) blueberry, bilberry.

bleuir /bløiʀ/ [3] I *vtr* to turn [sth] blue.
II *vi* to turn blue.

bleuté, ~e /bløte/ ► 141 | *adj* bluish.

blindage /blɛ̃daʒ/ *nm* armour^GB plating, security reinforcement.

blindé, ~e /blɛ̃de/ I *adj* 1 [*division, unité, corps*] armoured^GB; 2 (renforcé) **porte ~e** security door.
II *nm* armoured^GB vehicle.

blinder /blɛ̃de/ [1] *vtr* **~ une porte** to put security fittings on a door; **~ un véhicule** to armour-plate^GB a vehicle.

blinquer /blɛ̃ke/ [1] *vi* B (briller) to shine; **faire ~ to** polish.

blizzard /blizaʀ/ *nm* blizzard.

bloc /blɔk/ I *nm* 1 (masse solide) block (**de** of); **se retourner tout d'un ~** to pivot round GB ou around US; 2 (de personnes) group (**de** of); POL bloc; **faire ~ to** side together; **faire ~ contre qn** (s'unir) to unite against sb; (être unis) to be united against sb; 3 (pour écrire) notepad; **~ de papier à lettres** writing pad; 4 (d'actions, de titres) block; 5 ORDINAT block.
II **à bloc** *loc adv* [*serrer, visser, fermer*] tightly; [*charger, gonfler*] fully.
III **en bloc** *loc adv* (entièrement) outright.
■ **~ de départ** starting block; **~ opératoire** surgical unit.

blocage /blɔkaʒ/ *nm* (de route, véhicule, marchandise) blocking; **~ des vins dans le port** blockade of wines in the port; **~ de la vente des armes** ban on sales of arms; (situation de) **~ deadlock; ~ des prix/**

salaires price/wage freeze; **faire un ~ mental** to have a mental block.

bloc-note, *pl* **blocs-notes** /blɔknɔt/ *nm* notepad.

blocus /blɔkys/ *nm inv* blockade.

blond, ~e[1] /blɔ̃, ɔ̃d/ ► 141 | I *adj* [*cheveux, barbe*] fair; [*personne*] fair-haired; [*caramel, épi*] golden; [*tabac*] light; **cigarette ~e** Virginia tobacco cigarette; **nos chères têtes ~es** our little darlings.
II *nm,f* (femme) blonde GB, blond US; (homme) blond; ► **faux**[1].

blonde[2] /blɔ̃d/ I *adj f* ► **blond** I.
II *nf* 1 (cigarette) Virginia tobacco cigarette; 2 (bière) lager.

blondinet, -ette /blɔ̃dinɛ, ɛt/ *nm,f* fair-haired boy/girl.

blondir /blɔ̃diʀ/ [3] *vi* [*cheveux, personne*] to go blonde GB ou blond US; [*épi, champ*] to turn golden; **faire ~ qch** CULIN to brown [sth] lightly [*beurre, caramel*].

bloqué, ~e /blɔke/ I *pp* ► **bloquer**.
II *pp adj* 1 (obstrué) blocked; **avoir les reins ~s** to have a blockage in the kidneys; 2 (immobilisé) [*mécanisme, porte*] jammed; **elle/la voiture est ~e** she/the car is stuck; **~ par la neige** snowbound; [*fonds, compte*] frozen; **il a le dos ~** his back has seized up; 3 FIG **être ~** [*activité, carrière, négociations*] to be at a standstill; [*situation*] to be deadlocked; 4 (mentalement) **être ~** to have a (mental) block (**sur** about).

bloquer /blɔke/ [1] I *vtr* 1 (obstruer) to block [*route, entrée, porte*]; MIL to blockade [*ville, port*]; **~ la route** LIT to block the road; FIG to block the way; 2 (coincer) (accidentellement) to jam [*mécanisme, porte*]; (volontairement) to lock [*volant*]; to wedge [*porte*]; to secure [*écrou*]; 3 (immobiliser) to stop [*véhicule, voyageur, circulation, marchandise*]; SPORT to catch [*ballon*]; 4 ÉCON to freeze [*compte, salaires, crédit, dépenses, prix*]; to stop [*chèque*]; **~ des capitaux** to lock up capital; 5 (enrayer) to stop [*projet, contrat*]; to prevent [*ovulation*]; 6 (grouper) to lump [*sth*] together [*heures, jours, personnes*]; to bulk [*commandes*].
II *vi* 1 **il y a quelque chose qui bloque** something is jamming; 2° B students' slang (étudier) to swot° GB, to bone up° US.
III **se bloquer** *vpr* 1 [*frein, mécanisme, porte*] to jam; [*volant, roue*] to lock; 2 [*personne*] to retreat.

bloqueur, -euse /blɔkœʀ, øz/ *nm,f* B students' slang (étudiant zélé) swot° GB, grind° US.

blottir: se blottir /blɔtiʀ/ [3] *vpr* **se ~ contre qn/qch** (par affection) to snuggle up against sb/sth; (par peur, froid) to huddle up against sb/sth; **se ~ dans les bras de qn** to huddle up in sb's arms; **blotti contre mon épaule** buried in my shoulder; **blotti au pied de la montagne** nestled at the foot of the mountain.

blousant, ~e /bluzã, ãt/ *adj* [*robe, chemisier*] full.

blouse /bluz/ *nf* 1 (tablier) overall; **~ blanche** white coat; 2 (chemisier) blouse; 3 (de paysan) smock.

blouson /bluzɔ̃/ *nm* blouson.
■ **~ d'aviateur** bomber jacket; **~ noir** ~ rocker.

blue-jean, *pl* **~s** /bludʒin/ *nm* jeans (*pl*).

bluet /blyɛ/ *nm* cornflower.

bluffer° /blœfe/ [1] *vtr, vi* to bluff.

BN /been/ *nf* (*abbr* = **Bibliothèque nationale**) national library in Paris.

boa /bɔa/ *nm* (serpent, parure) boa.

bob /bɔb/ *nm* (chapeau) (sailor's) sunhat.

bobard° /bɔbaʀ/ *nm* fib°, tall story.

bobine /bɔbin/ *nf* 1 (de fil, câble, film) reel; (de métier à tisser) bobbin; (de machine à écrire) spool; 2 ÉLECTROTECH coil.

bobo° /bobo/ *nm* BABY TALK 1 (douleur physique) pain; **se faire ~** to hurt oneself; **j'ai** ou **ça fait ~** it hurts; 2 (petite plaie) scratch.

bobsleigh /bɔbslɛg/ ► 329 | *nm* 1 (engin) bobsleigh, bobsled US; 2 (activité) bobsleighing.

bocage /bɔkaʒ/ *nm* hedged farmland.

bocal, *pl* **-aux** /bɔkal, o/ *nm* 1 (récipient) jar; **mettre en bocaux** to preserve; 2 (aquarium) (fish)bowl.

■ **~ gradué** measuring jug.

bock /bɔk/ *nm* **1** (chope) beer glass; **2** (bière) glass of beer.

bœuf /bœf, *pl* bø/ *nm* **1** (animal) (de boucherie) bullock GB, steer US; (de trait) ox; **2** (viande) beef; **3**° MUS jam (session); **faire un ~**° LIT to have a jam; FIG to be a great success.

■ **~ gros sel** boiled beef; **~ mode** braised beef.

IDIOMES **qui vole un œuf vole un ~** PROV once a thief, always a thief; **fort comme un ~**° as strong as an ox; **souffler comme un ~**° to huff and puff; **faire un effet ~**° to make a fantastic° impression.

bof° /bɔf/ *excl* **'tu aimes la soupe?'—'~, pas vraiment!'** 'do you like soup?'—'hmm, not particularly'; **'tu préfères la mer ou la montagne?'—'~!'** 'which do you prefer the sea or the mountains?'—'I don't mind'.

bogue /bɔg/ *nf* ORDINAT bug.

bohème /bɔɛm/ I *adj* [*personne, caractère*] bohemian. II *nf* (milieu artiste) **la ~** bohemia; **vie de ~** bohemian lifestyle.

bohémien, -ienne /bɔemjɛ̃, ɛn/ *nm,f* **1** (tzigane) Bohemian, Romany; **2** (vagabond) tramp.

boire[1] /bwaʀ/ [70] I *vtr* **1** (consommer) [*personne*] to drink; **~ dans un verre** to drink out of a glass; **ce vin bon à ~** this wine is ready to drink; **il m'a fait ~** he got me drunk; **allons ~ un verre** let's go for a drink; **il y a à ~ et à manger dans leur théorie** FIG there's both good and bad in their theory; **2** (absorber) [*plante*] to drink; [*papier, buvard, moquette*] to soak [sth] up [*liquide*].
II **se boire** *vpr* **ce vin se boit frais** this wine should be drunk chilled; **ce porto se boit bien** this port is very drinkable.
IDIOMES **~ comme un trou**° to drink like a fish°; **qui a bu boira** PROV once a drinker, always a drinker.

boire[2] /bwaʀ/ *nm* drink; **le ~ et le manger** food and drink; **il en a perdu le ~ et le manger** FIG it has taken over his whole life.

bois /bwa/ I *nm inv* **1** (lieu) wood; **2** (matière) wood; **de chêne** oak; **c'est en ~?** is it made of wood?; **~ massif** solid wood; **table en ~** wooden table; **travailler le ~** to work in wood; **~ de construction** timber; ▶ **petit**; **3** ART (gravure sur) **~** woodcut.
II *nmpl* **1** ZOOL (de cerf) antlers; **2** MUS **les ~** (dans un orchestre) the woodwind section.

■ **~ aggloméré** chipboard; **~ de chauffage** firewood; **~ mort** firewood; **~ de placage** wood veneer; **~ de rose** rosewood.

IDIOMES **être de ~** to be insensitive; **ne pas être de ~** to be only human; **il va voir de quel ~ je me chauffe**° I'll show him; **faire feu** or **flèche de tout ~** to turn anything to good account.

boisé, ~e /bwaze/ *adj* [*terrain*] wooded; **dans les régions ~es** in the woodlands.

boisement /bwazmɑ̃/ *nm* afforestation.

boiser /bwaze/ [1] *vtr* (planter) to plant [sth] with trees [*terrain*].

boiserie /bwazʀi/ *nf* (lambris) **~(s)** panelling°GB ℂ.

boisson /bwasɔ̃/ *nf* drink; **~ alcoolisée/non alcoolisée** alcoholic/soft drink; **être pris de ~** to be under the influence.

boîte /bwat/ *nf* **1** GÉN box; (en métal) tin; (de conserve) tin GB, can; **petits pois en ~** tinned peas GB, canned peas; **mettre des fruits en ~** to can fruit; **mise en ~** IND canning ℂ; **2**° (cabaret) nightclub; **aller** or **sortir en ~** (une fois) to go out to a nightclub; (d'habitude) to go clubbing; **3**° (entreprise) firm; (bureau) office; (école) school.

■ **~ d'allumettes** (pleine) box of matches; (vide) matchbox; **~ automatique** AUT automatic gearbox GB ou transmission; **~ de conserve** tin GB, can; **~ de couleurs** ART paint box; **~ crânienne** ANAT cranium; **~ à gants** AUT glove compartment; **~ à** or **aux lettres** POSTES post box GB, mailbox US; FIG (personne) go-between; (adresse fictive) accommodation address; **~ à** or **aux lettres électronique** electronic mailbox; **~ à malice** bag of tricks; **~ à**

musique MUS musical box GB, music box US; **~ noire** AVIAT black box; **~ de nuit** nightclub; **~ à ordures** (d'intérieur) rubbish bin GB, garbage can US; **~ à outils** toolbox; **~ postale, BP** PO Box; **~ de raccordement** junction box; **~ de vitesses** (**automatique**/**mécanique**) (automatic/manual) gearbox.

IDIOMES **mettre qn en ~**° to tease sb.

boiter /bwate/ [1] *vi* [*personne*] to limp; [*meuble*] to wobble; [*raisonnement*] to be shaky; [*phrase*] (incorrecte) to be badly put together; (maladroite) to be clumsy.

boiteux, -euse /bwatø, øz/ I *adj* **1** [*personne*] lame; [*meuble*] wobbly; **2** [*raisonnement, alliance, paix*] shaky; [*vers*] lame.
II *nm,f* lame person.

boîtier /bwatje/ *nm* GÉN case; (d'appareil photo) body; (de téléphone) casing.

boitiller /bwatije/ [1] *vi* to limp slightly.

bol /bɔl/ *nm* **1** (récipient, contenu) bowl; **un ~ de café** a bowl of coffee; **2**° (chance) luck; **coup de ~** stroke of luck; **avoir du ~** to be lucky.
■ **~ d'air** breath of fresh air.

bolée /bɔle/ *nf* **~ de cidre** bowl of cider.

bolet /bɔlɛ/ *nm* boletus.

bolide /bɔlid/ *nm* (véhicule) high-powered car; **comme un ~** at high speed; **passer comme un ~** to shoot past.

bolivien, -ienne /bɔlivjɛ̃, ɛn/ [▶ 394] *adj* Bolivian.

bolle° /bɔl/ *nf* C (personne intelligente) brain°.

bolognaise /bɔlɔɲɛz/ *adj inv* [*spaghetti*] bolognese (*épith, après n*) GB, with meat sauce (*après n*) US.

bombage /bɔ̃baʒ/ *nm* **1** (action) graffiti spraying; **2** (résultat) sprayed graffiti.

bombance /bɔ̃bɑ̃s/ *nf* **faire ~** to have a feast.

bombarde /bɔ̃baʀd/ *nf* **1** HIST MIL bombard; **2** MUS (bois) bombardon; (jeu d'orgue) bombarde.

bombardement /bɔ̃baʀdəmɑ̃/ *nm* **1** MIL GÉN bombardment; (avec des bombes) bombing; (d'artillerie) shelling ℂ; **~ aérien** air raid; **2** (jet) (de projectiles) pelting; (de questions, critiques) bombardment; **être soumis à un ~ de critiques** to get bombarded with criticism.

bombarder /bɔ̃baʀde/ [1] *vtr* **1** MIL GÉN to bombard; (avec des bombes) to bomb; (avec des obus) to shell; **2** (harceler) **~ qn de tomates** to pelt sb with tomatoes; **~ qn de questions** to bombard sb with questions; **~ qn de coups de fil/lettres** to inundate sb with phone calls/letters; **3** PHYS to bombard; **4**° (nommer) **~ qn à un poste** to catapult sb into a job.

bombardier /bɔ̃baʀdje/ *nm* **1** (avion) bomber; **2** (aviateur) bombardier.

bombe /bɔ̃b/ *nf* **1** MIL bomb; **~ artisanale** homemade bomb; **attaque/attentat à la ~** bomb attack; **faire l'effet d'une ~** to come as a bombshell; **2** (atomiseur) **~** (aérosol) spray; **~ de peinture** paint spray; **3**° (coiffure) riding hat.

■ **~ A** A-bomb; **~ atomique** atomic bomb; **~ à billes** shrapnel bomb; **~ au cobalt** MÉD cobalt therapy unit; **~ éclairante** flare bomb; **~ gigogne** cluster bomb; **~ glacée** CULIN bombe (glacée); **~ guidée** smart bomb; **~ H** H-bomb; **~ à hydrogène** hydrogen bomb; **~ incendiaire** MIL incendiary bomb; (artisanale) incendiary device; **~ insecticide** insecticide spray; **~ lacrymogène** MIL teargas grenade; **~ à neutrons** neutron bomb; **~ perforante** penetration bomb; **~ à retardement** time bomb; **~ soufflante** air-blast bomb.

IDIOMES **arriver/partir à toute ~**° [*personne*] to rush in/off; **faire la ~**° (s'amuser) to live it up; (dans l'eau) to dive-bomb.

bombé, ~e /bɔ̃be/ *adj* [*front*] domed; [*forme, vase*] rounded; [*lentille*] convex; [*route*] cambered; [*parquet, mur*] bulging.

bomber /bɔ̃be/ [1] I *vtr* **1** (gonfler) **~ le torse** LIT to thrust out one's chest; FIG to swell with pride; **2**° (peindre) to spray-paint [*inscription, mur*].

II *vi* **1** [*planche, mur*] to bulge out; **2**° (rouler vite) to belt along°.
bombyx /bɔ̃biks/ *nm inv* bombyx.
■ ~ **du mûrier** silk-worm moth.
bôme /bom/ *nf* NAUT boom.
bon, bonne¹ /bɔ̃, bɔn/ **I** *adj* **1** (de qualité, compétent, remarquable, utile) good; **prends un** ~ **pull** take a warm jumper; **il a encore de bonnes jambes** he can still get around; **elle est (bien) bonne, celle-là**°! (amusé) that's a good one!; (indigné) I like that!; **ça fait un** ~ **bout de chemin** it's quite a way; **voilà une bonne chose de faite!** that's that out of the way!; **j'ai un** ~ **rhume** I've got a rotten cold; **nous sommes** ~**s derniers** we're well and truly last; **il n'est pas** ~ **à grand-chose** he's pretty useless; **il serait** ~ **qu'elle le sache** she ought to know; **à quoi** ~? what's the point?; **tous les moyens leur sont** ~**s** they'll stop at nothing; **2** (gentil) [*personne, paroles, geste*] kind (**avec, envers** to); [*sourire*] nice; **un homme** ~ **et généreux** a kind and generous man; **il a une bonne tête** he looks like a nice person; **tu es trop** ~ **avec lui** you're too good to him; **avoir** ~ **cœur** to be good-hearted; **il est** ~, **lui**°! IRON it's all very well for him to say that!; **3** (correct) [*moment, endroit, réponse, prix*] right; **c'est** ~, **vous pouvez y aller** it's OK, you can go; **c'est** ~ **pour les riches** it's all right for the rich; **c'est tout juste** ~ **pour les chiens!** it's only fit for dogs!; **4** (utilisable) [*billet, bon*] valid; **le lait ne sera plus** ~ **demain** the milk will have gone off by tomorrow; **tu es** ~ **pour la vaisselle, ce soir!** you're in line for the dishes tonight!; **me voilà** ~ **pour une amende** I'm in for a fine°; **5** (dans les souhaits) **bonne nuit/chance** good night/luck; ~ **anniversaire** happy birthday; **bonne journée/soirée!** have a nice day/evening!
II *nm,f* (personne) **les** ~**s et les méchants** good people and bad people; (au cinéma) the good guys and the bad guys°, the goodies and the baddies° GB.
III *nm* **1** (ce qui est de qualité) **il y a du** ~ **dans cet article** there are some good things in this article; **la concurrence peut avoir du** ~ competition can be a good thing; **2** (sur un emballage) coupon; (contremarque) voucher; **cadeau gratuit contre 50** ~**s** free gift with 50 coupons; ~ **à valoir sur l'achat de** voucher valid for the purchase of; **3** FIN bond.
IV *excl* (satisfaction) good; (accord) all right, OK; (intervention, interruption) right, well; ~, **on va pouvoir y aller** good, we can go; ~, **il faut que je parte** right, I must go now; ~, ~, **ça va!** OK, OK!; **allons** ~! oh dear!
V *adv* **ça sent** ~! that smells good!; **il fait** ~ (à l'extérieur) the weather's mild; **il fait** ~ **vivre ici** it's nice living here; **il ne fait pas** ~ **le déranger** it's not a good idea to disturb him.
VI **pour de bon** *loc adv* (vraiment) really; (définitivement) for good; **j'ai cru qu'il allait le faire pour de** ~ I thought he'd really do it; **je suis ici pour de** ~ I'm here for good; **tu dis ça pour de** ~? are you serious?
■ ~ **de commande** order form; ~ **enfant** good-natured; ~ **d'essence** petrol GB ou gas US coupon; ~ **de garantie** guarantee slip; ~ **garçon** nice chap; ~ **marché** cheap; ~ **mot** witticism; ~ **de réduction** COMM discount voucher; ~ **à rien** good-for-nothing; ~ **sens** common sense; ~ **teint** dyed-in-the-wool (*épith*); ~ **à tirer** pass for press; ~ **de transport** travel voucher; ~ **du Trésor** Treasury bond; ~ **usage** good usage; ~ **vivant** *adj* jovial; *nm* bon viveur; **bonne action** good deed; **bonne femme**° PEJ (femme) woman; (épouse) wife; **bonne parole** word of God; **bonne pâte** good sort; **bonne sœur**° nun; **bonnes mœurs** JUR public decency ⊄; ~**s offices** good offices.
IDIOMES **il m'a à la bonne** I'm in his good books.
bonasse /bɔnas/ *adj* PEJ meek.
bonbon /bɔ̃bɔ̃/ *nm* sweet GB, candy US; **des** ~**s** sweets GB, candy US; ~**s fourrés** sweets GB ou candy US with a soft centre.
■ ~ **acidulé** acid drop GB, sour ball US; ~ **à la menthe** mint.

bonbonne /bɔ̃bɔn/ *nf* (en verre) demijohn; (plus grand) carboy; ~ **de gaz** gas cylinder; .
bonbonnière /bɔ̃bɔnjɛR/ *nf* (boîte) sweet dish GB, candy dish US.
bond /bɔ̃/ *nm* **1** LIT, GÉN (de personne, d'animal) leap, bound; FIG (dans le temps) jump; **franchir qch d'un** ~ to leap across sth; **se lever d'un** ~ to leap to one's feet; **faire un** ~ **en avant** to leap forward; **2** FIG (progrès) leap; (hausse) (de prix) jump (**de** in); (de bénéfices, d'exportations) leap (**de** in); ~ **en avant** leap forward; (découverte) breakthrough; **3** MIL thrust; **progresser par** ~**s** to progress through a series of thrusts.
IDIOMES **saisir la balle au** ~ to seize the opportunity; **faire faux** ~ **à qn** to let sb down.
bonde /bɔ̃d/ *nf* **1** (orifice) (de piscine) outlet; (d'étang) sluice; (de lavabo) plughole; (de tonneau) bunghole; **2** (bouchon) (de piscine) outlet cover; (d'étang) sluicegate; (de lavabo) plug; (de tonneau) bung.
bondé, ~e /bɔ̃de/ *adj* packed (**with**).
bondieuserie° /bɔ̃djøzRi/ *nf* PEJ (objet) religious souvenir.
bondir /bɔ̃diR/ [3] *vi* **1** (sauter) [*personne, animal, flamme, torrent*] to leap; ~ **de joie** to jump for joy; **2** (s'élancer) ~ **sur qn/qch** to pounce on sb/sth; **3** (gambader) [*animal*] to leap about; **4** (s'indigner) to react furiously, to hit the roof°.
bondissement /bɔ̃dismã/ *nm* leap, bound.
bonheur /bɔnœR/ *nm* **1** (état de plénitude) happiness; **être au comble du** ~ to be ecstatic; **2** (moment heureux) pleasure; **faire le** ~ **de** [*personne, cadeau*] to make [sb] happy [*personne, enfant*]; [*exposition, événement*] to delight [*spectateur, touriste*]; **pour le plus grand** ~ **de qn** to the great delight of sb; **3** (chance) pleasure; **par** ~ fortunately; **au petit** ~ (**la chance**) [*répondre, décider, chercher*] at random; **tu ne connais pas ton** ~! you don't realize how lucky you are!; **4** FML (réussite) **il manie la métaphore avec** ~ he uses metaphor to great effect.
IDIOMES **le malheur des uns fait le** ~ **des autres** PROV one man's meat is another man's poison PROV; **l'argent ne fait pas le** ~ PROV money can't buy happiness; **alors, tu as trouvé ton** ~°? did you find what you wanted?
bonhomie /bɔnɔmi/ *nf* good-nature.
bonhomme, *pl* ~**s**, **bonshommes** /bɔnɔm, bɔzɔm/ **I** *adj* [*air, propos, gendarme*] good-natured.
II *nm* (homme) fellow, chap°; (mari) old man°; **découper des** ~**s de carton** to cut out little cardboard people.
■ ~ **de neige** snowman.
IDIOMES **aller** or **suivre son petit** ~ **de chemin** to go peacefully along.
bonification /bɔnifikasjɔ̃/ *nf* **1** SPORT bonus points; **2** FIN bonus.
boniment /bɔnimã/ **I** *nm* (de camelot) sales patter.
II boniments *nmpl* stories; **raconter des** ~**s à qn** (mensonges) to give sb some story° (**à propos de qch** about sth); (flatteries) to smooth-talk sb.
bonjour /bɔ̃ʒuR/ *nm* GÉN hello; (le matin) good morning, hello; (l'après-midi) good afternoon, hello; **bien le** ~ **à votre sœur** say hello to your sister for me; **allô,** ~! hello!
IDIOMES **être simple** or **facile comme** ~° to be dead easy° GB, to be easy as pie° US.
bonne² /bɔn/ **I** *adj f* ▶ **bon I.**
II ▶ **374** *nf* **1** (domestique) maid; **je ne suis pas ta** ~! I'm not the maid!; **2** (plaisanterie) **tu en as de** ~**s, toi!** you must be joking!; **une bien** ~ a good joke.
■ ~ **d'enfants** nanny; ~ **à tout faire** PEJ skivvy° GB PEJ, maid.
bonne-maman, *pl* **bonnes-mamans** /bɔnmamã/ *nf* grandma.
bonnement /bɔnmã/ *adv* **tout** ~ (quite) simply.
bonnet /bɔnɛ/ *nm* **1** (coiffe) hat; (de bébé) bonnet; **2** (de soutien-gorge) cup; **3** ZOOL reticulum.
■ ~ **d'âne** SCOL dunce's cap; ~ **de bain** bathing cap; ~ **de nuit** LIT nightcap; FIG wet blanket°.

IDIOMES **prendre qch sous son ~** to make sth one's concern; **avoir la tête près du ~** to be hot-tempered GB ou hotheaded.

bonneterie /bɔnɛtʀi/ *nf* (activité) **la ~** hosiery; (magasin) hosiery shop.

bonnetier, -ière /bɔntje, ɛʀ/ ▶ 374 *nm,f* COMM hosier.

bon-papa, *pl* **bons-papas** /bɔ̃papa/ *nm* granddad○, grandpapa○.

bonshommes ▶ **bonhomme.**

bonsoir /bɔ̃swaʀ/ *nm* (à l'arrivée) good evening, hello; (au départ) good night; (avant le coucher) good night.

bonté /bɔ̃te/ **I** *nf* (de personne) kindness (**envers** toward(s)); (de Dieu, Ciel) goodness; **c'est mon jour de ~** HUM I'm feeling generous today; **voudriez-vous avoir la ~ de faire** FML would you please be kind enough to do; **~ divine!** good heavens!
II bontés *nfpl* (gentillesses) kindness ₵ (**pour** toward(s)).

bonus /bɔnys/ *nm inv* no-claims bonus.

bonzerie /bɔ̃zʀi/ *nf* buddhist monastery.

booléen, -éenne /bɔleɛ̃, ɛn/ *adj* boolean.

boom /bum/ *nm* **~ économique** economic boom; **une industrie en plein ~** a booming industry.

boqueteau, *pl* **~x** /bɔkto/ *nm* copse.

borborygme /bɔʀbɔʀigm/ *nm* (bruit) (de faim) rumbling ₵; (de digestion) gurgling ₵.

bord /bɔʀ/ *nm* **1** (limite) GÉN edge; (de route) side; (de cours d'eau) bank; **le ~ de l'assiette** the edge of the plate; **au ~ de** LIT on ou at the edge of [chemin, lac, rivière]; FIG on the brink of [drame]; on the verge of [faillite]; **ils se sont assis au ~ du lac** they sat down by the lake; **au ~ de l'eau** [restaurant] waterside (épith); [manger, jouer] by the waterside; **au ~ de la mer** [maison, village, terrain] by the sea (après n); [activité, vacances] at the seaside (après n) ; **le ~ de la mer** the seaside; **du ~ de mer** [avenue, village, activité] seaside (épith); **~ à ~** edge-to-edge; **2** (pourtour) (de tasse, verre, cratère , lunettes) rim; (de chapeau) brim; **~s relevés** [chapeau] with a turned-up brim; **soucoupe à large ~** wide-rimmed saucer; **3** (dans un véhicule) **à ~** [être, travailler, dîner, dormir] on board, aboard; **monter à ~** to go aboard, to board; **à ~ d'un navire/avion** on board a ship/plane; **par-dessus ~** [tomber, jeter] overboard; **de ~** [instrument, personnel] on board (après n); **on fera○ avec les moyens du ~** we'll make do with what we've got; **4** FIG (tendance) side; **ils sont du même ~** they're on the same side; **de tous ~s** from all sides; **il est un peu anarchiste sur les ~s** he has slightly anarchic tendencies; **5** (côté) side; **d'un ~ à l'autre** from one side to the other; **tirer des ~s** (en bateau) to tack.

bordeaux /bɔʀdo/ **I** ▶ 141 *adj inv* burgundy.
II *nm* Bordeaux; **~ rouge** claret.

bordée /bɔʀde/ *nf* **1** MIL (décharge) broadside; (canons) broadside; **tirer une ~** LIT to fire a broadside; FIG to go on a binge○; **2** NAUT (route) tack.
IDIOMES **lâcher une ~ d'injures** to let out a volley of abuse.

border /bɔʀde/ [1] *vtr* **1** (suivre un contour) to line (**de** with); **route bordée d'arbres** road lined with trees; **2** (entourer) [plage] to skirt [côte]; [plantes] to border [massif, lac]; **3** (longer) [chemin, cours d'eau] to border, to run alongside [maison, terrain]; [marin, navire] to sail along [côte]; **4** (arranger la literie) to tuck [sb] in [personne]; **5** (garnir) to edge [vêtement] (**de** with); **un mouchoir bordé de dentelle** a lace-trimmed handkerchief; **6** NAUT to take up the slack in [voile]; to ship [avirons]; **~ un navire** (en bois) to plank; (en metal) to plate.

bordereau, *pl* **~x** /bɔʀdəʀo/ *nm* **1** (feuille) GEN form, slip; (de commerce, banque) note; (en informatique) sheet; **~ de commande** order form; **2** (en Bourse) contract; **3** (de dossier juridique) docket.

bordure /bɔʀdyʀ/ **I** *nf* **1** (de terrain, tapis, vêtement) border; **2** (contour externe) (de route, quai) edge; (de trottoir) kerb GB, curb US; **3** NAUT (de voile) foot.
II en bordure de *loc prép* **1** (sur le bord) (en un point)

next to [parc, terrain]; (en entourant) on the edge of [parc, terrain]; (en longeant) next to, running alongside [canal, voie ferrée]; on the side of [route, chemin]; **2** (à proximité) just outside [village, ville].

boréal, ~e, *mpl* **-aux** /bɔʀeal, o/ *adj* boreal.

borgne /bɔʀɲ/ **I** *adj* **1** [personne] one-eyed (épith); **il est ~** he has only one eye; **2** (bouché) **fenêtre ~** obstructed window; **3** (mal famé) seedy.
II *nmf* one-eyed man/woman.

borne /bɔʀn/ **I** *nf* **1** (sur une route) **~ (kilométrique)** kilometre GB marker; **2** (autour d'une propriété) boundary stone; (autour d'un édifice) post; **3** (pour bloquer le passage) bollard GB, post US; **4**○ (kilomètre) kilometre GB; **5** ÉLECTROTECH terminal; **6** MATH limit; **~ supérieure/inférieure** upper/lower bound.
II bornes *nfpl* FIG (limites) limits, boundaries; **une stupidité sans ~s** boundless stupidity; **leur ambition est sans ~s** their ambition knows no bounds.
■ **~ d'incendie** fire hydrant; **~ téléphonique** (sur l'autoroute) emergency telephone; (pour taxis) taxi stand telephone.
IDIOMES **dépasser les ~s** to go too far.

borné, ~e /bɔʀne/ *adj* [personne] narrow-minded; [esprit, existence] narrow; [intelligence] limited.

borner /bɔʀne/ [1] **I** *vtr* **1** (marquer la limite de) JUR to mark out the boundaries of [propriété]; [rivière, montagne] to border [pays, région]; **2** (limiter) to limit [ambition, désirs] (**à qch** to sth; **à faire** to doing).
II se borner *vpr* **1** (se contenter) **se ~ à faire** [personne] to content oneself with doing; **2** (se limiter) **notre rôle se borne à analyser** our role is limited to analysing GB.

bosniaque /bɔsnjak/ ▶ 509 *adj* Bosnian.

bosquet /bɔskɛ/ *nm* grove.

bosse /bɔs/ *nf* **1** (difformité) (sur le dos) hump; (sur le nez, un terrain) bump; **2** (après un choc) (sur la tête) bump; **3** (sur un objet) dent.
IDIOMES **avoir la ~ de**○ to have a flair for; **rouler sa ~** to knock about.

bosseler /bɔsle/ [19] *vtr* GEN to dent; (en orfèvrerie) to emboss.

bosser○ /bɔse/ [1] *vi* to work.

bossoir /bɔswaʀ/ *nm* (d'embarcation) davit; (d'ancre) cathead.

bossu, ~e /bɔsy/ **I** *adj* (infirme) hunchbacked; (qui se tient mal) round-shouldered.
II *nm,f* hunchback.
IDIOMES **rire comme un ~** to laugh like a drain.

bot /bo/ *adj m* **pied ~** club foot.

botanique /bɔtanik/ **I** *adj* botanical.
II *nf* botany.

botaniste /bɔtanist/ ▶ 374 *nmf* botanist.

botte /bɔt/ *nf* **1** (chaussure) boot; ▶ **plein; 2** (de fleurs) bunch; (de foin, paille) bale; **3** (en escrime) thrust.
■ **~s de caoutchouc** wellington boots, wellingtons; **~s de cheval** riding boots; **~s d'égoutier** waders; **~s de sept lieues** seven league boots.
IDIOMES **être à la ~ de qn** to be under sb's heel.

botté, ~e /bɔte/ **I** *pp* ▶ **botter.**
II *pp adj* with boots on; **~ de cuir** leather-booted.

botter /bɔte/ [1] *vtr* **1** (chausser de bottes) to put [sb's] boots on; **2**○ (plaire) **ça le botte!** he loves it, he really digs it○; **3** (frapper du pied) to kick; **~ le derrière**○ **de qn** to boot sb up the backside○.

botteur, -euse /bɔtœʀ/ *nm,f* SPORT striker.

bottier /bɔtje/ *nm* bootmaker.

bottillon /bɔtijɔ̃/ *nm* bootee.

bottin® /bɔtɛ̃/ *nm* telephone directory, phone book.

bottine /bɔtin/ *nf* ankle-boot.

bouc /buk/ *nm* (animal) billy goat; (barbe) goatee.
■ **~ émissaire** scapegoat.
IDIOMES **sentir le ~** to stink.

boucan○ /bukɑ̃/ *nm* (bruit) din, racket○.

boucaner /bukane/ [1] *vtr* to smoke-dry.

boucanier /bukanje/ *nm* **1** (pirate) buccaneer; **2** (chasseur) hunter of wild ox.

bouche /buʃ/ *nf* **1** (cavité buccale) mouth; **2** (lèvre) mouth, lips (*pl*); **s'embrasser sur la ~** to kiss on the lips; **3** (organe de la parole) **ouvrir la ~** to speak; **il n'a pas ouvert la ~ de toute la soirée** he hasn't said a word all evening; **il n'a que ce mot à la ~** that word is never off his lips; **dans sa ~, ce n'est pas une insulte** coming from him, that's not an insult; **apprendre qch de la ~ de qn** to hear sth from sb; **se transmettre de ~ à oreille** [*nouvelle*] to be spread by word of mouth; **4** (personne) **avoir trois ~s à nourrir** to have three mouths to feed.
■ **~ d'aération** air vent; **~ de chaleur** hot-air vent; **~ d 'égout** manhole; **~ d'incendie** fire hydrant; **~ de métro** tube entrance GB, subway entrance US.
IDIOMES **faire la fine ~ devant qch** to turn one's nose up at sth.

bouché, **~e¹** /buʃe/ I *pp* ▶ **boucher¹**.
II *pp adj* **1** FIG [*profession, secteur*] oversubscribed; **2°** PEJ (stupide) stupid; **3** (en bouteille) [*cidre*] bottled.

bouche-à-bouche /buʃabuʃ/ *nm inv* **faire le ~** to give mouth-to-mouth resuscitation (**à qn** to sb).

bouche-à-oreille /buʃaɔʀɛj/ *nm inv* **le ~** word of mouth.

bouchée² /buʃe/ I *pp adj f* ▶ **bouché**.
II *nf* (contenu de la bouche) mouthful; **pour une ~ de pain** FIG for next to nothing; **ne faire qu'une ~ d'un gâteau** to wolf a cake down; **ne faire qu'une ~ d'un adversaire** FIG to make short work of an opponent; **mettre les ~s doubles** FIG to double one's efforts.
■ **~ à la reine** vol-au-vent.

boucher¹ /buʃe/ [1] I *vtr* **1** (mettre un bouchon à) to cork; **2** (obstruer) to block; (en encrassant) to clog (up); (en comblant) to fill; **~ les trous** LIT to fill the holes; FIG to fill the gaps.
II **se boucher** *vpr* **1** (se fermer) **se ~ le nez** LIT to hold one's nose; **se ~ les oreilles** LIT to put one's fingers in one's ears; **2** (s'obstruer) [*lavabo*] to get blocked; [*artères*] to get clogged up; [*oreilles*] to feel blocked; [*nez*] to get blocked; **tu as les oreilles bouchées ou quoi?** IRON are you deaf or what°?; **3** MÉTÉO **temps/ciel bouché** overcast weather/sky.
IDIOMES **en ~ un coin à qn°** to amaze sb.

boucher², **-ère¹** /buʃe, ɛʀ/ ▶ **374**| *nm,f* butcher.

bouchère² /buʃɛʀ/ *nf* (épouse de boucher) butcher's wife.

boucherie /buʃʀi/ *nf* **1** ▶ **374**| (magasin) butcher's shop, butcher's; (commerce) butcher's trade, butchery; **2** FIG (tuerie) slaughter.
■ **~ chevaline** horsemeat butcher's.

bouche-trou, *pl* **~s** /buʃtʀu/ *nm* stand-in.

bouchon /buʃɔ̃/ *nm* **1** (qu'on enfonce) (en liège) cork; (autre) stopper; (de baignoire) plug; **2** (qui se visse) (de bidon) cap; (de tube, d'encrier) top, cap; **3** (de cire, cérumen) plug; **4** (de la circulation) traffic jam; **5** (pour la pêche) float.
IDIOMES **pousser le ~ trop loin** to push it a bit°.

bouchonner /buʃɔne/ [1] I *vtr* (frotter) to rub down [*cheval*].
II° *vi* **ça bouchonne partout** there are traffic jams everywhere.

bouclage /buklaʒ/ *nm* **1** (de ceinture) fastening; **2** (achèvement) completion; **3** (dans la presse) **la nouvelle de sa mort est arrivée après le ~** the news of his death arrived after the newspaper had been put to bed; **4** (encerclement) cordoning off; **5** ORDINAT wraparound.

boucle /bukl/ *nf* **1** (de ceinture, chaussure) buckle; **2** (de cheveux) curl; (de lacet, corde) loop; (de lettre) loop; **3** TV, VIDÉO **en ~** in a continuous loop; **4** ORDINAT loop.
■ **~ d'oreille** earring.

bouclé, **~e** /bukle/ *adj* [*cheveux, perruque*] curly.

boucler /bukle/ [1] I *vtr* **1** (attacher) to fasten [*ceinture de sécurité, bagages*]; **2°** (fermer) to lock [*porte, coffre*]; **3°** (encercler) [*police*] to cordon off [*quartier*]; to close [*frontière*]; **4** (achever) to complete [*enquête*]; to close [*dossier*]; to sign [*accord*]; **5** (en finance) to balance [*budget*]; **~ les fins de mois** to make ends meet at the end of each month; **6** (dans la presse) to put [sth] to

bed [*journal, édition*]; **7°** (mettre en prison) to lock [sb] up; **faire ~ qn** to get sb locked up.
II *vi* [*cheveux*] to curl.
IDIOMES **la ~** to shut up; **~ la boucle** to come full circle.

bouclette /buklɛt/ *nf* **1** (de cheveux) small curl; **2** (tissu) (**laine**) **~ bouclé** (wool).

bouclier /buklije/ *nm* shield.

bouddha /buda/ *nm* (représentation) buddha.

bouddhisme /budism/ *nm* Buddhism.

bouddhiste /budist/ *adj, nmf* Buddhist.

bouder /bude/ [1] I *vtr* to avoid [*personne*]; to stay away from [*spectacle*]; to steer clear of [*marchandise*].
II *vi* to sulk.

bouderie /budʀi/ *nf* (action) sulking.

boudeur, **-euse** /budœʀ, øz/ *adj* sulky.

boudin /budɛ̃/ *nm* **1** CULIN **~** black pudding GB, blood sausage; **2°** PEJ (femme) lump°.
IDIOMES **s'en aller** *or* **partir** *or* **finir en eau de ~** to come to nothing.

boudiné, **~e** /budine/ *adj* (gros) [*doigt, main*] podgy.

boudiner /budine/ [1] I *vtr* **1** TECH to coil [*fil de fer*]; **2** (serrer) **sa robe la boudine** her dress shows every bulge; **être boudiné dans qch** to be squeezed into sth.

boudoir /budwaʀ/ *nm* (salon) boudoir; (biscuit) ladyfinger.

boue /bu/ *nf* **1** (terre) mud; (sédiment) silt; **2** (scandale) **traîner qn dans la ~** to drag sb's name through the mud.

bouée /bwe/ *nf* **1** (gonflable) rubber ring; **2** (balise) buoy.
■ **~ de sauvetage** LIT lifebelt GB, life preserver US.

boueux, **-euse** /buø, øz/ *adj* [*terrain, chemin*] muddy.

bouffant, **~e** /bufɑ̃, ɑ̃t/ *adj* [*chemisier, pantalon*] baggy; [*manche*] puffed; [*coiffure*] bouffant.

bouffe° /buf/ *nf* (activité de manger) eating; (nourriture) food, grub°; (repas) meal.

bouffée /bufe/ *nf* **1** (souffle) (d'odeur) whiff; (de tabac, vapeur, vent) puff; **une ~ d'air frais** LIT, FIG a breath of fresh air; **tirer une ~** to have a puff *ou* drag°; **2** (accès) rush [de of]; **~ d'orgueil** surge of pride.
■ **~ de chaleur** MÉD hot flush GB, hot flash US.

bouffer /bufe/ [1] I° *vtr* **1** (manger) to eat; **2** (accaparer) **se faire ~** to be taken over (**par** by); **3** (consommer) to guzzle [*essence*]; to burn [*huile*]; **4** (dépenser) to throw [sth] away [*argent*]; **5** (utiliser) to take up [*espace*].
II *vi* **1°** (manger) to eat; (beaucoup) to eat a lot, to stuff oneself°; **2** (gonfler) [*vêtement*] to billow out.
IDIOMES **se ~ le nez°** to be at each other's throats.

bouffi, **~e** /bufi/ *adj* (physiquement) puffy; **il a le visage ~ par l'alcool** his face is puffy with drink.

bouffon, **-onne** /bufɔ̃, ɔn/ I *adj* farcical.
II *nm* **1** (plaisantin) clown; **faire le ~** to clown about *ou* around; **2** HIST (de cour) jester; (de théâtre) buffoon.

bouffonnerie /bufɔnʀi/ *nf* **1** (acte) antics (*pl*); **2** (effets comiques) buffoonery; **3** (caractère) ridiculousness; **4** THÉÂT farce.

bouge /buʒ/ *nm* (logement) hovel; (café) dive.

bougeoir /buʒwaʀ/ *nm* candleholder; (haut) candlestick.

bougeotte° /buʒɔt/ *nf* restlessness; **avoir la ~** to be restless.

bouger /buʒe/ [13] I *vtr* (tous contextes) to move.
II *vi* **1** (faire un mouvement, se déplacer) to move; **ne bougez plus, je prends une photo!** keep still, I'm taking a photo!; **c'est malin, tu m'as fait ~!** that's great, you jogged me!; **2°** (évoluer) [*secteur, entreprise, pays*] to be on the move; **3°** (être animé) **ville qui bouge** lively town; **4°** (réagir) to show signs of unrest; **5°** (varier) [*prix, score, prévision*] to change; **tu peux le laver à la machine, ça ne bougera pas** you can wash it in the machine, it won't shrink.
III **se bouger°** *vpr* [*personne*] (se pousser) to get out of the way; (se dépêcher) to get a move on°; (se donner du mal) to put some effort in.

bougie /buʒi/ *nf* **1** (de cire) candle; **2** TECH sparking plug GB, spark plug.

bougon, -onne /bugɔ̃, ɔn/ **I** *adj* grumpy.
II *nm,f* grouch.

bougonner /bugɔne/ [1] *vi* to grumble.

bougre° /bugʀ/ *nm* (type) bloke°; **bon** ~ good sort; **pauvre** ~ poor devil; ~ **d'imbécile** you damn° idiot.

bougrement° /bugʀəmɑ̃/ *adv* ~ **difficile** damn° hard.

bougresse° /bugʀɛs/ *nf* bird° GB, chick°, woman.

bouillabaisse /bujabɛs/ *nf* bouillabaisse, fish soup.

bouillant, ~e /bujɑ̃, ɑ̃t/ *adj* **1** (qui bout) boiling; **2**° (très chaud) boiling (hot).

bouille° /buj/ *nf* face.

bouillie /buji/ *nf* CULIN gruel; (pour bébés) baby cereal; **en** ~ [*légumes*] PEJ mushy.

bouillir /bujiʀ/ [31] *vi* **1** GÉN [*eau, lait*] to boil; **faire** ~ to boil; **2** FIG (s'emporter) [*personne*] to seethe.

bouilloire /bujwaʀ/ *nf* kettle.

bouillon /bujɔ̃/ *nm* **1** (potage) broth; **2** (liquide de cuisson, concentré) stock; **3** (de liquide qui bout) bubble; **bouillir à gros** ~**s** to boil, to bubble.
■ ~ **de culture** BIOL nutrient broth; FIG hotbed (**pour** of); ~ **gras** CULIN meat stock.
IDIOMES **boire un** ~ (en nageant) to get a mouthful; (en affaires) to come a cropper°, to sustain losses.

bouillonnant, ~e /bujɔnɑ̃, ɑ̃t/ *adj* [*eaux*] foaming; [*personne*] lively.

bouillonnement /bujɔnmɑ̃/ *nm* **1** (de vagues) foaming; **2** FIG **le** ~ **du marché** the frentic activity of the market.

bouillonner /bujɔne/ [1] *vi* **1** [*liquide chaud*] to bubble; [*eaux*] to foam; **2** [*personne*] ~ **d'activité** to be bustling with activity.

bouillotte /bujɔt/ *nf* hot-water bottle.

boulanger, -ère[1] /bulɑ̃ʒe, ɛʀ/ ▶ 374 *nm,f* baker.

boulangère[2] /bulɑ̃ʒɛʀ/ *nf* (épouse de boulanger) baker's wife.

boulangerie /bulɑ̃ʒʀi/ ▶ 374 *nf* **1** (magasin) bakery, baker's; **2** (activité) bakery trade.

boulangerie-pâtisserie, *pl* **boulangeries-pâtisseries** /bulɑ̃ʒʀipɑtisʀi/ *nf* bakery (*selling cakes and pastries*).

boule /bul/ **I** *nf* (de bowling) bowl; (de jeu de boules) boule; (de rampe d'escalier) knob; **mettre qch en** ~ to roll sth up into a ball; **avoir une** ~ **dans la gorge** to have a lump in one's throat.
II boules ▶ 329 *nfpl* boules.
■ ~ **de cristal** crystal ball; ~ **de naphtaline** mothball; ~ **puante** stink bomb; ~ **Quiès**® earplug; ~ **à thé** tea infuser GB, tea ball US.
IDIOMES **avoir la** ~ **à zéro**° to have no hair left; **perdre la** ~° to go mad; **mettre qn en** ~° to make sb furious.

bouleau, *pl* ~**x** /bulo/ *nm* birch.

bouledogue /buldɔg/ *nm* bulldog.

bouler /bule/ [1] *vi* **envoyer qn** ~° to send sb packing°.

boulet /bulɛ/ *nm* **1** (projectile) ~ **(de canon)** cannonball; **2** (de bagnard) ball and chain; **3** FIG millstone; **être un** ~ **pour qn** to be a millstone around sb's neck; **4** (de charbon) coal nut.
IDIOMES **tirer à** ~**s rouges sur qn/qch** to launch a fierce attack on sb/sth.

boulette /bulɛt/ *nf* **1** (de pain, papier) pellet; **2**° (bourde) blunder.

boulevard /bulvaʀ/ *nm* **1** (avenue) boulevard; **2** THÉÂT farce; **théâtre de** ~ farce.
■ ~ **périphérique** ring road GB, beltway US.

bouleversant, ~e /bulvɛʀsɑ̃, ɑ̃t/ *adj* (émouvant) deeply moving; (pénible) distressing.

bouleversement /bulvɛʀsəmɑ̃/ *nm* upheaval.

bouleverser /bulvɛʀse/ [1] *vtr* **1** (émouvoir) to move [sb] deeply; (affliger) to shatter; **2** (mettre en désordre) to wreak havoc in [*paysage, ville*]; to turn [sth] upside down [*maison, dossiers*]; **3** (désorganiser) to disrupt; **4** (changer) to change.

boulier /bulje/ *nm* abacus.

boulimie /bulimi/ *nf* MÉD bulimia.

bouliste /bulist/ *nmf* boules player.

boulodrome /bulɔdʀom/ *nm* area for playing boules.

boulon /bulɔ̃/ *nm* bolt.

boulonnage /bulɔnaʒ/ *nm* TECH (d'un élément) bolting; (d'éléments entre eux) bolting together.

boulonner /bulɔne/ [1] **I** *vtr* to bolt [sth] on [*élément*]; to bolt together [*éléments*].
II° *vi* to work, to slave away.

boulot, -otte /bulo, ɔt/ **I** *adj* tubby.
II° *nm* **1** (tâche) work; **au** ~! (toi) get to work!; (moi, nous) let's get to work!; **2** (emploi) job.

boulotter° /bulɔte/ [1] *vtr* to eat.

boum[1] /bum/ **I** *nm* **1** (bruit) bang; **2**° (développement) **être en plein** ~ [*économie, ventes, affaires*] to be booming; **faire un** ~ [*naissances*] to boom.
II *excl* (explosion) bang!

boum[2] /bum/ *nf* (fête) party.

bouquet /bukɛ/ *nm* **1** (floral) ~ **(de fleurs)** bunch of flowers; (composé) bouquet; (petit) posy; **2** (de feu d'artifice) final flourish; ~ **final** crowning piece; **3** (d'arbres) clump; **4** (de fines herbes) bunch; **5** (de vin) bouquet.
IDIOMES **c'est le** ~°! (le comble) that's the limit°!

bouquetin /buktɛ̃/ *nm* ibex.

bouquin° /bukɛ̃/ *nm* book.

bouquiner° /bukine/ [1] *vtr, vi* to read.

bouquiniste /bukinist/ ▶ 374 *nmf* secondhand bookseller.

bourbeux, -euse /buʀbø, øz/ *adj* muddy.

bourbier /buʀbje/ *nm* **1** LIT quagmire; **2** FIG tangle, quagmire.

bourde /buʀd/ *nf* (bévue) blunder.

bourdon /buʀdɔ̃/ *nm* **1** ZOOL bumblebee; **2** (cloche) tenor bell; **3** MUS (d'orgue) bourdon.

bourdonnement /buʀdɔnmɑ̃/ *nm* (d'insecte) buzzing ¢; (de ruche) humming ¢; (de moteur) hum; (d'hélicoptère, avion) drone.

bourdonner /buʀdɔne/ [1] *vi* [*insecte*] to buzz; [*moteur*] to hum; [*avion, hélicoptère*] to drone; [*foule*] to murmur.

bourg /buʀ/ *nm* market town.

bourgade /buʀgad/ *nf* small town.

bourgeois, ~e /buʀʒwa, az/ **I** *adj* **1** [*libéralisme*] bourgeois; PÉJ [*morale*] middle-class; **2** (cossu) **quartier** ~ wealthy residential district; **3** JUR [*habitation*] for private use (*après n*).
II *nm,f* **1** (personne de la classe moyenne) middle-class person, bourgeois PÉJ; **2** HIST (sous l'Ancien Régime) bourgeois; (au Moyen Âge) burgher.

bourgeoisie /buʀʒwazi/ *nf* **1** (classe moyenne) middle classes (*pl*); **2** HIST, POL bourgeoisie.

bourgeon /buʀʒɔ̃/ *nm* (en botanique) bud.

bourgeonner /buʀʒɔne/ [1] *vi* (en botanique) to bud, to burgeon.

bourgogne /buʀgɔɲ/ *nm* (vin) Burgundy.

Bourgogne /buʀgɔɲ/ ▶ 509 *nprf* **la** ~ Burgundy.

bourguignon, -onne /buʀgiɲɔ̃, ɔn/ **I** *adj* of Burgundy.
II *nm* CULIN beef bourguignon, beef casserole cooked in red wine.

bourlinguer° /buʀlɛ̃ge/ [1] *vi* (beaucoup naviguer) to sail the seven seas; (beaucoup voyager) to travel around a lot.

bourrache /buʀaʃ/ *nf* borage.

bourrade /buʀad/ *nf* (avec la main, l'épaule) shove; (avec le coude) (sharp) nudge.

bourrage /buʀaʒ/ *nm* (remplissage) (de fauteuil, coussin) stuffing; (de pipe) filling; (de cartouche) wadding.
■ ~ **de crâne** brainwashing.

bourrasque /buʀask/ *nf* (de vent) gust; (de neige) flurry.

bourratif, -ive /buʀatif, iv/ *adj* very filling, stodgy.

bourre /buʀ/ *nf* **1** (pour remplissage) stuffing; (déchets textiles) flock; (de cartouche) wad; **2** (en botanique) down. IDIOMES **être à la ~**○ to be pushed for time.

bourré, ~e /buʀe/ *adj* [*train, musée*] packed; [*valise, sac*] bulging (**de** with); **~ de fric**○ stinking rich○.

bourreau, *pl* **~x** /buʀo/ *nm* **1** (exécuteur) executioner; **2** (criminel) butcher; (persécuteur) tormenter. ■ **~ d'enfant** child beater; **~ de travail** workaholic.

bourrelet /buʀlɛ/ *nm* **1** TECH (d'étanchéité) weather strip; (amortisseur) pad; **2** (adiposité) **~ (de graisse)** roll of fat.

bourrelier, -ière /buʀəlje, ɛʀ/ ▶374 *nm,f* (sellier) saddler; (maroquinier) leather craftsman/craftswoman.

bourrellerie /buʀɛlʀi/ *nf* **1** (sellerie) (fabrication) saddlery; (produits) tack; **2** (maroquinerie) (fabrication) making of leather goods; (produits) leather goods (*pl*).

bourrer /buʀe/ [1] I *vtr* **1** (remplir) to cram [sth] full [*valise, caisse*]; to fill [*pipe*]; to wad [*arme à feu*]; **~ qch de** to cram sth with; **2** (gaver) **~ qu de** to stuff sb with [*nourriture*]; to dose sb up with [*médicaments*]; **3**○ (frapper) **~ qn de coups** to lay into sb○. II *vi* (remplir l'estomac)○ [*aliment*] to be filling. III **se bourrer** *vpr* (se gaver) **se ~ de** to stuff oneself with [*aliments*]; to dose oneself up with [*médicaments*].

bourricot /buʀiko/ *nm* donkey.

bourrique /buʀik/ *nf* **1** (ânesse) donkey; **2**○ (entêté) pig-headed person.

bourru, ~e /buʀy/ *adj* gruff.

bourse /buʀs/ I *nf* **1** (de soutien financier) grant GB, scholarship US; (pour le mérite) scholarship; (pour un projet particulier) grant; **2** (porte-monnaie) purse; **3** FIG budget; **pour les petites ~s** for limited budgets; **4** (vente d'objets d'occasion) **~ aux livres** second-hand book sale. II **bourses** *nfpl* ANAT scrotum (*sg*). ■ **~ d'étude** grant.

Bourse /buʀs/ *nf* FIN stock exchange; (valeurs cotées) shares (*pl*); **la ~ de Paris a monté** shares on the Paris Stock Exchange have gone up; **faire son entrée à la ~ de Milan** to be listed on the Milan Stock Exchange for the first time; **une société de ~** a broking GB ou brokerage US firm. ■ **~ de commerce** commodity exchange; **~ du travail** IND *local trade union offices*.

boursicoter /buʀsikɔte/ [1] *vi* [*personne*] to dabble in stocks and shares.

boursier, -ière /buʀsje, ɛʀ/ I *adj* (financier) [*cotation, valeur*] stock exchange, stock market (*épith*); [*semaine, mois*] trading (*épith*); **le marché ~** share prices. II *nm,f* (bénéficiaire d'une bourse) (pour raisons financières) grant holder GB, scholarship student US; (pour mérite) scholar GB, scholarship student US.

boursouflé, ~e /buʀsufle/ *adj* (enflé) [*peau, surface*] blistered; [*visage, paupière*] puffy; [*corps*] bloated.

boursouflure /buʀsuflyʀ/ *nf* (de peau) swelling ¢; (de papier, peinture) blister.

bousculade /buskylad/ *nf* **1** (choc) (volontaire) jostling; (involontaire) crush; **2** (précipitation) rush.

bousculer /buskyle/ [1] I *vtr* **1** (heurter) (involontairement) to bump into [*personne*]; (volontairement) to knock about [*personne*]; **2** (malmener) to jostle [*équipe*]; **3** (presser) to rush [*personne, programme*]. II **se bousculer** *vpr* **1** (se heurter) to bump into each other; **2** (être nombreux) to fall over each other (**pour faire** to do).

bouse /buz/ *nf* cow dung ¢; **une ~ (de vache)** a cowpat.

bousiller○ /buzije/ [1] *vtr* **1** (gâcher) to botch [*travail*]; **2** (détériorer) to wreck [*appareil, moteur*]; to smash up [*véhicule*]; to bust○ [*mécanisme*]. II **se bousiller** *vpr* **se ~ la santé/la vue** to ruin one's health/eyesight.

boussole /busɔl/ *nf* compass.

bout¹ /bu/ *nm* **1** (dernière partie) (de nez, branche, ficelle, table, rue, processus) end; (pointe) (d'épée, aile, de langue, doigt) tip; (de chaussure) toe; **en ~ de piste** AVIAT at the end of the runway; **tout au ~ de la rue** at the very end of the street; **ciseaux à ~s ronds** round-ended scissors; **à ~ carré/rond** [*bâton, doigt, aile*] square-/red-tipped; **au ~ du jardin/champ** at the bottom of the garden/field; **siège en ~ de rangée** aisle seat; **lire un livre de ~ en ~** to read a book from cover to cover; **parcourir une liste d'un ~ à l'autre** to scour a list; **d'un ~ à l'autre du spectacle/de l'année** throughout the show/the year; **marcher d'un ~ à l'autre de la ville** to walk across the city; **coller ~ à ~** to stick [sth] end to end; **être incapable de mettre deux phrases ~ à ~** to be unable to string two sentences together; **rester jusqu'au ~** to stay until the end; **aller jusqu'au ~** to go all the way; **aller (jusqu')au ~ de** to follow through [*idée, exigence*]; **aller au ~ de soi-même** to push oneself to the limit; **écouter qn jusqu'au ~** to hear sb out; **lutter jusqu'au ~** to fight to the last drop of blood; **elle est à ~** she can't take any more; **je suis à ~ de forces** I can do no more; **ne me pousse pas à ~** don't push me; **être à ~ d'arguments** to run out of arguments; **venir à ~ de** to overcome [*problème, difficultés*]; to get through [*tâche, repas*]; **au ~ d'une semaine/d'un certain temps** after a week/a while; **au ~ du compte** ultimately; **à ~ portant** at point-blank range; **2** (morceau) (de pain, chiffon, fil, papier) piece; (de terrain) bit; **~ de bois** GÉN piece of wood; (allongé) stick; **~s de papier/ferraille** scraps of paper/metal; **par petits ~s** [*apprendre, manger*] a bit at a time; [*payer, recevoir*] in dribs and drabs; [*occuper, progresser*] little by little; **un petit ~ de femme**○ a tiny woman. ■ **~ de chou**○ sweet little thing○; **~ d'essai** CIN screen test; **~ filtre** (de cigarette) filter tip. IDIOMES **tenir le bon ~**○ to be on the right track; **voir le ~ de qch** to get through sth; **ne pas être au ~ de ses peines** or **ennuis** not to be out of the woods yet; **ne pas savoir par quel ~ commencer** not to know where to begin; **mettre les ~s**○ to leave, to clear off○ GB, to split○ US.

bout² /but/ *nm* NAUT rope; **filer par le ~** to slip anchor.

boutade /butad/ *nf* (trait d'esprit) witticism.

boute-en-train /butɑ̃tʀɛ̃/ *nmf inv* live wire FIG.

bouteille /butɛj/ *nf* **1** (emballage) bottle; **~ de lait** (contenant) milk bottle; (contenu) bottle of milk; **~ de gaz** cylinder ou bottle of gas; **mettre le vin en ~s** to bottle wine; **boire à la ~** to drink out of the bottle; **2** (produit vinicole) bottle; **une bonne ~** a good bottle of wine; **3** SPORT **faire de la plongée avec des ~s** to dive with breathing equipment. ■ **~ d'oxygène** oxygen cylinder. IDIOMES **prendre de la ~**○ (âge) to be getting on; **jeter** or **lancer une ~ à la mer** to make a last despairing bid for help.

bouteur /butœʀ/ *nm* bulldozer.

boutique /butik/ *nf* **1** (d'artisan, de commerçant) shop GB, store US; (de prêt-à-porter) boutique; **plier ~** LIT, FIG to shut up shop; **2**○ (maison, entreprise) place.

boutiquier, -ière /butikje, ɛʀ/ I *adj* PEJ small-minded. II *nm,f* COMM shopkeeper.

boutoir /butwaʀ/ *nm* snout; **coup de ~** attack.

bouton /butɔ̃/ *nm* **1** (en couture) button; **sans ~s** buttonless; **2** TECH (d'appareil) (à tourner) knob; (à presser) button; **3** MÉD spot GB, pimple US; **4** (de fleur) bud. ■ **~ de fièvre** MÉD cold sore; **~ de manchette** cuff link; **~ de porte** doorknob.

bouton-d'or, *pl* **boutons-d'or** /butɔ̃dɔʀ/ *nm* buttercup.

boutonner /butɔne/ [1] I *vtr* to button [*vêtement*]; **~ qn** to do up sb's buttons. II **se boutonner** *vpr* [*vêtement*] to button up.

boutonneux, -euse /butɔnø, øz/ *adj* [*visage*] spotty GB, pimply US.

boutonnière /butɔnjɛʀ/ *nf* (de vêtement) buttonhole; **il porte une fleur rouge à la ~** he's wearing a red buttonhole GB ou boutonniere US.

bouture /butyʀ/ *nf* cutting.

bouturer /butyʀe/ [1] **I** *vtr* to take a cutting from [*plante*].

II *vi* [*plante*] to propagate from cuttings.

bouvier /buvje/ *nm* **1** ▶ 374] (personne) oxherd; **2** (chien) bouvier.

bouvreuil /buvʀœj/ *nm* bullfinch.

bovidé /bɔvide/ *nm* bovid; **les ~s** the Bovidae.

bovin, **~e** /bɔvɛ̃, in/ **I** *adj* bovine.

II *nm* bovine; **des ~s** cattle (+ *v pl*); **150 ~s** 150 head of cattle.

box, *pl* **boxes** /bɔks/ *nm* (pour véhicule) lock-up garage; (pour cheval) stall; (dans un bar) alcove; (dans un dortoir, parloir) cubicle; (de travail) section.
■ **~ des accusés** JUR dock.

boxe /bɔks/ ▶ 329] *nf* boxing; **champion de ~** boxing champion; **faire de la ~** to do boxing, to box.
■ **~ française** savate.

boxer[1] /bɔksɛʀ/ *nm* (chien) boxer.

boxer[2] /bɔkse/ [1] **I**° *vtr* (frapper) to punch.

II *vi* **1** (pratiquer la boxe) to box; **2** (livrer un match de boxe) to have a fight on.

boxeur /bɔksœʀ/ ▶ 374] *nm* boxer.

boyau, *pl* **~x** /bwajo/ **I** *nm* **1** (intestin) gut; **2** (pour raquette, violon) catgut; **3** (pour saucisse) casing; **4** (pneu) tubeless tyre GB ou tire US; **5** (passage) back alley; **6** (tuyau flexible) hose.

II° **boyaux** *nmpl* (intestins) insides°.

boycotter /bɔjkɔte/ [1] *vtr* to boycott.

BP *written abbr* ▶ **boîte**.

bracelet /bʀaslɛ/ *nm* (au poignet) GÉN bracelet; (large) bangle; (souple) wristband; (au bras, à la cheville) bangle.
■ **~ de montre** watchstrap.

bracelet-montre, *pl* **bracelets-montres** /bʀaslɛmɔ̃tʀ/ *nm* wristwatch.

braconner /bʀakɔne/ [1] *vi* to poach.

braconnier /bʀakɔnje/ *nm* poacher.

bradé, **~e** /bʀade/ *adj* **prix ~s** knockdown prices.

brader /bʀade/ [1] **I** *vtr* **1** (vendre à bas prix) to sell [sth] cheaply; **2** (liquider) to sell off.

II *vi* to slash prices.

braderie /bʀadʀi/ *nf* **1** COMM (marché) street market; (magasin) discount store; **2** (vente) clearance sale; (liquidation) selling off.

braguette /bʀagɛt/ *nf* flies GB (*pl*), fly US.

braillard°, **~e** /bʀajaʀ, aʀd/ **I** *adj* (qui crie) yelling (*épith*); (qui pleure) bawling (*épith*).

II *nm,f* loudmouth.

braille /bʀaj/ *nm* Braille; **en ~** in Braille.

brailler° /bʀaje/ [1] **I** *vtr* to yell out [*injure*]; to bawl out [*chanson*].

II *vi* (crier) to yell; (chanter fort, pleurer) to bawl.

braiment /bʀɛmɑ̃/ *nm* braying ¢.

braire /bʀɛʀ/ [58] *vi* to bray.

braise /bʀɛz/ *nf* live embers (*pl*).

braiser /bʀeze/ [1] *vtr* CULIN to braise.

bramer /bʀame/ [1] *vi* [*cerf*] to bell.

brancard /bʀɑ̃kaʀ/ *nm* (civière) stretcher; (de charrette) shaft.
IDIOMES **ruer dans les ~s** to rebel.

brancardier /bʀɑ̃kaʀdje/ ▶ 374] *nm* stretcher-bearer.

branchage /bʀɑ̃ʃaʒ/ **I** *nm* branches (*pl*).

II branchages *nmpl* (branches coupées) cut branches.

branche /bʀɑ̃ʃ/ *nf* **1** (d'arbre) branch; **~ maîtresse** limb; **2** CULIN **céleri en ~s** sticks of celery; **épinards en ~s** spinach on the stalk; **3** (secteur) field; **4** (de famille) branch; **5** (de chandelier) branch; (de lunettes) arm; (d'étoile) point.

branché°, **~e** /bʀɑ̃ʃe/ *adj* trendy°.

branchement /bʀɑ̃ʃmɑ̃/ *nm* **1** (à un réseau, à une prise) connection; **2** (conduite d'eau) branch pipe; (ligne électrique) lead GB, cable US.

brancher /bʀɑ̃ʃe/ [1] **I** *vtr* **1** (avec prise) to plug in [*télévision, téléphone*]; **2** (au réseau) to connect (up) [*eau, gaz, électricité, téléphone*]; to connect [*usager, maison*];

faire ~ le téléphone to have the phone connected; **3** (aiguiller) **~ qn sur** to get sb onto [*sujet*]; **4** (intéresser) **je vais au cinéma, ça te branche?** I'm going to the cinema, are you interested?

II se brancher *vpr* RADIO, TV (capter) **se ~ sur** to tune into [*poste, station*].

branchie /bʀɑ̃ʃi/ *nf* gill, branchia SPÉC.

brandade /bʀɑ̃dad/ *nf* **~ (de morue)** brandade, dish of flaked salt cod.

brandir /bʀɑ̃diʀ/ [3] *vtr* to brandish [*arme, objet*].

brandon /bʀɑ̃dɔ̃/ *nm* firebrand.
■ **~ de discorde** bone of contention.

branlant, **-e** /bʀɑ̃lɑ̃, ɑ̃t/ *adj* [*meuble, construction*] rickety; [*mur, mât*] unstable; [*dent*] loose; [*raisonnement, régime*] shaky.

branle /bʀɑ̃l/ *nm* (oscillation) swing; **mettre qch en ~** to set [sth] in motion [*mesure, projet, convoi*]; **se mettre en ~** [*convoi, personnes*] to get going; [*processus*] to be set in motion.

branle-bas /bʀɑ̃lba/ *nm inv* (agitation) commotion.
■ **~ de combat** MIL, FIG action stations.

branler /bʀɑ̃le/ [1] **I** *vtr* **~ la tête** or **du chef** to nod one's head.

II *vi* (osciller) [*mur*] to wobble; [*escalier, construction, échafaudage, chaise*] to be rickety; [*dent*] to be loose.

braquage /bʀakaʒ/ *nm* **1**° (de supermarché, banque) robbery; **2** AUT (steering) lock, turning circle.

braque /bʀak/ **I**° *adj* crazy.

II *nm* ZOOL **~ allemand** German shorthaired pointer.

braquer /bʀake/ [1] **I** *vtr* **1** (diriger) to point [*arme, caméra*] (**sur, vers** at); to train [*télescope, projecteur*] (**sur, vers** on); to turn ou fix [*yeux*] (**sur, vers** on); **tous les projecteurs sont braqués sur lui** FIG he's in the spotlight, the spotlight is on him; **tous les regards sont braqués sur vous** LIT, FIG all eyes are upon you; **2** AUT to turn [*volant, roues*] (**à gauche/droite** hard left/right); **3**° (viser) to point a gun at; **4**° (attaquer) to rob [*banque*]; **5**° (buter) **~ qn contre qch/qn** to turn sb against sth/sb; **ne le braque pas** don't get his back up; **il est braqué** he's dug his heels in.

II *vi* AUT [*chauffeur*] to turn the wheel full lock GB ou all the way US; [*véhicule*] **bien/mal ~** to have a good/poor lock GB, to turn well/badly; **braque à gauche** turn (the wheel) sharply to the left.

III se braquer *vpr* (viser) **se ~ sur/vers** [*arme, caméra*] to be pointed at; [*télescope, projecteur*] to be trained on; [*yeux*] to be turned on; (se buter) to dig one's heels in; **se ~ contre qn** to turn against sb.

braqueur° /bʀakœʀ/ *nm* robber.

bras /bʀa/ ▶ 137] *nm inv* **1** ANAT arm; **prendre qn dans ses ~** to take sb in one's arms; **avoir les ~ en croix** to have one's arms outstretched; **par le ~** [*tenir, prendre*] by the arm; **au ~ de qn** on sb's arm; **~ dessus ~ dessous** LIT, FIG arm in arm; **porter qch à bout de ~** LIT to carry sth with one's arms straight out; FIG to keep sth afloat; **baisser les ~** FIG to give up; **en ~ de chemise** in one's shirtsleeves; **rester les ~ croisés** to stand idly; **croiser les ~** LIT to fold one's arms; FIG to twiddle one's thumbs; **2** (main-d'œuvre) manpower, labour^{GB}; **3** GÉOG (de fleuve) branch; **4** TECH (de fauteuil, d'électrophone, ancre) arm ; (de brancard) pole; **5** (de mollusque) tentacle.
■ **~ droit** FIG right hand man; **~ de fer** (épreuve physique) arm wrestling; (lutte d'influence) trial of strength; **~ de mer** sound.
IDIOMES **les ~ m'en tombent** I'm absolutely speechless; **avoir le ~ long** to have a lot of influence.

brasier /bʀazje/ *nm* inferno.

bras-le-corps: à bras-le-corps /abʀalkɔʀ/ *loc adv* **1** LIT [*soulever*] bodily; **2** FIG head-on.

brassage /bʀasaʒ/ *nm* **1** IND (de bière) brewing; **2** (mélange) (de personnes) intermingling; (d'idées, de cultures) cross-fertilization; (d'air) mixture.

brassard /bʀasaʀ/ *nm* **1** GÉN armband; **2** (d'armure) arm-piece.

brasse /bʀas/ *nf* SPORT (style) breaststroke; (mouvement) stroke; **à la ~** in breaststroke.

■ **~ papillon** butterfly (stroke).

brassée /bʀase/ *nf* **1** (de fleurs, papier, bois) armful (**de** of); **2** (de chiffres, personnalités) (whole) host (**de** of).

brasser /bʀase/ [1] *vtr* **1** (remuer) [*personne*] to toss [*salade*]; to toss [sth] around [*idées*]; to shuffle [*cartes à jouer*]; to shuffle [sth] around [*papier*]; to gather [sth] up [*feuilles mortes, linge*]; [*vent*] to blow about [*feuilles*]; to intermingle [*population*]; **il brasse des millions** he handles big money; **2** to brew [*bière*].
IDIOMES **~ de l'air**° to talk a lot of hot air°.

brasserie /bʀasʀi/ ▶374 *nf* **1** (café, restaurant) brasserie; **2** (usine) brewery; **3** (secteur) brewing industry.

brasseur, -euse /bʀasœʀ, øz/ *nm,f* (de bière) brewer.

brassière /bʀasjɛʀ/ *nf* **1** (de bébé) (en coton) baby's vest; (en tricot) baby's top; **2** (soutien-gorge) crop top.

bravade /bʀavad/ *nf* (attitude) bravado.

brave /bʀav/ *adj* (gentil) nice; (courageux) brave.

bravement /bʀavmɑ̃/ *adv* **1** (avec courage) bravely; **2** (sans hésiter) boldly.

braver /bʀave/ [1] *vtr* to defy [*personne, ordre, tabou*]; to brave [*tempête, danger*].

bravo /bʀavo/ **I** *nm* **un grand ~ à** a big cheer for GB, let's hear it for.
II *excl* (pour applaudir) bravo!; (pour féliciter) well done!

bravoure /bʀavuʀ/ *nf* bravery.

break /bʀɛk/ *nm* **1** AUT estate car GB, station wagon US; **2** (d'attelage) (shooting) break.

brebis /bʀəbi/ *nf inv* ZOOL ewe; **les ~** the flock.

brèche /bʀɛʃ/ *nf* **1** (trou) (dans un mur) hole; (dans une haie) gap; **2** MIL (trouée) breach.
IDIOMES **battre qn/qch en ~** to give sb/sth a pounding; **être sur la ~** to be on the go.

bréchet /bʀeʃɛ/ *nm* wishbone.

bredouille /bʀəduj/ *adj* LIT, FIG empty-handed.

bredouiller /bʀəduje/ [1] *vtr, vi* to mumble.

bref, brève¹ /bʀɛf, bʀɛv/ **I** *adj* **1** (court) [*apparition, séjour*] brief; [*son*] short; **soyez ~** be brief; **2** (sec) [*ton*] curt.
II *adv* (pour résumer) (**en**) **~** in short.

brelan /bʀəlɑ̃/ *nm* JEUX three of a kind; **~ de 10** three tens.

breloque /bʀələk/ *nf* (objet) charm.

brème /bʀɛm/ *nf* (poisson) bream.

Brésil /bʀezil/ ▶232 *nprm* Brazil.

brésilien, -ienne /bʀeziljɛ̃, ɛn/ ▶394 *adj* **1** GÉOG Brazilian; **2** [*slip, maillot de bain*] high-cut.

Bretagne /bʀətaɲ/ ▶509 *nprf* **la ~** Brittany.

bretelle /bʀətɛl/ **I** *nf* **1** (de robe, maillot, sac à dos, d'accordéon) strap; **2** (de fusil) sling; **porter l'arme à la ~** to carry a weapon slung over one's shoulder; **3** (d'autoroute) slip road GB, ramp US.
II bretelles *nfpl* braces.
IDIOMES **se faire remonter les ~s**° to get told off°.

breton, -onne /bʀətɔ̃, ɔn/ **I** *adj* Breton; **être ~** to be from Brittany.
II ▶338 *nm* LING Breton.

breuvage /bʀœvaʒ/ *nm* **1** (boisson étrange) PEJ brew; **2** C (boisson) beverage.

brève² /bʀɛv/ **I** *adj f* ▶ **bref I**.
II *nf* **1** (information) news flash; **2** (voyelle, syllabe) short.

brevet /bʀəvɛ/ *nm* **1** (d'invention) **~ (d'invention)** patent; **après le dépôt du ~** after patenting; **2** (diplôme) **~ de secourisme** first aid certificate.
■ **~ des collèges** SCOL certificate of general education; **~ de pilote** AVIAT pilot's licence^GB; **~ de technicien supérieur, BTS** UNIV advanced vocational diploma.

brevetable /bʀəvtabl/ *adj* [*invention*] patentable.

breveté, ~e /bʀəvte/ **I** *pp* ▶ **breveter**.
II *pp adj* (diplômé) [*pilote*] qualified.

breveter /bʀəvte/ [20] *vtr* (faire) **~** to patent [*invention*].

bréviaire /bʀevjɛʀ/ *nm* **1** RELIG breviary; **2** FIG bible.

bribes /bʀib/ *nfpl* (de conversation) snatches; (d'histoire) bits and pieces; **par ~** bit by bit.

bric: de bric et de broc /dəbʀiked(ə)bʀɔk/ *loc adv* [*s'habiller*] any old how; [*meublé*] with bits and pieces.

bricolage /bʀikɔlaʒ/ *nm* **1** (activité) DIY, do-it-yourself; **2** (travail non professionnel) makeshift job.

bricole /bʀikɔl/ *nf* **1** (menu objet) **acheter une ~** to buy a little something; **des ~s** bits and pieces; **2** (de harnais) breast harness.

bricoler /bʀikɔle/ [1] **I** *vtr* (tenter de réparer) to tinker with [*moteur, appareil*]; (confectionner) to knock up GB, to throw together [*étagère, système*]; (truquer) to fiddle GB ou tamper with US [*compteur, machine*].
II *vi* (faire du bricolage) to do DIY GB, to fix things US.

bricoleur, -euse /bʀikɔlœʀ, øz/ **I** *adj* **être ~** to be good with one's hands.
II *nm,f* (personne habile) handyman/handywoman; (personne qui fait du bricolage) DIY enthusiast GB, do-it-yourselfer.

bride /bʀid/ *nf* **1** (de cheval) bridle; **2** (de boutonnage) button loop.
IDIOMES **partir à ~ abattue** to dash off; **avoir la ~ sur le cou** to have free rein.

bridé, ~e /bʀide/ *adj* **yeux ~s** slanting eyes.

brider /bʀide/ [1] *vtr* **1** to bridle [*cheval*]; **2** (contenir) to control [*personne*]; to curb [*élan, liberté, spontanéité*].

bridgeur, -euse /bʀidʒœʀ, øz/ *nm,f* JEUX bridge player.

brièvement /bʀijɛvmɑ̃/ *adv* briefly.

brièveté /bʀijɛvte/ *nf* brevity.

brigade /bʀigad/ *nf* **1** MIL brigade; **~ d'infanterie** infantry unit; **2** (dans la police) squad; **3** ADMIN (groupe de travailleurs) team.
■ **~ de gendarmerie** small unit of gendarmes; **~ de sapeurs-pompiers** fire brigade GB, fire department US.

brigadier /bʀigadje/ ▶284 *nm* **1** MIL (caporal) **~** corporal (in tank, artillery or transport division); **2** (de sapeurs-pompiers) fire chief.

brigand /bʀigɑ̃/ *nm* (bandit) brigand, bandit.

brigandage /bʀigɑ̃daʒ/ *nm* (armed) robbery, banditry†.

briguer /bʀige/ [1] *vtr* to crave [*honneur*]; to set one's sights on [*poste*].

brillamment /bʀijamɑ̃/ *adv* GÉN brilliantly.

brillance /bʀijɑ̃s/ *nf* (d'astre, de diamant) brilliance; (de tissu, papier) sheen.

brillant, ~e /bʀijɑ̃, ɑ̃t/ *adj* **1** (luisant) [*yeux, plumage*] bright; [*cheveux, surface polie, métal*] shiny; [*surface mouillée*] glistening; **regard ~ de joie** eyes shining with joy; **2** (admirable) brilliant; **pas ~** EUPH [*résultat*] not brilliant; [*situation*] quite bad; [*santé, affaires*] none too good, rather poor.
II *nm* **1** (éclat) (de surface polie, cheveux) shine (**de** of); **2** (diamant) (oval diamond), brilliant.

briller /bʀije/ [1] *vi* **1** (luire) [*soleil, lampe, métal*] to shine; [*flamme*] to burn brightly; [*diamant*] to sparkle; [*surface mouillée, neige, larme*] to glisten; [*nez*] to be shiny; (pétiller) to sparkle; **tout brillait de propreté** everything was sparkling clean; **faire ~ ses chaussures** to shine one's shoes; **shampooing qui fait ~ les cheveux** shampoo which makes your hair shine; **les étoiles brillent** the stars are out; **2** (exprimer) [*yeux, regard*] **~ de** to blaze with [*colère*]; to burn with [*fièvre, désir*]; **3** (se distinguer) [*mondain, causeur*] to shine; [*élève*] (dans une matière) to be brilliant (**en** at), to shine (**en** in).

brimade /bʀimad/ *nf* bullying ℂ; **être victime de ~s** to be bullied.

brimer /bʀime/ [1] *vtr* **1** (maltraiter) to bully [*personne*]; **2** (frustrer) **se sentir brimé** to feel picked on.

brin /bʀɛ̃/ *nm* **1** (tige) **un ~ de muguet/persil** a sprig of lily-of-the-valley/parsley; **un ~ de paille** a wisp of straw; **un ~ d'herbe** a blade of grass; **2** (peu) **un ~ de** a bit of; **faire un ~ de causette** to have a little chat; **un ~ exagéré** a touch exaggerated.

brindille /bʀɛ̃dij/ *nf* twig.

bringue○ /bʀɛ̃g/ *nf* **1** (beuverie) drinking party; (fête) rave-up○; **2** (fille) (**grande**) ~ beanpole.

brinquebaler /bʀɛ̃kbale/ [1] *vi* [*chargement*] to rattle about; [*véhicule*] to jolt along; [*personne*] to be shaken.

brio /bʀijo/ *nm* (talent) brilliance; MUS brio.

brioche /bʀijɔʃ/ *nf* **1** CULIN brioche, (sweet) bun; **2**○ (ventre) paunch.

brioché, ~**e** /bʀijɔʃe/ *adj* CULIN brioche (*épith*).

brique /bʀik/ *nf* **1** CONSTR brick; **2** (emballage de lait, jus de fruit) carton.

briquer /bʀike/ [1] *vtr* to polish up; NAUT to scrub down.

briquet /bʀikɛ/ *nm* (de fumeur) (cigarette) lighter.

briqueterie /bʀikɛtʀi/ *nf* (industrie) brickworks (+ *v sg* ou *pl*); (usine) brickyard.

bris /bʀi/ *nm inv* (rupture) GÉN, JUR (de matériel, scellés) breaking; **la police d'assurance ne couvre pas le ~ de glaces** the insurance policy does not cover broken windows or mirrors.

brisant, ~**e** /bʀizɑ̃, ɑ̃t/ **I** *adj* high explosive; **explosif** ~ high-explosive charge.
II *nm* (haut-fond) shoal.
III brisants *nmpl* (vagues) breakers.

brise /bʀiz/ *nf* breeze; **légère/bonne** ~ light/fresh breeze.

brise-bise /bʀizbiz/ *nm inv* half-curtain.

brise-fer /bʀizfɛʀ/ *nm inv* destructive child.

brise-glace /bʀizglas/ *nm inv* **1** (navire) icebreaker; **2** (de pont) ice-breaker.

brise-jet /bʀizʒɛ/ *nm inv* (rubber) spout.

brise-lames /bʀizlam/ *nm inv* breakwater.

briser /bʀize/ [1] **I** *vtr* **1** (rompre) to break [*objet, jambe*]; **2** (interrompre) to break [*rythme, élan*]; to stop [*tentative, attaque, ascension*]; to break down [*résistance*]; to crush [*révolte*]; [*travailleur*] to break [*grève*]; [*police*] to stop [*grève*]; **3** (mettre fin à) to break [*silence, monopole*]; to break down [*tabou*]; to shatter [*rêve, idylle*]; **4** (détruire) to destroy [*pays, structure*]; to break [*personne*]; to wreck [*carrière, vie*]; to shatter [*image*]; **l'émotion lui brisait la voix** his/her voice was breaking with emotion; **avoir le cœur brisé** to be broken-hearted; **5** (épuiser) to shatter [*personne*].
II se briser *vpr* **1** (se rompre) [*vitre, os*] to break; [*vague*] to break (**sur, contre** against); **2** (s'interrompre) [*rêve*] to be shattered; **3** (s'altérer) [*voix*] to break.

brise-tout /bʀiztu/ *nm inv* (personne) butterfingers (*sg*).

briseur, -**euse** /bʀizœʀ, øz/ *nm,f* wrecker.
■ ~ **de grève** strike breaker.

brise-vent /bʀizvɑ̃/ *nm inv* AGRIC windbreak.

bristol /bʀistɔl/ *nm* (carton) Bristol (board).

brisure /bʀizyʀ/ *nf* (fêlure) crack; (débris) fragment.

britannique /bʀitanik/ ▶394 *adj* British.

Britannique /bʀitanik/ ▶394 *nmf* **un/une** ~ a British man/woman; **les** ~**s** the British (people).

Britanniques /bʀitanik/ ▶305 *adj fpl* **les îles** ~ the British Isles.

broc /bʀo/ *nm* ewer.

brocante /bʀɔkɑ̃t/ *nf* **1** (activité) bric-à-brac trade; **2** (marché) flea market.

brocanteur, -**euse** /bʀɔkɑ̃tœʀ, øz/ ▶374 *nm,f* bric-à-brac trader.

brocarder /bʀɔkaʀde/ [1] *vtr* to ridicule, to gibe at.

brocart /bʀɔkaʀ/ *nm* (étoffe) brocade.

broche /bʀɔʃ/ *nf* **1** (bijou) brooch; **2** CULIN spit; **faire cuire qch à la** ~ to spit-roast sth; **3** MÉD pin.

broché, ~**e** /bʀɔʃe/ **I** *pp* ▶ **brocher**.
II *pp adj* [*livre*] paperback (*épith*), softcover (*épith*).

brocher /bʀɔʃe/ [1] *vtr* **1** (en imprimerie) to bind [sth] (with paper) [*livre*]; **2** (tisser) to brocade.

brochet /bʀɔʃɛ/ *nm* ZOOL pike.

brochette /bʀɔʃɛt/ *nf* CULIN (tige) skewer; (mets) kebab, brochette.

brocheur, -**euse**[1] /bʀɔʃœʀ, øz/ ▶374 *nm,f* book binder.

brocheuse[2] /bʀɔʃøz/ *nf* (machine) binder, binding machine.

brochure /bʀɔʃyʀ/ *nf* (fascicule) booklet; (de voyage) brochure.

brocoli /bʀɔkɔli/ *nm* broccoli ¢.

brodequin /bʀɔdkɛ̃/ *nm* **1** (laced) boot; **2** (autrefois) buskin.

broder /bʀɔde/ [1] *vtr, vi* to embroider.

broderie /bʀɔdʀi/ *nf* **1** (art) embroidery; **2** (ouvrage) piece of embroidery, embroidery ¢.

brodeuse /bʀɔdøz/ *nf* (personne) embroiderer.

brome /bʀom/ *nm* CHIMIE bromine.

bromure /bʀɔmyʀ/ *nm* bromide.

bronche /bʀɔ̃ʃ/ *nf* bronchus; **les** ~**s** the bronchial tubes; **avoir les** ~**s fragiles** to have a weak chest.

broncher /bʀɔ̃ʃe/ [1] *vi* [*obéir*] **sans** ~ without a murmur.

bronchite /bʀɔ̃ʃit/ ▶196 *nf* bronchitis ¢.

bronzage /bʀɔ̃zaʒ/ *nm* **1** (activité) (sun-)tanning; (hâle) tan; **2** TECH (de matière) bronzing.

bronze /bʀɔ̃z/ *nm* (matière, objet) bronze.

bronzé, ~**e** /bʀɔ̃ze/ *adj* [*personne*] (sun-)tanned.

bronzer /bʀɔ̃ze/ [1] **I** *vtr* (hâler) to tan [*peau*].
II *vi* [*personne*] to get a tan, to go brown; [*peau*] to tan.

bronzeur /bʀɔ̃zœʀ/ *nm* (ouvrier) bronze-smelter, bronzer.

brossage /bʀɔsaʒ/ *nm* (des cheveux, dents) brushing ¢; (du dos) scrubbing ¢

brosse /bʀɔs/ *nf* **1** GÉN brush; **donner un coup de** ~ **à qch** to give sth a brush; **avoir les cheveux** (**taillés**) **en** ~ to have a crew cut; **2** B (balai) broom.
■ ~ **à cheveux** hairbrush; ~ **à dents** toothbrush; ~ **à habits** clothesbrush; ~ **à ongles** nailbrush.

brosser /bʀɔse/ [1] **I** *vtr* **1** (frotter) to brush [*vêtements, cheveux, dents*]; to scrub [*dos*]; to brush [sb] down [*personne*]; **2** (peindre) to paint [*toile, paysage*]; **3** (décrire) to give a quick outline of.
II○ *vi* B schoolchildren's slang (s'absenter) to skip school.
III se brosser *vpr* to brush oneself down; **se** ~ **les dents/cheveux** to brush one's teeth/hair.

brou /bʀu/ *nm* (écale) husk.
■ ~ **de noix** walnut stain.

broue /bʀu/ *nf* C **1** (bière) beer; **2** (mousse) (de bière) head; (de lait) froth.

brouette /bʀuɛt/ *nf* (véhicule) wheelbarrow; (contenu) barrowful.

brouhaha /bʀuaa/ *nm* hubbub; **un grand** ~ a loud hubbub.

brouillage /bʀujaʒ/ *nm* **1** RADIO, TÉLÉCOM (provoqué) jamming; (involontaire) interference; **2** FIG (de pistes) covering up; (de données) mixing up.

brouillard /bʀujaʀ/ *nm* **1** MÉTÉO fog; **il y a du** ~ it's foggy; **un** ~ **à couper au couteau** a pea souper GB, a thick fog; **2** (pulvérisation) spray; **3** COMM (livre) daybook.
■ ~ **givrant** MÉTÉO freezing fog.

brouillasser /bʀujase/ [1] *v impers* to drizzle.

brouille /bʀuj/ *nf* (momentanée) quarrel; (durable) rift.

brouiller /bʀuje/ [1] **I** *vtr* **1** (rendre trouble) [*produit*] to make [sth] cloudy [*liquide*]; [*pluie*] to blur, to smudge [*nom, texte*]; [*larmes*] to blur [*vue*]; [*personne*] to cover (over) [*empreintes*]; ~ **les pistes** ou **les cartes** FIG to confuse ou cloud the issue; **2** RADIO, TÉLÉCOM [*personne*] to jam [*signaux, émission*]; [*parasites*] to interfere with [*émission, réception*].
II se brouiller *vpr* **1** (se fâcher) [*personnes, groupes*] to fall out; **se** ~ **avec qn** to fall out with sb; **être brouillé avec les chiffres** FIG to be hopeless with figures; **2** (devenir trouble) [*liquide*] to become cloudy; [*vue*] to become blurred; [*esprit, souvenirs*] to become confused; **avoir le teint brouillé** to look ill; **le temps se brouille** it's clouding over.

brouillon, -**onne** /bʀujɔ̃, ɔn/ **I** *adj* **1** (sans soin) [*personne, copie*] untidy; **2** (désorganisé) [*personne*

disorganized; [*esprit, style, discours*] muddled; [*émission, conférence*] disorganized.
II *nm* **1** (première rédaction) **C** (de texte, discours, devoir) rough draft; **faire qch au ~** to do sth in rough; **2** (papier) **¢** **(papier) ~** rough paper.

broussaille /bʀusaj/ *nf* (dans sous-bois) undergrowth **¢**; (sur terrain inculte) scrub **¢**; (dans jardin, parc) bushes (*pl*); **cheveux en ~** tousled hair.

broussailleux, -euse /bʀusajø, øz/ *adj* **1** [*terrain, région*] covered with bushes; [*jardin*] overgrown; **2** [*cheveux*] tousled.

brousse /bʀus/ *nf* BOT bush.

brouter /bʀute/ [1] **I** *vtr* [*chèvre*] to nibble [*herbe, feuilles*]; [*vache, mouton*] **~ (l'herbe)** to graze.
II *vi* AUT to judder.

broutille /bʀutij/ *nf* trifle.

broyer /bʀwaje/ [23] *vtr* (écraser) to grind [*grain, couleurs, aliments*]; to crush [*pierre, bras, pied*].
IDIOMES **~ du noir** [*personne*] to brood.

broyeur, -euse /bʀwajœʀ, øz/ **I** *adj* grinding, crushing.
II *nm* (machine) crusher, grinder.

bru /bʀy/ *nf* daughter-in-law.

brucellose /bʀysɛloz/ *nf* ▶ 196 brucellosis.

brugnon /bʀyɲɔ̃/ *nm* nectarine.

brugnonier /bʀyɲɔnje/ *nm* nectarine tree.

bruine /bʀɥin/ *nf* drizzle.

bruiner /bʀɥine/ [1] *v impers* to drizzle.

bruire /bʀɥiʀ/ [3] *vi* LITER [*feuille, papier, tissu*] to rustle; [*ruisseau*] to murmur; [*insecte*] to hum.

bruissement /bʀɥismɑ̃/ *nm* LITER (de feuille, papier, tissu, vent) rustle **¢**, rustling **¢**; (de ruisseau) murmur **¢**; (d'insecte) humming **¢**.

bruit /bʀɥi/ *nm* **1** (son) noise; **on n'entend pas un ~** you can't hear a sound; **~ étouffé** thud; **un ~ de marteau** hammering; **un ~ de casseroles/ d'assiettes** the clatter of saucepans/of plates; **un ~ de ferraille** a clang; **j'entends un ~ de pas/voix** I can hear footsteps/voices; **on dirait un ~ de moteur** it sounds like an engine; **2** (tapage) noise; **faire du ~** to make a noise, to be noisy; **il y a du ~** it's noisy; **faire un ~ infernal** or **d'enfer** [*machine*] to make a terrible din; [*voisins*] to make an awful racket; **sans ~** silently; **3** FIG (commotion) **son film a fait beaucoup de ~** his/her film attracted a lot of attention; **beaucoup de ~ pour rien** a lot of fuss about nothing; **une affaire qui a fait du ~** an affair that caused an uproar; **4** (rumeur) rumour GB; **le ~ court que** rumour GB has it that.
■ **~ de couloir** rumour GB; **~ de fond** background noise.

bruitage /bʀɥitaʒ/ *nm* CIN, THÉAT sound effects (*pl*).

bruiteur /bʀɥitœʀ/ *nm* sound effects engineer.

brûlant, -e /bʀylɑ̃, ɑ̃t/ *adj* **1** (très chaud) [*fer à repasser, casserole*] hot; [*thé, soupe*] boiling hot; [*vent, sable, asphalte, radiateur*] burning hot; [*soleil*] blazing; **2** (fiévreux) [*personne, front*] burning hot; **être ~ de fièvre** to be burning with fever; **3** (urgent) [*question, thème*] burning; **4** (ardent) [*passion*] burning; [*amour*] passionate; [*regard*] blazing.

brûlé, -e /bʀyle/ **I** *nm,f* MÉD **un grand ~** a third degree burns victim; **service des grands ~s** burns unit.
II *nm* **odeur de ~** smell of burning; **avoir un goût de ~** to taste burned; **ça sent le ~** LIT there's a smell of burning; FIG things are becoming unpleasant.

brûle-parfum(s) /bʀylpaʀfœ̃/ *nm inv* incense burner.

brûle-pourpoint   **à**   **brûle-pourpoint** /abʀylpuʀpwɛ̃/ *loc adv* point-blank.

brûler /bʀyle/ [1] **I** *vtr* **1** (mettre le feu) to burn [*papiers, broussailles, encens*]; to set fire to [*voiture, maison*]; **~ un cierge à** to light a candle to; **~ qn vif** to burn sb alive; **2** (consommer) to use [*combustible, calories*]; to use [*électricité*]; **3** (provoquer une brûlure) [*acide, flamme, huile*] to burn [*personne, peau*]; [*eau, thé*] to scald [*peau, corps*]; [*aliments, alcool*] to burn [*estomac, gorge*]; [*soleil*] to burn [*peau*];

to scorch [*herbe*]; **être brûlé par une explosion** to get burned in an explosion; **être brûlé au visage** to suffer burns to one's face; **attention, ça brûle!** careful, it's very hot!; **être brûlé par le soleil** [*personne*] to get sunburned; **l'argent te brûle les doigts** FIG money burns a hole in your pocket; **j'ai les yeux qui me brûlent** my eyes are stinging; **4** MÉD to cauterize [*verrue*] (à with); **5**° (ne pas respecter) to ignore [*stop, priorité*]; **~ un feu (rouge)** to jump° the lights.
II *vi* **1** (se consumer) [*bois, bougie*] to burn; [*forêt, maison, ville*] to be on fire; **bien/mal ~** [*combustible*] to burn well/badly; **3 000 hectares de forêt ont brûlé** 3,000 hectares of forest have been destroyed by fire; **faire ~** to burn [*papier, pneu*]; to burn [sth] down [*maison*]; **2** CULIN [*rôti, tarte*] to burn; **3** (flamber) [*feu*] to burn; **4** (désirer) **~ de faire, ~ d'envie de faire** to be longing to do; **~ (d'amour) pour qn** to be consumed with love for sb; **5** JEUX (à cache-tampon) **tu brûles!** you're getting very warm!
III **se brûler** *vpr* to burn oneself (avec with; en faisant doing); **se ~ la langue** to burn one's tongue.

brûlis /bʀyli/ *nm* **culture sur ~** slash-and-burn cultivation.

brûlure /bʀylyʀ/ *nf* **1** MÉD burn; **2** (marque) burn mark.
■ **~s d'estomac** MÉD heartburn **¢**.

brume /bʀym/ *nf* **1** (brouillard léger) mist; (en mer) (sea) mist; (brouillard épais) fog; **2** (vapeur) (d'aérosol) mist; **3** (état confus) haze.
■ **~ de chaleur** heat haze.

brumeux, -euse /bʀymø, øz/ *adj* **1** MÉTÉO (de chaleur) hazy; (de froid) misty, foggy; **2** (peu clair) [*esprit, idée*] hazy.

brun, ~e [1] /bʀœ̃, bʀyn/ **I** ▶ 141 *adj* [*peau, tissu, fourrure*] brown, dark; [*cheveux, barbe*] dark; [*yeux*] brown; [*personne*] dark-haired; [*tabac*] black; **cigarette ~e** black tobacco cigarette; **bière ~e** ~ stout GB.
II *nm,f* (homme) dark-haired man; (femme) dark-haired woman.
III *nm* (couleur) brown.

brunante /bʀynɑ̃t/ *nf* C (crépuscule) dusk; **à la ~** at dusk.

brunâtre /bʀynɑtʀ/ ▶ 141 *adj* brownish.

brune [2] /bʀyn/ **I** *adj f* ▶ **brun**.
II *nf* **1** (cigarette) black tobacco cigarette; **2** (bière) ~ stout GB.
III **à la brune** *loc prép* LITTÉR at dusk.

brunir /bʀyniʀ/ [3] **I** *vtr* (bronzer) to tan.
II *vi* **1** [*personne, peau*] to tan; [*cheveux*] to get darker; **2** CULIN to brown; **faire ~** to brown [*sauce, beurre*].

brushing /bʀœʃiŋ/ *nm* blow-dry.

brusque /bʀysk/ *adj* **1** [*personne, ton*] abrupt (avec qn with sb); **2** (imprévu) [*mouvement*] sudden; [*virage*] sharp.

brusquement /bʀyskəmɑ̃/ *adv* **1** [*dire, interrompre*] abruptly; **2** [*ralentir, entrer, mourir*] suddenly; [*freiner*] sharply.

brusquer /bʀyske/ [1] *vtr* **1** (traiter sans ménagement) to be brusque with; **2** (précipiter) to rush.

brusquerie /bʀyskəʀi/ *nf* (rudesse) brusqueness.

brut, ~e [1] /bʀyt/ **I** *adj* **1** (non traité) [*coton, soie, matière*] raw; [*minerai, pétrole*] crude; [*pierre précieuse*] rough, uncut; [*marbre, granit*] rough; [*laine*] untreated; [*sucre*] unrefined; **à l'état ~** in its natural state; **2** [*champagne, vin mousseux*] dry, brut; [*cidre*] dry; **3** [*salaire, bénéfice*] gross; **4** [*poids, charge*] gross.
II *adv* gross.
III *nm* (pétrole) crude (oil); (champagne) dry champagne.

brutal, ~e *mpl* **-aux** /bʀytal, o/ *adj* **1** (brusque) [*coup, choc*] violent; [*douleur, mort*] sudden; [*hausse, chute*] dramatic; [*coup de frein*] sharp; **2** (violent) [*ton, caractère, discours*] brutal; [*geste*] violent; **être ~ avec qn** (physiquement) to be rough with sb; (en paroles) to be brutal with sb; **3** (choquant) [*réalité*] stark.

brutalement /bʀytalmɑ̃/ *adv* **1** (avec violence) [*réprimer, frapper*] brutally; [*fermer, ouvrir*] violently;

2 (brusquement) [*changer, baisser*] dramatically; [*mourir, s'arrêter*] suddenly; [*freiner, accélérer*] sharply.

brutaliser /bʀytalize/ [1] *vtr* to ill-treat [*personne, animal*].

brutalité /bʀytalite/ *nf* **1** (violence) brutality; **2** (brusquerie) suddenness; **3** (acte de violence) (act of) brutality **C**; **les ~s policières** police brutality.

brute² /bʀyt/ I *adj f* ▶ **brut** I.

II *nf* **1** (personne violente) brute; **2** (personne sans culture) lout.

IDIOMES **comme une ~** [*taper*] savagely; [*dormir*] like a log; [*travailler*] like a horse.

Bruxelles /bʀysɛl/ ▶ 628 *npr* Brussels.

bruxellois, **~e** /bʀyselwa, az/ ▶ 628 *adj* Brussels (*épith*).

bruyamment /bʀɥijamɑ̃/ *adv* [*rire, éternuer, protester*] loudly; [*entrer, sortir*] noisily.

bruyant, **~e** /bʀɥijɑ̃, ɑ̃t/ *adj* **1** LIT [*conversation, musique*] loud; [*enfant, jeu*] noisy, boisterous; [*pièce, rue*] noisy; **2** FIG [*renommée, succès*] resounding.

bruyère /bʀyjɛʀ/ *nf* **1** (plante) heather; (racine) briar; **terre de ~** heath; **2** (lieu) heath.

BTP /betepe/ *nm* (*abbr* = **bâtiment et travaux publics**) building and civil engineering.

BTS /betɛs/ *nm*: *abbr* ▶ **brevet**.

bu, **~e** /by/ *pp* ▶ **boire**.

buanderie /bɥɑ̃dʀi/ *nf* **1** (dans une maison) laundry room; **2** C (laverie automatique) launderette GB, Laundromat® US.

buccal, **~e**, *mpl* -**aux** /bykal, o/ *adj* oral.

bucco-dentaire /bykodɑ̃tɛʀ/ *adj* [*hygiène*] oral.

bûche /byʃ/ *nf* **1** (de bois) log; **2**○ (chute) tumble; **prendre** or **ramasser une ~** to fall (flat on one's face).

■ **~ de Noël** CULIN yule log.

bûcher¹○ /byʃe/ [1] *vi* to slog away○.

bûcher² /byʃe/ *nm* **1** (de condamné) stake; **2** (de mort) (funeral) pyre; **3** (réserve) woodshed.

bûcheron /byʃʀɔ̃/ ▶ 374 *nm* lumberjack.

bûchette /byʃɛt/ *nf* **1** (objet) (pour le feu) stick; **des ~s pour allumer le feu** kindling **C**; **2** (pour compter) counting rod; **3** CULIN individual yule log.

bûcheur○, -**euse** /byʃœʀ, øz/ *adj* [*élève, étudiant*] industrious.

bucolique /bykɔlik/ *adj* bucolic, pastoral.

budget /bydʒɛ/ *nm* budget.

budgétaire /bydʒetɛʀ/ *adj* [*prévisions, déficit, excédent*] budget (*épith*); [*contrôle*] budgetary, budget (*épith*); [*contraintes, restrictions*] budgetary; [*année*] financial GB, fiscal US.

budgétiser /bydʒetize/ [1] *vtr* to include [sth] in the budget [*dépense, recette*].

buée /bɥe/ *nf* (de froid) condensation; (d'haleine) steam.

buffet /byfɛ/ *nm* **1** (meuble) (de salle à manger) sideboard; (de cuisine) dresser; **2** (de gare) buffet; **3** (table garnie) buffet.

buffle /byfl/ *nm* buffalo.

buis /bɥi/ *nm* (buisson) box tree; (haie) box hedge; (bois) boxwood.

buisson /bɥisɔ̃/ *nm* (sauvage) bush; (cultivé) shrub.

■ **~ ardent** BIBLE burning bush; BOT pyracantha.

buissonnière /bɥisɔnjɛʀ/ *adj* **faire l'école ~** to play truant GB, to play hooky○ US.

bulbe /bylb/ *nm* **1** (de plante) bulb; **2** (coupole) onion(-shaped) dome.

■ **~ dentaire** root of tooth; **~ pileux** hair bulb; **~ rachidien** medulla oblongata.

bulbeux, -**euse** /bylbø, øz/ *adj* bulbous.

bulgare /bylgaʀ/ ▶ 394, 338 *adj, nm* Bulgarian.

bulldozer /byldozœʀ/ *nm* bulldozer.

bulle¹ /byl/ *nm inv* **papier ~** unbleached paper.

bulle² /byl/ *nf* **1** (d'air, de gaz) bubble; **faire des ~s** to blow bubbles; **2** (de bande dessinée) speech bubble.

bulletin /byltɛ̃/ *nm* **1** (informations) bulletin, report; **~ météorologique** weather forecast; **~ scolaire** ou **de notes** school report GB, report card US; **2** (document)

certificate; (d'abonnement, adhésion) form; **~ de salaire** or **paie** payslip; **~ de naissance** birth certificate; **3** (bon) **~ de commande** order form; **~ de participation** (dans un jeu) entry form; **4** (publication) bulletin; **5** (rubrique de journal) (colonne) column; (page) page; **6** POL (de vote) ballot ou voting paper; **~ blanc** blank vote; **~ nul** spoiled ballot paper.

bulletin-réponse, *pl* **bulletins-réponse** /byltɛ̃ʀepɔ̃s/ *nm* reply coupon.

bulot /bylo/ *nm* whelk.

buraliste /byʀalist/ ▶ 374 *nmf* **1** (de bureau de tabac) (vendant des articles pour fumeurs) tobacconist; (vendant des cigarettes et journaux) newsagent GB, newsdealer US; **2** (de bureau de paiement) clerk.

bure /byʀ/ *nf* **1** (étoffe) frieze; **2** (vêtement) habit; **porter la ~** to be a monk.

bureau, *pl* **~x** /byʀo/ *nm* **1** (meuble) desk; **2** (pièce individuelle) (chez soi) study; (au travail) office; **heures d'ouverture** office hours; **3** (établissement) office; **ouvrir un ~ à Londres** to open an office in London; **4** (organe directeur) board; **~ exécutif** executive board.

■ **~ d'accueil** reception; **~ de change** bureau de change, foreign exchange office; **~ d'études** (recherche) research department; (conception) design office; **~ de poste** post office; **~ de tabac** (articles pour fumeurs) tobacconist's; (cigarettes, journaux) newsagent GB, news stand US; **~ de tri** sorting office; **~ de vote** polling station; **Bureau international du travail**, BIT International Labour Office, ILO.

bureaucrate /byʀokʀat/ *nmf* PEJ bureaucrat.

bureaucratie /byʀokʀasi/ *nf* (administration) bureaucracy; (pouvoir des bureaucrates) officialdom.

bureautique /byʀotik/ *nf* office automation.

burette /byʀɛt/ *nf* **1** (pour l'huile, le vinaigre) cruet; **2** (de messe) cruet; **3** TECH oil applicator; (plus grand) oilcan.

burin /byʀɛ̃/ *nm* chisel; **sculpter au ~** to chisel.

buriner /byʀine/ [1] *vtr* **1** (graver) to engrave; **2** (dégrossir) to chisel out [*statue, bloc*]; **3** (marquer) to furrow [*visage, traits*]; **avoir les traits burinés** to have a deeply furrowed face.

burlesque /byʀlɛsk/ I *adj* [*tenue, idée, histoire*] ludicrous; [*farce, film, scène*] farcical.

II *nm* CIN, LITTÉRAT **le ~** the burlesque.

bus /bys/ *nm inv* **1** (véhicule) bus; **2** ORDINAT bus.

busard /byzaʀ/ *nm* harrier.

buse /byz/ *nf* **1** ZOOL buzzard; **2**○ (idiot) clot○ GB, clod○; **triple ~!** you total ou prize idiot○!; **3** TECH (conduit) pipe, duct; (embout) nozzle.

busqué, **~e** /byske/ *adj* [*nez*] hooked.

buste /byst/ *nm* **1** (sculpture) bust; **2** (torse) chest; **3** (seins) bust.

bustier /bystje/ *nm* (sous-vêtement) long-line bra; (vêtement) bustier; **robe ~** bustier dress.

but /by(t)/ *nm* **1** (objectif) goal; (intention) aim, purpose; (ambition) aim; **atteindre son ~** to reach one's goal; **marcher sans ~** to walk aimlessly; **nous touchons au ~** our goal is in sight; **mon ~ dans la vie est de** my aim in life is to; **il s'est fixé pour ~ la présidence** he has set his sights on the presidency; **dans quel ~ est-il venu?** what was his purpose ou object in coming here?; **dans ce ~** with this aim in view; **faire qch dans un ~ désintéressé** to do sth with no ulterior motive; **aller droit au ~** to go straight to the point; **2** SPORT (au football) goal; (au tir) target.

IDIOMES **demander/déclarer de ~ en blanc** to ask/declare point-blank; **annoncer qch de ~ en blanc à qn** to spring sth on sb.

butane /bytan/ *nm* Calor gas® GB, butane.

buté, **~e**¹ /byte/ *adj* [*personne, air*] stubborn, obstinate.

butée² /byte/ *nf* **1** TECH stop; **~ d'une porte** doorstop; **2** ARCHIT buttress.

buter /byte/ [1] I *vtr* **1** (rendre têtu) to make [sb] even more stubborn; **2** CONSTR (étayer) to prop up [*mur*]; **3**○ (tuer) to kill [*personne*].

II *vi* **1** [*personne*] to trip, to stumble; **~ contre qch** (trébucher) to trip over sth; (se heurter) to bump into sth; **~ sur** or **contre** to come up against [*obstacle, difficulté*].

III se buter *vpr*(s'obstiner) **il va se ~** he'll be even more stubborn.

buteur /bytœʀ/ *nm* (au rugby) (place-)kicker; (au football) leading goal scorer.

butin /bytɛ̃/ *nm* **1** (de guerre) spoils (*pl*); **2** (de vol) haul, loot; **3** (de recherche) fruits (*pl*).

butiner /bytine/ [1] **I** *vtr* **1** [*abeilles*] to gather pollen from [*fleurs*]; **2** FIG (glaner) to glean, to pick up [*renseignements*].

II *vi* [*abeilles*] to gather pollen.

butoir /bytwaʀ/ *nm* **1** RAIL buffer; **2** TECH stop; **3** (date limite) (**date**) **~** deadline.

butte /byt/ *nf* mound.
IDIOMES **être en ~ à** to come up against [*difficultés*]; to be the butt of [*sarcasmes, moquerie*].

buvable /byvabl/ *adj* **1** (à boire) [*médicament*] to be taken orally (*après n*); **2** (pas mauvais) drinkable.

buvard /byvaʀ/ *nm* **1** (matière) (**papier**) **~** blotting paper **₵**; **2** (feuille) sheet of blotting paper; **3** (sous-main) blotter.

buvette /byvɛt/ *nf* (de gare, fête) refreshment area.

buveur, -euse /byvœʀ, øz/ *nm,f* **1** (alcoolique) drinker, alcoholic; **2** (personne qui boit) drinker.

byzantin, ~e /bizɑ̃tɛ̃, in/ *adj* Byzantine; **querelles ~es** FIG hairsplitting quarrels.

BZH (*written abbr* = **Breizh**) Brittany.

Cc

c, C /se/ *nm inv* c, C; **c cédille** c cedilla.

c' ▶ ce.

CA *written abbr* ▶ **chiffre**.

ça /sa/ *pron dém* ▶ 81 |
IDIOMES **elle est bête et méchante avec ~** she's stupid and what's more she's nasty; **et avec ~?** anything else?; **rien que ~!** IRON is that all! IRON; **c'est ~!** that's right!; **eh bien, c'est ~, ne te gêne pas!** IRON oh, carry on GB ou keep going, don't mind me! IRON; **~ va?** (la vie) how are things?; (l'affaire proposée) is that a deal?; **~ y est, ~ recommence!** here we go again!; **~ y est, j'ai fini!** that's it, I've finished!; **~ y est, il pleut!** here comes the rain!; **'alors, ~ y est, tu es prêt?'—'non, ~ n'y est pas!'** 'well, are you ready?'—'no, I'm not!'

çà /sa/ *adv* **~ et là** here and there.

cabale /kabal/ *nf* **1** (intrigue, intrigants) cabal; **monter une ~ contre qn** to form a cabal against sb; **2** RELIG cabbala.

caban /kabã/ *nm* sailor's jacket.

cabane /kaban/ *nf* **1** (habitation) hut; **2** (abri) shed; **3**⁰ (prison) nick○.

cabanon /kaban3/ *nm* (abri) shed.

cabaret /kabaʀɛ/ *nm* cabaret.

cabas /kaba/ *nm* shopping bag.

cabillaud /kabijo/ *nm* cod; **filet de ~** cod fillet.

cabine /kabin/ *nf* (de bateau, fusée) cabin; (de camion) cab; (de laboratoire de langue) booth; (de piscine) cubicle; (pour se changer) changing room.
■ **~ de douche** shower cubicle; **~ d'essayage** fitting room; **~ de pilotage** cockpit; **~ téléphonique** phone box GB, phone booth.

cabinet /kabinɛ/ I *nm* **1** (local) GÉN office; (de médecin, dentiste) surgery GB, office US; (de juge) chambers (*pl*); **2** (affaires et clientèle) practice; (cabinet collectif) firm; (de médecins, dentistes) practice; **ouvrir un ~** to set up in practice; **3** (agence) agency; **~ immobilier** estate agent's; **4** POL (gouvernement) cabinet; (de ministre, préfet) staff; **~ ministériel** minister's personal staff; **5** (de musée) exhibition room.
II **cabinets** *nmpl* toilet (*sg*), loo○ (*sg*) GB, bathroom (*sg*) US.
■ **~ de consultation** surgery GB, office US; **~ noir** cubbyhole; **~ de toilette** bathroom.

cabinet-conseil, *pl* cabinets-conseil /kabinɛk3sɛj/ *nm* firm of consultants.

câblage /kablaʒ/ *nm* **1** (connexions) wiring; **2** (mise en place) wiring; **3** TV cabling; **faire le ~ d'une ville** to install cable television in a town.

câble /kabl/ *nm* (en métal, synthétique) cable; (en fibres végétales) rope; **~ porteur** (de pont) suspension cable; (de téléphérique) carrying cable.
■ **~ d'amarrage** mooring rope; **~ de remorque** (de navire) towline.

câbler /kable/ [1] *vtr* **1** (connecter) to wire; **2** (télégraphier) to cable.

cabochard○, **~e** /kabɔʃaʀ, aʀd/ *adj* stubborn.

caboche○ /kabɔʃ/ *nf* (tête) head; **mets-toi ça dans la ~** get that into your thick skull.

cabosser /kabɔse/ [1] *vtr* to dent; **(tout) cabossé** battered.

cabot○ /kabo/ *nm* (chien) PÉJ dog, mutt○ PÉJ.

cabotage /kabɔtaʒ/ *nm* coastal shipping.

cabotin, **~e** /kabɔtɛ̃, in/ *adj* **être ~** to like playing to the gallery.

cabrer /kabʀe/ [1] I *vtr* to make [sth] rear [*cheval*].
II **se cabrer** *vpr* **1** [*cheval*] to rear (**devant** at); **2** [*personne*] to jib; **3** AVIAT [*avion*] to zoom.

cabri /kabʀi/ *nm* kid; **sauter comme un ~** to gambol like a lamb.

cabriole /kabʀijɔl/ *nf* **1** (de clown, d'enfant, animal) capering ¢; **faire des ~s** to caper about; **2** (de cheval) capriole; **3** (en danse) cabriole.

cabriolet /kabʀijɔlɛ/ *nm* AUT convertible, cabriolet; (voiture à cheval) cabriolet.

CAC® /kak/ *nm* (*abbr* = **Compagnie des agents de change**) **indice ~ 40**, **~ 40** Paris Stock Exchange index.

caca /kaka/ *nm* BABY TALK poo GB, poop US; **il a fait ~ dans sa culotte** he pooed GB ou pooped US in his pants.
■ **~ d'oie** (couleur) greenish yellow.

cacahuète /kakawɛt/ *nf* peanut.

cacao /kakao/ *nm* (poudre, boisson) cocoa.

cacaotier /kakaɔtje/, **cacaoyer** /kakaɔje/ *nm* cacao tree.

cacarder /kakaʀde/ [1] *vi* [*oie*] to honk.

cacatoès /kakatɔɛs/ *nm* cockatoo.

cachalot /kaʃalo/ *nm* sperm whale.

cache¹ /kaʃ/ *nm* (feuille opaque) mask.

cache² /kaʃ/ *nf* hiding place; **~ d'armes** arms cache.

caché, **~e** /kaʃe/ I *pp* ▶ **cacher**.
II *pp adj* [*trésor, charme, beauté, sens*] hidden; [*complot, douleur, désir, amour*] secret.

cache-cache /kaʃkaʃ/ ▶ 329 | *nm inv* hide and seek; **jouer à ~** LIT, FIG to play hide and seek.

cache-col /kaʃkɔl/ *nm inv* scarf.

cachemire /kaʃmiʀ/ *nm* cashmere; **de** or **en ~** cashmere (*épith*); **motif ~** paisley pattern.

Cachemire /kaʃmiʀ/ ▶ 509 | *nprm* **le ~** Kashmir.

cache-pot /kaʃpo/ *nm inv* flowerpot holder, planter.

cacher /kaʃe/ [1] I *vtr* to hide; **~ son visage dans ses mains** to hide ou bury one's face in one's hands; **~ sa nudité** to cover one's nakedness; **~ son jeu** FIG to keep one's cards close to one's chest; **~ qch à qn** to conceal ou hide sth from sb; **il leur a caché la mort de son chien** he didn't tell them his dog had died; **je ne vous cache pas que je suis inquiète** frankly, I'm worried; **pour ne rien vous ~** to be quite frank.
II **se cacher** *vpr* **1** GÉN to hide; (temporairement) [*personne*] to go into hiding; [*animal*] to go to ground; **il ne s'en cache pas** he makes no secret of it; **quelle organisation se cache derrière les émeutes?** which organization is behind these riots?; **2** (disparaître) [*soleil, objet*] to disappear.

cachet /kaʃɛ/ *nm* **1** (comprimé) tablet; **un ~ d'aspirine®** an aspirin; **2** (à l'encre) stamp; (de cire) seal; **de la poste** postmark; **'le ~ de la poste faisant foi'** 'as attested by date on postmark'; **3** (chic) style; (marque distinctive) cachet; **4** CIN, THÉÂT (paie) fee.

cacheter /kaʃte/ [20] *vtr* to seal.

cachette /kaʃɛt/ *nf* hiding place; **sortir de sa ~** GÉN to come out of one's hiding place; [*fugitif*] to come out of hiding; **en ~** on the sly.

cachot /kaʃo/ *nm* (de prison moderne) prison cell; (de prison ancienne) dungeon; **faire trois jours de ~** to be locked up alone for three days.

cachotterie /kaʃɔtʀi/ *nf* little secret; **faire des ~s à qn** to keep things from sb.

ça¹

I ça sert à désigner

Pour désigner un objet présent, on utilisera *this* si l'objet est proche, *that* s'il est plus éloigné:

aide-moi à plier ça = help me fold this

Pour récapituler, reprendre ce dont il s'agit, on utilisera *that*:

à part ça	= apart from that
et tout ça, parce que ...	= and all that because ...
tu n'en as pas envie, je vois ça	= you don't feel like it, I can see that
où as-tu entendu ça?	= where did you hear that?
me faire/dire ça, à moi!	= fancy doing/saying that to me (of all people)!
c'est pour ça qu'il est parti	= that's why he left
il ne manquait plus que ça!	= that's all we needed!
on dit ça !	= that's what they/you etc. say!

Attention:

sans ça = otherwise

II ça est sujet du verbe

(Voir également les verbes *aller*, *être*, *faire*, *marcher* ainsi que la note d'usage sur *la mesure du temps* pour l'expression *ça fait un an/deux mois que*)

ça représente un objet:

si ça flotte, ce n'est pas une pierre = if it floats, it can't be a stone
ça coûte cher? = is it expensive?

ça représente un fait, une déclaration, une idée déjà mentionnés: si le ton est neutre, on emploiera *it*, mais s'il est emphatique, on utilisera *that*:

ça fait mal = it hurts

lorsqu'il s'agit d'une simple constatation, mais quand il exprime la surprise, l'indignation:

ça fait mal = that hurts!

de même:

ça ne marchera pas = it won't work (est une affirmation neutre)

alors que:

ça ne marchera pas = that won't work (rejette avec force la solution proposée)
ça paraît incroyable = it seems incredible *ou* that seems incredible (selon l'emphase)

Dans les phrases ci-dessous, nettement emphatiques, *that* est la traduction qui s'impose:

ça suffit, voyons! = that's enough!
ça t'a étonné, n'est-ce pas? = that surprised you, didn't it?

ça représente ce qui va être explicité:

ça m'inquiète de la voir dans cet état = it worries me to see her in that state
ça vaut la peine qu'il y aille = it's worth his going
ça n'est pas pour me vanter, mais ... = I don't want to boast, but ...

On notera cependant:

la rue ça de bien qu'elle est calme = one good thing about the street is that it is quiet

ça a une valeur impersonnelle:

ça souffle aujourd'hui! = it's windy today!
ça chauffe aujourd'hui! = it's hot today!

ça représente une personne: dans ce cas on utilisera le pronom personnel approprié, *he*, *she* ou *they*:

et ça se croit malin! = and he/she etc. thinks he's/she's etc. clever!

La nature de *ça* n'est pas définie: on pourra souvent traduire par la tournure impersonnelle *there is/are*, comme dans les exemples suivants:

ça sent le brûlé = there's a smell of burning
ça tapait de tous les côtés = there was banging everywhere
ça criait de tous les côtés = there was shouting everywhere

Lorsque *ça* est sujet de rappel, il ne se traduit pas:

la télévision, ça m'ennuie = television bores me
voyager (ou les voyages),
ça revient cher = travelling is expensive
et le jardin, ça pousse? = how's the (*ou* your) garden doing?

ça a une valeur d'insistance. La tournure est emphatique:

qu'est-ce que c'est que ça? = what's that?
ça, je m'en moque! = I couldn't care less about that!
ça, ça ne compte pas! = that doesn't count!
c'est bizarre, ça
ou ça, c'est bizarre = that's strange

Pour renforcer une interrogation:

pourquoi ça? = why's that?
'je l'ai vu' 'quand/où ça?' = 'I saw him' 'when/where was that?'
'tu la connais?' 'qui ça?' = 'do you know her?' 'who do you mean?'
'je ne veux pas'—'comment ça, tu ne veux pas?' = 'I don't want to'—'what do you mean, you don't want to?'
'c'est faisable'—'comment ça?' = 'it can be done'—'how?'

Dans une comparaison (voir également *comme*):

ce n'est pas si facile que ça = it's not as easy as (all) that *ou* it's not that easy
la dernière fois que je l'ai vu, il n'était pas plus haut que ça! = last time I saw him, he was only so high!

Attention:

tu te lèves toujours aussi tard que ça? (l'heure qu'il est) = do you always get up this late? (l'heure mentionnée) = do you always get up that late?

Avec valeur d'interjection:

ça, par exemple! (indigné) = well, honestly! (surpris) = well I never!
ça, alors! (surpris) = well I never!
ça, oui! = definitely!
ça, non! = no way! *ou* absolutely not!
ça, pour se plaindre, il se plaint! = talk about complain, he does nothing else!
ça, comme bavard, il n'y a pas mieux! = he can certainly talk all right!
ça, mon vieux, débrouille-toi! = sort it out for yourself, mate!

---

cachottier, -ière /kaʃɔtje, ɛʀ/ *adj* secretive.

cacophonie /kakɔfɔni/ *nf* cacophony.

cactus /kaktys/ *nm inv* cactus.

c-à-d (*written abbr* = **c'est-à-dire**) ie.

cadastral, ~e, *mpl* **-aux** /kadastʀal, o/ *adj* [*plan*] cadastral; [*registre*] land (*épith*).

cadastre /kadastʀ/ *nm* (registre) land register, cadastre^GB; (administration) land registry.

cadavérique /kadaveʀik/ *adj* [*pâleur, odeur*] deathly (*épith*); [*teint*] deathly pale.

cadavre /kadavʀ/ *nm* **1** (de personne) GÉN corpse; (de victime) body; (d'animal) body, carcass; **~ ambulant**○ walking skeleton; **2**○ (bouteille vide) dead bottle.

caddie /kadi/ *nm* **1** (au golf) caddie; **2** ®(de supermarché) shopping trolley GB, shopping cart US.

cadeau, *pl* **~x** /kado/ **I** *nm* present, gift; **faire un ~ à qn** to give sb a present; **je t'en fais ~** (je te l'offre) I'm giving it to you; (je ne veux pas d'argent) I'm making you a present of it; (tu peux le garder) you can keep it; **il ne fait pas de ~x** (commerçant) he's not exactly cheap; (juge, examinateur) he's very strict; **ils ne se font pas de ~x** they don't do each other favours^GB; **se faire un ~** to treat oneself; **et, en ~,**

un disque and a record as a free gift; **mon chef c'est pas un ~**° my boss is a pain°.
II **(-)cadeau** (*in compounds*) gift; **papier(-)~** wrapping paper.
■ **~ empoisonné** poisoned chalice.

cadenas /kadna/ *nm* padlock.

cadence /kadãs/ *nf* **1** (de mouvements, pas) rhythm; **en ~** [*marcher*] in step; [*ramer*] rhythmically; **2** (de sons, poème) cadence; **3** (de travail, production) rate; **relâcher/tenir la ~** to slacken/to keep up the pace; **4** MIL (de tir) rate; **5** MUS (enchaînement d'accords) cadence.

cadencé, ~e /kadãse/ *adj* **les slogans cadencés des manifestants** the rhythmic chanting of the demonstrators.

cadet, -ette /kadɛ, ɛt/ **I** *adj* (de deux) younger; (de plus de deux) youngest.
II *nm,f* **1** (enfant) (dernier de deux) younger son/daughter, younger child; (dernier de plus de deux) youngest son/daughter, youngest child; **2** (frère, sœur) younger brother/sister; **3** (personne plus jeune) junior; (personne la plus jeune) youngest; **un homme de trente ans ton ~** a man thirty years your junior; **4** SPORT *athlete between the ages of 15 and 17*; **5** MIL cadet.

cadrage /kadraʒ/ *nm* **1** (action) framing; **2** (résultat) composition.

cadran /kadrã/ *nm* (de montre, boussole) face; (de compteur) dial; **~ solaire** sundial.
IDIOMES **faire le tour du ~**° to sleep round GB ou around US the clock.

cadre /kadR/ **I** *nm* **1** (de tableau, miroir) frame; **2** (lieu) setting; (milieu) surroundings (*pl*); **3** (domaine délimité) **cela sort du ~ de mes fonctions** that's not part of my duties; **sortir du ~ de la légalité** to go outside the law; **4** (structure) framework; **en dehors du ~ scolaire** outside a school context; **5** (employé) executive; **~ moyen/supérieur** middle ranking/senior executive; **les ~s moyens/supérieurs** middle/senior management (+ *v pl*); **6** (de bicyclette, moto) frame; **7** (dans un formulaire) space, box.
II **dans le cadre de** *loc prép* **1** (à l'occasion de) on the occasion of; **dans le ~ de cette journée particulière** on this special occasion; **2** (dans le contexte de) (de lutte, négociations, d'organisation) within the framework of; (de campagne, plan) as part of; **recevoir une formation dans le ~ d'une entreprise** to undergo training within a company.
■ **~ de vie** (living) environment.

cadrer /kadre/ [1] **I** *vtr* to centre^GB [*image, scène*]; **la photo est mal cadrée** the photo is off-centre^GB; **photo bien cadrée** well-composed photo.
II *vi* to tally, to fit (**avec** with); **ça ne cadre pas** it doesn't fit.

cadreur /kadrœR/ **▶ 374** *nm* CIN cameraman.

caduc, caduque /kadyk/ *adj* **1** (désuet) obsolete; (sans effet) null; **rendre qch ~** to render sth null and void; **2** [*feuille*] deciduous; **arbre à feuilles caduques** deciduous tree.

cafard /kafaR/ *nm* **1**° (mélancolie) depression; **avoir le ~** to be down in the dumps°; **un coup de ~** a fit of depression; **donner le ~ à qn** to get sb down°, to make sb depressed; **2** (insecte) cockroach.

cafardeux, -euse /kafardø, øz/ *adj* [*personne*] glum; [*nature, tempérament*] gloomy.

café /kafe/ **I ▶ 141** *adj inv* (couleur) dark brown.
II *nm* **1** (substance, boisson, arôme) coffee; **~ vert** unroasted coffee; **~ en grains** coffee beans (+ *v pl*); **~ soluble** instant coffee; **prendre un ~** to have a coffee; **glace au ~** coffee ice cream; **2** (établissement) café; **3** (fin d'un repas) **au ~** at the end of the meal.
■ **~ crème** espresso with milk; **~ au lait** coffee with milk; **peau ~ au lait** coffee-coloured^GB skin; **~ noir** black coffee.

café-concert, *pl* **cafés-concerts** /kafekɔ̃sɛR/ *nm* café with live music.

caféier /kafeje/ *nm* coffee tree.

caféine /kafein/ *nf* caffeine.

cafétéria /kafeteRja/ *nf* cafeteria.

café-théâtre, *pl* **cafés-théâtres** /kafeteatR/ *nm* café with live theatre^GB.

cafetière /kaftjɛR/ *nf* **1** (récipient) coffee pot; (appareil) coffee maker; **2**° (tête) head; **il n'a rien dans la ~** he's brainless.
■ **~ électrique** coffee machine.

cafouillage° /kafujaʒ/ *nm* (confusion) bungling° ¢.

cafouiller° /kafuje/ [1] *vi* [*personne*] to get flustered; [*appareil*] to be on the blink°; **il a fait ~ nos projets** he messed up our plans; **ça cafouille** things are in a mess.

cage /kaʒ/ *nf* **1** (pour animaux) cage; **en ~** caged; **mettre en ~** to cage [*animal*]; to put [sb] behind bars [*personne*]; **dans une ~ de verre** behind a glass screen; **vivre en ~** FIG to be cooped up°; **2**° SPORT goal.
■ **~ d'ascenseur** lift shaft GB, elevator shaft US; **~ d'escalier** stairwell; **~ à lapins** LIT, FIG° rabbit hutch; **~ à oiseaux** birdcage; **~ à poules** LIT hen coop; **~ thoracique** rib cage.
IDIOMES **tourner comme un ours** ou **lion en ~** to pace up and down like a caged animal.

cageot /kaʒo/ *nm* crate.

cagibi /kaʒibi/ *nm* store cupboard.

cagneux, -euse /kaɲø, øz/ *adj* **avoir les genoux ~** to be knock-kneed.

cagnotte /kaɲɔt/ *nf* **1** (caisse commune) kitty; **2** (de loterie) jackpot; **3** (économies) (pour plus tard) nest egg; (plus général) **une jolie ~** a nice little sum.

cagoule /kagul/ *nf* GÉN balaclava; **deux hommes en ~** two hooded men.

cahier /kaje/ **I** *nm* **1** (carnet) notebook; SCOL exercise book; **2** (en imprimerie) section.
II **cahiers** *nmpl* (revue) journal (*sg*).
■ **~ de brouillon** rough book; **~ de devoirs** homework book; **~ d'exercices** exercise book; **~ de textes** homework notebook; **~ de travaux pratiques** lab book, laboratory notebook.

cahin-caha° /kaɛ̃kaa/ *adv* [*marcher, avancer*] with difficulty; **les affaires vont ~** business isn't going too well.

cahot /kao/ *nm* jolt; **les ~s** FIG the ups and downs.

cahotant, ~e /kaotã, ãt/ *adj* [*route, carrière*] bumpy.

cahoté, ~e /kaote/ *adj* (secoué) shaken about; (éprouvé) buffeted; **~ par la vie** buffeted by life.

cahoter /kaote/ [1] *vi* [*véhicule*] to bounce along.

cahute /kayt/ *nf* (cabane) hut, shack.

caïd /kaid/ *nm* **1** (gangster) boss; **jouer les ~s** to act tough; **2**° (personne importante) big shot; (personne supérieure) star; (personne très compétente) wizard.

caillasse /kajas/ *nf* (cailloux) stones (*pl*).

caille /kaj/ *nf* ZOOL quail.

cailler /kaje/ [1] **I** *vtr* to curdle.
II *vi* (se figer) [*lait*] to curdle; [*sang*] to congeal.
III **se cailler** *vpr* **1** [*lait*] to curdle; [*sang*] to congeal; **2**° (avoir froid) [*personne*] to be freezing.
IV° *v impers* **ça caille** it's freezing.

caillot /kajo/ *nm* clot.

caillou, *pl* **~x** /kaju/ *nm* **1** (pierre) pebble; **gros ~** stone; **du ~**° rock ¢; **avoir un ~ à la place du cœur** FIG to have a heart of stone; **2**° (tête) **ne plus avoir un poil sur le ~** to be as bald as a coot°; **ne rien avoir dans le ~** to be brainless.

caillouteux, -euse /kajutø, øz/ *adj* [*sol, route*] stony.

caïman /kaimã/ *nm* cayman.

Caire /kɛR/ **▶ 628** *npr* **le ~** Cairo.

caisse /kɛs/ *nf* **1** (boîte) GÉN crate; (de champagne, vin) case, crate; (bac) planter; **2** (de voiture) shell, body; **3**° (voiture) car, old banger°; **4** (tambour) drum; **5** (pour l'argent) (tiroir) till; (appareil) cash register; (coffret) cash box; **les ~s de l'État** the Treasury coffers; **tenir la ~** (normalement) to be the cashier; (un moment) to be on the cash desk; FIG to hold the purse strings; **6** (guichet) (de magasin) cash desk; (de supermarché) checkout

(counter); (de banque) cashier' s desk; **7** (capital, organisme) fund; **~ de secours** relief fund.
■ **~ enregistreuse** cash register; **~ d'épargne**
~ savings bank; **~ noire** slush fund; **~ à outils**
toolbox.
IDIOMES **à fond la ~**○ [*partir, s'en aller*] at breakneck speed; [*mettre la musique*] at full blast.
caissette /kɛsɛt/ *nf* GÉN small box ou case; (pour fruits)
crate.
caissier, -ière /kesje, ɛʁ/ [▶ 374] *nm,f* cashier.
caisson /kɛsɔ̃/ *nm* (à bouteilles) crate.
■ **~ de décompression** decompression chamber.
cajoler /kaʒɔle/ [1] *vtr* (être tendre avec) to make a fuss
over; (flatter) to bring [sb] round GB ou around US.
cajolerie /kaʒɔlʁi/ *nf* (caresse) cuddle; (parole) compliment.
cajoleur, -euse /kaʒɔlœʁ, øz/ *adj* (tendre) affectionate.
cajou /kaʒu/ *nm* **noix de ~** cashew nut.
cake /kɛk/ *nm* fruit cake.
cal /kal/ *nm* callus; **des ~s** calluses.
calabrais, ~e /kalabʁɛ, ɛz/ [▶ 509] *adj* Calabrian.
calamar /kalamaʁ/ *nm* squid.
calaminer: se calaminer /kalamine/ [1] *vpr* to
carbonize, to coke up; **être calaminé** to be coked up.
calamité /kalamite/ *nf* **1** (malheur) disaster, calamity;
2○ (personne insupportable) pain○; (catastrophe ambulante)
walking disaster.
calandre /kalɑ̃dʁ/ *nf* AUT (radiator) grille GB.
calcaire /kalkɛʁ/ **I** *adj* [*sel*] calcium (*épith*); [*eau*]
hard; [*minéral*] calcareous; [*terrain*] chalky; [*plateau,
roche*] limestone (*épith*).
II *nm* **1** (roche) limestone; **2** (dépôt blanc) fur GB, sediment US; **enlever le ~ d'une bouilloire** to descale a
kettle.
calcification /kalsifikasjɔ̃/ *nf* calcification.
calciné, ~e /kalsine/ *adj* (carbonisé) charred; (soumis
à une chaleur intense) scorched.
calciner /kalsine/ [1] *vtr* (carboniser) to char; (au four) to
burn [sth] to a crisp; CHIMIE to calcine.
calcium /kalsjɔm/ *nm* calcium.
calcul /kalkyl/ **I** *nm* **1** (opération) calculation; **faire des
~s** to make some calculations; **faire le ~ de qch** to
calculate sth; **'à combien est-ce que ça va me revenir?'—'attends, il faut que je fasse le ~'** 'how
much will it come to?'—'wait, I'll have to work it out';
2 (matière) arithmetic; **3** (tactique) calculation; **agir par
~** to act out of self-interest; **être un bon ~** to be a
good move; **4** MÉD stone.
II calculs *nmpl* (estimations) calculations.
■ **~ mental** mental arithmetic; **~ rénal** kidney
stone; **~ urinaire** stone in the bladder.
calculateur, -trice[1] /kalkylatœʁ, tʁis/ **I** *adj* calculating.
II *nm,f* calculating person; **c'est un ~** he's very
calculating.
III *nm* ORDINAT computer.
calculatrice[2] /kalkylatʁis/ *nf* (pocket) calculator.
calculer /kalkyle/ [1] **I** *vtr* **1** (compter) to calculate, to
work out; **2** (évaluer) to weigh up [*avantages, chances*];
to gauge [*résultats, effort*]; **~ son rythme** SPORT to
pace oneself; **tout bien calculé** all things considered;
3 (préméditer) **~ son coup** to plan one's move.
II *vi* to calculate.
calculette /kalkylɛt/ *nf* pocket calculator.
Caldoche /kaldɔʃ/ *nmf* European New Caledonian.
cale /kal/ *nf* **1** (pour meuble, porte) wedge; (pour roue)
chock; (pour surélever) block; **2** NAUT (ship's) hold.
calé○, ~e /kale/ *adj* **1** (instruit) bright; **~ en qch**
brilliant at sth; **2** (complexe) difficult.
calebasse /kalbas/ *nf* **1** BOT calabash, gourd; **2**○ (tête)
head.
calèche /kalɛʃ/ *nf* barouche, calash.
caleçon /kalsɔ̃/ *nm* **1** (sous-vêtement masculin) boxer
shorts (*pl*), underpants (*pl*); **~ long** long johns○ (*pl*);
2 (vêtement féminin) leggings (*pl*).

calembour /kalɑ̃buʁ/ *nm* pun, play on words.
calendes /kalɑ̃d/ *nfpl* calends.
IDIOMES **aux ~ grecques** never in a month of
Sundays○; **renvoyer qch aux ~ grecques** to postpone sth indefinitely.
calendrier /kalɑ̃dʁije/ *nm* **1** calendar; **~ républicain** French Revolutionary calendar; **2** (programme)
schedule; **3** (dates) dates (*pl*).
calepin /kalpɛ̃/ *nm* notebook.
caler /kale/ [1] **I** *vtr* **1** (stabiliser) to wedge [*roue, pied de
table*]; to steady [*meuble*]; to support [*rangée de livres*];
~ sa tête sur un oreiller to rest one's head on a
pillow; **2**○ (remplir) **petit déjeuner qui cale l'estomac**
breakfast that fills you up.
II *vi* **1** (s'arrêter) to stall; **2** (abandonner) to give up; **j'ai
calé au dessert** I gave up when it came to the dessert;
~ sur un problème to get stuck on a problem.
III se caler *vpr* (s'installer) to settle (**dans** in).
calfeutrer /kalføtʁe/ [1] **I** *vtr* to stop up [*fissure*]; to
draughtproof [*porte, fenêtre*].
II se calfeutrer *vpr* to shut oneself away.
calibre /kalibʁ/ *nm* **1** (diamètre) (d'arme à feu, de tuyau,
balle) calibre GB; (de câble) diameter; **arme de gros ~**
large-bore weapon; **2** (d'œufs, de fruits, légumes) size; **3**
(étalon) gauge; **4** (mesure) template, pattern; **5**○ (pistolet)
gun; **6** (de personne) calibre GB.
calibrer /kalibʁe/ [1] *vtr* **1** (donner le calibre convenable
à) to calibrate; **2** (régler) to calibrate; **3** (classer) to size
[*œufs, fruits, légumes*].
calice /kalis/ *nm* RELIG chalice.
calife /kalif/ *nm* caliph.
califourchon: à califourchon /akalifuʁʃɔ̃/ *loc adv*
astride; **~ sur une chaise** astride a chair.
câlin, ~e /kalɛ̃, in/ **I** *adj* [*air, ton*] affectionate; [*personne*] cuddly.
II *nm* cuddle; **faire un ~ à qn** to give sb a cuddle.
câliner /kaline/ [1] *vtr* to cuddle.
calleux, -euse /kalø, øz/ *adj* calloused, rough-
skinned.
calligraphie /kaligʁafi/ *nf* calligraphy.
calligraphier /kaligʁafje/ [2] *vtr* to write [sth] in a
decorative hand.
callosité /kalozite/ *nf* callus.
calmant, ~e /kalmɑ̃, ɑ̃t/ **I** *adj* GÉN [*musique, parole*]
soothing; [*médicament*] sedative.
II *nm* sedative.
calmar /kalmaʁ/ *nm* squid.
calme /kalm/ **I** *adj* **1** (paisible) [*mer, temps*] calm; [*ciel,
nuit*] still; [*endroit, Bourse, vie, personne*] quiet;
2 (maître de soi) calm; **restons ~s!** let's keep calm!
II *nmf* (personne tranquille) calm person; **c'est un grand
~** he is unflappable.
III *nm* **1** (environnement paisible) peace (and quiet); **j'ai
besoin de ~** I need peace and quiet; **2** (absence d'agitation) calm; (de foule, d'assemblée) calmness; (de mer, nuit,
sanctuaire) stillness; **lancer un appel au ~** to appeal
for calm; **c'est le ~ avant la tempête** LIT, FIG it's the
calm before the storm; **le ~ est revenu** calm has
returned; **dans le ~** peacefully; **3** (maîtrise de soi)
composure; **avec le plus grand ~** with the greatest
composure; **garder** or **conserver son ~** to keep
calm; **avec ~** calmly; **du ~!** (reste tranquille) calm
down!; (fais moins de bruit) quiet!; **4** (sérénité) inner
peace; **5** MÉTÉO, NAUT calm.
calmement /kalməmɑ̃/ *adv* calmly.
calmer /kalme/ [1] **I** *vtr* **1** (apaiser) to calm [sb/sth]
down [*personne, animal*]; to defuse [*situation*]; to tone
down [*discussion*]; to subdue [*agitation, colère*]; to allay
[*inquiétude*]; **~ le jeu** FIG to calm things down; **~ les
esprits** to calm people down; **2** (atténuer) to ease [*douleur*]; to bring down [*fièvre*]; to dampen [*passions,
désir*]; to take the edge off [*faim, soif*].
II se calmer *vpr* **1** (s'apaiser) [*personne, situation*] to
calm down; [*tempête*] to die down; [*agitation, colère*] to
die down; [*discussion*] to quieten GB ou quiet US down;
[*inquiétude*] to subside; [*désir*] to cool; **calme-toi!** (reste
tranquille) calm down!; (fais moins de bruit) quieten GB ou

quiet US down!; **les esprits se sont calmés** tempers have cooled; **2** (s'atténuer) [*douleur*] to ease; [*fièvre, faim*] to die down; [*bruit*] to subside.

calomnie /kalɔmni/ *nf* slander.

calomnier /kalɔmnje/ [2] *vtr* to slander.

calomnieux, -ieuse /kalɔmnjø, øz/ *adj* slanderous.

calorie /kalɔʀi/ *nf* calorie; **régime (à) basses ~s** low-calorie diet.

calorifère /kalɔʀifɛʀ/ *adj* heat-conveying.

calorifique /kalɔʀifik/ *adj* calorific.

calorique /kalɔʀik/ *adj* calorie (*épith*); **ration/valeur ~** calorie intake/content.

calot /kalo/ *nm* (couvre-chef) MIL forage cap GB, overseas cap US; (pour femme) brimless hat.

calotte /kalɔt/ *nf* **1** (couvre-chef) skull cap; **2**◦ (tape) slap; FIG **prendre une bonne ~** to be given a slap.
■ **~ glaciaire** icecap.

calque /kalk/ *nm* (copie) tracing; (papier) tracing paper; (imitation) replica.

calquer /kalke/ [1] *vtr* **1** (imiter) to copy [*comportement*]; **~ qch sur qch** to model sth on sth; **2** (reproduire) to trace [*motif, dessin*].

calumet /kalymɛ/ *nm* calumet; **~ de la paix** peace pipe; **fumer le ~ de la paix avec qn**◦ FIG to make (one's) peace with sb.

calvados /kalvados/ *nm* calvados (*apple brandy distilled in Normandy*).

calvaire /kalvɛʀ/ *nm* (épreuves) ordeal; RELIG (monument) wayside cross; (lieu) Calvary; ART Calvary.

calvinisme /kalvinism/ *nm* Calvinism.

calvitie /kalvisi/ *nf* (affection) baldness; **avoir un début de ~** to be going bald.

camaïeu /kamajø/ *nm* **1** (pierre) cameo; **2** ART monochrome (painting); **en ~** in monochrome; **3** (de tissu) shades (*pl*); **en ~ vert** in green shades.

camarade /kamaʀad/ *nmf* **1** GÉN friend; **~ d'école** schoolfriend; **~ d'atelier** workmate; **~ de régiment** army pal◦ ou buddy◦; **2** POL comrade; **la ~ Markova** Comrade Markova.

camaraderie /kamaʀadʀi/ *nf* comradeship, camaraderie.

Cambodge /kɑ̃bɔdʒ/ **▶ 232 |** *nprm* Cambodia.

cambouis /kɑ̃bwi/ *nm* dirty grease.

cambré, ~e /kɑ̃bʀe/ *adj* [*dos*] arched; [*pied, chaussure*] with a high instep (*épith, après n*); **avoir le pied bien ~** to have a finely arched foot.

cambrer /kɑ̃bʀe/ [1] **I** *vtr* to curve [*objet*]; to arch [*chaussure*]; **~ les reins** or **le dos** to arch one's back.
II se cambrer *vpr* [*personne*] to arch one's back.

cambriolage /kɑ̃bʀijɔlaʒ/ *nm* burglary.

cambrioler /kɑ̃bʀijɔle/ [1] *vtr* to burgle GB, to burglarize US; **se faire ~** to be burgled GB, to be burglarized US.

cambrioleur, -euse /kɑ̃bʀijɔlœʀ, øz/ *nm,f* burglar.

cambrousse◦ /kɑ̃bʀus/ *nf* **la ~** the sticks◦ (*pl*), the country; **en pleine ~** in the middle of nowhere; **n'être jamais sorti de sa ~** to be a country bumpkin.

cambrure /kɑ̃bʀyʀ/ *nf* (état courbé) bending; (courbe) curve.
■ **~ des pieds** instep; **~ des reins** small of the back.

came /kam/ *nf* **1** (en mécanique) cam; **2**◦ (drogue) drugs (*pl*).

camé◦, ~e[1] /kame/ **I** *adj* **être ~** to be on drugs.
II *nm,f* junkie◦, drug addict.

camée[2] /kame/ *nm* cameo.

caméléon /kameleɔ̃/ *nm* LIT, FIG chameleon.

camelote◦ /kamlɔt/ *nf* PEJ junk◦, rubbish GB.

camembert /kamɑ̃bɛʀ/ *nm* **1** (fromage) Camembert; **2** (en statistique) pie chart.

camer◦: se camer /kame/ [1] *vpr* to be on drugs.

caméra /kameʀa/ *nf* (cine-)camera GB, movie camera US.

Cameroun /kamʀun/ **▶ 232 |** *nprm* Cameroon.

camerounais, ~e /kamʀunɛ, ɛz/ **▶ 394 |** *adj* Cameroonian.

caméscope® /kameskɔp/ *nm* camcorder.

camion /kamjɔ̃/ *nm* truck, lorry GB.
■ **~ à benne** tipper truck; **~ de déménagement** removal van; **~ frigorifique** refrigerated truck ou lorry GB; **~ militaire** military truck.

camion-citerne, *pl* **camions-citernes** /kamjɔ̃sitɛʀn/ *nm* tanker.

camionnette /kamjɔnɛt/ *nf* van.

camionneur /kamjɔnœʀ/ **▶ 374 |** *nm* (conducteur) lorry driver GB, truck driver.

camisole /kamizɔl/ *nf* camisole; **~ de force** straitjacket.

camomille /kamɔmij/ *nf* (plante) camomile; (infusion) camomile tea.

camouflage /kamuflaʒ/ *nm* **1** MIL (dispositif) camouflage; **tenue de ~** camouflage fatigues (*pl*); **2** FIG (de la vérité) concealing ¢; (transformation des faits) disguising ¢ (**en** as).

camoufler /kamufle/ [1] **I** *vtr* **1** MIL to camouflage; **2** (cacher) to cover up [*vérité*]; to conceal [*intention*]; to hide [*argent*].
II se camoufler *vpr* to hide; **se ~ le visage** to cover one's face.

camp /kɑ̃/ *nm* **1** MIL camp; **~ d'entraînement** training camp; **2** (prison) camp; **~ de prisonniers** prison camp; **~ de détention** or **réclusion** detention centreGB; **3** (campement provisoire) camp; **~ de réfugiés** refugee camp; **4** SPORT, POL side; **dans le ~ adverse** on the other side.
■ **~ de concentration** concentration camp; **~ d'extermination** extermination camp; **~ de la mort** death camp; **~ de travail** labourGB camp.
IDIOMES **ficher**◦ or **foutre**◦ **le ~** to split◦, to leave; **tout fout le ~**◦ everything is falling apart.

campagnard, ~e /kɑ̃paɲaʀ, aʀd/ **I** *adj* [*vie, fête*] country (*épith*); [*accent, repas, meuble*] rustic.
II *nm,f* country person; **les ~s** country people.

campagne /kɑ̃paɲ/ *nf* **1** (régions rurales) country; (paysage) (open) countryside; **habiter (à) la ~** to live in the country; **en pleine ~** in the countryside; **2** (opération) campaign; **~ électorale/publicitaire** election/advertising campaign; **~ de vaccination** vaccination drive; **faire ~** to campaign; **3** (période d'activité) year; **4** MIL campaign; **se mettre en ~ pour trouver qch** FIG to set about finding sth.
IDIOMES **battre la ~**◦ to be off one's rocker◦.

campagnol /kɑ̃paɲɔl/ *nm* vole.

campanule /kɑ̃panyl/ *nf* campanula, bellflower.

campement /kɑ̃pmɑ̃/ *nm* (lieu) camp; **établir un ~** to set up camp; **matériel de ~** camping equipment.

camper /kɑ̃pe/ [1] **I** *vtr* (décrire) to portray [*personnage*]; to depict [*paysage, scène*].
II *vi* to camp; **~ sur ses positions** FIG to stand firm.
III se camper *vpr* **se ~ devant qch/qn** to stand squarely in front of sth/sb.

campeur, -euse /kɑ̃pœʀ, øz/ *nm,f* camper.

camphre /kɑ̃fʀ/ *nm* camphor.

camping /kɑ̃piŋ/ *nm* **1** (activité) camping; **faire du ~** to go camping; **faire du ~ sauvage** to camp rough; **2** (lieu) campsite GB, campground US.

camping-gaz® /kɑ̃piŋgaz/ *nm inv* camping stove.

campus /kɑ̃pys/ *nm inv* campus; **hors ~** off-campus.

Canada /kanada/ **▶ 232 |** *nprm* Canada.

Canadair® /kanadɛʀ/ *nm* water bomber, air tanker.

canadien, -ienne[1] /kanadjɛ̃, ɛn/ **▶ 394 |** *adj* Canadian.

canadienne[2] /kanadjɛn/ *nf* (veste) sheepskin-lined jacket; (tente) ridge tent.

canaille /kanɑj/ **I** *adj* mischievous.
II *nf* (personne) villain; **petite ~** rascal.

canal, *pl* **-aux** /kanal, o/ *nm* **1** (voie navigable) canal; **le Grand Canal** the Grand Canal; **2** (moyen) channel; **3** ANAT (tube) duct; **4** TÉLÉCOM (fréquence) channel.

canalisation /kanalizasjɔ̃/ *nf* **1** (tuyau) pipe; (réseau) mains (*pl*); **2** (action de diriger) channelling^{GB}.

canaliser /kanalize/ [1] *vtr* **1** to canalize [*cours d'eau*]; **2** (diriger) to channel.

canapé /kanape/ *nm* **1** (siège) sofa, settee; ~ convertible sofa bed; **2** CULIN canapé.

canapé-lit, *pl* **canapés-lits** /kanapeli/ *nm* sofa bed.

canaque /kanak/ *adj* Kanak.

canard /kanaʀ/ *nm* **1** (animal) duck; **chasse aux ~s** duck shooting; **2**° (sucre) *sugar lump dipped in coffee or brandy*; **3**° (journal) rag°, newspaper; **4** MUS (fausse note) wrong note; **5**° (terme d'affection) darling.
■ ~ **de Barbarie** Muscovy duck; ~ **boîteux** FIG lame duck; ~ **laqué** Peking duck.
IDIOMES **ça ne casse pas trois** or **quatre pattes à un ~**° it's nothing to write home about.

canarder° /kanaʀde/ [1] *vtr* LIT, FIG to snipe at [*personne, positions*].

canari /kanaʀi/ *nm* (oiseau) canary.

canasson° /kanasɔ̃/ *nm* nag°, horse.

cancan /kɑ̃kɑ̃/ *nm* **1**° (commérage) gossip ¢; **faire** or **raconter des ~s** to gossip; **2** (danse) (French) ~ cancan.

cancaner° /kɑ̃kane/ [1] *vi* [*personne*] to gossip.

cancanier, -ière /kɑ̃kanje, ɛʀ/ *adj* [*personne*] gossipy (*épith*); **il est (très) ~** he's a (real) gossip.

cancer /kɑ̃sɛʀ/ *nm* **1** ▶196 MÉD cancer; **avoir un ~** to have cancer; **un ~ du sein** breast cancer; ~ **de l'estomac** cancer of the stomach; **2** FIG cancer.

Cancer /kɑ̃sɛʀ/ ▶641 *nprm* Cancer.

cancéreux, -euse /kɑ̃seʀø, øz/ **I** *adj* [*tumeur, cellule*] cancerous; [*personne*] with cancer (*épith, après n*).
II *nm,f* GÉN person with cancer; (sous traitement) cancer patient.

cancérigène /kɑ̃seʀiʒɛn/ *adj* carcinogenic.

cancérologie /kɑ̃seʀɔlɔʒi/ *nf* cancer research; **service de ~** cancer ward.

cancre /kɑ̃kʀ/ *nm* dunce.

cancrelat /kɑ̃kʀəla/ *nm* cockroach.

candélabre /kɑ̃delabʀ/ *nm* candelabra GB, candelabrum US.

candeur /kɑ̃dœʀ/ *nf* ingenuousness.

candi /kɑ̃di/ *adj m* **fruit ~** candied fruit; **sucre ~** sugar candy.

candidat, -e /kɑ̃dida, at/ *nm,f* **1** POL candidate; **être** or **se porter ~ aux élections** to stand for election GB, to run for office US; **~ désigné** or **officiel** nominee; **2** (à un examen) candidate; **les ~s au permis de conduire** people taking the driving test; **3** (à un poste, statut) applicant (**à** for); **le ~ retenu** the successful applicant; **être** or **se porter ~ (à un poste)** to apply (for a post); **4** JEUX contestant (**à** in); **5** (aspirant) **il n'est pas ~ au mariage** he's not the marrying type; **pour la vaisselle, il n'y a pas beaucoup de ~s** HUM when it comes to doing the dishes, there aren't many takers ou volunteers.

candidature /kɑ̃didatyʀ/ *nf* **1** (à une élection) candidacy; **retirer sa ~** to stand down GB, to drop out US; **2** (à un poste, statut) application; ~ **spontanée** unsolicited application; **faire acte de ~** to apply (**à** for).

candide /kɑ̃did/ *adj* ingenuous.

cane /kan/ *nf* (female) duck.

caneton /kantɔ̃/ *nm* duckling.

canette /kanɛt/ *nf* **1** (bouteille) ~ **(de bière)** (small) bottle of beer; **2** (boîte) ~ **de bière** can of beer; **3** (de machine à coudre) spool; **4** ZOOL (female) duckling.

canevas /kanva/ *nm inv* (toile) canvas; (ouvrage) tapestry work; FIG framework.

caniche /kaniʃ/ *nm* poodle; ~ **nain** toy poodle.

caniculaire /kanikylɛʀ/ *adj* scorching.

canicule /kanikyl/ *nf* **1** (chaleur) **hier, c'était la ~** yesterday was a real scorcher°; **sortir en pleine ~** to go out in the scorching heat°; **2** (période chaude) dog days (*pl*); (vague de chaleur) heatwave.

canif /kanif/ *nm* GÉN penknife, pocketknife.

canin, ~e[1] /kanɛ̃, in/ *adj* [*race*] canine; [*exposition, nourriture*] dog (*épith*).

canine[2] /kanin/ *nf* (dent) canine (tooth).

caniveau, *pl* ~**x** /kanivo/ *nm* (de chaussée) gutter.

canne /kan/ *nf* **1** (pour marcher) (walking) stick; **une ~ à pommeau** a stick with a knob; **2** BOT cane; **3**° (jambe) pin°, leg.
■ ~ **anglaise** (forearm) crutch; ~ **à pêche** fishing rod; ~ **à sucre** sugar cane.

canné, -e /kane/ *adj* [*fauteuil, chaise*] cane (*épith*).

canneberge /kanbɛʀʒ/ *nf* cranberry.

cannelé, -e /kanle/ *adj* [*colonne, verre*] fluted.

cannelle /kanɛl/ *nf* cinnamon.

cannelure /kanlyʀ/ *nf* (de colonne) flute; ~**s** fluting ¢.

cannette = **canette** 1, 2, 3.

cannibale /kanibal/ **I** *adj* cannibal (*épith*).
II *nmf* cannibal.

cannibalisme /kanibalism/ *nm* cannibalism.

canoë /kanɔe/ ▶329 *nm* **1** (embarcation) (Canadian) canoe; **descendre une rivière en ~** to canoe down a river; **2** (sport) canoeing; **faire du ~** to go canoeing.

canoë-kayak /kanɔekajak/ ▶329 *nm* canoeing.

canon /kanɔ̃/ **I** *adj m inv* JUR **droit ~** canon law.
II *nm* **1** MIL (arme) (big) gun; (sur un avion) cannon; HIST **cannon;** ~ **de 75 (mm)** 75-mm gun; **tirer un coup de ~** to fire a gun; **entendre des coups de ~** to hear cannon fire; **boulet de ~** cannonball; **2** MIL (tube d'arme) barrel; **à ~ lisse** smoothbore (*épith*); **à ~ rayé** rifled; **fusil à ~ double** double-barrelled^{GB} shotgun; **fusil à ~ scié** sawn-off GB ou sawed-off US shotgun; **3** MUS canon; **chanter en ~** to sing in a round; **4** (principe) canon; **5** RELIG canon.
■ ~ **antiaérien** antiaircraft gun; ~ **arroseur** sprinkler; ~ **à eau** water cannon; ~ **mitrailleur** heavy machine gun; ~ **à neige** snow-blower.

cañon /kanjɔ̃, kanjon/ *nm* canyon.

canonique /kanɔnik/ *adj* RELIG [*décret*] canonical; **droit ~** canon law; **d'âge ~** HUM of a venerable age.

canoniser /kanɔnize/ [1] *vtr* to canonize.

canonnière /kanɔnjɛʀ/ *nf* (navire) gunboat.

canot /kano/ *nm* (small) boat, dinghy; ~ **pneumatique** rubber ou inflatable dinghy; ~ **de sauvetage** NAUT lifeboat; AVIAT life raft.

canotier /kanɔtje/ *nm* (chapeau) boater.

canson® /kɑ̃sɔ̃/ *nm* drawing paper.

cantate /kɑ̃tat/ *nf* cantata.

cantatrice /kɑ̃tatʀis/ ▶374 *nf* (d'opéra) opera singer; (de musique classique) (professional) singer.

cantine /kɑ̃tin/ *nf* **1** (restaurant) canteen GB, cafeteria; **2** (malle) tin trunk.

cantique /kɑ̃tik/ *nm* canticle; **le Cantique des ~s** the Song of Songs.

canton /kɑ̃tɔ̃/ *nm* ADMIN canton.

cantonade : **à la cantonade** /alakɑ̃tɔnad/ *loc adv* **parler à la ~** to speak to no-one in particular; THÉÂT to speak off.

cantonais, ~e /kɑ̃tɔnɛ, ɛz/ ▶338, 628 **I** *adj* Cantonese.
II *nm* LING Cantonese.

cantonal, ~e[1], *mpl* -**aux** /kɑ̃tɔnal, o/ *adj* cantonal.

cantonale[2] /kɑ̃tɔnal/ *nf* POL ~ **(partielle)** by-election; **les ~s** cantonal elections.

cantonnement /kɑ̃tɔnmɑ̃/ *nm* MIL (stationnement) (dans une ville, région) stationing ¢; (chez l'habitant) billeting ¢; (lieu) GÉN quarters (*pl*); (camp) station.

cantonner /kɑ̃tɔne/ [1] **I** *vtr* **1** MIL GÉN to station; (chez l'habitant) to billet (**chez** with); **2** (restreindre) ~ **qn dans un lieu** to confine sb to a place; ~ **qn dans le rôle de** to reduce sb to the role.
II se cantonner *vpr* **se ~ dans un rôle** to restrict oneself to a role.

cantonnier /kɑ̃tɔnje/ ▶374 *nm* road-mender.

canular /kanylaʀ/ *nm* hoax.

canyon = **cañon**.

La capacité

Pour mesurer les liquides, on utilise traditionnellement les pints, les quarts (rares aujourd'hui) et les gallons en Grande-Bretagne et aux États-Unis. Les liquides comme le vin ou l'essence sont vendus de plus en plus au litre, mais cela n'a pas modifié les habitudes des consommateurs. L'automobiliste anglais ou américain achète donc désormais son essence en litres, mais compte toujours sa consommation en gallons.

Pour les mesures en cm^3, dm^3, m^3 etc. voir le volume ▶ 635|. Pour la prononciation des nombres, voir les nombres ▶ 399|.

Les mesures britanniques: équivalences

			dire
1 pint	= 0,57 ℓ		
1 quart	= 2 pints	= 1,13 ℓ	
1 gallon	= 8 pints	= 4,54 ℓ	
1 litre*	1 ℓ†	= 1.76‡ pt	pint
		0.88 qt	quarts
		0.22 galls	gallons

Les mesures américaines: équivalences

			dire
1 pint	= 0,47 ℓ		
1 quart	= 2 pints	= 0,94 ℓ	
1 gallon	= 8 pints	= 3,78 ℓ	
1 litre*	1 ℓ†	= 2.12 pts‡	pints
		1.06 qt	quart
		0.26 galls	gallons

* Attention: on écrit litre en anglais britannique, et liter en anglais américain.
† L'abréviation de litre (ℓ) est la même en anglais qu'en français.
‡ Noter que l'anglais utilise un point là où le français a une virgule.

il y a 1 000 centimètres cubes dans un litre	= there are 1,000 cubic centimetres in a litre
1 000 centimètres cubes font un litre	= 1,000 cubic centimetres make one litre
il y a huit pintes dans un gallon	= there are eight pints in a gallon
quelle est la contenance de la bouteille?	= what is the size of the bottle? ou (moins familier) what is the capacity of the bottle?

combien contient-elle?	= what does it hold?
elle contient 2 litres	= it holds two litres
elle a une contenance de 2 litres	= its capacity is two litres
la contenance de la bouteille est de 2 litres	= the capacity of the bottle is two litres

Noter l'absence d'équivalent anglais de la préposition française de avant le chiffre dans les deux derniers exemples.

la bouteille fait 2 litres	= the bottle holds 2 litres
elle fait à peu près 2 litres	= it holds about 2 litres
presque 3 litres	= almost 3 litres
plus de 2 litres	= more than 2 litres
moins de 3 litres	= less than 3 litres
A a une plus grande contenance que B	= A has a greater capacity than B
B a une moins grande contenance que A	= B has a smaller capacity than A
A a la même contenance que B	= A has the same capacity as B
A et B ont la même contenance	= A and B have the same capacity

Noter l'ordre des mots dans les adjectifs composés anglais, et l'utilisation du trait d'union. Noter aussi que litre, employé comme adjectif, ne prend pas la marque du pluriel.

une bouteille de deux litres	= a 2-litre bottle
un réservoir de 200 litres	= a 200-litre tank

Mais on peut également dire a tank 200 litres in capacity.

deux litres de vin	= two litres of wine
vendu au litre	= sold by the litre
ils utilisent 20 000 litres par jour	= they use 20,000 litres a day
elle fait 8 litres aux 100	= it does 28 miles to the gallon

En anglais, on compte la consommation d'une voiture en mesurant non pas le nombre de litres nécessaires pour parcourir 100 kilomètres, mais la distance parcourue (en miles) avec 4,54 litres (un gallon) de carburant.

---

caoutchouc /kautʃu/ nm **1** (matière): rubber; **de** or **en** ~ rubber (épith); **être en** ~ to be made of rubber; **2** (plante) rubber plant; **3** (élastique) rubber band.

caoutchouteux, -euse /kautʃutø, øz/ adj rubbery.

cap /kap/ nm **1** GÉOG (promontoire) cape; **le** ~ **Horn** Cape Horn; **doubler** or **franchir un** ~ to round a cape; **2** (obstacle) hurdle; **3** (limite) mark; **passer le** ~ **de la cinquantaine** to pass the fifty mark; **4** (orientation) course; **changer de** ~ to change course; **mettre le** ~ **sur** to head for; **mettre le** ~ **au sud** to head south.

Cap /kap/ ▶ 628| npr le ~ Capetown.

CAP /seape/ nm: abbr ▶ **certificat**.

capable /kapabl/ adj capable (**de faire** of doing); **c'est quelqu'un de très** ~ he's a very capable person; **il n'est même pas** ~ **de faire cuire un œuf** he can't even boil an egg!; **il est** ~ **de tout pour garder sa place** he would do anything to keep his job; **ils sont bien** ~s **de nous dénoncer** I wouldn't put it past them to turn us in; '**bon salaire si** ~' 'good salary for the right person'.

capacité /kapasite/ nf **1** (aptitude) ability; **un chercheur d'une grande** ~ a researcher of great ability; **2** (potentiel) capacity; ~ **de 100 mégawatts** 100 megawatt capacity; ~ **de mémoire** ORDINAT memory capacity ou size; ~ **d'accueil d'un hôtel** capacity of a hotel; **machine à laver à** ~ **variable** washing machine with variable load settings.
■ ~ **en droit** UNIV, JUR basic legal qualification.

cape /kap/ nf cape; **film de** ~ **et d'épée** swashbuckler.
IDIOMES **rire sous** ~ to laugh up one's sleeve.

capeline /kaplin/ nf wide-brimmed hat.

CAPES /kapɛs/ nm (abbr = **certificat d'aptitude professionnelle à l'enseignement secondaire**) secondary school teaching qualification.

capharnaüm /kafaRnaɔm/ nm shambles○ (+ v sg); **quel** ~, **ta chambre!** what a shambles your room is!

capillaire /kapilɛR/ **I** adj **1** (de vaisseau sanguin) capillary; **2** (de cheveu) hair (épith); **soins** ~s hair care.
II nm ANAT capillary.

capitaine /kapitɛn/ ▶ 284| nm **1** MIL (dans l'armée de terre, la marine) ~ captain; (dans l'armée de l'air) ~ flight lieutenant GB, ~ captain US; **2** SPORT captain.
■ ~ **de corvette** ~ lieutenant commander; ~ **de frégate** ~ commander; ~ **d'industrie** captain of industry; ~ **au long cours** fully-licensed captain; ~ **des pompiers** fire chief; ~ **de port** harbour GB master; ~ **de vaisseau** ~ captain.

capitainerie /kapitɛnRi/ nf **1** (administration) port authority; **2** (bâtiment) port authority buildings (pl).

capital, -e[1], mpl **-aux** /kapital, o/ **I** adj **1** (fondamental) GÉN key (épith), crucial; [importance] major; **une découverte** ~**e dans la recherche contre le cancer** a major breakthrough in cancer research; **c'est d'une importance** ~**e** it's of the utmost importance; **il est** ~ **de faire** it's essential to do; **2** [lettre] capital; **3** (de mort) **peine** ~**e** capital punishment.
II nm **1** FIN capital; **2** ÉCON capital; **le** ~ **et le travail**

capital and **labour**[GB]; **3** (ressource) **notre ~ santé** our health; **le ~ humain/industriel** human/industrial resources (pl). ■ **~ décès** death benefit.

capitale[2] /kapital/ nf **1** (d'un pays) capital (city); **2** (centre) capital; **Lyon, ~ des gourmets** Lyons, a paradise for gourmets; **3** (lettre) capital; **en ~s d'imprimerie** in block capitals.

capitaliser /kapitalize/ [1] vtr to capitalize.

capitalisme /kapitalism/ nm capitalism.

capitaliste /kapitalist/ adj, nmf capitalist.

Capitole /kapitɔl/ nprm **1** (de Rome) (colline) (**mont**) **~** Capitoline; (temple) Capitol; **2** (de Washington) Capitol.

capitonner /kapitɔne/ [1] vtr to pad.

capitulation /kapitylasjɔ̃/ nf capitulation (**devant** to); **~ sans conditions** unconditional surrender.

capituler /kapityle/ [1] vi to capitulate (**devant** to).

caporal, pl **-aux** /kapɔʀal, o/ ▶ 284 nm **1** MIL (armée de terre) ≈ corporal; (armée de l'air) ≈ corporal GB, ≈ sergeant US; **2** (tabac) caporal.

caporal-chef, pl **caporaux-chefs** /kapɔʀalʃɛf, kapɔʀoʃɛf/ ▶ 284 nm (armée de terre) rank between corporal and sergeant; (armée de l'air) rank between corporal and sergeant GB ou staff sergeant US.

capot /kapo/ nm AUT bonnet GB, hood US.

capotage /kapotaʒ/ nm (échec) collapse.

capote /kapɔt/ nf **1** (manteau) great-coat; **2** (de voiture, landau) hood GB, top; **3**○ (préservatif) **~ (anglaise)** condom, French letter†○.

capoter /kapɔte/ [1] vi **1** (échouer) to collapse; **faire ~** to ruin; **2** (se retourner) [voiture] to overturn.

câpre /kɑpʀ/ nf caper; **sauce aux ~s** caper sauce.

caprice /kapʀis/ nm **1** (fantaisie) (de personne) whim; (de temps, marché, nature, voiture) vagaries (pl); **sur un ~** on a whim; **céder aux ~s de qn** to indulge sb's whims; **2** (accès de colère) tantrum; **faire un ~** to throw a tantrum.

capricieusement /kapʀisjøzmɑ̃/ adv (comme un enfant gâté) capriciously; (avec fantaisie) whimsically.

capricieux, -ieuse /kapʀisjø, øz/ adj [personne] capricious; [mécanisme] temperamental; [temps, destin] fickle; [cours d'eau] irregular.

capricorne /kapʀikɔʀn/ nm capricorn beetle.

Capricorne /kapʀikɔʀn/ ▶ 641 nprm Capricorn.

câprier /kɑpʀije/ nm caper shrub.

capsule /kapsyl/ nf **1** (de bouteille) (bouchon) cap; (enveloppe du bouchon) capsule; **2** (médicament) capsule; **3** (de fusée) capsule; **4** (détonateur) cap.

capsuler /kapsyle/ [1] vtr to put a cap on [bouteille].

capter /kapte/ [1] vtr **1** (recevoir) to get [émission, chaîne]; to pick up; **2** (saisir) to capture [expression, image]; **3** (attirer) to catch [attention]; **4** (absorber) to soak up [lumière]; **5** (recueillir) to collect [eaux].

capteur /kaptœʀ/ nm sensor; **~ à infrarouges** infrared sensor. ■ **~ solaire** solar cell.

captif, -ive /kaptif, iv/ adj, nm,f captive.

captivant, ~e /kaptivɑ̃, ɑ̃t/ adj [livre] enthralling; [récit] gripping; [moment] riveting; [musique] captivating.

captiver /kaptive/ [1] vtr [beauté] to captivate; [voix, musique] to enthral[GB]; [histoire, personne] to fascinate.

captivité /kaptivite/ nf captivity; **vingt ans de ~** twenty years in captivity.

capture /kaptyʀ/ nf **1** (action d'attraper) capture; **2** (ce qui est attrapé) catch; **une belle ~** a good catch.

capturer /kaptyʀe/ [1] vtr LIT, FIG to capture.

capuche /kapyʃ/ nf hood.

capuchon /kapyʃɔ̃/ nm (de vêtement) hood; (de stylo) cap.

capucin /kapysɛ̃/ nm (moine) Capuchin friar.

capucine /kapysin/ nf nasturtium.

Cap-Vert /kapvɛʀ/ ▶ 305, 232 nprm **îles du ~** Cape Verde islands.

caquet /kakɛ/ nm (de bavard) prattle; **rabattre son ~**○ to stop crowing○; **rabattre le ~ à qn**○ to put sb in his/her place, to take sb down a peg or two.

caqueter /kakte/ [20] vi [poule] to cackle; [bavard] to prattle.

car[1] /kaʀ/ conj because, for.

car[2] /kaʀ/ nm (véhicule) coach GB, bus. ■ **~ de police** police van; **~ (de ramassage) scolaire** school bus.

carabine /kaʀabin/ nf **1** (arme) rifle; **~ 22 long rifle** .22 rifle; **~ à air comprimé** air gun; **~ à plombs** shotgun; **2** (jouet) toy gun; **~ à flèches** pop gun.

carabiné○, **~e** /kaʀabine/ adj [fièvre] raging; [migraine] ferocious; [rhume] stinking○.

carabinier /kaʀabinje/ nm **1** (policier italien) carabiniere; **les ~s** the carabinieri; **2** HIST carabineer.

Carabosse /kaʀabɔs/ npr **la fée ~** the wicked fairy.

caracoler /kaʀakɔle/ [1] vi **1** (avoir une position favorable) to be well ahead; **~ en tête** to be well in the lead; **2** [cheval] to prance; [cavalier] to parade.

caractère /kaʀaktɛʀ/ nm **1** (signe d'écriture) character; **~s d'imprimerie** (type d'écriture) block capitals; **en gros ~s** in large print; **en ~s gras** in bold type; **2** (tempérament) nature; **nous n'avons pas le même ~** we are different characters; **avoir bon ~** to be good-natured; **avoir mauvais ~** to be bad-tempered; **être d'un ~ facile** to have an easy-going nature; **avoir un sacré ~** (coléreux) to have a foul temper; (difficile) to be absolutely impossible; **3** (forte personnalité) character; **avoir du ~** to have character; **il n'a aucun ~** he's got no backbone; **4** (de maison, lieu) character; **'fermette de ~'** 'small farm with character'; **5** (type humain) character; **une étude de ~s** a study of character types; **6** (marque distinctive) characteristic; **7** (côté, valeur) nature; **avoir un ~ politique** to be of a political nature; **ma demande n'a aucun ~ définitif** my request has nothing definite about it; **film à ~ pornographique** pornographic film.
IDIOMES **avoir un ~ de chien** or **cochon**○, **avoir un sale ~** to have a vile temper; **avoir un ~ en or** to have a delightful nature.

caractériel, -ielle /kaʀakteʀjɛl/ adj [troubles] emotional; [personne] disturbed.

caractériser /kaʀakteʀize/ [1] **I** vtr to characterize.
II se caractériser vpr to be characterized (**par** by).

caractéristique /kaʀakteʀistik/ **I** adj characteristic.
II nf characteristics (pl).

carafe /kaʀaf/ nf **1** (récipient) carafe; **2**○ (tête) head; **ne rien avoir dans la ~**○ to have nothing upstairs○.

carafon /kaʀafɔ̃/ nm (récipient) small carafe.

caraïbe /kaʀaib/ adj Caribbean.

Caraïbes /kaʀaib/ **I** nmpl (peuple) Caribs.
II nprfpl **1** ▶ 305 (îles) Caribbean (islands); **2** ▶ 407 (mer) **mer des ~** Caribbean Sea.

carambolage /kaʀɑ̃bɔlaʒ/ nm (de voitures) pile-up.

caramboler /kaʀɑ̃bɔle/ [1] **I** vtr to collide with.
II se caramboler vpr to collide with each other.

caramel /kaʀamɛl/ nm **1** (liquide) caramel; **2** (bonbon) toffee GB, toffy US; **~ mou** ≈ fudge.

caraméliser /kaʀamelize/ [1] **I** vtr (transformer) to caramelize; (recouvrir) to coat [sth] with caramel.
II se caraméliser vpr to caramelize.

carapace /kaʀapas/ nf (d'animal) shell, carapace; (protection) **~ de béton** concrete shell; FIG armour[GB].

carapater○: **se carapater** /kaʀapate/ [1] vpr to beat it○.

carat /kaʀa/ nm carat; **or 18 ~s** 18-carat gold.
IDIOMES **dernier ~**⁹ at the latest.

caravane /kaʀavan/ nf (véhicule) caravan GB, trailer US; (de désert) caravan; **~ publicitaire** publicity cars (pl).
IDIOMES **les chiens aboient, la ~ passe** sticks and stones may break my bones (but words will never hurt me).

caravelle /kaʀavɛl/ *nf* (bateau) caravel.

carbonade /kaʀbɔnad/ *nf* (viande grillée) carbonado.

carbone /kaʀbɔn/ *nm* carbon; (papier) carbon paper; (feuille) sheet of carbon paper.
■ ~ **14** carbon 14; **dater qch au ~ 14** to carbon-date sth; **datation au ~ 14** (radio)carbon dating.

carbonique /kaʀbɔnik/ *adj* carbonic; **neige** ~ dry ice.

carbonisé, ~e /kaʀbɔnize/ *adj* **1** [*véhicule*] burned-out (*épith*), burned out (*jamais épith*); [*débris, arbre, corps*] charred; **2** CULIN burned to a cinder (*jamais épith*), burned.

carboniser /kaʀbɔnize/ [1] *vtr* **1** CHIMIE to carbonize; **2** (brûler complètement) to burn [sb] to death [*personne*]; to reduce [sth] to ashes [*forêt, maison, corps*]; to char [*objet, arbre, poutre*].

carburant /kaʀbyʀɑ̃/ *nm* fuel.

carburateur /kaʀbyʀatœʀ/ *nm* carburettor GB, carburetor US.

carbure /kaʀbyʀ/ *nm* carbide; **les ~s** carbides.

carburer /kaʀbyʀe/ [1] **I** *vtr* TECH to carburize.
II *vi* **1** AUT **bien/mal** ~ to be well/badly tuned; **2**○ (fonctionner) **il carbure au vin rouge** HUM he runs on red wine; **3**○ (travailler dur) to work flat out.

carcan /kaʀkɑ̃/ *nm* (entrave) ~ **administratif** administrative constraints (*pl*) ou straitjacket; **le ~ des institutions** institutional rigidity.

carcasse /kaʀkas/ *nf* **1** (squelette d'animal) carcass; **2**○ (corps humain) body; **promener** or **traîner sa ~** to bum○ around; **3**○ (épave de véhicule) shell; **4** (armature) (de navire) skeleton; (de bâtiment, hangar) frame.

carcéral, ~e, *mpl* **-aux** /kaʀseʀal, o/ *adj* prison (*épith*); **le milieu ~** the prison environment.

cardan /kaʀdɑ̃/ *nm* universal joint.

carder /kaʀde/ [1] *vtr* to card.

cardiaque /kaʀdjak/ **I** *adj* heart (*épith*); **avoir des ennuis ~s** to have heart trouble; **être ~** to have a heart condition.
II *nmf* person with a heart condition.

cardinal, ~e, *mpl* **-aux** /kaʀdinal, o/ **I** *adj* cardinal.
II *nm* **1** ▶596| RELIG cardinal; **le ~ Newman** Cardinal Newman; **2** LING, MATH cardinal number; **3** ZOOL cardinal (grosbeak), redbird US.

cardiologie /kaʀdjɔlɔʒi/ *nf* cardiology.

cardiologue /kaʀdjɔlɔg/ ▶374| *nmf* cardiologist.

cardiopathie /kaʀdjɔpati/ *nf* heart disorder.

cardon /kaʀdɔ̃/ *nm* cardoon.

carême /kaʀɛm/ *nm* **le ~** Lent; **observer le ~** to observe ou keep Lent.
IDIOMES **avoir une face de ~** to look as miserable as sin.

carence /kaʀɑ̃s/ *nf* **1** MÉD deficiency; **2** (absence) lack; **3** (manquement) shortcomings (*pl*); **les ~s de la loi** the shortcomings of the law.

carène /kaʀɛn/ *nf* hull (*below the waterline*).

caressant, ~e /kaʀɛsɑ̃, ɑ̃t/ *adj* [*enfant, geste, regard, parole*] affectionate; [*vent, rayon*] soft.

caresse /kaʀɛs/ *nf* (à un animal) stroke; (à une personne) caress, stroke; **couvrir qn de ~s** to caress sb all over; **il aime les ~s** he likes being stroked; **faire une ~** or **des ~s à** to stroke.

caresser /kaʀese/ [1] **I** *vtr* **1** (de la main) to stroke [*animal, joue, cheveux, barbe, objet*]; ~ **qn du regard** or **des yeux** to look at sb lovingly ou fondly; **2** (effleurer) [*soleil, vent, lumière*] to caress [*joue, cheveux*]; **3** (avoir en soi) to entertain [*rêve, idée*].
II se caresser *vpr* to stroke; **se ~ la barbe** to stroke one's beard.
IDIOMES ~ **qn dans le sens du poil** to stay on the right side of sb; ~ **la bouteille** to be on the bottle○.

cargaison /kaʀgɛzɔ̃/ *nf* **1** (chargement) cargo; **2**○ (grande quantité) load.

cargo /kaʀgo/ *nm* NAUT freighter, cargo ship; ~ **mixte** passenger-cargo ship.

cari /kaʀi/ = **curry**.

caricatural, ~e, *mpl* **-aux** /kaʀikatyʀal, o/ *adj* [*dessin*] (deliberately) grotesque; [*récit*] caricatural.

caricature /kaʀikatyʀ/ *nf* **1** (genre) caricature; **2** (dessin) (d'une personne) caricature; (de plusieurs personnes, situation) cartoon; **faire une ~** to draw a caricature ou cartoon; **3** (représentation déformée) caricature; **dans ses romans il fait une ~ de la société** his novels caricature society; **4** (parodie) mockery; ~ **de procès** mockery of a trial.

caricaturer /kaʀikatyʀe/ [1] *vtr* to caricature.

caricaturiste /kaʀikatyʀist/ ▶374| *nmf* caricaturist, cartoonist.

carie /kaʀi/ *nf* (lésion) decay ¢; (trou) cavity.

carié, ~e /kaʀje/ *adj* decayed.

carier /kaʀje/ [2] **I** *vtr* to cause [sth] to decay [*dent*].
II se carier *vpr* to decay.

carillon /kaʀijɔ̃/ *nm* **1** (d'église, de beffroi) (cloches) bells (*pl*); (sonnerie) chimes (*pl*); **2** (pendule) (chiming) clock; (sonnerie) chimes (*pl*); **une horloge à ~** a chiming clock; **3** (de porte) (door) chimes (*pl*).

carillonner /kaʀijɔne/ [1] **I** *vtr* **1** [*cloches*] to chime [*heure*]; to chime (out) [*air*]; to ring ou peal out for [*événement*]; **2**○ (faire savoir) to broadcast.
II *vi* **1** [*cloches*] to ring out; (très fort) to peal out; **2** (à une porte) to ring (loudly).

carillonneur /kaʀijɔnœʀ/ *nm* bell-ringer.

caritatif, -ive /kaʀitatif, iv/ *adj* charitable; **une association** or **organisation caritative** a charity.

carlingue /kaʀlɛ̃g/ *nf* AVIAT cabin; NAUT keelson.

carme /kaʀm/ *nm* Carmelite, white friar.

carmélite /kaʀmelit/ *nf* Carmelite nun.

carmin /kaʀmɛ̃/ **I** *adj inv* carmine.
II *nm* (matière) cochineal; (couleur) carmine.

carnage /kaʀnaʒ/ *nm* carnage ¢, massacre; **ils ont fait un véritable ~** they massacred everyone.

carnassier, -ière /kaʀnasje, ɛʀ/ **I** *adj* carnivorous.
II *nm* carnivore.

carnaval, *pl* **~s** /kaʀnaval/ *nm* (fête) carnival.

carnavalesque /kaʀnavalɛsk/ *adj* (grotesque) grotesque; (de carnaval) carnival (*épith*).

carne○ /kaʀn/ *nf* (viande) leathery meat.

carné, ~e /kaʀne/ *adj* meat-based (*épith*).

carnet /kaʀnɛ/ *nm* **1** (calepin) notebook; **2** (groupe de tickets, bons) book; **j'achète mes timbres en ~** I always buy a book of stamps.
■ ~ **d'adresses** address book; ~ **de chèques** chequebook GB, checkbook US; ~ **de correspondance** or **de notes** SCOL mark book; ~ **de rendez-vous** appointments diary; ~ **de route** travel journal; ~ **de santé** health record; ~ **à souches** counterfoil book.

carnivore /kaʀnivɔʀ/ **I** *adj* ZOOL carnivorous.
II *nm* carnivore; **les ~s** the carnivores.

carotène /kaʀɔtɛn/ *nf* carotene.

carotide /kaʀɔtid/ *adj, nf* carotid.

carotte /kaʀɔt/ **I** ▶141| *adj inv* (orange foncé) carrot-coloured GB; (roux) [*cheveux, poils*] carroty.
II *nf* (plante) carrot; ~**s râpées** grated carrot ¢.
IDIOMES **les ~s sont cuites**○ the game is up○; **manier la ~ et le bâton** to use stick-and-carrot tactics.

carpe[1] /kaʀp/ *nm* carpus.

carpe[2] /kaʀp/ *nf* carp.
IDIOMES **il est resté muet comme une ~** he never said a word.

carpette /kaʀpɛt/ *nf* **1** (tapis) rug; **2**○ (personne) PEJ doormat○.
IDIOMES **s'aplatir comme une ~ devant qn** to grovel to sb.

carquois /kaʀkwa/ *nm* quiver.

carre /kaʀ/ *nf* (de ski, patin) edge.

carré, ~e /kaʀe/ **I** *adj* **1** GÉN [*objet, forme*] square; **des chaussures à bout ~** square-toed shoes; **2** (anguleux) [*visage, menton, paume*] square; [*silhouette*] stocky; ~ **d'épaules** broad-shouldered; **3** (direct) [*personne*] straightforward; [*réponse*] straight; [*refus*] outright; **4** ▶575**|** (mesure) square; **prix du** or **au mètre ~** price per square metre^{GB}.

II *nm* **1** (figure) GÉN square; (de ciel, plantations) patch; (de chocolat) piece; **avoir une coupe au ~** [*femme*] to have one's hair cut in a bob; **je vais lui mettre la tête au ~**○ I'll beat the hell out of him/her○; **un lit (fait) au ~** a meticulously made bed; **~ blanc** '*suitable for adults only*' *sign on French TV*; **2** MATH square; **le ~ de deux** two squared; **deux au ~ égale quatre** two squared is four; **3** (de viande) **~ d'agneau** rack of lamb; **4** (aux cartes) **avoir un ~ de dix** to have the four tens; **5** C (place) square.

carreau, *pl* **~x** /kaʀo/ *nm* **1** (de sol) (floor) tile; (de mur) (wall) tile; **2** (carrelage) tiled floor; **3** (vitre) window-pane; **à petits ~x** with small panes; **faire les ~x** to clean the windows; **regarder à travers les ~x** to look out of the window; **4** (carré) (sur du papier) square; (sur du tissu) check; **papier à ~x** squared paper; **jupe à ~x** check(ed) skirt; **à ~x bleus et blancs** blue-and-white checked (*épith*); **papier à grands ~x** large-squared paper; **5** ▶329**|** JEUX (carte) diamonds (*pl*); **avoir du ~** to be holding diamonds; **6** HIST (marché) market (floor); **7** (de mine) pithead; **8** (d'arbalète) bolt.

IDIOMES **étendre qn sur le ~**○ to lay sb out○; **rester sur le ~**○ (dans une bagarre) to be killed; (dans une affaire) to be left high and dry○; **se tenir à ~**○ to watch one's step.

carrefour /kaʀfuʀ/ *nm* **1** (intersection) GÉN junction; (de deux routes) crossroads (+ *v sg*); **~ ferroviaire** railway junction ou intersection; **2** (lieu de passage) crossroads (+ *v sg*); (réseau de communications) transport hub; **~ international** international meeting point; **3** (moment stratégique) crossroads (*sg*); **être à un ~ de qch** to be at a crossroads in sth; **au ~ de la biologie et de la chimie** at the meeting point of biology and chemistry; **4** (forum) debate.

carrelage /kaʀlaʒ/ *nm* **1** (sol) tiled floor; **2** (ensemble de carreaux) tiles (*pl*); (pose) tiling.

carreler /kaʀle/ [19] *vtr* to tile.

carrelet /kaʀlɛ/ *nm* (poisson) plaice.

carreleur /kaʀlœʀ/ ▶374**|** *nm* tiler.

carrément /kaʀemɑ̃/ *adv* **la situation devient ~ inquiétante** the situation is becoming downright worrying; **il vaut ~ mieux les jeter** it would be better just to throw them out; **reprenons ~ depuis le début** let's start again right from the beginning; **elle m'a ~ accusé de mentir** she accused me straight out of lying; **il a ~ démissionné** he went straight ahead and resigned.

carrer: se carrer /kaʀe/ [1] *vpr* (s'installer) **se ~ dans un fauteuil** to ensconce oneself in an armchair.

carrière /kaʀjɛʀ/ *nf* **1** (profession) career; **une ~ d'écrivain** a career as a writer; **militaire de ~** career officer; **faire ~ dans l'armée** to make a career in the army; **2** (lieu d'extraction) quarry; **~ d'ardoise** slate quarry; **~ de sable** sandpit.

carriole /kaʀjɔl/ *nf* **1** (charrette) cart; **2**○ (voiture) PEJ jalopy○, car.

carrossable /kaʀɔsabl/ *adj* suitable for motor vehicles (*après n*).

carrosse /kaʀɔs/ *nm* (horse-drawn) coach; ▶**roue**.

carrosserie /kaʀɔsʀi/ *nf* (de voiture) bodywork; (conception) coachbuilding; (réparation) body repair work; **atelier de ~** body repair workshop.

carrossier /kaʀɔsje/ ▶374**|** *nm* (réparateur) coach-builder.

carrousel /kaʀusɛl/ *nm* (pour enfants) merry-go-round, carousel.

carrure /kaʀyʀ/ *nf* **1** LIT shoulders (*pl*); **avoir une ~ imposante** to have broad shoulders; **2** FIG innate qualities (*pl*), calibre^{GB}; **avoir la ~ d'un président** to have the necessary qualities to be a president.

cartable /kaʀtabl/ *nm* (d'écolier) schoolbag; (avec des bretelles) satchel; (d'adulte) briefcase.

carte /kaʀt/ *nf* **1** (pour écrire) card; **2** (document) GÉN card; (laissez-passer) pass; **3** ▶329**|** JEUX card; **~ à jouer** playing card; **jouer aux ~s** to play cards; **mettre ~s sur table** FIG to put one's cards on the table; **il possède plus d'une ~ dans son jeu** he's got other cards up his sleeve; **4** GÉOG map; **~ marine/du ciel** sea/astronomical chart; **5** BIOL **~ génétique** genetic map; **6** (au restaurant) menu; **manger à la ~** to eat à la carte, to order from the menu; **horaire à la ~** FIG personalized timetable; **activités sportives à la ~** choice (*sg*) of sporting activities.

■ **~ d'abonnement** RAIL season ticket; **~ d'adhérent** membership card; **~ d'assuré social** national insurance card; **~ bancaire** bank card; **~ bleue®** credit card; **~ de crédit** credit card; **~ d'électeur** polling card GB, voter registration card US; **~ d'étudiant** student card, student ID card; **~ de fidélité** discount card; **~ grise** car registration document ou (*pl*) papers US; **~ d'identité** identity card, ID card; **~ jeunes®** (young persons') railcard; COMM (young people's) discount card; **~ kiwi®** family railcard; **~ de lecteur** library card; **~ magnétique** GÉN magnetic card; (pour ouvrir une porte) swipe card; **~ maîtresse** LIT master card; FIG trump card; **~ à mémoire** ou à **microprocesseur** smart card; **~ orange®** season ticket (*in the Paris region*); **~ perforée** punch card; **~ postale** postcard; **~ de presse** press pass; **~ professionnelle** identity card (*showing occupation*); **~ à puce** smart card; **~ de réduction** discount card; **~ routière** roadmap; **~ de sécurité sociale = ~ d'assuré social**; **~ de séjour** resident's permit; **~ de téléphone** phonecard; **~ vermeil®** senior citizen's rail pass; **~ verte®** AUT = certificate of motor insurance; **~ des vins** wine list; **~ de visite** GÉN visiting card; (d'affaires) business card; **~ de vœux** greetings card.

IDIOMES **donner ~ blanche à qn** to give sb carte blanche ou a free hand.

cartel /kaʀtɛl/ *nm* **1** ÉCON cartel; **2** POL coalition.

carter /kaʀtɛʀ/ *nm* (de moteur) crankcase; (de boîte de vitesses) casing.

carte-réponse, *pl* **cartes-réponses** /kaʀtʀepɔ̃s/ *nf* reply card.

cartésien, -ienne /kaʀtezjɛ̃, ɛn/ *adj, nm,f* Cartesian.

cartilage /kaʀtilaʒ/ *nm* ANAT, ZOOL cartilage; CULIN gristle.

cartilagineux, -euse /kaʀtilaʒinø, øz/ *adj* ANAT, ZOOL cartilaginous; CULIN gristly.

cartomancie /kaʀtɔmɑ̃si/ *nf* fortune-telling.

cartomancien, -ienne /kaʀtɔmɑ̃sjɛ̃, ɛn/ ▶374**|** *nm,f* fortune-teller.

carton /kaʀtɔ̃/ *nm* **1** (matière) cardboard; **de** or **en ~** cardboard (*épith*); **2** (boîte) (cardboard) box; **c'est resté dans les ~s** LIT it's still in the box; FIG it didn't get past the drawing-board; **3** (carte) card.

■ **~ à dessin** portfolio; **~ d'invitation** invitation card; **~ jaune** SPORT yellow card; **~ ondulé** corrugated cardboard; **~ rouge** SPORT red card.

IDIOMES **faire un ~**○ (remporter un succès) to do great○; (tirer sur une cible) to shoot at a target.

cartonné, -e /kaʀtɔne/ *adj* **couverture ~e** (de livre) hard cover.

cartonner /kaʀtɔne/ [1] **I** *vtr* (en reliure) to bind.

II○ *vi* (marquer) to score.

carton-pâte /kaʀtɔ̃pɑt/ *nm inv* pasteboard; **en** or **de ~** LIT pasteboard (*épith*); FIG cardboard (*épith*).

cartouche¹ /kaʀtuʃ/ *nm* (sur un plan) title block; (sur une carte) legend.

cartouche² /kaʀtuʃ/ *nf* **1** (de fusil) cartridge; **2** (de stylo, d'imprimante) cartridge; (de gaz) refill; **une ~ d'encre** an ink cartridge; **3** (emballage) **~ de cigarettes** carton of cigarettes; **4** ORDINAT cartridge.

■ **~ à blanc** MIL blank cartridge.

IDIOMES **brûler ses dernières ~s** to play one's last cards.

cartoucherie /kaʀtuʃʀi/ *nf* cartridge factory.

cartouchière /kaʀtuʃjɛʀ/ *nf* cartridge belt.

cas /kɑ/ **I** *nm inv* **1** (circonstance) case; **en pareil ~** in such a case; **auquel ~** in which case; **dans tous les**

~ in every case; **au ~ où il viendrait** in case he comes; **prends ta voiture, au ~ où**○ take your car, just in case; **en ~ de besoin** if necessary, if need be; **en ~ d'incendie** in the event of a fire; **savoir être sévère ou pas selon les ~** to know how to be strict or not, as circumstances dictate; **ne pas déranger sauf pour un ~ grave** do not disturb except in an emergency; **le ~ échéant** if need be; **dans le ~ contraire, vous devrez...** should the opposite occur, you will have to...; **dans le meilleur/pire des ~** at best/worst; **c'est un ~ à envisager** it's a possibility we should bear in mind; **en aucun ~** on no account; **elle ne veut en aucun ~ quitter son domicile** she doesn't want to leave her home under any circumstances; **c'est le ~ de le dire!** you can say that again!; **2** (situation particulière) case; **étudier le ~ de qn** to look into sb's case; **le ~ de Sophie est spécial** Sophie's is a special case; **au ~ par ~** case by case; **être dans le même ~ que qn** to be in the same position as sb; **n'aggrave pas ton ~** don't make things worse for yourself; **3** (occurrence) case; **un ~ rare** a rare occurrence; **c'est vraiment un ~ ta sœur!** HUM your sister is a real case○!; **4** (en grammaire) case; **5** (cause) **c'est un ~ de renvoi** it's grounds for dismissal.
II en tout cas, en tous les cas loc adv **1** (assurément) in any case, at any rate; **ce n'est pas moi en tout ~** it's not me at any rate; **2** (du moins) at least.
■ **~ de conscience** moral dilemma; **~ de figure** scenario; **~ de force majeure** case of force majeure; **~ limite** borderline case; **~ social** socially disadvantaged person; **~ type** typical case.
IDIOMES **il a fait grand ~ de son avancement** he made a big thing of his promotion; **elle n'a fait aucun ~ de mon avancement** she didn't attach much importance to my promotion.

casanier, -ière /kazanje, ɛʀ/ adj [personne] stay-at-home (épith); [existence] unadventurous; **il est très ~** he's a real stay-at-home ou homebody US.

casaque /kazak/ nf (de jockey) jersey, silk.

casbah /kazba/ nf (citadelle, quartier) kasbah; (maison)○ pad○.

cascade /kaskad/ nf **1** (chute d'eau) waterfall; **2** CIN stunt; **3** (de rires) roar; (d'incidents, de réactions) series (+ v sg); **crises en ~** series of crises.

cascadeur, -euse /kaskadœʀ, øz/ nmf ▶374 stuntman/stuntwoman.

case /kɑz/ nf **1** (maison) hut, cabin; **2** (de damier, monopoly®) square; **sauter une ~** to jump a square; **reculer d'une ~** LIT to move ou go back a square; FIG to move backward(s); **3** (sur un formulaire) box.
■ **~ départ** LIT start; FIG square one; **retour à la ~ départ** back to square one; **repasser par la ~ départ** to pass go; **~ postale** C, H PO Box.
IDIOMES **il lui manque une ~**○ he's/she's got a screw loose○.

casemate /kazmat/ nf (abri) bunker.

caser○ /kɑze/ [1] **I** vtr **1** (placer) to put, to stick○; **tu as réussi à ~ ton expression favorite!** you've managed to slip in your favouriteGB expression!; **2** (marier) to marry off [enfant]; **3** (loger) to put [sb] up; **4** (trouver un emploi pour) to find a place for.
II se caser vpr to tie the knot○, to get married.

caserne /kazɛʀn/ nf MIL barracks.
■ **~ de sapeurs-pompiers** fire station.

casher /kaʃɛʀ/ adj inv kosher.

casier /kazje/ nm **1** (meuble) **~ (de rangement)** rack; **~ à bouteilles** bottle rack; **2** (pour le courrier) pigeon-hole; **3** (de pêche) pot; **~ à langoustes** lobster pot.
■ **~ judiciaire** police record; **avoir un ~** to have a (police) record; **mon ~ judiciaire est vierge** I don't have a police record.

casque /kask/ nm **1** (de motard, pilote) crash helmet; (d'ouvrier, de mineur) safety helmet, hard hat; (de cycliste) cycle helmet; **2** MIL helmet; **3** AUDIO, MUS headphones (pl); (sèche-cheveux) hairdrier GB, hairdryer US.
■ **~ de chantier** safety helmet, hard hat; **~ inté-**

gral full-face crash helmet; **~ de pompier** fireman's helmet; **Casque bleu** Blue Helmet.

casqué, ~e /kaske/ adj helmeted.

casquer○ /kaske/ [1] vi (payer la note) to foot the bill; (être puni) to carry the can○ GB, to take the rap○.

casquette /kaskɛt/ nf **1** (vêtement) cap; **~ de base-ball** base-ball cap; **2** (fonction) hat; (étiquette) label.

cassant, ~e /kasɑ̃, ɑ̃t/ adj **1** [bois, cheveux, métal] brittle; **2** (tranchant) [ton, personne] curt, abrupt.

casse¹○ /kɑs/ nm break-in, heist○ US.

casse² /kɑs/ nf **1** (objets cassés) breakage; **payer la ~** to pay for breakage ou for the damage; **il y a eu beaucoup de ~ pendant le déménagement** a lot of things got broken during the move; **2** (lieu) breaker's yard, scrap yard; **mettre à la ~** to scrap.

cassé, ~e /kase/ adj [voix] hoarse.

casse-cou /kasku/ **I** adj inv [personne] reckless; [lieu] dangerous.
II nmf inv (personne) daredevil.

casse-croûte /kaskʀut/ nm inv snack.

casse-noisettes /kasnwazɛt/, **casse-noix** /kasnwa/ nm inv nutcrackers (pl).

casse-pieds○ /kaspje/ **I** adj inv **être ~** [gêneur] to be a pain in the neck○; [raseur] to be a bore; [corvée] to be a drag○ ou bore.
II nmf inv (gêneur) pain in the neck○; (raseur) bore.

casser /kase/ [1] **I** vtr **1** (briser) to break [objet, os]; to crack [noix]; **les vandales ont tout cassé dans la maison** the vandals wrecked the house; **~ les prix** to slash prices; **~ le rythme d'une course** to slow down the pace of a race; **~ la figure**○ or **la gueule**○ **à qn** to beat sb up○; **2**○ (dégrader) to demote [militaire, employé]; **3** (annuler) to quash [jugement]; to annul [arrêt]; **4**○ (humilier) to cut [sb] down to size [personne].
II vi **1** (se briser) to break; **2** (se séparer)○ [couple] to split up.
III se casser vpr **1**○ (partir) to go away; **'bon, je me casse!'** 'right, I'm off○!'; **2** (se briser) to break; **la clé s'est cassée net** the key snapped in two; **3** (se blesser) **se ~ une** or **la jambe** to break one's leg; **se ~ la figure**○ (tomber par terre) [piéton] to fall over GB ou down; [cavalier, motard] to take a fall; (avoir un accident) to crash; (échouer) [entreprise, projet] to fail; (se battre) [personnes] to have a scrap○; **il ne s'est pas cassé la tête**○ he didn't exactly strain himself; **se ~ la tête** (sur un problème) to rack one's brain (over a problem); **se ~ la tête**○ **à faire qch** to go out of one's way to do sth.
IDIOMES **~ les pieds**○ **à qn** to annoy sb; **~ la croûte**○ or **la graine**○ to eat; **ça casse pas des briques**○ it's nothing to write home about○; **ça te prendra trois heures, à tout ~**○ it'll take you three hours at the very most ou at the outside; **qui casse (les verres) paie** if you cause damage, you pay for it.

casserole /kasʀɔl/ nf (récipient) saucepan, pan; **~ émaillée** enamelledGB saucepan ou pan.
IDIOMES **chanter/jouer comme une ~**○ to sing/to play atrociously.

casse-tête /kastɛt/ nm inv (problème) headache FIG; (jeu, devinette) puzzle; **~ chinois** Chinese puzzle.

cassette /kasɛt/ nf **1** (de bande) tape; **~ vierge** blank tape; **2** (petit coffret) casket.
■ **~ vidéo** video (cassette); **en ~ vidéo** on video.

casseur /kasœʀ/ nm **1** ▶374 (ferrailleur) scrap dealer; **2** (manifestant) rioting demonstrator; **3** (cambrioleur)○ burglar.

cassis /kasis/ nm inv **1** (arbre) blackcurrant (bush); (fruit) blackcurrant; **crème de ~** blackcurrant liqueur; **2** (sur la route) dip.

cassolette /kasɔlɛt/ nf (récipient) small ovenproof dish.

cassonade /kasɔnad/ nf soft brown sugar.

cassoulet /kasulɛ/ nm: meat and (haricot) bean stew.

cassure /kasyʀ/ nf **1** (endroit brisé) break; **2** (rupture) split, rupture; **3** (en géologie) fracture.

castagne○ /kastaɲ/ nf fight, scrap○; **il va y avoir de la ~** there's going to be a fight ou scrap○.

castagnettes /kastaɲɛt/ ▶392| *nfpl* castanets; **jouer des ~** to play the castanets.
caste /kast/ *nf* SOCIOL caste; PÉJ class.
castillan, **~e** /kastijɑ̃, an/ ▶338| I *adj* Castilian. II *nm* LING Castilian.
castor /kastɔʀ/ *nm* beaver.
castrer /kastʀe/ [1] *vtr* to castrate.
castrisme /kastʀism/ *nm* Castroism.
cataclysme /kataklism/ *nm* LIT, FIG cataclysm.
catacombes /katakɔ̃b/ *nfpl* catacombs.
catadioptre /katadjɔptʀ/ *nm* reflector.
catalan, **~e** /katalɑ̃, an/ ▶338| I *adj* Catalan. II *nm* Catalan.
catalogue /katalɔg/ *nm* catalogue^GB; **~ de l'exposition** exhibition catalogue^GB; **acheter qch sur ~** to buy sth by mail order.
cataloguer /katalɔge/ [1] *vtr* **1** (dresser la liste de) to catalogue^GB; **2** (juger définitivement) to label.
catalyser /katalize/ [1] *vtr* LIT, FIG to catalyse^GB.
catalyseur /katalizœʀ/ *nm* catalyst (**de** for, of).
catalytique /katalitik/ *adj* catalytic.
cataplasme /kataplasm/ *nm* poultice.
catapulter /katapylte/ [1] *vtr* to catapult.
cataracte /kataʀakt/ *nf* cataract.
catastrophe /katastʀɔf/ *nf* disaster; **~ aérienne** air disaster; **tourner à la ~** to end in disaster; **ce n'est pas une ~** it's not the end of the world; **en ~** in a (mad) panic; **atterrissage en ~** crash landing. ■ **~ naturelle** act of God.
catastrophé, **~e** /katastʀɔfe/ *adj* devastated.
catastrophique /katastʀɔfik/ *adj* disastrous.
catastrophisme /katastʀɔfism/ *nm* doomwatch.
catch /katʃ/ ▶329| *nm* wrestling; **faire du ~** to wrestle.
catcheur, **-euse** /katʃœʀ, øz/ ▶374| *nm,f* wrestler; **avoir des épaules de ~** to be built like a wrestler.
catéchisme /kateʃism/ *nm* catechism; **faire le ~ aux enfants** to teach children the catechism.
catégorie /kategɔʀi/ *nf* **1** (type) category; **de première/deuxième ~** top/low-grade; **2** ADMIN class; **3** SOCIOL group; **~ socioprofessionnelle** social and occupational group; **4** SPORT class; **hors ~** in a class of one's own; **toutes ~s** all-round.
catégorique /kategɔʀik/ *adj* **1** (inébranlable) adamant; **refus ~** adamant ou categoric refusal; **2** (sans ambiguïté) categoric.
catelle /katɛl/ *nf* H (carreau) tile.
cathare /kataʀ/ *adj, nmf* Cathar.
cathédrale /katedʀal/ *nf* cathedral.
catherinette /katʀinɛt/ *nf: single woman aged 25.*
cathodique /katɔdik/ *adj* PHYS cathodic; **tube ~** cathode-ray tube.
catholicisme /katɔlisism/ *nm* (Roman) Catholicism.
catholique /katɔlik/ I *adj* (Roman) Catholic; **ce n'est pas très ~**○ HUM it's a bit unorthodox; **ne pas avoir l'air très ~**○ to look a bit dubious. II *nmf* (Roman) Catholic.
catimini: en catimini /ɑ̃katimini/ *loc adv* on the sly.
cauchemar /koʃmaʀ/ *nm* nightmare; **faire un ~** to have a nightmare.
cauchemardesque /koʃmaʀdesk/ *adj* [expérience] nightmare (épith); [scène] nightmarish.
causal, **~e**, *mpl* **-aux** /kozal, o/ *adj* causal.
causalité /kozalite/ *nf* causality.
causant○, **~e** /kozɑ̃, ɑ̃t/ *adj* talkative, chatty○.
cause /koz/ *nf* **1** (origine) cause; **un rapport de ~ à effet** a relation of cause and effect; **il n'y a pas d'effet sans ~** there's no smoke without fire; **2** (raison) reason; **pour une ~ encore indéterminée** for a reason as yet unknown; **il s'est fâché et pour ~** he got angry and with good reason; **sans ~** groundless; **c'est une ~ de licenciement immédiat** it's a ground for immediate dismissal; **pour ~ de maladie** because of illness; **fermé pour ~ de travaux** closed for renovation; **avoir pour ~ qch** to be caused by sth; **à ~ de** because of; **3** (ensemble d'intérêts) cause; **une ~ perdue** a lost cause; **gagner qn à sa ~** to win sb over to one's cause; **prendre fait et ~ pour qn** to take up the cause of sb; **pour la bonne ~** for a good cause; **4** (affaire) case; **les ~s célèbres** the causes célèbres, the famous cases; **être en ~** [système, fait, organisme] to be at issue; [personne] to be involved; **être hors de ~** to be in the clear; **mettre qn en ~** to implicate sb/sth; **mettre hors de ~** to clear; **remettre en ~** to challenge [principe, hiérarchie, décision]; to cast doubt on [projet, efficacité, signification]; to undermine [efforts, proposition, processus]; **tout est remis en ~** everything has been thrown back into doubt; **se remettre en ~** to pass one's life under review; **remise en ~** (de système) reappraisal; **avoir** ou **obtenir gain de ~** to win one's case; **donner gain de ~ à** to decide in favour^GB of.
IDIOMES **en toute connaissance de ~** in full knowledge of the facts; **en tout état de ~** in any case; **en désespoir de ~** as a last resort.
causer /koze/ [1] I *vtr* **1** (provoquer) to cause; **~ de la peine à qn** to cause sb grief; **du tort à qn** to wrong sb; **ma santé m'a causé des soucis** my health has given me cause for concern; **2**○ (discuter de) to talk; **~ travail** to talk shop.
II **causer**○ **de** *vtr ind* to talk about; **~ de choses et d'autres** to talk about this and that.
III○ *vi* to talk; **à propos de** about); **cause toujours tu m'intéresses**○! IRON fascinating, I'm sure! IRON.
causerie /kozʀi/ *nf* (entretien organisé) talk; (entretien libre) chat; **une ~ au coin du feu** a fireside chat.
causette○ /kozɛt/ *nf* chat; **faire la ~ avec qn** to have a little chat with sb.
causse /kos/ *nm* limestone plateau.
caustique /kostik/ *adj* caustic.
cautériser /koteʀize/ [1] *vtr* to cauterize.
caution /kosjɔ̃/ *nf* **1** (garantie financière) COMM deposit; FIN guarantee, security; JUR bail; **libéré sous ~** released on bail; **2** (soutien) support; **apporter sa ~ à** to lend one's support to; **3** (garantie morale) guarantee; **sujet à ~** open to doubt.
cautionner /kosjɔne/ [1] *vtr* **1** (soutenir) to give one's support to; **être cautionné par** to have the support of; **2** COMM, FIN to stand surety for [personne, projet].
cavalcade /kavalkad/ *nf* **1** (course bruyante) stampede; **2** (défilé de cavaliers) cavalcade.
cavale○ /kaval/ *nf* (évasion) escape; **en ~** on the run.
cavaler○ /kavale/ [1] *vi* (courir) to rush about; **~ dans** to rush around; **~ après** to chase after; **~ après les femmes** to be a womanizer.
cavalerie /kavalʀi/ *nf* cavalry.
cavaleur○, **-euse** /kavalœʀ, øz/ PÉJ I *adj* womanizing (épith)/man-chasing (épith). II *nm,f* womanizer/man-chaser.
cavalier, **-ière** /kavalje, ɛʀ/ I *adj* **1** (impertinent) cavalier; **2** (en dessin) **vue cavalière** bird's eye view; **perspective cavalière** isometric projection; **3** (pour cheval) **allée cavalière** bridle path.
II *nm,f* **1** (en équitation) horseman/horsewoman; (en promenade) horse rider; **être bon ~** to be a good rider; **2** (pour danser) partner.
III *nm* **1** MIL cavalryman; **2** (aux échecs) knight.
IDIOMES **faire ~ seul** [personne, entreprise] to go it alone; SPORT to be ahead.
cavalièrement /kavaljɛʀmɑ̃/ *adv* in a cavalier fashion.
cave /kav/ *nf* **1** cellar; **de la ~ au grenier** high and low; **~ voûtée** vault; **avoir une bonne ~** [individu] to have a good cellar; [restaurant] to have a good winelist; **2** (entreprise vinicole) cellar; **3** (magasin) wine merchant.
caveau, *pl* **~x** /kavo/ *nm* vault; **~ de famille** family vault.
caverne /kavɛʀn/ *nf* (grotte) cavern.

ce

L'adjectif démonstratif: *ce, cet, cette, ces*

Lorsque *ce* (parfois renforcé par *-ci*) marque la proximité dans l'espace ou le temps, on le traduira par *this*:

prends ce livre(-ci) plutôt que celui-là = take this book, not that one
il a plu ce matin = it rained this morning
ce mois-ci = this month
un de ces jours = one of these days

Lorsque *ce* (parfois renforcé par *-là*) marque l'éloignement, on le traduira par *that*:

cet homme(-là) = that man
cette année-là = that year
en ces temps lointains = in those far-off days

Lorsque le nom n'est pas suivi de *-ci* ou *-là*, on prendra en compte le contexte pour choisir la traduction:

dans cette maison
(celle où l'on se trouve) = in this house
(celle dont on parle) = in that house
j'aime ces endroits calmes
(tels que celui où nous sommes)
= I like these quiet places
(tels que celui dont on parle)
= I like those quiet places
en ces temps difficiles
(maintenant) = in these difficult times
(autrefois) = in those difficult times

On notera que *that* sert aussi à indiquer que le locuteur se distancie d'une chose ou d'une personne, souvent pour marquer sa désapprobation:

tu es ridicule avec ce chapeau! = you look ridiculous in that hat!
ce garçon m'énerve! = that boy gets on my nerves!

Attention aux expressions suivantes:

cette nuit (passée) = last night
(à venir) = tonight
en ce moment = at the moment
(précis) = at this moment in time

Le pronom démonstratif: *ce, c'*

L'emploi du pronom démonstratif avec le verbe être est traité à l'entrée du verbe *être¹*.

Les autres emplois sont dans l'entrée, voir II.

caviar /kavjaʀ/ *nm* caviar.

cavité /kavite/ *nf* cavity; **~ buccale** oral cavity.

Cayenne /kajɛn/ *nf* GÉOG Cayenne; HIST Cayenne penal settlement.

CB /sebe/ *nf* (*abbr* = **Citizens' Band**) **bande ~** CB.

CCP /sesepe/ *nm*: *abbr* ▶ **compte**.

CD /sede/ *nm* (*abbr* = **compact disc**) CD.

CD-I /sedei/ *nm inv* (*abbr* = **compact disc interactif**) CD-I.

ce /sə/ (**c'** /s/ *before e*, **cet** /sɛt/ *before vowel or mute h*), **cette** /sɛt/, *pl* **ces** /se/ **I** *adj dém* **1**○ (avec un sujet redondant) **alors, ~ bébé, ça pousse?** how's the baby doing?; **et ces travaux, ça avance?** how's the work progressing?; **cet entretien, ça s'est bien passé?** how did the interview go?; **2** (de politesse) **et pour ces dames?** what are the ladies having?; **3** (suivi d'une précision) **il n'est pas de ces hommes qui disent** he's not the kind of man to say; **elle a eu cette chance que la corde a tenu** she was lucky in that the rope held; **4** (marquant le degré) **cette arrogance!** what arrogance!; **cette idée!** what an idea!; **quand on a ~ talent** when you are as talented as that; **j'ai un de ces rhumes!** I've got an awful cold!; **je ne pensais pas qu'il aurait cette audace** I never thought he would be so cheeky; **tu as de ces idées!** you've got some funny ideas!

II *pron dém* **1** (utilisé seul) **~ faisant** in so doing; **tout s'est bien passé, et ~, grâce à vos efforts** everything went well, and that was all thanks to you; **sur ~, je vous quitte** with that, I must take my leave;

2 (avec une proposition relative) **fais ~ que tu veux** do what you like; **~ dont tu as besoin** what you need; **il a fait faillite, ~ qui n'est pas surprenant** he's gone bankrupt, which is hardly surprising; **~ qui m'étonne, c'est qu'il ait accepté** what surprises me is that he accepted; **il s'étonne de ~ que tu ne le saches pas** he's surprised (that) you don't know; **il tient à ~ que vous veniez** he's very keen that you should come ou for you to come; **~ que c'est grand!** it's so big!; **c'est étonnant ~ qu'il te ressemble!** it's amazing how much he looks like you!; **~ que c'est que d'être vieux!** what it is to be old!; **~ que c'est que les enfants!** that's children for you!; **~ qu'il ne faut pas faire!** the things one has to do!; **~ que** or **qu'est-~ que**○ **j'ai faim!** I'm starving!; **~ qu'il**○ **pleut!** it's pouring!

CE /seə/ *nm*: *abbr* ▶ **cours**.

ceci /səsi/ *pron dém* this; **à ~ près** with one slight difference; **à ~ près que** except that; **~ n'empêche pas cela** the one doesn't necessarily exclude the other; **~ compense cela** things balance out; **cet hôtel a ~ de bien que** one good thing about this hotel is that.

cécité /sesite/ *nf* blindness; **atteint de ~** blind; **souffrir de ~ partielle** to be partially sighted.

céder /sede/ [14] **I** *vtr* **1** (laisser) to give up [*tour, siège, part*] (**à qn** to sb); to yield [*pouvoir, droit*] (**à qn** to sb); to make over [*bien*] (**à** to); **~ le passage** or **la priorité** to give way (**à** to); **il m'a cédé sa place** he let me have his seat; **~ la place** FIG to give way (**à** to); **2** (vendre) to sell (**à qn** to sb); **'cède villa bord de mer'** 'for sale: seaside house'; **3** (être inférieur) **ne le ~ en rien à** to be on a par with.

II céder à *vtr ind* **~ à** to give in to, to yield to.

III *vi* **1** (fléchir) [*personne*] to give in; **2** (casser) [*poignée, branche*] to give way; (ne plus résister) [*serrure, porte*] to yield; **faire ~ une porte** to force a door.

cedex /sedɛks/ *nm* (*abbr* = **courrier d'entreprise à distribution exceptionnelle**) *postal code for corporate users*.

cédille /sedij/ *nf* cedilla.

cèdre /sɛdʀ/ *nm* (arbre) cedar; (bois) cedar(wood).

CEE /seə/ *nf*: *abbr* ▶ **communauté**.

CEEA /seəa/ *nf* (*abbr* = **Communauté européenne de l'énergie atomique**) EAEC.

cégep /seʒɛp/ *nm* C (*abbr* = **collège d'enseignement général et professionnel**) *college of further education in Quebec offering two-year courses*.

CEI /seəi/ *nf*: *abbr* ▶ **communauté**.

ceindre /sɛdʀ/ [55] LITER **I** *vtr* **1** (entourer) **~ sa taille d'un ruban** to put ou tie a ribbon around one's waist; **2** (mettre) to put on [*armure*]; to gird [*épée*].

II se ceindre *vpr* **se ~ d'un pagne** to put a loincloth on; **se ~ la tête d'un bandeau** to put a headband on.

ceint, ~e /sɛ, sɛt/ ▶ **ceindre**.

ceinture /sɛtyʀ/ *nf* **1** (pour tenir) belt; **2** (en couture) waistband; **3** (gaine) girdle; **4** (taille) waist; **avoir de l'eau jusqu'à la ~** to be up to one's waist in water; **coup en dessous de la ~** blow below the belt; **5** SPORT (prise) waist hold; (lien) belt; **être ~ noire** to be a black belt (**de** in); **6** (ce qui entoure) ring; **boulevard de ~** ringroad.
■ **~ orthopédique** surgical corset; **~ de sauvetage** lifebelt; **~ de sécurité** safety ou seat belt.
IDIOMES **faire ~**○ to go without; **se serrer la ~** to tighten one's belt.

ceinturer /sɛtyʀe/ [1] *vtr* **1** (être autour) [*réseau, murailles*] to encircle [*ville, terrain*]; **2** (maîtriser) to collar○ [*malfaiteur*]; SPORT to tackle [*adversaire*].

ceinturon /sɛtyʀɔ̃/ *nm* belt.

cela /səla/ *pron dém*

■ **Note** Dans de nombreux emplois, *cela* et *ça* sont équivalents. On se reportera donc à cette entrée.

1 GÉN that; **il y a dix ans de ~** that was ten years ago; **quant à ~** as for that; **~ dit** having said that; **2** (sujet apparent ou réel) it; (emphatique) that; **~**

m'inquiète de la voir dans cet état it worries me to see her in that state; **mais ~ ne vous appartient pas!** but that doesn't belong to you!; **il est coupable, ~ est sûr!** he is guilty, that is certain! IDIOMES **voyez-vous ~!** did you ever hear of such a thing!

célébration /selebʀasjɔ̃/ *nf* celebration.

célèbre /selɛbʀ/ *adj* famous (**pour, par** for); **tristement ~** notorious.

célébrer /selebʀe/ [14] *vtr* **1** (fêter) to celebrate [*événement*]; **2** (accomplir) to celebrate [*messe, mariage, culte*]; to perform [*rite*]; **3** (vanter) to praise [*personne*]; to remember [*mort, disparu*]; to extol [*qualité*].

célébrissime /selebʀisim/ *adj* extremely famous.

célébrité /selebʀite/ *nf* (gloire) fame; (personnage) celebrity.

céleri /selʀi/ *nm* **1** (en branches) celery; **2** (céleri-rave) celeriac; **~ en branches** celery; **~ rémoulade** grated celeriac in a mayonnaise dressing.

céleri-rave, *pl* **céleris-raves** /selʀiʀav/ *nm* celeriac.

célérité /seleʀite/ *nf* (rapidité) FML promptness; **avec ~** promptly.

céleste /selɛst/ *adj* [*corps, phénomène, puissances*] celestial; [*gloire, esprit*] heavenly; [*colère, messager*] divine.

célibat /seliba/ *nm* (état) single status; (chasteté) celibacy.

célibataire /selibatɛʀ/ **I** *adj* single; **je suis ~ pour quelques jours** I'm on my own for a few days.
II *nmf* (homme) bachelor, single man; (femme) single woman; **mère ~** single mother; **~ endurci** confirmed bachelor.

celle ▶ **celui**.

celle-ci ▶ **celui-ci**.

celle-là ▶ **celui-là**.

celles-ci ▶ **celui-ci**.

celles-là ▶ **celui-là**.

cellier /selje/ *nm* cellar.

cellulaire /selylɛʀ/ *adj* **1** (de la cellule) cell (*épith*); (fait de cellules) cellular; **2** [*régime, système*] of solitary confinement.

cellule /selyl/ *nf* **1** (en biologie) cell; **~s nerveuses/sanguines** nerve/blood cells; **2** (de prison, monastère, ruche) cell; **3** (en sociologie) unit; **4** (de parti) cell; **5** (en photo, informatique) cell; **6** (d'électrophone) cartridge.

cellulite /selylit/ *nf* (graisse) cellulite; (inflammation) cellulitis.

cellulose /selyloz/ *nf* cellulose.

celte /sɛlt/ *adj, nm* Celtic.

Celte /sɛlt/ *nmf* Celt.

celtique /sɛltik/ *adj, nm* Celtic.

celui /səlɥi/, **celle** /sɛl/, *mpl* **ceux** /sø/, *fpl* **celles** /sɛl/ *pron dém*

■ **Note** Voir aussi *celui-ci* et *celui-là*.

the one; **ceux, celles** (personnes) those; (choses) those, the ones; **non, ~ qui parlait** no, the one who was talking; **~ des deux qui finira le premier** the first one to finish; **ceux d'entre vous qui veulent partir** those of you who want to leave; **tous ceux qui étaient absents** all those who were absent; **tes yeux sont bleus, ceux de ton frère sont gris** your eyes are blue, your brother's are grey GB ou gray US; **faire ~ qui n'entend pas** to pretend not to hear; **heureux ~/ceux qui...** happy is he/are they who...

celui-ci /səlɥisi/, **celle-ci** /sɛlsi/, *mpl* **ceux-ci** /søsi/, *fpl* **celles-ci** /sɛlsi/ *pron dém* **1** (désignant ce qui est proche dans l'espace) this one; **ceux-ci, celles-ci** these; **2** (annonçant ce qui suit) **je n'ai qu'une chose à dire et c'est celle-ci** I have only one thing to say and it's this; **3** (ce dernier) **elle essaya la fenêtre mais celle-ci était coincée** she tried the window but it was jammed; **il entra, suivi de son père et de son frère; ~ portait un paquet** he came in, followed by his father and his brother, the latter of whom was carrying a parcel; **celle-ci est très serviable mais celui-là est plus efficace** she is very obliging but he's more efficient;

4 (l'un) **ils ont tous apporté quelque chose: ~ une bouteille, celui-là un gâteau** they all brought something: one brought a bottle, another a cake.

celui-là /səlɥila/, **celle-là** /sɛlla/, *mpl* **ceux-là** /søla/, *fpl* **celles-là** /sɛlla/ *pron dém*

■ **Note** Pour les sens 1, 3 et 4 voir aussi *celui-ci*.

1 (désignant ce qui est plus éloigné) that one; **ceux-là, celles-là** those (ones); **2** (le suivant) **si je n'ai qu'un conseil à te donner, c'est ~** if I only have one piece of advice for you, it's this; **3** (le premier des deux) the former; **4** (l'autre) another; **5** (par rapport aux précédents) **il fit une autre proposition, plus réaliste celle-là** he made another proposal, a more realistic one this time; **6**° (emphatique) **il exagère, ~!** that fellow° GB ou guy° is pushing it a bit°!; **celle-là, alors, quelle idiote!** what an idiot that woman is!; **~, alors!** (admiratif) what a man!; (irrité) that man!; **regardez-moi ~: il n'est même pas rasé!** look at him! he hasn't even shaved!; **7**° **elle est bien bonne, celle-là!** that's a good one!; **je ne m'attendais pas à celle-là** I didn't expect that!; **~ même** the very one.

cendre /sɑ̃dʀ/ *nf* ash; **~ de cigarette** cigarette ash; **pommes de terre cuites sous la ~** potatoes baked in the embers; **réduire en ~s** to reduce to ashes.

cendré, ~e /sɑ̃dʀe/ [▶141] *adj* ash (grey); **des cheveux blond ~** ash blond hair.

cendrier /sɑ̃dʀije/ *nm* ashtray.

Cène /sɛn/ *nf* **la ~** the Last Supper.

censé, ~e /sɑ̃se/ *adj* **être ~ faire** to be supposed to do; **nul n'est ~ ignorer la loi** ignorance of the law is no excuse.

censeur /sɑ̃sœʀ/ *nm* **1** SCOL school official in charge of discipline; **2** (moraliste) **s'ériger en ~ de qch** to set oneself up as a critic of sth.

censure /sɑ̃syʀ/ *nf* **1** (interdiction) censorship; (**commission de**) **~** board of censors; **menacé par la ~** in danger of being censored; **2** POL censure.

censurer /sɑ̃syʀe/ [1] *vtr* **1** (expurger) to censor; (interdire) to ban; **2** POL to pass a vote of censure ou no confidence in [*gouvernement*].

cent /sɑ̃/ [▶399], 156] **I** *adj* GÉN a hundred, one hundred; **deux ~s** two hundred; **deux ~ trois/vingt-cinq** two hundred and three/twenty-five; **~ à deux ~s personnes** between a hundred and two hundred people.
II *pron* **ils sont venus tous les ~** all one hundred of them came.
III *nm* hundred; **un ~ d'œufs** a ou one hundred eggs; **vendre au ~** to sell by the hundred.
IV pour cent *loc adj* per cent; **un placement à sept pour ~** an investment at seven per cent; **dix à vingt pour ~** or 10 à 20% **des enseignants** between ten and twenty per cent of teachers; **une jupe ~ pour ~** ou **100% coton** a hundred per cent cotton skirt; **je ne suis pas sûr à 100%** I'm not a hundred per cent sure.
IDIOMES **faire les ~ pas** to pace up and down; **être aux ~ coups**° to be worried sick°, to be in a state°; **faire les quatre ~s coups** to be a real tearaway; **attendre ~ sept ans**° to wait for ages; **durer ~ sept ans**° to last for ages ou forever.

centaine /sɑ̃tɛn/ *nf* **1** (cent unités) hundred; **la colonne des ~s** the hundreds column; **2** (environ cent) about a hundred; **nous étions une ~** there were about a hundred of us; **une ~ de milliers de manifestants** about a hundred thousand protesters; **des ~s de femmes** hundreds of women; **quelques ~s de tonnes** a few hundred tons; **les victimes se comptent par ~s** there are hundreds of victims; **les lettres arrivent par ~s** letters are arriving in hundreds; **2** (âge) **avoir la ~** to be about a hundred; **approcher de la ~** to be getting on for a hundred; **dépasser la ~** to be over a hundred.

centenaire /sɑ̃tnɛʀ/ **I** *adj* **1** (de cent ans) [*arbre, objet*] hundred-year-old (*épith*); **plusieurs fois ~** several hundred years old; **2** [*personne*] centenarian; **elle est**

~ she's a hundred years old; **3** (se produisant une fois par siècle) **crue** ~ one-in-a-hundred-years flood.
II *nmf* **c'est une** ~ she's a hundred years old.
III *nm* (anniversaire) centenary GB, centennial US.

centième /sɑ̃tjɛm/ ▶399⌟ **I** *adj* hundredth.
II *nf* THÉÂT **la** ~ the hundredth performance.

centilitre /sɑ̃tilitʀ/ ▶86⌟ *nm* centilitre GB.

centime /sɑ̃tim/ ▶33⌟ *nm* (monnaie) centime; (somme infime) penny, cent US; **pas un** ~ not a penny; **calculer au** ~ **près** to work things out to the last penny; **dépenser jusqu'au dernier** ~ to spend one's last penny.

centimètre /sɑ̃timɛtʀ/ *nm* **1** ▶348⌟, 575⌟, 581⌟, 631⌟, 635⌟ (unité) centimetre GB; **2** (distance infime) inch; **ne pas avancer d'un** ~ not to move an inch; **3** (ruban) tape measure.
■ ~ **carré** square centimetre GB; ~ **cube** cubic centimetre GB.

centrafricain, ~**e** /sɑ̃tʀafʀikɛ̃, ɛn/ ▶394⌟ *adj* of the Central African Republic; **République** ~**e** Central African Republic.

Centrafrique /sɑ̃tʀafʀik/ ▶232⌟ *nprm* Central African Republic.

central, ~**e**[1], *mpl* -**aux** /sɑ̃tʀal, o/ **I** *adj* **1** (au centre) central; **l'Europe** ~**e** Central Europe; **court** ~ (en tennis) centre GB court; **ordinateur** ~ host computer; **chercher quelque chose de plus** ~ to look for something more central; **2** (principal) main.
II *nm* TÉLÉCOM ~ (**téléphonique**) (telephone) exchange.

centrale[2] /sɑ̃tʀal/ *nf* **1** (productrice d'énergie) power station; ~ **nucléaire** or **atomique** nuclear power station; ~ **hydraulique** hydroelectric power station; **2** (en politique) ~ **syndicale** or **ouvrière** confederation of trade unions; **les** ~**s syndicales** the trade unions; **3** (prison) prison; **4** COMM ~ **d'achat** (groupement) *central purchasing agency*.

centralisateur, -**trice** /sɑ̃tʀalizatœʀ, tʀis/ *adj* centralizing.

centraliser /sɑ̃tʀalize/ [1] *vtr* to centralize; **verrouillage centralisé** central locking.

centralisme /sɑ̃tʀalism/ *nm* centralism.

centre /sɑ̃tʀ/ *nm* **1** (milieu) centre GB; **au** ~ **de qch** in the centre GB of sth; **habiter dans le** ~ to live in the centre GB; **le** ~ (de la France) central France; **2** (lieu) centre GB; **un grand** ~ **industriel** a large industrial centre GB; **3** (établissement, organisme) centre GB; **4** (point essentiel) centre GB; **il se prend pour le** ~ **du monde** he thinks the whole world revolves around him; **5** POL **le** ~ the centre GB; **les partis du** ~ the centre GB parties; ~ **gauche/droit** centre GB left/right; **elle est au** ~ she's in the centre GB; **6** ANAT centre GB; ~ **nerveux** ANAT, FIG nerve centre GB; **les** ~**s vitaux** the vital organs; **7** (passe du ballon) centre GB pass.
■ ~ **d'accueil** reception centre GB; ~ **aéré** children's outdoor activity centre; ~ **antipoison** poisons unit; ~ **commercial** shopping centre GB; ~ **de dépistage** screening unit; ~ **de documentation** (dans une école) library; (pour professionnels) resource centre GB; ~ **de documentation et d'information**, **CDI** learning resources centre GB; ~ **dramatique** arts centre GB for theatre GB; ~ **équestre** riding school; ~ **d'examens** SCOL examination centre GB; ~ **de formation** training centre GB; ~ **de gériatrie** geriatric hospital; ~ **de gravité** centre GB of gravity; ~ **hospitalier** hospital complex; ~ **hospitalier universitaire**, **CHU** ~ teaching hospital; ~ **d'inertie** centre GB of inertia; ~ **de loisirs** leisure centre GB; ~ **médical** health centre GB; ~ **de recherches** research centre GB; ~ **de remise en forme** health farm; ~ **de soins** clinic; ~ **sportif** sports centre GB; ~ **de traitement** ORDINAT processing centre GB; ~ **de transfusion sanguine** blood transfusion centre GB; ~ **de tri** (**postal**) sorting office; ~ **universitaire** university; ~ **de vacances** holiday GB ou vacation US centre GB; **Centre d'information et d'orientation** SCOL national careers guidance centre GB; **Centre national**

d'enseignement à distance, **CNED** national centre GB for distance learning.

centrer /sɑ̃tʀe/ [1] *vtr* **1** (fixer par rapport au centre) to centre GB; **2** (diriger) **être centré sur qch** to be centred GB around sth; **école centrée sur l'enseignement de la musique** school which focuses on the teaching of music; **3** SPORT to centre GB.

centre-ville, *pl* **centres-villes** /sɑ̃tʀəvil/ *nm* town centre GB; (de grande ville) city centre GB.

centrifuge /sɑ̃tʀifyʒ/ *adj* centrifugal.

centrifugeur /sɑ̃tʀifyʒœʀ/ *nm* centrifuge.

centrifugeuse /sɑ̃tʀifyʒøz/ *nf* (en électroménager) juice extractor; (en chimie, mécanique) centrifuge.

centriste /sɑ̃tʀist/ *adj*, *nmf* centrist.

centuple /sɑ̃typl/ **I** *adj* **une somme** ~ **d'une autre** an amount a hundred times greater than another.
II *nm* **dix mille est le** ~ **de cent** ten thousand is a hundred times one hundred; **rendre au** ~ FIG to repay a hundred times over.

cep /sɛp/ *nm* ~ (**de vigne**) vine stock.

cépage /sepaʒ/ *nm* grape variety; ~ **cabernet** Cabernet grape.

cèpe /sɛp/ *nm* cep.

cependant /səpɑ̃dɑ̃/ **I** *conj* (pourtant) yet, however; **votre devoir est bon mais il y a** ~ **quelques erreurs** your work is good; however, there are a few mistakes; **une ambiguïté subsiste** ~ one ambiguity remains, however.
II **cependant que** *loc conj* (tandis que) whereas, while.

céphalée /sefale/ *nf* headache.

céramique /seʀamik/ *nf* **1** (matière) ceramic; **en** ~ ceramic (*épith*); **2** (objet) ceramic; **3** (art, industrie, technique) ceramics (+ *v sg*).

cerbère /sɛʀbɛʀ/ *nm* (garde du corps) minder; (gardien) watchdog.

cerceau, *pl* ~**x** /sɛʀso/ *nm* hoop; **pousser un** ~ to bowl a hoop.

cerclage /sɛʀklaʒ/ *nm* **1** (de tonneau) hooping; **2** MÉD **faire un** ~ **du col de l'utérus** to put in a cervical stitch.

cercle /sɛʀkl/ *nm* **1** (figure) circle; **en** ~ in a circle; **entourez le verbe d'un** ~ ring ou circle the verb; **décrire des** ~ [*avion, oiseau*] to circle (overhead); **faire** ~ **autour de qn** to gather around sb; **2** (groupe) circle; **3** (association) circle, society; JEUX, SPORT club; (local) club; **4** (de tonneau) hoop.
■ ~ **inscrit** inscribed circle; ~ **polaire** polar circle; ~ **polaire antarctique** Antarctic circle; ~ **polaire arctique** Arctic circle; ~ **vicieux** vicious circle.

cercler /sɛʀkle/ [1] *vtr* to hoop [*tonneau*]; **les noms cerclés de** or **en rouge** the names circled in red; **lunettes cerclées** rimmed glasses.

cercueil /sɛʀkœj/ *nm* coffin.

céréale /seʀeal/ **I** *nf* cereal, grain ¢; **cultiver des** ~**s** to grow cereals.
II **céréales** *nfpl* CULIN cereal ¢; **manger des** ~**s** to eat cereal.

céréalier, -**ière** /seʀealje, ɛʀ/ *adj* [*production*] cereal (*épith*); [*région*] cereal-growing (*épith*).

cérébral, ~**e**, *mpl* -**aux** /seʀebʀal, o/ **I** *adj* ANAT, MÉD cerebral; (intellectuel) [*travail*] intellectual; [*personne*] cerebral.
II *nm,f* cerebral type.

cérémonial, *pl* ~**s** /seʀemɔnjal/ *nm* ceremonial.

cérémonie /seʀemɔni/ **I** *nf* ceremony; **tenue** or **habit de** ~ ceremonial dress.
II **cérémonies** *nfpl* (politesse exagérée) ceremony ¢; **faire des** ~**s** to stand on ceremony; **sans** ~**s** [*repas, invitation*] informal; [*recevoir*] informally.

cérémonieux, -**ieuse** /seʀemɔnjø, øz/ *adj* ceremonious; **d'un air** ~ ceremoniously.

cerf /sɛʀ/ *nm* stag.

cerfeuil /sɛʀfœj/ *nm* chervil.

cerf-volant, *pl* **cerfs-volants** /sɛʀvɔlɑ̃/ *nm* (jouet) kite; (insecte) stag beetle.

cerise /s(ə)ʀiz/ **I** ▶ 141 | *adj inv* (**rouge**) ~ cherry-red, cerise.
II *nf* cherry.

cerisier /s(ə)ʀizje/ *nm* (arbre) cherry (tree); (bois) cherrywood.

cerne /sɛʀn/ *nm* ring.

cerné, ~**e** /sɛʀne/ *adj* **avoir les yeux** ~**s** to have rings under one's eyes.

cerneau, *pl* ~**x** /sɛʀno/ *nm* ~**x de noix** walnut halves.

cerner /sɛʀne/ [1] *vtr* **1** (encercler) to surround; **vous êtes cernés!** you're surrounded!; **2** (définir) to define [*question, problème*]; to make [sb] out [*personne*]; to determine [*personnalité, besoins*]; **3** (entourer d'un cercle) to outline [*figure, dessin*] (**de** with).

certain, ~**e** /sɛʀtɛ̃, ɛn/ **I** *adj* **1** (convaincu) ~ **de** certain ou sure of; **es-tu** ~ **d'avoir fermé le gaz?** are your certain ou sure that you turned off the gas?; **2** (indiscutable) certain, sure; **tenir qch pour** ~ to be certain of sth; **c'est sûr et** ~○ it's absolutely certain; **ils vont gagner, c'est** ~**!** they're bound to win!; **il est** ~ **qu'il n'aurait jamais pu faire ce qu'il a fait sans sa femme** he certainly couldn't have done what he did if it hadn't been for his wife; **ils vont à une mort** ~**e** they're heading for certain death; **une influence** ~**e** an undeniable ou a definite influence; **un homme d'un âge** ~ a man of advanced years; **3** (fixé) [*date, prix*] definite.
II *adj indéf* (*before n*) **1** (mal défini) **elle restera un** ~ **temps** she'll stay for some time ou for a while; **un** ~ **nombre d'erreurs** a (certain) number of mistakes; **une** ~**e image de la France** a certain image of France; **dans une** ~**e mesure** to a certain ou to some extent; **d'une** ~**e manière** in a way; **2** (devant un nom de personne) **un** ~ **M. Grovagnard** a (certain) Mr Grovagnard; **3** (intensif) some; **il faut un** ~ **culot**○ it takes some nerve○; **un homme d'un** ~ **âge** a man who's no longer young; **il avait déjà un** ~ **âge** he was already getting on in years.
III **certains**, **certaines** *adj indéf pl* some; **à** ~**s moments** sometimes, at times.
IV **certains**, **certaines** *pron indéf pl* some people; ~**s d'entre eux** some of them.

certainement /sɛʀtɛnmɑ̃/ *adv* **1** (sans certitude) most probably; **c'est** ~ **quelqu'un de très compétent** he/she must be a very competent person; **2** (avec certitude) certainly; **tu y es** ~ **pour quelque chose!** you have certainly got something to do with it!; **3** (pour renforcer) certainly; **mais** ~**!** certainly ou of course!; ~ **pas!** certainly not!

certes /sɛʀt/ *adv* (en signe de concession) admittedly; **ce ne sera** ~ **pas facile mais**... admittedly it won't be easy but...; **il est séduisant,** ~**, mais prétentieux** he is good-looking, certainly, but he is conceited; ~ **non!** certainly not!

certificat /sɛʀtifika/ *nm* **1** (document officiel) certificate; ~ **attestant que** certificate showing that; **2** (document privé) testimonial.
■ ~ **d'aptitude professionnelle, CAP** *vocational training qualification*; ~ **de bonne vie et mœurs** ~ character reference; ~ **de garantie** certificate of guarantee; ~ **de naissance** birth certificate; ~ **de résidence** proof of residence; ~ **de scolarité** proof of attendance (*at school or university*) ; ~ **de travail** *document from a previous employer giving dates and nature of employment*.

certifié, ~**e** /sɛʀtifje/ *adj* **professeur** ~ fully qualified teacher.

certifier /sɛʀtifje/ [2] *vtr* **1** GÉN to certify, to authenticate [*signature*]; ~ **conforme** to authenticate; **copie certifiée conforme** certified copy; **2** (affirmer) **elle m'a certifié que** she assured me that.

certitude /sɛʀtityd/ *nf* **1** (caractère indubitable) certainty; **on sait avec** ~ **que** we know for certain that; **seule** ~**, il est parti à midi** all we know for

certain is that he left at noon; **2** (conviction) conviction; **avoir la** ~ **que** to be certain that.

cérumen /seʀymɛn/ *nm* earwax; **bouchon de** ~ cerumen blockage.

cerveau, *pl* ~**x** /sɛʀvo/ *nm* **1** ANAT brain; **2** (siège de l'intelligence) mind; **3** (personne intelligente) brain○; **exode** or **fuite des** ~**x** brain drain; **la chasse aux** ~**x** talent hunting; **c'est un** ~ he/she has an outstanding mind; **4** (directeur) brains (+ *v sg*); (centre directeur) nerve centre.
IDIOMES **avoir le** ~ **fêlé**○ or **dérangé** to be deranged ou cracked○.

cervelas /sɛʀvəla/ *nm* saveloy.

cervelet /sɛʀvəlɛ/ *nm* cerebellum.

cervelle /sɛʀvɛl/ *nf* **1** (substance) brains (*pl*); **se brûler** or **se faire sauter la** ~○ to blow one's brains out○; ~ **de veau** CULIN calf's brains; **2**○ (tête) brain; **il n'a rien dans la** ~ he's brainless; **elle a une** ~ **d'oiseau** she's a birdbrain○.

cervical, ~**e**, *mpl* -**aux** /sɛʀvikal, o/ *adj* cervical.

cervoise /sɛʀvwaz/ *nf* (barley) beer.

ces ▶ **ce**.

CES /seəs/ *nm abbr* ▶ **collège**.

césar /sezaʀ/ *nm* **1** CIN César (*film award*); **2** (dictateur) caesar.

César /sezaʀ/ *npr* **Jules** ~ Julius Caesar; **rendons à** ~ **ce qui est à** ~ render unto Caesar that which is Caesar's.

césarienne /sezaʀjɛn/ *nf* caesarian (section).

cessante /sesɑ̃t/ *adj f* **toute(s) affaire(s)** ~**(s)** FML forthwith SOUT.

cessation /sesasjɔ̃/ *nf* suspension.
■ ~ **d'activité** GÉN suspension of activities; (retraite) retirement; COMM closing down.

cesse /sɛs/ *nf* **elle n'a de** ~ **de démontrer**... she's forever demonstrating...; **sans** ~ [*parler, changer*] constantly; **un nombre sans** ~ **grandissant** an ever increasing number; **des machines sans** ~ **plus puissantes** ever more powerful machines.

cesser /sese/ [1] **I** *vtr* to cease [*traitement, livraisons*]; to end [*soutien, répression*]; ~ **de faire** to stop doing; ~ **toute activité** [*entreprise*] to cease trading; ~ **les combats** to stop fighting; ~ **de fumer/d'espérer** to give up smoking/hope; ~ **d'exister** to cease to exist; ~ **de payer** to cease payment; **les prix ne cessent d'augmenter** prices keep (on) rising.
II *vi* [*activité*] to cease; [*vent*] to drop; [*pluie*] to stop; **faire** ~ to put an end to [*rumeur*]; to put a stop to [*combats*]; to end [*poursuites*].

cessez-le-feu /seselfø/ *nm inv* ceasefire.

cession /sesjɔ̃/ *nf* transfer.

c'est-à-dire /setadiʀ/ *loc conj* **1** (pour préciser) that is (to say); **2** (ce qui signifie) ~ **que** which means (that); **'j'ai presque fini'—'**~ **que tu viens de commencer'** 'I've nearly finished'—'what you mean is that you've barely started'; **'le travail est trop dur'—'**~**?'** 'the work is too hard'—'what do you mean?'; **3** (pour rectifier, excuser) ~ **que** well, actually; ~ **qu'il est jeune** well, you know, he's young.

césure /sezyʀ/ *nf* (de vers) caesura; (de fin de ligne) line break.

cet ▶ **ce**.

CET /seəte/ *nm: abbr* ▶ **collège**.

cette ▶ **ce**.

ceux ▶ **celui**.

ceux-ci ▶ **celui-ci**.

ceux-là ▶ **celui-là**.

Ceylan /selɑ̃/ *nprm* HIST Ceylon; **thé de** ~ Ceylon tea.

CFDT /seɛfdete/ *nf* (*abbr* = **Confédération française démocratique du travail**) CFDT (*French trade union*).

CFTC /seɛftese/ *nf* (*abbr* = **Confédération française des travailleurs chrétiens**) CFTC (*French trade union*).

CGC /seʒese/ *nf* (*abbr* = **Confédération générale des cadres**) CGC (*French trade union*).

CGT /seʒete/ *nf* (*abbr* = **Confédération générale du travail**) CGT (*French trade union*).

chacal, *pl* **~s** /ʃakal/ *nm* ZOOL, FIG jackal.

chacun, **~e** /ʃakœ̃, yn/ *pron indéf* **1** (chaque élément) each (one); **~ de** each one of, every one of; **~ d'entre nous** each (one) of us, every one of us; **ils ont ~ sa** or **leur chambre** they each have their own room; **vous avez droit à une boisson ~** you're each entitled to a drink; **nous avons ~ pris notre veste** we all took our jackets; **2** (tout le monde) everyone; **comme ~ sait** as everyone knows; **~ son tour** everyone in turn; **~ son tour!** wait your turn!; **~ ses goûts** every man to his own taste; **~ pour soi (et Dieu pour tous)** every man for himself (and God for us all); **tout un ~** everyone; **à ~ son métier** every man to his own trade.

chagrin, **~e** /ʃagʁɛ̃, in/ *I adj* [*personne*] despondent; *d'humeur* **~e** despondent.
II nm (peine) grief; **faire du ~ à qn** to cause sb grief; **accablé de ~** grief-stricken; **avoir du ~** to be sad; **elle a eu de nombreux ~s** she's had many sorrows; **mourir de ~** to die of a broken heart; **avoir un gros ~** [*enfant*] to be very upset; **~ d'amour** unhappy love affair.

chagriner /ʃagʁine/ [1] *vtr* **1** (peiner) to pain, to grieve; **2** (contrarier) to bother, to worry; **il y a quelque chose qui me chagrine dans cette histoire** there's something about this story which bothers me.

chahut /ʃay/ *nm* racket○; **faire du ~** [*fêtard*] to make a racket○; [*élève*] to play up the teacher.

chahuter /ʃayte/ [1] *I vtr* [*élève, classe*] to play up; [*personne, groupe*] to heckle [*orateur*]; **se faire ~ par qn** GÉN to be heckled by sb.
II vi to mess around (**avec** with).

chahuteur, **-euse** /ʃaytœʁ, øz/ *adj* disruptive.

chaîne /ʃɛn/ *I nf* **1** (entrave) chain; **mettre les ~s à qn** to put sb in chains; **attacher qn avec des ~s** to chain sb up; **2** (de transmission) chain; **~ de vélo** bicycle chain; **3** IND assembly line; **travailler à la ~** to work on the assembly line; **produire (qch) à la ~** to mass-produce (sth); **on n'est pas à la ~!** FIG we're not machines, you know!; **système éducatif à la ~** conveyor-belt education system; **4** (bijou) chain; **~ en or** gold chain; **5** (succession) chain; **des catastrophes en ~** a series of disasters; **réaction en ~** chain reaction; **6** (organisation) network ; **~ de solidarité** support network; **faire la ~** to make a chain; **7** GÉOG chain, range; **8** (de télévision) channel; **deuxième ~** channel 2; **9** COMM chain; **~ de magasins** chain of stores; **10** AUDIO system; **~ stéréo** stereo system; **11** CHIMIE chain.
II **chaînes** *nfpl* AUT snow chains.
■ **~ de fabrication** production line; **~ de montage** assembly line.

chaînette /ʃɛnɛt/ *nf* **1** (bijou) chain; **~ en argent** silver chain; **2** (de transmission) small chain.

chaînon /ʃɛnɔ̃/ *nm* link; **~ manquant** missing link.

chair /ʃɛʁ/ *I* ▶141 *adj inv* flesh-coloured○GB.
II nf **1** ANAT flesh *₵*; **~s meurtries** bruised flesh; **bien en ~** plump, well-padded○; **2** (de fruit, légume, poisson) flesh; (de volaille) meat; **~ à saucisses** sausage meat; **3** (corps) flesh; **être de ~** to be only human.
■ **~ à canon**○ cannon fodder; **~ fraîche** young bodies (*pl*); **~ de poule** gooseflesh, goose pimples (*pl*), goosebumps (*pl*); **donner la ~ de poule à qn** [*froid*] to give sb gooseflesh; [*peur*] to make sb's flesh creep.
IDIOMES **transformer qn en ~ à pâté** or **saucisses**○ to make mincemeat of sb○; **l'esprit est ardent mais la ~ est faible** BIBLE the spirit is willing but the flesh is weak BIBLE.

chaire /ʃɛʁ/ *nf* **1** RELIG (tribune) pulpit; (siège) throne; **2** UNIV (poste) chair; (tribune) rostrum.

chaise /ʃɛz/ *nf* (siège) chair; **~ pliante** folding chair.
■ **~ pour bébé** = **~ haute**; **~ électrique** electric chair; **~ haute** high-chair; **~ longue** deck-

chair; **~ percée** commode; **~ à porteurs** sedan chair; **~ roulante** wheelchair.
IDIOMES **être assis entre deux ~s** to be in an awkward position.

chaland, **~e** /ʃalɑ̃, ɑ̃d/ *I nm,f* (client) regular customer.
II nm NAUT barge.

chaldéen, **-éenne** /kaldeɛ̃, ɛn/ *I adj* Chaldean.
II nm LING Chaldean.

châle /ʃɑl/ *nm* shawl.

chalet /ʃalɛ/ *nm* (de montagne) chalet; (maison en bois) chalet-style house.

chaleur /ʃalœʁ/ *I nf* **1** (sensation physique) heat; (douce) warmth; **la ~ du soleil** the heat of the sun; **vague de ~** heatwave; **coup de ~** heat stroke; **il faisait une ~ moite** it was muggy; **il fait une de ces ~s**○!; **~ animale** body heat; **2** (de personne, voix, coloris, d'accueil) warmth; **3** ZOOL (être) **en ~** to be on heat; **les ~s** the heat *₵*.
II **chaleurs** *nfpl* MÉTÉO **les ~s** the hot season (*sg*); **les premières ~s** the first days of the hot season.

chaleureusement /ʃalœʁøzmɑ̃/ *adv* [*applaudir, remercier*] warmly; [*soutenir*] wholeheartedly; **accueillir qn ~** to give sb a warm welcome.

chaleureux, **-euse** /ʃalœʁø, øz/ *adj* [*personne, accueil, paroles*] warm; [*public, applaudissements*] enthusiastic; [*soutien*] wholehearted; [*atmosphère*] friendly; [*endroit*] welcoming.

challenge /ʃalɑ̃ʒ/ *nm* **1** (défi) challenge; **2** SPORT (épreuve) tournament; (trophée) trophy.

chaloir† /ʃalwaʁ/ *v impers* **peu me** or **m'en chaut** it matters little to me.

chaloupe /ʃalup/ *nf* (à rames) rowing boat GB, rowboat US; (à moteur) (motor) launch.

chalumeau, *pl* **~x** /ʃalymo/ *nm* **1** (outil) blowtorch; **~ à souder** welding torch; **2** ▶392 (flûte) pipe; **3** (pour boire) straw.

chalut /ʃaly/ *nm* trawl; **jeter le ~** to shoot the trawl; **pêcher (qch) au ~** to trawl (for sth).

chalutier /ʃalytje/ *nm* ▶374 (bateau) trawler; (marin) trawlerman.

chamade /ʃamad/ *nf* **battre la ~** to beat wildly.

chamailler○: **se chamailler** /ʃamaje/ [1] *vpr* to squabble.

chamarré, **~e** /ʃamaʁe/ *adj* (multicolore) brightly coloured○GB.

chambard○ /ʃɑ̃baʁ/ *nm* **1** (vacarme, désordre) din, racket○; **2** (bouleversement) upheaval.

chambardement○ /ʃɑ̃baʁdəmɑ̃/ *nm* (bouleversement) shake-up○; (désordre) mess.

chambarder○ /ʃɑ̃baʁde/ [1] *vtr* **1** (mettre sens dessus dessous) to turn [sth] upside down; **2** (modifier) to upset [*projets, habitudes*].

chambouler○ /ʃɑ̃bule/ [1] *vtr* **1** (bouleverser) to upset [*projet*]; to shake up [*vie, établissement*]; **~ les habitudes de qn** to upset sb's routine; **2** (mettre en désordre) to mess [sth] up [*meubles*]; (mélanger) to mix [sth] up [*photos, papiers*]; **ils ont tout chamboulé (dans la maison)** they turned the whole house upside down.

chambranle /ʃɑ̃bʁɑl/ *nm* (de porte, fenêtre) frame.

chambre /ʃɑ̃bʁ/ *nf* **1** (pour dormir) GÉN room; (chez soi) room, bedroom; **~ d'hôtel** hotel room; **~ pour une personne/pour deux personnes** single/double room; **~ à deux lits** twin room; **faire ~ à part** to sleep in separate rooms; **avez-vous une ~ de libre?** have you got any vacancies?; **politicien en ~** HUM armchair politician HUM; **2** MUS **musique de ~** chamber music; **3** (assemblée parlementaire) house; **4** ADMIN (organe professionnel) chamber; **5** TECH (enceinte close) chamber.
■ **~ à air** inner tube; **~ d'amis** guest room; **~ basse** Lower House; **~ de bonne** maid's room; **~ de commerce (et d'industrie)** chamber of commerce; **~ à coucher** (pièce) bedroom ; (mobilier) bedroom suite; **~ forte** strong room; **~ frigorifique** or **froide** cold (storage) room; **~ à gaz** gas

chamber; ~ **haute** Upper House; ~ **d'hôte** ~ room in a guest house; **'~s d'hôte'** 'bed and breakfast'; ~ **d'isolement** MÉD isolation room; ~ **noire** PHOT (boîte) camera obscura; (local) darkroom; ~ **de torture** torture chamber; **Chambre des communes** House of Commons; **Chambre des députés** Chamber of Deputies; **Chambre des lords** House of Lords.

chambrée /ʃɑ̃bʀe/ *nf* MIL (dortoir, soldats) barracks.

chambrer /ʃɑ̃bʀe/ [1] *vtr* **1** to bring [sth] to room temperature [*vin, bouteille*]; **ce vin rouge se boit chambré** this red wine should be drunk at room temperature; **2**○ (se moquer de) to tease.

chameau, *pl* ~**x** /ʃamo/ *nm* **1** ZOOL camel; **2**○ (personne désagréable) nasty person; **c'est un** ~ he's/she's really nasty.

chamelier /ʃaməlje/ ▶ 374 *nm* camel driver.

chamelle /ʃamɛl/ *nf* she-camel.

chamois /ʃamwa/ **I** ▶ 141 *adj inv* (ocre jaune) fawn.
II *nm* ZOOL chamois.

champ /ʃɑ̃/ **I** *nm* **1** (terre cultivable) field; **des ~s de coton** cotton fields; **prendre à travers ~s** to cut across the fields; **aux ~s** in the fields; **en pleins ~s** in open country; **2** (domaine) field; **le ~ culturel** the cultural arena; **le ~ des investigations** the scope of the investigations; **le ~ est libre, on peut y aller** the coast is clear, we can go ahead; **avoir le ~ libre** to have a free hand; **3** PHOT, CIN field; **le ~ visuel** the field of vision; **être dans le ~** to be in shot; **voix hors** ~ offscreen voice; **4** PHYS, LING, MATH field.
II à tout bout de champ○ *loc adv* all the time.
■ ~ **de bataille** MIL, FIG battlefield; ~ **de courses** racetrack; ~ **de foire** fairground; ~ **de manœuvre** training area; ~ **de mines** minefield; ~ **de tir** (terrain d'exercice) firing range; (portée) range.

champagne /ʃɑ̃paɲ/ *nm* champagne; **boire du** ~ to drink champagne; ~ **brut/sec/demi-sec** extra-dry/ dry/medium-dry champagne.

champagnisé /ʃɑ̃paɲize/ *adj* **vin champagnisé** sparkling wine.

champenois, ~**e** /ʃɑ̃pənwa, az/ *adj* **1** ▶ 509 GÉOG of the Champagne region; **2** IND **méthode** ~**e** champagne method.

champêtre /ʃɑ̃pɛtʀ/ *adj* [*fête, bal*] village (*épith*); [*scène, paysage*] rural; **déjeuner** ~ lunch in the country.

champignon /ʃɑ̃piɲɔ̃/ *nm* **1** CULIN mushroom; ~ **vénéneux** poisonous mushroom, toadstool; **aller aux** ~**s** to go mushroom picking; **2** BOT, MÉD fungus; **3** (ornement) (dans un jardin) toadstool; **4**○ (accélérateur) throttle, accelerator; **appuyer sur le** ~ to put one's foot down GB, to step on the gas US.
■ ~ **atomique** mushroom cloud; ~ **hallucinogène** hallucinogenic mushroom, magic mushroom○; ~ **de Paris** button mushroom GB, champignon US.
IDIOMES **pousser comme des** ~**s** to pop up like mushrooms.

champignonnière /ʃɑ̃piɲɔnjɛʀ/ *nf* mushroom bed.

champion, **-ionne** /ʃɑ̃pjɔ̃, ɔn/ *nm,f* **1** SPORT champion; **2**○ (qui excelle) **être** ~ to be in a class of one's own; ~ **de la gaffe** prize fool; **3**○ (leader) **pays** ~ **de la lutte contre la drogue** country which leads the field in the fight against drugs; **4**○ (défenseur) champion; **se faire le** ~ **d'une cause** to champion a cause.

championnat /ʃɑ̃pjɔna/ *nm* championship.

chance /ʃɑ̃s/ *nf* **1** (sort favorable) (good) luck; **c'est bien ma** ~! IRON just my luck!; **pas de** ~, **tu as perdu!** hard luck, you've lost!; **coup de** ~ stroke of luck; **la** ~ **a voulu que je le croise** as luck would have it, I bumped into him; **avoir de la** ~ to be lucky; **ne pas avoir de** ~ to be unlucky; **avoir une** ~ **du tonnerre**○ to have the luck of the devil; **c'est une** ~ **de pouvoir partir** we're lucky to be able to leave; **par** ~ luckily, fortunately; **2** (possibilité) chance; **il y a de fortes** ~**s** (pour) **qu'elle vienne** there's every chance that she will come; **il a ses** ~**s** he stands a good chance; **mettre toutes les** ~**s de**

son côté to take no chances; **conserver toutes ses** ~**s** still to have a chance; **'il va pleuvoir?'**—'il y a des ~**s**' 'is it going to rain?'—'probably'; **3** (fortune) luck; **4** (occasion favorable) chance, opportunity; **la** ~ **de ma vie** the chance ou opportunity of a lifetime; **laisser une** ~ **à qn** to give sb a chance; **saisir sa** ~ to seize the opportunity; **c'est la réunion de la dernière** ~ the meeting is the last hope.

chancelant, ~**e** /ʃɑ̃slɑ̃, ɑ̃t/ *adj* **1** (qui manque d'équilibre) [*démarche*] unsteady; [*objet*] rickety, shaky; [*personne*] staggering; ~ **de fatigue** staggering with tiredness; **avancer d'un pas** ~ to walk unsteadily; **2** (fragile) [*courage, pouvoir, foi*] wavering; [*moral*] flagging; [*volonté*] faltering; [*empire, trône*] tottering.

chanceler /ʃɑ̃sle/ [19] *vi* **1** (perdre l'équilibre) [*personne*] to stagger; [*objet*] to wobble; **2** (manquer de fermeté) to waver; **3** (être menacé) [*pouvoir, trône*] to totter; [*santé*] to be precarious.

chancelier /ʃɑ̃səlje/ *nm* GÉN chancellor; (d'ambassade) chancery.

chancellerie /ʃɑ̃sɛlʀi/ *nf* (en France) Ministry of Justice; (en Allemagne, Autriche) Chancellorship.

chanceux, **-euse** /ʃɑ̃sø, øz/ **I** *adj* (fortuné) lucky.
II *nm,f* C lucky man/woman.

chancre /ʃɑ̃kʀ/ *nm* canker.

chandail /ʃɑ̃daj/ *nm* sweater, jumper GB.

chandeleur /ʃɑ̃dlœʀ/ *nf* RELIG Candlemas.

chandelier /ʃɑ̃dəlje/ *nm* (à une branche) candlestick; (à plusieurs branches) candelabra GB.

chandelle /ʃɑ̃dɛl/ *nf* **1** (bougie) candle; **lire à la lueur d'une** ~ to read by candlelight; **s'éclairer à la** ~ to use candles for lighting; **un dîner aux** ~**s** a candlelit dinner; **2** SPORT **faire la** ~ to do a shoulder stand.
IDIOMES **devoir une fière** ~○ **à qn** to be hugely indebted to sb; **faire des économies de bouts de** ~**s** to make cheeseparing economies; **tenir la** ~○ to play gooseberry○; **brûler la** ~ **par les deux bouts** to burn the candle at both ends; **le jeu n'en vaut pas la** ~ the game isn't worth the candle; ▶ **trente-six**.

change /ʃɑ̃ʒ/ *nm* **1** (taux) exchange rate; **2** (opération) (foreign) exchange; **gagner/perdre au** ~ LIT to make/ to lose money on the exchange; **perdre au** ~ FIG to lose out; **en quittant son emploi précédent il a gagné** ou **il n'a pas perdu au** ~ when he left his previous job it was a change for the better.

changeant, ~**e** /ʃɑ̃ʒɑ̃, ɑ̃t/ *adj* **1** (inconstant) changeable, fickle; **d'humeur** ~**e** moody; **2** (chatoyant) [*tissu*] shimmering; [*couleur, reflet*] changing, shifting.

changement /ʃɑ̃ʒmɑ̃/ *nm* **1** (modification) change (**de** in); ~ **de température** change in temperature; ~ **en mieux/pire** change for the better/worse; **2** (de train, bus, d'avion) change; **Bordeaux-Bruxelles sans** ~ Bordeaux-Brussels straight through.
■ ~ **d'adresse** change of address; ~ **de décor** THÉÂT, CIN scene change; FIG change of scene.

changer /ʃɑ̃ʒe/ [13] **I** *vtr* **1** (échanger) to exchange [*objet*] (**pour, contre** for); to change [*secrétaire, emploi*] (**pour, contre** for); **2** (convertir) to change [*argent*]; ~ **des francs en dollars** to change francs into dollars; **3** (remplacer) to change [*objet*] (**par, pour** for); to replace [*personne*] (**par, pour** with); **4** (déplacer) ~ **qch de place** to move sth; ~ **un livre d'étagère** to move a book to another shelf; **5** (modifier) to change; **cette coiffure te change** you look different with your hair like that; **qu'est-ce que ça change?** what difference does it make?; **tu as changé quelque chose à ta coiffure** you've done something different with your hair; **ça n'a rien changé à mes habitudes** it hasn't changed my habits in any way; **cela ne change rien (à l'affaire)** that doesn't make any difference; **cela ne change rien au fait que** that doesn't alter the fact that; **on ne peut rien y** ~ we can't do anything about it; ~ **sa voix** to disguise one's voice; **6** (transformer) ~ **qch/qn en** to turn sth/sb into; **7** (rompre la monotonie) **cela nous change de la pluie** it makes a change from the rain; **ça va le** ~ **de sa vie tranquille à la campagne** it'll be a change from his

Le chant et les chanteurs

Les voix et les chanteurs

soprano	= soprano*
mezzo-soprano	= mezzo-soprano
contralto	= contralto
haute-contre	= counter-tenor
ténor	= tenor
baryton	= baritone
baryton-basse	= bass-baritone ([beɪs ˈbærɪtəʊn])
basse	= bass

* *Pour* une soprano, *on dira* a soprano, *et pour parler d'un jeune garçon on précisera* a boy soprano.

Dans les expressions suivantes, tenor *est pris comme exemple; les autres noms de voix s'utilisent de la même façon.*

il est ténor	= he's a tenor *ou* he sings tenor

Les expressions françaises avec de se traduisent par l'emploi du nom de la voix en position d'adjectif.

une voix de ténor	= a tenor voice
la tessiture de ténor	= the tenor range
un solo de ténor	= a tenor solo

quiet life in the country; **8** (renouveler les vêtements de) to change.
II changer de *vtr ind* **~ de** to change; **~ de travail** to change jobs; **~ de place** [*personne*] to change seats (**avec** with); [*objet*] to be moved; **nous avons changé de route au retour** we came back by a different route; **~ de rue** to move to another street; **~ d'adresse** to move to a new address; **quand il m'a vu il a changé de trottoir** when he saw me he crossed over to the other side of the road; **elle change de bonne tous les mois** she has a new maid every month; **~ d'opinion** or **d'avis** to change one's mind; **changeons de sujet** let's change the subject; **~ de sexe** to have a sex change; ▶ **chemise**.
III *vi* **1** (se modifier) [*situation, santé, temps*] to change; **il ne change pas** he never changes; **il a changé en bien/mal** he's changed for the better/worse; **il y a quelque chose de changé dans leur comportement** there's something different about their behaviourᴳᴮ; **pour ~ nous allons en Espagne cet été** for a change we are going to Spain this summer; **pour ne pas ~** as usual; **2** (être remplacé) [*personne, livre*] to be changed; [*horaire*] to change.
IV se changer *vpr* **1** (mettre d'autres vêtements) to get changed; **2** (se transformer) **se ~ en** to turn *ou* change into.
IDIOMES ~ d'air to have a change of air; **~ du tout au tout** to change completely.

changeur, -euse /ʃɑ̃ʒœʀ, øz/ I ▶ **374** *nm,f* FIN money changer.
II *nm* **1** HIST money changer; **2** COMM (appareil) change machine.

chanoine /ʃanwan/ ▶ **596** *nm* canon; **le ~ Kir** Canon Kir.
IDIOMES être gras comme un ~ to be as round as a barrel.

chanson /ʃɑ̃sɔ̃/ *nf* **1** (texte chanté) song; **~ folklorique** traditional folk song; **~ paillarde** bawdy song; **2** (genre) song; **la ~ française/pour enfants** French/children's song; **faire carrière dans la ~** to make a career as a singer; **vedette de la ~** singing star; **3**ᴼ (propos) **c'est toujours la même ~** it's always the same old story *ou* song; **je connais la ~** I've heard it all before; **4** LITTÉRAT song, epic (poem); **la Chanson de Roland** the Chanson de Roland.
■ **~ d'amour** love song; **~ à boire** drinking song; **~ de geste** chanson de geste; **~ de marin(s)** sea shanty; **~ à succès** hit (song).

chansonnette /ʃɑ̃sɔnɛt/ *nf* (frivole) light-hearted song.

chansonnier, -ière /ʃɑ̃sɔnje, ɛʀ/ ▶ **374** *nm,f* cabaret artist.

chant /ʃɑ̃/ *nm* **1** (activité) singing; **aimer le ~** (chanter) to like singing; (écouter) to like songs; **leçon de ~** singing lesson; **2** (sons caractéristiques) (d'oiseau, de

baleine) song; (de coq) crow(ing); (de grillon) chirp(ing); (de cigale) shrilling; (de vent, ruisseau, d'instrument) sound; **au ~ du coq** at cockcrow; **3** (composition musicale) song; **~ à plusieurs voix** part-song; **~s profanes** profane songs; **4** (poésie) ode; (division) canto; **~ funèbre** funeral lament.
■ **~ choral** choral singing; **~ du cygne** swansong; **~ d'église** hymn; **~ grégorien** Gregorian chant; **~ de Noël** Christmas carol.

chantage /ʃɑ̃taʒ/ *nm* blackmail; **faire du ~ à qn** to blackmail sb; **il me fait du ~ au suicide** he's using threats of suicide to blackmail me.

chantant, ~e /ʃɑ̃tɑ̃, ɑ̃t/ *adj* **1** (mélodieux) [*voix, accent*] singsong (*épith*), lilting; **2** (qui se chante aisément) [*mélodie*] tuneful.

chanter /ʃɑ̃te/ [1] I *vtr* **1** MUS to sing [*air*]; **spectacle chanté et dansé** musical spectacular; **2** (célébrer) to sing (of), to celebrate [*exploit, héros*]; **~ les louanges de qn** to sing sb's praises; **3**ᴼ (raconter) **qu'est-ce qu'il nous chante?** what's he talking about?; **~ qch sur tous les tons** to harp on about sth.
II chanter àᴼ *vtr ind* (plaire) **ça te chante d'aller à la campagne?** do you fancyᴼ going to the country?
III *vi* **1** [*personne*] to sing; **~ juste/faux** to sing in tune/out of tune; **une voix qui chante** a lilting voice; **2** [*oiseau*] to sing; [*coq*] to crow; [*grillon*] to chirp; [*cigale*] to shrill; [*bouilloire*] to sing; [*vent*] (dans les voiles) to sing; (dans les arbres) to rustle; [*source*] to bubble; **3** (subir du chantage) **faire ~ qn** to blackmail sb.

chanterelle /ʃɑ̃tʀɛl/ *nf* **1** BOT chanterelle; **2** MUS E-string.

chanteur, -euse /ʃɑ̃tœʀ, øz/ I *adj* oiseau **~** songbird.
II ▶ **374** *nm,f* singer; (de groupe) vocalist; **~ de charme** crooner; **~ des rues** street singer.

chantier /ʃɑ̃tje/ *nm* **1** (site) building *ou* construction site; **~ de démolition** demolition site; **le ~ a été ouvert l'été dernier** the construction work began last summer; **'~ interdit au public'** 'no admittance to the public'; **en ~** [*bâtiment*] under construction; [*loi, document*] in the process of being drafted; [*film*] in the process of being made; **notre maison sera en ~ tout l'hiver** the work on our house will go on all winter; **mettre en ~** to undertake [*projet*]; **remettre en ~** to resurrect, to dust [sth] off; **2** (entrepôt) builder's yard; **3**ᴼ (lieu en désordre) mess, shamblesᴼ (*sg*); **4** (de tonneau) gantry; **5** (dans une mine) face.
■ **~ naval** shipyard.

chantonner /ʃɑ̃tɔne/ [1] I *vtr* to hum [sth] to oneself.
II *vi* to hum to oneself.

chantre /ʃɑ̃tʀ/ *nm* **1** RELIG cantor; **voix de ~** rich and powerful voice; **2** (laudateur) eulogist (**de** of); (poète) bard.

chanvre /ʃɑ̃vʀ/ *nm* (plante, fibre) hemp; **toile de ~** hempen cloth.

chaos /kao/ *nm inv* **1** (désordre) chaos; **2** (de rochers) blockfield.

chaotique /kaɔtik/ *adj* chaotic.

chapardageᴼ /ʃapaʀdaʒ/ *nm* (action) pilfering; (petit vol) petty theft.

chaparderᴼ /ʃapaʀde/ [1] *vtr* to pinchᴼ.

chape /ʃap/ *nf* **1** CONSTR (surface étanche) screed GB, screed coat; **~ de béton** concrete screed; **2** (couche) FML **~ de nuages** blanket of cloud; **3** AUT (de pneu) tread; **4** RELIG (manteau) cope.

chapeau, *pl* **~x** /ʃapo/ I *nm* **1** (couvre-chef) hat; **2** (de gâteau) top; (de tuyau de cheminée) hood; **3** (en mécanique) cap; **4** PRESSE introductory paragraph; **5** (de champignon) cap.
IIᴼ *excl* well done!
■ **~ chinois** (coquillage) limpet; MUS Turkish Crescent; **~ claque** opera hat; **~ de gendarme** paper hat; **~ haut de forme** top hat; **~ de lampe** lampshade; **~ melon** bowler (hat) GB, derby (hat) US; **~ de paille** straw hat; **~ de plage** sun hat; **~ de roue** AUT hubcap; **démarrer sur les ~x de roues**ᴼ [*conducteur, voiture*] to shoot off at top

speed; [*film, roman, soirée*] to get off to a good ou cracking start.

IDIOMES **porter le ~**° to carry the can GB, to take the blame ou rap°; **coup de ~ à** hats off to; **tirer son ~ à** to take one's hat off to.

chapeauter° /ʃapote/ [1] *vtr* (contrôler) [*personne*] to head; **le ministère chapeaute notre équipe** our team works under the ministry.

chapelet /ʃaplɛ/ *nm* **1** RELIG (objet, prières) rosary; **2** (d'oignons, de saucisses, villages) string; (d'îlots) chain; (de jurons) stream; **en ~** in a string.

chapelier, -ière /ʃapəlje, ɛR/ **I** *adj* [*industrie, commerce*] hat (*épith*). **II ▶374‖** *nm,f* hatter.

chapelle /ʃapɛl/ *nf* **1** RELIG chapel; **la ~ de la Sainte Vierge** the Lady chapel; **2** (groupe) PEJ clique, coterie; **3** MUS choir.

■ **~ ardente** temporary mortuary.

chapelure /ʃaplyR/ *nf* breadcrumbs (*pl*).

chaperon /ʃapRɔ̃/ *nm* **1** (personne) chaperon(e); **2†** (coiffe) hood; **le Petit Chaperon rouge** Little Red Riding Hood.

chaperonner /ʃapRɔne/ [1] *vtr* to chaperone.

chapiteau, *pl* **~x** /ʃapito/ *nm* **1** (tente) marquee GB, tent; (de cirque) big top; **2** (de colonne) capital.

chapitre /ʃapitR/ *nm* **1** (division) (de livre) chapter; (de rapport) section; **2** (rubrique) **et au ~ des faits divers...** and now, other news...; **3** (sujet) subject; **sur ce ~** on this subject; **au ~ de** on the issue of; **4** (période) chapter; **5** (d'un budget) section, item; **~ des recettes** section on revenue; **6** RELIG chapter.

IDIOMES **avoir voix au ~** to have a say in the matter.

chapka /ʃapka/ *nf* fur hat.

chapon /ʃapɔ̃/ *nm* (jeune coq) capon.

chaque /ʃak/

■ **Note** Si l'on veut insister sur ce qui fait l'homogénéité d'un ensemble de phénomènes, d'individus ou d'objets on traduit *chaque* par *every*: *chaque année ils allaient faire du ski* = they used to go skiing every year; si l'on veut mettre l'accent sur les phénomènes ou les individus pris séparément on utilisera plutôt *each* (mais *every* ne serait pas faux pour autant): *la situation se détériore chaque année* = each year the situation gets worse.
– On remarquera que *every* ne s'utilise que pour parler de plus de deux personnes, objets ou phénomènes; dans l'exemple suivant, seul *each* est correct: *au volley-ball, chaque équipe est composée de six joueurs* = in volley-ball, each team is made up of six players.

I *adj indéf* each, every; **~ travailleur** (dans l'absolu) every worker; (dans un groupe particulier) each worker; **~ chose en son temps!** all in good time!; **la situation devient ~ jour plus compliquée** the situation becomes more and more complicated by the day ou each day ou every day; **il me dérange à ~ instant** he's always disturbing me.

II° *pron* (chacun) each; **il revend ses disques (à) 100 francs ~** he's selling his records for 100 francs each.

char /ʃaR/ *nm* **1** MIL tank; **~ léger** light tank; **2** (antique) chariot; **3** AGRIC cart, wagon; **~ à foin** haycart, haywagon; **4** (de carnaval) float; **5**° (bluff) bluff; **arrête ton ~!** come off it!; **6**° C (voiture) car.

■ **~ d'assaut** MIL tank; **~ à bancs** horse-drawn wagon with benches; **~ à bœufs** oxcart; **~ à voile** SPORT (sur roues) sand yacht; (sur patins) ice yacht.

charabia° /ʃaRabja/ *nm* gobbledygook°, double Dutch.

charade /ʃaRad/ *nf* riddle.

charançon /ʃaRɑ̃sɔ̃/ *nm* weevil.

charbon /ʃaRbɔ̃/ *nm* **1** IND coal; **faire griller qch sur des ~s** (de bois) to barbecue sth; **2** (médicament) charcoal; **3 ▶196‖** MÉD anthrax; **4** BOT smut; **5** ART charcoal; (dessin) charcoal drawing; **6** ÉLECTROTECH (balai) carbon brush; (électrode) carbon.

■ **~ de bois** charcoal.

IDIOMES **être sur des ~s ardents** to be like a cat on

a hot tin roof; **aller au ~**° (aller au travail) to get to work; (effectuer une tâche pénible) to do the menial work.

charbonner /ʃaRbɔne/ [1] **I** *vtr* to blacken [*visage, joue, mur*].
II se charbonner *vpr* se **~ le visage** to blacken one's face.

charbonneux, -euse /ʃaRbɔnø, øz/ *adj* **1** (évoquant le charbon) sooty; [*paupière*] black with make-up (*jamais épith*); **2** MÉD [*fièvre*] anthracic.

charbonnier, -ière /ʃaRbɔnje, ɛR/ **I** *adj* [*centre*] coalmining (*épith*); [*production, industrie*] coal (*épith*).
II ▶374‖ *nm,f* (marchand) coalman/coalwoman.
III *nm* NAUT collier GB, coaler.

charcuter° /ʃaRkyte/ [1] **I** *vtr* **1** (opérer) [*chirurgien*] to hack [sb] about [*malade*]; **2** (découper) to make a mess of carving [*viande*]; **3** (dénaturer) to carve up [*texte*].
II se charcuter *vpr* (se couper) to cut oneself badly.

charcuterie /ʃaRkytRi/ *nf* **1** CULIN (produits) cooked pork meats (*pl*); **2 ▶374‖ ~** (traiteur) (magasin) pork butcher's; (rayon dans un supermarché) delicatessen counter.

charcutier, -ière /ʃaRkytje, ɛR/ **▶374‖** *nm,f* (commerçant) pork butcher.

chardon /ʃaRdɔ̃/ *nm* thistle.

chardonneret /ʃaRdɔnRɛ/ *nm* goldfinch.

charentais, -e[1] /ʃaRɑ̃tɛ, ɛz/ **▶509‖** *adj* [*personne*] from the Charente region; [*melon*] Charentais.

charentaise[2] /ʃaRɑ̃tɛz/ *nf* (pantoufle) carpet slipper.

charge /ʃaRʒ/ *nf* **I 1** (fardeau) LIT, FIG burden, load; (cargaison) (de véhicule) load; (de navire) cargo, freight; NAUT (fait de charger) loading; **prendre qn en ~** [*taxi*] to take sb as a passenger ou fare; **prise en ~** (dans un taxi) minimum fare; **2** ARCHIT, CONSTR load; **3** (responsabilité) responsibility; **avoir la ~ de qn/qch** to be responsible for sb/sth; **trois enfants à ~** three dependent children; **il s'est bien acquitté de sa ~** he carried out his task well; **prendre en ~** [*tuteur*] to take charge of [*enfant*]; [*services sociaux*] to take [sb] into care [*enfant*]; [*sécurité sociale*] to accept financial responsibility for [*malade*]; to take care of [*frais, dépenses*]; **prise en ~** (par la sécurité sociale) agreement to bear medical costs; **la prise en ~ des réfugiés/dépenses sera assurée par...** the refugees/expenses will be taken care of ou looked after by...; **se prendre en ~** to take care of oneself; **mes neveux sont à ma ~** I support my nephews; **ces frais sont à la ~ du client** these expenses are payable by the customer; **à ~ pour lui de faire** it's up to him to do; **4** ADMIN (fonction) office; **occuper de hautes ~s** to hold high office; **~ de notaire** notary's office; **5** (preuve) evidence; **il n'y a aucune ~ contre lui** there's no evidence against him; **6** MIL (assaut) charge (contre against); (d'explosifs) charge; **7** ÉLECTROTECH, PHYS charge; **~ positive/négative** positive/negative charge; **8** (contenu) **~ émotionnelle** emotional charge; **~ symbolique** symbolic content.
II charges *nfpl* GÉN expenses, costs; (de locataire, copropriétaire) service charge (*sg*); **les ~s de l'État** government expenditure ¢.

■ **~ de travail** workload; **~s fiscales** tax expenses; **~s locatives** maintenance costs (*payable by a tenant*); **~s patronales** employer's social security contributions; **~s sociales** welfare costs.

IDIOMES **revenir à la ~** to try again; **revenir à la ~ contre qch** to renew one's attack on sth.

chargé, -e /ʃaRʒe/ **I** *pp* **▶ charger**.
II *pp adj* [*particule*] charged; **être ~ de** [*branches*] to be heavy ou laden (down) with [*fruits, neige*]; [*bras*] to be covered with [*bijoux*]; to be full of [*nuages, ratures*]; **un regard ~ de menaces** a threatening look; **être ~ de famille** to have dependents.
III *adj* [*personne, véhicule*] loaded; [*horaires, style*] heavy; [*journée*] busy; [*décorations*] over-ornate; [*langue*] coated; **trop ~** overloaded; **avoir un casier judiciaire ~** to have had several previous convictions.

■ **~ d'affaires** POL chargé d'affaires; **~ de cours**

UNIV part- time lecturer; **~ de mission** POL representative.

chargement /ʃaʀʒəmɑ̃/ *nm* **1** (objets transportés) GÉN load; (marchandises) (par avion, bateau) cargo, load; (par camion) load; **2** (mise à bord) loading; **3** (d'arme, appareil) loading; (de poêle) stoking; (de logiciel) loading; **4** ÉLECTROTECH (de batterie) charging.
■ **~ postal** registered mail ₵.

charger /ʃaʀʒe/ [13] **I** *vtr* **1** GÉN to load [*marchandises*] (**dans** into; **sur** onto); to load [*véhicule, navire, animal*] (**de** with); **~ un client** [*taxi*] to pick up a passenger ou fare; **trop ~ qch** to overload sth; **2** (remplir le chargeur) to load [*arme, appareil photo*]; **3** ORDINAT to load [*disquette, programme*] (**dans** into); **4** ÉLECTROTECH to charge [*batterie, accumulateur*]; **5** (outrer) to overdo [*description, aspect*]; **6** (confier une mission à) **~ qn de qch** to make sb responsible for sth; **~ qn de faire** to give sb the responsibility of doing; **elle m'a chargé de vous transmettre ses amitiés** she asked me to give you her regards; **c'est lui qui est chargé de l'enquête** he is in charge of the investigation; **7** (accabler) to bring evidence against [*accusé*]; **8** (attaquer) to charge at [*foule*].
II *vi* [*armée, taureau*] to charge.
III se charger *vpr* **1** (s'occuper) **se ~ de** to take responsibility for; **je m'en charge** I'll see to it; **je me charge de le leur dire** I'll tell them; **je me charge de la boisson** I'll take care of the drinks; **2** (prendre des bagages) to weigh oneself down; **3** MIL **se ~ facilement** [*arme*] to be easy to load.

chargeur /ʃaʀʒœʀ/ *nm* **1** MIL (objet) magazine; (personne) loader; **il a vidé son ~ sur le caissier** he fired a full round of bullets at the cashier; **2** ÉLECTROTECH charger; **3** PHOT cartridge; CIN film magazine; **4** ORDINAT loader; **5** (débardeur) loader; **6** (expéditeur) loader, shipper.

chariot /ʃaʀjo/ *nm* **1** (poussé à la main) trolley GB, cart US; **~ de supermarché** supermarket trolley GB, shopping cart US; **2** (motorisé) truck; **3** (tiré par des chevaux) waggon[GB]; **4** (de machine à écrire) carriage; **5** CIN (de caméra) dolly.

charisme /kaʀism/ *nm* charisma.

charitable /ʃaʀitabl/ *adj* charitable (**envers** toward(s), to); **tendre une main ~ à** FIG to lend a helping hand to.

charitablement /ʃaʀitabləmɑ̃/ *adv* (avec charité) charitably; (gentiment) kindly.

charité /ʃaʀite/ *nf* **1** (aumône) charity; **appel à la ~ publique** charity appeal; **vente de ~** charity sale; **la ~ s'il vous plaît** spare me some change, please; **2** (bienveillance) kindness; **il a eu la ~ de faire** he was kind enough to do; **3** RELIG charity.
IDIOMES **~ bien ordonnée commence par soi-même** PROV charity begins at home PROV.

charlatan /ʃaʀlatɑ̃/ *nm* (guérisseur) quack○; (vendeur) con man; (politicien) fraud.

Charles /ʃaʀl/ *npr* Charles.
■ **~ le Bel** Charles the Fair; **~ Quint** Charles the Fifth (of Spain); **~ le Téméraire** Charles the Bold.

charlot○ /ʃaʀlo/ *nm* clown; **arrête de faire le ~!** stop clowning!

Charlot /ʃaʀlo/ *npr* Charlie (Chaplin).

charlotte /ʃaʀlɔt/ *nf* **1** (dessert) charlotte; **2** (bonnet) mobcap.

charmant, ~e /ʃaʀmɑ̃, ɑ̃t/ *adj* **1** (plaisant) [*personne, sourire, lieu*] charming, delightful; [*soirée, enfant*] delightful; [*objet*] lovely; **c'est ~!** IRON charming ou wonderful! IRON; **un ~ bambin** IRON a little dear IRON; **2** (aimable) very nice (**avec** to).

charme /ʃaʀm/ **I** *nm* **1** (de personne, sourire, visage) charm; **une opération de ~** a public relations exercise; **c'est une véritable offensive de ~ pour convaincre les électeurs** they are really trying to woo the electorate; **faire du ~ à qn** to use one's charms on sb; **faire du ~** or **son numéro de ~ à qn pour qu'il fasse qch** to try to charm sb into doing sth; **2** (de lieu, musique) charm; **cela a le ~ de la nouveauté** it has (a certain) novelty value; **cela ne**

manque pas de ~ (mode de vie, roman) it is not without its charms; (proposition) it is not unattractive; **3** (qui envoûte) spell; **tomber sous le ~ de qn** to fall under sb's spell; **4** BOT hornbeam.
II charmes *nmpl* EUPH physical attributes EUPH.
IDIOMES **se porter comme un ~** to be as fit as a fiddle.

charmer /ʃaʀme/ [1] *vtr* to charm; **se laisser ~ par qn** to fall for ou succumb to sb's charms.

charmeur, -euse /ʃaʀmœʀ, øz/ **I** *adj* [*sourire*] winning, engaging; [*attitude*] charming, engaging; [*regard*] engaging.
II *nm,f* charmer.
■ **~ de serpents** snake charmer.

charnel, -elle /ʃaʀnɛl/ *adj* [*plaisirs, amour*] carnal.

charnier /ʃaʀnje/ *nm* GÉN mass grave; HIST (lieu couvert) charnel house.

charnière /ʃaʀnjɛʀ/ **I** *nf* **1** (de porte, coquillage) hinge; **2** FIG (lien important) bridge (**entre** between); **3** ANAT joint.
II (-)**charnière** (*in compounds*) **époque(-)~** transitional period; **rôle(-)~** pivotal role.

charnu, ~e /ʃaʀny/ *adj* [*bras, fruit, poulet*] plump; [*lèvre*] fleshy, thick; [*crabe*] meaty.

charognard /ʃaʀɔɲaʀ/ *nm* **1** (hyène, chacal) carrion feeder; (vautour) vulture; **2** (profiteur) PEJ vulture PÉJ.

charogne /ʃaʀɔɲ/ *nf* (d'animal) rotting carcass; (d'humain) rotting corpse.

charolais, ~e /ʃaʀɔlɛ, ɛz/ **▶509** *adj* Charolais.

charpente /ʃaʀpɑ̃t/ *nf* **1** CONSTR (de toit) roof structure; (de bâtiment) framework; (de bateau) structure; **bois de ~** timber; **2** ANAT (structure interne) framework; (constitution) build; **~ osseuse** skeleton; **3** (de livre, film) structure.

charpenté, ~e /ʃaʀpɑ̃te/ *adj* [*vin*] robust; **bien ~** [*personne*] well-built (*épith*).

charpentier /ʃaʀpɑ̃tje/ **▶374** *nm* carpenter.

charpie /ʃaʀpi/ *nf* FIG **être en ~** to be in shreds; **réduire** or **mettre qch en ~** to tear sth to shreds.

charretée /ʃaʀte/ *nf* cartload; **par ~s** LIT, FIG by the cartload.

charretier /ʃaʀtje/ **▶374** *nm* carter.
IDIOMES **jurer comme un ~** to swear like a trooper.

charrette /ʃaʀɛt/ *nf* **1** (voiture à deux roues) cart; **2** (série) **il a fait partie de la première ~ de licenciés** he went in the first wave ou round of layoffs.
■ **~ à bras** handcart, barrow; **~ des condamnés** HIST tumbril.

charrier /ʃaʀje/ [2] **I** *vtr* **1** (avec un chariot, une brouette) to cart; **2** (tirer avec effort) to haul [*troncs d'arbre, blocs de pierre*]; **3** (entraîner) [*cours d'eau*] to carry [*sth*] along; **4**○ (se moquer de) to tease [*sb*] unmercifully.
II○ *vi* to go too far; **faut pas ~** that's really pushing it○!

charrue /ʃaʀy/ *nf* plough, plow US.
IDIOMES **mettre la ~ avant les bœufs** to put the cart before the horse.

charte /ʃaʀt/ *nf* charter; **la ~ des droits de l'homme** the Charter of Human Rights.

charter /ʃaʀtɛʀ/ **I** *adj inv* charter (*épith*).
II *nm* charter plane.

chartreux /ʃaʀtʀø/ *nm* (moine) Carthusian monk.

Charybde /kaʀibd/ *npr* Charybdis.
IDIOMES **tomber de ~ en Scylla** to jump out of the frying pan into the fire.

chas /ʃa/ *nm inv* (d'aiguille) eye.

chasse /ʃas/ *nf* **1** (activité) GÉN hunting; (au fusil) shooting; **aller à la ~** to go shooting GB ou hunting US; (à cheval) to go hunting; **~ au lièvre** hare coursing; **la ~ aux papillons** catching butterflies; **~ au trésor** treasure hunt; **2** (saison) **la ~ est ouverte/fermée** it's the open/closed season; **3** (gibier) **faire (une) bonne ~** to get a good bag; **se partager la ~** to share the game; **4** (domaine) (pour le petit gibier) shoot; (pour le gros gibier) hunting ground; **~ gardée** LIT, FIG preserve; **5** (poursuite) chase; **donner la ~ à, prendre**

en ~ to chase; **faire la** ~ **aux araignées** to wage war on spiders; **faire la** ~ **aux trafiquants** to hunt down traffickers; **6** (recherche) hunting (à for); ~ **aux autographes** autograph-hunting; **être à la** ~ **de** or **à** to be hunting for; **7** MIL (avions) **la** ~, **l'aviation de** ~ fighter planes (pl); **8** (de WC) ~ **(d'eau)** (toilet) flush; **actionner la** ~ (manette) to flush the toilet; **tirer la** ~ (chaîne) to pull the chain.
■ ~ **à la baleine** whaling; ~ **aux cerveaux** head-hunting; ~ **à l'homme** manhunt; ~ **aux sorcières** witch-hunt; ~ **sous-marine** SPORT harpoon fishing, harpooning.
IDIOMES **qui va à la** ~ **perd sa place** PROV leave your place and you lose it.

chassé-croisé, pl **chassés-croisés** /ʃasekʀwaze/ nm **1** (manœuvres) continual coming and going (**entre** between); **chassés-croisés amoureux** romantic intrigue (sg); **2** (en danse) chassé-croisé, set to partners.

chasse-neige /ʃasnɛʒ/ nm inv snowplough GB, snowplow US; **faire du** ~ to snowplough GB, to snowplow US.

chasser /ʃase/ [1] **I** vtr **1** [animal] to hunt [proie]; **2** [personne] GÉN to hunt; (au fusil) to shoot GB, to hunt; ~ **le renard** to go (fox) hunting; ~ **la baleine** to go whaling; **3** (éloigner) [personne] to chase away [animal]; [police] to get rid of [badauds]; [bruit, mauvais temps] to drive away [touristes, client]; (expulser) to drive out [immigrant, ennemi]; (congédier) to fire [domestique]; ~ **qn de** (de place, rue, terrain) to drive sb out of ou from; (de lieu fermé) to throw sb out of; **le bruit nous a chassés de chez nous** we were driven out of our home by the noise; **être chassé du pouvoir** to be ousted from power; **4** (disperser) to dispel [fumée, odeur, doute]; ~ **une idée de son esprit** to banish a thought from one's mind; **5** (faire avancer) to herd [bétail, oies]; **6** (déloger) to force [sth] out [eau]; to knock [sth] out [tenon].
II vi **1** (aller à la chasse) GÉN to go hunting; (avec un fusil) to go shooting GB ou hunting US; **2** (déraper) [voiture, moto] to skid; **3** NAUT **le navire chasse sur ses ancres** the ship is dragging her anchor.

chasseresse /ʃasʀɛs/ nf LITER huntress LITTÉR.

chasseur, -euse /ʃasœʀ, øz/ **I** nm,f (animal, personne) hunter; ~ **de renards** fox hunter; **être un bon** ~ (au fusil) to be a good shot; (avec une meute) to be a good huntsman; **un groupe de** ~**s** (au fusil) a shooting party; (avec une meute) a hunt.
II nm **1** MIL (soldat) chasseur; **le 2ᵉ** ~ the 2nd (regiment of) chasseurs; **2** MIL (avion) fighter (aircraft); (pilote) fighter pilot; **3** (groom) bellboy GB, bellhop US.
■ ~ **alpin** soldier trained for mountainous terrain; ~ **de baleine** whaler; ~ **à cheval** light cavalryman; ~ **d'images** camera buff; ~ **de prime** bounty hunter; ~ **à réaction** jet fighter; ~ **de sons** recording buff; ~ **de têtes** LIT, FIG head-hunter.

châssis /ʃasi/ nm **1** (de fenêtre) frame; **2** AUT chassis; ~ **surbaissé** drop frame chassis; **3** AGRIC cold frame; **4** ART (pour tapisserie, broderie) frame; (en sculpture) pointing machine; **5** RAIL underframe.

chaste /ʃast/ adj GÉN chaste; [personne] celibate; [oreilles] innocent.

chastement /ʃastəmɑ̃/ adv [aimer] chastely, in a chaste fashion; [s'habiller] modestly, demurely; **vivre** ~ to lead a chaste life.

chasteté /ʃastəte/ nf chastity.

chat /ʃa/ nm **1** (animal) GÉN cat; (mâle) tomcat; **2** ▶329 JEUX **jouer à** ~ to play tag ou tig GB; **c'est toi le** ~ you're 'it'.
■ ~ **de gouttière** (tigré) tabby cat; (commun) ordinary cat, alley cat; ~ **perché** JEUX off-ground tag ou tig GB; ~ **sauvage** wildcat; **le Chat botté** Puss in Boots.
IDIOMES **donner sa langue au** ~ to give in; **il n'y a pas un** ~° the place is deserted; **avoir un** ~ **dans la gorge** to have a frog in one's throat; **il ne faut pas réveiller le** ~ **qui dort** PROV let sleeping dogs lie PROV; **être** or **s'entendre comme chien et** ~ to fight like

cat and dog; ▶ **échauder, fouetter, rat, souris**.

châtaigne /ʃatɛɲ/ nf **1** BOT (sweet) chestnut; **2**° (coup de poing) clout°, punch.

châtaignier /ʃatɛɲe/ nm (arbre) (sweet) chestnut (tree); **une table de** or **en** ~ a chestnut table.

châtain /ʃatɛ̃/ ▶141 adj m [cheveux, barbe] brown; **il est** ~ he's got brown hair.

château, pl ~**x** /ʃato/ nm **1** (forteresse) castle; **2** (résidence) (royale) palace; (seigneuriale) castle; **3** (grande demeure) manor.
■ ~ **de cartes** LIT, FIG house of cards; ~ **d'eau** water tower; ~ **fort** fortified castle; ~ **de sable** sand castle.
IDIOMES **mener la vie de** ~ to live the life of Riley GB, to live like a prince.

châtelain /ʃatlɛ̃/ ~**e** /ʃatlɛ, ɛn/ nm,f **1** (propriétaire) owner of a manor; **2** HIST lord/lady (of the manor).

chat-huant, pl **chats-huants** /ʃaɥɑ̃/ nm tawny owl.

châtier /ʃatje/ [2] vtr LITER **1** (punir) to punish [fautif, délit]; ~ **qn pour son insolence**, ~ **l'insolence de qn** to punish sb for his/her insolence; **2** (soigner) to polish [style]; to refine [langage].
IDIOMES **qui aime bien châtie bien** PROV spare the rod and spoil the child PROV.

chatière /ʃatjɛʀ/ nf **1** (porte) catflap; **2** (en spéléologie) crawl.

châtiment /ʃatimɑ̃/ nm punishment.

chatoiement /ʃatwamɑ̃/ nm shimmering.

chaton /ʃatɔ̃/ nm **1** (petit chat) kitten; **2** (sur les arbres) catkin; **3** (de bague) (monture) setting; (pierre) gem; **4**° (flocon de poussière) ball of fluff; **5** (terme d'affection) **mon** ~ my darling.

chatouille° /ʃatuj/ nf tickle ¢; **faire des** ~**s à qn** to tickle sb.

chatouiller /ʃatuje/ [1] vtr **1** LIT to tickle; **ça me chatouille dans le dos** my back is tickling; **2** (flatter) to titillate [palais]; to tickle [curiosité]; to flatter [orgueil]; **3**° (énerver) to nettle, to irritate [personne].
IDIOMES ~ **les côtes à qn** EUPH to tan sb's hide.

chatouilleux, -euse /ʃatujø, øz/ adj **1** (sensible aux chatouilles) ticklish; **2** (susceptible) [personne] touchy (**sur** about).

chatoyant, ~**e** /ʃatwajɑ̃, ɑ̃t/ adj **1** [mer, couleur] shimmering; [plumage] iridescent; **2** [style, écriture] sparkling.

chatoyer /ʃatwaje/ [23] vi [couleur, mer] to shimmer.

châtrer /ʃatʀe/ [1] vtr (castrer) to neuter [chat]; to geld [cheval]; to castrate [homme, taureau, chien].

chatte /ʃat/ nf (female) cat.
IDIOMES **être gourmand comme une** ~ to be a piggy°; **une** ~ **n'y retrouverait pas ses petits** it's a real mess.

chaud, -e /ʃo, ʃod/ **I** adj **1** (à température élevée) hot; (modérément) warm; **à four** ~/**très** ~ in a warm/hot oven; **on nous a servi des croissants tout** ~**s** we were served piping hot croissants; **2** (qui donne de la chaleur) [pièce] (agréablement) warm; (excessivement) hot; **3** (récent) **'ils sont mariés?'—'oui, c'est tout** ~' 'they're married?'—'yes, it's hot news'; **4** (enthousiaste) [félicitations] warm; [partisan] strong; **être** ~ **pour faire** to be keen on doing; **5** (agité) [région, période] turbulent; [sujet] sensitive; [discussion] heated; **un des points** ~**s du globe** one of the flash points of the world; ~**e ambiance ce soir chez les voisins!** HUM things are getting heated next door tonight!; **6** (attrayant) [coloris, voix] warm; **7**° (de prostitution) EUPH [quartier] red light (épith).
II adv **il fait** ~ (agréablement) it's warm; (excessivement) it's hot; **ça ne me fait ni** ~ **ni froid** it doesn't matter one way or the other to me; **manger** ~ to eat hot foods; **'servir** ~' 'serve hot'.
III nm (chaleur) heat; **on crève**° **de** ~ **ici!** we're roasting° in here!; **avoir** ~ (modérément) to be warm; (excessivement) to be hot; **nous avons eu** ~ LIT we were very hot; FIG we had a narrow escape; **donner**

~ à qn [*course, aventure*] to make sb sweat; **tenir ~ à qn** to keep sb warm; **ça me tient ~ aux pieds** it keeps my feet warm; **se tenir ~** [*personnes, animaux*] to keep warm; **~ devant**○! watch out!; **prendre un coup de ~** [*plante*] to wilt (in the sun); **tenir** or **garder au ~** LIT to keep [sb] warm [*personne*]; to keep [sth] hot [*plat, boisson*]; FIG (pour parer à une éventualité) to have [sth] on standby [*matériel, projet*].
IV à chaud *loc adv* **à ~** [*analyser*] on the spot; [*réaction*] immediate; TECH [*étirer*] under heat; **opérer à ~** to do an emergency operation.
■ **~ et froid** MÉD chill.

chaudement /ʃodmɑ̃/ *adv* **1** [*vêtu*] warmly; **2** (vivement) [*féliciter*] warmly; [*recommander*] heartily.

chaudière /ʃodjɛʀ/ *nf* boiler.

chaudron /ʃodʀɔ̃/ *nm* cauldron.

chaudronnerie /ʃodʀɔnʀi/ *nf* (industrie) boilermaking industry; (usine) boilerworks (+ *v sg*); (articles) **grosse ~** industrial boilers (*pl*); **petite ~** pots and pans (*pl*).

chaudronnier, -ière /ʃodʀɔnje, ɛʀ/ ▶374 *nm,f* (ouvrier) boilermaker.

chauffage /ʃofaʒ/ *nm* **1** (chaleur artificielle) heating; **une chambre sans ~** an unheated bedroom; **mettre le ~** to put the heating on; **le ~ de notre maison coûte très cher** the house is very expensive to heat; **2** (installations) heating; **~ par le sol** underfloor heating; **3** (appareil) heater; **~ d'appoint** extra heater GB, space heater US; **4** (élévation de la température) heating; **après un léger ~** after heating gently.

chauffagiste /ʃofaʒist/ ▶374 *nmf* heating engineer.

chauffant, ~e /ʃofɑ̃, ɑ̃t/ *adj* [*surface*] heating.

chauffard○ /ʃofaʀ/ *nm* PEJ reckless driver, road hog○.

chauffe /ʃof/ *nf* TECH **1** (opération) stoking; **2** (lieu) fire chamber.

chauffe-eau /ʃofo/ *nm inv* water-heater; **~ à gaz à accumulation** gas storage water-heater.

chauffe-plat /ʃofpla/ *nm inv* dish warmer.

chauffer /ʃofe/ [1] I *vtr* to heat [*pièce*]; to heat (up) [*métal, objet, liquide, plat*]; **trop chauffées** overheated; **~ du fer à blanc** to bring iron to a white heat; **~ l'auditoire à blanc** FIG to whip the audience into a frenzy; **~ le public** to warm up the audience.
II *vi* **1** (devenir chaud) [*plat*] to heat (up); [*moteur*] to warm up; [*four*] to heat up; **faire ~** to heat [*eau, aliment*]; to warm [*assiette, biberon*]; to heat (up) [*four*]; to warm (up) [*moteur*]; **mettre à ~** to put [sth] on to heat [*eau*]; to heat up [*plat*]; to warm [*biberon*]; **2** (devenir trop chaud) [*moteur*] to overheat; **ne laissez pas l'appareil ~ toute la nuit** don't leave the appliance running all night; **3** (produire de la chaleur) [*radiateur*] to give out heat; **4**○ FIG (être animé) **avec ce groupe, ça va ~**! this group's going to liven things up!; **si le patron l'apprend, ça va ~**! if the boss finds out, there'll be big trouble!; **5** JEUX to get warm.
III **se chauffer** *vpr* **se ~ au coin du feu** to warm oneself by the fire; **se ~ au soleil** [*personne, animal*] to bask in the sun; **nous nous chauffons au charbon** we have coal-fired heating.

chaufferie /ʃofʀi/ *nf* (de bâtiment) boiler room; (de bateau) stokehold.

chauffeur /ʃofœʀ/ *nm* **1** ▶374 AUT GÉN driver; (de particulier) chauffeur; **voiture avec/sans ~** chauffeur-driven/self-drive car; **faire le ~ pour qn** to chauffeur sb about; **2** (de chaudière) GÉN stoker; RAIL fireman.
■ **~ du dimanche** PEJ Sunday driver; **~ de maître** chauffeur.

chauffeuse /ʃoføz/ *nf* (fauteuil) low armless easy chair.

chaume /ʃom/ *nm* **1** AGRIC (tige) stubble ¢; (champ) stubble field; **2** (pour toiture) thatch.

chaumière /ʃomjɛʀ/ *nf* **1** (avec toit de chaume) thatched cottage; **2** (petite maison) LITER humble cottage; **faire jaser dans les ~s** HUM to cause tongues to wag.

chaussant, ~e /ʃosɑ̃, ɑ̃t/ *adj* well-fitting.

chaussée /ʃose/ *nf* **1** (route) road(way) GB, highway; (rue) street; **2** (revêtement) surface; **~ déformée** uneven road surface; **3** (chemin surélevé) causeway; (remblai) embankment.

chausse-pied, *pl* **~s** /ʃospje/ *nm* shoehorn.

chausser /ʃose/ [1] I *vtr* to put [sth] on [*chaussures, skis*]; to put [sth] on [*lunettes*]; to take [*étriers*]; **être mal chaussé** to be poorly shod; **elle était chaussée de pantoufles** she was wearing slippers; **se faire ~ sur mesure** to have one's shoes made to measure.
II ▶581 *vi* **je chausse du 41** I take a (size) 41; **ces mocassins chaussent grand** these loafers are large-fitting.
III **se chausser** *vpr* **1** (mettre ses chaussures) to put (one's) shoes on; **se ~ de qch** to put on sth; **2** (s'équiper) to get ou buy (one's) shoes.

chaussette /ʃosɛt/ *nf* (vêtement) sock.
IDIOMES **laisser tomber qn comme une vieille ~**○ to cast sb off like an old rag.

chausseur /ʃosœʀ/ *nm* **1** ▶374 (commerçant) shoe shop manager; **2** ▶374 (fabricant) shoemaker.

chausson /ʃosɔ̃/ *nm* (pantoufle) slipper; (de bébé) bootee; (de danse) ballet shoe ou pump; (de sport) pump.
■ **~ aux pommes** CULIN apple turnover.

chaussure /ʃosyʀ/ *nf* **1** (soulier) shoe; (à tige haute) boot; **~ basse** shoe; **~ montante** ankle boot; **~ de tennis** tennis shoe; **~ de ski** ski boot; **rayon ~s** shoe department; **2** (industrie) footwear industry; (commerce) footwear trade.
IDIOMES **trouver ~ à son pied** (compagnon) to find the right person.

chaut† ▶ **chaloir**.

chauve /ʃov/ I *adj* bald; FIG, LITER bare.
II *nm* bald(-headed) man.

chauve-souris, *pl* **chauves-souris** /ʃovsuʀi/ *nf* ZOOL bat.

chauvin, ~e /ʃovɛ̃, in/ I *adj* chauvinistic, jingoistic.
II *nm,f* chauvinist, jingoist.

chaux /ʃo/ *nf inv* lime; **lait de ~** whitewash; **blanchir** or **passer à la ~** to whitewash; **~ vive** quicklime.

chavirer /ʃaviʀe/ [1] *vi* [*navire*] to capsize; **faire ~ un navire** to capsize a ship; **faire ~ les cœurs** to be a heartbreaker.

chef¹ /ʃɛf/ *nm* **1** (meneur) leader; **qualités de ~** leadership qualities; **2** (supérieur) superior, boss○; MIL (sergent) sergeant; **3** (dirigeant) leader; COMM (d'un service) manager; **~ de l'Église** head of the Church; **l'exemple doit venir des ~s** the example must come from the top; **architecte en ~** chief architect; **commandant en ~** MIL commander-in-chief; **4** CULIN **~ (cuisinier** or **de cuisine)** chef; **5**○ (as, champion) ace; **se débrouiller comme un ~** to manage splendidly; **6†** (tête) head; **de mon/leur (propre) ~** on my/their own initiative; **7** (chapitre) **au premier ~** primarily, first and foremost.
■ **~ d'accusation** JUR count of indictment; **répondre à un ~ d'accusation** to answer a charge; **~ d'atelier** (shop) foreman; **~ de cabinet** principal private secretary; **~ de chantier** works GB ou site foreman; **~ d'équipe** foreman; **~ d'établissement** head teacher; **~ d'État** head of state; **~ d'état-major** Chief of Staff; **~ de fabrication** production manager; **~ de famille** head of the family ou household; **~ de file** GÉN leader; POL party leader; **~ de gare** stationmaster; **~ de gouvernement** head of government; **~ d'orchestre** conductor; **~ du personnel** personnel manager; **~ de plateau** CIN, TV floor manager; **~ de projet** project manager; **~ de publicité** (d'agence) account executive; (annonceur) advertising manager; (dans les médias) advertising (sales) manager; **~ de rayon** department supervisor ou manager; **~ de service** ADMIN section ou department head; MÉD clinical director GB, chief physician US; **~ de tribu** headman.

chef² /ʃɛf/ *nf* boss○; **c'est elle la ~** she's the boss○.

chef-d'œuvre, *pl* **chefs-d'œuvre** /ʃɛdœvʀ/ *nm* masterpiece.

chef-lieu, *pl* **chefs-lieux** /ʃɛfljø/ *nm* (ville) administrative centre.

cheik(h) /ʃɛk/ *nm* sheik(h).

chelem /ʃlɛm/ *nm* **1** (aux cartes) slam; **2** SPORT **gagner le grand ~** to win the Grand Slam.

chemin /ʃ(ə)mɛ̃/ *nm* **1** (route) country road; (étroit) lane; (de terre) (pour véhicule) track; (pour piétons) path; **être toujours sur les ~s** to be always on the road; **2** (passage) way; **les obstacles qui sont** or **se trouvent sur mon ~** LIT, FIG the obstacles which stand in my way; **3** (direction, itinéraire, trajet) way; **se tromper de ~** to go the wrong way; **sur le ~ du retour/de l'école** on the way back/to school; **reprendre le ~ du bureau** to go back to the office ou to work; **le ~ le plus court pour** the quickest way to; **le plus court ~ vers la paix** the shortest path to peace; **on a fait un bout de ~ ensemble** (à pied) we walked along together for a while; (dans la vie) we were together for a while; **~ faisant, en ~** on ou along the way; **faire tout le ~ à pied/en boitant** to walk/to limp all the way; **il a su trouver le ~ de mon cœur** FIG he's found the way to my heart; **cette femme fera/a fait du ~** this woman will go/has come a long way; **l'idée fait son ~** the idea is gaining ground; **montrer le ~** (donner l'exemple) to lead the way; **être sur le bon ~** GÉN to be heading in the right direction; **prendre le ~ de la faillite** to be heading for bankruptcy; **s'arrêter en ~** LIT to stop off on the way; FIG to stop; **tu ne vas pas t'arrêter en si bon ~!** don't stop when things are going so well!; **le ~ de la gloire** the path of glory; **le ~ de la célébrité/perdition** the road to fame/ruin; **le destin l'a mis sur mon ~** fate threw him in my path; **4** (tapis) (carpet) runner.

■ **le ~ des écoliers** the long way round GB ou around US; **prendre le ~ des écoliers** to take the long way round GB ou around US; **~ de fer** RAIL (infrastructure) railway, railroad US; (mode de transport) rail; **par ~ de fer** by rail; **~ de halage** towpath; **~ de table** (table) runner; **~ de terre** (pour véhicule) dirt track; (pour piétons) path; **~ de traverse** path across ou through the fields; **~ vicinal** country lane.

cheminée /ʃ(ə)mine/ *nf* **1** (de maison) (conduit complet) chimney; (sur le toit) chimney stack; (foyer) fireplace; (manteau) mantelpiece; **2** (d'usine) chimney; **3** (de fosse, cave) shaft; **4** (de bateau, locomotive) funnel, smokestack US; **5** (de mine) chute; **6** (en montagne) chimney.

cheminement /ʃ(ə)minmɑ̃/ *nm* **1** (avance) (slow) progression; **2** (voie suivie) course; **le ~ de sa pensée** his/her train of thought.

cheminer /ʃ(ə)mine/ [1] *vi* **1** (marcher) to walk (along); MIL (avancer à couvert) to advance (under cover); **2** (avancer) **~ à travers/entre** [ruisseau, sentier] to wend its way through/between LITTÉR; **3** (progresser) [idée, pensée] to progress, to develop.

cheminot /ʃ(ə)mino/ *nm* railway worker GB, railroader US.

chemise /ʃ(ə)miz/ *nf* **1** (pour hommes) shirt; **2** (lingerie) vest GB, undershirt US; **3** (en papeterie) folder; **4** TECH (intérieure) lining; (extérieure) jacket; **5** CONSTR facing.

■ **~ de nuit** (pour femme) nightgown, nightdress GB; (pour homme) nightshirt.

IDIOMES **j'y ai laissé ma ~**○ it broke the bank; **je m'en moque comme de ma première ~**○ I don't give two hoots○ GB ou a hoot○ US; **changer d'avis comme de ~**○ to change one's mind at the drop of a hat; **mouiller sa ~**○ to work hard.

chemiser /ʃ(ə)mize/ [1] *vtr* **1** CULIN to line [moule]; **2** TECH to jacket [pièce, conduit].

chemiserie /ʃ(ə)mizʀi/ *nf* (industrie) shirt-making trade; (fabrique) shirt factory; (magasin) shirt shop GB ou store US.

chemisier, -ière /ʃ(ə)mizje, ɛʀ/ *nm* (vêtement) blouse.

chenal, *pl* **-aux** /ʃənal, o/ *nm* (de fleuve, d'estuaire) channel, fairway; (d'usine) flume; (de moulin) millrace.

chenapan /ʃənapɑ̃/ *nm* HUM scallywag○, rascal.

chêne /ʃɛn/ *nm* (arbre) oak (tree); (bois) oak.

chenet /ʃənɛ/ *nm* firedog, andiron.

chenil /ʃənil/ *nm* **1** (niche) kennel; **2** (pension pour chiens) kennels (*sg*).

chenille /ʃənij/ *nf* **1** ZOOL caterpillar; **2** AUT caterpillar; **véhicule à ~s** tracked vehicle; **3** (fil à tricoter) chenille.

chenu, ~e /ʃəny/ *adj* LITER [vieillard, barbe] hoary; [arbre] leafless.

cheptel /ʃɛptɛl/ *nm* (bétail) **~ (vif)** livestock; **~ bovin** beef ou dairy herd; **~ ovin/porcin** sheep/pig population.

chèque /ʃɛk/ *nm* cheque GB, check US; **faire un ~ to** write a cheque GB ou check US; **~ à l'ordre de M. Daw** cheque GB ou check US payable to Mr Daw; **les ~s sont acceptés à partir de 100 francs** 'no cheques GB ou checks US under 100 francs'.

■ **~ bancaire** cheque GB, check US; **~ en blanc** blank cheque GB ou check US; **~ en bois**○ rubber cheque○ GB ou check US; **il m'a fait un ~ en bois** the cheque GB ou check US he wrote me bounced; **~ postal** ≈ giro cheque; **~ sans provision** bad cheque GB ou check US; **~ de voyage** traveller's cheque GB ou check US; **~s postaux** (service) ≈ National Girobank.

chèque-cadeau, *pl* **chèques-cadeaux** /ʃɛkkado/ *nm* gift-token.

chèque-voyage, *pl* **chèques-voyage** /ʃɛkvwajaʒ/ *nm* traveller's cheque GB ou check US.

chéquier /ʃekje/ *nm* chequebook GB, checkbook US.

cher, chère[1] /ʃɛʀ/ I *adj* **1** (aimé) [personne] dear; [objet, visage] beloved; **la mort d'un être ~** the death of a loved one; **2** (précieux) **~ à qn** [thème, principe, idée] dear to sb (épith, après n); **selon une formule qui lui est chère** as his/her favourite GB saying goes; **un site ~ au poète** a place the poet was fond of; **3** (pour interpeller) dear; **~ ami, vous avez tout à fait raison!** my dear friend, you're absolutely right!; **ah, mais c'est ce ~ Dupont!** well, if it isn't our dear old Dupont!; **4** (dans la correspondance) dear; **~s tous** dear all; **5** (onéreux) expensive, dear; **pas ~** cheap, inexpensive; **pas ~ du tout** reasonably-priced; **la vie est plus chère** the cost of living is higher.

II *nm,f* **mon ~** GÉN dear; (condescendant, à homme plus jeune) my dear boy; (à homme plus âgé) my dear sir; **ma chère** GÉN dear; (condescendant, à femme plus jeune) my dear girl; (à femme plus âgée) my dear lady.

III *adv* **1** LIT (en argent) a lot (of money); **les vêtements en cuir coûtent ~ à nettoyer** having leather clothes cleaned is expensive ou costly; **coûter plus/moins ~** to cost more/less; **acheter ~** to buy at a high price; **se vendre ~** [objet] to fetch a lot; **je l'ai eu pour moins ~** I got it cheaper; **ils font payer très ~ leur services** they charge an awful lot for their services; **2** FIG (en importance) [payer] dearly; **le blocus a coûté ~ à notre économie** our economy paid a high price for the blockade.

IDIOMES **ne pas donner ~ de qn** or **de la peau de qn**○ not to rate sb's chances (highly).

chercher /ʃɛʀʃe/ [1] I *vtr* **1** (essayer de trouver) to look for; **~ un mot dans le dictionnaire** to look up a word in the dictionary; **~ qn du regard dans la foule** to look (about) for sb in the crowd; **'cherchons vendeuses'** 'sales assistants wanted'; **son regard cherchait celui de sa femme** he sought his wife's eye; **elle chercha quelques pièces de monnaie dans sa poche** she felt for some coins in her pocket; **~ le sommeil** to try to get some sleep; **ne cherchez plus!** look no further!; **se ~ à faire** to try to do; **3** (prendre) **aller ~ qn/qch** GÉN to go and get sb/sth; (passer prendre) to pick sb/sth up; **aller ~ qch** [chien] to fetch sth; **envoyer qn ~ qch** to send sb to get sth; **4** (r éfléchir à) to try to find [réponse, idées]; to look for [prétexte, excuse]; (se souvenir de) to try to remember [nom]; **je cherche mes mots** I can't find my words; **j'ai beau ~, impossible de m'en souvenir** I've thought and thought and still can't remember it; **pas la peine de ~ bien loin** you don't have to look too far; **5** (imaginer) **où est-il allé ~ cela?** what made him think that?; **6** (atteindre) **ça va ~ dans les**

8000 francs it must fetch GB ou get US about 8,000 francs; **ça doit ~ dans les cinq ans de prison** it would get you about five years in prison; **7** (aller à la rencontre de) to look for [*complications*]; **elle t'a giflé mais tu l'as bien cherché** she slapped you but you asked for it.

II se chercher *vpr* **1 un écrivain qui se cherche** (raison d'être) a writer trying to find himself; (style, idées) a writer who is feeling his way; **2 se ~ des excuses** to try to find excuses for oneself; **3**° (se provoquer) to be out to get each other°.

chercheur, -euse /ʃɛRʃœR, øz/ ▶374| *nm,f* researcher.

■ **~ d'or** gold-digger.

chère² /ʃɛR/ I *adj f* ▶ **cher**.

II *nf* FML food, fare; **faire bonne ~** to eat well.

chèrement /ʃɛRmɑ̃/ *adv* (difficilement) **~ acquis** gained at great cost.

chéri, ~e /ʃeRi/ I *adj* beloved; **l'enfant ~ de** the darling of.

II *nm,f* **1** (en adresse) darling; **ma ~e** my darling; **2** (favori) darling; **3**° (amoureux) boyfriend/girlfriend.

chérir /ʃeRiR/ [3] *vtr* LITER to cherish [*personne*]; to hold [sth] dear [*principe, idée*].

cherra ▶ **choir**.

chérubin /ʃeRybɛ̃/ *nm* **1** RELIG des **~s** cherubim; **2** ART cherub; **3** (enfant) IRON little angel ou cherub.

chétif, -ive /ʃetif, iv/ *adj* [*enfant*] puny; [*plante*] scrawny.

cheval, pl -aux /ʃ(ə)val, o/ I *nm* **1** ZOOL horse; **~ sauvage** wild horse; **à (dos de) ~** on horseback; **monter à ~** to ride a horse; **à ~!** mount!; **promenade à ~** (horse) ride; **tenue de ~** riding clothes (*pl*); **remède de ~** strong medicine; **fièvre de ~** raging fever; **miser sur le bon ~** FIG to back the right horse; **2** ▶329| (activité) horse-riding; **3** (viande) horsemeat; **4** (personne) real Trojan; (vieux) **~ de retour** (homme politique) war horse; (récidiviste) habitual offender, old lag°; **5**° (femme masculine) PEJ **c'est un vrai ~** she's built like a horse.

II **à cheval** *sur loc prép* **à ~ sur un mur** astride a wall; **à ~ sur deux pays** spanning two countries; **le domaine est à ~ sur la route** the estate straddles the road; **à ~ sur le rouge et le violet** in between red and purple; **être à ~ sur les principes** to be a stickler for principles.

■ **~ d'arçons** pommel horse; **~ à bascule** JEUX rocking horse; **~ de bataille** hobbyhorse; **~ de course** racehorse; **~ fiscal**, *unit for car tax assessment*; **~ de labour** carthorse GB, drafthorse US; **~ marin** ZOOL sea horse; **~ de selle** saddle horse; **~ de Troie** Trojan horse; **chevaux de bois** merry-go-round horses.

IDIOMES **ne pas être un mauvais ~** not to be such a bad sort; **monter sur ses grands chevaux** to get on one's high horse.

chevaleresque /ʃ(ə)valRɛsk/ *adj* **1** LITTÉRAT [*littérature, poème*] chevaleresque; **2** (courtois) chivalrous.

chevalerie /ʃ(ə)valRi/ *nf* chivalry.

chevalet /ʃ(ə)valɛ/ *nm* **1** (de peintre) easel; (de menuisier) trestle, sawhorse; **2** (de violon) bridge.

chevalier /ʃ(ə)valje/ *nm* (tous contextes) knight; **armer qn ~** to knight sb.

■ **~ errant** knight errant; **~ noir** FIN black knight; **~ servant** HUM devoted admirer.

chevalière /ʃ(ə)valjɛR/ *nf* signet ring.

chevalin, ~e /ʃ(ə)valɛ̃, in/ *adj* **1** (ayant rapport au cheval) equine; **boucherie ~e** horse butcher's; **2** (ressemblant au cheval) horsey.

cheval-vapeur, pl chevaux-vapeur /ʃ(ə)valva pœR, ʃ(ə)vovapœR/ *nm* horsepower.

chevauchée /ʃ(ə)voʃe/ *nf* ride.

chevaucher /ʃ(ə)voʃe/ [1] I *vtr* **1** (être assis sur) to sit astride [*animal, objet*]; **2** (recouvrir en partie) to overlap.

II *vi* **1** (en imprimerie) [*caractères*] to become misaligned; **2** LITER to ride.

III **se chevaucher** *vpr* to overlap.

chevêche /ʃəvɛʃ/ *nf* ZOOL little owl.

chevelu, ~e /ʃəvly/ *adj* PEJ [*homme*] long-haired (*épith*).

chevelure /ʃəvlyR/ *nf* **1** (cheveux) hair ¢; **une abondante ~ bouclée** a mass of curly hair; **2** (de comète) tail.

chevet /ʃəvɛ/ *nm* **1** (de lit) bedhead; **être au ~ de qn** to be at sb's bedside; **2** (meuble) bedside table; **3** ARCHIT (d'église) chevet.

cheveu, pl ~x /ʃəvø/ I *nm* **1** (poil) hair; **avoir quelques ~x blancs** to have a few grey GB ou gray US hairs; **avoir le ~ rare** to be a bit thin on top; **2** (petite dimension) hair's breadth; **être à un ~ de qch/de faire** to be within a hair's breadth of sth/of doing; **ne tenir qu'à un ~** to hang by a thread.

II **cheveux** *nmpl* (chevelure) hair ¢; **avoir les ~x longs** to have long hair; **avoir les ~x blancs** to have grey GB ou gray US hair; **se laver les ~x** to wash one's hair; **se faire couper les ~x** to have one's hair cut; **avoir les ~x en bataille** to have tousled hair; **une histoire à vous faire dresser les ~x sur la tête** a story that makes your hair stand on end.

IDIOMES **avoir un ~ sur la langue** to have a lisp; **venir comme un ~ sur la soupe** to come at an awkward moment; **se faire des ~x°** (blancs) to worry oneself to death (pour about); **couper les ~x en quatre** to split hairs; **être tiré par les ~x** to be far-fetched.

cheville /ʃ(ə)vij/ ▶137| *nf* **1** ANAT ankle; **jupe qui arrive à la ~** ankle-length skirt; **on avait de l'eau jusqu'aux ~s** we were ankle-deep in water; **2** CONSTR (pour vis) Rawlplug®; (pour assemblage) peg; (en bois) dowel; **3** (d'instrument de musique) peg; **~ d'accord** tuning peg; **4** (de boucherie) butcher's hook; **5** (dans un poème) PEJ padding ¢ PÉJ.

■ **~ ouvrière** FIG kingpin; **être la ~ ouvrière de...** to play a key role in...

IDIOMES **il n'arrive pas à la ~ de Paul** he can't hold a candle to Paul; **avoir les ~s qui enflent** to get big-headed; **être en ~ avec°** to be in cahoots with°.

cheviller /ʃ(ə)vije/ [1] *vtr* to peg.

IDIOMES **avoir l'âme chevillée au corps** to have a tremendous hold on life.

chèvre¹ /ʃɛvR/ *nm* (fromage) goat's cheese.

chèvre² /ʃɛvR/ *nf* **1** ZOOL goat; (femelle du bouc) nanny-goat; **2** (peau) goatskin.

IDIOMES **devenir ~°** to go round the bend° GB, to go nuts°; **ménager la ~ et le chou** to tread the middle ground.

chevreau, pl ~x /ʃəvRo/ *nm* kid.

chèvrefeuille /ʃɛvRəfœj/ *nm* honeysuckle.

chevrette /ʃəvRɛt/ *nf* **1** ZOOL (chèvre) young nanny goat; (femelle du chevreuil) (female) roe deer; **2** (trépied) tripod.

chevreuil /ʃəvRœj/ *nm* **1** ZOOL roe (deer); (mâle) roebuck; **2** CULIN venison.

chevron /ʃəvRɔ̃/ *nm* **1** (poutre) rafter; **2** (motif) chevron; **les ~s** ou **le ~** (petits) herringbone pattern; (grands) chevron design; **3** ARCHIT chevron; **4** MIL (galon) chevron, stripe.

chevronné, ~e /ʃəvRɔne/ *adj* [*personne*] experienced.

chevrotant, ~e /ʃəvRɔtɑ̃, ɑ̃t/ *adj* [*voix*] quavering.

chevroter /ʃəvRɔte/ [1] *vtr, vi* to quaver.

chevrotine /ʃəvRɔtin/ *nf* buckshot.

chez /ʃe/ *prép* **1** (au domicile de) **~ qn** at sb's place; **~ David** at David's (place); **rentre ~ toi** go home; **je reste ~ moi** I stay at home; **tu peux dormir ~ moi** you can sleep at my place; **je ne veux pas de ça ~ moi!** I'll have none of that in my home!; **fais comme ~ toi** make yourself at home; **derrière ~ eux il y a une immense forêt** there is a huge forest behind their house; **vous habitez ~ vos parents?** do you live with your parents?; **2** ▶374| (au magasin, cabinet de) **la montre ne vient pas de ~ nous** this watch doesn't come from our shop GB ou store US; **en vente ~ tous les dépositaires** on sale at all agents; **va ~ Hallé, c'est un très bon médecin** go to Hallé, he's/she's a very good doctor; **une montre de ~ Lip** a Lip watch; **publié ~ Hachette** published by Hachette; **~ l'épicier du coin** at the local grocer's; **'~ Juliette'** (sur une enseigne) 'Juliette's'; **3** (dans la famille de) **~ moi/vous/eux** in my/your/their family; **comment ça va ~ les Pichon?** how are the Pichons doing? ; **ça va bien/mal ~ eux** things are going well/badly for them; **4** (dans le pays, la région de) **~ nous** (d'où je viens) where I come from; (où j'habite) where I live; **~ eux ils appellent ça...** in their part of the world they call this...; **un nom bien de ~ nous**○ (de France) a good old French name; (de notre région) a good old local name; **5** (parmi) among; **~ l'homme/ l'animal** in man/animals; **6** (dans la personnalité de) **ce que j'aime ~ elle, c'est son humour** what I like about her, is her sense of humour^{GB}; **c'est une obsession ~ elle!** it's an obsession with her!; **7** (dans l'œuvre de) in; **~ Cocteau** in Cocteau.

chic /ʃik/ **I** *adj* **1** (élégant) [*personne, vêtement*] smart GB, chic; **2**○ (sophistiqué) [*école, personne, hôtel, quartier*] chic; **3**○ (gentil) nice.
II *nm* chic; **avoir le ~ pour faire** to have a knack for doing; **avec ~** with style; **avoir du ~** to have style; **c'est du dernier ~** it's the height of sophistication.
III *adv* [*s'habiller*] smartly GB, stylishly.

chicane /ʃikan/ *nf* **1** (formée par obstacles) chicane; (tracé de route, piste) double bend; **en ~** on alternate sides; **2** (tracasserie) bickering ₵; **3** JUR (point de détail) delaying tactics (*pl*); (procédure) PEJ legal quibbling PEJ.
chicaner /ʃikane/ [1] **I** *vtr* (harceler) **~ qn sur qch** to argue with sb about sth.
II *vi* (discuter) to squabble (**sur, pour** over); (faire des manières) to fuss (**sur** about).
III se chicaner *vpr* to squabble (**pour** over).

chiche /ʃiʃ/ **I** *adj* **1** (parcimonieux) mean GB, stingy; **2**○ (capable) **être ~ de faire qch** to be able to do sth.
II○ *excl* **'je vais le faire'—'~!'** 'I'll do it'—'I dare you!'; **~ que je le fais!** bet you I can do it!

chichement /ʃiʃmã/ *adv* [*manger, vivre*] frugally, [*donner*] meanly GB, stingily; [*décorer*] sparsely; [*payer*] poorly.

chichi○ /ʃiʃi/ *nm* fuss ₵; **ne fais pas de ~s pour moi!** don't go to any trouble!; **sans ~(s)** [*personne*] straightforward; [*réception*] informal.

chicon /ʃikɔ̃/ *nm* (endive) chicory.

chicorée /ʃikɔʀe/ *nf* **1** BOT chicory; (salade) endive GB, chicory ₵ US; **2** CULIN (poudre) chicory; (boisson) chicory coffee.

chicot○ /ʃiko/ *nm* (dent) stump, snag.

chien, chienne[1] /ʃjɛ̃, ʃjɛn/ **I**○ *adj* bloody-minded GB, nasty; **~ de temps** wretched weather; **ma chienne de vie** my wretched life.
II *nm* **1** (animal) dog; **~ à poil ras/long** short-/long-haired dog; **'~ méchant'** 'beware of the dog'; **2** (fusil) hammer; **3** NAUT **coup de ~** fresh gale.
III de chien○ *loc adj* [*métier, temps*] rotten; **vie de ~** dog's life; **avoir un caractère de ~** to have a lousy○ character; **être d'une humeur de ~** to be in a foul mood; **ça me fait un mal de ~** it hurts like hell○; **avoir un mal de ~ à faire** to have an awful time doing.
■ **~ d'arrêt** pointer; **~ d'aveugle** guide dog; **~ de berger** sheepdog; **~ de chasse** retriever, gundog; **~ de garde** LIT guard dog; FIG watchdog; **~ de mer** dogfish; **~ policier** police dog; **~ de race** pedigree dog; **~s écrasés** PRESSE fillers; **~ de traîneau** sled dog.
IDIOMES **traiter qn comme un ~** to treat sb like a dog ou like dirt; **être couché en ~ de fusil** to be curled up; **entre ~ et loup** at dusk; **elle a du ~** she's got what it takes; **avoir un air de ~ battu** to have a hangdog look; **ce n'est pas fait pour les ~s**○ it's there to be used; **garder à qn un ~ de sa chienne** to bear a grudge against sb.

chiendent /ʃjɛ̃dã/ *nm* BOT couch grass, scutch grass; **brosse de ~** scrubbing brush.
IDIOMES **pousser comme du ~** to grow like a weed.

chienlit /ʃjãli/ *nf* havoc, chaos.

chien-loup, *pl* **chiens-loups** /ʃjɛ̃lu/ *nm* Alsatian GB, German shepherd.

chienne[2] /ʃjɛn/ **I** *adj f* ▶ **chien**.
II *nf* (animal) bitch.

chiffe /ʃif/ *nf* PEJ **~ molle** drip, wet blanket.

chiffon /ʃifɔ̃/ *nm* **1** (morceau d'étoffe) rag, (piece of) cloth; **une poupée de ~s** a rag doll; **2** (pour nettoyer) duster; **donner** or **passer un coup de ~ sur qch** to give sth a quick dust ou wipe; **donner** or **passer un coup de ~** to do some dusting; **3** (document sans valeur) scrap of paper.
IDIOMES **parler** or **causer**○ **~s** to talk (about) clothes.

chiffonné, ~e /ʃifɔne/ *adj* **1** (fatigué) [*visage*] tired-looking; **2**○ (chagriné) troubled, ruffled.

chiffonner /ʃifɔne/ [1] **I** *vtr* **1** (froisser) to crumple (up) [*feuille*]; to crease, to crumple [*tissu*]; **2**○ (chagriner) to bother [*personne*].
II se chiffonner *vpr* [*tissu*] to crease, to crumple.

chiffonnier, -ière /ʃifɔnje, ɛʀ/ **I** ▶ **374** *nm,f* rag-and-bone man/woman.
II *nm* (meuble) chiffonnier.
IDIOMES **se battre comme des ~s** to fight like cat and dog.

chiffrable /ʃifʀabl/ *adj* [*pertes, dégâts*] calculable; **les pertes ne sont pas ~s** it's impossible to put a figure on the losses.

chiffre /ʃifʀ/ *nm* **1** (symbole) figure; (numéro, nombre) number; **écrire le montant en ~s** to write the amount in figures; **un numéro à six ~s** a six-figure ou six-digit number; **2** (résultat) figure; **3** (statistique) statistic; **les ~s officiels** the official statistics; **4** (total) total; **~ global** total amount; **5** (code) (de message) code; (de coffre) combination; **le (service du) Chiffre** the cipher room; **6** (monogramme) monogram.
■ **~ d'affaires, CA** turnover GB, sales (*pl*) US; **~ arabe** Arabic numeral; **~ romain** Roman numeral; **~ de vente** sales (*pl*).

chiffrer /ʃifʀe/ [1] **I** *vtr* **1** (évaluer) to put a figure on, to assess [*coût, pertes*]; to cost [*travaux*]; **~ à** to put ou assess [sth] at [*coût, dépenses, pertes*]; to put the cost of [sth] at [*travaux*]; **données chiffrées** figures; **2** (coder) to encode [*message*]; **3** (marquer) to monogram [*linge, vaisselle*]; **4** (numéroter) to number [*pages*].
II○ *vi* (coûter cher) **ça chiffre vite** it soon adds up.
III se chiffrer *vpr* **se ~ à** to amount to, to come to.

chignole /ʃiɲɔl/ *nf* **1** (outil) hand drill; **2**○ (voiture) PEJ banger○ GB, junker○ US, car.

chignon /ʃiɲɔ̃/ *nm* bun; (plus élégant) chignon; **avoir un ~** to wear one's hair in a bun.

chiite /ʃiit/ RELIG *adj*, *nmf* Shiite.

chilien, -ienne /ʃiljɛ̃, ɛn/ ▶ **394** *adj* Chilean.

chimère /ʃimɛʀ/ *nf* **1** (rêve) wild dream, chim(a)era SOUT; **se complaire dans des ~s** to live in a dream world; **poursuivre des ~s** to chase rainbows; **de folles ~s** crazy fantasies; **2** MYTHOL Chim(a)era; **3** BIOL, BOT chim(a)era; ZOOL (poisson) chim(a)era.

chimérique /ʃimeʀik/ *adj* [*projet, espoir*] wild; [*animal*] fabulous; [*personne, esprit*] fanciful.

chimie /ʃimi/ *nf* **1** chemistry; **2** (transformation) LITER alchemy.

chimiothérapie /ʃimjoteʀapi/ *nf* chemotherapy.

chimique /ʃimik/ *adj* **1** [*produit*] chemical; [*fibre*] man-made; **2** PEJ [*nourriture*] synthetic; [*goût*] chemical.

chimiste /ʃimist/ ▶ **374** *nmf* chemist; **ingénieur ~** chemical engineer.

chimpanzé /ʃɛ̃pɑ̃ze/ *nm* chimpanzee.

Chine /ʃin/ ▶ **232** *nprf* China; **~ continentale** mainland China; **République populaire de ~** People's Republic of China.

chiner /ʃine/ [1] **I** *vtr* to dye the warp threads of [*tissu*]; **tissu chiné** chiné fabric.
II○ *vi* (chercher) to bargain-hunt, to antique US; (vendre) to deal in second-hand goods.

chinois, **~e** /ʃinwɑ, az/ I *adj* **1** ▶ 394 ɢéoɢ Chinese; **2**○ (tatillon) nitpicking○.

II *nm* **1** ▶ 338 ʟɪɴɢ Chinese; **2** cuʟɪɴ conical strainer.

ɪᴅɪoᴍᴇs **pour moi c'est du ~** it's double-Dutch ɢʙ ou Greek to me.

chiot /ʃjo/ *nm* puppy, pup.

chiper○ /ʃipe/ [1] *vtr* to pinch○ (**à** from).

chipie○ /ʃipi/ *nf* ᴘéJ cow○ ᴘéJ.

chipoter○ /ʃipɔte/ [1] *vi* **1** (faire des difficultés) to quibble (**sur** over); **2** (marchander) to haggle (**sur** over); **3** (pour manger) to pick at one's food.

chipoteur, **-euse**○ /ʃipɔtœr, øz/ I *adj* **1** (exigeant) difficult; **2** (sur le prix) **être ~** to haggle over everything; **3** (à table) fussy.

II *nm,f* **1** (personne exigeante) nit-picker; **2** (sur le prix) person who haggles over everything; **3** (à table) fussy ou picky○ us eater.

chips /ʃips/ *nf inv* crisp ɢʙ, potato chip us.

chique /ʃik/ *nf* plug ou quid ɢʙ (of tobacco).

ɪᴅɪoᴍᴇs **avaler sa ~**○ to kick the bucket; **couper la ~**○ **à qn** (faire taire) to shut sb up○; (surprendre) to leave sb speechless.

chiqué○ /ʃike/ *nm* **1** (bluff) **c'est du ~** it's a put-on ou sham○; **2** (affectation) airs (*pl*); **faire du ~** to put on ou give oneself airs; **sans ~** without affectation.

chiquenaude /ʃiknod/ *nf* flick.

chiquer /ʃike/ [1] *vtr* **tabac à ~** chewing tobacco.

chiromancie /kirɔmɑ̃si/ *nf* palmistry, chiromancy; **faire de la ~** to read palms.

chiropracteur /kiropraktœr/ ▶ 374 *nm* chiropractor.

chirurgical, **~e**, *mpl* **-aux** /ʃiryrʒikal, o/ *adj* surgical.

chirurgie /ʃiryrʒi/ *nf* surgery.

chirurgien /ʃiryrʒjɛ̃/ ▶ 374 *nm* surgeon.

chirurgien-dentiste, *pl* **chirurgiens-dentistes** /ʃiryrʒjɛ̃dɑ̃tist/ ▶ 374 *nm* dental surgeon.

chlore /klɔr/ *nm* chlorine.

chlorer /klɔre/ [1] *vtr* to chlorinate.

chlorhydrique /klɔridrik/ *adj* hydrochloric.

chloroforme /klɔrɔfɔrm/ *nm* chloroform.

chlorophylle /klɔrɔfil/ *nf* chlorophyll.

chlorure /klɔryr/ *nm* chloride.

choc /ʃɔk/ I *adj inv* **'prix ~!'** 'huge reductions'; **c'est l'argument ~!** there's no answer to that!; **le film ~ de l'année** the most sensational film of the year.

II *nm* **1** (rencontre brutale) (d'objets) impact, shock; (de vagues) crash; (de personnes) collision; ᴀuᴛ (collision) crash; (sans gravité) bump; **résister aux ~s** to be shock-resistant; **sous le ~** under the impact; **2** (bruit) (violent) crash, smash; (sourd) thud; (métallique) clang; (de vaisselle) clink; **3** (affrontement) **les troupes ont résisté au premier ~** the troops have weathered the first onslaught; **troupe** ou **unité de ~** ᴍɪʟ shock troops; **de ~** [*journaliste, patron*] ace○; **4** (commotion) shock; **être encore sous le ~** (après une nouvelle) to be still in a state of shock; (après un accident) to be still in shock; **tenir le ~** to cope; **traitement de ~** shock treatment.

■ **~ culturel** culture shock; **~ nerveux** (nervous) shock; **~ opératoire** post-operative shock; **~ pétrolier** oil crisis.

chocolat /ʃɔkɔla/ I ▶ 141 *adj inv* (couleur) chocolate-brown.

II *nm* **1** (substance) chocolate; **gâteau au ~** chocolate cake; **~ à croquer** plain chocolate; **tablette de ~** chocolate bar; **2** (friandise) chocolate; **une boîte de ~s** a box of chocolates; **3** (boisson) chocolate.

■ **~ à cuire** cooking chocolate; **~ en poudre** drinking chocolate.

chocolaterie /ʃɔkɔlatri/ *nf* chocolate factory.

chocolatier, **-ière** /ʃɔkɔlatje, ɛr/ ▶ 374 *nm,f* chocolate maker.

chœur /kœr/ *nm* **1** (groupe) choir; (d'opéra) chorus; **2** (morceau) chorus; **chanter en ~** to sing in chorus; **'reprenons tous en ~'** 'all together now'; **3** (de théâtre)

chorus; **4** ᴀʀᴄʜɪᴛ chancel, choir; **5** ꜰɪɢ chorus (**de** of); **le ~ des grévistes** all the strikers (*pl*); **en ~** [*dire, affirmer*] in unison; [*rire, souffrir*] all together.

choir /ʃwar/ [51] *vi* ʟɪᴛᴇʀ to fall; **la bobinette cherra** the latch will drop.

choisi, **~e** /ʃwazi/ *adj* **1** (sélectionné) [*morceaux, œuvres*] selected; **2** (recherché) [*expressions, terme*] carefully chosen; **3** (sélect) [*société, clientèle*] select.

choisir /ʃwazir/ [3] *vtr* to choose (**entre** between); **~ son camp** ꜰɪɢ to choose sides; **~ de faire** to choose to do; **bien/mal ~** to make the right/wrong choice; **~ qn comme ministre** to choose ou pick sb as a minister; **c'est à toi de ~** it's up to you.

choix /ʃwa/ *nm inv* **1** (option) choice (**entre** between; **parmi** among); **avoir/ne pas avoir le ~** to have a/no choice; **mon ~ est fait** I've made my choice; **faire le ~ de rester** to choose to stay; **je te laisse le ~ du jour** you decide on the date; **fixer** ou **arrêter** ou **porter son ~ sur** to settle ou decide on; **2** (assortiment) choice; **3** (sélection) selection; **un ~ d'instruments** a selection of instruments; **4** (qualité) **de ~** [*produit*] choice; [*candidat, collaborateur*] first-rate; **les places de ~ sont toutes réservées** the best seats are all reserved; **un morceau de ~** (en boucherie) a prime cut; **de second ~** poor quality (*avant n*).

choléra /kɔlera/ ▶ 196 *nm* cholera.

cholestérol /kɔlesterɔl/ *nm* cholesterol; **avoir du ~**○ to have a high cholesterol level.

chômage /ʃomaʒ/ *nm* unemployment; **être au** or **en ~** to be unemployed; **s'inscrire au ~** to register as unemployed; **mettre qn au** or **en ~** to make sb redundant ɢʙ, to lay sb off.

■ **~ partiel** short time (working); **~ technique** layoffs (*pl*).

chômé, **~e** /ʃome/ *adj* **jour ~** day off; **fête ~e** national holiday.

chômer /ʃome/ [1] I *vtr* not to work on [*journée*].

II *vi* **1** (être improductif) [*personne, machine, capital*] to be idle; **nous ne chômons pas en ce moment!** we're not short of work at the moment!; **2** (être sans travail) [*employé*] to be out of work; [*usine, machines*] to stand idle; [*industrie*] to be at a standstill.

chômeur, **-euse** /ʃomœr, øz/ *nm,f* unemployed person; **les ~s de longue durée** the long-term unemployed; **~s en fin de droit** unemployed people no longer eligible for benefit.

chope /ʃɔp/ *nf* beer mug, tankard.

choquant, **~e** /ʃɔkɑ̃, ɑ̃t/ *adj* shocking; **~ de franchise** shockingly frank.

choquer /ʃɔke/ [1] *vtr* **1** (scandaliser) to shock [*personne*]; **ça l'a choqué de voir ça** he was shocked to see it; **si le mot choque** if the word is shocking ou causes offence ɢʙ; **ça choque** it's shocking; **cela risque de ~** (comportement, film, remarque) it might cause offence ɢʙ; **2** (commotionner) [*événement, nouvelle*] to shake [*personne*]; [*chute, accident*] to shake [sb] (up); **être choqué** ᴍéᴅ to be in shock; **3** (blesser) to offend [*vue, sensibilité*]; to jar on [*oreille*]; to go against [*bon sens*].

choral, **~e¹**, *mpl* **~s** or **-aux** /kɔral, o/ I *adj* choral.

II (*pl* **~s**) *nm* chorale.

chorale² /kɔral/ *nf* choir.

chorégraphe /kɔregraf/ ▶ 374 *nmf* choreographer.

chorégraphie /kɔregrafi/ *nf* choreography.

choriste /kɔrist/ *nmf* (d'église) chorister; (d'opéra) member of the chorus; (de chorale) member of the choir.

chorus /kɔrys/ *nm inv* ᴍus chorus; **faire ~ avec qn** ꜰɪɢ to join in with sb.

chose /ʃoz/ I○ *adj* **se sentir tout ~** to feel out of sorts.

II *nf* **1** (objet) thing; **quelle autre ~ pourrais-je leur acheter?** what else could I buy them?; **'une bière'—'la même ~ (pour moi)'** 'a beer'—'the same for me'; **la même ~ s'il vous plaît** (pour être resservi) (the) same again, please; ▶ **quelque III**; **2** (entité)

thing; **et, ~ incroyable, il a dit oui** and the incredible thing is that he said yes; **de deux ~s l'une** it's got to be one thing or the other; **c'est toujours la même ~ ici/avec lui** it's always the same here/with him; **même ~ pour ta sœur** the same goes for your sister; **une ~ communément admise** a widely accepted fact; **je pense** or **j'ai pensé à une ~** I've thought of something; **c'est autre ~** that's different; **et si on parlait d'autre ~** let's talk about something else; **voilà autre ~○!** that's something else!; **3** (affaire, activité, message) thing; **j'ai une ~/deux ou trois ~s à vous dire** I've got something/two or three things to tell you; **(vous direz) bien des ~s à Madame Lemoine** give my regards to Mrs Lemoine; **c'est pas des ~s○ à dire** that's the last thing to say; **parler de ~s et d'autres** to talk about one thing and another ou this and that; **en mettant les ~s au mieux/au pire** at best/at (the) worst; **mettre les ~s au point** to clear things up; **on verra plus tard, chaque ~ en son temps** we' ll cross that bridge when we come to it; **avant toute ~** (auparavant) before anything else; (surtout) above all else; **'avez-vous déménagé?'—'c'est ~ faite'** 'have you moved?'—'it's all done'; **voilà** ou **c'est une bonne ~ de faite** that's one thing out of the way; **4** (ce dont il s'agit) matter; **la ~ en question** the matter in hand; **la ~ dont je vous parle** what I'm talking about; **il a pris la ~ avec humour** he saw the funny side of it; **il a bien/mal pris la ~** he took it well/badly; **5** (personne) **ce n'est qu'une pauvre ~** he/she is a poor little thing; **6○** (activités sexuelles) **être un peu porté sur la ~** to like it○, to be keen on sex; **7○** (nom de substitution) **Chose m'a dit qu'il...** what's-his-name/ what's-her-name ou thingummy told me that he...
III choses *nfpl* **1** (réalité) **les ~s étant ce qu'elles sont** things being what they are; **2** (domaine) **les ~s de l'esprit/de la chair** things of the mind/of the flesh; **les ~s de la religion** religious matters; **les ~s de la vie (quotidienne)** the little things in life.
■ **~ imprimée** printed word; **~ publique** LITER res publica, state.

chosifier /ʃozifje/ [2] *vtr* PHILOS to reify.

chou, *pl* **~x** /ʃu/ *nm* **1** (légume) cabbage; **soupe aux ~x** cabbage soup; **~ farci** stuffed cabbage; ▶ **chèvre²**; **2** (pâtisserie) choux bun GB, pastry shell US; **3○** (personne aimable) dear; **ferme la porte tu seras un ~** be a dear and close the door.
■ **~ de Bruxelles** Brussels sprout; **~ à la crème** cream puff; **~ rave** kohlrabi; **~ rouge** red cabbage; **~ vert** green cabbage.
IDIOMES **bête comme ~○** really easy; **faire ~ blanc○** to draw a blank; **faire ses ~x gras de qch○** to use sth to one's advantage; **être dans les ~x○** to bring up the rear; **aller planter ses ~x ailleurs** to go to pastures new; **rentrer dans le ~○ de qn** (physiquement) to beat sb up; (oralement) to give sb a piece of one's mind.

chouan /ʃwɑ̃/ *nm* Chouan (*Royalist insurgent from western France during the Revolution*).

choucas /ʃuka/ *nm* jackdaw.

chouchou○ /ʃuʃu/ *nm* **1** (du professeur) pet; (du public) darling; **2** (pour les cheveux) scrunchie.

chouchouter○ /ʃuʃute/ [1] *vtr* to pamper.

choucroute /ʃukʀut/ *nf* sauerkraut.

chouette /ʃwɛt/ **I○** *adj* great○, neat○ US; **être ~ avec qn** to be really nice to sb.
II *nf* ZOOL owl; **vieille ~** FIG PEJ old harridan.

chou-fleur, *pl* **choux-fleurs** /ʃuflœʀ/ *nm* cauliflower.

chou-rave, *pl* **choux-raves** /ʃuʀav/ *nm* kohlrabi.

chourer○ /ʃuʀe/ [1] *vtr* to pinch○; **se faire ~ qch** to have sth pinched.

choyer /ʃwaje/ [23] *vtr* to pamper [*enfant, client*].

chrétien, -ienne /kʀetjɛ̃, ɛn/ *adj, nm,f* Christian.

chrétienté /kʀetjɛ̃te/ *nf* **la ~** Christendom.

christ /kʀist/ *nm* ART **un ~** (sculpté) a sculpted Christ; (peint) a figure of Christ; (crucifix) a crucifix; **un ~ en croix** a crucifixion.

Christ /kʀist/ *npr* **le ~** Christ.

christianiser /kʀistjanize/ [1] *vtr* to Christianize.

christianisme /kʀistjanism/ *nm* **le ~** Christianity.

chromatique /kʀɔmatik/ *adj* **1** MUS chromatic; **2** (relatif aux couleurs) chromatic.

chrome /kʀom/ *nm* **1** CHIMIE chromium; **2** AUT **faire les ~s** to polish the chrome.

chromer /kʀome/ [1] *vtr* to chrome-plate.

chromosome /kʀɔmozom/ *nm* chromosome.

chromosomique /kʀɔmozomik/ *adj* chromosome (*épith*).

chronique /kʀɔnik/ **I** *adj* (tous contextes) chronic.
II *nf* PRESSE column, page; RADIO, TV programme[GB]; **tenir une ~** PRESSE to have a column; TV, RADIO to have a spot.

chroniqueur, -euse /kʀɔnikœʀ, øz/ ▶ **374** *nm,f* PRESSE columnist, editor; RADIO, TV commentator; **~ littéraire** book reviewer; **~ dramatique** drama critic.

chronologie /kʀɔnɔlɔʒi/ *nf* chronology.

chronologique /kʀɔnɔlɔʒik/ *adj* chronological.

chronométrage /kʀɔnɔmetʀaʒ/ *nm* timing.

chronomètre /kʀɔnɔmɛtʀ/ *nm* **1** (chronographe) stopwatch; **2** (montre de précision) chronometer.

chronométrer /kʀɔnɔmetʀe/ [14] *vtr* to time.

chrysalide /kʀizalid/ *nf* chrysalis; **sortir de sa ~** FIG to come out of one's shell.

chrysanthème /kʀizɑ̃tɛm/ *nm* chrysanthemum.

chu ▶ **choir**.

CHU /seaʃy/ *nm*: *abbr* ▶ **centre**.

chuchotement /ʃyʃɔtmɑ̃/ *nm* (de personnes) whisper.

chuchoter /ʃyʃɔte/ [1] **I** *vtr* to whisper.
II *vi* [*personne*] to whisper; [*ruisseau, vent*] to murmur.

chuintant, -e /ʃɥɛ̃tɑ̃, ɑ̃t/ *adj* bruit **~** (sifflement) hissing sound; (frottement) swishing sound.

chuintement /ʃɥɛ̃tmɑ̃/ *nm* **1** (de vapeur) hiss; (de pneus) swish; **2** (en prononciation) ~ lisp, pronunciation of *s* as *sh*.

chuinter /ʃɥɛ̃te/ [1] *vi* **1** [*vapeur*] to hiss gently; [*pneu*] to swish; **2** [*personne*] ~ to lisp, to pronounce *s* as *sh*; **3** [*chouette*] to hoot.

chum /tʃœm/ *nm* C (ami) friend; (petit ami) boyfriend.

chut /ʃyt/ *excl* shh!, hush!

chute /ʃyt/ *nf* **1** (action de tomber) fall; **faire une ~** [*personne*] to have ou take US a fall; [*objet*] to fall; **faire une ~ de moto** to fall off a motorbike; **faire une ~ de 5 mètres** to fall 5 metres[GB]; **2** (fait de se détacher) (de feuille) fall; **~ des cheveux** hair loss; **~s de pierres** falling rocks; **3** (cascade) **~ d'eau** waterfall; **les ~s du Niagara** Niagara Falls; **4** MÉTÉO fall; **fortes ~s de neige** heavy snowfall (*sg*); **5** (baisse) drop (**de** in); (de monnaie) fall; FIN **~ du franc** fall in the price of the franc; **~ de la Bourse** fall on the stock market; **~ de tension** MÉD sudden drop in blood pressure; **6** (de ministre, régime) fall (**de** of); (d'empire) collapse (**de** of); MIL (de ville, forteresse) fall (**de** of); **7** RELIG **la ~** the Fall; **8** (fin) (de texte, film) ending; (d'histoire) punch line; **9** (de tissu, papier, cuir) offcut.
■ **~ des corps** PHYS gravity; **~ libre** free-fall; **tomber en ~ libre** to fall through the air; **économie en ~ libre** FIG plummeting economy; **la ~ des reins** the small of the back; **~ du rideau** THÉÂT fall of the curtain.

chuter /ʃyte/ [1] *vi* (baisser) [*température, tension, prix*] to fall, to drop; [*ventes, production*] to fall; [*actions*] to fall; **~ de/à 10 francs** to fall ou drop by/to 10 francs; **faire ~ les cours** to cause prices to fall.

Chypre /ʃipʀ/ ▶ **305**, **232** *nprf* Cyprus.

chypriote /ʃipʀijɔt/ ▶ **394** *adj* Cypriot.

ci /si/ **I** *dét dém* **cette page-~** this page; **ces mots-~** these words; **ces jours-~** (récemment) these last few days; (bientôt) in the next few days; (en ce moment) at the moment; **ces temps-~** (récemment) lately; (à présent) at the moment; **à cette heure-~** (de la journée) at this time of day; (de la nuit) at this time of night; **il**

doit être arrivé à cette heure-~ he must have arrived by now; **vers cette heure-~** around this time.

II *pron dém* this; **~ et ça** this and that; ▶ **comme**.

ci-après /siapʀɛ/ *adv* GÉN below; **voir ~** see below.

cible /sibl/ *nf* target; **prendre qn/qch pour ~** FIG to pick on sb/sth; **servir de ~ aux moqueries de qn** to be the butt of sb's jokes.

cibler /sible/ [1] *vtr* COMM to target.

ciboulette /sibulɛt/ *nf* BOT chive; CULIN chives (*pl*).

cicatrice /sikatʀis/ *nf* LIT, FIG scar.

cicatrisant, **~e** /sikatʀizã, ãt/ *adj* [*substance*] healing.

cicatrisation /sikatʀizasjɔ̃/ *nf* LIT, FIG healing.

cicatriser /sikatʀize/ [1] *vtr*, **se cicatriser** *vpr* LIT, FIG to heal.

Cicéron /siseʀɔ̃/ *npr* Cicero.

ci-contre /sikɔ̃tʀ/ *adv* opposite.

ci-dessous /sidəsu/ *adv* below; **voir ~** see below, v. infra SOUT.

ci-dessus /sidəsy/ *adv* above; **voir ~** see above, v. supra SOUT.

ci-devant /sidəvã/ *adj inv* former.

cidre /sidʀ/ *nm* cider; **~ doux/sec** sweet/dry cider.

cidrerie /sidʀəʀi/ *nf* (local) cider-works.

ciel /sjɛl, sjø/ *nm* **1** (*pl* **ciels**) MÉTÉO sky; **~ clair** or **dégagé** clear sky; **les ~s d'Afrique** African skies; **carte du ~** star chart; **2** (*pl* **cieux**) (firmament) LITER sky; **les cieux étoilés** the starry skies; **entre ~ et terre** FIG between heaven and earth; **sous des cieux plus cléments** in kinder climes; **à ~ ouvert** [*piscine, musée*] open-air; [*égout*] open; [*mine*] open-cast GB, strip US; **3** (*pl* **cieux**) RELIG (paradis) heaven; **être au ~** to be in heaven; **le royaume des cieux** the kingdom of heaven; **4** (providence) LITER heaven; **remercier le ~** to thank heaven; **(juste) ~!** (good) heavens!; **c'est le ~ qui t'envoie** you are a godsend.

IDIOMES remuer ~ et terre to move heaven and earth (**pour faire** to do).

cierge /sjɛʀʒ/ *nm* (d'église) (church) candle.

cieux ▶ **ciel** 2, 3.

cigale /sigal/ *nf* cicada.

cigare /sigaʀ/ *nm* (à fumer) cigar.

cigarette /sigaʀɛt/ *nf* cigarette.

■ **~ (à) bout filtre** filter-tip (cigarette).

ci-gît /siʒi/ *loc verbale* here lies.

cigogne /sigɔɲ/ *nf* ZOOL stork.

ciguë /sigy/ *nf* (poison, plante) hemlock.

ci-inclus, **~e** /siɛ̃kly, yz/ *adj, adv* enclosed.

ci-joint, **~e** /siʒwɛ̃, ɛt/ **I** *adj* enclosed; **la copie ~e** the enclosed copy.

II *adv* enclosed.

cil /sil/ *nm* eyelash.

ciller /sije/ [1] *vi* **~ (des yeux)** to blink; **sans ~** LIT unblinkingly; FIG without batting an eyelid.

cimaise /simɛz/ *nf* (de corniche) cyma; (à mi-hauteur) picture rail.

cime /sim/ *nf* top.

ciment /simã/ *nm* LIT, FIG cement.

cimenter /simãte/ [1] **I** *vtr* **1** CONSTR to cement [*mur, briques*]; to concrete [*sol, allée*]; **2** FIG to cement [*amitié*].

II **se cimenter** *vpr* [*amitié*] to grow stronger.

cimenterie /simãtʀi/ *nf* (usine) cement works.

cimeterre /simtɛʀ/ *nm* scimitar.

cimetière /simtjɛʀ/ *nm* **1** LIT cemetery, graveyard; (d'église) churchyard, graveyard; **2** FIG graveyard.

■ **~ de voitures** scrapyard.

ciné○ /sine/ *nm* cinema GB, pictures○ (*pl*) GB, movies○ (*pl*) US.

cinéaste /sineast/ ▶ **374**| *nmf* film director.

ciné-club, *pl* **~s** /sineklœb/ *nm* film club.

cinéma /sinema/ *nm* **1** (bâtiment) (**salle de**) **~** cinema GB, movie theater US; **aller au ~** to go to the cinema

GB ou movies○ US; **2** (art, technique) cinema; (industrie) film industry; **de ~** film (*épith*) GB, movie (*épith*) US; **une école de ~** a film school; **faire du ~** to be in films; **adapté pour le ~** adapted for the screen; **3**○ FIG **c'est du ~** it's just play-acting; **arrête ton ~** (faire semblant) cut out the play-acting; (faire un drame) stop making such a fuss○; **se faire tout un ~** to start imagining things.

■ **~ d'animation** animation; **~ d'art et d'essai** (salle) cinema showing art films GB, art house US; (genre) art films (*pl*); **le ~ muet** silent films (*pl*); **le ~ parlant** the talkies○ (*pl*).

cinémathèque /sinematɛk/ *nf* cinematheque.

cinématographique /sinematɔgʀafik/ *adj* film (*épith*) GB, movie (*épith*) US.

cinéphile /sinefil/ *nmf* cinema enthusiast GB ou buff○.

cinéraire /sineʀɛʀ/ *adj* [*urne*] funerary.

cinétique /sinetik/ **I** *adj* kinetic.

II *nf* kinetics (+ *v sg*).

cing(h)alais, **~e** /sɛ̃galɛ, ɛz/ ▶ **338**| **I** *adj* Sinhalese.

II *nm* LING Sinhalese.

cinglant, **~e** /sɛ̃glã, ãt/ *adj* **1** LIT [*vent*] biting; [*pluie*] driving (*épith*); **2** FIG [*remarque*] scathing; [*démenti*] stinging; [*défaite, échec*] crushing, ignominious.

cinglé○, **~e** /sɛ̃gle/ **I** *adj* mad○, crazy○.

II *nm,f* (fou) loony○, nut○; (chauffeur) maniac.

cingler /sɛ̃gle/ [1] **I** *vtr* **1** [*pluie, vent*] to sting [*visage*]; **2** (avec un fouet) to lash.

II *vi* NAUT **~ vers** to head for.

cinoche○ /sinɔʃ/ *nm* **1** (art) cinema GB, pictures○ (*pl*) GB, movies (*pl*) US; **2** (salle) cinema GB, movie theater US.

cinq /sɛ̃k/ ▶ **399**|, **298**|, **156**| *adj inv, pron, nm inv* five.

IDIOMES il a dit les ~ lettres ~ he said a naughty word.

cinquantaine /sɛ̃kãtɛn/ *nf* about fifty; **avoir une ~ d'années** to be about fifty; **la ~ de passagers qui attendaient** the fifty or so passengers who were waiting; **une bonne ~** well over fifty; **nous étions plus d'une ~** there were more than fifty of us.

cinquante /sɛ̃kãt/ ▶ **399**|, **156**| *adj inv, pron* fifty.

cinquantenaire /sɛ̃kãtnɛʀ/ **I** *adj* fifty-year-old (*épith*), fifty years old (*jamais épith*).

II *nm* fiftieth anniversary.

cinquantième /sɛ̃kãtjɛm/ ▶ **399**| *adj* fiftieth.

cinquième /sɛ̃kjɛm/ ▶ **399**|, **156**| **I** *adj, nmf* fifth; ▶ **roue**.

II *nf* SCOL second year of secondary school, age 12–13.

cintre /sɛ̃tʀ/ **I** *nm* **1** (pour vêtement) hanger; **2** ARCHIT curve.

II **cintres** *nmpl* THÉÂT **les ~s** the flies.

cintré, **~e** /sɛ̃tʀe/ *adj* [*manteau*] waisted; [*chemise*] tailored.

cintrer /sɛ̃tʀe/ [1] *vtr* **1** (en couture) to take [sth] in at the waist [*veste*]; **2** ARCHIT to arch [*porte*]; to vault [*galerie*]; **3** TECH to bend [*tuyau*].

cirage /siʀaʒ/ *nm* (produit) (shoe) polish; **~ en crème** shoe cream.

IDIOMES être dans le ~○ (à demi conscient) to be half-conscious, to be out of it○; (désorienté) to be all at sea.

circoncire /siʀkɔ̃siʀ/ [64] *vtr* to circumcise.

circoncision /siʀkɔ̃sizjɔ̃/ *nf* male circumcision.

circonférence /siʀkɔ̃feʀɑ̃s/ *nf* circumference.

circonflexe /siʀkɔ̃flɛks/ *adj* **accent ~** circumflex (accent).

circonscription /siʀkɔ̃skʀipsjɔ̃/ *nf* ADMIN district.

■ **~ électorale** (de député) ~ electoral constituency GB ou district US; (de conseiller, maire) ~ electoral ward.

circonscrire /siʀkɔ̃skʀiʀ/ [67] *vtr* **1** (limiter) to contain [*incendie, épidémie*]; to limit [*sujet, domaine*] (**à** to); **2** (délimiter) to define.

circonspection /siʀkɔ̃spɛksjɔ̃/ *nf* caution (**envers qn** toward(s) sb; **envers qch** about sth); **avec ~** cautiously.

circonstance /siʀkɔ̃stɑ̃s/ **I** *nf* **1** (condition) circumstance; **en raison des ~s** under the circumstances; **2** (situation) situation; **en toute ~** in any event; **en la**

~ in this particular case; **pour la** ~ for the occasion; **être à la hauteur des** ~s to be equal to the occasion.
II de circonstance *loc adj* [*poème*] for the occasion (*after n*); [*blague, programme*] topical; [*sourire, attitude*] artificial; **faire une tête de** ~ to assume a fitting expression.
■ ~**s atténuantes** JUR extenuating circumstances.
circonstanciel, -ielle /siʀkɔ̃stɑ̃sjɛl/ *adj* LING [*complément, proposition*] adverbial.
circonvolution /siʀkɔ̃vɔlysjɔ̃/ *nf* convolution; **décrire des** ~s to twist and turn.
circuit /siʀkɥi/ *nm* **1** SPORT circuit; **2** (de tourisme) tour; **faire le** ~ **des châteaux de la Loire** to tour the Châteaux of the Loire; **ne pas suivre les** ~**s touristiques** to go off the beaten track; **3** (d'activité) circuit; ~ **économique** economic process; **être mis hors** ~ [*personne*] to be put on the sidelines; **remettre qch dans le** ~ to put sth back into circulation; **vivre en** ~ **fermé** to live in a closed world; **4** TECH circuit.
■ ~ **d'alimentation** feed system; ~ **hydraulique** hydraulic system; ~ **imprimé** printed circuit; ~ **intégré** integrated circuit.
circulaire /siʀkylɛʀ/ *adj, nf* circular.
circulation /siʀkylasjɔ̃/ *nf* **1** (de véhicules) traffic; **rue interdite à la** ~ street closed to traffic; **faire la** ~ [*agent*] to be on traffic duty; (en cas d'accident) to direct traffic; **2** (déplacement, échange) circulation; **la libre** ~ **des personnes, des marchandises et des capitaux** the free movement of people, goods and capital; **être en** ~ [*billets, produit*] to be in circulation; [*bateau*] to be in operation; [*train*] to be running; **mettre en** ~ to put [sth] into circulation [*billets, produit, modèle*]; **disparaître de la** ~ LIT, FIG [*personne, produit*] to disappear from circulation; **retirer de la** ~ to withdraw [sth] from circulation [*billet, produit*]; **3** (d'air, de gaz, sang) circulation; **avoir une mauvaise** ~ to have poor circulation.
circulatoire /siʀkylatwaʀ/ *adj* [*troubles*] circulatory.
circuler /siʀkyle/ [1] *vi* **1** (être en service) [*train, bus*] to run; [*bateau*] to operate; **'ne circule pas le dimanche'** (train, bus) 'does not run on Sundays'; **2** (aller d'un lieu à un autre) to get around; (sans but précis) to move about; (être en voiture) to travel; **circulez, il n'y a rien à voir!** move along, there's nothing to see!; **3** (se répandre) [*rumeur, plaisanterie, idée*] to circulate, to go around ou about; **faire** ~ to circulate [*information, idée*]; to spread, to put about [*rumeur*]; **4** (être distribué) [*marchandises, billets, journal*] to circulate; **5** [*sang, air*] to circulate; **faire** ~ to circulate.
cire /siʀ/ *nf* wax; **en** ~ wax (*épith*).
■ ~ **d'abeilles** beeswax; ~ **à cacheter** sealing wax.
ciré /siʀe/ *nm* oilskin.
cirer /siʀe/ [1] *vtr* to polish [*chaussures, parquet*].
IDIOMES ~ **les pompes**○ **de qn** to suck up to sb○.
cireuse[1] /siʀøz/ *nf* (appareil) (floor) polisher.
cireux, -euse[2] /siʀø, øz/ *adj* [*aspect*] waxen; [*consistance*] waxy.
cirque /siʀk/ *nm* **1** (spectacle) circus; **un numéro de** ~ a circus act; **2**○ (chahut) racket○; (désordre) shambles○ (*sg*); **arrête ton** ~! stop your nonsense!; **c'est le** ~ **pour se garer à Oxford** it's a real performance parking in Oxford; **3** (dans l'Antiquité) **les jeux du** ~ circus games.
cirrhose /siʀoz/ ▶ **196** *nf* cirrhosis.
■ ~ **du foie** cirrhosis of the liver.
cisaille /sizaj/ *nf* (de jardinier, d'orfèvre) pair of shears; ~**s** shears.
cisailler /sizaje/ [1] *vtr* **1** (avec une cisaille) to shear [*tôle*]; to cut [*câble*]; **2** (par usure) to shear off.
ciseau, pl ~**x** /sizo/ **I** *nm* **1** TECH chisel; **2** SPORT (saut) scissors jump; (prise de lutte) scissors hold.
II ciseaux *nmpl* scissors (*pl*); (gros et robustes) shears; **saut en** ~**x** scissors jump; **tailler à grands coups de** ~**x** to cut boldly.

ciseler /sizle/ [17] *vtr* TECH to chase [*métal*]; to chisel [*bois, pierre*].
ciselure /sizlyʀ/ *nf* (de métal) chasing; (de pierre, bois) carving.
Cisjordanie /sisʒɔʀdani/ ▶ **509** *nprf* **la** ~ the West Bank (of Jordan).
cistercien, -ienne /sistɛʀsjɛ̃, ɛn/ *adj, nm,f* Cistercian.
citadelle /sitadɛl/ *nf* LIT, FIG citadel.
citadin, ~e /sitadɛ̃, in/ **I** *adj* city (*épith*).
II *nm,f* city-dweller.
citation /sitasjɔ̃/ *nf* GÉN quotation.
cité /site/ *nf* **1** (ville) city; (plus petite) town; (antique) city; **2** (ensemble de logements) housing estate; ▶ **dortoir II**.
■ **la** ~ **des Papes** Avignon; ~ **universitaire** student halls (*pl*) of residence GB, dormitories (*pl*) US.
cité-jardin, pl cités-jardins /siteʒaʀdɛ̃/ *nf* garden city GB, planned town US.
citer /site/ [1] *vtr* **1** (rapporter exactement) to quote [*personne, phrase, passage*]; **je cite** I quote; **2** (mentionner) to name [*titre, œuvre*]; to cite [*personne, exemple, chiffres*]; **3** JUR to summon [*témoin*]; **être cité en justice** to be issued with a summons.
citerne /sitɛʀn/ *nf* tank.
cithare /sitaʀ/ ▶ **392** *nf* zither.
citoyen, -enne /sitwajɛ̃, ɛn/ *nm,f* citizen.
citoyenneté /sitwajɛnte/ *nf* citizenship.
citron /sitʀɔ̃/ **I** ▶ **141** *adj inv* **(jaune)** ~ lemon (yellow).
II *nm* **1** BOT, CULIN lemon; **goût de** ~ lemony taste; **2**○ (tête) **il n'a rien dans le** ~ he isn't all there○.
■ ~ **givré** lemon sorbet (*served inside a lemon*); ~ **vert** lime.
IDIOMES **presser qn comme un** ~○ to squeeze sb dry○; **se presser le** ~○ to rack one's brains.
citronnade /sitʀonad/ *nf* lemon squash GB, lemonade US.
citronné, ~e /sitʀone/ *adj* [*odeur*] lemony; [*crème*] lemon(-flavoured GB).
citronnelle /sitʀonɛl/ *nf* BOT citronella.
citronnier /sitʀonje/ *nm* lemon tree.
citrouille /sitʀuj/ *nf* **1** BOT, CULIN pumpkin; **2**○ (tête) head.
IDIOMES **avoir la tête comme une** ~○ to feel as if one's head was going to burst.
civet /sivɛ/ *nm* ~ stew; ~ **de lièvre** jugged hare *₵*.
civière /sivjɛʀ/ *nf* stretcher.
civil, ~e /sivil/ **I** *adj* (non militaire) civilian; (non religieux) [*mariage*] civil; [*enterrement*] non religious; (non pénal) civil.
II *nm* (personne) civilian; **se mettre en** ~ [*soldat*] to dress in civilian clothes; [*policier*] to dress in plain clothes; **dans le** ~ in civilian life.
civilisation /sivilizasjɔ̃/ *nf* civilization.
civiliser /sivilize/ [1] *vtr* LIT, FIG to civilize.
II se civiliser *vpr* to become civilized.
civique /sivik/ *adj* civic; **avoir l'esprit** ~ to have a sense of civic responsibility; **instruction** or **éducation** ~ civics (+ *v sg*).
clac /klak/ *nm* (de porte) slam; (de piège) snap; (de fouet) crack.
claie /klɛ/ *nf* **1** (à fromages, fruits) wicker rack; **2** (clôture) hurdle.
clair, ~e[1] /klɛʀ/ **I** *adj* **1** (pâle) [*couleur*] light; [*teint*] (rosé) fair; (frais) fresh; **avoir les yeux** ~**s** (bleus) to have pale blue-grey GB ou blue-gray US eyes; **2** (lumineux) [*logement, pièce*] light; **3** MÉTÉO [*nuit, temps*] clear; **par temps** ~ (de jour) on a clear day; **4** (limpide) clear; **à l'eau** ~**e** [*rincer*] in clear water; **5** (intelligible) [*texte, idées*] clear; **suis-je** ~? do I make myself clear?; **6** (sans équivoque) [*message, décision*] clear; **il faut que les choses soient (bien)** ~**es** let's get things straight; **c'est** ~ **net et précis** it's absolutely clear; **passer le plus** ~ **de son temps** to

spend most of one's time (**à faire** doing; **dans** in);
7 (pas touffu) [*forêt, blé*] sparse.

II *adv* **il faisait** ~ it was already light; **il fait** ~ **très
tôt** it gets light very early; **il fait** ~ **très tard** it stays
light very late; **voir** ~ LIT to see well; **j'aimerais y
voir** ~ **dans cette histoire** FIG I'd like to get to the
bottom of this story; **parler** ~ FIG to speak clearly.

III *nm* **1** (clarté) light; **en** ~ TV unscrambled; MIL, ORDI-
NAT in clear; (pour parler clairement) to put it clearly;
mettre ses idées au ~ FIG to get one's ideas straight;
tirer une affaire au ~ to get to the bottom of things;
2 (couleur) light colours^{GB} (*pl*).

■ ~ **de lune** moonlight.

IDIOMES **c'est** ~ **comme de l'eau de roche** it's crystal clear.

claire² /klɛʀ/ *nf* (bassin) oyster bed; **fine de** ~ CULIN
claire oyster.

clairement /klɛʀmɑ̃/ *adv* clearly.

clairet /klɛʀɛ/ *nm* (vin) light red wine.

claire-voie, *pl* **claires-voies** /klɛʀvwa/ *nf* à ~
[*volets, porte*] openwork.

clairière /klɛʀjɛʀ/ *nf* clearing, glade.

clairon /klɛʀɔ̃/ **▶ 392** *nm* **1** (instrument) bugle; **sonner
du** ~ to sound the bugle; **2** (personne) bugler.

claironnant, **~e** /klɛʀɔnɑ̃, ɑ̃t/ *adj* [*voix*] strident.

claironner /klɛʀɔne/ [1] *vtr* to shout [sth] from the
rooftops.

clairsemé, **~e** /klɛʀsəme/ *adj* [*arbres, maisons*] scattered; [*cheveux, public, foule*] thin.

clairvoyance /klɛʀvwajɑ̃s/ *nf* perceptiveness.

clairvoyant, **~e** /klɛʀvwajɑ̃, ɑ̃t/ *adj* FIG [*personne*]
perceptive.

clamer /klame/ [1] *vtr* to proclaim (**que** that); ~
haut et fort son soutien to loudly proclaim one's
support.

clameur /klamœʀ/ *nf* roar.

clan /klɑ̃/ *nm* LIT, FIG clan; **esprit de** ~ clan mentality,
clannishness.

clandestin, **~e** /klɑ̃dɛstɛ̃, in/ *adj* [*organisation,
journal*] underground (*épith*); [*immigration, commerce,
travail*] illegal; [*prostitution*] clandestine; **passager**
~ stowaway.

clandestinement /klɑ̃dɛstinmɑ̃/ *adv* (illégalement)
illegally.

clandestinité /klɑ̃dɛstinite/ *nf* (d'activité, organisation)
secret ou clandestine nature; **atmosphère de** ~
atmosphere of secrecy; **dans la** ~ [*passer, se réfugier*] underground; [*vivre*] in hiding; [*opérer*] in secret;
sortir de la ~ to come out into the open; **travailler
dans la** ~ to work illegally.

clap /klap/ *nm* clapperboard.

clapet /klapɛ/ *nm* **1** (soupape) valve; **2**° (bouche)
mouth, trap°.

clapier /klapje/ *nm* rabbit hutch.

clapoter /klapɔte/ [1] *vi* to lap.

clapotis /klapɔti/ *nm inv* lapping (**de** of).

claquage /klakaʒ/ *nm* pulled ou strained muscle; **se
faire un** ~ to pull a muscle.

claque¹ /klak/ *nm* (chapeau) (**chapeau**) ~ opera hat.

claque² /klak/ *nf* **1** (gifle) slap; **donner une** ~ **à qn**
to slap sb; **recevoir une** ~ to get a slap; **2**° (humiliation) slap in the face; (échec) beating; **se prendre une
~ aux élections** to take a beating at the elections;
3 THÉÂT claque.

IDIOMES **en avoir sa ~** to be fed up (to the back
teeth° GB).

claqué°, **~e** /klake/ *adj* (épuisé) knackered° GB, done
in°.

claquement /klakmɑ̃/ *nm* (de porte, fenêtre) bang; (de
fouet) crack; (de tonnerre) clap; (de langue, talons) click;
(répété) (de porte, fenêtre) banging **₵**; (de bannière, voile)
flapping **₵**; **le** ~ **des sabots** (de personne) the
clatter(ing) of clogs; (de chevaux) the clip-clop of hooves.

claquemurer: **se claquemurer** /klakmyʀe/ [1] *vpr*
to shut oneself away (**dans** in).

claquer /klake/ [1] **I** *vtr* **1** (fermer) to slam [*porte*]; ~

la porte au nez de qn LIT, FIG to slam the door in sb's
face; **partir** or **sortir en claquant la porte** LIT to storm
out slamming the door behind one; **ils sont partis en
claquant la porte** (pendant des négociations) they walked
out closing the door on further negotiations; **2**° (épuiser) to exhaust, to wear [sb] out [*personne*]; **3**° (dépenser) to blow° [*argent, paie*].

II *vi* **1** (faire un bruit) [*porte, volet*] to bang; [*coup de feu*]
to ring out; [*bannière, voile*] to flap; (se fermer) [*porte*]
to slam shut; **faire** ~ **la porte** to slam the door; **faire
~ son fouet** to crack one's whip; **2** (avec une partie du
corps) ~ **des doigts** to snap one's fingers; ~ **des
talons** MIL to click one's heels; ~ **des mains** to clap
(one's hands); **elle claque des dents** her teeth are
chattering; **faire** ~ **sa langue** to click one's tongue.

III **se claquer** *vpr* **1** (se distendre) **se** ~ **un muscle**
to pull ou strain a muscle; **2**° (s'épuiser) to wear
oneself out (**à faire** doing).

claquettes /klakɛt/ *nfpl* tap dancing (*sg*); **faire des
~** to tap dance.

clarifier /klaʀifje/ [2] *vtr* **1** FIG to clarify [*position, situation, débat*]; **2** LIT to clarify [*mélange, beurre*].

clarinette /klaʀinɛt/ **▶ 392** *nf* clarinet.

clarinettiste /klaʀinetist/ *nmf* clarinettist.

clarté /klaʀte/ *nf* **1** (lumière) light; **2** (de l'eau, du verre)
clarity; (de teint) fairness; **3** FIG (de style, d'exposé)
clarity; **avec** ~ clearly.

classe /klas/ *nf* **1** SCOL (groupe d'élèves) class, form GB;
(niveau) year, form GB, grade US; **redoubler une** ~ to
repeat a year; **passer dans la** ~ **supérieure** to go up
a year; **2** SCOL (cours) class, lesson; **les élèves de Mme
Dupont n'auront pas** ~ Mrs Dupont's class won't be
having any lessons; **après la** ~ after school; **3** SCOL
(salle) classroom; **4** SOCIOL, POL class; **les ~s sociales**
social classes; **une société sans ~s** a classless
society; **5** (catégorie) class (**de** of); **6** (rang) GÉN class;
ADMIN grade; **champagne de première** ~ first-class
champagne; **7** (élégance) class; **avoir de la** ~ to have
class; **c'est pas la ~**°! that's not very stylish!; **8** TOU-
RISME class; **billet de première/seconde** ~ first-/
second-class ou standard GB ticket; **voyager en
première** ~ to travel first class; **9** MIL **faire ses ~s**
LIT to do one's basic training; FIG to start out; **un
cinéaste qui a fait ses ~s à la télévision** FIG a film
director who started out in television.

■ ~ **d'adaptation** special needs class; ~ **d'âge**
age group; ~ **de neige** educational schooltrip in the
mountains including skiing lessons; **~s prépara-
toires** (**aux grandes écoles**) preparatory classes for
entrance to Grandes Écoles.

classement /klasmɑ̃/ *nm* **1** (en catégories) classification (**de** of); **faire un** ~ **alphabétique** to put into
alphabetical order; **2** (rangement) filing (**de** of); **faire
du** ~ **dans ses papiers** to sort one's papers out;
3 (d'élèves, employés) grading (**de** of); ~ **trimestriel** SCOL
termly position (in class); **avoir un mauvais** ~
[*élève*] to be in the bottom half of the class; **4** SPORT
ranking (**de** of); **prendre la tête du** ~ to get first
place; **5** (d'hôtel, de restaurant) rating (**de** of); ~ **deux
étoiles** two-star rating; **6** JUR ~ **d'une affaire** closing
of a case.

classer /klase/ [1] **I** *vtr* **1** (classifier) to classify; ~ **par
ordre alphabétique** to classify in alphabetical order;
~ **des nombres en ordre décroissant** to place
numbers in descending order; **être classé comme
dangereux** to be considered dangerous; **2** (ranger) to
file (away) [*documents*] (**dans** in); **3** JUR, POL to close
[*dossier, affaire*]; **c'est une affaire classée** FIG the
matter is closed; **4** ADMIN to list [*bâtiment*]; ~ **un château monument historique** to list a castle as a historic
monument; **5** (attribuer un rang à) to class [*pays,
élèves*]; to rank [*chanson, joueur*] (**parmi** among); **un
sportif classé au plan international** a world class
sportsman; **un joueur de tennis classé** a ranked ou
seeded tennis player; **non classé** unseeded; **6**° (juger)
to size [sb] up.

II **se classer** *vpr* to rank (**parmi** among); **se** ~
comme le pays le plus pauvre to be listed as the

world's poorest country; **se ~ deuxième** SPORT [*personne*] to rank second.

classeur /klasœʀ/ *nm* **1** (à anneaux) ring binder; (à compartiments) file; **2** (meuble de rangement) filing cabinet.

classicisme /klasisism/ *nm* **1** ART, LITTÉRAT classicism; **2** (conformisme) traditionalism, conservatism.

classification /klasifikasjɔ̃/ *nf* classification (**de** of).

classifier /klasifje/ [2] *vtr* to classify.

classique /klasik/ **I** *adj* **1** (gréco-latin) classical; **la littérature grecque ~** classical Greek literature; **faire des études ~s** SCOL, UNIV to do classics; **2** LING [*langue*] classical; **3** (pour une époque, un genre) classical; **théâtre ~ français** French classical theatre; **4** (consacré) [*auteur, œuvre*] classic; **5** (harmonieux, sobre) classic; **de coupe ~** of classic cut; **6** (courant) [*exemple, histoire, situation*] classic; [*traitement, méthode*] classic, standard; (habituel) [*symptôme, réaction*] classic; [*conséquence*] usual; **c'est ~**○! it's typical!; **c'est le coup ~**○! it's the same old story!; **7** (traditionnel) [*grammaire*] traditional; [*arme*] conventional.

II *nm* **1** (auteur) classical author; **2** (œuvre) classic; **un ~ du genre** a classic of its kind; **je connais mes ~s**○! I know my classics!

classiquement /klasikmɑ̃/ *adv* (de façon traditionnelle) traditionally.

claudicant, ~e /klodikɑ̃, ɑ̃t/ *adj* limping.

claudiquer /klodike/ [1] *vi* to limp.

clause /kloz/ *nf* clause (**sur** on).

claustrer /klostʀe/ [1] **I** *vtr* to confine.

II se claustrer *vpr* to shut oneself away (**dans** in).

claustrophobe /klostʀɔfɔb/ *adj* claustrophobic.

claustrophobie /klostʀɔfɔbi/ *nf* claustrophobia.

clavecin /klavsɛ̃/ ▶ 392| *nm* harpsichord.

claveciniste /klavsinist/ ▶ 374| *nmf* harpsichordist.

clavicule /klavikyl/ *nf* collarbone, clavicle SPÉC.

clavier /klavje/ *nm* (tous contextes) keyboard.

■ **~ numérique** numeric keypad.

claviériste /klavjeʀist/ *nmf* keyboard player.

claviste /klavist/ ▶ 374| *nmf* **1** (imprimeur) typesetter; **2** ORDINAT keyboarder.

clé /kle/ **I** *nf* **1** TECH (de serrure, mécanisme, conserve) key; **la ~ de ma chambre** the key to my bedroom; **laisser la ~ sur la porte** to leave the key in the door ou lock; **sous ~** under lock and key; **fermer à ~** to lock; **projet ~ en main** turnkey project; **solution ~s en main** ready-made solution; **prix ~s en main** AUT on the road price GB, sticker price US; **2** (condition, solution) key (**de** to); **détenir la ~ du bonheur** to know the secret of true happiness; **la ~ des songes** the key to the interpretation of dreams; **roman à ~** roman à clef; **3** (outil) spanner GB, wrench; **4** MUS (de flûte, clarinette) key; (de violon, guitare) peg; (de trompette) valve; (de tambour) tuning screw; (dans une notation) clef; **~ de fa/de sol/d'ut** bass ou F/treble ou G/alto ou C clef; **5** SPORT (prise) armlock; **faire une ~ à qn** to get sb in an armlock.

II (-)**clé** (in compounds) **poste/mot/document(-)~** key post/word/document.

III à la clé *loc adv* (comme enjeu) at stake; MUS in the key-signature; **avec, à la ~, une récompense** with a reward thrown in.

■ **~ d'accès électronique** TÉLÉCOM digital security coding; **~ d'accordeur** MUS tuning key; **~ anglaise** = **~ à molette**; **~ à bougie** AUT plug spanner GB, spark-plug wrench US; **~ de contact** AUT ignition key; **~ à molette** adjustable spanner GB ou wrench US; **~ plate** (de serrage) open end spanner GB ou wrench US; **~ à sardines** CULIN sardine tin key GB, sardine can key US; **~ de sûreté** (de serrure) Yale® key; **~ de voûte** ARCHIT, FIG keystone.

IDIOMES **prendre la ~ des champs** to escape; **mettre la ~ sous la porte** (partir) to leave; (faire faillite) to go bankrupt.

clef = **clé**.

clémence /klemɑ̃s/ *nf* **1** (indulgence) leniency (**envers** to); **2** (de climat) mildness (**de** of).

clément, ~e /klemɑ̃, ɑ̃t/ *adj* **1** [*juge*] lenient (**envers** to), clement SOUT (**envers** to); **se montrer ~** to show clemency (**envers** to); **2** [*température, hiver*] mild, clement SOUT.

clémentine /klemɑ̃tin/ *nf* clementine.

cleptomanie /klɛptɔmani/ *nf* kleptomania.

clerc /klɛʀ/ ▶ 374| *nm* ADMIN, JUR clerk; **~ (de notaire)** notary's clerk; **être (grand) ~ en la matière** to be an expert on the subject.

clergé /klɛʀʒe/ *nm* clergy.

clérical, ~e, *mpl* **-aux** /kleʀikal, o/ *adj* **1** [*vie, fonction*] clerical; **2** [*parti, presse*] that supports the Church (*épith, après n*).

cliché /kliʃe/ *nm* **1** PHOT (négatif) negative; (photo) snapshot; **prendre un ~** to take a snap; **2** (lieu commun) cliché; **3** (d'imprimerie) plate.

client, ~e /klijɑ̃, ɑ̃t/ *nm,f* (de magasin) customer; (d'avocat, de notaire) client; (d'hôtel) guest, patron; (de taxi) passenger, fare; **être ~ d'un magasin** to be a regular customer in a shop GB ou store US.

IDIOMES **c'est à la tête du ~** it depends whether they like the look of you.

clientèle /klijɑ̃tɛl/ *nf* **1** (de magasin, restaurant) customers (*pl*); (d'avocat, de notaire) clients (*pl*); (de médecin) patients (*pl*); **avoir une bonne ~** [*magasin, restaurant*] to have a lot of customers; [*avocat, médecin*] to have a large practice; **se faire une ~** to build up a clientele; **ils ont une ~ d'entreprises** they deal with firms; **2** (habitude d'achat) custom; (à plus grande échelle) business; **je vais lui retirer ma ~** I'll take my custom elsewhere, I'll take my business elsewhere.

clignement /klijnəmɑ̃/ *nm* **~** blinking ¢.

cligner: **cligner de** /kliɲe/ [1] *vtr ind* **~ des yeux** (plisser les yeux) to screw up one's eyes; (battre des paupières) to blink; **~ de l'œil** to wink.

clignotant, ~e /kliɲɔtɑ̃, ɑ̃t/ **I** *adj* flashing.

II *nm* AUT (pour tourner) indicator GB, turn signal US, blinker US; **mettre son ~** to indicate GB ou signal.

clignoter /kliɲɔte/ [1] *vi* [*lumière*] (une fois) to flash; (longtemps) to flash on and off; [*étoile*] to twinkle.

climat /klima/ *nm* MÉTÉO, GÉOG, FIG climate; **sous d'autres ~s** LITER in other climes.

climatique /klimatik/ *adj* climatic.

climatisation /klimatizasjɔ̃/ *nf* air-conditioning.

climatiser /klimatize/ [1] *vtr* (maintenir la température de) to air-condition [*pièce*]; (équiper) to install air-conditioning in [*maison*]; **hôtel climatisé** air-conditioned hotel.

climatiseur /klimatizœʀ/ *nm* air-conditioner.

climatologie /klimatɔlɔʒi/ *nf* climatology.

clin /klɛ̃/ *nm* **~ d'œil** LIT wink; FIG allusion; **faire un ~ d'œil à qn** LIT to wink at sb; **en un ~ d'œil** in a flash, in the wink of an eye LITTÉR.

clinicien, -ienne /klinisjɛ̃, ɛn/ *nm,f* clinician.

clinique /klinik/ **I** *adj* clinical.

II *nf* **1** (établissement) private hospital; **2** (médecine) clinical medecine.

■ **~ vétérinaire** veterinary clinic.

clinquant, ~e /klɛ̃kɑ̃, ɑ̃t/ *adj* flashy○.

clip /klip/ *nm* **1** (vidéoclip) videoclip; **2** (bijou) (broche) clip brooch; (boucle d'oreille) clip-on.

clique /klik/ *nf* (groupe) clique.

IDIOMES **prendre ses ~s et ses claques**○ to pack up and go.

cliquer /klike/ [1] *vi* ORDINAT to click (**sur** on).

cliqueter /klikte/ [20] *vi* [*clés*] to jingle; [*chaîne*] to rattle; [*mécanisme*] to go clickety-clack; [*aiguilles à tricoter*] to click.

cliquetis /klikti/ *nm inv* (d'aiguilles à tricoter) clicking; (d'épée) rattle; (de couverts) clinking.

clitoris /klitɔʀis/ *nm inv* clitoris.

clivage /klivaʒ/ *nm* GÉN, POL (division) divide (**entre** between); **le ~ Nord-Sud** the North-South divide; **~ d'opinion** division of opinion.

cloaque /klɔak/ *nm* **1** FIG cesspit; **2** ZOOL cloaca.

clochard, ~e /klɔʃaʀ, aʀd/ *nm,f* tramp.

clochardiser: **se clochardiser** /klɔʃaʀdize/ [1] *vpr* to be reduced to vagrancy.

cloche /klɔʃ/ *nf* **1** (instrument sonore) bell; **on a entendu dix coups de ~** we heard the bell ring ten times; **en (forme de) ~** bell-shaped; ▶ **déménager**; **2** (ustensile de jardinage) cloche; **3**○ (imbécile) clot○ GB, clod○, idiot; **4**○ (clochard) tramp; **la ~** the down-and-outs (*pl*).
■ **~ à fromage** cover of cheese dish.
IDIOMES **se taper la ~**○ to have a good *ou* slap-up GB meal, to pig out○; **entendre plusieurs sons de ~** to hear several different versions; **sonner les ~s**○ à qn to bawl sb out○; **se faire sonner les ~s**○ to get bawled out○.

cloche-pied: **à cloche-pied** /aklɔʃpje/ *loc adv* **sauter à ~** to hop.

clocher[1]○ /klɔʃe/ [1] *vi* (être défectueux) [*argumentation*] to be faulty; **il y a quelque chose qui cloche dans** there's something wrong with.

clocher[2] /klɔʃe/ *nm* **1** (d'église) (en pointe) steeple; (tour) church *ou* bell tower; **2** FIG (pays natal) home town; **esprit de ~** parochial *ou* small-town mentality; **querelle de ~** local quarrel.

clocheton /klɔʃtɔ̃/ *nm* **1** (ornement) pinnacle; **2** (petit clocher) little steeple.

clochette /klɔʃɛt/ *nf* **1** (petite cloche) (little) bell; **2** (fleur) bell.

cloison /klwazɔ̃/ *nf* **1** CONSTR partition; (mobile de bureau) screen; **étanche** LIT watertight bulkhead; FIG watertight compartment; **2** FIG (barrière) barrier (**entre** between).
■ **~ extensible** folding room-divider.

cloisonnement /klwazɔnmɑ̃/ *nm* (d'administration, de services) compartmentalization; **les ~s entre** the barriers between [*services, groupes*].

cloisonner /klwazɔne/ [1] *vtr* **1** CONSTR to partition [*pièce*]; to divide up [*espace*]; **2** FIG to divide up [*société*]; to compartmentalize [*secteurs, administration*]; to erect barriers between [*groupes*].

cloître /klwɑtʀ/ *nm* cloister.

cloîtrer /klwɑtʀe/ [1] **I** *vtr* (enfermer) to shut [sb] away.
II se cloîtrer *vpr* (s'enfermer) to shut oneself away; **se ~ dans le silence** to retreat into silence.

clone /klon/ *nm* clone.

clope○ /klɔp/ *nm ou f* fag○ GB, ciggy○, cigarette.

clopin-clopant○ /klɔpɛ̃klɔpɑ̃/ *loc adv* **1** (en boitant) **marcher ~** to hobble along; **partir ~** to hobble off; **2** (mal) **aller ~** [*économie, affaires*] to limp along.

clopinettes○ /klɔpinɛt/ *nfpl* **gagner des ~** to earn peanuts○.

cloporte /klɔpɔʀt/ *nm* woodlouse; **des ~s** woodlice.
IDIOMES **vivre comme un ~**○ to live like a hermit.

cloque /klɔk/ *nf* (sur la peau, de la peinture) blister.
IDIOMES **être en ~**⁹ to be up the spout○ GB, to be knocked up⁹, to be pregnant.

clore /klɔʀ/ [79] **I** *vtr* **1** (mettre fin à) to close [*débat, scrutin, compte*] (**par** with); **2** (être la fin de) to end, to conclude [*congrès*]; to end [*roman*]; **un dîner a clos le congrès** the conference ended with a dinner; **3** (fermer) LITER to close [*yeux*]; to block, to seal off [*passage*]; to seal [*enveloppe*]; **4** (enclore) to enclose [*terrain*] (**de** with); **5** (conclure) to conclude [*accord*].
II se clore *vpr* (se terminer) to end (**par** with).

clos, **~e** /klo, oz/ **I** *adj* (fermé) **monde ~** FIG self-contained world; **à la nuit ~e** LITER after nightfall.
II *nm inv* (terrain) fenced *ou* enclosed field.

clôture /klotyʀ/ *nf* **1** (barrière) (de bois) fence; (de fil de fer) wire fence; (de grillage) chain-link *ou* wire-mesh fence; (grille) railings (*pl*); (haie) hedge; **~ électrique** electric fence; **mur de ~** enclosing wall; **poser une ~ autour d'un terrain** to fence in *ou* enclose a field; **2** (de débat, scrutin) close; (de souscription) closing; (de magasin, bureau) closing; (de saison) close; **discours de ~** closing speech; **~ des inscriptions le 3 mai à midi** closing date for registration, noon on 3 May.

clôturer /klotyʀe/ [1] **I** *vtr* **1** (enclore) to enclose, to fence in [*terrain*]; **~ avec du fil de fer barbelé** to

surround [sth] with barbed wire; **2** (terminer) [*personne*] to close [*débat, liste, compte*]; [*discours, cérémonie*] to end, to bring [sth] to a close [*débat, festival*].
II *vi* FIN **~ à 3 francs** to close at 3 francs; **~ à la hausse/baisse** to close up/down.
III se clôturer *vpr* [*congrès*] to end (**par** with).

clou /klu/ **I** *nm* **1** TECH nail; **ceinture à ~s** studded belt; **2** (attraction) (de spectacle) star attraction; (de soirée) high point; **3** (furoncle) boil; **4**○ (mont-de-piété) **mettre qch au ~** to take sth to the pawnshop.
II clous *nmpl* **1** (passage pour piétons) pedestrian crossing (*sg*) GB, crosswalk (*sg*) US; **2**⁹ (rien) **des ~s!** no way!
■ **~ de girofle** BOT, CULIN clove.
IDIOMES **enfoncer le ~** to drive the point home; **ne pas valoir un ~**○ not to be worth a thing.

clouer /klue/ [1] *vtr* **1** (fixer avec de gros clous) to nail down [*caisse*]; to nail up [*pancarte*]; to tack together [*planches*]; **2** (fixer avec de petits clous) to tack [*moquette, affiche*]; **3** (immobiliser) **~ au sol** to pin [sb] down [*adversaire*]; **les avions sont restés cloués au sol** the planes were grounded; **4** (invalider) **~ au lit/chez soi** to confine [sb] to bed/to one's home.

clouté, **~e** /klute/ *adj* studded (**de** with); **passage ~** pedestrian crossing GB, crosswalk US.

clown /klun/ *nm* clown; **quel ~!** FIG what a co-median!; **faire le ~** to clown about.

clownerie /klunʀi/ *nf* **~s** clowning Ɛ; **arrête tes ~s** stop clowning about.

club /klœb/ *nm* (société, local) club; FIG (groupe) group.
■ **~ de vacances** holiday camp.

cm (*written abbr = centimètre*) cm; **cm²** (centimètre carré) cm²; **cm³** (centimètre cube) GÉN cm³; (moteurs) cc.

CM /seɛm/ *nm*: *abbr* ▶ **cours**.

CNED /knɛd/ *nm*: *abbr* ▶ **centre**.

CNPF /seɛnpeɛf/ *nm* (*abbr = Conseil national du patronat français*) national council of French employers.

CNRS /seɛnɛʀɛs/ *nm* (*abbr = Centre national de la recherche scientifique*) national centre for scientific research.

coaccusé, **~e** /koakyze/ *nm,f* codefendant.

coactionnaire /koaksjɔnɛʀ/ *nmf* joint shareholder.

coagulant, **~e** /kɔagylɑ̃, ɑ̃t/ **I** *adj* coagulative.
II *nm* coagulant.

coagulation /kɔagylasjɔ̃/ *nf* coagulation.

coaguler /kɔagyle/ [1] *vi*, **se coaguler** *vpr* [*sang*] to coagulate; [*lait*] to curdle.

coalisé, **~e** /kɔalize/ *adj* [*forces, pays, partis*] allied; [*intérêts*] combined.

coaliser: **se coaliser** /kɔalize/ [1] *vpr* GÉN to unite; POL to form a coalition; **se ~ contre la misère/pollution** to unite to combat poverty/pollution.

coalition /kɔalisjɔ̃/ *nf* coalition.

coaltar○ /kɔltaʀ/ *nm* **être dans le ~** to be in a daze.

coasser /kɔase/ [1] *vi* to croak.

cobalt /kɔbalt/ *nm* cobalt; **bleu ~** cobalt blue.

cobaye /kɔbaj/ *nm* LIT, FIG guinea pig.

cobra /kɔbʀa/ *nm* cobra.

coca /kɔka/ **I** *nm* BOT (arbuste) coca.
II *nm ou f* (extrait) coca extract.

cocagne /kɔkaɲ/ *nf* **mât de ~** ~ greasy pole; **pays de ~** land of Cockaigne.

cocaïne /kɔkain/ *nf* cocaine.

cocaïnomane /kɔkainɔman/ *nmf* cocaine addict.

cocarde /kɔkaʀd/ *nf* (sur uniforme) cockade; (emblème national) (sur un avion) roundel; (sur un véhicule) official badge; **~ tricolore** HIST revolutionary cockade; (en tissu) rosette.

cocasse /kɔkas/ *adj* comical.

cocasserie /kɔkasʀi/ *nf* (de propos) comical nature.

coccinelle /kɔksinɛl/ *nf* **1** (insecte) ladybird, ladybug US; **2**○ (voiture) beetle, Volkswagen® car.

coccyx /kɔksis/ *nm inv* coccyx.

coche /kɔʃ/ *nm* (diligence) (stage)coach.

IDIOMES **manquer le ~** to miss the boat.

cocher¹ /kɔʃe/ [1] *vtr* to tick GB, to check US.

cocher² /kɔʃe/ *nm* (de diligence) coachman; (de fiacre) cabman.

cochère /kɔʃɛʀ/ *adj f* **porte ~** carriage entrance.

cochon, -onne /kɔʃɔ̃, ɔn/ I° *adj* **1** (pornographique) [*film, magazine*] dirty; [*personne*] dirty-minded; **2** (malpropre) [*personne*] messy, dirty.
II° *nm,f* **1** (personne malpropre) PEJ pig°, slob°; **travail de ~** botched job; **2** (personne lubrique) sex maniac; **espèce de vieux ~!** you dirty old man!; **tu n'es qu'une cochonne** you've got a mind like a sewer.
III *nm* **1** ZOOL pig, hog; ▸ **confiture, perle**; **2** CULIN pork.
■ **~ d'Inde** ZOOL Guinea pig; **~ de lait** AGRIC, CULIN sucking pig.
IDIOMES **travailler comme un ~°** to make a mess of a job; **il ira loin, si les petits ~s ne le mangent pas** he'll go far, if nothing gets in his way; **un ~ n'y retrouverait pas ses petits** it's like a pigsty, it's a real shambles°.

cochonnaille° /kɔʃɔnɑj/ *nf*: products made from pork such as salami, bacon, pâté and ham.

cochonnerie° /kɔʃɔnʀi/ *nf* **1** (chose de mauvaise qualité) junk° ⊄; **il ne mange que des ~s** he only eats junk food; **c'est de la ~ ce stylo** this pen is crap° ou useless; **2** (saleté) mess ⊄; **faire des ~s** to make a mess; **3** (obscénité) obscenity; **dire des ~s** to say smutty° ou dirty things.

cochonnet /kɔʃɔnɛ/ *nm* **1** ZOOL piglet; **2** (à la pétanque) jack.

cocker /kɔkɛʀ/ *nm* (cocker) spaniel.

cocktail /kɔktɛl/ *nm* **1** (boisson) cocktail; (plat composé) **~ de fruits** fruit cocktail; **2** FIG (mélange) mixture; **3** (réception) cocktail party.
■ **~ Molotov** Molotov cocktail.

coco /koko/ *nm* **1** (noix) coconut; **huile de ~** coconut oil; **2°** (terme d'affection) darling; **3°** (individu) **c'est un drôle de ~ celui-là!** that guy's a bit of an oddball°; **4°** (communiste) PEJ commie° PEJ, red° PEJ.

cocon /kɔkɔ̃/ *nm* LIT, FIG cocoon.
IDIOMES **s'enfermer dans son ~** to withdraw into one's shell.

cocorico /kɔkɔʀiko/ *nm* (*also onomat*) cock-a-doodle-do.

cocotier /kɔkɔtje/ *nm* coconut palm.
IDIOMES **secouer le ~** to clean out the dead wood.

cocotte /kɔkɔt/ *nf* **1°** (poule) BABY TALK hen; **2°** (terme d'affection) **ma ~** honey; **3°** † PEJ (femme) loose woman; **4** CULIN (récipient) casserole dish GB, pot; **cuire qch à la ~** to casserole GB ou stew sth.
■ **~ en papier** paper hen (or *origami style*).

cocotte-minute®, *pl* **cocottes-minute** /kɔkɔtminyt/ *nf* pressure cooker.

cocotter° /kɔkɔte/ [1] *vi* to stink, to pong° GB.

cocu°, ~e /kɔky/ *nm,f* LIT deceived husband/wife; FIG dupe.

codage /kɔdaʒ/ *nm* coding, encoding.

code /kɔd/ I *nm* **1** (recueil) code; **~ de déontologie** code of practice; **2** (conventions) code; **3** (écriture, message) code; **~ chiffré** number code; **4** ORDINAT code; **~ de contrôle d'erreur** error-checking code.
II **codes** *nmpl* (phares) dipped GB ou dimmed US (head)lights, low beam (*sg*); **se mettre en ~s** to dip GB ou dim US one's headlights.
■ **~ (à) barres** COMM bar code; **~ civil** JUR civil code; **~ confidentiel (d'identification)** personal identification number, PIN; **~ génétique** BIOL genetic code; **~ de la nationalité** regulations (*pl*) as to nationality; **~ pénal** JUR penal code; **~ postal** post code GB, zip code US; **~ de la route** highway code GB, rules (*pl*) of the road US; **passer son ~°** AUT to take the written part of a driving test.

coder /kɔde/ [1] *vtr* to code, to encode.

codétenu, ~e /kodetny/ *nm,f* fellow prisoner.

codifier /kɔdifje/ [2] *vtr* to codify [*lois*]; to standardize [*langue, usage*].

codirecteur, -trice /kodiʀɛktœʀ, tʀis/ *nm,f* (responsable) joint manager; (administrateur) joint director.

coefficient /kɔefisjɑ̃/ *nm* **1** (proportion) ratio; **2** (pourcentage indéterminé) margin; **~ d'erreur** margin of error; **~ de sécurité** safety margin; **3** SCOL, UNIV weighting factor in an exam; **l'anglais a un ~ élevé** English results are heavily weighted; **la chimie est au ~ 4** chemistry results are multiplied by 4; **4** MATH coefficient; PHYS (d'expansion, absorption) coefficient; (d'élasticité, écrasement) modulus.

coentreprise /koɑ̃tʀəpʀiz/ *nf* joint venture.

coéquipier, -ière /koekipje, ɛʀ/ *nm,f* team-mate.

coercitif, -ive /kɔɛʀsitif, iv/ *adj* coercive.

coercition /kɔɛʀsisjɔ̃/ *nf* coercion.

cœur /kœʀ/ I *nm* **1** ANAT heart; **il a le ~ malade** he has a heart condition; **serrer qn sur** or **contre son ~** to hold sb close; **en forme de ~** heart-shaped (*épith*); **avoir mal au ~** to feel sick GB ou nauseous US; **lever** or **soulever le ~ de qn** to make sb feel sick GB ou nauseous US; ▸ **accrocher, joie, loin**; **2** CULIN heart; **~s de poulets** chicken hearts; **~ de palmier** palm heart; **3** FIG (de fruit, roche, matière, réacteur) core; (de problème, région, bâtiment) heart; (d'arbre) heartwood; **au ~ de** (de région, ville) in the middle of; (de bâtiment, problème, système) at the heart of; **au ~ de l'été** in the height of summer; **au ~ de l'hiver/la nuit** in the dead of winter/night; **4** (personne) **un ~ simple** a simple soul; **mon (petit) ~** sweetheart; **5** (siège des émotions) heart; **agir selon son ~** to follow one's heart; **écouter son ~** to go by feelings; **aller droit au ~ de qn** [*attentions, bienveillance*] to touch sb deeply; [*attaque, remarque*] to cut sb to the quick; **avoir un coup de ~ pour qch** to fall in love with sth; **faire mal au ~** to be heartbreaking; **ça me fait mal au ~ de voir** it makes me sick at heart to see; **ça me fait chaud au ~ de voir** it does my heart good to see; **mon ~ se serre quand...** I feel a pang when...; **problème de ~** emotional problem; ▸ **gros**; **6** (être intime) heart; **venir du ~** to come from the heart; **je suis de tout ~ avec vous** my heart goes out to you; **aimer qn de tout son ~** to love sb dearly; **parler à ~ ouvert** to speak openly; **7** (siège de la bonté) **avoir bon ~** to be kind-hearted; **ton bon ~ te perdra** you're too generous; **ne pas avoir de ~** to be heartless; **faire appel au bon ~ de qn** to appeal to sb's better nature; **une personne de ~** a kind-hearted person; ▸ **fortune**; **8** (courage) courage; **le ~ m'a manqué** my courage failed me; **redonner du ~ à qn** to give sb new heart; **9** (énergie) heart; **mettre tout son ~ dans qch/à faire** to put one's heart into sth/into doing; **10** (envie) mood; **je n'ai pas le ~ à plaisanter** I'm not in the mood for jokes; **je n'ai plus le ~ à rien** I don't feel like doing anything any more; ▸ **ouvrir**; **11** JEUX (carte) heart; (couleur) hearts (*pl*); **jouer (du) ~** to play hearts; **trois/dame de ~** three/Queen of hearts.
II **à cœur** *loc adv* **fait** or **moelleux à ~** [*fromage*] fully ripe; **avoir à ~ de faire** to be intent on doing; **prendre qch à ~** (être résolu) to take sth seriously.
III **de bon cœur** *loc adv* willingly; **pas de bon ~** (rather) unwillingly; **'merci!'—'c'est de bon ~'** 'thank you!'—'you're welcome'; **il brossait le sol et y allait de bon ~** he was scrubbing the floor with a will; **rire de bon ~** to laugh heartily.
IV **par cœur** *loc adv* by heart; **connaître qn par ~** to know sb inside out.
IDIOMES **avoir du ~ au ventre°** to be brave; **être beau** or **joli comme un ~** to be as pretty as a picture; **avoir le ~ sur la main** to be open-handed; **il a un ~ gros** or **grand comme ça°** he's very big-hearted; **avoir un ~ de pierre** or **marbre** to have a heart of stone; **il ne le porte pas dans son ~** he's not his favourite GB person EUPH; **le ~ n'y est pas** my/your etc heart isn't in it; **si le ~ t'en dit** if you feel like it; **avoir qch sur le ~** to be resentful about sth.

coexister /koegziste/ [1] *vi* to coexist.

coffrage /kɔfʀaʒ/ *nm* (habillage) box.

coffre /kɔfʀ/ *nm* **1** (meuble) chest; **~ à jouets** toy box; **2** (pour valeurs) GÉN safe; (individuel dans banque) safety deposit box; **la salle des ~s** the strongroom; **3** AUT boot GB, trunk US.

IDIOMES **avoir du ~**° (avoir une voix puissante) to have a powerful voice.

coffre-fort, *pl* **coffres-forts** /kɔfRəfɔR/ *nm* safe.

coffrer° /kɔfRe/ [1] *vtr* (arrêter) **~ qn** to put sb inside°.

coffret /kɔfRɛ/ *nm* **1** (petit coffre) casket; **~ à bijoux** jewellery GB ou jewelry US box; **2** (de disques, cassettes, livres) boxed set.

cofondateur, -trice /kofɔ̃datœR, tRis/ *nm,f* co-founder.

cogérer /koʒeRe/ [14] *vtr* to co-manage.

cogestion /koʒɛstjɔ̃/ *nf* joint management.

cogiter /koʒite/ [1] HUM **I**° *vtr* to dream up [*plan*].
II *vi* to cogitate, to think (**sur** about).

cognac /kɔɲak/ *nm* cognac (*brandy from the Cognac area*).

cognée /kɔɲe/ *nf* (woodman's) axe GB ou ax US.

IDIOMES **jeter le manche après la ~** to throw in the towel.

cogner /kɔɲe/ [1] **I** *vtr* **1** (heurter) (accidentellement) to knock (**contre** against, on); (volontairement) to bang (**contre** against, on); **tu as dû ~ la tasse** you must have given the cup a knock; **2**° (battre) to beat up.
II *vi* **1** (frapper) **~ contre** [*volet*] to bang against; [*branche*] to knock against; [*projectile*] to hit; **ma tête/la pierre est allée ~ contre la vitre** my head/the stone hit the window; **~ à la porte** to bang on the door; **2**° (frapper du poing) [*boxeur, agresseur*] to hit out; **~ dur** or **fort** to hit hard; **ça va ~** there's going to be a brawl; **3**° (être chaud) [*soleil*] to beat down; **ça cogne sur la plage** it's baking (hot) on the beach; **4** (battre) [*cœur, sang*] to pound.
III se cogner *vpr* **1** (se heurter) to bump into something; **se ~ contre** to hit; **se ~ le genou/la tête** to hit ou bump one's knee/head (**contre** on); **se ~ à la tête/au genou** to get a bump on the head/on the knee; **se ~ le pied contre une pierre** to stub one's toe on a stone; **2**° (se battre) to have a punch-up GB, to have a fistfight.

cognitif, -ive /kɔgnitif, iv/ *adj* cognitive.

cohabitation /koabitasjɔ̃/ *nf* **1** living with somebody; **2** POL *situation where the French President is in political opposition to the government.*

cohabiter /koabite/ [1] *vi* [*personnes*] to live together; [*choses*] to coexist.

cohérence /kɔeRɑ̃s/ *nf* **1** (de discours, raisonnement) (logique) coherence; (homogénéité) consistency; (de programme, d'attitude) consistency; **manquer de ~** to be inconsistent; **2** (de molécules, d'éléments) cohesion.

cohérent, -e /kɔeRɑ̃, ɑ̃t/ *adj* [*raisonnement*] (logique) coherent; (homogène) consistent; [*attitude, programme*] consistent.

cohésion /kɔezjɔ̃/ *nf* cohesion.

cohorte /kɔɔRt/ *nf* **1**° (groupe) crowd; **2** MIL cohort.

cohue /kɔy/ *nf* (monde) crowd; (désordre) **c'est la ~** it's a crush ou scramble.

coi, coite /kwa, kwat/ *adj* (silencieux) **rester** or **se tenir ~** to remain quiet; **j'en suis resté ~** it left me speechless.

coiffant, -e /kwafɑ̃, ɑ̃t/ *adj* **gel ~** styling gel.

coiffe /kwaf/ *nf* (couvre-chef) GÉN headgear; (de religieuse) wimple.

coiffer /kwafe/ [1] **I** *vtr* **1** (arranger les cheveux de) **~ qn** (mettre en forme) to do sb's hair; (peigner) to comb sb's hair; **il coiffe ses cheveux en arrière** he combs his hair back; **se faire ~ par qn** to have one's hair done by sb; **elle est bien coiffée** her hair is nicely done; **elle est mal coiffée** her hair is untidy; **elle est coiffée court** she has short hair; **2** (mettre) to put [sth] on [*chapeau, casque*]; **coiffé d'une casquette** wearing a cap; **3** (chapeauter) [*entreprise*] to control; [*personne*] to head.
II se coiffer *vpr* **1** (s'arranger les cheveux) to do one's hair; (se peigner) to comb one's hair; **tu t'es coiffé**

avec un clou! you look as if you've been dragged through a hedge backward(s)°!; **les cheveux frisés se coiffent mal** curly hair is difficult to keep tidy; **2** (se couvrir la tête) **se ~ de qch** to put sth on.

IDIOMES **être né coiffé** to be born with a silver spoon in one's mouth; **~ qn au poteau**° or **sur le fil**° to beat sb by a whisker.

coiffeur, -euse[1] /kwafœR, øz/ **►374**] *nm,f* hairdresser; **aller chez le ~** [*femme*] to go to the hairdresser's, to have one's hair done; [*homme*] to have one's hair cut.

coiffeuse[2] /kwaføz/ *nf* (meuble) dressing table.

coiffure /kwafyR/ *nf* **1** (coupe de cheveux) hairstyle; **faites-moi cette ~** do my hair like that; **2** (profession) hairdressing; **3** (élément de costume) headgear ₵.

coin /kwɛ̃/ **I** *nm* **1** (angle) corner; **un ~ de table** the corner of a table; **à tous les ~s de rue** everywhere, all over the place; **un placard qui fait le ~** a corner cupboard; **les ~s et les recoins** the nooks and crannies; **aux quatre ~s de la ville** all over the town; **j'ai dû poser mon sac dans un ~** I must have put my bag down somewhere; **assis au ~ du feu** sitting by the fire; **une causerie au ~ du feu** a fireside chat; **►petit**; **2** (extrémité) (d'œil, de bouche) corner; **regarder qch/qn du ~ de l'œil**° to watch sth/ sb out of the corner of one's eye; **un sourire en ~** a half-smile; **un regard en ~** (sournois) a sidelong glance; **3** (morceau) (de terre) plot; (de pelouse) patch; (d'ombre) spot; **un ~ ensoleillé** a sunny spot; **un ~ de paradis** an idyllic spot; **un ~ de ciel bleu** a patch of blue sky; **un ~ de verdure** a green bit; **dans un ~ de ma mémoire** in my memory; **4** (lieu d'habitation) part; **un ~ de France/de l'Ardèche** a part of France/of the Ardèche; **dans le ~** (ici) around here, in these parts; (là-bas) around there, in those parts; **nous étions dans le même ~** we were in the same area; **le café du ~** the local café; **je ne suis pas du ~** I'm not from around here; **de quel ~ est-il?** where does he come from?; **les gens du ~** the locals; **dans un ~ paumé**° or **perdu** in the middle of nowhere; **dans un ~ perdu de la Lozère** in a remote part of the Lozère; **connaître les bons ~s pour manger/ pour les champignons** to know all the good places to eat/to find mushrooms; **5** (en papeterie) (pour photos) corner; (pour classeur) reinforcing corner; **6** TECH (pour fendre) wedge.
II coin(-) (*in compounds*) **~-repas/-salon** dining/ living area; **~-bureau** work area.

IDIOMES **rencontrer qn au ~ d'un bois** to meet sb in a dark alley.

coincé, -e /kwɛ̃se/ *adj* **1** (incapable de bouger) stuck; (incapable de sortir) trapped; **rester ~ dans des embouteillages** to be stuck in traffic jams; **~ entre qch et qch** [*meuble, maison*] wedged between sth and sth; **il n'a pas pu se lever, il était ~**° he couldn't get up, his back had gone°; **2**° (incapable d'agir) stuck°; **sans mes outils je suis ~** without my tools I'm stuck; **il était ~ entre l'opposition et son propre parti** he was caught between the opposition and his own party; **3**° (collet monté) uptight°.

coincer /kwɛ̃se/ [12] **I** *vtr* **1** (immobiliser) to wedge [*objet*]; (pour maintenir ouvert) to wedge [sth] open; (pour maintenir fermé) to wedge [sth] shut; [*éboulement, neige*] to trap [*personne*]; **ils m'ont coincé contre le mur** they pinned me (up) against the wall; **2** (bloquer) to jam [*objet, clé, fermeture*]; **j'ai coincé ma fermeture** my zip GB ou zipper US is jammed ou caught; **3** (dans une porte, fermeture) to catch [*vêtement, doigt*]; **4**° (retenir) to catch, to corner [*personne*]; **5**⁰ (arrêter) [*police*] to pick [sb] up°, to nick° GB [*criminel*]; **6**° (prendre en défaut) to catch [sb] out [*personne*].
II *vi* **1** (résister au mouvement) [*fermeture, tiroir*] to stick; **la pellicule coince dans l'appareil** the film is sticking; **2**° (créer des problèmes) [*relations*] to cause problems; **ça coince** there's a problem.
III se coincer *vpr* **1** (se bloquer) [*objet*] to get stuck ou jammed; **2** (se prendre) **se ~ les doigts** to get one's fingers caught; **se ~ une vertèbre**° to trap a nerve in one's back.

coïncidence /kɔɛ̃sidɑ̃s/ nf (tous contextes) coincidence.

coïncider /kɔɛ̃side/ [1] vi [dates, dépositions] to coincide (avec with); [goûts] to be similar (avec with); **faire ~ l'offre et la demande** to make supply and demand match.

coin-coin /kwɛ̃kwɛ̃/ nm inv (also onomat) quack; **faire ~** to go quack quack.

coing /kwɛ̃/ nm quince.

coït /kɔit/ nm coitus; **~ interrompu** coitus interruptus.

coite ▶ coi.

coke /kɔk/ nm (charbon) coke.

cokéfaction /kɔkefaksjɔ̃/ nf coking.

col /kɔl/ nm 1 (de vêtement) collar; **~ de fourrure** fur collar; **sans ~** collarless; **~ rond** round neckline; **~ carré** square neckline; **~ en V** V neckline; ▶ faux[1]; 2 GÉOG pass; **le ~ du Lautaret** the Lautaret pass; 3 (d'objet, de bouteille, vase) neck; 4 ANAT (de vessie, fémur) neck; **il s'est cassé le ~ du fémur** he broke his hip(bone); 5† (cou) neck.
■ **~ blanc** SOCIOL white-collar worker; **~ bleu** SOCIOL blue-collar worker; **~ de l'utérus** cervix.

cola /kɔla/ nm BOT cola tree; **noix de ~** cola nut.

colchique /kɔlʃik/ nm autumn crocus.

coléoptère /kɔleɔptɛʀ/ nm beetle.

colère /kɔlɛʀ/ nf 1 (humeur) anger (**contre qch** at sth; **contre qn** with sb), wrath SOUT; **~ froide** contained anger; **être rouge de ~** to be flushed with anger; **avec ~** in anger; **être en ~** to be angry (**contre** with), to be mad○ (**contre** at); **se mettre en ~** to get angry (**contre** with), to get mad○ (**contre** at); **passer sa ~ sur qn** to take out ou vent one's anger on sb; **sous le coup de la ~** in a fit of anger; 2 (crise) fit; (caprice) tantrum; **faire ou piquer○ une ~** (crise) to have a fit; (caprice) to throw a tantrum; **il était dans une ~ noire** he was in a rage; 3 (de la mer) fury, wrath SOUT; (des cieux) wrath SOUT; (d'un volcan) fury.

coléreux, -euse /kɔleʀø, øz/ adj [personne] quick-tempered, irascible; [tempérament] irascible.

colibacille /kɔlibasil/ nm E coli, Escherichia coli.

colibri /kɔlibʀi/ nm hummingbird.

colifichet /kɔlifiʃɛ/ nm (bijou) trinket; (bibelot) knick-knack.

colimaçon /kɔlimasɔ̃/ nm snail.
■ **escalier en ~** spiral staircase.

colin /kɔlɛ̃/ nm (merlu) hake; (lieu noir) coley.

colin-maillard /kɔlɛ̃majaʀ/ ▶ 329 | nm **jouer à ~** to play blind man's buff.

colique /kɔlik/ nf 1 (diarrhée) diarrhoea; **avoir la ~** to have diarrhoea; 2 (douleur abdominale) stomach pain; (chez le bébé) colic ¢; **~s néphrétiques** renal colic.

colis /kɔli/ nm parcel.
■ **~ alimentaire** food parcel; **~ piégé** parcel bomb; **~ postal** parcel sent by mail; **~ postaux** (service) parcel post.

colistier, -ière /kɔlistje, ɛʀ/ nm,f fellow candidate GB, running mate US.

colite /kɔlit/ ▶ 196 | nf colitis.

collaborateur, -trice /kɔlabɔʀatœʀ, tʀis/ nm,f 1 (collègue) colleague; (assistant) assistant; **~ du ministre** adviser to the minister; 2 (employé) employee; 3 (journaliste) contributor (**de** to); 4 HIST PEJ collaborator.

collaboration /kɔlabɔʀasjɔ̃/ nf 1 (à une revue, un journal) contribution (**à** to); (à un ouvrage, un projet) collaboration (**à** on); **en ~ avec** in collaboration with; 2 HIST POL collaboration (**avec** with).

collaborationniste /kɔlabɔʀasjɔnist/ adj [journal, discours] collaborationist.

collaborer /kɔlabɔʀe/ [1] vi 1 (participer) **~ à** to contribute to [journal, revue]; to collaborate on [projet, ouvrage]; 2 (travailler) to collaborate (**avec** with).

collage /kɔlaʒ/ nm 1 ART (technique, œuvre) collage; **~s photographiques** photo montages; 2 (affichage) **le ~ des affiches** billposting GB, putting up posters; **~ sauvage** flyposting.

collagène /kɔlaʒɛn/ nm collagen.

collant, ~e /kɔlɑ̃, ɑ̃t/ I adj 1 (adhésif) [substance] sticky; 2 (gluant) [main, terre, riz, bonbon] sticky; 3 (moulant) [robe, pantalon] skintight, tight-fitting; 4○ (importun) [personne] clinging; [vendeur] persistant.
II nm tights (pl) GB, panty hose (+ v pl) US; **~ de danse** dance tights.

collatéral, ~e, mpl -aux /kɔlateʀal, o/ adj 1 ANAT [nerf] collateral; 2 JUR [succession, ligne] collateral; 3 (de côté) [nef, rue] side (épith).

collation /kɔlasjɔ̃/ nf (repas) light meal.

colle /kɔl/ nf 1 (adhésif) GÉN glue; (pour papier peint) (wall-paper) paste; **mettre de la ~ sur qch** to put glue on sth; **~ forte/à bois** strong/wood glue; 2○ (question difficile) poser○; **poser une ~ à qn** to set sb a poser○; 3○ (retenue) students' slang detention; **deux heures de ~** two hours' detention; 4○ (oral) students' slang oral test.
■ **~ blanche** paste.
IDIOMES **vivre à la ~**○ to live together.

collecte /kɔlɛkt/ nf (de fonds, vêtements) collection; **faire une ~** to raise funds (**pour** for).

collecter /kɔlɛkte/ [1] vtr to collect.

collecteur, -trice /kɔlɛktœʀ, tʀis/ I adj **centre ~** collection point.
II nm,f (personne) collector.
■ **~ de fonds** fundraiser; **~ d'impôts** tax collector.

collectif, -ive /kɔlɛktif, iv/ I adj 1 GÉN [travail, responsabilités] collective; [démissions, licenciements] mass (épith); [chauffage] shared; [billet, assurance] group (épith); **immeuble ~** block of flats GB, apartment building US; **donner une punition collective à toute la classe** to punish the whole class; **l'équipe pratique un bon jeu ~** the team plays well together; 2 LING collective.
II nm GÉN collective; (groupe de pression) action group.
■ **~ budgétaire** supplementary finance bill.

collection /kɔlɛksjɔ̃/ nf 1 (de timbres, photos) collection (**de** of); **~ de timbres/tableaux** stamp/art collection; **c'est un timbre/badge de ~** this stamp/badge is a collector's item; **j'ai acheté deux timbres de ~ pour mon frère** I bought two stamps for my brother's collection; **faire ~ de qch** to collect sth; ▶ pièce; 2 (ouvrages) (du même genre) series (+ v sg); (du même auteur) set; **toute la ~ de Tintin**® the whole set of Tintin® books; 3 (en couture, mode) collection.

collectionner /kɔlɛksjɔne/ [1] vtr to collect [timbres, papillons]; **~ les erreurs/les gaffes** to make one mistake/blunder after another.

collectionneur, -euse /kɔlɛksjɔnœʀ, øz/ nm,f collector.

collectivement /kɔlɛktivmɑ̃/ adv [gérer, négocier] collectively; [démissionner] en masse, as a body.

collectivité /kɔlɛktivite/ nf 1 (groupe) group; **~ professionnelle** professional body; 2 (ensemble des citoyens) community.
■ **~ locale** local authority GB, local government US; **~s publiques** state, regional and local authorities GB, federal, state and local government US; **~ territoriale** region with a measure of autonomy.

collège /kɔlɛʒ/ nm 1 (école) **~** (**d'enseignement secondaire**), CES secondary school GB, junior high school US (up to age 16); 2 (assemblée) college; **~ électoral** electoral college.
■ **~ d'enseignement technique**, CET technical secondary school in France.

collégial, ~e, mpl -iaux /kɔleʒjal, o/ adj [église] collegiate; [assemblée, pouvoir, système] collegial.

collégien, -ienne /kɔleʒjɛ̃, ɛn/ nm,f schoolboy/schoolgirl.
IDIOMES **se faire avoir**○ **comme un ~** to be completely taken in.

collègue /kɔlɛg/ nmf colleague; (dans une lettre) **Cher ~** Dear Sir.

coller /kɔle/ [1] I vtr 1 (faire adhérer) to stick, to glue [bois, papier, carton]; to paste up [affiche]; to hang [*papier peint, tissu mural*]; to stick [sth] on [*étiquette, timbre, rustine*®]; to stick down [*enveloppe*]; to stick [sth] together [*feuilles, morceaux*]; CIN to splice [*film, bande magnétique*]; **~ des affiches** to stick ou post bills; **il avait les cheveux collés par la peinture** his hair was matted with paint; **ta colle ne colle pas bien le carton** your glue isn't very good for sticking card; **2** (appuyer) **~ qch contre** or **à qch** to press sth against sth; **il avait un pistolet collé à la tempe** there was a pistol pressed to his head; **il la colla contre le parapet** he pushed her up against the parapet; **3**○ (mettre) to stick○; **je leur ai collé la facture sous le nez** I stuck○ the bill (right) under their noses; **tu vas te faire ~ une amende** you'll get landed○ with a fine; **si tu continues, je te colle une gifle** or **je vais t'en ~ une** if you keep on, I'm going to slap you; **on lui colle une étiquette de chanteur engagé** he's being labelled^{GB} as a political singer; **4**○ (dans un examen, un jeu) **je me suis fait ~ en physique** I failed ou flunked○ physics; **5**○ (donner une retenue à) to give [sb] detention [*élève*].

II *vi* **1** (adhérer) [*colle, timbre, enveloppe*] to stick; [*pâtes*] to stick together; [*boue, substance*] to stick; **~ à un véhicule** FIG to drive close behind a vehicle; **~ au sujet** to stick to the subject; **mon tee-shirt mouillé me collait à la peau** my wet T-shirt was clinging to my skin; **ton passé te colle à la peau** FIG your past never leaves you; **2**○ (être cohérent) **leur analyse ne colle pas à la réalité** their analysis doesn't fit with the facts; **leurs témoignages ne collent pas** their evidence doesn't tally; **tout colle!** it's all falling into place!

III se coller *vpr* **1** (s'appuyer) **se ~ à** or **contre qn/ qch** to press oneself against sb/sth; **ils se sont collés au sol** they lay flat on the ground; **l'alpiniste se collait à la paroi** the climber clung to the rockface; **2**○ (pour une activité) **dès qu'il rentre, il se colle devant son ordinateur** as soon as he comes in he's glued○ to his computer.

collerette /kɔlʀɛt/ *nf* (grand col) ruffle; (fraise) ruff.

collet /kɔlɛ/ *nm* (piège) snare.
IDIOMES **être ~ monté** to be prim; **mettre la main au ~ de qn** [*police*] to collar○ sb; **prendre** or **saisir qn par le ~** to grab sb by the collar.

colleur, -euse[1] /kɔlœʀ, øz/ ▶ 374| *nm,f* **~ (d'affiches)** billposter, billsticker.

colleuse[2] /kɔløz/ *nf* CIN splicer.

collier /kɔlje/ *nm* **1** (bijou) necklace; **~ de perles** string of pearls; **~ de fleurs** garland of flowers; **2** (d'animal) collar; **3** (barbe) beard.
IDIOMES **reprendre le ~** to get back into harness; **donner un coup de ~** (intellectuellement) to get one's head down; (manuellement) to put one's back into it.

collimateur /kɔlimatœʀ/ *nm* collimator.
IDIOMES **avoir qn dans le ~**○ to have it in for sb○.

colline /kɔlin/ *nf* hill.

collision /kɔlizjɔ̃/ *nf* **1** (choc) collision; **entrer en ~ avec** to collide with; **2** (affrontement) clash, conflict.

colloque /kɔl(l)ɔk/ *nm* conference, symposium.

collusion /kɔlyzjɔ̃/ *nf* collusion (**avec** with).

collyre /kɔliʀ/ *nm* eyedrops (*pl*).

colmater /kɔlmate/ [1] *vtr* **1** (boucher) to plug, to seal off [*fuite*]; to seal [*fente*]; **2** FIG **~ les brèches** to fill in the gaps.

Colomb /kɔlɔ̃/ *nprm* **Christophe ~** Christopher Columbus.

colombage /kɔlɔ̃baʒ/ *nm* half-timbering; **ferme à ~s** half-timbered farmhouse.

colombe /kɔlɔ̃b/ *nf* **1** (oiseau) dove; **2** (partisan de la paix) dove; **3** (terme d'affection) **ma ~** my little love; ▶ **crapaud**.

colombien, -ienne /kɔlɔ̃bjɛ̃, ɛn/ ▶ 394| *adj* Colombian.

colombier /kɔlɔ̃bje/ *nm* dovecote.

colon /kɔlɔ̃/ *nm* **1** (de terres inhabitées) colonist; **2** (de colonie de vacances) child (*at children's holiday camp*); **3**○ soldiers' slang colonel.

côlon /kolɔ̃, kɔlɔ̃/ *nm* colon.

colonel /kɔlɔnɛl/ ▶ 284| *nm* MIL (dans l'armée de terre) ≈ colonel; (dans l'armée de l'air) ≈ group captain GB, ≈ colonel US.

colonial, ~e, *mpl* **-iaux** /kɔlɔnjal, o/ *adj, nm,f* colonial.

colonialisme /kɔlɔnjalism/ *nm* colonialism.

colonialiste /kɔlɔnjalist/ *adj, nmf* colonialist.

colonie /kɔlɔni/ *nf* **1** POL colony; **les ~s** the colonies; **2** (groupe) (d'artistes) colony; (ethnique) community; **3** ZOOL, BIOL colony.
■ **~ de vacances** holiday camp (*for children*).

colonisateur, -trice /kɔlɔnizatœʀ, tʀis/ **I** *adj* colonizing.
II *nm,f* colonizer.

colonisation /kɔlɔnizasjɔ̃/ *nf* colonization.

coloniser /kɔlɔnize/ [1] *vtr* to colonize.

colonnade /kɔlɔnad/ *nf* colonnade.

colonne /kɔlɔn/ *nf* GÉN column; (de lit) (bed)post; ARCHIT column, pillar; **défiler ~ par cinq** to march in fives; **sur cinq ~s à la une** PRESSE splashed across the front page; **~ d'air** air stream.
■ **~ blindée** MIL armoured^{GB} column; **~ de direction** AUT steering column; **~ montante** CONSTR riser; **~ vertébrale** ANAT spinal column.

colonnette /kɔlɔnɛt/ *nf* small column.

colorant, ~e /kɔlɔʀɑ̃, ɑ̃t/ **I** *adj* colouring^{GB}.
II *nm* GÉN colouring^{GB} agent; (en teinture) dye; CHIMIE stain; CULIN colouring^{GB}; (pour cheveux) colourant^{GB}.

coloration /kɔlɔʀasjɔ̃/ *nf* **1** (action) colouring^{GB}; (de textiles) dyeing; (de bois, cellule) staining; (de cheveux) tinting; (permanente) dyeing; **2** (couleur) colour^{GB}; (de peau) colouring^{GB}; (nuance) shade.

coloré, ~e /kɔlɔʀe/ *adj* **1** (teinté) [*objet*] coloured^{GB}; [*visage*] (par l'air vif) ruddy; (par l'alcool) florid; **2** (pittoresque) [*vie, foule*] colourful^{GB}; [*style*] lively.

colorer /kɔlɔʀe/ [1] **I** *vtr* **1** (teinter) to colour^{GB} [*liquide, verre*]; to tint [*photo, cheveux*]; to stain [*bois, cellule*]; (teindre) to dye [*textiles, cheveux*]; **~ qch en vert** to colour^{GB} sth green; **2** (empreindre) [*nostalgie*] to tinge.
II se colorer *vpr* [*visage*] to flush.

coloriage /kɔlɔʀjaʒ/ *nm* (action) colouring^{GB}; (dessin colorié) coloured^{GB} picture; (dessin à colorier) picture for colouring^{GB} in.

colorier /kɔlɔʀje/ [2] *vtr* to colour in GB, to color US [*dessin*]; **~ qch en rouge** to colour^{GB} sth red.

coloris /kɔlɔʀi/ *nm inv* GÉN colour^{GB}; (nuance) shade.

colossal, ~e, *mpl* **-aux** /kɔlɔsal, o/ *adj* colossal, huge.

colosse /kɔlɔs/ *nm* giant.

colportage /kɔlpɔʀtaʒ/ *nm* hawking.

colporter /kɔlpɔʀte/ [1] *vtr* **1** (répandre) to spread [*ragots*]; **2** (vendre) to peddle [*marchandises*].

colporteur, -euse /kɔlpɔʀtœʀ, øz/ *nm,f* (marchand) pedlar.

colt /kɔlt/ *nm* (pistolet) gun, Colt®.

coltiner○: **se coltiner** /kɔltine/ [1] *vpr* **1** (porter) to lug○ [*objet lourd*]; **2** (devoir se charger de) to get lumbered with GB, to get stuck with○ [*corvée, personne*].

col-vert, *pl* **cols-verts**, **colvert** /kɔlvɛʀ/ *nm* mallard (*inv*).

colza /kɔlza/ *nm* rape; **huile de ~** rapeseed oil.

coma /kɔma/ *nm* coma; **dans le ~** in a coma.

comateux, -euse /kɔmatø, øz/ *adj* comatose.

combat /kɔ̃ba/ *nm* **1** MIL fighting ¢; **les ~s ont repris** the fighting has broken out again; **~s aériens/terrestres** air/land battles; **envoyer au ~** to send into combat; **mettre hors de ~** to disable; **partir au ~** to set off for battle; **2** POL struggle (**contre** against; **pour** for); **mener le ~** to lead the struggle; **livrer un ~** to campaign (**contre** against; **pour** for); **3** SPORT bout; **~ de boxe** boxing bout; **(mettre) hors de ~** (to put) out of action.
■ **~ de coqs** cock fight; **~ singulier** single combat.

combatif, -ive /kɔ̃batif, iv/ *adj* (déterminé) assertive; (agressif) aggressive; [*boxeur, armée*] full of fighting spirit.

combativité /kɔ̃bativite/ *nf* fighting spirit.

combattant, ~e /kɔ̃batɑ̃, ɑ̃t/ **I** *adj* **1** (combatif) [*esprit*] fighting; **2** (de combat) [*troupe, unité*] combat. **II** *nm,f* combatant; ▶ **ancien**.

combattre /kɔ̃batʀ/ [61] **I** *vtr* to fight. **II** *vi* to fight (**contre** against; **pour** for).

combien¹ /kɔ̃bjɛ̃/ **I** *adv* **1** ▶ 348 J, 455 J, 486 J, 581 J (dans une interrogation) **~ coûte une bouteille de vin?** how much ou what does a bottle of wine cost?; **~ mesure le salon?** how big is the lounge?; **~ êtes-vous/sont-ils?** how many of you/them are there?; **2** (modifiant un verbe) **il est triste de voir ~ la situation s'est dégradée** it's sad to see how the situation has deteriorated; **il est difficile d'expliquer ~ je les apprécie** it's difficult to explain how much I appreciate them; **3** (modifiant un adjectif) **c'est cher mais ~ efficace!** it's expensive but so effective!; **il souligne ~ est précieuse l'aide de ses collègues** he stresses how valuable his colleagues' help is to him; **4** (modifiant un adverbe) **~ peu d'idées** how few ideas; **~ peu d'or** how little gold. **II combien de** *dét inter* **1** (avec un nom dénombrable) how many; **~ d'élèves accueillerez-vous en septembre?** how many pupils will you receive in September?; **c'est à ~ de kilomètres?** how far away is it?; **~ de kilomètres y a-t-il entre les deux villes?** how far apart are the two towns?; **~ de fois** (nombre de fois) how many times; (fréquence) how often; **dans ~ d'années?** in how many years time?; **2** (avec un nom non dénombrable) how much; **de ~ de pain astu besoin?** how much bread do you need?; **~ de temps faut-il?** how long does it take?

combien² /kɔ̃bjɛ̃/ ▶ 581 J *nmf inv* **1** (ordre) **tu es la ~○?** (dans une queue) how many people are before you?; **2** (date) **le ~ sommes-nous?, on est le ~○?** what's the date today?; **vous arrivez le ~?** what date are you arriving?; **3** (mesure) **tu chausses du ~?** what size shoes do you take?; **4** (fréquence) **tu le vois tous les ~?** how often do you see him?

combinaison /kɔ̃binɛʒɔ̃/ *nf* **1** (agencement) (action) combining; (résultat) combination; **2** CHIMIE, MATH combination; **3** (de serrure, coffre-fort) combination; **4** (sousvêtement) (full-length) slip; (tenue de sport) jumpsuit; (d'ouvrier) overalls (*pl*) GB, coveralls (*pl*) US. ■ **~ d'aviateur** flying suit; **~ de plongée** wetsuit.

combinard○, ~e /kɔ̃binaʀ, aʀd/ PEJ **I** *adj* **il est ~** (débrouillard) he's a fixer○ ou wheeler-dealer○; (magouilleur) he's a schemer. **II** *nm,f* (débrouillard) fixer○; wheeler-dealer○; (magouilleur) schemer.

combine○ /kɔ̃bin/ *nf* (moyen) trick○; (intrigue) scheme; **être de** or **marcher dans la ~** to be in on it.

combiné /kɔ̃bine/ *nm* TÉLÉCOM handset, receiver.

combiner /kɔ̃bine/ [1] **I** *vtr* **1** (réunir) to combine (**à, avec** with); **2** (calculer) to work out [*horaire, plan*]. **II se combiner** *vpr* **1** (se mélanger) [*éléments*] to combine (**à, avec** with); **2** (s'harmoniser) [*couleurs, saveurs*] to go together.

comble /kɔ̃bl/ **I** *adj* [*salle*] packed; **faire salle ~** (pour une conférence) to have a capacity audience; (à un spectacle) to play to packed houses; **la mesure est ~, je démissionne!** that's the last straw, I resign! **II** *nm* **1** (point extrême) **le ~ de l'injustice** the height of injustice; **c'est le ~ de l'horreur** it's absolutely horrific; **il était au ~ de la joie** he was absolutely delighted; **être à son ~** [*émotion, suspense*] to be at its height; **porter qch à son ~** to take sth to its extreme; **être au ~ du désespoir** to be in the depths of despair; **pour ~ de malchance j'ai raté mon avion!** to crown it all, I missed my plane!; **et, ~ du raffinement, les draps étaient en soie!** and, as the ultimate in refinement, there were silk sheets!; **c'est un** or **le ~○!** that's the limit!; **2** ARCHIT roof space; **de fond en ~** [*fouiller, nettoyer*] from top to bottom; [*changer, détruire*] completely. **III combles** *nmpl* attic (*sg*).

combler /kɔ̃ble/ [1] *vtr* **1** (remplir) to fill (in) [*fossé, tranchée*]; **2** (pallier) to fill in [*lacunes*]; to make up [*déficit*]; to make up for [*manque, perte*]; **~ son retard** to make up (for) lost time; **~ son retard technologique** to catch up in the field of technology; **3** (satisfaire) to fulfil^GB, to satisfy [*besoin, désir*]; **la vie m'a comblé** I've had a wonderful life; **~ qn** to fill sb with joy ou delight; **~ qn de cadeaux/d'honneurs** to lavish presents/honours^GB on sb; **merci beaucoup, je suis comblé!** thank you very much, I don't know what to say!; **c'est une femme comblée** she has everything she could possibly want.

combustible /kɔ̃bystibl/ **I** *adj* combustible. **II** *nm* fuel; **~ nucléaire** nuclear fuel.

combustion /kɔ̃bystjɔ̃/ *nf* combustion.

comédie /kɔmedi/ *nf* **1** LITTÉRAT, THÉÂT comedy; **2** (attitude feinte) play-acting; **c'est de la ~** it's just an act; **jouer la ~** to put on an act; **3**○ (caprice) scene; **faire une ~** to make a scene; **4**○ (histoire) **quelle ~ pour avoir un visa** what a palaver○ to get a visa. ■ **~ de boulevard** light comedy; **~ musicale** musical.

comédien, -ienne /kɔmedjɛ̃, ɛn/ **I** *adj* **il est (un peu) ~** (simulateur) he puts it on; (hypocrite) he's a sham. **II** *nm,f* **1** ▶ 374 J (acteur) actor/actress; (acteur comique) comic actor/actress; **2** FIG **c'est un ~** (simulateur) he puts it on; (hypocrite) he's a sham.

comestible /kɔmɛstibl/ **I** *adj* edible. **II comestibles** *nmpl* food ₵; **marchand de ~s** grocer.

comète /kɔmɛt/ *nf* comet.

comique /kɔmik/ **I** *adj* **1** THÉÂT [*genre, personnage*] comic; **2** (amusant) funny. **II** *nmf* (humoriste) comedian. **III** *nm* **1** (pitre) clown; **2** (genre) comedy; **3** (drôlerie) **c'est d'un ~!** it's so funny!; **c'est du plus haut ~** it's absolutely hilarious.

comité /kɔmite/ *nm* **1** ADMIN committee; **~ exécutif** executive committee; **~ directeur** executive ou management committee; **2** (groupe) **~ restreint** small group; **dîner en petit ~** intimate little dinner. ■ **~ central** POL Central Committee.

commandant /kɔmɑ̃dɑ̃/ ▶ 284 J *nm* (dans l'armée de terre) major; (dans l'armée de l'air) squadron leader GB, ~ major US. ■ **~ de bord** AVIAT, NAUT captain; **~ en second** MIL ~ second-in-command.

commande /kɔmɑ̃d/ *nf* **1** COMM order; **passer une ~** (à qn) to place an order (with sb); **2** LITTÉRAT, ART commission; **passer ~ de qch à qn** to commission sb to do sth; **3** TECH control; **tableau de ~** control panel; **à distance** remote control; **à double ~** dual-control; **être aux** or **tenir les ~s** LIT to be at the controls; FIG to be in control; **se mettre aux** or **prendre les ~s de** LIT to take the controls of; FIG to take control of; **4** ORDINAT command.

commandement /kɔmɑ̃dmɑ̃/ *nm* **1** MIL (direction) command; **avoir le ~ de** to be in command of [*armée*]; **2** MIL (ordre) order, command; **à mon ~, feu!** at ou on my command, fire!; **3** (autorités militaires) command; **4** RELIG **les dix ~s** the Ten Commandments.

commander /kɔmɑ̃de/ [1] **I** *vtr* **1** COMM to order; **~ qch à qn** to order sth from sb; **2** (demander l'exécution de) to commission [*livre, tableau, sondage*]; **3** MIL (être à la direction de) to command, to be in command of [*armée*]; **4** (exercer une autorité sur) **il aime ~ tout le monde** he loves ordering everyone about; **5** (exiger) **les circonstances commandent la prudence** the circumstances call for caution; **6** (actionner) [*dispositif, ordinateur*] to control [*mécanisme*]. **II commander à** *vtr ind* (avoir autorité sur) **~ à** to be in command of.

comment¹

Lorsqu'il signifie 'de quelle manière', *comment* se traduit généralement par *how*:

comment vas-tu au travail?
= how do you get to work?
comment as-tu fait pour arriver avant moi?
= how did you manage to get here before me?
je ne comprends pas comment tu as pu te perdre
= I don't understand how you managed to get lost
dis-moi comment elle a réagi
= tell me how she reacted
comment résoudre le problème?
= how can this problem be solved?
as-tu compris comment faire?
= do you understand how to do it?
il ne sait même pas comment faire cuire un œuf au plat
= he doesn't even know how to fry an egg

Attention: certains verbes comme *appeler, nommer* etc. ont une construction différente en anglais:

comment appelles-tu cet objet?
= what do you call this object?
On se reportera au verbe.

Lorsqu'il peut être remplacé par 'pourquoi', *comment* se traduit par *why*:

comment ne m'a-t-on pas averti? = why wasn't I told?

Lorsqu'il sert à exprimer l'indignation ou la surprise, *comment* se traduit par *what*:

comment? il est marié? = what? he's married?

Lorsqu'il sert à faire répéter une information, *comment* se traduit par *pardon?*

comment? qu'est-ce que tu dis? = pardon? what did you say?

On trouvera exemples supplémentaires et exceptions ci-dessous.

III *vi* [*personne, chef*] to give the orders, to be in command; **c'est moi qui commande!** I'm in charge!
IV **se commander** *vpr* (être contrôlable) **la passion, ça ne se commande pas** passion doesn't come to order; **ces choses ne se commandent pas** you can't force these things.

commanditaire /kɔmɑ̃ditɛʀ/ *nmf* **1** (bailleur de fonds) sleeping partner GB, silent partner US; **2** (sponsor) backer, sponsor; **3** (d'un crime) **le ~ d'un assassinat** the person behind an assassination.

commanditer /kɔmɑ̃dite/ [1] *vtr* to finance [*société*]; to sponsor [*projet*]; to be behind [*crime*].

commando /kɔmɑ̃do/ *nm* commando.

comme /kɔm/ I *adv* how; **~ il a raison!** how right he is!
II *conj* **1** (de même que) **ici ~ en Italie** here as in Italy; **ils sont bêtes, lui ~ elle** he's as stupid as she is; **il est paresseux, ~ sa sœur d'ailleurs** he's lazy, just like his sister; **fais ~ moi** do as I do; **~ toujours** as always; **j'y étais allé ~ chaque matin** I'd gone there as I did every morning; **jolie ~ tout** ever so pretty GB, really pretty; **2** (dans une comparaison) **il est grand ~ sa sœur** he's as tall as his sister; **c'est tout ~**○ it comes to the same thing; **elle me traite ~ un enfant** she treats me like a child, she treats me as if I were a child; **je voudrais un manteau ~ le tien** I'd like a coat like yours; **elle a fait un geste ~ pour se protéger** she made a movement as if to protect herself; **3** (dans une explication) **des pays industrialisés ~ les États-Unis et le Japon** industrialized countries such as ou like the United States and Japan; **alors ~ ça tu vas travailler à l'étranger** so you're going to work abroad then?; **puisque c'est ~ ça** if that's the way it is, if that's how it is; **~ si je n'avais que ça à faire!** as if I had nothing better to do!; **~ si j'avais besoin de ça!** that's the last thing I needed!; **4**○ (dans une approximation) **elle a eu ~ un évanouissement** she sort of fainted, she had a kind of fainting fit; **5** (indiquant l'intensité) **avare ~ il est, il ne te donnera rien** he's

so mean, he won't give you anything; **6** (indiquant une fonction) as; **travailler ~ jardinier** to work as a gardener; **7** (puisque) as, since; **~ elle était seule** as ou since she was alone; **8** (au moment où) as; **~ il traversait la rue** as he was crossing the road.
IDIOMES **~ quoi!** which just shows!; **~ ci ~ ça**○ so-so○.

commémoratif, -ive /kɔmemɔʀatif, iv/ *adj* [*plaque, timbre*] commemorative; [*cérémonie*] memorial.

commémoration /kɔmemɔʀasjɔ̃/ *nf* commemoration.

commémorer /kɔmemɔʀe/ [1] *vtr* to commemorate.

commencement /kɔmɑ̃smɑ̃/ I *nm* (phase initiale) beginning; (point de départ) start; **au ~** at the beginning; **dès le ~** from the start; **du ~ à la fin** from start to finish, from beginning to end; **commencez par le ~** start ou begin at the beginning.
II **commencements** *nmpl* (premiers moments) beginnings (*pl*); **~s pénibles** difficult beginnings.

commencer /kɔmɑ̃se/ [12] I *vtr* **1** (entreprendre) to start, to begin [*travail, discours*]; **c'est lui qui a commencé!** (la dispute) he started it!; **elle a commencé le piano à six ans** she started playing the piano when she was six; **tu commences bien l'année!** that's a good start to the year!; **le film est commencé** the film has already started; **2 ~ à** or **de faire** to begin to do; **je commence à comprendre** I'm beginning to understand; **ça commence à bien faire**○ or **à suffire**○! it's getting a bit much!
II *vi* [*année, film, rue*] to start, to begin; [*processus*] to begin; **pour ~, c'est trop cher** for a start, it's too expensive; **commence par le plafond** start with the ceiling; **par où** or **quoi vais-je ~?** where shall I start?; **par qui vais-je ~?** who shall I start with?; **commence par obéir!** for a start you can do as you're told!; **~ comme secrétaire** to start (off) as a secretary.
III *v impers* **il commence à pleuvoir/neiger** it's starting ou beginning to rain/to snow.

comment¹ /kɔmɑ̃/ *adv* **1** (de quelle manière) how; **~ le sais-tu?** how do you know (that)?; **il faut voir ~ il nous a traités!** you should have seen the way he treated us!; **2** (pour faire répéter) **~, peux-tu répéter?** sorry, could you say that again?; **Paul ~?** Paul who?; **3** (évaluation) **~ est leur fils?** what's their son like?; **~ trouvez-vous ma robe?** what do you think of my dress?, how do you like my dress?; **4** (indignation, surprise) **~ cela?** what do you mean?; **ça se fait**○? how come○?, how is that?; **~? tu voudrais des excuses!** what? you expect me to apologize?; **5** (intensif) **~ donc!** but of course!; **'c'était bon?'—'et ~**○**!'** 'was it nice?'—'it certainly was!'

comment² /kɔmɑ̃/ *nm* **le ~** the how.

commentaire /kɔmɑ̃tɛʀ/ *nm* **1** (remarque) comment (sur about); **2** RADIO, TV commentary (**de** on); **~ en direct** live commentary; **3** LITTÉRAT commentary.

commentateur, -trice /kɔmɑ̃tatœʀ, tʀis/ **▶ 374**⌐ *nm,f* commentator.

commenter /kɔmɑ̃te/ [1] *vtr* **1** (dire son opinion sur) to comment on [*décision, déclaration, événement*]; **2** (donner des explications) to give a commentary on [*film, visite*]; **commenté par** with a commentary by; **3** RADIO, TV (décrire) to commentate on [*match, événement*]; **commenté par** commentated on by; **4** LITTÉRAT, SCOL to comment on [*texte*].

commérage /kɔmeʀaʒ/ *nm* gossip **⊄**.

commerçant, ~e /kɔmɛʀsɑ̃, ɑ̃t/ I *adj* **rue ~e** shopping street; **nation très ~e** great trading nation; **il n'est pas très ~** he's not interested in pleasing the customer.
II **▶ 374**⌐ *nm,f* shopkeeper, storekeeper US; **petit ~** small shopkeeper ou storekeeper US; **grand** or **gros ~** large retailer; **les ~s ferment en août** the shops ou stores US close in August.

commerce /kɔmɛʀs/ *nm* **1** (magasin) shop, store US; **dans le ~** in the shops ou stores US; **2** (entreprise commerciale) business; **3** (activité) trade; **faire le ~ de** to trade in; **faire ~ de** to sell; **faire du ~** to be in

business; **4** (fréquentation) LITER company; **être d'un ~ agréable** to be good company.
■ **~ de détail** retail trade; **~ extérieur** foreign trade; **~ de gros** wholesale trade.
commercer /kɔmɛʀse/ [12] *vi* to trade (**avec** with).
commercial, **~e**, *mpl* **-iaux** /kɔmɛʀsjal, o/ **I** *adj* **1** COMM commercial; **carrière ~e** career in sales and marketing; **2** ÉCON trade; **accord ~** trade agreement.
II *nm,f* sales and marketing person.
commercialisation /kɔmɛʀsjalizasjɔ̃/ *nf* marketing.
commercialiser /kɔmɛʀsjalize/ [1] *vtr* to market.
commère /kɔmɛʀ/ *nf* PEJ gossip; **c'est une vraie ~**! he/she is a real gossip!
commettre /kɔmɛtʀ/ [60] **I** *vtr* **1** (faire) to make [*erreur*]; to commit [*crime*]; to carry out [*attentat, massacre*]; **2** (préposer) **~ qn à un emploi** to appoint sb to a post.
II se commettre *vpr* FML **se ~ avec des indésirables** to associate with undesirable characters.
commis /kɔmi/ ▶374⟩ *nm inv* (employé) (de ferme) hand; (de bureau) clerk; (de commerce) shop assistant GB, salesclerk US.
■ **~ voyageur** travelling⟨GB⟩ salesman.
commisération /kɔmizeʀasjɔ̃/ *nf* commiseration.
commissaire /kɔmisɛʀ/ ▶374⟩ *nm* **1** (dans la police) **~ (de police)** ~ police superintendent; **2** (membre d'une commission) commissioner; **3** (surveillant, organisateur) steward.
■ **~ de bord** purser; **~ de la République** prefect.
commissaire-priseur, *pl* **commissaires-priseurs** /kɔmisɛʀpʀizœʀ/ ▶374⟩ *nm* auctioneer.
commissariat /kɔmisaʀja/ *nm* **1** (local) **~ (de police)** police station; **2** (commission) commission.
commission /kɔmisjɔ̃/ **I** *nf* **1** (groupe de travail) committee; **2** COMM, FIN commission; **être payé à la ~** to be payed on a commission basis; **3** (mission) **faire une ~ pour qn** to do ou run an errand for sb; **4** (message) **faire la ~ à qn** to give sb the message.
II commissions○ *nfpl* shopping ⊄; **faire les ~s** to do one's ou the shopping.
commissionnaire /kɔmisjɔnɛʀ/ ▶374⟩ *nm* **1** JUR, COMM agent, broker; **2** (coursier) messenger; **~ (d'hôtel)** doorman.
commissionner /kɔmisjɔne/ [1] *vtr* to commission.
commissure /kɔmisyʀ/ *nf* (de lèvres) corner.
commode /kɔmɔd/ **I** *adj* **1** (pratique) GÉN convenient; [*instrument, outil*] handy; **2** (aisé) easy; **ce serait trop ~** it would be too easy; **3 ne pas être ~** (être strict) to be strict; (être difficile) to be difficult (to deal with).
II *nf* (meuble) chest of drawers.
commodément /kɔmɔdemɑ̃/ *adv* [*situé*] conveniently; [*installé*] comfortably; [*se déplacer*] easily.
commodité /kɔmɔdite/ *nf* convenience.
commotion /kɔmɔsjɔ̃/ *nf* **1** MÉD (ébranlement) concussion; **~ cérébrale** concussion (*of the brain*); **2** FIG (émotion) shock.
commotionner /kɔmɔsjɔne/ [1] *vtr* **1** LIT to concuss; **2** FIG to shake.
commuer /kɔmɥe/ [1] *vtr* to commute [*peine*] (**en** to).
commun, **~e**[1] /kɔmœ̃, yn/ **I** *adj* **1** (venant de plusieurs personnes) [*travail, œuvre*] collaborative; [*désir, accord, conception*] common; [*candidat, politique, projet*] joint (*épith*); **d'un ~ accord** by mutual agreement; **2** (appartenant à plusieurs) [*pièce, équipement, souvenirs*] shared; [*langue, passé*] common; [*biens*] joint (*épith*); **nous avons des amis ~s** we have friends in common; **pour le bien ~** for the common good; **après dix ans de vie ~e** after living together for ten years; **3** (semblable) [*intérêts, traits*] common (**à** to); [*ambition, objectifs*] shared; **les événements d'hier sont sans ~e mesure avec les précédents** yesterday's events are on an altogether different scale from previous ones; **4** (courant) common; **elle est d'une beauté peu ~e** she's uncommonly beautiful; **5** (ordinaire) PEJ [*goût, personne*] common PÉJ; [*visage*] plain; **c'est/il est d'un ~**! it's/he's so common!

II *nm* ordinary; **sortir du ~** to be out of the ordinary; **le ~ des mortels** ordinary mortals (*pl*); **hors du ~** exceptional.
III en commun *loc adv* [*écrire, produire*] jointly, together; **avoir qch en ~** to have sth in common; **mettre ses moyens** or **ressources en ~** to pool one's resources; **nous mettons tout en ~** we share everything.
IV communs *nmpl* (bâtiment) outbuildings (*pl*).
communal, **~e**, *mpl* **-aux** /kɔmynal, o/ *adj* [*budget*] local council GB, local government US; [*bâtiment*] local council GB, community US; **chemin ~ ~** public track; **terrain ~** common land.
communautaire /kɔmynotɛʀ/ *adj* **1** POL [*budget, droit*] Community; [*population*] of the Community (*après n*); **2** (d'une collectivité) **la vie ~** life in a community; **les règles ~s** the rules of a community.
communauté /kɔmynote/ ▶232⟩ *nf* **1** (groupe humain) community; **2** (collectivité) commune; **vivre en ~** to live in a commune; **3** RELIG community; **4** JUR **~ (de biens)** joint ownership; **5** (identité) community; **une ~ d'idées/de valeurs** shared ideas/values.
■ **Communauté économique européenne**, **CEE** European Economic Community, EEC; **Communauté des États indépendants**, **CEI** Commonwealth of Independent States, CIS.
commune[2] /kɔmyn/ **I** *nf* **1** (village) village; (ville) town, district; **2** HIST **la Commune (de Paris)** the (Paris) Commune.
II communes *nfpl* POL **les Communes**, **la Chambre des ~s** the (House of) Commons.
communément /kɔmynemɑ̃/ *adv* [*admettre, désigner*] generally.
communiant, **~e** /kɔmynjɑ̃, ɑ̃t/ *nm,f* **1** (qui communie) communicant; **2** (qui fait sa première communion (**premier**) ~ child taking his/her first communion.
communicatif, **-ive** /kɔmynikatif, iv/ *adj* **1** [*personne, nature*] talkative; **2** [*gaieté, passion*] infectious.
communication /kɔmynikasjɔ̃/ *nf* **1** TÉLÉCOM call; **~ téléphonique** telephone call; **être en ~ avec qn** to be on the line to sb; **mettre qn en ~ avec qn** to put sb through to sb; **2** (relations sociales) communications (*pl*); **problème de ~** communications problem; **~ de masse** mass communications; **3** (transmission) communication; **demander ~ d'un dossier à qn** to ask sb for a file; **4** (au conseil des ministres) report; (à une conférence) paper; **faire une ~ sur** to give a paper on; **5** (relation personnelle) communication ⊄; **être en ~ avec qn** to be in communication with sb; **mettre qn en ~ avec qn** to put sb in touch with sb; **6** (média) communications (*pl*); **groupe de ~** communications group; **7** (liaison) **moyens** or **voies de ~** communications (*pl*).
communier /kɔmynje/ [2] *vi* **1** RELIG [*personne*] to receive Communion; **2** FIG to commune (**avec** with); **~ dans la douleur de qn** to share in sb's grief.
communion /kɔmynjɔ̃/ *nf* **1** RELIG Communion; **2** (accord) communion; **se sentir en ~ avec qch/qn** to feel in harmony with sth/sb.
■ **~ privée** RELIG first communion; **~ solennelle** RELIG *solemn declaration of faith made at the age of 11*.
communiqué /kɔmynike/ *nm* **1** (de presse) communiqué, press release; **2** (de parti, gouvernement) statement.
communiquer /kɔmynike/ [1] **I** *vtr* **1** (faire connaître) [*journaliste*] to announce [*date, décision*]; [*personne*] to give [*adresse, liste*] (**à** to); [*personne*] to declare [*intention*] (**à** to); **2** (transmettre) [*personne*] to pass on [*dossier*] (**à** to); to convey [*sentiment*] (**à** to).
II *vi* **1** LING, SOCIOL, TÉLÉCOM to communicate (**avec** with); **2** ARCHIT [*pièces*] to be adjoining; **~ avec** to adjoin [*pièce*].
III se communiquer *vpr* **1** (se transmettre) [*personnes*] to pass on [sth] to each other [*information*]; **2** (se répandre) [*feu, peur*] to spread (**à** to).
communisme /kɔmynism/ *nm* communism.
communiste /kɔmynist/ *adj, nmf* communist.
commutateur /kɔmytatœʀ/ *nm* switch.

commutatif, -ive /kɔmytatif, iv/ *adj* commutative.

commutation /kɔmytasjɔ̃/ *nf* **1** GÉN commutation; **2** ORDINAT message switching.

commuter /kɔmyte/ [1] *vtr* to commute.

comorien, -ienne /kɔmɔʀjɛ̃, ɛn/ ▶ **394** *adj* Comoran.

compact, ~e /kɔ̃pakt/ *adj* **1** (dense) [*brouillard, foule*] dense; [*terre*] compact; **2** (peu encombrant) [*meuble*] compact; **sous format ~** [*livre*] in pocket edition; **3** (solide) [*groupe*] monolithic; [*peloton*] compact.

compagne /kɔ̃paɲ/ *nf* **1** (amie) (female) companion; **2** (femelle) mate.

compagnie /kɔ̃paɲi/ *nf* **1** (présence) company; **tenir ~ à qn** to keep sb company; **en ~ de** together with; **2** (groupe) company; **salut la ~!** hello everybody!; **3** COMM company; **4** MIL company; **5** THÉÂT company; **6** (colonie animale) **~ de perdrix** covey of partridges.
■ **~ aérienne** airline; **~ d'assurance** insurance company; **~ pétrolière** oil company.

compagnon /kɔ̃paɲɔ̃/ *nm* **1** (ami) companion; **2** (amant) partner; **3** (mâle) mate; **4** (artisan) journeyman; **5** (franc-maçon) fellow of the craft.
■ **~ d'armes** comrade-in-arms; **~ d'infortune** companion in misfortune; **~ de route** fellow traveller^GB; **~ de voyage** travelling^GB companion.

comparable /kɔ̃paʀabl/ *adj* comparable (à to).

comparaison /kɔ̃paʀɛzɔ̃/ *nf* **1** (rapprochement) comparison (à, avec with); **c'est sans ~ le plus confortable** it's far and away the most comfortable; **2** (en rhétorique) simile; **3** LING comparison; **adjectif/ adverbe de ~** comparative adjective/adverb.

comparaître /kɔ̃paʀɛtʀ/ [73] *vi* to appear (**devant** before); **être appelé à ~** to be summoned to appear.

comparatif, -ive /kɔ̃paʀatif, iv/ **I** *adj* comparative.
II *nm* LING comparative.

comparé, ~e /kɔ̃paʀe/ *adj* comparative.

comparer /kɔ̃paʀe/ [1] **I** *vtr* to compare (**à, avec** with).
II se comparer *vpr* (soi-même) **se ~ à qn/qch** (pour évaluer) to compare oneself with sb/sth; (s'assimiler) to compare oneself to sb; (être comparable) to be comparable; **ça ne se compare pas** there's no comparison.

comparse /kɔ̃paʀs/ *nmf* **1** THÉÂT extra; **rôle de ~** walk-on part; PÉJ minor part; **2** (acolyte) sidekick^○; **on n'a arrêté que les ~s** they have only arrested the small fry.

compartiment /kɔ̃paʀtimɑ̃/ *nm* compartment.

compartimenter /kɔ̃paʀtimɑ̃te/ [1] *vtr* **1** LIT **~ un coffret** to divide a box into compartments; **~ un grenier** to divide up a loft with partitions; **2** FIG to compartmentalize [*administration, science*].

comparution /kɔ̃paʀysjɔ̃/ *nf* JUR appearance (**devant** before).

compas /kɔ̃pa/ *nm* **1** (de géométrie) compass, pair of compasses US; **2** AVIAT, NAUT compass.

compassion /kɔ̃pasjɔ̃/ *nf* compassion.

compatibilité /kɔ̃patibilite/ *nf* compatibility.

compatible /kɔ̃patibl/ *adj* compatible (**avec** with).

compatir /kɔ̃patiʀ/ [3] *vi* to sympathize; **je compatis à votre douleur** FML I feel for you in your sorrow SOUT.

compatissant, ~e /kɔ̃patisɑ̃, ɑ̃t/ *adj* compassionate.

compatriote /kɔ̃patʀiɔt/ *nmf* fellow-countryman/ fellow-countrywoman, compatriot.

compensation /kɔ̃pɑ̃sasjɔ̃/ *nf* compensation; **~s financières** financial compensation.

compensatoire /kɔ̃pɑ̃satwaʀ/ *adj* compensatory.

compensé, ~e /kɔ̃pɑ̃se/ *adj* **1** **semelle ~e** wedge heel; **2** MÉD compensated.

compenser /kɔ̃pɑ̃se/ [1] **I** *vtr* to compensate for [*défaut*]; to make up for [*dommages*]; to offset [*pertes*].
II se compenser *vpr* **les gains et pertes se compensent** the profits offset the losses; **ses défauts et ses qualités se compensent** his/her good qualities make up for his/her faults.

compère /kɔ̃pɛʀ/ *nm* **1** (partenaire) partner; (dans une tromperie) accomplice; **2** (camarade) mate^○ GB, buddy^○ US; **3** (individu) **joyeux/rusé ~** cheery/crafty fellow^○.

compétence /kɔ̃petɑ̃s/ *nf* **1** (aptitude) (dans une matière, un domaine) ability; (dans un emploi, une activité) competence, skill; **faire appel aux ~s de qn** to call upon sb's expertise; **2** (aptitude légale) competence; **relever de la ~ de qn** to fall within the competence of sb; **3** (fonction) domain, sphere; **être** or **entrer dans les ~s de qn** to be in sb's domain.

compétent, ~e /kɔ̃petɑ̃, ɑ̃t/ *adj* **1** (qualifié) competent; **2** (qui a l'autorité) [*autorité*] competent; [*service*] appropriate; **tribunal ~** court of competent jurisdiction; **le maire est seul ~ pour faire** the mayor is the only one with the authority to do; **le tribunal de Rennes n'est pas ~ pour juger cette affaire** this case does not come within the jurisdiction of the Rennes court.

compétitif, -ive /kɔ̃petitif, iv/ *adj* competitive.

compétition /kɔ̃petisjɔ̃/ *nf* **1** (concurrence) competition (**entre** between); **être en ~ avec** to be competing with; **l'esprit de ~** the competitive spirit; **2** (activité) competition; **voiture de ~** competition car; **faire de la ~** to compete; **sport de ~** competitive sport; **3** (épreuve) ~ (**sportive**) sporting event; **~ de natation** swimming event.

compétitivité /kɔ̃petitivite/ *nf* competitiveness.

compilation /kɔ̃pilasjɔ̃/ *nf* compilation.

complainte /kɔ̃plɛ̃t/ *nf* lament.

complaire: se complaire /kɔ̃plɛʀ/ [59] *vpr* **se ~ à faire** to take pleasure in doing; **se ~ dans le malheur** to wallow in misery; **se ~ dans son ignorance** to bask in one's own ignorance.

complaisamment /kɔ̃plɛzamɑ̃/ *adv* **1** (aimablement) obligingly; **2** (avec trop d'indulgence) indulgently; **3** (avec autosatisfaction) complacently.

complaisance /kɔ̃plɛzɑ̃s/ *nf* **1** (volonté de faire plaisir) kindness, readiness to oblige; **pavillon de ~** flag of convenience; **2** (indulgence excessive) **~ d'un père à l'égard de ses enfants** a father's indulgence toward(s) his children; **leur ~ à l'égard du régime** their soft attitude toward(s) the regime; **décrire la situation sans ~** to give an objective assessment of the situation; **3** (autosatisfaction) complacency, smugness.

complaisant, ~e /kɔ̃plɛzɑ̃, ɑ̃t/ *adj* **1** (prévenant) obliging; **2** (trop indulgent) indulgent (**avec** with); **sa description des faits est trop ~e** he's too uncritical in his account of the facts; **un mari ~** a husband who turns a blind eye; **3** (autosatisfait) PÉJ complacent PÉJ, self-satisfied PÉJ.

complément /kɔ̃plemɑ̃/ *nm* **1** (revenu) **~ de salaire** extra payment; **2** (de programme, travail, financement) supplement; **~ de formation** further training; **3** LING complement; **~ d'agent** agent; **~ d'objet direct** direct object.

complémentaire /kɔ̃plemɑ̃tɛʀ/ *adj* **1** (supplémentaire) [*formation*] further; [*activité, somme*] supplementary; **pour tous renseignements ~s** for further information; **2** (apparié) [*personne, qualité, équipement*] complementary (**de** to); **3** MATH complementary.

complet, -ète /kɔ̃plɛ, ɛt/ **I** *adj* **1** (total) [*arrêt, silence, révision*] complete; [*échec*] total; **2** (sans manques) [*œuvres*] complete; [*enquête, gamme*] full; **un artiste ~** an all-round artist; **3** (approfondi) comprehensive; **de façon (très) complète** (very) thoroughly; **4** (plein) [*train, hôtel, salle*] full; '~' (dans un hôtel) 'no vacancies'; (dans un théâtre) 'sold out'; (dans un parking) 'full'; **le gouvernement au ~** the entire government; **être (réuni) au (grand) ~** to be all present.
II *nm* (costume) suit; **~ trois pièces** three-piece suit.

complètement /kɔ̃plɛtmɑ̃/ *adv* **1** (totalement) completely; **pas ~** not entirely; **~ réveillé** fully awake; **je m'en moque ~** I couldn't care less; **2** (en entier) **j'ai ~ repeint la maison** I've repainted the whole house; **elle a ~ refait son article** she has rewritten her whole article ou her article in its entirety.

compléter /kɔ̃plete/ [14] **I** *vtr* **1** (s'ajouter à) to complete [*collection*]; to top up [*somme*]; to supplement [*connaissances*]; **pour ~ le tout** or **tableau**○ IRON to cap it all; **2** (être complémentaire de) to complement [*personne*]; **3** (remplir) [*personne*] to complete [*phrase*]; to complete, to fill in [*questionnaire*].

II se compléter *vpr* (l'un l'autre) [*éléments, personnes*] to complement each other.

complet-veston†, *pl* **complets-veston** /kɔ̃plɛ vɛstɔ̃/ *nm* suit.

complexe /kɔ̃plɛks/ **I** *adj* complex.
II *nm* **1** PSYCH complex; **il n'a pas de ~** he hasn't got any hang-ups○, he has no inhibitions; **2** (ensemble d'installations) complex; **~ sportif** sports complex.
■ **~ d'Œdipe** Oedipus complex.

complexé, ~e /kɔ̃plɛkse/ *adj* **il est très ~** he has a lot of hang-ups○.

complexer /kɔ̃plɛkse/ [1] *vtr* to give [sb] a complex [*personne*].

complexité /kɔ̃plɛksite/ *nf* complexity.

complication /kɔ̃plikasjɔ̃/ *nf* **1** (embarras) complication; **aimer les ~s** to like complicating matters; **2** MÉD complication.

complice /kɔ̃plis/ **I** *adj* **1** (qui aide) **être ~ de qch** to be a party to sth; **2** (de connivence) [*air, silence*] of complicity (*épith, après n*).
II *nmf* **1** (comparse) accomplice (**de qch** in sth); **se faire le ~ de qch** to be a party to sth.

complicité /kɔ̃plisite/ *nf* (collaboration) complicity; (entente) bond; **sourire de ~** smile of complicity.

compliment /kɔ̃plimɑ̃/ **I** *nm* **1** (parole de félicitations) compliment; **faire un ~ à qn** to compliment sb (**sur** on); **2** (petit discours) (nice little) speech.
II compliments *nmpl* **1** (félicitations) compliments; **(tous) mes ~s!** congratulations!; **faire des ~s à qn** to compliment sb (**sur, pour** on); **2** (formule de politesse) **avec les ~s de...** with the compliments of...; **mes ~s à votre mère** my regards to your mother.

complimenter /kɔ̃plimɑ̃te/ [1] *vtr* to compliment.

compliqué, ~e /kɔ̃plike/ *adj* **1** GÉN complicated; [*esprit*] tortuous; **si tu ne t'arrêtes pas de pleurer, ce n'est pas ~**○, **tu vas au lit!** it's quite simple, if you don't stop crying you'll go straight to bed!; **2** MÉD [*fracture*] compound.

compliquer /kɔ̃plike/ [1] **I** *vtr* to complicate; **~ la vie** or **l'existence de qn** to make life difficult for sb.
II se compliquer *vpr* **1** (devenir complexe) to get more complicated; **2** (rendre plus complexe) **se ~ la vie** or **l'existence** to make life difficult for oneself.

complot /kɔ̃plo/ *nm* plot.

comploter /kɔ̃plɔte/ [1] **I** *vtr* to plot [*attentat, ruine*]; to plan [*mauvais coup*].
II *vi* to plot (**contre** against; **de faire** to do).

comportement /kɔ̃pɔrtəmɑ̃/ *nm* GÉN behaviour^GB; (de sportif, voiture, Bourse) performance.

comporter /kɔ̃pɔrte/ [1] **I** *vtr* **1** (inclure) to include; **~ une bibliographie** to include a bibliography; **2** (être composé de) to comprise; **~ trois parties** to comprise three parts; **3** (présenter) to entail [*risque*].
II se comporter *vpr* **1** [*personne, animal*] to behave, to act; **se ~ en dictateur** to behave like a dictator; **2** (fonctionner) [*sportif, voiture, Bourse*] to perform.

composant /kɔ̃pozɑ̃/ *nm* **1** TECH (élément) component; **2** CHIMIE (élément simple) constituent.

composante /kɔ̃pozɑ̃t/ *nf* **1** GÉN (élément) element; **2** MATH, PHYS, LING component.

composé, ~e /kɔ̃poze/ **I** *adj* **1** (fait d'éléments divers) [*bouquet, style*] composite; [*salade*] mixed; **2** (affecté) affected.
II *nm* CHIMIE compound.

composer /kɔ̃poze/ [1] **I** *vtr* **1** (constituer) [*éléments, personnes*] to make up; **composé de** made up of; **le groupe est ~ à 90% de femmes** 90% of the group are women; **2** (réaliser) [*personne*] to put [sth] together [*menu*]; to select [*équipe*]; to make up [*bouquet*]; **3** ART, LITTÉRAT, MUS to compose [*morceau, texte*]; to paint [*tableau*]; **4** to dial [*numéro*]; **~ son code secret** to enter one's pin number; **5** (en imprimerie) to typeset [*page, texte*].

II FML *vi* (trouver un compromis) to compromise; **~ avec** to come to a compromise with [*personne*].
III se composer *vpr* **1** (être constitué) **se ~ de** to be made up of; **2** (adopter) to assume [*attitude, expression*].

composite /kɔ̃pozit/ *adj* **1** (divers) heterogeneous; **2** TECH [*matériau*] composite; **3** ARCHIT composite.

compositeur, -trice /kɔ̃pozitœr, tris/ **▶ 374** *nm,f* **1** MUS composer; **2** (typographe) typesetter.

composition /kɔ̃pozisjɔ̃/ *nf* **1** (éléments constitutifs) (de gouvernement, délégation) make-up, composition; (d'équipe) line-up, composition; (de produit, d'aliment) ingredients (*pl*); (chimique, pharmaceutique) composition; **2** (mise en place) (de gouvernement) formation; (de comité) setting up; (d'équipe) selection; (de liste, menu) drawing up; (de bouquet) making up; **de ma/leur ~** of my/their invention; **3** ART, LITTÉRAT, MUS composition (**de** by); **~ florale** flower arrangement; **4** CIN, THÉÂT (incarnation) performance (**de** as); **5** SCOL end-of-term test; **6** (en imprimerie) typesetting; **l'article est à la ~** the article is being typeset.
IDIOMES **être de bonne ~** to be good-natured.

composter /kɔ̃pɔste/ [1] *vtr* (au tampon) to (date) stamp; (au poinçon) to punch.

compote /kɔ̃pɔt/ *nf* CULIN stewed fruit, compote; **~ de pommes** stewed apples (*pl*); **mettre qn en ~**○ to beat sb black and blue.

compréhensible /kɔ̃preɑ̃sibl/ *adj* **1** (concevable) understandable; **2** (intelligible) comprehensible.

compréhensif, -ive /kɔ̃preɑ̃sif, iv/ *adj* understanding.

compréhension /kɔ̃preɑ̃sjɔ̃/ *nf* **1** (faculté, aptitude) understanding; **2** (de texte, paroles) comprehension; (de langue) understanding, comprehension; **pour aider à la ~** to make it easier to understand; **3** (indulgence) **faire preuve de ~** to show understanding; **attitude pleine de ~** sympathetic attitude.

comprendre /kɔ̃prɑ̃dr/ [52] **I** *vtr* **1** (saisir le sens de) to understand; **si je comprends bien** if I understand correctly; **il m'a dit son nom au téléphone mais je n'ai pas bien compris** he told me his name on the phone but I didn't quite catch it; **ne te mêles pas de cela, tu as compris** or **c'est compris!** keep out of it, do you hear ou understand?; **il ne comprend rien à rien** he hasn't got a clue; **c'est à n'y rien ~** it's completely baffling; **mal ~ qn/qch** to misunderstand sb/sth; **être compris comme une menace** to be interpreted as a threat; **~ qch de travers**○ to get sth all wrong; **se faire ~** to make oneself understood; **être lent à ~** to be slow on the uptake; **2** (se rendre compte de) to understand; **ce n'est pas facile, je comprends** it's not easy, I realize that; **je n'ai pas le temps, tu comprends** you see, I haven't got time; **3** (admettre) to understand [*attitude, sentiment*]; (faire preuve de compréhension envers) to understand [*person*]; **je comprends qu'il soit furieux** I can understand his anger; **comme je le comprends!** I understand him exactly; **4** (se faire une idée de) to see [*métier, vie*]; **5** (être totalement constitué de) to consist of, to comprise; **6** (être partiellement constitué de) to include.
II se comprendre *vpr* **1** [*personnes*] (l'un l'autre) to understand each other ou one another; **2** (soi-même) **je me comprends** I know what I'm trying to say; **3** (être compréhensible) [*attitude, sentiment*] to be understandable; **4** (être compris) **le terme doit se ~ ici dans son sens large** the term is to be understood ou taken in its broadest sense.

compresse /kɔ̃prɛs/ *nf* compress.

compresser /kɔ̃prese/ [1] *vtr* to compress.

compressible /kɔ̃presibl/ *adj* **1** PHYS, CHIMIE compressible; **2** (réductible) reducible.

compression /kɔ̃presjɔ̃/ *nf* **1** TECH compression; **2** (action de réduire) reduction; **3** (diminution effective) cut (**de** in); **~s budgétaires** budget cuts.

comprimé /kɔ̃prime/ *nm* tablet.

comprimer /kɔ̃prime/ [1] *vtr* **1** (serrer) to constrict [*ventre, buste*]; to squeeze [*pâte*]; **2** MÉD (appuyer sur) to compress, to constrict [*objet, organe*]; **3** TECH to compress [*liquide, gaz*]; **air comprimé** compressed air; **4** (réduire) to cut [*dépenses, budget*].

compris, **~e** /kɔ̃pʀi, iz/ **I** *pp* ▶ **comprendre**. **II** *pp adj* (inclus) including; **loyer de 3 000 francs charges ~es/non ~es** rent of 3,000 francs inclusive/exclusive; **service ~** service included; **TVA ~e/non ~e** including/not including VAT. **III tout compris** *loc adv* in total, all in○ GB; **prix tout ~** all-in GB ou inclusive price. **IV y compris** *loc adv* including; **y ~ à Paris** in Paris too.

compromettant, **~e** /kɔ̃pʀɔmetɑ̃, ɑ̃t/ *adj* compromising.

compromettre /kɔ̃pʀɔmetʀ/ [60] **I** *vtr* **1** (mettre en danger) to endanger, to jeopardize [*santé, chances*]; to compromise [*victoire*]; to impair [*efficacité*]; **2** (souiller) to compromise [*personne*]; to damage [*prestige*]. **II se compromettre** *vpr* (risquer sa réputation) to compromise oneself.

compromis, **~e** /kɔ̃pʀɔmi, iz/ **I** *adj* **1** (menacé) [*carrière, projet*] in jeopardy; **2** (souillé) [*personne*] compromised; [*réputation*] damaged; **être ~ dans un scandale** to be involved in a scandal. **II** *nm* compromise (**entre** between).

compromission /kɔ̃pʀɔmisjɔ̃/ *nf* (entre personnes) deal; (avec sa conscience) compromise of principle.

comptabiliser /kɔ̃tabilize/ [1] *vtr* **1** (additionner) to count (the number of) [*erreurs, entrées*]; **2** (en comptabilité) to enter ou record [sth] in the books.

comptabilité /kɔ̃tabilite/ *nf* **1** (concept, discipline) accountancy; **2** (profession, activité) accounting; **3** (tenue de livres) bookkeeping; **faire sa ~** to do one's accounts; **4** (ensemble des comptes) accounts (*pl*); **5** (service) accounts department.

comptable /kɔ̃tabl/ **I** *adj* **1** (de comptabilité) [*document, année*] accounting; [*service*] accounts; **agent ~** accountant; **2** LING countable; **non ~** uncountable. **II ▶ 374** *nmf* (spécialiste) accountant; (personne qui tient les livres) bookkeeper.

comptant /kɔ̃tɑ̃/ **I** *adv* [*payer*] cash; **acheter une maison ~** to pay cash for a house. **II au comptant** *loc adv* [*vendre*] for cash.

compte /kɔ̃t/ **I** *nm* **1** (calcul) count; **faire le ~ de qch** to work out [*dépenses, recettes*]; to count (up) [*personnes, objets*]; **si je fais le ~ de ce qu'il me doit** if I work out what he owes me; **le ~ est bon** that works out right; **tenir le ~ de qch** to keep count of sth; **comment fais-tu ton ~ pour faire...?** FIG how do you manage to do...?; **au bout du ~** (pour constater) in the end; **tout ~ fait** (tout bien considéré) all things considered; (en fait) when all is said and done; **en fin de ~** (pour conclure) at the end of the day; **tout ~ fait** or **en fin de ~, c'est lui qui avait raison** when all is said and done, HE was right; **2** (résultat) (d'argent) amount; (d'objets, heures, de personnes) number; **le ~ y est** (en argent) that's the right amount; (en objets, personnes) all present and correct; **le ~ n'y est pas, il n'y a pas le ~** (en argent) that's not the right amount; (en objets, personnes) that's not the right number; **il a son ~**○ (battu ou tué) he's done for○; (ivre) he's had a drop too much; **nous avons eu notre ~ d'ennuis** FIG we've had more than our fair share of problems; **à ce ~-là** (dans ces conditions) in that case; **3** (considération) **prendre qch en ~, tenir ~ de qch** to take sth into account; **~ tenu de** considering; **4** (intérêt personnel) **être** or **travailler à son ~** to be self-employed; **se mettre** or **s'installer** or **s'établir à son ~** to set up one's own business; **prendre des jours de congé à son ~** to take a few days off without pay; **pour le ~ de qn** on behalf of sb; **y trouver son ~** to get something out of it; **à ~ d'auteur** at the author's expense; **5** (en comptabilité) account; **tenir les ~s** to keep the accounts; **6** FIN account; **~ bancaire** or **~ en banque** bank account; **7** COMM (ardoise) account; **j'ai un ~ chez un libraire** I have an account with a bookshop GB ou bookstore; **mettre qch sur le ~ de qn** LIT to charge sth to sb's account; FIG to put sth down to sb; **8** (somme à payer) **voilà votre ~** here's your money;

9 (explication, rapport) **rendre ~ de qch à qn** (rapporter) to give an account of sth to sb; (justifier) to account for sth to sb; **rendre des ~s à qn** [*responsable*] to be answerable to sb; **demander des ~s à qn** to ask for an explanation from sb; **10** (notion nette) **se rendre ~ de** (être conscient) to realize; (remarquer) to notice; **11** (sujet) **je ne sais rien sur leur ~** I don't know anything about them; **12** SPORT (en boxe) count. **II à bon compte** *loc adv* LIT (à peu de frais) [*acheter*] cheap; [*acquérir, voyager*] cheaply; FIG (sans difficulté) the easy way; **s'en tirer à bon ~** to get off lightly. ■ **~ chèques** current account GB, checking account US; **~ chèque postal, CCP** post office account; **~ d'épargne** savings account; **~ à rebours** countdown; **le ~ à rebours de la campagne est commencé** FIG the run-up to the elections has started; **~s d'apothicaire** complicated calculations.

compté, **~e** /kɔ̃te/ *adj* **ses jours sont ~s, ses heures sont ~es** his/her days are numbered; **à pas ~s** LIT with measured steps; FIG cautiously.

compte-gouttes /kɔ̃tgut/ *nm inv* dropper; **au ~** LIT with a dropper; FIG (avec parcimonie) sparingly.

compter /kɔ̃te/ [1] **I** *vtr* **1** (dénombrer) to count; **on compte deux millions de chômeurs** there is a total of two million unemployed; **on ne compte plus ses victoires** he/she has had countless victories; **je ne compte plus les lettres anonymes que je reçois** I've lost count of the anonymous letters I have received; **il a toujours compté ses sous** he has always watched the pennies; **sans ~** [*donner, dépenser*] freely; **2** (évaluer) **~ une bouteille pour trois** to allow a bottle between three people; **il faut ~ environ 100 francs** you should reckon on GB ou count on paying about 100 francs; **je préfère ~ large** I prefer to be on the safe side; **3** (faire payer) **~ qch à qn** to charge sb for sth; **il m'a compté 250 francs de déplacement** he charged me a 250 francs call- out fee; **4** (inclure) to count; **je vous ai compté dans le nombre des participants** I've counted you as one of ou among the participants; **sans ~ les primes** not counting bonuses; **sans ~ les soucis** not to mention the worry; **notre club compte des gens célèbres** our club has some well-known people among its members; **5** (projeter) **~ faire** to intend to do; **je compte m'acheter un ordinateur** I'm hoping to buy myself a computer; **6** (s'attendre à) **il comptait que je lui prête de l'argent** he expected me to lend him some money; **'je vais t'aider'—'j'y compte bien'** 'I'll help you'—'I should hope so too'. **II** *vi* **1** (dire les nombres) to count; **il ne sait pas ~** he can't count; **2** (calculer) to count, to add up; **il sait très bien ~**, **il compte très bien** he's very good at counting; **3** (avoir de l'importance) to matter (**pour qn** to sb); **ce qui compte c'est qu'ils se sont réconciliés** what matters is that they have made it up; **c'est l'intention** or **le geste qui compte** it's the thought that counts; **ça compte beaucoup pour moi** it means a lot to me; **le salaire compte beaucoup dans le choix d'une carrière** pay is an important factor in the choice of a career; **4** (avoir une valeur) to count; **~ double/triple** to count double/triple; **5** (figurer) **~ au nombre de, ~ parmi** to be counted among; (faire face) **~ avec** to reckon with [*difficultés, concurrence*]; (ne pas oublier) to take [sb/sth] into account [*personne, chose*]; **il doit ~ avec les syndicats** he has to reckon with the unions; **il faut ~ avec l'opinion publique** one must take public opinion into account; **7** **~ sans** (négliger) not to take [sb/sth] into account [*personne, chose*]; **c'était ~ sans le brouillard** that was without allowing for the fog; **8** **~ sur** (attendre) to count on [*personne, aide*]; (dépendre, faire confiance) to rely on [*personne, ressource*]; (prévoir) to reckon on [*somme, revenu*]; **vous pouvez ~ sur moi, je vais m'en occuper** you can rely ou count on me, I'll see to it; **ne compte pas sur moi** (pour venir, participer) count me out; **je vais leur dire ce que j'en pense, tu peux ~ là- dessus**○ or **sur moi!** I'll tell them what I think, you can be sure of that!; **quand il s'agit de faire des bêtises, on peut ~ sur toi**○! HUM trust you to do something silly!.

III se compter *vpr* **leurs victoires se comptent par douzaines** they have had dozens of victories; **les faillites dans la région ne se comptent plus** there have been countless bankruptcies in the area. **IV à compter de** *loc prép* as from; **pendant 12 mois à ~ de la date de vente** for 12 months with effect from the date of sale. **V sans compter que** *loc conj* (en outre) and what is more; (d'autant plus que) especially as.

compte(-)rendu, *pl* **comptes(-)rendus** /kɔ̃trɑ̃dy/ *nm* (de débat, travaux, d'événement) report; (d'article, de livre) review.

compteur /kɔ̃tœr/ *nm* (de fluide) meter; (de distance) clock; **~ d'eau** water meter; **la voiture a 50 000 km au ~** the car has 50,000 km on the clock. ■ **~ kilométrique** ≈ milometer; **~ de vitesse** speedometer.

comptine /kɔ̃tin/ *nf* (pour choisir) counting rhyme; (chansonnette) nursery rhyme.

comptoir /kɔ̃twar/ *nm* **1** (de café) bar; **au ~** at the bar; **2** (de magasin) counter; **~ parfumerie** perfume counter; **3** HIST trading post; **4** FIN branch (*of the Banque de France*). ■ **~ d'enregistrement** check-in desk.

compulser /kɔ̃pylse/ [1] *vtr* to consult.

comte /kɔ̃t/ ▶596 *nm* GÉN count; (titre anglais) earl.

comté /kɔ̃te/ *nm* **1** ADMIN county; **2** HIST earldom (*land*).

comtesse /kɔ̃tɛs/ ▶596 *nf* countess.

comtois, **~e** /kɔ̃twa, az/ ▶509 *adj* of Franche-Comté.

con•, **conne** /kɔ̃, kɔn/ I *adj* **1** (bête) PEJ fucking• stupid, bloody◑ GB stupid; **2** (facile) dead○ easy. II *nm,f* OFFENSIVE bloody◑ idiot GB INJUR, stupid jerk○ INJUR; **faire le ~** to mess about, to arse around◑; **idée/voiture à la ~** lousy○ idea/car.

concasser /kɔ̃kase/ [1] *vtr* **1** CULIN, TECH to crush; **2** MUS to mix.

concave /kɔ̃kav/ *adj* concave.

concavité /kɔ̃kavite/ *nf* **1** (état) concavity; **2** (partie creuse) hollow.

concéder /kɔ̃sede/ [14] *vtr* **1** ADMIN, COMM, ÉCON to grant [*monopole, franchise*] (**à** to); to contract out [*travaux*] (**à** to); **autoroute concédée** motorway GB ou freeway US (which is) under private management; **2** (admettre) to concede.

concentration /kɔ̃sɑ̃trasjɔ̃/ *nf* **1** (attention) concentration; **j'ai besoin de quelques instants de ~** I need to concentrate for a few moments; **2** (accumulation) concentration (**de** of); **~ de troupes aux frontières du pays** build-up of troops on the country's borders; **3** CHIMIE concentration; **4** ÉCON concentration; **~ horizontale/verticale** horizontal/vertical integration. ■ **~ urbaine** conurbation.

concentré, **~e** /kɔ̃sɑ̃tre/ I *adj* **1** (attentif) **un air ~** a look of concentration; **2** (condensé, rassemblé) concentrated. II *nm* **1** CHIMIE (solution) concentrated solution; **2** (aliment) concentrate; **~ de tomate** tomato purée GB ou paste US.

concentrer /kɔ̃sɑ̃tre/ [1] I *vtr* **~ ses efforts sur qch** to concentrate one's efforts on sth. II **se concentrer** *vpr* **1** (être attentif) to concentrate (**sur** on); (se préparer mentalement) to gather one's thoughts; **2** (être dirigé) **se ~ sur qch** [*efforts, attention*] to be concentrated on sth; **3** (être rassemblé) [*population, erreurs, usines*] to be concentrated; **4** (se rassembler) **les grévistes se sont concentrés devant l'usine** the strikers gathered outside the factory.

concentrique /kɔ̃sɑ̃trik/ *adj* concentric.

concept /kɔ̃sɛpt/ *nm* concept.

conception /kɔ̃sɛpsjɔ̃/ *nf* **1** BIOL conception; **2** (formulation d'idée) conception; **3** (élaboration de la forme) design; **au stade de la ~** at the design stage; **4** (idée) idea; (façon de voir) conception.

conceptualiser /kɔ̃sɛptɥalize/ [1] *vtr* to conceptualize.

concernant /kɔ̃sɛrnɑ̃/ *prép* **1** (touchant) concerning; **2** (en ce qui concerne) as regards, with regard to.

concerner /kɔ̃sɛrne/ [1] *vtr* **1** (viser) to concern; **en ce qui me concerne** as far as I am concerned; **en ce qui concerne le salaire** as regards salary, as far as salary is concerned; **cela ne vous concerne pas** (ne vous vise pas) it does not concern you; (ne vous regarde pas) it's no concern of yours; **2** (toucher) to affect; **cette décision nous concerne tous** this decision affects all of us.

concert /kɔ̃sɛr/ I *nm* **1** MUS concert; **~ en plein air** open-air concert; **2** (bruits émis) **~ de klaxons®** a blaring of horns; **~ d'applaudissements** roar of applause; **~ de critiques** barrage of criticism; **3** (entente) **le ~ des nations** the alliance of nations. II **de concert** *loc adv* **ils ont agi de ~** they worked together.

concertation /kɔ̃sɛrtasjɔ̃/ *nf* **1** (discussions) consultation; **agir en ~ avec** to act in consultation with; **2** (fait de travailler de concert) cooperation.

concerté, **~e** /kɔ̃sɛrte/ *adj* [*plan, action*] concerted.

concerter /kɔ̃sɛrte/ [1] I *vtr* to plan. II **se concerter** *vpr* to consult each other.

concertiste /kɔ̃sɛrtist/ ▶374 *nmf* concert performer.

concerto /kɔ̃sɛrto/ *nm* concerto.

concession /kɔ̃sesjɔ̃/ *nf* **1** (compromis) concession (**à** to; **sur** on); **film sans ~s** uncompromising ou forthright film; **2** (attribution) concession; **~ de travaux** works contract; **3** (droit d'exploitation) (de mine, territoire) concession; (de produit) distributorship; AUT dealership; **4** (dans un cimetière) burial plot.

concessionnaire /kɔ̃sesjɔnɛr/ *nmf* **1** (détenteur d'un droit) GÉN concessionaire; **2** (commerçant) (pour un produit) distributor; (pour un service) agent; AUT dealer.

concevable /kɔ̃s(ə)vabl/ *adj* conceivable.

concevoir /kɔ̃s(ə)vwar/ [5] I *vtr* **1** (élaborer) to design [*produit, projet*]; **bien/mal conçu** well/badly designed; **2** (procréer) to conceive [*enfant*]; **3** (comprendre) to understand; **je conçois très bien que** I fully understand why; **je ne conçois pas de faire** I cannot conceive of ou imagine having to do; **4** (considérer) to see (**comme** as); **~ la politique comme un métier** to see politics as a job; **5** (ressentir) FML to conceive [*haine*]; to have [*doute*]. II **se concevoir** *vpr* **1** (être imaginable) to be conceivable; **2** (être compréhensible) to be understandable; **3** (s'élaborer) **se ~ sur ordinateur** to be designed on a computer.

concierge /kɔ̃sjɛrʒ/ ▶374 *nmf* caretaker GB, superintendant US; **c'est une vraie ~** FIG (bavard) she's a real gossip.

concile /kɔ̃sil/ *nm* RELIG council.

conciliable /kɔ̃siljabl/ *adj* reconcilable.

conciliabule /kɔ̃siljabyl/ *nm* consultation, confab○.

conciliant, **~e** /kɔ̃siljɑ̃, ɑ̃t/ *adj* conciliatory.

conciliateur, **-trice** /kɔ̃siljatœr, tris/ *nm,f* conciliator.

conciliation /kɔ̃siljasjɔ̃/ *nf* conciliation; (d'époux) reconciliation; **commission de ~** arbitration committee.

concilier /kɔ̃silje/ [2] I *vtr* **1** GÉN to reconcile; **2** (gagner) FML **cette loi lui a concilié l'opinion publique** this law won over public opinion to his/her side. II **se concilier** *vpr* (conquérir) to win [*bienveillance, soutien*]; to win over [*opinion publique, personne*].

concis, **~e** /kɔ̃si, iz/ *adj* concise.

concision /kɔ̃sizjɔ̃/ *nf* conciseness; **avec ~** concisely.

concitoyen, **-enne** /kɔ̃sitwajɛ̃, ɛn/ *nm,f* fellow-citizen.

concluant, **~e** /kɔ̃klyɑ̃, ɑ̃t/ *adj* conclusive.

conclure /kɔ̃klyr/ [78] I *vtr* **1** (déduire) to conclude (**que** that); **que concluez-vous de ces chiffres?** what conclusion do you draw from these figures?; **il ne faut pas se hâter d'en ~ que** we mustn't jump to the conclusion that; **2** (régler) to conclude [*accord*]; **~ un marché** to close ou clinch ou strike a deal; **'marché**

conclu!' 'it's a deal!'; **3** (mettre fin à) [*personne*] to conclude [*discours*] (**par** with); **4** (être la fin de) [*concert, match*] to bring [sth] to a close [*festival, journée*].
II conclure à *vtr ind* (décider) ~ **à la culpabilité de qn** to conclude that sb is guilty; [*jury*] to return a verdict of guilty.
III *vi* JUR ~ **en faveur de/contre qn** [*témoignage*] to go in favour^{GB} of/against sb; [*juge, jury*] to find in favour^{GB} of/against sb.

conclusion /kɔ̃klyzjɔ̃/ I *nf* **1** (déduction) conclusion; **en** ~ in conclusion; **~, il y a un problème**° in other words, there's a problem; **~, le dîner a été annulé**° so, the dinner was cancelled^{GB}; **tirer les ~s d'une expérience** to learn from an experience; **ne tire pas de ~s hâtives** don't jump to conclusions; **2** (de traité, marché) conclusion; **3** (dénouement) (de discours, session) close; (d'aventure) outcome.
II conclusions *nfpl* **1** (résultats) (d'analyse, autopsie) results; (d'enquête, de rapport) findings; **2** JUR (d'expert) opinion (*sg*); (de jury) verdict (*sg*); (de plaignant) pleadings, submissions.

concocter° /kɔ̃kɔkte/ [1] *vtr* to concoct [*dessert, sauce*]; to devise [*réponse, programme*].

concombre /kɔ̃kɔ̃bʀ/ *nm* cucumber.

concordance /kɔ̃kɔʀdɑ̃s/ *nf* (similarité) concordance (de between); (compatibilité) compatibility; **la parfaite ~ de leurs témoignages** the fact that their accounts agree in every respect; **s'il y a ~ entre les résultats** if the results tally.
■ **~ des temps** LING sequence of tenses.

concordant, ~e /kɔ̃kɔʀdɑ̃, ɑ̃t/ *adj* [*faits*] corroborating; [*témoignages, informations*] which are in agreement (*épith, après n*).

concordat /kɔ̃kɔʀda/ *nm* RELIG concordat.

concorde /kɔ̃kɔʀd/ *nf* FML harmony, concord.

concorder /kɔ̃kɔʀde/ [1] *vi* [*résultats, descriptions, témoignages*] to tally; [*évaluations*] to agree.

concourir /kɔ̃kuʀiʀ/ [26] **I** *vi* **1** (participer) [*athlète, candidat*] to compete (**pour** for; **dans** in); [*livre, film*] to be entered (**pour** for); **2** MATH (converger) to converge.
II concourir à *vtr ind* **1** (collaborer pour) ~ **à qch/à faire** [*facteurs*] to combine to bring about sth/to do; [*personnes*] to work together toward(s) sth/to do; **2** (contribuer à) [*facteur, personne*] ~ **à qch** to help bring about sth; ~ **à faire qch** to help do sth.

concours /kɔ̃kuʀ/ *nm inv* **1** (de piano) competition; (agricole) show; ~ **d'élégance** FIG fashion show; ~ **de beauté** beauty contest; **être hors** ~ to be ineligible to compete; **2** ADMIN, SCOL competitive examination; **3** (aide) help, assistance; (appui) support; (collaboration) cooperation; **avec le** ~ **de l'orchestre des Jeunes** (participation) with the Youth orchestra; **4** SPORT (en athlétisme) field event.
■ **~ de circonstances** combination of circumstances; ; ~ **hippique** (sport) show jumping; (épreuve) horse show.

concret, -ète /kɔ̃kʀɛ, ɛt/ *adj* **1** (réel) [*mesure, résultat*] concrete; [*présence*] tangible; **2** (pragmatique) [*esprit, personne*] practical.

concrètement /kɔ̃kʀɛtmɑ̃/ *adv* (en termes réels) in concrete terms; (en pratique) in practical terms.

concrétisation /kɔ̃kʀetizasjɔ̃/ *nf* (d'alliance) concrete expression; (d'espoir) fulfilment^{GB}; (d'ambition) achievement; **quant à la ~ de ce projet** as for turning this project into a reality.

concrétiser /kɔ̃kʀetize/ [1] **I** *vtr* **1** to make [sth] a reality [*projet*]; to give concrete expression to [*accord*]; to make [sth] concrete [*stratégie*]; **2** SPORT (marquer) to score.
II se concrétiser *vpr* [*projet*] to become a reality; [*offre*] to materialize; [*espoir*] to be fulfilled.

concubin, ~e /kɔ̃kybɛ̃, in/ *nm,f* JUR common law husband/wife.

concubinage /kɔ̃kybinaʒ/ *nm* cohabitation; **ils vivent en** ~ they live together (as husband and wife), they cohabit ADMIN.

concupiscent, ~e /kɔ̃kypisɑ̃, ɑ̃t/ *adj* lecherous, concupiscent SOUT.

concurrence /kɔ̃kyʀɑ̃s/ **I** *nf* **1** (rivalité) competition; **faire (de la)** ~ **à qn** to compete with sb; **prix défiant toute** ~ unbeatable price; **jeu de la** ~ free play of competition; **2** (concurrents) **la** ~ competitors (*pl*).
II jusqu'à ~ **de** *loc prép* up to a limit of.

concurrencer /kɔ̃kyʀɑ̃se/ [12] *vtr* [*personne, entreprise*] to compete with; **être rudement concurrencé par** to come up against fierce competition from.

concurrent, ~e /kɔ̃kyʀɑ̃, ɑ̃t/ **I** *adj* rival.
II *nm,f* (pour un poste) rival; COMM, SPORT competitor.

concurrentiel, -ielle /kɔ̃kyʀɑ̃sjɛl/ *adj* competitive.

condamnable /kɔ̃danabl/ *adj* reprehensible; **les parents sont** ~**s** the parents are to blame.

condamnation /kɔ̃danasjɔ̃/ *nf* **1** JUR (action) conviction; (peine) sentence; **2** (vive critique) condemnation; **3** AUT (verrouillage) ~ **électronique** or **centralisée des portières** central locking.

condamné, ~e /kɔ̃dane/ **I** *adj* **1** (très malade) terminally ill; **2** (fermé) [*porte, fenêtre*] sealed up.
II *nm,f* convicted prisoner.
■ ~ **à mort** condemned man/woman.

condamner /kɔ̃dane/ [1] *vtr* **1** JUR (infliger une peine à) to sentence; ~ **qn à une amende** to fine sb; **il a été condamné à quatre mois de prison avec sursis** he was given a four-month suspended sentence; ~ **qn pour vol** to convict sb of theft; **2** (interdire) [*loi, article*] to punish [*vol, trafic*]; **3** (désapprouver fortement) [*personne, pays*] to condemn [*acte, décision*]; **4** (astreindre à) ~ **qn à** to condemn sb to; **il se voit condamné à un choix difficile** he's being forced to make a difficult choice; ~ **qn à faire** to compel sb to do; **5** (sceller) to seal up [*fenêtre, porte*]; (fermer à clé) to shut up [*pièce*]; to lock [*portières*]; **6** (ruiner) to spell death for [*société, industrie*]; **7** (déclarer incurable) **les médecins l'ont condamné** the doctors have given up hope of saving him.

condensateur /kɔ̃dɑ̃satœʀ/ *nm* condenser.

condensation /kɔ̃dɑ̃sasjɔ̃/ *nf* condensation.

condensé /kɔ̃dɑ̃se/ *nm* (résumé) summary; (recueil) digest.

condenser /kɔ̃dɑ̃se/ [1] *vtr*, **se condenser** *vpr* to condense.

condescendance /kɔ̃desɑ̃dɑ̃s/ *nf* condescension.

condescendre /kɔ̃desɑ̃dʀ/ [6] *vtr ind* ~ **à** to condescend to.

condiment /kɔ̃dimɑ̃/ *nm* **1** CULIN (à la cuisson) seasoning; (à table) condiment; **2** FIG spice.

condisciple /kɔ̃disipl/ *nmf* fellow student.

condition /kɔ̃disjɔ̃/ **I** *nf* **1** (circonstance nécessaire) condition; **c'est possible à** ~ **d'avoir le temps** it's possible provided (that) one has the time; **je vous prêterai la somme, mais sous** ~ I'll lend you the money, but on certain conditions; **sous** ~ [*libéré*] conditionally; **achat sous** ~ purchase on approval; **sans** ~(s) [*capitulation*] unconditional; [*capituler*] unconditionally; **imposer ses** ~**s** to impose one's own terms; **le talent n'est pas la seule** ~ **du succès** talent is not the only requirement for success; ~ **préalable** precondition; ~**s d'attribution d'une bourse** eligibility for a grant; **2** JUR (clause) term; **3** (forme) condition; **être en mauvaise** ~ (physique) to be out of condition ou unfit; **mettre qn en** ~ (physiquement) to get sb fit; (mentalement) to prepare sb; **4** (situation sociale) condition; **la** ~ **ouvrière** the conditions of working-class life; **la** ~ **féminine** or **des femmes** women's position in society; **il s'intéresse beaucoup à la** ~ **féminine** he's very interested in women's affairs; **5** (niveau social) ~ (**sociale**) social status; **accepter sa** ~ to accept one's lot in life; **un jeune homme de** ~ **modeste** a young man from a humble background; **des personnes de toutes** ~**s** people from all walks of life; **6** LING conditionality.
II conditions *nfpl* **1** (ensemble de circonstances) conditions; **dans ces** ~**s** (dans cet environnement) in these conditions; (puisque c'est comme ça) in that case; **2** COMM

(modalités) terms; **~s de financement** methods of financing.

conditionnel, -elle /kɔ̃disjɔnɛl/ **I** *adj* GÉN, LING conditional.
II *nm* LING conditional.

conditionnement /kɔ̃disjɔnmɑ̃/ *nm* **1** (de personne) conditioning; **2** (emballage) packaging **₵**; **~s** forms of packaging.
■ **~ sous vide** vacuum packing.

conditionner /kɔ̃disjɔne/ [1] *vtr* **1** (influencer) to condition [*personne, comportement, animal*]; **2** (déterminer) **votre habileté conditionne votre réussite** your success depends on your skill; **3** (emballer) to package (**en** in); **conditionné sous vide** vacuum-packed.

condoléances /kɔ̃dɔleɑ̃s/ *nfpl* condolences; **toutes mes ~** please accept my deepest sympathy.

condom /kɔ̃dɔm/ *nm* condom.

conducteur, -trice /kɔ̃dyktœʀ, tʀis/ **I** *adj* **1** PHYS conductive; **un matériau peu ~** a poor conductor; **2** (qui guide) [*principe*] guiding.
II ▶ 374| *nm,f* **1** (de véhicule) driver; **2** (responsable) (de machine) operator; (de travaux) foreman.
III *nm* PHYS conductor.
■ **~ de bestiaux** drover; **~ d'engin** - bulldozer driver; **~ de travaux** foreman.

conductibilité /kɔ̃dyktibilite/ *nf* conductivity.

conductible /kɔ̃dyktibl/ *adj* conductive.

conduire /kɔ̃dɥiʀ/ [69] **I** *vtr* **1** (accompagner) to take [*personne*]; (en voiture) to drive [*personne*] (**à** to); **se faire ~ à la gare en taxi** to take a taxi to the station; **conduisez monsieur à sa chambre** show the gentleman to his room; **2** (mener à un lieu) **un bus vous conduira à l'hôtel** a bus will take you to the hotel; **le chemin conduit à l'église** the path leads to the church; **la route qui conduit à Oxford** the road that goes to Oxford; **3** (faire aboutir) **~ à qch** to lead to sth; **~ qn à la faillite** to make sb bankrupt; **~ qn à la folie/au désespoir** to drive sb to madness/to despair; **4** (être aux commandes de) to drive [*voiture, train*]; to ride [*moto*]; **5** (guider) to lead [*personne*] (**à** to); **6** (faire évoluer) to conduct [*recherches, négociations*]; to pursue [*politique*]; to carry out [*projet*]; to run [*affaire commerciale*]; **7** (être à la tête de) to lead [*délégation, troupe*]; **la liste conduite par le candidat socialiste** the list headed by the socialist candidate; **8** PHYS to conduct [*électricité, chaleur*].
II se conduire *vpr* to behave.

conduit /kɔ̃dɥi/ *nm* **1** CONSTR conduit; **2** ANAT canal.
■ **~ d'air chaud** hot-air duct; **~ de fumée** flue; **~ de ventilation** ventilation shaft.

conduite /kɔ̃dɥit/ *nf* **1** (manière d'être) GÉN behaviour^GB; (d'écolier) conduct; **zéro de ~** black mark for bad behaviour^GB; **avoir une ~ bizarre** to behave oddly; **ils n'accepteront pas qu'on leur dicte leur ~** they will not put up with being told what to do; **2** (d'enquête) conducting; (de travaux) supervision; (d'entreprise) management; (de nation) leadership; **mon père m'a laissé la ~ des affaires** my father left me to run the business; **3** (de voiture, train) driving; (de moto) riding; **4** AUT (colonne de direction) **voiture avec ~ à gauche** left-hand drive car; **5**° (examen) driving test; **6** (canalisation) pipe.
■ **~ accompagnée** driving accompanied by a qualified driver.

cône /kon/ *nm* cone.

confection /kɔ̃fɛksjɔ̃/ *nf* **1 la ~** (industrie) the clothing industry; (vêtements) ready-to-wear clothes (*pl*); **2** (élaboration) making.

confectionner /kɔ̃fɛksjɔne/ [1] *vtr* to make [*gâteau, vêtement*]; to prepare [*repas*].

confectionneur, -euse /kɔ̃fɛksjɔnœʀ, øz/ **▶374|** *nm,f* manufacturer of ready-to-wear clothing.

confédération /kɔ̃fedeʀasjɔ̃/ *nf* confederation.
■ **la Confédération helvétique** Switzerland.

confédéré, ~e /kɔ̃fedeʀe/ **I** *adj* [*États*] confederate; [*syndicats*] confederated.
II confédérés *nmpl* HIST **les ~s** the confederates.

confédérer /kɔ̃fedeʀe/ [14] *vtr* to confederate.

conférence /kɔ̃feʀɑ̃s/ *nf* **1** (discours, cours) lecture; **2** (congrès) conference; **3** (discussion) debate.
■ **~ de presse** press conference; **~ au sommet** summit meeting.

conférencier, -ière /kɔ̃feʀɑ̃sje, ɛʀ/ **▶374|** *nm,f* GÉN speaker; UNIV lecturer.

conférer /kɔ̃feʀe/ [14] *vtr* **1** to confer [*droit, statut*]; to award [*décoration*]; **~ le baptême à qn** to baptize sb; **2** FML [*fonction, âge*] to give [*droit, privilège*].

confesse° /kɔ̃fɛs/ *nf* confession.

confesser /kɔ̃fese/ [1] **I** *vtr* to confess [*péché, ignorance*]; **~** to hear sb's confession.
II se confesser *vpr* **1** RELIG to go to confession; **se ~ de qch** to confess (to) sth; **2** (se confier) **se ~ à un ami** to confide in a friend.

confesseur /kɔ̃fesœʀ/ *nm* confessor.

confession /kɔ̃fesjɔ̃/ *nf* **1** (aveu) confession; **2** RELIG confession; **3** (foi) faith.
IDIOMES **on te donnerait le bon Dieu sans ~** you look as if butter wouldn't melt in your mouth.

confessionnal, *pl* **-aux** /kɔ̃fesjɔnal, o/ *nm* confessional.

confessionnel, -elle /kɔ̃fesjɔnɛl/ *adj* GÉN denominational; [*école*] denominational GB, parochial US.

confetti /kɔ̃feti/ *nm* confetti **₵**; **un ~** a piece of confetti.

confiance /kɔ̃fjɑ̃s/ *nf* **1** (foi en l'honnêteté) trust (**en** in); **en toute ~** with complete confidence; **de ~** [*personne*] trustworthy; [*mission*] which requires (the utmost) trust; **avoir ~ en qn, faire ~ à qn** to trust sb; **il va tricher, tu peux lui faire ~!** IRON you can rely on him to cheat! IRON; **j'ai ~ en l'avenir** I feel confident about the future; **2** (foi en la compétence) confidence (**en** in); **faire ~ à** to have confidence in; **3** (assurance) confidence; **~ en soi** (self-)confidence; **ces champignons ne m'inspirent pas ~** I don't feel altogether happy about these mushrooms; **mettre qn en ~** to put sb at ease; **4** POL **voter la ~** to pass a vote of confidence.

confiant, ~e /kɔ̃fjɑ̃, ɑ̃t/ *adj* **1** (certain) confident; **2** (assuré) (self-)confident; **3** (se fiant aux autres) [*personne, regard*] trusting.

confidence /kɔ̃fidɑ̃s/ *nf* secret, confidence; **être dans la ~** to be in on the secret; **faire des ~s à qn sur qch** to confide in sb about sth; **sur le ton de la ~** confidentially.
■ **~s sur l'oreiller** pillow talk **₵**.

confident /kɔ̃fidɑ̃/ *nm* **1** GÉN, THÉÂT confidant; **2** (fauteuil) tête-à-tête.

confidente /kɔ̃fidɑ̃t/ *nf* GÉN, THÉÂT confidante.

confidentialité /kɔ̃fidɑ̃sjalite/ *nf* confidentiality.

confidentiel, -ielle /kɔ̃fidɑ̃sjɛl/ *adj* confidential.

confier /kɔ̃fje/ [2] **I** *vtr* **1** (remettre) **~ qch à qn** to entrust sb with sth [*mission, poste*]; to entrust sth to sb [*argent, valise*]; **~ (la garde d')un enfant à qn** to leave a child in sb's care; **on m'a confié la direction du projet** I have been put in charge of the project; **2** (dire en confidence) **~ à qn** to confide [sth] to sb [*peines, intentions*]; **~ un secret à qn** to tell sb a secret.
II se confier *vpr* to confide (**à** in).

configuration /kɔ̃figyʀasjɔ̃/ *nf* **1** LIT shape; **la ~ du terrain** the lie of the land; **la ~ des lieux** the layout of the premises; **2** FIG (disposition) configuration; (situation) set-up; **3** ORDINAT, PHYS configuration.

confiné, ~e /kɔ̃fine/ *adj* **1** (enfermé) **~ dans une pièce** confined to a room; **esprit ~ dans la routine** mind stuck in a rut; **2** [*atmosphère*] LIT, FIG stuffy; [*air*] stale; **3** [*espace*] confined, restricted.

confiner /kɔ̃fine/ [1] **I** *vtr* **1** (enfermer) **~ qn dans une pièce** to confine sb to a room; **2** (restreindre) **~ qn à une tâche** to restrict sb to a task.
II confiner à *vtr ind* **~ à** to border on.
III se confiner *vpr* to shut oneself away ou up; **se ~ dans un rôle** to restrict oneself to a role.

confins /kɔ̃fɛ̃/ *nmpl* (de territoire) boundaries; (de désert) edges; **aux ~ de l'Europe et de l'Asie** on the borders of Europe and Asia; **aux ~ de la psychologie** FIG on the borders of psychology.

confirmation /kɔ̃fiʀmasjɔ̃/ *nf* **1** (ratification) confirmation; **être la ~ de qch, apporter la ~ de qch** to confirm sth; **2** RELIG confirmation.

confirmer /kɔ̃fiʀme/ [1] **I** *vtr* **1** to confirm [*commande, fait*]; to uphold [*verdict*]; to bear out [*témoignage*]; **~ qn dans son opinion** to reinforce sb's opinion; **2** RELIG to confirm.
II se confirmer *vpr* [*bruit, nouvelle*] to be confirmed; [*témoignage*] to be corroborated; **il se confirme comme l'un de nos meilleurs acteurs** he has established himself as one of our best actors.

confiscation /kɔ̃fiskasjɔ̃/ *nf* confiscation, seizure JUR.

confiserie /kɔ̃fizʀi/ *nf* **1** ▶374⌐ (magasin) confectioner's (shop); **2** (fabrication, commerce) confectionery; **3** (produits) confectionery **¢**.

confiseur, -euse /kɔ̃fizœʀ, øz/ ▶374⌐ *nm,f* confectioner.

confisquer /kɔ̃fiske/ [1] *vtr* **1** (prendre) to confiscate [*bien, propriété*]; **2** FIG (accaparer) to monopolize [*gestion*]; **~ la direction de** to take control of.

confit, ~e /kɔ̃fi, it/ **I** *adj* CULIN [*fruits*] crystallized; [*cornichon*] pickled; [*canard*] preserved.
II *nm* confit; **~ de canard** confit of duck.

confiture /kɔ̃fityʀ/ *nf* CULIN jam, preserve; (d'agrumes) marmalade.
IDIOMES **donner de la ~ aux cochons** to cast pearls before swine; **mettre qch en ~**○ to wreck sth○.

confiturier /kɔ̃fityʀje/ *nm* (récipient) jam pot (*for serving*).

conflictuel, -elle /kɔ̃fliktɥɛl/ *adj* [*sujet*] controversial; [*tendances*] conflicting; **c'est une situation conflictuelle** it's a (potential) source of conflict.

conflit /kɔ̃fli/ *nm* GÉN conflict; (du travail) dispute; **~ de compétence** demarcation dispute.
■ **~ de générations** generation gap; **~ social** industrial strife; **~ du travail** industrial dispute.

confluent /kɔ̃flyɑ̃/ *nm* confluence.

confluer /kɔ̃flye/ [1] *vi* **1** GÉOG to meet, to join; **~ avec** to flow into; **2** FIG [*troupes*] to converge (**vers** on).

confondant, ~e /kɔ̃fɔ̃dɑ̃, ɑ̃t/ *adj* staggering.

confondre /kɔ̃fɔ̃dʀ/ [53] **I** *vtr* **1** (ne pas distinguer) to mix up, to confuse; **je l'ai confondu avec son cousin** I mistook him for his cousin; **tous secteurs confondus** all sectors taken together; **2** (mêler) LITER to merge; **3** (déconcenurer) FML to stagger; **leur ignorance me confondait** I found their ignorance staggering; **4** (démasquer) to expose [*accusé, traître*].
II se confondre *vpr* **1** (se mêler) [*formes, couleurs*] to merge; [*événements, faits*] to become confused; **2** (être identique) [*intérêts, espoirs*] to coincide; **notre avenir se confond avec celui de l'Europe** our future is bound up with that of Europe; **ma vie se confond avec mon œuvre** my life and my work are one; **3** (se répandre) FML **il s'est confondu en excuses** he apologized profusely; **il s'est confondu en remerciements** he was effusive in his thanks.

conforme /kɔ̃fɔʀm/ *adj* **1** (en accord) **être ~ à** to be in keeping with [*loi, tradition*]; to comply with [*règlement*]; **2** (identique) **être ~ à l'original** to conform to the original; **photocopie certifiée ~** ADMIN certified true copy.

conformé, ~e /kɔ̃fɔʀme/ *adj* **bien ~** normally formed; **mal ~** malformed.

conformément /kɔ̃fɔʀmemɑ̃/ *adv* **~ à** in accordance with.

conformer /kɔ̃fɔʀme/ [1] **I** *vtr* **1** (rendre conforme) **il doit ~ sa décision aux directives gouvernementales** his decision should comply with government directives; **2** TECH (donner une forme à) to shape.
II se conformer *vpr* (à un usage) to conform (**à** to); (à un règlement, une norme) to comply (**à** with).

conformisme /kɔ̃fɔʀmism/ *nm* **1** PÉJ conformity, conventionality; **elle est d'un ~!** she's such a conformist!, she's so conventional!; **2** RELIG conformity.

conformiste /kɔ̃fɔʀmist/ *adj, nmf* GÉN, RELIG conformist.

conformité /kɔ̃fɔʀmite/ *nf* **~ à la loi** compliance with the law; **en ~ avec** [*agir*] in accordance with; **mettre qch en ~ avec** to make sth comply with; **vérifier la ~ de la traduction à l'original** to check that the translation is faithful to the original.

confort /kɔ̃fɔʀ/ *nm* comfort; **le ~ moderne** modern conveniences (*pl*); **maison avec tout le ~, maison tout ~** house with all modern conveniences; **il me faut mon ~** I must have my creature comforts; **ça va déranger ton ~** it'll disturb your cosy GB ou cozy US existence; **~ d'écoute** quality of reception; **~ d'utilisation** user-friendliness.

confortable /kɔ̃fɔʀtabl/ *adj* comfortable; **pas ~** uncomfortable; **peu ~** rather uncomfortable.

confortablement /kɔ̃fɔʀtabləmɑ̃/ *adv* comfortably.

conforter /kɔ̃fɔʀte/ [1] *vtr* to consolidate [*position, régime*]; to reinforce [*situation*]; **~ qn dans une opinion** to confirm sb in his/her opinion.

confraternel, -elle /kɔ̃fʀatɛʀnɛl/ *adj* fraternal.

confraternellement /kɔ̃fʀatɛʀnɛlmɑ̃/ *adv* fraternally.

confrère /kɔ̃fʀɛʀ/ *nm* (de travail) colleague; (d'association) fellow member; **ses ~s musiciens** his/her fellow musicians; **dans un entretien accordé à un ~ de la presse écrite** in an interview given to a newspaper.

confrérie /kɔ̃fʀeʀi/ *nf* brotherhood.

confrontation /kɔ̃fʀɔ̃tasjɔ̃/ *nf* **1** (de témoins, d'idées) confrontation; (de textes) comparison; **2** (débat) debate; (affrontement) clash.

confronter /kɔ̃fʀɔ̃te/ [1] *vtr* to confront [*témoins, théories*]; to compare [*expériences, textes*]; **~ qch avec** (pour vérifier) to check sth against.

confus, ~e /kɔ̃fy, yz/ *adj* **1** (indistinct, obscur) confused; **un mélange ~** a hotchpotch GB, a hodgepodge US; **2** (vague) [*sentiment, crainte*] vague; **3** (navré) sorry; (gêné) embarrassed.

confusément /kɔ̃fyzemɑ̃/ *adv* [*requérir, expliquer*] confusedly; [*sentir*] vaguely.

confusion /kɔ̃fyzjɔ̃/ *nf* **1** (désordre) confusion; **jeter la ~ dans les esprits** to throw people into confusion; **2** (gêne) embarrassment; **3** (méprise) mix-up.
■ **~ de peines** JUR concurrency of sentences; **~ des pouvoirs** POL non-separation of powers.

congé /kɔ̃ʒe/ *nm* **1** (arrêt de travail) leave **¢**; **prendre quatre jours de ~** to take four days off; **avoir ~ le lundi** to have Mondays off; **2** SCOL holiday GB, vacation US; **en France les écoles ont ~ le mercredi** in France there is no school on Wednesdays; **3** (fin de contrat) notice; **donner (son)** or **signifier son ~ à qn** to give sb notice.
■ **~s payés** paid leave **¢**; **~s scolaires** school holidays GB ou vacation US (*sg*).
IDIOMES **prendre ~ de qn** to take leave of sb.

congédier /kɔ̃ʒedje/ [2] *vtr* to dismiss.

congelable /kɔ̃ʒlabl/ *adj* suitable for home freezing.

congélateur /kɔ̃ʒelatœʀ/ *nm* freezer, deep-freeze; (dans un réfrigérateur) freezer compartment.

congélation /kɔ̃ʒelasjɔ̃/ *nf* GÉN freezing; (d'huile) congelation.

congelé, ~e /kɔ̃ʒle/ **I** *adj* frozen; **produits ~s** frozen foods.
II *nm* frozen foods (*pl*).

congeler /kɔ̃ʒle/ [17] *vtr,* **se congeler** *vpr* to freeze.

congénère /kɔ̃ʒenɛʀ/ *nmf* (d'animal) fellow creature; (de personne) **vous et vos ~s** PÉJ you and your like.

congénital, ~e, mpl -aux /kɔ̃ʒenital, o/ *adj* congenital.

congère /kɔ̃ʒɛʀ/ *nf* snowdrift.

congestif, -ive /kɔ̃ʒɛstif, iv/ *adj* congestive.

congestion /kɔ̃ʒɛstjɔ̃/ *nf* congestion.
■ **~ cérébrale** stroke; **~ pulmonaire** congestion of the lungs.

congestionner /kɔ̃ʒɛstjɔne/ [1] *vtr* to congest; **il est tout congestionné** he's all flushed.

conglomérat /kɔ̃glɔmeʀa/ *nm* **1** (d'entreprises, de roches) conglomerate; **2** FIG (mélange) conglomeration.

Congo /kɔ̃go/ ▶ 232 ⌐, 260 ⌐ *nprm* Congo.

congolais, **~e** /kɔ̃gɔlɛ, ɛz/ I ▶ 394 ⌐ *adj* Congolese.
II *nm* CULIN (small) coconut cake.

congre /kɔ̃gʀ/ *nm* conger eel.

congrégation /kɔ̃gʀegasjɔ̃/ *nf* **1** RELIG congregation; **2** (assemblée) HUM assembly.

congrès /kɔ̃gʀɛ/ *nm inv* conference; **le Congrès** Congress.

congressiste /kɔ̃gʀesist/ *nmf* (conference) delegate.

congru, **~e** /kɔ̃gʀy/ *adj* MATH congruent (**à** with).

conifère /kɔnifɛʀ/ *nm* conifer.

conique /kɔnik/ *adj* MATH conical; **de forme ~** cone-shaped.

conjecture /kɔ̃ʒɛktyʀ/ *nf* conjecture ₵; **vaines ~s** idle speculation.

conjecturer /kɔ̃ʒɛktyʀe/ [1] *vtr* FML to speculate.

conjoint, **~e** /kɔ̃ʒwɛ̃, ɛ̃t/ I *adj* [démarche, déclaration] joint (épith); [questions, situations] linked.
II *nm,f* spouse; **les ~s** the husband and wife.

conjointement /kɔ̃ʒwɛ̃tmɑ̃/ *adv* **1** (de concert) jointly; **~ et solidairement** JUR jointly and severally; **2** (en même temps) at the same time; **~ avec** together with.

conjonctif, -ive /kɔ̃ʒɔ̃ktif, iv/ *adj* **1** ANAT conjunctival; **2** LING conjunctive.

conjonction /kɔ̃ʒɔ̃ksjɔ̃/ *nf* conjunction.

conjonctivite /kɔ̃ʒɔ̃ktivit/ ▶ 196 ⌐ *nf* conjunctivitis.

conjoncture /kɔ̃ʒɔ̃ktyʀ/ *nf* situation; **bonne ~** favourable[GB] conjunction of circumstances.

conjoncturel, -elle /kɔ̃ʒɔ̃ktyʀɛl/ *adj* [déficit, politique] short-term; [situation, fluctuations] economic; [crise] temporary, cyclical; [prélèvement] temporary; **évolution conjoncturelle** current trends.

conjugaison /kɔ̃ʒygɛzɔ̃/ *nf* **1** BIOL, LING conjugation; **2** FIG (réunion) combination; **la ~ de leurs efforts** their joint efforts (pl).

conjugal, **~e**, *mpl* **-aux** /kɔ̃ʒygal, o/ *adj* [amour, fidélité] conjugal; [drame] marital; [vie] married.

conjuguer /kɔ̃ʒyge/ [1] *vtr* **1** LING to conjugate [verbe]; **2** (combiner) to combine, to unite [efforts].

conjurateur, -trice /kɔ̃ʒyʀatœʀ, tʀis/ *nm,f* chief conspirator.

conjuration /kɔ̃ʒyʀasjɔ̃/ *nf* **1** (complot) conspiracy; **2** (d'influences maléfiques) conjuration.

conjuré, **~e** /kɔ̃ʒyʀe/ *nm,f* conspirator.

conjurer /kɔ̃ʒyʀe/ [1] *vtr* **1** to avert [crise, inflation]; to ward off [danger, sort]; to banish [angoisse, solitude]; **2 je vous en conjure** I beg you.

connaissance /kɔnɛsɑ̃s/ I *nf* **1** (savoir) knowledge (**de** of); **avoir ~ de qch** to know something about sth; **il a une profonde ~ de la psychologie humaine** he has a deep understanding of the way the human mind works; **prendre ~ d'un texte** to acquaint oneself with a text; **donner ~ de qch à qn** to inform sb of sth; **porter à la ~ de qn que** FML to advise sb that; **en ~ de cause** with full knowledge of the facts; **2** (conscience) consciousness; **rester sans ~** to be unconscious; **3** (sur le plan social) acquaintance; **j'ai fait leur ~ hier** I met them yesterday; **faire (plus ample) ~ avec qn** to get to know sb (better); **un visage de ~** a familiar face; **se retrouver en pays de ~** (avec des gens que l'on connaît) to be among familiar faces; (dans un domaine familier) to find oneself on familiar ground.
II **connaissances** *nfpl* (théoriques) knowledge ₵; (pratiques) experience ₵; '**~s en informatique souhaitées**' 'computing experience desirable'.

connaisseur, -euse /kɔnɛsœʀ, øz/ I *adj m* [air, œil] expert.
II *nm,f* expert, connoisseur; **regarder qch en ~** to look at sth with an expert eye.

connaître /kɔnɛtʀ/ [73] I *vtr* **1** to know [fait, nom, événement]; **il ne tient jamais ses promesses, c'est (bien) connu** it is common knowledge that he never

keeps his promises; **je ne leur connais aucun vice** I don't know them to have any vices; **tu connais la nouvelle?** have you heard the news?; **ne ~ que son devoir** to think of nothing but one's duty; **2** to know, to be acquainted with [sujet, méthode, auteur]; **la mécanique, je ne connais que ça** or **ça me connaît!** I know quite a bit about mechanics; **3** to know [faim]; to experience [crise]; to enjoy [gloire]; to have [difficultés]; **ils ont connu la défaite** they were defeated; **il a connu la prison** he's been to prison before; **les problèmes d'argent, ça me connaît**[○]! I could tell you a thing or two[○] about money problems!; **~ des hauts et des bas** to have one's/its ups and downs; **~ une fin tragique** to come to a tragic end; **~ une forte croissance** to show a rapid growth; **4** to know [personne, acteur]; **c'est bien mal la ~** they/you're misjudging her; **faire ~ qn à qn** to introduce sb to sb; **Bernadette? je ne connais qu'elle!** Bernadette? I know her very well!; **il ne me connaît plus depuis qu'il est passé officier** he ignores me now that he's an officer; **5**[†] (coucher avec) to know[†], to have a sexual relationship with; **6** JUR **~ de** to have jurisdiction over [affaire, cause]; **avoir à ~ de** to judge ou hear [cas].
II **se connaître** *vpr* **1** (soi-même) to know oneself; '**connais-toi toi-même**' 'know thyself'; **il ne se connaissait plus de joie** FML he was beside himself with joy; **2** (l'un l'autre) to know each other; **3** (être compétent) **s'y ~ en théâtre** to know all about theatre; **c'est le carburateur qui est bouché ou je ne m'y connais pas**[○] if I know anything about it, it's the carburettor GB ou carburetor US that's blocked.
IDIOMES **on connaît la chanson** or **musique!** we've heard it all before!; **~ qch comme sa poche** to know sth like the back of one's hand.

conne ▶ **con** I, II.

connecter /kɔnɛkte/ [1] *vtr* to connect (**à** to).

connétable /kɔnetabl/ *nm* HIST supreme commander of the French armies.

connexe /kɔnɛks/ *adj* related (**à** to).

connexion /kɔnɛksjɔ̃/ *nf* LIT, FIG connection.

connivence /kɔnivɑ̃s/ *nf* (complicité) connivance ₵; (accord tacite) tacit agreement; **signe de ~** sign of complicity; **être de ~ avec qn** to connive with sb.

connotation /kɔnɔtasjɔ̃/ *nf* connotation.

connoter /kɔnɔte/ [1] *vtr* to connote.

conque /kɔ̃k/ *nf* ZOOL, ARCHIT conch.

conquérant, **~e** /kɔ̃keʀɑ̃, ɑ̃t/ I *adj* [peuple] conquering; FIG [air] triumphant.
II *nm,f* (guerrier) conqueror.

conquérir /kɔ̃keʀiʀ/ [35] *vtr* to conquer [pays, sommet]; to capture [marché]; to gain [pouvoir]; to win [amitié, personne]; to win over [auditoire]; **leur talent a conquis Paris** they captivated Paris with their talent.
IDIOMES **se croire en pays** or **terrain conquis** to lord it over everyone.

conquête /kɔ̃kɛt/ *nf* conquest; **faire la ~ d'un pays** to conquer a country; **~s sociales** social victories; **partir à la ~ de** to set out to conquer [pays, sommet, pouvoir]; to set out to capture [marché]; to set out to achieve [bonheur]; **faire la ~ d'une femme** to win the heart of a lady.

conquis, **~e** /kɔ̃ki, iz/ ▶ **conquérir**.

consacré, **~e** /kɔ̃sakʀe/ *adj* **formule** or **expression ~e** time-honoured[GB] expression; **selon la formule ~e** as the expression goes; **artiste ~** recognized artist; **être ~ joueur de l'année** to be designated player of the year.

consacrer /kɔ̃sakʀe/ [1] I *vtr* **1** to devote [effort, vie, exposition] (**à** to); **2** to sanction [rupture, alliance]; **l'usage a consacré le mot** the word has gained acceptance through use; **3** RELIG to consecrate [basilique, évêque]; to ordain [prêtre]; **jour consacré** holy day.
II **se consacrer** *vpr* **se ~ à** to devote oneself to.

consanguin, **~e** /kɔ̃sɑ̃gɛ̃, in/ *adj* **union ~e**, **mariage ~** marriage between blood relations; **frère ~** half brother (having the same father).

consciemment /kɔ̃sjamã/ *adv* consciously.

conscience /kɔ̃sjɑ̃s/ *nf* **1** (morale) conscience; **écouter (la voix de) sa** ~ to follow one's conscience; **j'ai ma** ~ **pour moi** my conscience is clear; **2** (connaissance) awareness; **avoir** ~ **de** to be aware of; **prise de** ~ realization; ~ **de soi** self-awareness; **scruter les** ~**s** to read people's thoughts; **perdre/reprendre** ~ to lose/to regain consciousness; **avoir toute sa** ~ to be fully lucid.
■ ~ **professionnelle** conscientiousness.

consciencieusement /kɔ̃sjɑ̃sjøzmɑ̃/ *adv* **1** (avec sérieux) conscientiously; **2** (comme il se doit) dutifully.

consciencieux, -ieuse /kɔ̃sjɑ̃sjø, øz/ *adj* GÉN conscientious; [*enfant, époux*] dutiful.

conscient, ~e /kɔ̃sjɑ̃, ɑ̃t/ I *adj* **1** (au fait) aware; **2** (lucide) conscious; **de façon** ~**e** consciously.
II *nm* conscious.

conscription /kɔ̃skripsjɔ̃/ *nf* conscription GB, draft US.

conscrit /kɔ̃skri/ *nm* **1** MIL conscript GB, draftee US; **2**° (de la même année) **c'est mon** ~ he was born in the same year as me.

consécration /kɔ̃sekrasjɔ̃/ *nf* **1** (reconnaissance) recognition; **connaître la** ~ to win recognition; **2** RELIG (de basilique, d'évêque) consecration; (de prêtre) ordination.

consécutif, -ive /kɔ̃sekytif, iv/ *adj* GÉN, LING consecutive; **retards** ~**s à la modernisation** delays resulting from modernization; **série de procès** ~**s au scandale** series of court cases following the scandal.

consécutivement /kɔ̃sekytivmɑ̃/ *adv* consecutively.

conseil /kɔ̃sɛj/ *nm* **1** (avis) advice ¢; ~ **d'ami** piece of friendly advice; **quelques** ~**s de prudence** a few words of caution ou warning; **donner à qn le** ~ **de faire** to advise sb to do; **il est de bon** ~ he always gives good advice; **2** (assemblée) council; **tenir** ~ to hold a meeting; **3** (conseiller) consultant; ~ **en gestion** management consultant.
■ ~ **d'administration** board of directors; ~ **de classe** staff meeting (*for all those teaching a given class*); ~ **de discipline** disciplinary committee; ~ **de famille** JUR Board of Guardians; (non officiel) family meeting ou gathering; ~ **général** POL *council of a French department*; ~ **de guerre** council of war; ~ **des ministres** GÉN council of ministers; (en Grande-Bretagne) Cabinet meeting; ~ **de révision** MIL medical board (*assessing fitness for military service*); ~ **de surveillance** supervisory board; ~ **d'université** senate; **Conseil d'État** Council of State (*advising government on administrative matters*); **Conseil supérieur de l'audiovisuel, CSA** RADIO, TV *body which monitors broadcasting*; **Conseil supérieur de la magistrature** High Council for the Judiciary; ~**s d'entretien** cleaning ou care instructions.

conseillé, ~e /kɔ̃seje/ *adj* [*modèle, activité*] recommended; **il est** ~ **de faire** it is advisable to do.

conseiller, -ère /kɔ̃seje, ɛr/ [1] I *nm,f* **1** (expert) adviser^GB; ~ **du président** presidential adviser; ~ **en communication** communications adviser; **2** (guide) counsellor^GB.
II *nm* (membre de conseil) councillor^GB; (diplomate) counsellor^GB.
III *vtr* **1** (proposer) to recommend [*lieu, activité, prudence*]; ~ **à qn de faire** to advise sb to do; **2** (servir d'expert à) to advise [*personne*]; **se faire** ~ **par qn** to seek advice from sb.
■ ~ **commercial** commercial counsellor^GB; ~ **culturel** cultural counsellor^GB; ~ **(principal) d'éducation** chief supervisor; ~ **d'État** member of the Council of State; ~ **général** POL *councillor^GB for a French department*; ~ **municipal** town councillor^GB; ~ **d'orientation** careers adviser; ~ **régional** regional councillor^GB.

consensuel, -elle /kɔ̃sɛ̃sɥɛl/ *adj* [*politique*] consensual; [*réforme*] based on consensus.

consensus /kɔ̃sɛ̃sys/ *nm inv* consensus.

consentant, ~e /kɔ̃sɑ̃tɑ̃, ɑ̃t/ *adj* [*personne*] willing; JUR consenting; **les parents doivent être** ~**s** the parents must give their consent; **sourire** ~ smile of consent.

consentement /kɔ̃sɑ̃tmɑ̃/ *nm* consent (à to); **divorce par** ~ **mutuel** JUR divorce by consent GB, no-fault divorce US.

consentir /kɔ̃sɑ̃tir/ [30] I *vtr* to grant [*permission, prêt*]; to allow [*avantage*].
II **consentir à** *vtr ind* ~ **à qch/à faire** to agree to sth/to do.
IDIOMES **qui ne dit mot consent** PROV silence means consent PROV.

conséquence /kɔ̃sekɑ̃s/ *nf* consequence (**pour** for; **sur** to); **être lourd de** ~**s** to have serious consequences; **tirer les** ~**s de qch** to learn one's lesson from sth; **ne pas tirer à** ~ to be of no consequence; ~ **heureuse** happy result; **avoir pour** ~ **de faire** to have the effect of doing; **avoir pour** ~ **le chômage** to result in unemployment; **en** ~ **(de quoi)** as a result (of which); **agir en** ~ to act accordingly; **avoir des qualifications et un salaire en** ~ to have qualifications and a corresponding salary.

conséquent, ~e /kɔ̃sekɑ̃, ɑ̃t/ I *adj* **1** (important) substantial; **2** (cohérent) consistent; **3** GÉOG, LING, PHILOS consequent.
II **par conséquent** *loc adv* therefore, as a result.

conservateur, -trice /kɔ̃sɛrvatœr, tris/ I *adj* **1** POL conservative; **2** CHIMIE preservative.
II *nm,f* **1** POL conservative; **2** ▶ 374] (de musée) curator; (de bibliothèque) chief GB ou head US librarian.
III *nm* CHIMIE preservative; **'garanti sans** ~**s'** 'no preservatives'.
■ ~ **des hypothèques** land registrar.

conservation /kɔ̃sɛrvasjɔ̃/ *nf* **1** (protection) (d'espèce, de patrimoine) conservation; (de livres, tableaux) preservation; **2** (d'aliment) preservation; **lait longue** ~ long-life milk GB; **3** PHYS conservation.
■ ~ **des hypothèques** ADMIN land registry.

conservatisme /kɔ̃sɛrvatism/ *nm* conservatism ¢; **les** ~**s** conservative attitudes.

conservatoire /kɔ̃sɛrvatwar/ I *adj* JUR protective.
II *nm* academy; ~ **de musique** conservatoire of music.
■ **Conservatoire national des arts et métiers** (musée) *museum of technology*; (centre d'études) *institute for engineering studies*.

conserve /kɔ̃sɛrv/ I *nf* **1** IND canned food; ~**s de poissons** canned fish; **fruits en** ~ canned fruit; **boîte de** ~ can; **2** CULIN preserve.
II **de conserve** *loc adv* [*agir*] in concert; [*naviguer*] in convoy.

conserver /kɔ̃sɛrve/ [1] *vtr* **1** to keep [*brouillon, emploi*]; to retain [*influence, titre*]; ~ **son calme** to keep calm; ~ **l'anonymat** to remain anonymous; **2** CULIN to preserve [*aliment*]; ~ **dans du vinaigre** to pickle; **'à** ~ **au frais'** 'keep refrigerated'; **3** (maintenir jeune) [*sport*] to keep [sb] young [*personne*]; **homme bien conservé** well-preserved man.

conserverie /kɔ̃sɛrvəri/ *nf* **1** (usine) cannery; **2** (secteur) canning industry.

considérable /kɔ̃siderabl/ *adj* [*fortune, difficulté, retard*] considerable; [*rôle, événement*] significant; **l'enjeu est** ~ the stakes are high.

considérablement /kɔ̃siderablǝmɑ̃/ *adv* considerably, significantly.

considération /kɔ̃siderasjɔ̃/ *nf* **1** (facteur) consideration; **en** ~ **de** in view of; **sans** ~ **de** irrespective of; **2** (respect) consideration; **jouir d'une** ~ **unanime** to be respected by all; **3** (remarque) reflection.

considéré, ~e /kɔ̃sidere/ *adj* (en question) under consideration.

considérer /kɔ̃sidere/ [14] I *vtr* **1** (juger) ~ **qn/qch comme (étant)** to consider sb/sth to be; ~ **comme criminels ceux qui polluent l'atmosphère** to regard those who pollute the atmosphere as criminals; **il considère comme acquise sa victoire électorale** he sees himself as having already won the election; **2** (envisager) to regard [*personne*]; to consider [*chose*]; **à tout bien** ~ all things considered; **3** (respecter) to have a high regard for; **4** (examiner) to consider; **5** (regarder attentivement) to look at [*personne, spectacle*].

II se considérer *vpr* **1** (soi-même) **se ~ (comme)** to consider oneself (to be); **2** (l'un l'autre) **se ~ (comme)** to regard one another as being; (s'étudier) to gaze at each other.

consignation /kɔ̃siɲasjɔ̃/ *nf* **1** JUR, FIN deposit; **2** COMM **en ~** on consignment.

consigne /kɔ̃siɲ/ *nf* **1** (ordre) orders (*pl*), instructions (*pl*); **donner ~ de faire** to give orders to do; **donner** or **lancer une ~ de grève** to issue strike orders; **passer la ~ à qn** to pass the word on to sb; *'~s à suivre en cas d'incendie'* 'fire regulations'; **2** (pour les bagages) left luggage office GB, baggage checkroom US; **3** (de bouteilles, d'emballages) deposit. ■ **~ automatique** left luggage lockers (*pl*) GB, baggage lockers (*pl*) US.

consigné, **~e** /kɔ̃siɲe/ *adj* [*bouteille, emballage*] returnable; **non ~** nonreturnable.

consigner /kɔ̃siɲe/ [1] *vtr* **1** to record, to write [sth] down [*fait, souvenir*]; **2** MIL to confine [*soldat*]; SCOL to give [sb] detention [*élève*]; **3** to consign [*objet, marchandise*]; **4** to charge a deposit on [*bouteille*].

consistance /kɔ̃sistɑ̃s/ *nf* **1** (de pâte, sauce, peinture) consistency; **manquer de ~** [*sauce, peinture*] to be too runny; **prendre ~** to thicken; **2** (d'argument, de théorie) substance, weight; **sans ~** [*personne*] spineless; [*bonheur*] with no reality.

consistant, **~e** /kɔ̃sistɑ̃, ɑ̃t/ *adj* [*repas, investissement*] substantial; [*plat*] nourishing; [*sauce, peinture*] thick; [*livre*] with some substance; [*argument*] solid.

consister /kɔ̃siste/ [1] *vi* **1** (résider) **~ en** or **dans** to consist in; **en quoi consiste mon erreur?** where have I gone wrong?; **2** (être fait) **~ en** to consist of [*éléments, parties*]; **en quoi consiste cette aide?** what form does this aid take?

consœur /kɔ̃sœʀ/ *nf* **1** (d'une personne) female colleague; **2** (d'une banque, organisation) counterpart.

consolant, **~e** /kɔ̃sɔlɑ̃, ɑ̃t/ *adj* comforting.

consolation /kɔ̃sɔlasjɔ̃/ *nf* consolation.

console /kɔ̃sɔl/ *nf* console. ■ **~ de jeu vidéo** games console; **~ de mixage** mixing desk.

consoler /kɔ̃sɔle/ [1] *vtr* to console [*personne*] (**de** for); to soothe away [*peine*]; **cela console de savoir que** it is some consolation to know that; **si ça peut te ~** if it is any comfort to you.

II se consoler *vpr* **1** (soi-même) to find consolation; **se ~ de** to get over [*échec*]; **2** (réciproquement) to console each other.

consolidable /kɔ̃sɔlidabl/ *adj* **1** [*dette*] fundable; **2** [*structure*] reinforceable.

consolidation /kɔ̃sɔlidasjɔ̃/ *nf* **1** (de mur) strengthening; (de position) consolidation; **2** (de dette) consolidation, funding; (de chiffre d'affaires, bilan) consolidation; (de monnaie) strengthening; **3** (de fracture) mending.

consolider /kɔ̃sɔlide/ [1] I *vtr* (renforcer) to strengthen [*mur*]; to consolidate [*position, résultat, bénéfice, dette*]; to strengthen [*monnaie*]; MÉD to set [*fracture, tissus*].

II se consolider *vpr* **1** (se renforcer) GÉN to grow stronger; [*position*] to be consolidated; [*structure*] to be strengthened; **2** (s'affermir) to consolidate; **3** MÉD [*fracture, tissus*] to mend.

consommable /kɔ̃sɔmabl/ I *adj* **1** [*aliment*] edible; [*boisson*] drinkable; **2** TECH expendable.

II consommables *nmpl* COMM, ORDINAT consumables.

consommateur, **-trice** /kɔ̃sɔmatœʀ, tʀis/ I *adj* consumer (*épith*); **~ de pétrole/d'énergie** oil-/energy-consuming (*épith*).

II *nm,f* **1** ÉCON consumer; **défense des ~s** consumer protection; **2** (de café, bar) customer.

consommation /kɔ̃sɔmasjɔ̃/ *nf* **1** consumption; **~ intérieure** domestic consumption; **~ des ménages** household consumption; **pour ma ~ personnelle** for my personal use; **faire une grande** or **grosse ~ de** to use a lot of; **limitez la ~ de matières grasses** avoid eating fatty foods; **une réduction de la ~ de sodium** a reduction in sodium intake; **2** (boisson)

drink; **régler les ~s** to pay for the drinks; **3** (accomplissement) consummation SOUT.

consommé, **~e** /kɔ̃sɔme/ I *adj* [*art, artiste*] consummate; **avec un sens ~ du spectacle** with a consummate sense of the theatrical.

II *nm* CULIN consommé.

consommer /kɔ̃sɔme/ [1] I *vtr* **1** ▶**486** (utiliser) to consume; **ma voiture consomme énormément** my car consumes a lot of petrol GB ou gas US; **2** (manger) to eat; (boire) to drink; **~ de la drogue** to take drugs; **3** (accomplir) FML to consummate SOUT [*mariage*]; to complete [*rupture*].

II *vi* **1** ÉCON to consume; **2** COMM (boire) to drink.

III se consommer *vpr* **1** (être mangé) to be eaten; **le gaspacho se consomme froid** gazpacho is eaten cold; **2** (être utilisé) to be consumed.

consonance /kɔ̃sɔnɑ̃s/ *nf* consonance; **un mot aux ~s étrangères** a foreign-sounding word.

consonant, **~e** /kɔ̃sɔnɑ̃, ɑ̃t/ *adj* consonant.

consonantique /kɔ̃sɔnɑ̃tik/ *adj* [*langue*] consonantal; [*groupe*] consonant (*épith*).

consonne /kɔ̃sɔn/ *nf* consonant.

consortium /kɔ̃sɔʀsjɔm/ *nm* consortium.

conspirateur, **-trice** /kɔ̃spiʀatœʀ, tʀis/ I *adj* conspiratorial.

II *nm,f* conspirator.

conspiration /kɔ̃spiʀasjɔ̃/ *nf* conspiracy.

conspirer /kɔ̃spiʀe/ [1] I *vi* (comploter) to conspire, to plot (**contre** against).

II conspirer à *vtr ind* **~ à** to conspire to bring about [*malheur, succès*]; **~ à faire** to conspire to do.

conspuer /kɔ̃spɥe/ [1] *vtr* to boo.

constamment /kɔ̃stamɑ̃/ *adv* **1** (invariablement) always; **2** (sans interruption) [*augmenter*] continuously; [*maintenir*] consistently; **3** (très souvent) [*dérangé, malade*] constantly.

constance /kɔ̃stɑ̃s/ *nf* **1** (caractère stable) (de sentiment, phénomène) constancy; (d'opinion) consistency; **2** (persévérance) steadfastness; **affirmer avec ~ que...** to hold steadfastly that...; **travailler avec ~** to work steadily; **3**° (patience) patience.

constant, **~e**[1] /kɔ̃stɑ̃, ɑ̃t/ *adj* **1** GÉN constant; [*personne*] (dans ses affections) constant; (dans ses opinions) consistent; **2** (continu) [*progression*] continuous; [*hausse*] continual; **3** (persévérant) LITER [*personne*] steadfast; [*résolution*] firm.

■ Note On utilise *continuous* pour décrire une action qui ne cesse pas et *continual* pour décrire une action qui se répète.

constante[2] /kɔ̃stɑ̃t/ *nf* **1** MATH, PHYS constant; **2** FIG (trait) permanent feature.

constat /kɔ̃sta/ *nm* **1** (procès-verbal) certified ou official report; **2** (bilan) assessment; **3** (preuve) acknowledgement.

■ **~ (à l') amiable** accident report drawn up by the parties involved; **~ d'adultère** JUR record of adultery; **~ d'échec** FIG admission of failure; **~ d'huissier** JUR bailiff's report.

constatable /kɔ̃statabl/ *adj* observable.

constatation /kɔ̃statasjɔ̃/ I *nf* **1** (observation) observation; **c'est une simple ~** it's simply a statement of fact; **2** (enquête) investigation; (rapport d'enquête) report.

II constatations *nfpl* (conclusions) findings.

constater /kɔ̃state/ [1] *vtr* **1** (observer) to notice; **~ une amélioration** to note an improvement; **~ (par) soi-même** to see for oneself; **2** (établir) to ascertain, to establish [*fait*]; (consigner) to record [*délit*]; **~ le décès** to certify that death has occurred.

constellation /kɔ̃stɛlasjɔ̃/ *nf* **1** (en astronomie) constellation; **2** (groupe) (de partis, villes) cluster; (de firmes) group.

constellé, **~e** /kɔ̃stɛle/ *adj* **~ de** spangled with [*étoiles*]; scattered with [*fleurs*]; riddled with [*fautes*]; spotted with [*taches*]; **ciel ~ d'étoiles** starry sky.

consternant, **~e** /kɔ̃stɛʀnɑ̃, ɑ̃t/ *adj* [*fait*] distressing; [*bêtise*] appalling.

consternation /kɔ̃stɛʀnasjɔ̃/ *nf* consternation, dismay.

consterner /kɔ̃stɛʀne/ [1] *vtr* to fill [sb] with consternation; **mine consternée** look of dismay.

constipation /kɔ̃stipasjɔ̃/ *nf* constipation.

constipé, ~e /kɔ̃stipe/ *adj* **1** MÉD constipated; **2**° FIG (contraint) **avoir l'air ~** to look uptight.

constiper /kɔ̃stipe/ [1] *vtr* to make [sb] constipated; **le chocolat constipe** chocolate causes constipation.

constituant, ~e /kɔ̃stitɥɑ̃, ɑ̃t/ **I** *adj* constituent.
II *nm* GÉN, LING constituent.

Constituante /kɔ̃stitɥɑ̃t/ *nf* HIST, POL Constituent Assembly.

constitué, ~e /kɔ̃stitɥe/ *adj* **1** (physiquement) **personne bien/mal ~e** person of sound/unsound constitution; **2** POL constituted.

constituer /kɔ̃stitɥe/ [1] **I** *vtr* **1** (être) to be, to constitute; **le vol constitue un délit** theft constitutes an offence^{GB}; **2** (mettre en place) to form [*équipe, commission*]; **3** (composer) to make up [*ensemble*]; **4** JUR to settle [*dot, rente*] (à, pour on); **~ qn héritier** to appoint sb as heir.
II se constituer *vpr* **1** (se mettre en place) [*parti, réseau*] to be formed; **2** (créer pour soi) to build up [*réseau, clientèle, réserve*]; to get oneself [*alibi*]; **3** (se grouper) **se ~ en** to form [*parti, société*]; **4** (se faire) **se ~ prisonnier** to give oneself up; **se ~ partie civile** to institute a civil action.

constitutif, -ive /kɔ̃stitytif, iv/ *adj* **1** [*élément*] constituent; **2** POL [*assemblée*] constituent; [*congrès*] founding; [*réunion*] inaugural; [*texte*] constitutional.

constitution /kɔ̃stitysjɔ̃/ *nf* **1** (création) **~ d'une société** setting up of a company; **en voie de ~** currently being set up; **~ de capital** capital accumulation; **~ de stocks** stockpiling; **2** (physique) constitution; **bonne ~** sound constitution; **3** JUR (de rente, pension) settling ¢; **~ de partie civile** institution of civil action proceedings.

Constitution /kɔ̃stitysjɔ̃/ *nf* constitution.

constitutionnel, -elle /kɔ̃stitysjɔnɛl/ *adj* constitutional.

constructeur, -trice /kɔ̃stʀyktœʀ, tʀis/ **I** *adj* **1** (créateur) constructive; **2** CONSTR **société constructrice** construction company; **3** ZOOL **animal ~** builder.
II ▶ 374 *nm,f* **1** IND manufacturer; **~ automobile** or **d'automobiles** car manufacturer; **~ naval** shipwright; **2** CONSTR builder.

constructible /kɔ̃stʀyktibl/ *adj* building (*épith*), suitable for development (*après n*); **terrain ~** building land.

constructif, -ive /kɔ̃stʀyktif, iv/ *adj* constructive.

construction /kɔ̃stʀyksjɔ̃/ *nf* **1** GÉN building; **en (cours de) ~** under construction; **bâtiment de ~ ancienne** old building; **2** ÉCON (secteur industriel) **la ~** the construction industry; **3** IND manufacture; **~ de moteurs** engine manufacture; **de ~ japonaise** made in Japan ; **~ aéronautique** aircraft manufacturing; **~ électrique** electrical engineering; **~ ferroviaire** railway construction; **~ navale** shipbuilding; **4** POL, LING, MATH construction; **5** (élaboration) construction; **une pure ~ de l'esprit** pure imagination.

constructivisme /kɔ̃stʀyktivism/ *nm* constructivism.

construire /kɔ̃stʀɥiʀ/ [69] **I** *vtr* **1** LIT to build; **~ des voitures** to manufacture cars; **se faire ~ une villa** to have a villa built; **2** FIG to build [*Europe, avenir*]; to shape [*personnalité, image*]; **3** LING to construct [*phrase, théorie*]; **4** MATH to construct [*triangle*].
II se construire *vpr* **1** (bâtir pour soi) **se ~ une maison** to build a house for oneself; **se ~ son identité** FIG to shape one's own identity; **2** (être bâti) to be built; **3** LING to be constructed; **se ~ avec le subjonctif** to take the subjunctive.

consul /kɔ̃syl/ *nm* consul.

consulaire /kɔ̃sylɛʀ/ *adj* consular.

consulat /kɔ̃syla/ *nm* **1** ADMIN consulate; **2** HIST **le Consulat** the Consulate.

consultable /kɔ̃syltabl/ *adj* available for consultation (*après n*).

consultant, ~e /kɔ̃syltɑ̃, ɑ̃t/ ▶ 374 *nm,f* consultant.

consultatif, -ive /kɔ̃syltatif, iv/ *adj* consultative.

consultation /kɔ̃syltasjɔ̃/ *nf* **1** (heures de réception des malades) surgery hours (*pl*) GB, office hours (*pl*) US; **~ des nourrissons/de planning familial** baby/family planning clinic; **2** (examen médical) consultation; **3** (fait de prendre un avis) consulting; **après ~ des experts** after consulting the experts; **~ électorale** election; **~ juridique** legal consultation; **4** (délibération) consultation; **5** (de calendrier, livre, document) consultation; **'~ sur place'** (dans une bibliothèque) 'for reference use only'; **la ~ de l'annuaire n'a rien donné** we/they etc looked in the directory but in vain.

consulter /kɔ̃sylte/ [1] **I** *vtr* to consult [*personne, ouvrage*]; **~ le peuple** to hold a general election.
II *vi* MÉD (recevoir les patients) to hold surgery GB, to see patients.
III se consulter *vpr* **1** (échanger des vues) to consult together; **se ~ du regard** to exchange glances; **2** (être consultable) **'se consulte sur place'** 'for reference use only'.

consumer /kɔ̃syme/ [1] **I** *vtr* **1** (brûler) to consume [*forêt*]; **2** FIG, LITER **l'amour le consumait** he was consumed with love; **la maladie qui la consume** the illness which is eating away at her; **il a consumé son temps/sa vie en vains plaisirs** he wasted his time/his life in idle pleasures.
II se consumer *vpr* **1** (brûler) to be burning; **la mèche devrait se ~ en quelques minutes** the fuse should burn out in a few minutes; **2** FIG, LITER to waste away; **se ~ d'amour** to be consumed with love (**pour** for); **se ~ en vains efforts** to weary oneself in vain efforts.

contact /kɔ̃takt/ *nm* **1** (relation) contact ¢; **prendre ~ avec** to make contact with; **garder le ~** to keep in touch; **entrer en ~ avec** to get in touch with; **avoir un bon ~ avec qn** to get on well with sb; **être d'un ~ agréable** to be easy to get on with; **elle est devenue plus sociable à ton ~** she's become more sociable through spending time with you; **2** (toucher) contact; **3** ÉLECTROTECH contact; **couper le ~** AUT to switch off the ignition; ▶ **faux**¹; **4** (personne) contact.

contacter /kɔ̃takte/ [1] **I** *vtr* to contact.
II se contacter *vpr* to get in touch with each other.

contagieux, -ieuse /kɔ̃taʒjø, øz/ *adj* **1** MÉD contagious; **2** FIG [*rire, enthousiasme*] infectious, catching (*jamais épith*).

contagion /kɔ̃taʒjɔ̃/ *nf* **1** MÉD contagion; **2** FIG infectiousness; **craindre la ~ de certaines idées** to fear the spread of certain ideas.

contamination /kɔ̃taminasjɔ̃/ *nf* contamination.

contaminer /kɔ̃tamine/ [1] *vtr* GÉN to contaminate; [*virus*] to infect [*personne*]; to contaminate [*programme*].

conte /kɔ̃t/ *nm* **1** LITTÉRAT tale, story; **~ de fées** fairy tale; **2** (racontar) story.

contemplatif, -ive /kɔ̃tɑ̃platif, iv/ *adj* contemplative.

contemplation /kɔ̃tɑ̃plasjɔ̃/ *nf* contemplation.

contempler /kɔ̃tɑ̃ple/ [1] **I** *vtr* **1** (du regard) to survey [*spectacle*]; to contemplate [*paysage*]; to look at [*photo, vitrine*]; **2** (par la pensée) to reflect on [*théorie*].
II se contempler *vpr* to gaze at oneself.

contemporain, ~e /kɔ̃tɑ̃pɔʀɛ̃, ɛn/ **I** *adj* contemporary; **roman ~** novel contemporaneous with.
II *nm,f* contemporary (**de** of).

contenance /kɔ̃t(ə)nɑ̃s/ *nf* **1** ▶ 86, 635 (volume) capacity; **2** (allure) bearing; **essayer de se donner une ~** to try to appear composed; **perdre ~** to lose one's composure; **faire bonne ~** to keep an air of composure.

contenant /kɔ̃t(ə)nɑ̃/ *nm* packaging.

conteneur /kɔ̃t(ə)nœʀ/ *nm* container.

contenir /kɔ̃t(ə)niʀ/ [36] **I** *vtr* **1** to contain [*substance,* *erreur]*; **2 ▶ 86⏐**, **635⏐** *[tonneau]* to hold *[litre]*; *[salle]* to accommodate *[spectateur]*; **3** to contain *[foule, colère]*.

II se contenir *vpr* to contain oneself.

content, **~e** /kɔ̃tɑ̃, ɑ̃t/ **I** *adj* happy, pleased; **je suis ~e que tu sois là** I'm glad you're here; **il est toujours ~ de lui** he is always so self-satisfied; **non ~ de ne rien faire, il s'endette** not content with doing nothing, he is running up debts.

II *nm* **(tout) son ~** *[manger, dormir]* to one's heart's content; **avoir son ~ de** to have one's fill of.

contentement /kɔ̃tɑ̃tmɑ̃/ *nm* contentment, satisfaction.

II se contenter *vpr* se **~ de** to content oneself with; **je me contente de peu** I make do with very little; **il s'est contenté de rire** he just laughed.

contentieux, **-ieuse** /kɔ̃tɑ̃sjø, øz/ JUR **I** *adj* contentious.

II *nm inv* **1** (litige) bone of contention; **2** (service) legal department; (affaires) litigation.

contenu, **~e** /kɔ̃t(ə)ny/ **I** *adj* *[sentiment]* restrained; *[colère]* suppressed.

II *nm* **1** (de récipient) contents *(pl)*; **2** (d'œuvre) content.

conter /kɔ̃te/ [1] *vtr* LITER to tell *[histoire]*; to recount *[aventure]*.

IDIOMES **s'en laisser ~** (une fois) to be taken in; (toujours) to be easily taken in.

contestable /kɔ̃tɛstabl/ *adj* questionable.

contestataire /kɔ̃tɛstatɛʀ/ **I** *adj* *[mouvement, journal]* anti-authority, anti-establishment; **étudiant ~** student protester.

II *nmf* protester.

contestation /kɔ̃tɛstasjɔ̃/ *nf* **1** POL (de pouvoir) protest **(de** against); (dans une organisation) dissent **(de** from); **2** (de véracité, droit) challenging **(de** of); **il y a sujet ~**, **prêter à ~** to be questionable; **il y a sujet** ou **matière à ~** there are grounds for dispute ou contention; **sans ~ possible** beyond dispute.

conteste: **sans conteste** /sɑ̃kɔ̃tɛst/ *loc adv* unquestionably.

contesté, **~e** /kɔ̃tɛste/ *adj* controversial.

contester /kɔ̃tɛste/ [1] **I** *vtr* to question *[authenticité, décision, nécessité]*; to contest *[droit, testament]*; to dispute *[chiffre, frontière]*; to challenge *[impôt, projet]*.

II *vi* **1** (ne pas être d'accord) to raise objections; **2** (faire de l'opposition) to protest.

conteur, **-euse** /kɔ̃tœʀ, øz/ *nm,f* storyteller.

contexte /kɔ̃tɛkst/ *nm* **1** LING, FIG context **(de** of); **2** (conjoncture) situation.

contigu, **-uë** /kɔ̃tigy/ *adj* *[pièces, jardins]* adjoining.

contiguïté /kɔ̃tigɥite/ *nf* contiguity SOUT.

continence /kɔ̃tinɑ̃s/ *nf* continence, continency.

continent, **~e** /kɔ̃tinɑ̃, ɑ̃t/ **I** *adj* continent.

II *nm* GÉOG **1** (partie du monde) continent; **2** (par opposition à une île) mainland.

continental, **~e**, *mpl* **-aux** /kɔ̃tinɑ̃tal, o/ *adj* GÉN continental; (par opposition à un territoire insulaire) mainland *(épith)*.

contingence /kɔ̃tɛ̃ʒɑ̃s/ **I** *nf* PHILOS contingency.

II contingences *nfpl* (faits imprévus) contingencies; (faits sans importance) trivial circumstances.

contingent, **~e** /kɔ̃tɛ̃ʒɑ̃, ɑ̃t/ **I** *adj* contingent.

II *nm* **1** (groupe) contingent; MIL conscripts *(pl)*, draft US; **soldat du ~** conscript; **2** COMM, ÉCON quota; **3** JUR, FIG (quote-part) share.

contingenter /kɔ̃tɛ̃ʒɑ̃te/ [1] *vtr* (limiter) to fix a quota for *[importations]*; (répartir) to distribute [sth] using a quota system *[matière première]*.

continu, **~e** /kɔ̃tiny/ **I** *adj* continuous; **de façon ~e** continuously.

II en continu *loc adv* *[information]* nonstop; *[fabrication, travail]* continuous.

continuation /kɔ̃tinɥasjɔ̃/ *nf* continuation; **bonne ~!** all the best!

continuel, **-elle** /kɔ̃tinɥɛl/ *adj* continual.

continuellement /kɔ̃tinɥɛlmɑ̃/ *adv* continually.

continuer /kɔ̃tinɥe/ [1] **I** *vtr* to carry on, to continue *[combat, conversation]*; to continue *[études, voyage]*.

II *vi* to continue, tó go on; **c'est un bon début, continuez!** it's a good start, keep it up!

continuité /kɔ̃tinɥite/ *nf* continuity.

continûment /kɔ̃tinymɑ̃/ *adv* continuously.

contondant, **~e** /kɔ̃tɔ̃dɑ̃, ɑ̃t/ *adj* *[arme]* blunt.

contorsion /kɔ̃tɔʀsjɔ̃/ *nf* LIT, FIG contortion.

contorsionner: **se contorsionner** /kɔ̃tɔʀsjɔne/ [1] *vpr* *[personne]* to tie oneself in knots; (pour se dégager) to wriggle and writhe; *[serpent]* to writhe.

contorsionniste /kɔ̃tɔʀsjɔnist/ **▶ 374⏐** *nmf* contortionist.

contour /kɔ̃tuʀ/ **I** *nm* (d'objet, de montagne, bouche, dessin) outline; (de corps, visage, paysage) contour; (de meuble) line.

II contours *nmpl* (méandres) twists and turns.

contourner /kɔ̃tuʀne/ [1] *vtr* to by-pass *[ville]*; to skirt (around) *[colline]*; to get round *[difficulté]*.

contraceptif, **-ive** /kɔ̃tʀasɛptif, iv/ **I** *adj* contraceptive.

II *nm* contraceptive.

contraception /kɔ̃tʀasɛpsjɔ̃/ *nf* contraception; **~ orale** (moyen) oral contraception; (pilule) oral contraceptive.

contractant, **~e** /kɔ̃tʀaktɑ̃, ɑ̃t/ **I** *adj* contracting.

II *nm,f* contracting party.

contracter /kɔ̃tʀakte/ [1] **I** *vtr* **1** to contract, to tense *[muscle]*; to tense *[visage]*; **une grimace contracta sa bouche** or **ses traits** he/she grimaced; **l'émotion lui contracta la gorge** his/her throat tightened with emotion; **2** LING to contract *[forme]*; **3** (s'engager dans) to incur *[dette]*; to conclude *[marché]*; to take out *[emprunt]*; to enter into *[engagement]*; to form *[amitié]*; **4** MÉD to contract *[maladie]*.

II se contracter *vpr* **1** *[muscle]* to contract; *[visage, personne]* to tense up; *[gorge]* to tighten; **2** PHYS *[substance]* to contract; **3** LING *[forme]* (éventuellement) to contract; (obligatoirement) to be contracted.

contraction /kɔ̃tʀaksjɔ̃/ *nf* **1** (état) tenseness; (spasme) contraction; **2** LING, PHYS contraction.

contractuel, **-elle** /kɔ̃tʀaktɥɛl/ **I** *adj* **1** JUR *[obligation]* contractual; **2** ADMIN *[personnel]* contract *(épith)*.

II *nm,f* **1** (employé) contract employee; **2 ▶ 374⏐** (contrôlant le stationnement) traffic warden GB, meter reader US.

contracture /kɔ̃tʀaktyʀ/ *nf* **1** (de muscle) contracture, spasm; **2** ARCHIT contracture.

contradiction /kɔ̃tʀadiksjɔ̃/ *nf* contradiction; **être en ~ avec** to contradict *[personne, principe]*; **il ne supporte pas la ~** he can't bear to be contradicted.

contradictoire /kɔ̃tʀadiktwaʀ/ *adj* *[idée, témoignage]* contradictory; **être ~ à** to be in contradiction to.

contraignant, **~e** /kɔ̃tʀɛɲɑ̃, ɑ̃t/ *adj* restrictive.

contraindre /kɔ̃tʀɛ̃dʀ/ [54] **I** *vtr* **1** (obliger) **être contraint au repos** to be forced ou compelled to rest; **je me vois contraint de démissionner** I have no option but to resign; **2** (réprimer) to restrain *[sentiments, désir]*; to curb *[goût]*.

II se contraindre *vpr* **1** (se forcer) **se ~ à** to force oneself to; **2** (se contenir) LITER to exercise self-control.

contraint, **~e¹** /kɔ̃tʀɛ̃, ɛ̃t/ *adj* **1** (obligé) **~ et forcé** JUR under duress; **2** (gêné) *[air]* strained; *[sourire]* forced.

contrainte² /kɔ̃tʀɛ̃t/ *nf* **1** (pression) pressure; (coercition) coercion; **par la ~** forcibly prevented; **sous la ~** under duress; **2** (exigence) constraint; **3** (gêne) strain; **sans ~** without restraint.

contraire /kɔ̃tʀɛʀ/ **I** *adj* **1** *[effet, sens, décision]* opposite; NAUT *[vent]* contrary; (en conflit) *[avis, intérêts]* conflicting (à with); *[forces]* opposite (à to); **être ~ aux usages** to be contrary to custom; **dans le cas ~** (should it be) otherwise SOUT; **sauf avis ~** unless otherwise informed; **2** (défavorable) *[destin, force]* adverse; **le sort leur fut ~** fate was against them.

contre¹

En général la préposition *contre* se traduit par *against* lorsqu'elle sert à indiquer:

un contact entre des choses:

> *pousse le fauteuil contre le mur* = push the armchair (up) against the wall

(Les expressions telles que *joue contre joue*, *furieux contre* sont traitées sous l'élément principal, respectivement *joue*, *furieux* etc.)

une opposition:

> *lutter/réagir/voter contre le racisme* = to fight/react/vote against racism

une défense:

> *s'assurer contre le vol* = to insure against theft
> *se protéger contre une attaque* = to protect oneself against an attack

On aura toujours intérêt à consulter l'article de l'élément principal.

Lorsque *contre* sert à indiquer la proximité, il se traduit par *next to*:

> *leur jardin est contre le mien* = their garden is next to mine

Lorsque *contre* sert à indiquer un échange, il se traduit par *for*:

> *changer une chemise trop petite contre une plus grande* = to change a shirt which is too small for a larger one

Lorsque *contre* sert à indiquer une comparaison, il se traduit par *as against*:

> *22% contre 10% le mois dernier* = 22% as against 10% last month

On trouvera ci-dessous d'autres exemples de *contre* dans ses diverses fonctions.

II *nm* **le ~** the opposite (**de** of); **je pense** (**tout**) **le ~** I take the opposite view; **ne dites pas le ~** don't deny it; **au ~ de tes amis** unlike your friends; **dire tout et son ~** to keep contradicting oneself.

contrairement /kɔ̃tRɛRmɑ̃/ *adv* **~ à ce qu'on pourrait penser** contrary to what one might think; **~ à qn/à la France** unlike sb/France.

contralto¹ /kɔ̃tRalto/ ▶98 *nm* (voix) contralto.

contralto² ▶98 *nf* (femme) contralto.

contrariant, **~e** /kɔ̃tRaRjɑ̃, ɑ̃t/ *adj* **1** [*personne*] contrary (*jamais épith*); **il n'est pas ~** he is accommodating; **2** [*événement*] annoying.

contrarier /kɔ̃tRaRje/ [2] *vtr* **1** (chagriner) to upset; (fâcher) to annoy; **2** (contrecarrer) to frustrate, to thwart [*projet*]; to hinder [*progression*]; **~ un gaucher** to make a lefthanded person write with his/her right hand.

contrariété /kɔ̃tRaRjete/ *nf* upset; **éprouver une vive** or **grande ~** to feel very upset.

contraste /kɔ̃tRast/ **I** *nm* contrast; **faire ~ avec** to contrast with.

II **par contraste** *loc adv* in contrast (**avec** with), by way of contrast.

contrasté, **~e** /kɔ̃tRaste/ *adj* **1** [*couleurs*, *périodes*] contrasting; **2** [*image*, *photo*] with good contrast (*épith*, *après n*); [*tableau*] with sharp contrasts (*épith*, *après n*); **3** FIG [*résultats*] uneven; [*semaine*, *année*] of sharp contrasts (*épith*, *après n*).

contraster /kɔ̃tRaste/ [1] **I** *vtr* to contrast [*couleurs*, *motifs*]; to give contrast to [*photo*].

II *vi* to contrast (**avec** with).

contrat /kɔ̃tRa/ *nm* (accord) contract, agreement; JUR (document) contract; FIG (pacte) arrangement, understanding; **s'engager par ~ à** to contract to; **remplir son ~** to fulfil^{GB} one's pledge.

contravention /kɔ̃tRavɑ̃sjɔ̃/ *nf* **1** (amende) fine; (pour stationnement illicite) parking ticket; (pour excès de vitesse) speeding ticket; **dresser** (**une**) **~ à qn** GÉN to fine sb; (pour stationnement illicite) to issue a parking ticket; **2** JUR

(infraction) minor offence^{GB}; **être en ~** (**à la loi**) to be in breach of the law.

contre¹ /kɔ̃tR/ **I** *prép* **1** (marquant un contact entre personnes) **viens ~ moi** come to me; **ils étaient couchés l'un ~ l'autre** they were lying close together; **2** (marquant l'opposition) against; **être seul ~ tous** to stand alone against everyone else; **on ne peut rien ~ ce genre de choses** there's nothing one can do about that kind of thing; **dix ~ un** ten to one; **230 voix ~ 110** 230 votes to 110; **Nantes ~ Sochaux** SPORT Nantes versus Sochaux; **le procès Bedel ~ Caselli** the Bedel versus Caselli case.

II *adv* **1** (marquant un contact) **il y a un mur et une échelle appuyée ~** there's a wall and a ladder leaning against it; **2** (marquant l'opposition) **la majorité a voté ~** the majority voted against it.

III par contre *loc adv* on the other hand.

contre² /kɔ̃tR/ *nm* **1** (d'opposition) **le pour et le ~** the pros and cons (*pl*); **2** SPORT counter-attack; **faire un ~** to counter-attack; **3** JEUX (au bridge) double.

contre-accusation, *pl* **~s** /kɔ̃tRakyzasjɔ̃/ *nf* JUR counter-charge.

contre-allée, *pl* **~s** /kɔ̃tRale/ *nf* (de route) service road; (de parc) side path; (d'église) side aisle.

contre-amiral, *pl* **-aux** /kɔ̃tRamiral, o/ ▶284 *nm* ~ commodore.

contre-attaque, *pl* **~s** /kɔ̃tRatak/ *nf* counter-attack.

contre-autopsie, *pl* **~s** /kɔ̃tRotɔpsi/ *nf* second autopsy.

contrebalancer /kɔ̃tRəbalɑ̃se/ [12] **I** *vtr* **1** (faire équilibre à) to counterbalance [*poids*, *force*]; **2** (compenser) to offset [*importance*, *influence*].

II se contrebalancer *vpr* **1** (s'équilibrer) to counterbalance each other; **2°** (se moquer de) **se ~ de qch** not to give a damn° about.

contrebande /kɔ̃tRəbɑ̃d/ *nf* **1** (activité) smuggling; **faire de la ~ de vodka** to smuggle vodka; **la ~ d'armes** gun-running; **sortir qch en ~** (dans un pays) to smuggle sth out of the country; **2** (marchandises) smuggled goods (*pl*).

contrebandier, **-ière** /kɔ̃tRəbɑ̃dje, ɛR/ *nm,f* smuggler.

contrebas: en contrebas /ɑ̃kɔ̃tRəba/ *loc adv* (down) below; **en ~ de** (de montagne, hauteur) at the foot of; **la maison est en ~ de la route** the house is at a lower level than the road.

contrebasse /kɔ̃tRəbas/ *nf* **1** ▶392 (instrument) double bass; **2** ▶374 (musicien) double bass player.

contrebasson /kɔ̃tRəbasɔ̃/ *nm* **1** ▶392 (instrument) contrabassoon; **2** ▶374 (musicien) contrabassoon player.

contrecarrer /kɔ̃tRəkaRe/ [1] *vtr* to thwart, to foil [*effort*, *projet*]; to counteract [*influence*, *décision*].

contrechamp /kɔ̃tRəʃɑ̃/ *nm* (prise de vue) reverse angle; (plan) reverse shot.

contrecœur: à contrecœur /kɔ̃tRəkœR/ *loc adv* [*donner*, *prêter*] grudgingly, reluctantly; [*travailler*, *accepter*] reluctantly.

contrecoup /kɔ̃tRəku/ *nm* (conséquences) effects (*pl*); **le ~ d'une opération** the after-effects of an operation; **par ~** as a result.

contre-courant, *pl* **~s** /kɔ̃tRəkuRɑ̃/ *nm* counter-current; **nager à ~** to swim against the current; **aller à ~ de la mode** to go against the fashion.

contredanse /kɔ̃tRədɑ̃s/ *nf* **1°** parking ticket; **2** (danse) contredanse.

contredire /kɔ̃tRədiR/ [65] **I** *vtr* **1** (dire le contraire) to contradict; **2** (démentir) [*personne*, *fait*, *déclaration*] to contradict, to belie [*témoignage*, *thèse*]; [*document*] to belie [*témoignage*, *résultat*].

II se contredire *vpr* **1** (soi-même) to contradict oneself; **2** (l'un l'autre) [*personnes*] to contradict each other; [*témoignages*] to conflict.

contrée /kɔ̃tRe/ *nf* **1** (pays) LITER land, clime LITTÉR; **des ~s lointaines** far-off lands; **2** (région) region.

contre-enquête, *pl* ~**s** /kɔ̃tʀɑ̃kɛt/ *nf* second enquiry GB, second inquiry US.

contre-espionnage, *pl* ~**s** /kɔ̃tʀɛspjɔnaʒ/ *nm* **1** (lutte) counter-intelligence; **2** (organisation) counter-intelligence service.

contre-exemple, *pl* ~**s** /kɔ̃tʀɛɡzɑ̃pl/ *nm* exception, counter-example.

contre-expertise, *pl* ~**s** /kɔ̃tʀɛkspɛʀtiz/ *nf* second opinion.

contrefaçon /kɔ̃tʀəfasɔ̃/ *nf* **1** (action) (de signature, billet, carte de crédit) forging; (de pièces) counterfeiting; (d'invention, enregistrement) pirating; (de brevet) infringement; **2** (résultat) (signature, billet, gravure) forgery; (pièce, montre) counterfeit; (enregistrement, édition) pirated copy.

contrefacteur /kɔ̃tʀəfaktœʀ/ *nm* (de billets, cartes de crédit, tableau) forger; (de pièces) counterfeiter; (de logiciels, signatures, inventions) pirate.

contrefaire /kɔ̃tʀəfɛʀ/ [10] *vtr* **1** COMM, JUR (falsifier) to forge [*signature, billet, carte de crédit*]; to counterfeit [*pièce, montre*]; to pirate [*invention, enregistrement*]; to infringe [*brevet*]; **2** (imiter) to imitate [*personne, voix*]; **3** (déguiser) to disguise [*voix, écriture*].

contreficher○**: se contreficher** /kɔ̃tʀəfiʃe/ [1] *vpr* not to give a damn○ (**de** about; **que** if).

contrefort /kɔ̃tʀəfɔʀ/ *nm* **1** GÉOG foothills (*pl*); **2** ARCHIT buttress; **3** (de chaussure) back, counter SPÉC.

contre-indication, *pl* ~**s** /kɔ̃tʀɛ̃dikasjɔ̃/ *nf* contra-indication.

contre-indiqué, ~**e**, *mpl* ~**s** /kɔ̃tʀɛ̃dike/ *adj* [*médicament*] contraindicated; [*activité*] inadvisable.

contre-interrogatoire, *pl* ~**s** /kɔ̃tʀɛ̃tɛʀɔɡatwaʀ/ *nm* cross-examination.

contre-jour, *pl* ~**s** /kɔ̃tʀəʒuʀ/ *nm* PHOT, CIN **1** (effet) backlighting; **à** ~ against ou into the light; **2** (photo) contre-jour ou back-lit photograph.

contremaître, **-esse** /kɔ̃tʀəmɛtʀ, kɔ̃tʀəmɛtʀɛs/ ▸ 374┃ *nm,f* foreman/forewoman.

contremarque /kɔ̃tʀəmaʀk/ *nf* THÉAT, CIN pass (*for re-entry into theatre*); **2** (dans les transports) *voucher showing that the bearer is travelling* GB *on a group ticket*; **3** ADMIN, COMM counterseal.

contre-offensive, *pl* ~**s** /kɔ̃tʀɔfãsiv/ *nf* counter-offensive.

contrepartie /kɔ̃tʀəpaʀti/ *nf* **1** (équivalent) equivalent (**en** in); **2** (contrepoids) **c'est la** ~ **de la liberté** it is the price you have to pay for freedom; **mais la** ~ **est que le salaire est élevé** but this is offset by the high salary; **3** (dédommagement) compensation; **en** ~ (en compensation) in compensation (**de** for); (en échange) in return (**de** for).

contrepet /kɔ̃tʀəpɛ/ *nm*, **contrepèterie** /kɔ̃tʀəpɛtʀi/ *nf* (deliberate) spoonerism.

contre-pied, *pl* ~**s** /kɔ̃tʀəpje/ *nm* **1** FIG **prendre le** ~ **de ce que dit qn** (en paroles) to say the opposite of what sb says (**de** about, on); **2** SPORT **prendre qn à** ~ to wrong-foot sb.

contreplaqué /kɔ̃tʀəplake/ *nm* plywood.

contre-plongée, *pl* ~**s** /kɔ̃tʀəplɔ̃ʒe/ *nf* low-angle shot.

contrepoids /kɔ̃tʀəpwa/ *nm* **1** LIT, FIG counterweight, counterbalance; **faire** ~ to act as a counterbalance; **faire** ~ **à qch** LIT, FIG to counterbalance sth; **2** (de funambule) balancing pole.

contrepoint /kɔ̃tʀəpwɛ̃/ *nm* counterpoint.

contrepoison /kɔ̃tʀəpwazɔ̃/ *nm* LIT, FIG antidote.

contre-pouvoir, *pl* ~**s** /kɔ̃tʀəpuvwaʀ/ *nm* forces (*pl*) of opposition.

contre-publicité /kɔ̃tʀəpyblisite/ *nf* adverse publicity.

contrer /kɔ̃tʀe/ [1] *vtr* **1** (se dresser contre) to counter [*armée, délinquance*]; to fend off [*concurrent, opposition*]; to combat [*agressivité*]; to oppose [*parti*]; to block [*initiative*]; **2** SPORT to block [*adversaire*]. **II** *vi* JEUX (aux cartes) to double.

Contre-Réforme /kɔ̃tʀəʀefɔʀm/ *nf* Counter-Reformation.

contre-révolution, *pl* ~**s** /kɔ̃tʀəʀevɔlysjɔ̃/ *nf* counter-revolution.

contrescarpe /kɔ̃tʀɛskaʀp/ *nf* counterscarp.

contresens /kɔ̃tʀəsɑ̃s/ *nm* **1** (erreur) misinterpretation; (en traduisant) mistranslation; **faire un** ~ **sur qch** to misinterpret ou misconstrue sth; [*traducteur*] to mistranslate sth; **2** (absurdité) aberration; **3** (sens contraire) **à** ~ [*rouler, avancer*] in the opposite direction; (dans le mauvais sens) the wrong way; [*raboter*] against the grain.

contretemps /kɔ̃tʀətɑ̃/ *nm inv* **1** (difficulté) setback, contretemps SOUT; **2** MUS syncopation; **à** ~ LIT [*jouer*] GÉN on the off-beat; (par erreur) out of time; FIG [*agir, parler, intervenir*] at the wrong moment.

contre-terrorisme, *pl* ~**s** /kɔ̃tʀətɛʀɔʀism/ *nm* counter-terrorism.

contre-ut, *pl* ~(**s**) /kɔ̃tʀyt/ *nm* high C.

contre-valeur, *pl* ~**s** /kɔ̃tʀəvalœʀ/ *nf* FIN exchange value.

contrevenir /kɔ̃tʀəvəniʀ/ [36] *vtr ind* ~ **à** to contravene.

contre-vérité, *pl* ~**s** /kɔ̃tʀəveʀite/ *nf* untruth.

contre-voie, *pl* ~**s** /kɔ̃tʀəvwa/ *nf* **descendre à** ~ to get out on the wrong side of the track.

contribuable /kɔ̃tʀibɥabl/ *nmf* taxpayer.

contribuer /kɔ̃tʀibɥe/ [1] *vtr ind* ~ **à** to contribute to; **cela y a beaucoup contribué** it was a major factor; ~ **aux dépenses** to pay one's share of the expenses.

contribution /kɔ̃tʀibysjɔ̃/ **I** *nf* (participation) contribution; **mettre qn à** ~ to call upon sb's services. **II contributions** *nfpl* **1** (impôts) (à l'État) taxes; (à la commune) local taxes; ~ **directes** direct taxes; **2** (bureau) tax office (*sg*).

contrit, ~**e** /kɔ̃tʀi, it/ *adj* contrite, apologetic; **d'un air** ~ apologetically.

contrôlable /kɔ̃tʀolabl/ *adj* **1** (maîtrisable) [*situation, coût, variable, maladie*] controllable; **2** (pouvant être surveillé) which can be monitored (*après n*); **difficilement** ~ difficult to monitor (*après n*).

contrôle /kɔ̃tʀol/ *nm* **1** (maîtrise) control (**de** of; **sur** over); **prendre/perdre le** ~ to take/lose control; **prendre le** ~ **de** FIN to take a controlling interest in; **dispositif de** ~ control mechanism; **2** ADMIN check; ~ **de police/sécurité** police/security check; ~ **des billets** ticket inspection; ~ **douanier** customs control; **3** FIN audit; **4** (suivi) monitoring ¢; **5** SCOL, UNIV test; ~ **de géographie** geography test; **6** MED check-up; **sous** ~ **médical** under medical supervision. ■ ~ **antidopage** dope test; ~ **des changes** exchange controls (*pl*); ~ **des connaissances** assessment; ~ **continu** (**des connaissances**) continuous assessment; ~ **fiscal** tax investigation; ~ **d'identité** identity check; ~ **judiciaire** legal restrictions (*pl*) pending trial; ~ **des naissances** birth control; ~ **des passeports** passport control; ~ **sanitaire** health control; ~ **de soi** PSYCH self-control; ~ **technique** (**des véhicules**) AUT MOT (test) GB.

contrôler /kɔ̃tʀole/ [1] **I** *vtr* **1** (exercer son autorité sur) to control [*pays, organisation*]; **2** (maîtriser) to control [*prix, tremblement, ballon*]; **3** (superviser) to monitor [*opération*]; **4** (vérifier) [*inspecteur*] to check [*identité, billet*]; [*douanier*] to inspect [*bagage*]; [*comptable*] to audit [*comptes*]; [*contrôleur*] to inspect [*comptes*]; [*percepteur*] to check [*déclaration d'impôt*]; [*employé*] to test [*produit*]; [*chercheur*] to verify [*résultat*]; [*conducteur*] to check [*huile*]; ~ **que** to make sure that. **II se contrôler** *vpr* (se maîtriser) to control oneself.

contrôleur, **-euse** /kɔ̃tʀolœʀ, øz/ ▸ 374┃ *nm,f* GÉN inspector; ~ **aérien** air-traffic controller.

contrordre /kɔ̃tʀɔʀdʀ/ *nm* **1** GÉN **une série d'ordres et de** ~**s** a series of conflicting orders; **sauf** ~ unless I/you etc hear to the contrary; **2** MIL counter command.

controverse /kɔ̃tʀɔvɛʀs/ *nf* controversy (**sur** about).

controversé, ~**e** /kɔ̃tʀɔvɛʀse/ *adj* controversial.

contumace /kɔ̃tymas/ *nf* **par ~** in absentia.
contusion /kɔ̃tyzjɔ̃/ *nf* bruise, contusion SPÉC.
contusionner /kɔ̃tyzjɔne/ [1] *vtr* to bruise.
convaincant, **~e** /kɔ̃vɛ̃kɑ̃, ɑ̃t/ *adj* **1** (concluant) convincing; **2** (persuasif) persuasive; **3** SPORT [*tactique*] impressive.
convaincre /kɔ̃vɛ̃kR/ [57] **I** *vtr* **1** to convince [*incrédule*] (**de** of; **que** that); to persuade [*indécis*] (**de faire** to do); **je ne suis pas convaincu** I remain to be convinced; **se laisser ~** to let oneself be persuaded; (à tort) to allow oneself to be persuaded; **2** JUR to prove [sb] guilty (**de** of).
II se convaincre *vpr* to convince oneself (**de** of).
convaincu, **~e** /kɔ̃vɛ̃ky/ *adj* (résolu) [*partisan*] staunch; **d'un ton ~** with conviction.
convalescence /kɔ̃valesɑ̃s/ *nf* convalescence; **être en ~** to be convalescing; **sortir de ~** to finish convalescing.
convalescent, **~e** /kɔ̃valesɑ̃, ɑ̃t/ *adj*, *nm,f* convalescent.
convecteur /kɔ̃vɛktœR/ *nm* convector heater.
convenable /kɔ̃vnabl/ *adj* **1** (approprié) suitable; **2** (acceptable) [*résultat, salaire, travail*] reasonable, decent; [*vin, repas*] acceptable, decent; **tout juste ~** barely acceptable; **3** (bienséant) [*vêtement*] decent; [*conduite, manières*] proper; **pas ~** [*vêtement*] inappropriate; **4** (respectable) [*gens, famille*] respectable.
convenablement /kɔ̃vnabləmɑ̃/ *adv* **1** (sans erreur) [*fonctionner, s'exprimer*] properly; **2** (de façon acceptable) [*manger, travailler, payer*] reasonably well; **3** (de façon appropriée) [*vêtu*] properly; **4** (sans choquer) [*se vêtir*] decently; [*se conduire*] properly.
convenance /kɔ̃vnɑ̃s/ **I** *nf* **pour ~ personnelle** for personal reasons; **lundi ou mardi, à votre ~** on Monday or Tuesday, at your convenience.
II convenances *nfpl* (bienséance) (social) conventions; **respecter les ~s** to respect convention ou the conventions; **par souci des ~s** for propriety's sake.
convenir /kɔ̃vniR/ [36] **I** *vtr* **1** (concéder) to admit (**que** that); **2** (s'entendre) to agree (**que** that).
II convenir à *vtr ind* **~ à** to suit [*personne, goût*]; to be suitable for [*circonstance, activité*]; **si cela vous convient** if it suits you; **c'est tout à fait ce qui me convient** it's exactly what I need; **de la taille qui convient** of a suitable size; **de la façon qui convient** in the appropriate manner; **l'homme qui convient** the right man.
III convenir de *vtr ind* **1** (reconnaître) **~ de** to admit, to acknowledge [*faute*]; to acknowledge [*qualité*] ; **j'en conviens** I accept that; **2** (s'accorder sur) **~ de** [*personnes*] to agree on [*date, prix*]; **~ de faire** to agree to do.
IV se convenir *vpr* [*personnes*] (être assortis) to be well suited.
V *v impers* **1** (il est sage, correct, nécessaire) **il convient de faire** one should do ou ought to do; **il convient que vous fassiez** you should do ou ought to do; **2** (il est entendu) FML **il est convenu que** it is agreed that; **ce qu'il est convenu d'appeler le réalisme** what is commonly called realism.
convention /kɔ̃vɑ̃sjɔ̃/ **I** *nf* **1** (accord, contrat) GÉN agreement; (officiel) covenant; (entre nations) convention; (clause) article, clause; **2** (usage admis) convention; **de ~ conventional**; **3** (assemblée) POL convention.
II conventions *nfpl* (convenances) convention ₵
■ **~ collective** cf collective labour[GB] agreement; **Convention nationale** HIST National Convention.
conventionné, **~e** /kɔ̃vɑ̃sjɔne/ *adj* [*clinique*] registered; **médecin ~** doctor approved by the Department of Health (*whose fees are refunded*); **médecin non ~** private doctor; **les tarifs ~s** charges approved by the French Health Department.
conventionnel, **-elle** /kɔ̃vɑ̃sjɔnɛl/ *adj* **1** GÉN conventional; **armes non conventionnelles** nonconventional weapons; **2** JUR [*clause*] contractual.
convenu, **~e** /kɔ̃v(ə)ny/ **I** *pp* ▶ **convenir**.
II *pp adj* **1** (décidé) [*date, prix, termes*] agreed; **2**

(conventionnel) [*expression, tour*] conventional; [*sourire*] polite, forced.
convergence /kɔ̃vɛRʒɑ̃s/ *nf* **1** (d'idées, intérêts, de politiques) convergence; **la ~ des volontés a permis de...** a joint effort of will has made it possible to...; **2** (de faisceaux lumineux, lentille) convergence; (de chemins) meeting; **3** MATH convergence.
convergent, **~e** /kɔ̃vɛRʒɑ̃, ɑ̃t/ *adj* convergent.
converger /kɔ̃vɛRʒe/ [13] *vi* **1** (dans l'espace) [*chemins, véhicules, personnes*] to converge (**vers** on); **2** FIG **nos réflexions convergent vers les mêmes conclusions** our thoughts are leading us to the same conclusions; **nos opinions convergent** we're of the same opinion; **3** MATH, PHYS to converge.
conversation /kɔ̃vɛRsasjɔ̃/ *nf* conversation (**avec** with); **la ~ mondaine** or **de salon** polite conversation; **faire les frais de la ~** (en être l'objet) to be the chief topic ou subject of conversation; (la mener) to do all the talking; **avoir de la ~** to be a good conversationalist; **anglais de ~** conversational English; **dans la ~ courante** in everyday ou ordinary speech.
■ **~ à trois** TÉLÉCOM three-way calling.
converser /kɔ̃vɛRse/ [1] *vi* to converse SOUT (**avec** with).
conversion /kɔ̃vɛRsjɔ̃/ *nf* **1** RELIG, FIG conversion (à to); **2** (transformation) (d'entreprise) conversion (**en** into); (d'employé) re-training; **3** (de monnaie, dette) conversion (**en** into); **4** (de mesures, poids) conversion (**en** into); converting (**en** into); **5** SPORT (en ski) kick-turn.
converti, **~e** /kɔ̃vɛRti/ **I** *pp* ▶ **convertir**.
II *pp adj* converted.
III *nm,f* convert.
IDIOMES **prêcher un ~** to preach to the converted.
convertible /kɔ̃vɛRtibl/ *adj* **1** FIN [*devise*] convertible (**en** into); **2** MATH, ORDINAT convertible (**en** to); **3** (transformable) **canapé ~** sofa-bed.
convertir /kɔ̃vɛRtiR/ [3] **I** *vtr* **1** (faire changer d'idée) to convert [*personne, parti, gouvernement*] (**à** to); **2** (transformer) to convert [*industrie, logements*] (**en** into); **3** FIN to convert [*devise, dette*] (**en** into); **4** MATH, ORDINAT to convert [*fractions, texte*] (**en** to).
II se convertir *vpr* [*personne*] to convert, to become a convert (**à** to); [*entreprise*] to change products; **le pays doit se ~ au libéralisme** the country must adopt liberalism.
convertisseur /kɔ̃vɛRtisœR/ *nm* converter.
convexe /kɔ̃vɛks/ *adj* convex.
conviction /kɔ̃viksjɔ̃/ **I** *nf* **1** (certitude) conviction; **avoir la ~ que** to be convinced that; **2** (fougue, sérieux) conviction.
II convictions *nfpl* (opinions) convictions.
convier /kɔ̃vje/ [2] *vtr* **1** (inviter) to invite [*personne*] (à to); **2** (engager) to invite [*personne*] (**à faire** to do); to ask [*population, entreprise*] (**à faire** to do).
convive /kɔ̃viv/ *nmf* guest.
convivial, **~e**, *mpl* **-iaux** /kɔ̃vivjal, o/ *adj* **1** [*atmosphère, réunion*] friendly; **2** ORDINAT user-friendly.
convivialité /kɔ̃vivjalite/ *nf* **1** (de personne) friendliness; (d'atmosphère, de réunion) warmth, conviviality; **2** ORDINAT user-friendliness.
convocation /kɔ̃vɔkasjɔ̃/ *nf* **1** (appel) (d'assemblée) convening, convocation SOUT; (d'individu) GÉN summoning; MIL (de réserviste) calling up; (pour entrevue) invitation; **se rendre à une ~** GÉN to attend as instructed; JUR to obey a summons; **se présenter à un bureau sur ~** ADMIN to call at an office after being requested to do so; **2** (lettre) (ordre) GÉN notice to attend; JUR summons (+ *sg*); MIL call-up papers (*pl*); (invitation) invitation; **~ aux examens** notification of examination timetables.
convoi /kɔ̃vwa/ *nm* **1** (de véhicules, troupes) convoy; **'~ exceptionnel'** AUT 'abnormal load'; **2** RAIL train; **un ~ de marchandises** a goods train.
convoiter /kɔ̃vwate/ [1] *vtr* to covet.
convoitise /kɔ̃vwatiz/ *nf* GÉN desire; (péché) covetousness; (ambition, gourmandise) greed; (concupiscence) lust; (cupidité) lust for money; **regarder qch avec ~** to cast

covetous glances at sth; [*enfant*] to look longingly at sth.

convoquer /kɔ̃vɔke/ [1] *vtr* **1** (appeler à se réunir) to call, to convene [*réunion, assemblée*]; **2** (appeler à se présenter) to send for [*élève*]; JUR to summon [*témoin*]; MIL to call [sb] up [*soldat, officier*]; **être convoqué à un examen** to be asked to attend an exam; **être convoqué pour un entretien** to be called for interview.

convoyer /kɔ̃vwaje/ [23] *vtr* **1** (escorter) to escort [*prisonnier, navires*]; (transporter) to transport [*or, marchandises*]; **2** (jusqu'à son lieu d'utilisation) to ferry [*bateau, avion*].

convoyeur, -euse /kɔ̃vwajœr/ I ▶ 374 | *nm,f* (de prisonnier) prison escort; (de marchandise) courier; **~ de fonds** security guard.
II *nm* **1** IND conveyor; **2** NAUT **navire ~** escort ship.

convulser /kɔ̃vylse/ [1] FML *vtr* (tordre) [*peur, douleur*] to convulse, to contort [*visage*]; to grip [*estomac*].

convulsif, -ive /kɔ̃vylsif, iv/ *adj* **1** [*sanglots, mouvement*] convulsive; [*rire*] nervous; **2** MÉD [*toux, maladie*] convulsive.

convulsion /kɔ̃vylsjɔ̃/ *nf* **1** MÉD convulsion; **être pris de ~s** to be seized by convulsions; **2** POL (troubles) convulsions (*pl*), turmoil ¢.

cool /kul/ I *adj inv* cool◦, laidback◦.
II *adv* **s'habiller ~** to dress in a laidback◦ way.

coopérant /kɔɔperɑ̃/ *nm: young man working abroad in lieu of military service*.

coopérateur, -trice /kɔɔperatœr, tris/ I *adj* cooperating.
II *nm,f* **1** (associé) collaborator; **2** (membre d'une coopérative) member of a cooperative.

coopératif, -ive /kɔɔperatif, iv/ I *adj* cooperative.
II **coopérative** *nf* (groupement) cooperative; (magasin) co-op.

coopération /kɔɔperasjɔ̃/ *nf* **1** GÉN (collaboration) cooperation; **apporter sa ~ à un projet** to cooperate in a project; **2** *programme of aid to developing countries*.

coopérer /kɔɔpere/ [14] I **coopérer à** *vtr ind* **~ à** to cooperate (on ou in).
II *vi* to cooperate.

coopter /kɔɔpte/ [1] *vtr* to co-opt [*personne*].

coordinateur, -trice /kɔɔrdinatœr, tris/ I *adj* coordinating.
II *nm,f* (personne) coordinator.

coordination /kɔɔrdinasjɔ̃/ *nf* **1** GÉN coordination; **2** (groupe) joint committee.

coordonné, ~e /kɔɔrdɔne/ I *adj* **1** [*gestes, travail*] coordinated; [*vêtement*] coordinating (*épith*); **2** LING [*proposition*] coordinate.
II **coordonnés** *nmpl* (vêtements) coordinates.

coordonnées /kɔɔrdɔne/ *nfpl* **1** GÉOG, MATH coordinates; **2** (adresse) address and telephone number.

coordonner /kɔɔrdɔne/ [1] *vtr* to coordinate.

copain◦, copine /kɔpɛ̃, in/ *nm,f* (camarade) friend; (acolyte) PEJ crony; (amoureux) **son ~** her boyfriend; **sa copine** his girlfriend; **on sort en ~** we go out as friends.
■ **~ de classe** school friend; **~ de régiment** old army buddy◦.
IDIOMES **être ~s comme cochons◦** to be as thick as thieves.

copeau, *pl* **~x** /kɔpo/ *nm* **1** (de bois, métal) shaving; **des ~x de bois** wood shavings; **2** CULIN **~x de chocolat** chocolate shavings.

Copenhague /kɔpɛnag/ *npr* ▶ 628 | Copenhagen.

copie /kɔpi/ *nf* **1** (de document, tableau, logiciel, film) copy; **être la ~ conforme de qn** to be the spitting image of sb; **2** (duplication) copying ¢; **3** SCOL (feuille) sheet of paper; (devoir) paper; **ramasser les ~s** to collect the papers; **4** (en imprimerie) copy.
■ **~ certifiée conforme** JUR certified true copy; **~ de sauvegarde** ORDINAT back-up copy.
IDIOMES **revoir sa ~** to revise one's work.

copier /kɔpje/ [2] *vtr* **1** (transcrire) to copy [*lettre, texte*]; **vous copierez dix fois...** write out ten times...; **2** (reproduire) to copy [*tableau*]; **3** SCOL **~ sur qn** to copy ou crib from sb [*voisin*].
IDIOMES **tu me la copieras (celle-là)◦!** I'm not likely to forget that in a hurry!

copieur, -ieuse /kɔpjœr, øz/ I *nm,f* **1** SCOL cheat; **2** (plagiaire) imitator.
II *nm* photocopier.

copieusement /kɔpjøzmɑ̃/ *adv* [*manger*] heartily, a lot; [*illustrer*] lavishly; [*annoter*] copiously; **il m'a servi ~** he gave me a generous portion; **un repas ~ arrosé** a meal with lots to drink; **se faire ~ disputer** HUM to get well and truly told off.

copieux, -ieuse /kɔpjø, øz/ *adj* [*repas*] substantial, hearty; [*portion*] generous; [*notes*] copious; [*rapport*] weighty, substantial.

copilote /kɔpilɔt/ *nmf* **1** AVIAT, NAUT co-pilot; **2** AUT co-driver.

copinage◦ /kɔpinaʒ/ *nm* PEJ cronyism PÉJ.

copine ▶ **copain**.

coprésidence /kɔprezidɑ̃s/ *nf* (d'association, de club) joint presidency; (de comité) joint chairmanship.

coprésident /kɔprezidɑ̃/ *nm* (de société, d'association) joint president; (de comité, réunion) co-chair.

coprésidente /kɔprezidɑ̃t/ *nf* (de société, d'association) joint president, co-president; (de comité, réunion) co-chair, co-chairwoman.

coproducteur, -trice /kɔprɔdyktœr, tris/ *nm,f* co-producer.

coproduction /kɔprɔdyksjɔ̃/ *nf* co-production.

coproduire /kɔprɔdɥir/ [69] *vtr* to co-produce.

copropriétaire /kɔprɔprijetɛr/ *nmf* **1** (dans un immeuble) owner (*of a flat in a jointly-owned building*); **2** (de bien, cheval) joint owner, co-owner.

copropriété /kɔprɔprijete/ *nf* **1** (à deux) joint ownership; (à plus de deux) co-ownership; **posséder qch en ~** (à deux) to be joint owner of sth; (à plus de deux) to be co-owner of sth; **acheter qch en ~** to buy sth jointly with someone; **vendre des appartements en ~** to sell apartments in a block to individual buyers; **un immeuble en ~** a block of individually owned flats GB.

copulation /kɔpylasjɔ̃/ *nf* copulation.

copuler /kɔpyle/ [1] *vi* to copulate (**avec** with).

coq /kɔk/ *nm* **1** (de poulailler) cockerel, rooster US; (oiseau mâle) cock; **au chant du ~** at cockcrow; **rouge comme un ~** [*personne*] bright red in the face; **2** CULIN cockerel; **3** ARCHIT (de clocher) weathercock; **4** (séducteur) **le ~ du village** the local Casanova.
■ **~ de bruyère** grouse; **~ de combat** fighting cock; **~ au vin** coq au vin.
IDIOMES **être comme un ~ en pâte** to be in clover; **sauter du ~ à l'âne** to hop from one subject to another.

coquard◦, coquart◦ /kɔkar/ *nm* black eye.

coque /kɔk/ *nf* **1** NAUT hull; **2** AVIAT (d'hydravion) fuselage; AUT (car) body; **3** ZOOL (coquillage) cockle; **4** (coquille) shell.

coquelet /kɔklɛ/ *nm* young cockerel.

coquelicot /kɔkliko/ *nm* poppy.

coqueluche /kɔklyʃ/ *nf* **1** ▶ 196 | MÉD whooping-cough, pertussis SPÉC; **2**◦ FIG (chanteur, sportif) idol.

coquet, -ette /kɔkɛ, ɛt/ *adj* **1** [*personne*] (effet produit) well turned-out; (attitude) **être ~** to be particular about one's appearance; **2** (plaisant) pretty; **3**◦ [*somme*] tidy◦ (*épith*); [*héritage*] substantial.

coquetier /kɔktje/ *nm* eggcup.

coquettement /kɔkɛtmɑ̃/ *adv* [*regarder*] coquettishly; [*s'habiller*] stylishly; [*meubler*] prettily.

coquetterie /kɔkɛtri/ *nf* **1** (souci de plaire) interest in one's appearance; (excessif) vanity; **s'habiller avec ~** to dress stylishly; **par ~** out of vanity; **2** (envers les hommes) coquetry; **3** (maniérisme) affectation; **ses ~s** (minauderies) her coquettish ways.

IDIOMES avoir une ~ dans l'œil° to have a cast in one's eye.

coquillage /kɔkijaʒ/ *nm* **1** (mollusque) shellfish (*inv*); **2** (coquille) shell.

coquille /kɔkij/ *nf* **1** (d'œuf, de noix, mollusque) shell; **poussin à peine sorti de sa ~** newly-hatched chick; **2** CULIN (ravier) scallop-shaped dish; (mets) **~ de saumon** scalloped salmon GB, salmon served in a shell US; **3** (en imprimerie) misprint; **4** ARCHIT shell; (feston) scallop; **5** SPORT box GB, cup US; **6** (d'épée) guard; **7** MÉD (plâtre) spinal jacket.
■ **~ de beurre** butter curl; **~ Saint-Jacques** scallop; (écaille) scallop shell.

coquillette /kɔkijɛt/ *nf* CULIN small macaroni ¢; **des ~s** (small) macaroni.

coquin, ~e /kɔkɛ̃, in/ **I** *adj* **1** (espiègle) [*enfant, air*] mischievous; **2** (osé) [*coup d'œil, film*] naughty, saucy.
II *nm,f* (enfant) scamp; **petit ~!** you little monkey ou scamp!
III *nm* ‡(scélérat) scoundrel, rascal.

cor /kɔʀ/ *nm* **1** ▶392 MUS horn; **sonner** or **donner du ~** to blow the horn; **2** MÉD corn; **3** ZOOL (de cerf) tine; **(cerf de) 6 ~s** 6-point stag, 6-pointer.
■ **~ anglais** cor anglais; **~ basset** basset horn; **~ de chasse** hunting horn; **~ d'harmonie** French horn; **~ à pistons** valve horn.
IDIOMES réclamer or **demander qch à ~ et à cri** to clamour^{GB} for sth.

corail, pl -aux /kɔʀaj, o/ **I** *adj inv* ▶141 (couleur) coral(-pink).
II *nm* **1** ZOOL coral; **une barrière de ~** a coral reef; **2** (bijoux) coral; **3** CULIN (de crustacé) coral.

corallien, -ienne /kɔʀaljɛ̃, ɛn/ *adj* coral (*épith*).

Coran /kɔʀɑ̃/ *nm* **le ~** the Koran.

coranique /kɔʀanik/ *adj* [*loi*] Koranic; [*préceptes*] of the Koran.

corbeau, pl ~x /kɔʀbo/ *nm* **1** ZOOL crow; **grand ~** raven; **noir ~** raven black; **2**° (auteur de lettres anonymes) poison-pen letter writer; **3**° (prêtre) OFFENSIVE priest; **4** ARCHIT corbel.

corbeille /kɔʀbɛj/ *nf* **1** (en vannerie, plastique) basket; (de bureau) tray; **une ~ en osier** a wicker basket; **une ~ de fleurs** a basket of flowers; **2** THÉÂT dress circle; **3** (à la Bourse) trading floor; **4** ARCHIT bell.
■ **~ à papier** (à l'intérieur) (en osier) wastepaper basket; (en métal, en plastique) wastepaper bin.

corbillard /kɔʀbijaʀ/ *nm* hearse.

cordage /kɔʀdaʒ/ *nm* **1** NAUT (corde) rope; **~s** rigging ¢; **2** (de raquette) stringing.

corde /kɔʀd/ *nf* **1** (câble, lien) rope; **à semelles de ~** rope-soled; **2** (d'arc, de raquette) string; **3** (pendaison) **la ~** hanging; **4** SPORT **être à la ~** [*coureur*] to be on the inside; [*cheval*] to be on the rail; **prendre un virage à la ~** to hug a bend; **5** MUS (d'instrument) string; **6** (fil de chaîne) warp thread.
■ **~ à linge** clothes line; **~ lisse** SPORT climbing rope; **~ à nœuds** SPORT knotted (climbing) rope; **~ raide** LIT, FIG tightrope; **~ de rappel** SPORT abseiling rope; **~s vocales** vocal chords.
IDIOMES pleuvoir or **tomber des ~s**° to rain cats and dogs°; **tirer sur la ~** to push one's luck; **ce n'est pas dans mes ~s**° it's not my line; **c'est dans tes ~s**° it's just your sort of thing; **faire jouer la ~ sensible** to tug at the heartstrings; **quand la ~ est trop tendue, elle casse** PROV (d'une personne) if you push somebody too far, they'll snap; (d'une situation) if you allow a situation to reach a certain point, something's got to give; ▶**pendu**.

cordée /kɔʀde/ *nf* (en alpinisme) roped party (of climbers); **~ de secours** mountain rescue party; **premier de ~** leader.

cordelette /kɔʀdəlɛt/ *nf* thin cord.

cordelière /kɔʀdəljɛʀ/ *nf* (corde) cord.

corder /kɔʀde/ [1] *vtr* **1** SPORT to string [*raquette*]; **2** (lier) to tie up [sth] with rope [*malle*].

cordial, ~e, mpl -iaux /kɔʀdjal, o/ **I** *adj* [*accueil,*

relations] cordial; [*personne*] warm-hearted; [*sentiment*] warm.
II *nm* cordial.

cordialement /kɔʀdjalmɑ̃/ *adv* warmly; **détester qn ~** to dislike sb heartily; **~ (vôtre** or **à vous)** (dans une lettre) yours sincerely.

cordialité /kɔʀdjalite/ *nf* (de relations) warmth; (de personne) friendliness.

cordillère /kɔʀdijɛʀ/ *nf* cordillera.
■ **la Cordillère des Andes** the Andes Cordillera.

cordon /kɔʀdɔ̃/ *nm* **1** (de rideau) cord; (de tablier, bourse, sac) string; (de chaussure) lace; **tenir les ~s de la bourse** FIG to hold the purse-strings; **2** (d'appareil électrique) flex GB, cord US; **3** (ligne) (d'agents, de troupes) cordon; (d'arbres) row; **4** ANAT cord; **5** (décoration) (ruban) ribbon; (écharpe) sash.
■ **~ ombilical** umbilical cord.

cordonnerie /kɔʀdɔnʀi/ ▶374 *nf* **1** (fabrication) shoemaking; **2** (réparation) shoe repairing; **3** (boutique) cobbler's.

cordonnet /kɔʀdɔnɛ/ *nm* **1** (fil solide) buttonhole thread; **2** (petit cordon) thin cord.

cordonnier /kɔʀdɔnje/ ▶374 *nm* cobbler.
IDIOMES les ~s sont toujours les plus mal chaussés PROV it's always the baker's children who have no bread PROV.

Corée /kɔʀe/ ▶232 *nprf* Korea; **République démocratique populaire de ~** Democratic People's Republic of Korea.

coréen, -éenne /kɔʀeɛ̃, ɛn/ ▶338, 394 **I** *adj* Korean.
II *nm* LING Korean.

Corfou /kɔʀfu/ ▶628 *npr* Corfu.

coriace /kɔʀjas/ *adj* tough.

coriandre /kɔʀjɑ̃dʀ/ *nf* coriander.

Corinthe /kɔʀɛ̃t/ ▶628 *npr* Corinth; **raisins de ~** currants.

corinthien, -ienne /kɔʀɛ̃tjɛ̃, ɛn/ **I** ▶628 *adj* Corinthian.
II *nm* ARCHIT **le ~** the Corinthian order.

corne /kɔʀn/ *nf* **1** (de vache, chamois etc, d'escargot) horn; (de cerf) antler; **animal à ~s** horned animal; **donner un coup de ~ à qn** to butt sb; **blesser qn d'un coup de ~** to gore sb; ▶**taureau; 2** (substance) horn; **3** ▶392 (instrument) horn; **4** (de chapeau) point; **5**° (peau durcie) **avoir de la ~ aux pieds** to have calluses on one's feet.
■ **~ d'abondance** horn of plenty, cornucopia; **~ de brume** NAUT foghorn.
IDIOMES faire les ~s à qn to jeer at sb (*with a gesture of the hand*); **hou les ~s!** (dit par un enfant) you're no good!; **HUM shame on you!; avoir** or **porter des ~s** to be a cuckold†.

cornée /kɔʀne/ *nf* cornea.

corneille /kɔʀnɛj/ *nf* crow.

cornemuse /kɔʀnəmyz/ ▶392 *nf* bagpipes (*pl*).

corner /kɔʀne/ **[1] I** *vtr* to turn down the corner of [*page*]; **page cornée** dog-eared page.
II *vi* **1** (conducteur) to hoot GB, to honk; **2** (sonneur) to blow a horn.

cornet /kɔʀnɛ/ *nm* **1** (emballage conique) (paper) cone; **un ~ de dragées** a cornet of sugared almonds; **2** CULIN (pâtisserie) horn; (pour glace) cone; **3** MUS (d'orgue) cornet stop; (petit cor) post horn.
■ **~ acoustique** ear trumpet; **~ à dés** dice cup; **~ à pistons** cornet.

cornette /kɔʀnɛt/ *nf* (de religieuse) cornet, wimple.

cornettiste /kɔʀnɛtist/ ▶374 *nmf* cornet player, cornetist.

corniaud /kɔʀnjo/ *nm* (chien) mongrel.

corniche /kɔʀniʃ/ *nf* **1** (de bâtiment) cornice; (de meuble) moulding GB, molding US, beading; (de plafond) coving; **2** GÉOG (escarpement) ledge (of rock); **(route en) ~** cliff road.

cornichon /kɔʀniʃɔ̃/ *nm* **1** BOT, CULIN gherkin; **2**° (idiot) nitwit°.

cornière /kɔʀnjɛʀ/ *nf* **1** (de tuiles) valley; **2** (équerre) angle iron.

Cornouailles /kɔʀnuaj/ ▶ **509**⌐ *nprf* Cornwall.

cornu, ~e[1] /kɔʀny/ *adj* [*animal*] horned.

cornue[2] /kɔʀny/ *nf* retort.

corollaire /kɔʀɔlɛʀ/ *nm* corollary.

corolle /kɔʀɔl/ *nf* BOT corolla; **en ~** [*jupe*] flared; [*vase*] flower-shaped.

coron /kɔʀɔ̃/ *nm* miners' terraced houses (*pl*).

coronaire /kɔʀɔnɛʀ/ *adj* [*artère, veine*] coronary.

coronarien, -ienne /kɔʀɔnaʀjɛ̃, ɛn/ *adj* coronary.

corporatif, -ive /kɔʀpɔʀatif, iv/ *adj* corporate (*épith*).

corporation /kɔʀpɔʀasjɔ̃/ *nf* **1** GÉN corporation; **2** JUR corporate body, body corporate; **3** HIST guild.

corporatisme /kɔʀpɔʀatism/ *nm* corporatism.

corporel, -elle /kɔʀpɔʀɛl/ *adj* **1** (du corps) [*besoin, fonction*] bodily; [*température, lotion, soin*] body; [*châtiment*] corporal; **2** JUR (matériel) corporeal.

corps /kɔʀ/ *nm inv* **1** ANAT body; **~ humain** human body; **qu'est-ce qu'elle a dans le ~?** FIG what has got GB ou gotten US into her?; (**combat**) **~ à ~** hand-to-hand combat; **lutter** (**au**) **~ à ~** to fight hand to hand; **passer sur le ~ de qn** FIG to trample sb underfoot; **2** SOCIOL (groupe) body; (profession) profession; **~ d'ingénieurs** corps of engineers; **~ enseignant** teaching profession; **le ~ électoral** the electorate; **faire ~ avec** (avec sa famille, un groupe) to stand solidly behind; (avec la nature) to be at one with; **3** MIL corps; **~ d'armée** army corps; **~ expéditionnaire** expeditionary force; **4** (de doctrine, texte) body; **5** TECH (partie principale) (d'instrument, de machine) body; (de meuble) main part; (de bâtiment) (main) body; **6** (consistance) body; **prendre ~** to take shape; **7** (objet) body; **8** CHIMIE substance; **~ gras** fatty substance; **9** (de caractère d'imprimerie) type size; **10** (de vêtement) bodice; (de cuirasse) breastplate.

■ **~ de ballet** corps de ballet; **~ calleux** corpus callosum; **~ de chauffe** heater; **~ composé** compound; **~ constitué** constituent body; **~ du délit** JUR corpus delicti; **~ diplomatique** diplomatic corps; **~ et biens** NAUT with all hands; **~ de garde** guardroom; **~ gazeux** gas; **~ jaune** ANAT corpus luteum; **~ judiciaire** JUR judicature; **~ simple** element; **~ strié** corpus striatum.

IDIOMES **tenir au ~** to be nourishing.

corps-mort, *pl* **~s** /kɔʀmɔʀ/ *nm* NAUT mooring.

corpulence /kɔʀpylɑ̃s/ *nf* stoutness, corpulence; **de forte ~** of stout build.

corpulent, -e /kɔʀpylɑ̃, ɑ̃t/ *adj* stout, corpulent.

corpus /kɔʀpys/ *nm inv* corpus.

corpuscule /kɔʀpyskyl/ *nm* ANAT, PHYS corpuscle.

correct, -e /kɔʀɛkt/ *adj* **1** (sans erreur) [*calcul, réponse, interprétation*] correct; [*copie*] accurate; **2** (convenable) [*tenue*] proper; [*conduite*] correct; [*personne*] polite; **3**○ (de qualité suffisante) [*résultat, vin*] reasonable, decent; [*devoir*] adequate, reasonable; [*logement*] adequate; **4** (honnête) [*personne*] fair, correct.

correctement /kɔʀɛktəmɑ̃/ *adv* **1** (sans erreur) correctly; **2** (convenablement) properly; **3** (raisonnablement) [*manger, loger, traiter*] decently; [*travailler, être payé*] reasonably well.

correcteur, -trice /kɔʀɛktœʀ, tʀis/ **I** *adj* corrective.
II ▶ **374**⌐ *nm,f* **1** (d'examen) examiner GB, grader US; **2** (d'épreuves) proofreader.
■ **~ d'acidité** CHIMIE, IND acidity regulator; **~ automatique d'orthographe** ORDINAT automatic spellchecker.

correctif, -ive /kɔʀɛktif, iv/ *adj* corrective.

correction /kɔʀɛksjɔ̃/ *nf* **1** (action de corriger) GÉN correcting; (de manuscrit) proofreading; **apporter une ~ à qch** to correct sth; **2** (attribution d'une note) (d'examen) marking GB, grading US; **3** (modification) correction; **4** (punition) GÉN hiding○; (fessée) spanking; **5** (exactitude) accuracy; (justesse) correctness; **6** (convenance) (de tenue, conduite) correctness; (politesse) good manners (*pl*); **manquer de ~** to have no manners.

correctionnel, -elle[1] /kɔʀɛksjɔnɛl/ *adj* peine

correctionnelle penalty (imposed by court); **tribunal ~** magistrate's court.

correctionnelle[2] /kɔʀɛksjɔnɛl/ *nf* magistrate's court.

corrélation /kɔʀelasjɔ̃/ *nf* correlation (**entre** between); **être en** (**étroite**) **~ avec qn** to be (closely) related ou connected to sth.

correspondance /kɔʀɛspɔ̃dɑ̃s/ *nf* **1** (lettres) letters (*pl*); **2** (courrier) mail; (échange de courrier) correspondence (**entre** between); **faire des études par ~** to do a correspondence course; **3** (pour un journal) correspondence; **4** (lien, ressemblance) correspondence (**entre** between); **5** (dans les transports) connection; **vols en ~** connecting flights; **6** MATH correspondence.

correspondant, -e /kɔʀɛspɔ̃dɑ̃, ɑ̃t/ **I** *adj* [*avantage, chiffre, emploi, reçu*] corresponding; [*étiquette, boulon*] matching.
II *nm,f* **1** (par courrier) GÉN correspondent; (dans le cadre d'un passe-temps) penfriend GB, pen pal; **2** TÉLÉCOM **votre ~** the person you are calling; **3** ADMIN, COMM correspondent; **4** (pour un journal) correspondent.

correspondre /kɔʀɛspɔ̃dʀ/ [6] **I correspondre à** *vtr ind* **1** (être approprié à) **~ à** to match [*dimension, contenu, formation, programme*]; to suit [*goût*]; **2** (équivaloir à) **~ à** to correspond to [*chiffre, travail*]; (coïncider avec) [*élément*] to correspond to; **~ à la description** to match the description; **ce qu'il m'en a dit ne correspond pas du tout à la réalité** what he told me about it bears no relation to reality; **3** (être lié à) **~ à** to correspond to [*événement, caractéristique*].
II *vi* **1** (écrire) to correspond (**avec** with); **2 ~ par téléphone** to communicate by phone.
III se correspondre *vpr* [*éléments*] to correspond.

corrida /kɔʀida/ *nf* bullfight; **c'est la ~**○ **pour se**

Le corps humain

L'anglais utilise souvent l'adjectif possessif avec les noms des parties du corps, là où le français utilise l'article défini.

fermer les yeux	= to close one's eyes
je me suis frotté les mains	= I rubbed my hands
il a levé la main	= he put his hand up
elle se tenait la tête	= she was holding her head
il s'est cassé le nez	= he broke his nose
elle lui a cassé le nez	= she broke his nose

Pour décrire les gens

La tournure française avec avoir (il a le nez long) peut se traduire en anglais par une tournure avec to be (his nose is long), ou par une tournure avec to have (he has a long nose).

il a les mains sales	= his hands are dirty
	ou he has dirty hands
il a mal aux pieds	= his feet are sore
	ou he has sore feet
il a le nez qui coule	= his nose is running
	ou he has a runny nose
il a les cheveux longs	= his hair is long
	ou he has long hair
elle a les yeux bleus	= she has blue eyes
	ou her eyes are blue
elle a de beaux cheveux	= she has beautiful hair
	ou her hair is beautiful

Noter aussi:

l'homme avec une jambe cassée	= the man with a broken leg
l'homme à la jambe cassée	= the man with the broken leg
la fille aux yeux bleus	= the girl with blue eyes

Noter enfin que les tournures anglaises suivantes ne peuvent être utilisées que pour décrire des caractéristiques durables:

la fille aux yeux bleus	= the blue-eyed girl
ceux qui ont de longs cheveux	= long-haired people

Pour la taille des personnes, ▶ **581**⌐; *pour le poids,* ▶ **455**⌐; *pour la couleur des yeux, des cheveux* ▶ **141**⌐; *pour les maladies et douleurs* ▶ **196**⌐.

garer à Oxford it's a real performance parking in Oxford.

corridor /kɔʀidɔʀ/ *nm* corridor.

corrigé /kɔʀiʒe/ *nm* SCOL correct version; **recueil d'exercices avec ~s** collection of exercises with answers.

corriger /kɔʀiʒe/ [13] **I** *vtr* **1** (éliminer les erreurs) GÉN to correct [*texte*]; to proofread [*manuscrit, texte*]; to read [*épreuves*]; **2** (redresser) to correct [*erreur, défaut, jugement*]; to redress [*situation*]; to improve [*manières*]; to correct [*trajectoire, instrument*]; (adapter) to adjust [*position, chiffre*]; to modify [*théorie*]; **~ le tir** MIL to alter one's aim; FIG to adjust ou modify one's tactics; **3** SCOL to mark GB, to grade US [*copie, examen*]; **4** (châtier) GÉN to give [sb] a hiding○; (fesser) to give [sb] a spanking.
II se corriger *vpr* **1** (en parlant) to correct oneself; **2** (s'améliorer) to mend one's ways; **se ~ d'un défaut** to cure oneself of a fault.

corroborer /kɔʀɔbɔʀe/ [1] *vtr* to corroborate.

corroder /kɔʀɔde/ [1] *vtr* to corrode.

corrompre /kɔʀɔ̃pʀ/ [53] **I** *vtr* **1** (soudoyer) to bribe [*policier, juge*]; **2** (pervertir) to corrupt [*jeunesse, mœurs, goût*].
II se corrompre *vpr* [*mœurs, jeunesse*] to become corrupted.

corrompu, ~e /kɔʀɔ̃py/ *adj* [*société, juge, gouvernement*] corrupt.

corrosif, -ive /kɔʀozif, iv/ **I** *adj* [*substance*] corrosive; (mordant) [*esprit, remarque*] caustic.
II *nm* corrosive.

corrosion /kɔʀozjɔ̃/ *nf* (de métal) corrosion.

corrupteur, -trice /kɔʀyptœʀ, tʀis/ **I** *adj* corrupting.
II *nm,f* (qui soudoie) briber; (qui déprave) corrupter.

corruption /kɔʀypsjɔ̃/ *nf* **1** (avec de l'argent, des cadeaux) bribery (**de** of); **2** (état) corruption (**de** in); **3** (perversion) corruption (**de** of).

corsage /kɔʀsaʒ/ *nm* **1** (chemisier) blouse; **2** (de robe) bodice.

corsaire /kɔʀsɛʀ/ *nm* **1** (personne) corsair; **2** (pantalon) pedal pushers (*pl*).

corse /kɔʀs/ **I** ▶ 509 *adj* [*fromage, accent*] Corsican.
II ▶ 338 *nm* LING Corsican.

Corse /kɔʀs/ ▶ 305 *nprf* Corsica.

corsé, ~e /kɔʀse/ *adj* **1** CULIN [*café*] strong; [*vin*] full-bodied; [*sauce*] spicy; **2** (grivois) racy, spicy; **3**○ (difficile) [*problème*] tough; **4**○ (élevé) [*facture*] steep.

corser /kɔʀse/ [1] **I** *vtr* **1** (compliquer) to make [sth] more difficult [*exercice, problème*]; **pour ~ l'affaire** (just) to complicate matters; **2** (accentuer le goût) to strengthen the flavourᴳᴮ of [*sauce*]; (avec des épices) to make [sth] spicier [*sauce, plat*].
II se corser *vpr* to get more complicated.

corset /kɔʀsɛ/ *nm* corset.

corso /kɔʀso/ *nm* **~ fleuri** procession of floral floats.

cortège /kɔʀtɛʒ/ *nm* **1** (défilé) procession; **suivi d'un ~ d'enfants** followed by a troop of children; **2** (série) LITER **la guerre et son ~ de misères** war and its trail of misery.
■ ~ funèbre (funeral) cortège.

cortical, ~e, mpl -aux /kɔʀtikal, o/ *adj* cortical.

corvée /kɔʀve/ *nf* **1** (activité pénible) chore; **les ~s ménagères** household chores; **aller les voir, quelle ~!** it's a real bore ou grind○ to have to go and see them; **2** (travail obligatoire) duty; MIL fatigue (duty); **tu es de ~ de patates**○ it's your turn to peel the potatoes; **être de ~ pour faire** to have been roped into doing; **3** HIST corvée (*peasant's day of unpaid labour*ᴳᴮ *for feudal lord*).

coryza /kɔʀiza/ ▶ 196 *nm* head cold, coryza SPÉC.

cosaque /kɔzak/ *nm* Cossack.

coscénariste /cosenaʀist/ *nmf* co-writer.

cosinus /kosinys/ *nm inv* cosine.

cosmétique /kɔsmetik/ **I** *adj* LIT, FIG cosmetic.
II *nm* cosmetic ou beauty product; **des ~s** cosmetics.

cosmique /kɔsmik/ *adj* cosmic.

cosmologie /kɔsmɔlɔʒi/ *nf* cosmology.

cosmonaute /kɔsmɔnot/ ▶ 374 *nmf* cosmonaut.

cosmopolite /kɔsmɔpɔlit/ *adj* cosmopolitan.

cosmos /kɔsmos/ *nm* cosmos.

cossard○**, ~e** /kɔsaʀ, aʀd/ **I** *adj* [*personne*] lazy, bone idle○.
II *nm,f* idler, loafer○, lazybones○ (+ *v sg*).

cosse /kɔs/ *nf* **1** BOT (de fève, pois) pod; (de graine) husk; **2** (en électronique) terminal; **3**○ (paresse) laziness.

cossu, ~e /kɔsy/ *adj* [*personne*] well-to-do; [*intérieur*] plush; [*existence*] comfortable; [*maison*] smart, posh○.

costal, ~e, mpl -aux /kɔstal, o/ *adj* ANAT, ZOOL costal.

costard○ /kɔstaʀ/ *nm* (costume) suit.

Costa Rica /kɔsta ʀika/ ▶ 232 *nprm* Costa Rica.

costaricien, -ienne /kɔstaʀisjɛ̃, ɛn/ ▶ 394 *adj* Costa Rican.

costaud○ /kɔsto/ **I** *adj* **1** [*personne*] (fort) strong; (vigoureux) sturdy; **il est assez ~** EUPH (gros) he's pretty hefty○; **tu peux lui dire, elle est ~** (moralement) you can tell her, she can take it; **2** (solide) [*chaussures, bicyclette*] sturdy; [*matériau, assemblage*] strong; [*mur, maison*] sturdily built; (fort) [*alcool*] strong; [*aliment*] spicy, hot; **c'est du ~ ta machine!** that's a solid machine you have there!
II *nm* (homme) sturdily built man.

costume /kɔstym/ *nm* **1** (ensemble veste, pantalon) suit; **il est toujours en ~ cravate** he always wears a suit and tie; **2** THÉÂT, CIN costume; **répéter en ~** to have a dress rehearsal; **3** HIST costume.
■ ~ de bain† swimming costume; **~ de cérémonie** ceremonial dress ℭ; **~ marin** sailor suit; **~ trois pièces** three-piece suit.

costumer: se costumer /kɔstyme/ [1] *vpr* to put on fancy dress; **soirée costumée** fancy-dress party, costume party US.

costumier, -ière /kɔstymje, ɛʀ/ ▶ 374 *nm,f* (de troupe) wardrobe master/mistress; (indépendant) costumier.

cotation /kɔtasjɔ̃/ *nf* FIN quotation.

cote /kɔt/ *nf* **1** FIN (valeur en Bourse) quotation; (liste des valeurs) (stock exchange) list; **entrée** ou **admission à la ~** stock exchange listing; **inscrit** ou **admis à la ~** listed (on the stock exchange); **actions hors ~** unlisted shares; **2** COMM (de voiture d'occasion, timbre) quoted value; **3** (aux courses) odds (*pl*); **4** (de personne, lieu, film) rating; **avoir la ~**○ **auprès de qn** [*célébrité*] to be popular with sb; [*individu*] to be well thought of by sb; **ne plus avoir la ~**○ to have fallen from grace; **5** (sur un plan) dimension; **6** (sur une carte) spot height; **à la ~ plus/moins 20** 20 metres above/below sea level; **7** (marque de classement) classification mark; (numéro de livre) pressmark GB, call number US.
■ ~ d'alerte flood level; FIG danger level; **~ d'amour** ou **de popularité** popularity rating.

côte /kot/ **I** *nf* **1** GÉOG (littoral) coast; **2** GÉOG (pente) hill; **dans une ~** on a hill; **3** ANAT rib; **vraie/fausse ~** true/false rib; **4** CULIN chop; **~ de bœuf** rib roast; **5** (en tricot) rib; **col à ~s** ribbed collar; **tricoter les ~s** to do the ribbing; **6** BOT rib.
II côte à côte *loc adv* side by side.
■ Côte d'Azur French riviera.
IDIOMES **se tenir les ~s** to split one's sides with laughter.

coté, ~e /kɔte/ *adj* (prestigieux) **être (très) ~** to be (very) well thought of.

côté /kote/ **I** *nm* **1** ANAT (flanc) side; **2** (partie latérale) side (**de** of); **de l'autre ~ du mur** over (the other side of) the wall; **changer de ~** (au tennis) to change ends; **3** (direction) way, direction; **de quel ~ allez-vous?** which way are you going?; **ils sont arrivés des deux ~s** they came from both directions; **4** (aspect) side; **prendre** ou **voir les choses du bon ~** to look on the bright side of things; **par certains ~s** in some respects; **d'un ~** (d'une part) on the one hand; (en un sens) in one respect ou way; **d'un autre ~** (d'autre part) on the other hand; (dans un autre sens) in another respect ou way; **~ santé, ça va** healthwise ou on the health side, it's all right; **5** (branche familiale) side (**de** of); **6** (camp) side; **être du ~ de qn** to be on sb's side.

II à côté *loc adv* **1** (à proximité) **il habite à ~** he lives nearby ou close by; **les voisins d'à ~** the next-door neighbours^{GB}; **2** LIT, FIG (en dehors) **le ballon est passé à ~** the ball went wide; **répondre à ~** (par erreur) to miss the point; (volontairement) to sidestep the question; **3** (en comparaison) by comparison; **4** (simulta-nément) **elle est étudiante et travaille à ~** she's a student and she works on the side.

III à côté de *loc prép* **1** (à proximité de) next to; **2** (en dehors de) **le ballon est passé à ~ du but** LIT the ball went wide of the goal; **passer complètement à ~ de la question** FIG (par erreur) to miss the point com-pletely; (volontairement) to sidestep the issue; **3** (en com-paraison de) compared to; **4** (en plus de) besides; **à ~ de ça**○ (par ailleurs) for all that.

IV de côté *loc adv* **1** (obliquement) **faire un pas de ~** to step aside ou to one side; **2** (sur la partie latérale) side (*épith*); **des places de ~** THÉÂT side seats; **3** (en ré-serve) aside; **mettre de ~** to put [sth] aside ou on one side [*argent, livre*]; **mettre sa fierté de ~** to swallow one's pride.

V du côté de *loc prép* **1** (vers) **aller du ~ de Dijon** to head for Dijon; **mes parents habitent du ~ de Beaune** my parents live near Beaune; **2** (en ce qui concerne) as for; **le Président, de son ~, a dit...** the President, for his part, said...; **il s'amuse, de ce ~-là, il n'y a rien à craindre** he's having fun, as far as that's concerned, there's nothing to worry about; **indique-t-on du ~ de la Commission** people in the Commission are saying; **il se tourne du ~ des dramaturges américains** he's turning toward(s) the American dramatists; **10 morts du ~ des mani-festants** 10 dead among the demonstrators.

VI aux côtés de *loc prép* LIT, FIG (près de) **aux ~s de qn** [*être, rester*] beside sb, at sb's side; **aux ~s de qn/qch** [*se retrouver*] beside ou alongside sb/sth; [*siéger, s'engager, travailler*] alongside sb/sth.

VII de tous (les) côtés *loc adv* (partout) **regarder/courir de tous ~s** to look/to run all over the place; **une ville cernée de tous ~s** a town surrounded on all sides; **ils arrivent de tous ~s** they're coming from all directions.

coteau, ~x /kɔto/ *nm* **1** (pente) hillside; **à flanc de ~** on the hillside; **2** (colline) hill; **3** (vignoble) (sloping) vineyard.

Côte-d'Ivoire /kotdivwaʀ/ **▶ 232** *nprf* Ivory Coast.

côtelé, ~e /kotle/ *adj* **velours ~** corduroy, cord.

côtelette /kotlɛt/ *nf* CULIN chop.

coter /kɔte/ [1] **I** *vtr* **1** FIN (admettre à la cotation) to list [*titre*]; **action cotée en Bourse** share listed on the stock market; **2** (numéroter) to give a pressmark GB ou call number US to [*livre*]; **3** TECH to dimension [*dessin industriel*]; to put spot heights on [*carte*].

II *vi* **1** (valoir) **~ 100 francs** [*titre*] to be quoted at 100 francs; [*voiture, œuvre*] to be priced at 100 francs; **~ en hausse/en baisse à la clôture à 392** to close up/down at 392; **2** (aux courses) to be quoted at.

coterie /kɔtʀi/ *nf* PÉJ circle, clique PÉJ.

cothurne /kɔtyʀn/ *nm* buskin, cothurnus.

côtier, -ière /kotje, ɛʀ/ *adj* [*ville, navigation, chemin*] coastal; [*pêche*] inshore.

cotillon /kɔtijɔ̃/ *nm* **1** cotillion; **2**† petticoat.

cotisation /kɔtizasjɔ̃/ *nf* **1** (à la sécurité sociale, une caisse de retraite) contribution; **~ vieillesse** *contribu-tion to a pension fund*; **2** (à une association) subscrip-tion; (à un syndicat) dues (*pl*), subscription.

cotiser /kɔtize/ [1] **I** *vi* **1** (à un régime de protection) to pay one's contributions; **~ à une caisse de retraite** to pay one's superannuation contribution; **2** (à une association, un syndicat) to pay one's subscription (**à** to).

II se cotiser *vpr* to club together GB, to go in together.

coton /kɔtɔ̃/ *nm* **1** (plante, fibre) cotton; **drap de** ou **en ~** cotton sheet; **2** (ouate) cotton wool GB, cotton US; (morceau d'ouate) piece of cotton wool GB ou cotton US.

■ **~ hydrophile** cotton wool GB, absorbent cotton US.

IDIOMES **filer un mauvais ~** (être en mauvaise santé) to be in a bad way; **élever un enfant dans du ~** to give a child a very sheltered upbringing; **elle est ~**○, **ta question** it's a tricky question; **j'ai les jambes en ~** (après un choc) my legs have turned to jelly; (après une maladie) I am wobbly on my legs.

cotonnade /kɔtɔnad/ *nf* cotton fabric.

cotonneux, -euse /kɔtɔnø, øz/ *adj* [*brouillard*] like cotton-wool (*après n*); [*nuage*] fleecy; [*ciel*] full of fleecy clouds (*après n*).

cotonnier, -ière /kɔtɔnje, ɛʀ/ **I** *adj* cotton.

II *nm* BOT cotton plant.

côtoyer /kotwaje/ [23] **I** *vtr* (être près de) to be next to; (fréquenter) to move in [*milieu*]; to mix with [*per-sonnes*]; FIG to be in close contact with [*mort, danger*].

II se côtoyer *vpr* [*personnes*] to mix; [*extrêmes*] to be side by side.

cotte /kɔt/ *nf* (vêtement de travail) overalls (*pl*).

■ **~ d'armes** HIST surcoat; **~ de mailles** HIST coat of mail.

cou /ku/ **▶ 137**, **581** *nm* neck; **embrasser qn dans le ~** to kiss sb's neck; **avoir des ennuis** or **problèmes jusqu'au ~**○ FIG to be up to one's neck in problems; **être endetté jusqu'au ~**○ FIG to be up to one's eyes in debt.

IDIOMES **se casser** or **rompre le ~** to break one's neck; **se mettre/avoir la corde au ~**○ to tie/to have tied the knot○.

couac○ /kwak/ *nm* MUS wrong note; FIG jarring note.

couard, -e /kwaʀ, aʀd/ FML **I** *adj* cowardly.

II *nm,f* coward; **c'est un ~** he's a coward.

couchage /kuʃaʒ/ *nm* (organisation) sleeping arrange-ments (*pl*); (lit) bed; (matériel pour dormir) bedding; **un studio avec ~ pour six** a studio that sleeps six.

couchant /kuʃɑ̃/ **I** *adj m* **soleil ~** setting sun; **au soleil ~** at sunset.

II *nm* **1** (coucher du soleil) sunset; **2** (ouest) LITER west.

couche /kuʃ/ **I** *nf* **1** (de vernis, peinture, d'apprêt) coat; (d'aliments, de poussière, neige) layer; **une ~ d'huile** a film of oil; **2** (strate) stratum, layer; **la ~ d'ozone** the ozone layer; **'préserve la ~ d'ozone'** 'ozone-friendly'; **3** SOCIOL sector; **les ~s laborieuses** the working classes ou sectors; **4** (pour bébés) nappy GB, diaper US; **5** (lit) LITER bed.

II couches† *nfpl* (accouchement) childbirth (*sg*).

couché, -e /kuʃe/ *adj* (penché) [*écriture*] sloping.

couche-culotte, *pl* **couches-culottes** /kuʃkylɔt/ *nf* disposable nappy GB ou diaper US.

coucher¹ /kuʃe/ [1] **I** *vtr* **1** (allonger) to put [sb] to bed [*malade, enfant*]; to lay out [*blessé, mort*]; **2** (mettre à l'horizontale) to lay [sth] on its side [*armoire*]; to lay [sth] down [*échelle, planche*]; **3** (faire pencher) [*vent, pluie*] to flatten [*blés, herbes*]; **4** (écrire) LITER **~ qch par écrit** to put sth down in writing [*idées, phrases*]; **~ qn sur son testament** to name ou mention sb in one's will.

II *vi* **1** (dormir) to sleep; **~ avec qn** to sleep with sb; **2** (passer la nuit) **~ chez qn** to sleep at sb's (house); **~ sous la tente** to sleep in a tent; **~ sous les ponts** FIG to sleep rough GB ou outdoors.

III se coucher *vpr* **1** (s'allonger) [*personne, animal*] to lie (down); **se ~ sur/dans son lit** to lie (down) on/in one's bed; **se ~ sur le dos/côté** to lie on one's back/side; **se ~ sur le ventre** to lie flat on one's stomach; **je dois rester couchée** I have to stay in bed; **2** (aller dormir) [*personne*] to go to bed; **les enfants sont couchés** the children are in bed; **3** (se pencher) [*tige, blés*] to bend; [*voilier*] to list; (chavirer) to keel over; **se ~ sur** [*motard, cycliste*] to lean forward over [*guidon*]; **4** (disparaître à l'horizon) [*soleil*] to set, to go down.

coucher² /kuʃe/ *nm* bedtime; **à l'heure du ~** at bedtime.

■ **~ de soleil** sunset; **au ~ du soleil** at sunset.

couchette /kuʃɛt/ *nf* (de train) couchette, berth; (de

bateau) berth; **un train à ~s** a sleeper GB, a Pullman (car) US.

couci-couça○ /kusikusa/ *adv* so-so○.

coucou /kuku/ **I** *nm* **1** ZOOL cuckoo; **2** BOT cowslip; **3**○ (avion) (old) crate○; **4** (horloge) cuckoo clock. **II**○ *excl* (bonjour) cooee!; (en se cachant) peekaboo!

coude /kud/ ▶ **137**┃ *nm* **1** ANAT elbow; **~s au corps** with elbows tucked in; **donner un coup de ~ à qn** (pour attirer l'attention) to nudge sb, give sb a nudge; (en se battant) to jab sb with one's elbow; **jouer des ~s pour atteindre le buffet** to elbow one's way to the buffet; **2** (partie de manche) elbow; (pièce) elbow patch; **3** (de chemin, tuyau) bend; (de fleuve) bend, elbow.
IDIOMES **travailler ~ à ~** to work shoulder to shoulder; **être au ~ à ~** to be neck and neck; **se serrer** or **se tenir les ~s** to stick together; **lever le ~**○ to drink a bit; **garder qch sous le ~** to put sth on the back burner.

coudé, **~e**[1] /kude/ *adj* bent at an angle.

coudée[2] /kude/ *nf* (mesure) cubit.
IDIOMES **avoir les ~s franches** to have elbow room.

cou-de-pied, *pl* **cous-de-pied** /kudpje/ *nm* (dessus du pied) instep; (articulation) ankle joint.

couder /kude/ [1] *vtr* to bend.

coudre /kudʀ/ [76] **I** *vtr* (en couture) to sew [*ourlet*]; (en reliure) to stitch; to sew [sth] on [*bouton, pièce*]; to stitch [sth] on [*semelle*]; to stitch (up) [*robe, plaie*].
II *vi* to sew.
IDIOMES **leur histoire est cousue de fil blanc** you can see through their story.

couenne /kwan/ *nf* CULIN (bacon) rind.

couette /kwɛt/ *nf* **1** (couverture) duvet, continental quilt GB, comforter US; **2** (coiffure) **~s** bunches GB, pigtails US; **se faire des ~s** to put one's hair (up) in pigtails.

couffin /kufɛ̃/ *nm* Moses basket GB, bassinet US.

couic /kwik/ *nm* (*also onomat*) squeak.

couinement /kwinmɑ̃/ *nm* (de souris, chaton, jouet) squeak; (de lapin, porc, freins) squeal; (de porte, ressort) creak; (de chien, d'enfant) whine.

couiner /kwine/ [1] *vi* [*souris, chaton, jouet*] to squeak; [*lapin, porc, freins*] to squeal; [*ressort, porte*] to creak; [*chien, enfant*] to whine.

coulant, **~e** /kulɑ̃, ɑ̃t/ *adj* [*camembert*] runny; [*personne*] easy-going; [*style*] flowing.

coulé, **~e**[1] /kule/ **I** *adj* **1** (souple) [*mouvement*] fluid, flowing; [*graphisme, écriture*] flowing; [*style*] flowing, fluid; **2** NAUT [*navire*] sunken.
II *nm* MUS slide.

coulée[2] /kule/ *nf* **1** (en métallurgie) casting; **2** (d'une substance) **~ de boue/neige** mudslide/snowslide; **~ de lave** lava flow; **~ de peinture** drip of paint; **3** SPORT (en natation) glide.

couler /kule/ [1] **I** *vtr* **1** (verser) to cast [*métal, verre*]; to pour [*béton*]; **~ une dalle de béton** to make a concrete slab; **2** (fabriquer) to cast [*buste, cloche*]; **3** (faire sombrer) LIT to sink [*navire*]; FIG○ to put [sth] out of business [*entreprise, commerce*]; **4**○ (faire échouer) [*matière, épreuve*] to make [sb] fail [*élève, étudiant*]; **ce sont les maths qui l'ont coulé** it was his maths mark GB ou math grade US that brought him down; **les scandales l'ont coulé** the scandals ruined him○.
II *vi* **1** (se mouvoir) [*eau, ruisseau, boue, larmes, sang*] to flow; [*sève, peinture, colle, maquillage*] to run; **la sueur coulait sur mon front** sweat was running down my forehead; (s'écouler) to run ou flow from [*robinet, fontaine, réservoir*]; to run ou flow out of [*plaie*]; **faire ~ qch** to run [*eau*]; to pour [*vin, mazout*]; **2** (se fluidifier) [*fromage*] to go runny; **3** (glisser) [*neige*] to slide; **faire ~ du sable entre ses doigts** to let some sand run through one's fingers; **4** (fuir) [*robinet, stylo*] to leak; [*nez*] to run; **5** (sombrer) [*bateau, personne*] to sink; **je coule!** I'm drowning!; **6** (passer paisiblement) LITER [*vie, temps*] to slip by; **7** BOT [*fleur, fruit*] to drop; **8**○ (faire faillite) [*entreprise, projet*] to go under, to sink; **faire ~ une société** [*personne, concurrence*] to put a company out of business; **9** (être bien formulé) to flow.

III se couler *vpr* (se glisser) **se ~ dans** to slip into [*foule*]; to slip between [*draps*]; **se ~ entre** to slip between [*obstacles, gens*].
IDIOMES **~ des jours heureux** to lead a happy life.

couleur /kulœʀ/ **I** *nf* **1** GÉN colour GB; (de) **quelle ~ est ta voiture?** what colour GB is your car?; **une veste de ~ verte/~ abricot** a green/apricot-coloured GB jacket; **avoir la ~ de qch** to be the colour GB of sth; **faire prendre ~** CULIN to brown; **plein de ~** FIG [*récit, description*] vivid, colourful GB; **sans ~** LIT, FIG colourless; **2** CIN, PHOT, TV **photo en ~** colour GB photograph; **3** (substance colorante) colour GB, paint; **boîte de ~s** paintbox; **4** (coloration des joues) colour GB; **tu as pris des ~s!** you've got some colour GB in your cheeks!; **une personne de ~** a coloured GB person; **5** JEUX (aux cartes) suit; **6** (pour les cheveux) haircolour GB; **7** (tendance politique) **~ politique** political colour GB; **8** (aspect) light; **sous des ~s trompeuses** in a false light.
II couleurs *nfpl* **1** (drapeau) colours GB; **2** (marque) colours GB; **un avion aux ~s d'Air France** an aircraft with the Air France livery; **3** (vêtements de couleur) coloureds GB.
■ **~ locale** local colour GB.
IDIOMES **ne pas voir la ~ de qch** never to get a sniff of sth○; **il m'en a fait voir de toutes les ~s**○ he really gave me a hard time, he put me through the mill○; **passer par toutes les ~s (de l'arc-en-ciel)**○ to change colour GB.

couleuvre /kulœvʀ/ *nf* grass snake.
IDIOMES **avaler des ~s**○ (être humilié) to endure humiliation; (être trompé) to believe anything one is told.

coulissant, **~e** /kulisɑ̃, ɑ̃t/ *adj* sliding (*épith*).

coulisse /kulis/ *nf* **1** THÉÂT **les ~s, la ~** (côtés) the wings; (loges) the dressing rooms; **en ~, dans les ~s, dans la ~** (arrière-scène, loges) backstage; FIG behind the scenes; **2** (rainure) runner; **à ~** [*porte, cloison*] sliding; **3** (ourlet) casing; (cordon) drawstring.

coulissé, **~e** /kulise/ *adj* **points ~s** running stitches; **short ~** or **à la taille ~e** shorts with a drawstring waist.

coulisser /kulise/ [1] *vi* (dans une rainure) to slide; **faire ~ qch** (pour ouvrir/fermer) to slide sth open/shut.

couloir /kulwaʀ/ *nm* **1** (de bâtiment) corridor GB, hallway US; (de train) corridor; (de station de métro) passage; **bruits de ~s** rumours GB; **2** (sur la chaussée) **~ de circulation** ou **réservé** bus (and taxi) lane; **~ aérien** air (traffic) lane; **3** (sur stade, en piscine) lane; (sur court) tramlines (*pl*) GB, alley US; **4** GÉOG corridor.

coup /ku/ *nm*

■ Note Les expressions comme *coup de barre, coup de maître, coup de téléphone* etc seront normalement dans le dictionnaire sous le deuxième élément donc respectivement sous **barre**, **maître**, **téléphone** etc.

1 (choc physique) (neutre) knock; (brutal) blow, whack○; (dur, par accident) bang; (qui entaille) stroke; (d'un mouvement tranchant) chop; (du plat de la main) smack; (net et rapide) rap; (léger et direct) tap; (léger et fouettant) flick; (de la pointe) poke, prod, jab; **~ à la porte** knock at the door; **~ de marteau** hammer blow; **d'un ~ de hache** [*couper, tuer*] with a single blow from an axe GB ou ax US; **à ~s de hache** [*couper, tuer*] with an axe GB ou ax US; **casser la porte à (grands) ~s de marteau** to break down the door with a hammer; **à ~s de subventions** by means of subsidies; **fièvre combattue à ~s d'antibiotiques** fever controlled with antibiotics; **sous le ~ d'un embargo** under an embargo; **donner un ~ de qch à qn** GÉN to hit ou strike sb with sth; **donner un ~ de poing/pied/couteau à qn** to punch/kick/stab sb; **prendre un ~** [*personne, voiture*] to get a knock; **en avoir pris un**○ FIG (être très abîmé) to have taken (quite) a punishing; **rendre ~ pour ~** LIT to fight back; FIG to give tit for tat; **en venir aux ~s** to come to blows (**pour** over); **les trois ~s** THÉÂT *three knocks signalling* GB *that the curtain is about to rise*; **2** (choc moral) GÉN blow; (plus modéré) knock; **porter un ~ (sévère) à** to

Les couleurs

Attention: certains noms et adjectifs de couleur français ont plusieurs traductions possibles. Par ex., brun peut être brown, dark, black etc. Consulter les articles dans le dictionnaire.

La couleur des choses

Dans les expressions suivantes, vert est pris comme exemple; les autres adjectifs et noms de couleurs s'utilisent de la même façon.

Les adjectifs

de quelle couleur est-il?	= what colour is it?
il est vert	= it's green
une robe verte	= a green dress

Les noms

En anglais, les noms de couleurs n'ont en général pas d'article défini.

j'aime le vert	= I like green
je préfère le vert	= I prefer green
le vert me va bien	= green suits me
porter du vert	= to wear green
une gamme de verts	= a range of greens
le même vert	= the same green
en vert	= in green
je t'aime bien en vert	= I like you in green
s'habiller en vert	= to dress in green
habillé de vert	= dressed in green
avez-vous le même modèle en vert?	
	= have you got the same thing in green?

Avec les verbes to paint *(peindre) et* to dye *(teindre), le en français n'est pas traduit:*

peindre la porte en vert	= to paint the door green
teindre un chemisier en vert	= to dye a blouse green

Les nuances

très vert	= very green
vert foncé	= dark green
vert clair	= light green
vert vif	= bright green
vert pâle	= pale green
vert pastel	= pastel green
vert profond	= deep green
vert soutenu	= strong green
un chapeau vert foncé	= a dark green hat
une robe vert clair	= a light green dress
un vert plus foncé	= a darker green
la robe était d'un vert plus foncé	
	= the dress was a darker green
un joli vert	= a pretty green
un vert affreux	= a dreadful green
sa robe est d'un joli vert	= her dress is a pretty green

Noter l'absence d'équivalent du de français.

En anglais comme en français, on peut exprimer une nuance en utilisant le nom d'une chose dont la couleur est typique. Noter que l'adjectif prend un trait d'union (sky-blue), mais pas le nom (sky blue).

bleu ciel	= sky blue
une robe bleu ciel	= a sky-blue dress
vert tilleul	= sage green
vert pomme	= apple green
une veste vert pomme	= an apple-green jacket

De même, navy-blue *(bleu marine),* midnight-blue *(bleu nuit),* blood-red *(rouge sang) etc. En cas de doute, consulter le dictionnaire. En ajoutant* -coloured *(GB) ou* -colored *(US) à un nom, on obtient un adjectif composé qui correspond au français avec* couleur.

une robe couleur framboise	= a raspberry-coloured dress (GB), a raspberry-colored dress (US)
des collants couleur chair	= flesh-coloured tights (GB)
un papier peint couleur crème	= cream-coloured wallpaper (GB)

Noter enfin:

bleu-noir	= blue-black
verdâtre	= greenish
un jaune verdâtre	= a greenish yellow

Attention: ces adjectifs n'existent pas pour toutes les couleurs. En cas de doute, consulter le dictionnaire. On peut toujours utiliser shade, *comme on utilise* ton *ou* nuance *en français.*

un joli ton de vert	= a pretty shade of green

Les gens (▶ 137)

L'anglais n'utilise pas l'article défini dans les expressions suivantes:

avoir les cheveux blonds	= to have fair hair
avoir les yeux bleus	= to have blue eyes

Noter les adjectifs composés anglais:

un blond	= a fair-haired man
une brune	= a dark-haired woman
un enfant aux yeux bleus	= a blue-eyed child

Mais on peut aussi dire: a man with fair hair, a child with blue eyes *etc.*

La couleur des cheveux

Les adjectifs des deux langues ne sont pas exactement équivalents, mais les correspondances suivantes sont utiles. Noter que hair *est toujours au singulier.*

les cheveux noirs	= black hair
les cheveux bruns	= dark hair
les cheveux châtains	= brown hair
les cheveux blonds	= fair hair (ou blond(e): voir le mot français blond dans le dictionnaire)
les cheveux roux	= red hair
les cheveux gris	= grey (GB) ou gray (US) hair
les cheveux blancs	= white hair

La couleur des yeux

les yeux bleus	= blue eyes
les yeux bleu clair	= light blue eyes
les yeux gris	= grey (GB) ou gray (US) eyes
les yeux verts	= green eyes
les yeux gris-vert	= greyish green (GB) ou grayish green (US) eyes (grey-green et gray-green sont aussi possibles)
les yeux marron	= brown eyes
les yeux marron clair	= light brown eyes
les yeux noisette	= hazel eyes
les yeux clairs	= light-coloured (GB) ou light-colored (US) eyes
les yeux noirs	= dark eyes

deal [sb/sth] a (severe) blow [*personne, organisation*]; **en cas de ~ dur** (accident) should anything really bad happen; (difficulté) if things get rough; **ça m'a donné un** (sacré) **~**○ it gave me an awful shock; **sous le ~ de la colère** in (a fit of) anger; **sous le ~ de la fatigue/peur** out of tiredness/fear; **être sous le ~ d'une forte émotion** to be in a highly emotional state; **tomber sous le ~ d'une condamnation** to be liable to conviction; **3** (bruit) GÉN knock; (retentissant) bang; (sourd) thump, thud; **au douzième ~ de minuit** on the last stroke of midnight; **sur le ~ de dix heures**○ around ten; **~ de gong** stroke of a gong; **~ de sifflet** whistle blast; **4** (mouvement rapide) **se donner un** (petit) **~ de brosse/peigne** to give one's hair a (quick) brush/comb GB, to brush/comb one's hair (quickly); **donner un ~ sur la table** to dust the table; **les volets ont besoin d'un ~ de peinture** the shutters need a lick of paint; **d'un ~ d'aile** with a flap of its wings; **5** JEUX, SPORT (au tennis, golf, cricket) GÉN stroke; (qu'on juge) shot; (aux échecs, dames) move; (aux dés) throw; (à la boxe) blow, punch; (au karaté) (du poing) punch; (du tranchant) chop; (du pied) kick; **tous les ~s sont permis** LIT, FIG no holds barred; **~ défendu** JEUX, SPORT foul; **6** (d'arme à feu) (décharge, détonation) shot; (munition) round; **blesser qn d'un ~ de fusil** or **pistolet** to shoot and wound sb; **tuer qn d'un ~ de fusil** or **pistolet** to shoot sb dead; **7**○ (action organisée) (opération illégale) job○, racket○; (vilain tour) trick○; (manœuvre) move; **monter un ~** to plan a job○; **~ monté!** set-up○!; **mettre qn dans le**

~ to cut sb in on the deal○; **être sur un gros ~** to be onto something big○; **il a raté son ~**○ he blew it○; **réussir son ~** to pull it off; **être dans le ~** (impliqué) to be in on it; (au courant) to be up to date, to know what's going on; **tu n'es plus dans le ~!** FIG you're behind the times!; **être/rester hors du ~** (non impliqué) to have/to keep one's nose clean○; **8** (fois, moment) **essayer encore un ~** to have another shot; **du premier ~** (immédiatement) straight off; (à la première tentative) at the first attempt; (encore) **un ~ pour rien** no go again○; **à chaque ~**, **à tout ~**, **à tous les ~s** every time; **ce ~-ci/-là** this/that time; **du ~**○ as a result; **du même ~**○ by the same token; **pour le ~**○ this time; **après ~** afterwards, in restropect; **au ~ par ~** as things come; **~ sur ~** in succession; **tout d'un ~**, **tout à ~** suddenly, all of a sudden; **d'un ~**, **d'un seul ~** just like that; **en un seul ~** in one go○; **sur le ~** (à ce moment-là) at the time; (immédiatement) instantly, on the spot; **pleure un bon ~** have a good cry; **respire un grand ~** take a deep breath; **boire à petits ~s** to sip; **boire à grands ~s** to swig; **9**○ (boisson) drink; **je te paye un ~** (à boire) I'll buy you a drink; **donne-moi encore un petit ~ de gin** give me another shot○ of gin.

■ **~ bas** (en boxe) blow ou punch below the belt; **~s et blessures** JUR assault and battery; **~ droit** (au tennis) (forehand) drive; **faire un ~ droit** (au tennis) to drive; **~ fourré** dirty trick; **~ franc** (au football) free kick.

IDIOMES **tenir le ~** (résister à l'épreuve) [*personne*] to make it○; [*véhicule, chaussures*] to last out; [*lien, réparation*] to hold; (ne pas abandonner) [*personne*] to hold on; [*armée*] to hold out; (faire face) to cope; **j'ai vu venir le ~** I could see it coming; **faire ~ double** to kill two birds with one stone; **en mettre un ~**○ to give it all one's got○; **être aux cent ~s**○ to be worried sick○, to be in a state○; **faire les quatre cents ~s**○ to be up to no good; **attraper le ~ pour faire qch**○ to get the knack of doing sth; ▶ **pierre**.

coupable /kupabl/ **I** *adj* **1** GÉN, JUR [*personne, entreprise*] guilty (**de qch** of sth; **d'avoir fait** of doing); **s'être rendu ~ de qch** to have committed sth; **2** (répréhensible) [*pensées*] shameful; [*amour*] illicit.
II *nmf* GÉN, JUR culprit; (dans un procès) guilty party.

coupage /kupaʒ/ *nm* (de vin) blending.

coupant, **~e** /kupɑ̃, ɑ̃t/ *adj* sharp; FIG cutting.

coup-de-poing, *pl* **coups-de-poing** /kudpwɛ̃/ *nm* **~ américain** knuckle-duster GB, brass knuckles (*pl*) US.

coupe /kup/ *nf* **1** SPORT cup; **la ~ du Monde** the World Cup; **2** (coiffure) haircut; **faire une ~ à qn** to give sb a haircut; **3** (processus) cutting out; (façon) cut; **cours de ~ et couture** dressmaking course; **4** (diminution) cut; **annoncer une ~ de 10% dans le budget** to announce a cut of 10% in the budget; **5** (action de couper) cutting (**de** of); **vendu à la ~** not sold prepacked; **6** (surface d'exploitation) felling area; **7** CIN, LITTÉRAT, PRESSE (censure) (action) cutting; (résultat) cut; **8** (à fruits, dessert) bowl; (à champagne) glass; **9** BIOL section; **une (vue en) ~ de qch** a section of sth; **10** (aux cartes) void; **11** LING boundary; **~ syllabique** syllabic division.

■ **~ au bol** pudding GB ou dessert US bowl cut; **~ en brosse** crew cut; **~ dégradée** layered cut; **~ réglée** periodic felling.

IDIOMES **la ~ est pleine** enough is enough; **être sous la ~ de l'État** to be under the control of the State; **vivre sous la ~ de parents autoritaires** to live under the thumb of authoritarian parents.

coupe-cigare, *pl* **~s** /kupsigaʀ/ *nm* cigar cutter.

coupe-circuit /kupsiʀkɥi/ *nm inv* fuse.

coupée /kupe/ *nf* gangway.

coupe-faim /kupfɛ̃/ *nm inv* appetite suppressant.

coupe-feu /kupfø/ **I** *adj inv* fire-proof; **porte ~** fire door.
II *nm inv* (en forêt) firebreak.

coupe-gorge /kupgɔʀʒ/ *nm inv* (lieu) rough place; (quartier) rough area.

coupe-ongles /kupɔ̃gl/ *nm inv* nail clippers (*pl*).

coupe-papier /kuppapje/ *nm inv* paper knife, letter opener.

couper /kupe/ [1] **I** *vtr* **1** (sectionner) to cut [*ficelle, papier, fleur*] (**avec** with); to cut down [*arbre*]; to chop [*bois*]; (ôter) to cut [sth] off, to cut off [*frange, branche, membre*]; **~ un fil avec les dents** to bite a thread off; **~ la journée** FIG to break up the day; **j'ai coupé par le bois** FIG I cut through the wood; **2** CULIN to cut (up), to slice [*pain*]; to carve [*rôti*]; to cut (off) [*tranche*]; to cut, to chop [*légumes*]; **~ qch en tranches** to slice sth; **3** (en couture) (d'après un patron) to cut out [*vêtement*]; (raccourcir) to shorten; **4** (entamer) [*lanière*] to cut into [*chair*]; [*couteau, ciseaux*] to cut [os, métal]; **5** CIN to cut; (pour censurer) to cut (out) [*images*]; **6** (croiser) [*route, voie*] to cut across [*route*]; MATH [*droite, courbe*] to intersect with [*axe*]; **~ la route à qn/un véhicule** to cut in on sb/a vehicle; **7** (pour faire obstacle) [*barrage, police*] to cut off [*route*]; **une veste qui coupe bien du vent** a jacket that keeps out the wind; **8** (interrompre) [*agence*] GÉN to cut off [*électricité, eau*]; (pour non-paiement) to disconnect [*électricité, eau, téléphone*]; [*usager*] to turn off [*chauffage, eau, gaz*]; to switch off [*électricité, contact*]; **un œuf dur coupe la faim** a hard boiled egg takes the edge off your hunger; **~ les vivres à qn** LIT to cut off sb's food supply; FIG to stop giving sb money; **~ l'appétit à qn** to ruin ou spoil sb's appetite; **~ le souffle à qn** LIT, FIG to take sb's breath away; **~ la parole à qn** to interrupt sb; **9** (isoler) **~ qn de qn/qch** to cut sb off from sb/sth; **10** (mélanger) to dilute [*jus de fruit, vin*]; (à la fabrication) to blend [*vin*]; **11** (au tennis) to slice [*balle, revers*]; **12** JEUX (pour mélanger) to cut; (avec une carte) to trump; **13** (castrer) to neuter, to castrate [*chat, chien*].

II *vi* **attention ça coupe!** be careful, it's sharp ou you'll cut yourself!; **ça coupe beaucoup mieux** it cuts a lot better.

III se couper *vpr* **1** (se blesser) to cut oneself (**avec** with); **il s'est coupé le doigt** (entamé) he cut his finger; (amputé) he cut his finger off; **2** (s'isoler) **se ~ de qn/qch** to cut oneself off from sb/sth; **3** (se fendre) [*cuir*] to crack; [*étoffe*] to tear, to rip; **4** (se tailler) **ça se coupe facilement** it's easy to cut; **5** (se croiser) to cross, to intersect.

IDIOMES **tu n'y couperas pas** you won't get out of it; ▶ **main**.

couperet /kupʀɛ/ *nm* (de boucher) cleaver; (de guillotine) blade; **la nouvelle est tombée comme un ~** the news came as a bolt from the blue.

couperose /kupʀoz/ *nf* broken veins (*pl*).

coupe-vent /kupvɑ̃/ *nm inv* **1** (anorak) windcheater GB, windbreaker US; **2** (haie) windbreak.

couple /kupl/ *nm* **1** (avec lien amoureux) (personnes) couple; (relation) relationship; (de danseurs) couple, pair; (d'animaux) pair; **le ~ de marcheurs** the two walkers (*pl*); **2** ÉLECTROTECH, PHYS couple; **3** AVIAT, NAUT frame.
■ **~ moteur** engine torque; **~ résistant** resisting torque.

coupler /kuple/ [1] *vtr* to couple.

couplet /kuplɛ/ *nm* (de chanson) verse; LITTÉRAT (deux vers) couplet; **faire son ~ sur** PEJ to trot out the same old stuff about.

coupole /kupol/ *nf* ARCHIT cupola, dome.

coupon /kupɔ̃/ *nm* **1** (de tissu) remnant; **2** THÉÂT ticket voucher; **3** (de transport) multiuse ticket (*in travel pass*); **4** FIN coupon.

coupure /kupyʀ/ *nf* **1** (pause) break; **2** (fossé) gap (**entre** between); **3** (passage censuré ou éliminé) cut; **4** (rupture) break; **une ~ nette avec le passé** a clean break with the past; **5** (blessure) cut; **6** (d'eau, de gaz) **une ~ d'électricité** or **de courant** GÉN a power cut; (pour non-paiement) disconnection of electricity supply; **'~s d'eau pour travaux'** 'the water will be cut off several times during the repairs'; **7** FIN (billet de banque) (bank)note GB, bill US; **petites ~s** notes of small denomination.

■ **~ de journal** or **de presse** (newspaper) cutting ou clipping.

cour /kuʀ/ *nf* **1** (de maison, bâtiment) courtyard; (où l'on joue) playground; (de ferme) yard; **la ~ des grands** LIT the older children's playground; FIG the big league; **sur ~** overlooking the courtyard; **2** (de souverain) court; (de personne en vue) entourage; **3** (à une jeune fille) courtship; **faire la ~ à** to court; **4** JUR court; '**messieurs, la ~**' 'all rise'.
■ **~ d'appel** JUR court of appeal GB ou appeals US; **~ d'assises** JUR criminal court; **~ d'école** schoolyard; **~ d'honneur** main courtyard; **~ intérieure** inner courtyard; **~ martiale** MIL courtmartial; **passer en ~ martiale** to be courtmartialled; **~ des Miracles** HIST *area of a city frequented by beggars and thieves*; FIG den of thieves; **~ de récréation** playground; **Cour de cassation** court of cassation.

courage /kuʀaʒ/ *nm* **1** (bravoure) courage, bravery; **avec ~** bravely, courageously; **avoir du ~** to be brave ou courageous; **avoir le ~ de ses opinions** to have the courage of one's convictions; **2** (énergie) energy; **je n'ai même pas le ~ de me doucher** I don't even have the energy to have a shower; **bon ~!** good luck!; **perdre ~** to lose heart; **reprendre ~** to take fresh heart; **3** (dureté) **je n'ai pas eu le ~ de dire non** I didn't have the heart to say no.

courageusement /kuʀaʒøzmɑ̃/ *adv* **1** (bravement) courageously, bravely; **2** (avec décision) with a will.

courageux, -euse /kuʀaʒø, øz/ *adj* (vaillant) courageous, brave; **sois ~** be brave; **je ne me sens pas très ~ aujourd'hui** I haven't got much energy today.

couramment /kuʀamɑ̃/ *adv* **1** (avec aisance) [*parler, écrire*] fluently; **2** (communément) [*admis, utilisé*] widely; **cela se fait ~** it's very common.

courant¹ /kuʀɑ̃/ *prép* **~ janvier** some time in January.

courant², ~e /kuʀɑ̃, ɑ̃t/ **I** *adj* **1** (fréquent) [*mot, pratique, erreur*] common; **2** (ordinaire) [*langue*] everyday; [*procédure, fonctionnement*] usual, ordinary; COMM [*taille*] standard; **3** (avec référence temporelle) [*semaine, mois, année, prix*] current; **le 15 du mois ~** the 15th of this month.
II *nm* **1** (mouvement de l'eau, de l'air) current; **il y a beaucoup de ~** there's a strong current; **contre le ~** LIT against the current; FIG against the tide; **suivre le ~** LIT to go with the current, to go downstream; FIG to go with the flow; **remonter le ~** FIG to get back on one's feet; **2** ÉLECTROTECH current; **~ électrique** electric current; **il n'y a plus de ~** the power has gone off; **le ~ passe bien entre elle et lui** FIG they get on very well; **3** (tendance) trend; **un ~ de pensée** a current of thought; **4** (déplacement) movement; **les ~s migratoires** migratory; **5** (période) **dans le ~ de** in the course of.
III au courant *loc adj* **1** (informé) **être au ~** to know; **je ne suis pas du tout au ~ de ce qu'il veut faire** I really don't know what he wants to do; **mettre qn au ~** to put sb in the picture, to fill sb in (**de** about); **tenir qn au ~** to keep sb posted (**de** about); **2** (au fait) **être très au ~** to know all about it; **pour les questions techniques demande à Paul, il est très au ~** for technical questions ask Paul, he knows all about it; **mettre qn au ~** to bring sb up to date (**de** on); **se tenir au ~** to keep up to date (**de** on).
■ **~ d'air** draught GB, draft US; **leur fils est un vrai ~ d'air** HUM their son is never in one place for more than five minutes at a time.

courbatu, ~e /kuʀbaty/ *adj* stiff.

courbature /kuʀbatyʀ/ *nf* ache; **avoir des ~s** to be stiff; **être plein de ~s** to be stiff all over.

courbaturé, ~e /kuʀbatyʀe/ *adj* (après un effort) stiff; (pendant une grippe) aching.

courbe /kuʀb/ **I** *adj* curved.
II *nf* **1** (représentation graphique) curve; **~ ascendante des prix** rising price curve; **la ~ de popularité du ministre** the minister's popularity rating; **2** (de rivière)

bend; (de route) curve, bend; (de sourcil) arch; **faire une ~** [*route*] to curve, to bend.
■ **~ de niveau** contour line; **~ de température** temperature chart.

courber /kuʀbe/ [1] **I** *vtr* to bend [*rameau, barre, corps, partie du corps*]; **courbant la tête sur son livre** bending over her book; **courbant le dos** or **les épaules pour** bending down in order to; **~ la tête** or **le front** or **le dos** FIG to bow down.
II *vi* **~ sous le poids** to be bowed down under the weight.
III se courber *vpr* (se baisser) to bend down; (avec l'âge) to become bent with age.

courbette /kuʀbɛt/ *nf* **1** (low) bow; **faire des ~s** FIG to bow and scrape (**devant** to); **2** (en équitation) curvet.

courbure /kuʀbyʀ/ *nf* curve.

coureur, -euse /kuʀœʀ, øz/ *nm,f* **▶374** SPORT (en course à pied) runner.
■ **~ automobile** racing driver; **~ cycliste** racing cyclist; **~ de haies** hurdler; **~ de jupons** philanderer; **~ motocycliste** motorcycle racer.

courge /kuʀʒ/ *nf* BOT (terme générique) gourd; (fruit) (vegetable) marrow.

courgette /kuʀʒɛt/ *nf* courgette GB, zucchini US.

courir /kuʀiʀ/ [26] **I** *vtr* **1** SPORT to compete in [*épreuve*]; **2** (parcourir en tous sens) **~ la campagne/les océans/le monde** to roam the countryside/the oceans/the world; **j'ai couru tout Paris pour trouver ton cadeau** I searched the whole of Paris for your present; **3** (fréquenter) **~ les théâtres** to do the round of the theatres; **~ les boutiques** to go round the shops GB ou stores US; **4** (s'exposer à) **~ un (grand) danger** to be in (great) danger; **faire ~ un (grand) danger à qn** to put sb/sth in (serious) danger; **~ un (gros) risque** to run a (big) risk; **faire ~ un risque à qn** to put sb at risk; **c'est un risque à ~** it's a risk one has to take; **5** (chercher à séduire) **~ les filles/garçons** to chase after girls/boys.
II *vi* **1** GÉN [*personne, animal*] to run; **sortir en courant** to run out; **'va chercher ton frère'—'j'y cours'** 'go and get your brother'—'I'm going'; **tout le monde court voir leur spectacle** everybody is rushing to see their show; **les voleurs courent toujours** FIG the thieves are still at large; **2** SPORT (à pied) [*athlète, cheval*] to run; (en vélo, voiture, moto) to race; **~ sur une balle** (au tennis) to run for a ball; **3** (se presser) [*personne*] to rush; **en courant** hastily, in a rush; **~ (tout droit) à la catastrophe/faillite** to be heading (straight) for disaster/bankruptcy; **4** (chercher à rattraper) **~ après qn/qch** GÉN to run after sb/sth; (poursuivre) to chase after [*voleur, gloire*]; **s'il ne veut pas me voir je ne vais pas lui ~ après** FIG if he doesn't want to see me I'm not going to go chasing after him; **5** (se mouvoir rapidement) [*ruisseau*] to rush (**dans** through); [*nuages, flammes*] to race (**dans** across); **6** (parcourir) **~ le long de** [*sentier*] to run along; [*veine*] to run down; **7** (se propager) [*rumeur*] to go around; **c'est un bruit qui court** it's a rumour GB; **faire ~ un bruit** to spread a rumour GB; **8** (être en vigueur) [*intérêts*] to accrue; [*bail, contrat*] to run (**jusqu'à** to); **9** (s'écouler) **le mois/l'année qui court** the current ou present month/year; **10** [*navire*] to run, to sail.
IDIOMES **tu peux toujours ~!⚬** you can go whistle for it!⚬; **laisser ~⚬** to let things ride; **laisse ~⚬!** forget it!

courlis /kuʀli/ *nm inv* curlew.

couronne /kuʀɔn/ *nf* **1** (de roi) crown; (de noble) coronet; **2** (de fleurs, feuilles) **~ de fleurs** garland; (pour enterrement) wreath; **~ de lauriers** laurel wreath; **3** (de dent) crown; **4** (cercle) ring; **5** (pouvoir) **la ~** the Crown; **6** (monnaie) crown; **7** (pain) ring-shaped loaf; **8** (banlieue de Paris) **la petite ~** *the inner suburbs*; **la grande ~** *the outer suburbs*.

couronnement /kuʀɔnmɑ̃/ *nm* (de souverain) coronation; (de saint, héros) crowning; **c'est le ~ de leur carrière** FIG it's their crowning achievement.

couronner /kuʀɔne/ [1] *vtr* **1** (coiffer d'une couronne, sacrer) to crown [*roi*] (**de** with); **enfant à la tête**

couronnée de roses child wearing a garland of roses on his/her head; **pic couronné de neige** LITER snow-capped peak; **2** (donner un prix à) to award a prize to [*personne, œuvre*]; (récompenser) **être couronné de succès** to be crowned with success; **cela couronne dix années de recherches** this is the crowning achievement of ten years' research; **et pour ~ le tout** HUM and to crown it all; **3** (en dentisterie) to crown.

courre /kuʀ/ *vtr* **chasse à ~** hunting.

courrier /kuʀje/ *nm* (lettres) mail, post GB; (une lettre) letter; **faire son ~** to write some letters; **par retour du ~** by return (of post) GB, by return mail.

■ **~ du cœur** problem page; **~ de la mode/litté-raire** fashion/book page; **~ électronique** ORDINAT electronic mail; **~ des lecteurs** letters to the editor.

courriériste /kuʀjeʀist/ *nmf* columnist.

courroie /kuʀwa/ *nf* **1** (lien) strap; **2** (sur une machine) belt.

courroucé, ~e /kuʀuse/ *adj* LITER wrathful SOUT.

courroux /kuʀu/ *nm inv* LITER wrath SOUT, ire SOUT.

cours /kuʀ/ *nm inv* **1** (session d'enseignement) SCOL lesson, class; UNIV class; (magistral) lecture; (hors cadre scolaire) class; (en privé) lesson; (ensemble de sessions) course; **avoir ~** to have a class; **suivre un ~** to do ou take a course; **faire ~** to teach; **qui vous fait ~ en chimie?** who teaches chemistry; **faire un ~ sur qch** (une fois) to give a class in sth; (plusieurs fois) to teach a course in sth; **il nous a fait un véritable ~ sur la gastronomie** he gave us a real lecture on gastronomy; **donner des ~ de français** (dans l'ensei-gnement) to teach French; (en privé) to give French lessons; **2** (manuel) SCOL, UNIV course book, textbook; (notes) notes; **3** (établissement) school; **~ de théâtre** drama school; **4** FIN (taux de négociation) (de denrée, valeur) price; (de devise) exchange rate; **avoir ~** FIN [*monnaie*] to be legal tender; FIG [*théorie, pratique*] to be current; [*terme*] to be used; **ne plus avoir ~** FIN [*monnaie*] to be no longer legal tender; FIG [*théorie, pratique*] to be no longer accepted; [*terme*] to be no longer used; **5** (de rivière) (parcours) course; (débit) flow; **6** (enchaînement) (de récit, carrière, d'événements) course; (d'idées) flow; **les choses suivent leur ~** things are taking their course; **la vie reprend son ~** life returns to normal; **donner libre ~ à** to give free rein to [*imagination*]; to give way to [*peine*]; to give vent to [*colère*]; **au ou dans le ~ de** in the course of, during; **en ~** [*mois, semaine, année*] current; [*processus, projet*] under way (*après n*); [*travail, négociations, changements*] in progress (*après n*); **en ~ de journée/saison** in the course of the day/season; **en ~ de fabrication/réno-vation** in the process of being manufactured/renov-ated; **le pont en ~ de construction** the bridge being built ou under construction; **en ~ de route** along the way; **en ~ de cuisson** during cooking.

■ **~ d'eau** watercourse; **~ élémentaire deuxième année, CE2** third year of primary school, age 8–9; **~ élémentaire première année, CE1** second year of primary school, age 7–8; **~ magistral** lecture; **~ moyen deuxième année, CM2** fifth year of primary school, age 10–11; **~ moyen première année, CM1** fourth year of primary school, age 9–10; **~ d'initiation** introductory course; **~ par correspondance** correspondence course; **~ particulier(s)** private tuition ¢ GB, private tutoring ¢ US (en, de in); **~ de perfectionnement** improvers' course; **~ prépara-toire, CP** first year of primary school, age 6–7; **~ de rattrapage** remedial course; **~ de remise à niveau** refresher course; **~ du soir** evening class.

course /kuʀs/ *nf* **1** (mode de déplacement) running; **faire la ~ avec qn** LIT, FIG to race sb; **être rapide à la ~** to be a fast runner; **2** (trajet) (de personne) run; (de taxi) journey; **c'est 50 francs la ~** the fare is 50 francs; **3**° (précipitation) rush; **ça va être la ~ pour rendre le rapport dans les délais** it'll be a rush getting the report in before the deadline; **4** (compétition) race; **la ~ au profit/aux voix** the race for profit/for votes; **être en ~** SPORT to be in the race; FIG to be in

the running; **être hors ~** SPORT, FIG to be out of the race; **5** (activité) (en athlétisme) running; (avec un véhicule, animal) racing; (épreuve) race; (en alpinisme) climb; **6** (dé-marche) errand; **faire une ~** to run an errand; **7** (achat, commission) **j'ai une ~ à faire** I've got to go and get something; **j'ai deux ou trois ~s à faire** I've got some shopping to do; **8** (trajectoire) (d'astre, de planète, comète) path; (de nuages) passage; (de fusée, projectile) flight path; **9** (passage) LITER **la ~ du temps/des années** the passing of time/of the years.

II **courses** *nfpl* **1** (achats) shopping ¢; **je vais faire des ~s** I'm going shopping; **2** (de chevaux) races.

■ **~ de haies** (en athlétisme) hurdles (*pl*); (à cheval) steeplechase; **~ d'obstacles** obstacle race; FIG obstacle course; **~ à pied** running; **~ de taureaux** (corrida) bullfight; (dans la rue) bull run; **~ de vitesse** (en athlétisme) sprint; (en moto) speedway race.

IDIOMES **ne plus être dans la ~** to be out of touch; **être en fin de ~** to be on the decline; **être à bout de ~** to be worn out.

coursier, -ière /kuʀsje, ɛʀ/ I ▶374 *nm,f* messenger.
II *nm* HIST charger, warhorse.

coursive /kuʀsiv/ *nf* passageway.

court, ~e /kuʀ, kuʀt/ I *adj* **1** (de taille, en durée) short; **dans le délai le plus ~** in the shortest pos-sible time; **de ~e durée** [*victoire, joie, espoir*] short-lived; [*prêt, emploi, maladie*] short-term; **s'arrêter, souffle ~** to get out of breath and stop; **avoir le souffle ~** to get out of breath easily; **prendre au plus ~** to take the shortest route; **2** (insuffisant) [*connaissances*] limited; **une heure/trois pages c'est (un peu) ~** one hour/three pages, that's not really enough; **3** (faible) [*défaite, victoire, majorité*] narrow; **gagner d'une ~e tête** [*cheval*] to win by a short head; [*candidat*] to win by a narrow margin.
II *adv* **s'habiller ~** to wear short skirts; **jouer ~** to play short balls; **couper qch ~** to cut sth short; **couper ~** (en parlant) to cut the conversation short; **couper ~ à qch** (abréger) to cut sth short; (faire cesser) to put paid to sth; **tourner ~** to come to a sudden end; **s'arrêter ~** to stop short.
III *nm* **1** (style vestimentaire) **le ~** short skirts (*pl*); **2** SPORT **~ de tennis** tennis court.

■ **~ métrage** CIN short (film); **~e échelle** leg up°; **faire la ~e échelle à qn** to give sb a leg up°.
IDIOMES **être à ~ de** to be short of [*argent*]; to be short on [*idées*] ; **prendre qn de ~** to catch sb on the hop° GB ou unprepared.

courtaud, ~e /kuʀto, od/ *adj* [*personne*] shortish.

court-circuit, *pl* **~s** /kuʀsiʀkɥi/ *nm* shortcircuit.

court-circuiter /kuʀsiʀkɥite/ [1] *vtr* **1** LIT to short-circuit; **2**° FIG to bypass [*intermédiaire*].

courtier, -ière /kuʀtje, ɛʀ/ ▶374 *nm,f* broker.

courtisan /kuʀtizɑ̃/ *nm* **1** (flatteur) sycophant; **atti-tude de ~** fawning ¢; **2** HIST courtier.

courtisane /kuʀtizan/ *nf* courtesan.

courtiser /kuʀtize/ [1] *vtr* to woo.

courtois, ~e /kuʀtwa, az/ *adj* courteous; LITTÉRAT courtly.

courtoisie /kuʀtwazi/ *nf* courtesy.

court-vêtu, ~e, *mpl* **~s** /kuʀvety/ *adj* **une femme ~e** a woman in a short skirt.

couru, ~e /kuʀy/ *adj* **1** [*endroit*] popular; **2** (aux courses) **vingt partants, tous ~** twenty at the start, all ran.
IDIOMES **c'est ~° d'avance** it's a foregone conclu-sion.

cousin, ~e /kuzɛ̃, in/ I *nm,f* cousin; **~ germain** first cousin.
II *nm* ZOOL mosquito.
IDIOMES **être ~s à la mode de Bretagne** HUM to be distantly related; **le roi n'est pas son ~** he thinks he is the cat's whiskers.

coussin /kusɛ̃/ *nm* (pour divan) cushion.
■ **~ d'air** air cushion; **~ de sécurité** air bag.

coussinet /kusinɛ/ *nm* (de divan) small cushion.

■ ~ **plantaire** ZOOL pad.

cousu, ~e /kuzy/ ▶ **coudre**.

coût /ku/ nm cost (**de** of; **en** in).

coûtant /kutã/ adj **prix** ~ cost price.

couteau, pl ~**x** /kuto/ nm **1** GÉN knife; (de mixeur) blade; **c'est un coup de** ~ (blessure) it's a knife wound; **jouer** or **manier du** ~ to use a knife (*in a fight*); **donner un coup de** ~ **à qn** to stab sb; **tuer qn à coups de** ~ to stab sb to death; **2** (coquillage) razor shell GB ou clam US.
■ ~ **à cran d'arrêt** flick knife GB, switchblade US.
IDIOMES **être à** ~**x tirés**○ **avec qn** to be at daggers drawn with sb; **avoir le** ~ **sous la gorge** to have a pistol to one's head; **tendre la gorge au** ~ to lay one's head on the block.

coutelas /kutla/ nm (de cuisine) large (kitchen) knife; (sabre) cutlass.

coutelier, -ière /kutəlje, ɛR/ ▶ **374**| nm,f cutler.

coutellerie /kutɛlRi/ nf (magasin) cutlery shop; (fabrique) cutlery works (pl); (industrie) cutlery industry; (commerce) cutlery trade ou business; (objets) cutlery.

coûter /kute/ [1] **I** vtr to cost; ~ **la vie à qn** to cost sb his/her life.
II vi to cost; ~ **dix francs** to cost ten francs; **combien coûte ce livre?** how much is this book?; **cela me coûte d'aller le voir** FIG it's hard for me to go and see him; ~ **cher** to be expensive; **ne pas** ~ **cher** to be cheap, not to cost a lot; ~ **cher à qn** LIT to cost sb a lot; FIG [erreur, action] to cost sb dear(ly).
III v impers **il en coûte à qn de faire** it's hard for sb to do; **il t'en coûtera d'avoir fait cela** you will pay for doing this; **coûte que coûte, quoi qu'il en coûte** at all costs.
IDIOMES **il n'y a que le premier pas qui coûte** the first step is the hardest; ~ **les yeux de la tête**○ to cost an arm and a leg○.

coûteux, -euse /kutø, øz/ adj costly.

coutil /kuti/ nm (pour vêtement) (cotton) drill; (pour matelas) ticking.

coutume /kutym/ nf (habitude) custom; **selon la** ~ according to custom; **avoir** ~ **de faire qch** to be in the habit of doing sth; **la** ~ **le veut** it is the custom; **de** ~ as a rule; **comme de** ~ as usual.
IDIOMES **une fois n'est pas** ~ it does no harm just this once.

coutumier, -ière /kutymje, ɛR/ adj customary.

couture /kutyR/ nf **1** (activité, chose à coudre) sewing; (activité professionnelle) dressmaking; **faire de la** ~ to sew; **haute** ~ haute couture; **2** (bords cousus) seam.
IDIOMES **le petit doigt sur la** ~ **du pantalon** standing stiffly to attention; **regarder qch sous toutes les** ~**s** to examine sth from every angle; **battre qn à plates** ~**s** to beat sb hollow.

couturier /kutyRje/ nm ▶ **374**| dress designer; **grand** ~ couturier.

couturière /kutyRjɛR/ nf ▶ **374**| dressmaker.

couvée /kuve/ nf (d'oisillons, enfants) brood; (d'œufs) clutch.

couvent /kuvã/ nm **1** (pour femmes) convent; (pour hommes) monastery; **entrer au** ~ to enter a convent; **2** (école) convent school.

couver /kuve/ [1] **I** vtr **1** ZOOL to sit on [œufs]; **la poule couve** the hen is brooding; **2** (protéger) to overprotect; ~ **qn/qch du regard** (avec tendresse) to look fondly at sb/sth; (avec envie) to gaze longingly at sb/sth; **3** (être atteint de) to be coming down with [maladie]; **4** (préparer) to hatch [complot]; to plot [vengeance].
II vi [révolte] to brew; [feu, colère, jalousie] to smoulder; [racisme, fanatisme] to lie dormant.

couvercle /kuvɛRkl/ nm lid; (qui se visse) screwtop.

couvert, ~e /kuvɛR, ɛRt/ **I** pp ▶ **couvrir**.
II pp adj **1** (plein) covered (**de** in, with); **être** ~ **de diplômes** to have a lot of qualifications; **2** (en intérieur) [piscine] indoor; [marché, stade, passage] covered; **3** MÉTÉO [ciel, temps] overcast.
III nm **1** (accessoires pour un repas) place setting; **une table de 6** ~**s** a table set for 6; **mettre le** ~ to lay

the table; **avoir son** ~ **chez qn** FIG to be a frequent dinner guest at sb's house; **un** ~ **en argent** a silver knife, fork and spoon; **ils mangent avec des** ~**s en argent** they eat with silver cutlery; **2** (à payer au restaurant) cover charge; **3** (abri) cover; **sous le** ~ **d'un arbre/bois** under the cover of a tree/wood.
IV à couvert loc adv under cover; **se mettre à** ~ to take cover.
V sous le couvert de loc prép (apparence) under the pretence GB of; **sous** ~ **de la plaisanterie** under the guise of a joke.

couverture /kuvɛRtyR/ nf **1** (de lit) blanket; (plus petit) rug GB, lap robe US; **2** (de livre) cover; **3** (dans la presse) coverage; **assurer la** ~ **d'un événement** to cover an event; **4** (toiture) roofing ¢, roof; **5** (ce qui protège d'un risque, d'un danger) cover; ~ **aérienne** air cover; **taux de** ~ (dans les échanges commerciaux) import-export ratio.
■ ~ **chauffante** electric blanket; ~ **sociale** social security cover; ~ **végétale** plant cover; ~ **de voyage** travelling rug GB, lap robe US.
IDIOMES **tirer la** ~ **à soi** to turn a situation to one's own advantage.

couveuse /kuvøz/ nf **1** (appareil) incubator; **2** (poule) brood hen.

couvre-chef, pl ~**s** /kuvRəʃɛf/ nm HUM headgear ¢, hat.

couvre-feu, pl ~**x** /kuvRəfø/ nm curfew.

couvre-lit, pl ~**s** /kuvRəli/ nm bedspread.

couvre-pieds /kuvRəpje/ nm inv small quilt.

couvreur /kuvRœR/ ▶ **374**| nm roofer.

couvrir /kuvRiR/ [32] **I** vtr **1** (recouvrir) GÉN to cover (**de** with); to roof [maison]; (aux cartes) to cover; ~ **un toit d'ardoises/de tuiles** to slate/to tile a roof; ~ **des pages et des pages d'une écriture serrée** to fill page after page in closely written script; **une peinture qui couvre bien** a paint that gives good coverage; **2** (être plus fort que) [son, musique] to drown out; **3** (desservir) [émetteur, inspecteur] to cover [région]; **4** (contre le froid) (avec des vêtements) to wrap [sb] up; (au lit) to cover [sb] up; **il est trop couvert** (vêtu) he's got too many clothes on; (au lit) he's got too many blankets on; **5** (donner en grande quantité) ~ **qn de qch** (d'honneurs, de bijoux, compliments) to shower sb with sth, to shower sth on sb; (de baisers) to cover sb with sth; **6** (protéger) to cover up for [faute, personne]; (avec une arme) to cover [soldat, retraite]; **7** (parcourir) to cover [distance]; **8** (rendre compte de) [livre, auteur, presse] to cover [sujet, période, événement]; **9** (pourvoir à) ~ **les besoins de qn** to meet sb's needs; **10** FIN [somme] to cover [dépenses]; ~ **une enchère** to make a higher bid; **11** (garantir) to cover [dégât, risque, personne]; **12** ZOOL [mâle] to cover [femelle].
II se couvrir vpr **1** (s'habiller) to wrap up; (d'un chapeau) to put on a hat; **elle se couvrit les épaules d'un châle** she covered her shoulders with a shawl; **rester couvert** to keep one's hat on; **2** MÉTÉO [ciel] to become cloudy ou overcast; **3** (se remplir) **se** ~ **de** (de plaques, boutons) to become covered with; **l'arbre se couvre de fleurs/feuilles** the tree comes into bloom/leaf; **son visage se couvrit de larmes** tears poured down his/her face; **4** (se protéger) (de critiques, d'accusations) to cover oneself; (de coups) to protect oneself; **se** ~ **contre** to cover oneself against.

CP /sepe/ nm: abbr ▶ **cours**.

CQFD /sekyɛfde/ (abbr = **ce qu'il fallait démontrer**) QED.

crabe /kRab/ nm ZOOL crab; **marcher en** ~ to sidle along.

crac /kRak/ nm (also onomat) (cassure) crack; (déchirure) rip; (bruit) cracking sound; **et puis** ~**!** **elle a changé d'idée** and then, bang! she changed her mind.

crachat /kRaʃa/ nm spit ¢.

crachement /kRaʃmã/ nm **1** (de salive, etc) spitting ¢; **2** (de fumée) belching ¢; (d'étincelles) shower; (de flammes) burst; **3** (bruit) crackling ¢.

cracher /kRaʃe/ [1] **I** vtr **1** (ce qui est dans la bouche) to spit out [noyau, aliment]; ~ **du sang** to spit blood;

c'est le portrait de sa mère tout craché○ FIG she's the spitting image of her mother; **c'est lui tout craché**○ FIG that's just like him; **2** (dire) **~ des injures à qn** to hurl abuse at sb; **3** (émettre) to belch (out) [*flammes, fumée*]; to spit out [*balles*].

II *vi* **1** [*personne*] to spit; **je ne cracherais pas dessus**○ HUM I wouldn't turn up my nose at it; **2** [*robinet, stylo*] to splutter; [*radio*] to crackle.

IDIOMES **c'est comme si on crachait en l'air**○ it's a complete waste of time.

cracheur /kʀaʃœʀ/ *nm* **~ de feu** fire-eater.

crachin /kʀaʃɛ̃/ *nm* drizzle.

crachoir /kʀaʃwaʀ/ *nm* spittoon.
IDIOMES **tenir le ~ à qn** to talk on and on at sb.

crachoter /kʀaʃɔte/ [1] *vi* **1** [*personne*] to cough and splutter; **2** [*robinet*] to splutter; **3** [*micro*] to crackle.

crack /kʀak/ *nm* **1** (cheval) champion horse; **2**○ (génie) ace; **3**○ (drogue) crack○.

craie /kʀɛ/ *nf* (roche, bâton) chalk.

craindre /kʀɛ̃dʀ/ [54] *vtr* **1** (redouter) to fear, to be afraid of; **~ le pire** to fear the worst; **ne craignez rien** don't be afraid; **oui, je le crains** yes, I'm afraid so; **~ de faire** to be afraid of doing; **une explosion est à ~** there's some danger of an explosion; **2** (être sensible à) [*personne, peau*] to be sensitive to [*froid, savon*]; [*plante*] to dislike [*soleil*].

crainte /kʀɛ̃t/ *nf* **1** (peur) fear (**de** of; **de faire** of doing); **sans ~** without fear; **avec ~** fearfully; **2** (inquiétude) fear; **avoir des ~s au sujet de qn** to be worried about sb.
IDIOMES **la ~ est le commencement de la sagesse** PROV only a fool knows no fear.

craintif, -ive /kʀɛ̃tif, iv/ *adj* [*personne, voix*] timorous; [*animal*] timid.

craintivement /kʀɛ̃tivmɑ̃/ *adv* timidly.

cramoisi, ~e /kʀamwazi/ ▶ 141 *adj* crimson.

crampe /kʀɑ̃p/ *nf* cramp.

crampon /kʀɑ̃pɔ̃/ *nm* **1** (d'alpiniste) crampon; **chaussures à ~s** (de football) boots with studs GB ou cleats US; (de course) spiked shoes; **2** (pour assembler) cramp (iron), clamp.

cramponner: se cramponner /kʀɑ̃pɔne/ [1] *vpr* to hold on tightly; **se ~ à qch/qn** LIT, FIG to cling to sth/sb.

cran /kʀɑ̃/ **I** *nm* **1** (encoche) notch; (sur ceinture, courroie) hole; **se mettre un ~ à la ceinture** FIG to tighten one's belt; **monter d'un ~** FIG [*cote de popularité*] to go up a notch; [*personne*] (dans l'estime) to move up a notch; (dans une hiérarchie) to move up a rung; **poussetoi d'un ~** move up one (place); **2** (entaille repère) nick; **3**○ (courage) **avoir du ~** to have guts○; **4** (en coiffure) wave.

II à cran *loc adv* **être à ~, avoir les nerfs à ~** to be on edge.

■ **~ d'arrêt** flick knife GB, switchblade US; **~ de sûreté** safety catch.

crâne /kʀɑn/ ▶ 137 *nm* **1** ANAT skull; **2**○ (tête) head; **ne rien avoir dans le ~** to have no brains.
IDIOMES **bourrer le ~ à qn** to brainwash sb.

crânement /kʀɑnmɑ̃/ *adv* (bravement) gallantly; (fièrement) proudly.

crâner○ /kʀane/ [1] *vi* to show off.

crâneur, -euse /kʀanœʀ, øz/ **I** *adj* pretentious.
II *nm,f* show-off; **faire le ~** to show off.

crânien, -ienne /kʀanjɛ̃, ɛn/ *adj* cranial; **boîte crânienne** cranium.

cranter /kʀɑ̃te/ [1] *vtr* **1** (entailler) to notch; **2** (en coiffure) to crimp.

crapaud /kʀapo/ *nm* **1** ZOOL toad; **2** (de diamant) flaw.
IDIOMES **la bave du ~ n'atteint pas la blanche colombe** HUM ≈ sticks and stones (may break my bones but words will never hurt me).

crapule /kʀapyl/ *nf* PEJ (individu) crook.

crapuleux, -euse /kʀapylø, øz/ *adj* villainous.

craquant○, **~e** /kʀakɑ̃, ɑ̃t/ *adj* [*personne*] irresistible.

craqueler /kʀakle/ [19] **I** *vtr* to crackle [*céramique*].
II se craqueler *vpr* to crack.

craquelure /kʀaklyʀ/ *nf* crack; **~s** (en céramique) (accidentelles) crazing ¢; (délibérées) crackle ¢; ART craquelure ¢.

craquement /kʀakmɑ̃/ *nm* (grincement) creaking sound, creak; (bruit de cassure) cracking sound, crack; (de feuilles mortes) crackle ¢.

craquer /kʀake/ [1] **I** *vtr* **1** (déchirer) to split [*vêtement*]; to rip [*collant*]; to break [*sangle, poignée*]; **2** (frotter) to strike [*allumette*].

II *vi* **1** (se rompre) [*couture*] to split; [*vêtement*] to split (at the seams); [*collant*] to rip; [*branche, vitre*] to crack; [*sac*] to burst; **faire ~ une branche** to break a branch; **2** (faire un bruit) [*plancher, mât*] to creak; [*neige*] to crunch; [*feuilles*] to rustle; [*branchages*] to crack; **qui craque sous la dent** crunchy; **faire ~ ses articulations** to crack one's joints; **3** (pour allumer) **faire ~ une allumette** to strike a match; **4**○ (ne pas résister) [*entreprise*] to collapse; [*personne*] (de tension nerveuse) to crack up○; (dans un effort) to give up.

crasse /kʀas/ **I** *adj* [*ignorance, stupidité*] crass; [*impolitesse*] gross; **d'une ignorance ~** pig ignorant○.
II *nf* **1** (saleté) grime, filth; **2**○ (mauvais tour) dirty trick; **3** TECH (scorie) dross, slag; (résidus) scum ¢.

crasseux, -euse /kʀasø, øz/ *adj* filthy, grimy.

crassier /kʀasje/ *nm* slag heap.

cratère /kʀatɛʀ/ *nm* crater.

cravache /kʀavaʃ/ *nf* whip; **donner un coup de ~ à** to whip.

cravacher /kʀavaʃe/ [1] *vtr* to whip [*cheval*].

cravate /kʀavat/ *nf* **1** (pour chemise) tie; (insigne de décoration) ribbon; **2** (prise de catch) headlock.

cravater /kʀavate/ [1] *vtr* **1**○ (saisir par le cou) to grab [sb] round the neck; (en sport) to put [sb] in a headlock; **2** (d'une cravate) **cravaté de soie** wearing a silk tie.

crawl /kʀol/ *nm* crawl; **nager le ~** to do ou swim the crawl.

crawler /kʀole/ [1] *vi* to do ou swim the crawl; **dos crawlé** backstroke.

crayeux, -euse /kʀejø, øz/ *adj* GÉN chalky; [*teint*] chalk-white.

crayon /kʀejɔ̃/ *nm* **1** (pour écrire, se farder) pencil; **au ~** in pencil; **avoir un bon coup de ~** to be good at drawing; **faire un portrait en trois coups de ~** to quickly sketch a portrait; **2** (dessin) pencil drawing.
■ **~ à bille** ballpoint pen; **~ de couleur** coloured GB pencil; **~ feutre** felt-tip pen; **~ gras** soft pencil; **~ à lèvres** lip pencil; **~ noir** lead pencil; **~ optique** light pen; **~ à sourcils** eyebrow pencil; **~ pour les yeux** eyeliner.

crayon-feutre, *pl* **crayons-feutres** /kʀejɔ̃føtʀ/ *nm* felt-tip pen.

crayon-lecteur, *pl* **crayons-lecteurs** /kʀejɔ̃lɛktœʀ/ *nm* bar-code reader.

crayonnage /kʀejɔnaʒ/ *nm* (croquis) pencil sketch; (gribouillage) **des ~s** scribbles.

crayonner /kʀejɔne/ [1] *vtr* (dessiner) to make a pencil sketch of; (écrire) to scribble down.

créance /kʀeɑ̃s/ *nf* **1** (somme due) debt (*owed by a debtor*); (titre) letter of credit; **2** (foi) LITER credence SOUT; **perdre ~ auprès de qn** to lose credibility with sb.

créancier, -ière /kʀeɑ̃sje, ɛʀ/ *nm,f* creditor.

créateur, -trice /kʀeatœʀ, tʀis/ **I** *adj* creative.
II *nm,f* (de parfum, genre littéraire, rôle) creator; (de produit) designer.

Créateur /kʀeatœʀ/ *nm* RELIG **le ~** the Creator.

créatif, -ive /kʀeatif, iv/ *adj* creative.

création /kʀeasjɔ̃/ *nf* **1** (action de créer, produit original) creation; COMM (action) invention; (produit) product; **la ~ d'une société/d'un comité** setting up a company/a committee; **la ~ d'emplois** job creation; **il y aura des ~s d'emplois** new jobs will be created; **encourager les ~s d'entreprises** to encourage business startups; **2** THÉÂT **c'est une ~** (rôle) the part has never been acted before; (pièce) the play is being staged for the first time.

Création /kʀeasjɔ̃/ *nf* BIBLE **la ~ (du monde)** the Creation.

créativité /kʀeativite/ *nf* creativity.

créature /kʀeatyʀ/ *nf* GÉN creature.

crécelle /kʀesɛl/ *nf* rattle; **voix de ~** shrill voice.

crécerelle /kʀesʀɛl/ *nf* kestrel.

crèche /kʀɛʃ/ *nf* **1** (garderie) crèche GB, day-nursery; **2** (de Noël) crib GB, crèche US.

crédibilité /kʀedibilite/ *nf* credibility (**auprès de** with).

crédible /kʀedibl/ *adj* credible.

crédit /kʀedi/ *nm* **1** (somme allouée) funds (*pl*); **nous disposons d'un ~ de 20 000 francs** we have funds of 20,000 francs; **les ~s de la recherche/défense** research/defence GB funding ou budget; **2** (avance de fonds) credit **℄**; **accorder un ~ à qn** to grant credit terms ou facilities to sb; **faire ~ à qn** to give sb credit; **à ~** on credit; **3** FIN credit; **votre ~ est de 1500 francs** you are 1,500 francs in credit; **porter une somme au ~ de qn** or **d'un compte** to credit sb's account with a sum of money; **4** (considération) credibility; **mettre** or **porter qch au ~ de qn** FIG to give sb credit for sth.

■ **~ municipal** pawnshop.

créditer /kʀedite/ [1] *vtr* to credit (**de** with).

créditeur, -trice /kʀeditœʀ, tʀis/ *adj* [*compte, solde*] credit (*épith*); [*client, pays*] in credit (*après n*); **être ~** to be in credit.

crédit-relais, *pl* **crédits-relais** /kʀediʀəlɛ/ *nm* bridging loan.

credo /kʀedo/ *nm* **1** (principes) creed; **2** RELIG **le Credo** the Creed.

crédule /kʀedyl/ *adj* gullible, credulous.

crédulité /kʀedylite/ *nf* gullibility, credulity.

créer /kʀee/ [11] **I** *vtr* **1** GÉN to design, to invent [*produit*]; to set up [*compagnie, comité*]; to create [*problème*]; **2** THÉÂT to create [*rôle*]; to put on [sth] (for the first time) [*pièce, spectacle*].

II se créer *vpr* **se ~ du travail** to create work for oneself; **se ~ des problèmes** to create problems for oneself.

crémaillère /kʀemajɛʀ/ *nf* (de cheminée) trammel, chimney hook.

IDIOMES **pendre la ~** to have a house-warming (party).

crémation /kʀemasjɔ̃/ *nf* cremation.

crématoire /kʀematwaʀ/ *nm* crematorium; **four ~** crematorium furnace.

crème¹ /kʀɛm/ **I** ▶ 141 *adj inv* cream.

II *nm* **1**° (café) espresso with milk; ▶ **petit**; **2** ▶ 141 (couleur) cream.

crème² /kʀɛm/ *nf* **1** (matière grasse) cream; **escalope à la ~** escalope with cream; **2** (entremets) cream dessert; (pour fourrer un gâteau) cream; **3** (soupe) **~ d'asperges** asparagus soup; **4** (liqueur) **~ de cassis/menthe** crème de cassis/menthe; **5** (pour la peau) cream; **6**° (élite) **la ~** (socialement) the cream of society; **la ~ des linguistes** the very best linguists; **c'est la ~ des hommes** he's the perfect man.

■ **~ anglaise** ~ custard; **~ Chantilly** whipped cream; **~ fleurette** ~ whipping cream; **~ fouettée = ~ Chantilly**; **~ fraîche** crème fraîche, ~ cream; **~ glacée** dairy ice cream; **~ de gruyère** ~ cheese spread; **~ de marrons** chestnut purée; **~ pâtissière** confectioner's custard; **~ renversée** caramel custard.

crémerie /kʀɛmʀi/ ▶ 374 *nf* cheese shop GB ou store US; **changer de ~**° HUM to take one's custom ou business elsewhere.

crémeux, -euse /kʀemø, øz/ *adj* LIT, FIG creamy.

crémier, -ière /kʀemje, ɛʀ/ ▶ 374 *nm,f* cheese seller.

crémone /kʀemɔn/ *nf* espagnolette (bolt).

créneau, *pl* **~x** /kʀeno/ *nm* **1** AUT parallel parking **℄**; **2** (moment) **tu as un ~ demain?** do you have any

free time tomorrow?; **3** COMM market; (sur un marché) gap, niche (**sur** in); **4** ARCHIT crenel; **les ~x** crenellations.

■ **~ horaire** time slot; **~ de lancement** ASTRONAUT launch window; **~ publicitaire** RADIO, TV advertising slot.

IDIOMES **monter au ~** to intervene.

créneler /kʀenle/ [19] *vtr* to crenellate [*tour*]; to mill [*pièce de monnaie*].

créole¹ /kʀeɔl/ **I** *adj* [*accent, cuisine*] creole.

II ▶ 338 *nm* LING Creole.

créole² /kʀeɔl/ *nf* **1** (boucle d'oreille) hoop earring; **2** CULIN **à la ~** creole.

crêpage /kʀɛ(e)paʒ/ *nm* **~ de chignon**° fight.

crêpe¹ /kʀɛp/ *nm* **1** (tissu) crepe; **2** (de deuil) (voile) black veil; **3** (latex) crepe (rubber).

crêpe² /kʀɛp/ *nf* pancake, crêpe; **~ dentelle** very thin pancake; **faire sauter une ~** to toss a pancake.

IDIOMES **s'aplatir comme une ~**° PEJ to grovel (**devant qn** to sb).

crêper /kʀepe/ [1] **I** *vtr* to backcomb GB, to tease.

II se crêper *vpr* **se ~ les cheveux** to backcomb GB ou tease one's hair.

IDIOMES **se ~ le chignon**° (physiquement) to scratch each other's eyes out.

crépi /kʀepi/ *nm* rendering.

crépitement /kʀepitmɑ̃/ *nm* (de feu, flamme) crackling **℄**; (d'huile) sizzling **℄**; (de fusillade) crackle **℄**; (d'appareils photo) clicking **℄**.

crépiter /kʀepite/ [1] *vi* [*feu, bois*] to crackle; [*huile*] to sizzle; [*pluie, grêle*] to patter.

crépon /kʀepɔ̃/ *nm* (tissu) plissé; (papier) crepe paper.

crépu, -e /kʀepy/ *adj* [*cheveux*] frizzy.

crépusculaire /kʀepyskylɛʀ/ *adj* LIT, FIG crepuscular.

crépuscule /kʀepyskyl/ *nm* LIT twilight, dusk; FIG twilight.

crescendo /kʀeʃɛndo/ **I** *adv* MUS [*jouer*] crescendo; **aller ~** [*bruit, protestations, douleur*] to intensify; [*colère*] to grow, to mount.

II *nm* MUS crescendo.

cresson /kʀesɔ̃, kʀasɔ̃/ *nm* watercress.

crête /kʀɛt/ *nf* **1** ZOOL (de volaille) comb; (de lézard, d'oiseau) crest; **2** (de montagne, vague) crest; (de mur, toit) ridge; **3** ÉLECTROTECH peak value.

Crète /kʀɛt/ ▶ 305 *nprf* Crete.

crétin, -e /kʀetɛ̃, in/ *nm,f* PEJ moron° PEJ.

crétinerie /kʀetinʀi/ *nf* **1**° (acte) idiotic prank; (parole) idiotic remark; **2** (état) imbecillity.

crétinisme /kʀetinism/ *nm* MÉD cretinism.

crétois, -e /kʀetwa, az/ **I** *adj* Cretan.

II *nm* Cretan.

creusement /kʀøzmɑ̃/ *nm* (de sol) digging.

creuser /kʀøze/ [1] **I** *vtr* **1** (ôter de la matière dans) [*personne*] to dig a hole in [*terre*]; to hollow out [*tronc, fruit*]; to drill a hole in [*dent*]; to dig into [*roche*]; [*mer, eau*] to eat into, to erode [*falaise*]; **2** (pratiquer) to dig [*trou, canal, tombe, terrier*]; to sink [*puits*]; to plough GB, to plow US [*sillon*] (**dans** in); [*rivière*] to hollow out [*lit*]; **3** (marquer) [*rides*] to furrow [*front, visage*]; **elle avait le visage creusé par la faim/le chagrin** her face was gaunt with hunger/grief; **4** (accentuer la cambrure de) **~ le dos** or **les reins** to arch one's back; **5** (accentuer) to deepen, to increase [*déficit, fossé*] ; **~ l'écart entre** to widen the gap between; **6** (approfondir) [*personne*] to go into [sth] in depth [*sujet, théorie*].

II *vi* **~ dans la roche** to dig into the rock.

III se creuser *vpr* [*joues, visage*] to become hollow; [*mer, vagues*] to be whipped up; [*rides*] to deepen; [*écart*] to widen.

IDIOMES **ça creuse**° it really gives you an appetite; **se ~ (la tête** ou **la cervelle)**° to rack one's brains.

creuset /kʀøzɛ/ *nm* **1** (récipient) crucible; **2** FIG (mélange de cultures, d'influences) melting pot.

creux, -euse /kʀø, øz/ **I** *adj* **1** (vide à l'intérieur) [*tronc, dent, tube*] hollow; [*son, voix*] hollow; [*estomac*] empty; **2** (concave) [*joues, visage*] hollow; **un plat ~** a shallow dish; **assiette creuse** soup dish ou plate; **3** (vide de sens) [*discours*] empty; [*débat, analyse*] shallow; **4** (à l'activité réduite) [*jour, période*] slack, off-peak; **la saison creuse** the off-season.

II *adv* **sonner ~** LIT to make a hollow sound; FIG to ring hollow.

III *nm inv* **1** (dépression) hollow; **le ~ d'un arbre** the hollow of a tree; **le ~ de l'épaule** the hollow of one's shoulder; **le ~ des reins** ou **du dos** the small of the back; **le ~ de l'aisselle** the armpit; **au ~ de l'estomac** in the pit of the stomach; **ça tient dans le ~ de la main** it fits into the palm of the hand; **l'oiseau a mangé dans le ~ de ma main** the bird ate from my hand; **le ~ de la vague** LIT the trough of the wave; **être au ~ de la vague** FIG to be at rock bottom; **au ~ de la vallée** in the bottom of the valley; **2**° (petite faim) **avoir un (petit) ~** to feel peckish° GB, to have the munchies°; **3** ART **en ~** [*fresque, motif*] incised; **gravure en ~** intaglio engraving; **4** (sur un graphique) trough; **la courbe fait un ~** there is a trough in the curve; **5** (ralentissement d'activité) slack period.

crevaison /kʀəvɛzɔ̃/ *nf* puncture.

crevant°, **~e** /kʀəvɑ̃, ɑ̃t/ *adj* killing°.

crevasse /kʀəvas/ *nf* **1** (de glacier) crevasse; **2** (dans la terre, sur un mur) crack, fissure; **3** (gerçure) (sur les lèvres, mains) chapped skin; (sur les mamelons) crack.

crevasser /kʀəvase/ [1] **I** *vtr* to cause [sth] to crack [*terre, mur*]; to chap [*peau*].

II se crevasser *vpr* [*terre, mur*] to crack; [*peau*] to chap.

crève° /kʀɛv/ *nf* chill; **attraper la ~** to catch a chill ou une sale death (of cold).

crevé, **~e** /kʀəve/ *adj* **1** (percé) [*ballon, pneu*] punctured; [*tympan*] burst; **2**° (épuisé) done in° GB, exhausted.

crève-cœur /kʀɛvkœʀ/ *nm inv* heartbreak.

crève-la-faim° /kʀɛvlafɛ̃/ *nmf inv* down-and-out.

crever /kʀəve/ [16] **I** *vtr* **1** (percer) to puncture, to burst [*pneu, ballon*]; to burst [*bulle, abcès, tympan*]; **~ les yeux de qn** (accidentellement) to blind sb; (volontairement) to put sb's eyes out; **ça te crève les yeux** FIG it's staring you in the face; **ça crève les yeux** FIG it's blindingly obvious; **ça crève le cœur** FIG it's heartbreaking; **2**° (épuiser) [*travail, chaleur*] to wear [sb] out; [*patron*] to work [sb] into the ground; **~ un cheval** (au galop) to ride a horse into the ground.

II *vi* **1** (se percer) [*pneu, nuage, abcès, tympan*] to burst; [*paquet*] to burst open; **2** [*automobiliste, cycliste*] to have a puncture; **3** (mourir) [*plante, animal*] to die; **un chat crevé** a dead cat; **~ de faim/froid** to be starving/freezing; **4** (éclater) PEJ **~ d'envie/de jalousie** to be eaten up ou consumed with envy/with jealousy; **d'orgueil** to be terribly full of oneself.

III se crever *vpr* **se ~ un tympan** to burst an eardrum; **il s'est crevé un œil** he put his eye out.

IDIOMES **marche ou crève** sink or swim.

crevette /kʀəvɛt/ *nf* **~ grise** shrimp; **~ rose** prawn.

cri /kʀi/ *nm* **1** (de personne) cry; (plus fort) shout; (aigu) scream; **un ~ de douleur/surprise** a cry of pain/surprise; **un ~ de détresse** a cry for help; **un ~ perçant** a piercing scream; **un ~ aigu** a shriek; **à grands ~s** loudly; **pousser un grand ~** to scream loudly; **pousser des ~s de douleur/plaisir** to cry out in pain/pleasure; **2** (d'animal) GÉN cry; (d'oiseau) call.

IDIOMES **pousser** ou **jeter les hauts ~s** to protest loudly.

criaillement /kʀi(j)ajmɑ̃/ *nm* **1** (cri désagréable) squeal; **2** ZOOL (d'oie) honk; (de paon) screech.

criailler /kʀi(j)aje/ [1] *vi* **1** (crier souvent) [*enfants*] to shriek; **2** (rouspéter) to grouse (**après** at); **3** ZOOL [*oie*] to honk; [*paon*] to screech.

criant, **~e** /kʀijɑ̃, ɑ̃t/ *adj* **1** (manifeste) striking; **~ de vérité** [*description, peinture*] true to life (*jamais épith*); **il est ~ de vérité dans le rôle** he's extremely convincing in the role; **2** (scandaleux) [*inégalité,*

malhonnêteté] blatant; [*injustice*] glaring; [*abus*] flagrant.

criard, **~e** /kʀijaʀ, aʀd/ *adj* [*voix*] shrill; [*couleur, affiche*] garish; **un enfant ~** a squawking child.

crible /kʀibl/ *nm* TECH (pour minerai) screen; (pour sable) riddle; **passer au ~** FIG to sift through.

criblé, **~e** /kʀible/ *adj* **~ de** (de balles, trous, fautes) riddled with; (de flèches) bristling with; (de taches) covered in; (de dettes) crippled with.

cribler /kʀible/ [1] *vtr* **1** **~ qn/qch de balles** to riddle sb/sth with bullets; **~ qn de flèches/coups** to rain arrows/blows on sb; **2** (accabler) **~ qn de reproches** to heap reproaches on sb.

cric /kʀik/ *nm* (de voiture) jack.

cricket /kʀikɛ(t)/ **▶ 329** *nm* SPORT cricket.

cricri /kʀikʀi/ *nm* (*also onomat*) **1** (cri du grillon) chirping; **2** (grillon) cricket.

criée /kʀije/ *nf* (vente à la) **~** auction; **vendre qch à la ~** to auction sth.

crier /kʀije/ [2] **I** *vtr* **1** (pour dire) to shout (**à qn** to sb); **~ des slogans** to shout ou chant slogans; **2** (pour proclamer) to proclaim [*indignation*]; to protest [*innocence*].

II crier à *vtr ind* **ils criaient à l'injustice** they protested that it was injustice; **on a crié au génie quand il a proposé sa théorie** he was proclaimed a genius when he put forward his theory; **on a crié au scandale quand…** there was an outcry when…

III *vi* **1** [*personne*] to shout; (en pleurant) to cry; (de peur) to scream; **~ de joie** to shout for joy; **~ de peur/ plaisir** to cry out in fear/delight; **~ après**° **qn** to shout at sb; **2** [*animal*] to give a cry; [*singe*] to chatter; [*mouette*] to cry; [*porc*] to squeal; **3** [*craie, chaussure*] to squeak; [*planche, marche, gond*] to creak; [*pneu, frein*] to squeal.

IDIOMES **~ comme un cochon qu'on égorge** ou **un damné** to squeal like a stuck pig.

crieur, -ieuse /kʀijœʀ, øz/ *nm,f* **les ~s de slogans** slogan chanters.

■ **~ de journaux** news vendor; **~ public** HIST town crier.

crime /kʀim/ *nm* **1** (acte criminel répréhensible) GÉN, JUR crime; **ce serait un ~ de faire** it would be a crime to do; **2** (meurtre) murder; **~ crapuleux** murder for money; **~ passionnel** crime of passion, crime passionnel; **3** (actions criminelles) crime; **le ~ ne paie pas** crime does not pay.

■ **~ contre l'humanité** crime against humanity; **~ d'État** crime against the State; **~ organisé** organized crime; **~ de sang** murder; **~s de guerre** war crimes.

Crimée /kʀime/ **▶ 509** *nprf* Crimea; **guerre/presqu'île de ~** Crimean war/peninsula.

criminaliste /kʀiminalist/ **▶ 374** *nmf* criminologist.

criminalité /kʀiminalite/ *nf* crime.

criminel, -elle /kʀiminɛl/ **I** *adj* criminal.

II *nm,f* (coupable d'actes criminels) criminal; (meurtrier) murderer.

■ **~ de guerre** war criminal.

criminologie /kʀiminɔlɔʒi/ *nf* criminology.

criminologue /kʀiminɔlɔg/ **▶ 374** *nmf* criminologist.

crin /kʀɛ̃/ *nm* (de cheval) horsehair; **à tout ~** FIG dyed-in-the-wool.

■ **~ végétal** leaf fibre.

crincrin° /kʀɛ̃kʀɛ̃/ *nm* PEJ scratchy (old) violin.

crinière /kʀinjɛʀ/ *nf* **1** (de lion, cheval) mane; **2**° (chevelure) mane; **3** (de casque) plume.

crinoline /kʀinɔlin/ *nf* crinoline.

crique /kʀik/ *nf* GÉOG cove.

criquet /kʀikɛ/ *nm* locust.

crise /kʀiz/ *nf* **1** (phase difficile) crisis; **en (pleine) ~** [*secteur, pays*] in (the middle of a) crisis; **la ~ économique** the economic crisis; **la ~ de 1929** the Great Depression; **2** (pénurie) shortage; **~ de main-d'œuvre** shortage of labour GB; **~ de l'emploi** job shortage; **3** MÉD attack; **~ d'asthme** asthma attack; **~ d'appendicite** appendicitis; **~ d'épilepsie** epileptic

fit; **~ de rhumatisme** bout of rheumatism; **~ de toux** coughing fit; **4** (accès) fit; **~ de larmes** crying fit; **elle a été prise d'une ~ de rangement** she had a sudden urge to tidy up; **avoir une ~ de fou rire** to get the giggles; **faire/piquer° une** or **sa ~** [*enfant*] to have/to throw a tantrum; [*adulte*] to have/to throw a fit°.
■ **~ cardiaque** heart attack; **~ de foie** indigestion; **~ de nerfs** hysterics (*pl*).

crispant°, **~e** /kʀispɑ̃, ɑ̃t/ *adj* irritating.

crispation /kʀispasjɔ̃/ *nf* **1** (de muscle, visage) tensing; (de mâchoires, main) clenching; **2** (tension nerveuse) state of tension; **3** FIG (durcissement) tension.

crispé, **~e** /kʀispe/ *adj* **1** (contracté) [*doigts, mâchoires*] clenched; [*muscles, visage*] tensed; **traits ~s par la douleur/colère** features tense with pain/anger; **2** (tendu) [*personne, sourire*] tense, nervous.

crisper /kʀispe/ [1] **I** *vtr* **1** (contracter) **la colère crispait son visage** his/her face was tense with anger; **2°** (irriter) **~ qn** to irritate sb, to get on sb's nerves°.
II se crisper *vpr* **1** (se contracter) [*mains, doigts*] to clench; [*visage, personne*] to tense (up); [*sourire*] to freeze; **ne te crispe pas sur le volant!** don't clutch the wheel so hard!; **2** FIG (devenir tendu) [*personne*] to get nervous, to tense up; **3** (se raidir) [*régime, gouvernement*] to take a hard line (**sur** on).

crissement /kʀismɑ̃/ *nm* (de chaussures, craie) squeak; (de neige) crunch; (de freins, pneus) screech; (de plume) scratching.

crisser /kʀise/ [1] *vi* [*chaussures, craie, ongles*] to squeak; [*neige*] to crunch; [*pneus, freins*] to screech; [*plume*] to scratch.

cristal, *pl* **-aux** /kʀistal, o/ *nm* **1** (matière) crystal; **eaux d'une limpidité de ~** crystal-clear waters; **voix de ~** crystal-clear voice; **2** (objet) piece of crystalware; **les cristaux** the crystal(ware) ¢; **les cristaux du lustre** the crystal pendants of the chandelier.
■ **cristaux (de soude)** (pour laver) washing soda ¢.

cristallin, **~e** /kʀistalɛ̃, in/ *adj* **1** (en géologie) [*roche*] crystalline; [*massif*] of crystalline rock; **2** CHIMIE, PHYS [*zone, structure*] crystal; **3** (limpide) [*eau*] crystal clear; **elle avait un rire ~** her laugh was as clear as a bell.
II *nm* ANAT (crystalline) lens.

cristalliser /kʀistalize/ [1] *vtr, vi*, **se cristalliser** *vpr* to crystallize.

critère /kʀitɛʀ/ *nm* **1** (pour juger, pour sélectionner) criterion; (pour évaluer) standard; (pour identifier) indication, sign; **les ~s du succès/de l'intelligence** the criteria for success/intelligence; **~s de gestion/de confort** standards of management/comfort; **le prix n'est pas un ~ de qualité** price is no indication of quality; **le ~ déterminant** the crucial factor; **2** (stipulation) specification; **~s d'âge et de diplôme** specifications of age and qualifications; **remplir les ~s d'âge et de diplôme** to meet the requirements as far as age and qualifications are concerned.

critérium /kʀiteʀjɔm/ *nm* SPORT (cycliste) rally.

critiquable /kʀitikabl/ *adj* **1** (qu'on peut critiquer) open to criticism (*après n*); **2** (contestable) questionable.

critique[1] /kʀitik/ **I** *adj* critical (**à l'égard de, envers** of).
II ▶ 374 *nmf* (commentateur) critic.

critique[2] /kʀitik/ *nf* **1** (reproche) criticism; **accabler qn de ~s** to heap criticism on sb; **faire une ~** or **des ~s à qn** to criticize sb; **2** (désapprobation) criticism (**à l'égard de, à l'adresse de** of); **la ~ est aisée** it's easy to criticize; **3** (art de juger) criticism; **la nouvelle ~** the new criticism; **4** (de livre, film) review (**de** of); **avoir une bonne/mauvaise ~** to get good/ bad reviews; **faire la ~ d'une pièce/d'un film** to review a play/a film; **5** (commentateurs) **la ~** the critics (*pl*).

critiquer /kʀitike/ [1] *vtr* **1** (condamner) to criticize; **il ne fait que ~** he finds fault with everything, he criticizes everything; **usage critiqué** LING controversial usage; **2** (analyser) to make a critical study ou appraisal of [*ouvrage*].

croassement /kʀɔasmɑ̃/ *nm* cawing ¢.

croasser /kʀɔase/ [1] *vi* to caw.

croate /kʀɔat/ **▶ 394**, **338** **I** *adj* Croatian.
II *nm* LING Croatian.

Croatie /kʀɔasi/ **▶ 232** *nprf* Croatia.

croc /kʀo/ *nm* **1** (d'animal) fang; **montrer les ~s** FIG to bare one's teeth; **2** (crochet) butcher's hook.

croc-en-jambe, *pl* **crocs-en-jambe** /kʀɔkɑ̃ʒɑ̃b/ *nm* **faire un ~ à qn** LIT to trip sb up; FIG to set sb up.

croche /kʀɔʃ/ *nf* quaver GB, eighth note US; **double ~** semiquaver GB, sixteenth note US; **triple ~** demisemiquaver GB, thirty-second note US; **quadruple ~** hemidemisemiquaver GB, sixty-fourth note US.

croche-pied°, *pl* **~s** /kʀɔʃpje/ *nm* **faire un ~ à qn** to trip sb up.

crochet /kʀɔʃɛ/ *nm* **1** TECH hook; (d'appareil dentaire) clasp; **2** (de serrurier) picklock; **3** (en couture) (instrument) crochet hook; (technique) crochet; **faire qch au ~** to crochet sth; **4** (parenthèse) **mettre entre ~s** to put [sth] in square brackets; **5** (détour) LIT, FIG detour; **faire un ~** to make a detour (**par** via); **6** (écart) swerve; **faire un ~** to swerve; **7** SPORT (en boxe) hook; **8** RADIO (pour chanteur) talent contest; **9** (de serpent) fang.
IDIOMES **vivre aux ~s** ° **de qn** to sponge off° sb.

crocheter /kʀɔʃte/ [18] *vtr* **1** to crochet [*gilet*]; **2** to pick [*serrure*]; **3** SPORT to side-step.

crochu, **~e** /kʀɔʃy/ *adj* [*bec*] hooked; [*doigt*] clawed.
IDIOMES **avoir les doigts ~s** to be tight-fisted.

crocodile /kʀɔkɔdil/ *nm* (animal, peau) crocodile.

crocus /kʀɔkys/ *nm inv* crocus; **des ~** crocuses.

croire /kʀwaʀ/ [71] **I** *vtr* **1** (trouver crédible) to believe [*histoire, personne*]; **faire ~ à qn** to make sb believe; **tu me croiras si tu veux** believe it or not; **2** (penser) to think; **j'ai cru mourir** I thought I was dying; **je crois rêver!** I must be dreaming!; **je crois n'avoir rien oublié** I don't think I've forgotten anything; **je crois bien que non** I don't think so; **je crois savoir que** I happen to know that; **il faut ~ qu'il avait vraiment besoin de repos** it would seem that he really needed a rest; **il est malin, (il ne) faut pas° ~!** he's clever, believe me!; **c'est à ~ qu'elle le fait exprès** anyone would think she was doing it on purpose; **je ne suis pas celui que vous croyez** I'm not what you think I am; **tu ne crois pas si bien dire** you don't know how right you are; **on croirait de la soie/un diamant** it looks like silk/a diamond; **3** (se fier à) **en ~** to believe; **si l'on en croit l'auteur, à en ~ l'auteur** if we are to believe the author; **à en ~ les sondages, elle va remporter les élections** if the polls are anything to go by, she will win the election; **crois-en mon expérience** take my word for it.
II croire à *vtr ind* **~ à** to believe [*histoire*]; to believe in [*fantômes, justice, progrès*]; **~ à la médecine** to have faith in doctors; **nous avons cru à la victoire** we thought we'd win; **'veuillez ~ à ma sympathie'** 'with deepest sympathy'; **faire ~ à un accident** to make people believe ou think it was an accident.
III croire en *vtr ind* **~ en Dieu** to believe in God.
IV *vi* RELIG to believe.
V se croire *vpr* **il se croit beau** he thinks he's handsome; **il se croit quelqu'un** he thinks he's really somebody; **on se croirait à New York** you'd think you were in New York.

croisade /kʀwazad/ *nf* LIT, FIG crusade.

croisé, **~e**[1] /kʀwaze/ **I** *adj* **1** (se chevauchant) [*bâtons, fils, jambes*] crossed; [*bras, mains*] folded; **conversations ~es** TÉLÉCOM crossed lines; **2** (métissé) [*sang*] mixed; [*chien*] crossbred; **race ~e** crossbreed; **pollinisation ~e** cross-pollination; **3** (style vestimentaire) [*costume, veste*] double-breasted; [*dos, corsage*] crossover (*épith*); **4** (réciproque) [*accords, alliances*] reciprocal; [*taux*] cross (*épith*); **5** LITTÉRAT [*rimes, vers*] alternate; **6** SPORT **volée ~e** cross-court volley; **passe ~e** reverse pass.
II *nm* **1** HIST crusader; **2** (tissu) twill.

croisée[2] /kʀwaze/ *nf* **1** (intersection) junction (**de** of); **à**

la ~ **des chemins** LIT, FIG at the crossroads; **2** (fenêtre) LITER window.

croisement /kʀwazmã/ *nm* **1** (de routes) (carrefour) crossroads (+ *v sg*); (point d'intersection) crossing, junction; **au ~ de la route et de la voie ferrée** where the road crosses the railway line; **2** (de fils, lanières) crossing; **3** (de véhicules) **le ~ de deux trains** two trains passing one another; **4** (d'espèces) (méthode) crossing ¢ (**avec** with), crossbreeding ¢ (**avec** with); (spécimen obtenu) hybrid, cross(breed); **faire des ~s** (**d'espèces**) to crossbreed species; **faire un ~ entre A et B** to cross A with B.

croiser /kʀwaze/ [1] **I** *vtr* **1** (mettre l'un sur l'autre) to cross [*objets, jambes*]; ~ **les bras/mains** to fold one's arms/hands; ~ **les doigts** FIG to keep one's fingers crossed; **2** (couper) [*rue, voie*] to cross [*rue, voie*]; **3** (passer à côté de) [*véhicule, piéton*] ~ **qn/qch** to pass sb/sth (coming the other way); (rencontrer) to meet; **mon regard croisa le sien** our eyes met, my gaze met his/ hers; **4** BIOL to cross(breed) [*espèces, animaux*].

II *vi* **1** [*bretelles*] to cross; [*veste*] to cross over; **2** [*navire*] to cruise; (pour surveiller) to be on patrol.

III se croiser *vpr* [*piétons, véhicules*] to pass each other; [*lettres*] to cross (in the post GB ou mail US); [*routes*] to cross; **nos regards se sont croisés** our eyes met.

croiseur /kʀwazœʀ/ *nm* cruiser (warship).

croisière /kʀwazjɛʀ/ *nf* cruise; **faire une** or **partir en** ~ to go on a cruise; **régime de** ~ LIT cruising speed; **en régime de ~, nous produirons 10 tonnes par mois** FIG once we're up and running⁰ we'll produce 10 tons a month.

croisillon /kʀwazijɔ̃/ *nm* (de croix) crosspiece; **~s** (de fenêtre) lattice work; (sur une tarte) lattice pattern.

croissance /kʀwasɑ̃s/ *nf* growth; ~ **de 7%** 7% growth; **en pleine ~** [*enfant*] (secteur) [*secteur*] fast-growing (*épith*), growing fast (*jamais épith*).

croissant, **~e** /kʀwasɑ̃, ɑ̃t/ **I** *adj* **1** (en expansion) growing; **de manière ~e** increasingly; **2** MATH [*fonction, suite*] monotonic.

II *nm* **1** CULIN croissant; **2** (forme) crescent; **en forme de ~** crescent-shaped.

■ ~ **de lune** crescent moon.

croître /kʀwatʀ/ [72] *vi* **1** (se développer) [*animal, personne, plante*] to grow; **faire ~** to grow; **2** (en nombre, en importance) [*colère, abstentionnisme*] to grow; [*bruit*] to get ou grow louder; **aller ~** to increase; **3** (augmenter) [*production, vente*] to grow (**de** by); [*jour*] to get longer; ~ **de 3%** to grow by 3%; **4** MATH to increase; **faire ~** to increase.

croix /kʀwa/ *nf inv* cross; **disposé en ~** arranged crosswise; **bras en ~** arms out on either side of the body; **être mis en ~** [*condamné*] to be crucified; **chacun porte sa ~** FIG we all have our cross to bear.

■ ~ **gammée** swastika.

IDIOMES **ton argent, tu peux faire une ~ dessus**⁰ you can kiss your money goodbye; **faire une ~ sur son passé** to leave the past behind; **un jour à marquer d'une ~ blanche** a red-letter day, a day to remember; ~ **de bois, ~ de fer (si je mens, je vais en enfer)** cross my heart (and hope to die).

Croix-du-Sud /kʀwadysyd/ *nprf* **la ~** the Southern Cross.

Croix-Rouge /kʀwaʀuʒ/ *nf* **la ~** the Red Cross.

croquant, **~e** /kʀɔkɑ̃, ɑ̃t/ *adj* crunchy.

croque: à la croque au sel /alakʀɔkosɛl/ *loc adv* with just a sprinkling of salt.

croque-madame /kʀɔkmadam/ *nm inv*: toasted ham and cheese sandwich topped with a fried egg.

croquemitaine /kʀɔkmitɛn/ *nm* bogeyman; HUM ogre.

croque-monsieur /kʀɔkməsjø/ *nm inv*: toasted ham and cheese sandwich.

croque-mort⁰, *pl* **~s** /kʀɔkmɔʀ/ *nm* undertaker.

croquer /kʀɔke/ [1] **I** *vtr* **1** (manger) to crunch [*biscuit, pomme*]; **2**⁰ (dilapider) to squander [*fortune, argent*]; **3** (esquisser) to sketch [*personne*]; FIG (décrire) to give

a thumbnail sketch of [*personne*]; **elle est** (**jolie** ou **belle**) **à ~** she's as pretty as a picture.

II *vi* **1** [*pomme, biscuit*] to be crunchy; **2** [*personne*] ~ **dans une pomme** to bite into an apple.

croquet /kʀɔkɛ/ *nm* **1** ▶329] JEUX croquet; **2** (galon) rickrack braid GB, rickrack US; **3** (gâteau) almond biscuit GB ou cookie US.

croquis /kʀɔki/ *nm inv* **1** (dessin) sketch; **faire le ~ d'une maison** to draw a sketch of a house; **2** (description) outline; **faire un ~ de la situation** to give an outline of the situation.

cross(-country) /kʀɔs(kuntʀi)/ *nm inv* (course) (à pied, à cheval) cross country race; (à moto) motocross event.

crosse /kʀɔs/ *nf* **1** (de fusil) butt; (de revolver) grip; **à coups de ~** (de fusil) with the butt of a rifle; **2** (d'évêque) crozier; **3** SPORT stick; ~ **de hockey** hockey stick; **4** (extrémité recourbée) (de fougère) crozier; (de canne) crook; (de violon) head; (d'aorte) arch.

crotale /kʀɔtal/ *nm* rattlesnake.

crotte /kʀɔt/ *nf* **1** (de souris, lapin, chèvre) dropping; **ce sont des ~s** or **c'est de la ~ de souris** they're mouse droppings; **c'est de la ~ de chien/chat** it's dog/cat mess ¢ ou muck ¢; **2**† (boue) mud.

■ ~ **en chocolat** CULIN chocolate drop.

crotter /kʀɔte/ [1] *vtr* to muddy; **bottes crottées** muddy boots.

crottin /kʀɔtɛ̃/ *nm* **1** (de cheval) dung; **2** (fromage) (*small round*) goat's cheese.

croulant, **~e** /kʀulɑ̃, ɑ̃t/ *adj* [*bâtiment*] crumbling.

crouler /kʀule/ [1] *vi* **1** (s'effondrer) to collapse; (se désagréger) to crumble; **2** (être submergé) ~ **sous** [*personne*] to be weighed down by; ~ **sous les applaudissements** to resound with applause; ~ **sous le poids de** to groan under the weight of.

croupe /kʀup/ *nf* **1** (de cheval) croup; **monter en ~** to ride pillion; **2**⁰ (postérieur) behind⁰; **3** (de colline, montagne) (rounded) top.

croupetons: à croupetons /akʀuptɔ̃/ *loc adv* **être à ~** to be squatting; **se mettre à ~** to squat down.

croupi, **~e** /kʀupi/ *adj* [*eau*] stagnant.

croupier /kʀupje/ ▶374] *nm* croupier.

croupion /kʀupjɔ̃/ *nm* **1** (d'oiseau) rump; FIG **parti/parlement ~** rump party/parliament; **2** CULIN (de volaille) parson's nose.

croupir /kʀupiʀ/ [3] *vi* **1** [*eau*] to stagnate; [*détritus*] to rot; **2** [*personne*] ~ **en prison** to rot in jail; ~ **dans la misère** to languish in poverty.

croupissant, **~e** /kʀupisɑ̃, ɑ̃t/ *adj* [*eau*] stagnant.

croustillant, **~e** /kʀustijɑ̃, ɑ̃t/ *adj* **1** [*pain, peau grillée*] crispy; [*biscuit, toast*] crunchy; **2** [*histoire, détails*] spicy.

croustiller /kʀustije/ [1] *vi* [*pain*] to be crusty; [*viande grillée, chips*] to be crisp; [*chocolat*] to be crunchy.

croûte /kʀut/ *nf* **1** (surface épaisse) (de pain) crust; (de fromage) rind; **une ~ de pain** a crust; **2** (couche) (de peinture) (sur un mur) old layers (*pl*); (dans un pot) skin; (de glace) crust; **3** CULIN **pâté en ~** pâté en croute ou in pastry; **4** MÉD scab; **5**⁰ (tableau) daub.

■ **la ~ terrestre** the earth's crust.

IDIOMES **casser la ~**⁰ to have a bite to eat; **gagner sa ~**⁰ to earn a crust⁰.

croûton /kʀutɔ̃/ *nm* **1** (d'un pain) crust; **2** CULIN crouton.

croyable /kʀwajabl/ *adj* **pas ~** unbelievable.

croyance /kʀwajɑ̃s/ *nf* belief (**en** in).

croyant, **~e** /kʀwajɑ̃, ɑ̃t/ *adj* **être ~** to be a believer.

CRS /seɛʀɛs/ (*abbr* = **compagnie républicaine de sécurité**) *nm* **un ~** *a member of the French riot police*; **compagnie de ~** ≈ riot squad.

cru, **~e**¹ /kʀy/ **I** *adj* **1** CULIN GÉN raw; [*pâte à tarte*] uncooked; [*lait*] unpasteurized; **se faire manger** or **dévorer tout ~**⁰ FIG to be eaten alive⁰; **2** (intense) [*lumière, couleur*] harsh; **3** (direct) [*description, réalisme,*

réponse, termes] blunt; [*détail*] raw; [*représentation*] graphic; [*vérité*] harsh; **4** (osé) [*langage*] crude.
II *adv* **1** (sans ménagement) [*parler*] bluntly; **2** (en équitation) **monter à ~** to ride bareback.
III *nm* (vignoble) vineyard; (vin) vintage; (année) vintage year; **de grand** or **du meilleur ~** FIG [*disque, collection*] vintage (*épith*); **du ~** local; **de son (propre) ~** [*recette*] of one's own invention; [*expression*] of one's coinage.
cruauté /kʀyote/ *nf* **1** (caractère) cruelty (**envers** to); **2** (action cruelle) act of cruelty.
cruche /kʀyʃ/ *nf* **1** (contenant) jug GB, pitcher US; (contenu) jugful GB, pitcherful US; **2**○ (niais) dope○, twit○ GB.
IDIOMES **tant va la ~ à l'eau qu'à la fin elle se casse** PROV that's what comes of taking things for granted.
cruchon /kʀyʃɔ̃/ *nm* small jug GB, small pitcher US.
crucial, ~e, *mpl* **-iaux** /kʀysjal, o/ *adj* crucial.
crucifier /kʀysifje/ [2] *vtr* LIT, FIG to crucify.
crucifix /kʀysifi/ *nm* crucifix.
crucifixion /kʀysifiksjɔ̃/ *nf* crucifixion.
cruciforme /kʀysifɔʀm/ *adj* GÉN cruciform; [*vis, tournevis*] cross-head.
cruciverbiste /kʀysivɛʀbist/ *nmf* crossword fan.
crudité /kʀydite/ *nf* **1** CULIN **~s** raw vegetables, crudités; **2** (d'aliments) rawness; **3** (de couleur) garishness; (de lumière) harshness; **4** (de langage) crudeness.
crue² /kʀy/ **I** *adj f* ▶ **cru I**.
II *nf* (montée des eaux) rise in water level; (inondation) flood; **emporté par les ~s** swept away by the flood waters; **en ~** in spate.
cruel, -elle /kʀyɛl/ *adj* cruel (**envers, avec** to).
cruellement /kʀyɛlmɑ̃/ *adv* **1** (avec cruauté) cruelly; **2** (beaucoup) desperately; **manquer ~ de qch** to be desperately short of sth; **3** (douloureusement) [*ressentir*] terribly; **la pénurie de carburant se fait ~ sentir** the fuel shortage is being sorely felt; **être ~ ramené à la réalité** to be brought back to reality painfully.
crûment /kʀymɑ̃/ *adv* **1** (sans ménagement) bluntly; **2** (de façon choquante) crudely.
crustacé /kʀystase/ *nm* shellfish (*inv*).
crypte /kʀipt/ *nf* crypt.
crypté, ~e /kʀipte/ *adj* coded; ORDINAT encrypted; TV scrambled.
CSA /seɛsa/ *nm: abbr* ▶ **conseil**.
Cuba /kyba/ ▶ **305**|, **232**| *nprf* Cuba.
cubage /kybaʒ/ *nm* (d'eau, d'air) volume.
cubain, ~e /kybɛ̃, ɛn/ ▶ **394**| *adj* Cuban.
cube /kyb/ **I** ▶ **635**| *adj* cubic.
II *nm* GÉN, MATH cube; (jouet) building block; **le ~ de 3 est 27** 3 cubed is 27; **mettre au ~** to cube.
cubique /kybik/ *adj* **1** MATH [*racine*] cubic; **2 de forme ~** cube-shaped.
cubisme /kybism/ *nm* Cubism.
cubitus /kybitys/ *nm inv* ANAT ulna.
cucul○ /kyky/ **I** *adj* PÉJ [*histoire, film*] corny○; [*personne*] silly.
II *nmf* (personne) PÉJ twit○ GB, jerk○ US.
■ ~ la praline corny○.
cueillette /kœjɛt/ *nf* **1** (ramassage) (de fruits, fleurs) picking; FIG (d'idées, de chiffres) gathering together; **~ du coton** cotton-picking; **ils vivent de chasse et de ~** they are hunter-gatherers; **2** (produit) crop.
cueillir /kœjiʀ/ [27] *vtr* **1** (ramasser) to pick [*fruits, fleurs*]; **2** FIG to gather [*informations*]; **3**○ (prendre) to pick up○, to arrest [*malfaiteur*]; to pick up○ [*ami*]; **4** (atteindre) [*projectile*] to catch.
cui-cui /kɥikɥi/ *nm inv* (*also onomat*) twitter; **faire ~** to go tweet! tweet!
cuiller, cuillère /kɥijɛʀ/ *nf* **1** (pour manger) spoon; (contenu) spoonful; **petite ~ ≈** teaspoon; **2** MUS spoon; **jouer des ~s** to play the spoons; **3** (pour pêcher) spoon; **pêche à la ~** spoonbait fishing.
■ ~ à café ≈ teaspoon; (très petite) coffee spoon; **~ à dessert** dessertspoon; **~ à soupe** soupspoon; **~** (pour mesurer) **≈** tablespoon.

IDIOMES **il n'y va pas avec le dos de la ~**○ (en parlant) he doesn't pull his punches; (en agissant) he doesn't do things by halves; **on l'a ramassée à la petite ~** they had to scrape her up off the road; **faire qch en deux** or **trois coups de ~ à pot** to do sth in two shakes of a lamb's tail○.
cuillerée /kɥij(ə)ʀe/ *nf* spoonful.
cuir /kɥiʀ/ *nm* **1** (peau traitée) leather; **c'est du ~** it's leather; **sac en** or **de ~** leather bag; **le travail du ~** leatherwork; **2** (peau non traitée) rawhide; (peau de gros mammifère) hide; **~ de vache** cowhide; **3**○ (peau humaine) HUM hide; **avoir le ~ épais** to be thick-skinned.
■ ~ chevelu scalp; **~ naturel** natural leather.
cuirasse /kɥiʀas/ *nf* (armure) breast-plate; (blindage) armour^{GB} plating; FIG (d'indifférence) front.
cuirassé, ~e /kɥiʀase/ **I** *adj* [*véhicule, division*] armoured^{GB}.
II *nm* battleship.
cuirassier /kɥiʀasje/ *nm* (soldat) cuirassier; (régiment) **le premier ~** the first armoured^{GB} division.
cuire /kɥiʀ/ [69] **I** *vtr* **1** CULIN [*personne*] (sur le feu) to cook; (au four) to bake; to roast [*viande*]; to cook [*daube*]; **~ à la vapeur** to steam; **~ à la poêle** to fry; **~ au gril** to grill; **~ qch à feu doux** to cook sth gently; **2** to fire [*porcelaine, émaux*]; **3** (chauffer) [*soleil*] to bake [*terre*]; to burn [*peau*]; **le soleil me cuit le dos** the sun is burning my back.
II *vi* **1** [*aliment, repas*] to cook; **mets les légumes à ~** put the vegetables on (to cook); **faire** or **laisser ~ qch 20 minutes** to cook sth for 20 minutes; **laissez ~ à petit feu** allow to simmer gently; **tu l'as trop peu/trop fait ~** it's undercooked/overcooked; **à ~** [*chocolat, pomme*] cooking; [*fruit*] stewing; **2**○ (avoir chaud) [*personne*] **on cuit sur la plage** it's baking (hot) on the beach; **j'ai cuit au soleil toute la matinée** I spent the morning roasting in the sun; **3** (faire mal) **ça me cuit** it stings; **les joues me cuisaient** (de honte, après un coup de soleil) my cheeks were burning; (après des gifles) my cheeks were stinging ou smarting.
cuisant, ~e /kɥizɑ̃, ɑ̃t/ *adj* **1** (humiliant) [*défaite*] bitter; [*remarque*] stinging; **2** (douloureux) [*douleur*] (qui brûle) burning; (qui pique) stinging; [*froid*] biting.
cuisine /kɥizin/ **I** *nf* **1** (pièce) kitchen; NAUT galley; **2** (mobilier) kitchen furniture ¢; **3** (préparation des aliments) (art) cookery; (activité) cooking; **apprendre la ~** SCOL to do cookery; **il sait faire la ~** he can cook; **faire la ~** to do the cooking; **4** (méthode) cooking; (aliments) food; **tu n'aimes pas ma ~?** don't you like my cooking?; **~ au beurre** (méthode) cooking in butter; (aliments) food cooked in butter; **la ~ française** (méthode, art) French cooking; (aliments) French food; **5** (personnel) **la ~** the kitchen staff; **6**○ (magouillage) intrigues (*pl*); **~ électorale** dubious electioneering tactics; **faire sa petite ~** to be on the fiddle○ GB ou on the take○.
II cuisines *nfpl* (de restaurant, d'hôpital, d'école) kitchens.
■ ~ familiale home cooking; **~ intégrée** fully fitted kitchen; ▶ **grand**.
cuisiner /kɥizine/ [1] **I** *vtr* **1** CULIN to cook; **2**○ (interroger) to grill○.
II *vi* to cook; **bien ~** to be a good cook.
cuisinette /kɥizinɛt/ *nf* kitchenette.
cuisinier, -ière¹ /kɥizinje, ɛʀ/ ▶ **374**| *nm,f* (chez des particuliers) cook; (dans un restaurant) chef.
cuisinière² /kɥizinjɛʀ/ *nf* (à gaz, électrique) cooker.
cuissarde /kɥisaʀd/ *nf* (de caoutchouc) wader; (de cuir, daim) thighboot.
cuisse /kɥis/ ▶ **137**| *nf* **1** ANAT thigh; **2** CULIN (de poulet) thigh; (de chevreuil) haunch; **des ~s de grenouille** frogs' legs.
cuisseau, *pl* **~x** /kɥiso/ *nm* **~ de veau** haunch of veal.
cuissettes /kɥisɛt/ *nfpl* H (short) sports shorts.
cuisson /kɥisɔ̃/ *nf* **1** CULIN GÉN cooking; (au four) (de pain, gâteau, poisson) baking; (de rôti, poulet) roasting; **temps**

de ~ cooking time; **la** ~ **de la viande est très longue** meat takes a long time to cook; **2** (de poterie, d'émaux) firing; **mettre qch à la** ~ to fire sth.

cuissot /kɥiso/ *nm* (de chevreuil) haunch.

cuistot○ /kɥisto/ *nm* cook.

cuit, ~e¹ /kɥi, kɥit/ **I** *pp* ▶ **cuire**.

II *pp adj* **1** [*aliment*] cooked; [*viande, poisson, gâteau*] done (*jamais épith*); [*abricot*] stewed; **trop** ~ [*gigot, steak*] overdone; **bien** ~ well done; **pas assez** ~ underdone; **2** [*poterie, argile*] fired; **3**○ (par le soleil) [*gazon, plante*] scorched; [*peau*] burned.

IDIOMES **c'est** ~○ we've had it○; **sinon, on était** ~**s**○ otherwise, we were done for○; **c'est du tout** ~○ (facile) it's a piece of cake○; (assuré) it's in the bag○; **ce n'est pas du tout** ~○ it's not all cut and dried; **elle attend que ça (lui) tombe tout** ~○ she expects things to fall straight into her lap.

cuite² /kɥit/ *nf* **1**○ (ivresse) **quelle** ~! what a booze-up○ GB ou bender○!; **tenir/prendre une** ~ to be/to get plastered○; **2** TECH (cuisson) firing.

cuiter○: **se cuiter** /kɥite/ [1] *vpr* to get plastered○.

cuivre /kɥivʀ/ **I** *nm* (métal) ~ **(rouge)** copper; ~ **(jaune)** brass.

II cuivres *nmpl* **1** (objets) (en cuivre rouge) copperware; (en cuivre jaune) brass; **2** MUS **les** ~**s** the brass (*sg*); **ensemble de** ~**s** brass ensemble.

cuivré, ~e /kɥivʀe/ ▶141 *adj* [*peau*] copper-coloured^GB; (par le soleil) bronzed; **aux reflets** ~**s** with coppery glints.

cul /ky/ **I**◐ *adj inv* [*personne*] simple; [*film*] twee○.

II *nm* **1**◐ (postérieur) bottom, arse● GB, ass● US; ~ **nu** (à moitié nu) bare-bottomed; (entièrement nu) stark naked; **2**◐ (sexe) sex; **histoire de** ~ (blague) dirty joke; (texte) dirty story; (liaison) affair; **3** ZOOL rump; **4**○ (arrière) (de voiture, camion) back end; **5** (base) (de lampe, bouteille) bottom; ~ **de bouteille** bottom of a bottle; ~ **sec**○! bottoms up!○; **faire** ~ **sec**○ to down it in one.

IDIOMES **avoir qn au** ~○◐ to have sb on one's tail; **se bouger le** ~○◐ (se dépêcher) to get moving○; **en rester** or **tomber sur le** ~○◐ to be gobsmacked○.

culasse /kylas/ *nf* (de moteur) cylinder head; (d'arme) breechblock.

culbute /kylbyt/ *nf* **1** (galipette) somersault; **faire une** ~ to somersault; **2** (chute) tumble; **faire une** ~ **dans l'escalier** to tumble down the stairs.

culbuter /kylbyte/ [1] **I** *vtr* (faire tomber) to knock [sb/sth] over.

II *vi* (se renverser) [*personne*] to take a tumble; [*véhicule*] to overturn; **la voiture a culbuté dans le ravin** the car fell into the ravine.

cul-cul○ = **cucul**.

cul-de-jatte, *pl* **culs-de-jatte** /kydʒat/ *nmf* person who has had both legs amputated.

cul-de-poule, *pl* **culs-de-poule** /kydpul/ *nm* (récipient) mixing bowl; **avoir la bouche en** ~ to have a small pursed mouth.

cul-de-sac, *pl* **culs-de-sac** /kydsak/ *nm* (rue) cul-de-sac; (situation) dead end; (emploi sans avenir) dead-end job.

culinaire /kylinɛʀ/ *adj* culinary; **préparation** ~ dish.

culminant, ~e /kylminɑ̃, ɑ̃t/ *adj* **point** ~ (de montagne) highest point ou peak; (de carrière) peak; (de gloire) height; (de réunion, vacances, soirée) high point.

culminer /kylmine/ [1] *vi* **1** [*sommet, massif*] ~ **au-dessus de qch** to tower above sth; **2** FIG [*inflation, chômage*] to reach its peak; [*crise, carrière*] to reach its height; [*soirée*] to reach its climax; **l'inflation a culminé à 5% en mai** inflation peaked at 5% in May.

culot /kylo/ *nm* **1**○ (aplomb) cheek○; **avoir un sacré** ~ or **un** ~ **monstre** to have a hell○ of a nerve; **y aller au** ~ to bluff; **2** TECH (de bougie) AUT shell; (de douille, cartouche, d'ampoule) base.

culotte /kylɔt/ *nf* **1** (sous-vêtement féminin) pants (*pl*) GB, drawers (*pl*), panties (*pl*) US; **une** ~ (pour femme) a pair of pants GB ou panties US ou drawers; **où est la** ~ **de mon maillot de bain?** where are my bikini

bottoms?; **faire dans sa** ~○ (déféquer) to dirty one's pants; (uriner) to wet one's pants; FIG to wet oneself; **2** (pantalon mi-long) breeches (*pl*); (pantalon) trousers (*pl*), pants (*pl*) US; **en** ~**(s) courte(s)** in short trousers GB ou pants US.

■ ~ **bouffante** bloomers (*pl*); ~ **de cheval** (pantalon) riding breeches (*pl*); (cellulite) flabby thighs (*pl*); ~ **de golf** plus-fours (*pl*).

IDIOMES **c'est elle qui porte la** ~○ she's the one who wears the trousers GB ou pants US; **baisser** ~○ FIG to back down.

culotté○, ~**e** /kylɔte/ *adj* [*personne*] cheeky.

culpabilisation /kylpabilizasjɔ̃/ *nf* (action) making guilty; (résultat) feeling of guilt.

culpabiliser /kylpabilize/ [1] **I** *vtr* to make [sb] feel guilty.

II *vi* to feel guilty.

culpabilité /kylpabilite/ *nf* guilt.

culte /kylt/ **I** *nm* **1** RELIG GÉN cult; (adoration) worship; **rendre un** ~ **à** to worship; **2** (ensemble de pratiques) religion; **3** (adoration profane) cult, worship; **avoir le** ~ **de qch** to worship sth.

II (-)**culte** (*in compounds*) film-~ cult film.

cultivateur, -trice /kyltivatœʀ, tʀis/ **I** ▶374 *nm,f* farmer.

II *nm* (machine) cultivator.

cultivé, ~e /kyltive/ *adj* AGRIC cultivated; (raffiné) cultured, cultivated.

cultiver /kyltive/ [1] **I** *vtr* **1** AGRIC to grow [*plante*]; to cultivate [*champ*]; **2** (entretenir) to cultivate.

II se cultiver *vpr* **1** (devoir être entretenu) [*amitié, don*] to need to be cultivated; **2** (s'instruire) [*personne*] to improve one's mind; **3** [*plante*] to be grown; [*terre*] to be cultivated.

culture /kyltyʀ/ **I** *nf* **1** (action de cultiver) cultivation; **la** ~ **du blé** wheat growing; **2** (espèce cultivée) crop; ~ **d'hiver** winter crop; **3** BIOL culture; ~ **in vitro** in vitro culture; **4** (d'une civilisation) culture; ~ **de masse** mass culture; **5** (connaissances) knowledge; ~ **classique** classical education; **homme de (grande)** ~ man of (great) learning; **avoir de la** ~ to be cultured; **ne pas avoir de** ~ to be uncultured; **6** (arts) arts (*pl*); **subventionner la** ~ to subsidize the arts.

II cultures *nfpl* (terres cultivées) cultivated land ₵.

■ ~ **extensive** extensive farming; ~ **intensive** intensive farming; ~ **physique** SCOL physical education; SPORT physical exercise.

culturel, -elle /kyltyʀɛl/ *adj* cultural.

culturisme /kyltyʀism/ ▶329 *nm* body-building.

culturiste /kyltyʀist/ *nmf* body-builder.

cumin /kymɛ̃/ *nm* cumin.

cumul /kymyl/ *nm* **1** (accumulation) ~ **d'avantages** accumulation of advantages; ~ **de fonctions** holding of several posts concurrently; ~ **de salaires** drawing several salaries concurrently; **2** JUR ~ **des peines** ~ consecutive sentence.

cumulable /kymylabl/ *adj* [*fonctions, mandats*] which can be held concurrently (*après n*); [*traitement, allocations*] which can be drawn concurrently (*après n*).

cumulatif, -ive /kymylatif, iv/ *adj* cumulative.

cumuler /kymyle/ [1] **I** *vtr* **1** (avoir en même temps) to hold [sth] concurrently [*fonctions*]; to draw [sth] concurrently [*salaires*]; ~ **deux pensions** to draw two separate pensions; **il cumule les fonctions de gestionnaire avec celles de concepteur** he combines the post of manager with that of designer; **2** (accumuler) to accumulate [*handicaps, diplômes*]; **3** (réunir) to combine [*résultats*]; (ajouter) to add up [*sommes*]; **inté-rêts cumulés** accrued interest; ~ **qch avec qch** (réunir) to combine sth with sth; (ajouter) to add sth to sth.

II se cumuler *vpr* ces réductions ne peuvent pas se ~ you may claim only one of these discounts.

cumulus /kymylys/ *nm inv* cumulus.

cunéiforme /kyneifɔʀm/ *adj, nm* cuneiform.

cupide /kypid/ *adj* [*personne, esprit*] grasping.

cupidité /kypidite/ *nf* cupidity.

Cupidon /kypidɔ̃/ *npr* Cupid.

curable /kyrabl/ *adj* [*maladie*] curable.

curage /kyraʒ/ *nm* (de puits) cleaning out; (de rivière, d'étang) dredging.

curare /kyrar/ *nm* curare.

cure /kyr/ *nf* **1** (dans une station thermale) course of treatment in ou at a spa; **faire une ~** to go for a course of treatment in a spa; **2** (traitement) course of treatment; **faire une ~ de** to take a course of; **3** (grande consommation) **faire une ~ de raisin** to eat a lot of grapes; **j'ai fait une ~ de soleil** I did nothing but soak up the sun.
■ **~ d'amaigrissement** slimming course GB, reducing treatment US; **~ de désintoxication** detoxification; **~ de repos** rest cure; **~ de sommeil** sleep therapy.

curé /kyre/ *nm* (parish) priest; **se faire ~**○ to become a priest; **bouffer du ~**○ to be anticlerical.

cure-dents /kyrdɑ̃/ *nm inv* toothpick.

curée /kyre/ *nf* **1** (à la chasse) (portion of) quarry (*fed to hounds*); **2** FIG scramble for the spoils; **se précipiter à la ~** to scramble for the spoils.

cure-pipes /kyrpip/ *nm inv* pipe cleaner.

curer /kyre/ [1] **I** *vtr* to clean out [*pipe, étang*].
II se curer *vpr* **se ~ les ongles** to clean one's nails; **se ~ les dents/le nez** to pick one's teeth/nose.

curetage /kyrtaʒ/ *nm* MÉD D and C, curettage; **on lui a fait un ~** she's had a D and C SPÉC.

curie /kyri/ *nf* RELIG **la ~** the Curia.

curieusement /kyrjøzmɑ̃/ *adv* (modifiant un verbe ou un adjectif) oddly, strangely; (adverbe de phrase) curiously enough, oddly enough.

curieux, -ieuse /kyrjø, øz/ **I** *adj* **1** (comme défaut) [*personne*] inquisitive, curious; [*yeux*] inquisitive; **regarder qn d'un œil ~** to look curiously at sb; **2** (étrange) strange; **un ~ paradoxe** a curious paradox; **et, chose curieuse, elle était seule** and, curiously enough, she was alone; **3** (intellectuellement) **esprit ~** person with an inquiring mind; **être ~ de** to be very interested in; **être ~ d'apprendre** to be keen to learn; **je suis ~ de voir**... (une réaction) I am curious to see...; (une collection, un objet) I am keen to see...; **4** (intéressant) interesting.
II *nm,f* **1** (personne indiscrète) **c'est un ~** he's nosy○; **aller quelque part en ~** to go somewhere (just) out of curiosity; **2** (passant) onlooker.
III *nm* (chose étrange) **le ~ de l'histoire c'est que** the funny ou curious thing about it is that.

curiosité /kyrjozite/ *nf* **1** (défaut) curiosity; **par ~** out of curiosity; **il est d'une ~!** he is so curious!; **la ~ est un vilain défaut** curiosity killed the cat; **2** (désir de connaître) curiosity (**pour** about); **avec ~** [*dévisager, regarder*] curiously; **3** (objet) strange object; **4** (étrangeté) **objet d'une grande ~** very curious object.

curiste /kyrist/ *nmf* person having hydrotherapy.

curriculum vitae /kyrikylɔmvite/ *nm inv* curriculum vitae, résumé US.

curry /kyri/ *nm* **1** (assaisonnement) curry powder; **riz au ~** curried rice; **2** (plat) curry.

curseur /kyrsœr/ *nm* ORDINAT cursor; (de règle à calcul) cursor; (de fermeture à glissière) slider.

cursif, -ive /kyrsif, iv/ *adj* [*écriture*] cursive; [*lecture*] cursory.

cursus /kyrsys/ *nm inv* course.

cutané, ~e /kytane/ *adj* skin (*épith*).

cuti /kyti/ *nf* skin test; **virer sa ~** (changer de comportement sexuel) to switch over.

cutter /kytœr/ *nm* Stanley knife®.

cuve /kyv/ *nf* (pour fermentation, teinture, blanchissage) vat; (à eau, mazout) tank; (de lave-linge, lave-vaisselle) interior; PHOT developing tank.

cuvée /kyve/ *nf* **1** (vin de toute une vigne) vintage; **la ~**

1959 the 1959 vintage; **~ du patron** house wine; **2** (contenu) vatful; **3** FIG (de romans, films) crop; (d'élèves) year group.

cuver○ /kyve/ [1] *vtr* **~ son vin** to sleep it off○.

cuvette /kyvɛt/ *nf* **1** (en plastique, métal) bowl; **~ des wc** (lavatory) bowl ou pan; **2** GÉOG basin; **~ océanique** deep sea floor.

CV /seve/ *nm* **1** (*abbr* = **curriculum vitae**) CV GB, résumé US; **2** (*written abbr* = **cheval-vapeur**) HP.

cyanure /sjanyr/ *nm* cyanide.

cybernétique /sibɛrnetik/ **I** *adj* cybernetic.
II *nf* cybernetics (+ *v sg*).

cyclable /siklabl/ *adj* **piste ~** cycle track.

cyclamen /siklamɛn/ *nm* cyclamen.

cycle /sikl/ *nm* **1** (de phénomènes, changements) cycle; **~ infernal** FIG vicious cycle; **2** (série) GÉN series (+ *v sg*); **deux ~s de dix sessions** two series of ten sessions; **3** LITTÉRAT cycle; **~ de la Table ronde** Arthurian cycle; **~ de chansons** song cycle; **4** UNIV **premier ~** *first two years of a degree course leading to a diploma*; **deuxième ~** *final two years of a degree course*; **troisième ~** postgraduate GB ou graduate US studies; **5** (bicyclette) cycle; **magasin de ~s** cycle shop.
■ **~ de formation** training course.

cyclique /siklik/ *adj* cyclic.

cyclisme /siklism/ ▶329| *nm* GÉN cycling; (de compétition) cycle racing; **faire du ~** to go cycling or cycle racing.

cycliste /siklist/ **I** *adj* [*club, saison*] cycling (*épith*); [*course*] cycle (*épith*); **coureur ~** racing cyclist.
II *nmf* cyclist; **short de ~** cycling shorts (*pl*).

cyclo-cross /siklokrɔs/ ▶329| *nm inv* (sport) cyclo-cross; **faire du ~** to do cyclo-cross racing.

cyclomoteur /siklomotœr/ *nm* moped.

cyclomotoriste /siklomotorist/ *nmf* moped rider.

cyclone /siklon/ *nm* (typhon) cyclone; (zone de basse pression) depression; FIG whirlwind; **arriver comme un ~** to sweep in like a whirlwind.

Cyclope /siklɔp/ *npr* Cyclops.

cyclotourisme /sikloturism/ ▶329| *nm* cycle touring; **faire du ~** to go long-distance cycling.

cyclotouriste /sikloturist/ *nmf* (touring) cyclist.

cygne /siɲ/ *nm* GÉN swan; **~ mâle** cob; **~ femelle** pen; **jeune ~** cygnet; **chant du ~** swansong.

cylindrage /silɛ̃draʒ/ *nm* (de route) rolling; (au tour) turning.

cylindre /silɛ̃dr/ *nm* (objet cylindrique) cylinder; TECH (pour compresser, laminer) roller; (pour imprimer) cylinder; MATH, AUT cylinder.

cylindrée /silɛ̃dre/ *nf* **1** (volume) capacity, size; **~ de 1200 cm³** 1200 cc engine; **voiture de petite/grosse ~** car with a small/powerful engine; **2** (moto, voiture) **petite ~** (voiture) car with a small engine; (moto) light motorcycle; **grosse ~** (voiture) powerful car; (moto) powerful motorcycle.

cylindrique /silɛ̃drik/ *adj* cylindrical.

cymbale /sɛ̃bal/ ▶392| *nm* cymbal; **coup de ~s** clash of cymbals.

cymbalier, -ière /sɛ̃balje, ɛr/ ▶374| *nm,f* cymbal player.

cynique /sinik/ **I** *adj* GÉN cynical; PHILOS Cynic.
II *nm* GÉN cynic; PHILOS Cynic.

cynisme /sinism/ *nm* GÉN cynicism; PHILOS Cynicism.

cyprès /siprɛ/ *nm* cypress.

cypriote /siprijɔt/ ▶394| *adj* Cypriot.

cyrillique /sirilik/ *adj* Cyrillic.

cystite /sistit/ ▶196| *nf* cystitis *C*.

Cythère /sitɛr/ *npr* Cythera.

Dd

d, D /de/ *nm inv* d, D.

d' ▶ **de**.

DAB /deabe/ *nm*: *abbr* ▶ **distributeur**.

d'abord ▶ **abord**.

dactylo¹ /daktilo/ ▶ 374 ⌋ *nmf* (*abbr* = **dactylo-graphe**) typist.

dactylo² /daktilo/ *nf* (*abbr* = **dactylographie**) typing.

dactylographe /daktilɔgʀaf/ *nmf* typist.

dactylographie /daktilɔgʀafi/ *nf* (technique) typing.

dactylographier /daktilɔgʀafje/ [2] *vtr* to type (out).

dada /dada/ **I** *adj* ART, LITTÉRAT Dada.
II *nm* **1**° (cheval) BABY TALK horsie° LANG ENFANTIN; **2**° (passe-temps) hobby; (idée fixe) hobbyhorse; **enfourcher son ~** to get on one's hobbyhorse.

dadais° /dadɛ/ *nm inv* clumsy youth; **espèce de grand ~!** you great oaf!

dague /dag/ *nf* (épée courte) dagger; (de cerf) spike.

daigner /deɲe/ [1] *vtr* to deign (**faire** to do).

daim /dɛ̃/ *nm* **1** (animal) (fallow) deer; **2** (viande) venison; **3** (cuir de daim) buckskin; **4** (cuir de veau) suede; **chaussures en ~** suede shoes.

dalaï-lama /dalailama/ *nm* Dalai Lama.

dallage /dalaʒ/ *nm* **1** (revêtement) paving; **2** (action) flagging, paving.

dalle /dal/ *nf* **1** (de pierre, marbre) slab; (dans église, maison) flagstone; **2** CONSTR (à même le sol) concrete foundation slab; (d'étage) suspended slab; **~ de moquette** carpet tile; **3** (en alpinisme) wall; **4 que ~**° nothing at all, zilch°.
■ **~ funèbre** or **funéraire** tombstone.
IDIOMES **avoir** or **crever la ~**° to be ravenous; **casser la ~**° to eat.

daller /dale/ [1] *vtr* to pave.

dalmate /dalmat/ *adj, nm* Dalmatian.

dalmatien, -ienne /dalmasjɛ̃, ɛn/ *adj, nm* (chien) Dalmatian.

daltonien, -ienne /daltɔnjɛ̃, ɛn/ *adj* colour GB-blind.

dam /dɑm/ *nm* **au grand ~ de** to the great displeasure of.

damas /dama(s)/ *nm inv* **1** (tissu) damask; **2** (prune) damson.

Damas /damas/ ▶ 628 ⌋ *npr* Damascus.

dame /dam/ **I** *nf* **1** (femme) lady; (de la noblesse) lady; **la première ~ de France** France's First Lady; **la ~ de son cœur** LITER his lady-love; **de ~** lady's; **pour ~s** ladies'; **jouer les grandes ~s** to behave like a princess; **c'est une grande ~ du cinéma** she's a grande dame of the screen; **ma bonne** or **petite ~**° my dear; **2** (épouse)° lady; **3** (dans fables, contes) **~ belette** Old Mother Weasel; **Dame Nature** Mother Nature; **4** JEUX (aux cartes, échecs) queen; (aux dames) King; **5** JUR Mrs.
II° †*excl* **~ oui!/non!** my word yes!/no!
III dames *nfpl* **1** ▶ 329 ⌋ JEUX draughts (+ *v sg*) GB, checkers (+ *v sg*) US; **2** (inscription) ladies; **3** SPORT **le simple ~s** the women's singles.
■ **~ de compagnie** live-in companion; **~ d'honneur** lady-in-waiting; **une ~ de petite vertu** a woman of easy virtue.

damier /damje/ *nm* draughtboard GB, checkerboard US; **étoffe en** or **à ~** checked material.

damnation /danasjɔ̃/ *nf* (tous contextes) damnation.

damné, -e /dɑne/ **I** *pp* ▶ **damner**.
II *pp adj* **1**° (maudit) (*before n*) cursed; **2** RELIG damned.

III *nm,f* **1** RELIG damned soul; **les ~s** the damned; **2** (réprouvé) outcast.
IDIOMES **souffrir comme un ~** to suffer horribly.

damner /dɑne/ [1] **I** *vtr* to damn.
II se damner *vpr* **1** RELIG to damn oneself; **2**° HUM **se ~ pour qn/qch** to sell one's soul for sb/sth.

dancing /dɑ̃siŋ/ *nm* dance hall.

dandiner: se dandiner /dɑ̃dine/ [1] *vpr* [*canard*] to waddle; **se ~ d'un pied sur l'autre** to shift from one foot to the other.

Danemark /danmaʀk/ ▶ 232 ⌋ *nprm* Denmark.

danger /dɑ̃ʒe/ *nm* **1** (risque général) danger; **être en ~** to be in danger; **tout ~ est écarté maintenant** the danger is past now; **hors de ~** out of danger; **mettre qn/qch en ~** to endanger sb/sth; **sans ~** safe; **(en) ~ de faire** (in) danger of doing; **il y a ~ à faire** there's a danger in doing; **(il n'y a) pas de ~ qu'il fasse** no danger of him doing; **'~ de chute'** 'Danger: steep drop'; **'~ d'éboulement'** 'risk of landslide'; **'~ de noyade'** 'Danger: unsafe for bathing'; **'attention ~!'** 'Danger!'; **2** (risque ponctuel) danger; (personne) menace; **au volant c'est un vrai ~** he is a real menace at the wheel; **un ~ pour qn/qch** a danger to sb/sth; **courir un (grand) ~** to be in (great) danger; **faire courir un (grand) ~ à qn** to put sb in (serious) danger; **~ de la route** (obstacle) road hazard; (personne) menace behind the wheel.
■ **~ public** LIT danger to the public; FIG IRON menace.

dangereusement /dɑ̃ʒʀøzmɑ̃/ *adv* dangerously.

dangereux, -euse /dɑ̃ʒʀø, øz/ *adj* dangerous (**pour** to); **zone dangereuse** danger zone.

danois, -e /danwa, az/ **I** ▶ 394 ⌋ *adj* Danish.
II *nm* **1** ▶ 338 ⌋ LING Danish; **2** (chien) Great Dane.

Danois, ~e /danwa, az/ ▶ 394 ⌋ *nm,f* Dane.

dans /dɑ̃/

■ **Note** *Généralités*
– La préposition *dans* est présentée ici dans ses grandes lignes. Les expressions courantes comme *dans l'abondance*, *dans le genre*, *être dans le pétrin* etc sont traitées respectivement dans les articles **abondance**, **genre**, **pétrin** etc.
– On trouvera ci-dessous des exemples illustrant les principales utilisations de la préposition mais il sera toujours prudent de consulter l'entrée du nom introduit par *dans*.
– Par ailleurs, la consultation des notes d'usage dont la liste est donnée ▶ 1420 ⌋ pourra apporter des réponses à certains problèmes bien précis.

prép **1** (lieu, sans déplacement) in; **~ un avion/bus** on a plane/bus; **~ une voiture/ un taxi** in a car/a taxi; **boire ~ un verre** to drink out of a glass; **fouiller ~ un tiroir** to rummage through a drawer ; **prendre une casserole ~ un placard** to take a pan out of a cupboard; **vider qch ~ l'évier** to pour sth down the sink; **qu'est-ce que je fais ~ tout ça**°? what am I doing in all this?; **~ l'ensemble** by and large; **~ le fond** in fact; **2** (avec des verbes de mouvement) **aller ~ la cuisine** to go to the kitchen; **entrer ~ une pièce** to go into a room; **voler ~ les airs** to fly in the air; **descendre ~ un puits** to go down a well; **monter ~ un avion** to get on a plane; **3** (temps) **~ ma jeunesse** in my youth; **~ deux heures** in two hours; **je t'appellerai ~ la journée** I'll call you during the day; **~ la minute qui a suivi** the next moment; **~ l'heure qui suivit** within the hour; **finir qch ~ les temps**° to finish sth in time; **4** (domaine) in; **être ~ les affaires** to be in business; **5** (état) **~ la misère** to be

silence in poverty/silence; **6** (but) ~ **un esprit de vengeance** in a spirit of revenge; ~ **l'intention de faire** with the intention of doing; **7** (approximation) about; ~ **les 30 francs** about 30 francs.

dansant, ~**e** /dɑ̃sɑ̃, ɑ̃t/ *adj* (entraînant) [*reflet*] dancing; (où l'on danse) **thé** ~ tea dance.

danse /dɑ̃s/ *nf* **1** (style) dance; (activité) dancing; **faire de la** ~ to take dancing classes; **accorder une** ~ **à qn** to give sb a dance; **de** ~ [*festival*] of dance; [*club, piste, troupe*] dance (*épith*); **cours de** ~ (pour adultes) dance class; (pour enfants) dancing class; **école de** ~ school of dance; **professeur de** ~ GÉN dancing teacher; (de ballet) ballet teacher; **contempler la** ~ **des flammes dans l'âtre** to watch the flames dancing in the hearth; **2**○ (correction) hiding○.
■ ~ **classique** classical ballet; **faire de la** ~ **classique** to do ballet dancing; ~ **du feu/de la pluie** (ritual) fire-/rain-dance; ~ **guerrière** war dance; ~ **macabre** dance of death; ~ **nuptiale** ZOOL courtship display; ~ **du ventre** LIT belly dancing.
IDIOMES **entrer dans la** ~ LIT to join the dance; FIG to join in; **mener la** ~ FIG to run the show FIG; **avoir la** ~ **de Saint-Guy** FIG to have the fidgets; MÉD to have St Vitus's dance.

danser /dɑ̃se/ [1] **I** *vtr* to dance.
II *vi* GÉN to dance; [*barque*] to bob; ~ **sur une musique** to dance to a tune; ~ **de joie** to dance with joy; **faire** ~ **qn** to have a dance with sb.
IDIOMES **ne pas savoir sur quel pied** ~ not to know what to do.

danseur, **-euse** /dɑ̃sœʀ, øz/ *nm,f* dancer; **en danseuse** SPORT standing on the pedals.
■ ~ **étoile** principal dancer.

dard /daʀ/ *nm* (aiguillon) sting; (arme) spear.

darder /daʀde/ [1] *vtr* LITER **le soleil darde ses rayons** the sun is beaming down.

dare-dare○ /daʀdaʀ/ *adv* double quick.

darne /daʀn/ *nf* (fish) steak.

dartre /daʀtʀ/ *nf* scurf patch.

datation /datasjɔ̃/ *nf* (attribution d'une date) dating; (date attribuée) date.

date /dat/ ▶ **156** *nf* **1** (moment précis) date; ~ **de décès** date of death; ~ **d'expiration** expiry date GB, expiration date US; ~ **d'arrivée** date of arrival; ~ **de départ** departure date; ~ **de clôture** closing date; **prendre** ~ to set a date; **à une** ~ **ultérieure** at some future date; **à** ~ **fixe** on a set date; ~ **anniversaire** anniversary; **depuis 1962**, ~ **à laquelle**... since 1962, in which year...; ~ **limite** deadline; ~ **limite de consommation** vente eat-by sell-by date; ~ **limite d'envoi des dossiers** final date for sending the documents; ~ **limite d'inscription** closing date for registration; **2** (époque) time; **à/depuis cette** ~ at/ from that time; **jusqu'à une** ~ **récente** until recently; **un ami de fraîche/longue** ~ a recent/longstanding friend; **le dernier scandale en** ~ the latest scandal.

dater /date/ [1] **I** *vtr* **1** (donner une date à) to date; **la circulaire est datée du**... the circular is dated the...; **à** ~ **du 31 juillet** as from 31 July; **2** (attribuer une date à) to date [*fossile, objet*].
II *vi* **1** (exister depuis) ~ **de** to date from; **de quand date cette réforme?** what was the date of this reform?; **de quand date votre séparation?** when did you separate?; **cela ne date pas d'hier**○ it's not exactly new; **2** (être démodé) to be dated.

dateur /datœʀ, øz/ *adj* [*tampon, timbre*] date (*épith*).

datif /datif/ *nm* LING dative; **au** ~ in the dative.

dation /dasjɔ̃/ *nf* ~ (**en paiement**) payment in kind.

datte /dat/ *nf* date.

dattier /datje/ *nm* date palm.

daube /dob/ *nf* casserole.

dauphin /dofɛ̃/ *nm* **1** ZOOL dolphin; **2** (successeur) heir apparent; HIST dauphin.

daurade /doʀad/ *nf* ~ (**royale**) gilt-head bream.

davantage /davɑ̃taʒ/ **I** *adv* **1** (plus) more; **il est rusé mais elle l'est** ~ he's crafty but she's (even) more so; **il ne travaille pas** ~ (en effort) he isn't working

any harder; (en quantité) he doesn't do any more work; **après trois mois de cours je n'en sais pas** ~ after three months of classes I don't know any more than I did before; **je ne peux pas la supporter et ses enfants pas** ~ I can't stand her or her children either; **sinon** ~ if not more; **rien ne me plaît** ~ **que** CONTROV I like nothing better than; **2** (plus longtemps) longer; **le projet prendra cinq ans et peut-être** ~ the project will take five years and perhaps (even) more; **si vous vous exposez** ~ **aux radiations** if you are further exposed to radiation.
II *dét indéf* ~ **de** more; **en voulez-vous** ~? would you like some more?; **le système a** ~ **de succès à la campagne** the system is more successful in the country.

DCA /desea/ *nf* (*abbr* = **défense contre les aéronefs**) antiaircraft defence GB.

DDASS /das/ *nf* (*abbr* = **Direction départementale de l'action sanitaire et sociale**) regional social services department.

de (**d'** *before vowel or mute h*) /də, d/ ▶ **157** *prép* **1** (indiquant l'origine) from; **le train** ~ **Bruxelles** the train from Brussels; **il arrive du Japon** he's just come from Japan; **à 20 mètres** ~ **là** 20 metres GB from there; **un mari** ~ **mon premier mari** a child by my first husband; **un vin** ~ **Grèce** (rapporté de là-bas) a wine from Greece; (fait là-bas) a Greek wine; **né** ~ **parents immigrés** born of immigrant parents; **il est** ~ **père italien** his father is Italian; ~ **méfiant il est devenu paranoïaque** he went from being suspicious to being paranoid; **2** (indiquant la progression) ~...à, ~...en from...to; ~ **8 à 10 heures** from 8 to 10 (o'clock); **du matin au soir** from morning till night; **d'heure en heure** from hour to hour; **3** (indiquant la destination) to; **pleurer** ~ **rage** to cry with rage; **trembler** ~ **froid** to shiver with cold; **5** (indiquant la manière) in; **parler d'un ton monocorde** to speak in a monotone; **tirer** ~ **toutes ses forces** to pull with all one's might; **6** (indiquant le moyen) with; **pousser qch du pied** to push sth aside with one's foot; **vivre** ~ **saucisses** to live on sausages; **7** (indiquant l'agent) by; **un poème** ~ **Victor Hugo** a poem by Victor Hugo; **avoir un enfant** ~ **qn** to have a child by sb; **8** (indiquant la durée) **travailler** ~ **nuit/**~ **jour** to work at night/during the day; **ne rien faire** ~ **la journée** to do nothing all day; **9** (indiquant l'appartenance, la dépendance) **les chapeaux** ~ **Paul** Paul's hats; **un élève du professeur Talbin** one of professor Talbin's students; **l'immensité** ~ **la mer** the immensity of the sea; **le toit** ~ **la maison** the roof of the house; **la porte** ~ **la chambre** the bedroom door; **le cadran du téléphone** the dial on the telephone; **c'est bien** ~ **lui** it's just like him; **10** (détermination par le contenant) **le foin** ~ **la grange** the hay in the barn; **le vin du tonneau** (qui s'y trouve) the wine in the barrel; (qu'on a tiré) the wine from the barrel; **11** (détermination par le contenu) of; **une tasse** ~ **café** a cup of coffee; **12** (détermination par la quantité) of; **une minute** ~ **silence** one minute of silence, a minute's silence; **13** (détermination par le lieu) of; **les pyramides d'Égypte** the pyramids of Egypt; **14** (détermination par le temps) of; **le 20 du mois** the 20th of the month; **la réunion** ~ **samedi** Saturday's meeting; **la réunion du 20 juin** the meeting on 20 June; **le train** ~ **15 heures** the 3 o'clock train; **les ventes** ~ **juin** the June sales; **15** (détermination par la dimension, la mesure) **un livre** ~ **200 pages** a 200-page book; **être long** ~ **20 mètres** to be 20 metres GB long; **50 francs** ~ **l'heure** 50 francs an hour; **trop lourd** ~ **trois kilos** three kilos too heavy; **16** (détermination par la nature, fonction, matière) **un billet** ~ **train** a train ticket; **une robe** ~ **coton rouge** a red cotton dress; **une bulle d'air** an air bubble; **17** (apposition) of; **le mois** ~ **juillet** the month of July; **le nom** ~ **Flore** the name Flore; **18** (avec attribut du nom ou du pronom) **trois personnes** ~ **tuées** three people killed; **deux heures** ~ **libres** two hours free; **200 francs** ~ **plus** 200 francs more; **l'ourlet a deux centimètres** ~ **trop** the hem is two centimetres GB too long; **quelque chose/rien** ~ **nouveau** something/

La date

Noter

- Les noms de mois et les noms de jours prennent toujours une majuscule en anglais; pour les abréviations des noms de mois et de jours fréquemment utilisées en anglais, ▶ 382 | et ▶ 551 |.

- En anglais parlé, on utilise presque toujours le nombre ordinal (par ex. fifth et non five) pour indiquer le jour du mois; pour les abréviations des nombres ordinaux, ▶ 399 |.

En anglais, il y a quatre façons d'écrire la date, et trois façons de la dire: ces options sont toutes indiquées pour la première date du tableau suivant. Pour écrire la date, les deux premières façons (May 1st ou May 1) sont acceptées dans tous les pays anglophones. Dans le tableau on utilisera indifféremment l'une ou l'autre de ces deux formes.

Pour dire la date, la première des formes données (May the first) est acceptée partout, et c'est cette forme qu'on utilisera dans le tableau. Les deux autres ne sont pas aussi répandues.

	écrire	dire
1er mai	May 1 ou May 1st (US & GB) 1st May ou 1 May (GB)	May the first (GB & US) ou the first of May (GB) ou May first (US)
2 avril	April 2 (etc.) abrév. Apr 2	April the second (etc.)
lundi 3 mai	Monday, May 3	Monday, May the third
4 mai 1927	May 4th 1927	May the fourth, nineteen twenty-seven
31.7.65	31.7.65* (GB) ou 7.31.65* (US)	July the thirty-first nineteen sixty-five
jeudi 5 mai 1994	Thursday, May 5 1994	Thursday, May the fifth, nineteen ninety-four
1968	1968	nineteen sixty-eight
1900	1900	nineteen hundred
l'an 2000	the year 2000	the year two thousand
2001	2001	two thousand and one
45 ap. J.-C.	45 AD†	forty-five AD [eɪˈdiː]
250 av. J.-C.	250 BC‡	two hundred and fifty BC [biːˈsiː]
le XVIe siècle	the 16th§ century	the sixteenth century

* L'anglais britannique, comme le français, place le chiffre du jour avant celui du mois; l'anglais américain commence par le chiffre du mois.

† AD signifie anno domini (l'année de notre Seigneur).

‡ BC signifie before Christ (avant Jésus-Christ).

§ Noter que l'anglais utilise les chiffres arabes pour les siècles.

Pour les dates sur les lettres, voir **activités**.

Quel jour?

le combien sommes-nous aujourd'hui?	= what's the date today?
nous sommes le 10	= it's the tenth
nous sommes le lundi 10	= it's Monday 10th (dire Monday the tenth)
nous sommes le 10 mai	= it's May 10 (dire it's the tenth of May)

Pour indiquer la date à laquelle il s'est passé ou se passera quelque chose, l'anglais utilise normalement la préposition on devant le quantième du mois.

on se voit le 10	= see you on the 10th
c'est arrivé le 10	= it happened on the 10th
c'est arrivé le 10 décembre	= it happened on 10th December (dire the tenth of December)
le 10 de chaque mois	= on the 10th of every month

L'anglais emploie on même en début de phrase.

le lundi 5 mai, il atteignit Tombouctou	= on Monday May 5, he reached Timbuktu

Mais on peut aussi utiliser d'autres prépositions:

à partir du 10	= from the 10th onwards
jusqu'au 10	= till ou until the 10th
attendez le 10	= wait till the 10th
avant le 10 mai	= before May 10 (dire before May the tenth)
aux environs du 10 mai	= around 10 May (dire around the tenth of May)
du 10 au 16 mai	= from 10th to 16th May (GB) (dire from the tenth to the sixteenth of May) ou from 10th through 16th May (US) (dire from the tenth through the sixteenth of May)

Devant les noms de mois et les chiffres des années et des siècles, l'anglais utilise normalement in.

en mai	= in May
je suis né en mai 1914	= I was born in May 1914
en 1945	= in 1945
il est mort en 1616	= he died in 1616
Shakespeare (1564–1616)	= Shakespeare (1564–1616) (dire Shakespeare fifteen sixty-four to sixteen sixteen) ou Shakespeare, b. 1564– d. 1616 (dire Shakespeare born in fifteen sixty-four and died in sixteen sixteen)
la révolution de 1789	= the 1789 revolution
les émeutes de 68	= the riots of '68 (dire of sixty-eight)
en mai 45	= in May '45 (dire in May forty-five)
dans les années 50	= in the fifties ou in the 1950s (dire in the nineteen fifties)
au début des années 50	= in the early fifties
à la fin des années 50	= in the late fifties
au XVIIe siècle	= in the 17th century (dire in the seventeenth century)
au début du XIIe siècle	= in the early twelfth century
à la fin du XIIe siècle	= in the late twelfth century

Le mot century ne peut pas être omis en anglais:

à partir du XIIe	= from the 12th century onwards (dire from the twelfth century onwards)
les romanciers du XIXe	= 19th-century novelists (dire nineteenth century novelists)

---

nothing new; **c'est quelqu'un ~ célèbre** he's/she's famous; **c'est ça ~ fait**○ that's that out of the way; **19** (avec un infinitif) **ça me peinait ~ la voir ainsi** it upset me to see her like that; **et eux ~ rire** and they laughed; **20** (après un déverbal) **le filtrage ~ l'eau pose de gros problèmes** filtering water poses big problems; **21** (après un superlatif) GÉN of; (avec un lieu ou ensemble assimilé) in; **le plus grand restaurant ~ la ville** the biggest restaurant in the town; **22**○ (en corrélation avec le pronom un, une) **pour une gaffe, c'en est une, ~ gaffe!** as blunders go, that was a real one!; **23** (dans une comparaison chiffrée) than; **plus/moins ~ 10** more/ less than 10.

dé /de/ nm **1** JEUX dice (inv); **jeter les ~s** to throw the dice; **les ~s sont jetés** the die is cast; **couper de la viande en ~s** to dice meat; **coup de ~** LIT, FIG

throw of the dice; **2** (pour coudre) **~ (à coudre)** LIT thimble; (mesure) thimbleful.

DEA /deɑ/ nm (abbr = **diplôme d'études approfondies**) postgraduate certificate (prior to doctoral thesis).

déambulateur /deɑ̃bylatœʀ/ nm zimmer® (frame) GB, walker US.

déambuler /deɑ̃byle/ [1] vi to wander (about).

débâcle /debɑkl/ nf GÉOG breaking up; MIL rout; FIG collapse.

déballage○ /debalaʒ/ nm (désordre) jumble; (aveu public) outpouring.

déballer /debale/ [1] vtr to unpack [marchandise, caisse]; to open [paquet, cadeau]; (étaler) to display [marchandise].

débandade /debɑ̃dad/ nf **1** (déroute) stampede;

de

La préposition
Certains emplois de la préposition *de* sont traités ailleurs dans le dictionnaire, notamment:

lorsque *de* introduit le complément de verbes transitifs indirects comme *douter de, jouer de*, de verbes à double complément comme *recevoir qch de qn*, de certains noms comme *désir de, obligation de*, de certains adjectifs comme *fier de, plein de*;

lorsque *de* fait partie de locutions comme *d'abord, de travers* ou de composés comme *chemin de fer, pomme de terre*;

lorsque *de* est utilisé dans la structure de déterminants indéfinis comme *peu de, moins de* etc.;

lorsque *de* fait suite à *être* dans certaines tournures, voir *être*.

D'autres renvois essentiels apparaissent dans l'entrée ci-dessous, mais on se reportera également aux notes d'usage répertoriées ▶ **1420** pour certaines constructions.

L'article indéfini
de article indéfini pluriel est traité avec *un* I.

L'article partitif: *de, de l', de la, du*
Lorsqu'il exprime une généralité non quantifiée ou une alternative, *de* article partitif ne se traduit pas:

manger de la viande/du lapin/des œufs = to eat meat/rabbit/eggs
il ne boit jamais de vin = he never drinks wine

tu prends du café au petit déjeuner? = do you have coffee for breakfast?
voulez-vous de la bière ou du vin? = would you like beer or wine?
il ne veut pas de vin mais de la bière = he doesn't want wine, he wants beer

Lorsque l'idée de quantité est présente il se traduit par *some* ou *any*:

achète de la bière = buy some beer
achète des bananes = buy some bananas
voulez-vous de la bière? = would you like some beer?
évidemment, tu leur as donné de l'argent? = of course, you gave them some money?
y a-t-il du soleil? = is there any sun?
il n'y a pas de soleil = there isn't any sun, there's no sun
il y a rarement du soleil = there's seldom any sun
il n'y a jamais de soleil = there's never any sun
il n'y a plus de vin = there isn't any more wine

Et lorsqu'il s'agit d'une partie déterminée d'un tout, il se traduit par *some of* ou *any of*:

a-t-elle bu du vin que j'ai apporté? = did she drink any of the wine I brought?
je ne prendrai plus de ce mélange = I won't take any more of this mixture

---

soldats en pleine ~ soldiers fleeing in disarray; **2** FIG disarray.

débaptiser /debatize/ [1] *vtr* to rename [*rue, ville*].

débarbouiller /debaʀbuje/ [1] **I** *vtr* to wash.
II se débarbouiller *vpr* to wash one's face.

débarcadère /debaʀkadɛʀ/ *nm* landing stage, jetty.

débardeur /debaʀdœʀ/ *nm* (pull sans manches) tank top; (d'été) sleeveless tee-shirt.

débarquement /debaʀkəmɑ̃/ *nm* **1** (de marchandises) unloading; (de passagers) disembarkation; **2** MIL landing.

débarquer /debaʀke/ [1] **I** *vtr* to unload [*marchandise*] (**de** from; **sur** onto); to land [*personne*].
II *vi* **1** (descendre à terre) [*passagers*] to disembark; **~ du train** to get off the train; **2** MIL to land (**sur** on; **en** in); **3**○ (arriver) (en masse) to descend (**à** upon); (à l'improviste) to turn up○ (**chez qn** at sb's place); **4**○ (ne pas être au courant) **il débarque toujours** he never has a clue○ (what's going on).

débarras /debaʀa/ *nm inv* (endroit) junk room; **bon ~**○! good riddance!

débarrasser /debaʀase/ [1] **I** *vtr* **1** (vider) to clear out [*pièce, placard*]; to clear [*bureau, table, jardin*]; **~ une pièce de qch** to clear sth out of a room; **~ (la table)** (après le repas) to clear the table; **2** (libérer) **~ qn de** to free sb from [*complexe*]; to release sb from [obligation]; to rid sb of [*dictateur*]; **3 ~ qn (de son manteau)** to take sb's coat.
II se débarrasser *vpr* **1** (se séparer) **se ~ de** to get rid of; **se ~ des déchets** to dispose of waste; **2 se ~ (de son manteau)** to take off one's coat.
IDIOMES **~ le plancher**○ to clear off○.

débat /deba/ **I** *nm* **1** (discussion) debate (**sur** on); **entrer dans le cœur du ~** to get to the heart of the matter; **2** (conflit moral) crisis; **~ intérieur** crisis of conscience.
II débats *nmpl* **1** POL debates; **2** JUR closing submissions and summing-up.

débattre /debatʀ/ [61] **I** *vtr* (négocier) to negotiate; **prix à ~** price negotiable.
II débattre de or **sur** *vtr ind* (discuter) to discuss; (au Parlement, à la télévision) to debate.
III se débattre *vpr* **1** LIT [*animal*] to struggle; [*personne*] to put up a struggle; **se ~ contre** to struggle with; **2** FIG to struggle (**dans** with).

débauche /deboʃ/ *nf* **1** (dépravation) debauchery; **un lieu de ~** a den of vice; **2** (profusion) profusion.

débauché, ~e /deboʃe/ **I** *pp* ▶ **débaucher**.
II *pp adj* [*personne*] debauched.
III *nm,f* debauchee; **mener une vie de ~** to lead a dissolute life.

débaucher /deboʃe/ [1] *vtr* **1** (licencier) to lay off [*employé*]; **2**○ (distraire) to tempt [sb] away.

débile /debil/ **I**○ *adj* (idiot) [*personne*] moronic; [*film, raisonnement*] daft○; **c'est ~** it's daft○.
II *nmf* **~ mental** MÉD retarded person.

débilité /debilite/ *nf* **1** MÉD debility; **2**○ (de film, discours) stupidity.

débiner○ /debine/ [1] **I** *vtr* to badmouth○.
II se débiner *vpr* **1** (partir) to clear off○; (pour se dérober à qch) to make oneself scarce○; **2** (se disloquer) [*choses*] to fall apart.

débit /debi/ *nm* **1** (en comptabilité) debit; **la somme est inscrite au ~** GÉN the sum has been debited; **2** (en parlant, récitant) delivery; **il a un de ces ~s!** (bavard) he never stops talking!; **3** (de cours d'eau) rate of flow; **4** (de liquide) flow; (de gaz) output; **5** (de ligne d'assemblage) output; **6** (de magasin) turnover (of stock); (de restaurant) customer turnover; **produit qui a un bon ~** product which sells well.
■ **~ de boissons** (bar) bar; **~ de tabac** tobacconist GB.

débiter /debite/ [1] *vtr* **1** FIN to debit [*compte, client*]; **~ un compte de 100 francs** to debit an account with 100 francs; **2** (dire) PEJ to reel off [*texte*]; **~ des bêtises** to talk a lot of nonsense; **3** (découper) to cut up; **4** (vendre) to sell; **5** (produire) to produce; **6** (fournir en liquide) **~ tant par heure** [*fleuve*] to have a flow of so much per hour; [*pompe*] to discharge so much per hour.

débiteur, -trice /debitœʀ, tʀis/ **I** *adj* [*compte, solde*] debit (*épith*); [*entreprise, pays*] which is in debt.
II *nm,f* debtor.

déblais /deblɛ/ *nmpl* (décombres) rubble ¢; (sol) earth ¢.

déblayer /debleje/ [21] *vtr* (dégager) to clear away [*terre, neige*]; to clear [*lieu, porte*] (**de qch** of sth); (ranger) to tidy up [*pièce*]; **~ le plancher**○ to clear off○; **~ le terrain** to do the groundwork.

déblocage /deblɔkaʒ/ nm (de fonds) releasing; (de salaires) unfreezing; (de prix) deregulating.

débloquer /deblɔke/ [1] I vtr 1 to release [frein]; to unlock [volant, roue]; to unjam [machine, mécanisme]; 2 (libérer) to unfreeze [salaires, prix]; to release [fonds, crédits, dossiers, marchandises]; to end the deadlock in [situation, négociation]; 3 (dégager) to make [sth] available [crédits, subventions]; to create [poste]; 4 (ouvrir) to clear [rue, entrée].
II° vi to be off one's rocker°.
III se débloquer vpr la situation s'est débloquée the deadlock has been broken.

déboires /debwaʀ/ nmpl 1 (déceptions) disappointments; 2 (ennuis) trials; 3 (échecs) setbacks; essuyer des ~ to meet with setbacks.

déboiser /debwaze/ [1] vtr to clear [sth] of trees [terrain]; to deforest [région].

déboîtement /debwatmã/ nm 1 MÉD dislocation; 2 AUT accident dû au ~ d'une voiture accident caused by a car pulling out.

déboîter /debwate/ [1] I vtr (déloger) to dislocate [os]; to dislodge [objet]; to disconnect [tubes].
II vi (sortir d'un alignement) [personne] to move out of line; [groupe] to break out of column; [voiture] to pull out.
III se déboîter vpr se ~ le genou to dislocate one's knee.

débonnaire /debɔnɛʀ/ adj [personne] good-humoured^GB; [air] kindly.

débordant, ~e /debɔʀdã, ãt/ adj 1 (extrême) [imagination] overactive; [joie] overflowing; être d'une activité ~e to be extremely active; 2 (abondant) ~ de brimming with [vitalité, énergie]; bursting with [santé].

débordé, ~e /debɔʀde/ I pp ▶ déborder.
II pp adj 1 (dépassé) overwhelmed; 2 (surchargé) overloaded (de with).

débordement /debɔʀdəmã/ I nm (d'insultes, de protestations) flood; (d'enthousiasme) excess.
II débordements nmpl LITER excesses.

déborder /debɔʀde/ [1] I vtr 1 (sortir de) [problème]; to go beyond [domaine]; 2 (submerger) to overwhelm; se laisser ~ to let oneself be overwhelmed; 3 MIL, POL, SPORT to outflank; 4 (saillir de) to jut out from.
II déborder de vtr ind (être plein de) to be overflowing with [personnes, détails]; to be brimming over with [joie, amour]; to be bursting with [santé]; ~ de vie/d'activité to be full of life/of activity.
III vi 1 (sortir des bords) [liquide, rivière] to overflow; (en bouillant) to boil over; 2 (laisser répandre) [récipient] to overflow; (en bouillant) to boil over; la coupe déborde FIG it's the last straw; 3 (dépasser) to spill out (de of); la pierre déborde de dix centimètres the stone juts out ten centimetres^GB; elle déborde en coloriant she goes over the lines when she's colouring^GB in.
IV se déborder vpr (au lit) to become untucked.

débouché /debuʃe/ nm 1 (ouverture commerciale) (pays, région) market (dans in; pour for); (créneau) outlet (dans in; pour for); trouver de nouveaux ~s à l'exportation to find new export outlets; 2 (perspective d'avenir) job opportunity (en in); 3 (de vallée) mouth.

déboucher /debuʃe/ [1] I vtr (dégager) to unblock; (ouvrir) to open.
II vi 1 LIT, FIG (arriver) [personne, véhicule] to come out (de from; sur onto; dans into); (brusquement) to appear; 2 (ouvrir) ~ sur or dans [rue] to open onto; 3 (mener) ~ sur [études, débat] to lead to.
III se déboucher vpr 1 [évier, conduit] to come unblocked; 2 se ~ le nez to unblock one's nose.

déboucheur /debuʃœʀ/ nm (produit) drain clearing product.

déboucler /debukle/ [1] vtr to unbuckle [ceinture].

débouler /debule/ [1] I vtr to charge down.
II vi 1 (dégringoler) to tumble down; 2° (venir rapidement) ~ de [personne] to come charging along from; ~ sur qn to burst in on sb.

déboulonner /debulɔne/ [1] vtr to unbolt [roue]; ~

une statue [ouvrier] to remove a statue; [manifestants] to topple a statue.

déboursement /debuʀsəmã/ nm paying out (de of).

débourser /debuʀse/ [1] vtr to pay out.

déboussoler° /debusɔle/ [1] vtr to throw°, to confuse [personne].

debout /dəbu/ I adv, adj inv 1 (vertical, sur pied) [personne] standing; les personnes ~ the people standing; 'assis: 40, ~: 10' (dans un bus) 'seated: 40, standing: 10'; rester ~ to stand; (veiller) to stay up; j'ai dû voyager ~ I had to stand all the way; ne restez pas ~, asseyez-vous do take a seat; être or se tenir ~ to stand; se mettre ~ to stand up; ça bougeait tellement que personne ne pouvait se tenir ~ it was moving so much that no-one could stay on their feet; je ne tiens plus ~, je vais me coucher I'm falling asleep on my feet, I'm going to go to bed; aidez-la à se mettre ~ help her to get up; 2 (hors du lit) [personne] up; tu es déjà ~! you're already up!; 3 (qui se maintient) [bâtiment, mur] standing; le bâtiment ne tient plus ~ the building is falling down; ton histoire tient ~° your story seems likely; 4 (vertical, sur une extrémité) [animal] on its hind legs; [objet] upright; poser un tonneau ~ to put a barrel upright; nous avons remis la statue ~ we stood the statue back up; 5 (guéri) grâce à votre médicament, il était ~ en deux jours thanks to your medicine, he was up and about in two days.
II excl get up!

déboutonner /debutɔne/ [1] I vtr to unbutton [vêtement]; tu es déboutonné your buttons are undone.
II se déboutonner vpr [personne] to unbutton one's clothes; [vêtement] to come undone.

débraillé, ~e /debʀaje/ I adj [personne] dishevelled^GB; [tenue, style] sloppy.
II nm sortir en ~ to go out sloppily dressed.

débrancher /debʀãʃe/ [1] vtr to unplug [appareil]; to disconnect [système d'alarme]; to pull out [prise].

débrayage /debʀejaʒ/ nm 1 AUT declutching; pédale de ~ clutch pedal; 2 (grève) stoppage.

débrayer /debʀeje/ [21] vi AUT to declutch; (cesser le travail) to stop work.

débridé, ~e /debʀide/ adj [imagination] unbridled.

débris /debʀi/ I nm inv 1 (d'objet brisé) fragment; des ~ de verre broken glass ¢; 2 (de véhicule accidenté) piece of wreckage; parmi les ~ de l'avion among the wreckage from the plane.
II nmpl (ordures) rubbish GB (¢), garbage US (¢); (restes) scraps; (d'armée, de fortune) remnants.

débrouillard, ~e /debʀujaʀ, aʀd/ adj resourceful.

débrouillardise /debʀujaʀdiz/ nf resourcefulness.

débrouiller /debʀuje/ [1] I vtr (démêler) to disentangle; (éclaircir) to solve [énigme]; (enseigner les bases à)° to teach [sb] the basics (en, à of).
II se débrouiller vpr 1 (s'arranger) to manage; se ~ avec qn to sort it out with sb; se ~ pour faire to manage to do; se ~ pour que to arrange it so that; débrouille-toi pour que make sure that; se ~ pour ne pas faire to weasel out of doing sth°; 2 (s'en sortir) to get by; il faut savoir se ~ you have to learn to stand on your own two feet; il se débrouille en espagnol he gets by in Spanish; débrouille-toi tout seul you'll have to manage on your own.

débroussailler /debʀusaje/ [1] vtr AGRIC to clear the undergrowth from; (éclaircir) to do the groundwork on [texte, problème].

débusquer /debyske/ [1] vtr to flush out [animal, personne].

début /deby/ I nm (de film, mois, discours) beginning; (de crise, négociations, d'épidémie) start; au tout ~ at the very beginning; au ~ at first; au/en ~ de at the beginning of; ~ mars early in March; dès le ~ from the very beginning; depuis le ~ (de) since the beginning (of); je le savais depuis le ~ I knew all along; du ~ (jusqu')à la fin from start to finish; il y a un ~ à tout you have to start somewhere; pour un

~, ce n'est pas mal it's not bad for starters; **un ~ de solution** the beginnings of a solution.

II débuts *nmpl* **1** (de comédien, musicien) debut (*sg*); **à mes ~s** when I started out; **2** (de parti politique, média) early stages; **depuis ses ~s en 1962, le mouvement a évolué** since its inception in 1962, the movement has evolved.

débutant, ~e /debytɑ̃, ɑ̃t/ **I** *adj* [*conducteur, skieur, artiste*] novice (*épith*); [*ingénieur, cadre*] recently qualified; **elle est ~e** she's a beginner.

II *nm,f* GÉN beginner (**en** in); CIN, THÉÂT actor/actress making his/her debut; **c'est une ~e** she's a beginner.

débuter /debyte/ [1] **I** *vtr* CONTROV to begin.

II *vi* **1** (commencer) [*journée, roman, séance*] to begin, to start (**avec, par, sur** with); [*personne*] to start off (**avec, par, sur** with); **2** (faire ses premiers pas) GÉN to start out (**comme** as); [*acteur, comédien*] to make one's debut (**dans** in).

déca⚬ /deka/ *nm* decaf⚬, sanka® US.

deçà /dəsa/ **I** *adv* **~, delà** here and there.

II en deçà *loc adv* on this side.

III en deçà de *loc prép* **1** (de ce côté-ci de) on this side of [*montagne, rivière*]; **2** FIG (en dessous de) below; **le résultat est (très) en ~ de notre objectif** the result falls (far) short of our target.

décacheter /dekaʃte/ [20] *vtr* to unseal.

décade /dekad/ *nf* (dix jours) 10-day period; (décennie) CONTROV decade.

décadence /dekadɑ̃s/ *nf* (état) decadence; (déclin) decline.

décadent, ~e /dekadɑ̃, ɑ̃t/ *adj* (en état de dégénérescence) decadent; (en déclin) in decline (*après n*); LITTÉRAT Decadent.

décaféiné, ~e /dekafeine/ **I** *adj* decaffeinated.

II *nm* decaffeinated coffee.

décalage /dekalaʒ/ *nm* **1** (différence) (écart) gap; (désaccord) discrepancy; **se sentir en ~ (par rapport aux autres)** to feel out of step (with the others); **2** (intervalle dans le temps) interval; **3** (glissement dans le temps) (avance) move forward; (retard) move back; **4** (dans l'espace) shift; **~ des lignes de départ** SPORT staggering of starting lines; **il y a un ~ de 10 centimètres entre les deux tableaux** there's a 10 centimetre^{GB} difference in the height at which the two pictures are hung; **5** ORDINAT shift.

■ **~ horaire** (entre deux lieux) time difference; **mal supporter le ~ horaire** to suffer from jet-lag.

décalcifier /dekalsifje/ [1] **I** *vtr* to decalcify.

II se décalcifier *vpr* to be decalcified.

décalcomanie /dekalkɔmani/ *nf* transfer GB, decal US.

décaler /dekale/ [1] **I** *vtr* **1** (dans le temps) (avancer) to bring [sth] forward [*date, départ*]; (reculer) to put GB ou move US [sth] back; **les avions sont tous décalés d'une heure** (en retard) the planes are all taking off an hour later; **2** (dans l'espace) (avancer) to move [sth] forward [*objet*]; (reculer) to move [sth] back; **~ qn/ qch d'un rang** (reculer) to move sb/sth back a row; **poteau décalé (par rapport aux autres)** post out of line (with the others); **lignes décalées** staggered lines.

II se décaler *vpr* **se ~ sur la droite** to move ou shift to the right.

décalitre /dekalitʀ/ ▶ **86** *nm* (unité) decalitre^{GB}.

décalque /dekalk/ *nm* ART tracing; (imitation) carbon copy.

décalquer /dekalke/ [1] *vtr* **1** ART (par transparence) to trace (**sur** from); (reporter) to transfer (**sur** onto); **2** FIG (imiter) to copy (**sur** onto).

décamètre /dekamɛtʀ/ ▶ **348** *nm* (unité) decametre^{GB}.

décamper⚬ /dekɑ̃pe/ [1] *vi* (s'enfuir) to run off; (partir) to clear off⚬; **faire ~ qn** to chase sb away.

décantage /dekɑ̃taʒ/ *nm*, **décantation** /dekɑ̃tasjɔ̃/ *nf* (procédé) decantation; (action) (de liquide) (settling and) decanting.

décanter /dekɑ̃te/ [1] **I** *vtr* (laisser reposer) to allow [sth] to settle [*liquide*]; to clarify [*eaux usées*].

II se décanter *vpr* **1** [*liquide*] to settle; [*eaux usées*]

to clarify; **2** [*situation, idées*] to become clearer; **laisser les choses se ~** to allow the dust to settle.

décapage /dekapaʒ/ *nm* **1** (de meuble, plancher) GÉN cleaning; (avec un abrasif) scouring; (avec un produit) stripping; (à la brosse) scrubbing; (à la ponceuse) sanding; **2** TECH (de métal) pickling.

décapant, ~e /dekapɑ̃, ɑ̃t/ **I** *adj* **1** (abrasif) scouring; **produit ~** (produit pour enlever la peinture, le vernis) paint stripper; (acide) pickle; **2**⚬ FIG (caustique) [*humour*] abrasive, caustic.

II *nm* (abrasif) scouring agent; (pour peinture) paint stripper; (acide) pickle.

décaper /dekape/ [1] *vtr* **1** (nettoyer) GÉN to clean; (enlever la peinture) to strip; **~ à la brosse** to scrub; **~ avec un abrasif** to scour; **2**⚬ [*shampooing, savon*] to be harsh.

décapitation /dekapitasjɔ̃/ *nf* (de personne) (accident) decapitation; (exécution) beheading.

décapiter /dekapite/ [1] *vtr* (tuer) to behead; (accidentellement) to decapitate; FIG to remove the leaders from [*parti, organisation*].

décapotable /dekapɔtabl/ *adj* convertible.

décapsuler /dekapsyle/ [1] *vtr* to take the top off.

décapsuleur /dekapsylœʀ/ *nm* bottle-opener.

décarcasser⚬: **se décarcasser** /dekaʀkase/ [1] *vpr* to put oneself to a lot of trouble.

décathlon /dekatlɔ̃/ ▶ **329** *nm* decathlon.

décatir: se décatir /dekatiʀ/ [3] *vpr* to become decrepit; **décati** decrepit.

décéder /desede/ [14] *vi* to die; **X récemment décédé** X who died recently; **~ d'un cancer** to die of cancer.

décelable /deslabl/ *adj* detectable.

déceler /desle/ [17] *vtr* **1** (distinguer) to detect; **2** (indiquer) to reveal [*sentiment*]; to indicate [*présence*].

décélération /deseleʀasjɔ̃/ *nf* (de vitesse) deceleration.

décembre /desɑ̃bʀ/ ▶ **382** *nm* December.

décemment /desamɑ̃/ *adv* **1** (selon les normes) [*se conduire, être logé*] decently; **2** (avec compétence) [*travailler, jouer*] reasonably well; **3** (raisonnablement) reasonably.

décence /desɑ̃s/ *nf* (bienséance) decency.

décennal, ~e, mpl -aux /desenal, o/ *adj* ten-year.

décennie /deseni/ *nf* decade.

décent, ~e /desɑ̃, ɑ̃t/ *adj* **1** (bienséant) decent; **2** (correct) proper, right; **3** (acceptable) decent, reasonable.

décentraliser /desɑ̃tʀalize/ [1] **I** *vtr* to decentralize.

II se décentraliser *vpr* to become decentralized.

décentrer /desɑ̃tʀe/ [1] **I** *vtr* to move [sth] away from the centre^{GB}.

II se décentrer *vpr* to move away (**par rapport à** from); **décentré** off-centre^{GB}.

déception /desɛpsjɔ̃/ *nf* disappointment.

décerner /desɛʀne/ [1] *vtr* to award.

décès /desɛ/ *nm inv* death; **fermé pour cause de ~** closed owing to bereavement.

décevant, ~e /desəvɑ̃, ɑ̃t/ *adj* disappointing.

décevoir /desəvwaʀ/ [5] *vtr* **1** (ne pas répondre aux espoirs de) to disappoint; **tu me déçois (beaucoup)** I'm (very) disappointed in you; **ne pas ~** to live up to expectations; **2** (tromper) to fail to fulfil^{GB} [*espoir*].

déchaîné, ~e /deʃene/ **I** *pp* ▶ **déchaîner**.

II *pp adj* **1** (violent) [*mer, vent*] raging; **2** (très énervé) [*personne, foule*] wild; [*opinion*] stirred up (*jamais épith*); **~ contre** furious with.

déchaînement /deʃɛnmɑ̃/ *nm* **1** (de tempête) raging; **2** (explosion) **le ~ de l'opinion publique** the public outcry (**contre** against).

déchaîner /deʃene/ [1] **I** *vtr* to rouse [*sentiments*]; to excite [*personnes*].

II se déchaîner *vpr* **1** [*phénomènes naturels*] to rage; [*sentiments*] to burst out; **2** [*foule*] to go wild; **3** [*personne*] to fly into a rage.

déchanter /deʃɑ̃te/ [1] *vi* to become disenchanted; **elle a dû ~** she was brought down to earth; **faire ~** to disappoint.

décharge /deʃaʀʒ/ *nf* **1** (d'arme à feu) discharge; **2** (d'ordures) rubbish GB ou garbage US dump; **~ munici-pale** municipal dump; **3** (d'électricité) **recevoir une ~** to get an electric shock; **4** JUR (d'accusé) acquittal; **5** (de responsabilités) **signer une ~** to sign a discharge.

déchargement /deʃaʀʒəmɑ̃/ *nm* (de véhicule, d'arme à feu) unloading.

décharger /deʃaʀʒe/ [13] I *vtr* **1** (débarrasser de sa charge) to unload [*navire, véhicule*]; to relieve [*per-sonne*] (**de** of); **2** (enlever un chargement) to unload [*mar-chandises, passagers*]; **3** (ôter la charge de) to unload [*arme à feu*]; (tirer avec) to fire [*arme*]; **4** (libérer) **~ qn de** to relieve sb of [*tâche, obligation*]; **5** (en électricité) [*personne*] to discharge [*batterie*]; **6** (soulager) to unburden [*conscience, cœur*] (**auprès de qn** to sb).

II **se décharger** *vpr* **1** (se libérer) **se ~ de qch** to off-load sth (**sur qn** onto sb); **2** [*batterie*] to run down; **la batterie est déchargée** the battery is flat.

décharné, ~e /deʃaʀne/ *adj* [*corps, bras, visage*] emaciated; [*doigt*] bony.

décharner /deʃaʀne/ [1] *vtr* to emaciate.

déchaussé, ~e /deʃose/ I *pp* ▶ **déchausser**.

II *pp adj* [*personne*] barefoot; **dents ~es** receding gums.

déchausser /deʃose/ [1] I *vtr* GÉN **~ qn** to take sb's shoes off; SPORT **~ (ses skis)** to take off one's skis.

II **se déchausser** *vpr* **1** (enlever ses chaussures) to take off one's shoes; **2** [*dent*] to work loose due to receding gums.

dèche○ /dɛʃ/ *nf* **être dans la ~** to be broke○.

déchéance /deʃeɑ̃s/ *nf* **1** (décadence morale) decline; **tomber dans la ~** to go into total decline; **2** (décrépi-tude) degeneration; **3** (déclin) (d'une nation) decline.

déchet /deʃɛ/ I *nm* **1** (morceau inutilisé) scrap; **2** (perte) waste; **il y a du ~** (dans la marchandise) there's some waste; (parmi les candidats) there are failures ou duds○; **3** (épave) FIG wreck; **les ~s de la société** the dregs of society.

II **déchets** *nmpl* (résidus) waste material ¢; (ordures) waste ¢; **~s ménagers** household refuse ¢; **~s industriels** industrial waste.

déchetterie /deʃɛtʀi/ *nf* waste reception centre GB.

déchiffrage /deʃifʀaʒ/ *nm* GÉN deciphering; MUS sight-reading.

déchiffrement /deʃifʀəmɑ̃/ *nm* (de message codé) decoding; (de texte, d'écriture) deciphering.

déchiffrer /deʃifʀe/ [1] *vtr* (lire) to decipher; (interpré-ter) to fathom out; MUS to sight-read [*partition*].

déchiqueté, ~e /deʃikte/ *adj* [*côte, relief*] jagged, ragged.

déchiqueter /deʃikte/ [20] *vtr* **1** (réduire en lambeaux) to tear [sth] to shreds; **2** (mutiler) to mutilate [*membre*]; **3** (tuer) [*machine, animal*] to tear [sb] to pieces; [*ex-plosion*] to blow [sb] to pieces.

déchirant, ~e /deʃiʀɑ̃, ɑ̃t/ *adj* **1** (émouvant) heart-rending; **2** (difficile) agonizing; **3** [*lutte*] divisive.

déchirement /deʃiʀmɑ̃/ *nm* **1** (souffrance) heartbreak; **2** (conflit) (**entre** between).

déchirer /deʃiʀe/ [1] I *vtr* **1** (mettre en morceaux) to tear [sth] up [*papier, tissu*]; to rip [sth] up [*chair*]; to break [sth] up [*surface*]; **~ un contrat** FIG to go back on a contract; **2** (détériorer) to tear [*vêtement, sac*]; **3** (troubler) [*bruit*] to shatter [*silence*]; [*éclair*] to rend; **4** (diviser) [*conflit*] to split [*groupe, pays*]; **couple déchiré** divided couple; **déchiré entre son devoir et son désir de rester** torn between his duty and his desire to stay; **5** (faire souffrir) to torture [*personne*].

II **se déchirer** *vpr* **1** (se rompre) [*papier, tissu, vête-ment*] to tear; **2** MÉD **se ~ un muscle** to tear a muscle; **3** (s'affronter) [*personnes*] to tear each other apart; **4** LITER (souffrir) [*cœur*] to break.

déchirure /deʃiʀyʀ/ *nf* **1** MÉD tear; **~ à la cuisse** muscle tear in the thigh; **2** (accroc) tear (**de** in); **3** (rupture) break (**de** in); **4** (conflit) rift (**de** within).

déchoir /deʃwaʀ/ [51] I *vtr* JUR (priver) to strip [sb] of [*droit*].

II *vi* (tomber dans un état inférieur) [*personne*] to demean oneself; **~ de son rang** to come down in the world.

déchu, ~e /deʃy/ I *pp* ▶ **déchoir**.

II *pp adj* [*monarque, dictateur*] deposed; [*ange*] fallen.

de-ci /dəsi/ *adv* **~ de-là** here and there.

décibel /desibɛl/ *nm* decibel.

décidé, ~e /deside/ I *pp* ▶ **décider**.

II *pp adj* **1** (arrêté) **c'est ~, je m'en vais** it's settled, I'm leaving; **2** (résolu) [*personne*] determined; [*allure, air*] resolute.

décidément /desidemɑ̃/ *adv* really.

décider /deside/ [1] I *vtr* **1** (prendre la décision de) to decide; **~ une politique** to decide on a policy; **c'est toi qui décides, c'est à toi de ~** it's for you ou up to you to decide; **~ si** to decide whether; **~ qui contacter** to decide who to contact; **c'est ce qui a décidé sa perte** it's what led to his downfall; **2** (per-suader) to persuade (**à faire** to do).

II **décider de** *vtr ind* to decide on [*date, mesure, lieu*]; to fix [*prix*]; **le hasard en décida autrement** fate decided otherwise; **~ du sort de qn** to seal sb's fate.

III **se décider** *vpr* **1** (prendre une décision) to make up one's mind; **tu te décides à parler?** are you going to speak?; **elle s'est enfin décidée à s'excuser** she apolo-gized at last; **être décidé à faire** to be determined to do; **2** (choisir) **se ~ pour** to decide on; **3** (être fixé) [*accord, réunion*] to be decided on; [*date*] to be set; **tout s'est décidé très vite** it all happened very quickly.

décideur /desidœʀ/ *nm* decision-maker.

décigramme /desigʀam/ ▶455⟩ *nm* decigram.

décilitre /desilitʀ/ ▶86⟩ *nm* decilitre GB.

décimal, ~e, *mpl* -aux /desimal, o/ *adj* MATH deci-mal; CHIMIE decinormal.

décimer /desime/ [1] *vtr* to decimate.

décimètre /desimɛtʀ/ *nm* **1** ▶348⟩ (unité) decimetre GB; **2** (instrument) (decimetre GB) ruler; **double ~** (20 centi-metre GB) ruler.

décisif, -ive /desizif, iv/ *adj* GÉN decisive; [*preuve*] conclusive; [*ton, voix*] authoritative.

décision /desizjɔ̃/ *nf* **1** (résolution) decision; **prendre une ~** to make a decision; **prendre la ~ de faire** to decide to do; **2** (fait de décider) **avoir le pouvoir de ~** to be the one who makes the decisions; **3** (détermina-tion) decisiveness.

décisionnel, -elle /desizjɔnɛl/ *adj* [*système, processus*] decision-making (*épith*); **pouvoir ~** power to make decisions.

déclamer /deklame/ [1] *vtr* to declaim.

déclaration /deklaʀasjɔ̃/ *nf* **1** (communication publique) GÉN statement; (officielle) declaration (**sur** about); **~ de guerre** declaration of war; **~ (d'amour)** declaration of love; **faire sa ~ à qn** to declare one's love to sb; **2** ADMIN notification; **~ de naissance** (enregistrement) registration of birth; (information) notification of birth; **3** JUR statement; **~ de vol/perte** report of theft/loss; **~ sous serment** sworn statement.

■ **~ d'impôts** ou **de revenus** (income-)tax return.

déclaré, ~e /deklaʀe/ *adj* [*ennemi*] avowed; [*haine*] professed; [*maladie*] full-blown.

déclarer /deklaʀe/ [1] I *vtr* **1** (dire, proclamer) to declare [*indépendance, intentions*]; **~ son amour** to declare one's love; **~ qn vainqueur** to declare sb the winner; **il a été déclaré coupable** he was found guilty; **~ la séance ouverte** to declare the meeting open; **~ que** to declare that; **~ à qn que** to tell sb that; **~ la guerre à** to declare war on; **2** ADMIN to declare [*marchandise, revenus, employé*]; to report [*vol*]; to register [*naissance, décès*]; **non déclaré** [*somme*] undeclared; [*travail*] illegal.

II **se déclarer** *vpr* **1** (commencer) [*incendie, épidémie*] to break out; [*fièvre*] to start; [*maladie*] to manifest itself; **2** (se dire) **se ~ convaincu** to declare oneself convinced; **se ~ pour/contre qch** to come out for/against sth; **3** (avouer son amour) to declare one's love (**à qn** to sb).

déclasser /deklase/ [1] *vtr* **1** (rétrograder) to downgrade; **2** (mettre en désordre) to jumble up.

déclenchement /deklɑ̃ʃmɑ̃/ *nm* (de mécanisme) release; (d'avalanche) start; (de maladie) onset; (de réaction) start; (de conflit, grève) outbreak.

déclencher /deklɑ̃ʃe/ [1] **I** *vtr* **1** (entraîner) to spark (off) [*protestation*]; to prompt [*décision*]; to cause [*réaction, explosion*]; to start [*avalanche*]; to lead to [*larmes*]; **~ les larmes de qn** to make sb burst into tears; **~ un éclat de rire général** to provoke general laughter; **2** (commencer) to launch [*offensive*]; to begin [*hostilités*]; to start [*grève, polémique*]; **3** (actionner) to set off [*mécanisme*]; **4** ORDINAT to initiate [*opération*].
II se déclencher *vpr* **1** (se mettre en marche) [*alarme*] to go off; [*signal, mécanisme*] to be activated; **2** (commencer) [*douleur, réaction, contractions*] to start; [*grève, guerre*] to break out; [*opération*] to begin.

déclencheur /deklɑ̃ʃœʀ/ *nm* PHOT shutter release.

déclic /deklik/ *nm* **1** (mécanisme) trigger; **2** (bruit) click.

déclin /deklɛ̃/ *nm* GÉN decline; (de sentiment, passion) waning; **~ de la demande** decline in demand; **popularité en ~** declining popularity; **être en** or **sur le ~** [*civilisation, industrie*] to be in decline; [*popularité, prestige*] to be waning; **être sur le** or **son ~** [*homme d'État*] to be on the way out; **le soleil est à son ~** the sun is going down; **au ~ du jour** at the close of day; **au ~ de la vie** in the twilight of life.

déclinaison /deklinɛzɔ̃/ *nf* LING declension.

déclinant, ~e /deklinɑ̃, ɑ̃t/ *adj* [*forces*] waning; [*santé*] failing.

décliner /dekline/ [1] **I** *vtr* **1** (refuser) to decline [*invitation*]; to turn down [*offre*]; **~ toute responsabilité** to disclaim all responsibility; **2** LING to decline; **3** (dire) **~ son identité** to give one's name.
II *vi* [*lumière*] to fade; [*vue, santé*] to deteriorate; [*talent*] to fade; [*enthousiasme*] to wane; [*soleil*] to go down.
III se décliner *vpr* LING to decline.

déclivité /deklivite/ *nf* gradient; **habiter sur une ~** to live on a hill.

décocher /dekɔʃe/ [1] *vtr* to shoot [*flèche*] (à at); **~ un coup de poing à qn** to punch sb.

décoction /dekɔksjɔ̃/ *nf* brew, decoction.

décoder /dekɔde/ [1] *vtr* to decode.

décodeur /dekɔdœʀ/ *nm* (appareil) decoder.

décoiffer /dekwafe/ [1] **I** *vtr* (dépeigner) **~ qn** to ruffle sb's hair; **elle est toute décoiffée** her hair is in a mess; **tu me décoiffes** you are messing up my hair.
II se décoiffer *vpr* (se découvrir) to doff one's hat.

décoincer /dekwɛ̃se/ [12] **I** *vtr* (débloquer) to unjam [*mécanisme, tiroir, porte*]; to free [*clé*]; to get [sth] back to normal [*dos, cou*].
II se décoincer *vpr* [*mécanisme*] to come free.

décolérer /dekɔleʀe/ [14] *vi* **ne pas ~ de la soirée** to stay angry all evening; **sans ~** without letting up.

décollage /dekɔlaʒ/ *nm* **1** (d'avion) take-off; (de fusée) lift-off; **2** (d'enterprise) take-off; **3** (d'affiche, étiquette) peeling off.

décoller /dekɔle/ [1] **I** *vtr* (détacher) to peel off [*étiquette, affiche*]; to remove [*adhésif*]; **~ une étiquette en la laissant tremper** to soak a label off; **~ à la vapeur** to steam [sth] off [*étiquette, papier*]; to steam [sth] open [*enveloppe*].
II *vi* (s'envoler) [*avion*] to take off (**de** from); [*fusée*] to lift off (**de** from); **2** (démarrer) [*industrie*] to take off; [*spectacle*] to get going.
III se décoller *vpr* to come off.

décolleté, ~e /dekɔlte/ **I** *adj* [*vêtement*] low-cut; **pas assez ~** too high-cut; **une robe ~e en V** a V-neck dress.
II *nm* **1** (partie de vêtement) low neckline; **~ plongeant** plunging neckline; **2** (partie du corps) cleavage; **dans son ~** down her cleavage.

décolleter /dekɔlte/ [20] *vtr* IND to cut (from the bar) [*vis, boulons*].

décolleuse /dekɔløz/ *nf* steam stripper.

décolonisation /dekɔlɔnizasjɔ̃/ *nf* decolonization.

décolorant, ~e /dekɔlɔʀɑ̃, ɑ̃t/ **I** *adj* [*agent*] bleaching.
II *nm* bleaching agent.

décoloration /dekɔlɔʀasjɔ̃/ *nf* GÉN discoloration; (de tissu) fading.

décolorer /dekɔlɔʀe/ [1] **I** *vtr* [*substance*] to bleach [*tissu, cheveux*]; [*lumière, lavage*] to cause [sth] to fade.
II se décolorer *vpr* [*tapis, rideau*] to fade.

décombres /dekɔ̃bʀ/ *nmpl* rubble **¢**.

décommander /dekɔmɑ̃de/ [1] **I** *vtr* to call off [*rendez-vous*].
II se décommander *vpr* to cry off GB, to beg off.

décomposer /dekɔ̃poze/ [1] **I** *vtr* **1** (analyser) to break [sth] down [*raisonnement, phrase*] (**en** into); to break down [*eau*]; to disperse [*lumière*]; to resolve [*force*]; MATH to factorize [*expression*]; **2** (déformer) to distort [*traits, visage*]; **visage décomposé** distraught face.
II se décomposer *vpr* **1** (pourrir) [*matière organique*] to decompose; [*société, parti*] to fall apart; **2** (se déformer) [*visage, traits*] to become distorted

décomposition /dekɔ̃pozisjɔ̃/ *nf* **1** (de matière) decomposition; **en ~** decomposing; **2** (de société) disintegration; **en ~** decaying.

décompresser○ /dekɔ̃pʀese/ [1] *vi* to unwind.

décompte /dekɔ̃t/ *nm* **1** (déduction) discount; **2** (calcul détaillé) count; **faire le ~ de** to count [sth] up [*votes, points*]; **3** (relevé) statement.

décompter /dekɔ̃te/ [1] *vtr* **1** (déduire) to deduct (**de** from); **2** (calculer) to work out [*frais*]; to count [*votes, points, personnes*].

déconcentrer /dekɔ̃sɑ̃tʀe/ [1] **I** *vtr* (distraire) to distract.
II se déconcentrer *vpr* [*personne*] to lose one's concentration.

déconcertant, ~e /dekɔ̃sɛʀtɑ̃, ɑ̃t/ *adj* disconcerting; **d'une facilité ~e** ridiculously easy.

déconcerter /dekɔ̃sɛʀte/ [1] *vtr* to disconcert.

déconfit, ~e /dekɔ̃fi, it/ *adj* [*air, mine*] crestfallen.

déconfiture /dekɔ̃fityʀ/ *nf* **1** (échec) (de personne) failure; (de parti, d'équipe) defeat; **2** (faillite) (d'entreprise) collapse.

décongeler /dekɔ̃ʒle/ [17] *vtr, vi* to defrost.

décongestionner /dekɔ̃ʒɛstjɔne/ [1] **I** *vtr* **1** GÉN to ease the pressure on [*universités, services*]; (d'autoroute) to relieve congestion in [*rue, ville*]; **2** MÉD [*médicament*] to relieve congestion in [*organe*]; to clear [*nez*].
II se décongestionner *vpr* to clear.

déconnecté, ~e /dekɔnɛkte/ *adj* [*personne*] out of touch (**de** with).

déconnecter /dekɔnɛkte/ [1] *vtr* **1** to disconnect [*appareil*]; to break [*circuit*]; **2** FIG to dissociate (**de** from).

déconner○ /dekɔne/ [1] *vi* **1** [*personne*] (plaisanter) to kid around○; (dire des bêtises) to talk crap○; (faire l'idiot) to mess around○; **sans ~!** no kidding○!; **2** [*appareil*] to play up○.

déconseillé, ~e /dekɔ̃seje/ **I** *pp* ▶ **déconseiller**.
II *pp adj* [*action*] inadvisable; [*médicament, boisson, nourriture*] not recommended (**à** for); **départ ~ samedi** you are advised not to travel on Saturday.

déconseiller /dekɔ̃seje/ [1] *vtr* **~ qch à qn** to advise sb against sth; **~ à qn de faire** to advise sb against doing; **à ~ aux âmes sensibles** not for the squeamish.

déconsidérer /dekɔ̃sideʀe/ [14] *vtr* to discredit.
II se déconsidérer *vpr* [*journal*] to lower its tone; **tu t'es déconsidéré** it was unworthy of you.

décontaminer /dekɔ̃tamine/ [1] *vtr* to decontaminate.

décontenancer /dekɔ̃tnɑ̃se/ [12] *vtr* to disconcert.

décontractant, ~e /dekɔ̃tʀaktɑ̃, ɑ̃t/ **I** *adj* relaxing.
II *nm* relaxant.

décontracté, ~e /dekɔ̃tʀakte/ **I** *pp* ▶ **décontracter**.
II *pp adj* **1** (détendu) [*personne, soirée*] relaxed; [*mode*] casual; **2** (désinvolte) [*attitude*] laid-back○.

décontracter /dekɔ̃trakte/ [1] *vtr*, **se décontracter** *vpr* to relax.

décontraction /dekɔ̃traksjɔ̃/ *nf* **1** (relaxation) relaxation; **2** (aisance) ease; **3** (désinvolture) casual attitude.

déconvenue /dekɔ̃vəny/ *nf* disappointment.

décor /dekɔr/ *nm* **1** (de pièce) decor; (d'objet) decoration; **2** (cadre) setting; **j'ai besoin de changer de ~** I need a change of scene; **3** CIN, THÉÂT **le ~**, **les ~s** the set; **film tourné en ~ naturel** film shot on location.

décorateur, -trice /dekɔratœr, tris/ ▶374| *nm,f* **1** (de maison) interior decorator; (de vitrine) window dresser; **2** CIN, THÉÂT (concepteur) set designer; (peintre) scene painter.

décoratif, -ive /dekɔratif, iv/ *adj* **1** (destiné à la décoration) ornamental; **2** (qui décore bien) decorative.

décoration /dekɔrasjɔ̃/ *nf* **1** (action) decorating; **2** (garniture) decoration; **~s de Noël** Christmas decorations; **3** (médaille) decoration; **4** (métier) (d'intérieur) interior design; CIN set design; THÉÂT stage design.

décorer /dekɔre/ [1] *vtr* **1** (orner) to decorate (**de** with); (en couture) to trim (**de** with); **2** (médailler) to decorate; **il a été décoré de la médaille militaire** he has been awarded the military medal.

décortiquer /dekɔrtike/ [1] *vtr* **1** to shell [*noix, crabe*]; to peel [*crevette*]; to hull, to husk [*riz, graine*]; **2** to dissect [*texte*].

décorum /dekɔrɔm/ *nm* (bienséance) **observer le ~** to observe the proprieties.

décote /dekɔt/ *nf* FIN (baisse) drop.

découcher /dekuʃe/ [1] *vi* to spend the night away from home.

découdre /dekudʀ/ [76] *vtr* to take [sth] to pieces [*vêtement, rideau*]; to take off [*bouton*]; to undo [*ourlet*].
II *vi* **en ~** to have a fight (**avec** with).
III se découdre *vpr* [*couture, ourlet*] to come undone; [*bouton*] to come off.

découler /dekule/ [1] *vi* **1** (s'ensuivre) to follow (**de** from); **2** (provenir) to result (**de** from).

découpage /dekupaʒ/ *nm* **1** (image découpée) cut-out; **2** (de métal) cutting out; **3** CIN shooting script.
■ **~ électoral** POL division into constituencies GB, districting US.

découpé, ~e /dekupe/ *adj* [*feuille*] lobed; [*côte*] indented.

découper /dekupe/ [1] **I** *vtr* **1** (diviser) to cut up [*tarte*]; to carve [*rôti, volaille*]; to divide up [*territoire, domaine*]; **~ qch en tranches** to cut sth into slices; **2** (extraire) to cut out [*article, photo*]; **~ une photo dans un journal** to cut a photo out of a newspaper; **3** (délimiter) **la lampe découpe des ombres sur le mur** the lamp throws shadows on the wall.
II se découper *vpr* (se profiler) LITER **se ~ sur** to stand out against.

découragé, ~e /dekuraʒe/ *adj* [*personne*] disheartened; [*air*] despondent; [*ton*] dejected.

décourageant, ~e /dekuraʒɑ̃, ɑ̃t/ *adj* disheartening.

découragement /dekuraʒmɑ̃/ *nm* discouragement, despondency.

décourager /dekuraʒe/ [13] **I** *vtr* **1** (déprimer) to dishearten; **se laisser ~** to give up (**par** because of); **2** (déconseiller) **~ qn de faire** to discourage sb from doing; **3** (rebuter) to discourage [*épargne, initiative*]; to deter [*malfaiteur*]; **la pluie va en ~ plusieurs** the rain will put some people off.
II se décourager *vpr* to get discouraged; **ne te décourage pas** don't give up.

décousu, ~e /dekuzy/ **I** *pp* ▶ **découdre**.
II *pp adj* [*vêtement, ourlet*] which has come undone (*épith, après n*).
III *adj* (sans cohésion) [*histoire, discours, exposé*] rambling; (décontracté) [*conversation*] casual.

découvert, ~e¹ /dekuvɛr, ɛrt/ **I** *pp* ▶ **découvrir**.
II *pp adj* **1** (nu) [*épaules*] bare; **avoir la tête ~e** to be bare-headed; **2** (dégagé) [*terrain, pays*] open; **3** (non fermé) [*camion, wagon*] open; [*voiture*] open-topped.

III *nm* FIN overdraft; **~ budgétaire** budget deficit.
IV à découvert *loc adv* **1** FIN **être à ~** [*client, compte*] to be overdrawn; **2** (sans protection) [*combattre*] out in the open.

découverte² /dekuvɛrt/ *nf* discovery; **partir** or **aller à la ~ de** to set off to explore sth.

découvrir /dekuvʀir/ [32] **I** *vtr* **1** (trouver) GÉN to discover; to expose [*complot*]; **faire ~ qch à qn** to introduce sb to sth; **je vais leur faire ~ Paris** I'm going to show them Paris; **2** (montrer) to show [*partie du corps*]; to unveil [*statue*]; **~ son jeu** to show one's hand; **3** (priver de protection) to leave [sth] exposed [*frontière, pièce d'échec*]; (voir) to see [*château, vallée*].
II se découvrir *vpr* **1** (enlever son chapeau) to remove one's hat; **2** (trouver en soi) **elle s'est découvert un talent** she found she had a talent; **3** (s'exposer) (volontairement) **ne te découvre pas trop** keep covered up; (involontairement) [*dormeur*] to kick off one's bedclothes.

décrassage /dekrasaʒ/ *nm* (de moteur) cleaning; (de mur) scrubbing.

décrasser /dekrase/ [1] **I** *vtr* (nettoyer) to get [sb/sth] clean.
II se décrasser *vpr* (se laver) to clean oneself up; **se ~ les mains** to scrub one's hands clean; **se ~ les poumons**○ to get some fresh air into one's lungs.

décrêper /dekrepe/ [1] *vtr* to straighten [*cheveux*].

décrépit, ~e /dekrepi, it/ *adj* [*personne*] decrepit; [*bâtiment*] dilapidated; [*mur*] crumbling.

décrépitude /dekrepityd/ *nf* (de mœurs) degeneration; (de régime) decay; (de personne) decrepitude; **tomber en ~** [*idéologie, système*] to degenerate; [*lieu, monument*] to crumble.

décret /dekrɛ/ *nm* decree.

décréter /dekrete/ [14] *vtr* **1** (par décret) to order; **~ le couvre-feu** to impose a curfew; **2** (autoritairement) to decree (**que** that); (dire avec force) to declare.

décret-loi, *pl* **décrets-lois** /dekrɛlwa/ *nm* government decree.

décrier /dekrije/ [2] *vtr* **le roman a été très décrié** the novel met with a harsh reception; **après avoir été tant décrié, le mariage redevient à la mode** after getting a bad press for so long, marriage is back.

décrire /dekrir/ [67] *vtr* **1** (dépeindre) to describe; **2** (suivre) to describe [*courbe*]; to follow [*trajectoire*].

décrochement /dekrɔʃmɑ̃/ *nm* (discontinuité) (en creux) indentation; (en saillie) projection.

décrocher /dekrɔʃe/ [1] **I** *vtr* **1** (détacher) to take down [*tableau, jambon, tenture*]; to uncouple [*wagon*]; **~ son téléphone** (pour parler) to pick up the receiver; (pour ne pas être dérangé) to take the phone off the hook; **2**○ (obtenir) to clinch○, to get [*marché*]; to land○, to get [*contrat, poste, rôle*]; to get [*diplôme*]; to win [*titre*].
II *vi* **1**○ (cesser une activité) to give up; **2**○ (en parlant de tabac, drogue) to kick○ the habit; **3**○ (cesser de s'intéresser) to switch off GB, to tune out US; **4** MIL to disengage; **5** AVIAT to stall.
III se décrocher *vpr* [*tableau*] to come off its hook; [*rideau*] to come down; [*jupe*] to come undone.
IDIOMES ~ **le gros lot** to hit the jackpot.

décroiser /dekrwaze/ [1] *vtr* **~ les bras** to unfold one's arms; TECH to uncross [*fils*].

décroissant, ~e /dekrwasɑ̃, ɑ̃t/ *adj* [*bruit*] fading; [*intensité*] lessening; [*fortune, pouvoir*] declining; [*vitesse, nombre*] decreasing; [*lune*] waning; **par** or **en ordre ~** in descending order.

décroître /dekrwatr/ [72] *vi* **1** (baisser) [*niveau*] to fall; [*eau, rivière*] to go down; [*lune*] to wane; **2** (diminuer) [*jour*] to get shorter; [*lumière, bruit*] to fade; [*inflation, chômage*] to go down; [*influence, force*] to decline.

décrotter /dekrɔte/ [1] *vtr* **1** to scrape the dirt off [*chaussures*]; **2**○ to civilize○ [*personne*].

décrue /dekry/ *nf* (d'eaux) fall ou drop in the (water) level; **le fleuve est en ~** the level of the river is falling.

décrypter /dekripte/ [1] *vtr* **1** (décoder) to decipher [*signes, langue*]; **2** (interpréter) to interpret [*propos*].

déçu, ~e /desy/ **I** *pp* ▶ **décevoir**.

II *pp adj* [*personne*] disappointed (**de** or **par** by); [*espoir*] thwarted, foiled; **être ~ dans ses attentes** to feel let down.
III *nm,f* disillusioned person.

déculotter /dekylɔte/ [1] *vtr* **~ qn** to take off sb's trousers GB ou pants US.

déculpabiliser /dekylpabilize/ [1] **I** *vtr* to free [sb] of guilt [*personne*].
II se déculpabiliser *vpr* [*personne*] to stop feeling guilty.

décuple /dekypl/ **I** *adj* **une somme ~ d'une autre** a sum ten times greater than another.
II *nm* **ma mise m'a rapporté le ~** I got back ten times my original stake.

décupler /dekyple/ [1] **I** *vtr* **1** MATH to multiply [sth] by ten; **2** FIG to increase ou to multiply [sth] tenfold [*énergie, forces*]; **~ les forces de qn** to give sb the strength of ten.
II *vi* [*population, ressources*] to increase tenfold.

dédaigner /dedeɲe/ [1] *vtr* GÉN to despise [*personne, gloire, richesse*]; **ce n'est pas à ~** (somme, titre) it's not to be sneezed at ou despised; **dédaigné de ses contemporains** spurned by his/her contemporaries; **il ne dédaigne pas la bonne chère** he's not averse to good food.

dédaigneusement /dedeɲøzmɑ̃/ *adv* [*regarder, parler*] disdainfully; [*accueillir*] with disdain.

dédaigneux, -euse /dedeɲø, øz/ *adj* [*ton, sourire, air*] disdainful, scornful; **être ~ du danger** to be unmindful of danger; **être ~ des honneurs** to have no interest in glory.

dédain /dedɛ̃/ *nm* contempt (**de** for), disdain (**de** for).

dédale /dedal/ *nm* **1** (de couloirs, bâtiments) maze; **2** (de lois, formalités) labyrinth.

Dédale /dedal/ *npr* Daedalus.

dedans /dədɑ̃/ **I** *adv* inside; **il vaut mieux dîner ~** it would be better to eat inside ou indoors; **j'ai perdu mon sac et mes clés étaient ~** I've lost my bag and my keys were in it; **essaie ce fauteuil, on est très bien ~** try this armchair, it's very comfortable; **il n'y a rien ~** there's nothing in it ou inside.
II en dedans *loc adv* (à l'intérieur) inside.

dédicace /dedikas/ *nf* (inscription) (imprimée) dedication (**à qn** to sb); (manuscrite) inscription (**à qn** to sb); **faire une ~ à qn** to sign sth for sb.

dédicacer /dedikase/ [12] *vtr* **1** (dédier) to dedicate (**à** to); **2** (signer) to sign [*ouvrage, photographie*] (**à** for).

dédier /dedje/ [2] *vtr* **1** (offrir en hommage) to dedicate [*œuvre, pensées*] (**à** to); **2** (consacrer) to dedicate [*vie, efforts*] (**à** to); to devote [*soirée*] (**à** to); **3** RELIG to dedicate [*chapelle*] (**à** to).

dédire: se dédire /dediʀ/ [65] *vpr* to back out.

dédommagement /dedɔmaʒmɑ̃/ *nm* compensation ¢ (**de** for); **à titre de ~** in compensation (**pour** for).

dédommager /dedɔmaʒe/ [13] *vtr* **1** (indemniser) to compensate (**de** for); **être dédommagé** to get compensation; **2** (offrir une compensation à) **~ qn de qch** to make it up to sb for sth.

dédouanement /dedwanmɑ̃/ *nm* customs clearance.

dédouaner /dedwane/ [1] **I** *vtr* **1** COMM to clear [sth] through customs [*marchandises*]; **2** (disculper) to clear (**de** of; **auprès de** in the eyes of).
II se dédouaner *vpr* to rehabilitate oneself.

dédoublement /dedubləmɑ̃/ *nm* **~ de la personnalité** split personality.

dédoubler /deduble/ [1] **I** *vtr* (diviser) to split [sth] in two [*groupe*]; to separate [sth] into strands [*câble*].
II se dédoubler *vpr* (se diviser) [*groupe*] to split in two; [*ongle*] to split; [*rayon, image*] to split in two; [*fil, laine, câble*] to come apart.

dédramatiser /dedʀamatize/ [1] **I** *vtr* to make [sth] less traumatic [*divorce, examen*]; to play [sth] down [*maladie, situation*]; to play down the significance of [*événement*].
II *vi* to play things down.

déductible /dedyktibl/ *adj* deductible (**de** from); **~ des impôts** tax-deductible.

déduction /dedyksjɔ̃/ *nf* **1** (raisonnement) deduction; **par ~** by deduction; **2** (conclusion) deduction; **3** (soustraction) deduction; **après ~ de, ~ faite de** after deducting; **venir en ~** to be deducted (**de** from).

déduire /dedɥiʀ/ [69] **I** *vtr* **1** (tirer la conséquence) to deduce (**de** from; **que** that); **2** (supposer) to infer (**de** from; **que** that); **3** (soustraire) to deduct (**de** from); **frais déduits, une fois déduits les frais** after deduction of expenses.
II se déduire *vpr* **1** (être induit) to be inferred (**de** from); **2** (découler) to be deduced (**de** from); **3** (être soustrait) to be deducted (**de** from).

déesse /deɛs/ *nf* goddess.

défaillance /defajɑ̃s/ *nf* **1** (mauvais fonctionnement) failure; **2** (moment de faiblesse) **il a eu une ~ à 100 mètres de l'arrivée** he began to flag 100 metresGB from the line; **volonté sans ~** iron will.

défaillant, -e /defajɑ̃, ɑ̃t/ *adj* **1** (qui fonctionne mal) [*moteur, système*] faulty; **2** (inefficace) [*organisation, service, pouvoir*] inefficient; **3** (qui faiblit) [*santé, mémoire*] failing; (près de s'évanouir) [*personne*] fainting.

défaillir /defajiʀ/ [28] *vi* **1** (s'évanouir) to faint; **se sentir ~** to feel faint; **~ de faim** to feel faint with hunger; **~ de bonheur** to be overwhelmed with joy; **2** (faiblir) [*mémoire, santé*] to fail; **soutenir qn sans ~** to show unflinching support for sb.

défaire /defɛʀ/ [10] **I** *vtr* **1** (ce qui est fait) to undo [*paquet, chignon, ourlet, couture, assemblage*]; to unwind [*pelote*]; to unravel [*tricot, écheveau*]; to break [sth] up [*puzzle*]; to unpack [*valise*]; **le lit n'était pas défait** the bed hadn't been slept in; **2** (détacher) to undo [*cravate, bouton, ceinture, soutien-gorge*]; to untie [*lacet, nœud*]; **ta jupe est défaite** your skirt has come undone; **3** (casser) to break up [*union, alliance*]; **4** (infliger une défaite) to defeat [*armée, adversaire*]; **5** (délivrer) **~ qn de** to free sb from [*liens*]; to rid sb of [*habitudes, préjugés, illusions*].
II se défaire *vpr* **1** (ce qui était fait) [*nœud, ourlet*] to come undone; **2** (se casser) [*alliance, amitié*] to break up; **3** (se débarrasser) **se ~ de** (volontairement) to get rid of [*objet, animal, importun*]; to rid oneself of [*croyance, habitude*]; (à regret) to part with [*objet, animal*]; **4** (se troubler) [*visage, mine*] to fall; **le visage défait** looking haggard.

défaite /defɛt/ *nf* defeat.

défaitisme /defetism/ *nm* defeatism.

défalquer /defalke/ [1] *vtr* to deduct (**de** from).

défaut /defo/ **I** *nm* **1** (moral) fault; **n'avoir aucun ~** to be perfect; **se mettre en ~** to put oneself in the wrong; **prendre qn en ~** to catch sb out; **2** (physique, matériel, esthétique) GÉN defect; (de tissu, verre, gemme) flaw (**de** in); (de théorie, raisonnement, d'œuvre d'art) flaw (**de** in); **avoir** or **présenter des ~s** [*machine, construction*] to be faulty; **sans ~** [*système, machine*] perfect; [*rubis, raisonnement*] flawless; **le ~ de la cuirasse de qn** FIG the chink in sb's armourGB; **3** (insuffisance) shortage (**de** of); (absence) lack (**de** of); **faire ~** [*argent, ressources*] to be lacking; [*signature, document*] to be missing; **le talent leur fait ~** they lack talent; **le courage leur a fait ~** their courage failed them; **le temps m'a fait ~** I didn't have enough time; **4** JUR **~ de paiement** non-payment; **par ~** [*condamné, jugé*] in absentia; **faire ~** [*accusé, témoin*] to fail to appear in court.
II à défaut de *loc prép* **à ~ de miel, utilisez du sucre** if you have no honey, use sugar; **à ~ de paiement immédiat** failing prompt payment; **à ~ de quoi** failing which; **à ~ de mieux** for want of anything better.
■ **~ de construction** structural defect; **~ de fabrication** manufacturing fault; **~ de prononciation** speech impediment.

défaveur /defavœʀ/ *nf* **1** (perte d'estime) **être en ~ auprès de qn** to be out of favourGB with sb; **2** (désavantage) **il s'est trompé de 30 francs en ma ~** he overcharged me 30 francs; **mon âge a joué en ma ~** my age went against me.

défavorable /defavɔʀabl/ adj [situation, conditions] unfavourableGB (**à** to); [personne, gouvernement] opposed (**à** to).

défavorablement /defavɔʀabləmɑ̃/ adv unfavourablyGB; **juger ~** to have an unfavourableGB opinion of.

défavorisé, ~e /defavɔʀize/ **I** pp ▸ **défavoriser**.
II pp adj [milieu, personne] underprivileged; [région, pays] disadvantaged.
III nm,f underprivileged person.

défavoriser /defavɔʀize/ [1] vtr **1** (léser) [impôt, mesure sociale] to discriminate against; **2** (handicaper) [difformité physique, défaut] to put [sb] at a disadvantage; **3** (être injuste envers) [examinateur] to put [sb] at a disadvantage.

défection /defɛksjɔ̃/ nf **1** (abandon) (d'alliés) desertion; (pour un autre parti, pays) defection; **faire ~** to defect; **2** (absence) nonappearance; **faire ~** to back out.

défectueux, -euse /defɛktɥø, øz/ adj [matériel] faulty, defective; [raisonnement] flawed; [organisation] poor.

défendable /defɑ̃dabl/ adj MIL [position, ville] defensible; [point de vue] tenable; [conduite] justifiable; **pas ~** [ville] indefensible; [thèse] untenable; [conduite] indefensible, inexcusable; **l'accusé n'est pas ~** the defendant has no case.

défendant: **à son corps défendant** /asɔ̃kɔʀdefɑ̃dɑ̃/ loc adv unwillingly.

défendre /defɑ̃dʀ/ [6] **I** vtr **1** (interdire) **~ qch à qn** to forbid sb sth; **~ que qn fasse, ~ à qn de faire** to forbid sb to do; **ne fume pas ici, c'est défendu** you can't smoke here; **l'alcool/le tabac m'est défendu** I'm not allowed to drink/to smoke; **2** (protéger) (généralement) to defend [personne, pays, honneur, intérêts] (**contre** against); to fight for [droit]; (dans une circonstance) to stand up for [ami, idées, principe]; JUR to defend [accusé]; SPORT to defend [titre, but]; **~ qn/qch au péril de sa vie** to risk one's life in defenceGB of sb/ sth; **~ une cause** to champion a cause.
II se défendre vpr **1** (lutter) (généralement) to defend oneself (**contre** against); (dans une circonstance) to stand up for oneself (**contre** against); (être défendable) [argument, thèse] to be tenable; **cette opinion se défend** it's a valid opinion; **il préfère attendre, et ça se défend** he'd rather wait, and he's got a point; **3** (se protéger) to protect oneself (**de** or **contre** from ou against); **se ~ contre le désespoir** to ward off despair; **4**○ (se débrouiller) to get by; **se ~ en français** to be quite good at French; **se ~ bien en affaires** to do very well in business; **5** (nier) **se ~ d'être jaloux** to deny being jealous; **6** (s'empêcher) **se ~ de faire qch** to refrain from doing sth; **on ne peut se ~ de penser que...** one can't help thinking that...

défense /defɑ̃s/ nf **1** (interdiction) **'~ de pêcher/ fumer'** 'no fishing/smoking'; **'~ d'entrer'** 'no entry'; **'~ de toucher'** (please) do not touch'; **~ d'en parler devant lui** don't mention it in front of him; **2** (contre un agresseur) GÉN, MIL, SPORT defenceGB (**contre** against); (moyens, ouvrages) **~s** defencesGB; **courir à la ~ de qn** to leap to sb's defenceGB; **pour sa ~, elle a dit que...** in her defenceGB, she said that...; **le budget de la ~** (nationale) the defenceGB budget; **armes de ~** defensive weapons; **assurer la ~ du territoire** to defend the country; **sans ~** (faible) helpless; (sans protection) unprotected; **la ~ de l'environnement** the protection of the environment; **la ~ de la langue française** the preservation of the French language; **association pour la ~ des consommateurs** consumer rights organization; **faire grève pour la ~ de l'emploi** to strike against job cuts; **prendre la ~ de qn/qch** to stand up for sb/sth; **3** MÉD, PSYCH defenceGB; **les ~s de l'organisme** the body's defencesGB; **les ~s immunitaires** the immune system; **4** ZOOL (d'éléphant, de sanglier, morse) tusk.

défenseur /defɑ̃sœʀ/ nm defender; **se faire le ~ des faibles** to defend the weak.

défensive /defɑ̃siv/ nf **être** or **se tenir sur la ~** to be on the defensive.

déférence /defeʀɑ̃s/ nf deference (**pour, envers** to); **par ~ pour** out of ou in deference to.

déférent, ~e /defeʀɑ̃, ɑ̃t/ adj **se montrer ~** to show respect (**envers, à l'égard de** for).

déferlement /defɛʀləmɑ̃/ nm (d'articles, images) flood; (de violence, protestations) upsurge (**de** in); (de passion) surge; (de paroles) torrent; (de louanges) flood; **un ~ de critiques** a barrage of criticism.

déferler /defɛʀle/ [1] vi [vague] to break (**sur** on); [violence, protestations] to erupt; [injures] to pour out; [articles] to flood in; [personnes] to pour (**sur** into; **dans** through); **une vague de racisme déferle sur la France** a wave of racism is sweeping through France.

défi /defi/ nm **1** (gageure) challenge; **lancer un ~ à qn** to challenge sb; **relever un ~** to take up a challenge; **c'est un ~ aux lois de l'équilibre** it defies the laws of gravity; **2** (provocation) act of defiance.

défiance /defjɑ̃s/ nf distrust, mistrust; **avec ~** warily; **sans ~** unsuspectingly, trustingly.

défiant, ~e /defjɑ̃, ɑ̃t/ adj distrustful, wary.

déficeler /defisle/ [19] vtr to untie [paquet].

déficience /defisjɑ̃s/ nf **1** MÉD deficiency; **~ en calcium** calcium deficiency; **~ physique** physical handicap; **~ immunitaire** immunodeficiency; **2** (défaut) deficiency; **les ~s de l'intrigue** weaknesses in the plot.

déficient, ~e /defisjɑ̃, ɑ̃t/ adj **1** MÉD [cœur, muscle] deficient; **mentalement ~** mentally defective; **2** (insuffisant) [système, contrôle] inadequate.

déficit /defisit/ nm **1** COMM, ÉCON, FIN deficit; **2** MÉD deficiency.

déficitaire /defisitɛʀ/ adj [budget, compte] showing a deficit (jamais épith); [entreprise] showing a loss (jamais épith); [activité, secteur] loss-making (épith); [ressources] showing a shortfall (jamais épith).

défier /defje/ [2] vtr **1** (provoquer) to challenge [rival, adversaire]; **~ qn en combat singulier** to challenge sb to single combat; **~ qn de prouver** to defy sb to prove; **je te défie de plonger** I dare you to dive; **~ qn du regard** to stare defiantly at sb; **2** (braver) to defy [danger, mort, opinion]; **cela défie la raison et l'entendement** it is beyond belief; **prix défiant toute concurrence** unbeatable price.

défigurer /defigyʀe/ [1] vtr GÉN to disfigure; to mutilate [texte]; to distort [pensée, propos].

défilé /defile/ nm **1** (de fête) parade; (de manifestants) march; **2** (de visiteurs, candidats) stream; **3** GÉOG gorge.
■ **~ aérien** flypast GB, flyover US; **~ militaire** march-past; **~ de mode** fashion show.

défiler /defile/ [1] **I** vi **1** (marcher en rangs) (pour célébrer) to parade; (pour manifester) to march; **2** (se succéder) [personnes] to come and go; [minutes, kilomètres] to add up; **~ devant** (devant un cercueil, un lieu) to file past; [mannequin] to parade in front of; **les souvenirs défilaient dans ma mémoire** memories thronged in; **3** (se dérouler) [images, paysage] to unfold; **~ rapidement** to flash past; **voir ~ sa vie en quelques secondes** to see one's life flash before one's eyes; **4** ORDINAT [texte] to scroll (**vers le bas** down; **vers le haut** up).
II se défiler○ vpr **se ~ au moment de faire qch** to get out of doing sth.

défini, ~e /defini/ adj **1** GÉN clearly defined; **mal ~** [sentiment] vague; [contour, image, circonstances] ill-defined; **bien ~** well-defined (épith); **2** LING [article] definite.

définir /definiʀ/ [3] vtr to define [mot, politique]; to define [personne] (**comme** as); **~ qch comme une priorité** to make sth top priority; **~ la gestion comme un art** to see management as an art.

définitif, -ive /definitif, iv/ **I** adj [comptes, rapport, accord] final; [édition] definitive; [refus] final; **rien de ~** nothing definite; **renvoi ~** SCOL expulsion (**de** from); **'fermeture définitive'** COMM 'closing down'.
II en définitive loc adv at the end of the day.

définition /definisjɔ̃/ nf GÉN definition; (de mots croisés) clue; **par ~** by definition.

définitivement /definitivmɑ̃/ adv [fermer, séparer, cesser] for good.

défiscalisé, **~e** /defiskalize/ adj tax-exempt (épith).

déflagration /deflagrasjɔ̃/ nf (explosion) detonation.

défoncé, **~e** /defɔ̃se/ adj [fauteuil, divan] sagging (épith); [chaise] with a broken seat (épith, après n); [chemin] potholed, full of potholes (après n); [trottoir] full of holes (après n).

défoncer /defɔ̃se/ [12] vtr to smash [vitrine, barricade]; to break [sth] down [porte]; to break the springs of [divan, sommier]; to smash [sth] in [aile, arrière d'une voiture]; to dent [chapeau]; **il lui a défoncé la mâchoire**○ he broke his jaw; **la pluie a défoncé le terrain** the rain has churned up the ground.

déformant, **~e** /defɔʀmɑ̃, ɑ̃t/ adj [miroir] distorting.

déformation /defɔʀmasjɔ̃/ nf (d'objet, image, de fait, propos) distortion; **~ de la colonne vertébrale** spinal deformity; **c'est de la ~ professionnelle** it's a habit that comes from the job.

déformé, **~e** /defɔʀme/ adj [visage, traits, image, vérité] distorted; [objet] misshapen; [corps, membre] misshapen; [vêtement] shapeless; [esprit] warped; **traits ~s par la douleur/colère** features contorted with pain/anger; **mains ~es par l'âge** hands gnarled with age; **chaussée ~e** uneven (road) surface.

déformer /defɔʀme/ [1] **I** vtr **1** (endommager) to bend [sth] (out of shape) [pare-chocs, aile d'avion]; **tu vas le ~** you'll get it out of shape; **2** (transformer) to distort [image, traits]; **3** (fausser) to distort [vérité, faits]; **on a déformé mes propos** (par erreur) I've been misquoted; (à dessein) my words have been twisted.
II se déformer vpr GÉN to lose its shape; [pantalon] to go GB ou become baggy.

défoulement /defulmɑ̃/ nm letting off steam ⊄.

défouler /defule/ [1] **I** vtr **1** [activité] to release tension in [personne]; **2** [personne] **~ sa colère contre qn** to vent one's anger on sb.
II se défouler vpr (dépenser de l'énergie) to let off steam; (se détendre) to let one's hair down○; **se ~ sur qn** to take it out on sb.

défraîchi, **~e** /defʀeʃi/ adj [vêtement, rideau] worn; [tissu, beauté, couleur] faded.

défrayer /defʀeje/ [21] vtr **1** (être le sujet de) **~ la conversation** to be the main topic of conversation; **~ la chronique** to be the talk of the town; **2** (rembourser) **~ qn** to pay sb's expenses.

défricher /defʀiʃe/ [1] vtr to clear [bois, terre]; **~ le terrain** FIG to do the groundwork.

défriser /defʀize/ [1] vtr to straighten [cheveux].

défroisser /defʀwase/ [1] vtr to smooth out [vêtement, papier].

défroque /defʀɔk/ nf (vêtements ridicules) ridiculous outfit.

défroqué, **~e** /defʀɔke/ adj [prêtre] defrocked.

défunt, **~e** /defœ̃, œ̃t/ **I** adj [personne] late; [empire, grandeur] former; [idéologie] defunct.
II nm,f **le ~**, **la ~e** the deceased.

dégagé, **~e** /degaʒe/ adj [vue, passage, route, ciel] clear; [cou, front] bare; [air, allure] casual.

dégagement /degaʒmɑ̃/ nm **1** (d'un lieu) clearing (de of); **2** (de vestiges) digging out (de of); **3** SPORT (au football) clearance (de qn by sb).

dégager /degaʒe/ [13] **I** vtr **1** (libérer physiquement) to free; **2** (débarrasser) to clear [bureau, route, passage]; **'dégagez, s'il vous plaît'** (ordre de la police) 'move along please'; **dégage**○! clear off○! GB, get lost○!; **demande au coiffeur de te ~ les oreilles** ask the hairdresser to cut your hair away from your ears; **3** (extraire) to find [idée, morale, sens]; **~ les grands axes d'une politique** to highlight the main points of a policy; **4** (laisser échapper) [volcan, voiture] to emit [odeur, gaz]; [casserole] to let out [vapeur]; **~ de la chaleur** to give off heat; **5** FIN **~ des crédits pour la construction d'une école** to make funds available for

a school to be built; **~ des bénéfices** to make a profit; **~ un excédent commercial** to show a trade surplus; **6** (racheter ce qui était en gage) **~ une montre du mont-de-piété** to redeem a watch from the pawnbroker; **7** (libérer moralement) **~ qn d'une responsabilité** to relieve sb of a responsibility; **~ qn d'une obligation** to release sb from an obligation; **8** (au football, rugby) **~ la balle** to clear the ball; **9** (déboucher) to unblock [nez, sinus]; to clear [bronches].
II se dégager vpr **1** (se libérer) to free oneself/itself; **se ~ d'une situation piégée** to get out of a tricky situation; **2** MÉTÉO [temps, ciel] to clear; **3** (émaner) **se ~ de** [chaleur, gaz, fumée] to come out of; [odeur, parfum] to emanate from; **4** (apparaître) **un charme désuet se dégage du roman** the novel has an element of old world charm about it; **la conclusion qui se dégage de la discussion** the outcome of the debate.

dégaine○ /degɛn/ nf (allure) odd appearance; (démarche) odd walk; **avoir une ~ de cow-boy** (allure) to look like a cowboy; (démarche) to walk like a cowboy.

dégainer /degene/ [1] vtr **1** (sortir de son étui) to draw [arme]; **2** ÉLECTROTECH to strip [câble].

dégarni, **~e** /degaʀni/ adj **1** (sans cheveux) **avoir le crâne ~** to be balding; **front ~** receding hairline; **2** (vide) [rayons, magasin] bare; [compte] empty.

dégarnir /degaʀniʀ/ [3] **I** vtr to empty [rayon].
II se dégarnir vpr **1** (perdre ses cheveux) **il a le front qui se dégarnit** his hair is receding, he's got a receding hair line; **2** (se vider) [rue, salle] to empty.

dégât /dega/ nm damage ⊄; **limiter les ~s** to limit the damage; **faire des ~s** [personne] to do damage; [explosion] to cause damage.

dégel /deʒɛl/ nm **1** MÉTÉO thaw; **c'est le ~** it's thawing; **2** (de tensions) thaw; (de crédits) unfreezing.

dégeler /deʒle/ [17] **I** vtr **1** (détendre) to improve [relations]; to warm up [public]; **~ l'atmosphère** to break the ice; **2** (débloquer) to unfreeze [crédits].
II vi [sol, lac] to thaw (out).
III se dégeler vpr [relations, situation] to thaw; [public] to warm up; [personne] to thaw out.

dégénéré, **~e** /deʒeneʀe/ adj, nm,f degenerate.

dégénérer /deʒeneʀe/ [14] vi **1** (mal tourner) [bagarre, incident] to get out of hand; **~ en** to degenerate into; **2** (s'abâtardir) [race, plante, espèce] to degenerate.

dégénérescence /deʒeneʀesɑ̃s/ nf (d'organe, espèce) degeneration; **en pleine ~** [pays] in decline.

dégingandé, **~e** /deʒɛ̃gɑ̃de/ adj lanky.

dégivrage /deʒivʀaʒ/ nm **1** AUT, AVIAT de-icing; **2** (de réfrigérateur) defrosting.

dégivrer /deʒivʀe/ [1] vtr to de-ice [pare-brise, serrure]; to defrost [réfrigérateur].

déglacer /deglase/ [12] vtr CULIN to deglaze.

déglingué○, **~e** /deglɛ̃ge/ adj dilapidated.

déglinguer○ /deglɛ̃ge/ [1] **I** vtr to bust○, to break [appareil, objet].
II se déglinguer vpr [mécanisme] to go wrong; [appareil] to break down; **se ~ la santé** to wreck○ one's health.

déglutir /deglytiʀ/ [3] vtr, vi to swallow.

dégommer○ /degɔme/ [1] vtr **1** (licencier) to fire; **2** (décrier) **se faire ~** (en flèche) to get a terrible telling-off; **3** (atteindre) to hit (avec with).

dégonflé, **~e** /degɔ̃fle/ **I** adj [ballon] deflated; [pneu] flat.
II○ nm,f chicken○, coward.

dégonfler /degɔ̃fle/ [1] **I** vtr **1** (vider de son air) to deflate [pneu, ballon]; **2**○ (réduire) to streamline [effectifs]; to reduce [masse monétaire].
II vi (désenfler) [cheville, bosse] to go down.
III se dégonfler vpr **1** (se vider de son air) [bouée] to deflate; [pneu, ballon] to go down; **2**○ (manquer de courage) [personne] to chicken out○, to lose one's nerve.

dégot(t)er○ /degɔte/ [1] vtr to find.

dégouliner /deguline/ [1] vi **1** [liquide] to trickle; **2** [personne, objet] to drip (de with).

dégoupiller /degupije/ [1] *vtr* ~ **une grenade** to pull the pin out of a grenade.

dégourdi, **~e** /deguʀdi/ *adj* (débrouillard) smart.

dégourdir /deguʀdiʀ/ [3] **I** *vtr* **1** (réchauffer) to warm [sth] up [*doigts, pieds*]; **2** (assouplir) to loosen [sth] up [*doigts, membres*]; **3** (rendre plus hardi) ~ **des enfants** to bring children out of themselves.

II se dégourdir *vpr* **1** (se détendre) **se** ~ **(les jambes)** to stretch one's legs; **2** (devenir plus hardi) to come out of oneself.

dégoût /degu/ *nm* **1** (répulsion) disgust (**devant** at; **pour** for); **avec un profond** ~ with absolute disgust; **2** (lassitude) weariness; ~ **de la vie** world-weariness; **3** (satiété) nausea; **boire jusqu'au** ~ to drink until one feels sick.

dégoûtant, **~e** /degutɑ̃, ɑ̃t/ *adj* **1** (sale) filthy; **2**○ (scandaleux) disgusting; **3** (répugnant) [*habitude*] revolting; [*créature*] disgusting; **il fait un temps** ~ **aujourd'hui** the weather is foul today.

dégoûté, **~e** /degute/ *adj* [*commentaire, ton*] disgusted; **d'un air** ~ with disgust; **être** ~ **de qch** to have had enough of sth; **ne pas être** ~ to have a strong stomach; **faire le** ~ to turn one's nose up.

dégoûter /degute/ [1] **I** *vtr* **1** (répugner) to disgust; (écœurer) to make [sb] feel sick; **ça me dégoûte** it's disgusting; **2** (ôter l'envie) to put [sb] off; ~ **qn de qch/de faire** to put sb off sth/off doing; **3** (scandaliser) to sicken; **ça me dégoûte (de voir) que/de voir comment** it makes me sick (to see) that/the way.

II se dégoûter *vpr* (se lasser) **se** ~ **de** to get tired of.

dégradant, **~e** /degʀadɑ̃, ɑ̃t/ *adj* [*activité, travail*] degrading.

dégradation /degʀadasjɔ̃/ *nf* **1** (dégât provoqué) damage ¢; **la** ~ **du site** the damage caused to the area; **2** (usure naturelle) deterioration; **3** (détérioration) (de situation) deterioration (**de** in); (de mœurs) decline (**de** in); **la** ~ **des conditions de vie** the deterioration in the standard of living; **la** ~ **du pouvoir d'achat** the erosion in purchasing power.

■ ~ **civique** loss of civil rights; ~ **militaire** dishonourable[GB] discharge.

dégradé, **~e** /degʀade/ **I** *adj* **tons** **~s** shaded tones; **coupe ~e** layered cut.

II *nm* **1** (de couleurs) gradation; **peint en** ~ painted in shaded tones; **2** (en coiffure) layered cut.

dégrader /degʀade/ [1] **I** *vtr* **1** (détériorer) to damage; **2** MIL (destituer) to cashier [*officier*]; **3** ART to shade [sth] from dark to light [*tons, couleurs*]; **4** (avilir) [*vice*] to degrade [*personne*].

II se dégrader *vpr* (se détériorer) to deteriorate.

dégrafer /degʀafe/ [1] **I** *vtr* to undo.

II se dégrafer *vpr* to come undone.

dégraissage /degʀɛsaʒ/ *nm* (d'effectifs) reduction (**de** in); (d'entreprise) streamlining ¢ (**de** of); **~s de personnel** staff cuts.

dégraissant, **~e** /degʀɛsɑ̃, ɑ̃t/ *adj* [*produit, liquide*] grease-removing (*épith*).

dégraisser /degʀɛse/ [1] *vtr* **1**○ (réduire le personnel) to streamline [*effectifs*]; **2** (nettoyer) to dry-clean [*vêtement*].

degré /dəgʀe/ *nm* **1** ▶587 | (d'angle, de température) degree; **il fait 15 ~s dehors** it's 15 degrees outside; **2** (concentration) **ce vin fait 12°** this wine contains 12% alcohol; **cette boisson fait combien de ~s?** what is the alcohol content of this drink?; **3** (niveau) degree (**de** of); (stade d'une évolution) stage; **par ~s** gradually; **à un moindre** ~ to a lesser extent; **jusqu'à un certain** ~ up to a point; **susceptible au dernier** or **au plus haut** ~ extremely touchy; **un tel** ~ **de cruauté est-il possible?** is it possible that anyone could be so cruel?; **4** (dans un classement) degree; **brûlures du premier** ~ first-degree burns; **cousins au premier/second** ~ first/second cousins; **enseignement du premier/second** ~ primary/secondary education; **5** (dans une interprétation) **premier/deuxième** or **second** ~ literal/hidden meaning; **prendre ce que quelqu'un dit au premier** ~ to take what somebody

says literally; **tout discours politique est à interpréter au deuxième** or **second** ~ you need to read between the lines of any political speech; **6** (marche) step; **les ~s de l'échelle sociale** the rungs of the social ladder.

■ ~ **Celsius** degree Celsius; ~ **Fahrenheit** degree Fahrenheit; ~ **de parenté** degree of kinship.

dégressif, **-ive** /degʀesif, iv/ *adj* [*impôt*] graduated; **tarifs ~s** tapering charges.

dégrèvement /degʀɛvmɑ̃/ *nm* ~ **(fiscal)** tax relief.

dégriffé, **~e** /degʀife/ *adj* **robe/veste ~e** marked-down designer dress/jacket.

dégringolade○ /degʀɛ̃gɔlad/ *nf* **1** (de personne, d'objets) fall; **2** (de cours, prix) collapse.

dégringoler○ /degʀɛ̃gɔle/ [1] **I** *vtr* to race down [*escalier, pente*].

II *vi* **1** (tomber) [*personne*] to tumble; [*livres, tuiles*] to tumble down (**de** off); [*pluie*] to pour down; **2** (baisser) [*prix, température*] to fall sharply; [*production*] to drop sharply; [*popularité*] to slump.

dégripper /degʀipe/ [1] *vtr* to lubricate [*moteur*]; to unjam [*mécanisme*].

dégriser /degʀize/ [1] **I** *vtr* **1** (dessoûler) to sober [sb] up; **2** (ramener à la réalité) to bring [sb] to his/her senses.

II se dégriser *vpr* **1** (dessoûler) to sober up; **2** (revenir à la réalité) to come to one's senses.

dégrossi, **~e** /degʀosi/ *adj* [*planches*] rough-hewn; **mal** ~ [*personne*] coarse PÉJ.

dégrossir /degʀosiʀ/ [3] *vtr* to rough-hew [*pierre*]; to break the back of [*travail*]; to knock a few corners off [*personne*].

dégrouiller○: **se dégrouiller** /degʀuje/ [1] *vpr* to hurry up, to get a move on○.

déguerpir /degɛʀpiʀ/ [3] *vi* to leave; **faire** ~ **qn** to drive sb off.

déguisé, **~e** /degize/ *adj* **1** (vêtu d'un déguisement) (pour s'amuser) in fancy dress (*jamais épith*); (pour duper) in disguise (*jamais épith*); ~ **en pirate** dressed up as a pirate; **2** (où l'on se déguise) [*soirée, défilé*] fancy dress (*épith*); **3** (camouflé) [*appui, subvention, tentative*] concealed; [*compliment*] disguised; [*critique*] veiled; **une façon ~e de faire** a roundabout way of doing; **non** ~ undisguised.

déguisement /degizmɑ̃/ *nm* **1** (costume) (pour s'amuser) costume; (pour duper) disguise; **2** (de pensée, vérité) concealment; **sans** ~ openly.

déguiser /degize/ [1] **I** *vtr* **1** (mettre un déguisement à) (pour s'amuser) to dress [sb] up (**en** as); (pour duper) to disguise (**en** as); **2** (altérer) to disguise [*visage, voix, écriture*]; **3** (camoufler) to conceal [*intentions, ambition*].

II se déguiser *vpr* (pour s'amuser) to dress up (**en** as); (pour duper) to disguise oneself (**en** as).

dégurgiter /degyʀʒite/ [1] *vtr* **1** (vomir) to bring up [*aliment*]; **2** (dire) to spew out [*insultes*]; to regurgitate [*leçon*].

dégustation /degystasjɔ̃/ *nf* tasting.

déguster /degyste/ [1] *vtr* **1** (savourer) to savour[GB] [*boisson, aliment, victoire*]; to enjoy [*spectacle*].

déhanchement /deɑ̃ʃmɑ̃/ *nm* **1** (naturel) swaying hips (*pl*); **2** (d'infirme) lopsidedness; **3** MÉD dislocation of the hip.

déhancher: se déhancher /deɑ̃ʃe/ [1] *vpr* GÉN to sway one's hips; (exagérément) to wiggle one's hips.

dehors /dəɔʀ/ **I** *adv* outside; **passer la nuit** ~ (occasionnellement) to spend the night outdoors; [*clochard*] to sleep rough; **j'ai été** ~ **toute la journée** I was out all day; **mettre qn** ~ GÉN to throw sb out; (d'un travail) to fire sb; (d'un établissement scolaire) to expel [*élève*]; **de** ~ [*voir, arriver*] from outside.

II *excl* get out!

III *nm inv* **les bruits du** ~ noise from outside; **quelqu'un du** ~ **ne peut pas comprendre** an outsider can't understand; **ses** ~ **bourrus cachent un cœur d'or** his/her rough exterior hides a heart of gold.

IV en dehors *loc adv* **1** (à l'extérieur) outside; **2** FIG (non impliqu é) **rester en ~** to stay out of it.

V en dehors de *loc prép* **1** (à l'extérieur de) outside; **en ~ du pays** outside the country; **2** (mis à part) apart from; **3** (hors de) outside; **en ~ des heures de travail** outside working hours; **il est resté en ~ du coup** he stayed out of the whole business; **c'est en ~ du sujet** SCOL it's off the subject; **c'est en ~ de mes attributions** that's outside my jurisdiction SOUT, that's not my job; **en ~ des limites de la loi** beyond the limits of the law.

déifier /deifje/ [2] *vtr* **1** (diviniser) to deify [*personne, animal*]; **2** (vénérer) to worship [*argent, progrès*]; to idolize [*jeunesse, vedette*].

déjà /deʒa/ *adv* **1** (dès maintenant) already; **il est ~ tard** it is already late, it is late already; **sans cela, j'aurais ~ fini** if it hadn't been for that, I would have finished already ou I'd have finished by now; **elle serait ~ mariée, si elle l'avait voulu** she could have been married by now if she'd wanted; **2** (précédemment) before, already; **je te l'ai ~ dit** I told you before, I've already told you once; **3°** (pour renforcer) **c'est ~ un joli salaire!** that's a pretty good salary!; **être second, c'est ~ très bien!** even to come second is pretty good!; **c'est ~ beaucoup d'avoir la santé** good health is the main thing; **il s'est excusé, c'est ~ quelque chose** at least he apologized, that's something; **4°** (pour protester) **elle est ~ assez riche (comme ça)!** she's rich enough as it is; **5°** (pour faire répéter) again; **c'est combien, ~?** how much was it again?

déjà-vu /deʒavy/ *nm inv* **1°** **c'est du ~** we've seen it all before; **2** PSYCH déjà vu.

déjeuner¹ /deʒœne/ [1] *vi* **1** (à midi) to have lunch; **inviter qn à ~** to invite sb to lunch; **restez ~** stay for lunch; **~ d'un sandwich** to have a sandwich for lunch; **2** (le matin) DIAL, B, C to have breakfast.

déjeuner² /deʒœne/ *nm* **1** (repas de midi) lunch; **~ d'affaires** business lunch; **prendre son ~** to have lunch; **l'heure du ~** lunchtime; **le ~ est servi** lunch is ready; **après ~** after lunch; **2** (petit déjeuner) DIAL, B, C breakfast.

■ **~ sur l'herbe** picnic lunch.

déjouer /deʒwe/ [1] *vtr* to frustrate [*astuce, précaution*]; to foil [*plan, conspiration*]; to evade [*surveillance, contrôle*]; **~ les pièges de l'ennemi** to avoid the traps set by the enemy; **~ les manœuvres de qn** to outmanoeuvre sb.

déjuger: se déjuger /deʒyʒe/ [13] *vpr* to go back on one's decision.

delà /dəla/ *adv* **deçà, ~** here and there.

de-là /dəla/ *adv* **de-ci, ~** here and there.

délabré, ~e /delabʀe/ *adj* [*maison, équipement*] dilapidated; [*plafond, mur*] crumbling; [*vêtements*] ragged; [*santé, esprit*] damaged.

délabrement /delabʀəmɑ̃/ *nm* (de maison, d'équipement) dilapidation; (de santé, pays) poor state.

délabrer /delabʀe/ [1] I *vtr* to ruin [*maison, équipement*].

II **se délabrer** *vpr* [*maison, équipement, économie, pays*] to become run-down; [*affaires*] to go to rack and ruin; [*santé*] to deteriorate.

délacer /delase/ [12] I *vtr* to undo [*chaussures*]; to unlace [*corsage*].

II **se délacer** *vpr* [*chaussure*] to come undone.

délai /delɛ/ *nm* **1** (période accordée) **tu as un ~ de 20 jours pour payer** you have 20 days to pay; **dans un ~ de 24 heures** within 24 hours; **faire qch dans le ~ prescrit** to do sth within the allotted time; **rester dans les ~s** to meet the deadline; **les ~s sont trop courts** or **serrés** there isn't enough time; **fixer un ~** to set a deadline; **respecter un ~** to meet a deadline; **dernier ~ pour les inscriptions** final date for registration; **2** (période d'attente) **abaisser un ~** to cut the waiting time; **le ~ moyen tourne autour de six mois** the average wait is about six months; **comptez trois semaines de ~ pour la livraison** allow three weeks for delivery; **dans les meilleurs** or **plus brefs**

~s as soon as possible; **sans ~** [*agir*] immediately; **3** (période supplémentaire) extension; **obtenir un ~** to get an extension; **demander un ~** to ask for extra time; **proroger un ~** to extend a deadline.

■ **~ de grâce** grace period; **~ de livraison** delivery ou lead time (**pour** on); **~ de préavis** (period of) notice; **~ de réflexion** time to think.

délaissé, ~e /delese/ *adj* **1** (abandonné) [*épouse*] deserted; [*maîtresse, enfant, terres*] abandoned; **2** (négligé) [*personne*] neglected.

délaisser /delese/ [1] *vtr* **1** (abandonner) to leave [*épouse*]; to abandon [*lieu, activité*]; **2** (négliger) to neglect [*amis, études*].

délassant, ~e /delasɑ̃, ɑ̃t/ *adj* [*bain, activité physique*] relaxing; [*film*] entertaining.

délassement /delasmɑ̃/ *nm* relaxation.

délasser /delase/ [1] I *vtr* [*bain*] to relax [*corps*]; **cela m'a délassé de faire** I feel more relaxed after doing; **ça délasse** it's relaxing.

II **se délasser** *vpr* to relax (**en faisant** by doing).

délateur, -trice /delatœʀ, tʀis/ *nm,f* informer.

délation /delasjɔ̃/ *nf* informing.

délavé, ~e /delave/ *adj* **1** (décoloré) [*couleur, ciel*] washed-out; [*jean, affiche*] faded; **2** (imprégné d'eau) [*terre*] waterlogged.

délayer /deleje/ [21] *vtr* **1** (diluer) to thin [*peinture*] (**avec** with); to mix [*farine*] (**dans** with); **2** (trop étirer) **un rapport trop délayé** a waffling report°.

delco® /dɛlko/ *nm* distributor.

délectation /delɛktasjɔ̃/ *nf* (plaisir) delight.

délecter: se délecter /delɛkte/ [1] *vpr* **se ~ à faire/ en faisant** to delight in doing; **se ~ de qch** to enjoy sth thoroughly; **se ~ à l'avance de qch/de faire** to be thoroughly looking forward to sth/to doing.

délégation /delegasjɔ̃/ *nf* **1** (groupe) delegation (**auprès de** to); **aller voir qn en ~** to form a delegation to go and see sb; **2** JUR authority; **signer par ~** to sign on sb's authority; **recevoir ~ (de qn) pour faire qch** to be authorized to do sth (by sb); **3** (transmission) delegation (**à qn** to sb).

délégué, ~e /delege/ I *adj* [*administrateur, directeur*] acting (*épith*).

II *nm,f* **1** (à une réunion) delegate; **2** (responsable) director.

■ **~ du personnel** workers' representative; **~ syndical** union representative.

déléguer /delege/ [14] *vtr* **1** (charger d'une mission) to appoint [sb] as a delegate (**auprès de** to); **2** (transmettre) to delegate [*autorité, responsabilités*] (**à** to).

délestage /delɛstaʒ/ *nm* **1** (de navire, d'aérostat) unloading of the ballast; **2** (d'axe routier) diversion (*to relieve a road of heavy traffic*); **3** ÉLECTROTECH power cut.

délester /delɛste/ [1] I *vtr* **1** (alléger) to get rid of the ballast from [*navire, aérostat*]; **~ un véhicule de six sacs** to take six bags out of a vehicle; **se faire ~ de son portefeuille** HUM to have one's wallet pinched; **2** (décongestionner) to divert traffic away from [*route*].

II **se délester** *vpr* **se ~ de** [*personne*] to get rid of [*bagages*]; to off-load [*responsabilité*] (**sur** onto).

délibératif, -ive /deliberatif, iv/ *adj* **voix délibérative** voting powers (*pl*).

délibération /deliberasjɔ̃/ *nf* (discussion) deliberation; **être en ~** to be deliberating.

délibéré, ~e /delibeʀe/ I *adj* [*acte, violation*] deliberate; [*choix, volonté, politique*] conscious.

II *nm* JUR deliberation.

délibérément /deliberemɑ̃/ *adv* [*blesser, provoquer*] deliberately; [*accepter, choisir*] consciously.

délibérer /delibeʀe/ [14] I **délibérer de** or **sur** *vtr ind* to discuss.

II *vi* **1** (tenir conseil) [*assemblée*] to be in session; **2** (réfléchir) FML to think carefully.

délicat, ~e /delika, at/ I *adj* **1** (raffiné) [*mets*] subtle; [*palais*] discriminating; [*personne*] refined; **manières ~es** refinement (*sg*); **2** (plein de tact) tactful; (attentionné) thoughtful; **quelle attention ~e!** what a kind thought!; **des procédés peu ~s** unscrupulous

délicatement means; **3** (complexe, difficile) [*équilibre, négociations, tâche*] delicate; [*affaire, dossier, point, moment*] sensitive; [*mission, manœuvre*] tricky; **4** (fragile) [*peau, mécanisme, instrument*] delicate; [*estomac, oreille*] sensitive; **elle est de santé ~e** she's delicate.
II *nm,f* **faire le ~** to be fussy.

délicatement /delikatmã/ *adv* **1** (avec finesse, subtilité) [*dessiner, graver, sculpter*] finely, delicately; [*parfumer*] delicately; **2** (avec légèreté) [*appuyer, caresser, saisir*] delicately.

délicatesse /delikatɛs/ *nf* **1** (de saveur, coloris, parfum, sentiments) delicacy; **la ~ de ses traits** his/her fine features; **une œuvre sans ~** a crude piece of work; **un style sans ~** a coarse style; **2** (fragilité) GÉN delicacy; (de peau) sensitivity; **3** (tact) delicacy; **manquer de ~** to be heavy-handed; **il a eu la ~ de ne pas poser la question** he was tactful enough not to ask; **montrer de la ~ à l'égard de qn** to show kindness and consideration to sb; **4** (complexité) (d'opération, de négociations) delicacy; (de problème, cas, situation) trickiness; **5** (précaution) **manipuler qch avec ~** to handle sth with care; **6** (attention) **avoir des ~s pour qn** to be very attentive to sb.
IDIOMES **être en ~ avec qn** to be at odds with sb.

délice /delis/ *nm* delight; **avec ~** with delight; **un vrai ~ ton poulet** your chicken is quite delicious; **faire ses ~s de qch** to delight in sth; **faire les ~s de qn** to delight sb.

délicieusement /delisjøzmã/ *adv* GÉN delightfully; (au goût) deliciously; **~ parfumé** [*bain*] deliciously scented; [*fruit*] sweet-smelling (*épith*).

délicieux, -ieuse /delisjø, øz/ *adj* [*repas, goût, odeur, frisson*] delicious; [*sensation, endroit, humour, souvenir, musique*] delightful; [*joie*] exquisite; [*personne*] sweet.

délictueux, -euse /deliktɥø, øz/ *adj* [*acte*] criminal.

délié, ~e /delje/ **I** *adj* **1** [*taille*] slender; **2** [*mouvement*] loose; **3** [*esprit*] nimble.
II *nm* (en calligraphie) upstroke.
IDIOMES **avoir la langue ~e** to have the gift of the gab○.

délier /delje/ [2] *vtr* to untie [*personne, gerbe, poignets*]; **~ qn de** to release sb from [*promesse*].
IDIOMES **sans bourse ~** without paying a penny; **les langues se délient** people are starting to talk.

délimiter /delimite/ [1] *vtr* **1** (déterminer les limites de) [*clôture*] to mark the boundary of [*domaine*]; [*montagnes*] to form the boundary of [*pays*]; **2** (définir) to define [*rôle, frontière*]; to define the scope of [*sujet, question*].

délinquance /delɛ̃kɑ̃s/ *nf* crime; **la petite ~** petty crime; **la ~ juvénile** juvenile delinquency.

délinquant, ~e /delɛ̃kɑ̃, ɑ̃t/ **I** *adj* delinquent; **l'enfance ~e** child offenders (*pl*).
II *nm,f* offender; **un petit ~** a petty criminal.

déliquescence /delikesɑ̃s/ *nf* decline; **être en pleine ~** to be degenerating.

déliquescent, ~e /delikesɑ̃, ɑ̃t/ *adj* [*mœurs*] declining; [*style*] lifeless; [*esprit*] failing; [*industrie*] in decline (*après n*).

délirant, ~e /deliʀɑ̃, ɑ̃t/ *adj* **1** (exubérant) [*accueil, foule*] ecstatic; **2**○ (loufoque) [*personne, scénario, soirée*] crazy○; **3** (déraisonnable) [*prix*] outrageous; **4** MÉD [*personne, état*] delirious.

délire /deliʀ/ *nm* **1** MÉD, PSYCH delirium; **en proie au ~** suffering from delirium; **2**○ (folie) madness; **travailler autant, c'est du ~!** it's crazy○ to work that hard!; **3** (enthousiasme) frenzy; **salle en ~** ecstatic audience; **4** (frénésie) frenzy; **~ verbal** verbal excess.

délirer /deliʀe/ [1] *vi* **1** MÉD to be delirious; **2**○ FIG to be off one's rocker○.

délit /deli/ *nm* offence○.
■ **~ de fuite** hit-and-run offence○.

délivrance /delivʀɑ̃s/ *nf* **1** (soulagement) relief; **la mort fut pour elle une ~** her death was a merciful release; **2** (remise) (de certificat, brevet, passeport, d'ordonnance) issue; (de diplôme, prix) award.

délivrer /delivʀe/ [1] **I** *vtr* **1** (libérer) to free [*captif*]; to liberate [*pays, peuple*]; **~ qn de** to free sb from [*chaînes*]; to release sb from [*obligation*]; to relieve sb of [*souci*]; to rid sb of [*obsession*]; **vous me délivrez d'un grand poids** you have taken a great weight off my shoulders; (**délivre-nous du mal** RELIG deliver us from evil; **2** (donner) to issue document; to award [*diplôme, prix*]; to provide [*soins*].
II se délivrer *vpr* (se libérer) [*captif*] to free oneself; **se ~ de** to free oneself from [*chaînes, obligation*]; to rid oneself of [*angoisse*].

délocalisation /delɔkalizasjɔ̃/ *nf* relocation.

déloger /delɔʒe/ [13] *vtr* (chasser) to evict [*locataire*] (**de** from); to flush out [*rebelles, gibier*] (**de** from); to remove [*poussière*] (**de** from).

déloyal, ~e, *mpl* -aux /delwajal, o/ *adj* [*ami, collègue*] disloyal (**envers** to); [*concurrence*] unfair; [*acte, conduite, méthode, procédé*] underhand.

delta /dɛlta/ *nm inv* (tous contextes) delta.

deltaplane /dɛltaplan/ ► 329 *nm* **1** (engin) hang-glider; **2** (activité) hang-gliding.

déluge /delyʒ/ *nm* **1** (pluie) downpour, deluge; **2** (profusion) (de coups, d'insultes) hail (**de** of); (de larmes, plaintes) flood (**de** of); (de mots) torrent (**de** of); (de compliments) shower (**de** of); (de fleurs) profusion; (de malheurs) spate (**de** of).

Déluge /delyʒ/ *nm* **le ~** the Flood, the Deluge.
IDIOMES **ça remonte au ~** it goes back to the year dot OU one; **après moi le ~** I don't care what happens after I'm gone.

déluré, ~e /delyʀe/ *adj* **1** (dégourdi) smart; **2** (effronté) forward; PÉJ fast (*jamais épith*).

démagogie /demagɔʒi/ *nf* GÉN popularity seeking; (électoraliste) electioneering, demagogy SOUT; **faire de la ~** to try to gain popularity.

démagogique /demagɔʒik/ *adj* GÉN popularity-seeking (*épith*); (en politique) electioneering (*épith*).

démagogue /demagɔg/ *nmf* popularity-seeker, demagogue SOUT.

demain /dəmɛ̃/ **I** *adv* tomorrow; **~ toute la journée** all day tomorrow; **~ en huit/en quinze** a week/two weeks tomorrow.
II *nm* tomorrow; **à ~!** see you tomorrow; **de quoi ~ sera-t-il fait?** who knows what tomorrow may bring?; **l'Europe de ~** the Europe of the future.
IDIOMES **~ il fera jour** tomorrow is another day; **ce n'est pas ~ la veille** that's not going to happen in a hurry!

démancher /demɑ̃ʃe/ [1] **I** *vtr* **1** (ôter le manche de) to take the handle off; **2**○ (disloquer) to dislocate [*membre, mâchoire*].
II se démancher *vpr* **1** (perdre son manche) to come off its handle; **2**○ (se disloquer) [*membre, mâchoire*] to be dislocated.

demande /dəmɑ̃d/ *nf* **1** (sollicitation) request; **répondre à la ~ de qn** to grant sb's request; **2** (démarche) application; **faire une ~ de mutation** to apply for a transfer; **gratuit sur (simple) ~** free on request; **remboursement sur (simple) ~ écrite** refund on application; **3** ADMIN (formulaire) application form; **une ~ d'inscription** a registration form; **4** ÉCON demand; **5** JUR ~ (**en justice**) claim; **~ de divorce** petition for divorce.
■ **~ d'asile** application for asylum; **~ d'emploi** (démarche) job application; **'~s d'emploi'** (rubrique) 'situations wanted'; **~ en mariage** marriage proposal.

demandé, ~e /dəmɑ̃de/ *adj* très **~** [*destination, sport, personne*] very popular; [*service, qualification, produit*] in great demand.

demander /dəmɑ̃de/ [1] **I** *vtr* **1** (solliciter) to ask for [*conseil, argent, aide*]; **~ l'asile politique** to apply for political asylum; **~ la main de qn** to ask for sb's hand; **~ qn en mariage** to propose to sb; **'le numéro que vous demandez n'est plus en service'** 'the number you have dialled○ is unobtainable'; **on demande un plombier** (dans une offre d'emploi) plumber wanted; **fais ce qu'on te demande!** do as you're told!; **il n'en demandait pas tant** he didn't expect all that; **je ne demande pas mieux que de partir** there's nothing I would like better than to go; **je ne demande que ça!** that's exactly what I want!; **il ne demande qu'à te croire** he'd really like to believe you; **je demande à voir**○ that'll be the day○; **2** (interroger sur) ~ **qch à qn** to ask sb sth; **je ne t'ai rien demandé**○! I wasn't talking to you!; **3** (faire venir) to send for [*médecin, prêtre*]; **'un vendeur est demandé à l'accueil'** 'would a salesman please come to reception'; **le patron vous demande** (dans son bureau) the boss wants to see you; (au téléphone) the boss wants to speak to you; **4** (nécessiter) [*travail, tâche*] to require [*effort, qualification*]; [*plante, animal*] to need [*attention*] ; ~ **à être revu** [*sujet, texte*] to need revision; **5** (requérir) to call for [*peine, réformes*]; JUR to sue for [*divorce, dommages-intérêts*].

II se demander *vpr* **1** (s'interroger) **se** ~ **si/pourquoi** to wonder whether/why; **2** (être demandé) **ce genre de choses ne se demande pas** it's not the kind of thing you ask.

demandeur[1], **-euse** /dəmɑ̃dœr, øz/ **I** *adj* COMM, ÉCON **le pays est très** ~ **de matières premières** raw materials are very much in demand in the country.
II *nm,f* GÉN, ADMIN applicant
■ ~ **d'asile** asylum-seeker; ~ **d'emploi** job-seeker.

demandeur[2], **-eresse** /dəmɑ̃dœr, d(ə)rɛs/ *nm,f* JUR plaintiff.

démangeaison /demɑ̃ʒɛzɔ̃/ *nf* (irritation) itch ∅; **provoquer des** ~**s** to cause itching.

démanger /demɑ̃ʒe/ [13] *vtr* **1** LIT (irriter) **ça me démange** I'm itchy; **2** FIG **l'envie de le gifler me démangeait** I was itching to slap him.

démantèlement /demɑ̃tɛlmɑ̃/ *nm* (de laboratoire, service) dismantling (**de** of); (de forces nucléaires) destruction.

démanteler /demɑ̃tle/ [17] *vtr* to dismantle [*service, institution, armes, frontières*]; to break up [*gang*].

démantibuler○ /demɑ̃tibyle/ [1] *vtr* to bust○, to break up [*meuble*].

démaquillage /demakijaʒ/ *nm* make-up removal.

démaquillant, ~**e** /demakijɑ̃, ɑ̃t/ **I** *adj* [*lait, gel*] cleansing (*épith*).
II *nm* make-up remover.

démaquiller: se démaquiller /demakije/ [1] *vpr* to remove one's make-up.

démarcation /demarkasjɔ̃/ *nf* demarcation.

démarchage /demarʃaʒ/ *nm* door-to-door selling; ~ **électoral** canvassing; ~ **téléphonique** cold calling.

démarche /demarʃ/ *nf* **1** (allure) walk; **avoir une** ~ **assurée** to walk with a confident step; **avoir une** ~ **de canard** to waddle like a duck; **2** (tentative) step; **faire** OR **tenter une** ~ **auprès de qn** to approach sb; **faire des** ~**s pour obtenir qch** to take steps to obtain sth; ~ **commune** OR **collective** joint representation; **plusieurs** ~**s sont possibles** there are several possible courses of action open to you; **les** ~**s à effectuer sont les suivantes** the correct procedure is as follows; **3** (attitude) approach; **4** (raisonnement) reasoning; (évolution) ~ **de la pensée** thought process.

démarcher /demarʃe/ [1] *vtr* **1** (vendre) to sell [sth] door-to-door [*produit*]; **2** (solliciter) to canvass [*client, entreprise*].

démarcheur, **-euse** /demarʃœr, øz/ *nm,f* (door-to-door) salesman.

démarque /demark/ *nf* (de marchandises) mark-down (**de** of).

démarquer /demarke/ [1] *vtr* **1** (rendre anonyme) ~ **un article** to cut out the label from an item (*so as to lower the price*); **2** (solder) to mark down [*marchandises*]; **3** SPORT to free [sb] from a marker.
II se démarquer *vpr* **1** (se distinguer) **se** ~ **de qn/qch** to distance oneself from sb/sth; **2** SPORT to get free of one's marker.

démarrage /demaraʒ/ *nm* **1** LIT, FIG starting up; **j'ai**

peur de caler au ~ I'm afraid of stalling as I pull away; **2** (en course à pied) spurt, burst of speed.
■ ~ **en côte** hill start.

démarrer /demare/ [1] **I** *vtr* **1** LIT to start (up) [*moteur, véhicule*]; **2** FIG to start [*roman, émission*]; to get [sth] off the ground [*projet*].
II *vi* **1** (se mettre en marche) [*véhicule*] to pull away; [*moteur*] to start; **2** (mettre en marche) [*chauffeur*] to drive off; **3** (débuter) [*affaire, entreprise*] to start up; [*campagne électorale*] to get under way; [*personne*] to start off; **4** (en course à pied) to put on a spurt.

démarreur /demarœr/ *nm* AUT starter.

démasquer /demaske/ [1] **I** *vtr* **1** FIG to unmask [*traître*]; to expose [*hypocrisie*]; to uncover [*complot*]; **2** LIT ~ **qn** to remove sb's mask.
II se démasquer *vpr* **1** FIG (involontairement) to betray oneself; (volontairement) to reveal oneself; **2** LIT to remove one's mask.

démâter /demate/ [1] **I** *vtr* [*équipage*] to unstep the mast of [*navire*]; [*tempête*] to dismast [*navire*].
II *vi* [*voilier*] to lose its mast.

dématérialiser: se dématérialiser /dematerjalize/ [1] *vpr* to vanish, to disappear.

démazouter /demazute/ [1] *vtr* to clean the oil from [*plage*].

démêlant, ~**e** /demelɑ̃, ɑ̃t/ *adj* [*shampooing, baume*] detangling.

démêlé /demele/ *nm* wrangle; **avoir des** ~**s avec la justice** to get into trouble with the law.

démêler /demele/ [1] **I** *vtr* **1** LIT to disentangle [*fils, pelote*]; to untangle [*cheveux*]; **2** FIG (éclaircir) to sort out [*affaire, situation*]; ~ **les fils d'une intrigue** to unravel the threads of a plot.
II se démêler *vpr* **1** (être clarifié) [*situation*] to get sorted out; **2** (se dépêtrer) [*personne*] **se** ~ **de qch** to extricate oneself from sth.

démêloir /demelwar/ *nm* wide-toothed comb.

démembrement /demɑ̃brəmɑ̃/ *nm* **1** (de pays, compagnie) break-up (**de** of); **2** (de propriété) division (**de** of).

démembrer /demɑ̃bre/ [1] *vtr* (morceler) to divide up, to dismember [*domaine, empire*].

déménagement /demenaʒmɑ̃/ *nm* **1** (action de déménager) move; **2** (changement de domicile) moving house ∅; **3** (changement de bureaux) relocation; **4** (transport) removal; **5** (action de vider) clearing ∅.

déménager /demenaʒe/ [13] **I** *vtr* **1** (déplacer) to move [*meubles, livres*]; to relocate [*bureaux*]; **2** (vider) to clear [*pièce*].
II *vi* **1** (changer de domicile) to move house; **2** (changer de bureaux) to relocate; **3**○ (partir) to push off○, to leave; **4**○ (déraisonner) to be off one's rocker○.
IDIOMES ~ **à la cloche de bois** to do a moonlight flit GB.

déménageur, **-euse** /demenaʒœr, øz/ ▶ 374 *nm,f* (ouvrier) removal GB OU moving US man/woman; (patron) furniture remover GB OU mover US; **épaules de** ~ muscular shoulders.

démence /demɑ̃s/ *nf* madness, insanity.

démener: se démener /dem(ə)ne/ [16] *vpr* **1** (s'agiter) to thrash about; [*prisonnier*] to struggle; **2** (se donner du mal) to put oneself out; **se** ~ **pour faire** to put oneself to some trouble to do; **elle se démène du matin au soir** she slaves away from morning till night.
IDIOMES **se** ~ **comme un beau diable** (pour se libérer) to thrash about; (pour avoir qch) to do one's utmost.

dément, ~**e** /demɑ̃, ɑ̃t/ **I** *adj* **1** (fou) mad, insane; **2**○ [*spectacle*] terrific○; [*événement*] amazing; [*prix*] outrageous.
II *nm,f* mentally ill person.

démenti /demɑ̃ti/ *nm* denial; **cette rumeur est restée sans** ~ the rumour○ has not been denied.

démentiel, **-ielle** /demɑ̃sjɛl/ *adj* **1**○ [*inflation, rythme*] insane; [*prix*] outrageous; **2** PSYCH insane.

démentir /demɑ̃tir/ [30] **I** *vtr* **1** (nier) to deny [*information, accusation*]; **2** (contredire) [*personne*] to refute [*propos, déclaration*]; [*fait*] to give the lie to [*propos,* *déclaration*]; to contradict [*point de vue, prévision*]; to belie [*apparence*].

II se démentir *vpr* [*courage, intérêt*] to flag.

démerder³: **se démerder** /demɛʀde/ [1] *vpr* **1** (se débrouiller) to manage; **se ~ pour faire** to manage to do; **se ~ avec ses problèmes** to sort out one's own problems; **2** (se dépêcher) **démerde-toi un peu!** get your arse GB OU ass US in gear⊖!

démériter /demeʀite/ [1] *vi* to prove oneself unworthy.

démesure /demǝzyʀ/ *nf* **1** (d'ambition, de prétentions) excesses (*pl*); **2** (taille exagérée) excessive size.

démesuré, ~e /demǝzyʀe/ *adj* **1** [*taille*] excessive; **2** [*orgueil, appétit*] immoderate; [*ambition*] excessive.

démesurément /demǝzyʀemɑ̃/ *adv* excessively, inordinately.

démettre /demɛtʀ/ [60] **I** *vtr* **1** (déboîter) **~ l'épaule de qn** to dislocate sb's shoulder; **2** (révoquer) to dismiss [*personne*]; **~ qn de ses fonctions** to relieve sb of his/her duties.

II se démettre *vpr* **1** (se déboîter) **il s'est démis l'épaule** he dislocated his shoulder; **2** (démissionner) to resign.

demeurant: **au demeurant** /odǝmœʀɑ̃/ *loc adv* as it happens, besides, for all that.

demeure /dǝmœʀ/ **I** *nf* **1** (habitation) residence; **~ ancestrale** ancestral home; **2 mettre qn en ~ de faire** GÉN to require sb to do; JUR to give sb formal notice to do; **mise en ~** GÉN demand; JUR formal notice (**de faire** to do).

II à demeure *loc adv* permanently.

IDIOMES **il n'y a pas péril en la ~** there's no rush.

demeuré, ~e /dǝmœʀe/ **I** *adj* retarded.

II *nm,f* simpleton.

demeurer /dǝmœʀe/ [1] **I** *vi* **1** (+ *v avoir*) (résider) to reside; **2** (+ *v être*) (rester) to remain.

II *v impers* **il n'en demeure pas moins que** nonetheless, the fact remains that.

demi, ~e¹ /d(ǝ)mi/ **▶ 298 I et demi, et demie** *loc adj* and a half; **trois et ~ pour cent** three and a half per cent; **il est trois heures et ~e** it's half past three.

II *nm,f* half.

III *nm* **1** (verre de bière) glass of beer, ~ half-pint GB; **2** SPORT half; **~ de mêlée** scrum half; **~ d'ouverture** stand-off half.

IV à demi *loc adv* half; **je ne suis qu'à ~ éveillé** I'm only half awake; **je ne suis qu'à ~ satisfait** I'm not entirely satisfied.

V demi- (*in compounds*) **1** (à moitié) half; **une ~-pomme** half an apple; **trois ~-pommes** three half apples; **2** (incomplet) partial.

demi-botte, *pl* **~s** /d(ǝ)mibɔt/ *nf* calf-length boot.

demi-centre /d(ǝ)misɑ̃tʀ/ *nm* halfback.

demi-cercle, *pl* **~s** /d(ǝ)misɛʀkl/ *nm* semicircle; **en ~** [*objet*] semicircular.

demi-deuil, *pl* **~s** /d(ǝ)midœj/ *nm* half-mourning (*wearing grey*).

demi-dieu, *pl* **~x** /d(ǝ)midjø/ *nm* demigod.

demi-douzaine, *pl* **~s** /d(ǝ)miduzɛn/ *nf* half a dozen; **une ~ d'œufs** half a dozen eggs.

demi-droite, *pl* **~s** /d(ǝ)midʀwat/ *nf* half-line.

demie² /d(ǝ)mi/ **I** *adj f* **▶ demi I.**

II *nf* (d'heure) half hour; **il est déjà la ~** it's already half past.

demi-échec /d(ǝ)mieʃɛk/ *nm* **un ~** something of a failure.

demi-écrémé, ~e, *mpl* **~s** /d(ǝ)miekʀeme/ *adj* semi-skimmed.

demi-finale, *pl* **~s** /d(ǝ)mifinal/ *nf* semifinal.

demi-fond, *pl* **~s** /d(ǝ)mifɔ̃/ *nm* (spécialité) middle-distance running.

demi-franc, *pl* **~s** /d(ǝ)mifʀɑ̃/ *nm* half a franc, fifty centimes.

demi-frère, *pl* **~s** /d(ǝ)mifʀɛʀ/ *nm* half-brother.

demi-gros /d(ǝ)migʀo/ *nm inv* wholesale direct to the public.

demi-heure, *pl* **~s** /d(ǝ)mijœʀ/ *nf* half an hour.

demi-journée, *pl* **~s** /d(ǝ)miʒuʀne/ *nf* half a day; **à la ~** on a half-day basis.

démilitariser /demilitaʀize/ [1] *vtr* to demilitarize.

demi-litre, *pl* **~s** /d(ǝ)militʀ/ *nm* half a litre GB.

demi-longueur, *pl* **~s** /d(ǝ)milɔ̃gœʀ/ *nf* half-length.

demi-lune, *pl* **~s** /d(ǝ)milyn/ *nf* **1** LIT half-moon; **2** (objet) half-circle.

demi-mal /d(ǝ)mimal/ *nm* **il n'y a que ~** it's not as bad as all that.

demi-mesure, *pl* **~s** /d(ǝ)mim(ǝ)zyʀ/ *nf* LIT, FIG half-measure.

demi-mot: **à demi-mot** /ad(ǝ)mimo/ *loc adv* **j'ai compris à ~** I didn't need to have it spelt out.

déminage /deminaʒ/ *nm* (de terrain) (land)mine clearance; (de mer) minesweeping.

déminer /demine/ [1] *vtr* to clear [sth] of mines [*terrain*]; to sweep [sth] of mines [*estuaire*].

déminéraliser: **se déminéraliser** /demineʀalize/ [1] *vpr* [*personne*] to suffer from a mineral deficiency.

démineur /deminœʀ/ *nm* mine clearance expert.

demi-pause, *pl* **~s** /d(ǝ)mipoz/ *nf* minim rest GB, half rest US.

demi-pension /d(ǝ)mipɑ̃sjɔ̃/ *nf* (régime, prix) half board; **être en ~** (à l'hôtel) to stay half board; (à l'école) to have school lunches.

demi-pensionnaire, *pl* **~s** /d(ǝ)mipɑ̃sjɔnɛʀ/ *nmf* SCOL pupil who has school lunches.

demi-place, *pl* **~s** /d(ǝ)miplas/ *nf* **payer ~** (en voyage) to pay half-fare; (au spectacle) to pay half-price.

demi-queue, *pl* **~s** /d(ǝ)mikø/ *nm* (**piano**) **~** boudoir grand piano.

démis, ~e /demi, iz/ **I** *pp* **▶ démettre.**

II *pp adj* [*articulation*] dislocated.

demi-saison, *pl* **~s** /d(ǝ)misɛzɔ̃/ *nf* **manteau de ~** lightweight coat.

demi-sel /d(ǝ)misɛl/ *adj inv* [*beurre*] slightly salted.

demi-siècle, *pl* **~s** /d(ǝ)misjɛkl/ *nm* half a century.

demi-sœur, *pl* **~s** /d(ǝ)misœʀ/ *nf* half-sister.

demi-solde, *pl* **~s** /d(ǝ)misɔld/ *nf* half-pay.

demi-sommeil, *pl* **~s** /d(ǝ)misɔmɛj/ *nm* **être dans un ~** to be half-asleep.

demi-soupir, *pl* **~s** /d(ǝ)misupiʀ/ *nm* quaver GB OU eighth US rest.

démission /demisjɔ̃/ *nf* **1** LIT resignation (**de** from); **2** FIG failure to take responsibility.

démissionnaire /demisjɔnɛʀ/ *adj* resigning (*épith*).

démissionner /demisjɔne/ [1] **I**⊖ *vtr* HUM to oust.

II *vi* **1** (quitter son poste) to resign (**de** from); **2** (renoncer) to give up; (renier ses responsabilités) to abdicate one's responsibilities.

demi-succès /d(ǝ)misyksɛ/ *nm inv* qualified success.

demi-tarif, *pl* **~s** /d(ǝ)mitaʀif/ **I** *adj inv* half-price (*épith*).

II *adv* **payer ~** to pay half-price.

III *nm* (billet) half-price ticket; **voyager à ~** to travel half-fare.

demi-teinte, *pl* **~s** /d(ǝ)mitɛ̃t/ *nf* **en ~s** LIT in muted colours GB; FIG in a subdued style.

demi-ton, *pl* **~s** /d(ǝ)mitɔ̃/ *nm* semitone.

demi-tour, *pl* **~s** /d(ǝ)mituʀ/ *nm* (dans l'espace) AUT U-turn; MIL about-turn GB, about face US; **faire ~** GÉN to turn back.

demi-volée, *pl* **~s** /d(ǝ)mivɔle/ *nf* half-volley.

démobiliser /demɔbilize/ [1] *vtr* **1** MIL to demobilize; **2** FIG to demotivate [*électorat, partisan*].

démocrate /demɔkʀat/ **I** *adj* **1** GÉN democratic; **2** (aux États-Unis) [*parti, sénateur*] Democratic.

II *nmf* **1** GÉN democrat; **2** (aux États-Unis) Democrat.

démocrate-chrétien, -ienne, *pl* **démocrates-chrétiens, -iennes** /demɔkʀatkʀetjɛ̃, ɛn/ *adj, nm,f* Christian Democrat.

démocratie /demɔkʀasi/ nf democracy.

démocratique /demɔkʀatik/ adj **1** POL [régime, débat] democratic; **2** (accessible à tous) accessible.

démocratiser /demɔkʀatize/ [1] **I** vtr POL, FIG to democratize [régime, enseignement].
II se démocratiser vpr **1** POL [régime] to become more democratic; **2** [enseignement] to become more accessible.

démodé, **~e** /demɔde/ adj old-fashioned.

démoder: **se démoder** /demɔde/ [1] vpr to go out of fashion.

démographie /demɔgʀafi/ nf demography.

démographique /demɔgʀafik/ adj demographic.

demoiselle /d(ə)mwazɛl/ nf **1** (jeune fille) FML or IRON young lady; **2†** (célibataire) single lady; **elle est restée ~** she remained single; **3** (libellule) damselfly.
■ **~ de compagnie** female companion; **~ d'honneur** (de mariée) bridesmaid; (à la cour) maid of honour^GB.

démolir /demɔliʀ/ [3] **I** vtr **1** (détruire) to demolish [quartier, bâtiment]; (détériorer) to wreck [appareil, jouet]; **2** FIG to destroy [système, réputation]; to demolish [argumentation, politicien]; to wreck [carrière]; **3**○ (rosser) to beat [sb] up○ [personne]; (épuiser) [effort] to whack [sb] out○ [personne].
II se démolir vpr se **~**○ **la santé** to ruin one's health.

démolisseur, **-euse** /demɔlisœʀ, øz/ nm,f **1 ▶374** (personne) demolition worker; (entreprise) demolition contractor GB, wrecker US; **2** (destructeur) wrecker.

démolition /demɔlisjɔ̃/ **I** nf **1** (de construction) demolition; **2** FIG destruction.
II démolitions nfpl rubble ¢.

démon /demɔ̃/ nm **1** RELIG devil; **2** (esprit) spirit; **poussé par son ~ intérieur** (bon) prompted by his guiding spirit; (mauvais) driven by the demon inside him; **3** (personne) devil; **4** FIG **le ~ de la boisson** or **de l'alcool** the demon drink.
■ **~ de midi** ~ middle-age lust.

démoniaque /demɔnjak/ adj demonic.

démonstrateur, **-trice** /demɔ̃stʀatœʀ, tʀis/ **▶374** nm,f COMM demonstrator.

démonstratif, **-ive** /demɔ̃stʀatif, iv/ **I** adj GÉN, LING demonstrative; [geste] expressive; [joie] uninhibited.
II nm LING demonstrative.

démonstration /demɔ̃stʀasjɔ̃/ nf **1** (manifestation) display; **faire des ~s d'amitié à qn** to make a show of friendship toward(s) sb; **2** (leçon pratique) demonstration; **faire la ~ d'un appareil** to demonstrate an appliance; **3** (de théorie) demonstration; (de théorème) proof.

démontable /demɔ̃tabl/ adj [meuble] that can be taken apart.

démontage /demɔ̃taʒ/ nm **1** (d'échafaudage) taking down; (de meuble) taking apart; (de moteur) stripping down; (de pendule) dismantling; (de roue) removal; **2** FIG (explication) **procéder au ~ de mécanismes psychologiques** to describe the functioning of psychological mechanisms.

démonté, **~e** /demɔ̃te/ adj [mer] stormy.

démonte-pneu, pl **~s** /demɔ̃t(ə)pnø/ nm AUT tyre-lever GB, tire iron US.

démonter /demɔ̃te/ [1] **I** vtr **1** to dismantle [assemblage]; to take [sth] to pieces [machine]; **2** (enlever) to remove [roue]; to take off [porte]; to take down [rideau]; **3**○ (déconcerter) to fluster.
II se démonter vpr **1** (être démontable) **le buffet se démonte facilement** the sideboard can be taken apart GB ou knocked down US easily; **2** (se disloquer) to come apart; **3**○ (perdre son sang-froid) to become flustered.

démontrable /demɔ̃tʀabl/ adj demonstrable.

démontrer /demɔ̃tʀe/ [1] vtr **1** (avec preuve) to demonstrate [intérêt, absurdité]; to prove [théorème]; **2** (indiquer) to prove, to demonstrate.

démoraliser /demɔʀalize/ [1] **I** vtr to demoralize.
II se démoraliser vpr to get demoralized.

démordre: **démordre de** /demɔʀdʀ/ [6] vtr ind **je n'en démords pas** (d'une opinion) I stick by it; (d'une déclaration, décision) I'm sticking to it.

démoulage /demulaʒ/ nm **1** (de pâtisserie) turning out; **2** ART, TECH (d'objet) removal from the mould GB ou mold US; (de moule) turning out of the mould GB ou mold US.

démouler /demule/ [1] vtr to turn [sth] out of the tin GB ou pan US [gâteau]; to turn [sth] out of the mould GB ou mold US [flan]; to remove [sth] from the mould GB ou mold US [statue].

démultiplication /demyltiplikasjɔ̃/ nf (effet) gearing down; (rapport) reduction ratio.

démultiplier /demyltiplije/ [2] vtr **1** to reduce [vitesse]; **2** to increase [pouvoirs, capacité].

démuni, **~e** /demyni/ adj **1** (pauvre) impoverished; (à court d'argent) penniless; **2** (vulnérable) helpless; **3** (à court de stock) out of stock (jamais épith); **4** (privé) **~ de** devoid of [talent]; lacking [diplômes].

démunir /demyniʀ/ [3] **I** vtr (dégarnir) to divest (de of).
II se démunir vpr (se dessaisir) **se ~ de qch** to leave oneself without sth.

démystifier /demistifje/ [2] vtr **1 ~ qn** to dispel sb's illusions; **2** to demystify [discipline].

démythifier /demitifje/ [2] vtr to demythologize.

dénatalité /denatalite/ nf fall in the birthrate.

dénationaliser /denasjɔnalize/ [1] vtr to denationalize.

dénaturé, **~e** /denatyʀe/ adj **1** [alcool] denaturated; **2** (dépravé) warped; **3** (indigne) [parents, enfants] unnatural; **4** (déformé) distorted.

dénaturer /denatyʀe/ [1] vtr **1** TECH, IND to denature; **2** (déformer) to distort [faits]; **3** (altérer) to spoil [goût, sauce].

dénégation /denegasjɔ̃/ nf GÉN, JUR denial.

déneiger /deneʒe/ [13] vtr to clear the snow off [route].

déni /deni/ nm denial (**de** of).

déniaiser /denjeze/ [1] vtr **1** (dégourdir) to make [sb] more worldly-wise; **2**○ (initier sexuellement) to initiate [sb] sexually.

dénicher /denife/ [1] vtr **1**○ (découvrir) to dig out○ [objet]; to track down [personne]; to discover [bonne adresse]; **2** (faire sortir) to flush out [voleur, animal]; **3** LIT to take [sth] from the nest.

dénicheur, **-euse** /denifœʀ, øz/ nm,f **1** (d'objets, de talents) **~ de** person who is good at spotting [talent]; **2** (d'œufs) bird's-nester.

denier /dənje/ **I** nm **1** FIN, HIST (français) denier; (romain) denarius; **2** (de collants) denier.
II deniers nmpl money; **~s publics** or **de l'État** public funds.
■ **~ du culte** RELIG funds collected annually for a parish; **~ de saint Pierre** RELIG Peter's pence.

dénier /denje/ [2] vtr to deny.

dénigrement /denigʀəmɑ̃/ nm denigration; **par ~** disparagingly; **esprit de ~** disparaging mentality.

dénigrer /denigʀe/ [1] vtr to denigrate.

dénivelé /denivle/ nm, **dénivelée** nf difference in altitude.

dénivellation /denivɛlasjɔ̃/ nf **1** (écart d'altitude) difference in altitude; (écart de niveau) difference in level; **2** (inclinaison) gradient; **3** (inégalité de terrain) unevenness; **4** (changement du niveau) alteration of level.

dénombrable /denɔ̃bʀabl/ adj LING, MATH countable, count (épith); **non ~** uncountable.

dénombrer /denɔ̃bʀe/ [1] vtr to count.

dénominateur /denɔminatœʀ/ nm denominator.

dénomination /denɔminasjɔ̃/ nf **1** GÉN name; **2** RELIG denomination.
■ **~ commune** generic name; **~ sociale** ADMIN registered company name.

dénommé, **~e** /denɔme/ adj ADMIN **le ~ Pierre** the person by the name of Pierre.

dénommer /denɔme/ [1] vtr **1** JUR to name; **2** (appeler) to call; **3** (désigner) to designate.

dénoncer /denɔ̃se/ [12] **I** vtr **1** (signaler) to denounce [*personne, abus*]; **2** JUR (rompre) to break [*traité, contrat*].

II se dénoncer *vpr* to give oneself up.

dénonciateur, -trice /denɔ̃sjatœʀ, tʀis/ **I** *adj* [*lettre, article*] denunciatory.

II *nm,f* (de coupable) informer; (d'injustice) campaigner (**de** against).

dénonciation /denɔ̃sjasjɔ̃/ *nf* **1** (de coupable, d'injustice) denunciation; **2** JUR (de traité) (rupture) termination; (signification légale) notice.

dénoter /denɔte/ [1] *vtr* denote.

dénouement /denumɑ̃/ *nm* **1** THÉÂT denouement; **2** (d'une affaire, d'un conflit) outcome, conclusion; **un heureux ~** a happy ending.

dénouer /denwe/ [1] **I** *vtr* **1** (détacher) to undo [*nœud, cravate*]; to let down [*cheveux*]; to disentangle [*fils*]; **2** (débrouiller) to unravel [*intrigue*]; to resolve [*crise*].

II se dénouer *vpr* **1** [*lacet, corde*] to come undone; **2** [*crise*] to resolve itself; [*intrigue*] to unravel.

dénoyauter /denwajote/ [1] *vtr* to stone GB, to pit US.

denrée /dɑ̃ʀe/ *nf* **1** (produit) **~ de base** staple; **~s alimentaires** foodstuffs; **2** FIG commodity.

dense /dɑ̃s/ *adj* GÉN, PHYS dense; [*réseau*] concentrated; [*programme, tir*] heavy.

densité /dɑ̃site/ *nf* **1** GÉN, ORDINAT density; **~ démographique** density of population; **à forte ~** densely populated; **2** PHYS relative density; **3** (de végétation, brouillard) denseness.

dent /dɑ̃/ *nf* **1** ANAT, ZOOL tooth; **~s de devant** front teeth; **entre ses ~s** [*murmurer*] under one's breath; **parler entre ses ~s** to mumble; **mal** or **rage de ~s** toothache; **à pleines** or **à belles ~s** [*croquer*] with relish; **rire de toutes ses ~s** to laugh heartily; **manger du bout des ~s** to pick at one's food; **rire du bout des ~s** to laugh half-heartedly; **accepter du bout des ~s** to accept reluctantly; **faire ses (premières) ~s, percer ses ~s** to teethe; **elle vient de percer une ~** she has just cut a tooth; **jusqu'aux ~s** [*être armé*] to the teeth; **ne rien avoir à se mettre sous la ~** to have nothing to eat; **montrer les ~s** LIT, FIG to bare one's teeth; **serrer les ~s** to grit one's teeth; **2** (de peigne) tooth; (de fourchette) prong; (de timbre) serration; **en ~s de scie** [*bord, lame*] serrated; [*carrière*] full of ups and downs; [*résultats*] which go up and down; **3** (sommet) crag.

■ **~ de lait** milk tooth; **~ de sagesse** wisdom tooth.

IDIOMES **avoir** or **conserver une ~ contre qn** to bear sb a grudge; **avoir les ~s longues** to be ambitious; **avoir la ~ dure** to be scathing; **avoir la ~**○ to feel peckish○; **se casser les ~s (sur qch)** to come to grief (over sth); **être sur les ~s** to be on edge.

dentaire /dɑ̃tɛʀ/ *adj* dental.

denté, ~e /dɑ̃te/ *adj* TECH, ZOOL toothed; BOT dentate.

dentelé, ~e /dɑ̃t(ə)le/ *adj* [*côte*] indented; [*crête*] jagged; [*tissu*] pinked; [*papier, lame*] serrated; [*timbre*] perforated; BOT dentate.

dentelle /dɑ̃tɛl/ *nf* lace.

IDIOMES **il ne fait pas dans la ~** he's not one to bother with niceties.

dentellière /dɑ̃tɛljɛʀ/ *nf* **1** (personne) lacemaker; **2** (machine) lacemaking machine.

dentelure /dɑ̃tlyʀ/ *nf* (de timbre) perforation; (de tissu) pinked edge; (de papier, lame) serrated edge; (de côte) indentation; (de crête) jagged outline; BOT serration; ARCHIT dentils (*pl*).

dentier /dɑ̃tje/ *nm* dentures (*pl*).

dentifrice /dɑ̃tifʀis/ *nm* toothpaste.

dentiste /dɑ̃tist/ **▶ 374** *nmf* dentist.

dentition /dɑ̃tisjɔ̃/ *nf* dentition.

denture /dɑ̃tyʀ/ *nf* **1** (disposition) dentition; (dents) set of teeth; **2** TECH teeth (*pl*), cogs (*pl*).

dénucléariser /denykleaʀize/ [1] *vtr* to denuclearize.

dénuder /denyde/ [1] **I** *vtr* **1** ÉLECTROTECH to strip [*câble, fil*]; **2** [*mouvement*] to reveal [*corps*]; **3** MÉD to bare [*nerf, veine*]; to strip [*os*] (**de** of).

II se dénuder *vpr* **1** (se dévêtir) to strip (off); **2**

(perdre sa verdure) to become bare; **3** (perdre ses cheveux) **son crâne se dénude** he's going bald.

dénué, ~e /denɥe/ *adj* **~ de** lacking in; **un acte ~ de sens** a senseless act; **accusation ~e de fondement** groundless accusation; **~ de toute utilité** utterly useless; **~ de tout** destitute.

dénuement /denymɑ̃/ *nm* (de personne) destitution; (de pièce) bareness.

dénutrition /denytʀisjɔ̃/ *nf* malnutrition.

déodorant, ~e /deɔdɔʀɑ̃, ɑ̃t/ **I** *adj* deodorant. **II** *nm* deodorant.

déontologie /deɔ̃tɔlɔʒi/ *nf* (de profession) ethics (+ *v sg*); PHILOS deontology.

déontologique /deɔ̃tɔlɔʒik/ *adj* PHILOS deontological; MÉD ethical; **code ~ des médecins** code of practice governing doctors GB, medical code of ethics.

dépannage /depanaʒ/ *nm* (réparation) repair; **~s à domicile** home repairs; **~ 24 heures sur 24** 24 hour repair service; **faire un ~** to do a repair job.

dépanner /depane/ [1] *vtr* **1** (réparer) to fix [*voiture, appareil*]; **2** (remorquer) to tow away; **3**○ (aider) to help [sb] out.

dépanneur, -euse[1] /depanœʀ, øz/ **▶ 374** *nm,f* (personne) engineer.

dépanneuse[2] /depanøz/ *nf* (véhicule) breakdown truck GB, tow truck US.

dépaqueter /depakte/ [20] *vtr* to unpack.

dépareillé, ~e /depaʀeje/ *adj* **1** (isolé) odd (*épith*); **un volume ~** an odd volume; **articles ~s** oddments; **2** (disparate) [*service, ensemble*] odd; **un service de verres ~** a set of odd glasses; **3** (incomplet) incomplete.

déparer /depaʀe/ [1] *vtr* to spoil [*lieu*]; to mar [*beauté*].

départ /depaʀ/ *nm* **1** (d'un lieu) departure; **~ des grandes lignes/des lignes de banlieue** RAIL (platforms for) main line/suburban departures; **téléphone avant ton ~** phone before you leave; **se donner rendez-vous au ~ du car** (au lieu) to arrange to meet at the bus; **vols quotidiens au ~ de Nice** daily flights from Nice; **le train a pris du retard au ~ de Lyon** the train was late leaving Lyons; **être sur le ~** to be about to leave; **il n'y a qu'un ~ du courrier par jour** the post GB ou mail US only goes once a day; **2** (exode) exodus (**vers** to); **3** (d'une fonction, organisation) departure; (démission) resignation; **le ~ en retraite** retirement; **4** SPORT start; **~ arrêté/décalé/lancé** standing/staggered/flying start; **prendre le ~** (d'une course) to be among the starters; **prendre un nouveau ~** FIG to make a fresh start; **5** (début) start; **au ~** (d'abord) at first; (au début) at the outset; **langue de ~** source language; **salaire de ~** starting salary; **capital de ~** start-up capital.

départager /depaʀtaʒe/ [13] *vtr* to decide between [*concurrents*]; **le vote du président va ~ les voix** the chairman has the casting vote; **~ un jury** to bring the members of a jury to agreement.

département /depaʀtəmɑ̃/ *nm* **1** ADMIN (administrative) department (*French territorial division*); **2** (branche d'une administration) department.

départemental, ~e[1], *mpl* **-aux** /depaʀtəmɑ̃tal, o/ *adj* [*budget, élection*] local, regional.

départementale[2] /depaʀtəmɑ̃tal/ *nf* (route) secondary road, ≈ B road GB.

départir: se départir /depaʀtiʀ/ [30] *vpr* **se ~ de** to lose [*calme, sourire*]; to swerve from [*opinion*]; to abandon [*réserve*]; to break [*silence*].

dépassé, ~e /depase/ *adj* **1** (qui n'a plus cours) outdated, outmoded; **2** (vieux jeu) [*personne*] out-of-date (*épith*); **3**○ (débordé) [*personne*] overwhelmed; **être ~ par les événements** to be overtaken by events.

dépassement /depasmɑ̃/ *nm* **1** (sur route) overtaking GB, passing US; **2** (de budget) overrun; **~ d'horaire** overrunning the schedule; **le ~ de la dose prescrite peut entraîner des effets secondaires** exceeding the stated dose can produce side-effects; **3** (fait de se surpasser) **~ de soi** surpassing oneself.

■ **~ budgétaire** cost overrun; **~ de capacité** ORDINAT overflow.

dépasser /depɑse/ [1] **I** vtr **1** (passer devant) to overtake GB, to pass US; **2** (excéder) to exceed; **~ qch en hauteur** to be taller than sth; **certaines classes dépassent 30 élèves** some classes have over 30 pupils; **il a dépassé la cinquantaine** he's over ou past fifty; **3** (aller au-delà de) LIT to go past [cible, lieu]; FIG to exceed [espérances, attributions]; **quand vous aurez dépassé le village, tournez à droite** when you've gone through the village, turn right; **je ne peux pas acheter cette maison, elle dépasse mes moyens** I can't buy that house, it's more than I can afford; **nous avons dépassé les difficultés de base** we have got over the basic difficulties; **~ la mesure** or **les bornes** or **les limites** to go too far; **4** (montrer une supériorité sur) to be ahead of, to outstrip; **~ qn en bêtise** to surpass sb in stupidity; **ça me dépasse!** (incompréhensible) it's beyond me!; (choquant) it's beyond belief!

II vi **1** (être plus grand) to jut out; **2** (sortir) to stick out; **fais attention de ne pas ~ en coloriant** be careful not to colour GB over the lines; **3** (se faire voir) to show.

III se dépasser vpr **1** (soi-même) to surpass oneself; **2** (l'un l'autre) to overtake each other.

dépassionner /depɑsjɔne/ [1] vtr to defuse [débat, discussion]; **réflexion dépassionnée** dispassionate reflection.

dépatouiller○: **se dépatouiller** /depatuje/ [1] vpr to get by; **se ~ de** to pull oneself out of [situation].

dépaver /depave/ [1] vtr to take up the paving stones from [rue].

dépaysé, ~e /depeize/ adj **il est complètement ~** he's like a fish out of water; **il n'est pas ~ ici** he feels at home here.

dépaysement /depeizmɑ̃/ nm (changement volontaire) change of scenery; (changement désagréable) disorientation.

dépayser /depeize/ [1] vtr (agréablement) to provide [sb] with a pleasant change of scenery; (désagréablement) to disorient.

dépecer /dep(ə)se/ [16] vtr to tear [sth] apart [proie]; to cut up [victime]; to carve up [propriété].

dépêche /depɛʃ/ nf dispatch.

■ **~ d'Ems** HIST Ems telegram.

dépêcher /depeʃe/ [16] **I** vtr to dispatch (**à** to).

II se dépêcher vpr to hurry up.

dépeigné, ~e /depeɲe/ adj dishevelled GB.

dépeigner /depeɲe/ [1] vtr **~ qn** to make sb's hair untidy.

dépeindre /depɛ̃dʀ/ [55] vtr to depict (**comme** as).

dépenaillé, ~e /depɔnaje/ adj ragged.

dépénaliser /depenalize/ [1] vtr to decriminalize.

dépendance /depɑ̃dɑ̃s/ nf **1** (sujétion) dependence; **maintenir qn dans la ~** to keep sb dependent; **2** (lien) link; **3** (de malade, drogué) dependency; **4** (bâtiment) outbuilding; **5** HIST, POL dependency.

dépendant, ~e /depɑ̃dɑ̃, ɑ̃t/ adj GÉN dependent (**de** on); **être ~ de qn** (dans un emploi) to be responsible to sb; **organisme ~ du ministère** body which comes under the authority of the ministry; **les personnes ~es** dependants.

dépendre /depɑ̃dʀ/ [6] **I** vtr to take down [tableau].

II dépendre de vtr ind **1** (reposer sur) **~ de** to depend on; **ça dépend de toi** it's up to you; **2** (avoir besoin de) **~ de** to be dependent on; **3** (être sous l'autorité de) **~ de** [organisme, région] to come under the control of; [personne] to be responsible to; **4** (être la responsabilité de) **~ de** to be the responsibility of; **5** (être un territoire de) **~ de** to be a dependency of; **6** (être une dépendance de) **~ de** [bâtiment, terre] to belong to.

dépens /depɑ̃/ nmpl **1** (détriment) **aux ~ de** at the expense of; **victoire aux ~ de l'équipe favorite** win over the favourite GB team; **réussir aux ~ des autres** to walk over people to get to the top; **apprendre à ses ~ to learn to one's cost; **2** (frais) **vivre aux ~ des**

autres to live off other people; **3** JUR (frais de justice) legal costs.

dépense /depɑ̃s/ nf **1** (emploi d'argent) spending, expenditure; **pousser qn à la ~** to make sb spend money; **ça vaut la ~** it's worth the outlay; **regarder à la ~** to watch one's spending; **ne pas regarder à la ~** to spare no expense; **2** (somme déboursée) outlay; **avoir beaucoup de ~s** to have a lot of expenses; **faire des ~s inconsidérées** to indulge in reckless spending; **être une source de ~s** to be a drain on one's resources; **3** (quantité utilisée) (d'essence, électricité) consumption; **~ d'énergie physique** expenditure of physical energy; **cela représente une ~ de temps trop importante** it takes too much time.

■ **la ~ publique** public expenditure; **~s courantes** running costs.

dépenser /depɑ̃se/ [1] **I** vtr **1** (employer de l'argent) to spend [salaire, fortune]; **~ sans compter** to spend (money) freely; **2** (consommer) to use up [carburant]; to use [tissu, papier]; to spend [temps]; **ils ont dépensé des trésors d'imagination pour faire** they've really used their imagination doing.

II se dépenser vpr **1** (faire de l'exercice) to get (enough) exercise; **2** (se donner du mal) **se ~ pour faire** to put a lot of energy into doing.

dépensier, -ière /depɑ̃sje, ɛʀ/ **I** adj extravagant.

II nm,f spendthrift.

déperdition /depɛʀdisjɔ̃/ nf (perte) loss.

dépérir /depeʀiʀ/ [3] vi [personne, animal] LIT to waste away; FIG to fade away; [plante] to wilt; [économie] to be on the decline.

dépérissement /depeʀismɑ̃/ nm (de personne) deterioration; (de plante) wilting; (d'économie) decline.

dépêtrer /depɛtʀe/ [1] **I** vtr to extricate (**de** from).

II se dépêtrer vtr **se ~ de** to extricate oneself from [situation]; to get rid of [personne].

dépeuplement /depœpləmɑ̃/ nm depopulation.

dépeupler /depœple/ [1] vtr **1** GÉOG, SOCIOL to depopulate; **2** (vider temporairement) to empty; **3** ÉCOL to reduce the wildlife in [forêt, rivière].

déphasé, ~e /defaze/ adj **1**○ (décalé) out of step (**par rapport à** with); **je suis complètement ~e** I'm not with it at all; **2** PHYS out of phase.

déphaser /defaze/ [1] vtr **1**○ (décaler) to disorientate; **2** ÉLECTROTECH to shift phase.

dépiauter○ /depjote/ [1] vtr **1** (analyser) to dissect [document]; **2** (ôter la peau de) to skin [animal].

dépilation /depilasjɔ̃/ nf **1** (élimination) hair removal, depilation; **2** (chute) hair loss.

dépilatoire /depilatwaʀ/ adj, nm depilatory.

dépistable /depistabl/ adj detectable.

dépistage /depistaʒ/ nm (de maladie) screening; **~ systématique du sida** mass screening for Aids; **test de ~ du sida** Aids test; **~ précoce** early detection; **test de ~ génétique** genetic testing.

dépister /depiste/ [1] vtr **1** (découvrir) to track down [criminel]; to identify [problème]; to detect [maladie]; **2** (détourner) **~ les recherches** to put people off the scent; to deflect [soupçons]; **3** to spoor [gibier].

dépit /depi/ **I** nm (déception) bitter disappointment, chagrin; (ressentiment) pique; **par ~** in ou out of pique; **~ amoureux** on the rebound.

II en dépit de loc prép in spite of; **faire qch en ~ du bon sens** to do sth in a very illogical way.

dépité, ~e /depite/ adj piqued (**de** at); **avoir une mine ~e** to look really disappointed or upset.

dépiter /depite/ [1] vtr to upset [personne].

déplacé, ~e /deplase/ adj **1** SOCIOL [population] displaced; **2** (pas adapté) inappropriate; **c'est ~** (malséant) it's out of place; (inopportun) it's uncalled for; **3** (impoli) improper.

déplacement /deplasmɑ̃/ nm **1** (voyage) trip; **au cours de mes ~s** when I'm travelling GB around; **elle a fait le ~** she made the effort to go/to come; **2** (pour le travail) business trip; **3** (frais) **payer pour le ~** (de médecin, d'artisan) to pay a call-out fee; **4** (action de déplacer) moving; (d'attention, de problème) shifting; (de l'âge de la retraite) changing; **le ~ des voix sur un autre parti** the swing of votes to another party; **5** (de population) displacement (**vers** to); (de service) transfer (**vers** to); **6** LING, NAUT, PSYCH displacement.

déplacer /deplase/ [12] **I** *vtr* **1** (volontairement) to move [*objet, personne*]; (par accident) to dislodge [*tuile*]; to dislocate [*os*]; **2** to move [*réunion, cours*]; to change [*âge de la retraite*]; **3** (faire porter sur autre chose) to shift [*débat, problème, attention*]; **4** (muter) to move; (faire migrer) to displace; (attirer) to bring in [*foules*].

II se déplacer *vpr* **1** (changer de position) to move; **2** (être mis ailleurs) to be moved; [*tuile*] to be dislodged; **se ~ une vertèbre** to slip a disc; **3** (avancer) to get about; (voyager) to travel; (aller quelque part) to go; (venir) to come; **se ~ en fauteuil roulant** to be in a wheelchair; **se ~ avec difficulté** to have difficulty getting about; **4** [*médecin, artisan*] to go out on call.

IDIOMES **~ de l'air** or **beaucoup d'air**° to like to make one's presence felt.

déplafonner /deplafɔne/ [1] *vtr* FIG to lift the ceiling on.

déplaire /deplɛR/ [59] **I** *vi* **1** (ne pas avoir de succès) **le spectacle a déplu/n'a pas déplu** the show was not well received/was moderately successful; **2** (rebuter) **elle déplaît** she is not liked.

II déplaire à *vtr ind* **cela m'a déplu** I didn't like it.

III *v impers* **il me déplairait de vous voir partir** FML I should be sorry to see you go; **il ne me déplairait pas de les voir partir** I'd be quite happy to see them go; **je le ferai, ne vous en déplaise** IRON I shall do it whether you like it or not.

déplaisant, **~e** /deplɛzɑ̃, ɑ̃t/ *adj* unpleasant, disagreeable.

déplâtrer /deplɑtRe/ [1] *vtr* **1** CONSTR to strip the plaster off; **2** MÉD to remove the cast from [*membre*].

dépliant /deplijɑ̃/ *nm* (prospectus) leaflet; (dans un livre) gatefold; **~ hors-texte** foldout.

déplier /deplije/ [2] **I** *vtr* to unfold [*journal*]; to open out [*carte*]; to display [*marchandise*]; **~ les jambes** to stretch one's legs out.

II se déplier *vpr* **1** [*parachute*] to unfold; [*drapeau*] to unfurl; **2**° [*personne*] to rise to one's feet.

déploiement /deplwamɑ̃/ *nm* **1** (démonstration) (de solidarité) display; (de mesures) deployment; **2** MIL deployment; **3** (d'aile) spreading; (de voile) unfurling; (de panneau) opening out.

déplorable /deplɔRabl/ *adj* **1** (fâcheux) regrettable; **2** (très mauvais) appalling, deplorable.

déplorer /deplɔRe/ [1] *vtr* to deplore [*événement*]; **~ que** to bemoan the fact that.

déployer /deplwaje/ [23] **I** *vtr* **1** (montrer) to display [*talent*]; **~ toute son énergie pour faire** to expend all one's energy to do; **2** MIL to deploy [*troupes*]; **3** (déplier) to spread [*ailes*]; to unfurl [*voile*]; to open out [*panneau*].

II se déployer *vpr* **1** (s'éparpiller) [*policiers*] to fan out; **2** MIL [*troupes*] to be deployed; **3** (se déplier) [*ailes*] to spread; [*voile*] to unfurl; [*panneau*] to open out.

dépoli, **~e** /depɔli/ *adj* **verre ~** GÉN frosted glass; PHOT ground glass.

dépolir /depɔliR/ [3] *vtr* to frost [*verre*]; to take the gloss off [*vernis*]; to texture [*marbre*].

dépolitiser /depɔlitize/ [1] *vtr* to depoliticize [*débat, groupe*].

dépolluer /depɔlɥe/ [1] *vtr* to rid [sth] of pollution [*rivière*].

dépollution /depɔlysjɔ̃/ *nf* cleanup.

déportation /depɔRtasjɔ̃/ *nf* **1** (dans un camp de concentration) internment in a concentration camp; **2** (bannissement) deportation, transportation.

déporté, **~e** /depɔRte/ *nm,f* **1** (dans un camp de concentration) prisoner interned in a concentration camp; **2** (personne bannie) transported convict.

déporter /depɔRte/ [1] **I** *vtr* **1** (interner) to send [sb] to a concentration camp; **2** (faire dévier d'une trajectoire) to make [sth] swerve; **3** HIST (bannir) to deport.

II se déporter *vpr* to swerve.

déposant, **~e** /depozɑ̃, ɑ̃t/ *nm,f* **1** FIN depositor; **2** JUR (témoin) deponent.

déposer /depoze/ [1] **I** *vtr* **1** (poser) to put down [*fardeau*]; to dump [*ordures*]; to lay [*gerbe*]; **'défense de ~ des ordures'** 'no dumping'; **il déposa un baiser sur sa joue** he kissed his/her cheek; **~ les armes** FIG to lay down one's arms; **2** (laisser) to leave [*objet, lettre*]; (au passage) to drop off, to leave [*paquet, passager*]; **3** (verser) GÉN, FIN to deposit [*argent, bijoux*]; **~ sa signature à la banque** to give the bank a specimen signature; **4** (faire enregistrer) to register [*marque*]; to submit [*dossier, offre*]; to propose [*amendement*]; to introduce [*projet de loi*]; to file [*requête*]; to lodge [*plainte*]; **~ son bilan** FIN to file a petition in bankruptcy; **~ sa candidature** [*chercheur d'emploi*] to apply; [*homme politique*] to run; **~ une motion de censure** POL to move a vote of no confidence; **~ un préavis de grève** to give notice of strike action; **5** (laisser un dépôt) to deposit [*alluvions*]; **6** (destituer) to depose [*souverain*]; **7** (enlever) to remove [*moteur*]; to take up [*tapis*]; to take down [*rideau*].

II *vi* **1** JUR (devant un juge) to testify; (au commissariat) to make a statement; **2** [*vin*] to leave a sediment.

III se déposer *vpr* [*poussière*] to settle; [*calcaire*] to collect.

dépositaire /depozitɛR/ *nmf* **1** COMM **~ (exclusif)** (sole) agent; **~ agréé** authorized dealer; **2** (d'objet) trustee; JUR (de biens) bailee; FIG (de secret) guardian.

déposition /depozisjɔ̃/ *nf* **1** JUR (au tribunal) evidence ¢; (recueillie) statement; (par écrit) deposition; **2** (destitution) (de souverain) deposition; (de magistrat) removal from office; **3** ART **~ de croix** Deposition (from the Cross).

déposséder /deposede/ [14] *vtr* **~ qn de qch** to dispossess sb of sth.

dépossession /deposesjɔ̃/ *nf* dispossession.

dépôt /depo/ *nm* **1** (entrepôt) warehouse; (plus petit) store; RAIL depot; (à la douane) bonded warehouse; MIL (de garnison) depot; **2** COMM (succursale) outlet; **l'épicerie fait ~ de pain** the grocer's sells bread; **3** ADMIN, JUR (d'acte) filing ¢; (de marque) registration; (de projet de loi) introduction; (d'amendement) proposal; **4** (remise en un lieu) **nous recommandons le ~ des documents chez un notaire** we recommend that the documents be deposited with a notary; **5** FIN (de fonds) deposit; (de titres) lodging ¢; **en ~** [*fonds*] on deposit; [*bijoux*] in a safe at the bank; **6** (sédiment) deposit; **7** (prison) police cells.

■ **~ d'armes** arms store; (clandestin) arms cache; **~ de bilan** voluntary liquidation; **~ légal** *formal deposit of a copy of a book, film, record, etc with an institution*; **~ de marchandises** RAIL goods GB ou freight US depot; **~ de munitions** MIL munitions store; (au rebut) munitions dump; **~ d'ordures** (rubbish) tip ou dump GB, garbage dump US.

dépoter /depɔte/ [1] *vtr* **1** (en jardinage) to remove a plant from its pot; **2** TECH (décharger) to strip.

dépotoir /depɔtwaR/ *nm* **1** (d'ordures) rubbish dump, rubbish tip GB, garbage dump US; **2**° (lieu en désordre) shambles° (*sg*).

dépôt-vente, *pl* **dépôts-ventes** /depovɑ̃t/ *nm* secondhand shop GB ou store (*where goods are sold on commission*).

dépouille /depuj/ *nf* **1** (peau) skin; (de gros mammifère) hide; (de serpent) slough; **2** (cadavre) body; **~ (mortelle)** mortal remains (*pl*).

II dépouilles *nfpl* (butin) spoils.

dépouillé, **~e** /depuje/ *adj* **1** (sobre) [*style*] spare; **2** (écorché) [*animal*] skinned; **3** (dénudé) [*arbre*] bare.

dépouillement /depujmɑ̃/ *nm* **1** (examen) **assister au ~ du scrutin** to be present when the votes are counted; **procéder au ~ du courrier** to go through the mail; **2** (ascèse) asceticism; **vivre dans le plus grand ~** to live a very ascetic ou spartan life; **3** (sobriété) sobriety.

dépouiller /depuje/ [1] **I** *vtr* **1** (dépecer) to skin [*animal*]; **2** (dénuder) to lay [sth] bare [*champ, région*]; **3** (déposséder) to rob [*voyageur*]; HUM to fleece° [*contri-*

depuis

L'adverbe

depuis se traduit généralement par *since*:

elle a démontré, depuis, qu'elle pouvait le faire
= she has since demonstrated that she could do it

Lorsqu'on veut insister sur le temps qui s'est écoulé depuis l'action dont on parle on peut renforcer *since* par *ever*:

nous nous sommes disputés hier, depuis il me fait la tête
= we had an argument yesterday, he's been sulking ever since

Attention, cette construction ne marche pas à la forme négative:

depuis il ne me parle plus = he hasn't talked to me
since

La préposition

depuis préposition de temps se traduit par *since* lorsqu'il sert à indiquer un point de départ, une date, une heure précise:

depuis 1789 = since 1789
depuis 2 heures du matin = since 2 am
depuis le début = since the beginning

et par *for* lorsqu'il sert à indiquer une durée, un nombre de jours, d'heures:

depuis deux heures = for two hours
depuis six ans = for six years
depuis quelques mois = for a few months

depuis + date

j'apprends l'anglais depuis l'âge de 12 ans
= I've been learning English since I was 12
cette maison nous appartient depuis 1876
= we've owned this house since 1876
je le connais depuis l'été dernier
= I've known him since last summer

je n'ai pas mangé depuis hier soir
= I haven't eaten since yesterday evening
il a fait trois films depuis le début de sa carrière
= he's made three films since the beginning of his career
il neigeait depuis 2 h de l'après midi
= it had been snowing since 2 pm
il n'avait pas plu depuis dimanche
= it hadn't rained since Sunday

On notera l'emploi de la forme progressive:

il habite ici depuis 1990
= he's lived here since 1990
ou he's been living here since 1990
il habite ici depuis le mois de janvier
= he's been living here since January

depuis + durée

il travaille ici depuis quelques années
= he's worked here for a few years
il travaille ici depuis dix ans
= he's worked here for ten years
nous marchons depuis deux heures
= we've been walking for two hours
je n'ai pas eu de nouvelles depuis six mois
= I haven't had any news for six months
je dormais depuis une heure
= I had been sleeping for an hour
je ne les avais pas vus depuis cinq ans
= I hadn't seen them for five years

On trouvera des exemples supplémentaires et les autres emplois de la préposition *depuis* et de la locution conjonctive *depuis que* dans l'entrée ci-dessous.

---

buable]; **~ qn de ses biens** to strip sb of his/her possessions; **4** to open [*courrier*]; to count [*scrutin*]; to go through [*documents*].
II se dépouiller *vpr* **1** (se démunir) [*personne*] **se ~ de** to shed [*vêtements*]; to divest oneself of [*biens*]; FIG to cast off [*morgue*]; **2** ZOOL (muer) [*serpent*] to slough; **3** (se dénuder) [*arbre*] to shed its leaves; [*style*] to become spare.

dépourvu, ~e /depuʀvy/ **I** *adj* **~ de** devoid of, lacking in [*intérêt, charme, talent*]; devoid of [*arrière-pensées*]; without [*chauffage, rideaux, accessoire*].
II *nm* **prendre qn au ~** to take sb by surprise.

dépoussiérant /depusjeʀɑ̃/ *nm* furniture polish.

dépoussiérer /depusjere/ [14] *vtr* LIT to dust; FIG to revamp [*idéologie, loi*].

dépravation /depʀavasjɔ̃/ *nf* depravity.

dépravé, ~e /depʀave/ *adj* depraved.

dépraver /depʀave/ [1] *vtr* to deprave.

dépréciation /depʀesjasjɔ̃/ *nf* depreciation.

déprécier /depʀesje/ [2] *vtr* **1** ÉCON, FIN to depreciate; **2** (rabaisser) to disparage, to depreciate.

déprédateur -trice /depʀedatœʀ, tʀis/ **I** *adj* destructive.
II *nm,f* vandal.

déprédation /depʀedasjɔ̃/ *nf* **~s** (pillage) pillaging ¢; (dégâts) damage ¢.

dépressif, -ive /depʀesif, iv/ *adj, nm,f* depressive.

dépression /depʀesjɔ̃/ *nf* ▶ **196** (tous contextes) depression.
■ **~ nerveuse** nervous breakdown.

dépressionnaire /depʀesjɔnɛʀ/ *adj* **zone ~** area of low pressure.

dépressurisation /depʀesyʀizasjɔ̃/ *nf* (volontaire) depressurization; (accidentelle) loss of pressure.

dépressuriser /depʀesyʀize/ [1] *vtr* to depressurize.

déprimant, ~e /depʀimɑ̃, ɑ̃t/ *adj* depressing.

déprime° /depʀim/ *nf* depression; **il est en pleine ~** he's really depressed.

déprimer /depʀime/ [1] **I** *vtr* (démoraliser) to depress.

II° *vi* to be depressed.

déprogrammer /depʀɔgʀame/ [1] *vtr* to cancel.

depuis /dəpɥi/ **I** *adv* since.
II *prép* **1** (marquant le point de départ) since; **elle fait de la danse ~ l'âge de 6 ans** she has been dancing since she was 6 years old; **~ quand vis-tu là-bas?** how long have you been living there ?; **~ ta naissance** since you were born; **c'est ce que je te répète ~ le début** that's what I've been telling you all along; **~ le début jusqu'à la fin** from start to finish; **2** (marquant la durée) for; **il pleut ~ trois jours** it's been raining for three days; **~ quand** or **combien de temps est-ce qu'elle enseigne?** how long has she been teaching?; **~ longtemps** for a long time; **~ peu** recently; **~ toujours** always; **on pratique cette coutume ~ toujours** this custom has been observed from time immemorial; **3** (marquant le lieu) from; **~ ma fenêtre** from my window; **~ Dijon il faut deux heures** from Dijon it takes two hours; **4** (dans une série) from; **~ le premier jusqu'au dernier** from first to last.
III depuis que *loc conj* GÉN since; (pour renforcer) ever since; **il pleut ~ que nous sommes arrivés** it's been raining ever since we arrived.

députation /depytasjɔ̃/ *nf* **1** (délégation) deputation; **2** (mandat de député) post of deputy.

député /depyte/ *nm* **1** POL deputy; **~ britannique** (British) MP; **être ~ au Parlement européen** to be a Euro-MP GB ou member of the European Parliament; **2** (envoyé) representative, delegate.

député-maire, *pl* **députés-maires** /depytemɛʀ/ *nm* deputy and mayor.

députer /depyte/ [1] *vtr* **~ qn auprès d'un comité** to send sb as a representative to serve on a committee; **~ qn pour faire qch** to delegate sb to do sth.

déqualifier /dekalifje/ [2] *vtr* to deskill.

der° /dɛʀ/ *nf* last; **la ~ des ~s** HIST the war to end all wars; **dix de ~** JEUX bonus of 10 points awarded to player who takes the last trick in game of belote.

déraciné, ~e /deʀasine/ *nm,f* uprooted person.

déracinement /deʀasinmɑ̃/ *nm* **1** (d'arbre) uprooting; **2** (d'immigré) (processus) uprooting; (résultat) rootlessness.

déraciner /deʀasine/ [1] *vtr* **1** LIT to uproot [*arbre, plante*]; **2** FIG to uproot [*personne*]; **3** (faire disparaître) to eradicate [*préjugé, abus*].

déraillement /deʀajmɑ̃/ *nm* derailment.

dérailler /deʀaje/ [1] *vi* **1** RAIL to be derailed; **faire ~ un train** to derail a train; **2**○ (perdre l'esprit) [*vieillard*] to go senile, to lose one's marbles○; (tenir des propos incohérents) to rave, to ramble; (se tromper) to talk through one's hat○; **3** (*voix*) (chantée) to waver; (parlée) to crack; [*instrument*] to go out of pitch.

dérailleur /deʀajœʀ/ *nm* **1** (de bicyclette) derailleur; **2** RAIL derailing stop.

déraison /deʀɛzɔ̃/ *nf* LITER madness.

déraisonnable /deʀɛzɔnabl/ *adj* (impensable) unrealistic; (peu sage) senseless; (excessif) unreasonable.

déraisonner /deʀɛzɔne/ [1] *vi* LITER (dire des bêtises) to talk nonsense.

dérangé, ~e /deʀɑ̃ʒe/ *adj* **1** [*estomac*] upset; **2**○ (fou) **être ~**, **avoir l'esprit ~** to be deranged.

dérangeant, ~e /deʀɑ̃ʒɑ̃, ɑ̃t/ *adj* [*idée, livre, film*] disturbing.

dérangement /deʀɑ̃ʒmɑ̃/ **I** *nm* **1** (inconvénient) trouble, inconvenience; **excusez le ~** sorry to bother you; **2** (dérèglement) **~ intestinal** stomach upset; **être en ~** [*ascenseur, téléphone*] to be out of order.

II dérangements *nmpl* TÉLÉCOM fault reporting service (*sg*).

déranger /deʀɑ̃ʒe/ [13] **I** *vtr* **1** (importuner) [*visiteur, téléphone*] to disturb [*personne*]; **'(prière de) ne pas ~'** 'do not disturb'; **excusez-moi de vous ~** (I'm) sorry to bother you; **2** (gêner) [*bruit, fumée*] to bother [*personne*]; **et alors, ça te dérange que je sorte?** so, what's it to you if I go out?; **3** (surprendre) to disturb [*animal, voleur*]; **4** (faire déplacer) to disturb [*spectateurs assis*]; (faire venir) to call out [*médecin, plombier*]; **5** (contrarier) to upset [*personne, habitudes*]; (troubler) to disturb [*personne*]; **6** (mettre en désordre) to disturb [*livres*]; to ruffle, to mess up [*coiffure*]; to turn [sth] upside down [*pièce*]; **7** (dérégler) to upset [*estomac*]; to affect [*esprit*].

II se déranger *vpr* **1** (se déplacer) (aller) to go out; (venir) to come out; **2** (se lever) to get up; (changer de place) to move; **3** (faire un effort) to put oneself out; **ne te vous dérange pas pour moi** don't go to any trouble on my account.

dérapage /deʀapaʒ/ *nm* **1** (de véhicule) skid; **traces de ~** skid marks; **2** (erreur) blunder; **3** (augmentation) escalation; **~ des prix** escalation of prices; **4** (perte de contrôle) loss of control; **les risques de ~ demeurent** the risk of things getting out of control remains; **~ verbal** slip; **5** (sur skis) sideslip.

déraper /deʀape/ [1] *vi* **1** [*prix, débat*] to get out of control; **2** [*couteau*] to slip; **3** [*personne, voiture*] to skid; **4** (à skis) to sideslip.

dératé○, **~e** /deʀate/ *nm,f* **courir comme un ~** to run like crazy.

dératisation /deʀatizasjɔ̃/ *nf* pest control (*for rats*).

derechef /dəʀəʃɛf/ *adv* FML once again.

déréglé, ~e /deʀegle/ *adj* [*esprit*] unbalanced; [*vie*] irregular; **avoir le sommeil ~** to have a disrupted sleep pattern.

dérèglement /deʀɛɡləmɑ̃/ **I** *nm* (de machine) fault; MÉTÉO disturbance; (psychologique) disturbance; (physiologique) disorder; (socio-économique) imbalance.

II dérèglements *mpl* FML excesses.

déréglementation /deʀegləmɑ̃tasjɔ̃/ *nf* deregulation.

déréglementer /deʀegləmɑ̃te/ [1] *vtr* to deregulate.

dérégler /deʀegle/ [14] *vtr* to affect [*temps, organe*]; to upset [*déroulement*]; **~ la télévision** to lose the channel on the TV; **~ le réveil** to set the alarm clock wrong.

dérider /deʀide/ [1] **I** *vtr* to cheer [sb] up.

II se dérider *vpr* to start smiling.

dérision /deʀizjɔ̃/ *nf* scorn, derision; **avec ~** scornfully, derisively; **tourner qn/qch en ~** to ridicule sb/sth.

dérisoire /deʀizwaʀ/ *adj* [*pouvoir*] pathetic; [*somme*] trivial, derisory.

dérivatif, -ive /deʀivatif, iv/ **I** *adj* LING derivative.

II *nm* GÉN diversion (**à** from); **2** MÉD derivative.

dérivation /deʀivasjɔ̃/ *nf* **1** (de cours d'eau) diversion; **2** (routière) diversion GB, detour US; **3** ÉLECTROTECH shunt; **en ~** in parallel; **4** LING derivation.

dérive /deʀiv/ *nf* **1** FIG drift; **à la ~** drifting; **aller** or **partir à la ~** to drift away; **leur affaire va à la ~** their business is going downhill; **2** ÉCON slide; **3** NAUT (aileron) centreboard[GB]; (déviation) deviation; **être à la ~** to be adrift; **4** AVIAT (déviation) drift; (gouvernail) (vertical) fin.

dérivé, ~e /deʀive/ **I** *adj* CHIMIE, LING **corps/mot ~** derivative.

II *nm* **1** GÉN spin-off; **2** (produit) by-product; **3** CHIMIE, LING derivative.

dériver /deʀive/ [1] **I** *vtr* **1** (détourner) to divert [*rivière*]; **2** MATH to obtain the derivative of [*fonction*].

II dériver de *vtr ind* **1** GÉN **~ de** to stem from; **2** LING **~ de** to be derived from.

III *vi* **1** LIT, FIG to drift; **2** MATH to differentiate.

dériveur /deʀivœʀ/ *nm* **1** (de plaisance) (sailing) dinghy; **2** (de pêche) drifter; **3** (voile) stormsail.

dermatologie /dɛʀmatɔlɔʒi/ *nf* dermatology.

derme /dɛʀm/ *nm* dermis.

dernier, -ière[1] /dɛʀnje, ɛʀ/ **I** *adj* **1** (qui termine une série) GÉN last; [*étage, étagère*] top; **arriver ~** (dans une course) to come last; **être bon ~** to come well and truly last; **un ~ mot avant que vous ne partiez** a final word before you go; **la dissertation est pour le 20 juin ~ délai** the deadline for this essay is 20 June; **de la dernière chance** final; **2** (précédent) last; **l'an ~** last year; **3** (le plus récent) [*roman, nouvelles*] latest; **ces ~ temps** recently; **4** (extrême) **le ~ degré de** the height of; **être du ~ ridicule** to be utterly ridiculous; **c'était la dernière chose à faire** it was the worst possible thing to do; **le ~ choix** the poorest quality.

II *nm,f* **1** (qui est à la fin) last; **les ~s** the last; **arriver le ~** to arrive last; **tu es toujours le ~** you are always last; **c'est le ~ qui me reste** it's my last one; **le ~ qui** (personne) the last person who; **c'est bien le ~ de mes soucis** that is the least of my worries; **être le ~ de la classe** to be bottom of the class; **le petit ~** the youngest child; **est-ce votre ~?** is that your youngest?; **ce ~, ces ~s** (de plusieurs) the latter; **dans ce ~ cas** in the latter case; **2** (le pire) **c'est le ~ des imbéciles** or **idiots** he's a complete idiot; **le ~ des ~s** the lowest of the low.

III en dernier *loc adv* last.

■ **~ cri** latest fashion; **dernière demeure** final resting place; **dernières volontés** last requests.

dernière[2] /dɛʀnjɛʀ/ *nf* **1** (histoire, nouvelle) **la ~** the latest; **2** (d'un spectacle) last performance.

dernièrement /dɛʀnjɛʀmɑ̃/ *adv* recently, lately.

dernier-né, dernière-née, *mpl* **derniers-nés** /dɛʀnjene, dɛʀnjɛʀne/ *nm,f* **1** (enfant) youngest; **2** (modèle) latest model.

dérobade /deʀɔbad/ *nf* GÉN evasion; (d'un cheval) running out.

dérobé, ~e /deʀɔbe/ **I** *adj* [*porte, escalier*] concealed.

II à la dérobée *loc adv* furtively.

dérober /deʀɔbe/ [1] **I** *vtr* **1** LITER (voler) to steal; **2** LITER (cacher) to hide.

II se dérober *vpr* **1** (se soustraire aux questions) to be evasive; **2** (se soustraire à son devoir) to shirk responsibility; **3** (se soustraire) **se ~ à** to shirk [*responsabilités, devoir*]; to evade [*question, justice*]; **se ~ à un engagement** to get out of a commitment; **4** (céder) [*sol*] to give way (**sous** under).

dérogation /deʀɔgasjɔ̃/ *nf* **1** (autorisation) (special) dispensation; **2** (contravention) infringement (**à** of).

dérogatoire /deʀɔgatwaʀ/ *adj* [*régime, cas*] special; **clause** ~ derogation clause.

déroger /deʀɔʒe/ [13] *vtr ind* ~ **à** to infringe [*loi, droit*]; to depart from [*principes, politique*]; to ignore [*obligation*]; to break with [*tradition*].

dérouillée○ /deʀuje/ *nf* **1** (volée de coups) hiding○, beating; **2** (défaite sportive) thrashing○, defeat.

dérouiller○ /deʀuje/ [1] **I** *vtr* (dégourdir) [*sport*] to loosen up [*jambes*]; to limber [sb] up [*personne*].
II *vi* (recevoir des coups) to get a hiding○ ou beating; (souffrir) to suffer.
III se dérouiller *vpr* se ~ **les jambes** to loosen up one's legs.

déroulement /deʀulmɑ̃/ *nm* **le** ~ **des événements** the sequence of events; **veiller au bon** ~ **de** to make sure [sth] goes smoothly [*cérémonie, négociations*]; **expliquer le** ~ **de la cérémonie** to explain the procedure for the ceremony; ~ **de carrière** career development; **le** ~ **de l'intrigue** the unfolding of the plot.

dérouler /deʀule/ [1] **I** *vtr* (étendre) to unroll [*tapis, tuyau, manuscrit*]; to let down [*chevelure*]; to uncoil [*corde*]; (autour d'une bobine) to unwind [*fil, pellicule*].
II se dérouler *vpr* **1** (avoir lieu) to take place; **2** (progresser) [*négociations*] to proceed SOUT, to go; [*histoire, événements*] to unfold; **3** (être déroulé) [*tapis*] to be unrolled; [*pellicule*] to be unwound; [*carte*] to unroll; **les images qui se déroulent dans ma tête** the images going through my head.

dérouleur /deʀulœʀ/ *nm* **1** GÉN holder; **2** TECH (de câble, papier) unwinding machine; **3** ORDINAT ~ **de bande** tape drive.

déroutant, ~**e** /deʀutɑ̃, ɑ̃t/ *adj* puzzling.

déroute /deʀut/ *nf* **1** (défaite) crushing defeat; **mettre qn en** ~ to defeat sb; **2** (débandade) rout; **en** ~ in full flight; **mettre en** ~ to put [sb] to flight, to rout sb; **3** (crise profonde) disarray; **en** ~ in disarray.

dérouter /deʀute/ [1] *vtr* **1** (déconcerter) to puzzle; **2** AVIAT, NAUT to divert.

derrière[1] /deʀjɛʀ/ **I** *prép* **1** (en arrière de) behind; **l'un** ~ **l'autre** one behind the other; **il ne fait rien par lui-même, il faut toujours être** ~ **lui** FIG he never gets anything done unless you keep after him; **il a les syndicats** ~ **lui** the unions are behind him; **2** (sous) behind; ~ **les apparences** (de personne) behind the façade; (de situation) beneath the surface.
II *adv* (à l'arrière) behind; (dans le fond) at the back; (à l'arrière d'une voiture) in the back; **qu'y a-t-il** ~? FIG what's behind it?; **ne poussez pas** ~! stop pushing at the back!, stop pushing back there!

derrière[2] /deʀjɛʀ/ *nm* **1** (de maison, véhicule, d'objet) back; **de** ~ [*chambre, porte*] back; **2**○ (de personne, d'animal) behind○, backside○.

derviche /dɛʀviʃ/ *nm* dervish; ~ **tourneur** whirling dervish.

des /de/ *art indéf pl* ▶ **un** I.

dès /dɛ/ **I** *prép* **1** (indique le point de départ dans le temps) from; ~ **(l'âge de) huit ans** from the age of eight; ~ **aujourd'hui** [*faisable*] from today; [*écrire, se renseigner*] this very day; ~ **maintenant** [*s'inscrire, commencer*] straight away; ~ **le départ** or **début** (right) from the start ou beginning; ~ **l'instant** or **le moment** or **la minute où** from the very moment when; **je vous téléphone** ~ **mon arrivée** I'll phone ou call you as soon as I arrive; **je lui en parlerai** ~ **lundi** I'll talk to him about it on Monday; **2** (indique le point de départ dans l'espace) from; ~ **Versailles il y a des embouteillages** there are traffic jams from Versailles onwards; **vous serez pris en charge par les organisateurs** ~ **l'aéroport** organizers will take care of you as soon as you get to the airport.
II dès que *loc conj* as soon as; ~ **que possible** as soon as possible.
III dès lors *loc adv* (à partir de ce moment) from then on, from that time on, henceforth; (de ce fait) therefore, consequently.
IV dès lors que *loc conj* (à partir du moment où) once, from the moment that; (puisque) since.

désabusé, ~**e** /dezabyze/ **I** *pp* ▶ **désabuser**.
II *pp adj* [*personne*] disillusioned; [*air, ton, parole*] cynical.

désabuser /dezabyze/ [1] *vtr* **1** (désillusionner) to disenchant (**de** with); **2** (détromper) to disabuse (**de** about).

désaccord /dezakɔʀ/ *nm* **1** (divergence) disagreement (**avec** with; **sur** over); **exprimer son** ~ to express (one's) disagreement; **en** ~ in disagreement; **être en** ~ to disagree (**avec** with; **sur** over); **2** (contradiction) discrepancy.

désaccordé, ~**e** /dezakɔʀde/ *adj* MUS out-of-tune (*épith*); **ton piano est** ~ your piano is out of tune.

désaccoutumer /dezakutyme/ [1] **I** *vtr* ~ **qn de qch** to cure sb's addiction to sth [*tabac, drogue*]; ~ **qn de faire** to cure sb of doing.
II se désaccoutumer *vpr* se ~ **de qch** to break one's dependence on sth [*tabac, alcool*].

désaffecté, ~**e** /dezafɛkte/ *adj* disused.

désaffection /dezafɛksjɔ̃/ *nf* disaffection (**pour** with).

désagréable /dezagʀeabl/ *adj* unpleasant, disagreeable.

désagrégation /dezagʀegasjɔ̃/ *nf* **1** (décomposition) disintegration; (écroulement) collapse; (dislocation) break-up; **2** (de roche) disintegration; **3** PSYCH collapse.

désagréger /dezagʀeʒe/ [15] **I** *vtr* to disintegrate.
II se désagréger *vpr* **1** (se décomposer) to disintegrate; (s'écrouler) to collapse; (se disloquer) to break up; **2** [*roche*] to disintegrate.

désagrément /dezagʀemɑ̃/ *nm* **1** (gêne) inconvenience; **2** (embêtement) annoyance, inconvenience.

désaltérant, ~**e** /dezalteʀɑ̃, ɑ̃t/ *adj* thirst-quenching.

désaltérer /dezalteʀe/ [14] **I** *vtr* ~ **qn** to quench sb's thirst.
II se désaltérer *vpr* to quench one's thirst.

désamorçage /dezamɔʀsaʒ/ *nm* **1** (d'explosif, de crise) defusing; **2** (de pompe) draining.

désamorcer /dezamɔʀse/ [12] *vtr* to defuse [*explosif, crise*]; to drain [*pompe*].

désappointement /dezapwɛ̃tmɑ̃/ *nm* disappointment.

désappointer /dezapwɛ̃te/ [1] *vtr* to disappoint.

désapprobateur, -trice /dezapʀɔbatœʀ, tʀis/ *adj* disapproving; **d'un air** ~ disapprovingly.

désapprobation /dezapʀɔbasjɔ̃/ *nf* disapproval.

désapprouver /dezapʀuve/ [1] *vtr* to disapprove of.

désarçonner /dezaʀsɔne/ [1] *vtr* **1** (déséquilibrer) [*cheval*] to throw [*cavalier*]; **2** (déconcerter) to take [sb] aback [*personne*]; **se faire** ~ to be thrown (**par** by).

désargenté○, ~**e** /dezaʀʒɑ̃te/ *adj* (pauvre) hard up○, penniless.

désarmant, ~**e** /dezaʀmɑ̃, ɑ̃t/ *adj* disarming.

désarmement /dezaʀmemɑ̃/ *nm* **1** MIL (de pays, région) disarmament; **2** NAUT (de navire) laying up.

désarmer /dezaʀme/ [1] **I** *vtr* **1** (rendre inoffensif) GÉN, MIL to disarm; **2** (décontenancer) to disarm [*personne*]; (désamorcer) to defuse [*colère*]; **3** NAUT to lay up [*navire*]; to ship [*avirons*].
II *vi* **1** MIL to disarm; **2** (abandonner une lutte) [*personne*] to give up the fight; (cesser) [*colère, haine*] to abate.

désarroi /dezaʀwa/ *nm* (trouble moral) distress; (désordre) confusion; **au grand** ~ **de** much to the distress of; **jeter qn dans le** ~ to throw sb into confusion.

désarticulé, ~**e** /dezaʀtikyle/ **I** *pp* ▶ **désarticuler**.
II *pp adj* [*fauteuil*] wrecked; [*pantin*] with broken joints (*épith, après n*).

désarticuler /dezaʀtikyle/ [1] *vtr* **1** (déboîter) to dislocate [*membre*]; **2** MÉD (amputer) to amputate.

désastre /dezastʀ/ *nm* (tous contextes) disaster.

désastreux, -euse /dezastʀø, øz/ *adj* disastrous.

désavantage /dezavɑ̃taʒ/ *nm* **1** (handicap) disadvantage; **avoir un** ~ **par rapport à qn** to be at a disadvantage compared to sb; **être/tourner au** ~ **de qn** to be/to turn to sb's disadvantage; **2** (inconvénient) drawback, disadvantage.

désavantager /dezavɑ̃taʒe/ [13] *vtr* to put [sb/sth] at a disadvantage, to disadvantage [*personne, entreprise*].

désavantageux, -euse /dezavɑ̃taʒø, øz/ *adj* [*affaire, prix*] unfavourable[GB], disadvantageous.

désaveu /dezavø/ *nm* **1** (reniement) denial; **2** (condamnation) rejection.

désavouer /dezavwe/ [1] *vtr* **1** (ne pas reconnaître comme sien) to deny [*acte, propos*]; **2** (rejeter) to disown [*personne, candidat*]; **3** JUR to disown [*enfant*].

désaxé, ~e /dezakse/ I *adj* [*personne*] deranged.
II *nm,f* deranged person.

desceller /desele/ [1] I *vtr* **1** CONSTR to work [sth] free [*lavabo, pierre*]; **2** (ouvrir) to unseal [*acte, lettre*].
II **se desceller** *vpr* [*lavabo, pierre*] to work loose.

descendance /desɑ̃dɑ̃s/ *nf* **1** (lignée) descendants (*pl*); **2**† (origine familiale) descent.

descendant, ~e /desɑ̃dɑ̃, ɑ̃t/ I *adj* [*cabine, courbe*] downward; **train ~** RAIL down train.
II *nm,f* descendant (**de** of).

descendre /desɑ̃dʀ/ [6] I *vtr* (+ *avoir*) **1** (transporter) (en bas) GÉN to take [sb/sth] down (**à** to); (d'en haut) GÉN to bring [sb/sth] down (**de** from); **je peux vous ~ au village** I can take you down to the village; **descends-moi mes pantoufles** bring my slippers down for me; **2** (placer plus bas) to put [sth] down [*objet*]; (en abaissant) GÉN to lower (**de** by); (avec une manivelle) to wind [sth] down; **descends le store** put the blind down; **~ un seau dans un puits** to lower a bucket into a well; **3** (réussir à mettre plus bas) to get [sth] down [*objet*]; **comment va-t-on ~ le piano?** (de l'étage) how are we going to get the piano downstairs?; **4** (parcourir) (en allant) to go down; (en venant) to come down [*pente, rue, marches, fleuve*]; **~ la colline en rampant/à bicyclette** to crawl/to cycle down the hill; **~ la rivière en pagayant/à la nage** to paddle/to swim down the river; **5**° (éliminer) to bump off° [*personne*]; to shoot down [*avion*]; **on l'a descendu d'une balle dans la tête** he was shot in the head and killed; **6**° (malmener) to tear [sb/sth] to pieces; **7**° (boire) [*personne*] to down [*bouteille*].
II *vi* (+ *être*) **1** (se déplacer) [*personne*] (en allant) GÉN to go down (**à** to); (en venant) GÉN to come down (**de** from); [*ascenseur, avion*] (en allant) to go down; (en venant) to come down; [*oiseau, avion*] (en allant) to fly down; [*soleil*] to set (**sur** over); [*nuit*] to fall; [*brouillard*] to come down (**sur** over); **peux-tu ~ chercher mon sac?** can you go downstairs and get my bag?; **il est descendu fumer** he went downstairs to smoke; **tu es descendu à pied?** did you walk down?; **nous sommes descendus par la route** (à pied) we walked down by the road; (à cheval) we rode down by the road; **descends, je te suis** go on down, I'll follow you; **~ de** to step off [*trottoir, marche*]; to climb down from [*mur, tabouret, échelle*]; **~ aux Enfers** RELIG to descend into Hell; **descends de là!** get down from there!; **faites-les ~** send them down [*clients, marchandises*]; **faire ~ sa jupe** to pull one's skirt down; **2** (d'un moyen de transport) **~ d'une voiture** to get out of a car; **~ d'un train/bus/avion** to get off a train/bus/plane; **~ de bicyclette** to get off one's bicycle; **~ de cheval** to get off one's horse, to dismount SOUT; **~ à Marseille** (d'avion, de bateau, bus, train) to get off at Marseilles; **3** (s'étendre de haut en bas) [*route, voie ferrée*] to go downhill, to go down; [*terrain*] to go down; **jusqu'à la mer** [*route, rivière*] to go right down to the sea; **~ en lacets** [*route*] to wind its way down; **~ en pente douce** [*terrain, route*] to slope down gently; **~ en pente raide** [*terrain, route*] to drop steeply; **4** (atteindre) [*vêtement, cheveux*] to come down (**jusqu'à** to); **5** (baisser) [*niveau, baromètre, température, pression, prix, taux*] to drop, to go down (**à** to; **de** by); [*marée*] to go out; **le franc est** or **a descendu par rapport à la livre** the Franc has dropped ou gone down against the pound; **ça fait ~ la température** GÉN it lowers the temperature; MÉD it brings one's temperature down; **ça ne fera pas ~ le taux de chômage** it won't bring the unemployment rate down; **6** (se rendre, séjourner) **~ dans le Midi** to go down to the South (of France); **~ dans un hôtel** to stay at a hotel; **~ dans la rue** POL to take to the streets; **7** (être

issu) **~ de** GÉN to come from; (génétiquement) to be descended from.

descente /desɑ̃t/ *nf* **1** (parcours d'un véhicule, d'une personne) descent; **la ~ a pris une heure** it took an hour to come down; **freiner dans les ~s** to brake going downhill; **tomber dans la ~** to fall on the way down; **faire la ~ d'une rivière en canoë** to canoe down a river; **2** (sortie) **à ma ~ du train** when I got off the train; **accueillir qn à sa ~ d'avion** to meet sb off the plane; **3** SPORT (en ski) (épreuve) downhill (event); (parcours) run; **~ hommes/dames** men's/women's downhill; **4** SPORT (en alpinisme, cyclisme, spéléologie) descent; **5** (raid) raid (**dans** on); **la police a fait une ~ dans l'immeuble/le bar** the police raided the building/bar.
■ **~ de croix** ART, RELIG descent from the cross; **~ aux enfers** descent into hell; **~ de lit** (tapis) (bed-side) rug; **~ d'organe** MÉD prolapse.

descriptible /deskʀiptibl/ *adj* describable.

descriptif, -ive /deskʀiptif, iv/ I *adj* (tous contextes) descriptive.
II *nm* (notice explicative) GÉN detailed description; CONSTR specification.

description /deskʀipsjɔ̃/ *nf* GÉN description; **faire une ~ de qch** to give a description of sth, to describe sth.

désemparé, ~e /dezɑ̃paʀe/ I *pp* ▶ **désemparer**.
II *pp adj* **1** (dérouté) [*personne*] distraught, at a loss (*jamais épith*); **2** [*avion, navire*] in distress.

désemparer /dezɑ̃paʀe/ [1] I *vtr* (dérouter) to throw [sb] into confusion.
II *vi* **sans ~** without let-up.

désemplir /dezɑ̃pliʀ/ [3] *vi* **ce restaurant ne désemplit pas** this restaurant is always full.

désenchanté, ~e /dezɑ̃ʃɑ̃te/ *adj* disillusioned, disenchanted (**de** with).

désenchantement /dezɑ̃ʃɑ̃tmɑ̃/ *nm* disillusionment, disenchantment.

désenclaver /dezɑ̃klave/ [1] *vtr* to open up [*région*].

désendettement /dezɑ̃dɛtmɔ̃/ *nm* (partiel) reduction of the debt; (complet) rescuing from debt.

désenfler /dezɑ̃fle/ [1] *vi* to become less swollen, to go down.

désengagement /dezɑ̃gaʒmɑ̃/ *nm* **1** ÉCON, POL disengagement; **2** MIL withdrawal (**de** from).

désengager: se désengager /dezɑ̃gaʒe/ [13] *vpr* ÉCON, MIL, POL to withdraw (**de** from).

désensibiliser /desɑ̃sibilize/ [1] *vtr* PHOT, MÉD to desensitize.

désenvoûter /dezɑ̃vute/ [1] *vtr* to break the spell on.

désépaissir /dezepɛsiʀ/ [3] *vtr* **1** CULIN to thin [*sauce*]; **2** (en coiffure) to thin [sth] out [*chevelure*].

déséquilibre /dezekilibʀ/ *nm* **1** LIT (de personne) loss of balance; (de meuble, objet) rocking; **en ~** [*table*] unstable; [*personne*] off balance; **2** FIG (d'ordre économique, social, écologique) imbalance; **3** PSYCH lack of balance.

déséquilibré, ~e /dezekilibʀe/ I *pp* ▶ **déséquilibrer**.
II *pp adj* PSYCH (perturbé) unbalanced; (fou) crazy.
III *nm,f* PSYCH lunatic.

déséquilibrer /dezekilibʀe/ [1] *vtr* **1** LIT [*personne, choc, coup*] to make [sb] lose their balance [*personne*]; [*poids*] to make [sth] unstable [*barque, meuble*]; **être déséquilibré par qch** [*personne*] to be thrown off balance by sth; [*meuble, objet*] to be made unstable by sth; **2** FIG to destabilize [*pays*]; **3** PSYCH to unbalance [*personne*].

désert, ~e /dezɛʀ, ɛʀt/ I *adj* **1** (inhabité) uninhabited; **île ~e** desert island; **2** (vide) deserted.
II *nm* LIT, FIG desert.

déserter /dezɛʀte/ [1] *vtr* to desert.

déserteur /dezɛʀtœʀ/ *nm* deserter.

désertion /dezɛʀsjɔ̃/ *nf* **1** MIL desertion; **2** POL defection (**vers** to).

désertique /dezɛʀtik/ *adj* **1** (du désert) [*paysage, climat, région*] desert (*épith*); **2** (vide) [*étendue*] barren.

désespérant, **~e** /dezɛspeʀɑ̃, ɑ̃t/ adj [personne, situation] hopeless; [nouvelle] heart-breaking.

désespéré, **~e** /dezɛspeʀe/ I pp ▶ **désespérer**.
II pp adj [personne, population] in despair (épith, après n); [situation, cas] hopeless; [tentative, appel] desperate; [regard, geste] despairing.
III nm,f desperate person.

désespérément /dezɛspeʀemɑ̃/ adv 1 (avec désespoir) [attendre] despairingly; [regretter] desperately; 2 (avec acharnement) desperately; 3 (à en pleurer) hopelessly.

désespérer /dezɛspeʀe/ [14] I vtr to drive [sb] to despair (avec, par with); ça me désespère de voir... if fills me with despair to see...; il ne désespère pas qu'elle revienne un jour he has not given up hope that she will come back one day.
II **désespérer de** vtr ind **~ de qn/qch** to despair of sb/sth; il ne désespère pas de le sauver he hasn't given up hope of saving him.
III vi to despair, to lose hope; **c'est à ~** it's hopeless.
IV se **désespérer** vpr to despair.

désespoir /dezɛspwaʀ/ nm despair; **mettre** or **réduire qn au ~** to drive sb to despair; **être** or **faire le ~ de** [enfant, bêtise] to be the despair of; **en ~ de cause** out of ou in desperation.

déshabillé /dezabije/ nm (vêtement) negligee.

déshabiller /dezabije/ [1] I vtr to undress [personne].
II se **déshabiller** vpr 1 (complètement) to undress; 2 (ôter son manteau) to take one's coat off.

déshabituer /dezabitɥe/ [1] I vtr **~ qn du tabac/de fumer** to get sb out of the habit of smoking.
II se **déshabituer** vpr se **~ de l'alcool** to break oneself of the habit of drinking.

désherbant /dezɛʀbɑ̃/ nm weedkiller.

désherber /dezɛʀbe/ [1] vtr (à la main) to weed [allée]; (avec un désherbant) to apply weedkiller to [allée].

déshérité /dezeʀite/ I pp ▶ **déshériter**.
II pp adj (pauvre) [personne] underprivileged; [pays] disadvantaged; [région, quartier] deprived.
III nm,f **les ~s** the underprivileged.

déshériter /dezeʀite/ [1] vtr to disinherit.

déshonneur /dezɔnœʀ/ nm disgrace.

déshonorant, **~e** /dezɔnɔʀɑ̃, ɑ̃t/ adj dishonourable[GB], degrading.

déshonorer /dezɔnɔʀe/ [1] I vtr 1 (apporter le déshonneur à) to bring disgrace on [personne, famille]; to bring [sth] into disrepute [doctrine, pays]; 2† (séduire) to dishonour[GB] [femme, jeune fille].
II se **déshonorer** vpr to disgrace oneself.

déshumaniser /dezymanize/ [1] I vtr to dehumanize.
II se **déshumaniser** vpr to become dehumanized.

déshydratation /dezidʀatasjɔ̃/ nf 1 MÉD dehydration; 2 TECH drying; **~ à froid** freeze-drying.

déshydrater /dezidʀate/ [1] I vtr 1 MÉD to dehydrate; 2 TECH to dry [aliment].
II se **déshydrater** vpr [malade] to dehydrate; [peau] to dry out.

desiderata /dezideʀata/ nmpl wishes.

désigner /deziɲe/ [1] vtr 1 (faire référence à) [mot, expression] to designate; [triangle, couleur] to represent; 2 (indiquer) (d'un geste) to point out; (en nommant) to name; **~ qch du menton** or **d'un mouvement de tête** to indicate sth with a jerk of one's head; **~ du doigt** to point to; **~ nommément** to name; **~ qn comme responsable** to hold sb responsible; 3 (choisir) GÉN to choose, to designate (comme, en qualité de as); (à un emploi) to appoint (comme as); être tout désigné pour to be just right for.

désillusion /dezil(l)yzjɔ̃/ nf disillusion.

désincarcérer /dezɛ̃kaʀseʀe/ [14] vtr to free.

désincarné, **~e** /dezɛ̃kaʀne/ adj 1 LIT disembodied; 2 FIG LITER [théorie] not anchored in reality (jamais épith).

désinence /dezinɑ̃s/ nf LING ending.

désinfectant, **~e** /dezɛ̃fɛktɑ̃, ɑ̃t/ I adj disinfecting.
II nm disinfectant.

désinfecter /dezɛ̃fɛkte/ [1] vtr to disinfect.

désinformation /dezɛ̃fɔʀmasjɔ̃/ nf disinformation; il y a une **~ du public sur ce point** the public is being deliberately misinformed on that matter.

désinformer /dezɛ̃fɔʀme/ [1] vtr to misinform deliberately.

désintégration /dezɛ̃tegʀasjɔ̃/ nf 1 (destruction) disintegration; 2 PHYS disintegration; 3 (de roche) crumbling.

désintégrer /dezɛ̃tegʀe/ [14] vtr, se **désintégrer** vpr to disintegrate.

désintéressé, **~e** /dezɛ̃teʀese/ I pp ▶ **désintéresser**.
II pp adj [personne, acte] selfless, unselfish; [conseil, jugement] disinterested; il l'a aidée de façon **~e** he had no ulterior motive for helping her.

désintéressement /dezɛ̃teʀɛsmɑ̃/ nm 1 (détachement) disinterestedness; **agir avec ~** to act disinterestedly; 2 FIN (remboursement) paying off.

désintéresser /dezɛ̃teʀese/ [1] I vtr FIN to pay off [créancier].
II se **désintéresser** vpr se **~ de qch/qn** to lose interest in sth/sb.

désintérêt /dezɛ̃teʀɛ/ nm (indifférence) lack of interest (pour in); (baisse d'intérêt) loss of interest (pour in).

désintoxication /dezɛ̃tɔksikasjɔ̃/ nf detoxification.

désintoxiquer /dezɛ̃tɔksike/ [1] vtr MÉD to detoxify [alcoolique, toxicomane].

désinvestissement /dezɛ̃vɛstismɑ̃/ nm ÉCON (dans un secteur économique) divestiture; (dans les biens d'équipement) disinvestment.

désinvolte /dezɛ̃vɔlt/ adj [personne, remarque, geste] (cavalier) offhand; (à l'aise) casual.

désinvolture /dezɛ̃vɔltyʀ/ nf 1 (sans-gêne) offhand manner; **avec ~** in an offhand manner; 2 (manière dégagée) casual manner; **avec ~** casually.

désir /deziʀ/ nm 1 (souhait) desire (de for; de faire to do); **~s du défunt/public** wishes of the deceased/public; **prendre ses ~s pour des réalités** to delude oneself; 2 (attirance sexuelle) desire.

désirer /deziʀe/ [1] vtr 1 (vouloir) to want (faire to do); s'il le désire if he wants; effets non désirés unwanted effects; que désirez-vous? what would you like?; tu te fais **~** you don't come to see me/us etc very often; 2 (vouloir sexuellement) to want, to desire.

désireux, **-euse** /deziʀø, øz/ adj **~ de faire/que** anxious to do/that.

désistement /dezistəmɑ̃/ nm withdrawal.

désister: se **désister** /deziste/ [1] vpr to stand down GB, to withdraw (en faveur de in favour[GB] of).

désobéir /dezɔbeiʀ/ [3] vtr ind to be disobedient, to disobey; **~ à qn/à un ordre** to disobey sb/an order.

désobéissant, **~e** /dezɔbeisɑ̃, ɑ̃t/ adj disobedient.

désobligeant, **~e** /dezɔbliʒɑ̃, ɑ̃t/ adj disagreeable.

désobliger /dezɔbliʒe/ [13] vtr to offend.

désodorisant, **~e** /dezɔdɔʀizɑ̃, ɑ̃t/ I adj deodorant.
II nm (pour le corps) deodorant; (pour la maison) air freshener.

désodoriser /dezɔdɔʀize/ [1] vtr to freshen.

désœuvré, **~e** /dezœvʀe/ adj at a loose end○ GB, at loose ends○ US (jamais épith).

désœuvrement /dezœvʀəmɑ̃/ nm faire qch par **~** to do sth for lack of anything better to do.

désolant, **~e** /dezɔlɑ̃, ɑ̃t/ adj 1 (attristant) distressing, upsetting; 2 (consternant) depressing.

désolation /dezɔlasjɔ̃/ nf 1 (affliction) grief; 2 (caractère dévasté) desolation.

désolé, **~e** /dezɔle/ adj 1 (au regret) sorry; **être ~ que** to be sorry that; 2 (très affligé) [personne] desolate; 3 (vide) [village, plaine] desolate.

désoler /dezɔle/ [1] I vtr 1 (attrister) to upset, to distress; 2 (consterner) to depress.
II se **désoler** vpr to be upset (de qch about).

désolidariser: se **désolidariser** /desɔlidaʀize/ [1] vpr to dissociate oneself (de from).

désopilant, **~e** /dezɔpilɑ̃, ɑ̃t/ adj hilarious.

désordonné, **~e** /dezɔʀdɔne/ adj **1** (désorganisé) [personne] untidy; [article, paroles, pensée] muddled; [réunion, activité, combat] disorderly; [gestes] uncoordinated; **2** (déréglé) [conduite, existence] wild.

désordre /dezɔʀdʀ/ **I**° adj inv **faire ~** to look untidy ou messy; **être très ~** to be very untidy.
II nm **1** (fouillis) mess; **pièce/maison en ~** untidy room/house; **laisser tout en ~** to leave everything in a mess; **quel ~!** what a mess!; **2** (manque de cohérence) chaos ¢; **semer le ~** to cause chaos; **se retirer dans le ~** MIL to retreat in disorder; **3** (caractère peu soigné) untidiness; **le ~ de sa maison** his/her untidy house; **4** (ordre aléatoire) **dans le ~** in any order; **gagner dans le ~** (aux courses) to win with a combination forecast; **5** (trouble) disorder; **~s sociaux** social disorder; **~s mentaux** mental disorders.

désorganisation /dezɔʀganizasjɔ̃/ nf (action) disruption; (résultat) disorganization.

désorganisé, **~e** /dezɔʀganize/ adj disorganized.

désorienter /dezɔʀjɑ̃te/ [1] vtr **1** (déconcerter) to confuse, to bewilder; **2** (faire perdre le sens de l'orientation) to disorientate^{GB}.

désormais /dezɔʀmɛ/ adv (au présent) from now on, henceforth; (au passé) from then on, henceforth.

désosser /dezɔse/ [1] vtr CULIN to bone.

despote /dɛspɔt/ nm despot.

despotique /dɛspɔtik/ adj despotic.

desquelles ▶ **lequel**.

desquels ▶ **lequel**.

DESS /deɛsɛs/ nm (abbr = **diplôme d'études supérieures spécialisées**) postgraduate degree taken after Master's.

dessaisir /desɛziʀ/ [3] **I** vtr **1** (priver) to relieve sb of sth [responsabilité]; **~ un juge d'un dossier** to take a judge off a case; **~ un tribunal d'une affaire** JUR to remove a case from a court; **2** (déposséder) **~ qn de** to divest sb of [bien].
II se dessaisir vpr **se ~ de** to relinquish.

dessaler /desale/ [1] **I** vtr **1**° (initier) to teach [sb] the ways of the world; **2** (extraire le sel de) to desalinate [eau de mer]; to desalt [mets].
II vi **1** CULIN to desalt; **2**° NAUT to capsize.
III se dessaler° vpr to lose one's innocence.

dessèchement /desɛʃmɑ̃/ nm (état) dryness; (processus) drying out.

dessécher /deseʃe/ [14] **I** vtr **1** (déshydrater) to dry [sth] out; **le soleil dessèche la peau** the sun makes your skin dry; **arbre desséché** withered tree; **2** (rendre insensible) to harden [personne, cœur]; to deaden [imagination].
II se dessécher vpr **1** (se déshydrater) [cheveux, lèvres] to become dry; [végétation] to wither; [sol] to dry out; **2** FIG (maigrir) [personne] to wither.

dessein /desɛ̃/ nm (projet) design; (intention) intention; **grand ~** grand design; **noirs ~s** LITER dark designs; **avoir/former le ~ de faire** to have/form the intention of doing; **à ~** deliberately, by design.

desseller /desele/ [1] vtr to unsaddle.

desserré, **~e** /deseʀe/ adj loose.

desserrement /deseʀmɑ̃/ nm **1** TECH loosening; **2** ÉCON relaxation; **~ du crédit** relaxation of credit.

desserrer /deseʀe/ [1] **I** vtr **1** LIT to loosen [col, cravate, vis]; to release [frein]; to undo [nœud]; **2** FIG to relax [étau, étreinte, crédit]; **~ les rangs** to break ranks.
II se desserrer vpr **1** [ceinture, col, cravate] to come loose; [écrou, vis] to work loose; [nœud] to come undone; **2** [étau, étreinte] to slacken.
IDIOMES **il n'a pas desserré les dents** he never once opened his mouth.

dessert /desɛʀ/ nm **1** (plat) dessert; **en** or **comme ~** for dessert; **2** (moment) **au ~** at dessert.

desserte /desɛʀt/ nf **1** (service de transport) service; **ferroviaire** rail ou train service; **2** (fait de desservir une localité) **la ~ aérienne des Antilles** flights to and

from the Antilles; **chemin de ~** access road; **3** (meuble) sideboard.

desservir /desɛʀviʀ/ [30] vtr **1** (relier) to serve [ville, village]; **quartier bien/mal desservi** well-/badly-served district; **2** (conduire à) to lead to [chambre, étage]; **3** (être au service de) to serve.

dessin /desɛ̃/ nm **1** ART (activité) drawing; **~ au crayon/pinceau** pencil/brush drawing; **faire du ~** to draw; **école/professeur de ~** art school/teacher; **2** (résultat) drawing; **faire un ~** to do a drawing; **tu veux que je te fasse un ~?** FIG, IRON do I have to spell it out for you?; **3** ART, IND (conception) design; **4** (motif) pattern; **5** (organisation) layout; **6** (contour) outline; **7** (grandes lignes) outline.
■ **~ animé** CIN cartoon; **~ industriel** technical drawing.

dessinateur, **-trice** /desinatœʀ, tʀis/ ▶374 nmf **1** ART draughtsman GB, draftsman US; **2** IND **~ (industriel)** draughtsman GB; **3** ART, IND (concepteur) designer.
■ **~ de bande dessinée** ART (strip) cartoonist; **~ humoristique** PRESSE cartoonist; **~ de presse** illustrator.

dessiner /desine/ [1] **I** vtr **1** ART (représenter) to draw; **~ au crayon/à la plume** to draw in pencil/in pen and ink; **2** (concevoir) to design [tissu, décor, timbre]; to draw up [plans]; **~ les grandes lignes de** to outline [plan, programme]; **3** (faire ressortir) **robe qui dessine la silhouette** figure-hugging dress.
II vi ART to draw; **savoir ~** to be able to draw.
III se dessiner vpr **1** (se faire jour) to take shape; **2** (apparaître) **se ~ à l'horizon** [ruines, cavalier] to appear on the horizon.

dessoûler /desule/ [1] **I** vtr to sober up [personne].
II vi to sober up; **il n'a pas dessoûlé pendant trois jours** he's been drunk for three days.

dessous¹ /dəsu/ **I** adv underneath; **j'ai soulevé le livre, mes clés étaient ~** I lifted the book and my keys were underneath; **quand je vois une échelle, je ne passe jamais ~** when I see a ladder, I never walk under it.
II en dessous loc adj (inférieur) **la taille/le modèle en ~** the next size down.
III en dessous loc adv **1** (sous quelque chose) underneath; **mets une chemise en ~** put a shirt on underneath; **il habite juste en ~** he lives on the floor below; **va voir à l'étage en ~** go and have a look downstairs; **2** (sournoisement) **agir en ~** to act in an underhand way; **regarder qn en ~** to look at sb sidelong.
IV par en dessous loc adv underneath; **passer par en ~** to go underneath; **prendre qch par en ~** to lift sth up from underneath.
V en dessous de loc prép (sous) below; **en ~ de la fenêtre** below the window; **15 degrés en ~ de zéro** 15 degrees below zero; **les enfants en ~ de 13 ans** children under 13.

dessous² /dəsu/ **I** nm inv (de langue, vase) underside; (des bras) inside (part); **le ~ du pied** the sole of the foot; **de ~**, **du ~** [drap] bottom; **l'étagère de** or **du ~** (sous une autre) the shelf below; (la dernière) the bottom shelf; **l'étage du ~** the floor below.
II nmpl **1** (sous-vêtements) underwear ¢; **2** (la face cachée) (de scandale, cas, succès) inside story (sg) (**de** on); **on ignore les ~ de l'affaire** we don't know what's behind this affair.
IDIOMES **avoir le ~** to come off worst.

dessous-de-bouteille /d(ə)sudbutɛj/ nm inv drip mat (for bottle).

dessous-de-plat /d(ə)sudpla/ nm inv (en vannerie, en bois) table mat; (à pieds) plate stand; (en métal) trivet.

dessous-de-table /d(ə)sudtabl/ nm inv (entre particuliers) under-the-counter payment; (pot-de-vin) bribe, backhander° GB.

dessous-de-verre /d(ə)sudvɛʀ/ nm inv coaster.

dessus¹ /dəsy/

■ **Note** Lorsque dessus est utilisé avec un verbe d'action tel que marcher, taper, tirer, compter etc on se reportera au verbe correspondant; de même pour certaines expressions telles que *mettre la main dessus, avoir le nez dessus* etc on se reportera aux entrées **main, nez** etc. Les usages particuliers sont traités dans l'entrée ci-dessous.

adv passe ~ go over it; **tu vois la pile, le livre doit être ~** you see that pile over there, the book should be on top of it; **un gâteau avec du chocolat ~** a cake with chocolate on top; **le prix est marqué ~** the price is on it; **'ton rapport est fini?'—'non , je travaille** or **suis ~'** 'is your report finished?'—'no, I'm working on it'.

dessus² /dəsy/ *nm inv* (de chaussure) upper; (de table, tête, panier) top; **l'étage du ~** the floor above; **le drap de ~** the top sheet.
IDIOMES **reprendre le ~** (dans un débat, une lutte) to regain the upper hand; (après une maladie, un chagrin) to get back on one's feet.

dessus-de-lit /d(ə)sydli/ *nm inv* bedspread.

déstabiliser /destabilize/ [1] *vtr* to unsettle [*personne*]; to destabilize [*situation, pays*].

destin /dɛstɛ̃/ *nm* **1** (fatalité) fate; **c'est le ~!** that's life!; **2** (existence) destiny.

destinataire /dɛstinatɛʀ/ *nmf* **1** POSTES (de lettre) addressee; **2** (bénéficiaire de crédit, d'aide) beneficiary; (de mandat) payee.

destination /dɛstinasjɔ̃/ I *nf* **1** GÉN destination; **arriver à ~** [*personne*] to reach one's destination; [*lettre, train*] to reach its destination; **2** (rôle, fonction) purpose.
II **à destination de** *loc prép* [*avion, bateau, train*] bound for [*lieu*]; **'vol Air France 810 à ~ de Londres'** 'Air France flight 810 to London'.

destiné, ~e¹ /dɛstine/ I *pp* ▶ **destiner**.
II *pp adj* **1** (prévu) ~ **à faire** intended to do, meant to do; **2** (promis) ~ **à une belle carrière** destined for a successful career.

destinée² /dɛstine/ *nf* destiny.

destiner /dɛstine/ [1] I *vtr* **1** (concevoir pour) ~ **qch à qn** to design sth for sb; **être destiné à faire** [*objet, système*] to be designed ou intended to do; **2** (réserver) **l'argent destiné à mes enfants** the money intended for my children; **produits destinés à l'exportation** goods (destined) for export; **3** (adresser) **la bombe était destinée à quelqu'un d'autre** the bomb was meant ou intended for somebody else; **4** (vouer) **être destiné à qch/à faire** [*personne*] to be destined for sth/to do; **5** (par le destin) **on ne peut pas savoir ce qui nous est destiné** we never know what fate has in store for us.
II **se destiner** *vpr* **elle se destine à une carrière de juriste** she's decided on a legal career.

destituer /dɛstitɥe/ [1] *vtr* to discharge [*officier*]; to depose [*souverain*]; ~ **qn de ses fonctions** to relieve sb of their duties.

destitution /dɛstitysjɔ̃/ *nf* (d'officier) discharge; (d'homme politique) deposition.

destructeur, -trice /dɛstʀyktœʀ, tʀis/ I *adj* destructive.
II *nm,f* destroyer.

destruction /dɛstʀyksjɔ̃/ *nf* destruction ¢.

désuet, -ète /dezɥɛ, ɛt/ *adj* **1** (vieillot) [*décor, charme*] old-world, quaint; [*manière, style*] old-fashioned; **2** (dépassé) [*mot*] obsolete; [*technique*] outmoded.

désuétude /dezɥetyd/ *nf* obsolescence; **tomber en ~** to become obsolete.

désunion /dezynjɔ̃/ *nf* **1** (de parti) division, dissension; **2** (dans la famille, le couple) discord.

désunir /dezyniʀ/ [3] *vtr* (diviser) [*dispute*] to divide, to break up [*famille, groupe*].

détachant /detaʃɑ̃/ *nm* stain remover.

détaché, ~e /detaʃe/ I *pp* ▶ **détacher**.
II *pp adj* **1** (indifférent) detached, unconcerned; **2** ADMIN [*professeur, diplomate, militaire*] on secondment GB (*après n*), transferred (*jamais épith*) (**auprès de** to).

détachement /detaʃmɑ̃/ *nm* **1** (indifférence) detachment; **2** ADMIN (de fonctionnaire) secondment GB, transfer (**auprès de** to); **3** MIL (troupe) detachment.

détacher /detaʃe/ [1] I *vtr* **1** (ôter les liens de) to untie [*personne, animal, barque, cheveux, paquet*] (**de** from); **2** (défaire un lien) to unfasten [*ceinture, collier*]; to undo [*chaussure, bouton*]; to untie, to undo [*nœud, corde*]; **détachez-lui ses menottes** remove his/her handcuffs; **3** (défaire d'un support) [*personne*] to tear [sth] off [*timbre, coupon, chèque*]; to take down [*affiche*]; [*vent*] to tear [sth] off [*affiche*]; **détachez selon** or **suivant le pointillé** tear along the dotted line; **4** (éloigner) ~ **qn de** to turn ou drive sb away from [*personne, famille*]; **5** (détourner) ~ **les yeux** or **le regard de qch** to take one's eyes off sth; ~ **son attention de qch** to turn one's attention away from sth; **6** (affecter) [*administration*] to second GB, to transfer [*enseignant, diplomate, militaire*]; **demander à être détaché en Asie** to ask to be seconded to Asia; **7** (faire ressortir) [*orateur*] to articulate [*mot, syllabe*]; [*musicien*] to detach [*note*]; [*imprimeur, designer*] to make [sth] stand out [*lettre, titre, mot*]; **8** (enlever les taches de) to remove the stain(s) from [*vêtement*].
II **se détacher** *vpr* **1** (se défaire de ses liens) [*prisonnier, animal*] to break loose (**de** from); [*bateau*] to come untied (**de** from); **2** (se défaire) [*nœud, lien*] to come undone; (se séparer d'un support) [*coupon, feuillet*] to come out (**de** of); [*papier peint, affiche*] to come away (**de** from), to peel (**de** off); **les fruits se détachent facilement des branches** the fruit comes off the branches easily; **4** (se désintéresser) **se ~ de** to turn one's back on [*monde*]; to grow away from [*personne*]; **5** (ressortir) [*motif, titre, objet, silhouette*] to stand out (**dans** in; **sur** against); **6** (s'éloigner) **se ~ de** [*individu, invité*] to detach oneself from [*groupe*]; [*coureur, cheval*] to pull away from [*groupe*]; [*membre, pays*] to break away from [*organisation, union*].

détail /detaj/ *nm* **1** (petit élément) detail; **étudier dans les moindres ~s** to study in minute detail; **2** (analyse précise) breakdown; **expliquer en ~** to explain in detail; **entrer dans les ~s** to go into detail; **raconter qch en ~** to give a detailed account of sth; **analyse de ~** detailed analysis; **3** COMM retail; **acheter/vendre (qch) au ~** to buy/sell (sth) retail.

détaillant, -e /detajɑ̃, ɑ̃t/ *nm,f* retailer.

détaillé, ~e /detaje/ I *pp* ▶ **détailler**.
II *pp adj* [*analyse, liste, plan*] detailed; [*facture*] itemized; **très ~** very detailed.

détailler /detaje/ [1] *vtr* **1** (exposer) to detail [*projet, problème*]; **2** (regarder) to scrutinize [*personne, objet*].

détaler /detale/ [1] *vi* **1** [*lapin*] to bolt; **2** [*personne*] to scarper° GB, to decamp.

détartrer /detaʀtʀe/ [1] *vtr* **1** to descale [*bouilloire, chaudière*]; **2** to scale [*dents*].

détaxe /detaks/ *nf* (suppression de taxe) tax removal; (remboursement de taxe) tax refund; (ristourne d'exportation) export rebate.

détecter /detɛkte/ [1] *vtr* to detect.

détecteur /detɛktœʀ/ *nm* detector; ~ **de mines** mine detector.

détection /detɛksjɔ̃/ *nf* detection.

détective /detɛktiv/ **▶ 374 |** *nm* detective.

déteindre /detɛ̃dʀ/ [55] I *vtr* to fade [*tissu*].
II *vi* **1** LIT (au soleil) to fade; (dans l'eau) to run; **2** FIG (influer) to rub off (**sur** on).

dételer /detle/ [19] I *vtr* to unharness [*cheval*]; to unyoke [*bœuf*]; to unhitch [*charrue, wagon*].
II° *vi* (arrêter de travailler) to knock off°; **sans ~** without a break.

détendre /detɑ̃dʀ/ [6] I *vtr* **1** (faire jouer) to release [*ressort*]; **2** (relâcher) to slacken [*ressort, corde*]; **3** (reposer) to relax [*muscle*]; to calm [*atmosphère, esprit*]; **4** (distraire) to entertain [*public*].
II *vi* **1** (reposer) [*pause, thé*] to be relaxing; **2** (distraire) [*comédie*] to be entertaining.
III **se détendre** *vpr* **1** (s'étirer) [*corde, ressort*] to slacken; **2** (se relaxer) [*personne, muscle*] to relax.

détendu, ~e /detɑ̃dy/ I *pp* ▶ **détendre**.
II *pp adj* (étiré) [*ressort, corde*] slack.
III *adj* (calme) [*personne, ambiance, relation*] relaxed.

détenir /det(ə)niʀ/ [36] *vtr* **1** (posséder) to keep [*objets*]; to hold [*pouvoir, capital, record*]; to possess [*armes*]; to have [*moyen, secret, preuve*]; **~ la vérité** to possess the truth; **2** JUR to detain [*criminel, suspect*].

détente /detɑ̃t/ *nf* **1** (repos) relaxation; **2** POL détente; **3** TECH (d'arme) trigger; **4** SPORT **avoir une bonne ~** [*joueur de tennis, gardien de but*] to have quick reflexes; [*athlète*] to have a good take-off.
IDIOMES **être dur à la ~**○ to be slow on the uptake.

détention /detɑ̃sjɔ̃/ *nf* **1** (possession) (d'actions, de drogue, passeport, record) holding; (d'armes, de secret) possession; **2** JUR (privation de liberté) detention.
■ **~ préventive** or **provisoire** JUR custody; **placer qn en ~ préventive** to remand sb in custody.

détenu, **~e** /detəny/ *nm,f* prisoner.

détergent /detɛʀʒɑ̃/ *nm* detergent.

détérioration /deteʀjɔʀasjɔ̃/ *nf* **1** (dégât) damage (**de** to); **2** (usure) wear and tear (**de** on); **3** (déclin) deterioration (**de** in).

détériorer /deteʀjɔʀe/ [1] **I** *vtr* to damage.
II se détériorer *vpr* GÉN to deteriorate; [*denrée*] to go bad; [*monnaie*] to weaken.

déterminant, **~e** /detɛʀminɑ̃, ɑ̃t/ *adj* decisive.

détermination /detɛʀminasjɔ̃/ *nf* determination.

déterminé, **~e** /detɛʀmine/ **I** *pp* ▶ **déterminer**.
II *pp adj* **1** (résolu) [*personne*] determined; **2** (causé) determined (**par** by); **3** (établi) [*corrélation*] demonstrated (*jamais épith*); **il est mort dans des circonstances mal ~es** the circumstances in which he died are not yet clear ou established; **4** (donné) [*durée, objectif*] given.

déterminer /detɛʀmine/ [1] *vtr* **1** (établir) to determine [*raison, responsabilité*]; **2** (fixer) to work out [*mesures, modalités*]; **3** (causer) to determine [*attitude, choix*]; **4** (décider) **~ qn à faire** to make sb decide to do.

déterré, **~e** /detere/ *nm,f* **avoir une tête** or **mine de ~** to look like death warmed up.

déterrer /detere/ [1] *vtr* to dig up [*plante, os*].

détestable /detɛstabl/ *adj* [*caractère, style, temps*] appalling; [*habitudes*] revolting.

détester /detɛste/ [1] **I** *vtr* **1** (exécrer) to detest, to loathe [*personne*]; **se faire ~ de qn** to arouse sb's hatred; **2** (ne pas supporter) to hate.
II se détester *vpr* (soi-même) to hate oneself; **2** (l'un l'autre) to hate each other.

détonant, **~e** /detɔnɑ̃, ɑ̃t/ *adj* LIT, FIG explosive.

détonateur /detɔnatœʀ/ *nm* **1** (amorce d'explosif) detonator; **2** FIG catalyst.

détonation /detɔnasjɔ̃/ *nf* detonation.

détoner /detɔne/ [1] *vi* to go off, to detonate.

détonner /detɔne/ [1] *vi* (jurer) [*personne, comportement, meuble*] to be out of place (**au milieu de** among).

détordre /detɔʀdʀ/ [6] *vtr* to untwist [*barre de fer*]; to unwind [*câble*].

détour /detuʀ/ *nm* **1** (trajet) detour; **faire un ~ par Oxford** to make a detour via Oxford; **ça vaut le ~** it's worth the trip; **2** (moyen indirect) roundabout means; (dans le langage) circumlocution; **être sans ~s** (explication) to be straight and to the point; (personne) to be plain-speaking; **il me l'a dit sans ~s** he told me straight; **3** (tournant) bend.

détourné, **~e** /detuʀne/ **I** *pp* ▶ **détourner**.
II *pp adj* [*allusion*] oblique; [*moyen*] indirect; **d'une façon** or **manière ~e** in a roundabout way.

détournement /detuʀnəmɑ̃/ *nm* **1** (de recette, dividendes) misappropriation; **2** (d'avion, de navire) hijacking; **3** (de circulation, rivière) diversion.
■ **~ de fonds** embezzlement, misappropriation of funds; **~ de mineur** (incitation à la débauche) corruption of a minor.

détourner /detuʀne/ [1] **I** *vtr* **1** (écarter) to divert [*attention*] (**de** from); **~ les yeux** or **le regard** or **la tête** to look away (**de** from); **~ les soupçons sur qn d'autre** to make suspicion fall on sb else; **2** (éloigner) **~ de** to distract [sb] from [*objectif*]; **3** (modifier le cours de) to divert [*rivière, circulation*]; **~ la conversation**

to change the subject; **4** (modifier la destination de) to divert [*vol, navire, ressources*] (**sur, vers** to); **5** (à des fins criminelles) to hijack [*avion, navire*]; to misappropriate, to embezzle [*fonds*].
II se détourner *vpr* **1** (renoncer) **se ~ de** to turn away from [*client, ami*]; **2** (tourner la tête) to turn away; to look away.

détracteur, **-trice** /detʀaktœʀ, tʀis/ *nm,f* detractor.

détraqué, **~e** /detʀake/ **I** *pp* ▶ **détraquer**.
II *pp adj* **1** [*mécanisme, moteur*] broken down, on the blink○; [*organisation, système*] broken down; [*temps*] unsettled; **2**○ **être ~** or **avoir l'estomac ~** to have an upset stomach.
III○ *nm,f* deranged person.

détraquer /detʀake/ [1] **I** *vtr* **1** [*personne*] to bust○ [*mécanisme, montre*]; [*poussière, rouille, humidité*] to make [sth] go wrong [*mécanisme, montre*]; **2**○ [*médicament, alcool*] to upset [*estomac*]; to damage [*santé*].
II se détraquer *vpr* [*mécanisme, moteur*] to break down, to go on the blink○; [*montre, horloge*] to go wrong; [*temps*] to break.

détremper /detʀɑ̃pe/ [1] *vtr* (imprégner) to saturate [*sol*]; to soak [*vêtement*]; **le terrain est détrempé** the ground is waterlogged.

détresse /detʀɛs/ *nf* distress; **dans la ~** in distress; **lancer un appel de ~** to send out a distress call; **en ~** [*navire, avion*] in distress; [*entreprise, train*] in difficulties.

détriment: **au détriment de** /odetʀimɑ̃də/ *loc prép* to the detriment of.

détritus /detʀity(s)/ *nmpl* (ordures) refuse ¢, rubbish GB ¢, garbage US ¢.

détroit /detʀwa/ *nm* GÉOG straits (*pl*); **le ~ de Gibraltar** the Straits of Gibraltar.

détromper /detʀɔ̃pe/ [1] **I** *vtr* to set [sb] straight.
II se détromper *vpr* **si tu crois qu'il va nous attendre, détrompe-toi!** if you think he's going to wait for us, you'd better think again!

détrôner /detʀone/ [1] *vtr* LIT, FIG to dethrone.

détrousser† /detʀuse/ [1] *vtr* to rob.

détruire /detʀɥiʀ/ [69] **I** *vtr* LIT, FIG to destroy.
II se détruire *vpr* **1** (soi-même) to destroy oneself; **2** (l'un l'autre) to destroy each other.

dette /dɛt/ *nf* debt; **~ publique/extérieure** ÉCON national/foreign debt; **avoir 1000 francs de ~s** to have debts of 1,000 francs; **~ de jeu** gambling debt; **être en ~ envers qn** LIT, FIG to be indebted to sb.

DEUG /dœg/ *nm* (*abbr* = **diplôme d'études universitaires générales**) *university diploma taken after two years' study*.

deuil /dœj/ *nm* **1** (décès) bereavement; **être frappé par un ~** to be bereaved, to suffer a bereavement; **2** (douleur) mourning ¢, grief; **3** (tenue) mourning (clothes); **être/se mettre en ~** to be in/go into mourning; **prendre/porter le ~ de qn** to go into/wear mourning for sb; **4** (période) period of mourning; **5** (cortège) funeral procession.
IDIOMES **faire son ~ de qch**○ to kiss sth goodbye○.

deux /dø/ ▶ **399**⌐, **298**⌐, **156**⌐ **I** *adj inv* **1** (précisément) two; **prendre qch à ~ mains** to take sth with both hands; **~ fois** twice; **des ~ côtés de la rue** on either side ou both sides of the street; **tous les ~ jours** every other day, every two days; **'~ m'** (en épelant) 'double m' GB, 'two ms'; **à nous ~** (je suis à vous) I'm all yours; (parlons sérieusement) let's talk; (à un ennemi) it's just you and me now; **2** (quelques) a few, a couple of; **c'est à ~ minutes d'ici** it's a couple of ou two minutes from here; **l'arrêt de bus est à ~ pas** the bus stop is a stone's throw away; **3** (dans une date) second.
II *pron* **je vais essayer les ~** I'll try both of them.
III *nm inv* (chiffre) two; **une fois sur ~** 50% of the time; **il travaille un week-end sur ~** he works every other week-end; **faire qch en moins de ~**○ to do sth very quickly ou in two ticks○ GB.
IDIOMES **faire ~ poids, ~ mesures** to have double standards; **un tiens vaut mieux que ~ tu l'auras** PROV a bird in the hand is worth two in the bush PROV;

en ~ temps, trois mouvements very quickly, in two ticks° GB; **lui et moi, ça fait ~** we're two different people; **je n'ai fait ni une ni ~** I didn't have a second's hesitation.

deuxième /døzjɛm/ ▸ 399], 156] *adj* second; **dans un ~ temps nous étudierons...** subsequently, we will study...; **c'est à prendre au ~ degré** it is not to be taken literally. ■ ~ **classe** (soldat) private; (dans les transports) second class, standard class GB.

deuxièmement /døzjɛmmɑ̃/ *adv* secondly, second.

deux-points /døpwɛ̃/ *nm inv* LING colon.

deux-roues /døʀu/ *nm inv* two-wheeled vehicle, two-wheeler.

deux-temps /døtɑ̃/ *adj, nm inv* TECH two-stroke.

dévaler /devale/ [1] I *vtr* [*animal, rocher*] to hurtle down [*pente*]; [*personne*] to tear down [*pente, rue*]; ~ **les escaliers** to rush downstairs.
II *vi* **la lave dévale vers le village** the lava is pouring down toward(s) the village.

dévaliser /devalize/ [1] *vtr* 1 [*voleur*] to rob [*personne, banque, coffre*]; to clean out° [*appartement*]; 2 [*clients*] to clean out° [*boutique*].

dévalorisation /devalɔʀizasjɔ̃/ *nf* 1 (de monnaie, compétence) depreciation; 2 (de politique, diplôme) devaluation.

dévaloriser /devalɔʀize/ [1] I *vtr* 1 ÉCON, FIN (diminuer la valeur de) to reduce the value of [*monnaie, produit*]; 2 (diminuer le prestige de) to depreciate [*objet*]; to belittle [*personne*].
II **se dévaloriser** *vpr* 1 (en valeur) to lose value; (en prestige) to lose prestige; 2 (se déprécier soi-même) to put oneself down.

dévaluation /devalɥasjɔ̃/ *nf* ÉCON devaluation.

dévaluer /devalɥe/ [1] I *vtr* ÉCON to devalue [*monnaie*].
II **se dévaluer** *vpr* to become devalued.

devancer /dəvɑ̃se/ [12] *vtr* 1 (avoir de l'avance sur) to be ahead of, to outstrip [*adversaire, concurrent*]; 2 (précéder) **les pompiers ont devancé la police sur les lieux de l'accident** the fire brigade got to the scene of the accident ahead of ou before the police; 3 (anticiper sur) to anticipate [*revendication, désir*]; to forestall, to pre-empt [*attaque, critiques*]; 4 (faire avant la date prévue) ~ **l'appel** to enlist for military service before call-up.

devancier, -ière /dəvɑ̃sje, ɛʀ/ *nm,f* precursor.

devant¹ /dəvɑ̃/ I *prép* 1 (en face de) ~ **qn/qch** in front of sb/sth; **le bus est passé ~ moi sans s'arrêter** the bus went straight past me without stopping; **regarder/marcher droit ~ soi** to look/walk straight ahead; 2 (près de) outside; **cela s'est passé ~ chez moi** it happened in front of ou outside my house; **il attendait ~ la porte** (à l'extérieur) he was waiting outside the door; (à l'intérieur) he was waiting by the door; 3 (en présence de) **il l'a dit ~ moi** he said it in front of me; **tous les hommes sont égaux ~ la loi** all men are equal in the eyes of the law; **je jure ~ Dieu** I swear before God; **cela s'est passé ~ nous/nos yeux** it took place in front of us/before our very eyes; 4 (face à) **fuir ~ le danger** to run away from danger, to flee in the face of danger; **hésiter ~ le danger** to hesitate in the face of danger; **je recule ~ ce genre de responsabilité** I shy away from that kind of responsibility; ~ **l'inévitable** faced with the inevitable; **l'impuissance des mots ~ le malheur** the inadequacy of language when confronted with misfortune; 5 (en avant de) **la voiture ~ nous** the car ahead ou in front of us; **il était si fatigué qu'il ne pouvait plus mettre un pied ~ l'autre** he was so tired he could hardly put one foot in front of the other; **elle est passée ~ moi, elle m'est passée ~**° (dans une file) she jumped the queue GB ou cut in line US and went ahead of me ; **laisser passer quelqu'un ~ (soi)** to let somebody go first; 6 (de reste) **avoir du temps ~ soi** to have plenty of time; **avoir de l'argent ~ soi** to have some money to spare; **avoir toute la vie ~ soi** to have one's whole life ahead of one.
II *adv* 1 (en face) **où est la poste?'—'tu es juste ~'** 'where's the post office?'—'you're right in front of it';

2 (en tête) **je passe ~, si vous le permettez** (pour montrer le chemin) I'll go ahead of you, if you don't mind; 3 (à l'avant) (dans une salle, un théâtre) at the front; (dans une voiture) in the front.

devant² /dəvɑ̃/ *nm* (de vêtement, maison, scène) front; **une chambre sur le ~** a room at the front; **de ~** [*dents, chambre, porte*] front. IDIOMES **prendre les ~s** to take the initiative.

devanture /dəvɑ̃tyʀ/ *nf* 1 (façade de magasin) front, frontage; 2 (vitrine) shop ou store US window; 3 (étalage) window-dressing; **en ~** in the window.

dévastateur, -trice /devastatœʀ, tʀis/ *adj* devastating.

dévastation /devastasjɔ̃/ *nf* devastation ¢, havoc ¢.

dévaster /devaste/ [1] *vtr* 1 (détruire) [*armée*] to lay waste to [*pays*]; [*orage, feu*] to destroy [*récoltes*]; 2 (saccager) [*cambrioleur*] to wreck [*habitation*].

déveine° /devɛn/ *nf* rotten luck°, bad luck.

développement /devlɔpmɑ̃/ *nm* 1 (de faculté, science, pensée, d'organisme) development (**de** of); 2 (d'entreprise, économie, de pays) development, expansion (**de** of); **pays en voie de ~** developing nation; **l'entreprise a connu un fort ~ dans les années 80** the firm expanded greatly in the eighties; **en plein ~** [*pays*] rapidly developing (*épith*); [*industrie*] fast-growing (*épith*); [*ville, université*] rapidly expanding (*épith*); 3 (de produit, technique, stratégie) development; 4 PHOT developing; **détail qui est apparu au ~** detail which appeared when the picture was developed.

développer /devlɔpe/ [1] I *vtr* 1 (faire croître) to develop [*muscle, faculté, pays*]; to expand [*importations, réseau, connaissances*]; 2 (amplifier) to develop, to expand [*sujet, chapitre, récit*]; MUS to develop [*thème*]; 3 (innover) to develop [*stratégie, politique, modèle*]; 4 PHOT to develop [*cliché*]; **donner qch à ~** to have ou get sth developed.
II **se développer** *vpr* [*corps, faculté*] to develop; [*plante*] to grow; [*entreprise, ville, économie*] to grow, to expand; [*mœurs, usage*] to become widespread.

devenir¹ /dəvniʀ/ [36] *vi* to become; ~ **réalité** to become a reality; **qu'est-ce que je vais ~**°?, **que vais-je ~?** what is to become of me?; **et Paul, qu'est-ce qu'il devient**° ou **que devient-il?** and what is Paul up to these days?; **il devient urgent de faire** it has become necessary to do; **la concurrence devient sévère** the competition is getting fierce.

devenir² /dəvniʀ/ *nm* (avenir) future.

dévergonder: se dévergonder /devɛʀgɔ̃de/ [1] *vpr* to be going to the bad.

déversement /devɛʀsəmɑ̃/ *nm* 1 (de trop-plein) draining-off, pouring-out; (d'effluents, de pétrole) dumping; ~ **accidentel** spillage; 2 CONSTR deflection.

déverser /devɛʀse/ [1] I *vtr* 1 LIT to pour [*liquide*] (**dans** into); to drop [*bombes*] (**sur** on); to dump [*ordures, sable*] (**dans** into; **sur** on); to discharge [*effluents*] (**dans** into); to disgorge [*foule, touristes*] (**dans** onto); ~ **du pétrole** (volontairement) to dump oil (**dans** into); (accidentellement) to spill oil (**dans** into); 2 FIG to pour out [*insultes*].
II **se déverser** *vpr* [*fleuve, rivière*] to flow (**dans** into); [*égout, foule*] to pour (**dans** into).

dévêtir /devetiʀ/ [33] I *vtr* to undress.
II **se dévêtir** *vpr* to get undressed.

déviation /devjasjɔ̃/ *nf* 1 (de circulation, réseau) diversion GB, detour US; 2 (altération) departure (**par rapport à** from); 3 (de boussole) deviation; 4 (optique) deflection.

dévider /devide/ [1] *vtr* 1 (dérouler) to unwind [*fil, bobine*]; 2° (raconter) to pour out [*histoire, souvenirs*].

dévier /devje/ [2] I *vtr* to deflect [*ballon, trajectoire*]; to divert [*circulation*].
II *vi* 1 [*balle de fusil, ballon*] to deflect; [*véhicule*] to veer off course; ~ **d'une trajectoire** to veer off course; 2 FIG ~ **de** to deviate from, to depart from [*projet, plan*]; 3 [*outil*] to slip; 4 [*conversation*] to drift.

devin /dəvɛ̃/ *nm* soothsayer, seer; **je ne suis pas ~!** I'm not psychic°!

deviner /dəvine/ [1] *vtr* 1 (parvenir à connaître) to guess [*secret*]; to foresee, to tell [*avenir*]; **2** (soupçonner) to sense [*danger*]; **3** (apercevoir) to make out.

devinette /dəvinɛt/ *nf* riddle.

devis /d(ə)vi/ *nm inv* estimate, quote; **établir/faire faire un** ~ to draw up/to ask for an estimate ou quote.

dévisager /devizaʒe/ [13] *vtr* ~ **qn** to stare at sb.

devise /dəviz/ *nf* **1** (monnaie d'un pays) currency; **une** ~ **forte** a strong ou hard currency; **2** (monnaie étrangère) (foreign) currency **⊄**; **acheter des** ~**s** to buy foreign currency; **3** (maxime) motto.

deviser /dəvize/ [1] *vi* to converse (**de** about).

dévisser /devise/ [1] **I** *vtr* to unscrew [*boulon*].
II *vi* (en alpinisme) to fall.
III se dévisser *vtr* (être amovible) to unscrew.

dévitaliser /devitalize/ [1] *vtr* to do root canal work on [*dent*].

dévoiler /devwale/ [1] *vtr* **1** LIT to unveil [*statue*]; **2** FIG to reveal [*intentions*] (**à qn** to sb); to uncover [*scandale*].

devoir¹ /dəvwaʀ/ [44]

■ **Note** Lorsque *devoir* est utilisé comme auxiliaire pour exprimer une obligation posée comme directive, une recommandation, une hypothèse ou un objectif, il se traduit par *must* suivi de l'infinitif sans *to*: *je dois finir ma traduction aujourd'hui* = I must finish my translation today; *tu dois avoir faim!* = you must be hungry!
– Lorsqu'il exprime une obligation imposée par les circonstances extérieures, il se traduit par *to have* suivi de l'infinitif: *je dois me lever tous les matins à sept heures* = I have to get up at seven o'clock every morning.
– Les autres sens du verbe auxiliaire, et *devoir* verbe transitif et verbe pronominal, sont présentés ci-dessous.

I *v aux* **1** (obligation, recommandation, hypothèse) **tu dois te brosser les dents au moins deux fois par jour** you must brush your teeth at least twice a day; **je dois aller travailler** I've got to go to work; **il a dû accepter** (obligation) he had to accept; (hypothèse) he must have accepted; **tu ne dois pas montrer du doigt!** you shouldn't point!; **ces mesures doivent permettre une amélioration du niveau de vie** these measures should allow an improvement in the standard of living; **il doit absolument éviter l'alcool** it's imperative that he avoid alcohol, he really must avoid alcohol; **je dois dire/reconnaître que cela ne m'étonne pas** I have to ou I must say/admit I'm not surprised; **elle ne doit pas être fière!** she must be ashamed of herself; **je devais avoir 12 ans à ce moment-là** I must have been 12 at the time; **ils doivent arriver d'une minute à l'autre** they're due to arrive any minute; **2** (être dans la nécessité de) **l'entreprise va** ~ **fermer** the company will have to close; **dois-je prendre un parapluie?** do I need to take an umbrella?; **dussé-je en mourir** LITER even if I die for it; **il a cru** ~ **partir** he felt obliged to leave; **3** (exprime une prévision) **elles devaient en parler** they were to talk about it; **le contrat doit être signé à 16 h** the contract is to be signed at 4 pm; **à quelle heure doit-il rentrer?** what time should he be home?; **je dois m'absenter prochainement** I'll have to leave shortly; **4** (exprime la fatalité) **ce qui devait arriver arriva** the inevitable happened; **cela devait arriver** it was bound ou it had to happen; **nous devons tous mourir un jour** we all have to die some day; **elle devait mourir dans un accident de voiture** she was to die in a car crash.
II *vtr* **1** (avoir à payer) to owe [*argent, repas*]; ~ **qch à qn** to owe sth to sb, to owe sth by sb; **combien vous doisje?** (pour un service) how much do I owe you?; (pour un achat) how much is it?; **2** (être redevable de) ~ **qch à qn** to owe sth to sb, to owe sth by sb; **je te dois d'avoir gagné** it's thanks to you that I won; **3** (avoir une obligation morale) ~ **qch à qn** to owe sb sth; **il me doit des excuses** he owes me an apology.
III se devoir *vpr* **1** (avoir une obligation morale) **se** ~ **à qn/son pays** to have a duty to sb/one's country; **2** (réciproquement) **les époux se doivent fidélité** spouses owe it to each other to be faithful; **3** (par convention) **un**

homme de son rang se doit d'avoir un chauffeur a man of his standing has to have a chauffeur.
IV comme il se doit *loc adv* **1** (comme le veut l'usage) **faire qch/agir comme il se doit** to do sth/to act in the correct way; **2** (comme prévu) **comme il se doit, elle est en retard!** as you might expect, she's late!

devoir² /dəvwaʀ/ *nm* (obligation morale) duty; **faire son** ~ to do one's duty; **le** ~ **m'appelle!** duty calls!; **il est de mon** ~ **de** it's my duty to; SCOL (exercice fait en classe) test; (fait à la maison) homework **⊄**.
■ ~ **surveillé** or **sur table** SCOL written test.

dévolu, ~e /devɔly/ **I** *adj* **1** (échu par droit) devolved (**à** to); **2** (réservé) reserved (**à** for).
II *nm* **jeter son** ~ **sur** to set one's heart on [*objet*]; to set one's cap at [*personne*].

dévorant, ~e /devɔʀɑ̃, ɑ̃t/ *adj* [*faim*] voracious; [*soif*] raging; [*flamme, passion, amour*] all-consuming.

dévorer /devɔʀe/ [1] *vtr* **1** (consommer) to devour [*nourriture, proie, livre*]; **être dévoré par les moustiques** to be eaten alive by mosquitoes; ~ **qn de baisers** to smother sb with kisses; **2** (miner) [*obsession, sentiment*] to consume; **3** (consumer) to eat up [*kilomètres*].

dévot, ~e /devo, ɔt/ **I** *adj* (très pieux) devout.
II *nm,f* PEJ sanctimonious person.

dévotion /devɔsjɔ̃/ *nf* **1** (ferveur) devoutness; (culte) devotion (**à** to); **avec** ~ devotedly; **2** (adoration) passion.

dévoué, ~e /devwe/ *adj* devoted (**à** to).

dévouement /devumɑ̃/ *nm* devotion.

dévouer: se dévouer /devwe/ [1] *vpr* **1** (se consacrer) to devote oneself (**à** to); **2** (faire abnégation) to put oneself out (**pour qn/qch** for sb/sth; **pour faire** to do).

dévoyé, ~e /devwaje/ *nm,f* depraved person.

dévoyer /devwaje/ [23] **I** *vtr* to deprave, to lead [sb] astray [*personne*].
II se dévoyer *vpr* to go astray.

dextérité /dɛksteʀite/ *nf* (adresse manuelle) dexterity, skill; (adresse de l'esprit) skill; **avec** ~ with skill, skilfully GB.

diabète /djabɛt/ ▶ 196 ┃ *nm* diabetes.

diabétique /djabetik/ *adj, nmf* diabetic.

diable /djabl/ **I** *nm* **1** MYTHOL, RELIG diabolic; **le Diable** the Devil; **avoir un mal du** ~ or **de tous les** ~**s à faire** to have a devil ou a hell° of a job doing; **du** ~ [*courage, peur*] terrific; **il fait un froid du** ~ or **de tous les** ~**s** it's hellishly cold; **un** ~ **d'homme** quite a man; **en** ~ [*difficile*] diabolically; [*beau*] devastatingly; [*intelligent*] fiendishly; **2** (enfant) **un (petit)** ~ a little devil; **3** (individu) **un pauvre** ~ a poor devil; **4** (jouet) ~ **(en boîte)** jack-in-the-box; **5** TECH (chariot) two-wheeled trolley GB, hand truck US.
II *excl* **que** ~**!** damn it°!; **qui/où** ~ who/where on earth; **au** ~ **l'avarice!** hang the expense!; **au** ~ **les scrupules!** to hell° with scruples!
IDIOMES **habiter au** ~ or **à tous les** ~**s** to live miles from anywhere; **qu'il aille au** ~**!** he can go to the devil!; **que le** ~ **t'emporte!** to hell with you!; **(que) le** ~ **m'emporte si je me trompe** I'll eat my hat if I'm wrong; **ce n'est pas le** ~**!** it's not that difficult!; **ce serait tenter le** ~ that would be asking for it; **avoir le** ~ **au corps** to be like someone possessed; **tirer le** ~ **par la queue** to live from hand to mouth.

diablement /djabləmɑ̃/ *adv* [*courageux, sévère*] terrifically; [*intelligent*] fiendishly; [*beau*] devastatingly.

diabolique /djabɔlik/ *adj* **1** RELIG demonic; **2** (malveillant) [*personne, sourire*] demonic; [*machination, idée, ruse*] devilish; **3** (pénible, difficile) [*problème, situation*] diabolical; **4** (extrême) [*précision, habileté*] uncanny.

diaboliquement /djabɔlikmɑ̃/ *adv* fiendishly.

diabolo /djabɔlo/ *nm* **1** (jouet) diabolo; **2** ~ **menthe** mint cordial and lemonade GB ou soda US.

diacre /djakʀ/ *nm* deacon.

diadème /djadɛm/ *nm* **1** (parure) tiara; **2** HIST diadem.

diagnostic /djagnɔstik/ *nm* **1** MÉD diagnosis; **bon/mauvais** ~ correct/wrong diagnosis; **établir** or **poser un** ~ to make a diagnosis; **avoir un bon** ~

to be good at making diagnoses; **2** (évaluation) diagnosis; **~ d'un expert** expert opinion.

diagnostique /djagnɔstik/ *adj* diagnostic.

diagnostiquer /djagnɔstike/ [1] *vtr* LIT, FIG to diagnose.

diagonal, **~e**[1], *mpl* **-aux** /djagɔnal, o/ *adj* diagonal.

diagonale[2] /djagɔnal/ *nf* diagonal; **en ~** diagonally; **lire qch en ~** to skim through sth.

diagramme /djagʀam/ *nm* graph.

dialecte /djalɛkt/ *nm* dialect.

dialectique /djalɛktik/ **I** *adj* dialectical.
II *nf* dialectic.

dialogue /djalɔg/ *nm* dialogue[GB].
■ **un ~ de sourds** a dialogue[GB] of the deaf.

dialoguer /djalɔge/ [1] *vi* to have talks.

dialoguiste /djalɔgist/ ▶374 | *nmf* CIN screenwriter, dialogist.

dialyse /djaliz/ *nf* dialysis.

diamant /djamɑ̃/ *nm* **1** (pierre précieuse) diamond; **2** (de tête de lecture) stylus.

diamantaire /djamɑ̃tɛʀ/ ▶374 | *nm* (tailleur) diamond cutter; (commerçant) diamond merchant.

diamétralement /djametʀalmɑ̃/ *adv* diametrically.

diamètre /djamɛtʀ/ *nm* diameter.

diapason /djapazɔ̃/ *nm* MUS **1** (note) diapason; **2** (instrument) **~ (à branches)** tuning fork.
IDIOMES **se mettre au ~** to fall in step (**de** with); **être au ~** to be in tune.

diaphane /djafan/ *adj* LITER [*teint*] pallid; [*brume*] hazy; [*tissu*] diaphanous; [*papier*] translucent.

diaphragme /djafʀagm/ *nm* diaphragm.

diapo○ /djapo/ *nf* (*abbr* = **diapositive**) slide.

diaporama /djapoʀama/ *nm* slide show.

diapositive /djapozitiv/ *nf* slide.

diarrhée /djaʀe/ *nf* diarrhoea.

diatonique /djatɔnik/ *adj* diatonic.

diatribe /djatʀib/ *nf* diatribe (**contre** against).

dichotomie /dikɔtɔmi/ *nf* dichotomy.

dico○ /diko/ *nm* (*abbr* = **dictionnaire**) dictionary.

dictateur /diktatœʀ/ *nm* dictator.

dictatorial, **~e**, *mpl* **-iaux** /diktatɔʀjal, o/ *adj* dictatorial.

dictature /diktatyʀ/ *nf* dictatorship.

dictée /dikte/ *nf* **1** SCOL (exercice) dictation; **2** (action de dicter) **écrire sous la ~ de qn** [*élève, secrétaire*] to take down sb's dictation; (sous la contrainte) to write down what sb dictates.

dicter /dikte/ [1] *vtr* **1** (à haute voix) to dictate; **~ qch à qn** to dictate sth to sb; **2** (motiver) to motivate; **le souci d'aider autrui dicte notre action** our action is motivated by the desire to help others; **3** (imposer) to dictate (**à** to).

diction /diksjɔ̃/ *nf* **1** GÉN diction; **2** CIN, THÉÂT elocution.

dictionnaire /diksjɔnɛʀ/ *nm* GÉN dictionary.
■ **~ analogique** ~ thesaurus.

dicton /diktɔ̃/ *nm* saying; **comme le dit le ~** as the saying goes.

didacticiel /didaktisjɛl/ *nm* educational software program.

didactique /didaktik/ *adj* didactic.

dièse /djɛz/ *adj*, *nm* sharp; **do ~** C sharp.

diesel /djezɛl/ *nm* **1** (moteur) (**moteur**) **~** diesel (engine); **2** (véhicule) diesel; **voiture ~** diesel car.

diète /djɛt/ *nf* **1** MÉD light diet; **2** HIST diet.

diététicien, **-ienne** /djetetisjɛ̃, ɛn/ ▶374 | *nm,f* dietician.

diététique /djetetik/ **I** *adj* dietary (*épith*); **ce n'est pas très ~ de manger du pain avec des pâtes** it's not very healthy to eat bread with pasta.
II *nf* dietetics (+ *v sg*); **magasin de ~** health food shop GB ou store US.

dieu, *pl* **~x** /djø/ *nm* **1** MYTHOL, RELIG god; **le ~ des mers** the god of the sea; **2** (personne talentueuse) **le ~ du tennis** the greatest tennis player.

IDIOMES **être beau comme un ~** to look like a Greek god; **nager comme un ~** to be a superb swimmer; **jurer ses grands ~x que...** to swear to God that...; **être dans le secret des ~x** to be privy to the secrets of those on high.

Dieu /djø/ *nm* RELIG God; **~ le père** God the Father; **le bon ~** the good Lord; **mon ~!** my God!; **bon ~**○! for God's sake!; **~ merci!** thank God!; **~ me pardonne!** God forgive me!; **~ vous entende!** may God hear your prayer!; **~ soit loué** or **béni!** thanks be to God!; **~ m'en garde!** God forbid!; **~ ait son âme!** God rest his/her soul; **c'est pas ~ possible**○! good God, it's not possible!; **~ sait si je l'avais prévenu!** God knows I warned him!; **~ sait pourquoi/ quand!** God knows why/when; **~ seul le sait** goodness only knows; **si ~ le veut** God willing.
IDIOMES **se prendre pour ~ le père** to think one is God Almighty; **chaque jour que ~ fait** day in, day out; **il vaut mieux s'adresser à ~ qu'à ses saints** PROV always go straight to the top; **c'est la maison du bon ~ ici!** it's open house here!

diffamation /difamasjɔ̃/ *nf* GÉN, JUR (par écrit) libel; (oralement) slander.

diffamatoire /difamatwaʀ/ *adj* GÉN, JUR (par écrit) libellous[GB]; (oralement) slanderous; **écrit ~** libel.

diffamer /difame/ [1] *vtr* GÉN, JUR (par écrit) to libel; (oralement) to slander.

différé, **~e** /difeʀe/ **I** *pp* ▶ **différer**.
II *pp adj* **1** (remis) postponed; **2** FIN deferred; **3** RADIO, TV pre-recorded.
III *nm* recording; **match en ~** recording of the match; **en léger ~** recorded moments before.

différemment /difeʀamɑ̃/ *adv* differently (**de** from); **il en va ~ de** or **pour** it's a different matter for.

différence /difeʀɑ̃s/ *nf* **1** (écart) difference; **~ d'âge** age difference; **~ de taille/statut** difference in height/status; **~ d'opinion** difference of opinion; **à une ~ près** with one difference; **2** (distinction) difference; **faire la ~** to tell the difference; **à la ~ de** unlike; **à la ~ que**, **à cette ~ que** with the difference that; **3** (discrimination) differentiation ₵; **faire des ~s entre ses enfants** to differentiate between one's children; **4** (spécificité) difference; **le droit à la ~** the right to be different; **5** MATH difference.

différenciation /difeʀɑ̃sjasjɔ̃/ *nf* differentiation.

différencier /difeʀɑ̃sje/ [2] **I** *vtr* **1** (distinguer) to differentiate (**de** from); **rien ne les différencie** there's no way of telling them apart; **2** (créer une différence) to make [sb/sth] different (**de** from); **3** (voir une différence) to differentiate between.
II se différencier *vpr* **1** (se rendre différent) [*personne, organisation*] to differentiate oneself (**de** from); **2** (pouvoir être distingué) to differ (**de** from); **3** (devenir différent) to become different (**de** from).

différend /difeʀɑ̃/ *nm* disagreement (**entre** between; **sur** over).

différent, **~e** /difeʀɑ̃, ɑ̃t/ *adj* **1** (dissemblable) different (**de** from); **2** (varié) different, various; **pour ~es raisons** for various reasons; **à ~s moments** at various times; **en ~s endroits** in different places.

différentiel, **-ielle** /difeʀɑ̃sjɛl/ **I** *adj* (tous contextes) differential.
II *nm* ÉCON, TECH differential.

différer /difeʀe/ [14] **I** *vtr* to postpone [*départ, réunion, décision*]; to defer [*paiement, remboursement*].
II *vi* (être différent) to differ (**de** from); **~ peu** to differ little; **~ en ce que** to differ in that.

difficile /difisil/ *adj* **1** (malaisé, pénible) GÉN difficult; [*victoire*] hard-won (*épith*); **le plus ~ reste à faire** the worst is yet to come; **2** (indocile) [*personne, caractère*] difficult; **être ~ à vivre** to be difficult to live with; **3** (exigeant) fussy (*sur* about); **est-ce que ce cadeau va lui plaire? elle est si ~!** will she like this present? she's so hard to please!; **faire le ~** to be fussy.

difficilement /difisilmɑ̃/ *adv* with difficulty; **je pouvais ~ dire non** I couldn't very well say no; **~ supportable** hard to bear.

difficulté /difikylte/ *nf* **1** (peine) difficulty (**à faire** in doing); **aimer la ~** to enjoy difficulties; **reconnaître la ~ d'une tâche** to admit that a task is difficult; **avec ~** with difficulty; **en ~** in difficulties ou trouble; **2** (obstacle) difficulty; **avoir des ~s scolaires** to have problems at school; **sans ~(s)** without any difficulty; **non sans ~s** not without difficulty; **~s à** or **pour faire** difficulty (in) doing; **avoir des ~s de logement** to have problems with housing; **3** (objection) **faire des ~s** to raise objections.

difforme /difɔʀm/ *adj* [*corps, dos*] deformed; [*objet*] strangely shaped (*épith*); [*arbre*] twisted.

difformité /difɔʀmite/ *nf* deformity.

diffus, ~e /dify, yz/ *adj* [*lumière, chaleur*] diffuse; [*sentiment, impression*] vague; [*style, exposé*] PÉJ diffuse, loose.

diffuser /difyze/ [1] **I** *vtr* **1** RADIO, TV to broadcast; **diffusé en direct** broadcast live; **diffusé en différé** broadcast; **2** (propager) to spread; **~ le signalement de qn** to send out a description of sb; **3** (distribuer) to distribute [*article*]; **4** (émettre) to diffuse [*lumière, chaleur*].

II se diffuser *vpr* [*nouvelle, information*] to spread; [*chaleur, lumière*] to be diffused.

diffuseur /difyzœʀ/ *nm* (d'ouvrages) distributor.

diffusion /difyzjɔ̃/ *nf* **1** RADIO, TV, CIN broadcasting; **la ~ du film** the showing of the film; **2** (de connaissances) dissemination; **3** (distribution) distribution; **4** PRESSE circulation; **5** MÉD, PHYS diffusion.

digérer /diʒeʀe/ [14] *vtr* **1** (après un repas) to digest; **bien/mal ~** to have good/bad digestion; **2** (assimiler) to digest [*lecture, connaissances*]; **3**° (accepter) to swallow [*affront*]; to stomach [*défaite*]; **il a du mal à ~ son échec** he finds it hard to come to terms with his failure.

digeste /diʒɛst/ *adj* easily digestible, easy to digest.

digestif, -ive /diʒɛstif, iv/ **I** *adj* digestive.

II *nm* (liqueur) liqueur (*taken after dinner*); (eau-de-vie) brandy.

digestion /diʒɛstjɔ̃/ *nf* digestion.

digicode® /diʒikɔd/ *nm* digital (access) lock.

digital, ~e¹, ** *mpl* **-aux /diʒital, o/ *adj* digital.

digitale² /diʒital/ *nf* BOT digitalis; **~ pourprée** foxglove.

digne /diɲ/ *adj* **1** (plein de dignité) dignified; **2** (approprié) worthy; **3** (méritant) **~ de confiance** or **de foi** trustworthy; **~ d'être souligné** noteworthy; **~ d'envie** enviable; **4** (à la hauteur de) **~ de** worthy of.

dignement /diɲmɑ̃/ *adv* **1** (avec dignité) with dignity; **2** (comme il convient) fittingly.

dignitaire /diɲitɛʀ/ *nm* dignitary.

dignité /diɲite/ *nf* **1** (qualité) dignity; **rendre sa ~ à** to restore dignity to; **avoir sa ~** to have one's pride; **2** (fonction) dignity.

digramme /diɡʀam/ *nm* digraph.

digression /diɡʀesjɔ̃/ *nf* (s'écartant du sujet) digression (*sur* about); **faire une ~, faire des ~s** to digress.

digue /diɡ/ *nf* (au bord de la mer) sea wall; (pour polder) dyke GB, dike US; (autour d'un port) harbour^GB wall; (barrière morale) barrier.

dilapidateur, -trice /dilapidatœʀ, tʀis/ *adj, nm,f* spendthrift.

dilapider /dilapide/ [1] *vtr* to squander [*argent, fortune*].

dilatation /dilatasjɔ̃/ *nf* **1** (de corps, gaz) expansion; **2** (de pupille, vaisseau, d'organe, orifice) dilation.

dilater /dilate/ [1] **I** *vtr* (agrandir) to dilate [*orifice, pupille, vaisseau*]; to distend [*estomac*]; PHYS to expand [*corps, gaz*].

II se dilater *vpr* **1** (s'agrandir) [*pupille, vaisseau, orifice*] to dilate (**de** with); [*estomac*] to be distended; **2** PHYS [*corps, gaz*] to expand.

dilatoire /dilatwaʀ/ *adj* **1** (pour gagner du temps) [*tactique*] delaying; [*mesure, réponse, conduite*] intended to gain time; **2** JUR dilatory.

dilemme /dilɛm/ *nm* dilemma.

dilettante /diletɑ̃t/ *nmf* GÉN amateur, dilettante PÉJ; **écrire des romans en ~** to be an amateur novelist.

dilettantisme /diletɑ̃tism/ *nm* GÉN amateurism; PÉJ dilettantism.

diligence /diliʒɑ̃s/ *nf* **1** (véhicule) stagecoach; **2** (empressement) haste; **faire qch avec ~** to do sth post-haste.

diligent, ~e /diliʒɑ̃, ɑ̃t/ *adj* diligent.

diluant /dilɥɑ̃/ *nm* TECH thinner.

diluer /dilɥe/ [1] *vtr* **1** (diminuer la concentration de) to dilute (**avec** with; **dans** in); **2** (rendre plus liquide) to thin [sth] down.

dilution /dilysjɔ̃/ *nf* **1** (pour diminuer la concentration) dilution; (pour liquéfier) thinning down; **2** (solution) solution.

diluvien, -ienne /dilyvjɛ̃, ɛn/ *adj* **1** (torrentiel) **pluies diluviennes** torrential rain; **2** (du déluge) diluvian.

dimanche /dimɑ̃ʃ/ ▶ 551 *nm* Sunday; **habits** or **toilette du ~** Sunday best; **peintre du ~** weekend ou amateur painter.

IDIOMES **ce n'est pas tous les jours ~** not every day is a holiday.

dimension /dimɑ̃sjɔ̃/ *nf* **1** MATH, PHYS dimension; **object à trois ~s** three-dimensional object; **film en trois ~s** three-D film; **2** (mesure) dimension; **3** (taille, grandeur) size; **de toutes les ~s** of all sizes; **un objet de petite/grande ~** a small/large object; **de ~s standard** standard-size; **4** (aspect, caractère) dimension, aspect; **5** (importance, ampleur) dimensions (*pl*).

diminué, ~e /diminɥe/ **I** *pp* ▶ **diminuer**.

II *pp adj* (affaibli) [*personne, adversaire*] weak.

diminuer /diminɥe/ [1] **I** *vtr* **1** (réduire) to reduce [*quantité, durée, niveau, frais, risques*] (**à** to; **de** by); to lower [*taux, taxe, salaire*]; **2** (modérer) to dampen [*enthousiasme, courage*]; **3** (rabaisser) [*personne*] to belittle [*exploit, personne*]; [*fait*] **~ les mérites/le talent de qn** to detract from sb's merits/talent; **4** (affaiblir) to weaken [*personne*]; to sap [*forces*]; **5** (en tricot) to decrease [*mailles*].

II *vi* **1** (se réduire) [*facture, chômage, taux, prix*] to come ou go down (**de** by); [*pouvoir d'achat*] to be reduced; [*salaire*] to fall; [*écart*] to close; [*réserves, consommation, quantité*] to decrease; [*croissance, volume, déficit, différence*] to decrease; [*production, ventes, demande*] to fall off; [*bougie, bouteille*] to go down; **les jours diminuent** the days are getting shorter; **2** (faiblir) [*activité, intérêt, attaques, violence*] to fall off; [*pression, tension*] to decrease; [*bruit, flamme, orage, rire, rumeurs, colère*] to die down; [*forces, capacités*] to diminish; [*courage*] to fail; [*ardeur*] to cool; [*température, fièvre*] to go down.

diminutif, -ive /diminytif, iv/ **I** *adj* [*suffixe*] diminutive.

II *nm* GÉN diminutive; (familier) pet name.

diminution /diminysjɔ̃/ *nf* **1** (réduction) GÉN (provoquée ou contrôlée) reduction (**de** in); (constatée) decrease (**de** in); (de production, d'activités commerciales) fall-off (**de** in); **être en ~** GÉN to be decreasing; [*production, exportations*] to be falling off; **être en ~ de 7%** to be down by 7%; **2** (affaiblissement) diminishing; **3** (en tricot) **commencer les ~s** start decreasing.

dinde /dɛ̃d/ *nf* **1** ZOOL GÉN turkey; (femelle) turkey hen; **2** CULIN turkey; **~ aux marrons** turkey with chestnuts; **3**° (femme stupide) (silly) goose°.

dindon /dɛ̃dɔ̃/ *nm* **1** ZOOL turkey (cock); **2**° (homme stupide) dope°.

dindonneau, *pl* **~x** /dɛ̃dɔno/ *nm* turkey; **un rôti de ~** turkey roast.

dîner¹ /dine/ [1] *vi* **1** (prendre le repas du soir) to have dinner; **~ d'une soupe** to have soup for dinner; **2** (prendre le repas de midi) DIAL, B, C to have lunch.

IDIOMES **qui dort dîne** PROV when you're asleep you don't feel hungry.

dîner² /dine/ *nm* **1** (repas du soir) dinner; **l'heure du ~** dinner time; **préparer le ~** to get dinner ready; **le ~ est servi** dinner is ready; **après ~** after dinner; **2** (repas de midi) DIAL, B, C lunch.

dînette /dinɛt/ *nf* (service miniature) doll's tea set; **jouer à la ~** to play at tea parties.

dingo○ /dɛ̃go/ **I** *adj inv* crazy○.

II *nm* ZOOL dingo.

dingue /dɛ̃g/ **I** *adj* **1** (idiot) [*personne*] crazy○; **2** (fou) [*bruit, succès*] wild; [*prix, vitesse*] ridiculous; **c'est ~!** (inadmissible) it's crazy!; (incroyable) it's amazing!; **3** (passionné) **être ~ de qch** to be crazy○ about sth.

II *nmf* **1** (fou) nutcase○; **il est chez les ~s** he's in a loony bin○; **2** (passionné) **être un ~ de musique** to be a music freak○.

dinguer◑ /dɛ̃ge/ [1] *vi* **envoyer qn ~** (pousser) to send sb flying; [*chasser*] to send sb packing○.

dinosaure /dinozɔr/ *nm* dinosaur.

diocésain, ~e /djosezɛ̃, ɛn/ *adj, nm,f* diocesan.

diocèse /djosɛz/ *nm* diocese.

diphtérie /difteri/ **▶ 196】** *nf* MÉD diphtheria.

diphtongue /diftɔ̃g/ *nf* diphthong.

diplomate /diplɔmat/ **I** *adj* diplomatic.

II ▶ 374】 *nmf* diplomat.

III *nm* CULIN *dessert of glacé fruits and custard on a sponge base.*

diplomatie /diplɔmasi/ *nf* diplomacy.

diplomatique /diplɔmatik/ *adj* diplomatic.

diplôme /diplom/ *nm* **1** SCOL certificate, diploma; **il n'a aucun ~** he hasn't got any qualifications; **quels ~s faut-il pour faire?** what qualifications are needed to do?; **2** (d'université, de grande école) degree; (d'autre institution) diploma; **~ d'ingénieur** engineering degree; **~ d'architecte** degree in architecture; **3** (dans l'armée, la police) staff exam; **4** (nécessaire à l'exercice d'une activité) certificate; **5** (épreuves) exam; **passer un ~** to take an exam; **6** (document) certificate.

diplômé, ~e /diplome/ **I** *pp* **▶ diplômer.**

II *pp adj* **il est ~ de l'université de Lille** he's a graduate of the university of Lille; **elle est ~e en droit** she has a degree in law; **une infirmière ~e** a qualified nurse.

III *nm,f* graduate.

diplômer /diplome/ [1] *vtr* GÉN to award a diploma to; UNIV to award a degree to [*étudiant*].

dire[1] /dir/ [65] **I** *vtr* **1** (faire entendre) to say [*mots, prière*]; to tell [*histoire, blague*]; **'entrez' dit-elle** 'come in,' she said; **sans mot ~** without saying a word; **ce n'est pas une chose à ~** you don't say that sort of thing; **~ des bêtises** to talk nonsense; **~ qch à voix basse** to whisper sth; **~ qch entre ses dents** to mutter sth; **ne plus savoir que ~** to be at a loss for words; **j'ai mon mot à ~ là-dessus** I've got something to say about that; **~ ce qu'on a à ~** to say one's piece; **2** (faire savoir) to tell; **~ des mensonges** to tell lies; **~ qch à qn** to tell sb sth; **je vous l'avais bien dit!** I told you so!; **c'est ce qu'on m'a dit** so I've been told; **faire ~ à qn que** to let sb know that; **je me suis laissé ~ que...** I heard that...; **tenez-vous le pour dit!** I don't want to have to tell you again!; **c'est moi qui vous le dis** I'm telling you; **permets-moi de te ~ que tu vas le regretter**○! you'll regret this, I can tell you!; **je ne te dis que ça**○ I'll say no more; **c'est pas pour ~, mais**○ I don't want to make a big deal of it, but○...; **à qui le dites-vous**○! don't I know it!; **je ne vous le fais pas ~**○! you don't need to tell me!; **ne pas se le faire ~ deux fois**○ not to need to be told twice; **dis, tu me crois**○? tell me, do you believe me?; **dis donc, où tu te crois**○? hey! where do you think you are?; **à vous de ~** JEUX your bid; **3** (affirmer) to say (**que** that); **elle dit pouvoir le faire** she says she can do it; **ne fais pas attention, il ne sait pas ce qu'il dit** don't mind him, he doesn't know what he's talking about; **on dit que...** it is said that...; **on le dit marié** he is said to be married; **j'irai jusqu'à ~ que** I'd go as far as to say that; **c'est le moins qu'on puisse ~** that's the least one can say; **si l'on peut ~** if one might say so; **si je puis ~** if I may put it like that; **on peut ~ qu'elle a du toupet celle-là!** she's really got a nerve○!; **on ne peut pas ~ qu'il se soit fatigué!** he certainly didn't overtax himself; **autant ~ que** you might as well say that, in

other words; **si j'ose ~** if I may say so; **ce n'est pas à moi de le ~** it's not for me to say; **cela va sans ~** it goes without saying; **il faut ~ que** one should say that; **c'est (tout) ~!** need I say more?; **cela dit** having said that; **c'est vous qui le dites!** that's what you say!; **disons, demain** let's say tomorrow; **c'est difficile à ~** it's hard to tell; **je sais ce que je dis** I know what I'm talking about; **à vrai ~** actually; **entre nous soit dit** between you and me; **soit dit en passant** incidentally; **c'est ~ si j'ai raison** it just goes to show I'm right; **c'est beaucoup ~** that's going a bit far; **c'est peu ~** that's an understatement; **c'est vite dit** that's easy for you to say; **ce n'est pas dit** I'm not that sure; **c'est plus facile à ~ qu'à faire** it's easier said than done; **il est dit que je ne partirai jamais** I'm destined never to leave; **tu l'as dit**○!, **tune tu dis**○! you said it!; **4** (formuler) **voilà qui est bien dit!** well said!; **comment ~?** how shall I put it?; **tu ne crois pas si bien ~** you don't know how true that is; **pour ainsi ~** so to speak; **autrement dit** in other words; **lent, pour ne pas ~ ennuyeux** slow, not to say boring; **comme dirait l'autre**○ as they say; **disons que je suis préoccupé** let's say I'm worried; **un lien disons social** a link which we could call social; **5** (indiquer) [*loi*] to state (**que** that); [*appareil de mesure*] to show (**que** that); **vouloir ~** to mean; **quelque chose me dit que** something tells me that; **qu'est-ce que ça veut ~ tout ce bruit**○? what's the meaning of all this noise?; **6** (demander) **~ à qn de faire** to tell sb to do; **fais ce qu'on te dit!** do as you're told!; **7** (objecter) **qu'avez-vous à ~ à cela?** what have you got to say to that?; **je n'ai rien à ~** no comment; **il n'y a pas à ~**○, **elle est belle** you have to admit, she's beautiful; **il n'y a rien à ~, tout est en ordre** I have no complaint, everything's fine; **tu n'as rien à ~!** (ne te plains pas) don't complain!; (tais-toi) don't say a word!; **8** (penser) to think; **qu'en dites-vous?** what do you think?; **que diriez-vous d'une promenade?** how about a walk?; **on dirait qu'il va pleuvoir** it looks as if it's going to rain; **on dirait un fou** you'd think he was mad; **on dirait du Bach** it sounds like Bach; **~ qu'hier encore il était parmi nous!** it's odd to think (that) he was still with us yesterday!; **9** (inspirer) **ça ne me dit rien de faire** I don't feel like doing; **notre nouveau jardinier ne me dit rien (qui vaille)** I don't think much of our new gardener.

II se dire *vpr* **1** (penser) to tell oneself (**que** that); **il faut (bien) se ~ que...** one must realize that...; **il faut te ~ que...** you must understand that...; **2** (échanger) to exchange [*insultes, mots doux*]; **se ~ adieu** to say goodbye to each other; **3** (se prétendre) to claim to be; **4** (se déclarer) **il s'est dit favorable à** he says he's in favour○GB of; **5** (être exprimé) **ça ne se dit pas** you can't say that.

III se dire *v impers* **il ne s'est rien dit d'intéressant** nothing of interest was said.

dire[2] /dir/ **I** *nm* **au ~ de** according to; **au ~ de tous** by all accounts.

II dires *nmpl* statements; **selon les ~s de** according to.

direct /dirɛkt/ **I** *adj* **1** (sans intermédiaire) direct; (immédiat) [*supérieur*] immediate; **2** [*route, accès*] direct; **train ~** through train; **ce train est ~ pour Lille** this train is nonstop to Lille; **3** (franc) direct; **4** (en grammaire) direct.

II *nm* **1** RADIO, TV live broadcasting ¢; **en ~ de** live from; **2** (en boxe) jab; **~ du gauche** left jab; **3** (train) express (train).

directement /dirɛktəmɑ̃/ *adv* **1** (sans détour) straight; **je suis venu ~** I came straight here; **2** (personnellement) [*concerner, affecter*] directly; **ça ne dépend pas ~ de lui** it's not entirely up to him; **3** (sans intermédiaire) directly; **~ du producteur au consommateur** straight from the producer to the consumer.

directeur, -trice[1] /dirɛktœr, tris/ **I** *adj* (central) **principe ~** guiding principle; **idée directrice d'un ouvrage** central theme of a book; **les lignes directrices d'une politique** the guidelines of a policy.

II ▶374| *nm,f* **1** (d'école) headmaster/headmistress GB, principal US; (d'établissement privé) principal; **2** (d'hôtel, de cinéma) manager/manageress; **3** (administrateur) director; (chef) head (**de** of).
■ **~ de banque** bank manager; **~ commercial** sales manager; **~ général** managing director GB, chief executive officer US; ADMIN director general; **~ général adjoint** assistant general manager; **~ de journal** newspaper editor; **~ de prison** prison governor GB, warden US; **~ de la rédaction** PRESSE managing editor; **~ sportif** (team) manager; **~ d'usine** plant manager.

direction /diʀɛksjɔ̃/ *nf* **1** (chemin) direction; **se tromper de ~** to go in the wrong direction; **être** or **aller dans la bonne/mauvaise ~** LIT, FIG to be heading in the right/wrong direction; **quelle ~ ont-ils prise?** which way did they go?; **il a pris la ~ du nord** he headed north; **dans la ~ de**, **en ~ de** [*aller, regarder*] toward(s); **un village dans la ~ de Clermont** a village on the way to Clermont; **demander la ~ de** to ask the way to; **indiquer la ~ à qn** to tell sb the way; **prenez la ~ Nation** (d'autobus) take the bus going to 'Nation'; (de métro) take the train going to 'Nation'; **la ~ Lille** (route) the Lille road; **train en ~ de Toulouse** Toulouse train; **faire un pas** or **geste en ~ de qn** FIG to make an overture to sb; **2** (fonction de directeur) (gestion) management; (supervision) supervision; (de journal) editorship; (de parti, mouvement) leadership; **confier la ~ de qch à qn** to put sb in charge of sth; **nommé à la ~ de l'usine** appointed manager of the factory; **assurer la ~ de** (d'entreprise, de service) to manage, to run; (de projet, travaux) to be in charge of; **orchestre sous la ~ de** orchestra conducted by; **3** (personnes) management; **4** (lieu) manager's office; (siège social) head office; **5** (service) department; **6** (de véhicule) steering; **~ à crémaillère/assistée** rack-and-pinion/power steering.

directive /diʀɛktiv/ *nf* (instruction) directive.

directorial, **~e**, *mpl* **-iaux** /diʀɛktɔʀjal, o/ *adj* managerial.

directrice² /diʀɛktʀis/ I *adj f* ▶ **directeur** I.
II *nf* **1** MATH directrix; **2** (profession) ▶ **directeur** II.

dirigeable /diʀiʒabl/ *nm* dirigible, airship.

dirigeant, **~e** /diʀiʒɑ̃, ɑ̃t/ I *adj* [*classe*] ruling; [*rôle*] leading.
II *nm* (de pays, parti) leader; (gérant) manager.

diriger /diʀiʒe/ [13] I *vtr* **1** (être responsable de) to be in charge of [*personnes*]; to run [*service, école, journal, parti, pays*]; to manage [*usine, entreprise, théâtre*]; to lead [*discussion, débat, enquête*]; to direct [*opération*]; to supervise [*recherches, travaux*]; **mal ~ une entreprise** to mismanage a business; **il veut tout ~** he wants to be in charge of everything; **2** (conduire) to steer [*véhicule, navire*] (**vers** toward(s)); to pilot [*avion*] (**vers** toward(s)); **il vous dirigera dans la ville** he'll guide you around the town; **3** (orienter) LIT to turn [*lumière, lampe, jet, regard*] (**vers** toward(s), **sur** on); to point [*arme, télescope*] (**sur** at); FIG to direct [*critiques, attaques*] (**contre** against); **~ des étudiants dans leurs recherches** to guide students in their research; **~ qn sur un service** to send sb to a department; **4** (expédier) to dispatch [*marchandises*] (**vers, sur** to); to direct [*convoi*] (**vers, sur** to); **5** (motiver) **la volonté de plaire dirige tous leurs actes** all their actions are motivated by the desire to be liked; **6** MUS to conduct; **7** CIN, THÉÂT to direct [*acteurs*]; to manage [*troupe*].
II se diriger *vpr* **1** (aller) **se ~ vers** to make for; **se ~ droit sur** to head ou make straight for; **tu devrais te ~ dans cette voie** FIG that's the way to go; **2** (s'orienter) **se ~ d'après les étoiles** [*navigateur*] to sail by the stars; [*promeneur*] to be guided by the stars; **avoir du mal à se ~ dans le noir** to have difficulty finding one's way in the dark.

dirigisme /diʀiʒism/ *nm* planned economy.

discale /diskal/ *adj f* **hernie ~** slipped disc.

discernable /disɛʀnabl/ *adj* discernible, detectable.

discernement /disɛʀnəmɑ̃/ *nm* judgment; **choisir**

avec/sans ~ to be discriminating/undiscriminating in one's choice.

discerner /disɛʀne/ [1] *vtr* **1** (par un effort d'attention) to detect [*signe, odeur, expression*]; to make out [*silhouette, bruit*]; **2** (par un effort de réflexion) to make out [*mobiles, intentions*]; **~ le vrai du faux** to discriminate between truth and untruth; **~ le bien du mal** to be able to tell right from wrong.

disciple /disipl/ *nmf* **1** (partisan) follower; **2** (élève) disciple; **les ~s de Jésus** the disciples of Jesus.

disciplinaire /disiplinɛʀ/ *adj* disciplinary.

discipline /disiplin/ *nf* **1** (règle) discipline; **2** (spécialité) discipline; **3** SCOL (matière) subject; **4** SPORT sport.

discipliner /disipline/ [1] I *vtr* **1** (faire obéir) to discipline [*personne*]; **2** (maîtriser) to control [*troupes*]; to discipline [*pensées, passions*]; **3** (faire tenir en place) to keep [sth] under control [*cheveux*].
II se discipliner *vpr* to discipline oneself.

disco /disko/ I *adj inv* disco; **soirée ~** disco night.
II *nm* disco music.

discontinu, **~e** /diskɔ̃tiny/ *adj* **1** (intermittent) [*effort, mouvement*] intermittent; [*ligne*] broken; **2** LING, MATH discontinuous.

discordance /diskɔʀdɑ̃s/ *nf* (d'opinions) conflict; (de couleurs) clash; (de sons) dissonance.

discordant, **~e** /diskɔʀdɑ̃, ɑ̃t/ *adj* (qui ne s'accorde pas) [*couleurs*] clashing; (désagréable) [*son, instrument*] discordant; [*voix*] strident [*opinions, caractères*] conflicting.

discorde /diskɔʀd/ *nf* discord, dissension.

discothèque /diskɔtɛk/ *nf* (organisme de prêt) music library; (collection de disques) record collection; (boîte de nuit) discotheque.

discourir /diskuʀiʀ/ [26] *vi* **~ de** or **sur qch** to hold forth on sth.

discours /diskuʀ/ *nm inv* **1** (exposé) speech (**sur** on); **2** (paroles) talk; **assez de ~, des actes!** let's have less talk and more action!; **fais ce que je te dis et pas de ~!** do what I say and no argument!; **tenir de longs ~ sur qch** to talk at great length about sth; **3** (propos) views (*pl*); POL position; **il tient toujours le même ~** his views haven't changed; **4** LING (utilisation de la langue) speech; (énoncé) discourse.

discourtois, **~e** /diskuʀtwa, az/ *adj* discourteous.

discrédit /diskʀedi/ *nm* disrepute; **jeter le ~ sur** to discredit.

discréditer /diskʀedite/ [1] I *vtr* to discredit.
II se discréditer *vpr* to discredit oneself (**auprès de qn, aux yeux de qn** in sb's eyes).

discret, **-ète** /diskʀɛ, ɛt/ *adj* **1** (qu'on remarque peu) [*personne*] unassuming; [*vêtement, couleur*] sober; [*allusion, charme, maquillage*] subtle; [*éclairage*] subdued; [*sourire, signe, surveillance, parfum, bijou*] discreet; [*lieu*] quiet; **2** (qui garde les secrets) discreet (**sur** about); **3** (qui n'est pas curieux) not inquisitive.

discrètement /diskʀɛtmɑ̃/ *adv* (sans publicité) [*agir*] discreetly; (sobrement) [*se vêtir*] soberly; (sans bruit) quietly.

discrétion /diskʀesjɔ̃/ I *nf* (réserve) discretion; **dans la plus grande ~** in the greatest secrecy; **entourer qch de (la plus grande) ~** to shroud sth in (the greatest) secrecy; **garder la plus grande ~ sur qch** to keep sth a closely-guarded secret.
II à discrétion *loc* [*vin, pain*] unlimited.
III à la discrétion de *loc* at the discretion of.

discriminant, **~e** /diskʀiminɑ̃, ɑ̃t/ *adj* **1** (qui différencie) [*caractère, facteur*] differential; **2** (discriminatoire) discriminatory.

discrimination /diskʀiminasjɔ̃/ *nf* (principe) discrimination (**contre, envers, à l'égard de** against).

discriminatoire /diskʀiminatwaʀ/ *adj* discriminatory (**à l'encontre de** against).

discriminer /diskʀimine/ [1] *vtr* LITER to discriminate between [*choses, personnes*].

disculper /diskylpe/ [1] I *vtr* to exculpate.

II se disculper *vpr* to vindicate oneself; **se ~ auprès de qn** to vindicate oneself in sb's eyes.

discussion /diskysjɔ̃/ *nf* **1** (débat) discussion (**sur** about); **le texte est en ~** the text is under discussion; **nous sommes en ~ avec eux** we're having discussions with them; **relancer la ~** to revive the debate; **2** (échange de vues) discussion (**sur** about); **avoir une ~ avec qn** (conversation) to have a discussion with sb; (dispute) to have an argument with sb; **3** (contestation) argument; **pas de ~!** no argument!

discutable /diskytabl/ *adj* (prêtant à discussion) [*question, proportion*] debatable; (critiquable) [*manière, choix*] questionable.

discuté, ~e /diskyte/ I *pp* ▶ **discuter**.
II *pp adj* [*problème, programme, proposition*] controversial; **question très ~e** vexed question.

discuter /diskyte/ [1] **I** *vtr* **1** (examiner) to discuss [*question, problème, accord*]; to debate [*texte, mesure*]; **2** (contester) to question.
II discuter de *vtr ind* to discuss [*projet, prix*].
III *vi* **1** (converser) to talk (**avec qn** to sb); **2** (protester) to argue; **on ne discute pas!** no arguing!; **il a dit trois heures et il n'y a pas à ~** he said three o'clock and that's all there is to it.
IV se discuter *vpr* **ça se discute** that's debatable.

disette /dizɛt/ *nf* (famine) famine, food shortage.

diseur, -euse /dizœr, øz/ *nm,f* **~ de bonne aventure** fortune-teller.

disgrâce /disgrɑs/ *nf* (défaveur) disgrace; **tomber en ~** to fall into disgrace.

disgracier /disgrasje/ [2] *vtr* FML to dismiss [sb] from one's favour^{GB}.

disgracieux, -ieuse /disgrasjø, øz/ *adj* [*visage, enfant*] ugly; [*bouton, poil*] unsightly; [*démarche*] awkward.

disjoindre /disʒwɛ̃dr/ [56] **I** *vtr* **1** (écarter) to loosen; **2** (isoler) to separate.
II se disjoindre *vpr* to come loose.

disjoncter /disʒɔ̃kte/ [1] **I** *vtr* to trip.
II *vi* [*circuit*] to trip out; FIG [*système, usine*] to grind to a halt.

disjoncteur /disʒɔ̃ktœr/ *nm* circuit breaker.

dislocation /dislɔkasjɔ̃/ *nf* (d'empire) dismemberment; (de pacte, groupe) breaking up; MÉD **~ (articulaire)** dislocation (of a joint).

disloquer /dislɔke/ [1] **I** *vtr* **1** (démembrer) to dismember [*empire, État*]; **2** (déboîter) to dislocate [*membre*]; **3** (démonter) to break up.
II se disloquer *vpr* **1** (se démembrer) [*État, groupe*] to break up; **2** (se déboîter) [*personne*] **se ~ l'épaule** to dislocate one's shoulder; **3** (se casser) [*navire, mécanisme*] to break up.

disparaître /disparɛtr/ [73] *vi* **1** (devenir invisible) to disappear; **disparaissez!** out of my sight!; **le soleil disparaît à l'horizon** the sun is dipping below the horizon; **faire ~ tout un gâteau** to gobble up° a whole cake; **2** (devenir introuvable) [*objet, personne*] to disappear; (soudainement) to vanish; **des centaines de personnes disparaissent chaque année** hundreds of people go missing every year; **faire ~ qch** to remove sth [*objet*]; **3** (être supprimé) [*douleur, odeur*] to go; [*tache*] to come out; [*difficulté*] to disappear; [*craintes*] to vanish; [*fièvre*] to subside; **faire ~** to get rid of [*douleur, pellicules, pauvreté, trouble*]; to remove [*tache*]; to make [sth] extinct [*espèce*]; **4** EUPH (mourir) to die; (cesser d'exister) [*civilisation*] to die out; [*espèce*] to become extinct; **faire ~ qn** EUPH to get rid of sb; **voir ~** to witness the end of [*civilisation, culture*]; **quand j'aurai disparu** when I'm gone.

disparate /disparat/ *adj* [*ensemble, mobilier*] ill-assorted; [*foule*] mixed.

disparité /disparite/ *nf* (caractère différent) disparity SOUT (**de** in); (différence) difference.

disparition /disparisjɔ̃/ *nf* **1** GÉN disappearance; (d'espèce) extinction; **en voie de ~** [*civilisation, art*] dying (*épith*); [*espèce*] endangered; **2** EUPH (mort) death.

disparu, ~e /disparý/ **I** *pp* ▶ **disparaître**.

II *pp adj* **1** [*personne*] (enlevé, présumé mort etc) missing; **porté ~** MIL missing in action; **être porté ~** to be reported missing; **2** (perdu) GÉN lost; [*espèce*] extinct; **3** EUPH (mort) dead; **marin ~ en mer** sailor lost at sea.
III *nm,f* **1** (personne introuvable) missing person; **2** EUPH (mort) **les ~s** the dead.

dispendieux, -ieuse /dispɑ̃djø, øz/ *adj* expensive, extravagant.

dispense /dispɑ̃s/ *nf* (exemption) exemption (**de** from); (certificat d'exemption) certificate of exemption; RELIG dispensation.
■ **~ d'âge** exemption from statutory age limit.

dispenser /dispɑ̃se/ [1] **I** *vtr* **1** (donner) to hand out [*largesses*] (**à** to); to bestow SOUT [*honneurs, compliments*] (**à** on); **2** (exempter) **~ qn de (faire) qch** to exempt sb from doing sth; **3** (épargner) **~ qn de (faire) qch** to excuse sb from doing sth; **cela ne vous dispense pas d'étudier** this does not make it any the less necessary for you to study; **se faire ~ d'un cours** to be excused from a lesson; **je vous dispense de (tout) commentaire** I don't need any comment from you.
II se dispenser *vpr* (se passer de) **se ~ de (faire) qch** to spare oneself (the trouble of doing) sth; **j'ai décidé de me ~ de vos services** I've decided to dispense with your services.

disperser /dispɛrse/ [1] **I** *vtr* to scatter [*objets, famille*]; to disperse [*foule, fumée*]; to break up [*rassemblement, collection*]; **~ ses efforts** to spread oneself too thin.
II se disperser *vpr* [*famille, fumée*] to disperse; [*foule, manifestants*] (volontairement) to disperse; (par nécessité) to scatter; [*rassemblement*] to break up.

dispersion /dispɛrsjɔ̃/ *nf* (de manifestants, collection, fumée) dispersal; (de famille) scattering; (de tir, troupe) dispersion.

disponibilité /disponibilite/ **I** *nf* **1** (temps libre) availability; **2** COMM (d'un produit) availability; **3** ADMIN temporary leave of absence; **en ~** on leave of absence.
II disponibilités *nfpl* (argent) available funds.

disponible /disponibl/ *adj* **1** (libre) available (**pour** for); **2** COMM (à disposition) available (**auprès de** from).

dispos, ~e /dispo, oz/ *adj* (reposé) refreshed; (en bonne forme) in good form; **frais et ~** fresh as a daisy.

disposé, ~e /dispoze/ **I** *pp* ▶ **disposer**.

II *pp adj* **1** (agencé) [*meubles, fleurs*] arranged; [*appartement, pièce, jardin*] laid out; **2** (prêt) **~ à** willing to; **3** (favorable) **être bien/mal ~** to be in a good/bad mood; **être bien/mal ~ à l'égard de** or **envers qn** to be well-/ill-disposed toward(s) sb.

disposer /dispoze/ [1] **I** *vtr* **1** (placer) to arrange [*objets*]; to position [*personnes*].
II disposer de *vtr ind* **1** (avoir) **~ de** to have; **les machines dont nous disposons** the machines we have at our disposal; **je ne dispose que de quelques minutes pour vous recevoir** I can only spare you a few minutes; **2** (se servir de) **~ de** to use; **3** (partir) **merci, vous pouvez ~** thank you, you may go.
III se disposer *vpr* **1** (se préparer) **se ~ à faire** to be about to do; **2** (se placer) **se ~ en cercle autour de qn** to form a circle around sb.

dispositif /dispozitif/ *nm* **1** (mécanisme) device; (système) system; **2** (ensemble de mesures) operation.

disposition /dispozisjɔ̃/ **I** *nf* **1** (arrangement) arrangement; (d'appartement, de salle) layout; (place) position; **2** (possibilité d'utiliser) **c'est à ta ~** it's at your disposal; **à la ~ du public** for public use; **se tenir à la ~ de qn** to be at sb's disposal (**pour qch** for sth; **pour faire** to do); **je suis à votre entière ~** I am entirely at your disposal; **se mettre à la ~ de la justice** [*témoin*] to make oneself available to the court; **il a été mis à la ~ de la justice** he was remanded in custody; **3** (mesure) measure, step; **j'ai pris mes ~s pour arriver à l'heure** I made arrangements to arrive on time; **4** (tendance) FML tendency (**à** to); **5** (clause) clause.
II dispositions *nfpl* **1** (aptitudes) aptitude; **2** (humeur)

elle n'était pas dans de bonnes ~s ce jour-là she wasn't in a good mood that day.

disproportion /dispʀɔpɔʀsjɔ̃/ *nf* lack of proportion.

disproportionné, ~e /dispʀɔpɔʀsjɔne/ *adj* [*effort, demande, réaction*] disproportionate; [*nez, bouche*] disproportionately large; [*bras, jambes, tête*] out of proportion with one's body (*jamais épith*).

dispute /dispyt/ *nf* (querelle) argument (**sur** about); **un sujet de ~** a cause for argument.

disputé, ~e /dispyte/ *adj* **1** (objet de lutte) keenly contested (*épith*); **2** (recherché) sought-after (**de** by); **3** (contesté) controversial.

disputer /dispyte/ [1] **I** *vtr* **1** (participer à) to compete in [*épreuve, tournoi*]; to compete for [*coupe*]; to play [*match*]; to run [*course*]; to take part in [*combat*]; **2** (lutter pour obtenir) **~ qch à qn** to compete with sb for sth [*honneur, prix, titre*]; to contend with sb for sth [*trône, pouvoir*]; **3**○ (réprimander) to tell [sb] off.

II se disputer *vpr* **1** (se quereller) to argue (**à propos de, sur, au sujet de** about); **nous nous sommes disputés** we had an argument; **se ~ pour qch** to argue over sth; **2** (lutter pour obtenir) to fight over [*héritage, os*]; to contest [*siège*]; to compete for [*honneur, place*]; to contend for [*trône, titre, pouvoir*]; **3** (avoir lieu) to take place.

disquaire /diskɛʀ/ ▶374 *nmf* record dealer.

disqualifier /diskalifje/ [2] **I** *vtr* (exclure d'une compétition) to disqualify; **se faire ~ (par)** to be disqualified (by).

II se disqualifier *vpr* to discredit oneself (**en faisant** by doing).

disque /disk/ *nm* **1** MUS record; **passer un ~** to play a record; **change de ~**○! FIG give it a rest ou break○!; LIT put another record on; **2** TECH disc; **3** ▶329 SPORT discus; **le lancer du ~** the discus; **4** (objet rond) disc; **5** ORDINAT disk.
■ **~ compact** compact disc; **~ dur** ORDINAT hard disk; **~ d'embrayage** AUT clutch disc; **~ laser** laser disc; **~ numérique** digital disk; **~ d'or** gold disc; **~ souple** (de présentation, en cadeau) flexi disc; ORDINAT floppy disc; **~ de stationnement** AUT parking disc.

disquette /diskɛt/ *nf* diskette, floppy disk; **~ de sauvegarde** back-up disk; **lecteur de ~s** disk drive.

dissection /disɛksjɔ̃/ *nf* dissection.

dissemblable /disɑ̃blabl/ *adj* dissimilar, different.

dissémination /diseminasjɔ̃/ *nf* (de germe, virus) spread; (de pollen, troupes) dispersal; (de maisons) scattering; (d'idée) dissemination.

disséminé, ~e /disemine/ **I** *pp* ▶ **disséminer**.

II *pp adj* [*maisons, population, entreprises*] scattered.

disséminer /disemine/ [1] **I** *vtr* to spread [*germe, idée*]; to disperse [*pollen*]; to distribute [*personnes, troupes*].

II se disséminer *vpr* [*personnes*] to scatter; [*germe, idée*] to spread.

dissension /disɑ̃sjɔ̃/ *nf* **1** (discorde) dissension SOUT; **2** (désaccord) disagreement (**au sein de** within).

disséquer /diseke/ [14] *vtr* to dissect.

dissertation /disɛʀtasjɔ̃/ *nf* SCOL, UNIV (devoir) essay; **faire une ~** to write an essay.

disserter /disɛʀte/ [1] *vi* (discourir) to speak (**sur** on).

dissidence /disidɑ̃s/ *nf* **1** (opposition) PHILOS, RELIG dissent; POL dissidence; (insubordination civile) rebellion; **entrer en ~ contre** (contre un régime) to enter into rebellion against; (contre un parti) to break away from; **2** (opposants) **la ~** the dissidents.

dissident, ~e /disidɑ̃, ɑ̃t/ **I** *adj* **1** POL [*personne*] dissident; [*groupe*] break-away; **2** RELIG [*secte*] dissenting.

II *nm,f* **1** POL dissident; **2** PHILOS, RELIG dissenter.

dissimulateur, -trice /disimylatœʀ, tʀis/ **I** *adj* secretive.

II *nm,f* dissembler.

dissimulation /disimylasjɔ̃/ *nf* (de sentiment) dissimulation; (d'information) concealment; (caractère) secretiveness.

dissimulé, ~e /disimyle/ **I** *pp* ▶ **dissimuler**.

II *pp adj* concealed; **mal ~** ill-concealed; **fierté non ~e** undisguised pride.

dissimuler /disimyle/ [1] **I** *vtr* to conceal (**qch à qn** sth from sb); **mal ~** to conceal badly.

II se dissimuler *vpr* [*personne*] (se cacher) to hide; (ne pas vouloir voir) to close one's eyes to.

dissipation /disipasjɔ̃/ *nf* **1** (de malentendu) clearing up; **2** (de brouillard, nuages) clearing; **après ~ des brumes matinales** after the early morning mist has cleared; **3** (d'attention) wandering; **4** (d'élève) restlessness.

dissipé, ~e /disipe/ *adj* [*élève*] badly-behaved (*épith*); [*vie*] dissipated.

dissiper /disipe/ [1] **I** *vtr* to dispel [*doute, illusion, fatigue*]; to clear up [*malentendu*]; to disperse [*fumée*]; to distract [*personne*].

II se dissiper *vpr* **1** (disparaître) [*menace*] to recede; [*illusion, doute, malaise*] to vanish; [*malentendu*] to be cleared up; [*brume*] to clear; **2** (s'agiter) [*élève*] to behave badly.

dissociable /disɔsjabl/ *adj* [*questions, événements*] dissociable; **les deux causes ne sont pas ~s** the two causes can't be separated.

dissocier /disɔsje/ [2] **I** *vtr* (séparer) to separate (**de** from).

II se dissocier *vpr* **se ~ de** to dissociate oneself from.

dissolu, ~e /disɔly/ *adj* [*vie*] dissolute; [*mœurs*] loose.

dissolution /disɔlysjɔ̃/ *nf* (d'assemblée, organisation, de mariage) dissolution; (de substance) dissolution (**dans** in); (écroulement) (de système politique) disintegration; (de famille) break-up.

dissolvant, ~e /disɔlvɑ̃, ɑ̃t/ **I** *adj* solvent.

II *nm* (en cosmétique) nail varnish remover; CHIMIE solvent.

dissonant, ~e /disɔnɑ̃, ɑ̃t/ *adj* (discordant) [*voix, sons*] dissonant; [*couleurs, tons*] clashing, jarring.

dissoudre /disudʀ/ [75] **I** *vtr* **1** to dissolve [*assemblée, mariage, compagnie*]; to disband [*mouvement*]; **2** CHIMIE to dissolve [*substance*] (**dans** in); **faire ~** to dissolve; **3** (briser) to break up [*empire, institutions, alliance*]; to destroy [*cohésion, unité*].

II se dissoudre *vpr* **1** [*organisation, parti*] to disband; **2** [*substance*] to dissolve (**dans** in).

dissuader /disɥade/ [1] *vtr* **~ qn de faire** [*personne*] to dissuade sb from doing; [*publicité, maladie, temps*] to put sb off doing; **~ l'ennemi** to deter the enemy.

dissuasif, -ive /disɥazif, iv/ *adj* **1** (qui dissuade) [*argument, idée*] dissuasive; [*armes, force*] deterrent; **avoir un effet ~ sur qn** to act as a deterrent to sb; **2** (élevé) prohibitive.

dissuasion /disɥazjɔ̃/ *nf* **1** MIL, POL deterrence; **force de ~** deterrent force; **2** (action de dissuader) dissuasion.

dissymétrie /disimetʀi/ *nf* asymmetry.

distance /distɑ̃s/ ▶348 *nf* **1** (intervalle spatial) distance; **Paris est à quelle ~ de Londres?** how far is Paris from London?; **à quelle ~ est-ce?** how far is it?; **transporter 100 passagers sur une ~ de** to transport 100 passengers over a distance of; **j'ai couru sur une ~ de deux kilomètres** I ran for two kilometres^GB; **à une ~ de 10 kilomètres** 10 kilometres^GB away; **les deux frères vivent à 1 000 kilomètres de ~** the two brothers live 1,000 kilometres^GB apart; **être à faible ~** de not to be far (away) from; **gardez vos ~s** AUT keep your distance; **prendre ses ~s avec** FIG to distance oneself from; **tenir qn/qch à ~** FIG to keep sb/sth at a distance; **tenir ou garder ses ~s** FIG [*supérieur*] to stand aloof; [*inférieur*] to know one's place; **tenir la ~** [*sportif*] to stay the course; **appel longue ~** TÉLÉCOM long-distance call; **à ~** [*agir, communiquer, observer*] from a distance; [*commande, accès*] remote (*épith*); **se tenir à bonne ~ de qch** to keep a good distance from sth; **2** (intervalle temporel) gap; **à une semaine de ~** one week apart; **3** (recul) distance.

■ **~ focale** focal length; **~ de freinage** braking distance.

distancer /distɑ̃se/ [12] *vtr* SPORT GÉN to outdistance; (en course à pied, à cheval) to outrun; **il a largement distancé son rival** FIG he left his rival standing; **se faire** or **se laisser ~** to get left behind.

distancier: se distancier /distɑ̃sje/ [2] *vpr* to distance oneself (**de** from).

distant, ~e /distɑ̃, ɑ̃t/ *adj* **1** (éloigné dans l'espace) distant; **un village ~ de trois kilomètres** a village three kilometres^GB or three kilometres^GB apart; **2** (réservé) [*personne, regard*] distant; [*attitude*] reserved; [*rapports*] cool; **~ avec/envers** distant with/toward(s); **3** (éloigné dans le temps) **à une époque ~e de la nôtre** in the distant past; **des événements ~s de plusieurs années** (entre eux) events that are several years apart; (par rapport à aujourd'hui) events that took place several years ago.

distendre /distɑ̃dʀ/ [6] I *vtr* **1** (étirer) to distend [*estomac*]; to stretch [*peau*]; to over-stretch [*ressort*]; **2** (relâcher) to weaken [*liens*].
II **se distendre** *vpr* **1** (se relâcher) [*peau, ressort*] to slacken; **2** (s'affaiblir) [*liens*] to cool.

distendu, ~e /distɑ̃dy/ I *pp* ▶ **distendre**.
II *pp adj* **1** (étiré) [*estomac*] distended; **2** (relâché) [*peau, ressort, câble*] slack; **3** (affaibli) [*liens, relations*] cool.

distillation /distilasjɔ̃/ *nf* distillation.

distiller /distile/ [1] I *vtr* CHIMIE to distil^GB [*fruit, alcool*]; **2** (secréter) to secrete [*suc, poison, résine*]; **3** (répandre) to disclose [sth] little by little [*idée*].
II *vi* CHIMIE to evaporate (**à** at).

distillerie /distilʀi/ *nf* (usine) distillery; (production) distilling.

distinct, ~e /distɛ̃, ɛ̃kt/ *adj* **1** (différent) distinct (**de** from); **2** (qui se perçoit nettement) [*forme, son*] distinct; [*voix*] clear; **3** (sans liens) [*société, entreprise*] separate.

distinctement /distɛ̃ktəmɑ̃/ *adv* clearly.

distinctif, -ive /distɛ̃ktif, iv/ *adj* [*signe, caractère*] distinguishing; [*trait*] distinctive.

distinction /distɛ̃ksjɔ̃/ *nf* **1** (différence) distinction; **sans ~** [*agir, récompenser*] without discrimination; [*massacrer, nuire*] indiscriminately; **sans ~ d'origine ou de religion** irrespective of colour^GB or creed; **2** (récompense) honour^GB; **remettre/recevoir une ~** to confer/to be awarded an honour^GB; **~ honorifique** award; **3** (élégance) distinction; **il n'a aucune ~** he lacks refinement; **avoir de la ~** to be distinguished; **d'une grande ~** of great distinction (*épith, après n*).

distingué, ~e /distɛ̃ge/ I *pp* ▶ **distinguer**.
II *pp adj* **1** (élégant) distinguished; **2** (éminent) distinguished; **3** (en correspondance) **veuillez agréer mes salutations ~es** (à une personne non nommée) yours faithfully; (à une personne nommée) yours sincerely.

distinguer /distɛ̃ge/ [1] I *vtr* **1** (séparer) to distinguish between [*choses, personnes*]; **~ A de B** to distinguish A from B; **il est difficile de ~ les deux jumeaux** it's difficult to tell the twins apart; **2** (par la vue, l'ouïe) (percevoir les différences) to distinguish; (percevoir avec difficulté) to make out; **3** (percevoir intellectuellement) to discern; **je distinguerais trois points** (dans un exposé) I would like to bring out three main points; **4** (différencier) [*détail, trait*] to set [sb] apart [*personnes, animaux*]; to make [sth] different [*objets*] (**de** from); **aucune caractéristique physique ne les distingue** physically, they have no distinguishing features; **5** (récompenser) [*jury*] to single out [sb] for an honour^GB [*personne*]; [*prix*] to be awarded to [*personne, œuvre*].
II *vi* **il faut savoir ~** you have to be able to tell the difference; **~ s'il s'agit d'un besoin réel ou d'un caprice** to judge whether it's a question of real need or of a whim.
III **se distinguer** *vpr* **1** (différer) **se ~ de** (par ses qualités) to differ from; (par ses actes) to set oneself apart from; **il vaut mieux éviter de se ~** it's best not to be conspicuous; **2** (s'illustrer) [*chercheur, sportif, candidat*] to distinguish oneself; **l'auteur se distingue**

par son originalité the author is noted for his originality; **3** (être perçu) to be distinguishable; **4** (se faire remarquer) PEJ to draw attention to oneself.

distordre /distɔʀdʀ/ [6] I *vtr* [*colère, douleur*] to contort; **distordu par** contorted with.
II **se distordre** *vpr* [*visage*] to become contorted.

distorsion /distɔʀsjɔ̃/ *nf* distortion.

distraction /distʀaksjɔ̃/ *nf* **1** (activité) leisure ¢, entertainment ¢; **c'est ma seule ~** it's my only form of leisure; **cette ville manque de ~s** there's not much in the way of entertainment in this town; **2** (détente) recreation; **la lecture est un moyen de ~** reading is a means of relaxation; **j'ai besoin de ~** I need some form of relaxation; **3** (étourderie) absent-mindedness ¢; **par ~** through absent-mindedness; **avec ~** absent-mindedly.

distraire /distʀɛʀ/ [58] I *vtr* **1** (divertir) (en amusant) to amuse; (en occupant) to entertain; **cela m'a distrait un moment** (amusé) it kept me amused for a while; **2** (soulager) **~ qn de** to take sb's mind off [*problème*]; **3** (déconcentrer) to distract [*personne*] (**de** from; **par** by).
II **se distraire** *vpr* **1** (s'amuser) to amuse oneself; (prendre du bon temps) to enjoy oneself; **que fais-tu pour te ~?** what do you do for entertainment?; **2** (se changer les idées) **j'ai besoin de me ~** I need to take my mind off things.

distrait, ~e /distʀɛ, ɛt/ I *pp* ▶ **distraire**.
II *pp adj* [*personne*] (trait de caractère) absent-minded; (occasionnellement) inattentive; [*élève*] inattentive; [*air, manière*] distracted; [*regard, sourire*] vague; **regarder qn d'un œil ~** to look vaguely at sb.

distraitement /distʀɛtmɑ̃/ *adv* absent-mindedly; [*écouter*] with half an ear; [*lire*] with half an eye.

distrayant, ~e /distʀɛjɑ̃, ɑ̃t/ *adj* entertaining.

distribuer /distʀibɥe/ [1] *vtr* **1** (donner) to distribute [*prospectus*] (**à** to); to pay out [*dividende*] (**à** to); to hand out [*compliments, poignées de main*] (**à** to); to allocate [*crédits, tâches*] (**à** to); **~ les cartes** to deal; **~ le courrier** to deliver the mail; **~ les récompenses** to give out the awards; **2** (vendre) [*personne*] to distribute; [*machine*] to dispense; **3** to supply [*eau, chaleur*].

distributeur, -trice /distʀibytœʀ, tʀis/ ▶374 I *adj* COMM distributing.
II *nm,f* distributor; **~ exclusif** sole distributor.
III *nm* **1** (machine automatique) dispenser; (payant) vending machine; **~ de tickets** ticket machine; **~ de billets (de banque)** cash dispenser; **2** (compagnie du secteur ou de la distribution) retailing group.
■ **~ automatique de billets, DAB** automatic teller machine, ATM.

distributif, -ive /distʀibytif, iv/ *adj* distributive.

distribution /distʀibysjɔ̃/ *nf* **1** (secteur) retailing; **la ~ alimentaire** food retailing; **2** (commercialisation) distribution; **se réserver l'exclusivité de la ~** to keep exclusive distribution rights (**de** for); **3** (d'eau, électricité) supply; **4** (fourniture) (d'objets) distribution; (de tâches, rôles) allocation; **5** (disposition) distribution; **~ d'une maison** layout of a house; **6** CIN, THÉÂT (choix effectué) casting; (liste) cast.
■ **~ d'actions gratuites** allocation of bonus shares; **~ automatique** automatic dispensing; **~ des cartes** deal; **~ du courrier** postal delivery.

dithyrambique /ditiʀɑ̃bik/ *adj* [*discours, article, propos*] ecstatic; [*louange*] extravagant.

diurétique /djyʀetik/ *adj, nm* diuretic.

diurne /djyʀn/ *adj* [*fleur, animal*] diurnal.

divagation /divagasjɔ̃/ *nf* (de fou, malade) ravings (*pl*); (élucubration) rambling ¢.

divaguer /divage/ [1] *vi* **1** (délirer) [*malade*] to rave; **la fièvre le fait ~** he's delirious; **2** (déraisonner) to ramble; (dire des bêtises) to talk nonsense; **3** JUR [*animal*] to stray.

divan /divɑ̃/ *nm* (siège) divan; (de psychanaliste) couch.

divergence /divɛʀʒɑ̃s/ *nf* (d'opinions) divergence; (de politique, goûts) difference.

diverger /divɛʀʒe/ [13] *vi* **1** (être en désaccord) [*idées, intérêts*] to diverge (**de** from); [*lois, goûts*] to differ (**de**

from; **sur** on); **les témoignages divergent sur l'heure à laquelle le suspect a été vu** testimonies differ as to the time at which the suspect was seen; **2** (se séparer) to diverge.

divers, **~e** /divɛʀ, ɛʀs/ **I** adj **1** (varié, plusieurs) various; **à ~es reprises** on various ou several occasions; **les gens les plus ~** all sorts of people; **2** (indéfini) [frais] miscellaneous; **dépenses ~es** sundries. **II** nmpl (rubrique) miscellaneous.

■ **~ droite** POL minor right-wing parties; **~ gauche** POL minor left-wing parties.

diversement /divɛʀsəmɑ̃/ adv variously, in different ways; **le film a été ~ accueilli** the film had a mixed reception.

diversification /divɛʀsifikasjɔ̃/ nf diversification; **une entreprise en voie de ~** a company in the process of diversifying; **une ~ de la clientèle** targeting a wider clientele.

diversifier /divɛʀsifje/ [2] **I** vtr (varier) to vary [occupations, lectures]; to widen the range of [produits, activités]; to widen [clientèle]; to diversify [investissements]; **des méthodes diversifiées** varied methods. **II se diversifier** vpr [entreprise] to diversify; [produits, activités] to be diversified.

diversion /divɛʀsjɔ̃/ nf **1** MIL diversion; **une manœuvre de ~** a diversionary move; **une tentative de ~** an attempt at diversion; **2** LITER (distraction) diversion, distraction.

diversité /divɛʀsite/ nf (de personnes, paysages) diversity; (de couleurs, produits, cultures) diversity; (de goûts, d'opinions, intérêts) variety.

divertir /divɛʀtiʀ/ [3] **I** vtr (distraire) (en occupant) to entertain; (en amusant) to amuse. **II** vi LITER to entertain. **III se divertir** vpr (en s'amusant) to amuse oneself; (en prenant du bon temps) to enjoy oneself; **faire qch pour se ~** (en jouant, plaisantant) to do sth for fun; (à cause d'ennuis) to do sth to take one's mind off things.

divertissant, **~e** /divɛʀtisɑ̃, ɑ̃t/ adj (qui fait rire) amusing; (qui occupe) entertaining; (plaisant) enjoyable.

divertissement /divɛʀtismɑ̃/ nm (action) entertainment ¢; (distraction) recreation; MUS divertimento; THÉÂT divertissement.

dividende /dividɑ̃d/ nm dividend.

divin, **~e** /divɛ̃, in/ adj divine; **le ~ Enfant** the Holy Child.

diviniser /divinize/ [1] vtr (tous contextes) to deify.

divinité /divinite/ nf (être divin) deity; RELIG (nature) divinity.

diviser /divize/ [1] **I** vtr **1** (désunir) to divide; **être divisé sur** to be divided over; **~ pour régner** divide and rule; **2** MATH to divide (**en** into). **II se diviser** vpr **1** (se désunir) to become divided (**sur** over); **2** (être séparé) to be divided (**en** into); **3** MATH to be divisible (**par** by); **4** (se ramifier) [cellule, branche, fleuve] to divide; [route] to fork.

diviseur /divizœʀ/ nm divisor.

division /divizjɔ̃/ nf (tous contextes) division.

divisionnaire /divizjɔnɛʀ/ adj **commissaire ~** ADMIN ~ Chief Superintendent.

divorce /divɔʀs/ nm **1** JUR divorce (**d'avec** from); **prononcer le ~ entre deux époux** to grant a divorce to a couple; **gagner le ~** to win a divorce suit; **être en instance de ~** to be getting divorced ou a divorce; **2** FIG (rupture) divorce.

divorcé, **~e** /divɔʀse/ nm,f divorcee.

divorcer /divɔʀse/ [12] vi **1** JUR to get divorced; **il a divorcé d'avec** ou **de sa femme** he has divorced his wife; **elle veut ~** she wants a divorce; **2** FIG (rompre) to split (**d'avec, de** from).

divulgation /divylgasjɔ̃/ nf disclosure.

divulguer /divylge/ [1] **I** vtr to disclose. **II se divulguer** vpr to become known.

dix /dis, but before consonant di, before vowel diz/ ▶399¦, 298¦, 156¦ adj inv, pron ten. IDIOMES **ne rien savoir faire de ses ~ doigts** to be

useless; **un de perdu, ~ de retrouvés** PROV there's plenty more fish in the sea PROV.

dix-huit /dizɥit/ ▶399¦, 298¦, 156¦ adj inv, pron eighteen.

dix-huitième /dizɥitjɛm/ ▶156¦, 399¦ adj eighteenth.

dixième /dizjɛm/ ▶156¦, 399¦ adj tenth.

dix-neuf /diznœf/ ▶399¦, 298¦, 156¦ adj inv, pron nineteen.

dix-neuvième /diznœvjɛm/ ▶399¦ adj nineteenth.

dix-sept /dis(s)ɛt/ ▶399¦, 298¦, 156¦ adj inv, pron seventeen.

dix-septième /dis(s)ɛtjɛm/ ▶156¦, 399¦ adj seventeenth.

dizaine /dizɛn/ nf **1** (nombre) ten; **la colonne des ~** the tens column; **2** (environ dix) about ten; **ça a duré une bonne ~ d'années** it went on for over ten years; **plus d'une ~ de victimes** at least ten casualties; **des ~s de personnes** dozens of people.

dm written abbr = **décimètre** 1.

DM ▶33¦ (written abbr = **Deutsche Mark**) DM.

do /do/ nm inv MUS (note) C; (en solfiant) doh.

docile /dɔsil/ adj [animal, personne, élève] docile; [cheveux] manageable.

docilement /dɔsilmɑ̃/ adv [écouter] obediently; [sourire, obéir] meekly.

docilité /dɔsilite/ nf obedience.

dock /dɔk/ nm **1** (bassin de chargement) dock; **2** (entrepôt) warehouse.

docte /dɔkt/ adj [réflexions, personne] learned.

docteur /dɔktœʀ/ ▶596¦ nm **1** (en médecine) doctor; **le ~ Lagrange** Doctor Lagrange; **2** UNIV Doctor; **~ en droit** Doctor of Law.

doctoral, **~e**, mpl **-aux** /dɔktɔʀal, o/ adj (pédant) PÉJ pompous.

doctorat /dɔktɔʀa/ nm PhD, doctorate (**ès, en** in).

doctrinaire /dɔktʀinɛʀ/ adj [attitude] doctrinaire PEJ; [ton] sententious; [discussion] doctrinal.

doctrinal, **~e**, mpl **-aux** /dɔktʀinal, o/ adj [revirement, référence] RELIG doctrinal; POL ideological.

doctrine /dɔktʀin/ nf doctrine.

document /dɔkymɑ̃/ nm **1** (pour information, témoignage) document (**sur** on); **~ sonore/vidéo** audio/video material ¢; **avec ~s à l'appui** with documentary evidence; **l'exposition est un ~ sur notre époque** the exhibition is a record of our times; **2** (papier officiel) document, paper; **3** SCOL, UNIV **vous n'avez droit à aucun ~ pour cette épreuve** no books or notes are allowed for this exam.

documentaire /dɔkymɑ̃tɛʀ/ adj **I** [caractère, intérêt] documentary (épith); [centre] information (épith). **II** nm documentary (**sur** on, about).

documentaliste /dɔkymɑ̃talist/ ▶374¦ nmf (en entreprise) information officer; PRESSE, TV researcher; SCOL (school) librarian.

documentation /dɔkymɑ̃tasjɔ̃/ nf **1** (documents) material (**sur** on); **nous avons toute une ~ sur la ville** we can provide information about the town; **2** (information) research; **3** (brochures) brochures (pl) (**sur** on); **4** (activité) (en entreprise) research; (dans un journal, à la télévision) research; **centre de ~** resource centreᴳᴮ; **5** SCOL **la ~** the (school) library; **6** UNIV (discipline) studies in librarianship.

documenter /dɔkymɑ̃te/ [1] **I** vtr **1** (fournir des renseignements à) to provide [sb] with information; **2** (fournir des renseignements pour) to research. **II se documenter** vpr **se ~ sur qch** to research sth.

dodeliner /dɔdline/ [1] vi **il dodelinait de la tête** his head was nodding.

dodo /dodo/ nm BABY TALK **faire ~** to sleep.

dodu, **-e** /dɔdy/ adj plump.

dogmatique /dɔgmatik/ adj dogmatic.

dogme /dɔgm/ nm dogma.

dogue /dɔg/ nm mastiff.

doigt /dwa/ ▶ 137 │ *nm* (de main, gant) finger; **petit ~** little finger GB, pinkie US; **lever le ~** to put one's hand up; **bout des ~s** fingertips (*pl*); **du bout des ~s** LIT with one's fingertips; FIG reluctantly; **être français jusqu'au bout des ~s** to be French through and through; **connaître une ville sur le bout des ~s** to know a city like the back of one's hand; **savoir son vocabulaire sur le bout des ~s** to know one's vocabulary off pat; **désigner** or **montrer du ~** LIT to point at; FIG to point the finger at; **toucher du ~** (vraiment sentir) to experience at first hand; (atteindre) to come close to touching.
■ **~ de pied** ANAT toe.

IDIOMES **se brûler les ~s** to get one's fingers burned; **être à deux ~s de qch/de faire** to be a whisker away from sth/from doing; **filer entre les ~s** [*affaire, argent, voleur*] to slip through one's fingers; [*temps*] to slip away from sb; **ne pas lever le petit ~** not to lift a finger; **mon petit ~ me dit que** a little bird tells me that; **se faire taper sur les ~s** to get one's knuckles rapped.

doigté /dwate/ *nm* **1** (diplomatie) tact; **avoir du ~** to be tactful; **2** (adresse manuelle) light touch; **avoir du ~** to have a light touch; **manquer de ~** to be heavy-handed; **3** MUS fingering.

doigtier /dwatje/ *nm* fingerstall.

doléance /dɔleɑ̃s/ *nf* complaint.

dolent, **~e** /dɔlɑ̃, ɑ̃t/ *adj* [*air, personne*] doleful; [*ville*] lifeless.

dollar /dɔlaʀ/ ▶ 33 │ *nm* dollar.

DOM /dɔm/ *nm inv* (*abbr* = **département d'outre-mer**) *French overseas* (*administrative*) *department*.

domaine /dɔmɛn/ *nm* **1** (terres) estate; **~ vinicole** vineyards (*pl*); **2** (spécialité) field, domain; **dans le ~ financier** in the field of finance; **3**° (territoire) **le grenier c'est mon ~** (réservé) the attic is my territory; **4** ADMIN **le Domaine** state(-owned) property.
■ **~ public** public domain; **tomber dans le ~ public** JUR [*œuvres d'art, invention*] to be in the public domain; [*œuvre littéraire*] to be out of copyright; **~ réservé** POL, JUR reserved domain.

domanial, **~e**, *mpl* **-iaux** /dɔmanjal, o/ *adj* [*forêt, terrain, biens*] state-owned (*épith*).

dôme /dom/ *nm* dome; **une tente ~** a dome tent.

domesticité /dɔmɛstisite/ *nf* **1** (ensemble des domestiques) (household) staff; **2** (condition de domestique) domestic service.

domestique /dɔmɛstik/ **I** *adj* **1** [*soucis, vie, personnel, tâche*] domestic; **les travaux ~s** housework; **les accidents ~s** accidents in the home; **2** (domestiqué) [*animal*] domestic; **3** ÉCON, IND [*marché, consommation*] domestic, home.
II *nmf* servant.

domestiquer /dɔmɛstike/ [1] *vtr* to domesticate [*animal, espèce*]; to harness [*atome, marée*].

domicile /dɔmisil/ **I** *nm* (d'une personne) place of residence, domicile; (d'une société) registered address; **ils ont regagné leur ~** they went back home; **changer de ~** to move (house).
II à domicile *loc adj* **travail à ~** working at ou from home; **donner des soins à ~** to give home care; **'livraisons à ~'** 'home deliveries'.

domiciliaire /dɔmisiljɛʀ/ *adj* JUR **visite ~** domiciliary visit; **perquisition ~** house search.

domicilié, **~e** /dɔmisilje/ *être* **~ à Arras** to live in Arras; ADMIN to be resident in Arras; **j'habite à Paris, mais je suis ~e à Rennes** I live in Paris, but my official address is in Rennes.

dominance /dɔminɑ̃s/ *nf* dominance.

dominant, **~e**[1] /dɔminɑ̃, ɑ̃t/ *adj* **1** (principal) [*couleur, ton, rôle*] dominant; [*courant, opinion*] prevailing; [*trait, idée*] main; **2** (au pouvoir) [*classe*] ruling; **3** BIOL [*caractère, gène*] dominant.

dominante[2] /dɔminɑ̃t/ *nf* **1** (trait) dominant feature; (couleur) main colour GB; **2** MUS dominant (note); **3** UNIV main subject, major US.

dominateur, **-trice** /dɔminatœʀ, tʀis/ **I** *adj* [*per-*

sonne] domineering; [*manières, attitude*] overbearing; [*geste, ton*] imperious.
II *nmf* ruler.

domination /dɔminasjɔ̃/ *nf* domination; **être sous la ~ de** to be dominated by; **pays sous ~ étrangère** (influence) country dominated by a foreign power; (autorité) country under foreign rule; **il est sous la ~ de sa femme** he's completely under his wife's thumb.

dominer /dɔmine/ [1] **I** *vtr* **1** (surplomber) [*maison, montagne*] to dominate [*ville, vallée*]; (dépasser) [*gratte-ciel, sommet*] to tower above [*quartier, montagnes*]; **de là, on domine toute la vallée** from there you get a view of the whole valley; **il est tellement grand qu'il domine tout le monde** he's so tall that he towers over everyone; **2** (s'imposer dans, contre) to dominate [*match, sport, débat*]; to overshadow [*adversaire*]; **3** (prévaloir dans) [*thème, problème*] to dominate [*œuvre, débat*]; **4** (maîtriser) to master [*langue, technique, sujet*]; to overcome [*peur, timidité*]; to control [*colère*]; **~ la situation** to be in control of the situation; **5** (avoir la haute main sur) to dominate [*marché, secteur*]; **6** POL (gouverner) to rule [*pays*].
II *vi* **1** (exercer son pouvoir) [*pays, peuple*] to rule, to hold sway; **2** (être en tête) [*équipe, concurrent*] to be in the lead; **3** (prévaloir) [*impression, idée*] to prevail; [*couleur, goût, parfum*] to stand out; **c'est la persévérance qui domine chez lui** his chief characteristic is perseverance.
III se dominer *vpr* [*personne*] to control oneself.

dominicain, **~e** /dɔminikɛ̃, ɛn/ *adj* **1** ▶ 232 │, 394 │ Dominican; **2** RELIG Dominican.

dominical, **~e**, *mpl* **-aux** /dɔminikal, o/ *adj* Sunday (*épith*).

domino /dɔmino/ *nm* ▶ 329 │ JEUX domino.

dommage /dɔmaʒ/ *nm* **1** (chose regrettable) **c'est très ou vraiment ~** it's a great shame ou pity (**de faire** to do); **2** (dégât) damage ¢; **3** JUR (préjudice) tort.
■ **~s corporels** personal injury ¢; **~s et intérêts** JUR damages; **~s de guerre** JUR war damage ¢.

dommageable /dɔmaʒabl/ *adj* harmful (**pour** to).

dommages-intérêts /dɔmaʒɛtɛʀɛ/ *nmpl* damages; **10 000 francs de ~** 10,000 francs in damages.

domptage /dɔ̃taʒ/ *nm* taming (**de** of).

dompter /dɔ̃te/ [1] *vtr* to tame [*fauve, nature, eaux*]; to bring [sb] to heel [*indiscipliné*]; to crush, to put down [*insurgés, insurrection*]; to overcome, to master [*orgueil, passion*].

dompteur, **-euse** /dɔ̃tœʀ, øz/ ▶ 374 │ *nm,f* tamer.

DOM-TOM /dɔmtɔm/ *nmpl* (*abbr* = **départements et territoires d'outre-mer**) *French overseas administrative departments and territories*.

don /dɔ̃/ *nm* **1** (donation) donation; **faire ~ de** to give (**à** to); **~ de soi** self-sacrifice; **2** (talent) gift (**de qch** for sth); **avoir le ~ de faire** to have a talent for doing.
■ **~ du sang** blood donation.

donataire /dɔnatɛʀ/ *nmf* donee.

donateur, **-trice** /dɔnatœʀ, tʀis/ *nm,f* donor.

donation /dɔnasjɔ̃/ *nf* **1** (cadeau) donation; **2** JUR gift.

donc /dɔ̃k/ *conj* **1** (indiquant une conséquence) so, therefore; (dans une déduction logique, un syllogisme) therefore; **il avait une réunion, il n'a ~ pas pu venir** he had a meeting, so he was unable to come; **je pense ~ je suis** I think, therefore I am; **2** (marquant la surprise) so; **c'est ~ pour ça qu'il n'est pas venu!** so that's why he didn't come!; **3** (après interruption, digression) so; **nous disions ~?** so, where were we?; **je disais ~ que...** as I was saying...; **4** (pour renforcer une affirmation, un ordre, une question) **tais-toi ~!** be quiet, will you?; **entrez ~!** do come in!; **mais où est-il ~ passé?** where on earth has he gone?; **allons ~!** come on!

donjon /dɔ̃ʒɔ̃/ *nm* keep, donjon.

don Juan, *pl* **dons Juans** /dɔ̃ʒɥɑ̃/ *nm* **un ~** a Casanova.

Don Juan /dɔ̃ʒɥɑ̃/ *npr* **1** LITTÉRAT Don Juan; **2** MUS Don Giovanni.

donne /dɔn/ *nf* **1** (aux cartes) deal; **mauvaise** or **fausse ~** misdeal; **2** (rapport de ᴛᴏʀᴄᴇs) order.

donné, ~e¹ /dɔne/ **I** *pp* ▶ **donner**.
II *pp adj* **1** (possible) **il n'est pas ~ à tout le monde de faire** not everyone can do ou is capable of doing; **il m'a été ~ de travailler avec lui** I had the chance to work with him; **2** (déterminé) [*quantité, durée, endroit, situation*] given; **à un moment ~** ɢᴇ́ɴ at one point; (soudain) all of a sudden; **3** (bon marché) cheap.
III étant donné *loc adj* given.
IV étant donné que *loc conj* given that.

donnée² /dɔne/ *nf* **1** (élément d'information) fact, element; **nous n'avons aucune ~ sur cette question** we have no information on this issue; **2** (élément défini) data (+ *v pl* ou *sg*); **les ~s informatiques/statistiques** computer/statistical data; **en ~s brutes** in raw data; **après correction des ~s saisonnières** ᴇ́ᴄᴏɴ with seasonally adjusted figures.

donner /dɔne/ [1] **I** *vtr* **1** ɢᴇ́ɴ **~ qch à qn** to give sth to sb, to give sb sth [*livre, adresse, emploi, temps, autorisation, conseil, courage, rhume*]; ᴊᴇᴜx to deal [*cartes*] (à to); **~ pour les œuvres** to give to charity; **~ l'heure à qn** to tell sb the time; **je lui donne 40 ans** I'd say he/she was 40; **on ne lui donne pas d'âge** you can't tell how old he/she is; **~ froid/faim à qn** to make sb feel cold/hungry; **~ à croire** or **penser** or **comprendre que...** to suggest that...; **~ à qn à penser/croire que...** to make sb think/believe that...; **donne-moi ton genou que j'examine cette blessure** let me see your knee so that I can look at that wound; **2** (confier) to give [*objet, tâche*] (à **faire** to do); **elle donne sa fille à garder à mes parents** she has my parents look after her daughter; **j'ai donné ma voiture à réparer** I've taken my car in to be repaired; **3** (présenter) [*salle, cinéma*] to show [*film*]; [*théâtre*] to put on [*pièce*]; [*troupe*] to give [*spectacle, représentation*]; **qu'est-ce qu'on donne au Marignan?** ᴄɪɴ what's showing ou on at the Marignan?; ᴛʜᴇ́ᴀᴛ what's playing at the Marignan?; **4** (organiser) to give [*dîner, gala*] (**pour** for sb); **5** (assurer) to give [*cours, exposé*] (à, **devant** to); **6** (considérer) to give [*personne, œuvre*] (**comme, pour** as); **les sondages le donnent en tête** the polls put him in the lead; **7** (produire) to give [*sentiment, impression*]; to give [*ombre, aspect, teinte*]; to produce, to yield [*fruits, jus*]; to produce [*résultats*]; **leur intervention n'a rien donné** their intervention didn't have any effect; **8** (manifester) to show [*signes*] (à to); **9**⁰ (dénoncer) to inform on [*complice*] (à to); **10** (entreprendre) **~ l'assaut à qn** to attack sb; **~ la charge contre qn** to charge at sb.
II *vi* **1** (produire) **le poirier va bien ~ cette année** the pear tree will produce ɢʙ ou yield a good crop this year; **2** (émettre un son) [*radio*] to be playing; **~ du cor** (à la chasse) to sound the horn; **3** (heurter) **~ sur** ou **contre** [*personne, animal, véhicule*] to hit, to run into; **~ de la tête** ou **du front contre qch** to hit one's head against sth; **ne plus savoir où ~ de la tête** ғɪɢ not to know which way to turn; **4** (être orienté) **~ sur** [*chambre, fenêtre*] to overlook [*mer, rue*]; [*porte*] to give onto; **~ au nord/sud** [*façade, pièce*] to face ou look north/south; **la cuisine donne dans le salon** the kitchen leads into the living-room; **5** (avoir tendance à) **~ dans** to tend toward(s); **en ce moment, il donne dans la musique baroque** at the moment, he's into⁰ baroque music; **6** (se lancer) **~ dans un piège** to fall into a trap; **7** (consacrer) **~ de soi-même** or **de sa personne** to give of oneself; **8** (attaquer) [*troupe, chars*] to attack, to go into action.
III se donner *vpr* **1** (se livrer) **se ~ à** to devote oneself to [*travail, cause*]; **se ~ à fond dans qch** to give one's all to sth; **2** (s'octroyer) **se ~ le temps de faire** to give oneself time to do; **se ~ les moyens de faire** to find the means to do; **pays qui se donne un nouveau président** country which is getting a new president; **3** (s'imposer) **se ~ pour** or **comme but/ mission de faire** to make it one's aim/mission to do; **se ~ pour tâche de faire** to set oneself the task of doing; **4** (affecter) **se ~ pour intelligent/pacifiste** to make oneself out to be intelligent/a pacifist; **se ~ de**

grands airs to give oneself airs; **5** (échanger) **se ~ des coups** to exchange blows; **se ~ des baisers** to kiss one another; **se ~ rendez-vous** to arrange to meet; **se ~ le mot** to pass the word on.
ɪᴅɪᴏᴍᴇs **donnant donnant: je garde ton chat à Noël, tu gardes le mien à Pâques** fair's fair: I keep your cat at Christmas, you keep mine at Easter; **avec lui, c'est donnant donnant** he never does anything for nothing.

donneur, -euse /dɔnœʀ, øz/ *nm,f* **1** ᴍᴇ́ᴅ donor; **2** ᴊᴇᴜx dealer; **3** (personne qui aime donner) **les ~s de bons conseils** people who like to give advice.

don Quichotte /dɔ̃kiʃɔt/ *npr* Don Quixote.

dont /dɔ̃/ *pron rel*

■ **Note** Lorsque la traduction de *dont* fait intervenir une préposition en anglais, deux tournures sont possibles: *c'est un enfant dont je suis fier* = he's a child I'm proud of; = he's a child of whom I am proud. La première traduction est utilisée dans la langue courante, parlée ou écrite; la seconde traduction relève de la langue soutenue, surtout écrite, et n'est pas toujours acceptable: *le livre dont tu m'as parlé* = the book you told me about.

1 (en fonction d'objet indirect) **la jeune fille ~ on nous disait qu'elle avait 20 ans** the girl who they said was 20 ou who was said to be 20; **Sylvaine est quelqu'un ~ on se souvient** Sylvaine is somebody (that) you remember; **la maladie ~ il souffre** the illness which he's suffering from; **2** (en fonction de complément d'un adjectif) **des élèves ~ je suis satisfait** pupils I'm satisfied with, pupils with whom I am satisfied; **des renseignements ~ nous ne sommes pas certains** information which we are not sure about; **3** (en fonction de complément circonstanciel) **une voix ~ elle sait admirablement se servir** a voice which she really knows how to use; **la manière ~ elle s'habille** the way (in which) she dresses; **la façon ~ il a été traité** the way he has been treated; **la famille ~ il descend** the family from which he is descended; **4** (en fonction de nom) **un canapé ~ les housses sont amovibles** a sofa whose covers are removable; **un concours ~ le lauréat gagnera...** a competition the winner of which will receive...; **une personne ~ il prétend être l'ami** a person whose friend he claims to be; **5** (parmi lesquels) **il y a eu plusieurs victimes ~ mon père** there were several victims, one of whom was my father; **l'organisation propose diverses activités ~ l'équitation, la natation et le tricot** the organization offers various activities including horse riding, swimming and knitting; **des boîtes ~ la plupart sont vides** boxes, most of which are empty.

dopage /dɔpaʒ/ *nm* (de chevaux) doping; (d'athlète) illegal drug-taking ou drug use.

dopant /dɔpɑ̃/ *nm* drug.

doper /dɔpe/ [1] *vtr* ʟɪᴛ to dope [*cheval, sportif*]; ғɪɢ to boost [*monnaie, marché*].

dorade /dɔʀad/ *nf* sea bream.

doré, ~e /dɔʀe/ **I** *pp* ▶ **dorer**.
II ▶ 141 *pp adj* **1** (qui rappelle l'or) [*peinture, papier*] gold (*épith*); [*bronze*] gold-coloured ᴳʙ; [*cadre, chaise*] gilt (*épith*); **2** (avec de l'or) [*coupole*] gilded; **~ sur tranche** [*feuille, livre*] gilt-edged (*épith*); **3** (blond cuivré) [*cheveux, lumière*] golden; [*peau*] tanned; [*pain, poulet*] golden brown; **4** (dans la richesse) [*exil*] luxurious; **jeunesse ~e** gilded youth.
III *nm* gilt.

dorénavant /dɔʀenavɑ̃/ *adv* henceforth.

dorer /dɔʀe/ [1] **I** *vtr* **1** (couvrir d'or) to gild [*cadre*]; **~ qch à l'or fin** to gild sth with gold leaf; **2** ᴄᴜʟɪɴ to glaze [*tourte, pâte*]; **3** (changer la couleur de) [*soleil*] to turn [sth] to gold [*feuillage, blés*].
II *vi* **1** ᴄᴜʟɪɴ [*poulet*] to brown; **faire ~ qch** to brown sth; **2** ʟɪᴛᴇʀ [*moissons, raisins*] to turn golden.
III se dorer *vpr* **se ~ au soleil** to sunbathe.

doreur, -euse /dɔʀœʀ, øz/ ▶ 374 *nm,f* gilder.

dorique /dɔʀik/ *adj* Doric.

dorloter /dɔʀlɔte/ [1] *vtr* to pamper.

dormant, **~e** /dɔʀmɑ̃, ɑ̃t/ *adj* **eaux ~es** still waters.

dormeur, **-euse** /dɔʀmœʀ, øz/ **I** *nm,f* (personne) sleeper; **c'est un gros ~** he sleeps a lot. **II** *nm* ZOOL (tourteau) (edible) crab.

dormir /dɔʀmiʀ/ [30] *vi* **1** to sleep; **il dort** he's sleeping, he's asleep; **~ profondément** to sleep soundly; **~ d'un sommeil léger/lourd** to be in a light/deep sleep; **~ debout** [*animal*] to sleep standing up; [*personne*] to be asleep on one's feet; FIG (être épuisé) to be dead on one's feet; **ça m'empêche de ~** it keeps me awake; **il n'en dort plus** he's losing sleep over it; **2** FIN [*argent*] to lie idle.
IDIOMES **ne ~ que d'un œil** to sleep with one eye open; **~ sur ses deux oreilles**, **~ tranquille** to rest easy; **~ comme un loir** or **une marmotte** or **une souche** or **un bienheureux** to sleep like a log; **~ à poings fermés** to be fast asleep; **la fortune vient en dormant** PROV good luck comes when you're not looking for it.

dorsal, *mpl* **-aux** /dɔʀsal, o/ *adj* [*douleur, muscle*] back; [*vertèbre, nageoire*] dorsal.

dortoir /dɔʀtwaʀ/ **I** *nm* dormitory.
II (-)**dortoir** (*in compounds*) **ville-/banlieue-~** dormitory town/suburb.

dorure /dɔʀyʀ/ *nf* (revêtement) gilt **ℂ**; (technique) gilding.

doryphore /dɔʀifɔʀ/ *nm* Colorado beetle.

dos /do/ **▶ 137** *nm inv* GÉN back; (de livre) spine; (de lame) blunt edge; **être sur le ~** to be (lying) on one's back; **avoir le ~ rond** or **voûté** to stoop, to have round shoulders; **mal de ~** backache; **voir qn de ~** to see sb from behind; **au ~ de** (chèque, carte) on the back of; **robe décolletée dans le ~** dress with a low back; **voyager à ~ d'âne** to travel riding on a donkey; **faire qch dans** or **derrière le ~ de qn** to do sth when sb's back is turned; **ils sont arrivés, sac au ~** they arrived, with their rucksacks on their backs; **il n'a rien sur le ~**○ he's wearing hardly anything; **~ à ~** LIT back to back; **renvoyer deux parties ~ à ~** FIG to refuse to come out in favour^GB of either party; **tourner le ~ à** (position) to have one's back to; (mouvement) to turn one's back to; FIG to turn one's back on; **faire le gros ~** [*chat*] to arch its back; [*personne*] to keep one's head down.
IDIOMES **courber le ~** to bow and scrape; **mettre qch sur le ~ de qch/qn**○ to blame sth on sth/sb; **j'ai bon ~** it's always me; **se mettre qn à ~**○ to get on the wrong side of sb.

dosage /dozaʒ/ *nm* **1** (en chimie, pharmacie) (quantité) amount, proportion; (mesure) measurement; **2** (combinaison) mix; (action de mélanger) mixing; **3** FIG (contrôle) controlled use; **4** (proportions) proportions (*pl*).

dos-d'âne /dodɑn/ *nm inv* hump; **pont en ~** humpback bridge.

dose /doz/ *nf* **1** (quantité) LIT, FIG dose; **à petites ~s** in small doses; **à ~ homéopathique** in tiny doses; **avoir une bonne ~ de bêtise/d'égoïsme** not to be short on stupidity/selfishness; **forcer la ~**○ to go a bit far○; **2** (mesure) measure.

doser /doze/ [1] *vtr* **1** (déterminer la quantité) to measure; (introduire une quantité) to measure out; **dosé à 100 mg** containing 100 mg (**par** per); **2** (contrôler) to use [sth] in a controlled way; **~ ses efforts** to pace oneself.

doseur /dozœʀ/ *nm* measuring glass.

dossard /dosaʀ/ *nm* number (worn by an athlete).

dossier /dosje/ *nm* **1** GÉN file; **~ personnel** personal file; **constituer** or **établir un ~ sur qn/qch** [*policier*] to draw up a file on sb/sth; [*écolier, étudiant*] to do a project on sb/sth; **faire un ~ de demande de prêt** to make an application for a loan; **~ médical/scolaire** medical/school records (*pl*); **~ d'inscription** SCOL, UNIV registration form; **sélection sur ~** selection by written application; **2** JUR (documents) file; (affaire) case; **3** (sujet) **le ~ brûlant de la pollution** the controversial problem of pollution; **notre ~ sur l'alcoolisme** PRESSE our (special) feature on alcoholism; **4** (classeur) file, folder; **5** (de chaise, fauteuil) back.
■ **~ de presse** press pack.

dot /dɔt/ *nf* (de jeune fille, religieuse) dowry.

dotation /dɔtasjɔ̃/ *nf* **1** (somme allouée) allocation; (matériel) endowment; **2** (revenu de chef d'État) salary.

doté, **~e** /dɔte/ **I** *pp* ▶ **doter**.
II *pp adj* **richement ~** [*fondation*] richly endowed; [*fille*] with a large dowry (*after n*); **pays mal ~** poor country.

doter /dɔte/ [1] **I** *vtr* **1** (accorder une somme à) **~ qn de qch** to allocate sth to sb; **2** (fournir en équipement) **~ qn/qch de** to equip sb/sth with; **3** FIG (accorder) **~ qn/qch de** to endow sb/sth with; **elle est dotée d'un grand talent** she's endowed with great talent; **la CEE est dotée d'un président** the EEC has a president.
II se doter *vpr* **se ~ de** to acquire [*revenu*]; to create, set up [*service*].

douairière /dwɛʀjɛʀ/ *nf* dowager.

douane /dwan/ *nf* **1** (service) customs (+ *v sg* ou *pl*); **passer (à) la ~** to go through customs; **passer des marchandises en ~** to clear goods through customs; **marchandises (entreposées) en ~** bonded goods; **2** (taxe) duty; **exempt de ~** duty-free; **soumis aux droits de ~** dutiable.

douanier, **-ière** /dwanje, ɛʀ/ **I** *adj* customs (*épith*).
II ▶ 374 *nm* customs officer.

doublage /dublaʒ/ *nm* **1** CIN dubbing; **2** (de revêtement, fil) doubling; **3** (de vêtement, cloison) lining.

double /dubl/ **I** *adj* [*quantité, somme, dose, épaisseur, consonne*] double; **à ~ effet** dual ou double action (*épith*); **outil à ~ usage** dual-purpose tool; **cassette ~ durée** double-play cassette; **l'avantage est ~** the advantage is twofold; **rue à ~ sens** two-way street; **valise à ~ fond** suitcase with a false bottom; **mouchoirs ~ épaisseur** two-ply tissues GB ou Kleenex®; **~ nationalité** dual citizenship, dual nationality; **avoir le don de ~ vue** to have second sight; **en ~ exemplaire** in duplicate.
II *adv* [*compter, voir*] double.
III *nm* **1** (deux fois plus) double; **c'est le ~ de ce que j'ai payé!** that's double ou twice what I paid!; **30 est le ~ de 15** 30 is twice 15; **leur piscine fait le ~ de la nôtre** their swimming-pool is twice as big as ours ou is twice the size of ours; **2** (exemplaire supplémentaire) (de document) copy; (de personne) double; **avoir un ~ des clés** to have a spare set of keys; **prends ce livre, je l'ai en ~** take this book, I've got two copies of it; **3** SPORT (au tennis) doubles (*pl*).

doublé, **~e** /duble/ **I** *pp* ▶ **doubler**.
II *pp adj* **1** [*vêtement*] lined (**de** with); **2** CIN [*film*] dubbed; **3** (en plus de) **un imbécile ~ d'un lâche** a coward as well as a fool.
III *nm* SPORT (deux victoires successives) double.

double-crème, *pl* **doubles-crèmes** /dubləkʀɛm/ *nm* cream cheese.

doublement /dubləmɑ̃/ **I** *adv* (à double titre) in two ways; **il est ~ coupable** he's doubly guilty, he's guilty on two counts.
II *nm* (de quantité, chiffres) doubling.

doubler /duble/ [1] **I** *vtr* **1** (multiplier par deux) to double [*effectifs, prix, capacité*]; **~ le pas** to quicken one's pace; **~ la mise** JEUX to double the stakes; FIG to up the stakes; **2** (garnir d'une doublure, d'un revêtement) to line [*vêtement, cloison*] (**de** with); **3** (plier en deux) to fold [sth] in two [*papier, couverture*]; to double [*ficelle*]; **4** CIN to dub [*film, acteur*]; **5** CIN, THÉÂT (pour remplacement) (dans une scène périlleuse, un plan secondaire) to stand in for [*acteur*]; (pour indisponibilité) to understudy [*acteur*]; **6** (dépasser) to overtake GB, to pass US [*véhicule*]; **'défense de ~'** 'no overtaking' GB, 'no passing' US; **7** NAUT to double [*cap*]; **8** MUS to double; **~ une partie** to double a part.
II *vi* GÉN [*quantité, chiffre*] to double, to increase twofold; **~ de valeur** to double in value.
III se doubler *vpr* **se ~ de qch** to be coupled with sth.

doublure /dublyʀ/ *nf* **1** (pour un vêtement) lining; **2** THÉÂT understudy; CIN (dans une scène périlleuse) double; (dans un plan secondaire) stand-in.

Les douleurs et les maladies

Où est-ce que ça vous fait mal?

où avez-vous mal?	= where does it hurt?

Pour traduire avoir mal à, *l'anglais utilise un possessif devant le nom de la partie du corps (alors que le français a un article défini), et un verbe qui peut être* hurt *ou* ache *(faire mal).* hurt *est toujours possible:*

il a mal à la jambe	= his leg hurts
sa jambe lui fait mal	= his leg hurts
il a mal au dos	= his back hurts
il a mal aux yeux	= his eyes hurt
il a mal aux oreilles	= his ears hurt

ache *est utilisé avec les membres, les articulations, la tête, les dents et les oreilles:*

il a mal au bras	= his arm aches

On peut aussi traduire par have a pain in:

il a mal à la jambe	= he has a pain in his leg

Pour quelques parties du corps, l'anglais utilise un composé avec -ache:

avoir mal aux dents	= to have toothache
avoir mal au dos	= to have backache
avoir mal aux oreilles	= to have earache
avoir mal au ventre	= to have stomachache
avoir mal à la tête	= to have a headache
	(noter l'article indéfini)

Attention à:

il a mal au cœur	= he feels sick
il a mal aux reins	= he has backache

qui n'affectent pas la partie du corps désignée en français.

Les accidents

Là où le français a des formes pronominales (se faire mal à etc.) avec l'article défini, l'anglais utilise des verbes transitifs, avec des adjectifs possessifs:

il s'est cassé la jambe	= he broke his leg
il s'est fait mal au pied	= he hurt his foot

Noter:

il a eu la jambe cassée	= his leg was broken

Les faiblesses chroniques

Le français avoir le X fragile *peut se traduire par* to have something wrong with one's X *ou* to have X trouble:

avoir le cœur fragile	= to have something wrong with one's heart
	ou to have heart trouble
avoir les reins fragiles	= to have something wrong with one's kidneys
	ou to have kidney trouble

Pour certaines parties du corps (le cœur, les chevilles), on peut aussi utiliser l'adjectif weak:

avoir le cœur fragile	= to have a weak heart

Noter que l'anglais utilise l'article indéfini dans cette tournure.

Les maladies

L'anglais utilise tous les noms de maladie sans article:

avoir la grippe	= to have flu
avoir un cancer	= to have cancer
avoir une hépatite	= to have hepatitis
avoir de l'asthme	= to have asthma
avoir les oreillons	= to have mumps
être au lit avec la grippe	= to be in bed with flu
guérir de la grippe	= to recover from flu
mourir du choléra	= to die of cholera

Même les noms de maladies suivies d'un complément ne prennent pas toujours d'article:

avoir un cancer du foie	= to have cancer of the liver

Mais:

avoir un ulcère à l'estomac	= to have a stomach ulcer

Et attention à a cold (un rhume), *qui n'est pas vraiment une maladie:*

avoir un rhume	= to have a cold

L'anglais utilise moins volontiers les adjectifs dérivés des noms de maladies, si bien qu'on peut avoir:

être asthmatique	= to have asthma
	ou to be asthmatic
être épileptique	= to have epilepsy
	ou to be epileptic
être rachitique	= to have rickets

Noter:

quelqu'un qui a la malaria	= someone with malaria
quelqu'un qui a un cancer	= someone with cancer
les gens qui ont le Sida	= people with Aids

Les gens qui se font soigner pour une maladie sont désignés par a X patient:

quelqu'un qui se fait soigner pour un cancer	= a cancer patient

Les attaques de la maladie

Le français attraper *se traduit par* to get *ou* to catch.

attraper la grippe	= to get flu
	ou to catch flu
attraper une bronchite	= to get bronchitis
	ou to catch bronchitis

Mais get *est utilisable aussi pour ce qui n'est pas infectieux:*

développer un ulcère à l'estomac	= to get a stomach ulcer

Avoir peut se traduire par develop *lorsqu'il s'agit de l'apparition progressive d'une maladie:*

avoir un cancer	= to develop cancer
avoir un début d'ulcère	= to develop an ulcer

Pour une crise passagère, et qui peut se reproduire, on traduira avoir un/une ... *par* to have an attack of ... *ou a bout of ...:*

avoir une crise d'asthme	= to have an asthma attack
avoir une bronchite	= to have an attack of bronchitis
avoir une crise de malaria	= to have a bout of malaria

Noter aussi:

avoir une crise d'épilepsie	= to have an epileptic fit

Les traitements

Le français contre *ne se traduit pas toujours par* against.

prendre quelque chose contre le rhume des foins	= to take something for hay fever
prendre un médicament contre la toux	= to be taking something for a cough
prescrire un médicament contre la toux	= to prescribe something for a cough
des cachets contre la malaria	= malaria tablets
se faire vacciner contre la grippe	= to have a flu injection
vacciner qn contre le tétanos	= to give sb a tetanus injection
se faire vacciner contre le choléra	= to have a cholera vaccination
un vaccin contre la grippe	= a flu vaccine
	ou an anti-flu vaccine

Noter l'utilisation de la préposition anglaise on *avec le verbe* operate:

se faire opérer d'un cancer	= to be operated on for cancer
le chirurgien l'a opéré d'un cancer	= the surgeon operated on him for cancer

douce ▶ **doux**.

douce-amère ▶ **doux-amer**.

douceâtre /dusɑtʀ/ *adj* sickly sweet.

doucement /dusmɑ̃/ *adv* **1** (sans brusquer) GÉN gently; **il marchait ~ pour ne pas faire craquer le plancher** he walked softly so that the floorboards wouldn't creak; **holà! ~ avec le vin!** hey! go easy on the wine!; **~! je n'ai pas dit ça!** hang on a minute! I never said that!; **~, les enfants!** (calmez-vous) calm down, children!; (faites attention) careful, children!; **ça va ~, sans plus** things are so-so○; **2** (sans bruit) quietly; **3** (lentement) slowly, quietly.

doucereux, -euse /dusʀø, øz/ *adj* PEJ [*manières, personne*] smooth; [*paroles*] sugary; [*sourire*] sickly.

douceur /dusœʀ/ **I** *nf* **1** (de matière, tissu, cheveux, peau) softness, smoothness; (de saveur, d'odeur) mildness; (de fruit, vin) mellowness; (de liqueur, d'alcool) smoothness; (de lumière, couleur, musique, son) softness; **2** (de climat, temps, soleil) mildness; **~ de vivre** relaxed rhythm of life; **3** (de visage, traits, ton, voix, gestes, paroles) gentleness; **employer la ~ avec** to use the gentle approach with, to be gentle with; **avec ~** [*parler, agir*] gently; **en ~** [*conduire, atterrir*] smoothly; [*atterrissage, transition*] smooth; **4** (de relief, paysage) softness; **5** (friandise) sweet GB, candy US.

IDIOMES **plus fait ~ que violence** PROV gentleness works better than violence.

douche /duʃ/ *nf* **1** (pour se laver) shower; **prendre une ~** to have GB ou take US a shower; **être sous la ~** to be in the shower; **2**○ (déception) letdown○.

■ **~ écossaise** LIT alternating hot and cold shower; FIG bucket of cold water.

doucher /duʃe/ [1] **I** *vtr* **1** (laver) to give [sb] a shower [*personne*]; **2**○ (calmer) to dampen [*enthousiasme*]; to cool off [*personne*]; **3**○ (mouiller) [*pluie*] to soak [*personne*]; **se faire ~** to get a soaking.

II se doucher *vpr* to take a shower.

doué, -e /dwe/ *adj* **1** (talentueux) gifted, talented (**en** in, at); **être ~ pour** to have a gift for [*théâtre, études*]; **être ~ pour les chiffres** to have a good head for figures; **2** (pourvu) **~ de** endowed ou gifted with [*qualité*].

douille /duj/ *nf* **1** (de cartouche) cartridge (case); **2** ÉLEC-TROTECH socket.

douillet, -ette /dujɛ, ɛt/ *adj* **1** (sensible) PEJ [*personne*] oversensitive to pain (*jamais épith*); **2** (confortable) [*existence, appartement*] cosy GB, cozy US.

douleur /dulœʀ/ *nf* **1** ▶ 196 (physique) pain; **une ~ aiguë/sourde** a sharp/dull pain; **médicament contre la ~** a painkiller; **2** (morale) pain; (causée par un deuil) grief; **accablé de ~** grief-stricken; **nous avons la ~ de vous faire part du décès de** it is with great sorrow that we have to inform you of the death of.

douloureuse¹ /duluʀøz/ **I** *adj f* ▶ **douloureux**.

II○ *nf* bill.

douloureusement /duluʀøzmɑ̃/ *adv* **1** (avec douleur morale) grievously; **2** (avec douleur physique) painfully.

douloureux, -euse² /duluʀø, øz/ *adj* **1** [*sensation, piqûre*] painful; **2** [*dent, tête*] aching; **3** (moralement) [*spectacle, événement*] distressing; [*attente, décision, question*] painful; [*expression, sourire*] sorrowful.

doute /dut/ **I** *nm* **1** (incertitude) doubt; **laisser qn dans le ~** to leave sb in a state of uncertainty; **cela est hors de ~** it's beyond doubt; **jeter le ~ sur** to cast doubt on; **mettre qch en ~** to call sth into question; **être dans le ~** to be doubtful, to have misgivings (**au sujet de** about); **2** (soupçon) doubt; **avoir des ~s** to have doubts ou misgivings (**sur, au sujet de** about); **j'ai des ~s!** I have my doubts!; **il fait peu de ~ que, il ne fait guère de ~ que** there's little doubt that; **sa culpabilité ne fait aucun ~** there's no doubt as to his/her guilt; **3** PHILOS, RELIG doubt.

II sans doute *loc adv* probably; **sans aucun ~, sans nul ~** without any doubt.

douter /dute/ [1] **I** *vtr* **~ que** to doubt that ou whether.

II douter de *vtr ind* to have doubts about; **j'en doute!** I have my doubts!; **je n'ai jamais douté de toi**

I never doubted you; **à n'en pas ~** undoubtedly, without a doubt; **elle ne doute de rien**○! IRON she's so sure of herself!

III *vi* PHILOS, RELIG to doubt.

IV se douter *vpr* se **~ de qch** to suspect sth; **se ~ que** to suspect that; **je m'en doutais!** I thought so!, I suspected as much! ; **je m'en doute!** IRON (c'est évident) obviously! IRON; **je me doute (bien) qu'il devait être furieux** I can (well) imagine that he was furious; **nous étions loin de nous ~ que** we didn't have the least idea that; **il aurait dû se ~ que...** he should have known that...

douteux, -euse /dutø, øz/ *adj* **1** (peu certain) [*résultat, succès*] uncertain; **il est ~ qu'il ait pu s'échapper** it is unlikely that he was able to escape; **2** (ambigu) [*sens, réponse*] ambiguous; **3** (sujet à caution) [*honnêteté, renseignements*] dubious; **4** (suspect) [*affaire, individu*] shady; [*hygiène, viande*] dubious; **plaisanterie d'un goût ~** joke in dubious taste.

douve /duv/ *nf* **1** (fossé) (de château) moat; AGRIC drainage ditch; **2** (de tonneau) stave.

Douvres /duvʀ/ ▶ **628** *npr* Dover.

doux, douce /du, dus/ *adj* **1** (aux sens) [*matière, peau, lumière, voix*] soft; [*vin, cidre*] sweet; [*fromage, piment, tabac*] mild; [*shampooing*] mild; **2** (pas froid) [*climat, temps, saison, température*] mild; **il fait ~** it's mild; **3** (pas abrupt) [*relief, pente*] gentle; **4** (léger) [*punition*] mild; **5** (gentil) [*personne, animal, regard, geste, visage*] gentle; **6** LITER (agréable) [*pensée, souvenir, rêve*] pleasant; [*baisers, caresses*] sweet, gentle; **7** ÉCOL [*technologie, énergie*] environmentally friendly.

IDIOMES **filer ~**○ to keep a low profile; **se la couler douce**○ to take it easy; **faire qch en douce**○ to do sth on the sly.

doux-amer, douce-amère, *mpl* **~s**, *fpl* **douces-amères** /duzamɛʀ, dusamɛʀ/ *adj* FIG [*propos*] bittersweet, barbed.

douzaine /duzɛn/ *nf* **1** (douze) dozen (*inv*); **deux ~s d'œufs** two dozen eggs; **à la ~** by the dozen; **2** (environ douze) about twelve, a dozen or so.

douze /duz/ ▶ **399**, **298**, **156** *adj inv, pron* GÉN twelve.

douzième /duzjɛm/ ▶ **399**, **156** *adj* twelfth.

doyen, -enne /dwajɛ̃, ɛn/ *nmf* **1** (en âge) **~ (d'âge)** oldest person; **2** (en ancienneté) the (most) senior member; **3** RELIG, UNIV dean.

Dr (*written abbr* = **docteur**) Dr.

drachme /dʀakm/ ▶ **33** *nf* drachma.

draconien, -ienne /dʀakɔnjɛ̃, ɛn/ *adj* [*loi, attitude, punition*] draconian; [*régime, traitement*] very strict.

dragage /dʀagaʒ/ *nm* (nettoyage) dredging; (fouille) dragging; **~ de mines** minesweeping.

dragée /dʀaʒe/ *nf* **1** (bonbon) sugared almond; **2** (pilule) sugar-coated pill; **3** AGRIC mixed provender.

IDIOMES **la ~ est amère** it's a bitter pill to swallow; **tenir la ~ haute à qn** to hold out on sb.

dragon /dʀagɔ̃/ *nm* **1** (animal) dragon; **un ~ de vertu** FIG a dragon of virtue; **2** MIL, HIST dragoon.

drague /dʀag/ *nf* **1** TECH (machine) dredge; (chaland) dredger; **2** (filet de pêche) dragnet.

■ **~ télématique** *Minitel dating service*.

draguer /dʀage/ [1] *vtr* **1**○ to chat [sb] up○ GB, to come on to○; **2** TECH (pour nettoyer) to dredge; (pour fouiller) to drag; **3** (à la pêche) to catch [sth] with a dragnet; **~ au chalut** to trawl; **4** MIL to sweep [*mines*]; NAUT **l'ancre drague le fond** the ship is dragging its anchor.

dragueur, -euse /dʀagœʀ, øz/ **I**○ *nmf* **c'est un drôle de ~**○ he's a terrible flirt.

II *nm* (pêcheur) dragnet fisherman; (ouvrier) dredgeman; (chaland) dredger.

drain /dʀɛ̃/ *nm* drain.

drainage /dʀɛnaʒ/ *nm* **1** TECH, AGRIC drainage; **2** MÉD draining (off); **3** FIG drain; **~ des cerveaux** brain drain.

drainer /dʀene/ [1] *vtr* **1** AGRIC, MÉD to drain; **2** FIG to siphon off [*capitaux*] (**vers** to); [*spectacle, annonce*] to attract [*public*] (**vers** to).

dramatique /dʀamatik/ **I** *adj* **1** (tragique) [*problème, situation*] tragic; **2** THÉÂT, LITTÉRAT [*création, effet*] dramatic; **art ~** drama; **auteur ~** playwright.

II *nf* TV, RADIO play, drama.

dramatiquement /dʀamatikmɑ̃/ *adv* tragically.

dramatiser /dʀamatize/ [1] *vtr* to dramatize.

dramaturge /dʀamatyʀʒ/ ▶ 374 *nmf* playwright.

dramaturgie /dʀamatyʀʒi/ *nf* (art) dramatic art.

drame /dʀam/ *nm* **1** (événement tragique) tragedy; **tourner au ~** to take a tragic turn; **tu ne vas pas en faire un ~!** don't make a drama out of it!; **2** CIN, LITTÉRAT, THÉÂT (genre) drama; (pièce) play.
■ **~ lyrique** MUS opera.

drap /dʀa/ *nm* **1** (de lit) sheet; **2** (tissu) woollen^GB fabric.
■ **~ de bain** bath sheet; **~ funéraire** pall.
IDIOMES **se mettre dans de beaux ~s** to land oneself in a fine mess.

drapé /dʀape/ *nm* drape.

drapeau, *pl* **~x** /dʀapo/ *nm* flag; **être sous les ~x** to be doing military service.
■ **~ tricolore** (drapeau français) tricolour^GB.

draper /dʀape/ [1] **I** *vtr* to drape [*tissu*]; (envelopper) to drape [*personne*].
II se draper *vpr* **1** LIT **se ~ dans** to wrap oneself in [*châle*]; **2** FIG **se ~ dans sa dignité** to stand on one's dignity.

drap-housse, *pl* **draps-housses** /dʀaus/ *nm* fitted sheet.

drapier, **-ière** /dʀapje, ɛʀ/ ▶ 374 *nm,f* (fabricant) cloth manufacturer.

drastique /dʀastik/ *adj* FML [*mesure*] drastic.

dressage /dʀesaʒ/ *nm* **1** (d'animal) training; **2** (de jeune cheval) breaking in; (discipline) dressage.

dresser /dʀese/ [1] **I** *vtr* **1** (faire obéir) to train [*animal*]; to break in [*cheval*]; **2** (ériger) to put up [*tente, échafaudage, statue*]; **3** (lever) to raise [*tête, queue*]; **~ l'oreille** [*animal*] to prick up its ears; FIG to prick up one's ears; **4** (établir) to draw up [*carte géographique, inventaire, contrat*]; to write out [*procès-verbal*]; **5** (installer) to lay, to set [*table, piège*]; to lay out [*buffet*]; **6** (préparer) CULIN to garnish [*plat*]; **7** (influencer) **~ qn contre** to set sb against.
II se dresser *vpr* **1** (se mettre droit) to stand up; **2** (s'insurger) **se ~ contre** to rebel against [*injustice*]; **3** (s'élever) [*statue, obstacle*] to stand; (dominer) to tower up.

dresseur, **-euse** /dʀesœʀ, øz/ ▶ 374 *nm,f* (d'animal) trainer.

dribbler /dʀible/ [1] *vi* SPORT to dribble.

drille° /dʀij/ *nm* **joyeux ~** jolly fellow.

driver /dʀive/ [1] **I** *vtr* to drive [*balle, cheval*].
II *vi* (en tennis) to drive; (en golf) to drive off.

drogue /dʀɔg/ *nf* **1** (stupéfiant) drug; **la ~** drugs; **c'est devenu une ~** FIG it has become an addiction; **2†** (remède) drug; (de charlatan) quack remedy.

drogué, **~e** /dʀɔge/ *nm,f* drug-addict, junkie°.

droguer /dʀɔge/ [1] **I** *vtr* **1** PÉJ [*médecin*] (avec sédatif) to dope; (en prescrivant) to dish out° drugs to; **2** (illégalement) to dope [*animal, sportif*]; to drug [*victime*]; to doctor [*boisson*].
II se droguer *vpr* **1** PÉJ (avec des médicaments) to dope oneself (**à**, **de** with); **2** (avec des stupéfiants) to take drugs; **se ~ à l'héroïne** to be on heroin.

droguerie /dʀɔgʀi/ ▶ 374 *nf* (magasin) hardware shop GB ou store US; (commerce) hardware trade.

droguiste /dʀɔgist/ ▶ 374 *nmf* (propriétaire) owner of a hardware shop GB ou store US.

droit, **~e**^1 /dʀwa, at/ ▶ 326 **I** *adj* **1** (pas courbe, pas tordu) [*ligne, route, barre, cheveux, mur, nez*] straight; (pas penché) [*écriture*] up-and-down; **se tenir ~** (debout) to stand up straight; (assis) to sit up straight; **s'écarter du ~ chemin** FIG to stray from the straight and narrow; **descendre en ~e ligne de** to be a direct descendant of; **2** (contraire de gauche) right;

3 (honnête) [*personne*] straight, upright; [*vie*] blameless; **4** (sensé) [*jugement*] sound; **5** (en couture) [*jupe*] straight; [*veste*] single-breasted; **6** MATH [*cône, angle, prisme*] right.
II *adv* [*aller, rouler*] straight; **continuez tout ~** carry straight on; **aller ~ au but** ou **fait** FIG to go straight to the point; **aller ~ à la catastrophe** to be heading straight for disaster; **ça m'est allé ~ au cœur** FIG it really touched me; **marcher ou filer**° **~** FIG to toe the line; **venir tout ~ de** [*expression, citation*] to come straight out of [*auteur, œuvre*].
III *nm* **1** (prérogative) right; **avoir des ~s sur qn/qch** to have rights over sb/sth; **de quel ~ est-ce que tu me juges?** what gives you the right to judge me?; **être dans son** (**bon**) **~** to be within one's rights; **de** (**plein**) **~** by right(s); **de ~ divin** by divine right; **cela leur revient de ~** it's theirs by right; **avoir ~ à** to have the right to [*liberté, nationalité*]; to be entitled to [*bourse, indemnité*]; **il a eu ~ à une amende** IRON he got a fine; **avoir le ~ de faire** (la permission) to be allowed to do; (selon la morale, la justice) to have the right to do; **avoir le ~ de vie ou de mort sur qn** to have (the) power of life and death over sb; **il s'imagine qu'il a tous les ~s** he thinks he can do whatever he likes; **être en ~ de** to be entitled to; **à bon ~** [*se plaindre*] with good reason; **'à qui de ~'** to whom it may concern'; **j'en parlerai à qui de ~**° I'll speak to the appropriate person; **faire ~ à** to grant [*requête*]; **2** JUR (ensemble de lois) law; **faire son ~** to study law; **3** (redevance) fee; **~ d'inscription** registration fee; **4** (en boxe) right; **direct du ~** straight right; **crochet/uppercut du ~** right hook/uppercut.
■ **~ d'aînesse** JUR birthright, primogeniture; **~ d'antenne** broadcasting right; **~ de cité** JUR (right of) citizenship; FIG acceptance; **acquérir ~ de cité** FIG to gain acceptance; **avoir ~ de cité** FIG to be accepted; **~ commun** (prisonnier) nonpolitical; **~ d'entrée** COMM import duty; (pour une personne) entrance fee; **~ de passage** JUR right of way GB, easement US; **~ de port** FIN port dues; **~ de propriété** right of possession; **~ de regard** FIN right of inspection; GÉN **avoir ~ de regard sur** to have a say in; **~ de timbre** FIN stamp duty; **~ de vote** POL right to vote ; **~s d'auteur** royalties; **~s civiques** POL civil rights; **~s de douane** COMM, FIN customs duties; **les ~s de l'homme** human rights; **~s de succession** FIN inheritance tax.
IDIOMES **se tenir ~ comme un i** ou **un piquet** to hold oneself very erect.

droite^2 /dʀwat/ *nf* **1** (opposé à gauche) **la ~** the right; **rouler à ~** to drive on the right; **tenir sa ~** AUT to keep (to the) right; **à ta ~**, **sur ta ~** on your right; **à ~ de** to the right of; **demander à ~ et à gauche** (partout) to ask everywhere ou all over the place; (à tous) to ask everybody; **2** POL right; **voter à ~** to vote for the right; **de ~** [*parti, personne, gouvernement*] right-wing; **3** MATH straight line.

droitier, **-ière** /dʀwatje, ɛʀ/ *nm,f* **1** (qui se sert de la main droite) right-hander; **2**° POL right-winger.

droiture /dʀwatyʀ/ *nf* honesty, uprightness.

drôle /dʀol/ *adj* **1** (bizarre) funny, odd; **c'est un ~ de type** he's odd; **c'est ~ de faire/que** it's odd to do/that; **ce qui est** ou **ce qu'il y a de ~ c'est que** the funny thing is that; **faire** (**tout**) **~ à qn** to give sb a funny feeling; **faire une ~ de tête** to make a bit of a face; **~ de remerciement/consolation!** some thanks/consolation!; **2** (amusant) funny, amusing; **vous êtes ~, vous!** IRON don't make me laugh!; **3**° (grand) **un ~ de courage/travail** a lot of courage/work.
■ **~ de guerre** HIST phoney war.
IDIOMES **j'en ai entendu de ~s** I heard some funny things; **en faire voir de ~s à qn** to lead sb a merry dance.

drôlement /dʀolmɑ̃/ *adv* **1**° (très, beaucoup) really; **2** (bizarrement) oddly.

drôlerie /dʀolʀi/ *nf* **avec ~** amusingly.

dromadaire /dʀɔmadɛʀ/ *nm* dromedary.

dru, **~e** /dʀy/ **I** *adj* [*cheveux, blés*] thick; [*averse*] heavy.

II adv [pousser] thickly; [pleuvoir] heavily.

DS /dɛɛs/ nf: Citroen car of the 1950s.

DST /deɛste/ nf (abbr = **Direction de la surveil-lance du territoire**) French counterintelligence agency.

du /dy/ ▶ **de**.

dû, due, mpl **dus** /dy/ **I** pp ▶ **devoir**[1].

II pp adj **1** (à payer) owed (après n), owing (après n), due (après n) (à to); (exigible) due (après n); **les intérêts dus** the interest due; **respect ~ à qn/qch** respect due to sb/sth; **en bonne et due forme** in due form; **2** (attribuable) **~ à** due to.

III nm **réclamer son ~** to claim one's due; **payer son ~** to pay one's dues.

IDIOMES **chose promise chose due** a promise is a promise; **à chacun son ~** credit where credit is due.

dualisme /dɥalism/ nm **1** PHILOS dualism; **2** POL **le ~ des partis** the two-party system.

dualité /dɥalite/ nf duality.

dubitatif, -ive /dybitatif, iv/ adj sceptical GB, skeptical US.

duc /dyk/ ▶ **596** nm (titre) duke.

duché /dyʃe/ nm (seigneurie) dukedom; (domaine) duchy.

duchesse /dyʃɛs/ nf ▶ **596** duchess.

duègne /dɥɛɲ/ nf duenna.

duel /dɥɛl/ nm **1** (avec des armes) duel (à with); **se battre en ~** to fight a duel; **2** (en paroles) battle; **3** LING dual.

duettiste /dɥetist/ nmf duettist.

dulcinée /dylsine/ nf HUM lady-love.

dûment /dymɑ̃/ adv duly; **je vous ai ~ averti** I gave you due warning.

dune /dyn/ nf dune.

dunette /dynɛt/ nf poop.

duo /dyo, dɥo/ nm **1** MUS (œuvre) duet; (formation) **un ~ pour violon** a violin duet; **en ~** as a duo; **2** THÉÂT double act GB, duo US; **3**○ (couple) pair.

dupe /dyp/ **I** adj **être ~** to be fooled (**de** by).

II nf dupe; **un marché de ~s** a fool's bargain.

duper /dype/ [1] vtr to fool; **facile à ~** gullible.

duperie /dypri/ nf trickery ¢.

duplex /dyplɛks/ nm inv **1** (appartement) maisonette GB, duplex apartment US; **2** RADIO, TÉLÉCOM, TV duplex.

duplicata /dyplikata/ nm inv duplicate.

duplication /dyplikasjɔ̃/ nf TECH duplication; BIOL replication.

duplicité /dyplisite/ nf duplicity.

duquel ▶ **lequel**.

dur, ~e /dyʁ/ **I** adj **1** (difficile à entamer) [matériau, pain, siège, matelas] hard; [viande] tough; (rigide) [pinceau, poil, cuir, carton] stiff; [brosse à dents] hard; [plastique] rigid; [ressort] hard; **2** (malaisé à manipuler) [fermeture, poignée, pédale] stiff; [direction, volant] heavy; **3** (résistant) [personne] **~ au mal** tough; **elle est ~e à la tâche** or **au travail** she's a hard worker; **4** (anguleux) [profil, traits] hard; **5** (blessant) [son, voix, ton, parole, lumière, couleur] harsh; **6** (hostile) [visage, expression] severe; **7** (intransigeant) [parents, patron] (en général) hard; (à l'occasion) harsh; [régime] hard; [faction, politique] hard; **il est très ~ avec ses élèves** (comme défaut) he's very hard on his pupils; **il est ~ mais juste** (comme qualité) he's tough but fair; **la droite/gauche ~e** the hard Right/Left; **8** (contraignant) [loi naturelle, conditions de vie] harsh; [conditions de crédit, termes de sécurité] tough; **9** (éprouvant) [métier] GÉN hard; (physiquement) tough; [climat, nécessité] harsh; [concurrence, sport, ascension] hard, tough; **cela a été une ~e épreuve** it was quite an ordeal; **c'est la ~e réalité** it's the grim reality; **les temps sont ~s** times are hard; **10** (difficile) [examen, problème] hard; **il est ~ à supporter** he's heavy going; **11** (sans fard) [film, reportage] hard-hitting (épith); **12** (calcaire) [eau] hard.

II nm,f **1** (personne solide) tough nut○; **jouer les ~s** to act tough; **2** POL (partisan) hardliner.

III adv [travailler, frapper] hard.

IV nm permanent structure.

V à la dure loc adv the hard way.

IDIOMES **être ~ d'oreille**○ to be hard of hearing; **avoir la tête ~e** (obstiné) to be stubborn; (obtus) to be dense; **avoir la vie ~e** [insectes] to be difficult to get rid of; [habitude, préjugé] to die hard; **elle a la vie ~e** she has a hard life; **mener la vie ~e à qn** to give sb a hard time; **en faire voir de ~ à ses parents** to give one's parents a hard time.

durable /dyʁabl/ adj **1** (stable) [amélioration, amitié, impression, hausse, victoire] lasting; [attrait, intérêt] enduring; [situation] long-standing; [matériau] durable; **2** ÉCON [marchandise] durable.

durablement /dyʁabləmɑ̃/ adv [s'installer] on a permanent basis.

durant /dyʁɑ̃/ prép **1** (exprimant une durée) for; **des heures ~** for hours and hours, for hours on end; **l'été ~** the whole summer; **plus d'une heure ~** for over an hour; **sa vie ~** throughout his/her life; **2** (au cours de) during; **~ le match** during the match.

durcir /dyʁsiʁ/ [3] **I** vtr **1** (rendre dur) [sécheresse, froid] to harden [sol, pâte]; **2** (rendre sévère) [maquillage] to harden [traits]; **3** (radicaliser) to harden [position]; to intensify [mouvement de grève].

II vi [argile] to harden; [ciment, colle] to set; [pain] to go hard; [artères] to harden.

III se durcir vpr [argile, artères] to harden; [ton, régime] to become harsher; [conflit] to intensify.

durcissement /dyʁsismɑ̃/ nm **1** (d'argile, artère) hardening; (de ciment, colle) setting; **2** (d'attitude, de position) hardening; (de mouvement, grève) intensification.

durcisseur /dyʁsisœʁ/ nm hardener.

durée /dyʁe/ nf **1** (période) (de spectacle, séjour, règne, d'études) length; (de contrat) term; (de disque, cassette) playing time; **pour** or **pendant** (**toute**) **la ~ de** for the duration of; **séjour d'une ~ de trois mois** three-month stay; **ils n'ont pas précisé la ~ du projet** they didn't specify how long the project would last; **pendant une ~ limitée/fixée** over a limited/set period; **contrat à ~ déterminée** fixed-term contract; **de courte ~** [amitié, paix, reprise économique] short-lived; [orage, absence] brief; [bail, prêt] short-term; **de longue ~** [bail, prêt, chômage, contrat] long-term; [absence] long; **2** (longévité) **~ (de vie)** life; **~ d'utilisation** useful life; **pile longue ~** long-life battery; **3** MUS (de note) value; **4** PHILOS duration.

durement /dyʁmɑ̃/ adv **1** (de façon éprouvante) **être ~ touché** (affectivement) to be deeply affected; (économiquement) to be badly hit; **gagner ~ sa vie** to earn one's living the hard way; **2** (sans aménité) [punir, parler] harshly; [regarder] severely; **3** [frapper] hard.

durer /dyʁe/ [1] vi **1** (avoir une durée de) to last; **ne ~ qu'un instant** only to last a moment; **2** (se prolonger) to go on; **~ indéfiniment** to go on forever; **3** (se passer) [conférence, festival] to run; **4** (être durable) to last; **faire ~ ses vêtements** to make one's clothes last; **pourvu que ça dure** long may it last; **5** (se prolonger longtemps) to go on for long; **faire ~** to prolong [réunion]; **faire ~ le plaisir** IRON to prolong the agony.

dures /dyʁ/ nfpl **en faire voir de ~ à ses parents** to give one's parents a hard time.

dureté /dyʁte/ nf (fermeté) (de matériau, siège) hardness; (de viande) toughness; (de carton, poils, pinceau) stiffness; (de traits, visage) hardness; (d'expression, de ton, punition, paroles, métier, climat) harshness; (de regard) severity; (de tâche) difficulty; **avec ~** [regarder] severely.

durillon /dyʁijɔ̃/ nm callus.

durite /dyʁit/ nf radiator hose.

DUT /deyte/ nm (abbr = **diplôme universitaire de technologie**) two-year diploma from a university institute of technology.

duvet /dyvɛ/ nm **1** (plumes, poils) down; **le ~ d'oie** goosedown; **2** (sac de couchage) sleeping bag.

duveté, ~e /dyvte/ adj downy.

duveteux, -euse /dyvtø, øz/ adj [joue] downy; [pelage] fluffy; [fruit] downy GB, fuzzy US.

dynamique /dinamik/ I *adj* GÉN PHYS dynamic; [*match*] lively.
II *nf* **1** PHYS, PSYCH dynamics (+ *v sg*); **2** (processus) process.

dynamiser /dinamize/ [1] *vtr* to make [sb/sth] more dynamic; (de nouveau) to revitalize.

dynamisme /dinamism/ *nm* dynamism; **être plein de ~** to be very dynamic.

dynamite /dinamit/ *nf* LIT, FIG dynamite.

dynamiter /dinamite/ [1] *vtr* LIT to dynamite [*pont*]; FIG to destroy.

dynastie /dinasti/ *nf* dynasty.

dysfonctionnement /disfɔksjɔnmɑ̃/ *nm* **1** MÉD dysfunction; **2** (de système) malfunctioning.

dyslexie /dislɛksi/ *nf* dyslexia.

Ee

e, E /ə/ *nm inv* e, E; **e dans l'a** a and e joined together.

EAO /ɔao/ *nm: abbr* ▸ **enseignement**.

eau, *pl* **~x** /o/ **I** *nf* **1** GÉN water; **l'~ de source/du robinet** spring/tap water; **~ de pluie** rainwater ¢; **pastis sans ~** neat pastis; **2** (masse) water; **l'~ du lac** the water in the lake; **prendre l'~** [*chaussure*] to let in water; **être en ~** LIT [*réservoir*] to be full of water; FIG [*personne*] to be dripping with sweat; **mettre à l'~** to launch [*bateau*]; **se jeter à l'~** FIG to take the plunge; **tomber à l'~** FIG [*projet*] to fall through; **nettoyer le sol à grande ~** to sluice the floor down; **3** (approvisionnement) water; **~ courante** running water; **4** (pluie) rain; **5** (de pierre précieuse) water; **émeraude de la plus belle ~** emerald of the finest quality.
II eaux *nfpl* **1** GÉOG (niveau) water (*sg*); (masse) waters; **2** (liquide amniotique) waters; **elle a perdu ses ~x** her waters have broken.
■ **~ bénite** holy water; **~ de chaux** limewater; **~ douce** fresh water; **~ de Javel ~** (chloride) bleach; **~ lourde** heavy water; **~ de mer** seawater; **~ oxygénée** hydrogen peroxide; **~ plate** (du robinet) plain water ; (minérale) still mineral water; **~ de rose** rose water; **à l'~ de rose** [*roman*] sentimental; **~ de vaisselle** LIT, FIG dishwater; **~ vive** white water; **~x et forêts** ADMIN forestry commission (*sg*); **~x usées** waste water ¢.
IDIOMES **mettre l'~ à la bouche de qn** to make sb's mouth water; **c'est l'~ et le feu** they are like chalk and cheese; **être de la même ~** to be of the same ilk; **ou dans ces ~x-là**° or thereabouts; **vivre d'amour et d'~ fraîche** to live on love alone.

EAU *written abbr* ▸ **Émirats**.

eau-de-vie, *pl* **eaux-de-vie** /odvi/ *nf* brandy, eau de vie.

eau-forte, *pl* **eaux-fortes** /ofɔʀt/ *nf* etching.

ébahir /ebaiʀ/ [3] **I** *vtr* to dumbfound.
II s'ébahir *vpr* to be dumbfounded (**de, devant** by).

ébats /eba/ *nmpl* (d'enfants) frolics; (de sportifs) movements.

ébattre: s'ébattre /ebatʀ/ [61] *vpr* [*enfants*] to frolic (about); [*animaux*] to frisk about.

ébauche /eboʃ/ *nf* **1** (objet, sculpture) rough shape; (dessin) preliminary sketch; (roman, réforme) preliminary draft; **2** (action) (de sculpture) rough-hewing; (de dessin) sketching out; (de roman, réforme) drafting; **être encore à l'état d'~** to be still at an early stage; **3** FIG (début) **l'~ d'une amitié** the beginnings (*pl*) of a friendship; **l'~ d'un sourire** a hint of a smile; **l'~ d'un geste** an arrested gesture.

ébaucher /eboʃe/ [1] **I** *vtr* to sketch out [*tableau, solution*]; to draft [*roman, projet*]; to rough-hew [*statue*]; to begin [*conversation*].
II s'ébaucher *vpr* [*solution, roman*] to begin to take shape; [*amitié*] to begin to develop; [*négociations*] to start; [*image*] to begin to form.

ébène /ebɛn/ *nf* ebony; **des cheveux d'~** FIG jetblack hair.

ébéniste /ebenist/ ▸ **374** *nmf* cabinetmaker.

éberluer /ebɛʀlɥe/ [1] *vtr* [*nouvelle*] to dumbfound.

éblouir /ebluiʀ/ [3] *vtr* LIT, FIG to dazzle (**de** with).

éblouissant, ~e /ebluisɑ̃, ɑ̃t/ *adj* LIT, FIG dazzling.

éblouissement /ebluismɑ̃/ *nm* **1** (par une lumière vive) dazzle ¢; **2** FIG dazzling experience; **3** (vertige) dizzy spell.

éborgner /ebɔʀɲe/ [1] *vtr* (blesser) **~ qn** to blind sb in one eye.

éboueur /ebuœʀ/ ▸ **374** *nm* dustman GB, garbageman US.

ébouillanter /ebujɑ̃te/ [1] *vtr* to scald [*personne, volaille*]; to warm [*théière*]; to blanch [*légumes*].

éboulement /ebulmɑ̃/ *nm* (de mur, falaise) collapse; (de matériaux) fall; **~ (de rochers)** (chute) rockfall; (résultat) fallen rocks (*pl*).

ébouler: s'ébouler /ebule/ [1] *vpr* [*mur, falaise*] to collapse; [*rochers*] to fall.

éboulis /ebuli/ *nm inv* (rochers) mass of fallen rocks; (terre) heap of fallen earth.

ébouriffer /eburife/ [1] *vtr* [*vent*] to tousle [*cheveux*]; to ruffle [*plumes, poils*]; [*personne*] to ruffle [*cheveux*].

ébranler /ebʀɑ̃le/ [1] **I** *vtr* **1** LIT (faire vibrer) to rattle [*vitre*]; to shake [*maison*]; (rendre chancelant) to weaken [*construction*]; **2** (émouvoir) to shake [*personne, pays*]; (affaiblir) to undermine [*santé, régime*]; to shake [*personne, nerfs, conviction, confiance*]; to disturb [*esprit*].
II s'ébranler *vpr* [*convoi, train*] to move off.

ébrécher /ebʀeʃe/ [14] *vtr* **1** to chip [*vaisselle, dent*]; to make a nick in [*lame*]; to damage [*scie*]; FIG to tarnish [*réputation*]; **2** (entamer) to make a hole in [*économies*].

ébriété /ebʀijete/ *nf* intoxication; **en état d'~** in a state of intoxication, under the influence (of alcohol).

ébrouer: s'ébrouer /ebʀue/ [1] *vpr* **1** [*cheval*] to snort; **2** [*personne, chien*] to shake oneself/itself; [*gros oiseau*] to flap its wings; [*petit oiseau*] to flutter its wings.

ébruitement /ebʀɥitmɑ̃/ *nm* disclosure.

ébruiter /ebʀɥite/ [1] **I** *vtr* to divulge.
II s'ébruiter *vpr* [*nouvelle*] to get out.

ébullition /ebylisjɔ̃/ *nf* (de liquide) boiling; **porter à ~** to bring to the GB ou a US boil.
IDIOMES **être en ~** [*maisonnée, foule*] to be in a fever of excitement; [*pays, cerveau*] to be in a ferment.

écaille /ekaj/ *nf* **1** (de poisson) scale; (d'huître) shell; **2** (pour peignes) tortoiseshell; **lunettes en ~** horn-rimmed glasses; **3** (parcelle) flake; **4** BOT (de bourgeon, d'oignon) scale.

écailler¹ /ekaje/ [1] **I** *vtr* **1** CULIN to scale [*poisson*]; to open [*huître*]; **2** (endommager) **~ qch** [*personne*] to chip [sth] off.
II s'écailler *vpr* [*vernis, plâtre*] to flake away.

écailler², -ère /ekaje, ɛʀ/ ▸ **374** *nm,f* oyster seller.

écale /ekal/ *nf* (de noix) nutshell.

écaler /ekale/ [1] *vtr* to shell [*noix*].

écarlate /ekaʀlat/ ▸ **141** *nf* scarlet.

écarquiller /ekaʀkije/ [1] *vtr* **~ les yeux** to open one's eyes wide (**devant** at).

écart /ekaʀ/ **I** *nm* **1** (distance) (entre des objets) distance, gap (**entre** between); (entre des dates) interval; (entre des concepts) gap; (entre des versions) difference; **2** (variation) difference; **~ des salaires** pay differential; **~ par rapport à la normale** deviation from the norm; **3** (mouvement brusque) **faire un ~** [*cheval*] to shy; [*voiture*] to swerve; [*piéton*] to leap aside; **4** (faute) lapse; **il fait des ~s de régime** he doesn't stick to his diet; **~s de langage** bad language ¢; **5** (aux cartes) discard.
II à l'écart *loc adv* **être à l'~** to be isolated; **ils bavardaient dans le jardin, à l'~** they were talking in the garden GB ou yard US, off by themselves; **se tenir à l'~** (éloigné) to stand apart; (refuser de se mêler) to

keep oneself to oneself; (ne pas participer) not to join in; **mettre qn à l'~** (éloigner) to push sb aside; (mettre au ban) to ostracize sb.

III à l'écart de *loc prép* away from; **tenir qn à l'~ de** to keep sb away from [*lieu*]; to keep sb out of [*activité, négociations*].

écarté, ~e /ekaʀte/ **I** *pp* ▶ **écarter**.

II *pp adj* **1** (espacé) [*doigts*] spread (*épith, après n*); [*bras*] wide apart (*épith, après n*); [*jambes*] apart (*épith, après n*); [*yeux*] widely set; **2** (isolé) [*lieu*] isolated.

III ▶ 329 | *nm* JEUX écarté.

écarteler /ekaʀtəle/ [17] *vtr* **1** FIG (déchirer) **écartelé entre** torn between; **2** (supplicier) to quarter.

écartement /ekaʀtəmɑ̃/ *nm* (distance) distance, space.

écarter /ekaʀte/ [1] **I** *vtr* **1** (séparer) to move [sth] further apart [*objets*]; to open [*rideaux*]; to spread [*bras, jambes, doigts*]; to part [*lèvres, feuillage*]; **2** (éloigner) to move [sth] aside [*chaise*]; to brush [sth] aside [*mèche*]; to remove [*obstacle*]; to push [sb] aside [*personne*]; to move [sb] on [*badauds*]; **ce chemin nous écarte trop** this path takes us too far out of our way; **3** (détourner) **~ qn de son devoir** to distract sb from his duty; **4** (éliminer) to dispel [*soupçon*]; to remove [*tentation*]; to eliminate [*risque, concurrent*]; **tout danger est écarté** the danger is over; **5** (rejeter) to reject [*idée , candidature*]; to rule out [*possibilité*]; **~ qn de** (empêcher) to exclude sb from; (exclure) to remove sb from.

II s'écarter *vpr* **1** (se séparer) [*foule, nuages*] to part; [*volets*] to open; **2** (s'éloigner) to move away (**de** from); **écartez-vous** move out of the way; **écartez-vous les uns des autres** spread out a bit; **3** (dévier) LIT, FIG **s'~ de** to move away from [*direction, norme*]; to stray from [*chemin, sujet*]; to diverge from [*vérité*]; **s'~ de son devoir** to fail in one's duty.

ecchymose /ekimoz/ *nf* bruise.

ecclésiastique /eklezjastik/ **I** *adj* (du clergé) ecclesiastical; [*ordres, état*] holy.
II *nm* cleric.

écervelé, ~e /esεʀvəle/ **I** *adj* featherbrained.
II *nm,f* featherbrain.

échafaud /eʃafo/ *nm* **1** (lieu) scaffold; **2** (peine capitale) guillotine.

échafaudage /eʃafodaʒ/ *nm* **1** CONSTR scaffolding ¢; **2** (tas) stack; **3** FIG (montage) edifice.

échafauder /eʃafode/ [1] **I** *vtr* **1** (élaborer) to put [sth] together [*plan, théorie*]; to build up [*fortune*]; **2** (empiler) to stack [sth] up.
II *vi* CONSTR to put up scaffolding.

échalas /eʃala/ *nm inv* **1** (pieu) cane; **2**° (personne) beanpole°.
IDIOMES **maigre comme un ~** as thin as a rake.

échalote /eʃalɔt/ *nf* shallot.

échancré, ~e /eʃɑ̃kʀe/ **I** *pp* ▶ **échancrer**.
II *pp adj* **1** [*robe*] low-cut; [*culotte*] cut high on the thigh (*jamais épith*); **2** (ouvert) [*chemise*] open-necked; **3** [*côte*] indented.

échancrer /eʃɑ̃kʀe/ [1] *vtr* to cut away [*encolure, emmanchure*]; **~ une robe sur le devant/sous les bras** to cut a dress low at the front/under the arms.

échange /eʃɑ̃ʒ/ *nm* **1** GÉN exchange (**entre** between; **contre** for); **il y a eu un ~ de coups** blows were exchanged; **faire un ~ de prisonniers** to exchange prisoners; **en ~** in exchange, in return; **en ~ de quoi** in exchange for which; **2** ÉCON, COMM trade ¢; **~s commerciaux** trade ¢; **3** (relations, séjour linguistique) exchange; **4** BIOL, PHYS exchange; **5** (au tennis, tennis de table) rally; **6** (aux échecs) exchange.
■ **~ de bons procédés** quid pro quo; **~ standard** replacement by a reconditioned part.

échanger /eʃɑ̃ʒe/ [13] *vtr* **1** GÉN to exchange (**contre** for); **~ des insultes** to trade insults; **~ des remerciements** to thank each other; **elle et sa sœur échangent souvent leurs vêtements** she often swaps clothes with her sister; **'ni repris ni échangés'** 'no

exchanges or returns'; **2** (au tennis, tennis de table) **~ des balles** to rally.

échangeur /eʃɑ̃ʒœʀ/ *nm* **1** (intersection) interchange GB, grade separation US; **2** TECH exchanger.

échantillon /eʃɑ̃tijɔ̃/ *nm* sample.

échantillonnage /eʃɑ̃tijonaʒ/ *nm* **1** (prélèvement) sampling; (ensemble) selection; **2** MUS sampling.

échantillonner /eʃɑ̃tijone/ [1] *vtr* GÉN to take a sample of; ORDINAT, TÉLÉCOM to sample.

échappatoire /eʃapatwaʀ/ *nf* way out (**à** of); **répondre par une ~** to answer evasively.

échappée /eʃape/ *nf* SPORT break.

échappement /eʃapmɑ̃/ *nm* **1** (de gaz) (dispositif) **(tuyau d')~** exhaust (pipe); (expulsion) release; **en ~ libre** without a silencer GB ou muffler US; **2** (d'horlogerie) escapement.

échapper /eʃape/ [1] **I échapper à** *vtr ind* **1** (se dérober à) **~ à** (par la fuite) to get away from [*poursuivant*]; (par la ruse) to elude [*enquêteur, chasseur*]; **2** (éviter) **~ à** to escape [*mort, faillite*]; (to manage) to avoid [*accident, châtiment*]; **~ à tout contrôle** not to be subject to any control; **~ à une taxation** (légalement) to be exempt from tax; (illégalement) to evade a tax; **~ aux réunions de famille/à l'obligation de faire** to get out of family gatherings/of having to do; **3** (se libérer de) **~ à** to escape from [*milieu social*]; to shake off [*angoisse, désespoir*]; **je sens qu'il m'échappe** (mari, amant) I feel he is drifting away from me; (enfant) I feel he's growing away from me; **4** (tomber) **~ à qn** or **des mains de qn** [*objet*] to slip out of sb's hands; **5** (être produit involontairement) **un soupir m'a échappé** I let out a sigh; **6** (intellectuellement) **~ à** to escape; **le titre m'échappe** the title escapes me; **7** (ne pas suivre) **~ à** to defy [*classification, logique*]; **~ à la règle** to be an exception to the rule.

II s'échapper *vpr* **1** (s'enfuir) [*personne, animal*] to run away (**de** from); [*oiseau*] to fly away (**de** from); (d'un lieu clos) to escape (**de** from); (ne pas être pris) to get away; **laisser ~** [*personne*] to let [sb] get away [*personne, animal*]; to let [sth] slip between one's fingers [*victoire*]; to let [sth] slip [*occasion*]; **2** (se répandre) [*gaz, fumée*] to escape (**de, par** from); [*eau*] to leak (**de, par** from); **3** (partir) to get away; **4** (être produit) **laisser ~** to shed [*larmes*]; to let out [*parole, soupir*]; **5** SPORT to break away.
IDIOMES **l'~ belle** to have a narrow escape.

écharde /eʃaʀd/ *nf* splinter.

écharpe /eʃaʀp/ *nf* (cache-col) scarf; (d'officiel) sash; (bandage) sling.

écharper /eʃaʀpe/ [1] *vtr* to tear to pieces.

échasse /eʃas/ *nf* **1** (pour marcher) stilt; **2** (oiseau) stilt.

échassier /eʃasje/ *nm* wading bird.

échauder /eʃode/ [1] *vtr* **1** (décourager) to put [sb] off; **2** (ébouillanter) to scald.
IDIOMES **chat échaudé craint l'eau froide** PROV once bitten, twice shy PROV.

échauffement /eʃofmɑ̃/ *nm* **1** SPORT warm-up; **2** FIG (excitation) heat (**de** of); **3** TECH (de moteur) overheating; (de sol) warming; **4** BOT (de foin, bois) fermentation.

échauffer /eʃofe/ [1] *vtr* **1** SPORT to warm up; **2** FIG (animer) to stir [*imagination*]; to stir up [*personne, débat*]; **3** (rendre chaud) to overheat [*corps, liquide, pièce*]; to warm [*sol*]; **4** (produire une fermentation) to start [sth] fermenting.
IDIOMES **~ les oreilles** or **la bile de qn** to vex sb.

échauffourée /eʃofuʀe/ *nf* brawl.

échéance /eʃeɑ̃s/ *nf* **1** (date d'exigibilité) (de dette, facture) due date; (d'action, assurance) maturity date; (d'emprunt) redemption date; **arriver à ~** [*emprunt*] to fall due; [*assurance, placement*] to mature; **2** (date d'expiration) expiry date; **arriver à ~** to expire; **3** (délai) currency; **à longue/brève ~** [*bon, prévision*] long-/short-term (*avant n*); [*renforcer, changer*] in the long-/short-term; **4** (somme due) (de facture) payment; (d'emprunt) repayment; **faire face à de lourdes ~** to have to meet heavy financial commitments; **5** (d'événement) date; (date limite) deadline; **~ électorale** polling GB ou election day.

échéancier /eʃeɑ̃sje/ nm (ensemble d'échéances) schedule of due dates; (calendrier d'échéances) schedule of repayments.

échéant: **le cas échéant** /ləkazeʃeɑ̃/ loc adv if need be, should the case arise.

échec /eʃɛk/ I nm **1** SCOL, UNIV failure (**à** in GB, on US); **2** (fait de ne pas atteindre son but) failure; (remédiable) setback; **subir un ~** to fail; (temporairement) to suffer a setback; **voué à l'~** doomed to failure; **faire ~ à qn/aux projets de qn** to thwart sb/sb's plans; **tenir l'ennemi en ~** to hold the enemy in check; **3** (défaite) POL, SPORT defeat; MIL reverse; **essuyer** or **subir un ~** to suffer a defeat ou setback; **4** JEUX **~ au roi** check; **~ et mat** checkmate.
II ▶ **329**⏐ **échecs** nmpl **les ~s** (jeu) chess; (échiquier et pièces) chess set; (pièces) chessmen.

échelle /eʃɛl/ nf **1** (pour grimper) ladder; **monter à une ~** to climb a ladder; **faire la courte ~ à qn** to give sb a leg up; **plan à l'~** scale plan; (de plan, maquette) scale; **plan à l'~** scale plan; **carte à l'~ de 1/10 000e** map on a scale of 1:10,000; **3** (système de gradation) scale; **~ de Richter** Richter scale; **4** FIG (dans un milieu social) scale, ladder; (dans une entreprise) hierarchy, ladder; **s'élever dans l'~ sociale** to rise up the social scale; **~ des prix** scale of prices; **~ mobile des salaires** sliding pay-scale; **5** MUS scale; **6**○ (accroc à un collant) ladder.

échelon /eʃlɔ̃/ nm **1** (d'échelle) rung; **2** ADMIN (rang) grade; **sauter les ~s** to get accelerated promotion; **3** (niveau) level; **à l'~ ministériel** at ministerial level; **4** MIL (unité) echelon.

échelonner /eʃlɔne/ [1] I vtr **1** (espacer) to space [sth] out [balises]; **2** (répartir) to spread [paiements, travail] (**sur** over); to stagger [congés, départs] (**sur** over); **3** (graduer) to grade [exercices]; to build up [arguments]; **4** MIL to deploy [sth] in echelon [troupes].
II **s'échelonner** vpr **1** [objets, personnes] to be positioned at intervals (**sur** over); **2** [paiements, travaux] to be spread (**sur** over); [congés, départs] to be staggered (**sur** over).

écheveau, pl **~x** /eʃvo/ nm **1** (de laine) hank; (de fil) skein; **2** FIG (enchevêtrement) tangle.

échevelé, **~e** /eʃəvle/ adj **1** (décoiffé) tousled; **2** FIG [rythme] frenzied; [romantisme] unbridled.

échevin /eʃ(ə)vɛ̃/ nm **1** HIST municipal magistrate; **2** (en Belgique) deputy burgomaster.

échine /eʃin/ nf **1** (colonne vertébrale) spine; **2** CULIN (de porc) ~ spare rib.
IDIOMES **courber l'~ devant** to submit to.

échiner: **s'échiner** /eʃine/ [1] vpr **s'~ à faire** to make a great effort to do.

échiquier /eʃikje/ nm **1** (aux échecs) chessboard; **2** FIG (terrain) arena; **3** (motif) chequered GB ou checkered US pattern.

Échiquier /eʃikje/ nprm **l'~** the Exchequer.

écho /eko/ nm **1** (de son) echo; **faire ~ à qch, se faire l'~ de qch** to echo sth; **2** (réaction) response (**à** to); **ne trouver aucun ~** to fail to elicit any response; **3** (information) **nous n'avons eu aucun ~ des pourparlers** we have heard nothing about the talks; **4** (anecdote) piece of gossip.

échographie /ekografi/ nf scan.

échoir /eʃwaʀ/ [51] I vi [loyer] to fall due; [traite] to be payable.
II **échoir à** vtr ind **~ à qn** to fall to sb's share.

échoppe /eʃɔp/ nf stall.

échouer /eʃwe/ [1] I vtr NAUT to beach [bateau].
II **échouer à** vtr ind to fail [examen, épreuve].
III vi **1** (ne pas réussir) [personne, tentative] to fail; **faire ~** to cause [sth] to fail [négociations, projet]; **2** (se retrouver) [personne, dossier] to end up; **3** [bateau] to run aground; **un pétrolier échoué sur les récifs** an oil tanker stranded on the reef.
IV **s'échouer** vpr [bateau] to run aground (**sur** on); [baleine] to be beached.

échu, **~e** /eʃy/ I pp ▶ **échoir**.
II adj expired; **payer à terme ~** to pay in arrears.

éclabousser /eklabuse/ [1] vtr **1** (mouiller) to splash

(avec with); (salir) to spatter (**de** with); **2** (compromettre) **il a été éclaboussé par ces rumeurs** the rumoursGB have damaged his reputation.

éclair /eklɛʀ/ I adj inv **rencontre ~** brief meeting; **visite ~** flying visit; **attaque ~** lightning strike; **guerre ~** blitzkrieg; **repas ~** quick meal.
II nm **1** MÉTÉO flash of lightning; **passer comme un ~** to flash past; **2** (éclat) (d'explosion, de bijou) flash; (de regard) glint; **leurs yeux lançaient des ~s de colère** their eyes were flashing with anger; (de lucidité, triomphe) moment; **4** CULIN éclair.
■ **~ de chaleur** sheet lightning Ȼ.

éclairage /eklɛʀaʒ/ nm (manière d'éclairer) lighting; (lumière) light; **~ au gaz** gaslight; **faible ~** dim light.

éclairagiste /eklɛʀaʒist/ ▶ **374**⏐ nm electrician.

éclairant, **~e** /eklɛʀɑ̃, ɑ̃t/ adj [fusée, bombe] flare (épith).

éclaircie /eklɛʀsi/ nf **1** MÉTÉO (espace clair) sunny spell; (embellie) break in the weather; **2** (de situation, conflit) LITER respite SOUT.

éclaircir /eklɛʀsiʀ/ [3] I vtr **1** (rendre moins sombre) to lighten [couleur]; to lighten the colourGB of [cheveux]; to improve [teint]; **2** (élucider) to shed light on [mystère]; **3** (rendre moins épais) to thin [sauce, futaie].
II **s'éclaircir** vpr **1** MÉTÉO [temps] to clear; **l'horizon s'éclaircit** LIT the horizon is clearing; FIG the outlook is getting brighter; **2** (pâlir) [couleur] to fade; [teint] to improve; [cheveux] to get lighter; **3** (s'élucider) [situation, mystère] to become clearer; **4** (se clairsemer) [foule, forêt] to thin out; **5** (rendre clair) **s'~ les cheveux** to lighten one's hair; **s'~ la voix** or **la gorge** to clear one's throat.

éclaircissement /eklɛʀsismɑ̃/ nm (explication) explanation; (clarification) clarification Ȼ.

éclairé, **~e** /eklɛʀe/ adj [homme] enlightened; [amateur] well-informed.

éclairer /eklɛʀe/ [1] I vtr **1** (donner de la lumière à) [lampe] to light [lieu]; [soleil, phare] to light up [lieu, objet]; **2** (avec une lampe) to give [sb] some light; (pour montrer le chemin) to light the way for; **3** (expliquer) [remarque] to throw light on [texte, situation]; **4** (instruire) to enlighten [personne] (**sur** as to); **5** MIL to reconnoitreGB [route]; to reconnoitreGB for [convoi].
II vi [lampe, bougie] to give light.
III **s'éclairer** vpr **1** (s'illuminer) [écran] to light up; FIG [visage] to light up (**de** with); **2** (se donner de la lumière) **s'~ à l'électricité** to have electric lighting; **3** (s'éclaircir) [situation] to become clearer; [question] to be cleared up.

éclaireur, **-euse** /eklɛʀœʀ, øz/ nm,f **1** (en scoutisme) (garçon) scout GB, Boy Scout US; (fille) guide GB, Girl Guide US; **2** MIL scout.

éclat /ekla/ nm **1** (fragment) splinter; **un ~ d'obus** a piece of shrapnel; **voler en ~s** LIT, FIG to shatter; **2** (de lumière, d'astre) brightness; (de phare, projecteur) glare; (de neige, diamant) sparkle; **3** (de couleur, tissu) brilliance; (de fleur) brightness; (de cheveux, plumes) shine, sheen; (de métal) lustreGB; (du teint) radiance; (de chaussure, meuble) shine; **redonner de l'~ à** to make [sth] look like new [tissu]; to put the shine back into [meuble, cheveux]; **4** (de visage, sourire) radiance; (de regard) sparkle; **sans ~** [regard] dull; [beauté] lifeless; **5** (grandeur) splendourGB; **avec ~** [annoncer] dramatically; [fêter] with great pomp; **manquer d'~** [cérémonie, discours] to lack sparkle; **sans ~** [personnage, soirée] dull; **action** or **coup d'~** (admirable) remarkable feat; (qui attire l'attention) grand gesture; **6** (esclandre) scene.
■ **~ de colère** fit of anger; **~ de rire** roar of laughter; **des ~s de voix** raised voices.
IDIOMES **rire aux ~s** to roar with laughter.

éclatant, **~e** /eklatɑ̃, ɑ̃t/ adj **1** (très brillant) [lumière] dazzling; [soleil] blazing; **2** (vif) [couleur, teinte, plumage] bright; **dents d'une blancheur ~e** sparkling white teeth; **avoir une mine ~e** to be glowing with health; **3** (admirable) [beauté, sourire, santé] radiant; [victoire, réussite] brilliant; **4** (manifeste) [*preuve, démonstration*] striking; **5** (très bruyant) [*bruit, son*] deafening; [*rire, voix*] ringing.

éclaté, ~e /eklate/ *adj* **1** (fragmenté) GÉN fragmented; [*famille*] divided; **2** ART [*dessin, vue*] exploded.

éclatement /eklatmã/ *nm* **1** (rupture) (de tuyau) bursting; (de rate, foie) rupture; **2** (explosion) (de grenade) explosion; (de pneu) blow-out; **3** (de groupe) break-up (**en** into).

éclater /eklate/ [1] *vi* **1** (exploser) [*pneu, bulle, chaudière*] to burst; [*obus, pétard*] to explode; [*bouteille*] to shatter; **faire ~** [*personne*] to burst [*bulle, ballon*]; to detonate [*bombe, grenade*]; to let off [*pétard*]; **2** (se rompre) [*canalisation, abcès*] to burst; [*organe*] to rupture; **3** (retentir) [*applaudissements, rire, fusillade*] to break out; [*coup de feu*] to ring out; **4** (être révélé) [*scandale, nouvelle*] to break; [*vérité*] to come out; **faire ~ qch au grand jour** to bring sth to light; **5** (survenir) [*guerre, grève, polémique*] to break out; [*orage*] to break; [*crise*] to erupt; **6** (être exprimé) [*colère*] to erupt; **laisser ~ sa colère** to give vent to one's anger; **7** (se fragmenter) [*coalition, royaume*] to break up (**en** into); [*parti*] to split (**en** into); **8** (se mettre en colère) [*personne*] to lose one's temper; **~ de rire** to burst out laughing; **~ en sanglots** to burst into tears.

éclectisme /eklɛktism/ *nm* eclecticism.

éclipse /eklips/ *nf* LIT, FIG eclipse.

éclipser /eklipse/ [1] I *vtr* **1** (en astronomie) to eclipse; **2** (cacher) to obscure; **3** (surpasser) to outshine.
II **s'éclipser**○ *vpr* to slip away.

éclopé, ~e /eklɔpe/ I *adj* injured, lame.
II *nm,f* person with slight injuries.

éclore /eklɔʀ/ [79] *vi* **1** [*poussin, œuf*] to hatch; [*fleur*] to bloom; **2** [*idée*] to dawn; [*talent*] to bloom.

écluse /eklyz/ *nf* lock.

éclusier, -ière /eklyzje, ɛʀ/ ▶ 374 | *nm,f* lockkeeper.

écœurant, ~e /ekœʀã, ãt/ *adj* **1** (physiquement) [*gâteau, odeur, liqueur*] sickly; [*plat*] over-rich; **2** (révoltant) nauseating; **3** (décourageant) sickening.

écœurement /ekœʀmã/ *nm* LIT nausea; FIG disgust.

écœurer /ekœʀe/ [1] *vtr* **1** (physiquement) [*nourriture, odeur*] to make [sb] feel sick; **2** (moralement) to sicken.

école /ekɔl/ *nf* **1** SCOL (établissement, ensemble des élèves) school; **être à l'~** to be at GB ou in US school; **la grande/petite ~** primary/nursery school; **2** (enseignement) school; **dès l'~** from the very first days at school; **3** (système) education system; **4** UNIV (grande) **~** higher education institution with competitive entrance examination; **une ~ d'ingénieurs** a Grande École of Engineering; **5** (source de formation) training (**de** in); **l'~ de la vie** the university of life; **6** (mouvement) school; **~ flamande** Flemish school; **~ de pensée** school of thought; **faire ~** to gain a following.

■ **~ élémentaire** primary school; **~ de gestion** UNIV business school, school of business and management GB; **~ hôtelière** hotel management school; **~ d'infirmières** nursing college; **~ libre** (système) independent education; (établissement) independent school; **~ maternelle** nursery school; **~ militaire** military academy; **~ normale**, EN primary teacher training college; **~ de police** police college GB, police academy US; **~ primaire** primary school; **~ publique** (établissement) state school GB, public school US; (système) state education GB, public education US; **~ de secrétariat** secretarial college; **École nationale d'administration**, **ENA** Grande École for top civil servants; **École normale supérieure**, **ENS** Grande École from which the educational élite is recruited.

écolier, -ière /ekɔlje, ɛʀ/ *nm,f* schoolchild, schoolboy/schoolgirl.

écologie /ekɔlɔʒi/ *nf* (science) ecology.

écologique /ekɔlɔʒik/ *adj* **1** [*équilibre, catastrophe*] ecological; [*discours*] on the environment (*épith, après n*); **2** [*impact, intérêt, conscience*] environmental; **3** [*produit*] environment-friendly.

écologiste /ekɔlɔʒist/ I *adj* **1** [*candidat*] Green; **2** [*mesure*] ecological.
II *nmf* **1** (partisan) environmentalist; (candidat) Green; **2** (chercheur) ecologist.

écomusée /ekomyze/ *nm* ~ open air museum.

éconduire /ekɔ̃dɥiʀ/ [69] *vtr* to turn [sb] away.

économat /ekɔnɔma/ *nm* **1** (local) bursar's office; **2** (charge) office of bursar.

économe /ekɔnɔm/ I *adj* thrifty.
II ▶ 374 | *nmf* bursar.

économie /ekɔnɔmi/ I *nf* **1** (de pays, région) economy; **2** (discipline) economics (+ *v sg*); **3** (somme économisée) saving; **réaliser une ~ de 20 francs** to save 20 francs; **faire l'~ de** to save the cost of [*voyage, repas*]; **4** (action d'économiser) economy; **par ~** to save money; **5** (sobriété) economy.
II **économies** *nfpl* savings; **faire des ~s** (épargner) to save up; (dépenser moins) to cut back on spending.
■ **~ d'entreprise** managerial economics; **~ de marché** free market (economy).
IDIOMES **il n'y a pas de petites ~s** every little helps.

économique /ekɔnɔmik/ *adj* **1** ÉCON [*politique, crise*] economic; **2** (peu coûteux) economical.

économiser /ekɔnɔmize/ [1] *vtr* **1** (épargner) to save (up) [*argent*]; **~ ses forces** to pace oneself; **2** (réduire la consommation de) to save [*essence, eau, énergie*]; **3** (réduire ses dépenses) to economize (**sur** on).

économiste /ekɔnɔmist/ ▶ 374 | *nmf* economist.

écoper /ekɔpe/ [1] I *vtr* NAUT to bail out.
II **écoper**○ **de** *vtr ind* to get [*punition, amende*].
III○ *vi* to take the rap○.

écoproduit /ekopʀɔdɥi/ *nm* environment-friendly product.

écorce /ekɔʀs/ *nf* (d'arbre) bark; (de fruit) peel; (de châtaigne) skin.
■ **~ terrestre** earth's crust.

écorché, ~e /ekɔʀʃe/ I *nm,f* **c'est un ~ (vif)** FIG he's hypersensitive.
II *nm* **1** ANAT écorché; **2** TECH cutaway (diagram).

écorcher /ekɔʀʃe/ [1] *vtr* **1** (dépecer) to skin [*animal*]; to flay [*victime*]; **2** (blesser) to graze [*visage, jambe*]; **3** (estropier) to mispronounce [*mot*]; to murder [*chanson, langue*]; **4**○ (voler) to fleece○ [*client*].

écorchure /ekɔʀʃyʀ/ *nf* graze.

écorner /ekɔʀne/ [1] *vtr* **1** (entamer) to dent [*image de marque*]; to make a hole in [*capital*]; **2** (abîmer) to make [sth] dog-eared GB, to dogear [*livre*].

écossais, ~e /ekɔsɛ, ɛz/ ▶ 338 |, 509 | I *adj* [*caractère, personne, paysage*] Scottish; [*whisky*] Scotch; [*langue*] Scots; [*jupe*] tartan.
II *nm* **1** LING (dialecte anglais) Scots; (dialecte gaélique) (Scottish) Gaelic; **2** (tissu) tartan (cloth).

Écossais, ~e /ekɔsɛ, ɛz/ *nm,f* Scotsman/Scotswoman, Scot.

Écosse /ekɔs/ ▶ 509 | *nprf* Scotland.

écosser /ekɔse/ [1] *vtr* to shell.

écot /eko/ *nm* share.

écoulement /ekulmã/ *nm* **1** (d'eau, de circulation) flow; (de temps) passing; **2** MÉD discharge; **~ de sang** bleeding; **3** COMM distribution and sale.

écouler /ekule/ [1] I *vtr* **1** COMM to sell [*produit, stock*]; **les stocks sont écoulés** stocks are exhausted; **2** (trafiquer) to pass [*billet, drogue*]; to fence [*butin*].
II **s'écouler** *vpr* **1** (passer) [*temps, vie*] to pass; **la semaine écoulée** the past week; **le délai écoulé** the time which has elapsed; **2** (circuler) [*eau, rivière*] to flow; **3** (sortir accidentellement) [*pétrole, eau*] to escape (**de** from; **dans** into); **4** (être évacué) [*eau*] to drain away; **5** COMM [*produit*] to move.

écourter /ekuʀte/ [1] *vtr* (abréger) to cut short [*séjour*] (**de dix jours** by ten days); to shorten [*discours*].

écoute /ekut/ *nf* **1** (fait d'écouter) **l'~ de** listening to [*cassette, personne*]; **être à l'~ de** LIT to be listening to [*émission*]; (être attentif à) to be (always) ready to listen to [*problèmes*]; **restez à l'~ (de nos programmes)**

stay tuned; **la qualité d'~** (de réception d'un émetteur) reception; (du son) sound quality; **2** (audience) audience; **heure de grande ~** RADIO peak listening time; TV peak viewing time; **3** TECH **un appareil d'~** a listening device; **centre d'~(s)** monitoring centre^GB; **~s téléphoniques** phone-tapping ¢.

écouter /ekute/ [1] **I** *vtr* **1** (s'appliquer à entendre) to listen to [*conversation, musique*]; **~ qn chanter** to listen to sb singing; **écoute, ne sois pas ridicule!** come on, don't be ridiculous!; **~ aux portes** to eavesdrop; **2** (accepter d'entendre) to listen to [*explications, témoin*]; **3** (tenir compte de) to listen to [*conseil, personne*]; **4** (se laisser guider par) **~ son cœur** to follow one's own inclination; **~ sa conscience** to be guided by one's conscience.
II s'écouter *vpr* **1 s '~ parler** to like the sound of one's own voice; **2** (se dorloter) to cosset oneself; **3** (faire à sa guise) **si je m'écoutais** if I had my way.

écouteur /ekutœr/ *nm* **1** (de téléphone) earpiece; **2** (de stéréo) earphones (*pl*); (plus grand) headphones (*pl*).

écoutille /ekutij/ *nf* hatch.

écrabouiller° /ekRabuje/ [1] *vtr* to squash [*fruit, animal*].

écran /ekRɑ̃/ *nm* **1** CIN (surface) screen; (salle) cinema GB, movie theater US; (art) cinema; **porter une œuvre à l'~** to adapt a work for the cinema; **crever l'~** to have a great screen presence; **2** ORDINAT, TV screen; ÉLEC-TROTECH display; **une vedette du petit ~** a TV star; **3** (pour masquer) LIT, FIG screen; **crème ~ total** sun block; **4** (pour protéger) screen; (nucléaire) shielding.
■ **~ antibruit** soundproofing; **~ à cristaux liquides** liquid crystal display, LCD; **~ de fumée** LIT screen of smoke; FIG, MIL smokescreen; **~ solaire** sunscreen; **~ tactile** touch screen; **~ de visualisation** VDU screen.

écrasant, ~e /ekRazɑ̃, ɑ̃t/ *adj* **1** LIT [*poids*] enormous; **2** FIG [*chaleur*] sweltering; [*défaite, dette*] crushing; [*victoire*] resounding; [*supériorité*] overwhelming; [*responsabilité*] heavy.

écrasé, ~e /ekRaze/ *adj* (accablé) **~ de fatigue/remords** [*personne*] overcome with exhaustion/remorse; **~ par le travail** overwhelmed by work.

écraser /ekRaze/ [1] **I** *vtr* **1** (blesser, tuer) [*machine, porte*] to crush [*doigt, personne*]; [*personne*] to squash [*insecte*]; (avec un véhicule) to run over [*piéton, animal*]; **se faire ~** to get run over; **2** (endommager) [*personne*] to squash [*boîte, fruit*]; (plus endommagé) to crush; [*éléphant, tank*] to flatten [*végétation*]; **3** CULIN [*personne*] to mash [*légumes, fraises*]; to crush [*gousse d'ail*]; **4** (aplatir délibérément) GÉN to squash; **~ sa cigarette** to stub out one's cigarette; **~ une larme** to wipe away a tear; **5** (presser) [*personne*] to press [*nez, visage*] (contre against); **6** (anéantir) to crush [*révolte*]; to thrash° [*équipe*]; **7** (en étant meilleur) [*personne*] to outshine; **8** (humilier) to put [sb] down [*personne*]; **9** (accabler) [*chagrin, remords*] to overwhelm [*personne*]; [*fatigue, chaleur*] to overcome [*personne*].
II s'écraser *vpr* **1** (avoir un accident) [*voiture, train*] to crash (contre into); [*automobiliste, motocycliste*] to have a crash; [*insectes*] to splatter (contre on); **s'~ (au sol)** [*avion*] to crash (to the ground); **2**° (se taire) to shut up°; **3**° (se soumettre) to keep one's head down.

écrémer /ekReme/ [14] *vtr* **1** to skim [*lait*]; **2** to cream off the best of [*candidats*].

écrevisse /ekRəvis/ *nf* crayfish GB, crawfish US.
IDIOMES **rouge comme une ~** as red as a beetroot GB, as red as a beet US.

écrier: **s'écrier** /ekRije/ [2] *vpr* to exclaim.

écrin /ekRɛ̃/ *nm* **1** (boîte) case; **2** LITER (environnement) setting.

écrire /ekRiR/ [67] **I** *vtr* **1** (rédiger) to write (à to); **2** (orthographier) to spell.
II *vi* GÉN to write.
III s'écrire *vpr* **1** (être rédigé) to be written; **2** (être orthographié) to be spelled.

écrit, ~e /ekRi, it/ **I** *adj* written; **règle non ~e** unwritten rule; **c'était ~** FIG it was bound to happen.
II *nm* **1** (œuvre) work, piece of writing; **2** (document)

document; **par ~** in writing; **3** SCOL, UNIV (examen) written examination; (travail) written work.
IDIOMES **les paroles s'envolent, les ~s restent** (il ne faut pas s'engager par écrit) never put anything in writing; (faites promettre par écrit) get it in writing.

écriteau, *pl* **~x** /ekRito/ *nm* sign.

écritoire /ekRitwaR/ *nf* writing case.

écriture /ekRityR/ **I** *nf* **1** (manière) handwriting; **2** (en imprimerie) hand; **3** (texte) writing; **4** LING script; **~ phonétique** phonetic script; **5** LITTÉRAT (activité) writing; **6** (style) style; **7** COMM (inscription) entry.
II écritures *nfpl* COMM accounts.

Écriture /ekRityR/ *nf* RELIG Scripture.

écrivain /ekRivɛ̃/ ▶ 374 *nm* writer.
■ **~ public** letter-writer.

écrou /ekRu/ *nm* TECH nut.

écrouer /ekRue/ [1] *vtr* JUR to commit [sb] to prison.

écroulé, ~e /ekRule/ *adj* **1** [*personne*] overwhelmed; **2** [*maison, mur, pont*] in a state of collapse.

écrouler: **s'écrouler** /ekRule/ [1] *vpr* [*mur, personne, régime*] to collapse; [*espoir, espérance*] to fade; [*rêve, illusion*] to crumble.

écru, ~e /ekRy/ *adj* **1** (brut) [*toile*] unbleached; [*laine*] undyed; [*soie*] raw; **2** ▶ 141 (couleur) ecru.

ECU /eky/ ▶ 33 *nm* (*abbr* = **European currency unit**) ECU.

écu /eky/ *nm* **1** ▶ 33 (unité monétaire de la CEE) ecu; **2** (en numismatique) ~ crown; **3** (bouclier) shield; **4** (blason) escutcheon.

écueil /ekœj/ *nm* **1** NAUT reef; **2** FIG (danger) pitfall.

écuelle /ekɥɛl/ *nf* **1** (récipient) bowl; **2** (contenu) bowlful.

éculé, ~e /ekyle/ *adj* **1 chaussure ~e** shoe with a worn-down heel; **2** [*plaisanterie, théorie*] hackneyed.

écume /ekym/ *nf* **1** (sur l'eau) foam; (de bouillon, confiture) scum; (de bière, d'eau savonneuse) froth; (de métal) dross; **2** (bave) foam.
■ **~ de mer** (magnésite) meerschaum.

écumer /ekyme/ [1] **I** *vtr* **1** (enlever l'écume) to skim [*bouillon*]; to skim [*métal*]; **2** (parcourir) to scour.
II *vi* **1** (se couvrir d'écume) [*mer, lac*] to foam; [*vin*] to froth; **2** (baver) to foam.

écumoire /ekymwaR/ *nf* skimming ladle, skimmer.

écureuil /ekyRœj/ *nm* squirrel.

écurie /ekyRi/ *nf* **1** (de chevaux) stable; **2** (de voitures) stable; **3** (lieu sale) pigsty.
IDIOMES **sentir l'~** to know one is nearly there.

écusson /ekysɔ̃/ *nm* **1** GÉN badge; (de soldat) flash GB; (de voiture) insignia; **2** (en héraldique) escutcheon.

écuyer, -ère /ekɥije, ɛR/ ▶ 374 *nm,f* **1** (cavalier) horseman/horsewoman; (instructeur) riding instructor; **2** (dans un cirque) bareback rider.
II *nm* HIST (gentilhomme) squire; (responsable des écuries) equerry.

eczéma /egzema/ ▶ 196 *nm* eczema ¢.

éden /edɛn/ *nm* FIG paradise; **l'Éden** RELIG Eden.

édenté, ~e /edɑ̃te/ *adj* (sans dents) toothless; (avec des dents en moins) gap-toothed; [*peigne*] broken.

EDF /œdeɛf/ *nf* (*abbr* = **Électricité de France**) French electricity board.

édicter /edikte/ [1] *vtr* to enact [*loi, statut*]; to lay down [*peine, règle*].

édifiant, ~e /edifjɑ̃, ɑ̃t/ *adj* **1** (exemplaire) edifying; **2** (instructif) enlightening.

édification /edifikasjɔ̃/ *nf* **1** (de bâtiment, pays) building; **2** (d'œuvre) creation; **3** (instruction) enlightenment.

édifice /edifis/ *nm* **1** (bâtiment) building; **2** (vaste ensemble organisé) structure.

édifier /edifje/ [2] *vtr* **1** to build [*bâtiment, ville*]; **2** to build [*empire*]; to create [*œuvre*]; **3** (porter à la vertu) to edify; **4** (renseigner) to enlighten.

édile /edil/ *nm* **1** (conseiller municipal) town councillor^GB; **2** aedile.

Édimbourg /edɛ̃buR/ ▶ 628 *npr* Edinburgh.

édit /edi/ *nm* edict.

éditer /edite/ [1] *vtr* **1** (publier) to publish [*livre, auteur*]; to release [*disque*]; **2** (présenter et annoter) to edit; **3** ORDINAT to edit.

éditeur, -trice /editœr, tris/ ▶374 I *nm,f* (qui présente et annote des textes) editor.
II *nm* **1** (de livre, photo, musique) publisher; **2** ORDINAT editor.

édition /edisjɔ̃/ I *nf* **1** (action de publier et de diffuser) (de livre) publication; (de disque) release; **2** (texte, livre, gravure) edition; (disque) release; **3** (secteur) publishing; **société d'~** publishing firm; **4** (correction, annotation) editing; **5** (de journal) edition; **l'~ de 20 heures du journal télévisé** the eight o'clock (edition of the) news.
II éditions *nfpl* **les ~s Hachette** Hachette (*sg*).

éditorial, ~e, *mpl* **-iaux** /editɔrjal, o/ I *adj* [*politique, service*] editorial.
II *nm* PRESSE editorial, leader.

édredon /edrədɔ̃/ *nm* eiderdown.

éducateur, -trice /edykatœr, tris/ I *adj* educational.
II ▶374 *nm,f* ~ **(spécialisé)** youth worker.

éducatif, -ive /edykatif, iv/ *adj* educational.

éducation /edykasjɔ̃/ *nf* **1** (enseignement) education; **2** (formation de personne) education; **faire l'~ de** to educate; (entraînement) training; **4** (bonnes manières) manners (*pl*); **être sans ~** to be ill-mannered.
■ **Éducation nationale, EN** (ministère) Ministry of Education; (système) state education; ~ **physique** physical education, PE GB, phys ed US.

édulcorant, ~e /edylkɔrɑ̃, ɑ̃t/ *nm* sweetener.

édulcorer /edylkɔre/ [1] *vtr* **1** LIT to sweeten [*boisson, mets*]; **2** FIG (atténuer) to tone down [*propos*].

éduquer /edyke/ [1] *vtr* to educate [*personne, peuple*]; to train [*chien*]; **bien/mal éduqué** well/badly brought up.

effaçable /efasabl/ *adj* [*cassette*] erasable; [*tache*] removable.

effacé, ~e /efase/ *adj* [*personne*] retiring.

effacement /efasmɑ̃/ *nm* **1** (de mots) deletion; **touche d'~** delete key; **2** (de cassette) erasure; **3** (d'une personne) (en général) self-effacement; (devant un rival) withdrawal.

effacer /efase/ [12] I *vtr* **1** (faire disparaître) (avec une gomme, un chiffon) to rub out [*mot, dessin*]; (avec un effaceur) to remove [*mot, phrase*]; (sur un traitement de texte) to delete [*mot, paragraphe*]; to erase [*enregistrement, film*]; **2** (rendre propre) to wipe [*bande magnétique, cassette*]; to clear [*écran, fichier*]; to clean [*tableau noir*]; **3** (rendre moins visible) [*soleil*] to fade [*couleur*]; [*pluie*] to erase [*traces, pas*]; [*neige*] to cover (up) [*traces, pas*]; [*crème*] to remove [*rides*]; **l'usure** or **la temps a effacé l'inscription** the inscription has worn away with time; **4** (faire oublier) to blot out [*souvenir, image*]; to dispel [*doute, regret*]; to remove [*différence, distinctions*]; **on efface tout et on recommence** FIG (oublier, pardonner) let's wipe the slate clean and start all over again; (repartir à zéro) let's start afresh; **5** to write off [*dette, pertes*].
II s'effacer *vpr* **1** (avec une gomme) **ça s'efface** you can rub it out; **2** (avec le temps) [*inscription, couleur, dessin*] to fade; **3** (cesser) [*souvenir, sourire, haine*] to fade; [*impression*] to wear off; [*doute, crainte*] to disappear; **4** [*personne*] (pour laisser passer) to step aside; (rester discret) to stay in the background; **s'~ devant un rival** to give way to a rival.

effaceur /efasœr/ *nm* ~ **(d'encre)** correction pen.

effarant, ~e /efarɑ̃, ɑ̃t/ *adj* astounding.

effarement /efarmɑ̃/ *nm* alarm.

effarer /efare/ [1] *vtr* to alarm.

effaroucher /efaruʃe/ [1] I *vtr* **1** (faire fuir) to frighten [sth] away [*personne, animal*]; **2** (inquiéter) to alarm.
II s'effaroucher *vpr* to take fright (**de, à** at).

effectif, -ive /efɛktif, iv/ I *adj* (réel) [*contrôle, aide*] real; **durée effective du travail** actual time worked; **devenir ~** [*mesure*] to come into effect.
II *nm* (d'école) number of pupils; (d'entreprise) work-

force; (d'une armée) strength; **un ~ de 200 élèves** 200 pupils on the roll GB, an enrollment of 200 pupils US.

effectivement /efɛktivmɑ̃/ *adv* **1** (en effet) indeed; **2** (réellement) actually, really.

effectuer /efɛktɥe/ [1] *vtr* to do [*calcul, réparations, travail*]; to make [*paiement, changement, choix, atterrissage*]; to carry out [*transaction*]; to conduct [*sondage*]; to serve [*peine*]; to complete [*visite, voyage*]; ~ **son apprentissage** to serve an apprenticeship.

efféminé, ~e /efemine/ *adj* effeminate.

effervescence /efɛrvesɑ̃s/ *nf* **1** (bouillonnement) effervescence; **2** (émoi) turmoil; **il avait l'esprit en ~** his mind was in a ferment.

effervescent, ~e /efɛrvesɑ̃, ɑ̃t/ *adj* **1** LIT [*comprimé*] effervescent; **2** FIG [*foule*] seething; [*caractère*] effervescent.

effet /efɛ/ I *nm* **1** (conséquence) effect; **faire de l'~** [*médicament*] to work; [*commentaire*] to have some effect; **prendre ~** [*mesure*] to take effect; **sous l'~ de l'alcool** under the influence of alcohol; **sous l'~ de la passion** in a fit of passion; **sous l'~ de la colère** in a rage; **2** (impression) impression; **faire bonne/mauvaise ~** to make a good/bad impression; **être du meilleur ~** [*vêtement*] to look extremely nice; **être du plus mauvais ~** to be in the worst possible taste; **quel ~ cela te fait-il d'être père?** how does it feel to be a father?; **faire un drôle d'~** [*vitesse, alcool, rencontre*] to make one feel strange; **il me fait l'~ d'un homme honnête** he looks like an honest man to me; **leur réponse m'a fait l'~ d'une douche froide** their answer came as a real shock to me; **un ~ de surprise** an element of surprise; **3** (procédé) effect; **couper tous ses ~s à qn** to steal sb's thunder **4** (but) **à cet ~** for that purpose; **5** (phénomène) **l'~ Maastricht** the Maastricht effect; **6** SPORT spin.
II en effet *loc adv* indeed.
III effets *nmpl* (vêtements) things.
■ ~ **de serre** greenhouse effect; ~ **spécial** special effect; ~**s secondaires** side effects.

effeuiller /efœje/ [1] *vtr* [*personne*] to thin out the foliage of [*arbre*]; to strip the leaves off [*légume*]; [*vent*] to blow the leaves off [*arbre*].
IDIOMES ~ **la marguerite** to play 'he loves me, he loves me not'.

efficace /efikas/ *adj* [*action, méthode*] effective; [*remède*] effective; [*personne, dispositif*] efficient.

efficacement /efikasmɑ̃/ *adv* [*travailler, fonctionner*] efficiently; [*intervenir, soigner*] effectively.

efficacité /efikasite/ *nf* (d'action, de méthode, remède) effectiveness; (de personne, dispositif) efficiency.

efficience /efisjɑ̃s/ *nf* efficiency.

effigie /efiʒi/ *nf* **1** (représentation) effigy; **à l'~ de** [*médaille, timbre*] with the head of; **2** (symbole) logo.

effilé, ~e /efile/ *adj* **1** [*amandes*] flaked; **2** [*doigt*] slender.

effiler /efile/ [1] I *vtr* **1** to sharpen [*lame, pointe*]; **2** to thin out [*cheveux*]; **3** to string [*haricots verts*].
II s'effiler *vpr* (s'effranger) to fray.

effilocher: s'effilocher /efilɔʃe/ [1] *vpr* [*tissu*] to fray.

efflanqué, ~e /eflɑ̃ke/ *adj* emaciated.

effleurer /eflœre/ [1] *vtr* (frôler) to touch lightly, to brush (against); (égratigner) to graze; **l'idée ne m'a même pas effleuré** FIG the idea didn't even cross my mind; **le livre ne fait qu'~ la question** FIG the book only skims over the subject.

efflorescence /eflɔresɑ̃s/ *nf* **1** CHIMIE, MÉD efflorescence; **2** BOT bloom.

effluent /eflyɑ̃/ *nm* (eaux usées) effluent; ~**s radioactifs** radioactive discharge **¢**.

effluve /eflyv/ *nm* (nauséabond) unpleasant smell; (agréable) fragrance.

effondrement /efɔ̃drəmɑ̃/ *nm* **1** LIT (de toit, pont) collapse; **2** (de terrain) subsidence; **3** (de régime, d'économie) collapse.

effondrer: s'effondrer /efɔ̃dre/ [1] *vpr* **1** (s'écrouler) [*toit, personne, régime, prix*] to collapse; [*rêve*] to crumble; [*espoir*] to fall; [*popularité*] to fall drastically; **2** (nerveusement) (mise à collapse; **s'~ en larmes** to dissolve into tears; **s'~ de chagrin** to be distracted with grief; **être effondré par la nouvelle** to be distraught at the news.

efforcer: s'efforcer /efɔʀse/ [12] *vpr* to try hard (**de faire** to do).

effort /efɔʀ/ *nm* **1** (physique, intellectuel) effort; **après bien des ~s** after a great deal of effort; **un ~ de mémoire** an effort to remember; **fais un petit ~ d'imagination!** use a bit of imagination!; **avec mon dos, je ne peux pas faire d'~** with this back of mine, I can't do anything strenuous; **allons, encore un petit ~!** (près du bout) come on, you're almost there!; **sans ~** effortlessly; **2** (subvention, aide) financial aid; (mise de fonds) investment, (financial) outlay; **3** PHYS (force exercée) stress; (force subie) strain.

effraction /efʀaksjɔ̃/ *nf* JUR breaking and entering; **ils sont entrés dans la maison par ~** they broke into the house.
■ **~ informatique** computer hacking.

effranger /efʀɑ̃ʒe/ [13] *vtr*, **s'effranger** *vpr* to fray.

effrayant, ~e /efʀɛjɑ̃, ɑ̃t/ *adj* **1** (qui fait peur) [*vision, laideur*] frightening; [*maigreur, pâleur*] dreadful; **2**○ (excessif) [*chaleur, prix*] terrible.

effrayer /efʀeje/ [21] *vtr* **1** (faire peur à) to frighten; (alarmer) to alarm; **2** (rebuter) to put [sb] off.

effréné, ~e /efʀene/ *adj* [*course, rythme, concurrence*] frenzied; [*ambition, luxe, gaspillage*] wild.

effriter /efʀite/ [1] **I** *vtr* to crumble [*gâteau*]; to break up [*motte de terre*].
II s'effriter *vpr* LIT, FIG to crumble (away).

effroi /efʀwa/ *nm* dread, terror.

effronté, ~e /efʀɔ̃te/ **I** *adj* [*enfant, regard, remarque*] cheeky; [*adulte*] (éhonté) shameless; (hardi) cheeky.
II *nm,f* cheeky boy/girl.

effronterie /efʀɔ̃tʀi/ *nf* cheek, effrontery SOUT.

effroyable /efʀwajabl/ *adj* dreadful.

effusion /efyzjɔ̃/ *nf* effusion; **avec ~** [*remercier, parler*] effusively; **sans ~** [*parler*] unemotionally.
■ **~ de sang** bloodshed.

égailler: s'égailler /egaje/ [1] *vpr* to disperse.

égal, ~e, *mpl* **-aux** /egal, o/ **I** *adj* **1** (identique) equal (à to); **à travail ~, salaire ~** equal work for equal pay; **~ à lui-même, il...** true to form, he...; **2** (régulier) [*terrain*] level; [*lumière*] even; [*teinte*] uniform; [*temps*] settled; [*pouls, respiration*] steady; **d'un pas ~** at an even pace; **avoir un tempérament ~** to be even-tempered; **3** (indifférent) **ça m'est ~** (je n'ai pas de préférence) I don't mind either way; (je m'en moque) I don't care; **c'est ~**○ all the same; **4** (équitable) **la partie n'est pas ~e** (entre eux) they are not evenly matched.
II *adj* equal; **traiter d'~ à ~ avec qn** to deal with sb as an equal; **être d'une beauté sans ~e** to be supremely beautiful; **il fera un piètre ministre, à l'~ de son prédécesseur** he'll make a poor minister, just like his predecessor.
IDIOMES **rester ~ à soi-même** to be one's usual self; **combattre à armes ~es** to be on an equal footing.

égalable /egalabl/ *adj* **difficilement ~** [*beauté, bêtise*] unparalleled; [*technique*] incomparably superior.

également /egalmɑ̃/ *adv* **1** (aussi) also, too; **2** (au même degré) equally.

égaler /egale/ [1] *vtr* **1** (atteindre) to equal [*record*]; to be as good as [*personne*]; to be as high as [*prix*]; **~ les meilleurs** to rank with the best; **technique jamais encore égalée** hitherto unequalled[GB] technique; **2** (valoir) **rien n'égale un coucher de soleil** nothing can compare with a sunset; **leur intelligence égale leur charme** they're as clever as they're charming; **3** MATH **trois plus trois égalent six** three plus three equals six ou is six.

égalisation /egalizasjɔ̃/ *nf* **1** (des revenus, de surface,

sol) levelling[GB] out; **2** SPORT **rater l'~** to fail to score the equalizer.

égaliser /egalize/ [1] **I** *vtr* **1** (en nivelant) to level [*terrain*]; to level out [*prix, revenus*]; **2** (en taillant) to even up the ends of [*cheveux*]; to make [sth] the same size [*planches*].
II *vi* SPORT to equalize GB, to tie US.

égalitaire /egalitɛʀ/ *adj, nmf* egalitarian.

égalité /egalite/ *nf* **1** (parité) GÉN, POL equality; **2** SPORT **être à ~** to be level GB, to be tied US; **~!** (au tennis) deuce!; **3** (uniformité) (de terrain) flatness; (de climat) temperate nature; (d'humeur) evenness; **4** MATH equality.

égard /egaʀ/ **I** *nm* **1** (considération) **¢; sans ~ pour** without regard for; **par ~ pour** out of consideration for; **2** (rapport) **à l'~ de qn** toward(s) sb; **à l'~ de qch** regarding; **à cet ~** in this respect; **eu ~ à qch** in view of sth.
II égards *nmpl* (marques d'estime) **avec des ~s** with respect; **manquer d'~s envers qn** to be disrespectful toward(s) sb.

égaré, ~e /egaʀe/ *adj* **1** [*animal*] stray (*épith*); **2** [*air, yeux*] wild, distracted.

égarement /egaʀmɑ̃/ *nm* **1** (trouble) distraction; **2** (dérèglement) (état) confusion; (comportement) erratic behaviour[GB].

égarer /egaʀe/ [1] **I** *vtr* **1** LIT, FIG (faire perdre) to lead [sb] astray [*personne*]; **2** (perdre) to mislay [*objet*].
II s'égarer *vpr* **1** (se perdre) [*personne, animal*] to get lost; **2** (être perdu) [*lettre, colis*] to get lost; **3** (errer) [*esprit*] to wander; [*personne*] to ramble.

égayer /egeje/ [21] *vtr* to enliven [*conversation, soirée*]; to cheer [sb] up [*malade*]; to amuse [*convives, assemblée*]; to brighten [sth] up [*maison, robe*]; to lighten [*ouvrage, style*]; to brighten [*journée, vie*].

Égée /eʒe/ **▶ 407**| *npr* Aegeus; **mer ~** Aegean Sea.

égérie /eʒeʀi/ *nf* muse.

égide /eʒid/ *nf* aegis.

églantine /eglɑ̃tin/ *nf* wild rose, dog-rose.

églefin /egləfɛ̃/ *nm* haddock.

église /egliz/ *nf* church; **aller à l'~** to go to church.

Église /egliz/ *nf* Church; **homme d'~** cleric.

égocentrique /egosɑ̃tʀik/ *adj, nmf* egocentric.

égocentrisme /egosɑ̃tʀism/ *nm* self-centredness[GB].

égoïsme /egɔism/ *nm* selfishness.

égoïste /egɔist/ **I** *adj* selfish.
II *nmf* selfish man/woman.

égorger /egɔʀʒe/ [13] *vtr* **~ qn** to cut sb's throat.

égosiller: s'égosiller /egozije/ [1] *vpr* **1** (se fatiguer la voix) to shout oneself hoarse; **2** (chanter fort) to sing at the top of one's voice; (crier) to yell.

égotiste /egɔtist/ **I** *adj* egotistical.
II *nmf* egotist.

égout /egu/ *nm* sewer.

égoutier, -ière /egutje, ɛʀ/ **▶ 374**| *nm,f* sewage worker.

égoutter /egute/ [1] **I** *vtr* to drain [*vaisselle, riz, légumes, frites*]; to strain [*fromage*]; to hang up [sth] to drip dry [*linge*].
II *vi* [*vaisselle, riz, fromage*] to drain; [*linge*] to drip.
III s'égoutter *vpr* [*vaisselle, riz, légumes, fromage*] to drain; [*linge*] to drip dry.

égouttoir /egutwaʀ/ *nm* draining rack GB, (dish) drainer US.

égratigner /egʀatiɲe/ [1] **I** *vtr* **1** (griffer) to scratch [*jambe, meuble*]; (écorcher) to graze [*jambe*]; **2** FIG to hurt [*personne*].
II s'égratigner *vpr* (sur des ronces, un objet pointu) to scratch oneself; (par frottement) to graze oneself.

égratignure /egʀatiɲyʀ/ *nf* (en griffant) scratch; (par frottement) graze; **se sortir de qch sans une ~** LIT to come out of sth without a scratch; FIG to come out of sth with one's reputation unscathed.

égrener /egʀəne/ [16] *vtr* **1** CULIN to shell [*pois*]; to remove the seeds from [*tomate, melon*]; **2** to chime out [*notes, heures*]; to drone out [*chiffres, chanson*]; ~ **son chapelet** to tell one's beads.

égrillard, **~e** /egʀijaʀ, aʀd/ *adj* [*personne*] dirty-minded; [*air, histoire*] bawdy.

Égypte /eʒipt/ ▶ 232 | *nprf* Egypt.

égyptien, **-ienne** /eʒipsjɛ̃, ɛn/ ▶ 338 |, 394 | **I** *adj* Egyptian.
II *nm* LING Egyptian.

eh /e/ *excl* (pour attirer l'attention) hey; ~ **bien** well; ~ **oui** (ton résigné) so there we are; (pour insister) I'm afraid so.

éhonté, **~e** /eɔ̃te/ *adj* [*menteur, mensonge*] brazen; [*demande*] shameless.

Éire /eʀ/ *npr* Éire, Republic of Ireland.

éjaculer /eʒakyle/ [1] *vi* to ejaculate.

éjectable /eʒɛktabl/ *adj* **siège ~** ejector seat GB, ejection seat US.

éjecter /eʒɛkte/ [1] *vtr* **1** (dans un accident) to throw [sb/sth] out; **2**○ (expulser) to chuck○ [sb] out [*personne*] (**de** of); **3** TECH to eject.

éjection /eʒɛksjɔ̃/ *nf* **1** (de pilote, fluide, cartouche) ejection; **2**○ (expulsion) expulsion.

élaboration /elabɔʀasjɔ̃/ *nf* **1** (de projet) development; (de solution) working out; (de document) drafting; (de journal) putting together; **2** BOT elaboration.

élaboré, **~e** /elabɔʀe/ *adj* [*cuisine*] sophisticated.

élaborer /elabɔʀe/ [1] *vtr* (préparer) to work [sth] out [*stratégie, solution*]; to draw up [*document*]; to put [sth] together [*brochure*].

élaguer /elage/ [1] *vtr* LIT, FIG to prune.

élan /elɑ̃/ *nm* **1** SPORT (pour sauter) run up; **saut avec/sans ~** running/standing jump; **2** (force) LIT, FIG momentum; **3** (impulsion) impetus; **4** (enthousiasme) enthusiasm; **5** (mouvement affectif) impulse; **~ de colère** surge of anger; **6** ZOOL elk.

élancé, **~e** /elɑ̃se/ *adj* [*personne, édifice*] slender.

élancement /elɑ̃smɑ̃/ *nm* **1** (douleur) throbbing pain; **2** (aspiration) yearning.

élancer /elɑ̃se/ [12] **I** *vi* **mon doigt m'élance** I've got a throbbing pain in my finger.
II **s'élancer** *vpr* **1** (bondir) [*personne*] to dash forward; **s'~ à l'assaut** to launch an assault (**de** on); **2** (partir) [*personne, voiture*] to shoot off○; **3** (se dresser) **s'~ vers le ciel** [*arbre, cathédrale*] to soar up toward(s) the sky.

élargi, **~e** /elaʀʒi/ *adj* [*format*] enlarged; [*gouvernement*] expanded.

élargir /elaʀʒiʀ/ [3] **I** *vtr* **1** (rendre plus large) to widen [*chaussée*]; to let [sth] out [*vêtement*]; **2** (déformer) [*personne*] to stretch [*chaussures, pull*]; **3** (étendre) to widen [*débat*]; to extend [*contacts, audience, droit*]; to broaden [*connaissances, idées, activités*]; to increase [*majorité*]; to expand [*moyens, secteur*]; **4** JUR (libérer) to release [*détenu*].
II **s'élargir** *vpr* [*groupe*] to expand; [*écart*] to increase; [*débat, route, fleuve*] to widen; [*personne*] to fill out; [*épaules*] to become broader; [*vêtement*] to stretch.

élastique /elastik/ **I** *adj* **1** (extensible) [*bretelle, taille*] elasticated GB, elasticized US; **2** PHYS [*gaz, métal, fibre*] elastic; **une démarche ~** a springy walk; **3** [*règlement, horaire*] flexible; [*budget*] elastic.
II *nm* **1** (lien circulaire) rubber band; (en mercerie) elastic; **2** (jeu d'enfant) **jouer à l'~** to play elastics; **3** ▶ 329 | SPORT (pour sauter) bungee cord; **sauter à l'~** to do a bungee jump.

électeur, **-trice** /elɛktœʀ, tʀis/ *nm,f* voter.

élection /elɛksjɔ̃/ *nf* **1** POL election (**à** to); **~ partielle** by-election GB, off-year election US; **après son ~** after being elected; **2** (choix) choice; **mon pays d'~** my chosen country.

électoral, **~e**, *mpl* **-aux** /elɛktɔʀal, o/ *adj* [*programme, réforme, calendrier, promesse*] electoral; [*affiche, dépense, période*] election (*épith*); [*victoire, campagne*] election (*épith*), electoral.

électoralisme /elɛktɔʀalism/ *nm* electioneering.

électoraliste /elɛktɔʀalist/ *adj* electioneering.

électorat /elɛktɔʀa/ *nm* electorate, voters (*pl*).

électricien, **-ienne** /elɛktʀisjɛ̃, ɛn/ ▶ 374 | *nm,f* electrician.

électricité /elɛktʀisite/ *nf* LIT, FIG electricity; **marche à l'~** to run on electricity; **l'atmosphère était chargée d'~** FIG the atmosphere was electric.

électrifier /elɛktʀifje/ [2] *vtr* to bring electricity to [*village*]; to electrify [*voie ferrée*].

électrique /elɛktʀik/ *adj* **1** [*appareil*] electric; [*installation*] electrical; [*réseau*] electricity (*épith*); **2** FIG [*atmosphère*] electric.

électrisant, **~e** /elɛktʀizɑ̃, ɑ̃t/ *adj* FIG electrifying.

électriser /elɛktʀize/ [1] *vtr* **1** PHYS to charge [sth] with electricity; **2** (exalter) to electrify.

électro(-) /elɛktʀo/ *préf* electro; **~-aimant** electromagnet; **~cardiogramme** electrocardiogram.

électrochoc /elɛktʀoʃɔk/ *nm* **1** MÉD **~s** electroshock therapy (*sg*), EST; **2** FIG shock treatment **¢**.

électrocuter /elɛktʀɔkyte/ [1] **I** *vtr* to electrocute.
II **s'électrocuter** *vpr* (accidentellement) to be electrocuted.

électrode /elɛktʀɔd/ *nf* electrode.

électrogène /elɛktʀɔʒɛn/ *adj* **groupe ~** (electricity) generator.

électrolyse /elɛktʀɔliz/ *nf* electrolysis.

électromécanicien, **-ienne** /elɛktʀomekanisjɛ̃, ɛn/ ▶ 374 | *nm,f* electrical engineer.

électroménager /elɛktʀomenaʒe/ **I** *adj m* **appareil ~** electrical domestic ou household appliance.
II *nm* **1** (appareils) electrical domestic ou household appliances (*pl*); **2** (industrie) electrical goods industry.

électromoteur, **-trice** /elɛktʀomɔtœʀ, tʀis/ *adj* electromotive.

électron /elɛktʀɔ̃/ *nm* electron.

électronicien, **-ienne** /elɛktʀɔnisjɛ̃, ɛn/ ▶ 374 | *nm,f* electronics engineer.

électronique /elɛktʀɔnik/ **I** *adj* **1** [*circuit, composant*] electronic; **2** [*microscope, télescope*] electron (*épith*).
II *nf* electronics (+ *v sg*).

électrophone /elɛktʀɔfɔn/ *nm* record player.

électrostatique /elɛktʀostatik/ **I** *adj* electrostatic.
II *nf* electrostatics (+ *v sg*).

électrotechnique /elɛktʀotɛknik/ *nf* electrical engineering; (discipline) electrotechnology.

élégamment /elegamɑ̃/ *adv* [*s'habiller*] elegantly; [*se conduire*] courteously.

élégance /elegɑ̃s/ *nf* (qualité) elegance; **d'une grande ~** extremely elegant; **avec ~** [*s'habiller*] elegantly; [*perdre*] gracefully; [*se conduire*] honourably GB; [*résoudre un problème*] neatly.

élégant, **~e** /elegɑ̃, ɑ̃t/ **I** *adj* [*personne, vêtement, écriture*] elegant; [*solution*] neat, elegant; **ce n'est pas très ~ de ta part** it's not very decent of you.
II *nm,f* dandy/elegant lady.

élégie /eleʒi/ *nf* elegy.

élément /elemɑ̃/ **I** *nm* **1** (constituant) (d'ensemble, de structure) element; (d'appareil) component; (de mélange) ingredient; (de problème) element; (facteur) factor, element; **~ décisif** deciding factor; **l'~ humain** the human element ou factor; **~ moteur** (personne) driving force; **2** (de mobilier) unit; **~s de cuisine** kitchen units; **3** (fait) fact; **4** (individu) **bon ~** (élève) good pupil; (joueur) good player; **5** TECH (de pile) cell; **6** CHIMIE element.
II **éléments** *nmpl* **1** (rudiments) (premiers) **~s** basics; **2** MÉTÉO elements.

élémentaire /elemɑ̃tɛʀ/ *adj* (de base) [*principe, besoin*] basic; SCOL [*niveau*] elementary; (simple) elementary.

éléphant /elefɑ̃/ *nm* elephant.
IDIOMES **avoir une mémoire d'~** never to forget a thing.

éléphante /elefɑ̃t/ *nf* cow elephant.

éléphanteau, *pl* **~x** /elefɑ̃to/ *nm* (elephant) calf.

éléphantesque /elefɑ̃tɛsk/ *adj* elephantine, enormous.

élevage /elvaʒ/ *nm* **1** (de bétail) livestock farming; ~ **de saumons** salmon farming; **faire de l'~** to breed GB ou raise US livestock; **faire de l'~ de chevaux** to breed horses; **produits de l'~** meat and dairy products; **d'~** [*huîtres, poisson*] farmed; [*caille, faisan*] captive-bred; **2** (installation) farm; **un ~ de visons** a mink farm; **3** (ensemble des animaux) stock (**de** of).

élévateur /elevatœʀ/ *nm* (engin, muscle) elevator.

élévation /elevasjɔ̃/ *nf* **1** (de niveau) rise (**de** in); **2** (promotion) elevation; **3** (sur un plan) elevation; **4** GÉOG ~ **de terrain** rise in the ground; **5** RELIG Elevation (of the Host).

élève /elɛv/ *nmf* GÉN student; SCOL pupil.
■ ~ **officier** trainee officer.

élevé, ~e /elve/ *adj* **1** [*niveau, prix, grade, rang*] high; **plus** ~ higher; **moins** ~ lower; **peu** ~ low; **2** [*plateau*] high; **habiter un étage** ~ to live on an upper floor; **3** (noble) [*sentiment*] fine; [*principes*] high; [*idéal*] lofty; [*langage*] elevated.

élever /elve/ [16] **I** *vtr* **1** (construire) to put up [*barrière, mur*]; to erect [*statue*]; **des obstacles** FIG to make things difficult; **2** (porter à un degré supérieur) to raise [*température, taux, niveau*]; ~ **la voix** ou **le ton** LIT to raise one's voice; **3** (lever) to raise [*bras*]; (soulever) to raise, to lift [*chargement*]; **4** (ennoblir) **la poésie élève l'âme** ou **l'esprit** poetry is elevating; **5** (formuler) to raise [*objection*]; to voice [*doutes*]; **6** (éduquer) to bring up [*enfant*]; **enfant bien/mal élevé** well/badly brought up child; **c'est mal élevé** it's bad manners (**de faire** to do); **7** AGRIC to rear [*bétail*]; to keep [*volaille, abeilles*].
II s'élever *vpr* **1** (augmenter) [*température, taux*] to rise; **2** (atteindre) **s'~ à** [*bénéfices, dépenses*] to come to; [*chiffre d'affaires, nombre de victimes*] to stand at; **3** (se hausser) to rise; **s'~ dans les airs** ou **le ciel** [*fumée*] to rise up into the air; [*oiseau*] to soar into the air; **s'~ dans la hiérarchie** to rise in the hierarchy; **4** [*protestations, voix*] to be heard; **5** (prendre parti) **s'~ contre qch** to protest against sth; **6** (se dresser) [*clocher, statue*] to stand; **s'~ au-dessus de qch** [*clocher, falaise*] to rise above sth.

éleveur, -euse /elvœʀ, øz/ ▶374▎ *nm,f* breeder.

elfe /ɛlf/ *nm* elf.

élider /elide/ [1] *vtr*, **s'élider** *vpr* to elide.

éligibilité /eliʒibilite/ *nf* eligibility (**à** for election to).

éligible /eliʒibl/ *adj* eligible for office.

élimé /elime/ *adj* [*vêtement*] threadbare.

élimer /elime/ [1] *vtr* to wear [sth] thin [*tissu*].

éliminatoire /eliminatwaʀ/ **I** *adj* [*question, match*] qualifying (*épith*); [*note*] eliminatory.
II *nf* qualifier.

éliminer /elimine/ [1] *vtr* to eliminate [*candidat, équipe, toxines, erreurs*]; to rule out [*possibilité*].

élire /eliʀ/ [66] *vtr* to elect [*maire, représentant*]; ~ **qn président** to elect sb president; **se faire** ~ to be elected; **être élue Miss Monde** to be voted Miss World; ~ **domicile** GÉN to take up residence; JUR to elect domicile.

élisabéthain, ~e /elizabetɛ̃, ɛn/ *adj* Elizabethan.

élision /elizjɔ̃/ *nf* elision.

élite /elit/ *nf* **l'~** the elite; **d'~** [*troupes, unité*] elite (*épith*), crack; [*athlète, étudiant*] high-flying (*épith*); **sujet d'~** high-flier.

élitisme /elitism/ *nm* elitism.

elle /ɛl/ *pron pers f* **1** (sujet) (personne, animal familier) she; (objet, concept, pays, animal) it; ~**s** they; **ta mère est-~ arrivée?** has your mother arrived?; **j'aime le jazz,** ~ **aussi** I like jazz, so does she; ~ **qui aime tant le ballet, quel dommage qu'~ ne soit pas là** she loves ballet so much, it's a pity she isn't here; **est-ce** ~ **qui a bu le vin?** was she the one who drank the wine?; **ses collègues et** ~ **étaient enchantés** she and her colleagues were delighted; ~, ~ **ne dit rien** she never says a word; **'je n'aime pas ça!'—'~ non**

plus' 'I don't like that!'—'she doesn't either'; **la pie vole tout ce qu'~ trouve** the magpie steals everything it finds; **l'heure a-t-~ sonné?** has the clock struck the hour?; **le Portugal a signé, l'Espagne, ~, n'a pas encore donné son accord** Portugal has signed while Spain has not yet agreed; **2** (dans une comparaison) her; **je suis plus jeune qu'~** I'm younger than she is ou than her; **je les vois plus souvent qu'~** I see them more often than she does; (que je ne la vois) I see them more often than her; **3** (après une préposition) (personne, animal familier) her; (objet, animal) it; **à cause d'~** because of her; **pour ~, c'est un fou** she thinks he's mad; **je ne pense plus à ~** I don't think about her any more; **à ~** (dans une séquence) it's her turn; **c'est à ~ de choisir** (son tour) it's her turn to choose; (sa responsabilité) it's up to her to choose; (marquant la possession) **des amis à ~** friends of hers; **elle n'a pas de coin à ~ dans la maison** she doesn't have a room of her own in the house; **le bol bleu est à ~** the blue bowl is hers.

ellébore /elebɔʀ/ *nm* helebore.

elle-même, *pl* **elles-mêmes** /ɛlmɛm/ *pron pers f* **1** (personne) herself; **elles-mêmes** themselves; **en ~ elle se disait que** she told herself that; **'Madame Dubois?'—'~'** (au téléphone) 'Mrs Dubois?'—'speaking'; **2** (objet, idée, concept) itself; **elles-mêmes** themselves; **en ~** in itself; **les taches sont parties d'elles-mêmes** the stains came out by themselves.

elles *pron pers fpl* ▶ **elle**.

ellipse /elips/ *nf* **1** MATH ellipse; **2** LING ellipsis.

elliptique /eliptik/ *adj* MATH elliptic; LING elliptical.

élocution /elɔkysjɔ̃/ *nf* diction; **avoir une ~ lente** to speak slowly; **défaut d'~** speech impediment.

éloge /elɔʒ/ *nm* **1** (louange) praise; **faire l'~ de qn/qch** to sing the praises of sb/sth; **faire l'~ du crime/de la drogue** to extol GB crime/drugs; **être digne d'~s** [*personne*] to deserve praise; [*action*] to be praiseworthy; **il a été couvert d'~s par** he was showered with praise by; **décerner des ~s à qn** to commend sb; **être tout à l'~ de qn** to do sb great credit; **2** LITTÉRAT (discours) eulogy.
■ ~ **funèbre** funeral oration.

élogieux, -ieuse /elɔʒjø, øz/ *adj* [*personne*] full of praise; [*article*] laudatory; **en termes ~** in glowing terms.

éloigné, ~e /elwaɲe/ *adj* **1** (dans l'espace) distant; ~ **de tout** remote; **un hameau ~ de cinq kilomètres** a hamlet five kilometres GB away; **deux usines ~es de cinq kilomètres** two factories five kilometres GB apart; **c'est trop ~** it's too far away; **2** (dans le temps) [*souvenirs*] distant; [*événement*] remote (*jamais épith*); ~ **dans le temps** distant (in time); **dans un futur peu ~** in the not too distant future; **dans un passé peu ~** not (so) long ago; **3** (dans la famille) [*cousin*] distant; **éloignées** [*positions, opinions*] poles apart; **très ~ de la réalité** far removed from reality.

éloignement /elwaɲmɑ̃/ *nm* **1** (dans l'espace) distance; **2** (dans le temps) remoteness; **avec l'~, l'événement prend tout son sens** in retrospect, the full significance of the event becomes apparent; **3** (écart) **son ~ des milieux littéraires** his/her lack of contact with literary circles.

éloigner /elwaɲe/ [1] **I** *vtr* **1** LIT to move [sb/sth] away (**de** from); ~ **les badauds** to move onlookers on; **2** FIG **ils font tout pour l'~ de moi** they are doing everything to drive us apart; ~ **une menace/un danger** to remove a threat/a danger.
II s'éloigner *vpr* **1** LIT to move away (**de** from); **l'orage s'éloigne** the storm is moving away; **il s'éloigne à pas lents** he walks away slowly; **2** FIG **s'~ de** [*personne*] to move away from [*idéologie, ligne politique*]; to wander from, to stray from [*sujet*]; **le texte s'éloigne du schéma de base sur deux points** the text differs from the basic pattern on two points.

élongation /elɔ̃gasjɔ̃/ *nf* **1** MÉD (accidentelle) pulled

muscle; (thérapeutique) traction; **2** (en astronomie) elonga-
tion; **3** PHYS displacement.

éloquence /elɔkɑ̃s/ *nf* eloquence **¢**.

éloquent, **~e** /elɔkɑ̃, ɑ̃t/ *adj* [*personne, paroles*]
eloquent; **le score est ~** the score speaks for itself.

élu, **~e** /ely/ *nm,f* **1** POL elected representative; **2** (personne aimée) beloved; **l'~ de mon cœur** the one I
love; **3** (choisi par Dieu) **les ~s** the elect (+ *v pl*).

élucidation /elysidasjɔ̃/ *nf* clarification.

élucider /elyside/ [1] *vtr* to solve [*crime, problème*]; to
clarify [*circonstances, conditions*]; **crime non élucidé**
unsolved crime.

élucubrations /elykybrasjɔ̃/ *nfpl* rantings.

élucubrer /elykybre/ [1] *vtr* PEJ to dream up [*plan*].

éluder /elyde/ [1] *vtr* to evade.

Élysée /elize/ *nprm* **1** POL (**palais de l'**)**~** Élysée
Palace (*the official residence of the French President*);
2 MYTHOL Elysium.

élytre /elitr/ *nm* elytron.

émacier: s'émacier /emasje/ [2] *vpr* to become
emaciated.

émail, *pl* **-aux** /emaj, o/ *nm* (matière, objet) enamel.

émaillé, **~e** /emaje/ *adj* [*ustensile*] enamel (*épith*);
[*métal*] enamelled.

émailler /emaje/ [1] *vtr* **1** to enamel [*objet*]; **2** FIG **discours émaillé d'allusions** speech sprinkled with allu-
sions.

émanation /emanasjɔ̃/ *nf* (effluve) emanation; **~s de
gaz** gas fumes.

émancipateur, **-trice** /emɑ̃sipatœr, tris/ *adj* liberating.

émancipation /emɑ̃sipasjɔ̃/ *nf* emancipation.

émanciper /emɑ̃sipe/ [1] **I** *vtr* to emancipate [*peuple,
mineur*]; to liberate [*pays*] (**de** from).
II s'émanciper *vpr* to become emancipated; HUM to
become very independent; **femme émancipée**
liberated woman.

émaner /emane/ [1] **I** *vi* **~ de** [*chaleur, odeur*] to
emanate from; [*ordre*] to come from.
II *v impers* **il émane d'elle un charme fou** she exudes
charm.

émarger /emarʒe/ [13] **I** *vtr* **1** (rogner) to trim [*page*];
2 (signer) to sign.
II *vi* **~ à l'université** to be on the payroll of the
university; **~ à 20 000 francs** to draw 20,000 francs.

émasculer /emaskyle/ [1] *vtr* LIT, FIG to emasculate.

émaux ▶ **émail**.

emballage /ɑ̃balaʒ/ *nm* **1** (dans du carton) packaging;
(dans du papier) wrapping; (dans une caisse) packing;
2 (papier) wrapping; (carton) packaging.
■ **~ sous vide** vacuum packing.

emballant○, **~e** /ɑ̃balɑ̃, ɑ̃t/ *adj* exciting.

emballement /ɑ̃balmɑ̃/ *nm* **1** (enthousiasme) fit of
enthusiasm (**pour** for); (colère) outburst of anger; **2** (de
prix, d'inflation) rapid rise; **3** (de cheval) bolting; **4** (de
moteur) racing.

emballer /ɑ̃bale/ [1] **I** *vtr* **1** (dans une boîte) to pack;
(envelopper) to wrap; **2**○ (enthousiasmer) **cette idée
m'emballe** I am really taken with this idea; **être
emballé par** to be taken with; **3** to race [*moteur*].
II s'emballer *vpr* **1** [*cheval*] to bolt; **2**○ (se
passionner) to get carried away (**pour** by); **ça ne
m'emballe pas d'aller à Londres** I'm not too keen on
going to London; **3** (s'énerver) to get all worked up○;
4○ [*moteur*] to race; **5** [*prix, inflation*] to shoot up;
[*monnaie*] to shoot up in value.

embarcadère /ɑ̃barkadɛr/ *nm* (de passagers) pier; (de
marchandises) wharf.

embarcation /ɑ̃barkasjɔ̃/ *nf* boat.

embardée /ɑ̃barde/ *nf* (d'auto) swerve; (de bateau)
yaw; **faire une ~** [*auto*] to swerve; [*bateau*] to yaw.

embargo /ɑ̃bargo/ *nm* embargo (**contre, sur** on).

embarqué, **~e** /ɑ̃barke/ **I** *pp* ▶ **embarquer**.
II *pp adj* [*équipement, système*] on-board.

embarquement /ɑ̃barkəmɑ̃/ *nm* (de passagers) board-

ing; **formalités d'~** boarding procedures; **port d'~**
port of embarkation.

embarquer /ɑ̃barke/ [1] **I** *vtr* **1** AVIAT, NAUT (charger) to
load [*marchandises*]; to take on board [*passager*];
2○ (emmener) to take [*objet*]; [*police*] to pick up [*malfaiteur*]; **3**○ (engager) **~ qn dans un projet** to get
sb involved in a project.
II *vi* (monter à bord) to board; NAUT (partir en voyage) to
sail (**pour** for); **~ à bord de** to board.
III s'embarquer *vpr* **1** NAUT = **embarquer II**;
2○ (se lancer) **s'~ dans** to launch into [*explication*].

embarras /ɑ̃bara/ *nm inv* **1** (trouble) embarrassment;
2 (gêne financière) **~ d'argent** ou **financiers** financial
difficulties; **ton chèque m'a tiré d'~** your cheque GB
ou check US helped me out; **3** (situation délicate)
awkward position; **tirer qn d'~** to get sb out of a difficult situation; **4** (incertitude) **être dans l'~** to be in a
quandary; **je conçois votre ~** I understand your
dilemma; **n'avoir que l'~ du choix** to be spoiled for
choice GB, to have too much to choose from;
5† (obstacle) **il craint d'être un ~ pour vous** he's
afraid of being a nuisance (to you); **les ~ de la circulation** road congestion **¢**.
■ **~ gastrique** MÉD stomach upset.

embarrassant, **~e** /ɑ̃barasɑ̃, ɑ̃t/ *adj* **1** [*problème,
silence, choix*] awkward; [*situation*] embarrassing;
2 [*bagages*] cumbersome.

embarrassé, **~e** /ɑ̃barase/ **I** *pp* ▶ **embarrasser**.
II *pp adj* **1** [*personne, silence*] embarrassed; **être bien
~ pour répondre/expliquer** to be at a loss for an
answer/explanation; **2** [*explication*] confused; **3** [*pièce,
bureau*] cluttered (**de** with); **4** MÉD [*estomac*] upset.

embarrasser /ɑ̃barase/ [1] **I** *vtr* **1** (mettre mal à l'aise)
to embarrass [*personne*]; **ça m'embarrasse de te le
rappeler, mais...** I'm sorry to have to remind you,
but...; **2** (encombrer) to clutter (up) [*pièce, table*] (**de**
with); **cette armoire m'embarrasse plutôt qu'autre
chose** this wardrobe is more of a nuisance than
anything else.
II s'embarrasser *vpr* (s'encombrer) **s'~ de** to
burden oneself with [*paquet, personne*]; to weigh
oneself down with [*scrupules*]; to worry about [*détails*].

embauche /ɑ̃boʃ/ *nf* appointment GB, hiring **¢** US; **salaire d'~** starting salary; **aides à l'~** employment
incentives.

embaucher /ɑ̃boʃe/ [1] *vtr* **1** (pour un emploi) to hire
[*ouvrier*]; **2**○ (pour une corvée) to recruit.

embaumer /ɑ̃bome/ [1] **I** *vtr* **1** [*odeur*] to fill [*lieu*];
[*lieu*] to smell of [*lavande, cire*]; **2** to embalm [*cadavre*].
II *vi* [*air, fleurs*] to be fragrant.

embaumeur, **-euse** /ɑ̃bomœr, øz/ ▶ **374** *nm,f*
embalmer.

embellie /ɑ̃bɛli/ *nf* **1** (dans le temps) bright spell; NAUT
lull; **2** FIG improvement.

embellir /ɑ̃bɛlir/ [3] **I** *vtr* **1** to improve [*ville*]; to
make [sb] more attractive [*personne*]; **2** to embellish
[*récit, vérité*].
II *vi* to become more attractive.

embellissement /ɑ̃bɛlismɑ̃/ *nm* **1** (de pièce, maison)
improving; **travaux d'~** improvements; **2** (élément
amélioré) improvement, embellishment; **3** (inexactitude)
embellishment.

emberlificoté○, **~e** /ɑ̃bɛrlifikɔte/ *adj* [*texte*]
muddled; [*situation*] confused.

emberlificoter○ /ɑ̃bɛrlifikɔte/ [1] **I** *vtr* **1** (embrouiller)
to entangle [*fil*]; **2** (duper) to take [sb] in○ [*personne*].
II s'emberlificoter *vpr* **1** LIT to get entangled (**dans**
in); **2** FIG to get mixed up (**dans** in).

embêtant, **~e** /ɑ̃bɛtɑ̃, ɑ̃t/ *adj* **1** (fâcheux) GÉN annoying; [*situation*] awkward; **c'est ~ ça!** that's a real
nuisance!; **2** (agaçant) annoying; **3** (lassant) boring.

embêtement /ɑ̃bɛtmɑ̃/ *nm* problem.

embêter /ɑ̃bete/ [1] **I** *vtr* **1** (contrarier) to bother;
2 (importuner) to pester; (agacer) to annoy; **3** (lasser)
to bore.
II s'embêter *vpr* **1** (s'ennuyer) to be bored; **un hôtel
quatre étoiles! tu ne t'embêtes pas**○! a four-star

hotel! you're doing all right for yourself!; **2** (se compliquer la vie) **s'~ à faire** to go to all the bother of doing; **ne t'embête pas avec ça** don't bother with that!

emblée: **d'emblée** /dɑble/ *loc adv* (aussitôt) straightaway; [*détester*] at first sight.

emblématique /ɑblematik/ *adj* [*dessin, décoration*] emblematic; [*personnage, figure*] symbolic.

emblème /ɑblɛm/ *nm* emblem.

embobiner /ɑbɔbine/ [1] *vtr* **1**° (tromper) to hoodwink; **2** (enrouler) to wind.

emboîter /ɑbwate/ [1] **I** *vtr* to fit together [*pièces*].
II s'emboîter *vpr* to fit (**dans** into).
IDIOMES ~ le pas à qn LIT, FIG to fall in behind sb.

embolie /ɑbɔli/ ▶ **196** *nf* embolism.

embonpoint /ɑbɔpwɛ/ *nm* **avoir de l'~** to be stout.

embouché, **~e** /ɑbuʃe/ *adj* **mal ~** (grossier) coarse; (de mauvaise humeur) in a foul mood.

embouchure /ɑbuʃyʁ/ *nf* (de rivière) mouth; (d'instrument) mouthpiece; (de tuyau) opening.

embourber: **s'embourber** /ɑbuʁbe/ [1] *vpr* **1** (dans la boue) to get stuck in the mud; **2** (dans des difficultés) to get bogged down (**dans** in).

embourgeoiser: **s'embourgeoiser** /ɑbuʁʒwaze/ [1] *vpr* [*personne*] to become middle-class; [*quartier*] to become gentrified.

embout /ɑbu/ *nm* (de canne, cigare) tip; (de tuyau) nozzle; (de pipe) mouthpiece.

embouteillage /ɑbutɛjaʒ/ *nm* **1** (en ville) traffic jam; (sur l'autoroute) tailback; **2** (de système) bottleneck.

emboutir /ɑbutiʁ/ [3] *vtr* **1** TECH to stamp [*métal*]; **2** AUT to crash into [*véhicule, obstacle*].

embranchement /ɑbʁɑʃmɑ/ *nm* **1** (point de jonction) junction; **2** (voie) (routière) side road; (ferrée) branch line; **3** BOT, ZOOL branch.

embrasé, **~e** /ɑbʁaze/ *adj* **1** (en feu) burning; **2** (illuminé) glowing.

embrasement /ɑbʁazmɑ/ *nm* **1** (incendie) blaze; **2** (illumination) dazzling illumination; **3** (agitation sociale) unrest ₵.

embraser /ɑbʁaze/ [1] **I** *vtr* **1** (mettre le feu) to set [sth] ablaze [*bâtiment*]; **2** (agiter) to set [sth] alight [*ville, pays*]; **3** (illuminer) to set [sth] ablaze [*ciel, ville*]; **4** (emplir de passion) to set [sb] on fire [*personne*].
II s'embraser *vpr* **1** (prendre feu) to catch fire; **2** FIG [*pays, ville*] to erupt into violence; **3** (devenir illuminé) to be set ablaze; **4** (s'emplir de passion) to burn with desire.

embrassade /ɑbʁasad/ *nf* hugging and kissing ₵.

embrasse /ɑbʁas/ *nf* tieback.

embrasser /ɑbʁase/ [1] **I** *vtr* **1** (donner un baiser à) to kiss; **je t'embrasse** (en fin de lettre) lots of love; **2** (étreindre) to embrace [*personnalité*]; to hug [*ami*]; **3** (choisir) to take up [*carrière*]; to embrace [*cause, religion*]; **4** (inclure) [*étude*] to take in [*période, question*]; [*regard*] to take in [*paysage*]; [*auteur*] to cover [*sujet*].
II s'embrasser *vpr* to kiss (each other).

embrasure /ɑbʁazyʁ/ *nf* (dans un mur) opening.
■ **~ de fenêtre** window; **~ de porte** doorway.

embrayage /ɑbʁɛjaʒ/ *nm* **1** (dispositif) clutch; **2** (communication entre deux pièces) engaging; (par l'automobiliste) letting out the clutch; **3** (pédale) clutch pedal.

embrayer /ɑbʁeje/ [21] *vi* AUT to engage the clutch; TECH to engage.

embrigader /ɑbʁigade/ [1] *vtr* **1** (enrôler) to recruit (**dans** into; **comme** as); **2** MIL to brigade.

embrocher /ɑbʁɔʃe/ [1] **I** *vtr* **1** CULIN to put [sth] on a spit [*animal*]; to skewer [*morceau, gigot*]; **2**° (transpercer) to run [sb] through [*adversaire*].
II s'embrocher° *vpr* to impale oneself (**sur** on).

embrouillamini° /ɑbʁujamini/ *nm* muddle.

embrouille° /ɑbʁuj/ *nf* shady goings-on° (*pl*).

embrouillement /ɑbʁujmɑ/ *nm* (de fils) (action) tangling; (résultat) tangle.

embrouiller /ɑbʁuje/ [1] **I** *vtr* to tangle [*fils*]; to confuse [*affaire, personne*].
II s'embrouiller *vpr* [*fils, cheveux*] to become tangled; [*idées, affaire, personne*] to become confused;

s'~ dans to get into a muddle with [*comptes*]; to get tangled up in [*explications*].

embroussaillé, **~e** /ɑbʁusaje/ *adj* [*chemin*] overgrown; [*cheveux, sourcils*] bushy; [*barbe*] shaggy.

embrumé, **~e** /ɑbʁyme/ *adj* **1** [*temps*] misty; [*ciel, paysage*] hazy; **2** [*esprit*] befuddled; [*regard*] glazed; [*voix*] hoarse.

embruns /ɑbʁœ/ *nmpl* spray ₵.

embryon /ɑbʁijɔ/ *nm* embryo.

embryonnaire /ɑbʁijɔnɛʁ/ *adj* LIT, FIG embryonic.

embûche /ɑbyʃ/ *nf* **1** (machination) trap; **dresser des ~s** to set traps; **2** (danger) hazard; (difficulté) pitfall; **plein d'~s** LIT hazardous; FIG fraught with pitfalls.

embuer /ɑbɥe/ [1] **I** *vtr* to mist up, to fog up US [*vitre*].
II s'embuer *vpr* [*vitre*] to mist up, to fog up US; [*yeux*] to mist over.

embuscade /ɑbyskad/ *nf* ambush.

embusquer: **s'embusquer** /ɑbyske/ [1] *vpr* to lie in ambush.

éméché°, **~e** /emeʃe/ *adj* tipsy.

émeraude¹ /emʁod/ ▶ **141** *adj inv, nm* (couleur) emerald green.

émeraude² /emʁod/ *nf* (pierre) emerald.

émergence /emɛʁʒɑs/ *nf* emergence.

émerger /emɛʁʒe/ [13] *vi* **1** (apparaître) to emerge; **2**° (se réveiller) to surface.

émeri /emʁi/ *nm* emery; **bouché à l'~** FIG as thick as two short planks GB, dumb.

émérite /emeʁit/ *adj* **1** [*joueur, acteur*] outstanding; **2 professeur ~** (titre) emeritus professor.

émerveillement /emɛʁvɛjmɑ/ *nm* wonder (**devant** at); **il fait l'~ de ses professeurs** his teachers are greatly impressed by him; **la nature est un ~ perpétuel** nature is an eternal source of wonder.

émerveiller /emɛʁveje/ [1] **I** *vtr* **~ qn** to fill sb with wonder; **être émerveillé par** to marvel at, to be filled with wonder by.
II s'émerveiller *vpr* **s'~ de** or **devant qch** to marvel at; **il s'émerveillait qu'elle ait pu faire cela aussi vite** he was amazed ou impressed that she had been able to do it so quickly.

émétique /emetik/ *adj, nm* emetic.

émetteur, **-trice** /emetœʁ, tʁis/ **I** *adj* **1** RADIO, TV broadcasting; **2** [*banque, bureau*] issuing.
II *nm* **1** RADIO, TV transmitter; **2** (d'emprunt, de carte) issuer; **3** LING sender.

émettre /emɛtʁ/ [60] *vtr* **1** (exprimer) to express [*avis*]; to put forward [*hypothèse*]; to raise [*objection*]; **2** (produire) to utter [*cri*]; to produce [*son, chaleur*]; to give off [*odeur*]; **3** (mettre en circulation) to issue [*timbre, monnaie*]; **4** [*banque*] to float [*emprunt*]; **5** RADIO, TV to broadcast [*programme*]; **6** [*avion, bateau*] to send out [*signal*]; **7** PHYS to emit [*radiation*].

émeu /emø/ *nm* ZOOL emu.

émeute /emøt/ *nf* riot.

émeutier, **-ière** /emøtje, ɛʁ/ *nm,f* rioter.

émietter /emjete/ [1] **I** *vtr* **1** to crumble [*pain, motte de terre*]; **2** to split [sth] up [*domaine, fortune*]; **3** to dissipate [*forces, activités*]; to fritter away [*temps*].
II s'émietter *vpr* **1** [*pain, roche*] to crumble; **2** [*pouvoir*] to crumble; **3** [*héritage*] to be split up.

émigrant, **~e** /emigʁɑ, ɑt/ *nm,f* emigrant.

émigration /emigʁasjɔ/ *nf* emigration.

émigré, **~e** /emigʁe/ *nm,f* GÉN emigrant; HIST émigré.

émigrer /emigʁe/ [1] *vi* **1** [*personne*] to emigrate; **2** [*oiseau*] to migrate.

émincer /emɛse/ [12] *vtr* to slice [sth] thinly.

éminemment /eminamɑ/ *adv* eminently.

éminence /eminɑs/ *nf* **1** (monticule) hillock LITTÉR; **2** ANAT protuberance.

Éminence /eminɑs/ *nf* RELIG Eminence.
■ **~ grise** éminence grise, grey GB ou gray US eminence.

éminent, **~e** /eminɑ, ɑt/ *adj* distinguished, eminent.

émirat /emiʁa/ *nm* emirate.

Émirats /emiʀa/ ▶ 232┃ nprmpl ~ **arabes unis, EAU** United Arab Emirates.

émissaire /emiseʀ/ nm emissary.

émission /emisjɔ̃/ nf **1** RADIO, TV programme^GB (**sur** about, on); **2** (de document, monnaie, timbre) issue; **3** (d'ondes, de signaux) emission.

emmagasiner /ɑ̃magazine/ [1] vtr **1** (mettre en magasin) to store; **2** (accumuler) to stockpile [marchandises]; to store [énergie]; to store up [connaissances].

emmancher /ɑ̃mɑ̃ʃe/ [1] **I** vtr **1** to fit a handle to [outil]; **2**○ to set [sth] up [affaire, négociation].
II s'emmancher○ vpr s'~ **bien/mal** [affaire] to get off to a good/bad start.

emmanchure /ɑ̃mɑ̃ʃyʀ/ nf armhole.

emmêler /ɑ̃mɛle/ [1] **I** vtr **1** to tangle [cheveux, fils]; **2** to confuse [affaire].
II s'emmêler vpr [fils] to get tangled up; s'~ **les pieds dans** [personne] to get one's feet caught in.

emménager /ɑ̃menaʒe/ [13] vi to move in.

emmener /ɑ̃mne/ [16] vtr **1** (mener) to take [personne] (**à, jusqu'à** to); ~ **qn faire des courses/promener** to take sb shopping/for a walk; **emmène-moi chez toi!** take me home with you!; **veux-tu que je t'emmène en voiture?** do you want a lift GB ou a ride US?; **2** (emporter) CONTROV to take [parapluie, livre]; **3** (arrêter) [police] to take [sb] away [personne]; **4** (entraîner) [chef, capitaine] to lead [équipe, troupe].

emmerder⁹ /ɑ̃mɛʀde/ [1] **I** vtr **1** (importuner) to annoy, to hassle○; **tu m'emmerdes** you're a pain○; **je les emmerde** to hell○ with them; **2** (ennuyer) to bore [sb] stiff○.
II s'emmerder vpr **1** (s'ennuyer) to be bored (stiff)○; **2** (se compliquer la vie) s'~ **à faire** to go to the trouble ou bother of doing; **je n'ai pas envie de m'~ avec un chien** I don't want all the trouble ou hassle○ of a dog; **t'emmerde pas avec ça!** (avec la finition) don't bother with that!; (avec ce que les gens vont penser) don't waste your time worrying about that!; **un hôtel cinq étoiles, tu t'emmerdes pas!** a 5-star hotel! you're doing all right for yourself!; **tu as fouillé dans mes tiroirs, tu t'emmerdes pas!** you went through my drawers, you've got a nerve ou a bloody cheek○! GB

emmitoufler /ɑ̃mitufle/ [1] **I** vtr to wrap [sb/sth] up warmly.
II s'emmitoufler vpr to wrap (oneself) up warmly.

emmurer /ɑ̃myʀe/ [1] vtr to wall [sb/sth] in.

émoi /emwa/ nm agitation, turmoil; **la nouvelle a mis toute la ville en** ~ the news threw the whole city into turmoil; **l'arrivée du jeune homme l'avait mise en** ~ the young man's arrival had thrown her into a state of confusion.

émollient, ~e /emɔljɑ̃, ɑ̃t/ adj emollient.

émoluments /emolymɑ̃/ nmpl remuneration.

émonder /emɔ̃de/ [1] vtr to prune.

émotif, -ive /emɔtif, iv/ **I** adj emotional.
II nm,f emotional person.

émotion /emosjɔ̃/ nf (réaction affective) emotion; (peur) fright; (sensibilité) emotion; **rougir d'~** to blush with emotion; **donner des ~s**○ **à qn** to give sb a fright; **tu es remis de tes ~s**○? have you recovered from the shock?; **dans la salle d'audience, l'~ était à son comble** the atmosphere in the courtroom was extremely emotional.

émotivité /emɔtivite/ nf **enfant d'une grande ~** highly emotional child.

émoulu, ~e /emuly/ adj **frais ~ de** fresh from.

émousser /emuse/ [1] **I** vtr **1** to blunt [lame]; **2** to dull [curiosité, sensibilité].
II s'émousser vpr **1** [lame] to become ou get blunt; **2** [curiosité, sensibilité] to become dulled.

émoustiller /emustije/ [1] vtr **1** (égayer) to exhilarate; **2** (exciter) to titillate.

émouvant, ~e /emuvɑ̃, ɑ̃t/ adj moving.

émouvoir /emuvwaʀ/ [43] **I** vtr (attendrir) to move; (toucher) to touch; ~ **qn (jusqu')aux larmes** to move sb to tears; **se laisser** ~ **par les larmes de qn** to be swayed by sb's tears; ~ **l'opinion** to cause a stir.
II s'émouvoir vpr **1** (être touché) to be touched; s'~ **à la vue/au souvenir de** to be touched by the sight/memory of; **2** (s'inquiéter) **le gouvernement s'émeut des troubles paysans** the government is becoming concerned about the farmers' unrest; **répondre sans s'~** to reply calmly.

empailler /ɑ̃paje/ [1] vtr **1** to seat [sth] (with straw) [chaise]; **2** to stuff [animal].

empailleur, -euse /ɑ̃pajœʀ, øz/ ▶ 374┃ nm **1** (d'animaux) taxidermist; **2** (de chaise) chair seater.

empaler /ɑ̃pale/ [1] **I** vtr to impale [personne].
II s'empaler vpr to become impaled (**sur** on).

empaqueter /ɑ̃pakte/ [20] vtr (dans une boîte) to package; (dans du papier) to wrap [sth] up.

emparer: s'emparer /ɑ̃paʀe/ [1] vpr **1** (prendre) s'~ **de** [personne] to take over [ville, pays, record]; to seize [pouvoir, personne, prétexte]; to gain possession of [ballon]; to get hold of [rumeur, micro, volant]; **2** (envahir) s'~ **de** [torpeur] to take hold of [personne, pays].

empâter: s'empâter /ɑ̃pate/ vpr [1] [visage] to become puffy; [personne] to put on weight; [corps] to thicken out.

empêché, ~e /ɑ̃peʃe/ **I** pp ▶ **empêcher**.
II pp adj **1** (retenu) **le Président, ~, a dû se décommander** the President has been detained and has had to cancel; **2** (incapable) FML **l'électeur ~ d'aller voter** the voter unable to go and vote.

empêchement /ɑ̃pɛʃmɑ̃/ nm **1** (contretemps) unforeseen difficulty; **j'ai un ~, peux-tu reporter notre rendez-vous?** something's cropped up, can you make it another time?; **2** JUR impediment.

empêcher /ɑ̃peʃe/ [1] **I** vtr to prevent, to stop; ~ **un crime** to prevent a crime; ~ **qn de faire** to prevent ou stop sb (from) doing; **personne ne t'en empêche** no-one's stopping you; **la pauvreté n'empêche pas la générosité** poverty does not preclude generosity; **une disposition qui empêche les fonctionnaires de faire grève** a clause that prevents civil servants from striking; **pour ~ toute tentative d'OPA** to stave off ou ward off any takeover attempt.
II s'empêcher vpr **je n'ai pu m'~ de rire** I couldn't help laughing.
III v impers (il) **n'empêche** all the same; **il n'empêche que** nonetheless, the fact remains that.

empêcheur, -euse /ɑ̃peʃœʀ, øz/ nm,f ~ **de tourner** or **danser en rond** spoilsport, killjoy.

empeigne /ɑ̃pɛɲ/ nf upper.

empennage /ɑ̃penaʒ/ nm **1** (d'avion) tail; **2** (de flèche) flighting.

empereur /ɑ̃pʀœʀ/ ▶ 596┃ nm emperor.

empesé, ~e /ɑ̃pəze/ adj [col] starched; [air, style, personne] starchy.

empester /ɑ̃pɛste/ [16] **I** vtr to stink [sth] out GB, to stink up US [endroit].
II vi to stink; **ça empeste ici!** it stinks in here!

empêtrer: s'empêtrer /ɑ̃petʀe/ [1] vpr **1** s'~ **dans** to get entangled in [ronces, cordages]; to get tangled up in [mensonges, discours]; to get mixed up in [affaire]; to get bogged down in [comptes, problème]; **2**○ s'~ **de qn** to get stuck○ with sb.

emphase /ɑ̃faz/ nf **1** (exagération) grandiloquence; **plein d'~** grandiloquent; **parler sans ~** to speak without affectation; **2** LING emphasis.

emphatique /ɑ̃fatik/ adj **1** (pompeux) grandiloquent; **2** LING emphatic.

empiècement /ɑ̃pjɛsmɑ̃/ nm (de vêtement) yoke.

empierrer /ɑ̃pjeʀe/ [1] vtr to metal [route]; to ballast [voie ferrée].

empiéter /ɑ̃pjete/ [14] vtr ind ~ **sur** LIT, FIG to encroach upon.

empiffrer○: **s'empiffrer** /ɑ̃pifʀe/ [1] vpr to stuff oneself (**de** with).

empiler /ɑ̃pile/ [1] **I** vtr to pile [sth] (up).

II s'empiler *vpr* [*livres*] to pile up; **s'~ dans** [*personnes*] to pile into.

empire /ɑ̃pir/ *nm* **1** POL empire; **pas pour un ~**! not for the world!; **2** (entreprise) empire; **3** (ascendant) FML influence (**sur** over); **agir sous l'~ de la colère** to act in a fit of anger.

Empire /ɑ̃piʀ/ *nm* (règne de Napoléon Ier) **l'~** the Empire; **mobilier/style ~** Empire furniture/style.
■ **l'~ céleste** the Celestial Empire; **l'~ du Milieu** the Middle Kingdom; **l'~ d'Orient** the Byzantine Empire; **l'~ (romain) d'Occident** the Western (Roman) Empire; **l'~ du Soleil Levant** the land of the Rising Sun.

empirer /ɑ̃piʀe/ [1] *vi* to get worse.

empirique /ɑ̃piʀik/ *adj* GÉN empirical.

empirisme /ɑ̃piʀism/ *nm* empiricism.

emplacement /ɑ̃plasmɑ̃/ *nm* **1** (site) site; **2** (de stationnement) parking space.
■ **~ publicitaire** advertising space.

emplâtre /ɑ̃plɑtʀ/ *nm* **1** MÉD medicated plaster; **2**○ (personne) good-for-nothing○.

emplette /ɑ̃plɛt/ *nf* purchase; **faire quelques ~s** to make a few purchases.

emplir /ɑ̃pliʀ/ [3] *vtr*, **s'emplir** *vpr* to fill (**de** with).

emploi /ɑ̃plwa/ *nm* **1** (poste de travail) job; **changer d'~** to change jobs; **un ~ de chauffeur** a job as a driver; **sans ~** unemployed; **2** (embauche) employment; **stimuler l'~** to stimulate employment; **3** (utilisation) use; **l'~ d'armes/de fonds** the use of weapons/of funds; **téléviseur couleur à vendre, cause double ~** colour^GB TV for sale, surplus to requirements; **4** LING usage.
IDIOMES **avoir la tête de l'~** to look the part.

employé, ~e /ɑ̃plwaje/ ▸374 *nm,f* employee.
■ **~ de banque** bank clerk; **~ de bureau** office clerk; **~ aux écritures** ledger clerk; **~ de maison** domestic employee; **~ municipal** local authority employee.

employer /ɑ̃plwaje/ [23] **I** *vtr* to employ [*personne*] (**comme** as); to use [*mot, méthode, produit*].
II s'employer *vpr* **1** [*produit, mot*] to be used; **2 s'~ à faire** [*personne*] to apply oneself to doing.

employeur, -euse /ɑ̃plwajœʀ, øz/ *nm,f* employer.

empocher /ɑ̃pɔʃe/ [1] *vtr* to pocket.

empoignade○ /ɑ̃pwaɲad/ *nf* (bagarre) scrap○; (dispute) row.

empoigne /ɑ̃pwaɲ/ *nf* **c'était la foire d'~** it was a free-for-all.

empoigner /ɑ̃pwaɲe/ [1] **I** *vtr* to grab (hold of) (**par, au** by).
II s'empoigner *vpr* **1** (se battre) **s'~ avec qn** to grapple with sb; **2** (se quereller) to clash.

empoisonnant○, **~e** /ɑ̃pwazɔnɑ̃, ɑ̃t/ *adj* (fâcheux) annoying; (agaçant) irritating.

empoisonné, ~e /ɑ̃pwazɔne/ **I** *pp* ▸ **empoisonner**.
II *pp adj* [*aliment, flèche*] poisoned (**à** with); [*atmosphère, relations*] sour; [*querelle*] venomous; [*mot*] barbed.

empoisonnement /ɑ̃pwazɔnmɑ̃/ *nm* **1** LIT poisoning ¢; **~ au gaz** gas poisoning; **2**○ (ennui) trouble ¢.

empoisonner /ɑ̃pwazɔne/ [1] **I** *vtr* **1** (pour tuer) to poison [*personne, animal*]; **2** (intoxiquer) to poison [*sang*]; **être empoisonné par des champignons** to get food poisoning from mushrooms; **3** (polluer) to poison [*rivière*]; **4** FIG to poison [*relations, atmosphère*]; **arrête de m'~**○**!** stop bugging○ me!; **~ la vie de qn** to make sb's life a misery.
II s'empoisonner *vpr* **1** (volontairement) to poison oneself (**à** with); (accidentellement) **il s'est empoisonné avec une huître pas fraîche** he got food poisoning from eating a bad oyster; **2**○ (se rendre malheureux) **s'~ la vie** or **l'existence** to make one's life a misery.

empoisonneur, -euse /ɑ̃pwazɔnœʀ, øz/ *nm,f* **1** (criminel) poisoner; **2**○ (importun) nuisance.

emporté, ~e /ɑ̃pɔʀte/ *adj* **être ~, avoir un caractère ~** to be quick-tempered.

emportement /ɑ̃pɔʀtəmɑ̃/ *nm* fit of anger; **dans mon ~ je l'ai frappé** I hit him in a fit of anger.

emporte-pièce /ɑ̃pɔʀtəpjɛs/ *nm inv* **1** TECH punch; **découper qch à l'~** to punch sth; **jugement à l'~** FIG rash judgment; **2** CULIN pastry cutter.

emporter /ɑ̃pɔʀte/ [1] **I** *vtr* **1** (prendre avec soi) [*personne*] to take [*objet*]; **pizzas à ~** takeaway pizzas GB, pizzas to go US; **2** (transporter) [*ambulance, sauveteurs*] to take [sb] away [*blessé*]; [*bateau, train, avion*] to carry away [*passager, fret*]; **se laisser ~ par son élan** to get carried away; **se laisser ~ par la colère** to let one's anger get the better of one; **3** (entraîner, arracher) [*vent, rivière*] to sweep away [*personne, feuilles, pont*]; [*obus, balle*] to take [sth] off [*oreille, bras*]; **4** (causer la mort) **une leucémie l'a emporté** he died of leukaemia; **5** (conquérir) to take [*position*]; **~ l'adhésion de qn** to win sb over; **6** (triompher) **l'~** [*équipe, candidat*] to win; [*idée, bon sens*] to prevail; **l'~ sur qn** to beat sb; **l'~ sur qch** to overcome sth.
II s'emporter *vpr* to lose one's temper.
IDIOMES **~ la bouche**○ to take the roof off one's mouth○.

empoté○, **~e** /ɑ̃pɔte/ **I** *adj* clumsy, awkward.
II *nm,f* clumsy oaf○.

empourprer: s'empourprer /ɑ̃puʀpʀe/ [1] *vpr* [*ciel*] to turn crimson; [*visage*] to flush (**de** with).

empreindre /ɑ̃pʀɛ̃dʀ/ [55] **I** *vtr* **1** (marquer) to imprint; **2** (remplir de) to imbue SOUT (**de** with).
II s'empreindre *vpr* to become marked (**de** by), to become imbued (**de** with); **empreint de tristesse** [*personnalité*] imbued with sadness; [*visage*] marked by sadness.

empreinte /ɑ̃pʀɛ̃t/ *nf* **1** (de pas) footprint; (d'animal) track; **2** (de milieu, culture) stamp, mark.
■ **~s digitales** fingerprints; **~s génétiques** genetic fingerprints.

empressé, ~e /ɑ̃pʀese/ *adj* **1** (marquant la hâte) [*soins*] prompt; **2** (prévenant) [*admirateur*] attentive.

empressement /ɑ̃pʀɛsmɑ̃/ *nm* **1** (hâte) eagerness (**à faire** to do); **avec ~** eagerly; **2** (prévenance) attentiveness; **manifester de l'~** to be attentive.

empresser: s'empresser /ɑ̃pʀese/ [1] *vpr* **s'~ de faire** to hasten to do; **s'~ autour** or **auprès de qn** to fuss over sb.

emprise /ɑ̃pʀiz/ *nf* hold, influence.

emprisonnement /ɑ̃pʀizɔnmɑ̃/ *nm* imprisonment; **peine d'~** prison sentence.
■ **~ cellulaire** solitary confinement.

emprisonner /ɑ̃pʀizɔne/ [1] *vtr* **1** (mettre en prison) to imprison (**à, dans** in); FIG **être emprisonné dans** to be the prisoner of; **2** (retenir) to keep [sb] prisoner (**à, dans** in); **3** (enfermer) to clasp [*personne, main*].

emprunt /ɑ̃pʀœ̃/ *nm* **1** (somme) loan; **faire un ~ to** take out a loan; **un ~ à 10% sur 15 ans** a loan at 10% (repayable) over 15 years; **un ~ d'État** a public loan; **2** (action) borrowing; **financé par l'~** financed by borrowing; **d'~** [*voiture, nom*] borrowed; **3** (objet) loan; **un ~ fait à un musée** a loan from a museum; **4** (d'idée, de style, mot) borrowing.

emprunté, ~e /ɑ̃pʀœ̃te/ *adj* (embarrassé) awkward.

emprunter /ɑ̃pʀœ̃te/ [1] **I** *vtr* **1** to borrow [*argent, objet, idée*] (**à qn** from sb); **2** (imiter) to imitate [*voix, manière*]; **3** (prendre) to take [*route, métro*].

emprunteur, -euse /ɑ̃pʀœ̃tœʀ, øz/ **I** *adj* [*organisme*] borrowing the money (*après n*).
II *nm,f* borrower.

empuantir /ɑ̃pɥɑ̃tiʀ/ [3] *vtr* to stink out GB, to stink up US.

ému, ~e /emy/ **I** *pp* ▸ **émouvoir**.
II *pp adj* (attendri) moved; (reconnaissant) touched; (intimidé) nervous.
III *adj* [*paroles, regard*] full of emotion (*après n*); [*souvenir*] fond; **d'une voix ~e** with a catch in his/her voice.

en

Généralités

en, préposition et pronom, est présenté ici dans ses grandes lignes. Les expressions courantes du genre *en vitrine, être en colère, ne pas s'en faire, s'en aller* sont traitées respectivement dans les articles **vitrine, colère, faire, aller**; de même on trouvera les expressions avec *il y en a* sous **avoir** et les expressions avec *en être à* sous **être**.

Pour les traductions de *en*, préposition, associée à des noms de couleurs, pays, régions, et de *en*, pronom, quand il sert à exprimer des quantités, on consultera aussi les notes d'usage pertinentes. Voir la liste ▶ **1420**.

La préposition
en + gérondif

La traduction sera différente selon les nuances exprimées.

La simultanéité

L'action est brève
en ouvrant la porte, je me suis souvenue que
= as I opened the door, I remembered that
je l'ai croisé en sortant
= I met him as I was leaving

L'action dure
prends un café en attendant
= have a cup of coffee while you're waiting
elle travaille en chantant
= she sings while she works
il sifflait en lavant sa voiture
= he was whistling while he was cleaning his car

L'antériorité

en arrivant chez moi, je leur ai téléphoné
= when I got (*ou* on getting) back home,
I telephoned them
en la voyant, il rougit
= when he saw (*ou* on seeing) her, he blushed

Le déroulement d'une action 'cadre'

en faisant les courses, peux-tu acheter le journal?
= while you're doing the shopping, can you buy the paper?
en rangeant, j'ai retrouvé la lettre
= while (*ou* as) I was tidying up, I found the letter

La manière

il n'y a pas de traduction systématique:
l'enfant se réveilla en hurlant
= the child woke up screaming
il marchait en bombant le torse
= he was walking with his chest stuck out

Avec les verbes de mouvement, on optera pour un verbe suivi d'une postposition:
partir/entrer/monter/descendre en courant
= to run off/in/up/down

Le moyen

je m'en suis sorti en racontant un mensonge
= I got out of it by telling a lie
ouvrez cette caisse en soulevant le couvercle
= open this box by lifting the lid
endormir un enfant en lui chantant une berceuse
= to sing a child to sleep with a lullaby

Une explication

Dans ce cas, la traduction dépendra de la construction générée par ce qui précède:
elle a fait une erreur en acceptant ce poste
= she made a mistake in accepting the job
il a gâché sa vie en l'épousant
= he ruined his life by marrying her
il mentait en disant que c'était moi
= he was lying when he said it was me

La cause

la cause donnera lieu également à des traductions variées:
il s'est tordu le pied en tombant
= he twisted his foot when (*ou* as) he fell
il s'est étranglé en avalant
= he choked on his food
elle s'est enrouée en chantant
= she made herself hoarse with singing

La condition

tu aurais moins chaud en enlevant ta veste
= you'd be cooler (*ou* less hot)
if you took your jacket off
en prenant des vitamines, tu serais plus en forme
= if you took vitamins you'd feel fitter

Le pronom
en = de lui/d'elle/d'eux/d'elles

en représente un être humain ou un animal familier:
j'en suis content
= I am pleased with him/her/them
ils aiment leurs enfants et ils en sont aimés
= they love their children and they are loved by them
j'en suis fier (de mes enfants)
= I'm proud of them
je connais un bon coiffeur, je t'en donnerai l'adresse
= I know a good hairdresser, I'll give you his (*ou* the) address

en représente un animal, un concept, un objet:
j'en suis content = I am pleased with it/them
je m'en souviens = I remember it
deux ans après, on en parlait encore
= two years later, we were still talking about it
nous en sommes très peinés
= we're very upset about it
j'en suis fier = I'm proud of it
regarde cette robe, j'en aime beaucoup la forme
= look at that dress, I like its shape (*ou* the shape of it) a lot

Mais attention, le nom ne se traduit pas toujours littéralement en anglais:
j'ai reçu la facture de téléphone;
ça t'intéresserait d'en connaître le montant?
= I got the phone bill; would you like to know how much it was for?

Les locutions telles que *en voilà, de … en, en sorte que, en tant que* sont traitées sous **voilà, de, sorte, tant** etc.

en représente le lieu d'où l'on vient:
'tu as été voir ta mère?' 'oui, j'en viens'
= 'have you been to see your mother?'
'yes, I've just come from there'
il entra dans le café comme j'en sortais
= he entered the café as I was coming out

Expression de quantité

en, pronom, peut remplacer des noms dénombrables ou non-dénombrables:
'veux-tu des oranges?' = 'would you like some
'oui, j'en veux'   oranges?' 'yes, I'd like some'
'non, je n'en veux pas'   'no, I don't want any'
'veux-tu du vin?' = 'would you like some wine?'
'oui, j'en veux'   'yes, I'd like some'
'non, je n'en veux pas'   'no, I don't want any'
il en reste encore
(*des oranges*) = there are some left
(*du vin*) = there is some left
il n'en reste pas beaucoup
(*des oranges*) = there aren't many (of them) left
(*du vin*) = there isn't much (of it) left
il n'en reste plus
(*des oranges*) = there aren't any left
(*du vin*) = there isn't any left
prends-en plusieurs = take several *ou* take a few
prends-en un peu = take some
tu as emporté des livres?
= have you brought any books?
oui, j'en ai un passionnant
= yes, I've got one which is really good
oui, j'en ai deux = yes, I've got two
oui, j'en ai même trop = yes, too many in fact
il n'en a pas lu la moitié
(*du roman*) = he didn't even read half of it
(*des articles*) = he didn't even read half of them

émule /emyl/ *nmf* imitator; **être l'~ de qn** to model oneself on sb.

émuler /emyle/ [1] *vtr* ORDINAT to emulate.

émulsifiant, **~e** /emylsifjɑ̃, ɑ̃t/ **I** *adj* emulsifying. **II** *nm* emulsifier.

émulsion /emylsjɔ̃/ *nf* emulsion.

en /ɑ̃/ **I** *prép* **1** (lieu) (où l'on est) in; (où l'on va) to; (mouvement vers l'intérieur) into; **vivre ~ France/ville** to live in France/town; **aller ~ Allemagne** to go to Germany; **monter ~ voiture** to get into a car; **aller ~ ville** to go into town; **se promener ~ ville** to stroll around town; **2** (temps) (époque) in; (moment déterminé) in; (en l'espace de) in; **~ hiver/1991** in winter/1991; **~ semaine** during the week; **3** (moyens de transport) by; **voyager ~ train/voiture** to travel by train ou rail/car; **aller à Nice ~ avion/voiture** to fly/to drive to Nice; **descendre la rivière ~ canoë** to row down the river; **4** (manière, état) **elle était tout ~ vert** she was all in green; **il est toujours ~ manteau** he always wears a coat; **un ouvrage ~ vers/français/trois volumes** a work in verse/French/three volumes; **5** (comme) (en qualité de) as; (de la même manière que) like; **je vous parle ~ ami** I'm speaking (to you) as a friend; **agir ~ traître** to act like a traitor; **6** (transformation) into; **ils se séparèrent ~ plusieurs groupes** they broke up into several groups; **traduire ~ anglais** to translate into English; **changer des francs ~ dollars** to change francs into dollars; **7** (matière) made of; **c'est ~ quoi?** what is it made of?; **c'est ~ or** it's (made of) gold; **8** (pour indiquer une variante) **le même ~ plus grand** the same only bigger; **la même ~ bleu** the same in blue; **9** (indique le domaine, la discipline) in; **~ politique/affaires** in politics/business; **~ théorie** in theory; **licencié ~ droit** bachelor of law; **docteur ~ médecine** doctor of medicine; **être bon ~ histoire** to be good at history; **10** (mesures, dimensions) in; **compter ~ secondes** to count in seconds; **les draps se font ~ 90 et ~ 140** the sheets are available in single and double; **~ profondeur/hauteur, il y a assez d'espace** the space is deep/high enough; **~ largeur/longueur, il y a la place** widthwise/lengthwise, there's (enough) room.
II *pron* **1** (le moyen) **si les abricots sont abîmés, fais-~ de la confiture** if the apricots are bruised make jam with them; **prends cette couverture et couvre-t'~** take this blanket and cover yourself with it; **2** (la cause) **ça l'a tellement bouleversé qu'il ~ est tombé malade** it distressed him so much that he fell ill GB ou became sick US; **il a eu un cancer et il ~ est mort** he got cancer and died; **3**○ (emphatique) **tu ~ as un beau chapeau!** what a nice hat you've got!; **on s'~ souviendra de ce dimanche** we won't forget this Sunday in a hurry!; **et moi, je n'~ ai pas des soucis, peut-être?** do you think I haven't got worries too?; **j'~ connais qui seraient contents** I know some who would be pleased.

EN /ɛn/ *nf* **1** *abbr* ▶ **école**; **2** *abbr* ▶ **éducation**.

ENA /ena/ *nf: abbr* ▶ **école**.

enamourer: **s'enamourer** /ɑ̃namuʀe/ [1] *vpr* **s'~ de** to become enamoured^GB of LITTÉR.

énarque /enaʀk/ *nmf* graduate of the ENA.

en-avant /ɑ̃navɑ̃/ *nm inv* (au rugby) knock-on.

encablure /ɑ̃kablyʀ/ *nf* **à quelques ~s de là** a few hundred yards away.

encadré /ɑ̃kadʀe/ *nm* (dans un journal) box; **~ publicitaire** display ad.

encadrement /ɑ̃kadʀəmɑ̃/ *nm* **1** (supervision) supervision; **2** (personnel de supervision) supervisory staff; (cadres) managerial staff; MIL (officiers) officers (*pl*); **3** MIL (de tir) straddling; **4** ÉCON control; **5** ART (mise en cadre) framing; (cadre) frame; (tableau) framed picture; **6** ARCHIT frame.

encadrer /ɑ̃kadʀe/ [1] *vtr* **1** (superviser) to supervise [*personnel*]; to train [*soldat*]; **2** (entourer) to flank [*personne*]; to frame [*visage, fenêtre*]; to surround [*vallée*]; **~ de rouge** to outline [sth] in red; **3** (contrôler) to

restrict [*crédit*]; to control [*prix*]; **4** ART to frame [*tableau*]; **être à ~**○ HUM to be priceless○.

encadreur /ɑ̃kadʀœʀ/ ▶ **374** | *nm* picture framer.

encaissé, **~e** /ɑ̃kese/ *adj* [*vallée, rivière*] steep-sided; [*chemin*] cut deep into the hillside (*après n*).

encaissement /ɑ̃kesmɑ̃/ *nm* **1** (de cotisation) collection; (de chèque) cashing; (de dividende) receipt; **frais d'~** transaction costs; **2** GÉOG steeply sided setting.

encaisser /ɑ̃kese/ [1] **I** *vtr* **1** to cash [*somme, chèque*]; **2**○ (coup, défaite) **je ne peux pas ~ ton frère** I can't stand your brother.
II○ *vi* (résister) to take it; **il sait** ~ he can take it.
IDIOMES **~ le coup**○ to take it all in one's stride.

encaisseur, **-euse** /ɑ̃kesœʀ/ ▶ **374** | *nm,f* collector.

encanailler: **s'encanailler** /ɑ̃kanaje/ [1] *vpr* [*personne*] to slum it; [*style, ton*] to become vulgar.

encart /ɑ̃kaʀ/ *nm* insert.
■ **~ publicitaire** promotional insert.

en-cas /ɑ̃kɑ/ *nm inv* snack.

encastrable /ɑ̃kastʀabl/ *adj* [*four*] that can be built in (*épith, après n*); [*lavabo*] that can be fitted GB ou fit US (*épith, après n*).

encastrer /ɑ̃kastʀe/ [1] **I** *vtr* to build in [*four, réfrigérateur*]; to fit [*table de cuisson, lavabo*]; (en retrait) to recess; (dans le sol) to sink; **four encastré** built-in oven; **baignoire encastrée** (**dans le sol**) sunken bath.
II s'encastrer *vpr* [*élément*] to fit (**dans** into); **la voiture est venue s'~ sous le camion** the car crashed into the truck ou lorry GB and got jammed underneath it.

encaustique /ɑ̃kɔstik/ *nf* **1** (cire) wax polish; **passer à l'~** to wax; **2** ART (procédé) encaustic painting.

enceinte /ɑ̃sɛ̃t/ **I** *adj f* [*femme*] pregnant; **être ~ de trois mois** to be three months pregnant; **être ~ de jumeaux** to be pregnant with twins; **vêtements pour femmes ~s** maternity clothes.
II *nf* **1** (mur) surrounding wall; **~ de fossés/haies** surrounding ditches/hedges; **2** (espace) (de prison, palais, d'aéroport) compound; (de tribunal, d'église) interior; (dans une cérémonie, fête) enclosure.

encens /ɑ̃sɑ̃/ *nm inv* incense ¢.

encenser /ɑ̃sɑ̃se/ [1] *vtr* **1** RELIG to cense; **2** (flatter) to sing the praises of [*personne*]; to acclaim [*œuvre*].

encensoir /ɑ̃sɑ̃swaʀ/ *nm* censer.
IDIOMES **savoir manier l'~** to be good at flattery.

encéphale /ɑ̃sefal/ *nm* encephalon.

encéphalite /ɑ̃sefalit/ ▶ **196** | *nf* MÉD encephalitis.

encéphalopathie /ɑ̃sefalɔpati/ *nf* encephalopathy; **~ spongiforme bovine, ESB** Bovine Spongiform Encephalopathy.

encerclement /ɑ̃sɛʀkləmɑ̃/ *nm* surrounding, encirclement.

encercler /ɑ̃sɛʀkle/ [1] *vtr* **1** MIL to surround, to encircle; **2** (avec un trait) to circle.

enchaînement /ɑ̃ʃɛnmɑ̃/ *nm* **1** (d'événements liés entre eux) chain; **2** (suite) sequence; **~ de réponses** sequence of answers; **3** (coordination) coordination (**entre** between); **4** MUS, SPORT transition.

enchaîner /ɑ̃ʃene/ [1] **I** *vtr* **1** to chain up [*personne, animal*]; **~ à** to chain to; **2** to put [sth] together [*idées, mots*]; **3** to enslave [*humanité, peuple*]; to shackle [*presse*].
II *vi* (poursuivre) to go on; **~ sur l'économie** to move on to the economy.
III s'enchaîner *vpr* **1** [*personne*] to chain oneself (**à** to); **2** [*plans, séquences*] to follow on.

enchantement /ɑ̃ʃɑ̃tmɑ̃/ *nm* **1** (expérience agréable) delight; **2** (sortilège) enchantment, spell; **comme par ~** as if by magic.

enchanter /ɑ̃ʃɑ̃te/ [1] *vtr* **1** (faire plaisir à) **l'idée de te voir m'enchante** I'm delighted at the thought of seeing you; **ça ne m'enchante guère** it doesn't exactly thrill me; **enchanté (de faire votre connaissance)!** how do you do!; **2** (ensorceler) to enchant.

encore

Lorsqu'il signifie *toujours*, *encore* se traduit généralement par *still* dans une phrase affirmative ou interrogative:

il était encore étudiant

quand il s'est marié = he was still a student when he got married

habite-t-elle encore ici? = does she still live here?

pas encore se traduit par *not yet*:

elle n'était pas encore mariée quand elle a eu son premier bébé = she wasn't yet married when she had her first baby *ou* she was still unmarried when she had her first baby

il n'est pas encore rentré = he hasn't come home yet *ou* he still hasn't come home

Dans ce dernier cas, *still* marque l'étonnement ou l'exaspération, alors que *yet* indique un énoncé neutre des faits.

Des exceptions aux traductions fournies ci-dessus et les autres sens de *encore* sont traités dans l'entrée.

enchanteur, -eresse /ɑ̃ʃɑ̃tœʀ, tʀɛs/ **I** *adj* enchanting.

II *nm,f* **1** (magicien) enchanter/enchantress; **2** FIG charmer.

enchâsser /ɑ̃ʃase/ [1] *vtr* **1** to enshrine [*reliques*]; to set [*pierre précieuse*]; **2** LING to embed.

enchère /ɑ̃ʃɛʀ/ **I** *nf* (offre) bid; (activité) bidding; **faire une** ~ to bid, to make a bid.

II enchères *nfpl* **vente aux** ~**s** auction.

enchérir /ɑ̃ʃeʀiʀ/ [3] *vi* COMM, JEUX to bid; ~ **sur qn** to bid more than sb; ~ **sur une offre** to make a higher bid.

enchevêtrement /ɑ̃ʃ(ə)vɛtʀəmɑ̃/ *nm* (de fils, branches) tangle; (de couloirs, ruelles) labyrinth; (d'idées) muddle.

enchevêtrer /ɑ̃ʃ(ə)vetʀe/ [1] **I** *vtr* **1** LIT to tangle [sth] up [*fils*]; **2** FIG **être enchevêtré** [*phrase, intrigue*] to be muddled; [*problème, affaire*] to be complicated.

II s'enchevêtrer *vpr* **1** [*branches, fils*] to get tangled; **2** [*phrases, idées*] to become muddled; **3** [*personne*] **s'~ dans** to get tangled up in.

enclave /ɑ̃klav/ *nf* LIT, FIG enclave.

enclavement /ɑ̃klavmɑ̃/ *nm* (situation) enclosure; (processus) enclosing **℄**.

enclaver /ɑ̃klave/ [1] *vtr* to hem in [*terrain*]; **un pays enclavé** a landlocked country.

enclenchement /ɑ̃klɑ̃ʃmɑ̃/ *nm* (de mécanisme) engagement.

enclencher /ɑ̃klɑ̃ʃe/ [1] **I** *vtr* **1** FIG to launch, to set [sth] in motion [*processus*]; **2** LIT to set [*minuterie*]; to engage [*mécanisme*].

II s'enclencher *vpr* **1** FIG [*processus, cycle*] to get under way; **2** LIT [*mécanisme*] to engage.

enclin, ~e /ɑ̃klɛ̃, in/ *adj* inclined (**à** to; **à faire** to do).

enclos /ɑ̃klo/ *nm inv* GÉN enclosure; (pour animaux) pen.

enclume /ɑ̃klym/ *nf* ANAT, TECH anvil.

IDIOMES **être entre l'~ et le marteau** to be between the devil and the deep blue sea.

encoche /ɑ̃kɔʃ/ *nf* (entaille) notch.

encoder /ɑ̃kɔde/ [1] *vtr* to encode.

encodeur /ɑ̃kɔdœʀ/ *nm* ORDINAT encoder.

encoignure /ɑ̃kwaɲʀ/ *nf* **1** (angle) corner; **2** (placard) corner cupboard; (étagères) set of corner shelves.

encoller /ɑ̃kɔle/ [1] *vtr* to paste [*papier peint*].

encolure /ɑ̃kɔlyʀ/ *nf* **1** ▶**581**| (de vêtement) (partie échancrée) neckline; (dimension) collar size; **2** (d'animal) neck.

encombrant, ~e /ɑ̃kɔ̃bʀɑ̃, ɑ̃t/ *adj* **1** [*meuble*] bulky; [*paquet, valise*] cumbersome; **2** [*personne, affaire*] troublesome.

encombre: sans encombre /sɑ̃zɑ̃kɔ̃bʀ/ *loc adv* without a hitch.

encombré, ~e /ɑ̃kɔ̃bʀe/ *adj* [*route, ciel*] congested (**de** with); [*pièce, meuble*] cluttered (**de** with); [*conduit*] obstructed; [*lignes téléphoniques*] blocked; [*standard*] jammed; [*marché*] saturated (**de** with); [*profession*] overcrowded.

encombrement /ɑ̃kɔ̃bʀəmɑ̃/ *nm* **1** (de la circulation) (ralentissement) traffic congestion **℄**; (embouteillage) traffic jam; **2** (de standard, fréquences) jamming; **3** (de passage) obstruction; **4** (de pièce) cluttering; (des tribunaux) congestion; **5** (de profession) overcrowding; (de marché) saturation; **6** (volume) bulk; **d'un ~ réduit** compact.

encombrer /ɑ̃kɔ̃bʀe/ [1] **I** *vtr* to clutter up [*pièce, mémoire, esprit*]; (obstruer) to obstruct [*route, passage*]; TÉLÉCOM to block [*lignes*]; to overcrowd [*profession*]; to saturate [*marché*].

II s'encombrer *vpr* **s'~ de** LIT, FIG to burden oneself with; **s'~ l'esprit** to clutter up one's mind.

encontre: à l'encontre de /alɑ̃kɔ̃tʀədə/ *loc prép* **1** (contrairement à) contrary to; **2** (en opposition à) counter to; **3** (activement contre) against; **aller à l'~ de la politique gouvernementale** to go against government policy; **4** (envers) toward(s).

encorbellement /ɑ̃kɔʀbɛlmɑ̃/ *nm* (de fenêtre) corbel.

encorder: s'encorder /ɑ̃kɔʀde/ [1] *vpr* to rope up.

encore /ɑ̃kɔʀ/ **I** *adv* **1** (toujours) still; **je m'en souviens ~** I still remember; **il n'est ~ que midi** it's only midday; **tu en es ~ là?** FIG haven't you got GB *ou* gotten US beyond that by now?; **qu'il soit impoli passe ~, mais…** the fact that he's rude is one thing, but…; **~ heureux** *or* **une chance que je m'en sois aperçu** it's lucky that I realized; **2** (toujours pas) **pas ~** not yet; **tu n'as ~ rien vu** you haven't seen anything yet; **cela ne s'est ~ jamais vu/fait** it has never been seen/done before; **les abricots ne sont pas ~ assez mûrs** the apricots aren't ripe enough yet; **3** (de nouveau) again; **les prix ont ~ augmenté** prices have gone up again; **~ toi!** you again!; **~!** (à un spectacle) more!; **~ une fois** once more; **qu'est-ce que j'ai ~ fait?** what have I done now?; **elle s'est ~ acheté une nouvelle robe** she has bought herself yet another new dress; **4** (davantage) more; **j'en veux ~** I want some more; **tu devrais ~ raccourcir ta robe** you should take your dress up a little more; **cela va ~ aggraver les choses** it's going to make things even worse; **c'est ~ mieux/moins** it's even better/ less; **5** (en plus) **~ un gâteau?** another cake?; **pendant ~ trois jours** for another three days; **il me reste ~ 500 francs** I've still got 500 francs left; **que dois-je prendre ~?** what else shall I take?; **qu'est-ce qu'il te faut ~?** FIG what more do you need *ou* want?; **et puis quoi ~?** what next?!; **que dire ~?** what else can be said?; **ou ~** or else; **6** (toutefois) **il ne suffit pas d'avoir de bonnes idées, ~ faut-il savoir les exprimer** it's not enough to have good ideas, one must be able to articulate them; **~ faut-il qu'elle accepte** but she still has to accept; **si ~ il était généreux!** if he were at least generous!; **7** (seulement) only, just; **il y a ~ trois mois** only *ou* just three months ago.

II et encore *loc adv* if that.

III encore que *loc conj* (bien que) even though.

encoubler /ɑ̃kuble/ [1] **I** *vtr* (gêner) **tu m'encoubles** you're getting under my feet.

II s'encoubler *vpr* (se prendre les pieds) **s'~ dans qch** to catch one's feet in sth.

encourageant, ~e /ɑ̃kuʀaʒɑ̃, ɑ̃t/ *adj* encouraging.

encouragement /ɑ̃kuʀaʒmɑ̃/ *nm* encouragement **℄**.

encourager /ɑ̃kuʀaʒe/ [13] *vtr* **1** (pousser) to encourage (**à faire** to do); **2** (de la voix) to cheer [sb] on [*équipe, sportif*].

encourir /ɑ̃kuʀiʀ/ [26] *vtr* to incur.

encrasser /ɑ̃kʀase/ [1] **I** *vtr* **1** (obstruer) to clog [sth] (up) [*filtre, moteur, artère*]; to make [sth] sooty [*cheminée*]; **2** (salir) to dirty; AUT to foul up [*bougies*].

II s'encrasser *vpr* **1** (s'obstruer) to clog up; [*cheminée*] to get sooty; **2** (se salir) to get dirty; [*bougie*] to foul up.

encre /ɑ̃kʀ/ *nf* ink; **~ d'imprimerie** printer's ink.

■ **~ de Chine** Indian GB *ou* India US ink; **~ sympathique** invisible ink.

IDIOMES **cela a fait couler beaucoup d'~** a lot of ink has been spilled over this; **se faire un sang d'~** to be worried stiff.

encrer /ɑ̃kʀe/ [1] *vtr* to ink.

encrier /ɑ̃kʀije/ *nm* (encastré) inkwell; (pot) ink pot.

encroûter○: **s'encroûter** /ɑ̃kʀute/ [1] *vpr* [*personne*] to get in a rut; **il est complètement encroûté dans ses habitudes** he's very set in his ways.

encyclopédie /ɑ̃siklɔpedi/ *nf* encyclopedia.

endémique /ɑ̃demik/ *adj* endemic.

endetté, **~e** /ɑ̃dete/ *adj* in debt (*jamais épith*); **très ~** heavily in debt.

endettement /ɑ̃dɛtmɑ̃/ *nm* debt; **~ public/extérieur** national/foreign debt.

endetter /ɑ̃dete/ [1] **I** *vtr* to put [sb] into debt.
II s'endetter *vpr* to get into debt (**auprès de** with).

endeuiller /ɑ̃dœje/ [1] *vtr* to plunge [sb] into mourning [*famille*]; to cast a shadow over [*cérémonie, réunion sportive*]; **pays endeuillé** griefstricken country.

endiablé, **~e** /ɑ̃djable/ *adj* [*rythme*] (très vif) furious; [*enfant*] boisterous.

endiguer /ɑ̃dige/ [1] *vtr* to confine [*cours d'eau*]; to contain [*manifestants, groupe*]; to curb [*spéculation, mécontentement*].

endimanché, **~e** /ɑ̃dimɑ̃ʃe/ *adj* in one's Sunday best (*après n*).

endive /ɑ̃div/ *nf* chicory ⊄ GB, endive US.

endocrine /ɑ̃dɔkʀin/ *adj* endocrine.

endoctrinement /ɑ̃dɔktʀinmɑ̃/ *nm* indoctrination.

endoctriner /ɑ̃dɔktʀine/ [1] *vtr* to indoctrinate.

endolori, **~e** /ɑ̃dɔlɔʀi/ *adj* aching.

endommagement /ɑ̃dɔmaʒmɑ̃/ *nm* (action) damaging; (résultat) damage.

endommager /ɑ̃dɔmaʒe/ [13] *vtr* to damage.

endormant, **~e** /ɑ̃dɔʀmɑ̃, ɑ̃t/ *adj* [*travail, film*] mind-numbing.

endormi, **~e** /ɑ̃dɔʀmi/ *adj* **1** [*personne, animal*] sleeping (*épith*), asleep (*jamais épith*); **2** FIG [*village, yeux, cerveau, élève*] sleepy; [*économie, marché*] sluggish; [*public*] lethargic.

endormir /ɑ̃dɔʀmiʀ/ [30] **I** *vtr* **1** (naturellement) [*personne*] to send [sb] to sleep [*enfant*]; (chimiquement) [*personne, substance*] to put [sb] to sleep [*patient*]; **2** (donner envie de dormir) [*personne, discours*] to send [sb] to sleep [*personne*] (**avec** with); **3** (tromper) to dupe [*personne, opinion, ennemi*] (**avec** with); **4** (atténuer) to lessen [*vigilance*]; to allay [*soupçon*]; to numb [*faculté*].
II s'endormir *vpr* **1** (s'assoupir) to fall asleep; (trouver le sommeil) to get to sleep; **2** (se laisser aller) to sit back; **3** (décéder) FML to pass away.

endoscopie /ɑ̃dɔskɔpi/ *nf* endoscopy.

endossable /ɑ̃dosabl/ *adj* [*chèque*] endorsable.

endossement /ɑ̃dosmɑ̃/ *nm* FIN endorsement.

endosser /ɑ̃dose/ [1] *vtr* **1** (mettre) to put on; **2** (assumer) to take on [*responsabilité, rôle*]; to shoulder [*conséquence*]; **3** FIN to endorse [*chèque*]; **4** (en reliure) to back [*livre*].

endroit /ɑ̃dʀwa/ **I** *nm* **1** (lieu) place; **par ~s** in places; **à quel ~?** where?; **2** (de tissu, pull) right side.
II à l'endroit de *loc prep* toward(s).

enduire /ɑ̃dɥiʀ/ [69] **I** *vtr* to coat (**de** with).
II s'enduire *vpr* **s'~ de** to put [sth] on.

enduit /ɑ̃dɥi/ *nm* (pour couvrir) coating; (pour boucher) filler.

endurance /ɑ̃dyʀɑ̃s/ *nf* **1** (de personne) stamina; **2** (de véhicule) endurance.

endurant, **~e** /ɑ̃dyʀɑ̃, ɑ̃t/ *adj* [*personne*] tough, with stamina (*épith, après n*); [*moteur*] hard-wearing.

endurci, **~e** /ɑ̃dyʀsi/ *adj* **1** (dur) tough; **2** (invétéré) [*célibataire*] confirmed; [*criminel*] hardened.

endurcir /ɑ̃dyʀsiʀ/ [3] **I** *vtr* **1** (rendre plus robuste) [*travail, sport*] to strengthen [*corps, caractère*]; **~ qn contre** to build up sb's resistance to; **2** (rendre insensible) [*épreuve, égoïsme*] to harden.

II s'endurcir *vpr* **1** (devenir plus robuste) to become stronger; **2** (devenir insensible) to become hardened.

endurer /ɑ̃dyʀe/ [1] *vtr* **1** (supporter physiquement) to endure; **faire ~ qch à qn** to put sb through sth; **2** (tolérer) to put up with.

énergétique /enɛʀʒetik/ *adj* **1** ÉCON energy (*épith*); **besoins ~s** energy requirements; **2** [*aliment, produit*] high-calorie (*épith*); **aliment peu ~** low-calorie food; **3** PHYS energy; **bilan ~** energetics (+ *v sg*).

énergie /enɛʀʒi/ *nf* **1** ÉCON energy; **faire des économies d'~** to save energy; **2** PHYS energy; **tech** energy, power; **~ nucléaire** nuclear power ou energy; **~ éolienne** windpower; **3** (force) energy; **dépenser son ~ à faire** to use up one's energy doing; **avec l'~ du désespoir** driven on by despair; **avec ~** [*travailler*] energetically; [*agir*] forcefully; [*protester*] strongly.

énergique /enɛʀʒik/ *adj* **1** (physiquement) [*personne*] energetic; [*poignée de main*] vigorous; [*visage*] resolute; **2** FIG [*action*] tough; [*objection*] strong; [*refus*] firm; [*intervention, tentative*] forceful.

énergisant, **~e** /enɛʀʒizɑ̃, ɑ̃t/ **I** *adj* [*médicament, effet, activité*] energizing; **boisson ~e** energy drink.
II *nm* (stimulant) stimulant.

énergumène /enɛʀgymɛn/ *nmf* (personne exaltée) oddball.

énervant, **~e** /enɛʀvɑ̃, ɑ̃t/ *adj* irritating.

énervé, **~e** /enɛʀve/ *adj* **1** (irrité) irritated; **2** (agité) nervous; [*enfant*] overexcited.

énervement /enɛʀvəmɑ̃/ *nm* **1** (irritation) irritation; **2** (agitation) agitation; **elle pleura d'~** she was so on edge that she cried.

énerver /enɛʀve/ [1] **I** *vtr* **1** (agiter) to put [sb] on edge; **2** (irriter) **~ qn** to get on sb's nerves, to irritate sb.
II s'énerver *vpr* to get worked up (**pour** over).

enfance /ɑ̃fɑ̃s/ *nf* **1** (période) childhood; (de garçon) boyhood; (de fille) girlhood; **la petite ~** early childhood; **2** (enfants) children (*pl*); **3** (début) dawn.
IDIOMES **retomber en ~** to lapse into second childhood; **c'est l'~ de l'art** it's child's play.

enfant /ɑ̃fɑ̃/ *nmf* **1** (jeune être humain) child; (très jeune) infant; **c'est une ~ terrible** LIT she's an unruly child; **l'~ terrible du cinéma français** the enfant terrible of French cinema; **mes rêves d'~** my childhood dreams; **elle est restée très ~** she is still very childlike; ▶**vérité**; **2** (fils, fille) child; **être ~ unique** to be an only child; **couple sans ~** childless couple; **faire un ~** ○ (avoir) to have a child; **faire un ~ à qn** ○ to make sb pregnant; **ce roman, c'est son ~** that novel is his /her baby; **3** (terme d'affection) **mon ~** my child; **4** (marquant l'origine) child; **un ~ du peuple** a child of the people.
■ **~ de l'amour** love child; **~ de chœur** altar boy; **ce n'est pas un ~ de chœur** FIG he's no angel.

enfantement /ɑ̃fɑ̃tmɑ̃/ *nm* LIT childbirth; FIG giving birth (**de** to).

enfanter /ɑ̃fɑ̃te/ [1] *vtr* LIT, FIG to give birth to.

enfantillage /ɑ̃fɑ̃tijaʒ/ *nm* **1** (caprice) **cesse tes ~s!** stop being childish!; **2** (défaut) childishness.

enfantin, **~e** /ɑ̃fɑ̃tɛ̃, in/ *adj* **1** (simple) simple, easy; **2** (d'un enfant) [*geste*] childish; **les émotions ~es** children's emotions; **3** (pour enfant) [*classe*] infant GB, for young children; **mode ~e** children's fashion; **4** (digne d'un enfant) childish PÉJ, childlike.

enfarger: s'enfarger /ɑ̃faʀʒe/ [13] *vpr* C (trébucher) **s'~ dans qch** to catch one's foot in sth; **s'~ dans sa phrase** to get one's words mixed up.

enfariné, **~e** /ɑ̃faʀine/ *adj* **1** (saupoudré de farine) covered with flour; **2** (poudré) [*visage*] powdered.

enfer /ɑ̃fɛʀ/ *nm* **1** RELIG Hell; MYTHOL **les ~s** Hell (*sg*), the Underworld (*sg*); **2** FIG hell (**de** of); **un ~ de souffrance** a living hell; **l'~ de la guerre** the hell of war; **vision d'~** vision of hell, hellish sight; **aller à un train d'~**○ to go hell for leather○; **soirée d'~**○ hell of a○ party.
IDIOMES **croix de bois croix de fer, si je mens je vais en ~** ≈ cross my heart and hope to die.

enfermer /ɑ̃fɛʀme/ [1] **I** *vtr* **1** (dans un lieu) to shut

[sth] in [*animal*]; (à clé) to lock [sth] up [*bijou*] (**dans** in); to lock [sb] up, to put [sb] away○ [*criminel, aliéné*] (**dans** in); **elle est bonne à ~**○ she's stark raving mad○; **2** (bloquer) **~ qn dans une situation** to trap sb in a situation; **3** (contenir) **~ une théorie en une seule formule** to encapsulate a theory in a single formula; **4** MIL, SPORT to box [sb] in [*adversaire*].

II s'enfermer *vpr* **1** GÉN to lock oneself in; (pour s'isoler) to shut oneself away; (accidentellement) to get locked in; **ne reste pas enfermé toute la journée!** don't stay cooped up indoors all day!; **ça fait deux heures qu'ils sont enfermés dans le bureau à discuter** they've been closeted in the study for two hours; **2** (se confiner) **s'~ dans** to retreat into; **s'~ dans le mutisme** to remain obstinately silent.

enferrer: **s'enferrer** /ɑ̃feʀe/ [1] *vpr* **1** FIG to tie oneself up in knots; **s'~ dans des mensonges/une déposition** to get tangled up in lies/a statement; **2** LIT to impale oneself (**sur, à** on).

enfiévré, **~e** /ɑ̃fjevʀe/ *adj* [*imagination*] fevered (*épith*); [*atmosphère*] feverish; [*discours*] fiery.

enfilade /ɑ̃filad/ *nf* **1** (de pièces) succession; (de maisons, tables) row; **maison en ~** interconnecting house GB, shotgun house US; **2** ARCHIT enfilade.

enfiler /ɑ̃file/ [1] **I** *vtr* **1** (mettre) to slip on; **2** to thread [*aiguille*]; **3** (entrer dans) to take [*rue*]; **4** (dire) PEJ to spout [*phrases*].

II s'enfiler *vpr* **1**○ (avaler) to guzzle down; FIG to devour; **2**○ (faire) to get landed○ with [*corvée*].

enfin /ɑ̃fɛ̃/ *adv* **1** (en dernier lieu) (dans un développement, un discours) finally; (dans une énumération) lastly; **~ et surtout** last but not least; **2** (marquant le soulagement) at last; **~ seuls!** alone at last!; **3** (marquant la résignation) (oh) well; **~, puisque tu y tiens** oh well, as you insist; **4** (marquant l'impatience) for heaven's sake; **mais ~, cessez de vous disputer!** for heaven's sake, stop arguing!; **5** (en d'autres termes) in short, in other words; **6** (introduit un correctif) well, at least; **il pleut tous les jours, ~ presque** it rains every day, well almost; **7** (tout bien considéré) **car ~** after all; **8** (marquant la perplexité) (mais) **~, que signifie toute cette histoire?** what on earth does it all mean?

enflammé, **~e** /ɑ̃flame/ *adj* **1** LIT burning; **2** FIG [*personne, déclaration*] passionate; [*discours*] impassioned, fiery; **3** MÉD [*gorge, blessure*] inflamed; **4** (rouge) [*joues, visage*] burning (**de** with); [*ciel*] ablaze (*jamais épith*), blazing.

enflammer /ɑ̃flame/ [1] **I** *vtr* **1** (mettre le feu à) to set fire to; **2** (exciter) to inflame [*opinion, esprit, cœur*]; to fire [*imagination*]; to fuel [*colère*].

II s'enflammer *vpr* **1** (prendre feu) [*maison, papier*] to go up in flames; [*essence, bois*] to catch fire; **2** (s'exciter) [*regard*] to blaze; [*imagination*] to be fired (**de** with; **à la vue de** by); [*pays, peuple*] to explode; **s'~ pour qn** to become passionate about sb.

enflé, **~e** /ɑ̃fle/ *adj* **1** LIT [*poignet*] swollen; **2** [*style*] bombastic.

enfler /ɑ̃fle/ [1] **I** *vtr* **1** FIG to exaggerate [*récit, événements*]; **~ la voix** to raise one's voice; **2** LIT to swell.

II *vi* LIT [*partie du corps*] to swell (up); [*rivière, mer*] to swell.

enflure /ɑ̃flyʀ/ *nf* MÉD swelling.

enfoncé, **~e** /ɑ̃fɔ̃se/ *adj* **1** (défoncé) [*siège*] sagging; **2** (rentré) [*yeux*] deep-set.

enfoncement /ɑ̃fɔ̃smɑ̃/ *nm* **1** (creux) (dans un mur) recess; (sur un terrain) dip; **2** MÉD crushing ⊄; **3** MIL (déroute) collapse; **4** (enlisement) **l'~ du pays dans la récession** the country's slide into recession.

enfoncer /ɑ̃fɔ̃se/ [12] **I** *vtr* **1** (faire entrer sans outil) to push in [*piquet, bouchon*]; (avec un outil) **~ un clou dans qch** to knock a nail into sth; **~ les mains dans ses poches** to dig one's hands into one's pockets; **~ son chapeau jusqu'aux yeux** to pull one's hat down over one's eyes; **~ son doigt** to stick one's finger (**dans** into); **2** (faire céder) to break down [*porte*]; to break through [*adversaire*]; (accidentellement) to crash through [*obstacle*]; to break [*cage thoracique*]; to smash in [*aile de voiture*]; **~ des portes ouvertes** FIG

to state the obvious; **3** (vaincre) to defeat [*armée*]; to beat [*concurrent*]; **4** (abaisser) **ne m'enfonce pas davantage** don't rub it in.

II *vi* (s'enliser) to sink.

III s'enfoncer *vpr* **1** (s'enliser) **s'~ dans la neige/le sable** to sink in the snow/the sand; **être enfoncé dans un fauteuil** (confortablement) to be settled cosily GB ou cozily US in an armchair; **s'~ dans l'erreur** to make error after error; **2** (couler) **s'~ dans l'eau** to sink; **3** (pénétrer) **les piquets s'enfoncent facilement** the posts go in easily; **4** (se mettre) **s'~ une épine dans le doigt** to get a thorn in one's finger; **5** (aller) **s'~ dans la forêt** to go into the forest; **s '~ dans le brouillard** to disappear into the fog; **s'~ dans les ou à l'intérieur des terres** to go inland; **6** (se creuser) [*chaussée, terre*] to give way; **7**○ (aggraver son cas) to make things worse for oneself.

IDIOMES ~ qch dans le crâne○ or **la tête de qn** to get sth into sb's head.

enfouir /ɑ̃fwiʀ/ [3] **I** *vtr* **1** (enterrer) to bury; **2** (dissimuler) **~ son visage dans les coussins** to bury one's face in the cushions; **~ qch dans un sac** (sans soin) to shove sth into a bag; (avec soin) to tuck sth away in a bag.

II s'enfouir *vpr* (se blottir) **s'~ sous les couvertures** to burrow under the blankets; (s'enterrer) to bury oneself (**dans** in).

enfourcher /ɑ̃fuʀʃe/ [1] *vtr* to mount [*cheval*]; to get on [*moto*].

enfourner /ɑ̃fuʀne/ [1] *vtr* **1** (pour cuire) to put [sth] in the oven; **2**○ (manger) to stuff down; **3**○ (introduire) **~ qch dans** to stuff sth into.

enfreindre /ɑ̃fʀɛ̃dʀ/ [55] *vtr* to infringe, to break.

enfuir: **s'enfuir** /ɑ̃fɥiʀ/ [9] *vpr* **1** LIT to run away (**de** from); [*oiseau*] to fly away; (d'un lieu clos) to escape (**de** from); **s'~ à Paris** to run off to Paris; **s'~ vers la frontière** to make off toward(s) the border; **s'~ par les toits** to escape over the rooftops; **2** FIG [*temps*] to fly.

enfumer /ɑ̃fyme/ [1] *vtr* to fill [sth] with smoke.

engagé, **~e** /ɑ̃gaʒe/ **I** *adj* (politically) committed.

II *nm,f* enlisted man/woman.

engageant, **~e** /ɑ̃gaʒɑ̃, ɑ̃t/ *adj* [*personne, manières*] welcoming; [*offre*] attractive; [*plat, lieu*] inviting.

engagement /ɑ̃gaʒmɑ̃/ *nm* **1** (promesse) commitment; **prendre l'~ de faire** to undertake to do; **remplir ses ~s** to honour one's commitments; **sans ~ de votre part** with no obligation on your part; **2** (participation) involvement; **3** MIL (fait de s'engager, durée) enlistment; (combat) engagement; **4** (contrat) engagement.

■ **~ contractuel** contractual obligation; **~ volontaire** volunteering.

engager /ɑ̃gaʒe/ [13] **I** *vtr* **1** (recruter) to hire [*personnel*]; to enlist [*soldat*]; to engage [*artiste*]; **2** (commencer) to begin [*processus*]; **nous avons engagé la conversation** we struck up a conversation; **~ le combat** to go into combat; **~ la partie** (au football) to kick off; **~ une action judiciaire** to take legal action; **3** (obliger) to commit [*personne*]; **votre signature vous engage** your signature is binding; **4** (mettre en jeu) to stake [*réputation*]; **~ sa parole** to give one's word; **5** (introduire) **~ qch dans** to put sth in; **6** (amener) **~ une voiture dans une petite route** to take a car into a country road; **7** ÉCON to lay out [*capitaux*]; **~ des dépenses** to undertake expenditure; **8** **~ qn à faire** (exhorter) to urge sb to do; (conseiller) to advise sb to do; **9** SPORT **~ qn dans une compétition** to enter sb for a competition; **10** (donner en gage) to pawn [*objet précieux*].

II s'engager *vpr* **1** (promettre) to promise (**à faire** to do); **elle s'est engagée à fond** she is fully committed; **s'~ vis-à-vis de qn** to take on a commitment to sb; **2** (entreprendre) **s'~ dans un projet** to embark on a project; **s'~ dans la bataille** to go into action; **s'~ dans des dépenses** to incur expenses; **3** (s'impliquer) to get involved; **4** (p énétrer) **s'~ sur une route** to go into a road; **s'~ sur un pont** to go onto a bridge; **avant de s'~ dans un carrefour** before going across an intersection; **5** (être amorcé) [*action judiciaire, processus, négociations*] to begin; **6** (se faire recruter) to enlist; **s'~ dans l'armée/la police** to join the army/ the police; **s'~ dans une compétition** to enter a competition.

engelure /ãʒlyʀ/ *nf* chilblain (à on).

engendrer /ãʒãdʀe/ [1] *vtr* **1** (provoquer) to engender; **2** LING, MATH to generate; **3** (mettre au monde) FML [*femme*] to give birth to; [*homme*] to father.

engin /ãʒɛ̃/ *nm* **1** (machine, objet, instrument) device; **qu'est-ce que c'est que cet ~?** what's that contraption?; **2** (véhicule) vehicle; (machine) piece of equipment; **~s de levage** lifting equipment; **3** MIL (missile) missile; (bombe) device; (véhicule) vehicle.

englober /ãglɔbe/ [1] *vtr* to include.

engloutir /ãglutiʀ/ [3] *vtr* **1** (faire disparaître) [*mer, tempête, brouillard*] to engulf, to swallow up; **2**○ (dévorer) to gulp [sth] down; **3** (dépenser) to squander [*argent, somme*]; (coûter) to swallow up [*argent, somme*].

engloutissement /ãglutismã/ *nm* swallowing up.

engluer /ãglye/ [1] **I** *vtr* (pour attraper) to lime [*branche, oiseau*].
II s'engluer *vpr* **s'~ dans qch** to become bogged down in sth.

engoncé, ~e /ãgõse/ *adj* **il était ~ dans une veste trop étroite** he was squeezed into a tight jacket.

engorgement /ãgɔʀʒəmã/ *nm* (de canalisation) block- ing; (de route, d'organe) congestion.

engorger /ãgɔʀʒe/ [13] **I** *vtr* to block (up) [*canalisa- tion*]; to clog up [*routes*]; COMM to glut [*marché*]; MÉD to congest [*organe*].
II s'engorger *vpr* [*tuyau*] to be blocked (up).

engouement /ãgumã/ *nm* (pour une chose) passion (**pour** for); (pour une personne) infatuation (**pour** for).

engouer: s'engouer /ãgwe/ [1] *vpr* **s'~ de** to become infatuated with [*personne*]; to develop a passion for [*artiste, peinture, musique*].

engouffrer /ãgufʀe/ [1] **I** *vtr* **1**○ (manger) to gobble up; **2** (dépenser) to sink; (coûter) [*projet, affaire*] to swallow up; **3** (mettre) to stuff (**dans** into).
II s'engouffrer *vpr* **1** LIT (dans une pièce, un passage) [*personne, vent, eau*] to rush (**dans** in); (dans un taxi, le métro) to dive (**dans** into); **2** FIG **s'~ dans** (pour en profiter) to rush to take advantage of; (pour combler un vide) to rush into.

engourdi, ~e /ãguʀdi/ *adj* (ankylosé, transi) numb (**par, de** with); (somnolent) [*personne*] drowsy; FIG [*ville*] sleepy, drowsy; (hébété) [*cerveau*] dull(ed).

engourdir /ãguʀdiʀ/ [3] **I** *vtr* **1** (rendre gourd) to make [sb/sth] numb; **2** (endormir) to make [sb/sth] drowsy [*personne, esprit*]; to deaden [*douleur*]; **3** (hébéter) to dull.
II s'engourdir *vpr* [*membre*] to go numb, to go to sleep; [*corps*] to go numb; [*cerveau*] to grow dull.

engourdissement /ãguʀdismã/ *nm* **1** (état) (phy- sique) numbness; (mental) (torpeur) drowsiness; (affai- blissement) dullness; **2** (action) (du corps) numbing; (de l'esprit) dulling.

engrais /ãgʀɛ/ *nm inv* (animal) manure; (chimique) fertilizer.

engraissage /ãgʀɛsaʒ/ *nm*, **engraissement** /ãgʀɛsmã/ *nm* (de bétail) fattening.

engraisser /ãgʀɛse/ [1] **I** *vtr* **1** to fatten [*bétail*]; **2** to fertilize [*sol*]; **3**○ to make [sb] rich.
II *vi* (grossir) to get fat.
III s'engraisser○ *vpr* (s'enrichir) to grow fat○.

engranger /ãgʀãʒe/ [13] *vtr* LIT to gather in; FIG to store [*données*]; to store up [*souvenirs, argent*].

engrenage /ãgʀənaʒ/ *nm* **1** (mécanique) gears (*pl*); **2** FIG (de violence, difficultés) spiral; **être pris dans l'~ (de qch)** to get caught up in a spiral (of sth).

engueuler◗ /ãgœle/ [1] **I** *vtr* to tell [sb] off [*enfant*]; to give [sb] an earful○ [*adulte*].
II s'engueuler *vpr* to have a row (**avec qn** with sb).

enguirlander○ /ãgiʀlãde/ [1] **I** *vtr* to tell [sb] off

[*enfant*]; to give sb an earful○ [*adulte*]; **se faire ~** to get told off (**par** by), to get an earful○ (**par** from).
II s'enguirlander *vpr* to have a row.

enhardir /ãaʀdiʀ/ [3] **I** *vtr* to embolden.
II s'enhardir *vpr* to become bolder.

énième /ɛnjɛm/ *adj* umpteenth.

énigmatique /enigmatik/ *adj* enigmatic.

énigme /enigm/ *nf* **1** (mystère) enigma, mystery; **2** (de- vinette) riddle; **parler par ~s** to speak in riddles.

enivrant, ~e /ãnivʀã, ãt/ *adj* intoxicating.

enivrement /ãnivʀəmã/ *nm* intoxication.

enivrer /ãnivʀe/ [1] **I** *vtr* **1** [*alcool*] to intoxicate SOUT, make [sb] drunk; [*air, altitude, mer*] to intoxicate SOUT; **2 ~ qn** [*succès*] to go to sb's head.
II s'enivrer *vpr* **1** LIT (se soûler) to get intoxicated SOUT; **2** FIG to become intoxicated (**de** with).

enjambée /ãʒãbe/ *nf* stride; **s'éloigner à grandes ~s** to stride off.

enjamber /ãʒãbe/ [1] *vtr* **1** [*personne*] to step over [*obstacle*]; **2** [*pont*] to span [*rivière*].

enjeu, *pl* **~x** /ãʒø/ *nm* **1** JEUX stake; **2** (ce qui est en jeu) what is at stake; **3** (problème) issue; **un ~ écono- mique** an economic issue.

enjoindre /ãʒwɛ̃dʀ/ [56] *vtr* **~ à qn de faire** to enjoin SOUT sb to do.

enjôler /ãʒole/ [1] *vtr* to beguile; **se laisser ~ par** to be taken in ou beguiled (**par** by).

enjoliver /ãʒɔlive/ [1] *vtr* to embellish.

enjoliveur /ãʒɔlivœʀ/ *nm* hubcap.

enjoué, ~e /ãʒwe/ *adj* [*caractère*] cheerful; [*ton*] light-hearted.

enlacé, ~e /ãlase/ *adj* **1** [*corps, amants*] entwined (*jamais épith*); **2** [*fils, initiales*] interlacing.

enlacer /ãlase/ [12] **I** *vtr* **1** [*personne*] to embrace [*per- sonne*]; [*serpent*] to wrap itself around [*proie*].
II s'enlacer *vpr* [*personnes*] to embrace; [*corps*] to intertwine.

enlaidir /ãlediʀ/ [3] **I** *vtr* **1** to spoil [*paysage*]; to make [sb] look ugly [*personne*].
II *vi* to become ugly.
III s'enlaidir *vpr* [*personne*] to make oneself (look) ugly.

enlevé, ~e /ãlve/ *adj* [*morceau, rythme*] lively.

enlèvement /ãlɛvmã/ *nm* **1** (délit) kidnapping^GB, abduction; **2** (de colis) removal; (d'ordures) collection.

enlever /ãlve/ [16] **I** *vtr* **1** (ôter) GÉN to remove; to take [sth] down [*rideaux*]; to take [sth] off [*vêtement*]; to move [*véhicule*] (**de** from); **enlève tes affaires de là/tes pieds du fauteuil** get○ your things out of here/your feet off the armchair; **2** (supprimer) to remove (**de** from); **3** (priver de) to take [sb/sth] away [*personnes, objet*] (**à** from); **~ à qn l'envie de faire** to put sb off doing; **~ toute signification à qch** to make sth totally meaningless; **cela n'enlève rien à l'estime que j'ai pour elle** it doesn't make me think any the less of her; **4** (ravir) to kidnap; [*amant*] to carry [sb] off [*bien-aimée*]; **5** (gagner) to carry [sth] off [*coupe, prix*]; to capture [*marché*]; **6** (avec brio) to give a brilliant rendering of [*morceau de musique*].
II s'enlever *vpr* **1** (disparaître) [*vernis, papier peint*] to come off; [*tache*] to come out; **2** (être séparable) [*pièce*] to be detachable; **ça s'enlève comment?** [*vêtement*] how do you take it off?; **3**○ (partir) **enlève-toi de là** get off○.

enlisement /ãlizmã/ *nm* LIT sinking; FIG (de négocia- tions) stalemate; (de mouvement) collapse.

enliser /ãlize/ [1] *vtr* to get [sth] stuck (**dans** in).
II s'enliser *vpr* **1** [*bateau, véhicule*] to get stuck (**dans** in); **2** FIG [*enquête, négociations*] to drag on; **s'~ dans** to sink into; **être enlisé dans** (dans un conflit, des difficultés) to be embroiled in.

enluminure /ãlyminyʀ/ *nf* ART illumination.

enneigé, ~e /ãneʒe/ *adj* [*sommet, paysage*] snowy (*épith*); [*route*] covered in snow (*après n*).

enneigement /ãnɛʒmã/ *nm* **bulletin d'~** snow

report; **l'~ des pistes est insuffisant** there isn't enough snow on the slopes.

ennemi, **-e** /ɛnmi/ **I** *adj* **1** MIL enemy (*épith*); **2** (hostile) hostile; **être ~ de qch** to be opposed to sth.

II *nm,f* **1** (de personne, groupe) enemy; **se faire des ~s** to make enemies; **2** (d'idée) opponent; **3** (élément nocif) **la censure est l'~e de la liberté** censorship is the enemy of a free society.

III *nm* MIL enemy; **~ héréditaire** traditional enemy; **passer à l'~** to go over to the enemy.

IDIOMES **le mieux est l'~ du bien** perfectionism can be counter-productive.

ennoblir /ɑ̃nɔbliʀ/ [3] *vtr* to ennoble.

ennui /ɑ̃nɥi/ *nm* **1** (sentiment) boredom; **tromper l'~** to escape from boredom; **c'est à mourir d'~** it's enough to bore you stiff ou to death; **2** (problème) problem; **j'ai des ~s avec la police** I'm in trouble with the police; **créer des ~s à qn** to make trouble for sb; **s'attirer des ~s** to run into trouble.

ennuyé, **-e** /ɑ̃nɥije/ *adj* **1** (embarrassé) embarrassed; **j'étais très ~ de laisser les enfants seuls** I felt awful ou terrible about leaving the children on their own; **2** (dans une situation difficile) **j'aurais été très ~ si je n'avais pas eu la clé** I would have been in real trouble if I hadn't had the key.

ennuyer /ɑ̃nɥije/ [22] **I** *vtr* **1** (lasser) to bore; **voyager m'ennuie** I find travelling^{GB} boring; **2** (déranger) to bother; **ce qui m'ennuie avec lui c'est que** what bothers me about him is that; **si ça ne vous ennuie pas trop** if you don't mind; **3** (irriter) to annoy; **4** (harceler) to hassle○.

II s'ennuyer *vpr* **1** (être las) to be bored; **s'~ mortellement** to be bored stiff; **avoir l'air de s'~** to look bored; **2** (se lasser) to get bored; **je me suis franchement ennuyée** I got really bored; ▶**rat**, **sou**; **3** (languir) **s'~ de** to miss.

ennuyeux, **-euse** /ɑ̃nɥijø, øz/ *adj* **1** (lassant) boring; **2** (pénible) tedious; **3** (agaçant) annoying; **l'~ c'est que** the annoying thing is that.

IDIOMES **être ~ comme la pluie** to be as dull as ditchwater.

énoncé /enɔ̃se/ *nm* **1** (de problème, sujet) wording (**de** of); **l'~ d'une théorie** the exposition of a theory; **2** (de fait) statement (**de** of); **3** JUR pronouncement (**de** of); **à l'~ du verdict** when the verdict was pronounced; **4** LING utterance.

énoncer /enɔ̃se/ [12] *vtr* to pronounce [*jugement*]; to set out, to state [*faits, principes*]; to expound [*théorie*].

énorgueillir /ɑ̃nɔʀɡœjiʀ/ [3] **I** *vtr* to make [sb] proud [*personne*].

II s'enorgueillir *vpr* to pride oneself (**de** on).

énorme /enɔʀm/ *adj* **1** (par la taille, la quantité) [*objet, personne*] huge, enormous; [*dépense*] huge, vast; **2** (par l'intensité) [*succès, effort*] tremendous; [*erreur, gaffe*] terrible; [*mensonge*] outrageous; [*rire*] hearty; **la différence est ~** there's a world of difference; **ça vous ferait un bien ~** it would do you a power of good; **c'est déjà ~ qu'il les voie** for him to even see them is quite something.

énormément /enɔʀmemɑ̃/ *adv* [*manger, boire*] a tremendous amount; [*parler, changer*] a great deal; **il a ~ grossi** he's put on a tremendous amount of weight; **~ de temps** a tremendous amount of time; **ça m'a ~ plu** I liked it immensely; **ça l'a ~ fatigué** it made him tremendously tired; **ça a ~ progressé** it's come on a lot; **il travaille ~** he works very hard; **il gagne ~** he earns a fortune.

énormité /enɔʀmite/ *nf* **1** (de chiffre, taille) hugeness; (de faute, mensonge) enormity; **2** (propos aberrant) outrageous remark.

enquérir: **s'enquérir** /ɑ̃keʀiʀ/ [35] *vpr* **s'~ de** to inquire about sth.

enquête /ɑ̃kɛt/ *nf* **1** ADMIN, JUR inquiry, investigation (**sur** into); (après une mort) inquest (**sur** into); **ouvrir une ~** to open ou set up an investigation; **mener une ~** to lead an investigation; **2** PRESSE, SOCIOL (reportage) investigation (**sur** into); (sondage) survey (**sur** about).

■ **~ administrative** public inquiry; **~ d'opinion** GÉN survey; (pour des élections) opinion poll.

enquêter /ɑ̃kete/ [1] *vi* [*policier*] to carry out an investigation (**sur** into), to investigate; [*expert, commission*] to hold an inquiry (**sur** into).

enquêteur, **-trice** /ɑ̃ketœʀ, tʀis/ ▶**374**| *nm,f* **1** (de police) investigating officer; **2** (pour sondage politique) pollster; (pour sondage commercial) (market research) interviewer.

enquiquinant○, **-e** /ɑ̃kikinɑ̃, ɑ̃t/ *adj* **1** (agaçant) annoying; **2** (ennuyeux) boring.

enquiquiner○ /ɑ̃kikine/ [1] **I** *vtr* **~ qn** (agacer) to get on sb's nerves, to irritate sb; (importuner) to pester sb.

II s'enquiquiner *vpr* **s'~ à faire** to go to the trouble of doing.

enquiquineur○, **-euse** /ɑ̃kikinœʀ, øz/ *nm,f* pain○, nuisance.

enracinement /ɑ̃ʀasinmɑ̃/ *nm* **1** AGRIC, BOT taking root, rooting; **2** (de peuple) settling; **3** (d'habitude, idée, de parti) (processus) taking root; (situation) deep-rootedness.

enraciner /ɑ̃ʀasine/ [1] **I** *vtr* **1** AGRIC, BOT to root; **2** (installer) to establish [*peuple*]; **3** (fixer dans l'esprit) to implant [*idées*].

II s'enraciner *vpr* **1** AGRIC, BOT to take root; **2** (dans un lieu, pays) [*personne*] to put down roots; [*coutume, idée*] to take root.

enragé, **-e** /ɑ̃ʀaʒe/ **I** *adj* **1** (passionné) fanatical; **2** (furieux) enraged; **3** MÉD rabid.

II *nm,f* (passionné, révolté) fanatic.

IDIOMES **manger de la vache ~e**○ to go through hard times.

enrageant, **-e** /ɑ̃ʀaʒɑ̃, ɑ̃t/ *adj* infuriating.

enrager /ɑ̃ʀaʒe/ [13] *vi* to be furious; **j'enrage de voir** I'm furious to see; **faire ~ qn** (taquiner) to tease sb; (ennuyer) to annoy sb.

enrayer /ɑ̃ʀeje/ [21] **I** *vtr* **1** (maîtriser) to check [*épidémie, développement*]; to curb [*inflation, chômage*]; to stop [sth] escalating [*crise, violence*]; **2** (bloquer) to jam.

II s'enrayer *vpr* LIT, FIG to get jammed.

enregistrement /ɑ̃ʀəʒistʀəmɑ̃/ *nm* **1** AUDIO, VIDÉO recording; **2** (de plainte, données) recording; (de personnes, livres) registration; (de commande) taking down; **3** JUR registration; **4** (de bagages) check-in; **5** ORDINAT record.

enregistrer /ɑ̃ʀəʒistʀe/ [1] *vtr* **1** AUDIO, VIDÉO to record [*disque, cassette*]; **~ qch sur bande magnétique/vidéo** to tape/to videotape sth; **2** (constater) to note [*progrès, échec, phénomène*]; to record [*hausse, baisse*]; **3** (consigner) to make a record of [*dépenses*]; to take [*commande*]; to record [*données*]; to set [*record*]; **4** to register [*déclaration, naissance*]; **5** to check in [*bagages*]; **6** (mémoriser) to take in; **c'est enregistré** I've made a mental note of it.

enrhumer /ɑ̃ʀyme/ [1] **I** *vtr* to give [sb] a cold [*personne*].

II s'enrhumer *vpr* to catch a cold; **s'~ facilement** to catch colds easily; **être enrhumé** to have a cold.

enrichi, **-e** /ɑ̃ʀiʃi/ *adj* [*substance*] enriched (**en** with); **formule ~e** improved formula.

enrichir /ɑ̃ʀiʃiʀ/ [3] **I** *vtr* **1** (financièrement) to make [sb] rich [*personne*]; to bring wealth to [*pays*]; **2** (augmenter) to enrich, to enhance [*collection, ouvrage*] (**de** with); **3** TECH to enrich.

II s'enrichir *vpr* **1** (devenir riche) [*personne*] to become rich; **2** (être agrémenté) to be enriched (**de** with).

enrichissant, **-e** /ɑ̃ʀiʃisɑ̃, ɑ̃t/ *adj* [*expérience, lecture*] rewarding; [*relation*] fulfilling.

enrichissement /ɑ̃ʀiʃismɑ̃/ *nm* **1** (en argent) (de pays) enrichment; (de personne) accumulation of wealth; **2** TECH enrichment.

enrober /ɑ̃ʀɔbe/ [1] *vtr* **1** LIT to coat [*gâteau*] (**de** with); **2** FIG to wrap up [*paroles*] (**de** in).

enrôlement /ɑ̃ʀolmɑ̃/ *nm* (dans l'armée) enlistment (**dans** in); (dans un parti) enrolment^{GB} (**dans** in); **~ forcé** impressment.

enrôler /ɑ̃Role/ [1] **I** vtr GÉN to recruit; MIL to enlist, to recruit.
II s'enrôler vpr to enrol^{GB}, to enlist (**dans** in).

enroué, **~e** /ɑ̃Rwe/ adj hoarse, husky.

enrouer: **s'enrouer** /ɑ̃Rwe/ [1] vpr [voix] to go hoarse; [personne] to make oneself hoarse.

enroulement /ɑ̃Rulmɑ̃/ nm **1** (action de s'enrouler) winding, rolling up; **2** (disposition) curling (up); **3** ART, ARCHIT scroll; **4** ÉLECTROTECH coil.

enrouler /ɑ̃Rule/ [1] **I** vtr **1** (autour d'un axe) to wind (**autour de** round GB, around); **2** (envelopper) to wrap.
II s'enrouler vpr **1** [bande, fil] to wind (**sur** onto; **autour de** round GB, around); **2** [personne, animal] to curl up.

enrubanner /ɑ̃Rybane/ [1] vtr **1** (pour décorer) to decorate [sth] with ribbon; **2** (pour attacher) to tie [sth] up with ribbons.

ensabler /ɑ̃sable/ [1] **I** vtr **1** to get [sth] stuck in the sand [véhicule]; to strand [sth] on a sandbank [bateau]; **2** to silt up [port, canal].
II s'ensabler vpr **1** [véhicule] to get stuck in the sand; [bateau] to get stranded (on a sandbank); **2** [canal, port] to silt up.

ensanglanté, **~e** /ɑ̃sɑ̃glɑ̃te/ adj [corps, couteau] bloodstained, bloody; [blessure] bloody.

ensanglanter /ɑ̃sɑ̃glɑ̃te/ [1] vtr **1** (couvrir de sang) to cover [sth] with blood; **2** (ravager) to bring bloodshed to [pays, époque].

enseignant, **~e** /ɑ̃sɛɲɑ̃, ɑ̃t/ **▶374|** **I** adj **corps ~** teaching profession.
II nm,f SCOL teacher; UNIV lecturer.

enseigne /ɑ̃sɛɲ/ **I** nf **1** (de magasin) (shop) sign; **~ lumineuse** neon sign; **2** MIL, NAUT (drapeau) ensign.
II à telle enseigne que loc conj so much so that.
IDIOMES **nous sommes logés à la même ~** we are in the same boat.

enseignement /ɑ̃sɛɲmɑ̃/ nm **1** (institution) education; **l'~ supérieur** higher education; **réforme de l'~** educational reform; **2** (activité) teaching; **méthodes d'~** teaching methods; **entrer dans l'~** to enter the teaching profession; **3** (formation) instruction; **l'~ pratique** practical instruction; **4** (cours) tuition; **dispenser un ~** to give tuition; **5** (leçon) lesson.
■ **~ assisté par ordinateur**, **EAO** computer-aided learning, CAL; **~ par correspondance** or **à distance** distance learning; **~ général** mainstream education; **~ ménager** domestic science; **~ mixte** coeducation; **~ professionnel** vocational training ou education; **~ religieux** religious instruction; **~ technique** technical education.

enseigner /ɑ̃seɲe/ [1] vtr to teach; **~ qch à qn** to teach sth to sb, to teach sb sth.

ensemble /ɑ̃sɑ̃bl/ **I** adv **1** (l'un avec l'autre) together; **ils iraient bien ~ ces deux-là**○! they'd make a fine pair, those two○!; **2** (simultanément) at the same time; **3** (à la fois) LITER **tout ~** at once.
II nm **1** (éléments regroupés) group; **un ~ de personnes** a group of people; **l'~ des élèves de la classe** all the pupils (pl) in the class; **l'~ de l'œuvre d'un écrivain** the whole of a writer's work; **une vue d'~** an overall view; **plan d'~ d'une ville** general plan of a town; **dans l'~** by and large; **dans l'~ de** throughout; **dans son** ou **leur ~** as a whole; **2** (éléments assortis) set; **3** (cohésion) unity, cohesion; **former un bel ~** to form a harmonious whole; **4** (synchronisation) (de gestes) coordination; (de sons) unison; **5** MATH set; **théorie des ~s** set theory; **6** (formation musicale) ensemble; **7** CONSTR (de bureaux) complex; **~ industriel** industrial estate GB ou park US; **▶grand**; **8** (vêtements) outfit; (tailleur) suit.

ensemblier /ɑ̃sɑ̃blije/ **▶374|** nm (décorateur) interior designer; (au cinéma) assistant set designer.

ensemencer /ɑ̃smɑ̃se/ [12] vtr to sow; **~ une rivière** to stock a river with young fish.

enserrer /ɑ̃seRe/ [1] vtr **1** (mouler) to fit tightly round; **2** (serrer fortement) **il lui enserra la taille** he clasped

him/her around the waist; **la pieuvre enserra sa proie** the octopus gripped its prey tightly.

ensevelir /ɑ̃səvəliR/ [3] vtr **1** (enterrer) to bury, to inter SOUT; **2** (recouvrir) to bury; **3** (cacher) LITER [personne] to hide; [temps] to enshroud SOUT.

ensevelissement /ɑ̃səvəlismɑ̃/ nm **1** (enterrement) FML burial; **2** (recouvrement) LITER burying.

ensoleillé, **~e** /ɑ̃sɔleje/ adj sunny.

ensoleillement /ɑ̃sɔlejmɑ̃/ nm **1** (exposition au soleil) **la pièce jouit d'un bon ~** the room gets a lot of sun; **2** MÉTÉO **l'~ moyen de la région est de 2000 heures par an** on average the region gets 2,000 hours of sunshine a year.

ensommeillé, **~e** /ɑ̃sɔmeje/ adj [personne, voix] sleepy, drowsy.

ensorceler /ɑ̃sɔRsəle/ [19] vtr **1** (jeter un sort) to cast ou to put a spell on; **2** (captiver) to bewitch, to enchant.

ensorceleur, **-euse** /ɑ̃sɔRsəlœR, øz/ **I** adj **1** (séduisant) bewitching, enchanting; **2** (magique) magic.
II nm,f (personne séduisante) charmer.

ensorcellement /ɑ̃sɔRsɛlmɑ̃/ nm **1** (en jetant un sort) bewitchment; **2** (en séduisant) charm, enchantment.

ensuite /ɑ̃sɥit/ adv **1** (après) then; (ultérieurement) later, subsequently; **très bien, mais ~?** fine, but then what?; **2** (en second lieu) secondly.

ensuivre: **s'ensuivre** /ɑ̃sɥivR/ [19] vpr to follow, to ensue; **jusqu'à ce que mort s'ensuive** until one is dead.

entaché, **~e** /ɑ̃taʃe/ adj JUR **acte ~ d'un vice de forme** act vitiated by a formal flaw; **~ de nullité** JUR null and void.

entacher /ɑ̃taʃe/ [1] vtr FML to sully LITTÉR, to besmirch LITTÉR [réputation, honneur]; to mar [relations, rapports].

entaille /ɑ̃taj/ nf **1** (blessure) cut; (profonde) gash; (petite) nick; **2** (encoche) notch.

entailler /ɑ̃taje/ [1] **I** vtr to cut into; (profondément) to make a gash in.
II s'entailler vpr **s'~ le doigt** to cut one's finger; (profondément) to gash one's finger.

entame /ɑ̃tam/ nf (tranche) first slice; (carte) lead.

entamé, **~e** /ɑ̃tame/ adj **1** (avancé) under way; **2** (commencé) **le sandwich était à peine ~** the sandwich had hardly been touched.

entamer /ɑ̃tame/ [1] vtr **1** (démarrer) to start [activité, journée]; to initiate [procédure]; to enter into [bataille, entretien]; to open [réunion, négociation]; **2** (affaiblir) to undermine [crédibilité, moral]; to shake [détermination]; **3** (rogner) to eat into [économies]; **4** (commencer à consommer) to cut into [pain, rôti]; to open [bouteille, pot]; to start eating [dessert, sandwich]; **5** (entailler) to cut into; **6** (ronger) to eat into [métal].

entartrer /ɑ̃taRtRe/ [1] **I** vtr to fur up GB, to scale up.
II s'entartrer vpr to scale; [dents] to be covered in tartar.

entassement /ɑ̃tasmɑ̃/ nm **1** (action) (de choses) piling up; (de personnes) cramming together; **2** (résultat) (d'objets) pile; (plus gros) heap.

entasser /ɑ̃tase/ [1] **I** vtr **1** (empiler) to pile [livres, vêtements] (**dans** into; **sur** onto); **2** (amasser) to hoard [argent, vieilleries]; **3** (serrer) to pack, to cram [personnes, objets] (**dans** into).
II s'entasser vpr [objets] to pile up; [personnes] to crowd, to squeeze (**dans** into; **sur** onto).

entendement /ɑ̃tɑ̃dmɑ̃/ nm understanding; **cela dépasse l'~** it's beyond belief.

entendeur /ɑ̃tɑ̃dœR/ nm **à bon ~, salut!** you've been warned!

entendre /ɑ̃tɑ̃dR/ [6] **I** vtr **1** (percevoir par l'ouïe) to hear [bruit, mot]; **~ qn pleurer**, **~ qn qui pleure** to hear sb crying; **réussir à se faire ~** to manage to make oneself heard; **elle entend mal** she's hard of hearing; **faire ~ un cri** to give a cry; **j'ai entendu dire que** I've heard (say) that; **je n'en ai jamais entendu parler** I've never heard of it; **vous entendrez parler de moi** (menace) you haven't heard the last of it!; **2** (prêter attention à) [juge, police] to hear [*témoin, témoignage*]; [*dieu*] to hear [*prières, croyant*]; **à t'~**, **tout va bien** according to you, everything is fine; **raconter qch à qui veut l'~** to tell sth to anyone who'll listen; **(que) le ciel vous entende!** let's hope that's how it turns out!; **elle ne veut rien ~** she won't listen; **3** FML (comprendre) to understand; **il agit comme il l'entend** he does as he likes; **fais comme tu l'entends** do as you think best; **elle m'a laissé** or **donné à** or **fait ~ que** she gave me to understand that; **elle a laissé ~ que** she intimated that; **ils ne l'entendent pas de la sorte** or **de cette oreille** they don't see it that way; **4** (signifier) to mean; **qu'entends-tu par là?** what do you mean by that?; **5** FML (avoir l'intention de) **~ faire** to intend doing; **j'entends qu'on fasse ce que je dis** I expect people to do what I say.

II s'entendre *vpr* **1** (sympathiser) to get on ou along (**avec** with); **2** (se mettre d'accord) to agree (**sur** on); on **leur dit la vérité ou pas? il faudrait s'~** shall we tell them the truth or not? let's get it straight; **3** (être perçu par l'oreille) [*bruit*] to be heard; (soi-même) to hear oneself; (les uns les autres) to hear each other; **4** (être compris) **phrase qui peut s'~ de plusieurs façons** sentence which can be taken in several different ways; **5** (être compétent) **s'y ~ en meubles anciens** to know about antiques; **pour te faire culpabiliser, elle s'y entend!** when it comes to making you feel guilty, she's an expert!

entendu, **-e** /ɑ̃tɑ̃dy/ **I** *pp* ▶ **entendre**.
II *pp adj* (décidé) **c'est une affaire ~e** it's settled; **'tu viens demain?'—'~!'** 'will you come tomorrow?'—'OK○!'; **je fais ceci étant ~ que** I'm doing this on the understanding that.
III *adj* (de connivence) knowing; **d'un air ~** with a knowing look.
IV bien entendu *loc adv* of course; **elle a oublié, (comme de)○ bien ~** she's forgotten, of course; **il est bien ~ qu'elle ne sait rien** of course, she knows nothing.

entente /ɑ̃tɑ̃t/ *nf* **1** (bon rapport) harmony; **la bonne ~ de nos deux pays** the friendly relationship between our two countries; **vivre en bonne ~ avec qn** to be on good terms with sb; **2** (alliance) understanding; **3** (accord) arrangement.
■ **l'Entente cordiale** HIST the entente cordiale.

entériner /ɑ̃teʀine/ [1] *vtr* (ratifier) to ratify; (admettre) to confirm.

entérite /ɑ̃teʀit/ [▶ **196**] *nf* MÉD enteritis.

enterré, **-e** /ɑ̃teʀe/ *adj* **1** (sous terre) buried; **2** (oublié) **~ (depuis longtemps)** long-forgotten (*épith*).

enterrement /ɑ̃teʀmɑ̃/ *nm* **1** (inhumation) burial (**de** of); **2** (obsèques) funeral; **faire une tête d'~○** to look gloomy; **3** (mise à l'écart) shelving.

enterrer /ɑ̃teʀe/ [1] **I** *vtr* **1** (inhumer) to bury; **2** (mettre sous terre) to bury; ▶ **hache**; **3** (renoncer à) to say goodbye to; **4** (mettre à l'écart) to shelve.
II s'enterrer○ *vpr* to go and hole up○.
IDIOMES **~ sa vie de garçon** to have a stag party.

entêtant, **~e** /ɑ̃tɛtɑ̃, ɑ̃t/ *adj* [*parfum*] heady; [*musique*] insistent.

en-tête, *pl* **~s** /ɑ̃tɛt/ *nm* **1** (de papier) heading; **papier à lettres à ~** headed writing paper; **2** ORDINAT header-block.

entêté, **~e** /ɑ̃tete/ *adj* stubborn, obstinate.

entêtement /ɑ̃tɛtmɑ̃/ *nm* stubbornness, obstinacy.

entêter: **s'entêter** /ɑ̃tete/ [1] *vpr* to be stubborn; **s'~ dans qch/à faire** to persist in sth/in doing.

enthousiasmant, **~e** /ɑ̃tuzjasmɑ̃, ɑ̃t/ *adj* exciting.

enthousiasme /ɑ̃tuzjasm/ *nm* enthusiasm **¢** (**pour** for); **susciter l'~** to arouse enthusiasm; **refroidir les ~s** to dampen enthusiasm.

enthousiasmer /ɑ̃tuzjasme/ [1] **I** *vtr* to fill [sb] with enthusiasm; **j'ai été enthousiasmé par le concert** I found the concert exciting.
II s'enthousiasmer *vpr* to get enthusiastic (**pour** about).

enthousiaste /ɑ̃tuzjast/ **I** *adj* enthusiastic.
II *nmf* enthusiast.

enticher: **s'enticher** /ɑ̃tiʃe/ [1] *vpr* **s'~ de** to become infatuated with [*personne*]; to become passionate about [*objet, idée*].

entier, **-ière** /ɑ̃tje, ɛʀ/ **I** *adj* **1** (dans sa totalité) whole; **l'Europe (tout) entière** the whole of Europe; **il l'a fait cuire tout ~** he cooked it whole; (pendant) **des heures entières** for hours on end; **dans le monde ~** (partout dans le monde) all over the world; (au monde) in the whole world; **ils arrivent par trains ~s** they arrive by the trainload; **par caisses entières** by the crate; **lait ~** full-fat milk; **2** (complet) [*réussite, satisfaction*] complete; **avoir l'entière responsabilité de qch** to have full responsibility for sth; **avoir une entière confiance en qn** to have every confidence in sb; **3** (inaltéré) [*objet, réputation*] intact; **le problème de l'information reste ~** we have not even begun to address the information problem; **le mystère reste ~** the mystery remains unsolved; **4** (sans réserve) **donner** or **dévouer tout ~ à une cause** to devote oneself wholeheartedly to a cause; **avoir un caractère ~**, **être ~** to be uncompromising.
II *nm* **1** MATH (nombre) integer; **2** (totalité) **en ~, dans son ~** in its entirety; **le pays dans son ~** the whole ou entire country.

entièrement /ɑ̃tjɛʀmɑ̃/ *adv* entirely, completely; **~ équipé** fully equipped; **jouer ~ un morceau** to play a piece of music all the way through; **je partage ~ vos doutes** I share your doubts wholeheartedly.

entité /ɑ̃tite/ *nf* entity.

entoiler /ɑ̃twale/ [1] *vtr* **1** (en couture) to put interfacing in [*vêtement*]; **2** (fixer sur une toile) to mount [sth] on canvas; **3** (relier en toile) to bind [sth] in canvas [*livre*].

entomologie /ɑ̃tɔmɔlɔʒi/ *nf* entomology.

entonner /ɑ̃tɔne/ [1] *vtr* to start singing [*chanson, air*]; to launch into [*thème, discours*].

entonnoir /ɑ̃tɔnwaʀ/ *nm* (ustensile) funnel; (cavité) crater.

entorse /ɑ̃tɔʀs/ *nf* **1** MÉD sprain; **se faire une ~ à la cheville/au genou** to sprain one's ankle/knee; **2** FIG (manquement) infringement (**à** of); **faire une ~ au règlement** to bend ou stretch the rules.

entortillement /ɑ̃tɔʀtijmɑ̃/ *nm* **1** (de fils) (processus) tangling; (résultat) tangle; **2** (de phrases, style) muddle.

entortiller /ɑ̃tɔʀtije/ [1] **I** *vtr* **1** (pour entourer) to wind (**autour de qch** round GB sth); **2** (emmêler) to tangle up; **3○** FIG (embrouiller) to muddle up [*explications*]; **4○** FIG (embobiner) to get round GB [sb], to win [sb] over GB; **se faire ~** to let oneself be won over.
II s'entortiller *vpr* **1** (s'emmêler) [*fils, laine*] to get entangled (**dans** in); **2** (s'enrouler) [*plante*] to twist.

entourage /ɑ̃tuʀaʒ/ *nm* (famille) family circle; (amis) circle (of friends); (conseillers, courtisans) entourage.

entouré, **~e** /ɑ̃tuʀe/ *adj* **1** (populaire) [*président, femme*] popular; **2** (soutenu) **nos patients sont très ~s** our patients are well looked after.

entourer /ɑ̃tuʀe/ [1] **I** *vtr* **1** (être autour) [*bâtiments, clôture, personnes*] to surround; **entouré de** [*lieu*] surrounded by ou with; **les gens/objets qui nous entourent** the people/things around us; **2** (placer autour) **~ qch de qch** to put sth around sth; **~ qch de mystère** to shroud sth in mystery; **~ qn d'affection** to surround sb with love; **~ un mot** to circle a word; **3** (soutenir) to rally round GB ou around US [*malade, veuve*].
II s'entourer *vpr* **1** (réunir autour de soi) **s'~ d'amis** to surround oneself with friends; **s'~ de précautions** to take every possible precaution; **2** (se mettre) **s'~ d'un châle** to wrap oneself (up) in a shawl.

entourloupe○ /ɑ̃tuʀlup/ *nf* dirty trick.

entournure /ɑ̃tuʀnyʀ/ *nf* **être gêné aux ~s** FIG (mal à l'aise) to be in an awkward position; (financièrement) to feel the pinch○.

entracte /ɑ̃tʀakt/ *nm* **1** (au théâtre, concert) interval GB, intermission; (au cinéma) intermission; **2** (divertissement) interlude.

entraide /ɑ̃tʀɛd/ *nf* mutual aid (**entre** between).

entraider: **s'entraider** /ɑ̃tʀede/ [1] *vpr* to help each other ou one another.

entrailles /ɑ̃tʀɑj/ *nfpl* **1** (d'animal) innards, entrails; **2** (de mère) LITER womb; **3** (profondeurs) LITER bowels.

entrain /ɑ̃tʀɛ̃/ *nm* **1** (de personne) spirit, goᴼ GB; **elle est pleine d'~** she's full of go ou life; **manquer d'~** to have no go; **retrouver son ~** to cheer up; **2** (de soirée, musique, discussion) liveliness; **être plein/manquer d'~** to be/not to be very lively; **sans ~** half-hearted.

entraînant, ~e /ɑ̃tʀɛnɑ̃, ɑ̃t/ *adj* lively.

entraînement /ɑ̃tʀɛnmɑ̃/ *nm* **1** (formation) training; (séance) training session; **d'~** [*match, jours*] training (*épith*); **2** (habitude) practiceGB; **manquer d'~** (être inexpérimenté) to lack practiceGB; (avoir perdu l'habitude) to be out of practiceGB.

entraîner /ɑ̃tʀene/ **I** *vtr* **1** (provoquer) to lead to; **une panne a entraîné l'arrêt de la production** a breakdown brought production to a standstill; **2** (emporter) [*courant, rivière*] to carry [sth/sb] away; **il a entraîné qn/qch dans sa chute** LIT, FIG he dragged sb/sth down with him; **3** (conduire) to take [*personne*]; **~ qn à faire qch** [*personne*] to make sb do sth; [*circonstances*] to lead sb to do sth; **ce sont ses camarades qui l'ont entraîné** his friends dragged him into it; **4** FIG (stimuler) to carry [sb] away [*personne, groupe*]; **5** (former) to train, to coach [*sportif*] (**à** for); to train [*cheval, soldat*] (**à** for); **6** (actionner) [*moteur*] to drive [*machine*].

II s'entraîner *vpr* **1** (se former) [*sportif, soldats*] to train (**à** for); **s'~ au maniement des armes/au tir** to practiseGB handling weapons/shooting; **2** (s'exercer) to prepare oneself (**à qch** for sth); to train oneself (**à faire** to do); **3** (s'encourager) to encourage each other (**à faire** to do).

entraîneur, -euse¹ /ɑ̃tʀɛnœʀ, øz/ ▶374] *nm,f* (de sportif, d'équipe) coach, trainer; (de cheval) trainer.

entraîneuse² /ɑ̃tʀɛnøz/ *nf* (dans un bar) hostess.

entrapercevoir /ɑ̃tʀapɛʀsəvwaʀ/ [5] *vtr* to catch a glimpse of [*personne, phénomène*]; to glimpse [*solution, possibilité*].

entrave /ɑ̃tʀav/ **I** *nf* FIG (gêne) hindrance (**à** to); (à la liberté) restriction (**à** of); **s'exprimer sans ~** to speak freely; **pour ~ à la liberté du culte** JUR for failing to respect freedom of worship.

II entraves *nfpl* (d'animal) hobble (*sg*); (de forçat) shackles, fetters LITTÉR.

entraver /ɑ̃tʀave/ [1] *vtr* **1** (gêner) to hinder, to impede; **2** (attacher) to hobble [*animal*]; to shackle [*forçat*].

entre /ɑ̃tʀ/ *prép*

■ Note *entre* se traduit par *between* sauf lorsqu'il signifie *parmi* (▶4) auquel cas il se traduit généralement par *among*.
– Exemples et exceptions sont présentés dans l'article ci-dessous.
– Les expressions telles que *entre parenthèses*, *entre deux portes*, *lire entre les lignes* sont traitées respectivement sous *parenthèse*, *porte*, *lire¹*; de même *entre ciel et terre* se trouve sous *ciel*, *entre la vie et la mort* sous *vie* etc.

1 (dans l'espace, le temps) between; **~ midi et deux** at lunchtime; **2** (pour désigner un état intermédiaire) between; **'doux ou très épicé?'—'~ les deux'** 'mild or very spicy?'—'in between'; ▶**quatre**; **3** (à travers) between; **passer la main ~ les barreaux** to slip one's hand between ou through the bars; **4** (parmi) among; **choisir ~ plusieurs solutions** to choose between ou from among several solutions; **~ tous ces romans, lequel préfères-tu?** of all these novels, which one do you like best?; **chacune d'~ elles** each of them; **5** (pour désigner un groupe de personnes) **organiser une soirée ~ amis** to organize a party among friends; **~ hommes** as one man to another; **~ nous** between you and me, between ourselves; **nous sommes ~ nous** (deux personnes) there's just the two of us; (plus de deux) we're among friends; **6** (pour marquer la distribution) between; **son travail et l'informatique, il n'a pas**

le temps de sortir what with work and his computer he doesn't have time to go out; **7** (pour exprimer une relation) between; **les enfants sont souvent cruels ~ eux** children are often cruel to each other; **ces motifs peuvent se combiner ~ eux** these patterns can be combined (with each other); **deux d'~ eux sont cassés** two of them are broken.

entrebâillement /ɑ̃tʀəbajmɑ̃/ *nm* (de porte) gap (**de** in).

entrebâiller /ɑ̃tʀəbaje/ [1] *vtr* to half-open.

entrechoquer /ɑ̃tʀəʃɔke/ [1] **I** *vtr* to clatter [*vaisselle*]; to clink, to chink [*verres*]; to crash [*cymbales*]; to knock ou bang [sth] together [*cailloux, cuillères*].

II s'entrechoquer *vpr* **1** [*verres*] to clink, to chink; [*dents*] to chatter; [*casseroles*] to clatter; **2** [*idées, passions*] to clash.

entrecôte /ɑ̃tʀəkot/ *nf* (portion servie) entrecôte (steak); (pièce de boucherie) rib steak.

entrecouper /ɑ̃tʀəkupe/ [1] **I** *vtr* to punctuate (**de** by); **film entrecoupé de publicité** film interrupted by advertisements; **voix entrecoupée de sanglots** voice broken with sobs.

II s'entrecouper *vpr* [*lignes, routes*] to intersect.

entrecroiser /ɑ̃tʀəkʀwaze/ [1] *vtr*, **s'entrecroiser** *vpr* to intertwine.

entre-déchirer: **s'entre-déchirer** /ɑ̃tʀədeʃiʀe/ [1] *vpr* LIT to tear each other to pieces; FIG to tear each other apart.

entre-deux-guerres /ɑ̃tʀədøgɛʀ/ *nm* ou *f inv* inter-war period.

entrée /ɑ̃tʀe/ *nf* **1** (point d'accès) entrance (**de** to); **à l'~** at the entrance; **à l'~ de la ville** on the outskirts of the town; **il y a une pharmacie à l'~ de la rue** there's a chemist's where you turn into the street; **se retrouver à l'~ du bureau** to meet outside the office; **2** (d'autoroute) (entry) slip road GB, on-ramp US; **3** (vestibule) GÉN hall; (d'hôtel, de lieu public) lobby; (porte, grille) entry; **4** (moment initial) **trois mois après mon ~ à l'université** three months after I went to university; **5** (admission) **l'~ d'un pays dans une organisation** (accueil) the admission of a country to an organization; (adhésion) the entry of a country into an organization; **'~ libre'** (gratuite) 'admission free'; (publique) (dans un magasin) 'browsers welcome'; (dans un monument) 'visitors welcome'; **l'~ est payante** there's an admission charge; **refuser l'~ à qn** to refuse sb entry; **'~ interdite'** 'no admittance', 'no entry'; **6** (place) ticket; **nous avons eu 300 ~s** (d'exposition) we had 300 visitors; (de théâtre) we sold 300 tickets; **7** (arrivée) (de personne) GÉN, THÉÂT entrance; (de véhicule, marchandises) entry; **réussir son ~** [*acteur*] to enter on cue; **faire son ~ dans le monde** to enter society; **8** (commencement) **à l'~ de l'hiver** at the beginning of winter; **d'~ (de jeu)** from the very start; **9** CULIN (plat) starter; **10** TECH input ₵; **11** LING (de dictionnaire) entry; **12** (de capitaux) inflow; **13** (en comptabilité) **~s** receipts.

■ **~ des artistes** THÉÂT stage door; **~ en matière** introduction; **~ de service** tradesmen's entrance GB, service entrance.

IDIOMES **avoir ses ~s chez le ministre** to be an intimate of the minister.

entrée-sortie, *pl* **entrées-sorties** /ɑ̃tʀesɔʀti/ *nf* ORDINAT input-output.

entrefaites: **sur ces entrefaites** /syʀsezɑ̃tʀəfɛt/ *loc adv* at that moment, just then.

entrefilet /ɑ̃tʀəfilɛ/ *nm* PRESSE brief article.

entrejambes /ɑ̃tʀəʒɑ̃b/ *nm inv* **1** (de vêtement) (fond) crotch; (longueur de pantalon) inside leg GB, inseam US; **2** EUPH (partie du corps) crotch.

entrelacer /ɑ̃tʀəlase/ [12] *vtr*, **s'entrelacer** *vpr* to intertwine, to interlace.

entrelacs /ɑ̃tʀəla/ *nm inv* tracery.

entrelarder /ɑ̃tʀəlaʀde/ [1] *vtr* LIT, FIG **~ qch de qch** to lard sth with sth.

entremêler /ɑ̃tʀəmele/ [1] **I** *vtr* to mix [*objets*]; to interweave [*fils*].

II s'entremêler *vpr* GÉN to be mixed; [*branches, cheveux*] to get tangled.

entremets /ɑ̃tʀəmɛ/ *nm inv* dessert.

entremetteur, -euse /ɑ̃tʀəmɛtœʀ, øz/ *nm,f* **1** (marieur) matchmaker; (proxénète) procurer/procuress; **2** (intermédiaire) go-between.

entremettre: s'entremettre /ɑ̃tʀəmɛtʀ/ [60] *vpr* (intervenir) to act as mediator, to mediate (**dans** in; **entre** between).

entremise /ɑ̃tʀəmiz/ *nf* intervention (**auprès de** with); **il l'a su par mon ~** he heard of it through me.

entreposer /ɑ̃tʀəpoze/ [1] *vtr* **1** (dans un entrepôt) to store; (en douane) to bond; **2** (chez quelqu'un) to store (**chez** at).

entrepôt /ɑ̃tʀəpo/ *nm* (bâtiment) warehouse; (arrière-boutique) stockroom; **~ de douane** bonded warehouse; **~ frigorifique** cold storage plant.

entreprenant, -e /ɑ̃tʀəpʀənɑ̃, ɑ̃t/ *adj* (hardi) enterprising; (avec les femmes) **être ~** to be forward with the ladies.

entreprendre /ɑ̃tʀəpʀɑ̃dʀ/ [52] *vtr* **1** (commencer) to start, to undertake [*recherches, rénovation*]; **~ de faire** (se mettre à) to set about doing; (se donner pour tâche de) to undertake to do; **2** (adresser la parole à) **~ qn** (pour séduire) to set about seducing sb; (pour bavarder) to engage sb in conversation (**sur qch** about sth).

entrepreneur, -euse /ɑ̃tʀəpʀənœʀ, øz/ ▶374 *nm,f* **1** CONSTR builder; **2** (de travaux) contractor; **~ en bâtiment** building contractor; **~ de pompes funèbres** undertaker, mortician US; **3** (chef d'entreprise) owner-manager (*of a small firm*).

entreprise /ɑ̃tʀəpʀiz/ *nf* **1** (société) firm, business; **petites et moyennes ~s** small and medium enterprises; **~ de pompes funèbres** undertaker's GB, funeral home US; **~ de transports routiers** haulage contractor GB, trucking company US; **création d'~s** business start-ups; **la culture d'~** corporate culture; **2** (secteur) business, industry; **3** (projet) undertaking, enterprise; (risqué) venture; **la libre ~** free enterprise.

■ **~ unipersonnelle à responsabilité limitée, EURL** company owned by a sole proprietor.

entrer /ɑ̃tʀe/ [1] **I** *vtr* (+ *v avoir*) **1** (transporter) (vu de l'intérieur) to bring [sth] in; (vu de l'extérieur) to take [sth] in; **2** (enfoncer) to stick (**dans** into); **3** ORDINAT to enter; **4** SPORT to score [*but*].

II *vi* (+ *v être*) **1** (pénétrer) GÉN to get in, to enter; (en allant) to go in; (en venant) to come in; (en roulant) to drive in; **l'eau est entrée par une fissure** the water came in ou got in through a crack; **je suis entré dans Paris par le sud** (en voiture) I drove into Paris from the south; **entrez!** come in!; **'défense d'~'** (sur une porte) 'no entry'; (sur une barrière) 'no trespassing'; **je ne fais qu'~ et sortir** I can only stay a minute; **laisser ~ qn** to let sb in; **faire ~ la table par la fenêtre** (vu de l'intérieur) to bring the table in through the window; (vu de l'extérieur) to take the table in through the window; **fais-la ~** show her in; **2** (tenir, s'adapter) to fit; **faire ~ qch dans qch** to fit ou get sth into a sth; **je n'arrive pas à faire ~ la pièce dans la fente** I can't get the coin into the slot; **3** (s'intégrer, commencer) **~ dans** to enter [*débat, période*]; to join [*opposition, gouvernement, armée*]; **~ à** to enter [*école, hit-parade*]; to get into [*université*]; **~ en** to enter into [*pourparlers, négociations*]; **il entre en deuxième année** he's going into his second year; **il entre dans sa quarantième année** he's turned thirty-nine; **~ dans la vie de qn** to come into sb's life; **n'entrons pas dans les détails** let's not go into the details; **il m'a fait ~ au ministère** he got me into the ministry; **il entre dans la catégorie des...** he comes into the category of...; **expression entrée dans l'usage** expression which has come into the language; **~ dans l'histoire** to go down in history; **~ dans la légende** [*personne*] to become a legend; [*fait*] to become legendary; **j'ai fait ~ tes dépenses dans les frais généraux** I've included your expenses in the overheads; **~ en** fusion to begin to melt; **~ dans une colère noire** to fly into a blind rage; **4** (être un élément de) **le carbone entre pour moitié dans ce composé** carbon makes up half (of) this compound.

III *v impers* **il n'entre pas dans mes intentions de faire** I have no intention of doing.

entresol /ɑ̃tʀəsɔl/ *nm* mezzanine.

entre-temps /ɑ̃tʀətɑ̃/ *adv* meanwhile, in the meantime.

entretenir /ɑ̃tʀətniʀ/ [36] **I** *vtr* **1** (garder en bon état) to look after [*tapis, intérieur, vêtement*]; to maintain [*route, machine, édifice*]; **les mots croisés entretiennent la mémoire** crosswords keep the mind active; **~ sa forme** to keep in shape; **2** (faire vivre) to support [*famille, indigent*]; to keep [*maîtresse*]; **se faire ~ par qn** (par un amant) to be kept by sb; (par des amis, parents) to live off sb; **3** (maintenir) to keep up [*correspondance*]; **4** (alimenter) to keep [sth] going [*feu, conversation, rivalités*]; to keep [sth] alive [*amitié*] ; to fuel [*tensions*]; **5** (informer) **~ qn de qch** to speak to sb about sth.

II s'entretenir *vpr* (converser) **s'~ de qch** to discuss sth.

entretenu, -e /ɑ̃tʀətny/ *adj* [*personne*] kept (*épith*); **bien/mal ~** [*intérieur, plante*] well-/badly-kept; [*voiture, bâtiment*] well-/badly-maintained.

entretien /ɑ̃tʀətjɛ̃/ *nm* **1** (soins) (de maison, jardin) upkeep; (de voiture, route, d'immeuble) maintenance; (de vêtement, plante, peau) care; **frais d'~** maintenance costs; **demander peu d'~** [*plante, jardin, tapis*] to need little looking after; **d'un ~ facile** [*intérieur, jardin*] easy to look after; [*bâtiment, voiture*] easy to maintain; [*tissu*] easy-care (*épith*); **2** (nettoyage) cleaning; **3** (conversation) GÉN discussion; (pour un emploi) interview; PRESSE interview; POL talks (*pl*); **accorder un ~ à qn** to give sb an interview; **4** (soutien financier) **assurer l'~ d'un enfant** to support a child.

■ **~ d'appréciation** or **de carrière** job appraisal; **~ d'embauche** job interview; **faire passer un ~ d'embauche** to interview.

entre-tuer: s'entre-tuer /ɑ̃tʀətɥe/ [1] *vpr* to kill each other.

entrevoir /ɑ̃tʀəvwaʀ/ [46] *vtr* **1** (voir) (brièvement) to catch a glimpse of; (indistinctement) to make out; **2** (discerner, deviner) to glimpse; (présager) to foresee; **~ un espoir de paix** to see a glimmer of hope for peace; **commencer à ~...** to begin to see...; **laisser ~ que** [*signe, résultat*] to indicate that.

entrevue /ɑ̃tʀəvy/ *nf* (entretien) meeting; (discussion) POL talks (*pl*).

entrouvert, -e /ɑ̃tʀuvɛʀ/ *adj* [*porte*] ajar (*jamais épith*), half open; [*lèvres*] parted.

entrouvrir /ɑ̃tʀuvʀiʀ/ [32] **I** *vtr* to open [sth] a little.

II s'entrouvrir *vpr* GÉN [*porte, pays*] to half-open; [*lèvres*] to part.

énumération /enymeʀasjɔ̃/ *nf* (action) listing; (liste) catalogue^{GB}.

énumérer /enymeʀe/ [14] *vtr* to enumerate, to list.

envahir /ɑ̃vaiʀ/ [3] *vtr* (pénétrer dans) [*troupes, foule*] to invade; [*animal, plante*] to overrun; [*publicité*] to pervade; [*marchandise*] to flood [*marché*].

envahissant, -e /ɑ̃vaisɑ̃, ɑ̃t/ *adj* **1** (gênant) [*personne*] intrusive; **2** (doctrine, sentiment) pervasive; [*musique, odeur, plante*] invasive.

envahisseur /ɑ̃vaisœʀ/ *nm* invader.

envaser /ɑ̃vaze/ [1] **I** *vtr* to silt up [*estuaire, port*].

II s'envaser *vpr* [*estuaire, port*] to silt up; [*barque*] to get stuck in the mud.

enveloppant, -e /ɑ̃vlɔpɑ̃, ɑ̃t/ *adj* [*membrane*] enveloping; [*chaussure*] high-cut; [*manteau*] big and loose.

enveloppe /ɑ̃vlɔp/ *nf* **1** (de lettre) envelope; **sous ~** in an envelope; **2** (emballage) wrapping; (gaine) sheath; (tégument) husk; (cosse) pod; (d'organe) membrane; (peau) skin; (coquille, carapace) shell; **~ charnelle** or **mortelle** mortal coil; **3** (budget) budget; **4** (gratification) bonus; (indemnité de départ) golden handshake; (pot-de-vin) bribe.

enveloppé, **~e** /ɑ̃vlɔpe/ *adj* (gros) [*personne*] plump.

envelopper /ɑ̃vlɔpe/ [1] **I** *vtr* **1** (recouvrir) [*personne*] to wrap [sb/sth] (up); [*housse*] to cover; **le papier qui enveloppait le vase** the paper around the vase; **2** (entourer) [*brouillard, silence, nuit*] to envelop; [*brume*] to veil; [*mystère, secret*] to surround.
II s'envelopper *vpr* to wrap oneself (up); **s'~ la tête d'un turban** (le mettre) to wrap one's head in a turban; (le porter) to wear a turban.

enveloppe-réponse, *pl* **enveloppes-réponse** /ɑ̃vlɔprepɔ̃s/ *nf* freepost envelope GB, postpaid envelope US.

envenimé, **~e** /ɑ̃vnime/ *adj* [*plume, paroles*] poisoned; [*dispute*] bitter.

envenimer /ɑ̃vnime/ [1] **I** *vtr* (aviver) to inflame [*débat*]; to fan the flames of [*colère*]; to aggravate [*situation*]; **~ les choses** to make matters worse.
II s'envenimer *vpr* [*dispute*] to worsen; [*situation*] to turn ugly.

envergure /ɑ̃vɛrgyr/ *nf* **1** (d'ailes) wingspan; **de 20 mètres d'~** with a wingspan of 20 metres GB; **2** FIG (de personne) stature; (de projet, d'entreprise) scale; **un projet de grande ~** a large-scale project; **d'~ internationale** [*projet, œuvre*] of international scope; **prendre une ~ telle que** to swell to such proportions that...; **sans ~** [*projet, débat*] limited; [*personne*] of no account.

envers[1] /ɑ̃vɛr/ *prép* cruauté **~ qn** cruelty towards GB ou to sb; **méfiant/méprisant ~ qn** mistrustful/scornful of sb; **exigeant ~ qn** demanding with sb; **reconnaissance ~ qn** gratitude to sb; **cruel ~ qn** cruel to sb; **engagements ~** obligations towards GB ou to.
IDIOMES **~ et contre tous/tout** in spite of everyone/everything.

envers[2] /ɑ̃vɛr/ **I** *nm inv* (de papier) back; (de tissu) wrong side; (de vêtement) inside; (de monnaie) reverse; **l'~ du décor** FIG the other side (of the picture).
II à l'envers *loc adv* **1** (inadéquatement) the wrong way; **2** (le haut en bas) upside down; **3** (l'intérieur à l'extérieur) inside out; **4** (le devant derrière) back to front; **tenir des jumelles à l'~** to hold binoculars back to front; **5** (la droite à gauche) the wrong way round GB ou around US; **6** (à rebours) **passer un film à l'~** to run a film backward(s).

envi: à l'envi /alɑ̃vi/ *loc adv* [*répéter, souligner, rappeler*] at every possible opportunity.

enviable /ɑ̃vjabl/ *adj* [*situation, sort*] enviable; **une situation peu ~** an unenviable position.

envie /ɑ̃vi/ *nf* **1** GÉN urge (**de faire** to do); (de choses à manger) craving (**de** for); **~ folle** insane urge; **l'~ m'a prise de te téléphoner** I got the urge to phone you; **des ~s de femme enceinte** the cravings of a pregnant woman; **avoir des ~s de meurtre** to feel like killing somebody; **ce n'est pas l'~ qui me manque** don't think I haven't thought of it!; **avoir ~ de qch** to feel like sth; **avoir ~ de faire** (fortement) to want to do; (passagèrement) to feel like doing; **il n'a qu'une ~, (c'est de)** partir all he wants is to leave; **avoir ~ de rire** to feel like laughing; **avoir ~ de vomir** to feel sick; **il a ~ que je parte** he wants me to leave; **mourir d'~ de faire** to be dying to do; **donner (l')~ à qn de faire** to make sb want to do; **2** (convoitise) envy; **leur piscine fait ~ à** their swimming pool is the envy of; **il te fait ~ ce jouet?** would you like that toy?; **3** (angiome) birthmark; ▶ **pisser**.
IDIOMES **avoir une ~ pressante** to need to go to the toilet.

envier /ɑ̃vje/ [2] *vtr* to envy; **des musées que le monde entier nous envie** our museums that are the envy of the world.

envieux, -ieuse /ɑ̃vjø, øz/ **I** *adj* envious.
II *nm,f* envious person; **faire des ~** to make people jealous.

environ /ɑ̃virɔ̃/ *adv* about; **tous les deux ans ~**

about every two years; **à ~ dix mètres** about ten metres GB away.

environnant, **~e** /ɑ̃virɔnɑ̃, ɑ̃t/ *adj* surrounding.

environnement /ɑ̃virɔnmɑ̃/ *nm* environment.

environner /ɑ̃virɔne/ [1] *vtr* to surround.

environs /ɑ̃virɔ̃/ *nmpl* **être des ~** to be from the area; **aux ~ de** (dans l'espace) in the vicinity of; (dans le temps) around; (en grandeur) in the region of.

envisageable /ɑ̃vizaʒabl/ *adj* possible.

envisager /ɑ̃vizaʒe/ [13] *vtr* **1** (projeter) to plan (**de faire** to do); **2** (imaginer) to envisage [*hypothèse, situation*]; to foresee [*problème, possibilité*]; **~ le pire** to imagine the worst; **3** (considérer) to consider.

envoi /ɑ̃vwa/ *nm* **1** (expédition) **tous les ~s de colis sont suspendus** parcel post is suspended; **date d'~** dispatch date GB, mailing date US; **faire un ~ de** to send [*fleurs, livres*]; **date limite d'~ de qch** deadline for posting GB ou mailing US sth; **frais d'~** postage; **2** (ce qui est expédié) **nous attendons un ~ important** we're expecting a large consignment; **les ~s de plus de deux kilos** parcels over two kilos; **3** (déplacement) **demander l'~ (immédiat) de troupes** to ask for troops to be dispatched (immediately); **4** SPORT **coup d'~** kick-off; **donner le coup d'~ de** to kick off [*match, campagne*]; to open [*festival, fête*].
■ **~ en nombre** bulk dispatch GB ou mailing US; **~ recommandé** registered post ₵ GB ou mail ₵ US; **~ contre remboursement** cash on delivery, COD.

envol /ɑ̃vɔl/ *nm* (d'oiseau, imagination) flight; (d'avion) takeoff; **prendre son ~** [*oiseau*] to take flight; [*avion*] to take off; [*adolescent*] to leave the nest.

envolée /ɑ̃vɔle/ *nf* (discours) flight of fancy; (des prix) surge (**de** in); (de parti) rise.

envoler: s'envoler /ɑ̃vɔle/ [1] *vpr* **1** (partir) [*oiseau*] to fly off (**pour** to); [*avion, passager*] to take off (**pour** for); [*papier, chapeau*] to be blown away; **mon portefeuille ne s'est tout de même pas envolé**° my wallet didn't just disappear; **2** (augmenter) [*prix*] to soar; **3** (disparaître) to vanish; **4**° (s'enfuir) to do a runner°, to escape.

envoûtant, **~e** /ɑ̃vutɑ̃, ɑ̃t/ *adj* [*film, livre*] spellbinding; [*atmosphère, musique*] enchanting; [*sourire, beauté*] bewitching.

envoûtement /ɑ̃vutmɑ̃/ *nm* (action) bewitchment; (sortilège) spell.

envoûter /ɑ̃vute/ [1] *vtr* to bewitch; **~ son auditoire** FIG to hold the audience spellbound.

envoûteur, -euse /ɑ̃vutœr, øz/ *nm,f* sorcerer/sorceress.

envoyé, **~e** /ɑ̃vwaje/ **I** *adj* **ça c'est (bien) ~!**° well said!
II *nm,f* envoy; **~ spécial** (journaliste) special correspondent.

envoyer /ɑ̃vwaje/ [24] **I** *vtr* **1** (expédier, faire déplacer) to send (**à** to); **il vous envoie ses amitiés** he sends (you) his regards; **qui vous envoie?** who sent you?; **~ qn chercher le journal** to send sb out to get the paper; **2** (lancer) to throw [*caillou*]; to fire [*missile*] (**sur** at); **~ le ballon dans les buts** to put the ball in the net; **3** (asséner) **un coup de pied à qn** to kick sb; **m'a envoyé son poing dans la figure** he punched me in the face; **4** (transmettre) to send.
II s'envoyer *vpr* **1** (échanger) to exchange; **s'~ des baisers** (par gestes) to blow each other kisses; **2**° (avaler) to guzzle [*boisson*]; to wolf down [*repas*].
IDIOMES **~ qn promener**° to send sb packing°; **tout ~ promener**° to drop the lot°.

envoyeur /ɑ̃vwajœr/ *nm* **retour à l'~** return to sender.

éolien, -ienne[1] /eɔljɛ̃, ɛn/ *adj* [*érosion, générateur*] wind (*épith*).

éolienne[2] /eɔljɛn/ *nf* (aeolian) windmill.

épagneul /epaɲœl/ *nm* spaniel.

épais, épaisse /epɛ, ɛs/ **I** **▶ 348** *adj* **1** (pas mince) thick; **il n'est pas bien ~ ce petit**° **!** he's a skinny little fellow!; **2** (pas subtil) [*esprit*] dull; **3** (pâteux) thick; **4** (dense) thick; **5** (profond) [*nuit, silence*] deep.

II *adv* a lot, much; **tu en as mis trop ~** you've put too much on.

épaisseur /epɛsœʀ/ *nf* **1** ▶348│ (dimension, densité) thickness; **un mur de deux mètres d'~** a wall two metresᴳᴮ thick; **de faible ~** thin; **2** (de liquide) thickness; **3** (profondeur) depths (*pl*); **dans l'~ de la nuit** in the depths of night; **4** FIG (de personnage, projet) substance; **5** (couche) layer.

épaissir /epesiʀ/ [3] **I** *vtr* **1** (rendre consistant) to thicken; **2** (déformer) [*âge, graisse*] to thicken [*traits, taille*]; [*vêtement*] to broaden [*silhouette*]; **3** (obscurcir) to deepen [*mystère*].
II *vi* **1** (devenir plus consistant) [*sauce*] to thicken; [*gelée*] to set; **faire ~** cook mixture until it thickens; **2** (grossir) to put on weight.
III s'épaissir *vpr* [*sauce, brume, taille*] to thicken; [*mystère*] to deepen.

épanchement /epɑ̃ʃmɑ̃/ **I** *nm* MÉD (de sang) effusion; **avoir un ~ de synovie** to have water on the knee.
II épanchements *nmpl* (confidences) outpourings.

épancher: **s'épancher** /epɑ̃ʃe/ [1] *vpr* [*personne*] to open one's heart (**auprès de** to).

épandage /epɑ̃daʒ/ *nm* (action) spreading; TECH sewage farming.

épandre /epɑ̃dʀ/ [6] *vtr* to spread.

épanoui, **~e** /epanwi/ *adj* [*fleur*] in full bloom (*après n*); [*sourire, visage*] beaming; [*personne, personnalité*] well-adjusted; [*corps*] ample.

épanouir: **s'épanouir** /epanwiʀ/ [3] *vpr* [*fleur*] to bloom; [*visage*] to light up; [*personne*] to blossom; **permettre aux gens de s'~** to enable people to fulfilᴳᴮ their potential.

épanouissant, **~e** /epanwisɑ̃, ɑ̃t/ *adj* fulfilling.

épanouissement /epanwismɑ̃/ *nm* (de fleur) blooming; (développement) GÉN development; (de talent) flowering; **favoriser/empêcher l'~ de qn/qch** to foster/to hamper the development of sb/sth.

épargnant, **~e** /epaʀɲɑ̃, ɑ̃t/ *nm,f* saver.

épargne /epaʀɲ/ *nf* savings (*pl*); **un compte (d') ~** a savings account.

épargner /epaʀɲe/ [1] **I** *vtr* **1** to save [*argent*]; **2** (ne pas affecter) to spare [*lieu, personne, institution*]; **3** (éviter) **~ qch à qn** to spare sb sth.
II *vi* to save.
III s'épargner *vpr* to save oneself [*attente, effort*].

éparpillement /epaʀpijmɑ̃/ *nm* scattering.

éparpiller /epaʀpije/ [1] *vtr* LIT to scatter; FIG to fail to concentrate [*forces, attention*].
II s'éparpiller *vpr* [*cendres, foule*] to scatter.

épars, **~e** /epaʀ, aʀs/ *adj* scattered.

épatant○, **~e** /epatɑ̃, ɑ̃t/ *adj* marvellousᴳᴮ.

épate○ /epat/ *nf* showing off.

épaté, **~e** /epate/ *adj* **1 nez ~** pug nose, flat nose; **2**○ (surpris) amazed (**de** by).

épater○ /epate/ [1] **I** *vtr* **1** (impressionner) to impress; **ça t'épate, hein?** surprised, aren't you?; **2** (étonner) to amaze.
II s'épater *vpr* (s'étonner) to marvel (**de** at).

épaule /epol/ *nf* ▶137│ ANAT shoulder; **large d'~s** broad-shouldered; **rentrer la tête dans les ~s** to hunch one's shoulders; **~ d'agneau** shoulder of lamb.
IDIOMES **changer son fusil d'~** to change one's tactics; **avoir la tête sur les ~s** to have one's head screwed on○.

épauler /epole/ [1] **I** *vtr* **1** (aider) to help; **2** to take aim with [*fusil*].
II *vi* to take aim.

épaulette /epolɛt/ *nf* (rembourrage) shoulder-pad; (bretelle) (shoulder-)strap; MIL epaulette.

épave /epav/ *nf* **1** LIT, FIG wreck; **2** (débris) bit of wreckage.

épée /epe/ *nf* sword; **c'est un coup d'~ dans l'eau** FIG it was a complete waste of effort.

épeler /eple/ [19] *vtr* to spell [*mot*].

éperdu, **~e** /epɛʀdy/ *adj* [*besoin, désir*] overwhelm-ing; [*cri*] frantic; [*regard*] desperate; [*fuite*] headlong (*épith*); [*amour, reconnaissance*] boundless.

éperdument /epɛʀdymɑ̃/ *adv* [*crier*] frantically; [*amoureux*] madly; **je me moque ~ de ce qu'il pense** I couldn't care less about what he thinks.

éperon /epʀɔ̃/ *nm* spur.

éperonner /epʀɔne/ [1] *vtr* LIT, FIG to spur on.

épervier /epɛʀvje/ *nm* (oiseau) sparrowhawk.

éphèbe /efɛb/ *nm* **1** HUM Adonis; **2** HIST ephebe.

éphémère /efemɛʀ/ *adj* [*bonheur*] fleeting; [*succès, produit, insecte*] short-lived; **de manière ~** fleetingly.

éphéméride /efemeʀid/ *nf* (calendrier) block calendar.

épi /epi/ *nm* **1** BOT (de blé, d'avoine) ear; (de fleur) spike; **2** (mèche) (unmanageable) tuft of hair ᴳᴮ, cow-lick ᵁˢ.
■ **~ de maïs** corn cob.

épice /epis/ *nf* spice.

épicé, **~e** /epise/ *adj* (parfumé, grivois) spicy; (fort) hot.

épicéa /episea/ *nm* spruce.

épicentre /episɑ̃tʀ/ *nm* epicentre.

épicer /epise/ [12] *vtr* (en cuisine) to spice; FIG to add spice to.

épicerie /episʀi/ ▶374│ *nf* **1** (boutique) grocer's (shop) GB, grocery (store) US; **à l'~** at the grocer's; **2** (commerce) grocery trade; **3** (produits) groceries (*pl*).
■ **~ fine** delicatessen.

épicier, -ière /episje, ɛʀ/ ▶374│ *nm,f* grocer.

épicurien, -ienne /epikyʀjɛ̃, ɛn/ *adj* PHILOS Epicurean.

épidémie /epidemi/ *nf* MÉD, FIG epidemic.

épidémique /epidemik/ *adj* epidemic.

épiderme /epidɛʀm/ *nm* (peau) skin.

épidermique /epidɛʀmik/ *adj* LIT skin (*épith*); [*blessure*] skin-deep; FIG [*sensibilité*] extreme; **réaction ~** gut reaction.

épier /epje/ [2] *vtr* **1** (observer) to spy on [*personne, comportement*]; **2** (attendre) to be on the lookout for.

épigramme /epigʀam/ *nf* epigram.

épilation /epilasjɔ̃/ *nf* removal of unwanted hair; (à la cire) waxing.

épilepsie /epilɛpsi/ ▶196│ *nf* epilepsy; **crise d'~** epileptic fit.

épileptique /epilɛptik/ *adj, nmf* epileptic.

épiler /epile/ [1] **I** *vtr* to remove unwanted hair from [*jambe*]; (à la cire) to wax; to pluck [*sourcils*].
II s'épiler *vpr* **s'~ les sourcils** to pluck one's eyebrows; **s'~ le menton** to remove the hairs from one's chin.

épilogue /epilɔg/ *nm* LITTÉRAT epilogueᴳᴮ; FIG outcome.

épiloguer /epilɔge/ [1] *vi* to go on and on (**sur** about).

épinard /epinaʀ/ *nm* spinach ₵.
IDIOMES **ça met du beurre dans les ~s**○ it makes life that little bit easier.

épine /epin/ *nf* thorn; **sans ~s** thornless.
■ **~ dorsale** ANAT spine; FIG backbone.
IDIOMES **ôter à qn une ~ du pied** to take a weight off sb's shoulders.

épinette /epinɛt/ *nf* **1** MUS spinet; **2** BOT spruce.

épineux, -euse /epinø, øz/ *adj* [*tige*] prickly; [*problème, situation*] tricky; [*question*] vexed; [*caractère*] prickly.

épingle /epɛ̃gl/ *nf* pin.
■ **~ à chapeau** hatpin; **~ à cheveux** hairpin; **virage en ~ à cheveux** hairpin bend; **~ de** or **à nourrice**, **~ de sûreté** safety pin.
IDIOMES **monter qch en ~** to blow sth up out of proportion; **être tiré à quatre ~s**○ to be immaculately dressed; **tirer son ~ du jeu** to get out while the going is good.

épingler /epɛ̃gle/ [1] *vtr* **1** (fixer) to pin [*affiche*] (**à** to); to pin [sth] together [*billets*]; **2**○ (arrêter) to collar○.

épinière /epinjɛʀ/ *adj f* **moelle ~** spinal cord.

épiphyse /epifiz/ *nf* epiphysis.

épique /epik/ *adj* epic; **poème ~** epic; **c'était ~**○ HUM it was quite something○.

épiscopat /episkɔpa/ *nm* episcopate, episcopacy.

épiscope /episkɔp/ *nm* **1** (appareil optique) episcope GB, opaque projector US; **2** MIL periscope.

épisode /epizɔd/ *nm* episode; **roman à ~s** serialized novel.

épisodique /epizɔdik/ *adj* (secondaire) minor; (intermittent) [*crises*] sporadic; [*rôle*] occasional.

épisodiquement /epizɔdikmɑ̃/ *adv* sporadically.

épistémologie /epistemɔlɔʒi/ *nf* epistemology.

épistolaire /epistɔlɛR/ *adj* [*genre*] epistolary; **ils ont des relations ~s** they correspond.

épitaphe /epitaf/ *nf* epitaph; **en ~** as an epitaph.

épithète /epitɛt/ *nf* LING attributive adjective; (qualificatif) epithet.

épître /epitR/ *nf* epistle.

éploré, ~e /eplɔRe/ *adj* (affligé) grief-stricken; (en pleurs) tearful.

épluche-légume, *pl* **~s** /eplyʃlegym/ *nm* potato peeler.

éplucher /eplyʃe/ [1] *vtr* LIT to peel [*fruit*]; FIG to go through [sth] with a fine-tooth comb.

épluchure /eplyʃyR/ *nf* **~ de pomme** piece of apple peel; **~s** peelings.

éponge /epɔ̃ʒ/ *nf* **1** (animal) sponge; **2** (pour la maison) sponge; **3** (tissu) terry-towelling^GB.
■ **~ métallique** (pan) scourer.
IDIOMES **passer l'~** to forget the past; **passer l'~ sur qch** to forget all about sth.

éponger /epɔ̃ʒe/ [13] **I** *vtr* to mop up [*liquide*]; to mop [*sueur, surface*]; to absorb [*déficit*]; to pay off [*dettes*].
II s'éponger *vpr* **s'~ le front** to mop one's brow.

éponyme /epɔnim/ **I** *adj* eponymous.
II *nm* eponym.

épopée /epɔpe/ *nf* (en poésie) epic; (suite d'événements) saga.

époque /epɔk/ *nf* **1** (période quelconque) time; **à l'~** at that time; **à l'~ où** at the time when; **à cette ~ de l'année** (présent) at this time of the year; (passé, futur) at that time of the year; **d'une autre ~** from another time; **il est d'une autre ~** he belongs to another time; **vivre avec son ~** to move with the times; **l'~ est au pragmatisme** pragmatism is the order of the day; **quelle ~!** what's the world coming to!; **à mon ~** in my day; **à notre ~** (aujourd'hui) these days; **2** (période historique) era; **3** (période stylistique) period; **d'~ Renaissance** from the Renaissance period; **des meubles d'~** antique furniture; **4** (en géologie) epoch.

époumoner◦: **s'époumoner** /epumɔne/ [1] *vpr* LIT, FIG to shout oneself hoarse, to shout one's head off◦; (en chantant) to sing oneself hoarse.

épouse /epuz/ *nf* wife, spouse.

épouser /epuze/ [1] *vtr* **1** to marry [*personne*]; **2** to adopt [*cause, idée*].

épousseter /epuste/ [20] *vtr* to dust.

époustoufler◦ /epustufle/ [1] *vtr* to amaze.

épouvantable /epuvɑ̃tabl/ *adj* GÉN dreadful; (atroce) appalling.

épouvantail /epuvɑ̃taj/ *nm* (à oiseaux) scarecrow; (personne laide)◦ fright; (menace) spectre^GB.

épouvante /epuvɑ̃t/ *nf* (terreur) terror; (horreur) horror; **glacé d'~** paralyzed with terror; **film d'~** horror film; **vision d'~** terrifying vision.

épouvanter /epuvɑ̃te/ [1] *vtr* (terrifier) to terrify; (horrifier) to horrify.

époux /epu/ **I** *nm inv* husband.
II *nmpl* **les ~** the (married) couple; **les jeunes ~** the newly weds; **les ~ Martin** Mr and Mrs Martin.

éprendre: s'éprendre /eprɑ̃dR/ [52] *vpr* **s'~ de** to fall in love with [*personne*].

épreuve /eprœv/ *nf* **1** (moment pénible) ordeal; **subir de dures ~s** to go through terrible ordeals; **2** (testant la valeur, résistance) test; **mettre à l'~** to put [sth/sb] to the test; **mettre à rude ~** to put [sb] to a severe test; to be very hard on [*voiture, chaussures*]; to tax [*patience, nerfs*]; to put a strain on [*amitié, relation*]; **soumettre qch à l'~ de** to subject sth to the test of; **à**

toute ~ unfailing (*épith*); **résister à l'~ du temps** to stand the test of time; **à l'~ du feu/des balles** fire-/bullet-proof; **3** (partie d'examen) (part of an) examination; **~ écrite/orale** written/oral examination; **~ d'histoire** history examination; **4** SPORT **~ d'athlétisme** athletics event; **~s éliminatoires** heats; **~s de sélection** trials; **5** (photo, estampe) proof.
■ **~ de vérité** acid test.

épris, ~e /epri, iz/ *adj* (amoureux) in love (**de** with); (passionné) **être ~ de voyages** to have a great love of travelling.

éprouvant, ~e /epruvɑ̃, ɑ̃t/ *adj* [*attente, période, travail*] gruelling^GB; [*bruit, climat, situation*] trying.

éprouver /epruve/ [1] *vtr* **1** (ressentir) to feel [*regret, amour*]; to have [*sensation, doute, difficulté*]; **~ le désir de faire** to feel a desire to do; **~ de la colère contre** to feel angry with; **~ du plaisir à faire** to get pleasure out of doing; **2** (tester) to test [*sth*]; **une technique éprouvée** a tried and tested technique; **3** (toucher) [*décès, événement*] to distress; [*épidémie, tempête, crise*] to hit.

éprouvette /epruvɛt/ *nf* (tube) test tube; (échantillon) sample; **bébé ~** test-tube baby.

épuisant, ~e /epɥizɑ̃, ɑ̃t/ *adj* exhausting.

épuisé, ~e /epɥize/ *adj* (non disponible) [*livre*] out of print; [*article*] out of stock; **notre stock est ~** we're sold out; (consommé) [*stock, vivres*] exhausted.

épuisement /epɥizmɑ̃/ *nm* exhaustion; **jusqu'à ~ des stocks** while stocks last.

épuiser /epɥize/ [1] **I** *vtr* **1** (fatiguer) [*activité*] to exhaust; [*souci, personne*] to wear [sb] out; **épuisé nerveusement** emotionally drained; **2** (finir) to exhaust [*sujet, mine*]; **3** (appauvrir) to impoverish [*sol*].
II s'épuiser *vpr* **1** (se fatiguer) [*personne*] to exhaust oneself; **s'~ à faire qch** to wear oneself out doing sth; **2** (s'amenuiser) [*réserves*] to become exhausted.

épuisette /epɥizɛt/ *nf* landing net; (à crevettes) shrimp net.

épurateur /epyRatœR/ *nm* purifier.

épuration /epyRasjɔ̃/ *nf* (de gaz, liquide) purification; (de pétrole) refining; (d'eaux usées) treatment; (de groupe, parti) purge.

épurer /epyRe/ [1] *vtr* **1** CHIMIE to purify [*eau, gaz*]; **2** to purge [*parti*]; to clean up [*mœurs*]; to refine [*style, goût*]; to expurgate [*texte*].

équarrir /ekaRiR/ [3] *vtr* (tailler) to square (off) [*pierre, bois*]; **mal équarri** LIT, FIG rough-hewn.

équateur /ekwatœR/ *nm* Equator.

équation /ekwasjɔ̃/ *nf* equation.

équatorial, ~e, *mpl* **-iaux** /ekwatɔRjal, o/ *adj* equatorial.

équatorien, -ienne /ekwatɔRjɛ̃, ɛn/ ▶ 394 *adj* Ecuadorian, Ecuadoran.

équerre /ekɛR/ *nf* **1** (à dessin) set square; **2** (support) (en T) flat T-bracket; (en L) flat angle bracket.

équestre /ekɛstR/ *adj* equestrian.

équeuter /ekøte/ [1] *vtr* to remove the stalk from GB, to stem US [*cerise*]; to hull GB, to stem US [*fraise*].

équilibre /ekilibR/ *nm* **1** (fait de ne pas tomber) balance; **garder l'~** to keep one's balance; **être en ~ sur** [*objet*] to be balanced on; [*personne*] to balance on; **numéro d'~** balancing act; **2** (entre deux éléments, poids) balance; (stabilité) stability; **l'~ des forces** (en politique) the balance of power; **être en ~** [*objets*] to be balanced; **3** (bien-être, santé mentale) equilibrium; **manquer d'~** to be unstable; **4** (bonne combinaison) (de formes, phrase, d'alimentation) balance; **5** CHIMIE, PHYS equilibrium.

équilibrer /ekilibRe/ [1] **I** *vtr* to balance; **~ son alimentation** to have a balanced diet; **~ une façade** (en elle-même) to give balance to a façade; (avec un nouvel élément) to balance a façade; **un enfant équilibré** a well-balanced child; **le chargement est mal équilibré** the load is unevenly distributed.
II s'équilibrer *vpr* [*facteurs, coûts*] to balance each other.

équilibriste /ekilibRist/ *nmf* LIT, FIG acrobat.

équinoxe /ekinɔks/ *nm* equinox.

équipage /ekipaʒ/ *nm* GÉN crew; (attelage) horse and carriage.

équipe /ekip/ *nf* (groupe) team; (en usine) shift; (de rameurs) crew; **travailler en ~** to work as a team; **~ de secours** rescue team; **~ de dépannage** breakdown crew; **~ de télévision** television crew; **~ de tournage** CIN film unit; **faire ~ avec qn** to team up with sb (**pour faire** to do); **l'~ dirigeante** the management team; **l'~ de nuit** the night shift; **travailler en ~s** to work in shifts.

équipé, ~e¹ /ekipe/ *adj* equipped (**de, en** with; **pour** for; **pour faire** to do); **cuisine ~e** fitted kitchen.

équipée² /ekipe/ *nf* (aventure) escapade.

équipement /ekipmɑ̃/ *nm* **1** (matériel) (d'usine, de cuisine) equipment; (de sportif) kit; **2** (infrastructure) **~s** facilities; **~ hôtelier** accommodation facilities (*pl*); **~s collectifs** public facilities; **3** (processus) (d'armée) equipping; (de soldat, sportif) kitting out; **l'~ de la région a coûté...** improving the region's facilities cost...

équiper /ekipe/ [1] **I** *vtr* to equip [*hôpital, véhicule, armée*] (**de** with); to provide [*ville*] (**de** with); to fit out [*personne*] (**de** with).
II s'équiper *vpr* to equip oneself (**de, en** with; **pour** for; **pour faire** to do).

équipier, -ière /ekipje, ɛʀ/ *nm,f* GÉN team member; (rameur, marin) crew member.

équitable /ekitabl/ *adj* [*personne*] fair-minded; [*décision*] fair.

équitablement /ekitabləmɑ̃/ *adv* equitably, fairly.

équitation /ekitasjɔ̃/ ▸ 329│ *nf* (horse-)riding.

équité /ekite/ *nf* equity; **en toute ~** in all fairness.

équivalence /ekivalɑ̃s/ *nf* **1** (valeur identique) equivalence; **2** UNIV **demander une ~** to ask for recognition of one's qualifications GB, to ask for advanced standing US.

équivalent, ~e /ekivalɑ̃, ɑ̃t/ **I** *adj* (égal) equivalent (**à** to); (identique) identical (**à** to).
II *nm* equivalent.

équivaloir /ekivalwaʀ/ [45] *vtr ind* **~ à** to be equivalent to [*quantité*]; to amount to [*effet*]; to be tantamount to [*effet négatif*].

équivoque /ekivɔk/ **I** *adj* (ambigu) ambiguous; (suspect) [*réputation*] dubious; [*conduite*] questionable.
II *nf* (ambiguïté) ambiguity; **sans ~** [*réponse*] unequivocal; [*répondre*] unequivocally.

érable /eʀabl/ *nm* maple; **sirop d'~** maple syrup.

éradication /eʀadikasjɔ̃/ *nf* eradication.

érafler /eʀafle/ [1] *vtr* to scratch.

éraflure /eʀaflyʀ/ *nf* scratch.

éraillé, ~e /eʀaje/ *adj* [*voix*] rasping (*épith*).

érailler: s'érailler /eʀaje/ [1] *vpr* [*voix*] to become hoarse.

ère /ɛʀ/ *nf* **1** (historique, géologique) era; **cent ans avant notre ~** 100 years BC; **en l'an 10 de notre ~** in the year 10 AD; **2** (époque) age; **à l'~ atomique** in the nuclear age.

érection /eʀɛksjɔ̃/ *nf* erection.

éreintant, ~e /eʀɛ̃tɑ̃, ɑ̃t/ *adj* exhausting, killing○.

éreinter /eʀɛ̃te/ [1] **I** *vtr* (fatiguer) to exhaust.
II s'éreinter *vpr* to wear oneself out.

ergot /ɛʀgo/ *nm* (de coq) spur; (de chien) dewclaw; (de seigle) ergot.

ergoter /ɛʀgɔte/ [1] *vi* PÉJ to split hairs.

ériger /eʀiʒe/ [13] **I** *vtr* to erect [*statue, bâtiment*]; to establish, to set up [*tribunal, société*].
II s'ériger *vpr* **s'~ en** to set oneself up as.

ermitage /ɛʀmitaʒ/ *nm* LIT hermitage; FIG retreat.

ermite /ɛʀmit/ *nm* **1** LIT hermit; **2** FIG recluse; **vivre en ~** FIG to live the life of a recluse.

éroder /eʀɔde/ [1] **I** *vtr* LIT, FIG to erode; to erode the value of [*monnaie*]; to undermine [*argument*].
II s'éroder *vpr* FIG to become eroded.

érogène /eʀɔʒɛn/ *adj* erogenous.

érosion /eʀozjɔ̃/ *nf* erosion; **~ monétaire** depreciation of the currency.

érotique /eʀɔtik/ *adj* erotic.

érotisme /eʀɔtism/ *nm* eroticism.

errant, ~e /eʀɑ̃, ɑ̃t/ *adj* (par nécessité) wandering; (par choix) rootless; **chien ~** stray dog.

errements /eʀmɑ̃/ *nmpl* FML transgressions.

errer /eʀe/ [1] *vi* [*personne*] to wander (**par** about); [*imagination*] to wander (**sur** over); [*animal*] to roam.

erreur /eʀœʀ/ *nf* **1** (inexactitude, idée fausse) mistake; **~ de date** mistake about the date; **~ de jugement/de méthode** error of judgment/of method; **~ de calcul/de stratégie** calculation/strategic error; **~ de traduction** mistranslation; **je le croyais riche mais c'était une ~** I thought he was rich but I was mistaken; **sauf ~ ou omission** errors and omissions excepted; **2** (acte regrettable) mistake; **une ~ de jeunesse** a youthful mistake; **3** (confusion, fait de se tromper) **par ~** by mistake; **induire qn en ~** to mislead sb; **sauf ~ de ma part** if I'm not mistaken; **vous faites ~** you are mistaken; **il n'y a pas d'~ possible** there's no mistake; **il y a ~ sur la personne** it's a case of mistaken identity SOUT; **le droit à l'~** the right to make mistakes; (des scientifiques) the right to error; **4** JUR error.

erroné, ~e /eʀɔne/ *adj* incorrect; **'code ~'** 'code not valid'.

ersatz /ɛʀzats/ *nm* LIT, FIG ersatz.

éructer /eʀykte/ [1] **I** *vtr* to spit out [*injures*].
II *vi* to eructate.

érudit, ~e /eʀydi, it/ **I** *adj* erudite, scholarly.
II *nm,f* scholar, erudite person.

érudition /eʀydisjɔ̃/ *nf* erudition, scholarship.

éruption /eʀypsjɔ̃/ *nf* eruption; **entrer en ~** to erupt.

érythréen, -éenne /eʀitʀeɛ̃, ɛn/ *adj* Eritrean.

ès /ɛs/ *prép* **licence ~ lettres ~** arts degree, B.A. (degree).

esbroufe○ /ɛzbʀuf/ *nf* **c'est de l'~** it's all a lot of swank○; **faire de l'~** to swank○, to show off.

escabeau, pl ~x /ɛskabo/ *nm* (échelle) stepladder; (tabouret avec marches) kitchen steps.

escadre /ɛskadʀ/ *nf* squadron.

escadrille /ɛskadʀij/ *nf* squadron.

escadron /ɛskadʀɔ̃/ *nm* MIL company; **~ de la mort** death squad.

escalade /ɛskalad/ ▸ 329│ *nf* **1** (activité) climbing; (de montagne) ascent; **faire de l'~** to go climbing; **2** (intensification) MIL, GÉN escalation.

escalader /ɛskalade/ [1] *vtr* to scale [*mur, clôture*]; to climb [*montagne*].

escale /ɛskal/ *nf* **1** (arrêt, durée) GÉN stopover; **faire ~ à Rio** NAUT [*navire*] to call at Rio; [*passager*] to stop off in Rio; AVIAT [*avion, passager*] to stop over in Rio; **faire Londres-Rio sans ~** [*navire*] to sail London-Rio direct; [*avion*] to fly London-Rio nonstop; **2** (lieu) NAUT port of call; AVIAT stopover.
■ **~ technique** AVIAT refuelling GB stop; NAUT overhaul.

escalier /ɛskalje/ *nm* **1** (ensemble architectural) staircase; **2** (ensemble de marches) stairs (*pl*); **monter l'~** or **les ~s en courant** to run up the stairs.
■ **~ en colimaçon** spiral staircase; **~ d'honneur** grand staircase; **~ mécanique** or **roulant** escalator; **~ de secours** emergency staircase; **~ de service** backstairs (*pl*), service stairs (*pl*).

escamotable /ɛskamɔtabl/ *adj* (train d'atterrissage) retractable; [*meuble, échelle*] foldaway (*épith*).

escamotage /ɛskamɔtaʒ/ *nm* (de roues) retraction; (de fait, preuve) cover-up; (de personne) spiriting away.

escamoter /ɛskamɔte/ [1] *vtr* **1** [*illusionniste*] to make [sth] disappear; **2** (replier) to retract [*roues*]; **~ un lit** to fold a bed away; **3** [*fait, preuve*] to cover up; **4** (éluder) to evade [*problème*].

escampette○ /ɛskɑ̃pɛt/ *nf* **prendre la poudre d'~**
to scarper○ GB, to skedaddle○.

escapade /ɛskapad/ *nf* escapade; **faire une ~** (fugue)
to run away.

escargot /ɛskaʀgo/ *nm* snail.

escarpé, ~e /ɛskaʀpe/ *adj* [*chemin, pente*] steep;
[*rocher*] craggy.

escarpement /ɛskaʀpəmɑ̃/ *nm* (versant) steep slope;
(raideur) steepness.

escarpin /ɛskaʀpɛ̃/ *nm* court shoe GB, pump US.

escarre /ɛskaʀ/ *nf* bedsore.

escient /ɛsjɑ̃/ *nm* **à bon ~** [*agir*] wittingly, advisedly; **à mauvais ~** [*agir*] ill-advisedly.

esclaffer: **s'esclaffer** /ɛsklafe/ [1] *vpr* to guffaw.

esclandre /ɛsklɑ̃dʀ/ *nm* scene.

esclavage /ɛsklavaʒ/ *nm* **1** slavery; **réduire qn en
~** to reduce sb to slavery; **2** (contrainte) tyranny (de
of).

esclavagisme /ɛsklavaʒism/ *nm* (doctrine) pro-slavery
doctrine; (système) slavery.

esclavagiste /ɛsklavaʒist/ **I** *adj* [*politique*] pro-
slavery (*épith*); [*État*] slave (*épith*).
II *nmf* pro-slaver, person in favour GB of slavery.

esclave /ɛsklav/ **I** *adj* (asservi) enslaved; (servile)
servile; **être ~ de la mode** to be a slave to fashion.
II *nmf* slave.

escompte /ɛskɔ̃t/ *nm* discount.

escompter /ɛskɔ̃te/ [1] *vtr* **1** to discount [*effet, traite*];
2 (espérer) to anticipate; **~ faire** to count on doing.

escorte /ɛskɔʀt/ *nf* MIL, NAUT escort; (suite) retinue; FIG
accompaniment; **sous bonne ~** under escort.

escorter /ɛskɔʀte/ [1] *vtr* to escort.

escorteur /ɛskɔʀtœʀ/ *nm* escort vessel.

escrime /ɛskʀim/ ▶ **329** *nf* fencing.

escrimer○: **s'escrimer** /ɛskʀime/ [1] *vpr* **s'~ à
faire** to knock○ ou wear oneself out trying to do.

escrimeur, -euse /ɛskʀimœʀ, øz/ *nm,f* fencer.

escroc /ɛskʀo/ *nm* swindler, crook.

escroquer /ɛskʀoke/ [1] *vtr* to swindle; **~ qch à qn,
~ qn de qch** to swindle sb out of sth.

escroquerie /ɛskʀokʀi/ *nf* **1** (action) fraud, swindling;
tentative d'~ attempted fraud; **c'est de l'~!** it's
daylight robbery; **2** (résultat) swindle.

escudo /ɛskudo/ ▶ **33** *nm* escudo.

ESEU /ɛœsəy/ *nm*: *abbr* ▶ **examen**.

ésotérique /ezoteʀik/ *adj* [*propos*] esoteric; [*cercle*]
closed.

espace /ɛspas/ *nm* **1** (place, cosmos) space; **2** (lieu réservé à une activité) **~ de loisirs** leisure complex;
3 (sphère) arena; **4** (zone) area; **~ économique** economic area; **5** (intervalle) gap; **6** (laps de temps) **en l'~ de**
in the space of; **l'~ d'un instant** for a moment.
■ **~ aérien** airspace; **~ commercial** commercial
space *ⓒ*; **~ publicitaire** advertising space *ⓒ*.

espacement /ɛspasmɑ̃/ *nm* **1** GÉN (processus) spacing
out; (situation) growing infrequency; **2** (dans un texte)
spacing; **barre d'~** space bar.

espacer /ɛspase/ [12] **I** *vtr* to space [sth] out.
II **s'espacer** *vpr* to become less frequent.

espadon /ɛspadɔ̃/ *nm* swordfish.

Espagne /ɛspaɲ/ ▶ **232** *nprf* Spain.
IDIOMES **bâtir des châteaux en ~** to build castles
in the air.

espagnol, ~e /ɛspaɲɔl/ ▶ **394** **I** *adj* Spanish.
II ▶ **338** *nm* LING Spanish.

espalier /ɛspalje/ *nm* (treillis) espalier; (mur) fruit-wall;
(méthode) espalier cultivation.

espèce /ɛspɛs/ **I** *nf* **1** (en biologie) species; **une ~ rare**
a rare species; **l'~ humaine** mankind; **2** (type) kind;
de toute ~ of every kind; **de la pire** or **de la plus
belle ~** of the worst sort; **3** (dans une description
approximative) sort; **il y avait des ~s de colonnes**
there were some kind ou sort of columns; **cela n'a
aucune ~ d'importance** that is of absolutely no
importance; **~ d'idiot!** you idiot!

II espèces *nfpl* **en ~s** [*payer, règlement*] in cash.

espérance /ɛspeʀɑ̃s/ **I** *nf* hope.
II espérances *nfpl* (aspirations) expectations.
■ **~ de vie** life expectancy.

espérer /ɛspeʀe/ [14] **I** *vtr* **1** (appeler de ses vœux) **~
qch** to hope for sth; **~ faire** to hope to do; **j'espère
avoir bien fait** I hope (that) I did the right thing;
j'espère que oui/que non I hope so/not; **que peut-on
~ de plus?** what more can you hope for?;
2 (escompter) to expect (de from); **je n'en espérais pas
tant** it's more than I expected; **je ne t'espérais plus** I
had given up on you.
II *vi* to hope.

espiègle /ɛspjɛgl/ **I** *adj* mischievous.
II *nmf* imp, little monkey○.

espièglerie /ɛspjɛgləʀi/ *nf* (caractère) mischievousness.

espion, -ionne /ɛspjɔ̃, ɔn/ ▶ **374** *nm,f* spy.

espionnage /ɛspjonaʒ/ *nm* espionage, spying; **film/
roman d'~** spy film/story.
■ **~ industriel** industrial espionage.

espionner /ɛspjone/ [1] *vtr* to spy on.

espionnite /ɛspjonit/ *nf* spy mania.

esplanade /ɛsplanad/ *nf* esplanade.

espoir /ɛspwaʀ/ *nm* (fait, raison d'espérer) hope (**de** of);
rendre ~ to rekindle hope; **reprendre ~** to feel
hopeful again; **dans l'~ de faire qch** in the hope of
doing sth; **dans l'~ de te lire bientôt** hoping to hear
from you soon; **avoir l'~ de faire qch** to hope to do
sth; **avec ~** hopefully, in a hopeful way; **c'est sans
~** it's hopeless; **je garde ~** I am still hopeful.
IDIOMES **tant qu'il y a de la vie il y a de l'~** where
there's life there's hope.

esprit /ɛspʀi/ *nm* **1** (caractère) mind; **avoir l'~ vif** to
have a quick mind; **avoir l'~ mal placé** to have a
dirty mind○; **avoir l'~ d'aventure** to be adventurous; **avoir un ~ de synthèse** to be good at synthesiz-
ing; **avoir l'~ de contradiction** to be contrary;
2 (cerveau) mind; **l'idée m'a traversé l'~** the idea
crossed my mind; **mettre un doute dans l'~ de qn**
to sow the seeds of doubt in sb's mind; **cela m'était
totalement sorti de l'~** it completely slipped my
mind; **garder qch à l'~** to keep sth in mind; **cela ne
t'est jamais venu à l'~?** didn't it ever occur to you?
; **avoir l'~ dérangé** to be disturbed; **avoir l'~
ailleurs** to be miles away; **3** (humour) wit; **avoir
de l'~** to be witty; **une réponse pleine d'~** a witty
reply; **faire de l'~** to try to be witty; **4** (humeur) mood;
(disposition) spirit; (ambiance) atmosphere; **je n'ai
pas l'~ à rire** I'm in no mood for laughing; **dans un
~ de vengeance** in a spirit of revenge; **5** (personne)
individual; **l'un des plus grands ~s de son temps**
one of the greatest minds of his/her time; **calmer les
~s** to calm people down; **6** (caractéristique) spirit;
conforme à l'~ de l'entreprise in accordance with
the company ethic; **7** PHILOS, RELIG, MYTHOL spirit; **les
choses de l'~** spiritual matters; **croire aux ~s** to
believe in ghosts; **'~ es-tu là?'** 'is there anybody
there?'.
■ **~ d'à-propos** ready wit; **~ de corps** solidarity; **~ d'équipe** team spirit; **~ de famille** family
solidarity; **ils ont l'~ de famille** they're a very close
family; **je n'ai pas l'~ de famille** I'm not very family-
oriented.
IDIOMES **perdre ses ~s** (s'évanouir) to faint; (être très
troublé) to take leave of one's senses; **retrouver** or
reprendre ses ~s (après un malaise) to regain
consciousness; (après une émotion) to collect one's wits;
les grands ~s se rencontrent great minds think
alike.

esquimau, -aude, *mpl* **~x** /ɛskimo, od/ **I** *adj*
Eskimo; **chien ~** husky.
II *nm* **1** LING Eskimo; **2** ®(glace) chocolate-covered ice
lolly GB, ice-cream bar US.

esquinter○ /ɛskɛ̃te/ [1] **I** *vtr* **1** (amocher) to damage
[*voiture*]; to hurt [*personne*]; **2** (critiquer) to slate
[*auteur*]; **3** (fatiguer) to wear [sb] out.
II **s'esquinter** *vpr* **1** (se blesser) to hurt oneself; **s'~**

la santé to ruin one's health; **2** (se fatiguer) to wear oneself out (**à faire** doing).

esquisse /ɛskis/ *nf* (de dessin) sketch; (de programme) outline.

esquisser /ɛskise/ [1] **I** *vtr* to sketch [*portrait*]; to outline [*programme*].

II s'esquisser *vpr* [*solution*] to emerge.

esquiver /ɛskive/ [1] **I** *vtr* to duck [*coup*]; to sidestep [*question, attaque*]; to dodge [*responsabilité, difficulté*].

II s'esquiver *vpr* (partir) to slip away; (se dérober) to shy away.

essai /ese/ **I** *nm* **1** TECH (expérimentation) trial; **faire des ~s** to run trials; **être à l'~** to undergo trials; **vol d'~** test flight; **~ sur route** road test; **2** TECH (analyse, expérience) test; **~ de laboratoire** laboratory test; **3** (tentative) try; **un coup d'~** a try; **faire un ~** to have a try; **je serai à l'~ pendant un mois** I'll work a month on a trial basis; **4** (en littérature) essay (**sur** on); **5** (en athlétisme) attempt; (au rugby) try; **transformer un ~** to convert (a try).

II essais *nmpl* (en courses) qualifying round (*sg*).

essaim /esɛ̃/ *nm* LIT, FIG swarm.

essayage /esejaʒ/ *nm* fitting.

essayer /eseje/ [21] **I** *vtr* **1** (tenter) to try; **~ une voiture** (pour le plaisir) to try a car; (avant d'acheter) to test-drive a car; **~ sa force** to test one's strength; **2** TECH (soumettre à des tests) [*technicien*] to test [*arme, avion, mécanisme, matériau*]; [*technicien*] to run trials on [*voiture, machine*]; [*client*] to try out [*voiture, arme*]; **3** to try on [*vêtement, chaussures*]; to try [*taille, couleur*]; **acheter sans ~** to buy without trying on.

II s'essayer *vpr* **s'~ à** to have a go at [*sport*] ; to try one's hand at [*art, littérature*].

essayiste /esejist/ ▶374⎪ *nmf* essayist.

esse /ɛs/ *nf* (crochet) (S-shaped) hook; (de violon) f-hole.

essence /esɑ̃s/ *nf* **1** (carburant) petrol GB, gasoline US; **2** (extrait) essential oil; **3** (espèce d'arbre) tree species. ■ **~ à briquet** lighter fuel GB, lighter fluid US; **~ ordinaire** ~ 2-star petrol GB, regular gasoline US; **~ sans plomb** unleaded petrol GB ou gasoline US; **~ super** ~ 4-star petrol GB, premium gasoline US.

essentiel, -ielle /esɑ̃sjɛl/ **I** *adj* **1** (très important) essential; **2** (central) key (*épith*), essential; **rôle ~** key role.

II *nm* **1** (chose principale) **c'est l'~** that's the main thing; **aller à l'~** to get to the heart of the matter; **2** (partie la plus importante) bulk; **pour l'~** mainly; **3** (objets indispensables) basics (*pl*); **en voyage je n'emporte que l'~** when travelling GB I only ever take the bare minimum.

essentiellement /esɑ̃sjɛlmɑ̃/ *adv* **1** (pour la plus grande partie) mainly; **2** (dans ses aspects les plus importants) essentially.

esseulé, -e /esœle/ *adj* forlorn.

essieu, *pl* **~x** /esjø/ *nm* axle.

essor /esɔʀ/ *nm* (d'oiseau, imagination) flight; (de commerce, région) development; (de mode, sport) increasing popularity; **prendre son ~** [*oiseau*] to fly off; [*entreprise*] to take off; **être en plein ~** to be booming.

essorage /esɔʀaʒ/ *nm* (à la main) wringing; (en machine) spin-drying.

essorer /esɔʀe/ [1] *vtr* (en tordant) to wring; (par centrifugation) to spin-dry [*linge*]; to spin [*salade*].

essoreuse /esɔʀøz/ *nf* (à tambour) spin-drier GB, spin-dryer US; **~ à salade** salad spinner.

essoufflement /esufləmɑ̃/ *nm* LIT breathlessness; FIG loss of impetus.

essouffler /esufle/ [1] **I** *vtr* LIT to leave [sb] breathless; **être essoufflé** to be out of breath.

II s'essouffler *vpr* LIT to get breathless; FIG [*économie, projet*] to run out of steam.

essuie-glace, *pl* **~s** /esɥiglas/ *nm* windscreen wiper GB, windshield wiper US.

essuie-mains /esɥimɛ̃/ *nm inv* hand towel.

essuie-tout /esɥitu/ *nm inv* (en rouleau) kitchen roll; (en feuilles) kitchen paper.

essuyer /esɥije/ [22] **I** *vtr* **1** (rendre sec) to dry [*verre,*

mains, enfant, chien]; to wipe [*table*]; **~ la vaisselle** to dry up; **2** (pour nettoyer) to wipe; **3** (éponger) to wipe up; **~ ses larmes** to wipe away one's tears; **4** (subir) to run into [*orage*]; to suffer [*défaite, pertes, affront*].

II s'essuyer *vpr* (tout le corps) to dry oneself, to towel off US; (une partie du corps) (sécher) to dry; (nettoyer) to wipe; **s'~ les mains** to dry one's hands.

est /ɛst/ **I** *adj inv* [*façade, versant, côte*] east; [*frontière, zone*] eastern.

II *nm* **1** (point cardinal, région) east; **2** (en géographie) **l'Est** the East; **de l'Est** [*ville, accent*] eastern.

estafette /ɛstafɛt/ *nf* **1** ®AUT van; **2** MIL dispatch rider.

estampe /ɛstɑ̃p/ *nf* ART (sur planche gravée) engraving; (par lithographie) print.

estamper○ /ɛstɑ̃pe/ [1] *vtr* (escroquer) to rip [sb] off○.

estampille /ɛstɑ̃pij/ *nf* LIT (cachet, signature) stamp; (label) trademark; FIG mark.

est-ce ▶ être¹.

esthète /ɛstɛt/ *nmf* aesthete.

esthéticienne /ɛstetisjɛn/ ▶374⎪ *nf* beautician.

esthétique /ɛstetik/ **I** *adj* [*sens*] aesthetic; [*décor*] aesthetically pleasing; [*pose, geste*] graceful.

II *nf* (théorie) aesthetics (+ *v sg*); (de décor) aesthetic quality; (de geste) grace.

esthétisme /ɛstetism/ *nm* aestheticism.

estimable /ɛstimabl/ *adj* **1** (honorable) [*personne*] worthy; **2** (admirable) [*travail, résultat, effort*] laudable; **3 difficilement ~** [*fortune*] hard to estimate.

estimation /ɛstimasjɔ̃/ *nf* **1** (de coût) estimate; (valeur) valuation; (de dégâts) assessment; **2** (de distance, temps, d'efficacité) estimate; **3** (en statistique) estimate.

estime /ɛstim/ *nf* respect; **baisser dans l'~ de qn** to go down in sb's estimation.

estimer /ɛstime/ [1] **I** *vtr* **1** (penser) to consider (**que** that); **~ nécessaire/de son devoir de faire** to consider it necessary/one's duty to do; **2** (respecter) to think highly of [*ami, artiste*]; **3** (chiffrer) to value [*tableau, propriété*]; to assess [*dégâts*]; **~ qch au-dessus/au-dessous de sa valeur** to overvalue/under-value sth; **~ qch à** to value sth at; **~ qn à sa juste valeur** to recognize sb's real worth; **4** (calculer approximativement) to estimate (**à** at); **une vitesse estimée à 150 km/h** an estimated speed of 150 kph; **5** (deviner) to reckon.

II s'estimer *vpr* **estimez-vous heureux** think yourself lucky; **je m'estime satisfait de lui** I am satisfied with him.

estival, ~e, *mpl* **-aux** /ɛstival, o/ *adj* (d'été) summer (*épith*); (évoquant l'été) summery.

estivant, -e /ɛstivɑ̃, ɑ̃t/ *nmf* summer visitor.

estocade /ɛstɔkad/ *nf* LIT fatal sword thrust; FIG final blow.

estomac /ɛstɔma/ *nm* **1** ANAT stomach; **avoir mal à l'~** to have stomach ache GB ou a stomachache US; **~ bien rempli** full stomach; **j'ai un poids sur l'~** my stomach feels heavy; **avoir l'~ bien accroché** to have a strong stomach; **leur refus m'est resté sur l'~**○ their refusal left a nasty taste in my mouth; **2**○ FIG (courage) guts○ (*pl*).

IDIOMES avoir l'~ dans les talons○ to be famished.

estomaquer○ /ɛstɔmake/ [1] *vtr* to flabbergast.

estomper /ɛstɔ̃pe/ [1] **I** *vtr* to blur [*paysage, formes*]; FIG to gloss over [*détails*].

II s'estomper *vpr* [*paysage*] to become blurred; [*couleur, haine, souvenirs*] to fade.

estonien, -ienne /ɛstɔnjɛ̃, ɛn/ ▶394⎪, 338⎪ **I** *adj* Estonian.

II *nm* LING Estonian.

estrade /ɛstʀad/ *nf* platform.

estragon /ɛstʀagɔ̃/ *nm* tarragon.

estropié, ~e /ɛstʀɔpje/ **I** *adj* crippled.

II *nm,f* cripple.

estropier /ɛstʀɔpje/ [2] *vtr* **1** LIT to maim; **2** FIG (en prononçant) to mispronounce; (en écrivant) to misspell; (en jouant) to mangle [*sonate*].

estuaire /ɛstɥɛʀ/ *nm* estuary.

esturgeon /ɛstyRʒɔ̃/ *nm* sturgeon.

et /e/ *conj* and; **mon père ~ ma mère** my father and mother; **lui ~ son frère sont alcooliques** both he and his brother are alcoholics; **un homme grand ~ fort** a tall strong man; **~ voilà qu'il sort un couteau de sa poche!** and next thing he whips a knife out of his pocket!; **il y a expert ~ expert** (ils ne se valent pas tous) there are experts and experts; **et tu en es fier?** (exprimant la désapprobation) and you're proud of it?; **~ moi de répondre...** so I replied...; **~ le pourboire (alors)?** what about the tip?; **moi j'y vais, ~ toi?** I'm going, are you? ou what about you?; **~ alors?**, **~ après?** so what?

étable /etabl/ *nf* cowshed.

établi, **~e** /etabli/ I *pp* ▶ **établir**.

II *pp adj* **1** (solide, ancré) [*réputation, usage*] established; **il est/a été ~ que** it has been/was established that; **2** (en place) [*pouvoir*] ruling; [*ordre, autorité*] established.

III *nm* (table de travail) workbench.

établir /etabliʀ/ [3] I *vtr* **1** (fixer) to set up [*résidence*]; **~ son domicile à Londres** to set up home in London; **~ le prix (de vente) de** to price; **2** (instituer) to establish [*règlement, hiérarchie, régime, lien*]; to introduce [*impôt, discipline*]; to set up [*gouvernement*]; to set [*record, norme*]; **3** (mettre en forme) to draw up [*liste, plan, bilan, budget, dossier*]; to make out [*compte, chèque, facture*]; to prepare [*devis*]; to set up [*fiches*]; to make [*diagnostic*]; to draw [*parallèle*]; **4** (assurer) to establish [*réputation, fortune, influence*]; **5** (prouver) to establish [*fait, identité, innocence*].

II **s'établir** *vpr* **1** (se fixer) [*personne*] to settle (**à, en** in); [*organisme*] to set up; **s'~** (**comme**) **antiquaire** to set up as an antique dealer; **s'~ à son compte** to set up one's own business; **2** [*indice, taux, hausse*] to be set (**à** at); **3** (s'instituer) [*liens*] to develop (**sur** out of); [*domination, pouvoir*] to become established (**sur** on).

établissement /etablismɑ̃/ *nm* **1** (entreprise, organisme) GÉN organization; (institué) institution; (bâtiments) premises (*pl*); **2** (ville, village) settlement; **3** (mise en place) (de relations, hiérarchie, régime) establishment; (de norme) setting; (de gouvernement) formation; (de personne) settlement; (de taxe, sanction) introduction; **4** (mise en forme) (de liste, plan, dossier) drawing up; **5** (démonstration) **l'~ de leur culpabilité** proving they are guilty.

■ **~ commercial** commercial establishment; **~ de crédit** finance company; **~ d'enseignement supérieur** higher education institution; **~ hospitalier** hospital; **~ pénitentiaire** penal institution; **~ privé** (école) private school; **~ scolaire** school; **~ spécialisé** institution; **~ thermal** hydrotherapy centre^GB; **~ d'utilité publique** public service corporation.

étage /etaʒ/ *nm* **1** (d'immeuble) floor; **le premier ~** the first floor GB, the second floor US; **le dernier ~** the top floor; **à tous les ~s** on every floor; **à l'~ au-dessus/au-dessous** on the floor above/below; **dans les ~s** on (one of) the floors above; **à l'~** upstairs; **une maison sans ~** a single-storey(ed) house GB, a single-story house US; **2** (division) (de tour) level; (d'aqueduc, de gâteau, coiffure) tier; (de fusée) stage; **3** (de terrain) terrace; **terrain en ~s** terraced land.

étager /etaʒe/ [13] I *vtr* to plant [sth] in tiers [*fleurs*]; to stagger [*augmentations*].

II **s'étager** *vpr* [*cultures, jardins*] to rise in terraces.

étagère /etaʒɛʀ/ *nf* shelf; **des ~s** shelves.

étain /etɛ̃/ *nm* **1** (métal) tin; **2** (matière) pewter; **3** (objet) piece of pewter ware; **les ~s** pewter ware ₵.

étal /etal/ *nm* **1** (de marché) stall; **2** (de boucher) butcher's block.

étalage /etalaʒ/ *nm* **1** COMM (de magasin) window display; (de marché) stall; **2** (de luxe, richesses) display; **faire ~ de** to flaunt.

étalagiste /etalaʒist/ |▶**374**| *nmf* (décorateur) window dresser.

étalement /etalmɑ̃/ *nm* **1** (dans le temps) staggering; **2** (dans l'espace) sprawl.

étaler /etale/ [1] I *vtr* **1** (déployer) to spread out [*document, drap*]; to spread [*tapis*]; to roll [sth] out [*pâte*]; **2** (éparpiller) to scatter; **3** (répandre) to spread [*beurre, pâté, colle*]; to apply [*peinture, pommade*]; **4** (échelonner) to spread [*travaux, réformes, remboursements*] (**sur** over); to stagger [*départs, horaires*] (**sur** over); **5** (montrer) to display [*articles*]; PÉJ to flaunt [*richesse, savoir*]; **~ au grand jour** to bring [sth] out into the open [*vie privée*].

II **s'étaler** *vpr* **1** (s'échelonner) [*programme, paiement*] to be spread (**sur** over); [*départs*] to be staggered (**sur** over); **2** (s'exhiber) **s'~ en première page** to be splashed all over the front page; **s'~ (au grand jour)** to be plain for all to see; **3** (s'étendre) [*paysage*] to spread out; **4** (se vautrer) [*personne*] to sprawl; (prendre de la place) [*personne*] to spread out; **5**○ (tomber) to go sprawling○; **s'~ de tout son long** to fall flat on one's face; **6**○ (échouer) **s'~** ou **se faire ~ à un examen** to fail ou flunk ○ an exam.

étalon /etalɔ̃/ I *nm* **1** (cheval) stallion; **2** (modèle) standard; FIG yardstick.

II (-)**étalon** (*in compounds*) **métal(-)~** standard metal; **mètre(-)~** standard metre^GB.

étalonnage /etalɔnaʒ/ *nm*, **étalonnement** /etalɔnmɑ̃/ *nm* calibration.

étalonner /etalɔne/ [1] *vtr* (vérifier) to test; (graduer) to calibrate.

étalon-or /etalɔ̃ɔʀ/ *nm inv* gold standard.

étamer /etame/ [1] *vtr* to tin [*casserole*]; to tin-plate [*métal*].

étamine /etamin/ *nf* (de fleur) stamen.

étanche /etɑ̃ʃ/ *adj* **1** LIT ~ (à l'eau) [*montre, combinaison*] waterproof; [*tonneau, embarcation*] watertight; **~ à l'air**) airtight; **2** FIG impenetrable.

étanchéité /etɑ̃ʃeite/ *nf* ~ (à l'eau) (de montre) waterproof quality; (de citerne) watertightness; **~ (à l'air**) airtightness.

étancher /etɑ̃ʃe/ [1] *vtr* to quench [*soif*].

étang /etɑ̃/ *nm* pond.

étant /etɑ̃/ ▶ **donné** III, IV, **entendu**, **être**¹.

étape /etap/ *nf* **1** (lieu d'arrêt) stop; **2** (section de trajet) stage; (dans une course) leg; **3** FIG (phase) stage; (palier) step.

IDIOMES **brûler les ~s** to go too far too fast.

état /eta/ I *nm* **1** (condition physique) être/ne pas être en ~ de to be in a/no fit state to do; **mettre qn hors d'~ de faire qch** to render sb incapable of doing sth; **mettre qn hors d'~ de nuire** (légalement) to put sb out of harm's way; (physiquement) to incapacitate sb; **leur ~ de santé** their (state of) health; **en piteux**○ **~** in a pitiful state; **2** (condition psychique) state; **être dans un drôle**○ **d'~** to be in a hell of a state○; **ne pas être dans son ~ normal** not to be oneself; **ne te mets pas dans des ~s pareils!** don't get into such a state○!; **être dans un ~ second** to be in a trance; **3** (de voiture, livre, tapis) condition; **l'~ des routes** (conditions climatiques) road conditions (*pl*); (qualité) the state of the roads; **en bon/mauvais ~** [*maison, cœur*] in good/poor condition; **avoir les dents en mauvais ~** to have bad teeth; **hors d'~ de marche** [*voiture*] off the road; [*appareil*] out of order; **remettre qch en ~** to mend ou repair sth; **remettre une maison en ~** to do up a house; **j'ai laissé les choses en l'~** I left everything as it was; **à l'~ brut** [*pétrole*] in its raw state; **à l'~ de ruines** in a state of ruin; **à l'~ neuf** as good as new; **une voiture en ~ de rouler** a roadworthy car; **4** (d'affaires, économie, de finances, pays) state; **dans l'~ actuel des choses** in the present state of affairs; **5** (en sciences) (de corps) state; **6** (situation sociale) state; **être boulanger de son ~** to be a baker by trade; ▶ **tiers**; **7** SOCIOL state; **naissance d'un nouvel ~ social** birth of a new social order; **8** (en comptabilité) statement; **9** JUR (statut) status; **10** HIST (catégorie sociale) estate.

II **faire état de** *loc verbale* **1** (arguer) to cite [*document, loi*]; **2** (mentionner) to mention [*conversation,*

Les États, les pays et les continents

Les adjectifs comme anglais *peuvent aussi qualifier des personnes (par ex.* un touriste anglais, ▶ 394 |) *et des langues (par ex.* un mot anglais ▶ 338 |).

Les noms de pays

L'anglais n'utilise pas l'article défini devant les noms de pays et de continents, sauf pour les noms qui ont une forme de pluriel (the United States, the Netherlands, the Philippines *etc.) et quelques rares exceptions* (the Congo, the Gambia). *En cas de doute, consulter l'article dans le dictionnaire.*

la France	= France	Cuba	= Cuba
le Brésil	= Brazil	l'Afrique	= Africa

aimer la France = to like France
aimer l'Afrique = to like Africa

Attention: les noms qui ont une forme de pluriel se comportent en général comme des noms singuliers.

les États-Unis sont un pays riche = the United States is a rich country

Noter que les noms de continents et de pays qui utilisent les points cardinaux ne prennent pas d'article défini non plus:

l'Amérique du Nord = North America
la Corée du Sud = South Korea

À, au, aux, en

À, au, aux *et* en *se traduisent par* to *avec les verbes de mouvement (par ex.* aller, se rendre *etc.) et par* in *avec les autres verbes (par ex.* être, habiter *etc.).*

aller au Brésil = to go to Brazil
aller en Afrique = to go to Africa
vivre au Brésil = to live in Brazil
vivre en Afrique = to live in Africa

De avec les noms de pays et de continents

Les expressions françaises avec de se traduisent en général en anglais par l'emploi de l'adjectif. Mais voir ci-dessous quelques exceptions.

Attention: l'anglais emploie toujours la majuscule pour les adjectifs ethniques.

l'ambassade de France	= the French embassy
les campagnes de la France	= the French countryside
le climat de la France	= the French climate
l'équipe de France	= the French team
les fleuves et rivières de France	= French rivers
l'histoire de France	= French history

Mais noter:

l'ambassadeur de France	= the French ambassador
	ou the ambassador of France
la capitale de la France	= the capital of France
les peuples de l'Afrique	= the peoples of Africa
une carte de France	= a map of France

Traduction des adjectifs

l'argent français	= French money
l'armée française	= the French army
l'aviation française	= the French air force
la cuisine française	= French cooking
la douane française	= the French Customs
le gouvernement français	= the French government
la langue française	= the French language
la littérature française	= French literature
la marine française	= the French navy
le peuple français	= the French nation
la politique française	= French politics
les traditions françaises	= French traditions
la vie politique française	= French politics
une ville française	= a French town

En anglais, dans quelques rares cas, on trouve aussi le nom du pays ou du continent utilisé en position d'adjectif: the England team, the Africa question *etc. Il est préférable de ne pas imiter ces tournures.*

---

découverte]; **3** (exposer) to state [*préférences, privilèges*]; to air [*soupçon, idée*]; **4** (se prévaloir de) to make a point of mentioning [*succès, courage*].
■ ~ **d'alerte** MIL state of alert; ~ **d'âme** (scrupule) qualm; (sentiment) feeling; ~ **de choc** MÉD, PSYCH state of shock; ~ **civil** ADMIN (d'une personne) civil status; ~ **de crise** POL, SOCIOL state of crisis; ~ **d'esprit** state ou frame of mind; ~ **de fait** fact; ~ **de grâce** RELIG state of grace; **en ~ de grâce** FIG inspired; ~ **des lieux** JUR inventory and statement of state of repair; FIG appraisal; ~ **de siège** state of siege; **~s de service** service record; ~ **d'urgence** state of emergency; **les ~s généraux** HIST the Estates General.
IDIOMES **être/se mettre dans tous ses ~s**○ to be in/to get into a state○.

État /eta/ *nm* **1** (nation) state, State; **coup d'~** coup d'état; **2** (gouvernement) state, government; **demander une aide de l'~** to apply for state aid; **un emprunt d'~** a public loan; **3** (territoire autonome) state.
■ ~ **de droit** POL legally constituted state.

étatique /etatik/ *adj* [*financement, gestion*] state GB (*épith*), public US (*épith*); [*contrôle*] state (*épith*).

étatiser /etatize/ [1] *vtr* to bring [sth] under state control.

état-major, *pl* **états-majors** /etamaʒɔʀ/ *nm* **1** MIL (officiers) staff (+ *v pl*); (lieu) headquarters; **2** POL administrative staff.

États-Unis /etazyni/ ▶ 232 | *nprmpl* ~ **(d'Amérique)** United States (of America).

étau, *pl* **~x** /eto/ *nm* TECH vice GB, vise US; FIG stranglehold (**autour de** on); **être pris en ~** to be caught in a vice-like GB ou vise-like US grip; **l'~ se resserre** the net is tightening (**autour de** around).

étayer /eteje/ [21] *vtr* **1** CONSTR to shore up, to prop up [*mur, plafond*]; **2** FIG to support [*théorie, démonstration*] (**de, par** with).

été /ete/ ▶ 542 | *nm* summer; ~ **comme hiver** all year round.

éteignoir /etɛɲwaʀ/ *nm* (de bougie) snuffer.

éteindre /etɛ̃dʀ/ [55] **I** *vtr* **1** to put out [*feu, cigare, poêle*]; (en soufflant) to blow out [*bougie*]; **2** to switch off [*lampe, téléviseur, chauffage, phare*]; to turn off [*gaz*]; **c'est éteint chez elle** her lights are off; **tous feux éteints** [*rouler*] without lights; **3** (calmer) to subdue [*colère, désir*]; to quell [*ardeur*].
II s'éteindre *vpr* **1** [*cigare, feu*] to go out; (par accident) [*lumière*] to go out; [*radio*] to go off; **2** [*pièce, fenêtre*] to go dark; **3** (mourir) EUPH to pass away ou on; **4** [*famille, nom*] to die out; **5** [*son*] to die away; [*voix*] to become lifeless; [*désir, passion*] to fade; [*colère*] to subside.

éteint, **~e** /etɛ̃, ɛ̃t/ **I** *pp* ▶ éteindre.
II *pp adj* **1** [*regard*] dull; **2** [*volcan*] extinct; [*astre*] extinct, dead.

étendard /etɑ̃daʀ/ *nm* standard, flag; **se ranger sous l'~ de** to rally to the cause of.

étendre /etɑ̃dʀ/ [6] **I** *vtr* **1** (allonger) to stretch [*bras, jambe*]; **il a étendu les bras** he stretched his arms; **2** (déployer) to spread (out) [*bâche, nappe*]; ~ **du linge** (dehors) to hang out washing; (dedans) to hang up washing; **3** (coucher) to lay [sb] down; ~ **qn** (**sur le carreau**)○ (blesser) to lay sb out cold○, to floor GB sb; **4** (étaler) to spread [*enduit, peinture*]; CULIN to roll out [*pâte*]; **5** (accroître) to extend [*emprise, pouvoir*] (**sur** over); to extend [*allocation, embargo*] (**à** to).
II s'étendre *vpr* **1** (occuper un espace) to stretch (**sur** over); **2** (augmenter) [*grève, épidémie*] to spread (**à** to); [*ville*] to expand, to grow; **3** (s'appliquer) [*loi, mesure*] **s'~ à** to apply to; **4** (durer) to stretch (**sur** over), to last; **5** (s'allonger) to lie down; **6** (s'appesantir) **s'~ sur** to dwell on [*sujet, point*].

étendu, **~e**¹ /etɑ̃dy/ *adj* [*ville*] sprawling; [*région, plaine*] vast; [*connaissances, dégâts*] extensive.

étendue² /etɑ̃dy/ *nf* **1** (de terrain) expanse, area; (de sable, d'eau) expanse; **2** (de pays, collection) size; **sur**

toute l'~ **du pays** throughout the country; **3** (de dégâts) scale, extent; (de connaissances) range; (d'ignorance) depth.

■ ~ **territoriale** (de contrat) territorial limits (*pl*).

éternel, -elle /etɛʀnɛl/ I *adj* **1** [*problème*] endless; [*vérité*] eternal; [*optimiste*] eternal; [*sourire*] inevitable.

II *nm* eternal; l'~ **féminin** the eternal feminine.

Éternel /etɛʀnɛl/ *nm* Eternal; l'~ the Lord.

éternellement /etɛʀnɛlmɑ̃/ *adv* (jusqu'à la fin des temps) forever; (continûment) permanently; (de manière répétée) perpetually, continually; RELIG eternally.

éterniser: s'éterniser /etɛʀnize/ [1] *vpr* (se prolonger) to drag on; (s'attarder) to stay for ages○.

éternité /etɛʀnite/ *nf* eternity; **de toute ~** from time immemorial.

éternuement /etɛʀnymɑ̃/ *nm* sneeze.

éternuer /etɛʀnɥe/ [1] *vi* to sneeze.

étêter /etete/ [1] *vtr* **1** to top, to pollard [*arbre*]; **2** to remove the head of [*clou, sardine*].

éther /etɛʀ/ *nm* **1** CHIMIE ether; **2** (ciel) LITER l'~ the ether.

éthéré, -e /etere/ *adj* ethereal.

éthiopien, -ienne /etjɔpjɛ̃, ɛn/ ▶ 394 *adj* Ethiopian.

éthique /etik/ I *adj* ethical.

II *nf* PHILOS ethics (+ *v sg*); (conception morale) code of ethics; l'~ **capitaliste** the capitalist ethic.

ethnie /ɛtni/ *nf* ethnic group.

ethnique /ɛtnik/ *adj* ethnic.

ethnographie /ɛtnɔgʀafi/ *nf* ethnography.

ethnologie /ɛtnɔlɔʒi/ *nf* ethnology.

ethnologue /ɛtnɔlɔg/ ▶ 374 *nmf* ethnologist.

éthylique /etilik/ I *adj* **1** (alcoolique) alcoholic; **2** CHIMIE **alcool ~** ethyl alcohol.

II *nmf* alcoholic.

éthylisme /etilism/ ▶ 196 *nm* alcoholism.

étincelant, -e /etɛ̃slɑ̃, ɑ̃t/ *adj* **1** (lumineux) [*soleil*] blazing; [*étoile*] twinkling; [*pierreries, verre*] sparkling; [*plumage, couleur*] brilliant; **2** (remarquable) brilliant.

étinceler /etɛ̃sle/ [19] *vi* [*étoile*] to twinkle; [*soleil, pierre précieuse, métal*] to sparkle; [*yeux*] (de colère) to flash (**de** with); (de joie) to sparkle (**de** with).

étincelle /etɛ̃sɛl/ *nf* **1** (incandescence) spark; **2** (lueur) (sur une lame) flash; (sur un diamant) sparkle; (dans le regard) (d'humour) twinkle; (de colère) glint; **jeter des ~s** to glitter; **3** (manifestation fugitive) flash (**de** of).

IDIOMES **ça va faire des ~s**○ FIG that will make sparks fly; **faire des ~s** (dans l'action) to do brilliantly; **c'est l'~ qui a mis le feu aux poudres** FIG it's what sparked off the crisis.

étioler: s'étioler /etjɔle/ [1] *vpr* [*plante*] to witt.

étiquetage /etikta ʒ/ *nm* LIT, FIG labelling^GB.

■ ~ **génétique** gene tagging.

étiqueter /etikte/ [20] *vtr* LIT, FIG to label.

étiquette /etikɛt/ *nf* **1** (à coller) label; (à attacher) tag; **porter une ~** to be labelled^GB; **2** (protocole) etiquette; **3** ORDINAT tag.

étirement /etiʀmɑ̃/ *nm* SPORT stretching exercise.

étirer /etiʀe/ [1] I *vtr* (pour détendre) to stretch.

II **s'étirer** *vpr* **1** [*personne*] to stretch; **2** [*procession, chemin*] to stretch out; [*journée*] to seem endless.

étoffe /etɔf/ *nf* **1** (tissu) fabric; **2** FIG substance; **avoir l'~ d'un grand homme** to have the makings of a great man.

étoffer /etɔfe/ [1] I *vtr* to expand [*récit, développement*]; **un récit bien étoffé** a well-developed story.

II **s'étoffer** *vpr* [*personne*] to put on weight.

étoile /etwal/ *nf* **1** (astre) star; **ciel sans ~s** starless sky; **à la lueur des ~s** by starlight; **2** (forme) star; **~ à cinq branches** five-pointed star; **3** (artiste) star.

■ l'~ **du berger** the evening star; **~ filante** shooting star; **~ de mer** starfish; **~ polaire** Pole Star.

IDIOMES **être né sous une bonne/mauvaise ~** to be born under a lucky/an unlucky star; **coucher** or **dormir à la belle ~** to sleep out in the open.

étoilé, ~e /etwale/ *adj* **1** [*ciel*] starry; **2** [*verre*] crazed.

étole /etɔl/ *nf* stole.

étonnamment /etɔnamɑ̃/ *adv* surprisingly.

étonnant, ~e /etɔnɑ̃, ɑ̃t/ *adj* **1** (inattendu) surprising; **pas ~ qu'il soit malade**○ no wonder he's ill; **2** (extraordinaire) amazing.

étonnement /etɔnmɑ̃/ *nm* surprise; **à mon grand ~** to my amazement.

étonner /etɔne/ [1] I *vtr* to surprise; **ça m'étonnerait (fort)** I'd be (very) surprised; **tu m'étonneras toujours!** you never cease to amaze me!

II **s'étonner** *vpr* to be surprised (**que** that; **de qch** at sth); **il ne faut pas s'~ que** it should come as no surprise that.

étouffant, ~e /etufɑ̃, ɑ̃t/ *adj* **1** (suffocant) stifling; **2** (pesant) oppressive.

étouffé, ~e[1] /etufe/ *adj* **1** (assourdi) [*son, voix*] muffled (**par** by); **2** (retenu) [*sanglot*] choked; [*rire, cri*] suppressed; [*soupir*] discreet.

étouffée[2] /etufe/ *nf* **à l'~** [*légume, viande*] braised.

étouffer /etufe/ [1] I *vtr* **1** (entraver) to stifle [*carrière, création*]; to suppress [*protestation*]; **2** (dissimuler) to hush up [*scandale*]; **3** (asphyxier) to suffocate [*victime*]; [*bâillon*] to stifle; to choke [*plante*]; **la générosité ne les étouffe pas** they can't be accused of generosity; **4** (arrêter) to smother [*feu*]; **5** (retenir) to stifle [*bâillement*]; to hold back [*soupir*]; **6** (atténuer) to deaden [*bruits*].

II *vi* (être mal à l'aise) to feel stifled; **on étouffe ici**○ it's stifling in here!; **mourir étouffé** (par gaz etc) to die of suffocation; (par obstruction de la trachée) to choke to death.

III **s'étouffer** *vpr* (suffoquer) to choke.

étoupe /etup/ *nf* (de chanvre) tow; NAUT oakum.

étourderie /etuʀdəʀi/ *nf* absent-mindedness.

étourdi, ~e /etuʀdi/ I *adj* **1** [*personne*] absent-minded; **2** [*réponse, paroles*] unthinking.

II *nm,f* scatterbrain.

étourdir /etuʀdiʀ/ [3] I *vtr* **1** (assommer) to stun, to daze; **2** (fatiguer) **~ qn** [*vacarme, circulation*] to make sb's head spin.

II **s'étourdir** *vpr* **s'~ de paroles** to become intoxicated with words.

étourdissant, ~e /etuʀdisɑ̃, ɑ̃t/ *adj* [*bruit*] deafening; [*réussite*] stunning; [*vitesse*] dizzying.

étourdissement /etuʀdismɑ̃/ *nm* dizzy spell.

étourneau, *pl* **~x** /etuʀno/ *nm* **1** (oiseau) starling; **2**○ (étourdi) scatterbrain○.

étrange /etʀɑ̃ ʒ/ I *adj* strange; **trouver ~ que** to find it strange that; **chose ~ elle n'a pas répondu** strangely enough she didn't answer.

II *nm* (caractère surprenant) strangeness; (bizarrerie) bizarre.

étrangement /etʀɑ̃ ʒmɑ̃/ *adv* **1** (fort curieusement) curiously; **vous me rappelez ~ un ami** it's strange ou uncanny but you remind me of a friend; **2** (remarquablement) surprisingly.

étranger, -ère /etʀɑ̃ ʒe, ɛʀ/ I *adj* **1** (d'un autre pays) foreign; **2** (extérieur) **~ à** [*personne*] not involved in (*après n*); [*affaire*] outside (*après n*) [*groupe*]; [*fait*] with no bearing on (*après n*); [*comportement*] unrelated to (*après n*); **se sentir ~** to feel like an outsider; **3** (inconnu) [*personne, voix, théorie*] unfamiliar (**à** to); **votre visage ne m'est pas ~** I know your face; **le domaine ne m'est pas ~** I am quite familiar with the field; **la peur leur est étrangère** they know no fear.

II *nm,f* **1** (d'un autre pays) foreigner; **2** (d'un autre groupe) outsider; **3** (inconnu) stranger.

III *nm* **1** (autres pays) l'~ foreign countries (*pl*); **à l'~** [*aller*] abroad; **2** (gens d'ailleurs) foreigners (*pl*).

étrangeté /etʀɑ̃ ʒte/ *nf* strangeness.

étranglé, ~e /etʀɑ̃gle/ *adj* **1** [*voix*] choked; [*son*] muffled; **2** [*rue, vallée*] narrow.

étranglement /etʀɑ̃gləmɑ̃/ *nm* **1** (de victime) strangu-

être¹ (1)

Généralités

Dans la plupart des situations exprimant l'existence, l'identité, la localisation, la qualité, *être* sera traduit par *to be*:

je pense donc je suis	= I think therefore I am
le soleil est une étoile	= the sun is a star
j'étais chez moi	= I was at home
l'eau est froide	= the water is cold

Les locutions figées contenant *être* sont traitées sous l'entrée appropriée. Ainsi *être en train de/sur le point de/hors de soi* etc. sont respectivement sous **train**, **point**, **hors** etc.; *quoi qu'il en soit* sous **quoi**. De même, les expressions avec *si* et les questions commençant par *que* sont traitées sous **si** et **que**. Selon le même principe, l'emploi facultatif de *étant* après *considérer comme* et *présenter comme* est traité sous ces verbes; *étant donné (que)* et *étant entendu que* sont sous **donné** et **entendu**. La plupart des autres emplois de *étant* se traduisent par *being*:

> *cela* (ou *ceci*) *étant* = this being so

En revanche, *c'est-à-dire*, *n'est-ce pas*, *peut-être* et *soit* sont des entrées à part entière, traitées à leur place dans le dictionnaire.

Par ailleurs, on consultera utilement les notes d'usage répertoriées ▶ **1420 J**, notamment pour l'expression de *l'heure*, *la date*, *les nationalités*, *les métiers et les professions*, *les nombres* etc.

être = verbe auxiliaire
de la voix passive

être auxiliaire de la voix passive se traduit par *to be*. On notera l'emploi des divers temps en anglais.

Au présent

où sont les épreuves? elles sont révisées par le traducteur	= where are the proofs? they are being revised by the translator
votre voiture est réparée	= your car has been repaired
les portes sont repeintes chaque année	= the doors are repainted every year

Au passé

les épreuves ont été révisées en juin	= the proofs were revised in June
les épreuves ont été révisées plusieurs fois	= the proofs have been revised several times
les épreuves ont été révisées bien avant ma démission	= the proofs had been revised long before I resigned

Du passé dans les temps composés

être se traduit par *to have* si le temps est également composé en anglais – ce qui est beaucoup moins fréquent qu'en français (voir ci-dessus) – sauf avec *naître*. Dans certains contextes, on peut avoir:

elles sont tombées	= they have fallen
ils se sont enfuis	= they have escaped
elle s'était vengée	= she had taken her revenge

Les verbes traduits par une construction passive ou attributive en anglais (*se vendre* = to be sold; *s'indigner* = to be indignant) suivent les mêmes règles au passé:

tous les livres se sont vendus	= all the books have been sold
elle se serait indignée	= she would have been indignant

Noter que la forme pronominale à valeur passive est souvent mieux rendue en anglais par une forme intransitive:

les livres se sont bien vendus	= the books have sold well

être = aller

Lorsqu'il signifie *aller*, *être* se traduit par *to be* en anglais, mais seulement s'il est directement suivi d'un complément de lieu:

je n'ai jamais été en Chine	= I've never been to China

Suivi d'un infinitif, il se rend par *to go to*:

il a été voir son ami	= he's gone to see his friend
j'ai été manger au restaurant	= I went to eat in a restaurant

Dans le sens de *s'en aller*, on notera les tournures recherchées:

ils s'en furent au théâtre	= they went to the theatre
ils s'en furent (déçus)	= they left (disappointed)

c'est
Interrogation

est-ce, ou sa variante plus familière *c'est*, se traduit généralement par *is it*:

est-ce leur fils?	= is it their son?
est-ce leur voiture?	= is it their car?
c'est grave?	= is it serious?
c'est toi ou ton frère?	= is it you or your brother?

Quand *ce* garde sa valeur démonstrative, l'anglais précise la référence:

est-ce clair?	= is that clear?
qui est-ce?	= who is he/she?
(en montrant une personne)	= who is that?

Mais, en parlant de quelqu'un qui vous appelle au téléphone, ou à quelqu'un qui frappe à la porte:

qui est-ce?	= who is it?

est-ce n'est généralement pas traduit dans les tournures emphatiques ou permettant d'éviter l'inversion du sujet:

est-ce que tu parles russe?	= do you speak Russian?
est-ce leur fils, ce garçon?	= is this boy their son?
qui est-ce qui l'a fait?	= who did it?
qui est-ce que tu as rencontré?	= who did you meet?
quand est-ce que tu manges?	= when do you eat?
où est-ce que tu manges?	= where do you eat?
qu'est-ce que c'est?	= what is it?
(ou comme vu plus haut)	= what is this/that? (selon qu'on montre un objet proche ou éloigné)

Néanmoins, la tournure emphatique est également possible en anglais dans certaines expressions:

qu'est-ce que j'entends?	= what's this I hear?
est-ce bien ce qu'il a voulu dire?	= is that what he really meant?

Affirmation

c'est se traduit, selon les contextes, *it is* (*it's*), *this is*, *that is* (*that's*):

c'est facile (de critiquer)	= it's easy
(ce que tu me demandes, ce travail)	= that's easy
c'est moi (réponse à 'qui est-ce?')	= it's me
(réponse à 'qui le fait?')	= I do
(réponse à 'qui l'a fait?')	= I did
(pour me désigner sur une photo, ou comme étant le personnage dont il est question)	= that's me (*traduit également* ça, c'est moi)
c'est Mme Fox (qui téléphone, réponse à 'qui est-ce?')	= it's Mrs Fox
(réponse à 'qui le fait?')	= Mrs Fox *ou* Mrs Fox does
(réponse à 'qui l'a fait?')	= Mrs Fox did
(que je montre, dont vous voulez parler)	= that's Mrs Fox
c'est eux, ce sont eux	
(qui sont là-bas, que je montre)	= it's them
(qui le font)	= they do
(qui l'ont fait)	= they did
(qui arrivent)	= here they are
ce sont mes enfants	
(que je vous présente)	= these are my children
(qui sont là-bas)	= they are my children
c'est cela	= that's right
c'est ça! tu crois que je vais faire le travail tout seul?	= what's this! do you think I'm going to do the work all by myself?

☛ Voir page suivante

être¹ (2)

Lorsqu'il reprend un nom, un infinitif ou une proposition qui le précède *c'est* se traduit seulement par *is*:

une étoile, c'est un réacteur nucléaire
= a star is a nuclear reactor
réussir, c'est une question de volonté
= to succeed is a question of will
sortir par ce temps, c'est de la folie
= going out in this weather is sheer madness
eux, ce sont mes amis = they are my friends

De même, lorsque *c'est que* reprend un groupe nominal ou une proposition, il se traduit simplement par *is that*:

le comique, c'est que … = the funny thing is that …

On trouvera en général cette tournure sous l'entrée appropriée, comme **fort**, **importer** etc.

Lorsque *c'est que* sert à donner une explication il se rend généralement, et selon le temps, par *it is that, it was that*, mais aussi, pour insister sur l'explication, par *it is/was because*:

si j'ai fait ça, c'est que je ne pouvais pas faire autrement = if I did that, it was because I couldn't do otherwise

ce n'est pas que se traduit la plupart du temps *it is/was not that* (la contraction est *it's not* plutôt que *it isn't*):

ce n'est pas qu'il soit bête, mais … = it's not that he is stupid, but …

En corrélation avec un pronom relatif, *c'est* peut soit garder sa valeur de présentatif (voir plus haut) et se rendre par *that's*:

c'est le journaliste qui m'a interviewé = that's the journalist who interviewed me
c'est le journaliste que nous avons rencontré = that's the journalist (that) we met
c'est le journaliste dont je te parlais = that's the journalist I was telling you about
c'est le château où je suis né = that's the castle where I was born
c'est ce qui me fait croire que … = that's what makes me think that …
c'est justement ce que je disais = that's exactly what I was saying

soit constituer une tournure emphatique qui se rend en anglais selon la nuance:

c'est de la même femme que nous parlons = we're talking about the same woman
c'était d'en parler devant elle qui me gênait = talking about it in front of her was what made me feel uneasy *ou* what made me feel uneasy was talking about it in front of her
c'est lui/Paul qui l'a cassé
(je le dénonce) = **he/Paul** broke it
(je l'accuse) = **he/Paul** is the one who broke it
c'est mon frère qui l'a écrit = it was my brother who wrote it *ou* my brother's the one who wrote it
c'est de ta sœur que je parlais, pas de toi = it was your sister I was talking about, not you
c'est cette voiture qui m'intéresse = this is the car (that) I am interested in
c'est lui le coupable = **he** is the culprit
ce sont eux les meurtriers = **they** are the murderers

c'est à suivi d'un infinitif se traduit parfois par *it is* suivi de l'adjectif correspondant si cette même transformation est possible en français:

c'est à désespérer ou *c'est désespérant* = it's hopeless

Mais c'est rare, et il est conseillé de se reporter à l'infinitif en question ou à l'un des autres termes obtenus à partir de transformations semblables.

c'est à … de faire (ou parfois *à faire*) se traduira de deux manières:

c'est à Pierre/lui de choisir
(c'est son tour) = it's Pierre's/his turn to choose
(c'est sa responsabilité) = it's up to Pierre/to him to choose

La notion de rivalité contenue dans *c'est à qui* suivi du futur doit être rendue explicite en anglais:

c'est à qui proposera le plus de réformes = each is trying to suggest more reforms than the other
c'était à qui des deux aurait le dernier mot = they were each trying to get in the last word
c'était à qui trouverait le plus d'erreurs dans le texte = they were vying with each other to find the most mistakes in the text

c'est, équivalent de *ça fait* dans le compte d'une somme, se rend par *it is*:

c'est 200 francs = it's 200 francs
c'est combien? = how much is it?

ce sera avec valeur modale de *ce doit être* se traduit *it must be*:

ce sera mon professeur de piano = it must be my piano teacher

être = verbe impersonnel

il est facile de critiquer = it is easy to criticize
il serait nécessaire de faire = it would be necessary to do
il est des gens bizarres = there are some strange people
il n'est pas de jour/d'heure sans qu'il se plaigne = not a day/an hour goes by without him complaining

On se référera par ailleurs aux notes d'usage concernant l'heure et la date; voir aussi les entrées ***temps*** et ***fois***.

il est à suivi d'un infinitif se rend différemment, selon les nuances qu'imposent le contexte, par *it must be, it has to be, it should be, it can be* suivis du participe passé. Pour plus de sûreté, on se reportera à l'infinitif en question, où cette construction est généralement traitée.

il est de suivi d'un substantif ou d'un groupe nominal se rend souvent par *it is* suivi directement d'un adjectif ou d'un substantif précédé d'un déterminant (article, pronom):

il est de coutume de faire ou qu'on fasse = it is customary (*ou* the custom) to do
il est de notre responsabilité de faire = it is our responsibility to do

Mais ce n'est pas une règle absolue, et il est préférable de consulter des entrées telles que **règle**, **notoriété** etc. pour avoir des traductions adéquates. Voir également **1** ci-dessous pour des exemples supplémentaires.

Emplois avec en
en être

Certains cas sont traités sous la rubrique 'être = verbe impersonnel'; d'autres, expressions figées, le sont sous l'entrée appropriée; voir par exemple **poche** et **frais** pour *en être de sa poche/pour ses frais*. Enfin, quand l'antécédent de *en* est exprimé dans la phrase, l'expression est traitée plus bas sous *être de*:

où en étais-je? = where was I?
je ne sais plus où j'en suis = I'm lost
'où en es-tu de tes recherches?'
'j'en suis à mi-chemin/au début' = 'how far have you got in your research?' 'I'm halfway through/at the beginning'
elle a eu plusieurs amants/accidents: elle en est à son quatrième = she has had several lovers/accidents: this is her fourth
j'en suis à me demander si … = I'm beginning to wonder whether …
j'en étais à ne pouvoir distinguer le vrai du faux = I'd got to the point where I couldn't distinguish between truth and falsehood

☛ Voir page suivante

être¹ (3)

être en

Suivie d'un substantif représentant un vêtement, l'expression peut être traduite *to be in*, mais on consultera l'entrée appropriée pour s'en assurer. Si l'on dit *to be in uniform* ou éventuellement *to be wearing a uniform* pour *être en uniforme*, l'anglais préfère généralement *to be wearing a suit* à *to be in a suit* pour *être en costume* (de même pour *robe, tailleur* etc.). Dans le cas d'un déguisement, on a *to be dressed up as*:

  être en pirate = to be dressed up as a pirate.

emplois avec y

j'y suis (je vous comprends)	= I'm with you
(plus général mais un peu familier)	= I get it
je n'y suis pas (je ne comprends pas)	= I don't get it
vous y êtes? (vous comprenez?)	= are you with me?
(vous êtes prêt(e)?)	= are you ready?
20 000 francs? vous n'y êtes pas!	= 20,000 francs? you're a long way out!

tu n'y es pas, c'est plus complexe que ça = you don't realize, it's a lot more complicated than that

Voir aussi les entrées *y* et *pour*.

être + prépositions

La plupart des cas (*être dans, sur, devant, pour, après, avec* etc.) sont traités sous la préposition correspondante. Ne sont retenus ici que les cas particuliers de *être à* et *être de*.

être à

Les cas où l'on peut faire l'ellipse de *être* ou le remplacer par un autre verbe sont traités sous la préposition *à*; ceux de *en être à* sous la rubrique 'en être', et ceux de *c'est à* sous la rubrique 'c'est'.

Les emplois de *être à* suivi d'un groupe nominal et signifiant 'tendre vers' sont généralement traités sous le substantif approprié, comme *temps, hausse, agonie* etc. dans les expressions *le temps est à la pluie, être à la hausse, être à l'agonie*. De même, quand *être à* signifie un état, c'est sous le substantif ou l'adjectif approprié, comme *bout, disposition, quai, vif* etc., qu'on trouvera la ou les traductions de l'expression correspondante.

Suivi d'un infinitif et signifiant *devoir être*, *être à* peut généralement se traduire, en observant les mêmes nuances qu'avec *devoir*, par *must be, have to be* ou *should be* suivi du participe passé du verbe anglais. Il reste conseillé de consulter l'infinitif en question, comme *plaindre, prendre* etc. On en trouve également un traitement succinct sous les rubriques 'être = verbe impersonnel' et 'c'est'.

Au sens de *appartenir à*, l'anglais utilise *to be* suivi du cas possessif quand le possesseur est un être animé ou d'un pronom possessif quand celui-ci est représenté par un pronom objet. Si le cas possessif n'est pas d'usage, on utilise de préférence *to belong to*:

ce livre est à moi	= this book is mine
ce livre est à mon frère	= this book is my brother's
ces dictionnaires sont au service de traduction	= these dictionaries belong to the translation department

à qui est ce chien?	= who does this dog belong to? *ou* whose dog is this?

Voir **2** ci-dessous pour des exemples supplémentaires.

être de

Quand elle exprime un état ou une situation, la tournure *être de* suivie d'un substantif sans déterminant est traduite sous le substantif en question, notamment **avis, garde, service** etc. De même, certaines expressions où la présence de déterminant est variable, comme dans *être de mauvaise foi/d'une incroyable mauvaise foi* sont traitées sous l'entrée appropriée, en l'occurrence, **foi**; voir aussi **humeur, poil** etc.

La construction *être d'un/d'une* suivie d'un adjectif substantivé ou d'un substantif exprimant une qualité ou un défaut peut généralement être rendue par *to be so* suivi de l'adjectif correspondant en anglais, si le substantif est seul:

elle est d'un ridicule!	= she's so ridiculous!
elle est d'une prétention!	= she's so pretentious!

Si le substantif est qualifié, l'adjectif devient généralement un adverbe en anglais:

il est d'une exquise courtoisie	= he's exquisitely courteous
il est d'une incompétence rare	= he's exceptionally incompetent

Mais il n'est pas inutile de vérifier les traductions des adjectifs et substantifs à leur entrée avant de rendre cette construction.

Au sens de *participer à, faire partie de*, la tournure *être de* se traduit de façon très variable (voir aussi **partie**):

il est des nôtres (il vient avec nous)	= he's with us
(il est de notre clan, agit et pense comme nous)	= he's one of us
serez-vous des nôtres?	= will you be (coming) with us?
êtes-vous des nôtres?	= are you coming with us? (ici, *coming* est nécessaire, pour éviter l'ambiguïté de *are you with us?*)
les journalistes ne sont pas du voyage	= the journalists aren't coming on the trip
les journalistes ne seront pas du voyage	= the journalists won't be coming on the trip
ils ont organisé une expédition mais je n'en étais pas	= they organized an expedition but I wasn't part of it
il y avait un congrès mais il n'en était pas	= there was a congress but he didn't take part

Suivi d'un infinitif et précédé de noms abstraits avec l'article défini (*l'idéal, l'essentiel* etc.) ou de superlatifs (*le plus simple*), *être de* se traduit généralement par *to be* suivi de l'infinitif avec *to*:

le plus simple serait de tout recommencer	= the simplest thing to do would be to start all over again

---

lation; **2** (de vallée) (fait) narrowing; (endroit) narrow section.

étrangler /etʀɑ̃gle/ [1] **I** *vtr* **1** LIT to strangle [*victime*]; **j'ai envie de les ~!** FIG I feel like throttling them!; **2** (gêner) [*col, cravate*] to choke, to throttle; **3** (comprimer) to pinch in [*taille*]; **4** [*colère, émotion*] to choke [*personne*]; **5** (écraser) to cripple [*entreprise, économie*]; **6** (museler) to stifle [*groupe politique, presse*].
II s'étrangler *vpr* **1** (avec une corde, un foulard) to strangle oneself; **2** (ne pas pouvoir respirer) to choke; **s'~ de rage/de rire** to choke with rage/laughter; **3** [*cri*] to die in one's throat.

étrangleur, -euse /etʀɑ̃glœʀ, øz/ *nm,f* strangler.

être¹ /etʀ/ [7] *vi* (+ *v avoir*) **1** **il n'est pas jusqu'à l'Antarctique qui ne soit pollué** even the Antarctic is polluted; **il en est de Pierre comme de Paul** it is the same with Pierre as with Paul; **voilà ce qu'il en est** (présentation) this is how it is; (conclusion) that's how it is; **il n'en est rien** this isn't at all the case; **il en sera toujours ainsi** it will always be so; **il en a été de même** it was the same; **qu'en est-il de...?** what's the news on...?; **2 je suis à vous tout de suite/dans un instant** I'll be with you right away/in a minute; **je suis à vous** I'm all yours; **être à ce qu'on fait** to have one's mind on what one is doing; **elle est toujours à se plaindre** she's always complaining; **3 il n'est plus** EUPH he's no longer with us; **ce temps n'est plus** these days are gone; **fût-il duc/en cristal** even if he were a duke/it were made of crystal; **n'était leur grand âge**

were it not for their advanced age; **ne serait-ce qu'en faisant** if only by doing; **ne fût-ce qu'un instant** if only for a moment; **fût-ce pour des raisons humanitaires** if only on humanitarian grounds.

IDIOMES **on ne peut pas ~ et avoir été** PROV you can't stay young forever.

être² /ɛtʀ/ nm **1** (organisme vivant) being; **~ humain** human being; **les ~s animés et inanimés** animate and inanimate things; **les ~s et les choses** living things and objects; **un ~ sans défense** a defence-less^GB creature; **2** (personne) person; **un ~ d'exception** an exceptional person; **un ~ cher** or **aimé** a loved one; **un ~ sensible** a sensitive soul; **3** (nature intime) being; **de tout son ~** with one's whole being; **blessé au plus profond de son ~** hurt to the core; **4** PHILOS l'**~** being.

étreindre /etʀɛ̃dʀ/ [55] I vtr to embrace, to hug [ami]; to clasp [adversaire]; **la peur l'étreignait** he/she was constrained by fear.

II **s'étreindre** vpr [amis, amants] to embrace (each other).

IDIOMES **qui trop embrasse mal étreint** ≈ grasp all, lose all.

étreinte /etʀɛ̃t/ nf **1** (affectueuse) embrace; (violente) grip; **2** FIG grip.

■ **~ fatale** ORDINAT deadly embrace.

étrenner /etʀene/ [1] vtr to wear [sth] for the first time [vêtement]; to use [sth] for the first time [objet, voiture].

étrennes /etʀɛn/ nfpl (cadeau) gift; (argent) money.

étrier /etʀije/ nm (de cavalier) stirrup; (de ski) front binding.

IDIOMES **boire le coup de l'~**○ to have one for the road○; **mettre à qn le pied à l'~** to get sb started.

étriller /etʀije/ [1] vtr **1** (nettoyer) to curry; **2** (critiquer) to tear to pieces.

étriper /etʀipe/ [1] I vtr to gut [animal].

II **s'étriper**○ vpr to murder each other.

étriqué, ~e /etʀike/ adj [veste] skimpy; [vie] restricted.

étroit, ~e /etʀwa, at/ I adj **1** (pas large) narrow; **2** (restreint) [cercle d'amis, conception] narrow; **avoir l'esprit ~** to be narrow-minded; **3** (intime) [rapport, liaison] close (épith); **4** (rigoureux) **sous ~e surveillance** (de la police) under close surveillance.

II **à l'étroit** loc adv **nous sommes un peu à l'~** we're a bit cramped.

étroitement /etʀwatmɑ̃/ adv [surveiller] closely.

étroitesse /etʀwatɛs/ nf LIT, FIG narrowness; **~ d'esprit** narrow-mindedness.

étron /etʀɔ̃/ nm excreta (pl), turd○.

étrusque /etʀysk/ adj, nm Etruscan.

étude /etyd/ I nf **1** (recherche) study (**sur** on); (enquête) survey (**sur** of); **~ réalisée par** study carried out by; **2** (observation) study (**de** of); **3** (prise en considération) (**mise à** l')**~** consideration; **à l'~** under consideration; **4** (apprentissage) study; **5** (d'avoué, de notaire) (bureau) office; (charge) practice; **6** MUS étude; **7** ART study; **8** SCOL (salle) study room GB, study hall US; (période) study period.

II **études** nfpl SCOL, UNIV studies; **faire des ~s** to be a student; **faire** or **poursuivre des ~s de médecine** to study medicine; **je n'ai pas fait d'~s (supérieures)** I didn't go to university ou college; **~s primaires** primary education ¢.

■ **~ de cas** case study; **~ de marché** market research ¢.

étudiant, ~e /etydjɑ̃, ɑ̃t/ adj, nm,f student.

étudié, ~e /etydje/ adj **1** [discours] carefully prepared; **2** [démarche] studied.

étudier /etydje/ [2] I vtr **1** (se pencher sur) to examine [dossier, situation]; to study [carte, plan]; **2** (prendre en considération) to consider [création]; **3** (faire une recherche sur) to study; [science] to deal with [problème]; **4** (apprendre) to study [langue]; to learn [leçon]; **5** (observer) to study [personne, réaction]; **6** (concevoir) to design [nouveau moteur].

II vi **1** (faire des études) to be a student; **2** (apprendre) to be studying.

étui /etyi/ nm case; **~ à revolver** holster.

étuve /etyv/ nf **1** (bain de vapeur) steam room; **2** (en microbiologie) incubator.

étuvée /etyve/ nf **à l'~** braised.

étymologie /etimɔlɔʒi/ nf etymology.

étymologique /etimɔlɔʒik/ adj etymological.

eucharistie /økaʀisti/ nf (sacrifice) Eucharist; (pain, vin) Sacrament.

eugénique /øʒenik/ I adj eugenic.

II nf eugenics (+ v sg).

eunuque /ønyk/ nm eunuch.

euphémisme /øfemism/ nm euphemism.

euphorie /øfɔʀi/ nf euphoria.

euphorique /øfɔʀik/ adj [personne] euphoric; [marché] bullish.

euphorisant, ~e /øfɔʀizɑ̃, ɑ̃t/ I adj [boisson] stimulating; [qualité, atmosphère] uplifting; [substance, drogue] euphoriant.

II nm MÉD stimulant.

eurafricain, ~e /øʀafʀikɛ̃, ɛn/ adj [personne] Eurafrican; [entreprise] Euro-African.

eurasien, -ienne /øʀazjɛ̃, ɛn/ adj Eurasian.

Euratom /øʀatɔm/ nf (abbr = **European atomic energy commission**) Euratom.

EURL /œyɛʀɛl/ nf: abbr ▶ **entreprise**

eurochèque /øʀoʃɛk/ nm Eurocheque.

euroconnecteur /øʀokɔnɛktœʀ/ nm (femelle) scart socket; (mâle) scart plug.

euromarché /øʀomaʀʃe/ nm Euromarket.

Europe /øʀɔp/ nprf Europe; **▶ 232** l'**~ communautaire** the European community; l'**~ de l'espace** the joint European space venture; **faire l'~** to build Europe.

européaniser /øʀopeanize/ [1] I vtr to europeanize [pays]; **~ un débat** to broaden a debate to a European level.

II **s'européaniser** vpr [pays] to become europeanized; [économie] to become adapted to a European framework.

européen, -éenne /øʀopeɛ̃, ɛn/ adj European.

Européen, -éenne /øʀopeɛ̃, ɛn/ nm,f **1** GÉOG (habitant) European; **2** POL (partisan) pro-European.

Eurotunnel /øʀotynɛl/ nm Eurotunnel.

euthanasie /øtanazi/ nf euthanasia.

eux /ø/ pron pers **1** (sujet) they; **~ seuls ont le droit de parler** they alone have the right to speak; **ce sont ~, je les reconnais** it's them, I recognize them; **je sais que ce n'est pas ~ qui ont fait ça** I know they weren't the ones who did it; **2** (dans une comparaison) them; **3** (objet) **les inviter, ~, quelle idée!** invite THEM, what an idea!; **~, il faut les enfermer** they should be locked up; **4** (avec une préposition) **à cause d'~** because of them; **à ~, je peux dire la vérité** I can tell THEM the truth; **ce sont des amis à ~** they're friends of theirs; **ils n'ont pas encore de voiture à ~** they don't have their own car yet; **c'est à ~** (appartenance) it's theirs, it belongs to them; **c'est à ~ de faire** (leur tour) it's their turn to do; (leur responsabilité) it's up to them to do.

eux-mêmes /ømɛm/ pron pers themselves; **les experts ~ reconnaissent que...** even the experts admit that...; **ils me l'ont dit d'~** they volunteered the information, they told me themselves.

évacuateur, -trice /evakɥatœʀ, tʀis/ I adj [canal] discharge.

II nm sluice.

évacuation /evakɥasjɔ̃/ nf **1** (de liquide) discharge; **il y a un problème d'~ de l'eau** the water doesn't drain away; **2** (de lieu, personnes) evacuation.

■ **~ sanitaire** medical evacuation.

évacué, ~e /evakɥe/ nm,f evacuee.

évacuer /evakɥe/ [1] vtr **1** LIT to evacuate [personne];

to evacuate [*lieu*]; to drain off [*eaux usées*]; MÉD to evacuate [*excréments*]; **2** FIG to shrug off [*problème*].

évadé, ~e /evade/ *nm,f* escapee.

évader: s'évader /evade/ [1] *vpr* **1** (s'enfuir) to escape (**de** from); **2** FIG to get away (**de** from).

évaluable /evalɥabl/ *adj* assessable.

évaluation /evalɥasjɔ̃/ *nf* **1** (de collection, maison) valuation; **2** (de coûts, dégâts) (action) assessment; (résultat) estimate, appraisal US; **3** (d'employé) appraisal.

évaluer /evalɥe/ [1] *vtr* **1** (approximativement) to estimate [*grandeur, durée*] (**à** at); to assess [*risques, dégâts, coût*]; **2** (déterminer la valeur de) to value, to appraise US [*meuble, patrimoine*]; **3** (juger) to assess [*employé, élève*].

évangéliser /evɑ̃ʒelize/ [1] *vtr* evangelize.

Évangile /evɑ̃ʒil/ *nm* (message, livre) Gospel (**selon** according to); **parole d'~** FIG gospel truth.

évanouir: s'évanouir /evanwiʀ/ [3] *vpr* **1** LIT to faint (**de** with); **évanoui** unconscious; **2** FIG [*sentiment*] to fade.

évanouissement /evanwismɑ̃/ *nm* **1** MÉD blackout; **2** FIG fading.

évaporation /evapɔʀasjɔ̃/ *nf* evaporation.

évaporé, ~e /evapɔʀe/ **I** *adj* PEJ [*personne*] giddy.
II *nm,f* PEJ birdbrain○ PÉJ.

évaporer: s'évaporer /evapɔʀe/ [1] *vpr* to evaporate; ○FIG to vanish.

évaser /evaze/ [1] **I** *vtr* to widen [sth] at the mouth [*conduit, trou*]; to flare [*vêtement*].
II s'évaser *vpr* [*conduit*] to open out; [*jupe*] to flared.

évasif, -ive /evazif, iv/ *adj* evasive.

évasion /evazjɔ̃/ *nf* LIT, FIG escape.
■ **~ des capitaux** flight of capital; **~ fiscale** tax avoidance.

Ève /ɛv/ *nprf* Eve; **en tenue d'~** in one's birthday suit HUM.
IDIOMES **elle ne le connaît ni d'~ ni d'Adam** she doesn't know him from Adam.

évêché /eveʃe/ *nm* **1** (territoire) diocese; **2** (résidence) bishop's palace.

éveil /evɛj/ *nm* (de nature, dormeur, d'intelligence) awakening; (d'amour) dawning.

éveiller /eveje/ [1] **I** *vtr* **1** to arouse [*intérêt, curiosité, méfiance*]; to stimulate [*intelligence, imagination*]; to awaken [*conscience, goût*]; **sans ~ l'attention** without attracting attention; **un enfant éveillé** a bright child; **2** (du sommeil) to wake [*dormeur*].
II s'éveiller *vpr* **1** LIT to awake; **2** FIG [*imagination, intelligence*] to start to develop.

événement /evenmɑ̃/ *nm* event; **être dépassé par les ~s** to be overwhelmed; **riche en ~s** eventful.

événementiel, -ielle /evenmɑ̃sjɛl/ *adj* factual.

éventail /evɑ̃taj/ *nm* **1** (objet) fan; **2** (série) range.
IDIOMES **avoir les doigts de pied en ~**○ to laze about.

éventaire /evɑ̃tɛʀ/ *nm* (devanture) stall; (de marchand ambulant) tray.

éventer /evɑ̃te/ [1] **I** *vtr* **1** (révéler) to give away [*secret*]; **2** (avec un éventail) to fan.
II s'éventer *vpr* **1** (pour se rafraîchir) to fan oneself; **2** [*parfum, café*] to go stale; [*vin*] to pass its best; [*bière, limonade*] to go flat.

éventré, ~e /evɑ̃tʀe/ *adj* **1** [*animal*] gutted; **2** FIG [*fauteuil*] burst.

éventrer /evɑ̃tʀe/ [1] **I** *vtr* **1** (blesser) [*personne*] to disembowel; [*taureau*] to gore; **2** (ouvrir) to rip [sth] open [*matelas, sac*]; to burst [sth] open [*malle*]; to force [sth] open [*coffre*]; to shatter [*mur*].
II s'éventrer *vpr* **1** (se blesser) [*personne*] (dans un accident) to cut one's stomach open; **2** (s'ouvrir) [*sac*] to burst open.

éventreur /evɑ̃tʀœʀ/ *nm* Jack l'**~** Jack the Ripper.

éventualité /evɑ̃tɥalite/ *nf* **1** (événement possible) eventuality; **2** (hypothèse) possibility; **dans l'~ de** in the event of.

éventuel, -elle /evɑ̃tɥɛl/ *adj* **1** (possible) possible; **2** JUR conditional.

éventuellement /evɑ̃tɥɛlmɑ̃/ *adv* **1** (peut-être) possibly; **2** (si nécessaire) if necessary.

évêque /evɛk/ ▶ 596 *nm* bishop (**de** of).

évertuer: s'évertuer /evɛʀtɥe/ [1] *vpr* to try one's best (**à faire** to do), to strive (**à faire** to do).

éviction /eviksjɔ̃/ *nf* **1** (expulsion) ousting (**de** from); **2** JUR (dépossession) eviction.

évidemment /evidamɑ̃/ *adv* of course.

évidence /evidɑ̃s/ **I** *nf* (fait d'être évident) obviousness; (vérité évidente) obvious fact; **se rendre à l'~** to face the facts; **de toute ~, à l'~** obviously.
II en évidence *loc* **laisser/mettre qch en ~** LIT (pour être vu) to leave/put sth in an obvious ou a prominent place; **mettre en ~** FIG to highlight [*faiblesse, utilité*].

évident, ~e /evidɑ̃, ɑ̃t/ *adj* **1** GÉN obvious; [*progrès*] marked (*épith*); [*preuves*] clear (*épith*); **2**○ **ce n'est pas ~**○ (ce n'est pas si sûr) not necessarily; (ce n'est pas si facile) it's not so easy.

évider /evide/ [1] *vtr* (creuser) to hollow out; CULIN to scoop out.

évier /evje/ *nm* sink.

évincer /evɛ̃se/ [12] *vtr* (écarter) to oust [*rival*].

éviter /evite/ [1] *vtr* **1** (esquiver) to avoid [*obstacle, piéton*]; to dodge [*balle, coup*]; **2** (se soustraire à) to avoid [*crise, erreur*]; **3** (s'abstenir de) **~ qch/de faire** to avoid sth/doing; **4** (épargner) **~ qch à qn** to save sb sth; **je voulais t'~ une dépense** I wanted to spare you the expense; **~ à qn de faire** to save sb (from) doing.

évocateur, -trice /evɔkatœʀ, tʀis/ *adj* **1** (suggestif) evocative; **2** (significatif) significant.

évocation /evɔkasjɔ̃/ *nf* **1** (remémoration) (action) evocation; (résultat) reminiscence; **2** (mention) mention (**de** of).

évolué, ~e /evɔlɥe/ *adj* **1**○ (éclairé) **il n'est pas très ~!** he's not very bright!; **2** (avancé) [*pays, peuple*] civilized; **3** BIOL [*espèces*] evolved.

évoluer /evɔlɥe/ [1] *vi* **1** (progresser) [*groupe, individu, goûts*] to evolve, to change; [*idée*] to evolve; [*technique, science*] to advance, to evolve; [*situation*] to develop; **faire ~ la situation** to bring about some change in the situation; **2** (se déplacer gracieusement) [*danseurs*] to glide; [*avion*] to wheel.

évolutif, -ive /evɔlytif, iv/ *adj* GÉN, MÉD progressive; **une situation évolutive** a changing situation.

évolution /evɔlysjɔ̃/ *nf* **1** BIOL evolution; **2** (progrès) evolution (**de** of); (de langue, situation) development (**de** of); (de la science) advancement (**de** of); (d'enquête, étude) progress (**de** of); (de maladie) progression (**de** of); **~ démographique** demographical change; **~ de carrière** career advancement; **être en pleine ~** to be undergoing rapid change; **3** (changement) change.

évolutionniste /evɔlysjɔnist/ **I** *adj* evolutionary.
II *nmf* evolutionist.

évoquer /evɔke/ [1] *vtr* **1** (se remémorer) [*personne*] to recall [*passé, amis, souvenirs*]; **2** (mentionner) to mention, to bring up [*problème, question*]; **3** (faire penser à) [*objet, son, image*] to bring back [*souvenir*]; to conjure up [*image*]; to be reminiscent of [*printemps, enfance*]; **4** (raconter) [*auteur, musicien*] to evoke [*lieu, moment*]; **5** (par magie) to invoke.

ex /ɛks/ **I**○ *nmf inv* (ancien conjoint, concubin, compagnon) ex; (ancien membre) ex-member.
II *nm* **1** (written abbr = **exemple**) eg; **2** (written abbr = **exemplaire**) copy; **25 ~** 25 copies.

ex- /ɛks/ *préf* **~actrice/champion** former actress/champion.

exacerbation /ɛgzasɛʀbasjɔ̃/ *nf* exacerbation.

exacerber /ɛgzasɛʀbe/ [1] *vtr* to exacerbate.

exact, ~e /ɛgza(kt), akt/ *adj* **1** (juste) correct; **2** (précis) exact; **pour être plus ~** to be more precise; **3** (ponctuel) punctual.

exactement /ɛgzaktəmɑ̃/ *adv* GÉN exactly.

exaction /ɛgzaksjɔ̃/ I *nf* exaction.
  II **exactions** *nfpl* GÉN barbaric acts, acts of violence; (en temps de guerre) atrocities.

exactitude /ɛgzaktityd/ *nf* 1 (justesse) correctness; (de prévision) accuracy; 2 (précision) (de définition, description, dimension) accuracy; (de reproduction) exactness; (de montre) accuracy; **avec ~** [*mesurer, raconter*] accurately; 3 (ponctualité) punctuality; ▶ **politesse**.

ex æquo /ɛgzeko/ I *adj inv* (tous contextes) equally placed.
  II *adv* **ils sont premiers/deuxièmes ~** SPORT they've tied for first/second place.

exagération /ɛgzaʒeʀasjɔ̃/ *nf* exaggeration.

exagéré, ~e /ɛgzaʒeʀe/ *adj* 1 (outré) exaggerated; 2 (excessif) excessive; **d'une sensibilité ~e** oversensitive; **c'est un peu ~!** that's a bit much○!

exagérément /ɛgzaʒeʀemɑ̃/ *adv* excessively.

exagérer /ɛgzaʒeʀe/ [14] I *vtr* to exaggerate; **sans ~** without exaggeration.
  II *vi* to go too far, to push one's luck.
  III **s'exagérer** *vpr* [*personne*] to overestimate.

exaltant, ~e /ɛgzaltɑ̃, ɑ̃t/ *adj* [*aventure, lecture*] thrilling; [*projet, travail, musique*] inspiring.

exaltation /ɛgzaltasjɔ̃/ *nf* 1 (vive excitation) elation; **parler avec ~** to speak elatedly; 2 (intensification) (d'imagination) stimulation; (de différence) heightening; 3 (glorification) glorification.

exalté, ~e /ɛgzalte/ I *pp* ▶ **exalter**.
  II *pp adj* (surexcité) [*discours, esprit*] impassioned.
  III *nm,f* fanatic.

exalter /ɛgzalte/ [1] I *vtr* 1 (transporter) to elate, to thrill [*personne, foule*]; 2 (intensifier) to heighten [*qualité*]; 3 (glorifier) LITER to glorify [*personne*].
  II **s'exalter** *vpr* (s'enthousiasmer) to enthuse.

examen /ɛgzamɛ̃/ *nm* 1 SCOL, UNIV examination, exam○; **passer un ~** to take ou to sit (for) GB an exam○; **~ de rattrapage** retake, resit GB; 2 MÉD examination; **passer des ~s** to have some tests done; 3 (de cas, dossier) examination; (de question) consideration; (de situation) GÉN examination; (avant un changement) review; **à l'~** on examination; **être en cours d'~** [*dossier*] to be under review; [*question*] to be under consideration; [*cas*] to be under investigation; 4 (inspection) (de lieu) inspection; (d'objet) examination.
  ■ **~ blanc** mock (exam○); **~ de conscience** GÉN self-examination; **~ spécial d'entrée à l'université**, ESEU university entrance exam for students not having the baccalauréate.

examinateur, -trice /ɛgzaminatœʀ, tʀis/ *nm,f* examiner.

examiner /ɛgzamine/ [1] *vtr* 1 (étudier) GÉN to examine; (pour faire des changements) to review [*situation*]; **~ qch de près** to have a close look at sth; **~ qn de la tête aux pieds** to look sb up and down; 2 (observer) to examine [*marchandise, visage*]; **~ le ciel** to scan the sky; 3 MÉD to examine [*malade, blessure*].

exaspération /ɛgzaspeʀasjɔ̃/ *nf* 1 (d'humeur) exasperation; 2 (de besoin, douleur) intensification.

exaspérer /ɛgzaspeʀe/ [14] *vtr* 1 (irriter) to exasperate, to infuriate; 2 (exacerber) to exacerbate.

exaucer /ɛgzose/ [12] *vtr* to grant [*prière, requête*].

excavation /ɛkskavasjɔ̃/ *nf* excavation.

excavatrice /ɛkskavatʀis/ *nf* TECH excavator.

excédant, ~e /ɛksedɑ̃, ɑ̃t/ *adj* exasperating, infuriating.

excédent /ɛksedɑ̃/ *nm* surplus (**sur** over); **l'~ des dépenses sur les recettes** excess of expenditure over receipts; **~ de bagages** excess baggage.

excédentaire /ɛksedɑ̃tɛʀ/ *adj* surplus (*épith*).

excéder /ɛksede/ [14] *vtr* 1 (dépasser) to exceed [*quantité, durée*] (**de** by); 2 (agacer) to infuriate.

excellence /ɛksɛlɑ̃s/ *nf* excellence.

Excellence /ɛksɛlɑ̃s/ *nf* **Son ~, l'ambassadeur de France** His/Her Excellency, the French Ambassador.

excellent, ~e /ɛksɛlɑ̃, ɑ̃t/ *adj* excellent; **~!** great○!

exceller /ɛksele/ [1] *vi* to excel (**dans** in).

excentré, ~e /ɛksɑ̃tʀe/ *adj* 1 (loin du centre-ville) [*quartier*] outlying (*épith*); **l'école est (très) ~e** the school is (quite) some distance from the town centre GB; 2 TECH **être ~** [*axe*] to be off-centre GB.

excentricité /ɛksɑ̃tʀisite/ *nf* (de personne, comportement) eccentricity.

excentrique /ɛksɑ̃tʀik/ I *adj* 1 [*personne, idée*] eccentric; 2 [*quartier*] outlying; 3 [*courbe*] eccentric.
  II *nmf* eccentric.

excepté, ~e /ɛksɛpte/ I *pp* ▶ **excepter**.
  II *pp adj* (sauf) except.
  III *prép* (sauf) except; **~ quand** except when.

excepter /ɛksɛpte/ [1] *vtr* **si l'on excepte** except for, apart from.

exception /ɛksɛpsjɔ̃/ *nf* exception; **faire une ~** to make an exception; **faire ~** to be an exception; **~ à la règle** exception to the rule; **à l'~ de, ~ faite de** except for, with the exception of; **à quelques ~s près** with a few exceptions; **d'~** [*personne, destin*] exceptional; [*loi, tribunal*] emergency; **c'est l'~ qui confirme la règle** it's the exception that proves the rule.

exceptionnel, -elle /ɛksɛpsjɔnɛl/ *adj* 1 [*congé, subvention*] exceptional; [*autorisation*] special (*épith*); [*prix*] bargain (*épith*); [*réunion*] extraordinary (*épith*); **à titre ~** exceptionally; 2 [*circonstances, personne*] exceptional.

exceptionnellement /ɛksɛpsjɔnɛlmɑ̃/ *adv* exceptionally; **~, le magasin restera ouvert** today only the shop GB ou store US will stay open.

excès /ɛksɛ/ *nm inv* 1 (surplus) excess; **ôtez l'~ de colle** remove the excess glue; **en ~** excess (*épith*); 2 (abus) excess; **commettre des ~** to go too far; **faire des ~ de boisson** to drink excessively; **à l'~** excessively; 3 (extrême) **tomber dans l'~/dans l'~ inverse** to go too far/to the opposite extreme; **~ de confiance** overconfidence; **~ de prudence** excessive caution.
  ■ **~ de vitesse** JUR speeding; **faire un ~ de vitesse** to break the speed limit.

excessif, -ive /ɛksesif, iv/ *adj* 1 (qui dépasse la mesure) excessive; **être d'un optimisme ~** to be overoptimistic; **sans enthousiasme ~** without too much enthusiasm; 2 (qui manque de modération) extreme.

excessivement /ɛksesivmɑ̃/ *adv* (trop) excessively.

excipient /ɛksipjɑ̃/ *nm* excipient.

exciser /ɛksize/ [1] *vtr* 1 MÉD to excise; 2 (retirer le clitoris) to circumcise.

excision /ɛksizjɔ̃/ *nf* 1 MÉD excision; 2 (du clitoris) female circumcision.

excitable /ɛksitabl/ *adj* 1 (irritable) edgy; 2 [*muscle, organe*] excitable.

excitant, ~e /ɛksitɑ̃, ɑ̃t/ I *adj* 1 (stimulant) [*substance*] stimulating (*épith*); 2 (palpitant) [*perspective, époque*] exciting; [*roman, aventure*] thrilling.
  II *nm* (substance) stimulant.

excitation /ɛksitasjɔ̃/ *nf* 1 (enthousiasme) excitement; 2 (sexuelle) arousal; (stimulation) stimulation.

excité, ~e /ɛksite/ I *adj* 1 (déchaîné) [*foule, presse*] frenzied (*épith*), in a frenzy (*jamais épith*); [*atmosphère*] frenzied; 2 (enthousiaste) [*personne*] thrilled; 3 (émoustillé) (sexuellement) [*personne, sens*] aroused; (par l'alcool) elated.
  II *nm,f* PEJ 1 (fauteur de troubles) rowdy; 2 (fanatique) fanatic; 3 (nerveux) neurotic.
  IDIOMES **être ~ comme une puce**○ to be like a cat on a hot tin roof.

exciter /ɛksite/ [1] I *vtr* 1 (attiser) to stir up [*colère*]; kindle [*désir*]; 2 (enthousiasmer) to thrill; 3 (émoustiller) to arouse [*personne*]; 4 (énerver) [*personne*] to tease [*animal*]; to get [sb] excited [*enfant*]; [*café*] to make [sb] nervy [*personne*]; [*alcool*] to excite [*personne*]; 5 (stimuler) to stimulate [*palais*]; to excite [*nerf, tissu*].
  II **s'exciter** *vpr* (s'enthousiasmer) to get excited.

exclamatif, -ive /ɛksklamatif, iv/ *adj* exclamatory.

exclamation /ɛksklamasjɔ̃/ *nf* cry, exclamation.

exclamer: s'exclamer /ɛksklame/ [1] *vpr* (s'écrier) to

exclaim, to cry (**de** with); (avec admiration) **s'~ sur** to exclaim over.

exclu, **~e** /ɛkskly/ I *pp* ▶ **exclure**.
II *pp adj* (non admis) [*personne*] excluded (**de** from); [*hypothèse, idée*] ruled out; **c'est tout à fait ~!** it's absolutely out of the question!; **il n'est pas ~ que** it's not impossible that; **se sentir ~** to feel left out.

exclure /ɛsklyR/ [78] *vtr* **1** (ne pas inclure) to exclude [*personne*] (**de** from); to rule out [*hypothèse, possibilité*]; **~ que qn fasse** to prohibit sb from doing; **2** (rejeter) to expel [*membre de groupe*] (**de** from); to oust [*dirigeant, chef*]; to send [sb] down [*étudiant*].

exclusif, -ive /ɛsklyzif, iv/ *adj* **1** PRESSE [*document*] exclusive; **2** COMM [*concessionnaire*] sole; [*produit*] exclusive; **3** (d'un seul) [*propriété*] exclusive.

exclusion /ɛsklyzjɔ̃/ I *nf* **1** (non-admission) exclusion (**de** from); **2** (expulsion) (définitive) expulsion; (temporaire) suspension; **3** (clause contractuelle) exclusion.
II **à l'exclusion de** *loc prép* with the exception of.

exclusivement /ɛsklyzivmɑ̃/ *adv* exclusively.

exclusivité /ɛsklyzivite/ *nf* **1** (droits) COMM, CIN, PRESSE exclusive rights (*pl*); **l'~ d'une marque** the exclusive rights to a brand; **en ~** [*publier*] exclusively; [*produit*] exclusive; **2** (objet, produit) **c'est une ~ de notre entreprise** it's exclusive to our company.

excommunier /ɛkskɔmynje/ [2] *vtr* to excommunicate.

excrément /ɛkskRemɑ̃/ *nm* excrement ¢.

excrétion /ɛkskResjɔ̃/ *nf* (évacuation) excretion.

excroissance /ɛkskRwasɑ̃s/ *nf* **1** MÉD growth; **2** BOT outgrowth.

excursion /ɛkskyRsjɔ̃/ *nf* GÉN excursion, trip.

excusable /ɛkskyzabl/ *adj* excusable, forgivable.

excuse /ɛkskyz/ *nf* **1** (justification) excuse (**à qch** for sth); **ce n'est pas une ~ pour faire** it's no excuse for doing; **en guise d'~** by way of an excuse; **2** (regret) apology; **faire** or **présenter des ~s à qn** to offer one's apologies to sb; **exiger des ~s** (**de la part de qn**) to demand an apology from sb; **mille ~s** I'm terribly sorry.

excuser /ɛkskyze/ [1] I *vtr* **1** (pardonner) to forgive [*erreur, absence*]; to pardon [*faute*]; **excusez-moi** I'm sorry; **excusez mon retard** excuse me for being late; **vous êtes tout excusé** it's all right; **2** (justifier) to excuse; **rien n'excuse la cruauté** there is no excuse for cruelty; **3** (dispenser) to excuse [*personne*].
II **s'excuser** *vpr* to apologize (**auprès de**; **de** for; **d'avoir fait** for doing); **je m'excuse de vous déranger** I'm sorry to disturb you.

exécrable /ɛgzekRabl/ *adj* (épouvantable) dreadful.

exécrer /ɛgzekRe/ [14] *vtr* FML to loathe.

exécutable /ɛgzekytabl/ *adj* [*projet*] practicable; [*tâche*] manageable.

exécutant, ~e /ɛgzekytɑ̃, ɑ̃t/ *nm,f* **1** MUS performer; **orchestre de 60 ~s** 60-piece orchestra; **2** (agent) **il dit n'avoir été qu'un ~** he claims he was only obeying orders.

exécuter /ɛgzekyte/ [1] I *vtr* **1** (faire) to carry out [*tâche, travaux*]; to do [*exercice*]; **faire ~ des travaux** to have work done; **2** (appliquer) to carry out [*ordre, dessein, menace*]; to fulfil^GB [*promesse*]; COMM to fill [*commande*]; JUR to fulfil^GB [*contrat*]; to enforce [*loi, jugement*]; **3** (tuer) to execute [*condamné, otage*]; **4** MUS to perform, to play [*morceau*]; **5** ORDINAT to run [*programme*]; to execute [*instruction*].
II **s'exécuter** *vpr* (obéir) to comply.

exécutif, -ive /ɛgzekytif, iv/ I *adj* POL executive.
II *nm* executive.

exécution /ɛgzekysjɔ̃/ *nf* **1** (application) (d'ordre) execution; (de menace) carrying out ¢; (de décision, plan) implementation; JUR (de loi, jugement) enforcement; (d'obligation, de contrat) fulfilment^GB; **mettre à ~** to carry out [*menace*]; to implement [*programme*]; **2** (réalisation) (de travaux) execution; (de projet) implementation; ART (de tableau) painting ¢, execution; (de morceau) performance, execution; **veiller à la bonne ~ d'une tâche** to see that a job is done well; **d'~ facile** [*mou-*

vement*] easy to do; [*morceau*] easy to play; **3 (mise à mort) execution; **4** ORDINAT execution.

exemplaire /ɛgzɑ̃plɛʀ/ I *adj* **1** (modèle) [*conduite*] exemplary; [*élève*] model (*épith*); [*atterrissage*] textbook (*épith*); **de façon ~** in exemplary fashion; **la gestion de l'entreprise est ~** the firm is a model of good management; **2** (pour l'exemple) [*peine*] exemplary SOUT.
II *nm* **1** (livre, document) copy; **en deux/trois ~s** in duplicate/triplicate; **2** (spécimen) specimen, example.

exemplarité /ɛgzɑ̃plaʀite/ *nf* (de peine) deterrent nature (**de** of).

exemple /ɛgzɑ̃pl/ I *nm* **1** (cas) example; **prenez l'~ du Japon** take the case of Japan, take Japan for example; **sans ~** [*situation*] unprecedented; **2** (leçon) warning (**pour** to); **on a voulu faire de lui un ~** the intention was to make an example of him; **3** (image) example (**de** of); **donner l'~ du courage à qn** to set sb an example of courage; **prendre ~ sur qn, prendre qn en ~** to take sb as a model; **4** (idéal) model (**de** of); **être l'~ de la gentillesse** to be a model of kindness; **donner** or **citer qn en ~** to hold sb up as an example.
II **par exemple** *loc adv* **1** (pour illustrer) for example; **2** (marquant l'étonnement) (ça) **par ~!** how amazing!; **3** (marquant l'indignation) **ça par ~!** well, honestly!

exemplifier /ɛgzɑ̃plifje/ [2] *vtr* to exemplify.

exempt, ~e /ɛgzɑ̃, ɑ̃t/ *adj* **1** (dispensé) exempt (**de** from); **~ d'impôt** tax-free; **~ de droits de douane** duty-free; **2** (dépourvu) free (**de** from); **3** (à l'abri) immune (**de** to).

exempter /ɛgzɑ̃te/ [1] *vtr* **1** (dispenser) to exempt (**de** from; **de faire** from doing); **2** (mettre à l'abri) to preserve (**de** from).

exemption /ɛgzɑ̃psjɔ̃/ *nf* exemption.

exercé, ~e /ɛgzɛRse/ *adj* [*main*] deft, skilled; [*oreille*] trained; [*œil*] expert, practised^GB; [*personne*] experienced.

exercer /ɛgzɛRse/ [12] I *vtr* **1** (appliquer) to exercise [*droit, responsabilité*] (**sur** over); to exert [*pression, autorité*] (**sur** on); to have [*effet*] (**sur** on); **2** (pratiquer) to exercise [*profession*]; to practise^GB [*art*]; **~ un métier** to have a job; **3** (entraîner) to train, to exercise [*corps, esprit*]; (donner de l'exercice à) to exercise [*corps, muscle*].
II *vi* (travailler) [*travailleur, employé*] to work; [*médecin, juriste, architecte*] to practise^GB.
III **s'exercer** *vpr* **1** (s'entraîner) [*athlète*] to train; [*musicien*] to practise^GB; **s'~ à la plongée** to practise^GB diving; **s'~ au calme** to make an effort to stay calm; **2** (agir) [*influence, force*] to be exerted (**sur** on).

exercice /ɛgzɛRsis/ *nm* **1** (d'entraînement) exercise; **faire un ~** to do an exercise; **~ de prononciation** pronunciation drill; **2** (activité physique) exercise; **faire de l'~** to get some exercise; **3** (activité professionnelle) **avoir dix ans d'~** to have been working for ten years; **dans l'~ de ses fonctions** [*soldat, policier*] while on duty; [*travailleur*] while at work; **être en ~** [*fonctionnaire*] to be in office; [*médecin*] to be in practice; **en ~** [*ministre, président*] incumbent; **entrer en ~** to take up one's duties; **4** (usage) exercise (**de** of); **5** MIL (instruction) drill.
■ **~ d'application** practical exercise; **~ d'évacuation** GÉN emergency evacuation exercise; (en cas d'incendie) fire drill; **~ de tir** shooting practice ¢ GB, target practice ¢; **~s structuraux** LING structure drills.

exergue /ɛgzɛRg/ *nm* **1** (sur un ouvrage) epigraph; **2** (sur une médaille, une pièce) inscription.

exhaler /ɛgzale/ [1] FML I *vtr* (dégager) to exhale [*parfum*]; to give off [*relent*].
II **s'exhaler** *vpr* [*parfum*] to waft (**de** from).

exhausser /ɛgzose/ [1] *vtr* to raise.

exhaustif, -ive /ɛgzostif, iv/ *adj* exhaustive.

exhiber /ɛgzibe/ [1] I *vtr* to flaunt [*toilettes, richesse, objet*]; to show [*animal*]; to expose [*partie du corps*].
II **s'exhiber** *vpr* **1** PEJ (se montrer) to flaunt oneself; **2** (indécemment) to expose oneself.

exhibition /ɛgzibisjɔ̃/ *nf* **1** (d'animaux) display; **2** SPORT demonstration; **3** (étalage) (de richesse, toilettes) parade; (de sentiment) display.

exhibitionniste /ɛgzibisjɔnist/ *adj, nmf* exhibitionist.

exhortation /ɛgzɔrtasjɔ̃/ *nf* exhortation (**à faire** to do); **~ au calme** call for calm.

exhorter /ɛgzɔrte/ [1] *vtr* **~ qn à faire** [*personne*] to urge ou exhort sb to do; **~ qn au calme** to ask sb to remain calm.

exhumation /ɛgzymasjɔ̃/ *nf* **1** (de cadavre) exhumation; (de ruines) excavation; **2** (de document) unearthing; (du passé) resurrection.

exhumer /ɛgzyme/ [1] *vtr* **1** (déterrer) to exhume [*cadavre*]; to excavate [*ruines*]; **2** (tirer de l'oubli) to unearth [*document*] (**de** from); to resurrect [*souvenir*].

exigeant, ~e /ɛgziʒɑ̃, ɑ̃t/ *adj* demanding; **être ~ avec** or **envers qn** to demand a lot of sb.

exigence /ɛgziʒɑ̃s/ *nf* **1** (demande) demand (**de qch** for sth); **2** (obligation) demand; ADMIN requirement; **~s de sécurité** security requirements; **3** (trait de caractère) **le chef est d'une telle ~** the boss is so demanding.

exiger /ɛgziʒe/ [13] *vtr* **1** (demander impérativement) to demand [*réponse, réformes, excuses*]; **~ de qn qu'il fasse** to demand that sb do; **vous exigez trop d'eux** you're too demanding of them; **2** (nécessiter) to require; **3** (rendre obligatoire) to require; **comme l'exige la loi** as required by law; **'expérience exigée'** 'experience required'; **'anglais/permis de conduire exigé'** 'English/driver's licence^{GB} essential'; **'tenue de soirée exigée'** 'black tie'.

exigibilité /ɛgziʒibilite/ *nf* (d'impôt, de traite) payability; (de dette) repayability.

exigible /ɛgziʒibl/ *adj* [*impôt, traite*] due (*après n*).

exigu, -uë /ɛgzigy/ *adj* [*pièce, dimensions*] cramped; [*entrée*] narrow; [*espace*] confined.

exiguïté /ɛgziguite/ *nf* smallness, pokiness PÉJ.

exil /ɛgzil/ *nm* exile; **en ~** in exile.

exilé, ~e /ɛgzile/ *nm,f* exile.

exiler /ɛgzile/ [1] **I** *vtr* to exile.
II s'exiler *vpr* **1** (s'expatrier) to go into exile; **2** (se retirer) to bury oneself; **s'~ loin du monde** to cut oneself off from the world.

existant, ~e /ɛgzistɑ̃, ɑ̃t/ *adj* GÉN existing [*besoins, produits*] current; **non ~** nonexistent.

existence /ɛgzistɑ̃s/ *nf* **1** (réalité) existence; **2**⊙ (vie) life; **ne te complique pas la ~** don't make life difficult for yourself; **3** (mode de vie) lifestyle.

existentialisme /ɛgzistɑ̃sjalism/ *nm* existentialism.

exister /ɛgziste/ [1] **I** *vi* to exist; **ce risque existe** this is a very real risk; **le savon/la courtoisie, ça existe!** HUM there's such a thing as soap/manners, you know!; **si le paradis/la justice existe** if there is such a place as heaven/such a thing as justice; **la maison existe encore/n'existe plus** the house is still standing/is no longer standing; **la loi existe depuis dix ans** the law has been in existence for ten years; **~ en trois tailles** [*article, produit*] to be available in three sizes; **ces plantes n'existent que dans les Alpes** these plants are found only in the Alps; **les enfants me donnent une raison d'~** the children give me a reason for living.
II *v impers* to be; **il existe un lieu/des lieux où...** there is a place/there are places where...

exocet /ɛgzosɛ/ *nm* ZOOL flying fish.

exocrine /ɛgzokrin/ *adj* exocrine.

exode /ɛgzod/ *nm* LIT, FIG exodus.
■ **~ rural** rural depopulation.

exonération /ɛgzonerasjɔ̃/ *nf* exemption (**de** from).

exonérer /ɛgzonere/ [14] *vtr* to exempt (**de** from).

exorbitant, ~e /ɛgzorbitɑ̃, ɑ̃t/ *adj* [*prix, agios*] exorbitant; [*exigence, privilège*] outrageous; [*pouvoir*] inordinate (*épith*).

exorbité, ~e /ɛgzorbite/ *adj* bulging (**de** with).

exorciser /ɛgzorsize/ [1] *vtr* to exorcize.

exotique /ɛgzotik/ *adj* exotic.

expansible /ɛkspɑ̃sibl/ *adj* expansive.

expansif, -ive /ɛkspɑ̃sif, iv/ *adj* **1** [*personne*] communicative, outgoing; **2** TECH expansive.

expansion /ɛkspɑ̃sjɔ̃/ *nf* **1** (d'économie, de région) growth; **en (pleine) ~** [*organisme, filiale, marché*] (rapidly) growing; [*activité, monnaie*] (rapidly) increasing; **secteurs en ~** growth sectors; **2** (de corps, pays) expansion; **~ coloniale** colonial expansion; **3** (d'idées, épidémie) spread.

expansivité /ɛkspɑ̃sivite/ *nf* expansiveness.

expatriation /ɛkspatrijasjɔ̃/ *nf* expatriation.

expatrié, ~e /ɛkspatrije/ *adj, nm,f* expatriate.

expatrier /ɛkspatrije/ [2] **I** *vtr* to deport.
II s'expatrier *vpr* to emigrate (**en, à** to).

expectative /ɛkspɛktativ/ *nf* (attente prudente) prudent approach; **rester dans l'~** to wait and see.

expectorer /ɛkspɛktɔre/ [1] *vtr* to expectorate.

expédient /ɛkspedjɑ̃/ *nm* expedient; **user d'~s** to resort to expedients; **vivre d'~s** to live by one's wits.

expédier /ɛkspedje/ [2] *vtr* **1** GÉN to send; (par la poste) to post GB, to mail US [*lettres, colis*]; (faire partir) to dispatch [*marchandises, commande*]; **~ qch à qn** to send sb sth, to send sth to sb; **~ par bateau** to send [sth] by surface mail [*lettre, colis*]; to ship [*marchandises*]; **2** (envoyer) to send, to dispatch [*personne*] (**à** to); **3**⊙ (se débarrasser de) to get rid of [*importun*]; (bâcler) to polish off [*travail, repas*]; **~ un entretien en une heure** PÉJ to get an interview over within one hour; **4** (régler) to deal with; **~ les affaires courantes** to deal with ou dispatch daily business.

expéditeur, -trice /ɛkspeditœr, tris/ **I** *adj* [*bureau, gare*] of dispatch (*après n*).
II *nm,f* sender; **retour à l'~** return to sender.

expéditif, -ive /ɛkspeditif, iv/ *adj* [*personne*] brisk, efficient; [*méthode, procédé*] cursory, expeditious SOUT; **un jugement ~** a hasty verdict; **une justice expéditive** summary justice.

expédition /ɛkspedisjɔ̃/ *nf* **1** (de lettre, marchandises) dispatching, sending; (par bateau) shipping; **2** (chose expédiée) GÉN consignment, shipment US; (par bateau) shipment; **3** (mission) expedition; **4** JUR (de jugement, d'acte notarié) authenticated copy.

expéditionnaire /ɛkspedisjɔnɛr/ **I** *adj* [*corps, armée, forces*] expeditionary.
II ▶ 374 *nmf* **1** COMM forwarding agent; **2** ADMIN copyist.

expérience /ɛksperjɑ̃s/ *nf* **1** (pratique) experience; **je le sais par ~** I know from experience; **~ professionnelle** work experience; **avoir de l'~** to be experienced; **ne pas avoir d'~** to be inexperienced; **faire l'~ de qch** to experience sth; **j'en ai fait l'~ à mes dépens** I learned that lesson at my own expense; **2** (essai) experiment (**de** in).

expérimental, ~e, *mpl* **-aux** /ɛksperimɑ̃tal, o/ *adj* experimental.

expérimentateur, -trice /ɛksperimɑ̃tatœr, tris/ *nm,f* experimenter.

expérimentation /ɛksperimɑ̃tasjɔ̃/ *nf* experimentation.

expérimenté, ~e /ɛksperimɑ̃te/ *adj* experienced.

expérimenter /ɛksperimɑ̃te/ [1] *vtr* to test [*médicament*] (**sur** on); to try out [*méthode, procédé*].

expert, ~e /ɛkspɛr, ɛrt/ **I** *adj* expert.
II ▶ 374 *nm* **1** (spécialiste) expert (**en** on); **l'avis d'un ~** expert advice; **2** (dans les assurances) adjuster.

expert-comptable, *pl* **experts-comptables** /ɛkspɛrkɔ̃tabl/ **▶ 374** *nm* ~ chartered accountant GB, certified public accountant US.

expertise /ɛkspɛrtiz/ *nf* **1** (de bijou) valuation GB, appraisal US; (de dégâts) assessment; **rapport d'~** expert's report; **2** (compétence) expertise.

expertiser /ɛkspɛrtize/ [1] *vtr* **1** (évaluer) to value GB, to appraise US [*bijou*]; to assess [*dégâts*]; **2** (authentifier) to authenticate [*tableau*].

expiation /ɛkspjasjɔ̃/ *nf* atonement (**de** for), expiation (**de** of).

expier /ɛkspje/ [2] *vtr* **1** (réparer) to atone for, to expiate [*crime, faute*] (**par** with); **2** (être puni de) to pay for [*erreur*] (**par** with).

expiration /ɛkspiʀasjɔ̃/ *nf* **1** (d'air) exhalation; **2** (échéance) expiry GB, expiration US; **venir** or **arriver à** ~ to expire.

expirer /ɛkspiʀe/ [1] **I** *vtr* to exhale [*air*].
II *vi* **1** (arriver à son terme) to expire; **2** (souffler) to breathe out; **3** (mourir) LITER to expire.

explicatif, -ive /ɛksplikatif, iv/ *adj* [*note, lettre*] explanatory.

explication /ɛksplikasjɔ̃/ *nf* **1** (éclaircissement) explanation ¢; **je n'ai pas d'~s à vous donner** I don't have to explain; **nous avons eu une bonne** ~ we've talked things through; **2** (cause) explanation (**de** for); **3** (altercation) argument.
■ ~ **de texte** SCOL textual analysis.

explicite /ɛksplisit/ *adj* [*texte, titre, film*] explicit; [*réponse*] definite; **peu** or **pas très** ~ unclear.

explicitement /ɛksplisitmɑ̃/ *adv* [*mentionner*] explicitly; [*condamner*] unequivocally; [*demander*] specifically.

expliciter /ɛksplisite/ [1] *vtr* to clarify, to explain.

expliquer /ɛksplike/ [1] **I** *vtr* **1** (enseigner) to explain (à to); **2** (être la raison) to account for; **3** SCOL to analyze [*passage*].
II s'expliquer *vpr* **1** (comprendre) **s'~ qch** to understand sth; **2** (être compréhensible) to be understandable; **tout finira par s'~** everything will become clear; **la chose s'explique d'elle-même** it is self-explanatory; **3** (exposer sa pensée) **je m'explique** let me explain; **sans doute me suis-je mal expliqué** perhaps I didn't make myself clear; **4** (se justifier) to explain (oneself) (**auprès de, devant** to); **5** (résoudre un conflit) **ils se sont expliqués** they talked things through; **s'~ à coups de poings** to fight it out.

exploit /ɛksplwa/ *nm* exploit, feat.

exploitant, ~e /ɛksplwatɑ̃, ɑ̃t/ *nm,f* **1** (de ferme) farmer; **2** CIN cinema owner GB, exhibitor US; **3** COMM manager.
■ ~ **agricole** farmer.

exploitation /ɛksplwatasjɔ̃/ *nf* **1** (traitement injuste) exploitation; **2** (ferme) ~ (**agricole**) farm; **3** (entreprise) concern; **4** (de mine) working; (de gisement de charbon, de fer) mining; (de gisement, de forêt) exploitation; (de ferme, d'entreprise) running; (de réseau, liaison aérienne, maritime) operation; (de brevet) using.

exploiter /ɛksplwate/ [1] *vtr* **1** (abuser de) to exploit [*personne*]; **2** (faire valoir) to work [*mine*]; to mine [*gisement de charbon, fer*]; to exploit [*gisement, forêt, source thermale*]; to run [*entreprise*]; to operate [*réseau, liaison aérienne*]; to use [*brevet*]; **il exploite 17 hectares** he farms 17 hectares; **3** (utiliser) to make the most of [*don, connaissances*]; PÉJ to exploit [*crédulité, rivalités*]; ~ **une situation** to capitalize on a situation.

exploiteur, -euse /ɛksplwatœʀ, øz/ *nm,f* exploiter.

explorateur, -trice /ɛksplɔʀatœʀ, tʀis/ **I** ▶ 374⎪ *nm,f* (personne) explorer.
II *nm* MÉD endoscope.

exploration /ɛksplɔʀasjɔ̃/ *nf* exploration.

explorer /ɛksplɔʀe/ [1] *vtr* to explore.

exploser /ɛksploze/ [1] *vi* **1** LIT [*bombe, mine, appareil*] to explode; [*véhicule, immeuble*] to blow up; **faire** ~ [*personne, dispositif*] to blow up [*avion, voiture*]; to explode [*bombe, mine*]; [*gaz, court-circuit*] to cause [sth] to blow up [*immeuble*]; **2** FIG [*joie*] to burst forth; **laisser** ~ **sa colère** to give vent to one's anger; **3** (augmenter) [*prix*] to soar, to rocket○; [*ventes*] to boom, to rocket○.

explosif, -ive /ɛksplozif, iv/ **I** *adj* explosive.
II *nm* explosive.

explosion /ɛksplozjɔ̃/ *nf* **1** LIT explosion; **faire** ~ to explode; **2** (de haine, colère, violence) explosion; **3** (de population, fraudes) explosion (**de** of); **4** (de marché) boom (**de** in).

exponentiel, -ielle /ɛkspɔnɑ̃sjɛl/ *adj* exponential.

export /ɛkspɔʀ/ *nm* export.

exportateur, -trice /ɛkspɔʀtatœʀ, tʀis/ **I** *adj* [*pays*] exporting; [*marché, industrie, société*] export (*épith*).
II ▶ 374⎪ *nm,f* exporter.

exportation /ɛkspɔʀtasjɔ̃/ *nf* export; **faire l'~ de qch** to export sth.

exporter /ɛkspɔʀte/ [1] *vtr* to export.

exposant, ~e /ɛkspozɑ̃, ɑ̃t/ **I** *nm,f* exhibitor.
II *nm* MATH exponent.

exposé, ~e /ɛkspoze/ **I** *pp* ▶ **exposer**.
II *pp adj* **1** (situé) [*maison, endroit*] exposed; **maison** ~**e au sud** south-facing house; **maison bien** ~**e** house with a good aspect; **2** (montré) [*tableau*] on show (*après n*); [*denrée*] on display (*après n*); **liste des œuvres** ~**es** list of exhibits.
III *nm* **1** (compte rendu) ~ **de** account of [*situation*]; **faire l'~ des faits** to give a statement of the facts; **2** (conférence) talk (**sur** on); **faire un** ~ to give a talk.

exposer /ɛkspoze/ [1] **I** *vtr* **1** (montrer) to exhibit [*œuvre d'art*]; to display, to put [sth] on display [*marchandise*]; **2** (décrire) to state [*faits*]; to outline [*idée, plan*]; to list [*griefs*]; to explain [*situation*]; to expound [*argument*]; LITTÉRAT to set out [*sujet*]; **3** PHOT to expose; **4** (mettre en danger) to risk [*vie, réputation*]; JUR to abandon a child; **5** (soumettre à) to expose (**à** to); **ne reste pas exposé au soleil** stay out of the sun.
II s'exposer *vpr* **1** (se rendre vulnérable) to put oneself at risk; **s'~ à** to risk [*rechute, mort*]; to lay oneself open to [*poursuites, critiques*]; **2** (se placer) **s'~ au soleil** to go out in the sun.

exposition /ɛkspozisjɔ̃/ *nf* **1** (de tableaux, photos, d'objets d'art) exhibition; (d'animaux, de plantes, marchandises) show; (d'objets à vendre) fair; **2** (dans un magasin) display; **3** (de thèse, situation, faits) exposition; **4** (orientation) aspect; **la terrasse jouit d'une bonne** ~ the terrace has a pleasant aspect; **5** (soumission à un effet) PHOT exposure; **l'~ aux radiations/au soleil** exposure to radiation/to sunlight.

exprès[1] /ɛkspʀɛ/ *adv* **1** (délibérément) deliberately; **je ne l'ai pas fait** ~ I didn't do it on purpose; **'la porte se referme toute seule'—'c'est fait** ~**'** 'the door shuts itself'—'that's what it's designed to do!'; **comme par un fait** ~ as ill-luck would have it; **2** (spécialement) specially.

exprès[2], **-esse** /ɛkspʀɛs/ **I** *adj* [*ordre, condition, clause*] express; **défense expresse d'en parler** all mention of it is expressly forbidden.
II exprès *adj inv* POSTES special delivery.

express /ɛkspʀɛs/ **I** *adj inv* **1** [*train*] express; **2** [*nettoyage*] express; [*déjeuner*] quick.
II *nm inv* **1** RAIL express; **2** (café) espresso.

expressément /ɛkspʀɛsemɑ̃/ *adv* expressly.

expressif, -ive /ɛkspʀɛsif, iv/ *adj* expressive.

expression /ɛkspʀɛsjɔ̃/ *nf* **1** GÉN expression; **plein d'~** [*yeux, visage*] expressionless; **avec** ~ [*réciter, chanter*] with feeling; **réduire qch à sa plus simple** ~ FIG to reduce sth to a minimum; **2** (groupe de mots) expression; ~ **figée**, ~ **toute faite** set phrase; **passez-moi l'~!** if you'll pardon the expression!; **d'~ française/anglaise** French-speaking/English-speaking.
■ ~ **corporelle** self-expression through movement.

expressionnisme /ɛkspʀɛsjɔnism/ *nm* expressionism.

expressivité /ɛkspʀɛsivite/ *nf* expressiveness.

exprimable /ɛkspʀimabl/ *adj* possible to express; **difficilement** ~ [*sentiment, impression*] hard to express.

exprimer /ɛkspʀime/ [1] **I** *vtr* **1** (dire, montrer) to express; ~ **qch en pourcentage** to give sth as a percentage; **2** (extraire) to squeeze [*liquide*] (**de** out of).
II s'exprimer *vpr* **1** [*personne*] to express oneself; **si j'ose m'~ ainsi** if I can put it this way; **s'~ en français** to speak in French; **2** [*sentiment, état d'esprit*] to be expressed.

expropriation /ɛkspʀɔpʀijasjɔ̃/ *nf* (de propriété) compulsory purchase; (de personne) expropriation.

exproprier /ɛkspʀɔpʀije/ [2] *vtr* ~ **qn** to put a compulsory purchase order on sb's property.

expulser /ɛkspylse/ [1] *vtr* **1** (renvoyer) to evict [*locataire*] (**de** from); to deport [*immigré*] (**de** from; **en, vers** to); to expel [*élève, diplomate, dissident, membre*] (**de** from); **2** SPORT to send [sb] off [*joueur*]; **3** MÉD to expel [*calcul*]; to excrete [*déchets*].

expulsion /ɛkspylsjɔ̃/ *nf* **1** (de locataire) eviction (**de** from); (d'immigré) deportation (**de** from); (d'élève, de diplomate, dissident) expulsion (**de** from); (de locataire) eviction order; **2** SPORT sending-off (**de** from).

expurger /ɛkspyʀʒe/ [13] *vtr* **1** to expurgate, to bowdlerize [*texte*]; **2** POL to purge [*parti*].

exquis, ~**e** /ɛkski, iz/ *adj* GÉN exquisite; [*personne*] delightful.

exsangue /ɛgzɑ̃g/ *adj* LIT bloodless.

exsuder /ɛksyde/ [1] **I** *vtr* LIT, FIG to exude.
II *vi* LIT, FIG to ooze (**de** from).

extase /ɛkstɑz/ *nf* LIT, FIG ecstasy.

extasier: **s'extasier** /ɛkstazje/ [2] *vpr* to go into ecstasy ou raptures (**devant, sur** over).

extatique /ɛkstatik/ *adj* ecstatic.

extensible /ɛkstɑ̃sibl/ *adj* **1** LIT [*métal, tissu, matière*] extensible; **2** FIG [*liste*] elastic.

extensif, -ive /ɛkstɑ̃sif, iv/ *adj* **1** [*culture*] extensive; **2** [*sens*] wider; [*signification, usage*] extended.

extension /ɛkstɑ̃sjɔ̃/ *nf* **1** (de bras, jambe, muscle) stretching, extension; **faire des mouvements d'~ et de flexion** to stretch and bend; **quand votre jambe est en ~** when your leg is extended; **2** MÉD extension; **3** (d'industrie) expansion; (de grève, zone, pouvoirs, loi) extension (**à** to); **prendre de l'~** [*industrie*] to expand; [*grève*] to spread, to extend; **4** (de ressort, métal) stretching.

exténuer /ɛkstenɥe/ [1] **I** *vtr* to exhaust.
II **s'exténuer** *vpr* to wear oneself out (**à faire** doing).

extérieur, ~**e** /ɛksteʀjœʀ/ **I** *adj* **1** GÉN outside; **2** (périphérique) [*couche, mur*] outer; **3** (étranger) [*commerce, relations, aide*] foreign; **4** (apparent) [*joie, calme*] outward; **aspect** ~ (de personne) outward appearance; (de bâtiment) outside.
II *nm* **1** GÉN outside; **à l'~** outside, outdoors; **à l'~ de qch** outside sth; **d'~** outdoor (épith); **2** (monde autour de soi) outside world; **3** (étranger) foreign countries (+ *v pl*); **4** (apparence) exterior, appearance; **5** CIN **les ~s** outdoor location shots; **en ~** on location.

extérieurement /ɛksteʀjœʀmɑ̃/ *adv* **1** (vu du dehors) on the outside, externally; **2** (en apparence) outwardly.

extérioriser /ɛksteʀjɔʀize/ [1] **I** *vtr* to show.
II **s'extérioriser** *vpr* [*personne*] to express oneself.

extermination /ɛkstɛʀminasjɔ̃/ *nf* extermination.

exterminer /ɛkstɛʀmine/ [1] *vtr* to exterminate [*peuple, animaux*]; to wipe out [*armée, rebelles*].

externat /ɛkstɛʀna/ *nm* **1** SCOL (école) day school; **2** MÉD, UNIV **préparer l'~** to prepare for medical school entrance exams; **faire son ~** to be a nonresident student doctor (in a hospital) GB, to be an extern US.

externe /ɛkstɛʀn/ **I** *adj* **1** (extérieur) [*cause, problème, croissance*] external; [*face*] outside; [*partie*] exterior; **2** MÉD external.
II *nmf* **1** SCOL day pupil; **2** MÉD, UNIV ~ (**des hôpitaux**) non-residential medical student GB, extern US.

extincteur /ɛkstɛ̃ktœʀ/ *nm* fire extinguisher.

extinction /ɛkstɛ̃ksjɔ̃/ *nf* **1** MÉD **avoir une ~ de voix** to have lost one's voice; **2** (d'espèce, de race) extinction; **espèce en voie d'~** endangered species; **3** (action d'éteindre) **après l'~ de l'incendie** after the fire was put out; **après l'~ des feux** after lights out.

extirper /ɛkstiʀpe/ [1] *vtr* **1**○ (faire sortir) to drag [*personne*] (**de** out of, from); **2** (faire disparaître) to eradicate.

extorquer /ɛkstɔʀke/ [1] *vtr* to extort (**à qn** from sb).

extorsion /ɛkstɔʀsjɔ̃/ *nf* extortion.

extra /ɛkstʀa/ **I** *adj inv* **1**○ (remarquable) great○; **2** COMM **huile d'olive** ~ **vierge** extra virgin olive oil.
II *nm inv* **1** (dépense imprévue) extra; **se payer un petit** ~ to have a little treat; **2** (travail) **faire des** ~ (petits

travaux) to do bits and pieces; (travail supplémentaire) to do a few extra jobs; **3** (personne) extra worker.

extra-atmosphérique, *pl* ~**s** /ɛkstraatmɔsfeʀik/ *adj* **espace** ~ outer space.

extracommunautaire, *pl* ~**s** /ɛkstrakɔmynotɛʀ/ *adj* non-EEC (épith).

extraction /ɛkstraksjɔ̃/ *nf* **1** (de minerai, pétrole, gaz) extraction; (de charbon, diamants) mining; (d'ardoise, de marbre) quarrying; **2** MÉD (de balle, dent) extraction (**de** from); **3** (origine) extraction SOUT; **être d'~ bourgeoise** to be from a middle-class background.

extrader /ɛkstrade/ [1] *vtr* to extradite.

extra-fin, ~**e**, *mpl* ~**s** /ɛkstrafɛ̃, in/ *adj* [*collants*] ultra-fine; **petits pois** ~**s** petits pois.

extraire /ɛkstrɛʀ/ [58] **I** *vtr* **1** (exploiter) to extract [*minerai*]; to mine [*or, houille*]; to quarry [*ardoise, marbre*]; **2** (enlever) to extract, to pull out [*dent*]; to remove [*balle, épine*] (**de** from); to extract [*substance, élément*] (**de** from).
II **s'extraire** *vpr* **s'~ de** to climb out of [*fauteuil, cabine de pilotage*]; HUM to struggle out of [*vêtement*].

extrait /ɛkstrɛ/ *nm* **1** (de livre, film) extract, excerpt; (de discours) extract; **2** (substance) essence, extract.
■ ~ (**d'acte**) **de naissance** birth certificate; ~ **de casier judiciaire** (**de qn**) copy of (sb's) criminal record; ~ **de compte** abstract of accounts.

extra-long, -longue, *mpl* ~**s** /ɛkstralɔ̃, ɔ̃g/ *adj* [*cigarette*] king-size; [*vêtement*] extra-long.

extralucide /ɛkstralysid/ *adj* clairvoyant.

extraordinaire /ɛkstraɔʀdinɛʀ/ *adj* **1** (qui surprend) [*question, phénomène*] extraordinary; (qui plaît et surprend) [*sensation, paysage, personne*] amazing; (admirable) [*personne, film*] remarkable; (qui plaît beaucoup) [*personne, film*] fantastic○; **et si par** ~... and if by some extraordinary twist of fate...; **c'est quand même** ~! it's incredible!; **2** (non prévu) [*dépenses, mesure, assemblée*] extraordinary.

extraordinairement /ɛkstraɔʀdinɛʀmɑ̃/ *adv* amazingly, extraordinarily.

extrapoler /ɛkstrapole/ [1] *vtr, vi* to extrapolate.

extrascolaire /ɛkstraskɔlɛʀ/ *adj* [*activités*] extracurricular.

extraterrestre /ɛkstratɛʀɛstʀ/ **I** *adj* [*invasion*] extraterrestrial; **espace** ~ outer space.
II *nmf* extraterrestrial, alien.

extra-utérin, ~**e**, *mpl* ~**s** /ɛkstrayteʀɛ̃, in/ *adj* **grossesse** ~**e** ectopic pregnancy.

extravagance /ɛkstravagɑ̃s/ *nf* **1** (de personne) eccentricity; **2** (de projet, comportement, mode, d'idées) extravagance; **3** (acte) extravagance.

extravagant, ~**e** /ɛkstravagɑ̃, ɑ̃t/ *adj* **1** [*comportement*] eccentric; **2** [*idée, mode*] extravagant; **3** [*prix*] exorbitant.

extraverti, ~**e** /ɛkstravɛʀti/ *adj, nm,f* extrovert.

extrême /ɛkstrɛm/ **I** *adj* **1** (le plus distant) furthest; **dans l'~ sud du pays** in the extreme South of the country; **2** (très grand) [*simplicité, prudence*] extreme; [*pureté*] very great; **l'~ jeunesse du candidat** the candidate's extreme youth; **leur** ~ **vieillesse** their very great age; **avec un plaisir** ~ with the greatest pleasure; **d'une complexité** ~ extremely complex; **3** (immodéré) [*opinion, situation, comportement*] extreme; [*décision, remède*] drastic; **il est** ~ **en tout, c'est quelqu'un d'**~ he always goes to extremes; **4** POL [*parti*] extremist; [*droite, gauche*] far, extreme.
II *nm* **1** (ce qui est excessif) extreme; **c'est pousser la logique à l'~** that's taking logic to extremes; **courageux à l'~** extremely brave; **événement médiatisé à l'~** event which was given a lot of media hype○; **2** (opposé) extreme; **à l'~ opposé** or **inverse** at the other extreme; **3** MÉTÉO extreme.

extrêmement /ɛkstrɛmmɑ̃/ *adv* extremely.

extrême-onction, *pl* **extrêmes-onctions** /ɛkstrɛmɔ̃ksjɔ̃/ *nf* extreme unction.

Extrême-Orient /ɛkstrɛmɔʀjɑ̃/ ▶509 *nprm* **l'~** the Far East.

extrémiste /ɛkstremist/ *adj, nmf* extremist.

extrémité /ɛkstʀemite/ nf **1** GÉN end; (de doigt) tip; (de mât, clocher) top; (de surface, champ, ville) edge; **aux deux ~s** at both ends; **2** (mort) (**en**) **être à la dernière ~** to be on the point of death, to be close to death; **3** FIG (acte désespéré) extreme; **pousser qn jusqu'à la dernière ~** to push sb to the brink; **4** (de membre) extremity; **avoir de petites ~s** to have small hands and feet.

extrusion /ɛkstʀyzjɔ̃/ nf IND, TECH (procédé) extrusion.

exubérance /ɛgzybeʀɑ̃s/ nf exuberance.

exubérant, **~e** /ɛgzybeʀɑ̃, ɑ̃t/ adj exuberant.

exultation /ɛgzyltasjɔ̃/ nf exultation.

exulter /ɛgzylte/ [1] vi to be exultant (**de** with), to exult (**de faire** at doing).

exutoire /ɛgzytwaʀ/ nm **1** FIG outlet; **servir d'~ à** to be an outlet for; **2** TECH outlet.

ex-voto /ɛksvoto/ nm inv thanksgiving plaque.

f, F /ɛf/ *nm inv* **1** (lettre) f, F; **2** (appartement) **F3** 2-bedroom flat GB ou apartment; **3** (*written abbr* = **franc**) 50 F 50 F.

fa /fa/ *nm inv* (note) F, fa; (en solfiant) fa; **~ dièse** F sharp.

fable /fabl/ *nf* **1** (récit) tale; **2** LITTÉRAT fable; **3** (mensonge) tall story.

IDIOMES **être la ~ de la ville** (le sujet de conversation) to be the talk of the town; (la risée) to be a laughing stock.

fabricant /fabʀikɑ̃/ *nm* manufacturer.

fabrication /fabʀikasjɔ̃/ *nf* GÉN making; (pour le commerce) manufacture; **procédé de ~** manufacturing process; **il y a un défaut de ~** (tissu) it's imperfect; (machine) it's faulty; **de ~ française** French-made; **~ en série** mass production.

■ **~ assistée par ordinateur, FAO** computer-aided manufacturing, CAM.

fabrique /fabʀik/ *nf* (usine) factory.

fabriquer /fabʀike/ [1] **I** *vtr* **1** (produire) GÉN to make; (industriellement) to manufacture; **'fabriqué en France'** 'made in France'; **fabriqué en série** mass-produced; **2** (pour tromper) to forge [*faux papiers*]; to invent [*alibi*]; **c'est fabriqué de toutes pièces** it's a complete fabrication; **3**° (faire) **qu'est-ce que tu fabriques ici?** what are you doing here?

II se fabriquer *vpr* **1** (pour soi) to make [sth] for oneself; **2** COMM, IND to be manufactured.

fabulateur, -trice /fabylatœʀ, tʀis/ *nm,f* compulsive liar.

fabulation /fabylasjɔ̃/ *nf* **1** (fable) lie, tale; **2** (mythomanie) compulsive lying.

fabuler /fabyle/ [1] *vi* **1** (inventer) to make things up; **2** PSYCH to confabulate.

fabuleusement /fabyløzmɑ̃/ *adv* fabulously.

fabuleux, -euse /fabylø, øz/ *adj* [*beauté, temps, richesse*] fabulous; [*somme*] fantastic; [*être*] mythical.

fabuliste /fabylist/ *nmf* fabulist.

fac° /fak/ *nf* **1** (faculté) faculty; **2** (université) university.

façade /fasad/ *nf* **1** (de bâtiment) front; **chambres en ~** front bedrooms; **la ~ arrière** the back; **~ nord** north side; **2** (apparence) façade.

face /fas/ **I** *nf* **1** (visage) face; **~ à ~** face to face; (étendu) **~ contre terre** lying face downward(s); **à la ~ de qn** [*proclamer, jeter*] in sb's face; **les muscles/os de la ~** the facial muscles/bones; **le côté ~ d'une pièce** the heads side of a coin; **2** (côté) side; **3** (aspect) side; **une question à plusieurs ~s** a multifaceted question; **la ~ cachée de la politique** the underside of politics; **4** (front) **faire ~** (résister) to face up to things; **se faire ~** (*personnes*) to face each other; (*objets, maisons*) to be opposite one another; (s'affronter) to confront each other; **faire ~ à** [*maison, chambre*] to face [*lieu*]; [*personne*] to face [*adversaire, défi, accusation*]; to cope with [*exigences, dépenses*]; to meet [*besoin, dette*]; to measure up to [*concurrence*]; **faire ~ à l'inflation** to tackle inflation.

II de face *loc* [*photo*] fullface (*épith*); [*éclairage*] frontal; **elle est plus jolie de ~** she's prettier from the front; **aborder un problème de ~** to tackle a problem head-on; **prendre une loge de ~** THÉÂT to take a box facing the stage.

III en face *loc* **il habite en ~** he lives opposite; **les gens d'en ~** the people opposite; **avoir le soleil en ~** to have the sun in one's eyes; **voir les choses en ~** to see things as they are; **je leur ai dit la vérité en ~** I told them the truth straight out; **l'équipe d'en ~** the opposing team.

IV en face de *loc prép* **1** (devant) **en ~ de l'église** opposite the church GB, across from the church; **le couple en ~ de moi** the couple opposite me; **ils étaient assis l'un en ~ de l'autre** or **en ~ l'un de l'autre** they were sitting opposite ou facing each other; ▶ **trou; 2** (en présence de) **ne dis pas ça en ~ des enfants** don't say that in front of the children; **en ~ de difficultés imprévues** faced with unexpected difficulties; **3** (comparé à) compared with.

V face à *loc prép* **1** (devant) **parler ~ aux caméras** to speak facing the cameras; **mon lit est ~ à la fenêtre** my bed faces the window; **2** (confronté à) **~ à cette situation** in view of this situation.

IDIOMES **se voiler la ~** not to face facts.

face-à-face /fasafas/ *nm inv* (débat) one-to-one debate GB, one-on-one debate US; (confrontation) encounter.

facétie /fasesi/ *nf* (plaisanterie) facetious remark; (farce) practical joke.

facétieux, -ieuse /fasesjø, øz/ *adj* mischievous.

facette /fasɛt/ *nf* facet; **à plusieurs ~s** multifaceted.

fâché, ~e /faʃe/ *adj* **1** (en colère) angry (**contre** with); **2** (brouillé) **être ~ avec qn** to have fallen out with sb; **3**† (désolé) sorry (**de** about).

fâcher /faʃe/ [1] **I**† *vtr* (irriter) to make [sb] angry.

II se fâcher *vpr* **1** (se mettre en colère) to get angry (**contre qn** with sb; **pour qch** about sth); **2** (se brouiller) to fall out (**avec qn** with sb; **pour qch** over sth).

IDIOMES **se ~ tout rouge**° to be hopping mad°.

fâcheusement /faʃøzmɑ̃/ *adv* unfortunately.

fâcheux, -euse /faʃø, øz/ **I** *adj* [*influence, exemple*] detrimental; [*retard, initiative*] unfortunate; [*effet*] unpleasing; [*nouvelle, événement*] distressing.

II† *nm,f* irritating person.

facial, ~e, mpl -iaux /fasjal, o/ *adj* ANAT facial.

faciès /fasjɛs/ *nm inv* (expression) face.

facile /fasil/ **I** *adj* **1** (sans difficulté) easy; **rien de plus ~ (que)** nothing could be easier (than); **~ comme tout** as easy as pie; **c'est plus ~ à dire qu'à faire** that's easier said than done; **2** (spontané) **avoir la larme ~** to be quick to cry; **3** (docile) easy-going; **4** (médiocre) facile.

II° *adv* (facilement) easily; **il a soixante ans ~** he's easily sixty.

facilement /fasilmɑ̃/ *adv* **1** (sans difficultés) easily; **explicable** easy to explain; **elle rit très ~** she's very quick to laugh; **2**° (largement) **j'ai mis ~ deux heures** it took me a good two hours.

facilité /fasilite/ **I** *nf* **1** (de travail, jeu) easiness; (d'acte, utilisation, entretien) ease; **avec ~** with ease; **d'une ~ déconcertante** surprisingly easy; **2** (d'expression, de style) fluency; **avec ~** fluently; **3** (médiocrité) **tomber dans/éviter la ~** to tend to take/to tend not to take the easy way out.

II facilités *nfpl* **1** (possibilités) **~s d'importation** import opportunities; **toutes ~s pour faire** every opportunity to do; **2** FIN **~s (de paiement)** easy terms; **~s de caisse/prêt** overdraft/loan facility (*sg*).

faciliter /fasilite/ [1] *vtr* to make [sth] easier [*tâche, choses*] (**à** for).

façon /fasɔ̃/ **I** *nf* **1** (manière) way; **la ~ dont tu manges** the way you eat; **d'une ~ ou d'une autre** one way or another; **c'est une ~ comme une autre de faire** it's one way of doing; **d'une certaine ~** in a way; **de toute ~, de toutes les ~s** anyway; **de toutes les ~s possibles** in every possible way; **agir de la même ~** to do the same; **de telle ~ que personne n'a compris** so that nobody understood; **de ~ inattendue** unexpectedly; **à ma ~** my (own) way; **à la ~ de** like; **de ~ à faire** (en vue de) in order to do; (de telle manière que) in such a way as to do; **de ~ (à ce) qu'elle fasse** so (that) she does; **elle nous a joué un tour à sa ~** she played a trick of her own on us; **je vais leur dire ma ~ de penser** I'll tell them exactly what I think; **cette ~ de faire ne te/leur ressemble pas** that's not like you/them; **~ de parler** so to speak; **de quelle ~ est-il tombé?** how did he fall?; **2** (imitation) **un peigne ~ ivoire** an imitation ivory comb; **sac ~ sellier** saddle-stitched bag; **doublure ~ soie** silk-look lining; **3** (style) style; **spectacle ~ années 70** 70's-style show; **4** (main-d'œuvre) **on m'a donné le tissu et j'ai payé la ~** the cloth was a present and I paid for the making-up; **travailler à ~** to work to order (*with supplied materials*).

II façons *nfpl* **1** (attitude) **tes ~s me déplaisent** I don't like the way you behave; **en voilà des ~s!** what a way to behave!; **2** (excès de politesse) **faire des ~s** to stand on ceremony; **sans ~s** [*repas*] informal; [*personne*] unpretentious; **non merci, sans ~s** no thank you, really.

faconde /fakɔ̃d/ *nf* FML loquacity.

façonnage /fasɔnaʒ/ *nm* (du bois) hewing; (de la pierre) cutting; (du cuir) sleeking; (du papier) converting; (du pétrole) processing.

façonner /fasɔne/ [1] *vtr* **1** (fabriquer) to manufacture [*outil, pièce*]; to make [*chapeau, objet artisanal*]; **2** IND to hew [*bois*]; to cut [*pierre*]; to fashion [*argile*]; to sleek [*cuir*]; **3** (former) (par l'éducation) to shape; (par les épreuves) to mould GB, to mold US.

fac-similé, *pl* **~s** /faksimile/ *nm* facsimile.

facteur, -trice /faktœʀ, tʀis/ ► 374 ◄ **I** *nmf* postman/postwoman, mailman/mailwoman US.

II *nm* **1** (élément) factor; **~ de risque** risk factor; **le ~ chance** the element of chance; **2** MATH factor; **mettre en ~s** to factorize, to factor US; **3** MUS **~ d'orgues** organ builder; **~ de pianos** piano maker.

factice /faktis/ *adj* [*gaieté, sourire*] forced; [*style*] contrived; [*bijoux*] imitation (*épith*); [*fleur, beauté*] artificial; [*étalage*] dummy (*épith*).

factieux, -ieuse /faksjø, øz/ **I** *adj* seditious.

II *nmf* dissident.

faction /faksjɔ̃/ *nf* **1** POL faction; **2** MIL guard duty; **être de** or **en ~** GÉN to keep watch; MIL to be on guard duty; **3** (poste de travail) shift.

factoriel, -ielle[1] /faktɔʀjɛl/ *adj* factorial; **analyse factorielle** factor analysis.

factorielle[2] /faktɔʀjɛl/ *nf* factorial.

factotum /faktɔtɔm/ *nm* general handyman, factotum HUM.

factrice ► **facteur** I.

factuel, -elle /faktɥɛl/ *adj* factual.

facturation /faktyʀasjɔ̃/ *nf* **1** (opération) invoicing; **2** (service) invoicing department.

facture /faktyʀ/ *nf* **1** GÉN bill; (détaillée) invoice; **faire** or **établir une ~** to make out a bill ou an invoice; ► **faux**[1]; **2** (dépense) bill; **~ pétrolière** oil bill; **3** (technique) (d'artisan) craftsmanship; (d'artiste) technique; **4** MUS (d'orgues) building; (d'instruments) making.

■ **~ détaillée** itemized invoice.

facturer /faktyʀe/ [1] *vtr* **1** (dresser une facture pour) to invoice [*marchandises*]; **2** (faire payer) to charge for.

facturette /faktyʀɛt/ *nf* credit card slip.

facturier, -ière[1] /faktyʀje, ɛʀ/ ► 374 ◄ **I** *nmf* (employé) invoice clerk.

II *nm* (registre) invoice book.

facturière[2] /faktyʀjɛʀ/ *nf* (machine) invoicing machine.

facultatif, -ive /fakyltatif, iv/ *adj* optional.

faculté /fakylte/ *nf* **1** (aptitude) (sensorielle, intellectuelle) faculty; (physique) ability; **2** (liberté) option (**de faire** of

doing); **3** UNIV faculty; **4** JUR (droit) right (**de faire** to do).

fada○ /fada/ **I** *adj* crazy○ (**de** about), nuts○ (**de** about).

II *nmf* nutcase○.

fadaises○ /fadɛz/ *nfpl* twaddle○ ¢, silly chatter ¢.

fadasse○ /fadas/ *adj* tasteless, drab, dull.

fade /fad/ *adj* [*aliment*] tasteless; [*couleur*] drab; [*blondeur*] dull; [*odeur*] sickly; [*œuvre, personne*] dull.

fadeur /fadœʀ/ *nf* (de goût) blandness; (de style) dreariness.

fagot /fago/ *nm* bundle of firewood.

IDIOMES **de derrière les ~s**○ very special.

fagoter○ /fagɔte/ [1] **I** *vtr* (habiller) to do [sb] up○.

II se fagoter *vpr* to do oneself up○; (**être**) **mal fagoté** (to be) badly dressed.

faiblard○, **-e** /fɛblaʀ, aʀd/ *adj* PEJ [*personne, organisme*] weak; [*rendement, spectacle*] (pretty) poor.

faible /fɛbl/ **I** *adj* **1** (sans force) [*malade, structure, résistance, monnaie, marché*] weak; [*vue*] poor; **un enfant ~ de** or **de ~ constitution** a child with a frail constitution; **2** (sans fermeté) [*parents, gouvernement*] weak; **être ~ avec qn** to be soft with sb, to be too soft on sb; **3** (bas, léger, médiocre) [*proportion, progression*] small; [*coût, revenu*] low; [*moyens, portée*] limited; [*avantage*] slight; [*chance*] slim; [*bruit, lueur, vibrations*] faint; [*éclairage*] dim; [*vent, pluie*] light; [*résultat*] poor; [*score*] low; [*argument*] feeble; [*production*] weak; [*élève, classe*] slow; **à ~ vitesse** at a low speed; **à ~ profondeur** at a shallow depth; **de ~ profondeur** shallow; **il n'a qu'une ~ idée de** he has only a vague idea of; **de ~ importance** of little importance; **c'est une ~ consolation** it's small ou little consolation; **elle est ~ en anglais** she's weak in English; **~ d'esprit** feeble-minded; [*mot, expression*] inadequate; **c'est un imbécile et le mot est ~!** he's a fool and that's putting it mildly!.

II *nmf* weak-willed person.

III *nm* (penchant) weakness; **avoir un ~ pour** (pour un aliment, objet) to have a weakness for; (pour une personne) to have a soft spot for.

IV faibles *nmpl* **les ~s** the weak (+ *v pl*).

faiblement /fɛbləmɑ̃/ *adv* [*se défendre, sourire*] weakly; [*frapper*] gently; [*éclairer*] dimly; [*influencer, augmenter*] slightly; [*développé, qualifié*] poorly; [*fréquenté*] barely.

faiblesse /fɛblɛs/ *nf* **1** (manque de force) GÉN weakness; (d'infirme, de vieillard) frailty; **mes jambes tremblaient de ~** my legs were so weak they trembled; **2** (manque de fermeté) weakness (**envers** toward(s)); **sans ~** [*réprimer*] ruthlessly; [*répression*] ruthless; **avoir la ~ de faire** to be weak enough to do; **3** (insuffisance) inadequacy; **la ~ de nos revenus** our low level of income; **4** (de voix) faintness; (d'éclairage) dimness; (de précipitations) lightness; **5** (défaut, médiocrité) weakness; **6** (défaillance) **avoir une ~** or **des ~s** to feel faint; **être pris de ~(s)** to feel faint; **7** (acte réprouvé) moment of weakness.

faiblir /fɛbliʀ/ [3] *vi* **1** (perdre de sa force) to get weaker; **ma vue faiblit** my eyesight is failing; **2** (perdre de sa fermeté) to weaken; **3** (baisser de niveau) [*sportif*] to flag; [*roman, jeu*] to decline; [*mémoire*] to fail; [*attention, envie*] to wane; [*espoir*] to fade; [*rendement*] to dwindle; [*vitesse*] to slacken; **quel humour, ma parole, tu faiblis**○! that wasn't very funny, I think you're losing your touch!; **4** (diminuer d'intensité) [*pluie*] to abate; [*bruit*] to grow faint; [*éclairage*] to grow dim.

faïence /fajɑ̃s/ *nf* **1** (matière) earthenware; **de** or **en ~** earthenware (*épith*); **2** (objet) piece of earthenware.

IDIOMES **se regarder en chiens de ~** to look daggers at each other.

faïencerie /fajɑ̃sʀi/ ► 374 ◄ *nf* **1** (usine) pottery; **2** (objets) glazed earthenware ou pottery; **3** (magasin) china shop.

faille /faj/ *nf* **1** (cassure) fault; **2** (lacune) flaw; **sans ~** unfailing; **3** (rupture) rift.

faillir /fajiʀ/ [28] *vi* GÉN **elle a failli mourir** she almost ou (very) nearly died; **2** (manquer) LITER **sans ~**

faire

Un très grand nombre de tournures et locutions contenant ce verbe sont traitées ailleurs, généralement sous le terme qui suit *faire*, en particulier:

– les expressions décrivant les tâches domestiques, agricoles (*faire la cuisine/moisson*), les occupations manuelles (*faire du tricot/bricolage*), les activités professionnelles ou de loisir (*faire du théâtre, de la photo*), les types d'études (*faire médecine*). Pour ce qui est des jeux, sports et loisirs, voir également la note d'usage correspondante
– les locutions décrivant un mouvement, l'expression, un comportement (*faire un geste/une grimace/le pitre*)
– les expressions dans lesquelles *faire* signifie 'formuler' (*faire une promesse/offre* etc.)
– les expressions décrivant la qualité de la lumière (*il fait jour/sombre*) ou l'état du temps
– les expressions contenant une mesure (*faire 20 mètres de long/15 kilos/ 20°/15 kilomètres à l'heure* etc.) pour lesquelles on consultera les notes d'usage
– les expressions décrivant une démarche de l'esprit (*se faire une opinion/du souci* etc.)
– les expressions indiquant l'effet produit (*faire peur/mal/ plaisir/du tort* etc., *faire cuire/sécher/tomber* etc.)
– *faire + venir/entrer/sortir* etc.
– les locutions telles que *faire semblant/exprès, se faire avoir* etc.
– les expressions familières (*faire un enfant* etc.)

Par ailleurs pour les expressions décrivant:
– une activité sportive (*faire du tennis/de la marche/du parapente*)
– une durée (*ça fait 15 ans*)
la consultation des notes d'usage vous fournira des traductions utiles. Voir la liste ▶ **1420**. En outre, certaines entrées telles que **combien, ce, que, comment, laisser, rien, mieux, bien** etc. fourniront également des traductions utiles.

To make ou to do?

Les principales traductions de *faire* sont *to make* et *to do* mais elles ne sont pas interchangeables.

to make traduit *faire + objet* dénotant ce qui est créé, confectionné, composé, réalisé, obtenu; l'objet est le résultat de l'action:

faire son lit	= to make one's bed
faire des confitures	= to make jam
faire un discours	= to make a speech
faire une faute	= to make a mistake
faire un bénéfice	= to make a profit
je me suis fait un café	= I made myself a coffee

to do a le sens plus vague de se livrer à une activité, s'occuper à quelque chose; l'objet peut préciser la nature de l'activité:

faire de la recherche	= to do research
faire un exercice	= to do an exercise
faire son devoir	= to do one's duty

ou bien la nature de l'activité reste indéterminée:

que fait-il (dans la vie)?	= what does he do (for a living)?
qu'est-ce que tu fais ce soir?	= what are you doing tonight?
la science peut tout faire	= science can do anything
j'ai à faire	= I have things to do

ou encore le contexte suggère la nature de l'activité:

    faire une pièce   = to do a room

peut vouloir dire la nettoyer, la ranger, la peindre.

Si *faire* remplace un verbe plus précis, on traduira fréquemment par celui-ci:

faire une maison	= to build a house
faire un nid	= to build a nest
faire une lettre	= to write a letter
faire une visite	= to pay a visit
faire un numéro de téléphone	= to dial a number

Les périphrases verbales sont parfois rendues par un seul verbe:

faire voir (= *montrer*)	= to show
faire du tissage (= *tisser*)	= to weave

Mais:

faire un peu de tissage = to do a bit of weaving

Faire + infinitif + qn

faire + infinitive + qn, c'est-à-dire obtenir de quelqu'un qu'il agisse d'une certaine manière, se traduit selon le sens de *faire*, par:

to make sb do sth (forcer, être cause que):

fais-la lever	= make her get up
ça m'a fait rire	= it made me laugh
ça fait dormir	= it makes you sleep

to get sb to do sth (inciter):

fais-leur prendre un rendez-vous	= get them to make an appointment

to help sb to do sth (aider):

faire traverser la rue à un vieillard	= to help an old man across the street

Mais:

faire manger un bébé = to feed a child

Dans l'exemple *ça fait dormir* on notera qu'en anglais le sujet du verbe est toujours exprimé, ce qui n'est pas le cas en français.

(se) faire faire qch (par qn) se traduit par *to have sth done* ou *made (by sb)*, ou, dans une langue plus familière, *to get sth done* ou *made (by sb)*:

(se) faire construire une maison	= to have a house built
(se) faire réparer sa voiture	= to have ou get one's car repaired
c'est la table qu'il a fait faire	= it's the table he had made
elle fait exécuter les travaux par un ami	= she's having the work done by a friend

Ne faire que

exprime soit la continuité:

il ne fait que pleuvoir	= it never stops raining *ou* it rains all the time

soit la restriction:

je ne fais qu'obéir aux ordres	= I'm only obeying orders

Faire reprend un autre verbe

Dans ce cas il sera généralement traduit par *to do*:

'je peux regarder?' 'faites ou faites je vous en prie'	= 'may I look?' 'please do'
il souffla, comme il l'avait vu faire à son père	= he blew, as he had seen his father do
on veut que je parte, mais je n'en ferai rien	= they want me to leave, but I'll do nothing of the sort

Vous trouverez d'autres exemples dans l'entrée.

---

unfailingly; **~ à ses engagements** to fail in one's commitments; **~ à sa réputation** to fall short of one's reputation; **ne pas ~ à la tradition** to live up to the tradition.

faillite /fajit/ *nf* **1** COMM, JUR bankruptcy; **se mettre en ~** to file for bankruptcy; **être en ~** to be bankrupt; **faire ~** to go bankrupt; **2** (échec) failure.
■ **~ frauduleuse** fraudulent bankruptcy.

faim /fɛ̃/ *nf* hunger (**de** for); **avoir ~** to be hungry; **avoir ~ de** FIG to hunger for; **avoir une ~ de loup** to be ravenous; **donner ~ à qn** to give sb an appet-

ite; **manger à sa ~** to have enough to eat; **tromper sa ~** to stave off (one's) hunger; **mourir de ~** LIT to die of starvation; FIG to be starving; **je suis resté sur ma ~** FIG I was disappointed.

fainéant, ~e /feneɑ̃, ɑ̃t/ **I** *adj* lazy.
II *nm,f* layabout⁰ GB, lazybones (+ *v sg*).

fainéanter /feneɑ̃te/ [1] *vi* to laze about.

fainéantise /feneɑ̃tiz/ *nf* laziness.

faire /fɛʀ/ [10] **I** *vtr* **1** (produire) to make; **trois et deux font cinq** three and two make five; **combien font 13**

fois 13? what's 13 times 13?; **œil fait yeux au pluriel** œil is yeux in the plural; **2** (façonner) to shape [*histoire, période*]; **3** (étudier) to do [*licence, sujet*]; **~ du violon** to study ou play the violin; **tu as fait ton piano?** have you practised your piano?; **~ une école de commerce** to go to business school; **4** (préparer) to make [*soupe, thé*]; to prepare [*salade*]; **~ du poulet** to cook a chicken; **5** (nettoyer) to do, to clean [*vitres*]; to clean, to polish [*chaussures*]; **6** COMM (proposer) to do [*service, marque*]; (vendre) to do, to sell [*article*]; **ils ne font pas le petit déjeuner** they don't do breakfast; **l'hôtel fait-il restaurant?** does the hotel have a restaurant?; **7** (cultiver) **~ des céréales** [*personne*] to grow ou do cereals; [*région*] to produce cereals; **8** (se fournir en) **~ de l'eau** NAUT, RAIL to take on water; **~ (de) l'essence**○ AUT to get petrol GB ou gas US; **9** (parcourir) to do [*distance, trajet*]; to go round [*magasins, agences*]; (visiter) to do○ [*région, musées*]; **~ toute la ville** to go all over town; **~ l'Écosse** to visit Scotland; **j'ai fait tous les tiroirs** I went through all the drawers; **10** (souffrir de) to have [*diabète, tension, complexe*]; **~ une crise cardiaque** to have a heart attack; **11** (demander un prix) **~ qch à 30 francs** to sell sth for 30 francs, to charge 30 francs for sth; **12** (servir de) to serve as; **13** (user, disposer de) to do; **qu'as-tu fait du billet?** what have you done with the ticket?; **pour quoi ~?** what for?; **je n'ai que ~ de** I have no need for; **je n'en ai rien à ~**○ I couldn't care less; **14** (avoir un effet) **que veux-tu que j'y fasse?** what do you want me to do about it?, what am I supposed to do about it?; **ça y fait**○ it has an effect; **leur départ ne m'a rien fait** their departure didn't affect me at all; **ça me fait quelque chose de la voir dans cet état** it upsets me to see her in that state; **pour ce que ça fait**○! for all the good it does!; **ça ne fait rien à la chose** it makes no difference; **qu'est-ce que ça peut bien te ~**○? what is it to you?; **15** (entraîner, causer) **~ des jaloux** to make some people jealous; **l'explosion a fait 12 morts** the explosion killed 12 people, the explosion left 12 people dead; **ça ne fait rien!** (pas grave) it doesn't matter!; **ça fait ou ce qui fait que j'ai oublié**○ as a result I forgot; **16** (transformer) to make; **elle en a fait sa confidente** she's made her her confidante; **~ d'un garage un atelier** to make ou turn a garage into a workshop; **17** (proclamer) **~ qn général** to make sb a general; **18** (imiter) **~ le courageux** to pretend to be brave; **~ le dictateur** to act the dictator; **19** (tenir le rôle de) to be; **quel plaisantin vous faites!** what a joker you are!; **20** (dans un souhait) **mon Dieu, faites qu'il réussisse!** God, please let him succeed!; **21**○ (tromper) **il me l'a fait au baratin** he talked me into it; **on ne me la fait pas!** I'm not a fool!; **22** (dire) to say; **'bien sûr', fit-elle** 'of course,' she said; **le canard fait 'coin-coin'** the duck says ou goes 'quack'.

II *vi* **1** (agir) to do, to act; **fais comme tu veux** do as you like; **~ vite** to act quickly; **vas-y, mais fais vite!** go, but be quick about it!; **fais comme chez toi** LIT, IRON make yourself at home; **2** (paraître) to look; **~ jeune** to look young; **3**○ (être) to be; **il veut ~ pompier** he wants to be a fireman; **4** (durer) to last; **sa robe lui a fait deux ans** her dress lasted her two years; **5** (valoir) **ça fait cher** it's expensive; **6** (pour ses besoins naturels) to go; **tu as fait?** have you been?; **7**○ **~ avec** (se contenter de) to make do with; (supporter) to put up with.

III se faire *upr* **1** **se ~ un café** to make oneself a coffee; **se ~ des amis** to make friends; **se ~ la cuisine soi-même** to do one's own cooking; **combien se fait-il**○ **par mois?** how much does he make a month?; **2** (devenir) to get, to become; **il se fait tard** it's getting late; **3** (se rendre) **se ~ tout petit** to make oneself very small; **4** (s'inquiéter) **s'en ~** to worry; **il ne s'en fait pas!** (sans inquiétude) he's not the sort of person to worry about things!; (pas gêné) he's got a nerve!; **5** (s'habituer) **se ~ à** to get used to [*lieu, situation, idée*]; **6** (être d'usage) **ça se fait encore ici** it's still done here; **ça ne se fait pas** it's not the done thing (**de faire** to do); **7** (être à la mode) to be in (fashion); **ça ne se fait plus** it's no longer fashionable, it's out of fashion; **8** (être produit) **c'est ce qui se fait de**

mieux it's the best there is; **le pont se fera bien un jour** the bridge will be built one day; **9** (emploi impersonnel) **il se fit que** it (so) happened that; **il se fit un grand silence** there was complete silence; **comment se fait-il que...?** how is it that...?; **10** [*fromage*] to ripen; [*vin*] to mature; **11**○ **il faut se le ~, son copain!** his/her mate is a real pain○!; **12** (avec infinitif) **se ~ couler un bain** to run oneself a bath; **se ~ comprendre** to make oneself understood.

faire-part /fɛʀpaʀ/ *nm inv* announcement.

faire-valoir /fɛʀvalwaʀ/ *nm inv* **1** CIN, THÉÂT foil; **être le ~ de** to be a foil for; **2** AGRIC farming.

fair-play /fɛʀplɛ/ CONTROV **I** *adj inv* sporting.
II *nm* **le ~** sportsmanship, (sense of) fair play.

faisabilité /fəzabilite/ *nf* feasability; **étude de ~** feasability study.

faisable /fəzabl/ *adj* **c'est/ce n'est pas ~** it can/can't be done.

faisan /fəzã/ *nm* ZOOL (cock) pheasant.

faisandé, -e /fəzɑ̃de/ *adj* CULIN gamey, high.

faisane /fəzan/ *nf* (**poule**) **~** hen pheasant.

faisceau, *pl* **~x** /fɛso/ *nm* **1** (de rayon) beam; **~ lumineux** beam of light; **2** (gerbe) bundle; **3** (de preuves) body; (d'indices) array; **4** ANAT fasciculus; **5** MIL stack; **6** HIST fasces.
■ **~ hertzien** radio link.

faiseur, -euse /fəzœʀ, øz/ *nm,f* **~ de miracles** miracle-worker; **~ de rimes** rhymester PÉJ; **c'est un ~ d'histoires** he's a fusspot; **~ de bons mots** PEJ punster, wag; **~ d'intrigues** PEJ schemer; **~ de tours** conjuror.

fait, -e /fɛ, fɛt/ **I** *pp* ▶ **faire**.
II *pp adj* **1** (réalisé, accompli) [*tâche*] done; **bien/mal ~** well/badly done; **c'en est ~ de** that's the end of; **c'est bien ~**○ (**pour toi**)! it serves you right!; **2** (constitué) **~ de** or **en** (d'un élément) made of; (composite) made up of; **idée toute ~e** ready-made idea; **formules toutes ~es** clichés; **elle est bien ~e** she's got a great figure; **elle a la taille bien ~e** she has a shapely waist; **je suis ainsi ~** that's how I am; **la vie est ainsi ~e** life's like that!; **la vie est mal ~e** life is unfair!; **3** (adapté) **~ pour qch/pour faire** meant for sth/to do; **ta remarque n'était pas ~e pour arranger les choses** your comment certainly didn't help matters; **4** (conçu) [*programme, dispositif*] designed; **bien/mal ~** well/badly-designed; **5**○ (pris) done for; **6** (mûr) **un fromage bien ~** a ripe cheese.
III *nm* **1** (élément de réalité, acte) fact; **le ~ d'avoir** the fact of having; **le ~ d'être heureux** being happy; **le ~ est là** that's the fact of the matter; **il a réussi, c'est un ~, mais...** he has succeeded, certainly, but...; **les ~s et gestes de qn** sb's movements; **les menus ~s de la vie quotidienne** the tiny details of everyday life; **2** (cause) **de ce ~** because of this ou that; **du ~ de qch** due to sth; **du ~ même que** due to the very fact that; **être le ~ de** to be due to; **3** (événement) event; **au moment des ~s** at the time of (the) events; **4** (sujet) point; **au ~, je te prie!** get to the point, please!; **aller droit au ~** to go straight to the point; **elle lui a dit son ~** she told him/her straight; **5** (trait) **mentir n'est pas son ~** it isn't like him/her to lie; **6** (exploit) feat, exploit; **les hauts ~s** heroic deeds.
IV au fait /ofɛt/ *loc adv* by the way.
V de fait *loc* [*situation, pouvoir*] de facto (*épith*); [*exister, entraîner*] effectively; (en effet) indeed.
VI en fait *loc adv* in fact, actually.
VII en fait de *loc prép* as regards; **en ~ de réforme, il s'agit plutôt d'une...** it isn't so much a reform as a...; **en ~ de rénovation du système, ils (en) ont seulement changé quelques éléments** they haven't so much renovated the system as tinkered about at the edges.
■ **~ accompli** fait accompli; **~ d'actualité** news item; **~ d'armes** feat of arms; **~ divers** (short) news item; **la rubrique (des) '~s divers'** the 'news in brief' column; **~ de guerre** exploit of war; **~ du prince** fiat; **~ de société** fact of life.

IDIOMES **être au** ~ to be informed; **mettre qn au** ~ to inform sb; **être sûr de son** ~ to be sure of one's facts; **prendre qn sur le** ~ to catch sb in the act.

faîte /fɛt/ *nm* **1** (sommet) (de montagne) summit; (de maison) rooftop; (d'arbre) top; **2** CONSTR (faîtage) ridgepole; **3** FIG (apogée) pinnacle.

faitout /fɛtu/ *nm* stockpot.

falaise /falɛz/ *nf* cliff.

fallacieux, -ieuse /falasjø, øz/ *adj* [*argument*] fallacious; [*promesse, prétexte*] false; [*ressemblance*] deceptive; [*espoir*] illusory; **il est** ~ **de penser que**... it's a fallacy to think that...

falloir /falwaʀ/ [50] **I** *v impers* **1** il faut qch/qn GÉN we need sth/sb (**pour faire** to do); (sans bénéficiaire) sth/sb is needed (**pour faire** to do); **ce qu'il faut** what is needed; **il va** ~ **plusieurs personnes** it will take several people (**pour faire** to do); **il en faut pour qu'il se fâche** it takes a lot to make him angry; **c'est plus qu'il n'en faut** it's more than enough; **2** il leur faut qch they need sth; **il leur faut faire** they have to do, they must do; **il m'a fallu trois heures pour finir** it took me three hours to finish; **il me faut (absolument) ce livre!** I've got to have that book!; **pas assez grand! qu'est-ce qu'il te faut?** not big enough? what more do you want?; **3** il faut faire (nécessité) we've/you've etc got to do, we/you etc have to do; (autorité) we/you etc must do; (conseil, suggestion) we/you etc should do; (convenance, reproche) we/you etc ought to do; **il ne faut pas faire** (autorité) we/you etc mustn't do; (conseil) we/you etc shouldn't do; **'tu vas payer?'—'il faut bien!'** 'are you going to pay?'—'I have to!'; **il ne faut pas la déranger** she mustn't be disturbed; **faudrait pas me prendre pour un imbécile**○! do you think I'm a fool?; **qu'est-ce qu'il ne faut pas entendre!** what a lot of nonsense!; **s'il fallait croire tout ce qu'on raconte!** you can't believe everything people say!; **il faut dire que** I/you/we etc have to ou must say that; **il faut vous dire que** you should know that; **fallait le dire plus tôt**○! why didn't you say so before?; **nous ne savions pas encore, faut-il le rappeler, qu'il serait élu** it must be remembered that we didn't know then that he would be elected; **il fallait le faire** it had to be done; **(il) faut/fallait le faire**○! (c'est remarquable) it takes/took a bit of doing!; (c'est stupide) would you believe it?; **puisqu'il le faut** since it has to be done; **s'il le faut** (nécessité) if necessary; (obligation) if I/we/they etc have to; **il ne fallait pas!** (politesse) you shouldn't have!; **comme il faut** [*se tenir*] properly; **elle est très comme il faut** she's very proper; **encore faudra-t-il trouver de l'argent** we/you/they etc will still have to find the money; **encore faut-il préciser que** it should be added that; **4 il faut que tu fasses** (obligation) you must do, you've got to do, you have to do; (conseil) you should do; (convenance, reproche) you ought to do; **il fallait que ce soit fait** it had to be done; **faut-il qu'elle l'aime pour le croire!** she must love him to believe him!; **encore faut-il qu'elle accepte** she's still got to agree.

II *se falloir vpr* **loin** *ou* **tant s'en faut** far from it; **peu s'en faut** very nearly; **il s'en faut de beaucoup** very far from it; **elle a perdu, mais il s'en est fallu de peu** she lost, but only just; **il s'en est fallu d'un rien** *ou* **de presque rien** there was almost nothing in it.

IDIOMES **il faut ce qu'il faut!** there's no point in skimping!; **en moins de temps qu'il ne faut pour le dire** before you could say Jack Robinson.

falot, -e /falo, ɔt/ **I** *adj* [*personne*] insignificant. **II** *nm* lantern.

falsification /falsifikasjɔ̃/ *nf* **1** (altération) falsification; **2** (imitation) forging.

falsifier /falsifje/ [2] *vtr* **1** (altérer) to falsify, to tamper with [*document, chèque*]; to distort, to falsify [*faits*]; **2** (contrefaire) to forge [*signature, monnaie*].

famé, ~e /fame/ *adj* **un quartier mal** ~ a disreputable ou seedy area.

famélique /famelik/ *adj* [*personne*] emaciated; [*animal*] scrawny.

fameusement /famøzmɑ̃/ *adv* remarkably.

fameux, -euse /famø, øz/ *adj* **1** (dont on a parlé) much talked-about; **2** (connu de tous) famous; **3** (véritable) real, right; **4** (excellent) excellent; **pas** ~ not great.

familial, ~e[1], *mpl* **-iaux** /familjal, o/ *adj* **1** (de famille) family (*épith*); **la cellule** ~**e** the family unit; **2** AUT **berline** ~**e** estate car GB, station wagon US.

familiale[2] /familjal/ *nf* AUT estate car GB, station wagon US.

familiariser /familjaʀize/ [1] **I** *vtr* to familiarize. **II** *se familiariser vpr* to familiarize oneself.

familiarité /familjaʀite/ *nf* familiarity ¢; **il s'est permis des** ~**s** he was too familiar.

familier, -ière /familje, ɛʀ/ **I** *adj* **1** (connu) [*visage, paysage, nom*] familiar (**à** to); **2** LING [*mot, style*] informal, colloquial; **3** (sans façon) [*entretien, attitude*] informal; [*personne, geste*] familiar; **4** (domestique) **animal** ~ pet; **5** (informé) familiar (**de** with). **II** *nm* **1** (ami) close friend (**de** of); **2** (habitué) regular.

familièrement /familjɛʀmɑ̃/ *adv* (communément) commonly; (sans façon) informally; (de manière inconvenante) with undue familiarity.

famille /famij/ *nf* **1** SOCIOL family; **une** ~ **de musiciens** a musical family; **air de** ~ family resemblance; **c'est de** ~ it runs in the family; **faire partie de la** ~ to be one of the family; **nous partons en** ~ we're going as a family; **de** ~ [*photo, histoire*] family (*épith*); **ne pas avoir de** ~ to have no relatives; **ma seule** ~ **est un vieil oncle** my only relative is an old uncle; **rentrer dans sa** ~ **tous les samedis** to go back home every Saturday; **un petit vin des** ~**s**○ a nice little wine; **2** ART, POL, RELIG (communauté) body; **une** ~ **politique** a political persuasion; **3** BIOL, BOT, LING, ZOOL family.

■ ~ **d'accueil** host family; ~ **nombreuse** family with more than two children; ~ **de placement** foster family.

famine /famin/ *nf* famine; **salaire de** ~ starvation wages (*pl*); **crier** ~ to be starving.

fana /fana/ **I** *adj* mad keen○ GB (**de** about), crazy○ (**de** about). **II** *nmf* fanatic; **un** ~ **de cinéma** a film buff.

fanal, pl -aux /fanal, o/ *nm* GÉN lamp; NAUT lantern; RAIL headlamp.

fanatique /fanatik/ **I** *adj* [*militant, mouvement*] fanatical; [*admiration, amour*] ardent, unbridled. **II** *nmf* **1** (extrémiste) fanatic; **2** (enthousiaste)○ enthusiast, freak○.

fanatiser /fanatize/ [1] *vtr* to fanaticize, to inflame.

fanatisme /fanatism/ *nm* fanaticism.

faner /fane/ [1] **I** *vtr* **1** to wither [*plante*]; **2** to fade [*couleur*]; **3** to toss [*herbe*]. **II** *vi* **1** [*plantes*] to wither; **2** AGRIC to make hay. **III** *se faner vpr* **1** [*fleurs, plantes*] to wither, to wilt; **2** [*beauté, couleur*] to fade.

faneur, -euse[1] /fanœʀ, øz/ ▶ 374 *nm,f* haymaker.

faneuse[2] /fanøz/ *nf* (machine) tedder.

fanfare /fɑ̃faʀ/ *nf* **1** (orchestre) brass band; **annoncer qch en** ~ to trumpet sth, to give sth great publicity; **faire une entrée en** ~ to make a spectacular entry; **réveiller qn en** ~ to wake sb up with a great commotion; **2** (air) fanfare.

fanfaron, -onne /fɑ̃faʀɔ̃, ɔn/ **I** *adj* boastful. **II** *nm,f* boaster, swaggerer; **faire le** ~ to boast, to talk big○.

fanfaronnade /fɑ̃faʀɔnad/ *nf* boasting ¢.

fanfaronner /fɑ̃faʀɔne/ [1] *vi* to boast.

fanfreluches /fɑ̃fʀəlyʃ/ *nfpl* frills and flounces.

fange /fɑ̃ʒ/ *nf* mud, mire.

fanion /fanjɔ̃/ *nm* pennant.

fanon /fanɔ̃/ *nm* (de baleine) baleen plate; **les** ~**s** whalebone ¢; (de reptile, dindon) wattle; (de bovin, chien) dewlap; (de cheval) fetlock.

fantaisie /fɑ̃tezi/ *nf* **1** (qualité) imaginativeness; **être plein de** ~ [*personne*] to be full of marvellous[GB] ideas; [*roman*] to be highly imaginative; [*logement*] to be unconventional; **manquer de ~** [*personne*] to be staid; [*logement*] to be conventional; [*vie*] to be dull; **2** (caprice) whim, fancy; **vivre selon sa ~** to do as one pleases; **ne pouvoir se permettre aucune ~** (dans son habillement) to have to dress in a very conventional way; (dans ses dépenses) to be unable to afford any extra expenses; **3** (de peu de valeur) **s'offrir une petite ~** (objet) to buy oneself a little something; (sortie) to spoil oneself; **un bijou ~** a piece of costume jewellery GB ou jewelry US; **accessoires ~** fun accessories; **verres ~** novelty glasses; **4** MUS fantasia, fantasy; **5** LITTÉRAT fantasy.

fantaisiste /fɑ̃tezist/ **I** *adj* **1** (peu fiable) [*personne, renseignement, horaires*] unreliable; [*chiffres, analyse*] doubtful; **2** (excentrique) [*idée*] far-fetched; [*procédé*] odd; [*personne*] eccentric.
II *nmf* mildly eccentric person.

fantasmagorie /fɑ̃tasmagɔʀi/ *nf* phantasmagoria.

fantasme /fɑ̃tasm/ *nm* fantasy.

fantasmer /fɑ̃tasme/ [1] *vi* to fantasize (**sur** about).

fantasque /fɑ̃task/ *adj* [*personnage, comportement*] unpredictable; [*image, récit*] fanciful.

fantassin /fɑ̃tasɛ̃/ *nm* infantryman, footsoldier; **les ~s** the infantry (+ *v pl*).

fantastique /fɑ̃tastik/ **I** *adj* fantastic; **le cinéma ~** fantasy films (*pl*).
II *nm* ART, CIN, LITTÉRAT (genre) **le ~** fantasy.

fantoche /fɑ̃tɔʃ/ **I** *adj* puppet (*épith*).
II *nm* puppet.

fantomatique /fɑ̃tɔmatik/ *adj* ghostly.

fantôme /fɑ̃tom/ **I** *nm* ghost.
II (-)**fantôme** (*in compounds*) **cabinet-~** shadow cabinet GB, ~ minority leadership US; **image(-)~** TV ghost; **membre(-)~** MÉD phantom limb; **société(-)~** JUR dummy company; **train(-)~** ghost train; **ville(-)~** ghost town.

FAO /ɛfao/ *nf* **1** ÉCON, POL (*abbr* = Food and Agriculture Organization) FAO; **2** ORDINAT *abbr* ▶ **fabrication**.

faon /fɑ̃/ *nm* fawn.

faramineux°, -euse /faʀaminø, øz/ *adj* [*prix, somme*] colossal, staggering; [*bêtise*] incredible.

farandole /faʀɑ̃dɔl/ *nf* (folklorique) farandole; (de soirée) ~ conga.

farce /faʀs/ *nf* **1** (tour) practical joke; **faire une ~ à qn** to play a practical joke on sb; **magasin de ~s et attrapes** joke shop GB, novelty store US; **2** (plaisanterie) joke; **3** (bouffonnerie) farce; **4** THÉÂT farce; **5** CULIN stuffing, forcemeat.

farceur, -euse /faʀsœʀ, øz/ *nm,f* **1** (plaisantin) practical joker; **2** (personne peu sérieuse) joker°.

farcir /faʀsiʀ/ [3] **I** *vtr* **1** CULIN to stuff (**de** with); **2°** (surcharger) to cram (**de** with).
II se farcir *vpr* **1°** (accomplir) to get stuck with°; **2°** (supporter) to put up with; **il faut se le ~!** he's a real pain in the neck°!; **3°** (surcharger) to cram (**de** with); **elle se farcit la tête de détails inutiles** she crams her head with useless facts; **4°** (ingurgiter) to polish off°.

fard /faʀ/ *nm* make-up; **sans ~** [*beauté*] natural; [*vérité*] simple; [*avouer*] openly.
■ **~ à joues** blusher; **~ à paupières** eye-shadow.
IDIOMES **piquer un ~°** to go as red as a beetroot GB, to turn as red as a beet US.

farde /faʀd/ *nf* B (dossier) folder.

fardeau, *pl* **~x** /faʀdo/ *nm* LIT, FIG burden.

farder /faʀde/ [1] **I** *vtr* **1** FIG to disguise [*vérité*]; **2** LIT to put make-up on [*visage*]; **visage outrageusement fardé** face caked in make-up.
II se farder *vpr* [*acteur*] to make up; [*femme*] (tous les jours) to use make-up; (un jour) to put on make-up; **elle s'est fardé les joues** she's put blusher on her cheeks.

farfadet /faʀfadɛ/ *nm* elf; **des ~s** elves.

farfelu°, -e /faʀfəly/ **I** *adj* [*projet, idée*] harebrained°; [*histoire*] far-fetched; [*personne*] scatterbrained°; [*spectacle*] bizarre.
II *nm,f* scatterbrain°.

farfouiller° /faʀfuje/ [1] *vi* to rummage around ou about (**dans** in).

faribole† /faʀibɔl/ *nf* piece of nonsense; **des ~s** nonsense ¢.

farine /faʀin/ *nf* flour; (pour nourrisson) baby cereal.
■ **~ d'avoine** oatmeal; **~ de blé dur** durum wheat flour; **~ complète** wholemeal flour GB, wholewheat flour; **~ de froment** wheat flour; **~ lactée** ~ baby cereal; **~ de maïs** cornflour GB, cornstarch US; **~ d'orge** barley meal; **~ d'os** bone meal; **~ de poisson** fish meal; **~ de seigle** rye flour.
IDIOMES **de la même ~** as bad as each other; **rouler qn dans la ~°** to pull a fast one on sb°; **se faire rouler dans la ~°** to be had°.

farineux, -euse /faʀinø, øz/ *adj* [*aliment*] starchy; [*aspect, goût, pommes de terre, pain*] floury; [*fruit*] mealy.

farniente /faʀnjɛnte/ *nm* **le ~** lazing about, lazing around.

farouche /faʀuʃ/ *adj* **1** [*enfant, animal*] timid, shy; [*adulte*] unsociable; **2** [*regard*] fierce; [*guerrier*] savage; **3** [*ennemi, haine*] bitter; [*adversaire, résolution*] fierce; [*partisan*] staunch; [*ambition*] driving; [*volonté*] iron; **4** LITER [*paysage, côte*] wild.

farouchement /faʀuʃmɑ̃/ *adv* GÉN fiercely; [*refuser*] doggedly.

fart /faʀt/ *nm* (ski-)wax.

farter /faʀte/ [1] *vtr* to wax [*skis*].

fascicule /fasikyl/ *nm* (brochure) booklet; **paraître en ~s** to come out in parts.

fascinant, -e /fasinɑ̃, ɑ̃t/ *adj* [*personne, film*] fascinating; [*charme*] spellbinding; [*beauté*] bewitching.

fascination /fasinasjɔ̃/ *nf* fascination (**pour qch** with sth); **exercer une ~ sur qn** [*personne, musique*] to hold sb in one's ou its spell; [*télévision, mer*] to hold a fascination for sb.

fasciner /fasine/ [1] *vtr* **1** (captiver) to fascinate; **il regardait, fasciné** he watched in fascination; **2** (envoûter) [*orateur, musique*] to hold [sb] spellbound; [*mer, personne*] to fascinate; **3** (hypnotiser) [*regard, spectacle*] to mesmerize; [*serpent*] to hypnotize.

fascisant, ~e /faʃizɑ̃, ɑ̃t/ *adj* fascistic.

fascisme /faʃism/ *nm* fascism.

faste /fast/ **I** *adj* auspicious.
II *nm* splendour GB, pomp; **avec ~** with pomp.

fastidieux, -ieuse /fastidjø, øz/ *adj* tedious, tiresome.

fastueux, -euse /fastɥø, øz/ *adj* sumptuous.

fat, ~e /fa, at/ **I** *adj* [*homme, air, manières*] conceited.
II *nm* conceited man.

fatal, ~e /fatal/ *adj* **1** (inévitable) inevitable; **il était ~ que cela se produise** it was bound to happen; **2** (désastreux) fatal (**à qn/qch** to sb/sth), disastrous (**à qn/qch** for sb/sth); **3** (mortel) fatal; **4** (fatidique) [*moment, jour*] fateful.

fatalement /fatalmɑ̃/ *adv* inevitably.

fatalisme /fatalism/ *nm* fatalism.

fataliste /fatalist/ **I** *adj* fatalistic.
II *nmf* fatalist.

fatalité /fatalite/ *nf* **1** (sort) **la ~** fate; **2** (caractère inévitable) inevitability.

fatidique /fatidik/ *adj* fateful.

fatigant, ~e /fatigɑ̃, ɑ̃t/ *adj* **1** [*sport, voyage*] tiring; [*climat*] wearing; [*travail*] arduous; **mon travail est ~ pour les yeux** my job is a strain on the eyes; **2** [*personne*] tiresome; [*film, conversation*] tedious.

fatigue /fatig/ *nf* **1** GÉN tiredness; **excès de ~** overtiredness; **être mort de ~, tomber de ~** to be dead tired; **2** MÉD fatigue ¢; **~ visuelle** eyestrain; **3** TECH (de matériau) fatigue; (mécanique) wear and tear.

fatigué, ~e /fatige/ **I** *pp* ▶ **fatiguer**.
II *pp adj* **1** GÉN tired (**de faire** of doing); **2** MÉD [*personne*] suffering from fatigue (*après n*); [*cœur*] weak.
III *adj* **1** [*voix*] strained; [*visage, yeux, sourire*] weary; **2** [*vêtement, chaussure*] worn; [*moteur, voiture*] suffering from wear and tear (*après n*); [*couleur*] faded.

fatiguer /fatige/ [1] **I** *vtr* **1** (physiquement) to make [sb] tired [*personne*]; to strain [*yeux*]; to weaken [*cœur*]; to tire [*cheval*]; **2** (intellectuellement) to tire [sb] out; **3** (ennuyer) to wear [sb] out; **4** (mécaniquement) to wear out [*moteur*]; to put a strain on [*matériau, structure*]; **5** CULIN to toss [*salade*]; **6** AGRIC to exhaust [*terre*].

II *vi* **1**° (physiquement, intellectuellement) to get tired; **2** [*moteur, voiture*] to be labouring^GB; [*matériau, structure*] to show signs of strain.

III se fatiguer *vpr* **1** (devenir fatigué) to get tired (**de** of); **2** (se rendre fatigué) to tire oneself out; **se ~ en recherches/en démarches** to wear oneself out doing research/dealing with red tape; **3** (rendre fatigué) **se ~ les yeux** to strain one's eyes; **se ~ les jambes** to tire one's legs; **4** (s'évertuer) **se ~ à faire** to bother doing.

fatras /fatʀa/ *nm inv* jumble.

fatuité /fatɥite/ *nf* self-conceit; **avec ~** conceitedly.

faubourg /fobuʀ/ *nm* **1** (banlieue ouvrière) working class area (*on the outskirts*); **2** HIST *part of a town outside its walls or former walls*; **3** (artère) faubourg.

fauche /foʃ/ *nf* **1**° (vol) petty thieving; **2** = **fauchage**.

fauché°, **~e** /foʃe/ **I** *adj* (sans argent) broke° (*jamais épith*), penniless.

II *nm,f* **c'est un ~** he's always broke°.

IDIOMES **être ~ comme les blés** to be flat broke°.

faucher /foʃe/ [1] *vtr* **1** (couper) (avec une faucheuse) to mow, to cut; (à la faux) to scythe; **2** (abattre) [*cyclone, explosion*] to flatten [*arbres, bâtiment*]; [*véhicule, tir*] to mow down [*personne*]; **3**° (voler) to pinch° GB, to steal [*argent, place*].

faucheur, -euse¹ /foʃœʀ, øz/ **I** *nm,f* **1** (moissonneur) reaper; **2**° (voleur) petty thief.

II *nm* (araignée) harvestman.

faucheuse² /foʃøz/ *nf* (machine) mowing machine.

faucheux /foʃø/ *nm inv* (araignée) harvestman.

faucille /fosij/ *nf* sickle.

faucon /fokɔ̃/ *nm* **1** ZOOL falcon, hawk US; **2** POL hawk.

faudra /fodʀa/ ▶ **falloir**.

faufil /fofil/ *nm* basting thread.

faufiler /fofile/ [1] **I** *vtr* (en couture) to baste.

II se faufiler *vpr* **1** (se frayer un chemin) **se ~ à l'intérieur** to squeeze in; **se ~ à l'extérieur** to slip out; **se ~ à travers** to thread one's way through; **se ~ par une ouverture** to squeeze through an opening; **2** (s'insinuer) **se ~ dans** [*élément*] to creep into [*discours*]; **3** (serpenter) [*route*] to snake in and out (**entre** between).

faune¹ /fon/ *nm* faun.

faune² /fon/ *nf* **1** ZOOL wildlife, fauna; **la ~ du désert** desert wildlife ou fauna; **la ~ marine** marine life; **2** (personnes) PEJ set, crowd.

faussaire /fosɛʀ/ *nmf* forger.

fausse ▶ **faux¹** I.

faussement /fosmɑ̃/ *adv* **1** (à tort) falsely, wrongfully; **2** (hypocritement) deceptively; **attitude ~ soumise** attitude of feigned submission.

fausser /fose/ [1] *vtr* to distort [*résultat*]; to damage [*serrure*]; to bend [*clé, axe*]; to buckle [*lame*].

IDIOMES **~ compagnie à qn** to give sb the slip.

fausset /fosɛ/ *nm* MUS falsetto; **d'une voix de ~** in a falsetto.

fausseté /foste/ *nf* (d'argument, de nouvelle) falseness; (de personne) duplicity; (de sentiment) insincerity.

faut /fo/ ▶ **falloir**.

faute /fot/ *nf* **1** (erreur) mistake, error; **~ d'orthographe** spelling mistake; **~ d'étourderie** or **d'inattention** careless mistake; **~ de français** mistake in French; **~ de frappe** keying error; **~ d'impression** misprint; **~ de calcul** miscalculation; **~ de jugement** error of judgment; **il a fait un (parcours) sans ~** (en équitation) he had a clear round; FIG he's never put a foot wrong; **2** (action coupable) GÉN misdemeanour^GB, JUR civil wrong; RELIG sin; **être en ~** to be at fault; **prendre qn en ~** to catch sb out; **3** (responsabilité) fault; **c'est (de) ma ~**

it's my fault, I'm to blame; **par la ~ de qn** because of sb; **rejeter la ~ sur qn** to lay the blame on sb; **4** (manque) **~ de temps** through lack of time; **~ de preuves** for lack of evidence; **~ de garanties** in the absence of any guarantees; **~ de mieux** for want of anything better; **ce n'est pourtant pas ~ d'essayer** it's not for want of trying; **~ de quoi** otherwise, failing which; **sans ~** without fail; **5** SPORT GÉN foul; (au tennis) fault.

■ **~ contractuelle** breach of contract; **~ délictuelle** tort; **~ grave** gross misconduct; **~ professionnelle** professional misconduct ¢.

fauteuil /fotœj/ *nm* **1** (siège) chair; (bas, rembourré) armchair; **2** CIN, THÉÂT (place) seat; **3** FIG (siège) seat; (présidence d'une assemblée) **le ~** the chair; **~ de député** seat in parliament.

■ **~ à bascule** rocking chair; **~ crapaud** chunky armchair; **~ dentaire** dentist's chair; **~ relax** recliner; **~ roulant** wheelchair; **~ tournant** swivel chair.

fauteur, /fotœʀ/ *nm* **~ de troubles** troublemaker; **~ de guerre** warmonger.

fautif, -ive /fotif, iv/ **I** *adj* **1** (coupable) [*personne*] guilty, at fault [*véhicule*] at fault (*après n*), in the wrong (*après n*); **2** (erroné) [*mémoire, édition*] faulty; [*référence*] inaccurate; [*tournure*] incorrect.

II *nm,f* culprit.

fauve /fov/ **I** *adj* **1** ▶ **141** [*couleur*] tawny; **2** [*odeur*] musky; **3** ART [*période*] Fauve.

II *nm* **1** (animal féroce) wild animal; (félin) big cat; **les ~s** big cats; **sentir le ~**° to stink°; **2** (couleur) fawn; **3** ART Fauvist, Fauve.

fauvette /fovɛt/ *nf* warbler.

faux¹, fausse /fo, fos/ **I** *adj* **1** (résultat, numéro, idée) wrong; [*impression*] false; [*balance*] inaccurate; **il est ~ de dire** it's not true to say; **2** [*nez, barbe, dent, cils*] false; **3** [*bois, marbre, diamant*] imitation (*épith*); (pour tromper) fake (*épith*); [*porte, tiroir, cloison*] false; **c'est du ~ Louis XV** it's reproduction Louis Quinze; **4** (contrefait) [*billet, document*] forged; **5** [*science, savoir*] pseudo (*épith*); [*liberté, besoin*] false; [*policier, évêque*] bogus (*épith*); [*candeur, humilité*] feigned; **c'est un ~ problème** it's not really a problem at all; **6** [*espoir*] false; [*certitude*] mistaken; [*crainte*] groundless; [*réputation*] quite unfounded; **7** [*prétexte, promesse, accusation*] false; **8** [*personne, regard*] deceitful.

II *adv* [*jouer, chanter*] out of tune; **sonner ~** [*rire, parole*] to have a hollow ring; [*discours*] to sound false.

III à faux *loc adv* **porter à ~** to be off balance.

IV *nm inv* **1 le vrai et le ~** truth and falsehood; **2** (objet, tableau) fake; (document) forgery; **~ et usage de ~** JUR forgery and use of false documents.

■ **fausse alerte** false alarm; **fausse blonde** dyed blonde; **fausse couche** MÉD miscarriage; **fausse dent** false tooth; **fausse facture** bogus invoice; **fausse fenêtre** blind window; **fausse joie** ill-founded joy; **faire une fausse joie à qn** to raise sb's hopes in vain; **fausse manœuvre** false move; **fausse monnaie** forged ou counterfeit currency; **fausse note** MUS wrong note; FIG jarring note; **fausse nouvelle** false report; **fausse piste** wrong track; **~ ami** LING faux ami (*foreign word which looks deceptively like a word in one's own language*); **~ bruit** false rumour^GB; **~ col** (de chemise) detachable collar; (de bière) head; **~ contact** ÉLECTROTECH faulty connection; **~ débutant** false beginner; **~ départ** false start; **~ en écriture(s)** falsification ¢ of accounts; **~ frais** extras; **~ frère** HUM false friend; **~ jeton**° two-faced person; **~ jour** LIT deceptive light; FIG **sous un ~ jour** in a false light; **~ mouvement** false move; **~ nom** assumed name; **~ pas** LIT slip; FIG (erreur) mistake; (gaffe) faux pas; **~ plafond** false ceiling; **~ pli** crease; **~ seins** falsies°; **~ témoignage** JUR (déposition) false ou perjured evidence; (délit) perjury ¢; **faire un ~ témoignage** to bear false witness, to commit perjury.

faux² /fo/ *nf inv* scythe.

faux-bourdon, *pl* **~s** /fobuʀdɔ̃/ *nm* **1** ZOOL drone; **2** MUS faux bourdon.

faux-filet, *pl* ~**s** /fofilɛ/ *nm* sirloin.

faux-fuyant, *pl* ~**s** /fofɥijɑ̃/ *nm* **chercher un** ~ to try to evade the issue; **user de** ~**s** to evade the issue, to prevaricate.

faux-monnayeur, *pl* ~**s** /fomɔnɛjœr/ *nm* forger, counterfeiter.

faux-semblant, *pl* ~**s** /fosɑ̃blɑ̃/ *nm* **les** ~**s** pretence[GB] (*sg*); **user de** ~**s** to put up a pretence[GB], to put on an act.

faux-sens /fosɑ̃s/ *nm inv* mistranslation.

faveur /favœr/ *nf* **1** (bienfait) favour[GB]; **il nous a fait la** ~ **d'une visite** he honoured[GB] us with a visit; **avoir les** ~**s de qn** to be in favour[GB] with sb; **par** ~ as a favour[GB]; **régime** or **traitement de** ~ preferential treatment; **2** (ruban) favour[GB], ribbon.

II en faveur de *loc prép* (à l'avantage de) **le jugement a été rendu en sa** ~ the court decided in his/her favour[GB]; **les votes en** ~ **du candidat de l'opposition** the votes for the opposition candidate; **2** (pour aider) **en** ~ **des handicapés** to help the disabled; **en** ~ **de l'emploi** to promote employment; **intervenir en** ~ **de qn** to intervene on sb's behalf.

III à la faveur de *loc prép* thanks to; **à la** ~ **de la nuit** under cover of darkness.

favorable /favɔrabl/ *adj* favourable[GB]; **être** ~ **à** (partisan de) to be in favour[GB] of; (propice à) to be favourable[GB] to.

favorablement /favɔrabləmɑ̃/ *adv* favourably[GB].

favori, -ite /favɔri, it/ **I** *adj* favourite[GB].

II *nm,f* favourite[GB]; **c'est le** ~ **du professeur** he's the teacher's pet.

III *nm* (sportif, cheval) favourite[GB]; **partir** ~ to be the favourite[GB].

IV favoris *nmpl* (barbe) sideburns.

favoriser /favɔrize/ [1] *vtr* **1** (avantager) to favour[GB] (**par rapport à** over); **les circonstances l'ont favorisé** circumstances were in his favour[GB]; **les milieux favorisés** the privileged classes; **2** (encourager) to encourage; (activement) to promote.

favorite ▶ **favori** I, II.

favoritisme /favɔritism/ *nm* favouritism[GB].

fax /faks/ *nm inv* (document) fax; (machine) fax machine; **envoyer qch par** ~ to send sth by fax, to fax sth.

fayot[1]○ /fajo/ *nm* CULIN bean.

fayot[2]○, **-otte** /fajo, ɔt/ *nm,f* creep○, crawler○.

FB (*written abbr* = **franc belge**) BFr.

fébrile /febril/ *adj* **1** [*sentiment, geste, moment, œuvre*] feverish; [*personne, équipe*] nervous; **2** MÉD feverish.

fébrilement /febrilmɑ̃/ *adv* feverishly.

fébrilité /febrilite/ *nf* **1** (agitation) agitation; **avec** ~ agitatedly; **2** (nervosité) nervousness.

fécal, -e, *mpl* **-aux** /fekal, o/ *adj* faecal.

fécond, ~e /fekɔ̃, ɔ̃d/ *adj* [*femme, sol, esprit, imagination*] fertile; [*période, effort, travail, idée*] fruitful; **année** ~**e en incidents** eventful year.

fécondable /fekɔ̃dabl/ *adj* [*femelle*] fertile; [*ovule*] fertilizable.

fécondation /fekɔ̃dasjɔ̃/ *nf* (de femme, femelle) impregnation; (de plante) pollination; (d'œuf) fertilization.

■ ~ **artificielle** artificial insemination; ~ **croisée** cross-fertilization.

féconder /fekɔ̃de/ [1] *vtr* **1** to impregnate [*femme, femelle*]; (par insémination) to inseminate [*animal*]; to pollinate [*plante*]; to fertilize [*œuf*]; [*fleuve*] to make [sth] fertile [*terre*]; **2** FIG to enrich [*esprit*].

fécondité /fekɔ̃dite/ *nf* **1** (de femme, femelle, sol) fertility; **2** FIG (d'idée) potential; (d'auteur) productivity.

fécule /fekyl/ *nf* starch ¢.

féculent, ~e /fekylɑ̃, ɑ̃t/ **I** *adj* starchy.

II *nm* starch, starchy food ¢; **les** ~**s** starches.

fédéral, ~e, *mpl* **-aux** /federal, o/ *adj* [*république, police, budget*] federal; [*association*] federated.

fédéralisme /federalism/ *nm* federalism.

fédérateur, -trice /federatœr, tris/ **I** *adj* federal.

II *nm,f* unifier.

fédératif, -ive /federatif, iv/ *adj* federal.

fédération /federasjɔ̃/ *nf* federation.

fédérer /federe/ [14] **I** *vtr* to federate [*États*].

II se fédérer *vpr* [*États*] to federate; [*comités, entreprises*] to form an association.

fée /fe/ *nf* fairy; **méchante** ~ wicked fairy.

■ ~ **du logis** perfect housewife.

IDIOMES **avoir des doigts** or **mains de** ~ to have nimble fingers.

féerie /fe(e)ri/ *nf* **1** (spectacle merveilleux) **c'est une vraie** ~ it's magical; **2** CIN, THÉÂT extravaganza.

féerique /fe(e)rik/ *adj* [*beauté, vision*] enchanting; [*monde, paysage, moment*] enchanted.

feignant, ~e /fɛɲɑ̃, ɑ̃t/ = **fainéant**.

feindre /fɛ̃dr/ [55] **I** *vtr* to feign [*émotion, maladie*]; ~ **de faire/d'être** to pretend to do/to be.

II *vi* to pretend; **inutile de** ~ it's no use pretending.

feint, ~e[1] /fɛ̃, ɛ̃t/ *adj* [*émotion, état*] feigned; [*sourire*] false; **non** ~ genuine.

feinte[2] /fɛ̃t/ *nf* **1** (manœuvre) GÉN, MIL, SPORT feint; **2**○ (attrape) trick, ruse; **faire une** ~ **à qn** to trick sb.

feinter /fɛ̃te/ [1] **I** *vtr* **1** SPORT ~ **l'adversaire** (en boxe, escrime) to feint at one's opponent; (au football, rugby) to sell one's opponent a dummy GB, to fake out one's opponent US; **2**○ (tromper) to trick [*personne*].

II *vi* (en escrime) to make a feint; (en boxe) to feint; (au football, rugby) to dummy GB, to fake US.

fêlé○, ~**e** /fɛle/ **I** *adj* (fou) cracked○ (*jamais épith*).

II *nm,f* loony○; **un** ~ **du ski/jazz** a ski/jazz freak○.

fêler /fɛle/ [1] **I** *vtr* to crack [*tasse, os*].

II se fêler *vpr* [*tasse, os*] to crack; **d'une voix fêlée** in a cracked voice.

félicitations /felisitasjɔ̃/ *nfpl* congratulations (**pour** on; **à** to); **être reçu avec les** ~ **du jury** SCOL, UNIV to pass with distinction.

félicité /felisite/ *nf* bliss.

féliciter /felisite/ [1] **I** *vtr* to congratulate (**pour** on); **je te félicite!** congratulations!; **je ne te félicite pas!** it's nothing to be proud of!

II se féliciter *vpr* **se** ~ **de qch** to be very pleased about sth.

félin, ~e /felɛ̃, in/ **I** *adj* **1** ZOOL [*race*] feline; [*exposition*] cat (*épith*); **2** FIG [*grâce*] feline; [*yeux*] catlike.

II *nm* feline; **les** ~**s** felines, the cat family *sg*.

félon, -onne /felɔ̃, ɔn/ FML **I** *adj* perfidious.

II *nm,f* traitor/traitress.

fêlure /felyr/ *nf* crack.

femelle /fəmɛl/ **I** *adj* **1** BIOL, BOT female; **2** ZOOL GÉN female; [*baleine, éléphant*] cow; [*moineau, perroquet*] hen; **cygne** ~ pen; **3** ÉLECTROTECH [*prise*] female.

II *nf* female; (partenaire sexuel) mate.

féminin, ~e /feminɛ̃, in/ **I** *adj* [*corps, sexe, rôle, population*] female; [*activité, magazine, lingerie, record*] women's; [*allure*] feminine; [*nom, rime*] feminine.

II *nm* LING feminine; **au** ~ in the feminine.

féminiser /feminize/ [1] **I** *vtr* **1** to open [sth] up to women [*profession*]; **2** to make [sb/sth] more feminine [*personne, vêtement*]; **3** BIOL to feminize.

II se féminiser *vpr* [*profession*] (s'ouvrir aux femmes) to become more open to women; (avoir moins d'hommes) to become predominantly female.

féministe /feminist/ *adj, nmf* feminist.

féminité /feminite/ *nf* femininity.

femme /fam/ **I** *nf* **1** GÉN woman; **vêtements pour** ~**s** women's ou ladies' clothes; **c'est la** ~ **de sa vie** she's the love of his life; **elle fait très** ~ (jeune fille) she looks quite grown-up; **elle est très** ~ (adulte) she's very feminine; **elle n'est pas** ~ **à mentir** she's not a woman to lie; **2** (épouse) wife.

II femme(-) (*in compounds*) ~(-)**écrivain** woman writer; ~(-)**prêtre** woman priest; ~(-)**soldat** woman soldier; ~**-objet** sex object; **femme-femme**○ very feminine woman.

■ ~ **active** working woman; ~ **d'affaires** businesswoman; ~ **à barbe** (au cirque) bearded lady; ~ **battue** battered wife; ~ **de chambre** (employée d'hôtel, de maison) chambermaid; (attachée au service d'une dame) lady's maid, personal maid; **~ de charge** housekeeper; **~ de cœur** caring person; **~ enfant** little-girlish woman; **~ fatale** femme fatale; **~ au foyer** housewife; **~ galante** courtesan; **~ d'intérieur** homemaker; **~ de lettres** woman of letters; **~ de mauvaise vie** loose woman; **~ de ménage** cleaner, cleaning woman ou lady; **~ du monde** well-bred lady; **~ de petite vertu** woman of easy virtue; **~ de service** cleaner, cleaning lady; **~ de tête** assertive woman; ▶**bon, jeune**.

IDIOMES **ce que ~ veut, Dieu le veut** PROV what a woman wants, a woman gets; **souvent ~ varie (bien fol est celui qui s'y fie)** PROV woman is fickle.

femmelette /famlεt/ *nf* wimp°, weakling.

fémur /femyʀ/ *nm* thighbone; **se casser le col du ~** to break one's hip.

FEN /fɛn/ *nf* (*abbr* = **Fédération de l'éducation nationale**) FEN (*French teachers' union*).

fenaison /fənɛzɔ̃/ *nf* (saison) haymaking time; (action) haymaking.

fendiller /fādije/ [1] **I** *vtr* to chap [*peau, lèvres*]; to craze [*terre*]; to crack [*bois, meuble*].

II se fendiller *vpr* [*peau, lèvres*] to chap; [*terre*] to craze over; [*bois, meuble*] to crack.

fendre /fādʀ/ [6] **I** *vtr* **1** (couper) to chop [*bois*]; to split [*pierre*]; to slit [*tissu*]; **2** (ouvrir) (légèrement) to chap [*lèvre*]; to crack [*mur, pierre*]; (profondément) to split [*lèvre*]; to split [sth] open [*crâne*]; **3** FIG **~ le cœur à qn** to break sb's heart; **récit à ~ l'âme** heartbreaking story; **~ l'air** to slice through the air; **~ la foule** to push one's way through the crowd.

II se fendre *vpr* **1** (se craqueler) to crack; **2** FIG [*cœur*] to break; **3**° **tu ne t'es pas fendu!** that didn't break the bank!; **se ~ de** to manage [*sourire, discours*]; to come up with [*cadeau, brochure*]; to cough up° [*somme d'argent*]; **4** SPORT (en escrime) to lunge.

IDIOMES **~ la bise** to run like lightning; **se ~ la pêche**° or **poire**° to split one's sides°; **avoir la bouche fendue jusqu'aux oreilles** to be grinning from ear to ear.

fenêtre /fənɛtʀ/ *nf* **1** ARCHIT window; ▶**faux**¹; **2** (d'enveloppe) window; **3** (dans un document) space; **4** ORDINAT window.

■ **~ basculante** tilt-and-turn window; **~ à croisillons** lattice window; **~ à guillotine** sash window; **~ de lancement** ASTRONAUT launch window; **~ en saillie** bay window; (arrondie) bow window; **~ de toit** roof light.

IDIOMES **jeter l'argent par les ~s** to throw money away.

fenouil /fənuj/ *nm* fennel.

fente /fāt/ *nf* **1** (ouverture) GÉN slit; (pour insérer une pièce, carte, lettre) slot; (de veste) vent; **2** (fissure) GÉN crack; (de bois) split; (de rocher) crevice.

féodal, ~e, *mpl* **-aux** /feodal, o/ **I** *adj* feudal.

II *nm* feudal landowner.

féodalisme /feodalism/ *nm* feudalism.

féodalité /feodalite/ *nf* **1** HIST (caractère) feudalism; (système) feudal system; **2** POL (fief) fiefdom.

fer /fɛʀ/ **I** *nm* **1** (métal) iron; **2** FIG **de ~** [*discipline, volonté*] iron (*épith*); **3** (de chaussure) steel tip; (pour marquer) branding iron; (de relieur) blocking tool; **4** (épée) sword; (lame) blade; **croiser le ~ avec** to cross swords with; **5** (train) rail transport; **par ~** by rail.

II fers† *nmpl* **1** MÉD forceps; **2** (de prisonnier) irons; **être dans les ~s** LIT to be in irons; FIG to be in chains.

■ **~ à cheval** horseshoe; **en ~ à cheval** horseshoe-shaped; **~ forgé** wrought iron; **~ à friser** curling iron; **~ de lance** LIT, FIG spearhead; **~ à repasser** (pour les vêtements) iron; (pour carte de paiement) manual imprinter (*for credit card transactions*); **~ (à repasser) à vapeur** steam iron; **~ à souder** soldering iron.

IDIOMES **croire dur comme ~** to believe wholeheartedly; **il faut battre le ~ pendant** or **tant qu'il est**

chaud PROV strike while the iron is hot; **tomber les quatre ~s en l'air** to fall flat on one's back.

fer-blanc, *pl* **fers-blancs** /fɛʀblā/ *nm* tinplate.

ferblanterie /fɛʀblātʀi/ ▶374 *nf* **1** (ustensiles) tinware; **2** (secteur) tin trade; **3** (boutique) ironmonger's GB, hardware store US.

férié, ~e /feʀje/ *adj* **jour ~** public holiday GB, holiday US.

férir /feʀiʀ/ *vtr* **sans coup ~** meeting no resistance.

fermage /fɛʀmaʒ/ *nm* (mode) tenant farming; (bail) farm tenancy; (redevance) farm rent.

ferme¹ /fɛʀm/ **I** *adj* **1** (résistant) [*chair, sol*] firm; [*blanc d'œuf, crème*] stiff; **2** (assuré) [*pas, voix, attitude, écriture*] firm; [*geste, exécution*] confident; **être ~ sur ses jambes** to be steady on one's legs; **d'une main ~** [*diriger, saisir*] with a firm hand; [*écrire*] in a firm hand; **rester ~ dans ses résolutions** to be steadfast in one's resolutions; **3** (inflexible) firm; **4** [*marché, commande, prix*] firm; **5** JUR **peine de prison ~** custodial sentence; **cinq ans de prison ~, cinq ans ~**° a five-year sentence with no remission.

II *adv* **1** (discuter, batailler) vigorously; [*croire*] firmly; **tenir ~** to stand one's ground; **s'ennuyer ~** to be bored stiff; **2** (de façon définitive) **commander ~** to put in a firm order for [*avion, voiture*].

IDIOMES **attendre de pied ~** to be ready and waiting; **je les attends de pied ~** I'm ready for them.

ferme² /fɛʀm/ *nf* **1** (exploitation) farm; (maison) farmhouse; **à la ~** on the farm; **2** (contrat) **(bail à) ~** farming lease; (domaine affermé) leasehold; **donner qch à ~** to lease sth; **3** CONSTR truss.

■ **~ école** *farm attached to an agricultural college*.

fermé, ~e /fɛʀme/ **I** *pp* ▶**fermer**.

II *pp adj* **1** (hermétique) **être ~ à l'art moderne** to be totally uninterested in modern art; **visage ~** inscrutable face; **2** (élitiste) exclusive; **3** MATH closed.

fermement /fɛʀmmā/ *adv* firmly.

ferment /fɛʀmā/ *nm* LIT, FIG ferment.

fermentation /fɛʀmātasjɔ̃/ *nf* **1** BIOL fermentation; **2** (agitation) ferment.

fermenter /fɛʀmāte/ [1] *vi* **1** BIOL to ferment; **2** (être en effervescence) to be in ferment.

fermentescible /fɛʀmātɛsibl/ *adj* fermentable.

fermer /fɛʀme/ [1] **I** *vtr* **1** GÉN to close, to shut [*porte, fenêtre, livre, parapluie*]; to close, to shut [*yeux, bouche*]; to clench [*poing*]; to draw [*rideau*]; to seal [*lettre*]; to turn off [*robinet, gaz, radio*]; to switch off [*électricité*]; to do up [*vêtement*]; to close off [*passage*]; **~ à clé** to lock up [*maison*]; to lock [*voiture, valise*]; **~ à double tour** LIT to double-lock [*maison*]; FIG to lock securely [*voiture, valise*]; **~ le jeu** SPORT to play a defensive game; **2** ADMIN, COMM (temporairement) to close [*magasin, aéroport, frontière*]; (définitivement) to close down [*entreprise*]; to close [*mine, compte bancaire*]; **3** (terminer) to bring [sth] to a close [*débat*].

II *vi* (temporairement) to close; (définitivement) to close down.

III se fermer *vpr* **1** LIT [*porte*] to shut; [*fleur*] to close up; [*manteau, bracelet*] to fasten; **2** FIG [*personne*] to clam up; [*visage*] to harden.

IDIOMES **les yeux sur** to turn a blind eye to.

fermeté /fɛʀməte/ *nf* firmness.

fermette /fɛʀmɛt/ *nf* farmhouse-style cottage.

fermeture /fɛʀmətyʀ/ *nf* **1** GÉN (de magasin, d'usine) (brève) closing; (longue) closure; (définitive) closing down; (de compte en banque) closing; **'attention à la ~ des portes'** 'mind the doors'; **2** TECH (dispositif) (de porte) latch; (de fenêtre, meuble) catch; (de sac à main) clasp; (de vêtement) fastening; **~ automatique** automatic locking system; **3** (en phonétique) closure.

■ **~ à baïonnette** bayonet clutch; **~ éclair**® or **à glissière** zip GB, zipper US.

fermier, -ière¹ /fɛʀmje, ɛʀ/ **I** *adj* [*beurre, fromage*] farm (*épith*); [*poulet, œufs*] free-range (*épith*); **exploitation fermière** (activité) farming; (ferme) farm.

II ▶374 *nm,f* (agriculteur) farmer.

III *nm* COMM, JUR leaseholder.

fermière² /fɛʀmjɛʀ/ nf (épouse de fermier) farmer's wife.

fermoir /fɛʀmwaʀ/ nm (de bijou, sac, reliure) clasp.

féroce /feʀɔs/ adj **1** (cruel) [animal] ferocious; [rire, répression] savage; [personne, air] fierce; **2** (acharné) [bataille] fierce; **3** (violent) [appétit] voracious; [envie, désir] violent.

férocement /feʀɔsmɑ̃/ adv **1** (avec cruauté) savagely; **2** (violemment) fiercely.

férocité /feʀɔsite/ nf **1** (d'animal) ferociousness; **2** (de réplique, rire) savagery; **3** (de personne, regard) fierceness.

ferraille /fɛʀɑj/ nf **1** (morceaux de fer) scrap iron; (morceaux de métal) scrap metal; **2** (dépôt) scrapheap; **3**○ (monnaie) small change.

ferrailleur /feʀajœʀ/ nm **1** ▶374 (récupérateur) scrap (metal) dealer; **2** (batailleur) swashbuckler.

ferré, -e /feʀe/ **I** pp ▶ **ferrer**.
II pp adj **1** (muni de ferrures) [animal] shoed; [chaussure, bâton] steel-tipped; [roue] rimmed with steel; [lacet] tagged; [coffre] ironbound; **2**○ (instruit) **être ~ en** or **sur** to be well up on○.

ferrer /feʀe/ [1] vtr **1** to shoe [cheval]; (munir de ferrures) to fit steel tips to [chaussure]; to rim [sth] with steel [roue]; to tip [sth] with steel [bâton]; to tag [lacet]; to reinforce [sth] with steel [porte]; **2** to hook [poisson].

ferreux, -euse /feʀø, øz/ adj ferrous; **métaux non ~** nonferrous metals.

ferronnerie /feʀɔnʀi/ nf **1** (lieu) ironworks; **atelier de ~** wrought iron workshop; **2** (travail) (du fer forgé) wrought ironwork; (du fer) ironwork.

ferronnier /feʀɔnje/ ▶374 nm **1** (fabricant) iron craftsman; **2** (commerçant) iron work merchant.

ferroviaire /feʀɔvjɛʀ/ adj [transport, collision, trafic] rail (épith); [gare, tunnel, compagnie] railway GB (épith), railroad US (épith).

ferrugineux, -euse /feʀyʒinø, øz/ adj ferruginous.

ferrure /feʀyʀ/ nf **1** (de porte, fenêtre) metal fittings (pl); (de meuble, coffre) metal band; **2** (de cheval) shoes (pl).

ferry-boat, pl **~s** /feʀibot/ nm GÉN ferry; (pour véhicules) (car) ferry.

fertile /fɛʀtil/ adj [sol, plaine] fertile; [imagination] fertile; [année] productive; **année ~ en événements** eventful year; **journée ~ en émotions** day filled with emotion.

fertilisant /fɛʀtilizɑ̃/ nm (engrais) fertilizer.

fertiliser /fɛʀtilize/ [1] vtr to fertilize.

fertilité /fɛʀtilite/ nf fertility.

féru, ~e /feʀy/ adj **être ~ de qch** to be very keen on sth.

férule /feʀyl/ nf **être sous la ~ de qn** to be under sb's iron rule.

fervent, ~e /fɛʀvɑ̃, ɑ̃t/ **I** adj [croyant, prière] fervent; [admirateur, amour] ardent.
II nm,f **~ de tennis** tennis enthusiast GB, tennis buff US; **~ de musique/théâtre** music/theatre GB lover.

ferveur /fɛʀvœʀ/ nf (de prière) fervour GB; (d'amour) ardour GB.

fesse /fɛs/ nf ANAT buttock.
IDIOMES **attention à tes ~s**○ watch your step; **avoir la police aux ~s**○ to have the police hot on one's trail; **avoir chaud aux ~s**○ to have a narrow escape○; **coûter la peau des ~s**○ to cost an arm and a leg○; **pousse tes ~s**⚬! shove over○! GB, scoot over○! US; **serrer les ~s**⚬ to be scared stiff.

fessée /fese/ nf smack on the bottom, spanking.

fessier /fesje/ nm **1**○ (fesses) backside○, behind○; **2** ANAT (muscle) gluteus.

festin /fɛstɛ̃/ nm feast; **faire un ~** to have a feast.

festival /fɛstival/ nm festival; **pièce hors ~** play on the fringe.

festivalier, -ière /fɛstivalje, ɛʀ/ nm,f festival-goer.

festivités /fɛstivite/ nfpl festivities.

feston /fɛstɔ̃/ nm **1** (guirlande) festoon; **2** ARCHIT festoon; **3** (point de broderie) scallop; **à ~s** scalloped.

festoyer /fɛstwaje/ [23] vi to feast.

fêtard○, ~e /fɛtaʀ, aʀd/ nm,f reveller.

fête /fɛt/ nf **1** (jour chômé) public holiday GB, holiday US; **2** (jour du saint patron) **c'est ma ~** it's my (saint's) name-day; **ça va être ma ~**○! IRON I'm going to cop it○!; **la ~ des pompiers** the festival of the patron saint of firemen; **3** (solennité religieuse) festival; **4** (célébration) (day of) celebration; **5** (réjouissances privées) party; **faire la ~** to live it up○; **je serai de la ~**! I'll be there!; **air de ~** festive look; **avoir le cœur en ~** to feel incredibly happy; **être à la ~** FIG to have a field day; **ne pas être à la ~** FIG to be having a bad time; **6** (foire) fair; (kermesse) fête, fair; (manifestation culturelle) festival; (réjouissances officielles) celebrations (pl).
■ **~ de bienfaisance** charity bazaar; **~ fixe** fixed feast; **~ foraine** funfair; **~ légale** public holiday GB, legal holiday US; **~ des Mères** Mothers' Day; **~ mobile** movable feast; **la ~ des morts** All Souls' Day; **~ Nationale** national holiday; (en France) Bastille Day; **~ des Pères** Fathers' Day; **~ des Rois** (**Mages**) Twelfth Night, Epiphany; **~ du travail** Labour Day, 1 May.
IDIOMES **faire sa ~**○ **à qn** to give sb a working over○; **ce n'est pas tous les jours la ~** PROV life is not a bed of roses.

Fête-Dieu /fɛtdjø/ nf Corpus Christi.

fêter /fete/ [1] vtr to celebrate [anniversaire]; to fete [champion].

fétiche /fetiʃ/ **I** adj lucky; **jour ~** lucky day.
II nm **1** (mascotte) mascot; **2** PSYCH, RELIG fetish.

fétichiste /fetiʃist/ **I** adj fetishistic.
II nm,f fetishist.

fétide /fetid/ adj **1** (malodorant) [odeur] foul; [lieu] foul-smelling; **2** (répugnant) [personne] repulsive.

fétu /fety/ nm **~ (de paille)** wisp of straw.

feu¹, ~e /fø/ adj late; **~ la reine**, **la ~e reine** the late queen.

feu², pl **~x** /fø/ **I** ▶141 adj inv (de couleur) **~ flame-coloured** GB; **rouge ~** fiery red.
II nm **1** (combustion, incendie) fire; **~ de braises** glowing embers (pl); **au ~!** fire!; **mise à ~** (de fusée) blast-off; **au coin du ~** [s'asseoir, bavarder] by the fire; [causerie, rêverie] fireside (épith); ▶ **huile**, **marron**; **2** (lumière) light; **les ~x de la rampe** the footlights; **sous le ~ des projecteurs** LIT under the glare of the spotlights; FIG in the spotlight; **3** (éclat) **briller de mille ~x** [chandelier, diamant] to sparkle brilliantly; **les ~x du couchant** the fiery glow of the setting sun; **4** AUT, AVIAT, NAUT (signal) light; **tous ~x éteints** without lights; **5** (à un carrefour) traffic light; **~ orange** amber GB ou yellow US light; **j'ai le ~ vert de mon patron** my boss has given me the go-ahead; **6** CULIN (de cuisinière) ring GB, burner US; (chaleur) heat; **j'ai oublié la soupe sur le ~** I've left the soup on the stove; **j'ai quelque chose sur le ~** I've got something cooking; **7** (allumettes, briquet) **avez-vous du ~?** have you got a light?; **8** (sensation de brûlure) **épice qui met la bouche en ~** spice that burns your mouth; **elle avait les joues en ~** her cheeks were burning ou on fire; **pour apaiser le ~ du rasoir** to soothe shaving burn; **9** (enthousiasme) passion; **avoir un tempérament de ~** to have a fiery temperament; **dans le ~ de la discussion** in the heat of the discussion; **10** (tir) **~!** fire!; **faire ~** to fire (sur at); **coup de ~** shot; **le coup de ~ de midi** (dans un restaurant) the lunchtime rush; **être pris entre deux ~x** LIT, FIG to be caught in the crossfire; **11** (combat) action; **aller au ~** to go into action; **12**○ (pistolet) gun.
■ **~ d'artifice** (spectacle) fireworks display; (fusée) firework; **~ de Bengale** Bengal light; **~ de camp** campfire; **~ de cheminée** (incendie) chimney fire; (pour chauffer) open fire; **~ d'encombrement** marker lamp ou light; **~ follet** LIT, FIG will-o'-the-wisp; **~ de gabarit** = **~ d'encombrement**; **~ de joie** bonfire; **~ de paille** FIG flash in the pan; **~ de signalisation**, **~ tricolore** traffic light; **~x de croisement** dipped headlights GB, dimmed

headlights US; **~x de détresse** warning lights; **~x de position** AUT sidelights GB, parking lights US; **~x de recul** reversing GB ou back-up US lights; **~x de route** headlights; **~x de stationnement** sidelights GB, parking lights US.
IDIOMES **il n'y a pas le ~°!** there's no rush!; **jouer avec le ~** to play with fire; **faire long ~** [*projectile, projet*] to misfire; **ne pas faire long ~** not to last long; **il n'y a vu que du ~°** he fell for it; **mourir à petit ~** to die a slow death; **avoir le ~ au derrière°** ou **aux fesses°** (être pressé) to be in a rush.

feuillage /fœjaʒ/ nm **1** BOT foliage ¢, leaves (*pl*); **2** (décor) leafage ¢; (branches coupées) cut branches (*pl*).

feuille /fœj/ nf **1** (d'arbre) leaf; **~s d'érable** maple leaves; **arbre à ~s persistantes** evergreen; **arbre à ~s caduques** deciduous tree; **2** (de papier, carton) sheet; **3** (de métal, plastique) (plaque mince) sheet; (pellicule) foil ¢; **~ d'étain** tinfoil ¢; **~ d'argent** silver leaf ¢; **4** (de placage) veneer ¢; **5** (de dorure) **~ d'or**, **or en ~s** gold leaf ¢; **dorer à la ~** to gild; **6** (formulaire) form; **7°** (journal) paper.
■ **~ blanche** blank sheet; **~ de chêne** CULIN oak-leaf lettuce; **~ de chou°** (journal) rag°, newspaper; **~ de chou farcie** CULIN stuffed cabbage roll; **avoir les oreilles en ~ de chou** to have cauliflower ears; **~ d'impôts** (déclaration) tax return; (avis de débit) tax demand GB, tax statement US; **~ de maladie** *a form for reclaiming medical expenses from the social security office*; **~ de notes** school report; **~ de paie** payslip GB, pay stub US; **~ de présence** attendance sheet; **~ de vigne** BOT vine leaf; ART fig leaf; **~ volante** loose sheet.

feuillet /fœjɛ/ nm (feuille) leaf; (page) page.
■ **~ détachable** tear sheet; **bloc à ~s détachables** tear-off pad; **~ intercalaire** interleaf.

feuilleté, **~e** /fœjte/ **I** adj **1** (en géologie) [*roche*] foliated; **2** IND [*verre*] laminated; **3** CULIN **pâte ~e** puff pastry.
II nm CULIN savoury GB pasty (*made with puff pastry*); **~s au jambon/fromage** ham/cheese pasties.

feuilleter /fœjte/ [20] vtr to leaf through [*livre*].

feuilleton /fœjtɔ̃/ nm **1** RADIO, TV, LITTÉRAT serial; (à rebondissements) soap (opera); **publié en ~** serialized; **c'est un vrai ~** it's a real saga; **2** (chronique) column.

feuillu, **~e** /fœjy/ **I** adj **1** (touffu) leafy; **2** BOT [*arbre*] broad-leaved (*épith*).
II nm BOT broad-leaved tree.

feulement /følmɑ̃/ nm growl (*of a tiger*).

feutre /føtʀ/ nm **1** (matière) felt ¢; **2** (chapeau) felt hat; **3** (stylo) felt-tip (pen).

feutré, **~e** /føtʀe/ adj **1** (étouffé) [*ambiance, lieu*] hushed; [*son*] muffled; **marcher à pas ~s** to pad along; **2** (garni de feutre) [*bureau*] felt-topped.

feutrer /føtʀe/ [1] **I** vtr **1** (traiter) to felt [*poils, laine*]; **un tissu feutré** felt material; **2** (détériorer) to felt [*étoffe*]; **un pull feutré** a felted sweater; **3** (garnir) to felt [*selle*].
II vi [*lainage*] to become felted.

feutrine /føtʀin/ nf (pour vêtements) fine felt fabric; (pour ameublement, table de billard) baize.

fève /fɛv/ nf **1** BOT, CULIN broad bean; **2** C (haricot) bean; **~s au lard** baked beans; **3** (figurine) lucky charm (*hidden in Twelfth Night cake*).

février /fevʀije/ ▶382| nm February.

FF (*written abbr* = **franc français**) FFr.

fg *written abbr* = **faubourg** 3.

fi† /fi/ *excl* pooh!
IDIOMES **faire ~ de qch** to treat sth with disdain.

fiabilité /fjabilite/ nf reliability.

fiable /fjabl/ adj [*machine, compagnie*] reliable; [*personne*] (sérieuse) reliable; (de confiance) trustworthy.

fiançailles /fjɑ̃saj/ nfpl engagement (*sg*).

fiancé, **~e** /fjɑ̃se/ nm,f fiancé/fiancée.

fiancer: se fiancer /fjɑ̃se/ [12] vpr to get engaged (**à**, **avec** to).

fiasque /fjask/ nf straw-sheathed flask.

fibre /fibʀ/ nf **1** LIT fibre GB; **2** FIG (sensibilité) streak;

avoir la ~ maternelle to have a strong maternal streak.
■ **~ optique** fibre GB optics (+ *v sg*); **~ de verre** fibreglass GB.

fibreux, **-euse** /fibʀø, øz/ adj (texture) fibrous; (consistance) sinewy.

ficeler /fisle/ [19] vtr to tie up [*paquet*]; to tie [*mains, pieds*]; **bien/mal ficelé** [*intrigue, roman*] well/badly put together; [*projet, enquête*] badly organized.
IDIOMES **~ qn comme un saucisson** to truss sb up like a chicken GB, to hogtie sb US.

ficelle /fisɛl/ nf **1** (corde) string; **2** (astuce) trick; **la ~ est un peu grosse** it's a bit obvious; **3** CULIN (baguette mince) thin baguette.
IDIOMES **tirer sur la ~** to push one's luck.

fiche¹° /fiʃ/ vtr, **se fiche** vpr = **ficher** I 3, 4, 5; II 2, 3, 4.

fiche² /fiʃ/ nf **1** (à classer) (en carton) index card; (en papier) (petite) slip; (grande) sheet; **~ médicale** medical card; **~ pratique** card with practical hints; **2** (formulaire) form; **~ d'inscription** enrolment GB form; **3** ÉLECTROTECH (prise) plug; (broche) pin; **prise à trois ~s** three-pin plug.
■ **~ (individuelle) d'état civil** ADMIN *record of personal details for administrative purposes*; **~ de lecture** notes *pl* (*from a book*); **~ de paie** payslip GB, pay stub US; **~ technique** technical data sheet.

ficher /fiʃe/ **I** vtr **1** (répertorier) to put [sth] on a file [*œuvre*]; to open a file on [*personne*]; **être fiché par la police** to be on police files; **2** (enfoncer) to drive [*piquet, clou*] (**dans** into); **3°** (faire) to do; **ne rien ~** to do nothing; **n'en avoir rien à ~** not to give a damn°; **4°** (donner) **~ un coup à qn** LIT to wallop sb; FIG to be a real blow to sb; **~ la trouille°** à qn to scare the hell out° of sb; **5°** (mettre) **où est-ce qu'il a bien pu ~ mon journal?** where the hell° has he put my newspaper?; **son arrivée a fichu la soirée par terre** son en l'air his/her arrival ruined the party; **~ qn dehors** ou **à la porte** (congédier) to give sb the boot°; (faire sortir) to kick sb out°; **~ qn dedans** (induire en erreur) to make sb screw up°; **~ la paix à qn** to leave sb alone.
II se ficher vpr **1** (se planter) [*flèche, couteau*] to stick (**dans** in); **2°** (se mettre) **se ~ en colère** to fly off the handle°; **se ~ dedans** to screw up°; **3°** (ridiculiser) **se ~ de qn** (se moquer) to make fun of sb; (manquer de respect) to mess sb about°; **le repas était excellent, ils ne se sont pas fichus de nous** the meal was excellent, they did us proud; **se ~ du monde** [*personne*] to have a hell of a nerve°; **4°** (être indifférent) **se ~ de ce que qn fait** not to give a damn° (about) what sb does.

fichier /fiʃje/ nm **1** (liste) file; (plusieurs listes) files (*pl*); (dans une bibliothèque) index; **2** (meuble) filing cabinet; (boîte) card index file; **3** ORDINAT file.

fichu /fiʃy/ **I°** pp ▶ **ficher** I 3, 4, 5, II 2, 3, 4.
II° adj **1** (détestable) (*before n*) [*temps*] rotten°; [*pluie*] dreadful; [*voiture, télévision*] damned°, blasted°; [*caractère*] nasty; [*métier*] rotten°; **2** (condamné) [*personne*] done for°; (usé, cassé) [*vêtements, véhicule, machine*] done for°; **s'il pleut c'est ~** if it rains that's the end of that; **c'est la troisième ampoule de ~e** that's the third bulb that's gone; **3** (fait) **comment c'est ~ ce truc?** how's this thing made?; **être bien ~** [*femme*] to be shapely; [*homme*] to be well built; **être bien/mal ~** (conçu) [*dispositif*] to be well/badly designed; [*appartement*] to be well/badly laid out; [*vêtement*] to be well made/badly cut; **être mal ~** (malade) to feel lousy°; **4** (considérable) **une ~e différence** a heck° of a difference; **5** (capable) **être ~ de faire** to be quite capable of doing; **il n'est pas ~ d'écrire une lettre** he can't even write a letter.
III nm (châle) shawl.

fictif, **-ive** /fiktif, iv/ adj **1** (inventé) [*personnage, récit*] fictitious, imaginary; [*promesse, identité*] false; **2** FIN [*actif, dividende*] fictitious; [*valeur*] conventional.

fiction /fiksjɔ̃/ nf **1** GÉN fiction; **la réalité dépasse la**

~ truth is stranger than fiction; **2** TV (émission) (TV) drama.

ficus /fikys/ nm inv ficus.

fidèle /fidɛl/ **I** adj **1** (constant) [personne, chien] faithful (à to); **être ~ au poste** to be always there; **2** (loyal) loyal (à to); **3** (identique) true (à to); **4** (conforme) [traduction] faithful (à to); **5** (fiable) [instrument] reliable.

II nmf **1** (compagnon) loyal supporter; **2** (personne constante) faithful friend; **3** RELIG **les ~s** the faithful (+ v pl); **quelques ~s** some of the faithful.

fidèlement /fidɛlmɑ̃/ adv **1** (avec exactitude) faithfully; **2** (avec loyauté) loyally.

fidéliser /fidelize/ [1] vtr to secure the loyalty of [clients, adhérents].

fidélité /fidelite/ nf **1** (dans un couple) fidelity; **2** (d'ami, de client) loyalty (à to); **3** (de celui qui promet) faithfulness; **4** (de traduction) accuracy; **5** (de mesure) reliability.

fidjien, -ienne /fidʒjɛ̃, ɛn/ ▶ 394 | adj Fijian.

fiduciaire /fidysjɛʀ/ adj [émission, circulation] fiduciary; **société ~** trust company.

fief /fjɛf/ nm **1** HIST fief; **2** (espace) territory; (de parti) stronghold.

fieffé, ~e /fjefe/ adj **~ menteur** incorrigible liar.

fiel /fjɛl/ nm **1** (hargne) venom; **2** MÉD bile.

fielleux, -euse /fjɛlø, øz/ adj venomous.

fiente /fjɑ̃t/ nf droppings (pl).

fier¹, fière /fjɛʀ/ adj **1** (satisfait) proud; **tu peux être ~ de toi** LIT you have every right to be proud; IRON you must be very proud of yourself; **2** (hautain) proud, haughty; (prétentieux) stuck-up○; **il n'était pas si ~ à l'examen!** he wasn't so cocky○ in the exam!; **3** (noble) [caractère] proud; **avoir fière allure** to cut a fine figure.

IDIOMES **~ comme Artaban** or **un coq** or **un paon** proud as a peacock; **faire le ~** to be haughty.

fier²: se fier /fje/ [2] vpr **1** (placer sa confiance en) **se ~ à** to trust [personne, promesse]; **ne te fie pas à ce qu'il dit/aux apparences** don't go by what he says/by appearances; **2** (compter sur) **se ~ à** to rely on [personne, mémoire, calculs]; to trust to [chance, destin].

fier-à-bras, pl **fiers-à-bras** /fjɛʀabʀa/ nm braggart.

fièrement /fjɛʀmɑ̃/ adv proudly.

fierté /fjɛʀte/ nf pride; **tirer ~ de** to take pride in.

fiesta○ /fjɛsta/ nf party; **faire la ~** to rave it up○.

fièvre /fjɛvʀ/ nf **1** MÉD (high) temperature; **avoir de la ~** to have a (high) temperature; **2** (agitation) frenzy; **pris de ~** caught up in a frenzy; **3** (ardeur) fervour^{GB}; **4** (passion) fever; **~ électorale** election fever; **la ~ monte** the temperature is rising.

■ **~ de cheval**○ raging fever; **~ jaune** yellow fever.

fiévreusement /fjevʀøzmɑ̃/ adv [chercher, préparer] frantically; [parler] feverishly.

fiévreux, -euse /fjevʀø, øz/ adj **1** MÉD feverish; **2** (agité) frantic; **3** (passionné) feverish.

fifille○ /fifij/ nf little girl.

fifre /fifʀ/ nm **1** ▶ 392 | (instrument) fife; **2** (personne) fife player.

figé, ~e /fiʒe/ **I** pp ▶ **figer**.

II pp adj **1** (immobile) [attitude, personne] frozen; [situation, sourire] fixed; **2** (rigide) [société] fossilized; [situation] deadlocked; **être ~ dans ses habitudes** to be set in one's ways; **3** LING [expression] set.

figer /fiʒe/ [13] **I** vtr **1** (immobiliser) **la peur figeait leurs visages/traits** their faces/features were frozen with fear; **2** (solidifier) to congeal [graisse]; to thicken [sauce]; to clot [sang].

II se figer vpr **1** [attitude, sourire, personne] to freeze (**de** with); **2** (se scléroser) [idéologie, société, personne] to become fossilized; **3** (se solidifier) [graisse, sauce] to congeal; [sang] LIT to clot; FIG to freeze.

fignoler /fiɲɔle/ [1] **I** vtr **1** (terminer) to put the finishing touches to; **2** (soigner) to take great pains over.

II vi to fiddle about.

figue /fig/ nf fig.

■ **~ de Barbarie** prickly pear.

figuier /figje/ nm fig tree.

figurant, ~e /figyʀɑ̃, ɑ̃t/ nm,f (acteur) CIN extra; THÉÂT bit player; **n'être qu'un ~** FIG to have a token role.

figuratif, -ive /figyʀatif, iv/ adj ART figurative, representational; **artiste non ~** abstract artist; **poésie figurative** emblematic ou figured verse.

figuration /figyʀasjɔ̃/ nf **faire de la ~** THÉÂT to do bit parts; CIN to be an extra; FIG to have a token role.

figure /figyʀ/ nf **1** (visage, mine) face; **ma ~ s'allongea** my face fell; **elle changea de ~** her face fell; **2** (apparence) **faire ~ d'amateur** to look like an amateur; **ne plus avoir ~ humaine** to be unrecognizable; **reprendre ~ humaine** HUM to look half-human again; **3** (personnalité) figure; **4** (schéma, photo, dessin) figure; **5** JEUX (carte) court card.

■ **~ imposée** compulsory figure; **~ de proue** LIT figurehead; FIG key figure; **~ de rhétorique** GÉN figure of speech; LITTÉRAT rhetorical figure; **~ de style** stylistic device; **~s libres** freestyle ¢.

IDIOMES **prendre ~** to take shape; **faire bonne ~** (garder le sourire) to keep an air of composure; (faire bonne impression) to make the right impression; (réussir) to do well; **faire piètre** or **triste ~** (avoir l'air misérable) to look ou cut a sorry figure; (faire mauvaise impression) to make a bad impression.

figuré, ~e /figyʀe/ **I** adj **sens ~** figurative sense.

II nm LING figurative sense.

figurer /figyʀe/ [1] **I** vtr to represent.

II vi [nom, chose] to appear; **faire ~ qch dans un rapport** to include sth in a report; **un pompier figure parmi les victimes** a fireman is among the casualties.

III se figurer vpr to imagine; **j'avais compris, figurez-vous!** I had actually got the point!; **figure-toi que je l'ai revu dix ans après!** I saw him again ten years later, can you imagine!

figurine /figyʀin/ nf figurine.

fil /fil/ **I** nm **1** (brin) thread, cotton ¢ GB; **2** (fibre naturelle) yarn; (fibre synthétique) filament; **3** (câble, corde) (en fibre) string; (métallique) wire; (de câble) line; SPORT (d'arrivée) tape; **4** ÉLECTROTECH, TÉLÉCOM (ligne) wire; (de micro, combiné, d'appareil électrique) flex GB, cord US; (de téléphone) lead; **sans ~** [micro, téléphone] cordless; **coup de ~**○ (phone) call; **au bout du ~**○ on the phone; ▶ **inventer**; **5** (lin) linen ¢; **6** (enchaînement de texte, conversation) thread; **perdre le ~ des événements** to lose track of events; **~ de la pensée** train of thought; **7** CULIN (de haricot, céleri) string; **haricots sans ~s** stringless beans; **8** (d'araignée) thread; **9** (de bois) grain; **10** (tranchant) edge.

II au fil de loc prép **au ~ des ans** over the years; **au ~ de l'enquête** in the course of the investigation; **au ~ des kilomètres, le paysage change** the scenery changes as you travel along; **aller au ~ de l'eau** LIT, FIG to go with the flow.

■ **~ d'Ariane** MYTHOL Ariadne's thread; FIG vital clue; **~ conducteur** ÉLECTROTECH conductor; (de roman) thread; (d'enquête) lead; **~ à couper le beurre** CULIN cheese wire; **il n'a pas inventé le ~ à couper le beurre** FIG he's not very bright; **~ dentaire** dental floss; **~ directeur** guiding principle; **~ de fer** wire; **~ à plomb** plumb line; **~ de la Vierge** gossamer thread.

IDIOMES **ne tenir qu'à un ~** to hang by a thread; **être mince comme un ~** to be as thin as a rake; **être sur le ~ du rasoir** to be on a knife edge.

filage /filaʒ/ nm **1** (de laine etc) spinning; **2** THÉÂT run through.

filament /filamɑ̃/ nm **1** GÉN filament; **viande pleine de ~s** stringy meat; **2** ÉLECTROTECH filament.

filandreux, -euse /filɑ̃dʀø, øz/ adj **1** (plein de fils) [légume, viande] stringy; **2** (confus) rambling.

filasse /filas/ **I** adj inv **cheveux (blond) ~** dirty yellow hair ¢.

II nf (de lin, chanvre) tow.

filature /filatyʀ/ nf **1** (usine) textile mill; **2** (surveillance) tailing ¢; **prendre qn en ~** to tail sb○.

file /fil/ nf **1** (queue) **~ (d'attente)** queue GB, line US;

2 (alignement) line; **sortir/entrer en ~** to file out/in; **à la ~** (successivement) in a row; **3** (sur une chaussée) lane; **se garer en double ~** to double-park.
■ **~ indienne** single file.

filer /file/ [1] **I** *vtr* **1** (transformer en fil) to spin [*laine, coton*]; to draw [*métal*]; **2** ZOOL [*araignée, chenille*] to spin [*toile, cocon*]; **3** (démailler) to get a run in [*collant*]; **4** NAUT (dérouler) to pay out [*ligne*]; **~ 20 nœuds** [*navire*] to do 20 knots; **5** MUS to hold [*note*]; THÉÂT to run straight through [*scène*]; LITTÉRAT to extend [*métaphore*]; **6** (suivre) to tail○ [*suspect*]; **~ le train○ à qn** to be on sb's tail○; **7**○ (donner) to give.
II *vi* **1** CULIN (couler) [*sirop*] to thread; [*fromage fondu*] to go stringy; **2** (se démailler) [*collant*] to ladder GB, to run US; **3** NAUT (se dérouler) [*cordage*] to unwind; **laisser ~ un câble** to play out a cable; **4**○ (s'éloigner) [*véhicule, animal*] to go off; [*personne*] to leave; **~ à toute allure** [*véhicule*] to speed off; [*animal*] to run off; [*personne*] to dash off; **file, et que je ne te revoie plus!** clear off○, and don't come back!; **5**○ (aller) to rush; **6**○ (disparaître) [*temps, journée*] to fly past; [*prisonnier*] to get away; **~ entre les mains** [*personne, argent, occasion*] to slip through one's fingers.
IDIOMES **~ comme le vent** or **une flèche** to go like the wind; **~ des jours heureux** to lead a happy life.

filet /file/ *nm* **1** (objet en maille) net; **attirer** or **prendre qn dans ses ~s** FIG to get sb in one's clutches; **coup de ~** (par la police) raid; **travailler sans ~** FIG to take risks; **2** TECH (matériau) (textile) netting ¢; (métallique) mesh ¢; **3** CULIN (de viande, poisson) fillet; **4** (d'eau) trickle; (de gaz) breath; (de fumée) wisp; **~ de citron** dash of lemon juice; **un ~ de voix** a faint voice; **5** (trait fin) rule; (sur une reliure) fillet; ART thin line; **6** (article de presse) snippet.
■ **~ à bagages** luggage rack; **~ à papillons** butterfly net; **~ de pêche** fishing net; **~ de protection** safety net; **~ à provisions** string bag.

fileur, -euse /filœʀ, øz/ ▶374 *nm,f* (de laine, lin) spinner.

filial, ~e¹, *mpl* **-iaux** /filjal, o/ *adj* filial.

filiale² /filjal/ *nf* subsidiary.

filiation /filjasjɔ̃/ *nf* filiation; **descendre de qn par ~ directe** to be a direct descendant of sb.

filière /filjɛʀ/ *nf* **1** UNIV (domaine d'études) course of study; **suivre une ~ scientifique/littéraire** to study science/arts; **2** ÉCON (domaine d'activité) field; **3** (étapes de carrière) **la ~ habituelle** the usual career ladder; **4** (suite de formalités) official channels (*pl*); **5** (de la drogue) **~ (clandestine)** ring; **6** ORDINAT card throat.

filiforme /filifɔʀm/ *adj* (mince) [*personne, jambes, sculpture*] spindly; [*insecte, pattes*] threadlike.

filigrane /filigʀan/ *nm* **1** (de papier) watermark; **lire en ~** FIG to read between the lines; **être en ~ dans** FIG to be implicit in; **2** (en orfèvrerie, verrerie) filigree.

filin /filɛ̃/ *nm* NAUT rope.

fille /fij/ *nf* **1** (descendante) daughter; **elle a eu une petite ~** she's had a little girl; **ma ~** GÉN my girl; RELIG my child; ▶**superstition**; **2** (jeune femme) girl; **elle fait encore très petite ~** she's still very much a little girl.
■ **~ de (bonne) famille** girl from a good family; **~ de ferme** farm girl; **~ mère†** unmarried mother; **~ spirituelle** spiritual heir.
IDIOMES **jouer les ~s de l'air○** to vanish into thin air; **la plus belle ~ du monde ne peut donner que ce qu'elle a** with the best will in the world one can only go so far.

fillette /fijɛt/ *nf* **1** (petite fille) little girl; **rayon ~** COMM girlswear department; **2** (bouteille) half bottle.
IDIOMES **chausser du 45 ~○** to have feet like boats○.

filleul /fijœl/ *nm* godson, godchild.

filleule /fijœl/ *nf* goddaughter, godchild.

film /film/ *nm* **1** (œuvre) film, movie US; **un ~ à succès** a box-office success; **~ parlant** talking film; **~ muet** silent film; **2** (déroulement d'événements) course, sequence; **3** (pellicule) film; **4** (mince couche) film.

■ **~ d'animation** cartoon; **~ catastrophe** disaster film; **~ d'épouvante** or **d'horreur** horror film; **~ noir** film noir; **~ policier** detective film; **~ publicitaire** publicity film.

filmé, ~e /filme/ **I** *pp* ▶**filmer**.
II *pp adj* on film; **la version ~e de Hamlet** the film version of Hamlet.

filmer /filme/ [1] *vtr* to film.

filmique /filmik/ *adj* film (*épith*).

filon /filɔ̃/ *nm* **1** (de roches) vein, seam, lode; **~ d'or** vein of gold; **exploiter un ~** LIT, FIG to mine a seam; **2**○ (pactole) bonanza; (travail lucratif) cushy number○; **avoir trouvé le bon ~** to be on to a good thing.

filou /filu/ *nm* (escroc) crook; (tricheur) cheat; (enfant malin) rascal.

fils /fis/ *nm inv* son; **Alexandre Dumas ~** Alexandre Dumas the younger; **Dupont ~** (entreprise) Dupont Junior; **Dupont et ~** (entreprise) Dupont and Son(s); **mon ~** GÉN my boy; RELIG my son.
■ **~ de (bonne) famille** boy from a good family; **Fils de Dieu** RELIG Son of God; **Fils prodigue** BIBLE Prodigal Son; **~ spirituel** spiritual heir.

filtrant, ~e /filtʀɑ̃, ɑ̃t/ *adj* [*papier, corps, couche*] filter (*épith*).

filtre /filtʀ/ *nm* filter; **cigarette avec/sans ~** filter-tip/untipped cigarette.
■ **~ à air** air filter; **~ à café** coffee filter; **~ à huile** oil filter; **~ solaire** sun screen.

filtrer /filtʀe/ [1] **I** *vtr* **1** (purifier) to filter; **2** (tamiser) to filter [*bruit, lumière*]; **3** (sélectionner) to screen [*visiteurs, appels téléphoniques*].
II *vi* **1** (émerger) [*informations*] (lentement) to filter through; (malgré les précautions) to leak out; [*idée*] to filter through; **2** (s'écouler) [*liquide*] to filter through; **3** (passer) [*son, lumière*] to filter.

fin¹, fine¹ /fɛ̃, fin/ **I** *adj* **1** (*sable, pluie*) fine; [*fil, écriture, pinceau, pointe*] fine; [*tranche, couche, verre*] thin; **2** [*petit pois, haricots verts*] quality (*épith*); **très ~s** top-quality (*épith*); **3** (délicat) [*cheville, taille*] slender; [*traits*] fine; [*bijou, dentelle*] delicate, fine; [*vins, aliments*] fine; [*plat*] delicate; **4** (subtil) [*personne*] perceptive; [*esprit*] shrewd; [*allusion, interprétation, humour*] subtle; [*goût*] delicate, subtle; **vraiment c'est ~!** IRON that's really clever! IRON; **jouer au plus ~ avec qn** to try to outsmart sb; **avoir l'air ~○** to look a fool; **tu as l'air ~○ avec ce chapeau !** you look a sight○ in that hat!; **5** (sensible) [*odorat*] keen; **avoir l'ouïe ~e** to have a keen sense of hearing; **avoir le nez ~** to have a keen sense of smell; **6** (remarquable) excellent; **la ~e fleur des économistes** the top ou best economists; **7** (ultime) **au ~ fond de** in the remotest part of [*pays, région*]; at the very bottom of [*tiroir, armoire*]; **le ~ mot de l'histoire** the truth of the matter.
II *adv* **1** (complètement) **être ~ prêt** to be all set; **~ soûl○** completely drunk; **2** (finement) [*écrire, moudre*] finely; [*couper*] thinly.
III *nf* **le ~ du ~** the ultimate (**de** in).
■ **~ limier** super-sleuth; **~ renard** sly customer○; **~e gueule○** gourmet; **~e mouche** = **~ renard**; **~es herbes** mixed herbs, fines herbes.

fin² /fɛ̃/ *nf* **1** (terme) end; (de réunion, période) close, end; (façon dont se termine quelque chose) ending; **à la ~ des années 70** in the late '70s; **en ~ de matinée** late in the morning; **jusqu'à la ~** to the (very) end; **toucher** or **tirer à sa ~** to be coming ou drawing to an end; **prendre ~** to come to an end; **avoir des ~s de mois difficiles** to find it hard to make ends meet at the end of the month; **c'est la ~ de tout** it's the last straw; **mener qch à bonne ~** to bring sth to a successful conclusion; **sans ~** [*discussions*] endless; [*discuter*] endlessly; **tu vas te taire à la ~○!** for God's sake, be quiet!; **tu m'ennuies à la ~○!** you're really getting on my nerves!; **chômeur en ~ de droits** unemployed person no longer eligible for benefit; **~ de siècle** PEJ decadent, fin-de-siècle; **2** (mort) end, death; **3** (but) end, aim, purpose; **à toutes ~s utiles** for whatever purpose it may serve; **arriver à ses ~s** to achieve one's aims.

■ **~ de semaine** weekend; **~ de série** COMM oddment.

final, **~e**[1], mpl **-aux** /final, o/ adj final.

finale[2] /final/ nm MUS finale.

finale[3] /final/ nf **1** SPORT final; **quart de ~** quarterfinal; **2** LING final; **en ~** in final position.

finalement /finalmã/ adv **1** (à la fin) in the end, finally; **2** (en définitive) in fact, actually; **~ on a tout à y gagner** after all, we have everything to gain by it.

finaliser /finalize/ [1] vtr to finalize [accords]; to complete [transaction].

finaliste /finalist/ adj, nmf finalist.

finalité /finalite/ nf **1** GÉN purpose, aim; **2** PHILOS finality.

finance /finãs/ **I** nf **1** (activité) **la ~** finance; **un homme de ~** financier; **2** (milieu) financiers (pl).

II finances nfpl **les ~s** finances; **moyennant ~s** for a consideration; **les ~s sont à sec**○ funds are exhausted; **mes ~s sont à sec**○ I'm broke○; **les Finances**○ (ministère) the Ministry (sg) of Finance.

financement /finãsmã/ nm financing ₵.

financer /finãse/ [12] **I** vtr to finance.

II○ vi (payer) to fork out○.

financier, -ière /finãsje, ɛʀ/ **I** adj [directeur, crise] financial; **compagnie financière** finance company.

II nm **1** (personne) financier; **2** CULIN small cake (made with ground almonds and egg whites).

finasser /finase/ [1] vi to scheme, to use trickery.

finaud, ~e /fino, od/ **I** adj cunning, wily.

II nm,f (homme) wily bird○; (femme) crafty minx.

fine[2] /fin/ nf (boisson) brandy.

finement /finmã/ adv **1** [ouvragé, tissé] finely, delicately; [hacher, couper] finely; **2** (avec subtilité) cleverly; **c'est ~ joué!** that's a smart ou shrewd move!; **3** (avec précision) [mesurer] accurately, precisely.

finesse /finɛs/ nf **1** (minceur) (d'aiguille, écriture, de fil, cheveux) fineness; (de couche, papier) thinness; (de lame) keenness, sharpness; **2** (délicatesse) (de broderie, bijou, parfum, d'aliment) delicacy; (de visage) fineness, delicacy; (de chevilles, taille) slenderness; **3** (perspicacité) (de personne, remarque) perceptiveness; (d'acteur, interprétation) sensitivity, finesse; **4** (acuité des sens) keenness, sharpness; **5** (subtilité) **les ~s d'une langue** the subtleties of a language.

finette /finɛt/ nf brushed cotton.

fini, ~e /fini/ **I** pp ▶ **finir**.

II pp adj **1** (terminé) **être ~** to be over, to be finished; **~ de rire!**, **~e la rigolade**○! the party's over!; **c'en est ~ de leurs espoirs** it's the end of their hopes; **2** (ouvragé) finished; **produits ~s** finished products; **3**○ (invétéré) [menteur, alcoolique] out-and-out, complete; **4**○ (usé) [artiste, politicien] finished; **5** MATH [ensemble, univers] finite.

III nm finish.

finir /finir/ [3] **I** vtr **1** (achever) to finish (off), to complete [travail, tâche]; (conclure) to end [journée, nuit, discours]; **~ de faire** to finish doing; **finissez vos querelles!** put a stop to your quarrelling○GB!; **pour ~, je dirai que** in conclusion I'll say that; **vous n'avez pas fini de vous disputer?** for goodness sake stop arguing!; **tu n'as pas fini de te plaindre?** have you quite finished complaining?; **elle n'a pas fini de s'inquiéter** her worries are only just beginning; **tu n'as pas fini d'en entendre parler!** you haven't heard the last of it!; **2** (consommer jusqu'au bout) to use up [provisions, produit]; to finish [plat].

II vi to finish, to end; **le film finit bien/mal** the film has a happy/an unhappy ending; **ça va mal ~!** it'll end in tears!; **il finira mal ce garçon** that boy will come to a bad end; **sa barbe finit en pointe** his beard tapers to a point; **~ en prison** to end up in prison; **tu vas ~ par te blesser** you'll end up hurting yourself; **ils finiront bien par céder** they're bound to give in in the end; **il a fini par se décider** he eventually made up his mind; **finissons-en!** let's get it over with!; **il faut en ~ avec cette situation** we must put an end to this situation; **l'hiver n'en finit**

pas the winter seems endless; **il n'en finit pas ce feu rouge!** is this red light ever going to change?; **elle a des jambes qui n'en finissent pas** she's all legs; **elle n'en finit pas de se préparer** she takes ages○ to get ready; **des discussions à n'en plus ~** endless discussions; ▶ **queue**.

finish /finiʃ/ nm SPORT finish; **il l'a emporté au ~** he won at the finishing-line.

finissant, ~e /finisã, ãt/ adj **une époque ~e** an era which is drawing to an end; **à l'été ~** in the last days of the summer.

finition /finisjɔ̃/ nf (processus) finishing; (résultat) finish; **faire les ~s** to add the finishing touches (de to); **travaux de ~** finishing.

finlandais, ~e /fɛ̃lɑ̃dɛ, ɛz/ ▶ **394** | adj Finnish.

Finlandais, ~e /fɛ̃lɑ̃dɛ, ɛz/ ▶ **394** | nm,f Finn.

Finlande /fɛ̃lɑ̃d/ ▶ **232** | nprf Finland.

finnois, ~e /finwa, az/ ▶ **338** | **I** adj Finnish.

II nm LING Finnish.

fiole /fjɔl/ nf (flacon) phial.

fion○ /fjɔ̃/ nm H (mot blessant) cutting remark.

fioriture /fjɔrityr/ nf **1** (ornement) embellishment; **sans ~s** [meuble, pièce] unadorned; [écriture] plain; [parler, écrire] plainly; **2** MUS ornamentation.

fioul /fjul/ nm fuel oil.

■ **~ domestique** heating oil.

firmament /firmamã/ nm **1** (ciel) firmament; **2** FIG **au ~ du succès** at the pinnacle of success.

firme /firm/ nf firm.

fisc /fisk/ nm tax office.

fiscal, ~e, mpl **-aux** /fiskal, o/ adj fiscal, tax (épith).

fiscaliser /fiskalize/ [1] vtr **1** (imposer) to tax; **2** (financer par l'impôt) to fund [sth] by taxation.

fiscalité /fiskalite/ nf **1** (fait d'imposer) taxation; **2** (système) tax system.

fissible /fisibl/ adj fissionable, fissile.

fission /fisjɔ̃/ nf fission; **~ nucléaire** nuclear fission.

fissionner /fisjone/ [1] vtr, vi to split.

fissure /fisyr/ nf **1** (fente) crack; **2** ANAT fissure; **3** FIG rift.

fissurer /fisyre/ [1] vtr **1** (fendiller) to crack, to fissure SPÉC; **2** (diviser) to cause a rift in [amitié, union].

fiston○ /fistɔ̃/ nm sonny○, son.

fixateur /fiksatœr/ nm **1** ART, PHOT (produit) fixative; (appareil) (à main) fixative sprayer; (à bouche) fixative mouth blower; **2** (après une permanente) neutralizing solution; (laque) fixative; (de parfum) fixative; **3** BIOL (pour analyse) fixative.

fixation /fiksasjɔ̃/ nf **1** (mise en place) fixing; (attache) fastening; **2** (détermination) setting; **~ de la peine** JUR determination of penalty; **~ des cours** (en Bourse) fixing; **3** SPORT (de ski) binding; **4** (d'azote, oxygène) fixation; **5** BOT, ZOOL (processus) attachment; (attache) (de plante) stem; (de mollusque) foot; **6** ART, PHOT (de pastel, photo) fixing; **7** LING fossilization; **8** (de population) settling; **9** PSYCH fixation.

fixe /fiks/ **I** adj **1** (immobile) [caméra, point] fixed; **avoir le regard** or **l'œil ~** to have a fixed stare; **2** (invariable) [prix, taux] fixed; [poste, résidence] permanent; **à heures ~s** at set times.

II nm (salaire) basic salary GB, base pay US.

III excl MIL attention!

fixé, ~e /fikse/ **I** pp ▶ **fixer**.

II pp adj **1** (renseigné) **tu es ~ maintenant!** you've got the picture now○!; **nous ne sommes pas encore ~s sur leur sort** we are still uncertain about their fate; **2** (certain) **nous ne sommes pas encore très ~s** we haven't really decided yet; **3** (orienté) **le monde entier a les yeux ~s sur vous** the whole world is watching you; **4** (installé) [famille] settled.

III nm ART glass-picture.

fixement /fiksmã/ adv [regarder] fixedly.

fixer /fikse/ [1] **I** vtr **1** (attacher) to fix [objet] (à to; sur on); **~ avec des boulons/des vis/de la colle** to bolt/to screw/to stick (sur to); **2** (décider) to set [date, prix, conditions]; **~ son choix sur qch/qn** to decide on sth/sb; **au jour fixé** on the appointed day; **3** (établir) **~ son domicile en France** to make one's home in France; **~ le siège de l'organisation à Paris** to base the organization's headquarters in Paris; **4** (stabiliser) to fix [*couleur, émulsion*]; to establish [*frontières, forme littéraire*]; to regulate [*orthographe, langue*]; **~ ses idées par écrit** to set one's ideas down in writing; **5** (concentrer) to focus [*attention, regard*]; **6** (observer) to stare at [*personne, objet*].

II se fixer *vpr* **1** TECH (s'attacher) [*pièce*] to be attached (à to); **2** (décider) to set oneself [*but, limite*]; **3** (s'installer) [*personne*] to settle; (se ranger) [*personne*] to settle down; **4** (se figer) **se ~ dans l'esprit/la mémoire de qn** to stick in sb's mind/memory; **leur système d'écriture s'est fixé dès l'antiquité** their writing system was established in ancient times; **5** ZOOL [*coquillage, moule*] to attach itself (**à, sur** to).

fjord /fjɔʀd/ *nm* fjord.

flacon /flakɔ̃/ *nm* (bouteille) (small) bottle; (carafe) decanter; CHIMIE flask.

flagada◦ /flagada/ *adj inv* whacked◦, exhausted.

flagellation /flaʒɛlasjɔ̃/ *nf* GÉN flogging, scourging; RELIG flagellation.

flageller /flaʒele/ [1] *vtr* to flog; RELIG to flagellate.

flageoler /flaʒɔle/ [1] *vi* **~ avoir les jambes qui flageolent** to feel wobbly; **2** [*amitié*] to crumble.

flageolet /flaʒɔlɛ/ *nm* **1** (haricot) flageolet; **2** ▶392| (flûte) flageolet.

flagorner /flagɔʀne/ [1] *vtr* to fawn on, to toady to [*personne*]; to curry favour^{GB} with [*groupe, public*].

flagornerie /flagɔʀnəʀi/ *nf* toadying ℂ, sycophantic behaviour^{GB} ℂ.

flagrant, ~e /flagʀɑ̃, ɑ̃t/ *adj* [*preuve*] obvious; [*injustice*] flagrant; [*mensonge*] blatant; [*erreur, exemple*] glaring.
■ **~ délit** JUR *case requiring no further collection of evidence*; **en ~ délit** in flagrante delicto; **prendre qn en ~ délit** to catch sb red-handed.

flair /flɛʀ/ *nm* **1** (odorat) nose; **avoir du ~** to have a good nose; **2** (intuition) intuition.

flairer /fleʀe/ [1] *vtr* **1** (renifler) to sniff [*objet, vêtement*]; **le chien a flairé une piste** the dog has picked up a scent; **2** (sentir) [*animal*] to scent [*gibier, personne*]; [*personne*] to smell [*odeur*]; **3** (discerner) to sense [*danger*].
IDIOMES **~ le vent** to see which way the wind is blowing.

flamand, ~e /flamɑ̃, ɑ̃d/ *adj* Flemish.
II ▶338| *nm* LING Flemish.

flamant /flamɑ̃/ *nm* flamingo.
■ **~ rose** pink flamingo.

flambant /flɑ̃bɑ̃/ *adv* **~ neuf** brand new.

flambeau, *pl* **~x** /flɑ̃bo/ *nm* **1** (torche) torch; **retraite aux ~x** torchlight procession; **2** FIG torch (**de** of); **3** (chandelier) candlestick.

flambée /flɑ̃be/ *nf* **1** (feu) fire; **faire une ~** to light a fire; **2** (de violence) flare-up; (des prix) explosion (**de** in).

flamber /flɑ̃be/ [1] **I** *vtr* **1** CULIN (à la flamme) to singe [*volaille*]; (avec de l'alcool) to flambé [*crêpe, omelette*] (**à** in); **2** MÉD to sterilize [sth] in a flame; **3**◦ (dépenser) to blow◦ [*argent, économies*].
II *vi* **1** LIT [*combustible*] to burn; [*maison*] to burn down; **2** (augmenter) [*prix, cours*] to soar.

flambeur◦, **-euse** /flɑ̃bœʀ, øz/ *nm,f* **1** (dépensier) big spender; **2** (joueur) big-time gambler.

flamboiement /flɑ̃bwamɑ̃/ *nm* (de feu) blaze; **le ~ des arbres en automne** FIG the flaming colours^{GB} (*pl*) of the trees in autumn GB ou the fall US.

flamboyant, ~e /flɑ̃bwajɑ̃, ɑ̃t/ **I** *adj* **1** GÉN [*feu, lumière*] blazing; [*couleur*] flaming; [*ciel, coucher de soleil*] fiery; **chevelure ~e** flaming red hair; **2** ARCHIT gothique **~** Flamboyant Gothic.
II *nm* **1** BOT flame tree; **2** ARCHIT Flamboyant (Gothic) style.

flamboyer /flɑ̃bwaje/ [23] *vi* [*incendie, soleil, couleur*] to blaze; [*yeux*] GÉN to flash; (de colère) to blaze (**de** with); [*épée*] to gleam.

flamingant, ~e /flamɛ̃gɑ̃, ɑ̃t/ **I** *adj* LING [*population, région*] Flemish-speaking.
II *nm,f* **1** LING Flemish speaker; **2** POL Flemish nationalist.

flamme /flam/ **I** *nf* **1** (feu) flame; **passer une volaille à la ~** to singe a fowl; **2** (passion amoureuse) love; **3** (ardeur) **parler avec ~** to speak passionately; **ranimer la ~ d'une tradition** to rekindle a tradition; **4** (marque postale) postmark caption.
II flammes *nfpl* (feu) fire ℂ; **en ~s** on fire.
IDIOMES **descendre qn/qch en ~s**◦ to shoot sb/sth down; **jeter feu et ~** [*personne*] to be raging; **être tout feu tout ~** [*personne*] to be wildly enthusiastic.

flammèche /flamɛʃ/ *nf* spark.

flan /flɑ̃/ *nm* CULIN (crème) ≈ custard; (tarte) custard tart GB ou flan US.
IDIOMES **faire qch au ~**◦ to do sth brazenly; **y aller au ~**◦ to bluff; **en rester comme deux ronds de ~**◦ to be dumbfounded.

flanc /flɑ̃/ *nm* **1** ANAT (de personne) side; (d'animal) flank, side; **le cheval battait des ~s** the horse was panting; **être sur le ~**◦ to be exhausted; **2** (entrailles) GÉN entrails (*pl*); (de femme) womb; **3** (de montagne) side; **4** (de navire) side, beam end; **5** MIL flank.
IDIOMES **se battre les ~s**◦ to strive in vain; **tirer au ~**◦ to shirk, to skive◦ GB; **prêter le ~ à la critique** to lay oneself open to criticism.

flancher◦ /flɑ̃ʃe/ [1] *vi* **1** (manquer de courage) to lose one's nerve; (ne plus faire face) to crack up; (devant une décision) to crack; **2** (faiblir) [*cœur, moteur*] to give out; [*mémoire*] to let [sb] down; [*jambes*] to go wobbly.

flanchet /flɑ̃ʃɛ/ *nm* CULIN flank.

flanelle /flanɛl/ *nf* flannel; **jupe de ~** flannel skirt.
■ **~ de coton** flannelette.

flâner /flane/ [1] *vi* **1** (se promener) to stroll; (s'attarder) to dawdle; **2** (paresser) to loaf◦ around.

flânerie /flɑnʀi/ *nf* **1** (promenade) stroll; **2** (inaction) lazing around.

flâneur, -euse /flɑnœʀ, øz/ *nm,f* **1** (promeneur) stroller; **2** (paresseux) loafer◦ US.

flanquer /flɑ̃ke/ [1] **I** *vtr* **1** (garnir) to flank [*construction, meuble*] (**de** by); **il est toujours flanqué de son adjoint** his assistant never leaves his side; **2**◦ (mettre) to give [*coup, gifle, amende*]; **~ qch par terre** (jeter) to throw sth to the ground; (faire tomber) to knock sth to the ground; **~ la frousse**◦ ou **la trouille**◦ **à qn** to give sb a fright; **~ qn dehors** ou **à la porte** (d'un travail) to fire sb; (d'un lieu) to chuck◦ sb out.
II se flanquer◦ *vpr* **se ~ dans** to run into; **se ~ sous un train** to throw oneself under a train; **se ~ par terre** to fall flat on one's face.

flapi◦, **~e** /flapi/ *adj* fagged out◦ GB, shot◦ US, worn out.

flaque /flak/ *nf* **~ (d'eau)** puddle; **~ d'huile** pool of oil.

flash, *pl* **~es** /flaʃ/ *nm* **1** PHOT flash; **2** RADIO, TV **~ (d'information)** (programmé) news headlines (*pl*); (exceptionnel) news flash.
■ **~ publicitaire** advert GB, commercial US.

flasher◦ /flaʃe/ [1] *vi* **~ sur** to fall in love with.

flasque[1] /flask/ *adj* [*peau*] flabby; [*traits*] slack.

flasque[2] /flask/ *nf* (flacon) flask.

flatter /flate/ [1] **I** *vtr* **1** (complimenter) to flatter [*personne*]; **~ bassement qn** to toady to sb; **2** (honorer) **leur visite a flatté tout le village** the whole village felt honoured^{GB} by their visit; **3** (encourager) to encourage [*sentiment, vice*]; **~ qn dans son amour-propre** to boost sb's ego; **4** (caresser) to pat [*animal*]; **5** (être agréable) to delight [*narines, regard*]; **6** (avantager) [*vêtement, éclairage*] to flatter [*personne*].
II se flatter *vpr* **1** (prétendre) **je me flatte de m'exprimer au moins de façon claire** I flatter myself that I'm at least articulate; **2** (tirer vanité) to pride oneself (**de** on; **de faire** on doing).

flatterie /flatʀi/ *nf* flattery ℂ; **de basses ~s** toadying ℂ.

flatteur, -euse /flatœʀ, øz/ **I** *adj* **1** (avantageux)

Les fleuves et les rivières

L'anglais ne distingue pas entre fleuve *et* rivière; *dans les deux cas, c'est le mot* river *qui est utilisé, avec ou sans majuscule.*

Les noms de fleuves et de rivières

L'anglais utilise toujours l'article défini devant les noms de fleuves et de rivières.

le Nil = the Nile
l'Amazone = the Amazon
la Saône = the Saône

Le mot river *est parfois utilisé, mais n'est jamais obligatoire. En anglais britannique, il est avant le nom propre, en anglais américain il est après.*

la Tamise = the River Thames (*GB*)
              ou the river Thames
le Potomac = the Potomac River (*US*)
              ou the Potomac river

De avec les noms de fleuves et de rivières

Les expressions françaises avec de se traduisent en général par l'emploi des noms de fleuves et de rivières en position d'adjectifs.

un affluent de la Tamise = a Thames tributary
l'eau de la Seine = Seine water
l'estuaire de la Tamise = the Thames estuary
les industries de la Tamise = Thames industries
les péniches de la Tamise = Thames barges

Mais:

l'embouchure de la Tamise = the mouth of the Thames
la source de la Tamise = the source of the Thames

[*portrait, éclairage*] flattering; [*distinction, récompense*] gratifying; **sous un jour** ~ in a favourable^{GB} light; **2** (obséquieux) [*personne, paroles*] sycophantic.
II *nm,f* toady, sycophant.

flatulence /flatylɑ̃s/ *nf* wind **℄**, flatulence **℄** SPÉC.

fléau, *pl* ~**x** /fleo/ *nm* **1** (calamité) scourge; **le** ~ **de Dieu** the scourge of God; **2** (nuisance) (chose) curse; (personne) pest; **3** (outil agricole) flail; **4** (de balance) beam.
■ ~ **d'armes** HIST flail.

flèche /flɛʃ/ *nf* **1** (arme) arrow; **pointe de** ~ arrowhead; **les** ~**s de l'Amour** Love's darts; **partir/passer en** or **comme une** ~ to shoot off/to shoot past; **monter en** ~ [*fusée*] to shoot upward(s); [*prix*] to soar; ▶ **Parthe**; **2** (signe) arrow; **3** (raillerie) barbed remark; **4** (d'église) spire.
IDIOMES **il fait** ~ **de tout bois** it's all grist to his mill.

flécher /fleʃe/ [14] *vtr* to signpost.

fléchette /fleʃɛt/ ▶ 329 *nf* (objet) dart; (activité) darts (+ *v sg*).

fléchi, ~**e** /fleʃi/ *adj* LING inflected.

fléchir /fleʃiʀ/ [3] **I** *vtr* **1** (plier) to bend; **2** (ébranler) to sway [*personne, opinion*]; to weaken [*volonté*].
II *vi* **1** (ployer) [*poutre*] to sag; [*genoux*] to bend; [*jambes*] to give way; **2** (faiblir) [*attention*] to flag; [*courage*] to waver; [*volonté*] to weaken; [*production, demande*] to fall off; [*prix*] to fall (**de** by); **3** (céder) [*personne, armée*] to yield; (s'adoucir) [*personne*] to relent; **sans** ~ (stoïquement) unflinchingly; (obstinément) stubbornly.

flegmatique /flɛgmatik/ *adj* phlegmatic.

flegme /flɛgm/ *nm* (placidité) phlegm, composure.

flémingite○ /flemɛ̃ʒit/ *nf* HUM bone idleness; **il a une** ~ **aiguë** he's suffering from acute bone idleness.

flemmard○, ~**e** /flemaʀ, aʀd/ **I** *adj* bone idle (*jamais épith*).
II *nm,f* lazybones○ (+ *v sg*), lazy devil○.

flemmarder○ /flemaʀde/ [1] *vi* to loaf○ around; ~ **au lit** to lie in.

flemme○ /flɛm/ *nf* laziness; **j'ai la** ~ **de faire** I'm too lazy to do; **tirer sa** ~ to laze around.

flétan /fletɑ̃/ *nm* halibut.

flétrir /fletʀiʀ/ [3] **I** *vtr* **1** (faner) **le temps a flétri sa**

---

beauté her beauty has faded with time; **2** (stigmatiser) to blacken [*nom*]; **3** (souiller) to corrupt [*enfant*].
II se flétrir *vpr* **1** [*plante*] to wither; [*fleur*] to fade; [*fruit*] to shrivel; **2** [*beauté, peau*] to fade.

flétrissement /fletʀismɑ̃/ *nm* **1** (de peau) withering; **2** BOT wilt.

fleur /flœʀ/ *nf* **1** BOT flower; **être en** ~**s** [*jardin*] to be full of flowers; [*camélia*] to be in bloom ou flowering; [*poirier, lilas*] to be in blossom; **à** ~**s** flowery; **2** (le meilleur) **la** (**fine**) ~ **des arts** the flower of the art world; **dans la** ~ **de l'âge** in the prime of life; **3** (niveau) **à** ~ **d'eau** [*rocher*] just above the water; **4** (de cuir) grain; **côté** ~ grain layer.
■ ~ **des champs** wild flower; ~ **de farine** superfine white flour; ~ **de lys** fleur-de-lis, heraldic lily; ~ **d'oranger** (fleurs) orange blossom; (arôme) orange flower water.
IDIOMES **être** ~ **bleue** to be starry-eyed ou romantic; **avoir une sensibilité à** ~ **de peau** to be hypersensitive; **avoir les nerfs à** ~ **de peau** to be a bundle of nerves; **couvrir qn de** ~**s** to shower sb with compliments; **envoyer des** ~**s à qn**○ to pat sb on the back; **faire une** ~ **à qn**○ to do sb a favour^{GB}; **arriver** or **s'amener**○ **comme une** ~ to turn up just like that.

fleurdelisé, ~**e** /flœʀdəlize/ *adj* GÉN [*drapeau, manteau*] decorated with fleurs-de-lis (*après n*).

fleurer /flœʀe/ [1] *vtr* to be fragrant with.

fleuret /flœʀɛ/ ▶ 329 *nm* SPORT (épée) foil; (discipline) foil.
■ ~ **moucheté** buttoned foil.

fleurette /flœʀɛt/ *nf* CULIN **crème** ~ whipping cream.
IDIOMES **conter** ~† **à qn** to woo† sb.

fleurettiste /flœʀɛtist/ *nmf* SPORT foil fencer.

fleuri, ~**e** /flœʀi/ **I** *pp* ▶ **fleurir**.
II *pp adj* **1** [*champs, jardin*] full of flowers; [*arbre*] (de petites fleurs) in blossom; (de grosses fleurs) in bloom; **2** (décoré) [*table*] decorated with flowers; [*papier*] flowery; **3** [*teint*] florid, ruddy; [*nez*] spotty GB, pimply; **barbe** ~**e** hoary beard; **4** [*style*] flowery PÉJ.

fleurir /flœʀiʀ/ [3] **I** *vtr* to decorate [sth] with flowers [*maison, table*]; to put flowers on [*tombe*]; to put a flower in [*boutonnière*].
II *vi* **1** [*rosier*] to flower, to bloom; [*cerisier*] to blossom; **2** (apparaître) [*supermarchés*] to spring up; [*affiches*] to appear; **3** (prospérer) to thrive; **4** (se couvrir de boutons) [*visage*] to come out in spots GB ou pimples.

fleuriste /flœʀist/ ▶ 374 **I** *nmf* (commerçant) florist.
II *nm* (magasin) flower shop, florist's.

fleuron /flœʀɔ̃/ *nm* **1** FIG (joyau) jewel (in the crown); **2** GÉN, ARCHIT fleuron; (de pignon) finial; **3** BOT floret.

fleuve /flœv/ **I** *nm* **1** GÉOG river; **2** (flot de boue, lave) river (**de** of); ~ **de larmes** flood of tears.
II (-)**fleuve** (*in* compounds) **discours/procès**(-)~ interminable speech/trial.
■ ~ **Bleu** Yangtze, Chang Jiang; ~ **Jaune** Yellow River, Huang He; ~ **Rouge** Red River, Song Koi.

flexible /flɛksibl/ **I** *adj* **1** (souple) [*branche*] pliable; [*lame, tuyau*] flexible; [*corps*] supple; **2** (adaptable) flexible; **3** (docile) [*personne, caractère*] malleable.
II *nm* (tuyau souple) ~ **de cimentation** cementing hose; ~ **de douche** shower hose; ~ **de gaz** rubber gas pipe; ~ **de robinet** nozzle.

flexion /flɛksjɔ̃/ *nf* **1** (d'objet) bending; (de bras, jambe) flexing; **2** LING inflection.

flexionnel, -**elle** /flɛksjɔnɛl/ *adj* [*langue*] inflected; [*forme, marque*] inflectional.

flibustier /flibystje/ *nm* **1** HIST (pirate) freebooter; **2** (escroc) swindler.

flic○ /flik/ *nm* PÉJ cop○, policeman.

flip /flip/ *nm* **1**○ (dépression) **être le** ~ [*film*] to be a real downer○; [*lieu*] to be creepy○; **être en plein** ~ [*drogué*] to freak out○; **2 porto** ~ egg flip (*with port*).

flipper¹ /flipœʀ/ ▶ 329 *nm* JEUX (billard électrique) pinball machine; (pièce mobile) flipper; (jeu) pinball.

flipper²○ /flipe/ [1] *vi* (être perturbé) to freak out○; (être déprimé) to be depressed ou down○; **complètement**

flippé off his head○; **ta maison me fait ~** your house gives me the creeps○.

flirt /flœrt/ *nm* **1** (activité) flirting (**avec** with); **2** (relation) LIT flirtation, brief romance; FIG flirtation; **3** (personne) boyfriend/girlfriend.

flirter /flœrte/ [1] *vi* to flirt (**avec** with).

flocon /flɔkɔ̃/ *nm* (de neige, savon) flake; (de poussière) speck; (de laine) bit; (de fumée) wisp.
■ **~s d'avoine** oat flakes GB, oatmeal ¢ US; **~s de pomme de terre** instant mashed potato mix (*sg*).

floconneux, -euse /flɔkɔnø, øz/ *adj* **1** GÉN [*laine, nuage*] fleecy; [*neige*] powdery; **2** CHIMIE [*précipité*] flocculent.

flonflons /flɔ̃flɔ̃/ *nmpl* **1** MUS brass band music ¢; **2** FIG **il a été accueilli sous les ~** they put out the red carpet for him.

flop○ /flɔp/ *nm* (échec) flop; **faire un ~** to flop.

flopée○ /flɔpe/ *nf* (**toute) une ~ de gamins/livres** a whole load○ GB ou slew○ US of kids/books, masses (*pl*) of kids/books.

floraison /flɔrɛzɔ̃/ *nf* **1** (de fleurs) flowering, blooming; **2** (de talents) flowering; (d'entreprises) rash.

floral, ~e, *mpl* **-aux** /flɔral, o/ *adj* [*exposition, composition*] flower (*épith*); [*art, organe*] floral.

floralies /flɔrali/ *nfpl* flower show.

flore /flɔr/ *nf* **1** (végétation) flora; **2** (ouvrage) flora, botanical handbook.
■ **~ intestinale** intestinal flora.

florentin, ~e /flɔrɑ̃tɛ̃, in/ I ▶ **628** *adj* Florentine.
II *nm* CULIN Florentine.

florilège /flɔrilɛʒ/ *nm* anthology.

florin /flɔrɛ̃/ ▶ **33** *nm* **1** (monnaie des Pays-Bas) guilder; **2** HIST (ancienne monnaie) florin.

florissant, ~e /flɔrisɑ̃, ɑ̃t/ *adj* **1** [*activité, économie, pays*] thriving; [*théorie*] fashionable; **2** [*teint*] ruddy; **il est d'une santé ~e** he's blooming.

flot /flo/ I *nm* **1** (grande quantité) (de courrier, réfugiés) flood; (de questions, visiteurs) stream; (de critique) torrent; **2** (marée) LITER tide; **3** (en équitation) rosette.
II à flot *loc adv* **couler à ~(s)** LIT, FIG to flow; **être à ~** LIT, FIG to be buoyant; **remettre un navire à ~** to refloat a boat; **remettre qn/qch à ~** FIG to put sb/sth back on their/its feet.
III flots *nmpl* LITER **les ~s** the billows LITTÉR, the deep (*sg*) LITER.

flottaison /flɔtɛzɔ̃/ *nf* NAUT **ligne de ~** waterline.

flottant, ~e /flɔtɑ̃, ɑ̃t/ *adj* **1** [*bois, ligne, mine*] floating; [*nuage*] drifting; **2** [*vêtements, cheveux*] flowing.

flotte /flɔt/ *nf* **1** AVIAT, NAUT fleet; **2**○ (pluie) rain; **3**○ (eau) water; **4** (flotteur) float.
■ **~ aérienne** air fleet; **~ de guerre** MIL naval fleet.

flottement /flɔtmɑ̃/ *nm* (indécision) wavering ¢.

flotter /flɔte/ [1] I *vi* **1** (sur un liquide) to float (**sur** on; **dans** in); **~ à la dérive** to drift; **2** (dans l'air) [*brume*] to drift; [*drapeau*] to fly; **un sourire flottait sur ses lèvres** a smile hovered on his/her lips; **~ au vent** [*drapeau*] to flutter in the wind; [*cheveux*] to stream in the wind; **elle flotte dans ses vêtements** her clothes are hanging off her; **3** FIN [*monnaie*] to float.
II *v impers* (pleuvoir) to rain.

flotteur /flɔtœr/ *nm* (de ligne, filet, d'hydravion) float; (de chasse d'eau) ballcock.

flottille /flɔtij/ *nf* flotilla.
■ **~ de pêche** fishing fleet.

flou, ~e /flu/ I *adj* **1** LIT [*photo*] blurred; [*coiffure*] soft; [*vêtement*] loose; **2** FIG [*concept, style*] vague, woolly PÉJ; [*souvenir, personnage*] vague; [*passé*] hazy.
II *nm* **1** LIT (de contour) fuzziness; **2** FIG vagueness.
■ **~ artistique** CIN, PHOT soft focus; FIG artistry.

flouer○ /flue/ [1] *vtr* to cheat [*personne*]; **se faire ~** to be had○.

fluctuant, ~e /flyktɥɑ̃, ɑ̃t/ *adj* [*cours, opinion*] fluctuating; [*personne, temps*] fickle; [*opinion*] fluctuating.

fluet, -ette /flyɛ, ɛt/ *adj* [*corps, personne*] slight; [*bras, jambe*] frail; [*voix*] thin.

fluide /flɥid/ I *adj* [*huile, peinture*] fluid; [*style*] fluent; [*circulation*] moving freely (*jamais épith*); [*situation*] fluid.
II *nm* **1** PHYS fluid; **2** (de médium) (psychic) powers (*pl*).

fluidifier /flɥidifje/ [2] *vtr* to thin [*sang*]; to loosen [*mucosité*].

fluidité /flɥidite/ *nf* **1** PHYS fluidity; **2** (de style, diction) fluency; (de vêtement) flowing lines (*pl*).

fluo○ /flyo/ I ▶ **141** *adj inv* fluorescent.
II *nm* **la mode du ~** the fashion for Day-glo®.

fluor /flyɔr/ *nm* fluorine; **dentifrice au ~** fluoride toothpaste.

fluoré, ~e /flyɔre/ *adj* fluoride (*épith*).

fluorescent, ~e /flyɔrɛsɑ̃, ɑ̃t/ *adj* fluorescent.

flûte /flyt/ I *nf* **1** ▶ **392** MUS flute; **petite ~** piccolo; **2** (verre) (champagne) flute; **3** (pain) French loaf; **4**○ (jambe) leg.
II○ *excl* damn○!, darn it○!
■ **~ à bec** recorder; **~ de Pan** panpipes (*pl*); **~ traversière** (transverse) flute.

flûté, ~e /flyte/ *adj* [*voix, son*] piping (*épith*).

flûtiau, *pl* **~x** /flytjo/ ▶ **392** *nm* **1** (flûte champêtre) pipe; **2** (flûte d'enfant) penny whistle.

flûtiste /flytist/ ▶ **374** *nmf* flautist, flutist US.

fluvial, ~e, *mpl* **-iaux** /flyvjal, o/ *adj* [*érosion, plaine*] fluvial; [*port, bassin, transport*] river (*épith*).

flux /fly/ *nm inv* **1** (écoulement) flow; **2** PHYS flux; **3** ÉCON flow; **4** (marée) flood tide; **le ~ et le reflux** LIT flood tide and ebb tide; FIG the ebb and flow; **5** (mouvement) influx; **~ migratoire** influx of immigrants.

FMI /ɛfɛmi/ *nm*: *abbr* ▶ **fonds**.

FO /ɛfo/ *nf*: *abbr* ▶ **force**.

foc /fɔk/ *nm* jib.

focal, ~e¹, *mpl* **-aux** /fɔkal, o/ *adj* focal.

focale² /fɔkal/ *nf* (distance) focal length; (objectif)○ lens.

focaliser /fɔkalize/ [1] *vtr* **1** PHYS to focus [*rayons*]; to focalize [*faisceau d'électrons*]; **2** (concentrer) to focus [*espoirs, attention*]; to concentrate [*efforts*].

fœtus /fetys/ *nm inv* foetus.

fofolle /fɔfɔl/ ▶ **foufou**.

foi /fwa/ *nf* **1** RELIG faith; **avoir la ~** to be a believer; ▶ **montagne**; **2** (confiance) faith; **ajouter ~ à qch** to put faith in sth; **3** (sincérité) **ma ~ oui** well yes; **faire qch de bonne ~** or **en toute bonne ~** to do sth with the best intentions; **en toute bonne ~ je crois que** in all sincerity, I believe that; **il est de bonne ~** he is genuine; **bonne/mauvaise ~** PHILOS good/bad faith; **de bonne ~** JUR bona fide (*épith*); **elle est d'une incroyable mauvaise ~** she's so insincere; **4** (assurance) **sur la ~ de témoins** on the evidence of witnesses; **sur la ~ de documents** on the strength of documents; **en ~ de quoi** in witness whereof; **qui fait** or **faisant ~** [*texte, signature*] authentic; **sous la ~ du serment** under oath.
IDIOMES **voir avec les yeux de la ~** to see only what one wants to see; **sans ~ ni loi** fearing neither God nor man.

foie /fwa/ *nm* **1** ANAT liver; **avoir mal au ~** ≈ to have an upset stomach; **crise de ~** indigestion; **2** CULIN liver; **~ gras** foie gras.
IDIOMES **se ronger les ~s** to worry.

foin /fwɛ̃/ I *nm* **1** (herbe) hay ¢; **tas de ~** haystack; **faire les ~s** to make hay; **saison des ~s** haymaking season; ▶ **bête**; **2** (tabac sans goût) old socks○ (*pl*).
II‡ *excl* **~ de vos conseils/richesses!** I pour scorn on your advice/wealth!
■ **~ d'artichaut** choke.
IDIOMES **faire du ~**○ (faire du bruit) to make a hell of a racket ou noise○; (faire du scandale) to cause a scandal.

foire /fwar/ *nf* **1** COMM fair; **2** (fête foraine) fun fair; **3**○ (bruit, confusion) bedlam; **faire la ~**○ to live it up○; ▶ **larron**.

fois /fwa/ I *nf inv* time; **une ~** once; **deux ~** twice; **trois ~** three times; **deux ou trois ~** two or three times; **deux ~ et demie** two and a half times; **quatre ~ trois font douze** four times three is

twelve; **la plupart des** ~ most of the time, more often than not; **une (bonne)** ~ **pour toutes** once and for all; **il faudrait qu'il neige une bonne** ~ what we need is one good fall of snow; **une** ~ **sur deux** half the time; **une** ~ **sur trois** every third time; **deux** ~ **sur cinq** two times out of five; **toutes les** ~ **que** every time (that); **ça va pour cette** ~, **mais ne recommencez pas!** it's all right this once but don't do it again!; **comme (à) chaque** ~ as usual; **deux** ~ **plus petit** half as big; **deux** ~ **plus cher** twice as expensive; **deux** ~ **moins lourd** half the weight; **deux** ~ **moins cher** half as expensive; **par deux** ~ twice; **il vaut mieux le dire deux** ~ **plutôt qu'une** it needs saying twice; **c'est dix** ~ **trop lourd!** it's far too heavy!; **régler en trois** ~ to pay in three instalments^GB; **pour la énième** ~ for the hundredth time; **la première** ~ **que je vous ai parlé** when I first talked to you.
II à la fois loc **deux à la** ~ two at a time; **porter trois valises à la** ~ to carry three suitcases at the same time; **elle est à la** ~ **intelligente et travailleuse** she's both clever and hardworking; **pour des raisons à la** ~ **culturelles, sociales et religieuses** for cultural, social and religious reasons; **ne répondez pas tous à la** ~! LIT, IRON don't all answer at once! LIT, IRON.
III des fois^○ loc (parfois) sometimes; **y a des** ~ **où** there are times^○ when; **tu n'as pas vu mon chien, des** ~? you wouldn't have seen my dog, by any chance?; **des** ~ **que** in case; **non mais des** ~! (indignation) well really!
IDIOMES **il était** or **il y avait une** ~ once upon a time there was; **je t'ai déjà dit cent** or **trente-six** ~ **de ne pas faire ça!** I've already told you a hundred ou a thousand times not to do that!

foisonner /fwazɔne/ [1] vi [idées, erreurs] to abound; ~ **de** or **en** to have an abundance of.

fol ▶ fou I.

folâtre /fɔlɑtʀ/ adj [personne, humeur] playful.

folâtrer /fɔlɑtʀe/ [1] vi [personne] to romp about; [animal] to frisk.

folichon^○, **-onne** /fɔliʃɔ̃, ɔn/ adj **pas** ~ far from brilliant.

folie /fɔli/ nf **1** (déraison) madness; **crise** or **coup de** ~ brainstorm; **être pris de** ~ to go mad GB ou crazy; **aimer qn/qch à la** ~ to be mad GB ou crazy about sb/sth; **spectateurs en** ~ ecstatic crowd sg; **2** (acte déraisonnable) **cette** ~ **leur a coûté la vie** it was an act of folly which cost them their lives; **elle a fait une** ~ **en acceptant** she was mad to accept; **3** (passion) **avoir la** ~ **des antiquités** to be mad GB ou crazy about antiques; **4** (dépense inconsidérée) extravagance; **faire une** ~, **faire des** ~**s** to be extravagant.
■ ~ **douce** sheer madness; ~ **furieuse** stark raving madness; **être pris de** ~ **furieuse** to go berserk; ~ **des grandeurs** delusions (pl) of grandeur.

folk /fɔlk/ I adj inv [festival, musique] folk.
II nm **le** ~ folk music; **chanteur de** ~ folk singer.

folklo^○ /fɔlklo/ adj [personne] eccentric; [soirée] crazy^○; **ça va être** ~! it'll be some laugh^○!

folklore /fɔlklɔʀ/ nm **1** (traditions) folklore; **2**^○ (rituel) razzmatazz^○.

folklorique /fɔlklɔʀik/ adj **1** (traditionnel) [musique, coutume] folk (épith); [costume] traditional; **2**^○ (loufoque) [personnage] eccentric; [voiture, soirée] crazy^○.

folle ▶ fou I, II.

follement /fɔlmɑ̃/ adv **s'amuser** ~ to have a terrific time; **un spectacle** ~ **drôle** a terribly funny show.

follet /fɔlɛ/ adj m **feu** ~ will-o'-the-wisp; **esprit** ~ flighty creature.

follicule /fɔlikyl/ nm ANAT, BOT follicle.

fomenter /fɔmɑ̃te/ [1] vtr to instigate.

foncé, ~**e** /fɔ̃se/ ▶141 adj [couleur] GÉN dark; [rose, mauve] deep; **avoir la peau** ~**e/les cheveux** ~**s** to be dark-skinned/dark-haired.

foncer /fɔ̃se/ [12] **I** vtr (assombrir) to make [sth] darker [couleur]; to make [sth] deeper [rose, mauve].
II vi **1**^○ (aller très vite) [chauffeur, voiture, coureur] to tear along^○ (**vers** toward(s)); **fonce!** get a move on^○!; **il va falloir** ~ **pour terminer à temps** we'll have to rush to finish in time; **2**^○ (se précipiter) ~ **vers/dans** to rush toward(s)/into; ~ **sur qch/vers la sortie** to make a dash for sth/for the exit; ~ **sur qn** (en attaquant) to charge at sb; ~ **tête baissée dans la bagarre** to rush headlong into the fray; ~ **à New York** to dash over to New York; **il n'est pas du genre à** ~ (prudent) he's not the type to rush into things; **fonce!** (n'hésite pas) go for it^○!; **3** (s'assombrir) [couleur] to darken; [rose, mauve] to deepen; [tissu] to go darker; ~ **au soleil** [lunettes] to go darker in the sun.

fonceur^○, **-euse** /fɔ̃sœʀ, øz/ **I** adj dynamic.
II nm,f go-getter^○.

foncier, **-ière** /fɔ̃sje, ɛʀ/ adj **1** [impôt] land; [revenu] from land (après n); **propriétaire** ~ landowner; **2** (inhérent) intrinsic.

foncièrement /fɔ̃sjɛʀmɑ̃/ adv fundamentally.

fonction /fɔ̃ksjɔ̃/ nf **1** (dans l'administration, une entreprise) (poste) post; (activité) duties (pl); **prendre ses** ~**s, entrer en** ~**s** to take up one's post; **dans le cadre de mes** ~**s** as part of my duties; **occuper la** ~ **de** to hold the position of; **quitter ses** ~**s** to leave one's job; **logement de** ~ accommodation provided with the job; **voiture de** ~ company car; **occuper d'importantes** ~**s** to hold important office; **2** (dépendance) **en** ~ **de** according to; **être** ~ **de** to vary according to; **3** (rôle) function; ~ **d'une machine** function of a machine; **avoir pour** ~ **de faire** to be designed to do; **faire** ~ **de** to serve as; **4** MATH, ORDINAT, CHIMIE, BIOL function; ~ **acide** acid function; **la** ~ **crée l'organe** the organ is shaped by its function; **5** (secteur) profession; ~ **enseignante** teaching profession; **6** TECH function; **la** ~ **avance rapide est en panne** the fast forward function does not work; **7** LING function.
■ ~ **primitive** MATH primitive; ~ **publique** ADMIN civil service.

fonctionnaire /fɔ̃ksjɔnɛʀ/ ▶374 nmf (petit, moyen) civil servant; (haut) government official; **haut** ~ senior civil servant; ~ **international** international official.

fonctionnalité /fɔ̃ksjɔnalite/ nf ORDINAT functionality ℓ.

fonctionnariser /fɔ̃ksjɔnaʀize/ [1] vtr to make [sb] work for the state.

fonctionnel, **-elle** /fɔ̃ksjɔnɛl/ adj functional.

fonctionnement /fɔ̃ksjɔnmɑ̃/ nm **1** (d'institution, organe, du marché) functioning; ~ **quotidien** everyday functioning; **bon** ~ smooth functioning; **2** (d'équipement) working; **mauvais** ~ malfunction; **en** ~ in service; **entrer en** ~ to come into service; **en état de** ~ in working order.

fonctionner /fɔ̃ksjɔne/ [1] vi to work; ~ **à merveille** to work perfectly; ~ **à l'essence** to run on petrol GB ou gas US; ~ **comme un alibi** to be used as an excuse; ~ **comme une société anonyme** to operate as a public company; ~ **comme un système d'alarme** to serve as an alarm signal; ~ **à la vodka** HUM [personne] to live on vodka.

fond /fɔ̃/ **I** nm **1** (partie inférieure) bottom; **au** ~ **du verre** in the bottom of the glass; **au** ~ **du tiroir** at the bottom of the drawer; **vider les** ~**s de bouteilles** to empty out all the old bottles; **toucher le** ~ (dans l'eau) to touch the bottom; FIG to hit rock bottom; **descendre au** ~ **d'un puits** to go down a well; **2** (paroi) (horizontale) bottom; (verticale) back; **le** ~ **du placard** the back of the cupboard; **valise à double** ~ suitcase with a false bottom; ~ **de la mer** seabed; ~ **de l'océan** ocean floor; **3** (partie reculée) (de cour, magasin) back; (de couloir, pièce) far end; **au** ~ **de l'armoire** in the back of the wardrobe; **la chambre du** ~ the back bedroom; **au** ~ **des bois** deep in the woods; **avancer dans le** ~ (dans un bus) to move up the bus; **de**

en comble from top to bottom; **4** (essence) **quel est le ~ du problème?** what is the problem exactly?; **les problèmes de ~** the basic problems; **aller au ~ des choses** to get to the bottom of things; **un débat de ~** an in-depth debate; **au ~** or **dans le ~, le problème est simple** the problem is simple, in fact; **dans le ~, tu as raison** you're right, really; **5** (de texte) content; **le ~ et la forme** form and content; **6** (intérieur) **regarder qn au ~ des yeux** (avec amour) to look deep into sb's eyes; (avec suspicion) to give sb a searching look; **du ~ du cœur** from the bottom of my heart; **elle a un bon ~** she's very good at heart; **il a un mauvais ~** he's got a nasty streak; **7** (arrière-plan) background; **sur ~ noir** on a black background; **~ musical** background music; **8** (petite quantité) **un ~ de porto** a drop of port; **laisser un ~ de bouteille** to leave a drop in the bottle; **9** (hauteur d'eau) **il n'y a pas assez de ~** the water is not deep enough; **il y a 20 mètres de ~** the water is 20 metres^GB deep; **l'épave gisait par 30 mètres de ~** the wreck lay 30 metres^GB down; **10** SPORT **épreuve de ~** long-distance event; **11** (de pantalon) seat.

II à fond *loc adv* **1** (complètement) **connaître son domaine à ~** to be an expert in one's field; **s'engager à ~** to commit oneself totally; **soutenir qn/qch à ~, être à ~° pour qn/qch** to support sb/sth wholeheartedly; **nettoyer qch à ~** to give sth a thorough cleaning; **respirer à ~** to breathe deeply; **mettre la radio à ~** to turn the radio right up; **2°** (vite) **rouler à ~** to drive at top speed; **il est arrivé à ~** he came rushing in.

■ **~ d'artichaut** artichoke bottom; **~ de tarte** pastry case; **~ de teint** foundation GB, make-up base US; **~s marins** depths of the sea.

IDIOMES **user ses ~s de culotte sur le même banc** FIG to be at school together.

fondamental, ~e, *mpl* **-aux** /fɔ̃damɑ̃tal, o/ *adj* **1** (essentiel) [*droit, question, différence, élément*] basic; [*objectif, besoin, idée, raison, vocabulaire*] basic; [*cause, changement, conflit, importance, rôle*] fundamental; [*atout*] crucial; **libertés ~es** basic liberties, fundamental freedoms; **ce qui est ~ c'est que** the essential is that; **2** MUS [*note*] fundamental.

fondamentalement /fɔ̃damɑ̃talmɑ̃/ *adv* **1** (au fond) fundamentally; **2** (totalement) radically.

fondant, ~e /fɔ̃dɑ̃, ɑ̃t/ *adj* [*neige, glace*] melting; [*poire, biscuit*] which melts in the mouth (*épith, après n*); **bonbon ~** fondant.

fondateur, -trice /fɔ̃datœr, tris/ *nm,f* GÉN founder; **groupe ~** founding group; **membre ~** founder member; **les pères ~s** the founding fathers.

fondation /fɔ̃dasjɔ̃/ *nf* (action, organisme) foundation.

II fondations *nfpl* LIT, FIG foundations; **creuser les ~s de qch** to lay the foundations of sth.

fondé, ~e /fɔ̃de/ *adj* (légitime) [*réclamation*] justifiable; [*crainte*] well-founded; [*demande*] legitimate; **vos reproches ne sont pas ~s** your criticisms are unfounded; **ce que tu dis n'est pas ~** what you say has no justification; **non ~, mal ~** [*accusation*] groundless.

■ **~ de pouvoir** JUR (de personne) proxy; (de société) authorized representative; (de banque) manager.

fondement /fɔ̃dmɑ̃/ *nm* (bases) foundation; **être dénué de** or **sans ~** to be unfounded.

fonder /fɔ̃de/ [1] **I** *vtr* **1** (créer) to found [*ville, parti, journal*]; to establish [*prix, entreprise*]; **~ un foyer** to get married; **2** (baser) to base (**sur** on); **~ ses espoirs sur qch/qn** to place one's hopes in sth/sb.

II se fonder *vpr* **se ~ sur** [*théorie, méthode*] to be based on; [*personne*] to go on; **sur quoi te fondes-tu?** what have you got to go on?

fonderie /fɔ̃dri/ *nf* (atelier) foundry.

fondeur, -euse /fɔ̃dœr, øz/ **I** *nm,f* SPORT cross-country skier.

II ▶374 *nm* (ouvrier) foundry worker.

fondre /fɔ̃dr/ [6] **I** *vtr* **1** (liquéfier) to melt down [*métal*]; to smelt [*minerai*]; **2** (fabriquer) to cast [*statue, caractère, lingot*].

II *vi* **1** (se liquéfier) [*neige, métal, beurre*] to melt; **faire ~** to melt; **2** (se dissoudre) [*sucre*] to dissolve; **faire ~** to dissolve; **3** (baisser) [*réserve, économies*] to melt away; **4** (maigrir) [*personne*] to waste away; **avoir fondu de dix kilos** to have lost ten kilos; **5** (s'attendrir) to soften; **il fond devant sa petite-fille** his heart melts when he sees his granddaughter; **~ en larmes** or **pleurs** to dissolve into tears; **6** (s'abattre) FML **~ sur** [*troupe, oiseau*] to swoop down on; [*malheur*] to overwhelm; [*calamité*] to ravage.

III se fondre *vpr* **se ~ dans** [*personne, silhouette*] to blend in with.

fonds /fɔ̃/ **I** *nm inv* **1** (collection) collection; **2** (capital) fund.

II *nmpl* (capitaux) funds; **recueillir des ~** to raise money; **mise de ~** capital outlay; **rentrer dans ses ~** to recover outlay; **à ~ perdus** at a loss.

■ **~ d'amortissement** sinking fund; **~ bloqués** frozen assets; **~ de commerce** business; **~ de placement** investment fund; **~ de prévoyance** provident fund; **~ propres** equity capital; **~ de roulement** working capital; **~ de solidarité** mutual aid fund; **Fonds monétaire international, FMI** International Monetary Fund, IMF.

fondu, ~e¹ /fɔ̃dy/ **I** *pp* ▶ **fondre**.

II *pp adj* [*beurre*] melted; [*métal*] molten; [*sucre*] dissolved.

fondue² /fɔ̃dy/ *nf* CULIN fondue.

■ **~ bourguignonne** fondue bourguignonne (*meat dipped in hot oil*), meat fondue US; **~ savoyarde** cheese fondue.

fontaine /fɔ̃tɛn/ *nf* GÉN fountain; (pour boire) drinking fountain; (source) spring.

fonte /fɔ̃t/ *nf* **1** (métal) cast iron; **de** or **en ~** cast-iron (*épith*); **2** (liquéfaction) (de métal) melting down; (de minerai) smelting; **3** MÉTÉO (de cours d'eau, glace, neige) thawing; **4** (fabrication de cloche, statue) casting.

■ **~ des neiges** thaw; **à la ~ des neiges** when the snow thaws.

fonts /fɔ̃/ *nmpl* **~ baptismaux** font (*sg*).

foot° /fut/ *nm* = **football**.

football /futbol/ **▶329** *nm* football GB, soccer.

■ **~ américain** american football GB, football US.

footballeur, -euse /futbolœr, øz/ **▶374** *nm,f* football GB ou soccer player.

footing /futiŋ/ **▶329** *nm* jogging; **faire un ~** to go for a jog.

for /fɔr/ *nm* **dans** or **en son ~ intérieur** deep down.

forage /fɔraʒ/ *nm* drilling; **le ~ d'un puits** the sinking of a well; **faire des ~** to drill.

forain, -aine /fɔrɛ̃, ɛn/ **I** *adj* fairground.

II *nm* (marchand) stallkeeper; **les ~s** fairground people.

forçat /fɔrsa/ *nm* (bagnard) convict; (galérien) galley slave.

force /fɔrs/ **I** *nf* **1** (de personne) **~s** strength ¢; **avoir de la ~** to be strong; **ne plus avoir de ~** to have no strength left; **la ~ de marcher** the strength to walk; **mes ~s m'abandonnent** I'm getting weak; **être à bout de ~s** to feel drained; **c'est au-dessus de mes ~s** it's too much for me; **de toutes ses ~s** [*lancer*] with all one's might; [*désirer*] with all one's heart; **dans la ~ de l'âge** in the prime of life; **avec ~** [*nier*] strongly; [*affirmer*] firmly; **2** (contrainte) force; **~ armée** armed force; **de ~** by force; **faire faire qch à qn de ~** to force sb to do sth; **entrer de ~ dans un lieu** to force one's way into a place; **par la ~ des choses** through force of circumstance; **coup de ~** MIL strike; **3** (puissance) (de pays, groupe, secteur, personne) strength; (d'expression) force; **c'est ce qui fait leur ~** that's where their strength lies; **ils sont de même ~** or **de ~ égale aux échecs** they are evenly matched at chess; **être de ~ à faire** to be up to doing; **tu n'es pas de ~ à t'attaquer à lui** you're no match for him; **revenir en ~, faire un retour en ~** to make a strong comeback; **4** (poids) (d'argument, accusation, de conviction) force; **5** PHYS, FIG force; **les ~s du mal** the forces of evil; **6** (intensité) (de choc, séisme, vent) force; (de désir, sentiment) strength; **7** (ensemble humain) force; **~s d'opposition** opposition forces; **arriver en ~** to arrive in force; **8** MIL (corps) force; (effectifs) **~s** forces; **~s navales** navy (sg); **~s terrestres** army (sg); **d'importantes ~s de police** large numbers of police.

II à force○ loc adv **à ~, elle l'a cassé** she ended up breaking it.

III à force de loc prép **réussir à ~ de travail** to succeed by dint of hard work; **à ~ d'économiser, elle a pu l'acheter** by saving very hard, she was able to buy it; **il est aphone à ~ de crier** he shouted so much (that) he lost his voice; **à ~ de frotter, tu vas le déchirer** if you keep on rubbing it, you'll tear it.

■ **~ de dissuasion** MIL deterrent force; FIG deterrent; **~ de frappe** (arme nucléaire) nuclear weapons (pl); (groupe) strike force; **~ d'interposition** MIL peacekeeping force; **~ d'intervention** MIL task force; **~ de la nature** (real) Goliath; **~ publique** police force; **~s de l'ordre** forces of law and order; **~s vives** life blood ¢; **Force ouvrière**, FO French trade union.

forcé, ~e /fɔʀse/ **I** pp ▶ **forcer**.
II pp adj **1** (contraint) forced; (accidentel) unintentional; **2** (artificiel) [gaieté, sourire, comparaison] forced; **3**○ (inéluctable) **c'est ~!** there's no way around it○!; **c'est ~ qu'il/elle fasse** he's/she's bound to do.

forcément /fɔʀsemɑ̃/ adv inevitably; **elle viendra ~ tôt ou tard** she is bound to come sooner or later; **pas ~** not necessarily; **'j'ai faim'—'~, tu n'as pas déjeuné!'** 'I'm hungry'—'well, it's hardly surprising, you had no lunch!'

forcené, ~e /fɔʀsəne/ **I** adj [rythme] furious; [activité] frenzied.
II nm,f (enragé) maniac; (armé) crazed gunman.

forceps /fɔʀsɛps/ nm inv forceps (pl).

forcer /fɔʀse/ [12] **I** vtr **1** (contraindre) to force; **être forcé à l'exil** to be forced into exile; **2** (faire céder) to force [porte, serrure]; **~ la porte de qn** FIG to force one's way into sb's house; **3** (passer au travers) to break through [barrière]; **~ le passage** to force one's way through; **~ l'entrée** to force one's way in; **4** (imposer) to force [négociation, décision]; **5** (pousser) to force [allure]; **~ le ton** to raise one's voice.
II forcer sur vtr ind **1** (abuser) **~ sur** to overdo [vin, sel, couleur]; **2** TECH **~ sur** to overtighten [vis]; to force [mécanisme].
III vi **1** (faire trop d'efforts) **j'ai trop forcé** I overdid it; **gagner sans ~** to win easily; **2** (exercer une pression) **ne force pas, tu vas le casser** don't force it or you'll break it; **serrez sans ~** do not tighten too much.
IV se forcer vpr (se contraindre) to force oneself (à faire to do); (faire des efforts) **il se force pour manger** it's a real effort for him to eat.
IDIOMES **~ la main à qn** to force sb's hand.

forcing○ /fɔʀsiŋ/ nm **faire du ~** to go all out.

forcir /fɔʀsiʀ/ [3] vi [vent] to become stronger.

forer /fɔʀe/ [1] vtr to drill; **~ un puits** to sink a well.

forestier, -ière /fɔʀɛstje, ɛʀ/ adj **1** [région, massif] forested; [chemin, paysage, ressources] forest (épith); **exploitation forestière** (travail) forestry; (site) forestry plantation; **industrie forestière** timber industry; **2** CULIN [escalope] with mushrooms (après n).

foret /fɔʀɛ/ nm drill.

forêt /fɔʀɛ/ nf LIT, FIG forest; **~ tropicale** rain forest.
IDIOMES **c'est l'arbre qui cache la ~** you can't see the wood for the trees.

Forêt-Noire /fɔʀɛnwaʀ/ nprf **1 ▶ 509 |** (région) **la ~** the Black Forest; **2** (gâteau) Black Forest gâteau GB ou cake.

foreuse /fɔʀøz/ nf drill.

forfait /fɔʀfɛ/ nm **1** (prix global) fixed rate; **être payé au ~** to be paid a fixed rate; **~ hebdomadaire** weekly rate; **un ~ de 160 francs pour trois concerts** a 160 franc flat-rate ticket covering three concerts; **2** TOURISME (séjour) package; **~ avion-auto** fly-drive package; **le ~ comprend le voyage et cinq nuits d'hôtel** the all-in package covers travel and five

nights' hotel accommodation; **3** (carte d'accès) pass; **~ skieur** ski pass; **4** (d'un joueur, une équipe) withdrawal; **gagner par ~** to win by default; **déclarer ~** GÉN to give up; SPORT to withdraw; **5** (pour les impôts) **être au ~** to be taxed at a rate calculated according to estimated turnover.

■ **~ journalier** individual contribution to cost of state hospital care.

forfaitaire /fɔʀfɛtɛʀ/ adj **prix ~** contract ou all-inclusive price; **tarif ~** flat fare ou fee; **taxe ~** flat-rate tax; **somme ~** lump sum; **indemnité ~** basic allowance.

forge /fɔʀʒ/ nf (atelier) forge; (feu) forge; (aciérie) ironworks.

forgé, ~e /fɔʀʒe/ **I** pp ▶ **forger**.
II pp adj [objet, métal] wrought; **fer ~** wrought iron; **grille en fer ~** wrought-iron gate.

forger /fɔʀʒe/ [13] **I** vtr **1** (dans une forge) to forge; **2** to form [caractère]; to invent [théorie]; to create [métaphore]; **une histoire forgée de toutes pièces** a complete fabrication.
II se forger vpr **se ~ un alibi** to invent an alibi (for oneself).

forgeron /fɔʀʒəʀɔ̃/ **▶ 374 |** nm blacksmith.
IDIOMES **c'est en forgeant qu'on devient ~** PROV practice makes perfect PROV.

formaliser: se formaliser /fɔʀmalize/ [1] vpr to take offence GB (de to); **se ~ d'un rien** to be easily offended.

formalisme /fɔʀmalism/ nm **1** PÉJ formality; **2** (en art, philosophie) formalism.

formaliste /fɔʀmalist/ **I** adj **1** PÉJ [personne] formal; **il est très ~** he's a stickler for form; **2** (en art, philosophie) formalist.
II nmf formalist.

formalité /fɔʀmalite/ nf ADMIN formality; **les ~s à accomplir pour obtenir un visa** the necessary procedure to obtain a visa; **simplifier les ~s** to simplify procedure; **ce n'est qu'une ~** it's a mere formality; **par pure ~** as a matter of form.

format /fɔʀma/ nm **1** (de journal, disquette) format; (de livre, photo, d'objet) size; **de grand/très grand ~** large/extra large; **2** ORDINAT (mode d'enregistrement) format.

formatage /fɔʀmataʒ/ nm ORDINAT formatting; **faire le ~** to format.

formateur, -trice /fɔʀmatœʀ, tʀis/ adj formative.

formation /fɔʀmasjɔ̃/ nf **1** (instruction) (scolaire) education; (professionnelle) training (en in); **ingénieur de ~** engineer by training; **il a reçu une ~ d'ingénieur** he was trained as an engineer; **avoir une ~ littéraire** to have an arts background; **la ~ des jeunes** youth education; **en ~** undergoing training (après n); **'~ assurée'** 'training provided'; **2** (cours) training course; **3** (de gouvernement, parti, d'équipe) forming; **il a été chargé de la ~ du gouvernement** he was asked to form the government; **4** (apparition) formation; **au moment de la ~ des glaciers** when the glaciers were (being) formed; **5** (ensemble) formation; **une ~ nuageuse** a cloud formation; **6** (groupe) group; **7** MIL (détachement) detachment; (disposition) formation; **~ aérienne** aerial formation.

■ **~ continue**, **~ permanente** adult continuing education; **~ professionnelle** professional training; **~ sur le tas** on-the-job training.

forme /fɔʀm/ **I** nf **1** (concrète) shape; (abstraite) form; **une ~ de vie** a form of life; **prendre ~** to take shape; **de ~ ronde** round; **sous ~ de** in the form of; **sous une autre ~** in another form; **juger sur la ~** to judge on form; **sans ~** shapeless; **2** (modalité) (de gouvernement, contrat, violence) form; (de paiement, recrutement) method; **3** (procédé, condition) form; **en bonne et due ~** in due form; **pour la ~** as a matter of form; **pour la bonne ~** to formalize things; **de pure ~** purely formal; **4** (en grammaire) form; **à la ~ négative** in the negative (form); **5** (état général) form; **en ~** on form; **en grande ~** in peak form; **perdre/ne plus avoir la ~** to go off/to be off form; **en pleine ~** in great shape; **une séance de remise en ~** a fitness session.

II formes *nfpl* **1** (corps humain) figure (*sg*); **elle a des ~s rondes** she has a rounded figure; **pull qui moule les ~s** figure-hugging sweater; **2** (d'objet, de bâtiment) lines; **3** (règles) **faire qch dans les ~s** to do sth in the correct manner; **y mettre les ~s** to be tactful; **respecter les ~s** to respect convention.

formé, ~e /fɔrme/ **I** *pp* ▶ **former.**

II *pp adj* **1** (composé) made up (**de** of); (dessiné) formed (**de** from); **2** (instruit) educated; (professionnellement) trained; **3** (façonné) formed; **bien ~** well-formed; **mal ~** badly-formed; **4** (mûr) [*caractère, goût*] formed.

formel, -elle /fɔrmɛl/ *adj* **1** [*refus, démenti*] categorical, flat; [*promesse*] definite; [*ordre*] strict; **être ~ sur** [*personne*] to be definite about; [*loi*] to be clear on; **il a dit 20 heures, je suis ~** he said 8 pm, I'm quite positive about it; **2** (en art, philosophie) formal; **3** (superficiel) [*politesse*] formal.

formellement /fɔrmɛlmɑ̃/ *adv* **1** (expressément) [*démentir*] categorically; [*interdire*] strictly; **2** (de façon officielle) officially; **~ identifié** clearly identified.

former /fɔrme/ [1] **I** *vtr* **1** (prendre l'aspect de) to form [*rectangle*]; **2** (constituer) to form; **ils forment un couple très uni** they are a very close couple; **il forme avec son partenaire une brillante équipe** he and his partner make a brilliant team; **formez des groupes de cinq** get into groups of five; **3** (donner une formation à) to train [*personnel*] (**à faire** to do); (éduquer) to educate [*personne, goût*]; to develop [*intelligence*]; to form [*opinion*]; **~ qn au traitement de texte** to train sb in word processing; **4** (produire) to form [*abcès, pellicule*]; **5** (mettre en forme) to form [*lettres, phrases*].

II se former *vpr* **1** (se créer) to form; **un caillot s'est formé** a clot has formed; **2** (être créé) to be formed; **3** (acquérir une formation) to train, to be trained (**à** in); **se ~ à la vente** to train in sales; **4** (s'éduquer) [*caractère, personnalité, style*] to develop; [*personne*] to educate oneself; **5** (concevoir) to form.

formidable /fɔrmidabl/ *adj* **1** (considérable) [*force, croissance*] tremendous; [*explosion*] enormous; **2**○ (épatant) [*spectacle, livre*] great○; [*personne*] marvellous^{GB}; **être ~ de patience avec qn** to be wonderfully patient with sb; **être ~ avec qn** (généreux) to be wonderful to sb; (patient) to be wonderful with sb; **3**○ (incroyable) **c'est quand même ~ qu'elle n'ait pas téléphoné!** it's incredible she hasn't phoned!

formidablement /fɔrmidabləmɑ̃/ *adj* awfully; **il joue ~ bien**○ he plays tremendously well.

formol /fɔrmɔl/ *nm* formalin.

formulaire /fɔrmylɛr/ *nm* (imprimé) form.

formulation /fɔrmylasjɔ̃/ *nf* (action) formulation; (chose formulée) wording; **la ~ de cette idée est difficile** it's not easy to express that idea.

formule /fɔrmyl/ *nf* **1** (expression) expression; **~ toute faite** set phrase; **2** (option) option; **3** (méthode) method; **la bonne ~ pour s'enrichir** a good way of making money; **4** (conception) concept; **5** (en science) formula; **6** (automobile) **~ un/deux/trois** Formula One/Two/Three; **7** (d'émission, de magazine) format.

■ **~ magique** (en magie) magic words (*pl*); FIG magic formula; **~ de politesse** GÉN polite phrase; (à la fin d'une lettre) letter ending.

formuler /fɔrmyle/ [1] *vtr* GÉN to express [*réserves*]; to put [sth] into words [*idée*]; to set out [*grief*]; to draw up [*contrat*]; **~ une réponse** to give an answer.

forniquer /fɔrnike/ [1] *vi* to fornicate.

fort, ~e /fɔr, fɔrt/ **I** *adj* **1** (puissant) strong; **armée ~e de 10 000 hommes** 10,000-strong army; **~ d'un chiffre d'affaires en hausse** boasting an increased turnover; **~s de leur expérience...** boosted by their experience...; **le roi est plus ~ que la dame** a king is worth more than a queen; **trouver plus ~ que soi** to meet one's match; **s'attaquer à plus ~ que soi** to take on someone bigger than oneself; **2** (résistant) strong; **3** (intense) [*bruit*] loud; [*lumière*] bright; [*chaleur, activité, pression*] intense; [*crampe*] bad; [*fièvre*] high; [*soupçon*] strong; [*crainte, colère*] deep; **une ~e**

grippe a bad attack of flu; **avoir une ~e envie de faire** to feel a strong desire to do; **4** (violent) [*coup*] hard; [*pluie*] heavy; [*vent*] strong; **5** (concentré) [*café, cigarette, alcool*] strong; [*épice*] hot; **6** (net) [*accent, personnalité, odeur, tendance, impression*] strong; [*pente*] steep; [*somme, majorité, réduction*] large; [*taux, inflation, consommation*] high; [*expansion, pénurie*] great; [*baisse, augmentation*] sharp; [*différence*] big; [*contingent, dose, croissance*] strong; **~e émigration** high level of emigration; **7** (doué) good (**en, à** at); **pour faire** at doing); **il est ~ pour ne rien faire** HUM he's good at doing nothing; **8** (ferme) [*personne*] strong; **9** (gros) [*personne*] stout; [*hanches*] broad; [*poitrine*] large; [*cuisses*] big; **être ~ de poitrine** to have a large bust; **10**○ (exagéré) **c'est un peu ~!** that's a bit much○!; **le plus ~, c'est que...** (surprenant) the most amazing thing is that...; (absurde) the most ridiculous thing is that...

II *adv* **1** (très) [*bon, déçu, émouvant*] extremely; [*bien, vite*] very; **c'est ~ dommage** it's a great pity; **2** (beaucoup) [*douter*] very much; **j'ai eu ~ à faire**○ **pour le convaincre** I had a hard job convincing him; **3** (avec force) [*frapper, tirer, frotter*] hard; [*serrer*] tight; [*respirer*] deeply; [*parler, crier*] loudly; [*sentir*] strongly; **souffle ~!** blow hard!; **le vent souffle ~** there's a strong wind; **parler de plus en plus ~** to speak louder and louder; **mon cœur bat trop ~** my heart is beating too fast; **le chauffage marche trop ~** the heating is turned up too high; **y aller un peu ~**○ to go a bit too far; **y aller un peu ~ sur la moutarde** to overdo the mustard; **4** (bien) well; **il ne va pas très ~** he's not very well; **faire** or **frapper (très) ~**○ to do (really) well; **attaquer très ~**○ to start off really well.

III *nm* **1** (ouvrage fortifié) fort; **2** (personne puissante) strong person; **3** (domaine d'excellence) strong point, forte.

IV au plus fort de *loc prép* **au plus ~ de l'été** at the height of summer; **au plus ~ de l'hiver** in the depths of winter; **au plus ~ de la bataille** in the thick of the fighting.

■ **~ en thème** SCOL swot GB, grind○ US; **~e tête** rebel.

IDIOMES ~ comme un bœuf or **Turc** strong as an ox; **c'est plus ~ que moi/qu'elle** (incontrôlable) I/she just can't help it; **c'est plus ~ que l'as de pique**○ or **que de jouer au bouchon**○ that beats it all, that takes the biscuit○.

fortement /fɔrtəmɑ̃/ *adv* (avec force) [*encourager, critiquer*] strongly; (de façon très marquée) [*augmenter, accélérer*] sharply; (à un haut niveau) [*centralisé, industrialisé*] highly; (profondément) [*ébranlé*] deeply; [*endommagé, pollué*] badly; [*déplaire*] greatly; (lourdement) [*armé*] heavily; **il est ~ question de démolir l'usine** demolition of the factory is being seriously considered.

forteresse /fɔrtərɛs/ *nf* stronghold.

fortiche /fɔrtiʃ/ **I** *adj* smart, clever (**en** at).

II *nmf* brain○.

fortifiant, ~e /fɔrtifjɑ̃, ɑ̃t/ **I** *adj* [*boisson, médicament*] fortifying; [*air*] bracing.

II *nm* MÉD tonic.

fortification /fɔrtifikasjɔ̃/ *nf* fortification.

fortifier /fɔrtifje/ [2] **I** *vtr* **1** (donner de la robustesse) to strengthen [*cheveux*]; **2** (donner des forces) [*repas*] to fortify; [*vacances, vitamines*] to do [sb] good; **3** (consolider) to strengthen [*foi, régime*]; **4** MIL to fortify [*ville*].

II se fortifier *vpr* (se consolider) [*régime*] to get stronger; [*foi*] to grow stronger.

fortuit, ~e /fɔrtɥi, it/ *adj* [*rencontre*] accidental; [*incident, circonstance*] fortuitous; [*remarque, découverte*] fortuitous, chance (*épith*); [*occasion*] unexpected; **'toute ressemblance serait purement ~e'** 'any similarity is purely coincidental'.

fortune /fɔrtyn/ *nf* **1** (richesse) fortune; **grandes ~s** large fortunes; **faire ~** to make a fortune; **une des plus grosses ~s du Venezuela** one of Venezuela's wealthiest people; **2** (chance) **(bonne) ~** good fortune; **mauvaise ~** bad luck; **3** (destinée) fortunes (*pl*); **4 de ~** (improvisé) makeshift (*épith*).

IDIOMES **faire contre mauvaise ~ bon cœur** to put on a brave face.

fortuné, **~e** /fɔʀtyne/ *adj* (riche) wealthy.

fosse /fos/ *nf* **1** (cavité) pit; **2** (tombe) grave; **3** (pour le saut) sandpit; **4** (de garage) inspection pit.
■ **~ d'aisances** earth closet; **~ commune** communal grave; **~ aux lions** lions' den; **~ océanique** oceanic trench; **~ d'orchestre** orchestra pit; **~ septique** septic tank; **~s nasales** nasal passages.

fossé /fose/ *nm* **1** GÉN ditch; (de château) moat; **aller dans le** or **au ~** to go into the ditch; **2** FIG (écart) gap; (désaccord) rift; **ça a creusé un ~ entre eux** it caused a rift between them.
■ **~ des générations** generation gap.

fossette /fosɛt/ *nf* dimple.

fossile /fosil/ *adj*, *nm* fossil.

fossiliser /fosilize/ [1] *vtr*, **se fossiliser** *vpr* to fossilize.

fossoyeur /foswajœʀ/ *nm* LIT gravedigger; FIG destroyer (**de** of).

fou (**fol** *before vowel or mute h*), **folle** /fu, fɔl/ I *adj* **1** (dément) mad; **devenir ~** to go mad; **un tueur ~** a crazed killer; **2** (insensé) [*personne, idée*] mad GB, crazy; [*regard*] wild; [*soirée, histoire*] crazy; **tu n'es pas un peu ~?** are you mad ou crazy?; **réaliser ses rêves les plus ~s** to see one's wildest dreams come true; **être ~ furieux**○ to be raving mad; **être ~ à lier**○ to be stark raving mad○; **entre eux c'est l'amour ~** they're madly in love; **~ de colère** mad with rage; **~ de joie** wild with joy; **~ de qn** crazy about sb; **~ de musique** mad about music; **3** (considérable) [*gaieté, enthousiasme*] mad; [*succès*] huge; **un monde ~** a huge crowd; **à une vitesse folle** at a crazy speed; **avoir un mal ~ à faire** to find it incredibly difficult to do; **mettre un temps ~ pour faire** to take an incredibly long time to do; **coûter un prix ~** to cost a fortune; **gagner un argent ~** to earn a fortune; **c'est ~ ce que le temps passe vite!** it's amazing how time flies!; **4** (incontrôlable) [*véhicule, cheval*] runaway; [*terreur*] wild; [*mèche*] stray; [*cheveux*] straggly; [*course*] headlong; **avoir le ~ rire** to have a fit of the giggles.
II *nm,f* madman/madwoman; **envoyer qn chez les ~s**○ to send sb to the nuthouse○; **courir comme un ~** to run like mad; **rire comme un ~**○ to laugh one's head off; **c'est un ~ d'art contemporain** he's mad about contemporary art; **un ~ du volant**○ a car freak○; **une bande de ~s** a bunch of lunatics.
III *nm* HIST (à la cour) fool, court jester; JEUX (aux échecs) bishop.
IDIOMES **faire les ~s**○ to fool about; **plus on est de ~s plus on rit**○ the more the merrier.

foudre /fudʀ/ I *nf* lightning; **frappé par la ~** struck by lightning; **coup de ~** love at first sight; **avoir le coup de ~ pour qn/qch** to be really taken with sb/sth.
II **foudres** FML *nfpl* wrath ¢; **s'attirer les ~s de qn** to incur sb's wrath.

foudroyant, **~e** /fudʀwajɑ̃, ɑ̃t/ *adj* [*attaque, progrès*] lightning (épith.), sudden; [*succès*] meteoric; [*regard*] furious; [*mort*] sudden; **victime d'une leucémie ~e** struck down by leukemia.

foudroyer /fudʀwaje/ [23] *vtr* **1** (frapper) [*orage*] to strike [*arbre*]; **mort foudroyé** struck dead by lightning; **~ du regard** to look daggers○ at; **2** (abattre) [*maladie*] to strike down; [*nouvelle*] to devastate.

fouet /fwɛ/ *nm* **1** (à lanières) whip; **dix coups de ~** ten lashes of the whip; **donner le ~ à qn** to flog sb; **coup de ~** LIT whip lash; FIG boost; **le grand air m'a donné un coup de ~** the fresh air invigorated me; **se heurter de plein ~ à** to collide head-on; **2** CULIN whisk; **~ mécanique** hand whisk.

fouettard /fwɛtaʀ/ *adj m* **le père ~** ≈ the bogeyman.

fouetter /fwɛte/ [1] I *vtr* **1** (frapper avec un fouet) to flog [*personne*]; to whip [*animal*]; **~ jusqu'au sang** to flog [sb] until the blood runs; **2** (frapper) **la pluie leur fouettait le visage** the rain lashed their faces; **3** CUL to whisk GB, to beat US.
II *vi* (battre) **la pluie fouettait contre les vitres** the rain lashed the windows.
IDIOMES **il n'y a pas de quoi ~ un chat**○ it's no big deal○; **avoir d'autres chats à ~**○ to have other fish to fry.

foufou○, **fofolle** /fufu, fɔfɔl/ I *adj* scatterbrained.
II *nm,f* scatterbrain.

fougère /fuʒɛʀ/ *nf* (plante) fern; (végétation) bracken ¢.

fougue /fug/ *nf* enthusiasm.

fougueusement /fugøzmɑ̃/ *adv* enthusiastically.

fougueux, **-euse** /fugø, øz/ *adj* [*cheval*] spirited; [*personne, élan, déclaration*] enthusiastic.

fouille /fuj/ *nf* **1** (de lieu, personne, bagages) search; **~ corporelle** body search; **2** (en archéologie) excavation; **champ de ~s** archaeological site.

fouillé, **~e** /fuje/ I *pp* ▶ **fouiller**.
II *pp adj* [*travail, étude, portrait*] detailed; [*style*] elaborate.

fouiller /fuje/ [1] I *vtr* **1** (explorer) to search; **2** (en archéologie) to dig [*site*].
II *vi* (chercher) **~ dans** to rummage through [*poche, armoire*]; to search [*mémoire*]; to sift through [*souvenirs*]; to delve into [*passé*].

fouillis /fuji/ *nm inv* (désordre) mess; (ensemble désordonné) jumble; **~ d'idées** jumble of ideas.

fouine /fwin/ *nf* **1** ZOOL stone marten; **tête de ~** weasel face; **2** (curieux) snooper.

fouiner /fwine/ [1] *vi* **1** (sans but) to forage about; **2** **~ dans** to rummage through [*objets, papiers*]; to poke one's nose into [*vie, passé*].

fouineur, **-euse** /fwinœʀ, øz/ I *adj* inquisitive.
II *nm,f* **1** (chineur) bargain hunter; **2** (indiscret) snooper.

foulard /fulaʀ/ *nm* scarf, headscarf.

foule /ful/ *nf* **1** (multitude de personnes) GÉN crowd; (menaçante) mob; **la ~ des acheteurs** the crowds of shoppers; **il n'y a pas ~ aujourd'hui** there isn't exactly a crowd today; **il y avait ~ à la réunion** there were masses of people at the meeting; **attirer les ~s** [*spectacle, chanteur*] to be a crowd-puller; **ils sont venus en ~ à la conférence** they flocked to the lecture; **2** (grand nombre) mass; **une ~ de détails** mass of details; **une ~ de gens** a crowd of people.

foulée /fule/ *nf* (enjambée) stride; **rester** or **courir dans la ~ de qn** SPORT to tail sb; **dans la ~ de leurs prédécesseurs** FIG in the wake of their predecessors; **dans la ~ il a... ** while he was at it, he...

fouler /fule/ [1] I *vtr* **1** to tread [*raisin*]; **2** (marcher sur) **~ le sol de Mars** to set foot on Mars; **~ qch aux pieds** LIT to trample sth underfoot; **~ aux pieds les usages** to ride roughshod over customs.
II **se fouler** *vpr* **1** MÉD **se ~ le poignet** to sprain one's wrist; **avoir la cheville foulée** to have a sprained ankle; **2**○ (se fatiguer) to strain oneself; **tu ne t'es pas foulé** you didn't kill yourself○.

foulure /fulyʀ/ *nf* sprain; **une ~ du poignet** sprained wrist.

four /fuʀ/ *nm* **1** (de boulanger, cuisine) oven; **à ~ moyen** in a medium oven; **cuire au ~** to roast [*viande*]; to bake [*gâteau, poisson*]; **poulet au ~** roast chicken; **2** IND furnace; (à céramique) kiln.
■ **~ à catalyse** oven with self-clean linings; **~ à chaleur tournante** fan(-assisted) oven; **~ crématoire** crematory (furnace); **~ à micro-ondes** microwave oven; **~ à pyrolyse** self-cleaning oven.
IDIOMES **il fait noir comme dans un ~** it's pitch dark in here.

fourbi○ /fuʀbi/ *nm* (objets) gear○; (désordre) shambles (+ *v sg*).

fourbu, **~e** /fuʀby/ *adj* (épuisé) exhausted.

fourche /fuʀʃ/ *nf* fork; **faire une ~** to fork.

fourcher /fuʀʃe/ [1] *vi* **ma langue a fourché** it was a slip of the tongue.

fourchette /fuʀʃɛt/ *nf* **1** (de table) fork; **2** (gamme) (of) prix, température) range; (de revenus, d'âge) bracket; **~ horaire** period.

IDIOMES **avoir un bon coup de ~**○ to have a hearty appetite.

ourchu, ~e /furʃy/ *adj* [*langue, branche*] forked; [*sabot*] cloven; [*menton*] cleft; **cheveux ~s** split ends.

ourgon /furgɔ̃/ *nm* **1** (camion) van; **2** RAIL goods wagon GB, freight car US; **~ de tête** leading wagon GB, first car US; **~ de queue** last wagon GB, caboose US.
■ **~ à bagages** luggage van GB, baggage car US; **~ à bestiaux** cattle truck; **~ cellulaire** police van GB, patrol wagon US; **~ mortuaire** hearse; **~ postal** mail van GB, mail truck US.

ourgonnette /furgɔnɛt/ *nf* (small) van.

ourguer○ /furge/ [1] *vtr* to flog○ (**à** to) GB, to sell [sth] off (**à** to).

ourmi /furmi/ *nf* ZOOL ant; **~ volante** flying ant; **travail de ~** laborious task.

IDIOMES **avoir des ~s dans les jambes** (avoir des picotements) to have pins and needles in one's legs.

ourmilier /furmilje/ *nm* anteater.

ourmilière /furmiljɛr/ *nf* ZOOL ant hill; FIG hive of activity.

ourmillement /furmijmɑ̃/ *nm* **1** (abondance) **un ~ de gens** a mass of people; **un ~ d'idées** a host of ideas; **2** (picotement) tingling sensation.

ourmiller /furmije/ [1] **I fourmiller de** *vtr ind* **~ de** to be chock-full of [*erreurs*]; to be swarming with [*visiteurs*]; to be teeming with [*animaux*].
II *vi* **1** (abonder) to abound (**dans** in); **les rats fourmillent dans le quartier** the neighbourhood^{GB} is swarming with rats; **livre où fourmillent les exemples** book bursting with examples; **2** (picoter) **j'ai les jambes qui fourmillent** I've got pins and needles in my legs.

ournaise /furnɛz/ *nf* **1** (endroit chaud) blaze; **le bureau est une vraie ~!** the office is like an oven!; **la ville est une ~ en été** the town is baking hot in summer; **2** C (chaudière) boiler GB, furnace US.

ourneau, *pl* **~x** /furno/ *nm* TECH furnace; (cuisinière) stove; **être à ses ~x** to be doing the cooking.

ournée /furne/ *nf* batch.

ourni, ~e /furni/ **I** *pp* ▶ **fournir**.
II *pp adj* **bien ~** [*magasin*] well-stocked (**en** with).
III *adj* (dense) [*barbe*] bushy; [*chevelure*] thick; [*herbe*] lush; [*emploi du temps*] busy.

ourniment○ /furnimɑ̃/ *nm* clutter.

ournir /furnir/ [3] **I** *vtr* **1** (donner) to supply [*dossier, équipement, secours, information, argent*]; to give [*exemple, travail*]; to provide [*excuse, énergie, service*]; to contribute [*effort*]; to produce [*preuve, alibi*]; **~ à qn** to supply sb with [*biens, données*]; to give [sth] to sb [*exemple*]; to provide sb with [*occasion, moyen*]; **~ qn en** to supply sb with [*biens*].
II se fournir *vpr* **se ~ chez** or **auprès de** to get [sth] from.

ournisseur, -euse /furnisœr, øz/ **I** *adj* **pays ~** exporting country.
II *nm* supplier; **premier/deuxième ~ de** largest/ second-largest supplier of; **chez votre ~** from your supplier; **~ attitré** official supplier; **~ de drogue** drug dealer; **~ de la famille impériale** purveyor to the imperial family.

ourniture /furnityr/ *nf* **1** COMM (vente) supply ¢; **~ d'armes** supply of arms; **~s chinoises de coton** Chinese supply of cotton; **2** (équipement) **~s** equipment ¢. ■ **~s de bureau** office stationery ¢; **~s de laboratoire** (en sciences, dans l'industrie) laboratory equipment; **~s scolaires** school stationery.

ourrage /furaʒ/ *nm* forage; **~ sec** fodder.

ourre /fur/ *nf* H (couverture protectrice) cover.

ourré, ~e /fure/ **I** *pp* ▶ **fourrer**.
II *pp adj* **1** CULIN filled (**à** with); **~ au chocolat** with chocolate filling (*après n*); **2** (de fourrure) fur-lined; (d'étoffe, de peau) lined (**de, en** with); **3**○ (installé) **toujours ~ au café** always hanging about at the café; **où étais-tu ~?** where have you been hiding?
III *nm* (buisson) thicket.

fourrer /fure/ [1] **I** *vtr* **1** (mettre) to stick○; **~ qch dans la tête de qn** to put sth into sb's head; **2** (en cuisine) to fill (**avec, de** with); **3** to line [*vêtement*].
II se fourrer○ *vpr* (se mettre) **se ~ dans un coin** to get into a corner; **aller se ~** [*objet*] to get stuck in; **se ~ dans les jambes de qn** to get under sb's feet; **se ~ une idée dans la tête** to get an idea into one's head; **ne plus savoir où se ~** not to know where to put oneself; **se ~ dans une sale histoire** to get mixed up in a bad business.

fourre-tout /furtu/ **I** *adj inv* **1** [*solution*] cover-all; **groupe ~** ragbag; **2** [*pièce, placard*] storage; **sac ~** holdall GB, carryall US.
II *nm inv* (trousse) pencil case.

fourreur /furœr/ ▶ 374 *nm* furrier.

fourrière /furjɛr/ *nf* (pour animaux, véhicules) pound; **mettre une voiture à la ~** to impound a car.

fourrure /furyr/ *nf* **1** (pour vêtement) fur; **fausse ~** imitation fur; **~ polaire** fleece; **2** ZOOL coat.

fourvoyer: se fourvoyer /furvwaje/ [23] *vpr* (se tromper) to make a mistake.

foutoir○ /futwar/ *nm* (désordre) shambles○ (*sg*); (agitation) complete chaos.

foutre○ /futr/ [6] **I** *vtr* **1** (faire) to do; **qu'est-ce qu'il fout?** what the hell's he doing○?; **qu'est-ce que ça peut ~?** what the hell does it matter○?; **n'en avoir rien à ~** not to give a damn○ ou shit○; **2** (donner) **~ un coup à qn** LIT to wallop sb○; **sa mort nous a foutu un coup** his/her death was a terrible blow to us; **3** (mettre) **~ qch quelque part** to stick○ sth somewhere; **~ son nez partout** to stick one's nose into everything; **~ qn dehors** or **à la porte** to kick sb out○; **~ le camp** [*personne*] to bugger off○ GB, to split○ US; [*choses*] to fall apart; **fous(-moi) le camp d'ici!** get lost○!; **tout fout le camp** everything's falling apart; **ça la fout mal** it makes a lousy○ impression.
II se foutre *vpr* **1** (se mettre) **se ~ en colère** to fly off the handle○; **s'en ~ plein les poches** to rake it in○; **se ~ en l'air** (en voiture) to have an accident; (se suicider) to top oneself○; **2** (se donner) **je me foutrais des claques!** sometimes I could kick myself!; **3** (ridiculiser) **se ~ de (la gueule de) qn** to take the piss out of sb○; **il ne s'est pas foutu de toi!** he's been very generous!; **se ~ du monde** to have a bloody GB ou hell of a○ nerve; **4** (être indifférent) not to give a damn○ (**de** about); **je m'en fous** I don't give a damn○.

foutu○, **~e** /futy/ **I** *pp* ▶ **foutre**.
II *pp adj* **1** (mauvais) (*before n*) [*temps*] bloody awful○ GB, damned US; [*caractère*] bloody awful○ GB; **~e voiture** bloody○ car GB, damned US car; **2** (condamné) **être ~** [*personne, vêtement*] to have had it○; [*machine*] to be knackered○ GB, to be shot○ US; **s'il me trouve, je suis ~** if he finds me I've had it○; **être mal ~** (laid) [*personne*] to be unattractive; (malade) [*personne*] to feel lousy○; **3** (capable) **être ~ de faire** to be totally capable of doing; **il n'est même pas ~ de répondre** he can't even bloody○ well answer GB, he can't be bothered○ to answer.
IDIOMES **café bouillu café ~**○ boiled coffee is ruined coffee.

fox-terrier, *pl* **~s** /fɔkstɛrje/ *nm* fox terrier.

foyer /fwaje/ *nm* **1** (domicile) home; **rester au ~** to stay at home; **fonder un ~** to get married; **2** (famille) household; **3** (résidence) hostel; **4** (club) club; **5** CIN, THÉÂT (point de rencontre) foyer; **6** (de cheminée) hearth; **7** (centre actif) (de résistance) pocket; (d'intrigue) hotbed; **8** (centre de propagation) (d'incendie) seat; (d'épidémie) source; (de rébellion) seat; **9** PHYS focus; **lunettes à double ~** bifocals.
■ **~ fiscal** household for tax purposes; **~ de placement** foster home.

frac /frak/ *nm* morning coat.

fracas /fraka/ *nm inv* (de chute) crash; (de vagues) roar; (de ville, bataille) din; **tomber avec ~** to fall with a crash; **lancer un produit à grand ~** FIG to launch a product in a blaze of publicity; **renvoyé avec perte(s) et ~** summarily dismissed.

fracassant, **~e** /fʀakasɑ̃, ɑ̃t/ *adj* (violent) [*bruit*] deafening; (sensationnel) [*entrée, déclaration*] sensational; [*succès, débuts*] stunning.

fracasser /fʀakase/ [1] **I** *vtr* to smash [*vitrine, crâne*].
II se fracasser *vpr* to crash (**contre, sur** against).

fraction /fʀaksjɔ̃/ *nf* **1** MATH fraction; **2** (partie) (de terrain, somme) part; (de société, jeunesse) section; (de produits, d'électeurs) proportion; **en une ~ de seconde** in a split second, in a fraction of a second.

fractionnement /fʀaksjɔnmɑ̃/ *nm* (division) division; (morcellement) fragmentation.

fractionner /fʀaksjɔne/ [1] *vtr* **1** (diviser) to divide up [*travail, groupe*]; to split [*parti, opposition*]; **2** (échelonner) to stagger [*envois*]; to spread [*paiements*].

fracture /fʀaktyʀ/ *nf* fracture; **~ du poignet** fractured wrist; **~ ouverte** compound fracture.

fracturer /fʀaktyʀe/ [1] **I** *vtr* **1** to fracture [*os*]; **2** (pour pénétrer) to break down [*porte*]; to break [*fenêtre*]; to force [*serrure, coffre*].
II se fracturer *vpr* **se ~ la cheville** to break one's ankle.

fragile /fʀaʒil/ *adj* **1** (cassable) fragile; **2** (faible) [*personne, constitution*] frail; [*peau, œil*] sensitive; [*estomac, foie*] delicate; [*cœur*] weak; **il est ~ du foie** he has a delicate liver; **avoir une santé ~** to have poor health; **3** (instable) [*esprit, personne*] fragile.
IDIOMES **~ comme du verre** very fragile.

fragiliser /fʀaʒilize/ [1] *vtr* LIT, FIG to weaken.

fragilité /fʀaʒilite/ *nf* **1** (aptitude à se briser) fragility; **2** (de personne, constitution, santé) frailty.

fragment /fʀagmɑ̃/ *nm* **1** (morceau isolé) (de tasse, d'os) fragment; (de tissu) bit; **des ~s de conversation** snatches of conversation; **2** (d'œuvre) passage.

fragmentaire /fʀagmɑ̃tɛʀ/ *adj* [*connaissance*] patchy; [*vue, exposé*] sketchy; [*action, effort*] sporadic.

fragmentation /fʀagmɑ̃tasjɔ̃/ *nf* **1** FIG (division) division; (morcellement) splitting up; **2** LIT (de pierre) fragmentation.

fragmenter /fʀagmɑ̃te/ [1] **I** *vtr* (casser) to break up [*substance*]; (morceler) to split up [*domaine, parti*]; to divide up [*travail*]; to break up [*vacances, texte*].
II se fragmenter *vpr* [*pierre*] to break (**en** into).

fraîche ▸ **frais** I, V.

fraîchement /fʀɛʃmɑ̃/ *adv* **1** (récemment) [*creusé, repeint*] freshly; [*nommé*] newly; **~ cueillies** freshly cut; **2** (sans empressement) [*recevoir*] coldly; **elle a été ~ accueillie** she was given a cool welcome; **3**◦ 'comment allez-vous?'—'~' 'how are you?'—'cold'.

fraîcheur /fʀɛʃœʀ/ *nf* **1** (température) (agréable) coolness; (plus froide) coldness; **donner une sensation de ~ à** to make [sb] feel cool; **la ~ du soir** the cold evening air; **2** (d'aliment) freshness; **~ garantie** guaranteed fresh; **3** (jeunesse) freshness; **pour redonner de la ~ à votre teint** to rejuvenate your complexion.

frais, fraîche /fʀɛ, fʀɛʃ/ **I** *adj* **1** (légèrement froid) cool; (trop froid) cold; **'servir ~'** 'serve chilled'; **il fait ~ ce matin** (c'est agréable) it's cool this morning; (il fait froid) it's chilly this morning; **le fond de l'air est ~** there's a chill in the air; **2** (récent) [*nouvelles, traces, neige*] fresh; [*peinture*] wet; **de fraîche date** [*membre*] recent; [*produit*] fresh; **4** (jeune) [*teint, peau*] fresh; [*voix*] young; **une fraîche jeune fille** a fresh-faced girl; **5** (nouveau) [*troupes, équipe*] fresh; **apporter un peu d'air ~ à qch** to bring a breath of fresh air to sth; **de l'argent ~** more money; **6** (léger) [*parfum, décor, couleur*] fresh; **7** (sans chaleur) [*accueil, ambiance*] cool.
II *adv* (depuis peu) **~ rasé** freshly shaved; **un livre tout ~ paru** a newly-published book.
III *nm* (fraîcheur) **se tenir au ~** to stay in the cool; **prendre le ~** to get some fresh air; **mettre qch au ~** (pour le conserver) to put sth in a cool place; (pour le refroidir) to put sth to cool; **mettre qn au ~**◦ (en prison) to put sb inside◦.
IV *nmpl* **1** GÉN (dépenses) expenses; **aux ~ de l'entreprise** paid for by the company; **le voyage est à vos ~** you'll have to pay for the trip yourself; **vivre aux ~ de la société** to live off society; **aux ~ de qn** FIG

at sb's expense; **partager les ~** to share the cost; **faire des ~** [*personne*] to spend a lot of money; **rentrer dans ses ~** to cover one's expenses; **en être pour ses ~**◦ LIT to have to pay; FIG to get nothing for one's pains; **faire les ~ de qch** to bear the brunt of sth; **arrêter les ~** FIG to stop wasting one's time; **2** (coûts d'un service professionnel) fees; **~ d'agence** agency fees; **3** (coûts d'un service commercial, commission) charges; **4** (en comptabilité) (coûts) costs; **~ fixes/variables** fixed/variable costs.
V **à la fraîche** *loc adv* (le matin) in the cool of the morning; (le soir) in the cool of the evening.
■ **~ d'annulation** cancellation fees; **~ de déplacement** (d'employé) travel expenses; (de réparateur) call out charge (sg); **~ divers** miscellaneous costs; **~ d'expédition** (de colis) postage and packing; (de marchandise) freight; **~ de fonctionnement** running costs; **~ de garde** childminding fees; **~ généraux** overheads; **~ d'inscription** GÉN registration fees; UNIV tuition fees, academic fees GB; **~ de port** postage ¢; **~ professionnels** professional expenses; **~ de scolarité** tuition fees, school fees GB.
IDIOMES **être ~ comme une rose** to be as fresh as a daisy; **nous voilà ~**◦! now we're in a fix◦!

fraise /fʀɛz/ **I** ▸ **141** *adj inv* strawberry-pink.
II *nf* **1** (fruit) strawberry; **~ des bois** wild strawberry; **2** (en boucherie) **~ de veau** calf's caul; **3** (angiome) strawberry mark; **4** (collerette) ruff; **5** (outil) (pour aléser) reamer; (machine) (pour couper) milling-cutter; (pour forer) drill.
IDIOMES **ramener sa ~**◦ to stick one's nose in◦.

fraiser /fʀɛze/ [1] *vtr* to ream [*cylindre*]; to mill [*pièce*].

fraiseur, -euse¹ /fʀɛzœʀ, øz/ ▸ **374** *nm,f* (ouvrier) cutter.

fraiseuse² /fʀɛzøz/ *nf* (machine) milling machine.

fraisier /fʀɛzje/ *nm* (plante) strawberry plant; CULIN (gâteau) strawberry gateau.

framboise /fʀɑ̃bwaz/ **I** ▸ **141** *adj inv* (couleur)GB raspberry-coloured.
II *nf* (fruit) raspberry; (liqueur) raspberry liqueur.

framboisier /fʀɑ̃bwazje/ *nm* (cultivé) raspberry cane; (sauvage) raspberry bush.

franc¹, franche /fʀɑ̃, fʀɑ̃ʃ/ **I** *adj* **1** (honnête) [*personne*] frank, straight; [*réponse*] straight; [*rire, regard*] open, honest; **je vais être ~ avec vous** I'm going to be straight with you; **il n'est pas ~** he doesn't play straight; **jouer ~ jeu** to play fair; **2** (sans ambiguïté) (before n) [*victoire, aversion*] out-and-out; [*gaieté*] open, uninhibited; **3** (exempt) **~ de port** postage paid.
II *adv* **parler ~** to be perfectly frank.
III ▸ **33** *nm* (monnaie) franc; **un ~ symbolique de dommages et intérêts** JUR ≈ nominal damages (pl).
■ **~ belge** Belgian franc; **~ français** French franc; **~ lourd** new franc; **~ suisse** Swiss franc.

franc², franque /fʀɑ̃, fʀɑ̃k/ *adj* Frankish.

Franc, Franque /fʀɑ̃, fʀɑ̃k/ *nm,f* Frank.

français, -e /fʀɑ̃sɛ, ɛz/ ▸ **394**, **338** **I** *adj* French; **à la ~e** French-style (*épith*).
II *nm* LING French.

Français, ~e /fʀɑ̃sɛ, ɛz/ ▸ **394** *nm,f* Frenchman/Frenchwoman; **le ~ moyen** GÉN the average Frenchman; PÉJ the typical Frenchman.

France /fʀɑ̃s/ ▸ **232** *nprf* France; **la ~ libre** HIST Free France.

franche ▸ **franc¹** I.

franchement /fʀɑ̃ʃmɑ̃/ *adv* **1** (honnêtement) [*parler, dire*] frankly; [*répondre*] candidly; **je lui ai demandé ~ ce qu'il comptait faire** I asked him straight out what he intended to do; **~ non, je n'ai pas beaucoup aimé** to be frank ou honest I didn't like it very much; **2** (sans hésiter) [*appuyer*] firmly; [*entrer*] boldly; **servez-vous ~** take a good helping; **versez ~!** don't be afraid of pouring in too much!; **3** (complètement) really; **il m'a ~ agacé** he really annoyed me; **elle est ~ bête** she is downright ou plain stupid; **4** (exclamatif) really, honestly.

ranchir /fʀɑ̃ʃiʀ/ [3] *vtr* to cross [*fossé, seuil, montagne*]; to get over [*mur, barrière*]; to cover [*distance*]; ~ **un obstacle** LIT to clear an obstacle; FIG to overcome an obstacle; ~ **le cap des quarts de finale** to get past the quarterfinals; ~ **le cap de la cinquantaine** to turn fifty.

IDIOMES ~ **le pas** to take the plunge.

ranchise /fʀɑ̃ʃiz/ *nf* **1** (qualité) (de personne, regard, d'aveu) frankness; (de ton) sincerity; **2** (exemption) exemption; **3** (en assurance) excess GB, deductible US; **4** COMM franchise; **5** HIST (de ville) charter.

■ ~ **de bagages** AVIAT baggage allowance; ~ **fiscale** tax exemption; ~ **postale** (sur une enveloppe) 'postage paid'; **en** ~ **postale** post free.

ranchiser /fʀɑ̃ʃize/ [1] *vtr* to franchise.

ranchissement /fʀɑ̃ʃismɑ̃/ *nm* (de col, rivière, ravin, seuil) crossing ¢; (d'obstacle, de haie) clearing ¢; ~ **de la ligne continue** AUT crossing the white line.

rancisation /fʀɑ̃sizasjɔ̃/ *nf* (de mot) gallicization.

ranciser /fʀɑ̃size/ [1] *vtr* to gallicize [*mot*].

ranc-jeu /fʀɑ̃ʒø/ *nm* fair play.

ranc-maçon, -onne, *pl* **francs-maçons, franc-maçonnes** /fʀɑ̃masɔ̃, ɔn/ *nm,f* Freemason.

ranc-maçonnerie, *pl* ~**s** /fʀɑ̃masɔnʀi/ *nf* **la** ~ Freemasonry.

ranco /fʀɑ̃ko/ *adv* **1** COMM ~ **de port** [*lettre, colis*] postage paid; [*livraisons*] carriage paid; **2**° (sans hésiter) **y aller** ~ (explication) to go straight to the point; (action) to go right ahead.

rancophone /fʀɑ̃kɔfɔn/ **I** *adj* [*pays, personne*] French-speaking; **littérature** ~ literature in the French language.

II *nmf* French speaker.

rancophonie /fʀɑ̃kɔfɔni/ *nf* (ensemble des francophones) French-speaking world.

ranc-parler, *pl* **francs-parlers** /fʀɑ̃paʀle/ *nm* frankness; **avoir son** ~ to speak one's mind.

ranc-tireur, *pl* **francs-tireurs** /fʀɑ̃tiʀœʀ/ *nm* **1** (tireur isolé) sniper; **2** (personne indépendante) maverick.

range /fʀɑ̃ʒ/ *nf* **1** (en tissu, laine) fringe; **2** (de cheveux) fringe GB, bangs (*pl*) US.

rangin° /fʀɑ̃ʒɛ̃/ *nm* brother.

rangine° /fʀɑ̃ʒin/ *nf* sister.

ranque ▶ **franc²**.

ranquette°: **à la bonne franquette** /alabɔn fʀɑ̃kɛt/ *loc adv* **c'est à la bonne** ~ it's just an informal meal.

rappant, ~**e** /fʀapɑ̃, ɑ̃t/ *adj* striking.

rappe /fʀap/ *nf* **1** (de monnaie, médaille) (action) striking; (empreinte) impression; **2** (de texte) typing; **le texte est à la** ~ the text is being typed out; **3** SPORT (de footballeur) kick; (de boxeur) punch.

rappé, ~**e** /fʀape/ **I** *pp* ▶ **frapper**.

II *pp adj* **1** (rafraîchi) [*champagne, vin blanc*] chilled; [*cocktail*] frappé, mixed with crushed ice; [*café*] iced; **2**° (fou) crazy°, nuts°.

rapper /fʀape/ [1] **I** *vtr* **1** (taper sur) GÉN to hit, to strike; ~ **le sol du pied** to stamp one's foot; ~ **qn à coups de matraque** to club sb; ~ **qn/qch à coups de balle** to kick sb/sth; ~ **qn/qch à coups de poing** to punch sb/sth; ~ **un coup** (à la porte) to knock (once); ~ **fort** or **un grand coup** LIT to hit hard; (à la porte) to knock hard; FIG to pull out all the stops; **2** TECH to strike [*monnaie, médaille*]; **3** (affecter) [*chômage, épidémie, impôt*] to hit; **le malheur qui les frappe** the misfortune which has befallen them; **être frappé par le malheur** to be stricken by misfortune; **être frappé d'apoplexie** to have a stroke; **être frappé de mutisme** to be dumbstruck; **les taxes qui frappent les produits de luxe** duties imposed on luxury goods; **4** (marquer) to strike; **ce qui me frappe le plus c'est...** what strikes me most is...; **j'ai été frappé de voir que...** I was amazed to see that...; ~ **l'imagination de qn** to catch sb's imagination; **5** (rafraîchir) to chill [*champagne, vin*].

II *vi* **1** GÉN to hit, to strike; ~ **du poing sur la table** to bang one's fist on the table; ~ **du pied** to stamp

one's foot; ~ **dans ses mains** to clap one's hands; ~ **à** to knock on ou at [*porte, fenêtre*]; **on a frappé** there was a knock at the door; **2** (sévir) to strike.

frasque /fʀask/ *nf* escapade; **faire des** ~**s** to get up to mischief; ~**s de jeunesse** youthful indiscretions.

fraternel, -elle /fʀatɛʀnɛl/ *adj* fraternal, brotherly.

fraternellement /fʀatɛʀnɛlmɑ̃/ *adv* in a brotherly fashion.

fraternisation /fʀatɛʀnizasjɔ̃/ *nf* fraternizing.

fraterniser /fʀatɛʀnize/ [1] *vi* to fraternize.

fraternité /fʀatɛʀnite/ *nf* fraternity, brotherhood.

fratricide /fʀatʀisid/ **I** *adj* fratricidal.

II *nm* (crime) fratricide.

fraude /fʀod/ *nf* **1** JUR fraud ¢; ~ **fiscale** tax fraud; ~ **électorale** vote ou election rigging; **passer qch/qn en** ~ to smuggle sth/sb in; **sortir qch en** ~ to smuggle sth out; **entrer** or **passer en** ~ (dans un pays) to enter illegally; **2** SCOL, UNIV cheating ¢.

frauder /fʀode/ [1] *vi* (dans le métro) to travel without a ticket; (au cinéma) to slip in without paying.

fraudeur, -euse /fʀodœʀ, øz/ *nm,f* GÉN swindler; (du fisc) tax evader; (à un examen) cheat.

frauduleux, -euse /fʀodylø, øz/ *adj* fraudulent.

frayer /fʀeje/ [21] **I** *vtr* ~ **un passage à qn** to clear a path for sb; ~ **le chemin** or **la voie à qch** FIG to pave the way for sth.

II *vi* **1** (entretenir des relations) **il ne fraye pas avec ces gens-là** he doesn't mix with that sort of person; **2** ZOOL [*femelle*] to spawn; [*mâle*] to fertilize the eggs.

III se frayer *vpr* LIT (s'ouvrir) **se** ~ **un chemin dans** or **à travers** to make one's way through.

frayeur /fʀejœʀ/ *nf* **il poussait des cris de** ~ he was screaming in fear; **j'ai eu une de ces** ~**s!** I got such a fright!

fredaine /fʀodɛn/ *nf* **faire des** ~**s** to have amorous adventures.

fredonner /fʀodone/ [1] *vtr* to hum.

free-lance /fʀilɑ̃s/ *nmf* freelance, freelancer; **travailler en** ~ to work freelance ou as a freelancer.

freezer /fʀizœʀ/ *nm* freezer compartment GB, icebox.

frégate /fʀegat/ *nf* **1** NAUT frigate; **2** ZOOL frigate bird.

frein /fʀɛ̃/ *nm* **1** (de véhicule) brake; **la voiture n'a plus de** ~**s** the brakes are not working; **donner un coup de** ~ to brake hard; **utilisez le** ~ **moteur** keep in low gear; **2** (entrave) **mettre un** ~ **à** to curb [*expansion, optimisme*]; **3**† (mors) bit.

■ ~ **à disques** disc brake; ~ **à main** hand brake; ~ **à tambour** drum brake.

IDIOMES **ronger son** ~ to champ at the bit.

freinage /fʀɛnaʒ/ *nm* braking.

freiner /fʀɛne/ [1] **I** *vtr* **1** (faire ralentir) to slow down [*véhicule, parachute*]; **2** (gêner) to impede [*personne, avance*]; **3** (modérer) to curb [*consommation*].

II *vi* **1** (en voiture, à moto, vélo) to brake; ~ **à bloc** or **à fond** to slam on the brakes; **2** (à ski) to slow down.

frelaté, -e /fʀəlate/ *adj* **1** [*alcool*] adulterated; [*goût*] unnatural; **2** [*milieu, plaisirs*] dubious.

frêle /fʀɛl/ *adj* frail.

frelon /fʀəlɔ̃/ *nm* hornet.

freluquet† /fʀəlykɛ/ *nm* little squirt°, whippersnapper†.

frémir /fʀemiʀ/ [3] *vi* **1** (trembler) [*voile, feuille*] to quiver; [*eau du lac*] to ripple; **2** (sous l'effet d'une émotion) [*lèvre, narine*] to tremble; [*personne*] (d'impatience, de colère, plaisir) to quiver (**de** with); (de dégoût, d'effroi) to shudder (**de** with); **3** CULIN [*liquide*] to start to come to the boil.

frémissant, ~e /fʀemisɑ̃, ɑ̃t/ *adj* **faire cuire dans l'eau** ~**e** simmer gently in water.

frémissement /fʀemismɑ̃/ *nm* **1** (vibration) quiver, tremor; **le** ~ **du vent dans les arbres** the rustle of the wind in the trees; **2** (d'émotion) (de narine, lèvre, main) trembling ¢; (de personne, corps) (dû à la joie, la colère, au plaisir) quiver; (dû à l'effroi, au dégoût) shudder.

frêne /fʀɛn/ *nm* **1** (arbre) ash (tree); **2** (bois) ash (wood).

frénésie /fʀenezi/ *nf* frenzy; **avec ~** [*lutter*] frantically; [*danser*] frenziedly; [*applaudir*] wildly.

frénétique /fʀenetik/ *adj* [*applaudissements, lutte, activité*] frenzied; [*joueur*] frenetic.

frénétiquement /fʀenetikmɑ̃/ *adv* [*lutter, secouer*] frantically; [*danser*] frenziedly; [*applaudir*] wildly.

fréquemment /fʀekamɑ̃/ *adv* frequently.

fréquence /fʀekɑ̃s/ *nf* GÉN, PHYS frequency; **à ~ vocale** TÉLÉCOM tone dialling.

fréquent, **~e** /fʀekɑ̃, ɑ̃t/ *adj* **1** (dans le temps) frequent; **il est ~ que cela arrive** it happens frequently; **2** (répandu) [*maladie, attitude*] common.

fréquentable /fʀekɑ̃tabl/ *adj* (de bonne réputation) respectable; **ce ne sont pas des gens ~s** they are not the sort of people one should associate with.

fréquentation /fʀekɑ̃tasjɔ̃/ *nf* **1** (amis) company **¢**; **avoir de mauvaises ~s** to keep bad company; **c'est une mauvaise ~ pour toi** that's not the sort of person you should associate with; **2** (présence) **~ de l'église/des théâtres** churchgoing/theatregoing[GB]; **record de ~ des théâtres** record theatre[GB] audiences (*pl*); **la ~ des théâtres est en baisse/hausse** fewer/more people are going to the theatre[GB].

fréquenté, **~e** /fʀekɑ̃te/ **I** *pp* ▶ **fréquenter**.
II *pp adj* [*café, plage, théâtre*] popular; [*rue*] busy; **lieu bien/mal ~** place that attracts the right/wrong sort of people; **la plage/cantine est peu ~e** not many people go to the beach/canteen.

fréquenter /fʀekɑ̃te/ [1] **I** *vtr* **1** (côtoyer) to associate with [*genre de personne*]; to see [sb] frequently [*amis, famille*]; to move in [*milieu*]; **~ les grands auteurs** FML to read the works of great writers; **2** (sortir avec) to go out with; **3** (aller à) to attend [*école*]; to visit [*musée*]; to go to [*plage*]; to frequent [*clubs*]; **il fréquente les bars** he hangs about○ in bars.
II se fréquenter *vpr* **1** (se voir) [*amis*] to see one another; **2** (sortir ensemble) to go out together.

frère /fʀɛʀ/ *nm* GÉN, RELIG brother; **~s ennemis** rivals within the same camp; **mes biens chers ~s** RELIG my dear brethren; **vieux ~** old pal; **peuple** or **pays ~** fellow nation; **~ Jacques** RELIG Brother Jacques; **être élevé chez les ~s** RELIG to be educated by the brothers (*in a Catholic school*).
■ **~ d'armes** brother-in-arms; **~ de lait** foster brother.

fresque /fʀɛsk/ *nf* **1** ART fresco; **2** FIG panorama.

fret /fʀɛt/ *nm* freight.

fréter /fʀete/ [14] *vtr* **1** (donner en location) to charter out; **2** (prendre en location) to charter.

frétillement /fʀetijmɑ̃/ *nm* (de poisson) wriggling **¢**; (de queue de chien) wagging **¢**.

frétiller /fʀetije/ [1] *vi* **1** [*poisson*] to wriggle; **~ de la queue** [*chien*] to wag its tail; **2** FIG **~ d'aise** to be quivering with pleasure.

fretin /fʀətɛ̃/ *nm* LIT, FIG (menu) **~** small fry.

freudien, -ienne /fʀødjɛ̃, ɛn/ *adj, nm,f* Freudian.

freux /fʀø/ *nm inv* ZOOL rook.

friable /fʀijabl/ *adj* [*roche, pâte*] crumbly; [*terre*] friable.

friand, **~e** /fʀijɑ̃, ɑ̃d/ **I** *adj* **être ~ de qch** to be very fond of sth.
II *nm* CULIN puff; **~ au fromage** cheese puff.

friandise /fʀijɑ̃diz/ *nf* bonbon) sweet GB, candy US.

fric○ /fʀik/ *nm* dough○, money; **être bourré de ~** to be loaded○.

friche /fʀiʃ/ *nf* AGRIC waste land; **en ~** [*terre*] uncultivated, waste (*épith*).

friction /fʀiksjɔ̃/ *nf* **1** MÉD rub; **2** (désaccord) friction **¢**; **3** (en physique, mécanique) friction.

frictionner /fʀiksjɔne/ [1] **I** *vtr* to give [sb] a rub [*personne*]; to rub [*pieds, tête*].
II se frictionner *vpr* to rub oneself down.

frigidaire® /fʀiʒidɛʀ/ *nm* refrigerator.

frigide /fʀiʒid/ *adj* frigid.

frigidité /fʀiʒidite/ *nf* frigidity.

frigo○ /fʀigo/ *nm* fridge○.

frigorifié, **~e** /fʀigɔʀifje/ *adj* frozen.

frigorifier /fʀigɔʀifje/ [2] *vtr* to freeze.

frigorifique /fʀigɔʀifik/ *adj* [*vitrine, camion*] refrigerated; **machine ~** refrigeration system.

frileux, -euse /fʀilø, øz/ *adj* **1** (sensible au froid) sensitive to the cold; **être (très) ~** [*personne*] to feel the cold; **2** (timoré) [*attitude, politique*] cautious.

frimas /fʀima/ *nmpl* cold weather **¢**.

frime○ /fʀim/ *nf* **1** (ostentation) **pour la ~** for show; **arrête ta ~!** stop showing off; **2** (simulation) pretence[GB]; **c'est de la ~** it's all an act.

frimer○ /fʀime/ [1] *vi* to show off○.

frimousse○ /fʀimus/ *nf* little face.

fringale○ /fʀɛ̃gal/ *nf* **j'ai la ~** I'm absolutely starving○.

fringant, **~e** /fʀɛ̃gɑ̃, ɑ̃t/ *adj* [*cheval*] spirited; [*personne*] dashing; [*allure*] brisk.

fringuer○: **se fringuer** /fʀɛ̃ge/ [1] *vpr* to dress.

fringues○ /fʀɛ̃g/ *nfpl* gear○ **¢**, clothes.

fripé, **~e** /fʀipe/ *adj* [*tissu*] crumpled; [*visage, bébé*] wrinkled.

friper /fʀipe/ [1] *vtr*, **se friper** *vpr* to crease, crumple.

fripon○, **-onne** /fʀipɔ̃, ɔn/ **I** *adj* mischievous.
II *nm,f* rascal.

fripouille○ /fʀipuj/ *nf* **1** (escroc) crook○; **2** (affectueusement) **(petite) ~!** (little) monkey!

friqué○, **~e** /fʀike/ *adj* loaded○, very rich.

frire /fʀiʀ/ [64] *vtr, vi* to fry.

frisé, **~e**[1] /fʀize/ *adj* [*cheveux*] curly; **elle est frisée** she has curly hair.

frisée[2] /fʀize/ *nf* (salade) curly endive, frisée.

friser /fʀize/ [1] **I** *vtr* **1** (boucler) to curl [*cheveux, moustache*]; **se faire ~** to have one's hair curled; **2** (frôler) [*remarque, attitude*] to border on [*insolence, grossièreté*]; **il frise les quarante ans** he's getting on for forty; **cela frise les 10%** it's approaching 10%.
II *vi* [*cheveux*] to curl; [*personne*] to have curly hair.
III se friser *vpr* **se ~ les cheveux** to curl one's hair.

frisette○ /fʀizɛt/ *nf* little curl.

frisquet○, **-ette** /fʀiskɛ, ɛt/ *adj* chilly.

frisson /fʀisɔ̃/ *nm* **1** (de froid, fièvre, plaisir) shiver (of); (de peur) shudder; **avoir un ~ de** (de froid, fièvre) to shiver with; (de plaisir) to tremble with; (de peur) to shudder with; **j'ai des ~s** I keep shivering; **grand ~** great thrill; **2** (de feuillage) rustling; (de l'eau) rippling.

frissonnement /fʀisɔnmɑ̃/ *nm* **1** (de feuillage) rustling; **2** (de froid, fièvre, plaisir) shivering (de of); (de peur) shuddering (de of).

frissonner /fʀisɔne/ [1] *vi* **1** (de fièvre, froid) to shiver (de with); (de peur) to shudder (de with); (de plaisir) d'orgueil) to tremble (de with); **2** [*feuillage*] to tremble; [*lac*] to ripple; **3** (commencer à bouillir) to simmer.

frite /fʀit/ *nf* **1** CULIN chip GB, French fry US; **2**○ (forme) **avoir la ~** to be feeling great, to be feeling chipper○ US.

friterie /fʀitʀi/ *nf* chip shop GB, French-fries stall US.

friteuse /fʀitøz/ *nf* chip pan GB, deep fat fryer US.

friture /fʀityʀ/ *nf* **1** CULIN (méthode) frying; (huile) oil; (aliment) fried food; poissons) ~ whitebait (*pl*); **2** (parasites) crackling.

frivole /fʀivɔl/ *adj* frivolous.

frivolité /fʀivɔlite/ *nf* **1** (caractère) frivolousness; (chose sans importance) trivial matter; **3** (dentelle) tatting.

froc /fʀɔk/ *nm* **1**○ (pantalon) trousers (*pl*) GB, pants (*pl*) US; **2** RELIG habit.

froid, **~e** /fʀwa, fʀwad/ **I** *adj* **1** (à basse température) cold; **2** FIG [*personne, lumière, beauté*] [*accueil, manières, ton*] cool; [*humour*] deadpan; [*colère*] controlled; **laisser ~** to leave [sb] cold.
II *nm* **1** (basse température) cold; **il fait ~** it's cold; **avoir ~** to be cold; **avoir ~ aux pieds** to have cold feet; **attraper** or **prendre ~** to catch a cold; **coup**

~ MÉD chill; **2** (distance) coldness; **il y a un certain ~ dans nos relations** there's a certain coolness in our relationship; **ils sont en ~ avec moi** relations between them and me are strained; **jeter un ~** to cast a chill (**dans, sur** over).

III à froid loc adv **démarrage à ~** cold start; **plaisanterie à ~** spontaneous joke; **analyse à ~** impartial analysis.

IDIOMES **il fait un ~ de canard**° it is bitterly cold; **avoir/faire** or **donner ~ dans le dos** to feel/to send a shiver down the spine; **ne pas avoir ~ aux yeux** to be fearless; **garder la tête ~e** to keep a cool head.

roidement /fʀwadmɑ̃/ adv **1** (sans émotion) coolly; **abattre ~** to shoot [sb] down in cold blood [personne]; **2** (calmement) with a cool head; **regarder les choses ~** to look at things coolly.

roideur /fʀwadœʀ/ nf coolness.

roissement /fʀwasmɑ̃/ nm **1** (de tissu, papier, feuille) (action) crumpling; (bruit) rustling; **2** MÉD strain.

roisser /fʀwase/ [1] **I** vtr **1** LIT (chiffonner) to crease, to crumple [tissu, vêtement]; to crumple [papier]; **il n'y a eu que de la tôle froissée**° the car was damaged but no-one was hurt; **2** (blesser) to hurt [personne, sensibilité]; **3** MÉD to strain [muscle, nerf].

II se froisser vpr **1** (se chiffonner) [tissu, vêtement, papier] to crease; **2** (s'offusquer) to be hurt (**de** by); **3** MÉD to strain.

rôlement /fʀolmɑ̃/ nm **1** (contact) brushing ⊄; **2** (de feuille, papier, tissu) rustling; (d'ailes) fluttering.

rôler /fʀole/ [1] **I** vtr **1** (toucher) [personne, main, genou] to brush; [projectile] to graze; **2** (passer près) [balle, pierre, voiture] to miss narrowly; [personne] to brush past [personne]; to brush against [objet, mur]; **il a frôlé la mort** he very nearly died; **~ le mauvais goût** to border on bad taste; **~ les 200 km/h** to nearly touch 200km per hour.

II se frôler vpr **1** (se toucher) [personnes, mains, genoux] to brush against each other; **2** (sans se toucher) [objets, voitures, conducteurs] to just miss each other; [personnes] to brush past each other.

romage /fʀomaʒ/ nm **1** cheese; **2**° (situation rentable) **il a trouvé un bon ~** he's found a nice little earner GB, he's hit pay dirt US; **se partager le ~** to split the profits.

■ **~ blanc** or **frais** fromage frais; **~ maigre** low-fat cheese; **~ à tartiner** cheese spread; **~ de tête** brawn GB, head cheese US.

IDIOMES **faire un ~ de qch**° to make a big deal° out of sth.

romager, -ère /fʀomaʒe, ɛʀ/ **I** adj cheese (épith).

II ▶374 nm (fabricant) cheesemaker; (commerçant) cheese seller.

romagerie /fʀomaʒʀi/ **▶374** nf (fabrique) dairy; (magasin) cheese shop; (**rayon**) **~** cheese counter.

roment /fʀomɑ̃/ nm wheat.

ronce /fʀɔ̃s/ nf gather; **jupe à ~s** gathered skirt.

roncement /fʀɔ̃smɑ̃/ nm **avoir un léger ~ de sourcils** to frown slightly.

roncer /fʀɔ̃se/ [12] **I** vtr **1** (en couture) to gather; **2 ~ les sourcils** to frown; **~ le nez** to wrinkle one's nose.

II se froncer vpr **ses sourcils se froncèrent** he/she frowned.

rondaison /fʀɔ̃dɛzɔ̃/ nf **1** (feuillage) LITER foliage ⊄; **2** BOT foliation.

ronde /fʀɔ̃d/ nf **1** (arme) sling; (jouet) catapult GB, slingshot US; **2** (révolte) revolt.

rondeur, -euse /fʀɔ̃dœʀ, øz/ **I** adj [personne, esprit] rebellious; [propos] anti-authoritarian.

II nm troublemaker.

front /fʀɔ̃/ **I** nm **1** ANAT forehead, brow LITTÉR; **2** MIL front; **sur le ~ de l'emploi** FIG on the job front; **faire ~ commun contre l'ennemi** to make a united stand against the enemy; **3** (façade) façade; **4** MÉTÉO front; **5** (en politique) front.

II de front loc adv **aborder un problème de ~** to tackle a problem head-on; **les voitures se sont**

heurtées de ~ the cars collided head-on; **ils marchaient à quatre de ~** they were walking four abreast; **mener plusieurs tâches de ~** to have several jobs on the go.

■ **~ de mer** seafront; **Front populaire** HIST Popular Front.

IDIOMES **avoir le ~ de faire qch** to have the face ou effrontery to do sth.

frontal, ~e, mpl **-aux** /fʀɔ̃tal, o/ adj [attaque] frontal; [choc, collision] head-on (épith).

frontalier, -ière /fʀɔ̃talje, ɛʀ/ **I** adj border (épith); **travailleur ~** person who works across the border.

II nm,f person living near the border.

frontière /fʀɔ̃tjɛʀ/ nf **1** GÉOG, POL frontier, border; **à l'intérieur de nos ~s** at home; **hors de nos ~s** abroad; **2** (limite) **~s entre les disciplines** boundaries between disciplines; **faire reculer les ~s de la connaissance** to push back the frontiers of knowledge; **au-delà des ~s du possible** beyond the realms of possibility.

fronton /fʀɔ̃tɔ̃/ nm ARCHIT pediment.

frottement /fʀotmɑ̃/ nm **1** (mouvement) rubbing ⊄; **2** (bruit) **j'entends des ~s** I can hear something rubbing; **3** (en mécanique, physique) friction ⊄; **résistance de ~** frictional resistance.

frotter /fʀote/ [1] **I** vtr **1** (masser) to rub; **~ une allumette** to strike a match; **2** (nettoyer) to scrub [peau, parquet, linge, tapis]; to polish [argenterie].

II vi to rub; **le bas de la porte frotte** the bottom of the door is scraping against the floor.

III se frotter vpr **1** (se frictionner) **se ~ les yeux** to rub one's eyes; **se ~ les mains** LIT, FIG to rub one's hands; **2** (se nettoyer) **se ~ les mains** to scrub one's hands; **3** (se mesurer) **se ~ à** to take on.

IDIOMES **se faire ~ les oreilles**° to have one's ears boxed; **qui s'y frotte s'y pique** if you go looking for trouble, you'll find it.

frottis /fʀoti/ nm inv **1** (en biologie) smear; **2** ART scumble.

froussard°, **~e** /fʀusaʀ, aʀd/ nm,f chicken°, coward.

frousse° /fʀus/ nf fright; **avoir la ~** to be scared.

fructifier /fʀyktifje/ [2] vi [capital] to yield a profit; [affaire] to flourish; **faire ~ son argent** to make one's money grow.

fructueux, -euse /fʀyktɥø, øz/ adj (fécond) [relation, réunion] fruitful; [essai, carrière] successful; [travail] productive; (lucratif) profitable.

frugal, ~e, mpl **-aux** /fʀygal, o/ adj frugal.

frugalité /fʀygalite/ nf frugality; **avec ~** frugally.

fruit /fʀɥi/ nm **1** GÉN, CULIN fruit ⊄; **voulez-vous un ~?** would you like some fruit?; **aimer les ~s** to like fruit; **2** (résultat) fruit; **les ~s de ses efforts** the fruits of one's efforts; **le ~ de mes entrailles** the fruit of my womb; **porter ses ~s** to bear fruit.

■ **~ confit** candied ou glacé fruit; **~ défendu** BIBLE forbidden fruit; **~ de la passion** passion fruit; **~ sec** CULIN dried fruit; FIG (personne) disappointment; **~s de mer** seafood ⊄; **~s rouges** soft fruit ⊄ GB, berries US.

fruité, ~e /fʀɥite/ adj [alcool, parfum] fruity.

fruitier, -ière /fʀɥitje, ɛʀ/ **I** adj fruit (épith).

II ▶374 nm,f fruiterer GB, fruit seller US.

frusques° /fʀysk/ nfpl gear° ⊄, clothes; **de vieilles ~** old clothes.

fruste /fʀyst/ adj unsophisticated.

frustrant, ~e /fʀystʀɑ̃, ɑ̃t/ adj frustrating.

frustration /fʀystʀasjɔ̃/ nf frustration.

frustré, ~e /fʀystʀe/ **I** adj frustrated.

II nm,f malcontent.

frustrer /fʀystʀe/ [1] vtr **1** (décevoir) **~ les efforts de qn** to thwart sb's efforts; **~ qn dans son attente** to disappoint sb's hopes; **2** (priver) **~ qn de qch** to deprive sb of sth; (malhonnêtement) to cheat sb (out) of sth; **3** PSYCH to frustrate.

fuel /fjul/ nm = **fioul**.

fugace /fygas/ *adj* [*sensation, souvenir, reflet, instant, odeur*] fleeting; [*symptôme*] elusive.

fugitif, -ive /fyʒitif, iv/ I *adj* **1** (échappé) [*prisonnier*] escaped; [*esclave*] runaway (*épith*); **2** (bref) [*sensation, pensée, ombre, espoir*] fleeting; [*plaisir, joie*] elusive.
II *nmf* fugitive.

fugue /fyg/ *nf* **1** (escapade) **faire une ~** to run away; **c'est sa première ~** it's the first time he/she has run away; **2** MUS fugue.

fuguer /fyge/ [1] *vi* to run away.

fugueur, -euse /fygœʀ, øz/ *nmf* runaway (child).

fuir /fɥiʀ/ [29] I *vtr* **1** (quitter) to flee [*pays, ville, oppression*]; to flee from [*combats, amour*]; **2** (éviter) to escape [*hiver*]; to avoid [*responsabilité, personne*]; to steer clear of [*problème, foule*]; to stay out of [*soleil*].
II *vi* **1** (partir) [*personne, soldat, capitaux*] to flee; [*animal*] to run away; **~ à toutes jambes** to run for it; **faire ~** to scare [sb] off [*personne*]; **2** (suinter) [*robinet, gaz, toit, stylo*] to leak; **3** (se dérober) **~ devant ses responsabilités** not to face up to one's responsibilities; **4** (défiler et disparaître) [*nuages*] to sail by; [*temps*] to fly by.

fuite /fɥit/ *nf* **1** (mouvement) GÉN flight; (de fugitif) escape; **prendre la ~** [*personne*] to flee; [*fugitif*] to escape; **~ des cerveaux** brain drain; **~ de capitaux** outflow of capital; **2** (d'information) leak; **~s avant l'examen** leaks before the examination; **3** TECH (suintement) leak; **~ d'eau** water leak.

fulgurant, ~e /fylgyʀɑ̃, ɑ̃t/ *adj* [*réflexes, attaque*] lightning (*épith*); [*ascension, progression*] dazzling; [*imagination*] brilliant; [*douleur*] searing (*épith*); **ses progrès ont été ~s** he/she has made terrific progress; **regards ~s** blazing eyes.

fulminer /fylmine/ [1] *vi* (enrager) to fulminate (**contre** against); **il fulminait intérieurement** he was seething.

fumant, ~e /fymɑ̃, ɑ̃t/ *adj* **1** (dégageant de la fumée) smoking; (dégageant de la vapeur) steaming; **2**○ (sensationnel) terrific○; **faire un coup ~** to pull off a real coup (**à qn** on sb); **préparer un coup ~ contre** or **à qn** to have a nasty surprise in store for sb.

fumasseᵒ /fymas/ *adj* **être ~** to be fuming.

fumé, ~e¹ /fyme/ I *pp* ▶ **fumer**.
II *pp adj* **1** [*viande, poisson*] smoked; **2** (teinté) [*vitre, lunettes*] tinted; [*verre*] smoked; **des lunettes à verres ~s** tinted glasses.

fume-cigarette /fymsigaʀɛt/ *nm inv* cigarette holder.

fumée² /fyme/ I *pp adj f* ▶ **fumé**.
II *nf* **1** (de feu) smoke; (d'usine, d'échappement) **~s** fumes; **partir en ~** FIG to go up in smoke; **2** (vapeur) steam.
IDIOMES **il n'y a pas de ~ sans feu** PROV there's no smoke without fire.

fumer /fyme/ [1] I *vtr* **1** [*fumeur*] to smoke; **2** CULIN to smoke [*viande, poisson*]; **3** AGRIC to manure [*sol*].
II *vi* **1** [*fumeur*] to smoke; **2** [*volcan, cheminée*] to smoke; [*potage*] to steam; [*acide*] to give off fumes.
IDIOMES **~ comme un pompier** or **sapeur** to smoke like a chimney.

fumet /fymɛ/ *nm* **1** CULIN (de viande) aroma; (de vin) bouquet; (sauce) fumet; **2** (forte odeur) smell, odour^GB.

fumeur, -euse¹ /fymœʀ, øz/ *nmf* smoker; **un grand ~** a heavy smoker; **zone ~s/non ~s** smoking/non-smoking area.

fumeux, -euse² /fymø, øz/ *adj* [*théorie, propos*] woolly GB, wooly US; [*personne*] woolly-minded.

fumier /fymje/ *nm* **1** AGRIC manure; **tas de ~** dunghill; **2**ᵒ (salaud) OFFENSIVE bastard INJUR.

fumigène /fymiʒɛn/ I *adj* MIL [*grenade*] smoke.
II *nm* MIL smoke device; AGRIC fumigator.

fumiste /fymist/ *nmf* **1**○ (charlatan) phoney○; (paresseux) ▶374| **2** ▶374| (technicien) (pour cheminées) chimney specialist; (de chauffage) stove fitter.

fumisterie /fymistəʀi/ *nf* **1**○ (action peu sérieuse) joke; **c'est une** or **de la ~** it's a joke; **2** (profession) (pour cheminées) chimney engineering; (pour les appareils de chauffage) stove fitting.

fumoir /fymwaʀ/ *nm* smoking-room.

funambule /fynɑ̃byl/ ▶374| *nmf* tightrope walke... **un numéro de ~(s)** a tightrope act.

funèbre /fynɛbʀ/ *adj* **1** (funéraire) funeral; **2** (lugubr... gloomy.

funérailles /fyneʀaj/ *nfpl* funeral (*sg*).

funéraire /fyneʀɛʀ/ *adj* [*cérémonie, frais*] funera... [*objet, monument*] funerary; **dalle** or **stèle ~** toml... stone, gravestone GB.

funeste /fynɛst/ *adj* [*erreur, conseil*] fatal; [*décisio...* jour] fateful; [*conséquence*] dire; **être ~ à qn/qch** ... be fatal to sb/sth; **cela nous a été ~** it was fatal.

funiculaire /fynikylɛʀ/ *nm* funicular.

fur: **au fur et à mesure** /ofyʀeaməzyʀ/ *loc a*... **passe-moi les livres, je les rangerai au ~ et** ... **mesure** pass me the books, I'll put them away as I g... along; **au ~ et à mesure de leurs besoins** as an... when they need it; **la championne joue de mieux e**... **mieux au ~ et à mesure des rencontres** th... champion is playing better and better with eac... match; **au ~ et à mesure que la soirée avançait,** ... **devenait de plus en plus animé** as the evening wer... on, he became more and more animated.

furax○ /fyʀaks/ *adj inv* (hopping) mad○ (*jamais épith*... **être ~ de devoir faire qch** to be mad○ at having t... do sth; **je suis ~ d'avoir dit ça** I could kick myse... for saying that○.

furet /fyʀɛ/ *nm* ferret.

fureter /fyʀte/ [18] *vi* to rummage, to ferret around.

fureur /fyʀœʀ/ *nf* **1** (colère) rage, fury; **~ aveugle**... **noire** blind/unholy rage; **être en ~ contre qn**... **contre qch** to be in a rage with sb/about sth; **s**... **mettre en ~ contre qn/qch** to fly into a rage wit... sb/sth; **2** (passion) frenzy; **s'adonner au jeu avec ~**... to gamble frenziedly; **~ de vivre** lust for life; **avoi**... **la ~ du jeu** to be addicted to gambling; **faire ~** t... be all the rage.

furibond, ~e /fyʀibɔ̃, ɔ̃d/ *adj* furious.

furie /fyʀi/ *nf* **1** (rage) rage, fury; **mettre qn en ~** t... make sb furious; **entrer en ~** to get furious, to fl... into a rage; **2** (harpie) fury.

furieusement /fyʀjøzmɑ̃/ *adv* **1** (violemment) [*atta*... quer, cogner] furiously; [*injurier*] violently; [*répondre*... angrily; **2**○ (extrêmement) **j'ai ~ envie de dormir** I'r... dying to go to sleep; **elle ressemble ~ à son père**... she's incredibly like her father.

furieux, -ieuse /fyʀjø, øz/ *adj* **1** (irrité) [*personne*... geste, air, ton] furious; [*foule, animal, cris*] angry; **être**... **~ contre qn** to be furious with sb; **être ~ de qch**... to be infuriated by sth; **2**○ (intense) [*envie*] terrible... **3** (violent) [*combat*] intense; [*tempête, torrent*] raging.

furoncle /fyʀɔ̃kl/ *nm* boil, furuncle SPÉC.

furtif, -ive /fyʀtif, iv/ *adj* **1** (discret, rapide) furtive... **marcher d'un pas ~** to creep along; **2** (passager... [soupçon, joie, émotion] fleeting; **3** MIL (indétectable... **avion ~** Stealth bomber.

furtivement /fyʀtivmɑ̃/ *adv* furtively.

fusain /fyzɛ̃/ *nm* **1** (arbuste) spindle tree; **2** ART (matière... charcoal, fusain SPÉC; (crayon) charcoal crayon; (dessin... charcoal drawing; **au ~** [*dessiner*] in charcoal... [*dessin*] charcoal (*épith*).

fuseau, pl ~x /fyzo/ *nm* **1** (pour filer) spindle; **en ~**... [*jambe de pantalon, muscle*] tapering; **2** (à dentelle) lace... bobbin; **3** (pantalon) **~(x)** (de ski) ski pants (*pl*).
■ **~ horaire** time zone.

fusée /fyze/ *nf* **1** (en astronautique, pyrotechnie) rocket... **2** MIL (missile) rocket, missile; **3** AUT stub axle.
■ **~ antichar** antitank rocket ou missile; **~ éclai**... **rante** flare; **~ porteuse** carrier rocket; **~ sol**... air surface-to-air missile.
IDIOMES **partir comme une ~** to set off like a... rocket.

fuselage /fyzlaʒ/ *nm* fuselage.

fuselé, ~e /fyzle/ *adj* [*muscle, doigt*] tapering; [*arbre*... colonne, structure*] spindle-shaped.

fuser /fyze/ [1] *vi* **1** (retentir) to ring out; **les rires**...

fusaient laughter came from all sides; **2** (jaillir) [*objet*] to rocket; [*lumière*] to stream out.

fusible /fyzibl/ **I** *adj* fusible.

II *nm* (fil, cartouche) fuse.

fusil /fyzi/ *nm* **1** (arme) gun, shotgun; MIL rifle; **coup de ~** LIT gunshot; **dans ce restaurant c'est le coup de ~**◦ FIG they really sting yo.. in that restaurant; **2** (tireur) **être un bon ~** to be a good shot; **3** (pour aiguiser) sharpening steel.

IDIOMES **partir la fleur au ~** to set off without a care in the world.

fusilier /fyzi(l)je/ *nm* rifleman, fusilier; HIST fusilier.
■ **~ marin** marine.

fusillade /fyzijad/ *nf* (bruit) gunfire ⊄; (bataille) shoot-out.

fusiller /fyzije/ [1] *vtr* **1** (exécuter) to shoot; **2**◦ (abîmer) to wreck.

IDIOMES **~ qn du regard** to look daggers at sb.

fusil-mitrailleur, *pl* **fusils-mitrailleurs** /fyzi mitrajœr/ *nm* light machine gun.

fusion /fyzjɔ̃/ *nf* **1** (liquéfaction) (de métal) melting, fusion SPÉC; (de glace) melting; **roche/métal en ~** molten rock/metal; **2** BIOL, PHYS fusion; **~ (thermo)nucléaire** nuclear fusion; **3** LING fusion; **4** (union) (d'entreprises, de partis, listes, professions) merger (**entre** between); (de systèmes, cultures, théories) fusion (**entre** of); (de peuples, races) mixing (**entre** of).

fusionner /fyzjone/ [1] *vtr*, *vi* to merge.

fustiger /fystiʒe/ [13] *vtr* **1** (condamner) to castigate, to lambast; **2** (battre) to thrash.

fût /fy/ *nm* **1** (tonneau) cask, barrel; (pour produits chimiques) drum; **2** (d'arbre) trunk; **3** (de colonne) shaft.

futaie /fytɛ/ *nf* (forêt) forest of tall trees.

futé, **~e** /fyte/ **I** *adj* [*personne, animal*] wily, crafty PÉJ; [*sourire, réponse*] crafty; **ce n'est pas très ~** that isn't/wasn't very clever.

II *nm,f* (petit) **~** cunning little devil.

futile /fytil/ *adj* [*projet, prétexte, distraction*] trivial; [*personne, existence, propos*] superficial.

futilité /fytilite/ **I** *nf* (insignifiance) superficiality.

II **futilités** *nfpl* (paroles) banalities; (objets) trifles; (actions) meaningless activities; (détails) trivial details.

futur, **~e** /fytyʀ/ **I** *adj* future; **son ~ mari** her future husband; **les ~s époux** the engaged couple (*sg*); **les ~es mères** expectant mothers; **cet enfant, c'est un ~ artiste/champion** that child has the makings of an artist/a champion.

II *nm* **1** (avenir) future; **le train du ~** the train of the future; **2** LING future; **au ~** in the future (tense).
■ **~ antérieur** LING future perfect; **~ simple** LING future tense.

futuriste /fytyʀist/ *adj* **1** (ultramoderne) [*décor, voiture, vision*] futuristic; **2** ART, LITTÉRAT futurist.

futurologue /fytyʀɔlɔg/ ▶374 *nmf* futurologist.

fuyant, **~e** /fɥijɑ̃, ɑ̃t/ *adj* [*regard*] shifty; [*caractère*] slippery◦; [*point, horizon*] receding; [*bonheur*] elusive; **front/profil ~** receding forehead/profile.

fuyard, **~e** /fɥijaʀ, aʀd/ *nmf* **1** (fugitif) runaway; **2** (déserteur) deserter.

Gg

g, G /ʒe/ *nm inv* **1** (lettre) g, G; **2** (*written abbr* = **gramme**) 250 g *250* g; **3 G7** *abbr* ▶ **groupe**.

gabardine /gabaʀdin/ *nf* gabardine.

gabarit /gabaʀi/ *nm* **1** (de véhicule) size; **véhicule hors ~** oversize vehicle; **2**° (de personne) (corpulence) build; (aptitudes) calibre^{GB}.

gabegie /gabʒi/ *nf* (gaspillage) waste (due to mismanagement); (désordre) muddle.

gabonais, -e /gabɔnɛ, ɛz/ ▶ **394** *adj* Gabonese.

gâcher /gɑʃe/ [1] *vtr* to waste [*nourriture*]; to throw away [*vie*]; to spoil [*spectacle*]; to ruin [*affaire*].
IDIOMES **~ le métier** to ruin the trade (*by undercutting prices*).

gâchette /gɑʃɛt/ *nf* (d'arme) tumbler; (détente) CONTROV trigger; **appuyer sur la ~** to pull the trigger; **avoir la ~ facile** to be trigger-happy.

gâchis /gɑʃi/ *nm inv* (gaspillage) waste ¢; (pagaille) mess.

gadget /gadʒɛt/ *nm* gadget.

gadin° /gadɛ̃/ *nm* **ramasser** or **prendre un ~** to fall flat on one's face.

gadoue° /gadu/ *nf* (boue) mud.

gaélique /gaelik/ ▶ **338** *adj, nm* Gaelic.

gaffe /gaf/ *nf* **1**° (acte) boob^{GB}, blooper^{US}, blunder; (parole) clanger^{GB}, blooper^{US}; **faire ~** to watch out (**à** for); **faire ~ que** to be careful that; **2** NAUT boathook; **3** (pour accrocher le poisson) gaff.

gaffeur, -euse /gafœʀ, øz/ *nm,f* blunderer.

gag /gag/ *nm* **1** gag; **2** (incident drôle) joke.

gaga° /gaga/ **I** *adj inv* (gâteux) gaga°; (débile) daft^{GB}, silly; **devenir ~** to go gaga.
II *nmf* dodderer°.

gage /gaʒ/ **I** *nm* **1** (garantie) security ¢, surety ¢; **prêter sur ~s** to lend against surety; **mettre qch en ~** to pawn sth; **ta ténacité est le ~ de ta réussite future** your tenacity is a guarantee of your future success; **2** JEUX (pénitence) forfeit; **3** (d'amour, de fidélité, bonne foi) pledge; **donner des ~s d'amitié à qn** to pledge friendship to sb.
II gages† *nmpl* (salaire) wages; **tueur à ~s** hired killer.

gager /gaʒe/ [13] *vtr* **1** (supposer) FML **~ que** to suppose that, to wager† that; **2** (mettre en gage) to pawn.

gageure /gaʒyʀ/ *nf* challenge.

gagnant, -e /gaɲɑ̃, ɑ̃t/ **I** *adj* [*numéro, équipe*] winning (*épith*); **donner un cheval/qn ~** to tip a horse/sb to win; **partir ~** to be on to a winner; **être** or **sortir ~** to come out on top (**de** in).
II *nm,f* (personne, cheval) winner.

gagne-pain /gaɲpɛ̃/ *nm inv* livelihood.

gagne-petit /gaɲpəti/ **I** *adj inv* PEJ **être ~** to be after every last penny.
II *nmf inv* low-wage earner.

gagner /gaɲe/ [1] **I** *vtr* **1** (remporter) to win [*compétition, guerre, procès*]; **~ aux points** to win on points; **pour lui, rien n'est encore gagné** FIG he's not there yet, he's still got a long way to go; **c'est gagné!** LIT we've done it!; IRON well done!; **à tous les coups on gagne!** every one a winner!; **2** (percevoir, mériter) to earn; **~ 10 000 francs par mois** to earn 10,000 francs a month; **il gagne bien sa vie** he makes a good living; **il a gagné une fortune sur la vente du tableau** he made a fortune from the sale of the picture; **les sommes gagnées au jeu** gambling gains; **c'est**

toujours ça de gagné! well, that's something anyway!; **3** (acquérir) to gain [*réputation, avantage*]; **~ du temps** (atermoyer) to gain time; **~ du terrain** [*personne, armée, idées*] to gain ground (**sur** on); [*incendie*] to spread; **~ de la vitesse** to gather speed; **il a gagné de l'assurance** he has gained in self-confidence; **elle a gagné 5 cm en un an** she's grown 5 cm in a year; **il a gagné 9 kilos** he's put on 9 kilos; **l'équipe a gagné trois places** the team has moved up three places; **4** (économiser) to save [*temps*]; **~ de la place en faisant** to make more room by doing; **5** (attirer) to win [*sb*] over (**à** to); **6** (atteindre) [*voyageur, véhicule*] to reach, to get to [*lieu*]; **7** (atteindre) [*incendie, maladie, troubles, chômage*] to spread to [*lieu*]; **8** (s'emparer de) [*peur, émotion, découragement*] to overcome [*personne*]; **la fatigue me gagnait peu à peu** I was gradually overcome with fatigue; **je sentais le froid me ~** I started to feel cold; **9** (battre) **~ qn de vitesse** to outstrip sb.
II *vi* **1** (réussir) to win; **~ aux élections** to win the election; **2** (tirer avantage) **le film gagne à être vu en version originale** the film is best seen in the original version; **vous gagneriez à diversifier vos produits** it would be to your advantage to diversify; **elle gagne à être connue** she improves on acquaintance; **3** (acquérir plus) to gain (**en** in); **les entreprises ont gagné en productivité** firms have improved their productivity; **4** (être bénéficiaire) **y ~** to come off better; **y ~ en** to gain in; **5** (recouvrir) [*mer*] to encroach (**sur** on).

gagneur, -euse /gaɲœʀ, øz/ *nm,f* winner.

gai, -e /gɛ/ **I** *adj* **1** (joyeux) [*personne, visage*] happy; [*caractère, regard*] cheerful; [*réunion, œuvre*] light-hearted; [*couleur*] bright, cheerful; **2** (plaisant) IRON **c'est ~** great! IRON; **ça promet d'être ~** that'll be fun! IRON; **3** (éméché) merry; **4**° (homosexuel) CONTROV gay.
II° *nm* (homosexuel) CONTROV gay.

gaiement /gɛmɑ̃/ *adv* [*partir, chanter*] cheerfully, merrily; [*décoré*] gaily; **allons-y ~** HUM let's get on with it.

gaieté /gete/ *nf* (de personne, lieu, d'histoire) gaiety, cheerfulness; **il ne l'a pas fait de ~ de cœur** he wasn't very happy about doing it.

gaillard, -e /gajaʀ, aʀd/ **I** *adj* **1** (vigoureux) [*personne*] strapping; **2** (grivois) [*chanson*] ribald.
II *nm,f* strapping lad/girl; **viens ici, mon ~°!** come here, lad^{GB}, over here buddy^{US}!
III° *nm* (lascar) sly customer°.
■ **~ d'arrière** NAUT poop; **~ d'avant** NAUT (en marine ancienne) forecastle; (en marine moderne) forward superstructure.

gain /gɛ̃/ *nm* **1** (argent) earnings (*pl*); **tirer un ~ médiocre de ses efforts** to get a meagre^{GB} return for one's efforts; **cette maison représente ses ~s de toute une vie de labeur** this house represents the fruits of a lifetime's hard work; **mes ~s au jeu** my gambling gains; **2** (profit en Bourse) gain; **3** (économie) saving; **c'est un ~ de temps considérable** it saves a considerable amount of time.

gaine /gɛn/ *nf* **1** (de poignard) sheath; **2** (sous-vêtement) girdle; **3** TECH (de fil électrique) sheathing; (de tuyau) casing; **4** BOT sheath.

gainer /gene/ [1] *vtr* **1** (mouler) [*robe*] to sheathe [*corps*]; **2** TECH to sheathe [*fil électrique*].

gala /gala/ *nm* gala; **tenue de ~** evening dress ¢.

galamment /galamɑ̃/ *adv* gallantly.

galant, **~e** /galɑ̃, ɑ̃t/ **I** *adj* **1** (délicat envers les femmes) gallant, gentlemanly; **2** (obligeant) **soyez ~** be a gentleman; **3** (amoureux) [*rendez-vous*] romantic; **elle était en ~e compagnie** she was in the company of a gentleman; **4** ART, MUS [*style*] galant.
II† *nm* (fiancé) beau†.

galanterie /galɑ̃tʀi/ *nf* **1** (courtoisie) gallantry; **2†** (propos flatteur) flattering remark.

galaxie /galaksi/ *nf* galaxy.

galbe /galb/ *nm* curve.

galbé, **~e** /galbe/ *adj* [*colonne*] with entasis (*épith, après n*); [*pied de meuble*] curved; **épaule bien ~e** shapely shoulder.

galber /galbe/ [1] *vtr* to shape.

gale /gal/ ▶ **196** *nf* **1** (de personne) scabies ¢; **je n'ai pas la ~**○ HUM I'm not contagious; **2** (du chien, chat) mange; (du mouton) scab; **3** BOT scab.
IDIOMES **il est mauvais** or **méchant comme la ~**○ he's a nasty customer○.

galéjade /galeʒad/ *nf* tall story.

galère /galɛʀ/ *nf* **1** HIST (vaisseau) galley; **condamné aux ~s** (à ramer) sentenced to the galleys; (aux travaux forcés) sentenced to hard labour○GB; **2**○ (situation pénible) hell○; **c'est (la) ~!** it's a real pain○!; **être dans la même ~** to be in the same boat.

galérer○ /galeʀe/ [14] *vi* **1** (peiner) to have a hard time; **2** (travailler) to slave away, to slog away○.

galerie /galʀi/ *nf* **1** ARCHIT (de maison, musée) gallery; **2** ART (magasin, musée) gallery; **3** (de mine, grotte) gallery; (de taupe) tunnel; **4** AUT (pour bagages) **~ (de toit)** roof rack; **5** (de théâtre) gallery; **amuser la ~**○ to play to the gallery; **pour épater la ~**○ (in order) to impress the crowd.
■ **~ marchande** shopping arcade; **Galerie des Glaces** hall of mirrors.

galérien /galeʀjɛ̃/ *nm* HIST (sur une galère) galley slave; (au bagne) convict.

galet /galɛ/ *nm* **1** (caillou) pebble; **2** TECH roller.

galette /galɛt/ *nf* (gâteau) plain round flat cake; (crêpe) pancake.
■ **~ des Rois** Twelfth Night cake (*containing bean or lucky charm*).

galeux, **-euse** /galø, øz/ **I** *adj* **1** (atteint de gale) [*personne*] with scabies (*épith, après n*); [*chien*] mangy; [*mouton*] scabby; [*arbre*] covered with scab (*après n*); **2** (décrépit) [*mur*] peeling; [*bâtiment, quartier*] slummy.
II *nm,f* **1** LIT person with scabies; **2**○ FIG scum○ ¢.

galimatias /galimatja/ *nm inv* (parlé) gibberish; (écrit) rubbish.

galipette○ /galipɛt/ *nf* (cabriole) somersault.

Galles /gal/ ▶ **509** *nprfpl* **le pays de ~** Wales (*sg*).

gallicisme /galisism/ *nm* (dans une langue étrangère) gallicism; (en français) French idiom.

gallois, **~e** /galwɑ, ɑz/ ▶ **338** **I** *adj* Welsh.
II *nm* LING Welsh.

Gallois, **~e** /galwɑ, ɑz/ *nm,f* Welshman/Welshwoman; **les ~** the Welsh.

gallon /galɔ̃/ ▶ **86** *nm* gallon.

galoche /galɔʃ/ *nf* (sabot, godillot) clog; **menton en ~** protruding chin.

galon /galɔ̃/ *nm* **1** (ruban) braid ¢; **2** MIL stripe; **gagner ses ~s** to win promotion; **prendre du ~** to be promoted.

galonné, **~e** /galɔne/ **I** *adj* **1** (bordé de galon) trimmed with braid; **2** MIL [*militaire*] of officer class (*épith, après n*); [*manche*] displaying the insignia of rank (*épith, après n*).
II○ *nm* soldiers' slang brass hat○.

galop /galo/ *nm* **1** (d'équidé) gallop; **petit ~** canter; **grand ~** full gallop; **cheval au ~** galloping horse; **partir au ~** to set off at a gallop; **faire du ~** to gallop; **au ~!** gallop!; **s'enfuir au (triple) ~**○ [*personne*] to run off double-quick; **au ~**○! hurry up!; **2** MUS galop.
■ **~ d'essai** trial run.

IDIOMES **chassez le naturel il revient au ~** PROV what's bred in the bone will come out in the flesh PROV.

galopade /galɔpad/ *nf* **1** (de chevaux) gallop; **2**○ FIG (course précipitée) stampede.

galopant, **~e** /galɔpɑ̃, ɑ̃t/ *adj* [*inflation*] galloping; [*prolifération, démographie*] soaring.

galoper /galɔpe/ [1] *vi* **1** [*cheval, cavalier*] to gallop; **ne laisse pas ~ ton imagination** FIG don't let your imagination run away with you; **2**○ (en faisant du bruit) [*enfant*] to charge (around); **3**○ (se dépêcher) to dash (around).

galopin /galɔpɛ̃/ *nm* (enfant) rascal.

galvaniser /galvanize/ [1] *vtr* LIT, FIG to galvanize.

galvauder /galvode/ [1] *vtr* to sully [*réputation*]; to dull [*gloire*]; to waste [*talent*]; to overwork [*idée*]; to squander [*fortune*]; **expression galvaudée** hackneyed expression.

gamba /gɑ̃ba/ *pl as/ *nf* large (Mediterranean) prawn.

gambader /gɑ̃bade/ [1] *vi* [*animal, enfant*] to gambol.

gamberger /gɑ̃bɛʀʒe/ [13] *vi* to think hard.

gamelle /gamɛl/ *nf* (de soldat) dixie GB, mess kit; (de campeur) billycan GB, tin dish; (d'ouvrier) lunchbox; (d'animal) dish.
IDIOMES **prendre** or **ramasser une ~**○ (tomber) to fall flat on one's face○; (échouer) to come a cropper.

gamin, **~e** /gamɛ̃, in/ **I** *adj* [*air, allure*] youthful; [*caractère, attitude*] childish.
II *nm,f* kid○; **~ des rues** street urchin.

gaminerie /gaminʀi/ *nf* (action, propos) childish behaviour GB ¢.

gamme /gam/ *nf* **1** MUS scale; **2** (série) range; **produit (de) bas de ~** (en qualité) low quality product; (en prix) cheap product; **modèle (de) haut de ~** upmarket model; **viser le haut/bas de ~** to aim at the top/lower end of the market.

gammée /game/ *adj f* **croix ~** swastika.

ganache /ganaʃ/ *nf* **1** CULIN chocolate cream filling; **2** (de cheval) lower jaw; **3†** (idiot) **vieille ~** old fool.

Gand /gɑ̃/ ▶ **628** *npr* Ghent.

ganglion /gɑ̃glijɔ̃/ *nm* ganglion; **avoir des ~s**○ to have swollen glands.

gangrène /gɑ̃gʀɛn/ ▶ **196** *nf* **1** (maladie) gangrene; **2** FIG (corruption) canker.

gangrener /gɑ̃gʀəne/ [16] **I** *vtr* FIG to corrupt [*pays, société*].
II **se gangrener** *vpr* **1** [*plaie*] to become gangrenous; **2** FIG [*société*] to become corrupt.

gangster /gɑ̃gstɛʀ/ *nm* **1** (bandit) gangster; **2** (escroc) swindler.

gangstérisme /gɑ̃gsteʀism/ *nm* organized crime.

gangue /gɑ̃g/ *nf* **1** LIT (substance) gangue; **~ de boue** coating of mud; **2** FIG **extraire les idées de leur ~** to pick out the good ideas and discard the dross.

gant /gɑ̃/ *nm* glove; **~s de cuir** leather gloves.
■ **~ de boxe** boxing glove; **~ de crin** massage glove; **~ de ménage** rubber glove; **~ de toilette ~** (face) flannel GB, wash cloth US.
IDIOMES **son tailleur lui va comme un ~** her suit fits her like a glove; **tes nouvelles fonctions te vont comme un ~** your new duties suit you down to the ground; **mettre** or **prendre des ~s avec qn** to handle sb with kid gloves; **elle n'a pas pris de ~s pour m'annoncer mon renvoi** she didn't pull any punches when telling me I was fired; **jeter/relever le ~** to throw down/to take up the gauntlet; ▶ **velours**.

ganté, **~e** /gɑ̃te/ *adj* [*main*] gloved; [*personne*] wearing gloves (*après n*).

gantelet /gɑ̃tlɛ/ *nm* **1** HIST MIL gauntlet; **2** (en fauconnerie) hawking glove.

garage /gaʀaʒ/ *nm* **1** (pour se garer) garage; **2** ▶ **374** (station-service) garage.
■ **~ d'autobus** bus depot; **~ à vélos** bicycle shed; (dans un bâtiment) bicycle storage area.

garagiste /gaʀaʒist/ ▶ **374** *nmf* (propriétaire) garage owner; (ouvrier) car mechanic.

garant, **~e** /gaʀɑ̃, ɑ̃t/ **I** adj être or se porter **~** de qch/qn to vouch for sth/sb.
II nm,f JUR, POL guarantor; être le **~** d'un prêt to stand guarantor for a loan.

garanti, **~e**[1] /gaʀɑ̃ti/ adj **1** (protégé) with a guarantee (épith, après n); **c'est ~ six mois** it has a six-month guarantee; **2** (certifié) guaranteed; **fromage ~ pur chèvre** guaranteed pure goat's milk cheese; **prix ~** guaranteed price.

garantie[2] /gaʀɑ̃ti/ nf **1** COMM guarantee, warranty; **bon de ~** guarantee; **2** (en finance) (négociable) security ⊄; (fiduciaire) guarantee; **en ~** as security; **3** (en assurance) cover ⊄; **~ responsabilité civile** third-party cover; **montant des ~s** sum insured; **4** (certitude) guarantee (**de** of); **5** JUR guarantee.

garantir /gaʀɑ̃tiʀ/ [3] vtr **1** (promettre) to guarantee; **~ à qn qch/que** to guarantee sb sth/that; **2** (protéger) to safeguard [sécurité, indépendance, droit]; **3** (assurer) **~ qch à qn** to guarantee sb sth; **4** to guarantee [emprunt, paiement]; **5** COMM to guarantee [produit].

garçon /gaʀsɔ̃/ nm **1** (enfant, fils) boy; **2** (jeune homme) young man; **un brave** or **gentil ~** a nice chap GB ou guy US; **être beau** or **joli ~** to be good-looking; ▶ **bon**, **mauvais**; **3** (célibataire) bachelor; **4** ▶ **374** (serveur) **~ (de café)** waiter; (employé de magasin) (shop) assistant GB, salesclerk US.
■ **~ d'ascenseur** lift GB ou elevator US attendant; **~ de cabine** NAUT cabin steward; **~ de courses** messenger; **~ d'écurie** stableboy; **~ d'étage** floor supervisor; **~ de ferme** farmhand; **~ d'honneur** best man; **~ manqué** tomboy.

garçonne /gaʀsɔn/ nf être coiffée à la **~** to have an urchin cut.

garçonnet /gaʀsɔnɛ/ nm little boy; **taille/rayon ~** boys' size/department.

garçonnière /gaʀsɔnjɛʀ/ nf bachelor flat GB ou apartment US.

garde[1] /gaʀd/ ▶ **374** nm **1** (soldat, policier) guard; **2** (de malade) carer; (de prison) warder.
■ **~ champêtre** ≈ local policeman (appointed by the municipality); **~ du corps** bodyguard; **~ forestier** forest warden, forest ranger; **Garde des Sceaux** French Minister of Justice.

garde[2] /gaʀd/ nf **1** (infirmière) nurse; **2** (groupe) guard; **3** (surveillance, protection) **monter la ~** [soldat] to mount guard; **monter la ~ auprès de** to keep watch over [prisonnier, malade]; to stand guard over [enfant, homme politique]; **mettre sous bonne ~** to put [sb] under guard [suspect, prisonnier]; **être sous la ~ de qn** [prisonnier] to be guarded by sb; [enfant, objet de valeur] to be looked after by sb; JUR to be in sb's custody; **4** (service) **être de ~** [médecin] to be on call; [soldat, sentinelle] to be on guard duty; **pharmacie de ~** duty chemist's GB, emergency drugstore US; **5** (position de défense) guard, on-guard position; **en ~!** on guard!; **se mettre en ~** to square up; **mettre qn en ~** to warn sb; **mise en ~** warning; **prendre ~** (se méfier) to watch out (**à** for); (se soucier) to be careful (**de faire** to do); **sans y prendre ~** inadvertently; **n'avoir ~ de faire** FML to be careful not to do; **6** (d'épée) hilt; **jusqu'à la ~** up to the hilt; **7** (de livre, cahier) (page de) **~** endpaper.
■ **~ d'enfant** childminder GB, day-care lady US; **~ à vue** ≈ police custody; **placer qn en ~ à vue** to hold sb for questioning.

garde-à-vous /gaʀdavu/ nm inv se mettre au **~** to stand to attention.

garde-barrière, pl **~s** /gaʀdbaʀjɛʀ/ ▶ **374** nm,f level-crossing keeper GB, gateman (at grade crossing) US.

garde-boue /gaʀdəbu/ nm inv mudguard.

garde-chasse, pl **~s** /gaʀdəʃas/ ▶ **374** nm (de domaine public) game warden; (de domaine privé) gamekeeper.

garde-chiourme /gaʀdəʃjuʀm/ nm inv **1** HIST overseer; **2** (surveillant) prison warder.

garde-côte, pl **~s** /gaʀdəkot/ nm (bateau) coastguard ship.

garde-feu /gaʀdəfø/ nm inv fire screen.

garde-fou, pl **~s** /gaʀdəfu/ nm **1** (parapet) parapet; **2** FIG safeguard.

garde-frontière, pl **gardes-frontières** /gaʀdfʀɔ̃tjɛʀ/ ▶ **374** nm (personne) border guard.

garde-malade, pl **gardes-malades** /gaʀdmalad/ ▶ **374** nm,f home nurse.

garde-manger /gaʀdmɑ̃ʒe/ nm inv **1** (armoire grillagée) meat safe; **2** (placard) pantry, larder.

garde-meubles /gaʀdəmœbl/ nm inv furniture storage warehouse; **mettre qch au ~** to put sth in store ou storage.

garder /gaʀde/ [1] **I** vtr **1** (conserver) to keep [argent, objet]; to keep [sth] on [chapeau, vêtement]; to keep [sb] on [employé]; **~ pour soi** to keep [sth] to oneself [secret, critiques]; **gardez à votre teint toute sa fraîcheur** keep your complexion fresh; **un secret bien gardé** a well-kept secret; **ils gardent la suprématie en matière d'électronique** they retain the lead in electronics; **ils nous ont gentiment gardés à dîner** they kindly asked us to stay on for dinner; **~ le lit/la chambre** to stay in bed/in one's room; **2** (surveiller, protéger) [gardien] to guard; [personne] to look after [maison, enfant]; **parking gardé** supervised ou attended car park; **l'entrepôt est gardé** there's a security guard at the warehouse.
II se garder vpr **1** (éviter) **se ~ de faire** to be careful not to do; **je me garde de toute interprétation hâtive** I'm wary of making any hasty interpretation; **2** (se conserver) [aliment] to keep.

garderie /gaʀdəʀi/ nf **1** (local) day nursery; **2** (service) after-school child-minding facility.

garde-robe, pl **~s** /gaʀdəʀɔb/ nf (vêtements, armoire) wardrobe.

gardien, **-ienne**[1] /gaʀdjɛ̃, ɛn/ nm,f **1** (de locaux) security guard; (d'immeuble) caretaker GB, janitor US; (de parc) keeper; (de prison) warder; (de musée, parking) attendant; **2** SPORT keeper; **3** (personne qui préserve) FML guardian; **se faire le ~ des traditions** to set oneself up as a guardian of tradition.
■ **~ de but** goalkeeper; **~ de nuit** night watchman; **~ de la paix** police officer.

gardiennage /gaʀdjɛnaʒ/ nm (de locaux) security; (d'immeuble) caretaking; **société de ~** security firm.

gardienne[2] /gaʀdjɛn/ nf **~ (d'enfant)** childminder GB, day-care lady US.

gardon /gaʀdɔ̃/ nm roach.
IDIOMES **être frais comme un ~** to be as fresh as a daisy.

gare /gaʀ/ **I** nf (railway) station; **être en ~** [train] to be in the station; **entrer en ~** [train] to arrive.
II excl **1** (pour prévenir) **~ (à toi)!** watch out!; **~ à ton portefeuille!** watch your wallet!; **~ aux voleurs!** watch out for thieves!; **~ à ta réputation!** mind your reputation!; **2** (pour menacer) **~ à toi!** careful!, watch it○!; **~ aux tricheurs!** anyone who cheats will be in trouble!
■ **~ de marchandises** goods station GB, freight station US; **~ maritime** harbour GB station; **~ routière** (cars) coach station GB, bus station US; (camions) truck depot; **~ de triage** marshalling GB yard; **~ de voyageurs** passenger station.
IDIOMES **sans crier ~** without any warning.

garenne /gaʀɛn/ nf (de lapins) (rabbit) warren.

garer /gaʀe/ [1] **I** vtr to park [véhicule].
II se garer vpr **1** (stationner) to park; **2** (s'écarter) [véhicule] to pull over; [piéton] to move out of the way.

gargantuesque /gaʀgɑ̃tɥɛsk/ adj gargantuan.

gargariser: se gargariser /gaʀgaʀize/ [1] vpr **1** MÉD to gargle; **2**○ FIG **se ~ de** to revel in.

gargarisme /gaʀgaʀism/ nm (action) gargling; (solution) gargle, mouthwash.

gargote /gaʀgɔt/ nf cheap eating place, greasy spoon○.

gargouille /gaʀguj/ nf (décoratif) gargoyle; (pour la pluie) waterspout.

gargouiller /gaʀguje/ [1] *vi* [*eau, fontaine*] to gurgle; [*ventre*] to rumble, to growl US.

garnement /gaʀnəmã/ *nm* tearaway GB, brat○.

garni, ~e /gaʀni/ *adj* (rempli) **bien ~** [*portefeuille*] full; [*réfrigérateur*] well-stocked (*épith*); [*buffet*] copious; **une assiette bien ~e** a plateful; **plat ~** dish served with trimmings.

garnir /gaʀniʀ/ [3] **I** *vtr* **1** (remplir) [*objets*] to fill [*pièce*]; [*personne*] to stock [*rayons, congélateur*]; **2** (rembourrer) to stuff [*coussin, fauteuil*]; **3** (couvrir) to cover [*siège*]; **4** (orner) to trim [*robe*]; (doubler) to line [*vêtement, tiroir*]; **5** CULIN (décorer) to decorate [*gâteau, table*]; to garnish [*viande, poisson*]; (accompagner) to serve [*plat*].

II se garnir *vpr* [*salle, stade*] to fill up (**de** with).

garnison /gaʀnizɔ̃/ *nf* MIL garrison; **ville de ~** garrison town.

garniture /gaʀnityʀ/ *nf* **1** CULIN (accompagnement) side dish; (décoration) (de dessert) decoration; (de viande, poisson) garnish; **servir avec une ~ de légumes** serve with vegetables as a side dish; **2** (sur un chapeau, une robe) trimming; (dans un coffret, tiroir) lining.
■ **~ de bureau** desk accessories (*pl*); **~ de cheminée** mantelpiece ornaments (*pl*); **~ de foyer** fire irons (*pl*).

garrigue /gaʀig/ *nf* garrigue, scrubland (*in southern France*).

garrot /gaʀo/ *nm* **1** MÉD tourniquet; **2** ZOOL (de quadrupède) withers (*pl*); **le cheval mesure 1, 50 m au ~** the horse is 15 hands; **3** (instrument de supplice) garrotte.

garrotter /gaʀɔte/ [1] *vtr* **1** (lier) to tie up [*prisonnier*]; to bind [*bras, jambes*]; **2** FIG (bâillonner) to muzzle [*peuple*]; to stifle [*opposition*]; **3** (supplicier) to garrotte.

gars○ /ga/ *nm inv* (garçon, jeune homme) lad GB, boy; (adulte) chap○ GB, guy○ US.

Gascogne /gaskɔɲ/ ▶509│ *nprf* **la ~** Gascony; **le golfe de ~** the Bay of Biscay.

Gascon, -onne /gaskɔ̃, ɔn/ *nm,f* Gascon.
IDIOMES **c'est une offre de ~** it's not a serious offer.

gas-oil /gazwal/ *nm* diesel (oil) GB, fuel oil US.

gaspacho /gaspatʃo/ *nm* gazpacho.

gaspillage /gaspijaʒ/ *nm* **1** (par négligence) (action) wasting; (conséquence) waste; **quel ~!** what a waste!; **c'est du ~** it's wasteful; **2** (par prodigalité) squandering.

gaspiller /gaspije/ [1] *vtr* **1** (gâcher) to waste [*temps, argent, nourriture*]; **ne gaspille pas tant** don't be so wasteful; **2** (dissiper) to squander [*forces, ressources*].

gastrite /gastʀit/ ▶196│ *nf* gastritis ¢.

gastronome /gastʀɔnɔm/ *nmf* gourmet, gastronome.

gastronomie /gastʀɔnɔmi/ *nf* gastronomy.

gâteau, pl ~x /gɑto/ **I** *adj inv* [*papa*] doting.

II *nm* cake; **~ d'anniversaire** birthday cake; **se tailler une part du ~**○ FIG to take one's share of the loot.
■ **~ apéritif** cocktail biscuit; **~ de cire** honeycomb; **~ marbré** marble cake; **~ de miel** = **~ de cire**; **~ de riz** ≈ rice pudding; **~ salé** = **apéritif**; **~ sec** biscuit GB, cookie US; **~ de semoule** semolina pudding.
IDIOMES **c'est du ~**○! it's a piece of cake○!; **c'est pas du ~**○! it's no picnic!

gâter /gɑte/ [1] *vtr* **1** (choyer) to spoil [*personne*]; **enfant gâté** spoiled child; **on a été gâtés côté temps** we've been very lucky with the weather; **il n'a pas été gâté par la nature** HUM he hasn't been blessed by Nature; **2** (abîmer) to spoil [*fruit*]; to ruin [*dent*]; to spoil [*paysage*]; **3** (gâcher) to spoil [*plaisir*].

II se gâter *vpr* **1** (s'abîmer) [*viande*] to go bad; [*fruit, dent*] to rot; **avoir les dents gâtées** to have bad teeth; **2** (se détériorer) [*situation*] to take a turn for the worse; [*temps*] to change for the worse; **ça se gâte!** (situation) there's going to be trouble!

gâterie /gɑtʀi/ *nf* little treat.

gâteux, -euse /gɑtø, øz/ **I** *adj* (avec l'âge) senile; **il est ~**○ **avec sa fille** FIG he's dotty about his daughter○.

II *nm,f* senile person; **vieux ~**○ old dodderer○.

gauche¹ /goʃ/ **I** *adj* **1** GÉN [*œil, main etc*] left; **le**

côté ~ de qch the left-hand side of sth; **2** (maladroit) [*personne, manières*] awkward; [*style*] clumsy.

II *nm* (en boxe) left-hander.
IDIOMES **se lever du pied ~**○ to get out of bed on the wrong side GB, to get up on the wrong side of the bed US.

gauche² /goʃ/ ▶326│ *nf* **1** (côté) **la ~** the left; **à ~** [*rouler*] on the left; [*aller, regarder*] to the left; [*tourner*] left; **tenir sa ~** to keep to the left; **en bas à ~** in the bottom left-hand corner; **de ~** [*page, mur, file*] left-hand; **2** POL Left; **de ~** left-wing; **la ~ du parti libéral** the left wing of the liberal party.
IDIOMES **passer l'arme à ~**○ to kick the bucket○; **jusqu'à la ~**○ completely, thoroughly; **avoir de l'argent à ~**○ to have money stashed away; **mettre de l'argent à ~**○ to put money aside.

gauchement /goʃmã/ *adv* awkwardly.

gaucher, -ère /goʃe, ɛʀ/ **I** *adj* left-handed.

II *nm,f* left-handed person; **~ contrarié** naturally left-handed person (*forced to write with their right hand*).

gaucherie /goʃʀi/ *nf* awkwardness.

gauchisant, ~e /goʃizã, ãt/ *adj* [*journal, groupe*] leftish (*épith*); **être ~** to have leftish tendencies.

gauchiste /goʃist/ *adj, nm,f* leftist.

gaufre /gofʀ/ *nf* **1** CULIN waffle; **2** ZOOL honeycomb.

gaufrer /gofʀe/ [1] *vtr* (imprimer en relief) to emboss; (donner un aspect froissé) to crinkle.

gaufrette /gofʀɛt/ *nf* wafer.

gaufrier /gofʀije/ *nm* waffle iron US.

gaule /gol/ *nf* **1** (pour récolter les noix) long thin pole; (de bouvier, vacher) switch; **2** (de pêcheur) fishing rod.

Gaule /gol/ *nprf* Gaul.

gauler /gole/ [1] *vtr* **1** **~ les noix** to knock the nuts out of a walnut tree; **2**○ (prendre) to catch; **se faire ~** to get caught.

gaulois, ~e /golwa, az/ **I** *adj* Gallic.

II ▶338│ *nm* LING Gaulish.

Gaulois, ~e /golwa, az/ *nm,f* Gaul.

gausser: se gausser /gose/ [1] *vpr* (railler) LITER **se ~ de** to laugh at, to mock.

gavage /gavaʒ/ *nm* (des oies) force-feeding.

gaver /gave/ [1] **I** *vtr* to force-feed [*oies*]; to stuff [sb] with food [*personne*]; **être gavé** to be full up; **~ qn d'âneries** to cram sb's head with silly ideas; **~ qn de publicité** to bombard sb with advertising.

II se gaver *vpr* **1** (se nourrir) to stuff oneself (**de** with); **2** FIG **se ~ de** to devour [*romans, émissions*].

gavroche /gavʀɔʃ/ *nm* street urchin.

gay /gɛ/ *adj inv, nm* gay, homosexual.

gaz /gaz/ **I** *nm inv* **1** (domestique) gas; **baisser le ~** to turn down the gas; **se chauffer au ~** to have gas heating; **2** CHIMIE gas; **à l'état de ~** in its gaseous state.

II *nmpl* **1** AUT air-fuel mixture (*sg*); **mettre les ~**○ to step on the gas○; **rouler à pleins ~**○ to go at full throttle; **2** (flatulence) wind (*sg*).
■ **~ butane** butane gas; **~ carbonique** carbon dioxide; **~ de combat** poison gas, ¢; **~ d'échappement** exhaust fumes (*pl*); **~ hilarant** laughing gas; **~ lacrymogène** teargas; **~ de ville** mains gas.
IDIOMES **il y a de l'eau dans le ~**○ there's trouble brewing.

gaze /gaz/ *nf* gauze; **une bande de ~** a gauze bandage.

gazé, ~e /gaze/ *nm,f* gas victim.

gazéifier /gazeifje/ [2] *vtr* **1** (rendre pétillant) to carbonate [*boisson*]; **2** (transformer en gaz) to gasify.

gazelle /gazɛl/ *nf* gazelle; **des yeux de ~** doe eyes.

gazer /gaze/ [1] **I** *vtr* (asphyxier) to gas.

II○ *v impers* **ça gaze?** how's things○?; **oui, ça gaze** things are fine.

gazette /gazɛt/ *nf* **1** (journal) newspaper; HUM rag; **2** (personne) gossip; **la ~ du quartier** the local gossip.

gazeux, -euse /gazø, øz/ *adj* **1** [*boisson*] fizzy; **eau**

gazeuse (naturelle) sparkling mineral water; (gazéifiée) carbonated water; **2** CHIMIE, PHYS gaseous.

gazinière /gazinjɛʀ/ *nf* gas cooker GB, gas stove.

gazoduc /gazɔdyk/ *nm* gas pipeline.

gazogène /gazɔʒɛn/ *nm* (générateur) gas generator.

gazole /gazɔl/ *nm* diesel (oil) GB, fuel oil US.

gazon /gazɔ̃/ *nm* **1** (herbe) grass, turf; (en plaque) turf; **2** (pelouse) lawn; **tennis sur ~** lawn tennis; **jouer sur ~** to play on grass courts.

gazouillement /gazujmɑ̃/ *nm* (d'oiseau) twittering **¢**; (de bébé, source) babbling **¢**.

gazouiller /gazuje/ [1] *vi* [*oiseau*] to twitter; [*bébé, source*] to babble.

gazouillis /gazuji/ *nm inv* = **gazouillement**.

GDF /ʒedeɛf/ (*abbr* = **Gaz de France**) French gas board.

geai /ʒɛ/ *nm* jay.

géant, ~e /ʒeɑ̃, ɑ̃t/ **I** *adj* **1** (démesuré) huge, enormous; **2** (de grande taille) giant; **raie ~e** giant ray; **3** COMM [*paquet*] jumbo; **4**° (extraordinaire) **c'est ~!** it's brilliant GB ou great!
II *nm,f* giant/giantess; **~ de l'industrie** industrial giant.

geignard, ~e /ʒɛɲaʀ, aʀd/ *adj* [*personne*] moaning; [*enfant*] whining; [*ton, musique*] wailing.

geignement /ʒɛɲəmɑ̃/ *nm* (plainte) moan, groan.

geindre /ʒɛ̃dʀ/ [55] *vi* [*malade*] to moan, to groan; (faiblement) to whimper; [*pleurnichard*] to whine; [*mécontent*] to moan; [*violon*] to wail; [*meuble*] to creak.

gel /ʒɛl/ *nm* **1** MÉTÉO frost; **résistant au ~** frost-resistant; **2** ÉCON **~ des subventions** freeze on subsidies; **~ des prix/salaires** price/wage freeze; **~ des terres** set-aside **~ des avoirs** freezing of assets; **3** (suspension) **après le ~ du projet** after the project had been put on ice; **4** (produit) gel.

gélatine /ʒelatin/ *nf* gelatine GB, gelatin US.

gélatineux, -euse /ʒelatinø, øz/ *adj* gelatinous.

gelé, ~e¹ /ʒəle/ **I** *pp* ▶ **geler**.
II *pp adj* **1** (durci par le froid) [*eau, sol*] frozen; MÉD [*orteil*] frost-bitten; **2** (très froid) **j'ai les oreilles ~es** my ears are frozen; **3** (bloqué) [*prix, négociation*] frozen.

gelée² /ʒəle/ *nf* **1** CULIN (de fruit) jelly; (de viande, poisson) (suc naturel) gelatinous stock; (préparation) aspic; **œuf/poulet en ~** egg/chicken in aspic; **2** (cosmétique) gel; **3** MÉTÉO frost.
■ **~ blanche** hoarfrost; **~ royale** royal jelly.

geler /ʒəle/ [17] **I** *vtr* **1** (durcir) to freeze [*eau, sol*]; **2** (endommager) to freeze [*doigt*]; to nip [*plante*]; **3** (bloquer) to freeze [*salaire, prix, avoirs*]; to suspend [*projet, production*].
II *vi* **1** (se solidifier) [*eau, sol*] to freeze; **2** (être endommagé) [*doigt, pied*] to freeze; [*plante*] to be frosted; **3**° (avoir froid) to be freezing; **on gèle** it's freezing.
III se geler° *vpr* (avoir froid) to freeze.
IV *v impers* **il** or **ça gèle** it's freezing; **il gèle à pierre fendre** it's absolutely freezing.

gélifiant /ʒelifjɑ̃/ *nm* gelling agent.

gélule /ʒelyl/ *nf* capsule.

Gémeaux /ʒemo/ ▶ **641** *nprmpl* Gemini.

gémir /ʒemiʀ/ [3] *vi* [*malade*] to moan, to groan (**de** with); (faiblement) to whimper; [*pleurnichard*] to moan; [*plancher, meuble*] to creak; (sous un poids) to groan; [*vent*] to moan.

gémissement /ʒemismɑ̃/ *nm* (de personne) moan; (prolongé) moaning **¢**; (de plancher) creak; (prolongé) creaking **¢**; (du vent) moaning.

gemme /ʒɛm/ *nf* **1** (pierre) gem, gemstone; **2** (résine) resin.

gémonies /ʒemɔni/ *nfpl* **vouer qn aux ~** to expose sb to public contempt.

gênant, ~e /ʒɛnɑ̃, ɑ̃t/ *adj* **1** (incommode) [*meuble, carton*] cumbersome; [*problème, bruit*] annoying; [*odeur*] unpleasant; **2** (qui met mal à l'aise) [*question, témoin*] embarrassing; **c'est gênant** it's awkward.

gencive /ʒɑ̃siv/ *nf* gum.
IDIOMES **prendre un coup dans les ~s**° to be kicked in the teeth°.

gendarme /ʒɑ̃daʀm/ ▶ **374** *nm* **1** MIL gendarme, French policeman; **jouer aux ~s et aux voleurs** to play cops and robbers; **la peur du ~** FIG the fear of authority; **jouer les ~s du monde** FIG to act the role of world policeman; **2** (personne autoritaire) **quel ~!** what a bossy person!; **je n'ai pas envie de faire le ~** I don't want to have to lay down the law; **3** (organe de surveillance) watchdog; **4** ZOOL (punaise) stinkbug; **5** CULIN (saucisson) dried sausage.
■ **~ couché** road hump, sleeping policeman GB; **~ mobile** member of mobile police unit.

gendarmerie /ʒɑ̃daʀm(ə)ʀi/ *nf* **1** (bureaux) police station; **2** (logement) police quarters (*pl*); **3** (corps) **~ (nationale)** gendarmerie, French police force.
■ **~ mobile** mobile police unit.

gendre /ʒɑ̃dʀ/ *nm* son-in-law.

gène /ʒɛn/ *nm* gene.

gêne /ʒɛn/ *nf* **1** (embarras) embarrassment; **il n'y a pas de ~ à avoir** there's nothing to be embarrassed about; **2** (physique) discomfort; **éprouver une ~ en avalant** to have difficulty swallowing; **~ respiratoire** breathing difficulties (*pl*); **3** (nuisance) convenience; **~ visuelle** visual disturbance; **4** (pauvreté) poverty.
IDIOMES **là où il y a de la ~ il n'y a pas de plaisir**° you can't have fun if you're minding your p's and q's.

gêné, ~e /ʒɛne/ *adj* **1** (mal à l'aise) embarrassed; **2** (engoncé) **il est ~ dans sa veste** his jacket is too tight for him; **3** (désargenté) short of money.

généalogie /ʒenealɔʒi/ *nf* genealogy.

généalogique /ʒenealɔʒik/ *adj* genealogical; **livre ~** BIOL herd book, stud book; **arbre ~** family tree.

gêner /ʒɛne/ [1] **I** *vtr* **1** [*personne*] (déranger sérieusement) to disturb; (déranger par sa présence) to bother; **ça te gêne si j'allume?** do you mind if I switch the light on?; **2** (incommoder) [*fumée, bruit*] to bother; **3** (mettre mal à l'aise) [*question, personne*] to embarrass; **cela me gêne d'avoir à te le rappeler mais...** I hate to have to remind you, but...; **4** (entraver) to disrupt [*événement*]; to block [*circulation*]; to restrict [*respiration*]; to get in the way of [*discussion, progrès*]; to hamper [*progression*]; **pousse-toi, tu me gênes** get out of my way; **les chiffres gênent la compréhension du texte** the figures make the text difficult to understand; **5** (faire mal) [*caillou, ceinture*] to hurt [*personne*]; **quelque chose dans ma chaussure me gêne** I've something in my shoe.
II se gêner *vpr* **1** (se bousculer) [*personnes*] to get in each other's way; **on tient à quatre sans se ~** it can hold four people comfortably; **2** (faire des façons) **pourquoi se ~?** why hesitate?; **je ne me suis pas gênée pour le lui rappeler**° I made a point of reminding them; **je vais me ~, tiens** IRON see if I don't; **ne vous gênez pas pour moi, continuez** IRON don't mind me, carry on GB ou continue.

général, ~e¹, *mpl* **-aux** /ʒeneʀal, o/ **I** *adj* **1** (collectif) general; **de l'avis ~** in most people's opinion; **dans l'intérêt ~** in the public interest; **à la surprise ~e** to everyone's surprise; **2** (d'ensemble) general; **en ~, de façon** or **d'une manière ~e** generally, in general; **en règle ~e** as a rule.
II *nm* **1** ▶ **284** MIL general; **mon ~!** general!; **2** RELIG (supérieur) general; **3** PHILOS **le ~ et le particulier** the general and the particular.

générale² /ʒeneʀal/ *nf* **1** THÉÂT dress rehearsal; **2** (épouse de général) general's wife.

généralement /ʒeneʀalmɑ̃/ *adv* generally.

généralisable /ʒeneʀalizabl/ *adj* **l'expérience est ~ à d'autres domaines** the experiment can be applied to other fields.

généralisation /ʒeneʀalizasjɔ̃/ *nf* **1** (systématisation) (de politique) general implementation; (de vaccination) widespread use; (de langue) general use; **2** (déduction) generalization; **3** (de maladie, grève) spread.

généralisé, ~e /ʒeneʀalize/ *adj* [*conflit, pessimisme,* *corruption*] widespread; [*surproduction*] general; [*cancer*] generalized.

généraliser /ʒeneralize/ [1] **I** *vtr* to bring [sth] into general use [*impôt, vaccination, examen*]; to put [sth] into general use [*méthode*].

II *vi* to generalize.

III se généraliser *vpr* [*technique*] to become standard; [*impôt*] to become widely applicable; [*grève, maladie*] to spread (à to).

généraliste /ʒeneralist/ **I** *adj* [*chaîne, revue, ingénieur*] non-specialized; [*conception*] broad; **médecin ~** general practitioner.

II ▶ 374] *nmf* general practitioner, GP GB.

généralité /ʒeneralite/ *nf* **1** (notion générale) generality; **2** (règle générale) **devenir ~** to become general.

générateur, -trice /ʒeneratœr, tris/ **I** *adj* **1** (créateur) **être ~ de** to generate; **2** (servant à engendrer) generative.

II *nm* ORDINAT, TECH generator.

génération /ʒenerasjɔ̃/ *nf* **1** (dans une famille) generation; **le fossé des ~s** the generation gap; **2** (personnes du même âge) generation; **la nouvelle ~** the new generation; **3** (d'avions, ordinateurs) generation; **4** (d'énergie, électricité) generation; **5** BIOL generation.

générer /ʒenere/ [14] *vtr* to generate.

généreusement /ʒenerøzmɑ̃/ *adv* (noblement) generously; (libéralement) liberally.

généreux, -euse /ʒenerø, øz/ *adj* **1** (plein de largesse) generous (**envers** to); **2** (plein de grandeur d'âme) [*personne, caractère*] generous; [*idée, geste*] noble; **3** (copieux) [*portion*] generous; **poitrine généreuse** large bust; **femme aux formes généreuses** well-rounded woman; **4** (fertile) [*terre*] bountiful LITTÉR.

générique /ʒenerik/ **I** *adj* generic.

II *nm* CIN, RADIO, TV **1** (liste) credits (*pl*); **le ~ de début/fin** opening/closing credits; **2** (présentation) titles (*pl*).

générosité /ʒenerozite/ *nf* **1** (largesse) generosity (**envers** to, toward(s)); **2** (grandeur d'âme) generosity of spirit; **agir avec ~** to show generosity of spirit.

Gênes /ʒɛn/ **▶ 628]** *npr* Genoa.

genèse /ʒənɛz/ *nf* **1** (d'œuvre d'art, de projet) genesis; (d'État) birth; **2** BIBLE **la Genèse** Genesis.

genêt /ʒənɛ/ *nm* BOT broom.

généticien, -ienne /ʒenetisjɛ̃, ɛn/ **▶ 374]** *nm,f* geneticist.

génétique /ʒenetik/ **I** *adj* genetic.

II *nf* genetics (+ *v sg*).

gêneur, -euse /ʒɛnœr, øz/ *nm,f* troublemaker.

Genève /ʒənɛv/ **▶ 628]** *npr* Geneva.

genévrier /ʒənevrije/ *nm* juniper.

génial, ~e, *mpl* **-iaux** /ʒenjal, o/ *adj* **1** (ayant du génie) brilliant; **2** (inspiré par le génie) [*idée, invention, découverte*] brilliant; **3**° (fantastique) [*spectacle, livre*] brilliant° GB, great°; [*personne*] great°.

génie /ʒeni/ *nm* **1** (aptitude) genius; **avoir du ~** to be a genius; **avoir un coup de ~** to have a flash of inspiration; **idée de ~** brainwave; **2** (personne) genius; **3** (talent) **avoir le ~ du commerce** to have a great gift for business; **4** MYTHOL (esprit) spirit; (dans les contes) genie; **être le bon/mauvais ~ de qn** to be sb's guiding/evil spirit; **5** (ingénierie) engineering; **6** MIL (activité) military engineering; (personnel) **le ~** the Engineers (*pl*).

■ ~ civil (activité) civil engineering; (personnel) civil engineers (*pl*); **~ génétique** genetic engineering.

genièvre /ʒənjɛvr/ *nm* (arbuste) juniper; (baie) juniper berry; (eau-de-vie) Dutch gin.

génisse /ʒenis/ *nf* heifer; **foie de ~** beef liver.

génital, ~e, *mpl* **-aux** /ʒenital, o/ *adj* genital.

géniteur, -trice /ʒenitœr, tris/ **I** *nm,f* (parent) HUM parent, pater/mater HUM.

II *nm* ZOOL (reproducteur) sire.

génitif /ʒenitif/ *nm* LING genitive.

génocide /ʒenɔsid/ *nm* genocide.

génoise /ʒenwaz/ *nf* CULIN ≈ sponge cake.

genou, *pl* **~x** /ʒ(ə)nu/ **▶ 137]** **I** *nm* **1** (d'homme, animal) knee; **donner un coup de ~ à qn** to knee sb; **mettre (un) ~ à terre devant qn** LIT to kneel down in front of sb; FIG to pay homage to sb; **2** (de pantalon, collant) knee; **3** NAUT, TECH knee.

II à genoux *loc adv* **se mettre à ~x** GÉN to kneel down; (pour implorer) to go down on one's knees; **être à ~x devant qn** FIG to worship sb.

IDIOMES **faire du ~ à qn**° to play footsie° with sb; **être sur les ~x**° [*personne*] to be on one's last legs; **mettre qn sur les ~x**° to wear sb out.

genouillère /ʒənujɛr/ *nf* SPORT knee pad; MÉD knee support ou bandage; (pour un animal) knee boot.

genre /ʒɑ̃r/ *nm* **1** (sorte) sort, kind, type (**de** of); **c'est ce qu'on fait de mieux dans le ~** it's the best of its kind; **c'est le ~ rabat-joie** he/she's a killjoy; **tu vois le ~!** you know the type!; **elle n'est pas mal dans son ~** she's quite pretty in her way; **un peu dans le ~ de ta robe** a bit like your dress; **2** (comportement) **ce n'est pas mon ~ de tricher** cheating is not my style; **c'est bien son ~** it's just like him/her; **3** (allure) **pour se donner un ~** (in order) to make oneself look different; **4** LING gender; **5** ART, LITTÉRAT genre; **peinture de ~** genre painting; **6** BOT, ZOOL genus.

■ le ~ humain mankind.

gens /ʒɑ̃/ *nmpl* **1** (personnes) people; **les ~ du coin** the local people, the locals PÉJ; **les ~ sans histoires** ordinary people; **2** (domestiques) servants, household (*sg*); (escorte) retinue (*sg*).

■ ~ d'église clergymen; **~ de lettres** writers; **~ de loi** lawyers; **~ de maison** servants; **~ du monde** polite society (*sg*); **~ de théâtre** actors; **~ du voyage** travelling^GB people.

■ Note When used with *gens*, the adjectives *bon, mauvais, petit, vieux, vilain* are placed before *gens* and in the feminine: (*toutes*) *les vieilles gens*. But the gender of *gens* itself does not change: *les bonnes gens sont heureux*. All other adjectives behave normally: (*tous*) *les braves gens*.

gent† /ʒɑ̃/ *nf* **la ~ masculine/féminine** mankind/ womankind, men (*pl*)/women (*pl*).

gentiane /ʒɑ̃sjan/ *nf* **1** (fleur) gentian; **2** (liqueur) gentian liqueur.

gentil, -ille /ʒɑ̃ti, ij/ **I** *adj* **1** (agréable) kind, nice (**avec** to); **aide-moi, tu seras ~** give me a hand, will you?; **c'est ~, je vous remercie** that's very kind of you, thank you; **sois ~, réponds au téléphone** do me a favour^GB, answer the phone; **2** (obéissant) good; **3** PÉJ **le spectacle/film était ~** the show/film was harmless enough; **c'est bien ~ tout ça, mais...** that's all very well, but...; **il est (bien) ~** he's nice enough; **4** (non négligeable) [*somme, récompense*] fair.

II *nm* HIST RELIG gentile.

gentilhomme, *pl* **gentilshommes** /ʒɑ̃tijɔm, ʒɑ̃tizɔm/ *nm* HIST gentleman; **~ campagnard** country gentleman.

gentilhommière /ʒɑ̃tijɔmjɛr/ *nf* country house.

gentille ▶ gentil I.

gentillesse /ʒɑ̃tijɛs/ *nf* kindness (**envers** to); **faites-moi la ~ de...** would you do me the favour^GB of...?; **échanger des ~s** IRON to exchange insults; **dire des ~s sur qn** IRON to say unpleasant things about sb.

gentillet, -ette /ʒɑ̃tijɛ, ɛt/ *adj* **1** (agréable) **être ~** [*enfant*] to be a sweetie; **2** PÉJ [*personne, livre, film*] nice enough.

gentiment /ʒɑ̃timɑ̃/ *adv* **1** (aimablement) kindly; **se moquer ~ de qn** to tease sb playfully; **je leur ai fait ~ comprendre** in the nicest possible way I made them understand; **2** (sagement) quietly.

génuflexion /ʒenyflɛksjɔ̃/ *nf* genuflection.

géode /ʒeɔd/ *nf* geode.

géodésie /ʒeɔdezi/ *nf* geodesy.

géographe /ʒeɔgraf/ **▶ 374]** *nmf* geographer.

géographie /ʒeɔgrafi/ *nf* geography.

geôle /ʒol/ *nf* LITÉR jail.

geôlier, -ière /ʒolje, ɛʁ/ *nm,f* LITER jailer.

géologie /ʒeɔlɔʒi/ *nf* geology.

géologue /ʒeɔlɔg/ ▶ 374 *nmf* geologist.

géomètre /ʒeɔmɛtʁ/ ▶ 374 *nmf* **1** TECH land surveyor; **2**† MATH geometrician.

géométrie /ʒeɔmetʁi/ *nf* geometry; **~ dans l'espace** solid geometry; **à ~ variable** FIG [*doctrine*] flexible.

géométrique /ʒeɔmetʁik/ *adj* [*forme*] geometric; [*démonstration*] geometrical.

géophysique /ʒeofizik/ **I** *adj* geophysical.
II *nf* geophysics (+ *v sg*).

géopolitique /ʒeopɔlitik/ **I** *adj* geopolitical.
II *nf* geopolitics (+ *v sg*).

Géorgie /ʒeɔʁʒi/ *nprf* **1** ▶ 509 (État américain) Georgia; **2** ▶ 232 (État indépendant) Georgia.
■ **~ du Sud** (île) South Georgia.

géostationnaire /ʒeostasjɔnɛʁ/ *adj* geostationary.

géothermie /ʒeotɛʁmi/ *nf* (énergie) geothermal power.

gérable /ʒeʁabl/ *adj* manageable; **situation difficilement ~** a situation which is hard to handle.

gérance /ʒeʁɑ̃s/ *nf* management; **mettre en ~ to** appoint a manager for [*magasin, société*]; to appoint a managing agent for [*immeuble*].

géranium /ʒeʁanjɔm/ *nm* geranium.

gérant, ~e /ʒeʁɑ̃, ɑ̃t/ *nm,f* **1** (de magasin, d'usine) manager; (d'immeubles) (managing) agent; **'nouveau ~'** 'under new management'; **2** PRESSE editor.

gerbe /ʒɛʁb/ *nf* **1** (bouquet enveloppé) bouquet; **~ de fleurs** bunch of flowers; (mortuaire) wreath; **2** (d'eau) spray; **3** (de blé) sheaf.

gerboise /ʒɛʁbwaz/ *nf* jerboa.

gercer /ʒɛʁse/ [12] **I** *vtr* to chap [*main, lèvres*].
II *vi* [*lèvres, mains*] to become chapped.

gerçure /ʒɛʁsyʁ/ *nf* crack; **avoir les mains pleines de ~s** to have badly chapped hands.

gérer /ʒeʁe/ [14] *vtr* **1** (administrer) to manage [*production, temps*]; to manage, to run [*entreprise*]; to run [*pays*]; **2** (traiter) to handle [*situation, information*]; **3** ORDINAT to manage [*fichiers, bases de données*].

gerfaut /ʒɛʁfo/ *nm* gyrfalcon.

gériatrie /ʒeʁjatʁi/ *nf* geriatrics (+ *v sg*); **(service de) ~** geriatric ward.

germain, ~e /ʒɛʁmɛ̃, ɛn/ *adj* **1** (dans la famille) (cousin) **~** first cousin; **2** HIST Germanic.

germanique /ʒɛʁmanik/ *adj, nm* Germanic.

germaniste /ʒɛʁmanist/ *nmf* Germanist.

germanophone /ʒɛʁmanɔfɔn/ **I** *adj* German-speaking (*épith*); **être ~** to speak German.
II *nmf* German speaker.

germe /ʒɛʁm/ *nm* **1** (d'embryon, de graine) germ; (d'œuf) germinal disc; (de pomme de terre) sprout; **~ de blé** wheat germ; **~s de soja** bean sprouts; **2** (début) (de crise) seed; (d'idée) embryonic form, germ.
■ **~ dentaire** tooth bud.

germer /ʒɛʁme/ [1] *vi* FIG (naître) [*idée, soupçon*] to form; **2** BOT [*blé*] to germinate.

germination /ʒɛʁminasjɔ̃/ *nf* germination.

gérondif /ʒeʁɔ̃dif/ *nm* (nom verbal latin, anglais) gerund; (adjectif verbal latin) gerundive; (forme verbale en français) gerund.

gérontologie /ʒeʁɔ̃tɔlɔʒi/ *nf* gerontology.

gésier /ʒezje/ *nm* gizzard.

gésir /ʒeziʁ/ [37] *vi* FML **1** (être couché) [*personne*] to be lying; **elle gît/gisait sur son lit** she is/was lying on her bed; **2** (être abandonné) [*vêtements*] to be lying about ou around; **3** FIG (se trouver) [*solution*] to lie.

gestation /ʒɛstasjɔ̃/ *nf* gestation.

geste[1] /ʒɛst/ *nm* **1** (mouvement) movement; (mouvement expressif) gesture; **un ~ brusque** a sudden movement; **il nous a fait signe d'avancer d'un ~ de la main** he waved to us to come forward; **pas un ~!** don't move!; **il n'a pas fait un ~ pour m'aider** FIG he didn't make any move to help me; **il pourrait faire un ~ quand même!** FIG he could at least show that he cares; **joindre le ~ à la parole** to suit the action to

the word; **2** (acte) gesture, act; **un ~ désespéré** a desperate act; **un ~ symbolique** a token gesture; **un beau ~** a noble gesture.

geste[2] /ʒɛst/ *nf* LITTÉRAT *set of French epic poems of the Middle Ages.*

gesticuler /ʒɛstikyle/ [1] *vtr* **1** (en parlant) to gesticulate; **2** (s'agiter) to fidget.

gestion /ʒɛstjɔ̃/ *nf* **1** (administration) management; **la ~ de la production** production control; **2** (de situation, crise, d'information) handling; **3** (discipline) management; **faire de la ~** to study management; **4** ORDINAT management.
■ **~ administrative** administration; **~ prévisionnelle** (forward) planning; **~ de la production assistée par ordinateur** computer-aided production management; **~ des stocks** stock control GB, inventory control US.

gestionnaire /ʒɛstjɔnɛʁ/ **I** *adj* ÉCON [*technique, organisme*] administrative.
II *nmf* administrator.
■ **~ de fichiers** ORDINAT file-management system; **~ de portefeuille** FIN portfolio manager.

gestuel, -elle[1] /ʒɛstɥɛl/ *adj* gestural; **peinture gestuelle** action painting.

gestuelle[2] /ʒɛstɥɛl/ *nf* body language.

geyser /ʒezɛʁ/ *nm* geyser.

ghanéen, -éenne /ganeɛ̃, ɛn/ ▶ 394 *adj* Ghanaian.

ghetto /geto/ *nm* LIT, FIG ghetto.

gibecière /ʒibsjɛʁ/ *nf* gamebag; SCOL satchel.

gibet /ʒibɛ/ *nm* gallows (+ *v sg*).

gibier /ʒibje/ *nm* game; **gros ~** LIT big game; FIG big time criminals (*pl*); **être un ~ facile pour les escrocs** FIG to be an easy target for conmen; **c'est du ~ de potence** he'll/she'll/they'll come to a bad end.
■ **~ d'eau** water fowl (+ *v pl*); **~ à plumes** game birds (*pl*); **~ à poil** game animals (*pl*).

giboulée /ʒibule/ *nf* shower; **les ~s de mars** ≈ April showers GB.

giboyeux, -euse /ʒibwajø, øz/ *adj* [*région, plaine, réserve*] full of game (*après n*).

gibus /ʒibys/ *nm inv* opera hat.

GIC /ʒeise/ *nm: abbr* ▶ **grand**.

giclée /ʒikle/ *nf* (d'eau, de sang) spurt; (d'encre) squirt.

gicler /ʒikle/ [1] *vi* (jaillir) [*sang, eau*] to spurt (**de** from); [*jus*] to squirt (**sur** onto); **la voiture a fait ~ de la boue** the car sprayed up mud.

gicleur /ʒiklœʁ/ *nm* **1** (de carburateur) jet; **2** (de lave-vaisselle) spray.

gifle /ʒifl/ *nf* **1** (claque) slap in the face; **donner une bonne ~ à qn** to whack sb in the face; **flanquer° une paire de ~s à qn** to clip sb around the ears°; **2** (affront) slap in the face.

gifler /ʒifle/ [1] *vtr* **1** (frapper) to slap [*personne*]; **2** (cingler) [*pluie, vent*] to lash.

GIG /ʒeiʒe/ *nm: abbr* ▶ **grand**.

gigantesque /ʒigɑ̃tɛsk/ *adj* huge, gigantic.

gigantisme /ʒigɑ̃tism/ *nm* **1** (de bâtiment, ville, statue) colossal size; (de projet, spectacle) giant scale; **2** BOT, MÉD gigantism.

GIGN /ʒeiʒeɛn/ *nm* (*abbr* = **Groupe d'intervention de la gendarmerie nationale**) *branch of the police specialized in cases of armed robbery, terrorism etc.*

gigogne /ʒigɔɲ/ *adj* lit **~** hideaway bed; **tables ~s** nest *sg* of tables.

gigot /ʒigo/ *nm* (d'agneau) leg of lamb; **tranche de ~** slice of lamb; **~ de mouton** leg of mutton; **~ de chevreuil** haunch of venison.

gigoter /ʒigɔte/ [1] *vi* GÉN to wriggle; (nerveusement) to fidget.

gigue /ʒig/ *nf* **1** CULIN haunch; **2**° (fille) **une grande ~** a great beanpole° of a girl; **3** (air) gigue; (danse) jig.

gilet /ʒilɛ/ *nm* **1** (en tricot) cardigan; **~ sans manches** knitted waistcoat; **2** (en tissu, cuir) waistcoat GB, vest US.
■ **~ pare-balles** bulletproof vest; **~ de sauvetage** lifejacket.

gin /dʒin/ *nm* gin; **~ tonic** gin and tonic.

gingembre /ʒɛ̃ʒɑ̃bʀ/ *nm* ginger.

ginkgo /ʒinko/ *nm* ginkgo, maidenhair tree.

girafe /ʒiʀaf/ *nf* **1** ZOOL giraffe; **avoir un cou de ~** to have a long neck; **2**○ (personne) HUM beanpole○.

girafon /ʒiʀafɔ̃/ *nm* baby giraffe.

giratoire /ʒiʀatwaʀ/ *adj* [*mouvement*] gyratory; **carrefour ~** roundabout GB, traffic circle US.

girofle /ʒiʀɔfl/ *nm* clove; **clou de ~** clove.

giroflée /ʒiʀɔfle/ *nf* wallflower.

girolle /ʒiʀɔl/ *nf* chanterelle.

giron /ʒiʀɔ̃/ *nm* **1** (genoux) lap; **2** FIG (environnement) bosom.

girondin, ~e /ʒiʀɔ̃dɛ̃, in/ *adj* **1** GÉOG of the Gironde (*après n*); **2** HIST [*parti, politique*] Girondist.

girouette /ʒiʀwɛt/ *nf* **1** windvane; **2** FIG **c'est une vraie girouette** he/she is very capricious.

gisant /ʒizɑ̃/ *nm* recumbent effigy.

gisement /ʒizmɑ̃/ *nm* (de pétrole, minerai) deposit.

gît ▶ gésir.

gitan, ~e /ʒitɑ̃, an/ I *adj* gypsy.
II *nm,f* Gypsy^{GB}.

gîte /ʒit/ *nm* **1** (refuge) shelter; (demeure) home; (de lièvre) form; **le ~ et le couvert** board and lodging GB, room and lodging US; **2** (en boucherie) **~ (à la noix)** ~ top rump.
■ **~ rural** self-catering cottage.

givrant /ʒivʀɑ̃/ *adj m* **brouillard ~** freezing fog.

givre /ʒivʀ/ *nm* (sur le sol, une plante) frost; (sur un pare-brise, une hélice) ice.

givré, ~e /ʒivʀe/ *adj* **1** (couvert de givre) [*vitre*] frosty; [*branche, arbre*] covered in frost (*jamais épith*); [*neige*] frozen; **2**○ (fou) crazy; **3** (avec du sucre) [*verre*] frosted.

givrer /ʒivʀe/ [1] *vi,* **se givrer** *vpr* to frost over.

glabre /glabʀ/ *adj* (imberbe) beardless; (rasé) clean-shaven.

glaçage /glasaʒ/ *nm* **1** (de papier) glazing; **2** CULIN (de viande) glazing; (de dessert) (au sucre) icing; (au blanc d'œuf) glazing.

glace /glas/ I *nf* **1** (eau congelée) ice; **de ~** FIG [*accueil*] icy; [*visage*] stony; **2** (dessert) ice cream; **~ à l'eau** water ice; **3** (miroir) mirror; **tu ferais mieux de te regarder dans une ~** you'd better take a long hard look at yourself; **~ sans tain** two-way mirror; **4** (panneau de verre) (plaque) sheet of glass; (de vitrine) glass; (de voiture) window.
II **glaces** *nfpl* (de montagne) ice field (*sg*); (des pôles) ice sheet (*sg*); **pris dans les ~s** icebound.
IDIOMES **rester de ~** to remain unmoved.

glacé, ~e /glase/ *adj* **1** (très froid) [*pluie, vent, air*] ice-cold, icy; [*douche, boisson*] ice-cold; [*mains*] frozen; [*personne*] freezing; **thé/café ~** iced tea/coffee; **2** CULIN [*gâteau*] iced; [*fruit*] glacé (*épith*); **3** (intimidant) [*accueil, atmosphère*] frosty, icy; [*sourire*] chilly; [*voix*] cold; **4** (brillant) [*papier*] glossy; **5** (gelé) frozen

glacer /glase/ [12] I *vtr* **1** (transir) to freeze [*corps*]; to chill [sb] to the bone [*personne*]; **2** (rafraîchir) to chill [*boisson, fruit*]; **3** (intimider) [*personne, regard*] to intimidate; **~ qn d'effroi, ~ le sang de qn** to make sb's blood run cold; **~ qn de peur** to fill sb with fear.
II **se glacer** *vpr* [*sourire, expression*] to freeze; **mon sang se glaça dans mes veines** my blood froze.

glaciaire /glasjɛʀ/ *adj* glacial; **calotte ~** icecap.

glacial, ~e, *mpl* **~s** or **-iaux** /glasjal, o/ *adj* **1** (froid) [*froid, temps*] icy; [*pluie, journée, vent*] icy, freezing cold; **2** FIG (hostile) [*personne, accueil*] frosty; [*silence*] stony; [*regard*] icy.

glaciation /glasjasjɔ̃/ *nf* glaciation.

glacier /glasje/ *nm* **1** GÉOG glacier; **2** ▶ 374 (fabricant) ice-cream maker; (établissement) ice-cream parlour^{GB}.

glacière /glasjɛʀ/ *nf* coolbox GB, cooler, ice chest US.

glacis /glasi/ *nm inv* ART glacis.

glaçon /glasɔ̃/ *nm* **1** ice cube; **avec des/sans ~s** with/without ice; **2** (dans une rivière) block of ice; (sur un toit, arbre) icicle; **3**○ (personne) PEJ iceberg.

gladiateur /gladjatœʀ/ *nm* gladiator.

glaïeul /glajœl/ *nm* gladiolus.

glaire /glɛʀ/ *nf* **1** (sécrétion) mucus; **avoir des ~s** to have catarrh; **2** (blanc d'œuf) albumen.

glaise /glɛz/ *nf* clay.

glaive /glɛv/ *nm* double-edged sword; **le ~ et la balance** FIG the sword and the scales of justice.

gland /glɑ̃/ *nm* **1** BOT (de chêne) acorn; **2** ANAT glans; **3** (décoration) tassel.

glande /glɑ̃d/ *nf* gland.

glaner /glane/ [1] *vtr* to glean [*renseignements, grains, champ*].

glapir /glapiʀ/ [3] I *vtr* to screech [*injures*].
II *vi* **1** ZOOL [*chiot*] to yap; [*renard*] to bark; [*grue*] to whoop; **2** (hurler) [*personne*] to shriek; [*haut-parleur, radio*] to blare.

glas /glɑ/ *nm inv* toll, knell; **sonner le ~** LIT [*personne*] to toll the bell; [*cloche*] to toll; FIG to sound the death knell (**de** for).

glauque /glok/ *adj* [*eaux, lumière*] murky; [*rue*] squalid.

glissade /glisad/ *nf* **1** LIT (jeu) slide; (dérapage) skid; **faire une ~** [*enfant*] to slide; [*joueur*] to slip; [*véhicule*] to skid; **2** FIG (de prix, monnaie) slide.

glissant, ~e /glisɑ̃, ɑ̃t/ *adj* slippery.

glisse /glis/ *nf* **1** (de ski, skieur) glide; **2**○ (ski) skiing.

glissement /glismɑ̃/ *nm* **1** (déplacement) sliding; **les deux pièces se superposent par ~** the two parts slide over each other; **2** (évolution) (de sens) shift; (d'électorat, opinion) swing; (de prix) fall.
■ **~ de terrain** landslide.

glisser /glise/ [1] I *vtr* **1** (mettre) to slip [*objet*] (**dans** into); **~ un oreiller sous la tête d'un malade** to slide a pillow under a patient's head; **elle a glissé la main dans mes cheveux** she ran her fingers through my hair; **2** (introduire) to slip in [*remarque*]; **~ qch à l'oreille de qn** to whisper sth in sb's ear.
II *vi* **1** (être glissant) [*route, savon*] to be slippery; **2** (être déstabilisé) [*personne*] to slip; [*chapeau, écharpe*] to slip (down); [*outil*] to slip; [*véhicule*] to skid; **~ des mains de qn** [*savon, bouteille*] to slip out of sb's hands; **une tuile a glissé du toit** a tile fell off the roof; **3** (se déplacer) GÉN to slide; (avec grâce) to glide; **se laisser ~ le long d'une corde** to slide down a rope; **4** (ne pas accrocher) [*ski, tiroir, cloison*] to slide; **leur regard glissait sur l'assistance** they surveyed the people present; **~ sur** FIG (ne pas affecter) [*critique*] to have no effect on [*personne*]; (ne pas approfondir) [*personne*] to skate over [*sujet*]; **5** (passer) **~ dans l'ennui** to become bored; **l'électorat glisse à droite** there's a swing to the right among the electorate; **le roman glisse de la comédie au drame** the novel moves imperceptibly from comedy to drama.
III **se glisser** *vpr* **1** (s'introduire) to slip; **se ~ dans** GÉN to slip into; (furtivement) to sneak into; **se ~ dans la foule** to slip through the crowd; **se ~ parmi les invités** to slip in among the guests; **se ~ parmi les badauds** to edge through the onlookers; **le chat s'est glissé sous la voiture** the cat crept under the car; **2** (s'insinuer) [*sentiment, erreur*] to creep into [*personne, texte*].

glissière /glisjɛʀ/ *nf* TECH slide; (d'autoroute) **~ (de sécurité)** crash barrier; **à ~** [*porte, fenêtre*] sliding (*épith*); **fermeture à ~** zip GB, zipper US.

global, ~e, *mpl* **-aux** /glɔbal, o/ *adj* [*somme, effectif*] total; [*résultat, coût*] overall; [*accord, vision, solution*] global; [*étude*] comprehensive.

globalement /glɔbalmɑ̃/ *adv* on the whole.

globalité /glɔbalite/ *nf* **considérer qch dans sa ~** to consider sth in its entirety.

globe /glɔb/ *nm* **1** (Terre) earth, globe; **stratégie à l'échelle du ~** worldwide strategy; **parcourir le ~** to globe-trot; **2** (sphère en verre) (de lampe) round glass lampshade; (de protection) glass case; **3** ARCHIT dome.
■ **~ terrestre** (mappemonde) globe; (Terre) earth.

globulaire /glɔbylɛʀ/ *adj* **numération ~** blood count.

globule /glɔbyl/ *nm* (du sang) blood cell.

■ ~ **blanc** white cell; ~ **rouge** red cell.

globuleux, **-euse** /glɔbylø, øz/ adj [œil] protruding.

gloire /glwaʀ/ nf **1** (renom) glory, fame; **c'est ce qui a fait leur ~** that's what made them famous; **faire qch pour la ~** to do sth (just) for the sake of it; **2** (hommage) **~ à Dieu!** glory be to God; **rendre ~ à qn/au courage de qn** to pay tribute to sb/to sb's courage; **3** (sujet de fierté) **tirer ~ de** to pride oneself on; **4** (personne) celebrity; (dans le monde du spectacle) star; **5** (splendeur) glory; **le Christ en ~** ART Christ in majesty.

glorieusement /glɔʀjøzmɑ̃/ adv [combattre] with glory; **tomber ~ au champ d'honneur** to fall gloriously on the field of battle; **triompher ~** to have a great triumph.

glorieux, **-ieuse** /glɔʀjø, øz/ adj glorious.

glorifier /glɔʀifje/ [2] **I** vtr to glorify.
II se glorifier vpr to glory (**de** in), to boast (**de** about).

gloriole /glɔʀjɔl/ nf PEJ misplaced pride, vainglory LITTÉR.

glose /gloz/ nf (annotation, développement) gloss; (note explicative) note.

gloser /gloze/ [1] **I** vtr to annotate [texte].
II vi (discourir) to ramble on (**sur** about).

glossaire /glɔsɛʀ/ nm glossary.

glotte /glɔt/ nf glottis; **coup de ~** LING glottal stop.

glouglou /gluglu/ nm **1** ◦ (de liquide) gurgling sound; **2** (cri du dindon) gobbling sound.

glouglouter /gluglute/ [1] vi **1** ◦ [liquide] to gurgle; **2** [dindon] to gobble.

gloussement /glusmɑ̃/ nm (de poule) clucking ¢; (de personne) chuckle; **avec des ~s de satisfaction** with a satisfied chuckle.

glousser /gluse/ [1] vi [poule] to cluck; [personne] to chuckle.

glouton, **-onne** /glutɔ̃, ɔn/ **I** adj [personne] gluttonous; [appétit] voracious.
II nm,f glutton.
III nm ZOOL wolverine.

gloutonnerie /glutɔnʀi/ nf gluttony; **manger avec ~** to wolf down one's food.

glu /gly/ nf **1** bird lime; **prendre des oiseaux à la ~** to lime birds; **2** (colle) glue.

gluant, **-e** /glyɑ̃, ɑ̃t/ adj **1** (collant) [main, pâtes] sticky; [poisson, mur, boue] slimy; **2** ◦ (obséquieux) [personne] slimy.

glucide /glysid/ nm carbohydrate.

glycémie /glisemi/ nf **taux de ~** blood sugar level.

glycérine /gliseʀin/ nf glycerin.

glycine /glisin/ nf wisteria.

gnangnan /nɑ̃nɑ̃/ adj inv silly.

gnognotte /nɔɲɔt/ nf **c'est de la ~!** (c'est facile) it's dead easy ◦; **c'est pas de la ~!** (de bonne qualité) it's not your common or garden variety ◦; (difficile) it's quite a business ◦.

gnome /gnom/ nm gnome.

gnon ◦ /nɔ̃/ nm (bosse sur une voiture) dent; (ecchymose) bruise; **il m'a flanqué un ~** he socked me; **prendre un ~** to get hit.

gnostique /gnɔstik/ adj, nmf gnostic.

gnou /gnu/ nm gnu.

gnouf ◦ /nuf/ nm prison, nick ◦ GB.

go /go/ **I** ▶329 nm JEUX go.
II tout de go loc adv **tout de ~** [dire] straight out.

goal /gol/ nm goalkeeper, goalie ◦.

gobelet /gɔblɛ/ nm **1** (en plastique, carton) cup; (en verre) tumbler; (en métal) beaker; **~ en carton** paper cup; **2** JEUX shaker.

gobe-mouche, pl **~s** /gɔbmuʃ/ nm ZOOL flycatcher.

gober /gɔbe/ [1] vtr **1** (avaler) to suck [œuf]; to swallow [sth] whole [huître]; **2** ◦ (croire) to swallow, to fall for ◦ [mensonge]; **~ le morceau** to fall for it ◦.

godasse ◦ /gɔdas/ nf shoe.

goder /gɔde/ [1] vi (vêtement) to ruck up; (papier peint) to wrinkle.

godet /gɔdɛ/ nm **1** (pour boire) goblet; (petit récipient) pot; (à dés) shaker; **2** (faux pli) crease; (pan de jupe) gore.

godiche ◦ /gɔdiʃ/ adj **avoir un air ~** to look silly.

godille /gɔdij/ nf **1** (aviron) steering oar; **2** (à ski) wedeln.

godiller /gɔdije/ [1] vi (à skis) to wedeln.

godillot /gɔdijo/ nm **1** ◦ (soulier) clodhopper ◦; **2†** MIL (brodequin) combat boot.

goéland /gɔelɑ̃/ nm gull.

goélette /gɔelɛt/ nf schooner.

goémon /gɔemɔ̃/ nm (algues) wrack; (engrais) seaweed fertilizer.

gogo ◦ /gogo/ **I** nm (dupe) sucker ◦.
II à gogo loc adv **vin à ~** wine galore; **de l'argent, il en a à ~** he's got loads of money.

goguenard, **~e** /gɔgnaʀ, aʀd/ adj quietly ironic.

goguette ◦: **en goguette** /ɑ̃gɔgɛt/ **I** loc adj (ivre) tipsy.
II loc adv **partir en ~** to go on a spree.

goinfre /gwɛ̃fʀ/ nmf greedy pig ◦.

goinfrer ◦: **se goinfrer** /gwɛ̃fʀe/ [1] vpr to stuff oneself ◦ (**de** with).

goitre /gwatʀ/ nm goitre ᴳᴮ.

golden /gɔldɛn/ nf inv Golden Delicious (apple).

golf /gɔlf/ **▶329** nm **1** (sport) golf; **2** (terrain) golf course.

golfe /gɔlf/ nm (grand) gulf; (petit) bay.

golfeur, **-euse** /gɔlfœʀ, øz/ **▶374** nm,f golfer.

gomina® /gɔmina/ nf hair cream.

gominer: **se gominer** /gɔmine/ [1] vpr to slick one's hair back; **cheveux gominés** slicked-back hair.

gommage /gɔmaʒ/ nm **1** (action d'effacer) rubbing-out, erasing; **2** (action d'enduire) gumming; **3** (produit de beauté, action) scrub.

gomme /gɔm/ **I** nf **1** (pour effacer) eraser, rubber GB; **2** (substance) gum; **3** (bonbon) gum drop; **4** C (chewing-gum) **~ (à mâcher)** chewing gum; **5** MÉD gumma.
II à la gomme ◦ loc adj PEJ [idée, personne, renseignement, machine] useless; [projet] hopeless.
■ ~ **adhésive** blu-tack®; ~ **arabique** gum arabic; ~ **à encre** ink eraser.
IDIOMES mettre (toute) la ~ ◦ (en voiture, à moto) to step on it ◦; (en avion, bateau) to give it full throttle ◦; (avec une radio) to turn it up full blast.

gommer /gɔme/ [1] vtr **1** (effacer) to rub [sth] out [mot]; **2** (faire disparaître) to smooth out [ride]; to erase [passé, frontière]; to iron out [différence]; to soothe away [fatigue]; **3** (enduire) to gum; **papier gommé** gummed paper; **4** to scrub [peau].

gommier /gɔmje/ nm gum tree.

gond /gɔ̃/ nm hinge; **sortir de ses ~s** [porte] to come off its hinges, FIG [personne] to fly off the handle ◦.

gondole /gɔ̃dɔl/ nf **1** (embarcation) gondola; **en ~** in a gondola; **2** (de supermarché) sales shelf, gondola SPÉC.

gondoler: **se gondoler** /gɔ̃dɔle/ [1] vpr **1** [papier] to crinkle; [bois] to warp; [métal] to buckle; **2** ◦ (rire) to laugh.

gondolier /gɔ̃dɔlje/ **▶374** nm gondolier.

gonflable /gɔ̃flabl/ adj inflatable.

gonflage /gɔ̃flaʒ/ nm (de pneu, ballon) inflation; **station de ~** AUT air point (for pumping up tyres).

gonflé, **~e** /gɔ̃fle/ adj **1** (plein d'air) [pneu, ballon] inflated; [joue] puffed out; **2** (enflé) [bourgeon, veine, bras] swollen (**de** with); [ventre] (après un repas) bloated; (de malade) swollen; [yeux, visage] puffy, swollen; [muscle] bulging, flexed; [sac] bulging (**de** with); **yeux ~s de sommeil/de larmes** eyes heavy with sleep/swollen with tears; **éponge ~e d'eau** sponge saturated with water; **3** ◦ AUT [moteur] souped-up (épith); **voiture au moteur ~** hot rod GB, muscle car US; **4** ◦ (courageux) gutsy ◦; **être ~** to have guts ◦; **5** ◦ (impudent) cheeky ◦; **être ~** to have a nerve ◦.

gonfler /gɔ̃fle/ [1] **I** vtr **1** (remplir d'air) (avec la bouche)

to blow up [*ballon*]; to fill [*poumon*] (**de** with); to puff out [*joue*]; (avec une pompe) to inflate [*pneu*]; **être gonflé à bloc** [*pneu*] to be fully inflated; FIG [*personne*] to be raring○ to go; **le vent gonfle la voile** the wind swells ou fills the sail; **le vent gonfle ma chemise** the wind makes my shirt billow; **2** (faire grossir) [*personne*] to flex [*muscle*]; [*objet*] to make [sth] bulge [*poche*]; [*eau*] to saturate [*éponge*]; [*pluie*] to make [sth] swollen [*rivière*]; [*sève*] to swell [*bourgeon*]; **la limonade gonfle l'estomac** lemonade makes you feel bloated; **3** FIG **la joie gonflait mon cœur** my heart was bursting with joy; **il est gonflé d'orgueil** he's full of his own importance; **4** (augmenter) to increase [*effectifs*]; to push up [*prix*]; to inflate [*statistiques*]; to exaggerate [*importance*]; **5** AUT to soup up [*moteur, voiture*].
II *vi* **1** (enfler) [*pied, paupière*] to swell (up); [*riz, bois, éponge*] to swell; [*gâteau, pâte*] to rise; **2** (augmenter) [*effectifs*] to increase; **faire ~ les prix** to push prices up.

gonflette○ /gɔ̃flɛt/ *nf* PEJ **faire de la ~** to pump iron○, to go body-building.

gong /gɔ̃g/ *nm* **1** ▶ 392 | MUS gong; **2** (en boxe) bell.

gordien /gɔʀdjɛ̃/ *adj m* **trancher le nœud ~** to cut the Gordian knot.

goret /gɔʀɛ/ *nm* **1** ZOOL piglet; **2**○ (enfant) little pig○.

gorge /gɔʀʒ/ *nf* **1** ▶ 137 | ANAT throat; **avoir mal à la ~** to have a sore throat; **voix de ~** throaty voice; **je suis pris à la ~, je n'ai plus un sou** I'm in a fix○, I haven't got a penny; **tenir qn à la ~** FIG to have a stranglehold over sb; **avoir la ~ serrée** or **nouée** (d'émotion) to have a lump in one's throat; (de peur) to have one's heart in one's mouth; **à ~ déployée, à pleine ~** [*chanter*] at the top of one's voice; [*rire*] uproariously; **je te ferai rentrer tes mots dans la ~!** I'll make you eat your words!; **ta remarque m'est restée en travers de la ~** I found your comment hard to swallow ou very hard to take; **ma question m'est restée dans la ~** I couldn't get the question out; **2** (poitrine) bosom, breast; **3** GÉOG gorge.
IDIOMES **faire des ~s chaudes de qch** to laugh sth to scorn.

gorgé, ~e /gɔʀʒe/ **I** *pp* ▶ **gorger**.
II *pp adj* **~ de nourriture** glutted with food; **~ d'eau** [*terre*] waterlogged; [*éponge*] saturated with water (*jamais épith*); **fruit ~ de soleil** fruit bursting with sunshine.

gorgée /gɔʀʒe/ *nf* (petite) sip; (grande) gulp.

gorger /gɔʀʒe/ [13] **I** *vtr* **~ qn de nourriture** to stuff○ sb with food.
II se gorger *vpr* **se ~ de nourriture** to gorge oneself; **la terre se gorge d'eau** the soil soaks up water.

gorille /gɔʀij/ *nm* **1** ZOOL gorilla; **2**○ (garde du corps) bodyguard.

gosier /gozje/ *nm* throat, gullet; **ce vin (m')écorche le ~**○ HUM this wine is like paint stripper; **ça m'est resté en travers du ~**○ it stuck in my throat.
IDIOMES **s'humecter le ~**○ to wet one's whistle; **chanter à plein ~** to sing at the top of one's voice.

gospel /gɔspɛl/ *nm* **1** (style) gospel music; **2** (chant) gospel song.

gosse /gɔs/ *nmf* (enfant) kid○, child; **sale ~** brat○; **c'est un grand ~** he's still a kid at heart; **il est beau ~** he's a good-looking fellow.

gotha /gɔta/ *nm* (noblesse) aristocracy; (haute société) high society.

gothique /gɔtik/ *adj, nm* Gothic.

gouache /gwaʃ/ *nf* (peinture, tableau) gouache.

gouaille /gwaj/ *nf* (esprit moqueur) cheek.

gouailleur, -euse /gwajœʀ, øz/ *adj* cheeky.

goudron /gudʀɔ̃/ *nm* **1** CHIMIE tar; **'~s 12 mg'** '12 mg tar'; **2**○ (pour revêtement) tar, tarmac® GB.

goudronner /gudʀɔne/ [1] *vtr* to tarmac.

gouffre /gufʀ/ *nm* **1** (fosse) chasm, abyss; **le ~ de Padirac** the caves (*pl*) of Padirac; **2** FIG **le ~ de l'oubli** the pit of oblivion; **le pays est au bord du ~** the

country is on the brink of the abyss; **leur maison est un ~** their house is a real drain on their finances.

gouille /guj/ *nf* H (flaque) puddle.

goujat /guʒa/ *nm* boor; **comme un ~** boorishly.

goujaterie /guʒatʀi/ *nf* boorishness.

goujon /guʒɔ̃/ *nm* ZOOL gudgeon; **taquiner le ~**○ to do the odd bit of fishing.

goulée○ /gule/ *nf* (de liquide) gulp.

goulet /gulɛ/ *nm* (de port) narrows (*pl*); (en montagne) gully.
■ **~ d'étranglement** bottleneck.

goulot /gulo/ *nm* (de bouteille) neck; **boire au ~** to drink from the bottle.
■ **~ d'étranglement** bottleneck.

goulu, ~e /guly/ **I** *adj* greedy.
II *nmf* glutton.

goulûment /gulymɑ̃/ *adv* greedily.

goupille /gupij/ *nf* pin.

goupiller: se goupiller /gupije/ [1] *vpr* **ça s'est bien/mal goupillé** it turned out well/badly.

goupillon /gupijɔ̃/ *nm* **1** (brosse) bottle brush; **2** RELIG holy water sprinkler, aspergillum.

gourd, ~e¹ /guʀ, guʀd/ *adj* (engourdi) numb.

gourde² /guʀd/ **I**○ *adj* (niais) dumb○, gormless○ GB.
II *nf* **1** (pour liquide) GÉN flask; (en cuir, écorce) gourd; **2**○ (sot) dope○.

gourdin /guʀdɛ̃/ *nm* bludgeon, cudgel; **frapper qn à coups de ~** to bludgeon sb.

gourer○**: se gourer** /guʀe/ [1] *vpr* (dans un calcul) to make a mistake; (dans une supposition) to be mistaken; **se ~ de jour** to get the day wrong.

gourmand, ~e /guʀmɑ̃, ɑ̃d/ *adj* **1** (amateur) fond of good food (*jamais épith*); (glouton) greedy; **je ne suis pas ~e** I'm not that interested in food; **il est ~ (de sucreries)** he has a sweet tooth; **2** (d'argent) grasping.

gourmander† /guʀmɑ̃de/ [1] *vtr* to scold.

gourmandise /guʀmɑ̃diz/ **I** *nf* (pour les sucreries) weakness for sweet things; (pour la nourriture) weakness for good food; (défaut) greed; (péché) gluttony; **avec ~** greedily.
II gourmandises *nfpl* (friandises) sweets GB, candies US.

gourme /guʀm/ *nf* **jeter sa ~** to sow one's wild oats.

gourmet /guʀmɛ/ *nm* gourmet.

gourmette /guʀmɛt/ *nf* (de poignet) chain bracelet.

gourou /guʀu/ *nm* guru.

gousse /gus/ *nf* BOT pod; **~ d'ail** clove of garlic.

gousset /gusɛ/ *nm* **1** (poche) fob; **2** (de collant) gusset; **3** TECH gusset.

goût /gu/ *nm* **1** (sens) taste; (appréciation) palate; **agréable au ~** pleasant-tasting; **2** (saveur) taste; **avoir un ~ sucré** to taste sweet, to have a sweet taste; **avoir un ~ de brûlé/de pêche** to taste burned/of peaches; **avoir mauvais ~** to taste unpleasant; **avoir un petit ~** to taste a bit strange; **donner du ~ à qch** to give sth flavour^GB; **n'avoir aucun ~** to be tasteless; **3** (discernement) taste; **avoir du ~** to have taste; **avoir un ~ très sûr** to have unfailingly good taste; **de bon/mauvais ~** in good/bad taste (*après n*); **d'un ~ douteux** [*décor, plaisanterie, scène*] in dubious taste (*après n*); **avec/sans ~** [*décorer*] tastefully/tastelessly; **s'habiller avec/sans ~** to have good/no dress sense; **avoir le mauvais ~ de faire** to be tactless enough to do; **4** (gré) liking; **avoir du ~ pour qch** to have a liking for sth; **ne pas être du ~ de tout le monde** [*situation*] not to be to everyone's liking; [*décor, aliment*] not to be everyone's cup of tea; **je n'ai rien trouvé à mon ~** I didn't find anything I liked; **je n'ai plus ~ à rien** I've lost interest in everything; **elle reprend ~ à la vie** she's starting to enjoy life again; **être au ~ du jour** to be trendy; **se mettre au ~ du jour** to update one's image; **remettre qch au ~ du jour** to bring sth back into fashion; **il a pris ~ à la pêche** he's taken to fishing; **faire qch par ~** to do sth for pleasure; **5** (préférence) taste; **avoir des**

Les grades

*La liste suivante regroupe les grades des trois armes,
armée de terre, marine et aviation du Royaume-Uni et des
États-Unis. Pour les traductions, consulter les articles dans
le dictionnaire.*

*En anglais comme en français, l'armée de terre et l'armée
de l'air distinguent deux catégories: les officiers,
commissioned officers (GB) ou warrant officers (US), à
partir du grade de Second Lieutenant/Pilot Officer, et tous
les autres, à l'exception de Private/Aircraftman/Airman,
non-commissioned officers (the NCOs, dire [ði ensi:'əuz]:*

Royaume-Uni	États-Unis
L'armée de terre	
the British Army	the United States Army
Field Marshal (FM)*	General of the Army (GEN)
General (Gen)	General (GEN)
Lieutenant†-General (Lt-Gen)	Lieutenant† General (LTG)
Major-General (Maj-Gen)	Major General (MG)
Brigadier (Brig)	Brigadier General (BG)
Colonel (Col)	Colonel (COL)
Lieutenant†-Colonel (Lt-Col)	Lieutenant† Colonel (LTC)
Major (Maj)	Major (MAJ)
Captain (Capt)	Captain (CAPT)
Lieutenant† (Lieut)	First Lieutenant† (1LT)
Second Lieutenant† (2nd Lt)	Second Lieutenant† (2LT)
—	Chief Warrant Officer (CWO)
—	Warrant Officer (WO)
Regimental Sergeant Major (RSM)	Command Sergeant Major (CSM)
Company Sergeant Major (CSM)	Staff Sergeant Major (SSM)
—	1st Sergeant (1 SG)
—	Master Sergeant (MSG)
—	Sergeant 1st Class (SFC)
Staff Sergeant‡ (S/Sgt) *ou* Colour Sergeant‡ (C/Sgt)‡	Staff Sergeant (SSG)
Sergeant (Sgt)	Sergeant (SGT)
Corporal (Cpl)	Corporal (CPL)
Lance Corporal (L/Cpl)	Private First Class (P1C)
Private (Pte) *ou* Rifleman (Rfm) *ou* Guardsman (Gdm)‡	Private (PVT)
La marine	
the Royal Navy (RN)§	the United States Navy (USN)§
Admiral of the Fleet	Fleet Admiral
Admiral (Adm)*	Admiral (ADM)
Vice-Admiral (V-Adm)	Vice Admiral (VADM)
Rear-Admiral (Rear-Adm)	Rear Admiral (RADM)
Commodore (Cdre)	Commodore (CDRE)
Captain (Capt)	Captain (CAPT)
Commander (Cdr)	Commander (CDR)
Lieutenant†-Commander (Lt-Cdr)	Lieutenant† Commander (LCDR)
Lieutenant† (Lt)	Lieutenant† (LT)
Sub-Lieutenant† (Sub-Lt)	Lieutenant† Junior Grade (LTJG)
Acting Sub-Lieutenant† (Act Sub-Lt)	Ensign (ENS)
	Chief Warrant Officer (CWO)
Midshipman	Midshipman
Fleet Chief Petty Officer (FCPO)	—
—	Master Chief Petty Officer (MCPO)
—	Senior Chief Petty Officer (SCPO)
Chief Petty Officer (CPO)	Chief Petty Officer (CPO)
—	Petty Officer 1st Class (PO1)
—	Petty Officer 2nd Class (PO2)
Petty Officer (PO)	Petty Officer 3rd Class (PO3)
Leading Seaman (LS)	Seaman (SN)
Able Seaman (AB)	—
Ordinary Seaman (OD)	—
Junior Seaman (JS)	Seaman Apprentice (SA)
	Seaman Recruit (SR)

Royaume-Uni	États-Unis
L'armée de l'air	
the Royal Air Force (RAF)¶	the United States Air Force (USAF)‖
Marshal of the Royal Air Force	General of the Air Force
Air Chief Marshal (ACM)*	General (GEN)
Air Marshal (AM)	Lieutenant† General (LTG)
Air Vice-Marshal (AVM)	Major General (MG)
Air Commodore (Air Cdre)	Brigadier General (BG)
Group Captain (Gp Capt)	Colonel (COL)
Wing Commander (Wing Cdr)	Lieutenant† Colonel (LTC)
Squadron Leader (Sqn Ldr)	Major (MAJ)
Flight Lieutenant† (Flt Lt)	Captain (CAPT)
Flying Officer (FO)	First Lieutenant† (1LT)
Pilot Officer (PO)	Second Lieutenant† (2LT)
Warrant Officer (WO)	—
Flight Sergeant (FS)	Chief Master Sergeant (CMSGT)
—	Senior Master Sergeant (SMSGT)
—	Master Sergeant (MSGT)
Chief Technician (Chf Tech)	Technical Sergeant (TSGT)
Sergeant (Sgt)	Staff Sergeant (SSGT)
Corporal (Cpl)	Sergeant (SGT)
Junior Technician (Jnr Tech)	—
Senior Aircraftman (SAC) *ou* Senior Aircraftwoman	—
Leading Aircraftman (LAC) *ou* Leading Aircraftwoman	Airman First Class (A1C) *ou* Airwoman First Class
Aircraftman *ou* Aircraftwoman	Airman Basic (AB)

Comment parler des militaires

*L'anglais emploie l'article indéfini pour les noms de grades
utilisés avec les verbes* to be *(être),* to become *(devenir),*
to make *(faire) etc.*

Dans les expressions suivantes, colonel *est pris comme
exemple; les autres noms de grades s'utilisent de la même
façon.*

il est colonel	= he is a colonel
il est colonel dans l'armée de terre	= he is a colonel in the army
devenir colonel	= to become a colonel
on l'a nommé colonel	= he was made a colonel

Mais avec le verbe to promote *ou dans l'expression the
rank of ..., l'anglais n'emploie pas l'article indéfini:*

être promu colonel	= to be promoted colonel *ou* to be promoted to colonel
il a le grade de colonel	= he has the rank of colonel

*L'anglais n'emploie pas non plus l'article défini lorsque le
grade est suivi du nom propre:*

le colonel Jones est arrivé = Colonel Jones has arrived

Comparer:

le colonel est arrivé   = the colonel has arrived

Noter que le mot Colonel *prend une majuscule en anglais
devant le nom propre, mais rarement dans les autres cas.*

Comment s'adresser aux militaires

D'un militaire à son supérieur:

oui, mon colonel	= yes, sir
oui, colonel	= yes, ma'am

D'un militaire à son inférieur en grade:

oui, sergent   = yes, sergeant

---

* *Les abréviations sont utilisées uniquement par écrit et
avec les noms propres, par ex.: Capt. Jones.*
† *Noter la prononciation (GB):* [lef'tenənt], *(US):*
[lu:'tenənt].
‡ *Le nom varie selon le régiment.*
§ *Les abréviations* RN *et* USN *ne sont utilisées que par
écrit.*
¶ *Pour la* RAF, *dire* [ðɪɑ:reɪ'ef].
‖ *L'abréviation* USAF *n'est utilisée que par écrit. Dire* the
US Air Force.

~s **de luxe** to have expensive tastes; **chacun ses ~s** each to his own.

IDIOMES **avoir un ~ de trop peu** or **pas assez** to be on the stingy side; **tous les ~s sont dans la nature** PROV it takes all sorts to make a world PROV; **des ~s et des couleurs on ne discute pas** PROV there's no accounting for taste.

goûter[1] /gute/ [1] I *vtr* **1** (essayer) to taste, to try; **2** (apprécier) to enjoy [*paix, solitude, spectacle*]; **je goûte fort peu ce genre de plaisanterie** I don't appreciate that kind of joke at all.

II **goûter à** *vtr ind* **1** (essayer) **~ à** to try [*aliment, boisson*]; **mais tu y as à peine goûté!** but you've hardly touched it!; **2** (faire l'expérience de) **~ à** to have a taste of [*liberté, pouvoir*]; **~ aux joies de qch** to sample the joys of sth.

III **goûter de** *vtr ind* **~ de** to have a taste of; **avoir goûté de la prison** to have had a taste of life in prison.

IV *vi* to have one's mid-afternoon snack.

goûter[2] /gute/ *nm* **1** (nourriture) snack; **2** (réunion d'enfants) children's party; **~ d'anniversaire** children's birthday party.

goûteur, -euse /gutœʀ, øz/ ▶374 *nm,f* taster; **~ d'eau** water taster.

goutte /gut/ I *nf* **1** (de liquide) drop (**de** of); **~ de pluie** raindrop; **~ de rosée** dewdrop; **~ à ~** drop by drop; **couler** or **tomber ~ à ~** to drip; **à grosses ~s** [*pleuvoir*] heavily; [*transpirer*] profusely; **hier il est tombé quelques ~s** there were a few spots of rain yesterday; **~ de sueur** bead of sweat; ▶ **vase**[1]; **2**[○] (eau-de-vie) eau-de-vie; **3** ▶196 MÉD gout.

II **gouttes** *nfpl* (médicament) drops.

IDIOMES **se ressembler comme deux ~s d'eau** to be as alike as two peas in a pod; **c'est une ~ d'eau dans la mer** or **l'océan** it's a drop in the ocean; **avoir la ~ au nez** to have a runny nose; **on n'y voit ~** you can't see a thing.

goutte-à-goutte /gutagut/ *nm inv* MÉD drip.

gouttelette /gutlɛt/ *nf* droplet.

goutter /gute/ [1] *vi* to drip (**de** from).

gouttière /gutjɛʀ/ *nf* (de toit) gutter; (de descente) drainpipe.

gouvernail /guvɛʀnaj/ *nm* **1** NAUT rudder; **2** FIG helm; **tenir le ~** to be at the helm.

gouvernant, ~e[1] /guvɛʀnɑ̃, ɑ̃t/ I *adj* [*classe, parti*] ruling.

II **gouvernants** *nmpl* **les ~s** the government (*sg*).

gouvernante[2] /guvɛʀnɑ̃t/ *nf* **1** (institutrice) governess; **2** (domestique) housekeeper.

gouverne /guvɛʀn/ *nf* **pour votre ~** for your information.

gouvernement /guvɛʀnəmɑ̃/ *nm* government; **être au ~** to be a member of the government.

gouvernemental, ~e, mpl -aux /guvɛʀnəmɑ̃tal, o/ *adj* (du gouvernement) [*arrêté, politique*] government (*épith*); [*responsabilité*] governmental; **l'équipe ~e** the government; **non ~** non-governmental.

gouverner /guvɛʀne/ [1] I *vtr* **1** POL to govern, to rule [*pays, peuple*]; **le parti qui gouverne** the ruling party; **2** (dominer) [*intérêt*] to rule [*hommes*]; **3** NAUT to steer [*ship*].

II **se gouverner** *vpr* **le droit des peuples à se ~** the right of peoples to self-government.

gouverneur /guvɛʀnœʀ/ ▶596 *nm* governor.

goyave /gɔjav/ *nf* guava.

Graal /gʀal/ *nm* Grail.

grabat /gʀaba/ *nm* pallet.

grabataire /gʀabatɛʀ/ I *adj* bedridden.

II *nmf* bedridden invalid; **les ~s** the bedridden.

grabuge[○] /gʀabyʒ/ *nm* **il va y avoir du ~** there's going to be trouble; **faire du ~** to raise hell[○].

grâce /gʀɑs/ I *nf* **1** (de geste, personne) grace; (de paysage) charm; (de style) elegance; **sans ~** [*geste*] ungraceful; [*style*] inelegant; **se mouvoir avec/sans ~** to move gracefully/awkwardly; **2** (volonté) **bonne/**

mauvaise ~ good/bad grace; **de bonne/mauvaise ~** willingly/grudgingly; **3** (faveur) favour[GB]; **chercher/gagner les bonnes ~s de qn** to seek/to win sb's favour[GB]; **faire à qn la ~ d'accepter** FML to do sb the honour[GB] of accepting; **à la ~ de Dieu!** it's in God's hands!; **de ~** FML please; (avec impatience) for pity's sake; **donner le coup de ~ à qn** LIT, FIG to deal sb the death blow; **ce fut le coup de ~** that was the final stroke; **4** (pardon) mercy; JUR (free) pardon; **demander/crier ~** to beg/to cry for mercy; **~ présidentielle** JUR presidential pardon; **~!** (have) mercy!; **je vous fais ~ des détails** I'll spare you the details; **5** (bonté divine) grace; **être touché par la ~** to be touched by God's grace; **~ à Dieu!** thank God!; **dire les ~s** to say grace (after a meal).

II **grâce à** *loc prép* thanks to.

Grâce /gʀɑs/ *nf* Grace; **votre ~** your Grace.

gracier /gʀasje/ [2] *vtr* to pardon, to reprieve.

gracieusement /gʀasjøzmɑ̃/ *adv* **1** (gratuitement) free of charge; **un billet vous sera ~ offert** you will be given a free ticket; **2** (élégamment) [*danser*] gracefully.

gracieux, -ieuse /gʀasjø, øz/ *adj* **1** (beau) [*geste, personne*] graceful; **Sa gracieuse Majesté** FML his/her gracious Majesty; **2** (avenant) [*personne, sourire*] gracious.

gracile /gʀasil/ *adj* slender.

gradation /gʀadasjɔ̃/ *nf* GÉN, ART, PHOT gradation; **~ descendante** anticlimax.

grade /gʀad/ *nm* rank; **monter en ~** to be promoted; **en prendre pour son ~**[○] to be hauled over the coals.

gradé, ~e /gʀade/ *nm,f* MIL noncommissioned officer.

gradin /gʀadɛ̃/ *nm* (de salle) tier; (d'arène) terrace; (de stade) **les ~s** the terraces GB, the bleachers US; **en ~s** [*terrain*] terraced.

graduation /gʀaduasjɔ̃/ *nf* (d'instrument) graduation.

gradué, ~e /gʀadye/ *adj* **règle ~e** ruler; **verre ~** measuring cup; (avec bec verseur) measuring jug.

graduel, -elle /gʀaduɛl/ *adj* gradual.

graduer /gʀadue/ [1] *vtr* **1** GÉN to increase [*difficulté*]; to grade GB, to graduate US [*exercices*]; **2** TECH to graduate [*instrument*].

graffiti /gʀafiti/ *nmpl* graffiti.

graillon[○] /gʀajɔ̃/ *nm* **ça sent le ~** it smells of stale fat.

grain /gʀɛ̃/ *nm* **1** (céréales) grain; **nourri au ~** corn-fed, grain-fed; **2** (de céréale, sel, sable) grain; **~ de poivre** peppercorn; **~ de café** coffee bean; **~ de moutarde** mustard seed; **~ de cassis** blackcurrant; **~ de raisin** grape; **3** (de chapelet) bead; **4** (de poussière) speck (**de** of); **5** FIG **un ~ de folie** a touch of madness; **6** (texture) **le ~ de la peau** the grain; **7** (averse) heavy shower; **8** NAUT squall.

■ **~ de beauté** beauty spot, mole.

IDIOMES **avoir un ~**[○] to be loony[○]; **mettre son ~ de sel**[○] to put ou stick one's oar in[○].

graine /gʀɛn/ *nf* seed; **~s** (grosses ou individuelles) seeds; (pour semence) seed ¢; (pour oiseaux) birdseed ¢; **monter en ~** [*légume*] to run to seed; HUM [*enfant*] to shoot up; **ton fils, c'est de la mauvaise ~** your son is a bad lot[○].

IDIOMES **casser la ~**[○] to have a bite to eat; **prends-en de la ~**[○] let that be an example to you.

grainetier /gʀɛntje/ ▶374 *nm* seedsman GB, feedstore manager US.

graissage /gʀɛsaʒ/ *nm* lubrication.

graisse /gʀɛs/ *nf* **1** (tissu adipeux) fat; (de baleine, phoque) blubber; **2** CULIN fat; **mangez moins de ~s** eat less fat; **3** (lubrifiant) grease.

graisser /gʀɛse/ [1] *vtr* to grease [*poêle*]; to lubricate [*rouage*]; **~ la patte**[○] **à qn** FIG to grease sb's palm FIG.

graisseux, -euse /gʀɛsø, øz/ *adj* GÉN greasy; MÉD [*tissu*] fatty.

graminée /gʀamine/ *nf* **une ~** a grass; **les ~s** grasses.

grammaire /gʀamɛʀ/ *nf* **1** (science) grammar; **2** (manuel) grammar.

grammairien, **-ienne** /gʀamɛʀjɛ̃, ɛn/ ▶ 374 *nm,f* grammarian.

grammatical, **~e**, *mpl* **-aux** /gʀamatikal, o/ *adj* grammatical.

gramme /gʀam/ ▶ 455 *nm* gram; **il n'a pas un ~ de bon sens** he hasn't an ounce of common sense.

grand, **~e** /gʀɑ̃, gʀɑ̃d/ **I** *adj* **1** (de dimensions importantes) (en hauteur) tall; (en longueur, durée) long; (en largeur) wide; (en étendue, volume) big; **plus ~ que nature** larger than life; **ouvrir de ~s yeux** to open one's eyes wide; **2** (nombreux, abondant) large, big; **pas ~ monde** not many people; **il fait ~ jour** it's broad daylight; **laver à ~e eau** to wash [sth] in plenty of running water [*légumes*]; to wash [sth] down [*sol*]; **3** (à un degré élevé) [*rêveur, collectionneur, ami*] great; [*tricheur, joueur*] big; [*buveur, fumeur*] heavy; **c'est un ~ timide** he's very shy; **les ~s malades** very sick people; **les ~s blessés** the seriously injured; **4** (important) [*découverte, expédition, nouvelle*] great; [*date*] important; [*rôle*] major; [*problème, décision*] big; **c'est un ~ jour pour elle** it's a big day for her; **la ~e majorité** the great ou vast majority; **5** (principal) main; **les ~es lignes d'une politique** the broad lines of a policy; **6** (de premier plan) [*société, marque*] leading; **les ~es industries** the big industries; **7** (brillant, remarquable) [*peintre, vin, cause*] great; [*cœur, âme*] noble; **c'est un ~ homme** he's a great man; **Louis le Grand** Louis the Great; ▶ **esprit**; **8** (âgé) [*frère, sœur*] elder; [*élève*] senior GB, older; (adulte) **les ~es personnes** grown-ups; **les ~es classes** SCOL the senior forms GB, the upper classes US; **une ~e fille comme toi!** a big girl like you!; **assez ~ pour faire** old enough to do; **9** (qualifiant une mesure) [*hauteur, longueur, distance, valeur*] great; [*pointure, quantité, étendue*] large; [*vitesse*] high; **il est ~ temps que tu partes** it's high time you went; **10** (extrême, fort) [*bonté, amitié, danger, intérêt*] great; [*bruit*] loud; [*froid*] severe; [*chaleur*] intense; [*vent*] strong, high; [*tempête*] big, violent; **d'une ~e timidité** very shy; **à ma ~ surprise** much to my surprise; **sans ~ espoir** without much hope; **ça te ferait le plus ~ bien** it would do you a world of good; **à ~s cris** loudly; ▶ **cas**, **remède**; **11** (de rang social élevé) [*famille, nom*] great; **la ~e bourgeoisie** the upper middle class; **12** (grandiose) [*réception, projet*] grand; **avoir ~e allure** to look very impressive; **13** (emphatique) [*mot*] big; [*phrase*] high-sounding; **un ~ merci** a big thank you; **faire de ~s gestes** to wave one's arms about; **et voilà, tout de suite les ~s mots** there you go, straight off the deep end.

II *nm,f* (enfant) big boy/girl; SCOL senior GB ou older pupil; **pour les ~s et les petits** for old and young alike.

III *adv* wide; **ouvrir ~ les bras** to throw one's arms open; **ouvrir la porte toute ~e** to open the door wide; **ouvrir ~ ses oreilles** FIG to prick up one's ears; **leurs vêtements taillent ~** their clothes are cut on the large side; **voir ~** to think big.

IV *nm* **les ~s de ce monde** the great and the good; **les cinq ~s** POL the Big Five; **les ~s de l'automobile** the top car manufacturers.

V en grand *loc adv* **faire de l'élevage en ~** to breed animals on a large scale; **faire les choses en ~** to do things on the grand scale.

■ **~ banditisme** organized crime; **~ bassin** (de piscine) main pool; **~ couturier** couturier; **~ duc** ZOOL eagle owl; **~ écart** SPORT splits (*sg*); **~ ensemble** high-density housing complex; **~ invalide civil**, **GIC** civilian *who is registered severely disabled*; **~ invalide de guerre**, **GIG** *ex-serviceman who is registered severely disabled*; **le ~ large** NAUT the high seas (*pl*); **~ magasin** department store; **~ maître** (aux échecs) grand master; **~ mât** mainmast; **le ~ monde** high society; **le Grand Nord** the Far North; **~ panda** giant panda; **Grand Pardon** Day of Atonement; **~ patron** MÉD senior consultant GB, head doctor US; **~ prêtre** RELIG, FIG high priest; **le ~ public** the general public; COMM **produit ~ public** consumer product; **~ quotidien**

big national daily; **~ teint** colourfast GB; **~ tourisme** AUT GT, gran turismo; **la ~e banlieue** the outer suburbs (*pl*); **la ~e cuisine** haute cuisine; **~e distribution** volume retailing; **la Grande Guerre** the First World War; **~e gueule** loud mouth○; **la ~e muraille de Chine** the Great Wall of China; **~e personne** grown-up, adult; **la ~e presse** the popular dailies (*pl*); **~e puissance** POL superpower; **~e roue** (de foire) big wheel GB, Ferris wheel US; **~e série** COMM mass production; **fabriqué en ~e série** mass-produced; **~e surface** COMM supermarket; **~es eaux** fountains; **dès qu'on la gronde, ce sont les ~es eaux** FIG the minute you tell her off, she turns on the waterworks; **~es lignes** RAIL main train routes; **~es marées** spring tides; **~es ondes** long wave (*sg*); **~s espaces** open spaces; **~s fauves** big cats; **~s fonds** ocean depths; **Grands Lacs** Great Lakes; **~s singes** great apes; ▶ **voyage**.

grand-angle, *pl* **grands-angles** /gʀɑ̃tɑ̃gl, gʀɑ̃zɑ̃gl/, **grand-angulaire**, *pl* **grands-angulaires** /gʀɑ̃tɑ̃gylɛʀ, gʀɑ̃zɑ̃gylɛʀ/ *adj* wide-angle; **un (objectif) ~** a wide-angle lens.

grand-chose /gʀɑ̃ʃoz/ *pron indéf* **pas ~** not much, not a lot; **ça ne sert pas à ~** it's not much use; **je n'ai pas vu ~ d'intéressant** I didn't see anything much of interest; **il n'y a plus ~ à faire** there isn't much left to do; **'tu t'es fait mal?'—'ce n'est pas ~'** 'have you hurt yourself?'—'it's nothing much'.

grand-duc, *pl* **grands-ducs** /gʀɑ̃dyk/ ▶ 596 *nm* grand duke; **faire la tournée des grands-ducs** FIG to have a night on the town.

grand-duché, *pl* **grands-duchés** /gʀɑ̃dyʃe/ *nm* grand duchy.

Grande-Bretagne /gʀɑ̃dbʀətaɲ/ ▶ 305 *nprf* Great Britain.

grande-duchesse, *pl* **grandes-duchesses** /gʀɑ̃ddyʃɛs/ ▶ 596 *nf* grand duchess.

grandement /gʀɑ̃dmɑ̃/ *adv* [*intéresser*] greatly; [*aider*] a great deal; [*reconnaissant*] extremely.

grandeur /gʀɑ̃dœʀ/ *nf* **1** (taille) size; **être de la ~ de** to be the size of; **~ nature** [*reproduction*] full-scale; [*portrait*] life-size; **de première ~** LIT, FIG of the first magnitude; **2** (énormité) scale; **3** (élévation, gloire) greatness; **la ~ de leur sacrifice** their great sacrifice; **politique de ~** politics of national greatness; **par ~ d'âme** out of generosity of spirit.

IDIOMES **regarder qn du haut de sa ~** to look down one's nose at sb.

Grand-Guignol /gʀɑ̃giɲol/ *nm* **le ~** Grand Guignol; **c'est du ~** FIG it's farcical.

grandiloquence /gʀɑ̃dilɔkɑ̃s/ *nf* pomposity, grandiloquence SOUT.

grandiloquent, **~e** /gʀɑ̃dilɔkɑ̃, ɑ̃t/ *adj* pompous, grandiloquent.

grandiose /gʀɑ̃djoz/ *adj* [*site, édifice*] grandiose; [*réussite, fête*] spectacular; [*personnage*] grand.

grandir /gʀɑ̃diʀ/ [3] **I** *vtr* [*loupe*] to magnify; [*talons*] to make [sb] look taller; **sortir grandi d'une épreuve** to come out of an ordeal with increased stature.

II *vi* **1** (en taille) [*plante, enfant*] to grow; (en âge) [*enfant*] to grow up; **~ de 20 cm** to grow 20 cms; **~ dans l'estime de qn** FIG to go up in sb's esteem; **2** (en importance) [*entreprise*] to expand; [*rumeur, foule*] to grow; **aller grandissant** LITER [*inquiétude*] to become greater and greater; [*bruit*] to become louder and louder.

III se grandir *vpr* LIT to make oneself (look) taller.

grandissant, **~e** /gʀɑ̃disɑ̃, ɑ̃t/ *adj* growing.

grand-maman, *pl* **grands-mamans** /gʀɑ̃mamɑ̃/ *nf* grandma.

grand-mère, *pl* **grands-mères** /gʀɑ̃mɛʀ/ *nf* grandmother.

grand-messe, *pl* **~s** /gʀɑ̃mɛs/ *nf* **1** RELIG High Mass; **2** FIG ritual gathering.

grand-oncle, *pl* **grands-oncles** /gʀɑ̃tɔ̃kl, gʀɑ̃zɔ̃kl/ *nm* great-uncle.

grand-papa, *pl* **grands-papas** /gʀɑ̃papa/ *nm* grandpa○, granddad○.

grand-peine /gʀɑ̃pɛn/ **I** *nf* **avoir ~ à faire** to have great difficulty doing.
II à grand-peine *loc adv* **à ~** with great difficulty.

grand-père, *pl* **grands-pères** /gʀɑ̃pɛʀ/ *nm* grandfather.

grand-route, *pl* **~s** /gʀɑ̃ʀut/ *nf* main road.

grand-rue, *pl* **~s** /gʀɑ̃ʀy/ *nf* High Street GB, Main Street US.

grands-parents /gʀɑ̃paʀɑ̃/ *nmpl* grandparents.

grand-tante, *pl* **grand(s)-tantes** /gʀɑ̃tɑ̃t/ *nf* great-aunt.

grand-voile, *pl* **grand(s)-voiles** /gʀɑ̃vwal/ *nf* mainsail.

grange /gʀɑ̃ʒ/ *nf* barn.

granit(e) /gʀanit/ *nm* granite.

granité, **~e** /gʀanite/ *adj* grained.

granitique /gʀanitik/ *adj* granite (*épith*), granitic.

granule /gʀanyl/ *nm* granule.

granulé /gʀanyle/ *nm* granule.

granuleux, -euse /gʀanylø, øz/ *adj* [*roche*] granular; [*papier*] grained; [*peau, cuir*] grainy.

graphie /gʀafi/ *nf* **1** (*écriture*) written form; **2** (orthographe) spelling.

graphique /gʀafik/ **I** *adj* **1** ART, MATH [*forme, œuvre*] graphic; [*écran, tablette*] graphic; [*mode, mémoire, logiciel*] graphics (*épith*).
II *nm* graph; **~ à bandes** or **en colonnes** bar chart ou graph.

graphisme /gʀafism/ *nm* **1** (d'un artiste) style of drawing; **2** (écriture) handwriting; **3** (design) graphic design.

graphiste /gʀafist/ ▶374❘ *nmf* graphic designer.

graphite /gʀafit/ *nm* graphite.

graphologie /gʀafɔlɔʒi/ *nf* graphology.

graphologue /gʀafɔlɔg/ ▶374❘ *nmf* graphologist.

grappe /gʀap/ *nf* (de fruits) bunch; (de fleurs) cluster.

grappiller /gʀapije/ [1] *vtr* to pick up [*fruits*]; to glean [*renseignements*]; **~ quelques sous** to scrape together some money.

grappin /gʀapɛ̃/ *nm* (crochet) grappling irons (*pl*).
IDIOMES **mettre le ~**○ **sur qn** to get sb in one's clutches.

gras, grasse /gʀɑ, gʀɑs/ **I** *adj* **1** GÉN [*substance*] fatty; [*poisson*] oily; [*fromage*] full fat; [*papier, cheveux*] greasy; ▶**veau**; **2** (vulgaire) coarse; **3** (abondant) LITER [*salaire*] fat; [*récolte*] bumper (*épith*); **4** (en typographie) [*caractère*] bold.
II *adv* **cuisiner ~** to use a lot of fat in cooking; **manger ~** to eat fatty foods.
III *nm* **1** (de viande) fat; **2** (corps huileux) grease; **3** (de bras, mollet) **le ~** the fleshy part (**de** of).

grassement /gʀɑsmɑ̃/ *adv* (généreusement) [*payer*] handsomely; [*noter*] generously; [*nourrir*] lavishly.

grasseyement /gʀasɛjmɑ̃/ *nm* guttural pronunciation.

grassouillet○, **-ette** /gʀasujɛ, ɛt/ *adj* chubby, plump.

gratifiant, **~e** /gʀatifjɑ̃, ɑ̃t/ *adj* gratifying; **travail ~** rewarding job.

gratification /gʀatifikasjɔ̃/ *nf* **1** (satisfaction) gratification; **2** (prime) bonus.

gratifier /gʀatifje/ [2] *vtr* **~ qn de qch** to give sb sth; **se sentir gratifié** to feel gratified.

gratin /gʀatɛ̃/ *nm* **1** CULIN gratin (*breadcrumbs and cheese*); **macaroni au ~** macaroni cheese GB, macaroni and cheese US; **~ de pommes de terre** potatoes au gratin; **2**○ (élite) **le ~** the upper crust.

gratiné, **~e** /gʀatine/ *adj* **1** CULIN au gratin (*après n*); **2**○ FIG [*personne, style*] weird; [*problème*] mind-bending○.

gratiner /gʀatine/ [1] *vtr* (faire) **~ un plat** to brown a dish.

gratis /gʀatis/ **I** *adj inv* free.
II *adv* free GB, for free.

gratitude /gʀatityd/ *nf* gratitude; **éprouver de la ~ envers qn** to be grateful to sb.

gratouiller○ /gʀatuje/ [1] *vtr* **j'ai la gorge qui me gratouille** I've got a tickle in my throat.

grattage /gʀataʒ/ *nm* **1** (pour modifier) (de papier) scratching; (de métal, bois) scraping; **2** (pour enlever) (sur papier) scratching out; (sur métal, bois) scraping off; (de case sur un coupon) scratching.

gratte-ciel /gʀatsjɛl/ *nm inv* skyscraper.

gratte-cul○, *pl* **~s** /gʀatky/ *nm* rosehip.

gratte-papier○ /gʀatpapje/ *nm inv* pen pusher○ GB, pencil pusher○ US.

gratter /gʀate/ [1] **I** *vtr* **1** (frotter) to scratch; (pour nettoyer) to scrape; (pour enlever) to scrape off [*peinture, boue*]; **2** (démanger) **ça me gratte partout** I'm itching all over; **3**○ (gagner) **~ quelques francs** to fiddle a few francs (**sur** from); **~ un quart d'heure sur son temps de travail** to work a quarter of an hour less than one is supposed to.
II gratter de○ *vtr ind* **~ de la guitare** to strum the guitar.
III *vi* **~ à la porte** to scratch at the door.
IV se gratter *vpr* to scratch.
IDIOMES **il peut (toujours) se ~**○ he can go and jump in a lake.

grattoir /gʀatwaʀ/ *nm* **1** GÉN scraper; **2** (de boîte d'allumettes) striking strip.

gratuit, **~e** /gʀatɥi, it/ *adj* **1** (non payant) free; **numéro d'appel ~** Freefone® number GB, toll-free number US; **2** (injustifié) [*violence, remarque*] gratuitous; [*accusation*] spurious; [*exercice*] pointless; **3** (désintéressé) [*compliment*] disinterested.

gratuité /gʀatɥite/ *nf* **1** (caractère non payant) **la ~ de l'enseignement** free education; **2** (caractère injustifié) unwarranted nature, gratuitous nature.

gratuitement /gʀatɥitmɑ̃/ *adv* **1** (gratis) free GB, for free US; **2** (sans rétribution) [*travailler, réparer*] for nothing; **3** (sans motif) gratuitously.

gravats /gʀava/ *nmpl* rubble ₵.

grave /gʀav/ **I** *adj* **1** (préoccupant) [*problème, blessure*] serious; **deux blessés ~s** two people seriously injured; **2** (digne) [*air, visage*] grave, solemn; **3** (de basse fréquence) [*voix*] deep; [*note, registre*] low; [*son*] low-pitched.
II graves *nmpl* (d'amplificateur) **les ~s** the bass (*sg*).

graveleux, -euse /gʀavlø, øz/ *adj* (obscène) [*histoire*] smutty; [*propos*] indecent.

gravement /gʀavmɑ̃/ *adv* **1** (avec solennité) gravely, solemnly; **2** (de façon importante) seriously.

graver /gʀave/ [1] *vtr* to engrave [*inscription, motif*] (**sur** on); **il a gravé son nom sur l'arbre** he carved his name on the tree; **l'épisode est gravé à jamais dans leur mémoire** the episode is engraved on their memory forever.

graveur, -euse /gʀavœʀ, øz/ ▶374❘ *nm,f* engraver; **~ sur bois** wood engraver.

gravier /gʀavje/ *nm* **du ~** gravel ₵.

gravillon /gʀavijɔ̃/ *nm* (petits cailloux) grit ₵; **un ~** a bit of grit.

gravir /gʀaviʀ/ [3] *vtr* to climb up; **~ les échelons de la hiérarchie** to move up through the hierarchy.

gravissime /gʀavisim/ *adj* extremely serious.

gravitation /gʀavitasjɔ̃/ *nf* gravitation.
■ **~ universelle** PHYS Newton's law of gravitation.

gravité /gʀavite/ *nf* **1** (caractère préoccupant) seriousness; **une blessure sans ~** a minor injury; **2** (caractère solennel) solemnity; **3** PHYS gravity.

graviter /gʀavite/ [1] *vi* [*astre*] to orbit.

gravure /gʀavyʀ/ *nf* **1** (procédé) **la ~** engraving; **2** (estampe) engraving; **3** (reproduction) print.
■ **~ à l'eau-forte** etching.

gré /gʀe/ *nm* **1** (convenance) **être au ~ de qn** [*qualité, objet*] to be to sb's liking; **contre le ~ de qn** against sb's will; **de plein ~** willingly; **de mon/ton plein ~** of my/your own free will; **de bon ~** gladly; **de mauvais ~** reluctantly; **bon ~ mal ~** willy-nilly;

de ~ ou de force one way or another; **2** (gratitude) FML **savoir ~ à qn de qch** to be grateful to sb for sth; **3** (hasard) **j'ai flâné au ~ de mon humeur** I strolled where the mood took me; **au ~ des circonstances** as circumstances dictate.

grec, grecque¹ /gʀɛk/ I ▶ 394 adj **1** [île, art] Greek; **2** [nez, profil] Grecian.

II ▶ 338 nm LING Greek; **le ~ ancien/moderne** Ancient/Modern Greek.

Grèce /gʀɛs/ ▶ 232 nprf Greece; **~ antique** Ancient Greece.

gréco-romain, ~e, mpl ~**s** /gʀekoʀɔmɛ̃, ɛn/ adj Graeco-Roman GB, Greco-Roman US; **lutte ~e** Graeco-Roman.

grecque² /gʀɛk/ I adj ▶ **grec.**

II nf **1** ART Greek key; **2** CULIN **à la ~** à la grecque.

gredin, ~e /gʀədɛ̃, in/ nmf **1** HUM rascal; **2**† (crapule) scoundrel†.

gréer /gʀee/ [11] vtr to rig.

greffe /gʀɛf/ nf **1** MÉD (d'organe) transplant; (de peau) graft; **2** AGRIC (opération) grafting ₵; (résultat) graft.

greffer /gʀefe/ [1] I vtr **1** MÉD to transplant [organe]; to graft [tissu]; **on lui a greffé un rein** he's/she's had a kidney transplant; **2** AGRIC to graft.

II **se greffer** vpr se **~ sur qch** FIG to come along on top of sth.

greffier, -ière /gʀefje, ɛʀ/ ▶ 374 nmf clerk of the court GB, court clerk US.

greffon /gʀefɔ̃/ nm AGRIC graft, scion.

grégaire /gʀegɛʀ/ adj **instinct ~** herd instinct.

grège /gʀɛʒ/ ▶ 141 adj, nm oatmeal.

grégorien, -ienne /gʀegɔʀjɛ̃, ɛn/ adj Gregorian.

grêle /gʀɛl/ I adj **1** (mince) [silhouette] skinny; [jambes] spindly; **2** (aigu) [voix] reedy; [son] thin.

II nf **1** MÉTÉO hail ₵; **orage de ~** hailstorm; **il tombe de la ~** it's hailing; **2** (volée) **recevoir une ~ de coups** to be showered with blows.

grêlé, ~e /gʀɛle/ adj [visage, peau] pockmarked.

grêler /gʀɛle/ [1] v impers to hail; **il grêle** it's hailing; **il a grêlé sur les vignes** the vines were hit by hail.

grêlon /gʀɛlɔ̃/ nm hailstone.

grelot /gʀəlo/ nm small bell.

grelotter /gʀəlɔte/ [1] vi to shiver (**de** with); **on grelotte ici**○**!** we're freezing in here!

grenade /gʀənad/ nf **1** MIL (engin) grenade; **2** BOT, CULIN pomegranate.

Grenade /gʀənad/ I ▶ 628 npr (en Espagne) Granada.

II ▶ 232 nprf (État) **la ~** Grenada.

grenadier /gʀənadje/ nm **1** BOT pomegranate tree; **2** MIL grenadier.

grenadine /gʀənadin/ nf (sirop de) **~** grenadine.

grenaille /gʀənaj/ nf (de plomb) lead shot.

grenat /gʀəna/ ▶ 141 I adj inv dark red.

II nm **1** (pierre) garnet; **2** (couleur) dark red.

grenier /gʀənje/ nm (de maison) attic, loft; (grange) loft; **~ à foin** hay loft; **~ à grain** granary; **~ (à blé)** FIG breadbasket.

grenouille /gʀənuj/ nf frog.

■ **~ de bénitier**○ holy Joe○.

grenouillère /gʀənujɛʀ/ nf stretch suit GB, creepers (pl) US.

grenu, ~e /gʀəny/ adj [papier, peau] grained.

grès /gʀɛ/ nm inv **1** (roche) sandstone; **2** (céramique) stoneware; **3** (objet) piece of stoneware.

grésil /gʀezil/ nm hail.

grésillement /gʀezijmɑ̃/ nm **1** (à la radio) crackling; **2** (de beurre) sizzling.

grésiller /gʀezije/ [1] I vi **1** [radio, téléphone] to crackle; **2** [beurre, huile] to sizzle.

II v impers to hail.

grève /gʀɛv/ nf **1** (cessation du travail) strike; **être en ~** to be on strike; **se mettre en ~** to go on strike; **déclencher un mouvement de ~** to take industrial action; **2** (rivage) shore.

■ **~ de la faim** hunger strike; **~ sur le tas** sit-down strike; **~ tournante** staggered strike; **~ du zèle** work-to-rule.

grever /gʀəve/ [16] vtr to be a burden on [pays, contribuable]; to put a strain on [budget]; **l'entreprise est grevée de charges** the company has crippling overheads.

gréviste /gʀevist/ nmf striker; **les mineurs ~s** the striking miners.

■ **~ de la faim** hunger striker.

gribiche /gʀibiʃ/ adj **sauce ~** mayonnaise made of a chopped hard-boiled egg, capers and herbs.

gribouillage○ /gʀibujaʒ/ nm scribble; **faire des ~s** to doodle.

gribouiller○ /gʀibuje/ [1] I vtr to scribble (**sur** on).

II vi to doodle (**sur** on).

gribouillis○ /gʀibuji/ nm inv = gribouillage.

grief /gʀijɛf/ nm grievance; **je ne t'en fais pas ~** I don't hold it against you.

grièvement /gʀijɛvmɑ̃/ adv [blessé] seriously; [brûlé] badly; [atteint] severely; **être ~ blessé à la tête** to sustain serious head injuries.

griffe /gʀif/ nf **1** ZOOL claw; **coup de ~** scratch; **toutes ~s dehors** LIT, FIG ready to pounce; **tomber entre les ~s de qn** FIG to fall into sb's clutches; **2** COMM (marque) label; **3** (empreinte) signature stamp; **4** (en bijouterie) claw.

griffé, ~e /gʀife/ adj [vêtements] designer (épith).

griffer /gʀife/ [1] I vtr (égratigner) to scratch.

II **se griffer** vpr [personne] to scratch oneself.

griffonnage /gʀifɔnaʒ/ nm scribble.

griffonner /gʀifɔne/ [1] vtr **1** (écrire) to scrawl; **2** (dessiner) to sketch; **~ un plan** to draw a rough map.

griffure /gʀifyʀ/ nf scratch.

grignotage /gʀiɲɔtaʒ/ nm **1** (fait de manger) nibbling ₵; **2** (de libertés, capital) erosion (**de** of); (de terres) encroachment (**de** on).

grignoter /gʀiɲɔte/ [1] I vtr **1** (manger un peu) to nibble; **tu n'as pas quelque chose à ~?** have you got anything to nibble? GB, do you have anything to snack on? US; **2** (empiéter) to encroach on [terres]; to conquer [part de marché]; **3** (entamer) to fritter away [héritage]; **4** (gagner) [coureur] to gain [secondes].

II vi to nibble.

gri-gri, pl **gris-gris** /gʀigʀi/ nm lucky charm, talisman.

gril /gʀil/ nm (de cuisinière) grill GB, broiler US; (plaque) grill pan GB, broiler US; **être sur le ~** FIG to be on tenterhooks.

grillade /gʀijad/ nf grilled meat (₵).

grillage /gʀijaʒ/ nm (pour clôture) wire netting; (à gros trous hexagonaux) chicken wire; (à trous fins) wire mesh.

grillagé, ~e /gʀijaʒe/ adj [enclos] fenced with wire (après n); [porte] covered with wire mesh (après n).

grillager /gʀijaʒe/ [13] vtr to fit a screen to [fenêtre]; to put chicken wire around [poulailler].

grille /gʀij/ nf **1** (clôture) railings (pl); (porte) (iron) gate; (d'évier, égout) drain; (de bouche d'aération, confessionnal) grille; (de four) shelf; (de poêle) grate; **2** (de mots croisés, d'horaires) grid; **3** RADIO, TV programme^GB; **4** (système d'interprétation) model; **5** ADMIN scale.

grillé, ~e /gʀije/ I pp ▶ **griller.**

II pp adj **1** (cuit) [viande, maïs] grilled; [pain] toasted; [amandes] roasted; **2** (hors d'usage) burned out; **l'ampoule est ~e** the bulb has blown; **3**○ (révélé) [espion] exposed; **je suis ~** my cover is blown.

grille-pain /gʀijpɛ̃/ nm inv toaster.

griller /gʀije/ [1] I vtr **1** CULIN to grill [viande, maïs]; to toast [pain]; to roast [amandes]; **2**○ (fumer) to smoke [cigarette]; **3** (mettre hors d'usage) to burn out [appareil électrique]; to blow [ampoule]; **4**○ (ne pas respecter) to jump○ [feu rouge]; to ignore [priorité]; **5**○ (révéler) **il s'est fait ~** they blew his cover; **6**○ (dépasser) **~ un adversaire** to manage to get ahead of one's opponent.

II vi **1** CULIN **faire ~e** to grill [viande, maïs]; to toast [pain]; to roast [amandes]; **2** [ampoule] to blow.

grillon /gʀijɔ̃/ nm cricket.

grimaçant, **~e** /ɡʀimasɑ̃, ɑ̃t/ *adj* grimacing.

grimace /ɡʀimas/ *nf* (expression) grimace; (comique) funny face; **faire des ~s** LIT to make faces; FIG to be fussy; **faire une ~ à qn** to make ou pull a face at sb; **faire la ~** (devant un prix élevé) to wince; (de réticence) to make ou pull a face; ▶ **singe**.

grimacer /ɡʀimase/ [12] **I** *vtr* **~ un sourire** to force a smile.
II *vi* to grimace; **le soleil le faisait ~** he screwed up his eyes in the sun.

grimer: **se grimer** /ɡʀime/ [1] *vpr* to make oneself up (**en** as).

grimoire /ɡʀimwaʀ/ *nm* (écrit obscur) arcane text.

grimpant, **~e** /ɡʀɛ̃pɑ̃, ɑ̃t/ *adj* [*plante*] climbing.

grimpée /ɡʀɛ̃pe/ *nf* climb.

grimper[1] /ɡʀɛ̃pe/ [1] **I** *vtr* (gravir) to climb.
II *vi* **1** (escalader) **~ aux arbres** to climb (up) trees; **dans un arbre** to climb up a tree; **~ à la corde** to climb the rope; **~ sur la scène/les genoux de qn** to climb up onto the stage/sb's knees; **grimpe sur mon dos** get on my back; **grimpe dans ton lit** get into bed; **2**○ (suivre une pente raide) [*route*] to be steep; **3**○ (augmenter) [*température, prix*] to climb (**de** by); **4**○ (progresser) **~ de sept places** to go up seven places.

grimper[2] /ɡʀɛ̃pe/ *nm* **~** (**à la corde**) rope-climbing *C*.

grimpeur, **-euse** /ɡʀɛ̃pœʀ, øz/ *nm,f* (alpiniste) rock climber.

grinçant, **~e** /ɡʀɛ̃sɑ̃, ɑ̃t/ *adj* **1** (bruyant) [*serrure*] creaking; [*musique*] grating; **2** (acerbe) [*ton*] scathing; [*plaisanterie*] caustic; [*rire*] nasty.

grincement /ɡʀɛ̃smɑ̃/ *nm* **1** (type de bruit) (de porte) creaking *C*; (de craie) squeaking *C*; (de violon) screeching *C*; **2** (bruit) (de porte) creak; (de craie) squeak; (de violon) screech.

grincer /ɡʀɛ̃se/ [12] *vi* [*porte*] to creak; [*violon*] to screech; [*craie*] to squeak; **~ des dents** LIT to grind one's teeth; FIG to gnash one's teeth; **faire ~ les dents à qn** [*bruit*] to set sb's teeth on edge.

grincheux, **-euse** /ɡʀɛ̃ʃø, øz/ **I** *adj* grumpy GB, grouchy○.
II *nm,f* (old) misery○ GB, grouch○.

gringalet /ɡʀɛ̃ɡalɛ/ **I** *adj m* puny.
II *nm* runt.

griotte /ɡʀijɔt/ *nf* BOT, CULIN morello cherry.

grippal, **~e**, *mpl* **-aux** /ɡʀipal, o/ *adj* **affection ~e, état ~** flu.

grippe /ɡʀip/ ▶ **196** *nf* flu *C*; **avoir la ~** to have flu GB, to have the flu.
■ **~ intestinale** gastric flu GB, intestinal flu US.
IDIOMES **prendre qn/qch en ~**○ to take a sudden dislike to sb/sth.

grippé, **~e** /ɡʀipe/ *adj* MÉD **être ~** to have flu GB, to have the flu.

gripper /ɡʀipe/ [1] *vtr* to make [sth] seize up [*piston*]; **le moteur est grippé** the engine has seized up.

grippe-sou○, *pl* **~s** /ɡʀipsu/ *nm* skinflint○ GB, tightwad○ US.

gris, **~e** /ɡʀi, iz/ ▶ **141** **I** *adj* **1** (couleur) grey GB, gray US; **~ bleu** blue-grey GB, blue-gray US; **2** (morne) [*banlieue, rue*] dreary; [*existence*] dull; **il fait ~** it's a grey GB ou gray US day; **3** (ivre) tipsy.
II *nm inv* **1** (couleur) grey GB, gray US; **2** (tabac) cheap tobacco.
■ **~ anthracite** charcoal grey GB ou gray US; **~ ardoise** slate grey GB ou gray US; **~ perle** pearl grey GB ou gray US; **~ souris** mid-grey GB, mid-gray US; **~ tourterelle** dove grey GB ou gray US.
IDIOMES **faire ~e mine** to be none too pleased; **la nuit tous les chats sont ~** PROV all cats are grey GB ou gray US in the dark.

grisaille /ɡʀizaj/ *nf* **1** (ennui) **la ~ quotidienne** the daily grind; **2** (temps gris) greyness GB, grayness US.

grisant, **~e** /ɡʀizɑ̃, ɑ̃t/ *adj* **1** (exaltant) [*vitesse, plaisir*] exhilarating; [*succès, danger*] intoxicating; **2** (enivrant) [*parfum*] heady.

grisâtre /ɡʀizɑtʀ/ ▶ **141** *adj* [*couleur, ciel*] greyish GB, grayish US; [*linge*] dirty white; [*matin*] dull.

griser /ɡʀize/ [1] **I** *vtr* [*vitesse, plaisir*] to exhilarate; [*succès, danger, parfum*] to intoxicate; **se laisser ~ par le pouvoir** to let power go to one's head.
II se griser *vpr* **se ~ de** to get drunk on [*vin, succès, pouvoir*].

griserie /ɡʀizʀi/ *nf* (exaltation) exhilaration (**de** of).

grisonnant, **~e** /ɡʀizɔnɑ̃, ɑ̃t/ *adj* greying GB, graying US.

grisonner /ɡʀizɔne/ [1] *vi* to go grey GB, to gray US.

Grisons /ɡʀizɔ̃/ ▶ **509** *nprmpl* GÉOG **le canton des ~, les ~** the canton of Graubünden; **viande des ~** dried beef (*served in thin slices*).

grisou /ɡʀizu/ *nm* firedamp; **coup de ~** firedamp explosion.

grive /ɡʀiv/ *nf* thrush.
IDIOMES **faute de ~s on mange des merles** PROV half a loaf is better than no bread PROV.

grivois, **~e** /ɡʀivwa, az/ *adj* [*chanson*] bawdy; [*plaisanterie*] coarse; **être d'humeur ~e** to be in a saucy mood.

grivoiserie /ɡʀivwazʀi/ *nf* (propos) suggestive remark.

grizzli, **grizzly** /ɡʀizli/ *nm* grizzly bear.

Groenland /ɡʀɔenlɑ̃d/ *nprm* Greenland.

groenlandais, **~e** /ɡʀɔenlɑ̃dɛ, ɛz/ *adj* Greenland (*épith*).

grogne○ /ɡʀɔɲ/ *nf* discontent.

grognement /ɡʀɔɲəmɑ̃/ *nm* (de personne) grunt; (de chien, lion, d'ours) growl; (cri du cochon) grunt; **pousser des ~s de plaisir** to grunt with pleasure.

grogner /ɡʀɔɲe/ [1] **I** *vtr* to mutter [*insultes*].
II *vi* **1** [*personne*] LIT to groan; FIG to grumble; **~ de douleur** to groan with pain; **2** ZOOL [*cochon*] to grunt; [*ours, chien, lion*] to growl.

grognon /ɡʀɔɲɔ̃/ *nm* moaner GB, grouch○.

groin /ɡʀwɛ̃/ *nm* snout.

grommeler /ɡʀɔmle/ [19] **I** *vtr* to mutter [*insultes*]; to murmur [*compliment*].
II *vi* **1** [*personne*] to grumble (**contre** about); **2** [*sanglier*] to snort.

grommellement /ɡʀɔmɛlmɑ̃/ *nm* (de personne) groan; (de sanglier) snort.

grondement /ɡʀɔ̃dmɑ̃/ *nm* (d'avalanche, canon) rumble; (de torrent, machine) roar; (de chien, d'ours) growl; (de foule) angry murmur.

gronder /ɡʀɔ̃de/ [1] **I** *vtr* (réprimander) to tell [sb] off.
II *vi* **1** (tonner) [*tonnerre*] to rumble; [*machine, vent*] to roar; **2** (être menaçant) [*révolte*] to be brewing.

groom /ɡʀum/ ▶ **374** *nm* (valet) bellboy GB, bellhop US.

gros, **grosse** /ɡʀo, ɡʀos/ **I** *adj* **1** GÉN big, large; **2** (épais) thick; **3** (gras) fat; **4** (important) big, large; **5** (grave) [*problème, erreur*] serious, big; [*déception, défaut*] big, major; **6** (fort) [*rhume*] bad; [*sanglots*] loud; [*soupir, voix*] deep; [*pluie, chute de neige*] heavy; [*orage*] big; [*temps, mer*] rough; [*buveur, fumeur*] heavy; **avoir une grosse fièvre** to have a very high temperature; **avoir une grosse faim** to be very hungry; **pendant les grosses chaleurs** when the weather is at its hottest; **~ malin**○! you silly fool○!; **7** (rude) [*rire*] coarse; [*drap, laine*] coarse.
II *nm,f* fat man/woman.
III *adv* **1** (en grands caractères) [*écrire*] big; **écrire moins ~** to write smaller; **2** (beaucoup) [*miser, perdre*] LIT a lot of money; FIG a lot; **jouer ~** LIT, FIG to play for high stakes; **il y a ~ à parier que...** it's a good bet that...
IV *nm inv* **1** (plupart) **le ~ de** the majority ou bulk of [*spectateurs, passagers*]; the main body of [*manifestants, expédition*]; the bulk of [*travail*]; most of [*hiver, saison*]; most of [*déficit*]; **2** COMM wholesale trade; **de ~** [*magasin, prix*] wholesale; **3 la pêche au ~** game fishing.
V en gros *loc adv* **1** (dans les grandes lignes) roughly; **en ~ je suis d'accord** basically, I agree; **2** COMM

[*acheter*] wholesale; **3** (en grands caractères) in big letters.

■ **~ bétail** large livestock; **~ bonnet**○ big shot○; **~ lot** JEUX first prize, jackpot; **gagner** or **décrocher le ~ lot** LIT, FIG to hit the jackpot; **~ mot** swearword; **dire des ~ mots** to swear; **~ œuvre** shell (of a building); **~ plan** CIN close-up; **~ sel** cooking salt; **~ titre** headline; **être en ~ titres dans les journaux** to hit the headlines; **grosse caisse** bass drum; **grosse légume**○ = **~ bonnet**; **grosse tête**○ brain box○ GB, brain○.

IDIOMES **avoir le cœur ~** to have a heavy heart; **en avoir ~ sur le cœur** or **la patate**○ to be very upset; **~ comme le poing** as big as my fist; **~ comme une tête d'épingle** no bigger than a pinhead; **c'est un peu ~ comme histoire!** that's a bit of a tall story!; **il dit des bêtises grosses comme lui** he says the most ridiculous things.

groseille /gʀozɛj/ I ▶ 141 *adj inv* red.
II *nf* redcurrant.
■ **~ blanche** white currant; **~ à maquereau** gooseberry.

groseillier /gʀozeje/ *nm* redcurrant bush.

Gros-Jean /gʀoʒɑ̃/ *nm* **être ~ comme devant** to be left feeling a real mug○.

gros-porteur, *pl* **~s** /gʀopɔʀtœʀ/ *nm* AVIAT jumbo jet.

grosse ▶ gros.

grossesse /gʀosɛs/ *nf* pregnancy; **~ à risques** risk pregnancy; **robe de ~** maternity dress.
■ **~ nerveuse** phantom pregnancy GB, false pregnancy.

grosseur /gʀosœʀ/ *nf* **1** (volume) size; **de la ~ d'une orange** the size of an orange; **2** (épaisseur) thickness; **3** (bosse, kyste) lump.

grossier, -ière /gʀosje, ɛʀ/ *adj* **1** (impoli) [*personne, geste*] rude; [*langage*] bad; **2** (sans finesse) [*esprit, rire, traits*] coarse; [*formes*] crude; **3** (médiocre) [*copie, imitation*] crude; [*étoffe*] coarse; [*mobilier*] basic; **4** (rudimentaire) [*nettoyage*] cursory; [*ébauche, idée, estimation*] rough; [*travail*] crude; **5** (flagrant) [*ignorance*] crass; [*erreur*] glaring; [*procédé*] crude.

grossièrement /gʀosjɛʀmɑ̃/ *adv* **1** (de façon sommaire) roughly; **2** (sans soin particulier) crudely; **3** (avec impolitesse) rudely; **4** (lourdement) **se tromper ~** to be utterly mistaken.

grossièreté /gʀosjɛʀte/ *nf* **1** (inconvenance) rudeness; **ils sont d'une ~!** they're so rude!; **2** (mot grossier) rude word GB, dirty word; **dire des ~s** to use bad language GB, to talk dirty.

grossir /gʀosiʀ/ [3] I *vtr* **1** (agrandir) to enlarge [*image*]; **2** (faire augmenter) to increase [*effectifs*]; to boost [*nombre, profits*]; **~ les rangs** or **la foule** to swell the ranks; **3** (exagérer) to exaggerate [*incident*]; **4** (faire paraître plus gros) to make [sb] look fat [*personne*].
II *vi* **1** (prendre du poids) to put on weight; **~ de cinq kilos** to put on five kilos; **ça fait ~** it's fattening; **2** (devenir plus grand) GÉN to grow; [*fleuve*] to swell; **3** (s'intensifier) [*tempête*] to get worse; [*rumeur*] to grow.

grossissant, ~e /gʀosisɑ̃, ɑ̃t/ *adj* **1** [*verre*] magnifying; **2** [*flot*] swelling.

grossissement /gʀosismɑ̃/ *nm* **1** (fait de grossir) enlargement; **un ~ anormal du foie** an abnormally enlarged liver; **2** (exagération) exaggeration; **le ~ des faits par la presse** distortion of the facts in the press; **3** (en optique) magnification.

grossiste /gʀosist/ ▶ 374 *nmf* wholesaler.

grosso modo /gʀosomodo/ *adv* roughly; **~, je suis satisfaite** broadly speaking I am satisfied.

grotesque /gʀotɛsk/ I *adj* **1** (risible) [*personne, coiffure*] ridiculous; [*idée, histoire, remarque*] ridiculous, preposterous; **2** ART, LITTÉRAT grotesque.
II *nm* **1** (caractère risible) ridiculous aspect; **être d'un ~ absolu** [*histoire, situation*] to be utterly ridiculous; [*personne*] to be absolutely ludicrous; **2** ART, LITTÉRAT **le ~** the grotesque.

grotte /gʀot/ *nf* **1** GÉOG cave; **2** ARCHIT grotto.

grouillement /gʀujmɑ̃/ *nm* swarming ℂ.

grouiller /gʀuje/ [1] I *vi* [*vers, insectes*] to swarm about; [*gens*] to mill about; **~ de** to be swarming with; **~ d'asticots** to be crawling with maggots.
II **se grouiller** *vpr* to get a move on○.

groupage /gʀupaʒ/ *nm* (pour transporter) bulking; **envoi en ~** collective shipment.

groupe /gʀup/ *nm* **1** (ensemble de personnes) group (**de** of); **en ~** in a group; **par ~s de deux** in pairs, in twos; **former un ~ autour de qn** [*badauds*] to form a group around sb; **2** (ensemble d'objets) group; (plus petit) cluster (**de** of); **un ~ d'arbres** a cluster ou clump of trees; **3** FIN, IND, PRESSE group.
■ **~ d'autodéfense** vigilante group, vigilance committee; **~ de combat** combat unit; **~ électrogène** (electricity) generator; **~ de presse** newspaper group; **~ de pression** pressure group; **~ sanguin** blood group; **~ scolaire** school; **~ des Sept, G7** Group of Seven, G7 countries (*pl*); **~ de travail** working party.

groupement /gʀupmɑ̃/ *nm* **1** (association) association, group; **un ~ politique** a political grouping; **2** (classification) grouping (**de** of).

grouper /gʀupe/ [1] I *vtr* to put [sth] together [*factures, chèques*]; **~ ses achats** (dans un même magasin) to make all one's purchases in the same store; (à plusieurs acheteurs) to make a group purchase; **sauter en groupant les genoux** to jump with one's knees held against one's chest.
II **se grouper** *vpr* **1** (physiquement) [*personnes*] to gather (**autour de** around); **groupez-vous par classes** get into your class groups; **se ~ par trois** to form groups of three; **2** (s'organiser) to form a group (**autour de** around); **restez groupés** keep together; **ne restez pas groupés** scatter; **avancer groupés** to march in a group.

groupuscule /gʀupyskyl/ *nm* (very) small group.

gruau, *pl* **~x** /gʀyo/ *nm* **1** CULIN (bouillie) gruel; **2** (fleur de froment) fine wheat flour.

grue /gʀy/ *nf* **1** TECH crane; **2** ZOOL crane.
IDIOMES **faire le pied de ~**○ to hang around.

gruger○ /gʀyʒe/ [13] *vtr* to dupe; **se faire ~** to be duped.

grumeau, *pl* **~x** /gʀymo/ *nm* lump; **faire des ~x** [*sauce*] to go lumpy.

grumeleux, -euse /gʀymlø, øz/ *adj* [*sauce, pâte*] lumpy.

grutier, -ière /gʀytje, ɛʀ/ ▶ 374 *nm,f* crane operator.

Guadeloupe /gwadlup/ ▶ 305 , 509 *nprf* **la ~** Guadeloupe.

guadeloupéen, -éenne /gwadlupeɛ̃, ɛn/ *adj* Guadeloupian.

guatémaltèque /gwatemaltɛk/ ▶ 394 *adj* Guatemalan.

gué /ge/ *nm* ford; **passer un ruisseau à ~** to ford a stream.
IDIOMES **on ne change pas de chevaux au milieu du ~** PROV you can't swap horses in midstream.

guenille /gənij/ *nf* rag; **en ~s** in rags.

guenon /gənɔ̃/ *nf* female monkey.

guépard /gepaʀ/ *nm* cheetah.

guêpe /gɛp/ *nf* wasp.
IDIOMES **pas folle la ~**○! I'm/she's etc not just a pretty face○!

guêpier /gepje/ *nm* **1** (nid de guêpes) wasps' nest; **2** (situation difficile) tight corner; **dans quel ~ es-tu allé te fourrer**○? what kind of mess have you got GB ou gotten US yourself into?

guêpière /gepjɛʀ/ *nf* basque, bodyshaper with suspenders GB ou garters US.

guère /gɛʀ/ *adv* **1** (modifiant un adjectif) hardly; **les résultats n'étaient ~ meilleurs** the results were hardly any better; **les étudiants ne sont ~ préparés** the students aren't really prepared; **2** (modifiant un adverbe) **ça n'a ~ été mieux** it was hardly any better; **l'appareil ne coûte ~ plus de 500 francs** the appliance doesn't cost much more than 500 francs;

3 (avec un verbe) hardly; **il n'a ~ mangé** he hardly ate anything; **je n'ai ~ eu de mal à les convaincre** I didn't have much trouble convincing them; **il n'apprécie ~ ta décontraction** he doesn't much care for your casual attitude; **il n'avait ~ le choix** he didn't really have a choice, he had little choice; **ils ne se font ~ d'illusions sur leur avenir** they don't hold out much hope for their future; **il ne fait ~ de doute que** there is little doubt that.

guéridon /geʀidɔ̃/ *nm* pedestal table.

guérilla /geʀija/ *nf* (forme de combat) guerilla warfare.

guérillero /geʀijeʀo/ *nm* guerilla.

guérir /geʀiʀ/ [3] **I** *vtr* **1** MÉD to cure [*personne, maladie*]; to heal [*blessure*]; **cela soulage mais ne guérit pas** it brings relief but it isn't a cure; **2** FIG **~ qn de** to cure sb of.
II *vi* MÉD [*personne, animal*] to recover, to get well; [*blessure*] to heal; [*entorse, rhume*] to get better; **~ de qch** to recover from sth.
III se guérir *vpr* FIG **se ~ de** to overcome [*timidité*].

guérison /geʀizɔ̃/ *nf* (de malade, maladie) recovery; (de blessure) healing.

guérissable /geʀisabl/ *adj* [*malade, maladie*] curable.

guérisseur, -euse /geʀisœʀ, øz/ ▶ 374] *nm,f* healer.

guérite /geʀit/ *nf* (de sentinelle) sentry box; (de péage) booth.

guerre /gɛʀ/ *nf* (conflit) war; (technique) warfare; **entrer en ~** to go to war (**contre** against); **être en ~** to be at war (**avec** with); **faire la ~** to wage war (**à** against, on); **mon grand-père a fait la ~** my grandfather was ou fought in the war; **les pays en ~** the warring nations; **c'est la ~ ouverte** it's open warfare; **les candidats se livrent une ~ sans merci** it's out-and-out war between the candidates; **elle lui fait la ~** she's fighting a running battle with him; **les enfants jouent à la ~** the children are playing at GB ou playing soldiers; ▶ **grand**.
■ **~ chimique** (conflit) chemical war; (technique) chemical warfare; **~ éclair** blitzkrieg, lightning war; **~ d'Espagne** Spanish Civil War; **~ des étoiles** Star Wars; **~ froide** Cold War; **~ mondiale** world war; **Première/Deuxième** or **Seconde Guerre mondiale** World War I/II, First/Second World War; **~ des nerfs** war of nerves; **~ psychologique** psychological warfare; **~ de 14** 1914–18 war; **~ de Sécession** American Civil War; **~ de Troie** Trojan War; **~ d'usure** war of attrition.
IDIOMES **à la ~ comme à la ~** in time of hardship you have to make the best of things; **c'est de bonne ~** it's only fair, it's fair enough; **être sur le pied de ~** to be on a war footing; **de ~ lasse, elle renonça à le convaincre** realizing that she was fighting a losing battle, she gave up trying to convince him.

guerrier, -ière /geʀje, ɛʀ/ **I** *adj* [*peuple*] warlike; [*exploit*] war (*épith*).
II *nm,f* warrior.

guerroyer /geʀwaje/ [23] *vi* to wage war (**contre** against, on).

guet /gɛ/ *nm* **1** GÉN lookout; **faire le ~** to be on the lookout; **2** MIL watch.

guet-apens, *pl* **guets-apens** /gɛtapɑ̃/ *nm* LIT ambush; FIG trap; **tomber dans un ~** LIT to be caught in an ambush; FIG to fall into a trap.

guêtre /gɛtʀ/ *nf* (de laine) leggings (*pl*); (de cuir, tissu) gaiter.

guetter /gete/ [1] *vtr* **1** (surveiller) to watch [*proie, malfaiteur, réaction*]; to watch out for [*signe*]; to look out for [*facteur, ami*]; **je guettais le moindre bruit** I was alert for the slightest noise; **~ l'arrivée de l'ennemi** to lie in wait for the enemy; **2** (menacer) [*déclin, danger*] to threaten; **la folie le guette** he is on the brink of madness; **la fatigue guette les conducteurs** tiredness is a threat for drivers.

guetteur, -euse /gɛtœʀ, øz/ **I** *nm,f* lookout.
II *nm* HIST watchman.

gueule /gœl/ *nf* **1⁰** (visage) face; **casser la ~ à qn** to

beat sb up; **c'est bien fait pour leur ~** (it) serves them right; **il en fait une ~!** (mélancolique) he looks really down; (furieux) he looks absolutely livid!; **il a la ~ de l'emploi** he really looks the part; **2⁰** (bouche humaine) mouth; (ferme) **ta ~!** shut your face○ GB ou mouth○!; **être** or **avoir une grande ~** to be a bigmouth○; ▶ **fin¹**; **3⁰** (aspect) look; **le gâteau a une drôle de ~** the cake looks weird; **4** ZOOL (bouche d'animal) mouth; ▶ **loup**; **5** (de tunnel, four, canon) mouth.
■ **~ de bois** hangover.
IDIOMES **faire** or **tirer la ~○** to be sulking; **se bourrer** or **soûler la ~○** to get blind drunk.

gueule-de-loup, *pl* **gueules-de-loup** /gœldəlu/ *nf* snapdragon.

gueuler⁰ /gœle/ [1] **I** *vtr* (crier) to yell [*insultes*]; to bawl out [*réponse*]; (chanter) to bellow out.
II *vi* [*personne*] (crier) to yell, to bawl; (chanter) to bawl, to howl; (protester) to kick up a real fuss; **~ de douleur** to scream with pain; **après qn** to have a go at sb○; **~ contre qch** to moan about sth.
IDIOMES **~ comme un âne** or **putois** or **perdu** to scream blue GB ou bloody US murder○.

gueux†, gueuse /gø, gøz/ *nm,f* (pauvre) beggar; (personne vile) rogue.
IDIOMES **courir la gueuse○** to go looking for a bit of skirt○.

gui /gi/ *nm* **1** BOT mistletoe; **2** NAUT boom.

guichet /giʃɛ/ *nm* **1** (comptoir vitré) window; (comptoir ouvert) (de banque) counter; (de stade, musée, gare) ticket office; (de théâtre, cinéma) box office, ticket office; **la pièce se jouera à ~s fermés** the play is sold out; **2** (dans mur, porte) grille.
■ **~ automatique** automatic teller machine, ATM.

guichetier, -ière /giʃtje, ɛʀ/ ▶ 374] *nm,f* ticket clerk.

guidage /gidaʒ/ *nm* **1** AVIAT guidance; **2** TECH guide.

guide /gid/ *nm* **1** (accompagnateur) guide; **~ de haute montagne** mountain guide; **2** (ouvrage) guide; **~ pratique** practical guide.

guide-interprète, *pl* **guides-interprètes** /gidɛ̃tɛʀpʀɛt, gidzɛ̃tɛʀpʀɛt/ ▶ 374] *nmf* tour guide and interpreter.

guider /gide/ [1] **I** *vtr* **1** (montrer le chemin) to show [sb] the way (**vers** to); **~ jusque** to take [sb] to, to lead [sb] to; **~ à travers** to take [sb] around; **il m'a guidé dans les couloirs** he showed me the way through the corridors; **2** (orienter) [*étoile*] to guide; [*flair, trace*] to lead; [*panneau indicateur*] to guide, to direct; **le chien guide l'aveugle** the dog guides the blind man; **3** (diriger) to guide [*cheval, avion*]; **4** (conseiller) to guide.
II se guider *vpr* **se ~ sur qch** to set one's course by sth.

guidon /gidɔ̃/ *nm* (de bicyclette, moto) handlebars (*pl*).

guigne○ /giɲ/ *nf* bad luck; **avoir la ~** to be dogged by bad luck.
IDIOMES **se soucier** or **se moquer de qch/qn comme d'une ~** not to give a fig○ about sth/sb.

guignol /giɲɔl/ *nm* **1** (spectacle de marionnettes) puppet show, **~** Punch and Judy show; **c'est du ~** FIG it's farcical, it's a complete farce; **2** (personne peu sérieuse) PEJ clown, joker; **faire le ~** to clown around.

guilde /gild/ *nf* guild.

Guillaume /gijom/ *npr* **~ le Conquérant** William the Conqueror; **~ d'Orange** William of Orange; **~ Tell** William Tell.

guillemets /gijmɛ/ *nmpl* inverted commas GB, quotation marks; **entre ~** in inverted commas.

guilleret, -ette /gijʀɛ, ɛt/ *adj* [*personne, air*] perky, jaunty.

guillotine /gijɔtin/ *nf* guillotine.

guimauve /gimov/ *nf* BOT (marsh) mallow; CULIN marshmallow.

guimbarde /gɛ̃baʀd/ *nf* **1○** (vieille voiture) old banger GB ou crate○; **2** MUS Jew's harp.

guindé, -e /gɛ̃de/ *adj* formal.

guingois: de guingois /dəgɛ̃gwa/ *loc adv* **être de ~** [*meuble, maison*] to be lopsided; **aller de ~** to go askew.

guinguette /gɛ̃gɛt/ *nf*: *small restaurant with music and dancing.*

guirlande /giʀlɑ̃d/ *nf* (de fleurs) garland; (de Noël) tinsel; (de papier) paper chain; (en plein air) bunting ¢.
■ ~ **électrique** set ou string of fairy lights.

guise /giz/ *nf* **1** '**à votre ~**' 'just as you like ou please'; **n'en faire qu'à sa ~** to do exactly as one pleases ou likes; **2 en ~ de** by way of.

guitare /gitaʀ/ ▶ 392 *nf* guitar.

guitariste /gitaʀist/ ▶ 374 *nmf* guitarist.

gustatif, -ive /gystatif, iv/ *adj* [*organe*] taste.

guttural, ~e, *mpl* **-aux** /gytyʀal, o/ *adj* guttural.

Guyana /gɥijana/ ▶ 232 *nprf* Guyana; **République de ~** Republic of Guyana.

Guyane /gɥijan/ ▶ 509 *nprf* Guyana; **~ française** French Guyana; **~ hollandaise** HIST Dutch Guiana.

gym○ /ʒim/ ▶ 329 *nf* SCOL physical education, PE, phys ed○ US; SPORT gymnastics (+ *v sg*).

gymkhana /ʒimkana/ *nm* **1** (en voiture, à moto) rally; **2** (à pied) LIT obstacle race; FIG obstacle course.

gymnase /ʒimnɑz/ *nm* gymnasium.

gymnaste /ʒimnast/ *nmf* gymnast.

gymnastique /ʒimnastik/ ▶ 329 *nf* (discipline) gymnastics (+ *v sg*); (exercices) exercises (*pl*); **je fais 20 minutes de ~ tous les matins** I exercise for 20 minutes every morning; **~ de l'esprit** FIG mental exercise.
■ ~ **aquatique** aquagym; ~ **corrective** - physiotherapy exercises (*pl*); ~ **d'entretien** keep fit; ~ **rythmique et sportive** eurythmics (+ *v sg*); ~ **suédoise** callisthenics (+ *v sg*).

gymnique /ʒimnik/ *adj* [*exercice*] gymnastic.

gynécologie /ʒinekɔlɔʒi/ *nf* gynaecology.

gynécologue /ʒinekɔlɔg/ ▶ 374 *nmf* gynaecologist.

gyrophare /ʒiʀɔfaʀ/ *nm* flashing light, emergency rotating light.

gyroscope /ʒiʀɔskɔp/ *nm* gyroscope.

h, H /aʃ/ *nm inv* **1** (lettre) h, H; **h aspiré** aspirate, aspirated h; **h muet** mute h, silent h; **2** (*written abbr* = **heure**) 9 h 10 9.10.

ha /ˈa/ (*written abbr* = **hectare**) ha.

habile /abil/ *adj* **1** (adroit) [*bricoleur, policier, écrivain*] clever; [*avocat, diplomate*] skilful^{GB}; [*politicien*] smart; **~ à** good at; **être ~ de ses mains** or **doigts** to be clever with one's hands; **2** (fait avec adresse) clever.

habilement /abilmɑ̃/ *adv* (adroitement) skilfully^{GB}; **1** (intelligemment) cleverly.

habileté /abilte/ *nf* (de personne) skill; (de discours, manœuvre) skilfulness^{GB}.

habiliter /abilite/ [1] *vtr* to authorize (**à faire** to do).

habillé, ~e /abije/ *adj* [*robe*] smart; [*soirée*] formal.

habillement /abijmɑ̃/ *nm* **1** (activité) clothing; **2** (vêtements) clothing.

habiller /abije/ [1] **I** *vtr* **1** (mettre des vêtements à) to dress [*personne*] (**de** in); **2** (déguiser) to dress [sb] up (**en** as); **3** (fournir en vêtements) to clothe [*enfant*]; to provide [sb] with clothing [*acteur, personnel*]; **4** (faire des vêtements pour) to clothe [*enfant, famille*]; to dress [*acteur, personnel*]; **5** (convenir) [*vêtements*] to suit [*personne*]; **6** (revêtir) to cover [*mur, siège*] (**de** with); to encase [*appareil, tuyauterie*].

II s'habiller *vpr* **1** (mettre ses vêtements) to get dressed; **2** (choisir son style) to dress; **s'~ long/court** to wear long/short clothes; **3** (se vêtir élégamment) to dress up; **4** (se fournir en vêtements) to get one's clothes; **s'~ sur mesure** to have one's clothes made to measure; **5** (se travestir) to dress up (**en** as).

habilleur, -euse /abijœr, øz/ ▶ 374 *nm,f* dresser.

habit /abi/ **I** *nm* **1** (de marié) (queue-de-pie) tails (*pl*), morning coat; (tenue) morning dress; **2** (déguisement) (de professionnel) outfit; (de personnage) costume; **3** RELIG (de moine, nonne) habit; **prendre l'~** to take the cloth; **quitter l'~** to leave the priesthood.

II habits *nmpl* clothes.

■ **~ ecclésiastique** RELIG clerical dress; **~s du dimanche** Sunday best.

habitable /abitabl/ *adj* **1** (pouvant être habité) habitable; **logement ~ immédiatement** accommodation ready to move into; **2** (servant à l'habitation) **surface** or **espace ~** living space.

habitacle /abitakl/ *nm* **1** AVIAT cockpit; ASTRONAUT cabin; **2** AUT interior; **3** NAUT binnacle.

habitant, ~e /abitɑ̃, ɑ̃t/ *nm,f* **1** (personne) (de ville, pays, région) inhabitant; (de quartier, d'immeuble) resident; **loger chez l'~** TOURISME to stay as a paying guest; **2** LITER (personne) dweller; (animal) beast.

habitat /abita/ *nm* **1** (milieu) habitat; **2** (mode de peuplement) settlement; **3** (mode de logement) housing.

habitation /abitasjɔ̃/ *nf* **1** (construction) house, dwelling; **2** (résidence) home; **3** (fait d'habiter) living; **immeuble d'~** block of flats GB, apartment building US.

■ **~ à loyer modéré, HLM** (appartement) ≈ council flat GB, low-rent apartment US; (immeuble) ≈ block of council flats GB, low-rent apartment building US; (maison) ≈ council house GB, low rent house US.

habité, ~e /abite/ *adj* **1** [*territoire*] inhabited; **2** ASTRONAUT manned.

habiter /abite/ [1] **I** *vtr* **1** (résider à) to live in; **il habite une maison/Paris/la campagne** he lives in a house/in Paris/in the country; **2** FML [*sentiment*] to dwell in [*personne, cœur*].

II *vi* **1** (résider) **~ à** or **en** to live in; **~ à l'étranger** to live abroad; **~ au 6 rue de la Paix** to live at 6 rue de la Paix; **~ chez ses parents** to live with one's parents; **2** FIG **être habité par** to be filled with.

habitude /abityd/ **I** *nf* **1** (manière d'agir) habit; **faire qch par ~** to do sth out of habit; **ce n'est pas dans mes ~s d'être en retard** it's not like me to be late; **avoir ses (petites) ~s** (routine) to have got GB ou gotten US into a routine; (manière de faire) to have one's own way of doing things; **ne perdons pas les bonnes ~s** let's stick to what we usually do; **comme à leur ~, suivant leur ~** as they usually do; **2** (fait d'être accoutumé) habit; **avoir l'~ de** to be used to; **3** (coutume) (de pays, région) custom; (de personnes) habit.

II d'habitude *loc adv* usually.

habitué, ~e /abitye/ *nm,f* (de café) regular (customer); (de stade, musée) regular; (ami) regular (visitor).

habituel, -elle /abityɛl/ *adj* usual.

habituellement /abityɛlmɑ̃/ *adv* usually, generally.

habituer /abitye/ [1] **I** *vtr* **1** (accoutumer) to get [sb/sth] used (**à** to; **à faire** to doing); **2** (former) to teach (**à faire** to do).

II s'habituer *vpr* to get used ou accustomed (**à** to).

hâbleur, -euse /ˈɑblœr, øz/ **I** *adj* boastful.

II *nm,f* boaster; **c'est un ~** he's always boasting.

hache /ˈaʃ/ *nf* axe GB, ax US; **visage taillé à la ~** angular face.

■ **~ d'abordage** poleaxe; **~ de guerre** GÉN battle-axe GB ou ax US; (d'indien) tomahawk.

IDIOMES **enterrer la ~ de guerre** to bury the hatchet; **déterrer la ~ de guerre** to go on the warpath.

haché, ~e /ˈaʃe/ *adj* **1** CULIN **bifteck ~** hamburger; **viande ~e** mince; **2** (saccadé) [*style, phrase, discours*] disjointed.

hacher /ˈaʃe/ [1] *vtr* **1** (couper) to mince [*viande*]; to chop [*oignon, persil*]; **~ au couteau** to chop [sth] up with a knife; **2** (broyer) to crush [*récolte, feuille*]; **~ [sb/sth] en morceaux** to cut [sb/sth] to pieces [*personne, chair*].

hachette /ˈaʃɛt/ *nf* hatchet.

hachis /ˈaʃi/ *nm inv* CULIN **~ de viande** minced meat; **~ d'échalotes** chopped shallots.

■ **~ Parmentier** ≈ shepherd's pie.

hachisch /ˈaʃiʃ/ *nm* hashish.

hachoir /ˈaʃwar/ *nm* **1** (appareil) mincer; **~ électrique** electric mincer; **2** (couteau) (food) chopper, mincing knife; **3** (planche) chopping board.

hachurer /ˈaʃyre/ [1] *vtr* ART to hatch.

haddock /ˈadɔk/ *nm* smoked haddock.

hagard, ~e /ˈagar, ard/ *adj* [*air, personne*] dazed; [*yeux*] wild.

haie /ˈɛ/ *nf* **1** BOT hedge; **une ~ de cyprès** a cypress hedge; **2** SPORT (en athlétisme) hurdle; (en hippisme) fence; **course de ~s** (en athlétisme) hurdle race, hurdles; (en hippisme) steeple chase; **3** (rangée) (de personnes) line; (d'objets) row.

IDIOMES **former** or **faire une ~ d'honneur** to form a guard of honour^{GB}.

haillon /ˈajɔ̃/ *nm* rag; **vêtu de ~s** dressed in rags.

haine /ˈɛn/ *nf* hatred; **s'attirer la ~ de qn** to earn oneself sb's hatred.

haineux, -euse /ˈɛnø, øz/ *adj* full of hatred (*après n*).

haïr /ˈair/ [25] **I** *vtr* to hate [*personne, chose*] (**de faire** for doing); **~ que** to hate it when.

II se haïr *vpr* **1** [*ennemis*] to hate each other; **2** [*soi-même*] to hate oneself.

haïssable /'aisabl/ *adj* detestable, hateful.

haïtien, -ienne /aisjɛ̃, ɛn/ ▶ **394**], **338**] **I** *adj* Haitian.
II *nm* LING Haitian.

halage /'alaʒ/ *nm* towing; **chemin de ~** towpath.

hâle /'ɑl/ *nm* (sun)tan.

hâlé, ~e /'ɑle/ *adj* (par le soleil) suntanned; (par l'air, une lampe) tanned.

haleine /alɛn/ *nf* **1** (air expiré) breath; **2** (respiration) breathing; **être hors d'~** to be out of breath; **à perdre ~** until one is out of breath; **reprendre ~** LIT to get one's breath back; FIG to have a rest; **tenir qn en ~** (fasciné) to hold sb spellbound; (dans l'incertitude) to keep sb in suspense; **un travail de longue ~** a long-drawn-out job.

haler /'ale/ [1] *vtr* to tow [*bateau*]; to haul in [*chaîne*].

haletant, ~e /'altɑ̃, ɑ̃t/ *adj* [*personne*] panting, breathless; [*animal*] panting; [*voix*] breathless.

haleter /'alte/ [18] *vi* **1** to pant (**de** with); **2** [*machine*] to puff; [*poitrine*] to heave.

hall /'ol/ *nm* entrance hall GB, lobby US; **~ (de gare)** LIT concourse; **on dirait un ~ de gare** PEJ it looks like the inside of a railway station.
■ **~ d'accueil** reception; **~ d'exposition** exhibition hall.

hallali /'alali/ *nm* (en chasse à courre) mort.

halle /'al/ **I** *nf* market hall.
II halles *nfpl* covered market.
■ **~ aux grains** corn exchange; **~ à marchandises** goods depot.

hallebarde /'albard/ *nf* halberd.
IDIOMES **il pleut des ~s** it's raining cats and dogs.

hallucinant°, ~e /alysinɑ̃, ɑ̃t/ *adj* astounding.

hallucination /alysinasjɔ̃/ *nf* hallucination; **avoir des ~s** LIT to hallucinate; FIG to be seeing things.

halluciné, ~e /alysine/ **I** *adj* **1** (hagard) [*regard*] wild; **2** [*malade*] suffering from hallucinations (*après n*).
II *nm,f* **1°** (illuminé) crank; **2** person suffering from hallucinations.

hallucinogène /alysinɔʒɛn/ *adj* hallucinogenic.

halo /'alo/ *nm* **1** (de phares, lampe) **~ (de lumière)** circle of light; **entouré d'un ~ de mystère** shrouded in mystery; **2** (d'astre) halo.

halogène /alɔʒɛn/ *nm* **1** CHIMIE halogenous; **2** [*lampe, éclairage*] halogen (*épith*).

halte /'alt/ **I** *nf* **1** (temps d'arrêt) stop; **faire une ~** to stop somewhere; **2** (lieu d'arrêt) stop.
II *excl* GÉN stop!; MIL halt!; **~ à la vivisection!** stop vivisection!

halte-garderie, *pl* **haltes-garderies** /'altəɡardəri/ *nf* ≈ playgroup.

haltère /'altɛr/ *nm* (pour une main) dumbbell; (à deux mains) barbell; **faire des ~s** to do weightlifting.

haltérophilie /'alterɔfili/ ▶ **329**] *nf* weightlifting.

hamac /'amak/ *nm* hammock.

hameau, *pl* **~x** /'amo/ *nm* hamlet.

hameçon /'amsɔ̃/ *nm* hook.
IDIOMES **mordre à l'~** to take the bait.

hampe /'ɑ̃p/ *nf* **1** (de drapeau, parasol) pole; (d'arme) shaft; **2** BOT scape; **3** (de lettre) vertical stroke; **4** (de bœuf) flank.

hanche /'ɑ̃ʃ/ ▶ **137**], **581**] *nf* **1** ANAT hip; **prothèse de la ~** hip replacement; **2** (de cheval) haunch.

handball /'ɑdbal, 'ɑdbol/ ▶ **329**] *nm* handball.

handicap /'ɑdikap/ *nm* LIT, FIG handicap; (course) handicap (race).

handicapant, ~e /'ɑdikapɑ̃, ɑ̃t/ *adj* disabling.

handicapé, ~e /'ɑdikape/ **I** *adj* **1** (infirme) disabled, handicapped; **~ à vie** permanently disabled; **2** (désavantagé) **être ~** to be at a disadvantage.
II *nm,f* disabled person; **~ moteur** person with motor disability.

handicaper /'ɑdikape/ [1] *vtr* to handicap.

handisport /ɑdispɔr/ *adj* wheelchair (*épith*).

hangar /'ɑɡar/ *nm* GÉN (large) shed; (entrepôt) warehouse.
■ **~ d'aviation** hangar; **~ à bateaux** boathouse.

hanneton /'antɔ̃/ *nm* cockchafer GB, June bug US; ▶ **piquer**.

hanter /'ɑte/ [1] *vtr* (tous contextes) to haunt; **lieu hanté** haunted place.

hantise /'ɑtiz/ *nf* dread; **avoir la ~ de qch** to dread sth.

happer /'ape/ [1] *vtr* to catch [*nourriture, insecte*]; to seize [*animal, bras*]; **être happé par** (pris) to be caught up in [*machine*]; (fauché) to be hit by [*voiture, train*]; FIG to be swallowed up by [*bouche de métro, foule*].

haranguer /'arɑ̃ɡe/ [1] *vtr* to harangue.

haras /'ara/ *nm inv* stud farm.

harassement /'arasmɑ̃/ *nm* FML exhaustion.

harasser /'arase/ [1] *vtr* to exhaust.

harcèlement /'arsɛlmɑ̃/ *nm* harassment.
■ **~ sexuel** sexual harassment.

harceler /'arsəle/ [17] *vtr* **1** (importuner) [*démarcheur, mendiant, journaliste*] to pester [*personne*] (**de** with; **pour faire** to do); **les remords le harcèlent** he's plagued by remorse; **2** (poursuivre) to harass [*ennemi*].

harde /'ard/ **I** *nf* **1** (d'animaux sauvages) herd; **2** (de chiens) pack.
II hardes *nfpl* LITER rags.

hardi, ~e /'ardi/ *adj* **1** (intrépide, osé) bold; **2** [*plaisanterie*] risqué.

hardiesse /'ardjɛs/ *nf* **1** (intrépidité, originalité) boldness; **2** LITER (impudence) brazenness.

hareng /'arɑ̃/ *nm* herring.
■ **~ saur** smoked herring.
IDIOMES **sec comme un ~ saur** as thin as a rake.

hargne /'arɲ/ *nf* aggression; **avec ~** aggressively.

hargneux, -euse /'arɲø, øz/ *adj* aggressive.

haricot /'ariko/ *nm* (plante, graine) bean.
■ **~ beurre** wax bean; **~ blanc** haricot bean; **~ à écosser** bean for shelling; **~ rouge** red kidney bean; **~ vert** French bean.
IDIOMES **c'est la fin des ~s°** we've had it°.

harki /'arki/ *nm*: Algerian soldier who fought on the French side in the war of independence.

harmonica /armɔnika/ ▶ **392**] *nm* mouth organ.

harmonie /armɔni/ *nf* **1** (entente) harmony; **en ~ avec** GÉN in harmony with; **2** MUS (connaissance des accords) harmony; (fanfare) brass band.
■ **~ imitative** LITTÉRAT onomatopoeia; **~ vocalique** LING vowel harmony.

harmonieux, -ieuse /armɔnjø, øz/ *adj* **1** (agréable) harmonious; **2** (en accord) [*couleurs, courbes*] harmonious; [*gestes*] graceful; [*vie, mélange*] harmonious; **ils forment un couple ~** they are very well suited.

harmonique /armɔnik/ *adj, nm* harmonic.

harmonisation /armɔnizasjɔ̃/ *nf* GÉN harmonization; LING vowel harmony.

harmoniser /armɔnize/ [1] **I** *vtr* **1** (rendre harmonieux) to coordinate [*couleurs*]; **2** (rendre cohérents) to make [sth] consistent [*règles*]; **3** MUS to harmonize.
II s'harmoniser *vpr* **bien s'~** to go together well.

harnachement /'arnaʃmɑ̃/ *nm* **1** (de cheval) (pièces) harness; (action) harnessing; **2°** (de personne) get-up°.

harnacher /'arnaʃe/ [1] *vtr* **1** to harness [*cheval*]; **2°** (équiper) to rig out° [*personne*].

harnais /'arnɛ/ *nm inv* harness.

harpagon /arpagɔ̃/ *nm* LITER miser, Scrooge.

harpe /'arp/ ▶ **392**] *nf* harp.

harpie /'arpi/ *nf* **1** MYTHOL harpy; **les Harpies** the Harpies; **2** (femme acariâtre) harpy; **3** (aigle) harpy eagle.

harpon /'arpɔ̃/ *nm* harpoon.

harponner /'arpɔne/ [1] *vtr* **1** to harpoon [*baleine*]; **2** (arrêter)° to waylay [*badaud*]; to nab° [*malfaiteur*].

hasard /'azar/ *nm* (cause imprévisible) chance; **le ~ nous a fait découvrir que…** we discovered by chance that…; **ce n'est pas un ~ si…** it's no accident that…; **s'en remettre au ~, compter sur le ~** to

trust to luck (**pour** as regards; **pour faire** to do); **au ~** [*choisir, tirer*] at random; [*marcher*] aimlessly; **répondre au ~** to answer off the top of one's head; **au ~ de mes promenades** on my walks; **par ~** by chance; **par un curieux ~** by a curious coincidence; **par un heureux ~** by a stroke of luck; **comme par ~, il a oublié son argent** IRON surprise, surprise, he's forgotten his money; **à tout ~** (par précaution) just in case; (pour une tentative) on the off chance; **les ~s de la vie** the fortunes of life.
IDIOMES **le ~ fait bien les choses** fate is a great provider.

hasarder /'azaʀde/ [1] **I** *vtr* **1** (avancer) to venture [*conseil, explication*]; **2** LITER (risquer) to risk [*vie*].
II se hasarder *vpr* to venture (**à faire** to do).

hasardeux, -euse /'azaʀdø, øz/ *adj* (peu sûr) risky; (dangereux) hazardous.

hase /'az/ *nf* doe-hare.

hâte /'at/ *nf* **1** (précipitation) haste; **en toute ~** in great haste; **à la ~** hastily; **2** (impatience) **j'ai ~ de partir/qu'elle vienne** I can't wait to leave/for her to come.

hâter /'ate/ [1] **I** *vtr* to hasten; **~ le pas** to quicken one's step.
II se hâter *vpr* to hurry, to rush.

hâtif, -ive /'atif, iv/ *adj* **1** (rapide) [*jugement, recrutement*] hasty, hurried; **2** [*variété, plante*] early.

hâtivement /'ativmɑ̃/ *adv* hurriedly, hastily.

hauban /'obɑ̃/ *nm* **1** NAUT shroud; **2** TECH (souple) stay; (rigide) brace.

hausse /'os/ *nf* **1** (augmentation) (de prix, salaires) increase (**de** in); (de dépenses, chômage, température) rise (**de** in); **être en ~** [*prix, température*] to be rising; [*marchandise*] to be going up in price; **subir une forte ~** to rocket; **en ~ de 10%** up 10%; **réviser à la ~** to revise upward(s); **2** (en Bourse) rise (**de** in); **être à la ~** [*devise*] to be rising; [*tendance*] to be upward(s); [*marché*] to be on the uptrend.

haussement /'osmɑ̃/ *nm* (d'épaules) shrug; **il marqua son intérêt par un ~ de sourcils** he raised his eyebrows in an interested way.

hausser /'ose/ [1] **I** *vtr* **1** (élever) to shrug [*épaules*]; to raise [*sourcils*]; **~ le ton** or **la voix** LIT to raise one's voice; FIG to adopt an aggressive tone; **2** (augmenter) to raise [*prix*]; to increase [*exigences, prétentions*]; **3** (surélever) to raise [*mur, maison*].
II se hausser *vpr* **se ~ au niveau de** to rise up to the level of; **se ~ sur la pointe des pieds** to stand on tiptoe.

haut, ~e[1] /'o, 'ot/ **I** *adj* **1** ▶348 [*montagne, mur, talon*] high; [*arbre, monument*] tall; [*herbe*] long, tall; **attention, la première marche est ~e** be careful, the first step is steep; **2** (situé en altitude) high; **la partie ~e d'un mur** the top part of a wall; **l'étagère la plus ~e** the top shelf; **une robe à taille ~e** a high-waisted dress; **3** (dans une échelle de valeurs) [*température, salaires, précision*] high; [*note, ton*] high, high-pitched; **parler à ~e voix** to speak loudly; **lire à ~e voix** to read out loud; **au plus ~ point** immensely; **4** (dans une hiérarchie) (*before n*) [*personnage, poste*] high-ranking; [*clergé, magistrat*] senior; [*société*] high; [*responsabilités*] big; [*dirigeant, responsable*] senior, high-ranking; **~ Comité/Conseil** National Committee/Council; **~e surveillance** close supervision; **5** GÉOG upper; **la ~e Égypte** Upper Egypt; **6** HIST **de la plus ~e antiquité** from earliest antiquity; **le ~ Moyen Âge** the early Middle Ages.
II *adv* **1** (à un niveau élevé) [*monter, voler*] high; **un personnage ~ placé** a person in a high position; **de ~** from above; **2** (dans le temps) far back; **3** (dans un texte) **plus ~** above; **colle-le plus ~ sur la page** stick it higher up on the page; **4** (fort) loudly; **dire qch bien ~** to say sth loud(ly); **mettre la radio plus ~** to turn the radio up; **tout ~** out loud; **parler ~ et clair** FIG to speak unambiguously; **n'avoir jamais un mot plus ~ que l'autre** never to raise one's voice.
III *nm* **1** (partie élevée) top; **le ~ du visage** the top part of the face; **le ~ du corps** the top half of the

body; **l'étagère du ~** the top shelf; **les pièces du ~** the upstairs rooms; **prendre qch par le ~** to get hold of the top of sth; **parler du ~ d'un balcon** to speak from a balcony; **2** (hauteur) **faire 50 mètres de ~** to be 50 metres[GB] high.
IV en haut *loc* (à l'étage supérieur) upstairs; (à un étage supérieur) on an upper floor; (de rideau, mur, page) at the top; (le ciel, le paradis) above; **passer par en ~** (par la route) to take the top road; **les voleurs sont entrés par en ~** (par l'étage) the thieves got in upstairs.
V hauts *nmpl* GÉOG heights.
■ **~ en couleur** [*personnage, tableau, texte*] colourful[GB]; **~ fait** heroic deed; **~ fonctionnaire** senior civil servant; **~ lieu de** centre[GB] of ou for; **en ~ lieu** in high places; **une décision prise en ~ lieu** a decision taken at a high level; **~e mer** NAUT open sea; **~es eaux** high water (*sg*); **~es sphères** high social circles; **~es terres** GÉOG highlands.
IDIOMES **marcher la tête ~e** to walk with one's head held high; **voir les choses de ~** (avec sérénité) to have a detached view of things; **tomber de ~** to be dumbfounded; **regarder qn de ~ en bas** to look sb up and down; **avoir** ou **connaître des ~s et des bas** to have one's ups and downs; **~ les mains!** hands up!; **l'emporter** ou **gagner** ou **vaincre ~ la main** to win hands down; **prendre qn de ~** to look down one's nose at sb; **▶ cri, pavé**.

hautain, ~e /'otɛ̃, ɛn/ *adj* haughty.

hautbois /'obwa/ ▶392 *nm inv* **1** (instrument) oboe; **2** (instrumentiste) oboist.

hautboïste /'oboist/ ▶392, 374 *nmf* oboist.

haut-de-chausse(s), *pl* **hauts-de-chausses** /'odʃos/ *nm* (knee) breeches.

haut-de-forme, *pl* **hauts-de-formes** /'odfɔʀm/ *nm* top hat.

haute[2] /'ot/ **I** *adj f* ▶ **haut I**.
II○ *nf* (**les gens de**) **la ~** the upper crust.

haute-contre, *pl* **hautes-contre** /'otkɔ̃tʀ/ ▶98 *nf* MUS counter tenor.

haute(-)fidélité /'otfidelite/ *nf* ÉLECTROTECH **1** (qualité) **chaîne ~** hi-fi system; **2** (technique) ₵ **la ~** hi-fi, high fidelity.

hautement /'otmɑ̃/ *adv* (à un haut degré) highly.

hauteur /'otœʀ/ **I** *nf* **1** ▶348 (dimension verticale) height; **prendre de la ~** LIT [*avion, oiseau*] to climb; **dans le sens de la ~** upright; **à ~ d'homme** at about the height of a person; **à ~ des yeux** at eye level; **2** (profondeur) depth; **~ d'eau** NAUT depth of water; **3** SPORT **le saut en ~** high jump; **4** (de robe, jupe) length; **5** (éminence) hill; **gagner les ~s** to reach high ground; **il y a encore de la neige sur les ~s** there is still some snow on the upper slopes; **les ~s de la ville** the upper part of the town; **6** MATH height; **7** (qualité morale) nobility; **8** PÉJ (arrogance) haughtiness; **9** (en acoustique) pitch; **10** (d'astre) altitude.
II à la hauteur de *loc* **1** (au niveau) **arriver à la ~ de** to come up to; **raccourcir une jupe à la ~ des genoux** to shorten a dress to knee-level; **2** (à côté) **arriver à la ~ de** to draw level with; **un déraillement s'est produit à la ~ de Rouen** there was a derailment near Rouen; **3** FIG **être à la ~** to measure up; **être à la ~ de qn** to match up to sb; **être à la ~ de sa tâche** to be equal to one's job; **être à la ~ des espérances de qn** to live up to sb's hopes; **être à la ~ du talent de qn** [*scénario*] to do justice to sb's talent; **4** (en valeur, quantité) **à (la) ~ de 10%** up to 10%.
IDIOMES **tomber de toute sa ~** to fall headlong; **se dresser de toute sa ~** [*personne*] to draw oneself up to one's full height; [*animal*] to stand on its hind legs.

Haute-Volta /'otvɔlta/ *nprf* HIST Upper Volta.

haut-fond, *pl* **hauts-fonds** /'ofɔ̃/ *nm* NAUT shallows (*pl*).

haut(-)fourneau, *pl* **hauts(-)fourneaux** /'ofuʀno/ *nm* IND blast furnace.

haut-le-cœur /'olkœʀ/ *nm inv* retching ₵, heaving ₵; **en voyant les images nous avons eu un ~** FIG the pictures turned our stomachs.

haut-le-corps /'olkɔʀ/ *nm inv* start, jump.

haut-parleur, *pl* **~s** /'opaʀlœʀ/ *nm* loudspeaker. ■ **~ d'aigus** tweeter; **~ de graves** boomer.

haut-relief, *pl* **hauts-reliefs** /'oʀəljɛf/ *nm* ARCHIT, ART high relief.

hauturier, -ière /'otyʀje, ɛʀ/ *adj* [*pêche*] deep-sea; [*navire*] ocean-going.

havane /'avan/ **I** ▶ 141 *adj inv* tobacco-brown. **II** *nm* **1** (tabac) Havana tobacco; **2** (cigare) Havana cigar.

hâve /'av/ *adj* FML [*visage*] haggard, gaunt.

havre /'avʀ/ *nm* LITER, FIG haven.

Haye /'ɛ/ ▶ 628 *npr* **la ~** the Hague.

heaume /'om/ *nm* helmet.

hebdomadaire /ɛbdomadɛʀ/ **I** *adj* [*départ*] weekly. **II** *nm* weekly (magazine).

hébergement /ebɛʀʒəmɑ̃/ *nm* **1** (commercial) accommodation; **2** (social) housing.

héberger /ebɛʀʒe/ [13] *vtr* **1** (loger) [*personne*] to put [sb] up [*amis*]; to accommodate [*touristes*]; **2** (donner asile) [*pays*] to take [sb] in [*réfugiés*]; **3** (abriter) [*bâtiment*] to accommodate [*touristes*]; [*refuge*] to provide shelter for [*montagnards, sans-abri*].

hébété, ~e /ebete/ *adj* [*regard*] stupid; **d'un air ~** stupidly; **~ par** stupefied by [*alcool, travail*]; **~ de douleur** numb with grief.

hébraïque /ebʀaik/ *adj* [*études*] Hebrew.

hébreu, *pl* **~x** /ebʀø/ ▶ 338 **I** *adj m* Hebrew; **l'État ~** the State of Israel. **II** *nm* LING Hebrew. IDIOMES **pour moi, c'est de l'~** it's all Greek to me.

Hébreu, *pl* **~x** /ebʀø/ *nm* Hebrew.

HEC /aʃəse/ *nf* (*abbr* = **Hautes études commerciales**) *major business school.*

hécatombe /ekatɔ̃b/ *nf* **1** (massacre) massacre, slaughter; **l'examen a été une ~** FIG lots of people failed the exam; **2** (dans l'antiquité) hecatomb.

hectare /ɛktaʀ/ ▶ 575 *nm* hectare.

hecto /ɛkto/ **I** *nm* (*abbr* = **hectogramme**) hectogram. **II hecto(-)** (*in compounds*) hecto.

hectolitre /ɛktolitʀ/ ▶ 86 *nm* hectolitre[GB].

hectopascal /ɛktopaskal/ *nm* milibar.

hégémonie /eʒemoni/ *nf* hegemony.

hein◦ /'ɛ̃/ *excl* (pour faire répéter) what◦?, sorry?; **ça t'étonne, ~?** that's surprised you, hasn't it?

hélas /'elas/ *excl* alas; **~ non!** unfortunately not!

héler /'ele/ [14] *vtr* to hail [*taxi*]; to call [*personne*].

hélice /elis/ *nf* **1** NAUT, AVIAT (screw) propeller; **2** ARCHIT, BIOL, MATH helix; **3** TECH (de ventilateur) blades (*pl*).

hélicoïdal, ~e, *mpl* **-aux** /elikɔidal, o/ *adj* **1** MATH, TECH [*mouvement, axe*] helical; [*escalier*] spiral; **2** BOT helicoid.

hélicoptère /elikɔptɛʀ/ *nm* helicopter.

héliogravure /eljɔɡʀavyʀ/ *nf* **1** (procédé) gravure printing; **2** (image) gravure.

héliport /elipɔʀ/ *nm* heliport.

héliporté, ~e /elipɔʀte/ *adj* helicopter-borne.

hélitreuiller /elitʀœje/ [1] *vtr* to winch [sb] to safety (*by helicopter*).

hellène /ellɛn/ *adj* [*peuple, voilier*] Hellenic.

helvète /ɛlvɛt/ *adj* Helvetian.

helvétique /ɛlvetik/ *adj* Helvetic, Swiss; **la Confédération ~** Switzerland.

helvétisme /ɛlvetism/ *nm* Swiss French expression.

hématie /emati, emasi/ *nf* red blood cell.

hématome /ematom/ *nm* **1** bruise; **2** haematoma.

hémicycle /emisikl/ *nm* (de théâtre) semicircular auditorium; (salle quelconque) semicircular room.

hémiplégie /emipleʒi/ *nf* paralysis of one side of the body, hemiplegia SPÉC.

hémisphère /emisfɛʀ/ *nm* ANAT, GÉOG hemisphere; **l'~ Nord** GÉOG the northern hemisphere.

hémisphérique /emisfeʀik/ *adj* hemispherical.

hémistiche /emistiʃ/ *nm* (moitié de vers) hemistich; **coupe à l'~** caesura.

hémoglobine /emoɡlɔbin/ *nf* **1** (pigment des globules rouges) haemoglobin; **2**◦ (sang) blood.

hémophile /emofil/ **I** *adj* haemophilic. **II** *nmf* haemophiliac.

hémorragie /emoʀaʒi/ *nf* **1** MÉD bleeding ¢; **2** (fuite) (de capitaux) massive outflow; (de populations, clients) exodus; **3** (pertes humaines) massive loss of (human) life.

hémorroïdes /emoʀɔid/ ▶ 196 *nfpl* piles, haemorrhoids.

henné /'ene/ *nm* henna.

hennir /'eniʀ/ [3] *vi* [*cheval*] to neigh, to whinny.

hennissement /'enismɑ̃/ *nm* neigh, whinnying ¢.

hépatique /epatik/ **I** *adj* hepatic. **II** *nmf* person with a liver complaint.

hépatite /epatit/ ▶ 196 *nf* hepatitis.

héraldique /eʀaldik/ **I** *adj* heraldic. **II** *nf* heraldry.

héraut /'eʀo/ *nm* **1** (annonciateur) LITER harbinger; **2** HIST (officier) **~ d'armes** herald.

herbage /ɛʀbaʒ/ *nm* pasture.

herbe /ɛʀb/ **I** *nf* **1** (revêtement végétal) grass; **2** BOT (plante) **C hautes ~s** tall grass ¢; **mauvaise ~** weed; **3** BOT, CULIN aromatic herb. **II en herbe** *loc adj* **1** (encore vert) [*blé, avoine*] in the blade (*après n*); **2** (jeune) [*musicien*] budding. ■ **~s folles** wild grass. IDIOMES **couper l'~ sous le pied de qn** to pull the rug from under sb's feet.

herbeux, -euse /ɛʀbø, øz/ *adj* grassy.

herbicide /ɛʀbisid/ **I** *adj* [*produit*] herbicidal. **II** *nm* weed killer, herbicide.

herbier /ɛʀbje/ *nm* (de plantes séchées) herbarium.

herbivore /ɛʀbivɔʀ/ **I** *adj* herbivorous. **II** *nm* herbivore.

herboriste /ɛʀbɔʀist/ ▶ 374 *nmf* herbalist.

herboristerie /ɛʀbɔʀistəʀi/ ▶ 374 *nf* **1** (vente) herb trade; **2** (boutique) herbalist's shop GB ou store US.

Hercule /ɛʀkyl/ *npr* Hercules; **les travaux d'~** MYTHOL the Labours of Hercules; **c'est un travail d'~** FIG it's a Herculean task.

hère /'ɛʀ/ *nm* LITER **un pauvre ~** a poor wretch.

héréditaire /eʀeditɛʀ/ *adj* BIOL, JUR, MÉD hereditary; **l'ennemi ~** FIG the traditional enemy.

hérédité /eʀedite/ *nf* **1** BIOL heredity; **2** (origines) background; **3** JUR (de possession) hereditary nature.

hérésie /eʀezi/ *nf* **1** RELIG heresy; **tomber en ~** to become a heretic; **2** (opinion, théorie) heresy; HUM (action) sacrilege.

hérétique /eʀetik/ **I** *adj* heretical. **II** *nmf* heretic.

hérissé, ~e /'eʀise/ *adj* **il a les cheveux ~s** (volontairement) he's got spiky hair; (involontairement) his hair sticks up.

hérisser /'eʀise/ [1] **I** *vtr* **1** (dresser) [*oiseau*] to ruffle (up) [*plumes*]; [*hérisson*] to raise [*piquants*]; **2** (garnir) **~ qch de** to spike sth with; **question hérissée de difficultés** FIG question fraught with difficulties; **3**◦ (irriter) **~ qn** to make sb's hackles rise. **II se hérisser** *vpr* **1** (se dresser) [*poils, cheveux*] to stand on end; [*animal*] to bristle; **2**◦ (s'irriter) to bristle.

hérisson /'eʀisɔ̃/ *nm* **1** ZOOL hedgehog; **2** (de ramoneur) (chimney sweep's) brush; **3** (égouttoir à bouteilles) bottle-drainer; **4** MIL hedgehog.

héritage /eʀitaʒ/ *nm* **1** (biens légués) inheritance; **faire un ~** to come into an inheritance; **une tante à ~** a wealthy aunt; **recevoir qch en ~** to inherit sth; **2** (survivance du passé) (concret) inheritance; (abstrait) heritage, legacy.

hériter /eʀite/ [1] **I** *vtr* to inherit. **II hériter de** *vtr ind* **1** JUR to inherit [*argent, bien*]; **la maison dont il a hérité** the house he inherited; **2**◦ (se retrouver encombré de) to be landed with.

III *vi* (être légataire) to inherit; (faire un héritage) to come into an inheritance; **~ de qn** to receive an inheritance from sb.

héritier, -ière /eritje, ɛʀ/ *nm,f* JUR heir/heiress (**de** to).

■ **~ testamentaire** JUR legatee.

hermaphrodite /ɛʀmafʀɔdit/ *nm* hermaphrodite.

hermétique /ɛʀmetik/ *adj* **1** LIT (étanche) [*joint, récipient*] hermetic; [*fermeture*] (aux gaz) airtight; (aux liquides) watertight; **2** (impénétrable) [*frontière*] closed, sealed-off (*jamais épith*); [*milieu, société*] impenetrable; [*blocus, embargo*] solid; **3** (indéchiffrable) [*poésie, auteur*] abstruse; [*visage, expression*] inscrutable; **il est ~ au cricket** cricket is a closed book to him.

hermétiquement /ɛʀmetikmɑ̃/ *adv* **1** [*fermé*] hermetically; **2** [*s'exprimer*] abstrusely.

hermétisme /ɛʀmetism/ *nm* **1** (caractère indéchiffrable) abstruseness; **2** (doctrine) hermeticism.

hermine /ɛʀmin/ *nf* **1** (animal) stoat; **2** (fourrure) ermine.

hernie /'ɛʀni/ *nf* **1** MÉD hernia; **2** (de pneu) bulge.

héroïne /eʀɔin/ *nf* **1** (personnage) heroine; **2** (drogue) heroin.

héroïnomane /eʀɔinɔman/ *nm,f* heroin addict.

héroïque /eʀɔik/ *adj* [*personne*] heroic; [*poème*] epic.

héroïsme /eʀɔism/ *nm* heroism.

héron /eʀɔ̃/ *nm* heron.

héros /'eʀo/ *nm inv* hero; **mourir en ~** to die a hero's death.

herse /'ɛʀs/ *nf* **1** AGRIC harrow; **2** (grille d'entrée) portcullis; **3** THÉÂT (éclairage) batten GB, bank of floodlights US; **4** MIL (barrage routier) caltrop barrier.

hertzien, -ienne /ɛʀtzjɛ̃, ɛn/ *adj* [*onde*] Hertzian; [*station, système, liaison*] radio-relay.

hésitant, ~e /ezitɑ̃, ɑ̃t/ *adj* [*geste, dessin*] hesitant; [*pas, voix*] hesitant, faltering; [*démarrage*] shaky.

hésitation /ezitasjɔ̃/ *nf* **1** (indécision) indecision, hesitancy; **il a eu une seconde d'~** he hesitated for a second; **2** (signe d'incertitude) hesitation ¢; **lever les dernières ~s de qn** to overcome sb's final doubts.

hésiter /ezite/ [1] *vi* to hesitate (**sur** over; **devant** before); **elle hésite encore** she's still undecided; **il n'y a pas à ~** it's got to be done; **'alors, tu viens?'—'j'hésite'** 'are you coming?'—'I can't make up my mind'; **j'hésite entre plusieurs possibilités** I can't decide between several possibilities; **j'hésite à interrompre leur conversation** I don't like to interrupt their conversation; **les docteurs hésitent à l'opérer** the doctors are reluctant to operate on him/her.

hétéroclite /eteʀɔklit/ *adj* [*population, œuvre*] heterogeneous; [*objets, matériaux*] miscellaneous.

hétérogène /eteʀɔʒɛn/ *adj* [*groupe, ensemble*] mixed, heterogeneous SOUT; [*nombre*] mixed.

hétérosexuel, -elle /eteʀɔsɛksɥɛl/ *adj, nm,f* heterosexual.

hêtre /'ɛtʀ/ *nm* **1** (arbre) beech (tree); **2** (bois) beechwood.

heure /œʀ/ ► 298|, 588|, 631| *nf* **1** (soixante minutes) hour; **24 ~s sur 24** LIT, FIG 24 hours a day; **dans l'~ qui a suivi** within the hour; **d'~ en ~** [*augmenter, empirer*] by the hour; **deux ~s d'attente** a two-hour wait; **toutes les deux ~s** every two hours; **toutes les ~s** every hour; **après trois ~s d'avion** after three hours on the plane; **être à trois ~s d'avion de Paris** to be three hours away from Paris by plane; **faire trois ~s de bateau** to be on the boat for three hours; **faire du 60 à l'~**○, **faire 60 km à l'~** to do 60 km per hour; **payé à l'~** paid by the hour; **200 francs de l'~** 200 francs an hour; **la semaine de 35 ~s** the 35-hour week; **une petite ~** an hour at the most; **une bonne ~** a good hour; **2** (indication) time; **à 11 ~s, ~ de Paris** at 11, Paris time; **il ne sait pas lire l'~** he can't tell the time; **se tromper d'~** to get the time wrong; **il est 10 ~s** it's 10 (o'clock); **il est 10 ~s 20** it's 20 past 10; **il est 10 ~s moins 20** it's 20 to 10; **à 4 ~s pile** or **tapantes**○ at 4 o'clock sharp; **mettre sa montre à l'~** to set one's watch;

l'~ tourne time is passing; **3** (point dans le temps) time; **l'~ d'arrivée** the arrival time; **~s d'ouverture** opening times; **être à l'~** to be on time; **'sandwiches à toute ~'** 'sandwiches available at any time'; **à une ~ avancée (de la nuit)** late at night; **de bonne ~** [*se lever, partir*] early; **il doit être loin à l'~ qu'il est** he must be a long way off by now; **c'est son ~** it's his/her usual time; **à l'~ où je te parle** while I'm speaking to you; **de la première ~** [*résistant, militant*] from the very beginning; **à la première ~** at first light; **de dernière ~** [*manœuvre, décision*] last-minute; **un résistant de la dernière ~** a late convert to the resistance; **ta dernière ~ est arrivée** your time has come; **4** (période, époque) time; **à l'~ actuelle, pour l'~** at the present time; **à l'~ de la pause** during the break; **l'~ du déjeuner/thé/d îner** lunchtime/teatime/dinnertime; **aux ~s des repas** at mealtimes; **l'~ n'est pas à la polémique** this is no time for controversy; **l'~ est grave** the situation is serious; **il est peintre à ses ~s** he paints in his spare time; **à la bonne ~!** well done!; **5** (ère) era; **vivre à l'~ des satellites** to live in the satellite era.

■ **~ d'affluence** peak hour; **~ d'été** ADMIN summer time GB, daylight saving(s) time; **~ H** MIL, FIG zero hour; **~ d'hiver** ADMIN winter time GB, standard time; **~ légale** ADMIN standard time; **~ de pointe** rush hour; **~s supplémentaires** overtime.

IDIOMES **avant l'~, c'est pas l'~, après l'~, c'est plus l'~**○ there's no time but the right time; **vivre à cent à l'~**○ FIG to be always on the go○.

heureusement /œʀøzmɑ̃/ *adv* **1** (par chance) fortunately (**pour** for); **~ que tu es là!** it's a good job you're here!; **2** (avec bonheur) FML [*réparti*] successfully; [*terminé, conclu*] nicely.

heureux, -euse /œʀø, øz/ *adj* **1** (satisfait) [*personne, visage, enfance*] happy; **être ~ de vivre** to be happy with life; **~ en ménage** happily married; **très ~ de faire votre connaissance** (very) pleased to meet you; **2** (satisfaisant) [*fin*] happy; [*surprise*] pleasant; **3** (optimiste) [*nature, caractère*] happy; **4** (chanceux) lucky; **'il a réussi!'—'encore ~!'** 'he succeeded!'—'just as well!'; **l'~ propriétaire de...** the proud owner of...; **5** (réussi) [*idée*] happy; [*proportions*] pleasing; [*formulation*] happy, felicitous SOUT; **ce n'est pas très ~ comme choix de mots** it's an unfortunate ou unhappy choice of words.

■ **l'~ élu** (en amour) the lucky man; (à un jeu) the lucky winner.

IDIOMES **être ~ comme un roi** or **un pape** to be happy as a lark ou as Larry.

heurt /'œʀ/ *nm* **1** (friction) (différend) conflict; (accrochage) clash; **faire qch sans ~** to do sth smoothly; **leur relation ne va pas sans ~s** their relationship has its ups and downs; **2** (contraste) clash.

heurté, ~e /'œʀte/ *adj* [*style, rythme*] jerky, uneven; [*sons, couleurs, tons*] clashing.

heurter /'œʀte/ [1] **I** *vtr* **1** (cogner contre) [*objet*] to hit; [*personne*] to collide with [*passant, véhicule*]; to bump into [*objet, personne à l'arrêt*]; **~ qn avec qch** to knock sb with sth; **il a heurté la table avec sa valise** he knocked against the table with his suitcase; **2** (cogner) **~ qch avec** ou **contre qch** to knock sth against sth; **3** (offenser) to offend [*personne, morale*]; to go against [*convenances*]; to hurt [*sentiment*]; **~ l'opinion publique** [*action*] to run counter to public opinion; [*personne*] to conflict with public opinion; **~ qn de front** to clash with sb head-on.

II *vi* **~ contre** to strike.

III se heurter *vpr* **1** (se cogner) [*véhicules, personnes*] to collide; [*tasses*] to knock against each other; **les idées se heurtaient dans sa tête** ideas were whirling about in his head; **se ~ contre** ou **à qn/qch** to bump into sb/sth; **2** (rencontrer) **se ~ à** to come up against [*préjugé, refus*]; **3** (s'affronter) to clash (**à** with).

heurtoir /'œʀtwaʀ/ *nm* **1** (marteau de porte) (door) knocker; **2** RAIL buffers (*pl*).

hévéa /evea/ *nm* rubber tree, hevea SPÉC.

L'heure

Quelle heure est-il?

En anglais, on donne l'heure en utilisant les prépositions past et to (ou after et of aux États-Unis). Par ex., pour 4 h 05, five past four, five after four (US), pour 4 h 50, ten to five, ten of five (US) etc. Dans un style plus officiel, on juxtapose les chiffres des heures et des minutes: par ex., pour 4 h 10, four ten. Dans les horaires de trains etc, on utilise aussi l'horloge de vingt-quatre heures: par ex, pour 16 h 23, sixteen twenty-three. Dans le tableau suivant, past peut être remplacé par after (US) et to peut être remplacé par of (US).

il est ...	it is ...	dire
4 h	4 o'clock	four o'clock *ou* four
4 h du matin	4 am	four o'clock*
		ou four [eɪ em]
		ou four o'clock in the morning
4 h de l'après-midi	4 pm	four o'clock
		ou four [pi: em]
		ou four o'clock in the afternoon
4 h 02	4.02	two minutes past four†
		ou four oh two
4 h 05	4.05	five past four†
		ou four oh five
4 h 10	4.10	ten past four
		ou four ten
quatre heures et quart	4.15	a quarter past four
4 h 15	4.15	four fifteen
4 h 20	4.20	twenty past four
		ou four twenty
4 h 23	4.23	twenty-three minutes past four
		ou four twenty-three
4 h 25	4.25	twenty-five past four
		ou four twenty-five
quatre heures et demie	4.30	half past four
4 h 30	4.30	four thirty
4 h 37	4.37	four thirty-seven
cinq heures moins vingt	4.40	twenty to five
4 h 40	4.40	four forty
cinq heures moins le quart	4.45	a quarter to five
4 h 45	4.45	four forty-five
cinq heures moins dix	4.50	ten to five
4 h 50	4.50	four fifty
cinq heures moins cinq	4.55	five to five
4 h 55	4.55	four fifty-five
17 h 00	5 pm	five o'clock in the afternoon*
17 h 15	5.15 pm	a quarter past five
		ou five fifteen
17 h 23	5.23 pm	twenty-three minutes past five
		ou five twenty-three
18 h 00	6 pm	six o'clock
		ou six [pi: em]
12 h	12.00	twelve o'clock
midi	12.00	noon *ou* twelve noon
minuit	12.00	midnight
		ou twelve midnight
zéro heure *ou* 00 h 00	00.00	midnight

quelle heure est-il?	= what time is it?
il est quatre heures à ma montre	= my watch says four o'clock
pouvez-vous me donner l'heure?	= could you tell me the time?
il est quatre heures juste	= it's exactly four o'clock
il est environ quatre heures	= it's about four o'clock *ou* it's about four‡
il va être quatre heures	= it's nearly four o'clock
il est presque quatre heures	= it's almost four o'clock
il est à peine plus de quatre heures	= it's just after four o'clock
il est quatre heures passées	= it's gone four*

Quand?

à quelle heure cela est-il arrivé?	= what time did it happen? *ou* what time did it happen at?
à quelle heure va-t-il venir?	= what time will he come? *ou* what time will he come at?
c'est arrivé à quatre heures	= it happened at four o'clock
il viendra à quatre heures	= he's coming at four o'clock
à quatre heures dix	= at ten past four
à quatre heures et demie	= at half past four (GB), at half after four (US)
à quatre heures précises	= at four o'clock exactly
soyez là à quatre heures pile	= be there at four o'clock on the dot
aux environs de quatre heures	= at about four o'clock
à quatre heures au plus tard	= at four o'clock at the latest
un peu après quatre heures	= shortly after four o'clock
il faut que ce soit prêt avant quatre heures	= it must be ready by four
je serai là jusqu'à quatre heures	= I'll be there until four
je ne serai pas là avant quatre heures	= I won't be there until four
de 7 h à 9 h	= from seven till nine
ouvert de 9 h à 5 h	= open from nine to five
fermé entre treize et quatorze heures	= closed from 1 to 2 pm
toutes les heures à l'heure juste	= every hour on the hour
toutes les heures à dix	= at ten past every hour

---

* *Lorsqu'il s'agit d'horaires de trains, d'avions etc, on peut écrire 0400, qui est prononcé oh four hundred hours, de même sixteen hundred hours, twenty-four hundred hours etc.*

† *Le mot minutes ne peut être omis qu'avec les multiples de 5.*

‡ *Dans la conversation, o'clock est souvent omis.*

---

hexagonal, **-e**, *mpl* **-aux** /ɛgzagɔnal, o/ *adj* **1** MATH hexagonal; **2**° (français) French.

hexagone /ɛgzagon/ *nm* **1** MATH hexagon; **2**° (France métropolitaine) **l'Hexagone** France.

hiatus /'jatys/ *nm inv* **1** ANAT, LING hiatus; **2** FIG (interruption) hiatus, break; (décalage) discrepancy.

hibernation /ibɛrnasjɔ̃/ *nf* BIOL, ZOOL hibernation.

hiberner /ibɛrne/ [1] *vi* to hibernate.

hibou, *pl* **-x** /'ibu/ *nm* owl.

hic° /'ik/ *nm* snag; **c'est bien là le ~** there's the snag.

hideux, **-euse** /'idø, øz/ *adj* hideous.

hier /jɛr/ *adv* yesterday; **toute la journée d'~** all day yesterday; **ce problème ne date pas d'~** this problem is nothing new.

hiérarchie /'jerarʃi/ *nf* hierarchy.

hiérarchique /'jerarʃik/ *adj* [organisation] hierarchical; **mon supérieur ~** my immediate superior; **mes supérieurs ~s** my superiors; **par la voie ~** through the correct channels.

hiérarchiser /'jerarʃize/ [1] *vtr* to organize [sth] into a hierarchy [structure]; to prioritize [tâches]; **~ les salaires** to establish a wages hierarchy.

hiératique /jeratik/ *adj* hieratic.

hiéroglyphe /'jerɔglif/ *nm* **1** (caractère) hieroglyph; **2** (système) **les ~s** hieroglyphics (+ *v sg*).

hi-fi /'ifi/ **I** *adj inv* hi-fi; **une chaîne ~** a hi-fi system. **II** *nf inv* **la ~** hi-fi equipment.

hilarant, **~e** /ilarɑ̃, ɑ̃t/ *adj* hilarious; **gaz ~** laughing gas.

hilare /ilaʀ/ *adj* **être ~** to be laughing.

hilarité /ilaʀite/ *nf* mirth, hilarity.

hindi /'indi/ ▶ 338 | *adj, nm* Hindi.

hindou, **~e** /ɛ̃du/ *adj, nm,f* Hindu.

hindouisme /ɛ̃duism/ *nm* Hinduism.

hippique /ipik/ *adj* [*sport*] equestrian; **concours ~** showjumping event GB, horse show US; **club ~** riding school; **journaliste ~** racing journalist.

hippisme /ipism/ *nm* equestrianism.

hippocampe /ipokɑ̃p/ *nm* ZOOL sea horse.

hippodrome /ipodʀom/ *nm* racecourse GB, racetrack US.

hippopotame /ipopotam/ *nm* hippopotamus.

hirondelle /iʀɔ̃dɛl/ *nf* ZOOL swallow.

hirsute /'iʀsyt/ *adj* (peu soigné) [*personne, apparence*] dishevelled^GB, tousled; [*cheveux, barbe*] unkempt.

hispanique /ispanik/ ▶ 338 | *adj, nm,f* Hispanic.

hispaniste /ispanist/ *nm,f* Hispanicist.

hispano-américain, **~e**, *mpl* **~s** /ispanoameʀikɛ̃, ɛn/ ▶ 338 | *adj* Hispanic-American, Spanish-American.

hispanophone /ispanofɔn/ **I** *adj* Spanish-speaking. **II** *nm,f* Spanish speaker.

hisse /'is/ *excl* **oh ~!** heave-ho!

hisser /'ise/ [1] **I** *vtr* **1** (faire monter) to hoist [*charge, drapeau*]; to hoist [sb] (up) [*personne*]; **2** FIG **~ qn au rang de** to push sb to the rank of.
II se hisser *vpr* **1** (monter avec effort) to heave oneself up; **2** FIG (parvenir) to pull oneself up (**jusqu'à** to (the level of)).

histoire /istwaʀ/ *nf* **1** (discipline) history; **l'~ de France/Chine** French/Chinese history; **l'~ de l'art/ de la littérature** the history of art/of literature; **entrer dans** or **marquer l'~** to go down in history; **un lieu chargé d'~** a place steeped in history; **l'~ jugera** posterity will be the judge; **c'est de l'~ ancienne** (c'est sans intérêt) that's ancient history; (mieux vaut l'oublier) that was a long time ago; **la petite ~ veut que...** it is said that...; **pour la petite ~...** history has it that...; **2** (récit) story; **tout ça, c'est des ~s**○! that's all fiction!; **une ~ à dormir debout** a tall story; **raconter des ~s** to tell fibs; **c'est une ~ de fous** (c'est incroyable) it's absolutely crazy!; (sur les fous) it's a joke about mad people; **3** (aventure, affaire) **~ d'amour** love affair; **~ de famille** family matter; **c'est sûrement une ~ d'argent** there must be money involved; **il m'est arrivé une drôle d'~** a funny thing happened to me; **4** (embarras) fuss ¢; (ennuis) trouble ¢; **en voilà des ~s!** what a to-do!, what a fuss!; **elle fait toujours des ~s** she's always making a fuss; **ça va faire des ~s** it will cause trouble; **il n'y a pas de quoi en faire une ~** there's no need to get worked up about it; **c'est une femme à ~s** she's a troublemaker; **une vie sans ~s** an uneventful life; **ça va faire des ~s avec elle si...** she'll be upset if...; **ça a été toute une ~ pour faire** it was a terrible job doing; **chercher des ~s à qn** to go on○ at sb; **au travail, et pas d'~s**○! get on with it, no messing about○!; **5**○ **prends quelques jours de repos, ~ de te changer les idées** take a few days' rest, just to have a break from everything; **~ de rire** or **s'amuser** just for fun.

historien, **-ienne** /istɔʀjɛ̃, ɛn/ ▶ 374 | *nm,f* historian.

historique /istɔʀik/ **I** *adj* **1** (relatif au passé) historical; **2** (important) historic; **3** LING **passé ~** past historic; **présent ~** historic present.
II *nm* **faire l'~ du cinéma** to trace the history of the cinema; **faire l'~ d'une institution** to tell the story of an institution.

hitlérien, **-ienne** /itleʀjɛ̃, ɛn/ **I** *adj* Hitlerian.
II *nm,f* Hitlerite.

hit-parade, *pl* **~s** /'itpaʀad/ *nm* charts (*pl*).

hiver /iveʀ/ ▶ 542 | *nm* winter; **au cœur de l'~**, **au plus fort de l'~** in the depths of winter; **été comme ~** in summer and winter alike.

hivernage /ivɛʀnaʒ/ *nm* **1** (de bétail) wintering; **2** (de navires) over wintering.

hivernal, **~e**, *mpl* **-aux** /ivɛʀnal, o/ *adj* **1** (d'hiver) winter (*épith*); **2** (comme en hiver) [*jour, temps*] wintry.

hiverner /ivɛʀne/ [1] **I** *vtr* to winter [*bétail*].
II *vi* **1** (passer l'hiver) [*animaux, bateaux*] to winter; [*personnes*] to spend the winter.

HLM /aʃɛlɛm/ *nm* ou *f: abbr* ▶ **habitation**.

hobereau, *pl* **~x** /ɔbʀo/ *nm* **1** (gentilhomme) country squire; **2** (faucon) hobby.

hochement /'ɔʃmɑ̃/ *nm* **~ (de tête)** (de haut en bas) nod; (de droite à gauche) shake of the head.

hocher /'ɔʃe/ [1] *vtr* **~ la tête** (de haut en bas) to nod; (de droite à gauche) to shake one's head.

hochet /'ɔʃɛ/ *nm* rattle.

hockey /'ɔkɛ/ ▶ 329 | *nm* **~ (sur glace)** ice hockey; **~ sur gazon** hockey GB, field hockey US.

hockeyeur, **-euse** /'ɔkɛjœʀ, øz/ *nm,f* hockey player.

holà /'ɔla/ *excl* **1** (pour appeler) hey (there)!; **2** (pour arrêter un animal) whoa!
IDIOMES **mettre le ~ à qch** to put an end ou to sth.

holding /'ɔldiŋ/ *nm* ou *f* holding company.

hold-up /'ɔldœp/ *nm* ou **~s** /'ɔldœp/ *nm* hold-up (**de qch** at sth); **commettre un ~** to stage a hold-up.

hollandais, **~e** /'ɔlɑ̃dɛ, ɛz/ ▶ 338 | **I** *adj* Dutch.
II *nm* LING Dutch.

Hollandais, **~e** /'ɔlɑ̃dɛ, ɛz/ ▶ 394 |, 338 | *nm,f* Dutchman/Dutchwoman; **les ~** the Dutch.

Hollande /'ɔlɑ̃d/ ▶ 509 | *nprf* Holland.

holocauste /ɔlɔkost/ *nm* **1** HIST (génocide) holocaust; **2** RELIG holocaust, burned offering; **3** FIG (total) sacrifice.

homard /'ɔmaʀ/ *nm* lobster.
IDIOMES **rouge comme un ~** as red as a beetroot.

homélie /ɔmeli/ *nf* homily.

homéopathie /ɔmeopati/ *nf* homeopathy.

homéopathique /ɔmeopatik/ *adj* [*traitement, préparation*] homeopathic; **à doses ~s** FIG in small doses.

homérique /ɔmeʀik/ *adj* Homeric.

homicide /ɔmisid/ **I** *adj* homicidal.
II *nm,f* (personne) homicide.
III *nm* (crime) homicide.
■ **~ involontaire** JUR unintentional manslaughter; **~ avec préméditation** JUR premeditated murder; **~ volontaire** JUR intentional manslaughter.

hommage /ɔmaʒ/ **I** *nm* **1** (témoignage de respect) homage, tribute; **rendre ~ à qn/qch** to pay tribute to sb/sth; **c'est lui faire trop d'~** it's making too much of him/her; **2** (don) **faire ~ de qch à qn** to present sb with sth; **'~ de l'auteur'** 'with the author's compliments'; **3** HIST homage.
II hommages *nmpl* **1** (salutations) respects; **2** (compliments) compliments.

hommasse /ɔmas/ *adj* mannish.

homme /ɔm/ *nm* **1** (espèce) **l'~** man; **l'~ de Néanderthal** Neanderthal man; **2** (genre humain) **l'~** mankind; **3** (être humain) human being; **un ~ à la mer!** man overboard!; **comme un seul ~** as one; **4** (adulte de sexe masculin) man; **l'~ de la réunification** the man who achieved reunification; **l'~ de la situation** the right man for the job; **être l'~ de confiance de qn** to be sb's right-hand man; **il n'est pas ~ à se venger** he's not the type to want revenge; **l'~ du jour** the man of the moment.
■ **~ d'affaires** businessman; **~ de bien** philanthropist; **~ des bois** wild man; **~ des cavernes** caveman; **~ d'Église** man of the cloth; **~ d'équipage** NAUT crewman; **~ d'esprit** wit; **~ d'État** POL statesman; **~ à femmes** womanizer; **~ au foyer** house-husband; **~ de loi** lawyer; **~ de main** hired hand; **~ du monde** gentleman; **~ de l'ombre** behind-the-scenes operator; **~ de paille** front, straw man US; **~ de peine** labourer^GB; **~ de plume** writer; **~ politique** POL politician; **~ de robe** lawyer; **~ de terrain** man with practical

experience; POL grass-roots politician; **~ à tout faire** handyman; **~ de troupe** MIL private; **~s en blanc** surgeons.

IDIOMES **un ~ averti en vaut deux** PROV forewarned is forearmed.

homme-grenouille, *pl* **hommes-grenouilles** /ɔmgrənuj/ *nm* frogman.

homme-orchestre, *pl* **hommes-orchestres** /ɔmɔrkɛstr/ *nm* LIT, FIG one-man band.

homogène /ɔmɔʒɛn/ *adj* **1** (uniforme) homogeneous; **2** (cohérent) [*équipe*] united, harmonious; [*base*] consistent.

homogénéiser /ɔmɔʒeneize/ [1] *vtr* to homogenize.

homogénéité /ɔmɔʒeneite/ *nf* homogeneity.

homographe /ɔmɔgraf/ **I** *adj* [*mots*] homographic.
II *nm* homograph.

homologue /ɔmɔlɔg/ **I** *adj* homologous.
II *nmf* **1** (personne) counterpart, opposite number; **2** CHIMIE (composé) homologue[GB].

homologuer /ɔmɔlɔge/ [1] *vtr* **1** ADMIN (déclarer conforme) to approve [*produit, appareil*]; **2** SPORT (enregistrer) to recognize officially [*record, performance*].

homonyme /ɔmɔnim/ **I** *adj* LING homonymous.
II *nm* **1** LING homonym; **2** (personne) namesake.

homophone /ɔmɔfɔn/ **I** *adj* **1** LING homophonous; **2** MUS homophonic.
II *nm* LING homophone.

homosexualité /ɔmɔsɛksɥalite/ *nf* homosexuality.

homosexuel, **~elle** /ɔmɔsɛksɥɛl/ *adj, nm,f* homosexual.

hongrois, **~e** /ˈɔ̃grwa, az/ [I ▶ **394**] *adj* Hungarian.
II [▶ **338**] *nm* LING Hungarian.

honnête /ɔnɛt/ *adj* **1** (intègre) [*personne, réponse*] honest; [*élections*] fair; **2** (honorable) [*personne*] decent; [*vie*] respectable; [*moyens*] honest; [*intention*] honourable[GB]; **c'est une proposition ~** it's a genuine offer; **3** (juste) [*arbitre, prix, marché*] fair; **4** (moyen) [*travail, salaire, repas*] reasonable; [*résultat*] fair.
■ **~ femme**† respectable woman; **~ homme**† gentleman.

honnêtement /ɔnɛtmɑ̃/ *adv* **1** (avec probité) [*gérer, dire*] honestly; [*répondre*] frankly; [*agir*] properly; [*juger*] fairly; [*reconnaître*] freely; **2** (convenablement) [*rétribuer*] fairly; **gagner ~ sa vie** to earn a decent living; **travail ~ payé** reasonably well-paid job.

honnêteté /ɔnɛtte/ *nf* (probité) honesty.

honneur /ɔnœr/ *nm* **1** (fierté) honour[GB] ¢; **s'être engagé sur l'~ à faire** to be honour[GB] bound to do; **l'~ national** national pride; **sauver l'~** to save face; **faire ~ à sa parole** to honour[GB] one's promise; **avec ~** [*servir*] honourably[GB]; **dans l'~** [*capituler, se réconcilier*] honourably[GB]; **jouer pour l'~** to play for the love of it; **combattre pour l'~** to fight as a matter of honour[GB]; **être l'~ de sa famille** [*personne*] to be a credit to one's family; **2** (mérite) credit; **ce fut tout à leur ~** it was all credit to them; **3** (privilège) honour[GB]; **se disputer l'~ de faire** to fight over the honour[GB] of; **à qui ai-je l'~?** FML to whom do I have the honour[GB] of speaking? SOUT; **~ au perdant!** loser goes first!; **à toi l'~!** you do the honours[GB]!; **vous me faites trop d'~** you flatter me; **j'ai l'~ de vous informer que** I beg to inform you that; **d'~** [*escalier, cour*] main; ▶ **seigneur**; **2** (célébration) **être (mis) à l'~** [*personne*] to be honoured[GB]; **mettre qn à l'~** to honour[GB] sb; **être à l'** or **en ~** [*chose*] to be in favour[GB]; **être remis à l'~** [*tradition, usage, discipline*] to regain favour[GB]; **faire** or **rendre ~ à qn** to honour[GB] sb; **faire ~ à un repas** to do justice to a meal; **~ à ceux qui** all praise to those who; **en quel ~?** IRON any particular reason why?; **5** JEUX (carte haute) honour[GB].
II honneurs *nmpl* (distinction) honours[GB]; **être accueilli avec les ~s réservés aux chefs d'État** to be received with the ceremony reserved for heads of State; **rendre les ~s à** MIL (funèbres) to pay the last honours[GB] to; (militaires) to honour[GB] [sb]; **la richesse et les ~s** wealth and glory; **faire les ~s de la maison à**

qn to show sb around the house; **avoir les ~s de la presse** to be mentioned in the press.

IDIOMES **en tout bien tout ~** (sans arrière-pensées) with no hidden motive; **il est venu prendre un verre, mais c'était en tout bien tout ~** he came round for a drink but that's all there was to it.

honnir /ˈɔnir/ [3] *vtr* LITER to execrate.

IDIOMES **honni soit qui mal y pense** evil unto him who evil thinks.

honorabilité /ɔnɔrabilite/ *nf* integrity.

honorable /ɔnɔrabl/ *adj* **1** (respectable) [*personne, métier, reddition*] honourable[GB]; [*compagnie, marque*] venerable; **2** (suffisant) [*classement, score*] creditable; [*moyens financiers, nombre, proportion*] sizable; [*salaire*] decent.

honorablement /ɔnɔrabləmɑ̃/ *adv* **1** (de façon respectable) honourably; **~ connu** [*famille*] highly respected; [*compagnie*] venerable; **2** (suffisamment) decently; **gagner ~ sa vie** to earn a decent living.

honoraire /ɔnɔrɛr/ **I** *adj* [*membre*] honorary.
II honoraires *nmpl* (rétributions) fee (*sg*).

honorer /ɔnɔre/ [1] **I** *vtr* **1** (rendre hommage) to honour[GB] [*Dieu, personne, équipe, mémoire*]; **~ qn de sa confiance** to honour[GB] sb with one's trust; **2** (acquitter) to honour[GB] [*promesse, dette*]; **3** (procurer de la fierté) [*personne*] to be a credit to [*pays, profession, parents*]; **4** (donner du mérite) **votre courage vous honore** your bravery does you credit.
II s'honorer *vpr* **1** (être fier) to be proud; **2** (s'attirer de la considération) to bring credit on oneself.

honorifique /ɔnɔrifik/ *adj* honorary; **nommé président à titre ~** appointed honorary president.

honoris causa /ɔnɔriskoza/ *loc adj* [*docteur*] honorary; **être nommé docteur ~** to be awarded an honorary doctorate.

honte /ˈɔ̃t/ *nf* **1** (gêne) shame; **rougir de ~** to blush with shame; **avoir ~ de** to be ashamed of; **faire ~ à qn** to make sb ashamed; **sans ~** FML shamelessly; **à ma (grande) ~** to my (great) embarrassment; **avouer qch sans ~** to acknowledge sth openly; **2** (discrédit) disgrace; **faire la ~ de** to be a disgrace to; **jeter la ~ sur** to bring disgrace upon.

honteusement /ˈɔ̃tøzmɑ̃/ *adv* (ignoblement) [*traiter, trahir*] shamefully; (sans honte) [*tricher*] shamelessly.

honteux, **-euse** /ˈɔ̃tø, øz/ *adj* **1** (déshonorant) [*conduite, secret*] disgraceful; **2** (gêné) [*personne*] ashamed (**de qn/qch** of sb/sth).

hôpital, *pl* **-aux** /ɔpital, o/ *nm* hospital; **~ de campagne** field hospital.
■ **~ de jour** outpatient clinic.

IDIOMES **c'est l'~ qui se moque de la charité** it's the pot calling the kettle black.

hoquet /ˈɔkɛ/ *nm* hiccup; **avoir le ~** to have hiccups; **avoir un ~ de frayeur** to gulp with fright.

hoqueter /ˈɔkte/ [20] *vi* [*personne*] to hiccup; [*moteur*] to sputter.

horaire /ɔrɛr/ **I** *adj* [*salaire, débit, tarif*] per hour; **tranche** or **plage ~** time-slot.
II *nm* **1** (de train, bus) timetable GB, schedule US; (d'avion, de vols) schedule; **les ~s de train** the train times; **2** (emploi du temps) timetable, schedule; **les ~s de travail** working hours; **les ~s libres** or **à la carte** flexitime.

horde /ˈɔrd/ *nf* (de barbares) horde; (de chiens, loups) pack.

horizon /ɔrizɔ̃/ *nm* **1** (limite de la vue) horizon; **l'~ est bouché** LIT there are clouds on the horizon; FIG the road ahead is not clear; FIG (avenir) outlook; **des réformes se profilent à l'~** reforms are appearing on the horizon; **cet emploi m'ouvre de nouveaux ~s** this job opens up new horizons for me; **3** FIG (univers) horizons (*pl*); **changer d'~** to have a change of scene; **ils viennent d'~s très divers** they come from very varied backgrounds.

horizontal, **~e**[1], *mpl* **-aux** /ɔrizɔ̃tal, o/ *adj* horizontal.

horizontale² /ɔrizɔ̃tal/ *nf* MATH (ligne) horizontal; **à l'~** in a horizontal position.

horloge /ɔrlɔʒ/ *nf* clock.

horloger, -ère /ɔrlɔʒe, ɛr/ I *adj* watchmaking (*épith*). II ▶ 374|, 374| *nm,f* watchmaker.

horlogerie /ɔrlɔʒri/ ▶ 374| *nf* (industrie) watchmaking; (boutique) watchmaker's (shop); (produits) clocks and watches (*pl*); **pièce d'~** watch component.

hormis /ˈɔrmi/ *prép* FML save (for).

hormonal, -e, *mpl* **-aux** /ɔrmɔnal, o/ *adj* [*problème*] hormonal; [*traitement*] hormone (*épith*).

hormone /ɔrmɔn/ *nf* hormone.

horodateur /ɔrɔdatœr/ *nm* parking ticket machine.

horoscope /ɔrɔskɔp/ *nm* horoscope.

horreur /ɔrœr/ *nf* 1 (atrocité) horror; 2 (parole méchante) awful thing; 3 (épouvante) horror; **être glacé d'~** to be frozen with horror; **être saisi d'~** to be horror-struck; **être une ~** [*personne, chose, œuvre*] to be horrible; **quelle ~!** how horrible!; 4 (aversion) loathing; **avoir ~ de qn/qch**, **avoir qn/qch en ~** to loathe sb/sth; **avoir ~ de faire** to hate doing; **ton attitude me fait ~** your attitude horrifies me.
IDIOMES **c'est (vraiment) l'~**○ it's (really) the pits○.

horrible /ɔribl/ *adj* 1 (abominable) [*cri, maladie*] horrible; [*temps*] filthy; [*moment, séjour*] dreadful; [*meurtre, scène*] horrific; [*douleur, bruit*] terrible; [*pensée*] horrible; [*paroles, personne*] nasty; 2 (répugnant) [*goût, odeur*] revolting; [*créature*] horrid; [*nourriture*] dreadful; 3 (laid) [*visage, objet, cicatrice*] hideous.

horriblement /ɔribləmɑ̃/ *adv* 1 (effroyablement) [*brûlé*] horribly; 2 (terriblement) [*dangereux, froid*] terribly.

horrifier /ɔrifje/ [2] *vtr* to horrify.

horripiler /ɔripile/ [1] *vtr* to exasperate.

hors /ˈɔr/

■ Note Lorsque *hors* et *hors de* sont suivis d'un nom sans article reportez-vous à ce nom. Ainsi *hors catégorie* est traité sous **catégorie** et *hors d'atteinte* sous **atteinte**. Une expression telle que *mettre qn hors la loi* figure sous **loi**. *hors-la-loi* est une entrée à part.
– Les autres emplois de *hors* sont présentés dans l'article ci-dessous.

I *prép* LITER apart from, save SOUT.
II **hors de** *loc prép* (dans l'espace) (position fixe) outside; (avec mouvement) out of; FIG outside; **~ d'ici!** get out of here!; **~ de chez soi** away from home.
■ **~ tout** overall; **longueur ~ tout** overall length.
IDIOMES **être ~ de soi** to be beside oneself; **cela m'a mis ~ de moi** it infuriated me.

hors-bord /ˈɔrbɔr/ I *adj* [*moteur*] outboard.
II *nm inv* powerboat, speedboat; **faire du ~** to go speedboating.

hors-d'œuvre /ˈɔrdœvr/ *nm inv* 1 CULIN starter, hors d'oeuvre; 2○ FIG foretaste.

hors-jeu /ˈɔrʒø/ *nm inv* (pour) **~** for offside.

hors-la-loi /ˈɔrlalwa/ *nm inv* outlaw.

hors-piste /ˈɔrpist/ *nm inv* off-piste skiing.

hortensia /ɔrtɑ̃sja/ *nm* hydrangea.

horticole /ɔrtikɔl/ *adj* horticultural.

horticulteur, -trice /ɔrtikyltœr, tris/ ▶ 374| *nm,f* horticulturist.

hospice /ɔspis/ *nm* 1 (asile) home; **finir à l'~** to end up in the poorhouse; 2† RELIG hospice†.
■ **~ de vieillards** old people's home.

hospitalier, -ière /ɔspitalje, ɛr/ *adj* 1 MÉD hospital (*épith*); **centre ~** hospital; 2 (accueillant) hospitable; 3 RELIG [*ordre*] charitable.

hospitalisation /ɔspitalizasjɔ̃/ *nf* hospitalization.
■ **~ à domicile** home (medical) care.

hospitaliser /ɔspitalize/ [1] *vtr* to hospitalize.

hospitalité /ɔspitalite/ *nf* hospitality; **demander l'~ à qn** to ask sb for shelter.

hospitalo-universitaire, *pl* **~s** /ɔspitaloyniversitɛr/ *adj* **centre ~** teaching hospital.

hostellerie /ɔstɛlri/ *nf* (country) inn.

hostie /ɔsti/ *nf* RELIG Host.

hostile /ɔstil/ *adj* hostile (à to).

hostilité /ɔstilite/ *nf* hostility; **les ~s** MIL hostilities.

hôte /ot/ I *nm* 1 (personne qui invite) host; 2 (résident) (personne) occupant; (animal) inhabitant; 3 BIOL host.
II *nmf* 1 (personne invitée) guest; 2 (d'appartement) occupant; (d'hôtel) guest.

hôtel /otɛl/ *nm* hotel.
■ **~ des impôts** tax office; **~ de la Monnaie** ADMIN (French) Mint; **~ particulier** ARCHIT town house; **~ de tourisme** TOURISME tourist hotel; **~ des ventes** COMM saleroom; **~ de ville** ADMIN ~ town hall.

hôtel-club, *pl* **hôtels-clubs** /otɛlklœb/ *nm* (hotel-based) holiday club.

hôtel-Dieu, *pl* **hôtels-Dieu** /otɛldjø/ *nm* main hospital.

hôtelier, -ière /otəlje, ɛr/ ▶ 374| I *adj* [*industrie, chaîne*] hotel (*épith*); [*école*] hotel management.
II *nmf* hotelkeeper.

hôtellerie /otɛlri/ *nf* (profession) hotel business.

hôtesse /otɛs/ ▶ 374| *nf* 1 (professionnelle) (de société, magasin) receptionist; (d'exposition) hostess; (de train, bateau) stewardess; 2 (personne qui invite) hostess.
■ **~ d'accueil** receptionist; **~ de l'air** AVIAT stewardess; **~ au sol** AVIAT ground attendant.

hotte /ˈɔt/ *nf* 1 (de vendangeur) basket (*carried on the back*); 2 (de cheminée) hood; 3 (de cuisinière) hood GB, range hood US.
■ **~ aspirante** extractor hood GB, ventilator US; **la ~ du Père Noël** Father Christmas's sack GB, Santa Claus's sack US.

houblon /ˈublɔ̃/ *nm* hop C.

houe /ˈu/ *nf* hoe.

houille /ˈuj/ *nf* (charbon) coal.
■ **~ blanche** hydroelectric power.

houiller, -ère¹ /ˈuje, ɛr/ *adj* [*gisement, industrie*] coal (*épith*); [*terrain*] coal-bearing; [*région*] coalmining.

houillère² /ˈujɛr/ *nf* 1 (dépôt) coalmine; 2 (exploitation) colliery.

houle /ˈul/ *nf* swell.

houlette /ˈulɛt/ *nf* 1 (de berger) crook; **sous la ~ de** FIG under the leadership of; 2 (de jardinier) trowel.

houleux, -euse /ˈulø, øz/ *adj* 1 [*mer*] rough; 2 [*réunion, débat*] stormy.

houppe /ˈup/ *nf* 1 (de cheveux) tuft; (de fils) tassel; 2 (à poudrer) powder puff.

houppelande /ˈuplɑ̃d/ *nf* greatcoat.

houppette /ˈupɛt/ *nf* 1 (à poudrer) powder puff; 2 (de cheveux) little tuft (of hair).

hourra /ˈura/ I *nm* (acclamation) cheer; **pousser des ~s** to cheer; **pousser un ~ de joie** to give a shout of joy.
II *excl* hurrah!; **hip hip hip ~!** hip hip hurrah!

houspiller /ˈuspije/ [1] *vtr* to scold; **se faire ~** to be scolded.

housse /ˈus/ *nf* GÉN cover; (de chaise, sofa) slipcover; (de siège de voiture) seat cover; (de vêtements) garment bag; (de machine à écrire) dust cover.
■ **~ de couette** duvet cover, quilt cover.

houx /ˈu/ *nm inv* holly.

HS○ /ˈaʃɛs/ *adj* (*abbr* = **hors service**) [*machine*] on the blink○; [*personne*] knackered➒ GB, shot○ US.

HT 1 (*written abbr* = **hors taxes**) exclusive of tax; **2** (*written abbr* = **haute tension**) HV.

hublot /ˈyblo/ *nm* (de bateau) porthole; (d'avion) window; (de machine à laver) door.

huche /ˈyʃ/ *nf* (coffre) chest.
■ **~ à pain** bread bin.

huées /ˈɥe/ *nfpl* booing ⊄.

huer /ˈɥe/ [1] I *vtr* to boo [*auteur, discours*].
II *vi* (hibou) to hoot.

huile /ˈɥil/ *nf* 1 (substance) oil; **sardines à l'~** sardines in vegetable oil; **pommes à l'~** potato salad; **2** ART (tableau) oil painting; **3**° (personnage important) big shot°, bigwig°.

■ **~ d'arachide** peanut oil; **~ de coude** HUM elbow grease; **~ de graissage** lubricating oil; **~ de paraffine** liquid paraffin; **~ de ricin** castor oil; **~ solaire** suntan oil.

IDIOMES **tout/ça baigne dans l'~**° everything/it is going smoothly; **jeter** or **verser de l'~ sur le feu** to add fuel to the fire.

huiler /ɥile/ [1] *vtr* to oil [*peau, mécanisme, poêle*]; **bien huilé** [*mécanisme, machine*] LIT, FIG well-oiled; [*reportage, scénario*] FIG slick.

huilerie /ɥilʀi/ *nf* **1** (usine) oil mill; **2** (commerce) oil trade.

huileux, -euse /ɥilø, øz/ *adj* oily.

huilier /ɥilje/ *nm* (oil and vinegar) cruet.

huis /'ɥi/ *nm inv* JUR **~ clos** closed hearing; **à ~ clos** JUR in camera; FIG behind closed doors.

huisserie /ɥisʀi/ *nf* (de porte) doorframe; (de fenêtre) window frame.

huissier /ɥisje/ ▶374 *nm* **1** JUR **~ (de justice)** bailiff; **2** (portier) porter; (de tribunal) usher.

huit /'ɥit, but before consonant 'ɥi/ ▶399, 298, 156 **I** *adj inv* eight; **~ jours** (semaine) a week; (précisément) eight days; **mardi en ~** a week on Tuesday; **donner ses ~ jours à qn** to give sb a week's notice.

II *pron* eight.

III *nm inv* **1** (numéro) eight; **2** (trajectoire) a figure of eight.

huitaine /ɥitɛn/ *nf* **1** (semaine) about a week; **sous ~** within a week; **2** (environ huit) about eight.

huitième /ɥitjɛm/ ▶399, 156 **I** *adj* eighth.

II *nf* SCOL *fourth year of primary school, age 9–10*.

■ **le ~ art** television; **~ de finale** SPORT *round before the quarter finals*.

huître /ɥitʀ/ *nf* oyster.

huîtrier, -ière[1] /ɥitʀije, ɛʀ/ **I** *adj* oyster (*épith*).

II *nm* (oiseau) oystercatcher.

huîtrière[2] /ɥitʀijɛʀ/ *nf* (banc) oyster bed; (parc) oyster farm.

hululement /'ylylmɑ̃/ *nm* hooting ¢.

hululer /'ylyle/ [1] *vi* to hoot.

humain, ~e /ymɛ̃, ɛn/ **I** *adj* **1** GÉN human; **pertes ~es** loss of life ¢; **marée ~e** tide of humanity; **2** (clément) [*solution, régime*] humane; [*personne*] human.

II *nm* **1** (personne) human being; **2** (être terrestre) human; **3** PHILOS **l'~ et le divin** the human and the divine.

IDIOMES **l'erreur est ~e** to err is human.

humainement /ymɛnmɑ̃/ *adv* **1** [*possible, impossible*] humanly; **2** [*traiter, se comporter*] humanely.

humanisation /ymanizasjɔ̃/ *nf* (de prison, conditions de vie) humanization; (de politique) softening.

humaniser /ymanize/ [1] **I** *vtr* to humanize [*conditions de vie*]; to make [sb/sth] more human [*ville*].

II **s'humaniser** *vpr* to become more human.

humaniste /ymanist/ *adj, nmf* humanist.

humanitaire /ymanitɛʀ/ *adj* humanitarian.

humanité /ymanite/ *nf* **1** (genre humain) humanity; **2** (altruisme) humanity; **avec ~** [*traiter*] humanely.

humble /œbl/ **I** *adj* [*personne*] (par soi-même) unassuming; (vis-à-vis d'autres) humble; [*ton, manières*] unassuming; [*travail, origine*] humble; [*maison*] modest; **se faire ~ devant qn** to humble oneself before sb.

II humbles *nmpl* **les ~s** the common people.

humblement /œbləmɑ̃/ *adv* humbly.

humecter /ymɛkte/ [1] *vtr* to moisten [*visage, gâteau*] (**de, avec** with); to dampen [*linge*].

humer /'yme/ [1] *vtr* **1** to sniff [*air*]; **2** LITER to smell [*fleur, potage*].

humérus /ymeʀys/ *nm inv* humerus.

humeur /ymœʀ/ *nf* **1** (disposition passagère) mood; **être de bonne/mauvaise ~** to be in a good/bad mood; **être/ne pas être d'~ à faire** to be in the mood/in no mood to do; **2** (disposition dominante) temper; **d'~ égale** even-tempered; **d'~ inégale** moody; **un**

spectacle plein de bonne ~ a fun-filled show; **1** (mauvaise disposition) bad temper; **geste d'~** bad-tempered gesture.

humide /ymid/ *adj* **1** [*linge, cheveux, maison*] damp; **il avait le regard ~** his eyes were moist with tears; **2** [*région, air*] humid; [*saison*] rainy; **il fait froid et ~** it's cold and damp; **il fait une chaleur ~** it's muggy.

humidificateur /ymidifikatœʀ/ *nm* humidifier.

humidifier /ymidifje/ [2] *vtr* to dampen [*linge, papier*]; to spray [sth] (with water) [*peau*]; to humidify [*air*].

humidité /ymidite/ *nf* **1** (de lieu) dampness, damp; **'craint l'~'** 'should be stored in a dry place'; **le livre est resté à l'~** the book has been left in a damp place; **2** (résultat) damp; **prendre l'~** to be affected by damp; **3** (de climat, région) humidity.

humiliation /ymiljasjɔ̃/ *nf* humiliation.

humilier /ymilje/ [2] *vtr* to humiliate; **se sentir humilié** to feel humiliated (**par** by; **de faire** doing).

humilité /ymilite/ *nf* **1** (de personne) humility; **en toute/avec ~** in all/with humility; **2** (de condition, tâche) humble nature.

humoriste /ymɔʀist/ ▶374 *nmf* **1** (auteur) humorist; **2** (farceur) joker.

humoristique /ymɔʀistik/ *adj* humorous; **dessin ~** cartoon.

humour /ymuʀ/ *nm* (de personne, situation) humour^{GB}; **~ noir** black humour^{GB}; **ne pas avoir** to have no sense of humour^{GB}; **avec ~** humorously; **savoir faire preuve d'~** to take things in good part; **il n'a pas su apprécier l'~ de la situation** he couldn't see the funny side of it; **faire de l'~** to make jokes.

huppé, ~e /'ype/ *adj* **1**° (mondain) upper-crust (*épith*); **2** [*oiseau*] crested.

hure /'yʀ/ *nf* (tête, trophée) head.

hurlement /'yʀləmɑ̃/ *nm* (d'animal) howl, howling ¢; (de personne) yell, howl; (de sirène) wail, wailing ¢; **pousser un ~ de douleur** to howl with pain.

hurler /'yʀle/ [1] **I** *vtr* **1** [*personne*] to yell (**à qn** at sb); **2** [*télévision, radio, magnétophone*] to blare out.

II *vi* **1** (pousser des cris) to howl; **~ de douleur** to howl with pain; **~ de rire** to roar with laughter; **~ au scandale** to be outraged; **2** (parler fort) to yell; **3** (faire du bruit) [*sirène*] to wail; [*vent*] to roar; [*radio*] to blare.

IDIOMES **~ avec les loups** to follow the crowd; **~ à la mort** to bay at the moon.

hurluberlu, ~e /yʀlybɛʀly/ *nm,f* oddball°.

hutte /'yt/ *nf* hut.

hybride /ibʀid/ *adj, nm* LIT, FIG hybrid.

hydratant, ~e /idʀatɑ̃, ɑ̃t/ **I** *adj* moisturizing.

II *nm* moisturizer.

hydratation /idʀatasjɔ̃/ *nf* **1** (de la peau) moisturizing; **2** (du corps) hydration; **3** CHIMIE hydration.

hydrate /idʀat/ *nm* hydrate.

■ **~ de carbone** carbohydrate.

hydrater /idʀate/ [1] **I** *vtr* **1** to moisturize [*peau*]; **2** to hydrate [*tissu, organisme*]; **3** CHIMIE to hydrate.

II **s'hydrater** *vpr* **1** [*personne*] **bien s'~** to take plenty of fluids; **2** CHIMIE to undergo hydration.

hydraulique /idʀolik/ **I** *adj* hydraulic.

II *nf* hydraulics (+ *v sg*).

hydravion /idʀavjɔ̃/ *nm* seaplane, hydroplane.

hydre /idʀ/ *nf* MYTHOL Hydra.

hydro /idʀo/ *préf* hydro; **~céphale** hydrocephalic; **~électrique** hydroelectric.

hydrocarbure /idʀokaʀbyʀ/ *nm* hydrocarbon.

hydrocution /idʀokysjɔ̃/ *nf* immersion hypothermia.

hydrofuge /idʀofyʒ/ *adj* [*mastic*] water-repellent.

hydrogène /idʀoʒɛn/ *nm* hydrogen.

■ **~ lourd** CHIMIE deuterium.

hydroglisseur /idʀoglisœʀ/ *nm* hydroplane.

hydromel /idʀomɛl/ *nm* mead.

hydrophile /idʀofil/ *adj* [*tissu, matière*] absorbent.

hydroptère /idʀoptɛʀ/ *nm* hydrofoil.

hydrorésistant, **~e** /idroʀezistɑ̃, ɑ̃t/ *adj* water resistant.

hydroxyde /idroksid/ *nm* hydroxide.

hyène /'jɛn/ *nf* hyena.

hygiaphone® /iʒjafɔn/ *nm* grill (*perforated communication panel*).

hygiène /iʒjɛn/ *nf* hygiene; **contraire à l'~** unhygienic; **par mesure d'~** for (the sake of) hygiene; **~ scolaire** health guidelines for schools; **une bonne ~ alimentaire** a healthy diet.
■ **~ corporelle** personal hygiene; **~ mentale** mental health.

hygiénique /iʒjenik/ *adj* **1** (propre) hygienic; **2** (sain) healthy; **promenade ~** constitutional.

hymen /imɛn/ *nm* **1** ANAT hymen; **2** (mariage) LITER nuptial bond.

hymne /imn/ *nm* LITTÉRAT, MUS, FIG hymn; **~ à la vie** FIG hymn to life.
■ **~ national** national anthem.

hyperactif, **-ive** /ipeʀaktif, iv/ *adj* hyperactive.

hyperbole /ipeʀbɔl/ *nf* **1** MATH hyperbola; **2** LITTÉRAT hyperbole.

hypercalorique /ipeʀkalɔʀik/ *adj* high in calories (*jamais épith*), high-calorie (*épith*).

hyperclassique /ipeʀklasik/ *adj* [*situation, réaction*] absolutely classic; **roman** or **pièce** or **film ~** great classic.

hyperconnu, **~e** /ipeʀkɔny/ *adj* extremely famous.

hyperdoué, **~e** /ipeʀdwe/ *adj* exceptionally gifted.

hyperinformé, **~e** /ipeʀɛ̃fɔʀme/ *adj* very well informed.

hypermarché /ipeʀmaʀʃe/ *nm* large supermarket.

hypermétrope /ipeʀmetʀɔp/ *adj* longsighted.

hypernerveux, **-euse** /ipeʀnɛʀvø, øz/ *adj* highly strung.

hyperpuissant, **~e** /ipeʀpɥisɑ̃, ɑ̃t/ *adj* [*voiture, moteur*] extremely powerful.

hypersensible /ipeʀsɑ̃sibl/ *adj* hypersensitive.

hypersophistiqué, **~e** /ipeʀsofistike/ *adj* [*personne, vêtement*] very sophisticated; [*théorie*] highly sophisticated.

hyperspécialisé, **~e** /ipeʀspesjalize/ *adj* highly specialized.

hypertendu, **~e** /ipeʀtɑ̃dy/ *adj* **1°** extremely tense; **2** MÉD suffering from high blood pressure.

hypertension /ipeʀtɑ̃sjɔ̃/ *nf* **~ (artérielle)** high blood pressure, hypertension SPÉC.

hypertrophie /ipeʀtʀɔfi/ *nf* **1** MÉD enlargement, hypertrophy SPÉC; **2** (de ville) overdevelopment.

hypertrophier: **s'hypertrophier** /ipeʀtʀɔfje/ [2]

vpr **1** MÉD to hypertrophy; **2** [*administration, ville, sentiment*] to become overdeveloped.

hypnose /ipnoz/ *nf* hypnosis.

hypnotiser /ipnotize/ [1] *vtr* LIT to hypnotize; FIG to mesmerize.

hypnotiseur, **-euse** /ipnotizœr, øz/ **▶374** *nm,f* hypnotist.

hypocagne = **hypokhâgne**.

hypocalorique /ipokalɔʀik/ *adj* low-calorie (*épith*), low in calories (*jamais épith*).

hypocondriaque /ipokɔ̃dʀijak/ *adj*, *nmf* hypochondriac.

hypocrisie /ipokʀizi/ *nf* hypocrisy.

hypocrite /ipokʀit/ **I** *adj* hypocritical.
II *nmf* hypocrite.

hypodermique /ipodɛʀmik/ *adj* hypodermic.

hypoglucidique /ipoglysidik/ *adj* [*aliment*] low-carbohydrate (*épith*).

hypokhâgne /ipokaɲ/ *nf* students' slang *first year preparatory class in humanities for entrance to École normale supérieure.*

hypophyse /ipofiz/ *nf* pituitary gland.

hyposodé, **~e** /iposode/ *adj* low-salt (*épith*).

hypotaupe /ipotop/ *nf* students' slang *first year preparatory class in mathematics and science for entrance to Grandes Écoles.*

hypotendu, **~e** /ipotɑ̃dy/ *adj* suffering from low blood pressure ou hypotension SPÉC.

hypotension /ipotɑ̃sjɔ̃/ *nf* **~ (artérielle)** low blood pressure, hypotension SPÉC.

hypoténuse /ipotenyz/ *nf* hypotenuse.

hypothécaire /ipotekɛʀ/ *adj* mortgage (*épith*); **créancier/débiteur ~** mortgagee/mortgager.

hypothèque /ipotɛk/ *nf* **1** mortgage; **2** FIG (obstacle) obstacle.

hypothéquer /ipoteke/ [14] *vtr* to mortgage; FIG to endanger [*chances*]; **~ l'avenir** FIG to mortgage one's future.

hypothèse /ipotɛz/ *nf* hypothesis; **~ de travail** working hypothesis; **se refuser à la moindre ~** to refuse to speculate; **écarter l'~ de l'accident** to rule out the possibility of an accident.

hypothétique /ipotetik/ *adj* hypothetical.

hystérie /isteʀi/ *nf* hysteria; **~ collective** mass hysteria.

hystérique /isteʀik/ **I** *adj* hysterical.
II *nmf* **1** (nerveux) PEJ bundle of nerves; **2** MÉD, PSYCH hysteric.

i, I /i/ *nm inv* i, I.
IDIOMES **mettre les points sur les i** to dot the i's and cross the t's.

ibérique /iberik/ *adj* Iberian; **la péninsule ~** the Iberian peninsula.

iceberg /ajsbɛʀg, isbɛʀg/ *nm* iceberg; **la partie visible de l'~** FIG the tip of the iceberg.

ici /isi/ *adv* **1** (dans l'espace) here; **c'est ~ que...** this is where...; **c'est ~ même que...** it was in this very place that...; **par ~ la sortie** this way out; **par ~!** **j'ai trouvé quelque chose!** over here! I've found something!; **les gens sont plutôt méfiants par ~** the people around here are a bit wary; **il y a une belle église par ~** there is a beautiful church near here; **les gens d'~** the locals; **~ Grovagnard** (au téléphone, à la radio) this is Grovagnard; **je vois ça d'~!** I can just picture it!; **vous êtes ~ chez vous!** make yourself at home!; **2** (dans le temps) **jusqu'~** (au présent) until now; (dans le passé) until then; **d'~ peu** shortly; **d'~ demain** by tomorrow; **d'~ deux jours** two days from now; **je te téléphone ce soir, d'~ là,** **tâche de te reposer** I'll phone you tonight, in the meantime try and rest; **d'~ là, on sera tous morts** by then, we'll all be dead; **d'~ à ce qu'il change d'avis, il n'y a pas loin** it won't be long before he changes his mind; **il l'aime bien, mais d'~ à ce qu'il l'épouse...** he likes her, but as for marrying her...

ici-bas /isiba/ *adv* here below.

icône /ikon/ *nf* icon.

iconographie /ikɔnɔgʀafi/ *nf* (sur un thème) iconography; (illustrations) illustrations (*pl*).

idéal, ~e, *mpl* **-aux** /ideal, o/ **I** *adj* ideal.
II *nm* ideal; **ce n'est pas l'~** it's not ideal; **dans l'~** ideally.

idéalement /idealmã/ *adv* ideally.

idée /ide/ *nf* **1** (inspiration, projet) idea (**de faire** of doing); **une ~ de cadeau** an idea for a present; **il y a de l'~ dans ce projet** there are some good ideas in the project; **avoir de l'~** to be inventive; **avoir une ~ derrière la tête** to have something in mind; **il n'a qu'une ~ en tête, apprendre à piloter** all he can think about is learning to fly; **2** (opinion) idea (**sur** about); (réflexion) thought; **j'ai ma petite ~ sur le sujet** I have my own theory about that; **avoir ~ que** to think that; **se faire une haute ~ de** to think a lot of; **se faire des ~s** to imagine things; **mettre de l'ordre dans ses ~s** (dans l'immédiat) to gather one's thoughts; (à long terme) to order one's thoughts; **avoir les ~s larges** to be broad-minded; **ça te changera les ~s** it'll take your mind off things; **changer d'~** to change one's mind; **avoir de la suite dans les ~s** (savoir ce que l'on veut) to be single-minded; (être entêté) not to be easily deterred; **faire à son ~** to do as one thinks best; **3** (esprit) **avoir dans l'~ que** to have an idea that; **avoir dans l'~ de faire** to plan to do; **il n'est venu à l'~ de personne de faire** nobody has thought of doing; **il ne leur viendrait jamais à l'~ de faire** it would never occur to them to do; **tu ne m'ôteras pas de l'~ que...** I still think that...; **il s'est mis dans l'~ de faire** he's taken it into his head to do.
■ **~ fixe** idée fixe, obsession; **c'est une ~ fixe chez lui** he's got a fixation about it; **~ force** key idea; **~ de génie** brainwave°; **~ noire** dark thought; **~ toute faite** second-hand idea.

idem /idɛm/ *adv* ditto; **tu seras puni et lui ~°** you'll be punished and so will he.

identification /idātifikasjɔ̃/ *nf* identification.

identifier /idātifje/ [2] **I** *vtr* **1** (reconnaître) to identify; **non identifié** unidentified; **2** (assimiler) to identify (**à, avec, et** with).
II s'identifier *vpr* (être comparable) to become identified (**à** with); (vouloir ressembler) to identify (**à** with).

identique /idātik/ *adj* **1** (pareil) identical (**à** to); **2** (constant) unchanged.

identiquement /idātikmã/ *adv* identically.

identité /idātite/ *nf* **1** MATH, PHILOS, PSYCH identity; **2** (état civil) identity; **~ d'emprunt** assumed identity; **(les services de) l'~ judiciaire** the French criminal records office; **3** (similarité) similarity; **~ de vues** similar views (*pl*).

idéogramme /ideɔgram/ *nm* ideogram.

idéologie /ideɔlɔʒi/ *nf* ideology.

idéologue /ideɔlɔg/ *nmf* ideologist.

idiomatique /idjɔmatik/ *adj* idiomatic.

idiome /idjom/ *nm* idiom.

idiosyncrasie /idjosɛ̃krazi/ *nf* idiosyncrasy.

idiot, ~e /idjo, ɔt/ **I** *adj* stupid.
II *nm* **1** GÉN idiot; **l'~ du village** the village idiot; **faire l'~** (sans simuler) to behave like an idiot; (en simulant) to act innocent GB, to act dumb; **2†** MÉD idiot†.

idiotie /idjɔsi/ *nf* **1** (parole) stupid thing; **2** (ânerie) rubbish *C* GB, garbage *C* US; **3** (caractère) stupidity; **4†** MÉD idiocy†.

idiotisme /idjɔtism/ *nm* LING idiom.

idoine /idwan/ *adj* suitable.

idolâtre /idolɑtʀ/ **I** *adj* idolatrous.
II *nmf* idolator.

idolâtrer /idolɑtʀe/ [1] *vtr* to idolize.

idolâtrie /idolɑtʀi/ *nf* idolatry.

idole /idɔl/ *nf* idol.

idylle /idil/ *nf* **1** (liaison) love affair; **2** (poème) idyll.

idyllique /idilik/ *adj* idyllic.

if /if/ *nm* **1** (arbre) yew; **2** (bois) yew.

IFOP /ifɔp/ *nm* (*abbr* = **Institut français d'opinion publique**) French institute for opinion polls.

ignare /iɲaʀ/ **I** *adj* ignorant.
II *nmf* ignoramus.

ignifuge /iɲifyʒ/ *adj* [*produit*] fireproofing (*épith*).

ignifuger /iɲifyʒe/ [13] *vtr* to fireproof; **un mur ignifugé** a fireproof wall.

ignoble /iɲɔbl/ *adj* **1** [*personne, procédé*] vile; **2** [*lieu*] squalid; [*nourriture, œuvre*] revolting.

ignominie /iɲomini/ *nf* **1** (état) ignominy; **traiter qn avec ~** to treat sb abominably; **2** (acte, parole) dreadful thing; **c'est une ~!** it's an outrage!

ignorance /iɲoʀɑ̃s/ *nf* ignorance; **être dans l'~** to be in the dark (**de** about).

ignorant, ~e /iɲoʀɑ̃, ɑ̃t/ **I** *adj* ignorant; **être ~ de tout** to know nothing about anything.
II *nm,f* ignoramus; **faire l'~** to feign ignorance.

ignoré, ~e /iɲoʀe/ *adj* (inconnu) unknown (**de** to); (méprisé) ignored (**de** by); **vivre ~** to live in obscurity.

ignorer /iɲoʀe/ [1] *vtr* **1** (ne pas savoir) not to know; **~ tout de qch** to know nothing of ou about sth; **ne rien ~ de qch** to know everything about sth; **2** (ne pas connaître) **il ignore le savon** HUM he's never heard of soap; **~ l'existence de** to be unaware of the

Les îles

Article ou pas article?

En anglais, les noms d'îles se comportent comme les noms de pays: seuls les noms pluriels prennent un article (pour les îles qui sont aussi des pays, ▶ 232 *).*

Chypre	= Cyprus
aimer Chypre	= to like Cyprus
la Corse	= Corsica
aimer la Corse	= to like Corsica
les Baléares	= the Balearics
aimer les Baléares	= to like the Balearics

Noter que certains noms d'îles sont pluriels en français mais singuliers en anglais, et ne prennent donc pas d'article.

les îles Fidji	= Fiji
j'aime les îles Fidji	= I like Fiji
les Samoas occidentales	= Western Samoa

En, à, aux

En, à et *aux se traduisent par* to *avec les verbes de mouvement (par ex. aller, se rendre etc.):*

aller à Chypre	= to go to Cyprus
aller à Sainte-Hélène	= to go to St Helena
aller en Corse	= to go to Corsica
aller aux Baléares	= to go to the Balearics

Avec les autres verbes (par ex. être, habiter, etc.), en, à et aux se traduisent normalement par in. *Cependant, pour les toutes petites îles, on traduira par* on.

vivre en Corse	= to live in Corsica
vivre à Chypre	= to live in Cyprus
vivre aux Baléares	= to live in the Balearics
vivre à Naxos	= to live on Naxos

Pour la traduction des expressions avec de, ▶ 157 *.*

Avec ou sans *island*

L'anglais utilise toujours les mots island *ou* islands *dans les cas où le français utilise* île *ou* îles.

l'île de Guernesey	= the island of Guernsey
les îles Baléares	= the Balearic Islands
les Baléares	= the Balearics

Noter que isle *n'est plus utilisé que dans quelques noms d'îles, comme* the Isle of Man, the Isle of Wight, the Orkney Isles, *etc.*

---

existence of; **3** (ne pas tenir compte de) to ignore [*personne, règle, recherches*]; **tu n'as qu'à l'~** just ignore him/her; **4** (ne pas éprouver) not to feel [*émotion, sentiment*]; **il ignorait la peur** he didn't know what fear was.
II s'ignorer *vpr* **vous êtes un poète qui s'ignore** you are a poet without knowing it.

iguane /igwan/ *nm* iguana.

il /il/

■ **Note** il pronom personnel masculin représentant une personne du sexe masculin ou un animal familier mâle se traduit par *he* (1); lorsqu'il représente un objet, un concept, un animal non familier, *il* se traduit par *it*; *il* peut également se traduire par *she* lorsqu'il représente un navire.
– *il* pronom personnel neutre sujet d'un verbe impersonnel se traduit généralement par *it*. On se reportera au verbe.

I *pron pers m* **1** (personne, animal familier) he; **~s** they; **Pierre a-t-~ téléphoné?** has Pierre phoned?; **2** (objet, concept, animal) it; **~s** they; **le Japon a annoncé qu'~ participerait à la réunion** Japan announced that it would be taking part in the meeting.
II *pron pers neutre* it; **~ pleut** it's raining.

île /il/ *nf* island.
■ **l'~ de Beauté** Corsica; **~ flottante** CULIN floating island.

illégal, **~e**, *mpl* **-aux** /ilegal, o/ *adj* illegal.

illégalité /ilegalite/ *nf* **1** (caractère) illegality ¢; **être dans l'~** to be in breach of the law; **entrer dans l'~** to start breaking the law; **2** (acte illégal) breach of the law.

illégitime /ileʒitim/ *adj* **1** (hors mariage) [*union, amour*] illicit; [*enfant*] illegitimate; **2** (injustifié) [*prétention, revendication*] unjustified.

illégitimité /ileʒitimite/ *nf* GÉN illegitimacy; (d'amour) illicitness.

illettré, **~e** /iletre/ *adj, nm,f* illiterate.

illettrisme /iletrism/ *nm* illiteracy.

illicite /ilisit/ *adj* [*vente, gain, amour, plaisir*] illicit; [*pratique, contrat, trafic*] unlawful.

illico○ /iliko/ *adv* straightaway, sharpish○; **~ presto** pronto○.

illimité, **~e** /ilimite/ *adj* unlimited.

illisible /ilizibl/ *adj* **1** [*écriture, mot, document*] illegible; **2** [*œuvre, auteur*] unreadable.

illogique /ilɔʒik/ *adj* illogical.

illumination /ilyminasjɔ̃/ **I** *nf* **1** (action d'éclairer) floodlighting; **2** (inspiration) GÉN flash of inspiration; RELIG spiritual enlightenment ¢.
II illuminations *nfpl* (de ville, rue, bâtiment) illuminations; (de sapin, fête) lights.

illuminé, **~e** /ilymine/ **I** *adj* **1** [*monument, site*] flood-lit; **2** [*regard, visage*] radiant; **3** [*poète, prédicateur*] inspired.
II *nm,f* GÉN visionary; PÉJ crank.

illuminer /ilymine/ [1] **I** *vtr* **1** GÉN to illuminate; (avec des projecteurs) to floodlight; **2** FIG [*sourire*] to light up [*visage*]; [*foi, passion*] to illuminate.
II s'illuminer *vpr* **1** (s'éclairer) [*ville, rue*] to light up; **2** (prendre de l'éclat) [*visage*] to light up (**de** with).

illusion /ilyzjɔ̃/ *nf* **1** (croyance) illusions (*pl*) (**sur** about); **ne pas se faire d'~s** to have no illusions; **je ne me fais guère ou pas trop d'~s** I don't hold out much hope; **se faire des ~s** to delude oneself (**sur** about); **il se donne l'~ de dominer la situation** he likes to think that he's in control of the situation; **entretenir qn dans l'~ que...** to let sb labour under the illusion that...; **2** (apparence trompeuse) illusion; **il ne fait pas ~** he doesn't fool anyone.
■ **~ d'optique** optical illusion.

illusionner: s'illusionner /ilyzjɔne/ [1] *vpr* to delude oneself (**sur qch/qn** about sth/sb).

illusionnisme /ilyzjɔnism/ *nm* **1** (art du prestidigitateur) conjuring; **2** ART, POL (effet) illusionism.

illusionniste /ilyzjɔnist/ *nmf* ▶ 374 (prestidigitateur) conjuror, illusionist.

illusoire /ilyzwar/ *adj* illusory; **il serait ~ de croire que...** it would be an illusion to believe that...

illustrateur, -trice /ilystratœr, tris/ ▶ 374 *nm,f* illustrator.

illustration /ilystrasjɔ̃/ *nf* illustration.

illustre /ilystr/ *adj* illustrious; **un ~ inconnu** a perfect nobody.

illustré /ilystre/ *nm* (journal) comic.

illustrer /ilystre/ [1] **I** *vtr* to illustrate (**de** with).
II s'illustrer *vpr* [*personne*] to distinguish oneself.

îlot /ilo/ *nm* **1** (petite île) islet; **2** (espace réduit) **~s de végétation** isolated patches of vegetation; **~ de paix** haven of peace; **3** (habitations) block.
■ **~ directionnel** traffic island.

ilote /ilɔt/ *nmf* Helot.

îlotier /ilotje/ *nm* ADMIN community policeman.

ils ▶ **il**.

image /imaʒ/ *nf* **1** (reproduction) picture; **2** (sur une pellicule) frame; (qualité de réglage) picture; (qualité artistique) photography; **3** (reflet) reflection, image; PHYS image; **4** (représentation) picture; **à l'~ de ses prédécesseurs...** just like his/her predecessors...; **5** LITTÉRAT image.
■ **~ d'Épinal** LIT *simplistic print of traditional French life*; FIG clichéd image; **~ de marque** (de produit) brand image; (de société) corporate image; (de politicien, personnalité) (public) image.

imagé, **~e** /imaʒe/ *adj* [*langage, style*] colourful[GB].

imagerie /imaʒʀi/ nf **1** (thématique) imagery; **2** (scientifique) imaging; **~ médicale** medical imaging.

imaginable /imaʒinabl/ adj conceivable, imaginable.

imaginaire /imaʒinɛʀ/ **I** adj GÉN, MATH imaginary.
II nm imagination; **l'~ d'un auteur** the imaginative world of an author.

imaginatif, -ive /imaʒinatif, iv/ adj imaginative.

imagination /imaʒinasjɔ̃/ nf imagination; **un enfant plein d'~** a very imaginative child; **des chiffres qui dépassent** or **défient l'~** mind-boggling° figures.

imaginer /imaʒine/ [1] **I** vtr **1** (se représenter) to imagine, to picture [personne, chose, scène]; **je l'imaginais plus grand** I imagined him to be taller; **imagine sa tête quand...** just picture his/her face when...; **2** (supposer) to suppose; **3** (inventer) to devise, to think up [méthode, moyen]; **que vas-tu ~?** how can you think such a thing?
II s'imaginer vpr **1** (se représenter) to imagine, to picture [chose, personne]; **2** (se voir) to picture oneself; **3** (croire) to think (**que** that).

imbattable /ɛ̃batabl/ adj unbeatable.

imbécile /ɛ̃besil/ **I** adj idiotic.
II nmf fool; **passer pour un ~** to look a fool; **faire l'~** to play the fool; **jouer les ~s** to play dumb; **un ~ heureux** a happy idiot.

imbécillité /ɛ̃besilite/ nf stupidity; **avoir l'~ de faire** to be stupid enough to do; **quelle ~!** (acte) what a stupid thing to do!; (œuvre) what rubbish! GB, what garbage! US; (propos) what nonsense!

imberbe /ɛ̃bɛʀb/ adj beardless.

imbiber /ɛ̃bibe/ [1] **I** vtr to soak (**de** in).
II s'imbiber vpr to become soaked (**de** with).

imbrication /ɛ̃bʀikasjɔ̃/ nf **1** (d'objets) interlocking ⊄; (de tuiles) overlapping ⊄; **2** ORDINAT interleaving.

imbriquer /ɛ̃bʀike/ [1] **I** vtr **1** (faire se chevaucher) to overlap; **tuiles imbriquées** overlapping tiles; **2** (faire s'enchevêtrer) to interlock; **3** ORDINAT to interleave.
II s'imbriquer vpr [tuiles, écailles] to overlap; [chapitres] to be interwoven; [questions] to be interlinked; [pièces] to interlock.

imbroglio /ɛ̃bʀɔ(g)lijo/ nm imbroglio.

imbu, ~e /ɛ̃by/ adj **~ de sa personne** full of oneself.

imbuvable /ɛ̃byvabl/ adj **1** [liquide] undrinkable; **2°** [personne, discours, spectacle] unbearable.

imitable /imitabl/ adj **facilement ~** easy to imitate (jamais épith).

imitateur, -trice /imitatœʀ, tʀis/ nmf **1** ▶374| (comédien) impressionist; **2** ART imitator.

imitation /imitasjɔ̃/ nf **1** GÉN imitation; (de personne) impression; **faire un numéro d'~** to do impressions; **2** COMM imitation; **sac ~ crocodile** imitation crocodile handbag.

imiter /imite/ [1] vtr **1** (copier) to imitate [geste, cri, maître]; to forge [signature]; **un revêtement de sol qui imite le bois** an imitation parquet flooring; **2** THÉÂT to do an impression of [personne]; **3** (faire pareil) **il part, je vais l'~** he's leaving and I'm going to do the same.

immaculé, ~e /imakyle/ adj immaculate.

immanent, ~e /imanɑ̃, ɑ̃t/ adj immanent.

immangeable /ɛ̃mɑ̃ʒabl/ adj inedible.

immanquable /ɛ̃mɑ̃kabl/ adj [panneau, cible] impossible to miss (jamais épith); [succès] guaranteed.

immanquablement /ɛ̃mɑ̃kabləmɑ̃/ adv inevitably.

immatériel, -ielle /imateʀjɛl/ adj immaterial; **biens ~s** JUR intangible assets.

immatriculation /imatʀikylasjɔ̃/ nf GÉN, ADMIN registration; **d'~** [numéro] registration (épith) GB, license (épith) US.

immatriculer /imatʀikyle/ [1] vtr GÉN, ADMIN to register [personne, société]; to register GB ou license US [véhicule]; **se faire ~ au consulat** to register with the consulate; **faire ~ un véhicule** to have a vehicle registered GB ou licensed US.

immédiat, ~e /imedja, at/ **I** adj immediate.
II nm **l'~** the present; **dans l'~** for the time being.

immédiatement /imedjatmɑ̃/ adv immediately.

immense /imɑ̃s/ adj GÉN huge; [douleur, regret] immense; [joie, courage] great; **l'~ majorité des gens** the vast majority of people.

immensément /imɑ̃semɑ̃/ adv immensely.

immensité /imɑ̃site/ nf (de lieu) immensity; (de connaissances) breadth.

immergé, ~e /imɛʀʒe/ adj [corps, objet] submerged; [terres, récifs] sunken.

immerger /imɛʀʒe/ [13] **I** vtr to immerse [objet]; to bury [sth] at sea [cadavre]; to dump [sth] in the sea [déchets].
II s'immerger vpr **1** LIT [sous-marin] to dive; **2** FIG [personne] to immerse oneself (**dans** in).

immérité, ~e /imerite/ adj undeserved.

immersion /imɛʀsjɔ̃/ nf **1** (de corps, d'objet) immersion; (de cadavre) burial at sea; (de déchets) dumping; **2** GÉOG (de terres) flooding; **3** SCOL immersion (**dans** in).

immettable° /ɛ̃metabl/ adj [vêtement] unwearable.

immeuble /imœbl/ nm **1** (bâtiment) building; **2** JUR real asset.
■ **~ de bureaux** office block GB, office building; **~ d'habitation** residential block GB, apartment building US; **~ de rapport** rented property GB, rental building US.

immigrant, ~e /imigʀɑ̃, ɑ̃t/ adj, nm,f immigrant.

immigration /imigʀasjɔ̃/ nf immigration.

immigré, ~e /imigʀe/ adj, nm,f immigrant.

immigrer /imigʀe/ [1] vi to immigrate.

imminent, ~e /iminɑ̃, ɑ̃t/ adj imminent.

immiscer: s'immiscer /imise/ [12] vpr to interfere (**dans** in).

immobile /imɔbil/ adj GÉN motionless; [véhicule] stationary; [regard] fixed.

immobilier, -ière /imɔbilje, ɛʀ/ **I** adj property (épith) GB, real-estate (épith) US.
II nm **~** property GB, real estate US.

immobilisation /imɔbilizasjɔ̃/ nf **1** LIT (action) immobilization; (résultat) immobility; **2** FIN (de capital) tying up.

immobiliser /imɔbilize/ [1] **I** vtr **1** (arrêter) to bring [sth] to a standstill [véhicule]; to stop [machine, cheval]; to immobilize [armée]; **2** (maintenir immobile) to immobilize [personne, membre]; **3** (paralyser) to bring [sth] to a halt [économie, pays]; **4** FIN to tie up [capitaux].
II s'immobiliser vpr (volontairement) to stop; (involontairement) to come to a halt.

immobilisme /imɔbilism/ nm opposition to change.

immobilité /imɔbilite/ nf (de personne, d'animal) immobility; (d'eau, air, de paysage, feuillage) stillness.

immodéré, ~e /imɔdere/ adj [besoin, goût, amour, dépenses] excessive; [propos, attitude] immoderate; **faire un usage ~ de l'alcool** to abuse alcohol.

immolation /imɔlasjɔ̃/ nf immolation.

immoler /imɔle/ [1] vtr to sacrifice (**à** to).

immonde /imɔ̃d/ adj **1** (sale) filthy; **2** (révoltant) revolting.

immondices /imɔ̃dis/ nfpl refuse ⊄ GB, trash ⊄ US.

immoral, ~e, mpl **-aux** /imɔʀal, o/ adj immoral.

immortaliser /imɔʀtalize/ [1] **I** vtr to immortalize.
II s'immortaliser vpr to achieve immortality.

immortalité /imɔʀtalite/ nf immortality.

immortel, -elle[1] /imɔʀtɛl/ adj immortal.

immortelle[2] /imɔʀtɛl/ nf BOT everlasting (flower).

immotivé, ~e /imɔtive/ adj [colère, action] unmotivated; [réclamation, crainte] groundless.

immuable /imɥabl/ adj [loi, cycle, geste] immutable; [tradition, paysage] unchanging; [bonheur] perpetual.

immuniser /imynize/ [1] vtr **1** MÉD to immunize (**contre** against); **2** FIG **~ qn contre** to make sb immune to.

immunitaire /imynitɛʀ/ adj MÉD immune.

immunité /imynite/ nf immunity.

immunologie /imynɔlɔʒi/ nf immunology.

impact /ɛ̃pakt/ *nm* (choc, effet) impact; (trace) mark; **des ~s de balles** bullet holes.

impair, **-e** /ɛ̃pɛʀ/ I *adj* **1** MATH [*nombre, numéro*] odd; [*jour, année*] odd-numbered; **2** ANAT unpaired.
II *nm* (gaffe) indiscretion, faux pas.

imparable /ɛ̃paʀabl/ *adj* [*coup*] unstoppable; [*riposte*] unanswerable; [*argument*] irrefutable.

impardonnable /ɛ̃paʀdɔnabl/ *adj* unforgivable.

imparfait, **-e** /ɛ̃paʀfɛ, ɛt/ I *adj* **1** (défectueux) imperfect; **2** (incomplet) [*connaissance, guérison*] partial; [*travail*] unfinished; **3** LING imperfect.
II *nm* LING imperfect.

impartial, **~e**, *mpl* **-iaux** /ɛ̃paʀsjal, o/ *adj* impartial.

impartir /ɛ̃paʀtiʀ/ [3] *vtr* **~ un délai à qn** to give sb a set time; **dans les temps impartis** within the given time.

impasse /ɛ̃pas/ *nf* **1** (cul-de-sac) dead end, cul-de-sac GB; **2** (situation sans issue) deadlock; **3** SCOL, UNIV **faire une ~** to skip parts of one's revision GB ou review US; **4** JEUX finesse.

impassibilité /ɛ̃pasibilite/ *nf* impassivity.

impassible /ɛ̃pasibl/ *adj* impassive.

impatience /ɛ̃pasjɑ̃s/ *nf* impatience; **avec ~** impatiently; **mourir** or **brûler d'~ de faire** to be dying to do.

impatient, **~e**[1] /ɛ̃pasjɑ̃, ɑ̃t/ *adj* impatient.

impatiente[2] /ɛ̃pasjɑ̃t/ *nf* BOT busy lizzie.

impatienter /ɛ̃pasjɑ̃te/ [1] I *vtr* to irritate.
II **s'impatienter** *vpr* to get impatient.

impavide /ɛ̃pavid/ *adj* unperturbed.

impayable○ /ɛ̃pɛjabl/ *adj* (drôle) priceless.

impayé, **~e** /ɛ̃pɛje/ I *adj* unpaid.
II *nm* **les ~s** unpaid debts, outstanding debts.

impeccable /ɛ̃pekabl/ *adj* [*travail, style*] perfect, faultless; [*vêtement*] impeccable; [*maison*] spotless; [*rue*] spotlessly clean; [*tapis*] in perfect condition; **il est toujours ~** he's always impeccably dressed.

impeccablement /ɛ̃pekabləmɑ̃/ *adv* [*repassé, vêtu*] impeccably; [*enveloppé*] beautifully; **~ nettoyé** spotlessly clean; **travail ~ fait** perfect ou faultless job; **il parle ~ le français** he speaks perfect French.

impénétrable /ɛ̃penetʀabl/ *adj* **1** [*végétation, mystère*] impenetrable; **2** [*personne, visage*] inscrutable.
IDIOMES **les voies du Seigneur sont ~s** God moves in mysterious ways.

impénitent, **~e** /ɛ̃penitɑ̃, ɑ̃t/ *adj* **1** [*buveur, fumeur*] inveterate; [*célibataire*] confirmed; **2** RELIG impenitent SOUT, unrepentant.

impensable /ɛ̃pɑ̃sabl/ *adj* unthinkable, unimaginable.

imper○ /ɛ̃pɛʀ/ *nm* raincoat, mac○ GB.

impératif, **-ive** /ɛ̃peʀatif, iv/ I *adj* imperative.
II *nm* **1** (de situation) imperative; (de qualité) necessity; (d'emploi du temps) constraint; **2** LING imperative.

impérativement /ɛ̃peʀativmɑ̃/ *adv* **il faut ~ faire** it is imperative ou absolutely necessary to do.

impératrice /ɛ̃peʀatʀis/ *nf* empress.

imperceptible /ɛ̃pɛʀsɛptibl/ *adj* imperceptible.

imperceptiblement /ɛ̃pɛʀsɛptibləmɑ̃/ *adv* imperceptibly.

imperfection /ɛ̃pɛʀfɛksjɔ̃/ *nf* (état) imperfection; (petit défaut) flaw.

impérial, **~e**[1], *mpl* **-iaux** /ɛ̃peʀjal, o/ *adj* imperial.

impériale[2] /ɛ̃peʀjal/ *nf* **1** (de bus) upper deck; **autobus à ~** double-decker bus; **2** (barbe) imperial.

impérialisme /ɛ̃peʀjalism/ *nm* imperialism.

impérieux, **-ieuse** /ɛ̃peʀjø, øz/ *adj* **1** (autoritaire) imperious; **2** (urgent) pressing.

impérissable /ɛ̃peʀisabl/ *adj* imperishable.

imperméabiliser /ɛ̃pɛʀmeabilize/ [1] *vtr* to waterproof.

imperméable /ɛ̃pɛʀmeabl/ I *adj* **1** [*tissu, peinture*] waterproof; [*sol*] impermeable; **2** (insensible) impervious (**à** to).
II *nm* raincoat.

impersonnel, **-elle** /ɛ̃pɛʀsɔnɛl/ *adj* impersonal.

impertinence /ɛ̃pɛʀtinɑ̃s/ *nf* **1** (caractère) impertinence; **avec ~** impertinently; **2** (parole) impertinent remark.

impertinent, **~e** /ɛ̃pɛʀtinɑ̃, ɑ̃t/ I *adj* impertinent (**envers** to).
II *nm,f* impertinent person.

imperturbable /ɛ̃pɛʀtyʀbabl/ *adj* imperturbable, unruffled.

imperturbablement /ɛ̃pɛʀtyʀbabləmɑ̃/ *adv* [*continuer, écouter*] unperturbed; [*sérieux*] invariably.

impétrant, **~e** /ɛ̃petʀɑ̃, ɑ̃t/ *nm,f* **1** (de diplôme) *person receiving a qualification*; **2** (candidat) CONTROV applicant.

impétueusement /ɛ̃petɥøzmɑ̃/ *adv* impetuously.

impétueux, **-euse** /ɛ̃petɥø, øz/ *adj* [*orateur*] impassioned; [*caractère, jeunesse*] impetuous; [*vent, torrent*] raging.

impétuosité /ɛ̃petɥozite/ *nf* (de personnes) impetuousness; (de vent, torrent) fury.

impie /ɛ̃pi/ I *adj* [*paroles, actes*] impious.
II *nmf* impious person.

impiété /ɛ̃pjete/ *nf* impiousness.

impitoyable /ɛ̃pitwajabl/ *adj* [*personne, tribunal*] merciless, pitiless; [*lutte, loi*] relentless; [*sélection, châtiment*] ruthless.

implacable /ɛ̃plakabl/ *adj* [*logique, critique*] implacable; [*négociateur*] tough; [*répression, verdict*] harsh.

implacablement /ɛ̃plakabləmɑ̃/ *adv* [*progresser, continuer*] relentlessly; [*réprimer*] ruthlessly.

implantation /ɛ̃plɑ̃tasjɔ̃/ *nf* **1** (mise en place) (de secte, d'industrie) establishment; (d'entreprise) setting up; (d'équipement) installation; (de cheveux) implantation; (de personnes) settlement; **2** (entreprise) site; **3** (disposition) (de bâtiments, machines) layout; **4** MÉD implantation.

implanté, **~e** /ɛ̃plɑ̃te/ *adj* [*usine, parti, personne*] established; [*population*] settled; **préjugé solidement ~ chez** a deeply rooted prejudice; **dents bien/mal ~es** straight/crooked teeth.

implanter /ɛ̃plɑ̃te/ [1] I *vtr* **1** (établir) to establish [*usine*]; to build [*hypermarché, cinéma*]; to open [*agence, cafétéria*]; to install [*équipements*]; to introduce [*produit, système, mode*]; **2** MÉD to implant.
II **s'implanter** *vpr* [*entreprise, système*] to establish itself; [*usine*] to be built; [*personne*] to settle; [*parti, doctrine*] to gain a following; **s'~ sur un marché** to gain a foothold in a market.

implication /ɛ̃plikasjɔ̃/ *nf* **1** (participation) involvement; **2** (conséquence) implication; **3** (engagement personnel) commitment.

implicite /ɛ̃plisit/ *adj* implicit.

implicitement /ɛ̃plisitmɑ̃/ *adv* GÉN implicitly; ORDINAT by default.

impliquer /ɛ̃plike/ [1] I *vtr* **1** (mêler) to implicate [*personne*]; **2** (faire participer) to involve [*personnel*]; **3** (imposer) to involve (**de faire** doing); **4** (signifier) to mean.
II **s'impliquer** *vpr* to get involved.

implorer /ɛ̃plɔʀe/ [1] *vtr* **1** (supplier) to beseech, to implore [*personne, dieux*]; **2** (demander) to beg for [*délai, faveur*].

imploser /ɛ̃ploze/ [1] *vi* to implode.

implosion /ɛ̃plozjɔ̃/ *nf* **1** TECH implosion; **2** FIG collapse.

impoli, **~e** /ɛ̃poli/ *adj* rude, impolite.

impolitesse /ɛ̃polites/ *nf* rudeness; **avec ~** rudely; **commettre de graves ~s** to behave very rudely.

impopulaire /ɛ̃popylɛʀ/ *adj* unpopular.

impopularité /ɛ̃popylaʀite/ *nf* unpopularity.

importance /ɛ̃poʀtɑ̃s/ *nf* **1** (gravité) importance; **prendre de l'~** [*événement*] to gain in importance; **sans ~** [*détail*] unimportant; **cela est sans ~** it's not important; **d'~** [*problème*] important; **quelle ~?** what does it matter?; **2** (taille) (de réduction, société) size; (de travail, d'effort) amount; (de massacres, dégâts) extent; **prendre de l'~** [*société, ville*] to increase in size; **ville d'~ moyenne** medium-sized town; **d'une certaine ~** sizeable; **3** (influence) importance; **prendre de l'~** [*personne*] to become more important; **pour se donner de l'~** to make oneself look important.

important, ~e /ɛpɔʀtɑ̃, ɑ̃t/ I *adj* **1** (essentiel) important; **2** (considérable) [*hausse, baisse*] significant; [*nombre, effort, écart*] considerable; [*communauté, héritage*] sizeable; [*ville, société*] large; [*retard*] lengthy; [*actionnaire*] major; **3** (influent) important; **prendre un air ~** to adopt a self-important manner.

II *nm,f* **faire l'~**, **jouer les ~s** to act important○.

importateur, -trice /ɛpɔʀtatœʀ, tʀis/ I *adj* [*pays*] importing (*épith*); [*société*] import (*épith*); **pays ~s de pétrole** oil-importing countries.

II *nm,f* importer.

importation /ɛpɔʀtasjɔ̃/ *nf* **1** (introduction) importation; **d'~** [*coûts, compagnie, quotas*] import (*épith*); [*produit, article*] imported; **2** (produit) import; **~s de luxe** luxury imports.

importer /ɛpɔʀte/ [1] I *vtr* to import [*marchandise, main-d'œuvre, mode*]; to introduce [*espèce végétale*].

II *v impers* **cela importe peu** it doesn't really matter; **ce qui importe c'est que**... what matters is that...; **peu importe** or **qu'importe que**... it doesn't matter ou what does it matter if...; **'il pleut!'—'peu importe!'** 'it's raining!'—'never mind!'; **'lequel?'—'n'importe'** 'which one?'—'it doesn't matter'; **n'importe quel enfant** any child; **à n'importe quel moment** at any time; **n'importe qui** anybody, anyone; **n'importe lequel** any; **n'importe où** anywhere; **viens n'importe quand** come anytime; **prends n'importe quoi** take anything; **n'importe quoi de tranchant** any sharp object; **elle dit n'importe quoi** she talks nonsense; **c'est (du) n'importe quoi**○ it's rubbish; **c'est fait n'importe comment** it's done any old how○.

import-export /ɛpɔʀɛkspɔʀ/ *nm inv* import-export trade.

importun, ~e /ɛpɔʀtœ̃, yn/ I *adj* **1** [*personne*] (gênant) troublesome; (irritant) tiresome; (indésirable) unwelcome; **je ne voudrais pas être ~** I don't wish to intrude; **2** [*visite, intervention*] ill-timed; [*remarque*] ill-chosen; [*question*] awkward.

II *nm,f* (visiteur) unwelcome visitor; (gêneur) tiresome individual.

importuner /ɛpɔʀtyne/ [1] *vtr* **1** (ennuyer) to bother; **2** (déranger) to disturb.

imposable /ɛpozabl/ *adj* [*personne*] liable to tax (*après n*); [*revenu, bénéfice*] taxable.

imposant, ~e /ɛpozɑ̃, ɑ̃t/ *adj* [*stature, monument*] imposing; [*cérémonie, œuvre*] impressive.

imposé, ~e /ɛpoze/ *adj* **1** (fixé) [*tarif, délai*] fixed; **2** (obligatoire) [*thème, travail, figure*] set.

imposer /ɛpoze/ [1] I *vtr* **1** (rendre obligatoire) [*personne*] to impose [*sanctions, délai, personne*] (**à** on); to lay down [*règlement*]; [*situation*] to require [*mesures, changement*]; **~ le port de lunettes protectrices** to make it obligatory to wear protective goggles; **il nous a imposé sa présence** he forced his presence on us; **elle nous a imposé le silence** she made us be quiet; **2** (faire admettre) to impose [*idée, volonté*]; to set; **3** (inspirer) to command [*respect, admiration*]; **4** (soumettre à l'impôt) to tax.

II **en imposer** *vtr ind* **elle en impose par son calme** her calm is impressive; **elle en impose à ses élèves** she inspires respect in her pupils; **ne t'en laisse pas ~** don't let yourself be overawed.

III **s'imposer** *vpr* **1** (être évident) [*choix, solution*] to be obvious (**à** to); (être requis) [*prudence, mesure, changement*] to be called for; **une visite au Louvre s'impose** a visit to the Louvre is a must; **s'~ comme évident** to be obvious; **2** (s'astreindre à) to impose [sth] on oneself [*horaires, discipline*]; **s'~ un sacrifice** to force oneself to make a sacrifice; **s'~ de travailler le soir** to make it a rule to work in the evening; **3** (déranger) to impose (**à qn** on sb); **4** (se faire

admettre) **s'~ comme leader** to establish oneself as the leader; **s'~ comme langue officielle** to become established as the official language; **s'~ dans un domaine** [*personne*] to make a name for oneself in a field; **s'~ sur un marché** [*personne, goût, firme*] to establish itself in a market; **s'~ par son intelligence** to stand out because of one's intelligence; **s'~ comme le plus grand architecte contemporain** to be universally acknowledged as the greatest contemporary architect; **5** (pour dominer) [*personne*] to make one's presence felt; [*volonté*] to impose itself.

imposition /ɛpozisjɔ̃/ *nf* taxation.

impossibilité /ɛposibilite/ *nf* impossibility; **être dans l'~ de faire** to be unable to do; **mettre qn dans l'~ de faire** to make it impossible for sb to do.

impossible /ɛposibl/ I *adj* **1** GÉN impossible (**à faire** to do); **il est ~ qu'il soit déjà arrivé** he cannot possibly have arrived yet; **cela m'est ~** I really can't; **~!** out of the question!; **2**○ *l'~* [*personne, goût, heure, habitude, nom*] impossible; **rendre la vie ~ à qn** to make life impossible for sb.

II *nm* **l'~** the impossible; **faire** or **tenter l'~** to do everything one can.

IDIOMES **à l'~ nul n'est tenu** PROV nobody can be expected to do the impossible; **~ n'est pas français** there's no such word as 'can't'.

imposteur /ɛpostœʀ/ *nm* impostor.

imposture /ɛpostyʀ/ *nf* **1** (action de tromper) deception, imposture SOUT; **2** (acte de tromperie) fraud.

impôt /ɛpo/ *nm* tax; **payer ses ~** to pay one's taxes; **avant/après ~** before/after tax; **payer des ~s** to pay tax.

■ **~ additionnel** surtax; **~ foncier** property tax; **~ sur les plus-values** capital gains tax; **~ sur le revenu** income tax; **~ sur les sociétés** corporate tax, company tax; **~s locaux** local taxes.

impotence /ɛpotɑ̃s/ *nf* lack of mobility.

impotent, ~e /ɛpotɑ̃, ɑ̃t/ I *adj* infirm.

II *nm,f* person with impaired mobility.

impraticable /ɛpʀatikabl/ *adj* **1** [*chemin, route*] impassable; **2** [*projet*] unworkable, impracticable.

imprécis, ~e /ɛpʀesi, iz/ *adj* [*forme, souvenir, renseignement*] vague; [*idée*] hazy; [*résultats, statistiques*] imprecise; [*personne*] vague.

imprécision /ɛpʀesizjɔ̃/ *nf* (de connaissances) imprecision; (de données, document) vagueness; (de tir, coup) inaccuracy.

imprégnation /ɛpʀeɲasjɔ̃/ *nf* **1** (de bois, tissu) impregnation; **2** FIG **apprendre une langue par ~** to learn a language by immersing oneself in it.

imprégner /ɛpʀeɲe/ [14] I *vtr* **1** to impregnate [*tissu, bois*] (**de** with); to dye [*cuir*]; **une forte odeur de tabac imprégnait leurs vêtements** their clothes smelled strongly of tobacco; **2** FIG **une doctrine imprégnée de christianisme** a doctrine heavily influenced by Christian thinking.

II **s'imprégner** *vpr* [*étudiant*] to immerse oneself.

imprenable /ɛpʀənabl/ *adj* [*citadelle*] impregnable; **avec vue ~** with unobstructed view guaranteed.

imprésario /ɛpʀesaʀjo/ **▶ 374** *nm* agent, impresario.

impression /ɛpʀesjɔ̃/ *nf* **1** (sentiment, sensation) impression; **avoir l'~ de faire** to feel one is doing; **j'ai l'~ d'être surveillé** I feel I am being watched; **j'ai (comme○) l'~ que/d'avoir**... I've got a (funny) feeling that/I have...; **le film laisse une ~ de malaise** this film leaves one feeling uneasy; **ça m'a fait une drôle d'~ de les revoir** it was a strange feeling seeing them again; **2** (de textes, tissus) printing; **faire de l'~ sur tissu** to print on fabric; **l'ouvrage est à l'~** the book is with the printers; **3** (motif imprimé) pattern; **4** PHOT exposure.

impressionnable /ɛpʀesjɔnabl/ *adj* **1** (sensible) sensitive; (influençable) impressionable; **il est peu ~** he's not easily shocked; **2** PHOT [*papier, plaque*] sensitized.

impressionnant, ~e /ɛpʀesjɔnɑ̃, ɑ̃t/ *adj* **1** (remarquable) [*résultat, spectacle, joueur*] impressive;

[*arsenal, défi*] formidable; **~ de bêtise** amazingly stupid; **2** (troublant) disturbing.

impressionner /ɛpʀesjɔne/ [1] *vtr* **1** (faire de l'effet) [*personne, qualité, spectacle*] to impress; **se laisser facilement ~** to be easily impressed; **ne te laisse pas ~ par les examinateurs** don't be overawed by the examiners; **2** (troubler) to disturb; **3** (sensibiliser) to act on [*rétine, pellicule*].

impressionnisme /ɛpʀesjɔnism/ *nm* Impressionism.

impressionniste /ɛpʀesjɔnist/ **I** *adj* ART Impressionist; **2** LITTÉRAT, MUS impressionistic.

II *nmf* Impressionist.

imprévisible /ɛpʀevizibl/ *adj* unpredictable.

imprévoyance /ɛpʀevwajɑ̃s/ *nf* lack of foresight.

imprévoyant, **~e** /ɛpʀevwajɑ̃, ɑ̃t/ **I** *adj* improvident.

II *nm,f* improvident person.

imprévu, **~e** /ɛpʀevy/ **I** *adj* **1** (non prévu) unforeseen; **2** (non prévisible) unexpected.

II *nm* **1** (incident) hitch; **~ de dernière minute** last-minute hitch; **sauf ~** barring accidents; **2** (choses inattendues) **l'~** the unexpected; **plein d'~** [*personne, film*] quirky [*vacances, voyage*] with a few surprises (*épith, après n*); [*métier*] never dull (*jamais épith*), which is never dull (*épith, après n*); **3** (dépense exceptionnelle) unforeseen expense.

imprimante /ɛpʀimɑ̃t/ *nf* printer.

■ **~ à jet d'encre** ink-jet printer; **~ (à) laser** laser printer; **~ à marguerite** daisywheel printer; **~ matricielle** dot matrix printer.

imprimé, **~e** /ɛpʀime/ **I** *pp* ▶ **imprimer**.

II *pp adj* [*image, papier, tissu*] printed (**de** with).

III *nm* **1** (formulaire) form; **2** (papier imprimé) printed matter **¢**; **3** (tissu) print; **un ~ à fleurs** a floral print; **l'~ et l'uni** printed and plain fabrics.

imprimer /ɛpʀime/ [1] *vtr* **1** (marquer d'un motif) to print [*texte, étiquettes*]; to print a design on [*tissu*]; **2** (publier) to publish [*texte, auteur*]; **3** (reproduire) to put [*cachet*] (**sur** on); to print [*initiales*] (**sur** on); **4** (transmettre) [*personne*] to give [*style, direction, cadence*] (**à** to); to transmit [*impulsion*] (**à** to); **5** (laisser une empreinte) [*personne*] to leave an imprint of [*forme*]; **6** (graver) **être imprimé dans la mémoire de qn** to be engraved in sb's memory; **être imprimé sur le visage de qn** to be written all over sb's face.

imprimerie /ɛpʀimʀi/ *nf* **1** (technique) printing; **atelier d'~** printing shop; **2** (entreprise) printing works (+ *v sg*); **~ d'étiquettes** label-printing company; **une ~ clandestine** an underground printing press.

■ **Imprimerie nationale** government publications office.

imprimeur /ɛpʀimœʀ/ **▶ 374** *nm* **1** (directeur) printer; **~ éditeur** printer and publisher; **2** (ouvrier) (**ouvrier**) **~** print worker, printer.

improbable /ɛpʀɔbabl/ *adj* unlikely, improbable.

improductif, **-ive** /ɛpʀɔdyktif, iv/ *adj* unproductive; **capitaux ~s** idle capital (*sg*).

impromptu, **~e** /ɛpʀɔ̃pty/ *adj, adv, nm* impromptu.

imprononçable /ɛpʀɔnɔ̃sabl/ *adj* unpronounceable.

impropre /ɛpʀɔpʀ/ *adj* [*terme, tournure, usage*] incorrect; **~ à** unfit for [*consommation*].

improprement /ɛpʀɔpʀəmɑ̃/ *adv* incorrectly.

impropriété /ɛpʀɔpʀijete/ *nf* **1** (caractère impropre) incorrectness; **2** (mot impropre) incorrect usage.

improvisation /ɛpʀɔvizasjɔ̃/ *nf* improvisation; **tout laisser à l'~** to improvise all the way through.

improvisé, **~e** /ɛpʀɔvize/ *adj* (non préparé) [*discours, civière*] improvised; [*repas, rencontre*] impromptu (*épith*); [*moyens, réforme*] makeshift (*épith*); [*solution*] ad hoc; [*chauffeur, cuisinier*] stand-in (*épith*).

improviser /ɛpʀɔvize/ [1] **I** *vtr* to improvise [*civière, repas, discours*]; to concoct [*excuse, alibi*]; **~ un hôpital** to set up a makeshift hospital; **~ une rencontre** to set up an impromptu meeting.

II *vi* to improvise; **~ à l'orgue** to improvise on the organ.

III s'improviser *vpr* **1** (se faire) [*personne*] **s'~**

cuisinier/avocat to act as a cook/lawyer; **2** (se créer) **un camp pour réfugiés ne s'improvise pas** you can't create a refugee camp just like that.

improviste: **à l'improviste** /alɛpʀɔvist/ *loc adv* unexpectedly.

imprudemment /ɛpʀydamɑ̃/ *adv* [*parler, traverser*] carelessly; [*agir, annoncer*] unwisely; [*conduire*] recklessly.

imprudence /ɛpʀydɑ̃s/ *nf* **1** (témérité) carelessness; **avoir l'~ de faire** to be foolish enough to do; **être d'une grande ~** to be very careless; **2** (acte) **commettre une ~** to do something foolish; **pas d'~s surtout** make sure you don't do anything foolish.

imprudent, **~e** /ɛpʀydɑ̃, ɑ̃t/ **I** *adj* [*personne, parole*] careless; [*action, comportement*] rash.

II *nm,f* foolhardy person; **les ~s** the foolhardy.

impubère /ɛpybɛʀ/ *adj* pre-pubescent.

impudence /ɛpydɑ̃s/ *nf* (effronterie) impudence.

impudent, **~e** /ɛpydɑ̃, ɑ̃t/ *adj* impudent.

impudeur /ɛpydœʀ/ *nf* (physique) immodesty; (de sentiments) shamelessness.

impudique /ɛpydik/ *adj* [*geste, parole*] obscene; [*vêtement*] indecent; [*personne*] shameless.

impudiquement /ɛpydikmɑ̃/ *adv* shamelessly, brazenly.

impuissance /ɛpɥisɑ̃s/ *nf* **1** GÉN impotence; **~ à faire** inability to do; **réduire qn à l'~** to render sb powerless; **2** MÉD impotence.

impuissant, **~e** /ɛpɥisɑ̃, ɑ̃t/ **I** *adj* **1** GÉN powerless, helpless; [*effort*] vain; **~ à faire** powerless to do; **assister ~ à qch** to watch sth helplessly; **2** MÉD impotent.

II *nm* MÉD impotent man.

impulsif, **-ive** /ɛpylsif, iv/ *adj* impulsive.

impulsion /ɛpylsjɔ̃/ *nf* **1** (force) impetus; **donner une (nouvelle) ~ à** to give fresh impetus to; **2** (désir) impulse; **~ brusque** sudden impulse; **3** PSYCH drive; **4** (en dynamique) impulse; **5** ÉLECTROTECH, PHYS, TÉLÉCOM pulse.

impulsivité /ɛpylsivite/ *nf* impulsiveness; **avec ~** impulsively.

impunément /ɛpynemɑ̃/ *adv* with impunity; **on ne joue pas ~ avec sa santé** you don't play fast and loose with your health and get away with it.

impuni, **~e** /ɛpyni/ *adj* unpunished; **rester ~** to go unpunished.

impunité /ɛpynite/ *nf* impunity; **en toute ~** with complete impunity; **bénéficier d'une totale ~** to be granted immunity from prosecution.

impur, **~e** /ɛpyʀ/ *adj* **1** [*cœur, pensées*] impure; **2** [*eau, air*] dirty; [*sang*] tainted; **3** [*minerai*] impure; **4** RELIG unclean.

impureté /ɛpyʀte/ *nf* impurity.

imputable /ɛpytabl/ *adj* **1** [*erreur, accident, échec*] attributable (**à** to); **2** [*somme*] chargeable (**sur** to).

imputation /ɛpytasjɔ̃/ *nf* (accusation) accusation, imputation SOUT.

imputer /ɛpyte/ [1] *vtr* **1** (attribuer) to attribute, to impute SOUT; **2** (en comptabilité) to charge (**sur** to).

imputrescible /ɛpytʀesibl/ *adj* rotproof.

inabordable /inabɔʀdabl/ *adj* **1** [*sommet*] inaccessible; [*personne*] unapproachable; **2** [*prix*] prohibitive; [*produit, service*] prohibitively priced.

inacceptable /inaksɛptabl/ *adj* unacceptable.

inaccessible /inaksesibl/ *adj* [*lieu*] inaccessible; [*personne*] unapproachable; [*vérité*] unattainable; [*rêve*] impossible; **ce livre est ~ pour lui** this book is beyond him; **~ à la pitié** incapable of pity.

inaccompli, **~e** /inakɔ̃pli/ *adj* **1** GÉN [*travail*] unfinished; [*désir*] unfulfilled; **2** LING imperfective.

inaccoutumé, **~e** /inakutyme/ *adj* unusual.

inachevé, **~e** /inaʃve/ *adj* unfinished.

inachèvement /inaʃɛvmɑ̃/ *nm* incompleteness.

inactif, **-ive** /inaktif, iv/ **I** *adj* **1** GÉN [*personne,* *cerveau, journée*] idle; **2** SOCIOL [*personne*] inactive; [*population*] non-working; **3** FIN [*capital*] idle; [*marché*] slow; [*compte*] dormant; **4** [*volcan*] inactive.

II *nm,f* SOCIOL non-worker; **les ~s** the non-working population **⊄**.

inaction /inaksjɔ̃/ *nf* inactivity.

inactivité /inaktivite/ *nf* **1** (manque d'activité) inactivity; **~ forcée** enforced inactivity; **2** ADMIN, MIL inactivity; **être en ~** to be out of active service.

inadaptation /inadaptasjɔ̃/ *nf* **1** GÉN (de loi, d'équipement) inappropriateness (**à** for); **2** PSYCH, SOCIOL maladjustment (**à** to).

inadapté, ~e /inadapte/ **I** *adj* **1** PSYCH, SOCIOL [*enfant*] maladjusted; **2** (qui ne convient pas) [*moyen*] inappropriate (**à** for); [*outil*] unsuitable (**à** for); [*système, loi*] ill-adapted (**à** to); **3** (mal préparé) [*personne*] ill-equipped (**à** for).

II *nm,f* maladjusted person.

inadéquat, ~e /inadekwa, at/ *adj* [*système, moyen, réponse*] inadequate; [*structure, bâtiment*] unsuitable.

inadéquation /inadekwasjɔ̃/ *nf* (inadaptation) unsuitability; (décalage) disparity, discrepancy.

inadmissible /inadmisibl/ *adj* **1** (intolérable) [*comportement, erreur, situation*] intolerable; (inacceptable) [*proposition*] unacceptable; **3** JUR [*preuve*] inadmissible.

inadvertance: par inadvertance /paʁinadvɛʁtɑ̃s/ *loc adv* inadvertently.

inaliénable /inaljenabl/ *adj* JUR inalienable.

inaltérabilité /inalteʁabilite/ *nf* **1** (résistance) (de matière, substance) unalterability; (de couleur) fastness; **2** (permanence) permanence, immutability.

inaltérable /inalteʁabl/ *adj* **1** (résistant) [*matériau*] unalterable, non-corroding; [*couleur*] fade-resistant; **~ à** resistant to the effects of; **2** (immuable) [*ciel*] unchanging; [*caractère*] constant; [*principe*] immutable; [*espoir, règle*] steadfast; [*sentiment, humour*] unfailing.

inamical, ~e, *mpl* **-aux** /inamikal, o/ *adj* unfriendly.

inamovible /inamɔvibl/ *adj* **1** [*fonctionnaire, magistrat*] irremovable; [*poste, charge*] for life (*après n*); **être ~** HUM [*personne*] to be a permanent fixture; **2** [*panneau, élément*] fixed; **3** [*règle*] immutable.

inanimé, ~e /inanime/ *adj* [*matière*] inanimate; [*personne*] (inconscient) unconscious; (sans vie) lifeless.

inanité /inanite/ *nf* **1** (vanité) inanity; **2** (inutilité) futility, pointlessness.

inanition /inanisjɔ̃/ *nf* starvation.

inaperçu, ~e /inapɛʁsy/ *adj* **passer ~** to go unnoticed.

inapplicable /inaplikabl/ *adj* [*théorie, réforme*] unworkable; [*clause, traité*] unenforceable.

inapplication /inaplikasjɔ̃/ *nf* (de loi, réglementation) **~ de** failure to enforce GB, nonenforcement of US.

inappliqué, ~e /inaplike/ *adj* **1** [*élève*] lacking application (*après n*); **2** [*loi, réglementation*] unenforced.

inappréciable /inapʁesjabl/ *adj* (exceptionnel) [*service, soutien*] invaluable; [*avantage*] inestimable.

inapte /inapt/ *adj* **1** GÉN unfit (**à** for; **à faire** to do); **2** MIL **~ (au service militaire)** unfit (for military service).

inaptitude /inaptityd/ *nf* unfitness.

inarticulé, ~e /inaʁtikyle/ *adj* inarticulate.

inassouvi, ~e /inasuvi/ *adj* [*appétit*] insatiable; [*soif*] unquenchable (*épith*); [*personne, corps*] unsatisfied; [*ambition, âme*] unfulfilled; [*haine*] enduring.

inattaquable /inatakabl/ *adj* **1** MIL unassailable; **2** [*personne, conduite, réputation*] irreproachable; **3** [*argumentation, jugement*] irrefutable; [*droit*] unchallengeable; [*honnêteté*] indisputable; **4** [*matériau, substance*] (par la rouille) rust-proof; (par les vers) woodworm-proof; (par le temps) weatherproof.

inattendu, ~e /inatɑ̃dy/ **I** *adj* unexpected.

II *nm* **l'~** (ce qui est imprévu) the unexpected; (caractère imprévisible) the unexpectedness.

inattentif, -ive /inatɑ̃tif, iv/ *adj* **1** (distrait) [*enfant*]

inattentive; [*air*] distracted; **2** (indifférent) [*personne*] heedless (**à** of).

inattention /inatɑ̃sjɔ̃/ *nf* inattention; **moment d'~ (de qn)** lapse of concentration (on the part of sb); **faute d'~** careless mistake.

inaudible /inodibl/ *adj* inaudible.

inaugural, ~e, *mpl* **-aux** /inogyʁal, o/ *adj* **1** (d'ouverture) [*cérémonie*] inauguration (*épith*); [*discours, séance*] inaugural; **2** (tout premier) [*vol, voyage*] maiden.

inauguration /inogyʁasjɔ̃/ *nf* (statue) unveiling; (de route, bâtiment) inauguration; (de congrès) opening; (de politique) launching; **discours d'~** inaugural speech.

inaugurer /inogyʁe/ [1] *vtr* **1** (par une cérémonie) to unveil [*statue, plaque*]; to open [*autoroute, musée, école*]; **2** (ouvrir) to open [*congrès, débat, exposition*]; to inaugurate [*série d'articles*]; to launch [*politique*]; **3** (marquer le début) [*événement, politique*] to mark the start of [*période*]; **4**° to christen° [*vêtement, voiture*].

inavouable /inavwabl/ *adj* shameful.

inavoué, ~e /inavwe/ *adj* [*vice*] unconfessed; [*but*] undisclosed; [*peur*] hidden; [*amour*] undeclared.

incalculable /ɛ̃kalkylabl/ *adj* **1** (impossible à compter) innumerable; **2** (considérable) incalculable.

incandescence /ɛ̃kɑ̃desɑ̃s/ *nf* incandescence; **porter qch à ~** to heat sth until it's red hot.

incandescent, ~e /ɛ̃kɑ̃desɑ̃, ɑ̃t/ *adj* [*filament*] incandescent; [*métal*] white-hot; [*braises, lave*] glowing.

incapable /ɛ̃kapabl/ **I** *adj* **1** (par nature) incapable (**de faire** of doing); (temporairement) unable (**de faire** to do); **2** (incompétent) incompetent.

II *nmf* incompetent; **c'est un ~!** he's useless!

incapacité /ɛ̃kapasite/ *nf* **1** (impossibilité) inability (**à faire** to do); **être dans l'~ de faire** to be unable to do; **2** (incompétence) incompetence (**en matière de** as regards); **3** (invalidité) disability; **4** JUR incapacity; **~ de travail** unfitness for work; **~s électorales** *cases leading to disenfranchisement*.

incarcération /ɛ̃kaʁseʁasjɔ̃/ *nf* imprisonment.

incarcérer /ɛ̃kaʁseʁe/ [14] *vtr* to imprison, to jail.

incarnat, ~e /ɛ̃kaʁna, at/ **▶ 141** **I** *adj* incarnadine.

II *nm* incarnadine.

incarnation /ɛ̃kaʁnasjɔ̃/ *nf* incarnation; **être l'~ du mal** to be evil personified.

incarné, ~e /ɛ̃kaʁne/ *adj* **1** (personnifié) incarnate (*après n*); **c'est la bêtise ~e** he/she is stupidity itself; **2** RELIG incarnate (*après n*); **3** [*ongle*] ingrowing.

incarner /ɛ̃kaʁne/ [1] **I** *vtr* **1** to embody [*tendance, espoir*]; **2** to play, to portray [*personnage*].

II s'incarner *vpr* **1** (être représenté) to be embodied (**dans** in); **2** RELIG to become incarnate (**dans** in).

incartade /ɛ̃kaʁtad/ *nf* **1** (écart de conduite) misdemeanour^GB; **2** (de cheval) shy; **faire une ~** to shy.

incassable /ɛ̃kasabl/ *adj* unbreakable.

incendiaire /ɛ̃sɑ̃djɛʁ/ **I** *adj* **1** [*matière, bombe*] incendiary; **2** [*déclaration*] inflammatory.

II *nmf* arsonist.

incendie /ɛ̃sɑ̃di/ *nm* fire; **lutte contre l'~** firefighting.

■ **~ criminel** arson.

incendié, ~e /ɛ̃sɑ̃dje/ **I** *adj* [*bâtiment*] burned-out; [*forêt*] burned.

II *nm,f* person affected by the fire.

incendier /ɛ̃sɑ̃dje/ [2] *vtr* **1** (brûler) to burn down, to torch [*bâtiment*]; to burn, to torch [*véhicule, ville, forêt, récolte*]; **2**° (réprimander) to give [sb] a talking-to; **se faire ~** to be hauled over the coals; **~ qn du regard** to glower at sb.

incertain, ~e /ɛ̃sɛʁtɛ̃, ɛn/ *adj* **1** (indéterminé) [*date, durée, origine*] uncertain; [*effet*] unknown; [*contours*] blurred; [*couleur*] indeterminate; [*sourire, sentiment*] vague; **2** (aléatoire) [*résultat, entreprise, profit*] uncertain; [*temps*] unsettled; **3** (hésitant) [*personne*] uncertain; [*électeur*] undecided; [*pas, voix*] hesitant.

incertitude /ɛ̃sɛʁtityd/ *nf* uncertainty; **vivre dans l'~** to live in a state of uncertainty; **vivre dans l'~**

du lendemain to live from day to day; **être dans l'~ sur ce que l'on doit faire** not to be sure what to do.

incessamment /ɛsesamɑ̃/ *adv* very shortly; **sous peu**○ HUM in next to no time.

incessant, ~e /ɛsesɑ̃, ɑ̃t/ *adj* [*bruit, pluie, appels, querelles*] incessant; [*effort, activité*] unceasing; [*critiques*] unremitting; [*changements*] constant.

inceste /ɛsɛst/ *nm* incest; **commettre un ~** to commit incest.

incestueux, -euse /ɛsɛstɥø, øz/ *adj* **1** (coupable ou entaché d'inceste) incestuous; **2** (né d'un inceste) born of an incestuous liaison.

inchangé, ~e /ɛʃɑ̃ʒe/ *adj* unchanged.

incidemment /ɛsidamɑ̃/ *adv* **1** (au passage) in passing; **2** (par hasard) by chance.

incidence /ɛsidɑ̃s/ *nf* **1** (effet) impact; **2** MÉD, PHYS incidence.

incident, ~e[1] /ɛsidɑ̃, ɑ̃t/ **I** *adj* **1** (peu important) incidental; **2** LING [*proposition*] parenthetical; **3** PHYS [*lumière*] incident.
II *nm* **1** (événement fortuit) incident; **en cas d'~** if anything should happen; **2** (perturbation) **~ (de parcours)** hitch; **~ de séance** procedural hitch; **l'~ est clos** the matter is closed.

incidente[2] /ɛsidɑ̃t/ *nf* LING **1** (parenthèse) parenthetical clause; **2** (dans un discours rapporté) comment clause.

incinérateur /ɛsineʀatœʀ/ *nm* **1** (pour déchets) incinerator; **2** (crématoire) crematorium GB, crematory US.

incinération /ɛsineʀasjɔ̃/ *nf* (de déchets) incineration; (de corps) cremation.

incinérer /ɛsineʀe/ [14] *vtr* to burn [*bois*]; to incinerate [*déchets*]; to cremate [*corps*]; **choisir de se faire ~** to choose to be cremated.

incise /ɛsiz/ *nf* **1** MUS phrase; **2** LING (parenthèse) parenthetical clause; (dans un discours) comment clause.

inciser /ɛsize/ [1] *vtr* to make an incision in [*bois, peau*]; to lance [*abcès*].

incisif, -ive[1] /ɛsizif, iv/ *adj* [*critique*] incisive; [*portrait*] telling; [*regard*] piercing; [*instrument*] sharp.

incision /ɛsizjɔ̃/ *nf* (de peau, d'écorce) incision; (d'abcès) lancing ℂ.

incisive[2] /ɛsiziv/ *nf* (dent) incisor.

incitatif, -ive /ɛsitatif, iv/ *adj* incentive (*épith*).

incitation /ɛsitasjɔ̃/ *nf* **1** (encouragement) incentive (à to); **2** JUR incitement (à to).

inciter /ɛsite/ [1] *vtr* [*personne, situation, attitude*] to encourage; [*événement, décision*] to prompt; **~ qn à la prudence** to make sb cautious; **~ vivement** to urge; **~ à la haine raciale** to stir up racial hatred.

inclassable /ɛklasabl/ *adj* unclassifiable.

inclinable /ɛklinabl/ *adj* [*dossier*] adjustable; **fauteuil (à dossier) ~** reclining chair GB, recliner US.

inclinaison /ɛklinɛzɔ̃/ *nf* **1** (de route, pente) incline; (de mur, siège) angle; (de toit) slope; (de bateau) list; **2** MATH angle.

inclination /ɛklinasjɔ̃/ *nf* **1** (disposition naturelle) inclination (**à faire** to do); **2** (de la tête) nod; (du buste) bow; **3** (amour) LITER inclination.

incliné, ~e /ɛkline/ *adj* **1** (non horizontal) [*plateau, fonds marins*] sloping; [*toit*] steep; **le plancher est ~** the floor slopes; **2** (non vertical) [*mur, tour*] leaning; **tenir qch ~** to hold sth at an angle.

incliner /ɛkline/ [1] **I** *vtr* **1** (pencher) to tilt [*parasol*]; to tip up [*flacon*]; **~ le buste** to lean forward; **2** (inciter) FML **cela m'incline à penser que** this leads me to think that.
II *vi* FML to be inclined (**à faire** to do).
III s'incliner *vpr* **1** (se pencher en avant) to lean forward; (par politesse) to bow; **2** (ne pas contester) **s'~ devant qch** to bow to sth, to accept sth; **s'~ devant les faits** to accept the facts; **3** (s'avouer vaincu) to give in○ (**devant** to); **Pau s'incline devant Dax** SPORT Pau lost to Dax; **4** (témoigner du respect) **s'~ devant le courage de qn** to admire sb's courage; **5** (se pencher sur le côté) [*moto*] to lean over.

inclure /ɛklyʀ/ [78] *vtr* **1** (intégrer) to include [*nom,*

personne]; **2** (contenir) [*liste, prix*] to include; **3** (joindre) to enclose [*document, argent*]; **4** (ajouter) to insert [*correction, clause*]; **5** MATH to include.

inclus, ~e /ɛkly, yz/ **I** *pp* ▶ **inclure**.
II *pp adj* **1** (compris) **il y avait 20 personnes, enfants ~** there were 20 people, including children; **jusqu'au second chapitre ~** up to and including chapter two; **jusqu'à jeudi ~** up to and including Thursday GB, through Thursday US; **les taxes sont ~es dans le prix** taxes are included in the price; **2** (joint) enclosed; **3** MATH **B est ~ dans A** B is a subset of A.

inclusion /ɛklyzjɔ̃/ *nf* inclusion.

inclusivement /ɛklyzivmɑ̃/ *adv* **jusqu'au 4 mai ~** till 4 May inclusive.

incognito /ɛkɔnito/ **I** *adv* incognito.
II *nm* **garder l'~** to remain incognito.

incohérence /ɛkɔeʀɑ̃s/ *nf* **1** (manque de logique) incoherence ℂ; **avec ~** incoherently; **2** (contradiction) discrepancy.

incohérent, ~e /ɛkɔeʀɑ̃, ɑ̃t/ *adj* [*propos, comportement, personne*] incoherent; [*attitude, raisonnement*] illogical; **il se montre plutôt ~ dans ses décisions** he tends to be inconsistent in his decisions.

incollable /ɛkɔlabl/ *adj* **1**○ (qui a réponse à tout) [*personne*] impossible to catch out (*jamais épith*); **elle est ~ en latin** you can't catch her out in Latin; **2** CULIN **riz ~** easy-cook rice.

incolore /ɛkɔlɔʀ/ *adj* **1** (sans couleur) [*liquide, gaz, gel*] colourlessGB; [*vernis, verre*] clear; **2** (sans originalité) colourlessGB.

incomber /ɛkɔ̃be/ [1] **I** *vtr ind* **~ à** [*devoir, tâche, mission, dépense*] to fall to; [*responsabilité, faute*] to lie with; **la faute en incombe à...** the fault lies with...
II *v impers* **il incombe à qn de faire** it is incumbent upon sb to do SOUT; JUR it rests with sb to do.

incommensurable /ɛkɔmɑ̃syʀabl/ *adj* **1** (immense) boundless; **2** MATH incommensurable.

incommode /ɛkɔmɔd/ *adj* **1** (peu pratique) [*équipement*] inconvenient; [*installation*] awkward; [*horaire*] unsatisfactory; **2** (inconfortable) uncomfortable.

incommodé, ~e /ɛkɔmɔde/ *adj* unwell, indisposed SOUT.

incommoder /ɛkɔmɔde/ [1] *vtr* to bother.

incomparable /ɛkɔ̃paʀabl/ *adj* [*site, mérite, artiste*] incomparable; **d'un charme ~** extremely charming.

incompatibilité /ɛkɔ̃patibilite/ *nf* incompatibility (**de qch et qch** of sth with sth); **il y a ~ entre leur politique et la nôtre** our policies are incompatible.

incompatible /ɛkɔ̃patibl/ *adj* incompatible.

incompétence /ɛkɔ̃petɑ̃s/ *nf* GÉN incompetence; JUR incompetency.

incompétent, ~e /ɛkɔ̃petɑ̃, ɑ̃t/ *adj* incompetent.

incomplet, -ète /ɛkɔ̃plɛ, ɛt/ *adj* incomplete.

incompréhensible /ɛkɔ̃pʀeɑ̃sibl/ *adj* incomprehensible (**à, pour** to).

incompréhension /ɛkɔ̃pʀeɑ̃sjɔ̃/ *nf* (intellectuelle) incomprehension; (affective) lack of understanding.

incompressible /ɛkɔ̃pʀɛsibl/ *adj* **1** PHYS [*matière*] incompressible; **2** ÉCON [*dépenses, charges*] fixed; **3** JUR **peine ~** sentence without possibility of remittance.

incompris, ~e /ɛkɔ̃pʀi, iz/ **I** *adj* **un artiste ~** an artist whose work is not understood.
II *nm,f* misunderstood person.

inconcevable /ɛkɔ̃svabl/ *adj* inconceivable.

inconditionnel, -elle /ɛkɔ̃disjɔnɛl/ **I** *adj* [*reddition*] unconditional; [*appui*] unqualified; [*obéissance*] absolute; [*adhésion*] wholehearted; [*amateur*] dedicated.
II *nm,f* (fanatique) fan; **je suis un ~ de Mozart** I'm absolutely mad○ about Mozart.

inconduite /ɛkɔ̃dɥit/ *nf* GÉN misbehaviourGB; JUR misconduct.

inconfort /ɛkɔ̃fɔʀ/ *nm* lack of comfort.

inconfortable /ɛkɔ̃fɔʀtabl/ *adj* **1** (sans confort) uncomfortable; **2** (désagréable) awkward.

incongru, ~e /ɛkɔ̃gʀy/ *adj* [*comportement*] unseemly; [*remarque*] incongruous, unseemly.

incongruité /ɛ̃kɔ̃gʀɥite/ *nf* **1** (étrangeté) incongruity; **2** (acte) faux-pas; (parole) incongruous remark.

inconnu, **~e**[1] /ɛ̃kɔny/ **I** *adj* GÉN unknown (**de** to); [*territoires*] unexplored; **~ à cette adresse** not known at this address; **votre visage ne m'est pas ~** your face is familiar.
II *nm,f* **1** (personne non célèbre) unknown (person); **2** (étranger) stranger; **il s'est épris d'une ~e** he fell in love with a complete stranger.
III *nm* **l'~** the unknown.

inconnue[2] /ɛ̃kɔny/ *nf* GÉN, MATH unknown.

inconsciemment /ɛ̃kɔ̃sjamɑ̃/ *adv* (sans le savoir) subconsciously; (sans le vouloir) unintentionally, unconsciously.

inconscience /ɛ̃kɔ̃sjɑ̃s/ *nf* **1** (absence de jugement) recklessness; **c'est de l'~!** it's sheer madness!; **2** MÉD unconsciousness.

inconscient, **~e** /ɛ̃kɔ̃sjɑ̃, ɑ̃t/ **I** *adj* **1** (sans jugement) unthinking; (devant un danger) foolhardy; **être ~ de** to be unaware of; **il faut être ~ pour rouler à cette vitesse** you have to be mad○ to drive at that speed; **2** MÉD (sans connaissance) unconscious; **3** PSYCH [*acte, geste*] unconscious, automatic; [*sentiment*] subconscious; [*réaction*] unconscious.
II *nm,f* **c'est un ~** he's totally irresponsible.
III *nm* PSYCH **l'~** the unconscious.

inconséquence /ɛ̃kɔ̃sekɑ̃s/ *nf* (de raisonnement) inconsistency; (de conduite) fecklessness.

inconséquent, **~e** /ɛ̃kɔ̃sekɑ̃, ɑ̃t/ *adj* inconsistent.

inconsidéré, **~e** /ɛ̃kɔ̃sideʀe/ *adj* **1** (irréfléchi) [*propos, geste, action*] ill-considered; [*prêt*] ill-advised; **2** (excessif) [*usage, consommation*] excessive.

inconsidérément /ɛ̃kɔ̃sideʀemɑ̃/ *adv* **1** (imprudemment) [*dire, promettre*] rashly; [*prêter*] ill-advisedly; **2** (excessivement) [*boire*] to excess; [*dépenser*] wildly.

inconsistance /ɛ̃kɔ̃sistɑ̃s/ *nf* (d'œuvre) lack of substance; (de personne) lack of character.

inconsistant, **~e** /ɛ̃kɔ̃sistɑ̃, ɑ̃t/ *adj* [*raisonnement, argumentation, scénario*] flimsy; [*programme*] lacking in substance (*épith*); [*personne*] characterless.

inconsolable /ɛ̃kɔ̃sɔlabl/ *adj* inconsolable.

inconstance /ɛ̃kɔ̃stɑ̃s/ *nf* fickleness.

inconstant, **~e** /ɛ̃kɔ̃stɑ̃, ɑ̃t/ *adj* fickle.

incontestable /ɛ̃kɔ̃tɛstabl/ *adj* unquestionable, indisputable.

incontestablement /ɛ̃kɔ̃tɛstabləmɑ̃/ *adv* unquestionably.

incontesté, **~e** /ɛ̃kɔ̃tɛste/ *adj* [*victoire, champion*] undisputed; [*droit, fait*] uncontested.

incontinence /ɛ̃kɔ̃tinɑ̃s/ *nf* MÉD incontinence.

incontournable /ɛ̃kɔ̃tuʀnabl/ *adj* [*question, problème*] that must be addressed (*épith, après n*); [*chiffres, faits*] that cannot be ignored (*épith, après n*); [*personne*] to be reckoned with (*épith, après n*); [*livre*] considered to be essential reading (*épith, après n*).

incontrôlable /ɛ̃kɔ̃tʀolabl/ *adj* **1** (invérifiable) unverifiable; **2** (que l'on ne peut maîtriser) uncontrollable.

incontrôlé, **~e** /ɛ̃kɔ̃tʀole/ *adj* **1** (non vérifié) [*information, affirmation*] unverified, unchecked; **2** (non maîtrisé) [*individus, actes, violence*] uncontrolled.

inconvenance /ɛ̃kɔ̃vnɑ̃s/ *nf* **1** (de discours, proposition) impropriety, unseemliness; **2** (acte) impropriety.

inconvenant, **~e** /ɛ̃kɔ̃vnɑ̃, ɑ̃t/ *adj* [*terme*] unsuitable; [*attitude, propos, discours*] improper, unseemly.

inconvénient /ɛ̃kɔ̃venjɑ̃/ *nm* drawback, disadvantage; **si vous n'y voyez pas d'~** if you have no objection; **je ne vois pas d'~ à ce qu'il reste dîner** I see no reason why he should not stay for dinner; **il n'y a aucun ~ à reporter la réunion** the meeting can easily be postponed.

incorporation /ɛ̃kɔʀpɔʀasjɔ̃/ *nf* MIL enlistment GB, induction US.

incorporé, **~e** /ɛ̃kɔʀpɔʀe/ *adj* [*micro, antenne, cellule*] built-in.

incorporer /ɛ̃kɔʀpɔʀe/ [1] *vtr* **1** CULIN to blend (**à** into;

dans with); **2** (faire entrer dans un ensemble) to incorporate [*chapitre*]; **3** MIL to enlist GB, to induct US [*recrue*].

incorrect, **~e** /ɛ̃kɔʀɛkt/ *adj* **1** (comportant des fautes) [*terme, langue, interprétation*] incorrect; [*montage*] faulty, incorrect; [*prévisions*] inaccurate; **2** (inconvenant) [*conduite*] improper; [*terme*] unsuitable; [*personne*] impolite; **être ~ avec qn** to be rude ou impolite to sb; **3** (déloyal) [*personne, procédé*] unfair.

incorrection /ɛ̃kɔʀɛksjɔ̃/ *nf* **1** (de style, langue) incorrectness; (de conduite, comportement) impropriety; **2** (faute) inaccuracy.

incorrigible /ɛ̃kɔʀiʒibl/ *adj* incorrigible.

incorruptible /ɛ̃kɔʀyptibl/ **I** *adj* incorruptible.
II *nmf* incorruptible person.

incrédule /ɛ̃kʀedyl/ **I** *adj* **1** (sceptique) [*personne*] incredulous; [*expression, air*] of disbelief (*après n*), incredulous; **2** (en matière religieuse) unbelieving (*épith*).
II *nmf* unbeliever, nonbeliever.

incrédulité /ɛ̃kʀedylite/ *nf* **1** GÉN incredulity; **faire preuve d'~** to be incredulous; **un sourire d'~** an incredulous smile; **2** RELIG lack of belief.

incrémenter /ɛ̃kʀemɑ̃te/ [1] *vtr* to increment.

increvable /ɛ̃kʀəvabl/ *adj* **1**○ (inépuisable) [*personne*] tireless; **2** (qui ne peut être crevé) [*pneu*] puncture-proof.

incriminer /ɛ̃kʀimine/ [1] *vtr* [*personne*] to accuse [*personne*]; [*preuve, indice*] to incriminate [*personne*]; **l'article incriminé** the offending article.

incroyable /ɛ̃kʀwajabl/ *adj* **1** (impossible ou difficile à croire) [*récit, nouvelle*] incredible, unbelievable; **~ mais vrai** strange but true; **2** (hors du commun) [*chance, courage*] incredible, amazing; [*cruauté, paresse, bêtise*] incredible; **il est d'une intelligence/ignorance ~** he's incredibly intelligent/ignorant.

incroyablement /ɛ̃kʀwajabləmɑ̃/ *adv* incredibly, unbelievably.

incroyance /ɛ̃kʀwajɑ̃s/ *nf* unbelief.

incrustation /ɛ̃kʀystasjɔ̃/ *nf* **1** ART (procédé) inlaying; (résultat) inlay; **2** (dépôt) encrustation.

incruster /ɛ̃kʀyste/ [1] **I** *vtr* **1** ART to inlay [*objet*] (**de** with); **2** (en couture) **robe incrustée de diamants** dress encrusted with diamonds.
II s'incruster *vpr* (s'agglomérer) [*caillou, coquillage*] to become embedded ou encrusted (**dans** in).

incubateur /ɛ̃kybatœʀ/ *nm* incubator.

incubation /ɛ̃kybasjɔ̃/ *nf* **1** (de maladie, d'œuf) incubation; **2** (de révolution, d'insurrection) hatching.

incuber /ɛ̃kybe/ [1] *vtr* to incubate, to hatch.

inculpation /ɛ̃kylpasjɔ̃/ *nf* JUR charge (**de, pour** of); **être sous le coup d'une ~** to be facing charges.

inculpé, **~e** /ɛ̃kylpe/ *nm,f* **~** accused; **les ~s** the accused.

inculper /ɛ̃kylpe/ [1] *vtr* to charge (**de, pour** with).

inculquer /ɛ̃kylke/ [1] *vtr* to inculcate (**à** in), to instil[GB] (**à** in).

inculte /ɛ̃kylt/ *adj* **1** [*personne*] uncultivated; **2** [*terres*] uncultivated.

incultivable /ɛ̃kyltivabl/ *adj* unworkable, unfarmable.

inculture /ɛ̃kyltyʀ/ *nf* lack of culture.

incurable /ɛ̃kyʀabl/ *adj, nmf* incurable.

incurie /ɛ̃kyʀi/ *nf* negligence, carelessness.

incursion /ɛ̃kyʀsjɔ̃/ *nf* incursion, foray.

incurver /ɛ̃kyʀve/ [1] *vtr*, **s'incurver** *vpr* to curve, to bend.

Inde /ɛ̃d/ ▶ **232** *nprf* India.

indécemment /ɛ̃desamɑ̃/ *adv* indecently.

indécence /ɛ̃desɑ̃s/ *nf* **1** (manque de décence) (de tenue, attitude) indecency; (de propos) impropriety; **ce luxe, quelle ~!** such luxury is quite obscene; **2** (acte) act of indecency; (parole) obscenity.

indécent, **~e** /ɛ̃desɑ̃, ɑ̃t/ *adj* **1** [*joie*] improper, indecent; **2** [*tenue, geste, propos, spectacle*] indecent; **3** [*chance, succès, luxe*] obscene, indecent; **avoir une chance ~e** to be disgustingly lucky.

indéchiffrable /ɛ̃deʃifʀabl/ adj **1** (indécryptable) indecipherable; **2** (énigmatique) incomprehensible.

indécis, **~e** /ɛ̃desi, iz/ I adj **1** (ponctuellement) **il est encore ~** he hasn't decided yet; **2** (de nature) [personne, caractère] indecisive; **3** (incertain) [résultats, victoire] uncertain.

II nm,f indecisive person; (électeur) floating voter.

indécision /ɛ̃desizjɔ̃/ nf **1** (hésitation) indecision, uncertainty; **2** (trait de caractère) indecisiveness.

indécrottable○ /ɛ̃dekʀɔtabl/ adj (incorrigible) hopeless○.

indéfectible /ɛ̃defɛktibl/ adj [attachement, amitié, lien] indissoluble, indefectible; [soutien] unfailing.

indéfendable /ɛ̃defɑ̃dabl/ adj indefensible.

indéfini, **~e** /ɛ̃defini/ adj **1** (sans limites) [nombre] indeterminate; **2** (vague) [tristesse, mélancolie] undefined; [malaise] vague; [durée] indeterminate, indefinite; **3** LING indefinite.

indéfiniment /ɛ̃definimɑ̃/ adv indefinitely.

indéfinissable /ɛ̃definisabl/ adj undefinable.

indélébile /ɛ̃delebil/ adj indelible.

indélicat, **~e** /ɛ̃delika, at/ adj **1** (impoli) tactless; **2** (malhonnête) dishonest.

indélicatesse /ɛ̃delikatɛs/ nf **1** (impolitesse) indelicacy, tactlessness; **2** (malhonnêteté) dishonesty; **3** (acte malhonnête) act of dishonesty.

indemne /ɛ̃dɛmn/ adj unscathed, unharmed.

indemnisation /ɛ̃dɛmnizasjɔ̃/ nf **1** (paiement) indemnification; **2** (somme versée) indemnity, compensation ¢.

indemniser /ɛ̃dɛmnize/ [1] vtr to indemnify (**de** for), to compensate (**de** for); **se faire ~** to receive compensation.

indemnité /ɛ̃dɛmnite/ nf **1** JUR (dédommagement) indemnity, compensation ¢; **verser des ~s** to pay compensation; **2** (allocation) allowance.

■ **~ de chômage** unemployment benefit; **~ de déménagement** relocation expenses (+ v pl); **~ journalière** sick pay; **~ de licenciement** severance pay ¢, redundancy payment GB; **~ parlementaire** French deputy's allowances (pl).

indémontrable /ɛ̃demɔ̃trabl/ adj undemonstrable.

indéniable /ɛ̃denjabl/ adj undeniable, unquestionable.

indentation /ɛ̃dɑ̃tasjɔ̃/ nf indentation.

indépendamment /ɛ̃depɑ̃damɑ̃/ I adv independently.

II **indépendamment de** loc prép **1** (en faisant abstraction de) regardless of; **2** (outre) in addition to.

indépendance /ɛ̃depɑ̃dɑ̃s/ nf independence; **elle tient à son ~** she likes her independence.

indépendant, **~e** /ɛ̃depɑ̃dɑ̃, ɑ̃t/ I adj **1** [personne] independent (**de** of); **2** [chambre, entrée] separate; **maison ~e** detached house.

II nm,f **1** (travailleur) self-employed person; **travailler en ~** to be self-employed; **2** (candidat) independent.

indépendantiste /ɛ̃depɑ̃dɑ̃tist/ I adj [mouvement, organisation] (pro-)independence (épith).

II nmf **1** (combattant) freedom fighter; **2** (militant) member of an independence movement.

indéracinable /ɛ̃deʀasinabl/ adj ineradicable.

Indes† /ɛ̃d/ nprfpl HIST **les ~** the Indies.

■ **~ occidentales** HIST West Indies; **~ orientales** HIST East Indies.

indescriptible /ɛ̃dɛskʀiptibl/ adj indescribable.

indésirable /ɛ̃deziʀabl/ I adj [personne] undesirable; **effets ~s** MÉD adverse reactions.

II nmf undesirable.

indestructible /ɛ̃dɛstʀyktibl/ adj indestructible.

indétermination /ɛ̃detɛʀminasjɔ̃/ nf **1** (indécision) indecision; **2** (imprécision) vagueness.

indéterminé, **~e** /ɛ̃dctɛʀmine/ adj **1** (non précisé) [forme, quantité] indeterminate; [raison, nombre] unspecified; **l'origine de l'incendie reste ~e** the cause of the fire has not yet been identified; **2** (hésitant) (de caractère) indecisive; (ponctuellement) undecided; **3** MATH indeterminate.

index /ɛ̃dɛks/ nm inv **1** (table alphabétique) index; **mettre qch/qn à l'~** to blacklist sth/sb; **2** ORDINAT index; **3** ▶137| ANAT forefinger; **4** TECH pointer.

indexation /ɛ̃dɛksasjɔ̃/ nf **1** ÉCON indexation; **2** (pour classer) indexing.

indexer /ɛ̃dɛkse/ [1] vtr **1** ÉCON to index-link [salaire, taux]; **~ qch sur qch** to index sth to sth; **2** (classer) to index; **3** ORDINAT to index.

indicateur, **-trice** /ɛ̃dikatœʀ, tʀis/ I adj **panneau** or **poteau ~** signpost.

II nm **1** (délateur) informer; **2** (indice) indicator; **~ de tendance** market indicator; **3** (brochure) (de rues) directory; (d'horaires) timetable; **4** TECH gauge, indicator; **~ de niveau d'huile** oil gauge; **~ lumineux** (warning) light; **~ de vitesse** speed indicator; **~ (de changement) de direction** AUT (direction) indicator.

indicatif, **-ive** /ɛ̃dikatif, iv/ I adj indicative.

II nm **1** LING indicative; **à l'~** in the indicative; **le futur de l'~** the future indicative; **2** TÉLÉCOM **~ (téléphonique)** dialling^GB code; **~ de pays** country code; **3** RADIO, TV (d'émission) theme tune.

indication /ɛ̃dikasjɔ̃/ nf **1** (action d'indiquer) indication; **il n'y a pas d'~ d'origine** the place of origin is not indicated; **il n'y a pas d'~ de date/lieu** no date/ place is specified; **2** (renseignement) information ¢; **sauf ~ contraire** unless otherwise indicated; **3** (instruction) instruction; **se conformer aux** or **suivre les ~s** to follow the instructions; **4** (indice) indication.

■ **~ scénique** stage direction.

indice /ɛ̃dis/ nm **1** (signe apparent) sign, indication; **2** (dans une enquête) clue; **3** ÉCON, FIN index; **4** (évaluation) **~ de popularité** popularity rating; **l'~ d'écoute** audience ratings (pl).

indicible /ɛ̃disibl/ adj inexpressible.

indien, **-ienne**¹ /ɛ̃djɛ̃, ɛn/ ▶394| adj (d'Inde, d'Amérique) Indian.

Indien /ɛ̃djɛ̃/ ▶407| adj **l'océan ~** the Indian Ocean.

indienne² /ɛ̃djɛn/ nf **1** (tissu) (printed) calico; **2** (nage) sidestroke.

indifféremment /ɛ̃difeʀamɑ̃/ adv **1** (sans distinction) equally; **2** (selon les cas) **servir ~ de salon ou de bureau** to be used either as a living room or a study.

indifférence /ɛ̃difeʀɑ̃s/ nf indifference.

indifférencié, **~e** /ɛ̃difeʀɑ̃sje/ adj **1** (indistinct) indistinct; **2** BIOL undifferentiated.

indifférent, **~e** /ɛ̃difeʀɑ̃, ɑ̃t/ adj **1** (impassible) indifferent (à to); **laisser qn ~** [œuvre, événement] to leave sb cold; **ça m'est tout à fait ~** it makes absolutely no difference to me; **2** (sans importance) [âge, sexe] irrelevant.

indifférer /ɛ̃difeʀe/ [14] vtr to leave [sb] indifferent.

indigence /ɛ̃diʒɑ̃s/ nf destitution, extreme poverty.

indigène /ɛ̃diʒɛn/ I adj **1** BOT, ZOOL [faune, flore] indigenous; **2** [population, coutume, langue] (du pays) local; (d'une colonie) native.

II nmf (natif du pays) local, native HUM; (d'une colonie) native.

indigent, **~e** /ɛ̃diʒɑ̃, ɑ̃t/ I adj destitute.

II nm,f pauper; **les ~s** the destitute, the poor.

indigeste /ɛ̃diʒɛst/ adj [aliment, roman] indigestible.

indigestion /ɛ̃diʒɛstjɔ̃/ nf **1** MÉD indigestion ¢; **2** FIG **avoir une ~ de qch** to be fed up○ with sth.

indignation /ɛ̃diɲasjɔ̃/ nf indignation (devant at).

indigne /ɛ̃diɲ/ adj **1** (méprisable) [conduite, procédé] disgraceful; [mère, fils] bad; **2** (pas digne) **~ de qn** [propos, acte] unworthy of sb; **elle est ~ de ton amitié** she is unworthy of your friendship, she doesn't deserve your friendship; **il est ~ de représenter son pays** he's unfit to represent his country.

indigné, **~e** /ɛ̃diɲe/ adj indignant (de at).

indigner /ɛ̃diɲe/ [1] I vtr to make [sb] indignant, to outrage [personne].

II **s'indigner** vpr to be indignant (de about).

indignité /ɛ̃diɲite/ nf **1** (caractère) despicableness; **2** (action) despicable act, disgraceful act.

indigo /ɛ̃digo/ ▶141| adj inv, nm indigo.

indiqué, **~e** /ɛ̃dike/ I *pp* ▶ **indiquer**.

II *pp adj* **1** (recommandé) [*traitement*] recommended; **ça n'est pas très ~** [*aliment, trajet*] it's better avoided; **le moyen tout ~ d'échouer** the sure way to fail; **2** (convenu) **à l'heure ~e** at the specified time; (signalisé) **le village est très mal/bien indiqué** the village is very badly/well signposted.

indiquer /ɛ̃dike/ [1] *vtr* **1** (montrer où se trouve) [*personne*] to point out, to point to [*objet, lieu*]; [*pancarte*] to show the way to [*ville, magasin*]; **il indiqua l'endroit du doigt** he pointed out the place; **la carte n'indique que les grandes routes** the map only shows the main roads; **pouvez-vous m'~ la banque la plus proche?** can you tell me where the nearest bank is?; **2** (être un indice de) to indicate (**que** that); **rien n'indique que les deux affaires soient liées** there is nothing to indicate *ou* suggest that the two matters are connected; **les chiffres indiquent une légère reprise** the figures show a slight recovery; **3** (conseiller) **je peux t'~ un bon médecin** I can give you the name of a good doctor; **4** (signaler, dire) **indique-moi ton heure d'arrivée** tell me what time you are arriving; **l'heure indiquée sur le programme est fausse** the time given on the programme^GB is wrong; **comme il l'indique dans son introduction...** as he says in his introduction...; **on m'a indiqué la marche à suivre** I've been told the procedure.

indirect, **~e** /ɛ̃diʀɛkt/ *adj* indirect.

indirectement /ɛ̃diʀɛktəmɑ̃/ *adv* indirectly.

indiscipline /ɛ̃disiplin/ *nf* lack of discipline.

indiscipliné, **~e** /ɛ̃disipline/ *adj* undisciplined, unruly.

indiscret, **-ète** /ɛ̃diskʀɛ, ɛt/ *adj* **1** (trop curieux) [*question*] indiscreet; [*personne*] inquisitive; **combien gagnez-vous, si ce n'est pas ~?** how much do you earn, if you don't mind my asking?; **à l'abri des regards ~s** away from prying eyes; **2** (qui ne sait pas garder un secret) [*propos, personne*] indiscreet.

indiscrètement /ɛ̃diskʀɛtmɑ̃/ *adv* (révéler) indiscreetly; [*demander*] inquisitively.

indiscrétion /ɛ̃diskʀesjɔ̃/ *nf* **1** (curiosité) inquisitiveness; **sans ~, combien gagnez-vous?** if you don't mind my asking, how much do you earn?; **2** (tendance à trop parler) lack of discretion; **elle est d'une grande ~** she's very indiscreet; **3** (parole indiscrète) indiscreet remark.

indiscutable /ɛ̃diskytabl/ *adj* indisputable, unquestionable.

indiscutablement /ɛ̃diskytabləmɑ̃/ *adv* unquestionably.

indispensable /ɛ̃dispɑ̃sabl/ I *adj* GÉN essential (**à** to; **pour** for); [*argent*] necessary (*épith*), essential (*jamais épith*); **être ~ à qn** to be indispensable to sb; **c'est ~** it's essential.

II *nm* **l'~** essentials (*pl*); **n'emporte que l'~** only take the essentials with you; **faire l'~** to do what is necessary.

indisponible /ɛ̃disponibl/ *adj* unavailable.

indisposé, **~e** /ɛ̃dispoze/ *adj* unwell, indisposed SOUT.

indisposer /ɛ̃dispoze/ [1] *vtr* **1** (agacer) to annoy; **2** (rendre légèrement malade) to upset, to make [sb] feel ill.

indisposition /ɛ̃dispozisjɔ̃/ *nf* indisposition; **souffrir d'une légère ~** to be slightly indisposed.

indissociable /ɛ̃disosjabl/ *adj* inseparable (**de** from).

indistinct, **~e** /ɛ̃distɛ̃, ɛ̃kt/ *adj* indistinct.

individu /ɛ̃dividy/ *nm* **1** (personne privée) individual; **la société écrase l'~** society crushes the individual; **2** (personne physique) human being, person; **3** (homme suspect) individual; **un sinistre/dangereux ~** a sinister/dangerous individual *ou* character; **un ~ armé** an armed man; **4** (unité) subject.

individualisé, **~e** /ɛ̃dividɥalize/ *adj* [*enseignement, formation*] tailored to individual needs (*après n*), individualized US; [*salaire*] negotiated on an individual basis (*après n*).

individualiser /ɛ̃dividɥalize/ [1] I *vtr* (adapter) to

tailor [sth] to individual needs, to individualize US [*enseignement, horaire*].

II **s'individualiser** *vpr* to become more individual.

individualiste /ɛ̃dividɥalist/ I *adj* individualistic.

II *nmf* individualist.

individuel, **-elle** /ɛ̃dividɥɛl/ I *adj* **1** (pour personne) [*portion, cours*] individual; [*voiture*] private; [*chambre*] single (*épith*); **maison individuelle** (detached) house; **2** (d'une seule personne) [*initiative, réussite*] individual; **3** (qui concerne l'individu) [*propriété*] private; [*responsabilité*] personal.

II *nm* **1** SPORT **il a obtenu de bons résultats en ~** he did well in the individual events; **2** TOURISME **voyage en groupe ou en ~** group or individual travel.

individuellement /ɛ̃dividɥɛlmɑ̃/ *adv* individually.

indivisible /ɛ̃divizibl/ *adj* indivisible; **une et ~** one and indivisible.

indochinois, **~e** /ɛ̃dɔʃinwa, az/ *adj* Indochinese.

indo-européen, **-éenne**, *mpl* **~s** /ɛ̃doøʀɔpeɛ̃, ɛn/ I *adj* Indo-European.

II *nm* LING Indo-European.

indolence /ɛ̃dɔlɑ̃s/ *nf* (de personne) laziness, indolence SOUT; (d'administration) apathy, indifference.

indolent, **~e** /ɛ̃dɔlɑ̃, ɑ̃t/ *adj* lazy, indolent.

indolore /ɛ̃dɔlɔʀ/ *adj* painless.

indomptable /ɛ̃dɔ̃tabl/ *adj* [*tempérament, peuple, courage*] indomitable; [*colère, passion*] uncontrollable, ungovernable; [*personnes*] uncontrollable; [*animaux*] untamable; **avec une énergie ~** with tireless energy.

indompté, **~e** /ɛ̃dɔ̃te/ *adj* unsubdued, untamed.

indonésien, **-ienne** /ɛ̃dɔnezjɛ̃, ɛn/ ▶ **338**, **394** I *adj* Indonesian.

II *nm* LING Indonesian.

indu, **~e** /ɛ̃dy/ *adj* **1** (inconvenant) [*heure*] ungodly°, unearthly; [*propos, réaction*] inappropriate, unseemly; **2** (sans fondement) [*somme*] unwarranted, unjustified.

indubitable /ɛ̃dybitabl/ *adj* indubitable; **il nous cache quelque chose, c'est ~** he's hiding something from us, there's no doubt about it.

indubitablement /ɛ̃dybitabləmɑ̃/ *adv* undoubtedly.

induction /ɛ̃dyksjɔ̃/ *nf* induction.

induire /ɛ̃dɥiʀ/ [69] *vtr* **1** (entraîner) [*événement, mesures, phénomène*] to lead to, to bring about; **2** (conclure) to infer, to conclude (**de qch** from sth); **3** (inciter) to induce (**à faire** to do); **~ qn en erreur** to mislead sb; **4** (en électricité) to induce [*courant*].

indulgence /ɛ̃dylʒɑ̃s/ *nf* **1** (de parent, public) indulgence; **2** (de jury, d'examinateur) leniency.

indulgent, **~e** /ɛ̃dylʒɑ̃, ɑ̃t/ *adj* [*parent, public*] indulgent; [*jury, examinateur*] lenient.

industrialisation /ɛ̃dystʀializasjɔ̃/ *nf* industrialization.

industrialisé, **~e** /ɛ̃dystʀijalize/ *adj* **pays ~s** industrialized countries.

industrialiser /ɛ̃dystʀijalize/ [1] I *vtr* to industrialize.

II **s'industrialiser** *vpr* to become industrialized.

industrie /ɛ̃dystʀi/ *nf* **1** (secteur) industry; **~ automobile/d'armement** car/arms industry; **l'~ hôtelière** the hotel trade; **2** (entreprise) industrial concern *ou* firm.

industriel, **-ielle** /ɛ̃dystʀijɛl/ I *adj* industrial; [*pain*] factory-made, factory-baked; **en quantité industrielle** in vast *ou* huge amounts.

II *nm,f* industrialist, manufacturer.

industriellement /ɛ̃dystʀijɛlmɑ̃/ *adv* industrially.

industrieux, **-ieuse** /ɛ̃dystʀijø, øz/ *adj* LITER industrious.

inébranlable /inebʀɑ̃labl/ *adj* **1** [*personne, conviction, résolution*] unshakeable, unwavering; **rester ~ dans ses convictions** to stick firmly to one's convictions; **2** [*roc, construction*] immovable.

inédit, **~e** /inedi, it/ I *adj* **1** (jamais publié) [*livre, pièce, traduction*] (previously) unpublished; [*disque,*

film] (previously) unreleased; **2** (original) [*procédé,*
information, spectacle, situation] (totally) new.
II *nm* **1** (ouvrage) (previously) unpublished work ou
article; **un ~ de Diderot** a previously unpublished
work by Diderot; **2** (nouveau) **voilà de l'~** that's something completely new.
ineffable /inefabl/ *adj* ineffable, unutterable.
inefficace /inefikas/ *adj* [*traitement, médicament,*
mesure] ineffective; [*méthode, système, service, appareil,*
travailleur] inefficient.
inefficacité /inefikasite/ *nf* **1** (absence de résultats)
ineffectiveness, inefficacy SOUT; **2** (rendement insuffisant)
inefficiency.
inégal, **~e**, *mpl* **-aux** /inegal, o/ *adj* **1** (dissemblable)
unequal; **de force ~e** of unequal strength; **2** (déséquilibré) [*lutte, partage*] unequal; [*partie*] uneven; **3** (irrégulier) [*rythme*] irregular, uneven; [*surface*] uneven; **4** (variable) [*humeur*] changeable, erratic; [*auteur, œuvre*]
uneven; **il a un jeu ~** he is an inconsistent player;
avec un bonheur ~ with mixed success.
inégalable /inegalabl/ *adj* incomparable, matchless.
inégalé, **~e** /inegale/ *adj* unequalled^GB, unrivalled^GB.
inégalement /inegalmɑ̃/ *adv* (de manière dissemblable)
unequally; (de manière irrégulière) unevenly; **une œuvre**
~ appréciée a work which received a mixed reception.
inégalité /inegalite/ *nf* **1** (disproportion) disparity
(**entre** between; **de** in); **2** (iniquité) inequality; **les ~s**
sociales social inequalities; **3** (irrégularité) (d'humeur)
changeability; (de terrain, surface) unevenness.
inélégant, **~e** /inelegɑ̃, ɑ̃t/ *adj* **1** (mal habillé) inelegant; **2** (mesquin) [*procédé, comportement*] shabby.
inéligible /ineliʒibl/ *adj* ineligible.
inéluctable /inelyktabl/ *adj, nm* inevitable, ineluct-
able SOUT.
inénarrable /inenaʀabl/ *adj* hilarious.
inepte /inɛpt/ *adj* [*personne, gouvernement*] inept; [*jugement*] inane; [*film, remarque*] idiotic.
ineptie /inɛpsi/ *nf* **1** (caractère inepte) inanity; **des**
propos d'une ~ totale totally idiotic remarks;
2 (parole stupide) idiotic remark.
inépuisable /inepɥizabl/ *adj* inexhaustible.
inerte /inɛʀt/ *adj* **1** (sans réaction) [*corps, membre,*
personne] inert; **2** CHIMIE, PHYS inert; **3** (apathique) [*personne, groupe*] apathetic.
inertie /inɛʀsi/ *nf* **1** CHIMIE, PHYS inertia; **2** (passivité)
apathy, inertia.
inespéré, **~e** /inɛspeʀe/ *adj* [*victoire*] unhoped for;
c'est une occasion ~e de faire this is a heaven-sent
opportunity to do.
inesthétique /inɛstetik/ *adj* (laid) unsightly; (au niveau
artistique) unaesthetic.
inestimable /inɛstimabl/ *adj* [*fortune, valeur*] inestimable; [*dommages*] incalculable; [*tableau, cadeau*] priceless; [*aide, service*] invaluable.
inévitable /inevitabl/ **I** *adj* **1** (certain) inevitable; **2**
(incontournable) HUM **l'~ Paul était là** Paul was there,
as always; **il y avait l'~ clown** there was the inevitable clown.
II *nm* **l'~** the inevitable.
inévitablement /inevitabləmɑ̃/ *adv* inevitably.
inexact, **~e** /inɛgza, akt/ *adj* inaccurate; **c'est ~!**
that's not accurate!
inexactitude /inɛgzaktityd/ *nf* **1** (erreur) inaccuracy;
2 (manque de ponctualité) unpunctuality.
inexcusable /inɛkskyzabl/ *adj* inexcusable; **tu es ~**
there's no excuse for it!
inexistant, **~e** /inɛgzistɑ̃, ɑ̃t/ *adj* [*moyens, aide*]
nonexistent; **les risques ne sont pas ~s** there are
certain risks.
inexorable /inɛgzɔʀabl/ *adj* inexorable.
inexpérimenté, **~e** /inɛkspeʀimɑ̃te/ *adj* inexperienced.
inexplicable /inɛksplikabl/ *adj* inexplicable.
inexpliqué, **~e** /inɛksplike/ *adj* unexplained.

inexploitable /inɛksplwatabl/ *adj* [*gisement*] unworkable; [*renseignements, documents*] unusable.
inexploité, **~e** /inɛksplwate/ *adj* [*richesses, sol*]
unexploited; [*ressources, marché, créneau*] untapped,
unexploited; [*documents*] unused.
inexploré, **~e** /inɛksplɔʀe/ *adj* unexplored.
inexprimable /inɛkspʀimabl/ *adj* inexpressible.
inextinguible /inɛkstɛ̃gibl/ *adj* **1** [*feu, incendie*]
inextinguishable; **2** [*passion, ardeur*] inextinguishable; [*soif*] unquenchable.
in extremis /inɛkstʀemis/ **I** *loc adj inv* (de dernière
minute) [*sauvetage, accord*] last-minute.
II *loc adv* (au dernier moment) at the last minute.
inextricable /inɛkstʀikabl/ *adj* inextricable.
inextricablement /inɛkstʀikabləmɑ̃/ *adv* inextricably.
infaillible /ɛ̃fajibl/ *adj* infallible.
infaisable /ɛ̃fəzabl/ *adj* unfeasible, impossible.
infamant, **~e** /ɛ̃famɑ̃, ɑ̃t/ *adj* **1** [*propos*] defamatory
SOUT; **2** [*acte*] infamous.
infâme /ɛ̃fam/ *adj* **1** (répugnant) [*nourriture, odeur,*
boisson] revolting, disgusting; **2** (ignoble) [*individu*]
despicable; [*trahison*] base; [*crime*] odious.
infamie /ɛ̃fami/ *nf* **1** (caractère) infamy; **2** (acte vil) act
of infamy; (calomnie) slanderous remark.
infanterie /ɛ̃fɑ̃tʀi/ *nf* infantry.
infantile /ɛ̃fɑ̃til/ *adj* **1** (relatif aux enfants) [*maladie*]
childhood; [*mortalité*] infant; [*psychologie, protection*]
child; **2** (puéril) infantile, childish.
infantilisme /ɛ̃fɑ̃tilism/ *nm* **1** PÉJ childishness; **2** MÉD
infantilism.
infarctus /ɛ̃faʀktys/ ▶196 *nm inv* MÉD (du myocarde)
heart attack, myocardial infarction SPÉC; **faire**° or
avoir un ~ to have a coronary, to have a heart
attack.
infatigable /ɛ̃fatigabl/ *adj* [*personne, esprit*] tireless.
infatigablement /ɛ̃fatigabləmɑ̃/ *adv* tirelessly.
infatué, **~e** /ɛ̃fatɥe/ *adj* **être ~ de sa personne** or
soi-même to be full of oneself.
infatuer: s'infatuer /ɛ̃fatɥe/ [1] *vpr* FML to become
infatuated (**de qn** with sb).
infect, **~e** /ɛ̃fɛkt/ *adj* [*temps, odeur, humeur*] foul;
[*plat*] revolting; [*personne, attitude, lieu*] horrible.
infecter /ɛ̃fɛkte/ [1] **I** *vtr* **1** MÉD to infect; **2** FIG to
poison.
II s'infecter *vpr* to become infected, to go septic.
infectieux, -ieuse /ɛ̃fɛksjø, øz/ *adj* infectious.
infection /ɛ̃fɛksjɔ̃/ *nf* **1** MÉD infection; **2** FIG **c'est une**
~! (puanteur) it stinks to high heaven°!; (chose répugnante) it's disgusting!
inférer /ɛ̃feʀe/ [14] *vtr* to infer (**de** from).
inférieur, **~e** /ɛ̃feʀjœʀ/ **I** *adj* **1** (dans l'espace, dans
une hiérarchie) lower; **dans le coin ~ gauche** in the
bottom left-hand corner; **on l'a rétrogradé au rang**
~ he was demoted to the next rank down; **2** (en
valeur) [*température, vitesse, coût, salaire, nombre*]
lower (**à** than); [*taille*] smaller (**à** than); [*durée*]
shorter (**à** than); **~ à la moyenne** below average;
des coûts de production ~s à la moyenne lower
than average production costs; **être en nombre**
~ to be fewer in number; **3** (de qualité moindre)
[*travail, ouvrage, qualité*] inferior (**à** to); **4** MATH
si a est ~ à b if a is less than b.
II *nm,f* inferior.
infériorité /ɛ̃feʀjɔʀite/ *nf* inferiority; **être en position d'~** to be in an inferior position.
infernal, **~e**, *mpl* **-aux** /ɛ̃fɛʀnal, o/ *adj* **1**
(insupportable) [*bruit, cadence, chaleur*] infernal; **cycle**
~ unstoppable chain of events; **2** [*situation, circulation*] diabolical; **ce gosse est ~**° that child is a
monster; **3** MYTHOL infernal.
infertile /ɛ̃fɛʀtil/ *adj* barren, infertile.
infester /ɛ̃fɛste/ [1] *vtr* to infest, to overrun; **infesté**
de rats/requins rat-/shark-infested; **infesté de puces**
flea-ridden (*épith*); **jardin infesté d'orties** garden overrun with nettles.

infidèle /ɛ̃fidɛl/ I *adj* **1** (inconstant) [*mari, maîtresse*] unfaithful (**à qn** to sb); [*ami*] disloyal; **2** (non conforme) [*traduction, récit*] inaccurate; **3** RELIG infidel.
II *nmf* RELIG infidel.

infidélité /ɛ̃fidelite/ *nf* **1** (dans un couple) infidelity (**à** to); **faire des ~s à** to be unfaithful to; **2** (d'ami, allié) disloyalty (**à** to); **3** (de traduction) inaccuracy.

infiltration /ɛ̃filtʀasjɔ̃/ *nf* **1** (de liquide) **~s d'eau** water seepage ¢; **il y a des ~s dans le mur** water is seeping into the wall; **2** (d'espions) infiltration (**dans** into); **3** (piqûre) **~s de cortisone** cortisone injections.

infiltrer /ɛ̃filtʀe/ [1] I *vtr* to infiltrate [*organisation*].
II **s'infiltrer** *vpr* **1** [*liquide*] to leak (**dans** into); [*lumière, froid*] to filter in; **le doute s'infiltra dans mon esprit** I began to have doubts; **2** [*personne*] **s'~ dans** to infiltrate [*groupe, lieu*].

infime /ɛ̃fim/ *adj* (petit) tiny, minute; **chance ~** very remote chance.

infini, ~e /ɛ̃fini/ I *adj* infinite; **avec d'~es précautions** with infinite care.
II *nm* MATH, PHOT **l'~** infinity.

infiniment /ɛ̃finimɑ̃/ *adv* (énormément) immensely; **~ reconnaissant** immensely grateful; **~ plus** infinitely more.

infinité /ɛ̃finite/ *nf* **l'~** infinity; **une ~ de** an endless number of.

infinitésimal, ~e, *mpl* **-aux** /ɛ̃finitezimal, o/ *adj* infinitésimal.

infinitif, -ive /ɛ̃finitif, iv/ I *adj* infinitive.
II *nm* infinitive; **à l'~** in the infinitive.

infirmation /ɛ̃fiʀmasjɔ̃/ *nf* quashing, invalidation.

infirme /ɛ̃fiʀm/ I *adj* GÉN disabled; (par l'âge) infirm.
II *nmf* disabled person; **les ~s** the disabled.

infirmer /ɛ̃fiʀme/ [1] *vtr* GÉN, JUR to invalidate.

infirmerie /ɛ̃fiʀmɔʀi/ *nf* GÉN infirmary; (d'école) sick room; (de bateau) sick bay.

infirmier /ɛ̃fiʀmje/ ▶ 374 *nm* male nurse.

infirmière /ɛ̃fiʀmjɛʀ/ ▶ 374 *nf* nurse.

infirmité /ɛ̃fiʀmite/ *nf* **1** GÉN disability; (de vieillesse) infirmity; **2** (imperfection) weakness.

inflammable /ɛ̃flamabl/ *adj* flammable.

inflammation /ɛ̃flamasjɔ̃/ *nf* MÉD inflammation.

inflammatoire /ɛ̃flamatwaʀ/ *adj* MÉD inflammatory.

inflation /ɛ̃flasjɔ̃/ *nf* inflation.

inflationniste /ɛ̃flasjɔnist/ *adj* inflationary; **tensions ~s** inflationary pressures.

infléchir /ɛ̃fleʃiʀ/ [3] I *vtr* (assouplir) to soften [*position, politique*]; **2** (faire dévier) to deflect [*trajectoire*]; **~ la courbe des dépenses** to curb spending.
II **s'infléchir** *vpr* **1** (s'assouplir) [*position, politique*] to soften; **2** (se courber) [*tige, route*] to bend; [*poutre*] to sag; **3** (dévier) [*trajectoire*] to deflect; **4** (commencer à baisser) [*courbe*] to level off; **5** MATH [*courbe*] to inflect.

inflexibilité /ɛ̃flɛksibilite/ *nf* inflexibility.

inflexible /ɛ̃flɛksibl/ *adj* inflexible.

inflexion /ɛ̃flɛksjɔ̃/ *nf* **1** (changement) change (**de, dans** in); **2** (baisse) slight drop (**de** in); **3** (mouvement) **~ du corps** bow; **~ de la tête** bow; **~** (vocale) inflection.

infliger /ɛ̃fliʒe/ [13] *vtr* **1** (faire subir) to inflict [*défaite, mauvais traitements*] (**à** on); **2** JUR to impose [*amende, punition*] (**à** on); to give [*avertissement*] (**à** to).

influençable /ɛ̃flyɑ̃sabl/ *adj* impressionable.

influence /ɛ̃flyɑ̃s/ *nf* **1** (effet) influence (**sur** on); **il a une mauvaise ~ sur son frère** he is a bad influence on his brother; **avoir une ~ néfaste** [*facteur, phénomène*] to have a detrimental effect (**sur** on); **2** (pouvoir) influence ¢; **3** ART, LITTÉRAT influence (**sur** on); **4** POL (rôle) influence ¢.

influencer /ɛ̃flyɑ̃se/ [12] *vtr* to influence [*enfant, électeur, artiste*]; to affect [*économie, situation*].

influent, ~e /ɛ̃flyɑ̃, ɑ̃t/ *adj* influential.

influer /ɛ̃flye/ [1] *vtr ind* **~ sur** to have an influence on.

influx /ɛ̃fly/ *nm inv* **~ nerveux** nerve impulse.

infographie® /ɛ̃fogʀafi/ *nf* computer graphics (+ *v sg*).

informateur, -trice /ɛ̃fɔʀmatœʀ, tʀis/ *nm,f* **1** GÉN informant; **2** (indicateur de police) informer.

informaticien, -ienne /ɛ̃fɔʀmatisjɛ̃, ɛn/ ▶ 374 *nm,f* computer scientist.

information /ɛ̃fɔʀmasjɔ̃/ *nf* **1** (renseignement) information ¢; **une ~** a piece of information; **ces ~s sont confidentielles** this is confidential information; **2** PRESSE, RADIO, TV (nouvelle) piece of news, news item; **écouter les ~s** to listen to the news; **3** PRESSE, RADIO, TV (activité) reporting; (résultat) information; (médias) media; **de meilleurs journalistes pour une meilleure ~** better journalists for a better standard of reporting; **défendre le droit à l'~** to defend freedom of information; **contrôler l'~** to control the media; **4** ORDINAT information; **le traitement de l'~** data ou information processing; **5** JUR inquiry; **~ judiciaire** judicial inquiry.

informatique /ɛ̃fɔʀmatik/ I *adj* [*système, équipement*] computer.
II *nf* (science) computer science, computing; (techniques) information technology.

informatisation /ɛ̃fɔʀmatizasjɔ̃/ *nf* computerization.

informatiser /ɛ̃fɔʀmatize/ [1] I *vtr* to computerize.
II **s'informatiser** *vpr* to become computerized.

informe /ɛ̃fɔʀm/ *adj* shapeless.

informer /ɛ̃fɔʀme/ [1] I *vtr* (mettre au courant) to inform [*personne, groupe*] (**de** about; **que** that); **les journaux bien informés** the serious press; **les milieux bien informés** well-informed circles; **de source bien informée** from a reliable source.
II *vi* JUR to hold an inquiry ou investigation.
III **s'informer** *vpr* **1** (suivre l'actualité) to keep oneself informed; **2** (se mettre au courant) **s'~ de qch** to inquire about sth; **3** (prendre des renseignements) **s'~ sur qn** to make inquiries about sb.

infortune /ɛ̃fɔʀtyn/ *nf* misfortune; **compagnon d'~** companion in adversity.

infortuné, ~e /ɛ̃fɔʀtyne/ I *adj* ill-fated.
II *nm,f* unfortunate.

infra /ɛ̃fʀa/ *adv* below; **voir ~** see below.

infraction /ɛ̃fʀaksjɔ̃/ *nf* JUR offence^GB; **être en ~ avec la loi** [*personne*] to be in breach of the law.

infranchissable /ɛ̃fʀɑ̃ʃisabl/ *adj* [*obstacle*] insurmountable; [*frontière*] impassable.

infrarouge /ɛ̃fʀaʀuʒ/ *adj, nm* infrared; **missile guidé par ~** heat-seeking missile.

infrastructure /ɛ̃fʀastʀyktyʀ/ *nf* **1** (équipements) facilities (*pl*); **~ hôtelière/médicale** hotel/medical facilities; **2** ÉCON infrastructure; **3** CONSTR substructure.

infructueux, -euse /ɛ̃fʀyktɥø, øz/ *adj* fruitless.

infuser /ɛ̃fyze/ [1] I *vtr* CULIN to brew, to infuse [*thé*]; to infuse [*tisane*].
II *vi* [*thé*] to brew, to infuse; [*tisane*] to infuse.

infusion /ɛ̃fyzjɔ̃/ *nf* **1** (tisane) herbal tea; **~ de camomille** camomile tea; **boîte de 20 ~s** box of 20 herbal tea bags; **2** (processus) infusion.

ingénier: s'ingénier /ɛ̃ʒenje/ [2] *vpr* to do one's utmost (**à faire** to do).

ingénierie /ɛ̃ʒeniʀi/ *nf* engineering.

ingénieur /ɛ̃ʒenjœʀ/ ▶ 374 *nm* engineer; **~ agronome/chimiste/électricien** agricultural/chemical/ electrical/sound engineer; **~ des travaux publics** civil engineer.

ingénieur-conseil, *pl* **ingénieurs-conseils** /ɛ̃ʒenjœʀkɔ̃sɛj/ *nm* consulting engineer.

ingénieux, -ieuse /ɛ̃ʒenjø, øz/ *adj* ingenious.

ingéniosité /ɛ̃ʒenjozite/ *nf* ingenuity.

ingénu, ~e /ɛ̃ʒeny/ I *adj* ingenuous.
II *nm,f* **un ~** an ingenuous man; **une ~e** an ingénue.

ingénuité /ɛ̃ʒenɥite/ *nf* ingenuousness; **avec ~** ingenuously; **en toute ~** in all innocence.

ingérence /ɛ̃ʒeʀɑ̃s/ *nf* interference ¢ (**dans** in).

ingérer /ɛ̃ʒeʀe/ [14] I *vtr* to ingest.

II **s'ingérer** *vpr* to interfere (**dans** in).

ngestion /ε̃ʒεstjɔ̃/ *nf* ingestion.

ngrat, **~e** /ε̃gʀa, at/ I *adj* **1** (sans reconnaissance) ungrateful; **2** (sans agrément) [*œuvre*] arid; [*lieu, paysage*] unwelcoming; [*visage, physique*] unattractive; **3** (sans récompense) [*métier, tâche, rôle*] thankless; [*terre*] unproductive.
II *nm,f* ungrateful person.

ngratitude /ε̃gʀatityd/ *nf* (manque de reconnaissance) ingratitude (**envers** to); **faire preuve d'~** to show ingratitude, to be ungrateful.

ngrédient /ε̃gʀedjɑ̃/ *nm* ingredient.

ngurgiter /ε̃gyʀʒite/ [1] *vtr* **1** (avaler) to gulp down [*boisson, aliment*]; to swallow [*médicament*]; **2** (assimiler) to take in [*donnée*]; to learn [*programme*].

nhabitable /inabitabl/ *adj* uninhabitable.

nhabité, **~e** /inabite/ *adj* **1** (sans habitants) [*maison, région*] uninhabited; **2** ASTRONAUT [*engin, vol*] unmanned.

nhabituel, **-elle** /inabityεl/ *adj* unusual (**de la part de** for).

nhalateur /inalatœʀ/ *nm* inhaler.

nhalation /inalasjɔ̃/ *nf* inhalation; **faire des ~s** to have inhalations.

nhaler /inale/ [1] *vtr* to inhale.

nhérent, **~e** /ineʀɑ̃, ɑ̃t/ *adj* inherent (**à** in).

nhiber /inibe/ [1] *vtr* to inhibit.

nhibition /inibisjɔ̃/ *nf* inhibition.

nhospitalier, **-ière** /inɔspitalje, εʀ/ *adj* inhospitable.

nhumain, **~e** /inymε̃, εn/ *adj* inhuman.

nhumation /inymasjɔ̃/ *nf* **1** (mise en terre) burial; **2** (cérémonie) funeral.

nhumer /inyme/ [1] *vtr* to bury.

nimaginable /inimaʒinabl/ *adj* **1** (impossible à imaginer) unimaginable; **2** (impossible à concevoir) unthinkable.

nimitable /inimitabl/ *adj* inimitable.

ninflammable /inε̃flamabl/ *adj* nonflammable.

nintelligible /inε̃teliʒibl/ *adj* unintelligible.

nintéressant, **~e** /inε̃teʀesɑ̃, ɑ̃t/ *adj* uninteresting; **pas ~** not without interest.

ninterrompu, **~e** /inε̃teʀɔ̃py/ *adj* **1** (continu dans le temps) [*processus*] uninterrupted; [*chute, hausse*] continuous; [*bruit, circulation*] endless; **2** (continu dans l'espace) [*procession*] unbroken.

niquité /inikite/ *nf* iniquity.

nitial, **~e**[1], *mpl* **-iaux** /inisjal, o/ *adj* initial.

nitiale[2] /inisjal/ *nf* initial; **à l'~** in initial position (*après n*).

nitiateur, **-trice** /inisjatœʀ, tʀis/ *nm,f* **1** (de projet, mode) originator; (de publication, mobilisation) instigator; **2** (de personne) instructor.

nitiation /inisjasjɔ̃/ *nf* **1** (formation) introduction (**à** to); **~ à l'anglais/la gestion** introduction to English/management; **2** (admission à la connaissance) initiation; **rites d'~** initiation rites.

nitiatique /inisjatik/ *adj* initiatory.

nitiative /inisjativ/ *nf* initiative; **à l'~ de qn** on sb's initiative; **avoir de l'~**, **avoir l'esprit d'~** to have initiative.

nitié, **~e** /inisje/ *nm,f* **1** (formé et admis) initiate; **2** FIN insider trader.

nitier /inisje/ [2] I *vtr* **1** (former) to introduce (**à** to); **2** (admettre à la connaissance) to initiate (**à** into); **3** (être à l'origine de) to initiate [*projet, réforme*].
II **s'initier** *vpr* **s'~ à qch** to learn sth.

njectable /ε̃ʒεktabl/ *adj* injectable.

njecter /ε̃ʒεkte/ [1] I *vtr* to inject (**dans** into); **~ qch à qn** to inject sb with sth.
II **s'injecter** *vpr* [*personne*] to inject oneself with; [*médicament*] to be injected; **injecté de sang** bloodshot.

njection /ε̃ʒεksjɔ̃/ *nf* injection; **en ~(s)** by injection;

~ de capitaux or **crédits** injection of funds; **se faire une ~ de** to inject oneself with.

injoignable /ε̃ʒwaɲabl/ *adj* incommunicado.

injonction /ε̃ʒɔ̃ksjɔ̃/ *nf* injunction.

injure /ε̃ʒyʀ/ *nf* (insulte) abuse ¢; (offense) insult; **couvrir qn d'~s** to heap abuse on sb; **faire ~ à qn** to insult sb.

injurier /ε̃ʒyʀje/ [1] *vtr* to insult, to swear at; **se faire ~** to be sworn at (**par** by).

injurieux, **-ieuse** /ε̃ʒyʀjø, øz/ *adj* [*parole, écrit*] abusive, offensive; [*attitude*] insulting.

injuste /ε̃ʒyst/ *adj* unfair (**envers** to).

injustement /ε̃ʒystəmɑ̃/ *adv* [*accusé, condamné*] unjustly; [*méconnu, négligé*] unfairly.

injustice /ε̃ʒystis/ *nf* **1** (caractère injuste) (d'impôt, de société) injustice; (de personne) unfairness; **2** (absence de justice) injustice; **combattre l'~** to fight injustice; **3** (acte injuste) injustice; **réparer une ~** to right a wrong; **quelle ~!** how unfair!

injustifiable /ε̃ʒystifjabl/ *adj* unjustifiable.

injustifié, **~e** /ε̃ʒystifje/ *adj* unjustified.

inlassable /ε̃lasabl/ *adj* [*personne*] tireless; [*curiosité*] insatiable; [*efforts*] unremitting.

inlassablement /ε̃lasabləmɑ̃/ *adv* tirelessly.

inné, **~e** /inne/ *adj* innate.

innocemment /inɔsamɑ̃/ *adv* innocently; **pas ~** disingenuously.

innocence /inɔsɑ̃s/ *nf* innocence.

innocent, **~e** /inɔsɑ̃, ɑ̃t/ I *adj* innocent (**de** of).
II *nm,f* **1** (être pur) innocent; **2** (personne non coupable) innocent person; **une ~e** an innocent woman.

innocenter /inɔsɑ̃te/ [1] *vtr* to prove [sb] innocent (**de** of), to clear (**de** of).

innocuité /inɔkɥite/ *nf* harmlessness; **en toute ~** without any risks.

innombrable /inɔ̃bʀabl/ *adj* **1** (multiple) countless; **2** (immense) [*foule, armée*] vast.

innommable /inɔmabl/ *adj* [*comportement, saleté, terreur*] unspeakable; [*plat, boisson*] revolting.

innovateur, **-trice** /inɔvatœʀ, tʀis/ I *adj* innovative.
II *nm,f* innovator.

innovation /inɔvasjɔ̃/ *nf* innovation.

innover /inɔve/ [1] *vi* [*personne, entreprise*] to innovate (**en matière de** in); [*équipement*] to break new ground.

inoccupé, **~e** /inɔkype/ *adj* unoccupied.

inoculer /inɔkyle/ [1] *vtr* **1** (vacciner) to inoculate (**contre** against); **~ qch à qn** to inoculate sb with sth; **2** (contaminer) **~ à qn** to infect sb with [*virus, maladie, idée*].

inodore /inɔdɔʀ/ *adj* [*substance*] odourless[GB]; [*fleur*] scentless.

inoffensif, **-ive** /inɔfɑ̃sif, iv/ *adj* harmless.

inondation /inɔ̃dasjɔ̃/ *nf* **1** (situation) flood; **2** (processus) flooding.

inonder /inɔ̃de/ [1] *vtr* **1** (submerger) to flood [*lieu*]; **2** (baigner) [*soleil, lumière*] to flood [*lieu*]; **inondé de sueur/sang** bathed in sweat/blood; **les larmes lui inondaient le visage**, **il avait le visage inondé de larmes** tears were streaming down his face; **3** (envahir) [*commerçants, marque*] to flood [*marché*] (**de** with); to inundate [*clients*] (**de** with); [*produit*] to flood [*marché*].

inopérant, **~e** /inɔpeʀɑ̃, ɑ̃t/ *adj* ineffective.

inopiné, **~e** /inɔpine/ *adj* unexpected.

inopinément /inɔpinemɑ̃/ *adv* unexpectedly.

inopportun, **~e** /inɔpɔʀtœ̃, yn/ *adj* **1** (non souhaitable) inappropriate; **2** (mal à propos) ill-timed.

inoubliable /inublijabl/ *adj* unforgettable.

inouï, **~e** /inwi/ *adj* [*événement*] unprecedented; [*succès, violence*] incredible, tremendous; **c'est ~** that's unheard of; **chose ~e** something unheard of.

inox /inɔks/ *nm inv* stainless steel.

inoxydable /inɔksidabl/ I *adj* [*métal*] non-oxidizing; **acier ~** stainless steel.

II *nm* stainless steel.

inqualifiable /ɛ̃kalifjabl/ *adj* unspeakable.

inquiet, -iète /ɛ̃kjɛ, ɛt/ I *adj* **1** (de nature) anxious; **2** (alarmé) worried (**pour** about); **3** (empli de crainte) [*air, regard*] anxious, worried.
II *nm,f* worrier; **c'est un (éternel) ~** he's a (perpetual) worrier.

inquiétant, ~e /ɛ̃kjetɑ̃, ɑ̃t/ *adj* **1** (alarmant) worrying; **2** (effrayant) frightening.

inquiéter /ɛ̃kjete/ [14] I *vtr* **1** (soucier) to worry; **ce que vous venez de me dire m'inquiète un peu** I find what you've just told me rather worrying; **le phénomène commence à ~ les spécialistes** specialists are beginning to be concerned about the phenomenon; **2** (demander des comptes à) **les douaniers ne l'ont pas inquiété** the customs officers didn't bother him; **quitter le pays sans être inquiété** to leave the country without any trouble; **3** (harceler) FML to harass [*pays, région*]; **4**° (mettre en difficulté) to threaten [*adversaire*].
II **s'inquiéter** *vpr* **1** (s'alarmer) to worry, to get worried; **il n'y a pas de quoi s'~** there's nothing to get worried about ou to worry about; **2** (se soucier) **ne t'inquiète pas pour elle** don't worry about her; **3** (s'enquérir) **s'~ de qch** to inquire about sth; **s'~ de savoir si/combien** to inquire whether/how much.

inquiétude /ɛ̃kjetyd/ *nf* **1** (état) anxiety, concern; **être un sujet d'~** to give cause for concern ou anxiety; **être fou d'~** to be beside oneself with worry; **soyez sans ~** don't worry; **2** (trouble) worry; **il n'y a pas d'~ à avoir** there's nothing to worry ou be concerned about.

inquisiteur, -trice /ɛ̃kizitœr, tris/ I *adj* inquisitive.
II *nm,f* inquisitor; **grand ~** Grand Inquisitor.

inquisition /ɛ̃kizisjɔ̃/ *nf* inquisition.

insaisissable /ɛ̃sɛzisabl/ *adj* [*voleur, animal, caractère*] elusive; [*nuance, image*] imperceptible.

insalubre /ɛ̃salybʀ/ *adj* insanitary.

insanité /ɛ̃sanite/ *nf* (propos insensé) rubbish ¢; **c'est une ~** it's rubbish; **proférer** or **débiter des ~s** to come out with a lot of rubbish (**sur** about).

insatiable /ɛ̃sasjabl/ *adj* insatiable.

insatisfaction /ɛ̃satisfaksjɔ̃/ *nf* dissatisfaction ¢ (**quant à** with).

insatisfait, ~e /ɛ̃satisfɛ, ɛt/ I *adj* [*personne*] dissatisfied (**de** with); [*désir, ambition, requête*] unsatisfied.
II *nm,f* **c'est un ~** he's never satisfied.

inscription /ɛ̃skʀipsjɔ̃/ *nf* **1** SCOL enrolment^GB; UNIV registration; **il y a mille nouvelles ~s par an** a thousand new students register every year; **2** (enregistrement) **~ à un tournoi** entering for a tournament; **l'~ coûte 200 francs** the membership fee costs 200 francs; **~ électorale** registration as a voter; **3** (chose écrite, gravée) (élaborée) inscription; (graffiti) graffiti.

inscrire /ɛ̃skʀiʀ/ [67] I *vtr* **1** (enregistrer) [*institution, enseignant*] to enrol^GB [*élève*]; to register [*étudiant*]; **~ qn sur une liste** to enter sb's name on a list; **~ une question à l'ordre du jour** to place an item on the agenda; **faites-vous ~ à la mairie pour le tournoi** put your name down at the Town Hall for the tournament; **2** (écrire) to write down [*nom, rendez-vous*].
II **s'inscrire** *vpr* **1** (faire enregistrer) SCOL to enrol^GB; UNIV to register; **s'~ à un parti/club** to join a party/club; **s'~ à un examen** to enter for an exam; **s'~ au chômage** to register as unemployed; **s'~ sur les listes électorales** to get oneself put on the electoral roll; **2** (faire partie de) **s'~ dans le cadre de** to be in line with; **s'~ dans la logique de** to fit into the scheme of; **s'~ dans une stratégie** to be part of a strategy; **3 s'~ en faux contre qch** to dispute the validity of sth.

inscrit, ~e /ɛ̃skʀi, it/ I *pp* ▶ **inscrire**.
II *pp adj* LIT SCOL enrolled; UNIV registered; **les personnes ~es sur la liste d'attente** those on the waiting list; **le débat ~ à l'ordre du jour** the debate on the agenda; **les personnes non ~es au club** non-members of the club; **60% des électeurs ~s** 60% of

registered voters; **les députés non ~s** *independen* members of the French Parliament.
III *nm,f* (élève) registered student; (électeur) registere voter.

insecte /ɛ̃sɛkt/ *nm* insect.

insecticide /ɛ̃sɛktisid/ I *adj* insecticidal.
II *nm* insecticide.

insécurité /ɛ̃sekyʀite/ *nf* insecurity ¢.

insémination /ɛ̃seminasjɔ̃/ *nf* insemination; **~ artifi** **cielle** artificial insemination.

inséminer /ɛ̃semine/ [1] *vtr* to inseminate.

insensé, ~e /ɛ̃sɑ̃se/ *adj* **1** (extravagant) [*pari, histoire projet*] insane; **c'est ~!** that's insane!; **tenir de** **discours ~s** to talk complete nonsense; **2**° (excessif [*cohue, embouteillage, gains*] phenomenal.

insensibilisation /ɛ̃sɑ̃sibilizasjɔ̃/ *nf* anaesthetization

insensibiliser /ɛ̃sɑ̃sibilize/ [1] *vtr* to anaesthetize.

insensibilité /ɛ̃sɑ̃sibilite/ *nf* insensitivity (**à** to).

insensible /ɛ̃sɑ̃sibl/ *adj* **1** (sans réaction) impervious (à to); **2** (indifférent) insensitive (**à** to).

insensiblement /ɛ̃sɑ̃sibləmɑ̃/ *adv* imperceptibly.

inséparable /ɛ̃sepaʀabl/ *adj* inseparable.

insérer /ɛ̃seʀe/ [14] I *vtr* to insert (**dans** in).
II **s'insérer** *vpr* [*encart, disquette*] to be inserted **cette mesure s'insère dans un contexte de rigueur** this measure is to be seen in the context of austerity.

insertion /ɛ̃sɛʀsjɔ̃/ *nf* **1** (d'objet, annonce, de clause insertion; **2** (intégration) integration; **faciliter l'~ des immigrés** to facilitate the integration of immigrants **~ sociale** social integration.

insidieusement /ɛ̃sidjøzmɑ̃/ *adv* insidiously.

insidieux, -ieuse /ɛ̃sidjø, øz/ *adj* insidious.

insigne /ɛ̃siɲ/ I *adj* FML [*honneur, faveur, privilège* great, signal SOUT (*épith*); [*service*] distinguished; [*mala dresse*] remarkable IRON; **avoir l'~ honneur de faire** to have the great honour^GB of doing.
II *nm* (signe distinctif) badge.
III **insignes** *nmpl* (emblème) insignia (*pl*).

insignifiance /ɛ̃siɲifjɑ̃s/ *nf* insignificance.

insignifiant, ~e /ɛ̃siɲifjɑ̃, ɑ̃t/ *adj* insignificant.

insinuation /ɛ̃sinɥasjɔ̃/ *nf* insinuation.

insinuer /ɛ̃sinɥe/ [1] I *vtr* **1** (suggérer) to insinuate (**que** that); **2** (introduire) to slip (**dans** into).
II **s'insinuer** *vpr* [*personne*] (physiquement) to slip; (*so* cialement) to ingratiate oneself (**auprès de qn** with sb) [*sentiment, idée*] to creep; [*liquide, odeur*] to seep; **le doute s'insinuait en eux** or **dans leur esprit** doub crept into their minds.

insipide /ɛ̃sipid/ *adj* LIT, FIG insipid.

insistance /ɛ̃sistɑ̃s/ *nf* insistence; **avec ~** insist ently.

insistant, ~e /ɛ̃sistɑ̃, ɑ̃t/ *adj* insistent.

insister /ɛ̃siste/ [1] *vi* **1** (persévérer) to insist; **entendu je n'insiste pas!** all right ou OK, I won't insist!; **j'a dû ~ pour qu'il vienne** I had to press him to come **inutile d'~, ils doivent être sortis** it's pointless to keep on trying, they must be out; **inutile d'~, il es têtu** there's no point in insisting, he's stubborn; **il es parti sans ~** he left without further ado; **2** (mettre l'accent) **~ sur** to stress [*danger, besoin*]; to put the emphasis on [*orthographe, attitude*]; **n'insistons pas sur cette question** let's not dwell on this question **3** (repasser plusieurs fois) **~ sur** to pay particular at tention to [*tache, défaut, aspérité*].

insolation /ɛ̃solasjɔ̃/ *nf* **1** ▶ **196** (coup de soleil sunstroke ¢; **2** (exposition) exposure to the sun, insola tion SPÉC; PHOT (de plaque, film) exposure; **3** MÉTÉO (ensolei lement) sunny period.

insolence /ɛ̃solɑ̃s/ *nf* (irrespect) insolence.

insolent, ~e /ɛ̃solɑ̃, ɑ̃t/ I *adj* **1** (irrespectueux) [*enfan ton, attitude*] insolent, cheeky; **2** (arrogant) [*rival vainqueur*] arrogant; **3** (provocant) [*personne, jeunesse* brazen; [*luxe, succès, fortune, joie*] unashamed.
II *nm,f* insolent person.

insolite /ɛ̃solit/ *adj, nm* unusual; **goût de l'~** tast for the unusual.

nsoluble /ɛ̃sɔlybl/ *adj* **1** [*matière*] insoluble; **2** [*problème, question*] insoluble.

nsolvabilité /ɛ̃sɔlvabilite/ *nf* insolvency.

nsolvable /ɛ̃sɔlvabl/ *adj* insolvent.

nsomniaque /ɛ̃sɔmnjak/ *adj, nmf* insomniac.

nsomnie /ɛ̃sɔmni/ *nf* **1** ▶ **196** (trouble) insomnia **¢**; **avoir des ~s** to have insomnia; **2** (nuit sans sommeil) sleepless night.

nsondable /ɛ̃sɔ̃dabl/ *adj* [*abîme, mystère*] unfathomable; [*tristesse, désespoir, bêtise*] immense.

nsonorisation /ɛ̃sɔnɔʀizasjɔ̃/ *nf* soundproofing.

nsonoriser /ɛ̃sɔnɔʀize/ [1] *vtr* to soundproof; **mal insonorisé** poorly soundproofed.

nsouciance /ɛ̃susjɑ̃s/ *nf* carefreeness, insouciance SOUT; **vivre dans l'~** to lead a carefree life.

nsouciant, **~e** /ɛ̃susjɑ̃, ɑ̃t/ *adj* carefree; **~ du lendemain** without a thought for the future (*épith, après n*).

nsoumis, **~e** /ɛ̃sumi, iz/ **I** *adj* (rebelle) [*contrée, peuple*] unsubdued; **soldat ~** draft dodger.
II *nm,f* MIL draft dodger.

nsoumission /ɛ̃sumisjɔ̃/ *nf* **1** (rébellion) insubordination; **2** MIL avoidance of the draft.

nsoupçonnable /ɛ̃supsɔnabl/ *adj* beyond suspicion (*après n*).

nsoupçonné, **~e** /ɛ̃supsɔne/ *adj* [*ressources, force, menace, difficultés*] unsuspected; [*richesses, perspectives, horizons*] undreamed of.

nsoutenable /ɛ̃sutnabl/ *adj* **1** (intolérable) [*violence, douleur*] unbearable; **un film d'une violence ~** an unbearably violent film; **2** (impossible à suivre) [*cadence*] impossible; **3** (indéfendable) [*opinion*] untenable.

nspecter /ɛ̃spɛkte/ [1] *vtr* to inspect.

nspecteur, **-trice** /ɛ̃spɛktœʀ, tʀis/ ▶ **374**, **596** *nm,f* inspector.
■ **~ de police** ~ detective constable GB; **~ du travail** ADMIN government inspector (*concerned with health and safety and respect of labour laws*); **~ des travaux finis**○ HUM skiver○ GB, shirker○.

nspection /ɛ̃spɛksjɔ̃/ *nf* **1** (contrôle) inspection; **faire l'~ de qch** to inspect sth; **2** (ensemble d'inspecteurs) inspectorate.
■ **~ académique** ~ local schools inspectorate; **~ du travail** ~ labour^GB inspectorate.

nspirateur, **-trice** /ɛ̃spiʀatœʀ, tʀis/ *nm,f* **1** (d'idée, de théorie) initiator; (de complot) instigator; **2** (d'artiste, œuvre) inspiration.

nspiration /ɛ̃spiʀasjɔ̃/ *nf* **1** (souffle créateur) inspiration **¢**; **auteur sans ~** uninspired author; **2** (influence) inspiration; **œuvre d'~ romantique** work of romantic inspiration; **3** (idée) inspiration; **soudain, il eut une ~** he had a sudden inspiration, he had a brainwave○; **4** (inhalation) inspiration.

nspiré, **~e** /ɛ̃spiʀe/ *adj* [*auteur, artiste, œuvre*] inspired; **être bien/mal ~ de faire** to be well-/ill-advised to do; **un roman ~ des vieux contes populaires** a novel based on old folk tales.

nspirer /ɛ̃spiʀe/ [1] **I** *vtr* **1** (donner de l'inspiration à) to inspire [*personne*]; **2** (donner envie à) to appeal to; **ça ne m'inspire pas** that doesn't appeal to me; **3** (susciter) to inspire; **~ la méfiance à qn** to inspire distrust in sb; **il ne m'inspire pas confiance** I don't have much confidence in him; **vos remarques m'ont inspiré plusieurs réflexions** your remarks made me think of several things.
II *vi* (inhaler) to breathe in, to inhale.
III s'inspirer *vpr* **1** (prendre son inspiration) **s'~ de** to draw one's inspiration from; **la révolution s'est inspirée de ces idéaux** the revolution was inspired by these ideals; **2** (prendre exemple) **s'~ de qn** to follow sb's example, to take a leaf out of sb's book; **inspirez-vous d'elle!** follow her example!

nstabilité /ɛ̃stabilite/ *nf* **1** (de situation, pays, prix) instability; (de temps) changeability; **2** (de personne) (emotional) instability; **3** CHIMIE, PHYS instability.

nstable /ɛ̃stabl/ *adj* **1** [*monnaie, économie*] unstable;

[*construction*] unstable, unsteady; [*temps*] unsettled; **2** [*personne, caractère*] unstable, unsteady.

installateur, **-trice** /ɛ̃stalatœʀ, tʀis/ ▶ **374** *nm,f* fitter.

installation /ɛ̃stalasjɔ̃/ *nf* **1** (mise en place) (d'appareil ménager, de téléphone, gaz) installation, putting in; (de toilettes publiques, douches, canalisations) putting in; (de système de sécurité, d'équipement informatique, usine) installation; (de table pliante, chevalet) putting up; **~ gratuite** 'free installation'; **2** (appareils) system; **3** (manière d'être installé) **notre ~ est temporaire** we're not permanently settled; **4** (usine) plant; **5** (arrivée) **depuis mon ~ à Paris** since I moved to Paris; **dès leur ~ au pouvoir, les insurgés...** as soon as they came to power, the rebels...; **quelques jours après l'~ du nouveau gouvernement** a few days after the new government took office.
II installations *nfpl* (équipements) facilities.
■ **~ électrique** electric wiring; **~ téléphonique** telephone system; **~s militaires** military installations.

installé, **~e** /ɛ̃stale/ **I** *pp* ▶ **installer**.
II *pp adj* (établi) [*personne*] living (**à** in); [*organisme, société*] based (**à** in); **être bien ~ dans un fauteuil** to be ensconced ou comfortably installed in an armchair; **ils sont bien ~s dans leur nouvelle maison** they're very snug in their new home; **c'est un homme ~** FIG he's very nicely set up.

installer /ɛ̃stale/ [1] **I** *vtr* **1** (mettre en place) to install, to put in [*lave-vaisselle, évier, chauffage central*]; to put up [*table pliante, étagère*]; to set up [*infrastructure militaire*]; (raccorder) to connect [*gaz, téléphone, électricité*]; **faire ~ une antenne parabolique** to have a satellite dish put up ou installed; **~ le bureau près de la fenêtre** to put the desk near the window; **2** (aménager) to do up [*cuisine*]; **~ une chambre dans le grenier** to make a bedroom in the attic; **3** (implanter) to set up [*usine*]; **4** (loger) to put [*invité*] (**dans** in); **~ qn dans un fauteuil** to sit sb in an armchair; **5** ADMIN **il a été installé dans ses fonctions** he took up his duties; **~ qn à un poste** to appoint sb to a post.
II s'installer *vpr* **1** (devenir durable) [*régime*] to become established; [*morosité, récession*] to set in; **le doute s'installe dans leur esprit** they're beginning to have doubts; **2** (professionnellement) to set oneself up in business; **s'~ à son compte** to set up one's own business; **3** (pour vivre) to settle; **partir s'~ à l'étranger** to go and live abroad; **s'~ temporairement chez des amis** to move in temporarily with friends; **je viendrai te voir quand tu seras installé** I'll come and see you when you're settled in; **4** (se mettre à l'aise) **s'~ dans un fauteuil** to settle into an armchair; **s'~ au soleil** to sit in the sun; **s'~ pour travailler/à son bureau** to settle down to work/at one's desk; **tu es bien installé?** are you sitting comfortably?; **installe-toi, j'arrive!** make yourself at home, I'm coming!; **on est mal installé sur ces chaises** these chairs are uncomfortable; **5** (être mis en place) **l'appareil s'installe facilement** the appliance is easy to install; **des usines étrangères vont s'~ dans la région** foreign companies are going to open factories in the area.

instamment /ɛ̃stamɑ̃/ *adv* insistently.

instance /ɛ̃stɑ̃s/ *nf* **1** (autorité) authority; **l'~ supérieure** the higher authority; **en dernière ~** in the final analysis; **les ~s d'un parti politique** the leaders of a political party; **2** (demande) entreaty; **il m'a demandé avec ~ de venir** he pleaded with me to come; **3** JUR (action) legal proceedings (*pl*); (juridiction) level of jurisdiction; **être en ~ de divorce** to be engaged in divorce proceedings; **en seconde ~** on appeal; **4** (attente) **l'affaire est en ~** the matter is pending; **courrier en ~** mail pending attention.

instant, **~e** /ɛ̃stɑ̃, ɑ̃t/ **I** *adj* [*demande*] insistent.
II *nm* moment, instant; **un ~! just a minute!; à tout** ou **chaque ~** all the time; **ne pas perdre un ~** not to waste any time; **d'~ en ~** every minute; **par ~s** at times; **pour l'~** for the moment; **il devrait arriver d'un ~ à l'autre** he should arrive any minute

now; **à l'~ (même)** this instant ou minute; **à l'~ même où** just when; **au même ~** at that very moment.

instantané, **~e** /ɛ̃stɑ̃tane/ **I** adj [réponse, effet] instantaneous, instant (épith); [mort] instantaneous; [boisson, potage] instant; [vision, lueur] momentary.
II nm PHOT snapshot.

instar: **à l'instar de** /alɛ̃staʁdə/ loc prép following the example of.

instaurer /ɛ̃stoʀe/ [1] **I** vtr to institute [taxe, contrôle]; to establish [régime, dialogue]; to impose [couvre-feu].
II s'instaurer vpr to be established.

instigateur /ɛ̃stigatœʀ, tʀis/ nm,f (de troubles) instigator; (de mouvement) originator.

instigation /ɛ̃stigasjɔ̃/ nf **à l'~ de qn** at sb's instigation.

instiller /ɛ̃stile/ [1] vtr to instil GB **(à, dans** into).

instinct /ɛ̃stɛ̃/ nm instinct; **d'~** instinctively; **l'~ de conservation** the instinct of self-preservation.

instinctif, **-ive** /ɛ̃stɛ̃ktif, iv/ adj instinctive; **c'est quelqu'un d'~** he/she's someone who relies on instinct.

instituer /ɛ̃stitɥe/ [1] vtr (créer) to institute.

institut /ɛ̃stity/ nm institute.
■ **~ de beauté** beauty salon ou parlour GB.

instituteur, **-trice** /ɛ̃stitytœʀ, tʀis/ ▶ 374 | nm,f (d'école primaire) (primary school) teacher; (d'école maternelle) (nursery school) teacher.

institution /ɛ̃stitysjɔ̃/ **I** nf **1** (administration) institution; **2** (établissement d'enseignement) private school; **3** (action) institution (**de** of); **4** (établissement pour enfants, vieillards, malades) institution.
II institutions nfpl POL institutions.

institutionnel, **-elle** /ɛ̃stitysjɔnɛl/ adj institutional.

institutrice ▶ **instituteur**.

instructeur /ɛ̃stʀyktœʀ/ **I** adj JUR examining; MIL drill.
II nm GÉN, MIL instructor.

instructif, **-ive** /ɛ̃stʀyktif, iv/ adj [rencontre, histoire] instructive; [voyage, livre] informative; [expérience] enlightening.

instruction /ɛ̃stʀyksjɔ̃/ **I** nf **1** (formation) education ¢; MIL training; **2** (connaissances) education ¢; **niveau d'~ insuffisant** poor level of education; **homme sans ~** uneducated man; **manquer d'~** to be uneducated; **avoir de l'~** to be well-educated; **3** (circulaire) directive; **4** JUR preparation of a case for eventual judgment.
II instructions nfpl (directives) instructions.
■ **~ civique** civics (+ v sg); **~ religieuse** religious instruction.

instruire /ɛ̃stʀɥiʀ/ [69] **I** vtr **1** (former) [personne] to teach [enfant]; to train [soldats]; **ce film ne vise pas à ~** this film is not intended to be educational; **2** JUR **~ une affaire** to prepare a case for judgment; **3** (informer) FML **~ qn de qch** to inform sb of sth.
II s'instruire vpr (apprendre) to learn; **on s'instruit à tout âge** it's never too late to learn.

instruit, **~e** /ɛ̃stʀɥi, it/ **I** pp ▶ **instruire**.
II pp adj [personne] educated.

instrument /ɛ̃stʀymɑ̃/ nm **1** (objet) instrument; **~s de chirurgie** surgical instruments; **2** MUS instrument; **~ à cordes** string instrument; **3** (agent) tool; (moyen) instrument; **être l'~ de qn** to be sb's tool; **être l'~ de la vengeance de qn** to be the instrument of sb's revenge.
■ **~ ancien** MUS period instrument; **~ de musique** musical instrument; **~s de bord** controls.

insu: **à l'insu de** /alɛ̃sydə/ loc prép **1** (sans le dire) **je suis parti à leur ~** I left without their knowing; **2** (sans le savoir) without knowing it; **ils ont été filmés à leur ~** they were filmed without (their) knowing it.

insubmersible /ɛ̃sybmɛʀsibl/ adj unsinkable.

insubordonné, **~e** /ɛ̃sybɔʀdɔne/ adj GÉN rebellious, insubordinate SOUT; MIL insubordinate.

insuffisamment /ɛ̃syfizamɑ̃/ adv (pas assez) insufficiently; (mal) inadequately.

insuffisance /ɛ̃syfizɑ̃s/ nf **1** (pénurie) insufficiency shortage; **2** (médiocrité) poor standard; **3** (déficit) shorfall; **l'~ de la production** the shortfall in production; **4** (lacune) shortcoming; **5** MÉD insufficiency.

insuffisant, **~e** /ɛ̃syfizɑ̃, ɑ̃t/ adj **1** (quantitativement) insufficient; **ils sont en nombre ~** there aren enough of them; **2** (qualitativement) inadequate; **tes ré sultats sont ~s** your results are not good enough.

insuffler /ɛ̃syfle/ [1] vtr **1** to instil GB (**à** into); **~ la vi à qn** to breathe life into sb; **2** MÉD to insufflate [oxy gène] (**à, dans** into).

insulaire /ɛ̃sylɛʀ/ **I** adj [population, traditions] islan (épith); [mentalité] insular PÉJ.
II nmf islander.

insuline /ɛ̃sylin/ nf insulin.

insultant, **~e** /ɛ̃syltɑ̃, ɑ̃t/ adj insulting.

insulte /ɛ̃sylt/ nf insult; **c'est une ~ à leur mé moire** it is an insult to their memory; **une lettr d'~s** an insulting letter; **dire des ~s à qn t** insult sb; **faire à qn l'~ de refuser** to insult sb b refusing.

insulter /ɛ̃sylte/ [1] **I** vtr (injurier) to insult, to shou abuse at [personne]; (offenser) [personne] to insult; [att tude] to be an insult to; **se faire ~** to get a stream o abuse (**par** from).
II s'insulter vpr to exchange insults.

insupportable /ɛ̃sypɔʀtabl/ adj unbearable.

insurgé, **~e** /ɛ̃syʀʒe/ adj, nm,f insurgent, rebel.

insurger: **s'insurger** /ɛ̃syʀʒe/ [13] vpr (se soulever) rise up; (protester) to protest.

insurmontable /ɛ̃syʀmɔ̃tabl/ adj [problème, dett insurmountable; [désaccord] insuperable; [timidit unconquerable.

insurrection /ɛ̃syʀɛksjɔ̃/ nf **1** (de population) insurre tion, uprising; **mouvements d'~** rebel movement **2** FIG revolt (**contre** against).

insurrectionnel, **-elle** /ɛ̃syʀɛksjɔnɛl/ adj insurre tionary.

intact, **~e** /ɛ̃takt/ adj intact (jamais épith).

intangible /ɛ̃tɑ̃ʒibl/ adj (inviolable) [lois, principe inviolable.

intarissable /ɛ̃taʀisabl/ adj [imagination, bavar inexhaustible; [bavardage, larmes] endless; [source] ƒ never-ending; **elle est ~** she can go on forever (su about).

intégral, **~e¹**, mpl **-aux** /ɛ̃tegʀal, o/ adj **1** [pai ment] full, in full (après n); [bronzage] all-over (épith **2** [édition, texte] complete, unabridged; **voir un film e version ~e** to see the uncut version of a film.

intégrale² /ɛ̃tegʀal/ nf **1** MUS **l'~ des concerto pour piano** the complete piano concertos (pl); **2** MA integral.

intégralement /ɛ̃tegʀalmɑ̃/ adv [payer, citer, publie in full; [refuser, rejeter] completely.

intégralité /ɛ̃tegʀalite/ nf **l'~ de leur salaire** the entire salary; **payer une dette dans son ~** to pay debt in full; **diffuser un opéra dans son ~** to broa cast an opera in its entirety.

intégrante /ɛ̃tegʀɑ̃t/ adj f **faire partie ~ de qch** be an integral part of sth.

intégration /ɛ̃tegʀasjɔ̃/ nf GÉN integration (**à, dan** into); **~ sociale** integration into society.

intègre /ɛ̃tɛgʀ/ adj [personne, caractère, vie] hones **un homme ~** a man of integrity.

intégrer /ɛ̃tegʀe/ [14] **I** vtr **1** (insérer) to insert (**à, dan** into); **une architecture bien intégrée dans l'env ronnement** architecture which blends with the surroundings; **2** (assimiler) to integrate [communauté population] (**à, dans** into); **3°** (entrer dans) **il a intégr la garde présidentielle** he joined the presidentia guard; **il vient d'~ Harvard** he has just got int Harvard.
II s'intégrer vpr **1** [population] to integrate (**à, dan** with); **2** [immeuble] to fit in (**à, dans** with).

intégrisme /ɛ̃tegʀism/ *nm* fundamentalism.

intégrité /ɛ̃tegʀite/ *nf* integrity.

intellect /ɛ̃telɛkt/ *nm* intellect.

intellectuel, -elle /ɛ̃telɛktɥɛl/ **I** *adj* [*travail, facultés, milieu*] intellectual; [*fatigue, effort*] mental; [*goût, musique*] highbrow.
II *nm,f* intellectual.

intelligence /ɛ̃teliʒɑ̃s/ *nf* **1** (aptitude) intelligence **avec ~** intelligently; **2** (compréhension) understanding; **3** agreement; **agir d'~ avec qn** to act in agreement with sb; **faire des signes d'~ à qn** to make signs of complicity to sb.
■ **~ artificielle** ORDINAT artificial intelligence.

intelligent, ~e /ɛ̃teliʒɑ̃, ɑ̃t/ *adj* [*personne*] intelligent, clever; [*réponse, regard*] intelligent; **ce n'est pas ~ de ta part d'avoir fait** it wasn't very clever of you to do; **c'est ~!** IRON that's clever!

intelligible /ɛ̃teliʒibl/ *adj* intelligible (à to); **parler à haute et ~ voix** to speak loudly and clearly.

intempéries /ɛ̃tɑ̃peʀi/ *nfpl* bad weather ¢.

intempestif, -ive /ɛ̃tɑ̃pɛstif, iv/ *adj* [*démarche, arrivée*] untimely; [*curiosité, joie, zèle*] misplaced.

intemporel, -elle /ɛ̃tɑ̃pɔʀɛl/ *adj* (immuable) timeless.

intenable /ɛ̃t(ə)nabl/ *adj* [*odeur, chaleur, situation*] unbearable; (indiscipliné) difficult; (indéfendable) untenable.

intendance /ɛ̃tɑ̃dɑ̃s/ *nf* SCOL (service) administration; (bureau, personnel) administrative offices (*pl*); **l'~ ne suit pas** the backup is not forthcoming.

intendant, ~e /ɛ̃tɑ̃dɑ̃, ɑ̃t/ **I** *nm,f* SCOL bursar.
II *nm* MIL (général) quartermaster; (financier) paymaster.

intense /ɛ̃tɑ̃s/ *adj* intense.

intensif, -ive /ɛ̃tɑ̃sif, iv/ *adj* intensive.

intensification /ɛ̃tɑ̃sifikasjɔ̃/ *nf* intensification.

intensifier /ɛ̃tɑ̃sifje/ [2] *vtr*, **s'intensifier** *vpr* to intensify.

intensité /ɛ̃tɑ̃site/ *nf* **1** (force) intensity; **la tempête diminue d'~** the storm is dying down; **2** PHYS (électrique) current.

intensivement /ɛ̃tɑ̃sivmɑ̃/ *adv* intensively.

intenter /ɛ̃tɑ̃te/ [1] *vtr* **~ un procès à qn** to sue sb; **~ une action contre** to bring an action against.

intention /ɛ̃tɑ̃sjɔ̃/ *nf* intention; **les meilleures ~s du monde** the best of intentions; **avoir l'~ de faire** to intend to do; **c'est l'~ qui compte** it's the thought that counts; **dans l'~ de faire** with the intention of doing; **à l'~ de qn** [*déclaration, geste*] aimed at sb; [*œuvre*] intended for sb; [*fête*] in sb's honour^GB.

intentionné, ~e /ɛ̃tɑ̃sjɔne/ *adj* **bien/mal ~** well-/ill-intentioned.

intentionnel, -elle /ɛ̃tɑ̃sjɔnɛl/ *adj* intentional.

interactif, -ive /ɛ̃tɛʀaktif, iv/ *adj* interactive.

interaction /ɛ̃tɛʀaksjɔ̃/ *nf* interaction.

interallié, ~e /ɛ̃tɛʀalje/ *adj* [*état-major, force*] joint allied.

interarmées /ɛ̃tɛʀaʀme/ *adj inv* [*état-major, force*] joint.

interbancaire /ɛ̃tɛʀbɑ̃kɛʀ/ *adj* interbank (*épith*).

interbibliothèques /ɛ̃tɛʀbiblijɔtɛk/ *adj inv* **prêt ~** interlibrary loan.

intercalaire /ɛ̃tɛʀkalɛʀ/ **I** *adj* **feuille** or **feuillet ~** insert.
II *nm* (de séparation) divider.

intercaler /ɛ̃tɛʀkale/ [1] **I** *vtr* **1** (insérer) to insert (**dans** into); **2** (ajouter) to intercalate [*jour, mois*].
II **s'intercaler** *vpr* [*rendez-vous*] to fit; [*feuillet, exemple*] to be inserted; [*personne, véhicule*] to come.

intercéder /ɛ̃tɛʀsede/ [14] *vi* to intercede (**auprès de qn** with sb); **en faveur de qn** on sb's behalf.

intercepter /ɛ̃tɛʀsɛpte/ [1] *vtr* to intercept.

interception /ɛ̃tɛʀsɛpsjɔ̃/ *nf* interception.

intercession /ɛ̃tɛʀsesjɔ̃/ *nf* intercession.

interchangeable /ɛ̃tɛʀʃɑ̃ʒabl/ *adj* interchangeable.

interclasse /ɛ̃tɛʀklas/ *nm* break (between classes).

intercommunal, ~e, mpl -aux /ɛ̃tɛʀkɔmynal, o/ *adj* [*coopération*] between local councils (*épith, après n*); [*équipement*] district (*épith*).

intercommunautaire /ɛ̃tɛʀkɔmynotɛʀ/ *adj* within the EU (*après n*).

intercontinental, ~e, mpl -aux /ɛ̃tɛʀkɔ̃tinɑ̃tal, o/ *adj* intercontinental.

intercostal, ~e, mpl -aux /ɛ̃tɛʀkɔstal, o/ *adj* [*nerf*] intercostal; [*douleur*] in the ribs (*après n*).

interdiction /ɛ̃tɛʀdiksjɔ̃/ *nf* **1** (action d'interdire) banning; **demander l'~ de qch** to ask for sth to be banned; **'~ de fumer'** 'no smoking'; **condamné avec ~ d'exercer sa profession** found guilty and banned from practising^GB; **2** (chose interdite) ban; **lever une ~** to lift a ban.
■ **~ de séjour** prohibition on residence.

interdire /ɛ̃tɛʀdiʀ/ [65] **I** *vtr* **1** (ne pas autoriser) to ban; **~ à qn l'entrée de sa maison** to refuse sb entry to one's house; **le médecin m'a interdit l'alcool** the doctor has told me not to drink alcohol; **interdit d'antenne** banned from broadcasting; **~ à qn de faire, ~ que qn fasse** to forbid sb to do; **il est interdit de parler au chauffeur** it is forbidden to talk to the driver; **il est interdit de fumer** (sur une pancarte) no smoking; **2** (rendre impossible) **mon état de santé m'interdit l'alcool** I can't drink alcohol on account of my health; **~ à qn de faire** to prevent sb from doing.
II **s'interdire** *vpr* **s'~ le chocolat** to keep off chocolate; **s'~ les sorties** to refrain from going out.

interdisciplinaire /ɛ̃tɛʀdisiplinɛʀ/ *adj* SCOL [*cours, activité*] cross-curricular; UNIV interdisciplinary.

interdit, ~e /ɛ̃tɛʀdi, it/ **I** *pp* ▶ **interdire**.
II *pp adj* **1** (défendu) prohibited, forbidden; **baignade/chasse ~e** swimming/hunting prohibited; **entrée ~e** no entry ou admittance; **film ~ aux moins de 13 ans** film unsuitable for children under 13; **film ~ aux moins de 18 ans** film for adults over 18 only; **être ~ de séjour** JUR to be subject to a prohibition on residence; FIG to be banned (**dans** from).
III *adj* (stupéfait) dumbfounded.
IV *nm* **1** (chose interdite) (par les lois) proscription; (par les conventions) taboo; **2** (condamnation) bar; **jeter l'~ sur qn** to debar ou bar sb.

intéressant, ~e /ɛ̃teʀesɑ̃, ɑ̃t/ **I** *adj* **1** (qui retient l'attention) interesting (**de faire** to do); **2** (qui offre des ressources) interesting; **3** (avantageux) [*prix, conditions*] attractive; **c'est une affaire ~e** it's an attractive proposition; **il est plus ~ de payer au comptant** it's better to pay in cash.
II *nm,f* **faire l'~** ou **son ~** to show off.

intéressé, ~e /ɛ̃teʀese/ **I** *pp* ▶ **intéresser**.
II *pp adj* **1** (attiré) interested (**par** in); **il est peu ~ par l'affaire** he has little interest in the matter; **se dire ~ par qch** to express an interest in sth; **2** (captivé) attentive; **3** (concerné) **les parties ~es** those concerned; **toute personne ~e** all those interested (+ *v pl*); **les personnes ~es aux bénéfices** people with a share in the profits; **4** (qui vise un profit) [*personne, avis, démarche*] self-interested (*épith*); **il est ~** he acts out of self-interest; **ses conseils étaient ~s** he/she had a selfish motive for giving that advice.
III *nm,f* person concerned; **les ~s** people concerned; **le principal ~** the person most directly concerned; **les principaux ~s** those most directly concerned.

intéressement /ɛ̃teʀesmɑ̃/ *nm* (système) profit-sharing; (revenu) share in the profits.

intéresser /ɛ̃teʀese/ [1] **I** *vtr* **1** (retenir l'attention) to interest; **ça ne m'intéresse pas** I'm not interested (**de faire** in doing); **2** (concerner) [*problème, décision, mesures*] to concern; **la protection du site intéresse tout le monde** the protection of the site is of concern to all; **3** **~ les salariés aux bénéfices** to offer a profit-sharing scheme to employees.
II **s'intéresser** *vpr* **s'~ à** GÉN to be interested in; (en s'engageant) to take an interest in; **ils s'intéressent à l'environnement** they are taking an interest in the environment.

intérêt /ɛ̃teʀɛ/ *nm* **1** (attention) interest (**pour** in); **2** (attrait) interest; **recherche digne d'~** worthwhile research; **livre plein d'~** book of exceptional interest; **sans ~** uninteresting; **n'avoir pas grand ~** not to have much to recommend it; **3** (avantage, utilité) interest; **d'~ général** of general interest; **l'~ supérieur de la nation** the higher good of the country; **elle a tout ~ à faire** it is in her best interest to do; **être du plus grand ~** to be of particular interest (**pour**) to; **tu as ~ à faire**○ you'd be well advised to do; **quel ~ auraient-ils à faire?** what would be the point in their doing?; **y a ~**○**!** you bet○!; **je ne vois pas l'~ de cette réforme/de faire** I can't see the point of this reform/of doing; **par ~** [*agir*] out of self-interest; [*se marier*] for money; **4** FIN interest **¢**; **prêt sans ~s** interest-free loan; **5** (part) interest; **des ~s dans le sucre** interests in sugar.

interethnique /ɛ̃tɛʀɛtnik/ adj [*relations*] between ethnic communities (*après n*); [*violence, affrontements*] (entre tribus) intertribal; (entre communautés) racial.

interférence /ɛ̃tɛʀfeʀɑ̃s/ nf interference.

interférer /ɛ̃tɛʀfeʀe/ [14] vi to interfere (**avec** with).

intérieur, ~e /ɛ̃teʀjœʀ/ **I** adj **1** (au-dedans) [*mur, escalier, température*] internal, interior; [*cour*] inner; [*mer*] inland; [*poche*] inside; [*frontière*] internal; **le côté ~** the inside; **pour l'aménagement ~ de votre maison** for the interior decoration of your house; **lire notre article en pages ~es** read our article inside; **2** (d'un pays) domestic; **sur le plan ~** on the domestic front; **3** (d'une organisation) internal; **4** (intime) inner. **II** nm **1** (de boîte, journal, d'enveloppe, armoire) inside; (de voiture) interior; **fermé de l'~** locked from the inside; **à l'~** inside, indoors; **à l'~ de** inside; **à l'~ des terres** inland; **2** (habitation) interior; **fière de son ~** proud of her home; **d'~** [*jeu*] indoor; **plante d'~** houseplant, indoor plant; **3** (de pays) interior; **à l'~ du pays** inland; **les villes de l'~** the inland towns.

intérieurement /ɛ̃teʀjœʀmɑ̃/ adv (en soi-même) inwardly; (au-dedans) **verrouillé/doublé ~** bolted from the/lined on the inside.

intérim /ɛ̃teʀim/ nm **1** (période) interim (period); **par ~** on an interim basis; **président par ~** acting president; **2** (fonction) interim duties (pl); **assurer l'~ de** to stand in for; **3** (travail temporaire) temporary work; **société** or **agence d'~** GÉN temporary employment agency; (de secrétariat) temping agency; **travailler en ~** to do temporary work, to temp○.

intérimaire /ɛ̃teʀimɛʀ/ **I** adj [*fonction, comité*] interim; [*ministre*] acting, interim; [*emploi, personnel*] temporary. **II** nmf GÉN worker from a temporary employment agency; (secrétaire) temporary secretary, temp○.

intérioriser /ɛ̃teʀjɔʀize/ [1] vtr to internalize.

interjection /ɛ̃tɛʀ3ɛksjɔ̃/ nf LING interjection.

interligne /ɛ̃tɛʀliɲ/ nm (espace) line space; **ajouter un mot dans l'~** to add a word between the lines; **double ~** double spacing.

interlocuteur, -trice /ɛ̃tɛʀlɔkytœʀ, tʀis/ nm,f **1** (dans une conversation) interlocutor SOUT; **mon ~** the person I am talking to; **2** (dans une négociation) representative; **reconnaître qn comme un ~ valable** to acknowledge sb as a recognized spokesperson; **3** (contact) **Louis est notre seul ~** Louis is our only contact; **l'~ privilégié du gouvernement** the person the government prefers to deal with.

interloquer /ɛ̃tɛʀlɔke/ [1] vtr to take [sb] aback; **rester interloqué** to be taken aback.

interlude /ɛ̃tɛʀlyd/ nm TV, MUS interlude.

intermède /ɛ̃tɛʀmɛd/ nm interlude.

intermédiaire /ɛ̃tɛʀmedjɛʀ/ **I** adj [*taux, étape*] intermediate; **il n'existe pas de structure ~ entre la prison et l'hôpital psychiatrique** there's no halfway house between prison and a psychiatric hospital; **avez-vous la taille ~?** do you have a size in between? **II** nmf (dans des négociations) go-between; (dans l'industrie) middleman. **III** nm **sans ~** [*faire, agir*] without any intermediary; [*traiter, vendre*] direct; **par l'~ de** through.

interminable /ɛ̃tɛʀminabl/ adj (qui dure) interminable, never-ending; (long) [*lettre, file, plage*] endless.

intermittence /ɛ̃tɛʀmitɑ̃s/ nf **1 par ~** [*pleuvoir*] on and off; [*travailler*] intermittently; **2** MÉD (rémission) remission.

intermittent, ~e /ɛ̃tɛʀmitɑ̃, ɑ̃t/ adj [*pluie, fièvre*] intermittent; [*bruit, efforts*] sporadic.

internat /ɛ̃tɛʀna/ nm **1** (école) boarding school; (dortoirs) dormitories (pl); (élèves) boarders (pl); **2** UNIV (concours) examination for the post of houseman GB ou intern US; (stage) period as houseman GB, internship US.

international, ~e, mpl **-aux** /ɛ̃tɛʀnasjɔnal, o/ **I** adj international. **II** nm,f (athlète) international. **III internationaux** nmpl SPORT internationals.

internationalisme /ɛ̃tɛʀnasjɔnalism/ nm internationalism.

interne /ɛ̃tɛʀn/ **I** adj **1** (intérieur) [*crise, règlement, concours*] internal; [*formation*] in-house (épith); **~ à** within; **2** ANAT, MÉD [*paroi, organe, hémorragie*] internal; [*oreille*] inner; **à usage ~** for internal use. **II** nmf **1** SCOL boarder; **je suis ~** I'm a boarder; **2** UNIV ou (**en médecine**) houseman GB, intern US.

internement /ɛ̃tɛʀnəmɑ̃/ nm (de prisonnier, dissident) internment; (de malade mental) committal (to a psychiatric institution); **demander l'~ de qn** to request that sb be committed.

interner /ɛ̃tɛʀne/ [1] vtr to intern [*prisonnier politique*]; to commit [*malade*]; **faire ~ qn** to have sb committed; **il est bon à ~** HUM he ought to be in a loony bin○.

interparlementaire /ɛ̃tɛʀpaʀləmɑ̃tɛʀ/ adj interparliamentary GB, joint (épith).

interpellation /ɛ̃tɛʀpelasjɔ̃/ nf **1** (action policière) questioning **¢**; **il y a eu quinze ~s** fifteen people have been questioned by the police; **procéder à des ~s** to take people in for questioning; **2** (adresse) calling out (**de** to); **3** POL interpellation.

interpeller /ɛ̃tɛʀpəle/ [1] **I** vtr **1** (appeler) to call out to; (apostropher) to shout at; **2** (interroger sur place) to question; (emmener au poste) to take [sb] in for questioning; **3** POL to interpellate. **II s'interpeller** vpr [*personnes*] (amicalement) to shout to one another; (agressivement) to shout at one another.

interphone® /ɛ̃tɛʀfɔn/ nm **1** (dans un bureau) intercom; **parler par l'~** to speak over the intercom; **2** (dans un immeuble) entry phone.

interplanétaire /ɛ̃tɛʀplanetɛʀ/ adj interplanetary.

interposer /ɛ̃tɛʀpoze/ [1] **I** vtr to interpose SOUT (**entre** between); **par personne interposée** through an intermediary. **II s'interposer** vpr to intervene.

interprétariat /ɛ̃tɛʀpʀetaʀja/ nm interpreting.

interprétation /ɛ̃tɛʀpʀetasjɔ̃/ nf **1** (explication) interpretation (**de** of); **mauvaise ~** misinterpretation; **on peut donner plusieurs ~s à ce phénomène** this phenomenon can be interpreted in several ways; **2** MUS, THÉÂT interpretation; **3** (métier) interpreting.

interprète /ɛ̃tɛʀpʀɛt/ nmf **1** ▶374 (traducteur) interpreter; **servir d'~ à qn** to act as an interpreter for sb; **2** MUS (exécutant) performer; (soliste) soloist; **3** CIN, THÉÂT performer; **les ~s d'une pièce** the cast (sg) of a play; **4** (porte-parole) spokesperson; **se faire l'~ de qn** to act as sb's spokesperson; **5** (de texte) exponent; (de présage, rêve) interpreter.

interpréter /ɛ̃tɛʀpʀete/ [14] **I** vtr **1** to play [*rôle*]; to sing [*chanson*]; to perform [*sonate, morceau*]; **2** (tirer une signification de) to interpret; **ne pas savoir comment ~ qch** not to know what to make of sth; **mal ~ qch** to misinterpret sth. **II s'interpréter** vpr to be interpreted.

interpréteur /ɛ̃tɛʀpʀetœʀ/ nm ORDINAT interpreter.

interrogateur, -trice /ɛ̃tɛʀɔgatœʀ, tʀis/ adj inquiring; **d'un air ~** inquiringly.

interrogatif, -ive /ɛ̃tɛʀɔgatif, iv/ adj interrogative.

interrogation /ɛ̃tɛʀɔgasjɔ̃/ nf **1** (de témoin) questioning (**sur** about); **2** LING question; **3** SCOL test; **~ orale** oral test; **4** ORDINAT query.

interrogatoire /ɛ̃tɛʀɔgatwaʀ/ *nm* GÉN interrogation; (par la police) questioning.

interrogeable /ɛ̃tɛʀɔʒabl/ *adj* which can be interrogated; **répondeur ~ à distance** remote-access answering machine.

interroger /ɛ̃tɛʀɔʒe/ [13] I *vtr* **1** (questionner) GÉN to question (**sur** about); (pour un renseignement) to ask; [*police*] to question, to interrogate [*suspect*]; [*journaliste*] to put questions to (**sur** on); FIG to search [*mémoire*]; to examine [*conscience*]; **50% des personnes interrogées** 50% of those questioned; **quand on l'a interrogé sur ses intentions** when he was asked about his intentions; **être interrogé comme témoin** to be called as a witness; **2** (consulter) to query [*ordinateur*]; **~ son répondeur** to check one's calls; **3** SCOL to test (**sur** on).
II **s'interroger** *vpr* **s'~ sur** to wonder about.

interrompre /ɛ̃tɛʀɔ̃pʀ/ [53] I *vtr* **1** (momentanément) to interrupt [*émission, repas, conversation*]; to break off [*relations, dialogue*]; to disrupt [*circulation*]; to cut off [*distribution d'eau*]; to cease [*activité*]; **~ son repas pour faire** to stop eating to do; **2** (définitivement) to put an end to [*carrière, études, vacances*]; to stop [*traitement*]; **3** (couper la parole à) to interrupt; **ne m'interromps pas tout le temps!** stop interrupting all the time!
II **s'interrompre** *vpr* **1** (soi-même) **s'~ dans son travail** to stop working (**pour faire** to do); **2** (l'un l'autre) to interrupt each other; **3** (s'arrêter) [*pluie, fête*] to stop.

interrupteur /ɛ̃tɛʀyptœʀ/ *nm* switch.

interruption /ɛ̃tɛʀypsjɔ̃/ *nf* **1** (arrêt) break (**de** in); **une ~ de trois mois** a three-month break; **sans ~** continuously; **j'ai travaillé sans ~ jusqu'à minuit** I worked nonstop until midnight; **2** (fin) ending (**de** of); **l'~ du dialogue entre** the breaking off of the dialogue[GB] between.
■ **~ volontaire de grossesse, IVG** termination of pregnancy.

intersection /ɛ̃tɛʀsɛksjɔ̃/ *nf* intersection.

intersidéral, ~e, *mpl* **-aux** /ɛ̃tɛʀsideʀal, o/ *adj* interstellar.

interstellaire /ɛ̃tɛʀstɛllɛʀ/ *adj* interstellar.

interstice /ɛ̃tɛʀstis/ *nm* (de plancher) crack; (de volets, stores) chink.

intersyndical, ~e, *mpl* **-aux** /ɛ̃tɛʀsɛ̃dikal, o/ *adj* inter-union.

intertitre /ɛ̃tɛʀtitʀ/ *nm* CIN insert title.

interurbain, ~e /ɛ̃tɛʀyʀbɛ̃, ɛn/ I *adj* [*liaisons, transports*] interurban; (au téléphone) [*communications*] trunk; [*appel*] trunk, long distance.
II *nm* **l'~** long distance telephone service.

intervalle /ɛ̃tɛʀval/ *nm* **1** (dans l'espace) space; **à ~s réguliers** at regular intervals; **2** (dans le temps) interval; **dans l'~** meanwhile, in the meantime; **3** MUS interval.

intervenir /ɛ̃tɛʀvəniʀ/ [36] *vi* (+ *v* être) **1** (se produire) [*changements*] to take place; [*accord*] to be reached; [*augmentation*] to occur; **2** (prendre part) [*orateur*] to speak (**dans** in); **~ sur le marché** to intervene in the market; **3** (agir en urgence) [*armée, police, pompiers*] to intervene; **le chirurgien a décidé d'~** the surgeon decided to operate; **4** (intercéder) to intercede; **~ auprès de qn** to intercede with sb; **~ comme médiateur** to play the role of mediator.

intervention /ɛ̃tɛʀvɑ̃sjɔ̃/ *nf* **1** (engagement) intervention (**en faveur de** on behalf of; **auprès de** with); **~ de l'armée** military intervention; **2** (d'orateur) speech; (de conférencier) lecture; **3** (opération) operation; **~ chirurgicale** operation (**sur qn** on sb); **une petite ~** a minor operation.

interventionnisme /ɛ̃tɛʀvɑ̃sjɔnism/ *nm* interventionism.

interversion /ɛ̃tɛʀvɛʀsjɔ̃/ *nf* inversion.

intervertir /ɛ̃tɛʀvɛʀtiʀ/ [3] *vtr* to invert [*objets, mots*].

interviewer /ɛ̃tɛʀvjuve/ [1] *vtr* to interview.

intestin /ɛ̃tɛstɛ̃/ *nm* bowel, intestine.

intestinal, ~e, *mpl* **-aux** /ɛ̃tɛstinal, o/ *adj* intestinal; **problèmes intestinaux** bowel problems.

intime /ɛ̃tim/ I *adj* **1** (personnel) [*vie, journal*] private; [*ami, rapports*] intimate; [*hygiène*] personal; **avoir des relations ~s avec qn** to be on intimate terms with sb; **2** (entre proches) [*fête, dîner*] intimate; [*conversation*] private; [*cérémonie*] quiet; **3** (douillet) [*pièce*] cosy; **4** (profond) [*connaissance*] intimate; [*conviction*] deep; **j'ai la conviction ~ que...** I firmly believe that...
II *nmf* close friend, intimate; **c'est Jojo pour les ~s** my friends call me/him Jojo.

intimement /ɛ̃timmã/ *adv* intimately; **je suis ~ convaincu que...** I'm absolutely convinced that...

intimer /ɛ̃time/ [1] *vtr* **~ à qn l'ordre de faire** to order sb to do.

intimidable /ɛ̃timidabl/ *adj* **être ~** to be easily intimidated.

intimidation /ɛ̃timidasjɔ̃/ *nf* intimidation; **d'~** [*mesure, parole*] intimidatory; **céder à des mesures d'~** to allow oneself to be intimidated.

intimider /ɛ̃timide/ [1] *vtr* to intimidate; **se laisser ~ par** to be intimidated by.

intimité /ɛ̃timite/ *nf* **1** (lien) intimacy; **2** (privé) privacy; **ils ont fêté Noël dans l'~** they had a quiet Christmas; **dans l'~ il est beaucoup plus chaleureux** in private he is much warmer; **3** (vie privée) private life; **4** (de maison, pièce, cadre) cosiness.

intitulé /ɛ̃tityle/ *nm* title, heading.

intituler /ɛ̃tityle/ [1] I *vtr* to call.
II **s'intituler** *vpr* to be called, to be entitled.

intolérable /ɛ̃tɔleʀabl/ *adj* [*souffrance, vacarme, attitude*] intolerable; [*images*] deeply shocking; **de façon ~** intolerably.

intolérance /ɛ̃tɔleʀɑ̃s/ *nf* intolerance; MÉD allergy.

intolérant, ~e /ɛ̃tɔleʀɑ̃, ɑ̃t/ *adj* intolerant.

intonation /ɛ̃tɔnasjɔ̃/ *nf* intonation.

intouchable /ɛ̃tuʃabl/ *adj, nmf* untouchable.

intox(e)° /ɛ̃tɔks/ *nf inv* disinformation; **faire de l'~** to spread disinformation.

intoxication /ɛ̃tɔksikasjɔ̃/ *nf* **1** MÉD poisoning; **~ alimentaire** MÉD food poisoning; **~ par les champignons** poisoning caused by eating fungi; **17 ~s mortelles** 17 deaths due to poisoning; **2** (propagande) disinformation.

intoxiquer /ɛ̃tɔksike/ [1] I *vtr* (empoisonner) to poison; FIG (abrutir) to brainwash.
II **s'intoxiquer** *vpr* to poison oneself.

intraduisible /ɛ̃tʀadɥizibl/ *adj* **1** (qu'on ne peut traduire) untranslatable; **2** (inexprimable) inexpressible.

intraitable /ɛ̃tʀɛtabl/ *adj* inflexible; **je serai ~ là-dessus** I will not budge on this.

intra-muros /ɛ̃tʀamyʀos/ I *loc adj inv* **Paris ~** Paris itself.
II *loc adv* [*habiter*] in ou within the town itself.

intransigeance /ɛ̃tʀɑ̃ziʒɑ̃s/ *nf* intransigence.

intransigeant, ~e /ɛ̃tʀɑ̃ziʒɑ̃, ɑ̃t/ *adj* [*attitude, principe*] uncompromising; [*personne*] intransigent (**sur** on); [*partisan*] staunch.

intransitif, -ive /ɛ̃tʀɑ̃zitif, iv/ I *adj* intransitive.
II *nm* intransitive verb.

intransmissible /ɛ̃tʀɑ̃smisibl/ *adj* [*maladie*] non-infectious; [*savoir*] incommunicable.

intransportable /ɛ̃tʀɑ̃spɔʀtabl/ *adj* [*marchandises*] untransportable; [*blessé*] who should not be moved (*épith, après n*).

intra-utérin, ~e, *mpl* **~s** /ɛ̃tʀaytøʀɛ̃, in/ *adj* intra-uterine.

intraveineuse[1] /ɛ̃tʀavɛnøz/ *nf* intravenous injection.

intraveineux, -euse[2] /ɛ̃tʀavɛnø, øz/ *adj* intravenous.

intrépide /ɛ̃tʀepid/ *adj* intrepid, bold.

intrépidité /ɛ̃tʀepidite/ *nf* boldness, intrepidity; **avec ~** boldly.

intrigant, ~e /ɛ̃tʀigã, ãt/ *nm,f* schemer.

intrigue /ɛ̃trig/ *nf* **1** (machination) intrigue; **2** LITTÉRAT plot; **une ~ policière** a detective story.

intriguer /ɛ̃trige/ [1] *vtr* to intrigue; **elle m'intrigue** I find her intriguing.

intrinsèque /ɛ̃trɛ̃sɛk/ *adj* [*valeur, contenu*] intrinsic.

introducteur, -trice /ɛ̃trɔdyktœr, tris/ *nm,f* (personne qui introduit) **l'~ du tabac en France** the man who introduced tobacco to France.

introduction /ɛ̃trɔdyksjɔ̃/ *nf* **1** LITTÉRAT, MUS (préliminaire) introduction (**à, de** to); **2** (d'objet, sonde, clé) insertion (**dans** into); **3** (de visiteur) ushering (**dans** into); **4** (présentation) **une lettre d'~ auprès de qn** a letter of introduction to sb; **5** (de mode, produit, mesure) introduction; **6** (importation illicite) **~ de substances illicites** smuggling in illegal substances; **7** (initiation) introduction (**à** to).

introduire /ɛ̃trɔdɥir/ [69] **I** *vtr* **1** (insérer) to insert [*objet*]; **2** (faire entrer) (en grande pompe) to usher [sb] in [*personne*]; (clandestinement) to smuggle; **3** (présenter) to introduce [*personne*] (**auprès de** to); **4** (faire adopter) to introduce [*produit, idée*] (**dans** into); **5** (importer illicitement) to smuggle.

II s'introduire *vpr* **1** (pénétrer) **s'~ dans** to get into; **s'~ dans une maison par effraction** to break into a house; **2** (se faire admettre) [*personne*] to gain admittance (**dans** to).

introduit, ~e /ɛ̃trɔdɥi, it/ **I** *pp* ▶ **introduire**.
II *pp adj* **être ~ dans les milieux bancaires** to know a lot of people in banking circles; **être bien ~ auprès de qn** to have access to sb.

introniser /ɛ̃trɔnize/ [1] *vtr* to enthrone [*évêque*].

introspection /ɛ̃trɔspɛksjɔ̃/ *nf* introspection.

introuvable /ɛ̃truvabl/ *adj* **1** (qu'on ne peut trouver) [*personne*] untraceable; [*objet*] that cannot be found (*épith, après n*); [*endroit*] that is impossible to find (*épith, après n*); **le voleur reste ~** the thief has still not been found; **mon portefeuille est ~** I can't find my wallet anywhere; **2** (rare) [*spécialiste*] that is hard to come by (*épith, après n*); [*livre, antiquité*] that is impossible to get hold of (*épith, après n*).

introversion /ɛ̃trɔvɛrsjɔ̃/ *nf* introversion.

introverti, ~e /ɛ̃trɔvɛrti/ **I** *adj* introverted.
II *nm,f* introvert.

intrus, ~e /ɛ̃try, yz/ *nm,f* intruder; **'cherchez l'~'** JEUX 'spot the odd one out' GB, 'pick the one that doesn't fit' US.

intrusion /ɛ̃tryzjɔ̃/ *nf* (irruption) intrusion (**dans** into); (ingérence) (de personne, pays) interference (**dans** in); (d'objet, idée) intrusion.

intuitif, -ive /ɛ̃tɥitif, iv/ *adj* intuitive; **connaissance intuitive de qch** intuitive understanding of sth.

intuition /ɛ̃tɥisjɔ̃/ *nf* intuition; **avoir l'~ de** to have an intuition about.

inusable /inyzabl/ *adj* hardwearing.

inusité, ~e /inyzite/ *adj* LING (non utilisé) not used (*jamais épith*); (rare) uncommon, not in common use (*jamais épith*).

inutile /inytil/ *adj* **1** [*objet, développement*] useless; [*travail, discussion*] pointless; [*crainte*] needless; (**il est**) **~ de faire** there's no point in doing; **~ de dire que** needless to say; **~ de me demander si** it's no use asking me whether; **~ de rincer** no need to rinse; **sans risques ~s** without unnecessary risks; **mes efforts sont restés ~s** my efforts were in vain; **2** [*personne*] useless.

inutilement /inytilmɑ̃/ *adv* [*se fatiguer*] unnecessarily; [*s'inquiéter, souffrir*] needlessly; [*attendre, chercher*] in vain.

inutilisable /inytilizabl/ *adj* unusable.

inutilisé, ~e /inytilize/ *adj* unused.

inutilité /inytilite/ *nf* (d'objet, effort, de personne) uselessness; (de démarche, dépense) pointlessness.

invalide /ɛ̃valid/ **I** *adj* disabled.
II *nmf* disabled person; **les ~s** the disabled.
■ **~ de guerre** registered disabled ex-serviceman.

invalider /ɛ̃valide/ [1] *vtr* to invalidate.

invalidité /ɛ̃validite/ *nf* MÉD disability; JUR invalidity.

invariable /ɛ̃varjabl/ *adj* invariable.

invasion /ɛ̃vazjɔ̃/ *nf* MIL, FIG invasion.

invective /ɛ̃vɛktiv/ *nf* invective **C**, abuse **C**; **se répandre en ~s** to pour out abuse (**contre** against).

invendable /ɛ̃vɑ̃dabl/ *adj* unsaleable.

invendu, ~e /ɛ̃vɑ̃dy/ **I** *adj* unsold.
II *nm* GÉN unsold item; (journal) unsold copy; (livre) remaindered copy.

inventaire /ɛ̃vɑ̃tɛr/ *nm* **1** COMM (opération) stocktaking GB, inventory US; (liste) stocklist GB, inventory US; **faire l'~** to do the stocktaking GB, to take inventory US; **2** (de valise, garde-robe) list of contents; (de collection) inventory; **faire l'~ de sa valise** (vérifier le contenu) to go through one's suitcase.

inventer /ɛ̃vɑ̃te/ [1] **I** *vtr* to invent [*machine, technique, remède*]; to devise [*moyen*]; to invent [*excuse, raison*]; **histoire inventée** made-up story; **tu inventes** you're making it up; **je n'invente rien** I'm not making it up; **je ne sais plus quoi ~ pour te faire plaisir**○ I can't think what else to do to make you happy.
II s'inventer *vpr* **il s'est inventé une enfance malheureuse** he's invented an unhappy childhood for himself; **elle s'invente toujours des excuses** she can always find an excuse; **ça ne s'invente pas** that has to be true.
IDIOMES **il n'a pas inventé la poudre**○ or **l'eau tiède**○ or **le fil à couper le beurre**○ he is not very bright.

inventeur, -trice /ɛ̃vɑ̃tœr, tris/ *nm,f* **1** ▶ **374** inventor; **2** JUR (découvreur d'un bien) finder.

inventif, -ive /ɛ̃vɑ̃tif, iv/ *adj* (novateur) inventive; (débrouillard) resourceful.

invention /ɛ̃vɑ̃sjɔ̃/ *nf* **1** (création) invention; **elle nous a servi un plat de son ~** she served us a dish she'd invented herself; **2** (mensonge) fabrication; **c'est de l'~ pure** it's a complete fabrication; **ce ne sont que des ~s** it's not true at all.

inventorier /ɛ̃vɑ̃tɔrje/ [2] *vtr* to make out a stocklist GB ou an inventory US of [*marchandises*]; to draw up an inventory of [*biens, succession*].

inverse /ɛ̃vɛrs/ **I** *adj* GÉN [*direction, effet, démarche*] opposite; **on s'est retrouvé dans la situation ~** (de la vôtre) the exact opposite happened to us; (de la précédente) the situation was reversed; **en sens ~** [*aller, repartir*] in the opposite direction; [*venir, arriver*] from the opposite direction; **attention aux voitures qui arrivent en sens ~** beware of oncoming traffic; **une voiture a heurté un camion roulant en sens ~** a car was in collision with a truck coming the opposite way; **dans l'ordre ~** (sur une liste) in reverse order.
II *nm* **1** GÉN **l'~** the opposite; **à l'~** conversely; **aller à l'~ de** to be the opposite of; **à l'~ de ce qui s'est passé l'an dernier** unlike last year; **à l'~ de ce qu'il croyait** contrary to what he thought; **c'est comme ça qu'il faut faire et non l'~** that's how it should be done, not the other way around; **2** MATH inverse.

inversement /ɛ̃vɛrsəmɑ̃/ *adv* conversely; MATH inversely; **et ~** and vice-versa; **~ proportionnel** in inverse proportion (**à** to).

inverser /ɛ̃vɛrse/ [1] **I** *vtr* **1** (intervertir) to invert [*position, termes*]; to reverse [*tendance, rôles, ordre*]; **image inversée** mirror image; **2** to reverse [*courant*].
II s'inverser *vpr* to be reversed.

inversion /ɛ̃vɛrsjɔ̃/ *nf* **1** (d'éléments, de rôles, valeurs) inversion; (de tendance, processus) reversal; **2** ANAT, CHIMIE, LING, PSYCH inversion; **3** ÉLECTROTECH reversal.

invertébré, ~e /ɛ̃vɛrtebre/ **I** *adj* invertebrate.
II *nm* invertebrate; **les ~s** invertebrates.

invertir /ɛ̃vɛrtir/ [3] *vtr* **1** (inverser) to switch [sth] round [*termes*]; to reverse [*ordre*]; **2** to reverse [*courant*].

investigateur, -trice /ɛ̃vɛstigatœr, tris/ **I** *adj* inquiring.
II *nm,f* investigator.

investigation /ɛ̃vɛstigasjɔ̃/ *nf* investigation; **d'~** investigative.

investir /ɛ̃vɛstiʀ/ [3] I *vtr* **1** (placer) to invest [*capitaux*] (**dans** in); **~ en Bourse** to invest on the Stock Exchange; **2** (charger) to invest [*personne, ambassadeur*] (**de** with); **3** (se répandre dans) [*policiers*] to go into; [*touristes, manifestants*] to take over; **4** (encercler) [*armée*] to besiege.

II s'investir *vpr* **s'~ dans** (énergiquement) to put a lot of oneself into; (sentimentalement) to invest emotionally in.

investissement /ɛ̃vɛstismɑ̃/ *nm* **1** GÉN investment (**dans** in); **un énorme ~ de temps** an enormous investment in terms of time; **2** MIL (encerclement) investing (**de** of).

investisseur /ɛ̃vɛstisœʀ/ *nm* investor.

investiture /ɛ̃vɛstityʀ/ *nf* investiture.

invétéré, ~e /ɛ̃vetere/ *adj* [*buveur, voleur, tricheur*] inveterate; [*menteur*] compulsive; [*haine, habitude, mal*] deep-rooted.

invincibilité /ɛ̃vɛ̃sibilite/ *nf* invincibility.

invincible /ɛ̃vɛ̃sibl/ *adj* (qui ne peut être vaincu) invincible; (irréfutable) irrefutable.

inviolabilité /ɛ̃vjɔlabilite/ *nf* **1** (de règle, frontière, territoire) inviolability; **2** (de forteresse, coffre) impregnability.

inviolable /ɛ̃vjɔlabl/ *adj* [*loi, secret, frontière, refuge*] inviolable; [*coffre, porte*] impregnable.

invisible /ɛ̃vizibl/ I *adj* **1** (non perceptible) invisible; **2** (hors de vue) **la route était ~ depuis la maison** the road could not be seen from the house; **3** (non disponible) [*personne*] unavailable; **4** (caché, secret) [*vestiges*] hidden; [*danger, menace*] unseen.

II *nm* **l'~** the invisible.

invitation /ɛ̃vitasjɔ̃/ *nf* (prière, exhortation) invitation (**à** to); (document) invitation; **à** or **sur l'~ de qn** at sb's invitation; **carte** or **carton d'~** invitation card; **c'est une ~ à la révolte** it's an open invitation to revolt.

invité, ~e /ɛ̃vite/ *nm,f* guest; **~ d'honneur** guest of honour^GB; **~ de marque** distinguished guest.

inviter /ɛ̃vite/ [1] I *vtr* **1** (prier de venir) to invite; **2** (payer) **~ qn à déjeuner/à prendre un verre** to take sb out for lunch/for a drink; **3** (engager) to invite (**à faire** to do); (demander) to ask (**à faire** to do); **le temps n'invite guère à la promenade** it's not particularly nice weather for a walk; **cela invite à la réflexion** it is thought-provoking.

II s'inviter *vpr* [*personne*] to invite oneself.

in vitro /invitʀo/ *loc adj, loc adv* in vitro.

invivable /ɛ̃vivabl/ *adj* unbearable.

invocation /ɛ̃vɔkasjɔ̃/ *nf* invocation (**de** of).

involontaire /ɛ̃vɔlɔ̃tɛʀ/ *adj* (incontrôlé) [*réaction, cri, geste*] involuntary; [*mensonge, faute*] unintentional; (fortuit) [*intermédiaire, héros, témoin*] unwitting.

involontairement /ɛ̃vɔlɔ̃tɛʀmɑ̃/ *adv* (sans le vouloir) [*soupirer, crier, sourire*] involuntarily; (sans préméditation) [*blesser, casser*] unintentionally; **si je vous ai blessé, c'est bien ~** I didn't mean to hurt you.

invoquer /ɛ̃vɔke/ [1] *vtr* to invoke.

invraisemblable /ɛ̃vʀɛsɑ̃blabl/ *adj* **1** (non crédible) [*événement, histoire*] unlikely; [*hypothèse, aventure*] improbable; [*explication*] implausible; **2**° (inouï) fantastic, incredible.

invraisemblance /ɛ̃vʀɛsɑ̃blɑ̃s/ *nf* (caractère) unlikelihood; (détail) improbability.

invulnérabilité /ɛ̃vylneʀabilite/ *nf* invulnerability.

invulnérable /ɛ̃vylneʀabl/ *adj* invulnerable.

iode /jɔd/ *nm* iodine.

ioder /jɔde/ [1] *vtr* to iodize; **eau iodée** iodized water.

ion /jɔ̃/ *nm* ion.

iota /jɔta/ *nm inv* iota.
  IDIOMES **ne pas changer d'un ~** not to change one iota; **ne pas bouger d'un ~** not to move an inch.

irakien, -ienne /iʀakjɛ̃, ɛn/ ▶ **394** *adj* Iraqi.

iranien, -ienne /iʀanjɛ̃, ɛn/ ▶ **338**, **394** I *adj* Iranian.

II *nm* LING Iranian.

irascible /iʀasibl/ *adj* [*personne*] irascible SOUT, quick-

tempered; **avoir un caractère ~** to be quick-tempered.

iris /iʀis/ *nm inv* (fleur) iris; (de l'œil) iris; (diaphragme) iris diaphragm.

irisé, ~e /iʀize/ *adj* iridescent.

irlandais, ~e /iʀlɑ̃dɛ, ɛz/ ▶ **338**, **394** I *adj* Irish.

II *nm* LING Irish.

Irlandais, ~e /iʀlɑ̃dɛ, ɛz/ ▶ **394** *nm,f* Irishman/Irishwoman; **les ~ du Nord** the northern Irish.

Irlande /iʀlɑ̃d/ ▶ **232** *nprf* Ireland; **la République d'~** the Republic of Ireland; **l'~ du Nord** Northern Ireland.

ironie /iʀɔni/ *nf* irony; **l'~ du sort** the irony of fate; **faire de l'~** to be ironic.

ironique /iʀɔnik/ *adj* ironic.

ironiser /iʀɔnize/ [1] *vi* to be ironic (**sur** about); **'tu es déjà prête!' ironisa-t-il** 'ready so soon!' he said ironically.

iroquois, ~e /iʀɔkwa, az/ ▶ **338** I *adj* Iroquois.

II *nm* LING Iroquois.

irradiation /iʀadjasjɔ̃/ *nf* **1** (nucléaire) radiation; **dix morts par ~** ten deaths through ou from radiation; **2** IND, PHYS irradiation.

irradier /iʀadje/ [2] I *vtr* (exposer aux radiations) to irradiate; **déchets irradiés** radioactive waste ¢.

II *vi* (se propager) to radiate (**dans** through).

irrationnel, -elle /iʀasjɔnɛl/ I *adj* irrational.

II *nm* **l'~** the irrational.

irréalisable /iʀealizabl/ *adj* [*entreprise, idée, rêve*] impossible; [*projet*] unworkable.

irrecevable /iʀəsəvabl/ *adj* JUR inadmissible.

irréconciliable /iʀekɔ̃siljabl/ *adj* irreconcilable.

irrécupérable /iʀekypeʀabl/ *adj* **1** (que l'on ne peut recouvrer) irrecoverable; (que l'on ne peut réparer) damaged beyond repair (*après n*); **voiture ~** write-off; **2** [*délinquant*] beyond help (*après n*).

irrécusable /iʀekyzabl/ *adj* [*preuve*] indisputable; [*témoin*] unimpeachable.

irréductible /iʀedyktibl/ I *adj* [*opposition, volonté*] implacable; [*personne*] indomitable; [*conflit*] relentless.

II *nmf* diehard.

irréel, -elle /iʀeɛl/ I *adj* unreal.

II *nm* **l'~** the unreal.

irréfléchi, ~e /iʀefleʃi/ *adj* (précipité) [*action, propos*] ill-considered; (étourdi) [*personne*] careless.

irréfutable /iʀefytabl/ *adj* irrefutable.

irrégularité /iʀegylaʀite/ *nf* **1** (acte critiquable) irregularity; **2** (en quantité) **l'~ de la production** the irregular production; **3** (en qualité) irregularity, unevenness; **4** (défaut) irregularity; (de surface) unevenness; **les ~s du sol** the uneven ground (*sg*); **5** LING irregularity.

irrégulier, -ière /iʀegylje, ɛʀ/ *adj* **1** (sans régularité) [*forme, traits, croissance, pouls, respiration*] irregular; [*écriture, résultats, qualité, sol*] uneven; **2** (illégal) [*procédure, transaction*] irregular; [*travailleur, vente*] illegal; **immigré en situation irrégulière** illegal immigrant; **être en situation irrégulière** to be in breach of the regulations; **3** (inégal) [*élève, athlète*] whose performance is uneven (*épith, après n*); **4** MIL irregular; **5** LING [*verbe, pluriel*] irregular.

irrégulièrement /iʀegyljɛʀmɑ̃/ *adv* **1** (illégalement) illegally; **2** (sans régularité) [*découper, se conjuguer*] irregularly; [*répartir*] unevenly; [*travailler*] erratically.

irrémédiable /iʀ(ʀ)emedjabl/ *adj* [*perte, faute*] irreparable; [*déclin, situation*] irremediable SOUT.

irremplaçable /iʀɑ̃plasabl/ *adj* irreplaceable.

irréparable /iʀepaʀabl/ I *adj* [*voiture, appareil*] beyond repair (*après n*); [*dégât*] irreparable; [*tort, crime*] irreparable.

II *nm* **commettre l'~** to go beyond the point of no return.

irrépressible /iʀepʀesibl/ *adj* [*sourire, désir, rire*] irrepressible; [*larmes*] uncontrollable.

irréprochable /iʀepʀɔʃabl/ *adj* [*conduite, vie, employé*] irreproachable, beyond reproach (*après n*);

Les itinéraires

Comment s'y rendre

OK, you come out of the station. Go straight across the car park into Main Street. Keep straight on for several hundred yards over the first two sets of traffic lights and turn right at the third set into Grant Street. Take the third street on the left and walk down to the end – you'll find yourself facing the theatre. Go down the alleyway to the left of the theatre and you'll come out in West Street, with a bank on the right-hand corner as you reach the end. Cross over the road, going right towards a piece of open ground. The last shop before the open space is a tailor's with a coffee shop on the first floor. I'll be there with the gold and two single first-class tickets to Bali. Don't be late – I shan't wait!

[*travail*] perfect, impeccable; [*goût, manières*] impeccable.

irrésistible /iʀezistibl/ *adj* [*séducteur, charme, essor*] irresistible; [*besoin*] compelling; [*envie, passion*] overpowering; [*personne, blague*] hilarious.

irrésolu, ~e /iʀʀezɔly/ *adj* (indécis) [*personne*] indecisive; (sans solution) unsolved.

irrespectueux, -euse /iʀɛspɛktɥø, øz/ *adj* disrespectful (**envers** to, toward(s)).

irrespirable /iʀɛspiʀabl/ *adj* [*air, gaz*] unbreathable; [*climat, ambiance, atmosphère*] stifling.

irresponsable /iʀɛspɔ̃sabl/ *adj* **1** (qui agit avec légèreté) [*personne, attitude*] irresponsible; **de façon ~** irresponsibly; **2** JUR non-accountable.

irrévérencieux, -ieuse /iʀʀeveʀɑ̃sjø, øz/ *adj* irreverent (**envers** to, toward(s)).

irréversible /iʀeveʀsibl/ *adj* GÉN, CHIMIE, PHYS irreversible; [*engrenage, mécanisme*] non-reversible.

irrévocable /iʀevɔkabl/ *adj* irrevocable.

irrigateur /iʀigatœʀ/ I *adj m* irrigating.
II *nm* irrigator.

irrigation /iʀigasjɔ̃/ *nf* **1** AGRIC irrigation; **2** MÉD (de plaie, cavité) irrigation; (en sang) supply of blood; **une mauvaise ~ du cerveau** an insufficient blood supply to the brain.

irriguer /iʀige/ [1] *vtr* AGRIC, MÉD to irrigate; **le sang irrigue les organes** organs are supplied with blood.

irritable /iʀitabl/ *adj* irritable.

irritant, ~e /iʀitɑ̃, ɑ̃t/ *adj* (agaçant) irritating; MÉD irritant.

irritation /iʀitasjɔ̃/ *nf* (agacement) irritation; MÉD irritation.

irriter /iʀite/ [1] I *vtr* **1** (agacer) to irritate, to annoy; **très irrité** very annoyed; **2** MÉD to irritate.
II **s'irriter** *vpr* **1** (s'énerver) to get annoyed (**de** about, over), to get angry (**de** about, over); **2** MÉD to become irritated, to become inflamed.

irruption /iʀypsjɔ̃/ *nf* (apparition) irruption SOUT; **faire ~ dans** to burst into; **ils ont fait ~ dans le monde du rock il y a dix ans** they burst onto the rock scene ten years ago.

islam /islam/ *nm* **l'~** Islam.

islamique /islamik/ *adj* Islamic.

islamisme /islamism/ *nm* Islamism.

islandais, ~e /islɑ̃dɛ, ɛz/ ▶ **338**|, **394**| I *adj* Icelandic.
II *nm* LING Icelandic.

Islande /islɑ̃d/ ▶ **232**| *nprf* Iceland.

isocèle /izɔsɛl/ *adj* **triangle ~** isosceles triangle.

isolant, ~e /izɔlɑ̃, ɑ̃t/ I *adj* [*matériau*] insulating; **la laine de verre est très ~e** fibreglass^GB is a very good insulator.
II *nm* insulating material; **~ thermique** thermal insulator.

isolation /izɔlasjɔ̃/ *nf* **1** insulation; **~ acoustique** soundproofing; **2** PSYCH isolation.

isolé, ~e /izɔle/ I *pp* ▶ **isoler**.
II *pp adj* **1** (très éloigné) remote; **2** (un peu à l'écart) isolated (**de** from); **3** [*cas, événement*] isolated; **tireur**

~ lone gunman, sniper; **des tirs ~s** sniper fire ℂ; **4** (seul, sans alliés) isolated.

isolement /izɔlmɑ̃/ *nm* **1** (de village, région) remoteness; (de maison) isolated location; **2** (absence de contacts) (de malade, chômeur) isolation; (de pays, politicien) isolation; **3** (mise à l'écart) (de malade) isolation; (de prisonnier) solitary confinement; **4** (de gêne, substance, virus) isolation; **5** (en électricité) insulation.

isolément /izɔlemɑ̃/ *adv* in isolation.

isoler /izɔle/ [1] I *vtr* **1** to isolate [*malade, politicien, dissident*] (**de** from); to put [sb] in solitary confinement [*prisonnier*]; **2** (séparer d'un ensemble) to isolate [*gène, substance, élément*]; **~ une citation de son contexte** to take a quote out of context; **3** (contre le bruit) to soundproof; (contre la chaleur, le froid) to insulate (**contre** against); **4** (en électricité) to insulate.
II **s'isoler** *vpr* to isolate oneself (**de** from); **s'~ dans un coin pour lire une lettre** to withdraw into a corner to read a letter.

isoloir /izɔlwaʀ/ *nm* voting ou polling GB booth.

isomère /izɔmɛʀ/ I *adj* isomeric.
II *nm* isomer.

isomorphe /izɔmɔʀf/ *adj* isomorphic.

isorel® /izɔʀɛl/ *nm* hardboard.

isotherme /izɔtɛʀm/ *adj* [*camion, wagon*] refrigerated; **boîte ~** ice box; **bouteille ~** insulated bottle; **sac ~** cool bag.

isotope /izɔtɔp/ *nm* isotope.

Israël /isʀael/ ▶ **232**| *nprm* Israel; **en ~** in Israel.

israélien, -ienne /isʀaeljɛ̃, ɛn/ ▶ **394**| *adj* Israeli.

israélite /isʀaelit/ I *adj* Jewish.
II *nmf* HIST Israelite; (juif) Jew.

issu, ~e[1] /isy/ *adj* **1** (originaire) **être ~ de** to come from; **les jeunes ~s de familles pauvres** young people from poor families; **2** (résultant) **être ~ de** to result from.

issue[2] /isy/ *nf* **1** (sortie) exit; **'sans ~'** 'no exit'; **2** (solution) solution (**à** to); **situation sans ~** situation with no solution; **3** (dénouement) outcome; **à l'~ de** at the end of; **à l'~ de trois jours de pourparlers** at the close of three days of talks.
■ **~ de secours** emergency exit.

isthme /ism/ *nm* isthmus.

Italie /itali/ ▶ **232**| *nprf* Italy.

italien, -ienne /italjɛ̃, ɛn/ ▶ **338**|, **394**| I *adj* Italian.
II *nm* LING Italian.

italique /italik/ *nm* italics (*pl*).

item /itɛm/ *adv* ditto.

itinéraire /itineʀɛʀ/ *nm* **1** (de voyage) route; (détaillé) itinerary; **2** FIG career.
■ **~ bis** alternative route, holiday GB ou vacation US route; **~ de délestage** relief route.

itinérant, ~e /itineʀɑ̃, ɑ̃t/ *adj* [*musicien, artiste*] itinerant; [*spectacle, exposition*] touring; [*vie, personnel*] peripatetic; [*cirque*] travelling^GB.

IUT /iyte/ *nm* (abbr = **Institut universitaire de technologie**) university institute of technology.

IVG /iveʒe/ *nf: abbr* ▶ **interruption**.

ivoire /ivwaʀ/ ▶ **141**| I *adj inv* ivory.
II *nm* **1** (d'éléphant) ivory; **en ~, d'~** ivory (*épith*); **2** (de dent) dentine GB, dentin US.

ivoirien, -ienne /ivwaʀjɛ̃, ɛn/ ▶ **394**| *adj* of the Ivory Coast.

ivraie /ivʀɛ/ *nf* rye-grass; **séparer le bon grain de l'~** FIG to separate the wheat from the chaff.

ivre /ivʀ/ *adj* **1** (par l'alcool) intoxicated, drunk; **~ mort** dead drunk; **2** (transporté) drunk (**de** with); **~ de liberté** exhilarated ou intoxicated by freedom; **~ de bonheur** drunk with happiness; **~ de rage** wild with rage.

ivresse /ivʀɛs/ *nf* **1** (ébriété) intoxication; **conduite en état d'~** driving while intoxicated, drunken driving; **2** (exaltation) exhilaration.
■ **~ des profondeurs** decompression sickness.

ivrogne /ivʀɔɲ/ *nmf* drunkard.

ivrognerie /ivʀɔɲəʀi/ *nf* drinking.

i, J /ʒi/ *nm inv* j, J; **le jour J** D-day; **jour J moins dix** ten days to D-day.

j' ▸ je.

jabot /ʒabo/ *nm* (d'oiseau, abeille) crop; (de chemise) jabot.

jacasser /ʒakase/ [1] *vi* to chatter.

jachère /ʒaʃɛʀ/ *nf* (pratique, état) fallow; (terrain) fallow land **⊄**; **en ~** lying fallow.

jacinthe /ʒasɛ̃t/ *nf* (fleur) hyacinth.

jackpot /(d)ʒakpɔt/ *nm* **1** (combinaison gagnante) jackpot; **gagner le ~** to hit the jackpot; **2** (machine) slot machine.

jacobin, ~e /ʒakɔbɛ̃, in/ *adj, nm,f* HIST Jacobin; POL radical.

jacquerie /ʒakʀi/ *nf* HIST peasant revolt, jacquerie.

Jacques /ʒak/ **I** *nm* **faire le ~** to play the fool.

II *npr* James.

jacquet /ʒakɛ/ ▸ **329** *nm* (jeu) backgammon; (tablette) backgammon board.

jacter /ʒakte/ [1] *vi* (parler) to jaw, to talk.

jacuzzi® /ʒakyzi/ *nm* jacuzzi®.

jade /ʒad/ *nm* **1** (pierre) jade; **2** (objet) piece of jade.

jadis /ʒadis/ *adv* formerly, in the past; **~, la vie était différente** in the past, life was different; **les mœurs de ~** the customs of long ago.

jaguar /ʒagwaʀ/ *nm* jaguar.

jaillir /ʒajiʀ/ [3] *vi* **1** (sortir impétueusement) [*liquide, gaz*] to gush out (**de** of); [*larmes*] to flow (**de** from); [*flamme, étincelle*] to shoot up (**de** from); **2** (apparaître subitement) [*personne, animal*] to spring up (**de** from); (en sortant) to spring out (**de** from); [*voiture*] to shoot out (**de** from); **3** [*rires, cris, plaisanteries*] to burst out (**de** from); **4** (s'élever) [*clocher, arbre*] to thrust up, to tower up (**au-dessus de** above); **5** (se révéler) [*idée, vérité*] to emerge (**de** from).

jais /ʒɛ/ *nm inv* **1** (pierre) jet; **2** ▸ **141** (couleur) **(noir) de ~** jet-black (*épith*), jet black (*jamais épith*).

jalon /ʒalɔ̃/ *nm* (piquet) marker; FIG **poser les ~s de** to prepare the ground for; **~ important** milestone.

jalonner /ʒalɔne/ [1] *vtr* **1** (marquer) to punctuate [*vie, histoire*]; **une journée jalonnée de péripéties** a day full of incidents; **2** (border) to line [*route*]; **3** (délimiter avec une marque) [*personne*] to mark out [*route*].

jalousement /ʒaluzmɑ̃/ *adv* **1** (avec jalousie) jealously; (avec envie) enviously; **2** (avec un soin inquiet) jealously.

jalouser /ʒaluze/ [1] *vtr* to be jealous of.

jalousie /ʒaluzi/ *nf* **1** (sentiment) jealousy **⊄** (**à l'égard de, envers** toward(s)); **susciter des ~s chez les concurrents** to arouse jealousy among competitors; **2** (persienne) (à lattes verticales) vertical blind; (à lattes horizontales) Venetian blind; **3** (œillet) sweet william.

jaloux, -ouse /ʒalu, uz/ **I** *adj* jealous (**de** of); **avec un soin ~** with meticulous care.

II *nm,f* jealous man/woman; **faire des ~** to make people jealous.

jamais /ʒamɛ/ *adv* **1** (à aucun moment) never; **il n'écrit ~** he never writes; **il n'écrit-il ~?** doesn't he ever write?; **je n'écrirai ~ plus** or **plus ~** I'll never write again; **ce n'est ~ assez** it's never enough; **~ plus!** never again!; **rien n'est ~ certain** nothing is ever certain; **sans ~ comprendre** without ever understanding; **sait-on ~?** you never know; **~ de la vie!** never!; **c'est le moment ou ~** it's now or never; **2** (à tout autre moment) ever; **plus belle que ~** prettier than ever; **si ~ tu passes à Oxford, viens me voir**

if you are ever in Oxford, come and see me; **on a ce qu'il faut si ~ il pleut** we have everything we need in case it rains; **3** (toujours) **à ~, à tout ~** forever; **4** (seulement) **ce n'est ~ que** it is only.

jambage /ʒɑ̃baʒ/ *nm* (de lettre) downstroke; (support) jamb.

jambe /ʒɑ̃b/ *nf* **1** ▸ **137** leg; **avoir des ~s bien faites** to have nice ou good legs; **avoir de bonnes ~s** to have strong legs; **plier les ~s** (debout) to bend one's knees; (assis) to draw one's legs up; **croiser les ~s** to cross one's legs; **il avait les ~s écartées** his legs were wide apart; **aller** or **courir à toutes ~s** to run as fast as one's legs can carry one; **j'ai mal aux ~s** my legs are hurting; **j'ai les ~s lourdes** my legs feel heavy; **tomber les ~s en l'air** to fall flat on one's back; **j'ai les ~s comme du coton**○ I feel weak at the knees; **traîner la ~**○ to trudge along.

■ **~ de bois** wooden leg.

IDIOMES **cela me fait une belle ~**○ a fat lot of good○ that does me; **il ne tient plus sur ses ~s** he can hardly stand up; **prendre ses ~s à son cou** to take to one's heels; **parlez-lui de mariage et il prendra les ~s à son cou** mention marriage and you won't see him for dust○; **avoir qn dans les ~s** to have sb under one's feet; **tenir la ~ à qn** to keep talking to sb; **faire qch par-dessus** or **par-dessous la ~** to do sth in a slipshod manner.

jambière /ʒɑ̃bjɛʀ/ *nf* (de randonneur) legging; (de joueur de hockey) pad; (de danseur) leg-warmer; (de soldat) greave.

jambon /ʒɑ̃bɔ̃/ *nm* ham.

■ **~ beurre** (buttered) ham sandwich; **~ blanc** or **cuit** cooked ham; **~ fumé** smoked ham; **~ de Paris = ~ blanc**.

jambonneau, *pl* **~x** /ʒɑ̃bɔno/ *nm* knuckle of ham.

jansénisme /ʒɑ̃senism/ *nm* Jansenism.

jante /ʒɑ̃t/ *nf* (bord de roue) rim; (roue sans pneu) wheel.

janvier /ʒɑ̃vje/ ▸ **382** *nm* January; **du premier ~ à la Saint-Sylvestre** from New Year's Day to New Year's Eve.

Japon /ʒapɔ̃/ ▸ **232** *nprm* Japan.

japonais, ~e /ʒapɔnɛ, ɛz/ ▸ **394**, **338** **I** *adj* Japanese.

II *nm* LING Japanese.

jappement /ʒapmɑ̃/ *nm* yapping **⊄**.

japper /ʒape/ [1] *vi* to yap.

jaquette /ʒakɛt/ *nf* (d'homme) morning coat; (de livre) dust jacket; (de dent) crown.

jardin /ʒaʀdɛ̃/ *nm* **1** (privé) garden GB, yard US; **faire son ~** to work in one's garden GB ou in the yard US; **2** (parc) gardens (*pl*), park; **le ~ des Oliviers** the Garden of Gethsemane.

■ **~ d'acclimatation = ~ zoologique**; **~ d'agrément** ornamental ou pleasure garden; **~ anglais** landscape garden; **~ d'enfants** kindergarten; **~ à la française** formal garden; **~ japonais** Japanese garden; **~ potager** vegetable garden; **~ public** park; **~ secret** private domain; **~ zoologique** zoo.

jardinage /ʒaʀdinaʒ/ *nm* gardening.

jardiner /ʒaʀdine/ [1] *vi* to do some gardening; **il aime ~** he enjoys gardening.

jardinier, -ière¹ /ʒaʀdinje, ɛʀ/ **I** *adj* garden.

II ▸ **374** *nm,f* (personne) gardener; **outils de ~** garden tools; **~ paysagiste** landscape gardener.

jardinière² /ʒaʀdinjɛʀ/ *nf* (plat) ~ **(de légumes)** jardinière; (bac à fleurs) jardinière; ~ **d'enfants** SCOL kindergarten teacher.

jargon /ʒaʀgɔ̃/ *nm* **1** (langue de métier) jargon; ~ **administratif** officialese; **2** (langage incorrect) ungrammatical language; (langue étrangère) foreign language.

Jarnac /ʒaʀnak/ *npr* **coup de ~** decisive and unexpected blow.

jarre /ʒaʀ/ *nf* (earthenware) jar.

jarret /ʒaʀɛ/ *nm* **1** (d'humain) ham, hollow of the knee; **2** (d'animal) hock; **3** (en cuisine) ~ **de veau/porc** knuckle of veal/pork.

jarretelle /ʒaʀtɛl/ *nf* suspender GB, garter US.

jars /ʒaʀ/ *nm inv* gander.

jaser /ʒaze/ [1] *vi* **1** (médire) to gossip (**sur** about); **ça fait ~** it sets people talking; **2** C (bavarder) to chat.

jasmin /ʒasmɛ̃/ *nm* (arbuste, parfum) jasmine.

jaspe /ʒasp/ *nm* (pierre) jasper.

jatte /ʒat/ *nf* bowl, basin.

jauge /ʒoʒ/ *nf* gauge; ~ **d'huile** dipstick.

jauger /ʒoʒe/ [13] *vtr* **1** (évaluer) to get the measure of [*candidat, élève*]; **2** to measure [*capacité, volume*]; ~ **un réservoir** to measure the capacity of a tank.

jaunâtre /ʒonɑtʀ/ ▶ 141 | *adj* yellowish; [*teint, peau*] sallow.

jaune /ʒon/ ▶ 141 | **I** *adj* **1** (couleur) yellow; ~ **orange** orangy^{GB} yellow; ~ **canari/citron/moutarde** canary/lemon/mustard yellow; ~ **d'or** golden yellow; ~ **paille** straw-coloured^{GB}; ~ **poussin/safran** bright/saffron yellow; **il a le teint ~** he's got a sallow complexion; **2** (asiatique) East Asian.
II *nm* **1** (couleur) yellow; **2** CULIN ~ **(d'œuf)** (egg) yolk; **3** (briseur de grève) PÉJ blackleg PÉJ GB, scab PÉJ.
IDIOMES **rire ~**○ to give a forced laugh.

jaunir /ʒoniʀ/ [3] **I** *vtr* [*soleil*] to turn [sth] yellow [*papier, herbe*]; [*thé*] to make [sth] go yellow [*dents*]; [*nicotine*] to stain [*doigts*]; **le temps a jauni les photos** the photos have gone yellow with age; **doigts jaunis par la nicotine** nicotine-stained fingers.
II *vi* to go yellow.

jaunisse /ʒonis/ ▶ 196 | *nf* MÉD jaundice; **il va en faire une ~**○! that'll put his nose out of joint!

java /ʒava/ *nf* **1** (danse) popular dance; **2**○ (fête) rave-up○; **faire la ~** to rave it up○.

javanais, ~e /ʒavanɛ, ɛz/ ▶ 338 | **I** *adj* Javanese.
II *nm* LING Javanese.

Javel /ʒavɛl/ *nf* **(eau de) ~** ≈ bleach.

javelliser /ʒavelize/ [1] *vtr* to chlorinate.

javelot /ʒavlo/ ▶ 329 | *nm* (objet) javelin; (discipline) **(lancer du) ~** javelin.

jazz /dʒaz/ *nm* jazz; **musique de ~** jazz (music).

J-C (*written abbr* = **Jésus-Christ**) **avant ~** BC; **après ~** AD.

je (j' *before vowel or mute h*) /ʒ(ə)/ *pron pers* I.

jean /dʒin/ *nm* **1** (pantalon) jeans (*pl*); **un ~** a pair of jeans; **2** (tissu) denim.

Jean /ʒɑ̃/ *npr* John; **saint ~-Baptiste** St John the Baptist; **saint ~ de la Croix** St John of the Cross.

jeannette /ʒanɛt/ *nf* (pour repasser) sleeve board; (en scoutisme) ≈ Brownie.

je-ne-sais-quoi /ʒənsɛkwa/ *nm inv* **avoir un ~** to have a certain something.

jérémiades /ʒeʀemjad/ *nfpl* moaning ¢; **cesse tes ~** stop moaning.

jerrican /ʒeʀikan/ *nm* five-gallon container, jerrycan.

jersey /ʒɛʀzɛ/ *nm* **1** (point) stocking stitch; **2** (tissu) jersey; **jupe en ~** jersey skirt.

jésuite /ʒezɥit/ *adj, nm* RELIG Jesuit.

Jésus /ʒezy/ *npr* Jesus; **le petit ~** baby Jesus.

jet¹ /ʒɛ/ *nm* **1** (lancer) (action) throwing ¢; (distance) throw; **un ~ de 30 mètres au disque** SPORT a 30-metre^{GB} discus-throw; **à un ~ de pierre** a stone's throw away (**de** from); **2** (jaillissement) (de liquide, vapeur) jet; (de salive) spurt; (de flammes) burst; **premier ~** FIG

first sketch; **passer au ~** to hose down [*voiture, sol*] **3** TECH (coulage) cast(ing); **d'un seul ~** [*couler*] in one piece; [*écrire*] in one go.
■ ~ **d'eau** (fontaine, jaillissement) fountain; (de tuyau) hosepipe.

jet² /dʒɛt/ *nm* AVIAT jet.

jetable /ʒətabl/ *adj* [*briquet, rasoir, couche*] disposable.

jeté, ~e¹ /ʒəte/ **I**○ *adj* (fou) crazy.
II *nm* (en tricot) **une maille envers, un ~** purl one, wool round needle (once).
■ ~ **de lit** bedspread; ~ **de table** runner.

jetée² /ʒəte/ *nf* (sur l'eau) pier; (plus petite) jetty.

jeter /ʒəte/ [20] **I** *vtr* **1** (lancer) to throw [*caillou, dé*]; (avec force) to hurl, to fling [*objet*]; ~ **qch à qn** (pour qu'il l'attrape) to throw sth to sb; (pour faire mal, peur) to throw sth at sb; ~ **qch par terre/en l'air** to throw sth to the ground/(up) in the air; ~ **le buste en avant/la tête en arrière** to throw one's chest out/one's head back; **2** (placer rapidement) to throw (**dans** into; **sur** over); (étaler) ~ **une couverture sur un blessé** to throw a blanket over an injured person; ~ **quelques idées sur le papier** FIG to jot down a few ideas; **3** (mettre au rebut) to throw away ou out; ~ **qch à la poubelle** to throw sth out; **être bon à ~** to be fit for the bin GB ou the garbage US; ▶ **fenêtre**; **4** (expédier) ~ **qn dehors/par la fenêtre** to throw sb out/out of the window; ~ **qn en prison** to throw sb in jail; **se faire ~**○ to get thrown out; ~ **qn**○ to throw sb out; **5** (émettre) to give [*cri*]; ~ **un vif éclat** to shine brightly; **en ~**○ [*personne, voiture*] to be quite something○; **6** (construire) to lay [*fondations*]; **7** (causer) to create [*confusion*]; to cause [*consternation*]; to sow [*terreur*]; ~ **l'émoi dans la ville** to throw the town into turmoil; **8** (plonger) ~ **qn dans** to throw sb into [*despair*]; **9** (lancer en paroles) to hurl [*insultes*] (**à qn** to sb); **'tu es fou,' jeta-t-elle** 'you must be mad,' she said; ~ **quelques commentaires** (dans une discussion) to put in a few comments; ~ **à la tête** or **au visage de qn** to throw [sth] in sb's face [*vérité, défi*].
II se jeter *vpr* **1** (se précipiter) [*personne*] to throw oneself; **se ~ dans les bras de qn** to throw oneself into sb's arms; **se ~ sur** to fall upon [*adversaire*]; to pounce on [*proie, nourriture, journal*]; **se ~ au cou de qn** to fling oneself around sb's neck; **se ~ à l'eau** LIT to jump into the water; FIG to take the plunge; ~ **tête baissée dans qch** to rush headlong into sth; **2** (être jetable) to be disposable; **3** (être mis au rebut) to be disposed of; **4** [*cours d'eau*] to flow (**dans** into).
IDIOMES **n'en jetez plus (la cour est pleine)**○ hold your horses○.

jeteur, -euse /ʒətœʀ, øz/ *nm,f* thrower.
■ ~ **de sort** sorcerer; **jeteuse de sort** sorceress.

jeton /ʒ(ə)tɔ̃/ *nm* (pour un appareil) token; (pour un jeu de société) counter; (au casino) chip; ▶ **faux¹**.

jeu, *pl* ~**x** /ʒø/ ▶ 329 | *nm* **1** JEUX, SPORT (activité) **le ~** GÉN play ¢; (avec de l'argent) gambling ¢; (type) **un ~** a game; **on va faire un ~** let's play a game; **jouer (un) double ~** FIG to be guilty of double dealing; **à quel ~ joue-t-il?** FIG what's his game?; **il fait ça par ~** he does it for fun; **ton avenir est en ~** your future is at stake; **entrer en ~** FIG to come into the picture; **d'entrée de ~** right from the start; **se prendre au ~** to get hooked; **mettre en ~** to bring [sth] into play [*éléments*]; to stake [*somme, titre, honneur*]; **remise en ~** (au football, après une touche) throw; (au hockey, après un but) face-off; **être hors ~** (au football) to be offside; **ils ont beau ~ de me critiquer** it's easy for them to criticize me; **2** JEUX, SPORT (manche) game; **il a gagné (par) trois ~x à deux** he won by three games to two; **3** JEUX (main aux cartes) hand; **cacher bien son ~** FIG to keep it quiet; **4** COMM, JEUX (matériel) (d'échecs, de dames) set; (de cartes) deck; (de société) game; **5** (manière de jouer) (d'acteur) acting ¢; (de musicien) playing ¢; (de footballeur, joueur de tennis) game; **6** (série) set; ~ **de clés** set of keys; **7** (effet) (de reflets, vagues, d'ombres) play; (de forces, d'alliances) interplay; **8** TECH (possibilité de mouvement) play; **donner du ~ à** to loosen.

Les jeux et les sports

Les noms de jeux et de sports

En anglais, tous les noms de jeux et de sports sont singuliers. Ils ne prennent pas d'article défini.

le football	= football
j'aime le football	= I like football
les échecs	= chess
j'aime les échecs	= I like chess
les règles des échecs	= the rules of chess
jouer aux échecs	= to play chess
savez-vous jouer aux échecs?	= can you play chess?
faire une partie d'échecs	= to play a game of chess
faire un bridge	= to have a game of bridge

Certains noms de jeux et de sports ont une forme de pluriel, mais ils se comportent tout de même comme des singuliers: billiards, bowls, checkers, darts, dominoes, draughts *etc.*

les dominos sont un jeu facile	= dominoes is easy
le jeu de boules est pratiqué par les dames et les messieurs	= bowls is played both by men and women

Les noms des joueurs

Certains noms de sportifs en anglais se forment en ajoutant -er au nom du sport.

un footballeur	= a footballer
un golfeur	= a golfer
un coureur de 100 mètres	= a 100-metre runner
un coureur de haies	= a hurdler

Mais ceci n'est pas toujours possible. Par contre, pour les sports d'équipe, on peut toujours utiliser le mot player *précédé du nom du sport.*

un joueur de football	= a football player
un joueur de rugby	= a rugby player

En cas de doute, consulter l'article dans le dictionnaire.

Pour les noms de personnes qui jouent à des jeux, on utilise la même construction avec player.

un joueur d'échecs	= a chess player

Noter que dans les exemples suivants chess *peut être remplacé par presque tous les noms de sports et de jeux. En cas de doute, consulter l'article dans le dictionnaire.*

il joue très bien aux échecs	= he's very good at chess *ou* he's a very good chess player
un champion d'échecs	= a chess champion
le champion du monde d'échecs	= the world chess champion
je ne joue pas aux échecs	= I am not a chess player *ou* I don't play chess

Les événements

une partie d'échecs	= a game of chess
jouer aux échecs avec qn	= to play chess with sb
jouer aux échecs contre qn	= to play chess against sb
gagner une partie d'échecs	= to win a game of chess
battre qn aux échecs	= to beat sb at chess
perdre une partie d'échecs	= to lose a game of chess
jouer dans l'équipe d'Angleterre	= to play for England
gagner le championnat de Grande-Bretagne	= to win the British championship
j'espère que l'Angleterre va gagner	= I hope England wins
Douai a perdu 2 à zéro	= Douai lost 2 nil
Nantes 2—Lyon 0	= *dire* Nantes two, Douai nil
il est arrivé quatrième	= he came fourth

De avec les noms de jeux et de sports:

un championnat d'échecs	= a chess championship
un club d'échecs	= a chess club
l'équipe d'Angleterre d'échecs	= the English chess team
un fan d'échecs	= a chess enthusiast

L'anglais utilise la même construction dans des cas où le français a un mot différent, par ex.:

un échiquier	= a chess board

Mais:

les règles des échecs	= the rules of chess
une partie d'échecs	= a game of chess (a chess game est possible, mais moins fréquent)

En cas de doute, consulter l'article dans le dictionnaire.

Activités sportives

Les jeux:

faire du tennis/rugby	= to play tennis/rugby

Les arts martiaux et disciplines:

faire du judo/de la boxe/ de la gymnastique	= to do judo/boxing/gymnastics

Les activités de plein air:

faire de l'équitation/ de l'aviron/du jogging	= to go riding/rowing/jogging

Les jeux de cartes

Noter que dans les exemples suivants clubs *pourrait être remplacé par* hearts, spades *ou* diamonds.

le huit de trèfle	= the eight of clubs
l'as de trèfle	= the ace of clubs
jouer le huit de trèfle	= to play the eight of clubs
l'atout est trèfle	= clubs are trumps
demander du trèfle	= to call clubs
as-tu du trèfle?	= do you have clubs?

■ **~ d'adresse** game of skill; **~ d'argent** game played for money; **jouer à des ~x d'argent** to gamble; **~ de caractères** ORDINAT character set; **~ de construction** (pièces) construction set; **~ d'éveil** early-learning game; **~ de hasard** JEUX game of chance; **~ de jambes** SPORT footwork; **~ de massacre** JEUX ~ coconut shy GB; **~ de mots** pun; **~ de l'oie** ~ snakes and ladders GB; **~ radiophonique** radio game show; **~ de rôles** role playing ₡; **~ de société** (échecs, monopoly®️ etc) board game; (charades etc) party game; **~ télévisé** (TV) game show; **~ à XIII** SPORT rugby league; **~ vidéo** video game; **~x Olympiques, JO** Olympic Games, Olympics.
IDIOMES jouer le ~ to play the game; **jouer le grand ~** to pull all the stops out○; **c'est pas de** or **du ~**○! that's not fair!

eudi /ʒødi/ ▶ 551 | *nm* Thursday.
■ **~ de l'Ascension** Ascension day; **~ saint** Maundy Thursday.
IDIOMES ça aura lieu la semaine des quatre ~s○! never in a month of Sundays!

eun: à jeun /aʒœ̃/ *loc adv* **1** (l'estomac vide) [*partir, boire, fumer*] on an empty stomach; **soyez à ~** don't eat or drink anything; **2**○ (sans avoir bu d'alcool) sober.

jeune /ʒœn/ **I** *adj* **1** (non vieux) GÉN young; [*industrie*] new; [*allure, coiffure, visage*] youthful; **il est tout ~** he's very young; **elle n'est plus très ~** she's not so young any more; **nos ~s années** our youth; **le ~ âge** youth; **~ couple** young couple; **le ~ marié** the groom; **la ~ mariée** the bride; **2** (cadet) [*frère, sœur, fils, fille, génération*] younger; **être moins ~ que qn** to be older than sb; **Pline le Jeune** Pliny the Younger; **3** (nouveau dans son état) **les ~s mariés** the newlyweds.
II *nmf* young person; **un ~** a young man; **les ~s** young people.
III *adv* **s'habiller ~** to wear young styles; **faire ~** [*personne*] to look young.
■ **~ femme** young woman; **~ fille** girl; **~ homme** young man; **~ loup** up-and-coming executive; **~ premier** CIN, THÉÂT romantic lead.

jeûne /ʒøn/ *nm* **1** (privation) fasting; **observer le ~** to fast; **jour de ~** fast day; **2** (période) period of fasting.

jeûner /ʒøne/ [1] *vi* to fast.

jeunesse /ʒœnɛs/ *nf* **1** (période) youth; **la première** or **prime ~** early youth; **une seconde ~** a new lease of life; **il n'a pas eu de ~** he didn't have a proper youth; **mon amour de ~** my first love; **une erreur de ~** a youthful indiscretion; **il n'est plus de la**

première ~ HUM he's no longer in the first flush of youth HUM; **2** (état) youth; **quand on a la** ~ when you are young; **3** (les jeunes) young people (pl); **la** ~ **étudiante** students (pl).
IDIOMES **il faut que** ~ **se passe** youth will have its course; **les voyages forment la** ~ travel broadens the mind.

jeunet○, **-ette** /ʒœnɛ, ɛt/ **I** adj young.
II nm,f (garçon) young lad; (fille) young girl.

jf written abbr = **jeune femme** or **fille**.

jh written abbr = **jeune homme**.

JO /ʒio/ **I** nm: abbr ▶ **journal**.
II nmpl: abbr ▶ **jeu**.

joaillerie /ʒɔajʀi/ nf **1** ▶ 374 (magasin) jeweller's shop GB, jewelry store US; **2** (articles) jewellery GB, jewelry US.

joaillier, -ière /ʒɔalje, ɛʀ/ ▶ 374 nm,f jeweller.

Joconde /ʒɔkɔ̃d/ npr la ~ the Mona Lisa.

joggeur, -euse /dʒɔgœʀ, øz/ nm,f jogger.

joie /ʒwa/ nf **1** (bonheur) joy; **être au comble de la** ~ to be overjoyed; ~ **sans mélange** or **sans partage** pure joy; **faire la** ~ **de qn** to make sb happy; **cette enfant fait la** ~ **de ses parents** the child is her parents' pride and joy; **il y a eu des explosions de** ~ **dans toute la ville** the whole town erupted with joy; **quelle** ~! IRON wonderful! IRON; **être ivre de** ~ to be drunk with happiness ou delight; **pleurer de** ~ to cry for joy; **2** (plaisir) pleasure; **avoir la** ~ **de faire** to have the pleasure of doing; **se faire une** ~ **de faire** (envisager avec plaisir) to look forward to doing; (faire avec plaisir) to be delighted to do; **leurs seules** ~**s** their only pleasures; ▶ **faux**¹.
IDIOMES **s'en donner à cœur** ~ LIT to enjoy oneself to the full; FIG to have a field day.

joignable /ʒwaɲabl/ adj **il n'est pas** ~ **en ce moment** he's not available at the moment.

joindre /ʒwɛ̃dʀ/ [56] **I** vtr **1** (communiquer avec) to get hold of [personne]; ~ **qn au téléphone** to get sb on the phone; **2** (ajouter) (dans une lettre, un paquet) to enclose [timbre, chèque] (à with); (en agrafant, fixant) to attach (à to); ~ **sa voix au concert de protestations** to add one's voice to the chorus of protest; **3** (relier) [rue, pont, passage] ~ **qch à qch** to link sth with sth; **4** (mettre ensemble) to put [sth] together [planches, tôles]; ~ **les pieds** to put one's feet together.
II se joindre vpr **1** (se mêler) **se** ~ **à** to join [personne, groupe]; to join with [parti]; to mix with [sentiment, émotion]; **toute la famille se joint à moi pour vous souhaiter une bonne année** all the family join me in wishing you a happy New Year; **se** ~ **à la conversation** to join in the conversation; **2** (s'unir) [lèvres] to meet; [mains] to join.
IDIOMES ~ **les deux bouts**○ to make ends meet.

joint /ʒwɛ̃/ nm TECH (de planches, fenêtres) joint; (de robinet) washer; (de tuyauterie) seal; (de carrelage, briques) joint.
■ ~ **de cardan** cardan joint; ~ **de culasse** cylinder head gasket; ~ **de dilatation** expansion joint; ~ **d'étanchéité** seal.

jointoyer /ʒwɛ̃twaje/ [23] vtr CONSTR to point.

jointure /ʒwɛ̃tyʀ/ nf ANAT, TECH joint.

jojo○ /ʒoʒo/ **I** adj inv **il n'est pas** ~ **ton chapeau** your hat isn't very nice; **ce n'est pas** ~ **ce qu'ils lui ont fait** (moralement) what they did to him/her wasn't very nice; (physiquement) they made a mess of him/her○.
II nm **un affreux** ~ (enfant) a horrible brat○; (drôle d'individu) a weirdo○.

joli, ~e /ʒɔli/ **I** adj [personne, visage, fleur] pretty; [animal, objet, lieu, vêtement, visage, yeux] lovely; [somme, bénéfice] nice; [situation] good; [coup de publicité, résultat, but] great○; **faire** ~ to look nice, to look good; **ce n'est pas** ~ (**de faire**) it's not nice (to do); **ce n'était pas** ~ **à voir** it wasn't a pretty sight; **c'est** ~ **de dire du mal de ses parents** IRON that's a fine thing, saying nasty things about one's parents IRON.
II nm **le plus** ~ **c'est que** the funniest thing is (that); **c'est du** ~! IRON very nice! IRON.

■ ~ **cœur** smooth talker; **faire le** ~ **cœur** to pla[y] Romeo.
IDIOMES **être** ~ **à croquer** or **comme un cœur** to b[e] as pretty as a picture.

joliment /ʒɔlimɑ̃/ adv **1** (agréablement) [meublé, illustr[é] décoré] prettily, nicely; [dire] nicely; **comme l'a** [...] **dit Sue** as Sue put it so neatly; **2**○ (remarquablemen[t]) [content, bien] really; [manœuvrer] nicely; **il s'est fa**[...] ~ **recevoir** IRON he got a fine reception IRON.

jonc /ʒɔ̃/ nm BOT rush.

joncher /ʒɔ̃ʃe/ [1] vtr to be strewn over [sol]; **êt**[re] **jonché de** to be strewn with.

jonction /ʒɔ̃ksjɔ̃/ nf **1** (point de rencontre) junctio[n] **2** (rencontre) link-up; **établir** or **réaliser la** ~ **entre A e**[t] **B** to link up A and B; **opérer une** ~ [armée, man[...] festants] to link up; **point de** ~ meeting point.

jongler /ʒɔ̃gle/ [1] vi to juggle (**avec** with); ~ **ave**[c] **les chiffres/horaires** FIG to juggle figures/timetables.

jongleur, -euse /ʒɔ̃glœʀ, øz/ ▶ 374 nm,f juggler.

jonque /ʒɔ̃k/ nf junk.

jonquille /ʒɔ̃kij/ **I** ▶ 141 adj inv (couleur) daffod[il] yellow.
II nf BOT daffodil.

jouable /ʒwabl/ adj **1** (faisable) feasible; **le pari est** [...] the gamble might pay off; **2** (qu'on peut jouer) [musiqu[e] playable; **une pièce qui n'est pas** ~ a play that's impossible to stage.

joue /ʒu/ nf **1** ▶ 137 ANAT cheek; ~ **contre** ~ chee[k] to cheek; **avoir de bonnes** ~**s** to have plum[p] cheeks; **2** MIL **en** ~! aim!; **mettre qn en** ~ to tak[e] aim at sb; **tenir qn en** ~ to train one's gun on sb.

jouer /ʒwe/ [1] **I** vtr **1** JEUX, SPORT to play [match, carte]; to back [cheval, favori]; to stake [argent]; to ris[k] [réputation, vie]; **c'est joué d'avance** it's a foregon[e] conclusion; **tout n'est pas encore joué** the game isn[...] over yet; ~ **le tout pour le tout** to go for broke○; MUS to play [morceau, compositeur, disque]; **3** CIN, THÉA[...] [personne] to perform [pièce]; [personne] to act [Sh[a] kespeare]; [personne] to play [rôle]; [cinéma] to sho[w] [film]; [théâtre] to put on [pièce]; ~ **Figaro** to pla[y] Figaro; ~ **une pièce** to stage a play; **quel fil[m] joue-t-on au Rex?** what film is showing at the Rex[?] **4** (incarner) ~ **les imbéciles** to play dumb; ~ **l[a] surprise** to pretend to be surprised; ~ **les héros** [...] take unnecessary risks.
II jouer à vtr ind ~ **à** to play [tennis, échec[s] roulette]; to play with [poupée]; to play [cowbo[y] Tarzan]; **à quoi jouez-vous?** LIT what are you pla[y] ing?; FIG what are you playing at?; ~ **à qui per**[...] **gagne** to play 'loser takes all'; ~ **à la marchande** [...] **au docteur** to play shops/doctors and nurses.
III jouer de vtr ind **1** MUS ~ **de** to play [instr[...] ment]; ~ **du violon** to play the violin; **2** (se servir d[e] ~ **de** to use [influence] (**pour faire** to do).
IV vi **1** (s'amuser) [enfant, animal] to play (**avec** with[...] **allez** ~ **dehors!** go and play outside!; **arrête de** [...] **avec ta bague!** stop fiddling with your ring!; **c'éta**[it] **pour** ~, **ne le prenez pas mal!** I/he etc was on[ly] joking, don't be offended!; **2** (pratiquer un jeu) to pla[y] (avec de l'argent) to gamble; ~ **pour de l'argent** [...] play for money; **à toi de** ~! (au jeu) your turn!; FI[G] the ball's in your court!; **bien joué!** (au jeu) well played!; FIG well done!; **j'en ai assez, je ne joue plu[s]** I've had enough, count me out!; **3** (traiter à la légère) [...] **avec** to gamble with [vie, santé]; to put [sth] on th[e] line [réputation]; to play with [sentiments]; **4** (spécul[er] to gamble; ~ **en Bourse** to gamble on the sto[ck] exchange; ~ **aux courses** to bet on the horses; [...] **sur** to play on [crédulité, lassitude]; to speculate [...] [valeur boursière]; **5** CIN, MUS, THÉAT [acteur] to act; [musi[...] cien, radio] to play; **6** (produire des effets) [lumièr[e] flammes, vent] to play (**sur** on; **dans** in); **7** (interven[...] [argument, clause] to apply; [âge, qualification] [...] matter; **les questions d'argent ne jouent pas entr[e] eux** money is not a problem in their relationship; [...] **en faveur de qn** to work in sb's favour○GB; ~ **comm**[e] **un déclic** to serve as the trigger; **faire** ~ **la clé dan**[s] **la serrure** to jiggle the key in the lock; **faire** ~ **se**[...]

relations to make use of one's connections; **8** (être mal ajusté) to be loose; **le contrevent a joué** the shutter has worked loose.

V se jouer *vpr* **1** CIN, MUS, THÉÂT [*musique*] to be played; [*film*] to be shown; [*pièce*] to be performed; **2** JEUX, SPORT [*jeu, sport*] to be played; [*partie, rencontre*] (amicalement) to be played; (avec enjeu) to be played out; **3** (être en jeu) [*avenir, sort, paix*] to be at stake; **c'est l'avenir du pays qui se joue** the future of the country is at stake; **le sort des réfugiés va se ~ à la conférence sur la paix** the fate of the refugees hangs on the peace conference; **4** (triompher de) **se ~ de** to make light of [*difficulté*]; to defy [*pesanteur, gravité*]; to make light work of [*obstacle*].

ouet /ʒwɛ/ *nm* **1** (objet pour enfant) toy; **2** (victime) plaything; **être le ~ d'une hallucination** to be in the grip of an hallucination; **être le ~ des vagues** to be at the mercy of the waves.

oueur, -euse /ʒwœr, øz/ **I** *adj* **1** (qui aime s'amuser) playful; **2** (qui risque de l'argent) **être ~/joueuse** to be a gambling man/woman.

II ▶374 *nm,f* **1** MUS, JEUX, SPORT player; **une joueuse de tennis** a woman tennis player; **un ~ de mandoline** a mandolin player; **un ~ de cornemuse** a piper; **être beau/mauvais ~** to be a good/bad loser; **2** (personne qui joue de l'argent) gambler.

oufflu, -e /ʒufly/ *adj* [*personne*] chubby-cheeked; [*visage*] chubby.

oug /ʒu/ *nm* **1** AGRIC yoke; **2** (sujétion) yoke; **3** (de balance) beam.

ouir /ʒwir/ [3] **I** **jouir de** *vtr ind* (bénéficier) **~ de** [*personne*] to enjoy [*soutien, avantage*]; to enjoy the use of [*bien*]; [*lieu*] to have [*climat, vue*]; **~ de toutes ses facultés** to have the use of all one's faculties.

II *vi* (sexuellement) to have an orgasm.

ouissance /ʒwisãs/ *nf* **1** JUR (usage) use; **avoir la ~ de qch** to have the use of sth; **2** (plaisir) pleasure; **3** (orgasme) orgasm.

ouisseur, -euse /ʒwisœr, øz/ *nm,f* hedonist.

oujou, *pl* **~x** /ʒuʒu/ *nm* BABY TALK toy; **faire ~** to play (**avec** with).

our /ʒur/ ▶588 *nm* **1** (période de vingt-quatre heures) day; **en un ~** in one day; **dans les trois ~s** within three days; **ces derniers ~s** these last few days; **d'un ~** [*bonheur, espoir*] fleeting; [*mode*] passing; [*reine*] for a day; **des ~s et des ~s** for ever and ever; **dès le premier ~** right from the start; **~ après ~** (quotidiennement) day after day; (progressivement) little by little; **vivre au ~ le ~** to live one day at a time; ▶**ressembler, Rome; 2** (date) day; **ce ~-là** that day; **quel ~ sommes-nous?** what day is it today?; **un ~ ou l'autre** some day; **tous les ~s** every day; **~ pour ~** to the day; **de ~ en ~** from day to day; **à ce ~** to date; **à ~** up to date; **mettre à ~** (actualiser) to bring up to date [*courrier, travail*]; to revise [*édition*]; (révéler) to expose, to reveal [*mystère, secret, trafic, problème*]; **mise à ~** (actualisation) (d'édition, de données, statistiques) updating (**de** of); (découverte) (de secret, trafic) revelation (**de** of); **édition mise à ~** revised edition; **tenir à ~** to keep up to date; **jusqu'à ce ~** (maintenant) until now; (alors) until then; **de nos ~s** nowadays; **d'un ~ à l'autre** [*être attendu*] any day now; [*changer*] from one day to the next; **du ~ au lendemain** overnight; **nouvelle/mode du ~** latest news/fashion; **3** (du lever au coucher du soleil) day; **les ~s raccourcissent** the days are getting shorter; **pendant le ~** during the day; **nuit et ~** night and day; **le ~ se lève** it's getting light; **lumière du ~** daylight; **au lever** or **point du ~** at daybreak; **le petit ~** the early morning; **se lever avec le ~** to get up at the crack of dawn; **travailler de ~** to work days; **4** (clarté) daylight; **il fait ~** it's daylight; **en plein ~** in broad daylight; **faire qch au grand ~** to do sth for all to see; **se faire ~** [*vérité*] to come to light; **mettre au ~** to unearth [*vestige*]; to bring [sth] to light [*vérité*]; **jeter un ~ nouveau sur qch, éclairer qch d'un ~ nouveau** to shed new light on sth; ▶**faux¹; 5** (aspect) **sous ton meilleur/pire ~** at your best/worst; **je ne te connaissais pas sous ce**

~ I knew nothing of that side of you; **je t'ai vu sous ton vrai ~** I saw you in your true coloursᴳᴮ; **sous un ~ avantageux** in a favourableᴳᴮ light; **6** FIG **donner le ~ à qn** to bring sb into the world; **voir le ~** [*personne*] to come into the world; [*œuvre, projet*] to see the light of day; [*organisme*] to come into being; **mes ~s sont comptés** my days are numbered; **finir ses ~s à la campagne** to end one's days in the country; **des ~s difficiles** hard times; **attenter à ses ~s** to make a suicide attempt; **avoir encore de beaux ~s devant soi** still to have a future; **les beaux ~s reviennent** spring will soon be here; **7** CONSTR (ouverture) gap; **~ entre des tuiles** gap between tiles; **8** (de broderie) **~s** openwork (embroidery) ¢.

■ **~ de l'An** New Year's Day; **~ férié** bank holiday GB, legal holiday US; **~ de fermeture** closing day; **~ ouvrable** working day.

IDIOMES **Rome ne s'est pas faite en un ~** Rome wasn't built in a day; **beau comme le ~** very good-looking; **être dans un bon ~** to be in a good mood; **être dans un mauvais ~** to be having an off day; **il y a des ~s avec et des ~s sans**○ there are good days and bad days.

journal, pl -aux /ʒurnal, o/ *nm* **1** (quotidien) newspaper, paper; (revue) magazine; (bureaux) newspaper office; **2** RADIO, TV news bulletin, news ¢; **3** LITTÉRAT journal.

■ **~ de bord** logbook; **~ intime** diary; **Journal officiel, JO** *government publication listing new acts, laws etc.*

journalier, -ière /ʒurnalje, ɛr/ **I** *adj* [*taux, variation*] daily.

II *nm* day labourerᴳᴮ.

journalisme /ʒurnalism/ *nm* journalism.

journaliste /ʒurnalist/ ▶374 *nmf* journalist.

journalistique /ʒurnalistik/ *adj* journalistic; **style ~** journalese.

journée /ʒurne/ ▶588 *nf* day; **~ de repos** day off; **dans la ~** during the day; **à longueur de ~** all day long; **la ~ d'hier** yesterday; **la ~ de mardi** Tuesday; **faire des ~s de huit heures** to work an eight-hour day; **j'ai gagné ma ~!** IRON I may as well pack up and go home!

■ **~ d'études** conference; **~ d'information** awareness day; **~ portes ouvertes** open day GB, open house US.

journellement /ʒurnɛlmã/ *adv* (fréquemment) all the time.

joute /ʒut/ *nf* **1** (duel) FIG jousting ¢, battle; **~ oratoire** or **verbale** sparring match; **2** SPORT, HIST joust.

jouter /ʒute/ [1] *vi* (à cheval) to joust (**contre** against, with); (sur des barques) to joust (*in water tournament*).

jouvence /ʒuvãs/ *nf* **fontaine de ~** Fountain of Youth.

jouxter /ʒukste/ [1] *vtr* to adjoin [*bâtiment, terrain*].

jovial, ~e, *mpl* **~s** or **-iaux** /ʒɔvjal, o/ *adj* jovial.

jovialité /ʒɔvjalite/ *nf* joviality.

joyau, *pl* **~x** /ʒwajo/ *nm* LIT, FIG jewel, gem.

joyeusement /ʒwajøzmã/ *adv* **1** [*gambader*] merrily; [*saluer*] cheerfully; **2** IRON happily.

joyeux, -euse /ʒwajø, øz/ *adj* [*musique*] cheerful; **c'est ~!** IRON that's great! IRON.

jubilation /ʒybilasjɔ̃/ *nf* joy, jubilation.

jubilé /ʒybile/ *nm* jubilee.

jubiler /ʒybile/ [1] *vi* to be jubilant, to rejoice (**de faire** to do); (avec arrogance) to gloat.

jucher /ʒyʃe/ [1] **I** *vtr* to perch (**sur** on).

II se jucher *vpr* **se ~ sur** to perch on.

judaïsme /ʒydaism/ *nm* Judaism.

judas /ʒyda/ *nm inv* (dans une porte) peephole.

Judée /ʒyde/ ▶509 *nprf* Judaea; **arbre de ~** Judas tree.

judiciaire /ʒydisjɛr/ *adj* [*acte, institution, erreur*] judicial.

judicieux, -ieuse /ʒydisjø, øz/ *adj* [*conseil, idée,*

choix] sound; [*utilisation, critique*] judicious; **il semblerait ~ de faire** it would seem wise to do.

judo /ʒydo/ ▶ 329 *nm* judo.

juge /ʒyʒ/ *nm* **1** ▶ 374, 596 JUR judge; **elle est ~** she is a judge; **le ~ Morin** GÉN Judge Morin; (des juridictions supérieures) Mr ou Mrs Justice Morin; **oui, Monsieur le ~** yes, Your Honour^{GB}; **comparaître devant le ~** to appear before the court; **2** (de jeu, concours) judge; **3** (personne compétente) judge; **tu es seul ~** only you can tell.
■ **~ d'instruction** examining magistrate; **~ de touche** SPORT linesman.

jugé: **au jugé** /oʒyʒe/ *loc adv* [*évaluer*] by guesswork; **avancer au ~** to follow one's nose.

jugement /ʒyʒmɑ̃/ *nm* **1** (opinion) judgment; **~ de valeur** value judgment; **2** (aptitude) judgment; **n'avoir aucun ~** to lack judgment; **3** JUR (décision) (pour un crime) verdict; (pour un délit) judgment, decision; **passer en ~** [*affaire*] to come to court.

jugeote○ /ʒyʒɔt/ *nf* common sense.

juger /ʒyʒe/ [13] **I** *vtr* **1** (former une opinion sur) to judge; **ce n'est pas à moi de ~** how should I know?; **2** (considérer) to consider; **ne le juge pas mal** don't think badly of him; **je t'avais mal jugé** I misjudged you; **3** JUR (examiner) to try [*affaire, personne*]; (décider) to judge [*affaire*]; to arbitrate in [*différend, litige*]; **l'affaire sera jugée demain** the case will be heard ou tried tomorrow; **l'affaire est jugée** the case is closed; **le tribunal jugera** the court will decide; **4** (pour un concours) to judge [*candidats, films*].
II juger de *vtr ind* **1** (évaluer) **~ de** to assess [*niveau, valeur, capacité*]; **j'en jugerai par moi-même** I'll judge for myself; **à en ~ par tes réponses** judging by ou from your answers; **2** (imaginer) **jugez de ma colère** imagine my anger.
III se juger *vpr* **1** (se considérer) to consider oneself; **2** JUR [*affaire*] to be heard.

juguler /ʒygyle/ [1] *vtr* to stamp out [*épidémie, chômage, fléau*]; to check [*hémorragie*]; to curb [*inflation*].

juif, juive /ʒɥif, ʒɥiv/ **I** *adj* [*religion, communauté*] Jewish.
II *nm,f* Jew.

juillet /ʒɥijɛ/ ▶ 382 *nm* July; **le 14 ~** the Fourteenth of July, Bastille Day.

juin /ʒɥɛ̃/ ▶ 382 *nm* June.

juive ▶ juif.

jumeau, -elle[1], *mpl* **~x** /ʒymo, ɛl/ **I** *adj* **1** [*frère, sœur*] twin; [*fruits*] double; **2** [*lits*] twin; **3** [*ville*] twin.
II *nm,f* (personne) twin.

jumelage /ʒymlaʒ/ *nm* (de communes, clubs) twinning.

jumelé, ~e /ʒymle/ *adj* [*billet*] double; [*fenêtres, colonnes*] twin.

jumeler /ʒymle/ [19] *vtr* to twin [*communes, clubs*] (à with); to combine [*événements*].

jumelle[2] /ʒymɛl/ *nf* binoculars (*pl*); **une paire de ~s, des ~s** (a pair of) binoculars; **à la ~** through binoculars.
■ **~s de théâtre** opera glasses.

jument /ʒymɑ̃/ *nf* mare.

jumping /dʒœmpiŋ/ *nm* showjumping.

jungle /ʒɑ̃gl/ *nf* jungle.

junior /ʒynjɔr/ *adj inv*, *nmf* SPORT junior.

junte /ʒɛt̃/ *nf* junta.

jupe /ʒyp/ *nf* **1** (vêtement) skirt; **~ plissée** pleated skirt; **2** TECH skirt.
IDIOMES **il est toujours dans les ~s de sa mère** he's tied to his mother's apron strings.

jupe-culotte, *pl* **jupes-culottes** /ʒypkylɔt/ *nf* culottes (*pl*).

jupette /ʒypɛt/ *nf* short skirt; **~ de tennis** tennis skirt.

jupon /ʒypɔ̃/ *nm* petticoat.
IDIOMES **courir le ~** to womanize.

jurassien, -ienne /ʒyrasjɛ̃, ɛn/ *adj* of the Jura (Mountains).

jurassique /ʒyrasik/ *adj*, *nm* Jurassic.

juré, ~e /ʒyre/ **I** *pp* ▶ **jurer**.
II *pp adj* **1** (assermenté) [*expert*] on oath (*après n*); [*tr ducteur*] sworn-in (*épith*); **2** (éternel) [*fidélité, ennem* sworn.
III *nm* **1** JUR juror; **2** ART, SPORT judge.

jurer /ʒyre/ [1] **I** *vtr* to swear (**de faire** to do); **jur moi de ne rien dire** swear you won't say anything; **o leur a fait ~ le secret** they were sworn to secrecy **jure-le!** swear!; **on jurerait (que c'est) de la so** you'd swear it was silk; **~ de tuer qn** (à soi-même) to vow to kill sb; **ah mais je te jure**○**!** (indignation) hones ly○!
II jurer de *vtr ind* to swear to; **j'en jurerais** I wou swear to it.
III *vi* **1** (dire des jurons) to swear (**après, contre** at **2** (détonner) [*couleurs*] to clash (**avec** with); [*déta construction*] to look out of place (**avec** in); **3** (être partisa de) **ne ~ que par** to swear by.
IV se jurer *vpr* **1** (l'un l'autre) to swear [sth] to another [*fidélité*]; **2** (à soi-même) to vow.
IDIOMES **il ne faut ~ de rien** PROV never say never.

juridiction /ʒyridiksjɔ̃/ *nf* **1** (pouvoir) jurisdiction **sous ma ~** within my jurisdiction; **2** (tribuna courts (*pl*); **~ civile** civil courts (*pl*); **~ administr tive** administrative tribunals (*pl*).

juridique /ʒyridik/ *adj* [*statut, langue, formation* legal; **agir sur le plan ~** to take legal action; **vid ~ gap** in the law.

juridiquement /ʒyridikmɑ̃/ *adv* legally.

jurisprudence /ʒyrisprydɑ̃s/ *nf* case law; **faire ~** to set a legal precedent.

juriste /ʒyrist/ ▶ 374 *nmf* **1** (qui étudie le droit) juris **2** (qui pratique le droit) lawyer.

juron /ʒyrɔ̃/ *nm* swearword.

jury /ʒyri/ *nm* **1** JUR jury; **président du ~** foreman the jury; **2** ART, SPORT panel of judges; **3** UNIV board examiners.

jus /ʒy/ *nm inv* **1** (de fruit) juice; **~ de pomme** app juice; **2** (de viande) (qui exsude) juices (*pl*); (sauce servi gravy; **cuire qch au ~** to cook sth in the juices fro the meat; **laisser qn mijoter dans son ~**○ FIG to l sb stew in his own juice; **3**○ (café) coffee; **4**○ (coura électrique) juice○, electricity; **il n'y a plus de ~ th power's off; prendre le ~** to get a shock.

jusqu'au-boutiste, *pl* **~s** /ʒyskobutist/ *nmf* G hardliner; PÉJ extremist.

jusque (**jusqu'** *before vowel*) /ʒysk/ **I** *prép* **1** (da l'espace) **aller jusqu'à Paris/jusqu'en Amérique** (ins tant sur la destination atteinte) to go as far as Paris/Amer ca; (insistant sur la distance parcourue) to go all the way t Paris/America; **courir jusqu'au bout du jardin** to ru right down to the bottom of the garden GB ou the end the yard US; **suivre qn ~ dans sa chambre** to follo sb right into his/her room; **la nouvelle n'était pa officiellement arrivée jusqu'à nous** the news hadn reached us officially; **ils l'ont suivi ~ chez lui** the followed him all the way home ou right up to his fron door; **descendre jusqu'à 100 mètres de profonde** to go down to a depth of 100 metres^{GB}; **jusqu'o comptez-vous aller?** LIT, FIG how far do you intend go?; **2** (dans le temps) until, till; **je t'ai attendu jusqu' huit heures** I waited for you until ou till eight o'cloc **jusqu'alors** until then; **jusqu'à présent** ou **maint nant, jusqu'ici** (up) until now; **jusqu'à quand reste tu à Oxford?** how long are you staying in Oxford?; (limite supérieure) up to; (limite inférieure) down to; **il pe soulever jusqu'à dix kilos** he can lift up to ten kilos; **avoir de l'eau jusqu'aux chevilles** to be up to one ankles in water; **je le suivrai jusqu'au bout** FIG I follow him all the way; **4** (avec une notion d'exagérati to the point of; **aller jusqu'à faire** to go so far as to d **5** (y compris) even; **des détritus ~ sous la tabl** rubbish everywhere, even under the table; **ils son venus, jusqu'au dernier** every last one of them came
II jusqu'à ce que *loc conj* until; **jusqu'à ce qu' s'endorme** until he is asleep.

jusque-là /ʒyskəla/ *adv* **1** (dans le temps) until then, u to then; **~ je ne peux rien dire** until then ou in th meantime I have nothing to say; **2** (dans l'espace) up to here; (plus loin) up to there; **on avait de l'eau ~** (aux genoux etc) the water was up to here; **l'eau est montée ~** (en pointant vers un objet) the water came up to there.

IDIOMES en avoir ~ de qch/qn○ to have had it up to here with sth/sb○; **en avoir ~ de faire**○ to be sick and tired of doing○; **s'en mettre ~**○ to stuff one's face○.

usques LITER = **jusque**.

usquiame /ȝyskjam/ *nf* henbane.

ustaucorps /ȝystokɔʀ/ *nm inv* **1** (pour la danse) leotard; **2** (sous-vêtement) body stocking; **3** HIST doublet.

uste /ȝyst/ **I** *adj* **1** (impartial) [*personne*] fair; **2** (équitable) [*règlement, partage*] fair; [*récompense, sanction, cause*] just; **ce n'est pas ~!** it's not fair!; **~ retour des choses, il a été renvoyé** it was poetic justice that he got expelled; **trouver un ~ milieu** to find a happy medium; **~ ciel**†! good heavens!; **3** (légitime) [*colère, certitude*] righteous (*épith*); [*revendication*] legitimate; [*crainte*] justifiable; [*raisonnement, remarque, comparaison*] valid; **à ~ raison** or **titre** with good reason; **dire des choses ~s** to make some valid points; **4** (adéquat) right; **trouver le mot ~** to find the right word; **comme ce ~ il était en retard** of course , he was late; **5** (exact) [*calcul, proportion, heure, analyse*] correct; **avoir l'heure ~** to have the correct time; **le ~ prix des choses** FIG the true value of things; **apprécier qn à sa ~ valeur** to get a fair picture of sb; **6** (précis) [*instrument de mesure*] accurate; **7** MUS [*piano, voix*] in tune (*jamais épith*); [*note*] true; **ton piano n'est pas ~** your piano is out of tune; **8** (trop ajusté) [*vêtement, chaussure*] tight; **un peu ~** a bit tight; **9** (à la limite) **un poulet pour six c'est un peu ~** one chicken for six people is stretching it a bit; **une heure pour y aller c'est un peu ~** one hour to get there is cutting it a bit fine; **nous sommes un peu ~s**○ **en ce moment** money is a bit tight○ at the moment.

II *adv* **1** (sans erreur) [*chanter*] in tune; [*sonner*] true; [*deviner*] right; **elle a vu ~** she was right; **viser ~** LIT to aim straight; FIG to hit the nail on the head; **2** (précisément) just; **~ à temps** just in time; **3** (seulement) just; **~ un** just one; **4** (depuis peu) (tout) **~** only just; **j'arrive ~** I've only just arrived; **5** (à peine) hardly; **c'est tout ~ s'il sait lire** he can hardly read; **j'ai réussi à éviter le bus mais ça a été ~**○ I managed to avoid the bus but it was a close shave○.

III au juste *loc adv* exactly; **que s'est-il passé au ~?** what happened exactly?

IV *nm* righteous man; **les ~s** the righteous.

ustement /ȝystəmɑ̃/ *adv* **1** (précisément) precisely; **c'est ~ ce qu'il ne fallait pas dire** that's precisely what one shouldn't have said; **2** (à l'instant) just; **je parlais ~ de toi** I was just talking about you; **3** (avec justesse) [*dire, répondre*] correctly; **comme l'a fort ~ souligné Nina** as Nina so correctly pointed out; **4** (légitimement) [*se flatter, s'inquiéter*] justifiably.

ustesse /ȝystɛs/ **I** *nf* **1** (pertinence) **être convaincu de la ~ d'une décision** to be sure that a decision is

correct; **avec ~** [*souligner, remarquer*] correctly; **2** (précision) accuracy; **avec ~** [*analyser, prévoir, mesurer*] accurately.

II de justesse *loc adv* only just; **on a évité la catastrophe de ~** we only just avoided disaster; **s'en sortir de ~** to have a narrow escape.

justice /ȝystis/ *nf* **1** (principe) justice; (équité) fairness; **en toute ~** in all fairness; **ce n'est que ~** it is only fair; **2** (application) justice; **rendre la ~** to dispense justice; **il faut leur rendre** or **faire cette ~ qu'ils sont...** one has to acknowledge that they are...; **se faire ~** (à soi-même) (se venger) to take the law into one's own hands; (se suicider) to take one's own life; **3** (pouvoir) **la ~** (lois) the law; (institution) the legal system; (tribunaux) the courts (*pl*); **être livré à la ~** to be handed over to the law; **aller en ~** to go to court; **poursuivre qn en ~** to take sb to court; **être traduit en ~** to be brought before the courts; **action en ~** legal action.

■ **~ militaire** military law.

justicier, -ière /ȝystisje, ɛʀ/ *nm,f* righter of wrongs.

justificatif, -ive /ȝystifikatif, iv/ **I** *adj* [*facture, document*] supporting; **pièce justificative** documentary evidence ¢.

II *nm* documentary evidence ¢; **~ de domicile** proof of domicile; **~ de frais** receipt.

justification /ȝystifikasjɔ̃/ *nf* **1** (action) justification; **2** (preuve) (orale) explanation; (écrite) documentary evidence; **3** (en imprimerie) justification.

justifié, ~e /ȝystifje/ **I** *pp* ▶ **justifier**.

II *pp adj* **1** (légitime) [*inquiétude, choix*] justified; **non ~** unjustified; **2** (expliqué) justified.

justifier /ȝystifje/ [2] **I** *vtr* **1** (rendre acceptable) to justify [*méthode, politique, thèse, décision*] (**par** by); **2** (confirmer après coup) to vindicate; **les faits ont justifié nos craintes** events proved our fears to have been justified; **3** (excuser) to vindicate [*coupable*]; to justify [*comportement, retard, absence*]; to explain [*ignorance*]; **tu essaies toujours de la ~** you are always making excuses for her.

II justifier de *vtr ind* to give proof of [*domicile, identité*]; to have [*expérience, connaissance*].

III se justifier *vpr* **1** (se disculper) (devant un tribunal) to clear oneself; (devant une personne) to make excuses; **2** (être explicable) to be justified (**par** by); **ta décision peut se ~** there are good reasons for your decision.

jute /ȝyt/ *nm* **1** (fibre) jute; **toile de ~** hessian; **2** (tissu) hessian.

juteux, -euse /ȝytø, øz/ *adj* **1** [*fruit*] juicy; **2**○ [*affaire, projet*] profitable, juicy○.

juvénile /ȝyvenil/ *adj* [*sourire, caractère*] youthful; [*délinquance, mortalité*] juvenile; [*public*] young; [*assemblée*] of young people (*épith, après n*).

juxtaposer /ȝykstapoze/ [1] *vtr* to juxtapose [*termes, idées*].

juxtaposition /ȝykstapozisjɔ̃/ *nf* (de termes, d'idées) juxtaposition.

Kk

k, K /ka/ *nm inv* k, K.

kabbale /kabal/ *nf* cabala.

kafkaïen, -ïenne /kafkajɛ̃, ɛn/ *adj* **1** [*ambiance*] Kafkaesque; **2** [*études*] Kafka (*épith*).

kakatoès /kakatɔɛs/ *nm inv* cockatoo.

kaki /kaki/ **I** ▶ 141 *adj inv* khaki.
II *nm* **1** (fruit) persimmon; **2** (couleur) khaki.

kaléidoscope /kaleidɔskɔp/ *nm* kaleidoscope.

kanak = **canaque**.

kangourou /kɑ̃guʀu/ **I** *adj inv* **poche ~** front pocket; **slip ~** pouch-front briefs (*pl*).
II *nm* **1** ZOOL kangaroo; **2** ®(sac pour bébé) baby carrier.

kaput○ /kaput/ *adj inv* [*personne*] dog-tired○; [*objet, machine*] kaput○.

karaoké /kaʀaɔke/ *nm* karaoke.

karaté /kaʀate/ ▶ 329 *nm* karate.

karcher® /kaʀʃɛʀ/ *nm* pressurized water gun.

karité /kaʀite/ *nm* shea; **beurre de ~** shea butter.

kart /kaʀt/ *nm* go-kart.

karting /kaʀtiŋ/ ▶ 329 *nm* go-karting; **faire du ~** to go karting.

kasher /kaʃɛʀ/ *adj inv* kosher.

kayak /kajak/ ▶ 329 *nm* kayak; **faire du ~** to go canoeing.

kazakh, ~e /kazak/ **I** ▶ 394 *adj* Kazak.
II ▶ 338 *nm* Kazak.

kényan, ~e /kenjɑ̃, an/ ▶ 394 *adj* Kenyan.

képi /kepi/ *nm* kepi.

kératine /keʀatin/ *nf* keratin.

kermesse /kɛʀmɛs/ *nf* fête GB.

kérosène /keʀɔzɛn/ *nm* kerosene.

kF *written abbr* = **kilofranc**.

kg (*written abbr* = **kilogramme**) kg.

khi /ki/ *nm inv* chi.

Khmer, -ère /kmɛʀ/ *nm,f* Khmer; **les ~s rouges** Khmer Rouge (+ *v pl*).

kibboutz, *pl* **-tzim** /kibuts, kibutsim/ *nm* kibbutz.

kick /kik/ *nm* kick-start.

kidnapper /kidnape/ [1] *vtr* to kidnap; **se faire ~** to be kidnapped GB.

kidnappeur, -euse /kidnapœʀ, øz/ *nm,f* kidnapper GB.

kif-kif○ /kifkif/ *adj inv* **c'est ~ (bourricot)** it's all the same.

kilo[1] /kilo/ *préf* kilo.

kilo[2] /kilo/ ▶ 455 *nm* (*abbr* = **kilogramme**) kilo; **prendre des ~s** to put on weight.

kilofranc /kilɔfʀɑ̃/ *nm* 1,000 French francs.

kilogramme /kilɔgʀam/ ▶ 455 *nm* kilogram.

kilométrage /kilɔmetʀaʒ/ *nm* ~ mileage.

kilomètre /kilɔmɛtʀ/ ▶ 348, 575, 631 *nm* ki metre GB; **marcher des ~s** to walk for miles.

kilomètre-heure *pl* **kilomètres-heure** /k mɛtʀœʀ/ ▶ 631 kilometre GB per hour.

kilométrique /kilɔmetʀik/ *adj* [*distance*] in ki metres GB; [*prix, coût*] per kilometre GB.

kilo-octet /kilɔɔktɛ/ *nm* kilobyte.

kilotonne /kilɔtɔn/ *nf* kiloton.

kilowattheure /kilɔwatœʀ/ *nm* kilowatt-hour.

kimono /kimɔno/ *nm* GÉN kimono; SPORT = judo suit.

kinésithérapeute /kineziteʀapøt/ ▶ 374 n. physiotherapist GB, physical therapist US.

kinésithérapie /kineziteʀapi/ *nf* physiotherapy physical therapy US.

kinesthésie /kinɛstezi/ *nf* kinesthesia.

kiosque /kjɔsk/ *nm* (à journaux) kiosk.
■ **~ à musique** bandstand.

kirghiz, ~e /kiʀgiz/ **I** ▶ 394 *adj* Kirghiz.
II ▶ 338 *nm* Kirghiz.

kiwi /kiwi/ *nm* **1** (fruit) kiwi; **2** ZOOL kiwi.

klaxon® /klaksɔn/ *nm* (car) horn.

klaxonner /klaksɔne/ [1] **I** *vtr* to hoot GB, to honk.
II *vi* to sound one's horn GB, to honk the horn US.

kleptomane /klɛptɔman/ *adj, nmf* kleptomaniac.

kleptomanie /klɛptɔmani/ *nf* kleptomania.

km (*written abbr* = **kilomètre**) km.

knock-out /nɔkaut/ **I** *adj inv* [*boxeur*] knocked o (jamais épith).
II *nm* knockout; **gagner par ~** to win by a knoc out.

Ko (*written abbr* = **kilo-octet**) KB.

KO /kao/ **I** *adj inv* (*abbr* = **knocked out**) **1** SPO KO'd○; **mettre qn ~** to KO○ sb; **2**○ (épui exhausted.
II *nm* (*abbr* = **knockout**) KO○.

koala /kɔala/ *nm* koala (bear).

kôhl /kol/ *nm* kohl.

kolkhoze /kɔlkoz/ *nm* kolkhoz.

kopeck /kɔpɛk/ ▶ 33 *nm* kopeck; **ça ne vaut pas** **~** it's not worth a penny.

kouglof /kuglɔf/ *nm* kugelhopf.

koweïtien, -ienne /kɔwetjɛ̃, ɛn/ ▶ 394 *adj* Kuwait

krach /kʀak/ *nm* (boursier) crash.

kraft /kʀaft/ *nm* (**papier**) **~** brown paper.

kremlinologue /kʀɛmlinɔlɔg/ *nmf* Kremlinologist.

kurde /kyʀd/ ▶ 338 *adj, nm* Kurdish.

Kurde /kyʀd/ *nmf* Kurd.

kW (*written abbr* = **kilowatt**) kW.

K-way® /kawe/ *nm* windcheater GB, windbreaker US.

kyrielle /kiʀjɛl/ *nf* **une ~ de** a string of.

kyste /kist/ *nm* cyst.

L /ɛl/ *nm inv* **1** (lettre) l, L; **2** (*written abbr* = **litre**) 20 l = 20 l.
▶ **le**.

à /la/ I *art déf, pron* ▶ **le**.
II *nm* MUS (note) A; (en solfiant) lah; **donner le ~** LIT to give an A; FIG to set the tone.

là /la/

■ **Note** Lorsque *là* est employé par opposition à *ici* il se traduit par (*over*) *there*: *ne le mets pas ici, mets-le là* = don't put it here, put it there; lorsque *là* signifie ici il se traduit par (*over*) *here*: *viens là* = come (over) here.
– Lorsque *là* est utilisé avec un sens temporel il se traduit par *then*: *et là, le téléphone a sonné* = and then the phone rang.
– Pour les autres emplois voir l'article ci-dessous. *celle-là, celui-là* etc sont traités séparément à leur place dans l'ordre alphabétique.

adv **1** (désignant un lieu) (par opposition à ici) there; (ici) here; **tu étais ~ quand c'est arrivé?** were you there when it happened?; **il n'est pas ~ pour l'instant** he's not here at the moment; **~ où j'habite** where I live; **par ~** (par ici) here; (dans cette direction) this way; (dans cette zone) around there; **de ~** (de cet endroit) from there; (pour cette raison) hence; **rester ~ à ne rien faire** to hang around doing nothing; **2** (à ce moment) then; **d'ici ~** between now and then; **il n'en est pas encore ~** he hasn't yet reached that stage; **s'il en est (arrivé) ~, c'est que...** if he's reduced to that, it's because...; **3** (pour renforcer l'énoncé) **~ d'accord, j'ai eu tort** OK then, I was wrong; **alors ~ tu exagères!** now you're going too far!; **~, c'est fini, ne pleure plus** there now, it's over, don't cry; **~ c'est différent** that's a different matter; **~ c'est bien ~ ce qui me chagrine** that's precisely what's bothering me; **4** (dans cela, en cela) **je ne vois ~ rien d'anormal** I don't see anything unusual in that; **que me dites-vous ~?** what are you telling me?; **il veut réussir ~ où personne n'a osé se lancer** he wants to succeed where no-one has dared venture before; **il a fallu en passer par ~** there was no alternative; **qu'entendez-vous par ~?** what do you mean by that?; **5** (à ce point) **je vais m'en tenir ~** I'll leave it at that; **nous n'en sommes pas ~** (près du but) we haven't got that far; (ce n'est pas si catastrophique) we haven't reached that point yet; **6** (pour renforcer un adjectif démonstratif) **en ce temps-~** in those days; **ce jour-~** that day.

là-bas /laba/ *adv* **1** GÉN over there; **2** (pour renforcer) over; **~ au Pérou** over in Peru.

labeur /labœʀ/ *nm* LITER hard work.

labo○ /labo/ *nm* lab○.

laborantin, -e /labɔʀɑ̃tɛ̃, in/ ▶ 374 *nm,f* laboratory assistant.

laboratoire /labɔʀatwaʀ/ *nm* laboratory; **de ~** [*animal, appareil*] laboratory (*épith*).
■ **~ d'analyses médicales** medical laboratory; **~ de langues** language laboratory; **~ orbital** skylab; **~ pharmaceutique** pharmaceutical company.

laborieusement /labɔʀjøzmɑ̃/ *adv* laboriously.

laborieux, -ieuse /labɔʀjø, øz/ *adj* **1** GÉN [*travail, processus*] arduous; [*accouchement*] difficult; [*style*] laboured; [*victoire*] hard-won (*épith*); **c'est ~ de leur faire faire leurs devoirs!** it's hard work getting them to do their homework!; **2** SOCIOL [*classes*] working.

Les lacs

Les noms de lacs

L'anglais n'utilise pas l'article défini devant les noms de lacs. Le mot Lake prend une majuscule lorsqu'il est utilisé devant le nom propre.

le lac Supérieur = Lake Superior
le lac Victoria = Lake Victoria

Les mots Loch *et* Lough *s'utilisent de la même façon.*

le loch Ness = Loch Ness
le lough Erne = Lough Erne

Le de utilisé en français pour les lacs qui portent des noms de villes n'est pas traduit en anglais.

le lac de Constance = Lake Constance
le lac d'Annecy = Lake Annecy

Dans ce cas, l'anglais utilise toujours le mot Lake.
Dans d'autres cas, Lake *peut être omis:*

le lac Balaton = Balaton *ou* Lake Balaton
le lac Titicaca = Titicaca *ou* Lake Titicaca

En cas de doute, il est toujours préférable d'employer Lake.

---

labour /labuʀ/ *nm* (travail) ploughing ¢ GB, plowing ¢ US; **cheval de ~** plough GB ou plow US horse.

labourage /labuʀaʒ/ *nm* ploughing GB, plowing US.

labourer /labuʀe/ [1] *vtr* to plough GB, to plow US.

laboureur /labuʀœʀ/ ▶ 374 *nm* **1** ploughman GB, plowman US; **2**† (cultivateur) farmer.

labyrinthe /labiʀɛ̃t/ *nm* **1** ARCHIT maze; **2** MYTHOL labyrinth; **3** FIG labyrinth, maze.

lac /lak/ *nm* (naturel) lake; (artificiel) reservoir.

lacer /lase/ [12] *vtr* to lace up [*chaussures, corset*].

lacérer /laseʀe/ [14] *vtr* to lacerate [*peau, chair*]; to slash [*vêtement, tableau, affiche*].

lacet /lasɛ/ *nm* **1** (de soulier, corset) lace; **chaussures à ~s** lace-up shoes; **2** (de route) hairpin bend; **route en ~s** twisting road.

lâche /lɑʃ/ I *adj* **1** (sans courage) [*personne, attitude, crime*] cowardly; **2** (distendu) [*ceinture, nœud*] loose; **3** (sans rigueur) [*règlement*] lax; [*style, scénario*] woolly.
II *nmf* coward.

lâchement /lɑʃmɑ̃/ *adv* **ils se sont ~ enfuis** they fled like cowards; **il a été ~ assassiné** he was foully murdered.

lâcher[1] /lɑʃe/ [1] I *vtr* **1** (cesser de tenir) to drop [*objet*]; to let go of [*corde, main*]; **lâche-moi** LIT let go of me; FIG○ give me a break○, leave me alone; **~ prise** to lose one's grip; **2** (produire) to come out with [*mot*]; to reveal [*information*]; to let out [*cri*]; **il n'a pas lâché un mot de toute la soirée** he didn't utter a word all evening; **3** (laisser partir) to let [sb/sth] go [*personne, animal*]; **elle a lâché ses chiens sur lui** she set her dogs on him; **il ne la lâche pas des yeux** he never takes his eyes off her; **4** (abandonner) to drop [*ami, activité*]; **5** SPORT (distancer) to break away from [*concurrent*].
II *vi* (céder) [*lien, nœud*] to give way; [*freins*] to fail.

lâcher[2] /lɑʃe/ *nm* (de ballons, d'oiseaux) release.

lâcheté /lɑʃte/ *nf* **1** (défaut) cowardice ¢; **par ~** out of cowardice; **2** (acte) cowardly act.

lâcheur○, **-euse** /lɑʃœʀ, øz/ *nm,f* unreliable person.

laisser

Verbe transitif

laisser verbe transitif se traduit généralement par *to leave*.
On trouvera la traduction des expressions comme *laisser
la parole à qn, laisser qch en suspens, laisser à qn le soin
de, laisser qn pour mort* etc. sous le nom ou l'adjectif.
Attention, *to leave* verbe transitif ne s'utilise jamais sans
complément:

> *laisse, si tu n'as plus faim!*
> = leave it if you've had enough!
> *laisse, c'est trop lourd pour toi!*
> = leave it, it's too heavy for you!
> *non merci, je laisse, c'est trop cher*
> = no thank you, I think I'll leave it, it's too
> expensive

Voir **I**.

laisser + sujet + infinitif

On trouvera la traduction des expressions comme
laisser voir, laisser courir, laisser à penser etc. sous le
deuxième verbe.

Lorsque *laisser* signifie *permettre de* ou *ne pas empêcher
de*, on pourra le traduire par *to let*:

> *vous avez laissé pousser des mauvaises herbes*
> = you've let weeds grow
> *il ne laisse pas ses enfants regarder la télévision*
> = he doesn't let his children watch television

> *laisse-le pleurer/critiquer/dormir*
> = let him cry/criticize/sleep
> *ne laisse pas le chat monter sur le canapé*
> = don't let the cat climb on the settee
> *ne laisse pas brûler la sauce*
> = don't let the sauce burn
> *quand on laisse le repassage s'accumuler*
> = if you let the ironing mount up

Voir **II**.

se laisser + infinitif

De façon très générale, le verbe pronominal suivi d'un
verbe à l'infinitif peut se traduire par *to let oneself*:

> *laisse-toi couler jusqu'au fond* = let yourself sink to the
> bottom

Quand la structure signifie plus précisément *accepter
l'action d'autrui* on traduira par *to let sb do sth*:

> *il s'est laissé coiffer* = he let me/her etc. do his hair
> *il ne se laisse pas caresser* = he won't let you stroke hir

Quand *se laisser* peut être remplacé par *être* on traduira
par *to be*:

> *se laisser envahir par un sentiment de bien-être*
> = to be overcome by a feeling of well-being

Voir **III**.

---

laconique /lakɔnik/ *adj* [*style*] laconic; [*réponse*]
terse.

lacrymal, **~e**, *mpl* **-aux** /lakʀimal, o/ *adj* lach-
rymal.

lacrymogène /lakʀimɔʒɛn/ *adj* [*grenade, bombe*]
teargas; **gaz ~** teargas.

lacté, **~e** /lakte/ *adj* **1** (qui contient du lait) [*produit,
alimentation*] milk (*épith*); **2** (laiteux) [*liquide, blanc*]
milky; **la voie ~e** the Milky Way.

lacune /lakyn/ *nf* (dans un manuscrit) lacuna; (dans les
connaissances, la loi) gap; (dans une argumentation) hole.

lacustre /lakystʀ/ *adj* **cité ~** lake dwelling.

là-dedans /lad(ə)dɑ̃/ *adv*

■ **Note** De même que *là* se traduit soit par *here* soit par
there, *là-dedans*, au sens littéral, se traduit par *in here* ou
in there suivant que l'objet dont on parle se trouve près ou
non du locuteur.

(près) in here; (plus loin) in there; **mets ça ~**
(près) put this in here; (plus loin) put that in there;
debout ~○**!** get up!; **et moi ~ qu'est-ce que je
fais**○**?** and where do I come in?

là-dessous /lad(ə)su/ *adv*

■ **Note** De même que *là* se traduit soit par *here* soit par
there, *là-dessous*, au sens littéral, se traduit par *under
here* ou *under there* suivant que l'objet dont on parle se
trouve près ou non du locuteur.

(près) under here; (plus loin) under there; **il y a qch
de louche ~**○ there's something fishy○ about all
this.

là-dessus /lad(ə)sy/ *adv*

■ **Note** De même que *là* se traduit soit par *here* soit par
there, *là-dessus*, au sens littéral, se traduit par *on here* ou
on there suivant que l'objet dont on parle se trouve près
ou non du locuteur.

1 (sur une surface) (près) on here; (plus loin) on there;
2 (sur ce sujet) **nous sommes d'accord ~** we agree;
qu'as-tu à dire ~? what have you got to say about
it?; **il y a un bon livre ~** there's a good book on it;
3 (alors) **~ il a raccroché** with that he hung up;
nous nous sommes quittés ~ we parted at that
point.

ladite ▶ **ledit**.

ladre /ladʀ/ **I** *adj* LITER [*personne*] miserly.
II *nm* (avare) LITER miser.

lagon /lagɔ̃/ *nm* lagoon.

lagune /lagyn/ *nf* lagoon.

---

là-haut /lao/ *adv*

■ **Note** De même que *là* se traduit soit par *here* soit p
there, *là-haut*, au sens littéral, se traduit par *up here* ou
there suivant que l'objet dont on parle se trouve près
non du locuteur.

1 (en hauteur) (près) up here; (plus loin) up there;
dans le ciel up in the sky; **il veut grimper ~**
wants to climb up there; **de ~** from up there; **2**
l'étage) upstairs; **3** (au paradis) in heaven.

laïc /laik/ *nm* layman.

laïcité /laisite/ *nf* (concept) secularism; (nature) se
larity.

laid, **~e** /lɛ, lɛd/ *adj* **1** (pas beau) ugly; **2** (choqua
disgusting.

laideur /lɛdœʀ/ *nf* ugliness.

lainage /lɛnaʒ/ *nm* **1** (étoffe) woollen[GB] material; **2** (
tement) woollen[GB] garment.

laine /lɛn/ *nf* **1** wool; **de** or **en ~** woollen[GB], w
(*épith*); **2**○ (vêtement) **une (petite) ~** a woolly.
■ **~ peignée** worsted; **~ à repriser** darn
wool; **~ à tapisserie** tapestry wool; **~ à trico**
knitting wool; **~ de verre** glass wool; **~ vier**
new wool GB, virgin wool.

laineux, **-euse** /lɛnø, øz/ *adj* woolly.

lainier, **-ière** /lɛnje, ɛʀ/ *adj* [*industrie*] wool (*épith*
[*région*] wool-producing.

laïque /laik/ **I** *adj* [*école, enseignement*] nondenom
ational GB, public US; [*État, esprit*] secular.
II *nmf* layman/laywoman; **les ~s** lay people.

laisse /lɛs/ *nf* (pour chien) lead GB, leash US.

laissé-pour-compte, **laissée-pour-comp**
mpl **laissés-pour-compte** /lesepuʀkɔ̃t/ *n*
outcast.

laisser /lese/ [1] **I** *vtr* **1** to leave [*parapluie, pourbo*
marge, trace]; **~ qch à qn** to leave sb sth; **~
liberté à qn** to let sb go free; **je te laisse** I must
laisse tes livres et viens te balader put your boo
away and come for a stroll; **~ le choix à qn** to gi
sb the choice; **laisse ce jouet à ton frère** let yo
brother have the toy; **tu y laisseras ta santé** you
ruin your health; **je ne veux pas y ~ ma peau**○
don't want it to kill me; **laisse-le, ça lui passe**
ignore him, he'll get over it; **je te laisse à tes occu**
tions I'll let you get on; **cela me laisse sceptique** I
sceptical; **2** (cesser) LITER **cela ne laisse r**
d'étonner it is a continual source of amazement.
II *v aux* **~ qn/qch faire** to let sb/sth do; **laisse-m**
faire (ne m'aide pas) let me do it; (je m'en occupe) lea

it to me; **laisse-la faire!** (ne t'en mêle pas) let her get on with it!; **laisse-la faire, elle reviendra toute seule** just leave her, she'll come back of her own accord.
III se laisser *vpr* **se ~ bercer par les vagues** to be lulled by the waves; **il se laisse insulter** he puts up with insults; **elle n'est pas du genre à se ~ faire** (laisser abuser) she won't be pushed around; **il ne veut pas se ~ faire** (coiffer, laver etc) he won't let you touch him; **se ~ aller** to let oneself go; **ça se laisse manger**○! EUPH it's quite palatable.

laisser-aller /leseale/ *nm inv* **1** (dans la tenue) scruffiness; **2** (dans le travail) sloppiness.

laissez-passer /lesepase/ *nm inv* pass.

lait /lɛ/ *nm* milk; **frère/sœur de ~** foster brother/sister (*who has had the same wet nurse*); **~ de soja** soya milk.
■ **~ de chaux** whitewash; **~ concentré non sucré** evaporated milk; **~ concentré sucré** sweetened condensed milk; **~ condensé = ~ concentré**; **~ instantané** instant dried milk; **~ maternel** breastmilk; **~ de poule** CULIN eggnog.
IDIOMES **si on lui pressait le nez il en sortirait du ~**○ he's/she's still wet behind the ears.

laitage /lɛtaʒ/ *nm* dairy product.

laitance /lɛtɑ̃s/ *nf* CULIN, ZOOL soft roe.

laiterie /lɛtʀi/ *nf* **1** (usine) dairy; **2** (industrie) dairy industry; **3†** (crémerie) dairy.

laiteux, -euse /lɛtø, øz/ *adj* [*liquide, blanc, lueur*] milky; [*teint, peau*] creamy; [*mur, peinture*] milk-white.

laitier, -ière /lɛtje, ɛʀ/ **I** *adj* [*industrie, produit*] dairy (*épith*); [*production, vache*] milk.
II ▶ 374| *nm,f* **1** (livreur) milkman/milkwoman; **2†** (crémier) dairyman/dairymaid.

laiton /lɛtɔ̃/ *nm* brass.

laitue /lety/ *nf* lettuce.

laïus○ /lajys/ *nm inv* speech.

lama /lama/ *nm* **1** (animal) llama; **2** (religieux) lama.

lamantin /lamɑ̃tɛ̃/ *nm* manatee.

lambda /lɑ̃bda/ **I**○ *adj inv* [*individu, lecteur*] average.
II *nm inv* lambda.

lambeau, *pl* **~x** /lɑ̃bo/ *nm* **1** (d'étoffe) rag; (de papier, peau, cuir) strip; (de chair) bit; **mettre qch en ~x** to tear sth to pieces; **2** FIG (de patrimoine) scraps (*pl*); **fortune qui part en ~x** fortune which is being frittered away.

lambin○, **~e** /lɑ̃bɛ̃, in/ **I** *adj* slow.
II *nm,f* slowcoach○ GB, slowpoke○ US.

lambris /lɑ̃bʀi/ *nm inv* (en bois) panelling GB ¢; (en marbre) marble walls (*pl*); (au plafond) mouldings GB (*pl*).

lambrisser /lɑ̃bʀise/ [1] *vtr* (avec du bois) to panel.

lame /lam/ *nf* **1** (de couteau, scie, tournevis) blade; **visage en ~ de couteau** hatchet face; **2** (couteau) knife; (épée) sword; (personne) **une fine ~** an expert swordsman; **3** (plaque mince) (de métal, bois, etc) strip; (de store) slat; (de ressort) leaf; **4** (vague) breaker.
■ **~ de fond** LIT ground swell; FIG upheaval; **~ de parquet** (longue) parquet strip; (courte) parquet block; **~ de rasoir** razor blade.

lamé /lame/ *nm* lamé; **en ~** lamé (*épith*).

lamelle /lamɛl/ *nf* **1** (de bois, métal) small strip; **2** CULIN (de truffe, fromage) sliver; **découper en fines ~s** to slice thinly; **3** BOT (de champignon) gill.

lamentable /lamɑ̃tabl/ *adj* **1** (minable) [*résultat, jeu*] pathetic; **2** (pitoyable) [*spectacle, cri*] pitiful; [*mort, accident*] terrible; [*voix, ton*] plaintive.

lamentablement /lamɑ̃tabləmɑ̃/ *adv* [*échouer*] miserably; [*pleurer*] piteously.

lamentation /lamɑ̃tasjɔ̃/ *nf* wailing ¢.

lamenter: se lamenter /lamɑ̃te/ [1] *vpr* to moan.

laminer /lamine/ [1] *vtr* to roll.

laminoir /laminwaʀ/ *nm* rolling mill.

lampadaire /lɑ̃padɛʀ/ *nm* (de salon) standard lamp GB, floor lamp US; (de rue) streetlight.

lampe /lɑ̃p/ *nf* GÉN lamp, light; (ampoule) bulb; (tube électronique)† valve GB, electron tube US.
■ **~ à bronzer** sun lamp; **~ de bureau** desk light ou lamp; **~ de chevet** bedside light ou lamp; **~ électrique** torch GB, flashlight US; **~ à pétrole** paraffin lamp GB, kerosene lamp US; **~ de poche** pocket torch GB, flashlight US; **~ à souder** blow lamp GB, blow torch; **~ témoin** indicator light; **~ tempête** hurricane lamp.

lampion /lɑ̃pjɔ̃/ *nm* paper lantern.

lance /lɑ̃s/ *nf* (de chasse, guerre) spear; (de tournoi) lance.
■ **~ d'incendie** fire hose nozzle.

lancée /lɑ̃se/ *nf* **sur ma ~** while I was at it; **continuer sur sa ~** (dans une activité) to continue to forge ahead; (dans un discours) to continue in the same vein.

lance-flammes /lɑ̃sflam/ *nm inv* flame-thrower.

lancement /lɑ̃smɑ̃/ *nm* **1** (mise en route) (de navire, compagnie, campagne, d'offensive); (de programme, processus) setting up; **2** (mise sur le marché) (de produit, livre, film) launch; (d'emprunt) floating; (d'acteur, écrivain) promotion; **3** (de missile, satellite) (processus) launching; (action) launch.

lance-pierres /lɑ̃spjɛʀ/ *nm inv* catapult.
IDIOMES **manger au ~**○ to gobble one's food; **payer qn avec un ~**○ to pay sb peanuts○.

lancer[1] /lɑ̃se/ [12] **I** *vtr* **1** (jeter) to throw [*ballon, caillou, javelot*]; **~ un coup de pied/poing à qn** to kick/to punch sb; **2** (envoyer, mettre en route) to launch [*satellite, fusée, navire*]; to fire [*flèche, missile*] (**sur** at); to drop [*bombe*]; to launch [*offensive, projet, enquête, produit, chanteur*]; to start up [*engine*]; to take [*sth*] to full speed [*véhicule*]; **~ une voiture à 150 km/h** to take a car up to 150 kph; **3** (émettre) to throw out [*fumée, flammes*]; to give [*regard, cri*]; to put about [*rumeur*]; to issue [*avis, ultimatum*]; to send out [*invitation*]; to float [*emprunt*]; **4** (proférer) to hurl [*insulte*] (**à** at); to make [*menace, accusation*]; to let out [*juron*]; to crack [*plaisanterie*]; **~ une accusation à qn** to level an accusation at sb; **lança-t-il** he said.
II○ *vi* (élancer) to throb.
III se lancer *vpr* **1** (s'engager) **se ~ dans une explication** to launch into an explanation; **se ~ dans l'informatique** to take up computing; **se ~ dans les affaires** to go into business; **2** (sauter) **se ~ dans le vide** to jump; **3** (s'envoyer) (pour attraper) to throw [*sth*] to each other [*ballon*]; (pour faire mal) to throw [*sth*] at each other [*pierre*]; to exchange [*insultes*]; **4** (se faire connaître) [*acteur*] to make a name for oneself.

lancer[2] /lɑ̃se/ *nm* **1** SPORT **~ du disque** discus event; **~ du poids** shot put (event); **2** (à la pêche) **le ~, la pêche au ~** rod and reel fishing.

lance-roquettes /lɑ̃sʀɔkɛt/ *nm inv* rocket launcher.

lancinant, ~e /lɑ̃sinɑ̃, ɑ̃t/ *adj* [*douleur*] shooting (*épith*); [*musique*] insistent; [*problème*] nagging (*épith*).

lanciner /lɑ̃sine/ [1] *vtr* (tourmenter) [*idée, remords*] to torment.

landau /lɑ̃do/ *nm* (d'enfant) pram GB, baby carriage US.

lande /lɑ̃d/ *nf* moor.

langage /lɑ̃gaʒ/ *nm* language; **elle m'a tenu un tout autre ~** she said something completely different to me.
■ **~ administratif** official jargon; **~ journalistique** journalese; **~ des sourds-muets** sign language.

lange /lɑ̃ʒ/ *nm* **1** (pour emmailloter) swaddling clothes (*pl*); **2** (couche de change) nappy GB, diaper US.

langer /lɑ̃ʒe/ [13] *vtr* **1** (emmailloter) to wrap [*sb*] in swaddling clothes [*bébé*]; **2** (mettre une couche) to put a nappy GB ou diaper US on [*bébé*].

langoureux, -euse /lɑ̃guʀø, øz/ *adj* languorous.

langouste /lɑ̃gust/ *nf* spiny lobster.

langoustine /lɑ̃gustin/ *nf* langoustine.

Les langues

Les adjectifs comme anglais *peuvent qualifier des personnes:* un touriste anglais (▶ 394) *et des choses:* la cuisine anglaise (▶ 232). *Dans les expressions suivantes,* English *est pris comme exemple; les autres noms de langues s'utilisent de la même façon.*

Les noms de langues

L'anglais n'utilise pas l'article défini devant les noms de langues.
Noter aussi l'emploi de la majuscule, obligatoire en anglais.

apprendre l'anglais = to learn English
étudier l'anglais = to study English
l'anglais est facile = English is easy
j'aime l'anglais = I like English
parler anglais = to speak English
parler couramment l'anglais = to speak good English
ou to speak English fluently
je ne parle pas très bien l'anglais = I don't speak very good English *ou* my English isn't very good

En *avec les noms de langues*

Avec un verbe, en anglais *se traduit par* in English:
dis-le en anglais = say it in English

Après un nom, en anglais *se traduit par* in English *ou par l'adjectif* English. *Noter l'emploi de la majuscule, obligatoire pour l'adjectif et le nom.*

un livre en anglais = a book in English
ou an English book*
une émission en anglais = an English-language broadcast

Mais attention:
traduire en anglais = to translate into English

De *avec les noms de langues*

Les expressions françaises avec de se traduisent en général en utilisant l'adjectif.

un cours d'anglais = an English class
un dictionnaire d'anglais = an English dictionary
une leçon d'anglais = an English lesson
un manuel d'anglais = an English textbook
un professeur d'anglais = an English teacher

Noter que ceci peut signifier aussi un professeur anglais. *Pour éviter l'ambiguïté, on peut dire* a teacher of English.

La traduction de l'adjectif français

l'accent anglais = an English accent
une expression anglaise = an English expression
la langue anglaise = the English language
un mot anglais = an English word
un proverbe anglais = an English proverb

L'anglais a peu d'équivalents simples des adjectifs et des noms français en -phone.

un arabophone = an Arabic speaker
il est arabophone = he is an Arabic speaker
l'Afrique anglophone = English-speaking Africa

---

* *Noter que* an English book *est ambigu, tout comme* un livre français, *qui peut signifier* un livre en français *ou* un livre qui vient de France.

---

langue /lɑ̃g/ *nf* **1** ▶ 137 ANAT tongue; **tirer la ~** (comme insulte) to stick out one's tongue (**à qn** at sb); (au médecin) to put out one's tongue; (avoir soif) to be dying of thirst; (avoir des problèmes d'argent) to struggle financially; **2** LING (système) language; (discours) speech; **aimer les ~s** to love languages; **en ~ familière** in informal speech; **3** (personne) **les ~s vont aller bon train** people will talk; **mauvaise ~** malicious gossip; **4** (forme allongée) **~ de terre** spit of land.
■ **~ de bois** political cant; **~ maternelle** mother tongue; **~ d'origine** native language; **~ verte** slang.
IDIOMES **avoir la ~ bien pendue**○ to be very talkative; **avoir qch sur le bout de la ~** to have sth on the tip of one's tongue.

languette /lɑ̃gɛt/ *nf* (de soulier) tongue; (de cartable) strap; (de fermoir) flap; (de pain) long narrow strip.

langueur /lɑ̃gœʀ/ *nf* languor.

languir /lɑ̃giʀ/ [3] *I vi* **1** (manquer d'énergie) [*conversation*] to languish; [*économie*] to be sluggish; **2** (souffrir d'attendre) **~ après** or **pour qn** to pine for sb; **je languis de vous revoir** I'm longing to see you; **faire ~ qn** to keep sb in suspense.
II se languir vpr to pine (**de qn** for sb).

languissant, ~e /lɑ̃gisɑ̃, ɑ̃t/ *adj* [*personne*] listless; [*économie*] sluggish; [*conversation*] desultory.

lanière /lanjɛʀ/ *nf* (attache) strap; (de fouet) lash.

lanterne /lɑ̃tɛʀn/ *nf* **1** (lampe) lantern; **2** AUT (feu de position) sidelight GB, parking light US.
IDIOMES **être la ~ rouge** to bring up the rear; **éclairer la ~ de qn** to enlighten sb (**sur qch** about sth).

lapalissade /lapalisad/ *nf* truism.

laper /lape/ [1] *vtr* to lap (up) [*soupe, lait*].

lapidaire /lapidɛʀ/ *adj* [*formule, style*] pithy.

lapidation /lapidasjɔ̃/ *nf* stoning.

lapider /lapide/ [1] *vtr* **1** (tuer) to stone [sb] to death [*personne*]; **2** (attaquer) to throw stones at [*personne*].

lapin /lapɛ̃/ *nm* **1** (animal, viande) rabbit; **coup du ~** (coup asséné) rabbit punch; (choc en voiture) whiplash injury; **cage** or **cabane à ~s** LIT rabbit hutch; FIG○ (immeuble) tower block; **2** (fourrure) rabbit(skin).
■ **~ de garenne** wild rabbit.
IDIOMES **poser un ~ à qn**○ to stand sb up; **se faire**

tirer comme des ~s○ to be picked off like flies; **c'est un chaud ~**○ he's a randy devil.

lapine /lapin/ *nf* doe rabbit.

lapon, ~e /lapɔ̃, ɔn/ ▶ 338 *I adj* GÉOG Lapp.
II nm LING Lapp.

Laponie /laponi/ ▶ 509 *nprf* **la ~** Lapland.

laps /laps/ *nm inv* **~ de temps** period of time.

lapsus /lapsys/ *nm inv* slip; **~ révélateur** Freudian slip.

laquais /lakɛ/ *nm inv* lackey.

laque /lak/ *nf* **1** (pour cheveux) hairspray; **2** (résine, vernis) lacquer; (peinture) gloss paint GB, enamel US.

laqué, ~e /lake/ *adj* **1** [*peinture*] gloss; **2** CULIN **canard ~** Peking duck; **porc ~** roast glazed pork.

laquelle /lakɛl/ ▶ lequel.

laquer /lake/ [1] *I vtr* to lacquer [*meuble*]; to paint [sth] in gloss GB ou enamel US [*porte*].
II se laquer vpr se **~ les cheveux** to put hairspray on one's hair; **cheveux laqués** lacquered hair.

larbin○ /laʀbɛ̃/ *nm* (domestique) PEJ servant; FIG flunkey.

larcin /laʀsɛ̃/ *nm* **1** (vol) petty theft; **2** (produit du vol) loot.

lard /laʀ/ *nm* ≈ fat streaky bacon.
IDIOMES **je ne sais pas si c'est du ~ ou du cochon**○ I don't know what to think.

larder /laʀde/ [1] *vtr* CULIN to lard (**de** with); **~ qn de coups de couteau** FIG to stab sb repeatedly.

lardon /laʀdɔ̃/ *nm* CULIN bacon cube.

large /laʀʒ/ *I adj* **1** ▶ 348 (de grande dimension) [*épaules, hanches, paumes*] broad; [*couloir, avenue, rivière, lit*] wide; [*sillon*] broad; [*manteau*] loose-fitting; [*pantalon*] loose; [*jupe, cape*] full; [*chandail*] big; [*geste, mouvement*] sweeping; [*sourire*] broad; [*courbe, détour*] long; **un ~ cercle** a big circle; **~ de trois mètres** three metres^{GB} wide; **2** (important) [*avance, bénéfice*] substantial; [*choix, public*] wide; [*concertation, coalition*] broad; [*extrait, majorité*] large; **au sens ~** in a broad sense; **bénéficier d'un ~ soutien** to have widespread support; **3** (généreux) [*personne*] generous (**avec** to); **4** (aisé) [*vie*] comfortable; **5** (ouvert) **avoir les idées ~s, être ~ d'esprit** to be broad-minded.
II adv **1** (généreusement) [*prévoir*] on a generous scale;

[*calculer, mesurer*] on the generous side; **2 s'habiller ~** to wear loose-fitting clothes.

III *nm* **1** (largeur) **faire quatre mètres de ~** to be four metres^{GB} wide; **2** NAUT open sea; **au ~** offshore; **au ~ de Marseille** off Marseilles; **l'air du ~** the sea air; **prendre le ~** NAUT to sail; ▶ **grand**.
IDIOMES **ne pas en mener ~**○ to be worried stiff○.

largement /laʁʒəmɑ̃/ *adv* **1** (massivement) [*admis, approuvé, représenté*] widely; [*disperser, irriguer, répandre*] widely; **se prononcer ~ en faveur de/contre qch** to come out largely in favour^{GB} of/against sth; **2** (en grande partie) largely, to a large extent; **3** (nettement) **l'opposition a ~ remporté les élections** the opposition won the elections by a wide margin; **être ~ majoritaire** to have a comfortable majority; **arriver ~ en tête** to be a clear winner; **~ en dessous/au-dessus de la limite** well under/over the limit; **il dépasse ~ les autres** (en taille) he's much taller than the others; **4** (amplement) **tu as ~ le temps** you've got plenty of time; **c'est ~ suffisant, cela suffit ~** that's more than enough, that's plenty; **5** (au moins) easily; **une chaîne en or vaudrait ~ le double** a gold chain would easily be worth double; **6** (généreusement) [*indemniser, contribuer*] generously; **7** (dans l'aisance) [*vivre*] comfortably.

largesse /laʁʒɛs/ **I** *nf* generosity; **être d'une grande ~ avec qn** to be very generous with sb.
II largesses *nfpl* generous gifts.

largeur /laʁʒœʁ/ *nf* **1** ▶ **348** (dimension) GÉN width, breadth; (en géométrie) breadth; **occuper toute la ~ de qch** to take up the full width of sth; **en petite/grande ~** in a narrow/broad width; **être déchiré sur toute la ~** to be torn right across; **dans le sens de la ~** widthwise; **2** (ouverture) **~ d'esprit** or **de vues** broad-mindedness.

largué○, **~e** /laʁge/ *adj* **1** (dépassé) (par un raisonnement) lost; (par les événements) out of touch; **2** (marginal) spaced out○.

larguer /laʁge/ [1] *vtr* **1** MIL, AVIAT to drop [*bombe, missile*]; to drop [*parachutiste*]; to release [*satellite, navette*]; **2** NAUT to unfurl [*voile*]; **~ les amarres** LIT to cast off; FIG to set off; **3**○ (abandonner) to give up [*études, appartement*]; to leave [*travail*]; to chuck○, to leave [*petit ami*].

larme /laʁm/ *nf* **1** LIT tear; **elle a ri aux ~s** she laughed till she cried; **pleurer à chaudes ~s** to cry as though one's heart would break; **avoir la ~ à l'œil** to be a bit weepy; **pleurer toutes les ~s de son corps** to cry one's eyes out; **2**○ FIG (petite quantité) drop (**de** of).

larmoyant, **~e** /laʁmwajɑ̃, ɑ̃t/ *adj* **1** (qui pleure) [*personne*] tearful; [*yeux*] full of tears (*après* n); **2** (qui veut attendrir) [*ton, voix*] whining; [*discours*] maudlin; [*personne*] snivelling^{GB}.

larmoyer /laʁmwaje/ [23] *vi* **1** [*yeux*] to water; **2** (pleurnicher) to whine (**sur qch** about sth).

larron /laʁɔ̃/ *nm* **1** HUM scoundrel; **2** thief.
IDIOMES **s'entendre comme ~s en foire** to be as thick as thieves; **l'occasion fait le ~** PROV opportunity makes the thief.

larvaire /laʁvɛʁ/ *adj* FIG [*état*] embryonic.

larve /laʁv/ *nf* **1** ZOOL larva; **2** (être humain) PÉJ (sans volonté) wimp○; (sans dignité) worm PÉJ.

larvé, **~e** /laʁve/ *adj* **1** GÉN latent; **2** MÉD atypical.

laryngite /laʁɛ̃ʒit/ ▶ **196** *nf* laryngitis.

larynx /laʁɛ̃ks/ *nm inv* larynx.

las, **lasse** /lɑ, lɑs/ *adj* weary (**de** of).

lasagnes /lazaɲ/ *nfpl* lasagna ¢.

lascar○ /laskaʁ/ *nm* (gaillard) fellow; (enfant) devil.

lascif, **-ive** /lasif, iv/ *adj* LITER [*personne, pose, regard*] lascivious; [*tempérament*] lustful.

lascivité /lasivite/ *nf* LITER lasciviousness.

laser /lazɛʁ/ *nm* laser.

lassant, **~e** /lasɑ̃, ɑ̃t/ *adj* **1** (ennuyeux) [*discours*] tedious; [*reproches*] tiresome; **2** (fatigant) tiring.

lasser /lase/ [1] **I** *vtr* (ennuyer) to bore [*personne, audience*]; (excéder) to weary [*personne, audience*].

II se lasser *vpr* [*personne*] to grow tired (**de qn/qch** of sb/sth; **de faire** of doing); **sans se ~** (infatigablement) without tiring; (patiemment) patiently.

lassitude /lasityd/ *nf* weariness; **avec ~** wearily.

latence /latɑ̃s/ *nf* latency; PSYCH latency (period).

latent, **~e** /latɑ̃, ɑ̃t/ *adj* [*danger, maladie, possibilité*] latent; [*angoisse, jalousie*] underlying.

latéral, **~e**, *mpl* **-aux** /lateʁal, o/ *adj* (sur le côté) [*porte, sortie*] side (*épith*); (parallèle) [*nef, tunnel*] lateral.

latéralement /lateʁalmɑ̃/ *adv* LIT (de côté) [*arriver*] from the side; (sur le côté) [*placer*] sideways.

latin, **~e** /latɛ̃, in/ **I** *adj* **1** [*auteurs, textes*] Latin; **2** (méditerranéen) [*tempérament*] Latin; [*culture*] Mediterranean; **3** LING **langues ~es** Romance languages.
II ▶ **338** *nm* LING Latin.
IDIOMES **c'est à y perdre son ~** one can't make head or tail of it.

latinisme /latinism/ *nm* Latinism.

latiniste /latinist/ *nmf* Latinist.

latino-américain, **~e**, *mpl* **~s** /latinoameʁikɛ̃, ɛn/ *adj* Latin-American.

latitude /latityd/ **I** *nf* **1** GÉOG latitude; **par 38° de ~ nord** at latitude 38° north; **2** (liberté) latitude; **avoir toute ~ de faire** to be entirely free to do.
II latitudes *nfpl* (régions, climats) latitudes.

latte /lat/ *nf* **1** CONSTR (de plafond, mur) lath; (de plancher) board; (de sommier, siège) slat.

latter /late/ [1] *vtr* to lath.

laudateur, **-trice** /lodatœʁ, tʁis/ FML **I** *adj* laudatory SOUT.
II *nm,f* adulator.

laudatif, **-ive** /lodatif, iv/ *adj* laudatory.

lauréat, **~e** /loʁea, at/ *nm,f* **1** (de compétition) winner; **2** SCOL, UNIV successful candidate.

laurier /loʁje/ **I** *nm* **1** BOT laurel; **~ commun** bay (tree); **2** CULIN **feuille de ~** bay leaf.
II lauriers *nmpl* laurels; **se couvrir de ~s** [*soldat*] to distinguish oneself; [*écrivain*] to win many awards; [*candidat*] to perform outstandingly; **s'endormir** or **se reposer sur ses ~s** to rest on one's laurels.

laurier-rose, *pl* **lauriers-roses** /loʁjeʁoz/ *nm* oleander.

lavable /lavabl/ *adj* washable; **~ en machine** machine washable.

lavabo /lavabo/ *nm* (cuvette) washbasin, washbowl.

lavage /lavaʒ/ *nm* **1** (de linge, sol, mains) washing; (de plaie) cleaning; **le ~ des vitres** window cleaning; **2** (cycle de machine à laver) wash; **un ~** a wash.
■ **~ de cerveau** brainwashing; **faire un ~ d'estomac à qn** to pump sb's stomach (out).

lavande /lavɑ̃d/ ▶ **141** *adj inv*, *nf* lavender.

lavandière /lavɑ̃djɛʁ/ *nf* **1** (oiseau) wagtail; **2** ▶ **374** (blanchisseuse) washerwoman.

lavasse○ /lavas/ *nf* **c'est de la ~** (soupe, café) it tastes like dishwater.

lave /lav/ *nf* lava ¢; **coulée de ~** lava flow.

lave-auto, *pl* **~s** /lavoto/ *nm* C car wash.

lave-glace, *pl* **~s** /lavglas/ *nm* windscreen GB ou windshield US washer.

lave-linge /lavlɛ̃ʒ/ *nm inv* washing machine.

lavement /lavmɑ̃/ *nm* MÉD enema.

laver /lave/ [1] **I** *vtr* **1** (nettoyer) to wash [*vêtement, enfant, voiture*]; **~ son linge** to do one's washing; **~ la vaisselle** to do the dishes, to do the washing-up GB; **~ qch à grande eau** to wash sth down; **~ qch au jet** to hose sth down; **~ qch à la brosse** to scrub sth; **2** (désinfecter) to clean [*plaie*]; **3** LITER [*pluie, orage*] to wash [*rue, ciel*]; **4** (innocenter) to clear; **5** (venger) LITER to wash away [*humiliation, péché*]; **6** ART to wash.
II se laver *vpr* **1** (soi-même) to wash; **se ~ les dents** to brush one's teeth; **2** [*tissu, vêtement*] to be washable; **se ~ en machine** to be machine washable; **3** FIG, LITER **se ~ d'un affront** to take revenge for an insult.

le

Article

le, la, les article défini se traduit par *the* (invariable) quand le nom qu'il précède est déterminé par un contexte supposé connu de l'interlocuteur:

passe-moi le sel	= pass me the salt
le déjeuner d'anniversaire	= the birthday lunch
le courage de faire	= the courage to do

Il ne se traduit pas quand ce nom exprime une généralité ou que son contexte est indéterminé:

le sel de mer	= sea salt
pendant le déjeuner	= during lunch
le courage seul ne suffit pas	= courage alone isn't enough

the se prononce /ðə/ devant consonne et h aspiré, /ðɪ/ devant voyelle et h muet (hour, honest, honour, heir), et /ði:/ quand il est employé de manière emphatique pour indiquer l'excellence (comme **le** en français dans *c'est le poète de la liberté*).

Ne sont traités ci-dessous que les cas où l'article se traduit différemment de *the*, ou ne se traduit pas, ou se rend par une structure particulière, à l'exclusion de ceux qui sont développés dans les notes d'usage répertoriées ▶ **1420**│, notamment celles concernant *les jours de la semaine*, *les douleurs et les maladies*, *les jeux et les sports*, *les nationalités*, *les langues*, *les pays*, *les nombres*, *les titres de politesse* etc.

Dans la composition du superlatif, l'anglais ne répète pas l'article:

l'homme le plus riche du monde
= the richest man in the world
l'homme le plus intelligent du monde
= the most intelligent man in the world

Les noms de plat sur un menu ne prennent pas d'article:

le steak au poivre vert = steak with green peppercorns

Il n'y a pas d'article après *whose*:

les enfants dont la mère …= the children whose mother …

L'article se traduit avec les noms d'inventions:

la charrue = the plough   *l'ordinateur* = the computer

Noter:

la Terre est ronde   = the earth is round
sur la planète Terre = on planet Earth
au contraire de la Terre, Mars … = unlike Earth, Mars …

Pronom personnel

Le pronom personnel se traduit selon le genre et le nombre de l'antécédent en anglais: *him* pour représenter une personne de sexe masculin, un animal familier mâle; *her* pour une personne de sexe féminin, un animal familier femelle, un bateau, un véhicule qu'on aime bien ou dont on parle avec ironie; *it* pour une chose, un concept, un pays, une institution, un animal; *them* pour un antécédent régissant un verbe au pluriel.

IDIOMES **je m'en lave les mains** I'm washing my hands of it.

laverie /lavʀi/ ▶**374**│ *nf* ~ **(automatique)** launderette, laundromat® us.

lavette /lavɛt/ *nf* **1** (pour la vaisselle) dishcloth; **2**○ (personne) PEJ wimp○ PÉJ; **3** H (de toilette) flannel GB, wash cloth us.

laveur, -euse /lavœʀ, øz/ ▶**374**│ *nm,f* cleaner.

lave-vaisselle /lavvɛsɛl/ *nm inv* dishwasher.

lavis /lavi/ *nm inv* (technique) wash; (dessin) wash drawing.

lavoir /lavwaʀ/ *nm* (pour la lessive) wash house.

laxatif, -ive /laksatif, iv/ **I** *adj* laxative.
II *nm* laxative.

laxisme /laksism/ *nm* laxity.

laxiste /laksist/ *adj* lax (**à l'égard de, avec** with).

layette /lɛjɛt/ *nf* baby clothes (*pl*), layette.

lazaret /lazaʀɛ/ *nm* (dans un port) lazaretto; (dans un hôpital) isolation ward.

le, la¹ (**l'** *before vowel or mute h*), *pl* **les** /lə, la, l, lɛ/ **I** *art déf* **1** (avec complément de nom) **la jupe/fille de ma sœur** my sister's skirt/daughter; **les chapitres du livre** the chapters of the book; **la table de la cuisine** the kitchen table; **2** (en parlant d'une personne) **il est arrivé les mains dans les poches** he arrived with his hands in his pockets; **elle s'est cogné ~ bras** she banged her arm; **elle m'a pris par ~ bras** she took me by the arm; **3** (avec un nom d'espèce) **l'homme préhistorique/de Cro-Magnon** prehistoric/Cro-Magnon man; **les droits de l'enfant** children's rights; **elle aime les chevaux** she likes horses; **4** (avec un nom propre) **les Dupont** the Duponts; **la Noël** Christmas; **la Saint-Michel** St. Michael's day; **~ roi Olaf** King Olaf; **5** (avec un adjectif) **je prendrai la bleue** I'll take the blue one; **~ ridicule de cette affaire** what is ridiculous about this matter; **les pauvres** the poor; **6** (avec préposition et nombre) **dans les 20 francs** about 20 francs; **7** (pour donner un prix, une fréquence etc) a, an; **50 francs ~ kilo** 50 francs a kilo; **8** (dans les exclamations) **l'imbécile!** the fool!; **la pauvre!** the poor thing!; **(oh) la jolie robe!** what a pretty dress!
II *pron pers* **je ne ~/la/les comprends pas** I don't understand him/her/them.
III *pron neutre* **1** (complément) **je ~ savais** (j'étais au courant) I knew; (j'aurais dû m'en douter) I knew it; **je ne veux pas ~ savoir** I don't want to know (about it); **si je ne ~ fais pas, qui ~ fera?** if I don't do

it, who will?; **je ~ croyais aussi, mais**... I thought so too, but...; **si c'est lui qui ~ dit**... if HE says so...; **'ils auront fini demain'—'espérons-~!'** 'they'll have finished tomorrow'—'let's hope so!'; **2** (attribut) **'est-elle satisfaite?'—'je ne crois pas qu'elle ~ soit'** 'is she satisfied?'—'I don't think so'.

lé /le/ *nm* **1** (de papier peint) width; **2** (de jupe) panel.

LEA /ɛləa/ *nfpl* (*abbr* = **langues étrangères appliquées**) *university language course with emphasis on business and management.*

leadership /lidœʀʃip/ *nm* **1** (rôle de leader) leading role; **2** (suprématie) supremacy.

lèche-bottes○ /lɛʃbɔt/ *nm* (servilité) **le ~** crawling○ GB, bootlicking○; **faire du ~** to be a crawler GB ou bootlicker○.

lèchefrite /lɛʃfʀit/ *nf* dripping pan.

lécher /leʃe/ [1] **I** *vtr* **1** (avec la langue) to lick [*cuillère, assiette*]; **2** (effleurer) [*flamme*] to lick; [*mer*] to lap against; **3**○ (peaufiner) to polish [*œuvre*]; **4**○ **~ les vitrines** to go window-shopping.
II *se lécher* *vpr* **se ~ les doigts** to lick one's fingers.
IDIOMES **~ les bottes**○ **de qn** to lick sb's boots○, to brown-nose sb❶ us.

lécheur, -euse /leʃœʀ, øz/ *nm,f* PEJ crawler○ GB, brown-noser❶ us.

lèche-vitrines /lɛʃvitʀin/ *nm inv* window-shopping.

leçon /ləsɔ̃/ *nf* **1** SCOL lesson; **~ particulière** private lesson; **2** (punition, avis) lesson; **elle m'a fait la ~** she lectured me; **elle pourrait nous donner des ~s en matière de courage** she could teach us a thing or two about courage; **3** (conclusion) lesson; **la ~ de la fable** the moral of the story.

lecteur, -trice /lɛktœʀ, tʀis/ **I** ▶**374**│ *nm,f* **1** GÉN reader; **2** UNIV (language) teaching assistant.
II *nm* **1** ORDINAT reader; **~ optique** optical scanner ou reader; **2** AUDIO player; **~ de disquettes** disk drive; **~ laser** CD player.

lectorat /lɛktɔʀa/ *nm* **1** (public) readership; **2** UNIV post of lecteur/-trice.

lecture /lɛktyʀ/ *nf* **1** (de livre, journal) reading; **livre d'une ~ ardue** book which is difficult to read; **faire la ~ à qn** to read to sb; **donner ~ de qch** FML to read out sth; **2** (interprétation) reading, interpretation; **3** (ce qu'on lit) reading material; **ce sont mes ~s préférées** it's my favourite GB (kind of) reading; **4** (de musique, radiographie, graphique) reading; **5** POL reading; **6** AUDIO play; **7** ORDINAT reading.

ledit, **ladite**, *pl* **lesdits**, **lesdites** / lədi, ladit, ledi, ledit/ *adj* the aforementioned.

légal, **~e**, *mpl* **-aux** /legal, o/ *adj* [*âge, définition, voies*] legal; [*activité, possession*] lawful; **monnaie ~e** legal tender; **domicile ~** official residence.

légalement /legalmᾶ/ *adv* (selon la loi) legally; (sans enfreindre la loi) lawfully.

légaliser /legalize/ [1] *vtr* (rendre légal) to legalize; (certifier) to authenticate.

légalité /legalite/ *nf* (conformité à la loi) legality; (légitimité) lawfulness; **rester dans la ~** to remain within the law.

légat /lega/ *nm* legate.

légataire /legatɛR/ *nmf* legatee; **~ universel** sole legatee.

légendaire /leʒᾶdɛR/ *adj* legendary.

légende /leʒᾶd/ *nf* **1** (fable) legend; **entrer dans la ~** to become legendary; **2** (inscription) (d'illustration) caption; (de carte) key; **3** (mensonge) tall story.

léger, **-ère** /leʒe, ɛR/ **I** *adj* **1** (peu pesant) light; **se sentir plus ~** FIG to have a great weight off one's mind; **2** CULIN light; **3** (souple) [*danseur*] nimble; [*démarche*] light; [*pas*] springy; [*mouvement*] nimble; **4** (faible) [*rire*] gentle; [*coup*] soft, gentle; [*blessure, progrès, baisse, faute, retard*] slight; [*crainte, condamnation*] mild; [*goût, odeur, tremblement, espoir*] faint; [*vent, pluie, brume*] light; [*accent, bruit*] faint, slight; [*couche, nuage*] thin; [*blessure*] minor; **5** (peu concentré) [*café, thé, alcool*] weak; [*parfum, vin*] light; [*tabac*] mild GB, light US; **6** (superficiel) [*action, initiative*] ill-considered; [*jugement, propos*] thoughtless, careless; [*argument, preuve*] weak, flimsy; **7°** (insuffisant) **c'est un peu ~** it's a bit skimpy; **8** (frivole) [*femme*] loose; [*mœurs*] loose, lax; [*mari, caractère, humeur*] fickle; **9** MIL [*arme, division*] light.
II *adv* [*voyager*] light.
III à la légère *loc adv* [*agir*] without thinking; **prendre qch à la ~** not to take sth seriously.

légèrement /leʒɛRmᾶ/ *adv* **1** (faiblement) [*appuyer, bouger*] gently; [*masser, gratter*] gently, lightly; [*parfumer*] lightly, slightly; [*trembler, blessé, teinté*] slightly; **être habillé ~** to be dressed for warm weather; **2** CULIN [*manger*] lightly; **3** (avec souplesse) [*marcher, courir*] lightly, nimbly; **4** (avec désinvolture) [*agir, parler, se conduire*] without thinking.

légèreté /leʒɛRte/ *nf* **1** LIT lightness; **2** CULIN lightness; **3** (souplesse) (de personne) lightness, nimbleness; (de démarche, mouvement, style) lightness; **avec ~** lightly; **4** (superficialité) (de jugement, propos) lack of thought **(de qch** behind sth); **faire preuve de ~ dans qch** (dans la conduite) to show irresponsibility in sth; (dans les propos) to show a lack of depth in sth; **5** (frivolité) **la ~ de ses mœurs** his/her loose morals (*pl*); (caractère volage) fickleness.

légion /leʒjɔ̃/ *nf* **1** HIST, MIL legion; **2** (multitude) army **(de** of); **ils sont ~** they are legion.
■ **la Légion** (**étrangère**) the Foreign Legion; **la Légion d'honneur** the Legion of Honour^{GB}.

légionnaire /leʒjɔnɛR/ **I** *nmf* (qui a la Légion d'honneur) member of the Legion of Honour^{GB}.
II *nm* (romain) legionary; (de la Légion étrangère) legionnaire.

législateur, **-trice** /leʒislatœR, tRis/ *nm,f* legislator, law-maker.

législatif, **-ive** /leʒislatif, iv/ **I** *adj* legislative; **élections législatives** ≈ general election (*sg*).
II *nm* legislature.

législation /leʒislasjɔ̃/ *nf* legislation.

législature /leʒislatyR/ *nf* **1** (durée) term of office; **2** (assemblée) legislature.

légiste /leʒist/ ▶ **374** *nm* jurist.

légitime /leʒitim/ *adj* **1** (selon la loi) [*enfant, droit, pouvoir*] legitimate; [*union, époux, héritier*] lawful; **2** (justifié) [*grief, revendication, action*] legitimate;

[*colère*] justifiable; **3** (juste) [*salaire*] fair; [*récompense*] just.
■ **~ défense** self-defence^{GB}.

légitimité /leʒitimite/ *nf* **1** JUR legitimacy; **2** (d'une action) lawfulness.

legs /lɛg/ *nm inv* **1** JUR (de biens mobiliers) legacy; (de terres, biens immobiliers) devise; (d'effets personnels) bequest; (à une fondation) bequest; **2** FIG legacy.

léguer /lege/ [14] *vtr* **1** (par testament) to leave sth (**à qn** to sb); **2** (transmettre) to hand down [*traditions*]; to pass on [*qualité, défaut*].

légume /legym/ *nm* **1** LIT vegetable; **~s verts** green vegetables; **~s secs** pulses; **2°** FIG PEJ vegetable.

Léman /lemᾶ/ ▶ **335** *npr* **le lac ~** Lake Geneva.

lendemain /lᾶdəmɛ̃/ **I** *nm* **1** (jour suivant) **le ~**, **la journée du ~** the following day; **dès le ~** the (very) next day; **le ~ de l'accident** the day after the accident; **le ~ matin/soir** the following morning/evening; **du jour au ~** overnight; **2** (période qui suit) **au ~ de** (in the period) after; **3** (avenir) **le ~** tomorrow, the future; **sans ~** [*bonheur, succès*] short-lived.
II lendemains *nmpl* **1** (issue) outcome (*sg*); (conséquences) consequences; **2** (perspectives) future (*sg*); **des ~s difficiles** difficult days ahead.
IDIOMES **il ne faut jamais remettre au ~ ce qu'on peut faire le jour même** PROV never put off till tomorrow what you can do today.

lénifiant, **~e** /lenifjᾶ, ᾶt/ *adj* [*médicament, remarque*] soothing.

lent, **~e**¹ /lᾶ, ᾶt/ *adj* GÉN slow; [*film, véhicule*] slow-moving; [*poison*] slow-acting; **être ~ au travail** to be a slow worker; **avoir l'esprit ~** to be slow-witted.

lente² /lᾶt/ *nf* ZOOL nit.

lentement /lᾶt(ə)mᾶ/ *adv* slowly.
IDIOMES **qui va ~ va sûrement** PROV slowly but surely.

lenteur /lᾶtœR/ *nf* slowness (**à faire** to do, in doing); **avec ~** slowly.

lentille /lᾶtij/ *nf* **1** BOT, CULIN lentil; **2** (optique) lens; **~s de contact** contact lenses.

léopard /leopaR/ *nm* **1** (animal) leopard; **2** (fourrure) leopardskin.

lèpre /lɛpR/ ▶ **196** *nf* MÉD leprosy.

lépreux, **-euse** /lepRø, øz/ **I** *adj* MÉD leprous.
II *nm,f* leper.

léproserie /lepRozRi/ *nf* leper hospital.

lequel /ləkɛl/, **laquelle** /lakɛl/, **lesquels** *mpl*, **lesquelles** *fpl* /lekɛl/, (avec *à*) **auquel**, **auxquels** *mpl*, **auxquelles** *fpl* /okɛl/, (avec *de*) **duquel** /dykɛl/, **desquels** *mpl*, **desquelles** *fpl* /dekɛl/

■ **Note** Lorsque la traduction du verbe de la proposition relative introduite par *lequel, laquelle* etc fait intervenir une préposition en anglais, trois traductions sont possibles: *le carton dans lequel tu as mis les bouteilles* = the box you put the bottles in; = the box that ou which you put the bottles in; = the box in which you put the bottles. Les deux premières traductions relèvent de la langue courante, parlée ou écrite; la troisième traduction sera préférée dans une langue plus soutenue, surtout écrite.
– La forme interrogative fonctionne de la même façon, avec seulement deux possibilités, la seconde étant préférée dans la langue écrite soutenue: *dans lequel de ces cartons as-tu mis les bouteilles?* = which of these boxes did you put the bottles in?; = in which of these boxes did you put the bottles?

I lequel, **laquelle**, **lesquels**, **lesquelles** *adj* (avec personne) who; (autres cas) which; **elle a envoyé son dossier au service des inscriptions, ~ dossier a été perdu** she sent her file to the registration office, and it got lost; **auquel cas** in which case.
II *pron rel* **1** (en fonction de sujet) (représentant une personne) who; (dans les autres cas) which; **il a donné le colis au réceptionniste, ~ me l'a remis** he gave the package to the receptionist, who gave it to me; **2** (en fonction d'objet) (représentant une personne) whom;

(dans les autres cas) which; **l'ami auquel tu as écrit** the friend to whom you wrote, the friend (who) you wrote to; **les gens contre lesquels ils luttaient** the people against whom they were fighting; **la table sur laquelle tu as posé la tasse** the table (which) you put the cup on; **les gens chez lesquels nous sommes allés** the people whose house we went to.

III *pron inter* which; **de tous ces employés, lesquels sont les plus compétents?** of all these employees, which are the most competent?; **auquel de tes amis as-tu écrit?** which of your friends did you write to?; **'j'ai vu un film de Chaplin hier'—'~?'** 'I saw a Charlie Chaplin film yesterday'—'which one?'

les ▶ **le**.

lesbienne /lɛsbjɛn/ *nf* lesbian.

lesdites ▶ **ledit**.

lesdits ▶ **ledit**.

léser /leze/ [14] *vtr* **1** (causer du tort à) to wrong [*personne*]; to prejudice [*intérêts*]; **2** FIG to hurt [*sentiment*].

lésiner /lezine/ [1] *vi* **ne pas ~ sur** to be liberal with [*ingrédient, argent, compliments*]; **ne pas ~ sur la dépense** to spare no expense.

lésion /lezjɔ̃/ *nf* MÉD lesion.

lesquels, lesquelles /lekɛl/ ▶ **lequel**.

lessivable /lesivabl/ *adj* washable.

lessive /lesiv/ *nf* **1** (produit) (en poudre) washing powder; (liquide) washing liquid; **2** (tâche ménagère, linge) washing; **faire deux ~s par semaine** to do two washes a week.

lessiver /lesive/ [1] *vtr* **1** (laver) to wash; **2**○ (épuiser) **être lessivé** HUM to be washed out○.

lessiveuse /lesivøz/ *nf* boiler, copper GB.

lest /lɛst/ *nm* **1** NAUT, AVIAT ballast; **lâcher du ~** FIG to make concessions; **2** (sur un filet) weight.

leste /lɛste/ *adj* **1** (souple) [*personne, animal*] agile; [*démarche, pas*] nimble; **2** (osé) [*propos, plaisanterie*] risqué.

lestement /lɛstəmɑ̃/ *adv* (avec souplesse) nimbly.

lester /lɛste/ [1] *vtr* **1** NAUT, AVIAT to ballast; **2**○ (charger) to stuff sth (**de** with).

léthargie /letaʀʒi/ *nf* **1** (engourdissement) lethargy; **2** MÉD lethargy.

léthargique /letaʀʒik/ *adj* **1** [*personne*] lethargic; [*industrie, économie*] sluggish; **2** MÉD lethargic.

letton, -onne /lɛtɔ̃, ɔn/ **I** ▶ **394** *adj* Latvian.

II ▶ **338** *nm* LING **le ~** Latvian.

Lettonie /lɛtɔni/ *nprf* Latvia.

lettre /lɛtʀ/ **I** *nf* **1** (signe graphique) letter; **~ minuscule** small letter; **~ majuscule** or **capitale** capital letter; **~ d'imprimerie** block letter; **un mot de trois ~s** a three-letter word; **en toutes ~s** LIT in full; **c'est écrit en toutes ~s dans le rapport** FIG it's down in black and white in the report; **les Romains furent des urbanistes avant la ~** the Romans were city planners before the concept was invented; **2** (écrit adressé) letter; **~ de réclamation** letter of complaint; **une petite ~** a note; **3** (contenu d'un texte) letter; **à la ~**, **au pied de la ~** [*appliquer, suivre*] to the letter; **il prend à la ~ tout ce qu'on lui dit** he takes everything you say literally.

II lettres *nfpl* **1** UNIV, SCOL (français) French; (plus général) arts GB, humanities US; **étudiant en ~s** (français) student reading French GB, student majoring in French US; (plus général) arts GB or humanities US student; **docteur ès ~s** ≈ Doctor of Philosophy; **2** (culture littéraire) letters; **femme de ~s** woman of letters; **les gens de ~s** writers; **avoir des ~s** to be well read.

■ **~ ouverte** open letter (**à** to); **~ recommandée** registered letter; **~s classiques** French and Latin; **~s modernes** French language and literature.

IDIOMES **passer comme une ~ à la poste**○ [*réforme*] to go through smoothly; [*excuse*] to be accepted

without any questions; **devenir ~ morte** to become a dead letter; **rester ~ morte** to go unheeded.

lettré, ~e /letʀe/ **I** *adj* [*personne*] well-read; [*milieu*] literary.

II *nm,f* man/woman of letters.

leucémie /løsemi/ ▶ **196** *nf* leukaemia.

leucocyte /løkɔsit/ *nm* leucocyte GB, leukocyte US.

leur, (*pl* **leurs**) /lœʀ/

■ **Note** En anglais, on ne répète pas le possessif coordonné: *leur nom et leur adresse* = their names and addresses.

I *pron pers inv* them; **promesse ~ a été faite que** they were given a promise that; **il ~ a expliqué le fonctionnement de l'appareil** he told them how the machine worked; **il ~ a fallu faire** they had to do.

II *adj poss mf, pl* **~s** their; **elles ressemblent à ~ père** they look like their father; **un de ~s amis** a friend of theirs; **ils sont partis chacun de ~ côté** they went their separate ways; **à ~ arrivée/départ** when they arrived/left.

III le leur, la leur, les leurs *pron poss* theirs, celui-là, **c'est le ~** that's theirs; **qu'ils aient chacun le ~** let them have one each; **il est des ~s** (de un groupe) he's one of them; **ils vivent loin des ~s** (de leur famille) they live far away from their families.

leurre /lœʀ/ *nm* **1** (tromperie) illusion; **2** (à la pêche, chasse) lure; **3** MIL decoy.

leurrer /lœʀe/ [1] **I** *vtr* (tromper) to delude (**par** with).

II se leurrer *vpr* to delude oneself (**de** with; **au sujet de** about).

levage /ləvaʒ/ *nm* TECH (de charge) lifting.

levain /ləvɛ̃/ *nm* **1** CULIN leaven GB, sourdough US; **pain au/sans ~** leavened/unleavened bread; **2** BIOL, IND (agent de fermentation) starter; **3** (force) catalyst.

levant /ləvɑ̃/ **I** *adj m* **soleil ~** rising sun; **au soleil ~** at sunrise.

II *nm* east; **au ~** in the east.

levé, ~e¹ /ləve/ **I** *pp* ▶ **lever¹**.

II *pp adj* **1** (dressé) **voter à main ~e** to vote by a show of hands; **2** (hors du lit) up; **elle est toujours la première ~e** she's always the first up.

III *nm* GÉOG (relevé) survey.

IDIOMES **faire qch au pied ~** to do sth off the cuff.

levée² /ləve/ *nf* **1** (suppression) (d'embargo, de peine) martiale, préavis de grève, peine) lifting (**de** of); (de siège) raising; (de mesures, quotas) suspension (**de** of); (d'immunité parlementaire) removal (**de** of); (d'anonymat, de secret, tabou) ending (**de** of); (de séance) close (**de** of); **2** (de courrier) collection; **3** JEUX (aux cartes) trick; **4** GÉOG (remblai) levee; **5** MIL (recrutement) levying.

■ **~ de boucliers** outcry.

lever¹ /ləve/ [16] **I** *vtr* **1** (dresser) GÉN to raise; **~ la main** or **le doigt** (pour parler) to put up one's hand; **~ la main sur qn** (frapper) to raise a hand to sb; **~ les bras au ciel** to throw up one's hands (**de** in); **lève les pieds quand tu marches!** don't drag your feet!; **~ les yeux** or **la tête** (regarder) to look up (**sur, vers** at); **sans ~ les yeux** [*dire, répondre*] without looking up; [*travailler, étudier*] without a break; **2** (soulever) to lift [*objet*]; to raise [*barrière*]; **~ son verre** to raise one's glass (**à** to); **~ le rideau** THÉÂT to raise the curtain; **~ les filets** (à la pêche) to haul in the nets; **3** (sortir du lit) to get [sb] up [*enfants, malade*]; **4** (mettre fin à) to lift [*embargo, contrôle*]; to raise [*siège*]; to dispel [*doute, mystère*]; to end [*tabou, secret, audience*]; to remove [*obstacle, difficultés*]; to close [*séance*]; **5** (collecter) to raise [*capitaux, fonds*]; to levy [*impôt*]; **6** (recruter) to levy [*troupes*]; **7** (débusquer) to flush out [*gibier*]; **~ un lièvre** LIT to start a hare.

II *vi* **1** CULIN [*pâte*] to rise; **2** AGRIC [*semis, blé*] to come up.

III se lever *vpr* **1** (sortir du lit) to get up; **il faut se ~ de bonne heure**○ **pour comprendre ce qu'il dit** FIG you need to be pretty○ clever to understand what he says; **2** (se mettre debout) to stand up; **se ~ de sa**

chaise to rise from one's chair; **se ~ de table** to leave the table; **'accusé, levez-vous!'** JUR 'the accused will stand'; **3** (s'insurger) [*personne, peuple*] to rise up (**contre** against); **4** (apparaître) [*soleil, lune*] to rise (**sur** over); **le jour se lève** it's getting light; **5** (s'agiter) [*vent*] to rise; [*brise*] to get up; (s'éclaircir) [*nuages, brume*] to clear; [*temps*] to clear up.

lever² /ləve/ *nm* **1** (sortie du lit) **être là au ~ des enfants** to be there when the children get up; **2** GÉOG = **levé III.**
■ **~ du jour** daybreak; **au ~ du jour** at daybreak; **~ de rideau** (début de la représentation) curtain up; (prélude) curtain raiser; **~ du soleil** sunrise.

lève-tard /lɛvtaʀ/ *nmf inv* late riser.

lève-tôt /lɛvto/ *nmf inv* early riser, early bird○.

levier /ləvje/ *nm* LIT, FIG lever.
■ **~ de changement de vitesse** AUT gear lever GB, gear stick US; (de bicyclette) gear switch; **~ de commande** AVIAT control stick; **être aux ~s de commande** FIG to be in the driving seat.

levraut /ləvʀo/ *nm* leveret.

lèvre /lɛvʀ/ *nf* **1** (sur le visage) lip; **avoir le sourire aux ~s** to be smiling; **du bout des ~s** [*rire, manger*] half-heartedly; [*parler, répondre*] grudgingly; **2** (de la vulve) labium; **petites/grandes ~s** labia minora/majora; **3** (de faille, plaie) lip, edge.
IDIOMES **être suspendu aux ~s de qn** to hang on sb's every word.

levrette /ləvʀɛt/ *nf* **1** (femelle du lévrier) greyhound bitch; **2** (lévrier d'Italie) Italian greyhound.

lévrier /levʀije/ *nm* greyhound.
■ **~ afghan** Afghan hound.

levure /ləvyʀ/ *nf* yeast; **~ chimique** baking powder.

lexème /lɛksɛm/ *nm* lexeme.

lexical, ~e, *mpl* **-aux** /lɛksikal, o/ *adj* lexical.

lexicaliser /lɛksikalize/ [1] **I** *vtr* **1** LING to lexicalize; **2** ORDINAT to sort.
II se lexicaliser *vpr* LING to become lexicalized.

lexicographie /lɛksikɔgʀafi/ *nf* lexicography.

lexique /lɛksik/ *nm* **1** (unilingue) glossary; (bilingue) vocabulary (book); **2** LING lexicon, lexis.

lézard /lezaʀ/ *nm* **1** (animal) lizard; **2** (peau) lizard-(skin).

lézarde /lezaʀd/ *nf* LIT, FIG crack.

lézarder /lezaʀde/ [1] **I** *vtr* to crack.
II○ *vi* **~ au soleil** to bask in the sun.
III se lézarder *vpr* LIT, FIG to crack.

liaison /ljɛzɔ̃/ *nf* **1** (ligne) link; **la ~ Calais–Douvres** the Calais–Dover line ou route; **2** RADIO, TÉLÉCOM **~ radio** radio contact; **~ satellite/téléphonique** satellite/telephone link; **être en ~ avec qn** to be in contact with sb; **3** (contact) **assurer la ~ entre différents services** to liaise between different services; **travailler/agir en ~ avec** to work/act in collaboration with; **4** (rapport logique) connection; **5** (relation amoureuse) affair; **6** LING liaison.

liane /ljan/ *nf* creeper, liana.

liant, ~e /ljɑ̃, ɑ̃t/ *adj* (sociable) sociable.

liasse /ljas/ *nf* (de billets) wad; (de lettres, papiers, documents) bundle.

Liban /libɑ̃/ ▶ **232** *nprm* Lebanon.

libanais, ~e /libanɛ, ɛz/ ▶ **394** *adj* Lebanese.

libation /libasjɔ̃/ *nf* libation (**à** to).

libellé /libelle/ *nm* (de jugement, lettre) wording.

libeller /libɛlle/ [1] *vtr* **1** ADMIN to draw up [*acte, contrat*]; **2** FML to word [*lettre, demande, article*]; **3** to make out [*chèque, mandat*].

libellule /libɛllyl/ *nf* dragonfly.

libérable /libeʀabl/ *adj* **1** JUR **détenu ~** (à l'issue de sa peine) prisoner due for release; (par remise de peine) prisoner eligible for release; **prévenu ~** defendant to be discharged; **2** MIL [*conscrit, contingent*] to be discharged soon (*après n*).

libéral, ~e, *mpl* **-aux** /libeʀal, o/ **I** *adj* **1** (tolérant) [*personne, morale*] liberal; **2** (favorable aux libertés) liberal; **3** POL Liberal; **4** ÉCON free-market (*épith*).

II *nm,f* **1** POL Liberal; **2** ÉCON free marketeer.

libéralisation /libeʀalizasjɔ̃/ *nf* ÉCON, POL liberalization; **~ des mœurs** relaxation of moral standards.

libéraliser /libeʀalize/ [1] **I** *vtr* to liberalize [*commerce, économie, transports, loi, pays*].
II se libéraliser *vpr* [*pays, mœurs*] to become more liberal.

libéralisme /libeʀalism/ *nm* liberalism.

libéralité /libeʀalite/ *nf* (générosité) liberality.

libérateur, -trice /libeʀatœʀ, tʀis/ **I** *adj* liberating.
II *nm,f* (de pays, ville, personne) liberator.

libération /libeʀasjɔ̃/ *nf* **1** (de prisonnier, d'otage) release; **2** (de pays, ville, peuple) liberation; **3** (affranchissement) liberation; **4** (soulagement) relief; **5** ÉCON (de prix) deregulation; (d'échanges) freeing; **6** FIN (d'actions, de capital) paying up; **7** MIL discharge; **8** PHYS (d'énergie) release.

Libération /libeʀasjɔ̃/ *nf* HIST (de 1944) **la ~** the Liberation; **à la ~** at the time of the Liberation.

libéré, ~e /libeʀe/ **I** *pp* ▶ **libérer**.
II *pp adj* **1** (émancipé) [*homme, femme*] liberated; **2** (délivré) [*pays, zone, ville*] free; **3** (disponible) [*poste, lieux*] vacant; **4** (affranchi) [*personne, entreprise*] free.

libérer /libeʀe/ [14] **I** *vtr* **1** (délivrer) to liberate [*pays, ville*] (**de** from); to free [*compagnon, otage*] (**de** from); **2** (relâcher) to release [*otage, détenu*] (**de** from); to free [*esclave, animal*] (**de** from); **3** (laisser partir) to allow [sb] to go [*employé, élève*]; **4** (affranchir) (de contraintes) to liberate [*personne, imagination*] (**de** from); (de fonctions) to relieve [*ministre, employé*] (**de** of); (de service militaire) to discharge [*soldat*] (**de** from); **~ un associé de ses obligations** to release a partner from his obligations; **~ qn de l'emprise de qn** to get sb away from sb's influence; **5** (ne pas retenir) to release [*émotion, énergie*]; to give free rein to [*instinct, imagination*]; **6** (soulager) to relieve [*esprit, personne*] (**de** of); **~ sa conscience** to unburden oneself; **7** (débarrasser) to vacate [*appartement, bureau*]; to clear [*passage, trottoir*] (**de** of); **~ la chambre avant midi** (dans un hôtel) to check out before noon; **8** (dégager) to free [*bras, main*] (**de** from); to release [*ressort, cran*]; **9** ÉCON (libéraliser) to liberalize [*économie, échanges*]; (débloquer) to deregulate [*prix*]; **~ les loyers/tarifs** to lift rent/tariff controls; **10** CHIMIE, PHYS (produire) to release [*gaz, énergie, électrons*].
II se libérer *vpr* **1** (se délivrer) [*personne*] to free oneself (**de** from); [*pays, entreprise*] to free itself (**de** from); **2** (se rendre disponible) **j'essaierai de me ~ mercredi** I'll try and be free on Wednesday.

libertaire /libɛʀtɛʀ/ *adj, nmf* libertarian.

liberté /libɛʀte/ *nf* **1** (condition, état) freedom ¢; **Statue de la ~** Statue of Liberty; **~, égalité, fraternité** Liberty, Equality, Fraternity; **espèce vivant en ~** species in the wild; **être en ~** to be free; **l'assassin est toujours en ~** the killer is still at large; **2** (latitude) freedom ¢; **en toute ~** with complete freedom; **avoir toute ~ pour faire** to be quite free to do; **n'avoir aucune ~ de manœuvre** to have no room for manoeuvre GB ou maneuver US; **3** (hardiesse) freedom; **~ de ton** outspokenness; **prendre la ~ de faire** to take the liberty of doing; **4** (droit) freedom; **~ de pensée/d'expression** freedom of thought/of expression; **~s individuelles** individual liberties.
■ **~ conditionnelle** JUR parole; **~ de la presse** POL freedom of the press; **~ provisoire** JUR provisional release (*pending trial*); **mettre en ~ provisoire** to release provisionally; **~ surveillée** JUR probation; **mise en ~ surveillée** release on probation.

libertin, ~e /libɛʀtɛ̃, in/ *adj, nm,f* libertine.

libidineux, -euse /libidinø, øz/ *adj* libidinous, lustful.

libraire /libʀɛʀ/ ▶ **374** *nmf* bookseller.

librairie /libʀɛʀi/ ▶ **374** *nf* **1** (magasin) bookshop GB, bookstore; **2** (activité) bookselling business.

librairie-papeterie, *pl* **librairies-papeteries**

/librɛripapɛtri/ ▶374| *nf* stationer's and bookshop GB ou bookstore.

libre /libr/ *adj* **1** GÉN [*personne, condition, pays*] free (**de faire** to do); **être ~ de ses décisions/choix** to be free to decide/choose; **~ à elle de partir** it's up to her whether she goes or not; **être ~ de ses actes** to do as one wishes; **2** (dénué) free (**de** from); **~ de préjugés** free from prejudice; **être ~ de soucis** to enjoy peace of mind; **3** (direct) [*personne*] free and easy; [*manière*] free; [*allure*] easy; [*opinion*] candid; [*morale*] easygoing; **4** (dégagé) [*main, pouce*] free; [*route, voie*] LIT, FIG clear; **avoir les mains ~s** LIT to have one's hands free; FIG to be a free agent; **5** (disponible) [*personne, chambre*] available; [*siège, place*] free; '**~ de suite**' (dans une annonce) 'available immediately'; **6** (non occupé) [*WC*] vacant; **la ligne n'est pas ~** (au téléphone) the number is engaged GB ou busy US.
■ **~ arbitre** PHILOS free will; **~ concurrence** ÉCON free competition; **~ entreprise** ÉCON free enterprise.
IDIOMES **être ~ comme l'air** to be as free as a bird.

libre-échange /librɛʃɑ̃ʒ/ *nm* free trade.

librement /librəmɑ̃/ *adv* freely.

libre-penseur, *pl* **libres-penseurs** /librəpɑ̃sœr/ *nm* freethinker.

libre-service, *pl* **libres-services** /librəsɛrvis/ **I** *adj inv* self-service (*épith*).
II *nm* **1** (système) **le ~** self-service; **2** (magasin) self-service shop GB ou store US; (restaurant) self-service restaurant.
■ **~ bancaire** automatic teller.

lice /lis/ *nf* lists (*pl*); **entrer en ~** to enter the lists.

licence /lisɑ̃s/ *nf* **1** UNIV (bachelor's) degree; **~ en droit** law degree; **préparer une ~ d'anglais** to do a degree in English; **être en ~ d'anglais** to be in the final year of an English degree; **2** COMM, JUR licence GB; **~ de fabrication** manufacturing licence GB; **d'importation** import licence GB; **produit sous ~** licensed product; **3** SPORT **avoir sa ~ de tennis** to be a member of the national tennis federation; **4** (liberté) licence GB; **avoir toute ~ de faire** to have a free hand to do.

licencié, **~e** /lisɑ̃sje/ **I** *pp* ▶ **licencier**.
II *pp adj* [*étudiant*] graduate (*épith*).
III *nm,f* **1** UNIV graduate GB, college graduate US; **2** SPORT member (*of a sports federation*); **3** ÉCON ~ (**économique**) person made redundant GB, laid-off worker.

licenciement /lisɑ̃simɑ̃/ *nm* (pour faute) dismissal; **~ (économique)** redundancy GB, lay-off; **~ collectif** mass redundancy, mass lay-offs (*pl*).
■ **~ sec** compulsory redundancy (*without compensation*).

licencier /lisɑ̃sje/ [2] *vtr* (pour raisons économiques) to make [sb] redundant GB, to lay [sb] off; (pour faute) to dismiss GB, to let [sb] go.

licencieux, **-ieuse** /lisɑ̃sjø, øz/ *adj* licentious.

lichen /likɛn/ *nm* lichen.

licite /lisit/ *adj* lawful.

licorne /likɔrn/ *nf* MYTHOL unicorn.

lie /li/ *nf* LIT, FIG dregs (*pl*); **~ de vin** wine dregs.

lie-de-vin /lidvɛ̃/ ▶141| *adj inv* wine, wine-coloured GB.

liège /ljɛʒ/ *nm* cork; **bouchon en ~** cork.

liégeois, **~e** /ljeʒwa, az/ ▶628| *adj* of Liège; **café ~** iced coffee topped with whipped cream.

lien /ljɛ̃/ *nm* **1** (attache) strap; (plus fin) string; FIG bond; **se libérer de ses ~s** LIT to free oneself of one's bonds; FIG to shake off one's ties; **2** (rapport) connection, link; **3** (relation) GÉN link, tie; (d'ordre affectif) tie, bond; **ses ~s avec la pègre** his/her connections ou links with the underworld; **~ d'amitié** ties of friendship; **~s de parenté** family ties; **il n'a aucun ~ de parenté avec elle** he's not related to her at all; **être uni par les ~s du mariage** to be joined ou united in marriage.

lier /lje/ [1] **I** *vtr* **1** (attacher) to tie [sb/sth] up [*per-*

sonne, fleurs, paille*]; **il avait les mains liées** LIT, FIG his hands were tied; **être pieds et poings liés** LIT to be bound hand and foot; FIG to have one's hands tied; **2** (unir) to bind; **ils sont très liés** they are very close; **3** (établir un rapport) to link [*idées, événements*] (**à** to); **4** (commencer) **~ amitié avec qn** to strike up a friendship with sb; **5** CULIN to thicken [*sauce*]; **6** MUS to slur [*notes*].
II se lier *vpr* to make friends (**avec qn** with sb).

lierre /ljɛr/ *nm* ivy.

liesse /ljɛs/ *nf* jubilation; **en ~** jubilant.

lieu /ljø/ **I** *nm* **1** (*pl* **~s**) (poisson) **~ (noir)** coley, black pollock; **2** (*pl* **~x**) (endroit) place; **complément de ~** adverbial of place; **en ~ sûr** in a safe place; **~ de rendez-vous** or **de rencontre** meeting place; **~ d'habitation/de naissance** place of residence/of birth; **~ de vente** retail outlet, point of sale; **sur le ~ de travail** in the workplace; **~ de passage** thoroughfare; **sur le ~ du drame** at the scene of the tragedy; **en tous ~x** everywhere; **en ~ et place de qn** [*signer, agir*] on behalf of sb; **en premier ~** in the first place, firstly; **en second ~** secondly; **en dernier ~** lastly; **avoir ~** to take place; **tenir ~ de** to serve as [*réfectoire, chambre*]; **il y a ~ de s'inquiéter** there is cause for anxiety; **cela n'a pas ~ d'être** it shouldn't be so; **donner ~ à** to cause ou give rise to [*scandale*]; ▶ **haut**.
II au lieu de *loc prép* instead of.
III lieux *nmpl* **1** (endroit) parts; **repérer les ~x** to have a scout around; **sur les ~x** [*être*] at the scene; [*arriver*] on the scene; **2** (habitation) premises.
■ **~ commun** platitude; **~ jaune** yellow pollock; **~ public** public place; **~ saint** holy place.

lieue /ljø/ ▶348| *nf* HIST league; **~ marine** league.
IDIOMES **j'étais à cent** or **mille ~s d'imaginer** I never for a moment imagined.

lieutenant /ljøtnɑ̃/ ▶284| *nm* **1** MIL (dans l'armée de terre) ≈ lieutenant GB, ≈ first lieutenant US; (dans l'armée de l'air) ≈ flying officer GB, ≈ first lieutenant US; **2** NAUT first officer.

lieutenant-colonel, *pl* **lieutenants-colonels** /ljøtnɑ̃kɔlɔnɛl/ ▶284| *nm* (dans l'armée de terre) ≈ lieutenant-colonel; (dans l'armée de l'air) ≈ wing commander GB, ≈ lieutenant colonel US.

lièvre /ljɛvr/ *nm* **1** ZOOL hare; **2** SPORT pacemaker.
IDIOMES **courir plusieurs ~s à la fois** to have several irons in the fire.

lifter /lifte/ [1] *vtr* to put topspin on [*balle*].

lifting /liftiŋ/ *nm* MÉD, FIG face-lift.

ligament /ligamɑ̃/ *nm* ligament.

ligature /ligatyr/ *nf* MÉD (opération) tying; (résultat) ligature.

ligaturer /ligatyre/ [1] *vtr* MÉD to tie; **se faire ~ les trompes** to have one's tubes tied.

lignage /liɲaʒ/ *nm* **1** (de famille) lineage; **2** (en imprimerie) linage.

ligne /liɲ/ *nf* **1** (trait) line; **~ blanche/continue/discontinue** AUT white/solid/broken line; **~ de départ/d'arrivée** SPORT starting/finishing line; **lire les ~s de la main de qn** to read sb's palm; **~ droite** GÉN straight line; (de route) straight piece of road; **la dernière ~ droite avant l'arrivée** the home straight; **2** (d'écriture) line; **je vous écris ces quelques ~s pour vous dire...** this is just a quick note to tell you...; **à la ~!** (dans une dictée) new paragraph!; **3** (de bus, bateau, d'avion) (service) service; (parcours) route; (de métro, train) line; **la ~ Paris-Rome** AVIAT the Paris to Rome route; RAIL the Paris to Rome line; **~ de chemin de fer** railway line; **~s intérieures** AVIAT domestic flights; **4** ÉLECTROTECH (câble) cable; **5** TÉLÉCOM line; **la ~ est mauvaise** it's a bad line; **il y a quelqu'un d'autre sur la ~** we've got a crossed line; **avoir** or **obtenir la ~** to get through; **6** (silhouette) figure; **avoir/garder la ~** to be/to stay slim; **retrouver sa ~** to get back one's figure; **7** (contour) (de corps) contours (*pl*); (de visage) shape; (de collines) outline; **la ~ aérodynamique d'une voiture** the aerodynamic lines (*pl*) of a car; **8** (allure générale) (de mobilier, style, vêtement) look; **9** COMM (gamme) line; **10** (idée, point) outline; **raconter un événement dans ses grandes ~s** to give an outline of events; **11** (orientation) (de parti politique) line; **12** (à la pêche) fishing line; **pêche à la ~** angling; **13** (alignement) line; (rangée) row; **les ~s ennemies** MIL the enemy lines; **ils sont en ~ pour le départ** they are lined up for the start; **14** ORDINAT **en ~** on line; **15** (en généalogie) line; **16** TV (définition) line.

■ **~ de but** SPORT goal line; **~ de conduite** (politique) policy; (position) line; (attitude) attitude; (stratégie) strategy; **~ de démarcation** boundary; MIL demarcation line; **~ de mire** line of sight; **~ de tir** line of fire; **~ de touche** SPORT GÉN touchline; (au basket) boundary line.

IDIOMES **être en première ~** LIT, MIL to be in the front line; FIG to be in the firing line; **entrer en ~ de compte** to be taken into account ou consideration.

lignée /liɲe/ nf **1** (descendants) descendants (pl); (famille) line of descent; **de haute ~** of noble descent; **2** (filiation spirituelle) tradition.

lignite /liɲit/ nm brown coal, lignite SPÉC.

ligoter /ligɔte/ [1] vtr to truss [sb] up [personne].

ligue /lig/ nf league.

liguer /lige/ [1] I vtr **~ des gens/nations contre** to unite people/countries against.
II **se liguer** vpr [personnes] to join forces; **être ligué avec/contre** to be in league with/against.

lilas /lila/ ▶ **141** adj inv, nm inv lilac.

lilliputien, -ienne /lilipysjɛ̃, ɛn/ adj, nm,f Lilliputian.

limace /limas/ nf ZOOL slug.
IDIOMES **se traîner comme une ~** to crawl along at a snail's pace.

limaçon /limasɔ̃/ nm **1** ZOOL snail; **2** ANAT cochlea.

limaille /limaj/ nf filings (pl).

limande /limɑ̃d/ nf dab; **filet de ~** fillet of dab.

limande-sole, pl **limandes-soles** /limɑ̃dsɔl/ nf lemon sole.

lime /lim/ nf **1** TECH file; **à la ~** with a file; **~ à ongles** nail file; **2** BOT lime; **3** ZOOL lima.

limer /lime/ [1] I vtr **1** (façonner) to file [ongle, métal]; to file down [clé, aspérité]; **2** (couper) to file through [barreau].
II **se limer** vpr **se ~ les ongles** to file one's nails.

limier /limje/ nm **1** (chien) bloodhound; **2**° (détective, policier) sleuth; **un fin ~** a super-sleuth.

limitatif, -ive /limitatif, iv/ adj restrictive, restrictive.

limitation /limitasjɔ̃/ nf (de pouvoir, liberté) limitation, restriction; (de prix, taux d'intérêt) control ⊄.
■ **~ de vitesse** AUT speed limit.

limite /limit/ [1] I nf **1** (ligne de séparation) border; **2** (partie extrême) (de domaine, terrain) boundary; (de forêt, village) edge; **3** (borne) limit; **aller jusqu'à la ~ de ses forces** to push oneself to the limit; **ma patience a des ~s** there are limits to my patience; **connaître ses ~s** to know one's (own) limitations; **franchir les ~s de la décence** to go beyond the bounds of decency; **vraiment, il dépasse les ~s!** he's really going too far!; **à la ~, je préférerais qu'il refuse** I'd almost prefer it if he refused; **4** (bord) **à la ~ de** on the verge of; **plaisanterie à la ~ du mauvais goût** joke bordering on bad taste; **un spectacle à la ~ du supportable** an almost unbearable sight; **5** (cadre) **dans une certaine ~** up to a point, to a certain extent; **dans la ~ de, dans les ~s de** within the limits of; **nous vous aiderons dans la ~ de nos moyens** we will help you as much as we can; **accepter des spectateurs dans la ~ des places disponibles** to admit spectators subject to the availability of seats; **dans la ~ du possible** as far as possible.
II (-)**limite** (in compounds) **âge** (-)**~** maximum age; **date**(-)**~** deadline; **date**(-)**~ de vente** sell-by date.
■ **~ d'âge** age limit.

limité, ~e /limite/ I pp ▶ **limiter.**

II pp adj (restreint) [possibilité, conversation, ressources, intérêt, choix] limited; **devoir en temps ~** question to be answered within a set time limit.

limiter /limite/ [1] I vtr **1** (restreindre) to limit, to restrict [pouvoir, dépenses, durée, nombre] (à to); **la vitesse est limitée à 90 km/h** the speed limit is 90 kph; **~ les dégâts** to minimize the damage; **2** (border) **la clôture qui limite notre propriété** the enclosure which marks the boundaries of our property.
II **se limiter** vpr **1** (se restreindre) **se ~ à deux verres de bière par jour** to limit oneself to two glasses of beer a day; **2** (se résumer) **se ~ à** to be limited to; **la vie ne se limite pas au travail** there's more to life than work.

limitrophe /limitʀɔf/ adj [pays, État, département, province] adjacent; [ville] border (épith).

limoger /limɔʒe/ [13] vtr (destituer) to dismiss; (déplacer) to transfer.

limon /limɔ̃/ nm **1** (dépôt) silt; **2** (de voiture à cheval) shaft.

limonade /limɔnad/ nf lemonade GB, lemon soda US.

limoneux, -euse /limɔnø, øz/ adj [terre] silty; [eau] silt-laden.

limousine /limuzin/ nf AUT limousine.

limpide /lɛ̃pid/ adj **1** LIT clear, limpid; **2** FIG [explication, style] clear, lucid.

limpidité /lɛ̃pidite/ nf **1** LIT clarity; **2** FIG clarity, lucidity.

lin /lɛ̃/ nm **1** (fibre, plante) flax; **2** (tissu) linen.

linceul /lɛ̃sœl/ nm LIT, FIG shroud.

linéaire /lineɛʀ/ adj linear.

linge /lɛ̃ʒ/ nm **1** (domestique) linen; **~ sale** dirty linen; **~ de couleur** coloureds GB (pl); **2** (lessive) washing; **corde** or **fil à ~** clothes line; **3** (sous-vêtements) underwear; **4** (torchon) cloth.
■ **~ de corps** underwear; **~ de maison** household linen; **~ de toilette** bathroom linen.
IDIOMES **être blanc comme un ~** to be as white as a sheet; **déballer son ~ sale**° to reveal one's guilty secret.

lingère /lɛ̃ʒɛʀ/ nf (personne) laundry woman.

lingerie /lɛ̃ʒʀi/ nf **1** (local) linen room; **2** (linge de corps) **~ fine** fine lingerie; **3** (industrie) lingerie industry.

lingot /lɛ̃go/ nm ingot; **~ de métal** metal ingot.
■ **~ d'or** gold ingot (weighing 1 kg).

linguiste /lɛ̃gɥist/ ▶ **374** nmf linguist.

linguistique /lɛ̃gɥistik/ I adj linguistic; **communauté ~** speech community.
II nf linguistics (+ v sg).

linotte /linɔt/ nf linnet.

linteau, pl **~x** /lɛ̃to/ nm lintel.

lion /ljɔ̃/ nm lion; **la part du ~** the lion's share.
IDIOMES **se battre** ou **se défendre comme un ~** to fight like a tiger; **avoir mangé du ~**° to be full of beans° GB, to be full of pep° US.

Lion /ljɔ̃/ ▶ **641** nprm Leo.

lionceau, pl **~x** /ljɔ̃so/ nm lion cub.

lionne /ljɔn/ nf lioness.

lipide /lipid/ nm lipid.

lippu, ~e /lipy/ adj [bouche, personne] full-lipped; [lèvre] full.

liquéfier /likefje/ [2] I vtr to liquefy.
II **se liquéfier** vpr **1** LIT to liquefy; **2**° (avoir peur) to turn to jelly.

liquette° /likɛt/ nf shirt.

liquidation /likidasjɔ̃/ nf **1** COMM, JUR (d'entreprise, de bien) liquidation; (de dettes, comptes, succession) settlement, selling off; **~ judiciaire** or **forcée** compulsory liquidation; **société en ~** company in liquidation; **2** COMM (vente) clearance.

liquide /likid/ I adj liquid; **trop ~** [colle, sauce] too runny; **argent ~** cash; **miel ~** clear honey.
II nm **1** (substance) liquid; **2** (argent) cash.
■ **~ correcteur** correction fluid, white-out (fluid)

us; **~ de frein** brake fluid; **~ de refroidisse-ment** coolant.

liquider /likide/ [1] *vtr* **1** JUR to settle [*comptes*]; to liquidate [*société*, *commerce*]; to realize [*biens*]; to liquidate, to settle [*dettes*]; **2** COMM (vendre) to clear [*marchandises, stock*]; **3**° (régler) to settle [*problèmes, querelles*]; **4**° (se débarrasser de) to liquidate° [*adversaire, témoin*]; **5**° (consommer complètement) to demolish [*plat*]; to empty [*verre*]; to clear [*assiette*].

liquidité /likidite/ *nf* **1** (caractère liquide) liquidity; **2** FIN liquidity; **des ~s** liquid assets.

lire¹ /lir/ [66] *vtr* **1** (déchiffrer) to read; **~ qch à qn** to read sth to sb; **apprendre à ~** to learn to read; **elle sait ~** she can read; **~ à voix haute** to read aloud; **~ Platon dans le texte** to read Plato in the original; **'lu et approuvé'** 'read and approved'; **~ qch en diagonale** to skim through sth, to scan sth; **~ sur les lèvres de qn** to lip-read what sb is saying; **dans l'espoir de vous ~ bientôt** hoping to hear from you soon; **2** MÉD, MUS to read [*radiographie, musique*]; **3** AUDIO, ORDINAT to read; **4** (discerner) to read [*avenir*]; **~ les lignes de la main** to read palms; **~ dans les pensées de qn** to read sb's mind.

IDIOMES **~ entre les lignes** to read between the lines.

lire² /lir/ ▶ 33 *nf* lira.

lirette /liʀɛt/ *nf* **tapis en ~** rag rug.

lis /lis/ *nm inv* lily.

liséré /lizʀe/ *nm*, **liséré** /lizere/ *nm* (raie) edging; (ruban) piping.

liseron /lizʀɔ̃/ *nm* bindweed, convolvulus.

liseuse /lizøz/ *nf* **1** (veste) bed jacket; **2** (couvrant un livre) book cover; **3** (lampe) small reading lamp.

lisible /lizibl/ *adj* **1** [*écriture, manuscrit*] legible; **2** [*auteur, roman*] readable.

lisière /lizjɛʀ/ *nf* **1** (de bois, champ) edge; (de village) outskirts; FIG (bord) verge; **2** (de tissu) selvage.

lisse /lis/ *adj* [*surface, cheveux*] smooth; [*pneu*] worn.

lisser /lise/ [1] *vtr* to smooth [*cheveux*]; to stroke [*barbe, moustache*]; to smooth (out) [*vêtement, nappe*]; to smooth [*cuir*]; **l'oiseau lisse ses plumes** the bird is preening its feathers ou itself.

liste /list/ *nf* GÉN list (**de** of); POL list (of candidates) GB, ticket US; **dresser** or **établir une ~** to draw up a list; **faire la ~ de** to list, to make a list of.
■ **~ d'attente** waiting list; **~ de contrôle** checklist; **~ électorale** electoral roll.
IDIOMES **être sur (la) ~ rouge** to be ex-directory GB, to have an unlisted number US.

listel /listɛl/ *nm* **1** ARCHIT listel, fillet; **2** (de pièce, médaille) rim; **3** (de livre) fillet.

lister /liste/ [1] *vtr* to list.

lit /li/ *nm* **1** (meuble) bed; **~ à une place** or **d'une personne** single bed; **~ à deux places** or **de deux personnes** double bed; **aller** or **se mettre au ~** to go to bed; **garder le ~** to stay in bed; **mettre qn au ~** to put sb to bed; **tirer qn du ~** LIT to drag sb out of bed; **au ~!** (à un enfant) bedtime!; **2** (structure) bed; **~ métallique** iron bedstead; **3** (literie) bed; **le ~ n'était pas défait** the bed had not been slept in; **4** (unité d'accueil) bed; **un hôpital de 300 ~s** a 300-bed hospital; **5** JUR (mariage) marriage; **6** CULIN (couche) bed; **7** GÉOG (de cours d'eau) bed; **la rivière est sortie de son ~** the river has overflowed its banks.
■ **~ à baldaquin** four-poster bed; **~ de camp** camp bed GB, cot US; **~ d'enfant** cot GB, crib US; **~ de mort** death-bed; **~ en portefeuille** apple-pie bed; **~s superposés** bunk bed (*sg*).
IDIOMES **comme on fait son ~ on se couche** PROV as you make your bed so you must lie in it PROV.

litanie /litani/ *nf* LIT, FIG litany.

liteau, *pl* **~x** /lito/ *nm* **1** (en bois) (de toiture) batten; (d'étagère) bracket; **2** (de nappe) coloured^GB stripe.

literie /litʀi/ *nf* bedding.

lithographe /litɔgʀaf/ ▶ 374 *nmf* lithographer.

lithographie /litɔgʀafi/ *nf* **1** (technique) lithography; **2** (estampe) lithograph.

litière /litjɛʀ/ *nf* (de vaches) litter; (de chevaux) bedding; (pour chats) cat litter, kitty litter US.

litige /litiʒ/ *nm* dispute; **point de ~** GÉN bone of contention; JUR point at issue; **être en ~** JUR to be involved in litigation; **les parties en ~** the litigants.

litigieux, -ieuse /litiʒjø, øz/ *adj* [*affaire, point, hypothèse, argument*] contentious; [*personne*] litigious.

litote /litɔt/ *nf* GÉN, HUM understatement; (en rhétorique) litotes (+ *v sg*).

litre /litʀ/ ▶ 86 *nm* (mesure) litre^GB; (bouteille) litre^GB bottle; **être vendu au ~** to be sold by the litre^GB.

littéraire /literɛʀ/ **I** *adj* [*œuvre, critique, prix*] literary; [*études*] arts (*épith*), liberal arts (*épith*) US.
II *nm,f* (par penchant) literary person; (étudiant) arts ou liberal arts US student.

littéral, ~e, *mpl* **-aux** /literal, o/ *adj* GÉN literal.

littéralement /literalmɑ̃/ *adv* [*signifier, traduire*] literally; [*citer*] verbatim.

littérature /literatyr/ *nf* **1** GÉN literature; **2** (métier d'écrivain) **se lancer dans la ~** to become a writer; **3** (documentation) literature.

littoral, ~e, *mpl* **-aux** /litɔral/ **I** *adj* [*navigation, eaux*] coastal (*épith*); [*faune, flore*] inshore (*épith*).
II *nm* coast.

liturgie /lityʀʒi/ *nf* liturgy.

livide /livid/ *adj* [*personne, visage*] deathly pale; [*pâleur*] ghastly; LITER [*aube, teint, lueur*] livid.

living /liviŋ/ *nm* (pièce) living-room.

Livourne /livurn/ *npr* Leghorn, Livorno.

livraison /livʀɛzɔ̃/ *nf* **1** (de marchandise) delivery; **'~s à domicile'** 'we deliver'; **il est venu prendre ~ de la commande** he came to pick up the order; **2** (marchandises) delivery.

livre¹ /livʀ/ *nm* **1** (volume publié) book; **~ pour enfants** children's book; **~ de chevet** LIT bedside reading; FIG bible; **2** (registre) book; (de comptabilité) (account) book, ledger; **3** (tome) book; **4** (industrie) **le ~, l'industrie du ~** the book trade.
■ **~ blanc** blue book; **~ de bord** logbook; **~ de caisse** cash book; **~ de l'élève** pupil's book; **~ de lecture** reading book, reader; **~ du maître** teacher's book; **~ de messe** missal, mass book; **~ d'or** visitors' book; **~ de poche**® paperback; **~ scolaire** schoolbook, textbook.

livre² /livʀ/ *nf* **1** ▶ 33 (monnaie) pound; **~ sterling** pound sterling; **~ irlandaise** Irish pound, punt; **2** ▶ 455 (unité de masse) (demi-kilo) half a kilo; (anglo-saxonne) pound.

livrée /livʀe/ *nf* (de domestique) livery; **en ~** in livery.

livrer /livʀe/ [1] **I** *vtr* **1** COMM to deliver [*marchandises*] (**to** à); **se faire ~ qch** to have sth delivered; **~ qn** to deliver sb's order; **2** (remettre) to hand [sb] over [*criminel, prisonnier*] (à to); (en trahissant) to betray [*complice, secret*] (**to** à); to pass [sth] on [*document, renseignement*] (à to); **3** (abandonner) **ils ont livré le meurtrier à la colère de la foule** they turned the murderer over to the mob; **être livré à soi-même** to be left to one's own devices; **4** (confier) **il nous livre un peu de lui-même** he reveals something of himself.
II se livrer *vpr* **1** (s'adonner) **se ~ à un trafic de drogue** to engage in drug trafficking; **2** (se rendre) **se ~ à** [*terroristes, bandits*] to give oneself up to, to surrender to; **3** (se confier) **se ~ à un ami** to confide in a friend; **il ne se livre pas facilement** he doesn't open up easily.
IDIOMES **~ bataille (à qn)** to fight (sb).

livret /livʀɛ/ *nm* **1** (livre) booklet; **2** (d'opéra) libretto.
■ **~ de caisse d'épargne** ~ savings book GB, bankbook (*for a savings account*) US; **~ de famille** family record book (*of births, marriages and deaths*); **~ scolaire** school report book.

livreur, -euse ▶ 374 /livʀœʀ, øz/ *nm,f* delivery man/woman.

lobe /lɔb/ *nm* ANAT, BOT, GÉOG, ZOOL lobe.

lobé, **~e** /lɔbe/ *adj* **1** BOT lobed, sinuate; **2** ARCHIT foiled, foliated.

lober /lɔbe/ [1] *vtr, vi* to lob.

local, **~e**, *pl* **-aux** /lɔkal, o/ **I** *adj* GÉN local; [*journal, industrie, autorités*] local; [*douleur, averses*] localized; **contraceptif ~** *barrier method of contraception including spermicidal creams etc*; **22 heures heure ~e** 22.00 local time.

II *nm* **1** (pièce quelconque) place; **2** (pièce à usage déterminé) **~ (à usage) commercial** commercial premises (*pl*); **locaux habitables** residential units; **dans les locaux du lycée** on school premises; **dans les locaux de la gendarmerie** at the police station; **les locaux du journal** the newspaper offices.

localement /lɔkalmɑ̃/ *adv* GÉN on a local level; **appliquer la crème ~** apply the cream locally.

localisation /lɔkalizasjɔ̃/ *nf* **1** (emplacement) location; **2** (limitation) **la ~ d'un incendie** localizing a fire.

localiser /lɔkalize/ [1] *vtr* **1** (repérer) to locate [*personne, bruit, fuite, panne*]; **2** (circonscrire) to localize [*incendie, conflit*].

localité /lɔkalite/ *nf* BIOL, GÉOG locality.

locataire /lɔkatɛʀ/ *nmf* tenant; **être ~** to be renting.

locatif, -ive /lɔkatif, iv/ **I** *adj* [*revenu, secteur, valeur*] rental.

II *nm* LING locative; **au ~** in the locative.

location /lɔkasjɔ̃/ *nf* **1** (d'immobilier) (par le propriétaire) renting out; (par le locataire) renting; **agence de ~** rental agency; **donner** or **mettre en ~** to rent out, to let GB; **maison en ~** rented house; **2** (logement) rented accommodation ¢; **3** (loyer) rent; **4** (de matériel) hire ¢; **~ de voitures** car hire, car rental; **véhicule de ~** hire vehicle; **contrat de ~** rental agreement; **~ de téléviseurs/cassettes vidéos** TV/video rental; **coût de ~** cost of hiring; **5** (de spectacle) reservation, booking GB; **faire les ~s** to reserve, to book GB the seats; **guichet de ~** box office.

location-vente, *pl* **locations-ventes** /lɔkasjɔ̃vɑ̃t/ *nf* (d'immobilier) 100% mortgage scheme.

locomoteur, -trice /lɔkɔmɔtœʀ, tʀis/ *adj* locomotive.

locomotion /lɔkɔmɔsjɔ̃/ *nf* locomotion.

locomotive /lɔkɔmɔtiv/ *nf* **1** RAIL engine, locomotive; **~ à vapeur** steam engine; **2** FIG (meneur) driving force; (personne, région dynamique) powerhouse.

IDIOMES **souffler comme une ~**° to puff and pant.

locuteur, -trice /lɔkytœʀ, tʀis/ *nm,f* speaker.

locution /lɔkysjɔ̃/ *nf* (grammaticale) phrase; (expression) idiom; **~ toute faite** set phrase.

loden /lɔdɛn/ *nm* **1** (tissu) loden; **2** (manteau) loden coat.

logarithme /lɔgaʀitm/ *nm* logarithm, log.

loge /lɔʒ/ *nf* **1** (de gardien) lodge; **2** THÉÂT (d'artiste) dressing room; (de spectateur) box; **3** (de franc-maçons) Lodge; **4** ARCHIT loggia.

IDIOMES **être aux premières ~s**° to be in an ideal position.

logé, **~e** /lɔʒe/ **I** *pp* ▶ **loger**.

II *pp adj* housed; **être ~, nourri, blanchi** to have bed, board and one's laundry done.

logement /lɔʒmɑ̃/ *nm* **1** (local d'habitation) accommodation ¢; **l'achat d'un ~** (appartement) buying a flat GB ou an apartment US; (maison) buying a house; **2** (fait de loger) housing; **la crise du ~** the housing crisis.

■ **~ social** local authority housing GB, public housing US.

loger /lɔʒe/ [13] **I** *vtr* **1** (fournir un logement permanent à) [*mairie, service social*] to house [*famille, étudiant, réfugié*]; **2** (héberger temporairement) [*personne*] to put [sb] up [*ami*]; [*mairie, école*] to provide accommodation for [*sinistrés, stagiaires*]; **3** (contenir) [*hôtel, pensionnat*] to have accommodation for; **4** (placer) **~ qch dans un placard** to put sth in a cupboard [*objet, livres*]; **je n'ai pas pu ~ tous mes meubles dans le salon** I couldn't fit all my furniture in the living room; **5** (faire

pénétrer) **~ une balle dans la tête de qn** to shoot sb in the head.

II *vi* **1** (habiter) to live; **~ chez un particulier** to have a room in a private house; **2** (résider temporairement) to stay; **~ à l'hôtel** to stay at a hotel; **~ chez qn** to stay with sb.

III se loger *vpr* **1** (avoir un lieu d'habitation) **avec cette somme, je dois me nourrir et me ~** with that I have to pay for food and accommodation ou housing; **2** (se placer) **se ~ dans qch** (en se fixant) to get stuck in sth; [*poussière, saletés*] to collect in sth; **la balle est venue se ~ dans le genou** the bullet lodged in his/her knee.

logeur, -euse /lɔʒœʀ, øz/ *nm,f* lodger.

logiciel, -ielle /lɔʒisjɛl/ **I** *adj* software (*épith*).

II *nm* **1** (ensemble de programmes) software ¢; **~ de base** system(s) software; **~ contributif** shareware; **~ public** freeware; **2** (programme) program.

logicien, -ienne /lɔʒisjɛ̃, ɛn/ *nm,f* logician.

logique /lɔʒik/ **I** *adj* **1** GÉN logical; **il n'est pas ~ avec lui-même** he is not consistent; **2**° (compréhensible) reasonable.

II *nf* **1** GÉN logic (de of); **manquer de ~** to be illogical; **avec ~** in a logical way; **c'est dans la ~ des choses** it's in the nature of things; **~ déductive** deductive reasoning; **en toute ~** logically; **2** MATH, ORDINAT, PHILOS logic.

logiquement /lɔʒikmɑ̃/ *adv* logically.

logis /lɔʒi/ *nm inv* LITER home, dwelling.

logistique /lɔʒistik/ **I** *adj* logistical.

II *nf* logistics (+ *v sg*) (de of).

logo /lɔgo/ *nm*, **logotype** /lɔgotip/ *nm* logo.

loi /lwa/ *nf* **1** (règle) law (**sur** on; **contre** against); **voter/abroger une ~** to pass/to repeal a law; **être au-dessus des ~s** to be above the law; **2** (corps de textes) **la ~** the law; **enfreindre la ~** to break the law; **avoir la ~ pour soi** to have the law on one's side; **subir la ~ de qn** to be ruled by sb; **d'après la ~ française** under French law; **mettre qn/qch hors la ~** to outlaw sb/sth; **tomber sous le coup de la ~** to be ou constitute an offence^{GB}; **faire la ~** FIG to lay down the law; **3** (principe) law; **c'est la ~ des séries** things always happen in a row; **4** (convention) rule; **~s de l'hospitalité** the rules of hospitality; **~ du silence** (règle de conduite) code of silence; (pour protéger) conspiracy of silence.

■ **~ d'amnistie** *act granting amnesty to some offenders*; **~ communautaire** community law; **~ divine** divine law; **~ de la jungle** law of the jungle; **~ d'orientation** framework law; **~s d'exception** emergency legislation.

loin /lwɛ̃/ **I** *adv* **1** (dans l'espace) a long way, far (away); **c'est ~** it's a long way; **c'est trop ~** it's too far; **elle ne peut pas être bien ~** she can't be too far away ou off; **est-ce ~?** is it far (away)?; **il habite plus ~** he lives further ou farther away; **aussi ou du plus ~ que l'on regarde** however far you look; **aussi ~ que l'on pouvait voir** as far as the eye could see; **voir plus ~** (dans un texte) see below; **plus ~ dans le roman** at a later point in the novel; ▶ **monture**; **2** (dans le temps) **tout cela est bien ~** that was all a long time ago; **aussi ~ que je me souvienne** as far back ou as long as I can remember; **les vacances sont déjà ~** it's a long time since the holidays GB ou the vacation US now; **c'est encore ~** (dans l'avenir) it's still a long way off (in the future); **le temps n'est pas si ~ où...** it's not so long since...; **3** FIG **il y a ~ d'une idée à sa réalisation** there's a wide gap between an idea and its fulfilment^{GB}; **de là à dire qu'il est incompétent, il n'y a pas ~** that comes close to saying he's incompetent; **tu sembles si ~** (distant) you seem so distant; (absorbé) you seem miles away; **il n'est pas bête, ~ s'en faut!** he's not stupid, far from it!; **ce film ne va très pas ~** this film GB ou movie US is a bit shallow; **la décentralisation n'est pas allée très ~** decentralization didn't get very far; **votre fille est brillante, elle ira ~** your daughter is brilliant, she'll go far.

Les mesures de longueur (1)

Les unités

Le système métrique est de plus en plus utilisé en Grande-Bretagne et aux États-Unis pour les mesures de longueur. Mais les anciennes mesures ont encore cours, et sont quelquefois préférées, notamment pour les distances, exprimées en miles, et non en kilomètres. Les commerçants utilisent en général les deux systèmes.

Équivalences

1 inch	=	2,54 cm			
1 foot	=	12 inches	=	30,48 cm	
1 yard	=	3 feet	=	91,44 cm	
1 furlong	=	220 yards	=	201,17 m	
1 mile	=	1760 yards	=	1,61 km	

Pour la prononciation des nombres, voir **les nombres** ▶ 399 |.

dire			dire
one millimetre	1 mm	0.04 in*	*inches*
one centimetre	1 cm	0.39 in	
one metre	1 m	39.37 ins	
		3.28 ft†	*feet*
		1.09 yds	*yards*
one kilometre‡	1 km	1094 yds	
		0.62 ml	*miles*

* *Le symbole de inch est ": 4 inches = 4".*
† *Le symbole de foot et feet est ': 5 feet 4 inches = 5′ 4".*
‡ *Deux prononciations possibles:* /kɪˈlɒmɪtər/ *ou* /ˈkɪləmiːtər/

Pour l'écriture, noter:

– on écrit -metre en anglais britannique, mais -meter en anglais américain.
– pour le système métrique, les abréviations sont les mêmes en anglais qu'en français.
– l'anglais utilise un point là où le français a une virgule.

il y a 100 centimètres
dans un mètre = there are 100 centimetres in one metre
il y a douze pouces
dans un pied = there are twelve inches in one foot
il y a trois pieds
dans un yard = there are three feet in one yard

La distance

quelle distance y a-t-il entre A et B?
= what's the distance from A to B?
ou how far is it from A to B?
à quelle distance de l'église
se trouve l'école? = how far is the school from
the church?
il y a 2 km = it is 2 kilometres
il y a environ 2 km = it is about 2 kilometres
la distance est de 2 km = the distance is 2 kilometres
il y a 2 km entre A et B = it is 2 kilometres from A to B
A est à 2 km de B = A is 2 kilometres from B

(Noter l'absence d'équivalent anglais de la préposition française à avant le chiffre dans le dernier exemple.)

à peu près 2 km = about 2 kilometres
presque 3 km = almost 3 kilometres
plus de 2 km = more than 2 kilometres
ou over 2 kilometres
moins de 3 km = less than 3 kilometres
ou under 3 kilometres
A est plus loin de B que C de D = it is further from A to B
than from C to D
ou A is further away from
B than C is from D
C est plus près de B que A = C is nearer to B than A is
A est plus près de B que de C = A is nearer to B than to C
A est aussi loin que B = A is as far away as B
A et B sont à la même distance = A and B are the same
distance away

Noter l'ordre des mots dans l'adjectif composé anglais, et l'utilisation du trait d'union. Noter aussi que kilometre, employé comme adjectif, ne prend pas la marque du pluriel.

une promenade de 10 kilomètres = a 10-kilometre walk

☞ Voir page suivante

II loin de *loc prép* **1** (dans l'espace) far from; **est-ce encore ~ d'ici?** is it much further *ou* farther from here?; **2** (dans le temps) far from; **cette époque n'est pas si ~ de nous** we're not so far from that time; **ils veulent aller plus ~ dans leur coopération** they want to extend their cooperation; **il ne peut pas aller plus ~ dans son soutien** he can't increase his support; **on est encore ~ d'avoir fini** we're still far from finished, we're still a long way off finishing; **il n'est pas ~ de 11 heures** it's not far off 11 o'clock; **cela ne fait pas ~ de quatre ans que je suis ici** I've been here for almost four years now; **3** FIG far from, a long way from; **je me sens ~ de tout cela** I feel detached from all that; **~ de moi cette idée!** nothing could be further from my mind!; **avec l'imprimante, il faut compter pas ~ de 10 000 francs** if you include the printer, you're talking about 10,000 francs or thereabouts.

III de loin *loc adv* **1** (d'un endroit éloigné) from a distance, from afar LITTÉR; **je ne vois pas très bien de ~** I can't see very well at a distance; **2** FIG from a distance; **il voit les choses de ~** he sees things from a distance; **c'est de ~ ton meilleur roman** it's by far your best novel.

IV au loin *loc adv* (tout) au ~ (far away) in the distance.

V de loin en loin *loc adv* **1** (séparé dans l'espace) **on pouvait voir des maisons de ~ en ~** you could see houses scattered here and there; **2** (de temps en temps) every now and then.

IDIOMES **~ des yeux, ~ du cœur** PROV out of sight, out of mind PROV.

lointain, **~e** /lwɛ̃tɛ̃, ɛn/ I *adj* **1** (dans l'espace) distant; **2** (dans le temps) distant; **les jours ~s où…** the far-off days when…; **3** (indirect) [*ressemblance,*

rapport] remote; [*cause*] indirect; **4** (détaché) [*personne, air*] distant.

II *nm* background; **dans le ~** [*apercevoir, entendre*] in the distance.

loir /lwaʀ/ *nm* (edible) dormouse.

IDIOMES **être paresseux comme un ~** to be bone idle.

loisir /lwaziʀ/ *nm* **1** (temps libre) spare time ¢; **pendant mes ~s** in my spare time; **(tout) à** (great) leisure; **2** (possibilité) **avoir tout ~ de faire** to have plenty of time to do; **3** (activité) leisure activity; **civilisation des ~s** leisure society.

lombaire /lɔ̃bɛʀ/ *nf* lumbar vertebra.

londonien, **-ienne** /lɔ̃dɔnjɛ̃, ɛn/ ▶ 628 | *adj* of London.

Londonien, **-ienne** /lɔ̃dɔnjɛ̃, ɛn/ *nm,f* Londoner.

Londres /lɔ̃dʀ/ ▶ 628 | *npr* London.

long, **longue** /lɔ̃, lɔ̃g/ ▶ 348 | I *adj* **1** (dans l'espace) [*tige, cils, patte, lettre, robe, table, distance*] long; **une chemise à manches longues** a shirt with long sleeves, a long-sleeved shirt; **un tuyau ~ de trois mètres** a pipe three metres GB long, a three-metre GB long pipe; **au ~ cours** NAUT [*voyage, navigation*] ocean; [*capitaine*] fully-licensed; **2** (dans le temps) [*moment, vie, voyage, exil, film, silence*] long; [*amitié*] long-standing; **ta longue habitude des enfants** your great experience of children; **une traversée longue de 40 minutes** a 40 minute crossing; **être ~ (à faire)** [*personne*] to be slow (to do); **je ne serai pas ~** (pour aller quelque part) I won't be long; (pour un discours) I will be brief; **aliment ~ à cuire** food that takes a long time to cook; **être en longue maladie** to be on extended sick leave; **être ~ à la détente°** to be slow on the uptake°; **il trouve le temps ~** time hangs heavy on his hands; **pendant de longues**

Les mesures de longueur (2)

La longueur

combien mesure la corde?	= how long is the rope?
elle mesure 10 m de long	= it is 10 metres long
elle fait 10 m de long	= it is 10 metres in length
une corde d'environ 10 m de long	= a rope about 10 metres long *ou* 10 metres in length
à peu près 10 m	= about 10 metres
presque 11 m	= almost 11 metres
plus de 10 m	= more than 10 metres
moins de 11 m	= less than 11 metres
A est plus long que B	= A is longer than B
B est plus court que A	= B is shorter than A
A est aussi long que B	= A is as long as B
A et B ont la même longueur	= A and B are the same length
A a la même longueur que B	= A is the same length as B
10 mètres de corde	= 10 metres of rope
6 mètres de soie	= 6 metres of silk
vendu au mètre	= sold by the metre

Noter l'ordre des mots dans les adjectifs composés anglais, et l'utilisation du trait d'union. Noter aussi que metre *et* foot, *employés comme adjectifs, ne prennent pas la marque du pluriel.*

une corde de 10 mètres	= a 10-metre rope *ou* a rope 10 metres long
un python de six pieds de long	= a six-foot-long python *ou* a python six feet long

La hauteur
La taille des personnes

combien mesure-t-il?	= how tall is he? *ou (si l'on veut obtenir un chiffre précis)* what is his height?

En anglais, la taille des personnes est donnée en pieds (feet) *et en pouces* (inches), *jamais en yards. En gros, 1,50 m = cinq pieds, et 1,80 m = six pieds.*

il mesure 1,80 m	= he is 6 feet tall *ou* he is 6 feet *ou* he is 1.80 m
il mesure 1,75 m	= he is 5 feet 10 inches *ou* he is 5 feet 10 *ou* he is 1.75 m

Dans la conversation courante, on utilise souvent foot *au lieu de* feet: *on peut donc dire:* he is 5 foot 10 inches *ou* 5 foot 10.

à peu près 1,80 m	= about 6 ft
presque 1,80 m	= almost 6 ft
plus de 1,75 m	= more than 5 ft 10 ins
moins de 1,85 m	= less than 6 ft 3 ins
Pierre est plus grand que Paul	= Pierre is taller than Paul
Paul est plus petit que Pierre	= Paul is smaller than Pierre *ou* Paul is shorter than Pierre
Pierre est aussi grand que Paul	= Pierre is as tall as Paul
Pierre a la même taille que Paul	= Pierre is the same height as Paul
Pierre et Paul ont la même taille	= Pierre and Paul are the same height

Noter l'ordre des mots dans l'adjectif composé anglais, et l'utilisation du trait d'union. Noter également que foot, *employé comme adjectif, ne prend pas la marque du pluriel.*

un athlète d'un mètre quatre-vingts	= a six-foot athlete

On peut aussi dire an athlete six feet tall. *De même, a* footballer over six feet in height, *etc.*

La hauteur des choses

quelle est la hauteur de la tour?	= what is the height of the tower?
combien mesure la tour?	= what is the height of the tower?
elle fait 23 mètres de haut elle mesure 23 mètres de hauteur	= it is 23 metres high *ou* it is 23 metres in height
elle a une hauteur de 23 m	= its height is 23 metres
une tour d'environ 25 m de haut	= a tower about 25 metres high *ou* about 25 metres in height
à une hauteur de 20 mètres	= at a height of 20 metres

A est plus haut que B	= A is higher than B
B est moins haut que A	= B is lower than A
A est aussi haut que B	= A is as high as B
A et B sont de la même hauteur	= A and B are the same height
A est de la même hauteur que B	= A is the same height as B

Noter l'ordre des mots dans l'adjectif composé anglais, et l'utilisation du trait d'union. Noter aussi que metre, *employé comme adjectif, ne prend pas la marque du pluriel.*

une tour haute de 23 mètres	= a 23-metre-high tower

On peut aussi dire: a tower 23 metres high. *De même, a* mountain over 4,000 metres in height, *etc.*

à quelle altitude est l'avion?	= how high is the plane?
à quelle altitude vole l'avion?	= what height is the plane flying at?
l'avion vole à 5 000 m d'altitude	= the plane is flying at 5,000 metres
son altitude est de 5 000 m	= its altitude is 5,000 metres
à une altitude de 5 000 m	= at an altitude of 5,000 metres

La largeur

L'anglais dispose de deux mots pour la largeur: wide *mesure la distance entre deux limites* (a wider valley; *le nom est* width), *alors que* broad *décrit ce qui remplit un espace d'une certaine largeur* (a broad avenue; *le nom est* breadth).

Les expressions suivantes utilisent wide *et* width, *mais* broad *et* breadth *s'emploient de la même façon.*

quelle est la largeur de la rivière?	= how wide is the river? *ou* what width is the river?
elle fait 7 m	= it is 7 metres
elle fait 7 m de large	= it is 7 metres wide *ou* it is 7 metres in width *ou* it is 7 metres across
elle fait environ 7 m de large	= it is about 7 metres wide
A est plus large que B	= A is wider than B
B est plus étroit que A	= B is narrower than A
A est aussi large que B	= A is as wide as B
A et B sont de la même largeur	= A and B are the same width
A est de la même largeur que B	= A is the same width as B

Noter l'ordre des mots dans l'adjectif composé anglais, et l'utilisation du trait d'union. Noter aussi que metre, *employé comme adjectif, ne prend pas la marque du pluriel.*

une rivière de 7 m de large	= a seven-metre-wide river

On peut aussi dire: a river seven metres wide. *De même,* a ditch two metres wide, a piece of cloth two metres in width, *etc.*

La profondeur

quelle est la profondeur du lac?	= how deep is the lake *ou* what depth is the lake? *ou* what is the depth of the lake?
il fait 4 m	= it is 4 metres deep
il fait 4 m de profondeur	= it is 4 metres in depth
il fait environ 4 m de profondeur	= it is about 4 metres deep
un lac de 4 mètres de profondeur	= a lake four metres deep *ou* a lake four metres in depth

Noter l'absence d'équivalent anglais de la préposition française de *avant le chiffre dans les expressions de ce genre. Mais:*

à une profondeur de dix mètres	= at a depth of ten metres
A est plus profond que B	= A is deeper than B
B est moins profond que A	= B is shallower* than A
A est aussi profond que B	= A is as deep as B
A et B ont la même profondeur	= A and B are the same depth
A a la même profondeur que B	= A is the same depth as B
un puits de 7 m de profondeur	= a well seven metres deep

* *Noter que l'adjectif* shallow (peu profond) *n'a pas d'équivalent simple en français.*

heures/années for hours/years; **3** LING (voyelle) long.
II *adv* **1** (beaucoup) **en dire ~/trop ~/plus ~** to say a lot/too much/more (**sur qch/qn** about sth/sb); **2 s'habiller ~** to wear longer skirts.
III *nm* **1** (longueur) **un câble de six mètres de ~** a cable six metres ^{GB} long, a six-metre^{GB} long cable; **en ~** [*découper, fendre*] lengthwise; **en ~ et en large** [*raconter*] in great detail; **marcher de ~ en large** to pace up and down; **en ~, en large et en travers**○ [*raconter*] at great length; **le ~ du mur** (en longueur) along the wall; (en hauteur) up ou down the wall; **tout le ~ de qch** (dans l'espace) all along sth; (dans le temps) all the way through sth; **courir tout le ~ du chemin** to run all the way; **tomber de tout son ~** to fall flat (on one's face).
IV à la longue *loc adv* in the end, eventually.
■ **~ métrage** CIN feature-length film.

long-courrier, *pl* **~s** /lɔ̃kurje/ *nm* (navire) ocean-going ship; (avion) long-haul aircraft.

longe /lɔ̃ʒ/ *nf* (de cheval) (pour attacher) tether; (pour mener) rein; **mener un cheval à la ~** to lead a horse.

longer /lɔ̃ʒe/ [13] *vtr* **1** (aller le long de) [*personne, train*] to go along [*forêt, côte*]; to follow [*rivière*]; [*bateau*] to sail along [*côte*]; **2** (s'étendre le long de) [*jardin, route*] to run alongside [*lac, champ*].

longévité /lɔ̃ʒevite/ *nf* LIT, FIG longevity.

longiligne /lɔ̃ʒiliɲ/ *adj* lanky, rangy.

longitude /lɔ̃ʒityd/ *nf* longitude; **à** or **par 30° de ~ est/ouest** at longitude 30° east/west.

longitudinal, **~e**, *mpl* **-aux** /lɔ̃ʒitydinal, o/ *adj* GÉN longitudinal; [*axe, coupe, fibres, cassure*] longitudinal, lengthwise.

longtemps /lɔ̃tɑ̃/ *adv* **1** [*attendre, dormir etc*] (for) a long time; (avec négation, dans question) (for) long; **j'y ai vécu ~** I lived there for a long time; **il n'a pas mis ~** it didn't take him long; **tu en as pour ~/ encore pour ~?** (à te préparer) will you be long/ much longer?; **il n'en a plus pour ~** (à vivre) he won't last much longer; **prévoir qch ~ à l'avance** to plan sth a long time ahead; **~ avant/après** long before/after; **avant ~** (d'ici peu) before long; **pas avant ~** not for a long time; **j'ai attendu trop ~** I waited too long; **je peux le garder plus ~?** can I keep it a bit longer?; **durer assez ~** (suffisamment) to last long enough; (une longue période) to last quite a long time; **une lettre ~ attendue** a long-awaited letter; **2** (avec il y a, depuis, cela fait) (marquant la continuité) (for) a long time, (for) long; (quand l'action est terminée) a long time ago, long ago; **il y a** or **cela fait ~ que je le connais, je le connais depuis ~** I've known him for a long time; **il ne travaille pas ici depuis ~, il n'y a pas ~ qu'il travaille ici** he hasn't worked ou been working here (for) long; **ça fait ~ qu'il n'a pas téléphoné** he hasn't phoned for ages○; **il n'y a plus ~ à attendre** it won't be much longer now; **il est mort depuis ~** he died a long time ago; **il ne conduisait plus depuis ~** he had stopped driving long before then; **il n' y a pas si ~ c'était encore possible** it was still possible until quite recently.

longue ▶ **long** I, IV.

longuement /lɔ̃gmɑ̃/ *adv* (pendant longtemps) [*hésiter, cuire*] for a long time; (en détail) [*expliquer*] at length; **j'y ai ~ réfléchi** I've given it a lot of thought.

longueur /lɔ̃gœʀ/ **▶ 348** I *nf* **1** (dimension) length; **dans (le sens de) la ~** lengthways GB, lengthwise US; **être déchiré/fendu sur toute la ~** to be ripped/ cracked along the whole length; **la maison est tout en ~** the house is long and narrow; **un câble de trois mètres de ~** a cable three metres^{GB} long, a three-metre^{GB} long cable; **2** (distance entre deux concurrents) length; **avoir une ~ d'avance sur qn** SPORT to be one length ahead of sb; FIG to be ahead of sb; **3 ▶ 329** SPORT (en natation) length; (en athlétisme) **le saut en ~** the long ou broad US jump; **4** (durée) length; **traîner en ~** [*film*] to go on forever.

II longueurs *nfpl* (dans un film, livre, discours) over long passages.
III à longueur de *loc prép* **à ~ de journée** all day long; **à ~ d'année** all year round; **à ~ de temps** all the time.
■ **~ d'onde** PHYS, FIG wavelength.

longue-vue, *pl* **longues-vues** /lɔ̃gvy/ *nf* telescope.

look○ /luk/ *nm* (allure, style) look; (image) image.

looping /lupiŋ/ *nm* loop; **faire un ~** to loop the loop.

lopin /lɔpɛ̃/ *nm* **~ (de terre)** patch of land, plot.

loquace /lɔkas/ *adj* talkative, loquacious.

loque /lɔk/ I *nf* **~ (humaine)** (human) wreck.
II loques *nfpl* (guenilles) rags.

loquet /lɔkɛ/ *nm* latch.

loqueteux, **-euse** /lɔktø, øz/ *adj* FML [*vêtement, livre*] tattered; [*personne*] ragged (*épith*).

lorgner○ /lɔʀɲe/ [1] *vtr* to give [sb] the eye○ [*personne*]; to cast longing glances at [*bijou, gâteau*]; to have one's eye on [*héritage, poste*].

lorgnette /lɔʀɲɛt/ *nf* (d'opéra) opera-glasses (*pl*); (de marine) spy-glass.
IDIOMES **regarder la situation par le petit bout de la ~** to take a very simplistic view of the situation.

lorgnon /lɔʀɲɔ̃/ *nm* (face-à-main) lorgnette; (pince-nez) pince-nez.

loriot /lɔʀjo/ *nm* oriole.

lors /lɔʀ/ I **lors de** *loc prép* **1** (pendant) during; **2** (au moment de) at the time of.
II lors même que *loc conj* even if.

lorsque (lorsqu' *before vowel or mute h*) /lɔʀsk(ə)/ *conj* when.

■ Note *lorsque* se traduit par *when: lorsque je suis allé au Portugal* = when I went to Portugal; *lorsqu'elle travaille elle n'aime pas être dérangée* = she doesn't like to be disturbed when she's working.
– Attention, on n'utilise jamais le futur après *when: lorsqu'il aura terminé* = when he's finished.

losange /lɔzɑ̃ʒ/ *nm* rhomb, lozenge; **en ~** diamond shaped.

lot /lo/ *nm* **1** (portion) (de succession, partage) share, portion JUR; (d'émotions) share; (de terrain) plot; **2** (à la loterie) prize; **gagner le gros ~** LIT, FIG○ to hit the jackpot; **3** (d'objets en vente) GÉN batch; (aux enchères) lot; **4** (de personnes) **être au-dessus du ~** to be above the average; **5** ORDINAT batch; **6** (destin) fate, lot.

loterie /lɔtʀi/ *nf* (avec lots) raffle; (de fête foraine) tombola GB, raffle US; (à grande échelle) lottery; **jouer à la ~** to have a go○ on the lottery.

loti, **~e** /lɔti/ *adj* **bien/mal ~** well/badly off; **voilà bien ~e avec un patron pareil!** IRON just my luck to land up with a boss like him! IRON.

lotion /losjɔ̃/ *nf* lotion; **~ après rasage** after-shave.

lotir /lɔtiʀ/ [3] *vtr* **1** (répartir) to share out [*biens, immeubles*]; **terrain(s) à ~** plots ou lots US for sale; **2** (attribuer) to allot (**qn de qch** sth to sb).

lotissement /lɔtismɑ̃/ *nm* housing estate GB, subdivision US.

loto /lɔto/ **▶ 329** *nm* lotto; **le ~ sportif** ≈ the national sport lottery.

lotte /lɔt/ *nf* (de mer) monkfish, angler fish; (de rivière) burbot.

louable /luabl/ *adj* [*intention, effort*] commendable, praiseworthy.

louage /luaʒ/ *nm* **~ de services** contract of employment; **voiture de ~** rented car GB, rental car US.

louange /luɑ̃ʒ/ *nf* praise; **chanter les ~s de qn/ qch** to sing sb's/sth's praises; **à la ~ de** in praise of; **digne de ~** praiseworthy.

loubard○ /lubaʀ/ *nm* hooligan, delinquent youth.

louche /luʃ/ I *adj* (équivoque) [*individu, passé*] shady [*lieu*] seedy; **il y a quelque chose de ~ dans cette histoire** there is something fishy○ about this business.
II *nf* (ustensile) ladle; (contenu) ladleful.

loucher /luʃe/ [1] I *vi* to have a squint.

II loucher sur○ *vtr ind* (convoiter) to eye [*filles*]; to have one's eye on [*héritage*].

ouer /lue/ [1] **I** *vtr* **1** (donner en location) to let GB, to rent out [*maison, terrain*] (**à** to); to hire [*salle*]; to hire out GB, to rent out [*équipement, film*] (**à** to); **'à ~'** 'for rent', 'to let' GB; **2** (prendre en location) to rent [*maison, terrain*] (**à** from); to hire [*salle*]; to hire GB, to rent [*équipement, film*] (**à** from); **3** (embaucher) to hire [*personnel*]; **4** (rendre grâce à) to praise (**de, pour** for); **Dieu soit loué** thank God.

II se louer *vpr* **la chambre se loue à la semaine** the room is rented on a weekly basis; **l'appartement se loue 2 000 francs par mois** the rent for this apartment is 2,000 francs per month; (se féliciter) LITER **se ~ d'avoir fait** to congratulate oneself on doing.

oufoque○ /lufɔk/ *adj* crazy○.

oukoum /lukum/ *nm* Turkish delight ¢.

oulou /lulu/ *nm* **1** (chien) spitz; **2**○ (voyou) hooligan, delinquent youth; **3**○ (terme d'affection) pet○ GB, honey US.

oup /lu/ *nm* **1** (mammifère) wolf; **à pas de ~** stealthily; **crier au ~** LIT, FIG to cry wolf; **~ solitaire** lone wolf; ▶ **jeune**; **2** (poisson) **~ (de mer)** (sea) bass; **3** (masque) domino, mask.

■ **(vieux) ~ de mer** old salt, old tar.

IDIOMES **avoir une faim de ~** to be ravenous; **être connu comme le ~ blanc** to be known to everybody; **se jeter dans la gueule du ~** to stick one's head in the lion's mouth; **faire entrer le ~ dans la bergerie** to let the wolf into the fold; **elle a vu le ~** HUM she's lost her virginity; **les ~s ne se mangent pas entre eux** PROV (there is) honour^GB among thieves; **la faim fait sortir le ~ du bois** PROV needs must (when the devil drives); **quand on parle du ~ (on en voit la queue** or **il sort du bois)** PROV speak of the devil; **l'homme est un ~ pour l'homme** PROV dog eat dog.

oupe /lup/ *nf* (lentille) magnifying glass.

ouper○ /lupe/ [1] **I** *vtr* **1** (manquer) to miss [*train, occasion, personne*]; **la prochaine fois, ils ne te louperont pas** next time they'll get you; **il n'en loupe pas une** he's always opening his big mouth; **2** (ne pas réussir) to flunk○ [*examen*]; (to screw up○ [*sauce, ouvrage*]; to bungle [*entrée en scène*]; **il a loupé son coup** he botched it; **la soirée est complètement loupée** the evening is a wash-out.

II *vi* **j'avais dit que ça se casserait, ça n'a pas loupé** I said it would break, and sure enough it did; **tu vas tout faire ~** you'll mess everything up.

oup-garou, *pl* **loups-garous** /lugaʀu/ *nm* werewolf.

oupiote○ /lupjɔt/ *nf* small lamp.

ourd, **~e**[1] /luʀ, luʀd/ **I** *adj* **1** (d'un poids élevé) [*personne, objet, métal*] heavy; **~ à transporter** heavy to carry; **2** (donnant une sensation de pesanteur) [*estomac, jambe, tête, pas*] heavy; [*geste*] clumsy, ungainly; **j'ai les jambes ~es** my legs feel heavy, my legs ache; **il a les yeux ~s de sommeil** his eyes are heavy with sleep; **3** (indigeste) [*repas, aliment*] heavy; [*vin*] heady; **~ à digérer** heavy on the stomach; **4** (dense) [*protection*] heavy; [*chevelure*] thick; **5** IND, MIL [*armement, équipement*] heavy; **6** (onéreux) [*amende, fiscalité*] heavy; **7** (grave) [*perte, défaite, responsabilité*] heavy; [*présomption, erreur*] serious; **8** (encombrant) [*administration, structure*] unwieldy; [*effectifs*] great; **9** (massif) [*personne, animal*] ungainly; [*corps, objet, architecture, poitrine*] heavy; [*bâtiment*] squat; **10** (sans finesse) [*personne*] oafish; [*voix*] thick; [*plaisanterie*] flat; [*style*] clumsy; **11** (pénible) [*ciel, atmosphère, silence*] heavy; [*chaleur*] sultry; **12** (chargé) (de danger, conséquences) fraught (**de** with); (de menaces) charged (**de** with); **13** (difficilement praticable) [*piste, sol, terrain*] heavy; **14** FIN (médiocre) [*marché, tendance*] sluggish.

II *adv* **1** peser **~** (être d'un poids élevé) to weigh heavy; (compter beaucoup) **peser/ne pas peser ~** to carry a lot of/not to carry very much weight (**sur** with); **2** MÉTÉO **il fait ~** it's close; **3**○ (beaucoup) pas

~ not a lot, not much; **elle n'en fait/sait pas ~** she doesn't do/know a lot ou much; **rachète du beurre, il n'en reste pas ~** buy some more butter, there's hardly any left.

IDIOMES **avoir le cœur ~** to have a heavy heart; **être ~ comme du plomb** to be (as) heavy as lead; **avoir la main ~e** (avec taxes, punitions) to be heavy-handed; **avoir la main ~e avec le sel/le parfum** to overdo the salt/the perfume.

lourdaud, **~e** /luʀdo, od/ **I** *adj* [*personne*] oafish; [*esprit*] dull; [*discours*] clumsy.

II *nm,f* oaf.

lourde[2] /luʀd/ **I** *adj f* ▶ **lourd I**.

II○ *nf* (porte) door.

lourdement /luʀdəmɑ̃/ *adv* **1** (fortement) heavily; **se tromper ~** to be gravely mistaken; **2** (sans finesse) **marcher/se déplacer ~** to walk/move clumsily; **insister ~** to labour^GB the point; **insister ~ sur** to keep going on about.

lourder○ /luʀde/ [1] *vtr* (congédier) to kick [sb] out○.

lourdeur /luʀdœʀ/ *nf* **1** (d'organisation, de secteur, réseau) complexity; **2** (sensation de pesanteur) heaviness; **avoir des ~s d'estomac** to feel bloated; **3** (maladresse) (de style) clumsiness; (dans un texte) clumsy expression; **4** (importance) (de personne) heaviness, stiffness; **la ~ des subventions/impôts/pertes** the heavy subsidies (*pl*)/taxes (*pl*)/losses (*pl*); **5** (poids élevé) weight; **6** (manque de raffinement) (de personne) oafishness; (de plaisanterie) poorness; (d'architecture) ungainliness; **7** (de temps) closeness, mugginess; (d'ambiance) heaviness; **8** (de marché) sluggishness.

loustic○ /lustik/ *nm* PEJ chap, guy.

loutre /lutʀ/ *nf* **1** (animal) otter; **2** (fourrure) otterskin.

louve /luv/ *nf* she-wolf.

louveteau, *pl* **~x** /luvto/ *nm* ZOOL wolf cub.

louvoyer /luvwaje/ [23] *vi* **1** NAUT to beat to windward, to tack; **2** (biaiser) to manoeuvre GB, to maneuver US; (tergiverser) to hedge.

lover: se lover /lɔve/ [1] *vpr* [*serpent*] to coil itself up; [*personne*] to curl up.

loyal, **~e**, *mpl* **-aux** /lwajal, o/ *adj* **1** (fidèle) [*ami*] true; [*serviteur*] loyal, faithful; **bons et loyaux services** good and faithful service; **2** (honnête) [*procédé, conduite*] honest; [*concurrence, jeu*] fair.

loyalement /lwajalmɑ̃/ *adv* [*servir*] faithfully; [*se battre*] fairly; [*informer*] honestly.

loyalisme /lwajalism/ *nm* loyalty.

loyaliste /lwajalist/ *adj, nmf* loyalist.

loyauté /lwajote/ *nf* **1** (fidelité) loyalty (**envers** to); **2** (honnêteté) (de personne, conduite) honesty; (de procédé) honesty, fairness.

loyer /lwaje/ *nm* rent.

lubie /lybi/ *nf* whim; **avoir des ~s** to have whims.

lubricité /lybʀisite/ *nf* (de personne) lustfulness, lechery; (de propos, conduite) lewdness.

lubrifiant, **~e** /lybʀifjɑ̃, ɑ̃t/ *nm* lubricant.

lubrifier /lybʀifje/ [2] *vtr* to lubricate.

lubrique /lybʀik/ *adj* [*personne*] lecherous; [*œil, danse*] lewd.

lucarne /lykaʀn/ *nf* (fenêtre) (small) window; (dans un toit) skylight.

lucide /lysid/ *adj* [*personne, politique*] clear-sighted; MÉD lucid; [*esprit, analyse*] lucid.

lucidité /lysidite/ *nf* **1** MÉD lucidity; **moments de ~** lucid moments; **il a toute sa ~** he has all his wits about him; **2** (perspicacité) (de personne) clearheadedness; (d'esprit) clarity; **raisonner avec ~** to think clearly; **il a agi en toute ~** he knew perfectly well what he was doing.

luciole /lysjɔl/ *nf* firefly.

lucratif, **-ive** /lykʀatif, iv/ *adj* lucrative; **assez ~** [*emploi*] fairly well-paid; [*opération*] fairly profitable.

ludique /lydik/ *adj* **1** [*activité*] play (*épith*); **2** PSYCH ludic.

ludothèque /lydɔtɛk/ *nf* toy library.

luette /lyɛt/ *nf* uvula.

lueur /lɥœʀ/ *nf* **1** (faible clarté) (faint) light (**de** of); **les premières ~s de l'aube** the first light (*sg*) of dawn; **pas la moindre ~ d'espoir** FIG not the faintest glimmer of hope; **à la ~ des étoiles/d'une bougie** by starlight/candlelight; **à la ~ des événements d'hier** FIG in the light of yesterday's events; **jeter une faible ~** to cast a poor light; **2** (rougeoiement) glow; **les dernières ~s du soleil couchant** the dying glow of the sunset; **3** (éclat fugitif) LIT, FIG gleam, flash.

luge /lyʒ/ ▶329| *nf* **1** (objet) sledge GB, sled US; **2** (sport) luge.

lugubre /lygybʀ/ *adj* [*paysage, pensée*] gloomy; [*son, chant*] mournful.

lui /lɥi/ *pron pers*

■ **Note** Lorsqu'il représente une personne de sexe masculin ou un animal familier mâle, *lui* peut avoir plusieurs fonctions et se traduira différemment selon les cas: *lui, c'est un menteur* = HE'S a liar; *donne-lui à boire* = give him something to drink. Voir I.
– Lorsqu'il représente un objet, un concept, une plante, un animal mâle ou femelle, quel que soit le genre du mot, *lui* se traduira par *it* ou ne se traduira pas. Voir II.
– Lorsqu'il représente une personne de sexe féminin ou un animal familier femelle, *lui* = *à elle* se traduira par *her: je ne lui dirai rien* = I won't say anything to her. Voir III.

I *pron pers m* (personne, animal familier) **1** (en fonction sujet) **elle lit, ~ regarde la télévision** she's reading, HE'S watching TV; **~ et moi avons longuement discuté** he and I had a long chat; **~ seul a le droit de parler** he alone has the right to talk; **c'est ~** (à la porte) it's him; **~ c'est ~ et moi c'est moi**○ he and I are different; **je sais que ce n'est pas ~ qui a fait ça** I know it wasn't he ou him who did it; **2** (dans une comparaison) him; **je travaille plus que ~** I work more than him ou than he does; **je les vois plus souvent que ~** (qu' il ne les voit) I see them more often than he does; (que je ne le vois) I see them more often than I see him; **3** (en fonction d'objet) **le frapper, ~, quelle idée!** hit HIM? what a thought!; **~, il faut l'enfermer** HE should be locked away; **4** (après une préposition) him; **à cause de/autour de/après ~** because of/around/after him; **à ~** (en jouant) his turn; **ce sont des amis à ~** they're friends of his ; **il n'a pas encore de voiture à ~** he doesn't have his own car yet; **c'est à ~** (appartenance) it's his, it belongs to him; (tour de rôle) it's his turn; **c'est à ~ de choisir** (sa responsabilité) it's up to him to choose.

II *pron pers mf* (objet, concept, animal, plante) it; **le parti/l'association lance un appel, apportez-~ votre soutien** the party/the association is launching an appeal—give it your support; **l'Espagne a signé, le Portugal, ~, n'a pas encore donné son accord** Spain has signed while Portugal hasn't yet agreed; **le toit, ~, n'a pas besoin d'être réparé** the ROOF doesn't need to be repaired; **l'appartement, ~, a été vendu** the apartment was sold.

III *pron pers f* (personne, animal familier) her; **je l'ai rencontrée hier et ~ ai annoncé la nouvelle** I met her yesterday and told her the news.

lui-même /lɥimɛm/ *pron pers* **1** (personne) himself; **il me l'a dit ~** he told me himself; **en ~ il se disait que** he told himself that; **'M. Greiner?'—'~'** (au téléphone) 'Mr Greiner?'—'speaking'; **2** (objet, idée, concept) itself; **l'objet n'a pas de valeur en ~** the object has no value in itself.

luire /lɥiʀ/ [69] *vi* [*soleil, surface polie*] to shine; [*braises*] to glow; **les yeux du loup luisaient dans l'obscurité** the wolf's eyes gleamed in the dark; **~ de sueur** to glisten with sweat; **leur regard luisait de colère** their eyes shone with anger.

luisant, ~e /lɥizɑ̃, ɑ̃t/ *adj* GÉN [*surface polie*] shining (**de** with); [*surface mouillée*] glistening (**de** with); [*yeux*] gleaming.

lumbago /lœbago/ ▶196| *nm* back pain.

lumière /lymjɛʀ/ **I** *nf* **1** GÉN, PHYS light; **~ naturelle** natural light; **la ~ des étoiles** starlight; **la ~ du** soleil sunlight; **la ~ du jour** daylight; **il y a de la ~ dans la cuisine** there's a light on in the kitchen; **les ~ de la ville** the city lights; **il a éteint toutes les ~s** he put all the lights out; **à la ~ d'une chandelle** by candlelight; **2** FIG light; **à la ~ des ré cents événements** in the light of recent events **mettre qch en ~** (mettre en évidence) to highligh sth; (révéler) to bring sth to light; **agir en pleine ~** to act openly; **faire (toute) la ~ sur une affaire t** bring the truth about a matter to light; **3** (personne ce n'est pas une ~** he'll never set the world on fire.

II lumières *nfpl* **1** (feux d'un véhicule) lights; **2** (connaissances) **j'ai besoin de vos ~s** I need to pick your brains; **aider qn de ses ~s** to give sb the bene fit of one's wisdom; **avoir des ~s sur qch** to have some knowledge of a subject.

Lumières /lymjɛʀ/ *nfpl* **les ~** the Enlightenmen (*sg*); **le siècle des ~** the Age of Enlightenment.

lumignon /lymiɲɔ̃/ *nm* (lampe) (dim) lamp.

luminaire /lyminɛʀ/ *nm* (lampe) light (fitting).

lumineux, -euse /lyminø, øz/ *adj* **1** (qui émet de la lumière) [*corps, point*] luminous; **panneau ~** electronic display (board); **enseigne lumineuse** neon sign; **faisceau ~** beam of light, light beam; **rayon ~** ray of light; **2** (clair) [*exposé, explication*] clear, lucid; **idée lumineuse** brilliant idea, brainwave○; **3** (radieux) [*teint, regard*] radiant.

luminosité /lyminozite/ *nf* GÉN brightness, luminosity LITTÉR.

lump /lœmp/ *nm* **œufs de ~** lumpfish roe ℓ.

lunaire /lynɛʀ/ *adj* (de lune) lunar.

lunatique /lynatik/ *nmf* moody person.

lunch /lœʃ/ *nm* (dans la journée) buffet (lunch); (en soirée) buffet (supper).

lundi /lœdi/ ▶551| *nm* Monday; **le ~ de Pâques/de Pentecôte** Easter/Whit Monday.

lune /lyn/ *nf* moon; **pleine ~** full moon; **nuit sans ~** moonless night; **nouvelle ~** new moon.

■ **~ de miel** honeymoon; **~ rousse** ~ April moon.
IDIOMES **être dans la ~**○ to have one's head in the clouds; **avoir l'air de tomber de la ~** to look blank; **demander la ~**○ to cry for the moon; **promettre la ~**○ to promise the earth ou moon; **décrocher la ~**○ to do the impossible.

luné○, **~e** /lyne/ *adj* **bien ~** cheerful; **mal ~** grumpy.

lunette /lynɛt/ **I** *nf* **1** ARCHIT lunette; **2** (siège de toilettes) lavatory seat.
II lunettes *nfpl* **1** (optiques) glasses; **mettre ses ~s** to put on one's glasses; **porter des ~s** to wear glasses; **2** (de protection) goggles.
■ **~ d'approche** telescope; **~ arrière** AUT rear window; **~s noires** dark glasses; **~s de soleil** sunglasses.

lunule /lynyl/ *nf* (de l'ongle) half-moon.

lupanar /lypanaʀ/ *nm* house of ill repute.

lupin /lypɛ̃/ *nm* lupin GB, lupine US.

lurette○ /lyʀɛt/ *nf* **il y a** or **cela fait belle ~ qu'elle a tout dépensé** she spent it all ages○ ago; **il y a** or **cela fait belle ~ que je ne l'ai pas vue** it's been ages○ since I last saw her; **il n'a rien publié depuis belle ~** he has not published for ages○.

luron /lyʀɔ̃/ *nm* fellow; **gai** or **joyeux ~** jolly fellow.

lustrage /lystʀaʒ/ *nm* **1** (processus) (de bois, métal, cuir) buffing; (de textile) lustring; (de voiture) polishing; **2** (résultat) sheen.

lustre /lystʀ/ **I** *nm* **1** (au plafond) GÉN (decorative) ceiling light; (en cristal) chandelier; **2** (éclat) (de surface) sheen; (de cheveux) shine; **3** (de lieu, d'institution) prestigious image; **perdre de son ~** to become rather lacklustre.
II lustres○ *nmpl* **depuis des ~s** for a long time, for ages○.

lustré, ~e /lystʀe/ *adj* **1** (naturellement) glossy; (par l'usure) shiny; **2** [*tissu*] glazed.

lustrer /lystʀe/ [1] *vtr* (faire briller) to polish

[*chaussure, miroir*]; to make [sth] shine [*cheveux, vêtement*].

luth /lyt/ *nm* **1** ▶ 392 | MUS lute; **2** ZOOL leatherback.

luthérien, -ienne /lyteʀjɛ̃, ɛn/ *adj, nm,f* Lutheran.

luthier /lytje/ ▶ 374 | *nm* stringed instrument maker.

luthiste /lytist/ ▶ 392 | *nmf* lutenist.

lutin /lytɛ̃/ *nm* **1** (démon) goblin; **2** (enfant) imp.

lutte /lyt/ *nf* **1** (opposition entre personnes) conflict; (plus pénible) struggle; **~ d'influence** power struggle; **être en ~ contre qn** to be in conflict with sb; **une ~ sans merci** a ruthless battle; **2** (action énergique) fight; (plus pénible) struggle; **la ~ contre le cancer** the fight against cancer; **être en ~** to be fighting ou struggling; **de haute ~** FML [*gagner, obtenir*] after a hard-fought struggle; **3** ▶ 329 | SPORT wrestling; **faire de la ~** to wrestle.

■ **~ armée** armed conflict; **~ de classes** class war; **~ d'intérêts** clash of interests; **~ pour la vie** struggle for existence.

lutter /lyte/ [1] *vi* **1** (s'opposer) [*partie, peuple, pays*] to struggle; **~ contre qn** to fight against sb; **2** (agir énergiquement) [*personne, groupe*] to fight (**pour faire** to do); **~ contre** to fight [*crime, pollution, chômage*]; to fight against [*violence*]; to contend with [*intempéries, bruit*]; **aider le malade à ~ contre la maladie** to help the sick person fight back; **~ contre l'abus d'alcool** to combat alcohol abuse; **Louis luttait contre le sommeil** Louis was fighting off sleep.

lutteur, -euse /lytœʀ, øz/ *nm,f* **1** GÉN fighter; **2** SPORT wrestler.

luxation /lyksasjɔ̃/ *nf* MÉD dislocation.

luxe /lyks/ *nm* luxury; **vivre dans le ~** to live in luxury; **voitures de ~** luxury cars; **s'offrir le ~ de faire** (financièrement) to afford the luxury of doing; FIG to give oneself the satisfaction of doing; **il peut se payer ce ~** he can afford it; **ce n'est pas du ~**○ it has to be done; **je l'ai nettoyé et ce n'était pas du ~**○ I gave it a much needed clean; **avoir des goûts de ~** to have expensive tastes.

Luxembourg /lyksɑ̃buʀ/ ▶ 628 |, 232 |, 509 | *nprm* Luxembourg; **grand-duché de ~** Grand Duchy of Luxembourg.

luxembourgeois, ~e /lyksɑ̃buʀʒwa, az/ **I** *adj* **1** ▶ 394 | (du Luxembourg) of Luxembourg; **2** ▶ 628 | (de Luxembourg) Luxembourg.

II ▶ 338 | *nm* LING German dialect spoken in Luxembourg.

luxer /lykse/ [1] **I** *vtr* to dislocate.

II se luxer *vpr* **se ~ l'épaule** to dislocate one's shoulder.

luxueux, -euse /lyksɥø, øz/ *adj* [*appartement*] luxurious; [*magazine*] glossy.

luxure /lyksyʀ/ *nf* lust.

luxuriant, ~e /lyksyʀjɑ̃, ɑ̃t/ *adj* luxuriant.

luxurieux, -ieuse /lyksyʀjø, øz/ *adj* LITER lustful.

luzerne /lyzɛʀn/ *nf* alfalfa, lucerne GB.

lycée /lise/ *nm* secondary school (*school preparing students aged 15–18 for the baccalaureate*).

lycéen, -éenne /liseɛ̃, ɛn/ *nm,f* secondary school student.

lymphatique /lɛ̃fatik/ *adj* **1** (nonchalant) lethargic; **2** ANAT lymphatic.

lymphe /lɛ̃f/ *nf* lymph.

lyncher /lɛ̃ʃe/ [1] *vtr* to lynch.

lynx /lɛ̃ks/ *nm inv* lynx.
IDIOMES **avoir des yeux de ~** to be lynx-eyed.

lyophiliser /ljofilize/ [1] *vtr* to freeze-dry.

lyre /liʀ/ ▶ 392 | *nf* lyre.

lyrique /liʀik/ *adj* **1** MUS [*chant, compositeur*] operatic; [*chanteur, saison*] opera; **opéra ~** lyric opera; **2** LITTÉRAT [*poésie, poète*] lyric; [*contenu, élan*] lyrical.

lyrisme /liʀism/ *nm* lyricism; **avec ~** lyrically.

lys /lis/ *nm inv* lily.
IDIOMES **blanc comme un ~** lily-white.

Mm

m, **M** /ɛm/ *nm inv* **1** (lettre) m, M; **2** ▶348‖ (*written abbr* = **mètre**) 30 m 30 m.

m' ▶ **me**.

M. ▶596‖ (*written abbr* = **Monsieur**) Mr.

ma ▶ **mon**.

MA /ɛma/ *nmf* (*abbr* = **maître auxiliaire**) *secondary teacher without tenure*.

macabre /makabʀ/ *adj* macabre.

macadam /makadam/ *nm* tarmac®.

macaque /makak/ *nm* **1** ZOOL macaque; **2**○ (homme laid) ugly man.

macaron /makaʀɔ̃/ *nm* **1** (gâteau) macaroon; **2** (insigne) lapel badge; (étiquette autocollante) sticker; **3** (natte) coiled plait GB ou braid US.

maccarthysme /makkaʀtism/ *nm* McCarthyism.

macédoine /masedwan/ *nf* mixed diced vegetables (*pl*).

Macédoine /masedwan/ ▶509‖ *nprf* **la ~** Macedonia.

macédonien, **-ienne** /masedɔnjɛ̃, ɛn/ *adj* Macedonian.

macération /maseʀasjɔ̃/ *nf* (de fruits) soaking.

macérer /maseʀe/ [14] *vi* [*plante, fruit*] to soak; [*viande*] to marinate; (dans un vinaigre) [*cornichon*] to pickle; **faire ~** to steep, to soak.

Mach /mak/ *nm* Mach; **voler à ~ 2** to fly at Mach 2.

mâche /maʃ/ *nf* lamb's lettuce.

mâcher /maʃe/ [1] *vtr* to chew [*aliments, objet*].
IDIOMES **~ la besogne** or **le travail à qn** to break the back of the work for sb; **il ne mâche pas ses mots** he doesn't mince his words.

machette /maʃɛt/ *nf* machete.

machiavélique /makjavelik/ *adj* Machiavellian.

machin○ /maʃɛ̃/ *nm* **1** (objet dont on ne trouve pas le nom) thing, thingummy○, whatsit○; **qu'est-ce que c'est que ce ~-là?** what on earth's that?; **2** (chose) thing; **ce sont des ~s dangereux** they're dangerous things; **3** (personne) old fogey.

Machin○, **~e** /maʃɛ̃, in/ *nm,f* what's-his-name○/what's-her-name○; **la mère ~** Mrs whatsit.

machinal, **~e**, *mpl* **-aux** /maʃinal, o/ *adj* [*geste, réaction*] mechanical; **jeter un coup d'œil ~** to glance absent-mindedly.

machinalement /maʃinalmɑ̃/ *adv* mechanically, without thinking.

machination /maʃinasjɔ̃/ *nf* plot; **des ~s** plots, machinations.

machine /maʃin/ *nf* **1** TECH (appareil) machine; **taper une lettre à la ~** to type a letter; **coudre un ourlet à la ~** to machine-sew a hem; **lavable en ~** machine-washable; **langage ~** ORDINAT machine language; **2** (moteur) engine; **faire ~ arrière** NAUT to go astern; FIG to back-pedal; **3** (système) machine; **la ~ sociale/économique** the social/economic machine; **4**○ (lavage) **faire deux ~s (de linge)** to do two loads of washing.
■ **~ agricole** agricultural machine; **~ à calculer** calculating machine; **~ à coudre** sewing machine; **~ à écrire** typewriter; **~ infernale** (engin explosif) infernal machine; (bombe) time bomb; **~ à laver** washing machine; **~ à laver la vaisselle** dishwasher; **~ à sous** fruit machine GB, slot machine, one-armed bandit; **~ à vapeur** steam engine.

machine-outil, *pl* **machines-outils** /maʃinuti/ *nf* machine tool.

machinerie /maʃinʀi/ *nf* **1** (ensemble) machinery; **2** (local) GÉN machine room; NAUT engine room; **3** THÉÂT stage machinery.

machinisme /maʃinism/ *nm* mechanization.

machiniste /maʃinist/ ▶374‖ *nmf* **1** THÉÂT stagehand; CIN, TV scene shifter; **2** (conducteur) driver.

machisme /ma(t)ʃism/ *nm* male chauvinism.

macho○ /matʃo/ **I** *adj* macho.
II *nm* macho man.

mâchoire /maʃwaʀ/ *nf* jaw.
■ **~ de frein** AUT brake shoe.
IDIOMES **bâiller à s'en décrocher la ~** to yawn one's head off.

mâchonner /maʃɔne/ [1] *vtr* to chew.

mâchouiller○ /maʃuje/ [1] *vtr* to chew (on).

maçon /masɔ̃/ ▶374‖ *nm* GÉN, CONSTR bricklayer; (entrepreneur) builder; (qui construit en pierre) mason.

maçonnerie /masɔnʀi/ *nf* (travaux) building; **travaux de ~** building work ¢; (ouvrage) masonry-work ¢.

maçonnique /masɔnik/ *adj* masonic.

macramé /makʀame/ *nm* macramé.

macrobiotique /makʀɔbjɔtik/ **I** *adj* macrobiotic.
II *nf* macrobiotics (+ *v sg*).

macrocosme /makʀɔkɔsm/ *nm* macrocosm.

maculer /makyle/ [1] *vtr* to smudge [*devoir, feuille*]. (de with); **~ qch de sang/boue** to spatter sth with blood/mud.

madame, *pl* **mesdames** /madam, medam/ ▶596‖ *nf* **1** (titre donné à une inconnue) **Madame** (dans une lettre) Dear Madam; **Madame, Monsieur** Dear Sir or Madam; **bonsoir ~** good evening!; **mesdames et messieurs bonsoir** good evening ladies and gentlemen; **2** (titre donné à une femme dont on connaît le nom, par exemple Bon) **bonjour, ~** good morning, Ms ou Mrs Bon; **Chère Madame** (dans une lettre) Dear Ms. ou Mrs Bon; **Madame Blanc** (sur une enveloppe) Ms ou Mrs Blanc; **Madame le Ministre** (en lui parlant) Minister; (dans une lettre) Dear Minister; **3** (formule de respect) **oui, Madame** yes, madam; **veuillez m'annoncer à Madame** tell your mistress that I am here; **Madame est servie!** dinner is served; **4** HIST Madame.
■ Note L'anglais possède un équivalent féminin de monsieur, *Ms* /mɪz/, qui permet de faire référence à une femme dont on connaît le nom sans préciser sa situation de famille: *Ms X*.

madeleine /madlɛn/ *nf* madeleine.
IDIOMES **pleurer comme une Madeleine** to cry one's eyes out.

mademoiselle, *pl* **mesdemoiselles** /madmwazɛl, medmwazɛl/ ▶596‖ *nf* **1** (titre donné à une inconnue) **Mademoiselle** (dans une lettre) Dear Madam; **bonjour, ~** good morning; **entrez, mesdemoiselles** do come in; **occupez-vous de ~** (dans un magasin) could you attend to this lady, please?; **et pour ~, comme d'habitude?** (au café, bar etc) will it be the usual, madam?; **mesdames, mesdemoiselles, messieurs** ladies and gentlemen; **2** (titre donné à une jeune fille dont on connaît le nom, par exemple Bon) Ms Bon, Miss Bon; **Chère Mademoiselle** (dans une lettre) Dear Ms ou Miss Bon; **bonjour, ~** good morning Ms ou Miss Bon; **Mademoiselle Brun** (sur une enveloppe) Ms Brun, Miss Brun; **3** (formule de respect) **~ votre**

fille† your daughter; **~ boude?** HUM madam's sulking, is she? HUM.

■ Note L'anglais possède un équivalent féminin de monsieur, *Ms* /mɪz/, qui permet de faire référence à une femme dont on connaît le nom sans préciser sa situation de famille: *Ms X.*

madère /madɛʀ/ *nm* madeira.

madone /madɔn/ *nf* ART madonna; **un visage de ~** a serenely beautiful face.

madras /madʀas/ *nm inv* (tissu) madras cotton.

madrier /madʀije/ *nm* beam.

madrigal, *pl* **-aux** /madʀigal, o/ *nm* MUS madrigal.

madrilène /madʀilɛn/ **▶ 628** *adj* of Madrid.

maelström /malstʀɔm/ *nm* MÉTÉO, FIG maelstrom.

maestria /maɛstʀija/ *nf* brilliance, panache; **avec ~** with great panache.

maf(f)ia /mafja/ *nf* mafia; **la Mafia** the Mafia.

maf(f)ieux, **-ieuse** /mafjø, øz/ *adj* mafia (*épith*).

magasin /magazɛ̃/ *nm* **1** (boutique) shop GB, store US; (plus grand) **grand ~** department store; **~s spécialisés** specialist shops GB ou stores US; **faire les ~s** to go shopping; **~ d'alimentation** food shop GB ou store US; **2** IND store, storehouse; **avoir en ~** to have in stock.
■ **~ d'armes** MIL armoury GB; COMM gunsmith's.

magasiner /magazine/ [1] *vi* C **aller ~** to go shopping.

magasinier, **-ière** /magazinje, ɛʀ/ **▶ 374** *nm,f* **1** (dans une entreprise) stock controller; **2** (gardien de dépôt) warehouse keeper.

magazine /magazin/ *nm* (journal, émission) magazine.

mage /maʒ/ *nm* magus; **les rois ~s** the (Three) Wise Men.

magenta /maʒɛ̃ta/ **▶ 141** *adj*, *nm* magenta.

maghrébin, **~e** /magʀebɛ̃, in/ *adj* North African, Maghrebi.

magicien, **-ienne** /maʒisjɛ̃, ɛn/ **▶ 374** *nm,f* magician; **un ~ de l'économie** FIG an economic wizard.

magie /maʒi/ *nf* **1** (science, effet) magic; **comme par ~** as if by magic; **2** (dans un spectacle) conjuring.

magique /maʒik/ *adj* **1** LIT magic (*épith*), magical; **formule ~** magic words (*pl*); **2** FIG [*décor*] magical.

magistère /maʒistɛʀ/ *nm*: high-level University degree combining academic coursework with work experience in industry.

magistral, **~e**, *mpl* **-aux** /maʒistʀal, o/ *adj* **1** (remarquable) brilliant; **un coup ~** a masterstroke; **2** (doctoral) [*ton*] magisterial; **3** HUM [*gifle*] tremendous.

magistrat /maʒistʀa/ *nm* magistrate.

magistrature /maʒistʀatyʀ/ *nf* **1** JUR magistracy; **2** ADMIN (fonction) public office; **arriver à la ~ suprême** to reach the highest office in the land.

magma /magma/ *nm* **1** (en géologie) magma; **2** FIG jumble.

magnanime /maɲanim/ *adj* magnanimous.

magnanimité /maɲanimite/ *nf* magnanimity.

magnat /maɲa/ *nm* magnate, tycoon.

magner〇: **se magner** /maɲe/ [1] *vpr* to get a move on〇.

magnésie /maɲezi/ *nf* magnesia.

magnésium /maɲezjɔm/ *nm* magnesium.

magnétique /maɲetik/ *adj* magnetic.

magnétiser /maɲetize/ [1] *vtr* **1** PHYS, MÉD to magnetize; **2** (charmer) to hypnotize, to mesmerize.

magnétiseur, **-euse** /maɲetizœʀ, øz/ **▶ 374** *nm,f* (magnetic) healer.

magnétisme /maɲetism/ *nm* GÉN magnetism; **le ~ d'un discours** the magnetic power of a speech.

magnétophone /maɲetɔfɔn/ *nm* (à cassette) cassette (tape) recorder; (à bande) tape recorder.

magnétoscope /maɲetɔskɔp/ *nm* video recorder, VCR.

magnificence /maɲifisɑ̃s/ *nf* **1** (splendeur) magnifi-

cence, splendour GB; **2** (générosité) **recevoir qn avec ~** to entertain sb lavishly.

magnifier /maɲifje/ [1] *vtr* **1** (élever) to idealize [*souvenir, sentiment*]; **2** (célébrer) to glorify [*héroïsme, exploit*].

magnifique /maɲifik/ *adj* magnificent, splendid.

magnitude /maɲityd/ *nf* (de séisme) strength; **séisme de ~ 5,6** earthquake measuring 5.6 (on the Richter scale).

magnolia /maɲɔlja/ *nm* magnolia (tree).

magnum /magnɔm/ *nm* magnum (bottle).

magot〇 /mago/ *nm* pile〇 (of money).

magouillage〇 /magujaʒ/ *nm* wangling〇, fiddling〇.

magouille〇 /maguj/ *nf* **1** (procédé) wangling〇, fiddling〇; **2** (résultat) trick; **de sombres ~s** dirty tricks; **~s politiques** political skulduggery ¢; **~s électorales** election rigging ¢.

magouiller〇 /maguje/ [1] *vi* to wangle〇, to fiddle〇.

magret /magʀɛ/ *nm* **~ de canard** duck breast.

Mahomet /maɔme/ *npr* Mohammed.

mai /mɛ/ **▶ 382** *nm* May; **le premier ~** May Day.

maigre /mɛgʀ/ **I** *adj* **1** [*personne*] thin, skinny; **2** CULIN [*viande*] lean; [*fromage*] low-fat; **3** RELIG [*jour*] without meat; **faire** or **manger ~** to abstain from meat; **4** (médiocre) [*résultat*] poor; [*talents, repas, économies*] meagre GB; [*espoir*] slim; [*applaudissements*] scant; **5** (peu volumineux) [*filet d'eau*] thin; [*gazon, chevelure*] sparse, thin.
II *nmf* thin man/woman; **c'est une fausse ~** she looks thinner than she is.
IDIOMES **~ comme un clou**〇 as thin as a rake.

maigrement /mɛgʀəmɑ̃/ *adv* [*payé*] poorly.

maigreur /mɛgʀœʀ/ *nf* **1** (de personne) thinness; **d'une grande ~** very thin; **2** (faible quantité) meagreness GB.

maigrichon, **-onne** /mɛgʀiʃɔ̃, ɔn/ *adj* skinny.

maigrir /mɛgʀiʀ/ [3] *vi* to lose weight; **~ de trois kilos** to lose three kilos; **il a maigri du visage** his face has got GB ou gotten US thinner; **pour ~** [*cachet*] slimming GB, reducing US.

mail /maj/ *nm* **1** (allée) mall, avenue; **2** **▶ 329** (jeu) pall-mall.

mailing /meliŋ/ *nm* CONTROV **1** (principe) direct mail advertising; **2** (envoi) mail shot; **3** (document) mailing pack.

maillage /majaʒ/ *nm* **1** (de filet) mesh size; **2** (création de réseau) creation of a network; (réseau créé) network.

maille /maj/ *nf* **1** (de tricot) stitch; **~ (à l') endroit/envers** plain/purl stitch; **à fines/grosses ~s** fine-/loose-knit (*épith*); **une ~ qui file** (sur un collant) a ladder; **monter 20 ~s** to cast on 20 stitches; **2** (de filet) mesh; **passer à travers les ~s** LIT to pass through the net; FIG to slip through the net; **3** (de chaînette) link.
IDIOMES **avoir ~ à partir avec qn** to have a brush with sb.

maillet /majɛ/ *nm* mallet.

mailloche /majɔʃ/ *nf* **1** (maillet) mallet, beetle; **2** MUS beater.

maillon /majɔ̃/ *nm* link; **~ de la chaîne** link in the chain.

maillot /majo/ *nm* **1** **~ (de corps)** vest GB, undershirt US; **2** (de rugby) shirt; (de cyclisme) jersey; **3** **~ (de bain)** swimsuit.
■ **le ~ jaune** (cycliste) the leader in the Tour de France.

main /mɛ̃/ **▶ 137** *nf* **1** ANAT hand; **saluer qn de la ~** to wave at sb; **la ~ dans la ~** LIT hand in hand; **avoir les ~s liées** LIT, FIG to have one's hands tied; **haut les ~s!** hands up!; **se tenir la ~** to hold hands; **demander la ~ de qn** to ask for sb's hand in marriage; **ramasser qch à pleines ~s** to pick up handfuls of sth; **saisir qch à pleines ~s** to take a firm hold of sth; **avoir qch bien en ~(s)** LIT to hold sth firmly; FIG to have sth well in hand; **être adroit de**

ses ~s to be good with one's hands; **si tu lèves la ~ sur elle** if you lay a finger on her; **faire qch à la ~** to do sth by hand; **fait ~** [*produit*] handmade; **tricoté ~** hand-knitted; **à la ~** [*régler*] manually; **jouer du piano à quatre ~s** to play a duet on the piano; **à ~ levée** [*dessiner*] freehand; [*voter*] by a show of hands; **vol à ~ armée** armed robbery; **donner un coup de ~ à qn** to give sb a hand; **dix secondes montre en ~** ten seconds exactly; ▶**vilain**; **2** (personne) **une ~ secourable** a helping hand; **une ~ criminelle** someone with criminal intentions; **3** (dénotant le contrôle, la possession) **changer de ~s** to change hands; **avoir qch sous la ~** to have sth to hand; **cela m'est tombé sous la ~** I just happened to come across it; **mettre la ~ sur qch** (s'approprier) to get one's hands on sth; **je n'arrive pas à mettre la ~ dessus** I can't lay my hands on it; **je l'ai eu entre les ~s mais** I did have it but; **être entre les ~s de qn** [*pouvoir, responsabilité*] to be in the hands of sb; **prendre en ~s** to take [sth] in hand; **se prendre par la ~** (soi-même) to take oneself in hand; **prendre qn par la ~** LIT, FIG to take sb by the hand; **avoir la ~ haute sur** to have control over; **avoir les choses en ~** to have things in hand; **à ne pas mettre entre toutes les ~s** [*livre*] not for general reading; **tomber entre les ~s de qn** to fall into sb's hands; **repartir avec un contrat en ~(s)** to leave with a signed contract; **elle est arrivée preuve en ~** she had concrete proof; **les ~s vides** empty- handed; **je le lui ai remis en ~s propres** I gave it to him/her in person; **de la ~ à la ~** [*vendre, acheter*] privately; **être payé de la ~ à la ~** to be paid cash (in hand); **de seconde ~** secondhand; **de première ~** (dans une annonce) 'one owner'; **avoir des renseignements de première ~** to have first-hand information; ▶**velours**; **4** (origine) **écrit de la ~ du président** written by the president himself/herself; **reconnaître la ~ d'un artiste** to recognize an artist's style; **de ma plus belle ~** (écriture) in my best handwriting; **5** (dénotant l'habileté) **avoir le coup de ~** to have the knack; **il faut d'abord se faire la ~** you have to learn how to do it first; **avoir la ~ légère** to have a light touch; **6** ZOOL (de primate) hand; **7** (longueur) **une ~** a hand's width; **8** SPORT (au football) handball; **9** JEUX (cartes de chacun) hand; (tour de jeu) deal; **perdre la ~** FIG to lose one's touch; **garder la ~** FIG to keep one's hand in; **10** (direction) **à ~ droite/gauche** on the right/left.
■ **~ courante** CONSTR handrail; (en comptabilité) daybook.
IDIOMES **j'en mettrais ma ~ au feu** or **à couper** I'd swear to it; **d'une ~ de fer** [*gouverner*] with an iron rod; **il n'y est pas allé de ~ morte**○! he didn't pull his punches!; **avoir la ~ leste** to be always ready with a slap; **laisser les ~s libres à qn** to give sb a free hand ou rein; **passer la ~** to step down (**à** in favour^GB of); **faire ~ basse sur** to help oneself to [*biens*]; to take over [*marché*]; **en venir aux ~s** to come to blows; **avoir la ~ heureuse/malheureuse** to be lucky/unlucky; **mettre la dernière ~ à** to put the finishing touches to; **ils peuvent se donner la ~** PEJ (deux personnes) they're both the same.

mainate /mɛnat/ *nm* mynah bird.

main-d'œuvre, *pl* **mains-d'œuvre** /mɛ̃dœvʀ/ *nf* (travailleurs, travail) labour^GB ¢; **coût de la ~** labour^GB costs (*pl*).

main-forte /mɛ̃fɔʀt/ *nf inv* **prêter ~ à qn** to come to sb's aid.

mainmise /mɛ̃miz/ *nf* **1** (domination) control (**sur** over); **avoir la ~ sur qch** to have control over sth; **2** JUR seizure.

maint, **~e** /mɛ̃, mɛ̃t/ *adj indéf* many (+ *pl*), many a (+ *sg*); **pour ~ lecteur** for many a reader, for many readers; **dans ~e famille** in many families; **~es et ~es fois** time and (time) again; **à ~es reprises** many times.

maintenance /mɛ̃tnɑ̃s/ *nf* maintenance.

maintenant /mɛ̃t(ə)nɑ̃/ *adv* now; **jusqu'à ~** up

until now; **à partir de ~** from now on; **~ que** now that; **commence dès ~** start straightaway; **c'est ~ qu'il faut planter vos rosiers** now is the time to plant your rose bushes; **imaginons ~ que** now let's imagine that; **il doit avoir fini ~** he must have finished by now; **la jeunesse de ~** the youth of today; **les mœurs de ~** today's social mores; **~ les choses se font différemment** nowadays people do things differently; **je t'ai averti, ~ tu fais ce que tu veux** I've warned you, now do what you want.

maintenir /mɛ̃t(ə)niʀ/ [36] I *vtr* **1** (faire durer) to maintain [*situation, équilibre, privilège*]; to keep [*paix, cessez-le-feu*]; to keep up [*coutumes*]; **ils ont maintenu le secret** they kept it secret; **~ les prix** to keep prices stable; **2** (soutenir) to support [*mur, cheville*]; **3** (conserver en l'état) to keep; **~ la tête hors de l'eau** to keep one's head above the water; **~ qch debout** to hold sth upright; **~ la température** to maintain the temperature; **4** (ne pas retirer) to stand by [*décision, accusation*]; **~ que** to maintain that; **~ sa candidature** (pour un emploi) to go through with one's application; POL not to withdraw one's candidacy.
II **se maintenir** *vpr* [*amélioration, tendance*] to persist; [*prix*] to remain stable; [*système politique*] to remain in force; [*monnaie*] to hold steady (**à** at); [*temps*] to hold; [*personne*] to remain in good health; **se ~ au pouvoir** to remain in power.

maintien /mɛ̃tjɛ̃/ *nm* **1** (d'état de fait, de système) maintaining; **notre but c'est le ~ des prix** our aim is to keep prices stable; **assurer le ~ de l'ordre** to maintain order; **2** (de poitrine, tête) support; **3** POL **le ~ de sa candidature est peu probable** it is unlikely that he will continue to stand GB ou run US; **4** (allure) deportment.

maire /mɛʀ/ *nm* mayor.
■ **~ adjoint** deputy mayor.

mairie /meʀi/ *nf* **1** (administration) GÉN town council GB ou hall US; (dans une grande ville) city council; **être élu à la ~ de** to be elected mayor of; **2** (bureaux) town hall.

mais /mɛ/ *conj* but; **incroyable ~ vrai** strange but true; **~ ne t'inquiète donc pas!** don't you worry about it!; **il est bête, ~ bête**○! he's so incredibly stupid!; **je n'ai rien compris, ~ vraiment rien!** I understood absolutely nothing!; **'est-ce que je peux venir aussi?'—'~ oui!** 'can I come too?'—'of course!'; **~ où est-il passé?** where on earth○ has he got to?; **~ vas-tu te taire!** can't you just shut up○?; **~, vous pleurez!** good heavens, you're crying!; **~ alors, vous m'avez menti!** so you lied to me!; **~ j'y pense** now that I come to think of it; **~ dis-moi, tu le connais aussi?** so you know him too?; **il n'y a pas de ~** there are no buts about it.

maïs /mais/ *nm inv* **1** AGRIC maize GB, corn US; **2** CULIN sweetcorn; **épi de ~** corn on the cob.

maison /mɛzɔ̃/ I *adj inv* **1** (fait chez soi, comme chez soi) home-made; **2** (d'une entreprise) **notre formation ~** our very own training scheme.
II *nf* **1** (bâtisse) house; **2** (domicile familial) home; **rester à la ~** to stay at home; **elle tient la ~** she runs the house; **3** (maisonnée) household; (famille) family; **la ~ du roi** the royal household; **le fils de la ~** the son of the family; **faire la jeune fille de la ~** HUM to do the honours^GB; **gens de ~** domestic staff ¢; **c'est une ~ de fous!** it's a madhouse!; **4** (lignée) family; **~ d'Orange** House of Orange; **5** (société) firm; **avoir 15 ans de ~** to have been with the firm for 15 years; **~ d'édition** publishing house; **~ de production** production company; **~ de confiance** reliable company; **'la ~ ne fait pas crédit'** 'no credit given'; **6** (en astrologie) house.
■ **~ d'arrêt** prison; **~ bourgeoise** *imposing town house*; **~ de campagne** house in the country; **~ close** brothel; **~ de correction** institution for young offenders; **~ de la culture** ~ community arts centre^GB; **~ des jeunes et de la culture**, MJC ~ youth club; **~ de jeu** gaming house; **~ maternelle** home for single mothers; **~ mère** (siège) headquarters (*pl*); (établissement principal)

main branch; **~ de passe** brothel; **~ de poupée** doll's GB ou doll US house; **~ de retraite** old people's ou retirement home; **~ de santé** nursing home; **la Maison Blanche** the White House.
IDIOMES **c'est gros comme une ~**○ it sticks out a mile; **avoir un pied dans la ~** to have a foot in the door; **c'est la ~ du bon Dieu** it's open house.

maisonnée /mɛzɔne/ nf GÉN household; (famille) family.

maître, -esse[1] /mɛtʀ, ɛs/ ▶ 284 I adj 1 (en contrôle) **être ~ de soi** (calme) to have self-control; **être ~ de faire** to be free to do; **être ~ de ses émotions** to keep one's emotions under control; **être ~ chez soi** to be master in one's own house; **être ~ de son (propre) destin** to be master of one's destiny; **rester ~ de la décision** to retain control over the decision; **être ~ de son véhicule** to be in control of one's vehicle; **se rendre ~ d'une ville** to take over a city; **2** (principal) **idée maîtresse** key idea; **~ mot** catchword; **~ ouvrage** or **œuvre maîtresse** magnum opus; **qualité maîtresse** main quality.
II nm,f **1** SCOL teacher; **2** (de maison) master/mistress; **3** (d'animal) owner; **un chien et son ~** a dog and its master.
III nm **1** (dirigeant) **être (le) seul ~ à bord** LIT, FIG to be in sole command; **être le ~ du pays** to rule the country; **être son propre ~** to be one's own master/mistress; **régner en ~ absolu** to reign supreme (**sur** over); **être le ~ du jeu** to have the upper hand; **2** (expert) **tu es un ~** you're an expert; **Hitchcock, le ~ du suspense** Hitchcock, the master of suspense; **être passé ~ dans l'art de faire** to be a past master at doing; **en ~** masterfully; **de main de ~** in a masterly fashion; **coup de ~** masterstroke; ▶ **grand**; **3** (guide, enseignant) master; **4** ART, LITTÉRAT master; **5** (titre) Maître; **6** JEUX **être ~ à carreau** to hold the master card in diamonds.
■ **~ d'armes** SPORT fencing instructor; **~ d'hôtel** maître d'hôtel GB, maître d' US; **~ d'œuvre** CONSTR project manager; **~ d'ouvrage** (privé) employer; (public) contracting authority; **~ à penser** mentor; **maîtresse femme** strong-minded woman.
IDIOMES **trouver son ~** to meet one's match; **nul ne peut servir deux ~s** a man cannot serve two masters.

maître-assistant, ~e, mpl **maîtres-assistants** /mɛtʀasistɑ̃, ɑ̃t/ nm,f UNIV ~ senior lecturer GB, senior instructor US.

maître-autel, pl **maîtres-autels** /mɛtʀotɛl/ nm high altar.

maître-chanteur, pl **maîtres-chanteurs** /mɛtʀəʃɑ̃tœʀ/ nm blackmailer.

maître-chien, pl **maîtres-chiens** /mɛtʀəʃjɛ̃/ nm dog-handler.

maître-nageur, pl **maîtres-nageurs** /mɛtʀənaʒœʀ/ ▶ 374 nm (enseignant) swimming instructor; (surveillant) pool attendant.
■ **~ sauveteur** lifeguard.

maîtresse[2] /mɛtʀɛs/ I adj f ▶ **maître** I.
II nf (amante) mistress.

maîtrise /mɛtʀiz/ nf **1** (virtuosité) mastery ¢; **avec ~** masterfully; **2** (connaissance approfondie) perfect command; **3** (calme) **~ (de soi)** self-control ¢; **4** (contrôle) control; **5** (exploitation) harnessing; **~ de l'atome** harnessing of nuclear energy; **6** MIL (domination) supremacy; **7** UNIV master's degree.

maîtriser /mɛtʀize/ [1] I vtr **1** (contenir) to control [sentiment, rire, personne]; to get [sth] under control [épidémie]; to bring [sth] under control [incendie]; to overcome [adversaire]; to handle [problème]; **2** (connaître parfaitement) to master [langue, technique].
II **se maîtriser** vpr to have self-control; **ne plus se ~** to have lost one's self-control.

maïzena® /maizena/ nf cornflour.

majesté /maʒɛste/ nf majesty; **un air de ~** an air of dignity; **sa Majesté** His/Her Majesty.

majestueux, -euse /maʒɛstɥø, øz/ adj [bâtiment, avenue] majestic; [personne, démarche] stately.

majeur, ~e /maʒœʀ/ I adj **1 être ~** to be over 18 ou of age JUR; **elle sera ~e en mai** she will be 18 in May ou come of age in May; **2** (le plus important) [cause, défi] main, major; **un problème ~** a major problem; **le problème ~** the main problem; **en ~e partie** for the most part; **3** MUS major.
II nm (doigt) middle finger.

Majeur /maʒœʀ/ ▶ 335 npr **le lac ~** Lake Maggiore.

major /maʒɔʀ/ nm **1** UNIV **sortir ~ de sa promotion** to come first in one's year; **2** ▶ 284 MIL (dans l'armée de terre, de l'air) French rank above that of warrant officer GB ou chief warrant officer US; (dans la marine) French rank above that of fleet chief petty officer GB ou chief warrant officer US.

majoration /maʒɔʀasjɔ̃/ nf increase.

majordome /maʒɔʀdɔm/ nm butler, majordomo.

majorer /maʒɔʀe/ [1] vtr to increase.

majorette /maʒɔʀɛt/ nf majorette.

majoritaire /maʒɔʀitɛʀ/ adj majority (épith).

majoritairement /maʒɔʀitɛʀmɑ̃/ adv **1** (à la majorité) [décider] by a majority (vote); **2** (en majorité) **province ~ catholique** predominantly Catholic province.

majorité /maʒɔʀite/ nf **1** (dans un vote) majority; **avoir la ~** to have a majority; **la ~ silencieuse** the silent majority; **2** (des gens, choses) majority; **la ~ de la population** most of the population; **ils sont en ~** they are in the majority; **ce sont, en ~, des enfants** they are, for the most part, children; **3** (parti majoritaire) **la ~** the government, the party in power.

majuscule /maʒyskyl/ I adj capital.
II nf capital (letter).

mal, mpl **maux** /mal, mo/ I adj inv **1** (répréhensible) wrong; **qu'a-t-elle fait de ~?** what has she done wrong?; **2** (mauvais) bad; **ce ne serait pas ~ de déménager** it wouldn't be a bad idea to move out; ▶ **an**; **3**○ **un film pas ~** a rather good film; **elle est pas ~** (physiquement) she's rather good looking.
II nm **1** (peine) trouble, difficulty; **sans ~** easily; **avoir du ~ à faire** to have trouble doing; **se donner beaucoup de ~ pour qn** to go to a great deal of trouble on sb's account; **ne te donne pas ce ~!** don't bother!; **donne-toi un peu de ~!** make some effort!; **2** ▶ 196 (douleur) pain; **faire ~** LIT, FIG to hurt; **se faire ~** to hurt oneself; **j'ai ~** it hurts; **avoir ~ partout** to ache all over; **elle avait très ~** she was in pain; **ces bottes me font ~ aux pieds** these boots hurt my feet; **avoir ~ à la gorge** to have a sore throat; **j'ai ~ aux yeux** my eyes are sore; **ça me fait ~ au ventre** LIT it gives me a stomach-ache; **3** (maladie) illness, disease; **~ sans gravité** minor illness; **~ incurable** incurable disease; **tu vas attraper du ~**○ you'll catch something; ▶ **remède, patience**; **4** (manque) **être en ~ d'inspiration** to be short of inspiration; **être en ~ d'affection** to be lacking in affection; **5** (dommage) harm; **le ~ est fait** the harm is done; **faire du ~ à** (durablement) to harm; (momentanément) to hurt [personne, économie]; **il n'y a pas de ~** (formule de politesse) there's no harm done ; **une douche ne te ferait pas de ~** HUM a shower wouldn't do you any harm; **mettre à ~ qch** to damage sth; **6** (calamité) **qu'elle parte, est-ce vraiment un ~?** is it really a bad thing that she is leaving?; **un ~ à combattre** an evil that must be fought; **7** (méchanceté) **penser à ~** to have evil intentions; **sans penser à ~** without meaning any harm; **dire du ~ de qn** to speak ill of sb; **8** PHILOS, RELIG evil.
III adv **1** (avec incompétence) [fait, écrit] badly; **elle travaille ~** her work isn't good; **elle joue ~** (maintenant) she's playing badly; (en général) she's not a good player; **s'y prendre ~ avec qn** to deal with sb the wrong way; ▶ **étreindre; 2** (de manière défectueuse) **~ fonctionner** not to work properly; **elle est ~ en point** she's not too good; (très grave) she's in a bad way; **dire quelque chose ~ à propos** to make an inappropriate remark; **3** (difficilement) **on voit ~ comment** it's difficult to see how; **marcher ~** [personne] to walk with difficulty; **4** (insuffisamment)

[*éclairé, payé*] poorly; **je t'entends ~** I can't hear you very well; **~ entretenu** neglected; ▶**cordonnier**; **5** (sans goût) [*s'habiller*] badly; **6** (de manière erronée) [*diagnostiqué, adressé*] wrongly; **j'avais ~ compris** I had misunderstood; **~ informé** ill- informed; **7** (défavorablement) **aller ~** [*personne*] not to be well; [*affaires*] to go badly; [*vêtement*] not to fit well; **se trouver ~** to faint; **être ~** (assis or couché) not to be comfortable; **être au plus ~** to be critically ill; **ne le prenez pas ~** don't take it badly on the wrong way; **être ~ avec qn** to be on bad terms with sb; **se mettre ~ avec qn** to fall out with sb; **8** (de manière critiquable) [*se conduire*] badly; **~ faire** to do wrong; **se tenir ~** (grossièrement) to have bad manners; (voûté) to have a bad posture; **il serait ~ venu de faire** it would be unseemly to do; ▶**acquis**.
IV pas mal○ *loc adv* (beaucoup) **il a pas ~ bu** he's had quite a lot to drink; **elle a pas ~ d'amis** she has quite a few friends; **il est pas ~ violent** he's rather violent.
■ **~ de l'air** airsickness; **~ des grands ensembles** *social problems attendant on high-density housing*; **~ de mer** seasickness; **avoir le ~ de mer** (ponctuellement) to feel seasick; (généralement) to suffer from seasickness; **~ du pays** homesickness; **avoir le ~ du pays** to feel homesick; **~ du siècle** world-weariness; **~ des transports** travel sickness; **avoir le ~ des transports** to be prone to travel sickness.
IDIOMES **ça me ferait ~**○ (d'étonnement) I'd be amazed; (d'écœurement) it would really piss me off○; **entre** or **de deux maux il faut choisir le moindre** PROV it's a matter of choosing the lesser of two evils.

Malacca /malaka/ *npr* **presqu'île de ~** Malay peninsula.

malade /malad/ **I** *adj* **1** [*personne*] ill, sick; [*animal*] sick; [*plante*] diseased; **tomber ~** to fall ill ou sick, to get sick US; **être ~ en voiture/en avion** to get carsick/airsick; **j'en suis ~**○ FIG it makes me sick; **~ de peur** sick with fear; **être ~ d'inquiétude** to be worried sick; **se faire porter ~** to report sick; **2** [*poumons, œil*] diseased; [*dent*] bad; **3**○ (fou) **être ~ (de la tête)** to be crazy.
II *nmf* GÉN sick man/woman; (dans un cadre médical) patient; **les ~s** the sick (+ *v pl*), the patients.
■ **~ imaginaire** hypochondriac; **~ mental** mentally ill person; **les ~s mentaux** the mentally ill (+ *v pl*); **c'est un ~ mental** he's mentally ill.
IDIOMES **être ~ comme un chien**○ to be as sick as a dog.

maladie /maladi/ ▶**196** *nf* **1** (d'un malade) illness, disease; **pendant sa longue ~** during his/her long illness; **~s contagieuses** contagious diseases; **~ des poumons** lung disease; **une ~ mentale** a mental illness; **il va en faire une ~**○ FIG he'll have a fit○; **2** (de végétal, d'animal) disease; **3**○ (manie) **avoir la ~ du rangement** to have a mania for tidiness.
■ **~ honteuse** MÉD† venereal disease; FIG shameful disease; **~ professionnelle** occupational disease; **~ sexuellement transmissible, MST** sexually transmitted disease, STD.

maladif, -ive /maladif, iv/ *adj* [*enfant, air*] sickly; [*jalousie*] pathological; **être d'une pâleur maladive** to be unhealthily pale.

maladresse /maladRES/ *nf* **1** (manque d'adresse) clumsiness; **2** (manque de tact) tactlessness; **il a agi avec ~ envers elle** he was tactless with her; **3** (manque d'aisance) awkwardness; **avec ~** awkwardly; **4** (erreur) (de personne) mistake; (dans un texte) **des ~s de style** infelicities of style; **5** (bévue) blunder.

maladroit, ~e /maladRwa, wat/ **I** *adj* **1** (malhabile) [*personne, geste, traduction*] clumsy; [*écriture*] faltering; **2** (sans tact) tactless.
II *nm,f* (personne gauche) clumsy person; (gaffeur) tactless person.

maladroitement /maladRwatmã/ *adv* (sans adresse) clumsily; (sans tact) tactlessly; (sans aisance) awkwardly; (sans finesse) ineptly.

mal-aimé, ~e, *mpl* **~s** /malɛme/ *adj* **être ~** to be starved of affection.

malais, ~e[1] /malɛ, ɛz/ ▶**394**, **338** **I** *adj* Malay.
II *nm* Malay.

malaise[2] /malɛz/ *nm* **1** MÉD dizzy turn; **avoir un ~** to feel faint; **2** (gêne) uneasiness; **il y a (comme) un ~**○ there's a bit of a problem; **3** (état de crise) unrest (**chez** among).
■ **~ cardiaque** mild heart attack.

malaisé, ~e /malɛze/ *adj* difficult (**à faire, de faire** to do).

malapprist†, ~e /malapRi, iz/ *nm,f* lout.

malaria /malaRja/ ▶**196** *nf* malaria.

malawien, -ienne /malawjẽ, ɛn/ ▶**394** *adj* Malawian.

malaxer /malakse/ [1] *vtr* **1** (pétrir) to cream [*beurre*]; to knead [*pâte*]; **2** (mélanger) to mix.

malchance /malʃãs/ *nf* bad luck, misfortune; **jouer de ~** to be dogged by bad luck; **par ~** as ill luck would have it.

malchanceux, -euse /malʃãsø, øz/ *adj* unlucky.

maldonne /maldɔn/ *nf* (aux cartes) misdeal; (malentendu) misunderstanding.

mâle /mɑl/ **I** *adj* **1** BIOL, BOT male; **2** ZOOL GÉN male; [*éléphant, baleine*] bull; [*antilope, lièvre, lapin*] buck; [*moineau, perroquet*] cock; **cygne ~** cob; **canard ~** drake; **3** ÉLECTROTECH [*fiche, prise*] male; **4** (viril) manly.
II *nm* **1** ZOOL male; **2** (homme viril) HUM he-man○.

malédiction /malediksjɔ̃/ *nf* curse; **la ~ pèse sur eux** there's a curse on them.

maléfice /malefis/ *nm* evil spell.

maléfique /malefik/ *adj* evil.

malencontreusement /malãkɔ̃tRøzmã/ *adv* [*survenir*] inopportunely; [*annoncer*] inappropriately; [*oublier*] unfortunately.

malencontreux, -euse /malãkɔ̃tRø, øz/ *adj* unfortunate.

malentendant, ~e /malãtãdã, ãt/ **I** *adj* **être ~** to be hard of hearing.
II *nm,f* **les ~s** the hearing-impaired.

malentendu /malãtãdy/ *nm* misunderstanding.

malfaçon /malfasɔ̃/ *nf* defect (*caused by bad workmanship*).

malfaisant, ~e /malfəzã, ãt/ *adj* [*personne*] evil; [*influence, idéologie*] harmful.

malfaiteur /malfɛtœR/ *nm* criminal.

malformation /malfɔRmasjɔ̃/ *nf* malformation.

malgache /malgaʃ/ ▶**394**, **338** *adj, nm* Malagasy.

malgré /malgRe/ *prép* in spite of, despite; **~ les apparences** in spite of appearances; **elle l'a épousé ~ son âge** she married him in spite of his age; **~ le fait que** in spite of ou despite the fact that; **~ d'incontestables progrès** although there has been clear progress; **~ l'absence de liens diplomatiques entre les deux pays** although the two countries have no diplomatic ties; **~ cela, ~ tout** nevertheless; **~ qn** against sb's wishes; **(presque) ~ soi** reluctantly; **j'ai entendu leur conversation ~ moi** I overheard their conversation without wishing to ou by accident.

malhabile /malabil/ *adj* clumsy.

malheur /malœR/ *nm* **1** (adversité) adversity, misfortune; **tomber dans le ~** to be struck by misfortune; **faire le ~ de qn** to bring sb nothing but unhappiness; ▶**bonheur**; **2** (coup du sort) misfortune; (grave) tragedy; (accident) accident; **une série de ~s** a series of misfortunes; **le grand ~ de ma jeunesse** the great tragedy of my youth; **un ~ est si vite arrivé!** accidents can so easily happen!; **il leur arrivera ~!** something terrible will happen to them!; **raconter ses ~s à qn** to tell sb one's troubles; **le grand ~!** IRON so what!; **3** (malchance) misfortune; **ceux qui ont le ~ de faire** those who are unfortunate enough to do; **j'ai eu le ~ de le leur dire** I made the mistake of telling them; **pour mon ~** unfortunately for me; **par ~, le ~ a voulu que**

as bad ou ill luck would have it; **si par ~ la guerre éclatait** if, God forbid, war should break out; **porter ~** to be ou bring bad luck; **le ~, c'est que...** the trouble is,...
IDIOMES **il va faire un ~**⚬ (avoir du succès) he'll be a sensation; (faire un éclat) he'll cause a scene; **un ~ n'arrive jamais seul** PROV it never rains but it pours; **à quelque chose ~ est bon** PROV every cloud has a silver lining PROV.

malheureusement /malœʀøzmɑ̃/ *adv* unfortunately.

malheureux, -euse /malœʀø, øz/ **I** *adj* **1** (pas heureux) unhappy; (plus fort) miserable; **ne prends pas cet air ~!** don't look so miserable; **si c'est pas ~ de voir...** isn't it awful to see...; **2** (à plaindre) [*victime*] unfortunate; **3** (malchanceux) [*personne*] unlucky (**en** in); [*coïncidence*] unfortunate; [*passion*] ill-fated; **4** (regrettable) [*mot, geste, choix*] unfortunate; **c'est ~ que** it's a pity ou shame that; **5**⚬ (négligeable) paltry, pathetic; **pour trois ~ francs** for a paltry three francs; **seulement dix ~ visiteurs** only a pathetic ten visitors.
II *nm,f* **1** (personne peu chanceuse) **le ~!** poor man!; **ne fais pas cela, malheureuse!** don't do that, for heaven's sake!; **2** (indigent) poor person; **les ~** the poor.
IDIOMES **être ~ comme les pierres** to be as miserable as sin.

malhonnête /malɔnɛt/ **I** *adj* **1** (indélicat) dishonest; **2** (inconvenant) [*proposition*] improper.
II *nmf* **1** (personne indélicate) dishonest person; **2** (personne impolie) rude person.

malhonnêteté /malɔnɛtte/ *nf* dishonesty.

malice /malis/ *nf* **1** (taquinerie) mischief; **avec ~** mischievously; **2†** (malveillance) malice; **être sans ~** to be harmless.

malicieux, -ieuse /malisjø, øz/ *adj* mischievous.

malin, maligne /malɛ̃, maliɲ/ **I** *adj* **1** (intelligent) clever; **elle n'est pas très maligne** she isn't very bright; **j'ai eu l'air ~!** IRON I looked like a total fool!; **2**⚬ (difficile) **ce n'est pas bien ~** it's not exactly difficult; **3** (méchant) **prendre un ~ plaisir à faire** to take malicious pleasure in doing; **4** MÉD [*tumeur*] malignant.
II *nm,f* **1** (personne rusée) **c'est un ~** he's a crafty one; **faire le** ou **son ~**⚬ to show off; **jouer au plus ~**⚬ to play the wise guy⚬; **2** LITTÉRAT **le Malin** Satan, the Devil.
IDIOMES **à ~, ~ et demi** PROV there's always someone who will outwit you.

malingre /malɛ̃gʀ/ *adj* puny.

malintentionné, ~e /malɛ̃tɑ̃sjɔne/ *adj* malicious.

malle /mal/ *nf* **1** (coffre, valise) trunk; **se faire la ~**⚬ to clear off⚬; **2** AUT **~ (arrière)** boot GB, trunk US.

malléabilité /maleabilite/ *nf* malleability.

mallette /malɛt/ *nf* (pour le bureau) briefcase.

malmener /malmɔne/ [16] *vtr* **1** (maltraiter) to manhandle [*personne*]; **2** (mettre en difficulté) to give [sb] a rough ride; **3** [*auteur*] to misuse [*langue*].

malnutrition /malnytʀisjɔ̃/ *nf* malnutrition.

malodorant, ~e /malodɔʀɑ̃, ɑ̃t/ *adj* foul-smelling (épith).

malotru, ~e /malɔtʀy/ *nm,f* boor.

malouin, ~e /malwɛ̃, in/ ▶ 628 *adj* of Saint-Malo.

Malouines /malwin/ *nprfpl* **les (îles) ~** the Falklands, the Falkland Islands.

malpoli, ~e /malpɔli/ *adj* rude.

malpropre /malpʀɔpʀ/ **I** *adj* (sale) dirty.
II *nmf* **se faire renvoyer comme un ~** to be chucked out⚬.

malsain, ~e /malsɛ̃, ɛn/ *adj* LIT, FIG unhealthy.

malséant, ~e /malseɑ̃, ɑ̃t/ *adj* unseemly.

malt /malt/ *nm* malt; **de ~** malt (épith).

malthusianisme /maltyzjanism/ *nm* Malthusianism.

maltraiter /maltʀɛte/ [1] *vtr* to mistreat [*personne, animal*]; to misuse [*langue, grammaire*].

malus /malys/ *nm inv* (surprime) loaded premium.

malveillance /malvɛjɑ̃s/ *nf* **1** (antipathie) malice; **2** (intention de nuire) malicious intent; **incendie dû à la ~** arson.

malveillant, ~e /malvɛjɑ̃, ɑ̃t/ *adj* malicious.

malvenu, ~e /malvəny/ *adj* [*propos, intervention*] out of place (*jamais épith*); **tu es ~ de te plaindre** you're in no position to complain.

malversation /malvɛʀsasjɔ̃/ *nf* GÉN malpractice ₡; FIN embezzlement ₡.

malvoyant, ~e /malvwajɑ̃, ɑ̃t/ *nmf* partially sighted person.

maman /mamɑ̃/ *nf* mum⚬ GB, mom⚬ US, mummy⚬ GB, mommy⚬ US, mother.

mamelle /mamɛl/ *nf* ZOOL GÉN teat; (pis) udder.

mamelon /mamlɔ̃/ *nm* **1** ANAT nipple; **2** GÉOG hillock.

mamie /mami/ *nf* (grand-mère) granny⚬, grandma⚬.

mammaire /mamɛʀ/ *adj* mammary.

mammectomie /mamɛktɔmi/ *nf* mastectomy.

mammifère /mamifɛʀ/ *nm* mammal.

mammographie /mamɔgʀafi/ *nf* mammography.

mammouth /mamut/ *nm* mammoth.

mam'selle⚬, **mam'zelle**⚬ /mamzɛl/ *nf* miss.

mamy = **mamie**.

manager[1] /manaʒœʀ/ = **manageur**.

manager[2] /manaʒe/ [13] *vtr* to manage.

manageur /manaʒœʀ/ ▶ 374 *nm* manager.

manant† /manɑ̃/ *nm* HIST (paysan) peasant.

manche[1] /mɑ̃ʃ/ *nm* **1** (d'outil) handle; (de violon) neck; ▶ **cognée**; **2**⚬ (maladroit) clumsy idiot; **jouer comme un ~** to be a hopeless player; **il s'y est pris comme un ~** he set about it in a clumsy fashion.
■ **~ à balai** LIT broomhandle; (de sorcière) broomstick; AVIAT joystick.

manche[2] /mɑ̃ʃ/ *nf* **1** (de vêtement) sleeve; **à ~s longues** long-sleeved; **sans ~s** sleeveless; **2** SPORT round; (aux cartes) hand; (au bridge) game; **3**⚬ (quête) **faire la ~** [*mendiant*] to beg.
IDIOMES **avoir qn dans la ~** to have sb in one's pocket; **se faire tirer par la ~** to need coaxing; **c'est une autre paire de ~s**⚬ it's a different ball game⚬.

Manche /mɑ̃ʃ/ *nprf* **1** ▶ 407 (mer) **la ~** the (English) Channel; **le tunnel sous la ~** the Channel tunnel; **2** ▶ 509 (département) **la ~** the Manche.

manchette /mɑ̃ʃɛt/ *nf* **1** (de chemise) double cuff; (de protection) oversleeve; (garniture) cuff; **2** (titre) headline.

manchon /mɑ̃ʃɔ̃/ *nm* muff.

manchot, -otte /mɑ̃ʃo, ɔt/ **I** *adj* (d'un bras) one-armed; (d'une main) one-handed; **il est ~** (d'un bras) he's only got one arm; **ne pas être ~**⚬ to be pretty good with one's hands⚬.
II *nm,f* (personne) (d'un bras) one-armed person; (d'une main) one-handed person.
III *nm* ZOOL penguin.

mandarin /mɑ̃daʀɛ̃/ *nm* **1** HIST, FIG mandarin; **2** ▶ 338 LING Mandarin (Chinese).

mandarine /mɑ̃daʀin/ *nf* mandarin orange.

mandarinier /mɑ̃daʀinje/ *nm* mandarin tree.

mandat /mɑ̃da/ *nm* **1** **~ (postal)** money order; **2** (fonction, charge) term of office; **exercer son ~** to be in office; **3** (pouvoir) mandate, authorization; **donner ~ à qn de faire** to authorize sb to do.
■ **~ d'amener** summons (+ *v sg*); **~ d'arrêt** (arrest) warrant; **~ d'expulsion** (hors d'un pays) expulsion order; (hors d'une maison) eviction order; **~ international** JUR mandate; (postal) international money order; **~ de perquisition** search warrant; **~ télégraphique** telegraphic money order.

mandataire /mɑ̃datɛʀ/ *nmf* **1** JUR proxy; **2** (représentant) representative; COMM agent.

mandat-carte, *pl* **mandats-cartes** /mɑ̃dakaʀt/ *nm* postal order (*in the form of a postcard*).

mandater /mɑ̃date/ [1] *vtr* to appoint [sb] as one's representative [*personne*]; (pour une mission) to give a mandate to.

mandat-lettre, *pl* **mandats-lettres** /mɑ̃dalɛtʀ/ *nm* postal order.

mandchou, **~e** /mɑ̃dʃu/ **I** *adj* Manchu.

II ▶ 338 | *nm* LING Manchu.

mandibule /mɑ̃dibyl/ *nf* **1** ANAT, ZOOL mandible; **2**○ (mâchoire) jaw.

mandoline /mɑ̃dɔlin/ **▶ 392 |** *nf* mandolin.

mandrin /mɑ̃dʀɛ̃/ *nm* (de perceuse) chuck.

manège /manɛʒ/ *nm* **1** (de fête foraine) merry-go-round; **faire un tour de ~** to have a ride on the merry-go-round; **2** (centre équestre) riding school; (piste) **~** (**couvert**) indoor school *ou* arena; **3** (manœuvre habile) (little) trick, (little) game; **j'ai bien observé ton ~** I know what you are up to.

mânes /mɑn/ *nmpl* manes.

manette /manɛt/ *nf* **1** GÉN lever; (de jeu) joystick; **~ des gaz** throttle; **2** FIG (commande) **~s** controls.

manganèse /mɑ̃ganɛz/ *nm* manganese.

mangeable /mɑ̃ʒabl/ *adj* edible.

mangeoire /mɑ̃ʒwaʀ/ *nf* (pour chevaux, bovins) manger; (pour porcs) trough; (pour poules) feeding trough; (pour oiseaux) feeding tray.

manger /mɑ̃ʒe/ [13] **I** *vtr* **1** (consommer) to eat; **il n'y a rien à ~ dans la maison** there's no food in the house; **qu'est-ce qu'on mange à midi?** what's for lunch?; **je ne vais pas te ~**○! FIG I won't eat you○!; **▶ enragé**, **grive**, **soupe**; **2** (dépenser) to use up [*économies*]; to go through [*héritage*]; [*activité*] to take up [*temps*]; **3** (attaquer) [*rouille*, *acide*] to eat away [*métal*]; [*mites*] to eat [*laine*]; **être mangé aux** *ou* **par les rats** to be gnawed by rats; **se faire ~ par les moustiques** to be eaten alive by mosquitoes; **se faire ~ par son concurrent** to be devoured by one's competitor; **4** (mal articuler) **~ ses mots** to mumble.

II *vi* (se nourrir) to eat; **ils viendront te ~ dans la main** LIT, FIG you'll have them eating out of your hand; **~ à sa faim** to eat one's fill; **donner à ~ à** to feed [*bébé*]; to give [sb] something to eat [*pauvre*]; **faire à ~ to cook**; **~ froid** (un plat refroidi) to eat [sth] cold; (un repas froid) to have a cold meal; **inviter qn à ~** to invite sb for a meal; **je vous invite à ~ dimanche midi** (au restaurant) let me take you to lunch on Sunday; (chez soi) come to lunch on Sunday; **~ chinois** to have a Chinese meal; **~ au restaurant** to eat out; **on mange mal ici** the food is not good here.

III se manger *vpr* **le gaspacho se mange froid** gazpacho is served cold; **le poulet peut se ~ avec les doigts** you can eat chicken with your fingers; **▶ loup**.

IDIOMES **~ la consigne** to forget one's orders.

mangeur, **-euse** /mɑ̃ʒœʀ, øz/ *nm,f* **bon/gros ~** good/big eater.

■ **mangeuse d'hommes** man-eater.

mangouste /mɑ̃gust/ *nf* **1** ZOOL mongoose; **2** BOT mangosteen.

mangue /mɑ̃g/ *nf* mango.

manguier /mɑ̃gje/ *nm* mango (tree).

maniabilité /manjabilite/ *nf* (de véhicule) manoeuvrability GB, maneuverability US; **notre voiture allie la ~ à la puissance** our car is both easy to handle and powerful.

maniable /manjabl/ *adj* [*objet*, *voiture*] easy to handle (*jamais épith*).

maniaco-dépressif, **-ive**, *mpl* **~s** /manjakodepʀɛsif, iv/ *adj*, *nm,f* manic-depressive.

maniaque /manjak/ **I** *adj* **1** (tatillon) particular, fussy; (qui a des marottes) cranky; **2** MÉD manic.

II *nmf* **1** (tatillon) fusspot GB, fussbudget US; (personne excentrique) crank; (personne tatillonne) fusspot GB, fussbudget US; **2** (fanatique) fanatic; **c'est un ~ de l'ordre** he's obsessive about tidiness; **3** (détraqué) maniac.

■ **~ sexuel** sex maniac.

maniaquerie /manjakʀi/ *nf* (caractère) fussiness.

manichéen, **-éenne** /manikeɛ̃, ɛn/ *adj* PHILOS, RELIG Manichean; FIG dualistic.

manichéisme /manikeism/ *nm* Manicheism.

manie /mani/ *nf* **1** (habitude) habit (**de faire** of doing); **avoir la ~ de tout garder** to be a compulsive hoarder; **c'est une vraie ~** it's an absolute obsession; **2** (marotte) quirk, idiosyncrasy; **3** MÉD mania; **~ de la persécution** persecution mania.

maniement /manimɑ̃/ *nm* **1** (manipulation) GÉN handling; (de machine) operation; (de langue) command; **d'un ~ aisé** [*outil*] easy to handle; [*machine*] easy to operate; **2** (gestion) management.

■ **~ d'armes** MIL arms drill.

manier /manje/ [2] **I** *vtr* GÉN to handle; **bien ~ le pinceau** FIG to be a good painter.

II se manier *vpr* **se ~ aisément** [*outil*] to be easy to handle; [*voiture*] to handle well.

IDIOMES **~ la fourchette avec entrain**○ HUM to have a hearty appetite; **il sait ~ la brosse à reluire**○ he's good at buttering people up○.

manière /manjɛʀ/ **I** *nf* **1** (façon) way; **d'une ~ ou d'une autre** in one way or another; **d'une certaine ~** in a way; **la bonne ~ de s'y prendre** the right way to go about it; **leur ~ de vivre/penser** their way of life/thinking; **leur ~ d'être** the way they are; **de toutes les ~s possibles** in every possible way; **de telle ~ que** in such a way that; **de ~ à faire** so as to do; **en aucune ~** in no way; **de la même ~** [*travailler*] in the same way; [*agir*] the same way; **à ma ~** my (own) way; **de ~ décisive** in a decisive way; **de quelle ~ peut-on résoudre le problème?** how can one solve the problem?; **de toute ~**, **de toutes ~s** anyway, in any case; **2** (méthode) **employer la ~ forte** to use strong-arm tactics; **il ne reste plus que la ~ forte** there's no alternative but to use force; **utiliser la ~ douce** to use kid gloves; **3** (style) **à la ~ de qn/qch** in the style of sb/sth.

II manières *nfpl* **1** (savoir-vivre) manners; **bonnes/mauvaises ~s** good/bad manners; **il n'a pas de ~s** he has no manners; **qu'est-ce que c'est que ces ~s!** what manners!; **je vais t'apprendre les bonnes ~s** I'll teach you some manners; **2** (excès de politesse) **faire des ~s** to stand on ceremony.

maniéré, **~e** /manjeʀe/ *adj* PEJ affected.

maniérisme /manjeʀism/ *nm* ART mannerism.

manifestant, **~e** /manifɛstɑ̃, ɑ̃t/ *nm,f* demonstrator.

manifestation /manifɛstasjɔ̃/ *nf* **1** (pour protester) demonstration (**contre** against; **pour** for); **2** (réunion) event; **~s sportives** sporting events; **3** (de phénomène) appearance; **4** (de sentiment) expression, manifestation.

■ **~ silencieuse** vigil; **~ de soutien** rally (**en faveur de** for).

manifeste /manifɛst/ **I** *adj* obvious, manifest.

II *nm* ART, POL manifesto.

manifester /manifɛste/ [1] **I** *vtr* (faire connaître) to show, to demonstrate [*soutien*]; to show [*curiosité*, *sentiment*, *qualité*]; (exprimer) to express [*désir*, *crainte*]; **~ de l'humeur** to show irritation; **~ sa présence** to make one's presence known.

II *vi* to demonstrate.

III se manifester *vpr* **1** (devenir apparent) [*symptôme*] to manifest itself; [*phénomène*] to appear; [*maladie*, *inquiétude*] to show itself; **une tendance au changement se manifeste** a tendency for change can be seen; **2** (faire signe) **il ne s'est pas encore manifesté** (en personne) there is still no sign of him; (par lettre, téléphone) we still haven't heard from him; **3** (répondre à un appel) [*témoin*] to come forward.

manigance /manigɑ̃s/ *nf* little scheme.

manigancer /manigɑ̃se/ [12] *vtr* **~ quelque chose** to be up to something; **qu'est-ce qu'elle manigance encore?** what's she up to now?; **~ un mauvais coup** to hatch up a scheme.

manille /manij/ *nf* **▶ 329 |** JEUX manille.

manipulateur, **-trice** /manipylatœʀ, tʀis/ *nm,f*

1 ▶374⌋ (technicien) technician; **2** (provocateur) PEJ manipulator.

manipulation /manipylasjɔ̃/ *nf* **1** (d'objet, de produit) handling; **2** (d'opinion, de personne) manipulation *₵*; **~s électorales** electoral rigging *₵*; **3** MÉD manipulation *₵*; **4** (sur une substance) operation; SCOL, UNIV (expérience) experiment.

manipuler /manipyle/ [1] *vtr* **1** (avec les mains) to handle [*objet, véhicule*]; to manipulate [*bouton*]; **2** (utiliser) to handle [*chiffres*]; to use [*mots*]; **3** (falsifier) to massage [*données, chiffres*]; **4** (influencer) to manipulate [*opinion, personne*]; **5** THÉÂT to operate [*marionnettes*].

manitou /manitu/ *nm* **1**○ FIG big noise○; **un grand ~ de la finance** a big noise in the financial world; **2** RELIG manitou.

manivelle /manivɛl/ *nf* handle.

IDIOMES **donner le premier tour de ~** CIN to start filming.

manne /man/ *nf* (aubaine) godsend; **~ céleste** manna from Heaven.

mannequin /mankɛ̃/ *nm* **1** ▶374⌋ (de mode) model; **2** (de vitrine, musée) dummy.

manœuvre¹ /manœvʀ/ ▶374⌋ *nm* unskilled worker.

manœuvre² /manœvʀ/ *nf* **1** (avec véhicule) (opération) manoeuvre GB, maneuver US; (maniement) manoeuvring GB, maneuvering US; **effectuer** ou **faire une ~** to carry out a manoeuvre GB ou maneuver US; **fausse ~** mistake; ▶**faux¹**; **2** (d'appareil, de dispositif) operation; **3** (pour obtenir quelque chose) tactic; **~s électorales** electoral tactics; **4** MIL manoeuvre GB, maneuver US; **partir en ~s** to go on manoeuvres GB ou maneuvers US; **champ de ~s** military training area; **5** RAIL (mouvement) shunting GB, switching US.

manœuvrer /manœvʀe/ [1] **I** *vtr* **1** (déplacer) to manoeuvre GB, to maneuver US [*véhicule*]; **2** (actionner) to operate [*dispositif, machine*]; **3** (manipuler) to manipulate [*personne*].

II *vi* **j'ai dû ~ pour sortir la voiture** I had to carry out a tricky manoeuvre GB ou maneuver US to get the car out.

manoir /manwaʀ/ *nm* manor (house).

manomètre /manɔmɛtʀ/ *nm* pressure gauge.

manouche○ /manuʃ/ *nmf* gypsy.

manquant, ~e /mɑ̃kɑ̃, ɑ̃t/ *adj* missing.

manque /mɑ̃k/ **I** *nm* **1** (insuffisance) GÉN lack (**de** of); (de personnel) shortage (**de** of); **par ~ de ressources** for ou through lack of resources; **quel ~ de chance!** what bad luck!; **~ de chance, il est tombé malade** just his luck, he fell ill; **2** (lacune) gap; **3** (privation) **ressentir un ~** to feel an emptiness; **être en ~ d'affection** to be in need of affection; **être en (état de) ~** [*drogué*] to be suffering from withdrawal symptoms.

II à la manque○ *loc adj* **un héros à la ~** a would-be hero; **une idée à la ~** a useless idea.

■ **~ à gagner** loss of earnings.

manqué, ~e /mɑ̃ke/ **I** *pp* ▶**manquer**.

II *pp adj* [*tentative*] failed; [*occasion*] missed.

III *adj* **c'est un poète ~** he should have been a poet.

manquement /mɑ̃kmɑ̃/ *nm* **~ à la discipline** breach of discipline; **~ à une promesse** failure to keep a promise.

manquer /mɑ̃ke/ [1] **I** *vtr* **1** (ne pas atteindre, ne pas voir) to miss [*cible, spectacle, train, personne*]; **~ l'école** to miss school; **un film à ne pas ~** a film not to be missed; **vous l'avez manquée de cinq minutes** you missed her/it by five minutes; **2** (ne pas réussir) **elle a manqué son solo** she made a mess of her solo; **ça nous a fait ~ plusieurs contrats** it has lost us several contracts; **~ son coup**○ to fail; **3**○ (ne pas sanctionner) **la prochaine fois je ne le manquerai pas** next time I won't let him get away with it.

II manquer à *vtr ind* **1 la Bretagne/ma tante me manque** I miss Brittany/my aunt; **2 ~ à ses**

promesses to fail to keep one's promises; **~ à sa parole** to break one's word.

III manquer de *vtr ind* **1** (avoir en quantité insuffisante) **~ de** to lack [*patience, argent, expérience, pratique*]; **on ne manque de rien** we don't want ou lack for anything; **ma cousine ne manque pas d'humour**GB my cousin's got a good sense of humour GB; **elle ne manque pas de charme** she's not without charm; **on manque d'air ici** it's stuffy in here; **il manque de magnésium** he has a magnesium deficiency; **2** (toujours à la forme négative) **je ne manquerai pas de vous le faire savoir** I'll be sure to let you know; **'remercie-le de ma part'—'je n'y manquerai pas'** 'thank him for me'—'I won't forget'; **et évidemment, ça n'a pas manqué**○! and sure enough that's what happened!; **3** (faillir) **il a manqué (de) casser un carreau** he almost broke a windowpane.

IV *vi* **1** (faire défaut) **trois soldats manquaient à l'appel** three soldiers were missing at roll call; **les vivres vinrent à ~** supplies ran out ou short; **ce ne sont pas les occasions qui manquent** there's no lack of opportunity; **le courage leur manqua** their courage failed them; **les mots me manquent** words fail me; **les mots me manquent pour exprimer ma joie** I can't find the words to express my joy; **ce n'est pas l'envie qui me manque de faire** it's not that I don't want to do; **2** (être absent) [*élève, personne*] to be absent.

V *v impers* **il manquait deux fourchettes** two forks were missing; **il lui manque un doigt** he's got a finger missing; **il nous manque deux joueurs pour former une équipe** we're two players short of a team; **ça manque d'animation ici!** it's not very lively here!; **il ne manquerait plus que ça**○! that would be the last straw!; **il ne manquerait plus qu'il se mette à pleuvoir** all (that) we need now is for it to start raining.

VI se manquer *vpr* **1** (soi-même) to bungle one's suicide attempt; **2** (ne pas se voir) to miss each other.

mansarde /mɑ̃saʀd/ *nf* (pièce) attic room.

mansardé, ~e /mɑ̃saʀde/ *adj* [*pièce*] attic (*épith*).

mansuétude /mɑ̃sɥetyd/ *nf* indulgence.

mante /mɑ̃t/ *nf* **~ religieuse** ZOOL praying mantis; FIG man-eater.

manteau, *pl* **~x** /mɑ̃to/ *nm* **1** (vêtement) coat; **2** (de brume, de neige) blanket.

■ **~ de cheminée** mantelpiece.

IDIOMES **sous le ~** illicitly.

mantille /mɑ̃tij/ *nf* mantilla.

manucure /manykyʀ/ **I** ▶374⌋ *nmf* (personne) manicurist.

II *nf* (soins, technique) manicure; **se faire faire une ~** to have a manicure.

manuel, -elle /manɥɛl/ **I** *adj* manual.

II *nm,f* **1** (par métier) manual worker; **2** (par goût) **c'est une manuelle** she likes working with her hands; (par don) she is good with her hands.

III *nm* SCOL textbook.

■ **~ de conversation** phrase book; **~ d'utilisation** instruction manual; **~ scolaire** school textbook.

manuellement /manɥɛlmɑ̃/ *adv* **1** TECH manually; **2** (avec les mains) [*travailler*] with one's hands.

manufacture /manyfaktyʀ/ *nf* **1** (établissement) factory; **2** (fabrication) manufacture.

manufacturer /manyfaktyʀe/ [1] *vtr* to manufacture.

manu militari /manymilitaʀi/ *adv* forcibly.

manuscrit, ~e /manyskʀi, it/ **I** *adj* handwritten.

II *nm* manuscript.

manutention /manytɑ̃sjɔ̃/ *nf* (activité) handling.

manutentionnaire /manytɑ̃sjɔnɛʀ/ ▶374⌋ *nm* warehouseman.

maoïsme /maoism/ *nm* Maoism.

maori /maɔʀi/ ▶338⌋ *nm* LING Maori.

mappemonde /mapmɔ̃d/ *nf* **1** (carte) map of the world (in two hemispheres); **2** (globe) globe.

maquereau, *pl* **~x** /makʀo/ *nm* ZOOL mackerel.

maquette /makɛt/ *nf* **1** (modèle réduit) (scale) model; **2** (grandeur nature) mock-up.

maquignon /makiɲɔ̃/ *nm* **1** LIT horse dealer; **2** PÉJ shady operator.

maquignonnage /makiɲɔnaʒ/ *nm* **1** LIT horse dealing; **2** PÉJ sharp practice.

maquillage /makijaʒ/ *nm* **1** (action) making-up; (résultat) make-up; **2** (fard) make-up.
■ **~ de théâtre** greasepaint.

maquiller /makije/ [1] **I** *vtr* **1** (farder) to make [sb/sth] up [*acteur, visage*]; **2** (déguiser) to doctor [*document, vérité*]; **~ un crime en accident** to disguise a crime as an accident.
II se maquiller *vpr* (mettre du fard) to put make-up on; (porter du fard) to wear make-up.

maquilleur, -euse /makijœʀ, øz/ ▶374| *nm,f* THÉÂT make-up artist.

maquis /maki/ *nm inv* GÉOG, HIST maquis; **prendre le ~** [*résistant*] to join the maquis; [*fuyard*] to go underground.

maquisard, ~e /makizaʀ, aʀd/ *nm,f* HIST member of the Resistance.

marabout /maʀabu/ *nm* **1** ZOOL marabou; **2** RELIG marabout.

maraîchage /maʀɛʃaʒ/ *nm* market gardening GB, truck farming US.

maraîcher, -ère /maʀɛʃe, ɛʀ/ **I** *adj* **produits ~s** market garden produce ¢ GB, truck ¢ US; **la culture maraîchère** market gardening GB, truck farming US.
II ▶374| *nm,f* market gardener GB, truck farmer US.

marais /maʀɛ/ *nm inv* marsh, swamp.
■ **~ salant** saltern.

marasme /maʀasm/ *nm* ÉCON, POL stagnation; **être dans le** or **en plein ~** to be in the doldrums.

marathon /maʀatɔ̃/ *nm* marathon.

marathonien, -ienne /maʀatɔnjɛ̃, ɛn/ *nm,f* marathon runner.

marâtre /maʀɑtʀ/ *nf* PÉJ cruel mother.

maraude /maʀod/ *nf* (pillage) pilfering; **en ~** [*taxi*] cruising for fares (*après n*); [*voyou*] on the prowl (*jamais épith*)..

marauder /maʀode/ [1] *vi* **1** (voler) to pilfer; **2** (être à l'affût) [*taxi*] to cruise for fares; [*voyou*] to prowl around.

maraudeur, -euse /maʀodœʀ, øz/ *nm,f* petty thief.

marbre /maʀbʀ/ *nm* **1** (roche) marble; **2** (plaque de meuble) marble top; (statue) marble statue; **3** (en imprimerie) **livre sur le ~** book at press.
IDIOMES **rester de ~** (impassible) to remain stony-faced; **la nouvelle les laissa de ~** they were completely unmoved by the news.

marbrer /maʀbʀe/ [1] *vtr* **1** TECH to marble [*papier, cuir*]; **2** (marquer) **le froid lui marbrait le visage** his/her face was blotchy with the cold; **peau marbrée** mottled skin; **il avait le dos marbré de coups** or **de bleus** his back was mottled with bruises; **pelage roux marbré de noir** red coat mottled with black.

marbrerie /maʀbʀəʀi/ *nf* **1** (industrie) marble industry; (travail du marbre) marble masonry; **~ funéraire** monumental masonry; **2** (atelier) marble mason's workshop.

marbrier, -ière[1] /maʀbʀije, ɛʀ/ ▶374| *nm* (ouvrier, entrepreneur) marble mason; **~ funéraire** monumental mason; **~ d'art** artist in marble.

marbrière[2] /maʀbʀijɛʀ/ *nf* marble quarry.

marbrure /maʀbʀyʀ/ *nf* (sur papier, cuir) marbling ¢; (sur la peau) blotchiness ¢; (hématomes) mottling ¢.

marc /maʀ/ *nm* marc; **~ de raisin** grape marc.
■ **~ de café** coffee grounds (*pl*).

marcassin /maʀkasɛ̃/ *nm* young wild boar.

marchand, ~e /maʀʃɑ̃, ɑ̃d/ **I** *adj* COMM [*denrée, qualité*] marketable; [*secteur, économie*] trade; [*valeur*] market.
II ▶374| *nm,f* **1** (commerçant) trader; (négociant) dealer, merchant; (dans une boutique) shopkeeper; (sur un marché) stallholder; **~ d'armes/de bestiaux**

arms/cattle dealer; **~ de soie/vins** silk/wine merchant; **jouer à la ~e** to play shops; **2** HIST merchant.
■ **~ ambulant** hawker; **~ de couleurs** ironmonger GB, hardware merchant; **~ de glaces** ice cream vendor; **~ en gros** wholesaler; **~ de journaux** (dans un magasin) newsagent; (dans la rue) newsvendor; **~ des quatre saisons** costermonger GB, fruit and vegetable merchant; **~ de sable** FIG sandman; **le ~ de sable est passé** the sandman has been; **~ à la sauvette** street vendor; **~ de tableaux** art dealer; **~ de tapis** carpet salesman; **c'est un vrai ~ de tapis**○ PÉJ he's just a petty wrangler.

marchandage /maʀʃɑ̃daʒ/ *nm* (sur le prix) haggling (de over); **après un long ~** after lengthy haggling; **faire du ~** to haggle.

marchander /maʀʃɑ̃de/ [1] *vtr* **1** to haggle over [*marchandise, prix*]; to haggle for [*rabais*]; **sans ~** without haggling; **2** FIG **~ son accord** to give one's approval grudgingly; **~ sa peine** not to put oneself out; **il n'a pas marchandé ses éloges** he was not sparing in his praises.

marchandise /maʀʃɑ̃diz/ *nf* **1** (articles) **des ~s** goods, merchandise ¢; **~ en gros/au détail** wholesale/retail goods; **2** (produit) goods (*pl*); **livrer la ~** to deliver the goods; **tromper** or **voler qn sur la ~** to swindle sb.
IDIOMES **il a essayé de nous vendre sa ~**○ he tried to win us over; **vanter** or **étaler sa ~**○ to parade one's wares.

marche /maʀʃ/ *nf* **1** ▶329| (activité, sport) walking; (trajet) walk; **faire de la ~** to go walking; **la ~ à pied** walking; **faire une petite ~** to take a short walk; **à 10 minutes de ~** 10 minutes' walk away; **ralentir la ~** to walk slower; **2** MIL, POL march; **~ de protestation** protest march; **soldats en ~** soldiers on the march; **fermer la ~** to bring up the rear; **ouvrir la ~** to be at the head of the march; **3** (fonctionnement de véhicule) progress; **la ~ du train a été gênée** the progress of the train was hampered; **prendre un bus en ~** to climb aboard a moving bus; **dans le sens contraire de la ~** facing backward(s); **4** (fonctionnement de mécanisme) operation; **bonne ~** smooth operation; **en état de ~** in working order; **mettre en ~** to start [*machine, moteur*]; to start up [*chaudière, réacteur*]; to switch on [*téléviseur, ordinateur*]; **se mettre en ~** [*appareil, véhicule*] to start up; **être en ~** [*machine, moteur*] to be running; [*téléviseur, radio*] to be on; **5** (fonctionnement d'organisme) running; **bonne ~ de l'entreprise** smooth running of the company; **6** (déroulement) course; **la ~ du temps/du progrès** the march of time/of progress; **à suivre** procedure (**pour faire** for doing); **7** CONSTR (d'escalier, de train, bus) step; **les ~s** the stairs; **8** MUS march.
■ **~ arrière** AUT reverse; **passer la ~ arrière** to go into reverse; **sortir en ~ arrière** to reverse out; **faire ~ arrière** FIG to backpedal; **~ avant** forward; **~ forcée** MIL forced march.
IDIOMES **prendre le train en ~** (par hasard) to join halfway through; (par intérêt) to climb onto the bandwagon.

marché /maʀʃe/ *nm* **1** COMM market; **~ aux fleurs** flower market; **vendre ses pommes au ~** to sell one's apples at the market; **les jours de ~** market days; **faire son ~** to do one's shopping at the market; **il fait les ~s de la région** he does the rounds of the markets in the area; **mettre qch sur le ~** to put sth on the market; **2** ÉCON, FIN market; **~ boursier** stock market; **le ~ de l'immobilier** the property market; **pénétrer un ~** to break into a market; **3** (arrangement) deal; **conclure un ~ avec qn** to strike a deal with sb; **~ conclu!** it's a deal!; **bon/meilleur ~** [*produit*] cheap/cheaper; **par-dessus le ~**○ to top it all.
■ **~ de l'emploi** job market; **~ extérieur** foreign market; **~ intérieur** (national) domestic ou home market; (de l'UE) internal market; **~ libre**

free market; **~ noir** black market; **~ aux puces** flea market; **~ du travail** labour[GB] market; **Marché commun** Common Market.

IDIOMES **faire bon ~ de qch** to set little value on sth.

marchepied /maʀʃəpje/ *nm* **1** (de véhicule) step; **2** (escabeau) steps (*pl*); **3** FIG **servir de ~ à qn** to be a stepping stone for sb.

marcher /maʀʃe/ [1] *vi* **1** (utiliser ses pieds) [*personne, animal, robot*] to walk; **allons ~ un peu** let's go for a little walk; **2** (poser le pied) to tread (**dans** in; **sur** on); **~ sur les pieds de qn** to tread on sb's toes; **tu m'as marché sur le pied** you stood on my foot; **se laisser ~ sur les pieds** FIG to let oneself be walked over; **3** (avancer) to go; **~ sur les mains** [*gymnaste*] to walk on one's hands; **~ en tête de cortège** to march at the head of the procession; **~ sur le palais présidentiel** to march on the presidential palace; **4** (fonctionner) [*mécanisme, réforme, procédé*] to work; **ma radio marche bien/marche mal** my radio works well/doesn't work properly; **faire ~ qch** to get sth to work; **ma montre ne marche plus** my watch has stopped working; **la poste marche de mieux en mieux** the postal service is getting better and better; **~ au gaz** to run on gas; **les bus ne marchent pas le dimanche** the buses don't run on Sundays; **5**° (aller) **~ (bien)/~ mal** [*travail, relations, examen*] to go well/not to go well; [*affaires, film, élève*] to do well/ not to do well; **comment marchent les affaires?** how is business?; **6**° (être d'accord) to go for it; **je marche** I'll go for it; **c'est trop risqué, je ne marche pas** it's too risky, count me out; **ça marche!** (marché conclu) it's a deal!; (la commande est prise) coming up!; **7**° (croire naïvement) to fall for it; **tu verras, elle marchera à tous les coups** you'll see, she falls for it every time; **faire ~ qn** to pull sb's leg; **elle fait ~ sa mère comme elle veut** she's got her mother wrapped round her little finger; **8**° (obéir) **faire ~ son monde** to be good at giving orders.

IDIOMES **il ne marche pas, il court**°! he's as gullible as they come; **~ sur la tête de qn**° to walk all over sb.

marcheur, -euse /maʀʃœʀ, øz/ *nm,f* walker.

mardi /maʀdi/ ▶551| *nm* Tuesday; **~ gras** Shrove Tuesday.

mare /maʀ/ *nf* **1** (étang) pond; **~ aux canards** duck pond; **2** (grande quantité) pool (**de** of).

marécage /maʀekaʒ/ *nm* **1** LIT marsh; (sous les tropiques) swamp; **2** FIG quagmire.

marécageux, -euse /maʀekaʒø, øz/ *adj* **1** LIT [*sol*] marshy, swampy; [*faune, flore*] marsh (*épith*); **2** FIG [*terrain, situation*] sticky°.

maréchal, *pl* **-aux** /maʀeʃal, o/ ▶284| *nm* ~ field marshal GB, general of the army US.

■ **~ de France** marshal of France.

maréchal-ferrant, *pl* **maréchaux-ferrants** /maʀeʃalfeʀɑ̃, maʀeʃofeʀɑ̃/ ▶374| *nm* farrier.

maréchaussée /maʀeʃose/ *nf* HIST mounted police (+ *v pl*).

marée /maʀe/ *nf* **1** GÉOG tide; **la ~ monte/descend** the tide is coming in/is going out; **les grandes ~s** the spring tides; **à ~ haute/basse** at high/low tide; **la ~ montante/descendante** the rising/ebbing tide; **2** FIG **une ~ humaine** a human tide; **3** (produits pêchés) fresh fish.

■ **~ noire** oil slick.

IDIOMES **contre vents et ~s** (à l'avenir) come hell or high water; (dans le passé) against all odds.

marelle /maʀɛl/ ▶329| *nf* hopscotch.

marémoteur, -trice /maʀemɔtœʀ, tʀis/ *adj* tidal; **usine marémotrice** tidal power station.

mareyeur, -euse /maʀejœʀ, øz/ ▶374| *nm,f* fish wholesaler.

margarine /maʀgaʀin/ *nf* margarine.

marge /maʀʒ/ I *nf* **1** (espace) margin; **~ de gauche/du bas** left/bottom margin; **2** (écart) leeway; **on a 10 minutes de ~** we've got 10 minutes leeway; **le train n'est qu'à midi, on a de la ~** the train isn't

until midday, we've got plenty of leeway; **se sentir en ~** to feel like an outsider; **3** (latitude) scope; **tu devrais me laisser plus de ~ de décision** you should give me more scope for making decisions; **4** (profit) (écart) profit margin; (pourcentage) mark-up.

II **en marge de** *loc prép* **1** (à l'écart) **vivre en ~ de la société** to live on the fringes of society; **vivre en ~ de la loi** to live outside the law; **2** (parallèlement) **en ~ de la conférence** outside the conference proper; **en ~ de l'accord de septembre** alongside September's agreement.

■ **~ bénéficiaire** profit margin; **~ commerciale** gross profit; **~ d'erreur** margin of error; **~ de manœuvre** room for manoeuvre GB ou maneuver US; **~ de sécurité** safety margin; **~ de tolérance** tolerance margin.

margelle /maʀʒɛl/ *nf* edge, rim (**de** of).

margeur /maʀʒœʀ/ *nm* (de machine à écrire) margin stop; (machine) machine feeder.

marginal, ~e, *mpl* **-aux** /maʀʒinal, o/ I *adj* **1** (secondaire) [*occupations*] marginal; **2** (non conformiste) [*artiste*] fringe (*épith*); **3** (en marge de la société) on the margins of society (*après n*).

II *nm,f* dropout; **les marginaux** the fringe elements of society.

marginaliser /maʀʒinalize/ [1] I *vtr* to marginalize.

II **se marginaliser** *vpr* [*communauté*] to put itself on the fringes of society; [*artiste*] to put oneself on the fringe.

marginalité /maʀʒinalite/ *nf* marginality; **vivre dans la ~** to live on the fringes of society; **le parti est sorti de la ~** the party has come in from the cold.

marguerite /maʀgəʀit/ *nf* daisy.

IDIOMES **effeuiller la ~** to play he/she loves me, he/ she loves me not.

mari /maʀi/ *nm* husband.

mariage /maʀjaʒ/ *nm* **1** (union) marriage; **au début de leur ~** in the early days of their marriage; **né d'un premier ~** from a previous marriage; **faire un ~ de raison** to enter into a marriage of convenience; **faire un ~ d'amour/d'argent** to marry for love/ money; **faire un riche ~** to marry into money; **né hors ~** born out of wedlock; **2** (cérémonie) wedding; **un ~ en blanc** a white wedding; **le ~ a été célébré à la mairie** the wedding took place at the Town Hall; **leur ~ a été célébré à l'église** their marriage was followed by a church service; **3** FIG (association) (de couleurs) marriage; (d'entreprises) merger; (de partis) alliance; (de techniques) fusion.

■ **~ blanc** (contrat) marriage in name only; **faire un ~ blanc** (contractuel) to marry in name only; (ne pas le consommer) to have an unconsummated marriage; **~ civil** civil wedding; **~ religieux** church wedding.

IDIOMES **c'est le ~ de la carpe et du lapin**° it's a mismatch.

Marianne /maʀjan/ *npr* Marianne (*female figure personifying the French Republic*).

marié, ~e /maʀje/ I *pp* ▶ **marier**.

II *pp adj* [*personne, couple*] married (**à, avec** to); **être bien/mal ~** to have made a good/bad marriage.

III *nm,f* **le** (jeune) ~ the (bride)groom; **la** (jeune) **~e** the bride; **les** (jeunes) **~s** the newlyweds.

marier /maʀje/ [2] I *vtr* **1** (unir) to marry (**à, avec** to); **on l'a mariée de force** she was forced into marriage; **nous avons encore un fils à ~** we still have one unmarried son; **2** (associer) to marry [*couleurs, styles*].

II **se marier** *vpr* **1** [*personne*] to get married (**avec qn** to sb); **2** [*tissus, couleurs*] to go well together.

marigot /maʀigo/ *nm* marshland.

marijuana /maʀiʀwana/ *nf* marijuana.

marin, ~e[1] /maʀɛ̃, in/ I *adj* **1** (de mer) [*courant, faune*] marine (*épith*); [*air, sel, monstre*] sea (*épith*); [*prospection*] offshore (*épith*); [*bateau*] seaworthy;

2 (de marin) **pull ~** seaman's jersey; **costume ~** sailor suit.

II *nm* sailor; **peuple de ~s** seafaring nation.

■ **~ d'eau douce** fair-weather sailor; **~ pêcheur** fisherman.

IDIOMES **avoir le pied ~** to be a good sailor.

marine² /maʀin/ **I ▶ 141** *adj inv* (couleur) navy (blue).

II *nm* (soldat) marine.

marine³ /maʀin/ *nf* **1** MIL, NAUT navy; **~ marchande** merchant navy; **de ~** [*instrument*] nautical; **2** ART seascape.

mariner /maʀine/ [1] **I** *vtr* GÉN to marinate; **harengs marinés** pickled herrings.

II *vi* **1** CULIN to marinate; **2**° (attendre) **laisser** or **faire ~ qn** to let sb stew.

marinier /maʀinje/ **▶ 374** *nm* bargee GB, bargeman US.

marinière /maʀinjɛʀ/ *nf* (blouse) smock.

marionnette /maʀjɔnɛt/ **I** *nf* LIT, FIG puppet.

II marionnettes *nfpl* puppet show (*sg*).

marionnettiste /maʀjɔnetist/ **▶ 374** *nmf* puppeteer.

maritalement /maʀitalmɑ̃/ *adv* **vivre ~** to live as man and wife.

maritime /maʀitim/ *adj* GÉN maritime; [*région*] coastal; [*compagnie, droit*] shipping.

marivaudage /maʀivodaʒ/ *nm* **1** (badinage) gallant sophisticated banter; **2** LITTÉRAT refined affectation (*in the style of Marivaux*).

marjolaine /maʀʒɔlɛn/ *nf* marjoram.

mark /maʀk/ **▶ 33** *nm* mark.

marmaille° /maʀmaj/ *nf* rabble of kids° PÉJ.

marmelade /maʀməlad/ *nf* CULIN stewed fruit; **~ d'abricots** stewed apricots; **en ~** [*aliments cuits*] cooked to a mush; **réduire qn en ~**° to beat sb to a pulp°; **j'ai le dos en ~**° my back is killing° me.

marmite /maʀmit/ *nf* **1** (ustensile) pot; **2** (contenu) potful.

IDIOMES **faire bouillir la ~**° to bring home the bacon.

marmiton /maʀmitɔ̃/ *nm* chef's assistant.

marmonner /maʀmɔne/ [1] *vtr* to mumble [*excuse*]; to mutter [*injure*].

marmoréen, -éenne /maʀmɔʀeɛ̃, ɛn/ *adj* **1** [*roche*] marble; **2** [*beauté*] marble-like; [*froideur*] marmoreal.

marmot° /maʀmo/ *nm* kid°, brat° PÉJ.

marmotte /maʀmɔt/ *nf* **1** ZOOL marmot; **2** FIG sleepy-head°.

IDIOMES **dormir comme une ~** to sleep like a log.

marmotter /maʀmɔte/ [1] *vtr* to mumble [*excuse*]; to mutter [*injure*].

Maroc /maʀɔk/ **▶ 232** *nprm* Morocco.

marocain, ~e /maʀɔkɛ̃, ɛn/ **▶ 394** *adj* Moroccan.

maroquin /maʀɔkɛ̃/ *nm* (cuir) morocco (leather).

maroquinerie /maʀɔkinʀi/ **▶ 374** *nf* **1** (magasin) leather shop; **2** (commerce) leather trade; (articles) leather goods (*pl*).

maroquinier /maʀɔkinje/ **▶ 374** *nm* **1** (commerçant) trader in fine leather goods; **2** (artisan) fine leather craftsman.

marotte /maʀɔt/ *nf* **1** (thème favori) pet subject, hobby horse; (occupation) pet ou favourite^{GB} hobby; **il a la ~ des mots croisés** doing crosswords is his pet hobby.

marquant, ~e /maʀkɑ̃, ɑ̃t/ *adj* [*fait*] memorable; [*souvenir*] lasting; [*personnalité, œuvre*] outstanding.

marque /maʀk/ *nf* **1** COMM, IND (de produit) brand; (de machine, matériel, voiture) make; **des voitures de ~ japonaise** Japanese cars; **produits de ~** branded goods; **2** (trace) mark; (indice) sign; **faire une ~ au couteau** to make a notch with a knife; **les ~s du bétail** the brands on cattle; **on voit encore les ~s** (de coups) you can still see the bruises; **~s d'usure** signs of wear; **~ de naissance** birthmark; **~ de doigts** fingermarks (*pl*); **~ de pas** footprint; **~ de brûlure** (sur un tissu) scorch mark; (sur la peau) burn; **3** (preuve) sign; **il l'a fait en ~ d'estime** he did it as

a mark of his esteem; **4** (particularité) mark; **laisser sa ~** to make one's mark; **5** (haut niveau) **invité de ~** distinguished guest, VIP; **personnage de ~** eminent person; **6** JEUX, SPORT (décompte) score; **à vos ~s, prêts, partez!** on your marks, get set, go!; **7** LING marker; **~ du pluriel** plural marker.

■ **~ déposée** registered trademark; **~ de fabricant** or **fabrication** manufacturer's brand name; **~ de fabrique** trademark; **~ d'infamie** stigma.

marqué, ~e /maʀke/ **I** *pp* **▶ marquer**.

II *pp adj* **1** (affecté) **il a le corps ~ de traces de coups** he's bruised all over; **elle est restée ~e par la guerre** the war left its mark on her; **c'est un homme ~** he's been through the mill; **visage ~** worn face; **2** (affirmé) [*différence, préférence*] marked; **3** (jalonné) marked; **une époque ~e par les conflits sociaux** a period marked by social unrest; **4** LING marked; **non ~** unmarked.

marquer /maʀke/ [1] **I** *vtr* **1** (étiqueter) to mark [*article*]; to brand [*bétail*]; to mark out [*emplacement, limite*]; **~ des vêtements au nom d'un enfant** to put nametapes on a child's clothes; **~ d'une croix** to mark with a cross; **2** (signaler) to mark, to signal [*début, rupture*]; **3** (laisser une trace sur) [*personne, coup*] to mark [*corps, objet*]; **4** (influencer) [*événement, œuvre*] to leave its mark on [*personne, esprit*]; **c'est quelqu'un qui m'a beaucoup marqué** he/ she was a strong influence on me; **5** (écrire) to mark [*prix*]; to write [sth] (down) [*renseignement*]; **marquez cela sur mon compte** put it on my account; **qu'est-ce qu'il y a de marqué?** what does it say?; **6** (indiquer) [*montre*] to say [*heure*]; [*jauge, chiffres*] to show [*pression, température*]; **l'horloge marque dix heures** the clock says ten o'clock; **il marquait ses propos d'un hochement de tête** he nodded emphatically as he spoke; **~ la mesure** MUS to beat time; **7** (exprimer) to show [*volonté, désapprobation, sentiment*]; **il faut ~ le coup** (célébrer) let's celebrate; (exprimer le mécontentement) we can't let it go just like that; **8 ~ un temps (d'arrêt)** to pause; **~ un silence** to fall silent; **9** SPORT to score [*but, point*]; to mark [*adversaire*].

II *vi* **1** (laisser une trace) to leave a mark (**sur** on); **2** SPORT to score.

marqueterie /maʀkɛtʀi/ *nf* (art) marquetry; (produit) inlay; **en ~** inlaid.

marqueur /maʀkœʀ/ *nm* **1** (stylo) marker (pen); **2** BIOL, LING marker.

marquis, ~e¹ /maʀki, iz/ *nm,f* (titre) marquis/ marchioness.

marquise² /maʀkiz/ *nf* **1** (auvent) glass canopy GB, marquee US; **2** (siège) ≈ Gainsborough chair.

marraine /maʀɛn/ *nf* **1** RELIG (d'enfant) godmother; **être (la) ~ de qn** to be godmother to sb; **2** (d'enfant défavorisé) sponsor.

■ Note en anglais *godmother* n'est jamais une forme d'adresse.

■ **~ de guerre** *soldier's wartime female penfriend.*

marrant°, ~e /maʀɑ̃, ɑ̃t/ *adj* **1** (amusant) funny; **il/ce n'est pas ~** (ennuyeux) he's/it's not much fun; (pénible) he's/it's a real pain°; **2** (bizarre) funny, odd.

marre° /maʀ/ *adv* **en avoir ~** to be fed up° (**de** qch with sth; **de faire** with doing).

marrer°: se marrer /maʀe/ [1] *vpr* (s'amuser) to have a great time; (rire) to have a good laugh; **il n'y a pas de quoi se ~** there's nothing to laugh about.

marri†, ~e /maʀi/ *adj* saddened, grieved†.

marron, -onne /maʀɔ̃, ɔn/ **I** *adj* (malhonnête) bent°, crooked.

II ▶ 141 *adj inv* (couleur) brown.

III *nm* **1** BOT **~ (d'Inde)** horse chestnut; (châtaigne) chestnut; **2** (couleur) brown; **3**° (coup) thump°.

■ **~ glacé** marron glacé; **~s chauds** roast chestnuts.

IDIOMES **tirer les ~s du feu** (faire son profit) to reap the benefits; **je suis ~**° (dupé) I've been had°; (coincé) I'm stuck°.

marronnier /maʀɔnje/ nm chestnut (tree).
■ ~ **d'Inde** horse chestnut (tree).

mars /maʀs/ ▶ 382 | nm inv March.
IDIOMES **arriver comme ~ en carême** to come as sure as night follows day.

marseillais, ~e /maʀsɛjɛ, ɛz/ ▶ 628 | adj of Marseilles; **une histoire ~e** ~ a tall story.

Marseillaise /maʀsɛjɛz/ nf Marseillaise (French national anthem).

marsouin /maʀswɛ̃/ nm ZOOL porpoise.

marsupial, pl **-iaux** /maʀsypjal, o/ nm marsupial.

marteau, pl **~x** /maʀto/ I○ adj cracked○.
II nm GÉN, SPORT hammer; (de juge) gavel; (de porte) knocker; **un coup de ~** a blow from a hammer; **donner un coup de ~ à qch** to hit sth with a hammer; **enfoncer qch à coups de ~** to hammer sth in; **casser qch à coups de ~** to take a hammer to sth.

martel† /maʀtɛl/ nm **se mettre ~ en tête** to get worried.

marteler /maʀtəle/ [17] vtr **1** to beat [métal]; [poings, artillerie] to pound; **2** (scander) to rap out [syllabes].

martial, ~e, mpl **-iaux** /maʀsjal, o/ adj [air, pas] military.

martien, -ienne /maʀsjɛ̃, ɛn/ adj, nm,f Martian.

martinet /maʀtinɛ/ nm **1** ZOOL swift; **2** (fouet) ~ whip.

martingale /maʀtɛ̃gal/ nf **1** (de vêtement) half belt; **2** (de cheval) martingale.

Martinique /maʀtinik/ ▶ 509 |, 305 | nprf **la ~** Martinique.

martin-pêcheur, pl **martins-pêcheurs** /maʀtɛ̃pɛʃœʀ/ nm kingfisher.

martre /maʀtʀ/ nf **1** (animal) marten; **2** (fourrure) sable.

martyr, ~e¹ /maʀtiʀ/ I adj [héros, nation] martyred LITTÉR; **enfant ~** battered child.
II nm,f martyr (**d'une cause** to a cause); **se donner des airs de ~** to put on a martyred look.

martyre² /maʀtiʀ/ nm (supplice) RELIG, FIG martyrdom; (souffrance) agony, suffering; **souffrir le ~** to suffer agony; **je souffre le ~ dans ces chaussures** these shoes are sheer torture.

martyriser /maʀtiʀize/ [1] vtr **1** (torturer) to torment [victime, animal]; to batter [enfant]; **2** RELIG to martyr.

marxisme /maʀksism/ nm Marxism.

mas /mɑ/ nm inv farmhouse (in Provence).

mascara /maskaʀa/ nm mascara.

mascarade /maskaʀad/ nf **1** (pour duper) farce; ~ **de justice** travesty of justice; **2** (bal) masquerade; (accoutrement) PÉJ fancy dress.

mascotte /maskɔt/ nf mascot.

masculin, ~e /maskylɛ̃, in/ I adj **1** BIOL [sexualité, hormone] male; **le sexe ~** the male sex; **un enfant de sexe ~** a male child; **2** (pour hommes) [revue] men's; [activité] man's, for men; [contraception] male; **le seul rôle ~** the only male part; **3** (composé d'hommes) [population] male; SPORT [équipe, record] men's; **4** (viril) [visage, allure] masculine; **5** LING [nom, rime] masculine.
II nm LING masculine.

masculinité /maskylinite/ nf **1** (qualité) masculinity; **2** (en démographie) **rapport de ~** male to female ratio.

masochisme /mazɔʃism/ nm masochism.

masochiste /mazɔʃist/ I adj masochistic.
II nmf masochist.

masque /mask/ nm **1** (sur le visage) mask; **il portait un ~ de chien** he was wearing a dog mask; ~ **de gaze** surgical mask; **2** (de beauté) face-pack; **3** (expression) **prendre un ~ tragique** to put on a tragic expression; **se couvrir du ~ de la vertu** to hide behind the appearance of virtue; **4** ORDINAT mask.
■ ~ **d'apiculteur** beekeeper's veil; ~ **funéraire** funeral mask; ~ **à gaz** gas mask; ~ **de grossesse** mask of pregnancy; ~ **mortuaire** death mask; ~ **de plongée** diving mask; ~ **de**

soudeur face shield ; **le Masque de fer** the Iron Mask.
IDIOMES **jeter le ~** to show one's true colours GB; **bas les ~s!** no more pretending now.

masqué, ~e /maske/ I pp ▶ **masquer**.
II pp adj **1** (avec un masque) masked; **il est apparu le visage ~** he appeared wearing a mask; **2** FIG [défaut] concealed; [voix] disguised.

masquer /maske/ [1] I vtr **1** (cacher) to conceal [défaut] (à from); to hide [paysage] (à from); to mask [sentiment, problème, odeur]; **2** (couvrir) to block [orifice, lumière]; **3** MIL to mask [dispositif].
II **se masquer** vpr to hide [sth] from oneself [vérité].

massacrante /masakʀɑ̃t/ adj f **être d'humeur ~** to be in a foul mood.

massacre /masakʀ/ nm **1** (tuerie) (de personnes) massacre ℂ; (d'animaux) slaughter ℂ; **2○** SPORT, FIG massacre; **3○** (gâchis) botch(-up).
IDIOMES **faire un ~** [chanteur] to be a roaring○ success; [homme d'affaires] to make a killing; **arrêtez le ~!** stop making such a mess of things!

massacrer /masakʀe/ [1] vtr **1** (tuer) to slaughter; **2○** (écraser) to slaughter○ [adversaire]; **3○** (abîmer) to wreck; **4○** (maltraiter) to make a complete mess of [musique]; to botch [travail]; **5○** (critiquer) to savage GB, to trash US [auteur, œuvre].

massage /masaʒ/ nm massage; **faire un ~ à qn** to give sb a massage.
■ ~ **cardiaque** heart massage.

masse /mas/ nf **1** (ensemble) mass; ~ **rocheuse** rocky mass; ~ **d'air chaud** mass of warm air; ~ **d'eau** body of water; **une ~ humaine** a mass of humanity; **la ~ croissante des chômeurs** the swelling ranks (pl) of the unemployed; **2** (grande quantité) **une ~ de** a lot of; **départs/exécutions en ~** mass exodus (sg)/executions; **ils sont venus en ~** they came in droves; **produire qch en ~** to mass-produce sth; **production de ~** mass production; **la population a voté en ~** there was a high turnout at the election; **les manifestants ont envahi le stade en ~** the demonstrators invaded the stadium en masse; **il a des ~s○ d'argent/de copains** he's got masses ou loads○ of money/of friends; **'tu as aimé ce livre?'—'pas des ~s'○** 'did you like this book?'—'not much'; **la ~ des électeurs demeure indécise** the bulk of the electorate remains undecided; **3** (peuple) **la ~** the masses (pl); **~s laborieuses** working classes; **les ~s paysannes** the peasantry; **culture de ~** mass culture; **enseignement/loisirs de ~** education/leisure activities for the masses; **4** PHYS mass; ~ **atomique** atomic mass; **5** (en électricité) earth GB, ground US; **6** (maillet) sledgehammer.
■ ~ **d'armes** mace; ~ **monétaire** money supply; ~ **salariale** (total) wage bill.
IDIOMES **se noyer** ou **fondre dans la ~** to get lost in the crowd; (se laisser) **tomber comme une ~** to collapse; **dormir comme une ~** to sleep like a log○.

massepain /maspɛ̃/ nm marzipan cake.

masser /mase/ [1] I vtr **1** (assembler) to assemble [personnes]; to mass [troupes]; **2** (frictionner) to massage; **se faire ~** to have a massage.
II **se masser** vpr **1** (s'assembler) to mass; **2** (frictionner) **se ~ les jambes** to massage one's legs.

masseur, -euse /masœʀ, øz/ ▶ 374 | nm,f masseur/masseuse.

massicot /masiko/ nm (à papier) guillotine.

massif, -ive /masif, iv/ I adj **1** (d'aspect lourd) [meuble, traits] heavy; [personne] heavily built; [silhouette] massive; **2** (par la quantité, le nombre) [attaque, dose, foule, publicité] massive; [licenciements] mass (épith); **3** (pur) **or/argent/noyer ~** solid gold/silver/walnut.
II nm **1** GÉOG massif; **2** (de fleurs) (groupe) clump; (parterre) bed.

massivement /masivmɑ̃/ adv [embaucher, manifester] in great numbers; [injecter] in massive doses; [absorber] in large quantities; [approuver] overwhelmingly.

mass media /masmedja/ *nmpl* mass media.

massue /masy/ *nf* GÉN, SPORT club; **coup de ~** LIT blow with a club; (événement) crushing blow; (somme) staggering sum.

mastic /mastik/ I **▶141** *adj inv* (couleur) putty-coloured GB.

II *nm* **1** (pour vitres) putty; (pour trous) filler; (pour arbres) grafting wax; **2** (résine) mastic; **3** (erreur) transposition.

mastiquer /mastike/ [1] *vtr* **1** (mâcher) to chew, to masticate; **2** (boucher) to putty [*vitre*]; to fill in [*fente*]; to plug [*fuite*].

mastoc○ /mastɔk/ *adj inv* bulky.

mastodonte /mastɔdɔ̃t/ *nm* **1** FIG (personne) colossus; (animal) monster; (objet) huge thing; **2** ZOOL mastodon.

masturber /mastyʀbe/ [1] *vtr*, **se masturber** *vpr* to masturbate.

m'as-tu-vu○ /matyvy/ I *adj inv* showy.

II *nmf inv* show-off.

masure /mazyʀ/ *nf* hovel.

mat, **~e** /mat/ I *adj* **1** [*peinture, papier*] matt; **2** [*teint*] olive (*épith*); **3** [*son*] dull.

II *nm* (aux échecs) **~!**, **échec et ~!** checkmate!; **faire qn/être ~** to put sb/to be in checkmate.

mât /mɑ/ *nm* **1** NAUT mast; **▶ grand**; **2** (perche, pylône) GÉN pole; SPORT climbing pole; **~ de drapeau** flagpole.

■ **~ de cocagne** greasy pole.

matador /matadɔʀ/ **▶ 374** *nm* matador.

matamore /matamɔʀ/ *nm* braggart; **faire le ~** to swagger.

match /matʃ/ *nm* SPORT (jeux d'équipe) match GB, game US; (de boxe, lutte, tennis) match; **~ nul** draw GB, tie US; **faire ~ nul** to draw GB, to tie US.

■ **~ amical** friendly match; **~ avancé** match GB ou game that has been brought forward; **~ de classement** league match.

matelas /matla/ *nm inv* **1** (de lit) mattress; **~ à ressorts** spring mattress; **2** (de feuilles) bed.

■ **~ d'eau** water bed; **~ à langer** changing mat; **~ de plage** inflatable mattress, Lilo®; **~ pneumatique** air bed.

matelassé, **~e** /matlase/ I *pp* **▶ matelasser**.

II *pp adj* [*tissu*] quilted; **porte ~e** (de cuir) padded door; (de tissu) baize door.

matelasser /matlase/ [1] *vtr* to pad [*porte*]; to upholster [*siège*]; to quilt [*tissu, vêtement*].

matelot /matlo/ **▶ 284** *nm* seaman, sailor; MIL NAUT **~** ordinary seaman GB, **~** seaman apprentice US.

matelote /matlɔt/ *nf* **1** CULIN matelote, fish stew; **2** (danse) hornpipe.

mater /mate/ [1] *vtr* to put down [*révolte*]; to bring [sb] into line [*rebelles*]; to take [sb] in hand [*enfant, cheval*].

mâter /mɑte/ [1] *vtr* to mast.

matérialisation /mateʀjalizasjɔ̃/ *nf* **1** (de projet, d'idée, espoir) realization; **2** (signalisation) marking; **3** (en spiritisme) materialization.

matérialiser /mateʀjalize/ [1] I *vtr* **1** (concrétiser) to realize [*rêve*]; to fulfil GB [*espoir*]; to make [sth] happen [*projet*]; **des décisions qui seront matérialisées par un traité** decisions that will be embodied in a treaty; **le fleuve matérialise la frontière** the river forms the border; **2** (signaler) to mark; **'chaussée non matérialisée sur 3 km'** 'no road markings for 3 km'.

II **se matérialiser** *vpr* [*projet*] to materialize.

matérialisme /mateʀjalism/ *nm* materialism.

matérialiste /mateʀjalist/ I *adj* **1** PHILOS materialist; **2** (terre à terre) materialistic.

II *nmf* materialist.

matériau, *pl* **~x** /mateʀjo/ *nm* **1** (documentation) material **¢**; **2** CONSTR material; **~x de construction** building materials.

matériel, **-ielle** /mateʀjɛl/ I *adj* **1** GÉN [*conditions, biens, dégâts*] material; [*plaisirs*] worldly; [*problème, moyens*] practical; [*obstacle*] tangible, concrete; **sur le**

plan ~ in practical terms; **2** (matérialiste) materialistic; **3** PHILOS material.

II *nm* **1** (équipement) equipment; **~ agricole** farm machinery; **2** (documentation) material.

■ **~ informatique** hardware.

matériellement /mateʀjɛlmɑ̃/ *adv* **1** (physiquement) **c'est ~ possible** it can be done; **c'est impossible ~** it's a physical impossibility; **2** (financièrement) financially; **aider ~ qn** to give material assistance to sb; **~, c'est un peu difficile** things are a bit tight○ financially.

maternel, **-elle**[1] /mateʀnɛl/ *adj* **1** (d'une mère) [*instinct*] maternal; [*amour*] motherly; **2** (de la mère) **biens/conseils ~s** mother's property **¢**/advice **¢**; **3** (dans la famille) [*ligne, tante, grand-père*] maternal; **du côté ~** on the mother's ou maternal side.

maternelle[2] /mateʀnɛl/ *nf* SCOL nursery school.

materner /mateʀne/ [1] *vtr* to mother; (à l'excès) to mollycoddle, to baby.

maternité /mateʀnite/ *nf* **1** (état de mère) motherhood; **2** (grossesse) pregnancy; **de ~** [*allocation, congé*] maternity; **3** (établissement) maternity hospital; (service) maternity ward.

mathématicien, **-ienne** /matematisjɛ̃, ɛn/ **▶ 374** *nm,f* mathematician.

mathématique /matematik/ *adj* **1** MATH mathematical; **2** FIG **c'est ~** (logique) it follows; (certain) it's dead certain.

mathématiquement /matematikmɑ̃/ *adv* **1** MATH [*démontrer*] mathematically; **2** FIG (logiquement) logically.

mathématiques /matematik/ *nfpl* mathematics (+ *v sg*).

matheux○, **-euse** /matø, øz/ *nm,f* mathematician.

maths○ /mat/ *nfpl* maths○ (+ *v sg*) GB, math○ (*sg*) US.

matière /matjɛʀ/ *nf* **1** (substance) material; **mes voyages me fournissent la ~ de mes romans** my travels provide me with material for my novels; **2** BIOL, CHIMIE, PHILOS, PHYS matter; **la ~ vivante** organic matter; **3** (sujet) matter **¢**; **en ~ littéraire** as far as literature is concerned; **donner ~ à plaisanterie** to make people smile; **~ à réflexion** food for thought; **il n'y a pas là ~ à plaisanter** it's no laughing matter; **il n'y a pas là ~ à se féliciter** there's no call for complacency; **4** SCOL, UNIV (discipline) subject.

■ **~s fécales** faeces; **~s grasses** fat **¢**; **~ grise** grey GB ou gray US matter; **~ plastique** plastic; **~ première** raw material.

Matignon /matiɲɔ̃/ *npr*: *offices of the French Prime Minister.*

matin /matɛ̃/ *nm* morning; **travailler le ~** to work in the morning, to work mornings; **5 heures du ~** GÉN 5 (o'clock) in the morning; (pour un horaire) 5 am; **le ~ du 3, le 3 au ~** on the morning of the 3rd; **au ~ il avait oublié** by morning he had forgotten; **brume du ~** morning mist; **de bon ~** early in the morning; **de grand ~** at daybreak; **au petit ~** in the early hours; **à prendre ~, midi et soir** MÉD to be taken three times a day.

IDIOMES **être du ~** to be a morning person; **un de ces quatre ~s**○ one of these days.

matinal, **~e**, *mpl* **-aux** /matinal, o/ *adj* [*toilette, promenade*] morning (*épith*); [*brume, gelée*] (early) morning (*épith*); **heure ~e** early hour; **il est ~** (d'habitude) he is an early riser; (aujourd'hui) he's up early.

mâtiné, **~e** /mɑtine/ *adj* (mélangé) **un anglais ~ de français** a mixture of English and French.

matinée /matine/ *nf* **1** (période) morning; **dans la ~** in the morning; **(toute) une ~ de travail** a (whole) morning's work; **2** CIN, THÉÂT matinée.

IDIOMES **faire la grasse ~** to sleep in.

matines /matin/ *nfpl* matins.

matois, **~e** /matwa, az/ *adj* wily, sly.

matou /matu/ *nm* tomcat.

matraquage /matʀakaʒ/ *nm* **1** LIT bludgeoning; **2** FIG

~ **publicitaire** hype○; **faire du ~ pour un produit** to plug○ a product.

matraque /matʀak/ *nf* GÉN club; (de policier) truncheon GB, billy US; (de malfaiteur) cosh GB, blackjack US; **recevoir un coup de ~** [*manifestant*] to be hit with a truncheon; **il m'a donné deux coups de ~** he clubbed me twice; **c'est le coup de ~**○ FIG it costs a fortune.

matraquer /matʀake/ [1] *vtr* **1** (assommer) [*policier*] to club; [*malfaiteur*] to cosh GB, to blackjack US; **2** (étourdir) [*médias*] to bombard (**de** with); **3**○ (escroquer) to rip off○.

matriarcal, **~e**, *mpl* **-aux** /matʀijaʀkal, o/ *adj* matriarchal.

matrice /matʀis/ *nf* MATH, ORDINAT matrix; TECH (moule) die; (pour disque) matrix.

matriciel, **-ielle** /matʀisjɛl/ *adj* MATH matrix (*épith*).

matricule /matʀikyl/ *nm* (numéro) MIL service number; ADMIN reference number.

matrimonial, **~e**, *mpl*, **-iaux** /matʀimɔnjal, o/ *adj* marriage (*épith*), matrimonial.

matrone /matʀon/ *nf* matronly woman.

maturation /matyʀasjɔ̃/ *nf* (de fruit, fromage) ripening; (du vin) maturing; (de cellule, d'abcès) maturation; (d'idée) development.

maturité /matyʀite/ *nf* GÉN maturity; **~ d'esprit** (psychological) maturity; **manquer de ~** to be immature; **en pleine ~** [*homme*] of mature years (*épith*, *après n*); [*auteur*] at the height of one's powers (*après n*).

maudire /modiʀ/ [80] *vtr* to curse.

maudit, **~e** /modi, it/ **I** *pp* ▶ **maudire**.

II *adj* **1**○ (satané) (*before n*) blasted○; **2** (rejeté) (*after n*) [*écrivain*] cursed (**de** by); **~s soient-ils** a curse on them.

III *nm,f* damned soul; **les ~s** the damned.

Maudit /modi/ *nprm* **le ~** the evil one.

maugréer /mogʀee/ [11] *vi* to grumble (**contre** about).

naure /moʀ/ *adj* Moorish.

nauresque /moʀɛsk/ *adj* Moorish.

mauricien, **-ienne** /moʀisjɛ̃, ɛn/ ▶ **394** *adj* Mauritian.

mauritanien, **-ienne** /moʀitanjɛ̃, ɛn/ ▶ **394** *adj* Mauritanian.

mausolée /mozɔle/ *nm* mausoleum.

naussade /mosad/ *adj* [*voix, humeur*] sullen; [*temps*] dull; [*paysage, perspective*] bleak.

naussaderie /mosadʀi/ *nf* sullenness.

nauvais, **~e** /mɔvɛ, ɛz/ **I** *adj* **1** (d'un goût désagréable) **être ~** to be horrible; **ne pas être ~** to be quite good; **2** (de qualité inférieure) [*repas, restaurant*] poor; [*tabac, alcool, café*] cheap; [*spectacle*] terrible; [*nourriture, hébergement, livre*] bad; [*dictionnaire, lycée, enregistrement*] poor; **ne pas être ~** to be all right; **3** (mal fait) [*cuisine, travail, gestion, éducation*] poor; [*prononciation, départ*] bad; **4** (inadéquat) [*conseil, définition, exemple, conditions de travail*] bad; [*projet*] flawed; [*renseignement*] wrong; [*éclairage, vue, mémoire, santé*] poor; **il ne serait pas ~ de faire** it wouldn't be a bad idea to do; **~ pour la santé** bad for one's health; **5** (inapproprié) wrong; **6** (incompétent) [*auteur, cuisinier, menteur, équipe*] bad (**en** at); [*élève, nageur, chasseur*] poor; [*avocat, médecin*] incompetent; **être ~ en français** [*élève*] to be bad at French; **7** (déplaisant) [*nuit, rêve, nouvelle, journée, situation*] bad; [*surprise*] nasty; [*vacances*] terrible; **8** (méchant) [*animal*] vicious; [*personne, sourire, remarque*] nasty; **~ coup** (méchanceté) dirty trick; (blessure) nasty knock; (revers) terrible blow; **préparer un ~ coup** to be up to mischief; **9** (grave) [*fièvre, rhume*] nasty; **10** (peu lucratif) [*rendement, terre*] poor; [*salaire*] low; [*récolte, saison*] bad; **11** (peu flatteur) [*résultat, opinion*] poor; [*chiffres, critique*] bad; **12** (répréhensible) [*père, comportement*] bad; [*chrétien*] poor; [*instinct*] base; [*génie, intention, pensée*] evil; **13** (pénible) [*vent,*

pluie] nasty; [*traversée, mer*] rough; [*météo*] bad; ▶ **numéro, pas²**.

II *adv* **sentir ~** LIT to smell; FIG○ to look bad; **sentir très ~** LIT to stink; FIG to stink○; **ouvre la fenêtre, ça sent ~** open the window, there's a nasty smell; **il fait ~** the weather is bad.

III *nm* (mauvais côté) **le bon et le ~** the good and the bad; **il n'y a pas que du ~ dans le projet** the project isn't all bad.

■ **~ esprit** (personne) scoffing person; (attitude) scoffing attitude; **faire du ~ esprit** to scoff; **~ garçon** tough guy; **~ plaisant** person with a warped sense of humour GB; **~ traitements** ill-treatment ₵; **~e herbe** weed; **~es rencontres** bad company ₵; **faire de ~es rencontres** to get into bad company.

IDIOMES **la trouver** or **l'avoir ~e**○ to be furious.

mauve¹ /mov/ ▶ **141** *adj, nm* mauve.

mauve² /mov/ *nf* mallow.

mauviette /movjɛt/ *nf* PEJ wimp○.

maux ▶ **mal**.

maxi- /maksi/ *préf* **~-bouteille** one-and-a-half litre GB bottle; **il y a un ~-choix**○ there's a huge choice; **~-jupe** maxi-skirt.

maxillaire /maksilɛʀ/ **I** *adj* maxillary.

II *nm* jawbone; **~ inférieur/supérieur** lower/upper jawbone.

maxima ▶ **maximum**.

maximal, **~e**, *mpl* **-aux** /maksimal, o/ *adj* maximum.

maximaliser /maksimalize/ [1] *vtr* to maximize.

maximaliste /maksimalist/ *adj* [*discours*] uncompromising; [*attitude, personne*] hard-line (*épith*).

maxime /maksim/ *nf* maxim.

maximiser /maksimize/ [1] *vtr* to maximize.

maximum, *pl* **~s** or **maxima** /maksimɔm, maksima/ **I** *adj* maximum.

II *nm* **1** (limite supérieure) maximum; **un prêt jusqu'à un ~ de...** a loan for a maximum amount of...; **un ~ de 11 jours, 11 jours (au)** ~ eleven days at (the) most; **au grand ~** at the very most; **au ~** [*travailler, développer*] to the maximum; [*réduire*] as much as possible; **détenir 20% du capital au ~** to hold 20% of the capital at the outside ou at most; **rouler au ~**○ to drive flat out○; **obtenir le ~ d'avantages** to get as many advantages as possible; **faire le ~** to do one's utmost; **atteindre son ~** [*bruit, inflation*] to reach its peak; [*douleur*] to be at its worst; **2** MÉTÉO **~ (de température)** maximum temperature; **3**○ (grande quantité) **un ~** a lot; **faire un ~ de bruit** to be as noisy as possible; **coûter le** or **un ~** to cost a bundle○; **obtenir le** or **un ~** (dans une transaction) to get the best possible deal; **4** JUR maximum sentence.

maya /maja/ **I** *adj* Mayan.

II ▶ **338** *nm* LING Maya.

Maya /maja/ *nmf* Maya.

Mayence /majɑ̃s/ ▶ **628** *npr* Mainz.

mayonnaise /majɔnɛz/ *nf* mayonnaise.

mazagran /mazagʀɑ̃/ *nm*: thick china goblet for coffee.

mazout /mazut/ *nm* (fuel) oil; **cuve à ~** oil tank; **chauffage au ~** oil-fired heating.

me (**m'** *before vowel or mute h*) /m(ə)/ *pron pers* **1** (objet) me; **2** (à moi) me; **tu m'as fait mal** you hurt me; **3** (pronom réfléchi) myself; **je ~ lave** (**les mains**) I wash (my hands); **je m'en veux** I'm angry with myself.

Me *written abbr* = **maître** III 5.

méandre /meɑ̃dʀ/ *nm* **1** GÉOG meander. **2** FIG **les ~s de l'administration** the maze (*sg*) of officialdom; **les ~s de ta pensée** the rambling development (*sg*) of your ideas.

mec○ /mɛk/ *nm* guy○; **beau ~** gorgeous guy; **mon ~** my man○.

mécanicien, -ienne /mekanisjɛ̃, ɛn/ **I** *adj* mechanical.

II ▶374| *nm,f* (ouvrier) mechanic.

III *nm* RAIL engine driver GB, (locomotive) engineer US; AVIAT flight engineer; NAUT engineer; **~ navigant** AVIAT flight engineer.

mécanique /mekanik/ **I** *adj* **1** (manuel) [*hachoir, tondeuse*] hand (*épith*); [*jouet*] clockwork (*épith*); **2** (doté d'une machine) mechanical; **3** (fait à la machine) machine (*épith*); **4** (de machine) [*panne*] mechanical; **se déplacer de façon ~** to move mechanically; **industrie ~** engineering industry; **5** PHYS mechanical; **6** (irréfléchi) [*geste*] mechanical; [*rire*] empty.

II *nf* **1** (discipline) mechanics (+ *v sg*); **un terme de ~** a mechanical term; **une merveille de ~** a marvel of engineering; **2** (fonctionnement) mechanics (*pl*); **la ~ d'une campagne électorale** the mechanics of running a campaign; **3**° (machine, véhicule) machine.

mécaniquement /mekanikmɑ̃/ *adv* LIT, FIG mechanically; **fabriqué ~** machine-made.

mécaniser /mekanize/ [1] *vtr*, **se mécaniser** *vpr* to mechanize.

mécanisme /mekanism/ *nm* mechanism.

mécano° /mekano/ *nm* mechanic.

mécanographe /mekanɔgraf/ **▶374|** *nmf* punch-card operator.

meccano® /mekano/ *nm* Meccano® GB, erector set US.

mécénat /mesena/ *nm* **1** (artistique) patronage; **~ d'entreprise** corporate patronage; **2** (parrainage) sponsorship.

mécène /mesɛn/ *nm* (des arts) patron of the arts; (parrain) sponsor.

méchamment /meʃamɑ̃/ *adv* **1** (avec méchanceté) [*faire, parler, sourire*] spitefully, maliciously; [*frapper*] viciously; **traiter qn ~** to treat sb badly; **2**° (extrêmement) [*travailler*] terribly hard; [*abîmer*] badly; **ils nous en veulent ~** they're terribly angry with us.

méchanceté /meʃɑ̃ste/ *nf* **1** (de personne) nastiness; **par pure ~** out of pure spite ou malice; **avec ~** spitefully, nastily; **sans ~** without malice; **2** (de propos, regard, d'acte) maliciousness; (plus fort) viciousness; **3** (acte) malicious act; (propos) malicious remark; **dire des ~s** to say malicious ou nasty things.

méchant, -e /meʃɑ̃, ɑ̃t/ **I** *adj* **1** (malveillant) nasty, malicious; **ce n'est pas une ~e femme** she's not such a bad woman; **avoir l'air ~** to look mean; **être ~ avec qn** to be horrible ou mean to sb; **2** (dangereux) [*animal, personne*] vicious; **quand il a bu, il devient ~** he gets nasty when he's been drinking; **attention chien ~!** beware of the dog!; **3** (grave) [*blessure, grippe, affaire*] nasty, bad; **ce n'est pas bien ~** it's not very bad; **4**° (extraordinaire) fantastic°.

II *nm,f* (au cinéma) villain; (enfant) naughty boy/girl.

mèche /mɛʃ/ *nf* **1** (de cheveux) lock; (teinte) streak; **se faire faire des ~s** to have streaks put in one's hair; **2** (de bougie, lampe, briquet) wick; **3** MÉD packing ¢; **4** (d'explosif, arme, de fusée) fuse; **5** (outil) (drill) bit.

■ **~ folle** stray lock; **~ rebelle** wayward lock.

IDIOMES **être de ~ avec qn**° to be in cahoots° with sb; **vendre la ~** to let the cat out of the bag.

méchoui /meʃwi/ *nm* (repas) North African style barbecue; (viande grillée) spit-roast lamb; **faire un ~** to spit-roast a lamb.

méconnaissable /mekɔnɛsabl/ *adj* unrecognizable; (presque) barely recognizable.

méconnaissance /mekɔnɛsɑ̃s/ *nf* LITER **1** (ignorance) (total) ignorance; **2** (sous-estimation) misreading.

méconnaître /mekɔnɛtr/ [73] *vtr* (se méprendre sur) to misread [*situation*]; to be mistaken about [*cause*].

méconnu, ~e /mekɔny/ **I** *adj* [*artiste, œuvre*] neglected [*talent*] undervalued; [*valeur*] unrecognized.

II *nm,f* **un grand ~** a neglected genius.

mécontent, ~e /mekɔ̃tɑ̃, ɑ̃t/ **I** *adj* GÉN dissatisfied [*électeur*] discontented; **pas ~ de lui/d'avoir fin** rather pleased with him/to have finished.

II *nm,f* malcontent.

mécontentement /mekɔ̃tɑ̃tmɑ̃/ *nm* (insatisfaction) dissatisfaction; (déception) discontent; (irritation) annoyance; (déplaisir) displeasure.

mécontenter /mekɔ̃tɑ̃te/ [1] *vtr* (irriter) to annoy (courroucer) [*décision*] to anger [*peuple*].

Mecque /mɛk/ **▶628|** *npr* **la ~** Mecca.

médaille /medaj/ *nf* **1** (récompense) medal; **~ d'or** gold medal; **2** (pièce) coin; **3** (bijou) medallion.

médaillé, ~e /medaje/ **I** *pp* ▶ **médailler**.

II *pp adj* [*sportif*] medal-winning (*épith*); [*animal, vin*] prize-winning (*épith*); [*soldat*] decorated (*épith*); **un champion plusieurs fois ~** a champion with several medals to his credit.

III *nm,f* (sportif) medallist GB; GÉN person who has received a medal.

médailler /medaje/ [1] *vtr* **1** SPORT to award a medal to; **2** MIL to decorate; **3** to award a prize to [*animal, vin*].

médaillon /medajɔ̃/ *nm* **1** (bijou) locket; **2** ART, CULIN medallion; **3** (sur une image) **en ~** inset.

médecin /medsɛ̃/ **▶374|** *nm* doctor; **aller chez le ~** to go to the doctor's; **~ traitant** general practitioner, GP GB.

■ **~ acupuncteur** acupuncturist; **~ de famille** family doctor; **~ de garde** duty doctor; **~ homéopathe** homeopath; **~ légiste** forensic surgeon; **~ militaire** army doctor.

médecine /medsin/ *nf* **1** (discipline) medicine; **faire (des études de) ~** to study medicine; **étudiant en ~** medical student; **2** (profession) medicine.

■ **~ légale** forensic medicine; **~ par les plantes** herbal medicine; **~ scolaire** school health service; **~ sportive** sports medicine; **~ du travail** occupational medicine; **~s douces** alternative medicine ¢.

média /medja/ **I** *nm* medium.

II médias *nmpl* **les ~s** the media.

médian, ~e[1] /medjɑ̃, an/ *adj* median (*épith*).

médiane[2] /medjan/ *nf* MATH median.

médiateur, -trice[1] /medjatœr, tris/ **I** *adj* mediatory.

II *nm* GÉN mediator; (entre le public et l'administration) ombudsman.

médiathèque /medjatɛk/ *nf* multimedia library.

médiation /medjasjɔ̃/ *nf* mediation.

médiatique /medjatik/ *adj* **1** (par les médias) [*exploitation*] by the media; **2** (dans les médias) [*succès*] media (*épith*); **3** (attirant l'attention des médias) media (*épith*); **geste ~** publicity stunt; **4** (utilisant les médias) [*personne*] media-conscious; [*campagne électorale*] conducted through the media; **5** (des médias) [*milieu*] media (*pl*); **chef-d'œuvre ~** media success.

médiatisation /medjatizasjɔ̃/ *nf* media coverage.

médiatiser /medjatize/ [1] *vtr* to give [sth] publicity in the media.

médiatrice[2] /medjatris/ **I** *adj f* ▶ **médiateur**.

II *nf* MATH perpendicular bisector.

médical, ~e, *mpl* **-aux** /medikal, o/ *adj* medical.

médicament /medikamɑ̃/ *nm* medicine, drug (pour for; contre to prevent); **mes ~s** my medicine (*sg*).

médicamenteux, -euse /medikamɑ̃tø, øz/ *adj* [*produit*] medicinal; [*traitement*] drug (*épith*); [*eczéma, allergie*] drug-related.

médication /medikasjɔ̃/ *nf* medication ¢.

médicinal, ~e, *mpl* **-aux** /medisinal, o/ *adj* medicinal.

médico-légal, ~e, *mpl* **-aux** /medikolegal, o/ *adj* forensic; **certificat ~** autopsy report; **institut ~** forensic science laboratory.

médico-pédagogique, *pl* **~s** /medikopedagɔʒik/ *adj* **institut** ~ special school.

médico-social, **~e**, *mpl* **-iaux** /medikosɔsjal, o/ *adj* **centre** ~ ~ community health centre[GB].

médiéval, **~e**, *mpl* **-aux** /medjeval, o/ *adj* medieval.

médiocre /medjɔkʀ/ **I** *adj* **1** (aux capacités insuffisantes) [*personne, ouvrier*] mediocre, second-rate; [*élève, intelligence*] below-average; **2** (de qualité insuffisante) [*travail, qualité, résultat*] mediocre; [*terrain, nourriture, temps*] poor; (sans valeur) [*œuvre, carrière*] mediocre; [*vie*] humdrum; (sans intensité) [*plaisir, intérêt, succès, ambition*] limited; **3** (en quantité insuffisante) [*revenu, rentabilité*] meagre[GB]; [*lumière, résultat*] poor.
II *nmf* [*personne*] loser, no-hoper[o] GB.

médiocrement /medjɔkʀəmɑ̃/ *adv* rather badly.

médiocrité /medjɔkʀite/ *nf* **1** (de personne, travail, sentiment) mediocrity; **2** (de revenus, résultats, lumière) meagreness[GB].

médire /mediʀ/ [65] *vtr ind* ~ **de** to speak ill of.

médisance /medizɑ̃s/ *nf* malicious gossip ¢.

médisant, **~e** /medizɑ̃, ɑ̃t/ *adj* malicious.

méditatif, **-ive** /meditatif, iv/ *adj* meditative.

méditation /meditasjɔ̃/ *nf* meditation (**sur** on).

méditer /medite/ [1] **I** *vtr* (projeter) to contemplate (**de faire** doing); (évaluer) to mull over [*paroles*]; **un projet longuement médité** a carefully considered project.
II *vi* to meditate; ~ **sur** (sur l'existence, Dieu) to meditate on; (sur un problème) to ponder on ou over.

Méditerranée /mediteʀane/ **▶ 407** *nprf* **la (mer)** ~ the Mediterranean (Sea).

méditerranéen, **-éenne** /mediteʀaneɛ̃, ɛn/ *adj* Mediterranean.

médium /medjɔm/ *nm* **1** (voyant) medium; **2** MUS middle register.

médius /medjys/ *nm inv* middle finger.

méduse /medyz/ *nf* ZOOL jellyfish.

méduser /medyze/ [1] *vtr* to dumbfound; **en rester médusé** to be dumbfounded.

meeting /mitiŋ/ *nm* meeting; ~ **aérien** air show.

méfait /mefɛ/ *nm* **1** (de personne) misdemeanour[GB]; (plus grave) crime; **2** (du tabac, d'une politique) **~s** harmful effects.

méfiance /mefjɑ̃s/ *nf* mistrust, suspicion; **éveiller/apaiser la** ~ **de qn** to arouse/to allay sb's suspicions; **avoir de la** ~ **pour** to be wary of; **avec** ~ warily; **faire qch sans** ~ to do sth unsuspectingly; **être sans** ~ (de nature) to be naïve; ~ **de qn** **envers** sb's wariness of.

méfiant, **~e** /mefjɑ̃, ɑ̃t/ *adj* suspicious; **elle est d'un naturel** ou **caractère** ~ she's always very wary; **d'un œil** ~ suspiciously.

méfier: **se méfier** /mefje/ [2] *vpr* **1** (ne pas faire confiance) **se** ~ **de qn/qch** not to trust sb/sth; **sans se** ~ quite trustingly; **2** (faire attention) to be careful; **se** ~ **de qch** to be wary of sth; **ne pas se** ~ **de** not to watch out for; **méfie-toi! la route est glissante** be careful! the road is slippery; **méfie-toi, tu vas recevoir une gifle** watch it! you'll get a slap; **tu aurais dû te** ~ you should have been more careful.

méga¹ /mega/ *préf* **1** (un million) mega; **~watt** megawatt; **2**[o] mega; **~-entreprise** mega-firm.

méga²[o] /mega/ *adj inv* mega[o].

mégalo[o] /megalo/ *adj, nmf* megalomaniac.

mégalomane /megalɔman/ *adj, nmf* megalomaniac.

mégaphone /megafɔn/ *nm* (avec amplificateur) loudhailer; (porte-voix) megaphone.

mégarde: **par mégarde** /paʀmegaʀd/ *loc adv* inadvertently.

mégère /meʒɛʀ/ *nf* shrew.

mégot /mego/ *nm* (de cigarette) cigarette butt ou end; (de cigare) stub.

meilleur, **~e¹** /mɛjœʀ/ **I** *adj* **1** (comparatif) better (**que** than); **tu devrais en acheter une ~e** you should buy a better one; **en attendant des jours ~s**

hoping for better days; **jamais il n'avait mangé (de) ~e choucroute** he'd never eaten better sauerkraut; **2** (superlatif) best; **le** ~ **des deux** the better of the two; **c'est le** ~ **de l'équipe** he's the best in the team; **les ~s amis du monde** the best of friends; **ta plaisanterie n'était pas du** ~ **goût** your joke wasn't in the best of taste; **c'est le** ~ **des pères** he's the best of fathers; **c'est sur terre battue qu'il est le** ~ he's at his best on clay; **tu ne manges pas la croûte? c'est pourtant ce qu'il y a de** ~! aren't you going to eat the crust? but it's the best bit!; **au** ~ **prix** [*acheter*] at the lowest price; [*vendre*] at the highest price.
II *nm,f* **le** ~, **la ~e** the best one; **ce sont toujours les ~s qui s'en vont** it's always the best who go first; **que le** ~ **gagne** may the best man win.
III *adv* better; **il fait** ~ **qu'hier** the weather is better than it was yesterday.
IV *nm* **mange donc la croûte, c'est le ~!** eat the crust, it's the best bit!; **donner le** ~ **de soi-même** to give of one's best; **pour le** ~ **et pour le pire** for better or for worse; **garder le** ~ **pour la fin** to keep the best bit till last; **et le** ~ **c'est que...!** and the best bit of it is that...!

meilleure² /mɛjœʀ/ *nf* **tu connais la ~?** have you heard the best one yet?; **ça c'est la ~!** that's the best one yet!; **j'en passe et des ~s!** that's the least of it, I could go on!

mélancolie /melɑ̃kɔli/ *nf* melancholy; MÉD melancholia.

mélancolique /melɑ̃kɔlik/ **I** *adj* melancholy.
II *nmf* MÉD melancholic.

mélancoliquement /melɑ̃kɔlikmɑ̃/ *adv* melancholically, in a melancholy fashion.

mélange /melɑ̃ʒ/ *nm* **1** (action) GÉN mixing; (de thés, tabacs) blending; **bonheur/joie sans** ~ unadulterated happiness/joy; **2** (résultat) (de thés, tabacs) blend; (de légumes, produits, d'idées) combination; (de couleurs, céréales, sentiments) mixture; **un** ~ **explosif** an explosive mixture; **c'est un** ~ **(coton et synthétique)** it's a mix (of cotton and synthetic fibres[GB]).

mélanger /melɑ̃ʒe/ [13] **I** *vtr* **1** (pour former un tout) to blend [*tabacs, alcools, thés, huiles*]; to mix [*couleurs, peintures, liquides*]; ~ **les œufs et le sucre** to mix the eggs and the sugar together; **2** (associer) to put together [*styles, personnes*]; **3** (mettre en désordre) to mix up; ~ **les cartes** to shuffle (the cards); **4** (confondre) to mix up; **mais non! tu mélanges tout!** no! you're getting it all mixed up.
II **se mélanger** *vpr* **1** (pour former un tout) [*tabacs, thés, huiles*] to blend; [*couleurs, peintures*] to mix; **2** (en créant une confusion) **les souvenirs se mélangent dans ma tête** the memories are getting muddled (up) in my head.

mélangeur /melɑ̃ʒœʀ/ *nm* TECH **1** (appareil) mixer; **2** (robinet) **(robinet)** ~ mixer tap GB, mixer faucet US.

mélasse /melas/ *nf* **1** CULIN black treacle GB, molasses (*pl*); **2**[o] (boue) muck; (brouillard) murk; **3**[o] (confusion) shambles[o] (*sg*), mess.

mêlé, **~e¹** /mele/ **I** *pp* **▶ mêler**.
II *pp adj* [*éléments, public, société*] mixed; [*sons, eaux*] mingled; ~ **de** mingled with.

mêlée² /mele/ *nf* **1** (bataille, cohue) mêlée; ~ **générale** free-for-all; **la** ~ **devint générale** it turned into a free-for-all; **2** SPORT (au rugby) scrum; **3** FIG (contestation) fray; **rester en dehors** ou **au-dessus de la** ~ to keep out of the fray.

mêler /mele/ [1] **I** *vtr* **1** (mélanger) to mix [*produits, couleurs*]; to blend [*ingrédients, cultures*]; to combine [*thèmes, influences*]; ~ **le vrai et le faux** to mix truth and falsehood; ~ **ironie et tendresse** to combine irony and tenderness; **2** (allier en soi) ~ **l'utile à l'agréable** to be both useful and pleasurable; ~ **l'ironie à la colère** to be ironic and angry at the same time; **3** (impliquer) ~ **qn à** (à un scandale) to get sb involved in; (à des négociations) to involve sb in; (à une conversation) to bring sb into; **être mêlé à** (à un scandale, des négociations) to be involved in; (à une conversation) to be included in.

II se mêler *vpr* **1** (s'unir) [*cultures, religions*] to mix; [*odeurs, voix, eaux*] to mingle; **2 se ~ à** (se joindre à) to mingle with; (être sociable) to mix with; (participer à) to join in; **3** (s'occuper) **se ~ de** to meddle in; **il se mêle de tout** he interferes in everything; **mêle-toi de tes affaires** or **oignons ◑** mind your own business; **de quoi je me mêle**○! what's it got to do with you?; **se ~ de faire** to take it upon oneself to do; **quand l'amour s'en mêle** when love comes into it!

méli-mélo, *pl* **mélis-mélos** /melimelo/ *nm* (mélange) hotchpotch GB, hodgepodge US; (fouillis) jumble, mess; (imbroglio) muddle.

mélo /melo/ **I** *adj* slushy○, schmaltzy○; **feuilleton ~** soap (opera).

II *nm* melodrama; **c'est du pur ~** (film, pièce) it's pure schmaltz○.

mélodie /melɔdi/ *nf* **1** MUS melody; (air) tune; (pièce vocale) song; **2** (de vers) melodiousness.

mélodieux, -ieuse /melɔdjø, øz/ *adj* melodious.

mélodique /melɔdik/ *adj* melodic.

mélodrame /melɔdram/ *nm* melodrama.

mélomane /melɔman/ **I** *adj* **être ~** to be a music lover.

II *nmf* music lover.

melon /məlɔ̃/ *nm* **1** (fruit) melon; **~ d'hiver** honeydew melon; **2** (chapeau) bowler (hat) GB, derby (hat) US.

membrane /mɑ̃bran/ *nf* GÉN membrane.

membre /mɑ̃br/ *nm* **1** (personne) member; **devenir ~ d'un club** to join a club; **le parti a perdu beaucoup de ~s** the party's membership has fallen considerably; **les pays non ~s** the nonmember countries; **2** ANAT, ZOOL limb; **~ antérieur** forelimb; **3** (d'équation, expression) member.

■ **~ fantôme** MÉD phantom limb; **~ de phrase** part of a sentence; **~ viril** male member.

même /mɛm/ **I** *adj* **1** (identique) same; **en ~ temps** at the same time; **être de la ~ taille** to be the same size; **c'est toujours la ~ chose** it's always the same; **2** (suprême) [*bonté, dévouement*] itself; **il est la perfection ~** he's perfection itself; **3** (exact) **à l'heure ~ où** at the very moment when; **les lieux ~s du meurtre** the (actual) scene of the murder; **ce sont les termes ~s qu'il a employés** those were his very words.

II *adv* **1** (pour renchérir) even; **je ne m'en souviens ~ plus** I can't even remember now; **2** (précisément) very; **aujourd'hui ~** this very day; **c'est cela ~** that's it exactly; **3 à ~ la peau** next to the skin; **boire à ~ la bouteille** to drink straight from the bottle; **coucher à ~ le sol** to sleep on the bare ground.

III de même *loc adv* **agir de ~** to do the same; **il a refusé et sa sœur de ~** he refused and so did his sister; **il n'en est plus de ~ depuis 1970** this is no longer the case since 1970; **cette remarque ne s'adresse pas qu'à lui, il en est de ~ pour vous** this comment isn't just aimed at him, it goes for you too; (de la même manière) **de ~ en France l'armée...** similarly in France, the army...

IV de même que *loc conj* **~ que la première entreprise a fait faillite, la seconde n'a pas duré très longtemps** just as the first business went bankrupt, the second one didn't last very long either; **le prix du café, de ~ que celui du tabac, a augmenté de 10%** the price of coffee, as well as that of tobacco, has risen by 10%.

V à même de *loc prép* **être à ~ de faire** to be able ou in a position to do.

VI même si *loc conj* even if.

VII même que *loc conj* **il roulait à toute allure, ~ qu'il a failli avoir un accident** he was driving so fast that he nearly had an accident.

VIII *pron indéf* **le ~, la ~, les ~s** the same; **j'ai le ~** I've got the same one; **le ~ que celui de Pierre** the same as Pierre's; **le groupe est le ~**

qu'en **1980** the group is the same as it was in 1980; **ce sont les ~s qui disaient** these are the same people who said; **Smirnov, le ~ que l'on soupçonne aujourd'hui** Smirnov, the same person suspected today.

mémé○ /meme/ *nf* (grand-mère) gran○, granny○; (vieille femme) PEJ old granny○.

mémento /memɛ̃to/ *nm* guide.

mémère /memɛr/ *nf* (vieille femme) PEJ old granny○; (grand-mère) granny○.

mémo○ /memo/ *nm* note.

Mémo-Appel /memoapɛl/ *nm* TÉLÉCOM reminder call service (*in France*).

mémoire[1] /memwar/ *nm* **1** (rapport) memo; UNIV (exposé) dissertation (**sur** on); **2** (souvenirs) memoirs.

mémoire[2] /memwar/ *nf* **1** (faculté) memory; **avoir de la ~** to have a good memory; **si j'ai bonne ~** if I remember rightly; **ne pas avoir de ~** to have a bad memory; **avoir la ~ des dates** to have a good memory for dates; **gravé dans ma ~** engraved on my memory; **des faits qui sont dans toutes les ~s** facts that everyone remembers; **ça m'est soudain revenu en ~** it suddenly came back to me; **chacun a gardé en ~ cette image** everyone remembers that image; **citer de ~** to quote from memory; **de ~ d'homme** in living memory; **de ~ de journaliste, on n'avait jamais vu cela** no journalist could remember such a thing happening before; **2** (souvenir) memory (**de** of); (réputation) reputation (**de** of); **en ~ de** to the memory of, in memory of; **d'illustre ~** [*personnage, fait*] illustrious; **pour ~** (à titre de rappel) for the record; (pour conserver) for reference; **3** ORDINAT (espace adressable) memory; (unité fonctionnelle) storage; **mettre en ~** to input; **calculatrice à ~** calculator with a memory.

■ **~ centrale** main storage ou memory; **~ de maîtrise** UNIV dissertation (*which constitutes part of the French master's degree*); **~ morte** read-only memory, ROM; **~ vive** random access memory, RAM.

IDIOMES **avoir la ~ courte** to have a short memory.

Mémophone /memofɔn/ *nm* TÉLÉCOM public voice mail service.

mémorable /memorabl/ *adj* memorable.

mémorandum /memorɑ̃dɔm/ *nm* memorandum.

mémorial, ~e, *mpl* **-iaux** /memorjal, o/ *nm* ARCHIT memorial; LITTÉRAT memorials (*pl*).

mémoriser /memorize/ [1] *vtr* **1** to memorize; **2** ORDINAT to store.

menaçant, ~e /mənasɑ̃, ɑ̃t/ *adj* menacing; **être ~, dire des paroles ~es** to make threats; **se faire ~** [*personne*] to start to make threats; [*temps*] to look threatening.

menace /mənas/ *nf* threat; **~s de mort** death threats; **faire peser une ~ sur** to pose a threat to; **~s en l'air** idle threats; **obtenir de l'argent par la ~** to obtain money with menaces; **sous la ~** under duress; **sous la ~ d'une arme** at gunpoint.

menacer /mənase/ [12] *vtr* **1** (terroriser) to threaten (**de** with); **2** (agiter une menace) to threaten (**de faire** to do); **~ qn d'une amende** to threaten sb with a fine; **~ qn de mort** to threaten to kill sb; **la pluie menace** rain is threatening; **3** (mettre en danger) to pose a threat to; **être menacé** [*équilibre, économie*] to be in jeopardy; [*vie*] to be in danger; [*tranquillité*] to be threatened; [*carrière*] to be on the line; **toute la population est menacée** the entire population is at risk; **4** (risquer) **la chaudière menace d'exploser** the boiler could explode at any moment; **le retard menace d'être long** the delay threatens to be long.

ménage /menaʒ/ *nm* **1** (foyer) household; **2** (couple) couple; (rapports) relationship; **rien ne va plus dans leur ~** their relationship doesn't work any more; **se mettre en ~ avec qn** to set up home with sb; **ils sont** ou **vivent en ~** they're living together; **scènes de ~** domestic rows; **3** (administration domestique) **tenir son ~** to look after the house; **monter son ~**

to buy the household goods; **pain de ~** home-baked bread; **4** (entretien d'intérieur) housework; **faire le ~** LIT to do the cleaning; FIG (dans une organisation) to do the cleaning up; **faire des ~s** to do domestic cleaning work.

■ **~ à trois** ménage à trois.

IDIOMES **faire bon ~** [*personnes*] to get on well (**avec** with); [*choses*] to be compatible (**avec** with).

ménagement /menaʒmɑ̃/ *nm* **avec ~s** gently; **sans ~s** [*dire, annoncer, parler*] bluntly; [*jeter, pousser*] roughly, unceremoniously; **traite-le avec ~** (malade) be gentle with him; (personnage puissant) handle him very carefully; **la police l'a embarqué sans aucun ~** the police bundled him unceremoniously into the van.

ménager[1] /menaʒe/ [13] **I** *vtr* **1** (traiter avec précaution) to handle [sb] carefully [*collaborateur*]; to deal carefully with [*adversaire*]; to be gentle with, to treat [sb] gently [*personne âgée, malade*]; to be careful with [*machine*]; **ils savent ~ leurs alliés** they're careful not to upset their allies; **~ la susceptibilité de qn** to humour^GB sb; **les critiques n'ont pas ménagé le cinéaste** the critics didn't spare the film director; **~ sa santé** to look after one's health; **2** (employer avec économie) to be careful with [*vêtements, économies*]; to save [*forces*]; **elle ne nous a pas ménagé les critiques** she wasn't sparing in her criticism of us; **il ne ménage pas ses efforts** or **sa peine** he spares no effort; **3** (installer) **~ un passage** to make an opening; **~ un espace pour** to make some space for; **4** (régler avec soin) to organize [*entrevue*]; **~ un temps de pause entre les séquences** to allow for breaks between sequences; **je lui ménage une petite surprise** IRON I'm arranging a little surprise for him; **l'auteur ménage ses effets** the author saves his/her best effects until the end.

II se ménager *vpr* (s'économiser) [*personne*] to take it easy.

ménager[2], **-ère**[1] /menaʒe, ɛʀ/ *adj* [*tâches*] domestic; [*équipement*] household; **appareils ~s** domestic appliances; **travaux ~s** housework ¢.

ménagère[2] /menaʒɛʀ/ *nf* (personne) housewife; (couverts) canteen of cutlery.

ménagerie /menaʒʀi/ *nf* menagerie.

mendiant, **-e** /mɑ̃djɑ̃, ɑ̃t/ *nm,f* beggar.

mendicité /mɑ̃disite/ *nf* begging.

mendier /mɑ̃dje/ [2] **I** *vtr* to beg for; **~ qch auprès de qn** to beg sb for sth.

II *vi* to beg.

mener /məne/ [16] **I** *vtr* **1** (accompagner) GÉN **~ qn quelque part** to take sb somewhere; (en voiture) to drive sb somewhere; **2** (guider) to lead; **3** (commander) to lead [*hommes, pays*]; to run [*entreprise*]; **il ne se laisse pas ~ par sa grande sœur** he won't be bossed about^○ by his sister; **se laisser ~ par son seul intérêt** to be motivated by pure self-interest; **4** (avoir l'avantage) to lead; **la France mène le championnat devant l'Allemagne par trois points** France is leading the championship three points ahead of Germany; **5** (aller, faire aller) [*route*] **~ au village** to go ou lead to the village; **~ qn quelque part** to take sb somewhere; **6** (faire aboutir) **~ à** to lead to; **je ne vois pas où cela nous mène** I can't see where this is getting ou leading us; **cela mène à tout** it leads to all kinds of things; **parler ne mène à rien** it doesn't lead anywhere; **parler ne mène à rien** talking won't get you anywhere; **cette histoire peut te ~ loin** (avoir des conséquences graves) it could be a very nasty business; **50 francs, cela ne nous mènera pas loin** 50 francs, that won't get us very far; **~ à bien** or **à (son) terme** to complete [sth] successfully [*projet*]; to bring [sth] to a successful conclusion [*négociation, enquête*]; to handle [sth] successfully [*opération délicate*]; **7** (poursuivre) to carry out [*étude, réforme*]; to pursue [*politique*]; to run [*campagne*]; **~ une enquête** GÉN to hold an investigation; **~ une vie misérable** to lead a wretched existence; **~ sa vie comme on l'entend** to live as one pleases; **~ une guerre sans pitié** to wage a bitter war.

II *vi* SPORT to be in the lead; **~ par trois buts à un** to lead by three goals to one.

IDIOMES **~ la danse** or **le jeu** to call the tune; **~ la grande vie** to live it up.

ménestrel /menɛstʀɛl/ *nm* minstrel.

meneur, **-euse** /mənœʀ, øz/ *nm,f* leader; **qualités de ~** leadership qualities; **~ d'hommes** leader of men.

menhir /meniʀ/ *nm* menhir.

méninge /menɛ̃ʒ/ *nf* ANAT meninx.

II méninges^○ *nfpl* brains^○; **se creuser les ~s** to rack one's brains.

méningite /menɛ̃ʒit/ **▶196** *nf* meningitis.

ménisque /menisk/ *nm* meniscus.

ménopause /menopoz/ *nf* menopause.

menotte /mənɔt/ **I** *nf* (petite main) tiny hand.

II menottes *nfpl* handcuffs; **avoir les ~s aux poignets** to be handcuffed; **passer les ~s à qn** to handcuff sb.

mensonge /mɑ̃sɔ̃ʒ/ *nm* **1** (assertion fausse) lie; **dire des ~s à qn** to tell sb lies; **2** (principe) **le ~** lying.

mensonger, **-ère** /mɑ̃sɔ̃ʒe, ɛʀ/ *adj* [*propos, accusations*] false; [*publicité*] misleading; [*campagne*] dishonest.

mensualisé, **-e** /mɑ̃sɥalize/ *adj* [*paiement*] monthly (*épith*); [*salaire, employé*] paid monthly (*jamais épith*).

mensualiser /mɑ̃sɥalize/ [1] *vtr* (étaler) **~ des versements** to pay in monthly instalments^GB.

mensualité /mɑ̃sɥalite/ *nf* (versement) monthly instalment^GB; **par ~s** in monthly instalments^GB.

mensuel, **-elle** /mɑ̃sɥɛl/ **I** *adj* monthly.

II *nm* (revue) monthly magazine.

mensuellement /mɑ̃sɥɛlmɑ̃/ *adv* once a month, monthly.

mensurations /mɑ̃syʀasjɔ̃/ *nfpl* measurements.

mental, **~e**, *mpl* **-aux** /mɑ̃tal, o/ *adj* mental; **handicapé ~** mentally handicapped person.

mentalement /mɑ̃talmɑ̃/ *adv* (par la pensée) in one's head; (sur le plan mental) mentally.

mentalité /mɑ̃talite/ *nf* mentality; **belle ~!** IRON the mentality of some people!

menteur, **-euse** /mɑ̃tœʀ, øz/ **I** *adj* [*personne*] untruthful; **être ~** to be a liar.

II *nm,f* liar; **menteuse!** you liar!

menthe /mɑ̃t/ *nf* **1** (plante) mint; **à la ~** mint (*épith*); **~ poivrée** peppermint; **~ verte** spearmint; **2** (infusion) mint tea; **3** (sirop) **~ (à l'eau)** mint cordial.

menthol /mɛ̃tɔl/ *nm* menthol.

mentholé, **~e** /mɛ̃tɔle/ *adj* mentholated; [*bonbon, cigarette, dentifrice*] menthol (*épith*).

mention /mɑ̃sjɔ̃/ *nf* **1** (action de citer) mention; **sans ~ de** with no mention of; **faire ~ de qch** to mention sth; **ne pas faire ~ de qch** to make no mention of sth; **2** SCOL, UNIV **~ passable** *pass with 50 to 60%*; **~ assez bien** *pass with 60 to 70%*; **~ bien** *pass with 70 to 80%*; **~ très bien** *pass with 80% upwards*; **réussir avec ~** to pass with distinction; **3** (indication) note; **dossier portant la ~ 'secret'** file marked 'secret'; **rayer la ~ inutile** delete as appropriate.

mentionner /mɑ̃sjɔne/ [1] *vtr* to mention.

mentir /mɑ̃tiʀ/ [30] **I** *vi* **1** (ne pas dire la vérité) [*personne*] to lie (**sur** about), to tell lies (**sur** about, **à qn** to sb); **sans ~, le poisson était grand comme ça!** no lie, the fish was this big!; **▶arracheur**; **2** (être trompeur) to be misleading; **faire ~ le proverbe** to give the lie to the proverb.

II se mentir *vpr* **1** (à soi-même) to fool oneself (**sur** about); **2** (l'un à l'autre) to lie to one another (**sur** about).

menton /mɑ̃tɔ̃/ **▶137** *nm* chin.

mentonnière /mɑ̃tɔnjɛʀ/ *nf* (de couvre-chef) chin-strap; (de violon) chin rest.

menu, **~e** /məny/ **I** *adj* **1** (petit) [*personne*] slight;

[*pied, morceau*] tiny; [*brindille, écriture*] small; **2** (sans importance) [*corvées, travaux*] small; [*frais, soucis*] minor; [*détails*] minute.

II *adv* [*écrire*] small; [*hacher*] finely.

III *nm* **1** (liste) menu; **le ~ à 100 francs** the 100-franc menu; **~ dégustation** special house menu; **le ~ du jour** today's menu; **~ gastronomique/touristique** gourmet/middle-price menu; **au ~** on the menu; **2** (repas) meal; **3** (régime) diet; **4** (programme) programme^{GB}; **5** ORDINAT menu.

IV par le menu *loc adv* in (great) detail.
■ **~ fretin** LIT, FIG small fry; **~e monnaie** small change.

menuet /mənɥɛ/ *nm* minuet.

menuiserie /mənɥizʀi/ *nf* **1** (travail du bois, profession) joinery; (discipline, passe-temps) woodwork; **un atelier de ~** a joiner's workshop; **2** (boiseries) woodwork ₵.

menuisier /mənɥizje/ ▶374 *nm* joiner GB, finish carpenter.

méprendre: se méprendre /mepʀɑ̃dʀ/ [52] *vpr* FML to be mistaken (**sur** about); **elles se ressemblent tellement, c'est à s'y ~** they're so much alike, it's hard to tell them apart.

mépris /mepʀi/ *nm inv* **1** (dédain) contempt (**de** for); **avoir du ~ pour** to despise; **sourire de ~** contemptuous smile; **2** (indifférence) **~ de** (d'argent, de succès) contempt for; (de danger, des convenances) disregard for; **au ~ de la loi** regardless of the law.

méprisable /mepʀizabl/ *adj* contemptible; (plus fort) despicable.

méprisant, ~e /mepʀizɑ̃, ɑ̃t/ *adj* [*geste, sourire*] contemptuous; [*personne*] disdainful.

méprise /mepʀiz/ *nf* mistake; **par ~** by mistake.

mépriser /mepʀize/ [1] *vtr* to despise [*personne, argent*]; to scorn [*danger, conseils, offre*].

mer /mɛʀ/ ▶407 *nf* **1** (étendue d'eau) sea; **niveau de la ~** sea level; **~ d'huile** glassy sea; **en pleine ~** out at sea; **être en ~** to be at sea; **prendre la ~** to go to sea; **un homme à la ~!** man overboard!; **en bord de ~** by the sea; **mettre un bateau à la ~** to launch a boat; **eau de ~** seawater; **~ Morte** Dead Sea; **~ Noire** Black Sea; **~ du Nord** North Sea; **~ Rouge** Red Sea; **2** (zone côtière) seaside; **aller à la ~** to go to the seaside; **3** (marée) tide; **la ~ monte** the tide is coming in.

IDIOMES **ce n'est pas la ~ à boire** it's not all that difficult.

mercantile /mɛʀkɑ̃til/ *adj* PEJ mercenary PÉJ.

mercantilisme /mɛʀkɑ̃tilism/ *nm* (en économie) mercantilism; (mentalité) PEJ mercenary mentality.

mercenaire /mɛʀsənɛʀ/ *adj, nmf* mercenary.

mercerie /mɛʀsəʀi/ ▶374 *nf* (boutique) haberdasher's shop GB, notions store US.

merci¹ /mɛʀsi/ **I** *nm* thank you; **tu leur diras un grand ~ de ma part** give them a big thank you from me; **mille ~s** thank you so much.

II *excl* thank you, thanks○ (**à** to; **de, pour** for; **de faire, d'avoir fait** for doing); **~ beaucoup** thank you very much; **~ à vous!** (repartie) thank YOU!; **Dieu ~** thank God.

merci² /mɛʀsi/ *nf* mercy; **sans ~** [*lutte*] merciless (*épith*); **à leur ~** at their mercy; **on est toujours à la ~ d'un changement de dernière minute** there's always the risk of a last minute change.

mercredi /mɛʀkʀədi/ ▶551 *nm* Wednesday; **~ des Cendres** Ash Wednesday.

mercure /mɛʀkyʀ/ *nm* mercury.

mercurochrome® /mɛʀkyʀokʀom/ *nm* Mercurochrome®, antiseptic.

merde /mɛʀd/ **I●** *nf* **1** (matière) shit●; **2** (étron) turd○; **3** (objet de mauvaise qualité) crap●; **chaussures de ~** crap● shoes; **4** (pagaille) mess○.

II● *excl* shit●!; **dire ~ à qn** to tell sb to piss off●.

merdique /mɛʀdik/ *adj* [*film, livre*] crappy●; [*voiture, appareil, pays*] crap●.

mère /mɛʀ/ **I** *nf* **1** (génitrice) mother; **elles sont**

sages-femmes de ~ en fille they have been midwives for generations; **mariée et ~ de deux enfants** married with two children; **2**○ (femme) **la ~ Michel** old mother Michel; **3** (dans un couvent) **~ supérieure** Mother Superior.

II (-)**mère** (*in compounds*) **cellule/maison ~** parent cell/company.
■ **~ adoptive** foster mother; **~ célibataire** single mother; **~ de famille** GÉN mother; (ménagère) housewife; **~ patrie** motherland; **~ porteuse** surrogate mother; **~ poule** HUM mother hen.

IDIOMES **il tuerait père et ~ pour avoir qch** he'd kill to get sth.

merguez /mɛʀgɛz/ *nf inv* spicy sausage.

méridien, -ienne /meʀidjɛ̃, ɛn/ **I** *adj* meridian.

II *nm* meridian.

méridional, ~e, *mpl* **-aux** /meʀidjɔnal, o/ **I** *adj* (du Midi) Southern; [*versant, côte*] southern.

II *nm,f* Southerner.

meringue /məʀɛ̃g/ *nf* meringue.

mérinos /meʀinos/ *nm inv* merino.

merise /məʀiz/ *nf* wild cherry.

merisier /məʀizje/ *nm* (arbre) wild cherry tree; (bois) cherry wood.

méritant, ~e /meʀitɑ̃, ɑ̃t/ *adj* deserving.

mérite /meʀit/ *nm* (vertu permanente) merit; (pour un événement ponctuel) credit; (qualité) merit, quality; **il a au moins le ~ d'être sincère** but at least he's sincere; **au ~** according to merit; **avoir du ~ à faire qch** to deserve credit for doing sth; **il n'y a aucun ~ à faire** there's no merit in doing; **vous n'en avez que plus de ~** you deserve all the more credit for it; **cette voiture n'est pas très belle mais elle a le ~ de rouler** this car isn't much to look at but at least it goes GB ou runs US; **vanter les ~s de** to sing the praises of; **avoir le double ~ d'être confortable et puissant** to be both comfortable and powerful.

mériter /meʀite/ [1] **I** *vtr* to deserve; **il mériterait qu'on lui fasse subir le même sort** he deserves the same treatment; **tu n'as que ce que tu mérites** you've got GB ou gotten US what you deserve; **~ réflexion/d'être lu** to be worth considering/reading; **~ le détour** to be worth the detour; **il a reçu une gifle et il l'a bien méritée** he got a slap in the face and it was nothing less than he deserved; **succès (bien) mérité** well-deserved success; **sa lettre mérite une réponse** his/her letter merits a reply.

II se mériter *vpr* **c'est quelque chose qui se mérite** it's something that has to be earned.

méritoire /meʀitwaʀ/ *adj* praiseworthy.

merlan /mɛʀlɑ̃/ *nm* whiting.

merle /mɛʀl/ *nm* blackbird.

merlu /mɛʀly/ *nm* hake.

merluche /mɛʀlyʃ/ *nf* (merlu) hake; (morue séchée) stockfish.

mérou /meʀu/ *nm* grouper.

merveille /mɛʀvɛj/ **I** *nf* (chose admirable) marvel, wonder; **c'est une pure ~** it's marvellous^{GB}; **les sept ~s du monde** the seven wonders of the world; **la ~ des ~s** the most wonderful thing in the world; **une ~ de finesse** a marvel ou miracle of delicacy; **faire ~** ou **des ~s** to work wonders.

II à merveille *loc adv* wonderfully; **la voiture marche à ~** the car goes like a dream; **se porter à ~** to be in excellent health.

merveilleusement /mɛʀvɛjøzmɑ̃/ *adv* marvellously^{GB}, wonderfully.

merveilleux, -euse /mɛʀvɛjø, øz/ **I** *adj* (admirable) marvellous^{GB}, wonderful; [*conte*] fabulous.

II *nm* **le ~** the fabulous.

mes ▶ **mon**.

mésange /mezɑ̃ʒ/ *nf* tit; **~ bleue** blue tit.

mésaventure /mezavɑ̃tyʀ/ *nf* misadventure, unfortunate experience; **par ~** by some misfortune.

mesdames ▶ **madame**.

mesdemoiselles ▶ **mademoiselle**.

mésentente /mezɑ̃tɑ̃t/ *nf* dissension; (moins grave) disagreement.

mésestimer /mezɛstime/ [1] *vtr* LITER to underrate [*artiste, œuvre*]; to underestimate [*collaborateur, qualité, difficulté*].

mesquin, ~e /mɛskɛ̃, in/ *adj* **1** (vil) [*personne*] mean-minded, petty-minded; [*esprit, attitude*] petty; **2** (chiche) [*personne*] mean GB, cheap◦ US; [*récompense*] stingy.

mesquinerie /mɛskinʀi/ *nf* **1** (caractère) (bassesse) meanness; (avarice) stinginess; **2** (action) mean trick; (remarque) mean remark.

mess /mɛs/ *nm inv* MIL mess.

message /mesaʒ/ *nm* message; **~ de détresse** SOS message; ▶ **publicitaire** commercial.

messager, -ère /mesaʒe, ɛʀ/ *nm,f* (qui transmet) messenger; (en diplomatie) envoy; (qui présage) LITER herald.

messagerie /mesaʒʀi/ *nf* (transport de marchandises) freight forwarding; TÉLÉCOM messaging; **~ vocale** voice messaging, voice mail; **~s aériennes** air freight service (*sg*).

messe /mɛs/ *nf* RELIG, MUS mass (**en** in); **aller à la ~** to go to mass; **~ basse** low mass; FIG **~s basses**◦ whispering ₵; **arrêtez de faire des ~s basses**◦! stop whispering together!; **~ de minuit** midnight mass.

Messeigneurs ▶ **Monseigneur**.

messie /mesi/ *nm* messiah; **le Messie** the Messiah.

messieurs ▶ **monsieur**.

mesurable /məzyʀabl/ *adj* measurable; **non ~** unmeasurable; **ce n'est pas ~** it can't be measured.

mesure /məzyʀ/ *nf* **1** (initiative) measure; **par ~ d'économie** as an economy measure, to save money; **prendre des ~s** GÉN to take measures; (autoritairement) to take steps; **par ~ de sécurité** as a safety precaution; **2** (dimension) measurement; **prendre les ~s de qn** [*couturière*] to take sb's measurements; **faire prendre ses ~s** to be measured up; (**fait**) **sur ~** [*vêtement*] made-to-measure (épith); [*chaussures*] handmade; **le sur ~** made-to-measure clothes (*pl*); **tu as un emploi sur ~** the job is tailor-made for you; **emploi à la ~ de ses ambitions** job which is commensurate with one's ambition; **c'est une adversaire à ta ~** she is a match for you; **pour faire bonne ~** for good measure; **3** (évaluation) measurement; **unité de ~** unit of measurement; **instrument de ~** measuring device; **4** (unité) measure; ▶ **deux**; **5** (récipient, contenu) measure; **deux ~s de lait pour une ~ d'eau** two parts milk to one of water; **6** (modération) moderation; **parler avec ~** to weigh one's words; **agir avec ~** to behave in a moderate way; **sans ~** [*dépenser*] wildly; [*boire*] to excess; **dépasser la ~** to go too far; **7** MUS bar; **c'est une ~ à trois temps** it's in three time; **battre la ~** to beat time; **en ~** [*jouer*]; [*danser*] in time to the music; **8** (situation) **être en ~ de rembourser** to be in a position to reimburse; **le malade n'est pas en ~ de vous parler** the patient cannot talk to you; **9** (limite) **je t'aiderai, dans la ~ où je le pourrai or de mes moyens** I'll help you as much as I can; **dans la ~ du possible** as far as possible; **dans une certaine ~** to some extent; **dans une large ~** to a large extent; **dans la ~ où** insofar as.

mesuré, ~e /məzyʀe/ **I** *pp* ▶ **mesurer**.
II *pp adj* [*propos*] measured; [*attitude*] moderate; **être ~ dans ses propos** to weigh one's words.

mesurer /məzyʀe/ [1] ▶ **348|, 575|, 581|** **I** *vtr* **1** (avec un instrument) GÉN to measure [*longueur, quantité, objet, lieu*] (**en** in); (pour prélever une partie) to measure off [*longueur*]; to measure out [*poids, volume*]; (avant travaux) to measure up [*recoin*]; **~ le tour de cou de qn** to take sb's neck measurement; **2** (évaluer) to measure [*productivité, écart*]; to assess [*risques, effets*]; to consider [*conséquences*] ; **~ sa force contre or avec qn** to pit one's strength against sb; **mal ~ la portée de qch** to miscalculate the im-

plications of sth; **~ ses paroles** to weigh one's words; **ne pas ~ ses propos** to speak without restraint; **3** (donner sans générosité) **le temps nous est mesuré** our time is limited; **ne pas ~ ses efforts** to try one's utmost.
II *vi* **~ 20 mètres carrés** to be 20 metres GB square; **~ 2 mètres de haut** to be 2 metres GB high; **elle mesure 1,60 m** she's 1.60 m tall.
III se mesurer *vpr* **1** (se calculer) **se ~ en mètres** to be measured in metres GB; **2** (s'affronter) **se ~ à or avec qn** to pit one's strength against sb.

métabolique /metabɔlik/ *adj* metabolic.

métacarpe /metakaʀp/ *nm* metacarpus.

métal, pl -aux /metal, o/ *nm* metal; **pièce de or en ~ metal** coin; **~ jaune** gold.

métallique /metalik/ *adj* **1** LIT (en métal) metal (épith); (ressemblant au métal) metallic; **2** FIG metallic; **le bruit ~ des clés** the clink of keys.

métallisé /metalize/ *adj* [*vert, bleu*] metallic; **peinture ~e** paint with a metallic finish.

métalloïde /metalɔid/ *nm* metalloid.

métallurgie /metalyʀʒi/ *nf* (technique) metallurgy; (industrie) metalworking industry.

métallurgique /metalyʀʒik/ *adj* metallurgical.

métallurgiste /metalyʀʒist/ **▶ 374|** *nm* (ouvrier) metalworker; (industriel) metallurgist.

métamorphose /metamɔʀfoz/ *nf* metamorphosis.

métamorphoser /metamɔʀfoze/ [1] **I** *vtr* to transform completely; **~ qn en qch** to turn sb into sth.
II se métamorphoser *vpr* to be completely transformed; **se ~ en** to metamorphose into.

métaphore /metafɔʀ/ *nf* metaphor.

métaphorique /metafɔʀik/ *adj* metaphorical.

métaphysique /metafizik/ **I** *adj* metaphysical.
II *nf* PHILOS metaphysics (+ *v sg*).

métastase /metastɑz/ *nf* metastasis.

métatarse /metataʀs/ *nm* metatarsus.

métayage /metejaʒ/ *nm* tenant farming GB, share-cropping US.

métayer, -ère /meteje, ɛʀ/ *nm,f* tenant farmer GB, sharecropper US.

météo /meteo/ **I** *adj inv* weather (épith).
II *nf* **1** (organisme) Met Office GB, Weather Service US; **que dit la ~?** what's the forecast?; **2** (prévisions) weather forecast; **~ marine** shipping forecast.

météore /meteɔʀ/ *nm* meteor; **passer comme un ~** (avoir un bref succès) to be a flash in the pan; (faire une visite éclair) to be gone in a flash.

météorique /meteɔʀik/ *adj* meteoric.

météorite /meteɔʀit/ *nm or nf* meteorite.

météorologie /meteɔʀɔlɔʒi/ *nf* meteorology; **la ~ nationale** the Meteorological Office GB, the Weather Service US.

météorologique /meteɔʀɔlɔʒik/ *adj* [*phénomène*] meteorological; **conditions ~s** weather conditions.

météorologiste /meteɔʀɔlɔʒist/, **météorologue** /meteɔʀɔlɔg/ **▶ 374|** *nmf* meteorologist.

métèque /metɛk/ *nm* OFFENSIVE foreigner, dago ◦.

méthane /metan/ *nm* methane.

méthode /metɔd/ *nf* **1** GÉN, PHILOS method; **~ de gestion** management method; **2** (ordre) **procéder avec ~** to proceed methodically; **il manque de ~** he's not methodical; **avoir de la ~** to be methodical; **3** (manuel) (de musique) method; (de langues) course book GB, textbook US; **4** (système) way; **j'ai ma ~ pour le convaincre** I've got a way of convincing him; **il n'y a pas de ~ miracle pour réussir** there is no magic formula for success.

méthodique /metɔdik/ *adj* methodical.

méthodiquement /metɔdikmɑ̃/ *adv* methodically; **procédons ~** let's take things step by step.

méthodisme /metɔdism/ *nm* Methodism.

méthyle /metil/ *nm* methyl.

méthylique /metilik/ *adj* **alcool ~** methyl alcohol.

Les métiers et les professions

Les personnes

que fait-il dans la vie? = what does he do?
          ou what's his job?

Au singulier l'anglais emploie l'article indéfini devant les noms de métiers et de professions utilisés avec les verbes to be (*être*), to become (*devenir*), *etc., ou avec* as.

il est mécanicien	= he is a mechanic
elle est dentiste	= she is a dentist
elle est professeur d'histoire	= she is a history teacher
c'est un bon boucher	= he is a good butcher
il travaille comme boucher	= he works as a butcher
il est employé comme mécanicien	= he works as a mechanic
elle veut devenir architecte	= she wants to be an architect
ils sont bouchers	= they are butchers
ce sont de bons bouchers	= they are good butchers

Les lieux

S'il y a un nom en anglais pour désigner la personne (the butcher, the baker, the chemist *etc.*), *on peut utiliser ce nom pour désigner le lieu où elle travaille.*

aller chez le boucher = to go to the butcher's*
          ou to go to the butcher's shop†
travailler dans une boucherie
          = to work at a butcher's
          ou to work at a butcher's shop
acheter quelque chose chez le boucher
          = to buy something at the butcher's *ou* to buy something at the butcher's shop

Dans les cas où le lieu ne s'appelle pas shop *ou* store, *la première de ces deux formes est toujours possible.*

aller chez le coiffeur = to go to the hairdresser's

On peut aussi employer surgery *pour les professions médicales ou* office *pour les architectes, les avocats, les comptables, etc.*

aller chez le médecin	= to go to the doctor's surgery (*GB*) *ou* office (*US*)
aller chez l'avocat	= to go to the lawyer's office

On peut, dans certains cas, utiliser le nom particulier du lieu, s'il existe (bakery, grocery *etc.*).

aller à la boulangerie = to go to the bakery

Dans les cas où le français dit chez le marchand de X, *on peut, en général, dire en anglais* at/to the X shop.

aller chez le marchand de poissons	= to go to the fish shop
acheter quelque chose chez le marchand de fruits	= to buy something at the fruit shop

De même shoe shop (*chaussures*), toy shop (*jouets*), wine shop (*vin*) *etc.*

* *Au lieu de* to the butcher's, *on peut aussi dire* to the butcher. *Mais la forme avec* 's *est préférable.*

† *Attention: ce qui s'appelle* shop *en anglais britannique s'appelle en général* store *en anglais américain.*

---

méticuleux, **-euse** /metikylø, øz/ *adj* [*personne, soin*] meticulous; [*travail, choix*] painstaking.

métier /metje/ *nm* **1** (activité rémunérée) job; (intellectuel) profession; (manuel) trade; (artisanal) craft; **c'est mon ~ (de faire ça)**! it's my job!; **il a fait tous les ~s** he's tried his hand at everything; **apprendre un ~** (manuel) to learn a trade; **il est cuisinier de son ~** he's a cook by trade; **un maçon de ~** a professional mason; **terme de ~** specialized term; **les gens du ~** (manuels) people in the trade; (intellectuels) the professionals; **ne t'inquiète pas, elle est du ~** don't worry, she knows what she's doing; **2** (rôle) job; **faire son ~ de reine/mère** to do one's job as queen/ a mother; **3** (expérience) **avoir du ~** to be experienced; **avoir 20 ans de ~** to have 20 years' experience; **4** (objet) loom; **~ à tisser** weaving loom.
IDIOMES **faire le plus vieux ~ du monde** EUPH to practise^{GB} the oldest profession.

métis, **-isse** /metis/ **I** *adj* **1** [*famille, enfant*] mixed-race (*épith*); [*animal, plante*] hybrid; **2** [*toile*] union (*épith*).
II *nm,f* (personne) person of mixed-race.
III *nm inv* cotton and linen cloth.

métissage /metisaʒ/ *nm* (de personnes) miscegenation; (de plantes, d'animaux) crossing; **~ culturel** cultural cross-fertilization.

métrage /metʀaʒ/ *nm* **1** (de tissu) length; **2** (de mur, parquet) length in metres^{GB}; **3** (de film) length; **long/court ~** feature(-length)/short film.

mètre /mɛtʀ/ *nm* **1** ▶ 348|, 575|, 581|, 631|, 635| (unité de mesure) metre^{GB}; **ça se vend au ~** it's sold by the metre^{GB}; (en sport) **le 60 ~s** the 60 metres^{GB}; **piquer un cent ~s**○ FIG to break into a run; **2** (instrument de mesure) (metre^{GB}) rule GB, yardstick US; **3** LITTÉRAT metre^{GB}.
■ **~ carré** square metre^{GB}; **~ de couturière** tape measure; **~ cube** cubic metre^{GB}; **~ enrouleur** retractable tape measure; **~ étalon** standard metre^{GB}; **~ pliant** folding (metre^{GB}) rule; **~ ruban** tape measure.

métrique /metʀik/ *adj* metric.

métro /metʀo/ *nm* **1** (réseau) underground GB, subway US; **prendre le ~** to take the underground; **2** (rame) underground train GB, subway train US; **j'ai raté le**

dernier ~ I've missed the last train; **~ aérien** elevated railway.
IDIOMES **~, boulot, dodo**○ the daily grind.

métronome /metʀɔnɔm/ *nm* metronome.

métropole /metʀɔpɔl/ *nf* **1** (capitale) metropolis; (grande ville) major city; **2** (France métropolitaine) Metropolitan France.

métropolitain, **~e** /metʀɔpɔlitɛ̃, ɛn/ *adj* **1** [*réseau*] underground GB, subway US; **2** [*culture, investisseur*] from Metropolitan France.

métropolite /metʀɔpɔlit/ *nm* metropolitan.

mets /mɛ/ *nm inv* dish, delicacy.

mettable /mɛtabl/ *adj* [*vêtement*] wearable.

metteur /mɛtœʀ/ *nm* **~ en pages** make-up man; **~ en scène** director.

mettre /mɛtʀ/ [60] **I** *vtr* **1** (placer dans un endroit, une position) to put; **on m'a mis devant** they put me at the front; **je mets les enfants à la crèche** I send the children to a creche; **2** (projeter involontairement) to drop [*confiture, beurre*] (**sur** on); to spill [*liquide, poudre*] (**sur** on); **3** (placer sur le corps) to put on [*écharpe, fard*]; **4** (placer dans le corps) to put in; **on m'a mis un plombage** I had a filling; **5** (porter habituellement sur le corps) to wear; **je ne mets jamais de chapeau** I never wear a hat; **6** (placer dans une situation, un état) **~ qn en colère** to make sb angry; **~ qn de bonne humeur** to put sb in a good mood; **~ qn au travail** to put sb to work; **~ le riz à cuire** to put the rice on; **~ le linge à sécher** to put the washing out to dry; **7** (classer) **~ qch avant tout le reste** or **au-dessus de tout** to put sth; **8** (disposer) **~ les assiettes** to put the plates on the table; **~ les verres** to put out the glasses; **~ une autre chaise** to bring another chair; **~ une nappe** to put on a tablecloth; **je t'ai mis des draps propres** I've put clean sheets on for you; **9** (faire fonctionner) **~ la radio/les nouvelles** to put the radio/the news on; **mets plus/moins fort!** turn it up/down!; **~ les phares** to switch on the headlights; **~ le réveil** to set the alarm; **~ le verrou** to bolt the door; **10** (installer) to put in [*chauffage, douche, téléphone, placard*]; to put up [*rideau, lustre, étagère*]; **faire ~ le téléphone** to have a telephone put in; **~ du carrelage/de la moquette** to lay tiles/a carpet; **faire ~ de la moquette** (dans plusieurs pièces) to have carpets laid; **11** (écrire) to put up [*inscription*]; **il met que tout va bien** (dans une lettre) he says ou writes that everything's fine; **qu'est-ce que je dois ~?** what shall I put?; **~ au passif/en anglais** to put into the passive/into English; **est-ce qu'on met un trait d'union à 'multinational'?** is there a hyphen in 'multinational'?; **il faut ~ un trait d'union** you must put a hyphen in; **mettez votre signature ici** sign here; **mettez le pronom qui convient** (remplacez) replace with the appropriate pronoun; (bouchez les trous) insert the appropriate pronoun; **~ en musique** to set to music; (ajouter) to add [*ingrédient*] (**dans** to); to put [*accessoire*]; **~ du sel dans la soupe** to put some salt in the soup; **13** (consacrer) **~ tout son cœur dans son travail** to put one's heart into one's work; **y ~ du sien** to put oneself into it; **~ toute son énergie à faire** to put all one's energy into doing; **14** (investir, dépenser) to put [*argent*] (**dans, sur** into); **combien pouvez-vous ~?** (pour acheter) how much can you afford?; (pour contribuer) how much can you put in?; **15** (prendre) (du temps) **elle a (bien) mis une heure** it took her (easily) an hour; **~ un temps fou**○ to take ages○; **16**○ (vendre) **je vous mets des tomates?** would you like some tomatoes?; **17** (attribuer) to give [*note*]; **18**○ (dire) **mettons dix dollars/à dix heures** let's say ten dollars/at ten; **19**○ (supposer) **mettons qu'il vienne** supposing he comes; **20**○ (ficher) **tu peux te le ~ où je pense** or **quelque part** you know where you can put it○.

II *vi* **~ bas** GÉN [*vache*] to calve; [*brebis*] to lamb; [*jument*] to foal.

III se mettre *vpr* **1** (se placer dans un endroit, une position) **se ~ devant la fenêtre** (debout) to stand in front of the window; (assis) to sit down in front of the window; **se ~ sur les mains** to stand on one's hands; **se ~ sur le dos** to lie on one's back; **se ~ au lit** to go to bed; **se ~ debout** to stand up; **ne plus savoir où se ~** not to know where to put oneself; **se ~ les mains sur la tête** to put one's hands on one's head; **se ~ les doigts dans le nez** to pick one's nose; **où est-ce que ça se met?** where does this go?; **2** (projeter involontairement sur soi) to spill [sth] on oneself [*liquide, poudre*]; **se ~ de la confiture** to get jam on oneself; **s'en ~ partout** to get it all over oneself; **3** (placer sur son corps) to put on [*veste, fard*]; **je ne sais pas quoi me ~** I don't know what to put on; **4** (placer dans son corps) to put in; **5** (commencer) **se ~ à l'anglais** to take up English; **elle s'est mise à leur recherche** she started looking for them **il va se ~ à pleuvoir** it's going to start raining; **il s'est mis à faire du vent** it's starting to get windy; **6** (tourner) **le temps s'est mis au froid/à la pluie** the weather has turned cold/to rain; **7** (se placer dans une situation, un état) **se ~ en tort** to put oneself in the wrong; **se ~ dans une situation impossible** to get (oneself) into an impossible situation; **se ~ dans une sale affaire** to get involved in some shady business; **je me mets de ton côté** I'm on your side; **je préfère me ~ bien avec lui** I prefer to get on the right side of him; **se ~ à l'aise** to make oneself comfortable; **on va se ~ ensemble**○ (sous le même toit) we're going to live together; **8** (s'habiller) **se ~ en tenue d'été** to put on summer clothes; **se ~ en jaune** to wear yellow; **9** (se grouper) **ce n'est pas la peine de vous (y) ~ à dix** there's no need for ten of you; **ils s'y sont mis à au moins trente** there were at least thirty of them.

meuble /mœbl/ **I** *adj* [*sol*] loose.

II *nm* **un ~** a piece of furniture; **des ~s** furniture ℂ; **un ~ de jardin** a piece of garden furniture; **~ hi-fi** hi-fi unit; **~ de cuisine/salle de bains/rangement** kitchen/bathroom/storage unit.

IDIOMES **sauver les ~s** to salvage something; **faire partie des ~s** to be part of the furniture; **être dans ses ~s** to have a home of one's own.

meublé, ~e /mœble/ **I** *pp* ▶ **meubler**.

II *pp adj* furnished; **non ~** unfurnished.

III *nm* furnished flat GB ou apartment.

meubler /mœble/ [1] **I** *vtr* **1** [*personne*] to furnish (**de, avec** with); **2** (décorer) **un simple lit meuble la chambre** the room is furnished only with a bed; **la**

---

plante meuble bien la pièce the plant makes the room look more cosy GB ou cozy US.

II se meubler *vpr* to furnish one's home.

meuf○ /mœf/ *nf* GÉN woman; (petite amie) girlfriend.

meugler /møgle/ [1] *vi* to moo.

meuh /mø/ *nm* (*also onomat*) moo.

meule /møl/ *nf* **1** (de moulin) millstone; (pour aiguiser) grindstone; **2** (fromage) round; **3** AGRIC **~ de foin** haystack; **~ de paille** rick of straw.

meunier, -ière[1] /mønje, ɛʀ/ **I** *adj* flour-milling.

II ▶ **374** *nm,f* miller.

meunière[2] /mønjɛʀ/ *nf* **1** (épouse de meunier) miller's wife; **2** CULIN **sole (à la) ~** sole meunière.

meurtre /mœʀtʀ/ *nm* murder.

meurtrier, -ière /mœʀtʀije, ɛʀ/ **I** *adj* [*combats, répression*] bloody; [*explosion, accident*] fatal; [*épidémie*] deadly; [*arme*] lethal; [*rage*] murderous; [*route, carrefour*] very dangerous; **le lundi de Pâques a été très ~ sur la route** there were many deaths on the roads on Easter Monday; **les derniers séismes ont été très ~s** recent earthquakes have claimed many lives.

II *nm,f* murderer.

meurtrir /mœʀtʀiʀ/ [3] *vtr* **1** (faire mal) to hurt; (contusionner) to bruise; **2** (endommager) to bruise [*fruit*]; **3** (blesser moralement) to wound.

meurtrissure /mœʀtʀisyʀ/ *nf* LIT, FIG bruise.

meute /møt/ *nf* **1** (chiens) pack of hounds; **2** FIG pack; **la ~ des créanciers** the pack of creditors.

mexicain, ~e /mɛksikɛ̃, ɛn/ ▶ **394** *adj* Mexican.

Mexico /mɛksiko/ ▶ **628** *npr* Mexico City.

Mexique /mɛksik/ ▶ **232** *nprm* Mexico.

mezzanine /medzanin/ *nf* CONSTR mezzanine; CIN balcony; THÉÂT circle GB, mezzanine US.

MF /ɛmɛf/ *nf: abbr* ▶ **modulation**.

Mgr ▶ **596** (*written abbr* = **Monseigneur**) Mgr.

mi /mi/ *nm inv* (note) E; (en solfiant) mi, me.

mi- /mi/ *préf* **~-chinois, ~-français** [*personne*] half Chinese, half French; [*style, objet*] part Chinese, part French; **à ~-combat/carrière** in mid-fight/-career; **à la ~-journée** halfway through the day; **à la ~-mai/saison** in mid-May/-season; **à ~-parcours** in the middle; **à ~-pente** halfway up the hill.

miam-miam○ /mjammjam/ *excl* yum-yum○!, yummy○!

miaou /mjau/ *nm* (*also onomat*) miaow GB, meow; **faire ~** to go miaow GB ou meow.

miauler /mjole/ [1] *vi* to miaow GB, to meow.

mi-bas /miba/ *nm inv* knee sock, long sock.

mica /mika/ *nm* mica.

mi-carême /mikaʀɛm/ *nf: Thursday of the third week in Lent.*

miche /miʃ/ *nf* round loaf; H (petit pain) roll.

mi-chemin: à mi-chemin /amiʃmɛ̃/ *loc adv* LIT halfway; FIG halfway through; **à ~ de chez moi** halfway home.

mi-clos, ~e /miklo, oz/ *adj* half-closed.

micmac○ /mikmak/ *nm* **1** (intrigue) shady○ goings-on (*pl*); **faire des ~s** to wheel and deal○; **2** (désordre) mess○.

mi-côte: à mi-côte /amikot/ *loc adv* (en montant) halfway up; (en descendant) halfway down.

mi-course: à mi-course /amikuʀs/ *loc adv* SPORT halfway through the race; FIG halfway through.

micro[1] /mikʀo/ *préf* **~biologie** microbiology; **~chirurgie** microsurgery.

micro[2] /mikʀo/ *nm* **1** (microphone) microphone, mike○; **parler dans le ~** to speak into the microphone; **dire qch au ~** to say sth into the microphone; **une annonce au ~** an announcement over the microphone; **annoncer au ~ de la BBC que** to announce on the BBC that; **mettre des ~s dans une pièce** to bug a room; **2**○ (micro-ordinateur) micro○, microcomputer.

■ **~ caché** bug.

micro³ /mikʀo/ *nf* (micro-informatique) microcomputing.

microbe /mikʀɔb/ *nm* **1** (organisme) germ, bug○, microbe SPÉC; **2**○ (petite personne) OFFENSIVE squirt○.

microbien, -ienne /mikʀɔbjɛ̃, ɛn/ *adj* microbic.

microclimat /mikʀoklima/ *nm* microclimate.

microcosme /mikʀɔkɔsm/ *nm* microcosm.

micro-cravate, *pl* **micros-cravates** /mikʀokʀavat/ *nm* lapel-microphone.

micro-édition /mikʀoedisjɔ̃/ *nf* desktop publishing.

microfiche /mikʀɔfiʃ/ *nf* microfiche.

microfilm /mikʀɔfilm/ *nm* microfilm.

micro-informatique /mikʀoɛ̃fɔʀmatik/ *nf* microcomputing.

micron /mikʀɔ̃/ ▶348| *nm* micron.

micro-onde, *pl* **~s** /mikʀoɔ̃d/ *nf* microwave; **à ~s** microwave (*épith*).

micro-ondes /mikʀoɔ̃d/ *nm inv* (four) microwave○.

micro-ordinateur, *pl* **~s** /mikʀoɔʀdinatœʀ/ *nm* microcomputer.

microphone /mikʀɔfɔn/ *nm* microphone.

micropilule /mikʀopilyl/ *nf* mini-pill.

microprocesseur /mikʀopʀɔsɛsœʀ/ *nm* microprocessor.

microscope /mikʀɔskɔp/ *nm* microscope; **examiner qch au ~** LIT to examine sth under a microscope; FIG to scrutinize sth.

■ **~ électronique** electron microscope.

microscopique /mikʀɔskɔpik/ *adj* LIT microscopic; FIG tiny.

microsillon /mikʀɔsijɔ̃/ *nm* (disque) **~** microgroove record.

microtraumatisme /mikʀotʀomatism/ *nm* strain injury.

mi-cuisse: **à mi-cuisse** /amikɥis/ *loc adv* above one's knees.

midi /midi/ **I** *adj inv* midi; **chaîne ~** midi system.

II *nm* ▶298| **1** (heure) twelve o'clock, midday, noon; **je fais mes courses entre ~ et deux**○ I go shopping in my lunch hour; **2** (heure du déjeuner) lunchtime; **on mange ensemble à ~?** shall we have lunch together?; **qu'est-ce qu'on mange à ~?** what are we having for lunch?; **3** (point cardinal) south.

IDIOMES **chacun voit ~ à sa porte** everybody has their own way of looking at things.

Midi /midi/ ▶509| *nm* **le ~ (de la France)** the South (of France).

midinette /midinɛt/ *nf* feather-brained young girl, bimbo○; **elle a une âme** or **un cœur de ~** she's a romantic schoolgirl at heart.

mi-distance: **à mi-distance** /amidistɑ̃s/ *loc adv* halfway.

mie /mi/ *nf* bread without the crusts; **de la ~ (de pain)** fresh breadcrumbs (*pl*).

miel /mjɛl/ *nm* honey; **au ~** made with honey; **tes paroles sont de ~** FIG your words are soothing.

IDIOMES **être tout sucre tout ~** to be as sweet ou nice as pie○; **faire son ~ de qch** to turn sth to one's advantage.

mielleusement /mjɛløzmɑ̃/ *adv* unctuously.

mielleux, -euse /mjɛlø, øz/ *adj* FIG [*ton, paroles*] unctuous, honeyed; [*personne*] fawning.

mien, mienne /mjɛ̃, mjɛn/ **I** *adj poss* **ces idées, je les ai faites miennes** I adopted these ideas; **tu seras mienne** (mon épouse) you will be mine.

II le mien, la mienne, les miens, les miennes *pron poss* mine; **votre prix sera le ~** name your price; **les ~s** (ma famille) my family (*sg*).

miette /mjɛt/ *nf* crumb; **juste une ~** FIG just a little bit; **ne pas laisser une ~ de** not to leave a scrap of; **réduire en ~s** to smash [sth] to bits [*vase*]; to shatter [*bonheur*]; to shreds [*théorie*]; **elle n'en perd pas une ~**○ she's taking it all in; **nous n'avons eu que les ~s** we only had the leftovers.

mieux /mjø/ **I** *adj inv* better; **le ~, la ~, les ~** (de plusieurs) GÉN the best; (de caractère) the nicest; (d'aspect) the most attractive; **le ~ des deux** the better one; **ce qu'il y a de ~** the best.

II *adv* **1** (comparatif) better; **je ne peux pas te dire ~** that's all I can tell you; **qui dit ~?** GÉN any other offers?; (dans une vente aux enchères) any advance on that bid?; **tu serais ~ au lit** you'd be better off in bed; **elle est ~ portante** she's in better health; **j'aime ~ rester ici** I'd rather stay here; **il vaudrait ~ rester** it would be best to stay; **qui ~ est** moreover; **de ~ en ~** GÉN better and better; **parler anglais de ~ en ~** to get better and better at (speaking) English; **aller de ~ en ~** [*malade*] to be getting stronger all the time; **tu n'as pas d'argent? de ~ en ~** IRON you've no money now? that's absolutely great○! IRON; **ils criaient à qui ~ ~** they were all shouting, each one louder than the other; **on la critiquait à qui ~ ~** each person criticized her more harshly than the last; **c'est ~ que bien, c'est merveilleux** it's not just good, it's marvellous GB!; **c'est on ne peut ~** it couldn't be better; **2** (superlatif) **le ~, la ~, les ~** (de plusieurs) the best; (de deux) the better; **c'est ici qu'on mange le ~** this is the best place to eat; **je me porte le ~ du monde** I'm feeling absolutely fine; **être des ~ payés** to be extremely well paid.

III *nm inv* **le ~ est de refuser** the best thing is to refuse; **il y a du ~** there is some improvement; **il y a ~** it's nothing special; **il n'y a pas ~** it's the best there is; **tu ne trouveras pas ~** it's as good as you'll get; **je ne demande pas ~ que de rester ici** I'm perfectly happy staying here; **fais pour le ~, fais au ~** do whatever is best; **tout va pour le ~** everything's fine; **elle est au ~ avec sa voisine** she is on very good terms with her neighbour GB; **elle est au ~ de sa forme** she's on GB ou in US top form; **c'est le même, en ~** it's the same, only better; **changer en ~** to change for the better.

mieux-vivre /mjøvivʀ/ *nm inv* improved living standards (*pl*).

mièvre /mjɛvʀ/ *adj* [*personne, remarque*] vapid; [*sourire*] sickly; [*roman, musique*] soppy.

mièvrerie /mjɛvʀɑʀi/ *nf* **1** (de personne, parole, sourire) vapidity; (de roman, musique) soppiness; (de compliment, d'excuse) feebleness; **2** (parole, action) **tes ~s m'agacent** your simpering ways get on my nerves.

mi-figue /mifig/ *adj inv* **~ mi-raisin** [*sourire*] half-hearted; [*compliment*] ambiguous; [*remarque*] half-humourous GB; [*accueil*] mixed; **d'un ton ~ mi-raisin** half in jest half in earnest.

mi-fin, *pl* **~s** /mifɛ̃/ *adj m* [*haricot, petit pois*] medium-sized.

mignon, -onne /miɲɔ̃, ɔn/ *adj* **1** (joli) cute; **2** (gentil) sweet, kind; **sois ~, va fermer la porte** be a dear and close the door.

migraine /migʀɛn/ *nf* splitting headache; (plus fort) migraine; **donner la ~ à qn** FIG to give sb a headache.

migrant, ~e /migʀɑ̃, ɑ̃t/ *adj, nm,f* migrant.

migrateur, -trice /migʀatœʀ, tʀis/ *adj* migratory.

migration /migʀasjɔ̃/ *nf* migration; **~ saisonnière** (d'ouvriers) seasonal migration; (de vacanciers) seasonal departures (*pl*); **~ journalière** or **quotidienne** commuting.

migratoire /migʀatwaʀ/ *adj* migratory.

migrer /migʀe/ [1] *vi* to migrate (**à, en, vers** to).

mi-hauteur: **à mi-hauteur** /amiotœʀ/ *loc adv* (en montant) halfway up; (en descendant) halfway down.

mi-jambe: **à mi-jambe** /amiʒɑ̃b/ *loc adv* (up) to one's knees.

mijaurée /miʒɔʀe/ *nf* **ne fais pas ta ~** don't put on such airs; **petite ~!** little madam!

mijoter /miʒɔte/ [1] **I** *vtr* **1** CULIN to prepare [*plat*]; **2**○ (manigancer) to cook up.

II *vi* CULIN to simmer.

IDIOMES **laisser qn ~ dans son jus**○ to let sb stew in his/her own juice.

mijoteuse /mijɔtøz/ *nf* slow cooker.

mikado /mikado/ ▶329 *nm* spillikins (+ *v sg*).

mil /mil/ I *adj* = **mille** I.
II *nm* millet.

milan /milɑ̃/ *nm* ZOOL kite.

mildiou /mildju/ *nm* mildew.

milice /milis/ *nf* militia; ~ **de quartier** local vigilante group.

Milice /milis/ *nf* **la** ~ the Milice (*French wartime paramilitary organization which collaborated with the Germans against the Resistance*).

milicien, -ienne /milisjɛ̃, ɛn/ *nm,f* **1** MIL militiaman/ militiawoman; **2** HIST member of the Milice.

milieu, *pl* ~**x** /miljø/ I *nm* **1** (dans l'espace) middle; **au beau** or **en plein** ~ right in the middle; **2** (dans le temps) middle; **au** ~ **de** in the middle of, halfway through; **3** (moyen terme) middle ground; **c'est vrai ou faux, il n'y a pas de** ~ it's either right or wrong, there's no in-between; **4** (environnement) environment; **le** ~ **familial** the home environment; **en** ~ **rural** in the country; **en** ~ **urbain/scolaire** in towns/schools; **le** ~ **carcéral** prison life; **5** (origine sociale) background, milieu; (groupe) circle; **des gens de tous les** ~**x** people from every walk of life; **les** ~**x universitaires** academic circles; **un** ~ **professionnel très conservateur** a very conservative sector; **le** ~ **de l'édition** the world of publishing; **le** ~ (pègre) the underworld; **6** MATH (de segment) midpoint.
II **au milieu de** *loc prép* **1** (parmi) among; **être au** ~ **de ses amis** to be with one's friends; **2** (entouré de) surrounded by; **travailler au** ~ **du bruit** to work surrounded by noise; **au** ~ **du désastre** in the midst of disaster.
■ ~ **de culture** breeding ground; ~ **de terrain** (joueur) midfield player; (endroit) midfield.

militaire /militɛʀ/ I *adj* GÉN military; [*médecin, vie, camion*] army (*épith*); **école** ~ military academy.
II ▶374 *nm* serviceman; **un** ~ **de carrière** a career soldier; **être** ~ to be in the army.

militairement /militɛʀmɑ̃/ *adv* **1** LIT by military means; **zone occupée** ~ military occupied zone; **2** FIG (efficacement) with military efficiency; PÉJ along military lines.

militant, ~e /militɑ̃, ɑ̃t/ I *adj* militant.
II *nm,f* (de syndicat, parti) active member, activist; (de cause) campaigner; **les** ~**s de base** the rank-and-file members.

militantisme /militɑ̃tism/ *nm* political activism.

militarisation /militaʀizasjɔ̃/ *nf* militarization.

militariste /militaʀist/ I *adj* militaristic.
II *nmf* militarist.

militer /milite/ [1] *vi* **1** (agir) GÉN to campaign; (dans un parti) to be a political activist; **2** (constituer un argument) ~ **pour** or **en faveur de** to argue in favour of; ~ **contre** to militate against.

mille /mil/ I ▶399, 156 *adj inv* a thousand, one thousand; **deux/trois** ~ two/three thousand.
II *nm inv* **1** COMM, MATH a thousand, one thousand; **2** SPORT (cible) bull's eye; **mettre** or **taper dans le** ~ LIT to hit the bull's-eye; FIG to hit the nail on the head.
III ▶348, 631 *nm* NAUT ~ (**marin** or **nautique**) (nautical) mile; AVIAT (air) mile.
IV **pour mille** *loc adj* per thousand.
IDIOMES **je ne gagne pas des** ~ **et des cents** I don't earn very much; **je vous le donne en** ~ you'll never guess (in a million years).

millefeuille /milfœj/ *nm* millefeuille (*small layered cake made of puff pastry filled with custard and cream*).

millénaire /milenɛʀ/ I *adj* **1** (de mille ans) **un arbre** ~ a one thousand year old tree, a tree that is one thousand years old; **2** (vieux) [*tradition*] age-old.
II *nm* **1** (période) millennium; **pendant des** ~**s** for thousands of years; **2** (anniversaire) millennium, millenary.

mille-pattes /milpat/ *nm inv* centipede, millipede.

millésime /milezim/ *nm* **1** (de vin) vintage, year; (de

monnaie, médaille) date; 2 AUT year of manufacture; **3** (dans une date) millennial figure.

millésimé, ~e /milezime/ *adj* [*vin*] vintage (*épith*); [*monnaie*] bearing a date (*épith, après n*).

millet /mijɛ/ *nm* millet.
■ ~ **des oiseaux** birdseed, millet.

milli /mili/ *préf* milli-; ~**bar** millibar; ~**gramme** milligram; ~**litre** millilitre GB; ~**mètre** millimetre GB.

milliard /miljaʀ/ ▶399 *nm* billion.

milliardaire /miljaʀdɛʀ/ *nmf* multimillionaire, billionaire.

milliardième /miljaʀdjɛm/ ▶399 *adj* billionth.

millième /miljɛm/ ▶399 *adj* thousandth.

millier /milje/ *nm* **1** (mille) thousand; **2** (environ mille) **un** ~ about a thousand.

millimétré, ~e /milimetʀe/ *adj* graduated in millimetres GB; **papier** ~ graph paper.

million /miljɔ̃/ ▶399 *nm* million; **être riche à** ~**s** to be worth millions.

millionième /miljɔnjɛm/ ▶399 *adj* millionth; **au** ~ to the sixth decimal place.

millionnaire /miljɔnɛʀ/ I *adj* **être** ~ [*entreprise, société*] to be worth millions; [*personne*] to be a millionaire.
II *nmf* millionaire.

mi-lourd, *pl* ~**s** /miluʀ/ *nm* light heavyweight.

mime /mim/ ▶374 *nm* **1** THÉÂT mime; **2** (imitateur) mimic.

mimer /mime/ [1] *vtr* **1** THÉÂT to mime; **2** (imiter) to mimic.

mimétisme /mimetism/ *nm* **1** ZOOL mimicry; **2** (imitation) **par** ~ through unconscious imitation.

mimique /mimik/ *nf* **1** (expression comique) funny face; **2** (gestes et expressions) expressions and gestures (*pl*); (des sourds-muets) sign language.

mimodrame /mimɔdʀam/ *nm* mime.

mimosa /mimoza/ *nm* mimosa.

minable○ /minabl/ I *adj* **1** (médiocre) pathetic; [*délit*] petty; **2** (misérable) [*personne*] wretched; [*logement*] crummy○; [*existence*] miserable.
II *nmf* PÉJ (médiocre) pathetic○ character; (raté) loser○.

minage /minaʒ/ *nm* MIL mining.

minaret /minaʀɛ/ *nm* minaret.

minauder /minode/ [1] *vi* (dans l'allure) to mince about; (de la voix, du sourire) to simper.

minauderies /minodʀi/ *nfpl* affected mannerisms.

mince /mɛ̃s/ I *adj* **1** (fin) [*personne, jambe*] slim, slender; [*cou, bras*] slender; [*visage*] thin; [*tranche, lame*] thin; [*livre*] slim; **2** (faible) [*consolation*] small; [*espoir, chance*] slim; [*indice*] tenuous; [*revenus*] meagre; **ce n'est pas une** ~ **affaire** (difficile) that's no small task; (important) that's no trivial matter.
II○ *excl* ~ (**alors**)! (étonnement) wow○!; (dépit) damn○!

minceur /mɛ̃sœʀ/ I *adj inv* **cuisine** ~ low-calorie dishes (*pl*).
II *nf* **1** (de personne, jambes) slimness, slenderness; (de cou, bras) slenderness; (de visage, tranche) thinness; **2** (d'indice) tenuousness; (de revenus) meagreness GB.

mincir /mɛ̃siʀ/ [3] *vi* to lose weight; **il a minci de visage** his face has got GB ou gotten US thinner.

mine /min/ I *nf* **1** (expression) expression; (aspect) look; **faire triste** ~ to have a gloomy expression, to look gloomy; **juger sur la** ~ to judge by appearances; **faire** ~ **d'accepter** to pretend to accept; **faire** ~ **de partir** to make as if to go; **elle nous a dit,** ~ **de rien**○, **que** she told us, casually, that; **il est doué,** ~ **de rien**○ it may not be obvious, but he's very clever; **2** (apparence) **avoir mauvaise** ~, **avoir une sale**○ or **petite** ~ to look a bit off-colour GB; **avoir une** ~ **resplendissante** to be glowing with health; **avoir une** ~ **de papier mâché** to look washed out; **avoir bonne** ~ [*personne*] to look well; [*tarte, rôti*] to look appetizing; **j'aurais bonne** ~! IRON I would look really stupid!; **3** (pour dessiner) lead; **crayon à** ~

dure/grasse hard/soft pencil; **4** (gisement) mine; ~ **d'or** LIT, FIG gold mine; **5** (source) source; ~ **d'informations** FIG mine of information; **6** MIL mine.

II **mines** *nfpl* (minauderies) simpering ¢; **faire des** ~**s** to simper.

■ ~ **de crayon** lead; ~ **de plomb** graphite ¢.

IDIOMES **ne pas payer de** ~° not to look anything special°.

miner /mine/ [1] *vtr* **1** (affaiblir) to sap [*moral, énergie*]; to undermine [*santé, gouvernement*]; **cela me mine** it's wearing me down; (plus fort) it's eating me alive; **2** MIL to mine; **le terrain est miné** LIT the ground is mined; FIG it's a minefield.

minerai /minʀɛ/ *nm* ore; ~ **de fer** iron ore.

minéral, ~e, *mpl* **-aux** /mineral, o/ **I** *adj* **1** [*huile, eau, règne*] mineral; [*chimie*] inorganic; **2** FIG [*paysage*] barren.

II *nm* mineral.

minéralogie /mineralɔʒi/ *nf* mineralogy.

minéralogique /mineralɔʒik/ *adj* **1** (en géologie) mineralogical; **2** ADMIN, AUT **numéro** ~ registration number GB, license number US; **plaque** ~ number plate GB, license plate US.

minerve /minɛʀv/ *nf* MÉD surgical collar GB, neck brace US.

minet /minɛ/ *nm* **1** (chat) pussycat LANG ENFANTIN; **2°** (jeune dandy) pretty boy°.

minette /minɛt/ *nf* **1** (chatte) pussycat LANG ENFANTIN; **2°** (jeune fille) cool chick°.

mineur, ~e /minœʀ/ **I** *adj* **1** JUR under 18 (*après n*); **2** (peu important) minor; **3** MUS minor.

II *nm,f* JUR person under 18, minor SPÉC.

III *nm* **1** ▶**374** (ouvrier) miner; ~ **de fond** pit worker; **2** (soldat) soldier who lays mines.

mini /mini/ **I°** *adj inv* (minuscule) tiny.

II *nm* **1** (jupes courtes) **s'habiller en** ~ to wear miniskirts; **2°** ORDINAT minicomputer, mini°.

mini- /mini/ *préf* mini; ~**-révolution** mini-revolution.

miniature /minjatyʀ/ **I** *adj* miniature (*épith*).

II *nf* GÉN, ART miniature.

miniaturisation /minjatyʀizasjɔ̃/ *nf* miniaturization.

minibus /minibys/ *nm inv* minibus.

minicassette® /minikasɛt/ *nf* mini-cassette®.

minier, -ière /minje, ɛʀ/ *adj* mining.

mini-golf, *pl* ~**s** /minigɔlf/ ▶**329** *nm* mini-golf.

mini-informatique /miniɛ̃fɔʀmatik/ *nf* minicomputing.

mini-jupe, *pl* ~**s** /miniʒyp/ *nf* mini-skirt.

minima ▶ **minimum**.

minimal, ~e, *mpl* **-aux** /minimal, o/ *adj* minimal, minimum.

minimalisme /minimalism/ *nm* minimalism.

minime /minim/ **I** *adj* [*dégâts, différence, dépenses*] negligible; [*chance*] slim, slender; [*rôle*] minor.

II *nmf* SPORT junior (*7 to 13 years old*).

minimiser /minimize/ [1] *vtr* to minimize, to play down.

minimum, *pl* ~**s** or **minima** /minimɔm, minima/ **I** *adj* minimum; **un an, c'est le délai** ~ it will take one year at least.

II *nm* **1** (limite inférieure) minimum; **en faire un** ~ to do as little as possible; **il faut travailler un** ~ **si tu veux réussir** you have to do a bit of work if you want to succeed; **un** ~ **de bon sens** a certain amount of common sense; **un** ~ **d'hygiène** a basic level of hygiene; **avec un** ~ **d'efforts** with a minimum of effort; **prendre le** ~ **de risques** to take as few risks as possible; **il faut au** ~ **deux heures pour faire le trajet** the journey takes at least two hours; **2** JUR minimum sentence.

■ ~ **vital** subsistence level.

mini-ordinateur, *pl* ~**s** /miniɔʀdinatœʀ/ *nm* minicomputer.

minipilule /minipilyl/ *nf* low-dose combined pill.

ministère /ministɛʀ/ *nm* **1** POL GÉN ministry; (au Royaume-Uni, aux États-Unis) department; (charge) ministership; **2** POL (équipe gouvernementale) cabinet, government; **3** JUR **le** ~ **public** (service) the public prosecutor's office; (magistrat) the prosecuting magistrate, the prosecution; **4** RELIG ministry.

ministériel, -ielle /ministeʀjɛl/ *adj* ministerial.

ministre /ministʀ/ *nm* **1** POL GÉN minister; (au Royaume-Uni) Secretary of State; (aux États-Unis) Secretary; ~ **délégué** minister of state GB, under-secretary US (**auprès de** to); **les** ~**s** the cabinet; **Madame le** ~ Minister GB, Madam Secretary US; **Monsieur le** ~ Minister GB, Mr Secretary US; ▶**premier**; **2** (en diplomatie) envoy; **3** RELIG minister.

Minitel® /minitɛl/ *nm* Minitel (*terminal linking phone users to a database*); **sur** or **au** ~ on Minitel; **par le** ~ by Minitel.

minivague /minivag/ *nf* soft perm.

minois /minwa/ *nm inv* fresh young face; **joli petit** ~ pretty little face.

minon° /minɔ̃/ *nm* H (poussière) fluff ¢.

minoration /minɔʀasjɔ̃/ *nf* **1** (sous-estimation) undervaluation; (de prix) underestimation; **2** (réduction) reduction; ~ **des prix** cut in prices.

minorer /minɔʀe/ [1] *vtr* **1** (réduire) to reduce [*prix, taux*] (**de** by); **2** (sous-estimer) to undervalue [*biens*]; to underestimate [*montant*].

minoritaire /minɔʀitɛʀ/ **I** *adj* minority (*épith*).

II *nmf* member of a minority group; **les** ~**s** those in the minority.

minorité /minɔʀite/ *nf* **1** (groupe) minority; **être en** ~ to be in the minority; **être mis en** ~ to be defeated; **2** (petit nombre) minority (**de** of); **3** (d'âge) minority; ~ **pénale** JUR ≈ legal infancy.

■ ~ **de blocage** FIN blocking minority.

minoterie /minɔtʀi/ *nf* **1** (usine) flour mill; **2** (industrie) flour-milling (industry).

minotier /minɔtje/ ▶**374** *nm* miller.

minou /minu/ *nm* **1** (chat) pussycat LANG ENFANTIN; (pour appeler un chat) ~ ~! puss puss°!; **2°** (terme d'affection) **mon gros** ~ my sweetie°.

minuit /minɥi/ ▶**298** *nm* midnight; **de** ~ [*messe, soleil*] midnight (*épith*).

minus° /minys/ *nmf inv* PEJ moron°.

minuscule /minyskyl/ **I** *adj* **1** (tout petit) tiny; **2** (en écriture) small; (en imprimerie) lower-case.

II *nf* (en écriture) small letter; (en imprimerie) lower-case letter.

minutage /minytaʒ/ *nm* (precise) timing.

minute /minyt/ ▶**298**, **588** **I** *nf* **1** (unité de temps) minute; **2** (court moment) minute, moment; **hé!** ~°!, ~ **papillon°!** hang on a minute°!; **il peut arriver d'une** ~ **à l'autre** he may arrive any minute now; **j'en ai pour une** ~ I won't be a minute; **l'angoisse monte de** ~ **en** ~ fear is mounting by the minute; **on vient de me l'apporter à la** ~ it has just been brought to me this very second; **c'est pas à la** ~° it's not desperate ou urgent; **à la** ~ **où je vous parle** just as I'm speaking to you; **3** JUR ~ **d'un jugement** record of a decision; ~**s d'un procès** minutes of a trial; **4** (unité d'angle) minute.

II (-)**minute** (*in compounds*) **'clés-**~**'** 'keys cut while you wait'; **'nettoyage-**~**'** 'same day dry cleaning'.

■ ~ **de silence** minute's silence; **la** ~ **de vérité** the moment of truth.

minuter /minyte/ [1] *vtr* (chronométrer) to time; (prévoir) to work out the timing of; **l'opération doit être minutée à la seconde** the operation requires split-second timing.

minuterie /minytʀi/ *nf* (d'éclairage) (interrupteur) time-switch; (mécanisme) automatic lighting.

minuteur /minytœʀ/ *nm* timer.

minutie /minysi/ *nf* meticulousness.

minutieusement /minysjøzmɑ̃/ *adv* (avec soin) with meticulous care; (dans le détail) in great detail.

minutieux, -ieuse /minysjø, øz/ *adj* [*ouvrier, soin, travail*] meticulous; [*étude, description*] detailed.

mioche○ /mjɔʃ/ *nmf* kid○; **sale ~** horrible brat○.

mirabelle /miʀabɛl/ *nf* **1** (fruit) mirabelle (*small yellow plum*); **2** (eau-de-vie) plum brandy.

miracle /miʀakl/ **I** *adj inv* **un médicament ~** a wonder drug; **une méthode ~** a magic formula.

II *nm* **1** GÉN miracle; **accomplir** or **faire un ~** RELIG to work a miracle; FIG to work miracles; **tenir du ~** to be a miracle; **un ~ de l'architecture** an architectural wonder; **par ~** miraculously; **comme par ~** as if by magic; **2** (drame sacré) miracle play.

miraculé, ~e /miʀakyle/ RELIG **I** *adj* [*malade*] who is/was etc miraculously cured (*épith, après n*).

II *nm,f* **c'est un ~** he has been saved by a miracle; **les ~s de la route** people who have miraculously survived a road accident.

miraculeusement /miʀakyløzmã/ *adv* miraculously.

miraculeux, -euse /miʀakylø, øz/ *adj* GÉN miraculous; [*remède*] which works wonders (*épith, après n*).

mirador /miʀadɔʀ/ *nm* MIL watchtower.

mirage /miʀaʒ/ *nm* (vision) mirage.

mi-raisin /miʀɛzɛ̃/ *adj inv* ▶ **mi-figue**.

miraud○, **~e** /miʀo, od/ *adj* shortsighted.

mire /miʀ/ *nf* **1** TV test card GB, test pattern US; **2** (en topographie) levelling^{GB} staff.

mirer: se mirer /miʀe/ [1] *vpr* LITER [*personne*] to gaze at one's reflection; [*objet*] to be reflected.

mirifique /miʀifik/ *adj* HUM fabulous○.

mirobolant○, **~e** /miʀɔbɔlɑ̃, ɑ̃t/ *adj* fabulous○.

miroir /miʀwaʀ/ *nm* LIT, FIG mirror.

■ **~ aux alouettes** LIT, FIG lure.

miroitement /miʀwatmɑ̃/ *nm* LITER (de vitre) sparkling ¢; (de l'eau) shimmering ¢.

miroiter /miʀwate/ [1] *vi* [*objet*] to sparkle; [*eau*] to shimmer; **faire ~ qch à qn** to hold out the prospect of sth to sb.

mironton /miʀɔ̃tɔ̃/, **miroton** /miʀɔtɔ̃/ *nm* (**bœuf**) **~** beef stew (*with onion sauce*).

mis, ~e¹ /mi, miz/ **I** *pp* ▶ **mettre**.

II *pp adj* **être bien ~** to be well-dressed.

misaine /mizɛn/ *nf* (**voile de**) **~** foresail.

misanthrope /mizɑ̃tʀɔp/ **I** *adj* misanthropic.

II *nmf* misanthropist, misanthrope.

mise² /miz/ **I** *pp adj f* ▶ **mis**.

II *nf* **1** (dans un pari, jeu) **une ~ de cinq francs** a five-franc bet; **récupérer sa ~** to recover one's stake; **2** (tenue) **~ négligée** sloppy appearance.

■ **~ de fonds** investment; **~ en plis** set.

IDIOMES **être de ~** [*remarque*] to be appropriate; **ne pas être de ~** to be out of place; **je t'ai sauvé la ~** ○ I saved your bacon○.

■ Note Les expressions du type *mise en boîte, mise à feu, mise à mort* sont traitées sous le deuxième élément: on se reportera à *boîte, feu, mort* etc.

mise-bas, *pl* **mises-bas** /mizbɑ/ *nf* (d'animal) birth.

miser /mize/ [1] **I** *vtr* to bet [*argent*] (**sur** on).

II *vi* **1** (parier) **~ sur le 2** (au casino) to place a bet on the 2; **~ sur un cheval** to put money on a horse; **~ sur le mauvais cheval** FIG to make the wrong choice; **2** (compter) **~ sur la qualité d'un produit** to bank on the quality of a product; **~ sur un événement/sa chance/ses efforts** to count on an event/one's luck/one's efforts; **~ sur qn** to place all one's hopes in sb.

misérabilisme /mizeʀabilism/ *nm* **1** (d'écrivain) sordid realism; **2** (d'individu) tendency to dwell on the dark side.

misérable /mizeʀabl/ **I** *adj* **1** (très pauvre) [*personne*] destitute; [*habit*] shabby; [*vie, pays*] poor, wretched; [*maison*] squalid; **2** (dérisoire) [*salaire*] meagre^{GB}; [*affaire*] pathetic; **3** (pitoyable) pitiful, miserable.

II *nmf* **1** (indigent) pauper; **2**† (personne méprisable) scoundrel.

misérablement /mizeʀabləmɑ̃/ *adv* **1** (pauvrement) wretchedly, miserably; **2** (pitoyablement) miserably, pitifully.

misère /mizɛʀ/ *nf* **1** (pauvreté) destitution; **être dans la ~** to be destitute; **réduire qn à la ~** to reduce sb to poverty; **2** (détresse) misery, wretchedness; **quelle ~!** isn't it awful!; **3** (ennui) trouble, woe; **petites ~s** little troubles; **4** (somme dérisoire) pittance; **5** BOT wandering Jew, tradescantia.

■ **~ intellectuelle** intellectual poverty; **~ noire** dire poverty.

miséreux, -euse /mizeʀø, øz/ **I** *adj* destitute.

II *nm,f* destitute person; **les ~** the destitute.

miséricorde /mizeʀikɔʀd/ *nf* RELIG mercy.

miséricordieux, -ieuse /mizeʀikɔʀdjø, øz/ *adj* merciful.

misogyne /mizɔʒin/ **I** *adj* misogynous.

II *nmf* misogynist.

misogynie /mizɔʒini/ *nf* misogyny.

missel /misɛl/ *nm* missal.

missile /misil/ *nm* missile.

mission /misjɔ̃/ *nf* **1** (tâche) mission, task; **il s'est donné pour ~ de faire** he has taken it upon himself to do; **2** (fonction temporaire) mission, assignment; **~ d'information**, **~ d'enquête** special fact-finding mission; **être envoyé en ~ auprès de qn** to be sent to sb on special assignment; **être envoyé en ~ d'étude** to be sent to make a study; **3** (groupe) mission, team; **~ d'experts** team of experts; **4** MIL (but) mission; **5** RELIG GÉN mission; (groupe) missionary group.

missionnaire /misjɔnɛʀ/ *adj, nmf* missionary.

missive /misiv/ *nf* FML missive SOUT.

mistigri /mistigʀi/ *nm* **1** (aux cartes) mistigris; **2**○ (chat) pussycat○ LANG ENFANTIN.

mistral /mistʀal/ *nm* mistral.

mitaine /mitɛn/ *nf* fingerless mitt.

mite /mit/ *nf* (clothes) moth.

mi-temps¹ /mitɑ̃/ *nm inv* **1** (emploi) part-time job; **2** (système) part-time work ¢; **il est serveur à ~** he's a part-time waiter.

mi-temps² /mitɑ̃/ *nf inv* SPORT (arrêt) half-time; (moitié de match) half; **à la ~** at half-time.

miteux, -euse /mitø, øz/ *adj* [*quartier, hôtel*] seedy; [*vêtements*] shabby; [*personne*] down-at-heel.

mitigé, ~e /mitiʒe/ *adj* [*accueil*] lukewarm; [*succès*] qualified; [*conclusions*] ambivalent.

mitonner /mitɔne/ [1] **I** *vtr* to cook [sth] lovingly [*plat*]; to prepare the ground carefully for [*projet*].

II *vi* [*plat*] to cook slowly.

III se mitonner *vpr* **se ~ un petit plat** to cook a nice little meal for oneself; **se ~ un bel avenir** to carve out a nice future for oneself.

mitoyen, -enne /mitwajɛ̃, ɛn/ *adj* **1** JUR (en commun) [*haie*] dividing; **mur ~** party wall; **2** (contigu) CONTROV [*bâtiment*] adjoining.

mitraillage /mitʀajaʒ/ *nm* **1** MIL machine-gunning (de of); **2** FIG **~ (de questions)** quick-fire questioning.

■ **~ au sol** strafing.

mitraille /mitʀaj/ *nf* **1** MIL (d'artillerie) hail of bullets; **2**○ (monnaie) small change.

mitrailler /mitʀaje/ [1] *vtr* **1** MIL to machine-gun; **~ au sol** to strafe; **2** (bombarder) **~ qn de cailloux** to pelt sb with stones; **~ qn de questions** to fire questions at sb; **3**○ (photographier) to take photo after photo of [*tableau, personne*]; **se faire ~ par les photographes** to be besieged by photographers.

mitraillette /mitʀajɛt/ *nf* submachine gun.

mitrailleuse /mitʀajøz/ *nf* machine gun.

mitre /mitʀ/ *nf* RELIG mitre^{GB}.

mitron /mitʀɔ̃/ *nm* baker's boy.

mi-voix: à mi-voix /amivwa/ *loc adv* in a low voice.

mixage /miksaʒ/ *nm* sound mixing.

mixer¹ /mikse/ [1] *vtr* AUDIO to mix.

mixer² /miksɛʀ/ = **mixeur**.

mixeur /miksœʀ/ *nm* (batteur) mixer; (broyeur) blender.

mixité /miksite/ *nf* (à l'école) coeducation.

mixte /mikst/ *adj* **1** [*école*] coeducational; [*classe*] mixed; [*concours*] open to both sexes (*après n*); [*salon de coiffure*] unisex; **enseignement ~** coeducation; **2** (hétérogène) GÉN mixed; [*commission*] joint (*épith*); [*chaudière*] dual-system (*épith*); [*scrutin*] dual; **entreprise** or **société ~** joint venture.

mixture /mikstyʀ/ *nf* **1** (plat cuisiné) concoction; **2** (en pharmacie) mixture; **3** (mélange) mishmash○ PÉJ.

MJC /ɛmʒise/ *nf: abbr* ▶ **maison**.

MLF /ɛmɛlɛf/ *nm* (*abbr* = **mouvement de libération des femmes**) ~ Women's Lib.

Mlle ▶596| (*written abbr* = **Mademoiselle**) Ms, Miss; **~ Lévy** Ms Lévy, Miss Lévy.

Mlles ▶596| (*written abbr* = **Mesdemoiselles**) Misses.

mm (*written abbr* = **millimètre**) mm.

MM. ▶596| (*written abbr* = **Messieurs**) Messrs.

Mme ▶596| (*written abbr* = **Madame**) Ms, Mrs.

Mmes ▶596| (*written abbr* = **Mesdames**) ~ Huet et Cordelle Ms Huet and Ms Cordelle, Mrs Huet and Mrs Cordelle.

mnémotechnique /mnemɔtɛknik/ *adj* mnemonic.

Mo (*written abbr* = **mégaoctet**) Mb, MB.

mob○ /mɔb/ *nf* (vélomoteur) moped.

mobile /mɔbil/ **I** *adj* GÉN mobile; [*feuillet*] loose; [*fête*] movable.
II *nm* **1** (motif) motive; **2** PHYS moving body; **3** ART mobile.

mobilier, **-ière** /mɔbilje, ɛʀ/ **I** *adj* **biens ~s** movable property **₵**; **valeurs mobilières** securities.
II *nm* furniture; **~ urbain** street furniture.

mobilisateur, **-trice** /mɔbilizatœʀ, tʀis/ *adj* [*discours*] rousing; [*projet*] stimulating; [*personne*] inspiring.

mobilisation /mɔbilizasjɔ̃/ *nf* GÉN mobilization; **~ générale** MIL mobilization; FIG all-out effort.

mobiliser /mɔbilize/ [1] **I** *vtr* **1** MIL to mobilize [*militaire*]; to call up [*civil*]; **2** (rassembler) to mobilize [*militants*]; **le projet a mobilisé l'attention des étudiants** the project caught the attention of the students; **3** FIG to rally [*personne*]; to summon up [*courage*]; to call on [*raison*]; **~ les énergies** to mobilize people to act.
II se mobiliser *vpr* [*militants, étudiants*] to rally.

mobilité /mɔbilite/ *nf* GÉN mobility.

mobylette® /mɔbilɛt/ *nf* moped.

mocassin /mɔkasɛ̃/ *nm* (chaussure) moccasin.

moche○ /mɔʃ/ *adj* **1** (laid) [*personne*] ugly; [*vêtement*] ghastly; [*couleur*] awful; **2** (triste) dreadful; **3** (mesquin) nasty.
IDIOMES **~ comme un pou** as ugly as sin.

mocheté○ /mɔʃte/ *nf* (caractère) ugliness; (personne) horror.

modal, **-e**, *mpl* **-aux** /mɔdal, o/ **I** *adj* modal.
II *nm* modal verb.

modalité /mɔdalite/ **I** *nf* LING, MUS, PHILOS modality.
II modalités *nfpl* GÉN (conditions) terms; (façon de fonctionner) practical details; **~s de financement** methods of funding; **~s d'inscription** SCOL, UNIV enrolmentᴳᴮ procedure **₵**.

mode¹ /mɔd/ *nm* **1** (façon) way, mode; **~ de vie** way of life; **~ de transport** mode of transport; **~ de paiement** method of payment; **le ~ de fonctionnement de qch** the way sth operates; **traiter le sujet sur le ~ comique** to treat the subject in a comic vein; **2** LING mood; **3** MUS, ORDINAT, PHILOS mode.
■ **~ d'emploi** directions (*pl*) for use; (de plat cuisiné) cooking instructions (*pl*).

mode² /mɔd/ *nf* **1** (en matière d'habillement, d'idées) fashion; **lancer une ~** to start a trend; **une ~ passagère** a fad; **s'habiller à la dernière ~** to wear the latest fashions; **c'était une ~** it was fashionable;

coupe ~ fashionable cut; **à la ~** [*vêtement, restaurant, style*] fashionable; [*romancier*] who is in vogue (*épith, après n*); [*chanteur*] popular; **être à la ~** [*vêtement, style*] to be in fashion; **2** (secteur d'activité) fashion industry; **présentation de ~** fashion show.

modelage /mɔdlaʒ/ *nm* **1** (activité) modelling; **2** (objet) model.

modèle /mɔdɛl/ **I** *adj* GÉN model (*épith*).
II *nm* **1** (référence) GÉN model; (exemple) example; **prendre ~ sur qn** to do as sb does/did; **être un ~ de clarté** to be a model of clarity; **~ à suivre** (personne) somebody to look up to, role model; **2** COMM, IND (type) model; (taille) size; **grand/petit ~** large-/small-size (*épith*); **~ familial** family-size (*épith*); **construit sur le même ~** built to the same design; **3** (de v êtement) (création) model; (type d'article) style; **essaie ce ~** try this style; **4** (échantillon) **~ de signature** specimen signature; **compléter selon le ~** SCOL do the exercise following the example; **5** ▶374| ART, PHOT (personne) model; **6** (reproductible) pattern; **~ de conjugaison/tricot** conjugation/knitting pattern; **7** (prototype) model.
■ **~ déposé** JUR registered pattern; **~ réduit** scale model; **~ réduit d'avion** model plane.

modelé, **-e** /mɔdle/ **I** *adj* **bien ~** [*corps, jambe*] shapely; [*visage*] finely-sculpted.
II *nm* **1** ART, GÉOG relief; **2** (de visage, corps) contours (*pl*).

modeler /mɔdle/ [17] *vtr* (façonner) to model [*argile, statue*]; to shape [*personne, caractère*].

modélisme /mɔdelism/ *nm* modelling, model-making.

modéliste /mɔdelist/ ▶374| *nmf* **1** (de vêtements) (dress) designer; **2** (de maquettes) model-maker.

modérateur, **-trice** /mɔdeʀatœʀ, tʀis/ **I** *adj* moderating (*épith*).
II *nm,f* (personne) moderating influence; (fonction) moderator.
III *nm* (de pile atomique) moderator.

modération /mɔdeʀasjɔ̃/ *nf* **1** (sens de la mesure) moderation; **2** (de prix) reduction; **3** (de peine) mitigation.

modéré, **~e** /mɔdeʀe/ **I** *adj* GÉN moderate; [*prix*] reasonable; [*tempérament*] even; [*enthousiasme*] mild.
II *nm,f* moderate.

modérément /mɔdeʀemɑ̃/ *adv* **1** (moyennement) relatively; **2** (avec retenue) in moderation; **3** (légèrement) slightly.

modérer /mɔdeʀe/ [14] **I** *vtr* to curb [*dépenses, sentiments*]; to soften [*attitude*]; to moderate [*propos*]; to reduce [*vitesse*].
II se modérer *vpr* to exercise self-restraint.

moderne /mɔdɛʀn/ *adj* modern.

modernisateur, **-trice** /mɔdɛʀnizatœʀ, tʀis/ *adj*, *nm,f* progressive.

modernisation /mɔdɛʀnizasjɔ̃/ *nf* modernization.

moderniser /mɔdɛʀnize/ [1] *vtr* to modernize [*institution, secteur, matériel*]; to update [*loi, manuel*].

modernisme /mɔdɛʀnism/ *nm* **1** (goût) modernity; **2** (mouvement) modernism.

modernité /mɔdɛʀnite/ *nf* modernity.

modern style /mɔdɛʀnstil/ *nm inv* Art Deco style.

modeste /mɔdɛst/ *adj* GÉN modest; [*facture, coût*] moderate; [*famille, milieu*] humble.

modestement /mɔdɛstəmɑ̃/ *adv* **1** (sans superflu) modestly; **être ~ vêtu** to be wearing cheap clothes; **2** (sans orgueil) modestly.

modestie /mɔdɛsti/ *nf* modesty.

modicité /mɔdisite/ *nf* lowness; **la ~ des prix** the low prices (*pl*).

modificatif, **-ive** /mɔdifikatif, iv/ **I** *adj* **1** LING modifying; **2** ADMIN **texte ~** amendment.
II *nm* ADMIN amendment.

modification /mɔdifikasjɔ̃/ *nf* modification; (d'un projet de loi) amendments.

modifier /mɔdifje/ [2] *vtr* GÉN to change; TECH to alter, to modify [*moteur, système*]; POL to amend [*projet de loi*]; LING to modify.

nodique /mɔdik/ *adj* [*somme, ressources*] modest.

nodiste /mɔdist/ ▶ 374 *nf* milliner.

nodulable /mɔdylabl/ *adj* [*format, prélèvement*] adjustable; [*salle*] multi-purpose; [*horaire*] flexible.

nodulation /mɔdylasjɔ̃/ *nf* **1** PHYS, RADIO modulation; **2** (flexibilité) flexibility; **3** (adaptation) adjustment.
■ **~ de fréquence**, MF frequency modulation, FM.

nodule /mɔdyl/ *nm* **1** GÉN, UNIV module; (pour cuisine) unit; **2** MATH, PHYS modulus.

noduler /mɔdyle/ [1] *vtr* **1** GÉN, RADIO, TÉLÉCOM to modulate; **2** (adapter) to adjust [*prix*]; to adapt [*politique*].

noelle /mwal/ *nf* ANAT, CULIN, FIG marrow.
■ **~ épinière** spinal cord; **~ osseuse** bone marrow.

noelleux, -euse /mwalø, øz/ *adj* [*tissu, couleur, ton*] soft; [*voix*] mellifluous; [*vin*] mellow; [*dessert*] smooth; [*viande*] tender.

noellon /mwalɔ̃/ *nm* CONSTR breeze block GB, cinder block US.

nœurs /mœr(s)/ *nfpl* **1** (usages) GÉN customs; (de milieu social) lifestyle (*sg*); **entrer dans les ~** (*usage*) to become part of everyday life; **comédie de ~** LITTÉRAT comedy of manners; **l'évolution des ~** the change in attitudes; **2** (habitudes de conduite) habits; **les ~ des renards** the habits of foxes; **3** (moralité) morals; **la police des ~** the vice squad; **une sordide affaire de ~** a sordid sex case.
IDIOMES **autres temps, autres ~** other days, other ways.

nohair /mɔɛr/ *nm* mohair.

noi /mwa/ *pron pers* **1** (sujet) I, me; **c'est ~** (au téléphone) it's me; **c'est ~ qui ai cassé la vitre** I was the one who broke the windowpane; **il les voit plus souvent que ~** (que je ne les vois) he sees them more often than I do; (qu'il ne me voit) he sees them more often than me ou than he sees me; **2** (objet) me; **pour ~ il est fou** personally, I think he's mad; **à ~** (à l'aide) help!; (à mon tour) (it's) my turn!; **des amis à ~** friends of mine; **une pièce à ~** a room of my own; **c'est à ~** (appartenance) it's mine, it belongs to me; (tour) it's my turn; **c'est à ~ de choisir** (ma responsabilité) it's up to me to choose.

noignon /mwaɲɔ̃/ *nm* stump.

noi-même /mwamɛm/ *pron pers* myself; **en ~ je me disais que ça n'avait pas d'importance** I told myself that it didn't matter.

noindre /mwɛ̃dR/ *adj* **1** (comparatif) lesser; **dans une ~ mesure** to a lesser extent; **considérer qch comme un ~ mal** to consider sth as the lesser of two evils; **à ~ prix** more cheaply; **2** (superlatif) **le ~** the least; **c'est la ~ des choses** it's the least I/you etc could do; **ce serait la ~ des politesses de répondre à leur lettre** you/we etc could at least have the courtesy to reply to their letter; **je n'en ai pas la ~ idée** I haven't got the slightest idea; **de nombreux scientifiques, et non des ~s** many scientists, and highly respected ones at that; **dernier point à souligner et non des ~s** last but not least.

noine /mwan/ *nm* RELIG monk.
IDIOMES **l'habit ne fait pas le ~** PROV you can't judge a book by its cover.

noineau, *pl* **~x** /mwano/ *nm* (oiseau) sparrow.
IDIOMES **il a une cervelle de ~** he is a featherbrain.

noins¹ /mwɛ̃/ **I** *prép* **1** (dans une soustraction) minus; **2** (pour dire l'heure) to; **il est huit heures ~ dix** it's ten (minutes) to eight; **il est ~ vingt**° it's twenty to°; **il était ~ une**° ou **~ cinq**° it was a close shave°; **3** (dans une température) minus.
II *adv* **1** (modifiant un verbe) (comparatif) less; (superlatif) **le ~** the least; **ils sortent ~** they go out less often; **c'est ~ une question d'argent qu'une question de principe** it's not so much a question of money as a question of principle; **de ~ en ~** less and less; **~ je sors, ~ j'ai envie de sortir** the less I go out, the less I feel like going out; **qui travaille le ~ de**

---

moins¹

Généralités

La traduction en anglais de *moins* est *less*. Cependant, elle n'est utilisée que dans un nombre de cas assez restreint:

> en moins de trois jours = in less than three days

Très souvent, même quand une traduction avec *less* est possible, l'anglais a recours à d'autres moyens. Certains sont réguliers:

> ma chambre est moins grande que la tienne
>   = my bedroom isn't as big as yours
> j'ai moins d'expérience que toi
>   = I don't have as much experience as you (do)
>   *ou* I have less experience than you (do)
> c'est moins compliqué que vous ne le croyez
>   = it's not as complicated as you think
>   *ou* it's less complicated than you think

D'autres ne le sont pas:

> j'essaie de moins fumer
>   = I'm trying to cut down on my smoking
>   *ou* I'm trying to smoke less

moins de

Lorsque *moins de*, déterminant indéfini, est suivi d'un nom dénombrable, la règle voudrait que l'on traduise par *fewer* mais dans la langue parlée on utilise également *less*.

Les expressions telles que *le moins du monde* sont traitées sous *monde*.

On trouvera dans l'entrée exemples et exceptions illustrant les différentes fonctions de *moins*.

On pourra également se reporter aux notes d'usage portant notamment sur *les quantités*, l'expression de *l'âge* etc. Consulter l'index ▶ 1420.

---

tous? who works the least of all?; **le film qui m'a le ~ plu** the film I liked the least; **ce que j'aime le ~ chez lui** what I like least about him; **2** (modifiant un adjectif) (comparatif) less; (superlatif) **le ~, la ~, les ~** (de deux) the less; (de plus de deux) the least; **il est ~ grand que son père** he's not as tall as his father; **il est ~ menteur que sa sœur** he's less of a liar than his sister; **les jeunes et les ~ jeunes** the young and the not so young; **dans le livre il y a du bon et du ~ bon** in the book, there are bits that are good and bits that are not so good; **il n'en est pas ~ vrai que** it's nonetheless true that; **le même en ~ gros** the same, only thinner; **un individu des ~ recommandables** a most unsavoury individual; **3** (modifiant un adverbe) (comparatif) less; (superlatif) **le ~** least; **tu devrais rester ~ longtemps dans le sauna** you shouldn't stay so long in the sauna; **elle chante ~ bien qu'avant** she doesn't sing as well as she used to; **le ~ souvent** (the) least often.
III moins de *dét indéf* **1** (avec un nom) **~ de livres** fewer books; **~ de graisses** less fat; **~ de sucre/bruit** less sugar/noise; **il a parlé avec ~ de hargne** he spoke less aggressively; **il y a ~ de monde aujourd'hui qu'hier** there are fewer people today than there were yesterday; **c'est lui qui a le ~ d'expérience des trois** of the three he's the one with the least experience; **2** (avec un numéral) **en ~ de trois heures** in less than three hours; **il est ~ de 3 heures** it's not quite 3 o'clock; **les ~ de 20 ans** people under 20, the under-twenties.
IV à moins *loc adv* on serait furieux **à ~** it's more than enough to make one angry.
V à moins de *loc prép* **à ~ de partir maintenant** unless we/you etc leave now; **à ~ d'un miracle** unless there's a miracle.
VI à moins que *loc conj* **à ~ qu'il ne veuille venir** unless he wants to come.
VII à tout le moins *loc adv* to say the least.
VIII au moins *loc adv* at least; **tout au ~** at least; **tu l'as remercié, au ~?** you did thank him, didn't you?
IX de moins *loc adv* **ça m'a pris deux heures de**

Les mois de l'année

Les noms des mois

L'anglais emploie la majuscule pour les noms de mois. Les abréviations sont courantes en anglais familier écrit, par ex. dans une lettre à un ami: I'll see you on Mon 17 Sept.

		abréviation anglaise
janvier	January	Jan
février	February	Feb
mars	March	Mar
avril	April	Apr
mai	May	May
juin	June	Jun
juillet	July	Jul
août	August	Aug
septembre	September	Sept
octobre	October	Oct
novembre	November	Nov
décembre	December	Dec

Dans les expressions suivantes, May est pris comme exemple. Tous les autres noms de mois s'utilisent de la même façon.

mai a été pluvieux = May was wet

L'anglais peut utiliser les noms de mois même là où le français a recours à l'expression le mois de ...

j'aime le mois de mai	= I like May
le mois de mai le plus chaud	= the warmest May
nous avons eu un beau mois de mai	= we had a lovely May

Quand?

Pour l'expression de la date, ▶ 156 ⌋.
nous sommes en mai = it is May

Avec les autres verbes que be *(être), en se traduit normalement par* in.
en mai = in May *or* (*littéraire*) in the month of May

je suis né en mai	= I was born in May
je te verrai en mai	= I'll see you in May
l'an prochain en mai	= in May next year

Noter aussi:

cette année-là en mai	= that May
en mai prochain	= next May
l'année dernière en mai	= last May
dans deux ans en mai	= the May after next
il y a deux ans en mai	= the May before last
tous les ans en mai	= every May
tous les deux ans en mai	= every other May
presque tous les ans en mai	= most Mays

Comparer:

un matin en mai	= one morning in May
un matin de mai	= one May morning *ou* on a May morning
début mai	= in early May
au début de mai	= at the beginning of May
fin mai	= in late May
à la fin de mai	= at the end of May
à la mi-mai	= in mid-May
depuis mai	= since May
pendant tout le mois de mai	= for the whole of May *ou* for the whole month of May
tout au long du mois de mai	= all through May *ou* throughout May

De avec les noms de mois

Les expressions françaises avec de se traduisent par l'emploi du nom de mois en position d'adjectif.

les fleurs de mai	= May flowers
la pluie du mois de mai	= the May rain
le soleil de mai	= the May sunshine
le temps du mois de mai	= May weather
les soldes du mois de mai	= the May sales

~ it took me two hours less; **le kilo de pêches valait deux francs de ~ que la veille** a kilo of peaches cost two francs less than it had the day before; **j'ai un an de ~ que lui** I'm a year younger than he is; **il a obtenu 25% de voix de ~ que son adversaire** he got 25% fewer votes than his opponent; **X du moins** *loc adv* at least; **c'est du ~ ce qu'il m'a raconté** at least that's what he told me; **si du ~ tu es d'accord** that is if you agree; **XI en moins** *loc adv* **il y avait deux fourchettes en ~ dans la boîte** there were two forks missing from the box; **il est revenu du front avec une jambe en ~/avec un doigt en ~** he came back from the front with only one leg/with a finger missing; **c'est tout le portrait de son père, la moustache en ~** he's the spitting image of his father without the moustache GB ou mustache US. **XII pour le moins** *loc adv* to say the least.

moins² /mwɛ̃/ *nm inv* **1** MATH minus; **le signe ~** the minus sign; **2**○ (inconvénient) minus. ■ **~ que rien** good-for-nothing, nobody.

moins-value, *pl* **~s** /mwɛ̃valy/ *nf* **1** (diminution de valeur) depreciation; **2** (déficit des recettes fiscales) shortfall.

moire /mwaʀ/ *nf* (étoffe) moire.

moiré, ~e /mwaʀe/ *adj* [*tissu*] moiré; [*soie, papier*] watered.

mois /mwa/ ▶ 13 ⌋, 588 ⌋ *nm inv* **1** (division de l'année) month; **au ~ de juin** in June; **un bébé de trois ~** a three-month-old baby; **elle est enceinte de trois ~** she's three months pregnant; **à moins de deux ~ du premier tour** with the first round less than two months away; **2** (salaire) monthly salary.

Moïse /mɔiz/ *npr* Moses.

moisi /mwazi/ *nm* mould GB, mold US; **odeur/goût de ~** musty smell/taste.

moisir /mwaziʀ/ [3] *vi* **1** [*aliment*] to go mouldy GB ou moldy US; [*objet, plante*] to become mildewed; **2**○ [*personne*] to stagnate; [*argent, objet*] to gather dust;

on va pas ~ ici! we're not going to hang aroun here all day!

moisissure /mwazisyʀ/ *nf* mould ¢ GB, mold ¢ US mildew ¢.

moisson /mwasɔ̃/ *nf* **1** LIT, GÉN harvest; (époque harvest time; **faire la ~** to harvest; **2** FIG haul.

moissonner /mwasɔne/ [1] *vtr* **1** LIT to harvest; **2** FI to gather [*renseignements*]; to win [*médailles*].

moissonneur, -euse¹ /mwasɔnœʀ, øz/ *nm,f* (per sonne) harvester.

moissonneuse² /mwasɔnøz/ *nf* (machine) reaper.

moissonneuse-batteuse, *pl* **moissonneuses batteuses** /mwasɔnøzbatøz/ *nf* combine harvester.

moite /mwat/ *adj* [*chaleur*] muggy; [*mur*] damp [*peau*] sweaty.

moiteur /mwatœʀ/ *nf* (de l'air) mugginess; (de l peau) sweatiness.

moitié /mwatje/ *nf* **1** GÉN half; **la peinture, c'est ~ de ma vie** half of my life is devoted to painting; **~ vide** half empty; **dormir à ~**○ to be half asleep; **~ prix** half-price; **s'arrêter à la ~** to stop halfway through; **à ~ cassé** damaged; **je n'y crois qu'à ~** don't entirely believe it; **il fait toujours les choses ~** he never does anything properly; **être pour dans qch** to be instrumental in sth; **2**○ (époux) m **~** my better half○.

moitié-moitié /mwatjemwatje/ *adv* (en proportion égales) half-and-half; **partager ~ avec qn** (dépense to go halves with sb; (gains) to split the profits wit sb.

moka /mɔka/ *nm* **1** (café) mocha; **2** (gâteau) mocha cake.

mol ▶ **mou** I.

molaire /mɔlɛʀ/ *nf* (dent) molar.

môle /mol/ *nm* **1** (brise-lames) breakwater; **2** (pou s'amarrer) pier, jetty.

moléculaire /mɔlekylɛʀ/ *adj* molecular.

molécule /mɔlekyl/ *nf* molecule.

moleskine /mɔlɛskin/ *nf* **1** (imitant le cuir) imitation leather; **2** (pour doublures) moleskin; **3** (de café) wall seat.

molester /mɔlɛste/ [1] *vtr* to manhandle.

molette /mɔlɛt/ *nf* **1** TECH (de clé) adjusting knob; (pour découper) rotary cutter; **2** (de briquet) striker wheel.

mollasse○ /mɔlas/ *adj* (mou) PEJ LIT sluggish; FIG soft.

molle ▶ mou I.

mollement /mɔlmɑ̃/ *adv* [*allongé*] idly; [*travailler*] without much enthusiasm; [*protester*] half-heartedly; [*tomber*] softly; [*couler*] gently.

mollesse /mɔlɛs/ *nf* **1** (caractère moelleux) softness; **2** (de chair) flabbiness; (de trait du visage) weakness; **3** (de personne) listlessness; (de poignée de main) limpness; **4** (manque d'autorité) **la ~ du gouvernement face aux manifestants** the government's failure to stand up to the demonstrators; **5** FIG (de personne, réponse) lack of conviction; (d'idée, de style) woolliness; (d'opposition) weakness; (de croissance) sluggishness.

mollet /mɔlɛ/ **I** *adj m* **œuf ~** soft-boiled egg.
II ▶ 137 *nm* calf; **des ~s de coq** legs like sticks; **avoir des ~s de cycliste** to have muscular calves.

molletière /mɔltjɛʀ/ **I** *adj f* **bande ~** puttee.
II *nf* legging.

molleton /mɔltɔ̃/ *nm* **1** (en laine) flannel; (en coton) flannelette; **2** (pour une table) (table) felt; (pour une planche à repasser) (ironing board) cover.

molletonner /mɔltɔne/ [1] *vtr* to line with fleece.

mollir /mɔliʀ/ [3] *vi* **1** (céder) [*courage*] to fail; [*autorité*] to diminish; [*enthousiasme*] to cool; [*ténacité*] to flag; [*résistance*] to grow weaker; [*personne*] to soften; **2** MÉTÉO [*vent*] to die down, to abate.

mollusque /mɔlysk/ *nm* **1** ZOOL mollusc GB, mollusk US; **2**○ (personne) drip○, wimp○.

molosse /mɔlɔs/ *nm* huge dog.

Molotov /mɔlɔtɔf/ *npr* **cocktail ~** Molotov cocktail.

môme /mom/ *nmf* (enfant) kid○; PEJ brat○.

moment /mɔmɑ̃/ *nm* **1** (instant précis) moment; **le ~ venu** (dans l'avenir) when the time comes; (dans le passé) when the time came; **il devrait arriver d'un ~ à l'autre** he should arrive any minute now; **à aucun ~ il n'a abordé le sujet** at no time did he touch on the subject; **à un ~ donné** (quelconque) at some point; (fixé) at a given moment; **sur le ~ j'ai cru qu'il plaisantait** at first I thought he was joking; **à ce ~-là** (à l'époque) at that time; (au même instant) just then; (dans ce cas) in that case; **au ~ de l'accident** at the time of the accident; **au ~ où** GÉN at the time (when); **au ~ où il quittait son domicile** as he was leaving his home; **jusqu'au ~ où** until; **du ~ que** (pourvu que) as long as, provided; (puisque) since; **du ~ que tu le dis!** if you say so!; **ce n'est pas le ~** GÉN it's not the right moment; (inopportun) now is not the time; **il arrive toujours au bon** IRON **ou mauvais ~!** he certainly picks his moment to call! IRON; **choisir son ~ pour faire** IRON to pick one's moment to do IRON; **2** (temps bref) moment; **j'ai eu un ~ d'incertitude** I hesitated for a moment; **3** (temps long) **pour le ~** for the time being; **tu en as pour un ~ à avoir mal** you'll feel uncomfortable for quite some time; **ça va prendre un ~** it will take a while; **au bout d'un ~, après un ~** after a while; **du ~** (*ennemi, préoccupations*) of the moment; **en ce ~** at the moment; **par ~s** at times; **c'est le ~ de la journée où** it's the time of day when; **les ~s forts du film** the film's highlights; **cela a été un ~ fort émouvant** it was a moment of intense emotion; **dans ses meilleurs ~s, il fait penser à Orson Welles** at his best, he reminds one of Orson Welles; **à mes ~s perdus** in my spare time.

momentané, **~e** /mɔmɑ̃tane/ *adj* momentary; **interruption ~e du son** temporary loss of sound.

momentanément /mɔmɑ̃tanemɑ̃/ *adv* for a moment, momentarily.

momie /mɔmi/ *nf* mummy.

momifier /mɔmifje/ [2] *vtr*, **se momifier** *vpr* to mummify.

mon, ma, *pl* **mes** /mɔ̃, ma, mɛ/ *adj poss* my;

■ **Note** Au vocatif, on n'emploie généralement pas le possessif en anglais: *ma chérie!* = darling!; *oui mon général!* yes, sir!; *mes chers amis!* = dear friends! On ne répète pas le possessif coordonné: *mon café et mon cognac* = my coffee and my cognac.

ma mère à moi○ my mother; **un de mes amis** a friend of mine; **j'ai ~ idée** I have my own ideas about that; **à ~ arrivée** when I arrived; **pendant ~ absence** while I was away; **j'ai ~ lundi** (cette semaine) I'm off on Monday; (toutes les semaines) I have Mondays off.

monacal, **~e**, *mpl* **-aux** /mɔnakal, o/ *adj* LIT, FIG monastic.

monarchie /mɔnaʀʃi/ *nf* monarchy.

monarchiste /mɔnaʀʃist/ *adj*, *nmf* monarchist.

monarque /mɔnaʀk/ *nm* monarch.

monastère /mɔnastɛʀ/ *nm* monastery.

monastique /mɔnastik/ *adj* monastic.

monceau, *pl* **~x** /mɔ̃so/ *nm* pile.

mondain, **~e** /mɔ̃dɛ̃, ɛn/ **I** *adj* [*réception, vie*] society (*épith*); **conversation ~e** polite conversation; **il est très ~** he's a socialite.
II *nm,f* socialite.

mondanités /mɔ̃danite/ *nfpl* **1** (réceptions mondaines) society events; **2** (politesses) **se faire des ~** to stand on ceremony.

monde /mɔ̃d/ *nm* **1** GÉN world; **ce sont les meilleurs amis du ~** they are the best of friends; **le plus calmement du ~** quite calmly; **pas le moins du ~** not in the least; **si vous êtes le moins du ~ soucieux** if you are (in) the least bit worried; **s'il souffrait le moins du ~** if he felt any pain at all; **se porter le mieux du ~** to be absolutely fine; **aller** or **voyager de par le ~, parcourir le ~** to travel the world; **il irait jusqu'au bout du ~ pour la retrouver** he would go to the ends of the earth to find her again; **c'est le bout du ~!, c'est au bout du ~!** it's in the back of beyond!; **mon père habite à l'autre bout du ~** my father lives halfway around the world; **ce n'est pas le bout du ~!** FIG it' s not such a big deal!; **comme le ~ est petit!** it's a small world!; **la faim dans le ~** world famine; **à la face du ~** for all the world to see; **les biens de ce ~** worldly goods; **en ce bas ~** here below; **elle n'est plus de ce ~** EUPH she's no longer with us EUPH; **quand je ne serai plus de ce ~** EUPH when I have departed this world; **la perfection n'est pas de ce ~** there is no such thing as perfection; **le ~ des vivants** the land of the living; **je n'étais pas encore au ~** I wasn't yet born; **▶ grand; 2** (milieu) world; **le ~ médical** the medical world; **le ~ animal** the animal kingdom; **ils ne sont pas du même ~** they are from different social backgrounds; **cet événement marqua la fin d'un ~** this event marked the end of an era; **un ~ nous sépare** we are worlds apart; **▶ nouveau; 3** (gens) people; **il n'y a pas grand ~** there aren't many people; **tout le ~** everybody; **voir beaucoup de ~** to have a busy social life ; **j'ai du ~ ce soir**○ I'm having people round GB ou over US tonight; **elle se moque du ~!** what does she take us for?; **tout mon petit ~** my family and friends (*pl*); **4** (bonne société) society; **le beau** or **grand ~** high society.
IDIOMES **se faire (tout) un ~ de qch** to get all worked up about sth; **ainsi va le ~** that's the way it goes; **depuis que le ~ est ~** since the beginning of time; **c'est le ~ à l'envers!** whatever next!; **c 'est un ~ ~**○! that's a bit much!

mondial, **~e**, *mpl* **-iaux** /mɔ̃djal, o/ *adj* [*record, congrès, économie*] world (*épith*); [*problème, succès*] worldwide; **la capitale ~e du cinéma** the cinema capital of the world; **seconde guerre ~e** Second World War.

mondialement /mɔ̃djalmɑ̃/ *adv* **être ~ connu** to be known all over the world.

mondialisation /mɔ̃djalizasjɔ̃/ *nf* (de marché, sport,

phénomène) globalization; **la ~ d'un conflit** the worldwide spread of a conflict.

mondialiser /mɔ̃djalize/ [1] *vtr* to globalize [*marché, échanges*]; to cause [sth] to spread worldwide [*conflit*].

mondialisme /mɔ̃djalism/ *nm* internationalism.

mondovision /mɔ̃dovizjɔ̃/ *nf* satellite broadcasting; **retransmettre en ~** to broadcast worldwide via satellite.

monégasque /monegask/ ▶ **394** | *adj* Monegasque.

monème /monɛm/ *nm* moneme.

monétaire /monetɛʀ/ *adj* [*système*] monetary; [*marché*] money.

monétariste /monetaʀist/ *adj, nmf* monetarist.

monétique /monetik/ *nf* electronic banking.

monétiser /monetize/ [1] *vtr* to monetize.

mongol, ~e /mɔ̃gɔl/ **I** ▶ **394** | *adj* GÉOG Mongolian; **l'empire ~** HIST the Mongol Empire.
II ▶ **338** | *nm* LING Mongolian.

Mongolie /mɔ̃gɔli/ ▶ **232** | *nprf* Mongolia.

Mongolie-Intérieure /mɔ̃gɔliɛ̃teʀjœʀ/ ▶ **509** | *nprf* Inner Mongolia.

mongolien, -ienne /mɔ̃gɔljɛ̃, ɛn/ CONTROV **I** *adj* MÉD Down's syndrome (*épith*); **être ~** to have Down's syndrome.
II *nm,f* MÉD (enfant) Down's syndrome child.

mongolisme /mɔ̃gɔlism/ *nm* CONTROV MÉD **le ~** Down's syndrome.

moniteur, -trice /monitœʀ, tʀis/ **I** ▶ **374** | *nm,f* **1** (de sport, conduite) instructor; **2** (de colonie de vacances, centre aéré) group leader GB, counselor US.
II *nm* TV monitor; ORDINAT monitor system.
■ **~ cardiaque** heart monitor.

monitorat /monitoʀa/ *nm* UNIV (activité) tutoring; (système) tutorial system.

monnaie /monɛ/ *nf* **1** (unité monétaire) currency; **2** (pièces et billets de faible valeur) change; **faire de la ~** to get some change; **3** (appoint) change; **4** (pièce) coin; **battre ~** to mint ou strike coins; **frapper une ~** to strike coins ou a coinage; **5** (bâtiment) (**l'hôtel de**) **la Monnaie** the Mint; **6** ÉCON (argent) money.
IDIOMES **rendre à qn la ~ de sa pièce** to pay sb back in his/her own coin; **c'est ~ courante** it's commonplace.

monnaie-du-pape, *pl* **monnaies-du-pape** /monɛdypap/ *nf* BOT honesty.

monnayable /monɛjabl/ *adj* **1** [*bon, billet*] convertible; **2** [*diplôme, talent*] marketable.

monnayer /monɛje/ [21] *vtr* **1** LIT to convert [sth] into cash; **2** FIG to capitalize on [*talent, expérience*]; **~ qch contre qch** to exchange sth for sth; **~ son silence** to exact a price for one's silence.

mono¹ /mono/ *préf* mono; **~chrome** monochrome; **~culture** monoculture; **~graphie** monograph; **~lingue** monolingual; **~lithique** monolithic; **~syllabe** monosyllable.

mono² /mono/ *nf* AUDIO mono; **en ~** in mono.

monobloc /monoblɔk/ *adj inv* cast in one piece (*après n*).

monocellulaire /monosɛlylɛʀ/ *adj* **famille ~** nuclear family.

monocle /monɔkl/ *nm* monocle.

monocoque /monokɔk/ **I** *adj* [*bateau*] monohull; [*voiture*] monocoque.
II *nm* (bateau) monohull.

monocorde /monokɔʀd/ *adj* [*voix, discours*] monotonous; **sur un** or **d'un ton ~** in a monotone.

monocylindrique /monosilɛ̃dʀik/ *adj* single-cylinder (*épith*).

monogame /monogam/ **I** *adj* monogamous.
II *nmf* monogamist.

monogamie /monogami/ *nf* monogamy.

monolithisme /monolitism/ *nm* **1** (de parti) monolithic nature; **2** ARCHIT monolithic system.

monologue /monolɔg/ *nm* monologue.
■ **~ intérieur** stream of consciousness.

monologuer /monologe/ [1] *vi* (parler seul) to deliver a monologue; PÉJ to hold forth.

monôme /monom/ *nm* MATH monomial.

monomoteur /monomotœʀ/ *nm* AVIAT single-engine aircraft.

mononucléose /mononykleoz/ ▶ **196** | *nf* mononuc leosis.
■ **~ infectieuse** glandular fever.

monoparental, ~e, *mpl* **-aux** /monopaʀɑ̃tal, o‹ *adj* **famille ~e** single-parent family.

monoplace¹ /monoplas/ *nm* AVIAT single-seater (ai‹ craft).

monoplace² /monoplas/ *nf* AUT one-seater (car).

monoplan /monoplɑ̃/ *nm* monoplane.

monopole /monopɔl/ *nm* LIT, FIG monopoly.

monopoliser /monopolize/ [1] *vtr* to monopolize.

monoprocesseur /monopʀɔsɛsœʀ/ *nm* single-chi‹ computer.

monoski /monoski/ ▶ **329** | *nm* (ski) monoski; (sport‹ monoskiing.

monospace /monospas/ *nm* AUT space cruiser.

monothéiste /monoteist/ **I** *adj* monotheistic.
II *nmf* monotheist.

monotone /monoton/ *adj* monotonous.

monotonie /monotoni/ *nf* monotony.

monozygote /monozigot/ *adj* monozygotic.

Monseigneur, *pl* **Messeigneurs** /mɔ̃sɛɲœʀ, meseɲœʀ/ *nm* **1** (forme d'adresse) (à un prince‹ Your Highness; (à un membre de la famille royale) You‹ Royal Highness; (à un cardinal) Your Eminence; (à u‹ duc, archevêque) Your Grace; (à un évêque) Your Lor‹ ship, My Lord (Bishop); **2** (titre) **~ le duc d‹ Parme** His Grace, the duke of Parma.

monsieur, *pl* **messieurs** /məsjø, mesjø/ ▶ **596** | *nr‹* **1** (titre donné à un inconnu) **Monsieur** (dans une lettre‹ Dear Sir; **bonjour, ~** good morning; **2** (titre donné‹ un homme dont on connaît le nom, par exemple Bon‹ **bonjour, ~** good morning, Mr Bon; **cher Monsieu‹** (dans une lettre) Dear Mr Bon; **Monsieur le cur‹** Father Bon; **Monsieur le ministre** (en lui parlan‹ Minister; **merci Monsieur le président** (de club, d'asso‹ ciation) thank you Mr Chairman; (de la République‹ thank you Mr President; **moi Monsieur!** (à un ense‹ gnant) please sir!; **3** (homme) man; **c'était u‹ (grand) ~!** he was a (true) gentleman!; **4** (formu‹ de respect utilisée avec un homme dont on connaît le nom‹ **'Monsieur a sonné?'** 'you rang sir?'; **‹ comprends, Monsieur a ses habitudes!** IRON H‹ Lordship is rather set in his ways you see!; **5** HIS‹ **Monsieur, frère du roi** Monsieur, the king's brother.
■ **~ Tout le Monde** the man in the street.

monstre /mɔ̃stʀ/ **I**○ *adj* [*travail, succès*] huge; [*culo‹ publicité*] colossal; **'soldes ~s'** 'mammoth sales'.
II *nm* **1** LIT, FIG monster; **un ~ d'orgueil‹** monstrously arrogant person; **2** (être difforme) frea‹ (of nature).
■ **~ marin** sea monster; **~ sacré** superstar.

monstrueusement /mɔ̃stʀyøzmɑ̃/ *adv* LIT, FIG [*rich‹ bête, intelligent*] horrendously; **il est ~ gros** he's‹ monstrous size.

monstrueux, -euse /mɔ̃stʀyø, øz/ *adj* **1** (choquan‹ monstrous; **2** (hideux) hideous; **d'une laideur mon‹ trueuse** hideously ugly; **3** (énorme) colossal; **d'un‹ bêtise monstrueuse** incredibly stupid.

monstruosité /mɔ̃stʀyozite/ *nf* **1** (de crime‹ monstrousness; **2** (acte) atrocity; (objet) monstrosity‹ **dire des ~s** to say preposterous things; **3** (difformité‹ deformity.

mont /mɔ̃/ *nm* GÉOG GÉN mountain; (lieu) Mount; ▶ **pr‹ mettre, val**.
■ **le ~ Blanc** Mont Blanc; **le ~ Everest** Mour‹ Everest; **le ~ des Oliviers** the Mount of Olive‹ **~ de Vénus** ANAT mons veneris.

montage /mɔ̃taʒ/ *nm* **1** (organisation) set-up; **2** (‹ machine) assembly; (de tente) putting up; (en couture‹ (de col) putting on; (de manche) setting in; **ateli‹ de ~** assembly shop; **3** CIN (de film) editin‹

table de ~ cutting table; **4** (de pierre précieuse) setting, mounting.
■ **~ photo** photomontage; **~ sonore** sound montage.

montagnard, ~e /mɔ̃taɲaʀ, aʀd/ **I** *adj* [*peuple*] mountain (*épith*); [*coutume*] highland (*épith*); **la vie ~e** life in the mountains.
II *nm,f* mountain dweller.

montagne /mɔ̃taɲ/ *nf* **1** (élévation) mountain; **pays de ~s** mountainous country; **2** (région montagneuse) **la ~** the mountains (*pl*); **de ~** [*route, animal*] mountain (*épith*); **il neige en haute ~** it's snowing on the upper slopes; **village de basse ~** village in the foothills of the mountains; **3** FIG (grande quantité) mountain.
■ **les ~s Rocheuses** the Rocky Mountains, the Rockies; **~s russes** big dipper (*sg*) GB, roller coaster (*sg*); **~ à vaches**○ FIG easy walks (*pl*); (pour ski) easy slopes (*pl*).
IDIOMES **se faire une ~ de qch** to get really worked up about sth; **faire battre des ~s** to stir up trouble; **la foi déplace** or **soulève les ~s** faith can move mountains; **il n'y a que les ~s qui ne se rencontrent pas** PROV there are none so distant that fate cannot bring them together PROV; **c'est la ~ qui accouche d'une souris** HUM a great deal of effort leading to nothing much.

montagneux, -euse /mɔ̃taɲø, øz/ *adj* mountainous.

montant, ~e /mɔ̃tɑ̃, ɑ̃t/ **I** *adj* **1** [*cabine, groupe*] going up (*après n*); **2** [*rue*] uphill; [*courbe*] rising; **3** [*col*] high; [*chaussettes*] long; **chaussures ~es** ankle boots.
II *nm* **1** (somme) sum; **un ~ global** a sum total; **le ~ des pertes** the total losses (*pl*); **d'un** or **pour un ~ de** [*déficit, épargne*] amounting to; [*chèque*] to the amount of; [*marchandises*] for a total of; **2** (d'échafaudage) pole; (d'échelle, de porte) upright.
■ **~ de lit** bedpost; **~s compensatoires (monétaires)** (monetary) compensatory amounts.

mont-de-piété, *pl* **monts-de-piété** /mɔ̃dpjete/ *nm* pawnshop, pawnbroker's; **mettre qch au ~** to pawn sth.

monté○, **~e**[1] /mɔ̃te/ *adj* (équipé) equipped; **te voilà bien ~e avec un mari comme ça!** IRON you're in a bad way with a husband like that!

monte-charge /mɔ̃tʃaʀʒ/ *nm inv* goods lift GB ou elevator US.

montée[2] /mɔ̃te/ **I** *adj f* ▶ **monté**.
II *nf* **1** (action de grimper) (d'escalier, de pente) climb; (de montagne) ascent; **'ne pas gêner la ~ des voyageurs'** 'do not obstruct passengers boarding'; **2** (d'avion, de ballon) climb, ascent; **3** (élévation de niveau) (action) rising (**de** of); (résultat) rise (**de** in); **la ~ des eaux** the rise in the water level; **4** FIN rise (**de** in); (de coûts, frais) increase (**de** in); **5** (augmentation) AGR rise; (de dangers, risques) increase; **une ~ de l'inqui étude à travers le pays** a mounting concern throughout the country; **6** (pente) hill; **7** SPORT **~ de Papin** Papin moves up the field.

monte-plats /mɔ̃tpla/ *nm inv* dumbwaiter, small lift GB ou elevator US.

monter /mɔ̃te/ [1] **I** *vtr* (+ *v avoir*) **1** (transporter) (en haut) GÉN to take [sb/sth] up (**à** to); (à l'étage) to take [sb/sth] upstairs; **2** (placer plus haut) to put [sth] up [*objet*]; to raise [*étagère*] (**de** by); **3** (réussir à transporter) to get [sth] up [*objet*]; **impossible de ~ le piano par l'escalier** it's impossible to get the piano up the stairs; **4** (parcourir) to go up [*escalier, pente, rue*]; **~ la colline à bicyclette** to cycle up the hill; **5** (en valeur, intensité) to turn up [*volume, thermostat*]; MUS to raise the pitch of [*instrument*]; **6** CULIN to beat, to whisk [*blanc d'œuf, mayonnaise*]; **7** (rendre hostile) **~ qn contre qn** to turn sb set sb against sb; **8** (chevaucher) to ride [*cheval*]; **9** (couvrir, saillir) to mount, to cover; **10** (assembler) to assemble [*meuble, appareil*]; to put up [*tente, échafaudage*]; to set, to mount [*pierre précieuse*]; to mount [*gravure*]; MUS to string [*instrument*]; **~ un film** to edit a film; **11** (en couture) to put [sth]

in [*col*]; to set [sth] in [*manche*]; **12** (organiser) to hatch [*complot*]; to mount [*attaque*]; to set up [*société*]; THÉÂT to stage [*pièce*]; **~ une histoire de toutes pièces** to concoct ou fabricate a story from beginning to end; **13** (fournir) **~ son ménage** to set up home; **~ sa garde-robe** to build up one's wardrobe.
II *vi* (+ *v être*) **1** (se déplacer) (en allant) GÉN to go up; (à l'étage) to go upstairs; [*avion, hélicoptère*] to climb; [*oiseau*] to fly up; [*soleil, brume*] to rise; **tu es monté à pied?** GÉN did you walk up?; **il est monté au col à bicyclette/en voiture** he cycled/drove up to the pass; **~ sur** to get onto [*trottoir*]; to climb onto [*mur*] ; **~ sur le toit** [*enfant, chat*] to go up onto the roof; **~ à l'échelle/l'arbre** to climb (up) the ladder/the tree; **~ au ciel** to ascend into Heaven; **l'air chaud fait ~ les ballons** warm air makes balloons rise; **faites-les ~** (clients, marchandises) send them up; **2** (sur un moyen de transport) **~ dans une voiture** to get in a car; **~ dans un train/bus/avion** to get on a train/bus/plane; **il a peur de ~ en avion** he's afraid of flying; **~ à bord** to get on board; **~ sur** to get on [*cheval, bicyclette, tracteur*]; **3** (s'étendre de bas en haut) [*route, voie ferrée*] to go uphill, to climb; [*terrain*] to rise; [*canalisation, ligne téléphonique*] (en allant) to go up; **~ en lacets** [*route*] to wind its way up; **~ en pente douce** [*terrain , route*] to slope up gently; **~ en pente raide** [*terrain, route*] to climb steeply; **4** (atteindre) [*vêtement, liquide, neige*] to come up; **il avait des chaussettes qui lui montaient aux genoux** he was wearing knee socks; **5** (augmenter) GÉN to rise, to go up (**à** to; **de** by); [*marée*] to come in; MUS [*mélodie*] to rise; **faire ~ les cours de 2%** to push prices up by 2%; **6** (se rendre, séjourner) **~ à** or **sur Paris** (de province) to go up to Paris; **7** (chevaucher) **~** (**à cheval**) to ride; **~ à bicyclette/moto** to ride a bicycle/motorbike; **8** MIL **~ à l'assaut** or **l'attaque** to mount an attack (**de** on); **~ au front** to move up to the front; **~ en ligne** to move up the line; **~ au combat** to go into battle; **9** JEUX (aux cartes) to play a higher card; **10** (progresser) [*employé, artiste*] to rise; **à force de ~, il deviendra directeur** he'll work his way right up to director; **~ en puissance** [*parti, politicien*] to rise; **11** (gagner en intensité) [*colère, émotion*] to mount; [*sanglots*] to rise; [*larmes*] to well up; **le ton monta** (animation) the conversation became noisier; (énervement) the discussion became heated; **12** (saisir) **~ à la gorge de qn** [*sanglots, cri*] to rise (up) in sb's throat; **~ à la tête de qn** [*vin, succès*] to go to sb's head; **le rouge lui est monté au front** he/she went red in the face; **13** AUT, TECH **~ à 250 km/h** to go up to 250 kph.
III se monter *vpr* **1** (s'élever) **se ~ à** [*frais, facture*] to amount to; **2** (s'équiper) to get oneself set up (**en** with).
IDIOMES **se ~ la tête**○ to get worked up○.

monteur, -euse /mɔ̃tœʀ, øz/ ▶ **374** *nm,f* **1** IND fitter; **2** CIN editor; **3** (en typographie) paste-up artist.

montgolfière /mɔ̃gɔlfjɛʀ/ *nf* **1** (ballon) hot-air balloon; **2** ▶ **329** (sport) (hot-air) ballooning.

monticule /mɔ̃tikyl/ *nm* **1** (butte) hillock; **2** (amas) mound (**de** of).

montrable /mɔ̃tʀabl/ *adj* [*personne*] presentable; [*film*] suitable for viewing (*après n*).

montre /mɔ̃tʀ/ *nf* **1** (objet) watch; **il est 5 heures à ma ~** it's 5 o'clock by my watch; **trois heures ~ en main** FIG three hours exactly; **course contre la ~** race against the clock; **2** (action de montrer) FML **faire ~ de** to show [*prudence, courage*]; to display [*esprit, habileté*]; **3** (ostentation) LITER **pour la ~** for show, for the sake of appearances; **4** COMM (présentation) display, show; **articles en ~** articles on display.

Montréal /mɔ̃real/ ▶ **628** *npr* Montreal.

montrer /mɔ̃tʀe/ [1] **I** *vtr* **1** (faire voir) to show [*objet, passeport*]; **~ qch à qn** to show sth to sb, to show sth to sb; **2** (faire visiter) **laissez-moi vous ~ la maison** let me show you around the house; **3** (faire connaître) to show [*problème, sentiments, connaissances*]; to reveal [*intentions*]; **~ que** to show that; **~ à qn comment faire** to show sb how to do; **4** (indiquer) [*personne*] to point out [*trace, lieu, objet*]; [*panneau*] to point to [*direction*]; [*tableau, sondage*] to show [*évolution, résultats*]; **~ qch à qn** to point sth out to sb; **~ qch du doigt** or **d'un geste** to point to sth, to point sth out; **~ qn du doigt** LIT to point at sb; FIG to point the finger at sb; **~ le chemin à qn** LIT, FIG to show sb the way.

II se montrer *vpr* **1** (se révéler) [*personne*] to show oneself to be; [*choses*] to prove (to be); **il s'est montré serviable** he was very helpful; **il faut se ~ optimiste** we must try to be optimistic; **2** (se faire voir) [*personne*] to show oneself; [*soleil*] to come out; **il n'ose pas se ~** he doesn't dare show his face; **elle n'osait pas se ~ avec lui** she didn't dare be seen with him; **on n'est pas obligés de rester mais il faut au moins se ~** we don't have to stay but we should at least put in an appearance.

IDIOMES **~ le poing à qn** to shake one's fist at sb; **~ les dents** to bare one's teeth; **~ le bout de son** or **du nez** [*personne*] to show one's face; [*soleil*] to peep through; [*plantes*] to poke through.

montreur, -euse /mɔ̃trœr, øz/ ▶374 *nm,f* **~ d'animaux** animal trainer; **~ de marionnettes** puppeteer; **~ d'ours** bear tamer.

monture /mɔ̃tyr/ *nf* **1** (animal) mount; **2** TECH mount; (de lunettes) frames (*pl*); (de bague) setting.

IDIOMES **qui veut voyager loin ménage sa ~** PROV you have to learn to pace yourself.

monument /mɔnymɑ̃/ *nm* **1** (commémoratif) monument; **2** (édifice) (historic) building; **visiter les ~s de Paris** to see the sights of Paris; **3** FIG être un ~ de bêtise** [*personne*] to be monumentally stupid; **un des ~s de la littérature européenne** a masterpiece of European literature.

■ **~ historique** ancient monument; **~ aux morts** war memorial.

monumental, ~e, *mpl* **-aux** /mɔnymɑ̃tal, o/ *adj* monumental; **il est d'une ignorance ~e** he's monumentally ignorant.

moquer: se moquer /mɔke/ [1] *vpr* **1** (ridiculiser) to make fun (**de** of), to laugh (**de** at); **arrête de te ~!** stop poking fun!; **2** (être indifférent) **se ~ de** not to care about; **je me moque qu'ils viennent ou pas** I don't care whether they come or not; ▶**chemise, guigne**; **3** (tromper) **se ~ de qn** to fool sb; **se ~ des gens** to take people for fools.

moquerie /mɔkri/ *nf* **1** (remarque) mocking remark; **être en butte aux ~s** to be the target of mockery; **2** (action) mockery.

moquette /mɔkɛt/ *nf* **1** (tapis) fitted carpet GB, wall-to-wall carpet; **faire poser une** or **de la ~** to have a carpet laid ou fitted; **2** (tissu) moquette.

moquetter /mɔkete/ [1] *vtr* to carpet [*pièce*].

moqueur, -euse /mɔkœr, øz/ *adj* mocking.

moral, ~e¹, *mpl* **-aux** /mɔral, o/ **I** *adj* **1** (éthique) moral; **n'avoir aucun sens ~** to have no sense of right and wrong; **sur le plan ~** morally; **2** (mental) [*torture*] mental; [*courage, soutien*] moral; **douleur ~e** mental anguish; **force ~e** moral fibreGB; **3** (conforme aux bonnes mœurs) [*œuvre, personne*] moral; [*conduite*] ethical; **le conseil qu'il t'a donné n'était pas très ~** the advice he gave you was morally dubious; **ce n'est pas très ~ d'avoir fait cela** that was not a very ethical thing to do.

II *nm* **1** (disposition d'esprit) morale; **le ~ des troupes est bon/mauvais** the troops' morale is high/low; **avoir bon ~, avoir le ~** to be in good spirits; **ne pas avoir le ~** to feel down; **avoir le ~ à zéro**○ to feel very down; **remonter le ~ de qn** to raise sb's spirits ou morale, to cheer sb up; **garder le ~** to keep up one's morale; **saper le ~ de qn** to undermine sb's morale; **2** (psychique) mind; **au ~ comme au physique** mentally and physically.

morale² /mɔral/ *nf* **1** (règles de conduite) morality; **contraire à la ~** immoral; **leur ~** their moral code; **2** (enseignement) moral; **la ~ de tout ceci** the moral of all this; **faire la ~ à qn** FIG to give sb a lecture; **3** PHILOS **la ~** moral philosophy, ethics.

moralement /mɔralmɑ̃/ *adv* **1** (conformément à la morale) morally; **2** (psychiquement) psychologically.

moralisant, ~e /mɔralizɑ̃, ɑ̃t/ *adj* moralizing.

moralisateur, -trice /mɔralizatœr, tris/ *adj* [*personne, ton, discours*] moralizing, moralistic; [*histoire*] with a moral (*épith, après n*).

moraliser /mɔralize/ [1] **I** *vtr* to clean up [*campagne électorale*]; to reform [*vie publique*].

II *vi* to moralize (**sur** about).

moraliste /mɔralist/ *nmf* GÉN moralist; PÉJ moralizer; PHILOS moral philosopher.

moralité /mɔralite/ *nf* **1** (de personne, société) morals (*pl*), moral standards (*pl*); **un individu d'une ~ douteuse** an individual with dubious morals; **2** (d'œuvre, action) morality; **la ~ publique** public morality; **3** (leçon) moral; **~, ne faites confiance à personne** the moral is, don't trust anybody.

morbide /mɔrbid/ *adj* morbid.

morbidité /mɔrbidite/ *nf* morbidity.

morceau, *pl* **~x** /mɔrso/ *nm* **1** (fragment) piece, bit; **être en ~x** CULIN [*sucre*] to be in lumps; [*viande*] to be in cubes; (cassé) to be in pieces ou bits; **casser en mille ~x** to break into a thousand pieces; **manger un ~** to have a snack; **2** CULIN (en boucherie) cut; **bas ~** cheap cut; **3** MUS (œuvre) piece; **~ de piano** piano piece; **4** LITTÉRAT extract; **5**○ (partie) **le chapitre 8 est un sacré ~**○ chapter 8 is quite substantial.

IDIOMES **recoller les ~x** to patch things up.

morceler /mɔrsəle/ [19] *vtr* to divide up [*héritage, terrain*] (**en** into); to split up [*pays*].

morcellement /mɔrsɛlmɑ̃/ *nm* **1** (action) (d'héritage, de terrain) dividing up; (de pays) splitting up; **2** (résultat) division; **le ~ des terres** the division of land into smaller units.

mordant, ~e /mɔrdɑ̃, ɑ̃t/ **I** *adj* **1** [*ironie, ton*] caustic; [*personne*] scathing; **2** [*froid*] biting.

II *nm* **1** (causticité) sarcasm; **avec ~** sarcastically; **2**○ (énergie de personne, d'équipe) zip○.

mordicus○ /mɔrdikys/ *adv* pigheadedly○, stubbornly.

mordiller /mɔrdije/ [1] *vtr* to nibble at.

mordoré, ~e /mɔrdɔre/ *adj* golden brown.

mordre /mɔrdr/ [6] **I** *vtr* **1** [*animal, personne*] to bite; **~ qn au bras** to bite sb on the arm; **~ qn jusqu'au sang** to bite sb and draw blood; **se faire ~** to be bitten (**par** by); **2** (entamer) [*lime*] to bite; [*acide, rouille*] to eat into.

II mordre à *vtr ind* **~ à l'appât** or **l'hameçon** LIT, FIG to take the bait; **'ça mord?'** 'are the fish biting?'

III *vi* **1 ~ dans une pomme** to bite into an apple; **2** (empiéter) **~ sur** to go over [*ligne blanche*]; to encroach on [*territoire*]; **3**○ (croire naïvement) to fall for it○.

IV se mordre *vpr* **se ~ la langue** LIT, FIG to bite one's tongue.

IDIOMES **je m'en suis mordu les doigts** I could have kicked myself.

mordu, ~e /mɔrdy/ **I**○ *adj* **1** (passionné) **être ~ de qch** to be mad○ about sth; **2** (amoureux) smitten.

II○ *nm,f* fan; **les ~s du ski** skiing fans ou buffs○.

more, moresque = **maure**.

morfondre: se morfondre /mɔrfɔ̃dr/ [6] *vpr* **1** se ~ à attendre** or **en attendant** to wait dejectedly; **2** (languir) to pine; **le pays se morfond dans la crise** FIG the country is stagnating in recession.

morganatique /mɔrganatik/ *adj* morganatic.

morgue /mɔrg/ *nf* **1** (lieu) morgue; (dans un hôpital) mortuary; **2** arrogance.

moribond, ~e /mɔribɔ̃, ɔ̃d/ **I** *adj* LIT dying; FIG moribund.

II *nm,f* dying man/woman; **les ~s** the dying.

moricaud○, **~e** /mɔriko, od/ *adj* swarthy.

morigéner /mɔriʒene/ [14] *vtr* to reprimand.

morille /mɔrij/ *nf* morel (mushroom).

mormon, ~e /mɔrmɔ̃, ɔn/ *adj, nm,f* Mormon.

morne /mɔrn/ *adj* **1** [*personne, attitude, silence*] gloomy; [*visage*] glum; [*regard*] doleful; **2** [*paysage,* *lieu, existence, débat, vacances*] dreary; [*temps, journée*] dismal; **une rue ~** a drab street.

morose /mɔʀoz/ *adj* [*personne, vieillesse, humeur*] morose; [*journée, lieu, ton, atmosphère, vie*] gloomy.

morosité /mɔʀozite/ *nf* gloom.

Morphée /mɔʀfe/ *npr* Morpheus.
IDIOMES être dans les bras de ~ to be in the arms of Morpheus.

morphème /mɔʀfɛm/ *nm* morpheme.

morphine /mɔʀfin/ *nf* morphine.

morphinomane /mɔʀfinɔman/ *nmf* morphine addict.

morphologie /mɔʀfɔlɔʒi/ *nf* morphology.

morpion /mɔʀpjɔ̃/ *nm* ▶329⎹ (jeu) noughts and crosses GB, tick-tack-toe US.

mors /mɔʀ/ *nm inv* bit; **prendre le ~ aux dents** [*cheval*] to take the bit between its teeth; [*personne*] (colère subite) to fly off the handle○; (énergie subite) to take the bit between one's teeth.

morse /mɔʀs/ *nm* **1** ZOOL walrus; **2** TÉLÉCOM **(code) ~** Morse code.

morsure /mɔʀsyʀ/ *nf* **1** (plaie) bite; **~ de chien** dogbite; **2** (action) **la ~ du froid** the biting cold; **la ~ de l'acide** the bite of acid.

mort[1] /mɔʀ/ *nf* death; **mourir de ~ naturelle** to die of natural causes; **mourir de sa belle ~** to die peacefully in old age; **vouloir la ~ de qn** to wish sb dead; **il n'y a pas eu ~ d'homme** there were no fatalities; **être à deux doigts de la ~** to be at death's door; **j'ai vu la ~ de près** I saw death close up; **lutter jusqu'à la ~** to fight to the death; **jusqu'à ce que ~ s'ensuive** [*battre*] to death; **trouver la ~** LITER to die; **être en danger de ~** to be in mortal danger; **mettre qn à ~** to put sb to death; **mise à ~** (de condamné) killing; (de taureau) dispatch; **un engin de ~** a deadly contraption; **à ~** [*lutte*] to the death; [*guerre*] ruthless; [*freiner, serrer*] like mad○; [*frapper, lutter*] to death; [*blessé*] fatally; **je leur en veux à ~** I'll never forgive them; **on est fâchés à ~** we'll never have anything to do with each other again.
■ **~ cérébrale** brain death; **~ subite** sudden death; **~ subite du nourrisson** cot death GB, crib death US; **un ~ vivant** one of the living dead; **tu as l'air d'un ~ vivant** you look like death warmed up GB OU over US.
IDIOMES la ~ dans l'âme with a heavy heart.

mort[2], **~e** /mɔʀ, mɔʀt/ **I** *pp* ▶ **mourir**.
II *pp adj* **1** (sans vie) dead; **laisser qn pour ~** to leave sb for dead; **être ~ de faim** FIG to be starving; **je suis ~e de froid** I'm freezing to death; **il est ~ de sommeil** he's ready to drop; **2** (très fatigué) half-dead; **3** (partie du corps) [*dent*] dead; **mes orteils sont comme ~s** my toes have gone numb; **4** (sans activité) [*quartier*] dead; [*saison*] slack; **eaux ~es** stagnant water ⊄.
III *nm,f* (défunt) dead person, dead man/woman; **les ~s** the dead; **jour des ~s** RELIG All Souls' Day.
IV *nm* **1** (victime) fatality; **il y a eu 12 ~s** there were 12 dead; **il n'y a pas eu de ~s** there were no fatalities, nobody was killed; **l'attentat n'a fait qu'un ~** the attack claimed only one life; **2** (cadavre) body; **faire le ~** (être immobile) to play dead; (éviter les contacts) to lie low.
IDIOMES ne pas y aller de main ~e○ not to pull any punches; **être à la place du ~**○ (en voiture) to sit in the front passenger seat.

mortaise /mɔʀtɛz/ *nf* mortise.

mortalité /mɔʀtalite/ *nf* mortality.

mort-aux-rats /mɔʀoʀa/ *nf inv* rat poison.

morte-eau, *pl* **mortes-eaux** /mɔʀto, mɔʀtzo/ *nf* neap(-tide).

mortel, -elle /mɔʀtɛl/ **I** *adj* **1** [*coup, maladie, chute*] fatal; [*poison, dose, gaz*] lethal; [*venin*] deadly; [*champignon*] deadly poisonous; **2** [*froid, pâleur, silence*] deathly; [*angoisse, frayeur*] mortal; **3** [*ennemi*] mortal; **4** [*spectacle, personne, attente*] deadly boring; **5** (susceptible de mourir) [*être*] mortal.

II *nm,f* LITER mortal.

mortellement /mɔʀtɛlmɑ̃/ *adv* **1** [*blessé, atteint*] fatally; **2** [*ennuyeux*] deadly; [*pâle*] deathly.

morte-saison, *pl* **mortes-saisons** /mɔʀt(ə)sɛzɔ̃/ *nf* off season.

mortier /mɔʀtje/ *nm* (récipient, ciment, canon) mortar.

mortification /mɔʀtifikasjɔ̃/ *nf* mortification.

mortifier /mɔʀtifje/ [2] *vtr* to mortify.

mort-né, ~e, *mpl* **~s** /mɔʀne/ *adj* LIT stillborn; FIG abortive.

mortuaire /mɔʀtɥɛʀ/ *adj* [*cérémonie*] funeral; **veillée ~** wake.

morue /mɔʀy/ *nf* cod.

morutier /mɔʀytje/ *nm* **1** (navire) cod-fishing boat; **2** ▶374⎹ (pêcheur) cod fisherman.

morve /mɔʀv/ *nf* (sécrétion) nasal mucus.

morveux, -euse /mɔʀvø, øz/ *adj* [*enfant*] snotty-nosed○ (*épith*); **se sentir ~** to feel embarrassed.

mosaïque /mɔzaik/ *nf* (assemblage, art) mosaic.

Moscou /mɔsku/ ▶628⎹ *npr* Moscow.

mosquée /mɔske/ *nf* mosque.

mot /mo/ *nm* **1** GÉN word; **faire du ~ à ~** to translate word for word; **à ~s couverts** in veiled terms; **au bas ~** at least; **en un ~** in a word; **explique-moi en deux ~s** tell me briefly; **pour eux, l'amitié n'est pas un vain ~** they take friendship seriously; **'manger', il n'a que ce ~ à la bouche** all he can talk about is eating; ▶**gros**; **2** (parole) word; **dire un ~ à qn** to have a word with sb; **ne pas souffler** or **piper**○ ~ not to say a word; **ne pas pouvoir placer un ~** to be unable to get a word in edgeways; **prendre qn au ~** to take sb at their word; **toucher**○ **un ~ de qch à qn** to have a word with sb about sth; **glisser un ~ à qn** to have a quick word with sb; **des ~s que tout cela!** it's just hot air!; **si tu as besoin de moi tu n'as qu'un ~ à dire** if you need me you've only to say the word; **sur ces ~s il sortit** with that, he left; **il ne dit jamais un ~ plus haut que l'autre** he never raises his voice; **avoir son ~ à dire** to be entitled to one's say; **viens par ici, j'ai deux ~s à te dire!** EUPH come here, I've got a bone to pick with you!; **50 francs pour les deux c'est mon dernier ~** 50 francs the pair but that's my last offer; **avoir toujours le ~ pour rire** to be a born joker; **c'est un ~ d'enfant** it's something only a child could say; **3** (petite lettre) note; **4** ORDINAT word.
■ **~ d'auteur** literary quotation; **~ d'esprit** witticism, witty remark; **~ de la fin** closing words (*pl*); **avoir le ~ de la fin** to have the last word; **~ d'ordre** watchword; **~ d'ordre de grève** strike call; **~ de passe** password; **~s croisés** crossword; **~s doux** sweet nothings.
IDIOMES avoir or **échanger des ~s avec qn** EUPH to have words with sb; **ne pas avoir peur des ~s** to call a spade a spade; **se donner** or **passer le ~ to** pass the word around.

motard, ~e /mɔtaʀ, aʀd/ **I**○ *nm,f* motorcyclist, biker○.
II ▶374⎹ *nm* (de police) police motorcyclist.

mot-clé, *pl* **mots-clés** /mokle/ *nm* key word.

moteur, -trice[1] /mɔtœʀ, tʀis/ **I** *adj* **1** [*force, principe*] driving (*épith*); **être l'élément ~ de qch** to be the driving force behind sth; **jouer un rôle ~ dans** to play a dynamic role in; **la voiture a quatre roues motrices** the car has four-wheel drive; **les roues motrices sont à l'avant** it's a front-wheel drive (car); **2** [*trouble, fibre*] motor (*épith*).
II *nm* **1** LIT (électrique) motor; (autre) engine; **un véhicule à ~** a motor vehicle; **2** FIG driving force; **être le ~ de qch** to be the driving force behind sth.

motif /mɔtif/ *nm* **1** (raison) grounds (*pl*) (**de** for); **il y a des ~s d'espérer/de se réjouir** there are grounds for hope/for rejoicing; **2** (cause) reason (**de** for); **les ~s de notre retard** the reasons why we are/were late; **3** (motivation) motive; **sans ~ apparent** for no apparent motive; **4** (dessin) pattern; **à ~ floral** with a floral pattern; **5** (thème) motif.

motion /mɔsjɔ̃/ *nf* motion; **~ de censure** motion of censure.

motivant, **~e** /mɔtivɑ̃, ɑ̃t/ *adj* [*salaire*] attractive; [*travail*] rewarding; [*raison*] worthwhile.

motivation /mɔtivasjɔ̃/ *nf* **1** motivation; **2** motive.

motivé, **~e** /mɔtive/ *adj* **1** (enthousiaste) motivated (**pour** as regards; **pour faire** to do); **il est peu ~** he lacks motivation; **2** (légitime) [*plainte*] justifiable.

motiver /mɔtive/ [1] *vtr* **1** to motivate [*personne*] (**à faire** to do); **2** to lead to [*décision*, *action*]; **motivé par** caused by.

moto /mɔto/ *nf* **1** (véhicule) (motor)bike; **à ~** by motorbike; **2** (activité) motorcycling.

motocross /mɔtokrɔs/ ▶329 *nm inv* motocross, scramble GB.

motoculteur /mɔtokyltœr/ *nm* rotary cultivator.

motocyclette /mɔtosiklɛt/ *nf* motorcycle.

motocyclisme /mɔtosiklism/ ▶329 *nm* motorcycle racing.

motocycliste /mɔtosiklist/ **I** *adj* [*rallye*, *brigade*] motorcycle (*épith*); **le sport ~** the sport of motorcycling.
II *nmf* motorcyclist.

motonautisme /mɔtonotism/ ▶329 *nm* speedboat racing.

motoneige /mɔtonɛʒ/ *nf* snowmobile.

motopompe /mɔtopɔ̃p/ *nf* power-driven pump.

motorisation /mɔtɔrizasjɔ̃/ *nf* motorization; **taux de ~** rate of car ownership.

motoriser /mɔtɔrize/ [1] *vtr* to motorize [*véhicule*, *troupes*]; **être motorisé** to have transport GB ou transportation US.

motoriste /mɔtɔrist/ ▶374 *nmf* **1** (constructeur) engine builder; **2** (mécanicien) mechanic.

motrice² /mɔtris/ **I** *adj f* ▶ **moteur**.
II *nf* RAIL (locomotive) engine.

motte /mɔt/ *nf* **~ (de terre)** clod (of earth); **~ de gazon** sod, piece of turf; **~ (de beurre)** slab of butter; **acheter du beurre en ~** to buy butter by weight.

motus○ /mɔtys/ *excl* **~ (et bouche cousue)!** keep it under your hat!

mot-valise, *pl* **mots-valises** /movaliz/ *nm* portmanteau word.

mou (**mol** *before vowel or mute h*), **molle** /mu, mɔl/ **I** *adj* **1** (pas ferme) [*coussin*, *matière*] soft; [*tige*, *étoffe*] limp; [*choc*] dull; **2** (sans tenue) [*trait du visage*] weak; [*chair*, *ventre*] flabby; [*cheveux*] limp; **3** (apathique) [*personne*] listless; [*poignée de main*] limp; [*croissance*, *reprise économique*] sluggish; **4** (sans énergie) [*parent*, *professeur*] soft; **5** (sans conviction) PEJ [*version*, *libéralisme*] watered-down; [*discours*, *résistance*] feeble.
II *nm* **1** (personne) PEJ wimp○; **2** (en boucherie) lights (*pl*) GB, lungs (*pl*) US; **3** (de corde) **avoir du ~** to be slack; **donner du ~** to let (the rope) out a bit; **donner du ~ à qn**○ FIG to give sb a bit of leeway.

mouchard /muʃar, ard/ **I** *nm,f* (de police) grass○; SCOL sneak○.
II *nm* **1** (appareil) tachograph; **2** (orifice) spyhole.

moucharder○ /muʃarde/ [1] *vtr* **~ qn** (pour la police) to inform on sb, to squeal○ on sb; SCOL to sneak○ on sb.

mouche /muʃ/ *nf* **1** (insecte) fly; **2** (sur le visage) patch; **3** (de cible) bull's eye; **faire ~** LIT to hit the bull's eye; FIG to be right on target.
■ **~ bleue** bluebottle; **~ commune** or **domestique** housefly; **~ à miel** bee; **~ verte** greenbottle; **~ du vinaigre** fruit fly.
IDIOMES **on entendrait une ~ voler** you could hear a pin drop; **quelle ~ les a piqués**○? what's got GB ou gotten US into them?; **regarder voler les ~s** to stare into space; **prendre la ~** to fly off the handle.

moucher /muʃe/ [1] **I** *vtr* **1** **~ qn** LIT to blow sb's nose; FIG to put sb in their place; **2** to snuff (out) [*chandelle*].

II se moucher *vpr* to blow one's nose.
IDIOMES **il ne se mouche pas du pied**○ or **du coude**○ (mener grand train) he lives the high life; (être prétentieux) he's full of airs and graces.

moucheron /muʃrɔ̃/ *nm* (insecte) midge.

moucheté, **~e** /muʃte/ *adj* **1** [*étoffe*] flecked; [*œuf*] speckled; [*pelage*] spotted; [*cheval*] dappled; **2** [*fleuret*] buttoned.

mouchoir /muʃwar/ *nm* handkerchief; (en papier) tissue GB, Kleenex®.
IDIOMES **arriver dans un ~** [*candidats*, *concurrents*] to have a close finish.

Moudjahidin /mudʒaidin/ *nmpl* mujaheddin.

moudre /mudr/ [77] *vtr* to grind.

moue /mu/ *nf* pout; **faire la ~** (bouder) to pout; (pour exprimer un doute) to pull a face.

mouette /mwɛt/ *nf* (sea) gull.

mouf(f)ette /mufɛt/ *nf* skunk.

moufle /mufl/ *nf* (gant) mitten.

mouillage /mujaʒ/ *nm* NAUT (manœuvre) anchoring; (emplacement) anchorage; **être au ~** to lie ou ride at anchor; **~ de mines** MIL minelaying.

mouiller /muje/ [1] **I** *vtr* **1** to wet [*cheveux*, *linge*, *sol*]; to get [sth] wet [*vêtements*, *chaussures*]; **2** to drop [*ancre*]; to lay [*mine*]; to cast [*ligne*]; **3** CULIN to moisten; **4** to palatalize [*consonne*].
II *vi* NAUT to anchor, to drop anchor.
III se mouiller *vpr* **1** LIT to get wet; **2**○ FIG to stick one's neck out○.

mouillette○ /mujɛt/ *nf* soldier○ GB, finger of bread (*eaten with a boiled egg*).

mouilleur /mujœr/ *nm* **1** (stamp) sponge; **2** NAUT (dispositif) tumbler.
■ **~ de mines** minelayer.

moujik /muʒik/ *nm* muzhik.

moulage /mulaʒ/ *nm* (reproduction) casting; **faire un ~ de qch** to take a cast of sth.

moulant, **~e** /mulɑ̃, ɑ̃t/ *adj* [*vêtement*] skin-tight.

moule¹ /mul/ *nm* **1** ART, IND, TECH mould GB, mold US; **fait au ~** FIG perfectly shaped; **2** CULIN (pour gâteau, pain) tin, pan US; (pour gelées) mould GB, mold US.
■ **~ à gaufre** waffle iron.

moule² /mul/ *nf* ZOOL mussel.

mouler /mule/ [1] *vtr* **1** (fabriquer avec un moule) to mould GB, to mold US [*substance*]; to cast [*liquide*]; to mint [*médaille*]; **écriture moulée** FIG copperplate handwriting; **2** (prendre une empreinte) to take a cast of; **3** (coller à) [*vêtement*] to hug [*corps*]; **moulée dans une robe de cuir** in a skin-tight leather dress.

moulin /mulɛ̃/ *nm* (édifice, appareil) mill.
■ **~ à paroles**○ chatterbox; **~ à prières** prayer wheel; **~ à vent** windmill.
IDIOMES **apporter de l'eau au ~ de qn** to fuel sb's arguments; **on ne peut être à la fois au four et au ~** one can't be in two places at once; **on y entre comme dans un ~**○ one can just slip in; **se battre contre ~s à vent** to tilt at windmills; **jeter son bonnet par-dessus les ~s** to let one's hair down.

mouliner /muline/ [1] *vtr* **1** CULIN to purée [*pommes de terre*]; to grind [*café*]; **2** [*pêcheur*] to reel in [*ligne*].

moulinet /mulinɛ/ *nm* **1** (de canne à pêche) reel; **2** (mouvement) **faire des ~s avec les bras** GÉN to wave one's arms about; **faire des ~s avec un bâton** to twirl a stick.

moulinette® /mulinɛt/ *nf* (small) vegetable mill; **passer à la ~** LIT, FIG to put [sth/sb] through the mill.

moulu, **~e** /muly/ **I** *pp* ▶ **moudre**.
II *pp adj* [*café*, *poivre*] ground.
III○ *adj* FIG **~ (de fatigue)** worn out; **~ (de coups)** beaten black and blue.

moulure /mulyr/ *nf* moulding GB, molding US.

moumoute○ /mumut/ *nf* **1** (perruque) toupee; **2** (vêtement) sheepskin jacket.

mourant, **~e** /murɑ̃, ɑ̃t/ **I** *adj* [*personne*, *animal*] dying (**de** of); [*entreprise*] moribund; [*voix*] faint.
II *nm,f* dying person; **les ~s** the dying (+ *v pl*).

mourir /muʀiʀ/ [34] I *vi* **1** (cesser d'exister) to die (**de** of); **~ de vieillesse** to die of old age; **~ de froid** (dehors) to die of exposure; (sous un toit) to die of cold; **je meurs de soif** FIG I'm dying of thirst; **je meurs de faim** FIG I'm starving; **je meurs de froid** FIG I'm freezing to death; **je meurs de sommeil** FIG I'm ready to drop; **c'était à ~ (de rire)**! it was hilarious!; **~ assassiné** to be murdered; **je meurs d'envie de faire** I'm dying to do; **se laisser ~ de faim** to starve oneself to death; **faire ~ qn** to kill sb; **2** (faiblir) LITER [*jour*] to fade away LITTÉR; [*flamme*] to die down; [*conversation*] to die away; [*vagues*] to break and fall back.

II se mourir *vpr* LITER [*personne, civilisation*] to be dying; [*flamme, feu*] to die down.

IDIOMES **partir c'est ~ un peu** to say goodbye is to die a little; **je ne veux pas ~ idiot**○ HUM I want to know; **on n'en meurt pas**○!, **tu n'en mourras pas**○! HUM it won't kill you!; **je veux bien ~** or **que je meure si...** I'll eat my hat if...

mouroir /muʀwaʀ/ *nm* PEJ old people's home, twilight home PÉJ.

mouron /muʀɔ̃/ *nm* BOT pimpernel.

mousquetaire /muskətɛʀ/ *nm* musketeer.

mousqueton /muskətɔ̃/ *nm* **1** TECH snap clasp; **2** (d'alpinisme) carabiner; **3** MIL carbine.

moussaillon○ /musajɔ̃/ *nm* ship's apprentice.

moussant, ~e /musɑ̃, ɑ̃t/ *adj* [*gel*] foaming (*épith*); **non ~** [*savon, lessive*] low-lather.

mousse¹ /mus/ *nm* NAUT ship's apprentice.

mousse² /mus/ *nf* **1** BOT moss; **2** (bulles) GÉN foam; (de savon, lessive) lather; (sur le lait, le café) froth; (sur la bière) head; **3** CULIN mousse; **~ au chocolat** chocolate mousse; **4** (matière) (pour coussin) foam rubber; **chaussettes en ~** stretch socks.

■ **~ carbonique** (fire) foam; **~ de nylon**® stretch nylon; **~ à raser** shaving foam.

IDIOMES **pierre qui roule n'amasse pas ~** PROV a rolling stone gathers no moss PROV.

mousseline /muslin/ *nf* **1** (de coton) muslin; (de soie) chiffon; **2** CULIN **sauce ~** mousseline sauce.

mousser /muse/ [1] *vi* [*champagne*] to bubble; [*bière*] to foam; [*détergent, savon*] to lather; **faire ~** to work [sth] up into a lather [*savon, détergent*].

IDIOMES **se faire ~**○ to sing one's own praises.

mousseux, -euse /musø, øz/ *adj* **1** LIT [*vin*] sparkling; [*bière*] fizzy; **2** FIG [*dentelle*] frothy.

II *nm inv* (vin) sparkling wine.

mousson /musɔ̃/ *nf* monsoon.

moussu, ~e /musy/ *adj* mossy.

moustache /mustaʃ/ *nf* (d'homme) moustache GB, mustache US; (d'animal) **~s** whiskers.

■ **~ en brosse** toothbrush moustache GB ou mustache US; **~ à la gauloise** walrus moustache GB ou mustache US; **~ en guidon de vélo**○ handlebar moustache GB ou mustache US.

moustachu, ~e /mustaʃy/ *adj* with a moustache GB ou mustache US (*épith, après n*).

moustiquaire /mustikɛʀ/ *nf* mosquito net.

moustique /mustik/ *nm* ZOOL mosquito.

moût /mu/ *nm* (de raisin, pomme) must; (de houblon, d'orge) wort.

moutarde /mutaʀd/ *adj inv*, *nf* mustard.

IDIOMES **la ~ me monte au nez**○! I'm beginning to see red!

moutardier /mutaʀdje/ *nm* (récipient) mustard pot.

mouton /mutɔ̃/ I *nm* **1** ZOOL sheep; **2** CULIN mutton; **3** (peau) sheepskin; **4** (personne) PEJ sheep PÉJ.

II moutons *nmpl* **1** (nuages) small fleecy clouds; **2** (petites vagues) white horses GB, whitecaps; **3** (poussière) fluff ¢.

■ **~ à cinq pattes** rare bird; **~ de Panurge** PEJ sheep PÉJ; **ce sont des ~s de Panurge** they follow one another like sheep.

IDIOMES **revenons à nos ~s**○ let's get back to the subject ou point.

moutonnement /mutɔnmɑ̃/ *nm* **le ~ du ciel** the

sky breaking up into fleecy clouds; **le ~ des collines** the rolling hills (*pl*).

moutonneux, -euse /mutɔnø, øz/ *adj* [*toison*] curly; [*mer*] covered with white horses (*après n*).

moutonnier, -ière /mutɔnje, ɛʀ/ *adj* **1** [*élevage*] sheep (*épith*); **2** PEJ [*comportement*] sheeplike PÉJ.

mouvant, ~e /muvɑ̃, ɑ̃t/ *adj* **1** (qui s'enfonce) [*sol*] unstable; **2** (qui bouge) [*groupe*] shifting; **reflets ~s** shimmering reflections; **3** (qui évolue) [*situation, opinion*] changing; **électorat ~** floating voters.

mouvement /muvmɑ̃/ *nm* **1** (geste) movement; **faire un ~** to move, to make a move; **tu es libre de tes ~s** you can come and go as you please; ▶**faux¹**; **2** (déplacement) movement, motion; **le ~ des vagues** the movement of the waves; **~ perpétuel** perpetual motion; **le ~ de personnel dans une entreprise** staff changes in a company; **~ de retraite** withdrawal; **accélérer le ~** to speed up; **ralentir le ~** to slow down; **se mettre en ~** [*troupe*] to start moving; [*machine*] to start up; **mettre qch en ~**, **imprimer un ~ à qch** to set sth in motion; **3** (animation) bustle; **il y a du ~ dans la rue** there's a lot of bustle in the street; **une rue pleine de ~** a busy street; **suivre le ~** FIG to follow the crowd; **4** (élan) impulse, reaction; **mon premier ~ a été de me mettre en colère** my initial reaction ou my first impulse was to get angry; **dans un ~ de générosité** on a generous impulse; **un ~ de colère/pitié** a surge of anger/pity; **un ~ de panique** a panic reaction; **un bon ~** a kind ou nice gesture; **agir de son propre ~** to act of one's own accord; **5** (action collective) movement; **le ~ étudiant** the student protest movement; **~ surréaliste** surrealist movement; **~ de grève** strike; **6** (évolution) **le ~ des idées** the evolution of ideas; **être dans le ~** to move with the times; **un milieu en ~** a changing environment; **7** ÉCON, FIN (fluctuation) fluctuation; (échange) transaction; (tendance) trend; **le ~ du marché** market fluctuations; **~ de hausse** upward trend (**de** in); **un ~ de reprise** a movement toward(s) recovery; **~s financiers** financial transactions; **~ de fonds** movement of funds; **8** (de poème, d'œuvre musicale) movement; **9** (d'horloge) movement; **~ d'horlogerie** clockwork mechanism.

mouvementé, ~e /muvmɑ̃te/ *adj* **1** [*vie, semaine*] eventful, hectic; [*réunion*] lively; [*récit, voyage*] eventful; **l'histoire ~ d'un pays** a country's turbulent history; **2** [*relief, terrain*] rough.

mouvoir /muvwaʀ/ [43] FML I *vtr* **1** [*personne*] to move; [*énergie, mécanisme*] to drive [*machine*]; **2** [*sentiment, désir*] to move.

II se mouvoir *vpr* to move.

moyen, -enne¹ /mwajɛ̃, ɛn/ I *adj* **1** (intermédiaire en dimension, poids) [*taille, épaisseur*] medium; [*ville, entreprise, légume*] medium-sized; [*fil*] of medium thickness; [*prix*] moderate; **de grandeur moyenne** medium-sized; **de moyenne portée** medium-range; **le cours ~ d'un fleuve** the middle reaches of a river; **2** (passable) [*élève, résultat*] average (**en** in); **3** (dans une hiérarchie) [*cadre, revenu*] middle; [*échelon*] intermediate; **les salaires ~s** (personnes) people on middle incomes; **4** (ordinaire) average; **le Français /lecteur ~** the average Frenchman/reader; **5** (après évaluation, calcul) [*taux, température*] average, mean; **6** (de compromis) [*solution, position*] middle-of-the-road.

II *nm* **1** (façon de procéder) means (*sg*) (**de faire** of doing), way (**de faire** of doing); **c'est un ~ comme un autre** it's as good a way as any; **par tous les ~s** by every possible means; **par n'importe quel ~** by hook or by crook○; **tous les ~s sont bons** any means will do; **tous les ~s leur sont bons** they'll stop at nothing; **employer les grands ~s** to resort to drastic measures; **2** (d'action, expression, de production) means; (d'investigation, de paiement) method; **~ de communication** means of communication; **3** (possibilité) way; **il y a ~ de faire** there's a way of doing; **il y a ~ de s'en sortir** there's a way out; **n'y avait-il pas ~ de faire autrement?** was there no other way to go about it?; **(il n'y a) pas ~ de lui faire**

comprendre qu'il a tort it's impossible to make him realize he's wrong.

III au moyen de *loc prép* by means of, by using.

IV par le moyen de *loc prép* by means of, through.

V moyens *nmpl* **1** (financiers) means; **manquer de ~s** to lack the resources (**pour faire** to do); **faute de ~s** through lack of money; **vivre au-dessus de ses ~s** to live beyond one's means; **je n'ai pas les ~s de faire, mes ~s ne me permettent pas de faire** I can't afford to do; **avoir de petits/grands ~s** not to be/to be very well off; **2** (matériels) resources; **la ville a mis d'énormes ~s à notre disposition** the town put vast resources at our disposal; **je n'ai ni le temps ni les ~s de taper ce texte** I have neither the time nor the equipment to type this text; **donner à qn les ~s de faire** to give sb the means to do; **j'ai dû y aller par mes propres ~s** I had to make my own way there; **se débrouiller par ses propres ~s** to manage on one's own; **3** (intellectuels) ability; **il a de petits ~s** he has limited ability; **être en possession de tous ses ~s** to be at the height of one's powers; **perdre ses ~s** to go to pieces.

■ **~ de locomotion** or **transport** means of transport GB ou transportation US; **~ métrage** CIN medium-length film; **Moyen Âge** Middle Ages (*pl*); **le bas/haut Moyen Âge** the late/early Middle Ages; **Moyen Empire** Middle Kingdom.

moyenâgeux, -euse /mwajɛnaʒø, øz/ *adj* **1** [*château*] medieval; **2** PEJ [*idée*] antiquated.

moyen-courrier, *pl* **~s** /mwajɛ̃kurje/ *nm* medium-haul airliner.

moyennant /mwajɛnɑ̃/ *prép* for [*somme, rançon*]; in return for [*faveur*]; with [*effort, modification*]; **~ finances** for a fee ou a consideration; **~ quoi** (en conséquence de quoi) in view of which; (en échange de quoi) in return for which.

moyenne² /mwajɛn/ **I** *adj f* ▶ **moyen**.

II *nf* **1** (norme) average; **au-dessous/au-dessus de la ~** below/above average; **être dans la ~** to be average; **2** SCOL (moitié de la note maximale) half marks GB, 50%; **j'ai eu tout juste la ~** (à un examen) I barely passed; (à un devoir) I just got half marks GB, I just got 50%; **3** (après calcul) average; **la ~ d'âge** the average age; **en ~** on average; **4** (vitesse) average speed.

moyennement /mwajɛnmɑ̃/ *adv* [*intelligent, riche, cultivé*] moderately; [*réussir, comprendre*] moderately well; [*aimer, apprécier*] to a certain extent.

Moyen-Orient /mwajɛ̃ɔrjɑ̃/ ▶ **509** *nprm* Middle East.

moyeu, *pl* **~x** /mwajø/ *nm* hub.

MST /ɛmɛste/ *nf*: *abbr* ▶ **maladie**.

mû ▶ **mouvoir**.

mucosité /mykozite/ *nf* mucus ⊄.

mucoviscidose /mykovisidoz/ ▶ **196** *nf* cystic fibrosis.

mucus /mykys/ *nm inv* mucus.

mue¹ ▶ **mouvoir**.

mue² /my/ *nf* **1** ZOOL (renouvellement) (d'insecte) metamorphosis; (de serpent, lézard) sloughing of the skin; (d'oiseau, de mammifère) moulting GB; (de cerf) casting; **2** ZOOL (dépouille) (d'insecte, de serpent) slough, sloughed skin; **3** (de voix) breaking GB ou changing US of voice; **4** (transformation) LITER transformation.

muer /mɥe/ **I** *vtr* LITER to transform (**en** into).

II *vi* **1** ZOOL [*insecte*] to metamorphose; [*serpent, lézard*] to slough its skin; [*oiseau, mammifère*] to moult GB; [*cerf*] to cast its antlers; **2 sa voix mue, il mue** his voice is breaking GB ou changing US.

III se muer *vpr* (être transformé) to be transformed (**en** into); (activement) to transform oneself (**en** into).

muet, -ette¹ /mɥɛ, ɛt/ **I** *adj* **1** [*personne*] GÉN dumb; (momentanément) speechless; **sous le choc, elle resta muette** the shock left her speechless; **~ de** (d'admiration, de terreur) speechless with; **rester ~ de** to be struck dumb with; **2** (qui refuse de parler) [*témoin, presse, rapport*] silent (**sur, à propos de** on); **rester**

~ to remain silent; **3** (inexprimé) [*reproche, douleur, cloche*] silent; [*voyelle, consonne*] mute, silent; **4** CIN [*cinéma, film*] silent; [*rôle*] non-speaking (*épith*); **5** (sans inscription) [*carte de géographie, page*] blank; [*menu*] unpriced.

II *nm,f* MÉD mute; **les ~s** the dumb (+ *v pl*).

III *nm* CIN **le ~** the silent screen.

muette² /mɥɛt/ *nf* HIST **la grande ~** the army.

mufle /myfl/ **I** *adj* boorish, loutish.

II *nm* **1** ZOOL (museau) (de ruminant) muffle; (de carnassier) muzzle; **2** (malotru) boor, lout.

muflerie /myfləri/ *nf* boorishness.

mugir /myʒiʀ/ [3] *vi* **1** [*vache*] to low; [*taureau, bœuf*] to bellow; **2** [*vent*] to howl; [*sirène*] to wail; [*mer, torrent*] to roar.

mugissement /myʒismɑ̃/ *nm* **1** (de vache) lowing ⊄; (de taureau) bellowing ⊄; **pousser des ~s** [*vache*] to moo; **2** (de vent) howling ⊄; (de sirène) wailing ⊄; (de vagues) roar ⊄.

muguet /mygɛ/ *nm* (fleur) lily of the valley.

mulâtre /mylɑtr/ *adj, nm* mulatto.

mulâtresse /mylɑtrɛs/ *nf* mulatto.

mule /myl/ *nf* **1** ZOOL female mule; **2** (pantoufle) mule; **3** (passeur de drogue) mule; **~ aveugle** unwitting drugs carrier.

mulet /mylɛ/ *nm* **1** (équidé) (male) mule; **2** (poisson) grey mullet GB, mullet US; **3** SPORT back-up car.

muletier, -ière /myltje, ɛr/ **I** *adj* **sentier** or **chemin ~** mule track.

II ▶ **374** *nm* muleteer, mule skinner○ US.

mulot /mylo/ *nm* fieldmouse.

multi /mylti/ *préf* multi; **~colore** multicoloured GB; **~couche** multi-layered; **~latéral** multilateral; **~media** multimedia; **~programmation** multiple programming.

multicarte /myltikart/ *adj inv* **représentant ~** (sales) representative for several firms.

multifonction /myltifɔ̃ksjɔ̃/ *adj inv* GÉN multipurpose; ORDINAT multifunction.

multiforme /myltifɔrm/ *adj* [*aspect*] multiform; [*vie, danger*] many-sided; [*réalité*] multifaceted.

multipartite /myltipartit/ *adj* **1** [*réunion, traité*] multipartite; **2** [*élections*] multi-party (*épith*).

multiple /myltipl/ **I** *adj* **1** (nombreux) [*raisons, occasions*] numerous, many; [*naissances*] multiple; **après de ~s spéculations/tergiversations** after much speculation/hesitation; **à usages ~s** multipurpose; **à choix ~** multiple-choice (*épith*); **2** (divers) [*buts, causes, facettes*] many, various; **3** BOT, MATH, PHYS multiple.

II *nm* multiple.

multipliable /myltiplijabl/ *adj* multiplicable.

multiplicateur, -trice /myltiplikatœr, tris/ **I** *adj* multiplying.

II *nm* multiplier.

multiplication /myltiplikasjɔ̃/ *nf* **1** (augmentation) **~ de** increase in the number of; **2** MATH (processus) multiplication ⊄; (opération) multiplication C; **apprendre à faire des ~s** to learn to do multiplication; **il fait des ~s à longueur de journée** he does multiplications all day long; **faire une erreur de ~** to make a mistake in the multiplication; **3** BIOL, BOT multiplication.

multiplicité /myltiplisite/ *nf* multiplicity.

multiplier /myltiplije/ [2] **I** *vtr* **1** MATH to multiply [*chiffre*] (**par** by); **2** (augmenter) to increase [*risques, fortune*]; to increase the number of [*trains, accidents*]; **~ les bénéfices par cinq/par cent** to increase profits fivefold/a hundredfold; **~ les risques d'accident par trois/dix** to make the risk of accident three/ten times more likely; **3** (faire en grand nombre) **~ les excuses** to give endless excuses; **~ les visites** to make endless visits.

II se multiplier *vpr* **1** (augmenter) [*succursales, villas*] to grow in number; [*incidents, arrestations*] to be on the increase; [*difficultés, obstacles*] to increase;

[*contacts, disputes*] to become more frequent; **2** (se reproduire) [*animaux, microbes*] to multiply.

multiprise /myltipʀiz/ *adj* **pince ~** adjustable pliers (*pl*).

multipropriété /myltipʀɔpʀijete/ *nf* time-sharing; **acheter une villa en ~** to buy a time-share in a villa.

multirisque /myltiʀisk/ *adj* **assurance ~** comprehensive insurance.

multisalle /myltisal/ *adj inv* **cinéma ~** cinema complex GB, multiplex US.

multitude /myltityd/ *nf* **1** (grand nombre) **une ~ de** (d'objets, de touristes) a mass of; (d'idées, de raisons) a lot of, many; **2** (foule de gens) multitude, throng.

municipal, **~e**, *mpl* **-aux** /mynisipal, o/ *adj* ADMIN [*conseil, conseiller*] (de petite ville) local, town (*épith*); (de grande ville) city (*épith*); [*impôt, élections, arrêté*] local; [*parc, piscine, bibliothèque*] municipal.

municipales /mynisipal/ *nfpl* local elections.

municipalité /mynisipalite/ *nf* **1** (ville) municipality; **2** (conseil) (de petite ville) town council; (de grande ville) city council.

munificent, **~e** /mynifisɑ̃, ɑ̃t/ *adj* munificent.

munir /myniʀ/ [3] **I** *vtr* **1** to provide [*personne*] (**de** with); **2** (équiper) **~ un bâtiment d'un escalier de secours** to put a fire escape on a building; **muni de** fitted with.

II se munir *vpr* **se ~ de** (apporter) to bring [*argent, arme*]; (emporter) to take; **manifestants munis de barres de fer** demonstrators carrying iron bars; **se ~ de patience** to summon up one's patience.

munitions /mynisjɔ̃/ *nfpl* ammunition ¢, munitions.

muqueuse /mykøz/ *nf* mucous membrane.

mur /myʀ/ **I** *nm* wall; **rester** or **être entre quatre ~s** to be cooped up; **c'est à se taper**° or **cogner**° **la tête contre les ~s** you feel like banging your head against the wall; **un ~ de silence** a wall of silence; **parler à un ~** to be talking to a brick wall; **faire du ~** ° (au tennis) to practise GB hitting a ball against the wall; **faire les pieds au ~** LIT to do a handstand against the wall; FIG to tie oneself up in knots.

II murs *nmpl* (local) (d'entreprise) premises; (d'ambassade, de palais) confines; **être dans ses ~s** to own one's own house.

■ **~ d'appui** (de soutènement) retaining wall; (parapet) parapet; **~ portant** or **porteur** load-bearing wall; **~ du son** sound barrier; **franchir le ~ du son** to break the sound barrier; **~ de soutènement** retaining wall; **Mur des lamentations** Wailing Wall.

IDIOMES **faire le ~** (s'échapper) to go over the wall; (au football) to make a wall; **mettre qn au pied du ~** to call sb's bluff; **être au pied du ~** to be up against the wall.

mûr, **~e**[1] /myʀ/ *adj* **1** [*fruit, blé*] ripe; **2** (intellectuellement) mature; **être ~ pour son âge** to be mature for one's age; **l'âge ~** middle age; **après ~e réflexion** after careful consideration; **3** (psychologiquement) ready (**pour qch** for sth; **pour faire** to do); **il est ~ pour des aveux** he's ready to confess; **4** [*affaire, situation*] at a decisive stage (*jamais épith*); **5** [*abcès, bouton*] **être ~** to have come to a head.

IDIOMES **en voir des vertes et des pas ~es**° to go through a lot ou through some hard times; **en dire des vertes et des pas ~es**° (histoires osées) to tell some dirty jokes; (méchancetés) to say a lot of nasty things (**sur, au sujet de** about).

muraille /myʀɑj/ *nf* LIT, FIG great wall; **la Grande Muraille de Chine** the Great Wall of China.

mural, **~e**, *mpl* **-aux** /myʀal, o/ *adj* [*panneau, revêtement, carte*] wall (*épith*); [*plante*] climbing; [*four*] wall-mounted; **peinture ~e** ART mural.

mûre[2] /myʀ/ **I** *adj f* ▶ **mûr**.

II *nf* blackberry.

mûrement /myʀmɑ̃/ *adv* **~ réfléchi** carefully thought through.

murène /myʀɛn/ *nf* moray eel.

murer /myʀe/ [1] **I** *vtr* to build a wall around [*champ*]; to brick up [*porte*]; to block off [*pièce*]; to wall [sb] up [*personne*].

II se murer *vpr* **se ~ chez soi** to shut oneself away; **se ~ dans son obstination** to dig one's heels in; **se ~ dans la solitude** to retreat into isolation.

muret /myʀɛ/ *nm*, **murette** /myʀɛt/ *nf* low wall.

mûrier /myʀje/ *nm* mulberry tree.

mûrir /myʀiʀ/ [3] **I** *vtr* to ripen [*fruit*]; to mature [*personne*]; to develop [*projet*].

II *vi* [*fruit*] to ripen; **faire ~ des bananes** to ripen bananas; [*personne, talent*] to mature; [*projet, idée*] to evolve, to mature; [*passion*] to develop; [*abcès, bouton*] to come to a head.

murmure /myʀmyʀ/ *nm* **1** (chuchotement) murmur; **~ d'indignation** murmur of of protest; **2** (plainte sourde) **~s** mutterings; **3** (de vent) whisper; (de source) murmur, babbling; **4** (rumeur) rumour GB.

murmurer /myʀmyʀe/ [1] **I** *vtr* **1** (chuchoter) to murmur; **~ qch à qn/à l'oreille de qn** to murmur sth to sb/into sb's ear; **2** (dire) to say; **on murmure qu'il est riche** he is rumoured GB to be rich.

II *vi* **1** (chuchoter) [*personne*] to murmur; [*vent*] to whisper; [*ruisseau*] to babble; **2** (se plaindre) to mutter; **obéir sans ~** to obey without a murmur; **3** (faire courir des bruits) to spread rumours GB; **on murmure à leur sujet** there are rumours GB about them.

musaraigne /myzaʀɛɲ/ *nf* shrew.

musarder /myzaʀde/ [1] *vi* to wander around.

musc /mysk/ *nm* musk.

muscade /myskad/ *nf* BOT, CULIN nutmeg; **noix ~** nutmeg.

muscardin /myskaʀdɛ̃/ *nm* (common) dormouse.

muscle /myskl/ *nm* muscle.

musclé, **~e** /myskle/ *adj* **1** LIT muscular; **2** FIG (vigoureux) [*style*] sinewy; [*musique, discours*] powerful; [*réaction*] strong; (dur) [*discours, intervention, match*] tough; **3** ÉCON [*entreprise, économie*] competitive.

muscler /myskle/ [1] **I** *vtr* **1** LIT **~ les bras/jambes** to develop the arm/leg muscles; **2** FIG to strengthen; **~ l'industrie** to make industry more competitive.

II se muscler *vpr* **1** [*personne*] to develop one's muscles; **2** [*entreprise*] to become more competitive.

musculaire /myskylɛʀ/ *adj* [*tissu, fibre*] muscle (*épith*); [*force, faiblesse*] muscular.

musculation /myskylasjɔ̃/ *nf* (**exercices de**) **~** SPORT bodybuilding; (après une maladie) exercises to strengthen the muscles; **salle de ~** weights room.

musculature /myskylatyʀ/ *nf* musculature; **avoir une ~ bien développée** to have well developed muscles.

musculeux, **-euse** /myskylø, øz/ *adj* **1** [*bras, personne*] muscular; **2** ANAT [*tissu*] muscle (*épith*).

muse /myz/ *nf* **1** (divinité) Muse; **les neuf ~s** the Muses; **taquiner la ~** HUM to dabble in verse; **2** (inspiration) muse.

museau, *pl* **~x** /myzo/ *nm* **1** (de chien, bovin, d'ovin) muzzle; (de porc) snout; (de renard) nose; **2**° (visage) face.

musée /myze/ *nm* GÉN museum; (d'art) art gallery GB, art museum US; **leur maison, c'est le ~ des horreurs**° HUM everything in their house is indescribably ugly; **une ville ~** a city of great historical and artistic importance.

■ **~ de cire** waxworks, wax museum.

museler /myzle/ [19] *vtr* LIT, FIG to muzzle.

muselière /myzəljɛʀ/ *nf* muzzle.

muser[†] /myze/ [1] *vi* to wander around.

musette[1] /myzɛt/ *nm* **1** MUS (style) accordion music; **2** (bal) dance (*where accordion music is played*).

musette[2] /myzɛt/ *nf* **1** (sac) (de soldat) haversack; (d'ouvrier) lunchbag; **2** ZOOL common shrew.

muséum /myzeɔm/ *nm* **~ (d'histoire naturelle)** natural history museum.

Les instruments de musique

Les instruments

L'anglais emploie l'article défini devant les noms d'instruments de musique, même avec le verbe to play *(*jouer*).*

apprendre le piano	= to learn the piano
étudier le piano	= to study the piano
jouer du piano	= to play the piano

Les morceaux de musique

un arrangement pour piano	
	= an arrangement for piano
	ou a piano arrangement
une sonate pour violon	= a violin sonata
un concerto pour piano	
et orchestre	= a concerto for piano and
	orchestra
la partie pour piano	= the piano part

Les musiciens

Le suffixe anglais -ist *correspond au suffixe français* -iste.

un violoniste	= a violinist
un pianiste	= a pianist

Dans les autres cas, on peut toujours dire a — player.

un corniste = a horn player

De même, an oboe player, a piccolo player, *etc.*

En anglais comme en français, le nom de l'instrument est parfois utilisé pour parler des musiciens.

les trombones = the trombones

De avec les noms d'instruments de musique

un cours de violon	= a violin class
une leçon de violon	= a violin lesson
un professeur de violon	= a violin teacher
un solo de violon	= a violin solo

---

musical, **~e**, *mpl* **-aux** /myzikal, o/ *adj* [*événement*] musical; [*revue, critique*] music (*épith*); [*choix*] of music (*épith, après n*).

musicalité /myzikalite/ *nf* musicality.

music-hall, *pl* **~s** *nm* /mysikol/ music hall; **artiste/spectacle de ~** variety artist/show.

musicien, -ienne /myzisjɛ̃, ɛn/ **I** *adj* musical.
II ▶ 374 *nm,f* musician.

musicographie /myzikɔgrafi/ *nf* musicography.

musicologie /myzikɔlɔʒi/ *nf* musicology.

musique /myzik/ *nf* **1** (art, notes) music; **travailler en ~** to work with music in the background; **mettre en ~** to set [sth] to music; **faire de la ~** (savoir jouer) to play an instrument; **2** (œuvre) piece of music; **une ~ pour piano** a piece of piano music; **une ~ de film** a film score; **sur une ~ de** with music by; **3** (orchestre) band.
IDIOMES **c'est toujours la même ~**○ it's always the same old refrain; **connaître la ~**○ to know the score○; **je ne peux pas aller plus vite que la ~**○ I can't go any faster than I'm already going; **être réglé comme du papier à ~**○ [*personne*] to be as regular as clockwork; [*congrès, projet*] to go very smoothly.

musqué, ~e /myske/ *adj* **1** [*parfum*] musky; [*cheveux*] musk-scented; **2** ZOOL **bœuf ~** musk ox; **rat ~** muskrat.

musulman, ~e /myzylmɑ̃, an/ *adj, nm,f* Muslim.

mutabilité /mytabilite/ *nf* mutability.

mutant, ~e /mytɑ̃, ɑ̃t/ *adj, nm,f* BIOL, FIG mutant.

mutation /mytasjɔ̃/ *nf* **1** (transfert) transfer; **2** (transformation) transformation; **en pleine ~** undergoing radical transformation; **3** BIOL, LING, MUS mutation.

muter /myte/ [1] **I** *vtr* to transfer [*fonctionnaire*].
II *vi* BIOL to mutate.

mutilation /mytilasjɔ̃/ *nf* (d'arbre, de membre, texte) mutilation.
■ **~ volontaire** self-inflicted injury.

mutilé, ~e /mytile/ *nm,f* disabled person.
■ **~ de guerre** disabled war veteran; **~ du travail** *person disabled through an accident at work.*

mutiler /mytile/ [1] **I** *vtr* to mutilate.
II se mutiler *vpr* to inflict an injury on oneself.

mutin, ~e /mytɛ̃, in/ **I** *adj* mischievous.
II *nm* (soldat, marin) mutineer; (prisonnier) rioter.

mutiné, ~e /mytine/ *nm,f* (soldat, marin) mutineer; (prisonnier) rioter.

mutiner: se mutiner /mytine/ [1] *vpr* [*marins, soldats*] to mutiny; [*prisonniers*] to riot; **équipage mutiné** mutinous crew.

mutinerie /mytinri/ *nf* (de marins, soldats) mutiny; (de prisonniers) riot.

mutisme /mytism/ *nm* (silence) silence.

mutité /mytite/ *nf* muteness, dumbness.

mutualiste /mytɥalist/ **I** *adj* mutualist.
II *nmf* member of a mutual insurance company.

mutuel, -elle¹ /mytɥɛl/ *adj* mutual.

mutuelle² /mytɥɛl/ *nf* mutual insurance company.

mutuellement /mytɥɛlmɑ̃/ *adv* mutually; **s'aider ~** to help each other.

mycologie /mikɔlɔʒi/ *nf* mycology.

myocarde /mjɔkard/ *nm* myocardium.

myope /mjɔp/ *adj* short-sighted, myopic SPÉC.
IDIOMES **~ comme une taupe**○ as blind as a bat.

myopie /mjɔpi/ *nf* LIT, FIG short-sightedness.

myosotis /mjɔzɔtis/ *nm inv* forget-me-not.

myriade /mirjad/ *nf* LITER myriad (**de** of).

myrmidon /mirmidɔ̃/ *nm* pipsqueak○.

myrrhe /mir/ *nf* myrrh.

myrte /mirt/ *nm* myrtle.

myrtille /mirtij/ *nf* bilberry, blueberry.

mystère /mistɛr/ *nm* **1** (énigme) mystery; **auteur ~** mysterious author; **2** (fait de cacher) secrecy; **entourer qch de ~** to surround sth in secrecy; **je n'en fais pas (un) ~** I make no secret of it; **il n'est un ~ pour personne que** it's an open secret that; **3** RELIG mystery; LITTÉRAT Mystery play; **4** (rite antique) rite.

mystérieusement /misterjøzmɑ̃/ *adv* mysteriously.

mystérieux, -ieuse /misterjø, øz/ *adj* mysterious; **faire le ~** to assume an air of mystery.

mysticisme /mistisism/ *nm* mysticism.

mystificateur, -trice /mistifikatœr, tris/ **I** *adj* [*personne*] who likes playing tricks; [*lettre, coup de fil*] hoax (*épith*); [*attitude*] intended to dupe (*après n*); **dans un esprit ~** for a hoax.
II *nm,f* hoaxer.

mystification /mistifikasjɔ̃/ *nf* **1** (canular) hoax; **2** (illusion) myth.

mystifier /mistifje/ [2] *vtr* to hoodwink, to fool.

mystique /mistik/ **I** *adj* mystical.
II *nmf* mystic.
III *nf* **1** (doctrine) mysticism; **2** (mystère) mystique; **3** (passion) blind belief (**de** in); **avoir la ~ révolutionnaire** to have a blind belief in revolution.

mythe /mit/ *nm* GÉN myth; **le ~ d'Orphée** the myth of Orpheus; **le ~ de l'alcool qui fortifie** the myth that alcohol fortifies.

mythique /mitik/ *adj* mythical.

mythologie /mitɔlɔʒi/ *nf* mythology.

mythologique /mitɔlɔʒik/ *adj* mythological.

mythomane /mitɔman/ *adj, nmf* mythomaniac.

mythomanie /mitɔmani/ *nf* mythomania.

n, N /ɛn/ **I** *nm inv* **1** n, N; **2 n°** (*written abbr* = **numéro**) no.
II N *nf* (*abbr* = **nationale**) sur la N7 on the N7.

n' ▶ **ne**.

nabab /nabab/ *nm* **1** (homme riche) mogul; **2** (en Inde) nabob.

nabot, ~e /nabo, ɔt/ *nm,f* OFFENSIVE dwarf INJUR.

nacelle /nasɛl/ *nf* **1** (de ballon) gondola; **2** (de landau) carrycot GB, carrier US; **3** (d'ouvrier) cradle.

nacre /nakʀ/ *nf* mother-of-pearl; **de ~** [*teint, peau*] pearly.

nacré, ~e /nakʀe/ *adj* pearly.

nage /naʒ/ *nf* **1** (natation) swimming; **200 mètres quatre ~s** 200 metres^{GB} medley; **regagner la rive à la ~** to swim back to shore; **2** (sueur) **être en ~** to be in a sweat; **3** NAUT rowing; **4** CULIN **à la ~** à la nage (*après n*) (cooked in an aromatic court-bouillon).
■ **~ sur le dos** backstroke; **~ libre** freestyle.

nageoire /naʒwaʀ/ *nf* **1** (de poisson) fin; **2** (de phoque, pingouin) flipper.

nager /naʒe/ [13] **I** *vtr* to swim; **~ le cent mètres** to swim the hundred metres^{GB}; **~ le crawl** to do the crawl.
II *vi* **1** LIT to swim; **les tomates nagent dans l'huile** the tomatoes are swimming in oil; **2** FIG **~ dans le bonheur** to bask in contentment; **elle nage dans sa robe** her dress is far too big for her; **3**° (mal comprendre) to be absolutely lost; **4** NAUT to row.
IDIOMES **~ entre deux eaux** to run with the hare and hunt with the hounds.

nageur, -euse /naʒœʀ, øz/ *nm,f* **1** SPORT swimmer; **2** (rameur) oarsman/oarswoman.

naguère /nagɛʀ/ *adv* **1** (récemment) quite recently; **2** (autrefois) formerly.

naïade /najad/ *nf* naiad.

naïf, naïve /naif, iv/ **I** *adj* **1** [*personne*] (sans artifice) artless; (crédule) naïve; [*réponse*] naïve; **2** ART naïve.
II *nm,f* innocent, gullible fool PÉJ.

nain, ~e /nɛ̃, nɛn/ **I** *adj* [*arbre, étoile*] dwarf (*épith*); [*lapin, chien*] miniature.
II *nm,f* (personne) dwarf.
■ **le ~ jaune** JEUX pope Joan.

naissance /nesɑ̃s/ *nf* **1** (d'enfant) birth; **de ~** [*italien*] by birth; [*sourd*] from birth; **c'est de ~ chez lui**° he was born like that; **donner ~ à** to give birth to; **à la ~** at birth; **à ma/ta ~** when I was/you were born; **16% des ~s** 16% of births; **2** (d'œuvre, de courant, sentiment) birth; (de produit) first appearance; (de rumeur) start; **la ~ du jour** LITER daybreak; **le mouvement a pris ~ dans le milieu ouvrier** the movement sprang up in the working classes; **l'idée a donné ~ à de multiples œuvres** the idea gave rise to many works; **3** (base) **à la ~ du cou** at the base of the neck.

naissant, ~e /nesɑ̃, ɑ̃t/ *adj* [*barbe, art, pays*] new.

naître /nɛtʀ/ [74] *vi* **1** [*personne, animal*] to be born; **elle est née le 5 juin 92** she was born on 5 June 92; **le bébé doit ~ à la fin du mois** the baby is due at the end of the month; **elle vient de ~** she's only just been born; **les bébés qui viennent de ~** newborn babies; **l'enfant à ~** the unborn baby ou child; **~ sourd** to be born deaf; **2** (commencer d'exister) [*mouvement, projet*] to be born; [*entreprise*] to come into existence; [*amour, amitié*] to spring up; [*jour*] to break; [*soupçon*] to arise; **~ de** to arise out of [*désir*]; **faire**

~ à to give rise to [*espoir, conflit*]; **voir ~** to see the birth of [*journal*]; **3** LITER **~ à** to awaken to [*art, religion*].

naïve ▶ **naïf**.

naïvement /naivmɑ̃/ *adv* GÉN naively; (sans artifice) artlessly.

naïveté /naivte/ *nf* GÉN naivety; (naturel) artlessness; **avoir la ~ de croire que...** to be naïve enough to believe that...

naja /naʒa/ *nm* cobra.

nanisme /nanism/ *nm* dwarfism, nanism SPÉC.

nanti, ~e /nɑ̃ti/ **I** *adj* (riche) well-off.
II nantis *nmpl* **les ~s** PEJ the well-off (+ *v pl*).

nantir /nɑ̃tiʀ/ [3] **I** *vtr* (pourvoir) LITER **~ qn de** to provide sb with [*objet*]; to award [sth] to sb [*titre*].
II se nantir *vpr* (se munir de) LITER **se ~ de** to provide oneself with [*certificat, autorisation*]; to equip oneself with [*parapluie*].

naphtaline /naftalin/ *nf* mothballs (*pl*); **boule de ~** mothball.

napoléonien, -ienne /napɔleɔnjɛ̃, ɛn/ *adj* Napoleonic.

nappe /nap/ *nf* **1** (de table) tablecloth; **2** (couche) (de pétrole, gaz, d'huile) layer; (d'eau) sheet; CULIN layer; **~ de mazout** oil slick; **~ de feu** sheet of flames; **~ de brouillard** (en mer) fog bank; (sur terre) layer of fog.

napper /nape/ [1] *vtr* CULIN (avec de la sauce, du chocolat) to coat (**de** with); (avec de la confiture) to glaze.

napperon /napʀɔ̃/ *nm* (pour couvert) place mat; (pour vase, lampe) mat.

narcisse /naʀsis/ *nm* **1** (fleur) narcissus; **2** (vaniteux) PEJ narcissist.

narcissisme /naʀsisism/ *nm* narcissism.

narco(-) /naʀko/ *préf* drug; **~-dollars** drug money.

narcotique /naʀkɔtik/ *adj, nm* narcotic.

narghilé /naʀgile/ *nm* hookah.

narguer /naʀge/ [1] *vtr* to taunt [*personne*]; to flout [*autorité*].

narguilé /naʀgile/ *nm* hookah.

narine /naʀin/ ▶ 137 *nf* nostril.

narquois, ~e /naʀkwa, az/ *adj* mocking.

narquoisement /naʀkwazmɑ̃/ *adv* mockingly.

narrateur, -trice /naʀatœʀ, tʀis/ *nm,f* narrator.

narratif, -ive /naʀatif, iv/ *adj* narrative.

narration /naʀasjɔ̃/ *nf* narration.

narrer /naʀe/ [1] *vtr* LITER to relate.

nasal, ~e, mpl -aux /nazal, o/ *adj* [*cloison*] nasal; [*hémorragie, goutte*] nose; [*son, voix*] nasal.

naseau, pl ~x /nazo/ *nm* nostril.

nasillard, ~e /nazijaʀ, aʀd/ *adj* [*voix*] nasal; [*instrument*] tinny.

nasillement /nazijmɑ̃/ *nm* **1** (de personne) nasal twang; **2** (d'instrument) tinny sound; **3** (de canard) quack.

nasiller /nazije/ [1] *vi* **1** [*personne*] to speak with a nasal voice; **2** [*canard*] to quack.

nasse /nas/ *nf* **1** (pour la pêche) keepnet; **2** FIG net.

natal, ~e, mpl ~s /natal/ *adj* [*pays, langue*] native.

nataliste /natalist/ *adj* [*politique*] pro-birth (*épith*).

natalité /natalite/ *nf* (**taux de**) **~** birthrate.

natation /natasjɔ̃/ ▶ 329 *nf* swimming.

Les nationalités

Les adjectifs ethniques comme anglais *peuvent aussi qualifier des langues (par ex.* un mot anglais, ▶ **338** |) *et des choses (par ex.* la cuisine anglaise, ▶ **232** |).

En anglais, les noms et les adjectifs ethniques se forment de plusieurs manières. On peut distinguer cinq groupes. Noter que l'anglais emploie la majuscule dans tous les cas, pour l'adjectif et pour le nom.

1ᵉʳ groupe: le nom et l'adjectif ont la même forme. Le nom pluriel prend un s.

un Allemand	= a German *ou (s'il est nécessaire de distinguer)* a German man
une Allemande	= a German *ou* a German woman
les Allemands *(en général)*	= the Germans *ou* Germans *ou* German people
c'est un Allemand	he's German *ou* he's a German
il est allemand	= he's German

Dans ce groupe: American, Angolan, Belgian, Brazilian, Chilean, Cypriot, Czech, Egyptian, Greek, Indian, Iranian, Italian, Jamaican, Mexican, Moroccan, Norwegian, Pakistani, Russian, Thai *etc.*

2ᵉ groupe: le nom s'obtient en ajoutant le mot man *ou* woman *à l'adjectif.*

un Japonais	= a Japanese man
une Japonaise	= a Japanese woman
les Japonais *(en général)*	= the Japanese* *ou* Japanese people
c'est un Japonais	= he's Japanese
il est japonais	= he's Japanese

* Japanese *est un adjectif utilisé comme nom: il prend toujours l'article défini et ne prend jamais de* s.

Dans ce groupe: Burmese, Chinese, Congolese, Lebanese, Portuguese, Sudanese, Vietnamese *etc.*

3ᵉ groupe: le nom s'obtient en ajoutant le suffixe -man *ou* -woman *à l'adjectif.*

un Anglais	= an Englishman
une Anglaise	= an Englishwoman
les Anglais *(en général)*	= the English† *ou* English people
c'est un Anglais	= he's English *ou* he's an Englishman
il est anglais	= he's English

† English *est un adjectif utilisé comme nom: il prend toujours l'article défini et ne prend jamais de* s.

Dans ce groupe: French, Dutch, Irish, Welsh *etc.*

4ᵉ groupe: le nom et l'adjectif sont des mots différents. Le nom pluriel prend un s.

un Danois	= a Dane *ou* a Danish man
une Danoise	= a Dane *ou* a Danish woman
les Danois *(en général)*	= Danes *ou* the Danes *ou* Danish people
c'est un Danois	= he's Danish *ou* he's a Dane
il est danois	= he's Danish

Dans ce groupe: Finn (*nom*): Finnish (*adjectif*); Icelander: Icelandic; Pole: Polish; Scot: Scottish; Spaniard: Spanish; Swede: Swedish; Turk: Turkish *etc.*

5ᵉ groupe: quelques cas particuliers, qui n'ont pas d'adjectif, par ex. la Nouvelle-Zélande:

un Néo-Zélandais	= a New Zealander
une Néo-Zélandaise	= a New Zealander
les Néo-Zélandais *(en général)*	= New Zealanders
c'est un Néo-Zélandais	= he's a New Zealander
il est néo-zélandais	= he's a New Zealander

Quelques autres expressions permettant de parler de la nationalité de quelqu'un en anglais:

il est né en Angleterre	= he was born in England
il vient d'Angleterre	= he comes from England
il est d'origine anglaise	= he's of English extraction
il est citoyen britannique	= he's a British citizen
il est citoyen néo-zélandais	= he's a New Zealand citizen
c'est un ressortissant britannique	= he's a British national

natif, -ive /natif, iv/ *adj* (originaire) **~ de** native of.

nation /nasjɔ̃/ *nf* nation.

■ **les Nations unies** the United Nations.

national, ~e¹, *mpl* **-aux** /nasjɔnal, o/ **I** *adj* national.

II nationaux *nmpl* nationals; **nationaux autrichiens/danois** Austrian/Danish nationals.

nationale² /nasjɔnal/ *nf* (route) trunk road GB, ≈ A road GB, highway US.

nationalement /nasjɔnalmɑ̃/ *adv* nationally.

nationalisation /nasjɔnalizasjɔ̃/ *nf* nationalization.

nationaliser /nasjɔnalize/ [1] *vtr* to nationalize.

nationalisme /nasjɔnalism/ *nm* nationalism.

nationalité /nasjɔnalite/ *nf* nationality.

national-socialisme /nasjɔnalsɔsjalism/ *nm* National Socialism.

nativité /nativite/ *nf* **1** RELIG nativity; **2** ART Nativity scene.

natte /nat/ *nf* **1** (tresse) plait; **2** (sur le sol) mat.

natter /nate/ [1] *vtr* to plait.

naturalisation /natyralizasjɔ̃/ *nf* **1** JUR naturalization; **2** (acclimatation) naturalization; **3** (taxidermie) stuffing.

naturalisé, ~e /natyralize/ *adj* JUR naturalized.

naturaliser /natyralize/ [1] *vtr* **1** JUR to naturalize [*étranger*]; **elle est naturalisée française** she's acquired French nationality; **2** (adopter) to assimilate [*mot, coutume*]; **3** (acclimater) to naturalize [*espèce*]; **4** (empailler) to stuff [*animal*].

naturaliste /natyralist/ **I** *adj* naturalist.

II *nmf* **1** ART, LITTÉRAT, PHILOS naturalist; **2** ▶ **374** | (taxidermiste) taxidermist.

nature /natyr/ **I** *adj inv* **1** (sans additif) [*yaourt, fromage blanc*] natural; [*omelette*] plain; [*thé*] black; **à**

consommer avec du sucre ou ~ to be eaten with sugar or on its own; **2**○ (spontané) [*personne*] natural.

II *nf* **1** (forces nous gouvernant) nature; **laisser faire la ~** to let nature take its course; **la ~ fait bien les choses** the ways of nature are wonderful; **2** (environnement) nature; **une merveille de la ~** a wonder of nature; **protection de la ~** protection of the environment; **une ~ hostile** a hostile environment; **en pleine ~** in the heart of the countryside; **lâcher qn dans la ~** (en pleine campagne) to leave sb in the middle of nowhere; FIG to let sb loose; **3** (caractère) nature; **une ~ généreuse** a generous nature; **de ~ à faire** likely to do; **il est anxieux de ~, il est d'une ~ anxieuse** he's nervous by nature; **avoir une ~ fragile/robuste** to have a delicate/strong constitution; **de même ~** of the same nature; **des offres de toute ~** offers of all kinds; **4** (réalité) **peindre d'après ~** to paint from life; **plus petit/plus vrai que ~** smaller/more real than life; **5** (objets réels) **en ~** [*payer*] in kind; **avantages en ~** fringe benefits.

■ **~ morte** still life; ▶ **petit**.

IDIOMES **partir** or **disparaître dans la ~**○ to vanish into thin air.

naturel, -elle /natyrɛl/ **I** *adj* natural.

II *nm* **1** (caractère) nature; **être d'un ~ gai** to be naturally cheerful; **2** (spontanéité) **il manque de ~** he's not very natural; **avec le plus grand ~** in the most natural way; **3** CULIN **au ~** [*riz*] plain; [*thon*] in brine.

naturellement /natyrɛlmɑ̃/ *adv* naturally.

naturisme /natyrism/ *nm* **1** (nudisme) naturism GB, nudism; **faire du ~** to be a naturist GB ou nudist; **2** PHILOS, RELIG naturism.

naturiste /natyrist/ *nmf* (nudiste) naturist GB, nudist.

naufrage /nofraʒ/ *nm* shipwreck, sinking ¢; **le ~ de l'économie** FIG the collapse of the economy; **faire**

~ [*navire*] to be wrecked; [*marin*] to be shipwrecked; [*entreprise*] to collapse.

naufragé, **~e** /nofʀaʒe/ **I** *adj* [*marin*, *équipage*] shipwrecked; **retrouver le navire ~** to find the wreck of the ship.
II *nm,f* (rescapé) survivor (of a shipwreck); (sur une île, une côte déserte) castaway.

nauséabond, **~e** /nozeabɔ̃, ɔ̃d/ *adj* [*odeur*] sickening, nauseating.

nausée /noze/ *nf* (dégoût) nausea **C**; **avoir la ~** to feel sick GB ou nauseous.

nautique /notik/ *adj* [*science*] nautical; [*sports*] water (*épith*).

nautisme /notism/ *nm* (sports) water sports (*pl*).

naval, **~e**, *mpl* **~s** /naval/ *adj* **1** IND [*industrie*, *secteur*] shipbuilding; **2** MIL naval.

navet /navε/ *nm* **1** (légume) turnip; **2** (film) PEJ rubbishy film GB, turkey○ US.

navette /navεt/ *nf* **1** (véhicule) shuttle; (liaison) shuttle (service); **faire la ~ entre Paris et Dijon** [*personne*] (pour le travail) to commute between Paris and Dijon; (pour raison personnelle) to travel back and forth between Paris and Dijon; **il y a un car qui fait la ~** there is a shuttle service; **2** (en tissage) shuttle.
■ **~ spatiale** space shuttle.

navigabilité /navigabilite/ *nf* **1** (de rivière) navigability; **2** (de bateau) seaworthiness; (d'avion) airworthiness.

navigable /navigabl/ *adj* navigable.

navigant, **~e** /navigɑ̃, ɑ̃t/ *adj* [*personnel*] NAUT seagoing; AVIAT flying; **mécanicien ~** flight engineer.

navigateur, **-trice** /navigatœʀ, tʀis/ *nm,f* **1** (qui guide) navigator; **2** (marin) sailor; (au long cours) navigator.
■ **~ solitaire** solo yachtsman.

navigation /navigasjɔ̃/ *nf* **1** AVIAT, NAUT (techniques) navigation; **instrument de ~** navigational instrument; **2** (trafic sur l'eau) shipping, navigation; **~ intérieure** or **fluviale** inland navigation; **salon de la ~** boat show; **3** (voyage) **plusieurs semaines de ~** several weeks on the water; **4** ORDINAT browsing.
■ **~ de plaisance** GÉN boating; (en voilier) sailing.

naviguer /navige/ [1] *vi* **1** NAUT [*bateau*, *marin*, *passager*] to sail; **en état de ~** [*navire*] seaworthy; **2** (guider un bateau, un avion) to navigate; **3** (voler) to fly; **4** ORDINAT to browse.

navire /naviʀ/ **I** *nm* ship.
II **navire-** (*in compounds*) **~-école/-hôpital/-usine** training/hospital/factory ship; **~s-citernes** tankers.
■ **~ amiral** MIL flagship; **~ de commerce** merchant ship; **~ de guerre** warship; **~ marchand** merchant ship.

navrant, **~e** /navʀɑ̃, ɑ̃t/ *adj* **1** (consternant) depressing; **2** (attristant) distressing, upsetting.

navré, **~e** /navʀe/ *adj* **1** (dans une formule de politesse) **je suis vraiment ~** I am terribly sorry; **2** (triste, déçu) **avoir l'air ~** to look sad ou upset.

navrer /navʀe/ [1] *vtr* LITER (contrarier) to upset.

nazi, **~e** /nazi/ *adj*, *nm,f* Nazi.

nazisme /nazism/ *nm* Nazism.

NDLR *written abbr* ▶ **note**.

ne /nə/ (**n'** *before vowel or mute h*) *adv*

■ **Note** ne, adverbe de négation, n'a pas d'équivalent exact en anglais.
– Généralement, la forme négative se construit avec un auxiliaire ou un verbe modal accompagné d'une négation: *je ne sais pas* = I don't know; *je ne peux pas* = I can't, I cannot; *il n'a pas répondu* = he didn't answer.
– Pour ne utilisé avec *pas, jamais, guère, rien, plus, aucun, personne* etc, on se reportera à l'article correspondant.
– *ne + verbe + que* est traité dans l'article ci-dessous.

je n'ai que 100 francs I've only got 100 francs; **ce n'est qu'une égratignure** it's only a scratch; **il n'y avait que lui dans la salle** there was nobody but him

in the room; **tu n'avais qu'à le dire!** you only had to say so!; **il ne pense qu'à s'amuser** he only thinks of enjoying himself, he thinks of nothing but enjoying himself; **il n'y a qu'elle qui comprenne** only she understands; **il n'y a que lui pour être aussi désagréable** only he can be so unpleasant; **tu n'es qu'un raté** you're nothing but a loser○; **si l'avion est trop cher, il n'a qu'à prendre le train** if flying is too expensive he can take the train; **je n'ai que faire de tes conseils** you can keep your advice.

né, **~e** /ne/ **I** *pp* ▶ **naître**.
II *pp adj* **bien/mal ~** highborn/lowborn (*épith*); **Madame Masson ~e Roux** Mrs Masson née Roux.
III (-)**né** (*in compounds*) **un écrivain(-)~** a born writer.

néanmoins /neɑ̃mwɛ̃/ *adv* nevertheless.

néant /neɑ̃/ *nm* **1** PHILOS **le ~** nothingness; **2** (absence de valeur) emptiness; **réduire à ~** to negate [*efforts*, *progrès*]; to destroy [*argument*, *espoir*, *rêve*]; to wipe out [*majorité*]; **'revenus: ~'** 'income: nil'.

nébuleuse[1] /nebyløz/ *nf* **1** (objet céleste) nebula; **2** FIG amorphous grouping.

nébuleux, **-euse**[2] /nebylø, øz/ *adj* **1** (obscurci) [*ciel*] cloudy, overcast; [*masse*] nebulous; **2** FIG nebulous.

nébulosité /nebylozite/ *nf* (de ciel, concept) nebulosity.

nécessaire /nesesɛʀ/ **I** *adj* GÉN necessary (à for); **conditions ~s à la vie** conditions necessary for life; **juger ~ de faire** to consider it necessary to do; **~ ou pas** whether necessary or not; **il est ~ de faire** it is necessary to do; **il est ~ que tu y ailles** you have to go; **les voix ~s pour renverser le gouvernement** the votes needed in order to overthrow the government.
II *nm* **1** (ce qui s'impose) **faire le ~** to do what is necessary ou what needs to be done; **as-tu fait le ~ pour les billets?** did you see about the tickets?; **j'ai fait le ~** I've seen to it; **le ~ et le superflu** what is necessary and what is superfluous; **2** (biens et services) essentials (*pl*); **manquer du ~** to lack the essentials.
■ **~ de couture** sewing kit; **~ à ongles** manicure set; **~ de toilette** toiletries (*pl*).

nécessairement /nesesɛʀmɑ̃/ *adv* necessarily; **le progrès n'est pas ~ un bienfait** progress is not necessarily a blessing; **'y aura-t-il des licenciements?'—'pas ~/oui, ~'** 'will there be redundancies?'—'not necessarily/yes, it is unavoidable'; **cela finit ~ mal** it inevitably goes wrong; **passe-t-on ~ par Oslo?** do you have to go via Oslo?.

nécessité /nesesite/ *nf* **1** (ce qui s'impose) necessity; **le téléphone est devenu une ~** the telephone has become a necessity; **~ absolue** or **impérative** absolute necessity; **~ urgente/impérieuse** urgent/pressing need; **~ de qch/de faire/d'être** need for sth/to do/to be; **~ pour qn de faire** sb's need for sth/to do; **je n'en vois pas la ~** I don't see the need for it; **de première ~** vital; **par ~** out of necessity; **sans ~** unnecessarily; **être dans la ~ de faire** to have no choice but to do; **2** (pauvreté) need; **être dans la ~** to be in need; **3** (caractère inéluctable) necessity.
IDIOMES **~ fait loi** PROV necessity knows no law.

nécessiter /nesesite/ [1] *vtr* to require; **la situation nécessite qu'elle intervienne** the situation calls for her intervention.

nécessiteux, **-euse** /nesesitø, øz/ **I** *adj* needy.
II *nm,f* needy person; **les ~** the needy (+ *v pl*).

nec plus ultra /nɛkplyzyltʀa/ *nm inv* **le ~** the last word (**de** in).

nécrologie /nekʀɔlɔʒi/ *nf* **1** (liste) deaths column, obituary column; **2** (article) obituary.

nécrologique /nekʀɔlɔʒik/ *adj* obituary.

nécrophage /nekʀɔfaʒ/ *adj* necrophagous.

nécropole /nekʀɔpɔl/ *nf* necropolis.

nécrose /nekʀoz/ *nf* necrosis.

nécroser /nekʀoze/ [1] *vtr*, **se nécroser** *vpr* to necrose.

nectar /nɛktaʀ/ *nm* nectar.

néerlandais, **~e** /neɛʀlɑ̃dɛ, ɛz/ ▶338|, 394| I *adj* Dutch.

II *nm* LING Dutch.

Néerlandais, **~e** /neɛʀlɑ̃dɛ, ɛz/ ▶394| *nm,f* Dutchman/Dutchwoman; **les ~** the Dutch (+ *v pl*).

nef /nɛf/ *nf* **1** ARCHIT nave; **les ~s latérales** the side aisles; **2**† (embarcation) vessel, ship.

néfaste /nefast/ *adj* (nuisible) harmful (**à** to).

négatif, **-ive**[1] /negatif, iv/ I *adj* **1** (non positif) negative; **2** (néfaste) negative, adverse.

II *adv* AVIAT, MIL negative.

négation /negasjɔ̃/ *nf* **1** (action de nier) negation; **2** LING negative.

négative[2] /negativ/ I *adj f* ▶ **négatif**.

II *nf* **répondre par la ~** to reply in the negative; **dans la ~, nous aviserons** if not, we will think again.

négligé, **~e** /negliʒe/ I *adj* [*personne, vêtement*] sloppy, scruffy○; [*cheveux, barbe*] unkempt; [*maison*] neglected; [*travail*] careless, sloppy; [*blessure*] untreated.

II *nm* (vêtement) negligée.

négligeable /negliʒabl/ *adj* [*quantité, somme*] negligible, insignificant; [*personne*] insignificant; **non ~** [*somme, atout*] considerable; [*détail, rôle*] significant.

négligemment /negliʒamɑ̃/ *adv* (avec nonchalance) nonchalantly; (avec indifférence) carelessly.

négligence /negliʒɑ̃s/ *nf* **1** (faute) negligence ₵; **il y aurait eu des ~s** negligence is alleged; **2** (laisser-aller) negligence, carelessness.

négligent, **~e** /negliʒɑ̃, ɑ̃t/ *adj* [*employé*] negligent, careless; [*élève, démarche*] careless; [*geste*] casual.

négliger /negliʒe/ [13] I *vtr* **1** to neglect [*santé, travail, personne*]; to leave untreated [*affection, rhume*]; **2** to ignore, to disregard [*résultat, règle*]; **il n'a rien négligé pour réussir** he tried everything possible to succeed; **une offre qui n'est pas à ~** an offer which is worth considering; **~ de faire** to fail to do.

II **se négliger** *vpr* (dans sa tenue) not to take care over one's appearance; (pour sa santé) not to look after oneself.

négoce /negɔs/ *nm* trade (**avec** with).

négociable /negɔsjabl/ *adj* negotiable.

négociant, **~e** /negɔsjɑ̃, ɑ̃t/ ▶374| *nm,f* GÉN merchant; (grossiste) wholesaler.

négociateur, **-trice** /negɔsjatœʀ, tʀis/ *nm,f* negotiator.

négociation /negɔsjasjɔ̃/ *nf* negotiation; **la table de ~** the negotiating table.

négocier /negɔsje/ [2] I *vtr* **1** COMM, POL to negotiate (**avec** with); **2** SPORT **~ un virage** to negotiate a bend.

II *vi* to negotiate (**avec** with).

nègre /nɛgʀ/ I *adj* [*art, musique*] Negro.

II *nm* **1** (Noir) OFFENSIVE Negro INJUR; **2** (auteur occulte) ghostwriter.

négresse /negʀɛs/ *nf* OFFENSIVE Negress INJUR.

négrier /negʀije/ *nm* HIST (personne) slave trader; (navire) slave ship.

négritude /negʀityd/ *nf* black identity, negritude.

neige /nɛʒ/ *nf* MÉTÉO snow; **~ fondue** (au sol) slush; (pluie) sleet; **aller à la ~** to go skiing; **paysage de ~** snow-covered landscape; **blancs battus en ~** stiffly beaten eggwhites.

IDIOMES **être blanc comme ~** to be completely innocent; **fondre comme ~ au soleil** to melt away.

neiger /nɛʒe/ [13] *v impers* to snow; **il neige** it's snowing.

neigeux, **-euse** /nɛʒø, øz/ *adj* [*cime*] snow-covered; [*temps, hiver*] snowy.

nénuphar /nenyfaʀ/ *nm* waterlily.

néo /neo/ *préf* neo; **~classicisme** neoclassicism.

néo-calédonien, **-ienne**, *mpl* **~s** /neokaledɔnjɛ̃, ɛn/ *adj* New Caledonian.

néo-écossais, **~e** /neoekɔsɛ, ɛz/ *adj* Nova Scotian.

néologisme /neɔlɔʒism/ *nm* neologism.

néon /neɔ̃/ *nm* **1** (gaz) neon; **2** (tube) neon light.

néophyte /neɔfit/ *nmf* neophyte.

néo-zélandais, **~e** /neozelɑ̃dɛ, ɛz/ ▶394| *adj* New Zealand (*épith*).

Néo-Zélandais, **~e** /neozelɑ̃dɛ, ɛz/ ▶394| *nm,f* New Zealander.

népalais, **~e** /nepalɛ, ɛz/ ▶338|, 394| I *adj* Nepali.

II *nm* LING Nepali.

néphrétique /nefʀetik/ *adj* nephritic; **coliques ~s** renal colic ₵.

népotisme /nepɔtism/ *nm* nepotism.

nerf /nɛʀ/ I *nm* **1** ANAT nerve; **~ optique** optic nerve; **2** (vigueur) spirit, go○; **redonner du ~ à qn** to put new heart into sb; **allez, du ~○!** come on, buck up○!

II **nerfs** *nmpl* (système nerveux) nerves; **être malade des ~s** to suffer from nerves.

■ **~ de bœuf** pizzle.

IDIOMES **jouer avec les ~s de qn** to be deliberately annoying; **ses ~s ont lâché** he/she went to pieces; **avoir les ~s à fleur de peau** to have frayed nerves; **avoir les ~s en pelote○** or **en boule○** or **à vif** to be really wound up; **être sur les ~s, avoir ses ~s○** to be on edge; **vivre sur les ~s** to live on one's nerves; **taper○ sur les ~s de qn** to get on sb's nerves; **être à bout de ~s** to be at the end of one's tether; **passer ses ~s sur○ qn** to take it out on sb; **l'argent est le ~ de la guerre** money is the sinews of war.

nerveusement /nɛʀvøzmɑ̃/ *adv* **1** (avec impatience) nervously; **2** (psychologiquement) **être épuisé ~** to be suffering from nervous exhaustion; **il n'est pas solide ~** he's rather highly strung GB ou high-strung US; **il faut qu'il récupère ~** he needs to have a good rest and calm down.

nerveux, **-euse** /nɛʀvø, øz/ I *adj* **1** [*personne, animal, rire*] nervous; [*allure*] tense; **2** [*corps, main*] sinewy; [*moteur*] responsive; **3** (énergique) [*personne*] dynamic; [*style, écriture*] vigorous; **4** ANAT [*cellule, centre*] nerve (*épith*); [*système, tension*] nervous.

II *nm,f* MÉD nervous person.

nervosité /nɛʀvozite/ *nf* **1** (appréhension) nervousness; **on sentait la ~ ambiante** you could feel the tension in the air; **2** (surexcitation) excitability; **un cheval/enfant d'une grande ~** a very excitable horse/child; **3** AUT (de moteur) liveliness, bite○.

nervure /nɛʀvyʀ/ *nf* **1** BOT, ZOOL nervure; **2** ARCHIT rib.

nervuré, **~e** /nɛʀvyʀe/ *adj* [*feuille, aile*] veined.

n'est-ce pas /nɛspa/ *adv* **1** (appelant l'approbation) **c'est joli, ~?** it's pretty, isn't it?; **tu es d'accord, ~?** you agree, don't you?; **~ qu'il est gentil?** isn't he nice?; **2** (pour renforcer) of course.

net, **nette** /nɛt/ I *adj* **1** ÉCON, FIN (après déductions) net; **prix/salaire ~** net price/salary; **2** [*changement, augmentation*] marked; [*baisse*] sharp; [*tendance, odeur*] distinct; **3** [*personne, victoire, souvenir*] clear; [*situation*] clear-cut; [*écriture*] neat; [*cassure*] clean; **en avoir le cœur ~** to be clear in one's mind about it; **avoir la nette impression que** to have the distinct impression that; **4** (propre) LIT [*maison, vêtement*] neat; [*mains*] clean; FIG [*personne*] clean; [*conscience*] clear; **faire place nette** to clear everything away; **5○** (lucide) **pas (très) ~** not quite with it○.

II *adv* [*s'arrêter*] dead; [*tuer*] outright; [*refuser*] flatly; [*dire*] straight out; **refuser tout ~** to refuse point blank; **la corde a cassé ~** the rope snapped; **la clé s'est cassée ~** the key snapped in two.

III *nm* **1** ÉCON, FIN (revenu) net income; (bénéfices) earnings (*pl*); **2** (propre) **copie au ~** clean copy.

nettement /nɛtmɑ̃/ *adv* **1** [*augmenter, se détériorer*] markedly; [*devancer*] clearly; [*préférer*] definitely; **~ meilleur** decidedly better; **2** [*voir, dire*] clearly; [*refuser*] flatly; [*se souvenir*] distinctly.

netteté /nɛtte/ *nf* **1** (de voix, ciel) clarity; (d'image) sharpness; (de résultat) definite nature; (de cassure) cleanness; **2** (de lieu) cleanness; (de travail) neatness.

nettoiement /netwamɑ̃/ *nm* **1** (nettoyage) cleaning ¢; **2** (enlèvement des ordures) refuse collection GB, garbage collection US; **service de ~** cleansing department GB, sanitation department US.

nettoyage /netwajaʒ/ *nm* **1** (opération) cleanup; **~ de printemps** spring-cleaning ¢; **2** (action) cleaning ¢; **~ à sec** dry-cleaning; **produit de ~** cleaning product; **3** (de la peau) cleansing ¢; **4** MIL mopping-up ¢.

IDIOMES **faire le ~ par le vide**○ to have a good clearout○.

nettoyant /netwajɑ̃/ *nm* (produit) cleaning agent.

nettoyer /netwaje/ [23] I *vtr* **1** LIT to clean [*lieu, objet, mains*]; to clean up [*jardin*]; to clean out [*rivière*]; to clean off [*tache*]; **donner une robe à ~** to take a dress to the cleaner's; **faire ~ qch à sec** to have sth dry-cleaned; **2** FIG to clean up [*ville*]; (dévaliser, ruiner) to clean out○ [*appartement, personne*].

II **se nettoyer** *vpr* **1** (se laver soi-même) **se ~ les mains** to clean one's hands; **2** (pouvoir être lavé) **la tache se nettoie à l'eau** the stain can be cleaned with water.

neuf[1] /nœf/ ▶156|, 298|, 399| I *adj inv, pron* nine.
II *nm inv* nine; **faire la preuve par ~** MATH to cast out the nines.

neuf[2], **neuve** /nœf, nœv/ I *adj* new; **comme ~** as new; **tout ~** brand new; **porter un regard ~ sur qch** to look at sth in a new light; **'état ~'** 'as new'.
II *nm inv* new; **être habillé de ~** to be dressed in new clothes; **refaire qch à ~** to re-do sth completely; **faire du ~ avec du vieux** to revamp things.

IDIOMES **faire peau neuve** [*bâtiment*] to undergo a transformation; [*personne*] to transform one's image.

neurasthénie /nørasteni/ *nf* depression.

neurasthénique /nørastenik/ I *adj* depressed; (chroniquement) depressive.
II *nmf* depressive.

neuro /nøro/ *préf* neuro; **~biologie** neurobiology; **~logie** neurology.

neuronal, **~e**, *mpl* **-aux** /nørɔnal, o/ *adj* **1** MÉD neuronal; **2** ORDINAT neural.

neurone /nørɔn/ *nm* neurone.

neutralisation /nøtralizasjɔ̃/ *nf* neutralization.

neutraliser /nøtralize/ [1] *vtr* **1** GÉN, CHIMIE to neutralize; **2** (empêcher d'agir) to overpower [*forcené*].

neutralité /nøtralite/ *nf* (d'État) neutrality; (d'individu) impartiality.

neutre /nøtr/ I *adj* **1** GÉN, CHIMIE, PHYS, POL neutral; **2** LING, ZOOL neuter.
II *nm* LING **le ~** the neuter.

neutron /nøtrɔ̃/ *nm* neutron.

neuvième /nœvjɛm/ I ▶156|, 399| *adj* ninth.
II *nf* SCOL *third year of primary school, age 8–9.*

neveu, *pl* **~x** /n(ə)vø/ *nm* nephew.

névralgie /nevralʒi/ *nf* neuralgia ¢.

névralgique /nevralʒik/ *adj* **1** MÉD [*douleur*] neuralgic; **2** FIG **point ~** key point.

névropathe /nevrɔpat/ *adj, nmf* neurotic.

névrose /nevroz/ ▶196| *nf* neurosis.

névrosé, **~e** /nevroze/ *adj, nm,f* neurotic.

New York /njujɔrk/ *npr* **1** ▶628| (ville) New York City; **2** ▶509| **l'État de ~** New York (State).

nez /ne/ ▶137| *nm* nose; **~ en trompette** turned-up nose; **ça sent le parfum à plein ~**○ there's a strong smell of perfume; **je n'ai pas mis le ~ dehors**○ I didn't set foot outside; **mettre le ~ à la fenêtre**○ to show one's face at the window; **lever à peine le ~** barely to look up; **ne pas lever le ~ de qch** never to lift one's head from sth; **tu as le ~ dessus**○ it's staring you in the face; **avoir du ~**, **avoir le ~ fin** (odorat) to have a good sense of smell; (intuition) to be shrewd; **rire au ~ de qn** to laugh in sb's face.

IDIOMES **mener qn par le bout du ~**○ (dans un couple) to have sb under one's thumb; (plus général) to have sb wrapped round one 's little finger; **avoir qn dans le ~**○ to have it in for sb; **avoir un coup** or **verre dans le ~**○ to have had one too many○; **faire qch au ~** (**et à la barbe**) **de qn** to do sth right under sb's nose; **filer** or **passer sous le ~ de qn** to slip through sb's fingers; **avoir le ~ creux**○ to be canny; **se casser le ~**○ (trouver porte close) to find nobody at home; (échouer) to fail, to come a cropper○.

NF /ɛnɛf/ *adj, nf* (*abbr* = **norme française**) French manufacturing standard.

ni /ni/ *conj*

■ Note On observe que le français et l'anglais fonctionnent de la même façon: *il ne jure ni ne se met en colère* = he doesn't swear or lose his temper; *ni il jure ni il se met en colère* = he neither swears nor loses his temper; *elle ne veut pas le voir ni lui parler* = she doesn't wish to see him or talk to him; *elle ne veut ni le voir ni lui parler* = she neither wishes to see him nor talk to him.

elle ne veut ~ ne peut changer she doesn't want to change, nor can she; **il n'est ~ beau ~ laid** he's neither handsome nor ugly; **il ne parle ~ anglais, ~ allemand, ~ espagnol** he speaks neither English, nor German, nor Spanish; **~ l'un ~ l'autre** neither of them; **il ne m'a dit ~ oui ~ non** he didn't say yes or no; **~ plus ~ moins** no more and no less.

IDIOMES **faire qch ~ vu ~ connu**○ to do sth on the sly○; **c'est ~ fait ~ à faire**○ it's a botched○ job; **il n'a fait ~ une ~ deux**○ he didn't have a second's hesitation.

niais, **~e** /njɛ, njɛz/ I *adj* stupid.
II *nm,f* idiot, simpleton.

niaiserie /njɛzri/ *nf* **1** (caractère) stupidity, silliness; **2** (propos) stupid ou inane remark.

niaiseux, **-euse** /njɛzø, øz/ C I *adj* (stupide) moronic.
II *nm,f* (imbécile) moron○.

nicaraguayen, **-enne** /nikaragwajɛ̃, ɛn/ ▶394| *adj* Nicaraguan.

niche /niʃ/ *nf* **1** (de chien) kennel; **2** ARCHIT (de statue) niche; (alcôve) recess; **3**○ (farce) trick.

nichée /niʃe/ *nf* (d'oisillons, enfants) brood; (de souris) litter.

nicher /niʃe/ [1] I *vi* **1** ZOOL to nest; **2**○ (loger) to live.
II **se nicher** *vpr* **1** ZOOL to nest; **2** (se blottir) [*personne, chaumière*] to nestle (**dans** in).

nickel /nikɛl/ I○ *adj* [*objet*] spotless; [*logement*] spick and span (*jamais épith*).
II *nm* nickel.

nicotine /nikɔtin/ *nf* nicotine.

nid /ni/ *nm* nest.
■ **~ d'aigle** eyrie; **~ de brigands** den of thieves; **~ d'hirondelle** bird's nest; **~ à poussière** dust trap; **~ de résistance** pocket of resistance.

nid-d'abeilles, *pl* **nids-d'abeilles** /nidabɛj/ *nm* honeycomb weave.

nid-de-poule, *pl* **nids-de-poule** /nidpul/ *nm* pothole.

nidification /nidifikasjɔ̃/ *nf* nesting.

nièce /njɛs/ *nf* niece.

nième /ɛnjɛm/ = **énième**.

nier /nje/ [2] *vtr* to deny [*fait, existence, signature*]; to repudiate [*dette*]; **~ une faute** to deny having made a mistake; **~ l'évidence** to refuse to face up to the facts.

nigaud, **~e** /nigo, od/ I *adj* silly.
II *nm,f* (silly) twit○ GB, goof○ US.

nihiliste /niilist/ *adj, nmf* nihilist.

nimbe /nɛ̃b/ *nm* nimbus, halo.

nimber /nɛ̃be/ [1] *vtr* [*soleil*] to halo (**de** with); [*brume*] to swathe.

nîmois, **~e** /nimwa, az/ ▶628| *adj* of Nîmes.

nipper○: **se nipper** /nipe/ [1] *vpr* to get rigged out○ in one's Sunday best.

nippes○ /nip/ *nfpl* rags○, old clothes.

nippon, -onne /nipɔ̃, ɔn/ *adj* Japanese.

nitouche○ /nituʃ/ *nf* **sainte ~** goody-goody○.

nitrate /nitʀat/ *nm* nitrate.

nitrique /nitʀik/ *adj* nitric; **acide ~** nitric acid.

niveau, *pl* **~x** /nivo/ *nm* **1** (hauteur) level; **~ de l'eau/d'huile** water/oil level; **au ~ du sol** at ground level; **être de ~** to be level; **arrivé au ~ du bus** when he drew level with the bus; **au ~ du cou** [*blessures*] in the neck region; **accroc au ~ du genou** tear at the knee; **2** (étage) storey GB, story US; **bâtiment sur deux ~x** two-storey GB ou two-story US building; **3** (degré) (d'intelligence) level; (de connaissances) standard; **~ intellectuel** intellectual level; **'~ bac + 3'** baccalaureate or equivalent plus 3 years' higher education; **remettre qn à ~** to bring sb up to the required standard; **de haut ~** [*athlète*] top (*épith*); [*candidat*] high-calibreGB (*épith*); **~ des salaires** wage levels (*pl*); **4** (échelon) level; **au plus haut ~** [*discussion*] top-level (*épith*); **les négocia-tions se dérouleront au plus haut ~** there will be negotiations at the highest level; **5** LING register; **6** (ins-trument) level.
■ **~ de langue** register; **~ social** social status; **~ sonore** sound level; **~ de vie** standard of living, living standards (*pl*).

nivelage /nivlaʒ/ *nm* **1** (de sol) levellingGB; **2** (égalisa-tion) (économique) standardization; (social) levellingGB out.

niveler /nivle/ [19] *vtr* **1** (aplatir) to level [*sol*]; to flatten [*relief*]; **2** (égaliser) to bring [sth] to the same level [*revenus*]; **~ par le bas/haut** to level down/up.

nivellement /nivɛlmɑ̃/ *nm* **1** (du sol) levellingGB; **2** (mesure) land survey; **3** (économique) standardization; (social) levellingGB-out.

nobiliaire /nɔbiljɛʀ/ *adj* [*titre, particule*] nobiliary.

noble /nɔbl/ **I** *adj* **1** [*personne*] of noble birth; [*fa-mille*] aristocratic; **2** [*sentiments, maintien*] noble; [*cause*] worthy, noble; **3** [*matériau*] (naturel) natural, non-synthetic; (raffiné) fine; [*filière, section*] presti-gious; [*sport*] noble; **métaux ~s** precious metals.
II *nmf* (personne) nobleman/noblewoman; **les ~s** the nobility (*sg*).

noblement /nɔbləmɑ̃/ *adv* **1** (avec noblesse) nobly; **2** (avec générosité) handsomely.

noblesse /nɔblɛs/ *nf* **1** (qualité morale) nobility; **2** (aristocratie) **la ~** the nobility; **la petite ~** the gentry.

nobliau, *pl* **~x** /nɔblijo/ *nm* minor nobleman.

noce /nɔs/ **I** *nf* **1**○ (fête) party; **faire la ~**○ FIG to live it up○, to party○; **aujourd'hui je n'étais pas à la ~** FIG today was no picnic; **2** (invités) wedding party.
II noces *nfpl* wedding (*sg*); **nuit de ~s** wedding night; **en premières ~s, il a épousé**... his first wife was...

noceur○, **-euse** /nɔsœʀ, øz/ *nm,f* party animal○.

nocif, -ive /nɔsif, iv/ *adj* [*gaz*] noxious; [*théorie*] harmful.

nocivité /nɔsivite/ *nf* (de gaz) noxiousness.

noctambule /nɔktɑ̃byl/ **I** *adj* [*promeneur*] late-night (*épith*).
II *nmf* night owl.

nocturne[1] /nɔktyʀn/ **I** *adj* [*spectacle, attaque*] night (*épith*); [*animal*] nocturnal; [*sortie, promenade*] late-night (*épith*); **la vie ~ à Londres** nightlife in London.
II *nm* **1** ZOOL (oiseau) nocturnal bird; **2** MUS, RELIG nocturne.

nocturne[2] /nɔktyʀn/ *nf* **1** SPORT (course, match) evening fixture; **2** COMM (de magasin) late-night open-ing.

Noé /nɔe/ *npr* Noah.

noël /nɔɛl/ *nm* s2 (chant) Christmas carol.

Noël /nɔɛl/ *nm* Christmas; **'Joyeux ~'** 'Merry ou Happy Christmas'; **de ~** [*arbre, cadeau*] Christmas (*épith*).

nœud /nø/ **I** *nm* **1** (pour lier) knot; **faire un ~ d** **cravate** to tie a tie; **2** (pour orner) bow; **3 ▶ 631|** NA knot; **~s marins** sailors' knots; **4** BOT knot; **5** (poi essentiel) crux; **6** LITTÉRAT (de pièce, d'intrigue) crux.
II nœuds *nmpl* (d'amitié, affection) LITER bonds, ties.
■ **~ coulant** slipknot; **~ papillon** bow tie; **de vipères** nest of vipers; **~ vital** ANAT vita centreGB.

noir, ~e[1] /nwaʀ/ **▶ 141|** **I** *adj* **1** (couleur) [*peintur fumée, cheveux*] black; [*yeux*] dark; **être ~ de coup** to be black and blue; **être ~ de monde** [*rue, plag* to be swarming with people; **2** (sale) [*mains, co* black, filthy; **être ~ de crasse** to be black wit grime; **3** (obscur) [*ruelle, cachot*] dark; **il fait ~** it dark; **4** [*personne, race, peau, quartier*] black; (bronzé) **être ~, avoir la peau ~e** to have a dar tan; **6** (catastrophique) [*époque, année*] bad, blea [*misère*] dire, abject; [*désespoir*] deep; [*idée*] gloom dark; **7** (méchant) [*regard*] black; [*âme, dessein*] dar **entrer** or **se mettre dans une colère ~e** to fly into towering rage.
II *nm* **1** (couleur) black; **2** (crasse) dirt; (saleté, tac noire) **du ~** a black mark; **3** (obscurité) dar **4** (clandestinité) **au ~** [*acheter, vendre*] on the blac market; **travailler au ~** GÉN to work without decla ing one's earnings; (avoir un deuxième emploi, non d claré) to moonlight○; **5**○ (café) **un (petit) ~** a espresso.
IDIOMES voir tout en ~ to look on the black side (things).

Noir, ~e /nwaʀ/ *nm,f* black man/woman.

noirâtre /nwaʀɑtʀ/ **▶ 141|** *adj* blackish.

noiraud, ~e /nwaʀo, od/ *adj* [*personne, tein visage*] swarthy.

noirceur /nwaʀsœʀ/ *nf* **1** (d'encre) blackness; (cheveux, nuit, d'yeux) darkness; **2** (de personne, regar projets, d'intentions) blackness; **3** C (obscurité) dark.

noircir /nwaʀsiʀ/ [3] **I** *vtr* **1** (salir) [*charbon*] to mak [sth] dirty; [*fumée, pollution*] to blacken; [*encre*] t stain [sth] black; **~ du papier** FIG to scribble awa **2** (assombrir) **~ la situation** to paint a black pictu of the situation; **~ qn** to blacken sb's name.
II *vi* (devenir noir) [*banane*] to go black; [*mur*] to g dirty; [*métal*] to tarnish.
III se noircir *vpr* [*ciel*] to darken; [*temps*] to becom threatening; **se ~ le visage** to blacken one's face.

noircissure /nwaʀsisyʀ/ *nf* dark smudge.

noire[2] /nwaʀ/ **I** *adj f* ▶ **noir**.
II *nf* MUS crotchet GB, quarter note US.

noise /nwaz/ *nf* **chercher ~** or **des ~s à qn** to pic a quarrel with sb.

noisetier /nwaztje/ *nm* hazel (tree).

noisette /nwazɛt/ **I ▶ 141|** *adj inv* [*couleur, yeu* hazel; [*tissu*] light brown.
II *nf* **1** BOT, CULIN hazelnut; **2** (morceau) small knob.

noix /nwa/ *nf inv* BOT walnut GB, English walnut u **pain aux ~** walnut bread; **à la ~**○ [*histoir artiste*] crummy○; **une ~ de beurre** a knob butter.
■ **~ de cajou** cashew nut; **~ de coco** coconu **~ (de) muscade** nutmeg.

nom /nɔ̃/ **I** *nm* **1** (désignation) name; **connu sous ~ de** known as; **donner un ~ à** to name; **sans** PEJ unspeakable; **cela porte un ~:** **la fainéantis** there's a word for that: laziness; **~ de ~**○, **d'un chien**○ or **d'une pipe** hell○; **2** (nom propr name; (opposé à prénom) surname, second nam **porter le ~ de son mari** to use one's husband surname; **George Sand, de son vrai ~ Auror Dupin** George Sand, whose real name was Auror Dupin; **~ et prénom** full name; **~ à couch dehors**○ impossible name; **~ à rallonges**○ impos ibly long name; **parler en son propre ~** to spea for oneself; **3** (réputation) name; **il s'est fait un dans la publicité** he made his name in advertisin **4** LING (partie du discours) noun.
II au nom de *loc prép* **1** (en vertu de) in the nam of; **2** (de la part de) on behalf of.

Les nombres (1)

Les nombres cardinaux

0	nought (*GB*)	17	seventeen
	zero (*US*)*	18	eighteen
1	one	19	nineteen
2	two	20	twenty
3	three	21	twenty-one
4	four	22	twenty-two
5	five	30	thirty
6	six	31	thirty-one
7	seven	32	thirty-two
8	eight	40	forty†
9	nine	50	fifty
10	ten	60	sixty
11	eleven	70	seventy
12	twelve	73	seventy-three
13	thirteen	80	eighty
14	fourteen	84	eighty-four
15	fifteen	90	ninety
16	sixteen	95	ninety-five

100	a hundred
	ou one hundred‡
101	a hundred and one (*GB*)§
	a hundred one (*US*)
111	a hundred and eleven (*GB*)
	a hundred eleven (*US*)
123	a hundred and twenty-three (*GB*)
	a hundred twenty-three (*US*)
200	two hundred

Noter que l'anglais utilise une virgule là où le français a un espace.

1,000	a thousand
1,002	a thousand and two (*GB*)
	a thousand two (*US*)
1,020	a thousand and twenty (*GB*)
	a thousand twenty (*US*)
1,200	a thousand two hundred
10,000	ten thousand
10,200	ten thousand two hundred
100,000	a hundred thousand
102,000	a hundred and two thousand (*GB*)
	ou a hundred two thousand (*US*)
1,000,000	one million
1,200,000	one million two hundred thousand
1,264,932	one million two hundred and sixty-four thousand nine hundred and thirty-two (*GB*)
	ou one million two hundred sixty-four thousand nine hundred thirty-two (*US*)
2,000,000	two million¶
3,000,000,000	three thousand million (*GB*)
	ou three billion‖ (*US*)
4,000,000,000,000	four billion‖ (*GB*)
	four thousand billion (*US*)

les nombres jusqu'à dix	= numbers up to ten
compter jusqu'à dix	= to count up to ten

* *En anglais, lorsqu'on énonce les chiffres un à un, on prononce en général le zéro* oh: mon numéro de poste est le 403 = my extension number is 403 (*dire* four oh three).
Pour la température, on utilise zero: il fait zéro = it's zero.
Pour les scores dans les jeux et les sports, on utilise en général nil (*GB*), zero (*US*), *sauf au tennis, où zéro se dit* love.

† *Noter que* forty *s'écrit sans* u, *alors que* fourteen *et* fourth *s'écrivent comme* four.

‡ *Les formes avec* one *s'utilisent lorsqu'on veut insister sur la précision du chiffre. Dans les autres cas, on utilise plutôt* a.

§ *Noter que* and *s'utilise en anglais britannique entre* hundred *ou* thousand *et le chiffre des dizaines ou des unités (mais pas entre* thousand *et le chiffre des centaines). Il ne s'utilise pas en anglais américain.*

¶ *Noter que* million *est invariable en anglais dans ce cas.*

‖ *Attention: un* billion *américain vaut un milliard (1000 millions), alors qu'un* billion *britannique vaut 1000 milliards. Le* billion *américain est de plus en plus utilisé en Grande-Bretagne.*

Les adresses, les numéros de téléphone, les dates etc.

Les adresses

	dire
29 Park Road	twenty-nine Park Road
110 Park Road	a hundred and ten Park Road (*GB*)
	ou one ten Park Road (*US*)
1021 Park Road	one oh two one Park Road (*GB*)
	ou ten twenty-one Park Road (*US*)

Les numéros de téléphone

	dire
071 392 1011	oh seven one, three nine two; one oh one one *ou* ... one oh double one
1-415-243 7620	one, four one five, two four three, seven six two oh
78 02 75 27	seven eight, oh two, seven five, two seven

Les dates ▶ 156 |

Combien?

combien d'enfants y a-t-il?	= how many children are there?
il y a vingt-trois enfants	= there are twenty-three children

Noter que l'anglais n'a pas d'équivalent du pronom français en *dans:*

combien est-ce qu'il y en a?	= how many are there?
il y en a vingt-trois	= there are twenty-three
nous viendrons à 8	= there'll be 8 of us coming
ils sont 8	= there are 8 of them
ils étaient 10 au commencement	= there were 10 of them at the beginning
1 000 000 d'habitants	= 1,000,000 inhabitants (*dire* a million inhabitants *ou* one million inhabitants)
2 000 000 d'habitants	= two million inhabitants

L'anglais million *s'utilise ici comme adjectif. Noter l'absence d'équivalent anglais de la préposition de après* million.

L'anglais utilise aussi les mots hundreds, thousands, millions *etc. au pluriel, comme en français:*

j'en ai des centaines	= I've got hundreds
des milliers de livres	= thousands of books
les milliers de livres que j'ai lus	= the thousands of books I have read
des centaines et des centaines	= hundreds and hundreds
des milliers et des milliers	= thousands and thousands

Pour les numéraux français en -aine (dizaine, douzaine, quinzaine, vingtaine, trentaine, quarantaine, cinquantaine, soixantaine et centaine) *lorsqu'ils désignent une somme approximative, l'anglais utilise le chiffre avec la préposition* about *ou* around.

une dizaine de questions	= about ten questions
une quinzaine de personnes	= about fifteen people
une vingtaine	= about twenty
une centaine	= about a hundred
presque dix	= almost ten
	ou nearly ten
environ dix	= about ten
environ 400 pages	= about four hundred pages
moins de dix	= less than ten
plus de dix	= more than ten
tous les dix	= all ten of them
	ou all ten
ils s'y sont mis à cinq	= it took five of them *ou* (s'ils n'étaient que cinq en tout) it took all five of them

Noter l'ordre des mots dans:

les deux autres	= the other two
les cinq prochaines semaines	= the next five weeks
mes dix derniers dollars	= my last ten dollars

☞ Voir page suivante

Les nombres (2)

Quel numéro? Lequel?

le volume numéro 8 de la série	= volume 8 of the series *ou* the 8th volume of the series
le cheval numéro 11	= horse number 11
miser sur le 11	= to bet on number 11
le nombre 7 porte bonheur	= 7 is a lucky number
la ligne 8 du métro	= line number 8 of the underground (*GB*) *ou* subway (*US*)
la (chambre numéro) 8 est libre	= room 8 is free
le 8 de pique	= the 8 of spades
Louis XIV	= Louis the Fourteenth

Les opérations

	dire
10 + 3 = 13	ten and three are thirteen *ou* ten plus three make thirteen
10 − 3 = 7	ten minus three is seven *ou* three from ten leaves seven
10 × 3 = 30	ten times three is thirty *ou* ten threes are thirty
30 ÷ 3 = 10*	thirty divided by three is ten *ou* three into thirty is ten
3^2	three squared
3^3	three cubed *ou* three to the power of three
3^4	three to the fourth *ou* three to the power of four
3^{100}	three to the hundredth *ou* three to the power of a hundred
3^n	three to the nth (dire [enθ]) *ou* three to the power of n
$\sqrt{12}$	the square root of 12
$\sqrt{25} = 5$	the square root of twenty-five is 5
B > A	B is greater than A
A < B	A is less than B

Les nombres décimaux

Noter que l'anglais utilise un point (the decimal point) *là où le français a une virgule. Noter également qu'en anglais britannique* zéro *se dit* nought*, et en américain* zero.

	dire
0.25	nought point two five *ou* point two five
0.05	nought point nought five *ou* point oh five
0.75	nought point seven five *ou* point seven five
3.33	three point three three
8.195	eight point one nine five
9.1567	nine point one five six seven

Les pourcentages

	dire
25%	twenty-five per cent
50%	fifty per cent
100%	a hundred per cent *ou* one hundred per cent
200%	two hundred per cent
365%	three hundred and sixty-five per cent (*GB*) *ou* three hundred sixty-five per cent (*US*)
4.25%	four point two five per cent
4.025%	four point oh two five per cent

Les fractions

	dire
½	a half† *ou* one half
⅓	a third *ou* one third
¼	a quarter *ou* one quarter etc.
⅕	a fifth
⅙	a sixth
⅐	a seventh
⅛	an eighth
⅑	a ninth
⅒	a tenth
1/11	one eleventh
1/12	one twelfth (*etc.*)
⅔	two thirds
⅖	two fifths
2/10	two tenths (*etc.*)
¾	three quarters
⅝	five eighths
3/10	three tenths (*etc.*)

Noter l'utilisation en anglais de l'article indéfini dans les expressions suivantes:

1½	one and a half
1⅓	one and a third
1¼	one and a quarter
1⅙	one and a sixth
1⅐	one and a seventh (*etc.*)
5⅔	five and two thirds
5¾	five and three quarters
5⅘	five and four fifths (*etc.*)
45/100	forty-five hundredths

Noter que l'anglais n'utilise pas l'article défini dans:

les deux tiers d'entre eux = two thirds of them

Mais noter l'utilisation de l'article indéfini anglais dans:

quarante-cinq centièmes de seconde
    = forty-five hundredths of a second
dix sur cent = ten out of a hundred

Les nombres ordinaux

français	abréviation	en toutes lettres anglaises
1er	1st	first
2e	2nd	second
3e	3rd	third
4e	4th	fourth
5e	5th	fifth
6e	6th	sixth
7e	7th	seventh
8e	8th	eighth
9e	9th	ninth
10e	10th	tenth
11e	11th	eleventh
12e	12th	twelfth
13e	13th	thirteenth
20e	20th	twentieth
21e	21st	twenty-first
22e	22nd	twenty-second
23e	23rd	twenty-third
24e	24th	twenty-fourth
30e	30th	thirtieth
40e	40th	fortieth
50e	50th	fiftieth
60e	60th	sixtieth
70e	70th	seventieth
80e	80th	eightieth
90e	90th	ninetieth
99e	99th	ninety-ninth
100e	100th	hundredth
101e	101st	hundred and first
102e	102nd	hundred and second (*GB*) hundred second (*US*)
103e	103rd	hundred and third (*GB*) hundred third (*US*)
196e	196th	hundred and ninety-sixth (*GB*) hundred ninety-sixth (*US*)
1 000e	1,000th‡	thousandth
1 000 000e	1,000,000th	millionth

le premier	= the first *ou* the first one
le quarante-deuxième	= the forty-second *ou* the forty-second one
il y en a un deuxième	= there is a second one
le second des deux	= the second of the two

Noter l'ordre des mots dans:

les trois premiers	= the first three
le troisième pays le plus riche du monde	= the third richest nation in the world
les quatre derniers	= the last four

---

* *Noter que le signe divisé par est différent dans les deux langues: au* " : " *français correspond le* " ÷ " *anglais.*

† *Pour les fractions jusqu'à* 1/10*, on utilise normalement* a (a third)*; on utilise* one (one third) *en mathématiques et pour les calculs précis.*

‡ *Noter que l'anglais utilise une virgule là où le français a un espace.*

■ **~ de baptême** Christian name; **~ de code** code name; **~ commercial** corporate name; **~ d'emprunt** pseudonym; **~ de famille** surname; **~ de jeune fille** maiden name; **~ de lieu** place-name; **~ de théâtre** stage name.

IDIOMES **traiter qn de tous les ~s (d'oiseaux)**○ to call sb all the names under the sun; **appeler les choses par leur ~** to call a spade a spade.

nomade /nɔmad/ **I** *adj* [*personne, vie, tribu*] nomadic. **II** *nmf* (du désert) nomad; **mener une vie de ~** to lead a nomadic existence.

nombrable /nɔ̃bʀabl/ *adj* countable, numerable.

nombre /nɔ̃bʀ/ ▶399 *nm* **1** LING, MATH number; **un ~ à deux chiffres** a two-digit number; **2** (quantité) number; **un certain ~ de** some; **être en ~ inférieur** [*troupes, joueurs*] to be fewer in number; [*groupe*] to be smaller; **être en ~ supérieur** [*troupes, joueurs*] to be greater in number; [*groupe*] to be bigger; **dans le ~**○ **il y aura bien quelqu'un qui me prêtera de l'argent** surely one of them will lend me some money; **ils étaient au ~ de 30** there were 30 of them; **3** (grande quantité) numbers (*pl*); **être écrasé** or **succomber sous le ~** (de personnes) to be overcome by sheer weight of numbers; (de dossiers, lettres) to be defeated by the sheer volume; **sans ~** [*ennemis*] countless; [*ennuis*] endless; **bon ~ de** a good many; **~ de fois** many times.

■ **~ impair** odd number; **~ ordinal** ordinal number; **~ pair** even number; **~ premier** prime number.

nombrer /nɔ̃bʀe/ [1] *vtr* LITER to number, to count.

nombreux, -euse /nɔ̃bʀø, øz/ *adj* **1** (important) [*population, collection*] large; **la foule était nombreuse** there was a large ou vast crowd; **2** (en grand nombre) many (*épith*); **l'usine ne sera pas mise en service avant de nombreuses années** it will be many years before the factory is put into operation; **ils étaient peu ~** there were only a few of them; **ils ont répondu ~ à l'appel** numerous people responded to the appeal; **ils arrivent toujours plus ~** they are arriving in ever greater numbers; **les touristes deviennent trop ~** the number of tourists is becoming excessive.

nombril /nɔ̃bʀil/ *nm* navel; **elle se prend pour le ~ du monde**○ she thinks she's God's gift to mankind.

nombrilisme○ /nɔ̃bʀilism/ *nm* (de personne) PEJ navel-gazing○.

nombriliste○ /nɔ̃bʀilist/ *adj* PEJ [*personne*] egocentric; [*politique*] inward-looking.

nomenclature /nɔmɑ̃klatyʀ/ *nf* **1** (ensemble de termes) nomenclature; (de dictionnaire) word list; **2** ORDINAT nomenclature.

nominal, ~e, *mpl* **-aux** /nɔminal, o/ *adj* **1** ÉCON, FIN [*hausse, taux*] nominal; **salaire ~** (en valeur absolue) nominal wage; (avant déductions) gross salary ou pay; **valeur ~e** (d'action) par value; (de monnaie) face value; **2** (par nom) **liste ~e** list of names; **appel ~** roll call; **3** LING [*forme, emploi*] nominal.

nominatif, -ive /nɔminatif, iv/ **I** *adj* [*fichier, liste*] of names; [*invitation*] personal; FIN [*titre*] registered. **II** *nm* LING nominative; **au ~** in the nominative.

nomination /nɔminasjɔ̃/ *nf* **1** (affectation) appointment; (lettre d'affectation) letter of appointment; **3** (sélection) CONTROV nomination.

nominativement /nɔminativmɑ̃/ *adv* by name.

nominer /nɔmine/ [1] *vtr* CONTROV to nominate.

nommément /nɔmemɑ̃/ *adv* specifically, by name.

nommer /nɔme/ [1] **I** *vtr* **1** (désigner pour une fonction) to appoint; **être nommé à Paris** to be posted to Paris; **2** (dénommer) to name [*personne*]; to call [*chose*]; **comment l'ont-ils nommé?** what did they call him?; **3** (citer) to name [*complice, arbre, peintre*]. **II se nommer** *vpr* **1** (s'appeler) to be called; **2** (donner son nom) to give one's name.

non /nɔ̃/

■ **Note** En anglais la réponse *no* est renforcée en reprenant le verbe utilisé pour poser la question: '*tu es déçu?*'—'*non*' = 'are you disappointed?'—'no, I'm not'; '*est-ce que vous aimez les concombres?*'—'*non*' = 'do you like cucumber?'—'no, I don't'.

I *adv* **1** (marque le désaccord) no; **répondez par oui ou par ~** answer yes or no; **ah, ça ~!** definitely not!, no way○!; **alors, c'est ~?** so the answer is no?; **dire** ou **faire ~ de la tête** to shake one's head; **2** (remplace une proposition) **je pense que ~** I don't think so; **je te dis que ~** no, I tell you; **il paraît que ~** apparently not; **tu trouves ça drôle? moi ~** do you think that's funny? I don't; **3** (dans une double négation) **~ sans raison** not without reason; **une situation ~ moins triste** an equally sad situation; **4** (introduisant une rectification, nuance) **~ (pas) que je sois d'accord** not that I agree; **5** (dans une alternative) **qu'il soit d'accord ou ~** whether he agrees or not; **6** (interrogatif, exclamatif) **c'est difficile, ~?** (n'est-ce pas) it's difficult, isn't it?; **~?** (de scepticisme) oh no?; **~!** (de surprise) no!; **sois un peu plus poli, ~ mais** ○! be a bit more polite, for heaven's sake!; **7** (avec adjectif) non; **~ alcoolisé** nonalcoholic; **~ négligeable** [*somme*] considerable; [*rôle*] important; **objet ~ identifié** unidentified object. **II** *nm inv* **1** (désaccord) no; **un ~ catégorique** an emphatic no; **2** (vote négatif) 'no' vote. **III non plus** *loc adv* **~ plus** I don't agree either; **il n'a pas aimé le film, moi ~ plus** he didn't like the film and neither did I. **IV non(-)** (*in compounds*) **~-agression** non-aggression; **~-combattant** noncombatant; **~-dissémination** nonproliferation; **~-fumeur** nonsmoker; **~-responsabilité** nonliability; **~-syndiqué** non union member.

non-aligné, ~e, *mpl* **~s** /nɔnaliɲe/ *nm,f* nonaligned country.

nonante /nɔnɑ̃t/ ▶399, 156 *adj inv, pron* B, C, H ninety.

nonantième /nɔnɑ̃tjɛm/ *adj, nmf* B, C, H ninetieth.

non-assistance /nɔnasistɑ̃s/ *nf* **~ à personne en danger** failure to render assistance.

nonchalance /nɔ̃ʃalɑ̃s/ *nf* nonchalance; **avec ~** nonchalantly.

nonchalant, ~e /nɔ̃ʃalɑ̃, ɑ̃t/ *adj* (personne) nonchalant; (enfant, élève) apathetic; **c'est un ~** he shows no enthusiasm for anything.

non-dit /nɔ̃di/ *nm inv* **le ~** what is left unsaid.

non-figuratif, -ive, *mpl* **~s** /nɔ̃figyʀatif, iv/ *nm,f* abstract artist.

non-fonctionnement /nɔ̃fɔksjɔnmɑ̃/ *nm* failure to operate.

non-initié, ~e, *mpl* **~s** /nɔninisje/ *nm,f* GÉN layman, lay person; (dans une secte) uninitiated person.

non-inscrit, ~e, *mpl* **~s** /nɔnɛ̃skʀi, it/ *nm,f* independent.

non-lieu, *pl* **~x** /nɔ̃ljø/ *nm* JUR dismissal (of a charge); **il y a eu ~** the judge dismissed the case.

nonne† /nɔn/ *nf* 'nun.

nonnette /nɔnɛt/ *nf* CULIN small iced gingerbread.

nonobstant† /nɔnɔpstɑ̃/ *adv, prép* notwithstanding.

non-recevoir /nɔ̃ʀəsəvwaʀ/ *nm* **fin de ~** flat refusal.

non-reconduction, *pl* **~s** /nɔ̃ʀəkɔ̃dyksjɔ̃/ *nf* (de contrat, mesure) nonrenewal; (de personne) failure to reappoint.

non-respect /nɔ̃ʀɛspɛ/ *nm* **~ de** failure to comply with [*clause, accord*]; failure to respect [*personne*].

non-sens /nɔ̃sɑ̃s/ *nm inv* **1** (absurdité) nonsense ₵; **cette politique est un ~** this policy is nonsensical; **2** (dans une traduction) meaningless phrase.

non-spécialiste, *pl* **~s** /nɔ̃spesjalist/ *nmf* layman.

non-violent, ~e, *mpl* **~s** /nɔ̃vjɔlɑ̃, ɑ̃t/ *nm,f* advocate of nonviolence.

non-voyant, ~e, *mpl* **~s** /nɔ̃vwajɑ̃, ɑ̃t/ *nm,f*

visually handicapped person; **les ~s** the visually handicapped.

nord /nɔʀ/ ▶457 **I** *adj inv* [*façade, versant, côte*] north; [*frontière, zone*] northern.
II *nm* **1** (point cardinal) north; **2** (région) north; **le ~ de l'Europe** northern Europe; **3** GÉOG, POL **le Nord** the North; **du Nord** [*ville, accent*] northern.
IDIOMES **il ne perd pas le ~**○! he' s got his head screwed on○!

nord-africain, **~e**, *mpl* **~s** /nɔʀafʀikɛ̃, ɛn/ *adj* North African.

nord-américain, **~e**, *mpl* **~s** /nɔʀameʀikɛ̃, ɛn/ *adj* North American.

nord-coréen, **-éenne**, *mpl* **~s** /nɔʀkɔʀeɛ̃, ɛn/ ▶394 *adj* North Korean.

nord-est /nɔʀ(d)ɛst/ ▶457 **I** *adj inv* [*façade, versant*] northeast; [*frontière, zone*] northeastern.
II *nm* northeast; **vent de ~** northeasterly wind.

nordique /nɔʀdik/ *adj* [*pays, langue*] Nordic.

nord-ouest /nɔʀ(d)wɛst/ ▶457 **I** *adj inv* [*façade, versant*] northwest; [*frontière, zone*] northwestern.
II *nm* northwest; **vent de ~** northwesterly wind.

Nord-Sud /nɔʀsyd/ *adj inv* POL North-South.

nord-vietnamien, **-ienne**, *mpl* **~s** /nɔʀvjɛtna mjɛ̃, ɛn/ *adj* North Vietnamese.

normal, **~e¹**, *mpl* **-aux** /nɔʀmal, o/ *adj* normal; **ne pas être dans son état ~** not to be oneself; **il est ~ que** (+ *subj*) it is natural that; **il n'est pas ~ que** (+ *subj*) it is not right that.

normale² /nɔʀmal/ *nf* **1** (moyenne) average; **2** (norme) norm; **retour à la ~** return to normal.

normalement /nɔʀmalmã/ *adv* [*marcher*] normally; **~ elle devrait être là** she should be here by now.

normalien, **-ienne** /nɔʀmaljɛ̃, ɛn/ *nm,f* student at an École normale supérieure.

normalisation /nɔʀmalizasjɔ̃/ *nf* **1** POL (régularisation) normalization; **2** TECH (standardisation) standardization.

normaliser /nɔʀmalize/ [1] *vtr* **1** POL (régulariser) to normalize; **2** TECH (standardiser) to standardize.

normalité /nɔʀmalite/ *nf* normality.

normand, **~e** /nɔʀmã, ãd/ **I** ▶509 *adj* HIST [*conquête*] Norman.
II *nm* LING Norman (French).

Normand, **~e** /nɔʀmã, ãd/ *nm,f* (de Normandie) Norman.
IDIOMES **une réponse de ~** a noncommittal reply.

normatif, **-ive** /nɔʀmatif, iv/ *adj* normative.

norme /nɔʀm/ *nf* **1** (règle) norm; **2** COMM, TECH standard; **~s de sécurité** safety standards; **hors ~** LIT nonstandard; FIG extraordinary; **3** MATH norm.

Norvège /nɔʀvɛʒ/ ▶232 *nprf* Norway.

norvégien, **-ienne** /nɔʀveʒjɛ̃, ɛn/ ▶338, 394 *adj* Norwegian.
II *nm* LING Norwegian.

nos ▶ **notre**.

nostalgie /nɔstalʒi/ *nf* nostalgia (**de** for).

nostalgique /nɔstalʒik/ **I** *adj* (mélancolique) nostalgic (**de** for); (loin de son pays) homesick.
II *nmf* **les ~s des années 20** those who are nostalgic for the 1920's.

notabilité /nɔtabilite/ *nf* notability.

notable /nɔtabl/ **I** *adj* [*fait*] notable; [*progrès*] significant.
II *nm* notable.

notablement /nɔtabləmã/ *adv* significantly.

notaire /nɔtɛʀ/ ▶374 *nm* notary public.

notamment /nɔtamã/ *adv* **1** (entre autres) notably; **2** (plus particulièrement) in particular, more particularly.

notation /nɔtasjɔ̃/ *nf* **1** (système) notation; **2** (d'élève) marking GB, grading US; (de fonctionnaire) grading.

note /nɔt/ *nf* **1** (facture) bill, check US; **faire la ~ de qn** to write out sb's bill GB ou check US; **2** MUS note; **3** (évaluation) mark GB, grade US; **~ éliminatoire** fail

mark GB ou grade US; **c'est une bonne ~ pour lui** FIG that's a point in his favour^GB; **4** (communication écrite) note; **5** (transcription) **~s de cours** (lecture) notes; **prendre qch en ~** to make a note of sth; **prendre (bonne) ~ de qch** FIG to take (due) note of sth; **6** (détail) note; **une ~ d'originalité** a touch of originality; **forcer la ~** to overdo it; **7** (commentaire) note; **~ en bas de page** footnote.
■ **~ de frais** expense account; **~ d'honoraires** bill; **~ interne** memorandum, memo○; **~ de la rédaction**, **NDLR** editor's note; **~ de service** = **~ interne**.

noter /nɔte/ [1] *vtr* **1** (inscrire) to note down [*renseignement*]; to write down [*idée, citation*]; **c'est (bien) noté?** have you got that?; **2** (remarquer) to notice [*changement, progrès, erreur*]; **ceci est à ~** this should be noted; **il me déplaît, notez (bien) que je n'ai rien à lui reprocher** I don't like him, though mind you I haven't got anything particular against him; **il faut quand même ~** it has to be said; **3** (évaluer) to mark GB, to grade US [*devoir*]; to give a mark GB ou grade US to [*élève*]; to grade [*employé*]; **élève bien/mal noté** pupil who got good/bad marks GB ou grades US; **fonctionnaire bien/mal noté** civil servant who obtains a high/low rating in progress reports; **4** (marquer) to mark [*texte*]; **5** MUS to write down [*air, notes*].

notice /nɔtis/ *nf* **1** (exposé) note; **2** (instructions) instructions (*pl*).

notification /nɔtifikasjɔ̃/ *nf* GÉN notification; JUR notice.

notifier /nɔtifje/ [2] *vtr* **~ qch à qn** GÉN to notify sb of sth; JUR to give sb notice of sth.

notion /nɔsjɔ̃/ *nf* **1** (conscience) notion; **perdre la ~ de qch** to lose all sense of sth; **2** (concept) notion; **3** (de langue, science) **~s** basic knowledge ¢.

notoire /nɔtwaʀ/ *adj* [*fait, position*] well-known; [*escroc, bêtise*] notorious; JUR [*inconduite*] manifest.

notoirement /nɔtwaʀmã/ *adv* GÉN manifestly; PÉJ notoriously.

notoriété /nɔtɔʀjete/ *nf* **1** (de personne, lieu, d'œuvre) fame; (de produit) reputation; **il est de ~ (publique) que** it's common knowledge that; **2** (personne célèbre) celebrity.

notre, *pl* **nos** /nɔtʀ, no/ *adj poss*
■ **Note** En anglais, on ne répète pas le possessif coordonné: *notre adresse et notre numéro de téléphone* = our address and phone number.

our; **nos enfants à nous**○ our children; **à nos âges** at our age; **ils sont venus pendant ~ absence** they came while we were away; **~ retour s'est bien passé** we got back safely; **c'était ~ avis à tous** we all felt the same; **c'est ~ maître à tous** he's the master of us all.

nôtre /notʀ/ **I** *adj poss* **nous avons fait ~s ces idées** we've adopted these ideas.
II le nôtre, la nôtre, les nôtres *pron poss* ours; **quelle erreur était la ~!** how wrong we were!; **à la ~** cheers!; **soyez des ~s!** won't you join us?; **les ~s** (notre peuple) our own people; (notre équipe) our side (*sg*)

nouer /nwe/ [1] **I** *vtr* **1** (attacher) to tie [*lacets, cravate*]; to tie up [*chaussure, colis*]; **~ ses cheveux** to tie one's hair back; **~ ses bras autour du cou** to put one's arms around sb's neck; **2** (contracter) **avoir la gorge nouée** to have a lump in one's throat; **avoir l'estomac noué** to have a knot in one's stomach; **3** (établir) to establish [*relations*]; to engage in [*dialogue*]; **4** CIN, LITTÉRAT, THÉÂT to weave [*intrigue*].
II se nouer *vpr* **1** CIN, LITTÉRAT, THÉÂT [*intrigue*] to take shape; **2** [*relations diplomatiques*] to be established; [*dialogue, amitié*] to begin.

noueux, **-euse** /nwø, øz/ *adj* gnarled.

nougat /nuga/ *nm* nougat.

nouille /nuj/ *nf* **1** (pâtes alimentaires) **des ~s** noodles, pasta ¢; **2**○ (niais) noodle○.

nounou○ /nunu/ *nf* nanny GB, nurse.

nounours○ /nunuʀs/ *nm inv* BABY TALK teddy bear.

nourri, **~e** /nuʀi/ *adj* **1** [*tir*] heavy; [*applaudissements*] sustained; **2** [*conversation*] lively.

nourrice /nuʀis/ *nf* (gardienne) (chez elle) childminder GB, babysitter US; (chez l'enfant) nanny, babysitter US.

nourricier, -ière /nuʀisje, ɛʀ/ *adj* **1** LITER [*terre, sève*] nourishing; **2†** [*père*] foster.

nourrir /nuʀiʀ/ [3] **I** *vtr* **1** (fournir des aliments à) to feed [*personne, plante*]; to nourish [*cuir, peau*]; **bien nourri** well-fed; **mal nourri** undernourished; **~ au sein/au biberon** to breast-/to bottle-feed; **2** (subvenir aux besoins de) to keep [*famille*]; to provide a living for [*région*]; **mon travail ne me nourrit pas** I don't make enough to live on; **3** (entretenir) to harbour GB [*espoir*]; to nurture [*projet*]; to feed [*incendie*]; to fuel [*passion*]; to feed [*idéologie*]; **4** (enrichir) to fuel [*discussion*]; to feed [*esprit*]; **elle fut nourrie d'histoire classique** she was brought up on classical history.
II se nourrir *vpr* [*animal*] to feed (**de** on); [*personne*] to eat; **se ~ de** to live on [*légumes*]; to feed on [*illusions*].

nourrissant, **~e** /nuʀisɑ̃, ɑ̃t/ *adj* nourishing.

nourrisson /nuʀisɔ̃/ *nm* (nouveau-né) new-born baby; (enfant jusqu'à deux ans) infant.

nourriture /nuʀityʀ/ **I** *nf* **1** (aliments) food; **2** (régime) diet.
II nourritures *nfpl* LITER nourishment ¢.

nous /nu/ *pron pers* **1** (sujet) we; **c'est ~ les premiers**○ we're first; **2** (dans une comparaison) **il travaille plus que ~** he works more than we do ou than us; **ils les voient plus souvent que ~** (que nous ne les voyons) they see them more often than we do; (qu'ils ne nous voient) they see them more often than us; **3** (objet) us; **à cause de/autour de/après ~** because of/after us; **entre ~, il n'est pas très intelligent** between ourselves ou you and me, he isn't very intelligent; **à ~** (en jouant) our turn; **nous n'avons pas encore de maison à ~** we haven't got a house of our own yet; **c'est à ~** (appartenance) it's ours, it belongs to us; (séquence) it's our turn; **(c'est) à ~ de choisir** (notre tour) it's our turn to choose; (notre responsabilité) it's up to us to choose; **4** (pronom réfléchi) ourselves; **nous ne ~ soignons que par les plantes** we only use herbal medicines; **5** (nous-mêmes) ourselves.

nous-même, *pl* **nous-mêmes** /numɛm/ *pron pers* **1** (pluriel) ourselves; **2** (de majesté, modestie) we.

nouveau (**nouvel** *before vowel or mute h*), **nouvelle¹**, *mpl* **~x** /nuvo, nuvɛl/ **I** *adj* **1** (qui remplace, succède) [*modèle, locataire*] new; (qui s'ajoute) [*attentat, tentative*] fresh; **se faire faire un ~ costume** (pour remplacer) to have a new suit made; (supplémentaire) to have another suit made; **il a subi une nouvelle opération** he's had another operation; **faire une nouvelle tentative** to make another ou a fresh attempt; **procéder à de nouvelles arrestations** to make further arrests; **une nouvelle fois** once again; **2** (d'apparition récente) [*mot, virus, science, ville*] new; (de la saison) [*pommes de terre, vin*] new; **tout ~** brand-new; **les ~x élus** the newly-elected members; **les ~x mariés** the newlyweds; **la nouvelle venue** the newcomer; **3** (original) [*ligne, méthode*] new, original; **c'est une façon très nouvelle d'aborder le problème** it's a very novel approach to the problem; **4** (novice) **être ~ dans le métier** to be new to the job.
II *nm,f* (à l'école) new student; (dans une entreprise) new employee; (à l'armée) new recruit; **je ne sais pas, je suis ~** I don't know, I'm new here.
III *nm* **1** (rebondissement) **téléphone-moi s'il y a du ~** give me a call if there is anything new to report; **j'ai du ~ pour toi** I've got some news for you; **2** (nouveauté) **il nous faut du ~** we want something new.
IV à nouveau, de nouveau *loc adv* (once) again.
■ **~ franc** new franc; **~ riche** nouveau riche; **~ roman** nouveau roman; **Nouveau Monde** New World; **Nouvel An** New Year; **nouvelle année = Nouvel An**.
IDIOMES **tout ~ tout beau** the novelty will soon wear off.

nouveau-né, **~e**, *mpl* **~s** /nuvone/ **I** *adj* [*enfant, agneau*] newborn (*épith*).
II *nm,f* newborn baby.

nouveauté /nuvote/ *nf* **1** (caractère récent) newness, novelty; (originalité) novelty; **2** (chose nouvelle) novelty; **être à la recherche de/aimer la ~** to look for/to like novelty; **ce n'est pas une ~!** that's nothing new!; **3** (objet nouveau) GÉN new thing; (livre) new publication; (disque) new release; (appareil, voiture) new model.

nouvel ▶ nouveau I.

nouvelle² ** /nuvɛl/ **I *adj f* ▶ **nouveau**.
II *nf* **1** (annonce d'un événement) news ¢; **une ~** GÉN a piece of news; (aux informations) an item of news; **une bonne/mauvaise ~** some good/bad news; **tu connais la ~?** have you heard the news?; **première ~**○! that's news to me!; **2** LITTÉRAT short story.
III nouvelles *nfpl* **1** (renseignements) news (*sg*); **recevoir des ~s de qn** (par la personne elle-même) to hear from sb; (par un intermédiaire) to hear news of sb; **il m'a demandé de tes ~s** he asked after you; **je viens aux ~s**○ I've come to see what's happening; **il aura de mes ~s**○! he'll be hearing from me!; **goûte ce vin, tu m'en diras des ~s**○ have a taste of this wine, it's really good!; **2** (informations) **les ~s** the news (*sg*).

nouvellement /nuvɛlmɑ̃/ *adv* [*publié*] recently; [*bâti*] newly.

nouvelliste /nuvelist/ **▶ 374** *nmf* short-story writer.

novateur, -trice /nɔvatœʀ, tʀis/ **I** *adj* innovative.
II *nm,f* innovator, pioneer.

novembre /nɔvɑ̃bʀ/ **▶ 382** *nm* November.

novice /nɔvis/ **I** *adj* inexperienced, green.
II *nmf* **1** (débutant) novice; **2** RELIG novice.

noyade /nwajad/ *nf* (meurtre, accident) drowning ¢; **il y a eu 20 ~s** there were 20 people drowned.

noyau, *pl* **~x** /nwajo/ *nm* **1** (de fruit) stone GB, pit US; **fruits à ~** stone fruit GB, fruit with pits US; **2** (groupe humain) small group; **~x de résistance** pockets of resistance; **3** (partie centrale) BIOL, PHYS nucleus; (de la Terre) core; CONSTR newel; LING (de phrase) kernel; (d'intonation) nucleus; ORDINAT kernel.

noyauter /nwajote/ [1] *vtr* to infiltrate.

noyé, **~e** /nwaje/ **I** *adj* **1**○ (perdu) **mes enfants sont ~s en algèbre** my children are out of their depth in algebra; **2** (couvert) LITER **vallée ~e dans la brume** valley shrouded in mist; **visage ~ de larmes** face bathed in tears; **yeux ~s de larmes** eyes swimming with tears.
II *nm,f* drowned person.

noyer¹ /nwaje/ [23] **I** *vtr* **1** (tuer) to drown [*personne, animal*]; **2** (inonder) to flood [*village, champ*]; **3** (mettre trop de liquide) to flood [*moteur*]; to drown [*pastis, whisky*]; to douse [*feu, incendie*]; **~ son chagrin** or **sa peine dans l'alcool** to drown one's sorrows (in drink); **4** (accabler, étourdir) **~ qn sous un flot de paroles** to talk sb's head off; **5** (faire disparaître) **~ une idée dans qch** to lose ou bury an idea in sth; **6** ART to blend [*couleurs*]; to merge [*contours*].
II se noyer *vpr* **1** (accidentellement) to drown; (volontairement) to drown oneself; **mourir noyé** to die by drowning; **2** FIG **mes cris se sont noyés dans le brouhaha général** my shouts were drowned (out) in the general hubbub; **quelques acteurs connus noyés dans la foule** some well-known actors lost in the crowd; **se ~ dans des détails** to get bogged down in details.
IDIOMES **se ~ dans un verre d'eau** to make a mountain out of a molehill.

noyer² /nwaje/ *nm* **1** (arbre) walnut (tree); **2** (bois) walnut; **table en ~** walnut table.

nu, **~e** /ny/ **I** *adj* **1** (dévêtu) [*corps*] naked; [*partie du corps*] bare; **être ~** to be naked; **être tout ~** to be completely ou stark naked; **avoir la tête ~e** to be bare-headed; **avoir les pieds ~s** to be barefoot; **être torse ~** to be stripped to the waist; **2** [*mur, pièce, arbre, fil électrique*] bare; [*style*] unadorned; **voilà la vérité toute ~e** that is the plain truth.

II *nm inv* (lettre) nu.

III *nm* ART **le ~** the nudes (*pl*); **un ~** a nude.

IV à nu *loc adv* **être à ~** [*fil électrique*] to be bare ou exposed; [*personne, vice*] to be exposed; **mettre à ~** to strip [*fil électrique*]; to expose [*personne, vice*]; **mettre son cœur à ~** to open one's heart.

nuage /nɥaʒ/ *nm* LIT, FIG cloud; **sans ~s** [*ciel*] cloudless; [*bonheur*] unclouded; **~ de lait** dash of milk.

IDIOMES **être dans les ~s**○ to have one's head in the clouds; **descendre de son ~** to come back to earth.

nuageux, -euse /nɥaʒø, øz/ *adj* [*ciel*] cloudy; [*masse*] cloud (*épith*).

nuance /nɥɑ̃s/ *nf* **1** (de couleur) shade; **2** (de sens) nuance; **sans ~** [*commentaire, bilan*] clearcut; [*personnalité*] straightforward; PÉJ unsubtle; **3** (différence) slight ou subtle difference; **à cette ~ près que** with the small reservation that; **4** MUS nuance.

nuancer /nɥɑ̃se/ [12] *vtr* **1** (avec un élément nouveau) to qualify [*avis*]; to modify [*vision des choses*]; **peu nuancé** unsubtle; **2** (modérer) to moderate [*propos*].

nucléaire /nykleɛʀ/ **I** *adj* nuclear (*épith*).

II *nm* **le ~** (énergie) nuclear energy; (technologie) nuclear technology.

nudité /nydite/ *nf* **1** (de personne) nakedness, nudity; **2** (de lieu, mur) bareness.

nuée /nɥe/ *nf* **1** (multitude) (d'insectes) swarm; (de personnes) horde; **2** MÉTÉO dense cloud ⊄.

nues /ny/ *nfpl* **les ~** (cieux) LITER the heavens LITTÉR; (nuages) the clouds.

IDIOMES **tomber des ~**○ to be flabbergasted○; **porter qn aux ~** to praise sb to the skies.

nuire /nɥiʀ/ [69] **I** *vtr ind* **~ à** to harm [*voisin, famille*]; to be harmful to [*santé, intérêts, réputation*]; to damage [*récoltes*]; to take away from [*plaisir, qualité, beauté*]; to be detrimental to [*déroulement*].

II se nuire *vpr* (mutuellement) to do each other a lot of harm; (à soi-même) to do oneself a lot of harm.

IDIOMES **trop parler nuit** you should know when to keep your mouth shut.

nuisance /nɥizɑ̃s/ *nf* nuisance ⊄.

nuisible /nɥizibl/ *adj* [*déchets*] dangerous; [*influence*] harmful; **insecte ~** (insect) pest; **~ à** detrimental to.

nuit /nɥi/ *nf* **1** (période) night; **cette ~** tonight; **en pleine ~** in the middle of the night; **au cœur de la ~** at dead of night; **étudier la ~** to study at night; **une ~ d'hôtel** a night in a hotel; **voyager de ~** to travel by night; **vol/équipe de ~** night flight/shift; **faire sa ~** to sleep right through the night; **2** (date) night; **par une ~ d'orage** on a stormy night; **3** (obscurité) **la ~ tombe** night is falling; **avant la ~** before dark ou nightfall; **à la ~ tombante, à la tombée de la ~** at nightfall; **il fait ~** it's dark; **il faisait ~ noire, il faisait une ~ d'encre** it was pitch dark; **ça se perd dans la ~ des temps** it is lost in the mists of time; **depuis la ~ des temps** since the dawn of time; ▶ **gris**.

■ **~ américaine** CIN day for night; **~ blanche** sleepless night; **~ bleue** *night of terrorist bomb attacks*.

IDIOMES **c'est le jour et la ~** they're as different as chalk and cheese; **attends demain pour donner ta réponse: la ~ porte conseil** wait till tomorrow to give your answer: sleep on it first.

nul, nulle /nyl/ **I** *adj* **1**○ [*personne*] hopeless, useless; [*travail, étude*] worthless; [*film, roman*] trashy○; **il est trop ~ pour ce travail** he's too useless for the job; **2** JUR [*contrat, mariage*] void; [*testament*] invalid;

[*élections*] null and void; [*vote*] spoiled; **3** SPORT, JEUX **match ~** (égalité) tie, draw GB; (zéro partout) nil-all draw; **4** (qui n'existe pas) [*différence, effet*] nil (*jamais épith*); [*récolte*] nonexistent; **vent ~** no wind.

II *adj indéf* (aucun) [*homme, idée, pays*] no; **~ autre que vous** no-one else but you; **sans ~ doute** without any doubt.

III○ *nm,f* idiot○; **c'est un ~** he's a dead loss○, he's completely useless.

IV *pron indéf* no-one; **~ n'est censé ignorer la loi** ignorance of the law is no excuse; **~ n'ignore que** everyone knows that; ▶ **impossible**.

V nulle part *loc adv* nowhere.

nullement /nylmɑ̃/ *adv* not at all; **n'avoir ~ l'intention de faire** to have absolutely no intention of doing.

nullité /nylite/ *nf* **1** JUR nullity; **frapper de ~** to render void; **sous peine de ~** under pain of being declared null and void; **2** (d'argument, de théorie) invalidity; (d'œuvre, de personne)○ worthlessness; **c'est d'une totale ~** it's absolutely awful; **3**○ (personne incapable) idiot○.

numéraire /nymerɛʀ/ *nm* cash.

numéral, ~e, mpl -aux /nymeral, o/ ▶ **399** **I** *adj* numeral.

II *nm* numeral.

numération /nymerasjɔ̃/ *nf* MATH numeration.

■ **~ globulaire** blood count.

numérique /nymerik/ *adj* **1** TECH [*affichage*] digital; **clavier ~** TÉLÉCOM keypad; **commande ~** numerical control; **2** MATH [*valeur*] numerical.

numéro /nymero/ *nm* **1** (nombre) number; **~ de téléphone** telephone number; **2** (indiquant l'importance) **le ~ deux du parti** number two in the party; **objectif ~ un** primary objective; **le ~ un de l'opposition** the leader of the opposition; **3** (journal, magazine) issue; **un vieux ~** a back number ou issue; **suite au prochain ~** LIT to be continued; FIG watch this space; **4** (dans un spectacle) act; (de chant) number; **5**○ (personne drôle) **quel ~!** what a character!

■ **~ d'abonné** customer's number; **~ d'appel** telephone number; **~ d'appel gratuit** freefone number GB, toll-free number US; **~ de série** serial number; **~ vert** = **~ d'appel gratuit**; **~ zéro** (de périodique) trial issue.

IDIOMES **tirer le bon/mauvais ~** to be lucky/unlucky.

numérologie /nymerɔlɔʒi/ *nf* numerology.

numérotation /nymerɔtasjɔ̃/ *nf* numbering; **~ téléphonique** telephone numbering system.

numéroter /nymerɔte/ [1] *vtr* to number.

numerus clausus /nymeʀysklozys/ *nm inv* quota.

numismatique /nymismatik/ **I** *adj* numismatic.

II *nf* numismatics (+ *v sg*), numismatology.

nunuche○ /nynyʃ/ *adj* PÉJ bird-brained○, silly.

nu-pied, pl ~s /nypje/ *nm* (sandale) (open) sandal.

nuptial, ~e, mpl -iaux /nypsjal, o/ *adj* [*messe*] nuptial; [*chambre*] bridal; **cérémonie ~e** wedding.

nuque /nyk/ ▶ **137** *nf* nape (of the neck).

nurse /nœrs/ *nf* nanny GB, nurse.

nutritif, -ive /nytritif, iv/ *adj* [*aliment, repas*] nutritious; [*crème*] nourishing; [*valeur*] nutritive.

nutrition /nytrisjɔ̃/ *nf* nutrition.

nyctalopie /niktalɔpi/ *nf* night vision.

nylon® /nilɔ̃/ *nm* nylon.

nymphe /nɛ̃f/ *nf* MYTHOL, ZOOL nymph; ANAT nympha.

nymphéa /nɛ̃fea/ *nm* waterlily.

nymphomane /nɛ̃fɔman/ *adj, nf* nymphomaniac.

o, O /o/ *nm inv* o, O.
ô /o/ *excl* LITER o!

oasis /ɔazis/ *nf inv* oasis.

obédience /ɔbedjɑ̃s/ *nf* persuasion; **pays d'~ catholique** Catholic country.

obéir /ɔbeiʀ/ [3] *vtr ind* **1** (se soumettre) **~ à** to obey [*ordre, devoir*]; to follow [*norme*]; to observe [*coutume*]; to comply with [*décision*]; **~ à qn** [*soldat*] to obey sb; [*enfant, employé*] to do what one is told by sb; **elle se fait ~ de ses enfants** her children always do as she says; **2** (être soumis) [*freins*] to respond (**à** to).
IDIOMES **~ à qn au doigt et à l'œil** to obey sb slavishly.

obéissance /ɔbeisɑ̃s/ *nf* obedience (**à** to); **~ passive** blind obedience.

obéissant, ~e /ɔbeisɑ̃, ɑ̃t/ *adj* obedient.

obélisque /ɔbelisk/ *nm* obelisk.

obèse /ɔbɛz/ *adj* obese.

objecter /ɔbʒɛkte/ [1] *vtr* to object.

objecteur /ɔbʒɛktœʀ/ *nm* objector.
■ **~ de conscience** conscientious objector.

objectif, -ive /ɔbʒɛktif, iv/ **I** *adj* objective.
II *nm* **1** (dessein) objective; **se donner qch pour ~** to set oneself sth as an objective; **2** PHOT lens; (de microscope, jumelles, télescope) objective; **~ à focale variable** zoom lens; **braquer son ~ sur qn** to point one's camera at sb; **3** (cible) target; (position à saisir) objective.

objection /ɔbʒɛksjɔ̃/ *nf* objection.

objectivement /ɔbʒɛktivmɑ̃/ *adv* **1** (de façon objective) objectively; **2** (évidemment) clearly.

objectivité /ɔbʒɛktivite/ *nf* objectivity.

objet /ɔbʒɛ/ **I** *nm* **1** (chose) object; **~ en bois** wooden object; **~ fragile** fragile item; **~s personnels** GÉN personal possessions; ADMIN personal effects; **2** (sujet) (de débat, recherches, science) subject; (de haine, d'amour) object; (de désaccord) source; **faire l'~ de** to be the subject of [*enquête, recherche*]; to be subjected to [*moquerie, surveillance*]; to be the object of [*convoitise, haine, lutte*]; **être un ~ de respect pour qn** to be respected by sb; **3** (but) purpose, object; **cette lettre a pour ~ de faire** the purpose of this letter is to do; **'~: réponse à votre lettre du...'** (en haut d'une lettre) 're: your letter of...'; **être sans ~** [*réclamation, inquiétude*] to be groundless; **4** LING, PHILOS object; **5** JUR **~ d'un litige** matter at issue; **~ d'un procès** subject of an action.
II -objet (*in compounds*) as an object (*après n*); **femme-~** woman as an object.
■ **~ du culte** liturgical object; **~ du délit** HUM offending object; **~ sexuel** sex object; **~s trouvés** lost property ₡; **~ volant non identifié, ovni** unidentified flying object, UFO.

objurgations /ɔbʒyʀgasjɔ̃/ *nfpl* **1** (reproches) objurgations SOUT; **2** (prières) entreaties.

obligataire /ɔbligatɛʀ/ FIN **I** *adj* [*marché, émission, rendement*] bond; **emprunt ~** bond issue.
II *nmf* bondholder.

obligation /ɔbligasjɔ̃/ *nf* **1** (devoir) (professionnel, moral, familial) obligation, responsibility; (légal) obligation; (militaire) obligation, duty; **ce n'est pas une ~ de les inviter** you don't have to invite them; **se faire une ~ de** to feel it one's duty to; **avoir une ~ ou des ~s envers qn** to feel an obligation toward(s) sb; **2** (nécessité) necessity; **se voir** ou **trouver dans l'~ de faire** to be forced to do; **3** FIN bond; **4** JUR obligation; **5** (devoir de reconnaissance) LITER obligation (**envers** toward(s)).
■ **~ scolaire** compulsory school attendance; **~s militaires** military service ₡; **être dégagé des ~s militaires** to have done one's military service.

obligatoire /ɔbligatwaʀ/ *adj* **1** LIT compulsory, obligatory; **l'étude du latin n'est pas ~** Latin is not a compulsory subject; **tenue de soirée ~** evening dress is obligatory; **2°** (inévitable) inevitable.

obligatoirement /ɔbligatwaʀmɑ̃/ *adv* **1** (par règlement) **une lettre doit ~ accompagner la demande** the application must be accompanied by a letter; **2** (inévitablement) inevitably, necessarily.

obligé, ~e /ɔbliʒe/ **I** *pp* ▶ **obliger**.
II *pp adj* **1** (contraint) **je suis ~ de partir** I must go now, I have to go now; **se voir ~ de faire** to be forced to do; **je suis bien ~ de vous croire** I have no choice ou option but to believe you; **vous n'êtes pas ~ d'accepter** you don't have to accept; **2** (reconnaissant) **être ~ à qn de** to be obliged ou grateful to sb for; **3°** (fatal) inevitable; **4** (indispensable) essential; **un passage ~ (pour)** FIG a prerequisite (for).
III *nm,f* **1** FML (personne) **être l'~ de qn** to be obliged ou indebted to sb; **2** JUR (débiteur) obligor.

obligeamment /ɔbliʒamɑ̃/ *adv* obligingly.

obligeance /ɔbliʒɑ̃s/ *nf* **avec l'~ de qn** through sb's good offices; **avoir l'~ de** to be kind enough to.

obligeant, ~e /ɔbliʒɑ̃, ɑ̃t/ *adj* [*personne*] obliging; [*manières*] pleasing; [*offre, mot*] kind.

obliger /ɔbliʒe/ [13] **I** *vtr* **1** (contraindre) **~ qn à** [*personne, police*] to force sb to; [*autorité, règlement*] to make it compulsory for sb to; [*devoir, prudence*] to compel sb to; **comme la loi vous y oblige** as required by law; **rien ne t'oblige à accepter** you don't have to accept; **2** JUR [*bail, contrat, accord*] to bind [sb] legally [*personne*]; **le bail m'oblige à réparer les dégâts** the lease makes me legally responsible for repairs; **3** (rendre service à) to oblige.
II s'obliger *vpr* **s'~ à faire** to force oneself to do.

oblique /ɔblik/ *adj* [*trait, rayon*] slanting; [*regard*] sidelong (*épith*); **en ~** [*avancer*] diagonally; [*poser*] crosswise.

obliquement /ɔblikmɑ̃/ *adv* [*enfoncer, poser*] at an angle; [*déplacer*] diagonally.

obliquer /ɔblike/ [1] *vi* **~ vers la droite/gauche** (légèrement) to bear right/left; (nettement) to veer right/left.

oblitération /ɔbliterasjɔ̃/ *nf* **1** (de timbre) (action) cancelling^GB ₡; (cachet d')~ postmark; **2** MÉD occlusion.

oblitérer /ɔblitere/ [14] *vtr* **1** to cancel, to obliterate [*timbre*]; **2** MÉD to obstruct [*vaisseau*].

obnubiler /ɔbnybile/ [1] *vtr* **1** (obséder) to obsess [*personne*]; **2** (obscurcir) to cloud [*jugement, émotion*].

obole /ɔbɔl/ *nf* small donation.

obscène /ɔpsɛn/ *adj* obscene.

obscur, ~e /ɔpskyʀ/ *adj* **1** (sans lumière) dark; **2** (mystérieux) obscure; **3** (humble) lowly; **4** (vague) vague.

obscurcir /ɔpskyʀsiʀ/ [3] **I** *vtr* **1** LIT to make [sth] dark [*lieu*]; to deepen [*couleur*]; **2** (ternir) to overshadow [*relations*]; to blur [*situation*]; to make [sth] obscure [*texte, œuvre*]; [*fumée*] to obscure [*vue*].
II s'obscurcir *vpr* **1** LIT [*ciel, lieu*] to darken;

2 [*regard*] to become sombre^{GB}; [*situation*] to become confused.

obscurément /ɔpskyʀemɑ̃/ *adv* **1** [*sentir*] vaguely; **2** [*vivre*] in obscurity.

obscurité /ɔpskyʀite/ *nf* **1** (de lieu) darkness; **2** (d'œuvre, de personne) obscurity; (de situation) vagueness.

obsédant, **~e** /ɔpsedɑ̃, ɑ̃t/ *adj* [*souvenir, rêve, musique*] haunting; [*rythme*] insistent; [*problème*] nagging (*épith*).

obsédé, **~e** /ɔpsede/ *nm,f* **~** (**sexuel**) sex maniac; **un ~ du vélo/du ski** a cycling/ski freak○.

obséder /ɔpsede/ [14] *vtr* [*souvenir, rêve, remords*] to haunt; [*idée, problème*] to obsess; **il est obsédé** (sexuellement) he has sex on the brain○.

obsèques /ɔpsɛk/ *nfpl* funeral (*sg*).

obséquieux, **-ieuse** /ɔpsekjø, øz/ *adj* obsequious.

observateur, **-trice** /ɔpsɛʀvatœʀ, tʀis/ **I** *adj* observant.

II *nm,f* observer.

observation /ɔpsɛʀvasjɔ̃/ *nf* **1** GÉN, MÉD (étude, surveillance) observation; **mission d'~** POL observer mission; **l'~ des oiseaux** bird-watching; **2** (obéissance) observance; **3** (remarque) GÉN observation, remark; (sur un devoir) comment; **4** (reproche) reproach.

observatoire /ɔpsɛʀvatwaʀ/ *nm* **1** (astronomique) observatory; **2** MIL observation post, look-out post; **3** (organisme) watchdog.

observer /ɔpsɛʀve/ [1] **I** *vtr* **1** (regarder) GÉN to observe; to watch [*personne, mouvement*]; **je me sens observé** I feel I'm being watched; **~ qch au microscope** LIT to examine sth under a microscope; FIG to scrutinize sth; **2** (remarquer) to notice, to observe [*chose, phénomène, réaction*]; **faire ~ qch à qn** to point sth out to sb; **3** (suivre) to observe [*règle, usage, repos, traité*]; to keep, to observe [*jeûne*]; to maintain [*stratégie, politique, grève*]; **~ le silence** to keep ou remain quiet; **4** (contrôler) to watch [*propos, manières, gestes*].

II s'observer *vpr* **1** (se regarder) to watch each other; **2** (se surveiller) to keep a check on oneself.

obsession /ɔpsesjɔ̃/ *nf* obsession.

obsessionnel, **-elle** /ɔpsesjɔnɛl/ *adj* obsessional.

obsolète /ɔpsɔlɛt/ *adj* obsolete.

obstacle /ɔpstakl/ *nm* **1** (difficulté) obstacle (**à** to); **faire ~ aux négociations** to obstruct the negotiations; **elle a fait ~ à ma promotion** she stood in the way of my promotion; **2** (en équitation) fence.

obstétricien, **-ienne** /ɔpstetʀisjɛ̃, ɛn/ ▶374 *nm,f* obstetrician.

obstétrique /ɔpstetʀik/ *nf* obstetrics (+ *v sg*).

obstination /ɔpstinasjɔ̃/ *nf* obstinacy; **avec ~** stubbornly.

obstiné, **~e** /ɔpstine/ **I** *adj* **1** (entêté) [*personne, caractère, refus*] stubborn; **2** (acharné) [*efforts*] dogged; [*chercheur*] dedicated; **3** (durable) [*pluie*] persistent.

II *nm,f* pigheaded person PÉJ.

obstinément /ɔpstinemɑ̃/ *adv* obstinately.

obstiner: s'obstiner /ɔpstine/ [1] *vpr* to persist (**dans** in; **à faire** in doing); **s'~ à ne pas faire qch** to refuse obstinately to do sth; **s'~ dans une opinion** to cling stubbornly to an opinion.

obstruction /ɔpstʀyksjɔ̃/ *nf* GÉN, MÉD, POL, SPORT obstruction; TECH (de conduit, canalisation) blockage; **faire ~ à qch** to obstruct sth.

obstruer /ɔpstʀye/ [1] **I** *vtr* to obstruct, to block [*conduit, passage*]; **les valises obstruent le passage** the suitcases are in the way.

II s'obstruer *vpr* to get ou become blocked.

obtempérer /ɔptɑ̃peʀe/ [14] *vtr ind* **~ à** to comply with; **refus/refuser d'~** refusal/to refuse to comply.

obtenir /ɔptəniʀ/ [36] **I** *vtr* to get, to obtain [*informations, prix, diplôme*]; to secure [*silence*]; to get, to arrive at [*total, somme*]; **~ qch de/pour qn** to get ou

obtain sth from/for sb; **~ de faire** to gain ou get permission to do; **~ de qn qu'il fasse** to get sb to do.

II s'obtenir *vpr* [*total, résultat*] to be arrived at, to be obtained.

obtention /ɔptɑ̃sjɔ̃/ *nf* **l'~ d'un diplôme** getting a diploma; **l'~ d'un visa** obtaining a visa.

obturateur, **-trice** /ɔptyʀatœʀ, tʀis/ **I** *adj* TECH obturating (*épith*).

II *nm* PHOT shutter.

obturation /ɔptyʀasjɔ̃/ *nf* **1** (accidentelle) blocking (up); (volontaire) stopping up; **2** (résultat) blockage.

obturer /ɔptyʀe/ [1] *vtr* GÉN to block up [*trou*].

obtus, **~e** /ɔpty, yz/ *adj* obtuse.

obus /ɔby/ *nm inv* MIL shell; **un éclat d'~** a piece of shrapnel; **des éclats d'~** shrapnel ¢; **tirs d'~** shellfire ¢.

occasion /ɔkazjɔ̃/ *nf* **1** (circonstance) occasion; (moment favorable) opportunity, chance; **rater l'~** to miss one's opportunity ou chance; **à l'~** (si le cas se présente) some time; (parfois) occasionally; **à l'~ de** on the occasion of; **à** or **en plusieurs ~s** on several occasions; **par la même ~** at the same time; **pour l'~** for the occasion; **les grandes ~s** special occasions; **avoir l'~ de faire** to have the opportunity ou chance to do ou of doing; **être l'~ de qch** to give rise to sth; **être l'~ de faire** to be a chance ou an opportunity to do; **profiter de l'~ pour faire** to take the opportunity to do; **d'~** [*héroïsme*] incidental; [*rencontre, aventure*] chance; **j'ai encore raté une bonne ~ de me taire** I should have kept my mouth shut; **2** (marché) **une voiture d'~** a second-hand car; **je l'ai acheté d'~** I bought it second-hand; **3** (objet) second-hand buy; (bonne affaire) bargain.

occasionnel, **-elle** /ɔkazjɔnɛl/ *adj* occasional.

occasionner /ɔkazjɔne/ [1] *vtr* to cause, to occasion SOUT.

occident /ɔksidɑ̃/ *nm* **1** (direction) west; **2** (nations) **l'Occident** the West.

occidental, **~e**, *mpl* **-aux** /ɔksidɑ̃tal, o/ *adj* **1** GÉOG western; **2** POL Western.

Occidental, **~e**, *mpl* **-aux** /ɔksidɑ̃tal, o/ *nm,f* Westerner.

occitan, **~e** /ɔksitɑ̃, an/ *nm* LING langue d'oc.

occlusion /ɔklyzjɔ̃/ *nf* MÉD occlusion; **~ intestinale** intestinal obstruction, obstruction of the bowels.

occulte /ɔkylt/ *adj* **1** (relatif à l'occultisme) occult; **2** (secret) secret.

occulter /ɔkylte/ [1] *vtr* (involontairement) to eclipse, to overshadow; (volontairement) to obscure [*sujet, problème*]; to conceal [*vérité, fait*]; to conceal, to mask [*malaise*].

occultisme /ɔkyltism/ *nm* occultism.

occupant, **~e** /ɔkypɑ̃, ɑ̃t/ **I** *adj* [*troupes*] occupying.

II *nm,f* (de maison) occupier, occupant; (de siège, véhicule) occupant.

III *nm* MIL **l'~, les ~s** the occupying forces (*pl*).

occupation /ɔkypasjɔ̃/ *nf* **1** (passe-temps, tâche) occupation; (emploi) occupation, job; **mes ~s professionnelles** my professional activities; **2** (fait d'habiter un lieu) occupancy, occupation; **3** (pour protester) occupation; **décider l'~ des locaux** to decide to stage a sit-in; **4** MIL occupation; **l'armée d'~** the army of occupation; **l'Occupation** HIST the Occupation.

occupé, **~e** /ɔkype/ *pp* ▶ **occuper**.

II *pp adj* **1** [*personne, vie*] busy; **être très ~** to be very busy; **2** [*siège*] taken; [*ligne téléphonique*] engaged GB, busy; [*toilettes*] engaged; **3** MIL [*pays*] occupied.

occuper /ɔkype/ [1] **I** *vtr* **1** (se trouver dans) to live in, to occupy [*appartement, maison*]; to be in [*douche, cellule*]; to sit in, to occupy [*siège*]; **il occupe les lieux depuis six mois** he's been in the premises for six months; **2** (remplir) [*local, meuble*] to take up, to occupy [*espace*]; [*activité*] to take up, to fill [*temps*]; **le jardin potager occupe tout mon temps** the kitchen garden takes up all my time; **le sport oc-cupe une grande place dans ma vie** sport plays a large ou great part in my life; **~ son temps à faire** to spend one's time doing; **3** (donner une activité à) to occupy [*personne, esprit*]; **ça m'occupe!** it keeps me occupied ou busy!; **le sujet qui nous occupe** the matter which we are dealing with; **4** (exercer) to have [*emploi*]; to hold [*poste, fonctions*]; **5** (se rendre maître de) [*grévistes, armée*] to occupy [*lieu*]; **~ les locaux** to stage a sit-in.

II s'occuper *vpr* **1** (ne pas être oisif) to keep oneself busy ou occupied; **j'ai de quoi m'~** I've got plenty to do; **trouver à s'~** to find sth to do; **2** (prendre en charge) **s'~ de** to see to, to take care of [*dîner, billets*]; **3** (consacrer ses efforts à) **s'~ de** to be dealing with [*dossier*]; **4** (prodiguer des soins à) **s'~ de** to take care of [*enfant, animal, plante*]; to attend to [*client*]; **on s'occupe de vous?** COMM are you being served?; **je m'occupe de vous tout de suite** I'll be with you in a minute; **5** (avoir pour emploi) **s'~ de** to be in charge of [*financement, bibliothèque*]; to work with [*handicapés, enfants*]; **6** (se mêler) **occupe-toi de tes affaires**○ or **de ce qui te regarde**○! mind your own business○!; **ne t'occupe pas de ça!**, **t'occupe** ○! keep your nose out○! GB, keep your butt out○! US; **ne t'occupe pas d'elle** don't take any notice of her.

occurrence /ɔkyʀɑ̃s/ *nf* **1** (cas) case, instance; **en l'~** in this case ou instance; **2** LING occurrence.

OCDE /osedeə/ *nf* (*abbr* = **Organisation de coopé-ration et de développement économiques**) OECD.

océan /ɔseɑ̃/ ▶407 *nm* **1** LIT ocean; **2** (en France) **l'Océan** the Atlantic; **3** FIG **un ~ de** a sea of.

océanien, -ienne /ɔseanjɛ̃, ɛn/ *adj, nm,f* Oceanian.

océanique /ɔseanik/ *adj* oceanic.

océanographe /ɔseanɔɡʀaf/ ▶374 *nmf* oceanographer.

ocelle /ɔsɛl/ *nm* ocellus.

ocre[1] /ɔkʀ/ ▶141 *adj inv*, *nm* ochre GB, ocher US.

ocre[2] /ɔkʀ/ *nf* (pigment) ochre GB, ocher US.

octane /ɔktan/ *nm* octane.

octante /ɔktɑ̃t/ ▶399 *adj inv*, *pron* B, C, H eighty.

octave /ɔktav/ *nf* octave.

octet /ɔktɛt/ *nm* **1** ORDINAT byte; **2** PHYS octet.

octobre /ɔktɔbʀ/ ▶382 *nm* October; **à la mi-~** in mid-October.

octogénaire /ɔktɔʒenɛʀ/ **I** *adj* **être ~** to be in one's eighties, to be an octogenarian.

II *nmf* octogenarian.

octogonal, ~e, *mpl* -aux /ɔktɔɡɔnal, o/ *adj* octagonal.

octosyllabe /ɔktɔsilab/ **I** *adj* octosyllabic.

II *nm* octosyllable.

octroi /ɔktʀwa/ *nm* **1** (attribution) granting; **2** HIST octroi.

octroyer /ɔktʀwaje/ [23] **I** *vtr* **~ à qn** to grant sb [*pardon*]; to award sb [*bourse*]; to allocate sb [*budget*].

II s'octroyer *vpr* to allow oneself [*répit, sursis*]; to win [*victoire, place*]; to achieve [*succès*].

oculaire /ɔkylɛʀ/ *adj* **1** MÉD **avoir des troubles ~s** to have eye trouble; **2 témoin ~** eyewitness.

oculiste /ɔkylist/ ▶374 *nmf* oculist, ophthalmologist.

ode /ɔd/ *nf* ode (**à qn** to sb; **à qch** to sth, on sth).

odeur /ɔdœʀ/ *nf* smell (**de** of); (**bonne**) **~** nice smell; (**mauvaise**) **~** smell; **dégager** or **avoir une bonne ~** to smell nice; **dégager** or **avoir une mauvaise ~** to smell; **chasser les mauvaises ~s** to get rid of unpleasant odours(GB); **sans ~** [*crème, lotion*] fragrance-free; [*produit de nettoyage*] odourless(GB).

odieux, -ieuse /ɔdjø, øz/ *adj* **1** (abject) horrible, odious; **2** (insupportable) obnoxious (**avec qn** to sb).

odorant, ~e /ɔdɔʀɑ̃, ɑ̃t/ *adj* **1** (exhalant une odeur) odorous LITTÉR, which has a smell (*épith*); **2** (exhalant une bonne odeur) sweet-smelling.

Les océans et les mers

Les noms d'océans et de mers

En anglais, les mots Ocean et Sea prennent toujours une majuscule lorsqu'ils accompagnent un nom propre.

l'océan Atlantique	= the Atlantic Ocean
la mer Baltique	= the Baltic Sea

Ocean et Sea peuvent être omis en anglais dans la plupart des cas où océan et mer peuvent également être omis en français.

l'Atlantique	= the Atlantic
la Baltique	= the Baltic

En cas de doute, consulter l'article dans le dictionnaire.

De avec les noms de mers et d'océans

Les expressions françaises avec de se traduisent en général par l'emploi des noms de mers et d'océans en position d'adjectifs.

le climat de l'Atlantique	= the Atlantic climate
le climat de la mer du Nord	= the North Sea climate
une traversée de l'Atlantique	= an Atlantic crossing
une traversée de la mer du Nord	= a North Sea crossing

Noter aussi:

une croisière sur l'Atlantique	= an Atlantic cruise
une croisière en mer du Nord	= a North Sea cruise

---

odorat /ɔdɔʀa/ *nm* sense of smell; **l'organe de l'~** the olfactory organ.

OECE /ɔɛsɛ/ *nf* (*abbr* = **Organisation euro-péenne de coopération économique**) OEEC.

œdème /edɛm/ ▶196 *nm* MÉD oedema.

œdipe /edip/ *nm* (complexe) Oedipus complex.

œil, *pl* yeux /œj, jø/ *nm* ▶137 **1** ANAT eye; **avoir de bons yeux** to have good eyesight ou eyes; **ouvrir un ~** LIT to open one eye; **ouvrir l'~** FIG to keep one's eyes open; **ouvrir les yeux à qn** FIG to open sb's eyes; **fermer les yeux** LIT to shut one's eyes; **fermer les yeux sur qch** FIG to turn a blind eye to sth; **faire qch les yeux fermés** (très facilement) to be able to do sth with one's eyes closed; **acheter qch les yeux fermés** (avec confiance) to buy sth with complete confidence; **je n'ai pas fermé l'~ (de la nuit)** I didn't sleep a wink (all night); **il faut l'avoir à l'~** you have to keep an eye on him/her; **avoir l'~ à tout** to be vigilant; **cligner des yeux** to blink; **visible à l'~ nu** visible to the naked eye; **cela s'est passé sous mes yeux** it happened before my very eyes; **je n'en crois pas mes yeux** I can't believe my eyes; **il a suivie des yeux** his eyes followed her; **jeter un ~** à or **sur qch** to have a quick look at sth; **n'avoir d'yeux que pour qn** to have eyes only for sb; **sans lever les yeux** [*parler, répondre*] without looking up; [*travailler*] without a break; **lever les yeux sur qch** to look up at sth; **je l'ai sous les yeux** I have it in front of me; **faire qch aux yeux de tous** to do sth openly; **les yeux dans les yeux** gazing into each other's eyes; **être agréable à l'~** to be easy on the eye○ ou nice to look at; **coup d'~** (regard rapide) glance; (vue) view; **jette un coup d'~ pour voir s'il dort** have a quick look to see if he is asleep; **cela vaut le coup d'~** it's worth seeing; **avoir le coup d'~** to have a good eye; **yeux de biche** doe eyes; **yeux de chat** eyes like a cat; **yeux de cochon** piggy eyes; ▶ **obéir, taper**; **2** (exprimant des sentiments) eye; **des yeux rieurs/tristes** laughing/sad eyes; **elle le regardait d'un ~ amusé** she was looking at him with amusement in her eye; **d'un ~ mé-fiant** with a suspicious look, suspiciously; **d'un ~ inquiet** anxiously; **regarder qch d'un ~ neuf** to see sth in a new light; **voir qch d'un mauvais ~** to take a dim view of sth; **à mes yeux, il a tort** in my opinion he's wrong; **à leurs yeux, c'était un échec** in their eyes it was a failure; **voir qch d'un autre ~** to take a different view of sth; **3** (boucle, trou) GÉN eye; (dans une porte) peephole.

■ **~ poché**○ black eye; **~ de verre** glass eye.

IDIOMES **mon ~**○! (marquant l'incrédulité) my eye○, my foot○; **à l'~** ○ [*manger, voyager*] for nothing, for free○; **faire les gros yeux à qn** to glare at sb; **dévorer**

qch/qn des yeux to gaze longingly at sth/sb; **faire les yeux doux à qn** to make (sheep's) eyes at sb; **tourner de l'~**° to faint; **cela me sort par les yeux**° I 've had it up to here °; **avoir bon pied bon ~** to be as fit as a fiddle; **sauter aux yeux** to be obvious.

œil-de-bœuf, *pl* **œils-de-bœuf** /œjdəbœf/ *nm* (lucarne) bull's eye.

œillade /œjad/ *nf* (clin d'œil) wink; (regard furtif) glance.

œillère /œjɛʀ/ *nf* (du cheval) blinker, blinder US; **avoir** or **porter des ~s** FIG to have a blinkered attitude.

œillet /œjɛ/ *nm* **1** BOT carnation; **2** (de chaussure, bâche) eyelet; (de ceinture, bracelet) hole; (pour renforcer) reinforcement, reinforcing ring; (de métal) grommet.
■ **~ d'Inde** French marigold; **~ de poète** sweet william.

œilleton /œjtɔ̃/ *nm* (de porte) peephole.

œnologie /enɔlɔʒi/ *nf* oenology.

œsophage /ezɔfaʒ/ *nm* oesophagus.

œstrogène /ɛstrɔʒɛn/ **I** *adj* oestrogenic.
II *nm* oestrogen.

œuf /œf, *pl* ø/ *nm* **1** CULIN, ZOOL egg; **en forme d'~** eggshaped; **~s de cabillaud** cod's roe ₵; **2**° (imbécile) idiot°; **faire l'~** to play the fool.
■ **~ à la coque** boiled egg; **~ dur** hard-boiled egg; **~ en gelée** egg in aspic; **~ mimosa** egg mimosa (*chopped egg garnish*); **~ mollet** softboiled egg; **~ au plat** or **sur le plat** fried egg; **~ poché** poached egg; **~ à repriser** darning egg; **~s brouillés** scrambled eggs; **~s à la neige** floating islands.
IDIOMES **plein comme un ~** full to bursting; **va te faire cuire un ~**°**!** go and take a running jump°!; **marcher sur des ~s** to be walking on eggs.

œuvre /œvʀ/ *nf* **1** ART, LITTÉRAT, MUS (production unique) work; (production générale) works (*pl*) **les ~s complètes** the complete works; **il a laissé une ~ imposante** he left an imposing body of work; **2** (besogne) work; **se mettre à l'~** to get down to work; **voir qn à l'~** to see sb in action; **mettre en ~** to implement [*programme, réforme*]; to display [*grande ingéniosité*]; **mise en ~** (de programme) implementation; **tout mettre en ~ pour faire** to make every effort to do; **3** (résultat d'un travail) work; **être l'~ de** to be the work of.
■ **~ d'art** work of art; **~ de bienfaisance** or **de charité** charity.
IDIOMES **être à pied d'~** to be ready to get down to work.

off° /ɔf/ *adj inv* **1** CIN (hors écran) off-screen; **voix ~** voice-over; **2** (hors programme officiel) alternative; **le festival ~** the fringe festival.

offensant, ~e /ɔfɑ̃sɑ̃, ɑ̃t/ *adj* offensive (**pour** to).

offense /ɔfɑ̃s/ *nf* **1** (affront) insult; **faire ~ à qn** to offend sb; **2** RELIG trespass.

offenser /ɔfɑ̃se/ [1] **I** *vtr* **1** (blesser) to offend [*personne, sensibilité, délicatesse*]; to tarnish [*souvenir, réputation*]; **2** RELIG to offend against [*Dieu, ciel*].
II s'offenser *vpr* to take offence GB (**de** at).

offensif, -ive[1] /ɔfɑ̃sif, iv/ *adj* MIL offensive.

offensive[2] /ɔfɑ̃siv/ *nf* MIL, FIG offensive (**contre** against); **l'~ du froid** the onslaught of the cold.

office /ɔfis/ **I** *nm* **1** (rôle) **remplir son ~** [*objet*] to fulfil GB its purpose, to do the job°; [*employé*] to carry out one's duty; **faire ~ de table** to serve as a table; **faire ~ d'interprète** to act as an interpreter; **2** ADMIN, JUR (charge) office; **3** RELIG (cérémonie) service; (prières) office; **4** (salle) butlery.
II d'office *loc adv* **d'~** (autoritairement) without consultation; **on m'a muté d'~ aux archives** I was transferred to records without being consulted; **nos propositions ont été rejetées d'~** our proposals were dismissed out of hand; **commis** or **nommé d'~** [*avocat, expert*] appointed by the court (*après n*).

■ **~ du tourisme** tourist information office.

officialiser /ɔfisjalize/ [1] *vtr* to make [sth] official.

officiel, -ielle /ɔfisjɛl/ **I** *adj* GÉN official; **être en visite officielle** [*envoyé*] to be on an official visit; [*chef d'État*] to be on a state visit.
II *nm* (fonctionnaire, organisateur) official.

officier[1] /ɔfisje/ [2] *vi* RELIG, HUM to officiate.

officier[2] /ɔfisje/ *nm* officer.

officieusement /ɔfisjøzmɑ̃/ *adv* unofficially.

officieux, -ieuse /ɔfisjø, øz/ *adj* unofficial; **à titre ~** unofficially.

officinal, ~e, *mpl* **-aux** /ɔfisinal, o/ *adj* officinal.

officine /ɔfisin/ *nf* **1** (laboratoire) dispensary; (magasin) pharmacy; **2** (organisation) organization.

offrande /ɔfʀɑ̃d/ *nf* offering; **en ~** as an offering.

offrant /ɔfʀɑ̃/ *nm* **vendre qch au plus ~** to sell sth to the highest bidder.

offre /ɔfʀ/ *nf* **1** (proposition) offer; **faire une ~** to make an offer; **'~ d'emploi'** 'situation vacant'; **répondre à une ~ d'emploi** to reply to a job advertisement; **faire paraître une ~ d'emploi** to advertise a job; **'cadres: ~s d'emploi'** 'managerial appointments'; **'locations: ~s'** 'accommodation to let' GB, 'rentals' US; **2** ÉCON supply; **l'équilibre entre l'~ et la demande** the balance between supply and demand.
■ **~ d'achat** bid; **lancer une ~ d'achat** to launch a bid (**sur** for); **~ publique d'achat, OPA** takeover bid.

offrir /ɔfʀiʀ/ [4] **I** *vtr* **1** (en cadeau) **~ qch à qn** to give sth to sb, to give sb sth; **c'est pour ~?** (cadeau) do you want it gift-wrapped?; (fleurs) would you like them specially wrapped?; **2** (acheter) to buy (**à qn** for sb); **tu aimes ce chapeau? je te l'offre!** do you like this hat? I'll buy it for you!; **je t'offre un verre?** can I buy you a drink?; **j'offre la tournée** it's my round; **3** (mettre à la disposition) to offer [*rôle, crédit*]; **~ qch à qn** to offer sb sth; **~ à manger à qn** to offer sb something to eat; **il a offert de nous aider** he offered to help us; **4** (à titre d'échange) to offer [*récompense*]; **je t'en offre 200 francs** I'll give you 200 francs for it; **5** (présenter) to offer, to give [*choix*]; to offer [*démission*]; to present [*difficultés*]; **n'~ aucune résistance** to put up ou offer no resistance; **cela offre un avantage** there is one advantage; **6** (exposer) **~ son visage au vent** to turn one's face into the wind.
II s'offrir *vpr* **1** (se payer) **s'~** to buy oneself [*chapeau, fleurs*]; **ils ne peuvent pas s'~ le théâtre** GB they can't afford to go to the theatre GB; **je me suis offert le restaurant** I treated myself to a meal out; **2** (s'accorder) **s'~ un jour de vacances** to give oneself a day off; **3** (se présenter) [*solution*] to present itself (**à** to); **c'est une grande chance qui s'offre à toi** it's a wonderful opportunity for you; **le paysage qui s'offrait à nous était féerique** the landscape before us was magical; **s'~ en spectacle** to make an exhibition of oneself.

offusquer /ɔfyske/ [1] **I** *vtr* to offend.
II s'offusquer *vpr* to be offended (**de** by).

ogival, ~e, *mpl* **-aux** /ɔʒival, o/ *adj* [*arc, voûte*] ribbed, ogival SPÉC; [*architecture, art*] Gothic.

ogive /ɔʒiv/ *nf* **1** ARCHIT rib; **2** MIL nose cone.
■ **~ nucléaire** nuclear warhead.

ogre /ɔgʀ/ *nm* **1** (géant) ogre; **2** (gros mangeur) big eater.
IDIOMES **manger comme un ~** to eat like a horse.

ogresse /ɔgʀɛs/ *nf* **1** (géante) ogress; **2** (grosse mangeuse) big eater.

oh /o/ **I** *nm inv* **pousser un ~ de surprise** to give a cry of surprise; **pousser des ~** to cry out (**de** in).
II *excl* oh!; **~ hisse!** heave-ho!

oie /wa/ *nf* **1** ZOOL goose; **2**° (personne) goose.
■ **~ blanche** naïve young girl.

oignon /ɔɲɔ̃/ *nm* **1** BOT, CULIN onion; **2** BOT (de fleur) bulb; **3** (montre) fob watch; **4** MÉD bunion.
IDIOMES **faire qch aux petits ~s**° to do sth with great attention to detail; **ce n'est pas tes ~s**° it's

none of your business○; **occupe-toi de tes ~s**○ mind your own business○.

oindre /wɛdr/ [56] *vtr* **1** RELIG to anoint; **2** to rub [sb] with ointment [*athlète*].

oiseau, *pl* **~x** /wazo/ *nm* **1** ZOOL bird; **2**○ (personne) **un** (**drôle d'**)**~** an oddball○.

■ **~ de malheur** *or* **de mauvais augure** bird of ill omen; **~ de nuit** night owl; **~ de passage** LIT, FIG bird of passage; **~ de proie** bird of prey.

IDIOMES **trouver l'~ rare**○ to find the one person in a million; **petit à petit l'~ fait son nid** PROV with time and effort you achieve your goals.

oiseau-mouche, *pl* **oiseaux-mouches** /wazo muʃ/ *nm* hummingbird.

oiseleur /wazlœr/ *nm* bird-catcher.

oisellerie /wazɛlri/ *nf* (boutique) bird shop; (profession) selling of caged birds.

oiseux, -euse /wazø, øz/ *adj* [*propos*] idle (*épith*); [*dispute, explication*] pointless, unnecessary.

oisif, -ive /wazif, iv/ **I** *adj* idle.

II *nm,f* idler PÉJ; **les ~s** the idle rich.

oisillon /wazijɔ̃/ *nm* fledgling.

oisiveté /wazivte/ *nf* idleness.

IDIOMES **l'~ est** (**la**) **mère de tous les vices** PROV the devil makes work for idle hands (to do) PROV.

okapi /ɔkapi/ *nm* okapi.

olé○: **olé olé** /ɔleɔle/ *loc adj inv* [*plaisanterie*] naughty (*épith*); [*personne*] racy○.

oléagineux, -euse /ɔleaʒinø, øz/ **I** *adj* oleaginous.

II *nm inv* oleaginous plant.

oléiculture /ɔleikyltyr/ *nf* olive-growing.

oléoduc /ɔleɔdyk/ *nm* (oil) pipeline.

olfactif, -ive /ɔlfaktif, iv/ *adj* olfactory.

oligarchie /ɔligarʃi/ *nf* oligarchy.

oligo-élément, *pl* **~s** /ɔligoelemɑ̃/ *nm* trace element.

olivâtre /ɔlivɑtr/ **▶ 141** *adj* GÉN olive-greenish; [*teint*] sallow.

olive /ɔliv/ **I** **▶ 141** *adj inv* olive; **vert ~** olive green.

II *nf* **1** (fruit) olive; **2** (interrupteur) switch.

oliveraie /ɔlivrɛ/ *nf* olive grove.

olivette /ɔlivɛt/ *nf* (tomate) plum tomato.

olivier /ɔlivje/ *nm* (arbre) olive tree; (bois) olive wood.

Olympe /ɔlɛ̃p/ *nprm* **l'~** Mount Olympus.

olympiade /ɔlɛ̃pjad/ **I** *nf* (de l'antiquité) Olympiad.

II olympiades *nfpl* SPORT Olympics.

olympique /ɔlɛ̃pik/ *adj* Olympic.

ombilic /ɔ̃bilik/ *nm* ANAT umbilicus, navel.

ombilical, ~e, *mpl* **-aux** /ɔ̃bilikal, o/ *adj* umbilical.

ombrage /ɔ̃braʒ/ *nm* shade ¢.

IDIOMES **porter ~ à qn** to offend sb; **prendre ~ de qch** to take umbrage at sth.

ombrager /ɔ̃braʒe/ [13] *vtr* [*feuillage*] to shade; **route ombragée** shady road.

ombrageux, -euse /ɔ̃braʒø, øz/ *adj* [*personne*] tetchy.

ombre /ɔ̃br/ *nf* **1** (ombrage) shade; **30° à l'~** 30° in the shade; **à l'~ d'un figuier** in the shade of a fig tree; **tu leur fais de l'~** LIT you're (standing) in their light; FIG you're putting them in the shade; **rester dans l'~ de qn** to be in sb's shadow; **2** (forme portée) shadow; **suivre qn comme une ~** to be sb's shadow; **n'être plus que** *or* **être l'~ de soi-même** to be a shadow of one's former self; **3** (pénombre) LITER darkness; **4** (anonymat, clandestinité) **laisser certains détails dans l'~** to be deliberately vague about certain details; **agir dans l'~** to operate behind the scenes; **rester dans l'~** [*manipulateur*] to stay behind the scenes; [*poète*] to remain in obscurity; **5** (trace) LITER hint; **une ~ de moustache** a hint of a moustache; **l'~ d'un reproche/d'un accord** a hint of reproach/of an agreement; **une ~ de regret passa dans son**

regard a shadow of regret crossed his/her face; **sans l'~ d'un doute** without a shadow of a doubt; **sans l'~ d'une preuve** without the slightest shred of evidence; **6** ART **l'~** (procédé) shading ¢; **faire des ~s** to shade; **7** (silhouette indécise) shadowy figure.

■ **~ chinoise** shadow puppet; **~ à paupières** eye shadow.

IDIOMES **passer comme une ~** to be ephemeral; **courir après une ~** to chase rainbows; **il y a une ~ au tableau** there is only one thing wrong; **la seule ~ au tableau** the only snag.

ombrelle /ɔ̃brɛl/ *nf* (objet) parasol, sunshade.

omelette /ɔmlɛt/ *nf* CULIN omelette.

■ **~ norvégienne** baked Alaska.

IDIOMES **on ne fait pas d'~ sans casser des œufs** PROV your can't make an omelette without breaking eggs PROV.

omettre /ɔmɛtr/ [60] *vtr* to leave out, to omit.

omission /ɔmisjɔ̃/ *nf* omission.

omnibus /ɔmnibys/ *nm inv* RAIL slow *ou* local train.

omnipotent, ~e /ɔmnipɔtɑ̃, ɑ̃t/ *adj* omnipotent.

omnisports /ɔmnispɔr/ *adj inv* **salle ~** sports hall.

omnivore /ɔmnivɔr/ **I** *adj* omnivorous.

II *nmf* omnivore.

omoplate /ɔmɔplat/ *nf* shoulder blade.

OMS /ɔɛmɛs/ *nf* (*abbr* = **Organisation mondiale de la santé**) WHO.

on /ɔ̃/ *pron pers* **1** (complètement indéfini) **~ a refait la route** the road was resurfaced; **~ a prétendu que** it was claimed that; **une démission dont ~ a beaucoup parlé** a much talked-about resignation; **~ le dit très malade** he's said to be very ill; **~ dit qu'il a une maîtresse** it's said he has a mistress; **il pleut des cordes, comme ~ dit** it's raining cats and dogs, as they say; **2** (nous) we; **mon copain et moi, ~ va en Afrique** my boyfriend and I are going to Africa; **au lycée ~ n'a pas le droit de fumer** smoking is not allowed at school; **toi et moi, ~ est faits pour s'entendre** we're two of a kind; **~ en parlait avec Janet hier** I was discussing it with Janet yesterday; **qu'est-ce qu'~ mange ce soir?** what's for dinner tonight?; **~ recherche une secrétaire de direction bilingue** bilingual personal assistant required; **il y a tellement de bruit qu'~ ne s'entend plus** there's so much noise that you can't hear yourself think; **3** (tu, vous) you; **alors, ~ se promène?** so you're taking a stroll then?; **~ se calme**○! calm down!; **~ se dépêche**○! hurry up!; **quand ~ veut, ~ peut** where there's a will, there's a way; **4** (je) **~ fait ce qu'~ peut!** one does what one can!; **toi, ~ ne t'a rien demandé** nobody asked you for your opinion; **5** (ils, elles) they; **~ ne m'a pas demandé mon avis** they didn't ask me for my opinion; **est-ce qu'~ nous a livré le piano?** has the piano been delivered?; **6** (quelqu'un) **~ t'appelle** someone's calling you; **~ a refusé de me laisser entrer** I was refused admittance; **~ frappe** there's someone at the door; **si ~ me demande, dites que je ne suis pas là** if anyone asks for me, tell them I'm out; **7** (n'importe qui) **~ ne peut pas vivre avec 2000 francs par mois** you can't live on 2,000 francs a month; **~ peut le dire** you can say that.

onanisme /ɔnanism/ *nm* onanism.

once /ɔ̃s/ **▶ 455** *nf* ounce; **sans une ~ de méchanceté** without an ounce of malice.

oncle /ɔ̃kl/ *nm* uncle; **oui, mon ~** yes uncle; **l'~ Robert** Uncle Robert; **~ d'Amérique** FIG rich uncle.

onction /ɔ̃ksjɔ̃/ *nf* RELIG unction, anointing.

onctueux, -euse /ɔ̃ktɥø, øz/ *adj* **1** [*pâte, mélange*] smooth, creamy; [*couleur*] rich; **2** (mielleux) PEJ [*gestes, propos, personne*] unctuous.

onctuosité /ɔ̃ktɥozite/ *nf* smoothness.

onde /ɔ̃d/ *nf* **1** (vibration) wave; **grandes ~s** long wave (*sg*); **sur les ~s** on the air; **sur les ~s de la BBC** on the BBC; **2** (vague marine) wave; **3** (eau) LITER waters (*pl*) LITER.

■ **~ de choc** PHYS, FIG shock wave.

ondée /ɔde/ *nf* shower.

ondine /ɔdin/ *nf* **1** MYTHOL undine; **2** (nageuse) female swimmer.

on-dit /ɔdi/ *nm inv* **les ~** hearsay ¢.

ondoiement /ɔdwamɑ̃/ *nm* (de collines) undulation; (de blé, d'herbes) swaying.

ondoyant, **~e** /ɔdwajɑ̃, ɑ̃t/ *adj* [*blé, chevelure*] rippling; [*corps, personne*] lithe; [*démarche*] swaying.

ondoyer /ɔdwaje/ [23] *vi* [*paysage, chevelure*] to undulate; [*démarche, blé*] to sway; [*flamme*] to flutter.

ondulant, **~e** /ɔdylɑ̃, ɑ̃t/ *adj* [*démarche*] swaying; [*paysage*] undulating.

ondulation /ɔdylasjɔ̃/ *nf* **1** (mouvement) (de chevelure, musique) undulation; (de corps) swaying ¢; **~s du corps** swaying movements of the body; **2** (courbe) (de contour) curves (*pl*); (de chevelure) wave.

ondulatoire /ɔdylatwaʀ/ *adj* undulatory.

ondulé, **~e** /ɔdyle/ *adj* [*cheveux, forme*] wavy; [*collines, terrain*] undulating; [*carton, tôle*] corrugated.

onduler /ɔdyle/ [1] *vi* (ondoyer) [*route*] to roll; [*herbe*] to ripple; [*chevelure*] to fall in waves; [*corps*] to sway.

onéreux, **-euse** /ɔneʀø, øz/ *adj* (coûteux) [*dépense*] onerous, heavy; [*achat*] expensive; [*entretien*] costly.

ONG /ɔɛnʒe/ *nf* (*abbr* = **organisation non gouvernementale**) NGO.

ongle /ɔ̃gl/ *nm* (de personne) nail; (de quadrupède) claw; (de rapace) talon; **~s des mains** fingernails; **~s des pieds** toenails; **se faire les ~s** to do one's nails.

IDIOMES **défendre qch bec et ~s** to defend sth fiercely; **jusqu'au bout des ~s** through and through.

onglée /ɔ̃gle/ *nf* **avoir l'~** to have fingers numb with cold.

onglet /ɔ̃glɛ/ *nm* **1** (sur un livre) (échancré) thumb cutout; (qui déborde) tab; **avec ~s** (échancrés) with thumb-index; (qui débordent) with step index; **2** CULIN *prime cut of beef*; **3** (de lame, couvercle) groove.

onguent /ɔ̃gɑ̃/ *nm* ointment, salve.

onirique /ɔniʀik/ *adj* (analogue au rêve) [*scène, atmosphère*] dream-like, oneiric SOUT; (relatif au rêve) [*symbole*] dream (*épith*).

onomatopée /ɔnɔmatɔpe/ *nf* onomatopoeia.

ONU /ɔny, ɔɛny/ *nf* (*abbr* = **Organisation des Nations unies**) UN, UNO.

onyx /ɔniks/ *nm inv* onyx; **en ~** onyx (*épith*).

onze /ɔ̃z/ ▶399▶, 298▶, 156▶ *adj inv*, *pron* eleven.

onzième /ɔ̃zjɛm/ ▶399▶, 156▶ I *adj* eleventh.

II† *nf* SCOL *first year of primary school, age 6–7*.

OPA /opea/ *nf*: *abbr* ▶ **offre**.

opacité /ɔpasite/ *nf* **1** LIT opacity; **2** FIG (de texte) opacity; (de nuit) darkness; (de forêt) impenetrability.

opale /ɔpal/ *nf* opal.

opalescent, **~e** /ɔpalɛsɑ̃, ɑ̃t/ *adj* opalescent.

opaline /ɔpalin/ *nf* **1** (substance) opaline; **2** (objet) object made of opaline.

opaque /ɔpak/ *adj* **1** LIT opaque; **2** FIG [*texte*] opaque; [*nuit*] dark; [*forêt, brouillard*] impenetrable.

opéable /opeabl/ *adj* ripe for a takeover bid (*après n*); **une société ~** a potential takeover target.

OPEP /ɔpɛp/ *nf* (*abbr* = **Organisation des pays producteurs de pétrole**) OPEC; **pays membre de l'~** OPEC state.

opéra /ɔpeʀa/ *nm* **1** MUS opera; **2** (bâtiment) opera house.

opérable /ɔpeʀabl/ *adj* [*malade, tumeur*] operable.

opérateur, **-trice** /ɔpeʀatœʀ, tʀis/ I ▶374▶ *nm,f* operator.

II *nm* **1** LING, MATH operator; **2** TÉLÉCOM (exploitant) private telecommunications company.

■ **~ de saisie** keyboarder.

opération /ɔpeʀasjɔ̃/ *nf* **1** MÉD **~ (chirurgicale)** operation, surgery ¢; **2** MATH (type de calcul) operation; (calcul) calculation; **faire des ~s** (pour calculer) to do calculations; SCOL to do sums; **3** (étape d'un processus)

operation; **4** (fonctionnement) process; **l'~ de la digestion** the digestive process; **5** FIN (transaction) transaction; **~ boursière** stock transaction; **6** (suite d'actions concrètes) GÉN, MIL operation; **~ 'non à la misère'** anti-poverty campaign.

■ **~ à cœur ouvert** open-heart surgery ¢.

opérationnel, **-elle** /ɔpeʀasjɔnɛl/ *adj* operational.

opératoire /ɔpeʀatwaʀ/ *adj* **1** MÉD [*technique*] surgical; [*risque*] in operating (*après n*); **les suites ~s** the after-effects of surgery; **2** (qui fonctionne) operative.

opercule /ɔpɛʀkyl/ *nm* **1** BOT, ZOOL operculum; **2** (de hublot) deadlight; **3** (de pot) lid.

opéré, **~e** /ɔpeʀe/ *nm,f* person who has had an operation.

opérer /ɔpeʀe/ [14] I *vtr* **1** MÉD to operate on [*malade, organe*]; **~ qn du genou** to operate on sb's knee; **~ qn d'un kyste** to operate on sb to remove a cyst; **~ qn des amygdales** to remove sb's tonsils; **se faire ~** to have an operation; **on l'a opéré du cœur** he's had a heart operation; **2** (effectuer) to make [*choix, changement, distinction*]; to carry out [*restructuration*]; **3** (produire) to bring about [*changement*].

II *vi* **1** MÉD to operate; **il faut ~** an operation is necessary; **2** (avoir un effet) [*remède, charme*] to work (**sur** on); **3** (procéder) to proceed; **leur façon d'~** the way they go about things; **4** (mener des activités) [*voleur*] to operate.

III **s'opérer** *vpr* (se produire) to take place.

opérette /ɔpeʀɛt/ *nf* operetta, light opera ¢.

ophtalmologiste /ɔftalmɔlɔʒist/, **ophtalmologue** /ɔftalmɔlɔg/ ▶374▶ *nmf* ophthalmologist.

opiacé, **~e** /ɔpjase/ I *adj* [*médicament*] opiate (*épith*); [*odeur*] of opium (*épith*, *après n*).

II *nm* opiate.

opiner /ɔpine/ [1] *vi* **~ du bonnet** or **de la tête** to nod in agreement.

opiniâtre /ɔpinjatʀ/ *adj* [*résistance*] dogged; [*travail*] relentless; [*personne*] tenacious; [*toux*] persistent.

opinion /ɔpinjɔ̃/ *nf* **1** (jugement, idée) opinion; **il se moque de l'~ des autres** he doesn't care what other people think; **être de l'~ que** to be of the opinion that; **mon ~ est faite** my mind is made up; **se faire une ~** to form an opinion (**de, sur** on); **'sans ~'** (dans un sondage) 'don't know'; **2** (sentiment général) **l'~ (publique)** public opinion.

opiomane /ɔpjɔman/ *nmf* opium addict.

opium /ɔpjɔm/ *nm* opium.

opportun, **~e** /ɔpɔʀtœ̃, yn/ *adj* [*moment*] opportune, appropriate; [*remarque, visite*] opportune.

opportunisme /ɔpɔʀtynism/ *nm* opportunism.

opportuniste /ɔpɔʀtynist/ I *adj* opportunistic.

II *nmf* opportunist.

opportunité /ɔpɔʀtynite/ *nf* **1** (bien-fondé) appropriateness; **2** (occasion) CONTROV opportunity.

opposant, **~e** /ɔpozɑ̃, ɑ̃t/ I *adj* JUR opposing.

II *nm,f* POL opponent (**à** of).

opposé, **~e** /ɔpoze/ I *adj* **1** (inverse) [*direction*] opposite; **2** (en contradiction) [*avis, opinion*] opposite; [*partis, forces, côtés*] opposing; [*intérêts, buts, stratégies*] conflicting; **les deux partis restent ~s** the two parties remain opposed to each other; **3** (défavorable) opposed (**à** to).

II *nm* opposite; **elle est l'~ de sa sœur** she's the opposite of her sister.

III **à l'opposé** *loc* **1** (contrairement à) **à l'~ de mes frères** in contrast to my brothers; **à l'~ de ce qu'on pourrait croire** contrary to what one might think; **2** (dans l'autre sens) **il est parti exactement à l'~** he went off in exactly the opposite direction.

opposer /ɔpoze/ [1] I *vtr* **1** (poser en obstacle) to put up [*résistance, argument*]; **~ un refus à qn** to refuse sb; **~ un démenti à qch** to deny sth; **2** (mettre en compétition) **~ à** to match ou pit [sb] against [*personne, équipe*]; **la finale opposait deux Américains**

the final was between two Americans; **3** (séparer) [*litige*] to divide [*personnes*]; **le conflit qui a opposé les deux pays** the conflict which set the two countries against each other; **4** (comparer) to compare (**à** to, with).

II s'opposer *vpr* **1** (ne pas accepter) **s'~ à qch** (montrer son désaccord) to be opposed to sth; (désapprouver activement) to oppose sth; **ils s'opposent fermement à ce que l'usine se construise** they are strongly opposing the building of the factory; **2** (empêcher) to stand in the way of [*développement, changement*]; **3** (contraster) to contrast (**with** à); **4** (diverger) [*idées, opinions*] to conflict; [*personnes*] to disagree; [*partisans*] to be divided; **5** (s'affronter) [*équipes*] to confront each other.

opposition /ɔpozisjɔ̃/ *nf* **1** (en politique) opposition; **les partis de l'~** the opposition parties; **être dans l'~** to be in the opposition; **d'~** [*député, parti*] opposition (*épith*); **journal d'~** newspaper of the opposition; **2** (désaccord) opposition; **être en ~ avec** to be in opposition to; **3** (contraste) contrast (entre between); **~ de couleurs** contrast in colours^{GB}; **par ~ à** in contrast with ou to; **4** JUR objection; **faire ~ à un chèque** to stop a cheque GB ou check US.

oppressant, ~e /ɔpresɑ̃, ɑ̃t/ *adj* oppressive.

oppressé, ~e /ɔprese/ **I** *pp* ▶ **oppresser**.
II *pp adj* **être ~** (physiquement) to be breathless; (psychiquement) to be oppressed.

oppresser /ɔprese/ [1] *vtr* to oppress; **la chaleur l'oppresse** he/she finds the heat oppressive.

oppresseur /ɔprescœr/ *nm* oppressor.

oppression /ɔpresjɔ̃/ *nf* oppression.

opprimé, ~e /ɔprime/ **I** *adj* [*peuple, classe*] oppressed.
II *nm,f* **les ~s** the oppressed (+ *v pl*).

opprimer /ɔprime/ [1] *vtr* **1** to oppress [*peuple*]; **2** to stifle [*conscience*].

opprobre /ɔprɔbr/ *nm* FML (déshonneur) opprobrium SOUT; (déchéance) disgrace.

opter /ɔpte/ [1] *vi* to opt (**pour** for).

opticien, -ienne /ɔptisjɛ̃, ɛn/ ▶ **374**| *nm,f* optician.

optimal, ~e, mpl -aux /ɔptimal, o/ *adj* optimum.

optimiser /ɔptimize/ [1] *vtr* to optimize.

optimisme /ɔptimism/ *nm* optimism; **faire preuve d'un ~ prudent** to be cautiously optimistic.

optimiste /ɔptimist/ **I** *adj* optimistic (**sur** about).
II *nmf* optimist.

option /ɔpsjɔ̃/ *nf* **1** GÉN option (**sur** on); **le toit ouvrant est en ~** the sunroof is an optional extra ou an option US; **en ~** optional; **2** FIN option.

optionnel, -elle /ɔpsjɔnɛl/ *adj* optional.

optique /ɔptik/ **I** *adj* **1** ANAT optic; **2** PHYS, TECH optical.
II *nf* **1** (étude, industrie) optics (+ *v sg*); **2** (point de vue) perspective; **dans cette ~** from this perspective; **3** (partie d'instrument) optical components (*pl*).

optométriste /ɔptɔmetrist/ ▶ **374**| *nmf* ophthalmic optician GB, optometrist.

opulence /ɔpylɑ̃s/ *nf* (richesse) opulence.

opulent, ~e /ɔpylɑ̃, ɑ̃t/ *adj* **1** [*pays*] opulent, wealthy; [*train de vie*] affluent; **2** [*poitrine*] ample.

or¹ /ɔr/ *conj* **1** (indiquant une opposition) and yet; **tu m'as dit que tu serais à la bibliothèque, ~ tu n'y étais pas** you told me you'd be at the library and you weren't there; **2** (introduisant un nouvel élément) **les musées sont fermés le mardi, ~ c'était justement un mardi** museums are closed on Tuesdays, and it just so happened that it was a Tuesday; **3** (pour récapituler) **~ donc, c'était la nuit et nous étions perdus** now, it was night and we were lost.

or² /ɔr/ **I** ▶ **141**| *adj inv* [*couleur*] gold; [*cheveux*] golden.
II *nm* **1** (métal) gold ¢; **gravé à l'~ fin** engraved in fine gold; **en ~** [*dent, bague*] gold (*épith*); [*patron, mari*] marvellous^{GB}; [*occasion*] golden; **avoir un cœur d'~** or **en ~** to have a heart of gold; **2** ARCHIT, ART (d'encadrement, église, de dôme) gilding ¢; **3** (couleur)

cheveux d'~ golden hair (*sg*); **les ~s de l'automne** the golden tints of autumn.
■ **~ blanc** white gold; **~ jaune** yellow gold; **~ noir** black gold, oil.
IDIOMES **la parole est d'argent, le silence est d'~** PROV speech is silver, silence is golden PROV; **je ne le ferais pas pour tout l'~ du monde** I wouldn't do it for all the money in the world; **rouler sur l'~** to be rolling in it○ ou in money.

oracle /ɔrakl/ *nm* oracle.

orage /ɔraʒ/ *nm* storm; **le temps est à l'~, il y a de l'~ dans l'air** LIT, FIG there's a storm brewing; **pluie d'~** thundery shower GB, thundershower US; **ciel/vent d'~** stormy sky/wind; **~ de grêle** hailstorm; **l'~ de la passion** the tumult of passion.

orageux, -euse /ɔraʒø, øz/ *adj* **1** [*été*] stormy; [*temps*] thundery; **zone orageuse** storm belt; **2** (agité) [*discussion, réunion*] stormy; [*ambiance*] threatening; [*humeur*] angry.

oraison /ɔrezɔ̃/ *nf* prayer.
■ **~ funèbre** funeral oration.

oral, ~e, mpl -aux /ɔral, o/ **I** *adj* **1** (non écrit) oral; **2** MÉD **par voie ~e** orally.
II *nm* SCOL, UNIV oral (examination).

oralement /ɔralmɑ̃/ *adv* **1** MÉD orally; **2** (pas par écrit) verbally.

orange¹ /ɔrɑ̃ʒ/ ▶ **141**| **I** *adj inv* orange; [*feu*] amber GB, yellow US.
II *nm* (couleur) orange; **passer à l'~** to go through when the light is amber GB ou yellow US.

orange² /ɔrɑ̃ʒ/ *nf* (fruit) orange.

orangeade /ɔrɑ̃ʒad/ *nf* orangeade.

oranger /ɔrɑ̃ʒe/ *nm* orange tree; **fleur d'~** orange blossom.

orangeraie /ɔrɑ̃ʒrɛ/ *nf* orange grove.

orangerie /ɔrɑ̃ʒri/ *nf* orangery.

orateur, -trice /ɔratœr, tris/ *nm,f* (intervenant) speaker; (tribun) orator.

oratoire /ɔratwar/ **I** *adj* oratorical.
II *nm* RELIG oratory.

orbite /ɔrbit/ *nf* **1** (en astronomie) orbit; **en ~** in orbit; **mettre sur ~** to put into orbit [*satellite*]; FIG to launch; **2** ANAT eye-socket; **3** (zone d'influence) **être dans/tomber dans l'~ de** to be in/to fall within the sphere of influence of; **4** PHYS orbit.

orchestral, ~e, mpl -aux /ɔrkɛstral, o/ *adj* orchestral.

orchestre /ɔrkɛstr/ *nm* **1** (classique) orchestra; (de bal, d'harmonie) band; **~ de jazz** jazz band; **2** (fosse pour les musiciens) orchestra pit; **3** CIN, THÉÂT (partie de la salle) orchestra stalls (*pl*) GB, orchestra US.

orchestrer /ɔrkɛstre/ [1] *vtr* to orchestrate.

orchidée /ɔrkide/ *nf* orchid.

ordinaire /ɔrdinɛr/ **I** *adj* **1** (ni spécial, ni anormal) GÉN ordinary; [*qualité*] standard; [*lecteur, touriste*] average, ordinary; [*journée*] normal, ordinary; **l'(essence) ~** 2-star (petrol) GB, regular (gasoline) US; **en temps ~** in normal times; **journée peu ~** unusual day; **2** (médiocre) PEJ [*vie*] humdrum (*épith*); **très ~** [*repas, vin*] very average; [*personne*] very ordinary; **3** (coutumier) [*qualité, défaut*] usual.
II *nm* **1** (menu habituel) **l'~** everyday fare; **2** (moyenne) **l'~** the commonplace; **sortir de l'~** [*livre, film*] to be out of the ordinary.
III à l'ordinaire, d'ordinaire *loc adv* usually; **plus tard que d'~** or **qu'à l'~** later than usual; **comme à l'~** as usual.

ordinal, ~e, mpl -aux /ɔrdinal, o/ **I** *adj* ordinal.
II *nm* ordinal.

ordinateur /ɔrdinatœr/ *nm* computer; **travailler sur ~** to work with a computer; **~ central** mainframe; **création d'images par ~** computer-generated graphics; **assisté par ~** computer-aided.

ordination /ɔrdinasjɔ̃/ *nf* ordination.

ordonnance /ɔrdɔnɑ̃s/ *nf* **1** (document) prescription; **délivré uniquement sur ~** only available on prescription; **on peut l'acheter sans ~** you can buy it over the counter; **médicament vendu sans ~** over-the-counter medicine; **2** (agencement) (de salle, meubles) layout; (de cérémonie) order; **3** JUR ruling.

ordonné, **~e**[1] /ɔʀdɔne/ adj **1** (rangé) [chambre, armoire, personne] tidy; **2** (méthodique) [personne] methodical; **3** (pas désorganisé) [manifestation] orderly; **bien ~** [texte, vie] well-ordered; **4** MATH ordered.

ordonnée[2] /ɔʀdɔne/ nf MATH ordinate.

ordonner /ɔʀdɔne/ [1] vtr **1** (commander) GÉN to order; [médecin] to prescribe [repos]; **~ à qn de faire qch** to order sb to do sth; **2** (mettre en ordre) to put [sth] in order [objets]; to order [paragraphes]; **3** RELIG to ordain.

ordre /ɔʀdʀ/ nm **1** (commandement) order; **donner à qn l'~ de faire** to give sb the order to do; **je n'ai d'~ à recevoir de personne** I don't take orders from anybody; **j'ai des ~s** I'm acting under orders; **agir sur ~ de qn** to act on sb's orders; **travailler sous les ~s de qn** to work under sb; **elle a 30 personnes sous ses ~s** she has 30 people (working) under her; **prendre qn à ses ~s** to take sb on; **à vos ~s!** MIL yes, sir!; (à un ami, parent) HUM at your service! HUM; **jusqu'à nouvel ~** until further notice; **2** (disposition régulière) order; **par ~ alphabétique** in alphabetical order; **par ~ de préférence** in order of preference; **procédons par ~** let's do things in order; **en bon ~** [être aligné, avancer] in an orderly fashion; **avancer en ~ dispersé/serré** to advance in scattered/close formation; **3** ORDINAT command; **4** (fait d'être rangé) tidiness, orderliness; (fait d'être bien organisé) order; **être en ~** [maison, armoire] to be tidy; [comptes] to be in order; **tenir une pièce en ~** to keep a room tidy; **mettre de l'~ dans** to tidy up [pièce, placard]; **mettre de l'~ dans ses comptes** to get one's accounts in order; **mettre de l'~ dans ses idées** to get one's ideas straight; **mettre de l'~ dans sa vie** to set ou put one's life in order; **remettre une pièce en ~** to put everything back where it was in a room; **remise en ~** FIG rationalization; **5** (état stable et normal) order; **maintenir sa classe en ~** to keep order in the classroom; **rappeler qn à l'~** to reprimand sb; **tout est rentré dans l'~** GÉN everything is back to normal; (après des émeutes) order has been restored; **l'~ public** public order; **maintenir l'~ (public)** to maintain law and order; **6** (nature) nature; **c'est dans l'~ des choses** it's in the nature of things; **un problème de cet ~** a problem of that nature; **c'est un problème d'~ économique** it's a problem of an economic nature; **de l'~ de 30%** in the order of 30% GB, on the order of 30% US; **de premier ~** first-rate; **de second ~** second-rate; **dans le même ~ d'idées, je voudrais vous demander** talking of which, I would like to ask you; **c'est du même ~** it's the same kind of thing; **7** ARCHIT, BIOL, ZOOL order; **8** (confrérie) order; **9** RELIG order; **monastique** monastic order; **entrer dans les ~s** to take (holy) orders; **10** FIN order; **~ d'achat** order to buy; **libellez le chèque à l'~ de X** make the cheque GB ou check US payable to X. ■ **~ du jour** (de réunion) agenda; **être à l'~ du jour** LIT to be on the agenda; FIG to be talked about.

ordure /ɔʀdyʀ/ **I** nf (abjection) LITER filth; **se complaire dans l'~** to wallow in filth.
II ordures nfpl **1** (déchets) refuse ¢ GB, garbage ¢ US; **les ~s ménagères** household refuse GB ou garbage US; **mettre/jeter qch aux ~s** to put/to throw sth in the bin GB ou in the garbage US; **défense de déposer des ~s** no dumping; **tas d'~s** rubbish heap GB, pile of garbage US; **2** (grossièretés) filth ¢.

ordurier, -ière /ɔʀdyʀje, ɛʀ/ adj filthy.

orée /ɔʀe/ nf **1** LIT edge; **2** FIG start.

oreille /ɔʀɛj/ nf **1** ▶ 137 | ANAT ear; **avoir les ~s décollées** to have sticking out ears; **dire qch à l'~ de qn** to whisper sth in sb's ear; **dresser l'~** LIT, FIG to prick up one's ears; **emmitouflé jusqu'aux ~s** all wrapped up; **tendre l'~** to strain one's ears; **c'est arrivé à leurs ~s** they got to hear of it; **n'écouter**

que d'une ~, écouter d'une ~ distraite to half-listen, to listen with half an ear; **ouvre-bien les ~s!** listen carefully; **en avoir plein les ~s**○ **de qch** to have had an earful of sth; **arrête de crier, tu me casses les ~s**○ stop yelling, you're bursting my eardrums; **2** (ouïe) hearing; **avoir l' ~ fine** to have keen hearing ou sharp ears; **avoir de l'~** MUS to have a good ear (for music); **n'avoir pas d'~** MUS to be tone-deaf; **3** (personne) **à l'abri** ou **loin des ~s indiscrètes** where no-one can hear; **4** (de marmite, plat) handle; (de vis, fauteuil) wing.
IDIOMES **avoir l'~ basse** to look sheepish; **tirer** ou **frotter les ~s à qn** to tell sb off; **rougir jusqu'aux ~s** to blush to the roots of one's hair; **les ~s ont dû te siffler**○ or **tinter**○ or **sonner**○ your ears must have been burning.

oreiller /ɔʀeje/ nm pillow.

oreillette /ɔʀejɛt/ nf **1** ANAT auricle; **2** (de casquette) earflap.

oreillons /ɔʀejɔ̃/ ▶ 196 | nmpl mumps.

ores: d'ores et déjà /dɔʀdezeʒa/ loc adv already.

orfèvre /ɔʀfɛvʀ/ ▶ 374 | nmf goldsmith; **être ~ en la matière** FIG to be an expert in the field.

orfèvrerie /ɔʀfɛvʀəʀi/ nf (métier) goldsmith's art; (commerce) goldsmith's and silversmith's; **pièce d'~** (en argent) piece of silverware; (en or) piece of gold work.

organe /ɔʀgan/ nm **1** (de la vue, l'ouïe) organ; **2** (publication) organ; **~ officiel d'un parti** official organ of a party; **3** (institution) organ; **~ de presse** press organ; **4** (en mécanique) system; **~s de freinage/direction** braking/steering system (sg); **5** (voix) voice.

organigramme /ɔʀganigʀam/ nm **1** (d'entreprise) organization chart; **2** ORDINAT flowchart.

organique /ɔʀganik/ adj organic.

organisateur, -trice /ɔʀganizatœʀ, tʀis/ **I** adj organizing (épith).
II nm,f organizer.

organisation /ɔʀganizasjɔ̃/ nf organization; **tu devrais faire un effort d'~** you should try to be more organized; **comité d'~** organizing committee.

organiser /ɔʀganize/ [1] **I** vtr to organize.
II s'organiser vpr **1** (se regrouper) [dissidents, chômeurs, opposition] to get organized; **s'~ en** to organize oneself into; **2** (être méthodique) to organize oneself; **3** (être mis sur pied) [lutte, secours] to be organized; **4** (être conçu) to be organized; **l'histoire s'organise autour de deux thèmes principaux** the plot revolves ou is organized around two main themes.

organisme /ɔʀganism/ nm **1** (corps humain) body; **2** (être vivant) organism; **3** (organisation) organization.

organiste /ɔʀganist/ ▶ 374 | nmf organist.

orgasme /ɔʀgasm/ nm orgasm.

orge /ɔʀʒ/ nf barley.

orgelet /ɔʀʒəlɛ/ nm stye.

orgie /ɔʀʒi/ nf LIT, FIG orgy.

orgue /ɔʀg/ ▶ 392 | **I** nm MUS organ; **tenir l'~** to be at the organ.
II orgues nfpl MUS organ (sg).

orgueil /ɔʀgœj/ nm pride; **être l'~ de qn** to be sb's pride and joy; **pécher par ~** to be overproud.

orgueilleux, -euse /ɔʀgœjø, øz/ **I** adj overproud.
II nm,f **c'est un ~** he's overproud.

orient /ɔʀjɑ̃/ nm **1** (direction) east; **2** (pays) **l'Orient** the East.

oriental, ~e, mpl **-aux** /ɔʀjɑ̃tal, o/ adj [côte] eastern; [civilisation, langues, art, type] oriental.

Oriental, ~e, mpl **-aux** /ɔʀjɑ̃tal, o/ nm,f Asian; **les Orientaux** Asians.

orientation /ɔʀjɑ̃tasjɔ̃/ nf **1** (position) (de maison) aspect; (d'antenne) angle; (de projecteur) direction; **la maison a une ~ plein sud** the house faces directly south; **2** (d'enquête, de recherche, politique) direction; **les ~s de l'art moderne** trends in modern art; **3** SCOL, UNIV **l'~** (conseils) advice to students on which courses to follow; **changer d'~** to change courses;

4 (tendance politique) leanings (*pl*); **5** (action de s'orienter) finding one's bearings.
■ **~ scolaire** curriculum counselling GB, counseling US.

orienté, ~e /ɔʀjɑ̃te/ I *pp* ▶ **orienter**.
II *pp adj* **maison ~e d'est en ouest** house which has an east-west aspect; **bien/mal ~** [*maison*] in a good/bad position ou situation; **région ~e vers le tourisme** region geared to tourism.

orienter /ɔʀjɑ̃te/ [1] I *vtr* **1** (positionner) to decide on the aspect of [*maison*]; to adjust [*antenne, lampe*] (**vers** to); **~ la maison vers le sud** ou (**face**) **au sud** to make the house south-facing; **~ le spot vers le fond** to direct the spotlight toward(s) the back; **~ l'antenne vers l'ouest** to make the aerial face west; **2** (faire porter) to focus [*enquête*] (**sur** on); **~ la conversation sur** to bring the conversation around to; **3** (politiser) to slant [*cours*]; **4** (guider) to direct [*personne*] (**vers** to); **~ qn vers un spécialiste** to send sb to a specialist; **5** SCOL, UNIV (conseiller) to give [sb] some career advice.
II **s'orienter** *vpr* **1** (se repérer) to get ou find one's bearings; **2** (se diriger) **s'~ vers** LIT to turn toward(s); FIG [*pays, mouvement*] to move towards(s); [*conversation*] to turn to; **s'~ vers les carrières scientifiques** to go in for a career in science.

orifice /ɔʀifis/ *nm* **1** ANAT orifice; **2** GÉN (de tuyau) mouth; (de puits) opening; (de tube) neck.

originaire /ɔʀiʒinɛʀ/ *adj* **1** (provenant) [*plante, animal*] native (**de** to); **produit ~ d'Afrique** product from Africa; **famille ~ d'Asie** Asian family; **le pays dont il est ~** his native country; **2** (d'origine) [*tare, état*] original; [*déformation*] inherent.

original, ~e, *mpl* **-aux** /ɔʀiʒinal, o/ I *adj* **1** (authentique, créatif) original; **2** (bizarre) eccentric.
II *nm,f* (personne excentrique) eccentric, oddball○.
III *nm* (œuvre primitive) original.

originalité /ɔʀiʒinalite/ *nf* **1** (créativité) originality; **2** (aspect original) originality; **3** (excentricité) eccentricity.

origine /ɔʀiʒin/ *nf* **1** (provenance) origin; **être d'~ modeste/noble** to come from a modest/noble background; **être d'~ paysanne** [*personne*] to come from a farming family; **2** (commencement) origin; **l'~ de l'univers** the origin of the universe; **l'~ des temps** the beginning of time; **dès l'~** (de projet, technique) right from the start; (du monde) from the very beginning; **à l'~** originally; **d'~** [*pays*] of origin; [*moteur, vitraux*] original; **3** (source) origin; **produit d'~ végétale** product of vegetable origin; **à l'~ du conflit il y a un problème frontalier** the conflict has its origins in a border dispute; **4** MATH origin.

originel, -elle /ɔʀiʒinɛl/ *adj* original.

orignal, *pl* **-aux** /ɔʀinal, o/ *nm* moose (*inv*).

oripeaux /ɔʀipo/ *nmpl* faded finery ₵.

orme /ɔʀm/ *nm* **1** (arbre) elm (tree); **2** (bois) elm (wood).

ormeau, *pl* **~x** /ɔʀmo/ *nm* **1** BOT young elm tree; **2** ZOOL abalone.

orné, ~e /ɔʀne/ *adj* [*style*] ornate.

ornement /ɔʀnəmɑ̃/ *nm* **1** GÉN ornament; **jardin d'~** ornamental garden; **2** (de texte) embellishment; **3** ARCHIT, ART decorative detail; **4** MUS ornament.

ornemental, ~e, *mpl* **-aux** /ɔʀnəmɑ̃tal, o/ *adj* ornamental.

ornementer /ɔʀnəmɑ̃te/ [1] *vtr* to decorate (**de** with).

orner /ɔʀne/ [1] *vtr* **1** (décorer) [*personne*] to decorate [*maison*] (**de** with); to trim [*vêtement*] (**de** with); **2** (embellir) [*ornement*] to adorn [*maison, vêtement*]; [*personne*] to embellish [*style, texte*] (**de** with).

ornière /ɔʀnjɛʀ/ *nf* rut; **sortir de l'~** FIG (de la routine) to get out of a rut; (d'une situation difficile) to get out of a difficult ou tricky○ situation.

ornithologie /ɔʀnitɔlɔʒi/ *nf* ornithology.

ornithologue /ɔʀnitɔlɔg/ ▶ **374** *nmf* ornithologist.

ornithorynque /ɔʀnitɔʀɛ̃k/ *nm* (duck-billed) platypus, duckbill US.

oronge /ɔʀɔ̃ʒ/ *nf* agaric; **fausse ~** fly agaric.

orphelin, ~e /ɔʀfəlɛ̃, in/ I *adj* **1** (de père et mère) orphan; **être ~** to be an orphan; **être ~ de père** to be fatherless; **2** FIG **se sentir ~** to feel abandoned.
II *nm,f* orphan.
IDIOMES **défendre la veuve et l'~** to defend the weak.

orphelinat /ɔʀfəlina/ *nm* orphanage.

orque /ɔʀk/ *nm* ou *f* killer whale.

orteil /ɔʀtɛj/ ▶ **137** *nm* toe; **gros ~** big toe.

orthodoxe /ɔʀtɔdɔks/ I *adj* **1** (accepté) orthodox; **méthodes peu ~s** rather unorthodox methods; **2** RELIG Orthodox.
II *nmf* RELIG Orthodox.

orthographe /ɔʀtɔgʀaf/ ▶ **414** *nf* **1** (forme écrite) spelling; **quelle est l'~ de...?** how do you spell...?; **avoir une bonne/mauvaise ~** to be good/bad at spelling; **2** SCOL (matière) spelling ₵.

orthographier /ɔʀtɔgʀafje/ [2] I *vtr* to spell; **mot mal orthographié** misspelled word.
II **s'orthographier** *vpr* to be spelled.

orthographique /ɔʀtɔgʀafik/ *adj* [*règle*] spelling (*épith*), orthographic; **correcteur ~** ORDINAT spellchecker.

orthopédiste /ɔʀtɔpedist/ ▶ **374** *nmf* **1** MÉD orthopedic specialist, orthopedist; **2** (fabricant d'appareils) manufacturer of orthopedic appliances.

orthophoniste /ɔʀtɔfɔnist/ ▶ **374** *nmf* speech therapist.

ortie /ɔʀti/ *nf* (stinging) nettle; **se piquer aux ~s** to get stung in the nettles.

orvet /ɔʀvɛ/ *nm* slowworm, blindworm.

os /ɔs, *pl* o/ *nm inv* **1** (élément) bone; **en chair et en ~** in the flesh; **n'avoir que la peau sur les ~**○ to be all skin and bone; **se rompre les ~**○ to break one's neck○; **de la viande vendue avec/sans ~** meat sold on/off the bone; **2** (matière) bone; **un peigne en ~** a bone comb.
■ **~ à moelle** CULIN marrowbone; **~ de seiche** ZOOL cuttlebone.
IDIOMES **il y a un ~**○ there's a hitch; **jusqu'à l'~**○ completely; **tomber sur un ~**○ to come across a snag; **être trempé jusqu'aux ~**○ to be soaked to the skin○; **il ne va pas faire de vieux ~** he'll never make old bones.

oscillation /ɔsilasjɔ̃/ *nf* **1** PHYS, TÉLÉCOM oscillation; **2** (balancement) (de pendule) swinging; (de navire) rocking; (du corps) swaying; **3** (variation) fluctuation.

oscillatoire /ɔsilatwaʀ/ *adj* oscillatory.

osciller /ɔsile/ [1] *vi* **1** (se balancer) [*pendule*] to swing; [*navire*] to rock; [*foule*] to sway; **2** (fluctuer) [*monnaie*] to fluctuate; **3** (hésiter) to vacillate (**entre** between).

osé, ~e /oze/ *adj* **1** (licencieux) [*livre, film*] risqué; **2** (audacieux) [*comportement*] daring; [*paroles*] outspoken.

oseille /ozɛj/ *nf* **1** BOT, CULIN sorrel; **2**○ (argent) dough○, money; **avoir de l'~** to be rolling in it○.

oser /oze/ [1] *vtr* to dare; **je n'ose pas demander** I daren't ask, I don't dare ask; **il a osé rester** he dared to stay; **ils n'ont pas osé répondre** they didn't dare answer; **répète si tu l'oses!** don't you dare repeat that!; **je n'ose croire que** I hardly dare believe that; **j'ose espérer que** I would hope that; **si j'ose dire** if I may say so.

osier /ozje/ *nm* **1** (arbre) osier; **2** (bois) osier, wicker.

osmose /ɔsmoz/ *nf* LIT, FIG osmosis.

ossature /ɔsatyʀ/ *nf* skeleton; **avoir une forte ~** to be big-boned; **l'~ du visage** bone structure.

osselet /ɔslɛ/ *nm* **1** ANAT small bone; **~ de l'oreille** ossicle; **2** ▶ **329** JEUX (pièce) jack, knucklebone; (jeu) **les ~s** jacks.

ossements /ɔsmɑ̃/ *nmpl* remains.

osseux, -euse /ɔsø, øz/ *adj* **1** [*personne, visage, charpente*] bony; **2** [*croissance, maladie*] bone (*épith*).

L'orthographe et la ponctuation

L'alphabet anglais

La liste suivante indique la prononciation de chaque lettre, et donne pour chacune un moyen, parmi d'autres, d'épeler clairement en cas de difficultés. Certains utilisent pour cela l'alphabet des pilotes, d'autres celui des téléphonistes présenté ci-dessous.

A	[eɪ]	A for Alfred	O	[əʊ]	O for Oliver
B	[bi:]	B for beautiful	P	[pi:]	P for Peter
C	[si:]	C for cat	Q	[kju:]	Q for quite
D	[di:]	D for dog	R	[ɑ:]	R for Robert
E	[i:]	E for elephant	S	[es]	S for sugar
F	[ef]	F for father	T	[i:]	T for Tommy
G	[dʒi:]*	G for George	U	[ju:]	U for uncle
H	[eɪtʃ]	H for Harry	V	[vi:]	V for victory
I	[aɪ]	I for Ireland	W	[dʌbəlju:]	W for Walter
J	[dʒeɪ]*	J for John	X	[eks]	X for X-ray
K	[keɪ]	K for kangaroo	Y	[waɪ]	Y for yellow
L	[el]	L for London	Z	[zed] (GB)	Z for zoo
M	[em]	M for mother	*ou*	[zi:] (US)	
N	[en]	N for nothing			

Pour épeler

A majuscule	=	capital A
a minuscule	=	small a
ça s'écrit avec un A majuscule	=	it has got a capital A
en majuscules	=	in capital letters *ou* in capitals
en minuscules	=	in small letters
deux l	=	double l
deux n	=	double n
deux t	=	double t
à (a accent grave)	=	a grave [eɪ grɑ:v]
é (e accent aigu)	=	e acute [i: ə'kju:t]
è (e accent grave)	=	e grave [i: grɑ:v]
ê (e accent circonflexe)	=	e circumflex [i: 'sɜ:kəm‚fleks]
ë (e tréma)	=	e diaeresis [i: daɪ'ərɪsɪs] (*on dira parfois, plus simplement:* e with two dots)
ù (u accent grave)	=	u grave [ju: grɑ:v]
ç (c cédille)	=	c cedilla [si: sə'dɪlə]
l' (l apostrophe)	=	l apostrophe [el ə'pɒstrəfi]
d' (d apostrophe)	=	d apostrophe [di: ə'pɒstrəfi]
- (trait d'union)	=	hyphen [haɪfən]
"rase-mottes" s'écrit avec un trait d'union	=	"rase-mottes" has a hyphen

* *Noter que les francophones confondent souvent les prononciations anglaises de G et de J.*

† *Noter qu'en anglais les deux points, le point-virgule, le point d'exclamation et le point d'interrogation ne sont pas précédés par un espace. Il a dit oui ; je ne sais pas*

Pour dicter la ponctuation

un point	.	= full stop (GB) *ou* period (US)
à la ligne		= new paragraph
virgule	,	= comma
deux points	:	= colon†
point-virgule	;	= semi-colon†
point d'exclamation	!	= exclamation mark (GB) *ou* exclamation point (US)†
point d'interrogation	?	= question mark†
ouvrez la parenthèse	(	= open brackets
fermez la parenthèse	)	= close brackets
entre parenthèses	( )	= in brackets
entre crochets	[ ]	= in square brackets
tiret	-	= dash
points de suspension	...	= three dots (GB) *ou* suspension points (US)
ouvrez les guillemets	" *ou* ' ‡	= open inverted commas (GB) *ou* open quotation marks (US)
fermez les guillemets	" *ou* '	= close inverted commas (GB) *ou* close quotation marks (US)
entre guillemets	" " *ou* ' '	= in inverted commas (GB) *ou* in quotation marks (US) *ou* in quotes

La ponctuation des dialogues

La ponctuation des dialogues n'est pas la même dans les deux langues.

En français, le dialogue commence par le signe « (maintenant souvent remplacé par un tiret, ou par "), chaque prise de parole est signalée par un tiret, le dialogue est clos par » (ou par ") et les interventions du narrateur (dit-il, remarqua-t-elle etc.) ne sont pas séparées du dialogue par un quelconque signe de ponctuation. En anglais, chaque prise de parole commence par " ou ', et se termine par " ou '. Ces mêmes signes sont utilisés avant et après chaque intervention du narrateur à l'intérieur d'une réplique. Exemple:

"Well, I don't know," she said, "what to make of all this!"

pourquoi. = He said he would; I don't know why.
Voici pourquoi : je n'ai pas pu ! = This is why: I could not!

‡ *Noter que les guillemets anglais (" ou ' ') sont placés au dessus de la ligne.*

---

ossifier /ɔsifje/ [2] *vtr*, **s'ossifier** *vpr* to ossify.

ossu, ~e /ɔsy/ *adj* big-boned.

ossuaire /ɔsɥɛʀ/ *nm* ossuary.

ostensible /ɔstɑ̃sibl/ *adj* obvious.

ostentatoire /ɔstɑ̃tatwaʀ/ *adj* ostentatious.

ostéopathe /ɔsteɔpat/ **▶ 374** *nmf* osteopath.

ostracisme /ɔstʀasism/ *nm* ostracism; **être frappé d'~** POL to be ostracized.

ostréiculteur, -trice /ɔstʀeikyltœʀ, tʀis/ **▶ 374** *nm,f* oyster farmer.

ostréiculture /ɔstʀeikyltyʀ/ *nf* oyster farming.

otage /ɔtaʒ/ *nm* hostage; **être pris en ~** to be taken hostage; **prise d'~s** hostage-taking; **plusieurs prises d'~s** several instances of hostage-taking; **les grévistes tiennent les voyageurs en ~** FIG the strikers are holding the passengers to ransom.

OTAN /ɔtɑ̃/ *nf* (*abbr* = **Organisation du traité de l'Atlantique Nord**) NATO.

otarie /ɔtaʀi/ *nf* eared seal, otary.

ôter /ote/ [1] **I** *vtr* **1** (se débarrasser de) to take off [*vêtement, lunettes*]; to remove [*arête, tache*] (**de** from); **ôte tes pieds du fauteuil** take your feet off the chair; **2** (retirer) FML **~ qch à qn** to take sth away from sb; **~ tout espoir à qn** to dash sb's hopes; **~ la vie à qn** to take sb's life; **on ne m'ôtera pas de l'idée qu'ils le**

savaient I'm still convinced that they knew; **3** MATH (re trancher) to take [sth] (**à** away from); **4 ôté de 9, i reste 5** 9 minus ou less ou take away 4 leaves 5.

II s'ôter *vpr* **1** (s'enlever) **s'~ qch de l'esprit** or la tête to get sth out of one's mind ou head; **2** (se dépla cer) **ôte-toi de là!** move!

otite /ɔtit/ **▶ 196**] *nf* inflammation of the ear; **avoi une ~** to have earache.

oto-rhino-laryngologiste, *pl* **~s** /ɔtɔʀinɔlaʀɛ̃g lɔʒist/ **▶ 374**] *nmf* ENT specialist.

ou /u/ *conj* **1** (choix) or; **tu pourrais lui offrir ur collier, ~ (bien) une montre** you could give her a necklace, ou (else) a watch; **est-ce que tu viens ~ pas?** are you coming or not?; **tu te moques de mo ~ quoi○?** are you making fun of me or what?; **tu peux venir me prendre chez moi, ~ alors or s'attend devant le cinéma** you can pick me up a home or else we'll meet outside the cinema; **fatigu ~ pas, il faut bien rentrer à la maison** tired or not we have to go home; **que ça vous plaise ~ nor** whether you like it or not; **2** (choix unique) or; **~ (bien)... ~ (bien)**... either... or...; **~ bien il es très timide, ~ il est très impoli** he's either very sh or very rude; **3** (évaluation) or; **il y avait trois ~ quatre cents personnes** there were three or fou hundred people.

où /u/ **I** *adv* **1** LIT where; **je me demande ~...** i wonder where...; **~ est-ce que tu vas?** where are you going?; **~ ça?** where's that?; **je l'ai perdu je ne sais ~** I've lost it somewhere or other; **elle l'a rencontré je ne sais ~** God knows where she met him; **par ~ êtes-vous passés pour venir?** which way did you come?; **je ne sais pas d'~ elle vient** I don't know where she comes from; **2** FIG where; **~ en étais-je?** where was I?; **~ en êtes-vous?** (à quel stade) where have you got to?; (comment ça va) how is it going?; **~ allons-nous?** (quelle époque!) what are things coming to!; **d'~ tenez-vous que?** where did you get the idea that?

II *pron rel* **1** (locatif) where; **le quartier ~ nous habitons** the area we live in, the area in which we live; **trouver un endroit ~ dormir** to find a place ou somewhere to sleep; **d'~ s'élevait de la fumée** out of which smoke was rising; **les villes par ~ nous sommes passés** the towns we passed through; **~ tu iras, j'irai** where ou wherever you go, I'll go; **~ qu'ils aillent/qu'elle soit** wherever they go/she is; **2** (abstrait) **la misère ~ elle se trouvait** the poverty in which she was living, the poverty she was living in; **l'école d'~ elle sort est très réputée** the school she went to is very well-known; **au train** ou **au rythme** ou **à l'allure ~ vont les choses** (at) the rate things are going; **le travail s'est accumulé, d'~ ce retard** there is a backlog of work, hence the delay; **d'~ l'on peut conclure que** from which we can conclude that; **3** (temporel) when; **il fut un temps ~** there was a time when; **elle est à l'âge ~** she's at the age when ou where; **le matin ~ je l'ai rencontré** the morning I met him; **~ il se trompe, c'est lorsqu'il s'imagine que** where he goes wrong is in thinking that.

ouah⁰ /wa/ *excl* wow⁰!

ouailles /waj/ *nfpl* flock (*sg*); **une de mes ~** one of my flock.

ouate /wat/ *nf* **1** (de pharmacie) cotton wool GB, cotton US; **2** (garniture) wadding; **doublé d'~** wadded.

ouaté, ~e /wate/ *adj* **1** [*vêtement, tissu*] wadded; **2** FIG [*ambiance*] cocoon-like; [*bruit, pas*] muffled.

ouatine /watin/ *nf* wadding, padding.

oubli /ubli/ *nm* **1** GÉN **l'~ de qch** GÉN forgetting sth; (de devoir) neglect of sth; **l'~ des autres** forgetting other people; **elle cherche l'~ dans la boisson** she drinks to forget; **le temps apporte l'~** time passes and men forget; **2** (omission) omission; **3** (anonymat après la mort) oblivion; **tomber dans l'~** to be completely forgotten, to sink into oblivion.

oublier /ublije/ [2] **I** *vtr* **1** (ne pas se souvenir de) to forget [*nom, date, fait*]; (ne pas penser à) to forget about [*soucis, famille, incident*]; (ne pas prendre) to leave; **j'ai oublié mes clés chez elle** I've left my keys at her house; **rien ne pourra me faire ~ ce moment** I shall never forget that moment; **~ de faire/pourquoi/comment** to forget to do/why/how; **~ que** to forget that; **se faire ~** to keep a low profile, to lie low⁰; **2** (omettre) to leave [sth] out, to forget [*personne, détail*]; **tu oublies de dire que** you forget ou omit to mention that; **3** (négliger) to forget, to neglect [*devoir, ami*].

II s'oublier *vpr* **1** [*souvenir*] to be forgotten; **ce sont des choses qui ne s'oublient pas** it's not the sort of thing you forget; **2** (négliger de se servir) to leave oneself out.

oubliettes /ublijɛt/ *nfpl* oubliette (*sg*).

IDIOMES tomber dans les ~ to be forgotten; **mettre** ou **jeter qch aux ~** to consign sth to oblivion.

oued /wɛd/ *nm* wadi.

ouest /wɛst/ **▶ 457** **I** *adj inv* [*façade, versant, côte*] west; [*frontière, zone*] western.

II *nm* **1** (point cardinal) west; **2** (région) west; **3** GÉOG, POL **l'Ouest** the West; **de l'Ouest** [*ville, accent*] western.

ouest-allemand, ~e, *mpl* **~s** /wɛstalmɑ̃, ɑ̃d/ *adj* West German.

ouf /uf/ **I** *nm* **faire ~, pousser un ~** (de soulagement) to breathe a sigh of relief; **je n'ai pas eu le**

---

où

où adverbe de lieu se traduit généralement par *where* dans les interrogations directe ou indirecte:

> *où es-tu?* = where are you?
> *sais-tu où il est?* = do you know where he is?

Lorsque la traduction du verbe de la proposition relative introduite par *où* pronom relatif est un verbe avec postposition, quatre traductions sont possibles:

> *la ville où nous sommes passés*
> = the town we passed through
> *ou* the town that we passed through
> *ou* the town which we passed through
> *ou* the town through which we passed

Les trois premières traductions sont utilisées dans la langue courante, parlée ou écrite; la quatrième traduction sera préférée dans une langue plus soutenue, surtout écrite.

Pour simplifier la lecture des exemples, une seule traduction sera fournie mais il est toujours possible de générer les variantes sur les modèles donnés ci-dessus.

Lorsque *où* pronom relatif a une valeur temporelle, souvent il ne se traduit pas:

> *au moment où j'allais partir* = at the moment I was about to leave

ou bien il se traduit par *when*:

> *c'était l'époque où j'habitais à Oxford*
> = that was (the time) when I lived in Oxford

Attention, lorsque la proposition relative est au futur en français, elle est au présent en anglais:

> *le jour où elle arrivera* = the day she arrives
> *un jour où tu auras le temps* = one day when you have time

Pour les emplois abstraits et temporels de *où*, reportez-vous à l'article ci-contre.

---

temps de dire ~, il était déjà parti before I could say Jack Robinson, he'd gone.

II *excl* phew!

oui /wi/

■ **Note** En anglais la réponse *yes* est généralement renforcée en reprenant le verbe utilisé pour poser la question: *are you happy? yes, I am*; *do you like Brahms? yes, I do*.

I *adv* **1** (marque l'accord) yes; **mais ~!** yes!; **bien sûr que ~!** yes, of course!; **alors c'est ~?** so the answer is yes?; **acceptera-t-il ~ ou non de me rencontrer?** will he agree to meet me or not?; **découvrir si ~ ou non** to discover whether or not; **êtes-vous d'accord? si ~, dites pourquoi** do you agree? if so, say why; **dire ~ à qch** (par conviction) to welcome sth; (par nécessité) to agree to sth; **faire ~ de la tête** to nod; **2** (renforce une constatation) yes; **lui, prudent? un lâche, ~!** him, cautious? a coward, more like⁰!; **elle est radin⁰, ~, radin!** she's stingy, really stingy!; **eh ~, c'est comme ça!** well, that's just the way it is!; **eh bien ~, j'ai triché, et alors?** OK, I cheated, so what?; **3** (interrogatif) **tu viens, ~?** are you coming?; **tu viens, ~ ou non?** are you coming? yes or no?; **c'est bientôt fini, ~?** are you going to stop that or not?; **4** (marque une transition) yes; **~, tu disais?** yes, you were saying?; **~, ~, tu dis ça et puis tu ne le feras pas** yeah, yeah⁰, that's what you say, but you won't do it; **5** (remplace une proposition) **je crois que ~** I think so; **'ils sont partis?'—'je crains que ~'** 'have they left?'—'I'm afraid so'; **tu ne le crois pas, moi ~** you don't believe it, but I do.

II *nm inv* **1** (accord) yes; **le '~ mais' de M. Axel à notre proposition** Mr Axel's qualified 'yes' to our proposal; **2** (vote positif) 'yes' vote; **50 ~ sur 57 votants** 50 votes in favour⁰ᴮ out of 57 votes cast; **le ~ l'a emporté** the ayes have it.

IDIOMES pour un ~ pour un non [*s'énerver*] for the slightest thing; [*changer d'avis*] at the drop of a hat.

ouï-dire /widir/ *nm inv* hearsay; **par ~** by hearsay.

ouïe /wi/ *nf* **1** (sens) hearing **℃**; **avoir l'~ fine** to have good hearing; **être tout ~** to be all ears; **2** ZOOL (de poisson) gill; **3** MUS (de violon) sound hole.

ouïr† /wir/ [38] *vtr* **j'ai ouï dire que** word has reached me that; **oyez bonnes gens!** oyez! oyez! oyez!

ouistiti /wistiti/ *nm* **1** ZOOL marmoset; **2**° (personne) **un (drôle de) ~** a funny character.

ouragan /uragɑ̃/ *nm* **1** MÉTÉO hurricane; **2** (tumulte) storm; **déclencher un ~** to create a storm.
  IDIOMES **arriver/passer comme un ~** to arrive/to pass through like a hurricane.

Oural /ural/ *nprm* **1** ▶509 (région) **l'~** the Urals (*pl*); **2** ▶260 (fleuve) **l'~** the Ural.

ourler /urle/ [1] *vtr* to hem.

ourlet /urlɛ/ *nm* (en couture) hem; **faire un ~ à** to put a hem on.

ours /urs/ *nm inv* **1** ZOOL bear; **▶cage; 2** (personne) **il est un peu ~** he's a bit surly.
  ■ **~ blanc** polar bear; **~ brun** brown bear; **~ mal léché** boor; **~ de mer** Northern fur seal; **~ en peluche** teddy bear; **~ polaire** = **~ blanc**.
  IDIOMES **vendre la peau de l'~ avant de l'avoir tué** PROV to count one's chickens before they're hatched.

ourse /urs/ *nf* ZOOL she-bear.

Ourse /urs/ *nprf* **la Grande ~** the Plough GB, the Big Dipper US; **la Petite ~** the Little Bear GB, the Little Dipper US.

oursin /ursɛ̃/ *nm* (sea) urchin.

ourson /ursɔ̃/ *nm* bear cub.

outil /uti/ *nm* tool; **~ de travail** work tool.

outillage /utijaʒ/ *nm* tools (*pl*).

outiller /utije/ [1] *vtr* to equip [*personne, usine*].

outrage /utraʒ/ *nm* insult; **faire ~ à** to be an insult to [*personne, réputation, mémoire*]; to be an affront to [*raison, morale*].
  ■ **~ à agent** *verbal assault of a policeman*; **~ aux bonnes mœurs** affront to public decency; **~ à magistrat** contempt **℃** of court.

outragé, ~e /utraʒe/ I *pp* ▶ **outrager**.
  II *pp adj* [*personne, loyauté*] outraged; **prendre un air ~** to assume an air of outrage.

outrageant, ~e /utraʒɑ̃, ɑ̃t/ *adj* offensive.

outrager /utraʒe/ [13] *vtr* to offend [*personne*].

outrance /utrɑ̃s/ *nf* **1** (excès) excess; **2** (caractère excessif) excessiveness; **manger à ~** to eat excessively; **le sport à ~** excessive sport.

outrancier, -ière /utrɑ̃sje, ɛr/ *adj* extreme.

outre¹ /utr/ I *prép* (en plus de) in addition to; **~ (le fait) qu'il écrit, il illustre ses livres** as well as writing books, he also illustrates them.
  II *adv* **passer ~** to pay no heed; **passer ~ à** to disregard, to override [*loi, décision, objection*].
  III **outre mesure** *loc adv* unduly; **cela ne m'inquiète pas ~ mesure** it doesn't worry me unduly.
  IV **en outre** *loc adv* in addition.

outre² /utr/ *nf* goatskin.
  IDIOMES **être plein comme une ~**° to be full to bursting.

outré, ~e /utre/ I *pp* ▶ **outrer**.
  II *pp adj* **1** (indigné) outraged; **prendre un air ~** to look deeply offended; **2** (exagéré) extravagant.

outre-Atlantique /utratlɑ̃tik/ *adv* across the Atlantic; **d'~** American.

outre-Manche /utrəmɑ̃ʃ/ *adv* across the Channel, in Britain; **d'~** [*presse, chanteur*] British.

outremer /utrəmɛr/ ▶141 *adj inv*, *nm* ultramarine.

outre-mer /utrəmɛr/ *adv* overseas.

outrepasser /utrəpase/ [1] *vtr* to exceed [*droits, fonctions, devoir, pouvoir*]; to overstep [*limites, ordres*].

outrer /utre/ [1] *vtr* **1** (indigner) to outrage; **2** (exagérer) [*personne*] to exaggerate [*comportement, description*].

outre-tombe /utrətɔ̃b/ *adv* **d'~** [*pâleur*] deathly; **une voix d'~** a voice from beyond the grave.

ouvert, ~e /uvɛr, ɛrt/ I *pp* ▶ **ouvrir**.
  II *pp adj* **1** (non fermé) open; **rester ~** to stay open; **grand ~** wide open; **~ au public** open to the public; **~ à la circulation** open to traffic; **chemise à col ~** open-necked shirt; **(la) bouche ~e** [*rester, écouter*] GÉN with one's mouth open; (d'étonnement) open-mouthed; **avoir/garder les yeux ~s** (ne pas s'endormir) to be/to stay awake; (être attentif) to have to keep one's eyes open; **2** (en marche) [*lumière, gaz*] on (*jamais épith*); [*robinet*] running; **laisser le robinet ~** to leave the tap GB ou faucet US running; **3** (inauguré) [*séance, tunnel*] open; **4** (destiné) **~ à** [*centre, service*] open to; **5** (déclaré) [*guerre*] open; **6** (franc) [*personne, jeu, dialogue*] open; **7** (réceptif) [*personne, esprit*] open (à to); **8** (épanoui) [*fleur*] open; **9** (non résolu) [*question*] open; **10** (non limitatif) [*série, programme*] open-ended; **11** LING [*classe, voyelle, syllabe*] open.

ouvertement /uvɛrtəmɑ̃/ *adv* GÉN openly; (de manière éhontée) blatantly.

ouverture /uvɛrtyr/ *nf* **1** (action d'ouvrir) opening; **2** (fait de s'ouvrir) opening; **l'~ des vannes est automatique** the sluices open automatically; **3** (début) opening; **à l'~** at the opening; **~ de la chasse** opening of the shooting GB ou hunting US season; **4** (inauguration) opening; **cérémonie/jour d'~** opening ceremony/day; **5** ADMIN, COMM (fonctionnement) opening; **heures d'~** opening hours; **à l'~** at opening time; **6** (occasion) opportunity; **7** (mise en œuvre) opening; **~ de négociations** opening of negotiations; **8** CONST opening; **ménager une ~** to leave an opening; **9** (tolérance) openness (à to); **~ sur le monde** openness to the world; **~ d'esprit** open-mindedness; **10** POL (transparence) openness; **11** POL (libéralisation) opening-up; **~ à l'Ouest/à gauche** opening-up to the West/to the left; **12** ÉCON (de marché) opening (à to); **13** MUS overture; **14** JEUX (aux cartes) opening bid; (aux échecs) opening.

ouvrable /uvrabl/ *adj* [*jour*] working; [*heure*] business.

ouvrage /uvraʒ/ *nm* **1** (travail) work; **se mettre à l'~** to get down to work; **2** (livre) book, work; (œuvre) work; **~ de référence** reference book; **~ collectif** joint publication; **3** (produit par un artisan, ouvrier, un couturière) piece of work.
  IDIOMES **mettre** ou **avoir du cœur à l'~** to work with a will; **ne pas avoir le cœur à l'~** not to have one's heart in one's work.

ouvragé, ~e /uvraʒe/ *adj* finely wrought.

ouvrant, ~e /uvrɑ̃, ɑ̃t/ *adj* **toit ~** AUT sunroof.

ouvré, ~e /uvre/ *adj* **1** (ouvragé) finely worked; **2** ADMIN, JUR **jour ~** working day.

ouvre-boîtes /uvrəbwat/ *nm inv* tin-opener GB, can opener.

ouvre-bouteilles /uvrəbutɛj/ *nm inv* bottle-opener.

ouvreur, -euse /uvrœr, øz/ *nm,f* **1** ▶374 CIN, THÉÂ usher/usherette; **2** JEUX (joueur qui commence) opener.

ouvrier, -ière¹ /uvrije, ɛr/ I *adj* **1** POL, SOCIOL [*contestation*] of the workers (*après n*); **classe ouvrière** working class; **syndicat ~** trade union; **2** ZOOL [*abeille, fourmi*] worker (*épith*).
  II ▶374 *nm,f* GÉN worker; (dans le bâtiment) workman; **les ~s du bâtiment** the construction workers.
  ■ **~ agricole** agricultural labourer.

ouvrière² /uvrijɛr/ *nf* ZOOL worker.

ouvrir /uvrir/ [32] I *vtr* **1** GÉN to open [*boîte, porte, bouteille, tiroir, huître, lettre*]; to draw back [*verrou*]; to undo [*col, chemise*]; **ne pas ~ la bouche** ou **le bec** (ne rien dire) not to say a word; **~ ses oreilles** to keep one's ears open; **~ les bras** to open one's arms; **~ les bras à qn** (accueillir) to welcome sb with open arms; **~ sa maison à qn** to throw one's house open to sb; **2** (commencer) to open [*débat, spectacle, cérémonie, chantier*]; to initiate [*période, dialogue, processus*]; **3** (mettre en marche) to turn on [*radio, chauffage*]; **4** (créer) to open [*compte, magasin*, *école*]; to open up [*possibilité, marché, passage*]; to initiate [*cours*]; **~ une route** to build a road; **~ la route** or **voie à qch** to pave the way for sth; **5** (élargir) to open [*capital, rangs*] (**à** to); to open up [*compétition, marché*] (**à** to); **~ l'esprit à qn** to open sb's mind; **6** (entailler) to open [*abcès*]; to cut open [*joue*]; **~ le ventre**○ **à qn** (opérer) to cut sb open○.

II *vi* **1** (ouvrir la porte) to open the door (**à** to); **va ~** go and open the door; **ouvrez!** (injonction) open up!; **ouvre-moi!** let me in!; **se faire ~** to be let in; **2** (fonctionner) [*magasin, service*] to open; **~ le dimanche** to open on Sundays; **3** (être créé) [*magasin, service*] to be opened; **4** (déboucher) [*chambre, tunnel*] to open (**sur** onto); **5** FIN **la Bourse a ouvert en baisse** the exchange opened down; **6** (aux cartes, échecs) to open.

III s'ouvrir *vpr* **1** GÉN to open; (sous un souffle) [*fenêtre*] to blow open; (sous un choc) [*porte, boîte, sac*] to fly open; (inopinément) [*vêtement*] to come undone; **2** (commencer) [*négociation, spectacle, chantier*] to open (**sur, avec** with); [*période, dialogue, processus*] to be initiated (**sur, avec** with); **3** (s'élargir) [*pays, économie, capital, institution*] to open up (**à, vers** to); **4** (se confier) to open one's heart (**à** to); **5** (être ouvrant) [*fenêtre, toit*] to open; **ma jupe s'ouvre sur le côté** my skirt opens at the side; **6** (être créé) [*magasin, métro, possibilité*] to open; **un garage va s'~ ici** there's going to be a garage here; **7** (créer pour soi) [*personne*] to open up [*passage*]; **8** (se dérouler) [*chemin, voie, espace*] to open up; **9** (s'épanouir) [*fleur*] to open; **10** (se fendre) [*sol, cicatrice*] to open; **11** (se blesser) [*personne*] to cut open [*crâne, pied*]; **s'~ les veines** or **poignets** (pour se suicider) to slash one's wrists.

ovaire /ɔvɛʀ/ *nm* ovary; **un kyste de** or **à l'~** an ovarian cyst.

ovale /ɔval/ *adj, nm* oval.

ovation /ɔvasjɔ̃/ *nf* **1** (applaudissements) ovation; **faire une ~ à qn** to give sb an ovation; **il a fini son** discours sous les **~s de la foule** he finished his speech to wild applause from the crowd; **2** (reconnaissance) accolade.

ovationner /ɔvasjɔne/ [1] *vtr* to greet [sb/sth] with wild applause; **ils se levèrent pour ~ le candidat** they gave the candidate a standing ovation.

ovin, ~e /ɔvɛ̃, in/ **I** *adj* ovine; **la viande ~e** mutton; **les producteurs ~s** sheep farmers.
II *nm* sheep; **les ~s** sheep.

ovipare /ɔvipaʀ/ *nm* egg-laying animal.

ovni /ɔvni/ *nm: abbr* ▶ **objet**.

ovulation /ɔvylasjɔ̃/ *nf* ovulation.

ovule /ɔvyl/ *nm* **1** BIOL ovum; **2** BOT ovule; **3** (en pharmacie) pessary.

oxydable /ɔksidabl/ *adj* [*métal*] liable to rust (*après n*).

oxydant, ~e /ɔksidɑ̃, ɑ̃t/ **I** *adj* oxidizing.
II *nm* oxidizer, oxidizing agent.

oxydation /ɔksidasjɔ̃/ *nf* oxidation.

oxyde /ɔksid/ *nm* oxide.
■ **~ de carbone** carbon monoxide.

oxyder /ɔkside/ [1] *vtr*, **s'oxyder** *vpr* to oxidize.

oxygène /ɔksiʒɛn/ *nm* **1** CHIMIE oxygen; **à ~** [*masque, tente*] oxygen (*épith*); **2** (air) air; **je manque d'~ ici** I'm suffocating here.

oxygéné, ~e /ɔksiʒene/ **I** *pp* ▶ **oxygéner**.
II *pp adj* **cheveux ~s** peroxide (blond) hair; **eau ~e** hydrogen peroxide.

oxygéner /ɔksiʒene/ [14] **I** *vtr* to oxygenate.
II s'oxygéner *vpr* [*personne*] to get some fresh air.

oyez /ɔje/ ▶ **ouïr**.

ozone /ozon/ *nf* ozone; **la couche d'~** the ozone layer.

Pp

p, P /pe/ *nm inv* p, P.

pacage /pakaʒ/ *nm* **1** (lieu) pasture, grazing land; **2** (action) grazing.

pacha /paʃa/ *nm* pasha.
IDIOMES **mener une vie de ~**○ to live the life of Riley.

pachyderme /paʃidɛʀm/ *nm* **1** ZOOL pachyderm; **2** (personne massive) elephant; **de ~** [*physique, pas*] heavy.

pacificateur, -trice /pasifikatœʀ, tʀis/ **I** *adj* [*action, discours*] placatory; [*rôle*] peacemaking.
II *nm,f* peacemaker.

pacifier /pasifje/ [1] *vtr* to establish peace in, to pacify [*pays, région*]; **un monde pacifié** a world at peace.

pacifique /pasifik/ **I** *adj* **1** [*coexistence, solution, manifestation*] peaceful; [*peuple, personne*] peaceful, peace-loving; **2** GÉOG Pacific.
II *nmf* (personne) peace-loving person.

Pacifique /pasifik/ ▶ **407** *nprm* **l'océan ~, le ~** the Pacific (Ocean); **le ~ Sud** the South Pacific.

pacifiste /pasifist/ *adj, nmf* pacifist.

pacotille /pakɔtij/ *nf* PEJ **de la ~** cheap rubbish, junk○; **montre de ~** cheap watch; **héroïsme de ~** bogus heroism.

pacte /pakt/ *nm* pact.

pactiser /paktize/ [1] *vi* to treat (**avec qn** with sb).

pactole /paktɔl/ *nm* gold mine; **ramasser** or **toucher le ~**○ to make a fortune ou mint○.

PAF /paf/ **I** *nm: abbr* ▶ **paysage**.
II *nf: abbr* ▶ **police**.

pagaie /pagɛ/ *nf* paddle.

pagaille○ /pagɑj/ **I** *nf* mess; **elle a mis la ~ dans mes papiers** she messed up my papers; **la grève a semé la ~ dans le pays** the strike has caused chaos throughout the country.
II en pagaille *loc adv* **1** (en désordre) in a mess; **2** (à profusion) **du poisson en ~** loads○ of fish.

paganisme /paganism/ *nm* paganism.

pagayer /pageje/ [21] *vi* to paddle.

page¹ /paʒ/ *nm* page (boy).

page² /paʒ/ *nf* page; **tournez la ~ SVP** please turn over, PTO; **tourner la ~** FIG to turn over a new leaf; **faire la mise en ~** or **mettre en ~** to make up a page; **mise en ~** (résultat) layout; **une ~ sombre de leur existence** a dark chapter in their lives.
■ **~ de publicité** RADIO commercial break.
IDIOMES **être à la ~** to be up to date; **se mettre à la ~** to bring oneself up to date.

pagination /paʒinasjɔ̃/ *nf* **1** (numérotation) pagination; **2** ORDINAT paging.

pagne /paɲ/ *nm* **1** (en tissu) loincloth; **2** (en paille) grass skirt.

pagode /pagɔd/ *nf* pagoda.

paie /pɛ/ *nf* pay; **ma ~ me suffit pour vivre** I can live on my pay ou wages; **toucher une bonne ~** to be well paid, to get a good wage; **bulletin** or **fiche** or **feuille de ~** payslip.
IDIOMES **ça fait une ~**○ **que je ne l'ai pas vu** it's ages○ since I've seen him.

paiement /pɛmɑ̃/ *nm* payment; **le ~ de la dette extérieure** repayment of the foreign debt.

païen, -ïenne /pajɛ̃, ɛn/ *adj, nm,f* pagan.

paillard, ~e /pajaʀ, aʀd/ *adj* bawdy.

paillasse /pajas/ *nf* **1** (matelas) straw mattress; **2** (de laboratoire) lab bench; (d'évier) draining board.

paillasson /pajasɔ̃/ *nm* **1** (tapis) doormat; **2** (personne servile) doormat.

paille /pɑj/ **I** ▶ **141** *adj inv* (couleur) **cheveux (couleur) ~** straw-coloured^GB hair; **jaune ~** straw yellow.
II *nf* straw; **tapis de ~** straw mat; **~ de riz** rice straw; **boire avec une ~** to drink through a straw.
■ **~ de fer** steel wool.
IDIOMES **être sur la ~**○ to be penniless; **se retrouver sur la ~**○ to find oneself destitute; **tirer à la courte ~** to draw lots.

pailleté, ~e /pajte/ *adj* **1** (avec des disques brillants) sequined, spangled US; **2** (avec de la poudre brillante) [*tissu*] glittery.

paillette /pajɛt/ *nf* **1** (disque brillant) sequin, spangle US; **robe à ~s** a sequined ou spangled US dress; **2** (poudre brillante) glitter ¢; **3** (de roche) splinter; **savon en ~s** soap flakes (*pl*).

paillote /pajɔt/ *nf* grass hut.

pain /pɛ̃/ *nm* **1** (aliment) bread ¢; **miettes de ~** breadcrumbs; **2** (miche) loaf; **acheter deux ~s** to buy two loaves; **un petit ~** a (bread) roll; **3** CULIN **~ de légumes/viande** vegetable/meat loaf; **4** (bloc) (de savon, cire) bar; (de glace) block; (de dynamite) stick.
■ **~ blanc** white bread; **manger son ~ blanc (le premier)** to have it easy at the start; **~ brioché** brioche bread; **~ de campagne** farmhouse bread; (miche) farmhouse loaf; **~ complet** wholemeal bread; (miche) wholemeal loaf; **~ d'épices** gingerbread; **~ grillé** toast; **~ au lait** milk roll; **~ de mie** sandwich loaf; **~ perdu** French toast; **~ aux raisins** currant bun; **~ de seigle** rye bread; (miche) rye loaf; **~ de son** bran loaf; **~ de sucre** sugar loaf; **en ~ de sucre** (crâne) egg-shaped; (montagne) sugar loaf (*épith*).
IDIOMES **se vendre comme des petits ~s** to sell like hot cakes; **ça ne mange pas de ~**○ it doesn't cost anything; **je ne mange pas de ce ~-là**○ I won't have anything to do with it, I want no part of it; **enlever le ~ de la bouche à qn** to take the bread out of sb's mouth.

pair, ~e¹ /pɛʀ/ **I** *adj* [*nombre, jours, fonction*] even.
II *nm* **1** (égal) peer; **c'est une cuisinière hors ~** she's an excellent cook; **elle a un mari hors ~!** she has a marvellous^GB husband!; **aller** or **marcher de ~ avec** to go hand in hand with; **2** HIST, POL peer.
III au pair *loc* **travailler au ~** to work as an au pair; **jeune fille au ~** au pair (girl).

paire² /pɛʀ/ *nf* pair; **donner une ~ de gifles à qn** to box sb's ears.
IDIOMES **les deux font la ~!** they're two of a kind!

paisible /pɛzibl/ *adj* **1** (doux) gentle; **2** (tranquille) [*vie, quartier*] peaceful, quiet; [*personne*] calm, easy-going; [*eau*] calm, untroubled; [*sommeil*] peaceful; **il dormait d'un sommeil ~** he was sleeping peacefully.

paisiblement /pɛziblǝmɑ̃/ *adv* **1** (tranquillement) peacefully; **2** (sans s'inquiéter) quietly.

paître /pɛtʀ/ [74] *vi* to graze.
IDIOMES **envoyer ~**○ to send [sb] packing○.

paix /pɛ/ *nf inv* **1** MIL, POL peace; **en temps de ~** in peacetime, in times of peace; **2** (calme intérieur) peace; **avoir l'esprit en ~** to have peace of mind; **3** (tranquillité) peace; **avoir la ~** to get some peace; **laisser qn en ~** to leave sb alone, to leave sb in peace; **ficher**○ **la ~ à qn** to leave sb alone; **la ~**○! be quiet!.

pakistanais, **~e** /pakistanɛ, ɛz/ ▶394⟩ *adj* Pakistani.

palabre /palabʁ/ *nm* ou *f* (discussion) endless discussion.

palabrer /palabʁe/ [1] *vi* to discuss endlessly.

palace /palas/ *nm* luxury hotel.

palais /palɛ/ *nm inv* **1** ANAT palate; **2** (goût) palate; **3** ARCHIT (de souverain, particulier) palace; **4** JUR **~ de justice** law courts (*pl*).
■ **~ des sports** sports centre○GB.

palan /palɑ̃/ *nm* hoist.

pale /pal/ *nf* **1** (d'hélice, de rame, roue) blade; **2** TECH (vanne) paddle.

pâle /pal/ *adj* pale; **vert/bleu ~** pale green/blue; **tu es toute ~** you look really pale; **être ~ comme un linge** to be as white as a sheet; **une ~ imitation** a pale imitation; **faire ~ figure à côté de** to pale into insignificance beside.

palefrenier, **-ière** /palfʁənje, ɛʁ/ *nm,f* groom.

paléochrétien, **-ienne** /paleokʁetjɛ̃, ɛn/ *adj* [*art*] early Christian.

paléolithique /paleɔlitik/ *adj*, *nm* Paleolithic.

paléontologie /paleɔ̃tɔlɔʒi/ *nf* paleontology.

paléontologiste /paleɔ̃tɔlɔʒist/, **paléontologue** /paleɔ̃tɔlɔg/ ▶374⟩ *nmf* paleontologist.

palestinien, **-ienne** /palɛstinjɛ̃, ɛn/ ▶509⟩ *adj* Palestinian.

palet /palɛ/ *nm* **1** SPORT (au hockey sur glace) puck; **2** JEUX (pierre) quoit.

paletot /palto/ *nm* jacket.
IDIOMES **tomber sur le ~ de qn**○ to lay into sb○.

palette /palɛt/ *nf* **1** ART (objet, couleurs) palette; **2** FIG range; **une ~ d'activités** a range of activities; **la ~ d'un musicien/acteur** a musician's/an actor's range; **3** CULIN (de porc, mouton) ~ shoulder; **4** (plateau de chargement) pallet.
■ **~ de maquillage** make-up palette.

palétuvier /paletyvje/ *nm* mangrove.

pâleur /pɑlœʁ/ *nf* **1** (de ciel) paleness; **2** (de malade) pallor.

pâlichon○, **-onne** /paliʃɔ̃, ɔn/ *adj* [*personne, teint*] peaky○GB, peaked US; [*ciel, éclairage*] watery.

palier /palje/ *nm* **1** (d'escalier) landing; **mon voisin de ~** my neighbour○GB on the same floor; **2** (stade) level; (phase stable) plateau; **avancer par ~s** to proceed by stages; **3** SPORT (en plongée) ~ **(de décompression)** (decompression) stage.

palière /paljɛʁ/ *adj f* **porte ~** entry door.

pâlir /paliʁ/ [3] *vi* **1** [*coloris, photo, jour*] to fade; [*ciel, soleil*] to grow pale; [*personne*] to turn pale (**de** with); **faire ~ qn d'envie** or **de jalousie** to make sb green with envy; **2** [*gloire, prestige*] to fade.

palissade /palisad/ *nf* (de jardin) fence; MIL palisade.

pâlissant, **~e** /palisɑ̃, ɑ̃t/ *adj* [*jour, lueur*] fading.

palliatif, **-ive** /paljatif, iv/ **I** *adj* palliative.
II *nm* palliative.

pallier /palje/ [2] *vtr* to compensate for.

palmarès /palmaʁɛs/ *nm inv* **1** (classement) honours○GB list; (d'acteurs, auteurs) list of award winners; (de sportifs) list of winners; **2** (liste de succès) record of achievements; **il a trois tournois à son ~** he has three tournament wins to his credit; **3** (meilleures ventes) (de disques) hit parade; (de livres) bestsellers list.

palme /palm/ *nf* **1** BOT (feuille) palm leaf; (palmier) palm; **2** SPORT (pour nager) flipper; **3** MIL (décoration) ~ bar; **4** FIG prize; **remporter la ~** to take the prize.

palmé, **~e** /palme/ *adj* **1** ZOOL webbed; **2** BOT palmate.

palmeraie /palməʁɛ/ *nf* palm grove.

palmier /palmje/ *nm* **1** BOT palm (tree); **~ dattier** date palm; **2** CULIN (pâtisserie) large pastry biscuit.

palmipède /palmipɛd/ **I** *adj* web-footed.
II *nm* palmiped.

palombe /palɔ̃b/ *nf* wood pigeon.

pâlot○, **-otte** /palo, ɔt/ *adj* rather pale.

palourde /paluʁd/ *nf* clam.

palpable /palpabl/ *adj* [*objet, bonheur, brouillard*] palpable; [*vérité, preuve, avantage*] tangible.

palper /palpe/ [1] *vtr* [*médecin*] to palpate [*partie du corps*]; [*client, aveugle*] to feel [*objet, fruit*].

palpitant, **~e** /palpitɑ̃, ɑ̃t/ *adj* **1** (captivant) [*histoire, vie*] thrilling; **2** [*cœur*] fluttering; [*chair, corps*] twitching; **3** (qui respire par saccades) panting (**de** with).

palpitation /palpitasjɔ̃/ *nf* **1** MÉD palpitation; **avoir des ~s** to have palpitations; **2** (de paupière, muscle) twitching; **3** (de lumière, flamme, d'étoile) LITER flickering; (de feuille, voile) fluttering; (d'eau) quivering; **4** (exaltation) LITER thrill (**de** of).

palpiter /palpite/ [1] *vi* **1** (battre) [*cœur*] to beat; [*chair, corps*] to twitch; [*veine*] to pulse; **2** (avoir des mouvements convulsifs) [*cœur*] to flutter; [*paupière*] to twitch; **3** (frémir) LITER [*personne, eau*] to quiver (**de** with); [*lumière, flamme*] to flicker; [*feuille, voile*] to flutter.

paludisme /palydism/ ▶196⟩ *nm* malaria.

pâmer: **se pâmer** /pame/ [1] *vpr* † or HUM **se ~ de plaisir** to swoon with pleasure; **se ~ (d'admiration) devant qch** to swoon over sth.

pâmoison /pɑmwazɔ̃/ *nf* † or HUM swoon; **tomber en ~ (devant qch)** to swoon (over sth).

pamphlet /pɑ̃flɛ/ *nm* satirical tract.

pamphlétaire /pɑ̃fletɛʁ/ *nmf* pamphleteer.

pamplemousse /pɑ̃pləmus/ *nm* grapefruit.

pan /pɑ̃/ **I** *nm* **1** (partie) (de falaise, maison) section; (de vie, problème) part; (d'obscurité, de ciel) patch; **~ de mur** section of wall; **~ de vitre** glass panel; **2** (côté) (de tour, prisme) side; **relever les ~s d'un rideau** to tie back the curtains; **~s d'un manteau** coat-tails.
II *excl* (coup de feu) bang!; (coup de poing) thump!; (fessée) whack!
■ **~ de chemise** shirt-tail.

pan- /pɑ̃, pan/ *préf* POL Pan-; **~-européen** Pan-European; **~-russe** Pan-Russian.

panacée /panase/ *nf* panacea.

panache /panaʃ/ *nm* **1** (élégance) panache; **2** (plumes) plume.

panaché, **~e** /panaʃe/ **I** *adj* [*bouquet, salade*] mixed; [*tulipe, lierre*] variegated.
II *nm* (boisson) shandy.

panacher /panaʃe/ [1] *vtr* to mix.

panade /panad/ *nf* bread soup.
IDIOMES **être dans la ~**○ to be in the soup○.

panama /panama/ *nm* (chapeau) panama (hat).

panaméen, **-éenne** /panameɛ̃, ɛn/ ▶394⟩ *adj* Panamanian.

panaris /panaʁi/ ▶196⟩ *nm inv* whitlow.

pancarte /pɑ̃kaʁt/ *nf* **1** (sur un mur) notice GB, sign US; (sur un piquet) sign; **2** (dans une manifestation) placard GB, sign US.

pancréas /pɑ̃kʁeas/ *nm inv* pancreas.

panda /pɑ̃da/ *nm* panda.

panégyrique /paneʒiʁik/ *nm* panegyric.

paner /pane/ [1] *vtr* to coat with ou in breadcrumbs.

panier /panje/ *nm* **1** (en osier, rotin, etc) basket; (corbeille à papier) wastepaper basket; (dans un lave-vaisselle) rack; **mettre** or **jeter au ~** LIT to throw [sth] out; FIG to get rid of; **2** SPORT (au basket-ball) basket; **marquer un ~** to score a basket; **3** (de jupe, robe) pannier; **robe à ~s** dress with panniers.
■ **~ à salade** (ustensile) salad shaker; (fourgon de police)○ Black Maria GB, paddy wagon US.
IDIOMES **être un ~ percé**○ to spend money like water; **ils sont tous à mettre dans le même ~**○ they are all much of a muchness GB, they are all about the same; **mettre tous ses œufs dans le même**

~○ to put all one's eggs in one basket; **le haut** or **dessus du ~**○ the pick of the bunch.

panière /panjɛʀ/ *nf* large basket.

panier-repas, *pl* **paniers-repas** /panjeʀəpa/ *nm* packed lunch GB, box lunch US.

panique /panik/ **I** *adj* panic; **sensibilité ~ au bruit** panic reaction to noise; **peur ~ (de qch)** terror (of sth).

II *nf* panic; **mouvement de ~** panic; **début de ~** moment of panic; **pas de ~!** don't panic!; **être pris de ~** to panic.

paniquer○ /panike/ [1] **I** *vtr* to throw [sb] into a panic.

II *vi* to panic; **il a paniqué** he panicked.

panne /pan/ *nf* (de véhicule, machine) breakdown; (de moteur, d'électricité) failure; **~ de courant** power failure; **la machine/voiture est (tombée) en ~** the machine/car has broken down; **tomber en ~ sèche** or **d'essence** to run out of petrol GB ou gas US; **lorsque la ~ survint**... (de voiture) when the car broke down...; (d'électricité) when the power failed...; **être en ~ de**○ to be out of [objet, main-d'œuvre]; to have run out of [idées, imagination].

panneau, *pl* **~x** /pano/ *nm* **1** (permanent) sign; (temporaire) board; (d'information) notice board; **2** (élément) panel; **~ en bois** wooden panel; **3** ART panel.

■ **~ d'affichage** notice board GB, bulletin board; **~ indicateur** AUT signpost; **~ publicitaire** hoarding GB, billboard; **~ de signalisation routière** road sign; **~ solaire** solar panel.

IDIOMES **tomber** or **donner dans le ~**○ to fall for it○.

panonceau, *pl* **~x** /panɔso/ *nm* **1** (permanent) sign; (temporaire) board.

panoplie /panɔpli/ *nf* **1** JEUX (pour se déguiser) outfit; **2** (de professionnel) paraphernalia; **3** (ornementale) display of weapons; **4** (gamme) (d'objets usuels) array; (d'armements) arsenal; (de mesures, moyens) range.

panorama /panɔʀama/ *nm* **1** LIT panorama; **2** FIG (culturel) panorama; (politique) overview.

panoramique /panɔʀamik/ **I** *adj* GÉN [vue, visite, route] panoramic; **2** AUT [vitre, pare-brise] wraparound; **3** CIN [écran] wide.

II *nm* CIN pan (shot).

panosse /panɔs/ *nf* H **1** (serpillière) floor cloth; **2** (chiffon) cloth.

panse /pɑ̃s/ *nf* **1** ZOOL paunch; **2**○ (estomac) HUM belly○; **s'en mettre plein la ~**○ to stuff one's face○; **3** (de cruche) belly.

pansement /pɑ̃smɑ̃/ *nm* **1** (avec compresse) dressing; **~ (adhésif)** plaster GB, Band-Aid®; **faire un ~ à qn** to put a dressing on sb's wound; **2** (action) dressing.

panser /pɑ̃se/ [1] *vtr* **1** MÉD to dress [blessure]; to put a dressing on [partie du corps]; **2** FIG [temps] to heal [blessure morale]; **~ ses blessures** to lick one's wounds; **3** AGRIC (étriller) to groom [cheval].

pansu, **~e** /pɑ̃sy/ *adj* [personne, objet] pot-bellied.

pantagruélique /pɑ̃taɡʀyelik/ *adj* Pantagruelian.

pantalon /pɑ̃talɔ̃/ *nm* (culotte longue) trousers (pl) GB, pants (pl) US; **acheter un ~** to buy a pair of trousers GB ou pants US; **~ à pinces** pleat front trousers (pl) GB ou pants (pl) US; **~ de pyjama** pyjama GB ou pajama US bottoms (pl).

pantalonnade /pɑ̃talɔnad/ *nf* **1** THÉÂT slapstick comedy; **2** FIG play-acting ¢.

pantelant, **~e** /pɑ̃tlɑ̃, ɑ̃t/ *adj* **1** (haletant) [personne] panting; (palpitant) [chair] quivering; **2** (ému) overcome (de with).

panthère /pɑ̃tɛʀ/ *nf* **1** (animal) panther; **2** (fourrure) panther skin.

pantin /pɑ̃tɛ̃/ *nm* (jouet, fantoche) puppet.

pantois, **~e** /pɑ̃twa, az/ *adj* flabbergasted.

pantomime /pɑ̃tɔmim/ *nf* (art) mime; (spectacle) mime show; **faire la ~** FIG to play it up.

pantouflard○, **~e** /pɑ̃tuflaʀ, aʀd/ *adj* **qu'est-ce que tu es ~!** what a stay-at-home you are!

pantoufle /pɑ̃tufl/ *nf* slipper.

PAO /peao/ *nf* **1** *abbr* ▶ **production**; **2** *abbr* ▶ **publication**.

paon /pɑ̃/ *nm* peacock; **faire le ~** to strut around like a peacock.

IDIOMES **être fier comme un ~** to be as proud as a peacock.

papa /papa/ *nm* dad○, daddy○, father; **fils** or **fille à ~** spoiled little rich kid○.

papauté /papote/ *nf* papacy.

pape /pap/ *nm* **1** ▶ 596 RELIG pope; **le ~ Jean-Paul II** Pope John Paul II; **2** FIG (personne influente) high priest (de qch of sth).

IDIOMES **être sérieux comme un ~** to be solemn-faced.

paperasse○ /papʀas/ *nf* PÉJ **1** (papiers) bumph○ ¢ GB, documents (pl); **2** (activité) paperwork ¢.

paperasserie○ /papʀasʀi/ *nf* PÉJ paperwork.

papeterie /papɛtʀi/ *nf* **1** ▶ 374 (commerce) stationer's (shop), stationery shop GB ou store US; **2** (articles) stationery; **3** (industrie) papermaking industry; **4** (usine) paper mill.

papetier, -ière /paptje, ɛʀ/ **I** *adj* papermaking.

II ▶ 374 *nm,f* **1** (fabricant) papermaker; **2** (commerçant) stationer.

papi○ /papi/ *nm* **1** (grand-père) granddad○, grandpa○; **2** (vieil homme) granddad○, old man.

papier /papje/ **I** *nm* **1** (matière) paper; **sortie sur ~** ORDINAT hardcopy output; **pâte à ~** pulp; **2** (document) paper; **~s personnels** personal ou private papers; **3**○ (article de journal) article, piece○.

II papiers *nmpl* ADMIN documents, papers; **~s d'identité** (identity) papers ou documents.

■ **~ absorbant** kitchen towel, paper towel US; **~ alu**○, **~ (d')aluminium** (aluminium GB ou aluminum US) foil, kitchen foil; **~ brouillon** rough paper GB, scrap paper; **~ buvard** blotting paper; **~ cadeau** gift wrap, wrapping paper; **~ carbone** carbon paper; **~ à cigarettes** cigarette paper; **~ crépon** crepe paper; **~ à dessin** drawing paper; **~ d'emballage** wrapping paper; **~ glacé** glossy ou shiny paper; **~ hygiénique** toilet paper ou tissue; **~ journal** newsprint; **~ à lettres** writing paper, notepaper; **~ mâché** papier-mâché; **~ millimétré** graph paper; **~ à musique** music paper; **être réglé comme du ~ à musique**○ [vie] to be highly regimented; **~ peint** wallpaper; **~ pelure** onionskin (paper); **~ de verre** sandpaper, glasspaper; **~s gras** litter ¢.

IDIOMES **être dans les petits ~s de qn**○ to be in sb's good books.

papier-calque, *pl* **papiers-calque** /papjekalk/ *nm* tracing paper.

papille /papij/ *nf* papilla.

■ **~s gustatives** taste buds.

papillon /papijɔ̃/ *nm* **1** ZOOL butterfly; **~ de nuit** moth; **2**○ (contravention) parking ticket; **3** SPORT (brasse) butterfly (stroke); **4** (écrou) wing nut.

papillonner /papijɔne/ [1] *vi* **1** (voleter) to flit about; **2** (être volage) to flirt incessantly.

papillote /papijɔt/ *nf* **1** CULIN (papier aluminium) foil parcel; (confiserie) chocolate sweet GB ou candy US (wrapped in silver paper); (sur une côtelette) frill; **faire du saumon en ~** to cook salmon in a foil parcel; **2** (pour les cheveux) curlpaper; **3** (mèche) lock.

papilloter /papijɔte/ [1] *vi* [lumière] to flicker; [personne, yeux] to blink; **~ des paupières** to blink.

papoter○ /papɔte/ [1] *vi* to chatter.

paprika /papʀika/ *nm* paprika.

pâque /pak/ **I** *nf* **la ~ juive** Passover.

II pâques *nfpl* **faire ses ~s** to do one's Easter duty.

paquebot /pakbo/ *nm* liner.

pâquerette /pakʀɛt/ *nf* daisy.

IDIOMES **être au ras des ~s**○ to be very basic.

Pâques /pak/ **I** *nm* (date) Easter; **le lundi de ~** Easter Monday.

II *nfpl* (fête) Easter (*sg*).

III ▶305⎮ *nprf* GÉOG **île de ~** Easter Island.

paquet /pakɛ/ *nm* **1** COMM (de sucre, lessive, riz) packet GB, package US; (de cigarettes, café) packet GB, pack US; (d'enveloppes) pack; (de bonbons) bag; **mettre en ~** to package; **2** (colis) parcel; **3** (assemblage) (de vêtements, linge, billets) bundle; (de lettres) packet; **faire un ~ de journaux** to put together a bundle of newspapers; **4**○ (grande quantité) masses (*pl*); **5**○ (grosse somme) packet○ GB, bundle○ US; **6** ORDINAT, TÉLÉCOM packet.
■ **~ de muscles**○ muscleman; **~ de nerfs**○ bundle of nerves○.
IDIOMES **mettre le ~**○ to pull out all the stops.

paquetage /paktaʒ/ *nm* MIL pack.

paquet-cadeau, *pl* **paquets-cadeaux** /pakɛkado/ *nm* gift-wrapped present; **est-ce que vous pouvez faire un ~?** could you gift-wrap it?

par /paʀ/ **I** *prép* **1** (indiquant un trajet) **entre ~ le garage/~ la porte du garage** come in through the garage/by the garage door; **il a pris ~ les champs** he cut across the fields; **il est passé ~ tous les échelons** FIG he worked his way up through the ranks; **pour aller à Rome, je passe ~ Milan** to get to Rome, I go via *ou* through Milan; **elle est arrivée ~ la droite** she came from the right; **errer ~ les rues** to wander through the streets; **le peintre a terminé** *ou* **fini ~ la cuisine** the painter did the kitchen last; **2** (indiquant un lieu) **~ endroits** in places; **3** (indiquant une circonstance) **~ le passé** in the past; **~ une belle journée d'été** on a beautiful summer's day; **~ ce froid** in this cold weather; **ils sortent même ~ moins 40°** they go outdoors even when it's minus 40°; **~ deux/trois fois** on two/three occasions; **4** (indiquant une répartition) **~ jour/semaine/an** a day/week/year; **~ personne** *ou* **habitant** per person *ou* head; **~ petits groupes** in small groups; **deux ~ deux** [*travailler*] in twos; [*marcher*] two by two; **les touristes sont arrivés ~ centaines** tourists arrived by the hundred; **5** (introduit un complément d'agent) by; **être pris ~ son travail** to be taken up with one's work; **6** (indiquant le moyen) by; **payer ~ carte de crédit** to pay by credit card; **7** (indiquant la manière) in; **~ étapes** in stages; **~ rafales** in gusts; **8** (indiquant la cause) **l'accident est arrivé ~ sa faute** it was his/her fault that the accident happened; **~ ennui/jalousie** out of boredom/jealousy; **9** (indiquant un intermédiaire) through; **tu peux me faire passer le livre ~ ta sœur** you can get the book to me via your sister.
II de par *loc prép* FML **1** (partout dans) throughout, all over; **voyager de ~ le monde** to travel all over *ou* throughout the world; **2** (à cause de) **de ~ leurs origines** by virtue of their origins.

parabole /paʀabɔl/ *nf* **1** BIBLE parable; **2** MATH parabola.

parachever /paʀaʃve/ [16] *vtr* (terminer) to complete; (fignoler) to put the finishing touches to.

parachutage /paʀaʃytaʒ/ *nm* airdrop.

parachute /paʀaʃyt/ *nm* **1** (voile) parachute; **sauter en ~** to make a parachute jump; **2** ▶329⎮ (sport) parachuting.

parachuter /paʀaʃyte/ [1] *vtr* **1** MIL, SPORT to parachute [*soldat, vivres*]; **2**○ (envoyer) **je n'ai pas envie d'être parachuté en Normandie** I don't want to be shunted off○ to Normandy.

parachutisme /paʀaʃytism/ ▶329⎮ *nm* parachuting.

parachutiste /paʀaʃytist/ ▶374⎮ **I** *adj* [*troupes, escadron*] parachute.
II *nmf* **1** SPORT parachutist; **2** MIL paratrooper.

parade /paʀad/ *nf* **1** MIL, THÉÂT (défilé) parade; **de ~** [*costume, uniforme*] parade (*épith*); **faire une ~** to parade; **2** SPORT, FIG (défense) parry; **3** (étalage) parade; **faire ~ de** to flaunt; **4** (d'animal) display.

parader /paʀade/ [1] *vi* PEJ to strut about.

paradis /paʀadi/ *nm inv* **1** RELIG heaven; **2** (lieu idéal) paradise; **c'est le ~ sur terre** it's heavenly; **c'est un ~ perdu** it's a garden of Eden.

■ **~ fiscal** tax haven; **~ terrestre** Garden of Eden.
IDIOMES **tu ne l'emporteras pas au ~**○ you'll live to regret it.

paradisiaque /paʀadizjak/ *adj* heavenly.

paradoxal, ~e, *mpl* **-aux** /paʀadɔksal, o/ *adj* paradoxical.

paradoxe /paʀadɔks/ *nm* paradox.

paraffine /paʀafin/ *nf* (liquide) paraffin GB, kerosene US; (solide) paraffin wax; **huile de ~** paraffin oil GB, kerosene US.

parages /paʀaʒ/ *nmpl* neighbourhood^GB (*sg*); **dans les ~** around; **elle est dans les ~** she is around somewhere.

paragraphe /paʀagʀaf/ *nm* **1** (division) paragraph; **2** (signe typographique) section mark.

paraître /paʀɛtʀ/ [73] **I** *vi* **1** [*publication*] to come out, to be published; **faire ~ un article** to publish an article; **un article paru dans une revue** an article which appeared in a magazine; **'à ~'** 'forthcoming titles'; **prochains ouvrages à ~ dans cette collection** coming out soon in this collection; **2** (sembler) to appear, to seem; (avoir l'air) to look; **cela peut ~ ridicule** this may appear *ou* seem ridiculous; **il ne craint pas de ~ ridicule** he's not afraid of looking silly; **3** (devenir visible) [*personne, objet, véhicule, soleil*] to appear; **elle ne laisse rien ~ de ses sentiments** she doesn't let her feelings show at all; **sans qu'il n'y paraisse rien, elle a fini par gagner tout le monde à sa cause** without anyone realizing, she ended up winning everyone over to her cause; **4** (se montrer) to appear; **~ à son avantage** to look one's best; **chercher à/aimer ~** to try/to like to be noticed.
II *v impers* **il paraît qu'il/elle** apparently he/she; **il paraîtrait que** it would seem that; **il me paraît inutile de faire** it seems useless to me to do; **paraît-il** so it seems; **oui, il paraît** so I hear; **il paraît que les Français adorent la musique** the French are supposed to love music; **à ce qu'il paraît** apparently.

parallèle¹ /paʀalɛl/ **I** *adj* **1** [*lignes, plans*] parallel (**à** to); **la rue est ~ au fleuve** the street runs parallel to the river; **2** (distinct) parallel; (semblable) similar; **en ~ à** (distinctement) in parallel with; (semblablement) similarly to; **une manifestation ~** a parallel demonstration; **nos concurrents ont suivi une démarche ~** our competitors took similar steps; **3** (en marge) [*marché, police*] unofficial; [*médecine, éducation*] alternative; [*monde, univers*] parallel.
II *nm* **1** (comparaison) parallel; **établir** *ou* **dresser un ~** to draw a parallel (**entre** between); **mettre deux événements en ~** to draw a parallel between two events; **2** GÉOG parallel.

parallèle² /paʀalɛl/ *nf* MATH parallel line.

parallèlement /paʀalɛlmɑ̃/ *adv* **1** MATH **~ à** parallel to; **2** (simultanément) at the same time (**à** as).

parallélépipède /paʀalelepipɛd/ *nm* parallelepiped.

parallélisme /paʀalelism/ *nm* **1** MATH parallelism; **2** AUT (wheel) alignment; **3** (correspondance) parallelism (**entre** between).

parallélogramme /paʀalelogʀam/ *nm* parallelogram.

paralyser /paʀalize/ [1] *vtr* **1** MÉD to paralyse; **2** (bloquer) to paralyse [*pays, entreprise*]; to bring [sth] to a halt [*production*].

paralysie /paʀalizi/ *nf* paralysis; **être frappé de ~** to be paralysed.

paralytique /paʀalitik/ *adj, nmf* paralytic.

paramètre /paʀamɛtʀ/ *nm* parameter.

paranoïaque /paʀanɔjak/ *adj, nmf* paranoiac.

parapente /paʀapɑ̃t/ ▶329⎮ *nm* **1** (engin) paraglider; **2** (sport) paragliding.

parapet /paʀapɛ/ *nm* parapet.

paraphe /paʀaf/ *nm* (initiales) initials (*pl*); (trait de plume) flourish; (signature) signature.

parapher /paʀafe/ [1] *vtr* **1** (avec ses initiales) to initial; **2** (d'un trait de plume) to put a flourish to; **3** (avec sa signature) FML to sign.

paraphrase /paʀafʀɑz/ nf paraphrase.

paraphraser /paʀafʀɑze/ [1] vtr to paraphrase.

paraplégique /paʀapleʒik/ adj, nmf paraplegic.

parapluie /paʀaplɥi/ nm LIT, FIG umbrella.

parascolaire /paʀaskɔleʀ/ adj extracurricular.

parasismique /paʀasismik/ adj **construction ~** earthquake-resistant construction.

parasitaire /paʀaziteʀ/ adj parasitic(al).

parasite /paʀazit/ **I** adj [plante, organisme] parasitic(al); [idée] intrusive; **bruits ~s** RADIO, TV interference **℄**.

II nm **1** LIT, FIG parasite; **2** RADIO, TÉLÉCOM, TV **~s** (brouillage) interference **℄**; (électricité statique) static **℄**; **provoquer** or **faire des ~s dans la radio** to cause interference on the radio.

parasiter /paʀazite/ [1] vtr **1** BIOL, BOT, MÉD to live as a parasite on [plante, animal]; **2** (exploiter) to exploit.

parasol /paʀasɔl/ nm **1** (de plage) beach umbrella; (de café, jardin) sun umbrella; **2†** (ombrelle) parasol, sunshade.

paratonnerre /paʀatɔneʀ/ nm lightning conductor GB, lightning rod.

paravent /paʀavɑ̃/ nm LIT, FIG screen.

parc /paʀk/ nm **1** (jardin) park; **2** (enclos) (pour enfant) playpen; (pour bestiaux) pen; **3** (ensemble) (d'installations) (total) number (**de** of); (de biens d'équipement) stock (**de** of); **~ automobile** (d'une entreprise) fleet of cars; (d'un pays) number of cars (on the road); **~ ferroviaire** rolling stock; **~ immobilier** housing stock.
■ **~ d'attractions** amusement ou theme park; **~ de loisirs** theme park; **~ naturel** nature park.

parce: **parce que** /paʀs(ə)k(ə)/ loc conj because; **'pourquoi est-ce que je ne peux pas aller à la plage avec eux?'—'~ que!'** 'why can't I go to the beach with them?'—'because I say so ou you can't!'; **'pourquoi ne lui as-tu pas téléphoné?'—'~ que!'** 'why haven't you phoned him/her?'—'because I haven't, that's why'; **c'est bien ~ que c'est toi!** only because it's you!; **ne serait-ce que ~ que** if only because.

parcelle /paʀsɛl/ nf **1** (petit morceau) **~ de verre/plâtre** fragment of glass/plaster; **~ d'or** particle of gold; **2** (petite quantité) **une ~ de bonheur/d'autorité** a bit of happiness/of authority; **3** (terrain) plot (of land).

parchemin /paʀʃəmɛ̃/ nm (peau, document) parchment.

parcheminé, **-e** /paʀʃəmine/ adj **1** [papier] with a parchment finish (épith); **2** [peau] papery; **3** [visage, main] shrivelled GB.

par-ci /paʀsi/ adv **~ par-là** here and there; **un gâteau ~ un bonbon par-là** a cake here, a sweet GB ou candy US there.

parcimonie /paʀsimɔni/ nf parsimony SOUT; **avec ~** sparingly, parsimoniously.

parcimonieux, **-ieuse** /paʀsimɔnjø, øz/ adj [personne] sparing (jamais épith), parsimonious SOUT; [répartition] stingy (jamais épith).

parcmètre /paʀkmɛtʀ/ nm parking meter.

parcourir /paʀkuʀiʀ/ [26] vtr **1** (sillonner) to travel all over [pays, continent]; **~ la ville** to go all over town; **~ un lieu à la recherche de** to scour a place in search of; **2** (franchir) to cover [distance]; **il reste un long chemin à ~** there's still a long way to go; **3** (traverser) **la chemin de fer parcourt toute la région** the railway runs right across the region; **un frisson me parcourut le dos** a shiver ran down my spine; **4** (examiner rapidement) to glance through, to skim [lettre, offres d'emploi]; to scan [horizon]; **~ un endroit des yeux** to have a quick glance around a place.

parcours /paʀkuʀ/ nm inv **1** (trajet) (d'autobus, de personne) route; (de fleuve) course; **~ balisé** or **fléché** marked path; **2** SPORT course; **~ de golf** round of golf; **elle a fait un excellent ~** (dans une course) she had an excellent race; **3** (cheminement professionnel) career; **incident de ~** hitch.

par-delà /paʀdəla/ prép LITER **1** (de l'autre côté de)

beyond; **2** (à travers) **~ les siècles** down the centuries.

par-derrière /paʀdɛʀjeʀ/ adv **1** (par l'arrière) **passer ~** to go round GB ou to the back; **ils m'ont attaqué ~** they attacked me from behind; **2** (sournoisement) behind sb's back; **critiquer qn ~** to criticize sb behind their back.

par-dessous /paʀdəsu/ prép, adv underneath.

pardessus /paʀdəsy/ nm inv overcoat.

par-dessus /paʀdəsy/ **I** adv **1** (dessus) **tu vas avoir froid en chemise, mets un pull ~** you'll be cold in a shirt, put a sweater on; **pose ton sac dans un coin et mets ton manteau ~** put your bag in a corner and put your coat on top of it; **2** (par le dessus) **le mur n'est pas haut, passe/saute ~** the wall isn't high, climb/jump over it.

II prép over; **saute ~ le ruisseau** jump over the stream; **jeter qn/qch ~ bord** to throw sb/sth overboard; **ce que j'aime ~ tout, c'est voyager** what I like best of all is travelling GB.

par-devant /paʀdəvɑ̃/ **I** adv **1** (par l'avant) **passer ~** to come round by the front; **2** (en face) **il te fait des sourires ~ mais dit du mal de toi dans ton dos** he's all smiles to your face but says nasty things about you behind your back.

II prép **~ notaire** in the presence of a notary.

pardon /paʀdɔ̃/ nm **1** (fait de pardonner) forgiveness; RELIG pardon; **je te demande ~** I'm sorry; **tu lui as demandé ~?** did you apologize ou say you were sorry?; **2** (dans une formule de politesse) **~!** sorry!; **~? qu'est-ce que tu as dit?** sorry ou I beg your pardon GB, what did you say?; **~ madame, je cherche... excuse me please, I'm looking for...; **~ de vous avoir interrompu** I'm sorry for interrupting you.

pardonnable /paʀdɔnabl/ adj [faute, délit] forgivable; **ils ne sont pas ~s** it's unforgivable of them.

pardonner /paʀdɔne/ [1] **I** vtr **1** (accorder son pardon à) [personne] to forgive [faute, erreur, écart]; **~ à qn** to forgive sb; **~ qch à qn** to forgive sb sth; **~ à qn d'avoir fait** to forgive sb for doing; **2** (dans une formule de politesse) **pardonnez-moi, mais je voudrais intervenir** excuse me, but I'd like to say something.

II vi **ne pas ~** [maladie, erreur] to be fatal.

III **se pardonner** vpr **je ne me le pardonnerai jamais** I'll never forgive myself for that.
IDIOMES **faute avouée est à moitié pardonnée** PROV a fault confessed is half redressed PROV.

pare-balles /paʀbal/ adj inv bulletproof.

pare-brise /paʀbʀiz/ nm inv windscreen GB, windshield US.

pare-chocs /paʀʃɔk/ nm inv bumper.

pare-feu /paʀfø/ nm inv (bande déboisée) firebreak.

pareil, **-eille** /paʀɛj/ **I** adj **1** (semblable) similar (**à** to); **mon frère et ma sœur sont ~s** (l'un à l'autre) my brother and sister are alike; (que moi) my brother and sister are the same; **les deux chapeaux sont presque ~s** the two hats are almost identical; **je veux une robe pareille à la tienne** I want a dress the same as yours ou just like yours; **c'est toujours ~ avec toi** it's always the same with you; **pour moi, c'est ~** it's all the same to me; **ce n'est pas ~!** it's not the same thing!; **à nul autre ~** LITER without equal; **2** (de telle nature) such; **je n'ai jamais dit une chose pareille** I never said any such thing; **je n'ai jamais rien vu de ~** I've never seen anything like it; **tu travailles encore à une heure pareille!** you're still working at this hour!; **par un temps ~** in weather like this.

II nm,f (égal) equal; **c'est un homme sans ~** he's a man without equal; **il est d'un dynamisme sans ~** he's incredibly dynamic; **il n'a pas son ~ pour semer le doute** he's second to none for spreading doubt; **pour moi c'est du ~ au même**○ it makes no odds GB ou difference to me.

III○ adv **1** (identiquement) the same; **faire ~** to do the same; **nous étions habillées ~** we were dressed the same (way); **2**° C (néanmoins) all the same; **je l'ai fait ~** I did it all the same.

pareillement /paʀɛjmɑ̃/ *adv* **1** (de la même manière) (in) the same way; **2** (également) too; **vous le pensez et moi ~** you think so and so do I ou and me too.

parent, **-e** /paʀɑ̃, ɑ̃t/ **I** *adj* [*conceptions, langues*] similar; **~ avec** [*personne*] related to.

II *nm,f* relative, relation; **~s et amis** friends and relations; **plus proche ~(e)** next of kin.

III *nm* **1** (le père ou la mère) parent; **mes ~s** my parents; **2** (ancêtres) LITER **~s** forebears.

■ **~ pauvre** poor relation; **faire figure de ~ pauvre** to look like a poor relation; **~s d'élèves** (pupils') parents; **réunion de ~s d'élèves** parents' evening.

parental, **~e**, *mpl* **-aux** /paʀɑ̃tal, o/ *adj* parental.

parenté /paʀɑ̃te/ *nf* **1** (rapport) (entre personnes) blood relationship; (entre projets, histoires) connection; **l'importance des liens de ~** the importance of family ties; **il n'y a pas de lien de ~ entre eux** they are not related; **2** (parents et alliés) relations (*pl*).

parenthèse /paʀɑ̃tɛz/ *nf* **1** (digression) **ouvrir une ~** to digress; **refermons la ~** but to come back to what we were talking about; (**soit dit**) **par ~** or **entre ~s** incidentally; **2** ▶414 (signe typographique) bracket; **mettre qch entre ~s** LIT to put sth in brackets; FIG to put sth aside; **3** (épisode) interlude.

parer /paʀe/ [1] **I** *vtr* **1** (esquiver) to ward off [*coup, attaque*]; **2** (protéger) to protect; **3** (orner) [*objet*] to adorn [*chose, personne*]; [*personne*] to adorn [*chose, personne*] (**de** with).

II parer à *vtr ind* **~ à** (prévenir) to guard against; (remédier à) to deal with; **~ à toute éventualité** to be prepared for all contingencies; **~ au plus pressé** to deal with the most urgent matters first.

III se parer *vpr* **1** (se protéger) to take precautions (**contre** against); **2** (se vêtir) to adorn oneself; **3** (être recouvert) to be bedecked (**de** with).

pare-soleil /paʀsɔlɛj/ *nm inv* AUT visor.

paresse /paʀɛs/ *nf* laziness.

paresser /paʀese/ [1] *vi* to laze; **arrête de ~!** stop lazing around!

paresseux, **-euse** /paʀesø, øz/ **I** *adj* GÉN lazy; [*organe*] sluggish.

II *nm,f* lazy person.

III *nm* ZOOL sloth.

parfaire /paʀfɛʀ/ [10] *vtr* to complete, to round off [*éducation, œuvres*]; to perfect [*connaissance*].

parfait, **-e** /paʀfɛ, ɛt/ **I** *adj* **1** (insurpassable) [*personne, beauté, travail, accord*] perfect; **elle est d'une beauté ~e** she is absolutely beautiful; **2** (total) [*ressemblance*] exact; [*imbécile*] complete; [*discrétion, égalité*] absolute; [*ignorance*] total; **3** (typique) [*estivant, touriste*] archetypal; [*exemple*] classic.

II *nm* LING perfect.

IDIOMES **filer le ~ amour** to spin out love's sweet dream.

parfaitement /paʀfɛtmɑ̃/ *adv* **1** (à la perfection) perfectly; **2** (absolument) [*savoir*] perfectly well; [*tolérer, admettre*] fully; [*heureux, capable, simple*] perfectly; [*correct, égal*] absolutely; [*faux*] totally; [*absurde, choquant*] utterly; **3** (absolument) absolutely.

parfois /paʀfwa/ *adv* sometimes.

parfum /paʀfœ̃/ *nm* **1** (pour se parfumer) perfume, scent; **2** (senteur) (de fleur, forêt) scent; (de sels de bain) fragrance; (de vin) bouquet; (de fruit) scent, (sweet) smell; **3** (goût) flavour^GB; **4** FIG **un ~ du terroir** a rural flavour^GB; **un ~ de scandale** a whiff of scandal.

IDIOMES **mettre qn au ~**° to put sb in the picture, to clue sb in°.

parfumé, **~e** /paʀfyme/ *adj* **1** [*fleur*] sweet-scented; [*thé*] flavoured^GB; [*fruit*] fragrant; [*air, chambre*] fragrant; **2** [*mouchoir*] scented; **3** [*glace*] flavoured^GB.

parfumer /paʀfyme/ [1] **I** *vtr* **1** (embaumer) **les fleurs parfument la pièce** the room is fragrant with flowers; **2** (imprégner de parfum) to put scent on [*mouchoir*]; to

put scent in [*bain*]; **3** (aromatiser) to flavour^GB (**à** with).

II se parfumer *vpr* (en général) to wear perfume; (pour l'occasion) to put perfume on.

parfumerie /paʀfymʀi/ ▶374 *nf* perfumery.

parfumeur, **-euse** /paʀfymœʀ, øz/ ▶374 *nm,f* **1** (vendeur) perfume salesman/saleswoman; **2** (fabricant) perfumer.

pari /paʀi/ *nm* **1** SPORT bet; (gageure) bet, wager; **un ~ de 500 francs** a 500-franc bet; **2** (activité) betting ¢; **3** (défi) gamble.

parier /paʀje/ [2] *vtr* **1** (faire un pari) to bet; **tu paries?** do you want to bet?; **~ qch avec qn** to bet sb sth; **2** SPORT to bet [*argent*]; **~ sur** to bet on, to back [*cheval, boxeur*]; **~ gros sur un cheval** to bet heavily on a horse, to place a large bet on a horse; **il y a fort** or **gros à ~ que** it's a safe bet that, the odds are that; **3** (compter) to bank (**sur** on); **4** (être sûr) to bet; **je parie qu'il a encore oublié** I bet he has forgotten again; **je l'aurais parié!** I knew it!

parieur, **-ieuse** /paʀjœʀ, øz/ *nm,f* (joueur) gambler; (aux courses) better US, punter° GB.

Paris /paʀi/ ▶628 *npr* Paris.

IDIOMES **avec des si, on mettrait ~ en bouteille** ≈ if wishes were horses, beggars would ride PROV.

parisien, **-ienne** /paʀizjɛ̃, ɛn/ ▶628 *adj* [*agglomération, accent, vie*] Parisian; [*bassin, banlieue, région*] Paris (*épith*).

paritaire /paʀitɛʀ/ *adj* [*commission*] joint (*épith*).

parité /paʀite/ *nf* parity; **à ~** at parity.

parjure /paʀʒyʀ/ **I** *nmf* (personne) perjurer.

II *nm* (faux serment) perjury ¢; **commettre un ~** to commit perjury.

parking /paʀkiŋ/ *nm* **1** (parc de stationnement) car park GB, parking lot US; (place de stationnement) parking space; **2** (stationnement) CONTROV parking; **~ interdit** no parking.

par-là /paʀla/ *adv* ▶ **par-ci**.

parlant, **~e** /paʀlɑ̃, ɑ̃t/ *adj* **1** (éloquent) [*attitude, geste*] eloquent, meaningful; [*comparaison*] vivid; [*preuve, chiffre, résultat, fait*] which speaks for itself (*jamais épith, après n*); [*portrait*] lifelike; **les faits sont ~s** the facts speak for themselves; **ça me paraît suffisamment ~** it looks convincing enough to me; **2** (accompagné de paroles) **le cinéma ~** the talkies° (*pl*); **un film ~** a talking picture, a talkie°; **horloge ~** speaking clock.

parlé, **~e** /paʀle/ *adj* [*langue, style*] spoken; (familier) colloquial.

Parlement /paʀləmɑ̃/ *nm* Parliament.

parlementaire /paʀləmɑ̃tɛʀ/ **I** *adj* parliamentary.

II *nmf* (membre du Parlement) Member of Parliament.

parlementer /paʀləmɑ̃te/ [1] *vi* to negotiate.

parler¹ /paʀle/ [1] **I** *vtr* **1** (savoir manier) to speak [*langue*]; **~ (l')italien** to speak Italian; **2** (discuter) **~ affaires/politique** to talk (about) business/politics; **~ littérature/cinéma** to talk (about) books/films.

II parler à *vtr ind* **~ à** (s'adresser) to talk ou speak to; (ne pas être brouillé) to be on speaking terms with; **trouver à qui ~** FIG to meet one's match; **moi qui vous parle, je n'aurais jamais cru ça**°! I'm telling you, I'd never have believed it!

III parler de *vtr ind* **1** (discuter) **~ de** to talk about; (mentionner) **~ de** to mention; **~ de tout et de rien**, **~ de choses et d'autres** to talk about this and that ou one thing and another; **toute la ville en parle** it's the talk of the town; **les journaux en ont parlé** it was in the papers; **faire ~ de soi** GÉN to get oneself talked about; (dans les médias) to make the news; **c'est d'épidémie qu'il faut ~** we're talking about an epidemic here; **on parle d'un gymnase** there's talk of a gymnasium; **on en parle** there's talk of it; **qui parle de vous expulser?** who said anything about throwing you out?; **tu parles d'une aubaine**°! talk about a bargain°!; **ta promesse/son travail, parlons-en!** some promise/work!; **n'en**

parlons plus! (ça suffit) let's drop it; (c'est oublié, pardonné) that's the end of it; **finis-le, comme ça on n'en parle plus** finish it, then it's done; **2** (traiter) [*article, film, livre*] **~ de** to be about; **3** (s'entretenir) **~ de qch/qn avec qn** to talk to sb about sth/sb; **~ de qch/qn à qn** (l'entretenir de) to talk to sb about sth/ sb, to tell sb about sth/sb; **il va ~ de toi à son chef** he'll put in a word for you with his boss; **il nous a parlé de vous** he's told us about you; **il ne m'a jamais parlé de sa famille** he's never mentioned his family to me; **on m'a beaucoup parlé de vous** I've heard a lot about you; **la lecture? parle-lui plutôt de tennis!** books? he would rather hear about tennis!

IV *vi* **1** (articuler des mots) [*enfant, perroquet, poupée*] to talk; (d'une certaine façon) to speak, to talk; **elle a parlé à 14 mois** she started to talk at 14 months; **~ vite/fort/en russe** to speak ou talk fast/loudly/in Russian; **~ du nez/avec un accent** to speak with a nasal twang/with an accent; **2** (s'exprimer) to speak; **parle, on t'écoute** come on ou speak up, we're listening; **économiquement parlant** economically speaking; **laisser ~ son cœur** to speak from the heart; **~ par gestes** to communicate by means of gestures; **les muets parlent par signes** the speech-impaired use sign language; **~ en connaissance de cause** to know what one is talking about; **bien parlé!** well said!; **une prime? tu parles**○! a bonus? you must be joking○!; **tu parles si je viens**○! (bien sûr) you bet I'm coming○!; **3** (bavarder) to talk; **~ avec qn** to talk ou speak to sb (**de** about); **~ pour ne rien dire** to talk for the sake of talking; **il s'écoute** ~ he loves the sound of his own voice; **parlons peu et parlons bien** let's get down to business; **4** (faire des aveux) to talk.

V se parler *vpr* **1** (communiquer) to talk ou speak (to each other); **2** (ne pas être brouillés) to be on speaking terms; **ils ne se parlent pas** they're not on speaking terms; **3** (être utilisé) [*langue*] to be spoken.

parler² /paʀle/ *nm* **1** (manière de s'exprimer) way of talking; (langage) speech; **2** LING dialect.

parloir /paʀlwaʀ/ *nm* (d'école, hôpital) visitors' room; (de prison) visiting room; (pour avocat) interview room; (de maison, couvent) parlour^GB; (de théâtre) green-room.

parme /paʀm/ ▶141 *adj inv, nm* mauve.

Parmentier /paʀmɑ̃tje/ *npr* **hachis ~** cottage pie, shepherd's pie.

parmi /paʀmi/ *prép* among, amongst; **demain il sera ~ nous** he'll be with us tomorrow; **le plus important ~ les écrivains de ce siècle** the most important of this century's writers; **choisir ~ huit destinations** to choose from eight destinations.

parodie /paʀɔdi/ *nf* **1** (pastiche) parody; **2** (simulacre) mockery; **une ~ de procès** a travesty of justice.

parodier /paʀɔdje/ [2] *vtr* to parody.

paroi /paʀwa/ *nf* **1** (face interne) (de tunnel) side; (de grotte) wall; (de tube, tuyau) inner surface; **2** CONSTR (cloison) wall; **3** (de montagne) **~ rocheuse** rock face; **la ~ nord** the north face; **4** ANAT, BOT wall.

paroisse /paʀwas/ *nf* parish.

paroissial, ~e, *mpl* **-iaux** /paʀwasjal, o/ *adj* parish (*épith*).

paroissien, -ienne /paʀwasjɛ̃, ɛn/ *nm,f* parishioner.

parole /paʀɔl/ *nf* **1** (faculté) speech; **perdre/retrouver la ~** to lose/to regain the power of speech, to lose/to regain one's speech; **avoir la ~ facile** to have the gift of the gab○; **avoir le don de la ~** to be a good talker; **2** (possibilité de s'exprimer) **avoir droit à la ~** to have the right to speak; **prendre la ~** to speak; **laisser la ~ à qn** to let sb speak; **temps de ~** speaking time; **et maintenant, je donne ou laisse la ~ à mon collègue** and now I hand over to my colleague; **3** (mot) word; **il n'a pas dit une ~** he didn't say a word; **~s en l'air** empty words; **une ~ blessante** a hurtful remark; **joindre le geste à la ~** to suit the action to the word; **sur ces bonnes ~s, je**

m'en vais HUM on that (philosophical) note, I'm off; **4** (assurance verbale) word; **reprendre/manquer à/ donner sa ~** to go back on/to break/to give one's word; **tenir ~** to keep one's word; **il n'a qu'une ~, c'est un homme de ~** he's a man of his word; **il n'a aucune ~** you can't trust him; **je t'ai cru sur ~** I took you at your word; **~ d'honneur!** cross my heart!, I promise!; **je te donne ma ~ d'honneur que ce n'est pas vrai** I swear it's not true; **ma ~!** (upon) my word!; **5** (sentence, aphorisme) words (*pl*); **prêcher la bonne ~** to spread the good word; **c'est ~ d'évangile** it's gospel truth, it's gospel○; **6** (texte) **~s** (de chanson) words, lyrics; (de dessin) words; **film sans ~s** silent film; **7** LING speech.

parolier, -ière /paʀɔlje, ɛʀ/ ▶374 *nm,f* (de chansons) lyric writer; (d'opéra) librettist.

paroxysme /paʀɔksism/ *nm* **1** (plus haut degré) (de plaisir) paroxysm; (de bataille) climax; (de ridicule) height; **atteindre/être à son ~** [*douleur*] to reach/to be at its height; [*conflit, combat*] to reach/to be at its climax; **au ~ de la fureur** in a frenzy of rage; **2** MÉD crisis.

parpaing /paʀpɛ̃/ *nm* **1** (en béton) breeze-block GB, cinder block US; **2** (en pierre) perpend.

Parque /paʀk/ *npr* **la ~** Fate; **les trois ~s** the three Fates.

parquer /paʀke/ [1] *vtr* **1** (mettre dans un parc) to pen [*bestiaux*]; **2** (entasser) PEJ to coop up [*personnes*]; **3** (garer) to park [*voiture*].

parquet /paʀkɛ/ *nm* **1** (plancher) parquet (floor); **poser du** or **un ~** to lay parquet; **2** JUR **le ~** ~ the prosecution; **3** (à la Bourse) **le ~** the floor.

parrain /paʀɛ̃/ *nm* **1** RELIG godfather; **être (le) ~ de qn** to be godfather to sb; **2** (de candidat, projet, d'enfant défavorisé, initiative) sponsor; (d'œuvre, de fondation) patron; (de navire) *man who ceremonially launches a ship*; **4** (d'organisation criminelle) godfather.

■ Note En anglais *godfather* n'est jamais une forme d'adresse.

parrainage /paʀɛnaʒ/ *nm* **1** (caution morale) (de candidat, projet) sponsorship, backing ₵; (de fondation) patronage; **2** (soutien financier) sponsorship; **sous le ~ de...** sponsored by...

parrainer /paʀɛne/ [1] *vtr* **1** (moralement) to be patron of; **2** (financièrement) to sponsor.

parricide /paʀisid/ **I** *nmf* (personne) parricide.
II *nm* (crime) parricide.

parsemer /paʀsəme/ [16] *vtr* **parsemez-la de persil haché** sprinkle some chopped parsley over it; **une pelouse parsemée de fleurs** a lawn dotted with flowers; **les obstacles ont parsemé sa vie** his/her life was strewn with obstacles.

part /paʀ/ **I** *nf* **1** (portion) (de tarte, gâteau) slice, portion; (de viande, riz) helping, portion; (d'héritage, de marché) share; **une ~ du gâteau** FIG a slice ou share of the cake; **avoir sa ~ de misères** to have one's (fair) share of misfortunes; **2** (élément d'un tout) proportion; **une grande ~ de qch** a high proportion ou large part of sth; **une ~ de chance** an element of chance; **il y a une grande ~ de fiction dans son récit** his/her account is highly fictional; **le hasard n'a aucune ~ là-dedans** chance has nothing to do with it; **pour une bonne ou grande ~** to a large ou great extent; **faire la ~ de qch** to take sth into account ou consideration; **faire la ~ belle à qn** to give sb the best deal; **à ~ entière** [*membre, citoyen*] full (*épith*); [*science, sujet*] in its own right; **participer aux discussions à ~ entière** to participate fully in the discussions; **3** (contribution) share; **payer sa ~** to pay one's share; **prendre ~ à** to take part in; **il m'a fait ~ de ses projets/son inquiétude** he told me about his plans/his concern; **je vous ferai ~ de mes intentions** I'll let you know my intentions; **faire ~ d'une naissance** to announce a birth; **4** (partie d'un lieu) **de toute(s) ~(s)** [*surgir, arriver*] from all sides; **de ~ et d'autre** on both sides, on either side; **de ~ en ~** [*traverser, transpercer*] right ou straight through; **5** (point de vue) **pour ma ~** for my part; **d'une ~...**, **d'autre ~...** (marquant une énumération) firstly..., secondly...; (marquant une opposition) on (the) one hand..., on the other hand, **~** (de plus) moreover; **prendre qch en bonne/mauvaise ~** to take sth in good part/take sth badly.

II à part *loc* **1** (séparément) [*ranger, classer*] separately; **mettre qch à ~** to put sth to one side; **si on met à ~ cette partie de la population** leaving aside this section of the population; **prendre qn à ~** to take sb aside ou to one side; **2** (séparé) **une salle à ~** a separate room; **faire chambre à ~** to sleep in separate rooms; **3** (différent) **être un peu à ~** [*personne*] to be out of the ordinary; **un cas/lieu à ~** a special case/place; **4** (excepté) apart from; **à ~ ça, quoi de neuf○?** apart from that, what's new?; **à ~ que** apart from the fact that; **blague à ~** joking aside.

III de la part de *loc prép* **1** (à la place de) **de la ~ de** [*agir, écrire, téléphoner*] on behalf of; **2** (venant de) **de la ~ de qn** from sb; **il y a un message de la ~ de ton père** there's a message from your father; **donne-leur le bonjour de ma ~** say hello to them for me; **ce n'est pas très gentil de ta ~** that's not very nice of you; **sans engagement de votre ~** with no obligation on your part; **de leur ~, rien ne m'étonne** nothing they do surprises me; **c'est de la ~ de qui?** (au téléphone) who's calling please?

IDIOMES **faire la ~ du feu** to cut one's losses; **faire la ~ des choses** to put things in perspective.

partage /paʀtaʒ/ *nm* **1** (découpage) dividing, sharing; **le ~ des gains se fera entre 20 personnes** the profits will be split between ou shared out among 20 people; **des problèmes de ~ familial** problems in dividing up the inheritance; **2** (distribution) distribution; **le ~ des terres n'était pas équitable** the land had not been shared out fairly; **le ~ du pain** the breaking of the bread; **3** (répartition) sharing, division; **régner/gouverner sans ~** to reign/to govern absolutely; **victoire sans ~** total victory; **le ~ des voix** POL the division of votes; **4** (séparation) division, partition; **un plan de ~ d'un territoire en deux zones** a plan to divide ou partition a territory into two zones; **5** (part) **recevoir qch en ~** to be left sth (in a will); **il a reçu la malchance en ~** FIG his lot is an unhappy one.

partagé, **~e** /paʀtaʒe/ *adj* **1** (divisé) [*avis, presse, syndicats*] divided (**sur** on); **2** (ambivalent) [*réactions, sentiments*] mixed; **3** (indécis) **être ~** [*personne*] to be torn (**entre** between); **4** (commun) [*chagrin*] shared; **leurs torts sont ~s** they are both to blame; **5** (réciproque) [*tendresse*] mutual; **amour ~/non ~** requited/unrequited love.

partager /paʀtaʒe/ [13] **I** *vtr* **1** (donner une partie de ce qui est à soi) to share [*jouets, nourriture*]; **2** (séparer) to divide [*pays, pièce*]; **3** (diviser) to divide [sth] (up), to split; **je partage mon temps entre la lecture et la musique** I divide my time between reading and music; **4** (avoir en commun) to share; (prendre part à) to share [*émotion, angoisse*]; **~ les mêmes valeurs** to have common values, to share values; **je partage votre avis** I agree with you, I'm of the same opinion; **5** (communiquer) to share [*chagrin, problème, joie*]; **faire ~ qch à qn** to let sb share in sth; **il sait nous faire ~ ses émotions** he knows how to get his feelings across; **6** (opposer) [*problème, question*] to divide, to split [*opinion publique*].

II se partager *vpr* **1** (se répartir) to share [*argent, travail, responsabilité*]; **2** (être divisé) to be divided (**en** into; **entre** between); to be split (**en** into); **le mouvement se partage en deux grandes tendances** the movement is divided ou split into two broad tendencies; **3** (se diviser) [*frais, responsabilités, nourriture*] to be shared; [*gâteau, tarte*] to be cut (up) (**en** into); **4** (se communiquer) to be shared; **un tel chagrin ne peut se ~** such grief cannot be shared.

partance /paʀtɑ̃s/ *nf* **en ~** [*avion*] about to take off; [*navire*] about to sail; [*train, personne*] about to leave; **être en ~ pour** ou **vers** [*avion, navire, train, voyageurs*] to be bound for.

partant○, **~e** /paʀtɑ̃, ɑ̃t/ *adj* (enthousiaste) **être ~ to** be game○ (**pour faire** to do).

partenaire /paʀtənɛʀ/ **I** *nmf* partner; **qui était le ~ d'Arletty?** CIN, THÉÂT who played opposite Arletty? **II** *nm* FIN, POL partner.

■ **~s sociaux ~** unions and management.

partenariat /paʀtənaʀja/ *nm* partnership.

parterre /paʀtɛʀ/ *nm* **1** (de jardin) bed; **2** THÉÂT (places) stalls (*pl*) GB, orchestra US; (spectateurs) people in the stalls GB ou orchestra US; **3** (assemblée) panel; **devant un ~ de journalistes** before a panel of journalists.

Parthe /paʀt/ *nm* Parthian; **les ~s** the Parthians.

IDIOMES **décocher la flèche du ~** to fire a Parthian ou parting shot.

parti, **~e¹** /paʀti/ **I○** *adj* (ivre) **être ~** to be tight○; **être complètement ~** to be plastered○.

II *nm* **1** (groupe de personnes) group; POL party; **le ~ des mécontents** the malcontents (*pl*); **2** (solution) option; **prendre ~** to commit oneself; **prendre ~ contre qn** to side against sb; **prendre ~ pour/ contre qch** to be for/against sth; **prendre le ~ de qn** to side with sb; **prendre le ~ de qch** to opt for sth; **il a pris le ~ de ne rien dire** he decided not to say anything; **ne pas savoir quel ~ prendre** not to know what to do for the best; **3†** (personne à marier) suitable match.

■ **~ pris** bias; **~ pris de réalisme/modernité** bias toward(s) realism/modernity.

IDIOMES **prendre son ~ de qch** to come to terms with sth; **tirer ~ de** to take advantage of [*situation*]; to turn [sth] to good account [*leçon, invention*].

partial, **~e**, *mpl* **-iaux**, o/ *adj* biased^GB.

partialité /paʀsjalite/ *nf* (de personne, jugement) bias; **~ envers qn** (au profit de) bias toward(s) sb; (au détriment de) bias against sb; **avec ~** in a biased^GB way; **accuser qn de ~** to accuse sb of being biased^GB.

participant, **~e** /paʀtisipɑ̃, ɑ̃t/ *nm,f* (à un concours, une course) participant, entrant (**à** in); (à un débat, une cérémonie) participant, person taking part (**à** in).

participation /paʀtisipasjɔ̃/ *nf* **1** (à une réunion, un projet, festival, soulèvement) participation (**à** in); (à un complot, attentat) involvement (**à** in); **la ~ de plusieurs vedettes a attiré les photographes** the presence of several stars drew the photographers; **la ~ aux élections a été faible** there was a low turnout at the polls; **2** (contribution) contribution; **~ aux frais** (financial) contribution; **3** (part financière) stake, holding; **~ de 17%** 17% stake.

■ **~ aux bénéfices** profit-sharing.

participe /paʀtisip/ *nm* participle; **~ passé** past participle.

participer /paʀtisipe/ [1] **I participer à** *vtr ind* **1** (personnellement) **à** to participate in, to take part in [*réunion, soulèvement*]; to be involved in [*crime, complot*]; **il ne participe pas assez en classe** he doesn't participate enough in class; **ce projet est immoral, je n'y participerai pas** this project is immoral, I will have no part in it; **~ à la joie de qn** to share sb's joy; **2** (financièrement) **~ à** to contribute to; **~ aux frais** to share in the cost.

II participer de *vtr ind* FML **~ de la névrose** to be akin to ou to have some of the characteristics of neurosis; **~ de l'idéologie dominante** to draw on the dominant ideology.

particularisme /paʀtikylaʀism/ *nm* distinctive identity.

particularité /paʀtikylaʀite/ *nf* **1** (caractéristique) special feature; **les ~s historiques d'un pays** a country's particular historical background (*sg*); **2** (de maladie, régime politique, situation) particular nature; (de coutume) uniqueness.

particule /paʀtikyl/ *nf* **1** GÉN, PHYS particle; **2** LING particle; **nom à ~** aristocratic name.

particulier, **-ière** /paʀtikylje, ɛʀ/ **I** *adj* **1** (propre) **l'entreprise a une façon particulière de procéder** the company has its own (particular) procedures; **il a ceci de ~ qu'il aime son indépendance** the thing with him is that he likes his independence; **2** (spécifique)

[*droits, statut, privilèges, rôle*] special; [*exemple, thème, objectif*] specific; **3** (personnel) [*voiture, secrétaire, collection*] private; **4** (inhabituel) [*cas, situation, phénomène, épisode*] unusual; [*talent, jour, effort*] special; [*mœurs*] odd; [*accent, style*] distinctive, unusual; **il a examiné ce cas avec une attention particulière** he gave this case his particular attention; **c'est quelqu'un de très ~** (admiratif) he's/she's somebody out of the ordinary; PÉJ he's/she's weird; **'quoi de neuf?'—'rien de ~'** 'what's new?'—'nothing special'.
II en particulier *loc adv* **1** (en privé) in private; **2** (séparément) individually; **3** (notamment) in particular, particularly.
III *nm* (personne) (**simple**) ~ private individual; **loger chez des ~s** to stay with a family; **vendre de ~ à ~** to sell privately.

particulièrement /paʀtikyljɛʀmɑ̃/ *adv* **1** (hautement) [*fatigué, honteux, important*] particularly; [*intelligent*] exceptionally; [*aimer, souffrir*] really; **2** (spécialement) particularly, in particular; **plus or ~** more particularly; **je ne la connais pas ~** I don't know her particularly well.

partie² /paʀti/ **I** *adj f* ▶ **parti**.
II *nf* **1** (élément d'un tout) GÉN part; (d'une somme, d'un salaire) proportion, part; **une ~ des électeurs** a proportion of the voters; **une bonne** or **grande ~ de** a good ou large number of [*personnes, objets*]; a high proportion of [*masse, ressources*]; **la majeure ~ des gens** most people (*pl*); **la majeure ~ de la population** the majority of the population; **en ~** partly, in part; **en grande ~** to a large ou great extent; **il fait ~ de la famille** he's one of the family; **faire ~ des premiers/derniers** to be among the first/last; **2** (division de l'espace) part; **dans cette ~ du monde** in this part of the world; **3** (division temporelle) part; **il a plu une ~ de la nuit** it rained for part of the night; **elle passe la majeure ~ de son temps au travail/à dormir** she spends most of her time at work/sleeping; **4** (profession) line (of work); **dans ma ~** in my line (of work); **il est de la ~** it's in his line (of work); **5** ▶ **329** JEUX, SPORT game; **une ~ de tennis** a game of tennis; **une ~ de cache-cache** a game of hide-and-seek; **une ~ de golf** a round of golf; **faire une ~** to have a game; **gagner/perdre la ~** FIG to win/to lose the day; **je fête mes trente ans, j'espère que tu seras de la ~** I'm having a thirtieth birthday party, I hope you can come; **ce n'est que ~ remise** maybe next time; **6** (dans une négociation, un contrat) party; **les ~s en présence** the parties involved; **être ~ prenante dans qch** to be actively involved in [*conflit, contrat, négociation*]; **7** JUR party; **la ~ adverse** the opposing party; **8** MUS part; **9** MATH part.
III parties○ *nfpl* privates○.
■ **~ de chasse** hunting party; **~ civile** JUR plaintiff; **se constituer** or **porter ~ civile** to take civil action; **~ de pêche** fishing trip; **~ de plaisir** fun ¢; **tu parles d'une ~ de plaisir!** that's not my idea of fun!
IDIOMES **avoir affaire à forte ~** to have a tough opponent; **prendre qn à ~** to take sb to task.

partiel, -ielle¹ /paʀsjɛl/ **I** *adj* [*paiement*] part (*épith*); [*montant, remboursement, destruction, accord, résultat*] partial; **des solutions partielles** incomplete solutions.
II *nm* UNIV exam based on a module.

partielle² /paʀsjɛl/ *nf* by-election.

partiellement /paʀsjɛlmɑ̃/ *adv* partly, partially.

partir /paʀtiʀ/ [30] **I** *vi* **1** (quitter un lieu) [*personne*] to leave, to go; **partez devant, je vous rejoins** go on ahead, I'll catch you up; **est-ce qu'ils sont partis en avion ou en train?** did they fly or did they take the train?; **j'espère que je ne vous fais pas ~?** I hope I'm not driving you away?; **~ en courant/boitant/hurlant** to run off/to limp off/to go off screaming; **~ fâché** to go off in a huff○; **~ content** to go away happy; **~ sans laisser d'adresse** (sans laisser de traces) to disappear without trace; **2** (pour une destination) to go; **il est parti en ville à bicyclette** he went

to town on his bicycle; **~ pour le Mexique/l'Australie** to leave for Mexico/Australia; **ils sont partis en Écosse en stop** (ils sont encore en voyage) they're hitchhiking to Scotland; (dans le passé) they hitchhiked to Scotland; **~ à la guerre/au front** to go off to war/to the front; **~ en tournée** to set off on tour GB ou on a tour; **~ en retraite** to retire; **3** (se mettre en mouvement) [*personne, voiture, car, train*] to leave; [*avion*] to take off; [*moteur*] to start; **je pars** I'm off, I'm leaving; **les coureurs sont partis** the runners are off; **le train à destination de Dijon va ~** the train to Dijon is about to depart ou leave; **à vos marques, prêts, partez!** on your marks, get set, go!; **4** (être projeté) [*flèche, balle*] to be fired; [*bouchon*] to shoot out; [*capsule*] to shoot off; [*réplique*] to slip out; **le coup de feu est parti** the gun went off; **elle était tellement énervée que la gifle est partie toute seule** she was so angry that she slapped him/her before she realized what she was doing ou before she could stop herself; **5** (commencer) [*chemin, route*] to start; **les branches qui partent du tronc** the branches growing out from the trunk; **les avenues qui partent de la place de l'Étoile** the avenues which radiate outwards from the Place de l'Étoile; **~ favori** [*concurrent, candidat*] to start favourite GB; **~ battu d'avance** to be doomed from the start; **~ dernier** (dans une course) to start last; **le troisième en partant de la gauche** the third (starting) from the left; **~ de rien** to start from nothing; **c'est parti!** (ordre) go!; **et voilà, c'est parti**○, **il pleut!** here we go, it's raining!; **être bien parti** [*coureur, cheval, projet, travail, personne*] to have got GB ou gotten US off to a good start; **être bien parti pour gagner** to seem all set to win; **c'est mal parti**○ things don't look too good, it doesn't look too promising; **il a l'air parti**○ **pour réussir** he seems to be heading for success; **le mauvais temps est parti**○ **pour durer** it looks as if the bad weather is here to stay; **6** (se fonder) **~ de** to start from [*idée, observation*]; **~ du principe que** to work on the assumption that; **~ d'une bonne intention** to be well-meant; **7** (s'enlever) [*tache, saleté*] to come out; [*émail, peinture*] to come off; [*odeur*] to go; [*bouton, écusson, décoration*] to come off; **faire ~ une tache** to remove a stain; **8** (être expédié) [*colis, candidature*] to be sent (off); **9** (se lancer) **quand il est parti**○ **on ne l'arrête pas** once he starts ou gets going there's no stopping him; **~ dans des explications** to launch into explanations; **10** (mourir) EUPH to go, to pass away EUPH.
II à partir de *loc prép* from; **à ~ de maintenant** from now on; **à ~ du moment où** (sens temporel) as soon as; (sens conditionnel) as long as; **à ~ de là, tout a basculé** from then on everything changed radically; **les enfants ne sont admis qu'à ~ de huit ans** children under eight are not admitted; **faire une étude à ~ de statistiques** to base a study on statistics.

partisan, ~e /paʀtizɑ̃, an/ **I** *adj* **1** PÉJ [*esprit, querelle*] partisan; **2** (en faveur de) **~ de qch/de faire** in favour GB of sth/of doing; **être ~ du moindre effort** (être paresseux) to be lazy; (dans une décision) to go for the easy option.
II *nm,f* GÉN supporter, partisan; MIL partisan.

partitif, -ive /paʀtitif, iv/ **I** *adj* partitive.
II *nm* partitive.

partition /paʀtisjɔ̃/ *nf* **1** MUS score; **2** (partage) partition.

partout /paʀtu/ *adv* **1** (en tous lieux) [*sévir, traîner, chercher*] everywhere; [*avoir mal, s'enduire*] all over; **un peu ~ dans le monde** more or less all over the world; **il y avait de la boue ~** there was mud all over the place; **~ sur ton passage** wherever you go; **~ où je vais** wherever I go; **2** (dans tous les domaines) **il est le premier ~** he's the best at everything; **3** SPORT **trois (points** or **buts) ~** three all.
IDIOMES **fourrer son nez ~**○ to stick one's nose into everything○.

parure /paʀyʀ/ *nf* **1** (toilette) finery ¢; **2** (bijoux) set of jewels; **~ de diamants** set of diamonds; **3** (ensemble assorti) set; **~ de table** set of table linen.

parution /parysjɔ̃/ *nf* (de livre, journal, revue) publication; **à sa ~, le livre a fait scandale** when it came out, the book caused a scandal; **la ~ a été reportée** the publication date has been put back.

parvenir /parvənir/ [36] **I** *vtr ind* **1** (atteindre) **~ à** to reach; **un fruit parvenu à maturité** a fruit which has reached maturity; **faire ~ qch à qn** (par voie postale) to send sth to sb; (par messager) to get sth to sb; **2** (au prix d'efforts) **~ à** to reach [*accord, solution*]; to gain [*pouvoir*]; to get [*poste*]; to achieve [*équilibre*]; **~ à faire** to manage to do; **~ à ses fins** to achieve one's ends.
II *vi* (réussir socialement) to succeed.

parvenu, ~e /parvəny/ *nm,f* PEJ upstart.

parvis /parvi/ *nm inv* (d'église) square.

pas¹ /pa/ *adv*

■ **Note** Dans la langue parlée ou familière, *not* utilisé avec un auxiliaire prend parfois la forme *n't* qui est alors accolée à l'auxiliaire: *he hasn't finished, he couldn't come.* On notera que *will not* devient *won't*, que *shall not* devient *shan't* et *cannot* devient *can't*.

1 GÉN **c'est un Autrichien, ~ un Allemand** he's an Austrian, not a German; **je ne prends ~ de sucre avec mon café** I don't take sugar in coffee; **ce n'est ~ un lâche** GÉN he isn't a coward; (pour insister) he's no coward; **ce n'est ~ une raison pour crier comme ça!** that's no reason to shout like that!; **il n'est ~ plus intelligent qu'un autre** he's no brighter than anybody else; **je ne pense ~** I don't think so, I think not SOUT; **elle a aimé le film, mais lui ~** she liked the film but he didn't; **des tomates ~ mûres** unripe tomatoes; **des chaussures ~ cirées** unpolished shoes; **une radio ~ chère**○ a cheap radio; **non mais t'es ~ dingue**◑**?** are you mad or what?; **2** (dans des expressions, exclamations) **~ du tout** not at all; **~ le moins du monde** not in the slightest ou in the least; **absolument ~** absolutely not; **~ tellement** not much; **~ tant que ça** not all that much; **~ plus que ça** not all that much; **~ d'histoires!** I don't want any arguments ou fuss!; **~ de chance!** hard luck!; **~ possible!** Let's have it!; **~ vrai**○**?** GÉN isn't that so?; (n'est-ce pas) **on a bien travaillé, ~ vrai**○**?** we did good work, didn't we?

pas² /pa/ *nm inv* **1** (enjambée) step; **faire un grand ~** to take a small step; **avancer à grands ~** to stride along; **avancer à petits ~** to edge forward; **l'hiver arrive à grands ~** winter is fast approaching; **avancer à ~ de géant (dans qch)** to make giant strides (in sth); **marcher à ~ de loup** to move stealthily; **marcher à ~ feutrés** to walk softly; **faire ses premiers ~** [*enfant*] to take one's first steps; **faire ses premiers ~ dans la société mondaine** to make one's debut in society; **faire le premier ~** FIG to make the first move; **suivre qn à ~ à ~** to follow sb everywhere; **avancer ~ à ~** to proceed step by step; **de là à dire qu'il s'en fiche,** ○ **il n'y a qu'un ~** there's only a fine line between that and saying he doesn't care; **j'habite à deux ~ (d'ici)** I live just a step away (from here); **2** (allure) pace; **d'un bon ~** at a brisk pace; **d'un ~ lourd** with a heavy tread; **d'un ~ pressé** hurriedly; **marcher du même ~** to walk in step; **ralentir le ~** to slow down; **marcher au ~** (à pied) to march; (à cheval) to walk; **marquer le ~** MIL to mark time; **rouler au ~** to crawl (along); **'roulez au ~'** (panneau) 'dead slow' GB, '(very) slow' US; **mettre qn au ~** to bring sb to heel; **partir au ~ de course** to rush off, to race off; **faire qch au ~ de charge** to do sth in double-quick time; **j'y vais de ce ~** I'm on my way now; **3** (bruit) footstep; **reconnaître le ~ de qn** to recognize sb's footstep; **4** (trace de pied) footprint; **revenir** or **retourner sur ses ~** LIT to retrace one's steps; FIG to backtrack; **marcher sur les ~ de qn** FIG to follow in sb's footsteps; **5** (de danse) step; **apprendre les ~ du tango** to learn how to tango.

■ **~ de porte** doorstep.

IDIOMES **tirer qn/se tirer d'un mauvais ~** to get sb/

to get out of a tight corner; **faire** or **sauter le ~** to take the plunge; **céder le ~ à qn** to make way for sb; **prendre le ~ sur qch/qn** to overtake sth/sb.

pascal, ~e, *mpl* **~s** or **-aux** /paskal, o/ **I** *adj* RELIG [*fêtes*] Easter (*épith*); [*cierge, agneau*] paschal.
II *nm* (mesure) pascal.

pas-de-porte /padpɔrt/ *nm inv* (somme) key money.

passable /pasabl/ *adj* **1** [*film, soirée*] fairly good; [*production*] reasonable; **2** SCOL (notation) fair.

passablement /pasabləmɑ̃/ *adv* **1** (considérablement) [*livre, énervé, flou*] rather; [*boire, s'inquiéter*] quite a lot; **2** (moyennement) [*jouer au tennis*] reasonably well.

passade /pasad/ *nf* (engouement) fad.

passage /pasaʒ/ *nm* **1** (circulation) **interdire le ~ des camions dans la ville** to ban trucks from (driving through) the town; **une rue où il y a beaucoup de ~** (véhicules) a street where there's a lot of traffic; **2** (séjour) **ton ~ dans la ville a été bref** your stay in the town was brief; **un petit ~ chez le teinturier ne lui ferait pas de mal** a visit to the dry-cleaners' wouldn't do it any harm; **après un bref ~ dans la fonction publique** after a short spell in the civil service; **3** (visite en chemin) **était-ce après le ~ du facteur?** was it after the postman had come ou been?; **manquer le ~ des cigognes** to miss the storks going over; **je peux te prendre au ~** I can pick you up on the way; **des hôtes de ~** short-stay guests; **4** (franchissement) **'~ interdit, voie privée'** 'no entry, private road'; **pour permettre le ~ de la lumière** in order to let the light in; **pour empêcher le ~ de l'air** in order to prevent draughts GB ou drafts US; **pour laisser** or **céder le ~ à l'ambulance** in order to let the ambulance go past; **on se retourne sur leur ~** people's heads turn as they go past; **notons au ~ que...** FIG let's note in passing that...; **se servir au ~** LIT (en passant) to help oneself; FIG (légalement) to take a cut (of the profits); (illégalement) to pocket some of the profits; **~ en ferry** ferry crossing; **le ~ à gué du bras de mer est possible à marée basse** the sound can be forded at low tide; **5** (à la radio, télévision, au théâtre) **leur troisième ~ à l'Olympia** the third time they've been to the Olympia; **ton ~ sur scène a été remarqué** you made a great impact on stage; **chaque ~ de votre chanson à la radio** every time your song is played on the radio; **6** (chemin emprunté) (par une personne) way; (par une chose) path; **prévoir le ~ de câbles** to plan the route of cables; **7** (à une situation nouvelle) (de qch) à qch) transition (from sth) to sth; **~ à la phase suivante** progression to the next phase; **son ~ dans la classe supérieure est compromis** he/she won't be allowed to move up into the next year GB ou grade US; **rites de ~** rites of passage; **8** (petite rue) alley; (dans un bâtiment) passageway; **9** (de roman, symphonie) passage; (de film) sequence.

■ **~ à l'acte** PSYCH acting out; **~ clouté†** = **~ pour piétons**; **~ à niveau** level crossing GB, grade crossing US; **~ obligé** prerequisite; **~ pour piétons** pedestrian crossing; **~ protégé** right of way; **~ souterrain** underground passage; (sous une rue) subway; **~ à tabac** beating; **~ à vide** GÉN bad patch; (pour un artiste) unproductive period.

passager, -ère /pasaʒe, ɛr/ **I** *adj* (de courte durée) [*situation, crise*] temporary; [*sentiment*] passing; [*averse*] brief; [*malaise*] slight, short-lived (*épith*); [*amours*] casual; **sa mauvaise humeur n'est que passagère** his/her bad mood won't last long.
II *nm,f* passenger.

■ **~ clandestin** stowaway.

passant, ~e /pasɑ̃, ɑ̃t/ **I** *adj* [*rue*] busy.
II *nm,f* passer-by; **quelques ~s** a few passers-by.
III *nm* (anneau de ceinture, de bracelet-montre) loop.

passation /pasasjɔ̃/ *nf* **~ des pouvoirs** JUR, POL transfer of power.

passe¹○ /pas/ *nm* **1** (passe-partout) master key; **2** (laissez-passer) pass.

passe² /pas/ *nf* **1** SPORT pass; **faire une ~** to pass the ball (à to); **2** (de prestidigitateur, torero) pass; **3** (situation) être dans une ~ difficile/une mauvaise ~ to be going through a difficult/a bad patch; être en ~ de faire to be (well) on the way to doing; c'est une méthode révolue ou en ~ de l'être it's an outdated method or soon will be.

passé, ~e /pɑse/ **I** adj **1** (révolu) [années, amours] past; le temps ~ the past; ~ de mode dated; il était cinq heures ~es it was past five o'clock; **2** (dernier en date) [an, semaine] last; **3** (usé par le temps) [couleur, tissu] faded.
II nm **1** (division du temps) past; dans or par le ~ in the past; **2** (de civilisation, d'individu) past; mon ~ de syndicaliste/comédien my past as a trade unionist/an actor; **3** LING past (tense); au ~ in the past tense.
III prép after; ~ la poste c'est tout droit after the post office you go straight on; ~ 8 heures il s'endort dans son fauteuil come eight o'clock he goes to sleep in his armchair; ~ la rivière vous serez libre once you've crossed the river, you'll be free.
■ ~ antérieur past anterior; ~ composé present perfect; ~ simple past historic.

passe-droit, pl ~s /pɑsdʀwɑ/ nm bénéficier d'un ~ to get preferential treatment.

passéisme /paseism/ nm PEJ attachment to the past.

passéiste /paseist/ adj PEJ [méthode] old-fashioned; [organisation, idée] backward-looking PEJ.

passementerie /pasmɑ̃tʀi/ nf trimmings (pl).

passe-montagne, pl ~s /pasmɔ̃taɲ/ nm balaclava.

passe-partout /paspaʀtu/ **I** adj inv [formule, réponse] catch-all; [vêtement] for all occasions (après n).
II nm inv (clé) master key; (scie) two-man saw.

passe-passe /paspas/ nm inv tour de ~ conjuring trick; FIG sleight of hand; faire qch par des tours de ~ juridiques to do sth by legal sleight of hand.

passe-plat, pl ~s /paspla/ nm serving hatch.

passeport /paspɔʀ/ nm LIT, FIG passport.

passer /pɑse/ [1] **I** vtr **1** (franchir) to cross [fleuve, frontière]; to go through [porte, douane]; to get over [obstacle]; ils ont fait ~ la rivière au troupeau they took the herd across the river; il m'a fait ~ la frontière he got me across the border; **2** (faire franchir) ~ qch à la douane to get sth through customs; **3** (dépasser) to go past, to pass; quand vous aurez passé le feu, tournez à droite turn right after the lights; j'ai passé l'âge I'm too old; le malade ne passera pas la nuit the patient won't last the night; **4** (mettre) ~ le doigt sur la table to run one's finger over the table-top; ~ la tête à la fenêtre to stick one's head out of the window; elle m'a passé le bras autour des épaules she put her arm around my shoulders; **5** (transmettre) to pass [objet] (à to); to pass [sth] on [consigne, maladie] (à to); (prêter)○ to lend (à qn to sb); (donner)○ to give (à qn to sb); fais ~ la nouvelle à tes amis pass the news on to your friends; ~ sa colère sur ses collègues to take one's anger out on one's colleagues; **6** (au téléphone) tu peux me ~ Chris? can you put Chris on?; attends, je te la passe hold on, here she is, I'll put her on; je vous la passe (sur un autre poste) I'm putting you through; pourriez-vous me ~ le poste 4834? could you put me through to extension 4834 please?; **7** (se présenter à) to take, to sit [examen scolaire, test]; to have [visite médicale, entretien]; faire ~ un test à qn to give sb a test; c'est moi qui fais ~ l'oral de français aux nouveaux I'm taking the new pupils for the French oral; **8** (réussir) to pass [examen, test]; **9** (dans le temps) to spend [temps] (à faire doing); nous avons passé de bons moments ensemble we've had some good times together; dépêche-toi, on ne va pas y ~ la nuit○! hurry up, or we'll be here all night!; **10** (pardonner) elle leur passe tout she lets them get away with murder; il passe tous ses caprices à sa fille he indulges his daughter's every whim; passez-moi l'expression if you'll pardon the expression; **11** (omettre) to skip [mot, page, paragraphe]; je vous passe les détails I'll spare you the details; j'en passe et des meilleures○ (après énumération) and so on and so forth, I could go on; **12** (utiliser) ~ un chiffon sur

les meubles to go over the furniture with a cloth; ~ un coup de fer sur une chemise to give a shirt a quick iron; ~ l'aspirateur dans le salon to hoover® GB ou vacuum the lounge; **13** (étendre) ~ un peu de baume sur une brûlure to dab some ointment on a burn; ~ une couche de peinture sur qch to give sth a coat of paint; **14** (soumettre) ~ qch à la flamme to hold sth over a flame; qu'est-ce qu'elle nous a passé○! she really went for us○!; **15** (à travers une grille) to filter [café]; to strain [jus, sauce]; to purée [légumes]; **16** (enfiler) to slip [sth] on [vêtement, anneau]; to slip into [robe]; ils ont essayé de me ~ la camisole they tried to put me in a straitjacket; **17** (faire jouer) to play [disque, cassette audio]; (projeter) to show [film, diapositives, cassette vidéo]; (diffuser) to place [annonce]; **18** (signer) to sign [contrat]; to enter into [accord]; to place [commande]; to pass [loi, décret]; ~ un marché○ to make a deal; **19** AUT (enclencher) ~ la troisième/la marche arrière to go into third gear/into reverse; **20** JEUX ~ son tour to pass.
II vi **1** (parcourir son chemin) [personne, animal, véhicule, ballon] to go past ou by, to pass; ~ entre to pass between; nous sommes passés près du lac we went past the lake; ~ sur un pont to go over a bridge; l'autobus vient juste de ~ the bus has just gone; le facteur n'est pas encore passé the postman hasn't come ou been yet; je suis passé à côté du monument I passed the monument; nous sommes passés près de chez toi we were near your house; ~ à pied/à bicyclette to walk/to cycle past; un avion est passé a plane flew overhead; il est passé en courant he ran past; le ballon est passé tout près des buts the ball narrowly missed the goal; **2** (se trouver, s'étendre) la route passe à côté du lac the road runs alongside the lake; ils ont fait ~ la route devant chez nous they built the road in front of our house; ligne qui passe par les centres de deux cercles line that goes through the centres GB of two circles; en faisant ~ une ligne par ces deux villes drawing a line through these two towns; **3** (faire un saut) je ne fais que ~ I've just popped in GB ou dropped by for a minute; quand je suis passé au marché when I went down to the market; il est passé déposer un dossier he came to drop off a file; ~ dans la matinée to call in the morning GB, to come over in the morning; passe nous voir plus souvent! come and see us more often!; ~ prendre qn/qch to pick sb/sth up; **4** (se rendre) to go; les contrebandiers sont passés en Espagne the smugglers have crossed into Spain; passez derrière moi follow me; il est passé devant moi (dans une queue) he pushed in front of me; ~ devant une commission to come before a committee; **5** (aller au-delà) to get through; il est passé au rouge he went through the red lights; il n'a pas attendu le feu vert pour ~ he didn't wait for the lights to turn green; il m'a fait signe de ~ he waved me on; vas-y, ça passe! go on, there's plenty of room!; laisser ~ une ambulance to let an ambulance through; le volet laisse ~ un peu de lumière the shutter lets in a chink of light; la cloison laisse ~ le bruit the partition doesn't keep the noise out; ~ par-dessus bord to fall overboard; il est passé par la fenêtre (par accident) he fell out of the window; (pour entrer) he got in through the window; il est passé sous un train he was run over by a train; ~ derrière la maison to get round GB ou around US the back of the house; **6** (transiter) ~ par [personne] LIT to pass ou go through; FIG to go through; nous sommes passés par Édimbourg we went via Edinburgh; ~ par qn pour faire qch to go through sb to do; ~ par de rudes épreuves to go through the mill; ~ par une rue to go along a street; ~ au bord de la faillite to come very close to bankruptcy; la formation par laquelle il est passé the training (that) he had; il dit tout ce qui lui passe par la tête he always says the first thing that comes into his head; je ne sais jamais ce qui te passe par la tête I never know what's going on in your head; une idée m'est passée par la tête an idea occurred to me; qu'est-ce qui lui est passé par la tête? what

was he/she thinking of?; **un sourire passa sur ses lèvres** he/she smiled briefly; **des reptiles à l'homme, en passant par le singe** from reptiles to man, including apes; **7**○ (avoir son tour) **il accuse le patron, ses collègues, bref, tout le monde y passe** he's accusing the boss, his colleagues—in other words, everyone in sight; **que ça te plaise ou non, il va falloir y ~** whether you like it or not, there's no alternative; **on ne peut pas faire autrement que d'en ~ par là** there is no other way around it; **je sais, j'en suis déjà passé par là** I know all about that, I've been there○; **8** (négliger) **je préfère ~ sur ce point** I'd rather not dwell on that point; **il est passé sur les détails** he didn't go into the details; **si l'on passe sur les frais de déplacement** if we ignore the travel expenses; **passons!** (injonction) let's hear no more about it!; **~ à côté d'une question** (involontairement) to miss the point; **laisser ~ qch** (délibérément) to overlook sth; **laisser ~ une occasion** to miss an opportunity; **laisser ~ plusieurs fautes** (par inadvertance) to let several mistakes slip through; **9** (ne pas approfondir) **notons en passant que** we should note in passing that; **soit dit en ~** incidentally; **10** (être admis, supporté) [*aliment, repas*] to go down; [*commentaires, discours, critiques*] to go down well (**auprès de** with); [*loi, candidat*] to get through; [*attitude, pensée*] to be accepted; **ce doit être le concombre qui passe mal** it must be the cucumber; **prends un peu de cognac, ça fait ~!** have a drop of brandy, it's good for the digestion; **vos critiques sont mal passées** your criticism went down badly; **ils n'ont jamais pu faire ~ leurs idées** they never managed to get their ideas accepted; **que je sois critiqué, passe encore, mais calomnié, non!** criticism is one thing, but I draw the line at slander; **avec lui, la flatterie, ça ne passe pas** flattery won't work with him; **~ au premier tour** POL to be elected in the first round; **~ dans la classe supérieure** to move up to the next year ou grade US; **(ça) passe pour cette fois**○ I'll let it go this time; **11** (se déplacer) **~ de France en Espagne** to leave France and enter Spain; **~ de la salle à manger au salon** to move from the dining room to the lounge; **~ à l'ennemi** to go over to the enemy; **~ sous contrôle de l'ONU** to be taken over by the UN; **~ sous contrôle ennemi** to fall into enemy hands; **~ de main en main** to be passed around; **~ constamment d'un sujet à l'autre** to flit from one subject to another; **~ de la théorie à la pratique** to put theory into practice; **leur nombre pourrait ~ à 700** their number could reach 700; **~ à un taux supérieur** to go up to a higher rate; **faire ~ qch de 200 à 300** to increase sth from 200 to 300; **12** (être pris) **~ pour un imbécile** to look a fool; **il passe pour l'inventeur de l'ordinateur** he's supposed to have invented computers; **il pourrait ~ pour un Américain** he could be taken for an American; **il veut ~ pour un grand homme** he wants to be seen as a great man; **faire ~ qn/qch pour exceptionnel** to make sb/sth out to be exceptional; **se faire ~ pour malade** to pretend to be ill; **se faire ~ pour mort** to fake one's own death; **il se fait ~ pour mon frère** he passes himself off as my brother; **13** (disparaître) [*douleur, événement*] to pass; **quand l'orage sera ou aura passé** LIT when the storm is over; FIG when the storm dies down; **ça passera** (sa mauvaise humeur) it'll pass; (ton chagrin) you'll get over it; **la première réaction passée** once we/they calmed down; **nous avons dû attendre que sa colère soit passée** we had to wait for his/her anger to subside; **de mode** to go out of fashion; **cette mode est vite passée** that fashion was short-lived; **faire ~ à qn l'envie de faire** to cure sb of the desire to do; **je vais leur faire ~ l'envie de tirer sur ma sonnette!** I'll teach them to ring my bell!; **ce médicament fait ~ les maux d'estomac** this medicine relieves stomach ache; **cette mauvaise habitude te passera** it's a bad habit you'll grow out of; **14** (apparaître, être projeté, diffusé) [*artiste, groupe*] (sur une scène) to be appearing; (à la télévision, radio) to be on; [*spectacle, film*] to be on; [*cassette, musique*] to be playing; **15** (être placé) **~ avant/après** (en

importance) to come before/after; **la santé passe avant tout** health comes first; **il fait ~ sa famille avant ses amis** he puts his family before his friends; **16**○ (disparaître) **où étais-tu (encore) passé?** where (on earth) did you get to?; **où est passé mon livre?** where has my book got to?; **17** (s'écouler) [*temps*] to pass, to go by; **deux ans ont passé** two years have passed; **je ne vois pas le temps ~** I don't know where the time goes; **le week-end a passé trop vite** the weekend went too quickly; **18** (se mettre à) to turn to; **passons aux choses sérieuses** let's turn to serious matters; **~ à l'étape suivante** to move on to the next stage; **passons à autre chose** let's change the subject; **nous allons ~ au vote** let's vote now; **~ à l'offensive** to take the offensive; **19** (être transmis) **~ de père en fils** to be handed down from father to son; **l'expression est passée dans la langue** the expression has become part of the language; **ça finira par ~ dans les mœurs** it'll eventually become common practice; **il a fait ~ son émotion dans la salle** he transmitted his emotion to the audience; **20** (être promu) to be promoted to; **être passé maître dans l'art de faire** to be a past master at doing; **elle est passée maître dans l'art de mentir** she's an accomplished liar; **21** (être dépensé) [*argent, somme*] to go on ou in into; [*produit, matière*] to go into; **22**○ (mourir) **y ~** to die; **si tu continues à conduire comme ça, tu vas finir par y ~** if you keep driving like that, you'll kill yourself; **on y passera tous, mais le plus tard sera le mieux** we've all got to go sometime, the later the better; **23** (se décolorer) [*teinte, tissu*] to fade; **~ au soleil** to fade in the sun; **24** (filtrer) [*café*] to filter; **faire ~ la soupe** to put the soup through a sieve; **25** (changer de vitesse) **~ en troisième/marche arrière** to go into third/reverse; **la troisième passe mal ou a du mal à ~** third gear is a bit stiff; **26** JEUX (au bridge, poker) to pass.

III se passer *vpr* **1** (se produire) to happen; **tout se passe comme si le franc avait été dévalué** it's as if the franc had been devalued; **2** (être situé) to take place; **la scène se passe au Viêt Nam** the scene is set in Vietnam; **3** (se dérouler) [*opération, examen, négociations*] to go on; **tout s'est passé très vite** it all happened very fast; **ça va mal se ~ pour toi** you're going to be in trouble; **ça ne se passera pas comme ça!** I won't leave it at that!; **4** (s'écouler) [*période*] to go by, to pass; **deux ans se sont passés depuis** that was two years ago; **attendons que ça se passe** let's wait till it's over; **nos soirées se passaient à regarder la télévision** we spent the evenings watching television; **5** (se dispenser) **se ~ de** [*personne*] to do without [*objet, activité, personne*]; to go without [*repas, nourriture, sommeil*]; **se ~ de commentaires** to speak for itself; **ne pas pouvoir se ~ de faire** not to be able to help doing; **6** (se mettre) **se ~ la langue sur les lèvres** to run one's tongue over one's lips; **se ~ la main sur le front** to put a hand to one's forehead; **7** (l'un à l'autre) **ils se sont passé des documents** they exchanged some documents; **nous nous sommes passé le virus** we caught the virus from each other.

passereau, *pl* **~x** /pasʁo/ *nm* **1** GÉN passerine; **2**† (moineau) sparrow.

passerelle /pasʁɛl/ *nf* **1** (petit pont) footbridge; **2** FIG (lien) link; **jeter une ~ entre qch et qch** to provide a link between sth and sth; **3** (pour embarquer) NAUT gangway; AVIAT (escalier) steps (*pl*); (tunnel) gangway.

passe-temps /pastɑ̃/ *nm inv* pastime, hobby.

passeur, -euse /pasœʁ, øz/ *nm,f* **1** ▶374 NAUT ferryman/ferrywoman; **2** (pour passer une frontière) smuggler; (de drogue) courier, mule○.

passible /pasibl/ *adj* JUR **~ de** [*délit*] punishable by; [*personne*] liable to.

passif, -ive /pasif, iv/ **I** *adj* **1** GÉN [*personne*] passive (**devant, face à** in the face of); **2** LING passive.

II *nm* **1** LING passive (voice); **2** FIN debit; **mettre qch au ~ de qn** FIG to count sth amongst sb's failures.

passiflore /pasiflɔʁ/ *nf* passionflower.

passion /pasjɔ̃/ *nf* passion; **avoir la ~ d'écrire** to have a passion for writing; **aimer à la** or **avec ~** to love passionately; **sans ~** (objectivement) dispassionately; (sans enthousiasme) without enthusiasm; **se prendre de ~ pour qn** to become infatuated with sb; **se prendre de ~ pour qch** to develop a passion for sth.

passionnant, **~e** /pasjɔnɑ̃, ɑ̃t/ *adj* [*voyage, métier, match*] exciting; [*personne, roman, musée*] fascinating.

passionné, **~e** /pasjɔne/ **I** *adj* [*amour*] passionate; [*débat*] impassioned; **être ~ de** to have a passion for. **II** *nm,f* enthusiast; **un ~ de tennis** a tennis enthusiast.

passionnel, **-elle** /pasjɔnɛl/ *adj* [*débat*] passionate; [*sujet*] emotive; [*crime*] of passion (*après n*).

passionnément /pasjɔnemɑ̃/ *adv* passionately.

passionner /pasjɔne/ [1] **I** *vtr* **1** (intéresser) to fascinate; **la botanique le passionne** he has a passion for botany; **2** (rendre passionné) to inflame [*débat*]. **II se passionner** *vpr* to have a passion (**pour** for).

passivité /pasivite/ *nf* passivity.

passoire /paswar/ *nf* (pour légumes) colander; (pour infusion) strainer.

pastel /pastɛl/ **I** *adj inv* [*teinte*] pastel. **II** *nm* **1** (technique, crayon) pastel; (œuvre) pastel.

pastèque /pastɛk/ *nf* watermelon.

pasteur /pastœr/ ▶ **374** *nm* **1** (protestant) minister; **2** (prêtre) priest; **3** (berger) shepherd.

pasteuriser /pastœrize/ [1] *vtr* to pasteurize.

pastiche /pastiʃ/ *nm* pastiche.

pasticher /pastiʃe/ [1] *vtr* to imitate the style of [*auteur, œuvre*]; to imitate [*style*].

pastille /pastij/ *nf* **1** (médicament) pastille, lozenge; **~ contre la toux** cough drop; **2** (petit bonbon) **~ de chocolat** chocolate drop; **~ de menthe** peppermint; **3** (de tissu, caoutchouc) patch; (de plastique) disc.

pastoral, **~e**[1], *mpl* **-aux** /pastɔral, o/ *adj* pastoral.

pastorale[2] /pastɔral/ *nf* **1** LITTÉRAT, MUS pastoral; **2** RELIG pastoralia (*pl*).

patachon° /pataʃɔ̃/ *nm* **mener une vie de ~** to live in the fast lane.

patata° /patata/ *excl* ▶ **patati**.

patate /patat/ *nf* **1**° (pomme de terre) spud°; **2**° (idiot) blockhead°, idiot. ■ **~ douce** sweet potato. IDIOMES **se débrouiller comme une ~**° to make a complete hash of things; **ça m'est resté sur la ~**° it left me feeling bitter.

patati° /patati/ *excl* **~, patata** and so on and so forth.

patatras° /patatra/ *excl* crash°!

pataud, **~e** /pato, od/ *adj* clumsy.

pataugeoire /patoʒwar/ *nf* paddling pool GB, baby pool US.

patauger /patoʒe/ [13] *vi* **1** (jouer) (dans une flaque) to splash about; (au bord de la mer) to paddle; **~ dans la boue/neige** to flounder in the mud/snow; **2** (s'embrouiller) to flounder.

pâte /pat/ **I** *nf* **1** CULIN (à tarte) pastry; (levée) dough; (à friture, crêpes) batter; **2** (substance) (**produit en**) **~ paste.** **II pâtes** *nfpl* CULIN **~s** (**alimentaires**) pasta ¢. ■ **~ d'amandes** marzipan; **~ à beignets** batter; **~ de fruit(s)** fruit paste; **~ à modeler** modelling GB clay, Plasticine®; **~ à papier** pulp; **~ à tartiner** spread. IDIOMES **mettre la main à la ~** to pitch in.

pâté /pate/ *nm* **1** CULIN pâté; **~ de campagne** farmhouse pâté GB, coarse pâté; **~ en croûte ~** pie; **2** CONSTR **~ de maisons** block (of houses); **3** (tache d'encre) blot; **4** (à la plage) sandcastle.

pâtée /pate/ *nf* **1** (nourriture) (pour un chien) food; (pour les cochons) swill; (pour la volaille) mash; **2**° (râclée, défaite) hiding; **prendre la ~** to get a hiding.

patelin, **~e** /patlɛ̃, in/ **I**† *adj* [*manières, voix*] oily. **II**° *nm* small village.

patent, **~e**[1] /patɑ̃, ɑ̃t/ *adj* FML manifest, obvious.

patente[2] /patɑ̃t/ *nf* (permis) licence GB to exercise a trade or profession.

patenté, **~e** /patɑ̃te/ *adj* **1** (agréé) [*fournisseur, transporteur*] licensed, authorized; **2**° HUM [*critique, défenseur*] established.

patère /patɛr/ *nf* peg, hook.

paternalisme /patɛrnalism/ *nm* paternalism.

paternaliste /patɛrnalist/ *adj* paternalistic.

paternel, **-elle** /patɛrnɛl/ *adj* **1** (du père) paternal; **2** (affectueux) fatherly.

paternellement /patɛrnɛlmɑ̃/ *adv* in a fatherly way.

paternité /patɛrnite/ *nf* **1** (état de père) fatherhood; JUR paternity; **recherche de ~ naturelle** paternity suit; **2** (d'œuvre) authorship.

pâteux, **-euse** /patø, øz/ *adj* **1** [*substance*] doughy; [*bouillie*] mushy; **2** [*voix*] thick; **j'ai la bouche pâteuse** my mouth feels all furry.

pathétique /patetik/ **I** *adj* (émouvant) moving. **II** *nm* pathos.

pathétiquement /patetikmɑ̃/ *adv* touchingly.

pathologie /patɔlɔʒi/ *nf* pathology.

pathologique /patɔlɔʒik/ *adj* pathological.

pathos /patos/ *nm* pathos; **faire du ~** to pile° on the pathos.

patibulaire /patibylɛr/ *adj* [*individu*] sinister-looking.

patiemment /pasjamɑ̃/ *adv* patiently.

patience /pasjɑ̃s/ *nf* **1** (qualité) patience; **avoir de la ~** to be patient; **ma ~ a des limites** there are limits to my patience; **être d'une ~ infinie** to be endlessly patient; **2** ▶ **329** JEUX patience ¢ GB, solitaire ¢ US. IDIOMES **prendre son mal en ~** to resign oneself to one's fate.

patient, **~e** /pasjɑ̃, ɑ̃t/ *adj, nm,f* patient.

patienter /pasjɑ̃te/ [1] *vi* to wait; **puis-je vous demander de ~?** would you mind waiting?

patin /patɛ̃/ *nm* **1** ▶ **329** (de patineur) skate; **2** (pour parquet) *felt pad used for walking on parquet floors*; **3** TECH (de meuble) furniture glide; (d'hélicoptère) skid; (de luge) runner. ■ **~ à glace** (chaussure) ice skate; (activité) ice-skating; **~ de frein** AUT brake block; **~ à roulettes** (chaussure) roller skate; (activité) roller-skating.

patinage /patinaʒ/ ▶ **329** *nm* (sport) skating; **~ sur glace** ice-skating. ■ **~ artistique** figure skating; **~ de vitesse** speed skating.

patine /patin/ *nf* (naturelle) patina; (artificielle) finish, sheen; **la ~ du temps** or **de l'âge** the patina of age.

patiner /patine/ [1] **I** *vtr* (artificiellement) to apply a finish to [*métal, meuble*]. **II** *vi* **1** SPORT to skate; **2** AUT [*roue*] to spin; [*embrayage*] to slip; **faire ~ l'embrayage** to slip the clutch. **III se patiner** *vpr* [*bois, statue*] to acquire a patina; **chêne patiné** oak shiny with age.

patinette /patinɛt/ *nf* (child's) scooter.

patineur, **-euse** /patinœr, øz/ *nm,f* skater.

patinoire /patinwar/ *nf* ice rink.

pâtir /patir/ [3] *vi* **~ de** to suffer as a result of.

pâtisserie /patisri/ *nf* **1** ▶ **374** (magasin) cake shop, pâtisserie; **2** (gâteau) pastry, cake; **3** (gâteaux) **la ~** pastries (*pl*), cakes (*pl*); **faire de la ~** to do some baking; **4** (secteur) confectionery.

pâtissier, **-ière** /patisje, ɛr/ ▶ **374** *nm,f* confectioner, pastry cook.

patois /patwa/ *nm inv* patois, dialect; **parler ~** to speak patois.

patraque° /patrak/ *adj* under the weather°.

pâtre /patr/ *nm* shepherd.

patriarcal, **~e**, *mpl* **-aux** /patrijarkal, o/ *adj* patriarchal.

patriarcat /patrijarka/ *nm* **1** RELIG patriarchate; **2** SOCIOL patriarchy.

patriarche /patʁijaʁʃ/ *nm* patriarch.

patricien, -ienne /patʁisjɛ̃, ɛn/ *adj, nm,f* patrician.

patrie /patʁi/ *nf* homeland, country.

patrimoine /patʁimwan/ *nm* **1** (de personne, famille) patrimony; (d'une entreprise) capital; ~ **immobilier** property holdings (*pl*); **2** (biens communs) heritage.
■ ~ **génétique** gene pool; ~ **héréditaire** genetic inheritance.

patriote /patʁijɔt/ *nmf* patriot; **en** ~ patriotically.

patriotique /patʁijɔtik/ *adj* patriotic.

patriotisme /patʁijɔtism/ *nm* patriotism.

patron, -onne /patʁɔ̃, ɔn/ **I** *nm,f* (directeur, gérant) manager, boss○; (propriétaire) owner, boss○; **être son propre** ~ to be one's own boss○.
II *nm* **1** (en couture) pattern; **2** (taille) large; **grand** ~ extra-large.
■ ~ **d'industrie** captain of industry; ~ **de pêche** skipper, master.

patronage /patʁɔnaʒ/ *nm* **1** (soutien) patronage; **2**† (centre de loisirs) ≈ youth club.

patronal, -e, *mpl* **-aux** /patʁɔnal, o/ *adj* [*organisation, représentant*] employers'; [*cotisations*] employer.

patronat /patʁɔna/ *nm* employers (*pl*).

patronne ▶ **patron**.

patronner /patʁɔne/ [1] *vtr* to sponsor.

patronnesse /patʁɔnɛs/ *adj* **dame** ~ Lady Bountiful.

patronyme /patʁɔnim/ *nm* patronymic.

patrouille /patʁuj/ *nf* patrol; **en** ~ on patrol.

patrouiller /patʁuje/ [1] *vi* to be on patrol; ~ **dans la forêt** to patrol the forest.

patte /pat/ *nf* **1** ZOOL (jambe) leg; (pied) (de mammifère avec ongles ou griffes) paw; (d'oiseau) foot; ~ **de devant** (jambe) foreleg; ~ **de derrière** (jambe) hind leg; **donner la** ~ to give its paw; **retomber sur ses** ~**s** [*chat*] to fall on its feet; FIG [*personne*] to fall on one's feet; **2**○ (jambe) leg; (pied) foot; (main) hand; **tu es toujours dans mes** ~**s** you are always getting under my feet; **marcher à quatre** ~**s** [*enfant, adulte*] to walk on all fours; [*bébé*] to crawl; **traîner la** ~ to limp; **en avoir plein les** ~**s** to be dead on one's feet○; **bas les** ~**s!** (ne me touchez pas) keep your hands to yourself!; (n'y touchez pas) hands off!; **3**○ (style) hand; **on reconnaît ta** ~ one can recognize your hand; **4** (languette) tab; (d'attache) lug; (de vêtement, bonnet) flap; (de col) tab; (de chaussure) tongue; **5** (favori) sideburn.
■ ~ **d'éléphant** (de pantalon) flares; ~ **folle**○ gammy leg GB, game leg US; ~**s de mouche** (écriture) spidery scrawl ¢; **faire des** ~**s de mouche** to write in a spidery scrawl.
IDIOMES **faire** ~ **de velours** [*chat*] to draw in its claws; [*personne*] to switch on the charm; **tomber dans les** ~**s de qn** to fall into sb's clutches; **montrer** ~ **blanche** to prove one is acceptable; **avoir un fil à la** ~ to be tied down; **se tirer dans les** ~**s** to pull dirty tricks on each other.

patte-d'oie, *pl* **pattes-d'oie** /patdwa/ *nf* **1** (ride) crow's-foot; **2** (carrefour) junction.

pâturage /pɑtyʁaʒ/ *nm* **1** (terrain) pasture; **2** (droit) pasturage.

pâture /pɑtyʁ/ *nf* (nourriture animale) feed; (terrain) pasture; **un scandale donné en** ~ **au public** FIG a scandal used to satisfy the public's baser instincts; **être jeté en** ~ FIG to be thrown to the lions.

paume /pom/ ▶ **137** *nf* palm (of the hand).

paumé○, ~**e** /pome/ **I** *adj* **1** [*personne*] (perdu) lost; (inadapté) mixed up GB, out of it○ US; **2** PEJ [*endroit*] godforsaken, jerkwater US.
II *nm,f* misfit.

paumer○ /pome/ [1] **I** *vtr, vi* to lose.
II se paumer *vpr* to get lost.

paupière /popjɛʁ/ ▶ **137** *nf* eyelid; **battre des** ~**s** to flutter one's eyelashes.

paupiette /popjɛt/ *nf* ~ **de veau** stuffed escalope of veal.

pause /poz/ *nf* **1** (dans une activité) break; ~ **publicitaire** commercial break; **2** (période calme) pause; **3** MUS rest.

pauvre /povʁ/ **I** *adj* **1** (sans ressources) poor; **2** (déficient) [*sol, alimentation, vocabulaire*] poor; [*végétation*] sparse; [*langue, style*] impoverished; **régime** ~ **en sucre** (insuffisant) diet lacking in sugar; (conseillé) low-sugar diet; **minerai** ~ **en métal** ore with a low metal content; **3** (malheureux) [*personne*] poor; [*sourire*] weak; **un** ~ **type**○ (à plaindre) a poor chap○ GB ou guy○; (incapable) a dead loss○; ~ **de moi!** poor me!
II *nmf* **le/la** ~! (à plaindre) poor man/woman!; (attendri) poor thing!; **ma** ~, **si tu m'avais vu!** well, my dear, you should have seen me!
III *nm* (indigent) **un** ~ a poor man; **les** ~**s** the poor; **plat de** ~ humble dish; ~ **d'esprit** half-wit.

pauvrement /povʁəmɑ̃/ *adv* poorly.

pauvresse† /povʁɛs/ *nf* poor wretch, pauper.

pauvreté /povʁəte/ *nf* **1** (de personne, pays) poverty; **2** (de mobilier, vêtements) shabbiness; **3** (de sol, vocabulaire, d'imagination) poverty; (de débat, programme) poor quality; (de raisonnement) thinness; ~ **de moyens** lack of means; **la** ~ **de la récolte** the poor harvest.
IDIOMES ~ **n'est pas vice** PROV poverty is no disgrace ou sin PROV.

pavage /pavaʒ/ *nm* **1** (travail) paving; **2** (revêtement) paving.

pavaner: se pavaner /pavane/ [1] *vpr* [*personne*] to strut about; [*paon*] to strut.

pavé /pave/ *nm* cobblestone; **se retrouver sur le** ~ to find oneself out on the street; **battre le** ~ to wear out one's shoe leather.
IDIOMES **lancer un** ~ **dans la mare** to set the cat among the pigeons; **sous les** ~**s, la plage** beneath the harsh reality lies a brighter tomorrow; **tenir le haut du** ~ to head the field.

paver /pave/ [1] *vtr* to lay [sth] with cobblestones.
IDIOMES **l'enfer est pavé de bonnes intentions** the road to hell is paved with good intentions.

pavillon /pavijɔ̃/ *nm* **1** (maison) (detached) house; (d'exposition) pavilion; (d'hôpital) wing; (d'hôtel etc) chalet GB, bungalow US; **2** (d'oreille) auricle; (d'instrument) bell; (de haut-parleur, phonographe) horn; **3** NAUT flag; **baisser** ~ LIT to lower the flag; FIG to admit defeat (**devant qn** to sb); **battre** ~ **russe** NAUT to fly the Russian flag.
■ ~ **de chasse** hunting lodge.

pavillonnaire /pavijɔnɛʁ/ *adj* **zone** ~ residential area; **banlieue** ~ suburb consisting of houses (*as opposed to high-rise buildings*).

pavoiser /pavwaze/ [1] **I** *vtr* to decorate [sth] with flags [*édifice, rue*].
II○ *vi* (chanter victoire) to crow PEJ.

pavot /pavo/ *nm* poppy.

payable /pɛjabl/ *adj* [*somme*] payable; ~ **à la commande** cash with order.

payant, ~e /pɛjɑ̃, ɑ̃t/ *adj* **1** (qui paie) [*personne*] paying; **2** (qu'il faut payer) [*spectacle*] not free (*jamais épith*); **l'entrée est-elle** ~**e?** is there a charge for admission?; **chaîne** ~**e** subscription channel; **3** (avantageux) [*affaire*] lucrative, profitable; [*mesures*] worthwhile; [*effort*] which pays off (*épith, après n*); **notre attente a été** ~**e** it was worth the wait.

paye /pɛj/ = **paie**.

payement /pɛjmɑ̃/ = **paiement**.

payer /peje/ [21] **I** *vtr* **1** (régler) to pay for [*achat, travail*]; to pay, to settle [*facture*]; to pay [*somme*]; ~ **le téléphone** to pay the phone bill; **il m'a fait** ~ **10 francs** he charged me 10 francs; **être payé avec un lance-pierres**○ to be paid peanuts○; **2** (s'acquitter envers) to pay [*employé*]; **être payé à ne rien faire** to be paid for doing nothing; **être trop peu payé** to be underpaid; **il est payé pour le savoir!** FIG he knows that to his cost!; **3**○ (offrir) ~ **qch à qn** to buy sb sth; **je te paie le restaurant** I'll treat you to a meal; **4**

(subir des conséquences) to pay for [*faute, imprudence*];
il a payé sa témérité de sa vie his rashness cost him
his life; **~ pour les autres** to take the rap°; **5**
(compenser) to cover; **leur réussite la paie de tous
ses sacrifices** their success makes all her sacrifices
worthwhile.

II *vi* **1** (rapporter) [*efforts, peine, sacrifice*] to pay off;
[*profession, activité*] to pay; **c'est un métier qui paie
bien** it's a job that pays well; **2**° (prêter à rire) to look
funny; **il payait dans son imitation du patron** he did
a funny imitation of the boss.

III se payer *vpr* **1** (être payable) [*service,
marchandise*] to have to be paid for; [*personne, salaire*]
to have to be paid; **2**° (à soi-même) to treat oneself to
[*voyage, dîner*]; HUM to get [*rhume, mauvaise note*]; to
get landed with [*travail, importun*]; **se ~ une cuite**
to get plastered°; **se ~ un arbre** to crash into a tree;
3 (prendre son dû) **payez-vous sur ce billet** take what
I owe you out of this note GB ou bill US.

IDIOMES **~ qn de promesses** to fob sb off with
promises; **se ~ de mots** to talk a lot of rubbish°; **se
~ d'illusions** to delude oneself; **se ~ du bon
temps**° to have a good time; **se ~ la tête** de qn
(se moquer) to take the mickey° out of sb GB, to razz°
sb US; (duper) to take sb for a ride; **il me déteste et il
est payé de retour** he hates me and the feeling's
mutual; **il a payé de sa personne** it cost him dear.

payeur, -euse /pɛjœʀ, øz/ **I** *adj* **organisme ~**
paying authority.

II *nm* (trésorier) paymaster; **mauvais ~** bad debtor.

pays /pei/ *nm* **1** (État) country; **dans mon ~** where I
come from, in my country; **2** (région) **la Bourgogne
est le ~ du bon vin** Burgundy is the home of good
wine; **fromage du ~** locally-produced cheese; **gens/
produit du ~** local people/product; **rentrer au ~**
(vu du point de départ) to go back home; (vu du point
d'arrivée) to come back home; **3** (village) village.

■ **~ d'accueil** host country; **~ de cocagne** Cockaigne.

IDIOMES **voir du ~** to do some travelling^GB.

paysage /peizaʒ/ *nm* **1** (site) landscape; (vue) scenery **C**, landscape; **~ urbain** LIT, FIG urban landscape
GB, cityscape; **les cheminées gâchent le ~** the
chimneys spoil the view; **le ~ politique** the political
scene; **2** ART (genre, tableau) landscape (painting).

■ **~ audiovisuel français**, **PAF** French radio and
TV scene.

paysager, -ère /peizaʒe, ɛʀ/ *adj* **1** (relatif à l'environnement) environmental; **2** (aménagé) [*parc*] landscaped;
[*bureau*] open-plan.

paysagiste /peizaʒist/ *nmf* **1** (peintre) landscape
artist, landscapist; **2 ▶374** (concepteur) (**jardinier**)
~ landscape gardener.

paysan, -anne /peizɑ̃, an/ **I** *adj* **1** (agricole) [*milieu*]
farming; [*revendications*] farmers'; **2** (de la campagne)
[*monde, vie*] rural; [*allure, façons*] peasant; [*soupe,
pain*] country.

II *nm,f* **▶374** **1** (cultivateur) **~** small farmer; (dans le
tiers-monde) peasant farmer; HIST peasant/peasant
woman; **2** (campagnard) PEJ peasant PÉJ.

paysannerie /peizanʀi/ *nf* small farmers (*pl*); HIST
peasantry.

Pays-Bas /peibɑ/ **▶232** *nprmpl* **les ~** The Netherlands.

PC /pese/ *nm* **1** ORDINAT (*abbr* = **personal computer**) PC; **2** (*abbr* = **poste de commandement**)
(dans la police) division; MIL CP.

pcc (*written abbr* = **pour copie conforme**) ADMIN
certified true and accurate.

PCF /peseɛf/ *nm* (*abbr* = **parti communiste
français**) French Communist Party.

PCV /peseve/ *nm* (*abbr* = **paiement contre vérification**) reverse charge call GB, collect call US; **appelle-
moi en ~** phone me and reverse the charges GB, call
me collect US.

PDG /pedeʒe/ *nm* (*abbr* = **président-directeur général**) chairman and managing director GB, chief
executive officer, CEO.

péage /peaʒ/ *nm* **1** (taxe) toll; **à ~** toll (*épith*); **2**
(lieu) tollbooth.

peau, ~x /po/ *nf* **1** ANAT skin; **avoir la ~ dure** FIG
to be thick-skinned; **n'avoir que la ~ sur les os** to
be all skin and bone; **2** (d'animal) GÉN skin; (pour faire
du cuir) hide; (fourrure) pelt; **sac en ~ de porc**
pigskin bag; **gants/veste en** or **de ~** leather gloves/
jacket; **3** (de fruit, légume) skin, peel **C**; (d'orange, de
citron, pamplemousse) peel **C**; **les oranges ont une ~
épaisse** oranges have thick peel ou a thick rind; **enlever la ~ d'un fruit** to peel a fruit; **4** (pellicule sur le
lait, la peinture) skin; **5**° (vie) **risquer sa ~** to risk
one's life; **faire la ~ à qn** to kill sb; **tenir à sa ~** to
value one's life; **vouloir la ~ de qn** to want sb dead;
changer de ~ to turn over a new leaf; **▶ vieux**.

■ **~ de banane** LIT banana skin; FIG trap; **~ de
chagrin** shagreen **C**; **rétrécir comme une ~ de
chagrin** to shrink away to nothing; **~ de chamois**
chamois leather **C**, shammy (leather) **C**; **~
d'orange** (cellulite) orange peel skin, cellulite; **~ de
tambour** MUS drumhead; **~ de vache** LIT cowhide;
FIG° nasty piece of work GB, low-life°.

IDIOMES **je n'aimerais pas être dans sa ~** I
wouldn't like to be in his/her shoes; **être bien dans
sa ~**° (dans sa tête) to feel good about oneself; (dans
son corps) to feel good; **être mal dans sa ~**° (physiquement) to feel lousy°; (gêné) to feel ill-at-ease; **avoir
qn dans la ~**° to be crazy about sb; **prendre
douze balles dans la ~**° to be shot by a firing
squad.

peaufiner /pofine/ [1] *vtr* to refine [*politique,
système*]; to put the finishing touches to [*contrat,
travail, texte*].

Peau-Rouge, *pl* **Peaux-Rouges** /poʀuʒ/ *nmf* Red
Indian.

peausserie /posʀi/ *nf* leatherwork **C**; **les ~s**
leather goods.

peccadille /pekadij/ *nf* peccadillo.

pêche /pɛʃ/ **I ▶141** *adj inv* (couleur) peach.

II *nf* **1** BOT peach; **2** (activité) fishing; **la ~ est
ouverte** the fishing season is open; **3** (poissons captu-
rés) catch; **une belle ~** a good ou fine catch; **la ~
a été bonne?** LIT did you catch anything?; **4**°
(coup) clout°; **5**° (forme) **avoir la ~** to be feeling
great.

■ **~ à la baleine** whaling; **~ à la crevette**
shrimping; **~ au lancer** casting; **~ à la ligne**
angling; **~ miraculeuse** RELIG miraculous draught
of fishes; **~ à la mouche** fly-fishing; **~ aux
moules** mussel gathering ou picking.

péché /peʃe/ *nm* sin; **les sept ~s capitaux** the
seven deadly sins; **vivre dans le ~** to live a sinful
life; **~ de jeunesse** youthful indiscretion; **ce serait
un ~ de rater** ça it would be a crime to miss that.

■ **~ mignon** (little) weakness.

pécher /peʃe/ [14] *vi* **1** RELIG to sin; **2** (ne pas être
parfait) **~ par ignorance** to err through ignorance;
~ par excès de confiance to be overconfident; **le
roman pèche sur un point** the novel has one shortcoming.

pêcher[1] /peʃe/ [1] **I** *vtr* (chercher à prendre) to go fishing for [*poissons*]; to go catching [*crabes*]; (attraper) to
catch; **~ la truite** to go fishing for trout; **où est il
allé ~ cette idée?**° where did he get that idea
from?

II *vi* to fish; **~ à la mouche** to fly-fish; **~ au vif** to
fish with live bait; **~ en haute mer** to go deep-sea
fishing; **~ à la ligne** to angle.

IDIOMES **~ en eau trouble** to fish in troubled waters.

pêcher[2] /peʃe/ *nm* BOT peach tree.

pécheresse /peʃʀɛs/ *nf* sinner.

pêcherie /pɛʃʀi/ *nf* **1** (usine) fish factory; **2** (zone de
pêche) fishing ground.

pécheur /peʃœʀ/ *nm* sinner.

pêcheur /pɛʃœʀ/ **▶374** *nm* fisherman.

■ **~ de baleines** whaler; **~ de crevettes**
shrimper; **~ à la ligne** angler; **~ de perles** pearl
diver.

pectoral, **~e**, *mpl* **-aux** /pɛktɔʀal, o/ I *adj* pectoral.
II *nm* pectoral muscle; **gonfler les pectoraux** to stick out one's chest.

pécule /pekyl/ *nm* savings (*pl*), nest egg○; **amasser un petit ~** to put a little money by.

pécuniaire /pekynjɛʀ/ *adj* financial.

pédagogie /pedagɔʒi/ *nf* **1** (science) education, pedagogy; **2** (qualité de pédagogue) teaching skills (*pl*); **il a le sens de la ~** he's a born teacher; **3** (méthode) teaching method.

pédagogique /pedagɔʒik/ *adj* [*activité, but*] educational; [*système*] education (*épith*); [*matériel, méthode*] teaching (*épith*); **formation ~** teacher training.

pédagogue /pedagɔg/ I *adj* good at explaining (*jamais épith*).
II *nmf* **1** (enseignant) teacher; **2** (spécialiste) educationalist.

pédale /pedal/ *nf* (de bicyclette, piano, frein) pedal; (de machine à coudre, tour) treadle.
IDIOMES **perdre les ~s**○ (s'affoler) to lose one's grip.

pédaler /pedale/ [1] *vi* **1** LIT to pedal; **2**○ (se dépêcher) to get a move on○.
IDIOMES **~ dans la choucroute**○ or **semoule**○ to flounder around.

pédalier /pedalje/ *nm* (de bicyclette) chain transmission; (de piano) pedals (*pl*).

pédalo® /pedalo/ *nm* pedalo GB, pedal boat.

pédant, **~e** /pedɑ̃, ɑ̃t/ I *adj* pedantic.
II *nm,f* pedant.

pédantisme /pedɑ̃tism/ *nm* pedantry.

pédérastie /pederasti/ *nf* **1** (pédophilie) pederasty; **2** (homosexualité masculine) homosexuality.

pédestre /pedɛstʀ/ *adj* **randonnée ~** ramble; **itinéraire ~** ramblers' route; **circuit ~** (signed) walk.

pédiatre /pedjatʀ/ ▶ 374 *nmf* paediatrician.

pédiatrie /pedjatʀi/ *nf* paediatrics (+ *v sg*).

pédicure /pedikyʀ/ ▶ 374 *nmf* chiropodist GB, podiatrist US.

pedigree /pedigʀe/ *nm* pedigree.

pédologue /pedɔlɔg/ ▶ 374 *nmf* pedologist.

pédoncule /pedɔ̃kyl/ *nm* peduncle.

pédophilie /pedɔfili/ *nf* paedophilia.

peeling /piliŋ/ *nm* exfoliation.

pègre /pɛgʀ/ *nf* **la ~** the underworld.

peigne /pɛɲ/ *nm* **1** (à cheveux) comb; **se donner un coup de ~** to comb one's hair; **2** (de métier à tisser) reed; (pour carder) carder.
IDIOMES **passer qch au ~ fin** to go over sth with a fine-tooth comb.

peigner /peɲe/ [1] I *vtr* **1** to comb [*cheveux*]; **bien peignés** neatly combed; **mal peignés** tousled; **2** to card [*laine*].
II **se peigner** *vpr* to comb one's hair.
IDIOMES **~ la girafe**○ to fiddle about doing nothing GB, to do busy work US.

peignoir /peɲwaʀ/ *nm* (déshabillé) dressing gown GB, robe US; (de boxeur) dressing gown; **~ de bain** bathrobe.

peinard○, **~e** /penaʀ, aʀd/ *adj* [*travail*] cushy○; [*endroit*] snug; **être ~** to take things easy; **père ~** easy-going guy; **en père ~** indolently.

peindre /pɛ̃dʀ/ [55] I *vtr* **1** (avec de la peinture) to paint; **~ qch en blanc** to paint sth white; **2** (avec des mots) to depict [*personnage, situation, époque*] (**comme** as).
II *vi* to paint.
III **se peindre** *vpr* **1** [*peintre*] to paint a self-portrait; **2** [*auteur*] to depict oneself (**comme** as); **3** (apparaître) **se ~ sur** [*gêne, joie*] to be written on.

peine /pɛn/ I *nf* **1** (chagrin) sorrow, grief; **avoir de la ~** to feel sad ou upset; **faire de la ~ à qn** [*personne*] to hurt sb; [*événement, remarque*] to upset sb; **il faisait ~ à voir** he looked a sorry sight; **cela faisait ~ à voir** it was sad to see; **2** (effort) effort, trouble; **c'est**

~ perdue it's a waste of effort; **en être pour sa ~** to waste one's time and effort; **se donner de la ~ pour faire** to go to a lot of trouble to do; **il ne s'est même pas donné la ~ de nous prévenir** he didn't even bother to tell us; **donnez-vous** or **prenez la ~ d'entrer** FML please do come in; **il n'est pas au bout de ses ~s** (dans une situation pénible) his troubles are far from over; (pour accomplir une tâche) he's still got a long way to go; **se mettre en ~ pour qn** to go out of one's way for sb; **ce n'est pas la ~ de crier** (c'est inutile) there's no point shouting; (ton critique) there's no need to shout; **est-ce vraiment la ~ que je vienne?** do I really need to come?; **ce n'est pas la ~ d'aller voir ce film** that film's not worth seeing; **c'était bien la ~!** what was the point!; **ça en valait vraiment la ~** it was really worth it; **concentrez vos efforts sur ce qui en vaut la ~** concentrate on worthwhile activities; **pour la ~** or **ta/votre ~** (en récompense) for your trouble; **3** (difficulté) difficulty; **sans ~** easily; **j'ai ~ à le croire** I find it hard to believe; **l'allemand sans ~** German without tears; **il n'est pas en ~ pour trouver du travail** he has no difficulty finding work; **il serait bien en ~ de te prêter de l'argent** he would be hard put to lend you any money; **4** (punition) GÉN punishment; JUR penalty, sentence; **'défense de fumer sous ~ d'amende'** 'no smoking, offenders will be fined'; **sous ~ de perdre de l'argent** at the risk of losing money; **pour la** or **ta ~** as punishment.
II **à peine** *loc adv* hardly, barely; **une allusion à ~ voilée** a thinly veiled allusion; **c'est à ~ si je l'ai reconnu** I hardly recognized him; **il était à ~ arrivé qu'il pensait déjà à repartir** no sooner had he arrived than he was thinking of leaving again; **'je n'étais pas au courant'—'à ~○!'** (incrédulité) 'I didn't know about it!' ou 'I don't believe it!' ou 'I don't buy that○!'
■ **~ capitale** capital punishment; **condamné à la ~ capitale** sentenced to death; **~ de cœur** heartache ¢; **il a des ~s de cœur** he's unhappy in love; **~ de mort** death penalty.

peiner /pene/ [1] I *vtr* to sadden, to upset [*personne*].
II *vi* [*personne*] to struggle; [*machine, voiture*] to labour^GB.

peintre /pɛ̃tʀ/ ▶ 374 *nm* **1** (artiste, artisan) painter; **2** FIG (auteur) portrayer.
■ **~ en bâtiment** house painter.

peinture /pɛ̃tyʀ/ *nf* **1** (matériau) paint; **'~ fraîche'** 'wet paint'; **2** (revêtement) paintwork; **3** (art, technique) painting; **~ au pistolet** spray painting; **investir dans la ~** to invest in paintings; **faire de la ~** to paint; **je ne peux pas le voir en ~**○ FIG I can't stand the sight of him; **4** (tableau) painting; **5** FIG (description) portrayal.
■ **~ à l'eau** water-based paint; **~ de genre** genre painting; **~ gestuelle** action painting; **~ à l'huile** (revêtement) oil paint; (technique) painting in oils; (tableau) oil painting; **~ murale** mural.

peinturlurer /pɛ̃tyʀlyʀe/ [1] I *vtr* to daub; **un mur peinturluré** a wall that has been daubed with paint; **des clowns peinturlurés** clowns with their faces daubed in paint.
II **se peinturlurer** *vpr* **se ~ le visage** [*acteur, clown*] to cake one's face in greasepaint; PÉJ [*femme*] to cake one's face in make-up.

péjoratif, -ive /peʒɔʀatif, iv/ *adj* pejorative.

pékin○ = **péquin**.

Pékin /pekɛ̃/ ▶ 628 *npr* Beijing, Peking.

pékinois, **~e** /pekinwa, az/ I ▶ 628 *adj* of Beijing, Pekinese.
II *nm* **1** ▶ 338 LING Pekinese; **2** ZOOL Pekinese.

PEL /peɛl/ *nm: abbr* ▶ **plan**.

pelade /pəlad/ ▶ 196 *nf* alopecia.

pelage /pəlaʒ/ *nm* coat, fur.

pelé, **~e** /pəle/ *adj* [*animal*] mangy; [*vêtement*] threadbare; [*colline*] bare.
IDIOMES **il y avait quatre** or **trois ~s et un tondu**○ there was hardly anybody.

pêle-mêle /pɛlmɛl/ I *adv* [*entasser*] higgledy-piggledy.

II *nm inv* (désordre) jumble.

peler /pəle/ [17] **I** *vtr* to peel.
II *vi* **1** [*peau, nez*] to peel; **2**○ (avoir froid) to freeze.

pèlerin /pɛlʀɛ̃/ *nm* RELIG pilgrim.

pèlerinage /pɛlʀinaʒ/ *nm* **1** (voyage) pilgrimage; **2** (lieu) place of pilgrimage.

pèlerine /pɛlʀin/ *nf* cape.

pélican /pelikɑ̃/ *nm* pelican.

pelisse /pəlis/ *nf* fur-trimmed coat, pelisse.

pelle /pɛl/ *nf* GÉN shovel; (jouet) spade; (de boulanger) peel; **à la ~** ○ FIG by the dozen.
■ **~ à gâteau** cake slice; **~ à tarte** pie server.

pelletée /pɛlte/ *nf* **1** LIT shovelful; **2**○ FIG heap.

pelleterie /pɛltʀi/ *nf* (préparation) fur dressing; (commerce) fur trade; (fourrures) furs (*pl*).

pelleteuse /pɛltøz/ *nf* mechanical digger.

pellicule /pelikyl/ **I** *nf* **1** CIN, PHOT film; **2** (de poussière) film; (de givre) thin layer.
II **pellicules** *nfpl* (dans les cheveux) dandruff ¢.

pelote /p(ə)lɔt/ *nf* **1** (de laine) ball; **2** ▶ 329 | SPORT (balle) pelota ball; (jeu) pelota.
■ **~ basque** pelota; **~ à épingles** pin cushion.

peloton /p(ə)lɔtɔ̃/ *nm* **1** (de laine) ball; **2** MIL platoon; **3** (en cyclisme) pack; **dans le ~ de tête** SPORT in the leading pack; FIG [*entreprise*] up among the leaders.
■ **~ d'exécution** firing squad.

pelotonner: se pelotonner /pəlɔtɔne/ [1] *vpr* [*personne, chat*] (de bien-être) to snuggle up; (de peur) to huddle up.

pelouse /p(ə)luz/ *nf* **1** (gazon) lawn; **'~ interdite'** 'keep off the grass'; **2** SPORT (terrain) pitch GB, field US; (de champ de courses) public enclosure.

peluche /p(ə)lyʃ/ *nf* **1** (matière) plush; **jouet en ~** cuddly toy GB, stuffed animal US; **2** (sur un lainage) fluff.

pelucher /p(ə)lyʃe/ [1] *vi* [*lainage*] to become fluffy.

pelucheux, -euse /p(ə)lyʃø, øz/ *adj* fluffy.

pelure /p(ə)lyʀ/ *nf* **1** (de légume, fruit) peel ¢, piece of peel; (d'oignon) skin; **2**○ (manteau) coat.
■ **~ d'oignon** *adj inv* (couleur) pale rosé; *nm* (vin) rosé (wine).

pelvis /pɛlvis/ *nm inv* pelvis.

pénal, ~e, *mpl* **-aux** /penal, o/ **I** *adj* criminal.
II *nm* (juridiction) criminal courts (*pl*).

pénalisation /penalizasjɔ̃/ *nf* **1** SPORT (pénalité) penalty; (action) penalizing ¢; **2** (sanction) ~ **(fiscale)** taxation.

pénaliser /penalize/ [1] *vtr* to penalize.

pénalité /penalite/ *nf* **1** FIN, JUR (sanction) penalty; **2** SPORT penalty; **réussir une ~** (en rugby) to score a penalty goal.

penalty /penalti/ *nm* penalty; **siffler un ~** to award a penalty.

pénard, ~e = **peinard**.

pénates○ /penat/ *nmpl* (domicile) HUM home (*sg*).

penaud, ~e /pəno, od/ *adj* [*personne, air*] sheepish.

penchant /pɑ̃ʃɑ̃/ *nm* **1** (inclination) fondness; (faible) weakness; **2** (disposition) tendency, inclination; **donner libre cours à ses mauvais ~s** to give way to one's baser instincts.

penché, ~e /pɑ̃ʃe/ *adj* [*arbre, tour*] leaning; [*écriture*] slanting; **être ~** [*personne*] to be bent over; [*mur, arbre*] to be leaning.

pencher /pɑ̃ʃe/ [1] **I** *vtr* to tilt [*meuble*]; to tip [sth] up [*bouteille*]; **~ la tête en avant** to bend one's head forward(s); **~ la tête en arrière/sur le côté** to tilt one's head back/to one side.
II *vi* **1** (être incliné) [*tour, arbre, mur*] to lean; [*bateau*] to list; [*tableau*] to slant, to tilt; **2** (préférer) **~ pour** to incline toward(s) [*opinion, théorie*]; to be in favour GB of [*solution, fermeté*].
III **se pencher** *vpr* **1** (s'incliner) [*personne*] to lean; (se baisser) to bend down; **se ~ à la fenêtre** to lean out of the window; **se ~ sur qn/qch** to bend over sb/

sth; **2** (analyser) **se ~ sur** to look into [*problème, passé*].

pendable /pɑ̃dabl/ *adj* **c'est un cas ~** it's deplorable.
IDIOMES **jouer un tour ~ à qn** to play a rotten trick on sb.

pendaison /pɑ̃dɛzɔ̃/ *nf* hanging.
■ **~ de crémaillère** house-warming (party).

pendant¹ /pɑ̃dɑ̃/ **I** *prép* for; **je t'ai attendu ~ des heures** I waited for you for hours; **~ combien de temps avez-vous vécu à Versailles?** how long did you live in Versailles?; **avant la guerre et ~** before and during the war; **~ tout le trajet** throughout the journey; **~ ce temps(-là)** meanwhile.
II **pendant que** *loc conj* while; **voyage ~ qu'il est temps** travel while you have the chance; **~ que tu y es** while you're at it.

pendant², ~e /pɑ̃dɑ̃, ɑ̃t/ **I** *adj* **1** (qui pend) **être assis les jambes ~es** to be sitting with one's legs dangling; **l'oreille ~e** with one ear drooping; **le chien avait la langue ~e** the dog's tongue was hanging out; **2** (en instance) [*cas, procès*] pending; [*question*] outstanding.
II *nm* **1** (bijou) **~ (d'oreille)** drop earring; **2** (équivalent) **le ~ d'un vase** the matching vase.

pendeloque /pɑ̃dlɔk/ *nf* (de bijou) pendant, drop (*on earring*).

pendentif /pɑ̃dɑ̃tif/ *nm* (bijou) pendant; ARCHIT pendentive.

penderie /pɑ̃dʀi/ *nf* (meuble) wardrobe; (local) walk-in cupboard GB ou closet US.

Pendjab /pɛndʒab/ ▶ 509 | *nprm* Punjab.

pendouiller○ /pɑ̃duje/ [1] *vi* to dangle down.

pendre /pɑ̃dʀ/ [6] **I** *vtr* **1** (exécuter) to hang [*condamné*]; **~ qn haut et court** to hang sb; **va te faire ~** ○! go to hell○!; **je veux bien être pendu**○ **s'il rembourse ses dettes** if he pays off his debts I'll eat my hat; **2** (accrocher) to hang [*tableau, rideau*]; to hang up [*vêtement, clé*].
II *vi* **1** (être suspendu) [*objet, vêtement*] to hang (à from); [*jambe, bras*] to dangle; **2** (être tombant) [*lambeaux, mèche*] to hang down; [*joue, sein*] to sag; [*pan de jupe*] to droop.
III **se pendre** *vpr* **1** (se tuer) to hang oneself; **2** (s'accrocher) **se ~ à** to hang from [*branche*]; **se ~ au cou de qn** to throw one's arms around sb's neck.
IDIOMES **ça te pend au (bout du) nez**○ you've got it coming to you.

pendu, ~e /pɑ̃dy/ **I** *pp* ▶ **pendre**.
II *pp adj* **1** (mort) [*personne*] hanged; **2** (accroché) [*objet*] hung (à on), hanging (à from); **~ à son micro** FIG clutching the microphone; **~ au bras de sa femme** clinging to his wife's arm; **être ~ aux lèvres de qn** to hang on sb's every word; **être toujours ~ au téléphone** to spend all one's time on the telephone.
III *nm,f* hanged man/woman.
IV ▶ 329 | *nm* JEUX **jouer au ~** to play hangman.
IDIOMES **parler de corde dans la maison d'un ~** to make a tactless remark.

pendulaire /pɑ̃dylɛʀ/ *adj* [*mouvement*] pendular.

pendule¹ /pɑ̃dyl/ *nm* pendulum.

pendule² /pɑ̃dyl/ *nf* (horloge) clock.
IDIOMES **remettre les ~s à l'heure** to set the record straight.

pendulette /pɑ̃dylɛt/ *nf* small clock.

pêne /pɛn/ *nm* bolt.

pénétrant, ~e /penetʀɑ̃, ɑ̃t/ *adj* [*vent*] penetrating; [*pluie*] drenching; [*froid*] piercing; [*humidité*] pervasive; [*remarque*] shrewd; [*esprit, regard*] penetrating.

pénétration /penetʀasjɔ̃/ *nf* LIT, FIG penetration; (des eaux) seepage.

pénétré, ~e /penetʀe/ *adj* [*air, ton*] earnest, intense; **être ~ de** to be imbued with [*sentiment*]; **être ~ de son importance** to be full of one's own importance.

pénétrer /penetʀe/ [14] **I** *vtr* **1** (s'infiltrer dans) [*pluie*] to soak ou seep into [*terre*]; [*soleil*] to penetrate [*feuil-*

lage]; **le froid m'a pénétré jusqu'aux os** the cold went right through me; **2** (percer à jour) to fathom [*secret, pensée*]; **3** (sexuellement) to penetrate; **4** (atteindre) [*idée, mode*] to reach [*milieu*]; **5** (remplir) **~ qn d'admiration** to fill sb with admiration.

II *vi* **1** (entrer) **~ dans** or **à l'intérieur de** [*personne, animal*] to enter, to get into [*lieu*]; [*balle*] to penetrate [*organe*]; [*armée*] [*personne*] to penetrate [*cercle, organisation*] ; **~ dans une maison par effraction** to break into a house; **l'auteur nous fait ~ dans l'univers des sociétés secrètes** the author takes us into the world of secret societies; **2** (s'infiltrer) **~ dans** to get into; **3** (s'imprégner) **~ dans** to penetrate; **faire ~ la pommade** to rub the ointment in.

III se pénétrer *vpr* **se ~ d'une idée** to get an idea firmly rooted in one's mind.

pénible /penibl/ *adj* [*effort, impression*] painful; [*travail*] hard; [*voyage*] difficult; [*personne*] tiresome; **c'est un enfant ~** he's a difficult child; **c'est ~!** it's such a pain○!

péniblement /peniblǝmɑ̃/ *adv* **1** (tout juste) [*atteindre*] barely; **2** (avec peine) with difficulty.

péniche /peniʃ/ **I** *nf* barge.
II○ **péniches** *nfpl* (chaussures) clodhoppers○, shoes.

pénicilline /penisilin/ *nf* penicillin.

péninsulaire /penɛ̃sylɛʀ/ *adj* peninsular.

péninsule /penɛ̃syl/ *nf* peninsula.

pénis /penis/ **▶ 137**| *nm inv* penis.

pénitence /penitɑ̃s/ *nf* **1** RELIG (peine) penance; **2** (punition) punishment.

pénitencier /penitɑ̃sje/ *nm* prison, penitentiary US.

pénitent, ~e /penitɑ̃, ɑ̃t/ *adj, nm,f* penitent.

pénitentiaire /penitɑ̃sjɛʀ/ *adj* [*établissement*] penal; [*régime*] prison (*épith*).

penne /pɛn/ *nf* **1** (d'oiseau) quill, penna SPÉC; **2** (de flèche) feather.

pénombre /penɔ̃bʀ/ *nf* (obscurité) half-light.

pensable /pɑ̃sabl/ *adj*; **ce n'est pas ~** it's unthinkable.

pensant, ~e /pɑ̃sɑ̃, ɑ̃t/ *adj* thinking.

pense-bête, *pl* **pense-bêtes** /pɑ̃sbɛt/ *nm* reminder.

pensée /pɑ̃se/ *nf* **1** GÉN, PHILOS thought; **être perdu dans ses ~s** to be lost in thought; **j'aimerais connaître le fond de ta ~** I'd like to know what you really think deep down; **dire sa ~** to speak one's mind; **j'ai eu une ~ émue pour mes grands-parents** I thought fondly of my grandparents; **2** (esprit) mind; **en ~, par la ~** [*se représenter, voir*] in one's mind; **nous serons avec vous par la ~** we'll be with you in spirit; **3** (manière de penser) thinking; **~ claire** clear thinking; **4** (fleur) pansy.

penser /pɑ̃se/ [1] **I** *vtr* **1** (avoir une opinion) to think (de of, about); **~ du bien/du mal de qn/qch** to think well/badly ou ill of sb/sth; **je n'en pense rien** I have no opinion about it; **qu'est-ce que tu penserais d'un week-end en Normandie?** what would you say to a weekend in Normandy?; **il ne disait rien mais n'en pensait pas moins** he said nothing but it didn't mean that he agreed; **2** (croire) to think; **c'est bien ce que je pensais!** I thought as much!; **je te le dis comme je le pense** I'm telling you (just) what I think; **elle ne pense pas un mot de ce qu'elle dit** she doesn't believe a word of what she's saying; **tu penses vraiment ce que tu dis?** do you really mean what you're saying?; **tout laisse** ou **porte à ~ que** there's every indication that; **je pense bien!** you bet○!, for sure!; **vous pensez si j'étais content!** you can imagine how pleased I was!; **'il s'est excusé?'—'penses-tu!'** 'did he apologize?'—'you must be joking!' ou 'some hope!'; **pensez donc!** just imagine!; **3** (se rappeler) **pense que ça ne sera pas facile** remember that it won't be easy; **ça me fait ~ qu'il faut que je lui écrive** that reminds me that I must write to him/her; **4** (avoir l'intention de) **~ faire** to be thinking of doing, to intend to do; **5** (concevoir)

to think [sth] up [*dispositif, projet*]; **c'est bien pensé!** it's well thought out!

II penser à *vtr ind* **1** (songer) **~ à** to think of ou about [*personne, endroit*]; (réfléchir à) **~ à** to think about [*problème, proposition*]; **dire qch sans y ~** to say sth without thinking; **c'est simple, il fallait y ~** or **il suffisait d'y ~** it's simple, it just required some thinking; **regardez le pendule et ne pensez plus à rien** look at the pendulum and empty your mind; **sans ~ à mal** without meaning any harm; **tu n'y penses pas! c'est trop dangereux!** you can't be serious! it's too dangerous!; **n'y pensons plus!** let's forget about it!; **il a reçu le ballon où je pense**○ the ball hit him you know where○ or **il ne pense qu'à ça**○! he's got a one-track mind!; **2** (se souvenir) **~ à** to remember; **pense à ton rendez-vous** remember your appointment; **mais j'y pense, c'est ton anniversaire aujourd'hui!** now I come to think of it, it's your birthday today!; **il me fait ~ à mon père** he reminds me of my father; **3** (envisager) **~ à faire** to be thinking of doing.

III *vi* to think; **façon de ~** way of thinking; **je lui ai dit ma façon de ~!** I gave him/her a piece of my mind!; **je pense comme vous** I agree with you.

penseur /pɑ̃sœʀ/ *nm* thinker.

pensif, -ive /pɑ̃sif, iv/ *adj* pensive, thoughtful.

pension /pɑ̃sjɔ̃/ *nf* **1** (rente) pension; **2** (hôtel) boarding house; (séjour) board; **frais de ~** accommodation charges; **prendre qn en ~** to take sb as a lodger; **3** SCOL (école) boarding school; (frais) boarding fees (*pl*).
■ **~ alimentaire** alimony; **~ complète** full board; **~ de famille** family hotel; **~ de retraite** old-age pension.

pensionnaire /pɑ̃sjɔnɛʀ/ *nmf* **1** (résident) (d'hôtel) resident; (de prison) inmate; **2** SCOL boarder; **3** THÉÂT resident member.

pensionnat /pɑ̃sjɔna/ *nm* boarding school.

pensionné, ~e /pɑ̃sjɔne/ **I** *adj* pensioned-off.
II *nm,f* pensioner.

pensivement /pɑ̃sivmɑ̃/ *adv* pensively.

pensum† /pɛ̃sɔm/ *nm* (punition) imposition GB, punishment; (tâche pénible) chore; (ouvrage ennuyeux) laborious book.

pentagone /pɛ̃tagon/ *nm* pentagon.

pentathlon /pɛ̃tatlɔ̃/ *nm* pentathlon.

pente /pɑ̃t/ *nf* **1** (déclivité) slope; **une ~ de 10%** a gradient of 1 in 10 GB, a 10% gradient US; **toit en ~** sloping roof; **jardin en ~** garden on a slope; **descendre** or **aller en ~ douce** to slope gently down; **2** MATH gradient; **3** FIG (direction) direction; (tendance) trend.
IDIOMES **avoir la dalle** or **le gosier en ~**○ to drink like a fish○; **être sur la mauvaise ~, être sur une ~ savonneuse** [*délinquant*] to be on the slippery slope GB, to be going astray; [*entreprise*] to be going downhill; **remonter la ~** to get back on one's feet.

Pentecôte /pɑ̃tkot/ *nf* (événement) Pentecost; (période) Whitsun; **à la ~** at Whitsun; **lundi de ~** Whit Monday.

pentu, ~e /pɑ̃ty/ *adj* [*toit*] pitched (*épith*), sloping; [*chemin*] steep.

pénultième /penyltjɛm/ *nf* penultimate (syllable).

pénurie /penyʀi/ *nf* shortage.

pépé○ /pepe/ *nm* **1** (grand-père) grandpa○; **2** (vieil homme) old man.

pépère○ /pepɛʀ/ **I** *adj* [*vie*] cushy○; [*endroit*] nice.
II *nm* **1** (grand-père) granddad○, grandpa○; **2** (vieillard) granddad○, old man; **3** FIG (homme) PEJ fatty○ PEJ; (bébé) chubby little chap.

pépier /pepje/ [2] *vi* to chirp.

pépin /pepɛ̃/ *nm* **1** BOT pip; **sans ~s** seedless; **2**○ (ennui) slight problem; **3**○ (parapluie) brolly○ GB, umbrella.

pépinière /pepinjɛʀ/ *nf* **1** LIT nursery; **2** FIG breeding-ground.

pépiniériste /pepinjɛʀist/ ▶374❘ *nmf* nurseryman/ nurserywoman.

pépite /pepit/ *nf* (d'or) nugget.
■ ~**s de chocolat** chocolate chips.

péplum /peplɔm/ *nm* **1** (tunique) peplos; **2**° CIN historical epic.

péquenaud°, ~**e** /pɛkno, od/ *nm,f* PEJ country bumpkin°.

péquenot° /pɛkno/ *nm* PEJ country bumpkin°.

péquin° /pekɛ̃/ *nm* **1** soldiers' slang civvy°; **2** (individu) fellow°.

percale /pɛʀkal/ *nf* percale.

perçant, ~**e** /pɛʀsɑ̃, ɑ̃t/ *adj* **1** [*cri, voix*] shrill; [*regard*] piercing; **2** [*vue*] sharp.

percée /pɛʀse/ *nf* **1** LIT opening; **2** FIG, MIL breakthrough; **3** SPORT (au rugby) break.

percement /pɛʀsəmɑ̃/ *nm* (de tunnel) boring; (de route) (ouverture) cutting; (construction) building.

perce-neige /pɛʀsənɛʒ/ *nm* or *f inv* snowdrop.

perce-oreille, *pl* ~**s** /pɛʀsoʀɛj/ *nm* earwig.

percepteur /pɛʀsɛptœʀ/ ▶374❘ *nm* tax inspector.

perceptible /pɛʀsɛptibl/ *adj* **1** [*son*] perceptible; **2** [*impôt*] payable.

perception /pɛʀsɛpsjɔ̃/ *nf* **1** (bureau) tax office; **2** (d'impôt) collection; **3** PSYCH perception.

percer /pɛʀse/ [12] **1** *vtr* **1** (transpercer) to pierce [*corps, surface*]; (crever) to burst [*abcès, tympan*]; **cela me perce le cœur** it breaks my heart; **2** (faire un trou dans) ~ **un trou dans** GÉN to make a hole in; (avec une perceuse) to drill a hole through; (avec une pointe fine) to pierce a hole in; ~ **un coffre-fort** to break open a safe; **avoir des souliers percés** to have holes in one's shoes; **3** (créer) to make [*fenêtre, porte*]; to build [*route, tunnel*]; **4** (traverser) to pierce [*silence, air*]; to break through [*nuages*]; ~ **le front ennemi** to break through the enemy front lines; **5** (découvrir) to penetrate [*secret*]; to uncover [*complot*]; ~ **qn à jour** to see through sb; **6** ~ **ses dents** to be teething; ~ **une dent** to cut a tooth.
II *vi* **1** (apparaître) [*soleil*] to break through; [*plante*] to come up; [*dent*] to come through; **2** MIL, SPORT to break through; **3** (se révéler) [*inquiétude*] to show; **4** (réussir) [*acteur, écrivain*] to become known.

perceuse /pɛʀsøz/ *nf* drill.

percevable /pɛʀsəvabl/ *adj* [*impôt*] payable.

percevoir /pɛʀsəvwaʀ/ [5] *vtr* **1** (encaisser) to collect [*impôt*]; to receive [*pension, loyer*]; **2** (sentir) to perceive [*odeur, bruit*]; to experience [*sensation*]; to feel [*vibration*]; to appreciate [*signification*]; to perceive [*changement*]; **être perçu comme** to be seen as; **être bien/mal perçu** to be well/badly received.

perche /pɛʀʃ/ *nf* **1** (tige) GÉN pole; (de téléski) T-bar; (pour micro) (microphone) boom; **2**° (personne) (**grande**) ~ beanpole°; **3** ▶329❘ SPORT (activité) polevaulting; **4** (poisson) perch.
IDIOMES **tendre la ~ à qn** to throw sb a line.

perché, ~**e** /pɛʀʃe/ *adj* perched; **voix haut ~e** high-pitched voice; ~ **sur des échasses** standing on stilts; **ma valise est ~e en haut de l'armoire** my suitcase is on top of the wardrobe.

percher /pɛʀʃe/ [1] **I** *vtr* ~ **qch sur une étagère** to stick sth up on a shelf.
II *vi* **1** [*oiseau*] (se poser) to perch; (pour la nuit) to roost; **2**° [*personne*] (loger) to live; (passer la nuit) to crash°.
III se percher *vpr* to perch.

perchiste /pɛʀʃist/ ▶374❘ *nmf* **1** (sauteur) polevaulter; **2** CIN, RADIO, TV boom operator.

perchoir /pɛʀʃwaʀ/ *nm* **1** LIT, FIG perch; **2**° POL Speaker's Chair.

perclus, ~**e** /pɛʀkly, yz/ *adj* crippled; FIG paralysed.

percolateur /pɛʀkɔlatœʀ/ *nm* (espresso) coffee machine.

percussion /pɛʀkysjɔ̃/ *nf* MUS ~**s** (instruments) percussion instruments; (dans un orchestre) percussion section (*sg*); (tambours) drums.

percussionniste /pɛʀkysjɔnist/ *nmf* ▶374❘ percussionist.

percutant, ~**e** /pɛʀkytɑ̃, ɑ̃t/ *adj* **1** FIG [*critique*] hard-hitting; [*style*] trenchant; [*démonstration*] striking; [*personne*] forceful; [*slogan*] punchy°; **2** MUS [*son*] percussive.

percuter /pɛʀkyte/ [1] **I** *vtr* [*voiture, chauffeur*] to hit.
II *vi* ~ **contre** [*véhicule*] to crash into; [*obus*] to explode against.
III se percuter *vpr* [*véhicules*] to collide.

perdant, ~**e** /pɛʀdɑ̃, ɑ̃t/ **I** *adj* [*numéro*] losing (*épith*); **être** ~ (désavantagé) to have lost out; (ne pas gagner) to have lost; **partir** ~ (désavantagé) to be at a disadvantage from the word go; (défaitiste) to have a defeatist attitude from the word go.
II *nm,f* loser.

perdition /pɛʀdisjɔ̃/ *nf* **lieu de ~** den of iniquity; **en** ~ [*pays, entreprise*] in trouble (*après n*); [*navire*] in distress (*après n*).

perdre /pɛʀdʀ/ [6] **I** *vtr* **1** GÉN to lose; ~ **qch/qn de vue** LIT, FIG to lose sight of sth/sb; **il a perdu de son arrogance** he's become more humble; ~ **de l'importance** to become less important; **leurs actions ont perdu 9%** their shares have dropped 9%; **sans** ~ **le sourire, elle a continué** still smiling, she went on; **2** to shed [*feuilles, fleurs*]; **ton chien perd ses poils** your dog is moulting GB ou molting US; **la brosse perd ses poils** the brush is losing its bristles; **3** (manquer) to miss [*chance*]; **tu n'as rien perdu (en ne venant pas)** you didn't miss anything (by not coming); **ne pas** ~ **un mot de ce que qn dit** to hang on sb's every word; **4** (gaspiller) to waste [*journée, années*]; **perdre son temps** to waste one's time; **tu as de l'argent à ~!** you've got money to burn!; **elle a du temps à ~** she's got nothing better to do; **sans** ~ **un instant** immediately; **5** (mal retenir) **je perds mes chaussures** my shoes are too big; **je perds mon pantalon** my trousers are falling down; **6** (ruiner) to bring [sb] down; **cet homme te perdra** that man will be your undoing.
II *vi* **1** (être perdant) to lose; **j'y perds** I lose out; **2** (diminuer) ~ **en gentillesse** to be less kind.
III se perdre *vpr* **1** (s'égarer) to get lost; **2** (s'embrouiller) to get mixed up; **ne vous perdez pas dans des détails** don't get bogged down in details; **3** (être absorbé) **se** ~ **dans ses pensées** to be lost in thought; **4** (disparaître) (cesser d'être vu) to disappear; (cesser d'être entendu) to fade; **5** [*aliment, récolte*] to go to waste; **il y a des claques qui se perdent**°❘ somebody's looking for a good smack!; **6** [*tradition*] to die out.
IDIOMES ~ **la tête** or **la raison** or **l'esprit** (devenir fou) to go out of one's mind; (paniquer) to lose one's head.

perdreau, *pl* ~**x** /pɛʀdʀo/ *nm* **1** ZOOL young partridge; **2** CULIN partridge.

perdrix /pɛʀdʀi/ *nf inv* partridge.

perdu, ~**e** /pɛʀdy/ **I** *pp* ▶ **perdre**.
II *pp adj* **1** GÉN lost; **chien** ~ stray dog; **balle** ~**e** stray bullet; **tout est** ~ it's all over; **c'est** ~ **d'avance** it's hopeless; **2** [*journée, occasion*] wasted; **c'est du temps** ~ it's a waste of time; **à tes moments** ~**s** in your spare time; **3** [*récolte*] ruined; [*aliment*] spoiled; **il est** ~ (condamné) there's no hope for him; **le regard** ~ **dans le vide** staring into space.
III *adj* **1** (isolé) remote, isolated; **vivre dans un coin** ~ to live in a godforsaken spot; **salle** ~**e au bout d'un couloir** room tucked away at the end of a corridor; **2** (non réutilisable) disposable; (non consigné) non returnable.
IDIOMES **se lancer à corps** ~ **dans** to throw oneself headlong into; **ce n'est pas** ~ **pour tout le monde** somebody will do all right out of it; **crier/courir comme un** ~ to shout/to run like a madman.

perdurer /pɛʀdyʀe/ [1] *vi* LITER [*situation, conflit*] to continue; [*sentiment, phénomène*] to endure.

père /pɛʀ/ **I** *nm* **1** LIT, FIG, RELIG father; **ils sont**

banquiers de ~ en fils they have been bankers for generations; **Dupont ~** Dupont senior; **le ~**○ **Dupont** old○ Dupont; **2** (d'animal) GÉN male parent; (de chien, cheval) sire.

II pères *nmpl* (ancêtres) forefathers.

■ **~ abbé** abbot; **~ de famille** father; **être ~ de famille** to have a family to look after; **en bon ~ de famille** as a responsible person; **le ~ Noël** Santa Claus; **~ tranquille** mild-mannered fellow.

pérégrinations /peʀegʀinasjɔ̃/ *nfpl* travels, peregrinations SOUT.

péremps /peʀɑ̃psjɔ̃/ *nf* **date de ~** use-by date.

péremptoire /peʀɑ̃ptwaʀ/ *adj* peremptory.

pérennité /peʀenite/ *nf* LITER permanence.

péréquation /peʀekwasjɔ̃/ *nf* adjustment.

perfectif, -ive /pɛʀfɛktif, iv/ *adj* LING perfective.

perfection /pɛʀfɛksjɔ̃/ *nf* perfection.

perfectionné, ~e /pɛʀfɛksjɔne/ *adj* advanced.

perfectionnement /pɛʀfɛksjɔnmɑ̃/ *nm* improvement.

perfectionner /pɛʀfɛksjɔne/ [1] **I** *vtr* to perfect [*technique, machine*]; to refine [*art*].

II se perfectionner *vtr* [*technique, outils*] to improve; **se ~ en allemand** to improve one's German.

perfectionniste /pɛʀfɛksjɔnist/ *adj, nmf* perfectionist.

perfide /pɛʀfid/ **I** *adj* LITER perfidious, treacherous.

II *nmf* LITER GÉN traitor; (amant) faithless lover.

■ **la ~ Albion** perfidious Albion.

perfidie /pɛʀfidi/ *nf* LITER perfidy LITTÉR, treachery.

perforation /pɛʀfɔʀasjɔ̃/ *nf* **1** GÉN, MÉD perforation; **2** ORDINAT (opération) punching; (trou) punched hole.

perforatrice /pɛʀfɔʀatʀis/ *nf* **1** (pour papier, carton) punch; **2** TECH (outil) drill; (machine) drilling machine.

perforer /pɛʀfɔʀe/ [1] *vtr* **1** (percer) GÉN to pierce; (de trous réguliers) to perforate; **2** (poinçonner) to punch; **carte perforée** ORDINAT punch card.

performance /pɛʀfɔʀmɑ̃s/ *nf* (résultat) GÉN result, performance; (record, exploit) achievement; **~ d'acteur** acting performance.

performant, ~e /pɛʀfɔʀmɑ̃, ɑ̃t/ *adj* **1** TECH [*voiture, matériel*] high-performance (*épith*); [*personne, techniques*] efficient; **2** FIN [*action*] performing; [*investissement*] high-return (*épith*); **3** ÉCON [*entreprise*] competitive.

perfusion /pɛʀfyzjɔ̃/ *nm* MÉD drip GB, IV US.

péricliter /peʀiklite/ [1] *vi* to be going downhill.

péridurale /peʀidyʀal/ *nf* epidural.

péril /peʀil/ *nm* LITER peril LITTÉR, danger; **au ~ de sa vie** at the risk of his/her life; **à ses risques et ~s** at his/her own risk; **il n'y a pas ~ en la demeure** what's the hurry?; **mettre en ~** to jeopardize [*avenir, démocratie*]; to threaten [*survie, patrimoine*]; to endanger [*santé, qualité*].

périlleux, -euse /peʀijø, øz/ *adj* LITER perilous LITTÉR, dangerous.

périmé, ~e /peʀime/ *adj* **1** [*passeport, billet*] out-of-date (*épith*); **son passeport est ~** his/her passport has expired; **2** COMM **ce produit est ~** this product has passed its use-by date; **3** (désuet) [*idée, coutume, institution*] outdated.

périmètre /peʀimɛtʀ/ *nm* **1** MATH perimeter; **2** (espace enclos) area; **dans le ~ de l'usine** on the factory premises; **dans un ~ de 30 km** within a 30 km radius.

périnée /peʀine/ *nm* perineum.

période /peʀjɔd/ *nf* **1** GÉN period; **la ~ Brejnev** the Brezhnev era; **elle traverse une ~ Elvis** HUM she's going through an Elvis phase; **en ~ de crise** at times of crisis; **en ~ électorale** at election time; **nous sommes en pleine ~ de crise** we are right in the middle of a crisis; **par ~s** periodically; **2** MÉTÉO period; (plus court) spell; **3** SPORT (mi-temps) half.

périodique /peʀjɔdik/ **I** *adj* **1** CHIMIE, PHYS periodic;

2 MÉD [*fièvre*] recurring; **3** (hygiénique) [*protection*] sanitary.

II *nm* (publication) periodical.

périodiquement /peʀjɔdikmɑ̃/ *adv* periodically.

péripétie /peʀipesi/ *nf* **1** (incident) incident; (événement) event; (aventure) adventure; **les ~s de** the eventful moments of; **2** LITTÉRAT, THÉÂT **les ~s de l'intrigue** the twists and turns of the plot.

périphérie /peʀifeʀi/ *nf* periphery.

périphérique /peʀifeʀik/ **I** *adj* GÉN peripheral; [*quartier*] outlying (*épith*); **radio ~** broadcasting station situated outside the territory to which it transmits.

II *nm* **1** (boulevard) ring road GB, beltway US; **2** ORDINAT peripheral; **~ d'entrée/de sortie** input/output device.

périphrase /peʀifʀɑz/ *nf* circumlocution, periphrasis SPÉC.

périple /peʀipl/ *nm* GÉN journey; (en bateau) voyage.

périr /peʀiʀ/ [3] *vi* **1** (mourir) LITER to die, to perish LITTÉR; **2** NAUT [*navire*] to go down; **3** (disparaître) LITER [*œuvre*] to be destroyed; **4** (se détériorer) [*denrées*] to perish.

périscolaire /peʀiskɔlɛʀ/ *adj* extracurricular.

périscope /peʀiskɔp/ *nm* periscope.

périssable /peʀisabl/ *adj* **1** COMM perishable; **2** FIG [*œuvre*] ephemeral.

Péritel® /peʀitɛl/ *nf* **prise ~** (femelle) scart socket; (mâle) scart plug.

péritonite /peʀitɔnit/ [▶ 196] *nf* peritonitis.

perle /pɛʀl/ *nf* **1** LIT (d'huître, de bijouterie) pearl; (de verre) bead; **2** FIG gem; **épouser une ~** to marry a wonderful man/woman; **ma femme de ménage est une vraie ~** my cleaning lady is a real treasure; **3**○ (erreur grossière) howler○ (de in); **4** (goutte) LITER **~ de rosée** dewdrop; **~ de sang** drop(let) of blood; **~ de sueur** bead of sweat.

■ **~ de culture** cultured pearl; **~ fine** or **naturelle** real pearl; **~ rare** FIG real treasure.

IDIOMES **il n'est pas ici pour enfiler des ~s**○ he's not here to amuse himself; **jeter des ~s aux cochons** to cast one's pearls before swine.

perlé, ~e /pɛʀle/ *adj* **1** [*orge*] pearl (*épith*); [*riz*] polished; **2** [*laine*] pearlized; [*broderie*] beaded; **coton ~** pearl cotton; **3** FIG **rire ~** rippling laugh.

perler /pɛʀle/ [1] *vi* [*goutte, larme*] to appear; **la sueur perlait sur son front** beads of sweat stood out on his/her brow.

perlier, -ière /pɛʀlje, ɛʀ/ *adj* pearl (*épith*).

perlimpinpin /pɛʀlɛ̃pɛ̃pɛ̃/ *nm* **poudre de ~** HUM magical cure.

perm○ /pɛʀm/ *nf* **1** soldiers' slang = **permission 2**; **2** schoolchildren's slang = **permanence I 4**.

permanence /pɛʀmanɑ̃s/ **I** *nf* **1** (absence d'interruption) permanence; (répétition) persistence; **2** (service) **'~ de 8 à 9 heures'** 'open from 8 am till 9 am'; **~ téléphonique** manned line; **assurer** or **tenir une ~** [*personne*] to be on duty; [*député, avocat*] to hold a surgery GB, to have office hours US; **3** (local) permanently manned office; **~ du parti** party offices (*pl*); **4** SCOL (salle) (private) study room GB, study hall US; (période) (private) study period.

II en permanence *loc adv* **1** (sans interruption) permanently; **2** (très fréquemment) constantly.

permanent, ~e[1] /pɛʀmanɑ̃, ɑ̃t/ **I** *adj* **1** (durable) [*personnel, exposition*] permanent; [*comité, armée*] standing (*épith*); **2** (constant) [*danger*] constant; [*spectacle, formation*] continuous; [*invalidité*] permanent.

II *nm,f* (employé) permanent employee; (membre) permanent member.

permanente[2] /pɛʀmanɑ̃t/ *nf* (coiffure) perm; **se faire faire une ~** to have one's hair permed.

permanenter /pɛʀmanɑ̃te/ [1] *vtr* to perm [*cheveux*].

perméable /pɛʀmeabl/ *adj* **1** LIT permeable (à to); **2** FIG [*frontière*] easily crossed; [*marché*] easily penetrated; **être ~ à une influence** to be susceptible to an influence.

permettre /pɛRmɛtR/ [60] **I** vtr **1** (donner l'autorisation) **~ à qn de faire qch** to allow sb to do sth; **permets-moi de te dire que** let me tell you that; **permettez-moi d'ajouter que** I would like to add that; **vous permettez que j'ouvre la fenêtre?** do you mind if I open the window?; **(vous) permettez!** j'étais là **avant!** excuse me! I was here first!; **ça, permettez-moi d'en douter** I'm sorry, I have my doubts about that; **c'est pas permis**○ **d'être aussi hypocrite!** how can anyone be such a hypocrite?; **il est menteur comme c'est pas permis**○ he's an incredible liar; **il est permis de se poser des questions** one is entitled to wonder; **tous les espoirs sont permis** there is every hope of success; **2** (donner les moyens) **~ à qn de faire qch** to allow ou enable sb to do sth; **des mesures pour ~ une reprise rapide de l'économie** measures to ensure rapid economic recovery; **si le temps le permet** weather permitting; **je viendrai si mon emploi du temps (me) le permet** I'll come if my schedule allows ou permits; **ce procédé permet de consommer moins d'énergie** this system makes it possible to use less energy; **leurs moyens ne le leur permettent pas** they can't afford it; **ma santé ne me permet pas de faire du sport** my health prevents me from doing any sport; **autant qu'il est permis d'en juger** as far as one can tell.

II se permettre vpr **je peux me ~ ce genre de plaisanterie avec lui** I can get away with telling him that kind of joke; **puis-je me ~ une remarque?** might I say something?; **se ~ de faire** to take the liberty of doing; **je ne peux pas me ~ d'acheter une nouvelle voiture** I can't afford to buy a new car; **puis-je me ~ de vous offrir un verre?** would you care for a drink?; **puis-je me ~ de vous raccompagner?** might I be allowed to escort you home?; **'je me permets de vous écrire au sujet de...'** 'I'm writing to you about...'

permis, ~e /pɛRmi, iz/ **I** pp ▶ **permettre**.
II pp adj [limites] permitted.
III nm inv permit, licence GB, license US.
■ **~ de conduire** (document) driver's licence^GB; (examen) driving test; **~ de construire** planning permission GB, building permit US; **~ de démolition** demolition consent; **~ d'inhumer** burial certificate; **~ moto** motorcycle licence^GB; **~ de navigation** certificate of seaworthiness; **~ poids lourd** heavy goods vehicle licence GB, articulated-vehicle license US; **~ de port d'armes** gun licence^GB; **~ de séjour** residence permit; **~ de travail** work permit.

permissif, -ive /pɛRmisif, iv/ adj permissive.
permission /pɛRmisjɔ̃/ nf **1** GÉN permission; **2** MIL leave ¢; **partir en ~** to go on leave.
■ **la ~ de minuit** permission to stay out late.

permissionnaire /pɛRmisjɔnɛR/ nm soldier on leave.

permutable /pɛRmytabl/ adj [fonction] interchangeable.

permutation /pɛRmytasjɔ̃/ nf ADMIN, MIL exchange of posts.

permuter /pɛRmyte/ [1] **I** vtr **1** GÉN to switch [sth] around [lettres, étiquettes]; **2** MATH to permute.
II vi [personnes] to exchange posts (**avec** with).

pernicieux, -ieuse /pɛRnisjø, øz/ adj pernicious.

péroné /peRɔne/ nm fibula.

pérorer /peRɔRe/ [1] vi PÉJ to hold forth PÉJ.

Pérou /peRu/ ▶ 232 | nprm Peru.
IDIOMES **ce n'est pas le ~** it's not a fortune.

perpendiculaire /pɛRpɑ̃dikylɛR/ adj, nf perpendicular (**à** to).

perpendiculairement /pɛRpɑ̃dikylɛRmɑ̃/ adv **1** (à angle droit) at right angles (**à** to); **2** (verticalement) vertically.

perpète○ /pɛRpɛt/ nf **être condamné à ~**, **avoir la ~** prisoners' slang to get life○; **habiter à ~** to live miles away; **jusqu'à ~** forever and a day○.

perpétrer /pɛRpetRe/ [14] vtr to perpetrate.

perpette = **perpète**.

perpétuel, -elle /pɛRpetɥɛl/ adj **1** GÉN perpetual; **2** (à vie) [poste, secrétaire] permanent; **réclusion perpétuelle** life imprisonment.

perpétuellement /pɛRpetɥɛlmɑ̃/ adv constantly, perpetually.

perpétuer /pɛRpetɥe/ [1] vtr to perpetuate.

perpétuité /pɛRpetɥite/ nf (durée) perpetuity; **à ~** [réclusion] life; [concession] in perpetuity (après n).

perplexe /pɛRplɛks/ adj perplexed, baffled; **rendre ~** to perplex.

perplexité /pɛRplɛksite/ nf perplexity, confusion.

perquisition /pɛRkizisjɔ̃/ nf search.

perquisitionner /pɛRkizisjɔne/ [1] **I** vtr to search.
II vi to carry out a search.

perron /peRɔ̃/ nm flight of steps.

perroquet /peRɔkɛ/ nm **1** ZOOL parrot; **tout répéter comme un ~** to repeat everything parrot-fashion; **2** NAUT topgallant sail; **3** (apéritif) pastis with crème de menthe; **4** (porte-manteau) hat and coat stand.
■ **~ de mer** (oiseau) puffin; (poisson) parrotfish.

perruche /peRyʃ/ nf **1** ZOOL budgerigar GB, budgie○ GB, parakeet US; **2** NAUT mizzen topgallant sail.

perruque /peRyk/ nf (postiche) wig.

persan, ~e /pɛRsɑ̃, an/ adj [chat, tapis] Persian.

perse /pɛRs/ adj Persian.

persécuté, ~e /pɛRsekyte/ nm,f **1** LIT victim of persecution; **2** PSYCH person with a persecution complex.

persécuter /pɛRsekyte/ [1] vtr to persecute.

persécuteur, -trice /pɛRsekytœR, tRis/ nm,f persecutor.

persécution /pɛRsekysjɔ̃/ nf persecution.

persévérance /pɛRseveRɑ̃s/ nf perseverance.

persévérant, ~e /pɛRseveRɑ̃, ɑ̃t/ adj [personne] persevering (épith); **tu n'es pas très ~!** you give up too easily!

persévérer /pɛRseveRe/ [14] vi **1** [personne, équipe] to persevere; **2** (persister) LITER [fièvre] to persist.

persienne /pɛRsjɛn/ nf (louvred^GB) shutter.

persiflage /pɛRsiflaʒ/ nm mockery, persiflage.

persifleur, -euse /pɛRsiflœR, øz/ adj LITER [ton, propos] mocking.

persil /pɛRsi(l)/ nm parsley.

persillade /pɛRsijad/ nf parsley and garlic garnish.

persillé, ~e /pɛRsije/ adj garnished with chopped parsley (après n); **fromage ~** blue cheese; **viande ~e** marbled meat.

persique /pɛRsik/ adj Persian; **le golfe Persique** the Persian Gulf.

persistance /pɛRsistɑ̃s/ nf persistence; **avec ~** persistently.

persistant, ~e /pɛRsistɑ̃, ɑ̃t/ adj [chaleur, problème] continuing; [odeur, neige] lingering; [symptôme] persistent; **arbre à feuilles ~es** evergreen.

persister /pɛRsiste/ [1] vi **1** (durer) [symptôme, douleur] to persist; [mauvais temps, inflation] to continue; [doute, problème] to remain; [odeur] to linger; **2** (s'obstiner) **~ dans son erreur** to persist in one's error; **~ dans son refus** to continue to refuse; **je persiste à croire que...** I still think that...
IDIOMES **il persiste et signe**○ he's sticking to his guns○.

personnage /pɛRsɔnaʒ/ nm **1** (personne fictive) character; **la liste des ~s** THÉÂT the cast, the dramatis personae (pl); **2** (personne représentée) figure; **3** (personne importante) figure; **un ~ haut placé** a high-placed person; **les ~s importants de la ville** the local dignitaries; **4** (personne curieuse) character; **5** (personnalité que l'on se crée) **se composer un ~** to adopt a persona.

personnaliser /pɛRsɔnalize/ [1] vtr to add a personal touch to [maison]; to customize [voiture]; **~ un**

contrat to tailor a contract to an individual's needs; **lettre personnalisée** personal letter.

personnalité /pɛʀsɔnalite/ *nf* **1** PSYCH personality; **2** (personne influente) important person.

personne¹ /pɛʀsɔn/ *pron indéf* ~ **n'est parfait** nobody's ou no-one's perfect; **je n'ai parlé à** ~ I didn't talk to anybody ou anyone; ~ **de sensé ne ferait cela** no sensible person would do that; **ce n'est un mystère pour** ~ it's no mystery.

personne² /pɛʀsɔn/ *nf* **1** (individu) person; **dix** ~**s** ten people; **50% des** ~**s interrogées** 50% of those interviewed; **un voyage pour deux** ~**s** a trip for two; **lit/chambre d'une** ~ single bed/room; **la** ~ **aimée** the loved one; **les** ~**s âgées** the elderly; **une charmante jeune** ~ a charming young lady; **une** ~ **de confiance** someone trustworthy; **il doit y avoir erreur sur la** ~ it must be the wrong person ou a case of mistaken identity; **2** (individu en lui-même) **satisfait de sa (petite)** ~ satisfied with oneself; **bien fait de sa** ~ good-looking; **le respect de la** ~ **(humaine)** respect for the individual; **en** ~ personally; **c'est la cupidité en** ~ he/she is greed personified; **3** LING person.

■ ~ **à charge** dependant.

personnel, -elle /pɛʀsɔnɛl/ **I** *adj* **1** (individuel) [*ami, effets*] personal; [*engagement, papiers*] private; **adresse personnelle** home ou private address; **c'est** ~ it's confidential; **'personnelle'** (sur une lettre) 'private'; **'strictement personnelle'** (sur une lettre) 'private and confidential'; **2** (original) individual; **3** (égoïste) selfish; **4** LING [*forme, pronom*] personal; [*mode*] finite.

II *nm* (d'industrie, usine) workforce; (de compagnie, d'administration) employees (*pl*), personnel; (d'hôpital, hôtel) staff; **nous manquons de** ~ we are understaffed; ~ **navigant/au sol** flight/ground personnel.

personnellement /pɛʀsɔnɛlmɑ̃/ *adv* personally; **il nous a reçus** ~ he received us in person.

personnification /pɛʀsɔnifikasjɔ̃/ *nf* personification.

personnifier /pɛʀsɔnifje/ [2] *vtr* to personify.

perspective /pɛʀspɛktiv/ *nf* **1** ARCHIT, ART perspective; **en** ~ [*dessin*] perspective (*épith*); [*dessiner*] in perspective; **2** (vue) view; **3** (optique) perspective, angle; **4** (éventualité) prospect.

perspicace /pɛʀspikas/ *adj* perceptive, perspicacious.

perspicacité /pɛʀspikasite/ *nf* insight, perspicacity.

persuader /pɛʀsɥade/ [1] *vtr* to persuade; **j'en suis persuadé** I'm convinced of it.

persuasif, -ive /pɛʀsɥazif, iv/ *adj* persuasive.

persuasion /pɛʀsɥazjɔ̃/ *nf* persuasion.

perte /pɛʀt/ **I** *nf* **1** GÉN loss; **être en** ~ **de vitesse** LIT to be losing speed; FIG to be slowing down; **avoir des** ~**s de sang** to bleed; **à** ~ **de vue** as far as the eye can see; **vendre à** ~ to sell at a loss; **2** (gaspillage) waste; ~ **d'énergie** (de personne) waste of energy; (de machine) energy loss; **ce serait en pure** ~ (inutile) it would be futile; **agir en pure** ~ to do something that is a complete waste of time; **3** (ruine) ruin; **courir** ou **aller à sa (propre)** ~ to be heading for a fall; **vouloir la** ~ **de qn** to try to bring about sb's downfall.

II pertes *nfpl* losses; **causer des** ~**s en vies humaines** to take a heavy toll in human life.

■ ~ **sèche** FIN dead loss; ~**s blanches** vaginal discharge ¢; ~**s séminales** involuntary emission ¢ of semen.

pertinemment /pɛʀtinamɑ̃/ *adv* **1** (avec justesse) pertinently; **2** (parfaitement) [*savoir*] perfectly well.

pertinence /pɛʀtinɑ̃s/ *nf* pertinence.

pertinent, ~e /pɛʀtinɑ̃, ɑ̃t/ *adj* **1** (à propos) [*question*] pertinent; **2** LING **trait** ~ relevant feature.

perturbant, ~e /pɛʀtyʀbɑ̃, ɑ̃t/ *adj* disturbing.

perturbateur, -trice /pɛʀtyʀbatœʀ, tʀis/ *nm,f* troublemaker.

perturbation /pɛʀtyʀbasjɔ̃/ *nf* **1** (d'un service)

disruption; **2** MÉTÉO disturbance; **3** (politique) upheaval; (sociale) disturbance.

perturber /pɛʀtyʀbe/ [1] *vtr* **1** (dérégler) to disrupt [*trafic, marché*]; to interfere with [*sommeil, développement*]; **cela m'a un peu perturbé** it has unsettled me a bit; **être perturbé**○ (mentalement) to be very disturbed; **2** (inquiéter) to perturb SOUT; **cela ne m'a pas perturbé** it didn't bother me; **3** (semer le trouble) to disrupt [*réunion, ordre*].

péruvien, -ienne /peʀyvjɛ̃, ɛn/ ▶394 *adj* Peruvian.

pervenche /pɛʀvɑ̃ʃ/ **I** ▶141 *adj inv* (bleu) ~ periwinkle blue.

II *nf* **1** (fleur) periwinkle; **2**○ (contractuelle) (female) traffic warden GB, meter maid○ US.

pervers, ~e /pɛʀvɛʀ, ɛʀs/ **I** *adj* **1** (méchant) wicked; **2** (dépravé) perverted; **3** [*effet*] pernicious.

II *nm,f* pervert.

perversion /pɛʀvɛʀsjɔ̃/ *nf* perversion (**de** of).

perversité /pɛʀvɛʀsite/ *nf* perversity.

pervertir /pɛʀvɛʀtiʀ/ [3] *vtr* to corrupt.

pesamment /pəzamɑ̃/ *adv* [*tomber*] heavily; [*marcher*] with a heavy step.

pesant, ~e /pəzɑ̃, ɑ̃t/ *adj* **1** (lourd) heavy; **2** (pénible) [*réglementation*] cumbersome; [*contrainte*] burdensome; [*atmosphère, silence*] oppressive; [*incertitude*] heavy; **3** (inélégant) [*architecture, personne*] ungainly; [*style*] heavy; **4** (ennuyeux) [*écrivain*] dull, ponderous.

IDIOMES **valoir son** ~ **d'or** to be worth its weight in gold.

pesanteur /pəzɑ̃tœʀ/ *nf* **1** (de style) heaviness; (d'esprit) dullness; (de bureaucratie) inertia ¢; **2** PHYS gravity.

pèse-bébé, *pl* ~**s** /pɛzbebe/ *nm* baby scales (*pl*).

pesée /pəze/ ▶455 *nf* **1** (opération) weighing; **2** (poussée) shove; **3** (quantité) weight.

pèse-lettre, *pl* ~**s** /pɛzlɛtʀ/ *nm* letter scales (*pl*).

pèse-personne, *pl* ~**s** /pɛzpɛʀsɔn/ *nm* bathroom scales (*pl*).

peser /pəze/ [16] ▶455 **I** *vtr* **1** LIT to weigh [*personne, objet*]; **2** FIG to weigh up; ~ **le pour et le contre** to weigh up the pros and cons; ~ **ses mots** to choose one's words carefully; **tout bien pesé** all things considered.

II *vi* **1** (avoir un poids) to weigh; (être lourd) to be heavy; ~ **lourd** to weigh a lot; **2** (avoir de l'importance) to carry weight; ~ **dans/sur une décision** to have a decisive influence in/on a decision; **3** (faire sentir son poids) ~ **sur** [*soupçons, risques*] to hang over [*personne, projet*]; [*impôts, charges*] to weigh [sb/sth] down [*personne, pays*]; [*personne, décision*] to influence (greatly) [*politique, situation*]; **faire** ~ **un danger sur** to be a danger to; **faire** ~ **un risque sur** to threaten; **la solitude me pèse** FIG loneliness weighs heavily on me; **4** (exercer une poussée) ~ **contre/sur** to push against/down on.

III se peser *vpr* to weigh oneself.

IDIOMES **envoyez, c'est pesé**○! off it goes!

peseta /pezeta/ ▶33 *nf* peseta.

pessimisme /pesimism/ *nm* pessimism.

pessimiste /pesimist/ **I** *adj* pessimistic.

II *nmf* pessimist.

peste /pɛst/ *nf* **1** ▶196 MÉD plague; **2**○ (personne insupportable) pest○.

IDIOMES **je me méfie de lui comme de la** ~○ I don't trust him an inch.

pester /pɛste/ *vi* ~ **contre qn/qch** to curse sb/sth.

pesticide /pɛstisid/ **I** *adj* pesticidal.

II *nm* pesticide.

pestiféré, ~e /pɛstifeʀe/ *adj* [*personne*] plague-stricken; [*lieu*] plague-infested.

pestilence /pɛstilɑ̃s/ *nf* stench.

pet○ /pɛ/ *nm* fart○; **lâcher un** ~ to fart○.

IDIOMES **ça ne vaut pas un** ~ **(de lapin)** it's not worth a damn○; **il a toujours un** ~ **de travers** he's always got something wrong with him.

pétale /petal/ *nm* petal.

pétanque /petɑ̃k/ ▶ 329| *nf* petanque (*game of bowls played in the South of France*).

pétant○, **-e** /petɑ̃, ɑ̃t/ *adj* on the dot (*après n*).

pétarade /petaʀad/ *nf* backfiring ¢.

pétarader /petaʀade/ [1] *vi* to backfire, to sputter.

pétard /petaʀ/ *nm* **1** (explosif) banger GB, firecracker US; **un ~ mouillé** FIG a damp squib; **2**○ (tapage) racket○; **faire du ~** (faire scandale) to make a hell of a row○; (protester) to kick up a fuss○; **être en ~** (en colère) to be bursting with health.

pet-de-nonne, *pl* **pets-de-nonne** /pɛdnɔn/ *nm* CULIN fritter (*made from choux pastry*).

péter /pete/ [14] I○ *vtr* (casser) to bust○ [*appareil*]; to snap [*fil*].
II *vi* **1**○ (lâcher un pet) to fart○; **2**○ (éclater) LIT [*ballon, tuyau*] to burst; [*explosif*] to go off; FIG to blow up; **3** (casser) [*appareil, lampe*] to bust○; [*fil*] to snap; [*couture*] to burst.
IDIOMES **~ le feu**○ [*personne*] to be full of beans○; **~ la santé**○ to be bursting with health.

pète-sec○ /pɛtsɛk/ I *adj inv* [*ton, manières*] abrupt.
II *nmf inv* PEJ abrupt person.

péteux○, **-euse** /petø, øz/ I *adj* **1** (poltron) cowardly; **2** (prétentieux) stuck-up○.
II *nm,f* **1** (poltron) coward; **2** (prétentieux) cocky (little) upstart○.

pétillant, **~e** /petijɑ̃, ɑ̃t/ *adj* GÉN sparkling; [*personne*] bubbly.

pétillement /petijmɑ̃/ *nm* (de champagne) fizziness; (de feu) crackling.

pétiller /petije/ [1] *vi* [*champagne*] to fizz; [*bois*] to crackle; [*yeux, regard*] to sparkle (**de** with).

petiot○, **~e** /pətjo, ɔt/ I *adj* [*enfant*] tiny.
II *nm,f* (enfant) little boy/little girl.

petit, **~e** /p(ə)ti, it/ I *adj* **1** (en taille) small, little; **~ et trapu** short and stocky; **une toute ~e pièce** a tiny room; **se faire tout ~** FIG to try to make oneself inconspicuous; **c'est Versailles en plus ~** it's a miniature Versailles; **2** (en longueur, durée) short; **par ~es étapes** in easy stages; **3** (en âge) young, little; **je t'ai connu ~** I knew you when you were little; **le ~ Jésus** baby Jesus; **une ~e Française** a French girl; **le ~ nouveau** the new boy; **c'est notre ~ dernier** he's our youngest; **~ chat** kitten; **~ chien** puppy; **~ ours/renard/lion** bear/fox/lion cub; **4** [*appétit, quantité, groupe*] small; [*mangeur*] small; [*salaire*] low; [*averse*] light; [*cri, rire, souci*] little; [*chance, rhume*] slight; [*détail, défaut*] minor; **ça a un ~ goût de cerise** it tastes slightly of cherries; **avoir une ~e santé** to have poor health; **un (tout) ~ peu de sel** (just) a little salt; **5** (dans une hiérarchie) [*marque*] lesser known; [*emploi*] modest; [*fonctionnaire*] low-ranking; [*poète*] minor; **les ~es routes** minor roads; **le ~ personnel** low-grade staff; **les ~es gens** ordinary people; **un ~ escroc** a small-time crook; **6** FIG little; **mon ~ papa** darling daddy○; **un ~ imbécile** an idiot; **très préoccupée de sa ~e personne** very taken up with herself; **de bons ~s plats** tasty dishes; **un ~ coin tranquille** a quiet spot; **envoie-moi un ~ mot** drop me a line; **passe-moi un ~ coup de fil**○ give me a call; **j'en ai pour une ~e minute** it won't take me a minute; **une ~e trentaine de personnes** under thirty people; **7** (mesquin) [*personne, procédé*] petty, mean; (étroit) [*conception*] narrow.
II *nm,f* **1** (enfant) little boy/girl, child; (benjamin) **le ~** (de deux) the younger one; (de plus de deux) the youngest one; **mes ~s** my children; **pauvre ~!** poor thing!; **la ~e Martin** the Martin girl; **2** (adulte de petite taille) small man/woman.
III *adv* **voir ~** (sous-estimer) to underestimate; (être sans ambition) to have no ambition; **tailler ~** to be small-fitting; **~ à ~** little by little.
IV *nm* **1** (jeune animal) **~s** GÉN young (+ *v pl*); (chats) kittens; (chiens) puppies; **faire des ~s** [*chienne*] to have puppies; FIG [*argent*] to grow; **2** (per-

sonne modeste) **les ~s** ordinary people; **un ~ de la finance** a minor figure in the world of finance.
■ **~ ami** boyfriend; **~ bois** (d'allumage) kindling; **~ chef** petty tyrant; **jouer au ~ chef** to throw one's weight around○; **~ coin**○ (toilettes) EUPH loo○ GB, bathroom US; **~ crème** small espresso with milk; **~ déjeuner** breakfast; **~ linge** underwear; **~ noir**○ coffee; **~ nom**○ (prénom) first name; **~ pois** (garden) pea, petit pois; **~ pot** (pour bébés) jar of baby food; **~ rat (de l'Opéra)** pupil at Paris Opéra's ballet school; **~ salé** streaky salted pork; **~e amie** girlfriend; **~e annonce** classified advertisement; **~e école** ≈ nursery school; **~e main** seamstress (*at a top fashion house*); **~e nature** weakling; **~e souris** tooth fairy; **~e vérole** smallpox; **~e voiture** toy car; **~es annonces matrimoniales** personal ads; **~es et moyennes entreprises**, **PME** small and medium enterprises, SMEs; **~s chevaux** JEUX ≈ ludo (*sg*).

petit-beurre, *pl* **petits-beurre** /p(ə)tibœr/ *nm* petit beurre biscuit GB ou cookie US.

petite-fille, *pl* **petites-filles** /p(ə)titfij/ *nf* grand-daughter.

petitement /p(ə)titmɑ̃/ *adv* **1** (chichement) in a penny-pinching way; **2** (avec mesquinerie) pettily.

petitesse /p(ə)titɛs/ *nf* **1** (mesquinerie) pettiness; **2** (petite taille) small size.

petit-fils, *pl* **petits-fils** /p(ə)tifis/ *nm* grandson.

pétition /petisjɔ̃/ *nf* petition.

petit-lait /p(ə)tilɛ/ *nm* whey.
IDIOMES **ça se boit comme du ~**○! it slips down nicely!

petit-nègre○ /p(ə)tinɛgr/ *nm inv* OFFENSIVE pidgin French.

petits-enfants /p(ə)tizɑ̃fɑ̃/ *nmpl* grandchildren.

petit-suisse, *pl* **petits-suisses** /p(ə)tisɥis/ *nm* petit-suisse, individual fromage frais.

pétoire○ /petwaʀ/ *nf* (fusil) rusty old gun.

peton /pətɔ̃/ *nm* tootsie LANG ENFANTIN, foot.

pétoncle /petɔ̃kl/ *nm* small scallop.

pétouiller○ /petuje/ [1] *vi* H (avoir des problèmes) [*personne*] to be struggling; [*voiture*] to run rough.

pétri, **~e** /petri/ *adj* **~ de** PEJ steeped in [*ignorance*]; puffed up with [*orgueil*]; full of [*contradictions*].

pétrifiant, **~e** /petrifjɑ̃, ɑ̃t/ *adj* petrifying.

pétrifier /petrifje/ [2] I *vtr* **1** LIT to petrify; **2** FIG to transfix.
II **se pétrifier** *vpr* **1** LIT to become petrified; **2** FIG [*personne*] to be transfixed; [*cœur*] to harden; [*sourire*] to freeze.

pétrin /petrɛ̃/ *nm* dough trough; **~ mécanique** kneading machine; **être dans le ~**○ to be in a fix○.

pétrir /petrir/ [3] *vtr* **1** CULIN to knead [*pâte*]; **2** FIG to mould GB ou mold US [*personnalité*].

pétrochimique /petroʃimik/ *adj* petrochemical.

pétrole /petrɔl/ *nm* oil, petroleum SPÉC; **~ brut** crude oil.

pétrolette○ /petrɔlɛt/ *nf* (vélomoteur) moped.

pétroleuse /petrɔløz/ *nf* **1** HIST (female) fire-raiser (*during the Commune*); **2** (militante) (female) activist.

pétrolier, **-ière** /petrɔlje, ɛr/ I *adj* [*prospection*] oil; [*produits*] petroleum; [*pays*] oil-producing; [*port*] oil-exporting.
II *nm* **1** (navire) oil tanker; **2** ▶ 374| (industriel) oil man; (ingénieur) petroleum engineer.

pétrolifère /petrɔlifɛr/ *adj* [*roche*] oil-bearing; [*région*] oil-producing; **gisement ~** oilfield.

pétulant, **~e** /petylɑ̃, ɑ̃t/ *adj* exuberant.

pétunia /petynja/ *nm* petunia.

peu /pø/
■ **Note** Les emplois de *peu* avec *avant, d'ici, depuis, sous* sont traités respectivement sous chacun de ces mots.
– Il sera également utile de se reporter à la note d'usage sur les quantités ▶ 486|.

I *adv* **1** (modifiant un verbe) not much; **elle gagne**

assez ~ she doesn't earn very much; **elle gagne très** ~ she earns very little; **le radiateur chauffe** ~ the radiator doesn't give out much heat; **je sais me contenter de** ~ I'm satisfied with very little; **deux semaines c'est trop** ~ two weeks isn't long enough; **si** ~ **que ce soit** however little; **tu ne vas pas t'en faire pour si** ~ you're not going to worry about such a little thing; **la catastrophe a été évitée de** ~ disaster was only just avoided; **ça importe** ~ it doesn't really matter; **c'est** ~ **dire** to say the least; **il est aussi borné que son père et ce n'est pas** ~ **dire**⊘! he's as narrow-minded as his father and that's saying a lot!; **un homme comme on en voit** ~ the kind of man you don't often come across; **très** ~ **pour moi**⊘! FIG no thanks⊘!; **2** (modifiant un adjectif) not very; **assez** ~ **connu** little-known; **ils se sentent très** ~ **concernés par**... they feel quite unconcerned about...; **nous étions** ~ **nombreux** there weren't many of us; **un individu** ~ **recommandable** a disreputable character; **elle n'est pas** ~ **fière** she's more than a little proud.
II *pron indéf* ~ **leur font confiance** few ou not many people trust them.
III peu de *dét indéf* **1** (avec un nom dénombrable) ~ **de mots** few words; **2** (avec un nom non dénombrable) ~ **de temps** little time; **en** ~ **de temps** in next to no time; **il y a** ~ **de bruit** there's not much noise; **c'est** ~ **de chose** it's not much; **avec** ~ **de chose elle a fait un repas délicieux** with very little she made a delicious meal; **on est bien** ~ **de chose!** we're so insignificant!
IV *nm* **1** (petite quantité) **le** ~ **de** the little [*confiance, liberté*]; the few [*livres, amis*]; **il a voulu montrer le** ~ **d'importance qu'il attachait à l'affaire** he wanted to show how unimportant the matter was to him; **2** (manque) **le** ~ **de** the lack of.
V un peu *loc adv* **1** (dans une mesure faible) a little, a bit; **reste encore un** ~ stay a little longer; **'elle aime le fromage?'—'oui, pas qu'un** ~ ⊘!' 'does she like cheese?'—'does she ever⊘!'; **2** (modifiant un adverbe) a little, a bit; **parle un** ~ **moins fort** keep your voice down; **elle se maquille un** ~ **trop** she wears a bit too much make-up; **un** ~ **plus de gens** a few more people; **un** ~ **moins de** slightly less [*pluie*]; slightly fewer [*gens*]; **amène tes amis, un** ~ **plus un** ~ **moins**... bring your friends, another two or three people won't make much difference; **'il avait l'air un** ~ **contrarié'—'un** ~ **beaucoup même**⊘' 'he looked a bit annoyed'—'more than a bit'; **3** (emploi stylistique) just; **répète un** ~ **pour voir**⊘! you just try saying that again!; **je vous demande un** ~ ⊘! I ask you!; **il sait un** ~ ⊘ **de quoi il parle** he does know what he's talking about; **4** (emploi par antiphrase) a little; **tu ne serais pas un** ~ **jaloux toi?** aren't you just a little jealous?; **5**⊘ (pour renforcer une affirmation) **il est un** ~ **bien ton copain!** your boyfriend is a bit of all right⊘! GB ou a good-looker⊘!; **'tu le ferais toi?'—'un** ~ **(que je le ferais)!'** 'would you do it?'—'I sure would⊘!'
VI peu à peu *loc adv* gradually, little by little.
VII pour un peu *loc adv* **pour un** ~ **ils se seraient battus** they very nearly had a fight.
VIII pour peu que *loc conj* **if; pour** ~ **qu'il ait bu, il va nous raconter sa vie** if he's had anything at all to drink, he'll tell us his life story.

peuchère /pøʃɛʀ/ *excl* DIAL poor thing!
peuplade /pœplad/ *nf* small tribe.
peuple /pœpl/ *nm* **1** POL people; **le** ~ **de gauche** the left-wing element of the population; **2** SOCIOL **le** ~ the people (+ *v pl*); **le** ~ **des campagnes** country people (+ *v pl*); **le** ~ **des villes** townspeople (+ *v pl*); **3**⊘ (foule) lots of people (*pl*).
■ ~ **élu** Chosen People.
peuplement /pœpləmɑ̃/ *nm* **1** (d'une région) (en habitants) populating; (en arbres) planting (with trees); (d'un lac) stocking; **2** (habitants) population.
peupler /pœple/ [1] **I** *vtr* **1** (faire occuper) to populate [*pays*] (**de** with); to stock [*bois, étang*] (**de** with); **2** (occuper) [*personnes*] to populate [*pays*]; [*animaux,*

plantes] to colonize [*région*]; [*spectateurs, étudiants*] to fill [*salle, rue*]; **peuplé de** peopled with [*personnes*]; **3** (remplir) [*souvenirs, rêves*] to fill.
II se peupler *vpr* [*ville, région*] to fill up (**de** with).
peuplier /pøplije/ *nm* poplar.
peur /pœʀ/ *nf* GEN fear; (soudaine) fright, scare; **être mort** or **vert**⊘ **de** ~ to be scared to death; **une** ~ **panique s'empara de lui** he was panic-stricken; **avoir** ~ to be afraid; **j'en ai bien** ~ I'm afraid so; **il n'a** ~ **de rien** LIT he's not afraid of anything, he's fearless; **il veut courir le marathon sans s'être préparé? il n'a pas** ~ ⊘! he wants to run the marathon without having trained? he's being very optimistic!; **n'ayez pas** ~ (ne soyez pas effrayé) don't be afraid; (ne vous inquiétez pas) don't worry; **avoir plus de** ~ **que de mal** to be more frightened than hurt; **faire** ~ **à qn** to frighten sb; **tu ne me fais pas** ~! I'm not afraid of you!; **être laid à faire** ~ to be hideously ugly; **maigre** or **d'une maigreur à faire** ~ terribly thin; **le travail ne nous fait pas** ~ we're not afraid of hard work; **il est poli ça fait** ~ ⊘! IRON he's not exactly the most polite man in the world!
peureusement /pœʀøzmɑ̃/ *adv* fearfully.
peureux, -euse /pœʀø, øz/ **I** *adj* fearful.
II *nm,f* fearful person.
peut-être /pøtɛtʀ/ *adv* perhaps, maybe; **tu veux m'apprendre à conduire,** ~? IRON I do know how to drive, you know!; **elle travaille** ~ **lentement mais avec soin** she might work slowly, but she's careful.
pèze⊘ /pɛz/ *nm* dough⊘, money.
phacochère /fakoʃɛʀ/ *nm* warthog.
phagocyter /fagosite/ [1] *vtr* **1** BIOL to ingest by phagocytosis; **2** FIG to swallow up.
phalange /falɑ̃ʒ/ *nf* **1** ANAT phalanx; **2** HIST phalanx; **3** POL (en Espagne) Falange; (au Liban) **les** ~**s** (Christian) Phalangists.
phalangiste /falɑ̃ʒist/ *adj, nmf* (au Liban) Phalangist; (en Espagne) Falangist.
phalène /falɛn/ *nf* ou *m* geometer moth.
phallocrate /falɔkʀat/ *nm* male chauvinist, phallocrat.
phalloïde /falɔid/ *adj* **amanite** ~ death cap.
phallus /falys/ *nm inv* phallus.
phantasme = **fantasme**.
pharamineux, -euse = **faramineux**.
pharaon /faʀaɔ̃/ *nm* pharaoh.
phare /faʀ/ **I** *nm* **1** AUT headlight, headlamp; **2** NAUT lighthouse; **3** FIG (guide) beacon.
II (-)**phare** (*in compounds*) **société/industrie**(-)~ flagship company/industry; **œuvre**(-)~ seminal work; **pays**(-)~ leading country; **année**(-)~ key year.
■ ~ **antibrouillard** fog-light; ~ **à iode** quartz halogen light.
pharmaceutique /faʀmasøtik/ *adj* pharmaceutical.
pharmacie /faʀmasi/ *nf* **1** ▶374 COMM chemist's (shop) GB, drugstore US, pharmacy; ~ **de nuit** duty chemist's GB, night pharmacy US; ~ **de garde** duty chemist's GB, *pharmacy open on a Sunday or a holiday according to a rotating schedule*; **2** (dans un hôpital) dispensary, pharmacy; **3** (meuble) medicine cabinet; **4** (discipline) pharmacy; **elle est en troisième année de** ~ she's in her third year studying pharmacy; **5** (produits) **la** ~ medicines (*pl*); (dans un supermarché) health-care products (*pl*); IND pharmaceuticals (*pl*).
■ ~ **portative** or **de voyage** first-aid kit.
pharmacien, -ienne /faʀmasjɛ̃, ɛn/ ▶374 *nm,f* (dans un magasin) (dispensing) chemist GB, pharmacist; (ailleurs) pharmacist.
pharmacodépendance /faʀmakodepɑ̃dɑ̃s/ *nf* drug-dependence.
pharmacologie /faʀmakɔlɔʒi/ *nf* pharmacology.
pharmacopée /faʀmakɔpe/ *nf* pharmacopeia.
pharyngite /faʀɛ̃ʒit/ ▶196 *nf* pharyngitis.
pharynx /faʀɛ̃ks/ *nm inv* pharynx.

phase /faz/ *nf* **1** (d'évolution) stage; **2** CHIMIE, PHYS phase; **3** ÉLECTROTECH (conducteur de) ~ live wire; **en ~** in phase; **être en ~ avec qn** FIG to be on the same wavelength as sb.

phénicien, -ienne /fenisjɛ̃, ɛn/ **I** *adj* Phoenician. **II** *nm* LING Phoenician.

phénix /feniks/ *nm inv* MYTHOL phoenix.

phénoménal, ~e, *mpl* **-aux** /fenɔmenal, o/ *adj* phenomenal.

phénomène /fenɔmɛn/ *nm* **1** (fait) phenomenon; **des ~s de racisme** manifestations of racism; **2**° (original) character; **3** (de cirque) freak.

philanthropie /filɑ̃tʀɔpi/ *nf* philanthropy.

philatélie /filateli/ *nf* stamp collecting, philately SPÉC.

philatéliste /filatelist/ *nmf* stamp collector, philatelist SPÉC.

philharmonique /filaʀmɔnik/ *adj* philharmonic.

Philippe /filip/ *npr* Philip.
■ **~ Auguste** Philip Augustus; **~ le Bel** Philip the Fair; **~ le Bon** Philip the Good.

philippin, ~e /filipɛ̃, in/ ▶394 *adj* Philippine (*épith*).

Philippin, ~e /filipɛ̃, in/ ▶394 *nm,f* Filipino.

Philippines /filipin/ ▶407, 232 *nprfpl* **les ~** the Philippines; **mer des ~** Philippine Sea.

philosophale /filɔzɔfal/ *adj f* **la pierre ~** the philosopher's stone.

philosophe /filɔzɔf/ **I** *adj* philosophical. **II** *nmf* philosopher.

philosopher /filɔzɔfe/ [1] *vi* to philosophize.

philosophie /filɔzɔfi/ *nf* philosophy; **avec ~** philosophically.

philosophique /filɔzɔfik/ *adj* philosophical.

philtre /filtʀ/ *nm* philtre; **~ d'amour** love potion.

phlébite /flebit/ ▶196 *nf* phlebitis.

phlébologie /flebɔlɔʒi/ *nf* vascular medicine.

phlegmon /flɛgmɔ̃/ ▶196 *nm* acute inflammation.

phobie /fɔbi/ *nf* GÉN, PSYCH phobia (**de** about).

phocéen, -éenne /fɔseɛ̃, ɛn/ *nm,f* Phocean; **la cité phocéenne** Marseilles.

phonématique /fɔnematik/ *nf* phonemics (+ *v sg*).

phonème /fɔnɛm/ *nm* phoneme.

phonétique /fɔnetik/ **I** *adj* [*transcription, alphabet*] phonetic; **loi ~** sound law; **altération ~** sound change.
II *nf* phonetics (+ *v sg*).

phonographe /fɔnɔgʀaf/ *nm* gramophone GB, phonograph US.

phonothèque /fɔnɔtɛk/ *nf* sound archive.

phoque /fɔk/ *nm* **1** (animal) seal; **2** (peau) sealskin.
IDIOMES **souffler comme un ~**° to puff and pant.

phosphate /fɔsfat/ *nm* phosphate.

phosphore /fɔsfɔʀ/ *nm* phosphorus.

phosphorescent, ~e /fɔsfɔʀesɑ̃, ɑ̃t/ *adj* phosphorescent.

phosphoreux, -euse /fɔsfɔʀø, øz/ *adj* [*acide*] phosphorous; [*alliage*] phosphor (*épith*).

photo /fɔto/ *nf* **1** (technique) photography; **faire de la ~** (en amateur) to take photos; (en professionnel) to be a photographer; **2** (image) photo, picture; **être pris en ~** to be photographed.
■ **~ d'identité** passport photo; **~ de mode** fashion photo.

photocomposeuse /fɔtokɔ̃pozøz/ *nf* filmsetter GB, photocomposer US.

photocomposition /fɔtokɔ̃pozisjɔ̃/ *nf* film setting GB, photocomposition US.

photocopie /fɔtokɔpi/ *nf* **1** (copie) photocopy; **2** (procédé) photocopying; **3** (service) photocopying service.

photocopier /fɔtokɔpje/ [2] *vtr* to photocopy, to xerox® US.

photocopieur /fɔtokɔpjœʀ/ *nm* photocopier.

photocopieuse /fɔtokɔpjøz/ *nf* photocopier.

photoélectrique /fɔtoelɛktʀik/ *adj* photoelectric.

photogénique /fɔtoʒenik/ *adj* photogenic.

photographe /fɔtogʀaf/ ▶374 *nmf* **1** (qui prend des photos) photographer; **2** (commerçant) **aller chez le ~** to go to the camera shop GB ou store US.
■ **~ de plateau** stills man.

photographie /fɔtogʀafi/ *nf* **1** (technique) photography; **2** (image) photograph, picture; **3** FIG picture.
■ **~ aérienne** (technique) aerial photography; (cliché) aerial photograph; **~ d'art** art photography; **~ de plateau** CIN still.

photographier /fɔtogʀafje/ [2] *vtr* **1** (prendre en photo) to photograph, to take a photo of [*personne, lieu*]; **se faire ~** to have one's photo ou picture taken; **2** (mémoriser) to fix [sth/sb] in one's mind [*endroit, personne*].

photographique /fɔtogʀafik/ *adj* photographic.

photogravure /fɔtogʀavyʀ/ *nf* photoengraving.

photomaton® /fɔtomatɔ̃/ *nm* (appareil) photo booth.

photophore /fɔtofɔʀ/ *nm* (de mineur, spéléologue) miner's lamp; (décoratif) (decorative) candle holder.

photostyle /fɔtostil/ *nm* light pen.

photothèque /fɔtotɛk/ *nf* **1** (lieu) picture library; **2** (collection) photographic collection.

phrase /fʀaz/ *nf* **1** LING (assemblage de mots) sentence; **2** (propos) phrase; **avoir une ~ malheureuse** to say the wrong thing; **faire des ~s** or **de grandes ~s** to use flowery language; **pas de ~s** no fine phrases; **tour de ~** turn of phrase; **3** MUS phrase.
■ **~ toute faite** stock phrase, set expression.

phrasé /fʀaze/ *nm* MUS phrasing.

phrastique /fʀastik/ *adj* phrasal.

phréatique /fʀeatik/ *adj* **nappe ~** ground water ⊄.

phtisie† /ftizi/ *nf* consumption, phthisis SPÉC.

phylactère /filaktɛʀ/ *nm* **1** (de bande dessinée) speech ou thought bubble; **2** ART phylactery, scroll; **3** (étui) phylactery.

physicien, -ienne /fizisjɛ̃, ɛn/ ▶374 *nm,f* physicist.

physiologie /fizjɔlɔʒi/ *nf* **1** (science) physiology (**de** of); **2** (structure) LITER anatomy (**de** of).

physiologique /fizjɔlɔʒik/ *adj* physiological.

physiologiste /fizjɔlɔʒist/ ▶374 *nmf* physiologist.

physionomie /fizjɔnɔmi/ *nf* (traits du visage) facial appearance, physiognomy SOUT; (visage) face; FIG (de pays) face; (de quartier) appearance, look; **~ politique d'un pays** political complexion of a country; **~ du marché** FIN state of the market.

physionomiste /fizjɔnɔmist/ *nmf* **1** GÉN **c'est un bon ~** (doué de mémoire) he has a good memory for faces; (qui sait juger) he's a good judge of faces; **2** ▶374 (profession) *casino employee responsible for recognizing people who are banned from gaming halls.*

physiothérapie /fizjoteʀapi/ *nf* physiotherapy GB, physical therapy US.

physique¹ /fizik/ **I** *adj* physical; **pour les cyclistes, c'est une étape très ~** for cyclists, this stage is physically very taxing; **un acteur qui a un jeu très ~** an actor with a very physical way of acting; **le squash provoque une énorme dépense ~** squash is a very strenuous game.
II *nm* (apparence) physical appearance; (corps) physique; **avoir un ~ séduisant** to look attractive; **jouer de son ~** to play on one's good looks; **au ~** physically.
IDIOMES **avoir le ~ de l'emploi** to look the part.

physique² /fizik/ *nf* (discipline) physics (+ *v sg*).

physiquement /fizikmɑ̃/ *adv* physically.

phytothérapeute /fitoteʀapøt/ ▶374 *nmf* herbalist.

phytothérapie /fitoteʀapi/ *nf* herbal medicine.

piaf° /pjaf/ *nm* (petit oiseau) little bird.

piaffer /pjafe/ [1] *vi* **1** [*cheval*] to paw the ground; **2** [*personne*] to be impatient (**de faire** to do); **~ d'impatience** to be champing at the bit.

piailler /pjaje/ [1] *vi* **1** [*oiseau*] to chirp; **2**° [*personne*] to squeal.

pianiste /pjanist/ *nmf* **1** ▶374 (professionnel) pianist; **un ~ de talent** a talented pianist; **2** (amateur) piano player.

pianistique /pjanistik/ *adj* **1** (de pianiste) [*technique, qualité*] pianistic; **2** (de piano) [*musique, études*] piano.

piano /pjano/ **I** *nm* **1** ▶392 (instrument) piano; **jouer qch au ~** to play sth on the piano; **se mettre au ~** (s'asseoir) to sit down at the piano; (apprendre) to take up the piano; **2** (passage joué doucement) piano passage.

II *adv* **1** MUS piano; **2**° FIG gently; **vas-y ~** take it easy.

■ **~ bastringue** honky-tonk piano; **~ de concert** concert grand (piano); **~ crapaud** small baby grand; **~ demi-queue** boudoir grand GB, parlor grand US; **~ droit** upright piano; **~ numérique** player piano; **~ quart de queue** baby grand; **~ à queue** grand piano.

pianoforte /pjanofɔrte/ ▶392 *nm* pianoforte.

pianoter /pjanɔte/ [1] *vi* **1** (sur un piano) to tinkle; **2** (sur un ordinateur, une machine à écrire) to tap (**sur** at); **je pianote sur mon clavier toute la journée** I tap away at the keyboard all day long; **3** (sur une table) to drum one's fingers.

piastre /pjastr/ ▶33 *nf* **1** GÉN piastre^GB; **2** C (dollar) dollar.

piauler /pjole/ [1] *vi* **1** (oiseau) to cheep; **2**° (enfant) to bawl°.

PIB /peibe/ *nm: abbr* ▶ **produit**.

pic /pik/ **I** *nm* **1** (montagne, sommet) peak; **2** (outil) pick; (de mineur) pickaxe^GB; **3** (de courbe) peak; **4** (oiseau) woodpecker.

II à pic *loc adj* [*falaise*] sheer; [*ravin*] very steep.

III à pic *loc adv* **1** (en pente raide) **s'élever à ~** to rise sheer; **tomber à ~** to fall in a sheer drop; **couler à ~** [*personne, objet*] to go straight down; **2**° FIG **tomber à ~** to come just at the right time.

pichenette /piʃnɛt/ *nf* flick; **enlever une poussière d'une ~** to flick off a speck of dust.

pichet /piʃɛ/ *nm* **1** (cruche) jug GB, pitcher; **2** (contenu) jugful GB, pitcherful.

pick-up /pikœp/ *nm inv* record player.

picorer /pikɔre/ [1] **I** *vtr* [*oiseau*] to peck at [*graines*].

II *vi* [*oiseau*] to peck about; [*personne*] to nibble.

picotement /pikɔtmɑ̃/ *nm* (de peau, membres) tingling ¢; (de gorge) tickling ¢; (d'yeux) smarting ¢.

picoter /pikɔte/ [1] **I** *vtr* **1** (irriter) [*fumée, gaz, vent*] to sting, to make [sth] sting [*yeux, nez*]; to tickle [*gorge*]; **j'ai la gorge qui me picote** my throat is tickling; **2** (piquer) [*oiseau*] to peck [*fruit, pain*].

II *vi* [*gorge*] to tickle; [*yeux*] to sting.

picotin /pikɔtɛ̃/ *nm* **1** (ration) **~ d'avoine** ration of oats; **2** (mesure) peck.

picrate /pikrat/ *nm* **1**° (vin) plonk° GB, cheap wine; **2** CHIMIE picrate.

pictural, -e, *mpl* **-aux** /piktyral, o/ *adj* pictorial.

pie /pi/ **I** ▶141 *adj inv* [*vache*] black and white; **~ noir** [*cheval*] piebald; **~ alezan** [*cheval*] skewbald; **la race ~ rouge** (bovin) breed of red and white cattle.

II *nf* **1** (oiseau) magpie; **2**° (bavard) chatterbox°.

pièce /pjɛs/ **I** *nf* **1** (d'habitation) room; **maison de quatre ~s** four-room(ed) house (*excluding kitchen and bathroom*); **2** ▶33 (monnaie) **~ (de monnaie)** coin; **donner ou glisser la ~ à qn** to give sb a tip; **3** THÉÂT play; LITTÉRAT, MUS piece; **4** (morceau) bit, piece; **en ~s** in bits; **mettre en ~s** (briser) to smash [sth] to pieces; (déchirer) to pull [sth] to pieces; FIG to pull [sth/sb] to pieces; **5** (élément d'un assemblage) part; **créé de toutes ~s** FIG created from nothing; **c'est forgé** or **inventé de toutes ~s** FIG it's a complete fabrication; **6** (pour réparer) patch; **7** (document) document; **juger (avec) ~s à l'appui** to judge on the basis of supporting documents; **~s jointes** enclosures; **juger sur ~s** to judge on the actual evidence; **8** (unité, objet) piece, item; (de jeu d'échecs, puzzle)

piece; **vendu à la ~** sold separately ou individually; **travailler à la ~** or **aux ~s** to do piecework; **9** (d'étoffe) length; **~ de bois** piece of timber; **~ de viande** (large) piece of meat; **~ de terre** field, piece of land; **une belle ~ de poisson** a fine fish.

II -pièces (*in compounds*) **1** (habitation) **un trois-~s cuisine** a three-roomed flat GB ou apartment US with kitchen; **2** (vêtement) **un (maillot) deux-~s** a two-piece swimsuit.

■ **~ d'artillerie** cannon; **~ de collection** collector's item; **~ à conviction** exhibit; **~ d'eau** ornamental lake; (plus petit) ornamental pond; **~ détachée** spare part; **en ~s détachées** (en kit) in kit form; (démonté) dismantled; **~ d'identité** identity papers (*pl*); **~ maîtresse** (de collection) showpiece; (de plaidoyer) key element; (de politique) cornerstone; **~ montée** *pyramid-shaped arrangement of cream puffs*; **~ de musée** museum piece; **~ de théâtre** play; **~ de vin** cask of wine.

IDIOMES **il est tout d'une ~** he's a very straightforward man; **on n'est pas aux ~s**° we're not in a sweat-shop.

piécette /pjesɛt/ *nf* small coin.

pied /pje/ *nm* **1** ▶137 GÉN foot; **marcher avec les ~s tournés en dedans/en dehors** to be pigeon-toed/splay-footed; **être ~s nus** to be barefoot(ed); **il était ~s nus dans ses chaussures** his feet were bare inside his shoes; **sauter à ~s joints** LIT to jump with one's feet together; FIG to jump in with both feet; **coup de ~** kick; **donner un coup de ~ à qn** to kick sb; **casser qch à coups de ~** to kick sth to pieces; **écarter qch d'un coup de ~** to kick sth aside; **à ~** GÉN on foot; **promenade à ~** walk; **randonnée à ~** ramble; **bottes aux ~s** wearing boots; **traîner les ~s** LIT, FIG to drag one's feet; **ne plus tenir sur ses ~s** to be about to keel over; **taper du ~** (de colère) to stamp one's foot; (d'impatience) to tap one's foot; **mettre ~ à terre** to dismount; **de la tête aux ~s, des ~s à la tête, de ~ en cap** from head to foot, from top to toe; **portrait en ~** full-length portrait; **statue en ~** standing figure; **avoir un ~ dans l'édition** to have a foothold in publishing; **avoir conscience de là où on met les ~s**° FIG to be aware of what one is letting oneself in for; **sur un ~ d'égalité** on an equal footing; **2** (d'animal) GÉN foot; (de cheval) hoof; CULIN trotter; **animaux sur ~** livestock ¢ on the hoof; **3** (de colline, d'escalier) foot; (de colonne) foot, base; **4** (de meuble) (totalité) leg; (extrémité) foot; (de verre) stem; (de lampe) base; (d'appareil photo) GÉN stand; (trépied) tripod; (de champignon) stalk; **5** (plant) head; **~ de vigne** vine; **récolte sur ~** standing crop; **6** ▶348 (unité de longueur) foot.

■ **~ à coulisse** calliper rule; **~ de lit** footboard.

IDIOMES **~ à ~** inch by inch; **être sur ~** [*personne*] to be up and about; [*affaires*] to be up and running; **mettre qch sur ~** to set sth up; **j'ai ~** I can touch the bottom; **je n'ai plus ~** I'm out of my depth; **perdre ~** LIT to go out of one's depth; FIG to lose ground; **être à ~ d'œuvre** to be ready to get down to work; **je me suis débrouillé comme un ~**° I've made a mess of it; **elle joue au tennis comme un ~**° she's hopeless at tennis; **faire un ~ de nez à qn** to thumb one's nose at sb; **faire un ~ de nez aux conventions** to cock a snook at conventions; **faire du ~ à qn** to play footsy with sb°; **faire des ~s et des mains° pour obtenir qch** to work really hard at getting sth; **ça lui fera les ~s**° that will teach him/her a lesson; **c'est le ~**° (très bien) that's terrific°; **c'est pas le ~ aujourd'hui**° things aren't so hot today°; **prendre son ~**° to have a good time; **mettre à ~** (mesure disciplinaire) to suspend; (mesure économique) to lay [sb] off; **lever le ~**° (aller moins vite) to slow down; (s'arrêter) to stop.

pied-à-terre /pjetatɛr/ *nm inv* pied-à-terre.

pied-bot, *pl* **pieds-bots** /pjebo/ *nm* club-footed person.

pied-de-biche, *pl* **pieds-de-biche** /pjedbiʃ/ *nm* **1** (de machine à coudre) presser foot; **2** (levier) crowbar; **3** (arrache-clous) claw head.

pied-de-poule, *pl* **pieds-de-poule** /pjedpul/ *adj inv* houndstooth.

piédestal, *pl* **-aux** /pjedɛstal, o/ *nm* pedestal.

pied-noir○, *pl* **pieds-noirs** /pjenwaʀ/ *nmf* pied-noir (*French colonial born in Algeria*).

piège /pjɛʒ/ *nm* **1** LIT, FIG trap; **relever un ~** to check a trap; **pris au ~** trapped; **tendre un ~ à qn** to set a trap for sb; **être pris à son propre ~** to fall into one's own trap; **~ à loups** mantrap; **2** (difficulté) pitfall; **c'est un texte sans ~** it's a straightforward text; **~s orthographiques** tricky spellings.

piégé, **~e** /pjeʒe/ *adj* [*objet, valise*] booby-trapped; **lettre ~e** letter bomb; **colis ~** parcel GB ou package US bomb; **voiture ~e** car bomb.

piéger /pjeʒe/ [15] *vtr* **1** LIT to trap [*animal, criminel*]; **se faire** or **se laisser ~** to get trapped; **2** (tromper) to trick, to trap [*personne*]; **3** to booby-trap [*lettre, voiture*].

pie-grièche, *pl* **pies-grièches** /piɡʀijɛʃ/ *nf* shrike.

pierraille /pjɛʀaj/ *nf* loose stones (*pl*).

pierre /pjɛʀ/ *nf* **1** (matière) stone; **2** (morceau) stone, rock; **un désert de ~s** a rocky ou stony wilderness; **'chute de ~s'** 'falling rocks'; **poser la première ~** to lay the foundation stone; FIG to lay the foundations (**de** of); **être amateur de vieilles ~s** FIG to be fascinated by old buildings; **3** (immobilier) property GB, real-estate US.

■ **~ à aiguiser** whetstone; **~ angulaire** LIT, FIG cornerstone; **~ à briquet** flint; **~ fine** gemstone; **~ à fusil** gun flint; **~ de taille** dressed stone; **~ tombale** tombstone, gravestone.

IDIOMES **jeter la ~ à qn** to accuse sb; **apporter sa ~ à qch** to make one's contribution to sth; **faire d'une ~ deux coups** to kill two birds with one stone.

pierreries /pjɛʀʀi/ *nfpl* gems.

pierreux, -euse /pjɛʀø, øz/ *adj* stony (*épith*).

piétaille /pjetɑj/ *nf* PEJ **la ~** the underlings (*pl*) PÉJ.

piété /pjete/ *nf* piety; **de ~** [*articles*] devotional.

piétinement /pjetinmɑ̃/ *nm* **1** (mouvement) **le ~ de la foule dans les rues en fête** the crowd shuffling through the festive streets; **2** (bruit) **les ~s dans le couloir** the sound (*sg*) of feet in the corridor; **3** (de négociations, d'enquête) lack of progress.

piétiner /pjetine/ [1] **I** *vtr* LIT to trample [sth] underfoot [*bouquet, fraisiers*]; FIG to trample on [*droits, croyances*]; **~ le sol** to stamp one's feet.

II *vi* **1** (sur place) **~ d'impatience** to hop up and down with impatience; **2** (marcher lentement) (à cause de la foule) to shuffle along; (à cause de la neige) to trudge along; **3** FIG [*négociations, enquête*] to make no headway; **je piétine** I'm not getting anywhere.

piéton, -onne /pjetɔ̃, ɔn/ **I** *adj* [*rue, zone, voie*] pedestrianized.

II *nm,f* pedestrian; **passage pour ~s** pedestrian crossing.

piétonnier, -ière /pjetɔnje, ɛʀ/ *adj* **1** [*rue, zone, voie*] pedestrianized; **2** [*circulation*] pedestrian (*épith*).

piètre /pjɛtʀ/ *adj* [*acteur, écrivain*] very mediocre; [*santé, résultats*] very poor; [*avantage*] negligible; [*performance*] sorry; **c'est une ~ consolation** it's not much comfort; **avoir ~ allure** to cut a sorry figure.

pieu, *pl* **~x**¹ /pjø/ *nm* **1** (poteau pointu) stake; **2** ARCHIT, CONSTR pile.

pieuse ▸ pieux².

pieusement /pjøzmɑ̃/ *adv* **1** RELIG piously; **2** (avec respect) devotedly; **~ conservé** religiously kept.

pieuvre /pjœvʀ/ *nf* **1** ZOOL octopus; **2** (entreprise tentaculaire) octopus.

pieux², **pieuse** /pjø, øz/ *adj* **1** RELIG [*personne*] pious, religious; [*livre*] pious; [*peinture*] religious; **avoir une pensée pieuse pour qn** to remember sb in one's prayers; **2** LITER [*devoirs*] loving; [*affection, silence*] reverent.

■ **~ mensonge** white lie.

pif○ /pif/ *nm* **1** (nez) nose, conk○ GB, schnozzle○ US; **2** (flair) intuition; **j'ai eu du ~** I had a hunch○; [*mesurer*] roughly; [*trouver*] by chance; [*décider*] just like that.

IDIOMES **avoir qn dans le ~** to have it in for sb○.

pige /piʒ/ *nf* **1** (dans la presse) **travailler à la ~, faire des ~s** to do freelance work; **2** (tige) measuring rod; (longueur) length.

pigeon /piʒɔ̃/ *nm* **1** (oiseau) pigeon; **2**○ (naïf) sucker○.

■ **~ d'argile** clay pigeon; **~ ramier** wood pigeon ring dove; **~ vole** Simon says; **jouer à ~ vole** to play Simon says; **~ voyageur** carrier pigeon.

pigeonnant, ~e /piʒɔnɑ̃, ɑ̃t/ *adj* [*soutien-gorge*] uplift (*épith*); [*poitrine*] with a lot of cleavage (*épith, après n*).

pigeonneau, *pl* **~x** /piʒɔno/ *nm* young pigeon.

pigeonnier /piʒɔnje/ *nm* **1** (pour pigeons) GÉN pigeon house; (en haut d'un bâtiment) pigeon loft; (bâtiment circulaire) dovecote; **2** (appartement) HUM garret.

piger○ /piʒe/ [13] *vtr* (comprendre) to understand; **tu as pigé?** did you get it?; **je ne pige rien à l'informatique** I haven't got a clue○ about computing.

pigiste /piʒist/ *nmf* freelance.

pigment /pigmɑ̃/ *nm* pigment.

pigmenter /pigmɑ̃te/ [1] *vtr* [*soleil, maladie*] to alter the pigmentation of [*peau*].

pigne /piɲ/ *nf* pine cone.

pignon /piɲɔ̃/ *nm* **1** (de maison) gable; **2** (roue dentée) gearwheel, cogwheel; (petite roue) pinion; **3** (de pin) pine kernel.

IDIOMES **avoir ~ sur rue** to be well-established.

pilaf /pilaf/ *nm* pilau; **riz ~** pilau rice.

pile¹ ○ /pil/ *adv* **1** (brusquement) **s'arrêter ~** to stop dead; **2** (exactement) exactly; **à 10 heures et demie ~** at ten-thirty sharp ou on the dot○; **être ~ à l'heure** to be right on time; **tu tombes ~** (au bon moment) you've come just at the right time; (la personne qu'il faut) you're just the person I wanted to see; **tu es tombé ~** (en devinant) you hit the nail on the head○; **ça tombe ~** (au bon moment) that's lucky; **elle est arrivée ~ au moment où je devais partir** she turned up precisely as I was about to leave; **c'est tombé ~ dans mon assiette** it fell right into my plate.

pile² /pil/ *nf* **1** (tas) (désordonné) pile; (régulier) stack; **2** ÉLECTROTECH **~ (électrique)** battery; **à ~s** [*jouet, réveil*] battery-operated (*épith*); **3** ARCHIT (de pont) pier; **4** (de monnaie) **le côté ~** the reverse side; **jouer à ~ ou face** to play heads or tails; **ils ont décidé à ~ ou face** (choix de personne) they tossed for it; (choix d'option) they decided it on the flip ou toss of the coin.

■ **~ bouton** button battery; **~ solaire** solar cell.

piler /pile/ [1] **I** *vtr* to grind [*noix*]; to crush [*gousse d'ail, verre*].

II○ *vi* (s'arrêter net) [*voiture*] to pull up short, to stop suddenly; [*conducteur*] to slam on the brakes.

pileux, -euse /pilø, øz/ *adj* **système ~** hair.

pilier /pilje/ *nm* **1** CONSTR pillar; **2** FIG (d'économie) mainstay; (personne) (de communauté) pillar; (de parti) stalwart; **~ de bar**○ bar fly○; **3** (au rugby) prop forward.

pillage /pijaʒ/ *nm* **1** (de ville, région) pillage, plundering; (de magasins) looting; **2** (des caisses de l'État) pillaging; **3** (plagiat) plagiarism.

pillard, ~e /pijaʀ, aʀd/ **I** *adj* [*hordes, bandes*] pillaging, plundering; [*oiseaux*] thieving.

II *nm,f* looter.

piller /pije/ [1] *vtr* **1** (dépouiller) to pillage [*ville*]; to loot [*magasin*]; to ransack [*maison, réfrigérateur*]; **2** (voler) to pillage [*objets d'art*]; to plunder [*temple, caisse*]; **3** (plagier) to plagiarize [*œuvre, auteur*].

pilleur, -euse /pijœʀ, øz/ *nm,f* (de magasin) looter; (d'église) plunderer.

pilon /pilɔ̃/ *nm* **1** (outil) pestle; **2** (jambe de bois, wooden leg; **3** (de volaille) drumstick; **4** (dans l'édition) pulping; **mettre qch au ~** to pulp sth.

ilonnage /pilɔnaʒ/ *nm* MIL bombardment.

ilonner /pilɔne/ [1] *vtr* **1** MIL to bombard; **2** (écraser) to grind, to pound [*graines, céréales*]; **3**° SPORT to give [sb] a pounding° [*adversaire, équipe*]; to pound away at [*buts*]; **4** (dans l'édition) to pulp.

ilori /pilɔRi/ *nm* HIST stocks (*pl*); **mettre qn au ~** FIG to pillory sb.

ilosité /pilozite/ *nf* hairiness ₵.

ilotage /pilɔtaʒ/ *nm* **1** AVIAT, NAUT piloting ₵; AUT driving ₵; **erreur de ~** pilot error; **le ~ à trois** flying with two co-pilots; **2** (gestion) (d'entreprise) running ₵; (de négociation) leading ₵.

ilote /pilɔt/ I *nm* **1** ▸374 AVIAT, NAUT pilot; AUT driver; **2** (guide) guide; **servir de ~ à qn** to show sb around.
II **(-)pilote** (*in compounds*) **projet(-)~** pilot project.
▪ **~ automatique** automatic pilot; **~ automobile** racing driver; **~ de chasse** fighter pilot; **~ de course** = **~ automobile**; **~ d'essai** test pilot; **~ de ligne** airline pilot.

iloter /pilɔte/ [1] *vtr* **1** LIT to pilot [*avion, navire*]; to drive [*voiture*]; **2** FIG to show [sb] around [*personne*]; to run [*entreprise*]; to lead [*négociation*].
II *vi* **1** AVIAT to fly; **~ à deux** to fly with dual controls; **2** AUT to drive.

ilotis /pilɔti/ *nm inv* stilts (*pl*), pilotis (*pl*) SPÉC.

ilule /pilyl/ *nf* **1** (médicament) pill; **2** (contraceptif) **~** **(contraceptive)** (contraceptive) pill; **~** **abortive** abortion pill; **je prends la ~** I'm on the pill.
IDIOMES **avaler la ~**° to grin and bear it; **faire passer la ~**° to sweeten the pill; **dorer la ~ à qn** to butter sb up; **se dorer la ~**° to sunbathe.

imbêche /pɛ̃bɛʃ/ *nf* stuck-up madam°.

iment /pimɑ̃/ *nm* **1** (plante) capsicum; **2** (condiment) hot pepper; **le risque met du ~ dans la vie** FIG danger adds a bit of spice to life.
▪ **~ doux** sweet pepper; **~ rouge** red hot pepper, chilli; **~ vert** hot pepper.

imenter /pimɑ̃te/ [1] *vtr* **1** CULIN to put chillies GB in, to put chilli GB powder in [*plat*]; **un plat très pimenté** a very hot dish; **2** (animer) to give a bit of spice to [*situation, réunion, spectacle*].

impant, -e /pɛ̃pɑ̃, ɑ̃t/ *adj* [*personne*] spruce, smart; [*voiture*] smart.

imprenelle /pɛ̃pRɔnɛl/ *nf* burnet.

in /pɛ̃/ *nm* pine (tree); **du bois de ~** pine.

inacle /pinakl/ *nm* ARCHIT pinnacle.
IDIOMES **porter** or **mettre qn au ~** to praise sb to the skies; **être au ~** to be at the top.

inacothèque /pinakɔtɛk/ *nf* art gallery.

inailler° /pinaje/ [1] *vi* to split hairs, to quibble (**sur** about).

ince /pɛ̃s/ I *nf* **1** (outil) (de plombier, d'électricien) pliers (*pl*), pair of pliers; (de forgeron) tongs (*pl*), pair of tongs; **2** (en couture) dart; **un pantalon à ~s** pleat front trousers (*pl*) GB ou pants (*pl*) US; **3** (de crabe) pincer, claw; (dent de cheval) incisor; **4** (levier) crowbar.
II pinces° *nfpl* **être à ~s** to be on foot.
▪ **~ à cheveux** hair grip; **~ coupante** wire cutters (*pl*); **~ crocodile** crocodile clip; **~ à dessin** bulldog clip; **~ à épiler** tweezers (*pl*); **~ à escargot** snail tongs (*pl*); **~ à glaçons** ice tongs (*pl*); **~ à linge** clothes peg; **~ multiprise** adjustable pliers (*pl*); **~ à ongles** nail clippers (*pl*); **~ à sucre** sugar tongs (*pl*); **~ universelle** universal pliers (*pl*); **~ à vélo** bicycle clip.

incé, ~e[1] /pɛ̃se/ *adj* **1** (contraint) [*sourire*] tight-lipped; **prendre un air ~** to become stiff ou starchy; **2** (serré) [*lèvres*] thin; [*narines*] pinched.

inceau, pl ~x /pɛ̃so/ *nm* **1** (instrument) (paint) brush; **donner un coup de ~ à qch** to give sth a lick of paint; **2** (manière de peindre) brushwork; **3** (faisceau) **~ lumineux** pencil beam.

pincée[2] /pɛ̃se/ *nf* (de poivre, sel) pinch (**de** of).

pincement /pɛ̃smɑ̃/ *nm* **1** (de peau) pinch; **avoir un ~ de cœur** FIG to feel a twinge of sadness; **2** MUS (de corde) plucking.

pince-monseigneur, pl pinces-monseigneur /pɛ̃smɔ̃sɛɲœR/ *nf* (levier) jemmy GB, slim jim US.

pincer /pɛ̃se/ [12] I *vtr* **1** (pour faire mal) [*personne*] to pinch; [*crabe*] to nip; **2**° (attraper) to nab°, to catch [*voleur, criminel*]; **3** (serrer) **~ les lèvres** or **la bouche** to purse (up) one's lips; **une veste qui pince la taille** a jacket which hugs the waist; **4** MUS to pluck [*corde*].
II *vi* [*vent, froid*] to be nippy°.
III se pincer *vpr* **1** (accidentellement) to catch oneself; **elle s'est pincée en refermant le tiroir** she caught her fingers closing the drawer; **2** (volontairement) to pinch oneself; **j'ai dû me ~ pour y croire** I had to pinch myself to make sure I wasn't dreaming; **se ~ le nez** to hold one's nose.
IDIOMES **en ~**° **pour qn** to be stuck° on sb, to be in love with sb.

pince-sans-rire /pɛ̃ssɑ̃Rir/ *nmf inv* **c'est un ~** he has a deadpan sense of humour GB.

pincette /pɛ̃sɛt/ *nf* **1** (petite pince) tweezers (*pl*), pair of tweezers; **2** (de cheminée) fire tongs (*pl*).
IDIOMES **il n'est pas à prendre avec des ~s**° he's like a bear with a sore head.

pinçon /pɛ̃sɔ̃/ *nm* pinch-mark.

pinède /pinɛd/ *nf* pine forest.

pingouin /pɛ̃gwɛ̃/ *nm* auk; (manchot) CONTROV penguin; **grand ~** great auk; **petit ~** razorbill.

ping-pong®, *pl* **~s** /piŋpɔ̃/ ▸329 *nm* **1** (jeu) table tennis, ping-pong; **2** (table) table tennis table.

pingre /pɛ̃gR/ I *adj* stingy, niggardly.
II *nmf* skinflint.

pingrerie /pɛ̃gRəRi/ *nf* stinginess.

pin-pon /pɛ̃pɔ̃/ *nm* (*also onomat*) sound of a two-tone siren.

pin's /pins/ *nm inv* CONTROV lapel badge.

pinson /pɛ̃sɔ̃/ *nm* chaffinch.
IDIOMES **gai comme un ~** as happy as a lark.

pintade /pɛ̃tad/ *nf* guinea fowl.

pintadeau, pl ~x /pɛ̃tado/ *nm* young guinea fowl.

pinte /pɛ̃t/ *nf* ▸86 (mesure anglo-saxonne) pint; (ancienne mesure) = US quart (= 0,94 litre).
IDIOMES **se payer une ~ de bon sang**° (rire) to have a good laugh.

pinter°: **se pinter** /pɛ̃te/ [1] *vpr* (s'enivrer) to get plastered° ou drunk.

pin-up /pinœp/ *nf inv* (personne) glamour girl.

pioche /pjɔʃ/ *nf* **1** (de cultivateur) mattock; (de terrassier) pickaxe; **2** JEUX stock.

piocher /pjɔʃe/ [1] I *vtr* **1** (creuser) to dig [sth] over [*sol*]; **2**° (potasser) to work on [*sujet*]; **3** JEUX to take [sth] from the stock [*carte, domino*].
II *vi* **1** (creuser) to dig; **2**° (potasser) to study; **3** (prendre) to take [sth] from the stock [*carte, domino*]; **pioche!** (aux cartes) take a card!; (à table) help yourself!, dive in°!; **~ dans la caisse** to have one's hand in the till.

piolet /pjɔlɛ/ *nm* ice axe GB ou ax US.

pion, pionne /pjɔ̃, pjɔn/ I° *nm,f* SCOL *student paid to supervise pupils*.
II *nm* **1** (aux échecs) pawn; (aux dames) draught GB, checker US; **2** FIG pawn.

pionnier, -ière /pjɔnje, ɛR/ *adj, nm,f* pioneer.

pipe /pip/ *nf* (à fumer) pipe.
IDIOMES **casser sa ~**° to die, to kick the bucket°; **se fendre la ~**° to laugh one's head off°.

pipeau, pl ~x /pipo/ *nm* **1** ▸392 (petite flûte) (reed-) pipe; **2** (appeau) birdcall.
IDIOMES **c'est du ~**° it's no great shakes°; **c'est pas du ~**° it's for real°.

pipelette° /piplɛt/ *nf* (bavard) gossip(monger).

pipeline /piplin, pajplajn/ *nm* CONTROV pipeline.

piper /pipe/ [1] *vtr* **1**○ (dire) **ne pas ~ (mot)** not to say a word; **2** JEUX to load [*dés*]; to mark [*cartes*].

piperade /piperad/ *nf*: *omelette made with tomatoes and peppers*, ≈ Spanish omelette.

pipette /pipɛt/ *nf* pipette.

pipi○ /pipi/ *nm* wee○ GB, pee○; (langage enfantin) wee-wee○; **faire ~ dans sa culotte** to wet oneself; **c'est à faire ~ dans sa culotte** FIG it's hilarious.

IDIOMES **c'est du ~ de chat** (boisson) it's gnat's piss○; (spectacle, livre) it's as dull as dishwater.

piquant, **~e** /pikã, ãt/ **I** *adj* **1** [*tige, chardon*] prickly; [*clou*] sharp; [*barbe*] bristly; **2** [*moutarde, sauce*] hot; [*odeur*] pungent; [*vin, fromage*] sharp; **3** [*froid*] biting; [*air*] sharp; **4** [*remarque*] cutting, biting; **5** [*aventure*] spicy, piquant; [*charme*] heady.

II *nm* **1** (de tige, chardon) prickle; (de hérisson, cactus) spine; (de barbelés) spike, barb; **2** FIG (d'histoire) spiciness; (de situation) piquancy.

pique[1] /pik/ *nm* JEUX (carte) spade; (couleur) spades (*pl*).

pique[2] /pik/ *nf* **1** (parole) cutting remark; **2** (arme) pike; (de picador) lance; **3** (à cocktail) swizzle stick.

piqué, **~e** /pike/ **I** *pp* ▶ **piquer**.

II *pp adj* **1** [*couverture*] quilted; **2** (marqué) [*bois*] worm-eaten; [*linge, miroir, fruit*] spotted; [*papier, livre*] foxed; **un visage ~ de taches de rousseur** a face dotted with freckles; **3** (aigre) [*vin*] sour; **4**○ (fou) [*personne*] dotty○, eccentric; **5** MUS [*note, phrase*] staccato.

III○ *nm,f* (extravagant) nutcase○.

IV *nm* **1** (tissu) piqué; **2** .AVIAT (nose)dive; **3** (en danse) piqué; **4** (de photographie) sharpness.

pique-assiette○ /pikasjɛt/ *nmf inv* sponger○, freeloader○.

pique-feu /pikfø/ *nm inv* poker.

pique-nique, *pl* **~s** /piknik/ *nm* picnic.

pique-niquer /piknike/ [1] *vi* to have a picnic.

piquer /pike/ [1] **I** *vtr* **1** (blesser) [*guêpe, ortie*] to sting; [*moustique, serpent*] to bite; [*chardon, rosier*] to prick; **2** (enfoncer une pointe) [*personne*] to prick [*animal, fruit*]; **~ un couteau dans le gâteau** to prick the cake with a knife; **~ des petits pois avec sa fourchette** to stab peas with one's fork; **3** MÉD to give [sb] an injection; **je me suis fait ~ contre la grippe** I've had a flu injection; **faire ~ un animal** to have an animal put down; **4** CULIN **~ un gigot d'ail** to stud a leg of lamb with garlic; **~ un oignon de clous de girofle** to stick an onion with cloves; **5** (fixer) to stick [*épingle*]; **6** (de trous) [*insecte, ver*] to make holes in [*bois, meuble*]; **7** (irriter) **mon pull me pique la peau** my sweater feels scratchy; **le froid me pique le visage** the cold is making my face tingle; **la fumée me pique la gorge** the smoke is stinging my throat; **ses yeux la piquaient** her eyes were stinging; **ça me pique partout** I'm itchy all over; **8**○ (voler) to pinch○ GB, to steal [*livre, idée*] (à from); (emprunter) to pinch○ GB, to borrow [*crayon, pull*]; **il pique (dans les magasins** GB ou **stores** US) he's always pinching things (from shops GB ou stores US); **9**○ (arrêter) [*police*] to nab○, to nick○ GB [*bandit*]; (surprendre) to get [*personne*]; **ils se sont fait ~ à tricher pendant l'examen** they got caught cheating during the exam; **10**○ (attraper) to catch [*virus*]; **11** to stitch [*tissu, vêtement*]; **12** [*propos*] to needle [*personne*]; to sting [*orgueil, fierté*]; **~ qn au vif** to cut sb to the quick; **13** (éveiller) to arouse [*curiosité, intérêt*]; **14**○ (commencer) **~ un fou rire** to have a fit of the giggles; **~ une crise de nerfs** to throw a fit○; **~ un cent mètres** to break into a run; **~ un galop** to break into a gallop; **15** (plonger) **~ une tête** (dans l'eau) to dive (into the water); **16** MUS **~ une note** to play a note staccato.

II *vi* **1** (irriter) [*barbe*] to be bristly; [*vêtement, laine*] to be scratchy; [*gorge, yeux*] to sting; [*vent, froid*] to be biting; **2** (exciter les sens) [*moutarde, sauce*] to be hot; [*vin, fromage*] to be sharp; [*boisson, soda*]○ to be fizzy○ GB ou sparkling; **3** (descendre) [*oiseau*] to swoop down; [*avion*] to dive; **~ du nez** (s'endormir) to nod

off, to doze off; (baisser la tête) to look down; (chute) [*avion*] to go into a nosedive; [*marché, Bourse*] to take a nosedive; [*fleur*] to droop; **4**○ (prendre) **arrête de ~ dans le plat** stop picking (things out of the dish); **pique dans le tas si tu veux** help yourself from the pile; **5**○ (s'élancer) **le taureau piqua droit sur nous** the bull came straight for us; **il piqua à travers bois** he cut across the woods.

III se piquer *vpr* **1** (se blesser) to prick oneself; **se ~ aux ronces** to scratch oneself on the brambles; **se ~ aux orties** to get stung by nettles; **2** (se faire une piqûre) to inject oneself; (se droguer)○ to shoot up○; **3** (se couvrir de taches) [*miroir, linge, métal*] to become spotted; [*papier, livre*] to become foxed; **4** (par prétention) FML **se ~ d'être philosophe** to like to pretend one is a philosopher; **se ~ de pouvoir réussir** to claim that one can manage on one's own; **5** (se vexer) to take offence GB (**de** at).

IDIOMES **quelle mouche t'a piqué**○? what's eating you?; **son article n'était pas piqué des vers**○ or **hannetons**○ his/her article didn't pull any punches; **c'est une petite maison pas piquée des vers**○ or **hannetons**○ it's a really lovely little house.

piquet /pikɛ/ *nm* **1** (pieu) stake; (très court) peg; (po.. slalom) gate pole; (de parasol) pole; **2** (groupe de gen.. picket; **3** (punition) **mettre un élève au ~** to make a pupil stand in the corner; **4** ▶ **329**] (jeu de cartes piquet.

■ **~ de grève** (strike) picket, picket line.

IDIOMES **rester planté comme un ~**○ to stand lik a dummy; **raide comme un ~**○ stiff as a post.

piqueter /pikte/ [20] *vtr* **1** (pour délimiter) to stake ou **2** (parsemer) to dot; **piqueté de (taches de) rouill** spotted with rust; **ciel piqueté d'étoiles** sky spangle with stars.

piquette○ /pikɛt/ *nf* (vin) PEJ plonk○ GB, cheap wine.

piqûre /pikyʀ/ *nf* **1** (injection) injection, shot; **fair une ~ à qn** to give sb an injection; **2** (d'épin.. épingle) prick; (d'ortie, abeille) sting; (de moustiqu.. bite; **~ d'amour-propre** wound to one's pride; (dans le bois) hole; **4** (petite tache) spot; **~s d rouille** specks ou spots of rust; **5** (point) stitch; (co.. ture) stitching ℂ.

■ **~ de rappel** MÉD booster (injection).

piratage /piʀataʒ/ *nm* piracy, pirating; **~ de carte bancaires** credit card fraud; **~ informatiqu** computer hacking.

pirate /piʀat/ **I** *adj* [*édition, radio*] pirate (*épith*).

II *nm* NAUT pirate.

■ **~ de l'air** hijacker, skyjacker; **~ inform tique** computer hacker.

pirater /piʀate/ [1] *vtr* to pirate.

piraterie /piʀatʀi/ *nf* (activité) piracy ℂ; (acte) act piracy.

■ **~ aérienne** hijacking, skyjacking; **~ inform tique** computer hacking.

pire /piʀ/ **I** *adj* **1** (comparatif) worse (**que** than); (superlatif) worst; **les ~s mensonges** the mo wicked lies; **le ~ des imbéciles** the biggest fool; **~ des deux** the worse of the two.

II *nm* **le ~** the worst; **au ~** at the very worst.

IDIOMES **il n'y a ~ eau que l'eau qui dort** PROV st.. waters run deep PROV.

pirogue /piʀɔg/ *nf* dugout canoe, pirogue SPÉC.

pirouette /piʀwɛt/ *nf* **1** (tour) pirouette; **les ~ d'un clown** the cavortings of a clown; **2** FIG (répon évasive) skilful evasion; (revirement) U-turn, flip-flop US; **s'en tirer par une ~** to dodge the question sk fully.

pirouetter /piʀwɛte/ [1] *vi* **1** [*danseur*] to pirouett **~ sur ses talons** to spin on one's heels; **2** (faire volt face) to do a U-turn.

pis /pi/ **I** *adj inv* LITER worse.

II *adv* LITER worse.

III *nm inv* **1** (de vache) udder; **2** LITER **le ~** the worst.

IDIOMES **dire ~ que pendre de qn** to vilify sb.

pis-aller /pizale/ *nm inv* lesser evil; **ces matéria..**

sont des ~ we'll have to make do with these materials.

isciculteur, -trice /pisikyltœʀ, tʀis/ ▸ 374 *nm,f*
fish farmer, pisciculturist SPÉC.

isciculture /pisikyltyʀ/ *nf* fish farming, pisciculture SPÉC.

iscine /pisin/ *nf* swimming pool; **~ couverte**
indoor swimming pool.

ise /piz/ ▸ 628 *npr* Pisa.

isé /pize/ *nm* ~ adobe.

isse◦ /pis/ *nf* piss◦.

IDIOMES c'est de la ~ de chat or **d'âne** (boisson)
it's gnat's piss.

issenlit /pisãli/ *nm* dandelion.

IDIOMES manger les ~s par la racine◦ to be pushing up the daisies◦.

isser◦ /pise/ [1] **I** *vtr* **~ du sang** to pass blood; **~
le sang** [*personne, nez, blessure*] to pour with blood;
mon moteur pissait l'huile my engine was leaking
oil all over the place.

II *vi* **1** (uriner) [*personne, animal*] to pee◦, to piss◦;
rire à en ~ dans sa culotte to wet ou piss◦ one's
pants laughing; **~ au lit** to wet the bed; **2** (fuir) [*récipient*] to leak; **l'eau pisse de partout** water is pouring out from everywhere.

IDIOMES il pleut comme vache qui pisse it's pissing
down◦; **se regarder** or **s'écouter ~**, **ne plus se
sentir ~** to be full of oneself; **ça lui a pris comme
une envie de ~** he/she had a sudden urge to do it;
laisse ~! forget it!

isseux◦, **-euse** /pisø, øz/ *adj* (sale, terne) PEJ
dingy.

issotière◦ /pisɔtjɛʀ/ *nf* street urinal, pissoir US.

istache /pistaʃ/ *nf* pistachio; **une ~** a pistachio
nut.

iste /pist/ *nf* **1** (trace) LIT, FIG trail; **être sur une
fausse ~** to be on the wrong track; **2** (ensemble d'indices) lead; **3** (de stade, d'autodrome) track; (d'hippodrome) racecourse GB, racetrack US; (de danse) floor;
(de patinage) rink; (de cirque) ring; (de ski) slope; (de
ski de fond) trail; (pour course automobile) racetrack;
~ d'élan (au ski) take-off ramp; **~ (de ski) pour
débutants** nursery slope; **skier hors ~** to go off-
piste skiing; **épreuve sur ~** track event; **faire un
tour de ~** to do a lap; **entrer en ~** (au cirque) to
come into the ring; FIG to enter the fray; **en ~!** FIG get
cracking◦!; **être en ~** FIG to be in the running; **4**
(chemin) (de brousse) track; (de désert) trail; **5** AVIAT
runway; **6** (de disque, cassette) track.

■ ~ artificielle (avec neige artificielle) artificial
slope; (en matière plastique) dry ski slope; **~ cavalière** bridle path, bridleway; **~ cyclable** (sur une
route) cycle lane; (à côté d'une route) cycle way, cycle
path; (à la campagne) cycle track.

ister /piste/ [1] *vtr* to trail, to track.

istil /pistil/ *nm* pistil.

istolet /pistɔlɛ/ *nm* **1** (arme) pistol, gun; **tirer au ~**
to fire a pistol; **2** TECH (outil) gun.

■ ~ d'alarme alarm gun; **~ à peinture** spray
gun.

istolet-mitrailleur, *pl* **pistolets-
mitrailleurs** /pistɔlɛmitʀajœʀ/ *nm* submachine gun.

iston /pistɔ̃/ *nm* **1** TECH piston; **moteur à ~s** piston
engine; **2**◦ (relations) contacts (*pl*); **avoir du ~** to
have connections ou contacts in the right places; **il a
obtenu son poste par ~** someone pulled strings to
get him the job; **3** MUS (d'instrument) valve; **cornet à
~s** cornet.

istonner◦ /pistɔne/ [1] *vtr* PEJ to pull strings for.

itance† /pitãs/ *nf* fare ¢.

iteusement /pitøzmã/ *adv* pitifully, pathetically.

iteux, -euse /pitø, øz/ *adj* **1** (piètre) [*résultats*]
poor, pitiful; **en ~ état** in a sorry state; **2** (penaud)
[*personne, air*] crestfallen.

itié /pitje/ *nf* (compassion) pity; (indulgence) pity,
mercy; **avoir ~ de qn** (plaindre) to feel sorry for sb;
(se montrer charitable) to take pity on sb; **ayez ~ de**

nous! (soyez bon) take ou have pity on us!; (épargnez-
nous) have mercy on us!; **prendre qn en ~** to take
pity on sb; **il me fait ~** I feel sorry for him; **il fait
~ (à voir)** he's a pitiful sight; **maigre à faire ~**
pitifully thin; **ça me fait ~ de la voir dans cet état**
it makes me sad to see her in that state; **sans ~**
[*vainqueur*] merciless, pitiless; [*huer, critiquer*] mercilessly; [*concurrence*] ruthless; **un monde sans ~** a
cruel world; **par ~, tais-toi!** for pity's sake, be
quiet!; **~ pour nos forêts!** save our forests!; **~
pour mes pauvres oreilles!** think of my poor ears!;
regarder qn avec ~ to look pityingly at sb.

piton /pitɔ̃/ *nm* **1** (à crochet) hook; (à anneau) eye; **2**
(d'alpinisme) piton; **3** GÉOG peak.

pitoyable /pitwajabl/ *adv* **1** (digne de pitié) pitiful; **2**
(lamentable) pathetic.

pitoyablement /pitwajabləmã/ *adv* **1** (de façon
pitoyable) pitifully; **2** (lamentablement) [*échouer*] miserably; [*chanter*] pathetically.

pitre /pitʀ/ *nm* clown, buffoon.

pitrerie /pitʀəʀi/ *nf* clowning ¢.

pittoresque /pitɔʀɛsk/ **I** *adj* [*lieu*] picturesque; [*personnage, scène*] colourful GB; [*expression, œuvre*] vivid.

II *nm* **le ~** the picturesque; **le ~ de qch** the picturesque quality of sth, the vividness of sth; **le ~ dans
tout cela** the amusing thing about all that.

pivert /pivɛʀ/ *nm* green woodpecker.

pivoine /pivwan/ *nf* peony.

IDIOMES être rouge comme une ~ to be as red as a
beetroot GB ou a beet US.

pivot /pivo/ *nm* **1** TECH pivot; **2** FIG (d'économie)
linchpin; (de complot) kingpin; **société ~** key firm;
3 SPORT (joueur) pivot, post; **4** (de dent) post and core.

pivotant, -e /pivotã, ãt/ *adj* [*fauteuil*] swivel;
[*panneau*] pivoting; [*porte*] revolving.

pivoter /pivote/ [1] *vi* [*personne, animal*] to pivot, to
turn; [*panneau, mur*] to pivot; [*porte, table*] to revolve;
[*fauteuil, chaise*] to swivel.

PJ /peʒi/ *nf*: *abbr* ▸ **police**.

PL (*written abbr* = **poids lourd**) HGV GB, heavy
truck US.

placage /plakaʒ/ *nm* **1** (revêtement) (en bois) veneer;
(en métal) plating; (en pierre) facing; **2** SPORT tackling
¢.

placard /plakaʀ/ *nm* **1** (meuble) cupboard; **ranger** or
mettre au ~ FIG (de côté) to put [sth] on ice [*projet*];
to shunt [sb] aside [*personne*]; (au rebut) to ditch
[*projet*]; to pension [sb] off [*personne*]; **sortir du ~**
FIG to come in from the cold; **2** (affiche) poster, bill;
(dans un journal) **~ publicitaire** display advertisement; **3** (épreuve) galley (proof); **4**◦ (prison) clink◦.

placarder /plakaʀde/ [1] *vtr* **1** (afficher) to post, to
stick [*avis, affiche, photo*]; **2** (décorer) to cover [sth]
with posters [*mur*].

place /plas/ *nf* **1** (espace) room, space; **laisser de la
~** to leave enough space; **2** (emplacement, espace
défini) GÉN place; (pour s'asseoir) seat; **les dictionnaires ne sont pas à leur ~** the dictionaries aren't
where they should be; **deux ~s pour 'Le Lac des
Cygnes'** two tickets for 'Swan Lake'; **la ~ d'un mot
dans une phrase** the position of a word in a sentence;
il faut savoir rester à sa ~ you must know your
place; **tenir une grande ~ dans la vie de qn** to play
a large part in sb's life; **faire une large ~ à qch** to
put a lot of emphasis on sth; **notre travail laisse peu
de ~ à l'imagination** our work leaves little room for
the imagination; **faire ~ à** to give way to; **~ aux
jeunes** or **à la jeunesse!** LIT, FIG make way for the
young!; **il reste une ~ en première** there's one seat
left in first class; **une salle de 200 ~s** a 200 seat auditorium; **payer sa ~** (au cinéma, théâtre) to pay for
one's ticket; (dans un train etc) to pay one's fare; **les
~s sont chères** FIG (parking difficile) parking spaces
are hard to find; (âpre concurrence dans l'emploi) jobs
are hard to come by; **prenez ~** (sur un siège) take a
seat; (chacun à son siège) take your seats; (chacun à son
poste) take your places; **sur ~** [*aller*] to the scene;
[*arriver*] on the scene; [*étudier*] on the spot; [*enquête*]

on-the-spot; **on se retrouve sur ~** we'll meet up there; **ouvrage à consulter sur ~** reference book; **laisser qn sur ~** to leave sb standing; **de ~ en ~** here and there; **divan à trois ~s** three-seater sofa; **un parking de 500 ~s** a car park for 500 cars; **3** (dans un classement) place; (dans un ordre) position; **il est dans les premières ~s** he's up toward(s) the top; **4** (substitution) **à la ~ de** instead of, in place of; **il a mis de la vodka à la ~ du cognac** he's used vodka instead of brandy; **qu'aurais-tu fait à ma ~?** what would you have done in my place?; **(si j'étais) à ta ~** if I were in your position ou shoes; **je ne peux pas le faire à ta ~!** I can't do it for you!; **j'ai mis le vase à la ~ du cendrier** I put the vase where the ashtray was; **5** (situation définie) **en ~** [*système, structures*] in place (*après n*); [*troupes*] in position (*après n*); [*dirigeant, parti*] ruling (*épith*); **les gens en ~** the powers that be; **ne plus tenir en ~** to be restless ou fidgety; **mettre en ~** to put [sth] in place [*programme*]; to put [sth] in position [*équipe*]; to establish, to set up [*réseau, institution*]; to install [*ligne téléphonique*]; **6** (dans une agglomération) square; **la ~ du village** the village square; **la ~ du marché** the marketplace; **7** FIN market; **~ financière** financial market; **8** (emploi) job; **perdre sa ~** to lose one's job; **9** (forteresse) **être dans la ~** to be on the inside; **être maître de la ~** LIT to be in control; FIG to rule the roost; **avoir un pied dans la ~** FIG to have a foot in the door.

■ **~ d'armes** parade ground; **~ assise** seat; **~ forte** fortified town; **~ d'honneur** (à table) place ou seat of honour^GB; **sur la ~ publique** in public; **mettre qch sur la ~ publique** to bring sth out in the open.

placé, **~e** /plase/ **I** *pp* ▶ **placer**.
II *pp adj* **1** (situé géographiquement) **être ~** [*objet, robinet, fenêtre*] to be; [*chaise, table, statue*] to be placed; [*personne*] GÉN to be; (au théâtre, cinéma) to be sitting; **être bien/mal ~** [*objet*] to be in a good/bad position; [*bâtiment, boutique*] to be well/badly situated; [*personne*] (à table, à une cérémonie) to have a good/bad place; (au théâtre, cinéma) to have a good/bad seat; **être ~ face à** to be facing; (dans une hiérarchie) **être bien/mal ~** to be well/badly placed; **être bien ~ sur une liste** to have a good position on the list; **il est bien ~ pour le poste** he's a valid candidate for the job; **avoir des amis haut ~s** to have friends in high places; **être ~ sous la direction de** [*orchestre*] to be conducted by; [*troupe de théâtre*] to be directed by; **3** FIG **mal ~** [*orgueil, remarque*] misplaced; **être bien/mal ~ pour faire** (pour réussir) to be well/badly placed to do; (pour savoir, juger) to be in a (good)/in no position to do; **4** (aux courses) [*cheval*] placed; **jouer un cheval ~ et gagnant** to back a horse each way GB, to back a horse across the board US; **non ~** unplaced.

placebo /plasebo/ *nm* placebo.

placement /plasmɑ̃/ *nm* **1** FIN investment; **2** (emploi) **assurer le ~ des diplômés** to ensure that graduates find employment; **3** (d'enfant) fostering.

placenta /plasɛ̃ta/ *nm* placenta.

placer /plase/ [12] **I** *vtr* **1** (mettre à un endroit) to put, to place [*objet*]; to seat [*personne*]; **~ des gardes** to post guards; **~ des hommes autour d'une maison** to position men around a house; **2** (mettre dans une situation) to put, to place; **~ un service sous la responsabilité de qn** to make sb responsible for a department; **~ qn/être placé devant un choix difficile** to present sb/to be faced with a difficult choice; **3** (procurer un emploi) to place, to find a job for; **4** FIN (investir) to invest; (mettre en dépôt) to deposit, to put; **5** (attribuer) **~ sa confiance en qn** to put one's trust in sb; **6** (introduire) to slip in [*remarque, anecdote*]; **je n'arrive pas à en ~ une° avec elle!** I can't get a word in edgeways GB ou edgewise US with her!; **7** (prendre en charge) to place [sb] in care [*enfant*]; **8** (vendre) to place, to sell [*marchandise*].
II se placer *vpr* **1** (à un endroit) **se ~ près de** (debout) to stand next to; (assis) to sit next to; **se ~**

autour d'une maison [*policiers*] to position onese around a house; **où se placent les verres?** where d the glasses go?; **2** (dans une situation) **se ~ sous un perspective nouvelle** to look at things from a ne perspective; **il s'est placé comme apprenti** he foun himself an apprenticeship^GB; **notre démarche s place dans le cadre de l'aide au tiers-monde** ou action comes within the context of Third World aid; (dans une hiérarchie) **il s'est placé dans les premier** (en classe) he got one of the top places; (dans u course) he finished among the first.

placeur, **-euse** /plasœʀ, øz/ ▶374| *nm,f* usher/ushe ette.

placide /plasid/ *adj* placid, calm.

placier, **-ière** /plasje, ɛʀ/ ▶374| *nm,f* **1** (repr sentant) sales representative; **2** (sur un marché market superintendent.

plafond /plafɔ̃/ **I** *nm* **1** (de pièce) ceiling; (de tente, véh cule, souterrain) roof; **~ à caissons** coffered ceilin **salle haute de ~** high-ceilinged room; **~ nuageu** cloud ceiling; ▶ **faux¹**; **2** (limite) ceiling, limit; **creve le ~** (dépasser la limite) to go through the ceiling (battre les records) to break all previous records.
II (-)**plafond** (*in compounds*) **vitesse(-)~** max mum speed.

plafonnement /plafɔnmɑ̃/ *nm* **1** (action) setting ceiling on [*salaires*]; setting a limit on [*dépenses*]; (de salaires) ceiling (**de** on); (de dépenses) limitatio (**de** of).

plafonner /plafɔne/ [1] **I** *vtr* (limiter) to put a ceilin on [*prix, salaire, production*]; **l'augmentation de salaires est plafonnée à 3%** wage increases ar limited to a maximum of 3%; **loyer plafonn** protected rent; **salaire plafonné** upper limit of salar on which contributions are payable.
II *vi* (production, dépenses) to reach a ceiling; [*élèv employé*] to reach a maximum level of attainment; (s stabiliser) [*prix, chômage*] to level off; **la productio plafonne autour de 15 tonnes par an** productio remains constant at about 15 tons a year; **l'avio plafonne à 15 000 m** (est limité à) the plane has a absolute ceiling of 15,000 m; (culmine à) the plane ha reached its ceiling of 15,000 m.

plafonnier /plafɔnje/ *nm* (au plafond) flush-fitting cei ing light; (dans une voiture) interior light.

plage /plaʒ/ *nf* **1** GÉOG beach; **sac de ~** beach bag; (zone) range; **~ de prix** price range; **3** (tranch horaire) slot; **4** (de disque) track.
■ **~ arrière** AUT rear window shelf; NAUT quarte deck; **~ avant** NAUT forecastle; **~ horaire** RADIO, time slot; **~ musicale** RADIO, TV musical interval; **~ sous-marine** bank.

plagiaire /plaʒjɛʀ/ *nmf* plagiarist.

plagiat /plaʒja/ *nm* plagiarism.

plagier /plaʒje/ [2] *vtr* to plagiarize [*œuvre, auteur*].

plagiste /plaʒist/ ▶374| *nmf* (employé) beac attendant; (exploitant) beach manager.

plaid /plɛd/ *nm* (couverture) tartan rug GB, plai blanket us.

plaidant, **-e** /plɛdɑ̃, ɑ̃t/ *adj* JUR [*parties*] litigant.

plaider /plede/ [1] **I** *vtr* to plead [*cause, affaire*]; **la légitime défense** to plead self-defence^GB.
II *vi* **1** LIT to plead (contre against; pour qn on sb behalf); **2** FIG **~ en faveur de qn** [*circonstance qualités*] to speak in favour^GB of sb.

plaideur, **-euse** /plɛdœʀ, øz/ *nm,f* JUR litigant.

plaidoirie /plɛdwaʀi/ *nf* JUR plea.

plaidoyer /plɛdwaje/ *nm* **1** JUR speech for th defence^GB; **2** FIG plea.

plaie /plɛ/ *nf* **1** (blessure physique) wound; (ulcératio sore; (coupure) cut; **~ vive** open sore; **2** (blessu morale) wound; (calamité) scourge; **les sept ~ d'Égypte** the seven plagues of Egypt; **3°** (chose ou personne pénible) pain°; **cet enfant, quelle ~!** th child is such a pain!
IDIOMES **~ d'argent n'est pas mortelle** PROV mone

isn't everything; **mettre le doigt sur la ~** to put one's finger on the problem.

plaignant, **~e** /plɛɲɑ̃, ɑ̃t/ **I** *adj* JUR litigant.
II *nm,f* JUR plaintiff, complainant.

plaindre /plɛ̃dʀ/ [54] **I** *vtr* to pity, to feel sorry for [*personne, animal*]; **elle aime se faire ~** she likes to be pitied; **il est (bien) à ~** he's (very much) to be pitied; **il n'est vraiment pas à ~** (il mérite son sort) he got what he deserved; (il a de la chance) he's got nothing to complain about.
II se plaindre *vpr* **1** (protester) to complain; (pleurnicher) to whinge○ PÉJ, to complain; **se ~ à qn** to complain to sb; **je n'ai pas à me ~ de lui** I've no complaints about him; **2** (geindre) [*blessé, malade*] to moan.

plaine /plɛn/ *nf* plain.

plain-pied: **de plain-pied** /dəplɛ̃pje/ **I** *loc adj* **1** (à un étage) **un bâtiment/une maison de ~** a single-storey GB ou single-story US building/house; **la cuisine est de ~ avec le jardin** the kitchen is at the same level as the garden GB ou yard US; **2** (à égalité) **être de ~ avec qn** to be on an equal footing with sb.
II *loc adv* **entrer de ~ dans le monde politique** to have an easy passage into the world of politics.

plainte /plɛ̃t/ *nf* **1** GÉN, JUR complaint; **~ contre X** complaint against person or persons unknown; **2** (de malade) moan, groan; **la ~ du vent** the moaning of the wind; **la ~ des violons** the wail of the violins.

plaintif, -ive /plɛ̃tif, iv/ *adj* plaintive.

plaintivement /plɛ̃tivmɑ̃/ *adv* plaintively, dolefully.

plaire /plɛʀ/ [59] **I** **plaire à** *vtr ind* **elle plaît aux hommes** men find her attractive; **elle m'a plu tout de suite** I liked her straight away; **il a tout pour ~** LIT he is attractive in every way; IRON he is not exactly God's gift; **mon nouveau travail me plaît** I like my new job; **si ça ne te plaît pas, c'est pareil** or **c'est le même prix**○ if you don't like it, that's tough○ ou that's too bad; **offre-leur des fleurs, ça plaît toujours** give them flowers, they're always welcome; **un modèle qui plaît beaucoup** a very popular model.
II se plaire *vpr* **1** (à soi-même) to like oneself; **2** (l'un l'autre) [*personnes, couple*] to like each other; **3** (être bien) **ils se plaisent ici** they like it here; **cette plante se plaît dans un environnement marécageux** this plant thrives in a marshy environment; **4** (aimer) **se ~ à faire** to enjoy doing; **il se plaît à dire qu'il est issu du peuple** he likes to say that he's a son of the people.
III *v impers* **il me plaît de penser que** I like to think that; **s'il te plaît, s'il vous plaît** please; **plaît-il?** I beg your pardon?; **plût au ciel** or **à Dieu qu'il soit sain et sauf!** FML God grant he's safe and sound!

plaisamment /plɛzamɑ̃/ *adv* **1** (de manière agréable) agreeably; **2** (d'une manière comique) amusingly.

plaisance /plɛzɑ̃s/ *nf* **la** (**navigation de**) **~** GÉN boating; (sur un voilier) sailing; **bateau de ~** pleasure boat.

plaisancier, -ière /plɛzɑ̃sje, ɛʀ/ *nm,f* amateur sailor.

plaisant, ~e /plɛzɑ̃, ɑ̃t/ *adj* **1** (agréable) pleasant; **2** (amusant) amusing, funny; ▶ **mauvais**.

plaisanter /plɛzɑ̃te/ [1] **I** *vtr* (railler) to tease [*personne*] (**sur** about).
II *vi* to joke (**sur, de** about); **dire qch pour ~** to say sth as a joke; **on ne plaisante pas avec ces choses-là** these things are no laughing matter; **il ne faut pas ~ avec sa santé** one shouldn't take chances with one's health.

plaisanterie /plɛzɑ̃tʀi/ *nf* **1** GÉN joke; **il ne comprend pas la ~** he can't take a joke; **lancer des ~s** to crack jokes; **être l'objet des ~s de qn** to be a figure of fun to sb; **la ~ a assez duré!** this has gone on long enough!; **2** (chose facile à faire) **c'est une ~** it's a piece of cake○.

plaisantin /plɛzɑ̃tɛ̃/ *nm* **1** (blagueur) practical joker; **petit ~!** wise guy○!; **2** (fumiste) skiver○.

plaisir /plɛziʀ/ *nm* **1** (sensation agréable) pleasure; **le ~ des sens/des yeux** sensual/aesthetic pleasure; **prendre** or **avoir** (**du**) **~ à faire** to enjoy doing; **prendre un malin ~ à faire** to take a wicked delight in doing; **j'ai appris avec ~ que** I was delighted to hear that; **je ne te punis pas pour le ~ mais parce que tu le mérites** I'm not punishing you for the sake of it, but because you deserve it; **à ~** [*se tourmenter, exagérer, mentir*] for the sake of it; **pour le plus grand ~ des auditeurs** for the enjoyment of the listeners; **faire ~ à qn** to please sb; **qu'est-ce qui te ferait ~?** what would you like?; **si ça peut te faire ~** if it'll make you happy; **je viendrai, mais c'est bien pour te faire ~** I'll come, but only because you want me to; **ça fait toujours ~!** IRON isn't that nice!; **tu vas me faire le ~ de ranger ta chambre!** you'll tidy up your room if you know what's good for you!; **faites-moi le ~ de vous taire!** would you please shut up○!; **il se fera un ~ de vous aider** he will be delighted to help you; **faire durer le ~** LIT to make the pleasure last; IRON to prolong the agony; **je vous souhaite bien du ~** IRON I wish you joy of it!; **2** (source d'agrément) pleasure; **une vie de ~s** a life devoted to pleasure; **aimer les ~s de la table** to enjoy good food.

plan, ~e /plɑ̃, plan/ **I** *adj* **1** GÉN flat, even; **2** MATH, PHYS plane.
II *nm* **1** (carte) (de ville, métro) map; (dans un bâtiment) plan, map; **2** ARCHIT, CONSTR plan; **3** (de machine) (schéma directeur) blueprint; (après construction) plan; **4** MATH, PHYS plane; **5** (de dissertation) plan; **6** CIN, PHOT (image) shot; **montage ~ par ~** shot-to-shot editing; **premier ~** foreground; **second ~** middle-distance; ▶ **gros**; **7** (niveau) level; **au premier ~ de l'actualité** at the forefront of the news; **être relégué au second ~** [*personne, problème*] to be relegated to the background; **de (tout) premier ~** [*personnalité*] leading (*épith*); [*œuvre*] key, major; **de second ~** second-rate; **sur le ~ politique** from a political point of view; **8** (projet) plan, programme GB; **~ de relance économique** plan to boost the economy; **j'ai un bon ~**○ **pour voyager pas cher** I know a good way of travelling GB cheaply; **c'est (pas) le bon ~**○ it's (not) a good idea.
■ **~ américain** CIN medium shot; **~ directeur** ÉCON master plan; **~ d'eau** (artificiel) artificial lake; (naturel) smooth expanse of water; **~ d'ensemble** CIN long shot; **~ d'épargne** savings plan; **~ d'épargne-logement**, **PEL** *savings scheme entitling depositor to cheap mortgage*; **~ d'épargne retraite** top-up pensions scheme; **~ fixe** CIN static shot; **~ moyen** CIN medium close-up; **~ d'occupation des sols**, **POS** land use plan; **~ rapproché** CIN medium close-up; **~ social** ÉCON planned redundancy scheme GB, scheduled lay-off program US; **~ de travail** (pour projet) working schedule; (surface) worktop; **~ d'urbanisme** urban planning policy; **~ de vol** flight plan.
IDIOMES **laisser qn en ~**○ to leave sb in the lurch, to leave sb high and dry; **laisser qch en ~**○ to leave sth unfinished; **il a tout laissé en ~** he dropped everything.

planant○, **~e** /planɑ̃, ɑ̃t/ *adj* mind-blowing○.

planche /plɑ̃ʃ/ *nf* **1** (pièce de bois) plank; (pour pétrir, laver etc) board; **faire la ~** (en natation) to float on one's back; **2** (illustration) plate.
■ **~ à billets** minting plate; **faire marcher la ~ à billets**○ to print money; **~ à découper** chopping-board; (plus épaisse) butcher's block; **~ à dessin** drawing board; **~ à repasser** ironing-board; **~ à roulettes** SPORT skateboard; **~ de salut** lifeline; **~ de surf** surfboard; **~ à voile** (engin) windsurfing board; (activité) windsurfing.
IDIOMES **monter sur les ~s** THÉÂT to go on the stage, to tread the boards; **brûler les ~s** THÉÂT to bring the house down; **avoir du pain sur la ~**○ to have one's work cut out.

plancher[1]○ /plɑ̃ʃe/ [1] *vi* students' slang to work.

plancher[2] /plɑ̃ʃe/ **I** *nm* **1** (sol) floor; **2** ÉCON, FIN (seuil inférieur) floor, minimum; **atteindre un ~** [*prix, cours*] to bottom out.

II (-)**plancher** (*in compounds*) **prix**(-)~ bottom
price.
■ **le ~ des vaches**○ land, terra firma.
IDIOMES **mettre le pied au ~**○ to put one's foot
down on the accelerator.

planchette /plɑ̃ʃɛt/ *nf* **1** (petite planche) small board;
2 (rayon) (small) shelf.

planchiste /plɑ̃ʃist/ *nmf* windsurfer.

plancton /plɑ̃ktɔ̃/ *nm* plankton.

plané /plane/ *adj m* **vol ~** LIT glide; **faire un vol ~**
FIG to go flying.

planer /plane/ [1] *vi* **1** (avion, oiseau) to glide; [oiseau
de proie] to hover; [*vapeur*] to float; **2** [*tristesse,
menace*] to hang; **laisser ~ le doute** to allow
uncertainty to persist; **3**○ [*rêveur*] to have one's head
in the clouds; [*drogué*] to be spaced out○, to be high○.

planétaire /planetɛʀ/ *adj* PHYS, TECH planetary; FIG
global.

planète /planɛt/ *nf* planet.

planeur /planœʀ/ *nm* **1** (engin) glider; **2** ▶329|
(sport) gliding.

planification /planifikasjɔ̃/ *nf* planning.

planifier /planifje/ [2] *vtr* to plan [*production,
vacances*]; to schedule [*traitement*]; **~ à court terme**
to draw up a short-term plan.

planning○ /planiŋ/ *nm* CONTROV schedule.
■ **~ familial** family planning service.

planque○ /plɑ̃k/ *nf* **1** (cachette) (de personne) hideout; (de chose) hidey-hole○ GB, stash○ US; **2** (emploi
confortable) cushy number○.

planqué○ /plɑ̃ke/ *nm* soldiers' slang skiver.

planquer○ /plɑ̃ke/ [1] I *vtr* to hide [*personne*]; to
hide [sth] away [*objet*]; **~ de l'argent** to stash
money away.
II **se planquer** *vpr* GÉN to hide; (longtemps) to go
into hiding; (par lâcheté) to skive.

plan-relief, *pl* **plans-reliefs** /plɑ̃ʀəljɛf/ *nm* scale
model.

plan-séquence, *pl* **plans-séquences** /plɑ̃sekɑ̃s/
nm sequence shot.

plant /plɑ̃/ *nm* **1** (plante) young plant; (plus jeune)
seedling; **un ~ de vigne** a young vine; **des ~s de
fleurs** bedding plants; **2** (plantation) plantation; **~ de
légumes** vegetable patch; **~ de fleurs** flower bed.

plantaire /plɑ̃tɛʀ/ *adj* ANAT plantar.

plantation /plɑ̃tasjɔ̃/ *nf* (d'arbres, de café) plantation;
(de fleurs) bed; (de légumes) patch.

plante /plɑ̃t/ *nf* **1** BOT plant; **~ d'appartement** or
verte houseplant; **~ grasse** succulent; **~ de serre**
LIT, FIG hothouse plant; **~ vivace** perennial; **soigner
par les ~s** to use herbal medicine; **2** ANAT **~ (des
pieds)** sole (of the foot).

planté, ~e /plɑ̃te/ *adj* **1** (enraciné) **dents bien/mal
~es** regular/uneven teeth; **avoir les cheveux ~s
bas sur le front** to have a low forehead; **2**○ (debout)
standing; **ne reste pas ~ là!** don't just stand there!

planter /plɑ̃te/ [1] I *vtr* **1** to plant [*tomates, jardin*];
route plantée d'arbres road lined with trees; **2**
(enfoncer) to drive in [*pieu*]; to knock in [*clou*]; **~ un
couteau dans** to stick a knife into; **clou mal planté**
nail which has not gone in straight; **~ un drapeau**
to put a flag; **3** (dresser) to pitch [*tente*]; **~ un décor**
LIT to put up a set; FIG to set the scene; **~ une échelle
contre un mur** to stand a ladder against a wall; **4**○
(mettre) to put, to stick○; **~ la bouteille sur la table**
to stick the bottle on the table; **5**○ (abandonner) **~ là**
to drop [*outil*]; to abandon [*voiture*]; to pack in○ [*travail*]; to walk out on [*époux*]; **il m'a planté là** he left
me standing there.
II **se planter** *vpr* **1** [*fleur, parterre*] to be planted; **2**
(s'enfoncer) [*clou*] to go in; **3** [*personne*] **se ~ une
épine dans le pied** to get a thorn in one's foot; **4**○ (se
tenir) **aller se ~ devant qch** to go and stand in front
of sth; **5**○ (avoir un accident) **se ~ en vélo**
to have a bicycle accident; **6**○ (se tromper) to get it
wrong; (se perdre) to get lost; **il s'est planté en
histoire** he made a mess of the history exam.

planteur /plɑ̃tœʀ/ ▶374| *nm* (exploitant) planter.

plantoir /plɑ̃twaʀ/ *nm* dibble.

planton /plɑ̃tɔ̃/ *nm* (sentinelle) sentry; (ordonnance)
orderly; **faire le ~** FIG to wait around.

plantureux, -euse /plɑ̃tyʀø, øz/ *adj* **1** [*déjeuner*]
lavish; [*poitrine*] generous; [*femme*] buxom (*épith*),
well-endowed HUM; **2** [*terre*] fertile; [*année, récolte*]
bumper (*épith*).

plaquage /plakaʒ/ *nm* SPORT (technique) tackling ₵;
un ~ a tackle.

plaque /plak/ *nf* (de moisissure, d'humidité) patch; **~
de verglas** patch of ice; (sur la peau) blotch; (de verre,
métal) plate; (de marbre, chocolat) slab; (au jeu) chip;
(de cabinet médical, d'étude de notaire) brass plate; (de policier) badge.
■ **~ chauffante** hotplate; **~ de cheminée** fire-
back; **~ dentaire** plaque; **~ d'égout** manhole
cover; **~ d'identité** (de soldat) ID tag; (de chien)
name tag, dog tag; **~ d'immatriculation** or **minéralogique** number plate GB, license plate US; **~
tournante** LIT turntable; FIG crossroads (+ *v sg*).
IDIOMES **être à côté de la ~**○ (se tromper) to be
completely mistaken; **elle répond toujours à côté de
la ~**○ her answers are always slightly off beam○.

plaqué, ~e /plake/ I *adj* **~** or gold-plated; **~
acajou** with a mahogany veneer (*épith, après n*);
poche ~e patch pocket.
II *nm* **le ~** (bijoux) plated jewellery GB ou jewelry US;
(couverts) plated cutlery; **en ~** plated.

plaquer /plake/ [1] I *vtr* **1** (appuyer, aplatir) **~ qn
contre qch/au sol** to pin sb against sth/to the ground;
~ sa main sur to put one's hand on; **le vent
plaquait sa jupe contre ses cuisses** the wind made
her skirt cling to her legs; **~ une mèche sur son
front** to plaster a lock of hair onto one's forehead; **2**○
(quitter) to leave [*emploi, mari*]; **tout ~** to chuck it
all in○, to chuck everything○ US; **3** (en rugby) to
tackle; **4** (rajouter) PEJ to tack [*citation, commentaire*]
(**sur** onto); **5** TECH to veneer [*meuble, bois*]; to plate
[*bijou, métal*]; **6** MUS to strike [*accord*].
II **se plaquer** *vpr* **se ~ contre un mur** to flatten
oneself against a wall; **se ~ au sol** to lie flat on the
ground; **se ~ contre qn** to press oneself up against
sb.

plaquette /plakɛt/ *nf* **1** (de chocolat) bar; (de beurre)
packet; (de pilules) ~ blister strip; (de métal) small
plate; **2** (dans le sang) platelet; **3** (publicitaire)
brochure; (en prose) pamphlet.
■ **~ de frein** brake shoe.

plastic /plastik/ *nm* plastic explosive; **attentat au ~**
bomb attack.

plasticage /plastikaʒ/ *nm* bomb attack (**de** on).

plastifier /plastifje/ [2] *vtr* to coat [sth] with plastic.

plastiquage = **plasticage**.

plastique[1] /plastik/ I *adj* plastic.
II *nm* (matière) plastic; **c'est du ~** it's plastic.

plastique[2] /plastik/ *nf* **1** (arts) **la ~** the plastic arts
(*pl*); (sculpture) the art of sculpture; **2** (esthétique)
(d'objet, de statue) formal beauty; (de personne) physique.

plastiquer /plastike/ [1] *vtr* to carry out a bomb
attack on.

plastron /plastʀɔ̃/ *nm* **1** (de chemise) shirt front; **2**
(d'escrimeur) plastron; **3** (d'oiseau) breast-shield.

plastronner /plastʀɔne/ [1] *vi* to be full of oneself.

plat, ~e /pla, plat/ I *adj* **1** (sans relief) [*fond,
surface, pays*] flat; [*mer*] smooth; **être ~e, avoir la
poitrine ~e** to be flat-chested; **2** (peu profond) [*chapeau, caillou, paquet*] flat; [*bateau*] flat-bottomed;
[*montre, briquet*] slimline; [*cheveux*] limp; **3** (sans
talon) [*chaussure*] flat; **4** FIG [*goût*] bland; [*vin*] insipid; [*style, description*] lifeless; [*traduction*] flat; [*texte*]
dull; **faire de ~es excuses à qn** to apologize
abjectly to sb.
II *nm* **1** (pour cuire, servir) dish; **2** (aliments servis)
dish; **3** (partie d'un repas) course; **4** (partie plate) **le ~**

de la main the flat of one's hand; **5** (terrain plat) flat ground; **courir sur du ~** to run on the flat.

III à plat *loc adv* **1** (horizontalement) **poser** or **mettre qch à ~** to lay sth down flat; **dormir à ~** to sleep without a pillow; **à ~ ventre** LIT flat on one's stomach; **se mettre à ~ ventre devant qn** FIG to grovel in front of sb; **tomber à ~** [*plaisanterie*] to fall flat; **2** (hors d'usage) **à ~** [*pneu*] flat; [*batterie*] flat GB, dead; **3**○ (sans énergie) **être à ~** [*personne*] to be run down; **sa maladie l'a mis à ~**○ his illness really took it out of him○; **4** (en ordre) **mettre à ~** to review [sth] from scratch [*comptes, dossier*].

■ **~ de côtes** top rib of beef; **~ cuisiné** ready-cooked meal; **~ du jour** today's special; **~ à poisson** serving dish for fish; **~ de résistance** CULIN main course; FIG main item.

IDIOMES **faire un ~**○ (en natation) to do a belly flop○; **faire du ~ à qn**○ to chat sb up○ GB, to come on to sb○; **mettre les petits ~s dans les grands**○ to go to town on a meal○; **mettre les pieds dans le ~**○ to put one's foot in it; **faire tout un ~ de qch**○ to make a big deal about sth.

platane /platan/ *nm* plane tree; **se payer**○ **un ~** to crash into a tree.

plateau, *pl* **~x** /plato/ **I** *nm* **1** (pour servir, porter) tray; **2** THÉÂT stage; CIN, TV set; **et sur le ~ ici ce soir…** and in our panel tonight…; **3** (niveau constant) plateau; **arriver à un ~** [*fièvre, inflation*] to level off; [*talent, capacités*] to reach a plateau; **4** GÉOG plateau; **5** (de balance) pan; (de table) top; (de tourne-disques) turntable.

II plateau(-) (*in compounds*) **~(-)télé**○ TV dinner.

■ **~ continental** continental shelf; **~ à fromage** or **de fromages** cheeseboard; **~ de fruits de mer** seafood platter; **~ de tournage** film set.

IDIOMES **il faut qu'on t'apporte tout sur un ~?** do you expect everything to be handed to you on a plate?

plateau-repas, *pl* **plateaux-repas** /platoR(ə)pɑ/ *nm* meal tray.

plate-bande, *pl* **plates-bandes** /platbɑ̃d/ *nf* border, flower bed; **piétiner les plates-bandes de qn**○ FIG to encroach on sb's territory.

platée○ /plate/ *nf* plateful (**de** of).

plate-forme, *pl* **plates-formes** /platfɔrm/ *nf* GÉN platform; (pour marchandises) skid; **la ~ électorale** the party platform.

■ **~ de forage** drilling rig; **~ littorale** coastal shelf; **~ pétrolière** oil rig.

platement /platmɑ̃/ *adv* **s'excuser ~** to apologize abjectly.

platine[1] /platin/ ▶ 141 *adj inv, nm* platinum.

platine[2] /platin/ *nf* **1** (d'horloge, de serrure) plate; (de microscope) stage; **2** (tourne-disques) turntable.

platiné, **~e** /platine/ *adj* **1** (plaqué) platinum-plated; **2** ▶ 141 (blond) [*cheveux*] platinum blond.

platitude /platityd/ *nf* **1** (de texte) banality; (de personne) dreariness; (de style) triteness; **2** (propos) platitude.

platonique /platɔnik/ *adj* **1** [*amour*] platonic; **2** [*revendication*] token (*épith*).

plâtras /platRɑ/ *nm inv* CONSTR rubble ¢.

plâtre /platR/ *nm* **1** CONSTR (matériau) plaster; **les ~s** plasterwork ¢; **2** ART, MÉD (objet) plaster cast; **~ de marche** walking cast.

IDIOMES **battre qn comme ~**○ to beat the living daylights out of sb○; **essuyer les ~s** to put up with the initial problems.

plâtrer /platRe/ [1] *vtr* **1** CONSTR to plaster [*mur*]; **2** MÉD **~ le bras de qn** to put sb's arm in a cast.

plâtreux, **-euse** /platRø, øz/ *adj* **1** [*mur*] plastered; FIG [*teinte*] chalky; **2** CULIN [*fromage*] chalky.

plâtrier, **-ière**[1] /platRije, ɛR/ ▶ 374 *nm,f* plasterer.

plâtrière[2] /platRijɛR/ *nf* (carrière) gypsum quarry; (four) gypsum kiln; (usine) plasterworks.

plausible /plozibl/ *adj* plausible.

playback /plɛbak/ *nm inv* miming, lip syncing; **chanter en ~** to mime to a tape, to lip-sync (a song).

plébiscite /plebisit/ *nm* plebiscite.

plébisciter /plebisite/ [1] *vtr* **1** (élire) to elect [sb] with a huge majority; **2** (approuver) to vote overwhelmingly in favour GB of [*personne, mesure*]; to acclaim [*mode*].

pléiade /plejad/ *nf* LITER galaxy, pleiad.

plein, **~e** /plɛ̃, plɛn/ **I** *adj* **1** (rempli) full (**de** of); **une jupe ~e de taches** a skirt covered with stains; **2 un ~ verre/panier** a glassful/basketful (**de** of); **saisir à ~es mains** to take hold of [sth] with both hands [*objet massif*]; to pick up a handful of [*terre, sable, pièces*]; **3** (non creux) [*brique, mur*] solid; [*joues, visage*] plump; [*forme*] rounded; **4** (total) [*pouvoir, accord, effet*] full; [*succès, confiance*] complete; **avoir la responsabilité ~e et entière de qch** to have full responsibility for sth; **5** (entier) [*mois*] whole, full; [*lune*] full; **6** (milieu) **en ~e poitrine/réunion/forêt** (right) in the middle of the chest/meeting/forest; **en ~ cœur** right in the heart; **en ~ jour** in broad daylight; **en ~ été** at the height of summer; **en ~ hiver** in the depths of winter; **en ~e mer** on the open sea; **être en ~e mutation** to be experiencing radical change; **7** ZOOL **~e** [*femelle*] pregnant; [*vache*] in calf (*après n*); [*jument*] in foal (*après n*); [*truie*] in pig (*après n*); **8**○ (ivre) sloshed○, drunk; **9** (en parlant de cuir) **reliure ~ peau** full leather binding; **veste ~e peau** jacket made out of full skins.

II *adv* **1** (exprimant une grande quantité) **avoir des billes ~ les poches** to have one's pockets full of marbles; **il a des idées ~ la tête** he's full of ideas; **2** (directement) **être orienté ~ sud** to face due south.

III *nm* **1** (de réservoir) **faire le ~ de** LIT to fill up with [*eau, carburant*]; FIG to get a lot of [*idées, voix, visiteurs*]; **j'ai fait deux ~s** or **deux fois le ~ pour venir ici** I took two tankfuls to get here; **le ~ s'il vous plaît** fill it up please; **2** (en calligraphie) downstroke.

IV plein de○ *dét indéf* **~ de** lots of, loads○ of.

V à plein *loc adv* [*bénéficier, utiliser*] fully; **tourner** or **marcher à ~** to work flat out, to work to capacity.

VI en plein *loc adv* **l'avion s'est écrasé en ~ sur l'immeuble** the plane crashed straight into the building; **il m'est rentré en ~ dedans**○ he crashed right into me.

VII tout plein○ *loc adv* really; **mignon tout ~** really sweet.

■ **~e page** full page; **~e propriété** JUR freehold.

IDIOMES **en avoir ~ les jambes**○ or **pattes**○ to be worn out, to be fit to drop○; **en avoir ~ le dos**○ or **les bottes**❶ to be fed up (to the back teeth)○; **(s')en prendre ~ les gencives**❶ to get it in the neck○.

plein-air /plɛnɛR/ *nm inv* SCOL (outdoor) games (*pl*).

pleinement /plɛnmɑ̃/ *adv* fully.

plein-emploi /plɛnɑ̃plwa/ *nm inv* full employment.

plein-temps, *pl* **pleins-temps** /plɛ̃tɑ̃/ *nm* GÉN full-time job; MÉD full-time consultancy.

plénier, **-ière** /plenje, ɛR/ *adj* plenary.

plénipotentiaire /plenipɔtɑ̃sjɛR/ *adj, nm* plenipotentiary.

plénitude /plenityd/ *nf* **1** (intégrité) **exercer la ~ de ses fonctions** to exercise one's functions to the full; **garder la ~ de ses droits** to retain all one's rights; **2** (bien-être) **un sentiment de ~** a blissful feeling; **3** (ampleur) LITER fullness.

pléonasme /pleɔnasm/ *nm* pleonasm.

pléthore /pletɔR/ *nf* superabundance, plethora.

pléthorique /pletɔRik/ *adj* [*quantité, trafic*] excessive; [*classe*] overcrowded; [*personnel*] surplus to requirement (*jamais épith*); **aux effectifs ~s** [*société, service*] overstaffed.

pleurer /plœRe/ [1] **I** *vtr* **1** (regretter) to mourn [*ami*]; to lament [*absence*]; **2**○ (économiser) **ne pas ~ son argent** to spare no expense.

II *vi* **1** (après une émotion) to cry, to weep; **j'en aurais pleuré!** I could have wept!; **~ de rire, rire à en ~** to laugh until one cries; **c'est une histoire triste/bête à ~** this story is too sad/stupid for words; **2** (involontairement) [*yeux*] to water; **j'ai les yeux qui pleurent** my eyes are watering; **3** (s'affliger) **~ sur qch/qn** to shed tears over sth/sb; **arrête de ~ sur ton sort!** stop feeling sorry for yourself!; **4**○ (se plaindre) [*personne*] to whine; **aller ~ auprès de qn** to go whining to sb; **~ après** to beg for [*augmentation, faveur*]; **5** LITTÉR [*violon*] to sob; [*vent*] to sigh.
IDIOMES **elle n'a que ses yeux pour ~** all she can do is cry ou weep.

pleurésie /plœrezi/ ▶ **196 |** *nf* pleurisy.

pleureur /plœrœr/ *adj m* **saule ~** weeping willow.

pleureuse /plœrøz/ *nf* (hired) mourner.

pleurnichard○, **~e** /plœrniʃar, ard/ **I** *adj* whining.
II *nm,f* cry-baby○.

pleurnicher○ /plœrniʃe/ [1] *vi* to snivel.

pleurnicheur○, **-euse** /plœrniʃœr, øz/ *nm,f* sniveller^GB.

pleurs /plœr/ *nmpl* tears; **en ~** in tears; **il y aura des ~ et des grincements de dents** there will be wailing and gnashing of teeth.

pleutre /pløtr/ *nm* LITER coward.

pleuvoir /pløvwar/ [39] **I** *v impers* to rain; **il pleut** it's raining; **il pleut à torrents** ou **à seaux** it's pouring with rain; **il pleut des cordes**○ it's coming down in buckets; **des gâteaux comme s'il en pleuvait**○ loads○ of cakes.
II *vi* [*obus, coups*] to rain down; [*demandes d'emploi*] to pour in; [*questions, critiques*] to come thick and fast.

pli /pli/ *nm* **1** (de tissu, rideau, dépliant, soufflet) fold; (de pantalon) crease; (de jupe) pleat; **(faux) ~** crease; **ta veste fait des ~s** your jacket is all creased; **2** (de bouche, d'yeux) line; (de ventre, double menton) fold; **3** (de terrain) fold; **4** JEUX (levée) trick; **faire un ~** to take a trick; **5** (lettre) letter; **sous ~ cacheté** in a sealed envelope; **sous ~ séparé** under separate cover.
IDIOMES **ça ne fait pas un ~**○ there's no doubt about it; **c'est un ~ à prendre** it's something you've got to get used to; **il a pris un mauvais ~** he's got into a bad habit.

pliage /plijaʒ/ *nm* folding.

pliant, **~e** /plijɑ̃, ɑ̃t/ **I** *adj* folding.
II *nm* folding stool, campstool.

plie /pli/ *nf* plaice.

plier /plije/ [2] **I** *vtr* **1** (rabattre) to fold [*papier, vêtement, parapluie*]; to fold up [*meuble, tente*]; **~ qch en deux** to fold sth in two; **2** (courber) to bend [*tige, roseau*]; **je n'arrive pas à ~ le bras** I can't bend my arm; **3** (ranger) to pack [*affaires*]; **4** (soumettre) to submit (à to).
II *vi* **1** (ployer) [*arbre, branche, articulation*] to bend; [*planche, plancher*] to sag; **2** (céder) to give in; **faire ~ qn** to make sb give in; **~ sous les menaces de qn** to yield to sb's threats.
III se plier *vpr* **1** (être pliant) to fold; **2** (se soumettre) **se ~ à** to submit to; **se ~ à des exigences** to bow to necessity.
IDIOMES **être plié en deux**○ ou **quatre**○ (de rire) to be doubled up with laughter; (de douleur) to be doubled up with pain.

plinthe /plɛ̃t/ *nf* **1** (de mur) skirting board GB, baseboard US; **2** (de statue) plinth.

plissage /plisaʒ/ *nm* pleating.

plissé /plise/ *nm* pleats (*pl*).

plissement /plismɑ̃/ *nm* **1** **~ de terrain** fold; **~ alpin** Alpine orogeny; **2** (des yeux) screwing up; (de peau) wrinkling.

plisser /plise/ [1] **I** *vtr* **1** (volontairement) to fold [*papier*]; to pleat [*tissu*]; **2** (involontairement) to crease [*vêtement*]; **ta robe est toute plissée** your dress is all creased; **3** (froncer) **~ le front** to knit one's brows; **~ les yeux** to screw up one's eyes.

II *vi* [*bas*] to wrinkle; [*jupe, veste*] to be creased ou puckered.
III se plisser *vpr* **1** [*vêtement, tissu*] to crease, to get creased; **2** [*nez*] to wrinkle; [*bouche*] to pucker up.

pliure /plijyr/ *nf* (de feuille, tissu) fold; **la ~ du genou** the back of the knee; **la ~ du coude** the crook of the elbow.

plomb /plɔ̃/ *nm* **1** (métal) lead; **de** ou **en ~** lead (*épith*); **sans ~** [*essence*] unleaded; **soleil de ~** FIG burning sun; **ciel de ~** leaden sky; **2** (de chasse) **un ~** a lead pellet; **du ~** lead shot ¢; **du gros ~** buckshot ¢; **3** (fusible) fuse; **faire sauter les ~s** to blow the fuses; **4** (en couture) piece of lead; (pour la pêche) sinker; **5** (sur un compteur) **~s** seal (*sg*); **6** (de vitrail) lead; **7** (en typographie) type.
IDIOMES **avoir du ~ dans l'aile**○ to be in a bad way○; **cela va leur mettre du ~ dans la tête** ou **cervelle**○ that will knock some sense into them.

plombage /plɔ̃baʒ/ *nm* (dentaire) filling.

plombé, **~e** /plɔ̃be/ **I** *pp* ▶ **plomber**.
II *pp adj* [*dent*] with a filling (*épith, après n*).
III *adj* [*teint, visage*] ashen; [*couleur, ciel*] leaden.

plomber /plɔ̃be/ [1] **I** *vtr* **1** (sceller) to seal; **3** (pour alourdir) to weight [*filet, rideaux*].
II se plomber *vpr* LITER [*ciel*] to become leaden.

plomberie /plɔ̃bri/ *nf* (tuyaux, métier) plumbing.

plombier /plɔ̃bje/ ▶ **374 |** *nm* plumber.

plombières /plɔ̃bjɛr/ *nf inv* tutti-frutti ice cream.

plonge○ /plɔ̃ʒ/ *nf* washing up, dishwashing US.

plongeant, **~e** /plɔ̃ʒɑ̃, ɑ̃t/ *adj* [*tir, décolleté*] plunging; **une vue ~e** a bird's eye view (**sur** of).

plongée /plɔ̃ʒe/ *nf* **1** ▶ **329 |** (discipline) GÉN (skin) diving; (avec scaphandre) scuba diving; (avec tube) snorkelling^GB; **~ sous-marine** deep-sea diving; **faire de la ~** to go diving; **2** (séjour sous l'eau) dive; **un sous-marin en ~** a submerged submarine; **3** CIN high-angle shot.

plongeoir /plɔ̃ʒwar/ *nm* GÉN diving-board; (planche) springboard.

plongeon /plɔ̃ʒɔ̃/ *nm* **1** ▶ **329 |** (discipline) diving; **2** (de nageur, gardien de but) dive; **3** (chute) fall; **4** (oiseau) diver.

plonger /plɔ̃ʒe/ [13] **I** *vtr* to plunge; **elle plongea son regard dans le mien** she stared deep into my eyes; **il a plongé la tête dans le moteur** he stuck his head into the engine.
II *vi* **1** GÉN to dive (**dans** into); [*oiseau*] to swoop down (**sur** on); **2** (péricliter) [*affaire, commerce*] to flounder; [*action, monnaie*] to take a dive; [*élève*] to go downhill.
III se plonger *vpr* **1** LIT to plunge (**dans** into); **2** FIG to bury oneself (**dans** in); **être plongé dans ses pensées** to be deep in thought.

plongeur, **-euse** /plɔ̃ʒœr, øz/ **I** ▶ **374 |** *nm,f* SPORT diver; (laveur de vaisselle) dishwasher.
II *nm* **1** TECH plunger piston; **2** (oiseau) diver.

plot /plo/ *nm* **1** ÉLECTROTECH contact; **2** (de bois) block. **~ de départ** SPORT starting block.

plouc○ /pluk/ PEJ *nm* country bumpkin○.

plouf /pluf/ **I** *nm inv* splash; **faire un ~** to go splash.
II *excl* splash!

ployer /plwaje/ [23] LITER **I** *vtr* to bend [*genou, branche*]; to bow [*tête*]; **il ploya les épaules** his shoulders sagged.
II *vi* [*planche, toit*] to sag; [*branche, personne*] to bend; [*jambes, genoux*] to buckle, to give way; **~ sous un fardeau** to be weighed down by a burden; **~ sous le joug** to bend under the yoke; **faire ~ l'ennemi** to force the enemy to yield.

pluie /plɥi/ *nf* **1** MÉTÉO **la ~** rain; **sous une ~ battante** in driving rain; **il tombait une ~ fine** it was drizzling; **jour de ~** rainy day; **par temps de ~** when it rains, in rainy weather; **des ~s violentes** heavy showers; **la saison des ~s** the rainy season, the rains (*pl*); **2** (de missiles, d'injures) hail; (d'étincelles, de cadeaux, compliments) shower; (de

plus¹

Formation du comparatif des adjectifs et des adverbes en anglais

Deux cas peuvent se présenter:

1 *Adjectifs et adverbes courts*

En règle générale on ajoute '*-er*' à la fin de l'adjectif/adverbe:

plus grand	= taller	*plus longtemps*	= longer
plus petit	= smaller	*plus vite*	= faster
plus simple	= simpler		

Remarques:

Pour certains mots dont l'unique voyelle est une voyelle brève, on double la consonne finale:

big → *bigger*	*dim* → *dimmer*	
sad → *sadder*	*wet* → *wetter* etc.	

Attention aux adjectifs en '*y*':

sunny → *sunnier*	*happy* → *happier* etc.
pretty → *prettier*	

2 *Adjectifs et adverbes longs*

On ajoute *more* devant le mot:

plus beau	= more beautiful
plus compétent	= more competent
plus intéressant	= more interesting
plus facilement	= more easily
plus sérieusement	= more seriously

Remarques:

Certains mots de deux syllabes admettent les deux formes: *simple* peut produire *simpler* ou *more simple*; *handsome* → *handsomer* ou *more handsome* etc.

Certains mots de deux syllabes n'admettent que la forme avec *more*:

callous → *more callous*
cunning → *more cunning*

Les adverbes se terminant par '*-ly*' n'admettent que la forme avec *more*:

quickly → *more quickly*
slowly → *more slowly* etc.

Formation du superlatif des adjectifs et des adverbes en anglais

Deux cas peuvent se présenter:

1 *Adjectifs et adverbes courts*

En règle générale on ajoute '*(e)st*' à la fin du mot:

le plus grand	= the tallest
le plus petit	= the smallest
le plus simple	= the simplest
le plus longtemps	= the longest
le plus vite	= the fastest

Remarques:

Pour certains mots dont l'unique voyelle est une voyelle brève, on double la consonne finale:

big → *the biggest*
sad → *the saddest*
dim → *the dimmest* etc.

Attention aux adjectifs en '*y*':

sunny → *the sunniest*
pretty → *the prettiest*
happy → *the happiest* etc.

2 *Adjectifs et adverbes longs*

On ajoute *the most* devant le mot:

le plus beau	= the most beautiful
le plus compétent	= the most competent
le plus intéressant	= the most interesting
le plus facilement	= the most easily
le plus sérieusement	= the most seriously

Remarques:

Certains mots de deux syllabes admettent les deux formes:

simple → *the simplest* ou *the most simple*
clever → *the cleverest* ou *the most clever* etc.

Certains mots de deux syllabes n'admettent que la forme avec *the most*:

callous → *the most callous*
cunning → *the most cunning* etc.

Les adverbes en '*-ly*' n'admettent que la forme avec *the most*:

quickly → *the most quickly*
slowly → *the most slowly* etc.

Attention: lorsque la comparaison ne porte que sur deux éléments on utilise la forme du comparatif:

le plus doué des deux = the more gifted of the two
la voiture la plus rapide des deux = the faster car

L'expression *le plus possible* est traitée avec *possible*.

On trouvera dans l'entrée exemples et exceptions illustrant les différentes fonctions de *plus*. On trouvera également des exemples de *plus* dans les notes d'usage répertoriées ▶ 1420].

---

lettres, d'offres] lots (*pl*); **tomber en ~** [*projectiles, étincelles*] to rain down.

■ **~s acides** acid rain ¢.

IDIOMES **il n'est pas né** or **tombé de la dernière ~**° he wasn't born yesterday°; **parler de la ~ et du beau temps** to make small talk; **elle fait la ~ et le beau temps dans le parti** she calls the shots° in the party; **après la ~ le beau temps** PROV every cloud has a silver lining PROV.

plume /plym/ *nf* **1** (d'oiseau) feather; **chapeau à ~s** feathered hat; **oreiller de ~s** feather pillow; **2** (pour écrire) (d'oiseau) quill (pen); (en métal) (pen) nib; **prendre la ~ pour...** to put pen to paper to..., to take up one's pen to...; **d'un coup de ~** with a single stroke of the pen; **écrire au fil de la ~** to write as the thoughts come into one's head; **elle a la ~ facile** words flow easily from her pen; **vivre de sa ~** to earn a living by one's pen; **dessin à la ~** pen-and-ink drawing.

IDIOMES **elle y a laissé** or **perdu des ~s** she did not come off unscathed; **voler dans les ~s à** or **de qn**° to fly at sb.

plumeau, *pl* **~x** /plymo/ *nm* **1** (ustensile) feather duster; **2** (touffe) tuft.

plumer /plyme/ [1] *vtr* **1** to pluck [*oiseau*]; **2**° to fleece° [*personne*]; **se faire ~** to be ripped off° ou fleeced°.

plumier /plymje/ *nm* pencil box.

plupart: **la plupart** /laplypaʀ/ *nf inv* **la ~ des gens/oiseaux** most people/birds; **dans la ~ des cas** in most cases; **pour la ~** for the most part; **la ~ d'entre eux** most of them; **la ~ du temps** most of the time, mostly.

pluridisciplinaire /plyʀidisiplinɛʀ/ *adj* multidisciplinary.

pluriel, -elle /plyʀjɛl/ **I** *adj* plural.
II *nm* plural.

plurilinguisme /plyʀilɛ̃gµism/ *nm* multilingualism.

plus¹ /ply, plys, plyz/ **I** *prép* **8 ~ 3 égale 11** 8 and ou plus 3 equals 11; **un dessert ~ du café** a dessert and coffee (as well); **~ 10°** plus 10°.

II *adv de comparaison* **1** (modifiant un verbe) (comparatif) more; (superlatif) **le ~** the most; **je ne peux pas faire ~** I can do no more, I can't do any more; **elle est ~ que jolie** she's more than just pretty; **elle mange deux fois ~ que lui** she eats twice as much as he does; **~ j'y pense, moins je comprends** the more I think about it, the less I understand; **~ ça va** as time goes on; **qui ~ est** furthermore, what's more; **quel pays aimes-tu le ~?** which country do you like best?; **de ~ en ~** more and more; **2** (modifiant un adjectif) (comparatif) more; (superlatif) most; **deux fois ~ cher** twice as expensive (**que** as); **c'est**

le **même modèle en ~ petit** it's the same model, only smaller; **il est on ne peut ~ désagréable** he's as unpleasant as can be; **il est ~ ou moins artiste** he's an artist of sorts; **il a été ~ ou moins poli** he wasn't particularly polite; **ils étaient ~ ou moins ivres** they were a bit drunk; **un livre des ~ intéressants** a most interesting book; **de ~ en ~ difficile** more and more difficult; **3** (modifiant un adverbe) (comparatif) more; (superlatif) most; **trois heures ~ tôt/tard** three hours earlier/later; **deux fois ~ longtemps** twice as long (que as); **ils ne sont pas restés ~ longtemps que nous** they didn't stay any longer than we did ou than us; **il l'a fait ~ ou moins bien** he didn't do it very well; **de ~ en ~ loin** further and further; **~ tu te coucheras tôt, moins tu seras fatigué** the earlier you go to bed, the less tired you'll be.

III *adv de négation* **elle ne fume ~** she doesn't smoke any more ou any longer, she no longer smokes; **~ jamais ça!** never again!; **~ besoin de se presser**○ there's no need to hurry any more; **il n'y a ~ d'œufs** there are no more eggs, there aren't any eggs left; **j'entre dans le garage, ~ de voiture!** I went into the garage, the car was gone!; **il n'y a ~ que lui qui puisse nous aider** only he can help us now; **~ que trois jours avant Noël!** only three days left ou to go until Christmas!.

IV plus *de dét indéf* **1** (avec un nom dénombrable) **deux fois ~ de livres que** twice as many books as; **c'est lui qui a le ~ de livres** he's got the most books; **les gens qui posent le ~ de problèmes** the people who pose the most problems; **~ tu mangeras de bonbons, ~ tu auras de caries** the more sweets GB ou candy US you eat, the more cavities you'll have; **il y en a ~ d'un qui voudrait être à sa place** quite a few people would like to be in his/her position; **2** (avec un nom non dénombrable) **je n'ai pas pris ~ de crème que toi** I didn't take any more cream than you did, I took no more cream than you did; **deux fois ~ de vin** twice as much wine (**que** as); **3** (avec un numéral) **elle n'a pas ~ de 50 disques** she has no more than 50 records; **les gens de ~ de 60 ans** people over 60; **il était déjà bien ~ de onze heures** it was already well past ou after eleven o'clock.

V au plus *loc adv* at the most; **tout au ~** at the very most.

VI de plus *loc adv* **1** (en outre) furthermore, moreover, what's more; **2** (en supplément) **deux pommes de ~** two more apples; **une fois de ~** once more, once again; **9% de ~** 9% more.

VII en plus *loc* **en ~** (de cela) on top of that; **le même modèle avec le toit ouvrant en ~** the same model, only with a sunroof; **il a reçu 2 000 francs en ~ de son salaire** he got 2,000 francs on top of his salary; **les taxes en ~** plus tax, tax not included.

■ Note *A note on pronunciation*:
plus/le plus used in comparison (meaning more/the most) is pronounced [ply] before a consonant and [plyz] before a vowel. It is pronounced [plys] when at the end of a clause. In the *plus de* and *plus que* structures both [ply] and [plys] are generally used.
plus used in *ne plus* (meaning no longer/not any more) is always pronounced [ply] except before a vowel, in which case it is pronounced [plyz]: *il n'habite plus ici* [plyzisi].

plus² /plys/ *nm inv* **1** MATH plus; **le signe ~** the plus sign; **2**○ (avantage) plus○.

plusieurs /plyzjœr/ **I** *adj* several; **une ou ~ personnes** one or more people.

II *pron indéf* **~ ont déjà signé** several people have already signed; **vous êtes ~ à en vouloir** there are several of you who want some.

plus-que-parfait /plyskəparfɛ/ *nm inv* pluperfect.

plus-value, *pl* **~s** /plyvaly/ *nf* **1** FIN (de biens mobiliers) increase in value; (d'actif, de monnaie) appreciation; (profit à la vente) capital gain; **2** ÉCON surplus value.
■ **~ financière** capital gain.

plutôt /plyto/ *adv* **1** (de préférence) rather; **pourquoi lui ~ qu'un autre?** why him rather than anybody else?; **~ le matin** in the morning preferably; **2** (au lieu de) instead; **~ mourir (que d'accepter)!** I'd rather ou sooner die (than accept)!; **j'ai ~ tendance à ne pas m'en faire** I'm more the kind not to worry; **3** (plus précisément) rather; **elle est blonde ou ~ châtain clair** she's got blond, or rather light brown hair; **dis ~ que tu n'as pas envie de le faire** why don't you just say that you don't want to do it?; **4** (ayant une valeur intensive) rather; **la nouvelle a été ~ mal accueillie** the news went down rather badly; '**tu prends des vacances cet été?'—'~ oui○!**' 'are you taking a vacation this summer?'—'too right○!' ou 'you bet○!'

pluvial, **~e**, *mpl* **-iaux** /plyvjal, o/ *adj* pluvial.

pluvieux, **-ieuse** /plyvjø, øz/ *adj* wet, rainy.

PM /peɛm/ *nm* (*abbr* = **pistolet-mitrailleur**) submachine gun.

PME /peɛmə/ *nfpl*: *abbr* ▶ **petit**.

PMI /peɛmi/ *nfpl* (*abbr* = **petites et moyennes industries**) small and medium-sized industries.

PMU /peɛmy/ *nm* (*abbr* = **Pari mutuel urbain**) *French state-controlled betting system*; **un ~** a betting office.

PNB /peɛnbe/ *nm*: *abbr* ▶ **produit**.

pneu /pnø/ *nm* **1** AUT tyre GB, tire US; **~ clouté** or **à clous** studded tyre; **~ neige** snow tyre; **~ tendre** slick tyre; **2**○ = **pneumatique II 1**.

pneumatique /pnømatik/ **I** *adj* **1** TECH pneumatic; **2** (gonflable) inflatable.

II *nm* **1** (message) *letter sent by pneumatic tube*; **2†** = **pneu 1**.

pneumonie /pnømɔni/ (▶ **196**) *nf* pneumonia.

pochard○, **~e** /pɔʃar, ard/ *nm,f* soak○, drunk.

poche¹ /pɔʃ/ *nm* **1**○ (livre) paperback; **2** (format) pocket size; **paraître en ~** to come out in paperback.

poche² /pɔʃ/ *nf* **1** (de vêtement, sac, portefeuille) pocket; **il est revenu le contrat en ~** FIG he came back with the contract in the bag○ ou all sewn up○; **son diplôme en ~, il est parti aux États-Unis** armed with his diploma, he set off for the States; **il avait 1 000 francs en ~** LIT he had 1,000 francs on him; FIG (à sa disposition) he had 1,000 francs available; **avoir de l'argent plein les ~s**○ to be loaded○, to have plenty of money; **s'en mettre plein** or **se remplir les ~s**○ to line one's pockets; **faire les ~s de qn** (vider) to empty out sb's pockets; (voler) to pick sb's pocket; **format de ~** pocket-size (*épith*); **2** (sac) bag; **3** (accumulation) **~ de gaz/d'air** gas/air pocket; **4** (déformation) **avoir des ~s sous les yeux** to have bags under one's eyes; **mon pantalon fait des ~s aux genoux** my trousers GB ou pants US are baggy at the knees; **5** ZOOL (de kangourou, pélican) pouch.
■ **~ de glace** ice pack; **~ revolver** hip pocket.
IDIOMES **mettre qn dans sa ~**○ to get sb on one's side; **c'est dans la ~**○ it's in the bag○, it's all sewn up○; **en être de sa ~**○ to be out of pocket; **ne pas avoir les yeux dans sa ~**○ not to miss a thing○; **connaître un endroit comme sa ~**○ to know a place like the back of one's hand.

pocher /pɔʃe/ [1] *vtr* **1** CULIN to poach; **2** (meurtrir) **un œil à qn** to give sb a black eye; **se faire ~ un œil** to get a black eye.

pochette /pɔʃɛt/ *nf* **1** (de crayons, compas) case; (de document) folder; (de disque) sleeve; (d'allumettes) book; **vendu sous ~ plastique** sold in a plastic cover; **2** (mouchoir) pocket handkerchief; **3** (sac à main) clutch bag; (pour papiers d'identité, argent) pouch.

pochette-surprise, *pl* **pochettes-surprises** /pɔʃɛtsyrpriz/ *nf*: child's novelty consisting of several small surprise items in a cone.

pochoir /pɔʃwar/ *nm* stencil; **au ~** stencilled GB.

podium /pɔdjɔm/ *nm* GÉN podium; (de défilé de mannequins) catwalk GB, runway US; **monter sur le ~** to mount the podium.

Le poids

dire			dire
one gram	1 g*	= 0.35†oz	*ounces*
one hundred grams	100 g	= 0.22 lbs	*pounds‡*
		= 3.52 oz	*ounces*
one kilogram	1 kg	= 2.20 lbs	
		= 35.26 oz	
one hundred kilograms	100 kg	= 220 lbs	
		= 15.76 st§	*stones*
		= 1.96 cwt	*hundredweight*
One ton ou one metric ton		= 0.98 ton¶	*tons (GB)*
		= 1.10 tons‖	*tons (US)*

* Pour les mesures du système métrique, les abréviations sont les mêmes en anglais qu'en français. Mais attention à ton: voir ci-dessous.

† Noter que l'anglais a un point là où le français a une virgule. Pour la prononciation des nombres, voir **les nombres ▶ 399**].

‡ Noter que la pound anglaise, que nous appelons couramment livre, vaut en fait 454 grammes.

§ Les stones ne sont pas utilisées aux États-Unis.

¶ Il n'y a pas d'abréviation pour ton.

‖ La tonne anglaise et la tonne américaine ne correspondent pas au même poids. Attention, car les anglophones peuvent en outre utiliser le mot ton pour la tonne de 1 000 kilos; pour éviter cette ambiguïté, on peut dire metric ton.

Les équivalences suivantes peuvent être utiles:

1 oz	= 28,35 g					
1 lb	= 16 ozs		= 453,60 g			
1 st	= 14 lbs		= 6,35 kg			
1 cwt	= 8 st (GB)		= 112 lbs (GB)	= 50,73 kg		
	= 100 lbs (US)		= 45,36 kg			
1 ton	= 20 cwt (GB)		= 1014,6 kg			
	= 20 cwt (US)		= 907,2 kg			

Le poids des choses

combien pèse le colis?	= what does the parcel weigh?
	ou how much does the parcel weigh?
quel est son poids?	= how much does it weigh?
	ou how heavy is it?
	or what is its weight?
il pèse 5 kg	= it weighs 5 kilos
	ou it is 5 kilos in weight
le colis fait 5 kg	= the parcel weighs 5 kilos
il fait à peu près 5 kg	= it is about 5 kilos
presque 6 kg	= almost 6 kilos

plus de 5 kg	= more than 5 kilos
moins de 6 kg	= less than 6 kilos
A est plus lourd que B	= A is heavier than B
A pèse plus lourd que B	= A weighs more than B
B est plus léger que A	= B is lighter than A
B est moins lourd que A	= B is lighter than A
A est aussi lourd que B	= A is as heavy as B
A fait le même poids que B	= A is the same weight as B
A pèse autant que B	= A is the same weight as B
A et B font le même poids	= A and B are the same weight
A et B pèsent le même poids	= A and B are the same weight

Noter:

il pèse deux kilos de trop	= it is 2 kilos overweight
six kilos de sucre	= six kilos of sugar
vendu au kilo	= sold by the kilo

Noter l'ordre des mots dans l'adjectif composé anglais, et l'utilisation du trait d'union. Noter aussi que pound et kilo, employés comme adjectifs, ne prennent pas la marque du pluriel.

une pomme de terre de 3 livres	= a 3-lb potato (dire a three-pound potato)
un colis de 5 kg	= a 5-kilo parcel (dire a five-kilo parcel)

On peut aussi dire a parcel 5 kilos in weight.

Le poids des personnes

En anglais britannique, le poids des personnes est donné en stones, chaque stone valant 6,35 kilos; en anglais américain, on le donne en pounds (livres), chaque livre valant 454 grammes.

combien pèses-tu?	= how much do you weigh?
	ou what is your weight?
je pèse 63 kg 500	= I weigh 10 st (ten stone) (GB)
	ou I weigh 140 lbs (a hundred forty pounds) (US) ou I weigh 63 kg 500
il pèse 71 kg	= he weighs 10 st 3 (ten stone three) (GB)
	ou he weighs 160 lbs (a hundred sixty pounds) (US) ou he weighs 71 kg
il pèse 82 kg	= he weighs 13 st (thirteen stone) (GB)
	ou he weighs 180 lbs (a hundred eighty pounds) (US) ou he weighs 82 kg
il fait trois kilos de trop	= he is three kilos overweight

Noter l'ordre des mots dans l'adjectif composé anglais, et l'utilisation du trait d'union. Noter aussi que stone, employé comme adjectif, ne prend pas la marque du pluriel.

un athlète de 125 kg	= a 20-stone athlete
	ou a 125-kg athlete

---

poêle[1] /pwal/ *nm* **1** (pour chauffer) stove; **2** (de cercueil) pall.

poêle[2] /pwal/ *nf* frying pan; **passer à la ~** to fry.

poêlon /pwalɔ̃/ *nm* heavy saucepan (*earthenware or cast iron*).

poème /pɔɛm/ *nm* poem; **c'est tout un ~**° it's quite something.

poésie /pɔezi/ *nf* **1** (art) poetry; **2** (poème) poem; **3** (qualité) **la ~ de son œuvre** the poetic quality of his/her work.

poète /pɔɛt/ *nm* poet.

poétesse† /pɔetɛs/ *nf* poetess†.

poétique /pɔetik/ **I** *adj* [œuvre, lieu] poetic; [personne] romantic.
II *nf* poetics (+ *v sg*).

poétiquement /pɔetikmɑ̃/ *adv* poetically.

poids /pwa/ *nm inv* **1** PHYS weight; **peser son ~** to be very heavy; **2** (importance) (de personne, pays, parti, d'électorat) influence; (de paroles) weight; **argument de ~** weighty argument; **adversaire de ~** opponent to be reckoned with; **il n'a aucun ~ politique** he hasn't got any political stature; **il ne fait pas le ~ devant un adversaire aussi redoutable** he's no match for such a formidable opponent; **je ne crois pas qu'il fera le ~ à ce poste** I don't think he's up to this job; **3** (fardeau) LIT weight; FIG burden; **être un ~ pour qn** to be a burden on sb; **avoir un ~ sur la conscience** to have a guilty conscience; **4** (pour peser,

lester) weight; **des ~ en laiton** brass weights; **5** (en athlétisme) shot; **lancer le ~** to put the shot; **le lancer du ~** the shot put.
■ **~ atomique** atomic weight; **~ brut** gross weight; **~ coq** SPORT bantamweight; **~ et haltères** weightlifting **℃**; **~ léger** SPORT lightweight; **~ lourd** SPORT heavyweight; (camion) heavy goods vehicle GB, heavy truck; **~ mi-lourd** SPORT light heavyweight; **~ mi-moyen** SPORT welterweight; **~ mort** TECH, FIG dead weight; **~ mouche** SPORT flyweight; **~ moyen** SPORT middleweight; **~ net** net weight; **~ net égoutté** net weight drained; **~ plume** SPORT featherweight; **~ superléger** SPORT light middleweight; **~ total en charge, PTC** gross weight; **~ total à vide, PTAV** tare; **~ welter** SPORT welterweight.
IDIOMES **faire bon ~ bonne mesure** to be evenhanded; **avoir** or **faire deux ~ deux mesures** to have double standards.

poignant, **~e** /pwaɲɑ̃, ɑ̃t/ *adj* (émouvant) poignant; (déchirant) heart-rending, harrowing.

poignard /pwaɲaʀ/ *nm* dagger; **coup de ~** stab.

poignarder /pwaɲaʀde/ [1] *vtr* (blesser) to stab, to knife; (tuer) to stab [sb] to death; **~ qn dans le dos** LIT, FIG to stab sb in the back.

poigne /pwaɲ/ *nf* **avoir de la ~** LIT to have a strong grip; FIG to be firm-handed.

poignée /pwaɲe/ *nf* **1** (quantité) GÉN handful; (de

billets) fistful; **2** (de porte, tiroir, sac) handle; (de sabre) hilt.

■ **~ de main** handshake; **échanger une ~ de main** to shake hands.

poignet /pwaɲɛ/ *nm* **1** ▶ 137⌋ ANAT wrist; **au ~** on the wrist; **à la force des ~s** [*se hisser*] using the strength of one's arms; **à la force du ~** [*réussir*] by sheer hard work; **2** (de chemise) cuff.

poil /pwal/ *nm* **1** (chez l'être humain) hair; **avoir du ~ aux jambes** to have hairy legs; **avoir du ~ au menton** (être adulte) to be a grown man; **à ~**⚬ (nu) stark naked, starkers⚬; **se mettre à ~**⚬ to strip, to strip off GB; **de tout ~**⚬ of all kinds; **'au (petit) ~**⚬!' 'fine!'; **être au ~**⚬ [*objet*] to be just the ticket⚬; [*personne*] to be fantastic; **ça marche au ~**⚬ it works like a dream; **2**⚬ (cheveux) **avoir le ~ ras/rare** to have short/thin hair; **3** (d'animal) hair; **perdre ses ~s** to moult GB ou molt US, to shed (its) hairs; **animal à ~s** furry animal; **animal à ~ ras** short-haired animal; **animal au ~ soyeux** animal with a silky coat; **caresser dans le sens du ~** LIT to stroke [sth] the way the fur lies; FIG to butter [sb] up⚬; **4** BOT hair, down ₵; **5**⚬ (petite quantité) (d'humour, ironie) touch; (d'intelligence, de bon sens, courage) shred; **un ~ plus grand/trop petit** a shade larger/too small; **à un ~ près** by a whisker; **il s'en est fallu d'un ~ que je fasse** I was within a whisker of doing; **6** (de tapis) pile ₵; (de tissu) nap ₵; (de brosse, balai) bristle.

■ **~ à gratter** itching powder.

IDIOMES **être de bon/mauvais ~**⚬ to be in a good/bad mood; **j'ai le ~ qui se hérisse**⚬ my hackles rise; **hérisser le ~**⚬ **de qn** to put sb's back up⚬; **avoir un ~ dans la main**⚬ to be bone idle; **ne plus avoir un ~ sur le caillou**⚬ to be as bald as a coot⚬; **ne plus avoir un ~ de sec**⚬ to be soaked to the skin; **tomber sur le ~ de qn**⚬ (se fâcher contre) to have a real go at sb⚬; (frapper) to give sb what's coming to him/her.

poil-de-carotte /pwaldəkarɔt/ ▶ 141⌋ *adj inv* (couleur) [*cheveux*] ginger.

poilu, ~e /pwaly/ **I** *adj* hairy.
II⚬ *nm*: French soldier in World War I.

poinçon /pwɛ̃sɔ̃/ *nm* **1** (de brodeuse) stiletto; (de cordonnier) awl; (de menuisier) bradawl; (de graveur) burin; (de sculpteur) punch; (de scribe) stylus; **2** (pour marquer) die, stamp; (marque) hallmark; **3** (matrice) die.

poinçonner /pwɛ̃sɔne/ [1] *vtr* **1** (perforer) to punch, to clip [*billet*]; **2** (marquer) to hallmark [*or, argent*]; to stamp [*marchandise*].

poinçonneur, -euse[1] /pwɛ̃sɔnœR, øz/ ▶ 374⌋ *nm,f* (employé des transports) ticket-puncher; (ouvrier) punching-machine operator.

poinçonneuse[2] /pwɛ̃sɔnøz/ *nf* (à billets) ticket-punch; (machine-outil) punching machine.

poindre /pwɛ̃dR/ [56] *vi* [*jour*] to dawn, to break; [*aube*] to break; [*soleil*] to peep through; [*plante*] to peep through, to come up; [*idée, sentiment*] to dawn.

poing /pwɛ̃/ *nm* fist; **coup de ~** punch; **donner un coup de ~ à qn** to punch sb; **les ~s sur les hanches** with (one's) arms akimbo; **être pieds et ~s liés** LIT to be bound hand and foot; FIG to have one's hands tied; **l'épée au ~** sword in hand.

IDIOMES **dormir à ~s fermés** to sleep like a log.

point /pwɛ̃/ **I** *nm* **1** (endroit) point; **un ~ de rencontre** a meeting point; **~ de vente** (sales) outlet; **2** (situation) point; NAUT position; **être sur le ~ de faire** to be just about to do, to be on the point of doing; **j'en suis toujours au même ~ (qu'hier/qu'il y a un an)** I'm still exactly where I was (yesterday/last year); **au ~ où j'en suis, ça n'a pas d'importance!** I've reached the point where it doesn't matter any more!; **faire le ~** NAUT to take bearings; FIG to take stock of the situation; **3** (degré) **il m'agace au plus haut ~** he annoys me intensely; **je ne le pensais pas bête à ce ~** I didn't think he was that stupid; **'j'en aurais pleuré'—'ah bon, à ce ~?'** 'I could

have cried'—'really? it was that bad?'; **si tu savais à quel ~ il m'agace!** if you only knew how much he annoys me!; **au ~ que** to the extent that; **à tel ~ que** to such an extent that; **douloureux au ~ que** so painful that; **il est têtu à un ~**⚬! he's so incredibly stubborn!; **jusqu'à un certain ~** up to a (certain) point, to a certain extent; **4** (question particulière) point; (dans un ordre du jour) item, point; **programme en trois ~s** a three-point plan; **un ~ de détail** a minor point; **en tout ~, en tous ~s** in every respect ou way; **5** (marque visible) dot; **un ~ de colle** a spot of glue; **un ~ de rouille** a speck of rust; **6** JEUX, SPORT point; **marquer/perdre des ~s** LIT, FIG to score/to lose points; **compter les ~s** to keep (the score); **un ~ partout!** one all!; **gagner aux ~s** to win on points; **7** (pour évaluer) mark GB, point US; **avoir sept ~s d'avance/de retard** to be seven marks ahead/behind; **obtenir** ou **avoir 27 ~s sur 40** to get 27 out of 40; **être un bon ~ pour** to be a plus point for; **être un mauvais ~ pour qn/qch** to be a black mark against sb/sth; **8** (dans un système de calcul) point; **la livre a perdu trois ~s** the pound lost three points; **le permis à ~s** system whereby driving offender gets penalty points; **9** MATH point; **~ d'intersection** point of intersection; **10** ▶ 414⌋ LING (dans ponctuation) full stop GB, period US; **~ à la ligne** (dans une dictée) full stop, new paragraph; **~ final** (dans une dictée) full stop; **mettre un ~ final à qch** FIG to put a stop ou an end to sth; **je n'irai pas, ~ final**⚬! I'm not going, full stop GB ou period US!; **tu vas te coucher un ~ c'est tout**⚬! you're going to bed and that's final!; **11** MUS dot; **12** (en typographie) point; **13** MÉD (douleur) pain; **avoir un ~ à l'aine** to have a pain in the groin; **14** (en couture, tricot) stitch; **faire un ~ à qch** to put a few stitches in sth; **dentelle au ~ de Venise** Venetian lace.
II† *adv* not; **tu ne tueras ~** thou shalt not kill.
III à point *loc adv* **1** (en temps voulu) just in time; **~ nommé** just at the right moment; **2** CULIN (cuit) **~** medium rare; **le camembert est à ~** the camembert is ready to eat.
IV au point *loc* **être au ~** [*système, machine*] to be well designed; [*spectacle*] not yet put together; **leur système n'est pas encore très au ~** their system still needs some working on; **le prototype n'est pas encore au ~** the prototype isn't quite ready yet; **mettre au ~** (élaborer) to perfect [*système*]; to work out, to devise [*accord, plan*]; to develop [*vaccin, appareil*]; (régler) to adjust; **finir de mettre qch au ~** to put the finishing touches to sth; **mise au ~** (de système) perfecting; (de vaccin) development; (réglage) adjusting; PHOT focus; FIG (déclaration) clarifying statement; **faire la mise au ~** PHOT to focus; **faire une mise au ~** FIG to set the record straight (**sur** about).

■ **~ d'ancrage** AUT anchor; FIG base; **~ d'appui** MIL base of operations; PHYS fulcrum; GÉN support; **~ d'attache** base; **~ cardinal** compass ou cardinal point; **~ chaud** trouble ou hot spot; **~ de chute** FIG port of call; **~ commun** mutual interest; **nous avons beaucoup de ~s communs** we have a lot in common; **~ de côté** (douleur) stitch; **~ de départ** LIT, FIG starting point; **nous revoilà au ~ de départ** FIG we're back to square one; **~ d'eau** (naturel) watering place; (robinet) water tap GB ou faucet US; **~ d'exclamation** exclamation mark; **~ de fuite** vanishing point; **~ de fusion** melting point; **~ d'interrogation** question mark; **~ du jour** daybreak; **~ de mire** MIL target; FIG focal point; **~ mort** AUT neutral; **être au ~ mort** FIG [*affaire, consommation*] to be at a standstill; [*négociations*] to be in a state of deadlock; **~ noir** (comédon) blackhead; (problème) problem; (sur la route) blackspot; **~ d'orgue** MUS pause sign; **~ de penalty** penalty spot; **~ de repère** (spatial) landmark; (temporel, personnel) point of reference; **~ de suture** stitch; **~ de vue** (paysage) viewpoint; (opinion) point of view; **du ~ de vue du sens** as far as meaning is concerned; **~s de suspension** suspension points.
IDIOMES **être mal en ~** to be in a bad way.

pointage /pwɛ̃taʒ/ *nm* **1** (vérification) GÉN checking; (de

Les points cardinaux

nord	north	N
sud	south	S
est	east	E
ouest	west	W

Noter que la liste des quatre points cardinaux est traditionnellement donnée dans cet ordre dans les deux langues.

nord-est	northeast	NE
nord-ouest	northwest	NW
nord-nord-est	north northeast	NNE
est-nord-est	east northeast	ENE
etc.		

Dans les expressions suivantes, nord est pris comme exemple; les autres noms de points cardinaux s'utilisent de la même façon.

Où?

vivre dans le Nord	= to live in the North
dans le nord de l'Écosse	= in the north of Scotland
au nord du village	= north of the village *ou* to the north of the village
à 7 km au nord	= 7 kilometres north *ou* 7 kilometres to the north
droit au nord	= due north
la côte nord	= the north coast
la face nord (d'une montagne)	= the north face
le mur nord	= the north wall
la porte nord	= the north door
passer au nord d'Oxford	= to go north of Oxford

Les mots en -ern et -erner

Les mots anglais en -ern et -erner sont plus courants que les adjectifs français septentrional, occidental, oriental et méridional.

une ville du Nord	= a northern town
l'accent du Nord	= a northern accent
le dialecte du Nord	= the northern dialect
l'avant poste le plus au nord	= the most northerly outpost *ou* the northernmost outpost
quelqu'un qui habite dans le Nord	= a northerner
un homme du Nord	= a northerner
les gens du Nord	= northerners

Les adjectifs en -ern sont normalement utilisés pour désigner des régions à l'intérieur d'un pays ou d'un continent (▶ 509 |).

le nord de l'Europe	= northern Europe
l'est de la France	= eastern France
le sud de la Roumanie	= southern Romania
le nord d'Israël	= northern Israel

Mais noter:

l'Asie du Sud-Est	= South-East Asia

Pour les noms de pays qui utilisent les points cardinaux (Corée du Nord, Yemen du Sud) se reporter au dictionnaire.

Dans quelle direction?

Noter les adverbes en -ward ou -wards (GB) et les adjectifs en -ward, utilisés pour indiquer une direction vague.

aller vers le nord	= to go north *ou* to go northward *ou* to go in a northerly direction
naviguer vers le nord	= to sail north *ou* to sail northward
venir du nord	= to come from the north
un mouvement vers le nord	= a northward mouvement

Pour décrire le déplacement d'un object, on peut utiliser un composé avec -bound.

un bateau qui se dirige vers le nord	= a northbound ship
les véhicules qui se dirigent vers le nord	= northbound traffic

Noter aussi:

les véhicules qui viennent du nord	= traffic coming from the north
des fenêtres qui donnent au nord	= north-facing windows *ou* windows facing north
une pente orientée au nord	= a north-facing slope
nord quart nord-est	= north by northeast

Noter ces expressions servant à donner la direction des vents:

le vent du nord	= the north wind
un vent de nord	= a northerly wind *ou* a northerly
des vents dominants de nord	= prevailing north winds
le vent est au nord	= the wind is northerly *ou* the wind is in the north
le vent vient du nord	= the wind is blowing from the north

---

cochant) ticking off GB, checking off US; **le ~ des voix** (dans une vote) the tally of the votes; **2** (de salarié) (en entrant) clocking in; (en sortant) clocking off; **feuille de ~** time sheet.

ointe /pwɛ̃t/ I *nf* **1** (extrémité) (de couteau, crayon) point; (de chaussure) toe; (des cheveux) end; (de grille) spike; (de lance, flèche) tip, point; **en ~** pointed; **un casque à ~** a spiked helmet; **2** FIG **de ~** [*technologie*] advanced, state-of-the-art; [*secteur, industrie*] hightech; [*entreprise*] leading; **à la ~ du progrès** state-of-the-art (*épith*); **3** (maximum) high; **fortes ~s saisonnières** seasonal highs; **vitesse de ~** maximum ou top speed; **heure de ~** rush hour; **aux heures de ~** at peak time; **4** (petite quantité) (d'ail, de cannelle) touch; (d'accent, ironie) hint; **5** (clou) nail; **6** (outil) (pour tailler) cutter; (pour graver) metal point; **7** (de chausson de danse) blocked shoe; (extrémité de chausson) point; **8** (allusion désagréable) pointed ou barbed remark; **lancer des ~s à qn** to level cutting remarks at sb.

II **pointes** *nfpl* **1** SPORT (chaussures à) **~s** spikes; **courir avec des ~s** to run in spikes; **2** (en danse) **faire des ~s** to dance on points.

■ **~ d'asperge** asparagus tip; **~ de diamant** diamond cutter; **~ du pied** tiptoe; **elle est entrée sur la ~ des pieds** she tiptoed in; **aborder une question sur la ~ des pieds** FIG to broach a matter carefully; **~ sèche** metal point; **~ du sein** nipple. ◆IDIOMES **tailler les oreilles en ~**○ **à qn** to give sb a thick ear.

ointé, ~e /pwɛ̃te/ *adj* MUS [*note*] dotted.

ointer[1] /pwɛ̃te/ [1] I *vtr* **1** (en cochant) to tick off GB,

to check off US [*noms, mots, chiffres*]; to check [*liste*]; **2** (diriger) to point [*arme*] (**sur** at); **~ le doigt vers** to point at; **~ son museau** [*animal*] to peep out; **~ son nez**○ to show one's face; **3** (dresser) **~ ses oreilles** [*chien*] to prick up its ears.

II *vi* **1** [*employé*] (en arrivant) to clock in; (en sortant) to clock out; **~ à l'usine**○ to work in a factory; **~ à l'agence pour l'emploi** to sign on at the unemployment office; **2** (aux boules) *to aim at positioning a boule as close to the jack as possible*; **3** (se dresser) [*clocher, arbre, antenne*] to rise up; [*seins*] to stick out; **~ à l'horizon** to rise up on the horizon; **4** (apparaître) [*soleil*] to come up, to rise; [*aube, jour*] to break; [*fleur, plante*] to come up; [*bourgeon*] to open.

III **se pointer**○ *vpr* [*personne*] to turn up (**à** at).

pointer[2] /pwɛ̃tœʀ/ *nm* (chien) pointer.

pointeur, -euse[1] /pwɛ̃tœʀ, øz/ I *nm,f* GÉN checker; (en entreprise, sport) timekeeper; (aux boules) *player whose role is to position his own boule.*

II *nm* MIL gun-layer.

pointeuse[2] /pwɛ̃toz/ *nf* time clock.

pointillé, ~e /pwɛ̃tije/ I *adj* dotted (**de** with).

II *nm* **1** (ligne) dotted line; (perforation) perforation(s); **plier suivant le ~** fold along the dotted line; **en ~** LIT dotted; **message en ~** FIG underlying message; **2** ART stippling; **dessin au ~** stippled drawing.

pointilleux, -euse /pwɛ̃tijø, øz/ *adj* PEJ [*personne*] fussy (**sur** about), pernickety.

pointu, ~e /pwɛ̃ty/ I *adj* **1** [*bout*] pointed; [*ciseaux*] with a sharp point (*épith, après n*); [*toit, chapeau*] pointed; [*menton*] pointed, sharp PÉJ; **2** [*contrôle*] close, thorough; **3** [*secteur, travail*] highly specialized; [*question*] precise; **4** [*voix*] piercing; [*ton*] shrill.

II *adv* **parler ~** to sound like a Parisian to a native of the south of France.

pointure /pwɛ̃tyʀ/ ▶ 581 | *nf* (de gant, chaussure) size.

point-virgule, *pl* **points-virgules** /pwɛ̃viʀgyl/ ▶ 414 | *nm* semicolon.

poire /pwaʀ/ *nf* **1** (fruit) pear; **en forme de ~** pear-shaped; **2** (en boucherie) *cut of topside of beef used for steaks*; **3** (interrupteur) (pear-shaped) light switch; **4** (en bijouterie) pear-shaped stone; **5**⁰ (visage) face; **6**⁰ (personne naïve) mug⁰ GB, sucker⁰.
■ **~ à injections** or **à lavement** bulb syringe.
IDIOMES **couper la ~ en deux** to split the difference; **garder une ~ pour la soif** to save something for a rainy day.

poireau, *pl* **~x** /pwaʀo/ *nm* leek.

poireauter⁰ /pwaʀote/ [1] *vi* to hang about⁰.

poirier /pwaʀje/ *nm* **1** (arbre) pear (tree); **2** (bois) pear.
IDIOMES **faire le ~** to do a headstand.

pois /pwa/ *nm inv* **1** BOT, CULIN pea; **petit ~** (garden) pea, petit pois; **2** (motif) dot; **à ~** polka dot (*épith*), spotted.
■ **~ cassé** split pea; **~ chiche** chickpea; **~ de senteur** sweet pea.

poison /pwazɔ̃/ **I**⁰ *nmf* (personne agaçante) pest.
II *nm* LIT, FIG poison.

poisse⁰ /pwas/ *nf* (malchance) rotten luck⁰.

poisseux, -euse /pwaso, øz/ *adj* [*mains, table*] sticky; [*atmosphère*] muggy; [*restaurant*] greasy.

poisson /pwasɔ̃/ *nm* fish; **les ~s d'eau douce/de mer** freshwater/saltwater fish ₵.
■ **~ d'argent** (insecte) silverfish; **~ d'avril** (exclamation) April fool; (blague) April fool's joke; **faire un ~ d'avril à qn** to make an April fool of sb; **~ pané** breaded fish; (en bâtonnets) fish fingers (*pl*); **~ rouge** goldfish; **~ volant** flying fish.
IDIOMES **être comme un ~ dans l'eau** to be in one's element; **essayer de noyer le ~**⁰ to fudge the issue; **petit ~ deviendra grand** mighty oaks from little acorns grow; **les gros ~s mangent les petits** it is the survival of the fittest.

poissonnerie /pwasɔnʀi/ ▶ 374 | *nf* **1** (magasin) fishmonger's (shop) GB, fish shop US; (dans un supermarché) fish counter, fish market US; **2** (industrie) fish trade.

poissonneux, -euse /pwasɔnø, øz/ *adj* [*eaux, rivière*] well stocked with fish (*après n*).

poissonnier, -ière /pwasɔnje, ɛʀ/ ▶ 374 | *nm,f* fishmonger GB, fish vendor US.

Poissons /pwasɔ̃/ ▶ 641 | *nprmpl* Pisces.

poitrail /pwatʀaj/ *nm* breast; (poitrine) HUM chest.

poitrine /pwatʀin/ ▶ 137 |, 581 | *nf* **1** (thorax) chest; (seins) breasts (*pl*); **tour de ~** (pour un homme) chest size; (pour une femme) bust size; **se frapper la ~** FIG to beat one's breast; **elle n'a pas beaucoup de ~** she is rather flat-chested; **2** CULIN breast; **~ de bœuf** brisket; **~ de porc** ~ belly of pork.
■ **~ fumée/salée** ~ smoked/unsmoked streaky bacon.

poivre /pwavʀ/ *nm* pepper; **~ en grains** whole peppercorns (*pl*); **~ et sel** salt-and-pepper (*épith*).

poivré, -e /pwavʀe/ *adj* [*sauce, odeur*] peppery; [*plaisanterie*] racy.

poivrer /pwavʀe/ [1] *vtr* to add pepper to [*plat, sauce*].

poivrier /pwavʀije/ *nm* **1** CULIN (récipient) pepper-pot GB, pepper shaker US; (moulin) pepper mill; **2** BOT (arbuste) pepper tree.

poivron /pwavʀɔ̃/ *nm* sweet pepper.

poivrot⁰, **-e** /pwavʀo, ɔt/ *nm,f* drunk, drunkard.

poix /pwa/ *nf inv* pitch; **~ bitumineuse** coal-tar pitch.

poker /pokɛʀ/ ▶ 329 | *nm* poker; **une partie de ~** FIG a game of bluff; **coup de ~** FIG gamble.

polaire /polɛʀ/ *adj* **1** [*faune, flore, région*] polar; [*froid, paysage*] arctic; **2** CHIMIE, MATH polar.

polar⁰ /polaʀ/ *nm* detective novel.

polariser /polaʀize/ [1] **I** *vtr* **1** PHYS to polarize; **2** (concentrer) to focus [*débat, opinion*]; **3** (attirer à soi) to attract [*regards*]; to be a focus for [*soupçons*].
II se polariser *vpr* (se concentrer) [*attention, débat*] to focus; [*personne*] to focus one's attention.

pôle /pol/ *nm* **1** GÉOG, MATH, PHYS pole; **2** FIG (centre) centre^GB; (tendance) pole.

polémique /polemik/ **I** *adj* polemical.
II *nf* debate; **de violentes ~s** fierce debate ₵.

poli, ~e /poli/ **I** *pp* ▶ **polir**.
II *pp adj* LIT, FIG [*métal, style*] polished.
III *adj* (courtois) polite (**avec qn** to sb).
IV *nm* shine; **donner du ~ à qch** to polish sth up.

police /polis/ *nf* **1** (force) police (+ *v pl*); **toutes les ~s du pays** every police force in the country; **2** (organisme privé) security service; **3** (maintien de l'ordre) policing; **pouvoirs de ~** powers to enforce law and order; **faire la ~** to keep order; **4** (d'assurance) policy; **5** (en typographie) **~ (de caractères)** font (*pl*); **6** (tribunal) **passer en simple ~** to be tried in a police court.
■ **~ de l'air et des frontières, PAF** border police; **~ judiciaire, PJ** *detective division of the French police force*; **~ des mœurs** or **mondaine** vice squad; **~ montée** mounted police; **~ municipale** city police; **~ nationale** national police force; **~ privée** private police force; **~ de la route** traffic police; **~ secours** ~ emergency service (*pl*).

policer /polise/ [12] *vtr* LITER to civilize.

polichinelle /poliʃinɛl/ *nm* (jouet) Punch.

Polichinelle /poliʃinɛl/ *npr* Punchinello.

policier, -ière /polisje, ɛʀ/ **I** *adj* [*surveillance, chien, régime, mesure, enquête*] police; [*film, roman*] detective.
II *nm* **1** ▶ 374 | (personne) policeman; **femme ~** policewoman; **2**⁰ (film) detective film; (roman) detective novel.

policlinique /poliklinik/ *nf* ~ outpatients' clinic.

poliment /polimã/ *adv* politely.

polio /poljo/ ▶ 196 | *nf* polio.

poliomyélite /poljomjelit/ ▶ 196 | *nf* poliomyelitis.

poliomyélitique /poljomjelitik/ **I** *adj* handicappe by polio (*jamais épith*); [*virus*] polio (*épith*); **il est ~** he has polio.
II *nmf* polio sufferer.

polir /poliʀ/ [3] *vtr* to polish [*bois, pierre*]; to polis (up) [*style*]; **se ~ les ongles** to buff one's nails.

polisson, -onne /polisɔ̃, ɔn/ **I** *adj* **1** [*enfant*] naughty; **2** (licencieux) naughty, saucy.
II *nm,f* (enfant) naughty child.

polissonnerie /polisɔnʀi/ *nf* **1** (d'enfant) naughty trick; **2** (propos licencieux) naughty remark.

politesse /polites/ *nf* politeness; **par ~** out of politeness; **le 'vous' de ~** the polite 'vous' form; **tu pourrais avoir la ~ de t'excuser** you might have the decency to apologize; **rendre la ~ à qn** to return the compliment; **échanger des ~s** to exchange pleasantries; IRON to exchange insults.
IDIOMES **l'exactitude est la ~ des rois** PROV punctuality is the hallmark of a gentleman; **brûler** or **griller la ~ à qn** to push in ahead of sb.

politicard⁰ /politikaʀ/ *nm* PEJ political wheeler-dealer.

politicien, -ienne /politisjɛ̃, ɛn/ **I** *adj* (purely) political; **politique politicienne** PEJ politicking PÉJ.
II *nm,f* politician.

politique¹ /politik/ **I** *adj* **1** GÉN political; **2** (habile) [*concession*] tactical; [*comportement, acte*] calculating.
II *nm* **1** (aspect) political aspect; **2** (personne qui s'intéresse aux affaires de l'État) politician; **3** (personne habile) **un (fin) ~** a shrewd operator.

politique² /politik/ *nf* **1** (science, art) politics (+ *sg*); **faire de la ~** (en faire son métier) to go into pol

tics, to be in politics; (en tant que militant) to be involved in politics; **2** (manière de gouverner, stratégie) policy.
■ **~ de la terre brûlée** scorched earth policy.
IDIOMES **pratiquer la ~ de l'autruche** to stick one's head in the sand; **pratiquer la ~ du pire** to envisage the worst-case scenario.

•olitiquement /pɔlitikmɑ̃/ *adv* **1** LIT politically; **2** (habilement) shrewdly.

•olitiser /pɔlitize/ [1] **I** *vtr* to politicize.
II se politiser *vpr* to become politicized.

•olitologue /pɔlitɔlɔɡ/ ▶ 374 *nmf* political scientist.

•ollen /pɔl(l)ɛn/ *nm* pollen.

•olluant, ~e /pɔl(l)ɥɑ̃, ɑ̃t/ **I** *adj* polluting.
II *nm* pollutant.

•olluer /pɔl(l)ɥe/ [1] *vtr* to pollute.

•ollueur, -euse /pɔl(l)ɥœʀ, øz/ **I** *adj* polluting.
II *nm,f* (usine) polluter, factory responsible for pollution.

•ollution /pɔl(l)ysjɔ̃/ *nf* LIT, FIG pollution ¢.
■ **~ nocturne** wet dream, nocturnal emission SPÉC.

•olo /pɔlo/ *nm* **1** (vêtement) polo shirt; **2** ▶ 329 (sport) polo.

•olochon /pɔlɔʃɔ̃/ *nm* bolster; **bataille (à coups) de ~s** pillow fight.

•ologne /pɔlɔɲ/ ▶ 232 *nprf* Poland.

•olonais, ~e¹ /pɔlɔnɛ, ɛz/ **I** ▶ 394 *adj* Polish.
II ▶ 338 *nm* LING Polish.

•olonais, ~e /pɔlɔnɛ, ɛz/ ▶ 394 *nm,f* Pole.

•olonaise² /pɔlɔnɛz/ *nf* **1** MUS polonaise; **2** CULIN *pastry with meringue topping, flavoured*GB *with Kirsch*.

•oltron, -onne /pɔltʀɔ̃, ɔn/ **I** *adj* cowardly.
II *nm,f* coward.

•oltronnerie /pɔltʀɔnʀi/ *nf* cowardice.

•olyclinique /pɔliklinik/ *nf* private hospital.

•olycopie /pɔlikɔpi/ *nf* **1** (procédé) duplicating; **2** (feuille) duplicate copy.

•olycopié, ~e /pɔlikɔpje/ **I** *adj* duplicated.
II *nm* duplicated notes (*pl*).

•olycopier /pɔlikɔpje/ [2] *vtr* to duplicate.

•olyculture /pɔlikyltyʀ/ *nf* mixed farming.

•olyèdre /pɔljɛdʀ/ *nm* polyhedron.

•olyéthylène /pɔlietilɛn/ *nm* polythene GB, polyethylene US.

•olygame /pɔliɡam/ **I** *adj* polygamous.
II *nmf* polygamist.

•olyglotte /pɔliɡlɔt/ *adj, nmf* polyglot.

•olygone /pɔliɡon/ *nm* **1** MATH polygon; **2** MIL firing range.

•olyhandicapé, ~e /pɔliɑ̃dikape/ *nm,f* multiply handicapped person.

•olynésie /pɔlinezi/ ▶ 509 *nprf* Polynesia.

•olynésien, -ienne /pɔlinezjɛ̃, ɛn/ **I** *adj* Polynesian.
II *nm* LING Polynesian.

•olysémique /pɔlisemik/ *adj* polysemous.

•olytechnicien, -ienne /pɔliteknisjɛ̃, ɛn/ *nm,f: graduate of the École Polytechnique*.

•olytechnique /pɔliteknik/ *nf: Grande École of Science and Technology*.

•olyvalence /pɔlivalɑ̃s/ *nf* **1** (d'appareil, de matériel) versatility; **2** (d'employé, de professeur) flexibility; **3** CHIMIE, MÉD polyvalence.

•olyvalent, ~e¹ /pɔlivalɑ̃, ɑ̃t/ **I** *adj* CHIMIE, MÉD polyvalent; [*matériel*] multipurpose (*épith*); [*employé*] who does several jobs (*après n*); [*professeur*] teaching several subjects (*après n*).
II *nm* tax inspector (*checking company tax returns*).

•olyvalente² /pɔlivalɑ̃t/ *nf* C comprehensive school.

•ommade /pɔmad/ *nf* MÉD ointment.
IDIOMES **passer de la ~** à qn to butter sb up.

•omme /pɔm/ *nf* **1** (fruit) apple; **2** (d'arrosoir) rose; (de douche) shower-head; (de canne) pommel, knob; (de mât) truck; (d'escalier) knob; **3** (benêt) mug GB, sucker; **4** (personne) **ça va encore être pour ma**

~ (ennui) I'm in for it again; (tour de payer) it looks like it's my turn to pay again.
■ **~ d'Adam** Adam's apple; **~ d'amour** (confiserie) toffee apple GB, candy apple US; **~ d'api** ≈ small apple; **~ de discorde** bone of contention; **~ de pin** pine cone; **~ de terre** potato; **~ de terre en robe des champs** (bouillie) potato boiled in its skin; (au four) jacket potato; **~s allumettes** potato straws GB, shoestring potatoes US; **~s chips** crisps GB, potato chips US; **~s frites** chips GB, (French) fries; **~s à l'huile** ≈ potato salad; **~s vapeur** steamed potatoes.
IDIOMES **tomber dans les ~s** to faint, to pass out.

pommeau, *pl* **~x** /pɔmo/ *nm* (de canne, rampe) knob; (d'épée, de selle) pommel.

pommelé, ~e /pɔmle/ *adj* **cheval ~** dappled horse; **cheval gris ~** dapple-grey GB ou dapple-gray US horse; **un ciel ~** a mackerel sky.

pommeraie /pɔmʀɛ/ *nf* apple orchard.

pommette /pɔmɛt/ ▶ 137 *nf* cheekbone.

pommier /pɔmje/ *nm* (arbre) apple tree; (bois) apple, apple-wood.

pompage /pɔ̃paʒ/ *nm* pumping.

pompe /pɔ̃p/ **I** *nf* **1** (appareil) pump; **2** (chaussure) shoe; **3** (apparat) pomp; **4** SPORT (exercice) press-up GB, push-up.
II pompes *nfpl* RELIG vanities; **les ~s de Satan** Satan's pomps.
■ **~ à essence** petrol pump GB, gas pump US; **~ à incendie** fire engine; **~s funèbres** (lieu) undertaker's (*sg*) GB, funeral home (*sg*) US; (entreprise) undertaker's GB, funeral director's.
IDIOMES **avoir un coup de ~** to be knackered GB ou pooped; **à toute ~** at top speed, as quickly as possible; **marcher** or **être à côté de ses ~s** not to be with it, to be away with the fairies.

pomper /pɔ̃pe/ [1] *vtr* **1** (aspirer) to pump; (pour vider) to pump out; (pour faire monter) to pump up; **2** (copier) students' slang to copy (**sur** from), to crib (**sur** from).
IDIOMES **~ l'air** à qn to get on sb's nerves.

pompette /pɔ̃pɛt/ *adj* tipsy, drunk.

pompeux, -euse /pɔ̃pø, øz/ *adj* pompous.

pompier, -ière /pɔ̃pje, ɛʀ/ **I** *adj* pompous.
II ▶ 374 *nm* fireman, firefighter; **appeler les ~s** to call the fire brigade GB ou fire department US.

pompiste /pɔ̃pist/ ▶ 374 *nmf* petrol GB ou gas US pump attendant.

pompon /pɔ̃pɔ̃/ *nm* (de bonnet, frange) bobble; (de pantoufle) pompom.
IDIOMES **remporter** or **décrocher le ~** to come top, to win first prize.

pomponner /pɔ̃pɔne/ [1] **I** *vtr* **~ un bébé** to get a baby dressed up.
II se pomponner *vpr* to get dolled up.

ponçage /pɔ̃saʒ/ *nm* **1** TECH (de bois, mur) sanding; (de cuir) smoothing; **2** (à la pierre ponce) pumicing.

ponce /pɔ̃s/ *nf* **pierre ~** pumice stone.

poncer /pɔ̃se/ [12] *vtr* **1** TECH (pour décaper) to sand; **2** ART (pour reproduire) to pounce; **3** (à la pierre ponce) to pumice.

ponceuse /pɔ̃søz/ *nf* sander; **~ vibrante** orbital sander.

poncif /pɔ̃sif/ *nm* (banalité) cliché, commonplace.

ponction /pɔ̃ksjɔ̃/ *nf* **1** MÉD puncture; **2** (en argent) levy.

ponctionner /pɔ̃ksjɔne/ [1] *vtr* **1** MÉD (perforer) to puncture; (extraire) to tap [*liquide*]; **2** (prélever) to levy [*somme*].

ponctualité /pɔ̃ktɥalite/ *nf* punctuality; **avec ~** punctually.

ponctuation /pɔ̃ktɥasjɔ̃/ ▶ 414 *nf* LING punctuation.

ponctuel, -elle /pɔ̃ktɥɛl/ *adj* **1** (à l'heure) [*personne*] punctual, [*paiement*] prompt; **2** (ne portant pas sur l'ensemble) [*action*] limited; (localisé) localized; (ciblé) selective; [*problème*] isolated; **3** LING punctual.

ponctuellement /pɔ̃ktɥɛlmɑ̃/ *adj* **1** (à l'heure) [*arriver, répondre*] punctually; [*payer*] promptly; **2** (en ciblant) selectively.

ponctuer /pɔ̃ktɥe/ [1] *vtr* to punctuate (**de** with).

pondérateur, -trice /pɔ̃deratœr, tris/ *adj* [*élément*] stabilizing.

pondération /pɔ̃derasjɔ̃/ *nf* **1** (de personne) levelheadedness; **2** (équilibrage) balancing; (équilibre) balance (**entre** between); **3** (d'indice) weighting.

pondéré, ~e /pɔ̃dere/ *adj* **1** [*personne, attitude*] levelheaded; **2** [*indice*] weighted.

pondérer /pɔ̃dere/ [14] *vtr* **1** (équilibrer) to balance; **2** to weight [*indice*].

pondre /pɔ̃dr/ [6] *vtr* **1** ZOOL to lay [*œuf*]; **où les oiseaux pondent-ils?** where do birds lay their eggs?; **2**○ (produire) to produce [*poème, article*]; to churn out○ PÉJ [*poèmes, articles*]; to produce [*enfant*].

poney /pɔnɛ/ *nm* pony; **faire du ~** to go pony-riding.

pongiste /pɔ̃ʒist/ *nmf* table-tennis player.

pont /pɔ̃/ **I** *nm* **1** ARCHIT, CONSTR bridge; **2** (liens) link, tie; **couper les ~s** to break off all contact; **il a coupé les ~s avec sa famille** he has broken with his family; **3** (vacances) extended weekend (*including day(s) between a public holiday and a weekend*); **faire le ~** to make a long weekend of it; **lundi je fais le ~** I'm taking Monday off; **4** NAUT deck; **bâtiment à deux ~s** two-decker; **5** AUT axle; **6** SPORT crab; **faire le ~** to do the crab.

II ponts *nmpl* **~s (et chaussées)** highways department.

■ **~ aérien** airlift; **~ basculant** bascule bridge; **~ flottant** pontoon bridge; **~ levant** vertical-lift bridge; **~ roulant** (overhead) travelling GB crane; **~ suspendu** suspension bridge; **~ tournant** swing bridge.

IDIOMES **coucher sous les ~s** to sleep rough; **il coulera beaucoup d'eau sous les ~s avant que…** it will be a long time before…; **faire un ~ d'or à qn** to offer sb a large sum to accept a job.

pontage /pɔ̃taʒ/ *nm* MÉD bypass (operation).

ponte[1] /pɔ̃t/ *nm* **1**○ (personnage) big shot○; **2** (au jeu) punter.

ponte[2] /pɔ̃t/ *nf* (action) laying (*of eggs*); (œufs) clutch; **~ ovulaire** ovulation.

pontife /pɔ̃tif/ *nm* **1** RELIG pontiff; **le souverain ~** the pope; **2**○ (personnage important) pundit○.

pontifical, ~e, *mpl* **-aux** /pɔ̃tifikal, o/ *adj* [*trône, autorité, garde*] papal; [*messe, célébration*] pontifical.

pontifier /pɔ̃tifje/ [2] *vi* to pontificate.

pont-levis, *pl* **ponts-levis** /pɔ̃ləvi/ *nm* drawbridge.

ponton /pɔ̃tɔ̃/ *nm* NAUT (débarcadère) (floating) landing stage; (plate-forme) pontoon.

pope /pɔp/ *nm* pope, orthodox priest.

popeline /pɔplin/ *nf* poplin.

popote○ /pɔpɔt/ *nf* (cuisine) cooking.

popotin○ /pɔpɔtɛ̃/ *nm* bum○ GB, rear○, bottom.

populace /pɔpylas/ *nf* **la ~** the masses (*pl*).

populaire /pɔpylɛr/ *adj* **1** (ouvrier) [*quartier*] working-class; [*art, roman*] popular; [*édition*] cheap; [*restaurant*] basic; **classe ~** working class; **2** (entériné par la tradition) [*tradition*] folk; **culture ~** folklore; **le bon sens ~** popular wisdom; **3** (estimé) popular (**chez, parmi** with); **4** (venant du peuple) [*mouvement*] popular; [*volonté*] of the people (*après n*); **5** LING (utilisé par le peuple) popular; (grossier) vulgar; **6** GÉOG, POL **République ~** People's Republic.

populariser /pɔpylarize/ [1] **I** *vtr* to popularize.

II se populariser *vpr* to become very popular.

popularité /pɔpylarite/ *nf* popularity.

population /pɔpylasjɔ̃/ *nf* population; **~ active** working population.

populeux, -euse /pɔpylø, øz/ *adj* densely populated; populous.

porc /pɔr/ *nm* **1** (animal) pig, hog US; (viande) pork; (peau) pigskin; **2**○ (personne) PÉJ pig○.

porcelaine /pɔrsəlɛn/ *nf* **1** (matière) porcelain,

china; **~ de Chine** china; **~ de Sèvres** Sèvre china ou porcelain; **2** (objet) piece of porcelain; **3** ZOOL cowrie.

porcelet /pɔrsəlɛ/ *nm* piglet.

porc-épic, *pl* **~s** /pɔrkepik/ *nm* porcupine.

porche /pɔrʃ/ *nm* porch; **sous le ~** in the porch.

porcherie /pɔrʃəri/ *nf* LIT, FIG pigsty.

porcin, ~e /pɔrsɛ̃, in/ **I** *adj* **1** AGRIC [*race*] porcine **élevage ~** pig breeding; **viande ~e** pork; **2** FI [*visage, yeux*] piggy, porcine; [*manières*] swinish. **II** *nm* pig; **les ~s** pigs.

pore /pɔr/ *nm* pore; **suant la peur par tous les ~:** FIG exuding fear.

poreux, -euse /pɔrø, øz/ *adj* porous.

porno○ /pɔrno/ **I** *adj* porno○, porn○. **II** *nm* CIN (genre) porn○; (film) blue movie○.

pornographique /pɔrnɔgrafik/ *adj* pornographic.

port /pɔr/ *nm* **1** (pour accoster) harbour GB; (avec installations portuaires) port; **~ fluvial** river port; **les restaurants du ~** the restaurants along the harbour GB; **2** (ville portuaire) port; **3** (refuge) haven; **4** (fait de porter) **le ~ du casque est obligatoire** helmets must be worn at all times; **~ d'armes** carrying arms; **5** (maintien) carriage; (démarche) bearing; **un joli ~ de tête** a graceful carriage of the head; **6** (transport) carriage; (par la poste) postage; **~ dû/payé** GÉN carriage forward/paid; (par la poste) postage due/paid.

■ **~ d'aéroglisseurs** hoverport; **~ d'attache** NAUT port of registry; FIG home base; **~ d'escale** port of call; **~ franc** free port; **~ de pêche** (installations) fishing harbour GB; (ville) fishing port; **~ pétrolier** tanker terminal; **~ de plaisance** marina; **~ de salut** haven.

IDIOMES **arriver à bon ~** to arrive safe and sound.

portable /pɔrtabl/ *adj* **1** (portatif) portable; **2** (pas trop lourd) **c'est ~** it can be carried; **3** (mettable) wearable.

portail /pɔrtaj/ *nm* (de parc, jardin) gate; (d'église, de temple) great door.

portant, ~e /pɔrtɑ̃, ɑ̃t/ *adj* **1** [*mur*] load-bearing; [*roue*] carrying; **2** [*personne*] **bien ~** in good health; **être mieux ~** to be in better health.

IDIOMES **à bout ~** at point-blank range.

portatif, -ive /pɔrtatif, iv/ *adj* portable; **ordinateur ~** laptop computer.

porte /pɔrt/ **I** *adj* [*veine*] portal.

II *nf* **1** (entrée) (de bâtiment) door; (de parc, stade, ville) gate; **la ~ de derrière** the back door; **devant la ~ de l'hôpital** outside the hospital; **j'ai une gare à ma ~** I have a station on my doorstep; **aux ~s du désert** at the edge of the desert; **passer la ~** to enter the house; **ouvrir sa ~ à qn** to let sb in; **c'est la ~ ouverte à la criminalité** it's an open invitation to crime; **ouvrir ses ~s (au public)** [*salon, exposition, magasin*] to open (to the public); **l'entreprise a fermé ses ~s** the company has gone out of business; **mettre à la ~** (exclure d'un cours) to throw [sb] out; (renvoyer) to expel [*élève*]; to fire, to sack○ GB [*employé*]; **ce n'est pas la ~ à côté** it's quite far; **voir qn entre deux ~s** to see sb very briefly; **trouver ~ close** ou **de bois** to find nobody in; **tu frappes à la bonne/mauvaise ~** you've come to the right/wrong place; **2** (moyen d'accès) gateway; **la victoire leur ouvre la ~ de la finale** the victory clears the way to the final for them; **3** (possibilité) door; **cela ouvre bien des ~s** it opens many doors; **4** (dans un aéroport) gate; **5** SPORT (en ski) gate; **6** (portière) door; **une voiture à deux/cinq ~s** a two-/five-door car; **7** (en électronique) gate.

■ **~ basculante** up-and-over door; **~ battante** swing door; **~ d'écluse** lock gate; **~ d'entrée** (de maison) front door; (d'église, hôpital, immeuble) main entrance; **~ de service** tradesmen's entrance GB, service entrance; **~ de sortie** LIT exit; FIG escape route; **~ à tambour** revolving door; **~s ouvertes** open day GB, open house US.

IDIOMES **prendre la ~** to leave; **entrer par la petite/grande ~** to start at the bottom/top;

nfoncer une **~** ouverte to state the obvious; **il faut ju'une ~ soit ouverte ou fermée** PROV you've got to lecide one way or the other.

orté, **~e**[1] /pɔʀte/ *adj* **être ~ à se plaindre** to be nclined to complain; **être ~ sur qch** to be keen on th; **être ~ sur la chose** EUPH to like it°, to be keen n sex.

orte-à-faux /pɔʀtafo/ *nm inv* **être en porte à faux** T [*mur*] to be out of plumb; [*rocher*] to be precariously alanced; ARCHIT [*construction*] to be cantilevered; FIG [*personne*] to be in an awkward position.

orte-à-porte /pɔʀtapɔʀt/ *nm inv* COMM door-to-door elling; POL door-to-door canvassing.

orte-avions /pɔʀtavjɔ̃/ *nm inv* aircraft carrier.

orte-bagages /pɔʀt(ə)bagaʒ/ *nm inv* (sur un vélo) arrier; (dans un train) luggage rack; (sur un toit de oiture) roof rack.

orte-bébé /pɔʀt(ə)bebe/ *nm inv* (panier) carrycot B, carrier US; (kangourou®) (baby) sling, baby arrier; (sac à dos) baby carrier.

orte-bonheur /pɔʀt(ə)bɔnœʀ/ *nm inv* lucky harm.

orte-bouteilles /pɔʀt(ə)butɛj/ *nm inv* (panier) ottle-carrier, bottleholder; (égouttoir) bottle-drainer.

orte-clés, **porte-clefs** /pɔʀt(ə)kle/ *nm inv* key ing.

orte-couteau, *pl* **~x** /pɔʀt(ə)kuto/ *nm* knife est.

orte-documents /pɔʀt(ə)dɔkymɑ̃/ *nm inv* briefase, attaché case.

orte-drapeau /pɔʀt(ə)dʀapo/ *nm inv* standardearer.

ortée[2] /pɔʀte/ **I** *adj f* ▸ **porté**.

I *nf* **1** (distance) range; **être hors de ~** to be out of each; **être à ~ de main** ou **à la ~ de la main** (accesible) to be within reach; (dans endroit commode) to be o hand; **être à ~ de voix** to be within earshot; **2** niveau) **c'est à la ~ de n'importe qui** (faisable) nybody can do it; (compréhensible) anybody can undertand it; (en prix) anybody can afford it; **se mettre à a ~ de qn** to come down to sb's level; **3** (effet) mpact; **4** (d'animaux) litter; **5** MUS staff, stave GB.

orte-fenêtre, *pl* **portes-fenêtres** pɔʀt(ə)fənɛtʀ/ *nf* French window.

ortefeuille /pɔʀt(ə)fœj/ **I** *adj* **jupe/robe ~** wrapver skirt/dress.

I *nm* **1** (à billets) wallet, billfold US; **2** POL portfolio; **3** N portfolio.

DIOMES faire un lit en ~ to make an apple pie bed; **voir le ~ bien garni** to be well-off; **avoir toujours a main au ~** to be very generous.

orte-jarretelles /pɔʀt(ə)ʒaʀtɛl/ *nm inv* suspender elt GB, garter belt US.

ortemanteau, *pl* **~x** /pɔʀt(ə)mɑ̃to/ *nm* **1** (au patère) (coat) peg ou hook; (collectif) coat ack; (sur pied) coat stand, coat ou clothes tree US; **2** cintre) coat hanger.

ortemine /pɔʀt(ə)min/ *nm* propelling GB ou mechanal US pencil.

orte-monnaie /pɔʀt(ə)mɔnɛ/ *nm inv* purse GB, coin urse US.

orte-parapluies /pɔʀt(ə)paʀaplɥi/ *nm inv* mbrella stand.

orte-parole /pɔʀt(ə)paʀɔl/ *nm inv* (personne) pokesperson, spokesman/spokeswoman; (journal) 1outhpiece.

orte-plume /pɔʀt(ə)plym/ *nm inv* penholder.

orter /pɔʀte/ [1] **I** *vtr* **1** (transporter) to carry [*chose, ersonne*]; **~ qn sur son lit** to get sb into bed; **2** apporter) **~ qch quelque part** to take sth somewhere; **~ des messages** to run messages; **~ une ffaire devant les tribunaux** to bring a case to court; **‹** (soutenir) [*mur, chaise*] to carry, to bear [*poids*]; eau te portera the water will hold you up; **~ qn à out de bras** FIG to take on sb's problems; **~ l'espoir le millions d'hommes** to be the focus for the hopes f millions; **4** (avoir sur soi) to wear [*robe, bijou,*

verres de contact*]; to have [*cheveux longs, moustache*]; **~ les armes** to bear arms; **~ une arme** to be armed; **5** (avoir) to have [*initiales, date, titre*]; to bear [*sceau*]; **portant le numéro 300** with the number 300; **le document porte la mention 'secret'** the document is marked 'secret'; **ils ne portent pas le même nom** they have different names; **il porte bien son nom** the name suits him; **son âge** to look good for one's age; **~ des traces de sang** to be bloodstained; **portant une expression de découragement** looking discouraged; **~ en soi une grande volonté de réussir** to be full of ambition; **6** (produire) to bear [*fleurs*]; **~ des fruits** LIT, **~ ses fruits** FIG to bear fruit; **l'enfant qu'elle porte** the child she is carrying; **le roman qu'il porte en lui** his great unwritten novel; **7** (amener) **cela porte le prix du billet à...** this brings the price of the ticket to...; **~ un taux à** to put a rate up to; **~ la température de l'eau à 80°C** to heat the water to 80°C; **~ qn au pouvoir** to bring sb to power; **8** (diriger) **~ son regard vers** to look at; **~ qch à sa bouche** to raise sth to one's lips; **si tu portes la main sur elle** if you lay a finger on her; **l'estime qu'elle te porte** her respect for you; **~ ses efforts sur qch** to devote one's energies to sth; **~ un jugement sur qch** to pass judgment on sth; **9** (inscrire) **~ qch sur un registre** to enter sth on a register; **être porté disparu** to be reported missing; **se faire ~ malade** or **pâle°** to go° ou report sick; **10** (inciter) **~ qn à se méfier** to make sb cautious; **tout nous porte à croire que** everything leads us to believe that; **11** (donner, causer) **~ bonheur** or **chance** to be lucky; **~ malheur** to be unlucky; **ça m'a porté bonheur** it brought me luck; **ça m'a porté malheur** it was unlucky.

II porter sur *vtr ind* **1** (concerner) **~ sur** [*débat, article*] to be about; [*mesure, interdiction*] to apply to; **2** (reposer sur) **~ sur** [*structure*] to be resting on; **3** (heurter) **~ sur** to hit.

III *vi* **une voix qui porte** a voice that carries; **le coup a porté** the blow hit home; **un canon qui porte à 500 mètres** a cannon with a range of 500 metres GB.

IV se porter *vpr* **1** (se sentir) **se ~ bien/mal** [*personne*] to be well/ill; [*affaire*] to be going well/badly; **je ne m'en porte pas plus mal** I'm none the worse for it; **je me porte à merveille** I'm absolutely fine; **2** (être mis) **cela se porte avec des chaussures plates** you wear it with flat shoes; **cela ne se porte plus** it has gone out of fashion; **3** (se diriger) **se ~ sur** [*soupçon*] to fall on; **le choix se porta sur le vase** they/she etc chose the vase; **tous les regards se sont portés vers le ciel/vers lui** everyone looked toward(s) the sky/in his direction; **4** (se propager) **se ~ sur** to spread to.

porte-revues /pɔʀt(ə)ʀəvy/ *nm inv* magazine rack.

porte-savon /pɔʀt(ə)savɔ̃/ *nm inv* soapdish.

porte-serviettes /pɔʀt(ə)sɛʀvjɛt/ *nm inv* towel rail.

porteur, **-euse** /pɔʀtœʀ, øz/ **I** *adj* **1** GÉN **être ~ d'espoir** to bring hope; **être ~ d'un passeport grec** to hold a Greek passport; **être ~ d'un virus** to carry a virus; **2** TECH **mur/essieu ~** load-bearing wall/axle; **3** ÉCON (en expansion) [*marché*] buoyant; [*métier*] booming; **4** RADIO, TÉLÉCOM [*courant, onde*] carrier (*épith*); **5** LING **être ~ de sens** to have a meaning.

II *nm,f* **1** (possesseur) holder, bearer; **les ~s de diplômes étrangers** people who hold foreign qualifications; **2** MÉD carrier.

III *nm* **1** ▸374 (de bagages) porter; (coursier) messenger; **2** FIN (de chèque) bearer; **~ d'actions** shareholder.

■ **~ sain** MÉD symptom-free carrier.

porte-voix /pɔʀt(ə)vwa/ *nm inv* megaphone; **les mains en ~** his/her hands cupped around his/her mouth.

portier /pɔʀtje/ *nm* **1** ▸374 (concierge) porter; **2°** (gardien de but) goalkeeper.

portière /pɔʀtjɛʀ/ *nf* AUT door.

portillon /pɔʀtijɔ̃/ *nm* gate.

IDIOMES ça ne se bouscule pas au ~° people are not exactly queueing up GB ou lining up US.

portion /pɔʀsjɔ̃/ nf **1** CULIN (part) portion; (quantité servie) helping; **2** (dans un partage) share; **3** (partie) GÉN portion; (de route) stretch; (de territoire) part.
■ ~ **congrue** (nourriture) minute portion of food; (revenu) minimal income; **réduire qn à la ~ congrue** to give sb the strict minimum.

portique /pɔʀtik/ nm **1** ARCHIT portico; **2** SPORT frame (in gym); **3** (pour enfants) swing frame.

porto /pɔʀto/ nm port.

portoricain, ~e /pɔʀtɔʀikɛ̃, ɛn/ ▶394┃ adj Puerto Rican.

portrait /pɔʀtʀɛ/ nm **1** ART, PHOT portrait; **c'est un ~ fidèle** it's a good likeness; **2** GÉN, LITTÉRAT (description) description, picture; **faire le ~ de** to paint a picture of; **3** (réplique) **tu es tout le ~ de ton père** you're the spitting image of your father; **4**○ (visage) face; **se faire tirer le ~** to have one's photo taken.

portrait-robot, pl **portraits-robots** /pɔʀtʀeʀɔbo/ nm photofit® (picture), identikit®.

portuaire /pɔʀtɥɛʀ/ adj port (épith).

portugais, ~e /pɔʀtygɛ, ɛz/ I ▶394┃ adj Portuguese.
II ▶338┃ nm LING Portuguese.

Portugal /pɔʀtygal/ ▶232┃ nprm Portugal.

POS /peoɛs, pɔs/ nm: abbr ▶**plan**.

pose /poz/ nf **1** (mise en place) (de compteur, vitre) putting in, installation (**de** of); (de placard, dentier) fitting (**de** of); (de moquette) laying (**de** of); (de rideau) hanging, putting up (**de** of); MIL (de mine) laying (**de** of); **2** (manière de se tenir) pose; **prendre une ~ provocante** to strike a provocative pose; **3** ART pose; **une séance de ~** a sitting; **4** (affectation) pretention; **5** PHOT exposure.

posé, ~e /poze/ adj [air, personne] composed; [geste, voix] controlled.

posément /pozemɑ̃/ adv carefully, thoughtfully; **il parlait très ~** he weighed his words (carefully).

poser /poze/ [1] I vtr **1** (mettre) to put down; **pose ton manteau** put your coat somewhere; **ils ont posé un échafaudage contre le mur** they've put some scaffolding up against the wall; **~ la main sur le bras de qn** to lay ou place one's hand on sb's arm; **j'ai posé une lettre sur votre bureau** I've put a letter on your desk; **~ les yeux sur qn/qch** to look at sb/sth; **2** (mettre en place) to put in [compteur, vitre]; to install [signalisation, radiateur]; to fit [serrure, prothèse]; to lay [carrelage, mine, pierre, câble]; to plant [bombe]; to fit, to lay [moquette]; to put up [papier peint, tableau, rideau, cloison, affiches]; **3** (établir) to assert, to postulate SOUT [hypothèse]; to lay down [règles, limites]; **~ sa candidature à un poste** to apply for a job; **~ sa candidature à une élection** to stand GB ou run for election; **je pose 3 et je retiens 2** I put ou write down (the) 3 and carry (the) 2; **~ comme hypothèse que** to put forward the theory that; **4** (soulever) to ask [question]; to set [devinette]; **la question reste posée** the question (still) remains; **~ (un) problème à qn** to pose a problem for sb; **ça ne pose aucun problème** that's no problem at all; **5** MUS to place [voix].
II vi **1** ART, PHOT to pose; **~ nu** to pose (in the) nude; **2** (être affecté) to put on airs.
III se poser vpr **1** [oiseau, insecte] to settle, to alight; **2** [avion] to land, to touch down; **se ~ en catastrophe** to make an emergency landing; **3**○ (s'asseoir) to plant oneself; **pose-toi quelque part et attends-moi** park○ yourself somewhere and wait for me; **4** (s'arrêter) [yeux, regard] to fall (**sur** on); **5** (s'affirmer) **se ~ en** to claim to be; **se ~ en victime** to present oneself as a victim; **6** (se demander) **se ~ des questions** to ask oneself questions; **se ~ des questions au sujet de qn/qch** (s'interroger) to wonder about sb/sth; (douter) to have doubts about sb/sth; **ils vivent sans se ~ de questions** they accept things as they are; **7** (exister) [question] to arise; **la question ne se pose pas** (c'est impossible) there's no question of it; (c'est évident) it goes without saying.
IDIOMES **comme imbécile il se pose là**○! he's a prime example of an idiot!

poseur, **-euse** /pozœʀ, øz/ nm,f (snob) poser○.
■ ~ **d'affiches** billsticker, billposter; **~ de bombes** bomber, bomb planter; **~ de carrelage** tiler; **~ de moquette** carpet fitter.

positif, **-ive** /pozitif, iv/ I adj **1** (affirmatif) [répons] affirmative; **2** (constructif) [entretien, climat] constructive; [évolution, effet] positive; **3** (favorable) [réactic bilan] favourable^GB; [point, image] positive; **4** (réalis [personne, attitude] positive; **5** MÉD, MATH, ÉLECTROTEC PHOT positive.
II nm **1** (résultat concret) **je veux du ~** I need som thing positive; **2** (points favorables) positive poin (pl); **3** PHOT positive; **4** LING positive (degree).

position /pozisjɔ̃/ nf **1** (dans l'espace) position; **il fa revoir la ~ des joueurs** the positioning of th players has to be rethought; **en ~ horizontale/ver cale** horizontally/vertically; **attention, l'échelle es en ~ instable** be careful, the ladder isn't steady; MIL position; **3** (posture) position; **la ~ des doig sur une guitare** the positioning of the fingers on guitar; **rien de pire que de rester en ~ assi toute la journée** there's nothing worse than sitti down all day; **4** (situation) position; **une ~ délica** a tricky situation; **être en ~ dominante sur marché** to be a market leader; **5** (professionne sociale) position; **6** (au classement) place, position; (point de vue) position, stance; **prendre ~ sur problème** to take a stand on an issue; **prise de** stance, stand (**sur qch** on sth); **camper** ou **rester s ses ~s** to stand one's ground; **8** FIN (bank) balanc **être en ~ créditrice/débitrice** [compte] to be credit/debit; **9** (en danse) position.

positivement /pozitivmɑ̃/ adv [répondre] positive [réagir, juger] favourably^GB.

posologie /pozɔlɔʒi/ nf dosage.

possédant, ~e /posedɑ̃, ɑ̃t/ I adj wealthy.
II nm,f **les ~s** the rich (+ v pl), the wealthy (+ pl).

posséder /posede/ [14] I vtr **1** (détenir) GÉN to own, possess; to hold [charge]; **sa famille ne possède pl rien** his/her family has nothing left; **2** (être équipé c to have; **un jardin qui possède un bassin** a gard with a fish pond; **3** (jouir de) to have [connaissan qualité]; **4** (maîtriser) to speak [sth] fluently [langu to have a thorough knowledge of [sujet, technique]; (sexuellement) to have, to possess SOUT; **6** (domin [sentiment, douleur] to overwhelm; **7**○ (duper) **il no a bien possédés** he really had○ us there; **se faire par qn** to be had○ by sb.
II se posséder vpr (se dominer) LITER to contr oneself.

possesseur /posesœʀ/ nm (de biens, d'objets) own (de diplôme, carte d'identité, d'actions) holder; (de secr keeper; (de passeport) bearer.

possessif, **-ive** /posesif, iv/ I adj LING, PSYCH poss sive.
II nm LING possessive.

possession /posesjɔ̃/ nf **1** (de maison, terres, fortu possession, ownership; (de diplôme, drogue, d'arn possession; **la ~ d'un passeport est obligatoire** must have a passport; **prendre ~ d'un héritage** come into one's inheritance; **être en pleine ~ ses moyens** to be on top form; **2** (maîtrise) (de lang fluency (**de** in); (de métier, technique) mastery (of); **3** (chose possédée) possession; **4** (ensorcellem possession.

possibilité /posibilite/ I nf **1** (éventualité) possibili **2** (occasion) opportunity; (solution) option; **les ~ de trouver un emploi** the chances of finding a job; **réserver la ~ de faire** to reserve the right to do.
II **possibilités** nfpl **1** (potentiel) (de personne) at ities; (d'appareil) potential ou possible uses; **avoir nombreuses ~s** [personne, appareil] to be versati **2** (moyens) resources.

possible /posibl/ I adj **1** (réalisable) possible; **je vie drai chaque fois que cela sera ~** I'll come whe ever I can; **ce n'est pas ~ autrement** there's other way of doing it; **il ne me sera pas ~ de me**

lacer aujourd'hui I won't be able to get out today; **out le courage** ~ the utmost courage; **tous les cas ~s et imaginables** every conceivable case; **recule le lus** ~ go back as far as you can; **limiter les déplaements autant que** ~ to keep travelling^{GB} down to minimum; **2** (potentiel) possible; **il n'y a pas l'erreur** ~, **c'est lui** it's him, without a shadow of a oubt; **nous avons sélectionné de** ~**s candidats** ve have selected some potential candidates; (**ce 'est**) **pas** ~○! (surprise) I don't believe it!; ronie) you're joking!; **ce n'est pas** ~ **d'être aussi ête** how can anyone be so stupid?; **'tu vas acheter ine voiture?'—'~'** 'are you going to buy a ar?'—'maybe'; **3**○ (acceptable) **pas** ~ impossible, wful; (croyable) **pas** ~ unbelievable; **il a un accent as** ~ he has an atrocious accent; **être d'une enteur pas** ~ to be awfully slow; **il a une chance as** ~ he's incredibly lucky.

I *nm* **le** ~ that which is possible; **rester dans le lomaine du** ~ to be within the realms of possibility; **aire** (**tout**) **son** ~ to do one's best; **elle est bête au** ~○ she's as stupid as they come.

ost(-) /pɔst/ *préf* post(-); ~**-doctoral** postdocɔral; ~**-romantique** post-Romantic.

ostal, ~**e**, *mpl* **-aux** /pɔstal, o/ *adj* [*train, bateau, vion*] mail; [*fourgonnette, fourgon*] post office GB, iail US; [*services*] postal.

oste[1] /pɔst/ *nm* **1** (fonction) (dans une entreprise) posiion, job; (dans la fonction publique) post; **suppression le** ~ job cut; **trois** ~**s vacants** or **à pourvoir** three acancies; **être en** ~ **à Moscou** [*diplomate*] to be osted to Moscow; **2** SPORT position; **3** (lieu) post; ~ **de travail** work station; **4** (commissariat) ~ **de olice** police station; **5** RADIO, TV (appareil) set; ~ **de adio** radio (set); (station de radio) radio station; **6** ÉLÉCOM (appareil) (tele)phone; (ligne) extension; **7** périole de travail) shift; **8** (en comptabilité) item; **9** MIL ost; ~ **de garde** or **police** guardhouse; **il est oujours fidèle au** ~ you can always rely on him.

~ **d'aiguillage** signal box; ~ **budgétaire** udget item; ~ **de contrôle** control centre^{GB}; ~ **l'équipage** crew's quarters (*pl*); ~ **de péage** toll ooth; ~ **de pilotage** AVIAT flight deck; ~ **de ecours** first-aid post GB ou station; ~ **de soudure** ~ **à souder** welding equipment.

oste[2] /pɔst/ *nf* **1** (bureau) post office; **la Poste** the 'ost Office; **la** ~ (service) the post GB, the mail US; **nvoyer par la** ~ to send [sth] by post GB, to mail US; **rivatiser la** ~ to privatize postal services; **2** HIST iail.

~ **aérienne** airmail; ~ **restante** poste restante B, general delivery US.

oster[1] /pɔste/ [1] **I** *vtr* **1** (expédier) to post GB, to mail S; **2** (placer) to post, to station [*soldat, garde*]; to tation [*complice*]; to put [sb] in place [*espion*].

I se poster *vpr* **se** ~ **devant** (debout) to station neself in front of; (assis) to sit in front of.

oster[2] /pɔstɛʀ/ *nm* (affiche) poster.

ostérieur, ~**e** /pɔsteʀjœʀ/ **I** *adj* **1** (dans le temps) *late*] later (*épith*); [*événement, œuvre*] subsequent *épith*); **un écrivain** ~ **à Flaubert** a writer who ame after Flaubert; **un événement** ~ **à la guerre** n event which took place after the war; **2** (dans espace) [*partie, section*] posterior; [*pattes*] hind *épith*); **3** [*phonème*] back.

I○ *nm* behind○, posterior HUM.

ostérieurement /pɔsteʀjœʀmɑ̃/ *adv* subsequently; ~ **à** after, subsequent to SOUT.

ostérité /pɔsteʀite/ *nf* **1** (immortalité) posterity; **asser à** or **entrer dans la** ~ [*nom, personne*] to go own in history; [*œuvre*] to become part of the cultural eritage; **2** (lignée) descendants (*pl*).

osthume /pɔstym/ *adj* posthumous.

ostiche /pɔstiʃ/ **I** *adj* (faux) [*barbe*] false.

I *nm* (de cheveux) hairpiece; (pour un chauve) toupee; perruque) wig; (fausse moustache) false moustache GB u mustache US; (fausse barbe) false beard.

ostier, **-ière** /pɔstje, ɛʀ/ ▶ 374 *nm,f* postal worker.

postillon /pɔstijɔ̃/ *nm* **1**○ (de salive) drop of saliva; **2** ▶ 374 (cocher) postillion.

postillonner○ /pɔstijɔne/ [1] *vi* to spit (saliva).

postnatal, ~**e**, *mpl* ~**s** /pɔstnatal/ *adj* postnatal; **allocation** ~**e** maternity allowance.

postposer /pɔstpoze/ [1] *vtr* to place [sth] after the verb [*sujet*]; to place [sth] after the noun [*adjectif*].

postscolaire /pɔstskɔlɛʀ/ *adj* **enseignement** ~ continuing education.

post-scriptum /pɔstskʀiptɔm/ *nm inv* postscript.

postsynchroniser /pɔstsɛ̃kʀɔnize/ [1] *vtr* to dub, to add the soundtrack to.

postulant, ~**e** /pɔstylɑ̃, ɑ̃t/ *nm,f* **1** GÉN candidate (à for); **2** RELIG postulant.

postulat /pɔstyla/ *nm* GÉN premise; MATH, PHILOS postulate.

postuler /pɔstyle/ [1] **I** *vtr* **1** (solliciter) to apply for [*emploi*] (**auprès de** to); **2** (affirmer) to postulate.

II *vi* to apply (**à**, **pour** for).

posture /pɔstyʀ/ *nf* (pose) posture; (situation) position.

pot /po/ *nm* **1** (récipient, contenu) GÉN container; (en verre) jar; (en plastique) carton, tub; (en faïence, terre) pot; (pichet) jug; **mettre qch en** ~ to put [sth] into jars [*confiture, fruits*]; to pot [*plante*]; **plante en** ~ potted plant; **un** ~ **de peinture** a tin of paint; **2** (de chambre) pot; (de bébé) potty; **3**○ (boisson) drink; **prendre un** ~ to have a drink; **4**○ (réunion) do○ GB, drinks party; **5**○ (chance) luck; **avoir du** ~ to be lucky.

■ ~ **catalytique** catalytic converter; ~ **de colle** LIT pot of glue; FIG○ leech; ~ **à eau** water jug GB, pitcher US; ~ **d'échappement** (silencieux) silencer GB, muffler US; (système) exhaust; ~ **à tabac** LIT tobacco jar; FIG○ potbellied person.

IDIOMES **payer les** ~**s cassés** to pick up the pieces; **c'est le** ~ **de terre contre le** ~ **de fer** it's an unequal contest; **découvrir le** ~ **aux roses** to stumble on what's been going on; **être sourd comme un** ~○ to be as deaf as a post; **tourner autour du** ~○ to beat about the bush; **partir** or **démarrer plein** ~○ to be off ou go off like a shot○.

potable /pɔtabl/ *adj* **1** (buvable) **eau** ~ drinking water; **eau non** ~ water unsuitable for drinking; **2**○ (passable) decent.

potage /pɔtaʒ/ *nm* soup.

potager, **-ère** /pɔtaʒe, ɛʀ/ **I** *adj* [*plante, herbe, racine*] edible; **jardin** ~ kitchen garden.

II *nm* kitchen garden.

potasser○ /pɔtase/ [1] **I** *vtr* to mug up○ GB, to bone up on○ US [*dossier*]; to swot up○ GB, to bone up on○ US [*latin*].

II *vi* to swot○ GB, to bone up○ US.

pot-au-feu /potofø/ *nm inv* **1** (plat) boiled beef (*with vegetables*); **2** (viande) boiling beef.

pot-de-vin, *pl* **pots-de-vin** /podvɛ̃/ *nm* bribe, backhander○ GB.

pote○ /pɔt/ *nm* mate○ GB, pal○ US.

poteau, *pl* ~**x** /poto/ *nm* (grand piquet) post; (au football, rugby) goalpost; **coiffer qn au** ~ LIT, FIG to overtake GB ou pass US sb at the finishing line; **avoir des jambes comme des** ~**x**○ to have legs like tree trunks.

■ ~ **électrique** electricity pole (*supplying domestic power lines*); ~ **indicateur** signpost.

potelé, ~**e** /pɔtle/ *adj* chubby.

potence /pɔtɑ̃s/ *nf* **1** (gibet) gallows (+ *v sg*); (pendaison) gallows (+ *v sg*); **il mérite la** ~ he deserves to hang; **2** (équerre) bracket.

potentialité /pɔtɑ̃sjalite/ *nf* **1** (virtualité) potential; **2** (possibilité) potentiality.

potentiel, **-ielle** /pɔtɑ̃sjɛl/ **I** *adj* potential.

II *nm* **1** (possibilité) potential (**de** for); ~ **de production** production capacity; **2** PHYS potential.

poterie /pɔtʀi/ *nf* **1** (production) pottery; **2** (produit) piece of pottery; **des ~s** pottery ∉; **3** (atelier) pottery.

potiche /pɔtiʃ/ *nf* **1** (vase) vase; **2** (en politique) PEJ **n'être qu'une** or **faire figure de ~** to be a mere puppet; **3** (en société) PEJ **être une ~** to look merely decorative.

potier, -ière /pɔtje, ɛʁ/ ▶374 | *nm,f* potter.

potin○ /pɔtɛ̃/ *nm* **1** (commérage) gossip ∉; **2** (tapage) **faire du ~** to make a din○.

potion /posjɔ̃/ *nf* potion.

potiron /pɔtiʁɔ̃/ *nm* pumpkin GB, winter squash US.

pot-pourri, *pl* **pots-pourris** /popuʁi/ *nm* **1** MUS medley; **2** (pour parfumer) potpourri.

pou, *pl* **~x** /pu/ *nm* louse; **des ~x** lice.
IDIOMES **chercher des ~x**○ to nitpick○; **chercher des ~x dans la tête de qn**○ to find fault with sb; **être laid** or **moche**○ **comme un ~**○ to be as ugly as sin; **être vexé comme un ~**○ to be extremely offended.

poubelle /pubɛl/ *nf* (de cuisine, salle de bains) bin GB, trash can US; (d'extérieur) dustbin GB, garbage can US; **mettre** or **jeter qch à la ~** to throw sth away; **sortir la ~** to take the rubbish out; **faire les ~s** to go through dustbins GB ou trash cans US.

pouce /pus/ **I** *nm* **1** ▶137 | (de la main) thumb; (du pied) big toe; **2** ▶348 | (unité de mesure) inch; **ne pas bouger d'un ~** not to budge an inch.
II *excl* schoolchildren's slang pax!; truce!
IDIOMES **se tourner** or **rouler les ~s**○ to twiddle one's thumbs; **manger sur le ~** to have a quick bite to eat; **donner un coup de ~ à qn/à qch** (au départ) to help sb/sth get started; (pour relancer) to give sb/sth a boost.

Poucet /pusɛ/ *npr* **le petit ~** Hop o' my Thumb.

poudre /pudʁ/ *nf* **1** GÉN powder; **réduire qch en ~** to grind sth to a powder; **2** (cosmétique) powder; **~ compacte** pressed powder; **3** (explosif) **~ (à canon)** gunpowder.
■ **~ à éternuer** sneezing powder; **~ à récurer** scouring powder; **~ de riz** (cosmétique) rice powder.
IDIOMES **mettre le feu aux ~s** to bring things to a head; **jeter de la ~ aux yeux** to try to impress; **se répandre comme une traînée de ~** to spread like wildfire.

poudrer /pudʁe/ [1] *vtr* to powder.
II se poudrer *vpr* to powder oneself; **se ~ le visage/le nez** to powder one's face/one's nose.

poudrerie /pudʁəʁi/ *nf* (d'explosifs) explosives factory.

poudreuse[1] /pudʁøz/ *nf* (neige) powdery snow.

poudreux, -euse[2] /pudʁø, øz/ *adj* [neige] powdery.

poudrier /pudʁije/ *nm* powder compact.

poudrière /pudʁijɛʁ/ *nf* **1** (entrepôt) powder magazine; **2** FIG time bomb.

pouët-pouët /pwɛtpwɛt/ *nm inv* (also onomat) honk-honk.

pouf /puf/ *nm* **1** (siège) pouffe; **2** (bruit) **faire ~** to fall with a soft thud.

pouffer /pufe/ [1] *vi* **~ (de rire)** to burst out laughing.

Pouilles /puj/ ▶509 | *nprfpl* Apulia (*sg*).

pouilleux, -euse /pujø, øz/ *adj* **1**○ (sale) seedy; **2** (couvert de poux) flea-ridden.

poulailler /pulaje/ *nm* **1** AGRIC (abri) henhouse; (enclos) hen run; (oiseaux) hens (*pl*); **2**○ THÉÂT (lieu) **le ~** the Gods (*pl*) GB, the gallery; (spectateurs) the audience in the Gods (*pl*) GB, the gallery.

poulain /pulɛ̃/ *nm* **1** ZOOL colt; (très jeune) foal; **2** (débutant) protégé.

poularde /pulaʁd/ *nf* fattened chicken.

poule /pul/ *nf* **1** ZOOL hen; **2** CULIN boiling fowl; **3**○ (terme d'affection) **ma ~** my pet○, honey○ US; **4** SPORT (groupe d'adversaires) group; (tournoi) tournament; **5** JEUX pool, kitty.
■ **~ d'eau** moorhen; **~ faisane** hen pheasant; **~ mouillée**○ PEJ wimp○ PÉJ; **~ naine** bantam;

~ pondeuse laying hen; **~ au pot** CULIN boi chicken.
IDIOMES **quand les ~s auront des dents**○ wh pigs fly; **se coucher avec les ~s** to go to bed ear **tuer la ~ pour avoir l'œuf, tuer la ~ aux œu d'or** to kill the goose that lays the golden egg.

poulet /pulɛ/ *nm* **1** ZOOL, CULIN chicken; **2**○ (terme d'aff tion) **mon ~** my pet○, honey US.
■ **~ d'élevage ~** battery chicken; **~ fermier** free-range chicken.

poulette /pulɛt/ *nf* **1** ZOOL young hen; CULIN pullet; **2**○ (terme d'affection) **ma ~** my pet○, honey US.

pouliche /puliʃ/ *nf* filly.

poulie /puli/ *nf* pulley; **~ de tension** idler.

poulpe /pulp/ *nm* octopus.

pouls /pu/ *nm inv* pulse.

poumon /pumɔ̃/ *nm* ANAT lung; **à pleins ~s** [*crier*] the top of one's voice; [*aspirer*] deeply.

poupe /pup/ *nf* stern; **avoir le vent en ~** LIT, FIG have the wind in one's sails.

poupée /pupe/ *nf* **1** ▶329 | (jouet) doll; **jouer à la** to play dolls; **avoir un visage de ~** to have a do like face; **2**○ (forme d'adresse) poppet GB, toots○ US; **3** (pansement) finger bandage.
■ **~ mannequin** Barbie® doll; **~s gigognes russes** set (*sg*) of Russian dolls.

poupin, ~e /pupɛ̃, in/ *adj* chubby.

poupon /pupɔ̃/ *nm* (bébé) tiny baby; (jouet) bat doll.

pouponner○ /pupɔne/ [1] *vi* (s'occuper d'un bébé) play the doting father/mother.

pouponnière○ /pupɔnjɛʁ/ *nf* children's home (f under-threes).

pour[1] /puʁ/ *prép* **1** (indiquant le but) to; **~ cela,** **faudra faire** to do that, you'll have to do; **c'était** rire or **plaisanter** it was a joke; **il est seul mais il tout fait ~**○ he's on his own, but it's entirely h own doing; **~ que** so that; **~ ainsi dire** so to speal **c'est fait** or **étudié ~**○! (c'est sa fonction) that what it's for; **2** (indiquant une destination) for; **c'est l train ~ où?** where does this train go?; **il faut un heure ~ Oloron** it's an hour to Oloron; **3** (en ce qu concerne) **c'est bien payé mais ~ la sécurité de l'emploi...** the pay is good but as regards job secu ity...; **oui, c'est ~ quoi?** yes, what is it?; **~ mo il a tort** as far as I am concerned, he's wrong; **4** (e faveur de) for; **je suis ~**○ I'm in favour GB; **être ~ qch/faire qch** GÉN to be in favour GB of sth/doing sth; **5** (avec une indication de temps) for; **ce sera prêt ~ vendredi?** will it be ready by Friday?; **~ toujour** forever; **le bébé c'est ~ quand?** when is the bab due?; **6** (comme) **elle a ~ ambition d'être pilot** her ambition is to be a pilot; **ils ont ~ habitude d déjeuner tard** they usually have a late lunch; **7** (à l place de) for; **écrire qch ~ qch** to write sth instea of sth; **je l'ai pris ~ plus bête qu'il n'est** I though he was more stupid than he really is; **8** (à so avantage) **elle avait ~ elle de savoir écouter sh** had the merit of being a good listener; **9** (introduisar une concession) **~ intelligent qu'il soit** intelligen though he may be; **'il te parlera du Japon'—'~ c que ça m'intéresse!'** 'he'll talk to you abou Japan'—'I can't say I'm very interested'; **~ autan que je sache** as far as I know; **10** (marquant l'emphase **~ être intelligente, ça elle l'est!** she really i intelligent!, intelligent she certainly is!; **11** (indiquar une quantité) **j'ai mis ~ 200 francs d'essence** I've put in 200 francs' worth of petrol GB ou gas US; **je n' suis ~ rien** I had nothing to do with it; **elle y est ~ beaucoup s'il a réussi** if he has succeeded a lot of the credit should go to her; **je n'en ai pas ~ longtemps** it won't take long; **il n'en a plus ~ longtemps** (mou rant) he doesn't have long to live; **j'en ai encore ~ deux heures** it'll take another two hours; **12** (indiquan une cause) for; **se battre ~ une femme** to fight over a woman; **13** (introduisant une proportion) **dix ~ cen** ten per cent; **une cuillère de vinaigre ~ quatre**

pour¹

pour + verbe

Lorsque *pour* sert à indiquer un but il se traduit généralement par *to* devant un verbe à l'infinitif:

sortir pour acheter un journal = to go out to buy a newspaper
pour faire des meringues, il faut des œufs = to make meringues, you need eggs

Il peut également se traduire par *in order to*, qui est plus soutenu:

pour mettre fin aux hostilités = in order to put an end to hostilities

Quand *pour* est suivi d'une forme négative, il se traduira par *so as not to* ou *in order not to*:

pour ne pas oublier = so as not to forget
pour ne pas rater le train = so as not to miss the train *ou* in order not to miss the train

Lorsque *pour* relie deux actions distinctes sans relation de cause à effet, il sera traduit par *and* et le verbe conjugué normalement:

elle s'endormit pour se réveiller deux heures plus tard = she fell asleep and woke up two hours later

Quand la deuxième action n'est pas souhaitable ou qu'une notion de hasard malheureux est sous-entendue, on traduira par *only to*:

elle s'endormit pour se réveiller deux heures plus tard = she fell asleep only to wake up two hours later
il partit à la guerre pour se faire tuer trois jours plus tard = he went off to war only to be killed three days later

pour + nom ou pronom

Lorsque *pour* sert à indiquer la destination au sens large il se traduit généralement par *for*:

le train pour Pau = the train for Pau
pour vendredi = for Friday
il travaille pour elle = he works for her

Lorsque *pour* signifie *en ce qui concerne*, il se traduira le plus souvent par *about*:

tu te renseignes pour une assurance voiture? = will you find out about car insurance?
tu te renseignes pour samedi? = will you find out about Saturday?

Attention:
pour placé en début de phrase se traduira par *as regards*:

pour l'argent, rien n'est décidé = as regards the money, nothing has been decided *ou* nothing has been decided about the money

Lorsque *pour* signifie *comme* il se traduit souvent par *as*:

je l'ai eu pour professeur = I had him as a teacher

Attention à la présence de l'article en anglais.

Lorsque *pour* relie un terme redoublé il se traduit parfois par *for*:

mot pour mot = word for word

Mais ce n'est pas toujours le cas:

jour pour jour = to the day

On se reportera au nom dans le dictionnaire.

On trouvera dans l'entrée des exemples supplémentaires et exceptions.

---

d'huile one spoonful of vinegar to four of oil; **~ une large part** to a large extent.

pour² /puʀ/ *nm* **le ~ et le contre** pros and cons (*pl*).

pourboire /puʀbwaʀ/ *nm* tip; **donner un ~ à qn** to tip sb.

pourcentage /puʀsɑ̃taʒ/ *nm* **1** MATH percentage; **2** (rémunération) commission; **payer qn au ~** to pay sb by commission; **3** (profit illicite) PEJ cut○.

pourchasser /puʀʃase/ [1] *vtr* **1** (traquer) to hunt [*animal, criminel*]; **2** (harceler) to pursue.

pourparlers /puʀpaʀle/ *nmpl* talks; **être en ~** [*personnes*] to be engaged in talks; [*affaire*] to be under discussion.

pourpre¹ /puʀpʀ/ ▶ **141** I *adj* crimson.
II *nm* **1** (couleur) crimson; **2** ZOOL murex.

pourpre² /puʀpʀ/ *nf* (colorant) Tyrian purple; (étoffe, dignité) purple.

pourpré, ~e /puʀpʀe/ ▶ **141** *adj* crimson.

pourquoi¹ /puʀkwa/ I *adv, conj* **1** (dans une interrogation directe) why?; **~ ça?** why?; **~ donc?** but why?; **~ pas un week-end à Paris?** what ou how about a weekend in Paris?; **2** (dans une interrogation indirecte) why; **dis-moi ~ tu pleures** tell me why you are crying; **va donc savoir ~!** God knows why!
II **c'est pourquoi** *loc adv* that's why; **il semble que vous n'avez pas reçu ma première lettre, c'est ~ je vous adresse ci-joint une photocopie** it appears that you didn't receive my first letter, so I enclose a photocopy.

pourquoi² /puʀkwa/ *nm inv* **le ~ et le comment** the why and the wherefore; **quel est le ~ de toute cette agitation?** what is the reason for all this disturbance?

pourri, ~e /puʀi/ I *adj* **1** (avarié) [*aliment*] rotten; **2** (décomposé) [*végétal*] decayed, rotting; [*bois*] rotten; [*mur, roche*] rotten, crumbling; **3**○ (mauvais) [*temps*] rotten○, dismal; **4**○ (de mauvaise qualité) rotten○, lousy○; **5** (déplaisant) [*lieu*] awful; **6**○ (corrompu) [*personne, mentalité*] crooked○, corrupt; [*société*]

corrupt, rotten○; **7**○ (gâté) [*enfant*] spoiled rotten○ (*jamais épith*), spoiled.
II *nm* rotten part; **ça sent le ~** it smells rotten.

pourrir /puʀiʀ/ [3] I *vtr* **1** (faire se décomposer) [*eau, humidité*] to rot [*bois*]; **2** (corrompre) to spoil [*personne*]; **3**○ (gâter) to spoil [sb] rotten○ [*enfant*].
II *vi* **1** (s'abîmer) [*œuf, viande*] to go bad ou off GB; [*fruit*] to go bad, to rot; **2** (se décomposer) to rot; **3** (végéter) to rot; **4** (se dégrader) [*situation*] to deteriorate.

pourriture /puʀityʀ/ *nf* **1** (décomposition) rot, decay; **2** (corruption) corruption, rottenness; **3** AGRIC, BOT rot.

poursuite /puʀsɥit/ *nf* **1** (action de poursuivre) pursuit; **se lancer à la ~ de qn** to set off in pursuit of sb; **2** (chasse) chase; **une folle ~** a wild chase; **3** (continuation) continuation; **la ~ d'un dialogue** the continuation of a dialogue GB; **4** SPORT (en cyclisme) pursuit; **5** JUR ~ **(judiciaire)** (judicial) proceedings (*pl*); **abandonner les ~s** to drop the charges.

poursuivant, ~e /puʀsɥivɑ̃, ɑ̃t/ *nm,f* (personne qui poursuit) pursuer.

poursuivre /puʀsɥivʀ/ [62] I *vtr* **1** (traquer) to chase; **2** (harceler) [*personne*] to hound [*personne*]; [*cauchemar, rêve*] to haunt [*personne*]; **~ qn de ses assiduités** LITER to force one's attentions on sb; **cette histoire de vol m'a longtemps poursuivie** that stealing business dogged me for a long time; **3** (rechercher) to seek (after) [*honneurs, vérité*]; to pursue [*but*]; **4** (continuer) to continue [*chemin*]; to pursue [*négociations, réflexion, tâche*]; to continue [*efforts, conflit*]; **~ une enquête policière** to proceed with a police enquiry; **~ des** ou **ses études** to continue studying ou one's studies; **5** JUR **~ qn** (**en justice** or **devant les tribunaux**) (en droit civil) to sue sb; (en droit pénal) to take sb to court.
II *vi* (continuer) [*personne*] to continue; **poursuivez, nous vous écoutons** please continue, we're listening.
III **se poursuivre** *vpr* **1** (continuer) to continue; **les combats se sont poursuivis dans la nuit** fighting continued into the night; **2** (l'un l'autre) [*enfants, adultes*] to chase (after) each other.

pourtant /puʀtɑ̃/ *adv* though; **et ~** and yet; **c'était**

~ une bonne idée and yet it was a good idea, it was a good idea though; **ce n'est ~ pas difficile!** (and yet) it's not so difficult!; **techniquement ~, le film est parfait** technically, however, the film is perfect.

pourtour /puʀtuʀ/ *nm* **1** (bords extérieurs) perimeter; (de cercle) circumference; **2** (région avoisinante) surrounding area.

pourvoi /puʀvwa/ *nm* appeal.

pourvoir /puʀvwaʀ/ [40] **I** *vtr* **1** (attribuer) to fill [*poste, siège*]; **siège/poste à ~** available seat/position; **2** (doter) **~ qn de** to endow sb with [*qualité, trait, ressources*]; **~ une maison en équipement** to fit out a house.
II pourvoir à *vtr ind* (assurer) **~ à** to provide for [*besoin, dépense, sécurité*]; **j'y pourvoirai** I'll see to it.
III se pourvoir *vpr* **1** (se munir) **se ~ de** to provide oneself with [*monnaie*]; to equip oneself with [*véhicule, bottes*]; **2** JUR (faire appel) **se ~ en** or **devant** to appeal to.

pourvoyeur, -euse /puʀvwajœʀ, øz/ *nm,f* **1** (source) **~ de** source of; **2** (fournisseur) **~ de** purveyor of.

pourvu: pourvu que /puʀvyk(ə)/ *loc conj* **1** (à condition que) provided (that), as long as; **2** (espérons que) let's hope; **~ que ça dure!** let's hope it lasts!

pousse /pus/ *nf* **1** (rejet) BOT shoot; FIG offshoot; **~s de bambou** CULIN bamboo shoots; **2** (croissance) growth; **3** BOT (apparition) **la ~ des bourgeons/feuilles** the sprouting of buds/leaves.

poussé, ~e¹ /puse/ **I** *pp* ▶ **pousser**.
II *pp adj* **1** (de haut niveau) [*enquête*] thorough; [*formation, études*] advanced; **2** (exagéré) **être un peu ~** [*plaisanterie*] to go a bit too far; [*comparaison*] to be a bit forced; **3** AUT [*moteur*] modified, souped up°.

pousse-café /puskafe/ *nm inv* (after-dinner) liqueur.

poussée² /puse/ **I** *pp adj f* ▶ **poussé**.
II *nf* **1** (pression, poids) (d'eau, de foule) pressure; (de vent) force; PHYS (force) thrust; **~ verticale de l'eau** PHYS buoyancy in water; **sous la ~ de** LIT beneath the pressure of; FIG under the pressure of; **2** (bourrade) push, shove; MIL (avancée) thrust; **d'une ~** with a push ou shove; **3** MÉD (accès) attack (**de** of); **~ de fièvre** sudden high temperature; **~ d'urticaire** rash; **4** (augmentation) (de prix) (sharp) rise ou increase (**de** in); (de racisme, violence, nationalisme) upsurge (**de** of); **~ démographique** rise in population; **~ inflationniste** inflationary trend.

pousser /puse/ [1] **I** *vtr* **1** (déplacer) to push [*vélo, meuble, personne*]; (écarter ce qui gêne) to move, to shift, to push [sth] aside [*objet*]; **~ une porte** (pour la fermer) to push a door to; **~ un verrou** to push ou slide a bolt home; **le vent poussait le bateau vers la côte** the wind was driving the boat toward(s) the shore; **~ les enfants vers la sortie** to hustle the children toward(s) the exit; **~ qn du coude** to give sb a dig ou to nudge sb with one's elbow; **2** (entraîner) **poussé par la pitié** stirred by pity; **poussé par le désir de les aider** prompted by a desire to help them; **~ qn à faire qch** (encourager) to encourage sb to do sth; (vivement) to urge sb to do sth; (contraindre) [*faim, désespoir, haine*] to drive sb to do sth; **~ qn au suicide** to drive sb to suicide; **c'est ce qui m'a poussé vers l'enseignement** that's what made me take up teaching; **tout me pousse à croire que** everything leads me to believe that; **il n'a pas fallu le ~ beaucoup pour qu'il parle** he didn't need much prompting to talk; **3** (faire travailler plus) to push [*élève*]; to keep [sb] at it [*employé*]; to ride [sth] hard [*monture*]; to drive [sth] hard [*voiture*]; to flog° [*moteur*]; **4** (promouvoir) to push [*produit, protégé*]; **5** (porter plus avant) to pursue [*recherches, raisonnement*]; **c'est ~ un peu loin la plaisanterie** that's carrying ou taking the joke a bit far; **~ le perfectionnisme à l'extrême** to be too much of a perfectionist; **~ la bêtise jusqu'à faire** to be stupid enough to do; **6** (émettre) to let out [*cri*]; to heave [*soupir*]; **~ un hurlement/miaulement** to howl/to miaow; **~ une gueu-**

lante° to yell and scream°; **~ la chansonnette** to sing a song.
II *vi* **1** (croître) [*enfant, plante, barbe, ongle*] to grow; (apparaître) [*plante*] to sprout; [*dent*] to come through; [*immeuble, ville*] to spring up; **je fais ~ des légumes** I grow vegetables; **se laisser** or **se faire ~ les cheveux** to grow one's hair; **se laisser** or **se faire ~ la barbe** to grow a beard; **2** (aller) **~ plus loin/jusqu'à la ville** to go on further/as far as the town; **3** (pour accoucher, aller à la selle) to push; **4°** (exagérer) to overdo it, to go too far; **tu ne crois pas que tu pousses un peu?** don't you think you're overdoing it?
III se pousser *vpr* (pour faire de la place) to move over.
IDIOMES **à la va comme je te pousse°** any old how; **se ~ du col°** to push oneself forward, to be pushy°.

poussette /pusɛt/ *nf* (de bébé) pushchair GB, stroller US.

poussière /pusjɛʀ/ *nf* **1** (poudre) dust; **~ d'or** gold dust; **tomber en ~** LIT to crumble away; FIG to fall to bits; **~ d'étoiles** stardust; **2** (grain) speck of dust.
IDIOMES **10 francs/20 ans et des ~s°** just over 10 francs/20 years; **mordre la ~** to bite the dust.

poussiéreux, -euse /pusjeʀø, øz/ *adj* LIT dusty; FIG PEJ [*idée, bureaucratie*] outdated, fossilized.

poussif, -ive /pusif, iv/ *adj* **1** [*personne, véhicule*] wheezy; [*cheval*] broken-winded; **2** [*allure*] labouring^GB; **3** [*film, discours*] laboured^GB.

poussin /pusɛ̃/ *nm* **1** ZOOL chick; **2** CULIN poussin GB, spring chicken; **3°** (terme d'affection) **mon ~** my poppet° GB, honey(bunch) US.

poussoir /puswaʀ/ *nm* (bouton) (push) button.

poutre /putʀ/ *nf* **1** CONSTR (en bois, béton) beam; (en métal) girder; **~s apparentes** exposed beams; **2** SPORT beam.

poutrelle /putʀɛl/ *nf* girder.

pouvoir¹ /puvwaʀ/ [49]

■ **Note** *can* et *may* qui peuvent traduire le verbe *pouvoir* ne s'emploient ni à l'infinitif, ni au futur.

I *v aux* **1** (être capable de) to be able to; **peux-tu soulever cette boîte?** can you lift this box?; **dès que je pourrai** as soon as I can; **je suis content que vous ayez pu venir** I'm glad you could come; **il pourrait mieux faire** he could do better; **je n'en peux plus** (épuisement, exaspération) I've had it°; (satiété) I'm full°; **2** (être autorisé à) to be allowed to; **est-ce que je peux me servir de ta voiture?** can I use your car?; **puis-je m'asseoir?** may I sit down?; **est-ce qu'on peut fumer ici?** is smoking allowed here?; **3** (avoir le choix de) **on peut écrire clef ou clé** the word can be written clef or clé; **on peut ne pas faire l'accord** the agreement is optional; **il ne peut pas ne pas accepter** he has no option but to accept; **4** (avoir l'obligeance de) **pourriez-vous me tenir la porte s'il vous plaît?** can ou could you hold the door (open) for me please?; **5** (être susceptible de) **tout peut arriver** anything could happen; **il ne peut pas ne pas gagner** he's bound to win; **puisse cette nouvelle année exaucer vos vœux les plus chers** wishing you everything you could want for the new year; **qu'est-ce que cela peut (bien) te faire°?** what business is it of yours?; **on peut toujours espérer** there's no harm in wishing ou hoping; **s'il croit que je vais payer il peut toujours attendre** if he thinks I'm going to pay he's got another think coming; **ce qu'il peut être grand!** how tall he is!; **peux-tu être bête!** you can be so silly!
II *vtr* **que puis-je pour vous?** what can I do for you?; **je ne peux rien pour vous/contre eux** there's nothing I can do for you/about them; **je fais ce que je peux** I'm doing my best.
III *v impers* **il peut faire très froid en janvier** it can get very cold in January; **il pouvait être 10 heures** it was probably about 10 o'clock; **il peut neiger comme il peut faire beau** it might snow or it might be fine; **c'est inimaginable ce qu'il a pu pleuvoir!** you can't imagine ou wouldn't believe how much it rained!

IV il se peut *vpr impers* **il se peut que les prix augmentent en juin** prices may ou might rise in June; **se peut-il qu'il m'ait oublié?** can he really have forgotten me?; **'est-ce que tu viendras ce soir?'—'cela se peut** 'are you coming this evening?'—'I may do'; **ça ne se peut pas**○ it's impossible.

V on ne peut plus *loc adv* **il est on ne peut plus timide** he is as shy as can be; **il est on ne peut plus désagréable** he's thoroughly unpleasant.

VI on ne peut mieux *loc adv* **c'est on ne peut mieux** it couldn't be better; **ils s'entendent on ne peut mieux** they get on extremely well.

IDIOMES **autant que faire se peut** as far as possible.

pouvoir² /puvwaʀ/ *nm* **1** (puissance) power; **~s surnaturels** supernatural powers; **2** (faculté) ability; **avoir le ~ de faire** to be able to do; **3** (ascendant) power (**sur** over); **4** (autorité) power, authority; **je n'ai pas le ~ de décider** it's not up to me to decide; **5** POL power; **~ absolu** absolute power; **après 15 ans au ~** after 15 years in power; **donner tous ~ à qn** to give sb full powers; **le ~ en place** the government in power; **6** ADMIN, JUR power; **~ par-devant notaire** power of attorney.
■ **~ d'achat** purchasing power; **~ exécutif** executive power; **le ~ judiciaire** (corps) the judiciary; **~ législatif** legislative power; **les ~s constitués** the powers that be; **~s publics** authorities.

pragmatique /pʀagmatik/ *adj* pragmatic.

praire /pʀɛʀ/ *nf* clam.

prairie /pʀeʀi/ *nf* GÉN meadow; (aux États-Unis) **la ~** the prairie(s).

pralin /pʀalɛ̃/ *nm* CULIN praline.

praline /pʀalin/ *nf* (amande) sugared GB ou sugar-coated US almond.

praliné, **~e** /pʀaline/ **I** *adj* **1** (enrobé de sucre) sugared GB, sugar-coated US; **2** [*crème*] praline (*épith*).
II *nm* (mélange, arôme, bonbon) praline.

praticable /pʀatikabl/ *adj* **1** (où l'on peut passer) [*chemin, route*] passable; **2** (réalisable) [*sport*] that can be played (*épith, après n*); [*analyse*] practicable SOUT.

praticien, **-ienne** /pʀatisjɛ̃, ɛn/ *nm,f* **1** MÉD general practitioner, GP; **demandez à votre ~** ask your GP; **2** (personne de métier) practitioner.

pratiquant, **~e** /pʀatikɑ̃, ɑ̃t/ **I** *adj* RELIG [*personne, catholique*] practising GB; **il n'est pas ~** he doesn't practise GB (his religion); **être très ~** to be very devout.
II *nm,f* (catholique) practising GB Catholic; (musulman) practising GB Muslim; (juif) practising GB Jew.

pratique /pʀatik/ **I** *adj* **1** (commode) [*appareil, objet*] handy, practical; [*endroit, itinéraire*] convenient; [*technique, vêtement, meuble*] practical; **2** (utile) practical; **3** (non théorique, concret) practical; **4** (pragmatique) practical; **avoir le sens** or **l'esprit ~** to be practical.
II *nf* **1** (exercice d'une activité) **la ~ des arts martiaux est très répandue** many people practise GB martial arts; **cela nécessite de longues heures de ~** it takes hours of practice; **avoir une bonne ~ de l'anglais** to have a good working knowledge of English; **2** (expérience) practical experience; **avoir la ~ des affaires** to have practical business experience; **3** (application de principes) practice; **la théorie et la ~** theory and practice; **4** (habitude) practice; **une ~ courante** a common practice.

pratiquement /pʀatikmɑ̃/ *adv* **1** (en pratique) in practice; **2** (quasiment) practically, virtually; **~ jamais** hardly ever.

pratiquer /pʀatike/ [1] **I** *vtr* **1** (exercer régulièrement) to play [*tennis, basket*]; to do [*athlétisme, canoë, yoga*]; to take part in [*activité, discipline*]; to practise GB [*langue*]; **~ l'équitation/l'aviron/le ski** to ride/to row/to ski; **~ la médecine** to practise GB medicine; **il est croyant mais ne pratique pas** he believes in God but doesn't practise GB his religion; **2** (recourir à) to use [*méthode, chantage*]; to pursue [*politique*]; to charge

[*taux d'intérêt*]; **ils pratiquent des tarifs très compétitifs** they offer very competitive rates; **3** (effectuer) to carry out [*examen, greffe*]; to administer [*soins*]; to make [*trou*]; to clear [*chemin*]; to carry out [*expulsion*].
II se pratiquer *vpr* [*tennis, billard*] to be played; [*technique, politique*] to be used; [*prix*] to be charged; **un sport qui se pratique beaucoup** a very popular sport.

pré¹ /pʀe/ *préf* pre(-); **~accord** preliminary agreement; **~classique** preclassical; **~commande** advance order; **~victorien** pre-Victorian.

pré² /pʀe/ *nm* AGRIC meadow.

préadolescent, **~e** /pʀeadɔlesɑ̃, ɑ̃t/ *adj, nm,f* preteen.

préalable /pʀealabl/ **I** *adj* (qui précède) [*permission, avis*] prior; (qui prépare) [*entretien, étude*] preliminary; **les entretiens ~s aux négociations** the talks preceding the negotiations.
II *nm* (condition) precondition (**à** for, of); (préliminaire) preliminary; **en ~ à** (avant) prior to; (en préliminaire) as a preliminary to.
III au préalable *loc adv* first, beforehand.

préalablement /pʀealabləmɑ̃/ *adv* beforehand; **~ à toute décision** prior to ou before any decision; **coupez en petits dés les légumes ~ épluchés** dice the previously peeled vegetables.

préambule /pʀeɑ̃byl/ *nm* **1** (introduction) preamble; **2** (avertissement) **sans ~** with no forewarning.

préau, *pl* **~x** /pʀeo/ *nm* (d'école) covered playground; (de prison) exercise yard; (d'hôpital, de cloître) inner courtyard.

préavis /pʀeavi/ *nm inv* notice; **déposer un ~ de grève** to give notice of strike action.

précaire /pʀekɛʀ/ *adj* **1** [*existence, bonheur*] precarious; [*emploi*] insecure; [*construction*] flimsy; **le travail ~** casual work; **2** [*possession*] precarious.

précariser /pʀekaʀize/ [1] **I** *vtr* **~ l'emploi** to casualize labour GB; **~ la situation de qn** to make sb's position insecure.
II se précariser *vpr* [*emploi*] to become insecure.

précarité /pʀekaʀite/ *nf* GÉN, JUR precariousness; **la ~ de l'emploi** job insecurity.

précaution /pʀekosjɔ̃/ *nf* **1** (mesure) precaution; **~s d'hygiène** hygiene precautions; **les ~s d'emploi d'un médicament** the precautions to be taken in using a medicine; **prendre ses ~s** GÉN to take precautions; (en allant aux toilettes) EUPH to go to the toilet just in case; (avec un contraceptif) EUPH to take precautions EUPH; **2** (prévoyance) caution; **sans ~** without caution; **avec ~** (attention) with caution; (méfiance) cautiously; **par ~** as a precaution.
■ **~s oratoires** carefully chosen words.
IDIOMES **deux ~s valent mieux qu'une** PROV better safe than sorry PROV.

précautionneux, **-euse** /pʀekosjɔnø, øz/ *adj* FML careful.

précédemment /pʀesedamɑ̃/ *adv* previously, before.

précédent, **~e** /pʀesedɑ̃, ɑ̃t/ **I** *adj* previous.
II *nm,f* **le ~**, **la ~e** the previous one.
III *nm* precedent; **sans ~** without precedent.

précéder /pʀesede/ [14] *vtr* **1** (dans un groupe en mouvement) [*personne, groupe*] to go in front of, to precede; [*véhicule*] to be in front of, to precede; **2** (dans un lieu) **il m'avait précédé de cinq minutes** he'd got there five minutes ahead of me; **on l'avait précédé** someone had got there first; **3** (être placé avant) [*paragraphe, mot, chapitre*] to precede; **dans le paragraphe qui précède** in the above ou preceding paragraph; **4** (se produire avant) to precede; **la semaine qui a précédé votre départ** the week before you left; **les générations qui nous ont précédés** the generations that came before us; **5** (dans un classement) **Pierre précède Paul au classement** Pierre comes before Paul in the ranking; **Tours précède Grenoble de trois points** Tours is three points ahead of Grenoble.

précepte /pʀesɛpt/ *nm* precept.

précepteur, **-trice** /pʀesɛptœʀ, tʀis/ ▶374 *nm,f* (private) tutor.

préchauffer /pʀeʃofe/ [1] *vtr* to preheat [*aliment*]; to warm up [*moteur*]; to heat [*goudron, pièce à souder*].

prêcher /pʀeʃe/ [1] I *vtr* **1** RELIG to preach [*Évangile*]; **~ la bonne parole** to spread the Word; **2** (recommander) to advocate.

II *vi* to preach.

IDIOMES **~ le faux pour savoir le vrai** to tell a lie in order to get at the truth.

précieusement /pʀesjøzmɑ̃/ *adv* **1** [*garder, conserver*] carefully; [*graver*] minutely; **2** [*parler*] in an affected manner.

précieux, **-ieuse** /pʀesjø, øz/ *adj* **1** (coûteux) [*pierre, métal, livre*] precious; [*meuble*] valuable; **2** (utile) [*information*] very useful; [*collaborateur*] valued; **votre aide m'a été précieuse** your help was most valuable; **3** (chéri) [*amitié, droit, qualité*] precious; [*ami*] very dear; **4** (affecté) [*style, langage, geste*] precious; **5** LITTÉRAT [*littérature, salon*] précieuse.

précipice /pʀesipis/ *nm* precipice; **être au bord du ~** FIG to be on the brink of collapse.

précipitamment /pʀesipitamɑ̃/ *adv* [*partir, s'enfuir*] hurriedly; **il nous a quittés ~** he left us in a hurry.

précipitation /pʀesipitasjɔ̃/ I *nf* **1** (hâte) haste; **avec ~** hurriedly; **sans ~** unhurriedly; **2** CHIMIE precipitation.

II **précipitations** *nfpl* MÉTÉO rainfall ¢, precipitation ¢ SPÉC.

précipité, **-e** /pʀesipite/ I *adj* **1** (rapide) rapid; **2** (hâtif) hasty, precipitate; **un jugement ~** a snap judgment.

II *nm* CHIMIE precipitate.

précipiter /pʀesipite/ [1] I *vtr* **1** (jeter) **~ qn d'un balcon** to push sb off a balcony; **~ qn par la fenêtre** to push sb out of the window; **~ qn dans le vide** (du haut d'un bâtiment, palier) to push sb off; (du haut d'une falaise) to push sb over; (par la fenêtre) to push sb out; **~ qn contre** to throw sb against; **2** FIG (plonger) **~ qn dans le désarroi** to throw sb into confusion; **3** (hâter) to hasten [*départ, décision*]; to precipitate [*révolte, événement*]; **~ les choses** to rush things; **4** CHIMIE to precipitate [*solution*].

II *vi* CHIMIE to precipitate.

III **se précipiter** *vpr* **1** (se jeter) **il s'est précipité dans le vide** he jumped off; **2** (se ruer) to rush; **se ~ dans les bras de qn** to throw oneself into sb's arms; **se ~ sur** [*personne*] to rush at, to throw oneself on [*personne*]; [*animal*] to rush at [*personne*]; to rush for [*objet*], FIG to pounce on [*idée, théorie*]; **3** (se dépêcher) to rush, to hurry; **4** (affluer) [*clients*] to pour in; [*investisseurs*] to come running; **5** (s'accélérer) [*action, événement*] to move faster.

précis, **-e** /pʀesi, iz/ I *adj* **1** (bien défini) [*programme, critère, motif, réglementation*] specific; [*idée, engagement, date*] definite; [*moment*] particular; **2** (exact) [*personne, geste, langue, travail, horaire, réponse*] precise; [*chiffre, donnée*] accurate; [*souvenir*] clear; [*endroit, moment*] exact; **à deux heures ~es** at exactly two o'clock; **3** (de précision) [*instrument de mesure*] accurate.

II *nm inv* (manuel) handbook.

précisément /pʀesizemɑ̃/ *adv* **1** (justement) precisely; **2** (avec précision) precisely; **3** (pour être précis) **à la page 6 plus ~** on page 6 to be more precise; **l'Europe et plus ~ la France** Europe and more precisely France.

préciser /pʀesize/ [1] I *vtr* **1** (ajouter) [*personne, rapport*] to add (**que** that); **a-t-il précisé** he added; **faut-il** or **est-il besoin de ~** needless to say; **2** (faire état de) [*personne, communiqué*] to state (**que** that); **~ ses intentions** to state one's intentions; **3** (indiquer avec précision) to specify [*lieu, date, nombre*]; **pouvez-vous ~?** could you be more specific?; **4** (rendre plus précis) to clarify [*idées, programme*].

II **se préciser** *vpr* **1** (se concrétiser) [*danger, avenir, menace*] to become clearer; [*projet, mariage, voyage*]

to take shape; **2** (devenir apparent) [*forme, réalité*] to become clear.

précision /pʀesizjɔ̃/ *nf* **1** (minutie) precision; **~ du détail** detailed precision; **2** (justesse) accuracy; **avec une ~ d'un millimètre** with an accuracy to within one millimetre^GB; **avec ~** accurately; **localiser avec ~** to pinpoint; **instrument de ~** precision instrument; **3** (détail) detail; **apporter quelques ~s** to give a few details (**sur** about).

précité, **~e** /pʀesite/ *adj* aforementioned (*épith*).

précoce /pʀekɔs/ *adj* **1** (mûr avant l'âge) [*enfant, intelligence, sexualité*] precocious; **2** (en avance) [*légume, saison, diagnostic*] early (*épith*); **3** (prématuré) [*rides, sénilité*] premature.

précocité /pʀekɔsite/ *nf* **1** (d'enfant, intelligence) precociousness, precocity SOUT; **2** (d'action) **la ~ du dépistage** early detection; **3** (de fruit, saison) earliness.

précompte /pʀekɔ̃t/ *nm* deduction; **~ de l'impôt** deduction of tax at source.

préconçu, **~e** /pʀekɔ̃sy/ *adj* preconceived.

préconiser /pʀekɔnize/ [1] *vtr* **1** (conseiller) to recommend [*méthode, solution*]; (prôner) to advocate [*doctrine, jeûne*]; **2** RELIG to preconize [*évêque*].

précuit, **~e** /pʀekɥi, it/ *adj* precooked.

précurseur /pʀekyʀsœʀ/ I *adj m* precursory FML; **signes ~s de l'orage** signs that herald a storm.

II *nm* (dans un domaine) pioneer; **~ de** (discipline) forerunner of; (personne) precursor of.

prédateur, **-trice** /pʀedatœʀ, tʀis/ I *adj* predatory.

II *nm* **1** (animal) predator; **2** (homme préhistorique) hunter-gatherer.

prédécesseur /pʀedesesœʀ/ *nm* predecessor.

prédestiné, **~e** /pʀedɛstine/ *adj* [*nom, prénom*] appropriate.

prédestiner /pʀedɛstine/ [1] *vtr* to predestine.

prédicat /pʀedika/ *nm* predicate.

prédicateur, **-trice** /pʀedikatœʀ, tʀis/ *nm,f* preacher.

prédication /pʀedikasjɔ̃/ *nf* **1** LING, PHILOS predication; **2** RELIG (fait de prêcher) preaching; (sermon) sermon.

prédiction /pʀediksjɔ̃/ *nf* prediction.

prédilection /pʀedilɛksjɔ̃/ *nf* predilection (**pour** for), liking (**pour** for); **de ~** favourite^GB (*épith*).

prédire /pʀediʀ/ [65] *vtr* **1** (par divination) to predict [*avenir*]; **~ qch à qn** to predict sth for sb; **2** (par réflexion) to predict.

prédisposer /pʀedispoze/ [1] *vtr* to predispose (**à** to).

prédisposition /pʀedispozisjɔ̃/ *nf* predisposition (**à faire** to do); **montrer des ~s pour la musique** to show a talent for music.

prédominant, **~e** /pʀedɔminɑ̃, ɑ̃t/ *adj* predominant.

prédominer /pʀedɔmine/ [1] *vi* to predominate.

préélectoral, **~e**, *mpl* **-aux** /pʀeelɛktɔʀal, o/ *adj* pre-election (*épith*).

prééminent, **~e** /pʀeeminɑ̃, ɑ̃t/ *adj* preeminent.

préencollé, **~e** /pʀeɑ̃kɔle/ *adj* [*papier peint*] prepasted.

préétablir /pʀeetabliʀ/ [3] *vtr* to pre-establish.

préexister /pʀeɛgziste/ [1] *vi* to pre-exist; **~ à qch** to predate sth.

préfabriqué, **~e** /pʀefabʀike/ I *adj* prefabricated.

II *nm* **1** (matériau) prefabricated material; **2** (maison) prefabricated house, prefab^○; (bâtiment) prefabricated building, prefab^○.

préface /pʀefas/ *nf* preface.

préfacer /pʀefase/ [12] *vtr* to write a ou the preface to.

préfectoral, **~e**, *mpl* **-aux** /pʀefɛktɔʀal, o/ *adj* [*niveau, autorisation*] prefectorial; [*administration, locaux*] prefectural.

préfecture /pʀefɛktyʀ/ *nf* **1** ADMIN prefecture; **2** (chef-lieu) main city of a department; **3** NAUT **~ maritime** naval prefecture.

■ **~ de police** police headquarters in some large French cities.

préférable /pʁefeʁabl/ adj preferable; **il est ~ que** it is preferable ou better that; **~ à** preferable to.

préféré, ~e /pʁefeʁe/ adj, nm,f favourite^GB.

préférence /pʁefeʁɑ̃s/ nf preference; **de ~** preferably; **achète cette marque de ~** if you can, buy this brand.

préférentiel, -ielle /pʁefeʁɑ̃sjɛl/ adj preferential.

préférer /pʁefeʁe/ [14] vtr to prefer; **(c'est) comme tu préfères** (it's) as you prefer ou wish; **j'aurais préféré ne jamais l'apprendre** I wish I'd never heard it.

préfet /pʁefɛ/ nm prefect; **~ de police** prefect of police, police chief; **~ maritime** port admiral.

préfigurer /pʁefigyʁe/ [1] vtr to prefigure.

préfixe /pʁefiks/ nm prefix.

préhistoire /pʁeistwaʁ/ nf prehistory.

préhistorique /pʁeistɔʁik/ adj LIT, FIG prehistoric.

préinscription /pʁeɛ̃skʁipsjɔ̃/ nf preregistration.

préjudice /pʁeʒydis/ nm harm ¢, damage ¢; **un grave ~** serious harm ou damage; **~ matériel** material loss; **~ moral** moral wrong; **porter ~ à qn** to harm sb, to cause harm to sb; **porter ~ à qch** GÉN to damage sth, to be detrimental to sth; JUR to be prejudicial to sth; **subir un ~** to suffer harm; **au ~ de qn** to the detriment of sb; **sans ~ de** JUR without prejudice to.

préjugé /pʁeʒyʒe/ nm prejudice; **~(s) en faveur de qn** bias (sg) in favour^GB of sb.

préjuger /pʁeʒyʒe/ [13] **I** vtr to prejudge.
II préjuger de vtr ind **~ de** to prejudge; **nous ne pouvons ~ de l'avenir** we can't tell what the future holds.

prélasser: se prélasser /pʁelase/ [1] vpr to lounge; **se ~ au soleil** to laze in the sun.

prélat /pʁela/ nm prelate.

prélavage /pʁelavaʒ/ nm prewash.

prêle /pʁɛl/ nf BOT horsetail, equisetum.

prélèvement /pʁelɛvmɑ̃/ nm **1** (de roche, sang etc) sampling; **faire** ou **effectuer un ~ de sang** to take a blood sample; **2** (échantillon) sample; **3** FIN (opération) debiting; (somme) debit; **faire** ou **effectuer un ~ bancaire** to make a debit.
■ **~ automatique** direct debit; **~ exceptionnel** exceptional levy; **~ fiscal** deduction of tax; **~ à la source** deduction at source.

prélever /pʁelve/ [16] vtr **1** (extraire) (pour une analyse) to take a sample of [sang, eau]; (pour une greffe) to remove [organe]; **2** FIN (sur un compte bancaire) to debit; (sur un revenu) to deduct [cotisation, impôt]; **3** (prendre) to take [argent, pourcentage]; to remove [pièce, matériel].

préliminaire /pʁeliminɛʁ/ **I** adj preliminary (à to).
II préliminaires nmpl preliminaries.

prélude /pʁelyd/ nm MUS, FIG prelude.

préluder /pʁelyde/ [1] **préluder à** vtr ind **~ à** to be a prelude to.

prématuré, ~e /pʁematyʁe/ **I** adj premature.
II nm,f premature baby.

préméditation /pʁemeditasjɔ̃/ nf premeditation; **avec/sans ~** [agir] with/without premeditation; [crime] premeditated/unpremeditated.

préméditer /pʁemedite/ [1] vtr to premeditate.

prémices /pʁemis/ nfpl LITER beginnings.

premier, -ière¹ /pʁəmje, ɛʁ/ ▶156|, 399| **I** adj **1** (dans le temps) first; **(dans) les ~s temps** at first; **2** (dans l'espace) first; **3** (dans une série) first; **le ~ janvier** the first of January; **'livre ~'** 'book one'; **Napoléon Iᵉʳ** Napoleon I, Napoleon the First; **4** (dans une hiérarchie) [artiste, écrivain, puissance] leading; [élève, étudiant] top; **être ~** [élève, étudiant] to be top; [coureur] to be first; **une affaire de première urgence** a matter of the utmost urgency; **nos ~s prix** ou **tarifs** (pour voyages) our cheapest holidays^GB ou package tours US; (pour billets) our cheapest tickets; **5** (originel) [impression] first, initial; [éclat] initial; [aspect] original; **6** (essentiel) [qualité] prime; [objectif, consé-

quence] primary; **7** PHILOS [terme, notion, donnée] fundamental; [vérité, principe] first.
II nm,f **1** (dans le temps) first; **2** (dans une énumération) first; **je préfère le ~** I prefer the first one; **le ~ de mes fils** (sur deux fils) my elder son; (sur plus de deux fils) my eldest son; **3** (dans un classement) **arriver le ~** [coureur] to come first; **être le ~ de la classe** [élève] to be top of the class.
III nm **1** (dans un bâtiment) first floor GB, second floor US; **2** (jour du mois) first; **le ~ de l'an** New Year's Day; **3** (arrondissement) first arrondissement.
IV en premier loc adv **faire qch en ~** to do sth first; **citons en ~ le livre de notre collègue** first of all there's our colleague's book.
V de première○ loc adj first-rate; **c'est de première** it's first-class ou first-rate.
■ **~ âge** [produits, vêtements] for babies up to six months (après n); **~ de cordée** leader; **~ danseur** leading dancer; **~ jet** first ou rough draft; **~ ministre** prime minister; **le ~ venu** just anybody; **elle s'est jetée dans les bras du ~ venu** she threw herself at the first man to come along; **première nouvelle**○! that's the first I've heard about it; **~s secours** first aid ¢.

première² /pʁəmjɛʁ/ nf **1** (événement important, exploit) first; **~ mondiale** world first; **2** THÉÂT, CIN première; **3** SCOL sixth year of secondary school, age 16–17; **4** AUT first (gear); **5**○ (dans les transports) first class.

premièrement /pʁəmjɛʁmɑ̃/ adv **1** (dans une énumération) firstly, first; **2** (introduisant une objection) for a start, for one thing.

prémisse /pʁemis/ nf premise, premiss GB.

prémolaire /pʁemɔlɛʁ/ nf premolar.

prémonition /pʁemɔnisjɔ̃/ nf premonition.

prémonitoire /pʁemɔnitwaʁ/ adj premonitory.

prémunir /pʁemyniʁ/ [3] **I** vtr (protéger) to protect.
II se prémunir vpr to protect oneself.

prenant, ~e /pʁənɑ̃, ɑ̃t/ adj **1** (captivant) [intrigue, spectacle] fascinating; [voix] captivating; (absorbant) [travail, métier] absorbing; **2** ZOOL [queue] prehensile.

prénatal, ~e, mpl ~s /pʁenatal/ adj [chirurgie] prenatal; [surveillance] antenatal; **un examen ~** an antenatal○.

prendre /pʁɑ̃dʁ/ [52] **I** vtr **1** (saisir) to take; **~ un vase sur l'étagère/dans le placard** to take a vase off the shelf/out of the cupboard; **2** (se donner, acquérir) **~ un accent** (involontairement) to pick up an accent; (volontairement) to put on an accent; **~ une habitude** to develop ou pick up a habit; **~ une voix grave** to adopt a solemn tone; **~ un rôle** to assume a role; **3** (dérober) to take; **on m'a pris tous mes bijoux** I had all my jewellery GB ou jewelry US stolen; **la guerre leur a pris deux fils** the war lost two sons in the war; **4** (apporter) to bring; **je n'ai pas pris assez d'argent** I haven't brought enough money; **5** (emporter) to take; **j'ai pris ton parapluie** I took your umbrella; **6** (retirer) **~ de l'argent au distributeur** to get some money out of the cash dispenser; **~ de l'eau au puits** to get water from the well; **~ quelques livres à la bibliothèque** to get a few books out of the library; **7** (consommer) to have [boisson, aliment, repas]; to take [médicament, drogue]; **je vais ~ du poisson** I'll have fish; **aller ~ un café/une bière** to go for a coffee/a beer; **je prends des calmants depuis la guerre** I've been on tranquillizers^GB since the war; **je ne prends jamais d'alcool** I never touch alcohol; **8** (s'accorder) to take; **~ un congé** to take some time off; **je vais ~ mon mercredi**○ I'm going to take Wednesday off; **9** (choisir) to take [objet]; to choose [sujet, question]; **j'ai pris la question sur Zola** I chose the question on Zola; **~ qn pour époux/épouse** to take sb to be one's husband/wife; **10** (faire payer) to charge; **elle prend combien de l'heure?** how much does she charge an hour?; **il prend 15% au passage**○ he takes a cut of 15%; **11** (nécessiter) to take [temps]; (user) to take up [espace, temps]; **mes enfants me prennent tout mon temps** my children take up all my time; **12** (acheter , réserver, louer) to get [*aliments, essence, place*]; **~ une chambre en ville** to get a room in town; **13** (embaucher) (durablement) to take [sb] on [*employé, assistant, apprenti*]; (pour une mission) to engage [*personne*]; **ils ne m'ont pas pris** they didn't take me on; **~ qn comme nourrice** to take sb on as a nanny; **~ un avocat/guide** to engage a lawyer/guide; **14** (accueillir) to take; **ils ont pris la petite chez eux** they took the little girl in; **~ un client** [*taxi*] to pick up a customer; **15** (ramasser au passage) to pick up [*personne, pain, clé, journal, ticket*]; **~ les enfants à l'école** to collect the children from school; **16** (emmener) to take [*personne*]; **je peux te ~** (en voiture) I can give you a lift; **17** (attraper) to catch [*personne, animal*]; **elle s'est fait ~ en train de voler** she got caught stealing; **~ un papillon avec ses doigts** to pick up a butterfly; **je vous y prends○!** caught you!; **on ne m'y prendra plus○!** (à faire) you won't catch me doing that again!; (à croire) I won't be taken in○ again!; **je ne me suis pas laissé ~** (tromper) I wasn't going to be taken in○; **18○** (assaillir) **qu'est-ce qui te prend?** what's the matter with you?; **ça te/leur prend souvent?** are you/they often like this?; **19** (captiver) to involve [*spectateur, lecteur*]; **être pris par un livre/film** to get involved in a book/film; **20** (subir) to get [*gifle, coup de soleil, décharge, contravention*]; to catch [*rhume*]; **j'ai pris le marteau sur le pied** the hammer hit me on the foot; **21** (utiliser) to take [*autobus, métro, train, ferry, autoroute*]; **22** (envisager) to take; **prenons par exemple Nina** take Nina, for example; **à tout ~** all in all; **23** (considérer) to take; **ne le prends pas mal** don't take it the wrong way; **pour qui me prends-tu?** (grossière erreur) what do you take me for?; (manque de respect) who do you think you're talking to?; **excusez-moi, je vous ai pris pour quelqu'un d'autre** I'm sorry, I thought you were someone else; **24** (traiter) to handle; **il est très gentil quand on sait le ~** he's very nice when you know how to handle him; **25** (mesurer) to take [*mensurations, température, tension, pouls*]; **26** (noter) to take down; **je vais ~ votre adresse** let me just take down your address; **27** (apprendre) **~ que** to get the idea (that); **où a-t-il pris qu'ils allaient divorcer?** where did he get the idea they were going to get divorced?; **28** (accepter) to take; **il faut ~ les gens comme ils sont** you must take people as you find them; **29** (endosser) to take over [*direction, pouvoir*]; to assume [*contrôle, poste*]; **je prends ça sur moi** I'll see to it; **~ sur soi de faire** to take it upon oneself to do, to undertake to do; **30** (accumuler) to put on [*poids*]; to gain [*avance*]; **~ des forces** to build up one's strength; **31** (contracter) to take on [*bail*]; to take [*emploi*]; **32** (défier) to take [sb] on [*concurrent*]; **je prends le gagnant** I'll take on the winner; **33** (conquérir) MIL to take, to seize [*ville, forteresse*]; to capture [*navire, tank*]; JEUX to take [*pièce, carte*].

II *vi* **1** (aller) **~ à gauche/vers le nord** to go left/north; **prenez tout droit** keep straight on; **~ par le littoral** to follow the coast; **2** (s'enflammer) [*feu, bois, mèche*] to catch; [*incendie*] to break out; **3** (se solidifier) [*gelée, flan, glace, ciment, plâtre, colle*] to set; [*blancs d'œufs*] to stiffen; [*mayonnaise*] to thicken; **4** (réussir) [*greffe, innovation*] to be a success; [*idée, mode*] to catch on; [*teinture, bouture, vaccination, greffe*] to take; [*leçon*] to sink in; **5** (prélever) **~ sur son temps libre pour traduire un roman** to translate a novel in one's spare time; **6** (se contraindre) **j'ai pris sur moi pour les écouter** I made myself listen to them; **j'ai pris sur moi pour ne pas les insulter** I kept myself from insulting them; **7○** (être cru) **ça ne prend pas!** it won't wash○ ou work!; **8○** (subir) **c'est toujours moi qui prends!** I'm always the one who gets it in the neck○!; **il en a pris pour 20 ans** he got 20 years.

III se prendre *vpr* **1** (devoir être saisi, consommé, mesuré) **un marteau se prend par le manche** you hold a hammer by the handle; **en Chine le thé se prend sans sucre** in China they don't put sugar in their tea; **la vitamine C se prend de préférence le matin** vitamin C is best taken in the morning; **2** (pou-

voir être acquis) **les mauvaises habitudes se prennent vite** bad habits are easily picked up; **3** (se tenir l'un l'autre) **se ~ par la taille** to hold each other around the waist; **4** (se coincer) **se ~ les doigts dans la porte** to catch one's fingers in the door; **mon écharpe s'est prise dans les rayons** my scarf got caught in the spokes; **5○** (recevoir) **il s'est pris une gifle** he got a slap in the face; **je me suis pris une averse** I got caught in a shower; **6** (commencer) **~ à faire** to find oneself doing; **se ~ de sympathie pour qn** to take to sb; **7** (se considérer) **elle se prend pour un génie** she thinks she's a genius; **8 s'en ~** (par des reproches ou des critiques) to attack [*personne, presse, parti*]; (pour passer sa colère) to take it out on [*personne*]; (agresser verbalement ou physiquement) to go for [*personne*]; (blâmer) to blame [*personne, groupe, institution*]; **il ne pourra s'en ~ qu'à lui-même** he will have only himself to blame; **9** (se comporter) **savoir s'y ~ avec** to have a way with [*enfants, femmes, vieux*]; to know how to handle [*employés, élèves*]; **10** (agir) **il faut s'y ~ à l'avance pour avoir des places** you have to book ahead to get seats; **tu t'y es pris trop tard** you left it too late; **il s'y est pris à plusieurs fois** he tried several times; **regarde comment elle s'y prend** look how she's doing it; **elle s'y prend bien/mal** she goes about it the right/wrong way.

IDIOMES **c'est à ~ ou à laisser** take it or leave it; **tel est pris qui croyait ~** the tables are turned.

preneur, -euse /prənœr, øz/ *nm,f* COMM (acheteur, taker) **trouver ~** [*article*] to attract a buyer; [*personne*] to find a buyer (**pour** for); **ne pas trouver ~** [*article*] to remain unsold; **je suis ~** I'll take it.

prénom /prenɔ̃/ *nm* GÉN first name, christian name GB ADMIN forename, given name; **deuxième ~** middle name.

prénommé, ~e /prenɔme/ **I** *pp* ▶ **prénommer.**
II *pp adj* **un ~ Jules** somebody called Jules; **la ~e Isabelle** the girl known as Isabelle.
III *nm,f* JUR **le ~, la ~e** the aforementioned.

prénommer /prenɔme/ [1] **I** *vtr* to name, to call; **M Martin, prénommé Henri** Mr Martin, first name Henri.
II se prénommer *vpr* to be called.

prénuptial, ~e, *pl* **-iaux** /prenypsjal, o/ *adj* [*accord*] prenuptial; [*examen*] prior to marriage (*épith après n*).

préoccupant, ~e /preɔkypɑ̃, ɑ̃t/ *adj* worrying; **son état de santé est ~** his/her condition is giving cause for concern.

préoccupation /preɔkypasjɔ̃/ *nf* (souci) worry, concern; (pensée dominante) concern.

préoccupé, ~e /preɔkype/ **I** *pp* ▶ **préoccuper.**
II *pp adj* (soucieux) preoccupied; **être ~ par qch** to be concerned about sth; **il semble peu ~ par les problèmes de l'entreprise** he seems to have little concern for the company's problems.

préoccuper /preɔkype/ [1] **I** *vtr* **1** (inquiéter) to worry; **ma santé le préoccupe** he's been worried about my health; **2** (occuper) to concern.
II se préoccuper *vpr* **se ~ de** to be concerned about [*problème, situation*]; to think about [*avenir, opinion*]; **il ne s'est pas préoccupé de savoir si cela m'arrangeait** he didn't think to ask if it would suit me; **se ~ de sa petite personne** to think only of oneself, to be self-centred GB.

préparateur, -trice /preparatœr, tris/ ▶374 *nm,* **~ en pharmacie** pharmacist's assistant.

préparatifs /preparatif/ *nmpl* preparations (**de** for).

préparation /preparasjɔ̃/ *nf* **1** (mise au point) preparation; **2** (résultat) preparation; **~ pharmaceutique** pharmaceutical preparation; **3** SCOL homework.

préparatoire /preparatwar/ *adj* [*réunion, entretien, phase*] preliminary; [*travail*] preparatory, preliminary.

préparer /prepare/ [1] **I** *vtr* **1** (apprêter) to prepare [*affaires, chambre, cours, loi, plat, surprise*] (**pour** for); to get [sth] ready [*vêtements, outils, dossier*] (**pour** for); to prepare, to plan [*réunion, spectacle*]; to plan [*vacances, avenir*]; to prepare for [*rentrée*]; to draw up [*projet*]; to hatch [*complot*]; to prepare, to lay [*piège*]; **il est en train de ~ le dîner** he's getting dinner ready, he's fixing dinner US; **~ le terrain** FIG to prepare the ground; **il est en train de ~ un mauvais coup** he's up to no good; **il prépare un disque pour l'année prochaine** he's working on a record to be released next year; **des plats préparés** ready-to-eat meals; **je me demande ce que l'avenir nous prépare** I wonder what the future has in store for us; **2** (mettre en condition) to prepare [*personne, pays, économie*] (à for); **~ qn à une épreuve sportive** to coach sb for a (sports) competition; **essaie de la ~ avant de lui annoncer la nouvelle** try and break the news to her gently; **3** SCOL, UNIV to prepare for, to study for [*examen, concours*]; **4** TECH to dress [*laine, cuir*]; **5** CULIN to dress [*poisson, volaille*].

II se préparer *vpr* **1** (s'apprêter) [*personne*] to get ready; **2** (se mettre en condition) to prepare (à for); **je ne m'étais pas préparé à cette éventualité** I was not prepared for this to happen; **3** (être imminent) [*orage, malheurs*] to be brewing; [*changements*] to be in the offing; **un coup d'État se prépare** a coup d'état is imminent; **il se prépare quelque chose de louche** something fishy○ is going on; **4** (faire pour soi) **se ~ une tasse de thé** to make ou fix US oneself a cup of tea.

prépondérance /prepɔ̃derɑ̃s/ *nf* predominance.

prépondérant, ~e /prepɔ̃derɑ̃, ɑ̃t/ *adj* predominant.

préposé, ~e /prepoze/ *nm,f* **1** GÉN official; **~ à qch** official responsible for sth; **~ des douanes** customs official; **~ au vestiaire** cloakroom attendant; **2** (facteur) postman/postwoman.

préposer /prepoze/ [1] *vtr* **~ à** to assign to.

prépositif, -ive /prepozitif, iv/ *adj* prepositional.

préposition /prepozisjɔ̃/ *nf* preposition.

préprofessionnel, -elle /preprɔfesjɔnɛl/ *adj* vocational.

prépuce /prepys/ *nm* foreskin.

préretraite /preretrɛt/ *nf* **1** (situation) early retirement; **être en ~** to have taken early retirement; **2** (allocation) early retirement pension.

prérogative /preroɡativ/ *nf* prerogative; **~ de qn/ qch sur** primacy of sb/sth over; **s'arroger des ~s** to claim prerogatives.

près /prɛ/ **I** *adv* **1** (non loin dans l'espace) close; **la ville est tout ~** it's no distance to the town, the town is close by; **ce n'est pas tout ~** it's quite a way; **se raser de ~** to have a close shave; **2** FIG **10 kg, à quelques grammes ~** 10 kg, give or take a few grammes; **ce roman est plutôt bon, à quelques détails ~** this novel is quite good, apart from the odd detail; **à ceci** or **cela ~ que** except that; **il m'a remboursé au centime ~** he paid me back to the very last penny; **à une voix ~, le projet aurait été adopté** the project would have been adopted but for one vote; **gagner à deux voix ~** to win by two votes; **prends ton temps, on n'est pas à cinq minutes ~** take your time, five minutes won't make any difference; **précis au millimètre ~** accurate to within a millimetre GB; **à une exception ~** with only one exception; **à quelques exceptions ~** with a few rare exceptions.

II près de *loc prép* **1** (dans l'espace) near; **elle habite ~ d'ici** she lives nearby ou near here; **être ~ du but** FIG to be close to achieving one's goal; **j'aimerais être ~ de toi** I'd like to be with you; **elle est ~ de lui** (à ses côtés) she's at his side; **2** (dans le temps) near, nearly; **il est ~ de l'âge de la retraite** he's near retirement age; **il est ~ de minuit** it's nearly midnight; **être ~ de faire** to be about to do; **je suis ~ de penser que** I almost think that; **ils étaient ~ de la victoire** they were close to victory; **le problème n'est pas ~ d'être résolu** the problem is nowhere near solved; **3** (par les idées, les sentiments) close (de to); **ils sont très ~ l'un de l'autre** they are very close; **vivre ~ de la nature** to live close to

nature; **4** (presque) nearly, almost; **cela coûte ~ de 1 000 francs** it costs nearly ou almost 1,000 francs.

III de près *loc adv* closely; **regarder de plus ~** to take a closer look; **suivre qn de ~** to follow sb closely; **surveiller qn/qch de ~** to keep a close eye on sb/sth; **vu de ~, cela rassemble à...** seen from close quarters, it looks like...; **les concurrents se suivent de ~** the competitors are close together; **s'intéresser de ~ à qch** to take a close interest in sth; **voir la mort de ~** to look death in the face, to come close to death; **à y regarder de plus ~** on closer examination.

IV à peu près *loc adv* (presque) **la rue est à peu ~ vide** the street is practically ou virtually empty; **cela coûte à peu ~ 200 francs** it costs around ou around 200 francs; **il y a à peu ~ une heure qu'il est parti** he left about an hour ago; **à peu ~ de la même façon** in much the same way; **à peu ~ semblables** pretty much the same; **cela désigne à peu ~ n'importe quoi** it refers to just about anything.

présage /prezaʒ/ *nm* **1** (signe) omen; **2** (signe avant-coureur) harbinger; **3** (prédiction) prediction.

présager /prezaʒe/ [13] *vtr* (annoncer) [*événement, nouvelle*] to presage; (prévoir) [*personne*] to predict; **laisser ~** to suggest (à to); **cela ne présage rien de bon** this does not bode well.

presbyte /prɛsbit/ **I** *adj* longsighted GB, farsighted US.
II *nmf* longsighted person GB, farsighted person US.

presbytère /prɛsbitɛr/ *nm* presbytery.

presbytérien, -ienne /prɛsbiterjɛ̃, ɛn/ *adj, nm,f* Presbyterian.

presbytie /prɛsbisi/ *nf* longsightedness GB, farsightedness US.

prescience /presjɑ̃s/ *nf* **1** (connaissance de l'avenir) foresight, prescience; **2** (intuition) premonition; **3** RELIG prescience.

préscolaire /preskɔlɛr/ *adj* preschool.

prescriptible /prɛskriptibl/ *adj* [*dette, droit*] subject to limitation of action by lapse of time; [*peine, crime*] time-barred.

prescription /prɛskripsjɔ̃/ *nf* **1** MÉD prescription; (sur un emballage) **'se conformer aux ~s du médecin'** 'to be taken in accordance with doctor's instructions'; **2** (ordre) prescript.

prescrire /prɛskrir/ [67] *vtr* **1** MÉD to prescribe [*médicament, repos*] (à qn for sb); **'ne pas dépasser la dose prescrite'** (sur un emballage) 'do not exceed stated dose'; **2** (imposer) to stipulate; **au jour prescrit** on the day stipulated; **3** (requérir) [*circonstance, événement*] to call for; **4** JUR to subject [sth] to limitation by lapse of time [*peine, crime, dette, droit*].

préséance /preseɑ̃s/ *nf* precedence.

présélecteur /preselɛktœr/ *nm* **1** AUT preselector; **2** TECH preset device.

présélection /preselɛksjɔ̃/ *nf* **1** (de personnes, livres) shortlisting; **2** TECH presetting; **bouton de ~** preset button.

présélectionner /preselɛksjɔne/ [1] *vtr* **1** to shortlist [*personnes, livres*]; **2** TECH to preselect [*vitesse*]; TV, RADIO to preset.

présence /prezɑ̃s/ **I** *nf* **1** (de personne) presence; (au bureau, à l'usine) attendance; **il ignore ta ~** he doesn't know you are here; **il fait de la ~, c'est tout** he's present and not much else; **en ~ d'une foule énorme** in front of a huge crowd; **les forces en ~ dans le conflit** the forces involved in the conflict; **les parties en ~** JUR the litigants, the opposing parties; **mettre deux personnes en ~** to bring two people together ou face to face; **2** (de pays) presence; **3** (de substance, phénomène, d'industrie) presence (dans in); **4** (être animé) **sentir une ~** to feel a presence; **il a besoin d'une ~** he needs company; **5** (personnalité) presence.
■ **~ d'esprit** presence of mind.

présent, ~e[1] /prezɑ̃, ɑ̃t/ **I** *adj* **1** (sur les lieux) [*personne*] present; **les personnes ici ~es** the persons here present SOUT; **M. Glénat, ici ~** Mr Glénat, who

is here with us; **il ne sera pas ~ à l'audience** JUR he will not appear in court; **'~!'** (à l'école) 'here!', 'present!'; **j'étais ~ en pensée** or **par le cœur** I was there in spirit; **2** (existant) present; **la faim est toujours ~e dans cette partie du monde** there's still hunger in that part of the world; **avoir ~ à l'esprit** to have [sth] in mind [*conseil*]; to have [sth] fresh in one's mind [*souvenir*]; **le souvenir toujours ~ de** the ever present memory of; **gardez** or **ayez bien ~ à l'esprit que** bear in mind that; **3** (actif) actively involved; **un chanteur très ~ sur scène** a singer with a strong stage presence; **4** (actuel) [*moment, situation, état*] present; **5** (en cause) present; **par la ~e lettre** by the present (letter), hereby JUR; **6** LING [*temps, participe*] present.
II *nm,f* (personne) **il n'y avait que 20 ~s** there were only 20 people present; **la liste des ~s** the list of those present.
III *nm* **1** (période) **le ~** the present; **2** LING (temps) present (tense); **3** (cadeau) gift, present; **faire ~ de qch à qn** to present sb with sth.
IV à présent *loc adv* (en ce moment) at present; (maintenant) now; **d'à ~** of today; **à ~ que** now that.

présentable /pʀezɑ̃tabl/ *adj* presentable.

présentateur, -trice /pʀezɑ̃tatœʀ, tʀis/ ▶ **374**⏐ *nm,f* RADIO, TV (de spectacle, d'émission) presenter, anchor; **le ~ (du journal)** the newsreader GB, the newscaster US.

présentation /pʀezɑ̃tasjɔ̃/ *nf* **1** (d'ami, de conférencier) introduction; **faire les ~s** to make the introductions; **2** (apparence) appearance; **'excellente ~ exigée'** 'smart appearance required'; **3** (arrangement) presentation; **4** (manifestation, spectacle) show, showing; **~ de mode** fashion show; **5** (d'émission, de journal, jeu) presentation; **6** (de carte, ticket, bagage) production, showing; (de pièces justificatives) production, presentation; (de chèque) presentation; **sur ~ de** on production of; **7** (exposé) presentation; **8** RELIG **la Présentation de l'Enfant Jésus** Presentation of the Child.

présente² /pʀezɑ̃t/ **I** *adj f* ▶ **présent** I.
II *nf* **1** (lettre) **par la ~** hereby; **joint à la ~** herewith; **2** ▶ **présent** II.

présentement /pʀezɑ̃tmɑ̃/ *adv* at present GB, presently.

présenter /pʀezɑ̃te/ [1] **I** *vtr* **1** (faire connaître) to introduce (à to); (de manière officielle) to present (à qn to sb); **je vous présente mon fils** this is my son, may I introduce my son?; **il n'est pas nécessaire de vous ~ Pierre** Pierre needs no introduction from me; **2** (montrer) to show [*ticket, carte, menu*]; **~ une troupe à** to parade troops before; **'présentez armes!'** 'present arms!'; **3** (proposer au public) to present [*spectacle, vedette, rétrospective, collection*]; RADIO, TV to present [*journal, émission*]; COMM to display [*marchandises*]; **4** (soumettre) to present [*facture, addition*]; to submit [*devis, rapport*]; to table [*motion*]; to introduce [*proposition, projet de loi*]; **~ qn à** to put sb forward for [*poste, élection*]; **~ une liste pour les élections** to put forward a list (of candidates) for the elections; **~ une proposition à un comité** to put a proposal to a committee; **5** (exposer) to present [*situation, budget*]; to expound, to present [*théorie*]; to set out [*point de vue*]; **~ qn comme (étant) un monstre** to portray sb as a monster; **être présenté comme miraculeux** to be described as miraculous; **être présenté comme un modèle** to be held up as a model; **comment allez-vous leur ~ l'affaire?** how are you going to put the matter to them?; **6** (exprimer) to offer [*condoléances*] (à to); **~ des excuses** to apologize (à to); **7** (comporter) to involve, to present [*risque, difficulté*]; to show [*différences, trace*]; to show, to present [*symptôme*]; to offer [*avantage*]; to have [*aspect, particularité, défaut*]; **~ un grand intérêt/peu d'intérêt** to be of great interest/of little interest; **8** (orienter) **~ son visage au soleil** to turn one's face to the sun; **~ le flanc à l'ennemi** MIL to offer its flank to the enemy.

II *vi* **~ bien** to have a smart appearance; **~ ma[l]** not to have a smart appearance.
III se présenter *vpr* **1** (paraître) to appear; (aller) to go; (venir) to come; **se ~ à l'audience** JUR to appear in court; **en arrivant, il faut se ~ à la réception** when you arrive you must go ou report to reception; **comment oses-tu te ~ chez moi?** how dare you show your face at my house?; **2** (se faire connaître) to introduce oneself (à to); **se ~ comme le** or **en libérateur du pays** to make oneself out to be the country's saviour; **3** (se porter candidat) **se ~ à** to take [*examen, concours*]; to stand for [*élections*]; **se ~ sur la même liste que** to stand GB ou run alongside sb; **4** (survenir) [*occasion, difficulté, problème*] to arise, to present itself; [*solution*] to emerge; **lire/manger tout ce qu[i]** **se présente** to read /to eat anything that comes along; **les difficultés qui se présentent à nous** the difficul[ties] ties with which we are faced ou confronted; **[un]** **spectacle étonnant se présenta à mes yeux** a[n] amazing sight met my eyes; **5** (exister) [*médicament, produit*] **se ~ en, se ~ sous forme de** to come in the form of; **6** (s'annoncer) **l'affaire se présente bie[n]** things are looking good; **comment se présente l[a]** **situation sur le front?** what is the situation at the front?; **7** MÉD **comment se présente l'enfant?** how is the baby presenting?; **le bébé se présente par l[e]** **siège** the baby is in the breech position.

présentoir /pʀezɑ̃twaʀ/ *nm* (meuble) display stand o[u] unit; (rayon) display shelf.

préservatif /pʀezɛʀvatif/ *nm* condom.

préservation /pʀezɛʀvasjɔ̃/ *nf* preservation; **la ~** **de la nature** nature conservation.

préserver /pʀezɛʀve/ [1] **I** *vtr* to preserve [*tradition,* *patrimoine, paix*] (**de** from, against); to protect [*inté-* *rêt, droit, emploi, environnement, corps*] (**de** from, against).
II se préserver *vpr* **se ~ de** to protect onesel[f] against.

présidence /pʀezidɑ̃s/ *nf* **1** (fonction) (d'État, associa[-] tion, de club, syndicat, tribunal) presidency; (d'entrepris[e] de parti, commission, jury, cour) chairmanship; (d'un[i]-versité) vice-chancellorship GB, presidency US; **êtr[e]** **candidat à la ~** POL to stand GB ou run for president; **2** (résidence) presidential palace; (bureaux) presiden[-] tial offices (*pl*).

président /pʀezidɑ̃/ ▶ **596**⏐ *nm* (d'État, association, d[u] club, syndicat) president; (d'entreprise, de conseil d'adminis[-] tration, parti, commission, jury) chairman, chairperson (d'université) vice-chancellor GB, president US **Monsieur le Président** POL Mr President; (d'une entre[-] prise) Mr Chairman; JUR Your Honour^{GB}.

président-directeur, *pl* **présidents[-]** **directeurs** /pʀezidɑ̃diʀɛktœʀ/ *nm* **~ général** chair[-]man and managing director GB, chief executive officer.

présidente /pʀezidɑ̃t/ ▶ **596**⏐ *nf* **1** (d'État, de clu[b]** syndicat) president; (de parti, commission) chairwoman chairperson; (d'entreprise, de conseil d'administration chairman; **2** (épouse du chef d'État) First Lady.

présidentiel, -ielle¹ /pʀezidɑ̃sjɛl/ *adj* presidential **l'entourage ~** the president's entourage.

présidentielles² /pʀezidɑ̃sjɛl/ *nfpl* presidential elec[-] tion (*sg*), presidential elections.

présider /pʀezide/ [1] *vtr* **1** (diriger) to chair [*commi[-]* *sion, débat*]; **2** (être président de) to be the president o[f] [*association*]; to be the chairman/chairwoman o [*parti, conseil d'administration*]; JUR to preside ove [*cour*]; **~ un dîner** to be the guest of honour^{GB} at dinner.

présomption /pʀezɔ̃psjɔ̃/ *nf* **1** JUR presumption (d[e] of); **condamner qn sur de simples ~s** to condem[n] sb on presumptive grounds alone; **2** (supposition assumption; **3** (prétention) presumption.

présomptueux, -euse /pʀezɔ̃ptɥø, øz/ *adj* [*pe[r]-* *sonne, air*] arrogant; [*action, propos*] presumptuous.

presque /pʀɛsk/ *adv* almost, nearly; **la mêm[e]** **histoire ou ~** the same story or almost the same; **n'y avait personne ou ~, il n'y avait ~ personn[e]** there was hardly anyone there; **c'était le bonheur o[u]**

~ it was as close to happiness as one can get; **il ne reste ~ rien** there's hardly anything left.

presqu'île /pʀɛskil/ *nf* peninsula.

pressant, ~e /pʀɛsɑ̃, ɑ̃t/ *adj* [*besoin, invitation, danger*] pressing; [*appel*] urgent; [*vendeur*] insistent.

presse /pʀɛs/ **I** *nf* **1** (journaux) press; (journalistes) press; (magazines) magazines (*pl*); **que dit la ~?** what do the papers say?; **avoir bonne/mauvaise ~** FIG to be well/not well thought of (**auprès de** among); **2** (machine à presser) press; **3** (machine à imprimer) press; **mettre sous ~** to send [sth] to press; **être mis sous ~** to go to press; '**sous ~**' 'in preparation'.
II presses *nfpl* (maison d'édition) press (*sg*).

pressé, ~e /pʀɛse/ *adj* **1** (qui n'a pas le temps) [*personne*] in a hurry (*jamais épith*); [*pas, air*] hurried; **les gens ~s dans la rue** people rushing about in the street; **2** (désireux) **~ de faire** keen to do; **3** (urgent) [*affaire*] urgent; **elle n'a rien eu de plus ~ que de faire** she couldn't wait to do; **aller** or **parer au plus ~** to do the most urgent thing(s) first.

presse-citron /pʀɛsitʀɔ̃/ *nm inv* lemon squeezer.

pressentiment /pʀɛsɑ̃timɑ̃/ *nm* premonition; **mes ~s se confirment** it's all turning out as I expected.

pressentir /pʀɛsɑ̃tiʀ/ [30] *vtr* (deviner) to have a premonition about [*malheur, changement*]; **~ que** to have a premonition that.

presse-papiers /pʀɛspapje/ *nm inv* paperweight.

presse-purée /pʀɛspyʀe/ *nm inv* potato masher.

presser /pʀɛse/ [1] **I** *vtr* **1** (inciter) **~ qn de faire** to urge sb to do; **2** (harceler) [*personne*] to press [*personne, débiteur*]; [*armée*] to harry [*ennemi*]; **cessez de me ~** stop pestering me; **~ de questions** to ply [sb] with questions; **3** (éperonner) [*faim, nécessité*] to drive [sb] on [*personne*]; **4** (hâter) to increase [*cadence, rythme*]; **~ le pas** or **mouvement** to hurry; **5** (appuyer sur) to press [*bouton*]; **6** (serrer) to squeeze [*main, bras, objet*]; **~ qch contre** or **sur** to press sth against; **~ qn contre sa poitrine** to clasp sb to one's chest; **7** (comprimer) to squeeze [*orange, éponge, peau*]; to press [*raisin*]; **8** TECH to press [*disque*].
II *vi* (être urgent) [*affaire*] to be pressing; [*travail, tâche*] to be urgent; **le temps presse** time is running out.
III se presser *vpr* **1** (se serrer) **se ~ sur** or **contre** to press oneself against; **se ~ autour de qn/qch** to press around sb/sth; **2** (se hâter) to hurry up; **se ~ de faire** to hurry up and do; **pressons, pressons**○! get a move on○!; **3** (être en nombre) [*foule*] to throng; (aller en nombre) [*foule*] to flock (**à, dans, sur, vers** to).

pressing /pʀɛsiŋ/ ▶374 *nm* (teinturerie) dry-cleaner's.

pression /pʀɛsjɔ̃/ *nf* **1** (force physique) pressure ¢; **~ artérielle** blood pressure; **sous ~** (sans compression) under pressure; (avec compression) pressurized; **2** (contrainte) pressure ¢; **~ fiscale** tax burden; **3** (action d'appuyer) pressure; **exercer une (légère) ~ avec la main** to press (gently) with one's hand; **4** (bouton) press stud GB, popper GB, snap (fastener).

pressoir /pʀɛswaʀ/ *nm* **1** (bâtiment) pressing shed; **2** (machine) press.

pressurer /pʀɛsyʀe/ [1] *vtr* **1** AGRIC (presser) to press; **2**○ (exploiter) to milk○.

pressuriser /pʀɛsyʀize/ [1] *vtr* to pressurize.

prestance /pʀɛstɑ̃s/ *nf* **avoir de la ~** to have great presence; **noble ~** noble bearing.

prestataire /pʀɛstatɛʀ/ *nm* **1** COMM **~ de service** (service) contractor, service provider; **2** (bénéficiaire de prestations) recipient (*of a state benefit*).

prestation /pʀɛstasjɔ̃/ *nf* **1** ADMIN (aide) benefit; **2** MIL allowance (*paid to servicemen*); **3** (prêt, fourniture) provision; **~ de service** (provision of a) service; **4** (service) service; **5** (de personne) CONTROV performance; **~ télévisée** televised appearance.

prestement /pʀɛstəmɑ̃/ *adv* LITER [*agir, répliquer*] promptly; [*se mouvoir*] nimbly.

prestidigitateur, -trice /pʀɛstidiʒitatœʀ, tʀis/ ▶374 *nm,f* conjuror.

prestidigitation /pʀɛstidiʒitasjɔ̃/ *nf* conjuring.

prestige /pʀɛstiʒ/ *nm* prestige; **être sensible au ~ de l'uniforme** to be susceptible to the glamour of a uniform; **de ~** [*réalisation, voiture*] prestige.

prestigieux, -ieuse /pʀɛstiʒjø, øz/ *adj* prestigious.

présumer /pʀezyme/ [1] **I** *vtr* to presume, to assume; **le père présumé** the putative father; **le présumé coupable/terroriste** the alleged culprit/terrorist.
II présumer de *vtr ind* (**trop**) **~ de ses forces** to overestimate one's strength.

présupposer /pʀesypoze/ [1] *vtr* to presuppose.

présure /pʀezyʀ/ *nf* rennet.

prêt, ~e /pʀɛ, pʀɛt/ **I** *adj* **1** (préparé) ready; **être fin ~** [*personne*] to be all set; **2** (disposé) **être ~ à faire** to be ready ou prepared to do; **il est ~ à tout pour atteindre son but** he will stop at nothing ou he will do anything to get what he wants.
II *nm* **1** (action) lending; **le service de ~ de la bibliothèque** the library loans service; **2** (somme) loan; MIL soldier's pay.

prêt-à-porter /pʀɛtapɔʀte/ *nm* ready-to-wear, ready-to-wear clothes (*pl*); **acheter du ~** to buy clothes off the peg GB ou rack US.

prétendant, ~e /pʀetɑ̃dɑ̃, ɑ̃t/ **I** *nm,f* **1** (à un titre, poste) candidate (à for); **2** (royal) pretender.
II *nm* (soupirant) suitor.

prétendre /pʀetɑ̃dʀ/ [6] **I** *vtr* to claim; **à ce qu'il prétend** according to him; **on le prétend très spirituel** he is said to be very witty; **il ne prétend pas rivaliser avec les favoris** he does not expect to keep up with the favourites GB.
II prétendre à *vtr ind* **~ à des indemnités** to claim damages; **~ à un poste** to aspire to a job.
III se prétendre *vpr* **elle se prétend offensée** she claims she is offended; **il se prétend artiste** he makes out he is an artist.

prétendu, ~e /pʀetɑ̃dy/ *adj* [*coupable, terroriste*] alleged; [*démocratie, égalité, crise*] alleged, so-called; [*médecin, policier, expert, artiste*] would-be.

prétendument /pʀetɑ̃dymɑ̃/ *adv* supposedly, allegedly.

prête-nom, pl ~s /pʀɛtnɔ̃/ *nm* (personne) frontman, man of straw; **société ~** dummy ou fronting US company.

prétentieux, -ieuse /pʀetɑ̃sjø, øz/ **I** *adj* pretentious.
II *nm,f* pretentious person; **petit ~** pretentious twit.

prétention /pʀetɑ̃sjɔ̃/ **I** *nf* **1** (vanité) pretentiousness, conceit; **être plein de ~** to be very pretentious ou conceited; **être sans ~** to be unpretentious ou unassuming; **2** (revendication) claim; **avoir des ~s sur** or **à qch** to have a claim to sth; **3** (présomption) **avoir une ~ à l'élégance** to have pretentions to elegance; **avoir la ~ de faire** to claim to do.
II prétentions *nfpl* (salaire demandé) **quelles sont vos ~s?** what salary are you asking for?

prêter /pʀɛte/ [1] **I** *vtr* **1** (fournir un bien matériel) to lend [*argent, objet*]; **~ sur gages** to loan against security; **2** (accorder) **~ son assistance à qn** to give ou lend sb one's assistance; **~ attention à** to pay attention to; **~ la main à qn** to lend sb a hand; **~ l'oreille** to listen, to lend an ear HUM; **~ serment** to take an oath; **~ son nom à** to lend one's name to, to allow one's name to be used by; **si Dieu me prête vie** if God spares me; **3** (attribuer) **~ à qn** to attribute ou ascribe [sth] to sb; **les intentions que l'on prête au président** the president's supposed intentions; **on me prête des propos que je n'ai jamais tenus** I'm credited with remarks I never made.
II prêter à *vtr ind* **~ à** to give rise to, to cause; **sujet qui prête à l'inquiétude** issue which is cause for concern; **son attitude prête à rire** his/her attitude is laughable ou ridiculous; **tout prête à croire** or **penser que** all the indications would suggest that.
III se prêter *vpr* **1** (consentir) **se ~ à** to take part

in; **2** (convenir) **se ~ à** to lend itself to; **3** (se donner) **se ~ assistance** [*personnes*] to assist one another.

prétérit /pʀeteʀit/ *nm* preterite.

prêteur, -euse /pʀɛtœʀ, øz/ I *adj* **il n'est pas ~** he doesn't like lending his things.

II ▶ 374 *nm,f* lender.

■ **~ sur gages** pawnbroker.

prétexte /pʀetɛkst/ *nm* excuse, pretext; **être le ~ de** to be used as an excuse for; **n'ouvrez la porte sous aucun ~** don't open the door on any account.

prétexter /pʀetɛkste/ [1] I *vtr* to use [sth] as an excuse, to plead; **prétextant qu'il était trop vieux/ qu'il faisait froid** using his age/the cold as an excuse; **~ un rendez-vous urgent pour s'éclipser** to plead an urgent engagement in order to get away.

II **prétexter de** *vtr ind* **~ de qch pour faire** to use sth as an excuse for doing.

prétoire /pʀetwaʀ/ *nm* **1** JUR courtroom; **2** (tribunal) praetorium.

prêtre /pʀɛtʀ/ *nm* priest.

prêtresse /pʀɛtʀɛs/ *nf* priestess.

prêtrise /pʀetʀiz/ *nf* priesthood.

preuve /pʀœv/ *nf* **1** (argument) proof ¢; **une ~** a piece of evidence; **donner la ~ que** to prove that; **faire ses ~s** [*personne*] to prove oneself; [*chose*] to prove itself; **jusqu'à ~ du contraire** until proved otherwise; **il doit être malade, la ~, c'est qu'il n'a pas mangé** he must be ill, the fact that he has not eaten proves it; **2** (expression) demonstration; **~ d'amour** demonstration of love; **faire ~ de** to show; **~ de bonne volonté (de la part de)** goodwill gesture (from).

prévaloir /pʀevalwaʀ/ [45] I *vi* to prevail; **faire ~ son point de vue** to gain acceptance for one's point of view.

II **se prévaloir** *vpr* **1** (se fonder) **se ~ d'un règlement/précédent** to cite a rule/precedent (**auprès de** to; **pour faire** as grounds for doing); **se ~ de son ancienneté** to claim seniority (**pour faire** as grounds for doing); **2** (tirer vanité) **se ~ de** to boast [*succès, expérience, diplômes*].

prévenance /pʀevnɑ̃s/ *nf* consideration.

prévenant, -e /pʀevnɑ̃, ɑ̃t/ *adj* considerate.

prévenir /pʀevniʀ/ [36] *vtr* **1** (informer) to tell; **que** that); **partir sans ~** to leave without telling anybody; **2** (téléphoner à) to call [*médecin, police*]; **3** (donner un avertissement) to warn; **je vous aurai prévenu!** I have warned you!; **4** (éviter) to prevent [*catastrophe, maladie*]; **5** (aller au devant de) to anticipate [*désir*].

IDIOMES **mieux vaut ~ que guérir** PROV prevention is better than cure PROV.

préventif, -ive /pʀevɑ̃tif, iv/ *adj* preventive.

prévention /pʀevɑ̃sjɔ̃/ *nf* **1** (action préventive) prevention; **faire de la ~** to take preventive action; **2** (préjugé) FML prejudice (**contre** against); **3** JUR (détention préventive) detention on suspicion; (temps de détention préventive) detention.

préventivement /pʀevɑ̃tivmɑ̃/ *adv* as a precautionary measure; **agir ~** to take preventive action.

prévenu, -e /pʀevny/ I *adj* JUR **~ de** accused of.

II *nm,f* JUR defendant.

prévisible /pʀevizibl/ *adj* predictable; **un accident difficilement ~** an accident which could hardly have been foreseen.

prévision /pʀevizjɔ̃/ *nf* **1** (action de prévoir) forecasting; **faire des ~s** to make forecasts; **en ~ de** in anticipation of; **2** (ce qu'on prévoit) GÉN prediction; ÉCON, FIN forecast; **les résultats vont au-delà de toutes nos ~s** the results go beyond all our expectations; **~s météorologiques** weather forecast (*sg*).

prévisionnel, -elle /pʀevizjɔnɛl/ *adj* projected.

prévoir /pʀevwaʀ/ [42] *vtr* **1** (annoncer comme probable) to predict [*changement, arrivée, inflation*]; to foresee [*échec, victoire*]; to anticipate [*conséquence*]; to forecast [*résultat, temps*]; **c'était à ~!** that was predictable!; **2** JUR (envisager) [*loi*] to make provision for, to provide

for; [*législateur*] to make provision for, to allow for; **les cas prévus par la loi** cases provided for by the law; **3** (fixer dans le temps) to plan [*réunion*]; to set the date for [*déménagement*]; **rendez-vous comme prévu le 17** meeting on the 17th as planned ou arranged; **4** (planifier) [*concepteur*] to plan; [*propriétaire, client*] to plan to have [*pièce*]; **nous devons ~ une salle de conférence** we must make provision for a conference room; **ce n'était pas prévu!** that wasn't meant to happen!; **rien n'est prévu pour l'année prochaine** there's no plan for next year; **je dois ~ un repas pour 30 personnes** I have to organize a meal for 30 people; **un plan de réorganisation prévoyant 500 suppressions d'emploi** a reorganization plan which entails the projected loss of 500 jobs; **remplissez le formulaire prévu à cet effet** fill in the appropriate form; **tout a été prévu pour qch/pour faire** all the arrangements have been made for sth/to do; **la salle a été prévue pour 100 personnes** the room has been designed for 100 people; **5** (se munir de) to make sure one takes [*vêtement, parapluie*]; **~ le repas de midi** to bring a packed lunch; **6** (s'attendre à) to expect [*personne*]; to expect, to anticipate [*postes d'emploi, pénurie, grève*]; **7** (allouer) to allow [*argent, temps*].

prévoyance /pʀevwajɑ̃s/ *nf* foresight.

prévoyant, -e /pʀevwajɑ̃, ɑ̃t/ *adj* far-sighted.

prier /pʀije/ [2] I *vtr* **1** (demander à) **~ qn de faire** to ask sb to do; **je vous prie d'excuser mon retard** I'm so sorry I'm late; **je vous prie de vous taire** will you kindly be quiet; **vous êtes priés de vous abstenir de fumer** you are kindly requested to refrain from smoking; **vous êtes prié d'assister à l'inauguration** you are invited to attend the opening; **pouvez-vous me passer le sel, je vous prie?** would you mind passing the salt, please?; **je vous en prie, laissez-nous** please, leave us alone; **'puis-je entrer?'—'je vous en prie'** 'may I come in?'—'please do!'; **je vous en prie, ce n'est rien** don't mention it, it's nothing; **elle ne s'est pas fait ~** she didn't have to be asked twice; **il aime se faire ~** he likes to be coaxed; **il a accepté sans se faire ~** he accepted without hesitation; **2** RELIG to pray to [*Dieu, saint*]; **~ que** to pray that.

II *vi* RELIG to pray; **~ pour qn/qch** to pray for sb/sth; **~ sur la tombe de qn** to pray at sb's grave.

prière /pʀijɛʀ/ *nf* **1** RELIG prayer; **faire sa ~** to say one's prayers; **2** (demande) request; (plus insistant) plea, entreaty; **~ de ne pas fumer** no smoking please.

prieuré /pʀijœʀe/ *nm* (couvent) priory; (église) priory church; (maison du prieur) prior's house, priory.

primaire /pʀimɛʀ/ I *adj* **1** (par opposition à secondaire) primary; **2** (simpliste) [*personne*] limited, of limited outlook (*après n*); [*réaction*] kneejerk○ (*épith*); [*raisonnement, anticommunisme, opinion*] simplistic.

II *nm* **1** SCOL **le ~** primary education; **2** (en géologie) **le ~** the palaeozoic era.

primat /pʀima/ *nm* **1** (archevêque) primate; **2** (primauté) primacy.

primate /pʀimat/ *nm* primate; **les ~s** the primates.

primauté /pʀimote/ *nf* **1** (supériorité de fait) primacy, supremacy (**sur** over); **2** (autorité) primacy.

prime /pʀim/ I *adj* **1** (premier) **de ~ abord** at first, initially; **dans sa ~ jeunesse** in the early days of his/her youth; **la ~ enfance** early childhood; **2** MATH prime; **A~** A prime.

II *nf* **1** (récompense) bonus; **en ~ avec votre abonnement, recevez ce magnifique réveil** as a free gift to new subscribers, we're offering this fabulous alarm clock; **et en ~ il a reçu un coup de pied aux fesses** HUM and, for good measure, he got a kick in the backside; **2** (indemnité) allowance; **3** (subvention) subsidy; **4** (d'assurance) premium; **5** (en escrime) prime.

■ **~ de fin d'année** Christmas bonus; **~ de licenciement** redundancy payment GB, severance pay; **~ de risque** danger money; **~ de transport** transport allowance GB, transportation allowance US.

primer /pʀime/ [1] I *vtr* **1** (l'emporter sur) to take precedence over, to prevail over; **2** (récompenser) to award a prize to [*œuvre, animal*]; **film primé** award-winning film; **ce film a été primé** this film won an award.

II *primer sur* *vtr ind* CONTROV = **primer I 1**.

III *vi* (dominer) **pour moi, c'est la qualité qui prime** what counts for me is quality; **dans ce sorbet, c'est le cassis qui prime** blackcurrant is the dominant flavourᴳᴮ in this sorbet.

primesautier, -ière /pʀimsotje, ɛʀ/ *adj* impulsive.

primeur /pʀimœʀ/ **I** *nf* **1** (nouveauté) **avoir la ~ de qch** (apprendre) to be the first to hear sth; (bénéficier de) to be the first to benefit from sth; **2** COMM **fruits/légumes de ~** new season's fruit/vegetables.

II *primeurs* *nfpl* early fruit and vegetables, early produce ₵; **marchand de ~s** greengrocer (*specializing in early produce*).

primevère /pʀimvɛʀ/ *nf* primrose.

primitif, -ive /pʀimitif, iv/ **I** *adj* **1** (d'origine) [*budget, différence*] initial; [*projet, état*] original; **2** [*société, art*] primitive; **3** (peu évolué, rudimentaire) primitive; **4** (simpliste) [*personne*] primitive; [*raisonnement*] crude; **5** MATH [*fonction*] primitive; **6** LING [*temps*] basic.

II *nm,f* **1†** [*personne*] primitive; **2** (personne fruste) uncouth person.

III *nm* ART **~s italiens** Italian Primitives.

primordial, ~e, *mpl* **-iaux** /pʀimɔʀdjal, o/ *adj* essential, vital.

prince /pʀɛ̃s/ *nm* ▶ **596** prince; **le ~ de la mode** the king of fashion.

■ **le ~ charmant** Prince Charming; **~ héritier** crown prince.

IDIOMES **se montrer bon ~** to be magnanimous.

prince-de-galles /pʀɛ̃sdəgal/ *adj inv* prince-of-wales check.

princesse /pʀɛ̃sɛs/ ▶ **596** *nf* princess.

IDIOMES **aux frais de la ~°** (de l'État) at the taxpayer's expense; (d'une société) at the company's expense; (d'une personne) at sb's expense.

princier, -ière /pʀɛ̃sje, ɛʀ/ *adj* [*titre, goûts, somme*] princely; [*luxe*] dazzling.

principal, ~e¹, *mpl* **-aux** /pʀɛ̃sipal, o/ **I** *adj* **1** (le plus important) [*facteur, danger, souci*] main; [*tâche, objection, autorité*] principal; **c'est l'œuvre ~e de l'auteur** it's the author's major work; **2** (de tête) [*pays, rôle, personnage*] leading; **3** ADMIN [*commissaire, inspecteur*] chief; **4** LING [*proposition*] main.

II *nm* **1** (l'essentiel) **le ~** the main thing; **2** SCOL principal; **3** FIN principal.

principale² /pʀɛ̃sipal/ *nf* **1** LING main clause; **2** SCOL principal.

principalement /pʀɛ̃sipalmɑ̃/ *adv* mainly.

principauté /pʀɛ̃sipote/ *nf* principality.

principe /pʀɛ̃sip/ **I** *nm* **1** (règle) principle; **pour le ~** as a matter of principle; **objection de ~** objection on the grounds of principle; **accord de ~** provisional agreement; **2** (hypothèse) assumption; **partir du ~ que** to work on the assumption that; **3** (concept) principle; **quel est le ~ de la machine à vapeur?** how does a steam engine work?; **les ~s d'une science/d'un art** (rudiments) the rudiments of a science/an art; **4** CHIMIE principle.

II *en principe* *loc adv* **1** (habituellement) as a rule; **2** (en théorie) in theory.

printanier, -ière /pʀɛ̃tanje, ɛʀ/ *adj* [*fleur, soleil*] spring (*épith*); [*temps, tenue, couleur*] springlike.

printemps /pʀɛ̃tɑ̃/ ▶ **542** *nm inv* **1** (saison) spring; **au ~ de la vie** FIG in the springtime of life; **2°** (an) HUM **mes 60 ~** my 60 summers.

priori ▶ **a priori**.

prioritaire /pʀijɔʀitɛʀ/ *adj* **1** [*dossier, projet*] priority (*épith*); **être ~** to have priority; **2** [*voiture, chauffeur*] with right GB ou the right US of way (*épith, après n*); **être ~, être sur une route ~** to have right GB ou the right US of way.

priorité /pʀijɔʀite/ *nf* **1** (importance) priority; **en ~** (avant le reste) first; (par-dessus tout) first and fore-

most; **nous nous en occuperons en ~** we'll make it a priority; **2** (fait plus important) priority; **être la ~ numéro un** to be the top priority; **3** (en voiture) priority, right of way; **laisser/refuser la ~ à un véhicule** to give way/to refuse to give way to a vehicle.

pris, ~e¹ /pʀi, pʀiz/ **I** *pp* ▶ **prendre**.

II *pp adj* **1** (occupé) busy; **je suis ~** (pour l'instant) I'm busy; (pour la période qui vient) I've got something on; **j'ai les mains ~es** I've got my hands full; **les places sont toutes ~es** all the seats are taken; **2** (gelé) frozen; (encombré) [*nez*] stuffed up; [*bronches*] congested; **j'ai la gorge ~e** I'm hoarse; **4** (affecté) **~ de** overcome with; **~ de panique** panic-stricken; **être ~ de nausées** to feel sick GB ou nauseous US.

prise² /pʀiz/ *nf* **1** (assaut) storming; **2** (à la chasse, pêche) catching ₵; **une belle ~** a fine catch; **3** SPORT (au judo, catch) hold; **4** (point permettant de saisir) hold; **n'offrir aucune ~** (pour la main) to have no handholds; (pour le pied) to have no footholds; **avoir ~ sur qn** to have a hold over sb; **avoir ~ sur qch** to have leverage on sth; **donner** ou **laisser ~ à** [*personne*] to lay oneself open to; **être en ~ avec qch** [*personne*] to be in touch with sth; **5** (absorption) **la ~ d'alcool est déconseillée pendant le traitement** do not take alcohol during the course of treatment; **6** ÉLECTROTECH (femelle) socket GB, outlet US; (mâle) plug; **~ à deux fiches** two-pin plug; **~ multiple** (domino) (multiplug) adaptor; (sur une rallonge) trailing socket; **7** (en électronique) (femelle) jack; (mâle) plug.

■ **~ de bec°** row, argument; **~ en charge** (de frais) payment; **assurer la ~ en charge des frais de qn** to cover sb's expenses; **~ en compte** consideration (**de** of); **~ de conscience** realization; **~ de contact** initial contact; **~ de courant** (femelle) socket GB, outlet US; **~ de décision** decision-making ₵; **~ d'eau** water supply point; **~ d'otages** hostage-taking ₵; **~ de pouvoir** takeover; **~ de position** stand; **~ de sang** blood test; **faire une ~ de sang à qn** to take a blood sample from sb; **~ de vue** CIN, VIDÉO shooting ₵; PHOT shot.

IDIOMES **être aux ~s avec des difficultés** to be grappling with difficulties.

priser /pʀize/ **[1]** *vtr* **1** (apprécier) LITER to hold [sth] in esteem; **il prise fort/peu ce genre de divertissement** this kind of entertainment is very much/is not to his taste; **chanteur très prisé du public** singer very popular with the public; **2** (aspirer par le nez) to snort [*drogue*]; **~ (du tabac)** to take snuff.

prisme /pʀism/ *nm* prism.

prison /pʀizɔ̃/ *nf* LIT, FIG prison; **elle a fait de la ~** she has been in prison; **condamné à trois ans de ~** sentenced to three years' imprisonment.

prisonnier, -ière /pʀizɔnje, ɛʀ/ **I** *adj* **il est ~** he is a prisoner; **être ~ de** to be held prisoner by [*personne, groupe*]; to be a prisoner of [*éducation, croyance*]; **ma main était prisonnière** my hand was trapped.

II *nm,f* LIT, FIG prisoner.

privatif, -ive /pʀivatif, iv/ *adj* **1** (privé) private; **2** JUR (qui prive) privatory SOUT; **3** LING privative.

privation /pʀivasjɔ̃/ *nf* **1** (suppression) (de droit, liberté) deprivation; (de salaire) suspension; **2** (manque) want, privation SOUT; **s'imposer des ~s** to make sacrifices; **économiser à force de ~s** to scrimp and save.

privatisation /pʀivatizasjɔ̃/ *nf* privatization.

privatiser /pʀivatize/ **[1]** *vtr* to privatize.

privautés /pʀivote/ *nfpl* FML liberties.

privé, ~e /pʀive/ **I** *pp* ▶ **priver**.

II *pp adj* **~ de** deprived of; **un style ~ d'humour** a humourlessᴳᴮ style; **je suis resté ~ de téléphone pendant deux jours** I had to do without a phone for two days; **tu seras ~ de dessert!** you'll go without dessert!

III *adj* **1** (non étatique) private; **2** (non destiné au public) private; **3** (non officiel) unofficial; **à titre ~** unofficially; **4** (personnel) private.

IV *nm* **1** (secteur) ÉCON private sector; **2** SCOL **le ~**

(secteur) private schools (pl); **3** (activité) **dans le ~, le maire est directeur d'une société** apart from his official position, the mayor is a company director; **en ~** (seul à seul) in private; (non officiellement) off the record; **4**○ (détective) private eye○, private detective.

priver /pʀive/ [1] **I** vtr **~ qn/qch de** to deprive sb/ sth of; **~ qn de sorties** to forbid sb to go out; **son attaque l'a privée de l'usage d'un bras** she lost the use of an arm after her stroke; **l'orage nous a privés d'électricité** we had no electricity because of the thunderstorm.

II se priver vpr **1** (s'abstenir) **se ~ pour ses enfants** to go without for the sake of one's children; **pourquoi se ~?** why deprive ourselves?; **se ~ de qch/de faire** to go ou do without sth/doing; **c'est gratuit, j'aurais tort de m'en ~!** it's free, I'd be a fool not to take it!; **elle ne se privera pas du plaisir de le raconter à tout le monde** she will enjoy telling everyone about it; **elle ne s'est pas privée de leur dire les choses en face** she didn't hesitate to tell them a few home truths; **2** (se défaire) **se ~ de** to do without [personne]; to dispense with [services].

privilège /pʀivilɛʒ/ nm privilege; **j'ai le triste ~ de** it is my sad duty to.

privilégié, ~e /pʀivileʒje/ **I** adj **1** (avantagé) privileged; **être ~ par le sort** to be blessed by fortune; **2** (chanceux) fortunate; **3** (exceptionnel) [moment, liens] special; [traitement] preferential; [position, conditions de travail] privileged; **4** (préféré) [cible] preferred.

II nm,f (favorisé) **un ~** a privileged person; **les ~s** the privileged.

privilégier /pʀivileʒje/ [2] vtr **1** (favoriser) to favour^GB; **2** (donner priorité à) to give priority to.

prix /pʀi/ nm inv **1** ÉCON, FIG price; **~ de revient** cost price; **c'est à quel ~?** how much is it?; **ton ~ sera le mien** name your price; **c'est mon dernier ~** that's my final offer; **un ~ d'ami** a special price○; **qu'il soit d'accord ou pas, c'est le même ~○!** FIG it doesn't matter whether he agrees or not!; **trouver qch dans ses ~** (fourchette de prix) to find sth within one's price range; (dans ses moyens) to find sth one can afford; **acheter une maison au ~ fort** to pay the top price for a house; **hors de ~** extremely expensive; **cela n'a pas de ~** it's priceless; **acheter qch à ~ d'or** to pay a small fortune for sth; **y mettre le ~** to pay for it; **mettre qch à ~ à 50 francs** [commissaire-priseur] to start the bidding for sth at 50 francs; **mettre à ~ la tête de qn** to put a price on sb's head; **à tout ~** at all costs; **au ~ de nombreux sacrifices** by making many sacrifices; **son amitié n'a pas de ~ pour moi** his/her friendship is very precious to me; **j'attache beaucoup de ~ à son amitié** I value his/her friendship highly ou greatly; **2** (honneur, récompense) prize; **obtenir le premier ~ d'interprétation** to get the award for best actor; **~ Nobel** (récompense) Nobel prize; (personne) Nobel prizewinner; **3** (course hippique) race.

pro(-) /pʀo/ préf pro(-); **~-européen** pro-European.

probabilité /pʀobabilite/ nf **1** (d'événement, accident) probability, likelihood; **2** MATH probability ₵; **les ~s** probability theory (sg).

probable /pʀobabl/ adj **1** (vraisemblable) probable, likely; **c'est peu ~** it's unlikely; **il est ~ qu'il viendra** he'll probably come; **2** (prévisible) likely.

probablement /pʀobabləmɑ̃/ adv probably.

probant, ~e /pʀobɑ̃, ɑ̃t/ adj [argument, démonstration] convincing; [force, preuve] conclusive.

probation /pʀobasjɔ̃/ nf JUR, RELIG probation.

probatoire /pʀobatwaʀ/ adj **examen ~** assessment test; **épreuve ~** aptitude test; **stage ~** probation period; **délai ~** JUR probation.

probité /pʀobite/ nf integrity, probity.

problématique /pʀoblematik/ **I** adj [situation] problematic; [issue, dénouement] uncertain.

II nf problems (pl).

problème /pʀoblɛm/ nm (difficulté) problem; (sujet)

issue; **ça pose un ~** it is a problem; **~ mora**[l] moral issue; **peau à ~s** problem skin.

procédé /pʀosede/ nm **1** (méthode) process; **2** (manière d'agir) practice^GB; **échange de bons ~s** exchange o[f] courtesies; **3** LITTÉRAT device.

procéder /pʀosede/ [14] **I procéder à** vtr ind (se [livrer]) **~ à** to carry out [analyse, vérification[,] sondage]; to undertake [réforme, création d'emplois]; **~ à un tirage au sort/un vote** to hold a draw/a vote; **~ à l'arrestation de qn** to arrest sb.

II procéder de vtr ind **~ de** to be a product of.

III vi (agir) to go about things; **comment allez-vous ~?** how are you going to go about it?; **~ par éli**[mination] to use a process of elimination.

procédure /pʀosedyʀ/ nf **1** (action judiciaire) proceed[ings] (pl); **2** (méthode) procedure.

procédurier, -ière /pʀosedyʀje, ɛʀ/ PEJ **I** adj [per[sonne]] litigious.

II nm,f litigious person.

procès /pʀosɛ/ nm inv **1** JUR (pénal) trial; (civil[)] lawsuit, case; **intenter un ~ à qn** to take sb to court[,] to sue sb; **2** (critique) indictment; **faire le ~ de qch**[,] **qn** to put sth/sb in the dock; **faire un mauvais ~ [à]** **qn** to accuse sb unjustly; **faire un ~ d'intention [à]** **qn** to judge sb on mere intent; **3** LING process.

IDIOMES **sans autre forme de ~** without furthe[r] ado.

processeur /pʀosesœʀ/ nm ORDINAT processor.

procession /pʀosesjɔ̃/ nf **1** (file) procession; **2** (défilé) FIG stream; **3** RELIG procession.

processus /pʀosesys/ nm inv **1** GÉN process; **2** MÉD (évo[lution]) evolution.

procès-verbal, pl **-aux** /pʀosevɛʀbal, o/ nm **1** (de[réunion) minutes (pl); **2** JUR statement of offence^GB; **3** (amende) CONTROV fine; **avoir un ~** to get a ticket.

prochain, ~e /pʀoʃɛ̃, ɛn/ **I** adj **1** (suivant) next; **ce[sera pour une ~e fois** some other time, then!; **à la ~e○!** see you○!; **2** (imminent) [publication] forth[coming; [réunion] coming, forthcoming; [mort, départ[,] guerre] imminent, impending (épith); **un jour ~** on[e] day soon.

II nm GÉN fellow man; RELIG neighbour^GB.

prochainement /pʀoʃɛnmɑ̃/ adv soon, shortly.

proche /pʀoʃ/ **I** adj **1** (dans l'espace) [bâtiment[,] maison, rue] nearby (épith); **~ de** close to, near; **l[e] plus ~** the nearest; **assez ~** not far away; **le[s] bureaux sont très ~s les uns des autres** the desk[s] are very close together; **2** (dans le futur) [événement[]] imminent; **la victoire est ~** victory is at hand; **la fi[n] est ~** the end is (drawing) near; **3** (récent) [événe[ment] recent; [souvenir] real, vivid; **4** (voisin) GÉN simi[lar; [langues] closely related; **~ de** [chiffre, langue[]] close to; [idée, conclusion, parti] similar to; [attitude[]] verging on; **5** (sur le plan affectif) [personnes] close (de[to); ADMIN (sur un formulaire) (plus) **~ parent** next o[f] kin.

II de proche en proche loc adv little by little[,] gradually.

III nm (parent) close relative; (ami) close friend; (collè[gue, associé) close associate; **un ~ du président [a]** close aide to the president; **mes ~s** my nearest an[d] dearest.

Proche-Orient /pʀoʃoʀjɑ̃/ ►509 nprm **le ~** th[e] Near East.

proclamation /pʀoklamasjɔ̃/ nf proclamation.

proclamer /pʀoklame/ [1] vtr **1** (reconnaître officielle[ment) to proclaim; **2** (annoncer) to declare [confianc[e] intention, conviction]; to proclaim [innocence].

procréation /pʀokʀeasjɔ̃/ nf procreation.

procréer /pʀokʀee/ [11] vi to procreate.

procuration /pʀokyʀasjɔ̃/ nf **1** (pouvoir) power o[f] attorney; (pour une élection) proxy; **par ~** [voter] b[y] proxy; [vivre] vicariously; **2** (formulaire) power o[f] attorney; (pour une élection) proxy form.

procurer /pʀokyʀe/ [1] vtr **1** (apporter) to brin[g] [plaisir, sensation]; to give [argent, avantages]; **2** (fair[e] obtenir) [personne] **~ qch à qn** to get sb sth.

II se procurer *vpr* (obtenir) to obtain; (acheter) to buy.

procureur /prɔkyrœr/ ▶374⌋ *nm* prosecutor.

prodigalité /prɔdigalite/ *nf* **1** (trait de caractère) extravagance; **2** (abondance) LITER abundance (**de** of); **3** (dépenses) extravagance.

prodige /prɔdiʒ/ *nm* **1** (génie) prodigy; **guitariste ~** guitar prodigy; **2** (exploit) feat; **faire des ~s** to work wonders; **~ technique** technical miracle.

prodigieux, -ieuse /prɔdiʒjø, øz/ *adj* [*intelligence, mémoire, quantité*] prodigious; [*personne*] wonderful.

prodigue /prɔdig/ *adj* **1** (gaspilleur) extravagant; **2** (libéral) **être ~ de compliments/de son argent** to be lavish with one's praise/one's money; **être ~ de son temps/ses efforts** to be generous with one's time/one's efforts; **3** RELIG **le fils ~** the prodigal son.

prodiguer /prɔdige/ [1] *vtr* **1** (distribuer sans compter) to lavish [*affection, soins*]; to make lots of [*promesses*]; to give lots of [*conseils, encouragements*]; **malgré les efforts prodigués par l'équipe** despite the team's heroic efforts; **2** (donner) to give [*soins*].

producteur, -trice /prɔdyktœr, tris/ **I** *adj* **région productrice de thé/café** tea/coffee-growing area; **pays ~ de pétrole** oil-producing country.

II *nm,f* **1** ÉCON (de matériel, pétrole, d'objet) producer; (de café, coton) grower, producer; **2** ▶374⌋ CIN, TV (personne) producer; (société) production company.

productif, -ive /prɔdyktif, iv/ **I** *adj* [*travail, réunion, journée*] productive; [*investissement, capital*] profitable.

II *nm* **les ~s** people working in production.

production /prɔdyksjɔ̃/ *nf* **1** (fait de produire) (de produit) production; (d'énergie) generation; **la ~ du nouveau modèle débutera le mois prochain** the new model will go into production next month; **arrêter la ~ d'un modèle** to stop producing a model; **2** (produits) GÉN products (*pl*), goods (*pl*); (produits agricoles) produce ⊄; **3** (quantités produites) (de produits agricoles, matières premières) production; (de produits manufacturés, d'énergie) output, production; **4** (dans une entreprise) (**service de**) **la ~** production; **5** CIN, TV (processus, film) production; **6** (d'auteur) (ouvrage) work; (ensemble de l'œuvre) works (*pl*); **7** (présentation) presentation.

■ **~ assistée par ordinateur, PAO** computer-aided manufacturing, CAM.

productivité /prɔdyktivite/ *nf* productivity.

produire /prɔdɥir/ [69] **I** *vtr* **1** (fabriquer) to produce; **cette usine produit peu** this factory has a low output; **2** (cultiver) to produce, to grow [*céréales, café, coton*]; (donner) [*arbre, terre*] to yield; [*région, pays*] to produce; **3** (causer, provoquer) to produce, to have [*effet, résultat*]; to produce, to bring about [*changement*]; to create, to make [*impression*]; to cause, to create [*sensation, émotion*]; **4** (réaliser, créer) to produce; **un artiste/écrivain qui produit beaucoup** a prolific artist/writer; **5** FIN (rapporter) to bring in [*argent, richesse*]; to yield [*intérêt*]; **6** (montrer) to produce [*certificat*].

II se produire *vpr* **1** (survenir) [*catastrophe, changement*] to occur, to happen; **2** (donner un spectacle) [*groupe, chanteur*] to perform.

produit /prɔdɥi/ *nm* **1** (article) product; **des ~s** GÉN goods, products; AGRIC produce ⊄; **~s alimentaires** foodstuffs; **~s agricoles** agricultural ou farm produce ⊄; **2** FIN (revenu) income; (d'investissement) yield, return; (bénéfice) profit; **vivre du ~ de sa terre** to live off the land; **le ~ de la vente** the proceeds (*pl*) of the sale; **3** (résultat) (de recherche) result; (d'activité, état, de hasard) product; **c'est le ~ de ton imagination** it's a figment of your imagination; **c'est un pur ~ des médias** he's/she's a media creation; **4** BIOL, CHIMIE, PHYS product; **5** MATH product.

■ **~ de base** (aliment) staple food; **~ chimique** chemical; **~ d'entretien** cleaning product, household product; **~ intérieur brut, PIB** gross domestic product, GDP; **~ national brut, PNB** gross national product, GNP.

proéminent, ~e /prɔeminɑ̃, ɑ̃t/ *adj* prominent.

profanateur, -trice /prɔfanatœr, tris/ *nm,f* profaner.

profanation /prɔfanasjɔ̃/ *nf* (de temple, tombe) desecration; (de sentiment, mémoire, beauté) defilement; (de famille, d'institution) debasement.

profane /prɔfan/ **I** *adj* **1** (non religieux) secular; **2** (non initié) **être ~ en la matière** to know nothing about the subject.

II *nmf* **1** (non-initié) layman/laywoman; **2** RELIG nonbeliever.

III *nm* **le ~ et le sacré** the sacred and the profane.

profaner /prɔfane/ [1] *vtr* to desecrate [*temple, tombe*]; to defile [*mémoire, nom, beauté*]; to debase [*institution*].

proférer /prɔfere/ [14] *vtr* to hurl [*insultes, obscénités*]; to make [*menaces*] (**contre** against).

professer /prɔfese/ [1] *vtr* (déclarer) to declare [*admiration, amour*]; to profess [*théorie, idée*].

professeur /prɔfesœr/ ▶374⌋ *nm* **1** (enseignant) (de collège, lycée) teacher; (dans l'enseignement supérieur) lecturer GB, professor US; (titulaire d'une chaire) professor; **le ~ remplaçant** the supply GB ou substitute US teacher; **2** ▶596⌋ UNIV (titre) professor.

profession /prɔfesjɔ̃/ *nf* **1** (métier) occupation; **exercer la ~ d'infirmière** to be a nurse by profession; **être sans ~** GÉN to have no occupation; [*femme au foyer*] to be a housewife; **2** (corporation) profession; **3** (déclaration) declaration, profession; **faire ~ de libéralisme** to profess one's liberalism.

■ **~ libérale** profession.

professionnalisme /prɔfesjɔnalism/ *nm* (qualité) professionalism.

professionnel, -elle /prɔfesjɔnel/ **I** *adj* **1** (relatif au métier) GÉN professional; [*vie, milieu*] working (*épith*), professional; [*maladie*] occupational; [*enseignement, formation*] vocational; [*exposition, salon*] trade; **revendications professionnelles** workers' demands; **l'avenir ~** career prospects (*pl*); **activité professionnelle** occupation; **en dehors de mes activités professionnelles** outside my work; **il s'occupe de leur réinsertion professionnelle** he's responsible for finding them jobs; **local à usage ~** business premises (*pl*); **2** (non amateur) professional; **acteur/sportif non ~** amateur actor/sportsman.

II *nm,f* **1** (spécialiste d'un métier) professional; **le salon est réservé aux ~s** the fair is restricted to people in the trade; **un ~ du cinéma** a professional film-maker; **un ~ du bâtiment** a person working in the building trade; **2** (non-amateur) professional.

professionnellement /prɔfesjɔnelmɑ̃/ *adv* professionally.

professoral, ~e, *mpl* **-aux** /prɔfesɔral, o/ *adj* (dogmatique) professorial; (relatif aux professeurs) **le corps ~** the teaching profession.

profil /prɔfil/ *nm* **1** (contour, coupe) profile; **se mettre de ~** to turn sideways; **2** (qualifications) '**~ exigé**' 'qualifications required'; **avoir un ~ de gestionnaire** to have the right profile for a manager; **3** PSYCH profile.

profiler /prɔfile/ [1] **I** *vtr* (présenter) **la tour profile sa silhouette dans le ciel** the tower is silhouetted ou outlined against the sky.

II se profiler *vpr* [*forme*] to stand out (**contre, sur** against); [*candidat, problème*] to emerge; [*événements*] to approach.

profit /prɔfi/ *nm* **1** (avantage) benefit, advantage; **faire qch avec ~** to benefit from doing sth; **vous consulterez ce guide avec ~** you'll find this guide very useful; **tirer ~ de** to make the most of, to take advantage of; **faire du ~°** [*nourriture*] to go a long way; [*objet, appareil*] to be good value; **ce manteau m'a fait du ~°** I've had a lot of wear out of this coat; **concert au ~ des handicapés** concert in aid of the handicapped; **espionnage au ~ d'une puissance étrangère** spying for a foreign country; **la réforme s'est faite au ~ des grands propriétaires** the reform benefited land owners; **abandonner le**

charbon au ~ du nucléaire to drop coal in favour^{GB} of nuclear energy; **perdre des voix au ~ de** to lose votes to; **mettre à ~** to make the most of [*temps libre, stage*]; to turn [sth] to good account [*situation*]; to make good use of [*idée, résultat*]; **2** (gains) profit; **faire des ~s** to make a profit; **être une source de ~ pour** to be a source of wealth for.

IDIOMES **il n'y a pas de petits ~s** PROV look after the pennies and the pounds will look after themselves PROV GB, a dollar is a dollar US.

profitable /pʀɔfitabl/ adj (utile) beneficial (à to); **leur départ n'est ~ à personne** their leaving doesn't make things better for anybody.

profiter /pʀɔfite/ [1] **I profiter à** vtr ind (être utile) **~ à qn** to benefit sb; **ça profite toujours aux mêmes** it's always the same people who reap the benefit; **à qui profite le crime?** who benefits by ou from the crime?

II profiter de vtr ind **~ de** to use [*avantage*]; to make the most of [*situation*]; to take advantage of [*faiblesse, vente, personne*]; **profite bien de tes vacances!** have a good holiday!; **j'ai profité de ce qu'il était là pour lui demander de m'aider** since he was there I took the opportunity of asking him to help me; **il a profité de ce que je ne regardais pas** he took advantage of the fact that I was not looking; **~ de l'obscurité pour s'enfuir** to flee under cover of darkness; **les enfants ont profité de leurs vacances** the children got a lot out of their holidays GB ou vacation US.

III⊘ vi [*personne, animal*] to grow; [*plante*] to thrive.

profiteur, -euse /pʀɔfitœʀ, øz/ nm,f profiteer.

profond, ~e /pʀɔfɔ̃, 3d/ **I** adj **1** ▸348┃ (haut) deep; **peu ~** shallow; **au plus ~ de** in the depths of; **2** (intense) [*joie, désespoir*] overwhelming; [*ennui*] acute; [*soupir*] heavy; [*sentiment, sommeil*] deep; [*bleu*] deep; **3** (très grand) [*changement, désaccord*] profound; [*intérêt*] keen; [*mépris, ignorance*] profound; [*silence*] deep; **4** (pénétrant) [*esprit, remarque*] profound; [*regard*] penetrating; **5** (provincial) **la France ~e** provincial France; **l'Amérique ~e** small-town America.

II adv deeply, deep down; **creuser ~** to dig deeply.

profondément /pʀɔfɔ̃demã/ adv **1** (loin) [*creuser, s'enfoncer*] deeply; **2** (intensément) [*dormir, respirer, éprouver, aimer*] deeply; [*souffrir*] greatly; [*détester*] utterly; [*marqué, affecté*] profoundly; [*choqué, convaincu*] deeply; **s'ennuyer ~** to be profoundly bored.

profondeur /pʀɔfɔ̃dœʀ/ **I** nf **1** ▸348┃ (de mer, trou, d'armoire, étagères) depth; **avoir une ~ de 3 mètres** to be 3 metres deep; **creuser à 2 mètres de ~** to dig 2 metres down; **2** (de sentiment, d'amour) depth; (de remarque, d'œuvre) profundity; **en ~** [*analyse, réforme*] in-depth (épith); **travail en ~** thorough work.

II profondeurs nfpl (de mer, forêt) LITER depths.

profusion /pʀɔfyzjɔ̃/ nf (de détails, couleurs) profusion; (de nourriture, boisson) abundance; **à ~** in abundance.

progéniture /pʀɔʒenityʀ/ nf progeny.

programmateur, -trice /pʀɔgʀamatœʀ, tʀis/ **I** ▸374┃ nm,f RADIO, TV programme^{GB} planner.

II nm (mécanique) timer.

programmation /pʀɔgʀamasjɔ̃/ nf programming.

programme /pʀɔgʀam/ nm **1** CIN, RADIO, THÉÂT, TV programme^{GB}; **ce n'est pas au ~** LIT it's not on the programme^{GB}; FIG that wasn't planned; **changement de ~** LIT change in the programme^{GB}; FIG change of plan; **2** (emploi du temps) programme^{GB}; **quel est le ~ des réjouissances aujourd'hui?** HUM what delights are in store (for us) today?; **3** (projet) (d'action) plan; (de travail) programme^{GB}; **c'est tout un ~!** HUM that'll take some doing!; **4** SCOL, UNIV syllabus; **au ~** on the syllabus; **5** ORDINAT program.

programmer /pʀɔgʀame/ [1] vtr **1** (prévoir) to schedule [*émission*]; to plan [*travail, vacances*]; **2** ORDINAT to program.

programmeur, -euse /pʀɔgʀamœʀ, øz/ ▸374┃ nm,f (computer) programmer.

progrès /pʀɔgʀɛ/ nm inv **1** (pas en avant) progress ¢; **les ~ de la médecine** advances in medicine; **être en ~** [*personne*] to be making progress; [*résultats*] to be improving; **il y a du ~**○! things are improving!; **2** (résultat chiffré) increase; **être en ~ de 10%** to be up by 10%; **3** (concept) **le ~** progress; **on n'arrête pas le ~!** IRON that's progress for you!; **4** (de maladie) progression; (d'homme politique) progress; (d'armée) advance.

progresser /pʀɔgʀese/ [1] vi **1** (atteindre un niveau supérieur) [*taux, résultat, salaires, chômage*] to rise; [*pouvoir d'achat, budget*] to increase; [*économie*] to improve; [*entreprise*] to make progress; [*homme politique*] to make gains; **nos ventes ont bien progressé ce mois-ci** there has been a marked increase in our sales this month; **~ de 3%** [*production*] to rise by 3%; [*candidat, parti*] to gain 3%; **le franc a progressé de 3% par rapport à la lire** the franc has risen by 3% against the lira; **2** (dans son développement) [*relations*] to improve; [*pays, enquête, négociations*] to make progress; [*science*] to progress; [*connaissances*] to increase; **3** (gagner du terrain) [*marcheur*] to make progress; [*armée*] to move forward; **~ de 200 m** to advance 200 m; **~ dans sa carrière** to progress in one's career; **4** (se propager) [*maladie*] to spread; [*idéologie*] to gain ground; [*criminalité, toxicomanie*] to be on the increase; **5** (s'améliorer) to make progress.

progressif, -ive /pʀɔgʀesif, iv/ adj progressive.

progression /pʀɔgʀesjɔ̃/ nf **1** (avancée) (de marcheur, d'alpiniste) progress; (d'ennemi, orage) advance; **2** (propagation) (d'épidémie, idéologie) spread; (de criminalité) increase; **3** (résultats supérieurs) GÉN increase; (de candidat, parti) progress; **être en ~** [*résultat*] to be up; [*tendance*] to be increasing; **en ~ de 10%** up by 10%; **4** MATH, MUS progression.

progressiste /pʀɔgʀesist/ adj, nmf progressive.

progressivement /pʀɔgʀesivmɑ̃/ adv progressively.

prohibé, ~e /pʀɔibe/ adj [*marchandise, substance, arme*] prohibited; [*commerce, action*] illegal; **port d'arme ~** illegal possession of a firearm.

prohiber /pʀɔibe/ [1] vtr to prohibit.

prohibitif, -ive /pʀɔibitif, iv/ adj **1** (excessif) [*prix, taxe*] prohibitive; **2** (qui interdit) prohibition (épith).

prohibition /pʀɔibisjɔ̃/ nf prohibition.

proie /pʀwa/ nf LIT, FIG prey; **il a été la ~ des journaux à scandale** he fell prey to the gutter press; **être la ~ des flammes** to be in flames; **être en ~ à l'angoisse** to be racked by anguish; **pays en ~ à la guerre civile** country in the grip of civil war; **entreprise en ~ à des difficultés insurmontables** company beset by overwhelming difficulties.

projecteur /pʀɔʒɛktœʀ/ nm **1** (pour éclairer) (de DCA, mirador) searchlight; (de stade) floodlight; **être sous les ~s** FIG to be in the spotlight; **2** CIN projector.

projectile /pʀɔʒɛktil/ nm GÉN missile; (balle, obus) projectile.

projection /pʀɔʒɛksjɔ̃/ nf **1** (processus) **~ de cendres** discharge of ashes; **nettoyer qch par ~ de sable** to sandblast sth; **2** (éclaboussures) **le cuisinier a reçu des ~s d'huile bouillante** the cook got spattered with scalding oil; **3** CIN (fait de projeter) projection; (séance) showing; **salle de ~** screening room; **4** MATH, PSYCH projection (**sur** onto).

projectionniste /pʀɔʒɛksjɔnist/ ▸374┃ nmf projectionist.

projet /pʀɔʒɛ/ nm **1** (plan) plan; **en ~, à l'état de ~** at the planning stage, on the drawing board; **j'ai un film en ~** I'm planning a film; **2** (entreprise en cours) project; **3** (esquisse de roman, contrat) (rough) draft.

■ **~ de loi** (government) bill; **~ de réforme** POL reform bill.

projeter /pʀɔʒte/ [20] vtr **1** (lancer) [*véhicule*] to throw [*gravillon*] (**sur** up against); **~ du sable sur des bâtiments pour les nettoyer** to sandblast buildings; **le geyser projetait des gerbes d'eau** the geyser was spouting jets of water; **le choc l'a projeté par terre** the shock sent him hurtling to the ground; **par-dessus bord** the shock sent him hurtling to the ground/overboard; **~ des étincelles** to throw out sparks; **2** (jeter) to cast [*ombre, reflet*] (**sur** on); **3** CIN, PHOT to show [*film, diapositives*] (**sur** onto); **4** (prévoir) to plan; **5** MATH, PSYCH to project (**sur** onto).

prolétaire /pʀɔletɛʀ/ *adj, nmf* proletarian.

prolétariat /pʀɔletaʀja/ *nm* proletariat.

prolétarien, -ienne /pʀɔletaʀjɛ̃, ɛn/ *adj* proletarian.

proliférer /pʀɔlifeʀe/ [14] *vi* to proliferate.

prolifique /pʀɔlifik/ *adj* prolific.

prolixe /pʀɔliks/ *adj* verbose, prolix.

prolo○ /pʀɔlo/ **I** *adj* [*vêtement, style*] modest, cheap and nasty PÉJ; **ça fait ~** that's a bit common.
II *nmf* pleb○, prole.

prologue /pʀɔlɔg/ *nm* prologue.

prolongation /pʀɔlɔ̃gasjɔ̃/ *nf* **1** (de trêve, bataille) continuation; (de congé, spectacle) extension; **2** SPORT extra time; **jouer les ~s** to play ou go into extra time GB, to play overtime US.

prolongé, ~e /pʀɔlɔ̃ʒe/ *adj* [*effort*] sustained; [*arrêt*] lengthy; [*séjour*] extended; [*week-end*] long; [*exposition*] prolonged; **'pas d'utilisation ~e sans avis médical'** 'if symptoms persist, consult your doctor'.

prolongement /pʀɔlɔ̃ʒmɑ̃/ *nm* **1** (agrandissement) extension; **2** (direction) **la rue Berthollet se trouve dans le ~ de la rue de la Glacière** Rue de la Glacière becomes Rue Berthollet; **3** (suite) outcome; **une affaire aux ~s multiples** a case with wide-ranging repercussions.

prolonger /pʀɔlɔ̃ʒe/ [13] **I** *vtr* **1** (faire durer) to extend [*séjour, voyage*]; to prolong [*séance, vie*]; to continue [*traitement*] (**de** for); **2** (agrandir) to extend; **3** (être le prolongement de) to be an extension of.
II se prolonger *vpr* **1** (dans le temps) [*maladie, effet*] to persist; [*situation, réunion*] to go on; **2** (dans l'espace) **se ~ jusqu'à** to go as far as.

promenade /pʀɔmnad/ *nf* **1** (sortie) (à pied) walk; (à cheval, moto, bicyclette) ride; (en voiture) drive; (en bateau) boat-ride; **2** (lieu aménagé) GÉN walkway; (en bord de mer) promenade.

promener /pʀɔmne/ [16] **I** *vtr* **1** (faire sortir) to take [sb] out [*personne*]; **il est sorti ~ le chien** he's taken the dog out for a walk; **nous l'avons promené partout** we took him all over the place; **va chez le boulanger, ça te promènera**○ go to the baker's, it'll get you out; **2** (transporter) to carry; **il promène encore son ours en peluche** he still carries his teddy bear around with him; **~ son regard sur** to cast an eye over.
II se promener *vpr* (à pied) to go for a walk; (en voiture) to go for a drive; (en bateau) to go out in a boat; (à bicyclette, à cheval) to go for a ride; **le dossier s'est promené**○ **dans toute l'usine** the file did the rounds of the factory.

promeneur, -euse /pʀɔmnœʀ, øz/ *nm,f* walker; **quelques ~s attardés se trouvaient encore dans le parc** there were still a few people strolling in the park.

promesse /pʀɔmɛs/ *nf* **1** (engagement) promise; **faire de grandes ~s** to make fine promises; **avoir la ~ de qn** to have sb's word; **2** JUR, COMM **honorer ses ~s** to honour GB one's commitments; **~ de vente** agreement to sell; **3** (espérance) promise; **un magnifique coucher de soleil qui est la ~ de beau temps** a beautiful sunset which promises fine weather to come. ■ **~ en l'air** or **de Gascon** or **d'ivrogne** empty ou idle promise.

prometteur, -euse /pʀɔmɛtœʀ, øz/ *adj* promising.

promettre /pʀɔmɛtʀ/ [60] **I** *vtr* **1** (garantir) **~ qch à qn** to promise sb sth; **je ne (te) promets rien** I can't promise anything; **je te promets qu'il le regrettera** he'll regret it, I guarantee you; **2** (annoncer) **une soirée qui promet bien des surprises** an evening that holds a few surprises in store; **voilà qui nous promet de nombreux débats télévisés** it looks as though we'll be getting a lot of televised debates; **cette**

grève nous promet une belle pagaille this strike is guaranteed to cause chaos.
II *vi* **1** (avoir de l'avenir) to show promise; **un jeune musicien qui promet** a promising young musician; **un film qui promet** a film which sounds interesting; **2**○ (présager des ennuis) IRON **cet enfant promet!** that child is going to be a handful!; **ça promet!** that's going to be fun!; **ça promet pour l'hiver!** winter's got GB ou gotten US off to a good start!
III se promettre *vpr* **1** (à soi-même) to promise oneself; **se ~ du bon temps** to decide to have a bit of fun; **2** (être résolu) **se ~ de faire** to resolve to do; **3** (l'un à l'autre) [*personnes, couple*] **se ~ de faire** to promise each other to do; **ils se sont promis de ne plus se quitter** they (have) vowed never to be parted.
IDIOMES **~ monts et merveilles** or **la lune**○ (**à qn**) to promise (sb) the moon ou the earth.

promiscuité /pʀɔmiskɥite/ *nf* lack of privacy.

promo○ /pʀɔmo/ *nf* COMM (special) offer.

promontoire /pʀɔmɔ̃twaʀ/ *nm* promontory.

promoteur, -trice /pʀɔmɔtœʀ, tʀis/ *nm,f* **1** ▸374 CONSTR **~** (**immobilier**) property developer; **2** (de théorie) instigator; (de mouvement, d'exposition) promoter.

promotion /pʀɔmɔsjɔ̃/ *nf* **1** (avancement) promotion; (personnes promues) promotion list; **2** COMM (special) offer; **en ~** on (special) offer; **3** (développement) promotion; **assurer la ~ de** to promote.

promotionnel, -elle /pʀɔmɔsjɔnɛl/ *adj* promotional; **grande vente promotionnelle** big promotion GB, big sale US; **prix ~** special offer.

promouvoir /pʀɔmuvwaʀ/ [43] *vtr* (faire la promotion de) to promote; (dans la hiérarchie) to promote; (honorifiquement) to elevate.

prompt, ~e /pʀɔ̃, pʀɔ̃t/ *adj* [*réaction, coup d'œil*] swift; [*rétournement, départ*] sudden; **~ rétablissement** speedy recovery; **être ~ à agir** to act swiftly.

promptement /pʀɔ̃təmɑ̃/ *adv* (sans délai) [*expédier, remplacer, licencier*] promptly; [*réagir, intervenir*] swiftly; (vite) [*juger, comprendre*] quickly.

promptitude /pʀɔ̃tityd/ *nf* (de réponse, réaction, geste) swiftness; (de décision) rapidity; (de départ, changement) suddenness; **leur ~ à réagir** their quick reaction.

promulguer /pʀɔmylge/ [1] *vtr* to promulgate.

prôner /pʀone/ [1] *vtr* to advocate, to extol the virtues of.

pronom /pʀɔnɔ̃/ *nm* pronoun.

prononçable /pʀɔnɔ̃sabl/ *adj* pronounceable; **c'est difficilement ~** it's difficult to pronounce.

prononcé, ~e /pʀɔnɔ̃se/ *adj* [*accent, saveur, odeur*] strong; [*rides*] deep; **avoir un goût ~ pour** to be particularly fond of.

prononcer /pʀɔnɔ̃se/ [12] **I** *vtr* **1** (émettre) to pronounce [*mot*]; **mal ~** to mispronounce, to pronounce wrongly; **2** (proférer) to mention [*nom*]; to say [*mot, phrase*]; **3** (dire publiquement) to deliver [*discours*]; **4** JUR (déclarer) to pronounce [*peine de mort*]; to pass [*mesure*]; **~ le divorce** to grant a divorce.
II se prononcer *vpr* **1** (être émis) to be pronounced; **2** (faire connaître un avis) **se ~ contre/en faveur de** or **pour qch** to declare oneself against/in favour GB of sth; **se ~ sur qch** to give one's opinion on sth.

prononciation /pʀɔnɔ̃sjasjɔ̃/ *nf* pronunciation; **la mauvaise ~ du mot 'province'** the mispronunciation of the word 'province'.

pronostic /pʀɔnɔstik/ *nm* **1** (sportif, financier) forecast; **2** (dans un conflit) prediction; **3** (médical) prognosis.

pronostiquer /pʀɔnɔstike/ [1] *vtr* SPORT to forecast [*résultat*]; (prévoir) to herald.

pronostiqueur, -euse /pʀɔnɔstikœʀ, øz/ *nm,f* tipster.

propagande /pʀɔpagɑ̃d/ *nf* propaganda; **faire de la ~ pour** to campaign for [*cause*]; to plug, to push [*produit*].

propagateur, -trice /pʀɔpagatœʀ, tʀis/ *nm,f* proponent.

propagation /prɔpagasjɔ̃/ *nf* GÉN spread; (de son, d'onde) propagation; (d'espèce) propagation.

propager /prɔpaʒe/ [13] **I** *vtr* to spread [*rumeur, haine, maladie*]; to propagate [*espèce*]; PHYS to propagate [*onde, son*].

II se propager *vpr* GÉN to spread; PHYS to propagate.

propane /prɔpan/ *nm* propane.

propension /prɔpɑ̃sjɔ̃/ *nf* propensity.

prophète /prɔfɛt/ *nm* prophet; **~ de malheur** prophet of doom GB, doomsayer US.

IDIOMES **nul n'est ~ en son pays** PROV a prophet is not without honour, save in his own country.

prophétesse /prɔfetɛs/ *nf* prophetess.

prophétie /prɔfesi/ *nf* prophecy.

prophétique /prɔfetik/ *adj* prophetic.

prophétiser /prɔfetize/ [1] *vtr* to prophesy.

propice /prɔpis/ *adj* favourable^GB (à for); **peu ~** rather unfavourable^GB; **trouver le moment ~** to find the right moment.

proportion /prɔpɔrsjɔ̃/ *nf* **1** GÉN proportion; **une ~ de 10 chômeurs pour 35 salariés** 10 unemployed workers for every 35 in work; **dans une ~ de cinq contre un** in a ratio of five to one; **c'est calculé en ~** it is calculated proportionally; **ramener le débat à de plus justes ~s** to put things back in perspective; **cela a pris de telles ~s que** it has become so serious that; **dans des ~s considérables** considerably; **toutes ~s gardées** relatively speaking; **2** ART, ARCHIT proportion.

proportionné, ~e /prɔpɔrsjɔne/ *adj* **bien/mal ~** well-/badly-proportioned.

proportionnel, -elle[1] /prɔpɔrsjɔnɛl/ *adj* proportional.

proportionnelle[2] /prɔpɔrsjɔnɛl/ *nf* POL proportional representation.

proportionnellement /prɔpɔrsjɔnɛlmɑ̃/ *adv* proportionately.

propos /prɔpo/ **I** *nm inv* **1** (sujet) **à ~** by the way; **à ~ de** about; **à quel ~?** what about?; **à ~ de qui?** about who?; **à ~ de rien** about nothing in particular; **à ce ~** in this connection; **2** (moment) **à ~** at the right moment; **mal à ~** at (just) the wrong moment; **à tout ~** constantly.

II *nmpl* (paroles) comments; **'~ recueillis par J. Brun'** 'interview by J. Brun'.

proposer /prɔpoze/ [1] **I** *vtr* **1** (suggérer) to suggest; **2** (offrir) to offer; **'que veux-tu manger?'—'qu'est-ce que tu me proposes?'** 'what would you like to eat?'—'what is there?'; **je te propose de travailler avec nous** why don't you come and work with us?; **3** (soumettre) to put forward [*solution, mesure*]; to propose [*stratégie, projet*]; **~ la candidature de qn** to put sb's name forward as a candidate; **4** (à un examen) to set [*sujet*].

II se proposer *vpr* **1** (être volontaire) **se ~ pour faire** to offer to do; **2** (avoir l'intention) **se ~ de faire** to intend to do.

proposition /prɔpozisjɔ̃/ *nf* **1** (suggestion) suggestion; **2** (offre) proposal; **faire des ~s à qn** EUPH to proposition sb; **sur (la) ~ du maire** at the mayor's instigation; **3** LING clause; **~ principale** main clause.

■ **~ de loi** ≈ bill.

propre /prɔpr/ **I** *adj* **1** (sans souillure) clean; **la menuiserie est plus ~ que la plomberie** carpentry is not such a dirty job as plumbing; **nous voilà ~s!** FIG, IRON we're in a fine mess now!; **2** (soigné, soigneux) tidy, neat; **3** (moral) [*personne, vie*] decent; [*affaire*] honest; **des affaires pas très ~s** unsavoury^GB business (*sg*); **4** (personnel) own; **ce sont tes ~s paroles** (rapport) you said so yourself; (insistance) those were your very words; **5** (spécifique) of one's own; **chaque pays a des lois qui lui sont ~s** each country has its own particular laws; **6** (approprié) [*expression*] right; **7** (continent) [*bébé*] toilet-trained; [*animal*] housetrained GB, housebroken US.

II propre à *loc adj* **1** (spécifique) **~ à** peculiar to; **2** (capable de) **~ à faire** (résultat attendu) likely to do;

(résultat étonnant) liable to do; **mesures ~s à limiter le chômage** measures to curb unemployment; **3** (adapté) **~ à** appropriate for; **~ à la consommation** fit for consumption.

III *nm* **1** (nettoyé) **ça sent le ~** it smells nice and clean; **2** (recopié) **mettre qch au ~** to make a fair copy of sth; **3** (moral) **c'est du ~!** IRON that's very nice!; **4** (spécifique) **être le ~ de** to be peculiar to; **la maison leur appartient en ~** they are the sole owners of the house; **disposer en ~ d'un ordinateur** to have one's own individual computer; **~ à rien** good-for-nothing.

IDIOMES **bon à tout, ~ à rien** PROV Jack of all trades and master of none PROV.

proprement /prɔprəmɑ̃/ *adv* **1** (au sens strict) purely; **à ~ parler** strictly speaking; **~ dit** (sans considérations annexes) as such (*après n*); (au sens restreint) in the strict sense of the word (*après n*); **quant au procès ~ dit** as for the trial itself; **2** (absolument) absolutely; **3** (véritablement) really; **4** (littéralement) literally; **~ irrespirable** literally unbreathable; **5** (spécifiquement) specifically; **6** (comme il faut) **le professeur l'a ~ remis à sa place** he was well and truly put in his place by the teacher; **7** (avec soin) neatly; **travailler ~** to do a neat job; **mange ~!** don't make a mess when you eat!; **8** (honnêtement) [*gagner sa vie*] honestly; [*agir*] honestly.

propreté /prɔprəte/ *nf* **1** (absence de souillure) cleanliness; **d'une ~ douteuse** not very clean; **d'une ~ éblouissante** sparkling clean; **veiller à la ~ d'un bâtiment** to make sure that a building is kept clean; **2** (honnêteté) honesty.

propriétaire /prɔprijetɛr/ *nmf* **1** owner; **un petit ~** a small-scale property owner; **il y a plus de ~s que de locataires** there are more homeowners than tenants; **ils sont ~s de leur maison** they own their own house; **faire le tour du ~** to look round GB ou around US the house; **faire faire le tour du ~ à qn** to show sb round GB ou around US the house; **2** (de propriété louée) landlord/landlady.

propriété /prɔprijete/ *nf* **1** (droit) ownership; **2** (biens possédés) property; **3** (bien immobilier) GÉN property; (domaine) estate, property; (maison) house, property; **4** (caractéristique) property; **5** (exactitude) aptness.

■ **~ artistique et littéraire** intellectual property right, copyright; **~ foncière** landed estate; **~ immobilière** real estate ¢.

propulser /prɔpylse/ [1] *vtr* **1** (faire mouvoir) [*moteur*] to propel; **2**° (promouvoir) to propel; **3**° (déplacer violemment) to hurl [*personne, objet*].

propulseur /prɔpylsœr/ *nm* (moteur) engine.

■ **~ à hélice** propeller; **~ à réaction** jet engine.

propulsion /prɔpylsjɔ̃/ *nf* propulsion; **à ~ nucléaire** nuclear-powered.

prorata /prɔrata/ *nm inv* **au ~ de** in proportion to.

proroger /prɔrɔʒe/ [13] *vtr* (reculer) to defer [*date, échéance*]; (prolonger) to renew [*contrat, passeport*]; to extend [*validité, délai*].

prosaïque /prɔzaik/ *adj* prosaic.

prosaïsme /prɔzaism/ *nm* mundaneness.

prosateur /prɔzatœr/ *nm* prose writer.

proscription /prɔskripsjɔ̃/ *nf* **1** (interdiction) proscription; **2** POL (exil) banishment; **frapper qn de ~** to banish sb.

proscrire /prɔskrir/ [67] *vtr* (interdire) to ban; (bannir) to banish.

proscrit, ~e /prɔskri, it/ *nm,f* outcast.

prose /proz/ *nf* **1** (forme littéraire) prose; **2** (style personnel) HUM distinctive prose.

prosélyte /prɔzelit/ *nmf* proselyte.

prosélytisme /prɔzelitism/ *nm* proselytizing; **faire du ~ politique** to try to convert people to one's politics.

prosodie /prɔzɔdi/ *nf* prosody.

prospecter /prɔspɛkte/ [1] *vtr* **1** (pour vendre) to canvass; **2** (pour trouver) to prospect.

prospecteur, -trice /pʀɔspɛktœʀ, tʀis/ *nm,f* **1** COMM canvasser; **2** (de terrain) prospector; **3** (d'idées) explorer.

prospectif, -ive /pʀɔspɛktif, iv/ *adj* long-term.

prospection /pʀɔspɛksjɔ̃/ *nf* COMM canvassing; IND prospecting.

prospectus /pʀɔspɛktys/ *nm inv* leaflet.

prospère /pʀɔspɛʀ/ *adj* [*société, personne*] thriving; [*année, saison*] prosperous.

prospérer /pʀɔspeʀe/ [14] *vi* to thrive.

prospérité /pʀɔspeʀite/ *nf* prosperity; **en pleine ~** (fortune) prosperous; (santé) in flourishing health.

prostate /pʀɔstat/ *nf* prostate (gland).

prosternation /pʀɔstɛʀnasjɔ̃/ *nf* **1** LIT prostration (**devant** before); **2** FIG self-abasement.

prosterner: se prosterner /pʀɔstɛʀne/ [1] *vpr* **1** LIT to prostrate oneself; **prosterné devant l'autel** prostrate before the altar; **2** FIG to grovel (**devant** to).

prostitué /pʀɔstitɥe/ **▶374** *nm* male prostitute GB, prostitute US.

prostituée /pʀɔstitɥe/ **▶374** *nf* prostitute.

prostituer /pʀɔstitɥe/ [1] **I** *vtr* **1** LIT to send [sb] out to work as a prostitute; **2** FIG to prostitute [*talent*].

II se prostituer *vpr* LIT, FIG to prostitute oneself.

prostitution /pʀɔstitysjɔ̃/ *nf* LIT, FIG prostitution.

prostration /pʀɔstʀasjɔ̃/ *nf* MÉD, RELIG prostration; **un état de ~** a state of shock.

protagoniste /pʀɔtagɔnist/ *nmf* protagonist.

protecteur, -trice /pʀɔtɛktœʀ, tʀis/ **I** *adj* **1** (qui protège) protective; **sous l'œil ~ de** under the protective gaze of; **trop ~** overprotective; **2** (supérieur) patronizing.

II *nm,f* protector; **~ des arts** patron of the arts.

protection /pʀɔtɛksjɔ̃/ *nf* **1** (action de protéger) protection; **assurer la ~ de qn** to protect sb; **être sous haute ~** to be under tight security; **de ~** [*lunettes, mesures*] protective; [*zone, système*] protection; **2** (dispositif qui protège) protective device; **3** (appui) **bénéficier de ~s** to have friends in high places.

■ **~ civile** civil defence^GB; **~ rapprochée** bodyguard; **~ sociale** social welfare system.

protectionnisme /pʀɔtɛksjɔnism/ *nm* protectionism.

protectionniste /pʀɔtɛksjɔnist/ *adj, nmf* protectionist.

protège-cahier, *pl* **~s** /pʀɔtɛʒkaje/ *nm* exercise-book sleeve.

protège-matelas /pʀɔtɛʒmatla/ *nm inv* mattress cover.

protéger /pʀɔteʒe/ [15] **I** *vtr* **1** (préserver) to protect; **le vaccin protège pour dix ans** the vaccine provides protection for ten years; **2** (favoriser) to encourage [*art*].

II se protéger *vpr* to protect oneself.

protège-slip, *pl* **~s** /pʀɔtɛʒslip/ *nm* panty-liner.

protège-tibia, *pl* **~s** /pʀɔtɛʒtibja/ *nm* shinpad.

protéine /pʀɔtein/ *nf* protein.

protestant, ~e /pʀɔtɛstɑ̃, ɑ̃t/ *adj, nm,f* Protestant.

protestantisme /pʀɔtɛstɑ̃tism/ *nm* Protestantism.

protestataire /pʀɔtɛstatɛʀ/ **I** *adj* [*personne*] protesting (*épith*); [*défilé, mouvement*] protest (*épith*).

II *nmf* protester.

protestation /pʀɔtɛstasjɔ̃/ *nf* **1** (réclamation) protest; **2** (assurance) LITER protestation.

protester /pʀɔtɛste/ [1] **I protester de** *vtr ind* **~ de son innocence** to protest one's innocence.

II *vi* to protest.

prothèse /pʀɔtɛz/ *nf* GÉN prosthesis; (membre artificiel) artificial limb; (dentier) dentures (*pl*); **~ auditive** hearing aid; **~ de la hanche** hip replacement.

prothésiste /pʀɔtezist/ **▶374** *nmf* GÉN prosthetist; **~ dentaire** prosthodontist.

protide† /pʀɔtid/ *nm* protein.

protocolaire /pʀɔtɔkɔlɛʀ/ *adj* (cérémonieux) formal; (officiel) official; **question ~** question of protocol; **de façon peu ~** unceremoniously.

protocole /pʀɔtɔkɔl/ *nm* **1** (cérémonial) formalities (*pl*); (d'État) protocol; **sans ~** GÉN informally; HUM unceremoniously; **2** POL (accord) protocol; **~ d'accord** draft agreement.

prototype /pʀɔtɔtip/ *nm* prototype.

protubérance /pʀɔtybeʀɑ̃s/ *nf* GÉN bump; ANAT protuberance.

protubérant, ~e /pʀɔtybeʀɑ̃, ɑ̃t/ *adj* protruding.

prou /pʀu/ *adv* **peu ou ~** more or less.

proue /pʀu/ *nf* prow, bow(s).

prouesse /pʀuɛs/ *nf* LIT feat; IRON exploit.

prouver /pʀuve/ [1] **I** *vtr* **1** (établir la réalité de) to prove; **il faudrait qu'il accepte, et ça n'est pas prouvé**○ he has to accept and there's no guarantee that he will; **2** (indiquer) to show; **3** (exprimer) to demonstrate [*sentiment*].

II se prouver *vpr* **1** (à soi-même) to prove to oneself; **2** (être démontré) **un axiome ne se prouve pas** an axiom cannot be proved; **3** (l'un l'autre) **ils se sont prouvé qu'ils s'aimaient** they proved their love.

IDIOMES **n'avoir plus rien à ~** to have proved oneself.

provenance /pʀɔvnɑ̃s/ *nf* origin; **en ~ de** from.

provençal, ~e, *mpl* **-aux** /pʀɔvɑ̃sal, o/ **I** **▶509** *adj* Provençal; **à la ~e** CULIN (à la) provençale (*après n*).

II **▶338** *nm* LING Provençal.

provenir /pʀɔvniʀ/ [36] *vi* **1** (venir) to come (**de** from); **provenant de** from; **2** [*situation, déséquilibre*] to stem (**de** from).

proverbe /pʀɔvɛʀb/ *nm* proverb; **comme dit le ~** as the saying goes.

proverbial, ~e, *mpl* **-iaux** /pʀɔvɛʀbjal, o/ *adj* proverbial.

providence /pʀɔvidɑ̃s/ **I** *nf* salvation; (bonté divine) providence.

II (**-**)**providence** (*in compounds*) **État(-)~** welfare state.

providentiel, -ielle /pʀɔvidɑ̃sjɛl/ *adj* providential.

province /pʀɔvɛ̃s/ *nf* **1** (région) province; **2** (pays hormis la capitale) **la ~** the provinces (*pl*); **ville de ~** provincial town; **elle sort de sa ~** PEJ she's up from the country.

provincial, ~e, *mpl* **-iaux** /pʀɔvɛ̃sjal, o/ **I** *adj* provincial.

II *nm,f* provincial; **les provinciaux** people from ou in the provinces.

proviseur /pʀɔvizœʀ/ *nm* headteacher GB ou principal US (*of a lycée*).

provision /pʀɔviʒɔ̃/ **I** *nf* **1** (réserve) stock, supply; (d'eau) supply; **faire (une) ~ de qch** to stock up with sth; **faire (une) ~ d'énergie** [*personne*] to build up one's energy; **2** (acompte) deposit; (sur un compte en banque) credit (balance).

II provisions *nfpl* food shopping ¢; **faire ses ~s** to go food shopping.

provisoire /pʀɔvizwaʀ/ **I** *adj* [*accord, bilan, gouvernement*] provisional; [*construction, solution, situation*] temporary; **à titre ~** on a temporary basis.

II *nm* **s'installer dans le ~** to get stuck with what was originally temporary; **c'est du ~ qui dure** it was supposed to be only temporary.

provisoirement /pʀɔvizwaʀmɑ̃/ *adv* provisionally.

provocant, ~e /pʀɔvɔkɑ̃, ɑ̃t/ *adj* provocative.

provocateur, -trice /pʀɔvɔkatœʀ, tʀis/ **I** *adj* provocative.

II *nm,f* agitator.

provocation /pʀɔvɔkasjɔ̃/ *nf* provocation; **faire de la ~** to be provocative.

provoquer /pʀɔvɔke/ [1] *vtr* **1** (causer) to cause [*accident, mort*]; to arouse [*curiosité*]; to provoke [*réaction, gaieté, colère*]; to trigger off [*discussion*]; to prompt [*explications*]; **~ l'accouchement** to induce labour; **~ une rencontre entre** to set up a meeting between; **2** (défier) to provoke; **~ qn en duel** to challenge sb to a duel; **3** (exciter sexuellement) to arouse.

proxénète /pʀɔksenɛt/ *nm* procurer, pimp.

proxénétisme /pʀɔksenetism/ *nm* procuring SOUT; **inculpé de ~** JUR charged with living off immoral earnings.

proximité /pʀɔksimite/ *nf* **1** (voisinage) nearness, proximity; **à ~** nearby; **le commerce de ~** corner shops (*pl*) GB, convenience stores (*pl*) US; **à ~ de** near; **2** (imminence) imminence; **à cause de la ~ de Noël** because it is/was so close to Christmas.

prude /pʀyd/ *adj* prudish.

prudemment /pʀydamɑ̃/ *adv* [*conduire, observer*] carefully; [*réagir, progresser, attendre*] cautiously.

prudence /pʀydɑ̃s/ *nf* caution; **donner des conseils de ~** to advise caution; **avec ~** [*avancer, parler, réagir*] cautiously; [*utiliser*] with caution; **par ~** as a precaution; **redoubler de ~** to be doubly careful; **automobilistes, ~!** drive safely!

prudent, **~e** /pʀydɑ̃, ɑ̃t/ *adj* **1** (soucieux de sa sécurité) careful; **ce n'est pas ~ de faire** it isn't safe to do; **2** (réservé) cautious; **3** (sage) wise; **juger ~ de ne pas accepter** to think it wiser to decline.

prud'homme /pʀydɔm/ *nm* **Conseil des ~s ~** industrial tribunal GB, labor relations board US.

prune /pʀyn/ **I** ▶141 *adj inv* (couleur) plum-coloured^{GB}.
II *nf* (fruit) plum; (eau-de-vie) plum brandy.
IDIOMES **des ~s**⁰! no way⁰!; **pour des ~s**⁰ for nothing.

pruneau , *pl* **~x** /pʀyno/ *nm* **1** (fruit) prune; **2**⁰ (balle) slug⁰, bullet.

prunelle /pʀynɛl/ *nf* **1** (fruit) sloe; (liqueur) ~ sloe gin; **2** ANAT pupil.
IDIOMES **j'y tiens comme à la ~ de mes yeux** it's my pride and joy.

prunellier /pʀynelje/ *nm* blackthorn.

prunier /pʀynje/ *nm* plum (tree); **secouer qn comme un ~**⁰ to shake sb until their teeth rattle.

prurit /pʀyʀit/ *nm* pruritus.

Prusse /pʀys/ *nprf* Prussia.
IDIOMES **travailler pour le roi de ~** to work for nothing.

PS /peɛs/ *nm* (*abbr* = **post-scriptum**) PS.

psalmodier /psalmɔdje/ [2] **I** *vtr* to chant [*texte*].
II *vi* RELIG (réciter) to say psalms; (chanter) to chant psalms.

psaume /psom/ *nm* psalm.

pseudo- /psødo/ *préf* pseudo; **~-équilibre** so-called balance; **~-savant** self-styled scientist.

pseudonyme /psødɔnim/ *nm* pseudonym.

psy⁰ /psi/ *nmf* shrink⁰, therapist.

psychanalyse /psikanaliz/ *nf* psychoanalysis; **faire une ~** [*sujet*] to undergo analysis.

psychanalyser /psikanalize/ [1] *vtr* to psychoanalyse^{GB} [*personne*].

psychanalyste /psikanalist/ ▶374 *nmf* psychoanalyst.

psyché /psiʃe/ *nf* **1** (miroir) cheval glass; **2** PHILOS psyche.

psychiatre /psikjatʀ/ ▶374 *nmf* psychiatrist.

psychiatrie /psikjatʀi/ *nf* psychiatry.

psychiatrique /psikjatʀik/ *adj* psychiatric.

psychique /psiʃik/ *adj* [*activité, troubles*] mental.

psychisme /psiʃism/ *nm* psyche.

psychologie /psikɔlɔʒi/ *nf* (discipline) psychology; (intuition) (psychological) insight; (mentalité) psychology.

psychologique /psikɔlɔʒik/ *adj* psychological; **c'est ~!** it's all in the mind!

psychologue /psikɔlɔg/ **I** *adj* **il n'est pas très ~** he's not much of a psychologist; **être ~** to understand people very well.
II ▶374 *nmf* psychologist.

psychomoteur, **-trice** /psikomɔtœʀ, tʀis/ *adj* psychomotor.

psychopathe /psikɔpat/ *nmf* psychopath.

psychopédagogie /psikopedagɔʒi/ *nf* educational psychology.

psychose /psikoz/ *nf* **1** MÉD, PSYCH psychosis; **2** (obsession) **~ de la guerre** obsessive fear of war; **~ collective** mass panic.

psychosomatique /psikosɔmatik/ *adj* psychosomatic.

psychothérapeute /psikoteʀapøt/ ▶374 *nmf* psychotherapist.

psychothérapie /psikoteʀapi/ *nf* psychotherapy; **faire une ~** [*patient*] to be in ou have (psycho)therapy.

psychotique /psikɔtik/ *adj*, *nmf* psychotic.

PTAV *written abbr* ▶ **poids**.

PTC *written abbr* ▶ **poids**.

PTT /petete/ *nfpl* (*abbr* = **Administration des postes et télécommunications et de la télédiffusion**) *former French postal and telecommunications service.*

puant, **~e** /pɥɑ̃, ɑ̃t/ *adj* **1** LIT stinking, foul-smelling; [*fromage*] smelly; **2**⁰ FIG (déplaisant) PEJ **un type ~** an incredibly arrogant guy⁰.

puanteur /pɥɑ̃tœʀ/ *nf* stench.

pub⁰ /pyb/ *nf*: *abbr* ▶ **publicité**.

pubère /pybɛʀ/ *adj* pubescent.

puberté /pybɛʀte/ *nf* puberty; **à la ~** at puberty.

pubien, **-ienne** /pybjɛ̃, ɛn/ *adj* pubic.

pubis /pybis/ *nm inv* (région) pubes; (os) pubis.

public, **-ique** /pyblik/ **I** *adj* [*lieu, argent*] public; [*enseignement*] state (*épith*) GB, public US; [*entreprise, chaîne*] state-owned (*épith*); **la dette publique** the national debt; **les cours sont ~s** the lectures are open to the public; **homme** ou **personnage ~** public figure.
II *nm* **1** (tout le monde) public; **en ~** in public; **'interdit au ~'** 'no admittance'; **2** (de spectacle, conférence, d'émission) audience; (de manifestation sportive) spectators (*pl*); **être bon ~** to be a good audience; **être mauvais ~** to be hard to please; **tous ~s** for all ages; **3** (lecteurs) readership; **4** (adeptes) **avoir un ~** to have a following; **elle ne veut pas décevoir son ~** she doesn't want to disappoint her fans ou public; **5** (secteur) **le ~** the public sector.

publication /pyblikasjɔ̃/ *nf* **1** (parution) publication; **la ~ du livre est prévue pour mai** the book is due out in May; **2** (ouvrage) publication.
■ **~ assistée par ordinateur**, **PAO** desktop publishing, DTP.

publicitaire /pyblisitɛʀ/ **I** *adj* [*campagne, budget*] advertising; [*objet, vente*] promotional.
II ▶374 *nmf* (personne) advertising executive; **il est ~** he's in advertising.
III *nm* (société) advertising agency.

publicité /pyblisite/ *nf* **1** (activité, profession) advertising; **faire de la ~ pour** to advertise; **coup de ~** publicity stunt; **c'était un beau coup de ~** it was good publicity; **2** (annonce) advertisement, advert GB, ad⁰; **3** (diffusion) publicity; **faire une mauvaise ~ à qn/qch** to give sb/sth a bad press.
■ **~ comparative** knocking copy⁰; **~ mensongère** misleading advertising.

publier /pyblije/ [2] *vtr* to publish [*livre, auteur*]; to issue [*communiqué*]; **se faire ~** to get published.

publiquement /pyblikmɑ̃/ *adv* publicly.

puce /pys/ *nf* **1** ZOOL flea; **2**⁰ (terme d'affection) **ma ~** my pet⁰; **3** ▶329 JEUX **jeu de ~** tiddlywinks (+ *v sg*); **4** ORDINAT (silicon) chip.
IDIOMES **ça m'a mis la ~ à l'oreille** that set me thinking; **secoue-toi les ~s**⁰! get a move on⁰!; **secouer les ~s**⁰ **à qn** (gronder) to bawl sb out⁰.

puceau⁰, *pl* **~x** /pyso/ *nm* virgin.

pucelle⁰ /pysɛl/ *nf* virgin.

puceron /pysʀɔ̃/ *nm* aphid.

pudding /pudiŋ/ *nm* heavy fruit sponge.

pudeur /pydœʀ/ *nf* **1** (relative au corps) sense of modesty; **sans ~** shamelessly; **2** (relative aux sentiments) (considération) decency; (retenue) sense of propriety; **par ~ elle ne pleura pas** she did not like to cry in public.

pudibond, **~e** /pydibɔ̃, ɔ̃d/ *adj* PEJ prudish.

pudique /pydik/ *adj* modest; (discret) discreet.

pudiquement /pydikmɑ̃/ *adv* **1** (chastement) modestly; **2** (par timidité, discrétion) discreetly; **3** (en termes pudiques) discreetly.

puer /pɥe/ [1] **I** *vtr* to stink of [*essence, gaz*]; **il pue le parvenu** he is a real parvenu.
II *vi* to stink; **il puait des pieds** his feet stank.

puéricultrice /pɥerikyltRis/ ▶374 *nf* pediatric nurse.

puériculture /pɥerikyltyʀ/ *nf* childcare.

puéril, **~e** /pɥeril/ *adj* [*conduite, réaction*] childish; [*attitude, activité*] puerile.

puérilement /pɥerilmɑ̃/ *adv* childishly.

puis /pɥi/ *adv* **1** (ensuite) then; **et ~?** then what?; **des pommes, des poires et ~ des pêches** apples, pears and peaches; **et ~ quoi encore**○! what(ever) next?; **2** (d'ailleurs) **et ~ je m'en fiche**○! anyway, I don't care!; **il va être en colère? et ~ (après**○)? so what if he's angry!; **tu vas ranger ta chambre et ~ c'est tout!** you'll go and tidy your room and that's the end of the matter.

puisard /pɥizaʀ/ *nm* soakaway GB, sink hole US.

puiser /pɥize/ [1] *vtr* LIT, FIG **~ qch dans qch** to draw sth from sth; **~ à pleines mains dans qch** to draw heavily on sth; **~ ses informations aux meilleures sources** to get one's information from the most reliable sources.

puisque (**puisqu'** *before vowel or mute h*) /pɥisk(ə)/ *conj* since; **~ c'est comme ça, je m'en vais** if that's how it is, I'm off; **mais ~ je te dis que c'est impossible** but I'm telling you it's impossible.

puissance /pɥisɑ̃s/ **I** *nf* **1** PHYS, ÉLECTROTECH power; **un amplificateur d'une ~ de 60 watts** a 60-watt amplifier; **de forte ~** very powerful; **2** (intensité) (de lumière) intensity; (de son) volume; **3** MATH power; **dix ~ trois** ten to the power (of) three; **4** (pouvoir) power; **assassin en ~** potential killer; **5** (capacité) power; **la ~ militaire** the military strength ou might; **~ de concentration** powers (*pl*) of concentration; **il a une ~ de travail remarquable** his capacity for work is remarkable; **6** (vigueur) power, strength; **7** (pays) power; **une grande ~** a superpower.
II **puissances** *nfpl* RELIG **les ~s des ténèbres** the powers of darkness.

puissant, **~e** /pɥisɑ̃, ɑ̃t/ **I** *adj* GÉN powerful; [*sentiment*] strong.
II **puissants** *nmpl* **les ~s** the powerful (+ *v pl*), the mighty (+ *v pl*).

puits /pɥi/ *nm inv* **1** (d'eau) well; **~ de pétrole** oil well; **2** (conduit) shaft.
■ **~ de mine** mine shaft; **~ perdu** soakaway GB, sink hole US; **~ de science** fount of knowledge.

pull○ /pyl/ *nm* (tricot) sweater.

pull-over, *pl* **~s** /pylɔvɛʀ/ *nm* sweater.

pullulement /pylylmɑ̃/ *nm* **1** (multiplication) proliferation; **2** (grand nombre) (d'insectes, de gens) swarm; (de fautes, problèmes) multitude.

pulluler /pylyle/ [1] *vi* **1** (se multiplier) to proliferate; **depuis dix ans les romans de mauvaise qualité pullulent** over the last ten years there has been a glut of bad novels; **2** (grouiller) **les touristes pullulent dans la région** the area is swarming with tourists; **les poissons pullulent dans la rivière** the river is teeming with fish; **les erreurs pullulent dans le texte** the text is absolutely full of mistakes.

pulmonaire /pylmɔnɛʀ/ *adj* [*maladie, infection*] lung (*épith*); [*artère, veine*] pulmonary.

pulpe /pylp/ *nf* (de fruit) pulp; (de pomme de terre) flesh.

pulpeux, **-euse** /pylpø, øz/ *adj* [*corps, lèvres*] luscious; [*fruit*] fleshy.

pulsation /pylsasjɔ̃/ *nf* (battement) beat; **~s cardiaques** (rythme) heartbeat (*sg*); (battements) heartbeats.

pulsion /pylsjɔ̃/ *nf* impulse, urge; **~ de mort** death wish.

pulvérisateur /pylveʀizatœʀ/ *nm* GÉN spray; AGRIC sprayer.

pulvérisation /pylveʀizasjɔ̃/ *nf* **1** (de liquide) spraying; **'utiliser en ~s nasales'** 'for use as nasal spray'; **2** (de matériau) pulverization GB.

pulvériser /pylveʀize/ [1] *vtr* **1** (projeter) to spray [*liquide*]; **2** (broyer) to pulverize [*solide*]; **3** (anéantir) to pulverize [*bâtiment, ennemi*]; to demolish○ [*argument*]; **4** (battre) to shatter○ [*record*].

punaise /pynɛz/ **I** *nf* **1** (pointe) drawing pin GB, thumbtack US; **2** ZOOL bug.
II○ *excl* (de surprise) blimey○! GB, gee○! US; (de dépit) heck○!
■ **~ des bois** stink bug; **~ des lits** bedbug.

punaiser○ /pynɛze/ [1] *vtr* to pin ou tack US [sth] up.

punch[1] /pɔ̃ʃ/ *nm* (boisson) punch.

punch[2] /pœnʃ/ *nm* **1** (de boxeur) punch; **avoir du ~** to pack quite a punch; **2** (énergie) energy; (dynamisme) drive; **manquer de ~** [*slogan, film*] to lack punch; [*personne*] to lack drive; **avoir du ~** [*slogan, discours*] to be punchy○; [*personne*] to have drive.

punching-ball, *pl* **~s** /pœnʃiŋbɔl/ *nm* punchball GB, punching bag US.

punir /pyniʀ/ [3] *vtr* to punish.

punitif, **-ive** /pynitif, iv/ *adj* punitive; **expédition punitive** punitive strike.

punition /pynisjɔ̃/ *nf* **1** (châtiment) punishment; **infliger une ~ à qn** to punish sb; **avoir une ~** to be punished; **2** (tâche) **il n'a pas fait sa ~** he hasn't done the task he was given as punishment.

pupille[1] /pypij/ *nmf* (mineur sous tutelle) ward; **~ de l'État** child in care; **~ de la Nation** war orphan.

pupille[2] /pypij/ *nf* ANAT pupil.

pupitre /pypitʀ/ *nm* **1** (tableau de commande) control panel; (ORDINAT console; **2** (de musicien) music stand; (de piano) music rest; **qui est au ~?** who's conducting?; **3** (bureau) desk; **4** (d'orateur) lectern.

pupitreur, **-euse** /pypitʀœʀ, øz/ ▶374 *nm,f* computer operator.

pur, **~e** /pyʀ/ **I** *adj* **1** (sans mélange) pure; (non dilué) straight; **boire son vin ~** to drink one's wine undiluted; **2** (non altéré) [*eau, air*] pure; [*diamant*] flawless; [*ciel, voix*] clear; **3** (sans fioritures) [*ligne, style*] pure; **4** (total) [*méchanceté, vérité*] pure; [*coïncidence, plaisir, folie*] sheer; **en ~e perte** to no avail; **question de ~e forme** token question; **~ et simple** outright; **~ et dur** hardline; **5** (théorique) pure; **6** (d'origine) [*tradition*] true; **un ~ produit de** LIT, FIG a typical product of; **à l'état ~** [*génie, bêtise*] sheer; **7** (sans défaut moral) pure.
II *nm,f* **1** (personne irréprochable) virtuous person; **2** (fidèle à un parti) **~** (et dur) hardliner.

purée /pyʀe/ **I** *nf* CULIN (de fruits, légumes) purée; (aliment trop cuit) PEJ mush; **~ (de pommes de terre)** mashed potatoes (*pl*); **~ de marrons** chestnut purée.
II○ *excl* heck○!
■ **~ en flocons** instant mashed potatoes (*pl*); **~ de pois** (brouillard) pea souper GB, fog.
IDIOMES **être dans la ~**○ to be in a mess.

purement /pyʀmɑ̃/ *adv* purely.

pureté /pyʀte/ *nf* purity.

purgatif, **-ive** /pyʀgatif, iv/ **I** *adj* purgative.
II *nm* purgative.

purgatoire /pyʀgatwaʀ/ *nm* RELIG **le ~** purgatory; **faire son ~** FIG to do one's penance.

purge /pyʀ3/ *nf* MÉD purgative; POL purge.

purger /pyʀ3e/ [13] **I** *vtr* **1** MÉD to purge; **2** TECH to bleed [*radiateur, freins*]; to drain [*tuyau*]; to purify [*métal*]; **3** JUR to serve [*peine*].
II **se purger** *vpr* [*personne*] to take a laxative.

purificateur /pyʀifikatœʀ/ *nm* **~ d'atmosphère** or **d'air** air purifier.

purification /pyʀifikasjɔ̃/ *nf* purification.

purifier /pyʀifje/ [2] **I** vtr **1** GÉN to purify [eau, air, sang]; to cleanse [peau]; to purify [langage]; **2** (moralement) LITER to purify.

II se purifier vpr [personne] to cleanse oneself.

purin /pyʀɛ̃/ nm slurry.

puriste /pyʀist/ nmf purist.

puritain, **~e** /pyʀitɛ̃, ɛn/ **I** adj (austère) puritanical; RELIG Puritan.

II nm,f (rigoriste) puritan; RELIG Puritan.

puritanisme /pyʀitanism/ nm puritanism.

pur-sang /pyʀsɑ̃/ nm inv thoroughbred, purebred.

purulent, **~e** /pyʀylɑ̃, ɑ̃t/ adj purulent.

pus /py/ nm inv pus.

putois /pytwa/ nm inv (animal) polecat; (fourrure) skunk (fur).

IDIOMES **crier comme un ~**° to scream one's head off.

putréfaction /pytʀefaksjɔ̃/ nf putrefaction; **odeur de ~** smell of rotting; **cadavre en état de ~** decomposing body.

putréfier: **se putréfier** /pytʀefje/ [2] vpr [cadavre] to putrefy; [viande] to rot.

putsch /putʃ/ nm putsch.

putschiste /putʃist/ **I** adj involved in the putsch (après n).

II nmf **les ~s** those involved in the putsch.

puzzle /pœzl, pyzl/ nm JEUX jigsaw puzzle; FIG jigsaw.

PV° /peve/ nm (abbr = **procès-verbal**) GÉN fine;

(pour stationnement illégal) parking ticket; (pour excès de vitesse) speeding ticket.

pygmée /pigme/ nmf pygmy.

pyjama /piʒama/ nm pyjamas (pl) GB, pajamas (pl) US, pair of pyjamas GB ou pajamas US.

pylône /pilon/ nm pylon; RADIO, TV mast; (de pont) tower.

pyramidal, **~e**, mpl **-aux** /piʀamidal, o/ adj LIT pyramid-shaped; FIG [hiérarchie] structured like a pyramid (après n).

pyramide /piʀamid/ nf LIT, FIG pyramid; **~ des âges** age pyramid.

pyrograveur, **-euse** /piʀogʀavœʀ, øz/ ▶ 374 nm,f pokerwork artist.

pyrogravure /piʀogʀavyʀ/ nf pokerwork.

pyrolyse /piʀɔliz/ nf pyrolysis; **four à ~** self-cleaning oven.

pyromane /piʀɔman/ nmf GÉN pyromaniac; JUR arsonist.

pyrotechnicien, **-ienne** /piʀotɛknisjɛ̃, ɛn/ ▶ 374 nm,f fireworks manufacturer.

pyrotechnie /piʀotɛkni/ nf pyrotechnics (+ v sg).

Pyrrhus /piʀys/ npr Pyrrhus; **victoire à la ~** Pyrrhic victory.

Pythagore /pitagɔʀ/ npr Pythagoras; **théorème de ~** Pythagoras' theorem; **table de ~** multiplication table.

python /pitɔ̃/ nm python.

Qq

q, Q /ky/ *nm inv* q, Q.

qatari, ~e /katari/ **▶394** *adj* Qatari.

qcm /kyseɛm/ *nm* (*abbr* = **questionnaire à choix multiple**) multiple-choice questionnaire, mcq.

QI /kyi/ *nm: abbr* ▶ **quotient**.

qu' ▶ **que**.

quadragénaire /kwadraʒenɛr/ **I** *adj* **être ~** to be in one's forties.
II *nmf* person in his/her forties.

quadrature /kwadratyr/ *nf* quadrature; **c'est la ~ du cercle** it's like squaring the circle.

quadriennal, ~e, *mpl* **-aux** /kwadrijɛnal, o/ *adj* **1** (de quatre ans) [*plan*] four-year (*épith*); **2** (tous les quatre ans) quadrennial, four-yearly (*épith*).

quadrilatère /k(w)adrilatɛr/ *nm* quadrilateral.

quadrillage /kadrijaʒ/ *nm* **1** (de papier) cross-ruling; **2** (occupation) **le ~ de la ville par l'armée** the systematic military takeover of the town; **le ~ du terrain** MIL the chequering of the terrain.

quadrillé, ~e /kadrije/ **I** *pp* ▶ **quadriller**.
II *pp adj* [*papier*] squared.

quadriller /kadrije/ [1] *vtr* **1** (occuper) [*armée*] to take control of; [*police*] to spread one's net over; **2** (faire des carrés sur) to cross-rule [*papier*].

quadrimoteur /k(w)adrimɔtœr/ **I** *adj* four-engined.
II *nm* four-engined plane.

quadrupède /k(w)adrypɛd/ *adj, nm* quadruped.

quadruple /k(w)adrypl/ **I** *adj* [*nombre, rangée, somme*] quadruple.
II *nm* **le nombre des sans-abri est le ~ de ce qu'il était il y a 20 ans** the number of homeless people is four times what it was twenty years ago.

quadruplé, ~e /k(w)adryple/ *nm,f* quadruplet.

quadrupler /k(w)adryple/ [1] **I** *vtr* to quadruple.
II *vi* to quadruple, to increase fourfold.

quai /kɛ/ *nm* **1** NAUT quay; **le navire est à ~** the ship has docked; **2** (berge aménagée) bank; **3** (de gare, métro) platform.
■ **~ de débarquement** NAUT unloading dock; **~ d'embarquement** NAUT loading dock; **Quai des Orfèvres** criminal investigation department of the French police force; **Quai d'Orsay** French Foreign Office.

quaker, quakeresse /kwɛkœr, kwɛkərɛs/ *nm,f* Quaker/Quakeress.

qualifiable /kalifjabl/ *adj* SPORT able to qualify (*jamais épith*).

qualificatif, -ive /kalifikatif, iv/ **I** *adj* qualifying.
II *nm* LING qualifier; (mot) term.

qualification /kalifikasjɔ̃/ *nf* **1** SPORT qualification (**pour** for); **un match de ~** a qualifying match ou game; **2** (compétence pratique) skills (*pl*); (diplôme) qualification; **sans ~** unskilled.

qualifié, ~e /kalifje/ **I** *pp* ▶ **qualifier**.
II *pp adj* **1** (compétent) skilled; (diplômé) qualified; **les jeunes non ~s** (sans diplôme) young people without qualifications; (sans compétences) young people without skills; **je ne suis pas ~ pour vous répondre** I'm not qualified to give you an answer; **2** (demandant des compétences) skilled; **3** JUR [*vol*] aggravated.

qualifier /kalifje/ [2] **I** *vtr* **1** (caractériser) to describe (**de** as); **2** (donner la compétence à) to qualify; **3** SPORT [*victoire*] to qualify; **4** LING [*adjectif*] to qualify [*nom*].
II se qualifier *vpr* [*joueur, pays*] to qualify; **l'équipe s'est qualifiée pour la finale** the team has qualified for the final.

qualitatif, -ive /kalitatif, iv/ *adj* [*étude, enquête*] qualitative; **sur le plan ~** in terms of quality.

qualité /kalite/ *nf* **1** (valeur) quality; **de bonne ~** good quality (*épith*); **de ~** quality (*épith*); **de première ~** of the highest quality; **~ de la vie** quality of life; **2** (aptitude) quality; **avoir beaucoup de ~s** to have many (good) qualities; **ses ~s de gestionnaire** his/her skills as an administrator; **la franchise n'est pas sa ~ première** openness is not his/her strong point; **3** IND quality; **4** (statut) status; (fonction) position; **sa ~ de directeur l'autorise à faire** his/her position as manager allows him/her to do; **en (sa) ~ de représentant** in his/her capacity as a representative; **nom, prénom et ~** surname, first name and occupation; **5** (sorte) quality.

quand /kɑ̃, kɑ̃t/

■ **Note** when traduisant *quand* conjonction ne peut pas être suivi du futur: *quand il aura terminé* = when he has finished; *quand je serai guérie, j'irai te voir* = when I'm better, I'll come and see you.

I *conj* **1** (lorsque) when; **~ il arrivera, vous lui annoncerez la nouvelle** when he gets here, you can tell him the news; **~ il prend son poste en 1980, la situation est déjà catastrophique** when he took up his post in 1980, the situation was already catastrophic; **tu auras ton dessert ~ tu auras fini ta viande** you'll have your dessert when you have finished your meat; **emporte une pomme pour ~ tu auras faim**○ take an apple with you in case you get hungry; **2** (valeur exclamative) **~ je pense que ma fille va avoir dix ans!** to think that my daughter's almost ten (years old)!; **~ je vous le disais!** I told you so!; **3** (toutes les fois que) whenever; **~ il pleut plus de trois jours la cave est inondée** whenever it rains for more than three days, the cellar floods; **son attitude change ~ il s'agit de son fils** his/her attitude changes when it comes to his/her son; **4** (alors que) when; **tu oses te plaindre ~ des gens meurent de faim!** you dare to complain when there are people starving!; **5** (même si) even if; **~ (bien même) la terre s'écroulerait, il continuerait à dormir** he'd sleep through an earthquake.
II *adv* when; **~ arrive-t-il/viendras-tu?** when does he arrive/will you come?; **depuis ~ habitez-vous ici?** how long have you been living here?; **ça date de ~ cette histoire**○**?** when did all this happen?; **de ~ date votre dernière réunion?** when was your last meeting?; **de ~ est la lettre?** what is the date on the letter?; **c'est prévu pour ~?** when is it scheduled for?; **c'est pour ~ le bébé?** when is the baby due?; **à ~**○ **la semaine de 30 heures?** when will we get a 30-hour working week?
III quand même *loc adv* still; **ils étaient occupés mais ils nous ont ~ même rendu visite** they were busy but they still came to visit us; **ils ne veulent pas de moi, mais j'irai ~ même!** they don't want me, but I'm still going!; **elle est ~ même bête**○ **d'avoir fait ça!** it's really stupid of her to have done that!; **~ même**○**, tu exagères!** (tu n'es pas objectif) come on, you're exaggerating!; (tu vas trop loin) come on, that's going too far!; **tu ne vas pas faire ça ~ même**○**?** you're not going to do that, are you?

Les quantités

Dénombrables ou non-dénombrables?

L'anglais, comme le français, distingue deux catégories de noms: ceux qui désignent des éléments pouvant se compter par unités, se dénombrer (les dénombrables), comme les pommes, les chaises etc., et ceux qui désignent des éléments toujours à l'état de masse, non dénombrable en éléments séparés (les non-dénombrables), comme le lait ou le sable.

Comment distinguer un dénombrable d'un non-dénombrable? Précédés de «assez de», un dénombrable se met au pluriel (assez de pommes) et un non-dénombrable se met au singulier (assez de lait) (recette pour francophones uniquement). *«beaucoup», «peu» et «moins» exigent, en anglais, des traductions différentes, selon qu'ils spécifient un nom dénombrable, ou un nom non dénombrable.*

	pour les dénombrables	pour les non-dénombrables
beaucoup de =	a lot of ou lots of ou many*	a lot of ou lots of ou much*
peu =	few ou not many	little ou not much
plus =	more	more
moins =	fewer ou (familier) less	less less
assez =	enough	enough

* *Attention: not many et not much s'emploient couramment, mais many et much sont peu utilisés à la forme affirmative.*

Les noms dénombrables

combien y a-t-il de pommes? = how many apples are there?
il y a beaucoup de pommes = there are lots of apples

Noter l'absence d'équivalent anglais du français en dans les expressions suivantes:

combien y en a-t-il ? = how many are there?
il y en a beaucoup = there are a lot
il n'y en a pas beaucoup = there aren't many
il y en a deux kilos = there are two kilos (on peut aussi dire, dans la conversation, there's two kilos)
il y en a vingt = there are twenty
j'en ai vingt = I've got twenty
A a plus de pommes que B = A has got more apples than B

Noter l'ordre des mots dans:

quelques pommes de plus = a few more apples
quelques personnes de plus = a few more people
A a moins de pommes que B = A doesn't have as many apples as B
beaucoup moins de pommes = far fewer apples ou not nearly as many apples

Les noms non-dénombrables

combien y a-t-il de lait? = how much milk is there?
il y a beaucoup de lait = there is a lot of milk

Noter l'absence d'équivalent anglais du français en dans les expressions suivantes.

combien y en a-t-il? = how much is there?
il y en a beaucoup = there is a lot
il n'y en a pas beaucoup = there isn't much ou there's only a little
j'en ai deux kilos = I've got two kilos
A a plus de lait que B = A has got more milk than B
beaucoup plus de lait = much more milk
un peu plus de lait = a little more milk
A a moins de lait que B = A has got less milk than B
beaucoup moins de lait = much less milk ou far less milk
un peu moins de lait = a little less milk

Quantités relatives

combien y en a-t-il par kilo? = how many are there to the kilo?
il y en a dix par kilo = there are ten to the kilo
il y en a cinq pour dix francs = you get five for ten francs

Pour toutes les expressions utilisées pour donner un prix par unité de mesure (longueur, poids etc.), l'anglais utilise l'article indéfini là où le français utilise l'article défini.

combien coûte le litre? = how much does it cost a litre? ou how much does a litre cost?
vingt francs le litre = twenty francs a litre
combien coûte un kilo de pommes? = how much do apples cost a kilo? ou how much does a kilo of apples cost?
dix francs le kilo = ten francs a kilo
elles sont à dix francs le kilo = they are ten francs a kilo
combien coûte le mètre? = how much does it cost a metre?
dix livres le mètre = £10 a metre

Mais noter:

la voiture fait huit litres aux cent = the car does 35 miles to the gallon†
combien y a-t-il de verres par bouteille? = how many glasses are there to the bottle?
il y a six verres par bouteille = there are six glasses to the bottle

† *En anglais, on compte la consommation d'une voiture en mesurant non pas le nombre de litres nécessaires pour parcourir 100 kilomètres, mais la distance parcourue (en miles) avec 4,54 litres (un gallon) de carburant (mpg). Pour convertir la consommation exprimée en litres aux 100 km en mpg (miles per gallon) et vice versa il suffit de diviser 280 par le chiffre connu.*

quant: **quant à** /kɑ̃ta/ *loc prép* **1** (pour ce qui est de) as for; **la France, ~ à elle, n'a pas pris position** as for France, it did not take a stand; **~ à partir, jamais!** as for leaving, never!; **2** (au sujet de) about; **elle ne a rien dit ~ à l'heure de la réunion** she didn't say anything about what time the meeting would be.

quantifiable /kɑ̃tifjabl/ *adj* quantifiable.

quantifier /kɑ̃tifje/ [2] *vtr* ÉCON, MATH to quantify; PHYS to quantize.

quantique /kɑ̃tik/ *adj* PHYS quantum.

quantitatif, -ive /kɑ̃titatif, iv/ *adj* quantitative.

quantité /kɑ̃tite/ ▶486 *nf* **1** (mesure) quantity (de of), amount (de of); **en grande ~** in large quantities; **faire qch en ~s industrielles** IND to mass-produce sth; HUM to make vast quantities of sth; **~ négligeable** LIT small ou negligible quantity; **être une ~ négligeable** to be dispensable; **2** (grand nombre) **des ~s de** (de personnes) scores of; (de choses) a lot of; **il y avait une ~ de gens**

incroyable there was an incredible number of people; **du pain/vin en ~** plenty of bread/wine; **3** (en sciences, linguistique, musique) quantity.

quarantaine /kaʁɑ̃tɛn/ *nf* **1** (environ quarante) about forty; **2** (âge) **il a la ~** he's in his forties; **elle approche la ~** she's getting on for forty; **3** MÉD (isolement) quarantine; **être en ~** LIT to be in quarantine; FIG to be ostracized.

quarante /kaʁɑ̃t/ ▶399|, 156| *adj inv, pron* forty.

quarante-cinq /kaʁɑ̃tsɛ̃k/ ▶399|, 156| *adj inv, pron* forty-five.

■ **~ tours** AUDIO single.

quarantième /kaʁɑ̃tjɛm/ ▶399| *adj* fortieth.

quart /kaʁ/ ▶298| *nm* **1** (quatrième partie) quarter (de of); **un ~ d'heure** LIT a quarter of an hour; **faire passer un mauvais ~ d'heure à qn** to give sb a hard time; **un kilo un ~** a kilo and a quarter; **un ~ de siècle** a quarter of a century; **les trois ~s du temps**○ most of the time; **les trois ~s des gens**○ most people; **2** (bouteille) a quarter-litre^{GB} bottle (de

que

que conjonction de subordination se traduit généralement par *that*:

> *elle a dit qu'elle le ferait* = she said that she would do it
> *il est important qu'ils se rendent compte que*
> *ce n'est pas simple* = it's important that they should
> realize that it's not simple

On notera que *that* est souvent omis:

> *je pense qu'il devrait changer de métier*
> = I think he should change jobs

Quand *que* suit un verbe exprimant un souhait, une volonté l'anglais utilise un infinitif:

> *je voudrais que tu ranges ta chambre*
> = I'd like you to tidy your room
> *elle veut qu'il fasse un stage de formation*
> = she wants him to do a training course

On trouvera ci-dessous quelques exemples supplémentaires mais on pourra toujours se reporter aux verbes, adjectifs et substantifs qui peuvent être suivis de *que*, comme **montrer**, **comprendre**, **apparaître**, **certain**, **idée** etc. De même les locutions *ainsi que*, *alors que*, *bien que* sont traitées respectivement à **ainsi**, **alors**, **bien**. Pour les emplois de *que* avec *ne*, *plus*, *moins* etc. on se reportera à **ne**, **plus**, **moins** etc. Voir **I**.

que pronom relatif se traduit différemment selon qu'il a pour antécédent un nom de personne:

> *l'homme que je vois* = the man that I can see
> *ou* the man I can see
> *ou* the man who I can see
> *ou* the man whom I can see

> *les amis que j'ai invités*
> = the friends that I've invited
> *ou* the friends I've invited
> *ou* the friends who I have invited
> *ou* the friends whom I have invited

(dans les deux cas ci-dessus la traduction avec *whom* appartient au registre de la langue écrite); ou un nom de chose, concept, animal:

> *le chien que je vois* = the dog that I can see
> *ou* the dog I can see
> *ou* the dog which I can see

> *l'invitation que j'ai reçue*
> = the invitation that I received
> *ou* the invitation I received
> *ou* the invitation which I received

Voir **III**.

---

of); (pichet) a quarter-litre^{GB} pitcher (**de** of); **3** (gobelet) beaker (of a quarter-litre^{GB} capacity); **4** NAUT watch; **être de ~** to be on watch.
■ **~ de cercle** quadrant; **~ de tour** LIT 90° ou ninety-degree turn; **faire qch au ~ de tour**○ FIG to do sth immediately.

quarte /kaʀt/ *nf* MUS fourth.

quarté /kaʀte/ *nm*: *betting based on forecasting the first four horses in a race.*

quartier /kaʀtje/ *nm* **1** (partie d'une ville) area, district; (zone administrative) district; (zone ethnique) quarter; **le ~ des affaires** the business area ou district; **dans mon ~** in my area; **le plan du ~** a map of the area; **les beaux ~s** fashionable districts; **de ~** local; **la vie de ~** local community life; **les gens du ~** the locals; **êtes-vous du ~?** are you from around here?; **2** (portion) quarter; **un ~ de pommes** a slice of apple; **un ~ de bœuf** a quarter of beef; **un ~ d'orange** an orange segment; **3** (en astronomie) quarter; **le premier ~ de la lune** the moon's first quarter; **4** (de noblesse) quarter; **5** MIL **~s** quarters; **avoir ~ libre** MIL to be off duty ; FIG to have time off ou free time.
■ **~ général, QG** MIL, FIG headquarters, HQ.
IDIOMES **ne pas faire de ~** to show no mercy.

quartier-maître, *pl* **quartiers-maîtres** /kaʀtjemɛtʀ/ *nm* leading seaman GB, petty officer third class US.

quart-monde /kaʀmɔ̃d/ *nm inv* underclass.

---

quartz /kwaʀts/ *nm* quartz; **à ~** quartz (*épith*).

quasi /kazi/ **I** *adv* almost.
II *nm* CULIN **~ (de veau)** fillet of veal.
III quasi- (*in compounds*) **~-monopole/indifférence** virtual monopoly/indifference; **~-certitude** near certainty; **la ~-totalité de** almost all of.

quasiment○ /kazimã/ *adv* practically.

quaternaire /kwatɛʀnɛʀ/ *adj*, *nm* (en géologie) Quaternary.

quatorze /katɔʀz/ ▶399|, 298|, 156| *adj inv*, *pron* fourteen.
IDIOMES **chercher midi à ~ heures**○ to complicate matters; **c'est reparti comme en 14**○! here we go again!

quatorzième /katɔʀzjɛm/ ▶399|, 156| *adj* fourteenth.

quatrain /katʀɛ̃/ *nm* quatrain.

quatre /katʀ/ ▶399|, 298|, 156| *adj inv*, *pron*, *nm inv* four.
IDIOMES **dire ses ~ vérités**○ **à qn** to tell sb a few home truths; **faire les ~ volontés de qn** to give in to sb's every whim; **être tiré à ~ épingles** to be dressed up to the nines○; **manger comme ~** to eat like a horse; **ne pas y aller par ~ chemins** not to beat about the bush; **je vais leur parler entre ~ yeux** or **quat'zyeux**○ I'm going to talk to them face to face; **monter/descendre (un escalier) ~ à ~** to go up/to go down the stairs four at a time; **être entre ~ planches**○ to be six feet under.

quatre-cent-vingt-et-un /katsɑ̃vɛ̃teœ̃/ *nm inv*: *game of dice.*

quatre-heures /katʀœʀ/ *nm inv* afternoon snack (*for children*).

quatre-mâts /katʀəma/ *nm inv* four-master.

quatre-quarts /kat(ʀə)kaʀ/ *nm inv* pound cake.

quatre-vingt(s) /katʀəvɛ̃/ ▶399|, 156| *adj*, *pron* eighty.

quatre-vingt-dix /katʀəvɛ̃dis/ ▶399|, 156| *adj inv*, *pron* ninety.

quatre-vingt-dixième /katʀəvɛ̃dizjɛm/ ▶399| *adj* ninetieth.

quatre-vingtième /katʀəvɛ̃tjɛm/ ▶399| *adj* eightieth.

quatrième /katʀijɛm/ ▶399|, 156| **I** *adj* fourth.
II *nf* **1** SCOL third year of secondary school, age 13–14; **2** AUT fourth gear; **passer en ~** to change ou go into fourth gear.
■ **le ~ âge** very old people (+ *v pl*).
IDIOMES **faire qch en ~ vitesse** to do sth in double quick time○.

quatuor /kwatɥɔʀ/ *nm* (œuvre, formation) quartet.

quat'zyeux○ /katzjø/ ▶ **quatre**.

que (**qu'** *before vowel or mute h*) /kə/ **I** *conj* **1** (reprenant une autre conjonction) **comme tu ne veux pas venir et ~ tu ne veux pas dire pourquoi** since you refuse to come and (since you) refuse to say why; **si vous venez et ~ vous ayez le temps** if you come and (if) you have the time; **2 je crains ~ tu (ne) fasses une bêtise** I'm worried (that) you might do something silly; **qu'il soit le meilleur, nous nous en sommes déjà rendu compte** we were already well aware that he's the best; **approche, ~ je te regarde** come closer so I can look at you; **~ vous le vouliez ou non, ~ cela vous plaise ou non** whether you like it or not; **il n'était pas sitôt parti qu'elle appela la police** no sooner had he left than she called the police; **j'avais déjà lu dix pages qu'il n'avait toujours pas commencé** I had already read ten pages while he hadn't even started; **~ tout le monde sorte!** everyone must leave!; **qu'on veuille bien m'excuser mais...** you must excuse me but...; **~ ceux qui n'ont pas compris le disent** let anyone who hasn't understood say so; **qu'on le pende!** hang him!; **qu'il crève○!** let him rot○!; **~ je leur prête ma voiture!** you expect me to lend them my car!; **~ je sache** as far as I know.
II *pron inter* what; **~ dire?** what can you ou one

say?; ~ **faire?** (maintenant) what shall I/we do?; (au passé) what could I/we do?; **je ne sais pas ce qu'il a dit** I don't know what he said; **qu'est-ce que c'est que ça?** what's that?

III *pron rel* **1** (ayant un nom de personne pour antécédent) **Pierre, ~ je n'avais pas vu depuis 20 ans, est venu me voir hier** Pierre, whom I had not seen for 20 years, came to see me yesterday; **c'est la plus belle femme ~ j'aie jamais vue** she's the most beautiful woman (that) I've ever seen; **2** (ayant un nom de chose ou d'animal pour antécédent) **je n'aime pas la voiture ~ tu as achetée** I don't like the car (that) you've bought; **3** (employé comme attribut) that; **la vieille dame qu'elle est devenue** the old lady she is today.

IV *adv* ~ **vous êtes jolie!** how pretty you are!; ~ **c'est difficile!** how difficult it is!; ~ **c'est joli!** it's so pretty!; **ce ~ vous êtes jolie!** you're so pretty!; ~ **de monde!** what a lot of people!; **'vous ne leur en avez pas parlé?'—'oh ~ si!'** 'haven't you spoken to them about it?'—'yes I have!'; **'tu en as besoin?'—'~ oui!'** 'do you need it'—'I certainly do!'

Québec /kebɛk/ **I** ▶509▶ *nprm* (province) **le ~** Quebec.
II ▶628▶ *npr* (ville) Quebec.

québécois, ~e /kebekwa, az/ *adj* of Quebec.

Québécois, ~e /kebekwa, az/ *nm,f* Quebecois, Quebecker.

quel, quelle /kɛl/ **I** *dét inter* **~s sont les pays membres de l'UE?** what are the member countries of the EU?; **je me demande quelle est la meilleure solution** I wonder what the best solution is; **de ces deux médicaments, ~ est le plus efficace?** which of these two medicines is more effective?

II *adj inter* **dans ~s pays as-tu vécu?** what countries have you lived in?; **de ~ étage a-t-il sauté?** which floor did he jump from?; **quelle heure est-il?** what time is it?; **si tu savais à ~ point il m'agace!** if you only knew how much he irritates me!

III *adj excl* what; ~ **imbécile!** what an idiot!; **quelle coïncidence!** what a coincidence!; **quelle horreur!** how dreadful!

IV *adj rel* **quelles qu'aient pu être tes raisons, tu n'aurais jamais dû faire cela** whatever your reasons may have been, you should never have done that; **quelle que soit la route que l'on prenne** whatever road we take; ~ **que soit le vainqueur** whoever the winner may be; ~ **que soit l'endroit où il se sont arrêtés** wherever they stopped.

quelconque /kɛlkɔ̃k/ **I** *adj* (ordinaire) [*personne*] ordinary; [*livre, acteur*] poor; [*restaurant, produit*] second-rate; [*endroit, décor*] characterless; (qui manque de charme) [*personne*] ordinary-looking; **j'ai trouvé le film très ~** I thought the film was very poor.

II *adj indéf* (n'importe lequel) any; **je doute qu'il y ait un ~ rapport entre les deux événements** I doubt that there's any link between the two events; **si pour une raison ~** if for some reason or other.

quelle ▶ quel.

quelque /kɛlk/ **I** *adj indéf* **1** (au singulier) (dans les phrases affirmatives) some; (dans les phrases interrogatives) any; **il y aurait ~ contradiction à dire que** it would be somewhat contradictory to say that; **si pour ~ raison que ce soit** if for whatever reason; **de ~ côté que nous allions** whichever way we go; **2** (au pluriel) (dans les phrases affirmatives) some, a few; (dans les phrases interrogatives) any; **je voudrais ajouter ~s mots** I'd like to add a few words; **~s instants** a few moments; **est-ce qu'il vous reste ~s cartons?** do you have any boxes left?; **ça dure trois heures et ~s** it lasts over three hours.

II *adv* **1** (environ) **les ~ deux mille spectateurs** the two thousand odd spectators, the two thousand or so spectators; **ça lui a coûté ~ 300 francs** it cost him about 300 francs; **2** (si) however; ~ **admirable que soit son attitude** however admirable his/her attitude may be.

III **quelque chose** *pron indéf inv* (dans les phrases affirmatives) something; **il y a ~ chose qui ne va pas** something's wrong; **ils y sont pour ~ chose** they've

got something to do with it; **elle est restée ~ chose comme trois heures** she stayed for something like three hours; **il me reste ~ chose comme 200 francs** I've got about 200 francs left; ~ **chose de mieux** something better; **il y aurait ~ chose d'absurde à refuser sa proposition** it would be ridiculous to turn down his offer; **c'est ~ chose d'inimaginable!** it's unbelievable!; **il a ~ chose de son grand-père** he's got a look of his grandfather about him; **faire ~s chose à qn** [*événement, substance*] to have an effect on sb; **c'est ~ chose○! tu es toujours en retard!** for crying out loud! you're always late; **en ce temps-là, être instituteur, c'était ~ chose** in those days it was quite something to be a primary school teacher; **ça me dit ~ chose** it reminds me of something, it rings a bell.

IV **quelque part** *loc adv* somewhere; **il lui a mis son pied ~ part**○ EUPH he gave him/her a kick in the behind.

V **quelque peu** *loc adv* somewhat; **il a accepté après avoir ~ peu hésité** he accepted after some hesitation.

quelquefois /kɛlkəfwa/ *adv* sometimes.

quelques-uns, quelques-unes /kɛlkəzœ̃, yn/ *pron indéf pl* some, a few.

quelqu'un /kɛlkœ̃/ *pron indéf* **1** (dans les phrases affirmatives) someone, somebody; ~ **d'autre** somebody else, someone else; **c'est ~ de compétent/de très doué** he/she is competent/very gifted; **un jour, il deviendra ~**○ one day, he'll be somebody; **cette fille-là, c'est ~**○! that girl isn't just anybody;

2 (dans les phrases interrogatives et conditionnelles) **il y a ~?** is there anybody here?; **le téléphone sonne, est-ce que ~ pourrait répondre?** the telephone is ringing, could somebody answer?

quémander /kemɑ̃de/ [1] *vtr* to beg; **~ qch auprès de qn** to beg sth from sb, to beg sb for sth.

qu'en-dira-t-on /kɑ̃diʀatɔ̃/ *nm inv* gossip; **sans souci du ~** heedless of what people might say.

quenelle /kənɛl/ *nf*: *dumpling made of flour and egg, flavoured*GB *with meat or fish*.

quenotte○ /kənɔt/ *nf* toothy-peg○ GB LANG ENFANTIN; tooth.

quenouille /kənuj/ *nf* distaff.
IDIOMES **tomber en ~** to die out.

querelle /kəʀɛl/ *nf* **1** (dispute) quarrel (**entre** between); (chamaillerie) squabble; **chercher ~ à qn** to pick a quarrel with sb; **~s intestines** internal squabbling ⊄; **2** (débat) dispute.
■ **~ d'amoureux** lovers' tiff.

quereller /kəʀele/ [1] I† *vtr* (gronder) to tell [sb] off. II **se quereller** *vpr* to quarrel.

querelleur, -euse /kəʀɛlœʀ, øz/ *adj* quarrelsome.

question /kɛstjɔ̃/ *nf* **1** (interrogation) question (**sur** about); **je ne me suis jamais posé la ~** I've never really thought about it; **je me posais justement la ~** I was just wondering about that; **je ne sais pas, pose-leur la ~** I don't know, ask them; **sans se poser de ~s** unthinkingly; **2** (sujet) matter, question; (ensemble de problèmes) issue, question; **~ d'habitude** it's a matter of habit; **c'est une ~ de vie ou de mort** it's a matter of life and death; **il en fait une ~ de principe** he's making an issue of it; **la ~ n'est pas de savoir qui/comment/si** the question is not who/how/whether; **en ~** (dont il s'agit) in question; (qui pose problème) at issue; **(re)mettre en ~** (réexaminer) to reappraise; (repenser) to reassess; **se remettre en ~** to take a look at oneself; **la ~ n'est pas là** that's not the point; **les ~s à l'ordre du jour** the items on the agenda; **il est ~ d'elle dans l'article** she's mentioned in the article; **il est ~ qu'il prenne sa retraite** there's some talk of him retiring; **il n'est pas ~ que tu partes** (à un invité) you can't possibly leave; **pas ~!** no way○!; **3**○ (pour ce qui est de) **~ argent/santé, ça va** where money/health is concerned, things are OK; **la maison est jolie, mais ~ quartier...** the house is pretty, but as for the area...; **4** HIST (torture) question.
■ **~ de confiance** POL vote of confidence; **poser la ~ de confiance** to call for a vote of confidence.
IDIOMES **faire les ~s et les réponses** to do all the talking.

questionnaire /kɛstjɔnɛʀ/ *nm* questionnaire.

questionner /kɛstjɔne/ [1] *vtr* to question.

quête /kɛt/ *nf* **1** (d'aumônes) collection; **faire la ~** (à l'église) to take the collection; [*saltimbanque*] to pass the hat round; (pour une œuvre) to collect for charity; **2** (recherche) search (**de** for); **en ~ de nouvelles** in search of news; **être en ~ de qch** to be looking for sth; **la ~ du Graal** the quest for the Holy Grail.

quêter /kete/ [1] I *vtr* to look for, to seek [*approbation, pitié, soutien*]; to try to get [*sourire*].
II *vi* (à l'église) to take the collection; (pour une cause) **~ pour une œuvre** to collect for a charity.

quetsche /kwɛtʃ/ *nf* (sweet purple) plum.

queue /kø/ *nf* **1** ZOOL tail; **2** BOT (de feuille, fleur) stem; (de cerise, pomme) stalk GB, stem US; (de fraise) hull; **3** (manche) (de casserole, poêle) handle; **4** (de billard) cue; **5** (partie terminale) (d'animal, avion, de cerf-volant) tail; (de cortège, procession) tail(-end); (de train) rear, back; **6** (dans un classement) **ils arrivent en ~ (de peloton) des grandes entreprises** they come at the bottom of the league table of companies; **7** (file d'attente) queue GB, line US; **faire la ~** to stand in a queue GB, to stand in line US; **à la ~!** go to the back of the queue GB ou line US.
IDIOMES **une histoire sans ~ ni tête**○ a cock and bull story; **ce film n'a ni ~ ni tête**○ you can't make head or tail of this film; **la ~ basse** with one's tail

---

Remarques à propos de *quelque chose*

Dans les phrases affirmatives *quelque chose* se traduit par *something*:

> *quelque chose m'a frappé* = something struck me
> *j'ai vu quelque chose qui*
> *va te plaire* = I saw something that you will like

Dans les phrases interrogatives et conditionnelles, l'anglais fait une distinction entre une vraie question dont la réponse peut être *oui* ou *non* ou une vraie supposition:

> *avez-vous quelque chose à ajouter?*
> = have you got anything to add?
> *si tu vois quelque chose de louche*
> = if you see anything suspicious
> *si quelque chose leur arrivait*
> = if anything happened to them

et une supposition formulée sous forme de question:

> *tu fais une drôle de tête, tu as quelque chose à dire?*
> = you don't look too pleased, have you got something to say?

ou de suggestion:

> *si tu as vu quelque chose que tu aimerais pour ton anniversaire* = if you have seen something that you'd like for your birthday
> *si quelque chose te déplaît, dis-le*
> = if there's something you don't like, say so.

Voir exemples supplémentaires et exceptions dans l'entrée.

Dans les phrases affirmatives *quelqu'un* se traduit par *someone* ou *somebody*:

> *quelqu'un m'a dit qu'elle était malade*
> = someone told me she was ill
> *j'ai rencontré quelqu'un qui te connaissait*
> = I met someone who knew you

Dans les phrases interrogatives et conditionnelles l'anglais fait une distinction entre une vraie question dont la réponse peut être *oui* ou *non* ou une vraie supposition:

> *est-ce que quelqu'un parle grec?*
> = does anybody speak Greek?
> *est-ce que quelqu'un a vu mes clés?*
> = has anybody seen my keys?
> *est-ce que quelqu'un connaît la réponse?*
> = does anyone know the answer?
> *si quelqu'un téléphone, dites que je serai absent jusqu'à demain* = if anyone calls, say that I'll be away until tomorrow
> *si quelqu'un touche à mon ordinateur, il sera puni*
> = if anyone touches my computer, they'll be punished

et une supposition, un soupçon formulés sous forme de question:

> *est-ce que quelqu'un a touché à mon ordinateur?*
> = has somebody been playing with my computer?
> *est-ce que quelqu'un t'a donné la réponse?*
> = did someone give you the answer?

ou bien une requête ou une offre polie:

> *est-ce que quelqu'un pourrait fermer la fenêtre?*
> = could somebody close the window?
> *est-ce que quelqu'un veut encore du gâteau?*
> = would somebody like another piece of cake?
> *si quelqu'un voulait bien ouvrir la porte au chien*
> = if someone would please let the dog in

Dans les deux derniers cas, la réponse attendue est *oui*.

Voir exemples supplémentaires et exceptions dans l'entrée.

---

between one's legs; **il n'y en avait pas la ~ d'un(e)**○ there were none to be seen; **faire une ~ de poisson à qn** to cut in front of sb; **finir en ~ de poisson** to fizzle out, to peter out.

queue-de-cheval, *pl* **queues-de-cheval** /kød

qui

qui pronom interrogatif sujet se traduit par *who*:
   qui est-ce?   = who is it?
   qui a cassé la vitre? = who broke the window?
   qui vous a reçu?   = who met you?

qui pronom interrogatif dans des fonctions autres que sujet se traduit par *who* ou *whom*:
   qui avez-vous rencontré? = who did you meet?
           ou whom did you meet?
   qui vas-tu inviter? = who are you going to invite?
           ou whom are you going to invite?

La traduction avec *whom* appartient au registre de la langue écrite.

Lorsque le pronom interrogatif est utilisé avec une préposition, deux cas sont possibles:
   avec qui voulez-vous un rendez-vous?
       = who do you want an appointment with?
       ou with whom do you want an appointment?
   pour qui as-tu acheté cette montre?
       = who did you buy that watch for?
       ou for whom did you buy that watch?

Voir la remarque ci-dessus concernant *whom*.
Voir exemples supplémentaires et exceptions en **I** ci-dessous.

qui pronom relatif sujet se traduit par *who* lorsqu'il remplace un nom de personne:
   je remercie ceux qui m'ont aidé
       = my thanks to those who helped me
   j'ai rencontré Pierre qui m'a parlé de toi
       = I met Pierre who talked to me about you

et par *that* ou *which* (ce dernier étant plus spécifique à l'anglais britannique) dans la plupart des autres cas:
   le vase qui était sur la table
       = the vase that (*ou* which) was on the table
   une idée qui n'était pas mauvaise
       = an idea that (*ou* which) wasn't bad
   un chien qui avait l'air affamé
       = a dog that (*ou* which) looked hungry

Voir exemples supplémentaires et exceptions en **II 1** ci-dessous.

qui pronom relatif ayant une fonction autre que sujet et remplaçant un nom de personne se traduit par *that*, *who* ou *whom*, cette dernière traduction étant du domaine de la langue écrite:
   un ami en qui je peux avoir confiance
       = a friend that I can trust *ou* a friend who I can trust
       ou a friend whom I can trust *ou* (le pronom relatif peut parfois s'omettre en anglais) a friend I can trust

---

/ɔval/ *nf* ponytail; **elle se fait une ~** she puts her hair in a ponytail.

queue-de-pie°, *pl* **queues-de-pie** /kødpi/ *nf* tails (*pl*), tailcoat.

queux† /kø/ *nm inv* **maître ~** chef.

qui /ki/ **I** *pron inter* (fonction sujet) who; (fonction complément) whom; **~ veut-elle voir?** who does she want to speak to?; **à ~ sont ces livres?** whose books are these?; **de ~ est ce roman?** who is this novel by?; **dis-moi à ~ tu penses** tell me who you are thinking about.
II *pron rel* **1** (fonction sujet) (l'antécédent est un nom de personne) who; (autres cas) that, which; **le gouvernement ~ a été formé par** the government (which was) formed by; **le chien, ~ m'avait reconnu...** the dog, which recognized me...; **lui ~ s'intéresse aux armes à feu devrait aimer cette exposition** interested in firearms as he is, he should enjoy the exhibition; **toi ~ pensais faire des économies!** and you were the one who thought you were going to save money; **celui ~ a pris le livre aurait pu le dire** whoever took the book could have said so; **2** (fonction autre que sujet) **invitez ~ vous voulez** invite whoever ou anyone you like; **c'est à ~ des deux criera le plus fort** each (one) is trying to shout the other down; **quelqu'un en ~ j'ai confiance** someone I trust; **~ que vous soyez** whoever you are; **~ que ce soit** whoever it is, anybody; **je n'ai jamais frappé ~ que ce soit** I've never hit anybody; **~ que ce soit ~ a fait cela** whoever (it was who) did that; **~ que ce soit, je ne suis pas là** I'm not here for anybody; **3** FML **les enfants étaient déguisés ~ en indien, ~ en pirate** the children were dressed up, one as an Indian, one as a pirate.

quiche /kiʃ/ *nf* quiche, flan.
■ **~ lorraine** egg and bacon quiche.

quiconque /kikɔ̃k/ **I** *pron rel* whoever, anyone who.
II *pron indéf* anyone, anybody.

quiétude /kjetyd/ *nf* tranquillity (**de** of); **travailler en toute ~** to work undisturbed; **partez en toute ~, je m'occupe des chats** don't worry about a thing, I'll look after the cats while you're away.

quignon /kiɲɔ̃/ *nm* crusty end (of a loaf).

quille /kij/ *nf* **1** ▶329 (objet) skittle; **jouer aux ~s** to play skittles; **2** NAUT keel.
IDIOMES **être reçu comme un chien dans un jeu de ~s**° to be given a very unfriendly welcome.

quincaillerie /kɛ̃kajʀi/ *nf* **1** ▶374 (magasin) hardware shop GB ou store US, ironmonger's GB; **2** (articles) hardware; (industrie) hardware business.

quincaillier, -ère /kɛ̃kaje, ɛʀ/ ▶374 *nm,f* owner of a hardware shop GB ou store US, ironmonger GB.

quinconce /kɛ̃kɔ̃s/ *nm* **en ~** in staggered rows.

quinquagénaire /kɛ̃kaʒenɛʀ/ **I** *adj* **être ~** to be in one's fifties.
II *nmf* person in his/her fifties.

quinquennal, ~e, *mpl* -aux /kɛ̃kenal, o/ *adj* **1** (de cinq ans) [*plan*] five-year (*épith*); **2** (tous les cinq ans) five-yearly (*épith*).

quintal, *pl* -aux /kɛ̃tal, o/ ▶455 *nm* quintal.

quinte /kɛ̃t/ *nf* **1** MUS fifth; **2** JEUX (aux cartes) quint; **~ royale** royal flush; **3** SPORT (en escrime) quinte; **4** MÉD **une ~ (de toux)** a coughing fit.

quintessence /kɛ̃tesɑ̃s/ *nf* quintessence (**de** of).

quintette /kɛ̃tɛt/ *nm* MUS quintet.

quintuple /kɛ̃typl/ **I** *adj* [*nombre, rangée*] quintuple; **une somme ~ d'une autre** an amount five times more than another; **en ~ exemplaire** in five copies.
II *nm* **le ~ de cette quantité** five times the amount.

quintuplé, ~e /kɛ̃typle/ *nm,f* quintuplet.

quintupler /kɛ̃typle/ [1] *vtr, vi* to quintuple.

quinzaine /kɛ̃zɛn/ *nf* **1** (environ quinze) about fifteen; ▶ **cinquantaine**; **2** (deux semaines) fortnight GB, two weeks; **~ commerciale** two-week sale.

quinze /kɛ̃z/ ▶399, 298, 156 **I** *adj inv* fifteen; **~ jours** two weeks, a fortnight GB.
II *pron* fifteen.

quinzième /kɛ̃zjɛm/ ▶399, 156 *adj* fifteenth.

quiproquo /kipʀɔko/ *nm* (sur des personnes) case of mistaken identity; (sur des choses) misunderstanding.

quittance /kitɑ̃s/ *nf* (reçu) receipt; (facture) bill.

quitte /kit/ *adj* **1** (sans dette) **nous sommes ~s**, **je suis ~ avec lui** LIT, FIG we're quits; **2 en être ~ pour la peur/un rhume** to get off with a fright/a cold.
II quitte à *loc prép* **1** (au risque de) **nous voulons un barrage, ~ à inonder quelques fermes** we want a dam even if it means flooding a few farms; **2** (tant qu'à) **~ à aller à Londres, autant que ce soit pour quelques jours** if you're going to London anyway, you might as well go for a few days.
■ **~ ou double** double or quits.

quitter /kite/ [1] **I** *vtr* **1** (sortir de) [*personne*] to leave [*endroit, pays, ville, bureau*]; **il faut ~ la nationale 7 à Valence** you have to come off the nationale 7 at Valence; **2** (se séparer de) [*personne*] to leave [*personne, famille*]; **il faut que je vous quitte, j'ai une réunion** I must go now, I have a meeting; **3** (abandonner) to leave [*travail, poste, service, parti, entreprise*]; **~ l'enseignement** to give up teaching;

~ **la politique** to retire from politics; ~ **la scène** FIG [*acteur*] to give up acting; **tout en cuisinant, elle ne quittait pas ses enfants des yeux** while cooking, she didn' t let the children out of her sight; **il ne l'a pas quittée des yeux de tout le repas** he didn't take his eyes off her throughout the meal; **ne quittez pas** (au téléphone) hold the line, please; **4** (déménager) [*personne*] to leave [*lieu*]; [*entreprise*] to move from [*rue*]; to move out of [*bâtiment*]; **5** (laisser en mourant) EUPH **un grand homme nous a quittés** a great man has passed away EUPH; **quand je vous aurai quittés...** when I've gone...; **6** (enlever) [*personne*] to take off [*vêtement*]; ~ **le deuil** to come out of mourning.

II se quitter *vpr* (se séparer) to part; **nous nous sommes quittés bons amis** we parted the best of friends; **ils ne se quittent plus** they're inseparable now.

qui-vive /kiviv/ *nm inv* **être sur le** ~ to be on the alert.

quoi /kwa/ **I** *pron inter* what; ~**? je n'ai pas entendu** what? I didn't hear; **à** ~ **penses-tu?** what are you thinking about?; **à** ~ **bon recommencer?** what's the point of starting again?; **par** ~ **voulez-vous commencer?** (à table) what would you like to start with?; (tâche, travail) where would you like to start?; **pour** ~ **faire?** what for?; ~ **encore°?** what now?

II *pron rel* **il n'y a rien sur** ~ **vous puissiez fonder vos accusations** there's nothing on which you can base your accusations; **voilà sur** ~ **je fonde mes accusations** that's what I base my accusations on; **il prétend tout savoir, ce en** ~ **il se trompe** he claims he knows everything, and that's where he's wrong; **il se moque de tout ce en** ~ **elle croit** he laughs at everything she believes in; **ce en** ~ **il avait raison** and he was quite right; **à** ~ **il a répondu** to which he replied; **ce contre** ~ **ils se battent** what

they are fighting against; **(il n'y a) pas de** ~**!** (formule de politesse) think nothing of it, my pleasure; **il n'y a pas de** ~ **crier** there's no reason to shout; **il n'a (même) pas de** ~ **s'acheter un livre** he hasn't (even) got enough money to buy a book; **il a de** ~ **être satisfait** he's got good reason to feel satisfied; **dis-nous avec** ~ **tu as payé ta nouvelle voiture** tell us how you paid for your new car.

III *pron indéf* ~ **qu'elle puisse en dire** whatever she may say; **si je peux faire** ~ **que ce soit pour vous aider** if I can do anything to help you; **je ne m'étonne plus de** ~ **que ce soit** nothing surprises me any more; ~ **qu'il en soit** be that as it may.

IV *excl* really, basically; **alors,** ~°**!** really!; **il est prétentieux, stupide, pas du tout intéressant** ~°**!** he's pretentious, stupid, a dead loss° in fact!

quoique (**quoiqu'** *before vowel or mute* h) /kwak(ə)/ *conj* although, though; **nous sommes mieux ici qu'à Paris,** ~ we're better off here than in Paris, but then (again); **j'irai avec toi...,** ~**, c'est assez loin** I'll come with you...it's quite a long way though.

quota /kɔta/ *nm* quota (**sur** on).

quote-part, *pl* **quotes-parts** /kɔtpaʀ/ *nf* share.

quotidien, -ienne /kɔtidjɛ̃, ɛn/ **I** *adj* (de chaque jour) daily; (ordinaire) everyday (*épith*); **les tâches quotidiennes** daily tasks.

II *nm* **1** (journal) daily (paper); **2** (vie quotidienne) everyday life; **vivre la pauvreté au** ~ to experience real poverty on a daily basis.

quotidiennement /kɔtidjɛnmɑ̃/ *adv* every day, daily.

quotient /kɔsjɑ̃/ *nm* quotient.

■ ~ **intellectuel, QI** intelligence quotient, IQ.

Rr

r, R /ɛʀ/ *nm inv* r, R; **rouler les ~** to roll one's r's.

rab○ /ʀab/ *nm* **1** (ce qui est en trop) extra; **en ~** extra (*épith*); **faire du ~** (au travail) to do extra hours; **2** (portion supplémentaire) seconds.

rabâcher /ʀabaʃe/ [1] **I** *vtr* to keep repeating [*histoires, faits*].
II *vi* to keep harping on.

rabais /ʀabɛ/ *nm inv* discount; **obtenir un ~ de 20% sur qch** to get a 20% discount on sth; **au ~** [*achat, vente*] at a discount; [*matériel*] cheap; [*travail*] badly paid; [*chef, acteur*] third-rate.

rabaisser /ʀabese/ [1] **I** *vtr* to belittle [*mérite, personne*]; **~ les prétentions de qn** to humble sb's pride.
II se rabaisser *vpr* (en paroles) to run oneself down; (par son comportement) to demean oneself.

rabat /ʀaba/ *nm* (de sac, meuble, poche) flap.

rabat-joie /ʀabaʒwa/ *adj inv* **être ~** to be a killjoy.

rabattable /ʀabatabl/ *adj* [*siège*] folding (*épith*).

rabatteur, -euse /ʀabatœʀ, øz/ *nm,f* (à la chasse) beater.

rabattre /ʀabatʀ/ [61] **I** *vtr* **1** (refermer) [*personne*] to shut [*capot, couvercle*]; to fold [*tablette*]; to put up [*strapontin*]; [*vent*] to blow [sth] back [*volet*]; **2** (plier) to turn [sth] down [*col*]; to take in [*coutures*]; to take up [*ourlet*]; to turn [sth] back [*couverture*]; to turn [sth] down [*drap*] (**sur** over); **3** (faire descendre) [*personne*] to pull [sth] down [*chapeau, jupe*] (**sur** over); [*vent*] to blow [sth] down [*fumée*]; [*joueur*] to smash [*balle*]; **~ l'orgueil de qn** to humble sb's pride; **4** (retrancher) to knock [sth] off [*pourcentage, somme*]; **5** (à la chasse) to beat [*gibier*]; **6** (racoler) to tout for○ [*clientèle*].
II se rabattre *vpr* **1** (se refermer) [*capot, couvercle*] to shut; [*tablette*] to fold up; [*volet*] to bang to; **2** (rentrer dans sa file) [*automobiliste, véhicule*] to pull back in; **3** (s'accommoder) **se ~ sur** (faute de mieux) to make do with; (après réflexion) to settle for.

rabbin /ʀabɛ̃/ ▶596 *nm* rabbi; **grand ~** chief rabbi.

rabibocher○ /ʀabibɔʃe/ [1] **I** *vtr* **~ Pierre avec Paul** to bring Pierre and Paul together.
II se rabibocher *vpr* to make up.

râble /ʀabl/ *nm* (de lapin, lièvre) saddle.
IDIOMES **ils nous sont tombés sur le ~**○ they laid into us○.

râblé, ~e /ʀɑble/ *adj* **1** [*animal*] sturdy; **2** [*personne*] stocky.

rabot /ʀabo/ *nm* plane.

raboter /ʀabɔte/ [1] *vtr* TECH to plane.

rabougri, ~e /ʀabugʀi/ *adj* [*arbre, tronc*] stunted; [*fruit, adulte*] shrivelled^GB up; [*vieillard*] wizened.

rabougrir: se rabougrir /ʀabugʀiʀ/ [3] *vpr* [*plante*] to become stunted; [*vieillard*] to become wizened.

rabrouer /ʀabʀue/ [1] *vtr* to snub.

racaille /ʀakaj/ *nf* scum.

raccommoder /ʀakɔmɔde/ [1] **I** *vtr* **1** to mend [*filet*]; to darn [*bas*]; **2**○ to reconcile [*personnes*].
II○ **se raccommoder** *vpr* (se réconcilier) to make it up○ (**avec** with).

raccompagner /ʀakɔ̃paɲe/ [1] *vtr* (à pied) to walk [sb] (back) home; (en voiture) to drive [sb] (back) home.

raccord /ʀakɔʀ/ *nm* **1** (de planche, papier peint) join; **faire un ~** (en posant du papier peint) to line up the pattern; **2** (retouche en peinture) touch-up; **3** (transition) (dans un film) link shot; **4** TECH joint.

raccordement /ʀakɔʀdəmɑ̃/ *nm* (jonction) (de route) link road; (de voie ferrée) loop line; TÉLÉCOM connection, hookup US; (de tubes) joint.

raccorder /ʀakɔʀde/ [1] *vtr* **1** GÉN to connect (**à** to); to link together [*chapitres, parties*]; to line up [*motifs de papier peint*]; **2** TÉLÉCOM (par câble) to connect, to hook up US; (par satellite) to link up; **3** CIN to link [sth] together [*scènes, plans*].

raccourci /ʀakuʀsi/ *nm* **1** (chemin) shortcut; **prendre un ~** to take a shortcut; **2** (image réductrice) **c'est un peu un ~** it's a bit simplistic; **en ~** in short.

raccourcir /ʀakuʀsiʀ/ [3] **I** *vtr* GÉN to shorten (**de** by); to cut [*texte, discours*]; to cut short [*visite*].
II *vi* [*vêtement*] (au lavage) to shrink (**de** by); (avec la mode) to get shorter; US; (par satellite) [*jours*] to get shorter (**de** by), to draw in.
IDIOMES **tomber sur qn à bras ~s**○ FIG to lay into sb.

raccrocher /ʀakʀɔʃe/ [1] **I** *vtr* **1** (remettre) to hang [sth] back up [*rideaux, manteau, tableau*] (**à, sur** on); **2** TÉLÉCOM **le combiné** to put the telephone down.
II *vi* **1** TÉLÉCOM to hang up; **~ au nez de qn**○ to hang up on sb; **2**○ SPORT to give up competition.
III se raccrocher *vpr* **se ~ à** LIT to grab hold of [*bras, rebord*]; FIG to cling to [*personne, prétexte*].

race /ʀas/ *nf* **1** (d'êtres humains) race; **2** ZOOL breed; **cheval de ~** thoroughbred (horse); **chien de ~** pedigree (dog); **3**○ (catégorie de personnes) **une ~ guerrière** a race of warriors.

racé, ~e /ʀase/ *adj* **1** [*cheval*] thoroughbred; [*chien*] pedigree (*épith*); **2** [*objet*] classically elegant.

rachat /ʀaʃa/ *nm* **1** (d'objet vendu) buying back, buyback; **2** (de société) buyout; **3** (d'actions) repurchase; **4** (de dette) redemption; **5** (pardon) redemption.

racheter /ʀaʃte/ [18] **I** *vtr* **1** (récupérer un objet vendu) to buy [sth] back; **2** (acheter encore) **je vais ~ du vin** I'll buy some more wine; **3** (pour renouveler) **mes draps sont usés, il faut que j'en rachète** my sheets are worn out, I'll have to buy new ones; **4** (acheter) to buy out [*société, usine*]; to buy up [*ensemble d'actions*]; **5** [*pécheur*] to atone for [*faute*] (**par** by); [*qualité*] to make up for [*défaut*]; **6** [*examinateur*] to mark up [*candidat, copie*].
II se racheter *vpr* to redeem oneself (**par** through).

rachitique /ʀaʃitik/ *adj* **1** MÉD [*personne*] **il est ~** he suffers from rickets; **2** (maigre) [*animal, plante, personne*] scrawny.

rachitisme /ʀaʃitism/ *nm* rickets (+ *v sg*).

racial, ~e, mpl -iaux /ʀasjal, o/ *adj* racial; **émeutes/relations ~es** race riots/relations.

racine /ʀasin/ *nf* (tous contextes) root; **prendre ~** LIT, FIG to take root; **prendre** or **attaquer le mal à la ~** to strike at the root of the problem; **~ carrée/cubique** MATH square/cube root.

racisme /ʀasism/ *nm* **1** (doctrine) racism; **2** (discrimination) **~ anti-étudiants** prejudice against students.

raciste /ʀasist/ *adj, nm,f* racist.

racket /ʀakɛt/ *nm* (organisation) extortion racket; (activité) racketeering; **c'est du ~!** it's extortion!

raclée○ /ʀakle/ *nf* hiding○.

racler /ʀakle/ [1] **I** *vtr* **1** (nettoyer) to scrape [sth] clean [*plat*]; ▶tiroir; **2** (enlever) to scrape off [*rouille*]; **3** (frotter) [*pneu*] to scrape against [*trottoir*].

II **se racler** *vpr* se ~ **la gorge** to clear one's throat.

raclette /ʀɑklɛt/ *nf* **1** CULIN raclette; **2** (racloir) scraper.

racloir /ʀɑklwaʀ/ *nm* scraper.

racolage /ʀakɔlaʒ/ *nm* **1** (d'électeurs, de partisans) touting (**de** for); **le ~ publicitaire** canvassing; **2** (par une prostituée) soliciting (**de** for).

racoler /ʀakɔle/ [1] *vtr* **1** [*politicien*] to tout for [*électeurs*]; (pour un spectacle) to tout for, to bark for⚬ [*passants*]; **2** [*prostituée*] to solicit for [*clients*].

racoleur, -euse /ʀakɔlœʀ, øz/ *adj* [*affiche*] eye-catching; [*slogan*] catchy; [*regard, sourire*] enticing.

racontar⚬ /ʀakɔ̃taʀ/ *nm* piece of idle gossip.

raconter /ʀakɔ̃te/ [1] *vtr* **1** (relater) [*personne*] to tell [*histoire*]; [*film, livre*] to tell [*histoire*]; to describe [*fait, épisode, rencontre, amitié, vie, accident*]; **~ en détail** to describe in detail; **alors! raconte!** tell me all about it then!; **il raconte bien** he's a great storyteller; **je suis tombée en panne, je te raconte pas**⚬! my car broke down, I'll spare you the details!; **tu racontes n'importe quoi!** you're talking nonsense!; **2** (prétendre) to say; **on raconte que** they say that; **3** (dépeindre) LITER [*personne*] to describe [*époque, mœurs, pays*].

racornir /ʀakɔʀniʀ/ [3] **I** *vtr* (durcir) to harden [*peau*]; to stiffen [*cuir*]; FIG to harden [*personne, cœur*].

II **se racornir** *vpr* (devenir dur) [*peau*] to harden; FIG [*cœur*] to harden; [*cuir*] to stiffen.

radar /ʀadaʀ/ *nm* radar; **au ~** by radar; **effectuer des contrôles ~** to carry out radar speed checks; **marcher au ~**⚬ FIG to be on autopilot.

rade /ʀad/ *nf* NAUT roads (*pl*); **en ~ de Toulon** in the Toulon roads; **mouiller en ~** to lie at anchor.
IDIOMES **rester en ~**⚬ [*personne*] to be left stranded; [*projet*] to be shelved.

radeau, *pl* ~**x** /ʀado/ *nm* (embarcation) raft.

radiateur /ʀadjatœʀ/ *nm* radiator.

radiation /ʀadjasjɔ̃/ *nf* **1** PHYS radiation; **2** (de personne) GÉN expulsion; (de médecin) striking off from the register GB, loss of the license to practice medicine US; (d'avocat) disbarment.

radical, ~e, *mpl* **-aux** /ʀadikal, o/ *adj*, *nm,f* GÉN, POL radical.

radicalement /ʀadikalmɑ̃/ *adv* [*opposé, différent*] radically; [*nouveau*] completely; [*efficace*] extremely; [*changer*] radically.

radicaliser /ʀadikalize/ [1] **I** *vtr* [*syndicat, parti*] to toughen [*attitude*]; to harden [*politique*]; to step up [*revendications*].

II **se radicaliser** *vpr* [*personne*] to become more radical.

radicelle /ʀadisɛl/ *nf* rootlet.

radié, ~e /ʀadje/ *adj* BOT rayed.

radier /ʀadje/ [2] *vtr* ~ **qn d'une liste** to remove sb from a list; **~ un médecin** to strike off a doctor GB, to take away a doctor's license US; **~ un avocat** to disbar a lawyer.

radieux, -ieuse /ʀadjø, øz/ *adj* **1** (éclatant) [*soleil*] dazzling; (ensoleillé) [*temps, matinée*] glorious; **3** (heureux) [*visage, air, sourire*] radiant; [*personne*] radiant with joy (*jamais épith*); [*souvenir*] glorious; **4** (prometteur) [*avenir*] brilliant.

radin⚬, **~e** /ʀadɛ̃, in/ **I** *adj* stingy⚬.
II *nm,f* skinflint⚬.

radinerie⚬ /ʀadinʀi/ *nf* stinginess⚬.

radio[1] /ʀadjo/ **I** *adj inv* [*contact, signal*] radio.
II ▶ 374] *nm* (opérateur) radio operator.

radio[2] /ʀadjo/ *nf* **1** (appareil) radio; **2** (radiodiffusion) radio; **poste de ~** radio; **à la ~** on the radio; **3** (station) radio station; **4** (radiographie) X-ray; **passer une ~ des poumons** to have a chest X-ray.
■ **~ libre** independent local radio station.

radioactivité /ʀadjoaktivite/ *nf* radioactivity.

radiocassette /ʀadjokasɛt/ *nm ou f* (lecteur) radio cassette player; (enregistreur) radio cassette recorder.

radiocommande /ʀadjokɔmɑ̃d/ *nf* radio control.

radiodiffuser /ʀadjodifyze/ [1] *vtr* to broadcast.

radioélectricien, -ienne /ʀadjoelɛktʀisjɛ̃, ɛn/ ▶ 374] *nm,f* radio engineer.

radiographie /ʀadjogʀafi/ *nf* **1** (procédé) radiography, X-ray photography; **2** (cliché) X-ray (photograph).

radiographier /ʀadjogʀafje/ [2] *vtr* to X-ray.

radiographique /ʀadjogʀafik/ *adj* X-ray.

radioguidage /ʀadjogidaʒ/ *nm* AVIAT, NAUT radio control; **~ des automobilistes** traffic information service.

radioguider /ʀadjogide/ [1] *vtr* to control by radio.

radiologie /ʀadjolɔʒi/ *nf* radiology.

radiologiste /ʀadjolɔʒist/, **radiologue** /ʀadjolɔg/ ▶ 374] *nmf* radiologist.

radiophonique /ʀadjofɔnik/ *adj* [*programme, production*] radio (*épith*); **techniques ~s** (radio) broadcasting techniques.

radio-réveil, *pl* **radios-réveils** /ʀadjoʀevɛj/ *nm* clock radio.

radioscopie /ʀadjoskɔpi/ *nf* fluoroscopy.

radiothérapie /ʀadjoteʀapi/ *nf* radiotherapy.

radis /ʀadi/ *nm inv* radish; **~ noir** black radish.
IDIOMES **je n'ai plus un ~**⚬ I haven't got a penny.

radius /ʀadjys/ *nm inv* radius.

radotage /ʀadotaʒ/ *nm* drivel **C**.

radoter /ʀadote/ [1] **I** *vtr* to tell [sth] again and again.
II *vi* (se répéter) to repeat oneself; (dire des bêtises) to talk drivel⚬.

radoteur, -euse /ʀadotœʀ, øz/ *nm,f* driveller[GB].

radoucir /ʀadusiʀ/ [3] **I** *vtr* to soften up [*personne*].
II **se radoucir** *vpr* [*voix*] to become softer; [*personne*] to soften up; [*humeur*] to improve; [*temps*] to turn milder.

radoucissement /ʀadusismɑ̃/ *nm* **la météo annonce un ~** the forecast is for milder weather.

rafale /ʀafal/ *nf* **1** (de vent, pluie) gust; (de neige) flurry; **vent qui souffle en ~s** gusty wind; **2** (de mitraillette) burst; **tir en ~s** bursts (*pl*) of gunfire.

raffermir /ʀafɛʀmiʀ/ [3] **I** *vtr* **1** LIT to tone [*épiderme*]; to tone up [*musculature*]; **2** FIG [*personne*] to strengthen [*autorité, position*]; to steady [*marché*].
II **se raffermir** *vpr* [*tissus, peau*] to become firmer; [*voix*] to become more assured; [*cours boursier*] to become steady; [*sol*] to harden.

raffermissement /ʀafɛʀmismɑ̃/ *nm* **1** (de peau) firming up; **2** (de monnaie, taux) steadying; **le ~ du franc vis-à-vis du mark** the strengthening of the franc against the deutschmark.

raffinage /ʀafinaʒ/ *nm* refining.

raffiné, ~e /ʀafine/ *adj* [*personne, civilisation*] refined; [*cuisine*] sophisticated; **un type**⚬ **pas très ~** a rather uncouth character; **un mets ~** a delicacy.

raffinement /ʀafinmɑ̃/ *nm* **1** (de personne, civilisation) refinement; **2** (de décor, d'habillement) elegance (**de** of).

raffiner /ʀafine/ [1] *vtr* to refine.

raffinerie /ʀafinʀi/ *nf* refinery.

raffoler /ʀafɔle/ [1] *vtr ind* **~ de** to be crazy⚬ about.

raffut⚬ /ʀafy/ *nm* **1** (bruit) racket⚬; **2** (scandale) stink⚬; **faire du ~** to raise a stink.

rafiot⚬ /ʀafjo/ *nm* boat, (old) tub⚬.

rafistolage⚬ /ʀafistɔlaʒ/ *nm* **1** (action) patching up; **2** (réparation) makeshift repair; FIG stop-gap solution.

rafistoler⚬ /ʀafistɔle/ [1] *vtr* to patch up.

rafle /ʀɑfl/ *nf* (opération) raid; (arrestation massive) roundup; **faire une ~** to carry out a raid (**dans, chez** on).

rafler⚬ /ʀɑfle/ [1] *vtr* **1** (emporter) to make off with, to swipe⚬ [*bijoux, provisions*]; **2** (obtenir) to walk off with [*médaille, récompense*]; to snap up [*contrat, marché*].

rafraîchir /ʀafʀeʃiʀ/ [3] **I** *vtr* (refroidir) [*pluie*] to cool

[*atmosphère*]; [*glaçons*] to chill [*eau*]; **le thé glacé te rafraîchira** the iced tea will cool you down.
II se rafraîchir *vpr* [*temps, atmosphère*] to become ou get cooler; [*personne*] to refresh oneself.
IDIOMES **~ la mémoire○ de qn** to refresh sb's memory.

rafraîchissant, **-e** /ʀafʀɛʃisɑ̃, ɑ̃t/ *adj* refreshing.

rafraîchissement /ʀafʀɛʃismɑ̃/ *nm* **1** MÉTÉO drop in temperature; **2** (boisson) refreshment.

ragaillardir /ʀagajaʀdiʀ/ [3] *vtr* to cheer [sb] up; **je me sens (tout) ragaillardi** I feel much brighter.

rage /ʀaʒ/ *nf* **1** ▶196| MÉD rabies **¢**; **2** (fureur) rage; **être en ~ contre qn/contre qch** to be furious with sb/about sth; **être fou de ~** to be in a mad rage; **se mettre** or **entrer dans une ~ folle** to fly into a rage; **avoir la ~ au cœur** or **au ventre○** to (inwardly) seethe with rage; **mettre qn en ~** to make sb's blood boil; **faire ~** [*maladie, concurrence*] to be rife; [*épidémie, incendie, bataille*] to rage.
■ **~ de dents** raging toothache.
IDIOMES **qui veut noyer son chien l'accuse de la ~** give a dog a bad name and hang him.

rageant○, **-e** /ʀaʒɑ̃, ɑ̃t/ *adj* infuriating.

rageur, **-euse** /ʀaʒœʀ, øz/ *adj* furious.

rageusement /ʀaʒøzmɑ̃/ *adv* **1** (avec colère) [*s'écrier*] furiously; [*écrire*] angrily; **2○** (sans relâche) furiously.

ragondin /ʀagɔ̃dɛ̃/ *nm* (animal, fourrure) coypu.

ragot○ /ʀago/ *nm* malicious gossip **¢**.

ragoût /ʀagu/ *nm* stew, ragout.

ragoûtant, **-e** /ʀagutɑ̃, ɑ̃t/ *adj* **peu** or **pas très ~** [*cuisine, mets*] rather unappetizing; [*affaire*] rather unsavoury^GB.

rai /ʀɛ/ *nm* **~ de lumière** ray of light.

raï /ʀaj/ *nm*: *music from the Maghreb with Western influences.*

raid /ʀɛd/ *nm* **1** MIL raid; **~ aérien** air raid; **2** SPORT (à pied, ski, VTT) trek; **3** FIN raid (**sur** on).

raide /ʀɛd/ **I** *adj* **1** (sans souplesse) GÉN stiff; [*cheveux*] straight; (tendu) [*corde*] taut; **2** (à pic) [*pente, escalier*] steep; **3○** (exagéré) **je trouve ça un peu ~** that's a bit steep; **4○** (désargenté) broke○.
II *adv* [*monter, descendre*] steep.
IDIOMES **être/se tenir ~ comme un piquet** to be/to stand stiff as a ramrod; **tomber ~** (d'étonnement) to be flabbergasted; **tomber ~ mort** to drop dead.

raideur /ʀɛdœʀ/ *nf* **1** (de jambe, dos) stiffness; **avec ~** [*marcher, répondre*] stiffly; **2** (de pente) steepness.

raidir /ʀɛdiʀ/ [3] **I** *vtr* **1** LIT to tighten [*cordage*]; to tense [*bras, corps*]; **2** FIG to harden [*attitude*].
II se raidir *vpr* **1** LIT [*cordage*] to get tighter; [*bras, corps*] to tense up; [*tissu*] to stiffen; **2** FIG **se ~ contre la douleur** to brace oneself against pain.

raie /ʀɛ/ *nf* **1** (dans une coiffure) parting GB, part US; **2** (griffure) scratch; **3** (poisson) skate.

rail /ʀaj/ *nm* **1** (de chemin de fer) rail, track; **sortir des ~s** LIT to leave the track, to jump the track US; **2** (moyen de transport) **le ~** rail; **transport par ~** rail transport; **3** (de tringle, porte) rail.
■ **~ de sécurité** crash barrier.

railler /ʀaje/ [1] **I** *vtr* to make fun of.
II se railler *vpr* **se ~ de** to make fun of.

raillerie /ʀajʀi/ *nf* **1** (attitude) mockery **¢**; **dire qch sur le ton de la ~** to say sth in a mocking tone; **2** (propos) mocking remark; **être l'objet de ~s** to be a laughing stock; **être l'objet des ~s de qn** to be the butt of sb's jokes.

railleur, **-euse** /ʀajœʀ, øz/ **I** *adj* mocking.
II *nm,f* mocker.

rainette /ʀɛnɛt/ *nf* tree frog.

rainure /ʀenyʀ/ *nf* groove.

raisin /ʀezɛ̃/ *nm* **1** (fruit) grapes (*pl*); **une grappe de ~** a bunch of grapes; **un grain de ~** a grape; **2** (variété) grape; **un ~ sucré** a sweet grape.
■ **~s de Corinthe** currants; **~s secs** raisins.

raison /ʀezɔ̃/ *nf* **1** (motif) reason; **n'avoir aucune ~ de** to have no reason to; **pour ~(s) de santé** for

health reasons; **pour des ~s d'hygiène** for reasons of hygiene; **on ne sait pour quelle ~** for unknown reasons; **il y a une ~ à cela** there's a reason for that; **~ d'agir** reason for action; **~ de plus pour faire** all the more reason to do; **en ~ d'une panne** owing to a breakdown; **à plus forte ~** even more so; **à juste ~** quite rightly; **avec ~** justifiably; **comme de ~** as one might expect; **~ d'inquiétude** cause for alarm; **~ d'espoir** grounds (*pl*) for hope; **2** (opposé à tort) **avoir ~** to be right; **avoir un peu ~** to be partly right; **à** or **avec ~** rightly; **donner ~ à qn** to agree with sb; **obtenir ~** to obtain satisfaction; **3** (rationalité) reason **¢**; **la folie l'a emporté sur la ~** folly won the day; **se rendre à la ~** to see reason; **faire entendre ~ à qn** to make sb see reason; **ramener qn à la ~** to bring sb to his/her senses; **perdre la ~** to lose one's mind; **se faire une ~ de qch** to resign oneself to sth; **plus que de ~** more than is sensible; **avoir ~ de qn/qch** to get the better of sb/sth; **à ~ de** at the rate of; ▶ **rime**.
■ **~ d'État** reasons (*pl*) of State; **~ d'être** (de vivre) reason for living; **n'avoir aucune ~ d'être** to have no justification; **~ sociale** company ou corporate name.
IDIOMES **la ~ du plus fort est toujours la meilleure** PROV might is right PROV.

raisonnable /ʀɛzɔnabl/ *adj* **1** (pas trop élevé) [*prix, distance, délais*] reasonable; [*consommation, natalité*] moderate; **2** (mesuré) [*personne, objectif*] reasonable; [*politique, enthousiasme*] moderate; **3** (sensé) [*personne, idée*] sensible; **4** (doué de raison) rational.

raisonnablement /ʀɛzɔnabləmɑ̃/ *adv* [*expliquer*] reasonably; [*propre, confiant*] reasonably; [*boire, fumer*] in moderation; [*gérer, parler*] sensibly.

raisonné, **-e** /ʀɛzɔne/ **I** *pp* ▶ **raisonner**.
II *pp adj* **1** (prudent) [*attitude*] cautious; [*décision*] carefully thought out; **2** (contrôlé) [*passion*] controlled^GB; [*enthousiasme*] measured.

raisonnement /ʀɛzɔnmɑ̃/ *nm* **1** (suite d'arguments) reasoning **¢** ou *sg*; **selon le même ~** by the same token; **je ne tiens pas le même ~** I look at it differently; **avec ce genre de ~** with that sort of thinking; **2** (type de pensée) thinking; **~ économique** economic thinking.
■ **~ par l'absurde** reductio ad absurdum.

raisonner /ʀɛzɔne/ [1] **I** *vtr* to reason with [*personne, enfant*]; to rationalize [*sentiment, peur*]; **se laisser ~** to let oneself be talked round GB ou persuaded.
II *vi* to think; **~ à court terme** to think in the short term; **~ avant d'agir** to think carefully before acting.
III se raisonner *vpr* [*personne*] to be more sensible, to pull oneself together.

rajeunir /ʀaʒœniʀ/ [3] **I** *vtr* **1** (physiquement) to make [sb] look younger; (moralement) to make [sb] feel younger; **sa coiffure la rajeunit de cinq ans** that hairstyle makes her look five years younger ou takes five years off her; **2** (attribuer un âge moindre à) **~ qn** to make sb out to be younger; **votre fils a 25 ans! cela ne nous rajeunit pas** your son is 25! we're not getting any younger; **3** (rendre plus moderne) to give a new look to, to brighten up [*bâtiment, fauteuil*]; to modernize [*secteur économique, organisation, équipement*]; to update, to bring [sth] up to date [*livre, guide, règlement*]; **4** (abaisser la moyenne d'âge) to bring ou inject new blood into [*parti, profession*].
II *vi* **1** (physiquement) [*personne*] to look younger; **2** (moralement) [*personne*] to feel younger.
III se rajeunir *vpr* **1** (essayer de paraître plus jeune) to make oneself look younger; **2** (se dire plus jeune) to make oneself out to be younger (than one is).

rajeunissant, **-e** /ʀaʒœnisɑ̃, ɑ̃t/ *adj* rejuvenating.

rajeunissement /ʀaʒœnismɑ̃/ *nm* **1** (de groupe, population) **nous avons enregistré un ~ de la population** we see that the population is getting younger; **2** (d'entreprise, de bâtiment) modernization; (de livre, manuel, règlement) updating; **3** (de personnes) rejuvenation.

ajouter /aʒute/ [1] *vtr* to add (**à** to); **en ~** (mentir) to exaggerate; (en faire trop) to overdo it.

ajuster /aʒyste/ [1] *vtr* to straighten [*chapeau, vêtement*]; to push [sth] back up [*lunettes*].

âle /ɑl/ *nm* **1** (bruit pulmonaire) rale; **2** (de mourant) death rattle.

alenti, ~e /alɑ̃ti/ **I** *pp* ▶ **ralentir**.

II *pp adj* [*geste, rythme, croissance*] slower.

III *nm* CIN slow motion.

IV au ralenti *loc adv* **fonctionner au ~** [*machine, entreprise*] to be just ticking over; [*personne*] to be running at half-speed; **tourner au ~** [*moteur*] to be ticking over GB, to idle.

alentir /alɑ̃tiʀ/ [3] *vtr, vi*, **se ralentir** *vpr* to slow down.

alentissement /alɑ̃tismɑ̃/ *nm* **1** (processus) slowing down; **2** (sur les routes) tailback.

alentisseur /alɑ̃tisœʀ/ *nm* **1** (système de freins) engine brake; **2** (sur la chaussée) sleeping policeman GB, speed ramp.

âler /ɑle/ [1] *vi* **1** (protester) to moan (**contre** about); **ça me fait ~** it annoys ou bugs me; **2** [*mourant*] to give the death rattle.

âleur, -euse /ɑlœʀ, øz/ *nm,f* moaner.

alliement /alimɑ̃/ *nm* rallying (**de qn à qch** of sb to sth); **de ~** [*cri, point, signe*] rallying.

allier /alje/ [2] **I** *vtr* **1** (rassembler) to rally [*troupes, navires*]; **2** (convaincre) to rally [*partisans*]; to win over [*opposants*] (**à** to); **solution qui rallie tous les suffrages** solution that has unanimous support; **~ qn à sa cause** to win sb over; **3** (adhérer à) to rejoin [*groupe, parti*]; **4** (rejoindre) [*militaire*] to rejoin [*poste*]; [*diplomate, fonctionnaire*] to take up [*poste*]; **~ la terre** [*navire*] to make landfall.

II se rallier *vpr* **se ~ à** to rally to [*républicains*]; to come round to [*opinion*]; **elle s'est ralliée à notre cause** she was won over.

allonge /alɔ̃ʒ/ *nf* **1** (de fil électrique) extension cord, extension lead GB; (de table) leaf; **table à ~s** extending table; **nom à ~(s)** double-barrelled name GB, hyphenated name; **2** (d'argent) additional sum; (de temps) extension.

allonger /alɔ̃ʒe/ [13] **I** *vtr* to extend [*fil, table, période*] (**de** by); to make [sth] longer [*paragraphe*]; **~ une jupe** (par l'ourlet) to let a skirt down; **~ la paie** to increase wages (**de** by).

II *vi* **les jours rallongent** the days are drawing out.

III se rallonger *vpr* to lie down again.

allumer /alyme/ [1] **I** *vtr* to relight [*feu, pipe*]; **~ la lumière** to put the light on again.

II se rallumer *vpr* **1** [*incendie*] to flare up again; **les lumières se sont rallumées** the lights came back on; **2** FIG [*querelles, passions, guerre*] to flare up again.

allye /ali/ *nm* **1** SPORT (car) rally; **2** (réunion mondaine) party.

amadan /ramadɑ̃/ *nm* Ramadan; **faire le ~** to keep Ramadan.

amage /ramaʒ/ **I** *nm* (d'oiseau) LITER song.

II ramages *nmpl* (motif) foliage pattern.

amassage /ramasaʒ/ *nm* **1** (de coquillages, d'œufs) collecting; (de fruits, feuilles mortes, débris) picking up; **2** (fait de collecter) (de cahiers, copies) taking in, collection; (d'ordures ménagères) collection; (d'enfants) collection GB, picking up; **car de ~** (pour employés) works ou company bus; (scolaire) school bus.

amassé, ~e /ramase/ **I** *pp* ▶ **ramasser**.

II *pp adj* **1** (trapu) stocky, squat; **2** (recroquevillé) **~ sur lui-même** hunched up; **3** (concis) [*style, expression*] concise.

amasser /ramase/ [1] **I** *vtr* **1** (prendre par terre) to collect [*bois, œufs*]; to pick up [*crayon*]; to dig up [*pommes de terre*]; **~ à la pelle** LIT to shovel [sth] up [*terre*], FIG (en grande quantité) to get bucketfuls of [*argent*]; **2** (collecter) to take [sth] in, to collect [*cahiers, devoirs*]; to collect [*ordures ménagères*]; to collect GB, to pick up [*écoliers*]; **3** (rassembler) to pick up [*objets, jouets*]; **4** (relever) to pick up [*ivrogne*];

5 (recueillir) to collect GB, to take in [*personne, animal*]; **6** (arrêter) [*police*] to nick sb.

II se ramasser *vpr* **1** (se replier) to huddle up, to shrink into oneself; (se pelotonner) to curl up; **2** (échouer) to come a cropper.

ramassis /ramasi/ *nm inv* PEJ (de vauriens) bunch; (d'idées, objets) jumble.

rambarde /ʀɑ̃baʀd/ *nf* guardrail.

rame /ʀam/ *nf* **1** NAUT oar; **traversée à la ~** crossing in a rowing boat; **2** (de papier) ream; **3** (métro, train) train; **une ~ de métro** a metro train.

IDIOMES **il n'en fiche pas une ~** he doesn't do a stroke.

rameau, pl ~x /ramo/ *nm* GÉN branch; **~ d'olivier** olive branch.

Rameaux /ramo/ *nmpl* **les ~** Palm Sunday.

ramener /ramne/ [16] **I** *vtr* **1** (réduire) **~ l'inflation à 5%** to reduce inflation to 5 per cent; **~ qch à de justes proportions** or **à sa juste mesure** to get sth into proportion; **2** (faire revenir) to restore [*ordre, paix*]; **~ qn à la réalité** to bring sb back to reality; **~ qn à de meilleurs sentiments** to put sb into a better frame of mind; **~ qn sur terre** to bring sb down to earth; **~ qn à la vie** or **à soi** to bring sb round; **~ qn à la raison** to bring sb to his/her senses; **~ toujours tout à soi** always to relate everything to oneself; **3** (reconduire) to take [sb/sth] back; **~ qn en voiture** to give sb a lift GB ou ride US home; **4** (faire rentrer) to bring [sb/sth] back; **5** (rapporter) to bring back [*pain, photos, maladie*] (**de** from); to return [*objet prêté*]; to win [*médaille, titre*]; **6** (déplacer) '**~ les genoux vers le menton** 'draw your knees up to your chin'; **~ ses cheveux en arrière** (avec un peigne) to comb one's hair back; (avec la main) to sweep one's hair back; **~ son manteau sur ses genoux** to pull one's coat over one's knees.

II se ramener *vpr* **1** (être réductible) **se ~ à** to come down to, to boil down to; **2** (venir) to come over.

IDIOMES **la ~** (intervenir intempestivement) to stick one's oar in; (se vanter avec ostentation) to show off.

ramequin /ramkɛ̃/ *nm* ramekin.

ramer /rame/ [1] *vi* **1** NAUT to row; **2** (travailler dur) to work like a dog.

rameur, -euse /ramœʀ, øz/ *nm,f* GÉN rower; SPORT oarsman/oarswoman.

rameuter /ramøte/ [1] *vtr* to round up.

rami /rami/ ▶ **329** *nm* JEUX rummy.

ramier /ramje/ *nm* woodpigeon.

ramification /ramifikasjɔ̃/ *nf* **1** (de société secrète) network; (d'entreprise) several offshoots (*pl*); **2** (d'histoire, de complot) ramification; **3** (subdivision) subdivision; **4** BOT ramification.

ramifier: se ramifier /ramifje/ [2] *vpr* **1** LIT [*tronc, nerf, veine*] to branch (**en** into); [*branche*] to divide (**en** into); **2** FIG **famille très ramifiée** family with many branches; **problème très ramifié** problem with many ramifications.

ramolli, ~e /ramɔli/ *adj* **1** [*substance*] (devenu mou) soft; (rendu mou) softened; **2** [*personne*] (avachi) limp; (apathique) spineless; **avoir le cerveau ~** PEJ to be soft in the head.

ramollir /ramɔliʀ/ [3] **I** *vtr* **1** (rendre mou) to soften [*matière*]; **2** (affaiblir) to make [sb] soft [*personne*]; to weaken [*volonté*].

II se ramollir *vpr* **1** [*matière*] to become soft, to soften; **2** (s'avachir) [*personne*] to get soft.

ramollissement /ramɔlismɑ̃/ *nm* LIT, FIG softening.

ramoner /ramɔne/ [1] *vtr* to sweep [*cheminée*].

ramoneur /ramɔnœʀ/ ▶ **374** *nm* chimney sweep.

rampant, ~e /ʀɑ̃pɑ̃, ɑ̃t/ *adj* **1** [*animal*] crawling; [*tige*] prostrate; [*plante*] creeping; **2** (servile) [*manières, personne*] grovelling GB; **3** (insidieux) [*idéologie, mal, inflation*] creeping; **4** AVIAT **personnel ~** ground staff; **5** ARCHIT [*arc, voûte*] rampant.

rampe /ʀɑ̃p/ *nf* **1** (d'escalier) (sur balustres) banister;

(fixée au mur) hand-rail; **2** (plan incliné) ramp; **3** THÉÂT la ~ the footlights (pl).

■ ~ **d'accès** (d'autoroute) sliproad GB, entrance ramp US; (de bâtiment) ramp; ~ **d'arrosage** irrigation line; ~ **d'embarquement** embarcation ramp; ~ **de lancement** launchpad.

IDIOMES **passer la** ~ THÉÂT [dialogue] to work; [plaisanterie] to come off; **tenir bon la** ~○ to hold out; **lâcher la** ~○ to kick the bucket○.

ramper /ʀɑ̃pe/ [1] vi **1** [reptile, personne] to crawl; [chat, fauve] to creep; **s'éloigner en rampant** to crawl away; **2** [plante] to creep; **3** FIG (s'humilier) to grovel.

ramure /ʀamyʀ/ nf **1** (d'arbre) branches (pl); **2** (de cerf) antlers (pl).

rancard ⟨ /ʀɑ̃kaʀ/ nm **1** (rendez-vous) GÉN appointment; (amoureux) date; **2** (renseignement) tip.

rancart○ /ʀɑ̃kaʀ/ nm **mettre au** ~ to scrap [objet, projet]; to shunt [sb] aside [personne].

rance /ʀɑ̃s/ adj [odeur, graisse] rancid.

rancir /ʀɑ̃siʀ/ [3] vi [huile, graisse] to go rancid.

rancœur /ʀɑ̃kœʀ/ nf (grief) resentment **₵**.

rançon /ʀɑ̃sɔ̃/ nf **1** (somme d'argent) ransom; **2** (contrepartie) **la** ~ **de la gloire** the price of fame.

rançonner /ʀɑ̃sɔne/ [1] vtr (exiger de l'argent de) [brigand] to hold [voyageurs]; [racketteur] to extort money from [commerçants].

rancune /ʀɑ̃kyn/ nf (sentiment) resentment **₵**; (grief) grudge; **sans** ~! no hard feelings; **garder** ~ **à qn** to bear a grudge against sb.

rancunier, -ière /ʀɑ̃kynje, ɛʀ/ adj **être** ~ to be a person who holds grudges.

randonnée /ʀɑ̃dɔne/ nf **1** (activité) (à pied) hiking; (de plusieurs jours) backpacking; **la** ~ **à cheval** pony-trekking; **2** (promenade) (à pied) hike; ~ **équestre** pony trek; **faire une** ~ (à pied) to go hiking.

randonneur, -euse /ʀɑ̃dɔnœʀ, øz/ nm,f (à pied) hiker, rambler GB; (à bicyclette) cyclist.

rang /ʀɑ̃/ nm **1** (rangée) (de personnes, chaises, légumes) row; (de collier) strand; **en** ~s in rows; **mettre les enfants en** ~s to make the children line up; **se mettre en** ~s [enfants] to get into (a) line; (**mettez-vous**) **en** ~ **par deux** line up in twos; **2** MIL rank; **rompre les** ~s (sur ordre) to fall out; (sans ordre) to break ranks; **sortir du** ~ MIL, FIG to rise ou come up through the ranks; **serrer les** ~s MIL, FIG to close ranks; **rentrer dans le** ~ LIT to fall into line; FIG to toe the line; **les** ~s **des mécontents** FIG the ranks of the discontented; **3** (place) **arriver au 20ᵉ** ~ **mondial** to rank 20th in the world; **être au 5ᵉ** ~ **mondial des exportateurs** to be the 5th largest exporter in the world; **être sur les** ~s **pour un poste** to be in the running for a job; **acteur de second** ~ second-rate actor; **4** (ordre) order; **par** ~ **de taille** in order of height; **5** (dans une hiérarchie) rank; **accéder au** ~ **de** to rise to the rank of; **fonction de très haut** ~ high-ranking post; **des personnes de son** ~ people of one's own station; **tenir son** ~ to behave in a way appropriate to one's position; **6** (au tricot) row.

rangé, ~e¹ /ʀɑ̃ʒe/ adj (de bonne conduite) [vie] orderly; [personne] well-behaved.

rangée² /ʀɑ̃ʒe/ nf row.

rangement /ʀɑ̃ʒmɑ̃/ nm **1** (action) (de dossier, pièce) tidying up; (dans un meuble) putting away; **c'est un maniaque du** ~ he's obsessively tidy; **2** (meuble, espace) storage space **₵**.

ranger¹ /ʀɑ̃ʒe/ [13] I vtr **1** (remettre à sa place) to put away; ~ **un livre sur une étagère** to put a book back on a shelf; **le dossier était mal rangé** the file had been put in the wrong place; **où ranges-tu tes verres?** where do you keep the glasses?; **2** (ordonner) (par classement) to arrange; (en ligne) to line up; ~ **qch dans l'ordre alphabétique** to put sth in alphabetical order; **3** (situer) ~ **un animal dans les mammifères** to class an animal as a mammal; ~ **qn de son côté** to win sb over to one's side; **4** (mettre en ordre) to tidy [maison, meuble]; **tout est bien rangé** everything is nice and tidy.

II se ranger vpr **1** (se mettre en rang) to line up; **2** (se mettre sur le côté) [véhicule, conducteur] to pull over; [cycliste] to pull in; [piéton] to step aside; **3** (se garer) [véhicule, conducteur] to park; **se** ~ **à quai** [navire] to dock; **4** (se placer) **se** ~ **parmi** or **au côté de** to side with; **5** (être mis à sa place) [vaisselle, livres] to be kept; **un couteau ça se range!** there's a place for knives!; **6** (s'assagir) to settle down.

ranger² /ʀɑ̃dʒɛʀ/ nm (chaussure) heavy-duty boot.

ranimer /ʀanime/ [1] I vtr **1** (faire reprendre conscience à) to resuscitate [personne]; **2** (revigorer) [air, promenade] to revive [personne]; **3** (raviver) to rekindle [feu, ardeur, espoir, débat]; to stir up [querelle, inquiétude]; to restore [confiance]; to revive [marché financier, région]; to liven up [conversation].

II se ranimer vpr (se raviver) [feu] to flare up; [ardeur, flamme, débat] to be rekindled; [conversation] to liven up.

rapace /ʀapas/ I adj [personne] rapacious.

II nm ZOOL bird of prey.

rapacité /ʀapasite/ nf **1** (d'animal) ferocity; **2** (de marchand) greed.

rapatrié, ~e /ʀapatʀije/ nm,f repatriate (de from).

rapatriement /ʀapatʀimɑ̃/ nm repatriation.

rapatrier /ʀapatʀije/ [2] vtr to repatriate.

râpe /ʀɑp/ nf CULIN grater.

râpé, ~e /ʀɑpe/ I pp ▶ **râper**.

II pp adj [carotte, fromage] grated; [vêtement] worn.

III○ adj (loupé) **c'est** ~ it's off○.

râper /ʀɑpe/ [1] vtr to grate [fromage, carotte].

rapetisser /ʀap(ə)tise/ [1] I vtr LIT **la distance rapetisse les objets** distance makes things look smaller.

II vi to shrink.

III **se rapetisser** vpr to shrink.

râpeux, -euse /ʀɑpø, øz/ adj [langue, vin] rough; [voix] rasping.

raphia /ʀafja/ nm (fibre) raffia.

rapide /ʀapid/ I adj **1** (qui se déplace très vite) fast; **le plus** ~ the fastest; **le moins** ~ the slowest; **être** ~ **à la course** to be a fast runner; **2** (qui coule vite) [rivière, eau] fast-flowing; [courant] strong; **3** (fortement incliné) [pente, descente] steep; **4** (fait en peu de temps) [progrès, transformation, vieillissement] rapid; [moyen, victoire] quick; [livraison, succès, aggravation] quick, rapid; [réaction, intervention] quick, swift; [réponse, décision] prompt; [service] quick, speedy; **avec une machine c'est** ~ with a machine it's quick; **5** (au rythme soutenu) [mouvement, geste] quick; [allure] quick, rapid; [course] fast; [rythme, pouls] fast, rapid; [musique, danse] fast; **sa respiration était** ~ he/she was breathing rapidly; **6** (qui agit vite) [personne, esprit] quick; **à effet** ~ [médicament] quick-acting, fast-acting.

II nm **1** (cours d'eau) rapids (pl); **descendre un** ~ to shoot the rapids; **2** RAIL express.

IDIOMES **être** ~ **comme l'éclair** to be as quick as lightning.

rapidement /ʀapidmɑ̃/ adv **1** GÉN quickly; **2** MUS fast.

rapidité /ʀapidite/ nf (promptitude) speed; **la** ~ **avec laquelle il a réagi m'a surpris** his quick reaction surprised me.

rapiécer /ʀapjese/ [14] vtr to patch.

rappel /ʀapɛl/ nm **1** (remise en mémoire) reminder (de of; à to); ~ **à l'ordre** call to order; **2** (avis de facturation) (**lettre de**) ~ reminder; **'dernier** ~' 'final demand'; ~ **d'impôts** tax adjustment; **3** (salaire différé) back pay; **4** (appel à revenir) (d'ambassadeur) recall; (de réservistes) call-up; (d'acteurs) curtain call; **battre** or **sonner le** ~ LIT, FIG to give the call to arms; **5** MÉD (de vaccination) booster.

rappeler /ʀaple/ [19] I vtr **1** (remettre en mémoire) ~ **qch à qn** to remind sb of sth; ~ **(à qn) que** to remind (sb) that; ~ **le souvenir de qn** to evoke the memory of sb; ~ **le souvenir d'un événement** to recall an event; **rappelez-moi au bon souvenir de** remember me to; **2** (dire) to say; **rappelons-le** let's not forget; **3** (évoquer par ressemblance) to remind [sb] of; **vous me rappelez votre sœur** you remind me of your sister; **4** (par téléphone) to call back; **5** (appeler à revenir) to call [sb] back [*personne*]; MIL, POL to recall [*ambassadeur, réserviste*]; THÉÂT to call back [*acteur*]; **~ qn à l'ordre** to call sb to order.

II se rappeler *vpr* (se souvenir de) to remember (**avoir fait** doing).

rappliquer○ /ʀaplike/ [1] *vi* (arriver) to turn up○; (revenir) to come back.

rapport /ʀapɔʀ/ **I** *nm* **1** (lien) connection, link; **faire/ établir le ~ entre** to make/to establish the connection ou link between; **avoir ~ à qch** to have something to do with sth; **être sans ~ avec** to bear no relation to; **n'avoir aucun ~ avec** to have nothing to do with, to have no connection with; **les deux événements sont sans ~** the two events are unrelated ou unconnected; **je ne vois pas le ~!** I don't see the connection!; **un emploi en ~ avec tes goûts** a job suited to ou that matches your interests; **~ de cause à effet** relation of cause and effect; **2** (relations) **~s** relations (**entre** between); **avoir** or **entretenir de bons/mauvais ~s avec** to be on good/bad terms with sb; **il a des ~s difficiles avec sa mère** he has a difficult relationship with his mother; **3** (contact) **être/se mettre en ~ avec qn** to be/to get in touch with sb; **nous sommes en ~ avec d'autres entreprises** we have dealings with other companies; **mettre les gens en ~** to put people in touch with each other; **4** (point de vue) **sous tous les ~s** in every respect; **il est bien sous tous (les) ~s** he's a decent person in every way; **5** (compte rendu) report; **6** MIL daily briefing (*with roll-call*); **7** (rendement) return, yield; (de pari) **les ~s** the winnings (**de** on); **investissement d'un bon ~** investment that offers a good return ou yield; **être en plein ~** [*arbres, terres*] to be in full yield; **8** MATH, TECH ratio; **le ~ hommes/ femmes est de trois contre un** the ratio of men to women is three to one; **bon/mauvais ~ qualité prix** good/poor value for money.

II par rapport à *loc prép* **1** (comparé à) compared with; **par ~ au dollar** against the dollar; **2** (en fonction de) **le nombre de voitures par ~ au nombre d'habitants** the number of cars per head of the population; **un changement par ~ à la position habituelle du parti** a departure from the usual party line; **3** (vis-à-vis de) with regard to, toward(s); **l'attitude de la population par ~ à l'immigration** people's attitudes (*pl*) to immigration.

■ **~ de force** (équilibre) balance of power; (lutte) power struggle; **~s sexuels** sexual relations; **avoir des ~s (sexuels)** to have intercourse ou sex.

rapporter /ʀapɔʀte/ [1] **I** *vtr* **1** (remettre en place) (ici) to bring back; (là-bas) to take back; (rendre) (ici) to bring back (**à** to), to return (**à** to); (là-bas) to take back (**à** to), to return (**à** to); **2** (ramener avec soi) to bring back [*objet, cadeau, nouvelle*] (**à** to, **de** from); **3** (procurer un bénéfice) to bring in [*somme, revenu*] (**à** to); **la vente de la maison leur a rapporté beaucoup d'argent** they made a lot of money on the sale of the house; **les obligations rapportent 10%** the bonds yield ou return 10%; **mes terres me rapportent beaucoup d'argent** my land brings me in a good income; **leurs investissements leur rapportent beaucoup d'argent** their investments give them a high return on their money; **ça ne rapporte rien** it doesn't pay; **qu'est-ce que ça va te ~ sinon des ennuis?** you'll get nothing out of it except trouble; **4** (relater) to report (**à** to); (citer) to quote [*bon mot*]; **je ne fais que ~ ses propos** I'm only repeating what he said; **on m'a rapporté que** I was told that; **5**○ (moucharder) to tell (tales) on sb.

II *vi* **1** (procurer un bénéfice) to bring in money, to be lucrative; **un métier qui rapporte** a lucrative job; **2**○ (moucharder) to tell tales.

III se rapporter *vpr* **1** (être en relation avec) **se ~ à** to relate to, to bear a relation to; **2** (faire confiance à) **s'en ~ à qn/qch** to rely on sb/sth.

rapporteur○, **-euse** /ʀapɔʀtœʀ, øz/ *nm,f* (mouchard) telltale GB ou tattletale US.

rapproché, **~e** /ʀapʀɔʃe/ **I** *pp* ▶ **rapprocher**.

II *pp adj* **1** (dans l'espace) close together; **2** (dans le temps) close together; **à intervalles ~s** in quick succession.

rapprochement /ʀapʀɔʃmã/ *nm* **1** POL (entente) rapprochement; **2** (comparaison) connection.

rapprocher /ʀapʀɔʃe/ [1] **I** *vtr* **1** (rendre plus proche) to move [sth] closer [*objet*] (**de** to); **rapproche la chaise du mur** move the chair closer to the wall; **le courant nous rapproche de la côte** the current is taking us toward(s) the coast; **rapproche les deux vases** move the two vases closer together; **2** (dans le temps) to bring [sth] forward(s) [*date, rendez-vous*] (**de** to); **cette date nous rapproche trop des élections** that date brings us too close to the elections; **3** (disposer à l'entente) to bring [sb] (closer) together [*personnes*]; **leur passion pour la musique les rapproche** they are drawn together by their passion for music; **ses épreuves l'ont rapprochée des pauvres** having suffered herself, she feels for the poor; **ils ont réussi à ~ les deux pays** they managed to improve relations between the two countries; **4** (réunir) to bring together [*personnes*]; **5** (apparenter) to compare; **la situation est à ~ de ce qui s'est passé en 1951** the situation can be compared to that of 1951; **ses caractéristiques le rapprochent plus des mammifères** its characteristics make it closer to the mammals.

II se rapprocher *vpr* **1** (devenir plus proche) to get closer, to get nearer (**de** to); **l'orage se rapproche** the storm is getting closer; **j'ai choisi ce travail pour me ~ d'elle** I took this job so that I could be nearer to her; **2** (s'apparenter) **se ~ de** (processus) to get close to; (état) to be close to; **leurs peintures se rapprochent des fresques antiques** their paintings are similar to classical frescoes.

rapt /ʀapt/ *nm* (enlèvement) kidnapping GB, abduction.

raquette /ʀakɛt/ *nf* **1** (de tennis, badminton) racket; (de tennis de table) bat GB, paddle US; **2** (pour marcher dans la neige) snowshoe.

rare /ʀaʀ/ *adj* **1** (peu commun) [*personne, objet, animal, plante*] rare; [*denrée, main-d'œuvre, produit*] scarce; [*minerai*] rare, scarce; **devenir** or **se faire ~** to be ou become scarce; **être l'un des ~s qui** to be one of the few (people) who; **2** (peu fréquent) [*cas, mot, maladie*] rare; [*moment*] rare; [*visites*] infrequent; [*occasion*] rare, unusual; [*emploi, utilisation*] unusual, uncommon; [*voyages, trains*] infrequent; [*voitures, passants, clients, amis*] few; **les clients sont ~s** there are very few customers; **vous vous faites ~ ces temps-ci** you are not around much these days; **il est ~ de faire/qu'il fasse** it is unusual to do/for him to do; **cela n'a rien de ~** there's nothing unusual about it; **à de ~s exceptions près** with few exceptions; **3** (exceptionnel) [*qualité, beauté, talent*] rare; [*maîtrise, intelligence, énergie, courage*] exceptional; [*bêtise, impudence, inconséquence*] singular; **combat d'une ~ violence** exceptionally violent fight; **4** (clairsemé) [*cheveux, barbe, végétation*] sparse; [*air*] thin.

raréfaction /ʀaʀefaksjɔ̃/ *nf* (de gaz, d'air) rarefaction.

raréfier /ʀaʀefje/ [2] **I** *vtr* **1** (rendre moins dense) to rarefy [*air, gaz*]; **2** (rendre rare) to make [sth] rare.

II se raréfier *vpr* [*air*] to become thinner; [*gaz, atmosphère*] to rarefy; [*nourriture, denrée, argent*] to become scarce; [*espèce*] to become rare.

rarement /ʀaʀmã/ *adv* rarely, seldom.

rareté /ʀaʀte/ *nf* **1** (d'argent, de crédit, denrées) shortage, scarcity; (d'édition, de médaille, mot) rarity; (d'offre, de demande) shortage; **la ~ des visiteurs** the small number of visitors; **2** (de phénomène, d'événement) rarity; (de lettres, d'appels) infrequency.

rarissime /ʀaʀisim/ *adj* extremely rare.

ras, **~e** /ʀɑ, ʀɑz/ **I** *adj* **1** (naturellement court) [*poils, pelage*] short; [*végétation*] low-growing; **à poil ~** [*animal, fourrure*] short-haired; **2** (coupé court) [*barbe, gazon*] short; [*étoffe, tapis*] short-piled; **en**

~e campagne in (the) open country; **3** [*mesure*] level; **à ~ bord** to the brim (**de** with).

II *adv* short; **couper (à) ~** to cut [sth] very short.

III au ras de *loc prép* **au ~ de l'eau/des arbres** at water/tree level; **au ~ du sol** LIT at ground level.

IDIOMES **être à ~ du sol** or **des pâquerettes**○ to be rather basic; **faire table ~e de** to make a clean sweep of.

RAS /ɛRɑɛs/ (*abbr* = **rien à signaler**) nothing to report.

rasade /Rɑzad/ *nf* (dans un verre) glassful; (au goulot) swig○.

rasage /Rɑzaʒ/ *nm* **1** (action) shaving; **2** (résultat) shave.

rascasse /Raskas/ *nf* scorpion fish.

ras-de-cou /Rɑdku/, **ras-du-cou** /Rɑdyku/ *nm inv* **1** (pull) crew-neck sweater; **2** (collier) choker.

rasé, ~e /Rɑze/ **I** *pp* ▶ **raser**.

II *pp adj* **1** [*poil, cheveux, tête*] shaven; [*menton*] clean-shaven; [*jambe*] shaved; **2** (détruit) [*quartier*] demolished.

rase-mottes /Rɑzmɔt/ *nm inv* **le** (**vol en**) **~** low flying; **faire du ~, voler en ~** to fly low.

raser /Rɑze/ [1] **I** *vtr* **1** to shave [*personne, tête, joue, jambe*] (**à** with); to shave off [*cheveux, poils*]; **~ de près** to give [sb] a close shave; **crème/mousse à ~** shaving cream/foam; **2** (abattre) [*ouvriers*] to demolish [*bâtiment, quartier*]; [*soldats*] to raze [sth] to the ground; **3** (effleurer) [*projectile*] to graze; [*avion, oiseau*] to skim; **4**○ (ennuyer) to bore [sb] stiff○.

II se raser *vpr* to shave (**à** with); **se ~ la barbe** to shave off one's beard.

IDIOMES **~ les murs** to hug the walls.

raseur○, **-euse** /RɑzœR, øz/ *nm,f* bore.

ras-le-bol○ /Rɑlbɔl/ *nm inv* discontent.

rasoir /RɑzwaR/ **I**○ *adj inv* boring.

II *nm* (objet) razor; **~ mécanique** or **de sûreté** safety razor; **~ électrique** electric shaver; **une coupure de ~** a nick with a razor; **coupe au ~** razor cut.

rassasier /Rɑsazje/ [2] **I** *vtr* [*nourriture*] to fill [sb] up; [*personne*] to stuff (**de** with); **être rassasié** (de nourriture) to have eaten one's fill (**de** of).

II se rassasier *vpr* to eat one's fill (**de** of).

rassemblement /Rɑsɑ̃bləmɑ̃/ *nm* **1** (manifestation) rally; (attroupement) gathering; (organisé) meeting; **2** (fait de se rassembler) gathering.

rassembler /Rɑsɑ̃ble/ [1] **I** *vtr* **1** (pour former un groupe) to gather [sb] together [*personnes*]; (pour mettre en contact) to bring [sb] together [*personnes*]; MIL to muster, to assemble [*troupes*]; to round up [*moutons, troupeau*]; **2** (autour d'une cause commune) to unite [*citoyens, nation*]; **3** (réunir) to gather [sth] together [*effets personnels, documents*]; to gather, to collect [*informations, preuves*]; **~ ses forces** to summon up one's strength; **~ ses idées** to collect one's thoughts.

II se rassembler *vpr* [*personnes*] GÉN to gather; (dans un but précis) to assemble.

rasseoir: se rasseoir /Raswar/ [41] *vpr* to sit down (again).

rasséréner /RaseRene/ [14] **I** *vtr* to calm [sb] down [*personne*].

II se rasséréner *vpr* [*personne*] to calm down; [*visage*] to clear.

rassir /Rasir/ [3] *vi*, **se rassir** *vpr* to go stale.

rassis, ~e /Rasi, iz/ **I** *pp* **1** ▶ **rasseoir**; **2** ▶ **rassir**.

II *pp adj* [*pain, gâteau*] stale.

rassurant, ~e /RasyRɑ̃, ɑ̃t/ *adj* reassuring.

rassurer /RasyRe/ [1] **I** *vtr* to reassure; **~ qn** to reassure sb, to put sb's mind at rest (**sur qch** about sth).

II se rassurer *vpr* to reassure oneself; **rassure-toi, tout va bien maintenant** don't worry, everything's all right now; **je suis rassuré de te savoir guéri** I'm relieved to hear you're better; **je n'étais pas très rassuré** I was quite worried.

rat /Ra/ *nm* **1** ZOOL rat; **2**○ (terme d'affection) **mon petit ~** my little darling; **3** (avare) PEJ skinflint, cheapskate○; **quel ~**○! he is so tight-fisted○.

IDIOMES **on est fait comme des ~s** we're caught like rats in a trap; **s'ennuyer comme un ~ mort**○ to be bored stiff○; **à bon chat bon ~** PROV you/they etc have met your/their etc match.

ratatiner: se ratatiner /Ratatine/ [1] *vpr* **1** [*fruit*] to shrivel; **2** [*visage, personne*] to become wizened.

rate /Rat/ *nf* **1** ZOOL female rat; **2** ANAT spleen.

IDIOMES **se dilater la ~**○ to kill oneself laughing○.

raté, ~e /Rate/ **I** *pp* ▶ **rater**.

II *pp adj* **1** (pas réussi) [*acteur, politicien, peintre*] failed; **une vie ~e** a wasted life; **2** [*occasion*] missed.

III *nm,f* (personne) failure.

IV ratés *nmpl* **1** (de négociations, système) hiccups; **2** AUT **avoir des ~s** to backfire, to misfire GB.

râteau, pl ~x /Rato/ *nm* rake.

râtelier /Ratəlje/ *nm* AGRIC hayrack.

IDIOMES **manger à tous les ~s** to run with the hare and hunt with the hounds.

rater /Rate/ [1] **I** *vtr* **1** (ne pas réussir) to fail, to flunk○ US [*examen*]; **j'ai raté ma vie/ma photo** my life/my photo is a failure; **elle a raté son coup**○ she has failed; **2** (ne pas être présent pour) to miss [*train, début de film, rendez-vous*]; **3** (ne pas atteindre, ne pas voir) to miss [*cible, objectif, marche, personne*].

II *vi* [*plan, opération*] to fail, to flop○; **ça va tout faire ~**○ it'll spoil everything.

III se rater *vpr* (soi-même) to bungle one's suicide attempt; **2** (ne pas se voir) **nous nous sommes ratés** we missed each other.

ratière /RatjɛR/ *nf* rat trap.

ratification /Ratifikasjɔ̃/ *nf* (action) ratification (**de** of; **par** by); (document) instrument of ratification.

ratifier /Ratifje/ [2] *vtr* **1** ADMIN, JUR to ratify [*traité, contrat*]; **2** (confirmer) LITER to confirm [*projet, propos*].

ration /Rasjɔ̃/ *nf* **1** (portion) ration; **2** FIG share.

rationaliser /Rasjɔnalize/ [1] *vtr* to rationalize.

rationnel, -elle /Rasjɔnɛl/ **I** *adj* rational.

II *nm* **1** MATH rational number; **2** PHILOS **le ~** the rational.

rationnement /Rasjɔnmɑ̃/ *nm* rationing **₵**; **ticket/carte de ~** ration coupon/card.

rationner /Rasjɔne/ [1] **I** *vtr* ÉCON to ration [*essence*]; to impose rationing on [*population*].

II se rationner *vpr* to cut down (**en** on).

ratisser /Ratise/ [1] **I** *vtr* **1** (égaliser) to rake over [*allée*]; (enlever) to rake up [*feuilles mortes*]; **2** (fouiller) to comb [*région*]; **~ large**○ to cast one's net wide.

raton /Ratɔ̃/ *nm* ZOOL young rat.

■ **~ laveur** racoon.

raton(n)ade /Ratɔnad/ *nf* racial attack (*on Arabs or other minorities*).

rattachement /Rataʃmɑ̃/ *nm* **1** (de territoire) unification (**à** with); **2** ADMIN (de personne) **demander son ~ à** to ask to be posted to.

rattacher /Rataʃe/ [1] **I** *vtr* **1** (faire dépendre) to attach [*service, région*] (**à** to); to link [*devise*] (**à** to); to post [*employé*] (**à** to); **2** (associer) to associate [*œuvre, artiste*] (**à** with); **3** (attacher de nouveau) to retie [*lacets, poignets*]; to fasten [sth] again [*ceinture, collier*]; to re-attach [*remorque*]; **4** (affectivement) **plus rien ne la rattache à Lyon** she no longer has any ties with Lyons.

II se rattacher *vpr* [*œuvre, artiste*] to be linked (**à** to); [*thème, problème*] to relate (**à** to).

rattrapage /Ratrapaʒ/ *nm* **1** COMM, ÉCON (remise à jour) adjustment; (avec effet rétroactif) retroactive adjustment; **2** (de retard) catching up **₵** (**de** with); SCOL **cours/classe de ~** remedial lesson/class.

rattraper /Ratrape/ [1] **I** *vtr* **1** (rejoindre) to catch up with [*concurrent, passant, niveau*]; **2** (capturer) to catch [*fugitif, animal*]; **3** (compenser) to make up for [*absence, temps perdu, déficit, différence*]; to make up [*points, arriérés, temps de retard, distance*] (**on** sur);

~ son retard to catch up; **~ du sommeil en retard** to catch up on one's sleep; **4** (réparer) to make good [*dommage, omission*]; to put right [*problème, tort, erreur*]; to smooth over [*paroles, gaffe verbale*]; to get over [*inconvénient*]; to save [*situation*]; to pick up [*maille*]; **~ le coup**○ to put things right; **5** (saisir) to catch [*objet*]; **6**○ SCOL, UNIV (permettre de passer) to let [sb] through, to let [sb] pass [*élève, étudiant*].
II se rattraper *vpr* **1** (se faire pardonner) to redeem oneself (**auprès de qn** with sb); **2** (compenser son désavantage) to make up for it; **3** SCOL (atteindre le niveau requis) to catch up; **4** (compenser une perte) to make up one's losses (**avec** on); (compenser le temps perdu) to make up for lost time; **se ~ sur le dessert** to make up for it by eating a big dessert; **5** (éviter une catastrophe) **se ~ de justesse** to stop oneself just in time; **se ~ à une branche** to save oneself by catching hold of a branch.

rature /ʀatyʀ/ *nf* crossing-out.

raturer /ʀatyʀe/ [1] *vtr* **1** (barrer) to cross out; **2** (corriger) to correct.

rauque /ʀok/ *adj* [*voix*] (naturellement) husky; (momentanément) hoarse.

ravage /ʀavaʒ/ *nm* **les ~s de la guerre/du temps** the ravages of war/time; **faire des ~s** [*troupes, incendie, pollution*] to wreak havoc; [*épidémie*] to take a terrible toll; **tu vas faire des ~s avec ta mini-jupe** HUM you'll knock them dead in that mini-skirt.

ravagé○, **~e** /ʀavaʒe/ *adj* (fou) crazy.

ravager /ʀavaʒe/ [13] *vtr* **1** [*incendie, guerre*] to devastate, to ravage; **2** [*maladie, alcool*] to ravage [*personne, visage*]; [*chagrin*] to tear [sb] apart; [*passions*] to consume.

ravageur, -euse /ʀavaʒœʀ, øz/ *adj* **1** [*désir, passion*] all-consuming; [*humour*] crushing; [*sourire*] stunning; **2** [*insecte, animal*] destructive; [*incendie*] devastating.

ravalement /ʀavalmɑ̃/ *nm* **1** (de façades en pierre, brique) cleaning; (de façades crépies) refacing; **entreprise de ~** firm specializing in renovating façades; **2** FIG (amélioration) facelift.

ravaler /ʀavale/ [1] *vtr* **1** CONSTR to clean [*façade en pierre, brique*]; to reface [*façade crépie*]; to renovate [*bâtiment*]; **2** FIG to revamp [*image*]; **3** to swallow [*colère*]; **~ ses larmes** to hold back one's tears; **4** (déprécier) **~ qch au rang de** to reduce sth to the level of.

rave /ʀav/ *nf* turnip.

ravi, ~e /ʀavi/ **I** *pp* ▶ **ravir**.
II *pp adj* delighted (**de** with; **de faire** to do).

ravier /ʀavje/ *nm* small dish (*for hors-d'œuvre*).

ravigoter○ /ʀavigɔte/ [1] *vtr* [*air frais*] to invigorate; [*boisson*] to perk [sb] up.

ravin /ʀavɛ̃/ *nm* ravine.

raviner /ʀavine/ [1] *vtr* **1** (creuser) to furrow [*sol, terrain*]; **collines ravinées** hillsides full of ravines; **2** (marquer) to line [*visage*].

ravir /ʀaviʀ/ [3] *vtr* **1** (plaire beaucoup) to delight; **le bleu lui va à ~** blue really suits him/her; **2** (dérober) FML to abduct [*personne*]; to steal [*bien*].

raviser: se raviser /ʀavize/ [1] *vpr* to change one's mind.

ravissant, ~e /ʀavisɑ̃, ɑ̃t/ *adj* beautiful, delightful.

ravissement /ʀavismɑ̃/ *nm* **1** (enchantement) rapture; **2** (rapt) abduction.

ravisseur, -euse /ʀavisœʀ, øz/ *nm,f* abductor.

ravitaillement /ʀavitajmɑ̃/ *nm* **1** (activité) (en vivres) provision of fresh supplies (**de qn** to sb); **aller au ~** to go and stock up; **2** (vivres) supplies (*pl*).

ravitailler /ʀavitaje/ [1] **I** *vtr* (en vivres) to provide [sb] with fresh supplies [*armée, ville*] (**en qch** of sth); (en carburant) to refuel [*avion, navire*].
II se ravitailler *vpr* to obtain fresh supplies.

raviver /ʀavive/ [1] *vtr* [*personne*] to rekindle [*feu*]; [*produit*] to revive [*couleur*]; [*événement*] to rekindle [*colère, chagrin, passion, désir*]; to bring back [*mé-*

moire, souvenir]; to revive [*querelle, hostilité*]; **~ une douleur** (physique) to bring the pain back; (mentale) to re-open an old wound.

rayé, ~e /ʀeje/ **I** *pp* ▶ **rayer**.
II *pp adj* [*tissu*] striped; **~ blanc et jaune** with white and yellow stripes.

rayer /ʀeje/ [21] *vtr* **1** (barrer) to cross [sth] out; **'~ la mention inutile'** 'delete whichever does not apply'; **~ qch/qn d'une liste** to cross sth/sb's name off a list; **2** (supprimer) **la ville a été rayée de la carte** the town was wiped off the map; **3** (abîmer) to scratch [*meuble, disque*].

rayon /ʀɛjɔ̃/ *nm* **1** MATH radius; **2** (limite) radius; **dans un ~ de 10 km** within a 10 km radius; **~ d'action** LIT range; FIG sphere of activity ou activities; **3** (de lumière, lune) ray; **un ~ de soleil** LIT a ray of sunlight; FIG (personne) a ray of sunshine; **4** MÉD, PHYS (radiation) ray; **les ~s X** X-rays; **~ laser** laser beam; **être traité** or **soigné aux ~s** to undergo radiation treatment; **5** (de roue) spoke; **6** (étagère) shelf; **~ de bibliothèque** (book)shelf; **7** COMM (dans un grand magasin) department; **au ~ (des) jouets** in the toy department; **en ~** on display; **8**○ (domaine) **c'est mon ~** (responsabilité) that's my department○; **ce n'est pas mon ~** (compétence) that's not (really) my line; **il en connaît un ~ à ce sujet** he knows a lot about it; **9** ZOOL **un ~ (de ruche)** a honeycomb.

rayonnant, ~e /ʀɛjɔnɑ̃, ɑ̃t/ *adj* [*air, personne, beauté, joie, visage*] radiant; [*sourire*] beaming; **~ de** [*personne*] glowing with; [*visage*] shining ou radiant with.

rayonne /ʀɛjɔn/ *nf* rayon.

rayonnement /ʀɛjɔnmɑ̃/ *nm* **1** PHYS (radiation) radiation; **2** (éclat) radiance; **3** (influence de pays, personne, pensée) influence.

rayonner /ʀɛjɔne/ [1] *vi* **1** (se propager) [*lumière, chaleur*] to radiate (**de** from); **une chaleur qui rayonne** radiant heat; **2** (émettre de la lumière) LITER [*astre, étoile*] to shine (forth); [*mer*] to glisten, to sparkle; **3** (resplendir) [*personne*] to glow (**de** with); **4** (manifester son influence) [*personne, œuvre*] to be an influence (**sur** on; **dans** throughout); [*ville, pays*] to exert its influence, to hold sway (**sur** over; **dans** throughout); **5** (se déplacer) [*militaires, véhicule militaire*] to patrol; [*personnes, touristes*] to tour around; [*véhicule*] to tour; **6** (être disposé en rayons) [*avenues, lignes*] to radiate out (**de** from).

rayure /ʀɛjyʀ/ *nf* **1** (motif) stripe; **à ~s** striped; **~s jaunes** with yellow stripes (*épith, après n*); **2** (éraflure) scratch.

raz-de-marée /ʀadmaʀe/ *nm inv* LIT, FIG tidal wave; **~ électoral** electoral landslide.

razzia /ʀazja/ *nf* raid.

RDA /ɛʀdea/ *nprf* (*abbr* = **République démocratique allemande**) HIST German Democratic Republic, GDR.

ré /ʀe/ *nm inv* (note) D; (en solfiant) re.

réabonner /ʀeabɔne/ [1] *vtr* **~ qn** (à une revue) to renew sb's subscription (**à** to); THÉÂT to renew sb's season ticket.

réaccoutumer /ʀeakutyme/ [1] *vtr* **~ qn à qch** to get sb used to sth again.

réacteur /ʀeaktœʀ/ *nm* **1** **~ (nucléaire)** (nuclear) reactor; **2** AVIAT jet engine; **3** CHIMIE reactor.

réaction /ʀeaksjɔ̃/ *nf* **1** (en paroles, actions) reaction (**à** to; **contre** against); (plus posé, réfléchi) response; **en ~ à** in reaction to; **il est demeuré sans ~** he didn't react; **sans ~** [*moteur, instrument*] unresponsive; **sa ~ à la question fut de...** he/she responded to the question by...; **cela va provoquer des ~s** people are bound to react; **2** CHIMIE, MÉD, PHYS reaction; **moteur à ~** jet engine; **avion à ~** jet aircraft.

réactionnaire /ʀeaksjɔnɛʀ/ *adj, nmf* reactionary.

réactiver /ʀeaktive/ [1] *vtr* to rekindle [*feu*]; to reactivate [*appareil*]; to relaunch [*négociations*]; to increase [*emploi*].

réactualiser /ʀeaktyalize/ [1] *vtr* GÉN to update; to relaunch [*débat*].

réadapter /ʀeadapte/ [1] **I** *vtr* ~ **qn à qch** to help sb to readjust to sth.

II se réadapter *vpr* to readjust (**à qch** to sth).

réaffirmer /ʀeafiʀme/ [1] *vtr* to reaffirm, to reassert.

réagir /ʀeaʒiʀ/ [3] *vi* **1** [*personne, groupe*] to react (**à** to; **contre** against); (de façon plus posée, réfléchie) to respond (**à** to); **2** (avoir des répercussions) ~ **sur** to have an effect on; **3** CHIMIE to react (**à** to).

réajuster /ʀeaʒyste/ [1] *vtr* to readjust.

réaligner /ʀealiɲe/ [1] *vtr* FIN, POL to realign.

réalisable /ʀealizabl/ *adj* [*projet*] feasible; [*innovation*] workable.

réalisateur, **-trice** /ʀealizatœʀ, tʀis/ ▶ 374 | *nm,f* CIN, RADIO, TV director.

réalisation /ʀealizasjɔ̃/ *nf* **1** (de rêve, d'ambition) (action, résultat) fulfilment^{GB}; **2** (d'étude, de sondage) carrying out; **conception et** ~ (de meuble, satellite, hôtel) design and construction; **projet en cours de** ~ project in progress; **amener un projet jusqu'à sa** ~ (après sa conception) to get a project underway; (terminer) to bring a project to completion; **3** (ce qui est réalisé) achievement; **4** CIN, RADIO, TV production; (film) film.

réaliser /ʀealize/ [1] **I** *vtr* **1** (rendre réel) to fulfil^{GB} [*rêve, promesses*]; to achieve [*équilibre, idéal, exploit*]; ~ **des bénéfices** to make a profit; **elle a réalisé un exploit en faisant** it was no mean feat (for her) to do; **2** (exécuter, fabriquer) to make [*maquette, meuble*]; to carry out [*sondage, projet, tâche*]; **3** RADIO, TV, CIN to direct; **4** (se rendre compte de) CONTROV to realize.

II se réaliser *vpr* **1** (devenir réel) [*rêve*] to come true; [*promesses, prédictions*] to be fulfilled^{GB}; **2** (s'épanouir) **se** ~ (**dans qch**) to find fulfilment^{GB} (in sth).

réalisme /ʀealism/ *nm* realism.

réaliste /ʀealist/ **I** *adj* GÉN realistic; (en art) realist.

II *nmf* realist.

réalité /ʀealite/ *nf* **1** (réel) **la** ~ reality; **en** ~ in reality; **dans la** ~, **c'est impossible** in practice, it's impossible; **2** (caractère réel) **la** ~ **du problème/du marché** the real nature of the problem/of the market; **3** (fait réel) reality; **c'est déjà une** ~ (nouvelle autoroute, chômage) it is already a reality; **tenir compte des** ~**s** to take the facts into consideration.

réanimation /ʀeanimasjɔ̃/ *nf* **1** (service) intensive care; **service de** ~ intensive care unit; **être en** ~ to be in intensive care; **2** (technique) resuscitation.

réanimer /ʀeanime/ [1] *vtr* = **ranimer**.

réapparaître /ʀeapaʀɛtʀ/ [73] *vi* [*soleil*] to come out again; [*mot*] to reappear; [*phénomène*] to recur.

réapparition /ʀeapaʀisjɔ̃/ *nf* (de maladie, symptôme) recurrence; (de personne) reappearance.

réapprovisionner /ʀeapʀɔvizjɔne/ [1] **I** *vtr* to restock [*magasin*].

II se réapprovisionner *vpr* to stock up (**en** on).

réarmer /ʀeaʀme/ [1] *vtr* **1** (munir d'armes) to rearm; **2** (mettre en ordre de marche) to reload [*fusil, appareil photo*]; **3** NAUT (équiper) to refit [*navire*].

réassortiment /ʀeasɔʀtimɑ̃/ *nm* (de stock) replenishment; (de marchandises) restocking.

réassortir /ʀeasɔʀtiʀ/ [3] **I** *vtr* **1** to match up [*tissu*] (**avec** with); **2** COMM to replenish [*stock*].

II se réassortir *vpr* to stock up (**en** on).

rébarbatif, **-ive** /ʀebaʀbatif, iv/ *adj* [*travail*] off-putting; [*visage*] forbidding.

rebâtir /ʀ(ə)batiʀ/ [3] *vtr* to rebuild.

rebattre /ʀ(ə)batʀ/ [61] *vtr* to reshuffle [*cartes à jouer*].

IDIOMES ~ **les oreilles de qn avec une histoire** to go on (and on) about something.

rebattu, **-e** /ʀ(ə)baty/ **I** *pp* ▶ **rebattre**.

II *pp adj* [*histoire*] hackneyed.

rebelle /ʀabɛl/ **I** *adj* **1** MIL, POL rebel (*épith*); **2** (refusant l'autorité) rebellious; **être** ~ **à** to be resistant to

[*compromis*]; **3** [*mèche*] stray; [*tache*] stubborn; **4** MÉD resistant.

II *nmf* rebel.

rebeller: se rebeller /ʀəbɛle/ [1] *vpr* to rebel.

rébellion /ʀebeljɔ̃/ *nf* **1** (action) rebellion; **2** (groupe de personnes) **la** ~ the rebels (*pl*).

rebiffer[○]: **se rebiffer** /ʀ(ə)bife/ [1] *vpr* to rebel.

rebiquer[○] /ʀ(ə)bike/ [1] *vi* to stick up.

reboiser /ʀ(ə)bwaze/ [1] *vtr* to reafforest, to reforest.

rebond /ʀ(ə)bɔ̃/ *nm* **1** (de balle) bounce; **frapper la balle au** ~ to hit the ball on the rebound; **2** (ressaississement) recovery; (augmentation) increase.

rebondi, **~e** /ʀ(ə)bɔ̃di/ *adj* **1** [*vase, cruche, forme*] round, rounded; [*joue*] chubby; [*visage*] plump; [*ventre*] fat; [*poitrine*] ample; [*fesses, hanches*] generously proportioned; [*cuisse, muscle*] bulging; **2** FIG [*portefeuille*] bulging.

rebondir /ʀ(ə)bɔ̃diʀ/ [3] *vi* **1** [*balle, rayon, son, onde*] to bounce (**contre, sur** off); **fais** ~ **la balle par terre/contre le mur** bounce the ball on the ground/against the wall; **2** (repartir) [*conversation, polémique*] to start up again; [*économie, pays*] to pick up; [*procès, intrigue*] to take a new turn; **faire** ~ to start [sth] up again [*conversation, débat*]; to give a new twist to [*procès*].

rebondissement /ʀ(ə)bɔ̃dismɑ̃/ *nm* (de polémique) sudden revival (**de** of); (de procès, d'affaire) new development (**de** in); **les** ~**s de l'intrigue** the twists and turns of the plot.

rebord /ʀ(ə)bɔʀ/ *nm* **1** (partie en saillie) ledge; **2** (bord surélevé) GÉN raised edge; (d'objet rond) rim; **3** (bord arrondi) lip; **4** (bord) edge.

■ ~ **de fenêtre** windowsill; (plus large) (window) ledge.

reboucher /ʀ(ə)buʃe/ [1] *vtr* (avec un bouchon de liège) to recork [*bouteille*]; (avec un bouchon en verre) to replace the stopper of [*flacon*]; (avec un capuchon) to put the cap back on [*stylo*]; to put the top back on [*tube de dentifrice*]; ~ **un trou** to fill (up) a hole again.

rebours: à rebours /aʀ(ə)buʀ/ **I** *loc adv* [*compter, marcher*] backward(s).

II à rebours de *loc prép* **à** ~ **de la tendance actuelle** contrary to the current trend; **aller à** ~ **de** to go against [*mode, tendance*].

rebouteux[○], **-euse** /ʀ(ə)butø, øz/ ▶ 374 | *nm,f* bonesetter.

reboutonner /ʀ(ə)butɔne/ [1] *vtr* to button [sth] up again.

rebrousse-poil: à rebrousse-poil /aʀ(ə)bʀus pwal/ *loc adv* the wrong way; **caresser un chat à** ~ to stroke a cat's fur the wrong way; **prendre qn à** ~ FIG to rub sb up the wrong way.

rebrousser /ʀ(ə)bʀuse/ [1] *vtr* ~ **chemin** to turn back.

rébus /ʀebys/ *nm inv* rebus.

rebut /ʀ(ə)by/ *nm* **1** LIT (déchet) rubbish ¢; **bon pour le** ~ fit ou ready for the scrapheap; **mettre au** ~ to throw [sth/sb] on the scrapheap; **le** ~ **de la société** FIG the dregs (*pl*) of society; **2** POSTES dead mail.

rebutant, **~e** /ʀ(ə)bytɑ̃, ɑ̃t/ *adj* unpleasant.

rebuter /ʀ(ə)byte/ [1] *vtr* **1** (dégoûter) [*travail*] to disgust; [*personne*] to repel; **2** (décourager) to put [sb] off.

récalcitrant, **~e** /ʀekalsitʀɑ̃, ɑ̃t/ *adj* recalcitrant.

recaler[○] /ʀ(ə)kale/ [1] *vtr* SCOL, UNIV to fail [*candidat*]; **être recalé à une épreuve** to fail a test.

récapitulatif, **-ive** /ʀekapitylatif, iv/ **I** *adj* **tableau** ~ summary table.

II *nm* (texte) summary of the main points.

récapituler /ʀekapityle/ [1] *vtr* to sum up.

recaser[○] /ʀ(ə)kaze/ [1] **I** *vtr* (dans un emploi) to find another job for [*personne*].

II se recaser *vpr* **1** (dans un emploi) to find another job; **2** (se remarier) [*femme*] to find a new husband; [*homme*] to find a new wife.

receler /Rəs(ə)le, Rsəle/ [17] *vtr* **1** JUR to conceal [*criminel*]; ~ **des marchandises** (accepter) to receive stolen goods; (garder) to possess stolen goods; **2** (contenir) to contain; ~ **un trésor** to contain hidden treasure.

receleur, -euse /Rəs(ə)lœR, RsəlœR, øz/ *nm,f* (qui accepte) receiver of stolen goods, fence○; (qui garde) possessor of stolen goods.

récemment /Resamɑ̃/ *adv* recently.

recensement /R(ə)sɑ̃smɑ̃/ *nm* **1** SOCIOL census; **2** (inventaire) inventory.

recenser /R(ə)sɑ̃se/ [1] *vtr* **1** SOCIOL to take a census of [*population*]; **2** (inventorier) to list [*objets, problèmes*].

récent, ~e /Resɑ̃, ɑ̃t/ *adj* [*incident, nouvelle, découverte*] recent; [*maison*] new, newly built.

recentrer /Rəsɑ̃tRe/ [1] *vtr*, **se recentrer** *vpr* to refocus.

récépissé /Resepise/ *nm* receipt.

réceptacle /Reseptakl/ *nm* **1** (récepteur) **c'est le ~ des eaux fluviales** it receives the fluvial waters; **le ~ des immondices de la ville** the town tip; **2** GÉOG catchment basin; **3** BOT receptacle; **4** (récipient) container.

récepteur, -trice /ReseptœR, tRis/ **I** *adj* receiving.
II *nm* **1** BIOL receptor; **2** RADIO, TV (appareil) receiver.

réceptif, -ive /Reseptif, iv/ *adj* receptive (à to).

réception /Resepsjɔ̃/ *nf* **1** (réunion) reception; **2** (manière d'accueillir) reception, welcome; **discours de ~** welcoming speech; **3** (bureau d'accueil) reception; **4** (de courrier, marchandises) receipt; **s'occuper de la ~ des marchandises** to take delivery of the goods; **5** RADIO, TV (de signaux, d'ondes) reception; **6** SPORT (après un saut) landing; (de ballon) catching.

réceptionnaire /ResepsjɔnɛR/ ▶374❘ *nmf* **1** COMM receiving clerk; **2** (dans un hôtel) chief receptionist GB, head receptionist US.

réceptionner /Resepsjɔne/ [1] **I** *vtr* **1** COMM ~ **des marchandises** to take delivery of goods; **2** (accueillir) CONTROV to welcome [*personne, voyageur*]; **3** SPORT CONTROV to catch [*ballon*].
II **se réceptionner** *vpr* to land.

réceptionniste /Resepsjɔnist/ ▶374❘ *nmf* receptionist.

récession /Resesjɔ̃/ *nf* recession.

recette /R(ə)sɛt/ *nf* **1** CULIN ~ **(de cuisine)** recipe; **livre de ~s** recipe book; **2** (méthode) formula, recipe; **3** COMM (argent encaissé) takings (*pl*); **faire ~** LIT to bring in money; FIG to be a success; **4** (rentrée d'argent) **les ~s et (les) dépenses** receipts and expenses; **5** (d'impôts) (bureau) tax collector's office, revenue office; (recouvrement) collection.

recevable /Rəsvabl, R(ə)səvabl/ *adj* **1** GÉN [*excuse, offre*] acceptable; **2** JUR admissible.

receveur, -euse /Rəs(ə)vœR, øz/ *nm,f* **1** ▶374❘ (d'autobus, de tramway) conductor; **2** MÉD recipient.
■ ~ **des contributions** tax collector; ~ **des postes** postmaster.

recevoir /RəsvwaR, R(ə)səvwaR/ [5] **I** *vtr* **1** (être le destinataire de) to receive, to get (**de** from); **nous avons bien reçu votre lettre** we acknowledge receipt of your letter; **il a reçu le ballon dans le visage** he was hit in the face by the ball; **j'ai reçu le marteau sur le pied** the hammer landed on my foot; **je n'ai d'ordre à ~ de personne** I don't take orders from anyone; **la mesure a reçu un accueil favorable de la part des enseignants** the measure met with approval from teachers; **2** (accueillir) to welcome, to receive [*invités, délégation*]; **être bien/mal reçu** [*proposition*] to be well/badly received; [*invités*] to get a good/bad reception; ~ **qn froidement** to give sb a cold reception; **demain nous les recevons à dîner** we're having them to dinner tomorrow; **ils reçoivent beaucoup** they do a lot of entertaining; **Laval reçoit Caen** SPORT Laval is playing host to Caen; **il va se faire ~**○ he's going to get it○; **3** (pour consultation) to see [*patients, clients*]; **elle reçoit entre 14 et 17 heures** she's available for consultation between 2 and 5 pm; **4** RADIO, TV

(capter) to receive [*signal, ondes*]; **on reçoit mal cette chaîne** we get bad reception on that channel; **je vous reçois cinq sur cinq** RADIO I'm receiving you loud and clear; **5** (contenir) [*hôtel, refuge*] to accommodate [*personne*]; [*salle de spectacle, stade*] to hold [*spectateurs*]; **6** (recueillir) to get [*soleil, pluie*]; **des bassins reçoivent l'eau de pluie** pools collect the rainwater; **7** SCOL, UNIV (admettre) to pass [*élève, candidat*]; **être reçu à un examen** to pass an exam; **il a été reçu premier au concours** he came first in the examination.
II **se recevoir** *vpr* (après un saut, une chute) to land.

rechange: **de rechange** /dəR(ə)ʃɑ̃ʒ/ *loc adj* [*pièce, chemise*] spare; [*solution*] alternative; **j'ai pris une chemise de ~** I have a change of shirt.

réchapper /Reʃape/ [1] *vtr ind* ~ **de** to come through [*maladie, accident*]; **personne n'en a** o **est réchappé** nobody came through it alive.

recharge /R(ə)ʃaRʒ/ *nf* **1** (de briquet, stylo) refill; (d'arme) reload; **2** (processus) recharging.

rechargeable /R(ə)ʃaRʒabl/ *adj* [*briquet, stylo*] refillable; [*pile, appareil ménager*] rechargeable.

recharger /R(ə)ʃaRʒe/ [13] **I** *vtr* **1** (avec cargaison) to reload [*véhicule*]; **2** (regarnir) to reload [*arme, appareil photo*]; to refill [*stylo, briquet*]; **3** to recharge [*batterie*].
II **se recharger** *vpr* **1** (qualité) [*pile*] to be rechargeable; [*stylo*] to be refillable; **2** (processus) [*batterie, pile*] to recharge.

réchaud /Reʃo/ *nm* stove.
■ ~ **à alcool** spirit stove; ~ **électrique** electric ring GB, hotplate; ~ **à gaz** (d'appartement) gas ring; (de camping) camping stove.

réchauffé, ~e /Reʃofe/ **I** *pp* ▶ **réchauffer**.
II *pp adj* (rebattu) [*histoire, plaisanterie*] hackneyed.
III *nm* **c'est du ~** there's nothing new about it.

réchauffement /Reʃofmɑ̃/ *nm* warming (up); **le ~ de la planète** global warming.

réchauffer /Reʃofe/ [1] **I** *vtr* **1** CULIN to reheat, to heat [sth] up [*plat, nourriture*]; **2** (rendre chaud) to warm up [*personne, pieds*]; to heat up, to warm up [*pièce*]; **ça m'a réchauffé le cœur** FIG it warmed my heart; **3** (détendre) **ses plaisanteries ont réchauffé l'atmosphère** his/her jokes relaxed the atmosphere.
II *vi* CULIN **faire ~ qch** to heat sth up, to reheat sth.
III **se réchauffer** *vpr* **1** (soi-même) [*personne*] to warm oneself up; **2** (devenir chaud) [*temps*] to warm up; **les eaux du lac se sont réchauffées à cause de la pollution** the temperature of the water in the lake has risen because of pollution.

rechausser /R(ə)ʃose/ [1] *vtr* ~ **un enfant** to put a child's shoes back on; ~ **ses skis** to put one's skis on again.

rêche /Rɛʃ/ *adj* [*mains, tissu*] rough.

recherche /R(ə)ʃɛRʃ/ *nf* **1** (étude) research ¢; **travailler dans la ~** to work in research; **faire des ~s en biologie/sur le cancer** to do research in biology/into cancer; **2** (fouille) search; **après deux heures de ~** after a two-hour search; **tout le monde a participé aux ~s** everyone took part in the search; **être à la ~ de** to be looking for, to be in search of; **3** (volonté d'atteindre) ~ **de** pursuit of; **être à la ~ d'un bonheur idéal** to be in pursuit of ideal happiness; **4** (soin) (raffinement) meticulousness; (affectation) PÉJ affectation; **avec ~** [*habillé, décoré, écrit*] with meticulous care; **sans ~** (non affecté) without affectation; (négligé) carelessly.
■ ~ **d'emploi** job-hunting.

recherché, ~e /R(ə)ʃɛRʃe/ **I** *pp* ▶ **rechercher**.
II *pp adj* **1** (rare) sought-after (**pour** for); **un livre très ~** a much sought-after book; **2** (demandé) in demand (*après n*); **un mannequin très ~** a model very much in demand; **3** (soigné) [*toilette*] meticulous; PÉJ affected; [*style, écrit, expression*] original, inventive; PÉJ recherché; [*décor*] meticulously arranged (*épith*); **4** (visé) [*but, effet*] intended; **ce n'était pas le but ~** that wasn't the object of the exercise.

rechercher /R(ə)ʃɛRʃe/ [1] *vtr* **1** (tâcher de trouver) to search out [*objet convoité*]; to look for [*objet égaré*]; to look for [*logement, emploi, explication*]; ORDINAT to search for [*donnée*]; **~ les causes d'un accident** to look into the causes of an accident; **il est recherché par la police** he's wanted by the police; **'recherchons vendeuse qualifiée'** 'qualified sales assistant GB ou clerk US required'; **2** (tâcher d'obtenir) to seek [*sécurité, bonheur, paix*] (**auprès de qn** with sb); to seek, to look for [*alliés, soutien*]; to fish for [*compliments*].

rechigner /ʀ(ə)ʃiɲe/ [1] **I rechigner à** *vtr ind* **~ à qch/à faire** to balk at sth/at doing; **elle ne rechigne pas à la tâche** she's not afraid of hard work.
II *vi* to grumble.

rechute /ʀəʃyt/ *nf* MÉD, FIG relapse.

rechuter /ʀ(ə)ʃyte/ [1] *vi* **1** MÉD to have a relapse; FIG to relapse (**dans** into); **2** ÉCON [*prix, monnaie*] to fall again; [*ventes*] to fall off again.

récidive /ʀesidiv/ *nf* **1** JUR second offence GB; **il est accusé de vol avec ~** he has been charged with a second offence GB of theft; **2** FIG repetition; **3** MÉD recurrence.

récidiver /ʀesidive/ [1] *vi* **1** JUR (la première fois) to commit a second offence GB; (plusieurs fois) to commit subsequent offences; **2** (recommencer) FML to do it again; **3** MÉD to recur.

récidiviste /ʀesidivist/ *nmf* **1** JUR (au second délit) second offender, recidivist; (après plusieurs délits) habitual offender, recidivist; **2** FIG backslider.

récif /ʀesif/ *nm* reef.

récipient /ʀesipjɑ̃/ *nm* container (**à** for).

réciprocité /ʀesipʀɔsite/ *nf* reciprocity.

réciproque /ʀesipʀɔk/ **I** *adj* **1** GÉN [*aide, accord*] reciprocal, mutual; [*sentiment, confiance*] mutual; **2** LING, MATH reciprocal.
II *nf* **1** GÉN reverse; **2** MATH reciprocal.

réciproquement /ʀesipʀɔkmɑ̃/ *adv* **se respecter ~** to respect one another; **et ~** and vice versa.

récit /ʀesi/ *nm* **1** (narration) story; (genre) narrative; **un ~ d'aventures** an adventure story; **le ~ de mes aventures** the account of my adventures; **2** THÉÂT narrative monologue.

récital /ʀesital/ *nm* recital.

récitatif /ʀesitatif/ *nm* recitative.

récitation /ʀesitasjɔ̃/ *nf* **1** (texte littéraire) **apprendre une ~** to learn a text (off) by heart; **2** (matière) **être fort en ~** to be good at reciting (texts off by heart); **3** (action de réciter) reciting.

réciter /ʀesite/ [1] *vtr* **1** LIT to recite; **2** FIG, PEJ to trot out○ [*raisons, faits*].

réclamation /ʀeklamasjɔ̃/ *nf* **1** (plainte) complaint; **2** (demande) claim (**de** for); **sur ~** on request.

réclame /ʀeklam/ *nf* **1** (réputation) publicity; **2†** (annonce) advertisement; **3** (promotion) **'en ~'** 'on offer' GB, 'on sale'.

réclamer /ʀeklame/ [1] *vtr* **1** (demander) to ask for [*personne, chose, argent*]; to call for [*réforme, aide, silence, enquête*]; to beg [*indulgence*]; to claim [*dû, indemnité*]; to demand [*justice, augmentation*]; **~ que** to demand that; **~ la parole** GÉN to ask to speak; (dans un débat) to ask to take the floor; **se voir ~ qch** to be asked for sth; **2** (en pleurant) [*bébé*] to cry for; **3** (nécessiter) to require [*qualité*].
II *vi* (se plaindre) to complain.
III se réclamer *vpr* **1 se ~ de** (affirmer, représenter) [*parti*] to be an expression of [*démocratie*]; [*organisation, personne*] to claim to be representative of [*parti, organisme, religion*]; **2 se ~ de** (se fonder sur) [*personne*] to claim to follow [*principe, idéologie, personne*].

reclasser /ʀəklase/ [1] **I** *vtr* **1** (classer de nouveau) to reclassify [*dossiers*]; **2** (affecter à un nouveau poste) to redeploy (**dans** to); **3** (réajuster le salaire de) to regrade.
II se reclasser *vpr* to find new employment.

reclus, **~e** /ʀəkly, yz/ **I** *adj* reclusive; **vivre ~** to live as a recluse.
II *nm,f* recluse.

réclusion /ʀeklyzjɔ̃/ *nf* **1** JUR imprisonment; **~ à perpétuité** or **à vie** life sentence; **2** RELIG reclusion.

recoiffer: **se recoiffer** /ʀ(ə)kwafe/ [1] *vpr* to tidy one's hair.

recoin /ʀəkwɛ̃/ *nm* LIT corner; FIG recess; **tous les coins et les ~s** every nook and cranny (*sg*).

recoller /ʀ(ə)kɔle/ [1] *vtr* to stick [sth] together again [*morceaux*]; to reseal [*envelope*].

récolte /ʀekɔlt/ *nf* AGRIC (activité) harvest; (produits récoltés) crop, harvest.

récolter /ʀekɔlte/ [1] *vtr* **1** AGRIC to harvest [*maïs, raisin*]; to dig up [*pommes de terre*]; **2** (ramasser) [*abeille*] to collect [*pollen*]; [*personne*] to win [*voix, points*]; to collect [*somme d'argent, informations*]; to reap [*avantage*]; **à t'aider, je n'ai récolté que des ennuis**○ I got nothing but trouble in return for helping him/her; **~ les fruits de son travail** or **de ses efforts** to reap the fruits of one's labour GB.

recommandable /ʀəkɔmɑ̃dabl/ *adj* commendable; **un individu peu ~** a disreputable individual.

recommandation /ʀəkɔmɑ̃dasjɔ̃/ *nf* **1** (conseil) recommendation; **2** (parrainage) recommendation; **lettre de ~** letter of recommendation, reference; **3** POSTES registration.

recommandé, **~e** /ʀəkɔmɑ̃de/ **I** *pp* ▶**recommander**.
II *pp adj* [*colis, lettre*] registered.
III *nm* (lettre) registered letter; (colis) registered parcel; **en ~** [*envoyer*] by registered post GB ou mail.

recommander /ʀəkɔmɑ̃de/ [1] **I** *vtr* **1** (conseiller fortement) to advise; **~ la prudence à qn**, **~ à qn d'être prudent** to advise sb to be cautious; **la vaccination est recommandée pour les séjours en Afrique** vaccination is recommended for visits to Africa; **il est ~ de faire** it is advisable to do, you are advised to do; **2** (formuler un avis) [*président, organisme international*] to recommend (**qch à qn** sth to sb); **3** (signaler pour sa qualité) to recommend [*film, médecin, méthode, restaurant*] (**à qn** to sb); **4** (parrainer) to recommend (**à, auprès de** to); **5** POSTES to send [sth] by registered post GB ou mail.
II se recommander *vpr* (invoquer l'appui de) **se ~ de qn** to give sb's name as a reference.

recommencement /ʀəkɔmɑ̃smɑ̃/ *nm* **la vie n'est qu'une suite de ~s** life is just a series of new beginnings; **l'histoire est un éternel ~** history is constantly repeating itself.

recommencer /ʀəkɔmɑ̃se/ [12] **I** *vtr* **1** (complètement) to start [sth] again [*rapport, tâche*]; **tout est à ~** it will all have to be done again; **2** (après une pause) to start [sth] again; **~ à travailler/à vivre** to start working/living again; **3** (faire à nouveau) to do [sth] again [*rapport, action*]; to rewrite [*letter*]; **et ne recommence plus!** don't you ever do that again!
II *vi* to start again, to begin again.

récompense /ʀekɔ̃pɑ̃s/ *nf* (matérielle ou morale) reward; (honorifique) award; **en ~** as a reward.

récompenser /ʀekɔ̃pɑ̃se/ [1] *vtr* to reward (**de** for; **par** with).

recomposer /ʀ(ə)kɔ̃poze/ [1] **I** *vtr* GÉN to reconstruct [*scène*]; (en imprimerie) to reset [*page*]; TÉLÉCOM **~ un numéro** to dial a number again.
II se recomposer *vpr* to re-form.

recompter /ʀ(ə)kɔ̃te/ [1] *vtr* to count [sth] again [*argent*]; to add up [sth] again [*addition*].

réconciliation /ʀekɔ̃siljasjɔ̃/ *nf* reconciliation (**de X et de Y** of X with Y).

réconcilier /ʀekɔ̃silje/ [2] **I** *vtr* **~ Pierre et Paul**, **~ Pierre avec Paul** to bring Pierre and Paul back together; **~ la morale et la politique** to reconcile morality with politics.
II se réconcilier *vpr* [*couple, amis*] to make up; [*nations*] to be reconciled.

reconduction /ʀ(ə)kɔ̃dyksjɔ̃/ *nf* renewal.

reconduire /ʀ(ə)kɔ̃dɥiʀ/ [69] *vtr* **1** (accompagner) (à la porte) to see [sb] out; **~ qn chez lui/à la gare** GÉN to take sb home/to the station; (en voiture) to drive sb home/to the station; **la police l'a reconduit à la frontière** the police escorted him back to the border; **2** (prolonger) to extend [*grève, cessez-le-feu*]; (renouveler) to renew [*mandat, accord*]; **~ qn dans ses fonctions** to re-elect sb; **3** (piloter) to drive [sth] again.

réconfort /ʀekɔ̃fɔʀ/ *nm* comfort.

réconforter /ʀekɔ̃fɔʀte/ [1] **I** *vtr* **1** (consoler) to comfort; (rasséréner) **~ qn** to cheer sb up; **2** (revigorer) to fortify.
II se réconforter *vpr* to restore one's strength.

reconnaissable /ʀ(ə)kɔnɛsabl/ *adj* recognizable.

reconnaissance /ʀ(ə)kɔnɛsɑ̃s/ *nf* **1** (gratitude) gratitude; **geste de ~** mark of gratitude; **en ~ de** in appreciation of [*aide, services*]; **avoir** or **éprouver de la ~ pour qn** to be so feel grateful to sb; **2** (action d'identifier) recognition; **faire un signe de ~** to give a sign of recognition; **3** (fait d'admettre) (de torts, d'erreurs) admission, admitting; **4** (de droit, d'indépendance, d'un État) recognition, recognizing; **~ d'un enfant** legal recognition of a child; **5** (fait d'explorer) MIL reconnaissance, recon US; **aller** or **partir en ~** MIL to go on reconnaissance; FIG to go and have a look around, to go and have a recce○.

reconnaissant, **-e** /ʀ(ə)kɔnɛsɑ̃, ɑ̃t/ *adj* grateful; **je vous serais ~ de bien vouloir faire** FML I should ou would be grateful if you would do.

reconnaître /ʀ(ə)kɔnɛtʀ/ [73] **I** *vtr* **1** (retrouver) to recognize; (identifier) to identify; **je t'ai reconnu à ta voix** I recognized you by your voice; **je ne sais pas ~ les champignons** I can't identify different kinds of mushrooms; **je reconnais bien là leur grande générosité** it's just like them to be so generous; **2** (admettre) to admit [*faits, torts, erreurs*]; **il reconnaît avoir menti** or **qu'il a menti** he admits he lied; **~ qch comme une évidence** to accept sth as a fact; **~ qn comme le meilleur** to acknowledge sb to be the best; **~ qn coupable** to find sb guilty; **3** (considérer comme légitime ou valable) to recognize [*syndicat, régime, droit de grève, diplôme étranger*]; **~ un enfant** to recognize a child legally; **4** (explorer) **~ les lieux** MIL to reconnoitre^{GB} the area; FIG to have a look round^{GB}.
II se reconnaître *vpr* **1** (soi-même) to recognize oneself; **2** (l'un l'autre) to recognize each other; **3** (être identifiable) **se ~ à qch** to be recognizable by sth; **4** (s'orienter) to know where one is.

reconnu, **-e** /ʀ(ə)kɔny/ **I** *pp* ▶ **reconnaître**.
II *pp adj* [*fait, diplôme, médecin*] recognized; **être ~ fiable** [*méthode, machine*] to be known to be reliable.

reconquérir /ʀ(ə)kɔ̃keʀiʀ/ [35] *vtr* **1** MIL to reconquer, to recover [*territoire*]; **2** FIG to regain [*dignité, estime, liberté*]; to win back [*personne, droit*].

reconquête /ʀ(ə)kɔ̃kɛt/ *nf* **1** (de territoire) reconquest; **2** (de personne, droit) winning back; (de liberté) regaining.

reconstituant, **-e** /ʀ(ə)kɔ̃stityɑ̃, ɑ̃t/ **I** *adj* fortifying.
II *nm* tonic.

reconstituer /ʀ(ə)kɔ̃stitye/ [1] **I** *vtr* to re-form [*armée, association*]; to reconstruct [*crime, événement*]; to recreate [*époque, décor*]; to piece [sth] together again [*objet en morceaux*]; to build up again [*réserves, forces*].
II se reconstituer *vpr* to re-form.

reconstitution /ʀ(ə)kɔ̃stitysjɔ̃/ *nf* (d'armée, association) re-forming, reconstitution; (de crime, d'événement) reconstruction.

reconstruction /ʀ(ə)kɔ̃stʀyksjɔ̃/ *nf* (d'édifice, de ville) reconstruction; (de pays, société) rebuilding.

reconstruire /ʀ(ə)kɔ̃stʀɥiʀ/ [69] *vtr* to reconstruct [*édifice, ville*]; to rebuild [*pays, économie, société*].

reconversion /ʀ(ə)kɔ̃vɛʀsjɔ̃/ *nf* (de travailleur) redeployment; (de région) redevelopment; (d'économie) restructuring; (d'usine) conversion.

reconvertir /ʀ(ə)kɔ̃vɛʀtiʀ/ [3] **I** *vtr* to redeploy [*personnel*]; to redevelop [*région*]; to restructure [*économie,*

industrie]; to convert [*usine, bâtiment*]; to adapt [*équipement*].
II se reconvertir *vpr* [*personnel*] to switch to a new type of employment; [*entreprise*] to switch to a new type of production; **se ~ dans l'enseignement** to switch to teaching.

recopier /ʀ(ə)kɔpje/ [2] *vtr* **1** (retranscrire) to copy out [*texte, citations*]; **2** (mettre au propre) to write up [*brouillon, devoir*].

record /ʀ(ə)kɔʀ/ **I** *adj inv*; **en un temps ~** in record time.
II *nm* SPORT, FIG record (**de** for).

recoucher: **se recoucher** /ʀ(ə)kuʃe/ [1] *vpr* to go back to bed.

recoudre /ʀ(ə)kudʀ/ [76] *vtr* **1** to sew up [*ourlet, doublure*]; to sew [sth] back on [*bouton*]; **2** MÉD to stitch up [*plaie, blessé*].

recoupement /ʀ(ə)kupmɑ̃/ *nm* (vérification) cross-check, cross-checking **¢**.

recouper /ʀ(ə)kupe/ [1] **I** *vtr* **1** (de nouveau) to cut [sth] again [*cheveux, haie*]; (davantage) to cut some more [*viande*]; **2** (comparer) to tie in, to tally with [*version, témoignage*].
II se recouper *vpr* (s'accorder) [*versions*] to tally; [*résultats*] to add up; (se couper) [*lignes*] to intersect.

recourbé, **-e** /ʀ(ə)kuʀbe/ *adj* [*bec, nez*] hooked; [*cils, ongles*] curved; [*tige de métal*] curved.

recourir /ʀ(ə)kuʀiʀ/ [26] *vtr ind* **~ à** to use, to have recourse to [*remède, technique*]; to resort to [*expédient, stratagème, violence*]; to turn to [*parent, ami*]; to go to [*agence, expert*]; **~ à la justice** to go to court.

recours /ʀ(ə)kuʀ/ *nm inv* **1** (moyen quelconque) recourse; (moyen extrême) resort; **sans autre ~ que** with no other way out but; **avoir ~ à** to have recourse to [*remède, technique*]; to resort to [*expédient, stratagème*]; to turn to [*parent, ami*]; to go to [*agence, expert*]; **en dernier ~** as a last resort; **2** JUR appeal; **~ en grâce** petition for reprieve.

recouvrement /ʀ(ə)kuvʀəmɑ̃/ *nm* (d'impôt, de cotisation) collection; (de somme, dette) recovery.

recouvrer /ʀ(ə)kuvʀe/ [1] *vtr* **1** to recover [*somme, créance*]; to collect [*impôt, cotisation*]; **2** (retrouver) to recover [*santé, forces*]; to regain [*liberté*]; **~ la raison** to regain one's sanity.

recouvrir /ʀ(ə)kuvʀiʀ/ [32] **I** *vtr* **1** (couvrir complètement) to cover (**de** with); **2** (couvrir de nouveau) to cover [sb] up again [*malade, enfant*]; to re-cover [*chaise, fauteuil*]; **3** (masquer) to hide, to conceal; **4** (inclure) **cela recouvre en partie ce que j'allais dire** this partly covers what I was about to say.
II se recouvrir *vpr* **1** (devenir couvert) to become covered (**de** with); **2** (se chevaucher) [*tuiles*] to overlap; **3** (correspondre) [*concepts*] to overlap; **4** (remettre son chapeau) to put one's hat back on.

récréatif, **-ive** /ʀekʀeatif, iv/ *adj* [*jeu, activité, film, soirée*] recreational; [*zone, parc*] recreation (*épith*).

récréation /ʀekʀeasjɔ̃/ *nf* **1** (à l'école primaire) playtime GB, recess US; (dans le secondaire) break GB, recess US; **2** (loisir) recreation.

recréer /ʀ(ə)kʀee/ [11] *vtr* to recreate.

récrier: **se récrier** /ʀekʀije/ [2] *vpr* to exclaim.

récrimination /ʀekʀiminasjɔ̃/ *nf* recrimination.

récriminer /ʀekʀimine/ [1] *vi* to rail SOUT.

recroqueviller: **se recroqueviller** /ʀ(ə)kʀɔkvije/ [1] *vpr* **1** [*personne*] to huddle up; **2** [*objet, feuille*] to shrivel up.

recru, **~e**¹ /ʀəkʀy/ *adj* LITER **~ (de fatigue)** exhausted.

recrudescence /ʀ(ə)kʀydesɑ̃s/ *nf* (de violence, d'intérêt) fresh upsurge (**de** of); (de bombardements, peur, pessimisme, demandes, grèves) new wave (**de** of); (d'incendie, de combats) renewed outbreak (**de** of).

recrudescent, **-e** /ʀ(ə)kʀydesɑ̃, ɑ̃t/ *adj* **être ~** to be on the increase.

recrue² /ʀəkʀy/ *nf* recruit.

recrutement /ʀ(ə)kʀytmɑ̃/ *nm* recruitment.

recruter /ʀ(ə)kʀyte/ [1] *vtr* (engager) to recruit; ~ **qn comme enseignant** to take sb on as a teacher.

recruteur, -euse /ʀ(ə)kʀytœʀ, øz/ **I** *adj* [*officier, agent*] recruiting; [*bureau, agence*] recruitment (*épith*).

II *nm,f* GÉN recruitment specialist, recruiter US.

rectangle /ʀɛktɑ̃gl/ **I** *adj* MATH right-angled, right US.

II *nm* GÉN, MATH rectangle.

rectangulaire /ʀɛktɑ̃gylɛʀ/ *adj* rectangular, oblong.

recteur /ʀɛktœʀ/ *nm* SCOL, UNIV (d'académie) ≈ chief education officer GB, ≈ superintendent (of schools) US.

rectificatif /ʀɛktifikatif/ *nm* **1** (dans un journal) correction; **2** (à une loi) amendment (à to).

rectification /ʀɛktifikasjɔ̃/ *nf* **1** (correction) (d'erreur) correction; (de contrat) rectification; (modification de chiffres) adjustment; **2** (de tracé, route) straightening; (de virage) straightening out; **3** (rectificatif) correction.

rectifier /ʀɛktifje/ [2] *vtr* **1** (corriger) to correct, to rectify [*erreur*]; **2** (rendre conforme) to adjust [*position, chiffres*]; to rectify [*limites, contrat, ouvrage défectueux*]; to amend [*facture, document*]; ~ **le tir** LIT to adjust one's aim; FIG to change one's approach; **3** (redresser) to straighten [*tracé, route*]; to straighten out [*virage*].

rectiligne /ʀɛktilin/ *adj* GÉN straight; MATH rectilinear.

recto /ʀɛkto/ *nm* front; ~ **verso** on both sides.

rectorat /ʀɛktɔʀa/ *nm* **1** (administration) ≈ local education authority GB, ≈ board of education US; **2** (bureaux) local education offices (*pl*).

reçu, ~e /ʀ(ə)sy/ **I** *pp* ▶ **recevoir**.

II *pp adj* **1** [*candidat*] successful; **2** [*usage*] accepted; **3** RADIO **message ~** message received and understood.

III *nm,f* SCOL, UNIV successful candidate.

IV *nm* (quittance) receipt.

recueil /ʀ(ə)kœj/ *nm* (d'un auteur) collection; (de divers auteurs) anthology; (de documents, lois) compendium.

recueillement /ʀəkœjmɑ̃/ *nm* **1** (méditation) contemplation; **2** (attitude respectueuse) reverence.

recueilli, ~e /ʀəkœji/ **I** *pp* ▶ **recueillir**.

II *pp adj* [*air, visage*] rapt; [*fidèle*] rapt in prayer (*épith, après n*); [*foule, silence*] reverential.

recueillir /ʀəkœjiʀ/ [27] **I** *vtr* **1** (rassembler) to collect [*dons, signatures, anecdotes*]; to gather, to collect [*témoignages, renseignements*]; **2** (obtenir) to get [*voix, nouvelles*]; to gain [*consensus*]; to achieve [*unanimité*]; to win [*louanges*]; ~ **des applaudissements** [*personne, proposition*] to be greeted with applause; **3** (récupérer) to collect [*eau, résine*]; to gather [*miel*]; **cuvette pour ~ l'eau** bowl to catch the water; **4** (prendre avec soi) to take in [*orphelin*]; **5** (enregistrer) to record [*impression, opinions*]; (par écrit) to take down [*déposition*]; **6** (hériter) to inherit [*fortune*]; to receive [*héritage*].

II se recueillir *vpr* **1** (méditer) to commune with oneself; **2** (prier) to engage in private prayer.

recul /ʀ(ə)kyl/ *nm* **1** (détachement) detachment; **avec le ~** with hindsight, in retrospect; **manquer de ~** to be incapable of being objective; **prendre du ~** to stand back; **2** (baisse) (d'investissements, de production, nombre) drop (**de** in), fall (**de** in); (de doctrine, maladie) decline (**de** in); **être en ~** [*investissements, exportations, ventes*] to be dropping ou falling; [*racisme, tendance*] to be on the decline; [*parti*] to be in decline; **un ~ de 5%** a 5% drop; **3** (dans l'espace) (d'armée) pulling ou drawing back; (des eaux, de la mer) recession; **avoir un mouvement de ~** to recoil; **feu de ~** AUT reversing light; **le ~ de la forêt amazonienne** the gradual disappearance of the Amazonian forest; **4** (de date, réunion) postponement; (d'âge de la retraite) raising.

reculade /ʀəkylad/ *nf* climb-down.

reculé, ~e /ʀəkyle/ *adj* **1** [*quartier, zone, village*] remote; **2** [*temps, époque*] distant, remote.

reculer /ʀ(ə)kyle/ [1] **I** *vtr* **1** (pousser) to move back [*vase, lampe*]; to move ou push back [*meuble*]; ~ **les pendules d'une heure** to put the clocks back an hour; **2** (faisant marche arrière) to reverse GB, to back up;

3 (dans le temps) to put off [*moment du départ, événement, décision*]; to put back [*date*].

II *vi* **1** [*personne, groupe*] (aller en arrière) to move back; (pour mieux voir quelque chose, pour être vu) to stand back; [*chauffeur, voiture*] to reverse; ~ **d'un pas** to step back; ~ **de trois pas** to take three steps back(wards); **faire ~ un groupe de personnes** to move a group of people back; ~ **d'une case** JEUX to go back a square; **c'est ~ pour mieux sauter** FIG it's just putting off the inevitable; **2** [*armée*] to pull ou draw back; **3** [*falaise*] to be eroded; [*forêt*] to be gradually disappearing; [*eaux*] to go down; [*mer*] to recede; **4** (régresser) [*monnaie, production, exportations*] to fall; [*doctrine, mouvement*] to decline; [*parti, politicien*] to suffer a drop in popularity; **faire ~** to cause a fall in [*franc, exportation*]; **faire ~ le chômage** to reduce unemployment; ~ **de cinq places** [*élèves, sportif*] to fall back five places, to drop five places; **5** (céder, se dérober) to back down; (hésiter) to shrink back; **cela m'a fait ~** it put me off; ~ **devant une difficulté** to shrink from a difficulty; **ne ~ devant rien** to stop at nothing.

reculons: à reculons /aʀ(ə)kylɔ̃/ *loc adv* **aller à ~** LIT to go backward(s); FIG to go reluctantly.

récupérable /ʀekypeʀabl/ *adj* **1** (réutilisable) [*matériau*] reusable; **2** (réparable) [*objet, vêtement*] which can be made good again (*épith, après n*); **3** (réformable) [*délinquant*] who can be rehabilitated (*épith, après n*).

récupération /ʀekypeʀasjɔ̃/ *nf* **1** (de ferraille) salvage; (de chiffons) reclamation; **matériaux de ~** salvaged materials; **2** (de l'organisme) recovery; **capacité de ~** recuperative power; **3** (recouvrement) (d'argent, de prêt) recovery; **4** (d'heures de travail) making up; **5** POL (de mouvement) taking over, hijacking; (d'idées) appropriation.

récupérer /ʀekypeʀe/ [14] **I** *vtr* **1** (rentrer en possession de) to get back, to recover [*argent, objet, force*]; **2** (aller chercher) to fetch [*enfant*]; **il a récupéré le ticket de caisse au fond de la poubelle** he retrieved the receipt from the bottom of the bin GB ou garbage can US; **3** (ramasser pour réutiliser) to salvage [*ferraille*]; to reclaim [*chiffons, vieux journaux*]; **4** (garder) to save [*timbres, boîtes*]; **5** to make up [*journées, heures de travail*]; **6** POL to take over, to hijack [*mouvement, personnel*]; to appropriate [*idées*]; **7** (réinsérer) to rehabilitate [*délinquant*].

II *vi* (après un effort, une maladie) to recover (**de** from).

récurer /ʀekyʀe/ [1] *vtr* to scour [*casserole*]; to scrub [*lavabo*]; **poudre à ~** scouring powder.

récurrence /ʀekyʀɑ̃s/ *nf* **1** (répétition) recurrence; **2** MATH recursion.

récurrent, ~e /ʀekyʀɑ̃, ɑ̃t/ *adj* GÉN, ANAT, MÉD recurrent.

récusation /ʀekyzasjɔ̃/ *nf* challenging, challenge.

récuser /ʀekyze/ [1] **I** *vtr* to challenge, to object to [*juré, témoin*].

II se récuser *vpr* GÉN to declare oneself incompetent; JUR [*juge*] to decline to act in a case.

recyclable /ʀ(ə)siklabl/ *adj* [*matériau*] recyclable; [*personne*] retrainable.

recyclage /ʀ(ə)siklaʒ/ *nm* **1** (de matériau) recycling; **2** (de personnel) retraining; **3** FIN (de capitaux) recycling; (de profits) reinvestment.

recycler /ʀ(ə)sikle/ [1] **I** *vtr* **1** (pour réutiliser) to recycle [*matériau*]; **2** ~ **le personnel** (former de nouveau) to retrain the staff; (perfectionner) to provide refresher courses for the staff; **3** (réinvestir) to recycle [*capitaux*]; to reinvest [*profits*].

II se recycler *vpr* **1** (se perfectionner) to update one's skills; (faire un stage) to attend a refresher course; **2** (se reconvertir) to retrain; (changer d'emploi) to change jobs.

rédacteur, -trice /ʀedaktœʀ, tʀis/ ▶ 374 *nm,f* **1** (de texte) author, writer; **2** (de journal, magazine) editor.

rédaction /ʀedaksjɔ̃/ *nf* **1** (activité) (d'article, ouvrage) writing; (correction) editing; (de document, décret) drafting; **2** (dans la presse) (bureaux) editorial offices; (personnel) editorial staff; **3** SCOL essay GB, theme US.

rédactionnel, -elle /ʀedaksjɔnɛl/ *adj* editorial.

reddition /ʀɛdisjɔ̃/ *nf* (capitulation) surrender.

redemander /ʀədmɑ̃de, ʀ(ə)dəmɑ̃de/ [1] *vtr* **1** (demander de nouveau) **~ qch à qn** to ask sb for sth again; **2** (se faire rendre) **~ qch à qn** to ask sb for sth back; **3** (demander davantage) **~ des fruits à qn** to ask sb for more fruit.

redémarrer /ʀ(ə)demaʀe/ [1] *vi* **1** AUT [*chauffeur*] to drive off again; **2** ÉCON [*marché, économie*] to take off again; [*entreprise*] to relaunch itself.

rédemption /ʀedɑ̃psjɔ̃/ *nf* redemption.

redescendre /ʀədesɑ̃dʀ/ [6] **I** *vtr* **1** (transporter de nouveau) (en bas) GÉN to take [sb/sth] back down (à to); (à l'étage) to take [sb/sth] back downstairs; (d'en haut) GÉN to bring [sb/sth] back down (**de** from); (de l'étage) to bring [sb/sth] back downstairs; **je peux vous ~ au village** I can take you back down to the village; **2** (remettre en bas) to get [sth] back down [*valise, boîte*]; **3** (rabaisser) to lower [*étagère, tableau, store*] (**de** by); to wind [sth] back down [*vitre de véhicule*]; **4** (parcourir de nouveau) [*personne*] (en allant) to go back down [*pente, rue, étage*]; to go ou climb back down [*escalier, échelle*]; (en venant) to come back down [*rue, marches*]; [*voiture, automobiliste*] to drive back down [*route*].
II *vi* (descendre de nouveau) [*personne*] (en allant) GÉN to go back down, to go down again (**à** to); (de l'étage) to go back downstairs, to go downstairs again; (en venant) GÉN to come back down, to come down again (**de** from) ; (de l'étage) to come back downstairs, to come downstairs again; (après être remonté) (en allant) to go back down again; (en venant) to come back down again; [*ascenseur, avion*] (en allant) to go back down; (en venant) to come back down; [*oiseau*] to fly down again; [*prix, taux, monnaie*] to go down again; [*mer*] to go back out; [*température, baromètre*] to fall again, to go down again; **peux-tu ~ chercher mon sac?** can you go back downstairs and get my bag?; **tu es redescendu à pied?** GÉN did you walk back down?; **il est redescendu du col à bicyclette** he cycled back down from the pass; **~ de** to climb back down from [*mur*]; **~ de l'échelle** to climb back down the ladder; **il est redescendu du toit** [*enfant*] to come back down off the roof; **on nous a fait ~ de l'avion** we were made to get out of the plane again; **~ à Marseille** (retourner) to go back down to Marseilles; **~ dans les sondages** [*politicien, parti*] to drop ou to move down in the opinion polls; **les cours sont redescendus de 20%** prices have dropped again by 20%.
IDIOMES **~ sur terre** to come down to earth.

redevable /ʀədvabl, ʀ(ə)dəvabl/ *adj* **être ~ de qch à qn** to owe sth to sb, to be indebted to sb for sth; **être ~ de l'impôt** to be liable for tax.

redevance /ʀədvɑ̃s, ʀ(ə)dəvɑ̃s/ *nf* **1** (taxe) GÉN charge; (de télévision) licence GB ou license US fee; (de téléphone) rental charge; **2** (droit d'exploitation) royalty.

rédhibitoire /ʀedibitwaʀ/ *adj* [*coût*] prohibitive; [*obstacle*] insurmountable; [*condition*] unacceptable; [*timidité*] crippling.

rediffuser /ʀ(ə)difyze/ [1] *vtr* to repeat GB, to rerun [*émission*].

rédiger /ʀediʒe/ [13] *vtr* (écrire) to write [*article, texte*]; (en développant ses notes) to write up [*notes, thèse*]; to draft [*décret, contrat*].

redingote /ʀ(ə)dɛ̃ɡɔt/ *nf* (d'homme) frock coat; (de femme) fitted coat.

redire /ʀədiʀ/ [65] *vtr* to repeat; **~ qch à qn** (répéter) to tell sb sth again; **je le lui ai dit et redit** I've told him/her over and over again; **~ à qn de faire** to remind sb to do; **~ à qn que** to remind sb that; **avoir** ou **trouver quelque chose à ~ à qch** to find fault with sth; **côté qualité, (il n'y a) rien à ~** from the point of view of quality, it can't be faulted.

redistribuer /ʀ(ə)distʀibɥe/ [1] *vtr* to redistribute [*richesses*]; to reallocate [*tâches*].

redite /ʀ(ə)dit/ *nf* (needless) repetition.

redondance /ʀ(ə)dɔ̃dɑ̃s/ *nf* **1** (de style) verbosity; **2** (terme superflu) superfluous term; **3** LING redundancy.

redondant, ~e /ʀ(ə)dɔ̃dɑ̃, ɑ̃t/ *adj* **1** [*style*] verbose; [*terme*] superfluous, redundant; **2** LING redundant.

redonner /ʀ(ə)dɔne/ [1] *vtr* **1** (donner de nouveau) **~ qch à qn** to give sb sth again, to give sth to sb again; **il m'a redonné de la soupe** he gave me some more soup; **2** (rétablir) **~ confiance à qn** to restore sb's confidence; **~ espoir à qn** to give sb renewed hope; **~ des forces à qn** to restore sb's strength; **~ vie à un quartier** to breathe new life into an area; **3** (rendre) to give [sth] back [*objet, argent*] (**à** to); **4** (rediffuser) to show [sth] again [*film*].

redorer /ʀ(ə)dɔʀe/ [1] *vtr* to regild.
IDIOMES **~ son blason** [*personne*] to restore one's image; [*ville, groupe*] to restore its image.

redoublant, ~e /ʀ(ə)dublɑ̃, ɑ̃t/ *nm,f* student repeating a year.

redoublement /ʀ(ə)dubləmɑ̃/ *nm* **1** LING reduplication; **2** (intensification) intensification.

redoubler /ʀ(ə)duble/ [1] **I** *vtr* **1** SCOL **~ une classe** to repeat a year; **2** LING to reduplicate [*consonne, syllabe*].
II redoubler de *vtr ind* **~ de prudence/d'égards** to be twice as careful/attentive; **~ d'efforts** to redouble one's efforts; **la tempête a redoublé de violence** the storm has become even fiercer.
III *vi* **1** SCOL to repeat a year; **2** (s'intensifier) to intensify; **la pluie a redoublé** it's raining even harder.

redoutable /ʀ(ə)dutabl/ *adj* [*arme, examen, concurrent*] formidable; [*mal*] dreadful.

redouter /ʀ(ə)dute/ [1] *vtr* (craindre) to fear [*ennemi, mort*]; (appréhender) to dread [*événement, avenir*].

redressement /ʀədʀɛsmɑ̃/ *nm* **1** (reprise) recovery; **2** (remise sur pied) re-establishment; **plan de ~** recovery plan; **3** (remise en forme) straightening out; **4** (rééducation) **maison de ~** reformatory.

redresser /ʀ(ə)dʀese/ [1] **I** *vtr* **1** (remettre d'aplomb) to straighten up [*barrière, piquet*]; (remettre debout) to put [sth] up again [*barrière, piquet*]; (détordre) to straighten [sth] out [*barre de métal, pare-chocs*]; to straighten [*dent*]; **~ la tête** LIT to lift one's head up; FIG (tenir tête) to stand up for oneself; **2** (après une crise) to put [sth] back on its feet [*économie*]; to turn [sth] round GB ou around [*entreprise*]; **~ la situation** to put the situation right; **3** (après une baisse) to aid the recovery of [*monnaie*] ; to improve [*marge de bénéfices*]; **4** (après une manœuvre) to straighten up [*voilier, planeur, volant*]; **~ la barre** LIT to right the helm; FIG to put things back on an even keel; **5** (corriger) to rectify [*erreur*]; to redress [*injustices*]; **~ les torts** FML to right all wrongs.
II se redresser *vpr* **1** [*personne*] (se mettre debout) to stand up; (s'asseoir) to sit up; (se mettre droit) (en position debout) to stand up straight; (en position assise) to sit up straight; **2** (reprendre de la vigueur) [*industrie, économie, plante*] to pick up again, to recover; [*pays, compagnie*] to get back on its feet.

redresseur /ʀədʀesœʀ/ *nm* **~ de torts** redresser of wrongs.

réductible /ʀedyktibl/ *adj* **1** (en diminuant) [*frais*] which can be reduced ou cut (*après n*); **2** CHIMIE, MATH, MÉD reducible.

réduction /ʀedyksjɔ̃/ *nf* **1** (remise) discount, reduction; (consentie à un groupe particulier) concession (**sur** on); **~ de 5%** 5% reduction; **faire une ~ à qn** to give sb a discount; **~ étudiants** concession GB ou special price for students; **2** (action de diminuer) (de dépenses, coût, subventions, production) cutting, reducing; (de délais) shortening, reducing; (d'armements, inégalités) reducing; **3** (diminution) (de dépenses, coût, d'armements) reduction, cut (**de** in); **~ d'impôts** tax cut; **~s d'effectifs** staff cuts; **4** ART (reproduction réduite) small replica; **5** CHIMIE, CULIN, MATH, MÉD reduction.

réduire /ʀedɥiʀ/ [68] **I** *vtr* **1** (diminuer) to reduce; **~**

le personnel to cut (down on) staff; **~ un article de 3%** to reduce an article by 3%; **~ les subventions de moitié** to cut subsidies by half; **~ qch en taille** to make sth smaller, to reduce the size of sth; **~ le nombre de succursales** to reduce the number of branches; **je dois ~ mes dépenses** I must cut down on my spending; **~ l'écart entre** to narrow the gap between; **2** (en reproduisant) to reduce [*photographie*]; to scale down [*dessin*]; (en faisant des coupures) to cut [*texte*]; **3** (transformer) **~ qch en poudre** to crush sth to powder; **~ qch en bouillie** to reduce sth to a pulp; **être réduit en cendres** LIT [*ville*] to be reduced to ashes; FIG [*espoirs, rêves*] to turn to ashes; **être réduit à rien** ou **à néant** [*efforts, travail, fortune*] to be wiped out; **4** (en simplifiant) **~ qch à** to reduce sth to; **5** (obliger) **~ qn au silence** to reduce sb to silence; **6** (vaincre) to subdue [*ennemi*]; to silence [*opposition*]; to crush [*émeute*]; **7** CULIN, CHIMIE to reduce [*composé, sauce*]; **8** MATH to reduce [*fraction*].

II *vi* CULIN [*sauce*] to reduce; [*épinards*] to shrink.

III se réduire *vpr* **1** (diminuer) [*coûts*] to be reduced ou cut; [*délais*] to be reduced ou shortened; [*importations*] to be cut; [*écart*] to narrow; **2** (consister seulement en) **se ~ à** to consist merely of; **cela se réduit à bien peu de chose** it doesn't amount to very much.

réduit, ~e /ʀedɥi, it/ **I** *pp* ▶ **réduire**.

II *pp adj* **1** (diminué) [*taux, cotisation, vitesse*] reduced, lower; [*délai*] shorter; [*activité*] reduced; [*main-d'œuvre*] smaller, reduced; [*groupe*] smaller; **à vitesse ~e** at a lower speed; **billets à prix ~** tickets at a reduced price; **avec un personnel ~** with fewer staff; **à mobilité ~e** with restricted mobility; **2** (peu important) [*moyens, choix*] limited; [*groupe*] small; **3** (petit) [*taille*] small; **de taille ~e** small; **en format ~** [*objet*] in a scaled down or reduced format.

III *nm* (placard) cubbyhole.

réécrire /ʀeekʀiʀ/ [67] *vtr* to rewrite.

rééditer /ʀeedite/ [1] *vtr* to reissue [*livre*].

réédition /ʀeedisjɔ̃/ *nf* (de livre) reissue.

rééducation /ʀeedykasjɔ̃/ *nf* **1** MÉD (des mouvements) physiotherapy, physical therapy US; (de handicapé) rehabilitation; **~ de la parole** speech therapy; **2** (de délinquant) rehabilitation.

rééduquer /ʀeedyke/ [1] *vtr* **1** MÉD to restore normal functioning to [*membre*]; to rehabilitate [*handicapé*]; **~ la parole** to treat speech disorder; **2** JUR to rehabilitate [*délinquant*]; **3** (éduquer différemment) to re-educate [*personne*]; to retrain [*animal*].

réel, réelle /ʀeɛl/ **I** *adj* **1** (non imaginaire) [*besoin, risque, événement, être*] real; (véritable) [*cause, motif, coût*] true, actual; [*fait*] true; **2** (grand) [*émotion, difficultés, effort*] real; **3** FIN [*revenu*] real; [*taux d'intérêt*] effective; **4** MATH, ORDINAT, PHILOS, PHYS real.

II *nm* PHILOS **le ~** the real.

réélection /ʀeelɛksjɔ̃/ *nf* re-election.

réélire /ʀeeliʀ/ [66] *vtr* to reelect.

réellement /ʀeelmã/ *adv* really.

réembaucher /ʀeãboʃe/ [1] *vtr* to take [sb] on again.

réemployer /ʀeãplwaje/ [23] *vtr* to re-use [*matériaux*]; to reinvest [*fonds*]; to re-employ [*personnel*].

rééquilibrer /ʀeekilibʀe/ [1] *vtr* **1** TECH to readjust [*chargement*]; **2** AUT to balance [*wheels*]; **3** ÉCON to balance [*budget*]; **~ les pouvoirs** POL to restore the balance of power.

réessayer /ʀeɛseje/ [21] *vtr* to try [sth] on again [*robe*].

réévaluer /ʀeevalɥe/ [1] *vtr* **1** (relever) to revalue [*monnaie*]; to revise [*salaire, impôt*]; **2** (estimer à nouveau) to reappraise, to re-evaluate [*patrimoine, dépenses, forces, emploi*].

réexaminer /ʀeɛgzamine/ [1] *vtr* to re-examine [*dossier, budget*]; to reconsider [*décision, candidature*].

réexpédier /ʀeɛkspedje/ [2] *vtr* **1** (faire suivre) to forward, to redirect; **2** (retourner) to send [sth] back.

refaire /ʀəfɛʀ/ [10] **I** *vtr* **1** (faire de nouveau) to do [sth] again, to redo [*exercice, calcul, travail, vêtement*]; to

make [sth] again [*voyage, erreur*]; to repack [*bagage*]; **~ le même chemin** (en sens inverse) to go back the same way; **~ du cinéma** [*ancien acteur*] to get back into films GB ou movies US; **tout est à ~** it will have to be done all over again; **'à ~'** (sur une copie d'élève) 'do it again'; **~ un numéro de téléphone** to redial a number; **si c'était à ~** if I had to do it all over again; **je vais ~ les rideaux de ta chambre** I'll make some new curtains for your bedroom; **2** (faire en plus) **je vais ~ de la soupe** I'll make some more soup; **3** (changer complètement) **vouloir ~ le monde** to want to change the world; **se faire ~ le nez** to have one's nose re-modelled GB; **on ne le refera pas** there's no changing him; **~ sa vie** (avec quelqu'un d'autre) to start all over again (with somebody else); **4** (rénover) to redo [*toit, gouttière, sol*]; to redecorate [*pièce*]; to resurface [*route*]; **appartement refait à neuf** completely refurbished apartment.

II se refaire *vpr* **1** (fabriquer pour soi) **se ~ une robe** to make oneself another dress; **2** (retrouver) **se ~ une santé** to recuperate; **se ~ une beauté** to redo one's make- up; **3** (se réhabituer) **se ~ à** to get used to [sth] again; **4** (changer) **on ne se refait pas** a person can't change.

réfection /ʀefɛksjɔ̃/ *nf* (de toiture, façade, bâtiment) repairing; (de route) mending; (de pièce, maison) re-doing; **'en ~'** 'restoration work in progress'.

réfectoire /ʀefɛktwaʀ/ *nm* (d'institution) refectory; MIL mess.

référence /ʀefeʀãs/ **I** *nf* **1** (renvoi) reference (à to); **en** ou **par ~ à** in reference to; **faire ~ à** to refer to, to make reference to; **2** (modèle) (prime) example; **lui? ce n'est pas une ~!** who, him? well, he's not much of an example!; **date de ~** date of reference; **livre de ~** reference book; **3** (identification) reference; (numéro) reference number; **4** LING reference.

II références *nfpl* (pour emploi, location) references.

référendum /ʀefeʀɛ̃dɔm/ *nm* referendum (**sur** on).

référentiel, -ielle /ʀefeʀãsjɛl/ **I** *adj* GÉN, LING referential.

II *nm* FML frame of reference.

référer /ʀefeʀe/ [14] **I se référer à** *vtr ind* **1** **en ~ à** to consult; **2** LING **~ à** to refer to.

II se référer *vpr* **se ~ à** (faire référence à) to refer to; (consulter) to consult.

refermer /ʀ(ə)fɛʀme/ [1] **I** *vtr* (fermer) to close; (de nouveau) to close [sth] again.

II se refermer *vpr* [*piège, porte*] to close (**sur** on); [*eau*] to close (**sur** over); [*blessure*] to close up.

réfléchi, ~e /ʀefleʃi/ **I** *adj* **1** (posé) [*personne*] reflective, thoughtful; [*regard*] thoughtful; **2** (mûri) [*décision*] considered; [*action*] well-considered; **tout bien ~** all things considered; **c'est tout ~** my mind is made up; **3** PHYS reflected; **4** LING reflexive.

II *nm* LING reflexive.

réfléchir /ʀefleʃiʀ/ [3] **I** *vtr* to reflect [*onde, chaleur*].

II réfléchir à *vtr ind* **~ à** to think about.

III *vi* to think (**sur qch** about sth); **ça fait ~** it makes you think; **réfléchis et donne-moi ta réponse demain** think it over and give me your answer tomorrow; **mais réfléchis donc un peu!** use your brain!

IV se réfléchir *vpr* [*onde, image*] to be reflected.

réfléchissant, ~e /ʀefleʃisã, ãt/ *adj* reflective.

réflecteur, -trice /ʀeflɛktœʀ, tʀis/ **I** *adj* reflecting.

II *nm* reflector.

reflet /ʀ(ə)flɛ/ *nm* **1** (image) LIT, FIG reflection; **être le ~ d'une époque** to reflect a period; **2** (lueur) glint; (plus délicat) shimmer **C**; **~s dorés** golden glints; **feuillage à ~s argentés** foliage with a silvery shimmer; **3** (nuance de couleur) sheen **C**; **les ~s du satin** the sheen of satin; **cheveux châtains aux ~s roux** brown hair with (natural) auburn highlights.

refléter /ʀ(ə)flete/ [14] **I** *vtr* to reflect; **son visage reflétait son émotion** his/her emotion showed in his/her face.

II se refléter *vpr* LIT, FIG to be reflected (**dans** in).

refleurir /R(ə)flœRiR/ [3] *vi* **1** [*fleur*] to flower again; **2** [*arts*] to flourish again.

réflexe /Reflɛks/ **I** *adj* reflex.
II *nm* **1** (en physiologie) reflex; **2** (réaction, habitude) reaction; **manquer de ~** to be slow to react; **elle a eu le ~ de freiner** her instinctive reaction was to brake; **faire qch par ~** to do sth automatically.

réflexif, -ive /Reflɛksif, iv/ *adj* reflexive.

réflexion /Reflɛksjɔ̃/ *nf* **1** (pensée) thought, reflection; **2** (méditation) thinking, reflection; **cela demande ~** it needs thinking about; **sans ~** without thinking; **~ faite** or **à la ~, je n'irai pas** on reflection ou on second thoughts, I won't go; **donner matière à ~** to be food for thought; **3** (remarque) remark (**sur** about), comment (**sur** on); **s'attirer des ~s** to attract criticism ou adverse comment; **4** (étude) study (**sur** of); **document de ~** discussion paper; **5** PHYS reflection.

refluer /R(ə)flye/ [1] *vi* [*liquide*] to flow back; [*foule*] to surge back; **faire ~** to push back [*foule*].

reflux /R(ə)fly/ *nm inv* **1** (marée) ebb tide; **2** (de foule) surging away; (de chômage, devise) decline.

refondre /R(ə)fɔ̃dR/ [6] *vtr* LIT to melt down again [*métal*]; to recast [*objet*].

refonte /R(ə)fɔ̃t/ *nf* GÉN overhaul; (de contrat) rewriting.

reforestation /RəfɔRɛstasjɔ̃/ *nf* reafforestation.

réformateur, -trice /RefɔRmatœR, tRis/ **I** *adj* [*dirigeant, parti, idéologie*] reforming; [*milieu, courant, force*] of reform (*épith, après n*).
II *nm,f* reformer.

réforme /RefɔRm/ *nf* **1** (modification) reform; **2** MIL discharge; **3** RELIG **la Réforme** the Reformation.

réformé, ~e /RefɔRme/ **I** *adj* RELIG Reformed.
II *nm* MIL [*appelé*] person who has been declared unfit for service; [*soldat*] discharged soldier.
III *nm,f* RELIG Calvinist.

reformer /R(ə)fɔRme/ [1] **I** *vtr* to re-form; **~ les rangs** [*soldats*] to fall in again.
II **se reformer** *vpr* [*glace, équipe*] to re-form; [*soldats*] to form up again; [*peau*] to renew itself.

réformer /RefɔRme/ [1] **I** *vtr* **1** (changer) to reform; **2** MIL to declare [sb] unfit for service [*appelé*]; to discharge [*soldat*].
II **se réformer** *vpr* to mend one's ways.

réformiste /RefɔRmist/ *adj, nmf* reformist.

refoulé, ~e /R(ə)fule/ *nm,f* repressed person.

refoulement /R(ə)fulmɑ̃/ *nm* **1** PSYCH repression; **2** (expulsion) (d'ennemi) pushing back; (d'immigrant) turning back; (de la foule) driving back; (de liquide) forcing back.

refouler /R(ə)fule/ [1] *vtr* **1** (contenir) to suppress [*émotion, souvenir*]; to repress [*tendance*]; to hold back [*larmes*]; to stifle [*sanglots*]; **2** (repousser) to force [sth] back [*liquide*]; to push back [*ennemi*]; to turn back [*immigrant*]; to drive back [*foule*].

réfractaire /RefRaktɛR/ *adj* **1** [*personne*] **~ à** resistant to [*progrès, infection, influence*]; impervious to [*poésie, musique*]; **2** [*matériau*] refractory.

réfracter /RefRakte/ [1] **I** *vtr* to refract.
II **se réfracter** *vpr* to be refracted.

refrain /R(ə)fRɛ̃/ *nm* **1** (de chanson) chorus; **2** (rengaine) PEJ (old) refrain.

réfréner /RefRene/ [14] *vtr* to curb.

réfrigérant, ~e /RefRiʒeRɑ̃, ɑ̃t/ **I** *adj* **1** LIT [*appareil*] cooling; **2** FIG [*accueil*] frosty.
II *nm* (appareil) cooler.

réfrigérateur /RefRiʒeRatœR/ *nm* refrigerator.

réfrigérer /RefRiʒeRe/ [14] *vtr* to refrigerate [*aliment*]; to cool [*local*].

réfringent, ~e /RefRɛ̃ʒɑ̃, ɑ̃t/ *adj* refractive.

refroidir /RəfRwadiR/ [3] **I** *vtr* **1** LIT to cool down [*mélange, moteur*]; to cool [*atmosphère*]; **2** FIG to dampen [*ardeur, enthousiasme*]; **~ qn** to dampen sb's spirits
II *vi* (devenir moins chaud) to cool down; (devenir trop froid) to get cold.

III **se refroidir** *vpr* [*temps*] to get colder; [*muscle, articulation*] to stiffen up; [*personne*] to get cold.

refroidissement /RəfRwadismɑ̃/ *nm* **1** MÉTÉO drop in temperature; [*2*] GÉN, TECH cooling; **tuyau de ~** cooling pipe; **liquide de ~** coolant; **3** MÉD chill; **4** (de relations, sentiment) cooling.

refroidisseur /RəfRwadisœR/ *nm* coolant.

refuge /R(ə)fyʒ/ **I** *nm* **1** (abri, réconfort) refuge; **2** (en montagne) (mountain) refuge; **3** (pour animaux) sanctuary; **4** (de chaussée) traffic island; (de pont) refuge.
II (-)**refuge** (*in compounds*) **monnaie ~** safe currency; **pays ~** country of refuge.

réfugié, ~e /Refyʒje/ *nm,f* refugee.

réfugier: se réfugier /Refyʒje/ [2] *vpr* LIT, FIG to take refuge.

refus /R(ə)fy/ *nm inv* refusal (**de qch** of sth; **de faire** to do); **ce n'est pas de ~**○ I wouldn't say no○.
■ **~ d'obéissance** MIL insubordination; JUR contempt of court; **~ d'obtempérer** refusal to comply; **~ de priorité** failure to give way.

refuser /R(ə)fyze/ [1] **I** *vtr* **1** (ne pas accepter) to refuse [*offre, don, invitation*]; to turn down [*poste*]; **~ de faire qch** to refuse to do sth; **2** (ne pas accorder) to refuse [*permission, crédit, entrée*]; **~ qch à qn** to refuse sb sth; **se voir ~ qch** to be refused sth; **il a refusé qu'on vende la maison** he wouldn't allow the house to be sold; **~ sa porte à qn** to bar one's door to sb; **je lui refuse le droit de me juger** he/she has no right to judge me; **3** (rejeter) to reject [*budget, manuscrit, racisme*]; to refuse to accept [*fait, évidence*]; to turn away [*spectateur, client*]; **~ un candidat** (à un poste) to turn down a candidate; (à un examen) to fail a candidate; **être refusé à un concours** to fail an examination.
II **se refuser** *vpr* **1** (être décliné) **ça ne se refuse pas** (occasion) it's too good to pass up○ ou miss; (verre) I wouldn't say no○; **2** (se priver de) to deny oneself [*plaisir*]; **on ne se refuse rien**○! you're certainly not stinting yourself!; **3** (dire non) **se ~ à** to refuse to accept [*évidence*]; to refuse to adopt [*solution*]; **se ~ à faire** to refuse to do.

réfuter /Refyte/ [1] *vtr* to refute.

regagner /R(ə)gaɲe/ [1] *vtr* **1** (rejoindre) to get back to [*lieu, poste*]; **~ son domicile/sa place** to return home/to one's seat; **2** (recouvrer) to regain, to win back [*estime, confiance*]; to pick up [*point*]; **~ du terrain** MIL, FIG to regain ground.

regain /R(ə)gɛ̃/ *nm* **1** (reprise) (de marché) recovery (**de** of); (d'inflation, de chômage) rise (**de** in); **~ de la consommation** upturn in consumer spending; **2** (recrudescence) (d'intérêt) revival; (de violence, tension) resurgence, renewal; **connaître un ~ de popularité** to enjoy renewed popularity; **3** AGRIC second crop.

régal /Regal/ *nm* **1** (mets savoureux) culinary delight; **c'est un (vrai) ~!** it's (absolutely) delicious!; **2** FIG delight; **un ~ pour les yeux** a feast for the eyes.

régalade /Regalad/ *nf* **boire à la ~** to drink without letting one's lips touch the bottle.

régaler /Regale/ [1] **I** *vtr* [*personne*] to treat [sb] to a delicious meal; **~ qn de** to treat sb to [*vin, mets*]; FIG to regale sb with [*anecdotes*].
II **se régaler** *vpr* **1** (de nourriture) **je me régale** it's delicious; **les enfants se sont régalés avec ton dessert** the children really enjoyed your dessert; **2** FIG **se ~ avec** to enjoy [sth] thoroughly [*film, personnage*]; **se ~ de** to love [*anecdote*].

regard /R(ə)gaR/ **I** *nm* **1** (action de regarder) look; **porter son ~ sur qch** to look at sth; **détourner le ~** to look away; **chercher qn du ~** to look around for sb; **interroger qn du ~** to look enquiringly GB ou inquiringly US at sb; **suivre qch/qn du ~** to follow sth/sb with one's eyes; **elle attire tous les ~s** everyone looks at her; **jeter un ~ rapide à** or **sur qch** to glance at sth; **j'ai croisé son ~** our eyes met; **échanger des ~s** to exchange looks; **loin** or **à l'abri des ~s indiscrets** far from prying eyes; **soustraire qch aux ~s** to conceal sth from view; **2** (yeux) eyes (*pl*); **un ~ clair** light-coloured^{GB} eyes; **3** (expression)

expression; **son ~ triste** his/her sad expression; **elle a un ~ intelligent** she looks intelligent; **sous le ~ amusé de qn** under the amused eye of sb; **jeter un ~ noir à qn** to give sb a black look; **4** (manière de juger) eye; **le ~ des autres** other people's opinion; **porter un ~ nouveau sur qch** to take a fresh look at sth.

II au regard de *loc prép* FML with regard to; **au ~ du chômage** with regard to unemployment; **au ~ de la loi** in the eyes of the law.

III en regard de *loc prép* FML compared with.

IV en regard *loc adv* **avec une carte en ~** with a map on the opposite page.

regardant, **~e** /ʀəgaʀdɑ̃, ɑ̃t/ *adj* **ne pas être très ~** (exigeant) not to be very particular ou fussy (**sur** about); (économe) not to care about what things cost; **être ~** (**avec son argent**) to be careful with one's money.

regarder /ʀ(ə)gaʀde/ [1] **I** *vtr* **1** (diriger son regard vers) to look at; **~ qch par la fenêtre** to look out of the window at sth; **regarde qui vient!** look who's coming!; **~ qch méchamment** to glare at sth; **~ rapidement** to have a quick look at, to glance at [*bâtiment, paysage*]; to glance through [*document, livre*]; **~ qn en face** LIT, FIG to look sb in the face; **~ la réalité** or **les choses en face** to face facts; **~ qn de haut** FIG to look down one's nose at sb; **~ qn de travers** FIG to look askance at sb; **2** (fixer avec attention) to watch, to look at [*personne, scène*]; to look at [*tableau, paysage*]; to watch [*film, télévision*]; **~ qn faire** to watch sb doing; **regarde bien comment je fais** watch what I do carefully; **~ qch fixement** to stare at sth; **~ qn/qch longuement** to gaze at sb/sth; **~ qn dans les yeux** to look sb in the eye(s); **3** (pour vérifier, savoir) to look at [*montre, carte*]; to have a look at, to check [*pneus, niveau d'huile*]; **~ dans** to look up, to consult [*dictionnaire, annuaire*]; **~ si** to have a look to see if; **4** (examiner, considérer) to look at [*pays, situation*]; **~ pourquoi/si/qui** to see why/if/who; **5** (constater) to look; **regarde-moi ça!** just look at that!; **6°** (concerner) to concern [*personne*]; **ça ne vous regarde pas** that doesn't concern you; (moins poli) it's none of your business; **mêle-toi de ce qui te regarde!** mind your own business○!; **7** (prendre en compte, envisager) **elle ne regarde que ses intérêts** she thinks only of her own interests; **~ l'avenir avec confiance** to view the future with confidence; **8** (faire face à) [*maison*] to overlook [*baie, mer*].

II regarder à *vtr ind* to think about; **~ à la dépense** to watch what one spends; **ne pas ~ à la dépense** to spare no expense; **quand on y regarde de très près** when you look at it very closely; **tu devrais y ~ à deux fois avant de l'acheter** you should think twice before buying it.

III *vi* **1** (diriger son regard) to look; **~ en l'air** to look up; **~ par terre** to look down; **regarde autour de toi** LIT, FIG look around; **regarde bien** have a good look; **2** (en cherchant) to look; **3** (faire attention) to look; **regarde où tu mets les pieds** look ou watch where you put your feet.

IV se regarder *vpr* **1** (soi-même) to look at oneself; **2** (l'un l'autre) to look at one another.

regarnir /ʀəgaʀniʀ/ [3] *vtr* to restock [*étalage, réfrigérateur*]; to refill [*trousse de secours*].

régate /ʀegat/ *nf* regatta.

régence /ʀeʒɑ̃s/ **I** *adj inv* [*style*] French Regency; **~ anglais** Regency.

II *nf* **1** POL regency; **2** HIST **la Régence** the Regency.

régénérer /ʀeʒeneʀe/ [14] **I** *vtr* **1** BIOL, FIG to regenerate; **2** CHIMIE to reactivate.

II se régénérer *vpr* **1** BIOL [*cellules*] to regenerate; **2** FIG [*corps, personne*] to regain one's strength.

régent, **~e** /ʀeʒɑ̃, ɑ̃t/ *nm,f* POL regent.

régenter /ʀeʒɑ̃te/ [1] *vtr* (diriger) to rule, to regiment; (contrôler) to regulate.

régie /ʀeʒi/ *nf* **1** (gestion) (par l'État) state control; (par la commune) local government control; **2** (entreprise) **~ d'État** state-owned company; **3** (de

spectacle) THÉÂT stage management; CIN, TV production department; (salle) central control room.

regimber /ʀ(ə)ʒɛ̃be/ [1] *vi* **1** [*personne*] to balk (**contre** at); **2** [*cheval, âne*] to jib.

régime /ʀeʒim/ *nm* **1** (alimentation) diet; **être/se mettre au ~** to be/to go on a diet; **suivre un ~** to be on a diet; **produit de ~** dietary product; **2** POL (mode de gouvernement) system (of government); (gouvernement) government; (totalitaire) regime; **~ parlementaire** parliamentary system; **3** (conditions) system, regime; **~ pénitentiaire** prison system; **~ de faveur** preferential treatment; **4** ADMIN (organisation) scheme; (règlement) regulations (*pl*); **~ de retraite** pension scheme; **5** JUR **~ matrimonial** marriage settlement; **6** (rythme) (de moteur) running speed; **tourner à plein ~** [*moteur*] to run at top speed; [*usine*] to work at full capacity; **à ce ~** FIG at this rate; **7** PHYS (débit) rate of flow; **8** GÉOG, MÉTÉO regime; **9** (de bananes) bunch; (de dattes) cluster; **10** LING object.

régiment /ʀeʒimɑ̃/ *nm* **1** MIL (unité) regiment; **2°** (service militaire) military service; **3°** (multitude) army.

région /ʀeʒjɔ̃/ *nf* **1** ADMIN region; **la ~ parisienne** the Paris region; **2** GÉOG (territoire) region; (autour d'un lieu) area; **les ~s tropicales** tropical regions; **le Vésuve et sa ~** Vesuvius and the surrounding area; **le vin de la ~** the local wine; **3** ANAT region; **4** MIL district.

régional, **~e**, *mpl* **-aux** /ʀeʒjɔnal, o/ *adj* regional.

régionalisme /ʀeʒjɔnalism/ *nm* **1** POL regionalism; **2** LING regional expression, regionalism.

régir /ʀeʒiʀ/ [3] *vtr* to govern.

régisseur /ʀeʒisœʀ/ ▶ 374 *nm* **1** (de domaine) steward, manager; **2** THÉÂT stage manager.

■ **~ de plateau** CIN studio manager; TV floor manager.

registre /ʀ(ə)ʒistʀ/ *nm* **1** (cahier) register; **~ des absences** SCOL attendance register; **~ d'état civil** register of births, marriages and deaths; **les ~s de police** police records; **2** (de roman, film, discours) style; **3** (étendue) register; **cet acteur a un ~ limité** this actor has a limited range; **4** LING, ORDINAT, TECH register.

réglable /ʀeglabl/ *adj* **1** [*hauteur, pression*] adjustable; **2** (payable) payable.

réglage /ʀeglaʒ/ *nm* (mise au point) (de vitesse) regulating; (de compteur, thermostat) setting; (de moteur) tuning; (de pression, tir, volume, siège) adjustment; **avec ~ automatique** [*chauffage, four*] with a timing device.

règle /ʀɛgl/ **I** *nf* **1** (instrument) ruler, rule; **à la ~** with a ruler; **2** (consigne) rule; **~ de grammaire** grammatical rule; **~ de conduite** rule of conduct; **~s de sécurité** safety regulations; **respecter les ~s du jeu** LIT, FIG to play the game according to the rules; **dans** ou **selon les ~s de l'art** by the rule book; **il se fait une ~** ou **il a pour ~ de payer comptant** he makes it a rule to pay cash; **3** (usage établi) rule; **en ~ générale** as a (general) rule; **il est de ~ de répondre** ou **qu'on réponde** it is customary to reply.

II règles *nfpl* (menstruation) period (*sg*).

III en règle *loc adj* [*demande*] formal ; [*papiers, comptes*] in order; **subir un interrogatoire en ~** to be given a thorough interrogation.

IV en règle *loc adv* **pour passer la frontière, il faut être en ~** to cross the frontier, your papers must be in order; **se mettre en ~ avec le fisc** to get one's tax affairs properly sorted out.

réglé, **~e** /ʀegle/ *adj* **1** (à lignes) [*papier*] ruled, lined; **2** (organisé) [*vie, maison*] well-ordered; [*défilé*] well-organized; **3** (décidé) **l'affaire est ~e** the matter is settled; **4** (pubère) [*adolescente*] who has started having periods (*épith, après n*).

IDIOMES **être ~ comme du papier à musique**○ or **comme une horloge** to be as regular as clockwork.

règlement /ʀɛgləmɑ̃/ *nm* **1** (règles) regulations (*pl*), rules (*pl*); **2** (paiement) payment; **mode de ~** method of payment; **3** (résolution) settlement; **~ à**

Les régions

Les indications ci-dessous valent pour les noms des états américains, des provinces canadiennes, des comtés anglais, des départements français, des provinces françaises, des régions administratives d'autres pays comme les cantons suisses ou les provinces belges, et même pour les noms de régions géographiques qui ne sont pas des entités politiques.

Les noms de régions

En général, l'anglais n'utilise pas l'article défini devant les noms de régions.

aimer l'Alabama	= to like Alabama
aimer la Californie	= to like California
visiter le Nouveau-Mexique	= to visit New Mexico
visiter le Texas	= to visit Texas
le Lancashire	= Lancashire
la Bourgogne	= Burgundy
la Provence	= Provence
la Savoie	= Savoy

Mais l'article est utilisé pour les noms de certaines provinces ou régions françaises, certains cantons suisses et beaucoup de départements français. En cas de doute, consulter le dictionnaire.

le Berry	= the Berry
le Limousin	= the Limousin
le Valais	= the Valais
les Alpes-Maritimes	= the Alpes-Maritimes
l'Ardèche	= the Ardèche
les Landes	= the Landes
le Loir-et-Cher	= the Loir-et-Cher
le Loiret	= the Loiret
le Rhône	= the Rhône
le Var	= the Var

À, au, aux, dans, en

À, au, aux, dans et en se traduisent par to *avec les verbes de mouvement (par ex.* aller, se rendre *etc.) et par* in *avec les autres verbes (par ex.* être, habiter *etc.).*

vivre au Texas	= to live in Texas
aller au Texas	= to go to Texas
vivre en Californie	= to live in California
aller en Californie	= to go to California

vivre dans les Rocheuses	= to live in the Rockies
aller dans les Rocheuses	= to go to the Rockies

De avec les noms de régions

Quelques noms de régions ont donné naissance à des adjectifs, mais il y en a beaucoup moins qu'en français. En cas de doute, consulter le dictionnaire.

les habitants de la Californie	= Californian people
les vins de Californie	= Californian wines

Ces adjectifs sont tous utilisables comme des noms.

les habitants de la Californie	= Californians
	ou Californian people

Lorsqu'il n'y a pas d'adjectif, on peut, la plupart du temps, utiliser le nom de la région en position d'adjectif.

l'accent du Texas	= a Texas accent
le beurre de Normandie	= Normandy butter
les églises du Yorkshire	= Yorkshire churches
les paysages de la Californie	= the California countryside

Mais en cas de doute, il est plus sûr d'utiliser la tournure avec of, *toujours possible.*

la frontière du Texas	= the border of Texas
les habitants de l'Auvergne	= the inhabitants of the Auvergne
les rivières du Dorset	= the rivers of Dorset
les villes du Languedoc	= the towns of Languedoc

Les adjectifs dérivés

Les adjectifs dérivés des régions n'ont pas toujours d'équivalent en anglais. Plusieurs cas sont possibles mais on pourra presque toujours utiliser le nom de la région placé avant le nom qualifié:

la région dauphinoise = the Dauphiné region

Pour souligner la provenance on choisira from + *le nom de la région:*

l'équipe dauphinoise = the team from the Dauphiné region

Pour parler de l'environnement on optera pour of + *le nom de la région:*

l'économie vendéenne = the economy of the Vendée

Pour situer on utilisera in + *le nom de la région:*

mon séjour vendéen = my stay in the Vendée

---

l'amiable amicable settlement; JUR out-of-court settlement. ■ **~ de comptes** settling of scores; **~ direct** direct debit; **~ interne** rules and regulations (*pl*); **~ de sécurité** safety regulations (*pl*).

réglementaire /ʀeɡləmɑ̃tɛʀ/ *adj* **1** (requis) [*tenue, taille*] regulation (*épith*); [*format*] prescribed; [*procédure*] statutory; **2** (de réglementation) [*pouvoir*] regulatory; **les textes ~s** rules and regulations.

réglementation /ʀeɡləmɑ̃tasjɔ̃/ *nf* **1** (règles) rules (*pl*), regulations (*pl*); **2** (contrôle) regulation, control.

réglementer /ʀeɡləmɑ̃te/ [1] *vtr* to regulate.

régler /ʀeɡle/ [14] *vtr* **1** (payer) to settle [*compte, dette*]; to pay [*facture, montant, créancier, fournisseur*]; to pay for [*achat, travaux, fournitures*]; **réglons nos comptes** LIT let's settle up; **avoir des comptes à ~ avec qn** FIG to have a score ou account to settle with sb; **~ son compte à qn**° to sort sb out; **2** (résoudre) to settle [*litige, problème*]; **~ ses affaires** to sort out one's affairs; **3** (mettre au point) to settle [*détails, modalités, ordre*]; to fix, to decide on [*programme, calendrier*]; to arrange [*mise en scène, chorégraphie*]; to organize [*défilé*]; **4** (ajuster) to adjust [*hauteur, micro, chauffage*]; to regulate, to adjust [*vitesse, mécanisme*]; to tune [*moteur*]; (fixer d'avance) to set [*allumage, pression*]; **5** (adapter) **~ sa conduite sur celle de qn** to model one's behaviour°GB on sb's; **~ sa montre sur celle de qn** to set one's watch by sb's; **6** (tracer des lignes) to rule (lines on) [*papier*].

réglette /ʀeɡlɛt/ *nf* (de règle à calcul) slide; (de balance) graduated beam.

réglisse /ʀeɡlis/ *nf* liquorice GB, licorice US.

régnant, ~e /ʀeɲɑ̃, ɑ̃t/ *adj* [*dynastie*] reigning; [*idéologie*] prevailing.

règne /ʀɛɲ/ *nm* **1** POL (de monarque) reign; (de président) rule; **2** FIG (de peur, d'hypocrisie) reign; **3** BIOL kingdom.

régner /ʀeɲe/ [14] *vi* **1** POL [*souverain*] to reign, to rule; **~ sur** to reign over, to rule; **2** (imposer sa domination) [*chef, personnalité*] to be in control; **3** (prédominer) [*confusion, optimisme, harmonie*] to reign; [*ambiance*] to prevail; **la confiance règne!** IRON there's trust for you!; **faire ~** to give rise to [*insécurité, injustice*]; to impose [*ordre*]; **l'inquiétude règne chez les jeunes** there is a lot of anxiety among young people.

regonfler /ʀ(ə)ɡɔ̃fle/ [1] *vtr* **1** (gonfler de nouveau) to reinflate [*pneu*]; to blow [sth] up again [*ballon, bouée*]; **2** (gonfler davantage) to put more air into [*pneu, ballon*]; **3**° FIG to increase [*effectifs*]; to boost [*ventes, profits*].

regorger /ʀ(ə)ɡɔʀʒe/ [13] *vi* [*magasin, maison*] to be packed (**de** with); [*ville, région*] to have an abundance (**de** of); [*discours, film*] to be crammed (**de** with).

régresser /ʀeɡʀese/ [1] *vi* **1** (diminuer) [*eaux*] to recede; [*production*] to go down (**de** by); **faire ~ le chômage** to push down unemployment; **2** (décliner) [*culture*] to be in decline; [*personnalité*] to lose ground; **il a régressé en maths** his work in maths GB ou math US has deteriorated; **3** (disparaître) [*épidémie*] to die out.

régression /ʀeɡʀesjɔ̃/ *nf* GÉN decline; (en sciences) regression; **~ marine** marine regression; **de ~** [*courbe*] regression (*épith*).

regret /ʀəɡʀɛ/ *nm* **1** (remords) regret; **sans ~s** with no regrets; **je n'ai qu'un ~, c'est de ne pas l'avoir**

écouté my only regret is that I didn't listen to him; **2** (insatisfaction) regret; **il a remarqué avec ~ que** he observed with regret that; **j'apprends avec ~ que** I'm sorry to hear that; **à ~** [*consentir*] with regret; **à mon grand ~** to my great regret; **j'ai le** ou **je suis au ~ de vous annoncer** I regret to inform you; **j'ai le** ou **je suis au ~ de ne pouvoir vous aider** I regret that I cannot help you.

regrettable /ʀəgʀetabl/ *adj* regrettable.

regretter /ʀəgʀete/ [1] *vtr* **1** (déplorer) to regret [*situation, agissement*]; **~ que qn fasse** to regret ou to be sorry that sb does; **je regrette de ne pas pouvoir t'aider** I'm sorry I can't help you; **nous regrettons de ne pouvoir donner suite à votre demande** we regret to inform you that your application has been unsuccessful; **je regrette de partir** I'm sorry to be leaving; **j'ai beaucoup regretté leur départ** I was very sorry that they left; **'il n'y a pas de dialogue,' regrette un employé** 'there's no dialogueᴳᴮ,' complains one employee; **2** (se repentir de) to regret [*colère, erreur, décision*]; **~ son argent** to regret having spent one's money; **~ d'avoir fait** to regret doing, to be sorry for doing; **je ne regrette rien** I have no regrets; **3** (ressentir l'absence de) to miss [*passé, personne, lieu*]; **il a été beaucoup regretté** he was sorely ou greatly missed; **notre regretté collègue** FML our late lamented colleague; **4** (pour s'excuser) to be sorry; **je regrette, il est absent** I'm sorry but he's not here.

regroupement /ʀ(ə)gʀupmɑ̃/ *nm* **1** (rassemblement) (de mots, services, d'usines) grouping; (d'intérêts) pooling; (de personnes) bringing together; (de provinces, terrains) grouping together, regrouping; **2** (fusion) merger; **3** (fait de remettre ensemble) (de personnes, pièces de collection) getting [sth] back together; (de troupes) rallying; (de troupeau) rounding up.

regrouper /ʀ(ə)gʀupe/ [1] **I** *vtr* **1** (mettre ensemble) to group [sth] together [*objets, mots, services, terrains*]; to bring [sth] together [*personnes*]; to pool [*intérêts*]; (amalgamer) to merge; **l'exposition regroupe vingt tableaux de Monet** the exhibition brings together twenty pictures by Monet; **~ deux chapitres en un seul** to merge two chapters into one; **2** (remettre ensemble) to reassemble [*élèves*]; to rally [*partisans, armée*]; to regroup [*parti*]; to round up [*animaux*].
II se regrouper *vpr* **1** (se mettre ensemble) [*groupes, entreprises*] to group together; [*mécontents*] to gather (together); **2** (se remettre ensemble) [*personnes*] to regroup; [*coureurs*] to bunch together again.

régularisation /ʀegylaʀizasjɔ̃/ *nf* **1** (de situation) sorting out, regularization; **2** (de cours d'eau) regulation.

régulariser /ʀegylaʀize/ [1] *vtr* **1** (rendre légal) to sort out, to regularize [*situation*]; to put [sth] in order [*papiers*]; **2** (ajuster) to regulate [*flux, fonctionnement*]; to stabilize [*cours, marché*].

régularité /ʀegylaʀite/ *nf* **1** (caractère répétitif) regularity; **2** (caractère constant) (de rythme, production, progrès) steadiness; (de traits du visage) regularity; (d'écriture) neatness; (de surface) evenness; (de qualité) consistency; **avec ~** [*progresser*] steadily; [*tracer*] evenly; **3** (légalité) legality, correctness.

régulateur, -trice /ʀegylatœʀ, tʀis/ **I** *adj* regulating.
II *nm* (mécanisme) regulator.

régulation /ʀegylasjɔ̃/ *nf* regulation, control.
■ **~ des naissances** birth control.

régulier, -ière /ʀegylje, ɛʀ/ *adj* **1** (en fréquence) [*versements, intervalles, battement*] regular; **être en contact ~ avec qn** to be regularly in touch with sb; **2** (habituel) [*lecteur, client*] regular; [*train, ligne, service*] regular, scheduled; **vol ~** scheduled flight; **3** (de qualité constante) [*rythme, demande, hausse, effort, production*] steady; [*qualité, progrès*] consistent; [*épaisseur, surface, ligne*] even; [*écriture*] neat; [*vie*] (well-)ordered; **être ~ dans ses habitudes** to be regular in one's habits; **4** (symétrique) [*traits, polygone*] regular; [*façade*] symmetrical; **5** (honnête) [*affaire*] above board (*jamais épith*); [*personne*] honest; **6** (conforme) [*papiers, scrutin*] in order (*jamais épith*); [*gouvernement*] legitimate; **il est en**

situation régulière his official papers are in order; **7** LING [*pluriel, vers*] regular; **8** MIL [*troupes*] regular; **9** RELIG [*clergé*] regular.

régulièrement /ʀegyljɛʀmɑ̃/ *adv* **1** (périodiquement, habituellement) [*expédier, rencontrer, se produire*] regularly; **2** (sans à-coups) [*progresser, couler*] steadily; **3** (en formant un motif répété) [*disposer, espacer*] evenly; **4** (selon les règles) [*inscrit*] properly, duly; [*effectué*] in the proper manner; **5** (en principe, d'habitude) normally.

régurgiter /ʀegyʀʒite/ [1] *vtr* LIT, FIG to regurgitate.

réhabilitation /ʀeabilitasjɔ̃/ *nf* **1** (de personne) rehabilitation; **2** (d'immeuble) renovation.

réhabiliter /ʀeabilite/ [1] *vtr* **1** to rehabilitate [*personne*]; to redeem [*passé, institution*]; **2** to renovate [*immeuble, quartier*].
II se réhabiliter *vpr* [*personne*] to redeem oneself.

réhabituer /ʀeabitɥe/ [1] **I** *vtr* to reaccustom (**qn à qch** sb to sth; **qn à faire** sb to doing).
II se réhabituer *vpr* to become reaccustomed (à to).

rehausser /ʀəose/ [1] *vtr* **1** (surélever) to raise; **2** (accentuer) to enhance [*prestige, beauté*]; **3** (souligner) to set off [*contour, motif*].

réhydrater /ʀeidʀate/ [1] *vtr* to rehydrate [*plante, sol*]; to moisturize [*peau*].

réimplanter /ʀeɛ̃plɑ̃te/ [1] **I** *vtr* **1** to re-establish [*usine, industrie*]; **2** to reimplant [*dent, cellule*].
II se réimplanter *vpr* [*usine, industrie*] to re-establish itself.

réimpression /ʀeɛ̃pʀesjɔ̃/ *nf* **1** (activité) reprinting; **2** (ouvrage) reprint.

réimprimer /ʀeɛ̃pʀime/ [1] *vtr* to reprint.

rein /ʀɛ̃/ ANAT **I** *nm* (organe) kidney.
II reins *nmpl* **les ~s** (bas du dos) the small of the back; **mal aux ~s** backache; **une serviette autour des ~s** a towel around the waist; **avoir les ~s solides**○ FIG to be strong; **casser les ~s à qn**○ FIG to break sb.
■ **~ artificiel** kidney machine.

réincarner: se réincarner /ʀeɛ̃kaʀne/ [1] *vpr* to be reincarnated.

reine /ʀɛn/ *nf* **1** ▶ 596 POL, ZOOL, JEUX queen; **2** FIG **~ du bal** the belle of the ball; **être la ~ des imbéciles**○ to be a complete idiot.
■ **~ de beauté** beauty queen; **~ mère** queen mother.

reine-claude, *pl* **reines-claudes** /ʀɛnklod/ *nf* greengage.

reine-des-prés /ʀɛndepʀe/ *nf inv* BOT meadowsweet.

reine-marguerite, *pl* **reines-marguerites** /ʀɛnmaʀgəʀit/ *nf* China aster.

reinette /ʀɛnɛt/ *nf* rennet apple.

réinscrire: se réinscrire /ʀeɛ̃skʀiʀ/ [67] *vpr* to re-enrol.

réinsérer /ʀeɛ̃seʀe/ [14] **I** *vtr* **1** to reintegrate [*personne*]; **2** to reinsert [*annonce, objet*].
II se réinsérer *vpr* [*personne*] to become reintegrated.

réinstallation /ʀeɛ̃stalasjɔ̃/ *nf* **1** (dans un lieu) move, relocation; **2** (dans une fonction) reinstatement.

réinstaller /ʀeɛ̃stale/ [1] **I** *vtr* **1** (réaménager) to refit [*pièce*]; (changer de lieu) **~ les bureaux au premier étage** to move the offices back to the first GB ou second US floor; **2** (rétablir) (dans une ville, une région) to resettle [*personne*] (**dans** to); (dans une maison) to move [sb] back [*personne*] (**dans** to); (à un poste) **~ qn dans ses fonctions** to reinstate someone in his/her old job; (à un mandat) **~ qn à la présidence** to re-elect sb as president.
II se réinstaller *vpr* (dans un lieu) **se ~ dans un fauteuil** to settle (oneself) back into an armchair; **se ~ en banlieue** [*habitant*] to move back to the suburbs; [*compagnie, commerçant*] to set up business again in the suburbs.

réintégration /ʀeɛ̃tegʀasjɔ̃/ *nf* (réadmission) (au

travail) reinstatement (**de** of); (dans un système, un service) reintegration (**dans** into).

éintégrer /ʀeɛ̃tegʀe/ [14] vtr **1** (rejoindre) to return to [*lieu, groupe, système*]; **2** (rétablir) **~ qn** (**dans ses fonctions**) to reinstate sb (in his/her job); **~ qn dans la société** to reintegrate sb into society; **~ qn dans ses droits** to restore sb's rights.

éinventer /ʀeɛ̃vɑ̃te/ [1] vtr to reinvent.

éitération /ʀeiteʀasjɔ̃/ nf reiteration, repetition.

éitérer /ʀeiteʀe/ [14] vtr to repeat; **s'il réitère, ce sera la prison** if he re-offends, he will go to jail.

ejaillir /ʀ(ə)ʒajiʀ/ [3] vi **1** [*liquide*] to splash back (**sur** onto); (sous pression) to spurt back (**sur** onto); [*lumière*] to be reflected (**sur** on); **2** FIG **~ sur qn** [*succès*] to reflect on sb; [*scandale*] to affect sb adversely.

ejaillissement /ʀ(ə)ʒajismɑ̃/ nm (de liquide) splashing; (de scandale) adverse effect; (de succès) reflection.

ejet /ʀ(ə)ʒɛ/ nm **1** (refus) GÉN rejection; ADMIN, JUR (de recours, plainte, charges) dismissal; (de motion) defeat; (de requête) denial; (de demande) rejection; **2** (exclusion) rejection; **le ~ d'un enfant** the rejection of a child; **3** (de déchets industriels) (production) discharge **⊄**; (évacuation) disposal; (déchets) **~s** waste **⊄**; **les ~s en mer** (**de déchets**) dumping (of waste) at sea; **les ~s polluants** pollutants; **4** MÉD (de greffon) rejection; **5** AGRIC **~ de souche** shoot.

ejeter /ʀəʒ(ə)te, ʀʒəte/ [20] **I** vtr **1** (refuser) GÉN to reject [*théorie, initiative, alliance, conseil, pièce défectueuse, candidature*]; to turn down [*offre*]; ADMIN, JUR to dismiss [*plainte, charges, résolution*]; to defeat [*motion*]; to deny [*requête*]; to reject [*demande*]; to set aside [*décision, verdict*]; **~ une proposition de paix** to reject a peace proposal; **2** (exclure) to reject [*enfant, marginal*]; **3** (renvoyer) **~ qch sur qn** to shift sth onto sb [*tort, responsabilité*]; **4** (restituer) [*organisme*] to reject [*greffon*]; [*machine*] to reject [*jetons*]; **5** (produire) [*usine*] to discharge [*déchets*]; to eject [*fumée, gaz*]; [*volcan*] to spew out [*lave*]; **6** (se débarrasser de) [*personne, compagnie*] to dispose of [*déchets*]; [*pêcheur*] to throw [sth] back [*poisson*]; [*mer, marée*] to wash up [*corps, débris*]; **~ des déchets en mer** to dump waste at sea; **7** (déplacer) **~ un mot en fin de phrase** to put a word at the end of the sentence; **8** (chasser) [*armée*] to push ou drive back [*ennemi*] (**hors de** out of); **9** (bouger brutalement) [*personne*] to throw [*tête, cheveux, épaules*] (**en arrière** back).

II se rejeter vpr **1** (se reculer) **se ~ en arrière** to throw ou fling oneself back; **2** (se renvoyer) **se ~ la responsabilité de qch** to blame each other for sth.

ejeton /ʀəʒ(ə)tɔ̃, ʀʒətɔ̃/ nm **1**○ (enfant) HUM offspring (*inv*); **2** BOT, FIG offshoot.

ejoindre /ʀ(ə)ʒwɛ̃dʀ/ [56] **I** vtr **1** (à un rendez-vous) to meet up with; **2** (rattraper) to catch up with; **3** (se oindre à) to join [*personne, groupe, mouvement*]; (de nouveau) to rejoin; **le sentier rejoint la route** the path joins the road; **4** (aller à) [*personne*] to get to [*endroit*]; (de nouveau) to get back to [*endroit*]; to return to [*domicile, caserne*]; **~ son poste** to take up one's appointment; (de nouveau) to return to one's duties; **5** (s'accorder avec) [*personnes*] **~ qn sur qch** to concur with sb on sth; **ça rejoint ce qu'il a dit** it ties up with what he said.

II se rejoindre vpr **1** (se rencontrer) [*personnes*] to meet up; [*routes*] to meet; **2** (s'accorder) [*personnes*] to be in agreement (**sur** on); [*opinions, goûts*] to be similar; **3** (se fondre) **la musique et la poésie se rejoignent** music and poetry merge.

ejouer /ʀ(ə)ʒwe/ [1] vtr GÉN to play [sth] again; to replay [*match*]; **~ une pièce** to perform a play again.

ejoui, ~e /ʀeʒwi/ adj [*air, mine*] cheerful.

ejouir /ʀeʒwiʀ/ [3] **I** vtr **1** (faire plaisir à) to delight [*personne*]; to gladden [*cœur*]; **l'idée du départ me réjouit/ne me réjouit pas** I am delighted/less than delighted at the thought of leaving; **2** (divertir) to amuse.

II se réjouir vpr to rejoice; **se ~ de qch** to be delighted at [*nouvelle*]; to be delighted with [*succès*,

---

projet]; to delight in [*bonheur, malheur*]; **se ~ de faire** to be delighted to do; **se ~ à l'idée de** ou **à la pensée que** to be delighted at the thought that.

réjouissance /ʀeʒwisɑ̃s/ **I** nf rejoicing.

II réjouissances nfpl celebrations; **quel est le programme des ~s?**○ HUM what delights are in store for us?

réjouissant, ~e /ʀeʒwisɑ̃, ɑ̃t/ adj **1** (qui fait plaisir) heartening, delightful; **la nouvelle n'a rien de bien ~** it's not exactly cheerful news; **c'est ~!** IRON that's just wonderful!; **2** (divertissant) amusing.

relâche /ʀ(ə)lɑʃ/ nf **1** CIN, THÉÂT closure; (sur un panneau) '**~**' 'no performance'; **le jeudi est jour de ~** it's closed on Thursdays; **faire ~** to be closed; **2** (pause) break, rest; **sans ~** relentlessly; **3** NAUT port of call; **faire ~** (dans un port) to put in.

relâché, ~e /ʀ(ə)lɑʃe/ adj [*surveillance, discipline, morale, mœurs*] lax, slack; [*style*] slipshod.

relâchement /ʀ(ə)lɑʃmɑ̃/ nm **1** (de discipline, zèle, d'attention, effort) slackening; (de morale, mœurs) loosening, relaxation; **il y a du ~ dans le travail** the work is slacking off; **2** (de muscle) slackening.

relâcher /ʀ(ə)lɑʃe/ [1] **I** vtr **1** (desserrer) to loosen [*étreinte, lien, muscle, ressort*]; **2** (libérer) to release [*personne, animal*]; to let [sth] go [*poisson*]; **3** (diminuer) to relax, to let up on [*discipline, surveillance*]; **~ son attention** to let one's attention wander; **~ ses efforts** to let up.

II vi NAUT (dans un port) to put in; (au large) to drop anchor.

III se relâcher vpr **1** [*étreinte, lien, ressort*] to loosen; [*muscle*] to relax, to loosen up; **2** [*effort, discipline*] to slacken; [*zèle*] to flag; [*élève*] to grow slack.

relais /ʀ(ə)lɛ/ nm inv **1** (intermédiaire) intermediary; **prendre le ~** (**de qn/qch**) to take over (from sb/sth); **passer le ~ à** to hand over to; **2** SPORT relay; **course de ~** relay race; **3** (restaurant) restaurant; (hôtel) hotel; **4** TECH, TÉLÉCOM (dispositif) relay; **~ hertzien** radio relay station.

relance /ʀ(ə)lɑ̃s/ nf **1** (reprise) (d'industrie, idée) revival; (d'économie) reflation; (impulsion donnée) boost (**de** to); (de débat, négociations) reopening; (recrudescence) (de terrorisme) upsurge; (d'inflation) rise; **mesures de ~** reflationary measures; **entraîner la ~ de** to give a boost to [*construction, commerce*]; to lead to an upsurge of [*terrorisme*]; to lead to a rise in [*inflation*]; **2** (au poker) **faire une ~** to raise the stakes.

relancer /ʀ(ə)lɑ̃se/ [12] **I** vtr **1** (lancer de nouveau) to throw [sth] again [*balle*]; (renvoyer) to throw [sth] back (again) [*balle*]; **2** (faire repartir) to restart [*moteur*]; to relaunch [*compagnie, campagne*]; to revive [*idée, tradition*]; to reopen [*débat*]; to boost [*investissement, production*]; to reflate [*économie*]; **~ la mode de...** to bring back the fashion for...; **3** (poursuivre) [*créancier*] to chase [sb] up; [*importun*] to pester.

II vi (au poker) to raise the stakes (**de** by).

relaps, ~e /ʀəlaps/ nm,f (hérétique) relapsed heretic; (criminel) relapsed criminal.

relater /ʀ(ə)late/ [1] vtr FML to recount.

relatif, -ive /ʀ(ə)latif, iv/ adj **1** relative; **tout est ~** it's all relative; **le risque est très ~** the risk is relatively slight; **un confort très ~** limited comfort; **les lois relatives au divorce** the laws relating to divorce, divorce laws. **2** LING relative.

relation /ʀ(ə)lasjɔ̃/ **I** nf **1** (rapport) connection (**avec** with; **entre** between); **faire la ~ avec qch/qn** to make the connection with sth/sb; **un projet établi en ~ avec l'industrie** a project set up in partnership with industry; **2** (personne) acquaintance; **des ~s d'affaires** business acquaintances; **3** (personne puissante) connection; **avoir des ~s** to have connections; **4** (lien) relationship (**avec** with; **entre** between); **avoir de bonnes ~s avec qn** to have a good relationship with sb; **être/entrer en ~ avec qn** to be/to get in touch with sb; **être en ~ d'affaires avec qn** to have business dealings with sb; **5** MATH relation.

II relations nfpl (échanges) relations (**avec** with).

■ **~s extérieures** POL foreign affairs; **~s publiques** public relations.
relationnel, -elle /ʀ(ə)lasjɔnɛl/ *adj* relational.
relativement /ʀ(ə)lativmɑ̃/ I *adv* relatively.
II **relativement à** *loc prép* in relation to, relative
to.
relativiser /ʀ(ə)lativize/ [1] *vtr* to put [sth] into
perspective.
relativisme /ʀəlativism/ *nm* relativism.
relativité /ʀ(ə)lativite/ *nf* relativity.
relaver /ʀ(ə)lave/ [1] *vtr* to wash [sth] again.
relax○ /ʀəlaks/ *adj inv* [*personne*] relaxed, laid-
back○; [*tenue*] casual; [*soirée*] informal.
relaxant, ~e /ʀəlaksɑ̃, ɑ̃t/ *adj* [*bain, vacances*] relaxing; [*médicament*] relaxant.
relaxer /ʀəlakse/ [1] I *vtr* 1 (relâcher) to discharge
[*prévenu*]; 2 (détendre) to relax [*muscle, personne*].
II **se relaxer** *vpr* to relax.
relayer /ʀ(ə)leje/ [21] I *vtr* 1 (remplacer) to take over
from, to relieve; 2 TÉLÉCOM, TV to relay [*émission*].
II **se relayer** *vpr* 1 GÉN to take turns (**pour faire**
doing); 2 SPORT GÉN to take over from each other.
relecture /ʀ(ə)lɛktyʀ/ *nf* 1 (de livre) rereading; 2
(d'épreuves) proofreading; 3 (de cassette) replaying.
relégation /ʀ(ə)legasjɔ̃/ *nf* 1 SPORT relegation GB; 2
(travaux forcés) transportation; (prison) imprisonment.
reléguer /ʀ(ə)lege/ [14] *vtr* 1 FIG (mettre à l'écart) to
relegate [*personne, question, équipe*] (**à, dans, en** to);
to banish, to consign [*objet*] (**à, dans** to); 2 HIST, JUR
(bannir) to sentence [sb] to transportation.
relent /ʀ(ə)lɑ̃/ *nm* 1 (puanteur) lingering odourᴳᴮ; 2
FIG (trace) whiff.
relevable /ʀələvabl/ *adj* [*dossier*] adjustable.
relève /ʀ(ə)lɛv/ *nf* 1 (action) **la ~ de qn** relieving
sb; **la ~ de la garde** the changing of the guard;
prendre ou **assurer la ~** LIT, FIG to take over; 2
(personne) relief; (équipe) relief team.
relevé, ~e /ʀəlve, ʀləve/ I *adj* 1 CULIN spicy; 2
(raffiné) [*propos*] refined.
II *nm* 1 (action de noter) taking down, noting down;
faire le ~ de to list [*erreurs*]; **faire le ~ du
compteur** to read the meter; 2 (compte rendu) statement; **~ bancaire** bank statement; **~ de gaz** gas
bill.
relèvement /ʀ(ə)lɛvmɑ̃/ *nm* (hausse) (action)
increasing; (résultat) increase.
relever /ʀəl(ə)ve, ʀləve/ [16] I *vtr* 1 (remettre debout)
to pick up [*personne tombée, tabouret*]; to put [sth]
back up (again) [*statue, clôture*]; 2 (mettre à la verticale) to raise [*dossier de siège, manette*]; 3 (bouger à
nouveau) **~ la tête** (redresser) to raise one's head;
(pour voir) to look up; (ne pas être vaincu) to refuse to
accept defeat; 4 (mettre plus haut) to turn up [*col*]; to
lift [*jupe*]; to wind up [*vitre de voiture*]; to raise [*voile,
store*]; (à nouveau) to raise [sth] again; **~ ses
cheveux** to put one's hair up; 5 (constater) to note, to
notice [*erreur, signe*]; to notice [*fait, absence*]; (faire
remarquer) to point out [*erreur, contradiction*]; **~ que**
to note that; 6 (prendre note de) to take down, to note
down [*date, nom, dimensions, numéro*]; to take [*empreinte*]; to note down [*citation*]; **~ le compteur** to
read the meter; 7 (collecter) to take in [*copies d'examen*]; 8 (réagir à) to react to [*remarque*]; **~ le défi** to
take up the challenge; **'il t'a encore critiqué'—'je n'ai
pas relevé'** 'he criticized you again'—'I let it go'; 9 (reconstruire) to rebuild [*mur*]; to put [sth] back on its
feet [*pays, économie*]; 10 (augmenter) to raise [*niveau
de vie, prix, productivité*]; 11 (remplacer) to relieve
[*équipe*]; **~ la garde** to change the guard, to relieve
the guard; 12 (donner plus d'attrait à) LIT, FIG to spice up
[*plat, récit*]; 13 FML (libérer) **~ qn de** to release sb
from [*vœux, obligation*]; **~ qn de ses fonctions** to
relieve sb of their duties; 14 (en tricot) **~ une
maille** to pick up a stitch.
II **relever de** *vtr ind* 1 (dépendre de) **notre service
relève du ministère de la Défense** our department
comes under the Ministry of Defence; 2 (être de la

compétence de) **l'affaire relève de la Cour euro
péenne de justice** the case comes within the compe
tence of the European Court of Justice; **cela ne relève
pas de mes fonctions** this doesn't come within my
duties; 3 (s'apparenter à) **cela relève de la gageure**
this comes close to being impossible; 4 (se rétablir) **~
de** to be recovering from [*maladie*].
III **se relever** *vpr* 1 (après une chute) to pick onesel
up; (après avoir été assis, couché) to get up again; 2 (être
mis à la verticale) **se ~ facilement** [*dossier*] to be easy
to raise; 3 (être remonté) [*store*] to be raised; **la vitre
ne se relève plus** the window won't wind GB ou roll u
up; 4 (se remettre) **se ~ de** to recover from [*maladie,
chagrin, crise*].
relief /ʀəljɛf/ I *nm* 1 GÉOG relief ℭ; **le ~ sous-marin**
the relief of the sea bed; **un ~ accidenté** a hilly land
scape; **région au ~ accidenté** mountainous region
2 (de surface, paroi) relief ℭ; (de médaille, monnaie)
raised pattern; **en ~** [*globe terrestre*] in relief,
[*lettre, motif*] raised; **cinéma en ~** three dimensional
cinema; **carte en ~** relief map; **mettre qch en ~** to
accentuate sth, to throw sth into relief; 3 (profondeur)
depth; 4 (caractère) **personnage qui manque de ~**
one-dimensional ou flat character; **donner du ~ à un
texte** to enliven a text.
II **reliefs**† *nmpl* (de repas) leftovers.
relier /ʀəlje/ [2] *vtr* 1 (réunir) to link up, to link [sb
sth] together [*personnes, objets*] (**à** to); to join up
[*points*] (**à** to); to connect [*appareils électriques*] (**à** to;
par with); 2 (faire communiquer) to link [*ville, personne, organisme*] (**à** to); to link (up ou together)
[*lieux*]; 3 (rassembler) to link [*idées, faits*] (**à** to,
with); to link [sth] together [*mots, propositions*] (**par**
with); 4 to bind [*livre*]; **relié cuir** leather-bound.
relieur, -ieuse /ʀəljœʀ, øz/ ▶374 *nm,f* (book)-
binder.
religieuse¹ /ʀəliʒjøz/ *nf* CULIN round éclair.
religieusement /ʀəliʒjøzmɑ̃/ *adv* 1 [*obéir*] religiously; [*écouter*] with rapt attention; 2 (pieusement)
[*se marier*] in church.
religieux, -ieuse² /ʀəliʒjø, øz/ I *adj* 1 LIT [*culte, édifice, vie, personne, éducation, fête*] religious; [*école,
mariage*] (chrétien) church (*épith*); [*musique*] sacred;
l'habit ~ the monk's/nun's habit; 2 FIG [*silence*]
reverent; **avec un soin ~** most conscientiously.
II *nm,f* monk/nun.
religion /ʀ(ə)liʒjɔ̃/ *nf* 1 (croyance, culte) religion;
(piété) religion, (religious) faith; **avoir de la ~** to be
religious; **sa ~ est sincère** he is a sincere believer;
2 FIG **avoir la ~ du progrès** to be a great believer
in progress; **se faire une ~ de la ponctualité** to
make a fetish of punctuality; 3 (vie monastique) **entrer
en ~** to enter the Church.
reliquaire /ʀ(ə)likɛʀ/ *nm* reliquary.
reliquat /ʀ(ə)lika/ *nm* 1 (de somme) remainder; (de
compte) balance; (de dette) outstanding amount; 2 (de
maladie) after-effects (*pl*).
relique /ʀ(ə)lik/ *nf* RELIG, FIG relic.
relire /ʀ(ə)liʀ/ [66] *vtr* 1 (de nouveau) to reread; 2
(pour corriger) to read [sth] over [*texte*]; 3 to proofread
[*épreuves*].
reliure /ʀəljyʀ/ *nf* 1 (couverture) binding; 2 (travail)
bookbinding.
reloger /ʀ(ə)lɔʒe/ [13] *vtr* to rehouse.
reluire /ʀ(ə)lɥiʀ/ [69] *vi* [*bois, cuir*] to shine; [*surface
mouillée*] to glisten; [*métal*] to shine; (au soleil) to
glitter; **~ de propreté** to be sparkling clean.
IDIOMES **il sait passer la brosse à ~** he's a real
flatterer.
reluisant, ~e /ʀ(ə)lɥizɑ̃, ɑ̃t/ *adj* LIT [*meuble*] shining, shiny; [*surface mouillée*] glistening; [*métal*] shiny;
FIG **peu ~** [*situation*] far from brilliant.
remâcher /ʀ(ə)mɑʃe/ [1] *vtr* 1 [*ruminant*] to chew
[sth] again; 2○ (ressasser) to ruminate over [*problème,
passé*]; to nurse [*rancœur, dépit*].
remailler /ʀəmaje/ [1] *vtr* to mend the mesh of [*filet*];
to mend a ladder GB ou run US in [*bas*].

rémanent, **~e** /Remanɑ̃, ɑ̃t/ adj [magnétisme] residual; [odeur] persistent; **image ~e** after-image.

remaniement /R(ə)manimɑ̃/ nm (de plan, projet) modification; (de manuscrit) revision; (radical) redrafting; (d'équipe) reorganization.

■ **~ ministériel** cabinet reshuffle.

remanier /R(ə)manje/ [2] vtr to modify [plan, projet]; to alter [manuscrit]; (radicalement) to redraft; to reorganize [équipe]; to reshuffle [cabinet, ministère].

remaquiller: se remaquiller /R(ə)makije/ [1] vpr to redo one's make-up.

remarier: se remarier /R(ə)maRje/ [2] vpr to re-marry; **se ~ avec** to remarry.

remarquable /R(ə)maRkabl/ adj **1** (exceptionnel) [qualité, personne, œuvre, produit] remarkable (**par** for); **d'une beauté ~** remarkably beautiful; **2** (frappant) [caractère, trait] striking; **il est ~ que** it is amazing that; **3** (méritant mention) [événement, parole, produit] noteworthy; **je n'ai rien vu de ~** I haven't seen anything of note.

remarquablement /R(ə)maRkabləmɑ̃/ adv remarkably.

remarque /R(ə)maRk/ nf **1** (propos) remark; **faire des ~s** to comment; **elle m'en a fait la ~** she commented on it to me; **2** (note) comment.

remarqué, **~e** /R(ə)maRke/ adj [initiative] noteworthy; [hausse] noticeable; **leur entrée a été très ~e** their entrance attracted a lot of attention.

remarquer /R(ə)maRke/ [1] **I** vtr **1** (signaler) to point out; **faire ~ à qn que** to point out to sb that; **2** (dire) LITER to observe (**que** that); **3** (voir) to notice [personne, événement, objet]; **remarque, ce n'est pas très important** mind you, it's not very important; **remarquons que ce n'est pas la première fois** let us note that it is not the first time; **se faire ~** to draw attention to oneself; **le film mérite d'être remarqué** the film is worthy of attention; **4** (distinguer) to spot.

II se remarquer vpr **1** (attirer l'attention) [personne, vêtement, caractéristique] to attract attention; **2** (se voir) [qualité, défaut, sentiment] to show.

remballer /Rɑ̃bale/ [1] vtr **1** (emballer de nouveau) to pack [sth] up again; **2°** (rabrouer) to send [sb] packing°.

rembarrer° /Rɑ̃baRe/ [1] vtr to send [sb] packing°.

remblai /Rɑ̃blɛ/ nm **1** (talus) embankment; **route en ~** raised road; (dans un marais) causeway; **2** (action) (de fossé) filling in; (de talus) banking up; **3** (matériau) (**terre de ~**) (pour rail, route) ballast; (pour fossé) fill; (pour excavation) backfill.

remblayer /Rɑ̃bleje/ [21] vtr to fill in [fossé]; to bank up [route].

rembobiner /Rɑ̃bɔbine/ [1] vtr to rewind.

remboîter /Rɑ̃bwate/ [1] vtr **1** GÉN **~ qch dans qch** to fit sth back into sth; **2** MÉD to relocate [os].

rembourrer /Rɑ̃buRe/ [1] vtr to stuff [siège, coussin]; (en couture) to pad [épaules]; **bien rembourré** HUM [personne] well-padded.

remboursable /Rɑ̃buRsabl/ adj [emprunt, dette] repayable; [billet, médicament, soins] refundable.

remboursement /Rɑ̃buRsəmɑ̃/ nm **1** (de dette, d'emprunt) repayment; **2** (par un commerçant) refund; **3** (d'argent déboursé) reimbursement, refund; **faire une demande de ~** to claim for reimbursement ou a refund.

rembourser /Rɑ̃buRse/ [1] **I** vtr **1** (rendre de l'argent prêté par un organisme) to pay off, to repay [emprunt, dette]; **~ une dette sur 20 ans** to pay off a debt over 20 years; **2** (en reprenant des marchandises) to give a refund to [client]; to refund the price of [article]; **~ qch à qn** to give sb a refund on sth; **se faire ~ qch** to get a refund on sth; **3** (rendre de l'argent déboursé) to reimburse [frais professionnels, employé]; to reimburse ou refund the cost of [opération, médicament]; **~ qn de qch** to pay sb back for sth, to reimburse sb for sth; **~ les frais de qn** to reimburse sb; **~ un ami** to pay a friend back; **~ la différence** to refund the difference.

II se rembourser vpr **je me suis remboursé en gardant sa montre** I kept his/her watch by way of payment.

rembrunir: se rembrunir /Rɑ̃bRyniR/ [3] vpr [visage] to darken, to cloud over.

remède /R(ə)mɛd/ nm **1** (médicament) medicine; **un ~ universel** a panacea; **2** (solution) cure (**à, contre** for), remedy (**à, contre** for).

■ **~ de bonne femme** old wives' remedy; **~ de cheval** strong medicine; **~ miracle** miracle cure.

IDIOMES **aux grands maux les grands ~s** desperate times call for desperate measures.

remédier /R(ə)medje/ [2] vtr ind **~ à** to remedy.

remembrement /R(ə)mɑ̃bRəmɑ̃/ nm regrouping of lands.

remembrer /R(ə)mɑ̃bRe/ [1] vtr to regroup [terres]; to reconstitute [domaine].

remémorer: se remémorer /R(ə)memɔRe/ [1] vpr to recall, to recollect.

remerciement /R(ə)mɛRsimɑ̃/ nm thanks (pl); **je n'ai pas eu un seul ~** I didn't get a word of thanks; **tous mes ~s** many thanks; **lettre de ~** thank you letter; **adresser ses ~s à qn** to thank sb.

remercier /R(ə)mɛRsje/ [2] vtr **1** (dire merci à) to thank (**de, pour** for; **d'avoir fait** for doing); **je vous remercie** thank you; **tu peux me ~!** you have me to thank for that!; **remercions le ciel d'être encore en vie** thank God we are still alive; **nous vous remercions d'adresser votre courrier à...** please address your letters to...; **2** (congédier) IRON to dismiss, to let [sb] go.

remettre /R(ə)mɛtR/ [60] **I** vtr **1** (replacer) **~ qch dans/sur** to put sth back in/on; **remets ce livre là où tu l'as pris!** put that book back where you found it!; **~ qch à cuire** (sur la cuisinière) to put sth back on the ring; **~ la main sur qch** to put one's hands on sth again; **~ qch en mémoire à qn** to remind sb of sth; **2** (donner) **~ à qn** to hand [sth] over to sb [clés, rançon]; to hand [sth] in to sb [lettre, rapport]; to present [sth] to sb [récompense, trophée]; **~ sa démission** to hand in one's resignation (**à qn** to sb); **~ sa vie entre les mains de qn** to put one's life in sb's hands; **~ qn entre les mains de la justice** to hand sb over to the law; **3** (rétablir) **~ qch droit** or **d'aplomb** to put sth straight again; **~ qch à plat** to lay sth down again; **~ qch debout** to stand sth back up; **4** (différer) to postpone, to put off [visite, voyage]; to defer [jugement]; **~ qch à plus tard** to put sth off until later; **5** (faire fonctionner de nouveau) to put [sth] on again, to put [sth] back on [gaz, chauffage]; to play [sth] again [disque, chanson]; to turn [sth] on again [contact]; to switch on again [essuie-glaces, phares]; **6** (remplacer) **~ un bouton à qch** to put a new button on sth; **~ une vis** to put a new screw in; **7** (ajouter) to add some more [sel, bois, pl âtre]; to add another [bouton, clou]; **~ de l'argent dans qch** to put some more money in sth; **8** (porter de nouveau) (ce que l'on vient d'enlever) to put [sth] back on [chaussures, manteau, bijou]; (ce que l'on portait dans le passé) **il va falloir ~ les bottes, c'est l'hiver** we'll have to start wearing our boots again, it's winter; **9** MÉD to put [sth] back in place [épaule, cheville]; **10** (réconforter) [remontant, médicament] to make [sb] feel better; **11** (se souvenir de) **~ qn/le visage de qn** to remember sb/sb's face; **12** (faire grâce de) **~ une dette à qn** to let sb off a debt; **~ une peine à qn** to give sb remission; **13°** (recommencer) **~ ça** to start again; **on s'est bien amusé, quand est-ce qu'on remet ça?** that was fun, when are we going to do it again?

II se remettre vpr **1** (retourner) **se ~ à un endroit** to go ou get back to a place; **se ~ en selle** to get back in the saddle; **2** (s'appliquer à nouveau) **se ~ du rouge à lèvres** to put on some more lipstick; **3** (recommencer) **se ~ au travail** to go back to work; **se ~ au tennis** to start playing tennis again; **se ~ à faire** to start doing again; **4** (porter sur soi à nouveau) **se ~ en jean** to wear jeans again; **5** (se rétablir) **se ~ de** to recover from [maladie, accident]; to get over [émotion, échec]; **remets-toi vite!** get well soon!;

6 (faire confiance) **s'en ~ à qn** to leave it to sb; **s'en ~ à la décision de qn** to accept sb's decision; **7** (reprendre une vie de couple) **se ~ avec qn** to get back together with sb; **8** (se rappeler) **se ~ qn** to remember sb.

réminiscence /ʀeminisɑ̃s/ *nf* **1** (faculté de rappel) reminiscence; **2** (souvenir) recollection; **3** (rappel) **il y a dans cette œuvre des ~s de Bach** this work is reminiscent of Bach.

remise /ʀ(ə)miz/ *nf* **1** (transmission) **attendre la ~ des clés** to wait for the keys to be handed over; **la date limite de ~ des rapports** the deadline for handing in the reports; **~ des prix** prizegiving; **~ des médailles** medals ceremony; **~ des coupes** the presentation of the trophies; **2** COMM (rabais) discount; **3** (de dette, péchés) remission; **une ~ de peine** a remission; **4** FIN remittance; **5** (bâtiment) shed.
■ **~ de cause** JUR adjournment (of hearing).

remiser /ʀ(ə)mize/ **[1]** *vtr* to put [sth] away (**dans** in).

rémission /ʀemisjɔ̃/ *nf* (de maladie, péchés) remission; **sans ~** (sans indulgence) [*punir, condamner*] mercilessly; (sans interruption) [*pleuvoir, travailler*] without stopping.

remmener /ʀɑ̃mne/ **[16]** *vtr* to take [sb] back.

remodeler /ʀəmɔdle/ **[17]** *vtr* to restructure [*administration*]; to reshape [*nez, ébauche*]; to replan [*quartier*].

remontage /ʀ(ə)mɔ̃taʒ/ *nm* (de moteur, pièces) reassembly; (d'un tuyau) reconnection; (de mécanisme, montre) winding up.

remontant /ʀ(ə)mɔ̃tɑ̃/ *nm* pick-me-up○, tonic.

remontée /ʀ(ə)mɔ̃te/ *nf* **1** (action de remonter) climb up; **la ~ de la Saône en péniche** going up the Saône by barge; **2** (après une baisse) (d'influence, de prix, taux, parti) rise (**de** of); (de sportif, d'homme politique) recovery (**de** of); (de violence, d'incidents) increase (**de** in); **la ~ des eaux** the rise in the water levels.
■ **~ mécanique** SPORT ski lift.

remonte-pente, *pl* **~s** /ʀ(ə)mɔ̃tpɑ̃t/ *nm* ski-tow.

remonter /ʀəmɔ̃te/ **[1]** **I** *vtr* (+ *avoir*) **1** (transporter de nouveau) **~ qn/qch** (en haut) GÉN to take sb/sth back up (**à** to); (à l'étage) to take sb/sth back upstairs; (d'en bas) GÉN to bring sb/sth back up (**de** from); (de l'étage) to bring [sb/sth] back upstairs [*personne, objet*]; **~ les bouteilles de la cave** to bring the bottles back up from the cellar; **je peux vous ~ au village** I can take you back up to the village; **2** (replacer en haut) to put [sth] back up [*valise, boîte*]; **~ un seau d'un puits** to pull a bucket up from a well; **3** (relever) to raise [*étagère, store, tableau*] (**de** by); to wind [sth] back up [*vitre de véhicule*]; to roll up [*manches, jambes de pantalon*]; to hitch up [*jupe, pantalon*]; to turn up [*col*]; to pull up [*chaussettes*]; **4** (parcourir de nouveau) [*personne*] (en allant) to go back up [*pente, rue*]; to go ou climb back up [*escalier, échelle*]; (en venant) to come back up [*pente, rue, échelle*]; [*voiture, automobiliste*] to drive back up [*pente*]; **~ la colline à bicyclette** to cycle back up the hill; **il m'a fait ~ l'escalier en courant** he made me run back up the stairs; **5** (parcourir en sens inverse) [*bateau*] to sail up [*fleuve*]; [*poisson*] to swim up [*rivière*]; [*personne, voiture*] to go up [*rue*]; **~ une rivière à la nage** to swim up a river; **~ le flot de voyageurs** to walk against the flow of passengers; **~ une filière** ou **piste** FIG to follow a trail (**jusqu'à qn** to sb); **~ le temps par la pensée** to go back in time in one's imagination; **6** (rattraper dans un classement) [*cycliste*] to catch up with [*peloton, concurrent*]; **7** (réconforter) **~ qn** ou **le moral de qn** to cheer sb up, to raise sb's spirits; **8** (assembler de nouveau) to put [sth] back together again [*armoire, jouet*]; to put [sth] back [*roue*]; **9** (retendre le ressort de) to wind [sth] up [*mécanisme, réveil*]; **être remonté à bloc**○ FIG [*personne*] to be full of energy; **10** (remettre en scène) to revive [*pièce, spectacle*].
II *vi* (+ *être*) **1** (monter de nouveau) [*personne*] (en allant) GÉN to go back up, to go up again (**à** to); (en venant) GÉN to come back up, to come up again (**de**

from); (à l'étage) to go/to come back upstairs; (après être redescendu) to go/to come back up again; [*train, ascenseur*] to go back up; [*avion, hélicoptère*] to climb again; [*mer*] to come in again; [*prix, température, baromètre*] to rise again, to go up again; **reste ici, je remonte au grenier** stay here, I'm going back up to the attic; **peux-tu ~ chercher mon sac?** can you go back upstairs and get my bag?; **tu es remonté à pied?** did you walk back up?; **~ à l'échelle** to climb back up the ladder; **~ sur** [*personne*] to step back onto [*trottoir*]; to climb back onto [*mur*]; **~ à la surface** LIT [*plongeur*] to surface; [*huile, objet*] to rise to the surface; FIG [*scandale*] to resurface; [*souvenirs*] to surface again; **~ à cheval** to get back on a horse; **~ à bord d'un avion** to board a plane again; **~ dans les sondages** [*politicien, parti*] to move up in the opinion polls; **~ de la quinzième à la troisième place** [*sportif, équipe*] to move up from fifteenth to third position; **~ à Paris** (retourner) to go back up to Paris; **la criminalité remonte** crime is rising again; **faire ~ les cours** to put prices up again; **faire ~ la température** to raise the temperature; **2** (pour retrouver l'origine) **~ dans le temps** to go back in time; **~ à** [*historien*] to go back to [*époque, date*]; [*événement, œuvre, tradition*] to date back to [*époque, date, personnage historique*]; [*habitude*] to be carried over from [*enfance, période*]; [*enquêteur, police*] to follow the trail back to [*personne, chef de gang*]; **~ 20 ans en arrière** [*historien*] to go back 20 years; **faire ~** to trace (back) [*origines, ancêtres*] (**à** to); **3** (se retrousser) [*pull, jupe*] to ride up; **4** (se faire sentir) **les odeurs d'égout remontent dans la maison** the smell from the drains reaches our house; **5** NAUT **~ au** ou **dans le vent** to sail into the wind.
III **se remonter** *vpr* **1** (se réconforter) **se ~ le moral** (seul) to cheer oneself up; (à plusieurs) to cheer each other up; **2** (s'équiper de nouveau) **se ~ en meubles/draps** to get some new furniture/sheets.

remontoir /ʀ(ə)mɔ̃twaʀ/ *nm* winder.

remontrance /ʀəmɔ̃tʀɑ̃s/ *nf* (reproche) reprimand.

remontrer /ʀəmɔ̃tʀe/ **[1]** **I** *vtr* to show [sth] again.
II *vi* **en ~ à qn** (lui donner une leçon) to teach sb a thing or two; (montrer sa supériorité) to prove one's superiority to sb.

remords /ʀəmɔʀ/ *nm inv* remorse ¢; **plein de ~** filled with remorse, remorseful; **avoir du** ou **des ~** to feel remorse.

remorquage /ʀəmɔʀkaʒ/ *nm* towing.

remorque /ʀəmɔʀk/ *nf* (vehicle) trailer; (câble) towrope; **prendre une voiture en ~** to tow a car; **être à la ~** FIG to trail behind.

remorquer /ʀəmɔʀke/ **[1]** *vtr* **1** LIT to tow [*véhicule*]; **se faire ~** to be towed; **2** FIG to drag [sb] along.

remorqueur /ʀəmɔʀkœʀ/ *nm* tug.

rémoulade /ʀemulad/ *nf* mayonnaise-type dressing.

rémouleur /ʀemulœʀ/ **▶ 374** *nm* grinder.

remous /ʀ(ə)mu/ *nm inv* **1** (dans l'eau, l'air) eddy; **2** (sillage) backwash (*tjrs sg*); (contre la rive) wash (*tjrs sg*); **3** (agitation) (de sentiments, d'idées) turmoil ¢; (dans la foule) stir, movement; (dans l'opinion, l'auditoire) stir ¢.

rempailler /ʀɑ̃paje/ **[1]** *vtr* to reseat [*chaise*].

rempailleur, -euse /ʀɑ̃pajœʀ, øz/ **▶ 374** *nm,f* repairer of rush seats.

rempart /ʀɑ̃paʀ/ *nm* **1** (mur) rampart; (de château-fort) battlements (*pl*); **les ~s de la ville** the city walls, the ramparts; **2** (défense) defence^GB (**contre** against); **faire un ~ de son corps à qn** to shield sb with one's body.

rempiler /ʀɑ̃pile/ **[1]** **I** *vtr* to restack [*boîtes*].
II○ *vi* soldiers' slang to re-enlist.

remplaçable /ʀɑ̃plasabl/ *adj* replaceable.

remplaçant, ~e /ʀɑ̃plasɑ̃, ɑ̃t/ *nm,f* **1** (provisoire) GÉN substitute, replacement; (professeur, instituteur) supply GB ou substitute US teacher; (acteur) stand-in; SPORT substitute, reserve; **2** (définitif) successor.

remplacement /ʀɑ̃plasmɑ̃/ *nm* **1** (de personne)

replacement; **nommé en ~ de M. Robin** appointed as a replacement for Mr Robin; **assurer le ~ d'un collègue** to stand in for ou cover for a colleague; **faire des ~s** [*enseignant*] to do supply GB ou substitute US teaching; [*intérimaire*] to do temporary work, to do temping jobs○; **2** (de chose) replacement; **le ~ d'une pièce usée** the replacement of a worn part; **une télévision neuve en ~ de la vieille** a new television to replace the old one; **produit de ~** substitute.

remplacer /ʀɑ̃plase/ [12] **I** *vtr* **1** (momentanément) to stand in for, to cover for [*collègue, docteur, acteur*]; **elle s'est fait ~ par un collègue** she got a colleague to stand in for her; **2** (succéder à) to replace [*personne, méthode, tradition, appareil*]; **M. Bon remplace Mme Roux à la direction** Mr Bon is replacing ou succeeds Mrs Roux as director; **3** (changer) to replace [*pièce, matériel, personne*] (**par** with); **~ un carreau** to replace a windowpane; **4** (tenir lieu de) to replace; **le pronom remplace le nom** the pronoun takes the place of ou replaces the noun; **on peut ~ le vinaigre par du jus de citron** you can use lemon juice as a substitute for vinegar.

remplir /ʀɑ̃pliʀ/ [3] **I** *vtr* **1** (dans l'espace) to fill (up) [*récipient*] (**de** with); (de nouveau) to refill [*récipient*]; to fill in ou out [*formulaire*]; **~ qch à moitié** to half fill sth; **un verre à moitié rempli** a half-filled glass; **~ qch aux deux tiers** to fill sth two thirds full; **sa vie est remplie de petites contrariétés** FIG his/her life is full of small vexations; **~ qn de joie** FIG to fill sb with joy; **une journée bien remplie** a busy day; **avoir le portefeuille bien rempli**○ to be well-heeled○, to be rich; **2** (s'acquitter de) [*personne*] to carry out, to perform [*rôle, mission*]; to fulfil GB [*devoir, obligations, objectifs*]; to fulfil GB [*engagements*]; [*objet, dispositif*] to fulfil GB [*rôle, fonction*]; **~ les conditions** to fulfil GB ou meet the conditions.
II se remplir *vpr* to fill (up) (**de** with).

remplissage /ʀɑ̃plisaʒ/ *nm* **1** (de récipient) filling; **2** PEJ (dans un texte, film) padding.

remplumer: **se remplumer** /ʀɑ̃plyme/ [1] *vpr* **1**○ [*personne*] (en argent) to get back on one's feet; (en poids) to put some weight back on; **2** [*oiseau*] to grow new feathers.

rempocher /ʀɑ̃pɔʃe/ [1] *vtr* to put [sth] back in one's pocket.

remporter /ʀɑ̃pɔʀte/ [1] *vtr* **1** (gagner) to win [*épreuve, siège, titre, victoire*]; **la pièce a remporté un vif succès** the play was a great success; **2** (reprendre) to take [sth] away again.

rempoter /ʀɑ̃pɔte/ [1] *vtr* to repot.

remuant, ~e /ʀ(ə)mɥɑ̃, ɑ̃t/ *adj* **1** (agité) [*spectateur, adolescent, partisan*] rowdy; **2** (actif) [*enfant*] boisterous; [*adulte*] energetic.

remue-ménage /ʀ(ə)mymenaʒ/ *nm inv* **1** (désordre et confusion) commotion ¢; **faire du ~** to create a commotion; **2** (agitation) bustle ¢; **3** (changements) upheaval.

remuer /ʀ(ə)mɥe/ [1] **I** *vtr* **1** (mouvoir) to move [*doigt, main, tête*]; to wiggle [*orteil, oreille, hanches*]; **le chien remuait la queue** the dog was wagging its tail; **2** (secouer) to shake [*objet*]; **3** (déplacer) to move [*objet*]; **il a tout remué dans le tiroir pour retrouver la clé** he turned the whole drawer upside down to find the key; **4** CULIN to stir [*soupe, café, pâtes*]; to toss [*salade*]; **5** (brasser) LIT to turn over [*terre*]; to poke [*cendres*]; FIG to mull over [*pensées, chimères*]; to handle [*argent*]; **6** (évoquer) to rake up [*passé, vieille histoire*]; to stir up [*souvenirs*]; **7** (bouleverser) to upset [*personne*]; (émouvoir) to move.
II *vi* (bouger) [*personne*] to move; [*enfant*] to fidget; [*feuilles*] to flutter; [*bateau*] to bob up and down.
III se remuer○ *vpr* **1** (sortir de son apathie) to get a move on○; **2** (faire des efforts) **se ~ pour obtenir** to make an effort to get.

rémunérateur, -trice /ʀemyneʀatœʀ, tʀis/ *adj* lucrative.

rémunération /ʀemyneʀasjɔ̃/ *nf* (de travail) pay (**de** for); (de service) payment (**de** for).

rémunérer /ʀemyneʀe/ [14] *vtr* to pay [*personne*]; to pay for [*service, travail*].

renâcler /ʀ(ə)nakle/ [1] *vi* **1** [*personne*] to show reluctance; **~ à qch/à faire** to balk at sth/at doing; **sans ~** without complaining; **2** [*animal*] to snort.

renaissance /ʀ(ə)nɛsɑ̃s/ *nf* RELIG rebirth; FIG revival.

Renaissance /ʀ(ə)nɛsɑ̃s/ *nf* HIST Renaissance.

renaître /ʀ(ə)nɛtʀ/ [74] *vi* **1** [*personne, nature*] to come back to life; **faire ~ une région** to revive a region; **~ à la vie** to rediscover life; **~ de ses cendres** to rise from the ashes; **2** (réapparaître) [*désir, espoir*] to return; **faire ~ l'amour** to bring new love.

rénal, ~e, *mpl* **-aux** /ʀenal, o/ *adj* [*artère, veine*] renal; [*infection*] kidney (*épith*).

renard /ʀ(ə)naʀ/ *nm* **1** (animal, fourrure) fox; **2** (personne) cunning devil.

renarde /ʀ(ə)naʀd/ *nf* vixen.

renardeau, *pl* **~x** /ʀ(ə)naʀdo/ *nm* fox cub.

renchérir /ʀɑ̃ʃeʀiʀ/ [3] *vi* **1** (ajouter) to add; **~ sur ce que dit qn** to add something to what sb says; **2** (aller plus loin) to go one step further; **il a renchéri en envoyant l'armée** he went one step further and sent in the army; **3** (dans une vente) to raise the bidding; **~ sur le prix de qch** to make a higher bid for sth.

renchérissement /ʀɑ̃ʃeʀismɑ̃/ *nm* **le ~ des loyers** the increase in rents.

rencontre /ʀɑ̃kɔ̃tʀ/ *nf* **1** (réunion) meeting (**avec** with; **entre** between); **aller/venir à la rencontre de qn** to go/to come to meet sb; **aller à la ~ de problèmes** to be heading for trouble; **2** (contact) meeting; (non prévu) encounter; **~ inattendue** unexpected encounter; **faire la ~ de qn** to meet sb; **au hasard des ~s** through chance meetings ou encounters; **▶ mauvais**; **3** SPORT (match) match GB, game US; (réunion) meeting GB, meet US; **~ d'athlétisme** athletics meeting GB, track meet US; **4** MIL encounter.
■ **~ au sommet** POL summit meeting.

rencontrer /ʀɑ̃kɔ̃tʀe/ [1] **I** *vtr* **1** (voir) to meet [*personne*]; **~ qn sur son chemin** to come across sb; **2** (faire connaissance avec) to meet [*personne*]; **3** (être en présence de) to meet with [*réaction, opposition*]; to encounter [*obstacle, problème*]; **ma main a rencontré la sienne** my hand met his/hers; **4** (trouver) [*personne*] to come across [*objet, personne, mot*]; **5** SPORT to meet, to play [*joueur, équipe*]; to meet GB, to fight [*boxeur*].
II se rencontrer *vpr* **1** (se voir, faire connaissance) to meet; **leurs yeux se rencontrèrent** their eyes met; **2** (se trouver) [*qualité, objet, personne*] to be found; **3** SPORT [*joueurs, équipes*] to meet, to play each other.

rendement /ʀɑ̃dmɑ̃/ *nm* **1** (production) (de terre, d'investissement) yield; (de machine, travailleur) output ¢; **tourner à plein ~** to run at full capacity; **2** (productivité) (d'usine) productivity ¢; (de machine, travailleur) efficiency ¢; **3** (résultat) (de sportif, d'élève) performance.

rendez-vous /ʀɑ̃devu/ *nm inv* **1** (chez un médecin, coiffeur, avocat etc) appointment (**avec** with; **chez** at); **prendre ~ avec un spécialiste** to make an appointment with a specialist; **2** (avec des amis) **j'ai ~ avec un ami** I'm meeting a friend; **je leur ai donné ~ à minuit** I've arranged to meet them at midnight; **le soleil n'était pas au ~** the sun didn't shine; **3** (réunion professionnelle) meeting; **4** (rassemblement) gathering; (lieu) meeting place.

rendormir: **se rendormir** /ʀɑ̃dɔʀmiʀ/ [30] *vpr* to go back to sleep.

rendre /ʀɑ̃dʀ/ [6] **I** *vtr* **1** (retourner) (pour restituer) to give back, to return (**à** to); (pour refuser) to return, to give back [*cadeau*] (**à** to); (pour s'acquitter) to repay, to pay back [*somme*] (**à** to); to return [*article défectueux*] (**à** to); to return [*salut, invitation*] (**à** to); **elle m'a rendu mon livre** she gave me back my book; **prête-moi 500 francs, je te les rendrai demain** lend me 500 francs, I'll pay you back tomorrow; **elle ne m'a pas rendu la monnaie** she didn't give me my change; **~ la pareille à qn** to pay sb back;

2 (redonner) **~ la santé/vue à qn** to restore sb's health/sight; **~ le sourire à qn** to put the smile back on sb's face; **~ son indépendance à un pays** to restore a country's independence; **3** (faire devenir) **~ qn heureux** to make sb happy; **~ qch possible** to make sth possible; **~ qn fou** to drive sb mad; **4** (remettre) [*élève, étudiant*] to hand in, to give in [*copie, devoir*] (**à** to); **5** (produire) [*terre, champ*] to yield [*récolte, quantité*]; **6** (exprimer, traduire) [*auteur, mots*] to convey [*pensée, atmosphère*]; to convey, to render [*nuance*]; [*traduction, tableau*] to convey [*atmosphère , style*]; **~ l'expression d'un visage** [*peintre, photographe*] to capture the expression on a face; **un poème chinois merveilleusement rendu en anglais** a Chinese poem beautifully translated ou rendered into English; **ça ne rendra rien en couleurs** it won't come out in colour^{GB}; **7**$^\circ$ (vomir) to bring up [*aliment, bile*]; **8** (prononcer) to pronounce [*jugement, sentence, arrêt*]; to return [*verdict*]; to pronounce [*oracle*]; **9** (émettre) [*instrument, objet creux*] to give off [*son*]; **10** (exsuder) **les tomates rendent de l'eau (à la cuisson)** tomatoes give out water during cooking; **11** SPORT [*concurrent*] **~ du poids** to have a weight handicap (**à** compared with); **~ 10 mètres à qn** to give sb a 10-metre^{GB} handicap.

II *vi* **1** (produire) **~ (bien)** [*terre*] to be productive; [*plante*] to produce a good crop; [*activité, commerce*] to be profitable; **2**$^\circ$ (vomir) to be sick, to throw up$^\circ$.

III se rendre *vpr* **1** (aller) to go; **se ~ à Rome/en Chine** to go to Rome/to China; **se ~ chez des amis** to go to see friends; **2** (devenir) **se ~ malade** to make oneself ill; **se ~ ridicule** to make a fool of oneself; **3** (capituler) [*criminel*] to give oneself up (**à** to); [*armée, ville*] to surrender (**à** to); **4** (se soumettre) **se ~ à qch** to bow to [*argument, avis*]; to yield to [*prières, supplique*]; to answer [*appel*].

IDIOMES **~ l'âme** or **l'esprit** to pass away.

rendu /Rɑ̃dy/ *nm* **1** ART depiction; **2** COMM (objet rapporté) return, returned article.

rêne /Rɛn/ *nf* rein.

renégat, -e /Rənega, at/ *nm,f* RELIG, FIG renegade.

renfermé, ~e /Rɑ̃fɛʀme/ **I** *pp* ▸ **renfermer**.

II *pp adj* [*personne*] withdrawn; [*sentiment*] hidden.

III *nm* **ça sent le ~** it smells musty.

renfermer /Rɑ̃fɛʀme/ [1] **I** *vtr* (receler) to contain.

II se renfermer *vpr* [*personne*] to become withdrawn.

renflé, -e /Rɑ̃fle/ *adj* [*vase*] rounded; [*dome*] bulbous; [*estomac*] bulging.

renflement /Rɑ̃fləmɑ̃/ *nm* bulge.

renflouer /Rɑ̃flue/ [1] *vtr* **1** to raise [*navire*]; **2** to bail out [*personne, entreprise*].

renfoncement /Rɑ̃fɔ̃smɑ̃/ *nm* (de mur) recess; **~ de porte** doorway.

renforcer /Rɑ̃fɔʀse/ [12] **I** *vtr* **1** (rendre plus solide) to reinforce [*construction, vêtement*]; to strengthen [*muscles, tissus*]; **2** (accroître le nombre de) to strengthen [*équipe, effectifs*]; **3** (intensifier) to strengthen, to reinforce [*pouvoir, sanctions*]; to reinforce [*contrôle, déséquilibre*]; to step up [*surveillance*].

II se renforcer *vpr* [*pouvoir*] to increase; [*contrôle*] to become tighter; [*équipe, effectifs*] to grow; [*pays, secteur*] to grow stronger.

renfort /Rɑ̃fɔʀ/ *nm* **1** MIL reinforcement; **en ~** as reinforcements; **2** GÉN support ¢; **en ~** in support; **à grand ~ de qch** with a lot of sth; **annoncé à grand ~ de publicité** much heralded; **3** SPORT substitute; **4** TECH support; **une pièce de ~** a support piece.

renfrogné, ~e /Rɑ̃fʀɔɲe/ *adj* [*visage, air, personne*] sullen.

renfrogner: se renfrogner /Rɑ̃fʀɔɲe/ [1] *vpr* to become sullen.

rengager /Rɑ̃gaʒe/ [13] **I** *vtr* **1** (embaucher de nouveau) to take [sb] on again [*employé*]; MIL to re-enlist [*soldat*]; **2** (reprendre) to renew [*hostilités*]; to reopen [*discussion*].

II se rengager *vpr* MIL to re-enlist, to sign up again.

rengaine /Rɑ̃gɛn/ *nf* (chanson) corny old song$^\circ$; (air) corny old tune$^\circ$; FIG **c'est toujours la même ~** FIG it's the same old thing every time.

rengainer /Rɑ̃gɛne/ [1] *vtr* to sheathe [*épée, poignard*]; to put [sth] back in its holster [*pistolet*].

rengorger: se rengorger /Rɑ̃gɔʀʒe/ [13] *vpr* [*oiseau*] to puff out its breast; [*personne*] to swell with conceit (**de qch** at sth).

reniement /Rə nimɑ̃/ *nm* **1** GÉN disavowal; **2** RELIG denial.

renier /Rənje/ [2] **I** *vtr* to renounce [*religion, opinion*]; to disown [*enfant, œuvre*]; to disclaim [*obligation*].

II se renier *vpr* (désavouer ses opinions) to go back on one's opinions; (désavouer le passé) to go back on everything one has stood for.

reniflement /Rəniflə mɑ̃/ *nm* **1** (action) sniffing; **2** (bruit) sniff.

renifler /Rənifle/ [1] **I** *vtr* [*personne, animal*] to sniff [*odeur, piste*]; [*cochon*] to sniff for [*truffes*].

II *vi* to sniff.

renne /Rɛn/ *nm* reindeer.

renom /Rənɔ̃/ *nm* **1** (bonne reputation) fame, renown; **avoir du ~** to be famous ou renowned; **de** or **en ~** famous (*épith*); **2** (réputation) reputation.

renommé, ~e^1 /Rənɔme/ *adj* famous, renowned.

renommée^2 /Rənɔme/ *nf* **1** (réputation) reputation; **2** (célébrité) fame; **faire la ~ de qn** to make sb famous.

renoncement /Rənɔ̃smɑ̃/ *nm* renunciation.

renoncer /Rənɔ̃se/ [12] *vtr ind* **1** (après expérience) **~ à** to give up [*poste, activité, lutte*]; **je renonce à chercher une maison** I'm giving up looking for a house; **elle a renoncé à lui** she has finished with him; **2** (avant de commencer) **~ à** to abandon [*projet, objectif, principes*]; **~ à faire** to abandon the idea of doing; **3** (abandonner) **~ à** to relinquish [*pouvoir*]; to waive [*privilèges*]; to give up [*liberté*]; to renounce [*honneurs, couronne*].

renonciation /Rənɔ̃sjasjɔ̃/ *nf* **1** JUR, GÉN (à une fonction) giving up; **2** LITER renunciation.

renouer /Rənwe/ [1] **I** *vtr* **1** LIT to retie [*lacets, ficelle*]; **2** FIG to pick up the thread of [*conversation*].

II *vtr ind* **~ avec** (après une dispute) to make up with [*personne*]; (après avoir perdu contact) to get back in touch with [*personne*]; to revive [*tradition*]; to re-establish [*pratique*]; to go back to [*passé*].

renouveau, *pl* **~x** /Rənuvo/ *nm* **1** (renaissance) revival; **2** (regain) **un ~ d'intérêt** a renewal of interest.

renouvelable /Rənuvlabl/ *adj* renewable.

renouvelé, ~e /Rənuvle/ **I** *pp* ▸ **renouveler**.

II *pp adj* **1** (neuf) [*joie, vitalité, ardeur, énergie*] renewed; **2** (changé) [*équipe, édition*] remodelled^{GB}; **3** (répété) **controverse maintes fois ~e** recurring controversy.

renouveler /Rənuvle/ [19] **I** *vtr* **1** (proroger) to renew [*passeport, abonnement*]; **2** (refaire) to renew, to repeat [*suggestion, expérience, promesse*]; **3** (remplacer) to replace [*matériel, équipe*]; to change [*eau*]; to renew [*stocks*]; **~ l'air dans une chambre** to air a room **4** (redonner) to renew [*soutien, prêt*]; **5** (rendre nouveau) to revitalize [*genre, style*].

II se renouveler *vpr* **1** (être remplacé) **une pièce où l'air ne se renouvelle pas** a room which isn't aired **2** (varier) [*auteur, artiste*] to try out new ideas **3** (se reproduire) [*exploit, expérience*] to happen again.

renouvellement /Rənuvɛlmɑ̃/ *nm* **1** (de passeport d'abonnement) renewal; **2** (de matériel, d'équipe) replacement; **3** (de cellules, générations) renewal; **4** (de style doctrine) revitalization.

rénovateur, -trice /Renɔvatœʀ, tʀis/ **I** *adj* [*théorie attitude*] reforming.

II *nm,f* GÉN (de coutume) modernizer; (de science, religion) reformer.

rénovation /Renɔvasjɔ̃/ *nf* **1** CONSTR (de quartier) renovation; (de maison, d'immeuble) (pour gros travaux) renovation; (pour simples travaux) refurbishment; **2** FIG (de politique) reform; (de secteur économique) revitalization.

rénover /ʀenɔve/ [1] *vtr* **1** CONSTR (avec de gros travaux) to renovate [*quartier, maison*]; (avec des travaux simples) to refurbish [*maison*]; to restore [*meuble*]; **2** (remettre à jour) to reform [*institution, politique*]; to revamp [*projet, procédure*]; to overhaul [*système*].

renseignement /ʀɑ̃sɛɲmɑ̃/ **I** *nm* **1** (information) information **C**, piece of information; **des ~s** information; **prendre des ~s sur qch/qn** to find out about sth/sb; **demander des ~s à qn** to ask sb for information; **est-ce que je peux vous demander un ~?** can I ask you something?; **il est allé aux ~s** he went to find out (about it); **~s pris, il semblerait que** upon investigation, it would appear that; **'pour tous ~s, s'adresser à...'** 'all inquiries to...'; **2** MIL intelligence.

II renseignements *nmpl* (service, bureaux) information **C**; TÉLÉCOM directory enquiries GB, information US, directory assistance US.

renseigner /ʀɑ̃seɲe/ [1] **I** *vtr* **~ qn** to give information to sb (**sur** about); **être bien renseigné** to be well-informed; **demandez au rayon accessoires, ils vous renseigneront** ask at the accessories department, they'll be able to help you.

II se renseigner *vpr* (demander des informations) to find out, to enquire (**sur** about; **auprès de** from); (faire des recherches) to make enquiries (**sur** about; **auprès de** from); **se ~ sur les activités de qn** to make enquiries about ou to look into sb's activities.

rentabilisation /ʀɑ̃tabilizasjɔ̃/ *nf* **la ~ de l'entreprise est notre premier objectif** our primary aim is to make the company profitable.

rentabiliser /ʀɑ̃tabilize/ [1] *vtr* to secure a return on [*investissement*]; to make a profit on [*produit*]; to make [sth] profitable [*affaire*]; **l'isolation de ma maison sera vite rentabilisée** my home insulation will soon pay for itself.

rentabilité /ʀɑ̃tabilite/ *nf* **1** (caractère rentable) profitability; **2** (profit) return.

rentable /ʀɑ̃tabl/ *adj* profitable.

rente /ʀɑ̃t/ *nf* **1** (revenu personnel) private income; **2** (contrat financier) annuity; **~ viagère** life annuity; **~ mensuelle** monthly allowance; **3** FIN (emprunt d'État) government stock.

rentier, -ière /ʀɑ̃tje, ɛʀ/ *nm,f* person of independent means.

rentré, ~e[1] /ʀɑ̃tʀe/ *adj* **1** (retenu) [*colère*] suppressed; **2** (en retrait) [*joues, yeux*] sunken; [*ventre, fesses*] held in (*après n*).

rentrée[2] /ʀɑ̃tʀe/ *nf* **1** (reprise d'activité) (general) return to work (*after the slack period of the summer break, in France*); (début d'année scolaire) start of the (new) school year; (début de trimestre) beginning of term; **des grèves sont prévues pour la ~** strikes are expected after the summer break; **mon livre sera publié à la ~** my book will be published in the autumn GB ou fall US; **2** (retour) return (to work); **3** (réapparition publique) comeback; **~ politique** political comeback; **4** (d'argent) (recette) receipts (*pl*); (revenu) **~ (d' argent)** income **C**; (dans une caisse) takings (*pl*); **les ~s** receipts; **~s fiscales** (annuelles) tax revenues; **~s** (ponctuelles) tax revenues; **5** ASTRONAUT, MIL (de vaisseau, capsule, missile) re-entry.

■ **~ des classes** start of the school year; **~ parlementaire** reassembly of Parliament; **~ scolaire = ~ des classes**; **~ universitaire** start of the academic year.

rentrer /ʀɑ̃tʀe/ [1] **I** *vtr* **1** (mettre à l'abri) GÉN to put [sth] in [*objet, animal*]; (en venant) to bring [sth] in [*objet, animal*]; (en allant) to take [sth] in [*objet, animal*]; **2** (rétracter) [*pilote*] to raise [*train d'atterrissage*]; [*félin*] to draw in [*griffes*]; **rentrez le ventre!** hold your stomach in!; **3** (faire pénétrer) to put [*clé*] (**dans** in, into); to tuck [*pan de chemise*] (**dans** in).

II *vi* (+ *v être*) **1** (pénétrer) (dans une pièce, une cabine téléphonique) to go in; (dans une voiture, un ascenseur) to get in; (tenir, s'adapter) to fit; **~ dans un arbre**○ to hit a tree; **2** (entrer de nouveau) (en allant) to go back in; (en venant) to come back in; **~ dans** (en allant) to go back into; (en venant) to come back into; **la satellite va ~ dans l'atmosphère** the satellite is about to re-enter the atmosphere; **3** (revenir) GÉN to get back, to come back, to return (**de** from); (chez soi) to come home (**de** from); **il ne va pas tarder à ~ du travail** he'll be back from work soon; **4** (repartir) GÉN to get back, to go back, to return; (chez soi) to go home (**de** from); **il fait trop froid, je rentre** (à l'intérieur) it's too cold, I'm going (back) inside; (de plus loin) it's too cold, I'm going (back) home; **se dépêcher de ~** (chez soi) to hurry home; **5** (récupérer) **~ dans son argent** to recoup one's money; **6** (être encaissé) [*argent, loyer, créance*] to come in; **faire ~ l'argent** to bring money in; **7** (pouvoir trouver place) **mes chaussures ne rentrent pas dans ma valise** my shoes won't fit into my suitcase; **faire ~ qch dans la tête de qn** to get sth into sb's head; **~ dans la serrure** to fit the lock; **8**○ (être compris) **l'algèbre ça ne rentre pas!** I just can't understand ou get my head round○ algebra!

IDIOMES **je vais leur ~ dedans**○ (physiquement, oralement) I'm going to lay into them○; **il m'est rentré dedans**○ (en voiture) (légèrement) he bumped ou ran into me; (violemment) he crashed into me.

renversant, ~e /ʀɑ̃vɛʀsɑ̃, ɑ̃t/ *adj* astounding, astonishing.

renverse /ʀɑ̃vɛʀs/ *nf* **tomber à la ~** to fall flat on one's back; **il y a de quoi tomber à la ~!** it's absolutely astounding!

renversement /ʀɑ̃vɛʀsəmɑ̃/ *nm* **1** (inversion) (de situation, d'ordre) reversal; (d'image) inversion, reversal; **2** (de gouvernement, dirigeant) (par la force) overthrow; (par un vote) removal from office.

renverser /ʀɑ̃vɛʀse/ [1] **I** *vtr* **1** (faire tomber) to knock over [*personne, meuble, bouteille*]; [*automobiliste, véhicule*] to knock down [*piéton, cycliste*]; [*manifestants*] to topple [*statue*]; to overturn [*voiture*]; [*vague*] to overturn [*bateau*]; **2** (répandre) to spill [*liquide, contenu*]; **3** (mettre à l'envers) to turn [sth] upside down [*sablier, flacon*]; **4** (pencher) **~ la tête en arrière** to tip ou tilt one's head back; **~ le buste en arrière** to lean back; **5** (inverser) to reverse [*ordre, situation, rôles*]; PHYS to invert, to reverse [*image*]; ÉLECTROTECH to reverse [*courant*]; **6** POL (mettre fin à) (par la force) to overthrow, to topple [*régime, dirigeant*]; (par un vote) to vote [sb/sth] out of office [*dirigeant, gouvernement*]; **7**○ (stupéfier) [*événement, nouvelle*] to stagger, to astound [*personne*].

II se renverser *vpr* [*véhicule*] to overturn; [*bateau*] to capsize; [*objet, bouteille*] to fall over; [*liquide, contenu*] to spill.

renvoi /ʀɑ̃vwa/ *nm* **1** (d'élève, immigré, de joueur) expulsion (**de** from); (d'employé, ambassadeur) dismissal (**de** from); **~ d'un élève pour trois jours** suspension of a pupil from school for three days; **des immigrés dans leur pays** repatriation of immigrants to their own country; **2** (retour à l'expéditeur) return; **~ d'un colis** return of a parcel; **3** SPORT (au tennis, volley-ball) return; (au football, rugby) clearance; **4** (report) GÉN postponement; JUR, POL (envoi) referral (**devant** to); (ajournement) adjournment (**à** until) ; **~ de l'affaire devant la Cour d'appel** referral of the case to the court of appeal; **~ à huitaine** adjournment for a week; **5** (référence) (dans un dictionnaire, livre, fichier) cross-reference (**à** to); **6** (éructation) belch, burp○; **avoir un ~** GÉN to burp○; [*bébé*] to burp○, to bring up wind.

renvoyer /ʀɑ̃vwaje/ [24] *vtr* **1** (relancer) to throw [sth] back [*projectile, ballon*]; (répercuter) to reflect [*lumière, chaleur*]; to echo [*son*]; **2** (réexpédier) to return [*courrier, marchandises*]; **3** (faire retourner) to send [sb] back [*personne*]; **~ qn dans son pays** to send sb back to his/her own country; **~ qn chez lui** or **dans ses foyers** to send sb home; **~ un projet de loi en commission** to send a bill to committee, to commit a bill US; **4** (expulser) to expel [*élève, immigré, joueur*] (**de** from); to dismiss [*employé, ambassadeur*] (**de** from); **5** (ajourner) to postpone [*débat, décision*] (**à** until); to adjourn [*affaire*] (**à** until); **6** (faire se reporter) **~ à** to refer to; **~ le lecteur à un livre** to refer the reader to a book.

réorganisation /ReɔRganizasjɔ̃/ *nf* reorganization.

réorganiser /ReɔRganize/ [1] **I** *vtr* to reorganize. **II se réorganiser** *vpr* to reorganize oneself.

réorienter /ReɔRjɑ̃te/ [1] **I** *vtr* to reorientate [*élève, étudiant*] (**vers** toward(s)); to reshape [*politique*]; to reorientate [*fusée*]. **II se réorienter** *vpr* [*élève*] to transfer (**vers** to); [*étudiant*] to transfer (**vers** to) GB, to change majors US.

réouverture /ReuvɛRtyR/ *nf* reopening.

repaire /R(ə)pɛR/ *nm* (d'animal, de brigands) den; (de trafiquants, terroristes) hideout.

repaître: **se repaître** /RəpɛtR/ [74] *vpr* **se ~ de** [*animal*] to feed on; [*personne*] to revel in.

répandre /Repɑ̃dR/ [6] **I** *vtr* **1** (mettre) to spread [*substance, matériau*] (**sur** on; **dans** in); to pour [*liquide*] (**sur** on; **dans** in); (accidentellement) to spill [*liquide*]; **~ un chargement** to empty a load; **2** (disperser) to scatter [*graines, farine, déchets*]; **3** (propager) to spread [*nouvelle, religion*] (**dans, à travers** throughout); to give off [*chaleur, fumée, odeur*] (**dans** into); **~ la bonne parole** to spread the good word. **II se répandre** *vpr* **1** (se propager) [*nouvelle, religion, substance, odeur*] to spread (**dans, à travers** throughout); **2** (déverser) **se ~ en invectives** to let out a stream of abuse (**contre** at).

répandu, ~e /Repɑ̃dy/ *adj* (commun) widespread.

réparable /RepaRabl/ *adj* **1** [*objet*] repairable; **2** [*erreur*] which can be put right (*épith, après n*).

reparaître /R(ə)paRɛtR/ [73] *vi* **1** (apparaître de nouveau) = **réapparaître**; **2** (être publié à nouveau) [*journal*] to be back in print; [*œuvre, texte*] to be republished.

réparateur, -trice /RepaRatœR, tRis/ **I** *adj* [*repos, sommeil*] refreshing. **II ▶ 374** *nm,f* (d'appareil) engineer GB, fixer US.

réparation /RepaRasjɔ̃/ **I** *nf* **1** (de montre, machine) repairing, mending; (de véhicule, route, d'avarie) repairing; (de vêtement, chaussure) mending; **la ~ de la télévision m'a coûté 500 francs** it cost me 500 francs to get the television repaired; **être en ~** [*bâtiment, route*] to be under repair; **ma voiture est en ~** my car is being repaired; **2** JUR (de tort, préjudice) compensation (**de** for); **demander ~ de** to seek compensation for; **3** (d'injustice) redress (**de** for). **II réparations** *nfpl* **1** (travaux) repairs, repair work ¢; **2** (dommages et intérêts) compensation ¢.

réparer /RepaRe/ [1] *vtr* **1** (remettre en état) to repair [*bâtiment, véhicule, route, maison*]; to repair, to mend, to fix US [*appareil, accroc, vêtement*]; **~ sommairement qch** to patch sth up; **2** (compenser les effets de) to put [sth] right [*erreur, injustice*]; to make up for [*oubli*]; **3** JUR (dédommager) to compensate for [*dommage*].

reparler /R(ə)paRle/ [1] *vtr ind* **1** (après une interruption) **~ de** to discuss [sth] again (**à qn, avec qn** with sb); **on reparle de l'affaire de l'hôpital** the hospital scandal is in the news again; **2** (après une dispute) **~ à qn** to be back on speaking terms with sb.

repartie /RepaRti/ *nf* rejoinder FML; **elle a de la ~** she always has a ready reply; **avoir la ~ facile** or **l'esprit de ~** to have a quick wit.

repartir /R(ə)paRtiR/ [30] *vi* **1** (quitter un endroit) to leave again; (regagner un lieu) to go back; **tu repars déjà?** you're leaving already?; **2** (après un arrêt) [*personne*] to set off again; [*machine*] to start again; [*bus*] to leave; [*emploi, secteur économique*] to pick up again; **3** (recommencer) **~ sur de nouvelles bases** to start all over again; **~ à zéro** to start again from scratch; **c'est reparti pour un tour**○! here we go again○!

répartir /RepaRtiR/ [3] **I** *vtr* **1** (distribuer) to share [sth] out [*somme, travail, objets*] (**entre** among, between); to split [*bénéfices, frais*] (**entre** among, between); to distribute [*poids, bagages*]; **~ des gens dans des** **salles** to divide people into groups and put them in different rooms; **~ les rôles** to distribute the roles; **~ l'impôt** to spread taxes; **2** (étaler) to spread [*produit, crème*]. **II se répartir** *vpr* **1** (partager) to share out, to split [*travail, objets*]; **2** (être distribué) [*personnes*] to divide up; [*dépenses, travaux*] to be split ou shared; [*voix, votes*] to be split; **se ~ en** [*personnes, objets*] to divide (up) into, to split up into.

répartition /RepaRtisjɔ̃/ *nf* **1** (de biens, travail, rôles) sharing out (**entre** among, between; **en** into); (de personnes, terres, d'emplois) dividing up (**entre** among, **en** into); (de l'impôt) distribution (**de** of); **2** (résultat) distribution.

repas /R(ə)pɑ/ *nm inv* meal; **~ de noces** wedding breakfast; **~ d'affaires** (à midi) business lunch; (le soir) business dinner; **'téléphoner aux heures des ~'** 'please call at mealtimes'.

repassage /R(ə)pasaʒ/ *nm* ironing.

repasser /Rəpase/ [1] **I** *vtr* **1** (avec un fer) to iron [*vêtement*]; **'~ à fer doux'** 'cool iron'; **2** (franchir de nouveau) to cross [sth] again [*fleuve, frontière*]; **3** (se soumettre de nouveau à) to take [sth] again [*permis de conduire, oral*]; to retake, to resit GB [*examen écrit*]; **4** (donner de nouveau) to pass [sth] again [*outil, sel*] (**à qn** to sb); **je te repasse Jean** (au téléphone) I'll put you back on to Jean; **~ qch dans son esprit** to think back over sth; **5**○ (transmettre) to pass on [*virus*] (**à qn** to sb); to give [*rhume*] (**à qn** to sb). **II** *vi* **1** (dans un même lieu) [*cyclistes, procession*] to go past again; **~ devant qch** to go past sth again; **tu n'as pas besoin de ~ par Lyon** you don't have to go back through Lyons; **si tu repasses à Lyon, viens me voir** if you're ever back in Lyons, come and see me; **s'il croit que je vais accepter, il repassera**○ or **il peut toujours ~**○! if he thinks I'm going to agree, he's got another think coming○ GB ou he can think again!; **2** (être montré, diffusé) **~ au cinéma/à Paris** [*film*] to be showing again at the cinema GB ou movies US/ in Paris; **3** (pour terminer un travail) **quand elle fait la vaisselle, je dois ~ derrière elle** I always have to do the dishes again after she's done them.

repayer /R(ə)peje/ [21] *vtr* to pay [sth] again.

repêchage /R(ə)pɛʃaʒ/ *nm* **1** (dans l'eau) recovery (*from water*); **2** SCOL, UNIV **examen** or **épreuve de ~** resit GB, retest US; **question (de) ~** supplementary question (*giving another chance to pass*).

repêcher /R(ə)peʃe/ [1] *vtr* **1** (dans l'eau) to recover [*corps, véhicule*] (*from water*); to fish out [*objet*]; **2** SCOL, UNIV to award a discretionary pass to GB, to raise [sb] to a passing grade US [*candidat*]; SPORT to allow [sb] to qualify [*personne*].

repeindre /R(ə)pɛ̃dR/ [55] *vtr* to repaint.

repenser /R(ə)pɑ̃se/ [1] **I** *vtr* to rethink [*théorie*]. **II repenser à** *vtr ind* **~ à** to think back to [*enfance, vacances*]; to think again about [*discussion, anecdote*].

repenti, ~e /R(ə)pɑ̃ti/ **I** *adj* repentant. **II** *nm,f* penitent.

repentir[1]: **se repentir** /R(ə)pɑ̃tiR/ [30] *vpr* **1** GÉN to regret (**de qch** sth); **2** RELIG to repent (**de qch** of sth).

repentir[2] /R(ə)pɑ̃tiR/ *nm* GÉN, RELIG repentance.

repérable /R(ə)peRabl/ *adj* GÉN that can be spotted (*épith, après n*).

repérage /R(ə)peRaʒ/ *nm* AVIAT, MIL location (**de** of); CIN finding a location (**de** for).

répercussion /RepɛRkysjɔ̃/ *nf* repercussion.

répercuter /RepɛRkyte/ [1] **I** *vtr* **1** (transmettre) to pass [sth] on [*hausse, baisse*]; **2** PHYS to send back [*son*]. **II se répercuter** *vpr* **1** [*son*] to echo; [*augmentation, baisse*] to be reflected (**sur** in); **2** [*sentiment*] to have repercussions (**sur** on).

repère /R(ə)pɛR/ *nm* **1** (jalon) marker; (encoche, trait) (reference) mark; **la statue sert de ~** the statue is a useful landmark; **2** (événement) landmark; (date) reference point; (référence) reference point, criterion.

repérer /R(ə)peRe/ [14] **I** *vtr* **1**○ (discerner) to spot [*personne, erreur, endroit*]; **~ les lieux** to check out a place; **si tu ne veux pas te faire ~** if you don't want to get noticed; **se faire ~ par la police** to be spotted by the police; **2** (situer) to locate [*cible, ennemi*].

II se repérer◯ *vpr* LIT, FIG (dans un lieu) to get one's bearings; **2** (se remarquer) [*erreur*] to stand out.

répertoire /ʀepɛʀtwaʀ/ *nm* **1** (carnet) notebook with thumb index; **2** (liste) **~ téléphonique** (personnel) telephone book; **~ d'adresses** (personnel) address book; **3** MUS, THÉÂT repertoire; **une pièce du ~** a stock play; **avoir tout un ~ d'anecdotes** FIG to have an extensive repertoire of anecdotes.

répertorier /ʀepɛʀtɔʀje/ [2] *vtr* **1** (faire la liste de) to list [*entreprises, informations*]; to index [*ouvrages*]; **non répertorié** unlisted; **2** (recenser) to identify [*espèces, cas, risques*].

répéter /ʀepete/ [14] **I** *vtr* **1** (redire) to repeat; **~ qch à qn** to say sth to sb again, to tell sb sth again; **je ne me le suis pas fait ~ deux fois!** I didn't need to be told twice!; **répète (un peu pour voir**◯**)!** say that again!; **tu répètes toujours la même chose** you keep saying the same thing over and over again; **2** (rapporter) to tell; **ne le répète à personne** don't tell anyone; **elle répète tout ce qu'on lui dit** she repeats everything you tell her; **3** (refaire) to repeat [*expérience*]; **4** (rejouer) (pour harmoniser) to rehearse [*pièce*]; to rehearse for [*concert*]; (pour apprendre) to practise^GB [*passage*].

II se répéter *vpr* **1** (redire) (en rabâchant) to repeat oneself; (pour se rappeler) to repeat [sth] to oneself [*phrase, conseil*]; **j'ai beau me ~ que** no matter how often I tell myself that; **2** (se reproduire) [*phénomène, événement*] to be repeated; **si ce genre d'accident se répète...** if this kind of accident happens again...

répétitif, -ive /ʀepetitif, iv/ *adj* repetitive.

répétition /ʀepetisjɔ̃/ *nf* **1** (dans un texte) repetition; **2** (de geste, d'erreur) repetition; **3** MUS, THÉÂT (mise au point) rehearsal.

■ **~ générale** THÉÂT dress rehearsal; MUS final rehearsal.

repeuplement /ʀ(ə)pœpləmɑ̃/ *nm* **1** GÉOG repopulation; **2** (de forêt) reforestation (**en** with); **3** (de rivière) restocking (**en** with).

repeupler /ʀ(ə)pœple/ [1] **I** *vtr* **1** GÉOG to repopulate; **2** to restock [*étang, parc*] (**de** with); **3** AGRIC to reforest [*lieu*] (**en** with); **~ une forêt** to replant a forest.

II se repeupler *vpr* GÉOG to become repopulated.

repiquage /ʀ(ə)pikaʒ/ *nm* **1** (de riz) transplanting; (de salade, géranium) pricking out; **2** (de bande, disque) rerecording.

repiquer /ʀ(ə)pike/ [1] *vtr* **1** to transplant [*riz*]; to prick out [*salade, géranium*]; **2** (piquer encore) [*insecte*] to bite again; **3** to rerecord [*bande, disque*].

répit /ʀepi/ *nm* respite; **travailler sans ~** to work ceaselessly ou without respite; **leur travail ne leur laisse aucun ~** they never get a break from work; **laisser un ~ de cinq jours à qn** to give sb five days' grace.

replacer /ʀ(ə)plase/ [12] **I** *vtr* **1** (placer à nouveau) to put [sth] back, to replace [*objet*]; **2** FIG (situer) **~ qch dans son contexte** to set sth back in context.

II se replacer *vpr* FIG (s'imaginer) **se ~ dans un contexte** to imagine oneself back in a context.

replanter /ʀ(ə)plɑ̃te/ [1] *vtr* **1** (changer de terre) to transplant [*rosier, arbre*]; **2** (après destruction) to replant [*arbre*]; **3** (reboiser) to replant [*parc, forêt*] (**en** with).

replâtrer /ʀ(ə)plɑtʀe/ [1] *vtr* **1** CONSTR to replaster [*mur*]; **2** FIG to patch up [*groupe, union*].

replet, -ète /ʀəplɛ, ɛt/ *adj* [*personne*] plump; [*visage, joues*] plump, chubby.

repli /ʀ(ə)pli/ *nm* **1** (double pli) double fold; **2** (pli profond) fold; **les ~s de sa conscience** FIG the recesses of his/her conscience LITTÉR; **3** MIL (recul) (mouvement de) **~** withdrawal (**sur** to); **4** PSYCH **~ sur soi(-même)** withdrawal.

replier /ʀ(ə)plije/ [2] **I** *vtr* **1** (plier à nouveau) to fold

up [*dépliant, plan*]; **2** (rabattre) to fold [sth] back [*drap*] (**sur** over); **3** (refermer) to fold up [*chaise, éventail*]; to close [*parapluie, canif*]; **4** (siège, en place) **elle replia ses jambes** she tucked her legs under her; **~ ses ailes** [*oiseau*] to fold its wings.

II se replier *vpr* **1** [*lame, canapé-lit*] to fold up; **2** [*troupe, armée*] to withdraw (**sur** to; **dans** into); **3 se ~ sur soi-même** [*personne*] to become withdrawn; [*pays*] to shut itself off from the rest of the world.

réplique /ʀeplik/ *nf* **1** (riposte verbale) retort, rejoinder; **faire qch en ~ à un discours** to do sth in response to a speech; **il a la ~ facile** he's never stuck for an answer; **2** (objection) **faire qch sans ~** to do sth without arguing; **argument sans ~** irrefutable argument; **3** THÉÂT line; **donner la ~ à qn** (pour faire apprendre un rôle) to go through sb's lines with them; (dans une représentation) to play opposite sb; **les deux politiciens se sont donné la ~ pendant une heure** there was an hour-long sparring session between the two politicians; **4** (copie) ART replica; (personne) **elle est la ~ de sa mère** she is the image of her mother.

répliquer /ʀeplike/ [1] **I** *vtr* (répondre) to retort.

II répliquer à *vtr ind* **~ à qn** (en objectant) to argue with sb; **~ à** to respond to [*objections, critique, attaques*].

III *vi* **1** (verbalement) to answer back; **2** (par une action) to retaliate, to respond.

répondant, -e /ʀepɔ̃dɑ̃, ɑ̃t/ *nm,f* (d'une personne) referee; FIN, JUR (caution) surety, guarantor.

IDIOMES **avoir du ~**◯ (de l'argent) to have money.

répondeur /ʀepɔ̃dœʀ/ *nm* **~ (téléphonique)** (telephone) answering machine, answerphone GB.

répondre /ʀepɔ̃dʀ/ [6] **I** *vtr* to answer, to reply; **~ une bêtise** to give a silly answer ou reply; **tu réponds n'importe quoi** you just give any answer that comes into your head; **je me suis vu ~ que, il m'a été répondu que** I was told that; **qu'as-tu à ~ (à cela)?** what's your answer (to that)?; **qu'est-ce qu'il t'a répondu?** what was his answer?

II répondre à *vtr ind* **1** (être conforme à) **~ à** to answer, to meet [*besoin, exigences*]; to fulfil [*souhait*]; to answer, to fit [*signalement*]; to come up to, to meet [*espérances*]; **2** (agir en retour) **~ à** to respond to [*avances, appel, attaque*]; to return [*affection, salut, politesse*]; **~ aux critiques de qn par le mépris** to treat sb's criticism with contempt; **~ à un sourire** to smile back; **~ à la violence par la violence** to meet violence with violence.

III répondre de *vtr ind* (servir de caution) **~ de qn** to vouch for sb; FIN, JUR to stand surety for sb; **~ de ses actes** to answer for one's actions; **je ne réponds plus de rien** it's out of my hands from now on; **ça sera fini, j'en** ou **je vous en réponds**◯ it will be finished, take my word for it ou you can be sure of that.

IV *vi* **1** (donner une réponse) **~ à** to reply to, to answer [*personne, question, lettre*]; to reply to [*ultimatum*]; **~ à un questionnaire** to fill in a questionnaire; **~ par oui ou par non** to answer yes or no; **~ par un sourire** to answer with a smile; **2** (se manifester) **~ au téléphone/à la porte** to answer the phone/the door; **ça ne répond pas** there's no answer ou reply; **3** (être insolent) **~ à qn** to answer sb back GB, to talk back to sb; **4** (se nommer) LITER **elle répond au nom de Flore** she answers to the name of Flore; **5** (réagir) [*mécanisme, organe, muscle*] to respond (**à** to).

réponse /ʀepɔ̃s/ *nf* **1** (à une question, lettre, objection) answer (**à** to), reply (**à** to); (à un questionnaire) reply; **en ~ à votre lettre** in reply to your letter; **ma lettre est restée sans ~** my letter remained unanswered; **2** (solution) answer (**à** to); **3** (réaction) response (**à** to); **temps de ~** response time; **la ~ du public a été favorable** the public has responded favourably^GB.

■ **~ de Normand** noncommittal reply.

IDIOMES **avoir ~ à tout** to have an answer for everything.

report /ʀəpɔʀ/ *nm* **1** (de procès) adjournment (**à** until); (de rendez-vous, départ) postponement (**à** to, until); (de jugement) deferment (**à** to, until); **2** (de dessin, d'image) transfer (**sur** onto); **3** (aux élections) transfer; **4** (de somme) carrying forward; (somme reportée) amount carried forward.

reportage /ʀ(ə)pɔʀtaʒ/ *nm* **1** (dans les média) report (**sur** on); **2** (technique) reporting.

reporter[1] /ʀ(ə)pɔʀte/ [1] **I** *vtr* **1** (différer) to put back [*date*] (**à** to); to postpone, to put back [*rendez-vous, événement*] (**à** until); to postpone [*départ, match*] (**à** until); to defer [*jugement*] (**à** until); ~ **son départ d'une semaine** to postpone one's departure by a week; ~ **la réunion de lundi à vendredi** to postpone Monday's meeting until Friday; **2** (copier sur un autre support) to carry forward [*calcul, résultat*]; to copy out [*nom*]; **3** (déplacer) ~ **un paragraphe en début d'un texte** to move a paragraph to the beginning of a text; **4** (aller remettre) to take [sth] back [*marchandise, objet*]; **5** (dans le passé) **cela nous reporte longtemps en arrière** that's going back a long time; **6** (transférer) to transfer [*affection*] (**sur** to); ~ **des voix sur un autre candidat** to transfer votes to another candidate; ~ **son agressivité sur qn** to take one's aggression out on sb.

II se reporter *vpr* **1** (consulter) **se** ~ **à** to refer to; **2** (revenir en pensée) **se** ~ **à** to think back to; **3** (être transféré) [*voix*] to be transferred (**sur** to).

reporter[2] /ʀəpɔʀtɛʀ/ ▶ 374 | *nm* (journaliste) reporter; **un grand** ~ a special correspondent.

reporter-photographe, *pl* **reporters-photographes** /ʀ(ə)pɔʀtɛʀfɔtɔgʀaf/ ▶ 374 | *nm* photojournalist.

repos /ʀəpo/ *nm inv* **1** (inactivité, délassement) rest; **s'accorder du** ~ to have a rest; **mon jour de** ~ (sans travail) my day off; **ce n'est pas de tout** ~ it's no easy task, it's no picnic○; **muscle au** ~ relaxed muscle; ~**!** MIL at ease!; **soldats au** ~ soldiers standing at ease; **2** (absence de soucis) LITER peace; **chercher le** ~ to search for peace.

reposant, ~**e** /ʀəpozɑ̃, ɑ̃t/ *adj* [*occupation*] peaceful, restful; [*lumière*] soothing; [*position, lecture*] relaxing.

reposé, ~**e** /ʀəpoze/ **I** *pp* ▶ **reposer**.
II *pp adj* **avoir les traits** ~**s** to look rested; **lire qch à tête** ~**e** to read sth at one's leisure.

repose-pied, *pl* ~**s** /ʀ(ə)pozpje/ *nm* footrest.

reposer /ʀəpoze/ [1] **I** *vtr* **1** (d'une fatigue) to rest [*jambes, esprit*]; **cela me repose de mon travail habituel** it's a rest from my usual work; **2** (appuyer) ~ **sa tête sur qch** to rest one's head on sth; **3** (placer) to put [sth] down [*téléphone, verre*]; (à nouveau) to put [sth] down again [*bibelot*]; **4** (soulever à nouveau) to ask [sth] again [*question*]; **cela repose le problème du chômage** this raises the problem of unemployment again.

II *vi* **1** (être enterré) **qu'elle repose en paix** may she rest in peace; **où reposent de nombreux soldats** where many soldiers are buried; **'ici repose le Dr Grunard'** (sur une tombe) 'here lies Dr Grunard'; **2** (être inactif) **laisser** ~ **la terre** to rest the land; **3** [*navire, épave*] to lie; **4** CULIN **'laisser** ~ **la pâte'** 'let the dough rest'; **5** ~ **sur** [*idée, expérience*] to be based on; **la poutre repose sur...** the beam is supported by...; **tout repose sur elle** it all rests with her.

III se reposer *vpr* **1** (d'une fatigue) to have a rest, to rest; **repose-toi bien** have a good rest; **2** (faire confiance à, avoir besoin de) **se** ~ **sur qn** to rely on sb; **3** (à nouveau) **le problème va se** ~ the problem will recur.

repose-tête /ʀəpoztɛt/ *nm inv* **1** GÉN head rest; **2** AUT head restraint.

repoussant, ~**e** /ʀəpusɑ̃, ɑ̃t/ *adj* [*laideur*] hideous; [*saleté, odeur*] revolting; **être** ~ **de laideur**, **être d'une laideur** ~**e** to be hideously ugly.

repousser /ʀəpuse/ [1] **I** *vtr* **1** (remettre en place) to push [sth] back into [*tiroir*]; to push [sth] to [*verrou, porte*]; to push back [*meuble, objet*]; ~ **la porte d'un coup de pied** to kick the door to ou shut; **2** (déplacer, éloigner) to push away [*objets*]; to push back [*mèche de cheveux*]; **3** (obliger à reculer) to push ou drive back [*attaquant, foule*]; **4** (s'opposer avec succès à) to repel

[*attaque*]; **5** (rejeter) to dismiss [*argument*]; to decline [*aide*]; to turn down [*demande*]; ~ **les avances de qn** to spurn sb's advances; **6** (dégoûter) [*saleté*] to revolt **7** (différer) to postpone, to put [sth] back [*départ, rendez-vous*]; to put GB ou move [sth] back [*date*]; to postpone [*événement*]; ~ **une réunion du lundi au vendredi** to postpone a Monday meeting until Friday.

II *vi* [*cheveux, barbe, herbe*] (après une coupe) to grow again; (après disparition) to grow back; [*feuille*] to grow again; [*dent*] to come through.

répréhensible /ʀepʀeɑ̃sibl/ *adj* reprehensible.

reprendre /ʀ(ə)pʀɑ̃dʀ/ [52] **I** *vtr* **1** (se resservir) ~ **du pain/vin** to have some more bread/wine; **j'en ai repris deux fois** I had three helpings; **2** (prendre de nouveau) to pick [sth] up again [*objet, outil*]; to take [sth] back [*cadeau, objet prêté*]; to recapture [*ville, fugitif*]; to go back on [*parole, promesse*]; (aller chercher) to pick [sb/sth] up, to collect [*personne, voiture*]; **tu passes me** ~ **à quelle heure?** what time will you come back for me?; ~ **sa place** (son siège) to go back to one's seat; **j'ai repris les kilos que j'avais perdus** I've put back on the weight I'd lost; ~ **son nom de jeune fille** to revert to one's maiden name; **3** (accepter de nouveau) to take [sb] on again [*employé*]; COMM to take [sth] back [*article*]; (contre un nouvel achat) to take [sth] in part GB ou partial US exchange; **les marchandises ne sont ni reprises ni échangées** goods cannot be returned or exchanged; **4** (recommencer) to resume [*promenade, récit, fonctions, études*]; to pick up [sth] again, to go back to [*journal, tricot*]; to take up [sth] again [*lutte*]; to revive [*pièce, tradition*]; ~ **le travail** (après un congé, une grève) to go back to work; **on quitte à midi et on reprend à 14 heures** we stop at 12 and start again at 2; **tu reprends le train à quelle heure?** (de retour) what time is your train back?; ~ **la parole** to start speaking again; ~ **une histoire au début** to go back to the beginning of a story; **5** (acquérir) to take over [*cabinet, commerce, entreprise*]; **6** (surprendre de nouveau) **que je ne t'y reprenne plus!** don't let me catch you doing that again!; **on ne me reprendra plus à lui rendre service!** you won't catch me doing him/her any favours[GB] again!; **7** (recouvrer) ~ **confiance** to regain one's confidence; ~ **ses vieilles habitudes** to get back into one's old ways; **la nature reprend ses droits** nature reasserts itself; **elle a repris sa liberté** she's a free woman again; **8** (retoucher) to alter [*vêtement, couture*]; ~ **le travail de qn** to correct sb's work; **il y a tout à** ~ **dans ce chapitre** the whole chapter needs re-writing; **9** (utiliser de nouveau) to take up [*idée, politique*]; **10** (répéter) to repeat [*argument*]; to take up [*slogan, chant*]; **reprenons à la vingtième mesure** MUS let's take it again from bar 20; ~ **la leçon précédente** SCOL to go over the previous lesson again; **tous les médias ont repris la nouvelle** the news was taken up by all the media; **11** (corriger) to correct [*élève*]; **12** (resurgir) **mon mal de dents m'a repris** my toothache has come back; **voilà que ça le reprend**○! there he goes again!

II *vi* **1** (retrouver sa vigueur) [*commerce, affaires*] to pick up again; [*plante*] to recover; **la vie reprend peu à peu** life is gradually getting back to normal; **2** (recommencer) [*cours, bombardements*] to start again; [*négociations*] to resume; **nos émissions reprendront à 7 heures** RADIO, TV we shall be back on the air at 7 o'clock; **3** (continuer) **'c'est bien étrange,' reprit-il** 'it's very strange,' he continued.

III se reprendre *vpr* **1** (se corriger) to correct oneself; **2** (se ressaisir) [*personne*] to pull oneself together; **3** (recommencer) **s'y** ~ **à trois fois pour faire qch** to make three attempts to do ou at doing sth; **il se reprend à penser que c'est possible** he's gone back to thinking it might be possible.

représailles /ʀ(ə)pʀezaj/ *nfpl* GÉN, MIL, POL reprisals; (moins violentes) retaliation ¢; **en** ~ in retaliation.

représentant, ~**e** /ʀ(ə)pʀezɑ̃tɑ̃, ɑ̃t/ *nm,f* **1** (délégué) representative (**de** of); ~ **des forces de**

l'ordre police officer; **2** ▸374| COMM ~ (**de commerce**) sales representative, sales rep.

eprésentatif, -ive /ʀəpʀezãtatif, iv/ *adj* representative (**de** of).

eprésentation /ʀəpʀezãtasjɔ̃/ *nf* **1** (action de représenter) representation (**de** of); **2** THÉÂT (séance) performance; **3** (rôle de mandataire, délégué) representation; (mandataires, délégation) representatives (*pl*); **~ proportionnelle** proportional representation; **4** COMM (activité) commercial travelling^GB; **~ exclusive** sole agency; **faire de la ~** to be a sales representative ou rep.

eprésenter /ʀəpʀezãte/ [1] **I** *vtr* **1** (figurer) [*tableau, dessin*] to depict, to show; [*peintre*] to depict [*paysage, situation*]; to portray [*personne*]; **le décor représente un jardin** THÉÂT the scene shows a garden; **on l'a représenté comme un héros** he has been portrayed as a hero; **2** (exprimer) to represent; **que représente ce signe?** what does this sign represent?; **elle représente bien l'esprit de son époque** she typifies the spirit of her age; **3** (équivaloir à) to represent; (signifier) to mean; **le prix d'une voiture représente deux ans de salaire** a car represents two years' salary; **cela représente trop de sacrifices** it means too many sacrifices; **le vin représente 60% de la consommation d'alcool** wine accounts for 60% of alcohol consumption; **4** (être mandataire de) to represent; **5** THÉÂT (jouer) to perform [*pièce*]; to put on [*spectacle*].

II se représenter *vpr* **1** (s'imaginer) to imagine [*conséquences, scène, personne*]; **on se la représente très bien en premier ministre** one can just see her as Prime Minister; **2** (survenir à nouveau) [*occasion*] to arise again; [*problème*] to crop up again; **3** (être à nouveau candidat) **se ~ à un examen** to retake an examination; **se ~ aux élections** to stand GB ou run US for election again.

répressif, -ive /ʀepʀesif, iv/ *adj* repressive.

répression /ʀepʀesjɔ̃/ *nf* **1** POL, JUR suppression (**de, contre** of); **2** PSYCH (d'élan, de pulsion) repression.

réprimande /ʀepʀimãd/ *nf* reprimand.

réprimander /ʀepʀimãde/ [1] *vtr* to reprimand.

réprimer /ʀepʀime/ [1] *vtr* to repress [*envie, penchant*]; to suppress [*bâillement, sourire*]; to suppress [*révolte*]; to crack down on [*fraude, trafic*].

repris /ʀ(ə)pʀi/ *nm inv* **~ de justice** ex-convict.

reprise /ʀəpʀiz/ *nf* **1** JUR (récupération) repossession; **2** (recommencement) (de travaux, cours, vols, dialogue, négociations, d'hostilités) resumption (**de** of); (de pièce, film) rerun; (d'émission) RADIO, TV repeat; **~ du travail** resumption of work; (après une grève) return to work; **à deux ~s** on two occasions, twice; **3** ÉCON, FIN (de demande, production) increase (**de** in); (de commerce) revival (**de** of); **~ de la Bourse** stock market rally; **on assiste à une ~ de l'économie** we're seeing an upturn in the economy; **la ~ de l'emploi** the increase ou rise in employment; **4** COMM (de marchandise) return, taking back; (contre un nouvel achat) trade-in, part exchange GB; COMM, ÉCON (d'entreprise, de commerce) takeover; **250 francs de ~ sur votre vieille machine à laver contre achat d'une neuve** 250 francs for your old washing machine when you buy a new one; **5** (dans l'immobilier) key money; **6** AUT acceleration ¢; **7** (de tissu) mend; (de lainage) darn; **8** SPORT (en boxe) round; (au football) start of second half; (en escrime) bout.

repriser /ʀəpʀize/ [1] *vtr* to mend [*vêtement, rideau, accroc*]; to darn [*chaussette*].

réprobateur, -trice /ʀepʀɔbatœʀ, tʀis/ *adj* reproachful, disapproving.

réprobation /ʀepʀɔbasjɔ̃/ *nf* GÉN disapproval, reprobation SOUT.

reproche /ʀ(ə)pʀɔʃ/ *nm* reproach; **faire** ou **adresser des ~s à qn** to reproach sb (**sur, au sujet de** for); **j'ai un ou deux ~s à vous faire** I've one or two criticisms to make; **un ton de ~** a reproachful tone; **sans ~** beyond reproach; **elle est toujours en train**

de lui faire des ~s she's always finding fault with him/her.

reprocher /ʀəpʀɔʃe/ [1] **I** *vtr* **1** (parlant de personnes) **~ qch à qn** to criticize ou reproach sb for sth; **qu'est-ce que tu lui reproches?** what have you got against him/her?; **je ne vous reproche rien, mais...** I'm not criticizing ou reproaching you...; **on ne peut rien lui ~** he's/she's beyond reproach; **je lui reproche de ne jamais tenir compte des autres** I hate the way he/she never considers other people; **elle me reproche de ne jamais lui écrire** she complains that I never write to her; **2** (parlant de choses) **ce que je reproche à cette voiture c'est...** what I don't like about this car is...; **tu ne peux pas me ~ les erreurs des autres** you can't blame me for other people's mistakes; **qu'est-ce que tu reproches à ma cravate?** what's wrong with my tie?; **les faits qui lui sont reprochés** the charges against him/her.

II se reprocher *vpr* **se ~ qch** to blame ou reproach oneself for sth; **je n'ai rien à me ~** I've done nothing wrong.

reproducteur, -trice /ʀəpʀɔdyktœʀ, tʀis/ **I** *adj* **1** BIOL [*organe, appareil, fonction*] reproductive; **2** AGRIC [*animal*] breeding (*épith*).

II *nm* AGRIC breeding animal.

reproduction /ʀ(ə)pʀɔdyksjɔ̃/ *nf* **1** BIOL reproduction; **la ~ artificielle** assisted reproduction; **2** (action de copier) reproduction; (copie) reproduction, copy; **droit de ~** copyright; **droits de ~ réservés** all rights reserved; **~ interdite** no unauthorized reproduction ou copying.

reproduire /ʀ(ə)pʀɔdɥiʀ/ [69] **I** *vtr* **1** (répéter) to repeat [*erreur, expérience*]; to imitate, to copy [*habitude, geste*]; to recreate [*condition, milieu*]; to reproduce [*son*]; **2** (copier) to reproduce [*tableau, motif, texte, déclaration*]; to recreate [*style, condition*]; **sa déclaration sera reproduite dans les journaux** his/her declaration will be printed (in full) in the papers; **3** TECH (restituer) to reproduce [*son*].

II se reproduire *vpr* **1** BIOL [*homme, animal, plante*] to reproduce; **2** (se répéter) [*phénomène*] to recur; **et que cela ne se reproduise plus!** and don't let it happen again!

réprouvé, ~e /ʀepʀuve/ *nm,f* outcast.

réprouver /ʀepʀuve/ [1] *vtr* to condemn.

reptile /ʀɛptil/ *nm* ZOOL reptile.

repu, ~e /ʀəpy/ **I** *pp* ▸ **repaître**.

II *pp adj* full (*jamais épith*).

républicain, ~e /ʀepyblikɛ̃, ɛn/ *adj, nm,f* republican.

république /ʀepyblik/ *nf* republic; **après tout, on vit en ~** after all, it's a free country.

répudier /ʀepydje/ [2] *vtr* **1** to repudiate [*épouse*]; **2** to renounce [*droit, nationalité*]; **3** (rejeter) LITER to renege on [*engagement*]; to repudiate [*idée, opinion*]; to renounce [*foi, croyance*].

répugnance /ʀepyɲɑ̃s/ *nf* **1** (aversion) revulsion; **avoir ou éprouver de la ~ pour** to loathe [*aliment, idée, personne*]; **to find** [sth] revolting ou disgusting [*comportement, mensonge, violence*]; **to find** [sth] disgusting [*saleté*]; **2** (hésitation) reluctance (**à faire** to do); **avec ~** reluctantly, with reluctance.

répugnant, ~e /ʀepyɲɑ̃, ɑ̃t/ *adj* [*personne, laideur, saleté*] revolting; [*lieu*] disgusting; [*comportement, idée*] loathsome; **d'une saleté ~e** disgustingly dirty.

répugner /ʀepyɲe/ [1] **I** *vtr* [*nourriture, personne*] to be repugnant to, to disgust [*personne*]; **vivre ici me répugne** I loathe ou detest living here.

II répugner à *vtr ind* to be averse to [*tâche, violence*]; **~ à faire** to be reluctant to do, to be loath to do.

III *v impers* **il me répugne de vous le dire, mais...** I hate to have to tell you, but...; **il me répugne de devoir faire** I am loath to do.

répulsion /ʀepylsjɔ̃/ *nf* repulsion; **éprouver de la** ou **un sentiment de ~ pour qn** to be repelled by sb; **il m'inspire de la ~** I find him repulsive.

réputation /Repytasjɔ̃/ *nf* **1** (honorabilité) reputation; **2** (renom) reputation; **avoir bonne/mauvaise ~** to have a good/bad reputation; **se faire une ~** to make a name for oneself; **connaître qn de ~** to know sb by reputation; **sa ~ d'efficacité/de chanteur** his reputation for efficiency/as a singer; **avoir la ~ d'être honnête** to have a reputation for being honest.

réputé, ~e /Repyte/ *adj* **1** (renommé) [*compagnie, école*] reputable; [*écrivain, peintre*] of repute; [*produit*] well-known; **~ pour qch** renowned for sth; **c'est l'avocat le plus ~ de Paris** he's/she's regarded as the best lawyer in Paris; **2** (tenu pour) **~ cher** reputed ou reckoned to be expensive.

requérir /RəkeRiR/ [35] *vtr* **1** (solliciter) to request [*secours*]; **2** (nécessiter) (au besoin) to call for [*qualité*]; (impérativement) to require [*soin, compétences, unanimité, preuve*]; **le maire peut ~ la force publique** the mayor can summon the police; **3** JUR to call for [*peine*].

requête /Rəkɛt/ *nf* **1** (sollicitation) request; **à** ou **sur la ~ de qn** at sb's request; **2** JUR petition; **adresser une ~ au juge** to petition the judge.

requin /R(ə)kɛ̃/ *nm* ZOOL, FIG shark.

requinquer° /R(ə)kɛ̃ke/ [1] **I** *vtr* to buck [sb] up°; **ça (vous) requinque** [*boisson*] it peps you up°.

II se requinquer *vpr* to perk up°.

requis, ~e /Rəki, iz/ **I** *pp* ▶ **requérir**.

II *pp adj* (nécessaire) necessary; (exigé) required; **satisfaire aux conditions ~es** to meet the requirements.

réquisition /Rekizisjɔ̃/ *nf* ADMIN, MIL (de biens, locaux) (officiellement) requisitioning; (officieusement) commandeering; (de personnes) conscription (*for forced labour*GB).

réquisitionner /Rekizisjɔne/ [1] *vtr* ADMIN, MIL (officiellement) to requisition; (officieusement) to commandeer [*biens, locaux*]; to conscript [*ouvriers, civils*].

réquisitoire /Rekizitwar/ *nm* **1** (discours) closing speech for the prosecution (*requesting a specific sentence*); **2** (dénonciation) indictment (**contre** of).

RER /ɛRøeR/ *nm: abbr* ▶ **réseau**.

rescapé, ~e /Rɛskape/ **I** *adj* [*personne*] surviving.

II *nm,f* survivor (**de** from).

rescousse: à la rescousse /alaRɛskus/ *loc adv* **venir/aller à la ~ de qn** to come/to go to sb's rescue; **appeler qn à la ~** to call to sb for help.

réseau, *pl* **~x** /Rezo/ *nm* **1** TECH (de fils, conduits, routes) network; **sur l'ensemble du ~** throughout the network; **les abonnés du ~** TÉLÉCOM telephone customers; **2** (de personnes) network; **~ d'espions/de trafiquants de drogue** spy/drugs ring; **3** ORDINAT network; **~ local** local area network.

■ **~ express régional**, **RER** *rapid-transit rail system in the Paris region.*

réservation /RezɛRvasjɔ̃/ *nf* reservation, booking GB.

réserve /RezɛRv/ *nf* **1** (restriction) reservation (**au sujet de**, **à l'égard de** about); **je me range sans ~ de votre côté** you have my unreserved support; **sous ~ de disponibilité/de changement** subject to availability/alteration; **'sous (toute) ~'** (dans un programme) 'to be confirmed'; **je vous le dis sous toutes ~s** I'm telling you for what it's worth; **2** (provision) stock; **faire des ~s de farine** to lay in a stock of flour; **~(s) d'argent** money in reserve; **j'ai toujours une bonne bouteille en ~** I always have a good bottle put by; **3** ÉCON **~s de charbon/pétrole** coal/oil reserves; **~s d'eau** water supply (*sg*); **4** (discrétion) reserve; **manquer de ~** to be too outspoken; **garder une certaine ~ avec qn** to keep a certain distance with sb; **5** (local de stockage) stockroom; **6** (section de bibliothèque) stacks (*pl*); (section de musée) storerooms (*pl*); **7** (territoire protégé) reserve; **~ naturelle/de chasse/de pêche** nature/game/fishing reserve; **8** (territoire alloué) reservation; **~ indienne** Indian reservation; **9** MIL (réservistes) **la ~** the reserves (*pl*); **officier de ~** reserve officer.

réservé, ~e /RezɛRve/ **I** *pp* ▶ **réserver**.

II *pp adj* **1** (privé) [*chasse, pêche*] private; **2** (attribué) **~ à la clientèle** (reserved) for patrons only;

voie ~e aux taxis taxi lane; **'tous droits ~s'** JU 'all rights reserved'; **3** (réticent) [*personne, caractèr*] reserved; [*attitude, propos*] reticent; **se montrer ~ sur** to be guarded about.

réserver /RezɛRve/ [1] **I** *vtr* **1** (retenir à l'avance) t reserve [*chambre, place, billet*]; **2** (mettre de côté) t put aside [*journal, marchandise*] (**pour** for); **~ qc pour les grandes occasions** to keep sth for speci occasions; **3** (garder pour plus tard) to set aside [*argen* to save [*énergie, explications*]; **est-ce que tu peux m ~ une heure cet après-midi?** can you set aside a hour for me this afternoon?; **4** (destiner) **~ un bo accueil à qn** to give sb a warm welcome; **que nous r serve l'avenir?** what does the future hold?; **l (triste) sort qui lui était réservé** the sad fate th awaited him; **l'année passée m'a réservé bien de surprises** last year was full of surprises for me; **5** (mettre à plus tard) **~ son jugement** to reserve judg ment GB; **~ son diagnostic** to defer diagnosis.

II se réserver *vpr* **elle se réserve quelque instants de repos après le déjeuner** she sets aside few minutes after lunch to relax; **se ~ les meilleu morceaux** to save the best bits for oneself; **se ~ droit de faire** to reserve the right to do; **se ~ pou le dessert** to save some room for dessert.

réserviste /RezɛRvist/ *nmf* reservist.

réservoir /RezɛRvwar/ *nm* **1** (cuve) GÉN tank; **~ essence** petrol tank GB, gas tank US; **2** (lac artificie reservoir; **3** FIG (source) **~ de main-d'œuv** reservoir of labourGB.

résidant, ~e /Rezidɑ̃, ɑ̃t/ *adj* resident.

résidence /Rezidɑ̃s/ *nf* **1** (maison) residence; **2** (don cile) place of residence; **en ~ surveillée** under ho arrest; **3** (groupe d'immeubles) block of flats GB, apa ment complex US.

■ **~ principale/secondaire** main/second hom **~ universitaire** (university) hall of residence (residence hall US.

résident, ~e /Rezidɑ̃, ɑ̃t/ *nm,f* **1** (étranger) forei resident, resident alien US; **2** (diplomate) resident.

résidentiel, -ielle /Rezidɑ̃sjɛl/ *adj* residential.

résider /Rezide/ [1] *vi* **1** (vivre) to reside SOUT, to liv **2** (se trouver) **~ dans qch** to lie in sth.

résidu /Rezidy/ *nm* **1** (dépôt) residue ¢; **2** (res remnant; (détritus) waste ¢.

résiduel, -elle /Rezidɥɛl/ *adj* residual.

résignation /Rezinasjɔ̃/ *nf* resignation (**à** to).

résigner: se résigner /Rezine/ [1] *vpr* to resi oneself (**à qch** to sth; **à faire** to doing); **dans la vie, faut se ~** in life you have to learn to accept things.

résiliation /Reziljasjɔ̃/ *nf* (de contrat, bail) termin tion.

résilier /Rezilje/ [2] *vtr* to terminate [*contrat, bail*].

résine /Rezin/ *nf* resin.

résineux, -euse /Rezinø, øz/ **I** *adj* resinous.

II *nm* conifer.

résistance /Rezistɑ̃s/ *nf* **1** (opposition) resistance to); **faire de la ~** to resist; **opposer** or **offrir u ~ à** to put up resistance to; **2** (groupe de personne resistance; **la Résistance** HIST the Resistance; **3** (fait supporter physiquement) (de personne, microbe) resi ance (**à** to); (de plante) hardiness; **manquer de [***personne***]** to lack stamina; **4** (fait de supporter mora ment) resilience (**à** to); **5** PHYS (de matériau, d'appare strength; **~ à la corrosion** resistance to corrosio **~ au choc** shock-resistance; **~ de l'air** air ou wi resistance; **6** ÉLECTROTECH (propriété) résistanc (conducteur) resistance; (d'appareil ménager) element.

résistant, ~e /Rezistɑ̃, ɑ̃t/ **I** *adj* **1** [*person animal*] tough, resilient; [*plante*] hardy; **2** (solide) [*n tériau*] resistant; [*tissu, vêtement*] hard-wearing; **~ GÉN** resistant to; **~ à l'eau/la chaleur** waterpro heatproof.

II *nm,f* HIST Resistance fighter.

résister /Reziste/ [1] *vtr ind* **1** (s'opposer par la for **~ à** to resist [*agresseur, assaut, régime*]; **le voleu tenté de ~** the thief tried to resist arre

2 (supporter physiquement) ~ **à** [*personne, organe, animal*] to stand [*effort*]; [*matériau, bateau*] to withstand [*force, poussée*]; [*bâtiment, bois, objet*] to resist [*intempéries*]; **l'appareil ne résistera pas longtemps à un tel traitement** the machine won't last long if you treat it like that; **tissu qui résiste à des lavages fréquents** material that will stand frequent washing; **couleur qui résiste au soleil** colour^{GB} that won't fade in the sun; **le mur n'a pas résisté** the wall collapsed ou gave; **qui résiste à l'eau** waterproof; **qui résiste à la chaleur/rouille** heatproof/rustproof; **rien ne lui résiste, il casse tout** he breaks everything in sight, and I mean everything!; **3** (supporter moralement) ~ **à** to get through, to endure [*épreuve*]; **4** (être plus fort que) ~ **à** [*amour, amitié*] to withstand [*séparation*]; ~ **au temps** or **à l'épreuve du temps** to stand the test of time; **théorie qui ne résiste pas à l'analyse** theory that doesn't stand up to ou bear analysis, **5** (tenir tête) ~ **à** to resist [*personne, pression, charme, tentation*]; **il ne supporte pas qu'on lui résiste** he doesn't like it when people stand up to him.

résolu, ~e /ʀezɔly/ **I** pp ▶ **résoudre.**
II pp adj resolute, determined.

résolument /ʀezɔlymɑ̃/ adv [*opposé, favorable*] resolutely; [*confiant*] firmly; [*croire*] firmly.

résolution /ʀezɔlysjɔ̃/ nf **1** (décision) resolution; **prendre la ~ de faire** to make a resolution to do, to resolve to do; **2** POL (proposition retenue) resolution; **voter une ~** to pass a resolution; **3** (solution) resolution; **4** (fermeté) resolve; **5** MATH, MUS, MÉD, ORDINAT resolution.

résonance /ʀezɔnɑ̃s/ nf **1** GÉN, ÉLECTROTECH, PHYS, TÉLÉCOM resonance; **2** (de poème, musique) LITER echo.

résonner /ʀezɔne/ [1] vi **1** (faire du bruit) [*pas, rire, cloche*] to ring out; [*sonnerie*] to resound; [*cymbales*] to clash; **2** (renvoyer un bruit) [*salle*] to echo; ~ **de** to resound with.

résorber /ʀezɔʀbe/ [1] **I** vtr **1** FIG to absorb [*excédent, déficit*]; to reduce [*inflation, chômage*]; **2** MÉD to resorb.
II se résorber vpr **1** FIG [*excédent, déficit*] to be reduced; [*inflation, chômage*] to be coming down; **2** MÉD to be resorbed.

résorption /ʀezɔʀpsjɔ̃/ nf **1** MÉD resorption (**de** of); **2** FIG (de chômage, d'inflation) reduction (**de** of).

résoudre /ʀezudʀ/ [75] **I** vtr **1** (trouver la solution à) to solve [*équation, mystère, problème*]; to resolve [*crise, conflits*]; **ce n'est pas résolu** it's unresolved; **2** FML (décider) ~ **de faire** to resolve ou decide to do.
II se résoudre vpr **1** (se décider) **se ~ à faire** to resolve ou make up one's mind to do; **être résolu à faire** to be determined to do; **2** (se résigner) **je ne peux pas me ~ à la renvoyer** I can't bring myself to dismiss her.

respect /ʀɛspɛ/ **I** nm GÉN respect (**de, pour** for); **avoir peu/beaucoup de ~ pour** to have little/a lot of respect for; **avec tout le ~ qui lui est dû** with all the respect due to them; **malgré tout le ~ qu'on lui doit** with all due respect to him/her; **manquer de ~ à qn** to be disrespectful to ou toward(s) sb; **le ~ de soi** self-respect.
II respects nmpl respects; **présenter ses ~s à qn** to pay one's respects to sb.
IDIOMES **sauf votre ~** with all due respect; **tenir qn en ~** to keep sb at bay.

respectabilité /ʀɛspɛktabilite/ nf respectability.

respecter /ʀɛspɛkte/ [1] **I** vtr **1** (considérer avec respect) to respect [*personne, mémoire*]; **il s'est toujours fait ~ par ses élèves** he has always commanded the respect of his pupils; **2** (ne pas porter atteinte à) to respect, to have respect for [*opinion, action, nature, vie privée*]; to treat [sth] with respect [*objet, matériel*]; to respect [*promesse, loi, contrat*]; to honour^{GB} [*engagement*]; **en respectant l'ordre alphabétique** in alphabetical order; **faire ~ l'ordre** to enforce order; **respectez le sommeil des gens** remember people are sleeping.
II se respecter vpr to respect oneself; **tout homme qui se respecte** any self-respecting man.

respectif, -ive /ʀɛspɛktif, iv/ adj respective.

respectueusement /ʀɛspɛktɥøzmɑ̃/ adv respectfully.

respectueux, -euse /ʀɛspɛktɥø, øz/ adj respectful (**envers** to, toward(s)); **se montrer peu ~ de qch** to show little respect for sth; **des propos peu ~** some rather disrespectful remarks; ~ **de la loi** law-abiding; **salutations respectueuses** (dans une lettre) (à une personne non nommée) yours faithfully; (à une personne nommée) yours sincerely.

respirable /ʀɛspiʀabl/ adj **1** LIT [*air*] breathable; **2** FIG [*ambiance*] bearable.

respiration /ʀɛspiʀasjɔ̃/ nf (fonction) breathing; (souffle) breath; ~ **artificielle** artificial respiration; **avoir une ~ difficile** to have breathing difficulties; **retenir sa ~** to hold one's breath; **reprendre sa ~** to get one's breath back.

respiratoire /ʀɛspiʀatwaʀ/ adj respiratory.

respirer /ʀɛspiʀe/ [1] **I** vtr **1** (inhaler) to breathe in [*air, gaz, poussière*]; **2** (sentir) to smell [*parfum, odeur*]; **3** (exprimer) [*personne, endroit*] to exude; **il respire la santé** he's a picture of health.
II vi **1** LIT to breathe; **'respirez!'** 'breathe in!'; **'respirez bien fort'** 'take a deep breath'; ~ **avec difficulté** to have difficulty breathing; **2** FIG (se reposer) to catch one's breath; **laisse-moi ~** let me get my breath back; **3** (être soulagé) to breathe; **enfin je respire!** at last I can breathe again!

resplendir /ʀɛsplɑ̃diʀ/ [3] vi **1** (briller) [*lumière*] to shine brightly; [*neige*] to sparkle; [*surface métallique*] to gleam; **2** (rayonner) **la joie resplendissait sur son visage** his/her face was beaming with joy; ~ **de bonheur/santé** to be glowing with happiness/health.

resplendissant, ~e /ʀɛsplɑ̃disɑ̃, ɑ̃t/ adj **1** (brillant) [*soleil, lumière*] brilliant; [*neige*] sparkling; [*surface métallique*] gleaming; **2** (rayonnant) [*santé, beauté, mine*] radiant.

responsabiliser /ʀɛspɔ̃sabilize/ [1] vtr to give [sb] a sense of responsibility.

responsabilité /ʀɛspɔ̃sabilite/ nf GÉN responsibility (**de** for); (légalement) liability; **avoir sa part de ~ dans qch** to share some of the responsibility for sth; **il en porte l'entière ~** he bears full responsibility for it; **se renvoyer la ~** to blame each other; **avoir la ~ de qch** to be responsible for sth; **un poste à ~** a position of responsibility; **sous la ~ de qn** under the supervision of sb; **prendre ses ~s** to face up to one's responsibilities; **faute grave engageant la ~ de la société** serious mistake for which the company is liable.
■ ~ **civile** (assurance) personal liability.

responsable /ʀɛspɔ̃sabl/ **I** adj **1** (coupable) [*personne, défaillance, erreur*] responsible (*après n*) (**de qch** for sth); **l'alcool est ~ de nombreux accidents** alcohol is responsible ou is to blame for many accidents; **2** (devant répondre de ses actes) responsible, accountable (**de qch** for sth); (légalement) responsible, liable (**de qch** for sth); **3** (ayant la charge) **être ~ de qch/qn** to be responsible for sth/sb, to be in charge of sth/sb; **4** (raisonnable) [*personne, attitude, acte*] responsible; **un vote/rapport ~** a sensible vote/report.
II nmf **1** (personne en charge) GÉN person in charge; (gérant, directeur) manager; (chef de parti) leader; (chef de service) head; (administrateur) official; **des ~s de la police** senior police officers; **2** (personne coupable) **les ~s de la catastrophe** the people responsible ou to blame for the catastrophe; **3** (cause) **le grand ~ c'est le tabac/le manque d'amour** smoking/lack of love is the main cause.
■ ~ **de classe** SCOL form representative (*elected by the pupils*).

resquiller[○] /ʀɛskije/ [1] **I** vtr ~ **une place** to get in for free[○].
II vi (en train, métro) not to pay the fare; (au spectacle) to sneak in[○], to get in for free; (dans une queue) to queue-jump GB, to cut in line US.

resquilleur[○], **-euse** /ʀɛskijœʀ, øz/ nm,f **1** (en train, métro) fare dodger; **2** (dans une queue) queue-jumper GB, person who cuts in line US.

ressac /Rəsak/ *nm* backwash.

ressaisir /R(ə)sEziR/ [3] **I** *vtr* [*peur, rire, envie, passion*] to take hold of [sb] again [*personne*].

II se ressaisir *vpr* [*personne, candidat, sportif*] to pull oneself together; [*équipe sportive, marché*] to recover; **appeler l'opinion à se ~** to call on the public to come to their senses.

ressasser /R(ə)sase/ [1] *vtr* (ruminer) to brood over [*échec, pensées*]; to dwell on [*regrets, malheurs*]; (rabâcher) to keep trotting out○ [*griefs, conseils*] (**à qn** to sb); **théorie ressassée** hackneyed theory.

ressemblance /R(ə)sãblãs/ *nf* **1** (entre personnes) resemblance, likeness (**avec qn** to sb); **la ~ avec ton père est frappante** there's a striking resemblance between you and your father; **'toute ~ avec des personnes existant ou ayant existé...'** 'any similarity to persons living or dead...'; **2** (entre choses) similarity; **3** (de tableau, sculpture) likeness (**avec** to); **un portrait d'une grande ~** a portrait that is a very good likeness.

ressemblant, **-e** /R(ə)sãblã, ãt/ *adj* **un portrait ~/peu ~** a portrait which is a good likeness/isn't a very good likeness.

ressembler /R(ə)sãble/ [1] **I** **ressembler à** *vtr ind* **1** (en parlant de personnes) (physiquement) **~ à** to look like, to resemble [*personne, animal*]; (psychologiquement) **~ à** to be like [*personne*]; **tu as vu à quoi tu ressembles?** have you any idea what you look like?; **il ne ressemble pas à l'image que j'en avais** he's not how I imagined him; **cela ne te ressemble pas de perdre patience** it's not like you to get impatient; **2** (en parlant de choses) (par l'aspect) to look like; (par le contenu) to be like, to resemble; **~ fort à qch** to be very like sth; **cela ne ressemble à rien** (spectacle, robe) it's like nothing on earth; (n'avoir aucun sens) it makes no sense; **à quoi ça ressemble de dire cela**○? what a thing to say!

II se ressembler *vpr* **1** [*personnes*] (physiquement) to look alike; (psychologiquement) to be alike; **2** [*choses*] to be alike.

IDIOMES les jours se suivent et ne se ressemblent pas no two days are the same.

ressemeler /R(ə)səmle/ [19] *vtr* to resole.

ressentiment /R(ə)sãtimã/ *nm* resentment; **éprouver du ~** to feel resentful (**de** about).

ressentir /R(ə)sãtiR/ [30] **I** *vtr* to feel; **ressenti comme une urgence** felt to be an emergency.

II se ressentir *vpr* **se ~ de** [*personne, pays*] to feel the effects of, to suffer from; [*travail, performances, qualité*] to show the effects of, to suffer from; **la qualité s'en ressent** the quality is suffering.

resserrer /R(ə)seRe/ [1] **I** *vtr* **1** (serrer de nouveau) to tighten [*nœud, vis, étreinte*]; **2** (rendre plus étroit) to narrow [*route*]; to take [sth] in [*vêtement*]; to tighten [*pores*]; **3** (renforcer) to strengthen [*amitié, relation*]; **4** (faire regrouper) to make [sb/sth] draw closer; **resserrez les rangs!** close up a bit!; **5** (rendre plus sévère) to tighten up on [*discipline, surveillance*].

II se resserrer *vpr* **1** (devenir plus étroit) [*vallée*] to narrow; **2** (devenir plus fort) [*amitié*] to become stronger; **3** (devenir plus serré) [*lien, nœud*] to tighten; **4** (se refermer) [*troupes*] to close in; [*étreinte, piège*] to tighten; [*écart*] to close; **5** (se regrouper) [*personnes, cercle*] to draw closer together; **6** (devenir plus sévère) [*discipline*] to become stricter.

resservir /R(ə)seRviR/ [30] **I** *vtr* **1** (servir de nouveau) to serve [sth] (up) again; **~ qch à qn** to serve sb with sth again; **2** (à table) to give [sb] another helping; **3**○ (utiliser à nouveau) to trot○ [sth] out again [*thème*].

II *vi* [*objet, outil, vêtement*] to be used again; **cela peut toujours ~** it may come in handy again.

III se resservir *vpr* **1** (d'un plat) to take another helping; **se ~ du poulet** to help oneself to some more chicken; **2** (réutiliser) **se ~ de qch** to use sth again.

ressort /R(ə)sɔR/ *nm* **1** TECH spring; **un mécanisme à ~** a spring mechanism; **un matelas à ~** a sprung mattress; **2** (énergie) resilience; **avoir du/manquer de ~** to have/to lack resilience; **3** (force agissante) impulse; **les ~s psychologiques du personnage** the character's psychological motivation; **4** (compétence) **être du ~ de qn** to be within sb's province; **l'affaire est du ~ de la Cour européenne** the case falls within the jurisdiction of the European court; **en premier/dernier ~** in the first/last resort.

ressortir /R(ə)sɔRtiR/ [30] **I** *vtr* **1** (sortir à nouveau) to take [sth] out again, to get [sth] out again; **2** (ce qu'on ne sortait plus) to bring [sth] out again [*vieux vêtement*] (**de** from); to dig out○ [*affaire*] (**de** from); **3**○ (redire) **il nous ressort toujours les mêmes histoires** he's always coming out with the same stories; **4** (remettre sur le marché) to re-release [*disque, film*].

II *vi* **1** (sortir à nouveau) [*personne*] to go out again; **2** (après être entré) [*balle, tige*] to come out (**par** through); [*personne*] to come back out (**de** of); **3** (se distinguer nettement) to stand out; **cela ressort bien sur ce fond** it shows up very well against that background; **voici ce qui ressort de l'étude** the results of the study are as follows; **faire ~** to bring to light [*contradiction*]; [*maquillage*] to bring out [*yeux*]; to set [sth] off well [*tableau*]; **faire ~ que** [*étude, rapport*] to bring out the fact that; **4** (être remis sur le marché) [*film, disque*] to be re-released; [*revue*] to be back in circulation.

III *v impers* **il ressort que** it emerges that.

ressortissant, **~e** /R(ə)sɔRtisã, ãt/ *nm,f* national.

ressouder /R(ə)sude/ [1] **I** *vtr* to solder [sth] again [*joint*]; to solder [sth] together again [*pièces*].

II se ressouder *vpr* [*os*] to knit (together); [*fracture*] to mend.

ressource /R(ə)suRs/ *nf* **1** (richesse) resource; **les ~s énergétiques/forestières** energy/forest resources; **2** (option) option; **en dernière ~** as a last resort; **être à bout de ~** to be at one's wits' end; **3** (réserves) **avoir de la ~**○ to be resourceful; **puiser dans ses propres ~s** to fall back on one's inner resources; **4** (revenus) **~s** resources; **être sans ~s** to have no means of support; **5** (de lieu, technique) **~s** possibilities.

ressourcer: se ressourcer /R(ə)suRse/ [12] *vpr* to recharge one's batteries.

ressusciter /Resysite/ [1] **I** *vtr* **1** (exhumer du passé) to revive [*tradition, passé, auteur*]; to rekindle [*haine, amour*]; **2** RELIG to raise [sb] from the dead; FIG to bring [sb] back to life.

II *vi* **1** RELIG [*mort*] to rise from the dead; **2** (revenir à la vie) [*nature, ville*] to come back to life; [*passé, souvenir*] to come alive again.

restant, **~e** /REstã, ãt/ **I** *adj* remaining; **avec les 100 francs ~s** with the remaining 100 francs.

II *nm* **1** (ce qui est encore à venir) remainder; **mets-en trois ici et le ~ dans le jardin** put three here and the rest in the garden GB ou yard US; **passer le ~ de la journée à lire** to spend the rest of the day reading; **2** (ce qui subsiste) **un ~ de jambon** some left-over ham; **un ~ de clarté** a last glimmer of light.

restaurant /REstɔRã/ *nm* restaurant; **on mange** or **va souvent au ~** we often eat out.

■ **~ d'entreprise** staff canteen; **~ universitaire, RU** university canteen GB, cafeteria.

restaurateur, **-trice** /REstɔRatœR, tRis/ *nm,f* **1** (hôtelier) restaurant owner; (de restaurant gastronomique) restaurateur; **2 ▶ 374|** ART restorer.

restauration /REstɔRasjɔ̃/ *nf* **1** (hôtellerie) catering; **2** ART restoration; **3** (de monarchie, paix) restoration.

■ **~ rapide** fast-food industry.

restaurer /REstɔRe/ [1] **I** *vtr* **1** (nourrir) to feed; **2** to restore [*tableau, monarchie, paix*].

II se restaurer *vpr* to have something to eat.

reste /REst/ *nm* **1** (ce qui subsiste) **le ~** GÉN the rest (**de** of); MATH the remainder; **s'il y a un ~ de lait** if there is any milk left; **un ~ de tissu** some left-over material; **il a un ~ d'affection pour elle** he still feels a bit of affection for her; **2** (ce qui est encore à dire, faire etc) **le ~** the rest; **le loyer, les assurances et (tout) le ~**○ the rent, the insurance and everything else; **je te souhaite santé, bonheur et tout le ~** ○ I wish you health, happiness and all the rest; **au ~, du ~** besides.

II restes *nmpl* **1** (de fortune, bâtiment, d'armée) remains (**de** of); **2** (de repas) leftovers; **les ~s d'un gigot** the remains of a joint; **3** (cadavre) **les ~s de qn** the remains of sb.

IDIOMES **elle a encore de beaux ~s**○ HUM she's still well preserved; **sans demander** or **attendre son ~** without further ado; **être** or **demeurer en ~ avec qn** to feel indebted to sb; **pour ne pas être en ~** so as not to be outdone.

'ester /ʀɛste/ [1] (+ *v être*) **I** *vi* **1** (dans un lieu) to stay, to remain; **~ chez soi/en ville** to stay at home/in town; **les autres sont partis, mais elle est restée pour m'aider** the others left but she stayed behind to help me; **~ un moment à bavarder** to stay chatting for a while; **~ (à) dîner** to stay for dinner; **la clé est restée coincée dans la serrure** the key got stuck in the lock; **la bière est restée au soleil** the beer was left in the sun; **c'est resté dans ma mémoire** I still remember it; **cet enfant ne peut pas ~ en place!** the child can't keep still!; **que ça reste entre nous!** this is strictly between you and me!; **j'y suis, j'y reste** here I am and here I stay; **2** (dans une position, un état) to remain; **restez assis!** (par mesure de sécurité) remain seated!; (ne vous dérangez pas) don't get up!; **je suis resté debout pendant tout le voyage** I had to stand for the whole journey; **~ indécis** to remain undecided; **un auteur resté méconnu** an author who went unrecognized; **~ sans manger** to go without food; **elle est restée très naturelle** she's stayed very natural; **~ paralysé** to be left paralyzed; **~ veuve/orphelin** to be widowed/orphaned; **~ les bras croisés** FIG to stand idly by; **3** (subsister) to be left, to remain; **dis-moi ce qui reste à faire** tell me what there is left to do; **il reste 50 km à parcourir** there's still another 50 km to go; **4** (survivre) [*œuvre, souvenir*] to live on; **l'habitude lui en est restée** the habit stuck; **5** (s'arrêter) **~ sur une bonne impression** to be left with a good impression; **leur refus m'est resté sur le cœur** their refusal still rankles; **6** (ne pas aller au-delà de) **en ~ à** to go no further than; **l'affaire aurait pu en ~ là** the matter needn't have gone any further; **je compte bien ne pas en ~ là** I won't let the matter rest there; **nous en sommes restés aux préliminaires** we didn't get beyond the preliminaries; **restons-en là pour le moment** let's leave it at that for now.

II *v impers* **il reste encore quelques minutes** there are still a few minutes left; **il ne me reste plus que lui** he's all I've got left; **il me reste juste de quoi payer le loyer** I've just got enough left to pay the rent; **il me reste à peine le temps** I've barely got time; **il me reste beaucoup à faire** there's still a lot to do ou to be done; **il ne te reste plus qu'à t'excuser** it only remains for you to apologize; **reste à résoudre le problème du logement** the housing problem remains to be solved; **il reste que, il n'en reste pas moins que** the fact remains that.

IDIOMES **y ~**○ to meet one's end ou Maker.

restituer /ʀɛstitɥe/ [1] *vtr* **1** (rendre) to restore (**à qn** to sb); **2** (rétablir, recréer) to reconstruct [*texte*]; to restore [*fresque*]; to reproduce [*son, image*]; to recreate [*ambiance*].

restitution /ʀɛstitysjɔ̃/ *nf* **1** (action de rendre) (de bien, terre) return; (de droit, qualité) restoration; **2** (de son, d'image) reproduction.

restreindre /ʀɛstʀɛ̃dʀ/ [55] **I** *vtr* to curb [*dépenses*]; to limit [*possibilités, choix*]; to restrict [*champ d'action, subventions, nombre*].

II se restreindre *vpr* **1** (devenir plus petit) [*champ d'action, possibilités*] to become restricted; [*influence*] to wane; **2** (se limiter) **se ~ (dans ses dépenses)** to cut back (on one's expenses).

restreint, ~e /ʀɛstʀɛ̃, ɛ̃t/ *adj* [*public, vocabulaire*]

limited; [*équipe*] small; **être en nombre ~** to be few in number; **cela a été décidé en comité ~** it was decided by just a few people.

restrictif, -ive /ʀɛstʀiktif, iv/ *adj* restrictive.

restriction /ʀɛstʀiksjɔ̃/ *nf* **1** (limitation) restriction; **~s de crédit** credit restrictions; **~s salariales** wage restraints; **pendant les ~s** (de guerre) when there was rationing; **sans ~** [*voyager*] freely; [*commercialiser*] without restriction; **2** (réserve) qualification; **apporter une ~ à ce qui est dit** to qualify a statement; **sans ~** [*accepter, approuver*] without reservations; [*soutenir*] unreservedly.

restructuration /ʀəstʀyktyʀasjɔ̃/ *nf* restructuring; (en urbanisme) redevelopment.

restructurer /ʀəstʀyktyʀe/ [1] *vtr* to restructure [*service, organisation*]; to redevelop [*ville, quartier*].

résultat /ʀezylta/ **I** *nm* GÉN result; (de recherches) results (*pl*), findings (*pl*); (de négociations, d'enquête) result, outcome; **obtenir un ~** to get a result; **beau ~!** great work, well done!; **sans ~** without success; **avoir pour ~ de faire** to have the effect of doing.

II résultats *nmpl* **1** (chiffres) (d'examen, entreprise, de compétition) results (*pl*); SCOL, UNIV (d'élève, de mois) marks GB, grades US; **2** MÉD (d'analyse, examen) results.

résulter /ʀezylte/ [1] **I résulter de** *vtr ind* **~ de** to be the result of, to result from; **votre échec résulte d'un manque de travail** the reason for your failure is that you didn't do enough work; **la colère qui en résulte** the resulting anger.

II *v impers* **il résulte de ce que vous venez de dire que** it follows from what you have just said that; **il en résulte que** as a result; **qu'en résultera-t-il?** what will be the result of this?

résumé /ʀezyme/ *nm* **1** (version courte) summary, résumé; **faire le ~ de qch** to summarize sth; **en ~** (pour finir) to sum up; (en bref) in brief; **2** (exposé succinct) rundown; **faire un ~ de qch (à qn)** to give (sb) a rundown of ou on sth.

résumer /ʀezyme/ [1] **I** *vtr* **1** (raccourcir) to summarize [*texte, pensée*]; **2** (récapituler) to sum up [*nouvelle, match, état d'esprit*]; **cette anecdote résume le personnage** this anecdote sums up the character.

II se résumer *vpr* **1** [*personne*] to sum up; **2 se ~ à** to come down to.

résurgence /ʀezyʀʒɑ̃s/ *nf* **1** (de rivière) re-emergence; **2** (d'idéologie) resurgence; (de mode) revival.

resurgir /ʀ(ə)syʀʒiʀ/ [3] *vi* [*rivière*] to re-emerge; [*idéologie, problème, personne*] to reappear; [*souvenir*] to come back.

résurrection /ʀezyʀɛksjɔ̃/ *nf* **1** (de mort) resurrection; **2** (renaissance) (de cinéma, tradition) revival; (de personne) rebirth.

rétablir /ʀetabliʀ/ [3] **I** *vtr* **1** (ramener) to restore [*électricité, ordre, confiance, régime, impôt*]; **~ la situation** to restore normality; **~ la circulation** to get the traffic moving again; **2** (restituer) to re-establish [*vérité, faits*]; to restore [*texte*]; **3** (guérir) to restore [sb] to health [*malade*]; **4** (réintégrer) **~ qn dans ses fonctions** to reinstate sb in his/her job; **~ qn sur le trône** to restore sb to the throne.

II se rétablir *vpr* **1** LIT, FIG (s'améliorer) [*malade, monnaie, devise*] to recover; **2** (être restauré) [*ordre, silence*] to be restored; [*calme*] to return; [*situation*] to return to normal.

rétablissement /ʀetablismɑ̃/ *nm* **1** (de malade, monnaie) recovery; **2** SPORT pull-up; **faire un ~** to pull oneself up.

rétamer /ʀetame/ [1] **I** *vtr* **1** (réparer) to re-tin [*casseroles*]; **2**○ (épuiser) to wear [sb] out○; (battre) to hammer○.

II se rétamer○ *vpr* (tomber) to fall, to come a cropper○.

retape○ /ʀ(ə)tap/ *nf* (recrutement) **faire de la ~ pour qch** to beat the drum for sth.

retaper /ʀ(ə)tape/ [1] **I** *vtr* **1**○ (réparer) to do up [*maison, auto*]; **2**○ (rétablir) [*traitement*] to put [sb] on his/her feet again; **3** (arranger) to straighten [*lit*].

retard /R(ə)taR/ *nm* **1** (absence de ponctualité) lateness; (temps écoulé) delay; **vos ~s répétés** your continual lateness (*sg*); **trois ~s en une semaine c'est trop!** being late three times in a week is too much!; **un ~ de dix minutes** a ten-minute delay; **avoir du ~** to be late; **avoir un ~ d'une heure, avoir une heure de ~** (avant échéance) to be one hour behind schedule; (après échéance) to be one hour late; **arriver en ~** to arrive late; **être/se mettre en ~ dans son travail** to be/to fall behind with one's work; **être en ~ sur l'emploi du temps** to be behind schedule; **prendre du ~** to fall ou get behind (**dans** with); **rattraper** or **combler son ~** to catch up; **être en ~ pour faire qch** to be late doing sth; **il lui a souhaité son anniversaire en ~** he wished him/her a belated happy birthday; **avoir du courrier/travail en ~** to have a backlog of mail/work; **après bien des ~s** after a lot of delay; **sans ~** without delay, straight away; **2** (développement moins avancé) backwardness **¢**; **~ industriel** industrial backwardness; **il a deux ans de ~** SCOL he's two years behind at school; **être en ~ sur son temps** to be behind the times.

retardataire /R(ə)taRdatɛR/ **I** *adj* **1** (non ponctuel) **les élèves ~s** students who are late; **2** (qui date) outdated.

II *nmf* latecomer.

retardé, ~e /R(ə)taRde/ *adj* [*personne*] backward.

retardement: **à retardement** /aR(ə)taRdəmã/ **I** *loc adj* [*appareil photo, dispositif*] delayed-action (épith); **bombe à ~** time-bomb; **des applaudissements à ~** belated applause **¢**.

II *loc adv* [*se fâcher, agir*] after the event; **il comprend toujours à ~** he's slow on the uptake⁰.

retarder /R(ə)taRde/ [1] **I** *vtr* **1** (par rapport à une heure convenue) to make [sb] late; **être retardé** [*train, avion*] to be delayed; **2** (par rapport à un emploi du temps) to hold [sb] up; **il a été retardé par les embouteillages** he was held up by the traffic; **ça l'a retardé dans son travail** this held up his work; **3** (reporter) to put off, to postpone [*départ*]; **4** (reculer) to put back [*réveil*].

II *vi* **1** (être en retard) [*réveil*] to be slow; **ma montre retarde de cinq minutes par jour** my watch loses five minutes a day; **je retarde de cinq minutes** my watch is five minutes slow; **2** (être rétrograde) **~ sur son temps** or **son époque** to be behind the times; **3** (ne pas être au courant) to be out of touch.

retéléphoner /R(ə)telefone/ [1] *vi* to phone again.

retendre /R(ə)tãdR/ [6] *vtr* **1** (de nouveau) to tighten up (again) [*corde*]; **2** (davantage) to tighten up; **faire ~ les cordes** to have the strings tightened.

retenir /Rət(ə)niR, RtəniR/ [36] **I** *vtr* **1** (empêcher de partir) to keep [*personne*]; (retarder) to hold [sb] up, to detain [*personne*]; **il m'a retenu plus d'une heure avec ses bavardages** he kept me chatting for over an hour; **je ne vous retiens pas!** don't let me keep you!; **~ qn prisonnier** to hold sb captive ou prisoner; **~ qn à dîner** to ask sb to stay for dinner; **2** (maintenir fixe) LIT, FIG to hold [*objet, attention*]; (en arrière) to hold back [*cheveux, volet, chien, personne, foule*]; to retain [*sol*]; (empêcher une chute) to stop [*personne*]; to rein in [*cheval*]; **~ sa langue** to hold one's tongue; **si je ne l'avais pas retenu, il aurait tout avoué** if I hadn't held him back, he would have confessed everything; **retenez-moi ou je fais un malheur**⁰! hold me down or I'll go berserk⁰!; **~ qn par la manche** to catch hold of sb's sleeve; **votre réclamation a retenu toute notre attention** your complaint is receiving our full attention; **3** (réprimer) to hold back [*larmes*]; to hold [*souffle*]; to stifle [*cri, rire, soupir*]; to bite back [*exclamation*]; to suppress [*sourire*]; to contain [*colère*]; to check [*geste*]; **4** (capturer) to retain [*chaleur, eau, odeur*]; to absorb [*lumière*]; **5** (réserver) to reserve [*table, place*]; to set [*date*]; **6** (confisquer) to withhold [*caution, bagages*]; to stop [*salaire*]; (prélever) to deduct [*somme, impôt*] (**sur** from); **7** (mémoriser) to remember [*nom, date*]; **retiens-bien ceci** remember this; **cet enfant ne retient rien** that child doesn't take anything in; **je retiens qu'on peut leur faire confiance** I've learned that they can be trusted; **toi, je te retiens**⁰! I won't forget this!; **8** (agréer) to accep [*argument, proposition*]; JUR to uphold [*chef d'accusation*]; (considérer favorablement) **votre candidature a été retenue** you're being considered for the post; **êtr retenu comme critère** to be used as a criterion **9** MATH to carry (over); **je pose 5 et je retiens 1** I pu down 5 and carry 1.

II se retenir *vpr* **1** (se rattraper) to stop oneself; **s ~ à qch** to hang on to sth; **2** (réprimer une env psychique) to stop oneself; **je n'ai pas pu me ~ d pleurer** I couldn't hold back the tears; **il ne put se ~ de rire** he couldn't help laughing; **je me suis retenu de leur dire ce que je pensais** I refrained from tellin them what I thought; **j'ai dû me ~ pour ne pas l gifler** it was all I could do not to slap her; **3**⁰ (réprime un besoin physiologique) to control oneself.

rétention /Retãsjɔ̃/ *nf* **1** MÉD retention; **2** (refus d communiquer) withholding (**de** of).

retentir /R(ə)tãtiR/ [3] *vi* **1** (résonner) to ring out (plus fort) to resound; **~ aux oreilles de qn** to rin in sb's ears; **2** (affecter) **~ sur** [*fatigue, drogue, état*] to have an impact on; [*événement, situation*] to have repercussions on.

retentissant, ~e /R(ə)tãtisã, ãt/ *adj* **1** (éclatant [*déclaration, échec, succès*] resounding; [*procès, film, dé couverte, discours*] sensational; **2** (sonore) [*voix, bruit*] ringing; (plus fort) resounding.

retentissement /R(ə)tãtismã/ *nm* **1** (répercussions effect; (d'artiste, œuvre) impact; **2** (succès) sensation **avoir un (grand) ~** to cause a (great) sensation.

retenue /Rət(ə)ny/ *nf* **1** (modération) restraint **manquer de ~** to lack restraint; **perdre toute ~** t lose one's inhibitions; **n'avoir aucune ~ dans son langage** to use very immoderate language; **n'avoir aucune ~ dans sa conduite** to behave wildly; **sans ~** [*boire*] to excess; [*rire*] uproariously; **2** (prélève ment) deduction (**sur** from); **faire une ~ de 10% sur le salaire de qn** to deduct 10% from sb's salary **3** SCOL detention; **4** MATH **tu as oublié la ~ des dizaines** you forgot to carry over from the tens column; **5** (masse d'eau) reservoir; **ouvrage de ~** dam.

réticence /Retisãs/ *nf* **1** (répugnance) reluctance; **avec ~** reluctantly; **sans ~** [*parler*] openly; [*accepter*] unreservedly; **2** LITER (réserve) reticence **¢**; **ses ~s en ce qui concerne le passé** his/her reticence about the past; **3** (chose omise) non-disclosure, omission.

réticent, ~e /Retisã, ãt/ *adj* (qui hésite) hesitant (à faire about doing); (qui rechigne) reluctant (à faire to do); **se montrer/être ~ à une idée** to seem/to be hostile to an idea.

rétif, -ive /Retif, iv/ *adj* [*âne*] restive; [*personne, humeur*] rebellious.

rétine /Retin/ *nf* retina.

retiré, ~e /Rətire/ *adj* (solitaire) [*endroit, vie*] secluded; (éloigné) [*endroit*] remote.

retirer /Rətire/ [1] **I** *vtr* **1** (se débarrasser de) to take off [*vêtement, bijou*]; **2** (faire sortir) to take out, to remove (**de** from); **~ une balle d'une blessure** to remove ou extract a bullet from a wound; **~ les mains de ses poches** to take one's hands out of one's pockets; **~ un enfant d'une école** to take a child away from a school, to remove a child from a school; **~ qch de l'eau/des décombres** to pull sth out of the water/ from ou out of the rubble; **~ un gâteau d'un moule** to turn a cake out of a tin GB ou pan US; **~ ses troupes d'un pays** to withdraw one's troops from a country; **3** (écarter) to withdraw [*pied, main*]; **retire ta main, tu vas te brûler** move your hand away, you 'll burn yourself; **4** (supprimer, enlever) to withdraw [*permission*] (à from); to take away, to remove [*droit, bien, objet*] (à from); **~ un produit de la vente** COMM to recall a product; **~ la garde d'un enfant à qn** to withdraw custody of a child from sb; **on m'a retiré la garde de mon fils** I've lost custody of my son; **il s'est fait ~ son permis de conduire** he had his driver's licence^GB taken away from him; **~ de la**

irculation to withdraw [sth] from circulation
monnaie]; ~ **un livre du programme/de la table** to
ake a book off the syllabus/off the table; ~ **une
ièce de l'affiche** to close a play; **5** (ne pas maintenir)
o withdraw [*plainte, offre*]; ~ **sa candidature** (à un
oste) to withdraw one's application; (à une élection)
o stand down (**en faveur de** in favour^{GB} of); **je retire
e que j'ai dit** I take back what I said; **6** (rentrer en
ossession de) to collect, to pick up [*billet, bagages,
ossier*] ; to withdraw [*argent*]; **7** (recueillir) to get, to
erive [*bénéfice*] (**de** from); **il en retire 10 000 francs
ar an** he gets 10,000 francs a year out of it; **je n'en ai
etiré que des ennuis** I got nothing but trouble out of
: **8** (extraire) to extract [*minerai, huile*] (**de** from).
I se retirer *vpr* (partir) to withdraw, to leave; (aller
e coucher)† to retire to bed; **se ~ dans son
ureau** to withdraw to one's study; **se ~ sur ses
erres** to retire to one's estate; **se ~ du monde** to
vithdraw from society; **un homme retiré de la poli-
ique** a man retired from political life; **se ~ du
ombat** to pull out; **se ~ sur la pointe des pieds** to
iptoe out ou away; **se ~ sans bruit** to slip away
uietly; (reculer) [*eaux de crue*] to subside; [*personne*]
o step back; (pour laisser passer) to step aside; **la mer
e retire** the tide is going out.

tombée /rɔ̃tbe/ **I** *nf* ARCHIT springing.

retombées *nfpl* **1** (pluie) ~**s radioactives**
adioactive fallout *¢*; **2** (conséquences) effects (*pl*),
onsequences (*pl*); **3** (d'une invention) spin-offs (*pl*).

tomber /rɔ̃tbe/ [1] *vi* **1** (faire une nouvelle chute)
personne, objet] to fall again; ~ **malade/amoureux**
o fall ill/in love again; ~ **dans la misère/la facilité**
o sink back into poverty/a state of complacency; ~
n enfance to regress to childhood; **2** (retourner au sol
près s'être élevé) [*personne, chat, projectile*] to land;
allon, capot] to come down; [*brouillard*] to set in
gain; ~ **sur ses pattes** [*chat*] to land on its feet; ~
ur ses pieds ou **pattes** FIG to land on one's feet; **les
umées toxiques retombent en pluie acide** toxic
umes come down as acid rain; **ça va te ~ sur la
ez**$^\circ$ FIG it'll come down on your head; **3** (s'affaisser)
personne] to fall back; [*soufflé*] to collapse; FIG [*inté-
ết*] to wane; **4** (diminuer) [*monnaie*] to fall; [*tempéra-
ure*] to go down, to fall; **le dollar est retombé à 6
ancs** the dollar has fallen to 6 francs; **5** (incomber à)
~ **sur qn** [*responsabilité, ennui*] to fall on sb; **tu fais
es bêtises et c'est sur moi que ça retombe** you
ehave stupidly, and I'm the one who has to pay for it;
ire ~ la responsabilité sur qn to pass the buck$^\circ$
~ sb.

tordre /rɔ̃tɔrdr/ [6] *vtr* **donner du fil à ~ à** qn
give sb a hard time.

torquer /rɔ̃tɔrke/ [1] *vtr* (répliquer) to retort.

tors, ~e /rɔ̃tɔr, ɔrs/ *adj* PEJ [*personne*] crafty;
rgument] devious.

torsion /rɔ̃tɔrsjɔ̃/ *nf* retaliation; **mesure de ~**
etaliatory measure.

touche /rɔ̃tuʃ/ *nf* (de vêtement, texte) alteration;
e photo, tableau) retouch.

toucher /rɔ̃tuʃe/ [1] **I** *vtr* (modifier) to make
terations to [*vêtement, texte*]; to alter [*col, manches*];
touch up [*photographie*].

I retoucher à *vtr ind* **il a juré qu'il ne retoucherait
mais à l'alcool** he vowed that he would never touch
cohol again.

tour /rɔ̃tur/ *nm* **1** (trajet) return; (**billet de**) ~
turn ticket GB, round trip (ticket) US; **au ~** on the
ay back; **être sur le chemin du ~** to be on one's
ay back; **notre ~ s'est bien passé** we got back
ifely; **il pense déjà à son ~** he's already thinking
bout going back; **2** (au point de départ) return; **à mon
~** à Paris/de Paris on my return to Paris/from
aris; **être de ~** to be back; **de ~ à la maison**
ack home; **à son ~, elle m'a téléphoné** when she
ot back, she phoned me; **partir sans espoir de ~** to
ave for good; **3** (à un stade antérieur) return; ~ **à la
ormale** return to normal; **on attend le ~ au calme
ople** are waiting for things to calm down; ~ **à la
rre** going back to the land; '~ **à la case départ**'

'back to square one'; **il connaît maintenant le succès
et c'est un juste ~ des choses** he's successful now,
and deservedly so; **4** (réapparition) return; **le ~ de la
mode des années 60** the return of 60s fashions; **faire
un ~ en force** [*chanteur*] to make a big comeback;
[*idéologie*] to be back with a vengeance; [*cycliste,
coureur*] to make a strong comeback; **5** (échange) **elle
s'engage, en ~, à payer la facture** she undertakes
for her part to pay the bill; **aimer sans ~** LITER to
suffer from unrequited love; **6** COMM (objet invendu)
return; (de bouteille) return; '**sans ~ ni consigne**'
'no deposit or return'; **7** (renvoi) **par ~ du courrier**
by return of post GB, by the next mail US.
■ ~ **d'âge** change of life; ~ **en arrière** CIN, LITTÉRAT
flashback; **ce serait un ~ en arrière** (non souhaitable)
it would be a step backward(s); **un ~ en arrière
s'impose** (souhaitable) we must go back to the
previous state of affairs ; ~ **de balancier** ou **de
bâton**$^\circ$ ou **de manivelle**$^\circ$ backlash; ~ **de
marée** undertow.
IDIOMES **être sur le ~**$^\circ$ to be over the hill$^\circ$.

retournement /rɔ̃turnəmɑ̃/ *nm* (de situation)
reversal; **un ~ de l'opinion publique** a turn around
in public opinion.

retourner /rɔ̃turne/ [1] **I** *vtr* (+ *v avoir*) **1** (changer
de côté) to turn [sth] over [*seau, steak*]; to turn [*matelas*]; ~ **une carte à jouer** to turn over a playing
card; **2** (mettre à l'envers) to turn [sth] inside out [*vêtement, sac*]; **3** (tourner à plusieurs reprises) to turn over
[*terre*]; to toss [*salade, foin*]; ~ **une idée dans sa
tête** FIG to turn an idea over in one's mind; **4** (changer
d'orientation) to return [*compliment, critique*]; ~ **la
situation** to reverse the situation; **elle a retourné le
pistolet contre elle-même** she then turned the gun
on herself; **si tu retournes l'argument contre lui** if
you turn his own argument against him; **5** (bouleverser) [*personne*] to turn [sth] upside down
[*maison*]; [*nouvelle, spectacle*] to shake [*personne*]; **je
suis encore tout retourné**$^\circ$ I'm still quite shaken;
6 (renvoyer) to send [sth] back, to return [*colis, lettre*].
II *vi* (+ *v être*) to go back (**à** to), to return (**à** to).
III se retourner *vpr* **1** (tourner la tête) to turn
around; **partir sans se ~** LIT, FIG to leave without a
backward glance; **elle est tellement grande que
tout le monde se retourne sur son passage** she's so
tall that everybody turns to look as she goes past; **2** to
turn over; **se ~ sur le dos** to turn over onto one's
back; **il n'a pas arrêté de se ~** (dans son lit) he
kept tossing and turning; **la voiture s'est retournée
dans un fossé** the car overturned into a ditch;
3 (s'organiser) to get organized; **4** (prendre un tour inverse)
se ~ contre qn [*personne, animal*] to turn against
sb; [*situation, agissements*] to backfire on sb; **se ~
contre ses alliés** to turn on one's allies; **ses arguments se sont retournés contre lui** his arguments
backfired on him; **5** (se tordre) **elle s'est retourné le
doigt** she bent back her finger; **6** (repartir) **s'en ~** to
go back; **s'en ~ chez soi** to go back home.
IV *v impers* **j'aimerais savoir de quoi il retourne** I'd
like to know what's going on.
IDIOMES ~ **qn comme une crêpe**$^\circ$ ou **un gant**$^\circ$
to make sb change their mind completely.

retracer /rɔ̃trase/ [12] *vtr* **1** (marquer) to redraw;
2 (narrer) to recount.

rétractable /rɔ̃traktabl/ *adj* [*pointe*] retractable;
[*offre*] revocable.

rétracter /rɔ̃trakte/ [1] *vtr*, **se rétracter** *vpr* to
retract.

retrait /rɔ̃trɛ/ **I** *nm* **1** (de valise, commande, dossier)
collection; (d'argent) withdrawal; **2** (d'autorisation, de
soutien, monnaie) withdrawal (**de** of); COMM (d'article défectueux) recall (**de** of); **réclamer le ~ d'une
mesure** to call for a measure to be lifted; **après le ~
de la candidature du maire sortant** after the
outgoing mayor stood down; ~ **du permis (de
conduire)** disqualification from driving; **3** (départ)
withdrawal; **le ~ des eaux a révélé l'ampleur du
désastre** when the water went down ou subsided, the
scale of the disaster became apparent.

II en retrait *loc adv* (à l' écart) **maison (située) en ~ de** house set back from [*route*]; house a little way out of [*village*]; **se tenir en ~** LIT to stand back; FIG to occupy a back seat; **rester en ~** FIG to stay in the background.

retraite /R(ə)tRɛt/ *nf* **1** (cessation d'activité) retirement; **prendre sa ~** to retire; **mettre qn à la ~** to retire sb; **il a été mis à la ~ anticipée** he was made to take early retirement; **être en** or **à la ~** to be retired; **départ à la ~** retirement; **2** (pension) pension; **3** MIL retreat; **battre en ~** MIL to beat a retreat, to retreat; FIG to beat a hasty retreat; **4** RELIG retreat; **5** (lieu retiré) retreat; (de brigands) refuge.

retraité, ~e /Rətrete/ **I** *adj* [*personne*] retired.
II *nm,f* retired person; **les ~s** retired people (+ *v pl*).

retraiter /Rətrete/ [1] *vtr* to reprocess [*plutonium*].

retranché, ~e /R(ə)tRɑ̃ʃe/ *adj* [*village, cap, position*] entrenched.

retranchement /R(ə)tRɑ̃ʃmɑ̃/ *nm* entrenchment; **pousser qn dans ses derniers ~s** FIG to drive sb into a corner.

retrancher /R(ə)tRɑ̃ʃe/ [1] **I** *vtr* **1** (enlever) to cut out [*mot, phrase*] (**de** from); **2** (soustraire) to subtract, to take away [*montant*] (**de** from); to deduct [*frais*] (**de** from).
II se retrancher *vpr* **1** MIL (s'installer) to take up position; (pour être à l'abri) to entrench oneself; **être retranché dans un village** [*soldats*] to have taken up position in a village; **2** (se cacher) **se ~ derrière** to hide behind [*idéologie, loi*]; **il se retranche derrière le directeur** he says it's a matter for the manager; **se ~ dans** to take refuge in [*silence, rêve*].

retransmettre /RətRɑ̃smɛtr/ [60] *vtr* **1** RADIO, TV to broadcast [*émission*]; **2** (par relais) to relay; **3** TÉLÉCOM, RADIO to retransmit [*appel*].

retransmission /RətRɑ̃smisjɔ̃/ *nf* **1** (d'émission) broadcast; **2** (relais) relay; **assurer la ~ d'un signal** to relay a signal; **3** (de message, d'appel) retransmission.

retravailler /Rətravaje/ [1] **I** *vtr* to revise [*œuvre*].
II *vi* to start working again; (après des vacances, une maladie) to go back to work.

rétrécir /RetResiR/ [3] **I** *vtr* **1** [*lavage*] to shrink; **2** [*couturier*] to take in (**de** by); **3** to make [sth] narrower [*route, bague, orifice*]; to make [sth] smaller [*terrain, parc*].
II *vi* [*tissu*] to shrink (**de** by).
III se rétrécir *vpr* **1** [*route, champ d'investigation*] to narrow; [*groupe*] to shrink; **2** ANAT [*pupille*] to contract; **3** [*pensée*] to become more restricted.

rétrécissement /RetResismɑ̃/ *nm* **1** (après lavage) shrinkage; **2** (de route, vallée) narrowing; **3** (de pupille) contraction; (d'intestin) stricture.

rétribuer /RetRibɥe/ [1] *vtr* to remunerate [*personne, travail*].

rétribution /RetRibysjɔ̃/ *nf* **1** (paiement) remuneration; **2** (récompense) reward (**de** for).

rétro /RetRo/ *nm* **1** ARCHIT, ART (style) nostalgic style; **2** (mode) retro fashions (*pl*).

rétroactif, -ive /Retroaktif, iv/ *adj* ADMIN, JUR retroactive; [*augmentation*] backdated.

rétroaction /Retroaksjɔ̃/ *nf* **1** ADMIN, JUR retroactive effect; **2** BIOL, PHYS feedback.

rétroactivité /Retroaktivite/ *nf* ADMIN, JUR retroactivity; (de jugement) ex post facto effect.

rétrograde /RetRogRad/ *adj* **1** (réactionnaire) [*personne, gouvernement*] reactionary; [*loi, pensée*] retrograde; **2** (qui va en sens inverse) [*mouvement*] retrograde.

rétrograder /RetRogRade/ [1] **I** *vtr* **1** MIL, ADMIN to demote [*militaire, fonctionnaire*] (**à** to); **2** SPORT to relegate [*sportif, cheval*].
II *vi* AUT to change down GB, to downshift US.

rétrospectif, -ive¹ /RetRospɛktif, iv/ *adj* retrospective.

rétrospective² /RetRospɛktiv/ *nf* ART retrospectiv CIN festival.

rétrospectivement /RetRospɛktivmɑ̃/ *adv* **1** (apr coup) [*avoir peur*] after the event; **2** (après réflexio in retrospect.

retroussé, ~e /R(ə)tRuse/ *adj* [*nez*] turned u [*lèvre*] curling (*épith*).

retrousser /R(ə)tRuse/ [1] *vtr* to hitch up GB, to hi up US [*robe*]; to roll up [*pantalon*]; **~ ses manche** LIT, FIG to roll up one's sleeves; **le chien retroussa s babines** the dog bared its teeth.

retrouvailles /RətRuvaj/ *nfpl* (après une séparatio reunion (**avec** with); (après une brouille) reconcili tion (**avec** with).

retrouver /RətRuve/ [1] **I** *vtr* **1** (ce qui était perdu) find [*sac, cadavre, fugitif*]; **~ son chemin** to fir one's way; **2** (trouver à nouveau) to find [sth] again [*tr vail, objet*]; to come across [sth] again [*thème*]; **3** (red couvrir) to rediscover [*technique, recette*]; **4** (recouvre to get [sth] back [*assurance*]; to regain, to recove [*force, santé*]; **~ son sang-froid** to regain one composure; **il a retrouvé le sourire** he's smilin again; **~ le sommeil** to be able to sleep again; **5** (s rappeler) to remember [*nom, air*]; **6** (revoir) to me [sb] again [*connaissance*]; (regagner) to be back i [*lieu*]; **7** (reconnaître) to recognize [*personne, trai style*]; **je retrouve sa mère en elle** I can see he mother in her; **on le retrouve dans cette œuvre** yo can see his hand in this work; **quand tu souris, je t retrouve** that's more like you to be smiling; **8** (re joindre) to join, to meet [*personne*]; **je te retrouverai** (menace) I'll get my own back on you!
II se retrouver *vpr* **1** (se réunir) to meet; (se voir d nouveau) to meet again; **on se retrouvera devant l cinéma** let's meet (up) outside the cinema; **de temp en temps on se retrouve entre amis** we get togethe with a few friends once in a while; **on s'est retrouv en famille** the family got together; **2** (être) to fin oneself; **se ~ enceinte** to find oneself pregnant; **s ~ orphelin/sans argent/seul** to be left an orphan penniless/on one's own; **se ~ confronté à** to b faced with; **se ~ à l'hôpital** to end up in hospital; **s ~ au même point** to be back to square one **3** (s'orienter) **se** or **s'y ~ dans** LIT to find one's wa around in [*lieu, fouillis*]; FIG to follow [*explication*]; **t t'y retrouves entre tous ces emplois/amants?** ca you cope with all these jobs/lovers?; **il y a trop d changements, on ne s'y retrouve plus** there are to many changes, we don't know if we're coming o going; **4°** (rentrer dans ses frais) **s'y ~** to break even (faire un bénéfice) to do well; **5** (être présent) [*personn qualité*] to be found; [*problème*] to occur; **le mêm amour de la musique se retrouve chez les deu enfants** both children have the same love of music; **6** (se reconnaître) **se ~ dans qn/qch** to see ou recogniz oneself in sb/sth.
IDIOMES **un de perdu, dix de retrouvés** there ar plenty more fish in the sea.

rétroviseur /Retrovizœr/ *nm* **1** (intérieur) rear-view mirror; **2** (extérieur) wing mirror GB, outside rear-view mirror US.

réuni, ~e /Reyni/ *adj* **1** (mis ensemble) [*forces qualités, salaires*] combined; **2** (assemblé) [*conseil, per sonnes*] assembled; **3** (remis ensemble) reunited; **les deux Berlin ~s** (a) reunited Berlin; **4** COMM (asso ciés) associated.

réunification /Reynifikasjɔ̃/ *nf* reunification.
réunifier /Reynifje/ [2] **I** *vtr* to reunify.
II se réunifier *vpr* to be reunified, to reunite

réunion /Reynjɔ̃/ *nf* **1** (séance) meeting (**entre** between); **être en ~** [*personne*] to be at ou in a meet ing; [*comité*] to be meeting; **2** (rencontre) gathering; **~ familiale** family gathering; **3** (retrouvailles) (après une séparation) reunion; (après une brouille) reconcilia tion; **4** (groupement) (de talents, volontés) combination; (d'œuvres) collection; **5** (rattachement) union (**à** with); (après séparation) reunification; (de sociétés) merger.

Réunion /Reynjɔ̃/ **▶ 305** *nprf* **la ~** Reunion.

réunir /ʀeyniʀ/ [3] **I** vtr **1** (assembler) [congrès] to bring together [participants]; [organisateur] to get [sb] together [participants]; **2** (convoquer) to call [sb] together [délégués]; to convene [assemblée]; **3** (inviter) to have [sb] round GB ou over [amis]; **4** (rapprocher) to join [bords]; to bring [sb] together [personnes]; (après une brouille, une séparation) to reunite; **5** (fusionner) to merge [sociétés]; to unite [provinces] (à with); **6** (cumuler) ~ **les qualités nécessaires** to have all the necessary qualifications; **7** (recueillir) to raise [fonds]; to collect [preuves, articles]; **8** (regrouper) to assemble [éléments, preuves]; to gather [sth] together [documents]; **9** (relier) [route, canal] to connect [lieux].

II se réunir vpr **1** (s'assembler) [délégués, comité] to meet; [amis] to get together; **2** (se joindre) [routes, fleuves] to meet; **3** (s'associer) [sociétés] to merge; [nations] to unite.

réussi, **~e** /ʀeysi/ adj **1** (mené à bien) [opération] successful; **2** (apprécié) [soirée] successful; **3** (bien fait) [œuvre] accomplished; [photo] good.

réussir /ʀeysiʀ/ [3] **I** vtr to achieve [unification, modernisation]; to carry off [sth] successfully [coup politique]; to carry out [sth] successfully [fabrication, opération]; to make a success of [vie, éducation]; to win [pari]; to pass [examen]; **l'impossible** to manage the impossible; ~ **son coup**○ to pull it off○.

II réussir à vtr ind **1** (parvenir à) ~ **à faire** to succeed in doing, to manage to do; ~ **à ne pas tomber** to manage not to fall; ~ **à un examen** to pass an exam; **2** (être favorable à) ~ **à qn** [vie, méthode] to turn out well for sb; [aliment, repos] to do sb good; **le vin blanc ne me réussit pas** white wine doesn't agree with me.

III vi **1** (atteindre le but recherché) to succeed; **ça n'a pas réussi** it didn't work, it didn't come off; **2** (être couronné de succès) [opération chirurgicale, tentative] to be successful; **3** (obtenir un bon résultat) [personne] to do well (**en, dans** in).

réussite /ʀeysit/ nf **1** GÉN success (**dans** in); ~ **sociale** social success; ~ **scolaire** success at school; ~ **à un examen** success in an examination; **2** JEUX patience ¢ GB, solitaire ¢ US.

revaloir /ʀ(ə)valwaʀ/ [45] vtr **je te revaudrai ça** (hostile) I'll get even with you for that; (reconnaissant) I'll return the favour GB.

revalorisation /ʀ(ə)valɔʀizasjɔ̃/ nf **1** (augmentation) **une ~ des salaires de 3%** a 3% wage increase; **2** (retour de l'estime) **la ~ des enseignants** the enhanced prestige of teachers; **3** (amélioration) improvement (**de** in), enhancement (**de** of).

revaloriser /ʀ(ə)valɔʀize/ [1] vtr **1** (augmenter) to increase, to raise [salaire]; to revalue [monnaie]; **2** (rendre l'estime envers) to reassert the value of [travail manuel, traditions]; **3** (remettre en état) to renovate [bâtiment].

revanche /ʀ(ə)vɑ̃ʃ/ **I** nf **1** revenge; **désir de/esprit de ~** desire for/spirit of revenge; **avoir sa ~** to get one's revenge; **2** SPORT return match GB ou game US; JEUX return game.

II en revanche loc adv on the other hand.

IDIOMES à charge de ~ provided you'll let me return the favour GB.

rêvasser /ʀɛvase/ [1] vi to daydream.

rêve /ʀɛv/ nm **1** (de dormeur) (activité) dreaming; (résultat) dream; **faire un ~** to have a dream; **fais de beaux ~s!** sweet dreams!; **j'ai l'impression de vivre un ~** I feel as if I'm dreaming; **en ~** in a dream; **2** (fantasme) dream; **~ de jeunesse** youthful dream; **avoir des ~s de grandeur** to dream of greatness; **une maison de ~** a dream house; **3** (idéal) **c'est le ~** this is just perfect; **ce n'est pas le ~** it's not ideal.

■ **~ éveillé** daydream.

rêvé, **~e** /ʀeve/ adj ideal, perfect.

revêche /ʀəvɛʃ/ adj [air, ton] sour; [personne] crabby.

réveil /ʀevɛj/ nm **1** (après un somme) waking (up); **au ~/dès son ~** when he wakes up/as soon as he wakes up; **2** (après un malaise, une anesthésie) **j'ai eu**

des nausées au ~ I felt nauseous when I came to; **3** (de la nature, d'un sentiment) reawakening; (de nation, mouvement) resurgence; (de la foi) revival; (de douleurs) return, recurrence; (de la conscience) awakening; (de volcan) return to activity; **le ~ des minorités** the new activism of minorities; **4** (retour à la réalité) awakening; **5** MIL reveille; ~ **en fanfare** FIG rousing start to the day; **6** (pendule) alarm clock.

réveille-matin /ʀevɛjmatɛ̃/ nm inv alarm clock.

réveiller /ʀeveje/ [1] **I** vtr **1** (tirer du sommeil, de rêverie, d'hypnose) to wake [sb] up, to wake; **être réveillé en sursaut** to wake up with a start; **être réveillé par l'orage** to be woken by the storm; **faire un bruit à ~ les morts**○ to make enough noise to wake the dead; **2** (ranimer) to revive [malade]; to bring some sensation back into [membre ankylosé]; to whet [appétit]; to awaken [sentiment]; to arouse [crainte, curiosité, polémique]; to bring out [instinct]; to awaken, to stir up [souvenir]; ~ **la douleur** to bring back the pain.

II se réveiller vpr **1** (après un somme) to wake up; (après une rêverie, une hypnose) to awaken (**de** from); **se ~ en sursaut/en sueur** to wake up with a start/in a sweat; **2** (après une anesthésie, un malaise) [personne] to come round GB, to regain consciousness; **3** (après une période d'inertie) [personne, peuple] to wake up; [nature] to reawaken; [volcan] to become active again; **4** (se raviver) [douleur, appétit] to come back; [jalousie, souvenir] to be reawakened.

réveillon /ʀevɛjɔ̃/ nm ~ **de Noël/du Nouvel An** (fête) Christmas Eve/New Year's Eve party.

réveillonner /ʀevɛjɔne/ [1] vi (pour le Nouvel An) to see the New Year in.

révélateur, **-trice** /ʀevelatœʀ, tʀis/ **I** adj [détail, fait] revealing, telling.

II nm **1** PHOT developer; **2** (fait, détail) pointer (**de** to).

révélation /ʀevelasjɔ̃/ nf **1** (découverte, aveu) revelation; **2** (œuvre, auteur) discovery; **3** PHOT development.

révéler /ʀevele/ [14] **I** vtr **1** (dévoiler) to reveal, to disclose [fait, chiffres, nom] (**à** to); to give away [secret] (**à** to); **2** (indiquer) to show; **3** (faire connaître) [œuvre] to make [sb] known [auteur, acteur] (**à** to); [éditeur, imprésario] to discover, to launch [auteur, artiste]; **cela l'a révélée à elle-même** it gave her a great deal of personal insight; **4** PHOT to develop.

II se révéler vpr (être finalement) **se ~ faux** to turn out to be wrong; **se ~ comme un grand pianiste** to emerge as a great pianist.

revenant, **~e** /ʀəv(ə)nɑ̃, ɑ̃t/ nm,f ghost; **tiens, une ~e**○! HUM long time no see○!

revendeur, **-euse** /ʀ(ə)vɑ̃dœʀ, øz/ **▶ 374** nm,f **1** (détaillant) stockist; **un ~ de drogue** a drug dealer; **2** (d'objets volés) seller (of stolen goods).

revendicatif, **-ive** /ʀ(ə)vɑ̃dikatif, iv/ adj [action] protest (épith); [dossier] of demands; **journée revendicative** day of protest.

revendication /ʀ(ə)vɑ̃dikasjɔ̃/ nf (d'ouvrier, de catégorie sociale) demand; (de pays, population, d'héritier) claim (**sur, de** to).

revendiquer /ʀ(ə)vɑ̃dike/ [1] vtr **1** (réclamer) to demand [droit, augmentation]; to claim [héritage, trône, territoire]; **2** (s'affirmer l'auteur de) to claim responsibility for [attentat]; to claim authorship of [livre]; ~ **la paternité d'un enfant** to claim paternity of a child; ~ **la responsabilité de** to take (full) responsibility for; **3** (affirmer avoir) to claim; **4** (être fier de) to proclaim [origines].

revendre /ʀ(ə)vɑ̃dʀ/ [6] **I** vtr **1** (vendre au détail) to sell [sth] retail, to retail (**à** to); **2** (vendre ce qui est à soi) to sell [objet, maison] (**à** to); to sell (off) [actions, parts, or]; (vendre des objets volés) to sell on; **avoir des crayons à ~** FIG to have pencils galore; **avoir de l'énergie à ~** FIG to have energy to spare.

II se revendre vpr (se vendre d'occasion) to resell.

revenez-y /ʀəvnezi, ʀvənezi/ nm inv **le gâteau a un petit goût de ~** the cake is rather moreish○ GB, the cake is so good I'd like seconds.

revenir /ʀəvniʀ, ʀvəniʀ/ [36] **I** vi (+ v être) **1** (fréquenter de nouveau) to come back; (venir une fois encore) to come again; **2** (rentrer) [*personne, animal, véhicule*] to come back (**à** to; **de** from), to return (**à** to; **de** from); **~ sur terre** FIG to come down to earth; **partir pour ne jamais ~** to leave never to return; **~ de loin** LIT to come back from far away; FIG to have had a close shave; **en revenant du bureau** (en route) coming home from the office; (à l'arrivée) on getting home from the office; **je reviens tout de suite** I'll be back in a minute, I'll be right back○; **il en est revenu vivant** he got back in one piece; **elle est revenue en vitesse à la maison** she rushed back home; **mon chèque m'est revenu** my cheque GB ou check US was returned; **3** (reprendre, retourner à) **~ à** to return to, to come back to [*méthode, conception, histoire*]; **revenons à notre héros** let's return to our hero; **~ à la normale/au pouvoir** to return to normal/to power; **le dollar est revenu à 5 francs** the dollar has gone back to 5 francs; **~ à la politique** to come back into politics; **~ à ses habitudes/aux frontières d'avant la guerre** to revert to one's old habits/to pre-war borders; **pour (en) ~ à ce que je disais** to get back to what I was saying; **~ à de meilleurs sentiments** to return to a better frame of mind; **4** (réapparaître) [*tache, rhume, mode*] to come back; [*soleil*] to come out again; [*saison*] to return; [*date, fête*] to come round again GB, to come again US; [*idée, thème*] to recur; **cette idée me revenait souvent** the idea kept occurring to me; **le mot revient souvent sous sa plume** the word keeps cropping up in his/her writing; **le calme est revenu** calm has been restored, things have calmed down; **5** (être recouvré) [*appétit, mémoire*] to come back; **l'appétit me revient** I'm getting my appetite back; **6** (être remémoré) **~ à qn, ~ à la mémoire** or **l'esprit de qn** to come back to sb; **ça me revient!** now I remember!, now it's coming back!; **7** (coûter) **~ à 100 francs** to cost 100 francs, to cost 100 francs; **ça m'est revenu à 100 francs** it cost me 100 francs; **ça revient cher** it works out expensive; **8** (équivaloir à) **ça revient au même** it amounts ou comes to the same thing; **ce qui revient à dire que** which amounts to saying that; **9** (reconsidérer) **~ sur** to go back over [*question, passé*]; (changer d'avis) to go back on [*décision, promesse*]; to retract [*aveu*]; **10** (sortir d'un état) **~ de** to get over [*maladie, surprise*]; to lose [*illusion*]; to abandon [*théorie*]; **la vie à la campagne, j'en suis revenu** as for life in the country, I've seen it for what it is; **être revenu de tout** to be blasé; **je n'en reviens pas**○! I can't get over it!; **11** (être rapporté) **~ à qn, ~ aux oreilles de qn** [*propos*] to get back to sb, to reach sb's ears; **12** (être attribué) **~ à qn** [*bien, titre*] to go to sb; [*honneur*] to fall to sb; (de droit) to be due to sb; **ce poste pourrait revenir à un écologiste** this post could go to an ecologist; **ça leur revient de droit** it's theirs by right; **les 10% qui me reviennent** the 10% that's coming to me; **la décision revient au rédacteur** it is the editor's decision; **13** CULIN **faire ~** to brown.

II s'en revenir vpr LITER to return (**de** from).

III v impers **1** (incomber) **c'est à vous qu'il revient de trancher** it is for you to decide; **2** (parvenir à la connaissance de) **il m'est revenu certains propos** certain remarks have reached my ears; **3** (être remémoré) **il me revient que** I recall ou remember that.

IDIOMS **~ à soi** to come round GB, to come to; **~ à la vie** to come back to life; **il a une tête qui ne me revient pas** I don't like the look of him.

revenu /Rǝv(ǝ)ny, Rvǝny/ nm (de personne) income; (de l'État) revenue ⊄.

■ **~ minimum d'insertion, RMI** minimum benefit paid to those with no other source of income.

rêver /Reve/ [1] **I** vtr **1** (en dormant) to dream (**que** that); **2** (imaginer) to dream of [*succès, vengeance*].

II vi **1** [*dormeur*] to dream (**de** about); **~ tout éveillé** to be lost in a daydream; **on croit ~!** you'd think you were dreaming!; **2** (se faire des illusions) to dream; **3** (rêvasser, aspirer à) to dream.

réverbération /ReveRbeRasjɔ̃/ nf (de lumière) glare; (de chaleur) reflection; (de son) reverberation.

réverbère /ReveRbeR/ nm (lampadaire) street lamp.

réverbérer /ReveRbeRe/ [14] **I** vtr [*surface*] to reflect [*lumière, chaleur*]; to make [sth] reverberate [*son*].

II se réverbérer vpr [*lumière, chaleur*] to be reflected; [*son*] to reverberate.

révérence /ReveRɑ̃s/ nf **1** (salut) (de femme) curtsey; (d'homme) bow; **faire la ~** [*femme*] to curtsey (**à** to); [*homme*] to bow (**à** to); **2** (respect) LITER reverence; **traiter qn avec ~** to treat sb respectfully.

IDIOMS **tirer sa ~**○ to take one's leave (**à qn** of sb).

révérencieux, -ieuse /ReveRɑ̃sjø, øz/ adj LITER deferential (**envers** to); **attitude peu révérencieuse** irreverent attitude.

révérend, -e /ReveRɑ̃, ɑ̃d/ **I** adj reverend.

II ▶596 nm,f **1** (dans un couvent) Father/Mother Superior; **2** (pasteur) reverend.

révérer /ReveRe/ [14] vtr to revere.

rêverie /REvRi/ nf **1** (activité) daydreaming, reverie; **se laisser aller à la ~** to drift off into a dream; **2** (rêve éveillé) daydream.

revérifier /R(ǝ)veRifje/ [2] vtr to double-check.

revers /R(ǝ)vER/ nm inv **1** (dos) (de feuille) back, reverse; (de tissu) wrong side; (de médaille) reverse; **d'un ~ de la main** with the back of one's hand; **le ~ de la médaille** FIG the downside○; **2** (repli) (de veste) lapel; (de pantalon) turn-up GB, cuff US; (de manche) cuff; **3** (au tennis) backhand (stroke); **faire un ~** to play a backhand (stroke); **4** FIG (échec) setback, reversal.

■ **~ de fortune** reversal of fortune.

IDIOMS **toute médaille a son ~** PROV there is no rose without a thorn.

reverser /R(ǝ)vERse/ [1] vtr **1** FIN to transfer [*somme*] (**à** to); **2** (une autre fois) **~ à boire à qn** to pour sb another drink.

réversibilité /ReveRsibilite/ nf GÉN reversibility; JUR reversion.

réversible /ReveRsibl/ adj GÉN reversible; JUR reversionary.

revêtement /R(ǝ)vɛtmɑ̃/ nm **1** (de route, terrain de sport) surface; **~ routier** road surface; **2** (peinture, crépi, ciment) coating; (en vinyl, plastique) covering; **3** (surface protectrice) skin.

revêtir /R(ǝ)vetiR/ [33] **I** vtr **1** (avoir) to have [*caractère, intérêt*]; to assume [*gravité, solennité*]; to take on [*aspect, signification*]; to hold [*importance*]; to entail [*inconvénient*]; **~ la forme de** to take the form of; **2** (mettre) to put on [*vêtement*]; **3** (recouvrir) **~ qch de** to cover sth with [*moquette*].

II se revêtir vpr **se ~ de** (se vêtir) to put on; (se recouvrir) to become covered with [*neige*].

rêveur, -euse /REvœR, øz/ **I** adj [*air, personne*] dreamy; **cela laisse ~** it makes you wonder.

II nm,f dreamer.

revient /R(ǝ)vjɛ̃/ nm **prix de ~** cost price; **calculer** or **établir le prix de ~ de qch** to do the costing for sth.

revigorer /R(ǝ)vigɔRe/ [1] vtr **1** (physiquement) [*boisson*] to perk [sb] up, to revive; [*douche, air*] to revive; **2** (moralement) to hearten.

revirement /R(ǝ)viRmɑ̃/ nm (de situation, politique, d'opinion) turnaround (**de** in); **~ total** U-turn GB, flip-flop US.

réviser /Revize/ [1] vtr **1** (réexaminer) to revise [*position, contrat, tarifs*]; to review [*procès, Constitution*]; to redraw [*frontières*]; **~ qch à la hausse** to revise sth upward(s); **2** (vérifier) to service, to overhaul [*machine, auto*]; to revise [*manuscrit*]; to audit [*comptes*]; **3** SCOL, UNIV to revise GB, to review US.

réviseur /RevizœR/ ▶374 nm (dans l'édition) proofreader.

révision /Revizjɔ̃/ nf **1** (de position, tarifs) revision; (de procès) review; (de frontière) redrawing; **2** (de machine, voiture, chaudière) service; (de manuscrit) revision; (de comptes) audit; **3** SCOL, UNIV revision ⊄ GB, review ⊄ US.

révisionniste /Revizjɔnist/ adj, nmf revisionist.

revitaliser /R(ə)vitalize/ [1] *vtr* to revitalize.

revivifier /R(ə)vivifje/ [2] *vtr* LITER to revive [*sentiment*]; to revivify [*personne*].

revivre /R(ə)vivR/ [63] I *vtr* **1** (se remémorer) to go over, to relive [*événement, passé*]; **faire ~ qch à qn** to bring back memories of sth to sb; **2** (connaître à nouveau) to live through [sth] again [*guerre*].

II *vi* **1** (être ragaillardi) to come alive again; **2** (être soulagé) to be able to breathe again; **3** (renaître) [*idée, tradition*] to be reborn ou revived; **faire ~** to revive [*tradition*]; **4** (être ressuscité) to live again (**dans , à travers** in); **faire ~** FIG to bring [sth] back to life [*événement*].

révocation /Revɔkasjɔ̃/ *nf* (de testament, d'édit) revocation; (de personne) dismissal.

revoici○ /R(ə)vwasi/ *prép* **te ~!** so you're back!; **nous ~ au point de départ** we are back to ou at square one.

revoilà /R(ə)vwala/ = **revoici**.

revoir[1] /R(ə)vwaR/ [46] I *vtr* **1** (voir de nouveau) to see [sb/sth]; **il ne l'avait pas revu depuis 10 ans** he hadn't seen him for 10 years; **2** (en pensée) to see; **je la revois encore dans sa robe bleue** I can still see her in her blue dress; **3** (réexaminer) to go over [*devoir, épreuve*]; to review [*méthode, action*]; to check through [*compte*]; **'à ~'** 'go over again'; **4** (corriger) to correct; **5** (réviser) SCOL to revise GB, to review [*matière*]; to go over [*leçon*].

II se revoir *vpr* **1** (l'un l'autre) [*amis*] to see each other again; **2** (soi-même) **je me revois encore enfant** I can still see myself as a child.

revoir[2]: **au revoir** /ɔR(ə)vwaR/ *loc nom* goodbye, bye○; **au ~ Monsieur/Madame** goodbye; **faire au ~ de la main** to wave goodbye.

révolte /Revɔlt/ *nf* **1** (soulèvement) revolt; **la ~ gronde** there are murmurings of revolt; **2** (indignation, désobéissance) rebellion.

révolté, ~e /Revɔlte/ I *adj* **1** (qui s'est soulevé) rebel (*épith*); **2** (qui refuse d'obéir) rebellious; **3** (indigné) appalled.

II *nm,f* rebel.

révolter /Revɔlte/ [1] I *vtr* to appal GB.

II se révolter *vpr* **1** (se soulever, refuser d'obéir) to rebel; **2** (s'indigner) to be appalled (**contre, devant** by).

révolu, ~e /Revɔly/ *adj* **1** (passé) **ce temps est ~** those days are over ou past; **2** (achevé) **avoir 12 ans ~s** to be over 12 years of age; **après une année ~e** after a year has gone by.

révolution /Revɔlysjɔ̃/ *nf* **1** (changement radical) revolution; **faire ~ dans** to revolutionize; **2** (effervescence) turmoil; **être en ~** to be in turmoil; **3** (de planète) revolution; **4** MATH rotation.

révolutionnaire /RevɔlysjɔnɛR/ *adj, nmf* revolutionary.

révolutionner /Revɔlysjɔne/ [1] *vtr* **1** (transformer) to revolutionize [*sciences*] (**par** with); **2**○ (mettre en émoi) to upset; **3** (soulever) to revolutionize [*pays*].

revolver /RevɔlvɛR/ *nm* (à barillet) revolver; (arme de poing) handgun; **coup de ~** gunshot; **abattre qn à coups de ~** to shoot sb, to gun sb down.

révoquer /Revɔke/ [1] *vtr* **1** to revoke [*testament*]; **2** to dismiss [*personne*].

revue /R(ə)vy/ *nf* **1** (magazine) GÉN magazine; (spécialisé) journal; **2** MIL (parade) parade; (inspection) review; **passer en ~** to review [*troupes*]; to inspect [*équipement*]; **3** (spectacle) revue; **4** (examen) examination; **se livrer à une ~ minutieuse de ses papiers** to go through one's papers in minute detail; **passer qch en ~** to go over sth, to have a look at sth. ▪ ~ **de presse** TV, RADIO review of the papers. IDIOMES **être de la ~**○ to miss out○.

révulser /Revylse/ [1] I *vtr* (indigner) to appal GB.

II se révulser *vpr* [*yeux*] to roll (upward(s)); [*visage*] to contort.

rez-de-chaussée /Redʃose/ *nm inv* (niveau) ground floor GB, first floor US (**de** of); **au ~** on the ground GB ou first US floor.

RF (*written abbr* = **République française**) French Republic.

RFA /ɛRɛfa/ *nprf* (*abbr* = **République fédérale d'Allemagne**) HIST Federal Republic of Germany, FRG.

rhabiller: se rhabiller /Rabije/ [1] *vpr* to get dressed again. IDIOMES **il peut aller se ~**○! he can go back where he came from!

rhapsodie /Rapsɔdi/ *nf* rhapsody.

rhénan, ~e /Renɑ̃, an/ ▶509 *adj* of the Rhineland.

Rhénanie /Renani/ ▶509 *nprf* Rhineland.

rhésus /Rezys/ *nm inv* **1** BIOL **facteur ~** rhesus factor; **~ positif** rhesus positive; **2** (macaque) ~ rhesus monkey.

rhétorique /Retɔrik/ I *adj* [*procédé, effet*] rhetorical.

II *nf* rhetoric (**de** of).

Rhin /Rɛ̃/ ▶260 *nprm* **le ~** the Rhine.

rhinocéros /RinɔseRɔs/ *nm inv* rhinoceros.

rhino-pharyngite, *pl* **~s** /Rinofaʀɛ̃ʒit/ *nf* nasopharyngitis.

rhodanien, -ienne /Rɔdanjɛ̃, ɛn/ *adj* [*vallée, couloir*] Rhône (*épith*); [*capitale, club*] of the Rhône.

rhododendron /Rɔdɔdɛ̃dRɔ̃/ *nm* rhododendron.

rhubarbe /RybaRb/ *nf* rhubarb; **confiture de ~** rhubarb jam.

rhum /Rɔm/ *nm* rum.

rhumatismal, ~e, *mpl* **-aux** /Rymatismal, o/ *adj* rheumatic.

rhumatisme /Rymatism/ ▶196 *nm* rheumatism ¢.

rhumatologie /Rymatɔlɔʒi/ *nf* rheumatology.

rhume /Rym/ ▶196 *nm* cold; **un gros ~** a bad cold. ▪ ~ **de cerveau** head cold; **~ des foins** hay fever.

riant, ~e /Rijɑ̃, ɑ̃t/ *adj* [*visage*] happy; [*paysage*] pleasant.

ribambelle○ /Ribɑ̃bɛl/ *nf* (d'enfants) flock (**de** of); (d'amis) host (**de** of); (de noms) whole string (**de** of); (de procès) series (**de** of).

ricain, ~e○ /Rikɛ̃, ɛn/ OFFENSIVE *or* HUM I *adj* Yankee○.

II *nm,f* Yank○.

ricanement /Rikanmɑ̃/ *nm* (rire moqueur) snigger; (rire sot) giggle; **des ~s** (de moquerie) sniggering ¢; (de sottise) giggling ¢.

ricaner /Rikane/ [1] *vi* (méchamment) to snigger; (bêtement) to giggle.

richard, ~e○ /Riʃaʀ, aʀd/ *nm,f* PEJ well-heeled○ person.

Richard /Riʃaʀ/ *npr* Richard. ▪ ~ **Cœur de Lion** Richard the Lionheart GB, Richard the Lion-hearted US.

riche /Riʃ/ I *adj* **1** [*personne*] rich, wealthy, well-off; [*pays, ville*] rich; **à millions** extremely rich; **2** [*faune, collection, vocabulaire*] rich; [*bibliothèque*] well-stocked; **3** [*minerai, langue, aliment*] rich (**en** in); [*décor*] elaborate, rich; **4** [*bijoux, habit*] fine; [*étoffe*] rich; [*demeure*] sumptuous; [*cadeau*] magnificent; **une ~ idée** an excellent idea; **aliment ~ en fibres** food that is high ou rich in fibre GB; **un pays ~ en uranium** a uranium-rich country; **~ de promesses** full of promise.

II *nmf* rich man/woman; **les ~s** the rich (+ *v pl*) , the wealthy (+ *v pl*). IDIOMES **on ne prête qu'aux ~s** PROV unto those that have shall more be given.

richement /Riʃmɑ̃/ *adv* [*meublé, vêtu, décoré, illustré*] richly, lavishly; [*doté* [*fille*] provided with a large dowry; [*tombola*] with big prizes.

richesse /Riʃɛs/ I *nf* **1** (de personne, pays) wealth; **notre principale ~** our main source of wealth; **faire la ~ de** to bring wealth to; **c'est toute notre ~** it's all we have; **2** (de bijoux) magnificence; (d'étoffe, de

vêtement) richness; (de mobilier, demeure) sumptuousness;
décoration d'une trop grande ~ over-elaborate
decoration; **3** (teneur) richness (**en** in); **4** (de faune,
vocabulaire, collection) richness; (de documentation)
wealth.

II richesses *nfpl* **1** (biens matériels) wealth ¢; **2**
(objets de grande valeur) treasures; **les ~s d'un
musée** the treasures of a museum; **3** (ressources)
resources; **~s naturelles** natural resources.

richissime○ /ʀiʃisim/ *adj* fabulously rich ou
wealthy.

ricin /ʀisɛ̃/ *nf* castor-oil plant; **huile de ~** castor oil.

ricocher /ʀikɔʃe/ [1] *vi* [*balle*] to ricochet (**sur** off);
[*pierre*] (sur l'eau) to skim (**sur** on ou across); (sur un
obstacle) to rebound (**sur** off).

ricochet /ʀikɔʃɛ/ *nm* (de balle) ricochet; (de pierre)
(sur l'eau) bounce; (sur un obstacle) rebound; **faire des
~s** to skim stones (**sur** on ou across); **cela l'a
touché par ~** (projectile) he was hit on the rebound;
(chômage) he was indirectly affected.

ric-rac○ /ʀikʀak/ *loc adv* **1** (de justesse) by the skin
of one's teeth; **2** (rigoureusement) [*payer*] on the dot.

rictus /ʀiktys/ *nm inv* (fixed) grin, rictus.

ride /ʀid/ *nf* (de visage, fruit) wrinkle; (de lac) ripple;
ne pas avoir pris une ~ [*visage*] not to have aged;
[*œuvre*] not to have dated.

rideau, *pl* **~x** /ʀido/ *nm* **1** (dans une maison)
curtain; (voilage) net curtain; **doubles ~x** curtains;
2 THÉÂT curtain; **3** (de magasin, bâtiment) (plein) roller
shutter; (grille) security grille; **4** (d'arbres, de brouillard)
curtain; (de flammes) wall.
■ **~ de fer** HIST Iron Curtain; **~ de fumée** LIT
blanket of smoke; FIG smokescreen.
IDIOMES **tirer le ~ sur qch** to draw a veil over sth;
~! THÉÂT curtain!; FIG (let's) drop it!; **grimper aux
~x**○ to go up the wall○.

rider /ʀide/ [1] **I** *vtr* **1** to wrinkle [*peau*]; **2** to ripple
[*surface, lac*].

II se rider *vpr* **1** [*peau*] to wrinkle; **2** [*lac*] to ripple.

ridicule /ʀidikyl/ **I** *adj* **1** (grotesque, insensé) ridiculous; **2** (insignifiant) [*somme, salaire*] ridiculously low,
pathetic.

II *nm* **1** (le grotesque) **le ~** ridicule; **tourner qn en
~** to make sb look ridiculous; **2** (de situation) ridiculousness, absurdity; **il est d'un ~!** he looks so ridiculous!
IDIOMES **le ~ ne tue pas** PROV looking a fool never
killed anyone.

ridiculement /ʀidikylmɑ̃/ *adv* ridiculously.

ridiculiser /ʀidikylize/ [1] **I** *vtr* [*personne*] to ridicule
[*personne, théorie, propos*] (**auprès de** in front of); to
wipe the floor with [*équipe, concurrent*]; [*comportement, situation*] to make [sb] look ridiculous [*personne*].

II se ridiculiser *vpr* [*personne*] to make a fool of
oneself.

rien[1] /ʀjɛ̃/ **I** *pron indéf* **1** (nulle chose) **~ n'est
impossible** nothing is impossible; **un mois à ne ~
faire** a month doing nothing; **il n'y a ~ qui puisse la
consoler** nothing can console her; **il n'y a plus ~**
there's nothing left; **ce n'est ~** it's nothing; **elle
n'est ~** she's a nobody; **il n'est ~ pour moi** he
means ou is nothing to me; **il n'en est ~** it's nothing
of the sort; **elle ne t'a ~ fait** she hasn't done
anything to you; **~ n'y fait!** nothing's any good!; **il
n'a ~ d'un intrigant** there's nothing of the schemer
about him; **elle n'a ~ de sa sœur** she's nothing like
her sister; **~ de bon** nothing good; **~ d'autre**
nothing else; **il n'y a ~ eu de cassé** nothing was
broken; **~ à déclarer** nothing to declare; **partir de
~** to start from nothing; **pour ~** (en vain) for
nothing; (à bas prix) for next to nothing; **'pourquoi?'—'pour ~'** 'why?'—'no reason'; **parler pour
~** to waste one's breath; **'merci'—'de ~'** 'thank
you'—'you're welcome' ou 'not at all'; **en moins de ~**
in no time at all; **'que prends-tu?'—'~ du tout'**
'what are you having?'—'nothing at all'; **ça ou ~,
c'est pareil** it makes no odds; **c'est trois fois ~**○

it's next to nothing; **~ de ~**○ absolutely nothing;
faire qch comme ~ to do sth very easily; **2** (seulement) **~ que la bouteille pèse deux kilos** the bottle
alone weighs two kilos; **elle voudrait un bureau ~
qu'à elle**○ she would like an office all to herself; **la
vérité, ~ que la vérité** the truth and nothing but the
truth; **~ que pour te plaire** just to please you; **~
que ça**○**?** (en réponse) is that all?; **ils habitent un
château, ~ que ça!** IRON they live in a castle, no less!
ou if you please!; **3** (quoi que ce soit) anything; **avant
de ~ signer** before signing anything; **sans que j'en
sache** without my knowing anything about it;
4 SPORT GÉN nil; (au tennis) love.

II de rien (du tout) *loc adj* **fille de ~** worthless
girl; **un petit bleu de ~ (du tout)** a tiny bruise;
une affaire de ~ du tout a trivial matter.

III○ **un rien** *loc adv* a (tiny) bit; **un ~ pédant** a
bit pedantic.

IV en rien *loc adv* at all, in any way.

IDIOMES **~ à faire!** (c'est impossible) it's no good ou
use!; (refus) no way○!; **on n'a ~ pour ~** you get
nothing for nothing; **ce n'est pas ~!** (exploit) it's
quite something!; (tâche) it's no joke, it's not exactly a
picnic○!; (somme) it's not exactly peanuts○!

rien[2] /ʀjɛ̃/ *nm* **1** (vétille) **un ~ le fâche** the slightest
thing annoys him; **se disputer pour un ~** to quarrel
over nothing; **perdre son temps à des ~s** to waste
one's time on trivial things; **les petits ~s qui
rendent la vie agréable** the little things which make
life pleasant; **faire qch comme un ~**○ to do sth
very easily; **2** (petite quantité) **un ~ de** a touch of;
un ~ de cognac a dash of brandy; **en un ~ de
temps** in next to no time; **3**○ (personne) **un/une ~
du tout** (insignifiant) a nobody; (sans moralité) a no-
good○, a worthless person.

rieur, rieuse /ʀijœʀ, øz/ *adj* [*personne*] cheerful;
[*visage, yeux*] laughing; [*ton*] cheerful.
IDIOMES **mettre les ~s de son côté** to win the audience over.

rififi○ /ʀififi/ *nm* fight.

rigide /ʀiʒid/ *adj* **1** [*personne, règlement*] rigid; **2** [*matériau, support*] rigid; [*carton*] stiff.

rigidité /ʀiʒidite/ *nf* rigidity.

rigolade○ /ʀigɔlad/ *nf* **1** (amusement) **quelle ~!**
what a laugh○!, what fun!; **ça a été une partie de
(franche) ~** it was a really good laugh○; **prendre
qch à la ~** to make a joke of sth; **le moment n'est
pas à la ~** this is no time for laughter ou for fun and
games; **2** (plaisanterie) joke; **la conférence a été une
vaste ~** the conference was one big joke; **3** (chose
facile) **réparer ça, c'est de la ~!** repairing this is a
piece of cake○ ou is dead easy○.

rigole /ʀigɔl/ *nf* (conduit) channel; (écoulement) rivulet.

rigoler○ /ʀigɔle/ [1] *vi* **1** (rire) to laugh; **on a bien
rigolé** we had a good laugh; **2** (s'amuser) to have fun;
ça ne rigole pas tous les jours ici it's not much fun
here; **3** (plaisanter) to joke, to kid○; **il ne faut pas ~
avec la sécurité** you mustn't mess about ou fool
around with security; **il a dit ça pour ~** he said it as
a joke.

rigolo○, **-ote** /ʀigɔlo, ɔt/ **I** *adj* funny.

II *nm,f* **1** (fumiste) joker; **2** (personne amusante) **c'est
un petit ~** he's quite a little comedian.

rigoureusement /ʀiguʀøzmɑ̃/ *adv* [*vrai, inexact*]
completely; [*défendu, conforme*] strictly; [*punir, traiter*] harshly; [*obéir*] scrupulously; [*sélectionner,
mesurer*] carefully.

rigoureux, -euse /ʀiguʀø, øz/ *adj* **1** [*morale, discipline*] strict, rigorous; [*règlement, personne, application*] strict; **2** [*climat, hiver, conditions de travail*]
harsh, severe; [*froid*] severe; **3** [*observations, recherches, démonstration*] meticulous; [*analyse, gestion,
pensée, argumentation*] rigorous.

rigueur /ʀigœʀ/ **I** *nf* **1** (de sanction, loi, personne)
strictness; (de répression) harshness; **2** (de climat, condition) harshness; **3** (d'observation, de recherche, style, démonstration) rigour[GB]; **une analyse d'une grande ~**

a very rigorous analysis; **leur travail manque de ~** their work is not rigorous enough; **4** POL, ÉCON austerity; **plan de ~** austerity measures (pl).

II rigueurs nfpl (de saison, climat) LITER rigours^{GB}.

III de rigueur loc adj obligatory; **les gants blancs sont de ~** white gloves must be worn; **la prudence reste de ~ au ministère** caution is the order of the day at the ministry; **visite de ~** obligatory social call.

IV à la rigueur loc adv **nous pouvons à la ~ emprunter à mes parents** if we absolutely have to we can borrow from my parents; **à la ~ je peux te prêter 100 francs** at a pinch GB ou in a pinch US I can lend you 100 francs; **je peux venir trois jours ou cinq à la ~** I can come for three days or five at the very outside; **il est un peu excentrique à la ~, mais fou certainement pas** he may be a bit eccentric, but he's certainly not mad.

IDIOMES **tenir ~ à qn de qch** to bear sb a grudge for sth; **il ne t'en tiendra pas ~** he won't hold it against you.

rillettes /ʀijɛt/ nfpl ~ potted meat ¢.

rime /ʀim/ nf rhyme (**en** in).

rimer /ʀime/ [1] vi **1** (former une rime) to rhyme; **2** (signifier) **cela ne rime à rien** it makes no sense.

rimmel® /ʀimɛl/ nm mascara.

rinçage /ʀɛ̃saʒ/ nm (processus) rinsing; (de lave-linge, lave-vaisselle) rinse.

rince-doigts /ʀɛ̃sdwa/ nm inv **1** (récipient) finger bowl; **2** (en papier) finger wipe.

rincée⁰ /ʀɛ̃se/ nf **prendre une ~** (pluie) to get drenched; (coups) to get a thrashing⁰.

rincer /ʀɛ̃se/ [12] **I** vtr (ôter le savon) to rinse; (laver) to rinse [sth] out.

II se rincer vpr **se ~ les mains** to rinse one's hands; **se ~ la bouche** to rinse one's mouth out.

IDIOMES **se ~ l'œil**⁰ to get an eyeful.

ringard, ~e /ʀɛ̃gaʀ, aʀd/ **I**⁰ adj [vêtement] dated; [politique] out of date; [personne] behind the times (jamais épith).

II nm,f (individu démodé) PEJ, GÉN fuddy-duddy⁰ PÉJ; (artiste, politicien) has-been⁰ PÉJ.

ripaille⁰ /ʀipaj/ nf blow-out⁰, feast.

riper /ʀipe/ [1] vi [pied] to slip; [bicyclette] to skid.

riposte /ʀipɔst/ nf **1** (verbale) reply, riposte; **prompt à la ~** always ready with a reply; **2** (physique) response (à to); **3** SPORT (en escrime) riposte; (en lutte, boxe) counter.

riposter /ʀipɔste/ [1] **I** vtr to retort (**que** that).

II vi **1** (verbalement) to retort; **~ à qn/qch par** to counter sb/sth with; **2** (par des coups) to respond (**à** to; **par** with); **en faisant** by doing); **3** MIL to return fire, to shoot back; **~ à qch par qch** to counter sth with sth; **4** (en sport) to riposte.

riquiqui⁰ /ʀikiki/ adj inv [vêtement] ridiculously small; [logement] poky⁰.

rire¹ /ʀiʀ/ [68] **I** vi **1** (s'esclaffer) to laugh; **se mettre à ~** to burst out laughing; **tu nous feras toujours ~!** you're a real scream⁰!; **il n'y a pas de quoi ~!** that's not funny!, that's no laughing matter!; **il vaut mieux en ~ (qu'en pleurer)** you might as well laugh as cry; **on a ri un bon coup**⁰ we had a good laugh; **2** (s'amuser) to have fun; **il faut bien ~ un peu** you need a bit of fun now and again; **fini de ~** the fun's over; **tu veux ~!** you must be joking ou kidding⁰!; **j'ai fait ça pour ~** I was joking; **c'était pour ~** it was a joke; **sans ~**⁰ seriously, honestly; **laisse-moi ~**⁰, **ne me fais pas ~**⁰ don't make me laugh; **3** (se moquer) **~ de qch/qn** to laugh at sth/sb; **4** (avoir une expression gaie) LITER **elle a les yeux qui rient, ses yeux rient** she has laughing eyes.

II se rire vpr **se ~ de qn** FML to laugh at sb; **se ~ des difficultés** FML to make light of difficulties.

IDIOMES **rira bien qui rira le dernier** PROV he who laughs last laughs longest PROV; **être mort** ou **écroulé de ~**⁰ to be doubled up (with laughter).

rire² /ʀiʀ/ nm laughter; **un ~** a laugh; **avoir un ~**

forcé to give a forced laugh; **avoir le ~ facile** to laugh at the slightest thing; **il y eut des ~s dans le public** there was laughter in the audience; **il a eu un petit ~** he chuckled; **il éclata d'un gros ~** (bref) he let out a guffaw; (qui dure) he gave a hearty laugh.

■ **~s préenregistrés** RADIO, TV canned laughter ¢.

ris /ʀi/ nm inv **1** CULIN **~ (de veau)** calf's sweetbread; **2** NAUT reef.

risée /ʀize/ nf **1** (sujet de moquerie) **être la ~ de** to be the laughing stock of; **2** (vent) gust (of wind).

risette⁰ /ʀizɛt/ nf smile; **fais ~!** give me a smile!

risible /ʀizibl/ adj ridiculous, laughable.

risque /ʀisk/ nm risk (**de** of; **à faire** in doing); **comporter** or **présenter un ~** [processus] to carry a risk; [décision, action] to involve some risk; **c'est sans ~** it's safe; **au ~ de faire** at the risk of doing; **à ~s** [personne, prêt] high-risk (épith).

■ **les ~s du métier** occupational hazards.

risqué, ~e /ʀiske/ adj **1** (aléatoire) [entreprise, comportement] risky; [investissement] high-risk; **2** (osé) [plaisanterie] risqué; [hypothèse] daring.

risquer /ʀiske/ [1] **I** vtr **1** (être passible de) to face [condamnation]; **~ gros** to face a heavy sentence; **2** (s'exposer à) to risk [mort, critique]; **vas-y, tu ne risques rien** go ahead, you're safe; FIG go ahead, you've got nothing to lose; **qu'est-ce qu'on risque?** LIT what are the risks?; FIG what have we got to lose?; **~ gros** to take a major risk; **tu risques qu'on t'abîme ta voiture** you run the risk of having your car damaged; **3** (mettre en danger) to risk [vie, réputation, emploi]; **~ sa peau**⁰ to risk one's neck⁰; **4** (oser) to venture [regard, allusion, question]; to risk [geste]; to attempt [démarche, opération]; **~ un œil** to venture a glance; **~ le coup**⁰ to risk it, to chance it.

II risquer de vtr ind **1** (pouvoir) **tu risques de te brûler** you might burn yourself; **elle risque fort d'être déçue** she may well be disappointed; **ça ne risque pas de m'arriver!** there's no chance of that happening to me!; **2** (prendre le risque) **il ne veut pas ~ de perdre son travail** he doesn't want to risk losing his job.

III se risquer vpr **1** (s'aventurer) to venture (**à faire** to do); **je m'y risquerais pas!** I wouldn't risk it; **2** (oser) **se ~ à dire** to dare to say.

IV v impers **il risque de pleuvoir** it might rain; **il risque d'y avoir du monde** there may well be a lot of people there.

IDIOMES **qui ne risque rien n'a rien** nothing ventured, nothing gained; **~ le tout pour le tout** to stake no risk one's all.

risque-tout /ʀiskətu/ adj inv daredevil.

rissoler /ʀisɔle/ [1] vtr, vi CULIN to brown.

ristourne /ʀistuʀn/ nf discount, rebate.

rite /ʀit/ nm LIT, FIG rite.

ritournelle /ʀituʀnɛl/ nf **1** MUS ritornello; **2**⁰ FIG harping on.

rituel, -elle /ʀitɥɛl/ adj, nm ritual.

rivage /ʀivaʒ/ nm shore.

rival, ~e, mpl **-aux** /ʀival, o/ adj, nm,f rival.

rivaliser /ʀivalize/ [1] vi **~ avec** to compete with [personne]; **~ avec qch** to rival sth; **~ d'adresse/ d'esprit avec qn** to vie with sb in skill/wit.

rivalité /ʀivalite/ nf rivalry (**entre** between; **avec** with).

rive /ʀiv/ nf **1** (de fleuve) bank; **2** (de mer, lac) shore.

river /ʀive/ [1] vtr to clinch [clou]; to rivet [plaques de tôle]; to fasten [prisonnier] (**à** to); **être rivé à qch** FIG to be tied to [travail]; to be glued to [télévision]; **avoir les yeux rivés sur** to have one's eyes riveted on.

IDIOMES **~ son clou à qn**⁰ to leave sb speechless.

riverain, ~e /ʀivʀɛ̃, ɛn/ **I** adj **1** (de voie) [maison, propriété] bordering the street ou road; **2** (de cours d'eau) riverside (épith); **3** (de lac) lakeside (épith).

II nm,f **1** (habitant) (de rue) resident; (de cours d'eau) riverside resident; (de bord de lac) lakeside resident; **2** (propriétaire) riparian.

rivet /ʀivɛ/ nm rivet.

rivière /ʀivjɛʀ/ nf **1** (cours d'eau) river; **2** (en équitation) water jump.
■ ~ **de diamants** diamond necklace.
IDIOMES **les petits ruisseaux font les grandes ~s** PROV great oaks from little acorns grow PROV.

rixe /ʀiks/ nf brawl (**entre** between).

riz /ʀi/ nm rice.

rizière /ʀizjɛʀ/ nf paddy field.

RMI /ɛʀɛmi/ nm: abbr ▶ **revenu**.

RMIste /ɛʀɛmist/ nmf person receiving minimum benefit payment.

RN /ɛʀɛn/ nf (abbr = **route nationale**) ≈ A road GB, highway US.

robe /ʀɔb/ nf **1** (de femme) dress; **2** (d'avocat) gown; (de prêtre) robe; (de moine) frock; **la ~ the** Robe; **3** (couleur) (de cheval) coat; (de vin) colour^GB.
■ ~ **de bal** ball gown; ~ **de bure** habit; ~ **bustier** (boned) strapless dress; ~ **de chambre** dressing gown, robe US; ~ **chasuble** pinafore dress, jumper US; ~ **de grossesse** maternity dress ou smock; ~ **d'intérieur** housecoat; ~ **de mariée** wedding dress ou gown; ~ **du soir** evening dress ou gown.

Robin /ʀɔbɛ̃/ npr Robin.
■ ~ **des bois** Robin Hood.

robinet /ʀɔbinɛ/ nm (d'eau) tap GB, faucet US; (de gaz) tap GB, valve US.

robinetterie /ʀɔbinɛtʀi/ nf (dispositif) plumbing fixtures (pl).

robinier /ʀɔbinje/ nm locust tree, false acacia.

robot /ʀɔbo/ nm robot.
■ ~ **ménager** food processor.

robotique /ʀɔbɔtik/ nf robotics (+ v sg).

robotisation /ʀɔbɔtizasjɔ̃/ nf automation, robotization US.

robotiser /ʀɔbɔtize/ [1] vtr to automate, to robotize US.

robuste /ʀɔbyst/ adj [personne, machine] robust, sturdy; [plante] sturdy; [constitution, santé] robust, sound; [appétit] healthy; [foi] strong, firm.

robustesse /ʀɔbystɛs/ nf robustness.

roc /ʀɔk/ nm (roche, rocher) rock.

rocade /ʀɔkad/ nf **1** (de dérivation) bypass; (circulaire) ring road, beltway US; **2** MIL transversal route.

rocaille /ʀɔkaj/ nf **1** (pierres) loose stones (pl); **2** (terrain) rocky ou stony ground; **3** (décor de jardin) rockery, rock garden; **4** (pierre d'ornement) rocaille; **grotte en ~s** rock-work grotto.

rocailleux, -euse /ʀɔkajø, øz/ adj **1** [terrain] rocky, stony; **2** [voix, sonorités] harsh, grating.

rocambolesque /ʀɔkɑ̃bɔlɛsk/ adj fantastic, incredible.

roche /ʀɔʃ/ nf rock.

rocher /ʀɔʃe/ [1] nm **1** (pierre) rock; **2** (os) petrosal bone; **3** CULIN praline chocolate.

Rocheuses /ʀɔʃøz/ nprfpl **les ~** the Rocky Mountains, the Rockies.

rocheux, -euse /ʀɔʃø, øz/ adj rocky; **paroi rocheuse** rock face.

rock /ʀɔk/ nm **1** (musique) rock (music); **2** (danse) jive.
■ ~ **and roll**, **~'n'roll** rock and roll, rock'n'roll.

rocker = **rockeur**.

rockeur, -euse /ʀɔkœʀ, øz/ nm,f (chanteur) rock singer; (musicien) rock musician; (amateur) rock fan.

rococo /ʀɔkoko/ **I** adj inv **1** ART [art, style, objets] rococo; **2** (démodé) PEJ old-fashioned.
II nm rococo.

rodage /ʀɔdaʒ/ nm **1** (de véhicule, moteur) running in GB, breaking in US; **2** (de pièce, soupapes) grinding; **le spectacle/l'équipe est encore en ~** FIG the show/the team is still getting into its stride.

rodéo /ʀɔdeo/ nm rodeo; ~ **à la voiture volée** joyriding^○.

roder /ʀɔde/ [1] vtr **1** AUT to run in GB, to break in US

[véhicule]; **2** TECH to grind [pièce, soupapes]; **3** (mettre au point) to bring [sth] up to scratch [spectacle, méthode]; ~ **qn à** or **pour qch** SPORT to train sb for sth; **être (bien) rodé** [personne] to have the hang of things; [service] to be running smoothly.

rôder /ʀode/ [1] vi **1** (avec intention malfaisante) to prowl; ~ **autour de qn** to hang around sb; **2** (au hasard) to roam around, to wander about.

rôdeur, -euse /ʀodœʀ, øz/ nm,f PEJ prowler.

rogaton /ʀɔgatɔ̃/ nm **1** (reste de repas) ~**s** leftovers; **2** (objet de rebut) rubbish ¢, piece of junk.

rogne /ʀɔɲ/ nf anger; **se mettre en ~** to get mad^○.

rogner /ʀɔɲe/ [1] vtr **1** (couper les bords de) to trim [bâton, angle]; to clip [griffes, ongles]; ~ **les ailes à qn** FIG to clip sb's wings; **2** (prélever) to cut down ou back on sth [budget]; to whittle away [économies]; **3** (découper) to trim [feuille].

rognon /ʀɔɲɔ̃/ nm CULIN kidney.

rognure /ʀɔɲyʀ/ nf (de papier) trimming; (d'ongles, or) clipping.

rogue /ʀɔg/ adj haughty, contemptuous.

roi /ʀwa/ nm **1** ▶ 596 (souverain) king; **mets de ~** dish fit for a king; **2** (sans rival en son genre) **le ~ des animaux** the king of beasts; **le ~ des imbéciles^○** a complete idiot; **3** (magnat) tycoon; **4** JEUX king.
■ **les ~s fainéants** HIST the last Merovingian kings; **les ~s mages** BIBLE the (three) wise men, the three kings, the Magi.
IDIOMES **tirer les Rois** to eat Twelfth Night cake.

roitelet /ʀwatlɛ/ nm **1** (oiseau) goldcrest; **2** (petit roi) kinglet.

rôle /ʀol/ nm **1** (d'acteur) part, role; **premier ~** lead, leading role; **second ~** supporting part ou role; ~ **de composition** character part; **distribuer les ~s** to do the casting; **2** (fonction) GÉN role; (d'organe, de cœur, rein) function, role; **le comité a pour ~ de faire** the role of the committee is to do; **ils auront un ~ d'observateurs** they will act as observers; **faire qch à tour de ~** to take it in turns to do sth, to do sth in turn; **3** JUR (feuillet) roll; (registre) register.
IDIOMES **avoir** or **tenir le beau ~ ^○** to have the easy job.

rôle-titre, pl **rôles-titres** /ʀoltitʀ/ nm title role.

romain, ~e^1 /ʀɔmɛ̃, ɛn/ adj **1** (de Rome) Roman; **2** RELIG **l'Église ~e** the Roman Catholic Church; **3** (en typographie) **caractères ~s** roman typeface ¢.

romaine^2 /ʀɔmɛn/ nf **1** (salade) cos lettuce, romaine lettuce US; **2** (balance) steelyard.
IDIOMES **être bon comme la ~^○** to be soft^○ ou gullible.

roman, ~e /ʀɔmɑ̃, an/ **I** adj **1** ARCHIT Romanesque; (en Angleterre) Norman; **2** LING [langue] Romance (épith).
II nm **1** (œuvre en prose) novel; **sa vie est un vrai ~** his/her life is like something out of a novel; **ça n'existe que dans les ~s** that only happens in books; **2** (genre) **le ~** the novel; **3** (du Moyen Âge) romance; ~ **courtois** courtly romance; **4** ARCHIT **le ~** the Romanesque; **5** LING **le ~** (commun) late vulgar Latin.
■ ~ **d'amour** love story, romance; ~ **d'analyse** psychological novel; ~ **d'anticipation** (œuvre) science fiction novel; (genre) science fiction; ~ **de cape et d'épée** swashbuckling historical romance; ~ **à clé** roman à clef; **le ~ d'évasion** escapist fiction; ~ **de gare** airport novel; ~ **de mœurs** novel of manners; ~ **noir** roman noir, crime novel; ~ **policier** detective story, whodunnit^○; ~ **de série noire®** thriller; ~ **à thèse** philosophical novel; ~ **à tiroirs** episodic novel.

romance /ʀɔmɑ̃s/ nf **1** (chanson) love song; **2** LITTÉR romance.

romancer /ʀɔmɑ̃se/ [12] vtr **1** (déformer) to romanticize; **2** (présenter sous forme de roman) to fictionalize.

romanche /ʀɔmɑ̃ʃ/ ▶ 338 nm, adj LING Romans(c)h.

romancier, -ière /ʀɔmɑ̃sje, ɛʀ/ ▶ 374 nm,f novelist.

romand, ~e /ʀɔmɑ̃, ɑ̃d/ *adj* [*Suisse*] French-speaking.

romanesque /ʀɔmanɛsk/ **I** *adj* **1** [*personne*] romantic; [*situation, histoire*] like something out of a novel (*après n*); **2** [*récit, texte*] fictional; **c'est une œuvre ~** it's a work of fiction, it's a novel; **l'œuvre ~ de Balzac** Balzac's novels (*pl*).
II *nm* **1** (genre) **le ~** fiction; **2** (caractère) **le ~ d'une situation** the fantastical aspect of a situation.

roman-feuilleton, *pl* **romans-feuilletons** /ʀɔmɑ̃fœjtɔ̃/ *nm* serial.

roman-fleuve, *pl* **romans-fleuves** /ʀɔmɑ̃flœv/ *nm* roman-fleuve, saga.

romanichel, -elle /ʀɔmaniʃɛl/ *nm,f* **1** (tzigane) OFFENSIVE Romany, gypsy; **2** (vagabond) PEJ tramp.

romanisant, ~e /ʀɔmanizɑ̃, ɑ̃t/ *adj* **1** [*église*] Romanistic; **2** LING [*étudiant*] specializing in Romance languages (*épith, après n*).

roman-photo, *pl* **romans-photos** /ʀɔmɑ̃foto/ *nm* photo-story.

romantique /ʀɔmɑ̃tik/ *adj, nmf* romantic.

romantisme /ʀɔmɑ̃tism/ *nm* **1** (genre) Romanticism; **2** (sentimentalisme) romanticism.

romarin /ʀɔmaʀɛ̃/ *nm* rosemary.

rombière⁹ /ʀɔ̃bjɛʀ/ *nf* PEJ **une vieille ~** an old bag○.

Rome /ʀɔm/ ▶ 628 | *npr* Rome.
IDIOMES **tous les chemins mènent à ~** PROV all roads lead to Rome PROV; **~ ne s'est pas faite en un jour** PROV Rome wasn't built in a day PROV.

rompre /ʀɔ̃pʀ/ [53] **I** *vtr* GÉN to break, to break off [*fiançailles, relation*]; to upset [*équilibre*]; to disrupt [*harmonie*]; to end [*isolement*]; to break up [*unité*]; to interrupt [*uniformité*]; to break through [*ligne ennemie, barrage*]; **rompez (les rangs)!** fall out!
II *vi* **~ avec** to break with [*habitude, tradition, doctrine*]; to make a break from [*passé*]; to break away from [*parti, milieu*]; to break up with [*fiancé*]; **ils ont rompu** they've broken up.
III se rompre *vpr* GÉN to break.

rompu, ~e /ʀɔ̃py/ *adj* **1** (habitué) **~ à** well accustomed to; **~ aux techniques modernes** well-versed in modern techniques; **2** (fatigué) **~ (de fatigue)** worn-out.

romsteck /ʀɔmstɛk/ *nm* rump steak.

ronce /ʀɔ̃s/ *nf* **1** (plante, tige) bramble; **2** (nœud du bois) burr; **~ de noyer** burr walnut.

ronchon○, **-onne** /ʀɔ̃ʃɔ̃, ɔn/ *adj* grouchy○.

ronchonner○ /ʀɔ̃ʃɔne/ [1] *vi* to grumble (**après** about), to grouse○ (**après** about).

rond, ~e¹ /ʀɔ̃, ʀɔ̃d/ **I** *adj* **1** (en forme de cercle) GÉN round; [*bâtiment*] circular; **2** (arrondi) GÉN rounded; [*seins*] full; [*visage*] round; [*personne*] tubby; **un bébé tout ~** a chubby baby; **elle se trouve trop ~e** EUPH she thinks she's too fat; **3** (net) [*nombre*] round; **un compte ~** a round sum; **ça fait trois cents francs tout ~** that's three hundred francs exactly; **4**○ (ivre) drunk.
II *nm* (cercle) circle; **en ~** in a circle; **faire des ~s de fumée** to blow smoke rings; **faire des ~s dans l'eau** LIT to make ripples in the water.
■ **~ de jambe** (en danse) rond de jambe; **faire des ~s de jambe à qn** FIG to be overly polite to sb; **~ de serviette** napkin ring; **~ de sorcière** fairy ring.
IDIOMES **être ~ en affaires**○ to be honest, to be on the level○; **ouvrir les yeux ~s** to be wide-eyed with astonishment; **être ~ comme une barrique** or **une queue de pelle** or **un petit pois**○ to be blind drunk○.

rond-de-cuir, *pl* **ronds-de-cuir** /ʀɔ̃dkɥiʀ/ *nm* penpusher GB, pencil pusher US.

ronde² /ʀɔ̃d/ **I** *nf* **1** (danse) round dance; **faire une ~** to make ou form a circle; **entrer dans la ~** LIT, FIG to join the dance; **2** (va-et-vient) **la ~ des voitures sur le circuit** the cars whirling round the circuit; **3** (de policiers) patrol; (de soldats, gardiens) watch; **faire**

sa ~ to be on patrol ou watch; **4** MUS (note) semibreve GB, whole note US; **5** (écriture) roundhand.
II à la ronde *loc adv* around.

rondelet○, **-ette** /ʀɔ̃dlɛ, ɛt/ *adj* [*personne*] plump, tubby; [*visage*] chubby; **une somme rondelette** quite a tidy○ sum.

rondelle /ʀɔ̃dɛl/ *nf* **1** (tranche) slice; **2** TECH washer.

rondement /ʀɔ̃dmɑ̃/ *adv* promptly.

rondeur /ʀɔ̃dœʀ/ *nf* **1** (de femme, bras) curve; **2** (de caractère) openness; **avec ~** (franchement) frankly.

rondin /ʀɔ̃dɛ̃/ *nm* log; **cabane en ~s** log cabin.

rondouillard○, **~e** /ʀɔ̃dujaʀ, aʀd/ *adj* tubby○.

rond-point, *pl* **ronds-points** /ʀɔ̃pwɛ̃/ *nm* roundabout GB, traffic circle US.

ronéoter○ /ʀɔneɔte/, **ronéotyper** /ʀɔneɔtipe/ [1] *vtr* to duplicate, to Roneo®.

ronflant, ~e /ʀɔ̃flɑ̃, ɑ̃t/ *adj* **1** [*poêle*] roaring; **2** [*style*] high-flown (*épith*); [*discours*] grandiloquent; [*promesse*] fine-sounding (*épith*).

ronflement /ʀɔ̃fləmɑ̃/ *nm* **1** (de dormeur) snore; **2** (de chaudière, poêle) roar ₵; (moins fort) purr ₵; (de moteur) purr ₵; (de petit avion) drone.

ronfler /ʀɔ̃fle/ [1] *vi* **1** [*dormeur*] to snore; [*poêle*] to roar; [*moteur*] to purr; **2**○ (dormir) to be fast asleep.
IDIOMES **~ comme une toupie** or **un orgue** or **un sonneur** to snore like a pig.

ronfleur, -euse /ʀɔ̃flœʀ, øz/ *nm,f* **1** (personne) (qui ronfle) snorer; (qui aime dormir)○ great sleeper; **2** (de téléphone) electric buzzer.

ronger /ʀɔ̃ʒe/ [13] **I** *vtr* **1** (grignoter) [*souris, chien*] to gnaw; [*vers*] to eat into [*bois*]; [*chenille*] to eat away [*feuilles*]; **rongé par les vers** worm-eaten; **2** (attaquer) [*eau, acide, rouille*] to erode, to eat away at; **3** FIG [*maladie*] to wear down [*personne*].
II se ronger *vpr* **se ~ les ongles** to bite one's nails.
IDIOMES **se ~ les sangs**○ to worry oneself sick.

rongeur /ʀɔ̃ʒœʀ/ *nm* rodent.

ronron○ /ʀɔ̃ʀɔ̃/ *nm* (also onomat) **1** (de chat) purr, purring ₵; **faire ~** to purr; **2** (de moteur) purring ₵; **3** (routine) **le ~ de la vie quotidienne** the humdrum routine of daily life.

ronronnement /ʀɔ̃ʀɔnmɑ̃/ *nm* (de chat, moteur) purring ₵.

ronronner /ʀɔ̃ʀɔne/ [1] *vi* to purr.

roque /ʀɔk/ *nm* castling; **grand/petit ~** castling long/short.

roquer /ʀɔke/ [1] *vi* JEUX **1** (aux échecs) to castle; **2** (au croquet) to roquet.

roquet /ʀɔke/ *nm* **1** (chien) yappy little dog; **2**○ (personne) bad-tempered little runt○.

roquette /ʀɔkɛt/ *nf* MIL rocket.

rosace /ʀozas/ *nf* (figure géométrique) rosette; (vitrail) rose window; (au plafond) rose.

rosaire /ʀozɛʀ/ *nm* (chapelet, prières) rosary.

rosâtre /ʀozɑtʀ/ ▶ 141 | *adj* pinkish.

rosbif /ʀosbif/ *nm* **1** (viande) (crue) joint of beef GB, roast of beef US; (cuite) roast beef; **2**○† (Anglais) OFFENSIVE **les ~s** the English (+ *v pl*).

rose¹ /ʀoz/ ▶ 141 | **I** *adj* GÉN pink; (de santé) rosy.
II *nm* (couleur) pink.
IDIOMES **ce n'est pas (tout) ~** it's not all roses, it's not roses all the way; **la vie n'est pas ~** life isn't a bed of roses; **voir la vie en ~** to see life through rose-coloured GB spectacles.

rose² /ʀoz/ *nf* **1** BOT rose; **2** (vitrail) rose window; **3** (en bijouterie) **diamant en ~** rose diamond.
■ **~ d'Inde** African marigold; **~ pompon** button rose; **~ des sables** gypsum flower; **~ trémière** hollyhock; **~ des vents** compass rose.
IDIOMES **il n'y a pas de ~ sans épines** PROV there is no rose without a thorn; **envoyer qn sur les ~s**○ to send sb packing○; **découvrir le pot aux ~s** to find out what's going on.

rosé, ~e¹ /ʀoze/ **I** ▶ 141 | *adj* GÉN pinkish; [*vin*] rosé.
II *nm* rosé.

roseau, *pl* ~**x** /rozo/ *nm* BOT reed.

rosée[2] /roze/ *nf* dew.

roseraie /rozrɛ/ *nf* rose garden.

rosette /rozɛt/ *nf* **1** (insigne, ornement) rosette; (nœud) bow; **2** BOT rosette.

rosier /rozje/ *nm* BOT rosebush, rose.

rosière /rozjɛr/ *nf*: *young girl recognized for her virtue*.

rosir /rozir/ [3] **I** *vtr* to turn [sth] pink.
II *vi* [ciel, paysage] to turn pink; [visage] to go pink.

rosse /rɔs/ **I**[○] *adj* [professeur, critique] mean; [imitateur, humour] nasty.
II *nf* **1** (cheval) nag[○]; **2** (personne) heel[○], meanie[○].

rossée[○] /rose/ *nf* thrashing.

rosser[○] /rose/ [1] *vtr* **1** (battre) to give [sb] a good thrashing [personne]; to beat [animal]; **2** (vaincre) to thrash[○] [équipe, armée].

rosserie /rosri/ *nf* **1** (parole) nasty remark; (action) mean trick; **2** (caractère) (de professeur) meanness; (d'imitateur) nastiness.

rossignol /rosiɲɔl/ *nm* **1** (oiseau) nightingale; **2**[○] (de cambrioleur) picklock; **3**[○] (marchandise invendable) bit of junk.

rot[○] /ro/ *nm* burp[○]; **faire un** ~ to burp[○].

rotatif, -ive[1] /rotatif, iv/ *adj* rotary.

rotation /rotasjɔ̃/ *nf* **1** (mouvement sur soi) rotation; ~ **autour d'un axe** rotation about an axis; **mouvement de** ~ rotational movement; **effectuer une** ~ **complète** to rotate fully; **2** (voyage) round trip; (fréquence des voyages) round trip service; MIL, AVIAT, NAUT turn round GB, turnaround; **3** (de locataire, stock) turnover; (d'équipe, de médecin) rotation; **système de** ~ rota system; **4** AGRIC rotation; ~ **des cultures** crop rotation.

rotative[2] /rotativ/ *nf* rotary press.

rotatoire /rotatwar/ *adj* rotary.

roter[○] /rote/ [1] *vtr* to burp[○], to belch.

rôti, ~e[1] /roti/ **I** *adj* [poulet, lapin] roast (épith).
II *nm* **1** (avant la cuisson) joint; **2** (après la cuisson) roast.

rôtie[2] /roti/ *nf* piece of toast.

rotin /rotɛ̃/ *nm* (matériau) rattan.

rôtir /rotir/ [3] **I** *vtr* to roast [viande]; to toast [pain].
II *vi* **1** CULIN to roast; **2**[○] (être exposé au soleil) to roast; **se faire** ~ **au soleil** to roast in the sun; **3**[○] (subir une forte chaleur) [personne] to be roasting.
III se rôtir *vpr* [personne] (au soleil) to roast (oneself); (devant un feu) to toast (oneself).
IDIOMES **il attend que ça lui tombe tout rôti dans le bec**[○] he expects things to fall into his lap.

rôtisseur, -euse /rotisœr, øz/ [▶ 374] *nm,f* seller of roast meat.

rôtissoire /rotiswar/ *nf* rotisserie, roasting spit.

rotonde /rotɔ̃d/ *nf* **1** ARCHIT (édifice) rotunda; **2** (dans un bus) back seat; **3** RAIL roundhouse.

rotondité /rotɔ̃dite/ *nf* (caractère) roundness.

rotule /rotyl/ *nf* **1** ANAT kneecap; **2** TECH ball-and-socket joint.
IDIOMES **être sur les** ~**s**[○] to be on one's last legs; **mettre qn sur les** ~**s**[○] to wear sb out[○].

roture /rotyr/ *nf* (condition) common birth.

roturier, -ière /rotyrje, ɛr/ **I** *adj* common.
II *nm,f* HIST commoner.

rouage /rwaʒ/ *nm* **1** (de machine) wheel; **les** ~**s** the parts ou works; **2** (d'administration) machinery [C]; **les** ~**s bureaucratiques** the wheels of bureaucracy; **être un** ~ **parmi d'autres** to be a cog in a machine.

roublard[○], ~**e** /rublar, ard/ *adj* crafty, cunning.

roublardise[○] /rublardiz/ *nf* craftiness, cunning.

rouble /rubl/ [▶ 33] *nm* rouble.

roucoulades /rukulad/ *nfpl* (d'oiseau) cooing [C]; (de chanteur) crooning [C]; (d'amoureux) billing and cooing [C].

roucoulement /rukulmɑ̃/ *nm* **1** (d'oiseau) cooing [C];

2[○] (d'amoureux) billing and cooing [C]; (mots tendres) murmuring [C].

roucouler /rukule/ [1] **I** *vtr* to croon [chanson]; to coo [mots d'amour].
II *vi* **1** [oiseau] to coo; **2** [amoureux] to bill and coo.

roue /ru/ *nf* **1** (de véhicule, jeu) wheel; **être** ~(**s**) à ~(**s**) ou ~ **dans** ~ to be neck and neck; **avoir une** ~ **à plat** to have a flat tyre GB ou tire US; ▶ **grand**; **2** (en gymnastique) cartwheel; **3** (de mécanisme) wheel; ~ **dentée** cogwheel; **4** (supplice) wheel.
■ ~ **à aube** paddle wheel; ~ **libre** freewheel; **pédaler en** ~ **libre** to freewheel; ~ **motrice** driving wheel; **véhicule à quatre** ~**s motrices** four-wheel-drive vehicle; ~ **de secours** spare wheel GB ou tire US.
IDIOMES **être la cinquième** ~ **du carrosse** (inutile) to be superfluous; (de trop) to feel unwanted; **pousser qn à la** ~ to be behind sb; **faire la** ~ [paon] to spread its tail, to display; [personne] PEJ to strut around; (en gymnastique) to do a cartwheel.

roué, ~e /rwe/ **I** *adj* cunning.
II *nm,f* (personne rusée) PEJ cunning devil.

rouer /rwe/ [1] *vtr* ~ **qn de coups** to beat sb up.

rouerie /ruri/ *nf* **1** (caractère) cunning; **2** (action) cunning trick.

rouet /rwɛ/ *nm* (machine à filer) spinning wheel; **filer au** ~ to spin.

rouflaquettes[○] /ruflakɛt/ *nfpl* sideburns.

rouge /ruʒ/ [▶ 141] **I** *adj* **1** GÉN red (de with); (congestionné) red, flushed; **avoir le teint** ~ to have a high colour[GB]; **2** (roux) [cheveux, barbe] red, ginger; [pelage] ginger; **3** (incandescent) red-hot; **les braises sont encore** ~**s** the embers are still glowing; **4** (communiste) Red.
II *nmf* POL (communiste) Red.
III *adv* **voter** ~[○] to vote communist.
IV *nm* **1** ▶ **couleurs 99** (couleur) red; **2** (colorant) red; **les** ~**s organiques** natural red dyes; **3** (fard) ~ **à joues** blusher, rouge; ~ **à lèvres** lipstick; **4** (signal) red; **le feu est au** ~ the (traffic) lights are red, the (traffic) light is red; **passer au** ~ to jump the lights GB ou a red light; **5** (dû à l'incandescence) **chauffer** ou **porter un fer au** ~ to heat a piece of iron until it is red hot; **un fer porté au** ~ a red-hot iron; **6** (coloration) **le** ~ **lui monta au visage** he/she went red in the face; **7**[○] (vin) red (wine); **gros** ~ (**qui tache**)[○] cheap red wine, red plonk[○] GB; **un coup de** ~[○] a glass of red wine; **8** (indicateur) red; **être dans le** ~ (à la banque) to be in the red.
■ ~ **brique** brick red; ~ **sang** blood red.
IDIOMES **être** ~ **comme une tomate** or **un coq** or **une écrevisse** or **un coquelicot** (de timidité, honte) to be as red as a beetroot GB ou a beet US; (après avoir couru) to be red in the face; **voir** ~ to see red.

rougeâtre /ruʒatr/ [▶ 141] *adj* reddish.

rougeaud, ~e /ruʒo, od/ *adj* [personne] ruddy-faced, ruddy-cheeked; [visage, teint] ruddy.

rouge-gorge, *pl* **rouges-gorges** /ruʒgɔrʒ/ *nm* robin (redbreast).

rougeoiement /ruʒwamɑ̃/ *nm* red ou reddish glow.

rougeole /ruʒɔl/ [▶ 196] *nf* measles (+ *v sg*).

rougeoyant, ~e /ruʒwajɑ̃, ɑ̃t/ *adj* [reflet] reddish; [ciel] reddening (épith), glowing red (jamais épith).

rougeoyer /ruʒwaje/ [23] *vi* [ciel] to take on a red glow; [soleil couchant] to glow fiery red; [feu] to glow red.

rouget /ruʒɛ/ *nm* red mullet, goatfish US.

rougeur /ruʒœr/ *nf* **1** (couleur, teinte) redness; **2** (congestion) redness, flushing; **3** (sur la peau) red blotch.

rougir /ruʒir/ [3] **I** *vtr* **1** (teinter) GÉN to redden; ~ **son eau** to put a little red wine in one's water; ~ **la terre de son sang** to make the earth run red with one's blood; **2** (chauffer) to make [sth] red hot [métal].
II *vi* **1** [personne] (d'émotion, de honte) to blush (**de** with); (de colère) to flush (**de** with); (de chaleur) to go red; [peau, visage] to go ou turn red; ~ **jusqu'aux**

yeux or **oreilles** to turn ou go as red as a beetroot GB ou a beet US; **il n'a pas à en ~** that's nothing for him to be ashamed of; **sans ~** without shame; **ne ~ de rien** to have no shame; **2** [*fruit, feuille, forêt, ciel, crustacé, carapace*] to turn red; **3** [*métal, tison*] to become red hot.

rougissant, **~e** /ʀuʒisɑ̃, ɑ̃t/ *adj* [*personne*] blushing; [*feuille, forêt, ciel*] reddening.

rouille /ʀuj/ **I ▶141** *adj inv* red-brown, rust (-coloured GB).
II *nf* **1** CHIMIE, BOT rust; **2** CULIN rouille.

rouillé, **~e** /ʀuje/ *adj* **1** LIT [*objet, fer*] rusty, rusted; BOT rusty; **2** FIG [*athlète*] out of practice; [*corps, muscle, membre*] stiff; [*mémoire, personne, technique*] rusty.

rouiller /ʀuje/ [1] **I** *vtr* **1** LIT to rust, to make [sth] go rusty [*fer*]; **2** FIG to slow [sb] down; to dull [*esprit*].
II *vi* [*fer*] to rust, to go rusty.
III se rouiller *vpr* [*personne*] to slow down; [*sportif*] to get out of shape; [*muscle, corps*] to lose tone; [*mémoire, esprit, connaissances*] to get rusty.

roulade /ʀulad/ *nf* **1** CULIN (de viande) stuffed rolled meat, roulade; **2** SPORT roll; **3** (de chanteur) roulade; (d'oiseau) trill, trilling *Ȼ*.

roulant, **~e** /ʀulɑ̃, ɑ̃t/ *adj* **table ~e** trolley GB, serving cart US; **matériel ~** RAIL rolling stock; **personnel ~** (dans le train) train crew.

roulé, **~e** /ʀule/ **I** *adj* **1** CULIN **épaule ~e** rolled shoulder; **2** (en phonétique) **r ~** rolled r.
II *nm* CULIN roll; **~ au fromage** puff pastry filled with cheese.

rouleau, *pl* **~x** /ʀulo/ *nm* **1** (cylindre) roll; **2** (grosse vague) breaker, roller; **3** AGRIC, TECH roller; **4** (bigoudi) roller, curler; **~ ventral** straddle (roll); **~ dorsal** flop; **sauter en ~** (en ventral) to straddle; (en dorsal) to flop; **6** (pour peindre) roller.
■ **~ compresseur** TECH, FIG steamroller; **~ à pâtisserie** CULIN rolling pin; **~ de printemps** CULIN spring roll.
IDIOMES être au bout du ~○ (nerveusement) to be at the end of one's tether; (être mourant) to be at death's door.

roulé-boulé, *pl* **roulés-boulés** /ʀulebule/ *nm* roll.

roulement /ʀulmɑ̃/ *nm* **1** (bruit) (de train, tonnerre) rumble; (de tambour) roll; **2** FIN (de capital) circulation; **3** (alternance) rotation; **travailler par ~** to work (in) shifts; **faire** ou **établir un ~** to draw up a rota GB ou schedule; **4** TECH bearing; **~ à billes** ball bearing.

rouler /ʀule/ [1] **I** *vtr* **1** (entraîner) to roll [*tonneau, pneu, boulette*]; to wheel [*charrette, brouette*]; **le fleuve roule ses eaux boueuses** the muddy waters of the river swirl along; **les vagues roulent les galets** the waves shift the pebbles around; **2** (mettre en rouleau) to roll up [*tapis, manche, col*]; to roll [*cigarette*]; **~ qch en boule** to roll [sth] into a ball; **3** (faire bouger) **~ les** or **des épaules** to roll one's shoulders; **~ les** or **des hanches** to wiggle one's hips; **~ les** or **des yeux** to roll one's eyes; **4** (aplanir) to roll [*champ, gazon*]; to roll out [*pâte à tarte*]; **5** (en phonétique) **~ les r** to roll one's r's; **6**○ (tromper) **~ qn** to diddle○ GB ou to cheat sb.
II ▶631 *vi* **1** [*boule, pièce, pierre, tronc, personne*] to roll; **~ dans le ravin** to roll down into the ravine; **faire ~ les dés** to roll the dice; **2** [*véhicule*] to go; **ma voiture ne roule plus** my car won't go; **ma voiture n'a pas roulé depuis deux ans** my car hasn't been driven for two years; **les bus ne roulent pas le dimanche** buses don't run on Sundays; **~ à grande vitesse** [*voiture, train*] to travel at high speed; **~ au super**○ to run on 4-star GB ou premium US; **ça roule**○! FIG (c'est entendu) it's a deal!; **3** (conduire) to drive; **~ à gauche** to drive on the left; **~ en Cadillac**® to drive a Cadillac®; **4** (bouger) [*muscles*] to ripple; **faire ~ ses épaules** to roll one's shoulders; **faire ~ ses biceps** to flex one's biceps; **5** [*bateau*] to roll; **6** [*tonnerre, détonation*] to rumble.
III se rouler *vpr* **1** (se mettre) **se ~ dans** to roll in [*boue*]; **se ~ par terre** LIT to roll (about) on the floor;

FIG (rire) to fall about laughing; **c'était à se ~ par terre** it was hilarious; **se ~ en boule** to curl up in a ball; **2** (s'envelopper) **se ~ dans** to wrap oneself in [*couverture*].
IDIOMES ~ sous la table○ to be under the table; **~ la caisse**○ or **des mécaniques**○ to swagger along.

roulette /ʀulɛt/ *nf* **1** (petite roue) caster; **lit à ~s** bed on casters; **2 ▶329** JEUX roulette; **3** (de dentiste) (dentist's) drill; **4** CULIN pastry wheel; **5** (en couture) tracing wheel; **6** (en reliure) fillet.
IDIOMES marcher comme sur des ~s○ to go smoothly ou like a dream.

rouleur, **-euse** /ʀulœʀ, øz/ *nm,f* cyclist.

roulier /ʀulje/ *nm* **1** (navire) roll-on roll-off ship; **2** (personne) carter.

roulis /ʀuli/ *nm* (de bateau) rolling; (de voiture, train) swaying.

roulotte /ʀulɔt/ *nf* (horse-drawn) caravan GB, trailer US.

roumain, **~e** /ʀumɛ̃, ɛn/ **I ▶394** *adj* Romanian.
II ▶338 *nm* LING Romanian.

Roumanie /ʀumani/ **▶232** *nprf* Romania.

roupie /ʀupi/ **▶33** *nf* rupee.
IDIOMES c'est de la ~ de sansonnet○ it's a load of rubbish○.

roupiller○ /ʀupije/ [1] *vtr* to sleep.

roupillon○ /ʀupijɔ̃/ *nm* snooze○, nap.

rouquin, **~e** /ʀukɛ̃, in/ **I** *adj* [*personne*] red-haired; [*cheveux*] red.
II *nm,f* redhead.
III *nm* (vin) plonk○ GB, cheap red wine.

rouspéter○ /ʀuspete/ [14] *vi* to grumble (**contre** about; **après** at).

rouspéteur○, **-euse** /ʀuspetœʀ, øz/ *nm,f* grumbler.

roussâtre /ʀusɑtʀ/ **▶141** *adj* reddish.

rousse /ʀus/ *adj* ▶**roux** I, II.

rousseur /ʀusœʀ/ *nf* (de cheveux, barbe, feuille) redness; (de teinte, ton) russet colour GB.

roussi /ʀusi/ *nm* **ça sent le ~** LIT it smells of burning; FIG○ there's trouble brewing.

roussir /ʀusiʀ/ [3] **I** *vtr* **1** (colorer) LITER to turn [sth] brown; **2** (brûler) [*fer à repasser, soleil*] to scorch; [*flamme*] to singe.
II *vi* **1** (se colorer) to go brown; **2** CULIN **faire ~** to brown.

routage /ʀutaʒ/ *nm* **1** (de journaux, colis) sorting and mailing; **société de ~** mailing house; **2** ORDINAT routing.

routard○, **~e** /ʀutaʀ, aʀd/ *nm,f* backpacker.

route /ʀut/ *nf* **1** (voie terrestre) road, highway US; **demain je prends la ~** tomorrow I take to the road; **tenir la ~** LIT [*voiture*] to hold the road; FIG○ [*argument*] to hold water; [*équipement*] to be well-made; **2** (moyen de transport) road; **par la ~** by road; **il y a six heures de ~** it's a six-hour drive; **je préfère prendre la ~** I prefer to go by road; **faire de la ~**○ to do a lot of mileage; **~s maritimes** sea routes; **s'éloigner** or **dévier de sa ~** LIT [*avion, bateau*] to go off course; [*voiture, piéton*] to go the wrong way; FIG [*personne*] to stray from one's chosen path; **la ~ est toute tracée désormais** FIG from now on, it's all plain sailing; **nos ~s se sont croisées** FIG our paths crossed; **4** (parcours) LIT, FIG way; **la ~ sera longue** it will be a long journey; **être sur la ~ de qn** to be in sb's way; **rencontrer qch en ~** LIT to meet sth on the way; FIG to meet sth along the way; **j'ai changé d'avis en cours de ~** I changed my mind along the way; **je me suis arrêté en cours de ~** I stopped on the way; **finis ta phrase, ne t'arrête pas en (cours de) ~** finish your sentence, don't stop halfway through; **être en ~** [*personne*] to be on one's way; [*projet*] to be underway; [*plat*] to be cooking; **avoir qch en ~** to have sth underway; **remettre qn sur la bonne ~** to put sb right; **~ du succès** road to success; **faire ~ avec qn** to travel with sb;

faire ~ vers, **être en ~ pour** [*avion, passager*] to be en route to; [*bateau*] to be sailing to; [*voiture, train, piéton*] to be heading for; **faire fausse ~** LIT to go off course; FIG to be mistaken; **se mettre en ~** to set off; **en ~**! let's go!; **bonne ~**! have a good journey GB ou a nice trip!; **mettre en ~** to start [*machine, voiture*]; to get [sth] going [*projet, fabrication*]; **la mise en ~ des négociations a été difficile** it was difficult to get the negotiations going; **5** (cyclisme) **géants** ou **rois de la ~** road-cycling champions; **épreuve** or **course sur ~** road race.

■ **~ départementale** secondary road (*maintained by local authority*); **~ des épices** HIST spice route; **~ à grande circulation** trunk road GB, highway US; **~ nationale** trunk road GB, ~ A road GB, national highway US; **~ de navigation** shipping lane; **~ du rhum** SPORT Rum route race; **~ secondaire** minor road; **~ de la soie** HIST Silk Route ou Road; **~ du vin** wine trail.

router /Rute/ [1] *vtr* to sort [sth] for mailing [*magazines, journaux*].

routier, -ière[1] /Rutje, ɛR/ **I** *adj* road (*épith*).

II *nm* **1** ▶**374** (chauffeur) lorry driver GB, truck driver; **2** (restaurant) transport café GB, truck stop US; **3** (en cyclisme) road racer.

routière[2] /Rutjɛr/ *nf* **ma voiture n'est pas une très bonne ~** my car is not very good for long-distance driving.

routine /Rutin/ *nf* **1** (habitude) routine; **tomber dans la ~** to get into a rut; **2** ORDINAT routine.

routinier, -ière /Rutinje, ɛR/ *adj* [*personne*] set in one's ways (*jamais épith*); [*esprit, méthode, travail, vie*] routine (*épith*).

rouvrir /RuvRiR/ [32] **I** *vtr* **1** to open [sth] again [*porte, rideau, coffre, yeux*]; to reopen [*blessure*]; to turn [sth] back on [*gaz*]; **2** (remettre en service) to reopen [*magasin, route*]; **3** (après arrêt) to resume [*négociations, hostilités*]; to reopen [*débat, affaire*].

II *vi* [*magasin, école, route*] to reopen.

III **se rouvrir** *vpr* [*porte, fenêtre*] to open (again); [*blessure, parapluie*] to open up (again).

roux, rousse /Ru, Rus/ ▶**141** **I** *adj* [*couleur*] russet; [*cheveux, barbe*] red; (plus clair) ginger; [*feuilles*] russet; [*personne*] red-haired (*épith*); [*animal, pelage*] ginger; **il est ~** he's a redhead.

II *nm,f* red-haired person, redhead; **les ~** redheads.

royal, ~e[1], *mpl* **-aux** /Rwajal, o/ *adj* **1** (de souverain) royal; **2** (magnifique) [*accueil*] royal; [*cadeau*] fit for a king (*après n*); [*salaire*] princely; **3** (suprême) [*indifférence*] supreme; [*mépris*] majestic; [*paix*] blissful.

royale[2] /Rwajal/ *nf* **1** CULIN royale (*savoury egg custard*); **2** MIL **la Royale** the French Navy; **3** (barbe) imperial.

royalement /Rwajalmã/ *adv* **1** (avec magnificence) [*recevoir, traiter*] royally, like royalty; [*vivre*] royally, like a king; **être payé ~** to be paid handsomely; **2**○ (complètement) **il se moque ~ de son travail** he really couldn't care less about his work.

royaliste /Rwajalist/ *adj, nmf* royalist.

IDIOMES **être plus ~ que le roi** to be more Catholic than the pope.

royaume /Rwajom/ *nm* LIT, FIG kingdom.

IDIOMES **au ~ des aveugles, les borgnes sont rois** PROV in the country of the blind, the one-eyed man is king PROV.

Royaume-Uni /Rwajomyni/ ▶**232** *nprm* **~ de Grande-Bretagne et d'Irlande du Nord** United Kingdom of Great Britain and Northern Ireland; **le ~** the United Kingdom.

royauté /Rwajote/ *nf* **1** (dignité) kingship; **2** (régime) monarchy.

RSVP (*written abbr* = **répondez s'il vous plaît**) RSVP.

RU /Ry/ *nm: abbr* ▶ **restaurant**.

ruade /Ryad/ *nf* **1** (de cheval) buck; **2** FIG (de personne) attack.

ruban /Rybã/ *nm* ribbon.

■ **~ d'acier** steel band ou strip; **~ adhésif** adhesive tape; **~ de chapeau** hat band; **~ perforé** ORDINAT (punched) paper tape.

rubéole /Rybeɔl/ ▶**196** *nf* German measles (+ *v sg*).

rubis /Rybi/ *nm inv* **1** (pierre, bijou) ruby; **2** ▶**141** (couleur) ruby; **3** (de montre) jewel.

IDIOMES **payer ~ sur l'ongle**○ to pay cash on the nail.

rubrique /RybRik/ *nf* **1** (de journal) section; **tenir une ~ dans un journal** to have a column in a newspaper; **2** (catégorie) category; **classer des papiers sous la ~ 'à suivre'** to file papers under 'further action'; **3** RELIG rubric.

■ **~ mondaine** social column; **~ nécrologique** obituary column.

ruche /Ryʃ/ *nf* **1** (habitation) beehive, hive; **2** FIG hive of activity; **3** (en couture) ruche.

rucher /Ryʃe/ *nm* apiary.

rude /Ryd/ *adj* **1** [*métier, journée, combat*] hard, tough; [*climat, hiver*] harsh; [*épreuve*] severe; **2** [*étoffe, barbe, peau*] rough; **3** [*voix, manières*] harsh; [*traits, personne*] coarse; **4** [*appétit*] healthy; [*montagnard, marin*] rugged; **c'est un ~ gaillard** he's a strapping fellow; **5** [*adversaire*] tough, formidable.

IDIOMES **en voir de ~s**○ to have a hard ou tough time of it; **en faire voir de ~s**○ **à qn** to put sb through it.

rudement /Rydmã/ *adv* **1** (sans ménagements) roughly, harshly; **2**○ (très) really; **c'est ~ mieux!** it's a hell of a lot○ better!

rudesse /Rydɛs/ *nf* **1** (sévérité) harshness, severity; **2** (manque de raffinement) coarseness.

rudiment /Rydimã/ **I** *nm* ANAT rudiment; **un ~ de queue** a rudimentary tail.

II **rudiments** *nmpl* rudiments; **avoir quelques ~s de** to have a rudimentary knowledge of.

rudimentaire /RydimãtɛR/ *adj* **1** (de base) basic; **2** ANAT rudimentary.

rudoyer /Rydwaje/ [23] *vtr* to bully.

rue /Ry/ *nf* **1** (voie) street; **2** (peuple) PÉJ **la ~** the mob PÉJ; **3** BOT rue.

IDIOMES **ça ne court pas les ~s**○ it's pretty thin on the ground; **être à la ~** to be on the street, to be down-and-out; **jeter/mettre qn à la ~** to throw/to put sb out on the street; **descendre dans la ~** to take to the street.

ruée /Rɥe/ *nf* rush; **~ vers l'or** gold rush.

ruelle /Rɥɛl/ *nf* alleyway, back street.

ruer /Rɥe/ [1] **I** *vi* [*cheval*] to kick.

II **se ruer** *vpr* to rush; **se ~ sur qn/qch** to pounce on sb/sth; **se ~ à l'assaut de qch** to launch an attack on sth; **les gens se ruent à l'assaut des magasins** there is a rush on the shops GB ou stores US.

IDIOMES **~ dans les brancards** to kick over the traces, to rebel.

rufian○ /Ryfjã/ *nm* (aventurier) adventurer.

rugby /Rygbi/ ▶**329** *nm* rugby; **~ à treize** rugby league; **~ à quinze** rugby union.

rugbyman, *pl* **rugbymen** /Rygbiman, mɛn/ ▶**374** *nm* rugby player.

rugir /RyʒiR/ [3] **I** *vtr* to bellow (out), to growl.

II *vi* [*animal, moteur, mer*] to roar; [*personne, vent*] to howl.

rugissement /Ryʒismã/ *nm* (d'animal, de personne) roar; (de vent) howling; **pousser un ~ ou des ~s** to roar.

rugosité /Rygozite/ *nf* **1** (état) roughness; **2** (aspérité) rough patch.

rugueux, -euse /Rygø, øz/ *adj* rough.

ruine /Rɥin/ *nf* **1** (destruction) (de bâtiment, pays, réputation, personne, d'entreprise) ruin; (de civilisation) collapse; (d'espoir) death; **en ~(s)** ruined (*épith*); **être/tomber en ~(s)** to be in ruins/to fall into ruin; **menacer ~** to be threatening to collapse; **c'est la ~**○ FIG it's exorbitant; **ce n'est pas la ~**○ FIG it's not that expensive; **les femmes seront sa ~**

women will be the ruin of him/her; **être la ~ de** to ruin; **courir** or **aller à la ~** [*personne, entreprise*] to be heading for financial ruin; [*civilisation*] to be heading for collapse; **2** (restes) (bâtiment) ruin; (personne) PEJ wreck.

ruiner /ʀɥine/ [1] **I** *vtr* **1** (financièrement) to ruin [*pays, personne, entreprise, économie*]; **~ qn** to be a drain on sb's resources; **ça ne va pas le ~**° that's not going to break the bank; **2** (physiquement) to destroy, to wreck [*santé, forces*]; [*bombardement*] to reduce [sth] to rubble [*ville, bâtiment*]; [*éléments*] to ruin [*culture*]; **3** FIG to ruin [*vie, réputation*]; to destroy [*argument, théorie, bonheur*]; to shatter [*espérances, rêve*].

II se ruiner *vpr* (perdre ses biens) to be ruined, to lose everything; (dépenser excessivement) to ruin oneself (**en faisant** doing); **se ~ pour une femme** to spend everything one has on a woman.

ruineux, -euse /ʀɥinø, øz/ *adj* [*entretien, dépense*] exorbitant; [*goût, plaisir, sortie*] very expensive; [*achat, guerre, affaire, objet*] ruinously expensive.

ruisseau, *pl* **~x** /ʀɥiso/ *nm* **1** (cours d'eau) stream, brook; **2** (flot) **~ de larmes/lave** stream of tears/lava; **3**† (caniveau) gutter; **tirer** or **sortir qn du ~** FIG to pull sb out of the gutter.

ruisseler /ʀɥisle/ [19] *vi* **1** (s'écouler) [*eau, sang*] to stream; [*graisse*] to drip; **2** [*personne, surface, objet*] to be streaming (**de** with); **~ de sueur** to be dripping with sweat; **~ de lumière** to be flooded with light.

ruissellement /ʀɥisɛlmɑ̃/ *nm* (de pluie) streaming (**sur** down); (de produits toxiques) seepage.

rumeur /ʀymœʀ/ *nf* **1** (ouï-dire) rumour^GB (**sur** about); **selon certaines ~s, il aurait quitté le pays** rumour^GB has it that he may have left the country; **faire taire une ~** to put a stop to a rumour^GB; **2** (de voix, mer, vent) murmur.

ruminant /ʀyminɑ̃/ *nm* ruminant.

ruminer /ʀymine/ [1] **I** *vtr* **1** ZOOL to ruminate, to chew the cud; **2** (penser constamment à) to brood on [*malheur*]; to chew over° [*idée, projet*].

II *vi* **1** ZOOL to ruminate, to chew the cud; **2** [*personne*] to brood.

rumsteck /ʀɔmstɛk/ *nm* rump steak.

rupestre /ʀypɛstʀ/ *adj* **1** [*plante, flore*] rock (*épith*); **2** [*peinture, art, dessin*] cave (*épith*), rock (*épith*).

rupture /ʀyptyʀ/ *nf* **1** (de relations, d'accord) breaking-off; **2** (résultat) breakdown (**avec** in); **3** (de couple, coalition, d'amis) break-up; **lettre de ~** letter ending a relationship; **4** (opposition) **être en ~ avec** to be at odds with [*hiérarchie, groupe*]; to have broken away from [*idéologie, tradition*]; **5** (cassure) GÉN break; (de barrage, digue) breaking; (de conduite) fracture; (de muscle, d'artère) rupture; (d'organe mécanique ou électrique) failure.

■ **~ d'anévrisme** ruptured aneurysm; **~ de charge** transshipment; **~ de contrat** breach of

contract; **~ de stock** stock shortage; **être en ~ de stock** to be out of stock.

rural, -e, *mpl* **-aux** /ʀyʀal, o/ **I** *adj* [*exode, milieu*] rural; [*chemin, vie*] country; **l'espace ~** the countryside.

II *nm,f* **les ruraux** people who live in the country.

ruse /ʀyz/ *nf* **1** (procédé) trick, ruse; **c'est une ~ de guerre** HUM it's a cunning stratagem; **c'est une ~ de Sioux** HUM it's a crafty trick; **2** (habileté) cunning, craftiness; **avec ~** cunningly.

rusé, -e /ʀyze/ **I** *adj* cunning, crafty; **jouer au plus ~ avec qn** to try to outsmart sb.

II *nm,f* **c'est une ~e** she's a crafty one.

ruser /ʀyze/ [1] *vi* **1** (être rusé) to be crafty; **2** (être plus fin que) **~ avec** to trick [*ennemi*]; **3** (vaincre) **~ avec** to find a way around [*difficulté*].

rush, *pl* **rushes** /ʀœʃ/ **I** *nm* **1** SPORT (à la course) final burst; (en sport collectif) attack; **2**° (ruée) rush.

II rushes *nmpl* CIN rushes.

russe /ʀys/ **▶338**⌋, **394**⌋ *adj, nm* LING Russian.

Russie /ʀysi/ **▶232**⌋ *nprf* Russia.

rusticité /ʀystisite/ *nf* **1** (de matériau, lieu) rustic character (**de** of); **2** (de plante) hardiness (**de** of).

rustine® /ʀystin/ *nf* (puncture-repair) patch.

rustique /ʀystik/ **I** *adj* **1** (campagnard) rustic, country (*épith*); **2** [*plante*] hardy (*épith*).

II *nm* **le ~** rustic style.

rustre /ʀystʀ/ **I** *adj* uncouth.

II *nm* **1** (homme grossier) lout; **2**† (paysan) peasant.

rut /ʀyt/ *nm* rutting season; **être en ~** to be in rut.

rutabaga /ʀytabaga/ *nm* swede GB, rutabaga US.

rutilant, -e /ʀytilɑ̃, ɑ̃t/ *adj* [*diamant*] sparkling; [*carrosserie, chrome*] gleaming.

rwandais, -e /ʀwɑ̃dɛ, ɛz/ **▶394**⌋ *adj* Rwandan.

rythme /ʀitm/ *nm* **1** LITTÉRAT, MUS rhythm; **au ~ de** the rhythm of; **marquer le ~** to beat time; **avoir le ~ dans la peau**° to have a natural sense of rhythm; **2** (d'accroissement, de production) rate; (de vie, film) pace; **changer au ~ des saisons** to change with the seasons; **la situation se dégrade à un ~ accéléré** the situation is deteriorating rapidly; **au ~ de** at a rate of; **3** (mouvement régulier) rate; **~ cardiaque** heart rate.

■ **~ biologique** biorhythm; **~ de croissance** growth rate; **~s scolaires** school timetables.

rythmé, -e /ʀitme/ *adj* rhythmic; **la musique est très ~e** the music has a very good rhythm.

rythmer /ʀitme/ [1] *vtr* **1** (scander) to put rhythm into [*phrase, poème*]; to give rhythm to [*tâche, marche*]; **2** (ponctuer) to regulate [*vie, journée, travail*].

rythmique /ʀitmik/ **I** *adj* rhythmic.

II *nf* **1** LING rhythmics (+ *v sg*); **2** MUS rhythm section.

Ss

s, S /ɛs/ *nm inv* s, S.

s' 1 ▶ se; 2 ▶ si¹.

sa ▶ son¹.

sabbat /saba/ *nm* 1 RELIG Sabbath; 2 (des sorcières) witching hour.

sabbatique /sabatik/ *adj* 1 RELIG Sabbatical; 2 UNIV, ADMIN [*année*] sabbatical.

sabir /sabiʀ/ *nm* 1 (charabia) mumbo-jumbo; 2 (mélange) pidgin.

sable /sabl/ I ▶ 141 *adj inv* sand-coloured^GB.
II *nm* sand; **bâtir sur le ~** FIG to build on sand.
III **sables** *nmpl* sands.
■ **~s mouvants** quicksands.
IDIOMES **être sur le ~**○ to be on one's beam ends.

sablé, ~e /sable/ I *adj* 1 [*route, allée*] covered with sand; 2 CULIN **pâte ~e** rich shortcrust pastry.
II *nm* (biscuit) ≈ shortbread biscuit GB ou cookie US.

sabler /sable/ [1] *vtr* 1 to grit [*chaussée*]; 2 TECH (pour nettoyer) to sandblast; (pour mouler) to sand-cast.

sableuse¹ /sabløz/ *nf* 1 (pour la chaussée) gritter; 2 (pour décaper) sandblaster.

sableux, -euse² /sablø, øz/ *adj* sandy.

sablier /sablije/ *nm* hourglass; (pour cuire des œufs) egg timer.

sablonneux, -euse /sablɔnø, øz/ *adj* sandy.

sabord /sabɔʀ/ *nm* scuttle.

sabordage /sabɔʀdaʒ/ *nm* NAUT scuttling.

saborder /sabɔʀde/ [1] I *vtr* NAUT, FIG to scuttle.
II **se saborder** *vpr* NAUT to scuttle ou scupper one's/ its etc own ship; FIG to sink oneself/itself.

sabot /sabo/ *nm* 1 (chaussure) clog; 2 ZOOL hoof; **donner un coup de ~ à qn** to kick sb; 3 AUT shoe; 4 TECH (de pieu, poteau) shoe; (de pied de meuble) (metal) foot; 5○ (objet sans valeur) old contraption.
■ **~ de Denver®** wheel clamp.
IDIOMES **jouer comme un ~**○ to play very badly; **je te vois** or **t'entends venir avec tes gros ~s**○ I can see it coming a mile off○; **ne pas avoir les deux pieds dans le même ~** to be on one's toes.

sabotage /sabotaʒ/ *nm* 1 (méthode) sabotage; 2 (acte) (act of) sabotage.

saboter /sabote/ [1] *vtr* to sabotage; **~ un travail**○ to botch○ a job.

saboteur, -euse /sabotœʀ, øz/ *nm,f* 1 (de matériel) saboteur; 2 (de travail) botcher○.

sabotier, -ière /sabotje, ɛʀ/ ▶ 374 *nm,f* (fabricant) clog maker; (commerçant) clog seller.

sabre /sabʀ/ *nm* (à lame droite) sword; (à lame courbée) sabre^GB; **~ au clair** MIL with sword(s) drawn; **bruits de ~** FIG sabre^GB rattling ⊄.
■ **~ d'abattage** or **d'abattis** machete; **~ d'abordage** cutlass.

sabrer /sabʀe/ [1] *vtr* 1 MIL to cut down; 2○ (écourter) to cut chunks out of [*article, manuscrit*]; (supprimer) to cut out [*phrase, paragraphe*]; to axe^GB [*projet*]; 3○ (critiquer) to tear [sb] to pieces [*auteur*]; to pan○ [*livre, film*]; 4○ (recaler) to flunk○ [*étudiant*]; (licencier) to fire, to sack○ GB; 5 (rayer) to score [*page, dessin*] (de with); 6○ (bâcler) to rush through [*travail*].

sabreur /sabʀœʀ/ *nm* 1 MIL, SPORT swordsman; 2 (soldat) PEJ real fighter.

sac /sak/ *nm* 1 (contenant) GÉN bag; (grossier, à usage commercial) sack; 2 (contenu) bag(ful), sack(ful); 3 ANAT, BOT sac; 4 (pillage) sack; **mettre à ~** to sack [*ville, région*]; to ransack [*boutique, maison*].
■ **~ à bandoulière** shoulder bag; **~ de congéla-tion** freezer bag; **~ de couchage** sleeping bag; **~ à dos** rucksack, backpack; **~ d'embrouilles** can of worms; **~ isotherme** cool bag; **~ à main** handbag, purse US; **~ (de) marin** NAUT kitbag GB, duffel bag US; **~ de nœuds** = **~ d'embrouilles**; **~ en plastique** (sans poignées) polythene bag; (avec poignées) carrier bag; **~ postal** mail sack; **~ poubelle** bin liner GB, trash bag US, trash-can liner US; **~ à provisions** shopping bag, carry-all US; **~ à puces**○ fleabag○ GB, flea-infested animal; **~ à vin**○ (old) soak○.
IDIOMES **l'affaire est dans le ~**○ it's in the bag○; **avoir plus d'un tour dans son ~** to have more than one trick up one's sleeve; **vider son ~**○ to get it off one's chest; **se faire prendre la main dans le ~** to be caught red-handed; **mettre dans le même ~**○ to lump [sth] together.

saccade /sakad/ *nf* jerk.

saccadé, ~e /sakade/ *adj* [*mouvement, marche*] jerky; [*musique, rythme*] staccato; [*voix*] clipped.

saccage /sakaʒ/ *nm* (de région) devastation; (de bâti-ment) vandalizing.

saccager /sakaʒe/ [13] *vtr* 1 (abîmer) to wreck, to devastate [*région, site, arbres*]; to vandalize [*bâtiment, tombe*]; 2 (mettre à sac) to sack.

saccharine /sakaʀin/ *nf* saccharin.

SACEM /sasɛm/ *nf* (abbr = **Société des auteurs compositeurs et éditeurs de musique**) associa-tion of composers and music publishers to protect copyright and royalties.

sacerdoce /sasɛʀdɔs/ *nm* 1 RELIG priesthood; **30 ans de ~** 30 years in the priesthood; 2 FIG vocation.

sacerdotal, ~e, *mpl* **-aux** /sasɛʀdɔtal, o/ *adj* priestly.

sachet /saʃɛ/ *nm* (de poudre) packet; (d'aromates) sachet; (de confiseries) bag; **~ de thé** tea bag.

sacoche /sakɔʃ/ *nf* 1 (gros sac) bag; 2 (contre la roue arrière d'un vélo, d'une moto) pannier GB, saddlebag US; 3 (d'écolier) (school)bag; (avec bretelles) satchel.

sacquer○ /sake/ [1] *vtr* 1 [*employeur*] to sack○, to fire○ [*employé*]; 2 [*enseignant*] to mark [sb] strictly; **se faire ~ en anglais** to get a really low mark in English.
IDIOMES **je ne peux pas le ~** I can't stand the sight of him.

sacraliser /sakʀalize/ [1] *vtr* 1 (rendre sacré) to make [sth] sacred; 2 (considérer comme sacré) to regard [sth] as sacred.

sacre /sakʀ/ *nm* (de roi) coronation; (d'évêque) conse-cration; **le Sacre du Printemps** MUS The Rite of Spring.

sacré, ~e /sakʀe/ I *adj* 1 RELIG [*art, objet, lieu*] sacred; [*cause*] holy; 2 (à respecter) [*règle, droit*] sacred; 3○ (remarquable) **être un ~ menteur** to be a hell of○ a liar; **il a un ~ courage** he's really cour-ageous; 4○ (d'admiration, de surprise) **~ Paul, va!** Paul you old devil!
II *nm* **le ~** the sacred.
IDIOMES **avoir le feu ~** to be full of zeal ou enthu-siasm.

sacrement /sakʀəmɑ̃/ *nm* sacrament; **mourir muni des derniers ~s de l'Église** to die having received the last rites of the Church.

sacrément○ /sakʀemɑ̃/ *adv* incredibly○.

sacrer /sakʀe/ [1] *vtr* RELIG to crown [*roi*]; to consecrate [*évêque*].

sacrifice /sakʀifis/ *nm* sacrifice.

sacrifier /sakʀifje/ [1] I *vtr* **1** (immoler) LIT to sacrifice (à to); **2** (négliger) to sacrifice; **~ sa famille à son travail** to put one's work before one's family; **'prix sacrifiés'** COMM 'rock-bottom prices'.
II **sacrifier à** *vtr ind* to conform to [*rite, coutume*].
III **se sacrifier** *vpr* **1** LIT to sacrifice oneself (**pour qn** for sb); **2**○ FIG (financièrement) to make sacrifices.

sacrilège /sakʀilɛʒ/ I *adj* sacrilegious.
II *nm* RELIG sacrilege **₵**; **un ~** an act of sacrilege.

sacripant○ /sakʀipɑ̃/ *nm* tearaway○.

sacristain /sakʀistɛ̃/ **▶ 374** *nm* sexton.

sacristie /sakʀisti/ *nf* (d'église) sacristy; (de temple protestant) vestry.

sacro-saint, **~e**, *mpl* **~s** /sakʀosɛ̃, ɛ̃t/ *adj* sacrosanct.

sadique /sadik/ I *adj* sadistic.
II *nmf* sadist.

sadisme /sadism/ *nm* sadism.

sadomasochisme /sadomazɔʃism/ *nm* sadomasochism.

sadomasochiste /sadomazɔʃist/ I *adj* sadomasochistic.
II *nmf* sadomasochist.

safran /safʀɑ̃/ **▶ 141** I *adj inv* saffron (yellow).
II *nm* **1** (épice) saffron; **riz au ~** saffron rice; **2** (couleur) saffron.

sagace /sagas/ *adj* sagacious, shrewd.

sagacité /sagasite/ *nf* sagacity, shrewdness.

sagaie /sage/ *nf* assegai.

sage /saʒ/ I *adj* **1** (sensé) wise, sensible; **2** (docile) [*enfant, chien*] good, well-behaved; **sois ~!** be good!; **3** (modéré) [*goût, mode*] sober; [*prix*] moderate, reasonable; [*idées*] sensible; **4** (pudique) [*vêtement*] sober.
II *nm* **1** (homme avisé) wise man; (dans l'antiquité) sage; **2** (conseiller) expert.
IDIOMES **être ~ comme une image** to be as good as gold.

sage-femme, *pl* **sages-femmes** /saʒfam/ **▶ 374** *nf* midwife; **un homme ~** a male midwife.

sagement /saʒmɑ̃/ *adv* **1** (avec bon sens) wisely; **2** (avec docilité) quietly; **3** (avec décence) GÉN properly; [*s'habiller*] soberly; [*vivre*] quietly.

sagesse /saʒɛs/ *nf* **1** (de sage) wisdom; **▶ crainte**; **2** (bon sens) (de personne) wisdom, common sense; (de parole, décision, d'action) wisdom; (de conseil) soundness; **faire preuve de ~** to show common sense; **3** (docilité) good behaviour^{GB}.

Sagittaire /saʒitɛʀ/ **▶ 641** *nprm* Sagittarius.

saharienne /saaʀjɛn/ *nf* (veste) safari jacket.

saignant, **~e** /sɛɲɑ̃, ɑ̃t/ *adj* **1** [*viande*] rare; **2**○ FIG [*critique*] savage; SPORT [*rencontre*] bloody.

saignée /sɛɲe/ *nf* **1** MÉD bloodletting, bleeding; **2** (dans un budget) hole (**dans** in); **3** (entaille) cut.

saignement /sɛɲ(ə)mɑ̃/ *nm* bleeding **₵**.

saigner /sɛɲe/ [1] I *vtr* **1** MÉD to bleed; **2** (tuer) to kill [*animal*] (**by slitting its throat**).
II *vi* to bleed; **~ du nez** to have a nosebleed.
IDIOMES **~ comme un bœuf**○ to bleed heavily; **~ qn à blanc** to bleed sb dry ou white; **se ~ (aux quatre veines) pour qn** to make big sacrifices for sb.

saillant, **~e** /sajɑ̃, ɑ̃t/ *adj* **1** [*os*] prominent; [*muscle*] bulging; [*angle*] salient; **2** [*fait*] salient.

saillie /saji/ *nf* **1** (avancée) projection; **en ~** projecting (*épith*); **faire ~** to project; **2** ZOOL covering, serving; **3** (pointe d'esprit) sally.

saillir /sajiʀ/ [28] *vi* (avancer) to jut out; (ressortir) [*côtes, muscles*] to bulge.

sain, **~e** /sɛ̃, sɛn/ *adj* **1** (en bonne santé) LIT, FIG [*personne, corps, plante*] healthy; [*dent*] sound, healthy; **~ d'esprit** sane; **~ de corps et d'esprit** sound in body and mind; **~ et sauf** [*revenir*] safe and sound; [*s'en tirer, s'en sortir*] unscathed; **2** (bénéfique) [*climat, vie*] healthy; [*affaire, entreprise*] sound; [*lecture*] wholesome; **3** (en bon état) [*fruit, maison*] sound; [*plaie*] clean; **4** (solide) [*jugement, bases*] sound; [*économie*] healthy.

saindoux /sɛ̃du/ *nm inv* lard.

sainement /sɛnmɑ̃/ *adv* **1** [*vivre*] healthily; **2** [*raisonner*] soundly.

saint, **~e** /sɛ̃, sɛ̃t/ I *adj* **1** (sacré) holy; **vendredi ~** Good Friday; **jeudi ~** Maundy Thursday; **2** (canonisé) **~ Paul** Saint Paul; **3** (vertueux) good, godly.
II *nm,f* saint; **ce n'est pas une ~e!** she's no saint!; **se prendre pour un ~/une ~e** to think one is perfect; **▶ vouer**.
■ **~e nitouche** PEJ goody-goody○ PÉJ; **la Sainte Vierge** the Virgin Mary.

Saint-Barthélémy /sɛ̃baʀtelemi/ *nf* **la ~** the St Bartholomew's Day massacre.

saint-bernard /sɛ̃bɛʀnaʀ/ *nm inv* (chien) St Bernard; **c'est un vrai ~** FIG he's/she's a real Good Samaritan.

Saint-Cyr /sɛ̃siʀ/ *npr*: *French military academy*.

Saint-Esprit /sɛ̃tɛspʀi/ *nprm* Holy Spirit; (en formule) Holy Ghost; **par l'opération du ~**○ by magic.

sainteté /sɛ̃te/ *nf* (de personne) saintliness.
IDIOMES **ne pas être en odeur de ~ (auprès de qn)** to be in sb's bad books.

saint-frusquin○ /sɛ̃fʀyskɛ̃/ *nm inv* **tout le ~** the whole caboodle○.

saint-glinglin○: **à la saint-glinglin** /alasɛ̃glɛ̃glɛ̃/ *loc adv* probably never; **rester/attendre jusqu'à la ~** to stay/to wait till the cows come home○.

Saint-Guy /sɛ̃gi/ **▶ 196** *npr* **la danse de ~** MÉD Saint Vitus's dance; FIG the fidgets (*pl*).

saint-honoré /sɛ̃tɔnɔʀe/ *nm inv* CULIN Saint-Honoré (*cream-filled tart topped with choux and caramel*).

Saint-Jacques /sɛ̃ʒak/ *npr* **coquille ~** scallop.

Saint-Jean /sɛ̃ʒɑ̃/ *nf* **la ~** Midsummer Day; **feux de la ~** bonfires lit on Midsummer Night.

Saint-Martin /sɛ̃maʀtɛ̃/ **▶ 156** *nf* **été de la ~** Indian summer.

Saint-Sylvestre /sɛ̃silvɛstʀ/ *nf* **la ~** New Year's Eve.

Saint-Valentin /sɛ̃valɑ̃tɛ̃/ **▶ 156** *nf* **la ~** St Valentine's Day, Valentine's Day.

saisie /sezi/ *nf* **1** GÉN, JUR (confiscation) seizure; **2** ORDINAT **~ (informatique)** keyboarding; **~ de données** data capture.

saisir /seziʀ/ [3] I *vtr* **1** (prendre fermement) to grab [*objet, personne, bras*]; **~ qn par le bras** to grab sb by the arm; **2** (attraper) [*animal*] to seize [*proie*]; (prendre) to snatch [sth] up [*clés*]; **~ au vol** LIT to catch [*balle*]; FIG to jump at [*affaire*]; **3** (profiter de) to seize [*occasion*]; **'affaire à ~'** 'amazing bargain'; **4** (comprendre) to understand; **tu saisis?** do you get it?○; **5** (entendre) to catch [*bribes de conversation*]; **6** (s'emparer de) [*émotion, froid*] to grip [*personne*]; **7** (impressionner) to strike [*personne*]; **8** (confisquer) [*police, douane*] to seize [*drogue*]; **9** JUR to seize [*biens*]; **~ la justice d'une affaire** to refer a matter to a court; **10** ORDINAT to capture [*données*]; to keyboard [*texte*].
II **se saisir** *vpr* **se ~** to catch.

saisissable /sezisabl/ *adj* JUR [*biens*] distrainable; [*revenus*] attachable.

saisissant, **~e** /sezisɑ̃, ɑ̃t/ *adj* **1** [*froid*] piercing; **2** (frappant) [*effet, ressemblance, coïncidence*] striking.

saison /sezɔ̃/ **▶ 542** *nf* **1** (division de l'année) season; **en cette ~** at this time of year; **en toute ~** all (the) year round; **fruits de ~** seasonal fruits; **à la belle ~** in the summer months; **2** (période) season; **~ des pluies** rainy season; **~ des amours** mating season; **~ des foins** haymaking; **3** TOURISME, SPORT, THÉÂT season; **la haute/morte ~** the high/slack season; **prix hors ~** off-season prices.

saisonnier, **-ière** /sezɔnje, ɛʀ/ I *adj* seasonal.
II *nm,f* (ouvrier) seasonal worker.

Les saisons

En anglais, on trouve quelquefois les noms des saisons avec des majuscules, mais les minuscules sont préférables.

printemps	= spring
été	= summer
automne	= autumn (*GB*) *ou* fall (*US*)
hiver	= winter

Dans les expressions suivantes, summer est pris comme exemple; les autres noms de saisons s'utilisent de la même façon.

j'aime l'été	= I like the summer *ou* I like summer
l'été a été pluvieux	= the summer was wet *ou* summer was wet
un été pluvieux	= a rainy summer
l'été le plus chaud	= the warmest summer

Quand?

L'anglais emploie souvent in *devant les noms de saisons.*

en été	= in the summer *ou* in summer
au début de l'été	= in the early summer *ou* in early summer
à la fin de l'été	= in the late summer *ou* in late summer
à la mi-été	= in mid-summer

Mais in *peut être remplacé par une autre préposition, ou par* this, that, next, last *etc.*

pendant l'été	= during the summer
pendant tout l'été	= throughout the summer
tout au long de l'été	= all through the summer
avant l'été	= before the summer
jusqu'à l'été	= until the summer
cet été	= this summer

cet été-là	= that summer
l'été prochain	= next summer
l'été dernier	= last summer
l'année prochaine en été	
(c'est l'automne ou l'hiver)	= next summer
(c'est le printemps)	= the summer after next
l'année dernière en été	
(c'est le printemps)	= last summer
(c'est l'automne ou l'hiver)	= the summer before last
tous les ans en été	= every summer
un été sur deux	= every other summer *ou* every second summer
presque tous les étés	= most summers

De avec les noms de saisons

Les expressions françaises avec de se traduisent en anglais par l'emploi des noms de saisons en position d'adjectifs.

la collection d'été	= the summer collection
une journée d'été	= a summer day
une pluie d'été	= a summer shower
un soir d'été	= a summer evening
le soleil d'été	= summer sunshine
les soldes d'été	= the summer sales
des vêtements d'été	= summer clothes
un temps d'été	= summer weather

Enfin, comparer:

un matin d'été	= one summer morning
par un matin d'été	= on a summer morning
un matin en été	= one morning in summer

---

salace /salas/ *adj* salacious.

salade /salad/ *nf* **1** (plante) lettuce; **2** (plat) salad; **~ verte** green salad; **~ de tomates/riz** tomato/rice salad; **3**○ (embrouillamini) muddle; (mensonge) yarn; (boniment de vendeur) sales patter *ou* pitch○; **raconter des ~s** to spin yarns○.

saladier /saladje/ *nm* **1** (récipient) salad bowl; **2** (contenu) bowl.

salaire /salɛʀ/ *nm* **1** (paie) salary; (à la journée, à l'heure, à la semaine) (taux) wage; (somme) wages (*pl*); **~ annuel/mensuel** annual/monthly salary; **~ brut/net** gross/take-home pay; **~ de misère** *ou* **famine** starvation wage; **2** FIG (récompense) reward (**de** for); (châtiment) punishment (**de** for).
■ **~ de base** basic salary GB, base pay US; **~ d'embauche** starting salary; **~ minimum interprofessionnel de croissance**, **SMIC** guaranteed minimum wage; **~ unique** single income.
IDIOMES **toute peine mérite ~** PROV hard work deserves a reward.

salaison /salɛzɔ̃/ *nf* (viande) salt meat ₵; (poisson) salt fish ₵.

salamandre /salamɑ̃dʀ/ *nf* ZOOL salamander.

salami /salami/ *nm* salami GB, boloney US.

salant /salɑ̃/ *adj m* **marais ~** saltern.

salarial, **~e**, *mpl* **-iaux** /salaʀjal, o/ *adj* **1** (des salaires) [politique, augmentation] wage (*épith*); **2** (des salariés) **cotisation ~e** employee's contribution.

salarié, **~e** /salaʀje/ **I** *adj* [ouvrier, employé] wage-earning; [emploi, travail] salaried; **travailleur non ~** non-wage-earning worker.
II *nm,f* (ouvrier) wage earner; (employé) salaried employee.

salaud○ /salo/ **I** *adj m* rotten○.
II *nm* OFFENSIVE bastard❶ INJUR.

sale /sal/ **I** *adj* **1** (*after n*) (pas propre) dirty; (obscène) dirty; **2**○ (*before n*) (désagréable) [individu] horrible; [bête, maladie, affaire, habitude] nasty; [temps] foul, horrible; [travail, endroit] rotten○, dirty; **~ menteur!** you dirty liar!; **il a une ~ tête** (antipathique) he's got a nasty face; (maladif) he looks dreadful; **un ~ coup** LIT, FIG a very nasty blow; **jouer un ~ tour à qn** to play a dirty trick on sb; **un ~ caractère** a foul temper.

II *nm* **mettre qch au ~** to put sth in the wash.
IDIOMES **être ~ comme un peigne** *or* **un cochon** to be filthy dirty.

salé, **~e** /sale/ **I** *pp* ▶ **saler**.
II *pp adj* **1** (contenant du sel) salt (*épith*); salty (*jamais épith*); **2** (additionné de sel) [beurre, eau, plat] salted; [mets, amuse-gueule] savoury GB; (conservé avec du sel) [poisson, viande] salt (*épith*); **manger ~** to eat savoury GB things; **non ~** unsalted; **trop ~** too salty; **3** (de sel) salty; **goût ~** salty taste.
III *adj* (grivois) spicy; **propos ~s** spicy talk ₵.

salement /salmɑ̃/ *adv* **1** (en salissant) **manger ~** to be a messy eater; **2**○ (gravement) badly, seriously.

saler /sale/ [1] *vtr* **1** (mettre du sel sur) to salt [mets]; **2**○ (augmenter) to bump up○ [facture, note, prix]; **3** (en hiver) to grit GB, to salt US [route].

saleté /salte/ *nf* **1** (état) dirtiness; (crasse) dirt; **d'une ~ repoussante** to be filthy; **vivre dans la ~** to live in filth; **être couvert de ~** to be covered with dirt; **2** (impureté) dirt ₵; **il y a une ~ sur l'objectif** there's dirt on the lens; **3** (ordure) **ramasser les ~s** to pick up the rubbish GB *ou* trash US; **faire des ~s** LIT, EUPH to make a mess; **4**○ (chose de mauvaise qualité) (objet) piece of junk; (aliment) junk food ₵; **~ d'ordinateur!** damn○ computer!; **c'est une vraie ~ ce virus!** it's a rotten bug!

salière /saljɛʀ/ *nf* CULIN saltcellar, saltshaker US.

saligaud❶ /saligo/ *nm* OFFENSIVE dirty bastard❶ INJUR.

salir /saliʀ/ [3] **I** *vtr* **1** (rendre sale) to dirty [sol, assiette]; to soil [draps, lit]; **2** (flétrir) to sully [mémoire, amour, réputation]; to corrupt [artiste, imagination].
II *vi* [industrie, charbon] to pollute.
III se salir *vpr* (se couvrir de taches, de saleté) to get dirty, to dirty oneself.

salissant, **~e** /salisɑ̃, ɑ̃t/ *adj* **1** [couleur, tissu] which shows the dirt (*épith*, *après n*); **2** [travail] dirty.

salissure /salisyʀ/ *nf* (dirty) mark.

salive /saliv/ *nf* saliva.
IDIOMES **perdre** *or* **dépenser inutilement sa ~** to waste one's breath.

saliver /salive/ [1] *vi* to salivate; **~ devant qch** to drool over sth.

salle /sal/ *nf* **1** (pièce) GÉN room; (de château, palais) hall; (de restaurant) (dining) room; (de cinéma, théâtre) auditorium; (de grotte) chamber; **cinéma à cinq ~s** cinema with five screens; **faire ~ comble** [*spectacle*] to be packed; [*acteur*] to fill the house; **en ~** [*sport*] indoor; **2** (spectateurs) audience.
■ (entrepôt) armory; **~ d'attente** waiting room; **~ d'audience** JUR courtroom; **~ de bains** bathroom; **~ de cinéma** cinema GB, movie theater US; **~ de classe** classroom; **~ commune** (à l'hôpital) ward; **~ de concert** concert hall; **~ de conférences** (avec gradins) lecture theatre^GB, auditorium; **~ d'eau** shower room; **~ d'embarquement** AVIAT departure lounge; **~ d'études** SCOL private study room GB, study hall US; **~ des fêtes** (de village) village hall; (en ville) community centre^GB; **~ de garde** (d'hôpital) staff room; **~ de jeu(x)** (de casino) gaming room; (pour enfants) playroom; **~ des machines** NAUT engine room; **~ à manger** (pièce) dining room; (mobilier) dining-room suite; **~ omnisports** sports hall; **~ d'opération** MÉD operating theatre GB, operating room US; **~ des pas perdus** waiting hall; **~ polyvalente** multi-purpose hall; **~ de séjour** living room; **~ des ventes** auction room; **~s obscures** cinemas GB, movie theaters US.

saloir /salwaR/ *nm* salting tub.

salon /salɔ̃/ *nm* **1** (pièce) GÉN lounge; (dans un château, palais) drawing room; **~-salle à manger** living-cum-dining room; **2** (mobilier) living-room suite, sitting-room suite; **~ de jardin** garden furniture ¢; **3** (exposition) (pour professionnels) (trade) show; (pour grand public) fair; (artistique) exhibition; **le ~ de l'auto** the car show; **~ du livre** book fair; **4** (réunion mondaine, intellectuelle) salon; **faire ~** to hold a salon.
■ **~ de beauté** beauty salon; **~ de coiffure** hairdressing salon; **~ d'essayage** fitting room; **~ de thé** tearoom.

salope❶ /salɔp/ *nf* OFFENSIVE (garce) bitch❶ INJUR; (femme facile) tart❶ INJUR, whore.

saloper○ /salɔpe/ [1] *vtr* **1** (gâcher) to botch○ [*travail*]; **2** (salir) to muck up○ [*vêtement*].

saloperie❶ /salɔpRi/ *nf* **1** (saleté) muck○ ¢, FIG (produit nocif, drogue) muck○ ¢; **2** (microbe, maladie) bug○; **3** (nourriture) (infecte) muck○ ¢, slop○; (malsaine) junk (food)○ ¢; **4** (objet de rebut) junk○ ¢; **5** (procédé) dirty trick.

salopette /salɔpɛt/ *nf* (pour protéger) overalls (*pl*); (pour s'habiller) dungarees (*pl*) GB, overalls (*pl*) US.

salpêtre /salpɛtR/ *nm* saltpetre^GB.

salpingite /salpɛ̃ʒit/ **▶196|** *nf* salpingitis.

salsifis /salsifi/ *nm inv* salsify.

saltimbanque /saltɛ̃bɑ̃k/ *nmf* **1** (bateleur) street acrobat; **2** (comédien) PEJ entertainer.

salubre /salybR/ *adj* [*climat*] healthy; [*logement*] salubrious.

salubrité /salybRite/ *nf* (d'air, de climat) healthiness; (de logement) salubrity SOUT.
■ **~ publique** public health.

saluer /salɥe/ [1] *vtr* **1** (dire bonjour) to greet [*personne*]; **~ qn de la main** to wave to ou at sb; **~ qn de la tête** to nod to sb; **~ qn de loin/en passant** to acknowledge sb from a distance/in passing; **saluez-la de ma part** say hello to her from me; **le public** to take a bow; **2** (dire au revoir) to say goodbye to [*personne*]; **je vous salue** I'll say goodbye; **3** (accueillir) to greet [*personne*]; **4** MIL to salute [*soldat, officier, drapeau, navire*]; **5** (accueillir avec satisfaction) to welcome [*décision, résultat*]; **6** (rendre hommage) to salute [*héros*]; to pay tribute to [*défunt*]; to praise [*travail, attitude*]; **je vous salue Marie** hail Mary.

salut /saly/ *nm* **1** (salutation) greeting; **~!** (bonjour) hello!, hi!; (au revoir) bye!; **~ de la main** wave (of the hand); **~ de la tête** nod; **~ des acteurs** bow; **2** (geste) salute; **3** (secours) salvation (**dans** in); **4** RELIG (rédemption) salvation; **5** (hommage) homage (à to).

salutaire /salytɛR/ *adj* (bénéfique) [*choc, expérience*]

salutary; [*effet, environnement*] beneficial; [*air, habitude*] healthy; **cela leur a été ~** it did them good.

salutation /salytasjɔ̃/ **I** *nf* **1** GÉN greeting; **2** RELIG salutation.
II salutations *nfpl* **sincères ~s** (à une personne nommée) yours sincerely; (à une personne non nommée) yours faithfully.

salvateur, -trice /salvatœR, tRis/ *adj* saving (épith).

salve /salv/ *nf* **1** (d'armes à feu) salvo; **tirer une ~ d'honneur** to fire a salute; **2** (série) **~ d'applaudissements** burst of applause; **~ d'injures** volley of insults; **3** (attaque verbale) broadside.

Samaritain, -e /samaritɛ̃, ɛn/ *nm,f* Samaritan; **jouer les ~s** to act the good Samaritan.

samedi /samdi/ **▶551|** *nm* Saturday.

SAMU /samy/ *nm* (abbr = **Service d'assistance médicale d'urgence**) ≈ mobile accident unit GB, emergency medical service, EMS US.

sanctifier /sɑ̃ktifje/ [1] *vtr* to sanctify.

sanction /sɑ̃ksjɔ̃/ *nf* **1** (peine) JUR penalty, sanction; ADMIN disciplinary measure; SCOL punishment; **prendre des ~s contre qn** GÉN to discipline sb; ADMIN to take disciplinary action against sb; **2** (jugement) verdict.

sanctionner /sɑ̃ksjɔne/ [1] *vtr* **1** (punir) to punish [*faute, coupable*]; **2** (consacrer) to give official recognition to [*études, formation*].

sanctuaire /sɑ̃ktɥeR/ *nm* **1** (lieu saint) shrine; **2** (asile) sanctuary.

sandale /sɑ̃dal/ *nf* sandal.

sandalette /sɑ̃dalɛt/ *nf* light sandal.

sandow® /sɑ̃do/ *nm* **1** (sangle) luggage elastic; **2** AVIAT bungee.

sandwich, *pl* **~s** or **~es** /sɑ̃dwitʃ/ *nm* CULIN sandwich; (pris) **en ~** sandwiched.

sang /sɑ̃/ *nm* **1** BIOL blood; **donner son ~** to give blood; **~ contaminé** contaminated blood; **perte de ~** loss of blood; **être en ~** to be covered with blood; **couleur de ~** blood-red; **taché de ~** bloodstained; **mordre jusqu'au ~** to bite through the skin; **animal à ~ chaud/froid** warm-/cold-blooded animal; **avoir le ~ qui monte au visage** to blush; **faire couler le ~** FIG to shed blood; **le ~ a coulé** FIG blood flowed; **2** (vie) **au prix du ~** with loss of life; **▶pinte**; **3** (violence) bloodshed; **se terminer dans le ~** to end in bloodshed; **4** (hérédité) blood; **de ~** [*frère, liens*] blood (épith); **être du même ~** to be kin.
■ **~ bleu** blue blood; **~ rouge** arterial blood.
IDIOMES **avoir le ~ chaud** (être sensuel) to be hot-blooded; (être coléreux) to be hotheaded; **avoir un coup de ~** to have apoplexy; **il a ça dans le ~** it's in his blood; **mettre qch à feu et à ~** to put sth to fire and the sword; **mon ~ n'a fait qu'un tour** (d'émotion) my heart missed a beat; (de colère) I saw red; **se faire du mauvais ~**○ to worry; **bon ~** (de bonsoir○)! for God's sake○!

sang-froid /sɑ̃fRwa/ *nm inv* composure; **perdre son ~** to lose one's composure; **garde ton ~!** keep calm!; **faire qch de ~** to do sth in cold blood.

sanglant, -e /sɑ̃glɑ̃, ɑ̃t/ *adj* **1** (violent) [*affrontement, incident, répression, putsch, époque*] bloody; **2** (outrageant) [*affront, défaite*] cruel; **3** (couvert de sang) [*plaie, main*] bloody; [*couteau, vêtement*] blood-stained.

sangle /sɑ̃gl/ *nf* **1** (pour attacher) strap; **2** (pour un cheval) girth; **3** (de siège, lit) webbing ¢.
■ **~ abdominale** ANAT abdominal muscles (*pl*).

sangler /sɑ̃gle/ [1] *vtr* to girth [*cheval*].

sanglier /sɑ̃glije/ *nm* wild boar.

sanglot /sɑ̃glo/ *nm* sob; **éclater en ~s** to burst out sobbing; **avec des ~s dans la voix** with a sob in one's voice.

sangloter /sɑ̃glɔte/ [1] *vi* to sob.

sangsue /sɑ̃sy/ *nf* leech.

sanguin, -e¹ /sɑ̃gɛ̃, in/ *adj* **1** (de sang) blood; **examen/prélèvement ~** blood test/sample; **2** (rouge) [*visage*] ruddy; **3** (impétueux) impulsive.

II *nm,f* **c'est un ~** he's hotheaded.

sanguinaire /sɑ̃ginɛʀ/ *adj* [*régime, bataille, crime*] bloody; [*personne*] bloodthirsty.

sanguine² /sɑ̃gin/ **I** *adj f* ▶ **sanguin**.

II *nf* **1** (orange à pulpe rouge) blood orange; **2** ART (dessin) red chalk drawing; (crayon) red chalk.

sanguinolent, ~e /sɑ̃ginɔlɑ̃, ɑ̃t/ *adj* [*couteau, vêtement*] blood-stained; [*plaie*] from which blood is oozing (*épith, après n*).

sanisette® /sanizɛt/ *nf* automatic public toilet.

sanitaire /sanitɛʀ/ **I** *adj* [*règlement, personnel*] health (*épith*); [*conditions*] sanitary.

II sanitaires *nmpl* **les ~s** (dans un bâtiment) the bathroom (*sg*); (dans un camping) the toilet block (*sg*).

sans /sɑ̃/

■ **Note** Lorsque *sans* marque l'absence, le manque ou la privation, il se traduit généralement par *without*. Lorsqu'il fait partie d'une expression figée comme *sans concession, sans équivoque, sans emploi, sans intérêt* la traduction est donnée respectivement sous **concession, équivoque, emploi, intérêt** etc.
– De même, quand il est associé à un verbe, *compter sans, cela va sans dire* etc, la traduction est donnée respectivement sous les verbes **compter, dire¹** etc.
– La double négation *non sans* est traitée sous **non**.
– On trouvera ci-dessous d'autres exemples et les usages particuliers de *sans*.

I *adv* without; **faire ~** to do without.

II *prép* **1** (absence, manque) without [*personne, accord, permission*]; **une maison ~ téléphone** a house without a telephone; **je suis ~ voiture aujourd'hui** I don't have a car today; **je bois mon thé ~ sucre** I don't take sugar in my tea; **du chocolat noir ~ sucre** sugar-free dark chocolate; **un visage ~ charme** an unattractive face; **un couple ~ enfant** a childless couple; **c'est un couple ~ enfant** they have no children; **une personne ~ fierté/scrupules** a person who has no pride/scruples; **~ cela** or **ça**○ otherwise; **2** (pour écarter une circonstance) **il est resté trois mois ~ téléphoner** he didn't call for three months; **il est poli, ~ plus** he's polite, but that's as far as it goes; **~ plus tarder** without further delay; **3** (à l'exclusion de) **on sera douze ~ les enfants** there'll be twelve of us not counting the children; **3500 francs ~ le voyage** 3,500 francs not including transport GB ou transportation US.

III sans que *loc conj* without; **pars ~ qu'on te voie** leave without anyone seeing you.

■ **~ domicile fixe, SDF** no fixed abode, NFA.

sans-abri /sɑ̃zabʀi/ *nmf inv* **un ~** a homeless person; **les ~** the homeless.

sans-cœur /sɑ̃kœʀ/ *nmf inv* heartless person.

sans-emploi /sɑ̃zɑ̃plwa/ *nmf inv* unemployed person; **les ~** the unemployed, the jobless (+ *v pl*).

sans-faute /sɑ̃fot/ *nm inv* **1** (en équitation) clear round; **2** FIG faultless performance.

sans-gêne /sɑ̃ʒɛn/ **I** *adj inv* cheeky, bad-mannered (*épith*).

II *nmf inv* cheeky person, bad-mannered person.

III *nm* **faire preuve de ~** to be cheeky ou bad-mannered.

santal /sɑ̃tal/ *nm* sandalwood.

santé /sɑ̃te/ *nf* **1** (de personne, pays, d'organisation) health; **~ mentale** mental health; **être en bonne/mauvaise ~** to be in good/bad health; **avoir la ~** LIT to enjoy good health; FIG to be full of bounce; **il respire la ~** he's glowing with health; **avoir une ~ de fer** to have an iron constitution; **2** (en buvant) **à votre ~!** cheers!; **à la ~ de Janet!** here's to Janet!; **3** ADMIN health.

santon /sɑ̃tɔ̃/ *nm* Christmas crib figure.

saoudien, -ienne /saudjɛ̃, ɛn/ ▶ **394** *adj* Saudi (Arabian).

saoul, ~e ▶ **soûl**.

sape /sap/ *nf* **travail de ~** TECH sap digging; FIG sabo tage.

saper /sape/ [1] **I** *vtr* (détruire) to undermine [*mur, fa laise, moral*].

II○ **se saper** *vpr* **1** (s'habiller) to dress; **être bien/mal sapé** to be well/badly dressed; **2** (s'habiller bien) t dress up to the nines○.

sapeur /sapœʀ/ *nm* sapper.

IDIOMES fumer comme un ~ to smoke like chimney.

sapeur-pompier, *pl* **sapeurs-pompiers** /sapœʀpɔ̃pje/ *nm* fireman; **les sapeurs-pompiers d Paris** the Paris Fire Brigade.

saphir /safiʀ/ *nm* **1** (pierre) sapphire; **2** (pointe d lecture) stylus.

sapidité /sapidite/ *nf* sapidity; **agent de ~** flavour ing GB agent.

sapin /sapɛ̃/ *nm* **1** fir tree; **2** (bois) deal.

saquer○ = **sacquer**.

sarbacane /saʀbakan/ *nf* blowpipe.

sarcasme /saʀkasm/ *nm* **1** (dérision) sarcasm; **2** (re marque) sarcastic remark.

sarcastique /saʀkastik/ *adj* sarcastic.

sarcler /saʀkle/ [1] *vtr* to hoe.

sarcloir /saʀklwaʀ/ *nm* hoe.

sarcophage /saʀkɔfaʒ/ *nm* sarcophagus.

Sardaigne /saʀdɛɲ/ ▶ **305** *nprf* Sardinia.

sarde /saʀd/ ▶ **338** *adj, nm* Sardinian.

sardine /saʀdin/ *nf* **1** ZOOL sardine; **~ à l'huile** sardine in oil; **2**○ (piquet de tente) tent peg.

IDIOMES être serrés comme des ~s○ to be crammed together like sardines.

sardonique /saʀdɔnik/ *adj* sardonic.

sarment /saʀmɑ̃/ *nm* **~ (de vigne)** vine shoot.

sarrasin, ~e /saʀazɛ̃, in/ **I** *adj* HIST Saracen.

II *nm* BOT, CULIN buckwheat.

Sarre /saʀ/ ▶ **260**, **509** *nprf* (rivière, région) Saar.

sas /sas/ *nm inv* **1** (pièce étanche) airlock; **2** (d'écluse) lock.

satané○**, ~e** /satane/ *adj* damned○.

satanique /satanik/ *adj* **1** (démoniaque) [*sourire, ruse*] fiendish; **2** (de Satan) [*culte*] Satanic.

satelliser /satelize/ [1] *vtr* **1** ASTRONAUT to put [sth] into orbit [*engin*]; **2** FIG (assujettir) to turn [sth] into a satellite [*pays, entreprise*].

satellite /satelit/ *nm* **1** (astre, engin) satellite; **~ de transmission/météorologique** broadcasting/weather satellite; **2** POL (pays) satellite.

satiété /sasjete/ *nf* satiation, satiety.

II à satiété *loc adv* **1** (jusqu'à satisfaction) **manger à ~** to eat one's fill; **il avait mangé à ~** he was replete; **2** (jusqu'à saturation) [*répéter*] ad nauseam.

satin /satɛ̃/ *nm* satin; **une peau de ~** a satin-smooth skin.

satiné, ~e /satine/ *adj* [*étoffe*] satiny (*épith*); [*doublure*] satin (*épith*); [*peinture*] satin-finish (*épith*).

satire /satiʀ/ *nf* satire.

satirique /satiʀik/ *adj* satirical.

satisfaction /satisfaksjɔ̃/ *nf* **1** (plaisir) satisfaction ¢; **à la ~ générale** to everyone's satisfaction; **motif de ~** reason to feel satisfied; **2** (contentement) satisfaction; **la ~ de nos besoins** the fulfilment GB of our needs; **si le lave-vaisselle ne vous donne pas ~** if you are not entirely satisfied with the dishwasher; **3** (réparation) satisfaction; **obtenir ~ sur tout** to obtain complete satisfaction.

satisfaire /satisfɛʀ/ [10] **I** *vtr* (contenter) to satisfy [*personne, demande, curiosité*]; to please [*électorat, client*]; to meet [*besoin*]; to fulfil GB [*aspiration, exigence*]; **~ les besoins d'un enfant** to meet the needs of a child; **~ l'attente d'un client** to come up to a customer's expectations; **~ un besoin naturel** EUPH to answer a call of nature.

II satisfaire à *vtr ind* to fulfil GB [*obligation*]; to meet [*norme*].

III se satisfaire *vpr* (se contenter) **se ~ de** [*personne*] to be satisfied with [*explication, excuse*]; to be content with [*bas salaire*].

satisfaisant, **~e** /satisfəzɑ̃, ɑ̃t/ *adj* (adéquat) satisfactory; (gratifiant) satisfying.

satisfait, **~e** /satisfɛ, ɛt/ *adj* (contenté) [*client, besoin*] satisfied; [*désir, envie*] gratified; (content) [*personne*] happy; **être ~ de soi** to be pleased with oneself.

saturation /satyrasjɔ̃/ *nf* (de marché) saturation; (de trains, d'hôtels) overcrowding; (de réseau) overloading; **arriver à ~** [*marché, réseau*] to reach saturation point; [*personne*] to have had as much as one can take.

saturé, **~e** /satyre/ *adj* **1** (imprégné) saturated (**de** with); **terre ~e d'eau** waterlogged land; **atmosphère ~e d'humidité** saturated air; **2** (rassasié) **le public est ~ de publicité** the public has had its fill of advertising; **3** (surchargé) [*marché*] saturated; [*profession*] overcrowded; [*système, équipement*] overloaded; [*région, transports*] crowded out (**de** with); **le réseau est ~** TÉLÉCOM all the lines are busy.

saturer /satyre/ [1] I *vtr* **1** (imprégner) to saturate (**de** with); **2** (gorger) **on nous sature de feuilletons** we're being inundated with soap operas.
II° *vi* **je sature** I've had it up to here°.

satyre /satir/ *nm* **1** MYTHOL satyr; **2** (homme) lecher.

sauce /sos/ *nf* CULIN sauce; **~ tomate/au vin** tomato/wine sauce; **viande/plat en ~** meat/dish with sauce; **allonger une ~** to thin a sauce; **(r)allonger la ~** FIG to spin things out.
IDIOMES **mettre qch à toutes les ~s** to adapt sth to any purpose; **je me demande à quelle ~ on va me manger**° I wonder what's in store for me; **prendre la ~ °** to get soaked ou drenched.

saucer /sose/ [1] *vtr* **1** (éponger) to wipe [sth] with a piece of bread [*assiette, plat*]; **2**° (tremper) **se faire ~** to get soaked ou drenched.

saucière /sosjɛr/ *nf* sauceboat.

saucisse /sosis/ *nf* sausage; **chair à ~** sausage meat.
■ **~ de Francfort** frankfurter; **~ de Strasbourg** knackwurst ¢.

saucisson /sosisɔ̃/ *nm* (slicing) sausage; **~ à l'ail** garlic sausage; **~ sec ~** salami, summer sausage US.

sauf¹ /sof/ I *prép* **1** (excepté, hormis) except, but; **le film était bien ~ la fin** the film was good apart from the ending; **2** (sous réserve de) **~ contrordre** failing an order to the contrary; **~ avis contraire** unless otherwise stated; **~ imprévu** all things being equal, unless anything unforeseen happens; **~ dispositions contraires** JUR except as otherwise provided; **~ erreur de ma part** if I'm not mistaken.
II sauf si *loc conj* unless.
III sauf que *loc conj* except that.

sauf², **sauve** /sof, sov/ *adj* **1** (sauvé) safe; **laisser la vie sauve à qn** to spare sb's life; **2** FIG [*honneur, réputation*] intact.

sauf-conduit, *pl* **~s** /sofkɔ̃dɥi/ *nm* safe-conduct; **accorder un ~ à qn** to issue sb with a safe-conduct.

sauge /soʒ/ *nf* sage.

saugrenu, **~e** /sogrəny/ *adj* crazy, potty° GB.

saule /sol/ *nm* willow; **~ pleureur** weeping willow.

saumâtre /somatr/ *adj* [*eau*] brackish; [*goût*] bitter and salty.

saumon /somɔ̃/ I ▶ 141 *adj inv* salmon (pink).
II *nm* salmon; **~ fumé** smoked salmon.

saumure /somyr/ *nf* brine.

sauna /sona/ *nm* sauna.

saupoudrer /supudre/ [1] *vtr* **1** LIT to sprinkle (**de** with); **2** FIG to give [sth] sparingly.

saur /sɔr/ *adj m* **hareng ~** kipper, kippered herring.

saut /so/ *nm* **1** (mouvement) jump; **faire un petit ~** to skip; **faire un ~ sur place** to leap in the air; **faire un ~ de 10 ans** to skip 10 years; **faire un ~ de 2%** to shoot up by 2%; **faire un ~ dans l'inconnu** to take a leap into the unknown; **au ~ du lit** first thing

in the morning; **2** ▶ 329 SPORT (activité) **le ~** jumping; **être bon en ~** to be a good jumper; **3**° (visite) **faire un ~ à Paris** to make a flying visit to Paris; **faire un ~ chez qn** to pop in and see sb; **faire un ~ à la boulangerie** (de chez soi) to pop round to the baker's GB, to duck out to the bakery US; (en chemin) to pop in to the baker's; **4** ORDINAT jump; **~ de page** page break.
■ **~ de l'ange** swallow dive GB, swan dive US; **~ à la corde** skipping; **~ à l'élastique** bungee jumping; **~ en hauteur** high jump; **~ d'obstacles** show jumping; **~ à la perche** pole vault; **~ périlleux** mid-air somersault.
IDIOMES **faire le ~** to take the plunge; **faire le grand ~** (se suicider) to kill oneself.

saute /sot/ *nf* **~ de température** sudden change in temperature; **~ d'humeur** mood swing.

sauté, **~e** /sote/ I *adj* CULIN sautéed.
II *nm* CULIN **~ de veau** sautéed veal.

saute-mouton /sotmutɔ̃/ ▶ 329 *nm inv* **jouer à ~** to play leapfrog.

sauter /sote/ [1] I *vtr* **1** (franchir) to jump [*distance, hauteur*]; to jump over [*ruisseau, barrière*]; **~ quatre mètres en longueur** to do four metres GB in the long jump; **2** (omettre volontairement) to skip [*étape, repas, période*]; to leave out [*détails*]; **3** (omettre involontairement) to miss [*mot, ligne*]; **~ son tour** to miss one's turn; **4** SCOL **~ une classe** to skip a year.
II *vi* **1** (faire un saut) GÉN to jump; (vers le bas) to jump (down); (vers le haut) to jump (up); (vers l'extérieur) to jump (out); (vers l'intérieur) to jump (in); **~ sur le banc** to jump onto the bench; **~ du banc** to jump off the bench; **saute!** (de haut) jump (down)!; (dans une piscine) jump (in)!; **~ d'une branche à l'autre** to leap from branch to branch; **~ d'un pied sur l'autre** to hop from one foot to the other; **~ à pieds joints** LIT to jump with one's feet together; **~ à pieds joints dans un piège** FIG to fall straight into a trap; **~ dans le vide** to jump; **~ en hauteur/en longueur** to do the high/long jump; **~ à la perche** to pole vault; **~ en parachute** (une fois) to make a parachute jump; (régulièrement) to go parachute jumping; **~ à la corde** to skip; **faire ~ un enfant sur ses genoux** to dandle a child on one's knee; **~ dans l'inconnu** to take a leap into the unknown; **~ sur qn** to pounce on sb; **~ sur son téléphone/pistolet** to grab one's telephone/gun; **~ sur l'occasion/une offre** to jump at the chance/an offer; **~ à la gorge de qn** to go for sb's throat; **~ au cou de qn** to greet sb with a kiss; **2** (aller vivement) to jump; **~ du lit** to jump out of bed; **~ dans un taxi/dans un train** to jump ou hop into a taxi/onto a train; **3** (passer) **~ d'un sujet à l'autre** to skip from one subject to another; **4**° (être supprimé) **faire ~ un paragraphe** (délibérément) to take out a paragraph; (par erreur) to miss out GB ou miss a paragraph; **faire ~ une réunion** to cancel a meeting; **le poste va ~** the job is being axed ; **faire ~ une contravention** to get out of paying a parking ticket; **5** (être délogé, instable) [*courroie, chaîne de vélo*] to come off; [*images de télévision*] to jump; **la troisième vitesse saute** the third gear keeps slipping; **6** (céder) **faire ~ une serrure** to force a lock; **faire ~ une maille** to drop a stitch; **faire ~ les boutons** to burst one's buttons; **faire ~ les barrières** FIG to break down the barriers; **7** (exploser) [*bombe, mine*] to blow up, to go off; [*pont, bâtiment*] to be blown up, to go up; **faire ~ qch** to blow sth up; **faire ~ les plombs** to blow the fuses; **8** CULIN **faire ~ des oignons** to sauté onions; **faire ~ une crêpe** to toss a pancake; **faire ~ les bouchons de champagne** to make the champagne corks pop.
IDIOMES **~ aux yeux** to be blindingly obvious; **et que ça saute**°! make it snappy°!; **~ en l'air**° or **au plafond**° (de joie) to jump for joy; (de colère) to hit the roof°; (de surprise) to be staggered.

sauterelle /sotrɛl/ *nf* grasshopper.

sauterie† /sotri/ *nf* party, hop†.

sauteur, **-euse**¹ /sotœr, øz/ *nm* SPORT jumper; **~ en**

hauteur high jumper; **~ en longueur** long jumper; **~ à la perche** pole vaulter.

sauteuse² /sotøz/ *nf* **1** CULIN (deep) frying pan; **2** (scie) jigsaw.

sautillant, ~e /sotijã, ãt/ *adj* [*démarche, rythme*] bouncy; [*oiseau*] hopping.

sautiller /sotije/ [1] *vi* **1** [*oiseau*] to hop; (d'un lieu à l'autre) to hop around; **2** [*enfant*] (en avançant) to skip along; (d'un pied sur l'autre) to hop from one foot to the other; (sur place) to jump up and down.

sautoir /sotwaʀ/ *nm* (collier) long necklace.

sauvage /sovaʒ/ **I** *adj* **1** (non apprivoisé) [*animal, plante, enfant, rire*] wild; [*tribu*] primitive; **2** (cruel) [*mœurs*] savage; [*lutte*] fierce; **3** (timide) unsociable; **4** (illégal) illegal.
II *nmf* **1** (être primitif ou brutal) savage; **2** (être non sociable) unsociable person, loner.

sauvageon, -onne /sovaʒɔ̃, ɔn/ *nm,f* (enfant) wild child.

sauvagerie /sovaʒʀi/ *nf* **1** (brutalité) savagery; **2** (insociabilité) unsociability.

sauve ▶ sauf².

sauvegarde /sovgaʀd/ *nf* (de patrimoine, paix, valeurs) maintenance; (de droits, libertés) protection; **assurer la ~ de** to safeguard.

sauvegarder /sovgaʀde/ [1] *vtr* **1** GÉN to safeguard; **2** ORDINAT (provisoirement) to save; (recopier) to back [sth] up.

sauve-qui-peut /sovkipø/ *nm inv* stampede.

sauver /sove/ [1] **I** *vtr* **1** (garder en vie) to save; (porter secours à) to rescue; **~ la vie à qn** to save sb's life; **~ qn de la noyade** to save sb from drowning; **~ sa peau**○ to save one's skin○; **elle est sauvée** [*malade*] she has pulled through○; **2** (sauvegarder) to save (**de** from); to salvage [*marchandises*] (**de** from); **3** (rendre acceptable) **ce qui le sauve à mes yeux, c'est sa générosité** his redeeming feature for me is his generosity.
II se sauver *vpr* **1** (s'enfuir) (de prison, d'une cage) to escape (**de** from); (de chez ses parents, de l'école) to run away (**de** from); (face à une situation difficile) to run away (**de** from); (face à un danger) to run; **se ~ en bateau/avion** to escape by boat/plane; **sauvez-vous!** run (for it)!; **2**○ (s'en aller) **il faut que je me sauve** I've got to rush off now.
IDIOMES **~ la situation** to save the day; **sauve qui peut!** (à terre) run for your life!; (en mer) it's every man for himself.

sauvetage /sovtaʒ/ *nm* rescue.

sauveteur /sovtœʀ/ **▶ 374** *nm* rescuer.

sauvette: à la sauvette /alasovɛt/ *loc adv* **1** (en hâte) [*préparer, signer*] in a rush, hastily; **2** (à la dérobée) [*filmer, enregistrer*] on the sly; **3** (illégalement) **vendre qch à la ~** to sell sth illegally on the street.

sauveur /sovœʀ/ *nm* RELIG saviour^GB.

savamment /savamã/ *adv* **1** (avec érudition) learnedly, eruditely; **2** (avec habileté) [*mené*] adroitly; [*construit, choisi*] skilfully^GB.

savane /savan/ *nf* savannah.

savant, ~e /savã, ãt/ **I** *adj* **1** [*personne*] learned (**en** in), erudite; [*assemblée*] learned, scholarly; **2** [*édition, étude, émission*] scholarly; [*calcul*] complicated, involved; **3** (habile) [*manœuvre, action*] clever; [*mise en scène*] skilful^GB; **4** [*animal*] performing.
II *nm,f* (personne cultivée) scholar.
III *nm* (scientifique) scientist.

savate○ /savat/ *nf* (pantoufle) old slipper; (chaussure) old shoe.

saveur /savœʀ/ *nf* (d'aliment, de boisson) flavour^GB; **plein de ~** [*fruit*] full of flavour^GB; [*plat cuisiné*] flavoursome^GB, tasty; [*remarque*] pungent.

savoir¹ /savwaʀ/ [47] **I** *vtr* **1** (connaître) to know [*vérité, réponse*]; **~ son texte** to know one's lines; **~ qch par cœur** to know sth by heart; **~ que** to know (that); **vous n'êtes pas sans ~ que** you are no doubt aware that; **elle ne sait plus ce qu'elle dit** she doesn't know what she's saying; **~ qch sur qn** to know sth about sb; **ne rien ~ de qch** to know nothing about sth; **elle en sait plus/moins que moi** she knows more/less about it than I do; **il n'en saura rien** he'll never know (about it); **va** *ou* **allez ~!, qui sait!** who knows!; **on ne sait jamais** you never know; **est-ce que je sais, moi!** how should I know!; **elle n'a rien voulu ~** she just didn't want to know; **parler sans ~** to talk about things one knows nothing about; **sans le ~** without knowing (it); **pour autant que je sache** as far as I know; **pas que je sache** not as far as I know; **elle nous a fait ~ que** she informed us that; **comment l'as-tu su ?** how did you find out?; **je l'ai su par elle** she told me about it; **~ le chinois** to know Chinese; **on la savait riche** she was known to be rich; **reste à ~ si** it remains to be seen if *ou* whether; **ne ~ que faire pour…** to be at a loss as to how to…; **on croit ~ qu'elle est à Paris** she is understood *ou* thought to be in Paris; **sachant que** given that; **sache qu'il t'a menti** I'm telling you, he was lying; **la personne que vous savez, qui vous savez** you-know-who; **je ne sais quel journaliste** some journalist or other; **je ne sais qui** somebody or other; **tu viens ou pas, il faudrait ~!** are you coming or not? make your mind up!; **si tu savais** *ou* **tu ne peux pas ~ comme je suis content!** you can't imagine how happy I am!; **tu en sais des choses!** you really know a thing or two!; **2** (être capable de) **~ faire** to be able to do, to know how to do; **~ comment faire** to know how to do; **je sais conduire/nager/taper à la machine** I can drive/swim/type; **il ne sait pas dire non** he can't say no; **~ écouter** to be a good listener; **elle sait bien expliquer** she's good at explaining things; **il a su nous parler** he was able to talk to us; **on ne saurait mieux dire** I couldn't have put it better myself; **elle sait y faire avec les enfants** she's good with children; **il pleurait tout ce qu'il savait** he cried and cried; **3** B (pouvoir) **je ne sais pas soulever la valise** I can't lift the suitcase.
II se savoir *vpr* **1** (être connu) **ça se saurait** people would know about that; **tout se sait ici** people get to know everything in this place; **ça s'est su tout de suite** word immediately got around; **2** (être conscient d'être) **se savoir aimé** to know one is loved.
III à savoir *loc adv* that is to say.
IDIOMES **ne pas ~ où donner de la tête** not to know whether one is coming or going.

savoir² /savwaʀ/ *nm* **1** (érudition) learning; **un grand ~** great learning; **2** (science) knowledge; **3** (culture) body of knowledge.

savoir-faire /savwaʀfɛʀ/ *nm inv* know-how.

savoir-vivre /savwaʀvivʀ/ *nm inv* manners (*pl*).

savon /savɔ̃/ *nm* **1** (produit) soap; **2** (morceau) (bar of) soap.
■ **~ de Marseille** household soap; **~ noir** soft soap.
IDIOMES **passer un ~**○ **à qn** to give sb a telling-off.

savonner /savone/ [1] **I** *vtr* to rub soap on [*linge*]; to soap [sb] all over [*enfant*].
II se savonner *vpr* (pour se laver) to soap oneself all over; (pour se raser) to lather oneself.

savonnette /savonɛt/ *nf* small cake of soap.

savonneux, -euse /savonø, øz/ *adj* soapy.

savourer /savure/ [1] *vtr* to savour^GB [*succès, instant*].

savoureux, -euse /savurø, øz/ *adj* [*plat*] tasty; [*anecdote*] juicy.

saxe /saks/ *nm* Dresden china ₵.

Saxe /saks/ **▶ 509** *nprf* Saxony.

saxon, -onne /saksɔ̃, ɔn/ **I** *adj* Saxon.
II *nm* LING Saxon.

saxophone /saksofon/ **▶ 392** *nm* **1** (instrument) saxophone; **2** (instrumentiste) saxophone player.

saxophoniste /saksofonist/ **▶ 374** *nmf* saxophonist.

saynète /sɛnɛt/ *nf* playlet.

sbire /sbiʀ/ *nm* PEJ henchman PEJ.

scabreux, -euse /skabʀø, øz/ *adj* risqué.

scalp /skalp/ *nm* scalp.

scalper /skalpe/ [1] *vtr* to scalp.

scandale /skɑ̃dal/ *nm* scandal; **~ boursier** scandal on the Stock Exchange; **faire éclater un ~** to cause a scandal to break; **étouffer un ~** to hush up a scandal; **faire un** or **du ~** (réprobation générale) to cause a scandal; (scène individuelle) to cause a fuss; **au grand ~ de** to the great disgust of; **un journal à ~** a scandal sheet; **la presse à ~** the gutter press; **c'est un ~!** it's scandalous, it's outrageous!

scandaleux, -euse /skɑ̃dalø, øz/ *adj* scandalous, outrageous.

scandaliser /skɑ̃dalize/ [1] **I** *vtr* to outrage, to scandalize [*personne*]; **être scandalisé par** to be outraged by. **II se scandaliser** *vpr* to be shocked (**de** by).

scander /skɑ̃de/ [1] *vtr* **1** LITTÉRAT (faire l'analyse métrique) to scan; **2** to chant [*slogan, nom*].

scandinave /skɑ̃dinav/ *adj* Scandinavian.

Scandinavie /skɑ̃dinavi/ **▶509** *nprf* **la ~** Scandinavia.

scanneur /skanœʀ/ *nm* (appareil) scanner.

scaphandre /skafɑ̃dʀ/ *nm* **1** NAUT deep-sea diving suit; **2** ASTRONAUT spacesuit.

scaphandrier /skafɑ̃dʀije/ **▶374** *nm* deep-sea diver.

scarabée /skaʀabe/ *nm* **1** ZOOL beetle; **2** (bijou en archéologie) scarab.

scarlatine /skaʀlatin/ **▶196** *nf* scarlet fever.

scatologique /skatɔlɔʒik/ *adj* scatological.

sceau, *pl* **~x** /so/ *nm* **1** (objet, empreinte) seal; **sous le ~ du secret** in strictest secrecy; **2** (marque distinctive) stamp, hallmark.

scélérat, ~e /selera, at/ LITER **I** *adj* villainous. **II** *nm,f* villain.

scellé /sele/ *nm* seal; **apposer les ~s** to affix seals.

sceller /sele/ [1] *vtr* **1** (apposer un sceau) to seal [*document, acte*]; **2** (fixer solidement) to fix [sth] securely [*étagère, barreau*]; **3** (consacrer) to seal [*amitié, alliance, réconciliation*].

scénario /senaʀjo/ *nm* **1** CIN screenplay, script; **2** THÉÂT scenario; **3** (déroulement) scenario.

scénariste /senaʀist/ **▶374** *nmf* scriptwriter.

scène /sɛn/ *nf* **1** THÉÂT (plateau) stage; **'en ~!'** 'on stage!'; **entrer en ~** to come on; **entrée en ~** entrance; **sortir de ~** to go off; **le rideau de ~** the curtain; **2** (subdivision, action) scene; **la ~ se passe à Paris** the scene is set in Paris; **3** (activité théâtrale) stage; **quitter la ~** (métier) to give up the stage; **la ~ parisienne** Parisian theatre^GB; **musique de ~** music for the theatre^GB; **mettre 'Phèdre' en ~** [*troupe*] to stage 'Phèdre'; [*personne*] to direct 'Phèdre'; **mettre en ~ un film** to direct a film; **une excellente mise en ~** an excellent production; **à la ~ comme à la ville** on stage and off; **4** (actualité) scene; **occuper le devant de la ~** FIG to be in the news; **5** (esclandre) **faire (toute) une ~ (à qn)** to throw a fit^○; **6** (épisode, spectacle) scene; **~s de chasse** hunting scenes; **~s de panique** scenes of panic.
■ **~ de ménage** domestic dispute.

scepticisme /sɛptisism/ *nm* GÉN, PHILOS (incrédulité) scepticism GB, skepticism US.

sceptique /sɛptik/ **I** *adj* sceptical GB, skeptical US; **laisser qn ~** to leave sb unconvinced. **II** *nmf* GÉN, PHILOS sceptic GB, skeptic US.

sceptre /sɛptʀ/ *nm* sceptre^GB.

schéma /ʃema/ *nm* **1** (dessin) diagram; **2** (points principaux) outline; **3** (processus) pattern.

schématique /ʃematik/ *adj* **1** (simplifié) [*vision, raisonnement*] simplistic; **2** (de schéma) schematic.

schématiquement /ʃematikmɑ̃/ *adv* **1** (avec un schéma) [*représenter, reproduire*] in a diagram; **2** (en simplifiant) [*exposer, expliquer*] in broad outline.

schématisation /ʃematizasjɔ̃/ *nf* simplification; (excessive) oversimplification.

schématiser /ʃematize/ [1] *vtr* **1** (simplifier) to sim-

plify; (à l'excès) to oversimplify; **2** (faire un schéma) to make ou draw a diagram.

schilling /ʃiliŋ/ **▶33** *nm* schilling.

schisme /ʃism/ *nm* schism.

schizophrène /skizɔfʀɛn/ *adj, nmf* schizophrenic.

schizophrénie /skizɔfʀeni/ **▶196** *nf* schizophrenia.

sciatique /sjatik/ **I** *adj* **nerf ~** sciatic nerve. **II** **▶196** *nf* (douleur) sciatica.

scie /si/ *nf* (outil) saw; **~ sauteuse** jigsaw.

sciemment /sjamɑ̃/ *adv* knowingly.

science /sjɑ̃s/ *nf* **1** (savoir) science; **dans l'état actuel de la ~** in the present state of science; **2** (domaine du savoir) science; **les ~s et les lettres** science and the arts; **3** (érudition) knowledge, erudition; **épater qn avec sa ~** to blind sb with science.
■ **~s appliquées** applied sciences; **~s économiques** economics (+ *v sg*); **~s naturelles ~** biology (*sg*); **~s occultes** black arts; **~s politiques** political science (*sg*); **~s de la Terre** Earth sciences; **Sciences Po**○ *Institute of Political Science*.
IDIOMES **être un puits de ~** to be a fount of knowledge.

science-fiction /sjɑ̃sfiksjɔ̃/ *nf* science fiction.

scientifique /sjɑ̃tifik/ **I** *adj* scientific. **II** *nmf* scientist.

scier /sje/ [2] *vtr* **1** to saw; **2**○ (abasourdir) to stun.
IDIOMES **~ la branche sur laquelle on est assis** to shoot oneself in the foot.

scierie /siʀi/ *nf* sawmill.

scinder /sɛ̃de/ [1] **I** *vtr* to split [*organisation, groupe*]; to break down [*problème, question*]. **II se scinder** *vpr* [*organisation, parti*] to split up.

scintiller /sɛ̃tije/ [1] *vi* [*diamant*] to sparkle; [*regard, œil*] (de santé) to sparkle; (de malice) to twinkle; [*étoile*] to twinkle; [*eau*] to glisten.

scission /sisjɔ̃/ *nf* **1** (sécession) split, schism (**au sein de** within); **faire ~** to break away, to secede SOUT; **2** BIOL, PHYS fission.

sciure /sjyʀ/ *nf* **~ (de bois)** sawdust.

sclérosant, ~e /skleʀozɑ̃, ɑ̃t/ *adj* **1** MÉD [*traitement, substance*] sclerosant; **2** FIG [*mode de vie, travail*] mind-numbing.

sclérose /skleʀoz/ *nf* **1** **▶196** MÉD sclerosis; **2** (immobilisme) fossilization, ossification.
■ **~ en plaques** multiple sclerosis, MS.

scléroser /skleʀoze/ [1] **I** *vtr* MÉD to sclerose. **II se scléroser** *vpr* **1** FIG (se figer) [*institution, personne*] to become fossilized; **2** MÉD [*tissu, organe, veine*] to become hardened.

scolaire /skɔlɛʀ/ *adj* [*vacances, programme, livre*] school (*épith*); [*réforme, publication*] educational; [*échec, réussite*] academic; **établissement ~** school.

scolarisable /skɔlaʀizabl/ *adj* **1** (par l'âge) [*enfant*] ready to start school; **2** (ayant les capacités nécessaires) **il n'est pas ~** he needs special schooling.

scolarisation /skɔlaʀizasjɔ̃/ *nf* schooling, education.

scolariser /skɔlaʀize/ [1] *vtr* (envoyer à l'école) to send [sb] to school; **est-il scolarisé?** does he go to school?.

scolarité /skɔlaʀite/ *nf* **1** (études) schooling; **durant ma ~** when I was at school; **après une ~ à** having been educated at; **arrêter sa ~ à 13 ans** to leave school at 13; **avoir une ~ difficile** not to do well at school; **la ~ obligatoire** compulsory education; **allonger la ~** to raise the school-leaving age; **2** UNIV (service administratif) registrar's office.

scoliose /skɔljoz/ *nf* scoliosis.

scoop○ /skup/ *nm* (en journalisme) scoop.

scooter /skutœʀ/ *nm* (motor) scooter.
■ **~ des mers** or **nautique** jetski; **~ des neiges** snowmobile.

scorbut /skɔʀbyt/ **▶196** *nm* scurvy.

score /skɔʀ/ *nm* **1** SCOL, SPORT score; **réaliser un bon/mauvais ~** to get a good/bad score; **~ nul** draw GB, tie US; **2** POL result.

se

La traduction du pronom personnel *se* varie en fonction du verbe auquel il est associé et de son rôle; il sera traité automatiquement avec le verbe pronominal auquel on aura tout intérêt à se reporter.

se complément d'objet direct ou indirect d'un verbe pronominal réfléchi

se blesser	= to hurt oneself
il se regarde	= he's looking at himself
elle se regarde	= she's looking at herself
ils se sont brûlés	= they burnt themselves
elles se sont brûlées	= they burnt themselves
le chien s'est brûlé	= the dog burnt itself

Mais attention, très souvent en anglais le pronom ne sera pas exprimé:

se laver	= to wash *ou* to have a wash
elle s'habille	= she's getting dressed
il se rase	= he's shaving

Avec les parties du corps

il se lave les pieds	= he's washing his feet
elles se coupent les ongles	= they're cutting their nails
se ronger les ongles	= to bite one's nails
le chat se lèche les moustaches	= the cat is cleaning its whiskers
ils se bouchent les oreilles	= they put their fingers in their ears

se pronom réciproque

ils se détestent	= they hate each other

On trouvera des exemples supplémentaires et des cas non envisagés ici dans l'entrée. En cas de doute, se reporter à l'article du verbe.

scorie /skɔʀi/ *nf* **1** (géologique) scoria ℂ; **2** (minière) slag ℂ, scoria ℂ.

scorpion /skɔʀpjɔ̃/ *nm* ZOOL scorpion.

Scorpion /skɔʀpjɔ̃/ **▶ 641|** *nprm* Scorpio.

scotch, *pl* **~es** /skɔtʃ/ *nm* **1** (boisson) Scotch (whisky); **2** ®(ruban adhésif) Sellotape® GB, Scotch® tape US.

scout, **~e** /skut/ **I** *adj* scout (*épith*).
II *nm,f* (Catholic) boy scout/(Catholic) girl scout.

scoutisme /skutism/ *nm* scouting.

scribouillard○, **~e** /skʀibujaʀ, aʀd/ *nm,f* pen pusher○ GB, pencil pusher US.

script /skʀipt/ *nm* **1** (écriture) **écrire en ~** to print; **2** CIN, RADIO, TV script.

scripte /skʀipt/ *nmf* continuity man/girl.

scrupule /skʀypyl/ *nm* scruple; **avoir des ~s à faire** to have scruples about doing; **être dénué de ~s** to be completely unscrupulous; **une personne sans ~s** an unscrupulous person.

scrupuleusement /skʀypyløzmɑ̃/ *adv* GÉN [*respecter, appliquer*] scrupulously; **se comporter ~ en affaires** to be scrupulous in one's business dealings.

scrupuleux, **-euse** /skʀypylø, øz/ *adj* scrupulous.

scrutateur, **-trice** /skʀytatœʀ, tʀis/ **I** *adj* [*regard, air*] searching.
II *nm,f* (de vote) scrutineer.

scruter /skʀyte/ [1] *vtr* to scan [*mer, horizon, paysage*]; to scrutinize [*objet*]; to examine [*sol, personne, motif*].

scrutin /skʀytɛ̃/ *nm* **1** (vote) ballot; **par voie de ~** by ballot; **dépouiller le ~** to count the votes; **2** (élections) polls (*pl*); **jour du ~** polling day; **premier tour de ~** first ballot; **mode de ~** electoral system.
■ **~ de liste** list system; **~ majoritaire** election by majority vote; **~ proportionnel** proportional representation, PR.

sculpter /skylte/ [1] *vtr* **1** (réaliser) to sculpt, to carve [*statue*] (**dans** in); to carve [*ornements, meuble*] (**dans** out of); **2** (travailler) to sculpt, to carve [*pierre, marbre*]; to carve [*bois*]; **3** (éroder) to sculpt, to carve out [*roche*].

sculpteur /skyltœʀ/ **▶ 374|** *nm* sculptor; **elle est ~** she's a sculptor.

sculptural, **~e**, *mpl* **-aux** /skyltyʀal, o/ *adj* [*art*] sculptural; [*forme, beauté, corps*] statuesque.

sculpture /skyltyʀ/ *nf* sculpture; **faire de la ~** (comme passe-temps) to do sculpture; (comme travail) to be a sculptor; **la ~ sur bois** woodcarving.

Scylla /sila/ *npr* Scylla; **▶ Charybde**.

SDF /ɛsdeɛf/ *nmf: abbr* **▶ sans**.

se (**s'** *before vowel or mute h*) /sə, s/ *pron pers* **1** (verbe à valeur intransitive) **elle ~ comporte honorablement** she behaves honourably; **la voiture s'est bien comportée** the car performed well; **l'écart ~ creuse** the gap is widening; **2** (verbe à valeur passive) **les exemples ~ comptent sur les doigts de la main** the examples can be counted on the fingers of your hand; **le médicament ~ vend sans ordonnance** the medicine is sold without a prescription; **3** (avec un verbe impersonnel) **comment ~ fait-il que...?** how come...?, how is it that...?; **il ~ produit une réaction chimique** there is a chemical reaction.

séance /seɑ̃s/ *nf* **1** (réunion) (de tribunal, parlement, Bourse) session; (de comité, conseil municipal) meeting; **~ d'ouverture** opening session; **~ ordinaire/plénière** ordinary/plenary session; **tenir ~** to meet; **~ tenante** immediately; **2** (période d'activité) session; **organiser une ~ de travail** to organize a workshop; **3** CIN show; **une ~ privée** a private screening.

séant /seɑ̃/ *nm* **se mettre sur son ~** to sit up.

seau, *pl* **~x** /so/ *nm* (récipient) GÉN (pour enfant) bucket; (contenu) bucket(ful).
■ **~ à champagne** champagne bucket; **~ à charbon** coal scuttle; **~ à glace** ice bucket; **~ hygiénique** slop pail.
IDIOMES **pleuvoir à ~x**○ to rain buckets○, to pour.

sébile /sebil/ *nf* begging bowl; **tendre la ~** to beg.

sec, **sèche**[1] /sɛk, sɛʃ/ **I** *adj* **1** (sans humidité) [*temps, cheveux*] dry; [*fruit*] dried; **avoir la gorge sèche** to feel parched○; **à pied ~** without getting one's feet wet; **2** (pas doux) [*vin, cidre*] dry; (sans eau) **boire son gin ~** to like one's gin straight; **3** (austère) [*personne, communiqué*] terse; [*lettre, ton*] curt; [*style*] dry; **avoir un cœur ~** to be cold-hearted; **▶ trique**; **4** (net) [*bruit*] sharp; **se briser d'un coup ~** to snap.
II *nm* **être à ~** [*rivière, réservoir*] to have dried up; [*personne*] to have no money.
III *adv* **1** (avec netteté) **se briser ~** to snap; **2**○ (beaucoup) [*cogner, pleuvoir, boire*] a lot.
IDIOMES **aussi ~**○ immediately; **rester ~**○ to be unable to reply; **je l'ai eu ~**○ I was pretty choked○.

sécable /sekabl/ *adj* [*comprimé*] divisible.

sécateur /sekatœʀ/ *nm* clippers (*pl*).
■ **~ à haie** shears (*pl*).

sécession /sesesjɔ̃/ *nf* secession ℂ; **faire ~** to secede.

sécessionniste /sesesjɔnist/ *adj, nmf* secessionist.

sèche[2] /sɛʃ/ **I** *adj f* **▶ sec I**.
II○ *nf* (cigarette) fag GB, cig○.

sèche-cheveux /sɛʃʃəvø/ *nm inv* hairdrier GB, blow-dryer.

sèche-linge /sɛʃlɛ̃ʒ/ *nm inv* tumble-drier GB, tumble-dryer.

sèche-mains /sɛʃmɛ̃/ *nm inv* hand-drier GB, blower US.

sèchement /sɛʃmɑ̃/ *adv* drily, coldly; **très ~** curtly.

sécher /seʃe/ [1] **I** *vtr* GÉN to dry [*cheveux, fruit, larme, linge*]; **2**○ (manquer) to skip [*cours*].
II *vi* **1** (devenir sec) [*linge, cheveux*] to dry; [*plaie, herbe, boue*] to dry up; [*encre, peinture*] (normalement) to dry; (par négligence) to dry up; [*fleur*] to wither; [*jambon*] to get dried up; **fleur/viande/boue séchée** dried flower/meat/mud; **mettre le linge à ~** (dehors) to hang out the washing; **mettre des vêtements à ~** (après un lavage) to hang clothes up to dry; (après la pluie) to dry out clothes; **mettre du bois à ~** to

leave wood to season; **2**○ (ne pas savoir répondre) to dry up.

III se sécher *vpr* to dry oneself; **se ~ les cheveux** to dry one's hair.

sécheresse /seʃʀɛs/ *nf* **1** (manque de pluie) drought; **une grave ~** a severe drought; **2** (de climat) dryness ¢; **3** (austérité) (de personne) dryness ¢ (d'auteur, ouvrage) dryness; **la ~ de son ton** his/her curt tone.

séchoir /seʃwaʀ/ *nm* (pour le linge) clothes airer, clothes horse; (machine) tumble-drier GB, tumble-dryer.

second, ~e¹ /səgɔ̃, ɔ̃d/ **I** *adj* **1** (dans une séquence) second; **chapitre ~** chapter two; **en ~e lecture** at a second reading; **en ~ lieu** secondly; **dans un ~ temps, nous étudierons...** subsequently, we will study...; **c'est à prendre au ~ degré** it is not to be taken literally; **2** (dans une hiérarchie) second; **voyager en ~e classe** to travel second class; **de ~ ordre** second-rate; **politicien de ~ plan** minor politician; **de ~ choix** of inferior quality; **jouer un ~ rôle** THÉÂT to play a supporting role; **jouer les ~ rôles** FIG to play second fiddle.

II *nm,f* **le ~, la ~e** GÉN the second one.

III *nm* **1** (adjoint) second-in-command; **2** (étage) second floor GB, third floor US; **3** (dans un duel) second.

IV en second *loc adv* [*arriver, partir*] second; **passer en ~** [*travail, amis*] to come second.

secondaire /səgɔ̃dɛʀ/ **I** *adj* **1** (en deuxième position) secondary; **2** (de moindre importance) [*personnage, route*] minor; **3** SCOL **école ~** secondary school GB, high school US; **j'ai fait mes études ~s à...** I was in secondary school GB ou high school US at...; **4** MÉD **lésions ~s** secondary lesions; **syphilis ~** the second stage of syphilis; **effets ~s** side effects; **5** (en géologie) **ère ~** Mesozoic era; **6** TECH secondary.

II *nm* **1** SCOL secondary school GB ou high school US education; **les enseignants du ~** secondary GB ou high US school teachers; **2 le ~** the Mesozoic.

seconde² /səgɔ̃d/ **I** *adj f* ▶ **second I**.

II *nf* **1** ▶ **631** **1** (unité de temps) second; **11 mètres par ~** 11 metres^GB per ou a second; **à la ~ près** to the nearest second; **2** (court laps de temps) second; **en une fraction de ~** in a split second; **3** SCOL (classe) *fifth year of secondary school, age 15–16*; **4** (dans les transports en commun) **billet de ~** second-class ticket; **5** AUT second gear; **6** MUS second.

seconder /səgɔ̃de/ [1] *vtr* [*personne*] to assist; [*circonstance*] to aid.

secouer /səkwe/ [1] **I** *vtr* **1** (agiter) to shake [*bouteille, branche, personne*]; to shake out [*nappe, tapis, parapluie*]; **~ la tête** to shake one's head; **être un peu secoué** (dans une voiture, un avion) to have rather a bumpy ride; (sur un bateau) to have rather a rough trip; **2** (se débarrasser de) to shake off [*poussière, neige, joug*]; **3** (ébranler) [*crise*] to shake [*personne, pays*]; **4**○ (activer) to give [sb] a shaking-up○ [*personne*].

II se secouer *vpr* **1** (pour se dégager) [*personne*] to give oneself a shake; **2** (nerveusement) to jump about all over the place; **3**○ (contre le découragement) to pull oneself together; (contre l'inertie) to wake up, to get moving○.

secourable /səkuʀabl/ *adj* [*personne*] helpful.

secourir /səkuʀiʀ/ [26] *vtr* **1** (aider) to help [*personne*]; (sauver) to rescue [*marin*]; (soigner) to give first aid to [*accidenté*]; (assister) to provide aid for [*réfugié*].

secourisme /səkuʀism/ *nm* first aid.

secouriste /səkuʀist/ ▶ **374** *nmf* first-aid worker.

secours /səkuʀ/ **I** *nm inv* (aide) help; **au ~!** help!; **appeler** *or* **crier au ~** to shout for help; **appel au ~** cry for help; **être d'un grand ~** to be a great help; **il l'a appelée à son ~** he got her to help him; **porter ~ à, se porter au ~ de** to help [*blessé, réfugié*]; to come to the aid of [*personne critiquée, entreprise*]; to rescue [*animal*]; **voler au ~ de qn** to rush to sb's aid; **le ~ en mer** sea rescue operations (*pl*); **de ~** (de rechange) [*roue*] spare; (d'urgence) [*sortie*] emergency; (de soins) [*trousse*] first-aid; (de sauvetage) [*équipe*] rescue; (de sécurité) [*matériel*] back up.

II *nmpl* **1** (personnes) (secouristes) rescuers, rescue

team (*sg*); (renforts) reinforcements; **2** (vivres, médicaments) relief supplies; **~ humanitaires** humanitarian aid ¢; **premiers ~, ~ d'urgence** first aid ¢.

secousse /səkus/ *nf* (mouvement brusque) jolt; **éviter les ~s** (en voiture, avion) to avoid the bumps; **avancer par ~s** [*voiture, train*] to jerk forward; GÉOG **~ (sismique)** (earth) tremor.

secret, -ète /səkʀɛ, ɛt/ **I** *adj* **1** (non divulgué) [*dossier, code, rite, société*] secret; **tenir qch ~** to keep sth secret ou a secret; **2** (dissimulé) [*passage, mécanisme*] secret; **3** (intime, mystérieux) [*vie, sentiment, raisons*] secret; **4** (réservé) [*personne*] secretive.

II *nm* **1** (ce qu'on cache) secret; **c'est un ~ entre nous** it's our secret; **ne pas avoir de ~s pour qn** to have no secrets from sb; **confier un ~ à qn** to let sb into GB ou in on a secret; **ce n'est un ~ pour personne** it's no secret (**que** that); **2** (ce qui est caché) secret; **livrer ses ~s** [*nature, tombe*] to yield up (its) secrets (**à** to); **la mécanique n'a plus de ~s pour elle** mechanics holds no secrets for her; **3** (discrétion) secrecy; **être tenu au ~** to be sworn to secrecy; **dans le ~ de ton cœur** in your heart of hearts; **être dans le ~ (des dieux)** to be in on the secret; **mettre qn dans le ~** to let sb into GB ou in on the secret; **garder le ~ sur qch** to keep sth a secret; **en ~** in secret; **4** (recette) secret; **le ~ du bonheur** the secret of happiness; **avoir le ~ de qch** to know the secret of sth; **il a le ~ des solutions compliquées pour les problèmes simples** HUM he has a knack of finding complicated answers to simple problems; **5** (prison) solitary confinement.

■ **~ bancaire** FIN, JUR bank confidentiality; **~ de fabrication** industrial secret; **~ de Polichinelle** open secret; **~ professionnel** JUR professional confidentiality.

secrétaire /s(ə)kʀetɛʀ/ ▶ **374** **I** *nmf* (employé administratif) secretary.

II *nm* **1** (cadre politique, diplomatique) secretary; **2** (meuble) secretaire GB, secretary US; **3** ZOOL secretary bird.

■ **~ de direction** personal assistant; **~ d'État** (en France) minister; (en Grande-Bretagne, aux États-Unis) Secretary of State; **~ de rédaction** subeditor GB, copy-editor.

secrétariat /s(ə)kʀetaʀja/ *nm* (travail) secretarial work; (lieu) secretariat.

■ **~ d'État** ministry; **~ d'État à l'emploi** ministry for employment; **~ de rédaction** (activité) copy-editing; (bureau) copy-editors' room.

secrètement /səkʀɛtmã/ *adv* secretly.

sécréter /sekʀete/ [1] *vtr* **1** to secrete [*sève, bile*]; **2** (exuder) to exude [*liquide*]; **3** FIG to foster [*inégalités, idéologie*]; to hatch [*réforme*].

sécrétion /sekʀesjɔ̃/ *nf* secretion.

sectaire /sɛktɛʀ/ *adj, nmf* sectarian.

secte /sɛkt/ *nf* RELIG sect; (clan) faction.

secteur /sɛktœʀ/ *nm* **1** ÉCON (d'activités générales) sector; **~ primaire/secondaire/tertiaire** primary/manufacturing/service sector; **~ d'activité** sector; **2** ADMIN (subdivision) area, territory; MIL sector; **3**○ (parages) neighbourhood^GB; **4** ÉLECTROTECH **le ~** (réseau) the mains (*pl*); **appareil fonctionnant sur ~** mains-operated appliance; **panne de ~** power failure; **5** MATH sector.

section /sɛksjɔ̃/ *nf* **1** (division) ADMIN, MIL section; (de parti, syndicat) branch; (de route, chemin de fer) section; (de livre) part; **2** SCOL (selon les niveaux) stream GB, track US; **choisir une ~ littéraire** to choose a literary option; **3** UNIV department; **4** MATH, TECH (coupe) section.

■ **~ d'autobus** fare stage.

sectionnement /sɛksjɔnmã/ *nm* (de tendon, membre) severing; (de territoire, service) division (**en** into).

sectionner /sɛksjɔne/ [1] *vtr* to sever [*membre, artère*]; to divide up [*service, administration*] (**en** into); to cut [*tuyau, câble, fil*].

sectoriel, -ielle /sɛktɔʀjɛl/ *adj* sectoral.

sectorisation /sɛktɔʀizasjɔ̃/ *nf* division.

sectoriser /sɛktɔʀize/ [1] *vtr* to divide [sth] into sectors.

séculaire /sekylɛʀ/ *adj* **1** (vieux) [*tradition, arbre*] ancient; **2** (vieux de cent ans) [*arbre, maison*] hundred-year-old; [*personne*] centenarian; **3** (tous les cent ans) [*cérémonie*] centennial; **4** (en astronomie) secular.

séculariser /sekylaʀize/ [1] *vtr* **1** (rendre séculier) to secularize [*personne, monastère*]; **2** (rendre laïque) to laicize [*personne*]; to secularize [*biens, fonctions*].

séculier, -ière /sekylje, ɛʀ/ *adj* secular.

secundo /səɡɔ̃do/ *adv* secondly.

sécuriser /sekyʀize/ [1] *vtr* **1** GÉN (rassurer) to reassure; **2** PSYCH to make [sb] feel secure.

securit® /sekyʀit/ *nm* (**verre**) ~ Triplex® (glass) GB, safety glass.

sécurité /sekyʀite/ *nf* (absence de risques d'agression) security; (absence de danger fortuit) safety; ~ **de l'emploi** job security; **de** ~ [*système, forces*] security; [*dispositif, zone*] safety; [*raisons, problème*] of security (*après n*); **se sentir en** ~ to feel secure ou safe. ■ ~ **routière** road safety; ~ **sociale** French national health and pensions organization.

sédatif, -ive /sedatif, iv/ **I** *adj* [*propriété*] sedative; [*potion, effet*] soothing.
II *nm* sedative.

sédentaire /sedɑ̃tɛʀ/ **I** *adj* **1** GÉN [*vie, travail, personne*] sedentary; **2** [*population*] geographically stable; MIL [*troupes*] garrison(ed) (*épith*).
II *nmf* **1** (dans le travail) person with a sedentary ou desk job; (casanier) stay-at-home GB, homebody US; **2 les** ~**s** the indigenous population (*sg*).

sédentariser /sedɑ̃taʀize/ [1] *vtr* to settle.

sédiment /sedimɑ̃/ *nm* sediment.

sédimentation /sedimɑ̃tasjɔ̃/ *nf* sedimentation.

séditieux, -ieuse /sedisjø, øz/ *adj* **1** [*personne*] rebellious; **2** [*écrit, esprit, propos*] seditious.

séducteur, -trice /sedyktœʀ, tʀis/ **I** *adj* seductive.
II *nm,f* (trompeur) deceiver/seductress; (charmeur) charmer.

séduction /sedyksjɔ̃/ *nf* (manœuvre) seduction; (charme naturel) charm; (de l'argent) lure; (du luxe) enticement; (des mots) seductive power.

séduire /seduiʀ/ [1] *vtr* **1** (attirer) [*personne*] to captivate; **il aime** ~ to charm people; **les qualités qui séduisent le plus chez un homme** the most attractive qualities in a man; **2** (plaire à) to appeal to [*personne*]; **3** (convaincre) [*personne*] to win over; **4**† (pour des relations sexuelles) to seduce.

séduisant, ~e /seduizɑ̃, ɑ̃t/ *adj* [*personne, perspective*] attractive; [*projet, idée*] appealing.

segment /sɛɡmɑ̃/ *nm* LING, MATH, ORDINAT segment.

segmenter /sɛɡmɑ̃te/ [1] *vtr*, **se segmenter** *vpr* to segment.

ségrégation /seɡʀeɡasjɔ̃/ *nf* segregation.

seiche /sɛʃ/ *nf* cuttlefish.

seigle /sɛɡl/ *nm* rye; **farine de** ~ rye flour.

seigneur /sɛɲœʀ/ *nm* **1** HIST (propriétaire, noble) lord; **être grand** ~ to be full of largesse; **2** FIG (de la finance, l'industrie) heavyweight; (du sport) star. ■ ~ **de la guerre** warlord.
IDIOMES **à tout** ~ **tout honneur** PROV credit where credit is due.

Seigneur /sɛɲœʀ/ **I** *nm* Lord; **le** ~ **l'a rappelé à lui** EUPH he has gone to meet his Maker.
II *excl* Good Lord!

seigneurial, ~e, *mpl* **-iaux** /sɛɲœʀjal, o/ *adj* **1** [*château, terres*] (en France) seigneurial; (en Angleterre) manorial; **2** FIG [*demeure*] stately; [*manières*] lordly.

seigneurie /sɛɲœʀi/ *nf* **1** (terre) seigneury; **2** (autorité, droits) seigniory; **3** (titre) **votre** ~ your Lordship.

sein /sɛ̃/ *nm* **1** ANAT breast; **avoir les** ~**s nus** to be topless; **se faire refaire les** ~**s** to have plastic surgery on one's breasts; **nourrir au** ~ to breast-feed; **serrer qn contre** or **sur son** ~ to clasp sb to one's bosom; **2** (utérus) LITER womb; **porter un enfant dans**

son ~ to be carrying a child; **3** LITER, FIG bosom; **au** ~ **de** within; ▸ **faux¹**.

seing /sɛ̃/ *nm* JUR signature; **acte sous** ~ **privé** private agreement.

séisme /seism/ *nm* **1** LIT earthquake, seism; **2** FIG upheaval.

seize /sɛz/ ▸ **399**, **298**, **156** *adj inv, pron* sixteen.

seizième /sɛzjɛm/ ▸ **399**, **156** *adj* sixteenth.
■ ~ **de finale** SPORT *round in competition with thirty-two competitors or teams.*

séjour /seʒuʀ/ *nm* **1** (période) stay; **il a fait plusieurs** ~**s en prison** he has been in prison several times; ~**s à l'étranger** (dans un CV) time spent abroad; **2** (pièce) living room; **3** (lieu) FML abode SOUT. ■ ~ **culturel** cultural holiday GB ou vacation; ~ **linguistique** language study holiday GB ou vacation.

séjourner /seʒuʀne/ [1] *vi* to stay.

sel /sɛl/ **I** *nm* **1** LIT salt; **gros** ~ coarse salt; **régime sans** ~ salt-free diet; **pain sans** ~ unsalted bread; **2** FIG (esprit) savour^GB; (piquant) piquancy.
II sels *nmpl* smelling salts. ■ ~ **de cuisine** cooking salt; ~ **gemme** rock salt; ~ **marin** sea salt; ~**s de bain** bath salts.

sélect○, ~e /selɛkt/ *adj* [*club, bar*] exclusive; [*clientèle*] select.

sélecteur, -trice /selɛktœʀ, tʀis/ **I** *adj* selective.
II *nm* **1** ORDINAT, TÉLÉCOM, TV selector; **2** (de bicyclette, d'embrayage standard) gear lever, gearshift US; (de moto) gear change, gearshift US; (d'embrayage automatique) gearstick, gearshift US.

sélectif, -ive /selɛktif, iv/ *adj* selective.

sélection /selɛksjɔ̃/ *nf* **1** GÉN, BIOL selection; (pour un emploi) selection process; ~ **à l'entrée** selective entry; **2** (choix) selection, choice; **3** SPORT (choix) selection; (équipe) team; **épreuve de** ~ trial (**pour** for).

sélectionner /selɛksjɔne/ [1] *vtr* **1** (choisir) to select; ~ **des élèves pour un concours** to enter pupils for a competitive examination; **être sélectionné sur dossier** UNIV, SCOL to be selected on the basis of one's academic record; **2** ORDINAT to highlight [*texte*].

sélectionneur, -euse /selɛksjɔnœʀ, øz/ *nm,f* SPORT selector.

self○ /sɛlf/ *nm* (restaurant) self-service restaurant.

self-service, *pl* ~**s** /sɛlfsɛʀvis/ *nm* (restaurant) self-service restaurant.

selle /sɛl/ **I** *nf* **1** (siège) saddle; **2** (de sculpteur) turntable; **3**† (chaise percée) commode; **aller à la** ~ EUPH to have a bowel movement.
II selles *nfpl* MÉD stools.

seller /sele/ [1] *vtr* to saddle.

sellerie /sɛlʀi/ *nf* **1** COMM (bourrellerie) saddlery; (maroquinerie) leatherwork.

sellette /sɛlɛt/ *nf* **1** (pour plante, statue) stand; (de sculpteur) small turntable; **2** (d'ouvrier) cradle.
IDIOMES **être sur la** ~ to be in the hot seat.

sellier /selje/ ▸ **374** *nm* (bourrelier) saddler; (maroquinier) maker of fancy leather goods.

selon /səlɔ̃/ **I** *prép* **1** GÉN according to; ~ **moi, il va pleuvoir** in my opinion, it's going to rain; ~ **les termes du président** in the President's words; ~ **la formule** as people ou they say; ~ **la loi** under the law; **l'idée** ~ **laquelle** the idea that; ~ **une pratique courante** in accordance with ou following a common practice; **dépenser** ~ **ses moyens** to spend according to one's pocket; **2** (en fonction de) depending on [*heure, température, circonstances*]; **la situation varie** ~ **les régions** the situation varies from region to region; **c'est** ~○ it all depends.
II selon que *loc conj* depending on whether.

Seltz /sɛlts/ *npr* **eau de** ~ seltzer water.

semailles /səmaj/ *nfpl* (travail) sowing ¢; (époque) sowing season (*sg*); (graines semées) seeds.

semaine /s(ə)mɛn/ ▸ **588** *nf* **1** (de calendrier) week; **2** (salaire hebdomadaire) week's wages (*pl*); (argent de poche) (weekly) pocket money.
IDIOMES **vivre à la petite** ~ to live from day to day.

Les jours de la semaine

Les noms des jours

L'anglais emploie la majuscule pour les noms de jours.
Les abréviations sont courantes en anglais familier écrit,
par ex. dans une lettre à un ami: I'll see you on Mon
17 Sept.

		abréviation anglaise
dimanche	Sunday	Sun
lundi	Monday	Mon
mardi	Tuesday	Tue *ou* Tues
mercredi	Wednesday	Wed
jeudi	Thursday	Thur *ou* Thurs
vendredi	Friday	Fri
samedi	Saturday	Sat

Noter que dans les pays anglophones on considère en
général que la semaine commence le dimanche.
Dans les expressions suivantes, Monday est pris comme
exemple; les autres noms de jours s'utilisent de la même
façon.

quel jour sommes-nous?	= what day is it?
nous sommes lundi	= it's Monday
c'est aujourd'hui lundi	= today is Monday

Pour l'expression de la date, ▶ 156].
L'anglais emploie normalement on *devant les noms de*
jours, sauf lorsqu'il y a une autre préposition, ou un mot
comme this, that, next, last *etc.*

Lundi *ou* le lundi: *un jour précis, passé ou futur*

c'est arrivé lundi	= it happened on Monday
lundi matin	= on Monday morning
lundi après-midi	= on Monday afternoon
lundi matin de bonne heure	= early on Monday morning
lundi soir en fin de soirée	= late on Monday evening
lundi, on va au zoo	= on Monday, we're going to the zoo
lundi dernier	= last Monday
lundi dernier dans la soirée	= last Monday evening
lundi prochain	= next Monday
lundi en huit	= the Monday after next *ou* on Monday week
dans un mois lundi	= a month from Monday
dans un mois à dater de lundi dernier	= in a month from last Monday
à partir de lundi	= from Monday onwards
c'est arrivé le lundi	= it happened on the Monday
le lundi matin	= on the Monday morning
le lundi après-midi	= on the Monday afternoon
tard le lundi soir	= late on the Monday evening
tôt le lundi matin	= early on the Monday morning

elle est partie le lundi après-midi	= she left on the Monday afternoon
ce lundi	= this Monday
ce lundi-là	= that Monday
précisément ce lundi-là	= that very Monday

Le lundi: *un même jour chaque semaine*

quand est-ce que cela a lieu?	= when does it happen?
cela a lieu le lundi	= it happens on Mondays
le lundi, on va au zoo	= on Mondays, we go to the zoo
elle ne travaille jamais le lundi	= she never works on Mondays
le lundi après-midi, elle va à la piscine	= she goes swimming on Monday afternoons
tous les lundis	= every Monday
chaque lundi	= each Monday
un lundi sur deux	= every other Monday *ou* every second Monday
un lundi sur trois	= every third Monday
presque tous les lundis	= most Mondays
certains lundis	= some Mondays
un lundi de temps en temps	= on the occasional Monday
le deuxième lundi de chaque mois	= on the second Monday in the month

Un lundi: *un jour quelconque*

c'est arrivé un lundi	= it happened on a Monday *ou* it happened one Monday
un lundi matin	= on a Monday morning *ou* one Monday morning
un lundi après-midi	= on a Monday afternoon *ou* one Monday afternoon

Du *avec les noms des jours de la semaine*

Les expressions françaises avec du *se traduisent*
normalement par l'emploi du nom de jour en position
d'adjectif.

les cours du lundi	= Monday classes
la fermeture du lundi	= Monday closing
les programmes de télévision du lundi	= Monday TV programmes
les trains du lundi	= Monday trains
le vol du lundi	= the Monday flight

Et comparer:

le journal du lundi	= the Monday paper
le journal de lundi	= Monday's paper

et de même the Monday classes *et* Monday's classes *etc.*

---

semainier /səmɛnje/ *nm* (agenda) week-to-a-page diary.

sémantique /semɑ̃tik/ **I** *adj* semantic.
II *nf* semantics (+ *v sg*).

sémaphore /semafɔr/ *nm* NAUT, TÉLÉCOM semaphore.

semblable /sɑ̃blabl/ **I** *adj* **1** (comparable) similar (à to); **des résultats à peu près/tout à fait ~s** roughly/quite similar results; **ils sont ~s en tout** they are alike in all respects; **une journée ~ à tant d'autres** a day like any other; **j'en ai vu de ~s** I've seen similar ones; **2** (identique) identical; **3** (tel) (*before n*) such; **~ proposition** such a proposal.
II *nmf* fellow creature; **eux et leurs ~s** they and their kind.

semblant /sɑ̃blɑ̃/ *nm* **un ~ de légalité** a semblance of legality; **faire ~ d'être triste** to pretend to be sad; **elle fait ~ de rien, mais elle t'a vu** she's seen you but she's not letting on°.

sembler /sɑ̃ble/ [1] **I** *vi* to seem; **le temps m'a semblé long** the time seemed to me to pass slowly; **tout semble possible** it seems anything is possible.
II *v impers* **il semble bon de faire** it seems appropriate to do; **faites comme bon vous semble** do whatever you think best; **le problème est réglé à ce qu'il me semble** the problem has been solved, or so it seems to me; **il me semble important de faire** I think it is important to do; **il me semble l'avoir déjà rencontrée** I think I've met her before; **elle a, semble-t-il, refusé** apparently, she has refused; **si bon me semble** if I feel like it.

semelle /s(ə)mɛl/ *nf* **1** sole; **~ antidérapante** non-slip sole; **2** TECH (de fer à repasser) soleplate; (de machine) bedplate; (de rail) flange; (de ski) midsection.
■ **~ compensée** wedge heel; **~ intérieure** insole.
IDIOMES **être (dur comme) de la ~**° to be as tough as old boots° GB *ou* leather US; **ne pas quitter** or **lâcher qn d'une ~** to stick to sb like a leech.

semence /s(ə)mɑ̃s/ *nf* seed.

semer /s(ə)me/ [1] *vtr* **1** AGRIC to sow [*graines*]; **~ à la volée** to sow, to broadcast; **2** (apporter) to sow [*discorde, trouble*]; to spread [*confusion, panique*]; [*arme, ouragan*] to bring [*mort*]; **~ le doute** to sow doubt; **3** (parsemer) **~ des clous sur la route** to strew the road with nails; **mission semée de difficultés** mission bristling with difficulties; **copie semée de fautes** written work riddled with errors; **ciel semé d'étoiles** star-spangled sky; **on récolte ce qu'on a semé** as you sow so shall you reap; **4**° (perdre) to drop; **5**° (distancer) to shake off [*poursuivant, gêneur*]; to leave [sb] behind [*concurrent*].

semestre /s(ə)mɛstr/ ▶ 588] *nm* **1** (d'année civile) half-year; **tous les ~s** twice a year; **2** (d'année universitaire) semester; **3** (rente, pension) half-yearly payment.

semestriel, -ielle /səmɛstʀijɛl/ *adj* **1** [*revue*] biannual; [*réunion, prévisions*] twice-yearly (*épith*); [*résultats*] half-yearly (*épith*); **la présidence semestrielle de la CEE** the six-month presidency of the EEC; **2** UNIV [*examen*] end-of-semester (*épith*) GB, final US; [*cours*] one-semester (*épith*).

semeur, -euse /səmœʀ, øz/ *nm,f* LIT, FIG sower; **~ de troubles** troublemaker.

semi-circulaire, *pl* **~s** /səmisiʀkylɛʀ/ *adj* semicircular.

semi-conserve, *pl* **~s** /səmikɔ̃sɛʀv/ *nf* CULIN, IND partially preserved product.

semi-démocratique, *pl* **~s** /səmidemɔkʀatik/ *adj* relatively democratic.

semi-désertique, *pl* **~s** /səmidezɛʀtik/ *adj* semidesert.

semi-échec, *pl* **~s** /səmieʃɛk/ *nm* partial failure.

semi-liberté, *pl* **~s** /səmilibɛʀte/ *nf* relative freedom.

sémillant, ~e /semijɑ̃, ɑ̃t/ *adj* spirited; [*esprit*] sparkling.

séminaire /seminɛʀ/ *nm* **1** (réunion) seminar; **2** (institution) seminary.

séminal, ~e, *mpl* **-aux** /seminal, o/ *adj* seminal.

séminariste /seminaʀist/ *nm* seminarist, seminarian.

sémiologie /semjɔlɔʒi/ *nf* semiology.

sémiotique /semjɔtik/ **I** *adj* semiotic.
II *nf* semiotics (+ *v sg*).

semi-précieux, -ieuse /səmipʀesjø, øz/ *adj* [*pierre*] semiprecious.

semi-remorque, *pl* **~s** /səmiʀəmɔʀk/ *nm* (camion) articulated lorry GB, tractor-trailer US.

semis /s(ə)mi/ *nm inv* AGRIC (ensemencement) sowing; (jeune plant) seedling; (terrain) seedbed.

semoir /səmwaʀ/ *nm* **1** (machine) seed drill; **2†** (sac) seedbag.

semonce /səmɔ̃s/ *nf* reprimand; **coup de ~** LIT, FIG warning shot.

semoule /səmul/ *nf* semolina; **sucre ~** caster sugar.

sempiternel, -elle /sɑ̃pitɛʀnɛl/ *adj* perpetual, endless.

sénat /sena/ *nm* senate.

sénateur /senatœʀ/ **▶596** *nm* senator.

sénatorial, ~e, *mpl* **-iaux** /senatɔʀjal, o/ *adj* senatorial.

séné /sene/ *nm* senna.

sénile /senil/ *adj* senile.

sénilité /senilite/ *nf* senility.

sens /sɑ̃s/ **I** *nm inv* **1** (direction) LIT, FIG direction, way; **dans les deux ~** in both directions; **elle venait en ~ inverse** she was coming from the opposite direction; **mouvement en ~ contraire** backward movement; **en tous ~** in all directions; **dans le ~ Paris-Lyon** in the Paris to Lyons direction; **dans le ~ de la largeur** widthways, across; **dans le ~ de la longueur** lengthways, longways US; **être dans le bon/mauvais ~** to be the right/wrong way up; **des flèches dans tous les ~** arrows pointing in all directions; **retourner un problème dans tous les ~** to consider a problem from every angle; **courir dans tous les ~** to run all over the place; **dans le ~ de la marche** facing the engine; **dans le ~ des fils** (de tissu) with the grain; **~ dessus dessous** /sɑ̃dəsydəsu/ (à l'envers) upside down; (en désordre) upside down; (très troublé) very upset; **~ devant derrière** /sɑ̃dəvɑ̃dɛʀjɛʀ/ back to front; **aller dans le bon ~** [*réformes, mesures*] to be a step in the right direction; **des mesures qui vont dans le ~ de notre rapport** measures which are in line with our report; **le pays va dans le ~ d'une plus grande indépendance** the country is moving toward(s) greater independence; **le ~ de l'histoire** the tide of history; **2** (signification) meaning; **le ~ figuré d'un mot** the figurative sense of a word; **employer un mot au ~ propre** to use a word literally; **au ~ fort du terme** in the fullest sense of the word; **cela n'a pas**

de ~ GÉN it doesn't make sense; (idiot, ridicule) it's absurd; **3** (fonction physiologique) sense; **retrouver l'usage de ses ~** to regain consciousness; **4** (intuition) sense; **avoir le ~ de l'orientation** to have a good sense of direction; **avoir le ~ pratique** to be practical; **ne pas avoir le ~ du ridicule** not to realize when one looks silly; **avoir le ~ des affaires** to have a flair for business; **avoir le ~ des affaires** your business sense; **ne pas avoir le ~ de la langue** to have no feeling for language; **n'avoir aucun ~ des réalités** to live in a dream world.
II *nmpl* senses; **plaisirs des ~** sensual pleasures.
■ **~ giratoire** roundabout GB, traffic circle US; **~ interdit** (panneau) no-entry sign; (rue) one-way street; **~ obligatoire** (panneau) one-way sign ; **~ unique** (panneau) one-way sign; (rue) one-way street.
IDIOMES **tomber sous le ~** to be patently obvious.

sensation /sɑ̃sasjɔ̃/ *nf* **1** LIT, FIG feeling, sensation; **cela ne procure pas les mêmes ~s** it doesn't have the same effect; **on a la ~ de flotter** you feel as if you're floating; **aimer les ~s fortes** to like one's thrills; **2** (réaction) sensation; **la décision a fait ~** (a étonné) the decision caused a sensation; **reportages à ~** keyhole journalism ¢.

sensationnel, -elle /sɑ̃sasjɔnɛl/ *adj* **1°** (formidable) fantastic°; **2** (surprenant) sensational, astonishing; **3** (à sensation) sensational.

sensé, ~e /sɑ̃se/ *adj* sensible.

sensibilisation /sɑ̃sibilizasjɔ̃/ *nf* **1** **campagne de ~** awareness campaign; **une ~ des médecins au problème** making doctors aware of the problem; **2** MÉD, PHOT sensitizing, sensitization.

sensibiliser /sɑ̃sibilize/ [1] *vtr* **1** **~ le public à un problème** to increase public awareness of an issue; **2** CHIMIE, MÉD, PHOT to sensitize.

sensibilité /sɑ̃sibilite/ *nf* **1** (qualité) sensibility; **elle est d'une grande ~** she is very sensitive; **2** MÉD, PHOT sensitivity.

sensible /sɑ̃sibl/ **I** *adj* **1** GÉN sensitive; **être ~ aux compliments** to like compliments; **être ~ aux charmes de qn** to be susceptible to sb's charms; **j'ai été très ~ à votre gentille attention** I was most touched by your kindness; **je suis ~ au fait que** I am aware that; **avoir le cœur ~** to be sensitive; **être ~ à un argument** to be swayed by an argument; **les natures ~s** PÉJ the fainthearted; **avoir l'oreille ~** to have keen hearing; **un être ~** a sentient being; **je suis très ~ au froid** I really feel the cold; **2** [*peau*] sensitive; [*peau cicatrisée*] tender; [*membre blessé*] sore; **je suis ~ de la gorge, j'ai la gorge ~** I often get a sore throat; **j'ai les pieds ~s** my feet are very sensitive; **3** (notable) [*hausse, différence*] appreciable; [*effort*] real; **4** (perceptible) **le monde ~** the physical ou tangible world.
II *nmf* sensitive person.

sensiblement /sɑ̃sibləmɑ̃/ *adv* **1** (considérablement) [*réduire, augmenter*] appreciably, noticeably; [*différent*] perceptibly; **2** (plus ou moins) [*pareil*] roughly.

sensiblerie /sɑ̃sibləʀi/ *nf* PÉJ sentimentality PÉJ.

sensitif, -ive /sɑ̃sitif, iv/ *adj* sensory.

sensoriel, -ielle /sɑ̃sɔʀjɛl/ *adj* sensory.

sensualité /sɑ̃sɥalite/ *nf* sensuality.

sensuel, -elle /sɑ̃sɥɛl/ *adj* sensual.

sentence /sɑ̃tɑ̃s/ *nf* **1** (décision) sentence; **2** (propos) maxim.

sentencieux, -ieuse /sɑ̃tɑ̃sjø, øz/ *adj* sententious.

senteur /sɑ̃tœʀ/ *nf* LITER scent.

senti, ~e /sɑ̃ti/ *adj* **bien ~** [*remarques*] well-chosen; [*réponse*] blunt; [*discours*] forthright.

sentier /sɑ̃tje/ *nm* LIT, FIG path, track; **être sur le ~ de la guerre** FIG to be on the warpath; **hors des ~s battus** off the beaten track.
■ **~ de grande randonnée** long-distance footpath; **~ de petite randonnée** footpath.

sentiment /sɑ̃timɑ̃/ *nm* **1** GÉN feeling; **il est incapable de ~** he's incapable of emotion; **agir par ~ plus que par raison** to be guided by one's feelings rather than by reason; **faire du ~** to sentimentalize; **prendre qn par les ~s** to appeal to sb's better nature; **il ne fait pas de ~ en affaires** he doesn't let sentiment get in the way of business; **j'ai le ~ qu'il va pleuvoir** I've got a feeling it's going to rain; **donner le ~ de faire** to give the impression of doing; **2** (inclination) feeling, sentiment SOUT; **les beaux** or **bons ~s** fine sentiments; **être animé de mauvais ~s** to have bad intentions; **3** (dans les formules épistolaires) **~s affectueux** or **amicaux** best wishes; **veuillez croire à mes ~s les meilleurs** (à une personne non nommée) yours faithfully; (à une personne nommée) yours sincerely.

sentimental, **~e**, *mpl* **-aux** /sɑ̃timɑ̃tal, o/ I *adj* **1** [*attachement*] sentimental; [*vie*] love (*épith*); [*relations*] romantic; **sur le plan ~** (dans un horoscope) on the romance front; **2** (sensible) sentimental, romantic.
II *nm,f* sentimental person.

sentinelle /sɑ̃tinɛl/ *nf* **1** (soldat) sentry; **2** FIG lookout; **faire la ~** to stand guard, to keep watch.

sentir /sɑ̃tir/ [30] I *vtr* **1** (percevoir par l'odorat) to smell [*parfum, fleur*]; **on sent que tu fumes le cigare** one can tell that you smoke cigars by the smell; **2** (percevoir par le toucher, le corps, le goût) to feel; **j'ai marché trop longtemps, je ne sens plus mes pieds** I've been walking for too long, my feet are numb; **on sent qu'il y a du vin dans la sauce** the sauce tastes of wine; **~ d'où vient le vent** LIT, NAUT to see how the wind blows ou lies; FIG to see which way the wind is blowing; **3** (comprendre) to be conscious of [*importance*]; to feel [*beauté, force*]; to appreciate [*difficulté*]; to sense [*danger, désapprobation*]; **~ que** (percevoir) to feel that; (avoir l'idée) to have a feeling that; **on sent que l'hiver approche** it feels wintry; **je te sens inquiet, je sens que tu es inquiet** I can tell you're worried; **je leur ai fait ~ mon désaccord** I made it clear to them that I didn't agree; **faire ~ le rythme d'un poème** to bring out the rhythm of a poem; **se faire ~** [*besoin, présence, absence*] to be felt.
II *vi* **1** (avoir une odeur) to smell; **~ bon** to smell nice; **ça sent bon le café** there's a nice smell of coffee; **fleurs qui ne sentent rien** flowers which don't have a scent; **2** (puer) to smell; **~ des pieds** to have smelly feet; **3** (révéler) to smack of; **ta douleur sent la comédie** your grief seems put on; **ciel nuageux qui sent l'orage** cloudy sky that heralds a storm.
III *se sentir* *vpr* **1** to feel; **se ~ mieux** to feel better; **se ~ surveillé** to feel that one is being watched; **elle ne s'est pas sentie visée par ma remarque** she didn't feel that my remark was aimed at her; **ne plus se ~**° (de joie) to be overjoyed; (de vanité) to get above oneself; **2** (être perceptible) [*phénomène, amélioration, effet*] to be felt.
IDIOMES **je ne peux pas le ~** I can't stand him; **je l'ai senti passer!** (piqûre, addition) it really hurt!; (réprimande) I really got it in the neck!

séparable /separabl/ *adj* separable (**de** from); **être difficilement ~ de** to be difficult to separate from.

séparation /separasjɔ̃/ *nf* **1** GÉN, POL, JUR separation; **la ~ des pouvoirs** POL the separation of powers; **après la ~ des composants du mélange** after separating out the constituents of the mixture; **la ~ du pays en deux États** the division ou splitting of the country into two states; **après deux ans de ~** after two years' separation; **2** (division) (entre des jardins) boundary; (entre des pièces) partition; FIG boundary, dividing line; **mur de ~** (extérieur) boundary wall; (intérieur) dividing wall; **établir une ~ (nette) entre sa vie privée et professionnelle** to keep one's private life (completely) separate from one's work.
■ **~ de biens** JUR matrimonial division of property; **~ de corps** JUR judicial separation; **~ de fait** JUR de facto separation.

séparatisme /separatism/ *nm* separatism.

séparatiste /separatist/ *adj, nmf* separatist.

séparé, **~e** /separe/ *adj* **1** (sans contact) **vivre ~** to live apart (**de** from); **2** (éloigné) **les deux villages sont ~s de quelques kilomètres** the two villages are a few kilometres GB apart; **3** (distinct) separate.

séparément /separemɑ̃/ *adv* separately.

séparer /separe/ [1] I *vtr* **1** (ne pas laisser ensemble) to separate [*objets, rôles*]; to separate out [*composants*]; **~ l'aspect politique d'un problème de son aspect économique** to keep the political and economic aspects of a problem separate; **la mort les a séparés** they were parted by death; **la vie nous a séparés** we have gone our separate ways in life; **2** (distinguer) [*personne*] to distinguish between [*concepts, domaines, problèmes*]; **on ne peut ~ ces deux problèmes** one cannot dissociate these two problems; **3** (former une limite entre) to separate; **quelques kilomètres nous séparent de la mer** we are a few kilometres GB away from the sea; **deux ans séparent les deux événements** there is a gap of two years between the two events; **le temps qui sépare le passage de deux véhicules** the time lapse between the passage of two vehicles; **4** (diviser) LIT, FIG to divide; **l'âge les séparait** the age difference between them was a problem; **les qualités qui séparent un bon musicien d'un virtuose** the qualities that distinguish a good musician from a virtuoso; **tout les sépare** they are worlds apart.
II *se séparer* *vpr* **1** (se quitter) [*invités*] to part, to leave each other ; [*conjoints, amants*] to split up; [*mari, femme*] to separate; **2** (quitter) **se ~ de** to leave [*camarade, groupe, famille*]; to split up with; JUR to separate from [*mari, femme*]; **3** (se disperser) [*manifestants*] to disperse, to split (up); [*assemblée*] to break up; **4** (se passer de) **se ~ de** to let [sb] go [*employé, collaborateur*]; to part with [*objet personnel*]; **il ne se sépare jamais de son parapluie** he takes his umbrella everywhere; **5** (se diviser) to divide; **la route se sépare (en deux)** the road forks.

sept /sɛt/ ▶ **399**, **298**, **156** *adj inv, pron, nm inv* seven.
■ **les ~ Familles** JEUX Happy Families.
IDIOMES **tourne ~ fois ta langue dans ta bouche avant de parler** think before you speak.

septante /sɛptɑ̃t/ ▶ **399**, **156** *adj inv, pron* B, H seventy.

septantième /sɛptɑ̃tjɛm/ ▶ **399** *adj* B, H seventieth.

septembre /sɛptɑ̃br/ ▶ **382** *nm* September.

septennat /sɛptena/ *nm* seven-year term (of office).

septentrional, **~e**, *mpl* **-aux** /sɛptɑ̃trijonal, o/ *adj* northern.

septicémie /sɛptisemi/ ▶ **196** *nf* blood-poisoning, septicemia SPÉC.

septième /sɛtjɛm/ ▶ **399**, **156** I *adj* seventh.
II *nf* SCOL fifth year of primary school, age 10–11.
■ **le ~ art** cinematography.
IDIOMES **septième être au ~ ciel** to be on cloud nine.

septuagénaire /sɛptɥaʒenɛr/ I *adj* **être ~** to be in one's seventies.
II *nm,f* person in his/her seventies.

septuor /sɛptɥor/ *nm* (œuvre, formation) septet.

septupler /sɛptyple/ [1] I *vtr* to increase [sth] sevenfold.
II *vi* to increase sevenfold.

sépulcral, **~e**, *mpl* **-aux** /sepylkral, o/ *adj* **1** (funèbre) sepulchral; **silence ~** deathly silence; **2**† (funéraire) [*pierre, caveau*] funerary.

sépulcre /sepylkr/ *nm* sepulchre GB.

sépulture /sepyltyr/ *nf* **1** (tombe) grave; **2** (enterrement) burial.

séquelle /sekɛl/ *nf* **1** MÉD (d'accident, opération) aftereffect; **2** (retombées) repercussion; (conséquence) consequence.

séquence /sekɑ̃s/ *nf* **1** GÉN sequence; **2** CHIMIE (de polymère) block.

séquestration /sekɛstrasjɔ̃/ *nf* **1** (détention) GÉN confinement; JUR **~ (arbitraire)** illegal detention; **2** JUR, CHIMIE sequestration.

séquestre /sekɛstr/ *nm* JUR sequestration; **biens (mis) sous ~** sequestrated property ₵.

séquestrer /sekɛstre/ [1] *vtr* **1** (détenir) GÉN to hold [*otage*]; JUR to confine [sb] illegally [*personne*]; **2** JUR (saisir) to sequestrate [*biens*].

sérail /seʀaj/ *nm* **1** HIST seraglio; **2** (entourage) innermost circle.

séraphin /seʀafɛ̃/ *nm* (ange) seraph.

serbe /sɛʀb/ I ▶509 *adj* Serbian.
II ▶338 *nm* LING Serbian.

serbo-croate /sɛʀbokʀɔat/ ▶338 *nm* Serbo-Croatian.

Sercq /sɛʀk/ ▶305 *nprf* Sark.

serein, **~e** /sɔʀɛ̃, ɛn/ *adj* [*ciel, temps*] clear; [*personne, visage*] serene; [*jugement*] dispassionate; [*critique*] objective.

sereinement /sɔʀɛnmɑ̃/ *adv* [*regarder*] serenely; [*réfléchir, parler*] calmly; [*voir l'avenir*] with equanimity; [*juger*] dispassionately.

sérénade /seʀenad/ *nf* **1** (concert) serenade; **2**○ (tapage) racket○.

sérénissime /seʀenisim/ *adj* **son Altesse ~** His/Her Serene Highness.

sérénité /seʀenite/ *nf* **1** (de visage, d'esprit) serenity; (de personne) equanimity; **2** (de juge, jugement) impartiality; **3** (de ciel, temps) calmness.

serf, serve /sɛʀ, sɛʀv/ *nm,f* serf.

sergent /sɛʀʒɑ̃/ ▶284 *nm* MIL (de terre) ≈ sergeant; (de l'air) ≈ sergeant GB, ≈ staff sergeant US.

sergent-chef, *pl* **sergents-chefs** /sɛʀʒɑ̃ʃɛf/ ▶284 *nm* MIL (de terre) ≈ staff sergeant; (de l'air) ≈ flight sergeant GB, ≈ chief master sergeant US.

série /seʀi/ *nf* **1** (suite) series (+ *v sg*); **catastrophes en ~** a series of catastrophes; **avoir des problèmes en ~**, **avoir toute une ~ de problèmes** to have one problem after another; **2** (de production) **numéro de ~** serial number; **~ limitée** limited edition; **modèle de ~** GÉN mass-produced model; (voiture) production model; **fabriqués** or **faits en ~** mass-produced; **production en ~** mass production; **voiture hors ~** custom-built car; **numéro hors ~** special issue; ▶ **grand**; **3** (collection) set; **4** TV series (+ *v sg*); **5** CIN (**film de**) **~ B** B movie; **6** SPORT (catégorie) division; (épreuve) heat; **tête de ~ numéro un** (au tennis) number one seed; **7** CHIMIE, MATH, MUS series (*sg*); **8** SCOL option.
■ **~ noire** CIN, LITTÉRAT thriller; FIG (catastrophes) series of disasters (*pl*); (malchance) run of bad luck.

sérieusement /seʀjøzmɑ̃/ *adv* **1** GÉN seriously; **2** (considérablement) seriously, considerably.

sérieux, **-ieuse** /seʀjø, øz/ I *adj* **1** GÉN **être ~ dans son travail** [*personne*] to be serious about one's work; **2** (qui mérite considération) [*affaire, menace*] serious; [*piste, indice*] important; [*annonce, proposition*] genuine; **passer aux choses sérieuses** to move on to serious matters; **'pas ~ s'abstenir'** (dans une petite annonce) 'genuine inquiries only'; **3** (digne de confiance) reliable; (responsable) responsible; **cela ne fait pas très ~** that doesn't make a very good impression; **4** (grave) serious; **5** (considérable) [*effort, besoin*] real; [*progrès*] considerable; [*handicap*] serious.
II *nm* seriousness; **dire qch avec beaucoup de ~** to say sth very seriously; **garder son ~** to keep a straight face; **faire qch avec ~** to do sth carefully; **il a fait preuve de beaucoup de ~ dans ses études** he's really worked hard (at his studies); **se prendre au ~** to take oneself seriously.

sérigraphie /seʀigʀafi/ *nf* **1** (procédé) silkscreen printing; **2** (œuvre) silkscreen print.

serin /sɔʀɛ̃/ *nm* ZOOL canary.

seriner○ /sɔʀine/ [1] *vtr* **~ qch à qn** to drum sth into sb.

seringa /sɔʀɛ̃ga/ *nm* syringa, mock orange.

seringue /sɔʀɛ̃g/ *nf* syringe.

serment /sɛʀmɑ̃/ *nm* **1** (devant une autorité) oath; **déclarer sous ~** to declare under oath; **prêter ~** to take the oath; **2** (promesse) LITER vow.
■ **le ~ d'Hippocrate** MÉD the Hippocratic oath.

sermon /sɛʀmɔ̃/ *nm* **1** LITTÉRAT, RELIG sermon; **2** (discours) PEJ lecture; (remontrance) PEJ talking-to.

sermonner /sɛʀmɔne/ [1] *vtr* (conseiller) to lecture; (morigéner) to give [sb] a talking-to.

séronégatif, **-ive** /seʀonegatif, iv/ I *adj* HIV-negative.
II *nm,f* HIV-negative person.

séropositif, **-ive** /seʀopozitif, iv/ I *adj* GÉN seropositive (**à** for); (dans le cas du sida) HIV positive.
II *nm,f* HIV-positive person.

séropositivité /seʀopozitivite/ *nf* (dans le cas du sida) (HIV antibody) seropositivity.

sérosité /seʀozite/ *nf* serous fluid.

serpe /sɛʀp/ *nf* billhook.

serpent /sɛʀpɑ̃/ *nm* **1** ZOOL snake; **2** BIBLE serpent; **3** ▶392 MUS serpent.
■ **~ monétaire** FIN currency snake; **~ à sonnette** rattlesnake.

serpenter /sɛʀpɑ̃te/ [1] *vi* [*route, fleuve*] to wind.

serpentin /sɛʀpɑ̃tɛ̃/ *nm* (de fête) streamer.

serpette /sɛʀpɛt/ *nf* pruning knife.

serpillière /sɛʀpijɛʀ/ *nf* floorcloth.

serpolet /sɛʀpɔlɛ/ *nm* wild thyme.

serre /sɛʀ/ *nf* **1** (maison de verre) greenhouse; **mettre qch en ~** or **sous ~** to put sth in a greenhouse; **effet de ~** greenhouse effect; **2** (de rapace) talon, claw.

serré, **~e** /seʀe/ I *adj* **1** (ajusté) [*vis, écrou*] tight; [*jupe, pantalon*] tight; **je suis ~e dans ma veste** my jacket is too tight; **robe ~e à la taille** dress fitted at the waist; **2** (dense) [*herbe*] thick; [*écriture*] cramped; **en rangs ~s** in serried rows; **il tombait une pluie fine et ~e** it was drizzling; **3** FIG [*délais, budget*] tight; [*virage*] sharp; [*contrôle, gestion*] strict; [*lutte*] hard; [*débat, négociation*] heated; [*partie, match*] close; **4** (fort) [*café*] very strong.
II *adv* [*écrire*] in a cramped hand; [*tricoter*] tightly; **il va falloir jouer ~ si...** we can't take any chances if...

serre-livres /sɛʀlivʀ/ *nm inv* book end.

serrement /sɛʀmɑ̃/ *nm* **1** LIT **~ de main** handshake; **2** FIG **avoir** or **ressentir un ~ de cœur** to feel a pang.

serrer /seʀe/ [1] I *vtr* **1** (maintenir vigoureusement) [*personne*] to grip [*volant, rame*]; **~ qn/qch dans ses bras** to hug sb/sth; **~ qch entre ses dents** to clench sth between one's teeth; **~ la main de qn** to shake hands with sb; **~ les poings** to clench one's fists; **la peur me serrait la gorge** my throat was constricted with fear; **ça me serre le cœur de voir ça** it wrings my heart to see that; **2** (ajuster) to tighten [*nœud, corde*]; **serre bien tes lacets** do your shoelaces up tight; **tu as trop serré ton nœud de cravate** your tie is too tight; **mon chignon n'est pas assez serré** my bun is (too) loose; **3** (tenir à l'étroit) [*chaussures, vêtement*] to be too tight; **4** (bloquer) to tighten [*écrou, vis, boulon*]; to turn [sth] off tightly [*robinet*]; **sans ~** [*fixer, visser*] loosely; **5** (être près de) **~ le trottoir** [*automobiliste*] to hug the kerb GB ou curb US; **~ à droite** [*véhicule*] to get ou stay in the right-hand lane; **~ qn de près** [*concurrent*] to be hot on sb's tail; **~ un sujet de près** to study a subject closely; **6** (rapprocher) to push [sth] closer together [*livres, tables, objets*]; to squeeze [*personne*]; **être serré** [*livres, personnes*] to be packed together; **nous sommes trop serrés dans la cuisine** there are too many of us in the kitchen; **~ les rangs** LIT, FIG to close ranks; **7** (réduire) to cut [*dépenses, prix*]; **8** NAUT to furl [*voile*]; **~ le vent** to sail close to the wind; **9** (ranger) LITER, DIAL to stow [sth] away [*objet précieux, économies*].
II **se serrer** *vpr* **1** (se rapprocher de) [*personnes*] to squeeze up; **ils se sont serrés les uns contre les autres** they huddled together; **2** (se comprimer) **se ~ dans une jupe** to squeeze oneself into a skirt; **nous nous sommes serré la main** we shook hands; **3** (se contracter) **avoir le cœur qui se serre** to feel deeply upset; **avoir la gorge qui se serre** (d'émotion) to have a lump in one's throat; (de peur) to have one's heart in one's mouth.

serre-tête, *pl* **~s** /sɛʀtɛt/ *nm* hairband.

serrure /seʀyʀ/ *nf* lock; **trou de ~** keyhole.

serrurerie /seʀyʀʀi/ *nf* **1** ▶374‖ (boutique) locksmith's; **2** (corps de métier) locksmith's trade.

serrurier /seʀyʀje/ ▶374‖ *nm* locksmith.

sertir /seʀtiʀ/ [3] *vtr* (en joaillerie) to set [*pierre*].

sérum /seʀɔm/ *nm* serum; **~ antirabique** anti-rabies serum; **un ~ antivenimeux** an antivenin; **~ physiologique** saline solution; **~ sanguin** blood serum; **~ de vérité** truth drug.

servage /seʀvaʒ/ *nm* HIST serfdom.

servant /seʀvɑ̃/ **I** *adj m* **chevalier ~** devoted admirer.
II *nm* **1** RELIG server; **2** MIL (au canon) member of a gun crew.

servante /seʀvɑ̃t/ ▶374‖ *nf* (domestique) maidservant.

serve ▶ **serf**.

serveur, -euse /seʀvœʀ, øz/ ▶374‖ **I** *nm,f* (dans café, restaurant) waiter/waitress.
II *nm* **1** SPORT server; **2** (aux cartes) dealer; **3** ORDINAT server.

servi, ~e /seʀvi/ *adj* (à table) **'prends de la viande'—'merci je suis déjà ~'** 'have some meat'—'I already have some, thank you'; **nous voulions du soleil, nous sommes ~s**○ we wanted some sunshine and we've certainly got it.

serviable /seʀvjabl/ *adj* obliging, helpful.

service /seʀvis/ **I** *nm* **1** (action serviable, faveur) **je peux te demander un ~?** (action serviable) can I ask you to do something for me?; (faveur) can I ask you a favour^GB?; **elle m'a rendu de nombreux ~s** she's been very helpful; **il est toujours prêt à rendre ~** he is always ready to help; **2** (liaison) service; **~ de bus** bus service; **3** (fonctionnement) **être en ~** [*ascenseur*] (en train de fonctionner) to be working; (en état de fonctionner) to be in working order; [*autoroute*] to be open; [*ligne de métro, de bus*] to be running; **être hors ~** [*ascenseur*] to be out of order; **entrer en ~** [*ligne de métro, autoroute*] to be opened, to come into service; **mettre en ~** to bring [sth] into service [*appareil, véhicule*]; to open [*gare, autoroute, ligne de bus*]; **4** (aide) **rendre ~ à qn** [*machine, appareil*] to be a help to sb; [*route, passage, magasin*] to be convenient (for sb); **ça peut toujours rendre ~** it might come in handy; **5** (action de servir) service; **être au ~ de son pays** to serve one's country; **je suis à leur ~** (employé) I work for them; (dévoué) I'm at their disposal; **'à votre ~!'** (je vous en prie) 'don't mention it!', 'not at all!'; **'que puis- je faire** or **qu'y a-t-il pour votre ~?'** 'may I help you?'; **6** (à table) service; **12% pour le ~** 12% service charge; **faire le ~** (servir les plats) to serve; (desservir) to act as waiter; **manger au premier ~** to go to the first sitting; **7** (des gens de maison) (domestic) service; **entrer au ~ de qn** to go to work for sb; **prendre qn à son ~** to take sb on, to engage sb; **escalier de ~** backstairs (*pl*), service stairs (*pl*); **8** (obligations professionnelles) **avoir 20 ans de ~ dans une entreprise** to have been with a firm 20 years; **être de** or **en ~** to be on duty; **assurer le ~ de qn** to cover for sb; **son ~ se termine à** he/she comes off duty at; **être en ~ commandé** [*policier*] to be acting under orders; **état de ~**(s) record of service, service record; **le ~ de nuit** night duty; **pharmacie de ~** duty chemist; **être l'idiot de ~** to be the house clown; **9** (section administrative) department; **~ des urgences** casualty department GB, emergency room US; **~ de réanimation** intensive care unit; **les ~s secrets** the secret service (*sg*); **les ~s d'espionnage** or **de renseignements** the intelligence services; **~ de dépannage** breakdown service; **les ~s du Premier Ministre se refusent à tout commentaire** the Prime Minister's office has refused to comment; **chef de ~** (dans une administration) section head; (dans un hôpital) senior consultant; **10** MIL **~** (**militaire**) military ou national service; **~ national** national service; **~ civil** non-military national service; **partir au ~**○ to go off to do one's military service; **~ en temps de paix** peace time service; **être bon pour le ~** LIT to be passed fit for military service; FIG HUM to be passed fit; **reprendre du ~** to re-enlist, to sign up again; **11** (vaisselle) set; **un ~ à thé** a tea set; **~ de table** dinner service; **12** RELIG service; **13** SPORT service, serve; **être au ~** to serve ou be serving.
II services *nmpl* services; **se passer des ~s de qn** to dispense with sb's services.
■ **~ après-vente** (département) after-sales service department; (activité) after-sales service; **~ minimum** reduced service; **~ d'ordre** stewards (*pl*); **~ de presse** (de ministère, parti, d'entreprise) press office; (de maison d'édition) press and publicity department; (livre) review copy.

serviette /seʀvjɛt/ *nf* **1** (en tissu) **~** (**de toilette**) towel; **~** (**de table**) (table) napkin; **2** (cartable) briefcase.
■ **~ hygiénique** sanitary towel.
IDIOMES **il ne faut pas mélanger les torchons et les ~s**○ you've got to know what's what.

serviette-éponge, *pl* **serviettes-éponges** /seʀvjɛtepɔ̃ʒ/ *nf* terry towel.

servile /seʀvil/ *adj* **1** (soumis) [*personne, attitude*] servile; [*fidélité, obéissance*] slavish; **2** (peu original) [*adaptation*] slavish; [*traduction*] over-literal; **3** HIST (de serf) servile; (de domestique) menial.

servilement /seʀvilmɑ̃/ *adv* [*obéir*] slavishly; [*flatter*] obsequiously; (sans originalité) [*imiter, copier*] slavishly.

servilité /seʀvilite/ *nf* (soumission) servility.

servir /seʀviʀ/ [30] **I** *vtr* **1** GÉN to serve; **le boucher m'a mal servi aujourd'hui** the butcher didn't give me very good meat today; **~ qch à qn, ~ qn en qch** to serve sb (with) sth; **qu'est-ce que je vous sers (à boire)?** what would you like to drink?; **tu as été bien servi en gâteau** you've been given a generous helping of cake; **'Madame est servie'** 'dinner is served Madam'; **au moment de ~** before serving; **'~ frais'** 'serve chilled'; **~ la messe** to serve mass; **2** FIG (être utile à) [*situation*] to help [*personne, cause*]; to serve [*intérêt*]; [*personne*] to further [*ambition, intérêt*]; **3**○ (donner) **~ qch comme excuse** to use sth as an excuse; **4** JEUX to deal [*cartes*].
II servir à *vtr ind* **1** LIT **~ à qn** [*pièce, maison, salle*] to be used by sb; **cette casserole me sert pour faire des confitures** I use this pan for making jam; **~ à qch** to be used for sth; **les exercices m'ont servi à comprendre la règle** the exercises helped me to understand the rule; **2** FIG to come in useful; **cela ne sert à rien** (objet) it's useless; (action) it's no good; **cela ne sert à rien de faire** there's no point in doing; **~ à quelque chose** to serve a useful purpose; **~ à faire** to be good for doing.
III servir de *vtr ind* (avoir la fonction) **~ d'intermédiaire à qn** to act as an intermediary for sb; **~ d'arme** to be used as a weapon.
IV *vi* **1** MIL **~ dans** to serve in; **2** SPORT to serve; **3** (être employé) **il a servi dix ans chez nous** he was in our service for ten years; **~ dans un café** GÉN to work as a waiter in a café; (au bar) to work as a barman; **4** (être utilisé) to be used.
V se servir *vpr* **1** (à boire, à manger) to serve oneself; **se ~ un verre de vin** to pour oneself a glass of wine; **sers-toi bien** take plenty; **2** (dans un magasin) to serve oneself; (faire ses courses) **se ~ chez le boucher du coin** to shop at the local butcher's; **3** (faire usage de) **se ~ de qch/qn** to use sth/sb; **se ~ d'une situation** to make use of a situation; **4** CULIN to be served.
VI *v impers* **il ne sert à rien de crier** there's no point in shouting.
IDIOMES **on n'est jamais si bien servi que par soi-même** PROV if you want something done it's better to do it yourself.

serviteur /seʀvitœʀ/ *nm* servant; **'votre ~!'** (à votre service) 'at your service, sir ou madam!'; **votre ~** (moi-même) yours truly.

servitude /seʀvityd/ *nf* LIT servitude; FIG constraint.

servofrein /sɛʀvofʀɛ̃/ *nm* power(-assisted) brakes (*pl*).

ses ▸ **son**[1].

sésame /sezam/ *nm* sesame.
IDIOMES **Sésame ouvre-toi!** open sesame!

session /sesjɔ̃/ *nf* **1** (réunion) session; **2** SCOL, UNIV examination session; **~ de rattrapage** retakes (*pl*); **3** (stage) course.

sesterce /sɛstɛʀs/ *nm* sestertium.

set /sɛt/ *nm* SPORT set.
■ **~ de table** place mat.

seuil /sœj/ *nm* **1** (dalle) **~ (de la porte)** doorstep; (entrée) doorway; **franchir le ~** to cross the threshold; **2** FIG threshold; **au ~ de** (de saison, carrière) at the beginning of; (de la mort, l'adolescence) on the threshold of.
■ **~ de pauvreté** poverty line; **~ de rentabilité** break-even point.

seul, ~e /sœl/ *adj* **1** (sans compagnie) alone, on one's own; **elle est venue toute ~e** she came alone; **elle m'a laissé ~** she left me on my own; **vous êtes ~ dans la vie?** are you single?; **elle veut vous parler ~ à ~** or **~ à ~(e)** she wants to speak to you alone ou in private; **parler tout ~** to talk to oneself; **2** (sans aide) by oneself, on one's own; **je peux le faire ~** I can do it by myself ou on my own; **elle a mené la révolution à elle ~e** she single-handedly led the revolution; **il a mangé un poulet à lui tout ~** he ate a whole chicken all by himself; **ça va tout ~** (c'est facile) it's really easy; (c'est sans problèmes) things are running smoothly; **3** (unique) only; **une ~e femme** only one woman; **un ~ d'entre eux** only one of them; **la ~e et unique personne** the one and only person; **pas un ~ client** not a single customer; **l'espion et l'ambassadeur sont une ~e et même personne** the spy and the ambassador are one and the same person; **d'une ~e pièce** in one piece; **pour cette ~e raison** for this reason alone; **dans le ~ but de faire** with the sole aim of doing; **à la ~e idée de faire** at the very idea of doing; **~ de son espèce** unique; **ils ont parlé d'une ~e voix** they were unanimous; **4** (solitaire) lonely; **5** (avec valeur adverbiale) only; **elle ~e pourrait vous le dire** only she could tell you; **l'offre est réservée à nos ~s employés** the offer is open only to our employees; **6** (avec valeur nominale) **le ~, la ~e** the only one; **j'ai été le ~ à aimer le spectacle** I was the only one who enjoyed the show; **ils sont les ~s à croire que** they're alone in thinking that; **il n'y en a pas un ~ qui se soit levé** not a single person stood up.

seulement /sœlmɑ̃/ *adv* **1** GÉN only; **nous étions ~ deux** or **deux ~** there were only the two of us; **'nous étions dix'—'~?'** 'there were ten of us'—'is that all?'; **j'ai compris ~ plus tard** I only realized later; **elle revient ~ demain** she's not coming back until tomorrow; **il ne nous a pas ~ remerciés** he didn't even thank us; **2** (toutefois) only, but; **c'est possible, ~ je veux y réfléchir** it's possible, only ou but I'd like to think about it; **3** (au moins) **si ~** if only.

sève /sɛv/ *nf* **1** BOT sap; **2** FIG vigour[GB].

sévère /sevɛʀ/ *adj* GÉN severe; [*personne, éducation*] strict; [*sélection*] rigorous; [*jugement*] harsh; [*défaite, pertes*] heavy.

sévèrement /sevɛʀmɑ̃/ *adv* GÉN severely; [*punir*] harshly; [*réglementer*] strictly; [*regarder*] sternly.

sévérité /severite/ *nf* (dureté) strictness, harshness; (austérité) sternness, severity.

sévices /sevis/ *nmpl* physical abuse ¢.

sévir /seviʀ/ [3] *vi* **1** (punir) to clamp down (**contre** on); **2** (causer des ravages) [*tempête, guerre*] to rage; [*épidémie, pauvreté*] to be rife; [*voyous*] to be running wild; **la sécheresse sévit dans le pays** drought is ravaging the country; **3** FIG [*doctrine*] to hold sway; [*délation*] to be rife; **mon ancien professeur sévit toujours au lycée** HUM my former teacher is still pegging away at the school.

sevrage /səvʀaʒ/ *nm* weaning.

sevrer /səvʀe/ [16] *vtr* **1** LIT to wean [*enfant, animal*]; **2** (priver) HUM **~ qn de qch** to deprive sb of sth.

sexagénaire /sɛksaʒenɛʀ/ **I** *adj* **être ~** to be in one's sixties.
II *nmf* person in his/her sixties.

sexe /sɛks/ *nm* **1** BIOL sex; **indépendamment du ~, de l'ethnie, de l'âge** irrespective of gender, race or age; **un bébé de ~ féminin** a female baby; **2** (organes génitaux) genitals (*pl*); **3** (sexualité) sex.

sexiste /sɛksist/ *adj, nmf* sexist.

sexologue /sɛksɔlɔg/ ▸ 374 ╎ *nmf* sex therapist.

sextant /sɛkstɑ̃/ *nm* sextant.

sextuor /sɛkstɥɔʀ/ *nm* (œuvre, formation) sextet.

sextupler /sɛkstyple/ [1] **I** *vtr* to multiply [sth] by six.
II *vi* [*bénéfices*] to increase sixfold.

sexualité /sɛksɥalite/ *nf* sexuality.

sexué, ~e /sɛksɥe/ *adj* [*plante*] sexed; [*reproduction*] sexual.

sexuel, -elle /sɛksɥɛl/ *adj* GÉN sexual; [*éducation, glande*] sex.

seyant, ~e /sejɑ̃, ɑ̃t/ *adj* becoming.

SF /ɛsɛf/ *nf* (abbr = **science-fiction**) sci-fi.

SFP /ɛsɛfpe/ *nf* (abbr = **Société française de production et de création audiovisuelles**) television and video production company.

shampooing /ʃɑ̃pwɛ̃/ *nm* shampoo.

shampouiner /ʃɑ̃pwine/ [1] *vtr* to shampoo.

shampouineur, -euse /ʃɑ̃pwinœʀ, øz/ ▸ 374 ╎ *nm,f*: trainee hairdresser (who washes hair).

shérif /ʃeʀif/ *nm* sheriff.

shetland /ʃetlɑ̃d/ *nm* **1** (laine) Shetland wool; **2** (poney) Shetland pony.

shoot /ʃut/ *nm* **1** SPORT shot; **2**○ (de drogue) fix○.

shooter /ʃute/ [1] **I** *vi* to shoot.
II se shooter○ *vpr* to shoot up○.

short /ʃɔʀt/ *nm* shorts (*pl*).

si[1] /si/

■ **Note** si adverbe de degré modifiant un adjectif a deux traductions en anglais selon que l'adjectif modifié est attribut: *la maison est si jolie* = the house is so pretty, ou épithète: *une si jolie maison* = such a pretty house.
– Dans le cas de l'épithète il existe une deuxième possibilité, assez rare et littéraire, citée pour information: = so pretty a house.

I *nm inv* if; **des ~ et des mais** ifs and buts.
II *adv* **1** (marquant l'affirmation) yes; **'tu ne le veux pas?'—'~!'** 'don't you want it?'—'yes I do!'; **mais ~** yes, of course; **2** (marquant l'intensité) so; **de ~ bon matin** so early in the morning; **c'est un homme ~ agréable** he's such a pleasant man; **je suis heureux de visiter votre ~ jolie ville** I'm glad to visit your town, it's so pretty; **~ ce n'est pas ~ pretty**; **bien que** (par conséquent) so; (à tel point que) so much so that; **tant et ~ bien que** so much so that; **3** (pour marquer la comparaison) **rien n'est ~ beau qu'un coucher de soleil** there's nothing so beautiful as a sunset; **est-elle ~ bête qu'on le dit?** is she as stupid as people say (she is)?; **4** (pour marquer la concession) **~ peu que ce soit** however little it may be.
III *conj* (**s'** before il or ils) **1** (marquant l'éventualité) if; **~ ce n'est (pas) toi, qui est-ce?** if it wasn't you, who was it?, if not you, who?; **il n'a rien pris avec lui ~ ce n'est un livre** he didn't take anything with him apart from a book; **à quoi servent ces réunions ~ ce n'est à nous faire perdre notre temps?** what purpose do these meetings serve other than to waste our time?; **~ tant est qu'une telle distinction ait un sens** if such a distinction makes any sense; **c'est un brave homme s'il en est** he's a brave man if ever there was one; **2** (marquant l'hypothèse) if; **~ j'étais riche** if I were rich; **~ j'avais su!** if only I'd known!; **vous pensez ~ j'étais content!** you can imagine how happy I was!; **~ j'ai envie de partir? ah ça oui!** leave? I certainly do want to leave!; **je me demande s'il viendra** I wonder if ou whether he'll come; **3** (quand) if; **enfant, ~ je**

lisais, je n'aimais pas être dérangé when I was a child I used to hate being disturbed if ou when I was reading; **4** (introduit la suggestion) **~ tu venais avec moi?** how about coming with me?; **~ tu venais passer le week-end avec nous?** why don't you come and spend the weekend with us?; **et s'il décidait de ne pas venir?** and what if he decided not to come?; **5** (pour marquer l'opposition) whereas; **~ la France est favorable au projet, les autres pays y sont violemment opposés** whereas France is in favour^{GB} of the project, the other countries are violently opposed to it.

si² /si/ *nm inv* (note) B; (en solfiant) ti.

siamois, ~e /sjamwa, az/ **I** *adj* ZOOL [*chat*] Siamese; **2** MÉD **des frères ~** male Siamese twins; **des sœurs ~es** female Siamese twins.
II *nm inv* LING Siamese; **2** ZOOL Siamese cat.

sibyllin, ~e /sibilɛ̃, in/ *adj* LIT, FIG sibylline.

SICAV /sikav/ *nf* (*abbr* = **société d'investissement à capital variable**) unit trust GB, mutual fund US.

sicilien, -ienne /sisiljɛ̃, ɛn/ **► 509** **I** *adj* Sicilian.
II ► 338 *nm* LING Sicilian.

sida /sida/ **► 196** *nm* (*abbr* = **syndrome immunodéficitaire acquis**) Aids (+ *v sg*).

side-car, *pl* **~s** /sidkaʀ/ *nm* **1** (caisse) sidecar; **2** (moto et caisse) motorcycle combination.

sidéral, ~e, *mpl* **-aux** /sideʀal, o/ *adj* sidereal.

sidérer⚬ /sidere/ [14] *vtr* to stagger⚬, to astonish.

sidérurgie /sideʀyʀʒi/ *nf* steel industry.

sidérurgique /sideʀyʀʒik/ *adj* steel (*épith*).

siècle /sjɛkl/ **► 588** *nm* **1** (cent ans) century; **au Vᵉ ~ après J.-C.** in the 5th century AD; **l'art du XVIIᵉ ~** 17th-century art; **au ~ dernier** in the last century; **d'ici la fin du ~** by the turn of the century; **être né avec le ~** to be born at the turn of the century; **un ~ de photographie** one hundred years of photography; **il y a des ~s**⚬ **que je ne suis venu ici** I haven't been here for ages; **2** (époque) age; **le ~ de Louis XIV** the age of Louis XIV; **il est d'un autre ~** he belongs to another age; **il faut vivre avec son ~** one must move with the times; **3** RELIG world; **dans** or **pour les ~s des ~s** forever and ever.

siège /sjɛʒ/ *nm* **1** (pour s'asseoir) seat; **~ avant** front seat; **2** (d'entreprise) **~ (social)** head office; (d'organisation) headquarters (*pl*); (d'évêché) see; (de tribunal) seat; **3** POL (d'élu) seat; **perdre son ~** to lose one's seat; **4** MIL (de ville, forteresse) siege; **faire le ~ d'une ville** to besiege a town; **5** ANAT seat; **le bébé se présente par le ~** the baby is in the breech position.

siéger /sjeʒe/ [15] *vi* **1** (être membre) to sit; **~ au sénat** to sit in the senate; **2** (tenir séance) to be in session; **3** (résider) to have its headquarters.

sien, sienne /sjɛ̃, sjɛn/

■ **Note** En anglais, le choix du possessif de la troisième personne du singulier est déterminé par le genre du 'possesseur'. Sont du masculin: les personnes de sexe masculin et les animaux domestiques mâles; sont du féminin: les personnes de sexe féminin, les animaux domestiques femelles et souvent les navires; sont du neutre les animaux non domestiques et les non-animés. La forme masculine est *his: il m'a donné le sien/la sienne/les siens/les siennes* = he gave me his. La forme féminine est *hers: elle m'a donné le sien/la sienne/les siens/les siennes* = she gave me hers. Pour le neutre on répète le nom avec l'adjectif possessif *its*.

I *adj poss* **cette maison est sienne à présent** the house is now his/hers.
II le sien, la sienne, les siens, les siennes *pron poss* his/hers/its; **celui-là, c'est le ~** that's his/hers; **être de retour parmi les ~s** (sa famille) to be back with one's family; (ses amis) to be back among one's own friends; **elle a encore fait des siennes!** she's been up to mischief again!

sieste /sjɛst/ *nf* nap, siesta.

sifflant, ~e /siflɑ̃, ɑ̃t/ *adj* **1** GÉN [*voix, son*] hissing; [*respiration, toux*] wheezing; **2** [*consonne*] sibilant.

sifflement /sifləmɑ̃/ *nm* (de personne, train) whistle; (de bouilloire, vent) whistling ¢; (d'oiseau, insecte) chirping ¢; (de serpent) hissing ¢.

siffler /sifle/ [1] **I** *vtr* **1** (avec la bouche) to whistle [*air, chanson*]; (appeler) to whistle for [*personne, chien*]; (interpeller) to whistle at [*personne*]; **se faire ~** [*femme*] to get wolf-whistles; **2** SPORT [*arbitre*] to blow one's whistle for [*faute, fin*]; **3** (huer) to hiss, to boo [*vedette, politicien*].
II *vi* **1** GÉN to whistle; [*projectile*] to whistle through the air; [*oiseau*] to chirp; [*serpent*] to hiss; **2** (dans un sifflet) to blow one's whistle.

sifflet /siflɛ/ *nm* **1** (instrument) whistle; **2** (sifflement) (de locomotive) whistle; (de désapprobation) hiss, boo, catcalls (*pl*); (de bouilloire) whistling ¢.
IDIOMES **couper le ~ à qn**⚬ (faire taire) to shut sb up⚬; (interloquer) to take the wind out of sb's sails.

siffleur, -euse /siflœʀ, øz/ *adj* [*oiseau*] chirping; [*serpent*] hissing.

siffloter /siflɔte/ [1] **I** *vtr* to whistle [sth] to oneself.
II *vi* to whistle away to oneself.

sigle /sigl/ *nm* acronym.

signal, *pl* **-aux** /siɲal, o/ *nm* signal; **le ~ du départ** GÉN, MIL the signal to leave; SPORT the starting signal.
■ **~ d'alarme** alarm signal; **tirer le ~ d'alarme** LIT to pull the alarm; FIG to raise the alarm; **~ d'appel** TÉLÉCOM call waiting service; **~ de détresse** AVIAT, NAUT distress signal; AUT emergency signal; **~ sonore** (de répondeur) tone.

signalement /siɲalmɑ̃/ *nm* description.

signaler /siɲale/ [1] **I** *vtr* **1** (faire remarquer) to point sth out to sb; (faire savoir) to inform sb of sth; **2** (rappeler) **~ à qn que** to remind sb that; **3** (indiquer) to indicate [*travaux, danger*]; **un virage mal/bien signalé** a badly/well signposted bend; **4** (rapporter) to report [*fait, événement*].
II se signaler *vpr* **se ~ par qch** to distinguish oneself by sth.

signalétique /siɲaletik/ *adj* descriptive; **photo ~** identity photograph; **renseignement ~** detail of identity; **fiche ~** specification sheet.

signalisation /siɲalizasjɔ̃/ *nf* **1** (système) signalling^{GB}; **2** (réseau) signals (*pl*).
■ **~ horizontale** road markings (*pl*); **~ de piste** AVIAT runway lights and markings (*pl*); **~ routière** roadsigns and markings (*pl*); **~ verticale** roadsigns (*pl*).

signaliser /siɲalize/ [1] *vtr* to signpost [*route*]; to put up signals along [*voie ferrée*]; to mark out and light [*piste d'atterrissage*].

signataire /siɲatɛʀ/ *nmf* signatory.

signature /siɲatyʀ/ *nf* **1** (inscription) signature; **apposer sa ~** to append one's signature; **2** (droit de signer) **avoir la ~ de qn** to have the right to sign for sb; **avoir la ~ sur un compte** to be authorized to sign on an account; **3** (fait de signer) signing (**de** of); **4** (engagement) **il a donné sa ~** he signed, he put his signature to it; **5** (caractéristique) hallmarks (*pl*).

signe /siɲ/ *nm* **1** GÉN sign; **~ précurseur** omen; **c'est ~ de pluie** it's a sign of rain; **~ distinctif** or **particulier** distinguishing feature; **c'était un ~ du destin** it was fate; **2** (symbole) GÉN sign; (d'écriture) mark; **~s de ponctuation** punctuation marks; **marquer qch d'un ~** to put a mark against sth; **~ astral** star sign; **placé sous le ~ de** marked by [*violence, espoir*]; **3** (geste) sign; **faire ~ à qn** LIT to wave to sb; (contacter) to get in touch with sb; **faire de grands ~s à qn** to gesticulate to sb; **faire ~ à qn de** to motion sb to [*parler, commencer*]; to beckon sb to [*avancer, reculer*]; **il m'a fait ~ de la tête** (pour que je vienne) he beckoned to me; (pour me saluer) he nodded to me; (pour désapprouver) he shook his head; **d'un ~ de la main, elle m'a montré la cuisine** she pointed to the kitchen; **faire ~ que oui/que non** to indicate agreement/disagreement; **faire comprendre par un ~** to indicate that; **échanger des ~s d'intelligence avec qn** (regards) to exchange knowing looks with sb; (gestes) to make meaningful signs at sb.

IDIOMES **il n'a pas donné ~ de vie depuis six mois** there's been no sign of him for six months.

signer /siɲe/ [1] **I** *vtr* to sign; **il signe son troisième roman** he's written his third novel; **un parfum signé Fior** a perfume by Fior; **ça, c'est signé ta sœur**○! that's your sister all over○!; **~ son arrêt de mort** to sign one's own death warrant; **le disque compact a signé la fin du 33 tours** the compact disc signalled GB the end of the LP.

II se signer *vpr* to cross oneself.

signet /siɲɛ/ *nm* bookmark.

signifiant, ~e /siɲifjɑ̃, ɑ̃t/ **I** *adj* LING significant, meaningful.

II *nm* LING signifier.

significatif, -ive /siɲifikatif, iv/ *adj* significant.

signification /siɲifikasjɔ̃/ *nf* **1** (sens) GÉN meaning; LING signification; **2** (portée) importance; **avoir une ~ politique** to be politically significant; **3** JUR notification.

signifié /siɲifje/ *nm* LING signified.

signifier /siɲifje/ [1] *vtr* **1** to mean; **qu'est-ce que ça signifie?** (question normale) what does it mean?; (ton mécontent) what is the meaning of this?; **2** (notifier) **~ qch à qn** FML to inform sb of sth; JUR to notify sb of sth; **~ son congé à qn** to give sb notice.

silence /silɑ̃s/ *nm* **1** (absence de bruit) silence; **2** (fait de se taire) silence; **'un peu de ~ s'il vous plaît'** 'quiet please'; **en ~** in silence; **garder le ~** to keep silent; **réduire qn au ~** (empêcher de s'exprimer) to reduce sb to silence; (tuer) to silence sb; **réduire un mouvement au ~** to quell a movement; **passer qch sous ~** to say nothing about sth; **3** MUS rest.

silencieusement /silɑ̃sjøzmɑ̃/ *adv* silently.

silencieux, -ieuse /silɑ̃sjø, øz/ **I** *adj* **1** GÉN silent; **2** (peu bruyant) [*aspirateur, moteur*] quiet.

II *nm* **1** (sur une arme) silencer; **2** AUT (de pot d'échappement) silencer GB, muffler US.

silex /silɛks/ *nm inv* (roche, objet) flint.

silhouette /silwɛt/ *nf* (en contre-jour) silhouette; (dans l'obscurité) (de personne) figure; (d'objet) shape; (dans le lointain) outline.

silice /silis/ *nf* silica.

silicium /silisjɔm/ *nm* silicon.

silicone /silikɔn/ *nf* silicone.

sillage /sijaʒ/ *nm* **1** (de navire) wake; (d'avion) (visible) vapour GB trail; (invisible) slipstream; **2** (de personne) wake; (de parfum) trail; **3** PHYS wake.

sillon /sijɔ̃/ *nm* **1** AGRIC furrow; **2** (rainure) line; **3** (ride profonde) furrow; **4** ANAT, ZOOL fissure; **5** AUDIO (de disque) groove; **6** GÉOG line.

sillonner /sijɔne/ [1] *vtr* **1** (parcourir) [*personne, bicyclette, automobile*] to go up and down; [*aéronef*] to fly to and fro across; [*navire*] to sail to and fro across; [*réseau*] to criss-cross; **2** (creuser) to furrow.

simagrée /simagre/ *nf* play-acting ¢.

simiesque /simjɛsk/ *adj* ape-like.

similaire /similɛr/ *adj* similar (à to).

similicuir /similikɥir/ *nm* imitation leather, Leatherette®.

similitude /similityd/ *nf* GÉN, MATH similarity.

simple /sɛ̃pl/ **I** *adj* **1** (facile) **c'est (bien) ~, il ne fait plus rien** he simply doesn't do anything any more; **2** (sans prétention) [*repas, cérémonie, mariage, vie, goûts*] simple; [*décoration, intérieur*] plain; [*vêtement*] simple, plain; [*personne, air*] unaffected, unpretentious; **une jupe toute ~** a very plain skirt; **3** (modeste) [*origines*] modest; **venir d'un milieu ~** to come from a modest background; **4** (ordinaire) [*fonctionnaire, travailleur*] ordinary; **c'est une ~ question de bon sens** it's just common sense; **un ~ tour de clé suffit** just one turn of the key does it; **il est ~ garçon de café** he's just a waiter in a café; **même en hiver, il n'est vêtu que d'une ~ chemise** even in winter he only ou just wears a shirt; **pour la ~ raison que** for the simple reason that; **le ~ fait de poser la question** the mere fact of asking the question; **par ~ curiosité** out of pure curiosity; **sur ~**

présentation du passeport on presentation of one's passport; **ce ne sera qu'une ~ formalité/vérification** it will be a mere formality/a simple check; **réduire qch à sa plus ~ expression** to reduce sth to a minimum, to pare sth down to basics; **5** (peu intelligent) [*personne*] simple; **6** CHIMIE, BOT simple; **7** LING [*passé, futur*] simple; **8** (non multiple) [*cornet de glace, nœud*] single.

II *nm* **1** (dans un calcul) **le prix varie du ~ au double** the price can turn out to be twice as high; **2** SPORT **~ dames/messieurs** ladies'/men's singles (*pl*).

simplement /sɛ̃pləmɑ̃/ *adv* **1** (seulement) [*approuver, déclarer, rappeler*] just; **vas-y, ~ fais attention** you can go, only be careful; **2** (sans sophistication) [*se vêtir, vivre*] simply; (absolument) simply; **tout ~** quite simply; **3** (sans difficulté) easily.

simplet, -ette /sɛ̃plɛ, ɛt/ *adj* simple-minded.

simplicité /sɛ̃plisite/ *nf* **1** (facilité) simplicity; **grâce à sa ~ d'utilisation** because it's so easy to use; **2** (caractère) (de personne) unpretentiousness, lack of pretention; (de choses) simplicity; **recevoir qn en toute ~** to entertain sb very unpretentiously; **avec ~** simply.

■ **~ d'esprit** simple-mindedness.

simplifier /sɛ̃plifje/ [2] **I** *vtr* **1** GÉN to simplify; **2** MATH to reduce [*fraction*].

II se simplifier *vpr* **se ~ la vie** to make life easier for oneself.

simpliste /sɛ̃plist/ *adj* simplistic.

simulacre /simylakr/ *nm* LITER **1** (action simulée) pretence GB; **~ de procès** mock trial; **2** (travesti) PEJ sham; **~ de justice** travesty of justice; **~ de bonheur** illusion of happiness.

simulateur, -trice /simylatœr, tris/ **I** *nm,f* (personne qui feint) shammer, faker; (faux malade) malingerer.

II *nm* TECH simulator; **~ de vol** flight simulator.

simulation /simylasjɔ̃/ *nf* **1** GÉN, MÉD simulation; (pour éviter une corvée) malingering ¢; **2** (en science) (méthode) simulation.

simuler /simyle/ [1] *vtr* **1** (feindre) to feign, to simulate [*attaque, émotion, sentiment*]; **2** ORDINAT, TECH (reproduire) to simulate.

simultané, ~e /simyltane/ *adj* simultaneous.

simultanéité /simyltaneite/ *nf* simultaneity.

sincère /sɛ̃sɛr/ *adj* **1** (dont on ne peut douter) [*personne, confession, regret, affection*] sincere; [*ami*] true (*épith*); (non feint) [*émotion, offre, soutien*] genuine; (franc) [*opinion, portrait*] honest; **sois ~ pour une fois!** be honest for once!; **2** (en correspondance) **~s condoléances** sincere ou heartfelt sympathy ¢.

sincèrement /sɛ̃sɛrmɑ̃/ *adv* **1** (sans feindre) [*regretter, croire*] sincerely; [*penser*] really; [*remercier, parler, s'exprimer*] sincerely; **dis-moi ~ ce que tu en penses** tell me honestly what you think of it; **je suis ~ désolé** I'm truly sorry; **2** (franchement) frankly.

sincérité /sɛ̃serite/ *nf* (de personne, paroles, d'affection) sincerity; (de réponse, d'opinion) honesty; (d'offre, de soutien) genuineness.

sinécure /sinekyr/ *nf* sinecure.

singe /sɛ̃ʒ/ *nm* **1** ZOOL monkey; (sans queue) ape; **les grands ~s** the apes, the large primates; **2** FIG (imitateur) mimic; (personne agile) **c'est un vrai ~** he's very agile; **faire le ~** to clown about GB ou around.

IDIOMES **malin comme un ~** as cunning ou sly as a fox; **payer en monnaie de ~** to let sb whistle for his/her money; **ce n'est pas à un vieux ~ qu'on apprend à faire la grimace** PROV don't teach your grandmother to suck eggs.

singer /sɛ̃ʒe/ [13] *vtr* to ape [*personne, manière*]; to feign, to fake [*attitude, sentiment*].

singeries /sɛ̃ʒri/ *nfpl* (grimaces) faces; (pitreries) antics; **faire des ~** to monkey about GB ou around.

singulariser: se singulariser /sɛ̃gylarize/ [1] *vpr* to call attention to oneself; **se ~ par qch/en faisant qch** to distinguish oneself by sth/by doing sth.

singularité /sɛ̃gylaʀite/ *nf* **1** (chose anormale) peculiarity, singularity; **2** (caractère unique) uniqueness; **3** PHYS singularity.

singulier, -ière /sɛ̃gylje, ɛʀ/ **I** *adj* **1** (insolite) peculiar; **un personnage ~** an unusual character; **2** (individuel) **combat ~** single combat.
II *nm* **1** LING singular; **2** (caractère étonnant) singularity.

singulièrement /sɛ̃gyljɛʀmɑ̃/ *adv* **1** (curieusement) oddly; **2** (beaucoup) radically.

sinistre /sinistʀ/ **I** *adj* **1** [*personnage, projet*] sinister; [*bruit, lueur*] sinister, ominous; [*lieu, paysage, avenir*] bleak; [*soirée, invité*] dreary; **2** (*before n*) **de ~s crétins○/crapules** absolute idiots/crooks.
II *nm* (désastre) disaster; (accident) accident; (incendie) blaze.

sinistré, ~e /sinistʀe/ **I** *adj* [*personne, famille, pays*] stricken (*épith*); **région ~e** disaster area.
II *nm,f* disaster victim.

sinon /sin5/ **I** *conj* **1** (autrement) otherwise, or else; **arrête ~ je crie/je me fâche!** stop or (else) I'll scream/I'll get cross!; **2** (à part) except, apart from; **3** (pour ne pas dire) not to say; **c'est devenu difficile ~ impossible** it has become difficult if not impossible.
II sinon que *loc conj* except that, other than that.

sinueux, -euse /sinɥø, øz/ *adj* [*ligne*] sinuous; [*cours d'eau*] winding, meandering; [*sentier*] winding; [*approche*] tortuous.

sinus /sinys/ *nm inv* **1** ANAT sinus; **2** MATH sine.

sinusite /sinyzit/ ▶ **196** *nf* sinusitis ¢.

sionisme /sjɔnism/ *nm* Zionism.

siphon /sif5/ *nm* **1** (tuyau) GÉN siphon; (d'évier, de lavabo) U-bend; **2** (bouteille) siphon (bottle).

siphonné○, ~e /sifɔne/ *adj* nuts○, crazy○.

sire /siʀ/ *nm* HIST Sire; **un triste ~** a disreputable character.

sirène /siʀɛn/ *nf* **1** GÉN, MIL siren; (de bateau) foghorn; (d'usine) hooter GB, siren; **~ des pompiers** (dans la ville) fire siren; (sur un camion) fire engine siren; **2** (de mythologie) mermaid; (au chant fatal) siren.
■ ~ d'alarme fire alarm.

sirop /siʀo/ *nm* **1** CULIN (pour dessert) syrup GB ou sirup US; (boisson) cordial; **~ d'érable** maple syrup GB ou sirup US; **~ de fraise** strawberry cordial; **~ de citron/d'orange** ~lemon/orange squash; **2** (médicament) syrup GB ou sirup US, mixture; **~ pectoral** cough mixture.

siroter○ /siʀɔte/ [1] *vtr* to sip.

sirupeux, -euse /siʀypø, øz/ *adj* LIT, FIG syrupy GB, sirupy US.

sis, ~e /si, siz/ *adj* located.

sismique /sismik/ *adj* seismic.

sismologue /sismɔlɔg/ ▶ **374** *nmf* seismologist.

site /sit/ *nm* **1** (lieu pittoresque) GÉN area; **~ touristique** or **pittoresque** place of interest; **visitez les ~s d'Égypte** visit Egypt's historic sites; **les merveilleux ~s de la Côte d'Azur** the splendours GB of the Côte d'Azur; **~ archéologique** archeological site; **~ classé** conservation area; **2** IND, COMM (lieu d'une implantation particulière) site.

sitôt /sito/
■ Note *sitôt* conjonction et préposition se traduit le plus souvent par *as soon as*. Mais attention au choix du temps: *sitôt rentré de voyage* (qu'il rentrera) = as soon as he gets back from his trip; (qu'il est rentré) = as soon as he got back from his trip; *sitôt la fin du mauvais temps* (dans le passé) = as soon as the bad weather was over; (dans l'avenir) = as soon as the bad weather is over.
I *adv* **~ après** (tout de suite) immediately after; (peu de temps) soon after; **elle est arrivée ~ après** she arrived soon afterwards; **nous partirons ~ après** we'll leave immediately afterwards; **je n'y retournerai pas de ~** I won't go back there in a hurry○.
II *conj* **~ que** as soon as.
IDIOMES **~ dit, ~ fait†** no sooner said than done.

situation /situasjɔ̃/ *nf* **1** (ensemble de conditions) situation; **une population en ~ d'extrême pauvreté** a population suffering extreme poverty; **~ financière** financial standing ou status; **2** (emploi) job, position; **3** (emplacement) location (**de** of).
■ ~ de famille marital status, family status; **~ militaire** *status as regards military service*.

situer /situe/ [1] **I** *vtr* **1** (déterminer la position de) (dans l'espace) to locate [*ville, pays*]; (dans le temps) to place; **notre maison est située dans le nord d'Oxford** our house is on the north side of Oxford; **l'hôtel est bien situé** the hotel is in a good location; **~ un événement dans le temps** to situate an event historically; **2** (définir) to situate [*écrivain, œuvre*]; **3** (placer) **~ une histoire en 2001/à Palerme** to set a story in 2001/in Palermo.
II se situer *vpr* **1** (se dérouler) **se ~ à Paris/à l'époque de la Révolution** to be set in Paris/at the time of the Revolution; **2** (être) politiquement, **je me situe plutôt à gauche/droite** politically I'm more to the left/right.

six /sis, *but before consonant* si, *and before vowel* siz/ ▶ **399**, **298**, **156** *adj inv, pron, nm inv* six.

sixième /sizjɛm/ ▶ **399**, **156** **I** *adj* sixth.
II *nf* SCOL *first year of secondary school, age 11–12.*

skaï® /skaj/ *nm* imitation leather, Leatherette®.

skate-board, *pl* **~s** /skɛtbɔʀd/ ▶ **329** *nm* (objet) skateboard; (activité) skateboarding.

sketch, *pl* **~es** /skɛtʃ/ *nm* (au théâtre) sketch.

ski /ski/ ▶ **329** *nm* **1** (matériel) ski; **chausser des ~s** to put on skis; **2** (activité) **le ~** skiing; **faire du ~** to ski, to go skiing; **station de ~** ski resort.
■ ~ alpin Alpine skiing; **~ de descente** = **~ de piste**; **~ de fond** (activité) cross-country skiing; (matériel) cross-country ski; **~ nautique** water skiing; **~ nordique** Nordic skiing; **~ de piste** (activité) downhill skiing; (matériel) downhill ski.

skier /skje/ [2] *vi* to ski.

skieur, -ieuse /skjœʀ, øz/ *nm,f* skier.

slalom /slalɔm/ *nm* slalom; **faire du ~** LIT to slalom.

slalomer /slalɔme/ [1] *vi* **1** SPORT to slalom (**entre** between); **2** FIG to zigzag (**entre** between).

slave /slav/ *adj* Slavonic.

slip /slip/ *nm* **1** (d'homme) underpants (*pl*) GB, undershorts (*pl*) US; (de femme) knickers (*pl*), pants (*pl*) GB, panties (*pl*) US; **2** NAUT slipway.
■ ~ de bain (d'homme) bathing trunks (*pl*).

slogan /slɔgɑ̃/ *nm* slogan.

Slovaquie /slɔvaki/ ▶ **232** *nprf* Slovakia.

Slovénie /slɔveni/ ▶ **232** *nprf* Slovenia.

slow /slo/ *nm* slow dance; **danser un ~ avec qn** to dance a slow number with sb.

smala○ /smala/ *nf* (famille) tribe○.

smasher /smaʃe/ [1] **I** *vtr* to smash [*balle*].
II *vi* to play a smash.

SME /ɛsɛmə/ *nm: abbr* ▶ **système**.

SMIC /smik/ *nm: abbr* ▶ **salaire**.

smocks /smɔk/ *nmpl* smocking ¢.

smoking /smɔkiŋ/ *nm* dinner jacket GB, tuxedo.

SNCF /ɛsɛnseɛf/ *nf* (*abbr* = **Société nationale des chemins de fer français**) *French national railway company.*

snob /snɔb/ **I** *adj* [*personne*] stuck-up○; [*endroit, restaurant, soirée*] posh.
II *nmf* snob; **c'est un ~** he's a snob.

snober /snɔbe/ [1] *vtr* to snub [*personne*].

snobisme /snɔbism/ *nm* snobbery.

sobre /sɔbʀ/ *adj* **1** (qui mange et boit peu) abstemious; (qui ne boit jamais d'alcool) teetotal; (qui n'a pas trop bu) sober; **il est très ~ ce soir** he's being very abstemious tonight; **je suis ~, je peux conduire** I'm sober, so I can drive; **2** (mesuré) [*personne*] temperate, sober, moderate; [*discours, récit, langage*] sober, low-key; [*vie*] simple; **3** (simple) [*style*] plain, sober; [*architecture, décoration, vêtement, mise en scène*] sober.

sobrement /sɔbʀəmɑ̃/ *adv* **1** (avec modération)

[*manger, boire*] in moderation; **2** (simplement) [*s'habiller*] plainly, soberly; [*dire*] soberly.

sobriété /sɔbʀijete/ *nf* **1** (fait de ne pas boire) temperance, sobriety SOUT; **2** (réserve) (de personne) restraint, sobriety SOUT; (de discours, critique) moderation; **3** (de style, ligne, mise en scène, d'art) sobriety SOUT.

sobriquet /sɔbʀikɛ/ *nm* nickname.

soc /sɔk/ *nm* ploughshare GB, plowshare US.

sociabilité /sɔsjabilite/ *nf* sociability.

sociable /sɔsjabl/ *adj* **1** GÉN [*personne, tempérament*] sociable; **2** SOCIOL social.

social, **~e**, *mpl* **-iaux** /sɔsjal, o/ I *adj* **1** (relatif à la vie en société) social; **sur le plan ~** in social terms; **mesures ~es** social policy measures; **2** (propre à la société) social; **les origines ~es de qn, le milieu ~ de qn** sb's social background; **3** (relatif au travail) **conflit ~** industrial ou trade dispute.
II *nm* **le ~** social issues (*pl*); **faire du ~** [*gouvernement*] to take a keen interest in social issues.

social-démocratie /sɔsjaldemɔkʀasi/ *nf* social democracy.

socialement /sɔsjalmã/ *adv* socially; **être ~ pris en charge** to be in the care of the social services.

socialiser /sɔsjalize/ [1] *vtr* **1** SOCIOL to socialize [*individus*]; **2** ÉCON, POL to collectivize.

socialisme /sɔsjalism/ *nm* socialism.

socialiste /sɔsjalist/ *adj, nmf* socialist.

sociétaire /sɔsjetɛʀ/ *nmf* member.

société /sɔsjete/ *nf* **1** GÉN, SOCIOL society; **2** (groupe spécifique) society; **~ de chasse** hunting club; **3** (entreprise) company; **~ de nettoyage** cleaning company; **4** (vie mondaine) society; **en ~** in society; **la bonne/ haute ~** polite/high society; **5** (compagnie) FML company, society SOUT; **rechercher la ~ de qn** to seek sb's company.

socioculturel, **-elle** /sɔsjokyltyʀɛl/ *adj* [*rapports*] sociocultural; **centre ~** recreation centreGB.

socio-démocrate, *pl* **~s** /sɔsjodemɔkʀat/ I *adj* social democratic.
II *nmf* social democrat.

socio-éducatif, **-ive**, *mpl* **~s** /sɔsjoedykatif, iv/ *adj* [*programme, système*] socioeducational.

sociologie /sɔsjɔlɔʒi/ *nf* sociology.

sociologique /sɔsjɔlɔʒik/ *adj* sociological.

sociologue /sɔsjɔlɔg/ **▶ 374**| *nmf* sociologist.

socioprofessionnel, **-elle** /sɔsjopʀɔfɛsjɔnɛl/ *adj* social and occupational.

socle /sɔkl/ *nm* **1** (base) (de statue, pilier) pedestal, plinth; (de lampe, construction) base; (d'appareil) stand; **2** FIG (base) basis; **3** GÉOG platform.

socquette /sɔkɛt/ *nf* ankle sock, anklet US.

soda /sɔda/ *nm* (eau gazeuse) soda water; (boisson gazeuse sucrée) fizzy drink GB, soda US.

sodium /sɔdjɔm/ *nm* sodium.

sodomiser /sɔdɔmize/ [1] *vtr* to sodomize, to bugger.

sœur /sœʀ/ *nf* **1** (dans la famille) sister; **~ jumelle** twin sister; **2** RELIG sister; **une ~** a nun; **elle est allée à l'école chez les ~s** she went to a convent school.

sœurette○ /sœʀɛt/ *nf* sis○, sister.

soi /swa/ *pron pers* **1** (personne) autour de **~** around one; **pour une meilleure connaissance de ~** for better self-knowledge; **apprendre la maîtrise de ~** to learn self-control; **rester maître de ~** to keep one's self-control; **laisser la porte se refermer derrière ~** to let the door shut behind one; **développer sa confiance en ~** to build up one's self-confidence; **la haine de ~** self-loathing; **trouver en ~ les ressources nécessaires** to find the necessary inner resources; **garder qch pour ~** to keep sth to oneself; **malgré ~ on est ému** you can't help being moved; **2** (objet, concept, idée) **un épisode banal en ~** an episode that is in itself commonplace; **la logique n'est pas un objectif en ~** logic is not an end in itself; **aller de ~** to go without saying; **ça devrait aller de ~** it should be obvious; **le parallèle**

allait de ~ entre... there was an obvious paralle[l] between...; **publier une œuvre de cette nature ne v[a] pas de ~** publishing a work of this kind is a compli[ ]cated business.

soi-disant /swadizɑ̃/ I *adj inv* **1** (qui prétend être) self styled; **2** (prétendu) CONTROV [*démocratie, liberté miracle*] so-called (*épith*).
II *adv* (prétendument) supposedly; **elle a ~ l[a] migraine** she has a migraine, or so she says.

soie /swa/ *nf* **1** (tissu) silk; **2** (poil) bristle; **une brosse à cheveux en ~s naturelles** a bristle hair brush; **3** BOT awn; **4** TECH (de couteau) tang.

soierie /swaʀi/ *nf* **1** (étoffe) silk; **2** IND silk industry **3** COMM silk trade.

soif /swaf/ *nf* **1** (besoin de boire) thirst; **avoir ~** to be thirsty; **mourir de ~** LIT to die of thirst; FIG to be dying of thirst; **boire jusqu'à plus ~** to drink one's fill; **donner ~** to make one thirsty; **il fait ~** ○! HUM it's thirsty work! HUM; **2** (désir) **~ de** thirst for [*justice, liberté, revanche, amour*]; hunger ou lust for [*pouvoir, richesses*]; **la ~ d'apprendre** the thirst for knowledge; **avoir ~ d'affection** to crave affection.
IDIOMES **conserver une poire pour la ~** to save something for a rainy day.

soignant, **~e** /swaɲɑ̃, ɑ̃t/ *adj* [*personnel, équipe*] medical (*épith*); **médecin ~** doctor, GP.

soigné, **~e** /swaɲe/ I *pp* ▶ **soigner**.
II *pp adj* **1** (bien entretenu) [*mains, ongles*] well-manicured; [*coiffure, vêtements, tenue*] immaculate; **il est très ~ de sa personne** he's very well-groomed; **individu peu ~** unkempt person; **2** (bien fait) [*catalogue, revue, édition*] carefully produced; [*emballage, maquette*] carefully done; [*conception, organisation, tactique*] carefully thought out; [*travail*] meticulous.

soigner /swaɲe/ [1] I *vtr* **1** (chercher à guérir) to treat [*personne, animal, maladie*]; **faire ~ qn** to get sb treatment; **il faut te faire ~** ○! HUM you should have your head examined!; **2** (s'occuper de) to look after [*personne, animal, client*]; **3** (faire attention à) to take care over [*tenue, présentation*]; to look after [*mains*]; **soignez votre écriture** take care over your writing.
II **se soigner** *vpr* **1** (chercher à se guérir) to treat oneself; **soigne-toi bien!** look after yourself!; **2** (pouvoir être guéri) [*maladie*] to be treatable; **ça se soigne, tu sais!** HUM (time to) get the men in white coats! HUM; **3** (veiller à sa tenue) to take care over one's appearance; (veiller à son bien-être) to take care of oneself.

soigneusement /swaɲøzmɑ̃/ *adv* [*ranger, laver, examiner, décrire, choisir, préparer, éviter*] carefully; [*travailler*] meticulously; [*écrire, colorier*] neatly.

soigneux, **-euse** /swaɲø, øz/ *adj* **1** (consciencieux) conscientious; (précautionneux) careful; **2** (propre et ordonné) [*personne*] neat, tidy; **3** (bien fait) [*examen, recherche*] careful.

soi-même /swamɛm/ *pron pers* oneself; **être ~** to be oneself; **la connaissance de ~** knowing oneself, self-knowledge; **le plaisir de faire ~ des confitures** the pleasure of making one's own jam.

soin /swɛ̃/ I *nm* **1** (application) care; **avec ~** [*choisir, préparer, travailler*] carefully; **sans ~** carelessly; **prendre ~ de qch** to take care of sth; **prendre ~ de qn/sa santé** to look after sb/one's health; **nous avons pris ~ d'éviter toute confrontation** we were careful to avoid any confrontation; **prendre ~ de sa petite personne** to coddle oneself; **laisser à qn le ~ de faire** to leave it to sb to do; **2** (en cosmétique) (produit) **~ antipelliculaire** dandruff treatment.
II **soins** *nmpl* **1** MÉD (traitement) treatment ¢; (ensemble d'activités, service) care ¢; **recevoir des ~s** to receive treatment; **~s dentaires** dental care; **les premiers ~s** à donner aux brûlés first-aid treatment for burns; **~s à domicile** homecare ¢; **2** (en cosmétique) care ¢; **~s corporels** or **du corps** body care ¢; **~s du visage** skincare ¢; **3** (attention) care ¢; **'aux bons ~s de'** 'care of', 'c/o'; **publié par mes ~s** published by my good offices.
IDIOMES **être aux petits ~s pour qn** to attend to sb's every need.

soir /swaʀ/ *nm* **1** (fin du jour) evening; (partie de la nuit) night; **travailler le ~** to work in the evening, to work evenings; **le ~ du 3, le 3 au ~** on the evening of the 3ʳᵈ; **par un beau ~ d'été** on a fine summer evening; **le ~ venu** when evening fell; **nous partirons samedi ~** we'll leave on Saturday evening; **il sort tous les samedis ~** he goes out every Saturday night; **6 heures du ~** 6 (o'clock) in the evening; (pour un horaire) 6 pm; **à ce ~!** see you tonight!; **2** (soirée) evening; **3** (déclin) LITER twilight.

soirée /swaʀe/ *nf* **1** (période) evening; **dans** or **pendant la ~, en ~** in the evening; **en début/fin de ~** at the beginning/end of the evening; **la pièce sera jouée en ~** there will be an evening performance of the play; **2** (réception) party; **aller dans une** or **en ~** to go to a party; **donner une ~** to give a party; **3** (spectacle) evening performance ou show.

soit¹ /swa/ **I ▸ être**¹.
II *conj* **1** (marque une alternative) **~, ~** either, or; **~ du fromage, ~ un gâteau** either cheese, or a cake; **elle suggère ~ que vous veniez chez nous, ~ qu'on aille au restaurant** she suggests that either you come to our place, or that we eat out; **c'est ~ l'un ~ l'autre, pas les deux** it's got to be one thing or the other, not both; **2** (à savoir) that is, ie; **toutes mes économies, ~ 200 francs** all my savings, ie ou that is, 200 francs; **3** MATH **~ un triangle ABC** let ABC be a triangle.

■ Note L'usage hésite, en mathématiques, entre la forme invariable de la conjonction et la forme verbale qui se met facultativement au pluriel (*soit* ou *soient* deux vecteurs), mais la traduction reste la même.

soit² /swat/ *adv* very well; **je me suis trompé, ~, mais là n'est pas la question** all right, so I was wrong, but that's not the point.

soixantaine /swasɑ̃tɛn/ *nf* **avoir la ~** to be about sixty; **une ~ de kilomètres** about sixty kilometres ᴳᴮ.

soixante /swasɑ̃t/ **▸ 399**, **156** *adj inv, pron* sixty.

soixante-dix /swasɑ̃tdis/ **▸ 399**, **156** *adj inv, pron* seventy.

soixante-dixième /swasɑ̃tdizjɛm/ **▸ 399** *adj* seventieth.

soixantième /swasɑ̃tjɛm/ **▸ 399** *adj* sixtieth.

soja /sɔʒa/ *nm* soya bean ᴳᴮ, soybean ᵁˢ; **pâté de** or **au ~** soya ᴳᴮ ou soybean pâté; **sauce de ~** soy sauce; **salade de (pousses de) ~** bean sprout salad.

sol¹ /sɔl/ *nm* **1** (à l'extérieur) ground; (dans une maison) floor; **une maison au ~ en terre battue** a house with a trodden earth floor; **sentir le ~ se dérober sous ses pieds** LIT to feel the ground giving way; FIG to feel as if one is about to faint; **vitesse au ~ d'un avion** ground speed of an aeroplane; **la surface au ~ d'un bâtiment** the floor surface of a building; **exercices au ~** SPORT floor exercises; **2** (territoire) soil; **le ~ africain** African soil; **3** (terrain) soil; **~ argileux** clay soil; **4** MUS (note) G; (en solfiant) soh; **5** (monnaie) sol.

solaire /sɔlɛʀ/ **I** *adj* [*calendrier, énergie*] solar; [*moteur, radio*] solar-powered; [*lumière, crème*] sun (*épith*).
II *nm* (énergie) solar energy.

soldat /sɔlda/ **▸ 284**, **374** *nm* soldier, serviceman.

solde¹ /sɔld/ **I** *nm* FIN balance; **faire le ~ d'un compte** to settle an account; **reçu pour ~ de tout compte** received in full and final payment.
II en solde *loc adv* **acheter une veste en ~** to buy a jacket in a sale ou at sale price ᴳᴮ ou on sale ᵁˢ.
III soldes *nmpl* sales; (écrit en vitrine) sale (*sg*).

solde² /sɔld/ *nf* MIL pay; **avoir qn à sa ~** FIG to have sb in one's pay; **être à la ~ de l'ennemi** FIG to be in the pay of the enemy ou the enemy's pay.

solder /sɔlde/ [1] **I** *vtr* **1** COMM to sell off, to clear [*marchandises*]; **2** to settle the balance of [*compte*].
II se solder *vpr* (finir) **se ~ par qch** to end in sth; **se ~ par un échec** [*efforts*] to end in failure.

solderie /sɔldəʀi/ *nf* discount shop.

soldeur, -euse /sɔldœʀ, øz/ **▸ 374** *nm,f* discount trader.

soleil /sɔlɛj/ *nm* **1** GÉN sun; **~ de minuit** midnight sun; **au ~** in the sun; **se mettre au ~** [*personne, animal*] (s'exposer) to go into the sun; (rester) to sit in the sun; **le ~ se lève à l'est** the sun rises in the east; **en plein ~** [*travailler, marcher, être assis*] in hot sun; [*laisser un produit, exposer*] in direct sunlight; **la pièce était pleine de ~** the room was filled with sunlight; **nous avons eu deux jours de ~** we've had two sunny days; **quand il y a du ~** when it's sunny; **il fait ~** it's sunny; **attraper un coup** or **des coups de ~** to get sunburned.
IDIOMES **se faire une place au ~** to do well for oneself; **(il n'y a) rien de nouveau sous le ~** there is nothing new under the sun; **le ~ brille pour tout le monde** PROV the sun shines upon all alike.

solennel, -elle /sɔlanɛl/ *adj* **1** (empreint de gravité) solemn; **dire qch d'un ton ~** to say sth solemnly; **2** (officiel) [*cérémonie*] solemn; [*appel, cadre*] formal.

solennité /sɔlanite/ *nf* solemnity; **chef d'État reçu avec ~** head of state given a ceremonious reception.

solfège /sɔlfɛʒ/ *nm* music theory; **~ chanté** sol-fa.

solfier /sɔlfje/ [2] *vtr* to sing using the tonic sol-fa system.

solidaire /sɔlidɛʀ/ *adj* **1** (lié par des intérêts communs) [*équipe, groupe*] united; **ils forment un groupe très ~** they really stand together; **être ~ de qn** to be behind sb, to support sb; **se sentir ~ de qn** to feel solidarity with sb; **2** TECH [*pièces*] interdependent.

solidariser: se solidariser /sɔlidaʀize/ [1] *vpr* **se ~ avec qch/qn** to stand by sth/sb.

solidarité /sɔlidaʀite/ *nf* solidarity (**entre** between).

solide /sɔlid/ **I** *adj* **1** (consistant) solid; **2** (résistant) [*maison, amitié, lien*] solid; [*chaussures, sac*] sturdy; [*lien, fixation, lame, mécanisme*] strong; [*position, base*] firm; **la chaise n'est pas très ~** the chair is a bit rickety; **3** (vigoureux) [*personne, constitution*] strong; [*poignée de main*] firm; [*cœur, poumons*] strong, sound; **être ~ sur ses jambes** LIT, FIG to be steady on one's legs; **elle a les nerfs ~s** she's got nerves of steel; **avoir la tête ~** FIG to have one's head screwed on; **4** (sérieux) [*affaire, connaissances, expérience, raisons*] sound; [*garanties*] firm; [*qualités*] solid; [*partenaire*] dependable; **ton rapport n'est pas assez ~** your report isn't very convincing; **5** (substantiel) hearty; **un ~ appétit** a hearty appetite.
II *nm* **1** MATH, PHYS solid; **2** (fiable) **ce qu'il te dit, c'est du ~** what he says is sound; **3** (consistant) **manger du ~** to eat solids; **4** (durable) **les meubles anciens, c'est du ~** antique furniture is solidly built.

solidement /sɔlidmɑ̃/ *adv* **1** (fermement) [*lier, accrocher, soutenir*] firmly; **2** (fortement) [*s'établir, implanter, ancré*] firmly; [*barricadé*] securely; [*armé*] heavily; **un rapport ~ documenté** a soundly-documented report; **elle a ~ établi sa réputation** she has established quite a reputation (**de, en tant que** as).

solidifier /sɔlidifje/ [2] *vtr*, **se solidifier** *vpr* to solidify.

solidité /sɔlidite/ *nf* **1** (de construction) solidity; (de machine) strength; (de lien) firmness; (de vêtement) hard-wearing quality; **d'une grande ~** [*construction*] well-built; [*machine*] sturdy; [*lien*] strong; [*vêtement*] hard-wearing; **2** (de raisonnement) soundness.

soliloque /sɔlilɔk/ *nm* soliloquy (**sur** on ou about).

soliloquer /sɔlilɔke/ [1] *vi* to soliloquize.

soliste /sɔlist/ *nmf* soloist.

solitaire /sɔlitɛʀ/ **I** *adj* **1** (sans compagnie) [*personne, vie, promenade*] solitary (*épith*); [*vieillesse, enfance*] lonely; **navigateur ~** single-handed ou solo yachtsman; **2** (isolé) [*maison, hameau*] isolated.
II *nmf* (personne) solitary person, loner; (ermite) hermit; **vivre en ~** to live alone; **naviguer en ~** to sail solo; **course en ~** solo race.
III *nm* **1** (diamant) solitaire; **2** (sanglier) rogue boar; **3 ▸ 329** JEUX solitaire.

solitude /sɔlityd/ nf **1** (fait d'être seul) solitude; **aimer la ~** to enjoy solitude, to enjoy being on one's own; **2** (sentiment) loneliness.

solive /sɔliv/ nf joist.

sollicitation /sɔlisitasjɔ̃/ nf **1** (requête) appeal, request; **2** (impulsion donnée) (à un cheval) prompting; (à une machine) touch.

solliciter /sɔlisite/ [1] vtr **1** (demander) FML to seek [entretien, poste, avis]; to seek, to solicit SOUT [contributions]; to canvass, to solicit SOUT [voix]; **j'ai l'honneur de ~ de votre bienveillance l'autorisation de faire** I would respectfully request your permission to do; **son avis est très sollicité** his/her advice is much ou highly sought-after; **2** (démarcher) to approach, to call on ou upon [personne, organisation]; to canvass [client, électeur]; **être très sollicité** [député, bienfaiteur] to be assailed by requests; [chanteur] to be very much in demand; **3** (faire appel à) to attract [intérêt, regard]; to call upon [mémoire].

sollicitude /sɔlisityd/ nf concern, solicitude.

solstice /sɔlstis/ nm solstice.

soluble /sɔlybl/ adj **1** [comprimé] soluble; **2** [problème] solvable, soluble.

solution /sɔlysjɔ̃/ nf **1** (action de résoudre) (de difficulté, mots croisés, d'énigme) solution (**de** of), solving (**de** of); (de crise, conflit) resolution (**de** of); **2** (réponse) solution (**de, à** to); **tenir la ~ de qch** to have the solution to sth; **une ~ de facilité** an easy way out; **~ de compromis** compromise; **3** CHIMIE solution.

solutionner /sɔlysjɔne/ [1] vtr CONTROV to solve.

solvabilité /sɔlvabilite/ nf (de débiteur) solvency; (de client, d'emprunteur) creditworthiness.

solvable /sɔlvabl/ adj [débiteur] solvent; [emprunteur, client] creditworthy.

solvant /sɔlvɑ̃/ nm solvent.

somatique /sɔmatik/ adj BIOL, MÉD somatic.

somatiser /sɔmatize/ [1] vtr to have a psychosomatic reaction to [problème].

sombre /sɔ̃bʀ/ adj **1** (obscur) dark; **vert/rouge ~** dark green/red; **il fait ~** it's dark; **2** (triste) [pensée, avenir, période] dark, black; [tableau, conclusion] depressing, grim; [air, personne, visage] solemn, sombreᴳᴮ; **d'un air ~** [annoncer] in a sombreᴳᴮ tone; [regarder] gloomily; **3**° (déplorable) (before n) [crétin, brute] absolute; [affaire] murky; **c'est une ~ histoire d'inceste** it's a grim story of incest.

sombrer /sɔ̃bʀe/ [1] vi **1** (couler) [navire] to sink; **2** (s'engloutir) **~ dans** [personne] to sink into [désespoir, folie, oubli, débauche, alcoolisme]; **le pays est en train de ~** the country is going to the dogs.

sommaire /sɔmɛʀ/ **I** adj [enquête] perfunctory; [examen, analyse, explication] cursory; [description] rough; [installation, éducation, repas] rough and ready (épith); [vision, conception] shallow; [toilette] quick; [compte rendu, jugement, procès, exécution] summary.

II nm **1** (table des matières) contents (pl); **au ~ de notre numéro de juillet** featured in our July issue; **2**° (programme) **au ~:** **un débat sur le chômage** a debate on unemployment is on the programmeᴳᴮ.

sommairement /sɔmɛʀmɑ̃/ adv [exposer, juger, exécuter] summarily.

sommation /sɔmasjɔ̃/ nf **1** JUR (acte d'huissier) notice; **2** (avertissement) (de policier) warning; (de sentinelle) challenge.

somme¹ /sɔm/ nm nap, snooze°.

somme² /sɔm/ nf **1** (argent) sum; **ça fait**° **une ~!** it's quite a sum!; **2** (quantité) sum total; **la ~ de nos connaissances** the sum total of our knowledge; **en ~, ~ toute** all in all; **3** MATH sum; **4** (œuvre) summa.

sommeil /sɔmɛj/ nm **1** GÉN sleep ₡; **avoir ~** to be ou feel sleepy; **nuit sans ~** sleepless night; **avoir le ~ agité** to sleep fitfully; **avoir le ~ léger/lourd** to be a light/heavy sleeper; **tirer qn de son ~** to wake sb up, to rouse sb SOUT; **2** (attente) **être en ~** [projet, activité, affaire] to have been put on ice.

IDIOMES **dormir d'un ~ de plomb** to sleep like a log°.

sommeiller /sɔmeje/ [1] vi (somnoler) [personne, animal] to doze; [nature, désir] to lie dormant.

sommelier, -ière /sɔmelje, ɛʀ/ ▶374 nm,f wine steward, sommelier.

sommer /sɔme/ [1] vtr **~ qn de faire** to command sb to do; **~ qn de comparaître** JUR to summons sb to appear.

sommet /sɔmɛ/ nm **1** GÉOG (de montagne indéfinie) peak; (de montagne définie) summit; (montagne pointue) peak; **2** (d'arbre, de bâtiment, tour, mur, crâne, colline) top; (de vague) crest; (de courbe) peak; (de hiérarchie, d'organisation) top; (de carrière) summit; **3** (summum) (de gloire, réussite, bêtise) height; **atteindre un ~** or **des ~s** [prix, ventes] to peak; **4** (rencontre) summit; **conférence au ~** summit meeting; **se réunir au ~** to meet at the summit; **5** MATH (de triangle, d'angle) apex; (de cône, volume) vertex.

sommier /sɔmje/ nm (de lit) (bed) base; **~ tapissier** or **à ressorts** bed base GB, box spring US; **~ à lattes** slatted bed base.

sommité /sɔmite/ nf (expert) leading expert (**en** in).

somnambule /sɔmnɑ̃byl/ **I** adj **être ~** to sleepwalk.

II nmf sleepwalker.

somnifère /sɔmnifɛʀ/ **I** adj soporific.

II nm (médicament) somnifacient; (comprimé) sleeping pill.

somnolence /sɔmnɔlɑ̃s/ nf **1** LIT drowsiness; **en état de ~** in a drowsy state; **2** FIG lethargy.

somnolent, -e /sɔmnɔlɑ̃, ɑ̃t/ adj **1** LIT [personne] drowsy; **2** FIG [attention] flagging; [ville] sleepy; [industrie, pays, marché] lethargic.

somnoler /sɔmnɔle/ [1] vi **1** LIT [personne] to drowse; **2** FIG [ville] to be sleepy; [marché, industrie, pays] to be lethargic.

somptuaire /sɔ̃ptɥɛʀ/ adj **1** HIST [loi, édit] sumptuary; **2** (excessif) CONTROV [dépense] lavish.

somptueux, -euse /sɔ̃ptɥø, øz/ adj sumptuous.

somptuosité /sɔ̃ptɥozite/ nf LITER sumptuousness.

son¹, sa, pl **ses** /sɔ̃, sa, sɛ/ adj poss

■ **Note** En anglais, le choix du possessif de la troisième personne du singulier est déterminé par le genre du 'possesseur'. Sont du masculin: les personnes de sexe masculin et les animaux domestiques mâles; sont du féminin: les personnes de sexe féminin, les animaux domestiques femelles et souvent les navires; sont du neutre: les animaux non domestiques et les non-animés. La forme masculine est his: sa femme/moustache = his wife/moustache; son ordinateur = his computer; sa niche = his kennel. La forme féminine est her: son mari/ordinateur = her husband/computer; sa robe = her dress; sa niche = her kennel. La forme neutre est its. Quand le 'possesseur' est indéterminé on peut dire one's: faire ses devoirs = to do one's homework. On ne répète pas le possessif coordonné: sa robe et son manteau = her dress and coat.

ses enfants à elle° her children; **~ étourdie de sœur**° his/her absent-minded sister; **Sa Majesté** His/Her Majesty; **un de ses amis** a friend of his/hers; **elle a ~ lundi** (cette semaine) she's off on Monday; (toutes les semaines) she gets Mondays off.

son² /sɔ̃/ nm **1** (bruit) sound; **le timbre et la hauteur d'un ~** the tone and pitch of a sound; **2** (volume) volume; **baisser le ~** to turn the volume down; **3** RADIO, MUS, TV, CIN sound; **ingénieur du ~** sound engineer; **4** (enveloppe du blé) bran; **des céréales au ~** cereals with bran; **pain au ~** bran loaf.

IDIOMES **entendre plusieurs ~s de cloche** to hear several different versions (of the same thing).

■ **~ et lumière** son et lumière.

sonate /sɔnat/ nf sonata.

sondage /sɔ̃daʒ/ nm **1** (enquête) (pour opinion) poll; (pour étude) survey; **~ d'opinion** opinion poll; **2** MÉD (pour évacuer, introduire) catheterization; (pour examiner) probing; **3** MÉTÉO, NAUT sounding.

■ **~ d'écoute** RADIO, TV audience ratings poll.

sonde /sɔ̃d/ *nf* **1** MÉD (pour évacuer, introduire) catheter; (pour examiner) probe; **2** NAUT (plomb) sounding lead; (ligne) sounding line; **3** MÉTÉO sonde; **4** (de roche) drill; **5** IND (pour produits alimentaires) taster.

■ **~ spatiale** space probe.

sonder /sɔ̃de/ [1] *vtr* **1** (enquêter) (pour opinion) to poll [*personne, groupe*]; (pour étude) to survey [*personne, groupe*]; (pour dévoiler) to sound [sb] out [*personne*]; to sound out [*intentions*]; **2** (fouiller) to probe [*ballot, couche de neige, mare*]; **3** MÉD (pour évacuer, introduire dans) to catheterize [*organe*]; (pour examiner) to probe [*organe*]; **4** MÉTÉO to take soundings in [*atmosphère*]; **5** NAUT to sound [*fond*]; **6** TECH to make test drills in [*couche*].

sondeur, -euse /sɔ̃dœʀ, øz/ I *nm,f* **1 ▶ 374** (enquêteur) pollster; **2** NAUT (personne) sounder; **3** (de gisement) driller.

II *nm* MÉTÉO, NAUT (appareil) sounder; (de roche) driller.

songe /sɔ̃ʒ/ *nm* LITER dream.

songer /sɔ̃ʒe/ [13] I **songer à** *vtr ind* **~ à qch/qn** to think of sth/sb; **~ à faire** to think of doing; **~ que** to think that; **quand on** or **si l'on y songe** when you come to think of it; **il songe à changer de métier** he's contemplating a change of job; **tu n'y songes pas!** you can't be serious!; **songez-y** (n'oubliez pas) bear it in mind; (réfléchissez) think about it; **je n'y avais même pas songé** it hadn't even occurred to me; **songe à ton avenir** think of ou consider your future; **je songeais à lui pour ce poste** I was considering him for the post.

II† *vi* LITER to daydream.

songeur, -euse /sɔ̃ʒœʀ, øz/ *adj* pensive.

sonique /sonik/ *adj* [*barrière*] sound (*épith*).

sonnant, ~e /sɔnɑ̃, ɑ̃t/ *adj* **à trois heures ~es** on the stroke of three.

IDIOMES **payer en espèces ~es et trébuchantes** to pay in cash.

sonné, ~e /sone/ I *pp* ▶ **sonner**.

II *pp adj* **1** (étourdi) (physiquement) groggy; (moralement) shattered; **2** (révolu) **elle a quarante ans bien ~s**° she's well into her forties; **3**° (fou) nuts°.

sonner /sone/ [1] I *vtr* **1** (faire tinter) to ring [*cloche*]; **2** (annoncer) [*horloge*] to strike [*heure*]; [*personne*] to sound [*charge, retraite, alarme*]; to ring out [*vêpres, angélus*]; **3** (faire venir) to ring for; **on ne t'a pas sonné**°! did anyone ask you?; **4**° (faire vaciller) [*coup, boxeur*] to make [sb] dizzy [*personne*]; [*nouvelle, événement*] to stagger [*personne*]; [*vin, alcool*] to knock [sb] out [*personne*].

II **sonner de** *vtr ind* to sound [*cor, trompette*]; to play [*cornemuse*].

III *vi* **1** (se faire entendre) [*cloches, téléphone*] to ring; [*heure*] to strike; [*r éveil*] to go off; [*alerte, alarme, trompette*] to sound; **leur dernière heure a sonné** their last hour has come; **il fait ~ son réveil à 5 heures** he sets his alarm for 5 o'clock; **2** (rendre un son) [*mot, expression*] to sound; **ça sonne bien/mal** that sounds good/bad; **3** (actionner une sonnerie) to ring; **on a sonné à la porte** the doorbell has just rung; **va voir qui sonne** go and see who's at the door.

sonnerie /sɔnʀi/ *nf* **1** (son) ringing; (de carillon) chimes (*pl*); **je n'ai pas entendu la ~ du téléphone** I didn't hear the telephone ringing; **2** (de clairon, trompette) sounding.

sonnet /sɔnɛ/ *nm* sonnet.

sonnette /sɔnɛt/ *nf* (de bicyclette, d'intérieur) bell; (de porte) doorbell; **actionner la ~** to ring the bell; **tirer la ~ d'alarme** LIT to pull the emergency cord; FIG to sound the alarm.

sonneur /sɔnœʀ/ *nm* (de cloches) bell-ringer; (d'autres instruments) player.

IDIOMES **dormir** or **ronfler comme un ~**° to sleep like a log.

sonore /sɔnɔʀ/ *adj* **1** (éclatant) [*rire, baiser, gifle*] resounding; [*formules, paroles*] high-sounding; **2** (qui résonne) [*paroi*] resonant; [*pièce, couloir, voûte*] echoing; [*plancher*] hollow-sounding (*épith*); **3** (relatif au

son) sound (*épith*); **4** CIN, RADIO **effets ~s** sound effects; **un document ~** a recording; **5** (en phonétique) voiced.

sonorisation /sɔnɔʀizasjɔ̃/ *nf* **1** TECH (matériel) public address system, PA system; **2** CIN **la ~ d'un film** adding the soundtrack to a film.

sonoriser /sɔnɔʀize/ [1] *vtr* **1** (équiper d'une sonorisation) to install a public address system ou PA system in [*salle de conférences, rue*]; to install a sound system in [*salle de concert, cinéma*]; **2** CIN **~ un film** to add the soundtrack to a film; **3** (en phonétique) to voice.

sonorité /sɔnɔʀite/ *nf* **1** MUS (d'un instrument, d'une voix) tone (de of); **les ~s de l'italien** the sound of Italian; **2** AUDIO (d'une chaîne hi-fi) sound quality (de of); **3** (d'un plancher, mur) resonance (de of); **4** (en phonétique) voicing (de of).

sophisme /sɔfism/ *nm* sophism.

sophistication /sɔfistikasjɔ̃/ *nf* sophistication.

sophistiqué, ~e /sɔfistike/ *adj* (complexe) sophisticated; (artificiel) artificial, mannered.

sophrologie /sɔfʀɔlɔʒi/ *nf* relaxation therapy.

soporifique /sɔpɔʀifik/ I *adj* LIT, FIG soporific.

II *nm* (médicament) somnifacient.

soprano /sɔpʀano/ **▶ 98** I *nm* (voix) soprano.

II *nmf* (chanteur) (femme) soprano; (enfant) treble, soprano.

sorbet /sɔʀbɛ/ *nm* sorbet.

sorcellerie /sɔʀsɛlʀi/ *nf* witchcraft; (maléfique) sorcery.

sorcier /sɔʀsje/ I° *adj m* **ce n'est (pourtant) pas ~!** (but) it's dead° easy!

II *nm* **1** (magicien) wizard; (maléfique) sorcerer; **2** (guérisseur) witch doctor.

sorcière /sɔʀsjɛʀ/ *nf* witch.

sordide /sɔʀdid/ *adj* [*habitation, quartier*] squalid, sordid; [*conditions de vie, crime, détails*] sordid; [*avarice, égoïsme*] base.

sornettes /sɔʀnɛt/ *nfpl* tall stories.

sort /sɔʀ/ *nm* **1** (condition) lot; **2** (destin) fate ₵; **remettre son ~ entre les mains de qn** to put one's fate in sb's hands; **c'est un coup du ~** it's just one of those things; **le ~ est contre moi** I'm ill-fated; **il a eu un ~ tragique** he came to a tragic end; **tirer au ~** to draw lots; **tirer qch au ~** to draw lots for sth; **faire un ~ à**° **un plat** FIG to polish off° a dish.

IDIOMES **jeter un ~ à qn** to put a curse ou jinx on sb; **le ~ en est jeté** the die is cast.

sortable /sɔʀtabl/ *adj* **mon mari n'est pas ~** I can't take my husband anywhere.

sorte /sɔʀt/ I *nf* sort (de of), kind (de of); **d'aucune ~** of any sort ou kind ou type.

II **de la sorte** *loc adv* [*agir, se comporter, mentir*] in this way; **je n'ai rien fait de la ~** I haven't done anything of the kind ou sort.

III **de sorte que** *loc conj* **1** (de but) so that; **2** (de manière) **la toile est peinte de ~ que** the canvas is painted in such a way that; **3** (de conséquence) **de ~ que je n'ai pas pu venir** with the result that I couldn't come.

IV **en quelque sorte** *loc adv* in a way.

V **en sorte de** *loc prép* **fais en ~ d'être à l'heure** try to be on time.

VI **en sorte que** *loc conj* **1** (de but) **fais en ~ que tout soit en ordre** make sure everything is tidy; **2** (de conséquence) so; **en ~ qu'il n'a rien compris** so he understood nothing.

sortie /sɔʀti/ *nf* **1** (lieu) exit; **je t'attendrai à la ~** I'll wait for you outside (the building); **prenez la première ~** (sur une route) take the first exit; **'~'** (sur un panneau) 'exit', 'way out' GB; **à la ~ de la ville** (extra-muros) on the outskirts of the town; (intra-muros) on the edge of the town; **surveiller la ~ des écoles** to patrol the school gates; **2** (moment) **à ma ~ du tribunal/de l'armée** when I left the court/the army; **sa femme l'attendait à sa ~ de prison** his wife was waiting for him when he came out of prison; **prendre ses enfants à la ~ de l'école** to pick the children up after school; **mendier à la ~ des églises** to beg outside churches; **à la ~ de l'hiver** at the end of winter; **l'heure de la ~** SCOL home time; **(du travail)** knocking-off° time; **3 (départ) faire une ~ fracassante** [*personne*] to make a dramatic exit; **je suis las de tes entrées et ~s continuelles** I'm tired of your constant comings and goings; **~ d'un navire** sailing of a boat; **la ~ de la crise** the end of the crisis; **la ~ de la livre hors du SME** the withdrawal of the pound from the ERM; **le droit à la libre ~ du territoire** the right to travel freely abroad; **être interdit de ~ (du territoire)** to be forbidden to leave the country; **4 (activité) faire une ~ avec l'école** to go on a school outing; **ce soir, c'est mon soir de ~** tonight is my night out; **priver qn de ~** to keep sb in; **première ~ d'un convalescent** a convalescent's first time out; **5 (commercialisation) (de nouveau modèle)** launching ¢; (de film, disque) release; (de livre) publication; (de collection) showing; (de nouveau journal) publication; **le film a été interdit de sa ~** the film was banned as soon as it came out; **6°** (déclaration) remark; **7** ÉLECTROTECH, ORDINAT output; **~ sur imprimante** (processus) printing; **~ laser** (processus) hardcopy laser output; (feuille imprimée) laser hardcopy.

■ **~ des artistes** THÉÂT stage-door; **~ d'autoroute** exit; **~ de bain** bathrobe; **être en ~ de bain** to be wearing a bathrobe; **~ scolaire** (d'un jour) school outing; (de plus d'un jour) school trip.

sortilège /sɔʀtilɛʒ/ *nm* spell.

sortir¹ /sɔʀtiʀ/ [30] **I** *vtr* **1** (promener) to take [sb/sth] out [*personne, chien, cheval*]; **j'y vais moi-même, ça me sortira** I'll go myself, it'll give me a chance to get out; **2°** (inviter) to take [sb] out [*personne*]; **3°** (expulser) to throw [sb] out, to chuck° [sb] out [*personne*]; (de of); to send [sb] out [*élève*]; **se faire ~ en quart de finale** to be knocked out in the quarterfinal; **4** (mettre à l'extérieur) to get [sb/sth] out (de of); **~ qn du lit** to get sb out of bed; **~ sa voiture en marche arrière** to reverse one's car out; **~ les mains de ses poches** to take one's hands out of one's pockets; **~ un revolver** to pull out a revolver; **~ la poubelle** to put the bin out; **~ sa langue** to stick one's tongue out; **~ une carte** to bring out a card; **5** (délivrer) **~ qn de** to get sb out of; **~ une entreprise de ses difficultés** to get a company out of difficulties; **~ qn de sa léthargie** to shake sb out of his/her lethargy; **6** (commercialiser) to bring out [*livre, disque, modèle*]; to release [*film*]; to show [*collection*]; **7** (produire) to turn out [*livre, disque, film, produit*]; **8** (imprimer) to bring [sth] out [*exemplaire, numéro, journal*]; **9°** (dire) to come out with° [*remarques*]; **~ une blague** to crack a joke.

II *vi* (+ *v être*) **1** (aller dehors) [*personne, animal*] to go out; (venir dehors) [*personne, animal*] to come out (de of); **~ par la fenêtre** to go out through the window; **~ dans la rue/sur le balcon** to go out into the street/on the balcony; **~ faire un tour** (à pied) to go out for a walk; **~ faire des courses** to go out shopping; **~ déjeuner** to go out for lunch; **être sorti** to be out; **~ discrètement** to slip out (de of); **~ en courant** to run out; **~ en trombe de sa chambre** to burst out of one's room; **faire ~ qn** to get sb outside; **laisser ~ qn** to allow sb out; **empêcher de ~** to keep [sb/sth] in; **~ dans l'espace** to space-walk; **2** (passer du temps dehors) to go out; **~ au restaurant** to go out to a restaurant; **~ avec qn** to go out with sb; **inviter qn à sortir** to ask sb out; **3** (quitter un lieu) **~ de** to leave; **~ de chez qn** to leave sb's house; **~ d'une réunion** to leave a meeting; **~ du port** [*navire*] to leave port; **~ du pays** [*personne, marchandise*] to leave the country; **~ de chez soi** to go out; **~ de la pièce** to walk out of the room; **sortez d'ici/de là!** get out of here/of there!; **~ de la route** [*véhicule*] to leave the road; **~ de la famille** [*bijou, tableau*] to go out of the family; **~ tout chaud du four** to be hot from the oven; **4** (venir d'un lieu) **~ de** to come out of; **~ de chez le médecin** to come out of the doctor's; **5** (quitter un état, une situation) **~ d'un profond sommeil** to wake up from a

deep sleep; **~ de son mutisme** or **silence** to break one's silence; **~ de l'adolescence** to leave adolescence behind; **~ de la récession** to pull out of the recession; **6** (venir de quitter un état) **~ à peine de l'enfance** to be just emerging from childhood; **~ de maladie** to be recovering from an illness; **~ d'une guerre** to emerge from a war; **7** (émerger) to come out; **elle est sortie de sa dépression très affaiblie** after her depression she was a mere shadow of her former self; **8** (s'échapper) [*eau, air, étincelle, fumée*] to come out (de of; par through); **faire ~** to squeeze [sth] out [*pâte, colle, eau, jus*] (de of); to eject [*cassette*] (de from); **~ en masse** [*personnes*] to pour out; **9** (pousser) [*bourgeon, insecte*] to come out; [*dent*] to come through; **~ de terre** [*plante*] to come through; [*bâtiment*] to rise from the ground; **10** (dépasser) to stick out; **il y a un clou qui sort** there's a nail sticking out; **11** (être commercialisé) [*film, disque, livre, nouveau modèle*] to come out; **~ tous les jours** [*journal*] to be published daily; **12** (provenir) [*personne, produit*] to come from; **~ de Berkeley** UNIV to have graduated from Berkeley; **d'où sors-tu à cette heure**°? where have you been?; **d'où il sort celui-là**°? where's he been living°?; **13** (être en dehors) **~ du sujet** [*personne*] to wander off the subject; [*remarque*] to be beside the point; **14** (être tiré) [*numéro, sujet*] to come up; **15** ORDINAT to exit.

III se sortir *vpr* **1** (échapper) **se ~ d'une situation difficile** to get out of a predicament; **s'en ~** (situation difficile) to get out of it; (maladie) to get over it; **s'en ~ vivant** to escape with one's life; **2** (se débrouiller) **s'en ~** GÉN to pull through; (financièrement) to cope; (intellectuellement, manuellement, physiquement) to manage; **tu t'en sors?** can you manage?; **s'en ~ à peine** (financièrement) to scrape a living.

sortir² /sɔʀtiʀ/ *nm* **au ~ de** at the end of.

SOS /ɛsoɛs/ *nm* **1** (signal) SOS; **2** (service) emergency service; **~ médecins** emergency medical service; **3** (ligne téléphonique) helpline.

sosie /sɔzi/ *nm* double; **c'est ton ~!** he/she's the spitting image of you!

sot, sotte /so, sɔt/ *adj* silly.
IDIOMES **il n'y a pas de ~s métiers** PROV no profession is without merit.

sottise /sɔtiz/ *nf* **1** (manque de jugement) silliness, foolishness; **2** (parole) silly ou foolish remark; **dire des ~s** to talk rubbish; **3** (acte) **c'est une ~ de faire** it's silly to do; **faire une ~** to do something silly; **faire des ~s** [*enfants*] to be naughty.

sou /su/ *nm* **1** (petite monnaie) penny GB, cent US; **il est arrivé sans un ~** he arrived without a penny; **être sans le ~** to be penniless; **économiser ~ par ou à ~** to scrimp and save; **il est près de ses ~s** he's a penny-pincher; **c'est une affaire de gros ~s** there's big money involved; **un manteau de quatre ~s** a cheap coat; **2** (petite quantité) **il n'a pas un ~ de bon sens** he hasn't got a scrap of common sense; **3** HIST (pièce) sou.
IDIOMES **un ~ est un ~** every penny counts; **être propre comme un ~ neuf** to be clean as a new pin°; **s'ennuyer à cent ~s de l'heure** to be bored to death.

soubassement /subasmɑ̃/ *nm* **1** CONSTR (de bâtiment) base, base course; (de colonne) base; **2** (en géologie) bedrock.

soubresaut /subʀəso/ *nm* (de personne, d'animal) start; (de véhicule) jolt; **les derniers ~s** (de personne, d'animal, empire) the death throes.

soubrette /subʀɛt/ *nf* maid.

souche /suʃ/ *nf* **1** (d'arbre) (tree) stump; (de vigne) stock; **2** (origine) stock; **de ~ paysanne** of peasant stock; **faire ~** to establish a line; **3** BIOL strain; **4** (de carnet, livret) stub.
IDIOMES **dormir comme une ~** to sleep like a log.

souci /susi/ *nm* **1** (inquiétude) **se faire du ~** to worry; **tu te fais du ~ pour rien** there's nothing to worry about; **donner du ~ à qn** to be a worry to sb; **2** (problème) problem; **avoir des ~s** to have problems; **j'ai d'autres ~s (en tête)** I've got other things to worry about; **être sans ~s** to have no worries; **leur unique ~ est de faire** all they care about is doing; **3** (soin) FML **avoir le ~ de qch** to care about sth; **avoir le ~ de faire** to be anxious to do; **leur ~ du réalisme** their concern for realism; **dans le seul ~ de plaire** with the sole intention of pleasing; **4** BOT marigold.

soucier: se soucier /susje/ [2] *vpr* to care (**de qch** about sth; **de faire** about doing); **il ne se soucie guère de son avenir** he cares little about his future; **sans se ~ de qch/faire** without concerning oneself with sth/doing.

soucieux, -ieuse /susjø, øz/ *adj* worried; **ça me rend ~ de voir** it worries me to see; **être ~ de** to be concerned about [*réputation, santé*]; to care about [*indépendance, qualité, avenir*]; **être peu ~ de** to care little about; **être ~ de faire** to be anxious to do.

soucoupe /sukup/ *nf* saucer.
■ **~ volante** flying saucer.

soudain, -e /sudɛ̃, ɛn/ **I** *adj* sudden, unexpected.
II *adv* suddenly, all of a sudden.

soudainement /sudɛnmɑ̃/ *adv* suddenly.

soudaineté /sudɛnte/ *nf* suddenness.

soudard /sudaʀ/ *nm* **1** (individu grossier) LITER boor; **2** HIST soldier.

soude /sud/ *nf* soda; **~ caustique** caustic soda.

souder /sude/ [1] **I** *vtr* **1** TECH GÉN to weld [*pièces métalliques*]; (braser) to solder; **2** (réunir) to join [*bords, extrémités*] (**à** to); FIG to bind [sb] together [*personnes*].
II se souder *vpr* **1** LIT [*vertèbres*] to fuse; [*os*] to knit together; **2** FIG [*équipe*] to become united; [*personnes*] to be brought closer together.

soudoyer /sudwaje/ [23] *vtr* to bribe.

soudure /sudyʀ/ *nf* TECH (joint) weld, join; (fil à souder) solder; (opération) GÉN welding; (brasage) soldering; **~ à l'arc** arc welding.

soufflant, -e /suflɑ̃, ɑ̃t/ *adj* **1** TECH **machine ~e** blowing apparatus; **2**○ (étonnant) stunning.

souffle /sufl/ *nm* **1** (respiration) breath; **couper le ~ à qn** LIT to wind sb; FIG to take sb's breath away; **à couper le ~** [*beauté, vitesse*] breathtaking; [*beau*] breathtakingly; **(en) avoir le ~ coupé** LIT to be winded; FIG to be speechless; **être à bout de ~** [*personne*] to be out of breath; [*pays, économie*] to be running out of steam; **dire qch dans un ~** to say sth in a whisper; **retrouver un second ~** (après un effort) to get one's second wind; (après un marasme, vieillissement) to get a new lease of GB ou on US life; **donner un second** ou **nouveau ~ à qn/qch** to put new life into sb/sth; **avoir du ~** LIT [*trompettiste*] to have good lungs; [*acteur, chanteur*] to have a powerful voice; [*sportif*] to be fit; FIG (avoir de l'endurance) [*personne*] to have staying power; (avoir de l'esprit) [*auteur, œuvre*] to be inspired; (avoir de l'audace)○ to have nerve; **2** (bruit de respiration) breathing; **~ précipité** rapid breathing; **3** (brise) breeze; **pas un ~ (de vent)** not a breath (of wind); **4** (esprit) spirit; **~ de la révolte** spirit of rebellion; **5** (force) inspiration; **~ créateur** creative inspiration; **6** (élément) touch; **7** PHYS (d'explosion, de réacteur, ventilateur) blast; **8** MÉD (en cardiologie) murmur; **~ au cœur** heart murmur.

soufflé, -e /sufle/ **I** *pp* ▶ **souffler**.
II *pp adj* **1**○ (stupéfait) flabbergasted; **2** IND [*bitume, huile, pâte*] blown; **3** CULIN [*omelette*] souffléed.
III *nm* CULIN soufflé.

souffler /sufle/ [1] **I** *vtr* **1** (éteindre) to blow out [*bougie, lampe*]; **2** (envoyer) to blow [*air, odeur, poussière*]; **3** (chuchoter) to whisper [*mots, texte*] (**à qn** to sb; **que** that); **~ qch à l'oreille de qn** to whisper sth into sb's ear; **~ la réplique à un acteur** to prompt an actor, to give an actor a prompt; **4** (suggérer) to suggest [*idée, nom*] (**à** to); **on lui a soufflé la réponse** he/she was prompted; **5** IND to blow [*verre, bouteille*]; to blast [*métal*]; **6** (détruire) [*explosion, bombe*] to blow out [*vitre*]; to blow up [*construction*]; **7** JEUX (aux dames) to huff [*pièce*]; **8**○ (stupéfier) to flabbergast.

II *vi* **1** MÉTÉO [*vent*] to blow; **le vent souffle fort** there's a strong wind; **ça souffle** it's windy; **2** (se propager) [*vent de révolte, liberté*] to blow; **un vent de folie souffle sur le stade** frenzy is sweeping through the stadium; **3** (reprendre sa respiration) to get one's breath back; [*cheval*] to get its wind back; FIG [*personne, économie*] to take a breather○; **4** (respirer difficilement) to puff; **5** (produire un souffle) [*personne, animal*] to blow; **~ dans une trompette** to blow a trumpet; **~ sur une bougie** to blow out a candle; **~ sur le feu** LIT to blow on the fire; FIG to inflame the situation; **6** (donner la réponse) to tell sb the answer; **on ne souffle pas!** no prompting!
IDIOMES **~ comme un bœuf** or **un phoque** or **une locomotive** to puff and pant.

soufflerie /sufləʀi/ *nf* **1** TECH (d'expérimentation) wind tunnel; **2** (d'orgue, de forge, four) bellows (*pl*); **3** (machine) blower; (lieu) blower house; **4** (de verre) (machine) glassblower; (entreprise) glassblowing company.

soufflet /suflɛ/ *nm* **1** TECH (de forge, d'orgue, appareil photo) bellows (*pl*); **2** (de wagon) concertina vestibule; **3** (de chaussure, poche) gusset; **4**† (gifle) slap.

souffleur, -euse /suflœʀ, øz/ *nm,f* **1** ▶ **374** THÉÂT prompter; **2** IND ~ (**de verre**) glassblower.

souffrance /sufʀɑ̃s/ *nf* suffering ¢; **en ~** [*projet, dossier*] pending; **colis en ~** (non livré) parcel awaiting delivery; (non réclamé) unclaimed parcel.

souffrant, -e /sufʀɑ̃, ɑ̃t/ *adj* unwell.

souffre-douleur /sufʀədulœʀ/ *nm inv* punch-bag GB, punching-bag US.

souffreteux, -euse /sufʀətø, øz/ *adj* sickly.

souffrir /sufʀiʀ/ [4] **I** *vtr* **1** (supporter) **~ tout de qn** to put up with anything from sb; **il ne souffre pas d'être contredit** he can't stand being contradicted; **elle ne peut plus le ~** she can't stand him any more; **2** (permettre) **souffrez que je vous dise** allow me to tell you; **cette affaire ne peut ~ aucun retard** this matter brooks no delay.
II *vi* **1** (physiquement) [*personne, animal*] to suffer; **faire ~ qn** to cause sb suffering; **~ de qch** to suffer from [*diabète, malformation*]; **~ du dos** to suffer from back problems; **ma cheville me fait ~** my ankle hurts; **est-ce qu'il souffre?** is he in pain?; **2** (moralement) [*personne*] to suffer; **faire ~** [*personne*] to make [sb] suffer; [*situation*] to upset; **~ de** to suffer from [*trac*]; **~ du racisme** to be a victim of racism; **~ d'être rejeté** to suffer the pain of rejection; **ils souffrent de ne pas se voir** they find it painful to be separated; **elle souffre de voir que** it upsets her to see that; **3** (être endommagé) [*cultures, économie*] to be badly affected (**de** by); [*pays, ville*] to suffer (**de** from); **4**○ (peiner) [*personne, équipe*] to have a hard time (**pour faire** doing); **j'ai fini la course mais j'ai souffert!** I finished the race but it was tough!
III se souffrir *vpr* **ils ne peuvent pas se ~** they can't stand each other.

soufre /sufʀ/ *nm* sulphur GB.

soufrer /sufʀe/ [1] *vtr* to sulphurate GB [*étoffe, laine*]; to sulphur GB [*allumette*]; to treat [sth] with sulphur GB [*vigne*].

souhait /swɛ/ *nm* wish; **répondre aux ~s de qn** [*proposition*] to suit sb; **à ~** [*beau*] incredibly.
IDIOMES **à vos ~s!** bless you!

souhaitable /swɛtabl/ *adj* desirable.

souhaiter /swete/ [1] *vtr* **1** (espérer) to hope for; **~ que** to hope that; **2** (exprimer) **~ qch à qn** to wish sb sth; **~ bonne chance à qn** to wish sb luck; **je vous souhaite une bonne et heureuse année** I wish you a happy New Year; **~ la bienvenue à qn** to welcome sb; **~ beaucoup de bonheur à qn** to wish sb every happiness; **je vous souhaite d'obtenir très bientôt votre diplôme** I hope you get your degree very soon; **3** (désirer) **il souhaite se rendre là-bas en voiture** he would like to go by car.

souiller /suje/ [1] *vtr* **1** (salir, polluer) to soil, to make [sth] dirty; **2** (rendre impur) LITER to defile [*lieu, personne*]; to sully [*mémoire, réputation*].

souillon /sujɔ̃/ *nf* slattern†.

souillure /sujyʀ/ nf **1** (flétrissure morale) stain, taint; **2** (saleté) stain.

souk /suk/ nm **1** (marché) souk; **2**○ (désordre) mess; (bruit) racket○.

soûl, ~e /su, sul/ I adj drunk.
II **tout son soûl** loc adv [boire, manger] one's fill; **dormir tout son ~** to sleep as much as one wants.

soulagement /sulaʒmɑ̃/ nm relief.

soulager /sulaʒe/ [13] I vtr **1** (décharger) to relieve [personne, entreprise, étagère] (de of); **2** (apaiser) to relieve [personne]; to relieve, to ease [conscience, peine]; **~ qn d'un mal de tête** to relieve sb's headache; **pleure un bon coup, ça soulage** have a good cry, you'll feel better; **tu m'as soulagé d'un grand poids** you've taken a great weight off my shoulders; **3**○ FIG (voler) to relieve (de qch of sth).
II **se soulager** vpr **1**○ (satisfaire un besoin naturel) EUPH to relieve oneself; **2** (s'apaiser) **elle m'a raconté tout cela pour se ~** she told me the whole story to get it off her chest.

soûlant○, **~e** /sulɑ̃, ɑ̃t/ adj **elle est ~e!** she makes my head spin!

soûler /sule/ [1] I vtr **1** (rendre ivre) [personne] to get [sb] drunk [personne]; [alcool] to make [sb] drunk [personne]; **2** (griser) [odeur, parfum, grand air] to intoxicate [personne]; **3**○ (étourdir) **tu me soûles avec tes histoires** give me a break, my head is spinning!.
II **se soûler** vpr **1** (s'enivrer) to get drunk (à, avec on); **2** (se griser) **se ~ de** to become intoxicated with [paroles, musique].

soulèvement /sulɛvmɑ̃/ nm (insurrection) uprising.

soulever /sulve/ [16] I vtr **1** (déplacer vers le haut) [personne] to lift [objet]; [vent, tourbillon, véhicule] to whip up [feuilles, poussière]; **~ qn/qch de terre** [personne] to pick sb/sth up; [vent] to sweep sb/sth up into the air; **2** (entraîner) to arouse [enthousiasme, colère, dégoût]; to stir up [foule, peuple, opinion] (contre against); to raise [problèmes, difficultés, obstacles]; to give rise to [protestations, applaudissements]; **3** (faire considérer) to raise [question, problème, interrogation].
II **se soulever** vpr **1** (se dresser) to raise oneself up; **2** (se révolter) to rise up (contre against).
IDIOMES **ça me soulève le cœur** (odeur) it turns my stomach; (attitude) it makes me sick.

soulier /sulje/ nm shoe.
IDIOMES **être dans ses petits ~s** to feel uncomfortable.

souligner /suliɲe/ [1] vtr **1** (d'un trait) to underline [mot, titre]; to outline [yeux]; **2** (accentuer) to emphasize [attitude, remarque]; to set off [teint, éclat].

soumettre /sumɛtʀ/ [60] I vtr **1** (vaincre) to bring [sb/sth] to heel [personne, groupe, région]; to subdue [ennemi, rebelles, armée]; **2** (assujettir) **~ qn/qch à** to subject sb/sth to; **3** (proposer) to submit (à to); **~ une proposition à qn** to put forward a proposal to sb; **4** (faire subir) **~ un produit à une température élevée** to subject a product to a high temperature.
II **se soumettre** vpr **1** (se rendre) to submit; **2** (accepter) **se ~ à** to accept [règlement].

soumis, ~e /sumi, iz/ adj submissive.

soumission /sumisjɔ̃/ nf **1** (assujettissement) submission (à to); **2** (reddition) submission (à to); **3** ADMIN, COMM tender.

soumissionner /sumisjɔne/ [1] vtr to tender.

soupape /supap/ nf valve.

soupçon /supsɔ̃/ nm **1** (sur l'honnêteté, authenticité) suspicion; **avoir des ~s sur qn/qch** to have one's suspicions about sb/sth; **2** (idée vague) FML **ne pas avoir ~ de qch** to have no notion of sth; **3**○ (faible quantité) (de lait, vin) drop, spot○; (de cannelle, sel, d'herbes aromatiques) pinch; (dans un goût) hint.

soupçonner /supsɔne/ [1] vtr **1** (suspecter) to suspect; **~ qn de qch/d'avoir fait** to suspect sb of sth/of having done; **2** (conjecturer) to suspect [piège, coup bas].

soupçonneux, -euse /supsɔnø, øz/ adj suspicious, mistrustful.

soupe /sup/ nf **1** CULIN soup; **~ de légumes/aux oignons** vegetable/onion soup; **à la ~!** HUM grub up○!, come and get it!; **2**○ (neige) slush.
■ **~ populaire** soup kitchen.
IDIOMES **par ici la bonne ~!**○ come on, cough up○!, come on, hand over the money!; **être ~ au lait**○ to be quick-tempered; **cracher dans la ~**○ to bite the hand that feeds you; **il me mange la ~ sur la tête** he towers over me.

soupente /supɑ̃t/ nf **1** (sous un toit) loft, garret; **2** (sous un escalier) cupboard under the stairs.

souper¹ /supe/ [1] vi to have late dinner.
IDIOMES **en avoir soupé de qch**○ to have had it up to here with sth○.

souper² /supe/ nm late dinner, supper.

soupeser /supəze/ [16] vtr **1** LIT to heft, to feel the weight of [objet]; **2** FIG to weigh up [arguments].

soupière /supjɛʀ/ nf soup tureen.

soupir /supiʀ/ nm **1** (expiration) sigh (de of); **pousser un ~** to sigh ou heave a sigh; **~ de soulagement** sigh of relief; **2** (du vent) LITER sighing; (d'amoureux) **~s** sighs; **3** MUS crotchet rest GB, quarter rest US.

soupirail, pl **-aux** /supiʀaj, o/ nm cellar window.

soupirer /supiʀe/ [1] vi [personne, vent] to sigh (de with); **~ pour qn** to pine for sb.

souple /supl/ adj **1** (flexible) [corps, animal] supple; [tige, lame] flexible; [cheveux, matière] soft; **2** (aisé) [démarche, geste, style] flowing (épith); [forme, contour] smooth; **3** (adaptable) [règlement, horaire] flexible.

souplesse /suplɛs/ nf **1** (de tige, lame, disque) flexibility; (de cheveux, matière) softness; (de corps, d'animal) suppleness; **2** (de démarche) litheness; (de geste) grace; (de voiture, conduite) smoothness; (de style) fluidity; **3** (de règlement, d'esprit, horaire) flexibility; **en ~** smoothly; **4** SPORT (en gymnastique) walk-over.

source /suʀs/ nf **1** (d'eau) spring; **2** (de cours d'eau) source; **prendre sa ~ dans** or **à** to rise in ou at; **3** (origine) source; **être à la ~ de** to be at the root of; **être une ~ de** to be a source of [conflits, ennuis, profits]; **4** (référence) source; **citer/vérifier ses ~s** to give/to check one's sources.
IDIOMES **ça coule de ~** it's obvious; **retour aux ~s** return to basics.

sourcil /suʀsi/ nm eyebrow; **~s épais** bushy eyebrows.

sourcilier, -ière /suʀsilje, ɛʀ/ adj [muscle] superciliary.

sourciller /suʀsije/ [1] vi to raise one's eyebrows; **sans ~** without batting an eyelid.

sourd, ~e /suʀ, suʀd/ I adj **1** MÉD [personne] deaf; **être ~ d'une oreille** to be deaf in one ear; **2** (insensible) deaf (à to); **3** (étouffé) [bruit, explosion] dull, muffled; [voix] muffled; [plainte] faint, muted; **4** (diffus) [douleur] dull; **5** (secret) [lutte, machinations] secret, hidden; **6** LING voiceless, surd.
II nm,f deaf person; **les ~s** the deaf (+ v pl).
IDIOMES **faire la ~e oreille** to turn a deaf ear; **mieux vaut entendre ça que d'être ~**○! HUM what stupid things you hear!; **comme un ~** [crier, taper, frapper] like one possessed; **ce n'est pas tombé dans l'oreille d'un ~** it didn't go unheard.

sourdine /suʀdin/ nf MUS mute; (de piano) soft pedal; **jouer en ~** to play softly; **mettre une ~ à** FIG to tone down [critiques].

sourd-muet, sourde-muette, pl **sourds-muets, sourdes-muettes** /suʀmɥɛ, suʀdmɥɛt/ I adj deaf and dumb.
II nm,f deaf-mute.

souriant, ~e, /suʀjɑ̃, ɑ̃t/ adj smiling.

souriceau, pl **~x** /suʀiso/ nm young mouse.

souricière /suʀisjɛʀ/ nf **1** (pour souris) mousetrap; **2** (pour malfaiteur) trap.

sourire¹ /suʀiʀ/ [68] vi **1** (adresser un sourire) to smile (à qn at sb); **~ jusqu'aux oreilles** to grin from ear

to ear; **2** (être agréable) LITER [*destin, fortune*] to smile; [*idée, projet*] to appeal to [*personne*].
IDIOMES **~ aux anges** to have a silly smile on one's face.

sourire² /suRiR/ *nm* smile; **un bon/large ~** a kindly/ broad smile; **le ~ aux lèvres** with a smile on one's face; **être tout ~** to be all smiles; **garder le ~** to keep smiling (through); **faire un ~ à qn** to give sb a smile.

souris /suRi/ *nf inv* **1** ZOOL mouse; **2** ORDINAT mouse; **3**○ (femme) bird○ GB, chick○ US.
IDIOMES **jouer au chat et à la ~** to play cat and mouse; **quand le chat n'est pas là les ~ dansent** when the cat's away, the mice will play.

sournois, -e /suRnwa, az/ **I** *adj* [*personne, animal, air, regard*] sly; [*conduite, pensée, action*] underhand; [*douleur, mal*] insidious.
II *nm,f* sly person, underhand person.

sous /su/ *prép*

■ Note Lorsque *sous* indique une position dans l'espace il se traduit généralement par *under*: *sous la table/un arbre* = under the table/a tree.
– On trouvera ci-dessous des exemples supplémentaires et exceptions.
– Lorsque *sous* a une valeur figurée comme dans *sous le choc, sous la menace, sous aucun prétexte* etc la traduction de *sous* sera fournie sous le deuxième élément, respectivement **choc, menace, prétexte** etc, auquel on se reportera.

1 (en dessous de) under, underneath, beneath SOUT; **un journal ~ le bras** a newspaper under one's arm; **le jardin était ~ la neige** the garden GB ou yard US was covered in snow; **~ l'eau** under the water, underwater, below water; **~ la pluie** in the rain; **j'aurais voulu rentrer ~ terre** FIG I wished the ground would swallow me up; ▶ **étoile, herbe**; **2** (dans un classement) under; **~ le numéro 4757** under number 4757; **3** (pendant une période) during; **~ la présidence de Mitterrand** during Mitterrand's presidency; **4** (avant) within; **~ peu** before long; **5** (sous l'action de) **~ traitement** undergoing treatment; **~ antibiotiques** on antibiotics.

sous-alimenté, ~e, *mpl* **~s** /suzalimɑ̃te/ *adj* undernourished.

sous-bois /subwa/ *nm inv* undergrowth ¢.

sous-chef, *pl* **~s** /suʃɛf/ *nm* GÉN second-in-command.

souscripteur, -trice /suskRiptœR, tRis/ *nm,f* subscriber (**de** to).

souscription /suskRipsjɔ̃/ *nf* **1** (à une publication, une œuvre charitable) subscription (**à** to); **2** (d'assurance) **~ d'un contrat d'assurances** taking out an insurance policy; **~ collective** collective underwriting; **3** FIN (d'un emprunt, une émission) subscription (**à** to); **~ d'actions** application for shares; **taux de ~** take-up (of a rights issue).

souscrire /suskRiR/ [67] **I** *vtr* to take out [*assurance, abonnement, plan d'épargne*]; to sign [*contrat, traite*]; to subscribe [*somme*].
II souscrire à *vtr ind* **1** (en payant) **~ à** to subscribe to [*publication, emprunt, œuvre charitable*]; **2** (adhérer) **~ à** to subscribe to [*propos, décision*]; **j'y souscris entièrement** I go along with that completely.

souscrit, ~e /suskRi, it/ **I** *pp* ▶ **souscrire**.
II *pp adj* **1** FIN subscribed; **2** (en imprimerie) [*lettre*] subscript.

sous-cutané, ~e, *mpl* **~s** /sukytane/ *adj* subcutaneous.

sous-développé, ~e, *mpl* **~s** /sudevlɔpe/ *adj* [*pays, région, économie*] underdeveloped.

sous-directeur, -trice, *mpl* **~s** /sudiRɛktœR, tRis/ *nm,f* assistant manager.

sous-direction, *pl* **~s** /sudiRɛksjɔ̃/ *nf* division; **~ des affaires économiques et financières** economic and financial affairs division.

sous-effectif, *pl* **~s** /suzefɛktif/ *nm* understaffing ¢; **ils sont en ~** they're understaffed.

sous-employer /suzɑ̃plwaje/ [23] *vtr* to underemploy.

sous-entendre /suzɑ̃tɑ̃dR/ [6] *vtr* to imply.

sous-entendu, ~e, *mpl* **~s** /suzɑ̃tɑ̃dy/ **I** *pp* ▶ **sous-entendre**.
II *pp adj* understood.
III *nm* innuendo; **un sourire plein de ~s** a smile full of innuendo.

sous-entraîné, ~e, *mpl* **~s** /suzɑ̃tRene/ *adj* ill-prepared.

sous-équipé, ~e, *mpl* **~s** /suzekipe/ *adj* underequipped.

sous-espèce, *pl* **~s** /suzɛspɛs/ *nf* subspecies (+ *v sg*).

sous-estimer /suzestime/ [1] *vtr* to underestimate.

sous-évaluer /suzevalɥe/ [1] *vtr* to underestimate [*coût, problème*]; to undervalue [*maison, terrain*].

sous-exposer /suzekspoze/ [1] *vtr* PHOT to underexpose [*photo*].

sous-fifre○, *pl* **~s** /sufifR/ *nm* underling.

sous-jacent, ~e, *mpl* **~s** /suʒasɑ̃, ɑ̃t/ *adj* **1** FIG (latent) [*idée, problème, tension*] underlying; **2** (audessous) subjacent.

sous-lieutenant, *pl* **~s** /suljøtnɑ̃/ ▶ **284** *nm* (dans l'armée de terre) ≈ second lieutenant; (dans l'aviation) ≈ pilot officer GB, ≈ second lieutenant US.

sous-louer /sulwe/ [1] *vtr* **1** (donner en location) to sublet, to sublease [*appartement, pièce*]; **2** (prendre en location) to sublease [*appartement, pièce*].

sous-main /sumɛ̃/ **I** *nm inv* desk blotter.
II en sous-main *loc adv* under the table, secretly.

sous-marin, ~e, *mpl* **~s** /sumaRɛ̃, in/ **I** *adj* **1** [*relief, faune, flore*] submarine, underwater; **2** [*exploration, câble*] underwater; [*plongée*] deep-sea.
II *nm* **1** NAUT submarine; **2**○ (espion) spy.
■ **~ à propulsion nucléaire** nuclear-powered submarine.

sous-marinier, *pl* **~s** /sumaRinje/ ▶ **374** *nm* submariner.

sous-marque, *pl* **~s** /sumaRk/ *nf* sub-brand.

sous-officier, *pl* **~s** /suzɔfisje/ ▶ **284** *nm* noncommissioned officer.

sous-ordre, *pl* **~s** /suzɔRdR/ *nm* suborder.

sous-payer /supeje/ [21] *vtr* to underpay [*employé*].

sous-peuplé, ~e, *mpl* **~s** /supœple/ *adj* [*pays, région*] underpopulated.

sous-préfecture, *pl* **~s** /supRefɛktyR/ *nf*: administrative subdivision of a department in France.

sous-préfet, *pl* **~s** /supRefɛ/ *nm*: permanent ministerial representative in a department in France.

sous-produit, *pl* **~s** /supRɔdɥi/ *nm* **1** (produit secondaire) by-product; **2** (produit médiocre) second-rate product.

sous-prolétariat, *pl* **~s** /supRɔletaRja/ *nm* underclass.

sous-pull, *pl* **~s** /supyl/ *nm* thin polo-neck jumper.

sous-secrétaire, *pl* **~s** /sus(ə)kRetɛR/ *nmf* **~ d'État** Parliamentary Undersecretary of State.

soussigné, ~e /susiɲe/ **I** *adj* undersigned.
II *nm,f* **les ~s** the undersigned (+ *v pl*).

sous-sol, *pl* **~s** /susɔl/ *nm* **1** CONSTR basement; **2** GÉOG subsoil ¢.

sous-tasse, *pl* **~s** /sutas/ *nf* saucer.

sous-titrage, *pl* **~s** /sutitRaʒ/ *nm* subtitling.

sous-titre, *pl* **~s** /sutitR/ *nm* **1** (titre secondaire) subtitle; **2** CIN, TV, MUS (texte sous image) subtitle, caption.

sous-titrer /sutitRe/ [1] *vtr* CIN, TV, MUS to subtitle.

soustractif, -ive /sustRaktif, iv/ *adj* subtractive.

soustraction /sustRaksjɔ̃/ *nf* **1** MATH (processus) subtraction ¢; (opération) subtraction; **faire une erreur de ~** to make a mistake while subtracting; **2** JUR (vol) removal, taking away.

soustraire /sustRɛR/ [58] **I** *vtr* **1** MATH to subtract (**de** from); **2** (voler) to steal (**à** from); **3** (retirer) to take away [*personne*] (à from); ~ **qn/qch à la vue de qn** to hide sb/sth from sb; **4** (protéger) to shield [*personne*]; ~ **qn à la mort** to save sb's life.

II se soustraire *vpr* **1** (éviter) **se** ~ **à** to escape from [*tâche, ennui*]; **se** ~ **à ses obligations** to shirk one's duties; **2** (échapper à) **se** ~ **à** to avoid [*arrestation*]; **se** ~ **à la justice** to escape justice.

sous-traitance, *pl* ~**s** /sutʀɛtɑ̃s/ *nf* subcontracting; **travail donné en** ~ work contracted out.

sous-verre /suvɛʀ/ *nm inv* **1** (encadrement) frame; **2** (œuvre) framed picture.

sous-vêtement, *pl* ~**s** /suvɛtmɑ̃/ *nm* underwear ¢.

soutane /sutan/ *nf* cassock; **porter la** ~ to be a priest.

soute /sut/ *nf* NAUT hold.

soutenable /sutnabl/ *adj* **1** (supportable) bearable; **pas** ~ unbearable; **2** (défendable) [*hypothèse*] tenable.

soutenance /sutnɑ̃s/ *nf* UNIV (de mémoire, dossier) viva GB, orals (*pl*) US.

soutènement /sutɛnmɑ̃/ *nm* GÉN retaining structure; (dans une mine) props (*pl*).

souteneur /sutnœʀ/ *nm* pimp°, procurer.

soutenir /sutniʀ/ [36] **I** *vtr* **1** (donner son appui) to support; ~ **une grève** to support a strike; ~ **à bout de bras** to keep [sb/sth] afloat [*personne, projet*]; ~ **qn contre qn** to side with sb against sb; **2** ÉCON, FIN to support [*monnaie, marché, cours, économie*]; **3** (affirmer) to maintain [*contraire*]; to defend [*paradoxe*]; to uphold [*opinion*]; ~ **que** to maintain that; **4** (servir de support) to support [*personne, toit, monnaie*]; **mur soutenu par des étais** wall supported by props; **5** (donner des forces) to keep [sb] going [*personne*]; **6** (réconforter) [*personne*] to support; [*espoir*] to sustain; ~ **le moral de qn** to keep sb's spirits up; **7** (faire durer) to keep [sth] alive [*curiosité, intérêt*]; to keep [sth] going [*conversation*]; to keep up, to sustain [*effort, rythme*]; **8** (résister) to withstand [*choc, siège, assaut, regard*]; to bear [*comparaison*]; **9** UNIV ~ **sa thèse** to have one's viva GB ou defense US.

II se soutenir *vpr* **1** (s'entraider) to support each other; **2** (être défendable) [*argument, hypothèse*] to be tenable, to hold oneself up.

soutenu, ~**e** /sutny/ **I** *pp* ▶ **soutenir**.
II *pp adj* (intense) [*activité, effort*] sustained; [*attention*] close; [*rythme*] steady.
III *adj* **1** GÉN [*marché*] firm; [*couleur*] deep; [*style, langue*] formal, elevated; **2** MUS (maintenu) [*note, ton*] sustained, long-drawn-out.

souterrain, ~**e** /suteʀɛ̃, ɛn/ **I** *adj* **1** (sous terre) [*lac, ouvrage, explosion*] underground; **2** (secret) [*menées, accord*] secret; **économie** ~**e** black economy.
II *nm* underground passage, tunnel.

soutien /sutjɛ̃/ *nm* **1** (appui) support (à for); **le parti a manifesté son** ~ **à la majorité** the party showed its support for the majority; ~ **en anglais** SCOL extra help in English; **2** (agent) support; **3** (de voûte, plateforme) support.

soutien-gorge, *pl* **soutiens-gorge** /sutjɛ̃gɔʀʒ/ *nm* bra.

soutirer /sutiʀe/ [1] *vtr* **1** (dérober) ~ **à qn** to squeeze [sth] out of sb [*argent*]; to extract [sth] from sb [*aveu*]; **2** (clarifier) to rack [*vin*].

souvenance /suvnɑ̃s/ *nf* FML **à ma** ~ as far as I recall; **avoir** ~ **de qch** to remember sth.

souvenir[1] /suvniʀ/ [36] **I se souvenir** *vpr* **se** ~ **de qn/qch** to remember sb/sth; **se** ~ (**d'**)**avoir fait** to remember doing; **se** ~ **que** to remember that.
II *v impers* **il me souvient que** LITER I recollect that; **autant qu'il m'en souvienne** if my memory serves me right.

souvenir[2] /suvniʀ/ *nm* **1** (pensée du passé) memory; **garder un bon/mauvais** ~ **de qch** to have happy/bad ou unhappy memories of sth; **le** ~ **que je garde de lui est encore très clair** I still remember him very clearly; ~**s d'école** memories of schooldays; ~**s**

d'enfance childhood memories; **chercher dans ses** ~**s** to sift through one's memories; **avoir** (**le**) ~ **de qch** to remember sth; **ne pas avoir** ~ **de** to have no recollection of; **au** ~ **de** at the memory of; **2** (mémoire) memory; **3** (objet) (rappelant un lieu, un événement) souvenir (**de** of); (rappelant une personne) memento (**de** from); **en** ~ GÉN as a souvenir; (avec valeur affective) as a memento; (cadeau ayant valeur affective) as a keepsake; **boutique de** ~**s** souvenir shop GB ou store US; **4** (salutation) **croyez à mon bon** or **fidèle** or **meilleur** ~ yours ever; **mon bon** ~ **à** remember me to.

souvent /suvɑ̃/ *adv* often; **le plus** ~ more often than not.
IDIOMES **on a** ~ **besoin d'un plus petit que soi** PROV a mouse may help a lion.

souverain, ~**e** /suvʀɛ̃, ɛn/ **I** *adj* **1** (indépendant) [*État, peuple, droit, pouvoir*] sovereign; [*décision, autorité*] supreme; **2** (suprême) [*bonheur, talent, mépris*] supreme; **3** (infaillible) [*remède, potion*] sovereign; [*conseil, vertu*] sterling; **4** (hautain) [*personne*] haughty.
II *nm,f* sovereign, monarch.
III *nm* (monnaie) sovereign.

souverainement /suvʀɛnmɑ̃/ *adv* **1** (sans appel) [*décider, juger*] without appeal; **2** (suprêmement) **votre attitude me déplaît** ~ I dislike your attitude intensely.

souveraineté /suvʀɛnte/ *nf* sovereignty.

soviétique /sɔvjetik/ *adj* HIST Soviet.

soyeux, -euse /swajø, øz/ **I** *adj* silky.
II ▶ 374 *nm* (fabricant) silk manufacturer.

SPA /ɛspea/ *nf* (*abbr* = **Société protectrice des animaux**) society for the prevention of cruelty to animals.

spacieux, -ieuse /spasjø, øz/ *adj* spacious.

spaghetti /spageti/ *nm inv* spaghetti ¢.

sparadrap /spaʀadʀa/ *nm* **1** (bande adhésive) surgical ou adhesive tape; **2** (pansement) (sticking) plaster GB, Band-aid®.

spartiate /spaʀsjat/ *adj, nmf* Spartan.

spasme /spasm/ *nm* spasm.

spasmophilie /spasmɔfili/ *nf* spasmophilia.

spath /spat/ *nm* spar.

spatial, ~**e**, *mpl* **-iaux** /spasjal, o/ *adj* **1** GÉN, PSYCH [*repérage, perception, représentation*] spatial; **2** ASTRO-NAUT space (*épith*); **vaisseau** ~ spaceship.

spationaute /spasjɔnot/ ▶ 374 *nmf* astronaut.

spatule /spatyl/ *nf* **1** CULIN, ART spatula; (de plâtrier) filling-knife; **2** (de ski) tip; **3** ZOOL (poisson) paddlefish; (oiseau) spoonbill.

speaker, speakerine /spikœʀ, spikʀin/ ▶ 374 *nm,f* announcer.

spécial, ~**e**, *mpl* **-iaux** /spesjal, o/ *adj* **1** (non général) [*formation, tarif, statut*] special; **2** (adapté) [*appareil, chaussures, peigne*] special; **3** (bizarre) [*mentalité, personne*] odd.

spécialement /spesjalmɑ̃/ *adv* **1** (particulièrement) specially; **2** (très) especially; **pas** ~ not especially.

spécialisé, ~**e** /spesjalize/ **I** *pp* ▶ **spécialiser**.
II *pp adj* **être** ~ **dans** or **en** [*personne*] to be a specialist in; [*établissement, usine*] to specialize in.

spécialiser: se spécialiser /spesjalize/ [1] *vpr* to specialize (**en, dans** in).

spécialiste /spesjalist/ *nmf* specialist (**de, en** in).

spécialité /spesjalite/ *nf* **1** GÉN speciality GB, specialty US; ~ **médicale** specialized medical field; **2** CULIN speciality GB, specialty US.

spécieux, -ieuse /spesjø, øz/ *adj* specious.

spécificité /spesifisite/ *nf* **1** (de produit, maladie) specificity; **2** (caractéristique) characteristic; **3** (caractère unique) uniqueness.

spécifier /spesifje/ [2] *vtr* to specify.

spécifique /spesifik/ *adj* specific (**de** to).

spécimen /spesimɛn/ *nm* **1** (exemple) specimen;

2 (exemplaire) (free) sample; **3**○ (personne) odd specimen○.

spectacle /spɛktakl/ **I** nm **1** (vue) sight; (événement) sight; **au ~ de...** at the sight of...; **devant un tel ~** (affreux) at this awful sight; (merveilleux) at this amazing sight; **se donner en ~** PÉJ to make an exhibition ou a spectacle of oneself; **2** (divertissement) **avoir le sens du ~** [metteur en scène] to have a real sense of theatreGB; [politicien] to have an eye for effect; **3** THÉÂT (représentation) show; **~ de marionnettes** puppet show; '**~s**' (rubrique) 'entertainment'; **film à grand ~** spectacular; **4** (activité professionnelle) **le ~**, **l'industrie du ~** show business.
II -spectacle (in compounds) **1** PÉJ **politique-~** showbiz○ politics; **2** THÉÂT **dîner-~** dinner and floor show.

spectaculaire /spɛktakylɛʁ/ adj spectacular.

spectateur, -trice /spɛktatœʀ, tʀis/ nm,f **1** (au théâtre, cinéma) member of the audience; (dans un stade, la rue) spectator; **les ~s** (au théâtre) the audience (sg); (dans un stade, la rue) the spectators, the crowd (sg); **2** (curieux) onlooker; **assister à une réunion en ~** to sit in on a meeting.

spectral, ~e, mpl **-aux** /spɛktʀal, o/ adj **1** (de fantôme) LITER spectral, ghostly; **2** PHYS spectral.

spectre /spɛktʀ/ nm **1** (fantôme) ghost; **2** (de guerre, famine, mort) spectreGB (**de** of); **3** PHYS spectrum.

spectroscopie /spɛktʀɔskɔpi/ nf spectroscopy.

spéculateur, -trice /spekylatœʀ, tʀis/ nm,f speculator.

spéculatif, -ive /spekylatif, iv/ adj speculative.

spéculation /spekylasjɔ̃/ nf **1** FIN speculation; **~ sur** speculation in [actions, valeurs, or]; **2** GÉN, PHILOS speculation (**sur** on, about).

spéculer /spekyle/ [1] vi **1** FIN to speculate; **~ à la hausse/baisse** to bull/bear; **~ sur** to speculate in [valeurs, actions, or]; **2** PHILOS, GÉN to speculate (**sur** on, about).

spéléologie /speleɔlɔʒi/ nf **1** ▶329 (sport) potholing GB, caving, spelunking US; **2** (science) speleology.

spéléologue /speleɔlɔg/ nmf **1** (sportif) potholer GB, caver, spelunker US; **2** ▶374 (scientifique) speleologist SPÉC.

spermatozoïde /spɛʀmatozoid/ nm spermatozoon.

sperme /spɛʀm/ nm sperm.

spermicide /spɛʀmisid/ **I** adj (gelée) spermicidal.
II nm spermicide.

sphère /sfɛʀ/ nf **1** MATH sphere; **2** (domaine) sphere; **les hautes ~s de la finance** the higher echelons of finance.

sphérique /sferik/ adj spherical.

sphincter /sfɛ̃ktɛʀ/ nm sphincter.

sphinx /sfɛ̃ks/ nm inv **1** MYTHOL, ART Sphinx; **2** (papillon) hawkmoth.

spinal, ~e, mpl **-aux** /spinal, o/ adj spinal.

spirale /spiʀal/ nf **1** MATH spiral; **monter/descendre en ~** to spiral up/down; **2** (amplification) spiral; **la ~ des prix et des salaires** the wage-price spiral.

spire /spiʀ/ nf TECH, MATH turn.

spiritisme /spiʀitism/ nm spiritualism.

spiritualisme /spiʀitɥalism/ nm GÉN, PHILOS spiritualism.

spiritualité /spiʀitɥalite/ nf spirituality.

spirituel, -elle /spiʀitɥɛl/ adj **1** (de l'esprit) spiritual; **2** (amusant) witty.

spiritueux, -euse /spiʀitɥø, øz/ **I** adj [vin] with a high alcohol content.
II nm inv spirit; **vins et ~** wines and spirits.

spleen /splin/ nm spleen; **avoir le ~** to feel despondent.

splendeur /splɑ̃dœʀ/ nf (de paysage, site, jour) splendourGB; (d'époque, de règne) glory; **cette église est une ~** this church is truly magnificent.

splendide /splɑ̃did/ adj [objet, journée, victoire] splendid; [villa, pays] magnificent; [yeux, personne] stunning.

spoliation /spɔljasjɔ̃/ nf FML despoliation SOUT.

spolier /spɔlje/ [2] vtr FML to despoil SOUT (**de** of).

spongieux, -ieuse /spɔ̃ʒjø, øz/ adj spongy.

sponsoriser /spɔ̃sɔʀize/ [1] vtr to sponsor.

spontané, ~e /spɔ̃tane/ adj spontaneous; **candidature ~e** unsolicited application.

spontanéité /spɔ̃taneite/ nf spontaneity.

sporadique /spɔʀadik/ adj sporadic.

spore /spɔʀ/ nf spore.

sport /spɔʀ/ nm (activité générale) sport; (ensemble d'activités) sports (pl); **aimer le ~** to like sport; **vous faites du ~?** do you do any sports?; **je fais un peu de ~ tous les jours** I do some sport every day.
■ **~ automobile** motor sports (pl), car-racing; **~ cérébral** intellectual game; **~ de compétition** competitive sport; **~ d'équipe** team sport; **~ d'hiver** winter sport; **~ individuel** individual sport.
IDIOMES **ça c'est du ~!** this is no picnic○!; **il va y avoir du ~!** this is going to be fun ou interesting!; **faire qch pour le ~** to do sth for fun.

sportif, -ive /spɔʀtif, iv/ **I** adj **1** LIT [équipement, épreuve, journal, rencontre] sports (épith); **je ne suis pas ~** I'm not the sporty type; **2** FIG [allure] athletic, sporty○; **conduite sportive** AUT speeding; **3** (généreux) [personne, esprit, attitude] sporting; **faire preuve d'esprit ~** to be a good sport, to display sportsmanship.
II nm,f sportsman/sportswoman.

spot /spɔt/ nm **1** (pour éclairer) spotlight, spot; **2** (séquence) **~ (publicitaire)** commercial; **3** PHYS spot.

squale /skwal/ nm shark.

square /skwaʀ/ nm small public garden.

squash /skwaʃ/ ▶329 nm squash.

squatter /skwate/ [1], **squattériser** /skwateʀize/ [1] vtr to squat in [appartement]; to take over [escalier].

squelette /skɔlɛt/ nm **1** ANAT skeleton; **2**○ (personne maigre) bag of bones○, skeleton; **3** (de bateau) framework; **4** (d'une œuvre) outline.

squelettique /skɔletik/ adj [personne, jambes] scrawny; MÉD skeletal; FIG [arbre] skeletal; [rapport, article] sketchy.

stabilisateur, -trice /stabilizatœʀ, tʀis/ **I** adj stabilizing.
II nm stabilizer.

stabiliser /stabilize/ [1] **I** vtr to stabilize [prix, marché, monnaie, pays, personnes, véhicule, gaz]; to consolidate [accotements].
II se stabiliser vpr [chômage, prix, taux] to stabilize; [personne] to become stable.

stabilité /stabilite/ nf stability.

stable /stabl/ adj stable.

stade /stad/ nm **1** SPORT stadium; **2** (étape) stage; **les ~s de la production** the stages of production.

stage /staʒ/ nm **1** (pour obtenir diplôme, titre) professional training; **2** (pendant des études) work experience ¢; **3** (pour le travail, le sport, les loisirs) course; **suivre un ~** to go on a course; **~ de formation** training course.

stagiaire /staʒjɛʀ/ nmf GÉN trainee; (enseignant) student teacher; (infirmière) student nurse.

stagnation /stagnasjɔ̃/ nf LIT, FIG stagnation.

stagner /stagne/ [1] vi LIT, FIG to stagnate.

stalactite /stalaktit/ nf stalactite.

stalagmite /stalagmit/ nf stalagmite.

stalle /stal/ nf **1** (pour chevaux) stall; **2** (d'église) stall.

stand /stɑ̃d/ nm (d'exposition) stand; (de fête foraine) stall.
■ **~ de tir** (de club sportif) shooting range; (de fête foraine) shooting gallery.

standard /stɑ̃daʀ/ **I** adj inv standard.
II nm TÉLÉCOM switchboard.

standardisation /stɑ̃daʀdizasjɔ̃/ nf standardization.

standardiste /stɑ̃daʀdist/ ▶374 nmf switchboard operator.

standing /stɑ̃diŋ/ nm **1** (confort) **de (grand) ~**

[*appartement*] luxury (*épith*); **2** (niveau de vie) standard of living.

star /staʀ/ *nf* star.

starlette /staʀlɛt/ *nf* starlet.

starter /staʀtɛʀ/ *nm* AUT choke; **mettre le ~** to pull out the choke.

station /stasjɔ̃/ *nf* **1** (de métro) station; (de taxis) taxi-rank GB, taxi stand; **~ de métro** tube GB ou subway US station; **2** RADIO station; **~ de radio** radio station; **3** (lieu de séjour) resort; **~ balnéaire** seaside resort; **~ de sports d'hiver** winter sports resort; **~ thermale** spa; **4** (lieu d'observation scientifique) station; **~ météorologique** meteorological ou weather station; **~ orbitale** orbiting space station; **~ spatiale** space station; **5** (position) posture; **~ debout** ou **verticale** upright posture or position; **6** (pause) stop, pause; **7**○ AUT (station-service) service station; **~ de lavage** car wash.
■ **~ d'épuration** sewage treatment plant; **~ de travail** workstation.

stationnaire /stasjɔnɛʀ/ *adj* **1** [*planète, véhicule*] stationary; **2** [*situation, production*] stable; **être dans un état ~** [*malade*] to be in a stable condition.

stationnement /stasjɔnmɑ̃/ *nm* **1** AUT parking; **~ interdit** no parking; **~ payant** (dans la rue) metered parking; (dans un parking) pay and display parking; **~ à durée limitée** short-term parking; **'~ gênant'** 'no parking or waiting'; **une amende pour ~ gênant** a parking fine; **~ en épi** angle parking; **~ en bataille** perpendicular parking; **2** C AUT car park GB, parking lot US; **3** MIL (de troupes) stationing.

stationner /stasjɔne/ [1] *vi* **1** AUT to park; **~ en double file** to double-park; **2** MIL to station.

station-service, *pl* **stations-service** /stasjɔ̃sɛʀvis/ *nf* service station, filling station.

statique /statik/ *adj* static.

statistique /statistik/ **I** *adj* statistical.
II *nf* (méthode) statistics (+ *v sg*); (donnée) statistic.

statue /staty/ *nf* statue (**de** of).
IDIOMES **se changer en ~** to be frozen to the spot.

statuer /statɥe/ [1] *vi* to give a ruling (**sur** on).

statuette /statɥɛt/ *nf* statuette.

statu quo /statykwo/ *nm inv* status quo.

stature /statyʀ/ *nf* **1** LIT (gabarit) stature; (sur une étiquette de vêtements) height; **2** FIG (envergure) calibre GB.

statut /staty/ *nm* **1** (loi, règlement) statute; **2** (situation) status; **avoir un ~ d'immigrant** to have immigrant status.

statutaire /statytɛʀ/ *adj* statutory.

steak /stɛk/ *nm* steak.
■ **~ haché** (cru) minced beef GB, ground beef US; (cuit) hamburger.

stèle /stɛl/ *nf* stele.

sténo○ /steno/ ▶ **sténodactylo**.

sténodactylo /stenodaktilo/ **I** ▶374| *nmf* (personne) shorthand typist GB, stenographer US.
II *nf* (activité) shorthand typing GB, stenography US.

sténodactylographie /stenodaktilɔgʀafi/ *nf* shorthand typing GB, stenography US.

sténographier /stenɔgʀafje/ [2] *vtr* to take [sth] down in shorthand.

sténotypie /stenɔtipi/ *nf* stenotypy.

sténotypiste /stenɔtipist/ ▶374| *nmf* stenotypist.

stentor /stɑ̃tɔʀ/ *nm* **1** GÉN **voix de ~** stentorian voice; **2** ZOOL stentor.

steppe /stɛp/ *nf* steppe.

stère /stɛʀ/ ▶635| *nm* stere.

stéréo /steʀeo/ **I** *adj inv* (abbr = **stéréophonique**) stereo (*épith*).
II○ *nf* stereo.

stéréophonie /steʀeofɔni/ *nf* stereophony; **en ~** [*enregistrer*] in stereo; [*enregistrement*] stereophonic (*épith*).

stéréophonique /steʀeofɔnik/ *adj* stereophonic.

stéréotype /steʀeɔtip/ *nm* **1** (personne) stereotype; **2** (cliché) cliché.

stérile /steʀil/ *adj* **1** [*personne, animal, plante*] sterile; [*mariage*] childless; [*sol*] barren; **2** [*pansement, milieu*] sterile; **3** FIG [*artiste*] unproductive; [*imagination*] barren; [*discussion*] fruitless.

stérilet /steʀilɛ/ *nm* coil, intrauterine device SPÉC.

stériliser /steʀilize/ [1] *vtr* **1** LIT to sterilize [*personne, animal*]; to make [sth] barren [*sol*]; **2** FIG to stifle [*créativité, artiste*]; **3** (purifier) to sterilize [*biberon, appareil, bocal, pansement*].

stérilité /steʀilite/ *nf* **1** (de personne, d'animal) sterility; (de sol, région) barrenness; **2** FIG (d'artiste) lack of creativity; (de travail) fruitlessness; **3** (de milieu) sterility.

sterling /stɛʀliŋ/ *adj inv* sterling; **livre ~** pound sterling.

sternum /stɛʀnɔm/ *nm* breastbone, sternum SPÉC.

stéthoscope /stetɔskɔp/ *nm* stethoscope.

steward /stjuwaʀd/ *nm* steward.

stigmate /stigmat/ **I** *nm* **1** (trace sur la peau) scar; FIG (de vice, guerre) mark; **2** BOT, ZOOL stigma.
II stigmates *nmpl* RELIG stigmata.

stimulant, **~e** /stimylɑ̃, ɑ̃t/ **I** *adj* (physiquement) [*bain*] invigorating; [*air, climat*] bracing; (mentalement) stimulating.
II *nm* **1** (physique) (fortifiant) tonic; (excitant) stimulant; **2** (mental) stimulus.

stimulation /stimylasjɔ̃/ *nf* stimulation.

stimuler /stimyle/ [1] **I** *vtr* **1** to stimulate [*organe, fonction*]; **2** (motiver) to spur [sb] on.
II *vi* **1** [*air, froid*] to be bracing; **2**○ [*récompense*] to act as a spur.

stipuler /stipyle/ [1] *vtr* to stipulate (**que** that).

stock /stɔk/ *nm* LIT, FIG stock; **avoir des ~s de**○ FIG to have a whole stock of.

stockage /stɔkaʒ/ *nm* **1** (mise en réserve) COMM stocking; (accumulation excessive) stockpiling; **2** (conservation) COMM, ORDINAT storage.

stocker /stɔke/ [1] *vtr* **1** COMM to stock; (à l'excès) to stockpile; **2** ORDINAT to store [*données*].

stoïque /stɔik/ **I** *adj* stoical.
II *nmf* stoic.

stomacal, **~e**, *mpl* **-aux** /stɔmakal, o/ *adj* stomach.

stomatologie /stɔmatɔlɔʒi/ *nf* stomatology.

stop /stɔp/ **I** *nm* **1** AUT (panneau) stop sign; (feu arrière) brake light; **2**○ (auto-stop) hitching○; **faire la France en ~** to hitch○ round GB France; **prendre qn en ~** to give sb a lift GB ou ride US.
II *excl* stop!

stopper /stɔpe/ [1] **I** *vtr* **1** (arrêter) to stop [*personne, voiture, attaque*]; to halt [*maladie, évolution*]; **2** (en couture) to mend.
II *vi* to stop.

store /stɔʀ/ *nm* blind; (auvent) awning.

strabisme /stʀabism/ *nm* squint, strabismus SPÉC.

strapontin /stʀapɔ̃tɛ̃/ *nm* foldaway seat.

strass /stʀas/ *nm inv* (verroterie) paste.

stratagème /stʀataʒɛm/ *nm* stratagem.

strate /stʀat/ *nf* LIT, FIG stratum.

stratège /stʀatɛʒ/ *nm* strategist.

stratégie /stʀateʒi/ *nf* strategy.

stratégique /stʀateʒik/ *adj* strategic.

stratifié, **~e** /stʀatifje/ **I** *adj* **1** BIOL, SOCIOL stratified; **2** TECH laminated.
II *nm* (matériau) **du ~** laminate; **table en ~** laminated table.

stratosphère /stʀatɔsfɛʀ/ *nf* stratosphere.

stress /stʀɛs/ *nm inv* stress.

stressant, **~e** /stʀɛsɑ̃, ɑ̃t/ *adj* [*journée*] stressful; [*incident*] upsetting; [*perspective*] worrying.

stresser /stʀɛse/ [1] **I** *vtr* [*perspective*] to put [sb] on edge; [*travail*] to put [sb] under stress; **être stressé**

(tendu) to be stressed; (irritable) to be on edge; (sous pression) to be under stress.

II° *vi* to get worked up.

stretch /strɛtʃ/ *nm* stretch material.

strict, **~e** /strikt/ *adj* **1** (sévère) [*discipline, morale, professeur*] strict; **il est très ~ sur la propreté** he's very strict about cleanliness; **2** (complet) **au sens ~** in the strict sense of the word; **c'est la ~e vérité** it's the absolute truth; **le ~ nécessaire** what is strictly necessary; **3** (austère) [*tenue, robe*] severe, austere; [*coiffure*] severe.

stricto sensu /striktosɛ̃sy/ *loc adv* strictly speaking.

strident, **~e** /stridɑ̃, ɑ̃t/ *adj* **1** [*bruit*] piercing; [*voix*] strident; **2** LING strident.

strie /stri/ *nf* **1** (rayure) streak; **2** (sillon) GÉN groove; (de front, visage) furrow; ANAT, BIOL stria.

strié, **~e** /strije/ *adj* **1** (de couleur) streaked (**de** with); [*muscle*] striated; **2** (de sillons) [*roche*] striated; [*colonne*] fluted; [*coquille, tige*] grooved.

strier /strije/ [2] *vtr* **1** (de couleur) to streak (**de** with); **2** (faire des sillons) to make grooves in; **3** (en géologie) to striate.

strip-teaseur, **-euse** /striptizœr, øz/ ▶374 *nm,f* stripper.

stroboscope /stroboskop/ *nm* stroboscope.

strophe /strof/ *nf* **1** (de poème) stanza, verse; **2** (dans une tragédie grecque) strophe.

structural, **~e**, *mpl* **-aux** /stryktyral, o/ *adj* structural.

structuralisme /stryktyralism/ *nm* structuralism.

structure /stryktyr/ *nf* **1** (agencement) structure; **2** (organisme) organization; **~ d'accueil** shelter, refuge.

structuré, **~e** /stryktyre/ *adj* structured.

structurel, **-elle** /stryktyrɛl/ *adj* structural.

structurer /stryktyre/ [1] **I** *vtr* to structure.

II se structurer *vpr* to be structured.

stuc /styk/ *nm* stucco.

studieux, **-ieuse** /stydjø, øz/ *adj* [*élève*] studious; [*vacances*] study (*épith*); [*ambiance*] industrious.

studio /stydjo/ *nm* **1** (logement) studio flat GB, studio apartment US; **2** (atelier) studio; **3** CIN, RADIO, TV studio; **tourné en ~** filmed ou shot in the studio.

stupéfait, **~e** /stypefɛ, ɛt/ *adj* astounded, dumbfounded; **rester ~ de qch/d'apprendre** to be astounded at sth/to hear.

stupéfiant, **~e** /stypefjɑ̃, ɑ̃t/ **I** *adj* **1** (étonnant) stunning, astounding; **2** MÉD stupefying.

II *nm* (drogue) drug, narcotic.

stupéfier /stypefje/ [2] *vtr* **1** (étonner) to astound, to stun; **2** MÉD (hébéter) to stupefy.

stupeur /stypœr/ *nf* **1** (étonnement) astonishment; **2** MÉD (torpeur) stupor.

stupide /stypid/ *adj* stupid.

stupidité /stypidite/ *nf* **1** (caractère) stupidity; **2** (remarque) stupid remark.

style /stil/ *nm* **1** ART, LITTÉRAT, SPORT style; **~ de vie** lifestyle; **avoir du ~** to have style; **elle veut se donner le ~ Marilyn Monroe** she's trying to cultivate the Marilyn Monroe look; **c'est bien** (dans) **ton ~ de faire** it's typical of you to do; **elle est du ~ à passer une nuit blanche pour finir un article** she's the kind that would stay up all night to finish an article; **il m'a répondu qch du ~ 'on vous téléphonera'** he told me they'd phone me, or something like that; **2** (de mobilier) **meubles de ~** (anciens) period furniture; (copiés) reproduction period furniture; **3** LING speech form; **~ direct/indirect** direct/indirect ou reported speech; **4** (tige de cadran solaire) style; **5** BOT, ZOOL style.

styliser /stilize/ [1] *vtr* to stylize.

styliste /stilist/ *nmf* ▶374 (de mode) fashion designer.

stylistique /stilistik/ **I** *adj* stylistic.

II *nf* stylistics (+ *v sg*).

stylo /stilo/ *nm* pen.

■ **~** (**à**) **bille** ball-point pen; **~ à encre** fountain

pen; **~ feutre** felt-tip pen; **~** (**à**) **plume** = **~ à encre**.

su /sy/ *nm* **au ~ de qn** LITER to sb's knowledge; **au vu et au ~ de tous** openly, for all to see.

suaire /sɥɛr/ *nm* shroud.

suant, **~e** /sɥɑ̃, ɑ̃t/ *adj* **1** (qui sue) sweaty; **2**° (ennuyeux) deadly dull.

suave /sɥav/ *adj* LITER [*parfum, sourire*] sweet; [*coloris, regard*] soft; [*contours*] smooth; [*voix*] mellifluous; [*plaisir*] exquisite; [*personne, manière*] suave.

subalterne /sybaltɛrn/ **I** *adj* [*poste*] junior; [*rôle*] subordinate; (au théâtre) minor.

II *nmf* subordinate; MIL low-ranking officer.

subconscient, **~e** /sybkɔ̃sjɑ̃, ɑ̃t/ **I** *adj* subconscious.

II *nm* subconscious.

subdiviser /sybdivize/ [1] **I** *vtr* to subdivide (**en** into).

II se subdiviser *vpr* to be subdivided (**en** into).

subdivision /sybdivizjɔ̃/ *nf* subdivision.

subéquatorial, **~e**, *mpl* **-iaux** /sybekwatɔrjal, o/ *adj* subequatorial.

subir /sybir/ [3] *vtr* **1** (être victime de) to be subjected to [*mauvais traitements, violences, pressions*]; to suffer [*dégâts, discrimination, brimades*]; **faire ~ à qn** to subject sb to [*mauvais traitements*]; to inflict [sth] on sb [*défaite, pertes*]; **2** (être soumis à) to undergo, to be subjected to [*interrogatoire*]; to take [*examen scolaire*]; to have [*opération, examens médicaux*]; **~ l'influence de qn** to be under sb's influence; **3** (supporter) to put up with [*personne, épreuve*]; **4** (être l'objet de) to undergo [*changements*].

subit, **~e** /sybi, it/ *adj* sudden.

subitement /sybitmɑ̃/ *adv* suddenly, all of a sudden.

subjectif, **-ive** /sybʒɛktif, iv/ *adj* subjective.

subjectivité /sybʒɛktivite/ *nf* subjectivity.

subjonctif, **-ive** /sybʒɔ̃ktif, iv/ **I** *adj* subjunctive.

II *nm* subjunctive; **au ~** in the subjunctive.

subjuguer /sybʒyge/ [1] *vtr* **1** (séduire) to captivate, to enthral GB; **2** (asservir) LITER to subjugate.

sublime /syblim/ *adj* [*peinture, œuvre, acteur*] sublime; **~ de générosité** extraordinarily generous.

sublimer /syblime/ [1] *vtr*, *vi* to sublimate.

subliminal, **~e**, *mpl* **-aux** /sybliminal, o/ *adj* subliminal.

submerger /sybmɛrʒe/ [13] *vtr* **1** (inonder) LIT to submerge [*terre, récif*]; FIG to flood [*standard téléphonique, marché*] (**de** with); **2** (dominer) [*foule, ennemi, émotion*] to overwhelm [*personne, groupe*]; **3** (accabler) **~ qn de travail** to inundate sb with work.

submersible /sybmɛrsibl/ **I** *adj* **1** GÉOG [*terre*] liable to flooding (*après n*); **2** TECH [*machine, navire*] submersible.

II *nm* submersible.

submersion /sybmɛrsjɔ̃/ *nf* **1** AGRIC irrigation by flooding; **2** NAUT (de sous-marin) submersion; (naufrage) sinking.

subodorer /sybɔdɔre/ [1] *vtr* to detect [*piège*].

subordination /sybɔrdinasjɔ̃/ *nf* **1** (dépendance) subordination (**à** to); **2** LING subordination; **conjonction de ~** subordinating conjunction.

subordonné, **~e**[1] /sybɔrdɔne/ *nm,f* subordinate.

subordonnée[2] /sybɔrdɔne/ *nf* LING subordinate clause; **~ circonstancielle** adverbial clause.

subordonner /sybɔrdɔne/ [1] *vtr* **1** (dans une hiérarchie) **être subordonné à qn** [*soldat, fonctionnaire*] to be subordinate to sb; **2** (faire dépendre) **elle subordonne tout à son travail** everything else comes second to her job; **être subordonné à qch** [*réussite, réalisation*] to be subject to ou dependent on sth.

suborner /sybɔrne/ [1] *vtr* (corrompre) to bribe [*employé, garde*]; JUR to suborn [*témoin*].

subreptice /sybrɛptis/ *adj* surreptitious.

subside /sybsid/ *nm* (d'État, association) grant; (entre particuliers) allowance.

subsidiaire /sybzidjɛʀ/ *adj* [*moyens*] ancillary; [*motif*] subsidiary; **question ~** tiebreaker.

subsistance /sybzistɑ̃s/ *nf* (de personne) subsistence; (de plante) sustenance; (moyens de survie) (**moyens de**) **~** means of support, livelihood; **frais de ~** living expenses; **économie de ~** subsistence economy; **assurer la ~ de sa famille** to support one's family.

subsister /sybziste/ [1] **I** *vi* **1** (durer) [*crainte, trace*] to remain; **2** (survivre) [*personne, coutume*] to survive; **3** (subvenir à ses besoins) [*personne*] to subsist; **ça leur suffit à peine pour ~** it's barely enough for them to live on.
II *v impers* **il subsistera toujours un doute** a doubt will always remain.

substance /sypstɑ̃s/ *nf* substance; **en ~** in substance; **~s végétales** vegetable matter *¢*.

substantiel, -ielle /sypstɑ̃sjɛl/ *adj* **1** (nourrissant) [*repas*] substantial; FIG [*lecture*] solid; **2** (considérable) [*nombre, baisse*] substantial; [*progrès*] significant.

substantif, -ive /sypstɑ̃tif, iv/ **I** *adj* [*proposition*] noun; [*style*] nominal; [*emploi*] nominal, substantival.
II *nm* noun, substantive.

substantiver /sypstɑ̃tive/ [1] *vtr* to substantivize.

substituable /sypstitɥabl/ *adj* substitutable.

substituer /sypstitɥe/ [1] **I** *vtr* **1 ~ A à B** to substitute A for B; **2** JUR **~ un héritage** to entail an estate.
II se substituer *vpr* **se ~ à** [*personne*] (pour représenter) to deputize for, to stand in for [*personne, groupe*]; (pour remplacer) to take the place of [*personne*]; [*chose*] to take the place of, to replace [*chose*].

substitut /sypstity/ *nm* **1** (magistrat) deputy public prosecutor; **2** (remplacement) substitute (**de** for); **~ maternel** mother substitute.

substitution /sypstitysjɔ̃/ *nf* (remplacement) substitution (**de qn/qch à** of sb/sth for); **produit de ~ du sucre/café** sugar/coffee substitute.

subterfuge /syptɛʀfyʒ/ *nm* ploy, subterfuge *¢*.

subtil, ~e /syptil/ *adj* [*personne, argument, nuance, parfum*] subtle; [*négociateur, manœuvre*] skilful^{GB}.

subtiliser /syptilize/ [1] *vtr* (dérober) **~ qch à qn** to steal sth from sb.

subtilité /syptilite/ *nf* subtlety.

subvenir /sybvəniʀ/ [36] *vtr ind* **~ à** to meet [*dépenses, besoins*]; **~ aux besoins de sa famille** to provide for one's family.

subvention /sybvɑ̃sjɔ̃/ *nf* (allocation) grant; (pour que le public paie moins cher) subsidy.

subventionner /sybvɑ̃sjɔne/ [1] *vtr* to subsidize.

subversif, -ive /sybvɛʀsif, iv/ *adj* subversive.

subversion /sybvɛʀsjɔ̃/ *nf* subversion (**de** of).

suc /syk/ *nm* **1** LIT (de fruit, viande) juice; (de plante, fleur) sap; **2** FIG essence (**de** of).
■ **~s digestifs** or **gastriques** gastric juices.

succédané /syksedane/ *nm* LIT, FIG substitute, ersatz (**de** for); (en pharmacie) succedaneum.

succéder /syksede/ [14] **I succéder à** *vtr ind* **1** (remplacer) **~ à** [*personne*] to succeed [*personne*]; **~ à qn à la tête d'une entreprise** to succeed sb as head of a company; **2** (suivre) **~ à** [*chose*] to follow [*chose*].
II se succéder *vpr* (venir l'un après l'autre) [*personnes*] to succeed ou follow one another; [*choses*] to follow (one another); **les orages se succèdent sans interruption** there is storm after storm.

succès /syksɛ/ *nm inv* success; **une série de ~** a string of successes; **votre ~ aux élections/à l'école** your success in the elections/at school; **avoir du ~, être un ~** [*produit, livre, opération*] to be a success (**auprès de** with); [*disque, chanson*] to be a hit (**auprès de** with); **avoir du ~** [*artiste*] to be a success; **avoir du ~ auprès de qn** [*personne*] to be a hit with sb; **leur proposition n'a eu aucun ~** their proposal got nowhere; **connaître un grand ~** to be a great success; **faire le ~ de qn/qch** to make sb/sth successful; **à ~** [*acteur, pièce, film*] successful; **auteur à ~** best-selling author; **avec ~** successfully.

successeur /syksesœʀ/ *nm* successor.

successif, -ive /syksesif, iv/ *adj* successive.

succession /syksesjɔ̃/ *nf* **1** (série, suite) (de personnes, visiteurs) stream, succession; (d'événements) series (+ *v sg*), succession; (de jours, saisons) passage; (de nombres) series (+ *v sg*); (d'accidents, de malheurs) string, succession; **2** (transmission de pouvoir) succession; **prendre la ~ de** to succeed [*roi*]; to take over from [*ministre, directeur*]; **3** JUR (transmission) (de biens) succession; (de patrimoine) inheritance, estate.

succinct, ~e /syksɛ̃, ɛ̃t/ *adj* [*écrit*] succinct; [*discours*] brief.

succion /syksjɔ̃/ *nf* **1** (avec appareil) suction; **2** (avec la bouche) sucking.

succomber /sykɔ̃be/ [1] *vi* **1** (mourir) to die; **2** (fléchir) LITER to give way, to yield; **~ sous le poids** to collapse under the weight; **~ sous le nombre** to be overwhelmed by numbers; **3** (s'abandonner) **~ à** to succumb to [*charme, désespoir*]; to yield to [*tentation*].

succulent, ~e /sykylɑ̃, ɑ̃t/ *adj* **1** (savoureux) [*repas, cuisine, fruit*] delicious; **2** BOT **plante ~** succulent.

succursale /sykyʀsal/ *nf* branch, outlet.

sucer /syse/ [12] *vtr* to suck.

sucette /sysɛt/ *nf* **1** (bonbon) lollipop, lolly[○]; **2** (tétine) dummy GB, pacifier US.

suçoter /sysɔte/ [1] *vtr* to suck.

sucre /sykʀ/ *nm* **1** (substance) sugar; **je bois mon thé sans ~** I don't take sugar in my tea; **du chocolat noir sans ~** sugar-free dark chocolate; **2** (morceau) sugar lump; **combien de ~s dans ton café?** how many sugars in your coffee?
■ **~ blanc** white sugar; **~ brun** dark brown sugar; **~ de canne** cane sugar; **~ cristallisé** granulated sugar; **~ glace** icing sugar GB, powdered sugar US; **~ d'orge** (substance) barley sugar; (bâton) stick of barley sugar, **~ rock**; **~ en poudre** caster sugar GB, superfine sugar US; **~ roux** brown sugar; **~ vanillé** vanilla sugar.
IDIOMES **être tout ~ tout miel** to be all sweetness and light; **casser du ~ sur le dos de qn** to run sb down, to badmouth sb[○].

sucré, ~e /sykʀe/ **I** *adj* **1** LIT [*fruit, goût, vin, biscuit*] sweet; [*lait condensé, jus de fruit*] sweetened; **2** FIG [*ton*] honeyed.
II *nm* (aliments) sweet food; **je n'aime pas le ~** I don't like sweet things.

sucrer /sykʀe/ [1] *vtr* (rendre doux) [*personne*] to put sugar in [*café, compote*]; (en saupoudrant) to sprinkle sugar on [*fraises*]; [*miel, saccharine*] to sweeten.

sucrerie /sykʀəʀi/ **I** *nf* (usine) sugar refinery.
II sucreries *nfpl* sweets GB.

sucrier, -ière /sykʀije, ɛʀ/ **I** *adj* [*industrie*] sugar; [*région*] sugar-producing.
II *nm* (pot) sugar bowl; **~ verseur** sugar shaker.

sud /syd/ ► 457 **I** *adj inv* [*façade, versant, côté*] south; [*frontière, zone*] southern.
II *nm* **1** (point cardinal) south; **2** (région) south; **le ~ de la France** the south of France; **le ~ de l'Europe/du Japon** southern Europe/Japan; **3** GÉOG, POL **le Sud** the South; **du Sud** [*ville, accent*] southern.
■ **le Sud Viêt Nam** HIST South Vietnam.

sud-africain, ~e, *mpl* **~s** /sydafʀikɛ̃, ɛn/ ► 394 *adj* South African.

sudation /sydasjɔ̃/ *nf* sweating.

sud-coréen, -éenne, *mpl* **~s** /sydkɔʀeɛ̃, ɛn/ ► 394 *adj* South Korean.

sud-est /sydɛst/ ► 457 **I** *adj inv* [*façade, versant*] southeast; [*frontière, zone*] southeastern.
II *nm* southeast; **le Sud-Est asiatique** South East Asia.

sudiste /sydist/ *adj, nmf* HIST Confederate.

sud-ouest /sydwɛst/ ► 457 **I** *adj inv* [*façade, versant*] southwest; [*frontière, zone*] southwestern.
II *nm* southwest.

Suède /sɥɛd/ ► 232 *nprf* Sweden.

uédois, **~e** /sɥedwa, az/ ▶338|, 394| **I** *adj* Swedish.

II *nm* LING Swedish.

uédois, **~e** /sɥedwa, az/ ▶394| *nm,f* Swede.

uer /sɥe/ [1] **I** *vtr* **1** (exsuder) [*personne, peau*] to sweat; [*mur, roche*] to ooze [*eau, humidité*]; **~ sang et eau** FIG to sweat blood and tears (**pour faire** to do; **sur qch** over sth); **2** (dégager) [*personne*] to exude [*bêtise, ennui, misère*].

II *vi* to sweat (**sur** over); **~ à grosses gouttes** to sweat buckets; **faire ~ qn**○ (embêter) to bore sb stiff○ (**avec** with).

ueur /sɥœʀ/ *nf* sweat; **se mettre en ~** to break into a sweat; **j'en avais des ~s froides** I was in a cold sweat about it; **gagner son pain à la ~ de son front** to earn one's living by the sweat of one's brow; **il avait le dos en ~** his back was covered in sweat.

suffire /syfiʀ/ [64] **I** *vi* (être suffisant) [*somme, durée, quantité*] to be enough; **quelques gouttes suffisent** a few drops are enough; **ma retraite suffit à mes besoins** my pension is enough to cover my needs; **deux heures sufffisent amplement pour faire le trajet** two hours is ample time ou is easily enough for the journey; **un rien suffit à** or **pour le mettre en colère** it only takes the slightest thing to make him lose his temper.

II se suffire *vpr* **se ~ (à soi-même)** [*personne, pays*] to be self-sufficient; **le film se suffit à lui-même** the film speaks for itself.

III *v impers* **1** (être très simple) **il suffit de faire qch** all you have to do is do sth; **il suffit d'un coup de téléphone pour annuler son abonnement** it only takes one phone call to cancel your subscription; **2** (être suffisant) **il suffit d'une lampe pour éclairer la pièce** one lamp is enough to light the room; **il suffit d'une seconde d'inattention pour qu'un accident se produise** it only takes a second's carelessness to cause an accident; **3** (notion de cause à effet) **il suffit que je sorte sans parapluie pour qu'il pleuve!** every time I go out without my umbrella, it's guaranteed to rain; **4** (être satisfaisant) **ça suffit (comme ça)!**, **il suffit†!** that's enough!; **il ne leur a pas suffi de nous cambrioler, il a fallu qu'ils saccagent la maison** they weren't satisfied with burgling GB ou burglarizing US us, they had to wreck the house as well.

IDIOMES **à chaque jour suffit sa peine** PROV sufficient unto the day (is the evil thereof).

suffisamment /syfizamã/ *adv* enough; **~ intelligent pour** intelligent enough to; **nous avons ~ marché** we've walked enough; **il n'a pas ~ d'argent pour faire** he doesn't have enough money to do.

suffisance /syfizãs/ *nf* (vanité) self-importance, arrogance; **il est plein de ~** he's very self-important.

suffisant, **~e** /syfizã, ãt/ *adj* **1** (adéquat) sufficient; **deux heures, c'est ~ pour faire le trajet** two hours is enough for the journey; **l'éclairage n'est pas ~** the lighting is inadequate; **2** (vaniteux) [*personne, ton, air*] self-important.

suffixe /syfiks/ *nm* suffix.

suffocant, **~e** /syfɔkã, ãt/ *adj* **1** (étouffant) [*chaleur, atmosphère*] suffocating; **2** (stupéfiant) staggering.

suffocation /syfɔkasjɔ̃/ *nf* (action) suffocation; (sensation) suffocating feeling; **crise de ~** fit of choking.

suffoquer /syfɔke/ [1] **I** *vtr* **1** (étouffer) [*chaleur, fumée*] to suffocate; **2**○ (stupéfier) **son aplomb m'a suffoqué** I was staggered by his/her cheek○.

II *vi* **1** (étouffer) to suffocate; **on suffoque ici** it's suffocating in here; **2** (s'étrangler) to choke (**de** with).

suffrage /syfʀaʒ/ *nm* **1** POL (système) suffrage; **~ universel** universal suffrage; **2** POL (voix) vote; **~s exprimés** recorded votes; **remporter peu de ~s** to receive few votes; **3** FIG (approbation) approval ¢; **recueillir tous les ~s** to meet with universal approval.

suggérer /sygʒeʀe/ [14] *vtr* to suggest (**à** to); **je suggère qu'on s'en aille** I suggest (that) we leave; **elle a suggéré à la commission de modifier le projet** she suggested to the commission that they should modify the project.

suggestif, **-ive** /sygʒɛstif, iv/ *adj* [*texte*] evocative; [*pose, photos*] suggestive; [*décolleté*] provocative.

suggestion /sygʒɛstjɔ̃/ *nf* suggestion.

suicidaire /sɥisidɛʀ/ **I** *adj* LIT, FIG suicidal.

II *nmf* person with suicidal tendencies.

suicide /sɥisid/ *nm* LIT, FIG suicide; **c'est du** or **un ~** FIG it's suicide.

suicider: **se suicider** /sɥiside/ [1] *vpr* to commit suicide.

suie /sɥi/ *nf* soot.

suif /sɥif/ *nm* **1** (de chandelle) tallow; **2** CULIN suet.

suinter /sɥɛte/ [1] *vi* **1** [*eau*] to seep (**de** through); [*sang, sève*] to ooze (**de** from); **2** [*mur*] to sweat; [*plaie*] to weep.

suisse /sɥis/ **I** ▶394| *adj* Swiss; **~ allemand** Swiss German; **~ romand** French-speaking Swiss, of French-speaking Switzerland; **~ italien** Italian-speaking Swiss, of Italian-speaking Switzerland.

II *nm* **1** (au Vatican) Swiss Guard; **2** (d'église) verger.

IDIOMES **manger/boire en ~** to eat/drink alone.

Suisse /sɥis/ **I** ▶394| *nm,f* (habitant) Swiss; **~ allemand** Swiss German; **~ romand** French-speaking Swiss.

II ▶232| *nprf* Switzerland; **~ allemande/romande/italienne** German-speaking/French-speaking/Italian-speaking Switzerland.

suite /sɥit/ **I** *nf* **1** (reste) rest; **je te raconterai la ~ plus tard** I'll tell you the rest later; **la ~ des événements** (à venir) what happens next; (déjà survenue) what happened next; **lis la ~ pour comprendre** read on and you'll understand; **2** (partie suivante) (de récit) continuation; (de feuilleton) next instalment GB; (de repas) next course; **~ page 10/au prochain numéro** continued on page 10/in the next issue; **3** (nouveau film, roman) sequel (**à, de** to); (émission, article de suivi) follow-up (**à, de** to); **4** (résultat) result; **les ~s** (d'acte, de décision) the consequences; (d'affaire, incident) the repercussions; (de maladie, d'opération) the after-effects; **mourir des ~s d'une chute** to die as a result of a fall; **5** (réponse produite) **donner ~ à** to follow up [*plainte, affaire*]; to pursue [*projet*]; to act on [*requête*]; to respond to [*lettre*]; COMM to deal with [*commande*]; **ne pas donner ~ à une lettre** to fail to respond to a letter; **rester sans ~** [*demande*] not to be followed up; [*projet*] to be dropped; **6** (indiquant la position) **faire ~ à** to follow on from [*paragraphe*]; to follow upon [*incident*]; **la pièce qui fait ~ au bureau** the room which leads off the study; **prendre la ~ de qn** to take over from sb; **7** (cohérence) coherence; **avoir de la ~ dans les idées** (savoir ce que l'on veut) to be single-minded; (être entêté) IRON not to be easily deterred; **8** (série) (de sommets, d'incidents) series (+ *v sg*); (de malheurs) string, series (+ *v sg*); (de succès) run; **9** (dans un hôtel) suite; **10** (entourage) suite; **11** MATH series (+ *v sg*); **12** MUS suite; **13** LING string; **14** JEUX (aux cartes) run.

II de suite *loc adv* **1** (d'affilée) in succession, in a row; **il a plu trois jours de ~** it rained for three days running; **dormir dix heures de ~** to sleep for ten hours solid; **sur dix pages de ~** over ten consecutive pages; **et ainsi de ~** and so on; **2** (immédiatement) straight ou right away.

III par la suite *loc adv* (après) afterwards; (plus tard) later.

IV par suite *loc adv* consequently, as a result.

V par suite de *loc prép* due to; **par ~ d'encombrement, votre appel ne peut aboutir** all lines are engaged GB ou busy, please try later.

VI à la suite de *loc prép* **1** (en conséquence, après) following; **2** (derrière) behind; **à la ~ les uns des autres, l'un à la ~ de l'autre** one behind the other; **entraîner qn à sa ~** (derrière soi) to drag sb along behind one; (dans une chute) LIT, FIG to drag sb down with one.

VII suite à *loc prép* **~ à ma lettre** further to my letter; **~ à votre lettre** with reference to your letter.

suivant[1] /sɥivã/ **I** *prép* **1** (le long de) along [*axe, pointillé*]; **2** (conformément à) in accordance with

[*coutume, rituel*]; ~ **leur habitude** (au présent) as they usually do; (au passé) as they usually did; **3** (en fonction de) depending on [*temps, compétence, circonstances*]; **4** (selon) according to; ~ **le plan/leurs instructions** according to the map/their instructions.
II suivant que *loc conj* depending on whether.

suivant², ~**e¹** /sɥivɑ̃, ɑ̃t/ **I** *adj* **1** (ci-après) following; **de la manière** or **façon** ~**e** in the following manner; **2** (d'après) (dans le temps) following, next; (dans une série) next; **voir le chapitre** ~ see next chapter.
II *nm,f* **le** ~ (dans le temps) the following one, the next one; (dans une série) the next one; (**au**) ~**!** next!; **pas ce lundi, le** ~ not this Monday, the one after.
III le suivant, la suivante *loc adj* as follows (*jamais épith*); **la situation est la** ~**e** the situation is as follows.

suivante² /sɥivɑ̃t/ *nf* **1** THÉÂT, LITTÉRAT lady's maid; **2**† (dame de compagnie) companion.

suivi, ~**e** /sɥivi/ **I** *pp* ▶ **suivre**.
II *pp adj* **1** (maintenu) [*travail, demande*] steady; [*effort*] sustained; [*correspondance*] regular; [*habitudes*] regular; [*qualité*] consistent; [*relations*] close; **2** COMM [*article*] in general production (*après n*), that is always in stock (*épith, après n*); **3** (apprécié) **la boxe est le sport le plus** ~ boxing is the most popular sport; **quelle est l'émission la plus** ~**e?** which is the most popular programme GB?; **c'est une mode peu** ~**e** it's a fashion which hasn't really caught on; **4** (cohérent) [*politique*] consistent; [*argumentation*] coherent.
III *nm* (de procédure) monitoring; COMM (de commande) follow-up; **le** ~ **des malades** follow-up care for patients; **assurer le** ~ **des jeunes délinquants** to follow up (on) young delinquents; **assurer le** ~ **d'un produit** COMM to ensure the continued supply of a product.

suivre /sɥivʀ/ [62] **I** *vtr* **1** (aller derrière) to follow [*personne, voiture*]; (accompagner) to accompany [*personne*]; **faire** ~ **qn** to have sb followed; ~ **qn dans le jardin** to follow sb into the garden GB ou yard US; ~ **qn de près/de loin** LIT to follow sb closely/at a distance; ~ **de très près la voiture de tête** to be right behind the leading car; **il est mort en juin, et elle l'a suivi de près** he died in June and she followed not long after; **ta réputation t'a suivi jusqu'ici** your reputation has preceded you; **suivez le guide!** this way, please!; **2** (se situer après) to follow, to come after [*période, incident, dynastie*]; (succéder à) to follow; (résulter de) to follow; **le jour qui suivit** the next ou following day; **lis ce qui suit** read on; **'à** ~**'** 'to be continued'; **3** (aller selon) [*personne*] to follow [*flèche, sentier, itinéraire*]; [*police, chien*] to follow [*piste*]; [*bateau, route*] to follow, to hug [*côte*]; [*route*] to run alongside [*voie ferrée*]; **indiquer (à qn) la route à** ~ to give (sb) directions; **quelle est la marche à** ~**?** FIG what is the best way to go about it?; ~ **le droit chemin** FIG to keep to the straight and narrow; **lire en suivant (les lignes) du doigt dans son livre** to read with a finger under the line; **4** (se conformer à) to follow [*coutume, exemple, instinct*]; to obey [*caprice, impulsion*]; **décider de** ~ **un régime** to decide to go on a diet; **5** (être attentif à) to follow [*leçon, match, procès*]; to follow the progress of [*élève, malade*]; ~ **l'actualité** to keep up with the news; **c'est une affaire à** ~ it's something worth watching; **être suivi** or **se faire** ~ **par un spécialiste** MÉD to be treated by a specialist; **elle ne suit jamais en classe** she never pays attention in class; **un de nos collègues, suivez mon regard**° HUM one of our colleagues, not mentioning any names; **6** (assister à) ~ **un cours de cuisine** to do a cookery GB ou cooking US course; **7** (comprendre) to follow [*explication, raisonnement*]; **je vous suis** I'm with you; **8** FIG (ne pas se laisser distancer) to keep pace with [*personne*]; **tu vas trop vite, je ne peux pas (te)** ~ you're going too fast, I can't keep up; **les prix augmentent, mais les salaires ne suivent pas** prices are going up but wages are

not keeping pace; **9** COMM ~ **un article** to keep a lin[e] in stock; **10** SPORT to follow [sth] through [*ballon*].
II *vi* **1** POSTES **faire** ~ **son courrier** to have one's mai[l] forwarded; (**prière de**) **faire** ~ please forward; **2** JEUX (au poker) **je suis** I'm in.
III se suivre *vpr* **1** (être placés dans un ordre) [*numéros, pages*] to be in order; JEUX [*cartes*] to be consecu[tive]; **2** (se succéder) [*incidents*] to happen one after th[e] other; **les deux frères se suivent de près** the tw[o] brothers are close in age.
IV *v impers* **il suit** it follows (**de** from); **comme sui[t]** as follows.

sujet, -ette /syʒɛ, ɛt/ **I** *adj* **être** ~ **à** to be prone t[o] [*rhumes, migraine, vertige, accès de colère*]; ~ **[à]** **caution** [*information, témoignage*] questionable.
II *nm* **1** (question) subject; **traiter un** ~ to deal wit[h] a subject; **un** ~ **de conversation** a topic of conversa[-]tion; **leur vieille voiture est un** ~ **de plaisanteri[e]** **pour leurs amis** their friends joke about their old car; **un** ~ **d'actualité** a topical issue; **je n'ai rien à dire [à] ce** ~ I've nothing to say on that subject ou matter; **c'est à quel** ~**?** what is it about?; **au** ~ **[de]** about; **2** (thème) subject; **3** SCOL, UNIV question; **un** ~ **d'examen** an exam question ; **quel est ton** ~ **d[e] thèse ?** what's your thesis on?; **hors** ~ off th[e] subject; **4** (raison) cause; **c'est un** ~ **d'étonnemen[t]** it is amazing; **5** (individu) **les** ~**s qui se son[t] soumis au test médical** those who have had the me[d]ical; **c'est un brillant** ~ (étudiant) he's a brillian[t] student; **6** LING, PHILOS subject; **7** (ressortissant d'u[n] royaume) subject; **8** (d'expérience scientifique) subject.

sujétion /syʒesjɔ̃/ *nf* **1** (servitude) subjection (**à** to); **être tenu en** ~ to be held in subjection; **[2]** (contrainte) constraint.

sulfate /sylfat/ *nm* sulphate GB.

sulfite /sylfit/ *nm* sulphite GB.

sulfure /sylfyʀ/ *nm* **1** CHIMIE sulphide GB; **2** ART (en verr[e]rie) sulphide GB; (presse-papier) glass paperweight.

sulfuré, ~**e** /sylfyʀe/ *adj* sulphurated GB; **hydrogèn[e]** ~ hydrogen sulphide GB.

sulfureux, -euse /sylfyʀø, øz/ *adj* **1** CHIMIE [*ea[u], vapeur*] sulphurous GB; [*bain, source*] sulphur[e] (*épith*); [*odeur*] like sulphur GB (*après n*); **2** FIG [*personne, réputation, charme*] fiendish.

sulfurisé, ~**e** /sylfyʀize/ *adj* **papier** ~ greaseproo[f] paper.

sultan /syltɑ̃/ *nm* sultan.

summum /sɔm(m)ɔm/ *nm* height.

sumo /sumo, symo/ ▶ **329**⌡ *nm inv* sumo wrestling.

super¹ /sypɛʀ/ *préf* super.

super² /sypɛʀ/ **I**° *adj inv* great°.
II *nm* (essence) four-star (petrol) GB, super, hig[h] octane gasoline US.
III° *excl* great°!

superbe /sypɛʀb/ **I** *adj* [*fleurs, spectacle*] superb; [*pe[r]sonne*] superb-looking (*épith*); [*ville, pays*] magni[fi]cent.
II *nf* LITER haughtiness.

superbement /sypɛʀbəmɑ̃/ *adv* GÉN [*décorer, cuisine[r]*] superbly; [*ignorer*] haughtily.

supercarburant /sypɛʀkaʀbyʀɑ̃/ *nm* four-star high-octane petrol GB, super, high-octane gasoline US.

supercherie /sypɛʀʃəʀi/ *nf* **1** (tromperie) deceptio[n]; **2** (acte) hoax, act of deception; (faux) fake.

supérette /sypeʀɛt/ *nf* minimarket, superette US.

superficie /sypɛʀfisi/ *nf* **1** (aire) (de terrain, pays) area; (de pièce, bâtiment) floor area; **la** ~ **de la Terr[e]** the surface area of the Earth; **2** (aspect) superficie[s]; **en** ~ FIG superficially.

superficiel, -ielle /sypɛʀfisjɛl/ *adj* **1** LIT [*couch[e]*] surface (*épith*); [*blessure*] superficial; **2** FIG superf[i]cial, shallow.

superflu, ~**e** /sypɛʀfly/ **I** *adj* (de trop) superfluou[s], (inutile) unnecessary.
II *nm* (excédent) surplus; **s'offrir le** ~ to trea[t] oneself to luxuries.

La superficie

*Pour la prononciation des nombres, voir **les nombres** ▶ 399*.

Équivalences

1 sq in = 6,45 cm^2	1 acre = 40,47 ares *ou* 0,40 ha
1 sq ft = 929,03 cm^2	1 sq ml = 2,59 km^2
1 sq yd = 0,84 m^2	

dire			dire
one square centimetre	1 cm^2 = 0.15 sq in		square inches
one square metre	1 m^2 = 10.76 sq ft		square feet
		1.19 sq yds	square yards
one square kilometre	1 km^2 = 0.38 sq mls		square miles
one are	1 are = 119.6 sq yds		
one hectare	1 hectare = 2.47 acres		acres

Pour l'écriture, noter:
– *l'anglais utilise un point là où le français a une virgule:*
 0,15 *s'écrit* 0.15, *etc.*
– *on écrit* -metre *en anglais britannique et* -meter *en anglais américain.*
– *on peut écrire* sq in *ou* in^2, sq ft *ou* ft^2, *etc.*

il y a 10 000 centimètres carrés dans un mètre carré	= there are 10,000 square centimetres in a square metre
10 000 centimètres carrés font un mètre carré	= 10,000 square centimetres make one square metre

quelle est la superficie du jardin?	= what is the area of the garden? *ou* how big is the garden?
combien mesure le jardin?	= what size is the garden? *ou* what does the garden measure?
il fait 12 m^2	= it is 12 square metres
sa surface est de 12 m^2	= its area is 12 square metres
il a une surface de 12 m^2	= it is 12 square metres *ou* it is 12 square metres in area
il fait 20 m sur 10 m	= it is 20 metres by 10 metres
il fait à peu près 200 m^2	= it is about 200 square metres
presque 200 m^2	= almost 200 square metres
plus de 200 m^2	= more than 200 square metres
moins de 200 m^2	= less than 200 square metres
la superficie de A est égale à celle de B	
A et B ont la même surface	= A is the same area as B = A and B are the same area

Noter l'ordre des mots dans l'adjectif composé anglais, et l'utilisation du trait d'union. Noter aussi que metre, *employé comme adjectif, ne prend pas la marque du pluriel.*

un jardin de 200 m^2	= a 200-square-metre garden

On peut aussi dire: a garden 200 square metres in area.

6 mètres carrés de soie vendu au mètre carré	= six square metres of silk = sold by the square metre

supérieur, ~e /syperjœr/ **I** *adj* **1** (situé en haut dans l'espace) [*mâchoire, membre, lèvre*] upper; [*niveau, étage*] upper, top; **dans le coin ~ droit** in the top right-hand corner; **2** (dans une hiérarchie) [*grades, classes sociales*] upper; **il a été promu au rang ~** he was promoted to the next rank up; **3** (en valeur) [*vitesse, coût, salaire, nombre*] higher (**à** than); [*taille, dimensions*] bigger (**à** than); [*durée*] longer (**à** than); **mes notes sont ~es à la moyenne** my marks are above average; **être ~ en nombre** to be greater in number; **si a est ~ à b** if a is greater than b; **température ~e à 20°** temperature above 20°; **4** (de meilleure qualité) [*travail, qualité*] superior (**à** to); **leur ennemi leur était ~** their enemy was better than them; **5** (hautain) [*air, ton, sourire*] superior.
II *nm,f* **1** (chef) superior; **mon ~ hiérarchique** my immediate superior; **2** RELIG Superior.
III *nm* UNIV higher education.

supérieurement /syperjœrmɑ̃/ *adv* exceptionally.

supériorité /syperjɔrite/ *nf* superiority; **avoir un sentiment de ~** to feel superior.

superlatif, -ive /syperlatif, iv/ **I** *adj* superlative.
II *nm* superlative.

supermarché /sypermarʃe/ *nm* supermarket.

superposable /syperpozabl/ *adj* stackable.

superposer /syperpoze/ [1] *vtr* **1** (l'un sur l'autre) to stack (up) [*casiers, tabourets, caisses, briques, matelas*]; **des lits superposés** bunk beds; **2** (faire coïncider) to superimpose [*dessins, formes*] (**à** on (top of)); to juxtapose [*approches, théories*] (**à** with).

superproduction /syperprodyksjɔ̃/ *nf* CIN blockbuster○.

superpuissance /syperpɥisɑ̃s/ *nf* superpower.

supersonique /sypersonik/ *adj* supersonic.

superstitieux, -ieuse /syperstisjø, øz/ *adj* superstitious.

superstition /syperstisjɔ̃/ *nf* superstition.
IDIOMES **la ~ est fille de l'ignorance** PROV superstition is born of ignorance.

superviser /sypervize/ [1] *vtr* to supervise.

supplanter /syplɑ̃te/ [1] *vtr* to supplant (**dans** in).

suppléance /sypleɑ̃s/ *nf* GÉN temporary replacement post; SCOL supply GB *ou* substitute US post; **être chargé d'une ~** GÉN to fill in for sb.

suppléant, ~e /sypleɑ̃, ɑ̃t/ *nm,f* GÉN replacement; (de juge) deputy; (d'enseignant) supply GB *ou* substitute

US teacher; (de médecin) stand-in (doctor); **un poste de ~** GÉN temporary replacement post; SCOL supply GB ou substitute US post.

suppléer /syplee/ [11] *vtr ind* **~ à** to make up for, to compensate for.

supplément /syplemɑ̃/ *nm* **1** (somme d'argent) GÉN extra ou additional charge; (en voyage, à l'hôtel) supplement; **il y a un ~ à payer pour l'excédent de bagages** you have to pay a supplement ou you have to pay extra for excess baggage; **le vin est en ~** the wine is extra; **2** (complément) **~ d'informations** additional information; **3** (magazine) supplement (**à** to).

supplémentaire /syplemɑ̃ter/ *adj* additional, extra; **un obstacle ~** another obstacle; **un délai ~** another extension of the deadline; **train ~** relief train.

suppliant, ~e /syplijɑ̃, ɑ̃t/ *adj* [*voix*] pleading; [*air, regard*] imploring.

supplication /syplikasjɔ̃/ *nf* **1** GÉN plea; **2** RELIG supplication.

supplice /syplis/ *nm* torture; **les ~s au Moyen Âge** forms of torture in the Middle Ages; **subir un ~** LIT to be tortured; FIG to be in torment; **mettre qn au ~** FIG to torture sb; **j'étais au ~** FIG it was agony.

supplicié, ~e /syplisje/ *nm,f* torture victim.

supplicier /syplisje/ [2] *vtr* (torturer) to torture; (exécuter) to execute.

supplier /syplije/ [2] *vtr* to beg, to beseech (**de faire** to do).

supplique /syplik/ *nf* LITER petition; **présenter** or **adresser une ~ à qn** to petition sb; **céder aux ~s de qn** to give in to sb's entreaties.

support /sypor/ *nm* **1** (soutien) support; **servir de ~ à qch** to serve as a support for sth; **2** (objet) (pour des bibelots) stand; (pour des tubes à essai) rack; **3** (aide) back-up; **utiliser des diapositives comme ~** to use slides as backup material; **~ audiovisuel** audiovisual aid; **4** ART support.

supportable /syportabl/ *adj* bearable.

supporter¹ /syporte/ [1] **I** *vtr* **1** (soutenir) [*structure, colonne, pilier*] to support, to bear the weight of [*toiture, édifice*]; **2** (prendre en charge) to bear [*frais, dépenses*]; **3** (endurer) to put up with, to endure [*privations, malheur*]; to put up with [*personne, attitude, sarcasme*]; to bear, to endure [*souffrance, solitude*]; [*plante*] to withstand [*froid, chaleur*]; **elle ne supporte pas d'attendre/la vue du sang** she can't stand waiting/the sight of blood; **il a mal supporté tes critiques** he found your criticisms hard to take; **elle supporte bien la chaleur** she can take ou stand the heat; **il a bien supporté son opération** he came through the operation well; **il a bien supporté le voyage** he stood the journey well; **il ne supporterait pas le voyage** the journey would be too much for him.

II se supporter *vpr* **ils ne peuvent plus se ~** they can't stand each other any more.

supporter[2] /sypɔʀtœʀ/ *nmf* supporter.

supposer /sypoze/ [1] *vtr* **1** (comme base d'un raisonnement) GÉN to suppose; MATH, PHILOS to postulate; **en supposant** or **à ~ que** supposing (that); **la chaleur est supposée constante** the heat is taken to be constant; **2** (tenir pour probable) to assume; **on peut ~ que** we can assume that; **3** (impliquer) to presuppose; **cela suppose que** this presupposes that.

supposition /sypozisjɔ̃/ *nf* supposition, assumption.

suppositoire /sypozitwaʀ/ *nm* suppository.

suppôt /sypo/ *nm* LITER PEJ **le ~ du dictateur** the dictator's henchman; **un dangereux ~ de la subversion/réaction** a dangerous subversive/reactionary.

■ **~ de Satan** or **du diable** fiend.

suppression /sypʀesjɔ̃/ *nf* (d'impôt) abolition; (de droit) revocation; (de sanction, contrôle) lifting; (d'avantages) withdrawal; (de preuves, faits) suppression; (de chômage, défauts) elimination; (de monopole) breaking; (de mot, ligne) deletion; **la ~ du train de 8 heures 50** the discontinuation of the 8.50 service; **~s d'emplois** job cuts; **il y a eu 20 ~s de postes** 20 posts have gone.

supprimer /sypʀime/ [1] **I** *vtr* **1** to cut [*emploi, poste*]; to stop [*aide, vibration*]; to abolish [*impôt, rationnement, institution*]; to lift [*sanction, restriction*]; to lift, to abolish [*contrôle, censure*]; to remove [*effet, cause, obstacle, mur*]; to do away with [*examen, classe*]; to put an end to [*pauvreté*]; to withdraw [*avantage, subvention*]; to break, to end [*monopole*]; to eliminate [*nuisance, défaut*]; to repeal [*loi*]; to cease to allow [*dérogation*]; to cut off [*argent de poche*]; to cut out [*sucre, sel*]; to delete [*mot, ligne*]; to take [sth] away [*liberté*]; **~ un train** (annuler) to cancel a train; (définitivement) to discontinue a service; **2** (tuer) EUPH to eliminate.

II se supprimer *vpr* (se suicider) to do away with oneself.

suppurer /sypyʀe/ [1] *vi* to suppurate.

supputer /sypyte/ LITER [1] *vtr* to calculate, to work out (que that); **~ ses chances de réussite** to weigh up one's chances of success.

supranational, **~e**, *mpl* **-aux** /sypʀanasjɔnal, o/ *adj* supranational.

suprématie /sypʀemasi/ *nf* supremacy (**sur** over).

suprême /sypʀɛm/ **I** *adj* **1** (le plus élevé) [*fonction, autorité*] supreme; **2** (très grand) [*élégance, habileté*] supreme; [*insolence*] ultimate.

II *nm* CULIN **~ de foie gras** goose or duck liver pâté.

suprêmement /sypʀɛmmɑ̃/ *adv* supremely.

sur[1] /syʀ/ *prép*

■ **Note** Lorsque *sur* indique une position dans l'espace il se traduit généralement par *on*: *sur la table/une chaise* = on the table/a chair; *sur la côte/le lac* = on the coast/the lake.

– On trouvera ci-dessous exemples supplémentaires et exceptions.

– Lorsque *sur* a une valeur figurée comme dans *régner sur, pleurer sur, sur l'honneur, sur place* etc la traduction sera fournie dans l'article du deuxième élément, respectivement *régner, pleurer, honneur, place* etc.

1 (dessus) on; **prends un verre ~ la table** take a glass from the table; **applique la lotion ~ vos cheveux** apply the lotion to your hair; **la clé est ~ la porte** the key is in the door; **passer la main ~ une étoffe** to run one's hand over a fabric; **2** (audessus, sans contact) over; **un pont ~ la rivière** a bridge across ou over the river; **3** (étendue, surface) over; **150 hectares ~** over an area of 150 hectares; **une table**

d'un mètre ~ deux a table that measures one metr by two; **4** (direction) **se diriger ~ Valence** to hea for Valence; **une voiture déboucha ~ la droite** car pulled out on the right; **5** (support matériel) or **écrire ~ du papier** to write on paper; **elle est ~ l photo** she's in the photograph; **dessiner ~ le sabl** to draw in the sand; **6** (au sujet de) [*débat, thèse*] about [*étude, poème*] about; **7** (objet d'un travail) **être ~ un affaire** to be involved in a business deal; **8** (indique u rapport de proportion) **une personne ~ dix** one perso out of ou in ten; **une semaine ~ trois** one week i three; **un mardi ~ deux** every other Tuesday **9** (indique l'accumulation) LIT upon; FIG after; **faire propo sition ~ proposition** to make one offer after another **10** (juste après) **ils se sont quittés ~ ces mots** wit these words, they parted; **~ le moment** at the time **~ ce** or **quoi** upon which; **~ ce, je vous laisse** wit that, I must leave you; **11** (pendant) **on ne peut pa juger ~ une période aussi courte** you can't judg over ou in such a short period **12** RADIO, TV, TÉLÉCOM o [*radio, chaîne, ligne téléphonique*].

sur[2], **~e** /syʀ/ *adj* (aigre) (slightly) sour.

sûr, **~e** /syʀ/ **I** *adj* **1** (fiable) [*information, service* reliable; [*personne*] reliable; [*avis, base, investissemen* sound; **avoir la main ~e** to have a steady hand **2** (sans danger) safe; **le voleur a été mis en lieu ~** EUPH the thief has been put in prison; **le plus ~ est de faire** the safest thing is to do; **peu ~** unsafe; **3** (ga ranti) certain; **une chose est ~e, tu t'es fai avoir**○ one thing's certain ou for sure, you've been had○; **ce n'est pas si ~** it's not that certain, wouldn't be so sure; **c'est ~ et certain** it's definite à coup ~** definitely, for sure; **la victoire est ~e** victory is assured; **4** (convaincu) sure; **j'en suis ~ e certain** I'm positive (about it); **il est ~ de lui** (qua lité) he's self-confident; (ponctuellement) he's sure of it; **être ~ de ses possibilités** to be confident of one's abilities; **être ~ de qn** to trust sb; **j'en étais ~!** I knew it!

II *adv* (sûrement) **bien ~** (que oui) of course; **bien ~ que non** of course not.

IDIOMES **être ~ de son coup**○ to be confident of success.

surabondance /syʀabɔ̃dɑ̃s/ *nf* overabundance.

surabonder /syʀabɔ̃de/ [1] *vi* **1** (être en nombre) to abound; **2** (être rempli) **~ de** or **en** to abound in ou with.

suraigu, **-uë** /syʀegy/ *adj* [*son*] very shrill.

surajouter: **se surajouter** /syʀaʒute/ [1] *vpr* to be added on (à to).

suralimenter /syʀalimɑ̃te/ [1] *vtr* **1** to feed [sb] up [*personne*]; **2** to fatten [*volaille, bétail*]; **3** to supercharge, to boost [*moteur*].

suranné, **~e** /syʀane/ *adj* [*idées*] outmoded; [*style*] outdated.

surbaisser /syʀbese/ [1] *vtr* **1** ARCHIT to lower [*plafond*]; to surbase [*arc*]; **2** AUT to undersling.

surcharge /syʀʃaʀʒ/ *nf* (poids) excess load, overload; (fait d'être surchargé) overloading; **~ pondérale** excess weight; **un véhicule en ~** an overloaded vehicle; **une ~ de travail** an extra load of work.

surchargé, **~e** /syʀʃaʀʒe/ *adj* **1** (qui est trop chargé) [*personne, animal, ascenseur, étagère*] overloaded; **des voyageurs ~s de bagages** passengers weighed down ou overloaded with luggage; **décoration ~e** overabundant ou excessive decoration; **2** (aux activités trop nombreuses) [*personne*] overburdened; [*journée, emploi du temps*] overloaded, overfull; (aux effectifs trop nombreux) [*classe*] overcrowded.

surcharger /syʀʃaʀʒe/ [13] *vtr* **1** (charger à l'excès) to overload; **~ un texte de citations** to cram a text with quotations; **2** (accabler) to overburden (**de** with); **~ qn de travail** to overburden sb with work; **3** ORDINAT to overload.

surchauffe /syʀʃof/ *nf* **1** LIT superheating; **2** FIG (de l'économie) overheating.

surchauffer /syʀʃofe/ [1] **I** *vtr* **1** (chauffer) to overheat [*maison, pièce*]; **2** PHYS, TECH to superheat [*liquide*].

II *vi* [*voiture*] to be overheating.

surclasser /syʀklase/ [1] *vtr* to outclass.

surconsommation /syʀkɔ̃sɔmasjɔ̃/ *nf* ÉCON overconsumption; **~ de médicaments** excessive drug consumption.

surcroît /syʀkʀwa/ *nm* increase (**de** in); **un ~ de travail** extra work; **un ~ de prestige** increased prestige; **de ~** moreover.

surdéveloppement /syʀdevlɔpmɑ̃/ *nm* overdevelopment.

surdité /syʀdite/ *nf* deafness.

surdoué, ~e /syʀdwe/ **I** *adj* [*enfant*] gifted; [*pianiste, sportif*] exceptionally gifted.

II *nm,f* (enfant) gifted child; (pianiste) exceptionally gifted pianist.

sureau, *pl* **~x** /syʀo/ *nm* elder (tree).

sureffectif /syʀefɛktif/ *nm* (personnel) excess ou surplus staff **¢**; (situation) (en usine) overmanning; (dans un bureau) overstaffing.

surélever /syʀelve/ [16] *vtr* to raise the height of [*maison, route*].

sûrement /syʀmɑ̃/ *adv* **1** (très probablement) most probably; **elle est ~ malade** she must be ill; **elle sera ~ là demain** she should be there tomorrow; **2** (bien sûr) certainly; **~ pas** certainly not; **3** (sans risque) safely.

surenchère /syʀɑ̃ʃɛʀ/ *nf* **1** (enchère supérieure) higher bid; **faire une ~ sur qn** to bid higher than sb; **faire une ~ de 500 francs** to bid 500 francs more (**sur qn** than sb; **sur qch** for sth); **2** (exagération) escalation; **une ~ de violence** an escalation of violence; **faire de la ~** to try to go one better.

surenchérir /syʀɑ̃ʃeʀiʀ/ [3] *vi* **1** (faire une offre plus élevée) to make a higher bid; **~ sur une offre** or **quelqu'un** to raise the bidding; **2** (ajouter) (après soi) to add; (après autrui) to chime in.

surendetté, ~e /syʀɑ̃dete/ *adj* [*personne, pays*] deeply in debt [*après n*]; [*entreprise*] overextended.

surendettement /syʀɑ̃dɛtmɑ̃/ *nm* excessive debt.

suréquipement /syʀekipmɑ̃/ *nm* (en matériel) overequipment; (d'hôtels) over-provision.

surestimation /syʀɛstimasjɔ̃/ *nf* (de bien, propriété) overvaluation; (de coût, capacité, d'importance) overestimation; (de qualité, mérite) overrating.

surestimer /syʀɛstime/ [1] **I** *vtr* to overvalue [*propriété, tableau*]; to overestimate [*coût, capacités, importance*]; to overrate [*qualités, mérites*].

II se surestimer *vpr* to rate oneself too highly.

sûreté /syʀte/ *nf* **1** (sécurité) (d'équipement, de lieu, personne) safety; (d'investissement) soundness; (de pays) security; **être en ~** [*bijou, argent, personne*] to be in a safe place; **être en ~ à la banque** to be in safe keeping in the bank; **il se croyait en ~** he thought he was safe; **2** (assurance) (de jugement) soundness; (de geste) steadiness; (d'acteur, de musicien) confidence; **3** (dispositif de sécurité) (d'une arme) safety catch; (chaîne) safety chain; (serrure) safety lock.

surévaluer /syʀevalɥe/ [1] *vtr* to overvalue [*monnaie*]; to overestimate [*coût*].

surexciter /syʀɛksite/ [1] *vtr* to overexcite [*enfants*]; **foule surexcitée** highly excited crowd.

surexploiter /syʀɛksplwate/ [1] *vtr* to overexploit.

surexposer /syʀɛkspoze/ [1] *vtr* to overexpose.

surf /sœʀf/ ▶ 329 *nm* surfing.

surface /syʀfas/ *nf* **1** (partie externe) surface; **à la ~ de** LIT, FIG on the surface of; **en ~** (à l'extérieur) LIT, FIG on the surface; (au-dessus du sol) above ground; **de ~** LIT [*structure, tension*] surface; [*métro, installations*] above ground (*après n*); FIG [*amabilité*] superficial; **faire ~** LIT, FIG to surface; **refaire ~** LIT, FIG to resurface; **2** ▶ 575 (aire) surface area; **d'une ~ de** with a surface area of; **en ~** in area; **3** SPORT (au football) area; (au tennis) surface.

surfait, ~e /syʀfɛ, ɛt/ *adj* [*personne, œuvre*] overrated; [*réputation*] inflated.

surfer /sœʀfe/ [1] *vi* to go surfing.

surfiler /syʀfile/ [1] *vtr* to oversew.

surgelé, ~e /syʀʒəle/ **I** *adj* deep-frozen.

II *nm* **le ~, les ~s** frozen food **¢**.

surgeler /syʀʒəle/ [17] *vtr* to deep-freeze.

surgénérateur /syʀʒeneʀatœʀ/ *nm* fast-breeder reactor.

surgir /syʀʒiʀ/ [3] *vi* [*personne, animal*] to appear suddenly (**de** from); [*problème, difficulté*] to crop up (**de** from); **faire ~** to conjure up [*craintes, image*]; **faire ~ la vérité** to bring the truth to light.

surhomme /syʀɔm/ *nm* superman.

surhumain, ~e /syʀymɛ̃, ɛn/ *adj* superhuman.

surimpression /syʀɛ̃pʀesjɔ̃/ *nf* PHOT double exposure; **en ~** superimposed (**à** on).

surinformation /syʀɛ̃fɔʀmasjɔ̃/ *nf* surfeit of information.

surintendant /syʀɛ̃tɑ̃dɑ̃/ *nm* superintendent.

surjet /syʀʒɛ/ *nm* oversewing.

sur-le-champ /syʀləʃɑ̃/ *adv* right away.

surlendemain /syʀlɑ̃d(ə)mɛ̃/ *nm* **le ~** two days later; **le lendemain et le ~** the next day and the day after that.

surligner /syʀliɲe/ [1] *vtr* to highlight.

surligneur /syʀliɲœʀ/ *nm* highlighter (pen).

surmenage /syʀmənaʒ/ *nm* overwork.

surmener /syʀmene/ [16] **I** *vtr* to overwork.

II se surmener *vpr* to push oneself too hard.

surmontable /syʀmɔ̃tabl/ *adj* surmountable.

surmonter /syʀmɔ̃te/ [1] *vtr* **1** (dépasser) to overcome [*obstacle, crise*]; **~ l'épreuve de la séparation** to get through the ordeal of separation; **2** (être placé au-dessus de) **être surmonté de qch** to be topped by sth.

surmultiplié, ~e /syʀmyltiplije/ *adj* **vitesse ~e** overdrive.

surnager /syʀnaʒe/ [13] *vi* [*pétrole, débris*] to float.

surnaturel, -elle /syʀnatyʀɛl/ *adj* **1** (non naturel) supernatural; **2** (extraordinaire) eerie.

surnom /syʀnɔ̃/ *nm* nickname.

surnombre /syʀnɔ̃bʀ/ *nm* **en ~** [*objets*] surplus (*épith*); [*employé*] redundant; [*personnel*] excess (*épith*); [*passager*] extra (*épith*); **deux d'entre nous étaient en ~** there were two too many of us.

surnommer /syʀnɔme/ [1] *vtr* to nickname; **X, surnommé Y** X, known as ou dubbed Y

surnuméraire /syʀnymeʀɛʀ/ *adj, nmf* supernumerary.

suroît /syʀwa/ *nm* MÉTÉO, NAUT southwester.

surpasser /syʀpase/ [1] **I** *vtr* (faire mieux que) to surpass, to outdo [*adversaire, concurrent*]; **~ qn en habileté/érudition** to surpass ou outdo sb in skill/erudition.

II se surpasser *vpr* to surpass oneself.

surpeuplé, ~e /syʀpœple/ *adj* [*pays, région, ville*] overpopulated; [*local, train, rue*] overcrowded.

surpeuplement /syʀpœpləmɑ̃/ *nm* (de pays, région) overpopulation; (de ville, quartier) overcrowding.

surpiquer /syʀpike/ [1] *vtr* to topstitch.

surplace /syʀplas/ *nm inv* **faire du ~** (dans un embouteillage) to be stuck; (dans un travail) to be getting nowhere; (en cyclisme) to do a track stand; (dans le ciel) to hover.

surplis /syʀpli/ *nm inv* surplice.

surplomb /syʀplɔ̃/ *nm* overhang; **en ~** overhanging.

surplomber /syʀplɔ̃be/ [1] *vtr* to overhang.

surplus /syʀply/ *nm inv* surplus.

surpopulation /syʀpɔpylasjɔ̃/ *nf* overpopulation.

surprenant, ~e /syʀpʀənɑ̃, ɑ̃t/ *adj* [*aspect, nombre, qualité, lieu*] surprising; [*personne*] amazing; **n'avoir rien de ~** to be hardly surprising; **il serait ~ qu'il vienne** it would be surprising if he came; **il est ~ de voir comment/combien** it is surprising how/how much; **un enfant ~ d'intelligence** an amazingly intelligent child.

surprendre /syʀpʀɑ̃dʀ/ [52] **I** *vtr* **1** (étonner) to surprise; **il sait ~ son monde** he never fails to surprise; **en ~ plus d'un** to surprise more than a few; **2** (prendre par surprise) [*personne*] to take [sb] by surprise [*victime*]; **se laisser ~ par les événements** to be caught out by events; **se laisser ~ par la pluie** to get caught in the rain; **3** (prendre sur le fait) to catch [*malfaiteur*] (à faire doing); **4** (être témoin de) to overhear [*conversation*]; to intercept [*regard*].
II *vi* [*comportement*] to be surprising; [*spectacle*] to surprise; [*personne*] to surprise people; **avoir de quoi ~** to be somewhat surprising.

surprise /syʀpʀiz/ **I** *nf* **1** (événement étonnant) surprise; **quelle ~!** what a surprise!; **être une ~ to** come as a surprise; **c'est la ~ de la journée** that's a big surprise; **créer la ~** to cause a stir; **on veut leur faire une ~** we want it to be a surprise; **2** (étonnement) surprise; **à ma ~** to my surprise; **il m'a fait la ~ de venir me voir** he came to see me as a surprise; **prendre qn par ~** to take sb by surprise; **avoir la bonne ~/la mauvaise ~ d'apprendre que** to be pleasantly surprised/unpleasantly surprised to hear that; **discours sans ~** uneventful speech; **l'élection a été sans ~** the election went as expected.
II **(-)surprise** (*in compounds*) **invité/visite ~** surprise guest/visit; **voyage ~** unexpected trip; **grève ~** lightning strike.

surproduction /syʀpʀɔdyksjɔ̃/ *nf* overproduction.

surpuissant, ~e /syʀpɥisɑ̃, ɑ̃t/ *adj* [*moteur*] high-powered.

surqualifié, ~e /syʀkalifje/ *adj* overqualified.

surréalisme /syʀ(ʀ)ealism/ *nm* surrealism.

surréaliste /syʀ(ʀ)ealist/ **I** *adj* **1** [*œuvre, auteur*] surrealist; **2** [*décor, paysage, vision*] surreal.
II *nmf* surrealist.

surrégénérateur /syʀʀeʒeneʀatœʀ/ *nm* fast-breeder reactor.

surrénal, ~e, *mpl* **-aux** /syʀ(ʀ)enal, o/ *adj* suprarenal.

surréservation /syʀʀezɛʀvasjɔ̃/ *nf* overbooking.

sursaut /syʀso/ *nm* **1** LIT (mouvement) start; **en ~** with a start; **2** FIG (d'énergie, enthousiasme) sudden burst (de of); (d'orgueil, indignation) flash (de of); **dans un dernier ~** in a final spurt of effort.

sursauter /syʀsote/ [1] *vi* to jump, to start.

surseoir /syʀswaʀ/ [41] *vtr ind* **~ à** to postpone [*décision*]; to defer [*versement*]; to stay [*exécution*].

sursis /syʀsi/ *nm inv* **1** (délai) respite; **un ~ de trois mois** a three-month respite; **2** JUR suspended sentence; **trois mois de prison dont deux avec ~** prison sentence of three months, with two months suspended; **3** MIL deferment of military service.

sursitaire /syʀsitɛʀ/ *nmf* MIL *person whose military service has been deferred.*

surtaxe /syʀtaks/ *nf* surcharge.

surtaxer /syʀtakse/ [1] *vtr* to surcharge.

surtitre /syʀtitʀ/ *nm* (de journal) subheading.

surtout /syʀtu/ *adv* above all; **j'ai ~ besoin de repos** more than anything I need a rest; **~ quand/si/que** especially when/if/as; **~ pas!** certainly not!; **~ pas lui!** especially not him!; **~ pas de chien dans la maison** absolutely no dogs in the house.

surveillance /syʀvɛjɑ̃s/ *nf* **1** GÉN watch; (par la police) surveillance; **exercer une ~ étroite sur qn/qch** to keep a close watch over sb/sth; **placer qn sous haute ~** to put sb under tight surveillance; **déjouer la ~ de qn** to escape detection by sb; **2** SCOL, UNIV (d'examens, de récréation) supervision; **assurer la ~ d'épreuves** to supervise exams; **3** (contrôle) supervision; **médicament à prendre sous ~ médicale** drug to be taken under medical supervision; **4** MIL monitoring.

surveillant, ~e /syʀvɛjɑ̃, ɑ̃t/ ▶374 *nm,f* **1** SCOL supervisor; **2** ADMIN **~ de prison** prison warder GB OU guard; **3** (dans un magasin) store detective.

surveiller /syʀvɛje/ [1] **I** *vtr* **1** (veiller sur) to watch, to keep an eye on [*enfants, cuisson, affaires*]; to watch

(over) [*prisonnier, malade*]; **~ du coin de l'œil** to watch [sb/sth] out of the corner of one's eye; **2** (exercer une surveillance sur) to keep watch on, to keep [sb/sth] under surveillance [*adversaire, bâtiment*]; **c'est ton tour de ~** it's your turn to keep watch; **3** (contrôler) to supervise, to oversee [*travail, projet*]; to supervise [*sortie d'école*]; to monitor [*cessez-le-feu, finances*]; to man, to monitor [*machine*]; **~ les progrès d'un élève** to monitor a pupil's progress; **4** SCOL, UNIV to supervise, **5** (veiller à) **~ son langage/sa ligne** to watch one's language/one's figure; **~ sa santé** to take care of one's health.
II se surveiller *vpr* to watch oneself; **avec eux, il faut sans cesse se ~** with them, you have to be on your best behaviour GB.

survenir /syʀvəniʀ/ [36] *vi* [*décès, orage*] to occur; [*difficulté, conflit*] to arise; [*personne*] to arrive unexpectedly.

survêtement /syʀvɛtmɑ̃/ *nm* tracksuit.

survie /syʀvi/ *nf* LIT, FIG survival.

survitrage /syʀvitʀaʒ/ *nm* secondary (double) glazing.

survivance /syʀvivɑ̃s/ *nf* survival.

survivant, ~e /syʀvivɑ̃, ɑ̃t/ **I** *adj* surviving.
II *nm,f* survivor.

survivre /syʀvivʀ/ [63] **I** *vtr ind* **~ à** to survive [*événement, accident, blessures*]; **~ à qn** [*personne*] to outlive sb, survive sb; [*œuvre, influence*] to outlast sb.
II *vi* to survive.

survol /syʀvɔl/ *nm* **1** (en avion) flying over; **effectuer le ~ de qch** to fly over sth; **2** (de sujet) synopsis (**de** of); (de magazine, livre) quick glance (**de** at).

survoler /syʀvɔle/ [1] *vtr* **1** (en avion) [*avion, pilote*] to fly over [*lieu*]; **2** (voir superficiellement) to skim through [*livre, magazine*]; to do a quick review of [*problème*].

survolté○, ~e /syʀvɔlte/ *adj* [*personne*] over-excited; [*ambiance*] highly charged.

survolter /syʀvɔlte/ [1] *vtr* to boost [*circuit*].

sus: **en sus** /ɑ̃sys/ *loc adv* **être en ~** to be extra; **en ~ de** on top of [*salaire, location*]; in addition to [*choses, conseils*].

susceptibilité /sysɛptibilite/ *nf* touchiness; **être d'une grande ~** to be very touchy; **pour ménager les ~s** so as not to upset anybody.

susceptible /sysɛptibl/ *adj* **1** (ombrageux) touchy; **2 ~ de** likely to [*influencer, intéresser*]; **remarque ~ de plusieurs interprétations** remark open to several interpretations.

susciter /sysite/ [1] *vtr* **1** (provoquer) to spark off [*réaction, débat*]; **2** (éveiller) to arouse [*enthousiasme, intérêt*]; **3** (faire naître) to give rise to [*réticences, vocation*]; **4** (créer) to create [*problème*] (**à** for).

susdit, ~e /sysdi, it/ *adj* aforesaid.

susnommé, ~e /sysnɔme/ *adj, nm,f* aforementioned.

suspect, ~e /syspɛ, ɛkt/ **I** *adj* [*mort, odeur, allure, objet*] suspicious; [*information, logique*] dubious; [*aliment, honnêteté, enthousiasme*] suspect; [*personne*] suspicious-looking (épith).
II *nm,f* suspect; **le principal ~** the prime suspect.

suspecter /syspɛkte/ [1] *vtr* to suspect [*personne, groupe, institution*] (**de qch** of sth; **de faire** of doing).

suspendre /syspɑ̃dʀ/ [6] **I** *vtr* **1** (pendre) to hang up; **~ qch à qch** to hang sth on sth; **~ qch/qn par** to hang sth/sb by; **2** (interrompre) to suspend [*émission, publication, relations, paiement*]; to end [*grève*]; to adjourn [*séance, réunion, enquête, procès*]; to stop [*diffusion*]; **~ son souffle** to hold one's breath; **3** (destituer) to suspend [*fonctionnaire, médecin, sportif*] (**de** from).
II se suspendre *vpr* [*personne, animal*] to hang; **se ~ à une corde** to hang from a rope; **se ~ par les bras** to hang by one's arms.

suspendu, ~e /syspɑ̃dy/ *adj* **1** LIT hanging (**à** from; **par** by); **2** FIG **être ~ aux lèvres de qn** to be hanging on sb's every word; **des maisons ~es au-dessus de la vallée** houses perched above the valley.

suspens: **en suspens** /āsyspā/ *loc adv* **1** (en souffrance) [*problème*] outstanding (*épith*); **laisser un problème en ~** to leave a problem unresolved; **laisser des travaux en ~** to leave work unfinished; **2** (dans l'expectative) in suspense; **tenir qn en ~** to keep sb in suspense; **3** (en suspension) [*fumée*] hanging in the air.

suspense /syspɛns/ *nm* suspense; **maintenir le ~** to maintain the suspense; **le ~ reste entier** everything still hangs in the balance; **film** or **roman à ~** thriller.

suspension /syspɑ̃sjɔ̃/ *nf* **1** (attache) suspension; **2** AUT, TECH suspension; **3** (interruption) (d'aide, de relations, travaux) suspension; (d'enquête, de procès) adjournment; **demander la ~ de la séance** to ask for the session to be adjourned; **4** (sanction) suspension; **être condamné à deux ans de ~ du permis de conduire** to be disqualified GB ou suspended US from driving for two years; **5** CHIMIE suspension; **en ~** [*particules*] in suspension; **6** (éclairage) pendant.
■ **~ d'armes** MIL cease-fire.

suspensoir /syspɑ̃swaR/ *nm* SPORT athletic support GB, athletic supporter US, jockstrap○.

suspicieux, -ieuse /syspisjø, øz/ *adj* suspicious.

suspicion /syspisjɔ̃/ *nf* suspicion; **faire peser la ~ sur qn** to bring suspicion to bear on sb; **avec ~** suspiciously.

sustenter: **se sustenter** /systɑ̃te/ [1] *vpr* HUM to have a little snack.

susurrer /sysyRe/ [1] *vtr, vi* to whisper.

suture /sytyR/ *nf* suture; **point de ~** stitch.

suzerain, ~e /syzRɛ̃, ɛn/ *adj, nm,f* suzerain.

suzeraineté /syzRɛnte/ *nf* suzerainty.

svelte /svɛlt/ *adj* [*personne, taille*] slender.

sveltesse /svɛltɛs/ *nf* slenderness.

SVP (*written abbr* = **s'il vous plaît**) please.

sycomore /sikɔmɔR/ *nm* sycamore.

syllabe /sil(l)ab/ *nf* syllable.

syllabique /sil(l)abik/ *adj* [*écriture, vers*] syllabic.

syllogisme /silɔʒism/ *nm* syllogism.

sylphide /silfid/ *nf* sylph.

sylvestre /silvɛstR/ *adj* LITER sylvan LITTÉR.

sylvicole /silvikɔl/ *adj* silvicultural.

sylviculture /silvikyltyR/ *nf* forestry.

symbiose /sɛ̃bjoz/ *nf* symbiosis; **en ~** in symbiosis.

symbole /sɛ̃bɔl/ *nm* **1** GÉN, LING symbol; **2** RELIG creed.

symbolique /sɛ̃bɔlik/ *adj* **1** (significatif) [*œuvre, action, portée*] symbolic; **2** (pour la forme) [*geste, salaire, augmentation*] token (*épith*); [*prix*] nominal.

symboliser /sɛ̃bɔlize/ [1] *vtr* to symbolize.

symbolisme /sɛ̃bɔlism/ *nm* symbolism.

symétrie /simetRi/ *nf* symmetry (**par rapport à** in relation to).

symétrique /simetRik/ *adj* **1** (géométriquement) [*dessin, visage, points*] symmetrical; **2** (en logique) [*relation*] symmetric.

sympa○ /sɛ̃pa/ *adj inv* nice.

sympathie /sɛ̃pati/ *nf* **1** (amitié) **avoir** or **éprouver de la ~ pour qn** to like sb; **montrer** or **témoigner de la ~ à qn** to be friendly toward(s) sb; **elle inspire la ~** she's very likeable; **2** (d'un sympathisant) sympathy; **mes ~s vont aux...** my sympathies lie with...; **3** (compassion) sympathy; **croyez à toute ma ~** you have my deepest sympathy.

sympathique /sɛ̃patik/ *adj* [*personne*] nice, likeable; [*endroit*] nice, pleasant; [*soirée*] pleasant; [*idée*] nice.

sympathisant, ~e /sɛ̃patizɑ̃, ɑ̃t/ *nm,f* sympathizer.

sympathiser /sɛ̃patize/ [1] *vi* to get on well (**avec qn** with sb).

symphonie /sɛ̃fɔni/ *nf* LIT, FIG symphony.

symphonique /sɛ̃fɔnik/ *adj* symphonic.

symposium /sɛ̃pozjɔm/ *nm* symposium (**sur** on).

symptomatique /sɛ̃ptɔmatik/ *adj* symptomatic.

symptôme /sɛ̃ptom/ *nm* symptom (**de** of).

synagogue /sinagɔg/ *nf* synagogue.

synchronique /sɛ̃kRɔnik/ *adj* synchronic.

synchronisation /sɛ̃kRɔnizasjɔ̃/ *nf* synchronization.

synchroniser /sɛ̃kRɔnize/ [1] *vtr* to synchronize.

syncope /sɛ̃kɔp/ *nf* **1** fainting fit; **tomber en ~** to faint; **2** MUS syncopation.

syncopé, ~e /sɛ̃kɔpe/ *adj* [*rythme*] syncopated.

syndic /sɛ̃dik/ *nm* (d'immeuble) property manager.

syndical, ~e, *mpl* **-aux** /sɛ̃dikal, o/ *adj* (trade) union (*épith*); **droit ~** (trade) union law.

syndicalisme /sɛ̃dikalism/ *nm* (fait social) trade unionism; (activité) union activities (*pl*).

syndicaliste /sɛ̃dikalist/ **I** *adj* (trade) union (*épith*).
II *nmf* union activist.

syndicat /sɛ̃dika/ *nm* GÉN trade union; (d'employeurs) association.
■ **~ du crime** underworld; **~ d'initiative** tourist information office; **~ professionnel** trade association.

syndiqué, ~e /sɛ̃dike/ **I** *adj* **être ~** to be a union member; **main-d'œuvre non ~e** non-union labour GB.
II *nm,f* union member.

syndiquer /sɛ̃dike/ [1] **I** *vtr* to unionize.
II **se syndiquer** *vpr* [*personne*] to join a union.

syndrome /sɛ̃dRom/ *nm* syndrome.
■ **~ immunodéficitaire acquis** acquired immunodeficiency syndrome.

synergie /sinɛRʒi/ *nf* synergy (**entre** between).

synode /sinɔd/ *nm* synod.

synonyme /sinɔnim/ **I** *adj* synonymous (**de** with).
II *nm* synonym; **dictionnaire de ~s** ~ thesaurus.

synonymie /sinɔnimi/ *nf* synonymy.

synopsis /sinɔpsis/ *nm inv* CIN synopsis.

synovie /sinɔvi/ *nf* synovia; **avoir un épanchement de ~** to have water on the knee.

syntagme /sɛ̃tagm/ *nm* phrase, syntagm.

syntaxe /sɛ̃taks/ *nf* syntax.

syntaxique /sɛ̃taksik/ *adj* syntactic(al).

synthèse /sɛ̃tɛz/ *nf* **1** (d'idées) synthesis; (résumé) summary; **faire la ~ de plusieurs documents** to extract the essential facts from several documents; **esprit de ~** ability to synthesize; **2** CHIMIE synthesis; **produit de ~** synthetic product; **3** ORDINAT **images de ~** computer generated images.

synthétique /sɛ̃tetik/ *adj* **1** CHIMIE, TECH synthetic; **2** (non analytique) [*réflexion, vision*] global; [*ouvrage*] that gives a general picture (*épith, après n*); **3** MUS synthetic.

synthétiser /sɛ̃tetize/ [1] *vtr* to synthesize.

syphilis /sifilis/ ▶ 196 *nf inv* syphilis.

systématique /sistematik/ *adj* [*classification, refus*] systematic; [*aide, soutien*] unconditional.

systématiser /sistematize/ [1] **I** *vtr* to systematize.
II **se systématiser** *vpr* to become the rule.

système /sistɛm/ *nm* **1** (ensemble organisé, doctrine) system; **2** (dispositif, réunion d'éléments) system; **~ de canaux** canal system ou network; **3** (plan, méthode) system, scheme; **4** (moyen) system, way; (combine) dodge○; **5** ANAT system; **~ cardio-vasculaire** cardiovascular system; **~ pileux** hair; **6** ORDINAT system; **~ de gestion de bases de données** database (management) system; **7** (en astronomie) **~ solaire** solar system.
■ **~ d'alarme** burglar alarm, alarm system; **le ~ D**○ resourcefulness; **~ monétaire européen**, **SME** European Monetary System, EMS.
IDIOMES **taper** or **courir sur le ~ de qn**○ to get on sb's nerves ou wick○ GB.

systémique /sistemik/ **I** *adj* systematic.
II *nf* systematism.

Tt

t, T /te/ *nm inv* t, T; **en** (**forme de**) **T** T-shaped.

t' ▶**te**.

ta ▶**ton**[1].

tabac /taba/ *nm* **1** BOT, IND tobacco; **2** ▶**374**⏐ (magasin) tobacconist's GB, smoke shop US; **3**○ (succès) **faire un ~** to be a big hit; **4** NAUT **coup de ~** squall.
■ **~ blond** Virginia tobacco; **~ brun** dark tobacco; **~ à priser** snuff; **~ à rouler** rolling tobacco.
IDIOMES **passer qn à ~**○ to beat sb up.

tabagie /tabaʒi/ *nf* **c'est une vraie ~ ici!** it's really smoky in here!

tabagisme /tabaʒism/ *nm* tobacco addiction.

tabasser○ /tabase/ [1] **I** *vtr* to give [sb] a beating; **se faire ~** to get a beating.
II se tabasser *vpr* to lay into each other○.

tabatière /tabatjɛʀ/ *nf* **1** (boîte à tabac) snuffbox; **2** (lucarne) skylight.

table /tabl/ *nf* **1** (meuble) table; **2** (lieu du repas) table; **bien/mal se tenir à ~** to have good/bad table manners; **nous serons dix à ~ ce midi** there'll be ten of us for lunch today; **nous étions toujours à ~ quand...** we were still eating when...; **s'asseoir à ~** (pour manger) to sit down to eat; **passer** or **se mettre à ~** LIT to sit down at the table; (avouer)○ to spill the beans○; **3** (nourriture) table; **~ remarquable** or **de roi** marvellous GB spread; **4** (lieu de discussion) table; **s'asseoir autour d'une ~** to get round the table; **5** MATH table.
■ **~ basse** coffee table; **~ de chevet** bedside table GB, night stand US; **~ de cuisson** hob; **~ à dessin** drawing board; **~ d'école** school desk; **~ d'écoute** wiretapping set; **être mis sur ~ d'écoute** to have one's phone tapped; **~ des matières** (table of) contents; **~ de mixage** mixing desk; **~ de montage** editing bench ou table; **~ de nuit** bedside table GB, night stand US; **~ d'orientation** viewpoint diagram; **~ à repasser** ironing board; **~ roulante** trolley; **~ de toilette** washstand.
IDIOMES **mettre les pieds sous la ~** to let others wait on you.

tableau, *pl* **~x** /tablo/ *nm* **1** (œuvre d'art) GÉN picture; (peinture) painting; **2** (description) picture; **et pour achever le ~** and to cap it all; **3** (spectacle) picture; **en plus, il était ivre, tu vois un peu le ~**○! on top of that he was drunk, you can just imagine!; **4** (présentation graphique) table, chart; **présenter qch sous forme de ~** to present sth in tabular form; **5** SCOL blackboard; **6** (affichant des renseignements) GÉN board; RAIL indicator board; **~ horaire** timetable; **7** (support mural) board; **8** THÉÂT short scene.
■ **~ d'affichage** notice board; **~ de bord** AUT dashboard; AVIAT, RAIL instrument panel; **~ de chasse** (de chasseur) total number of kills; (de séducteur) list of conquests; **~ de commande** control panel; **~ d'honneur** honours board GB, honor roll US.
IDIOMES **jouer** or **miser sur les deux ~x** to hedge one's bets; **gagner/perdre sur tous les ~x** to win/to lose on all counts.

tablée /table/ *nf* table; **une grande ~** a large party.

tabler /table/ [1] *vi* **~ sur** to bank○ on.

tablette /tablɛt/ **I** *nf* **1** (de chocolat) bar; (de chewing-gum) stick; **2** (étagère) shelf.
II tablettes *nfpl* (archives) annals; **j'ai inscrit notre**

---

rendez-vous dans mes ~s I've made a note of our meeting in my diary.

tablier /tablije/ *nm* **1** (vêtement) apron; **2** (de pont) roadway.
IDIOMES **rendre son ~** to give in GB ou give US one's notice.

tabou /tabu/ **I** *adj* **1** (frappé d'interdit) taboo; (qu'on ne peut critiquer) untouchable, sacred; **2** RELIG taboo.
II *nm* taboo.

tabouret /taburɛ/ *nm* stool.

tac /tak/ *nm* **répondre du ~ au ~** to answer as quick as a flash.

tache /taʃ/ *nf* **1** LIT (salissure) stain; **~ d'encre** ink stain; (sur un manuscrit) ink blot; **~ d'humidité** damp patch; **~ de sang** bloodstain; **une ~ sur la table** a mark on the table; **faire ~** FIG to stick out like a sore thumb; **2** FIG (souillure) stain, blot (à on); **sans ~** [*réputation*] spotless; **3** (altération) (sur un fruit) mark; (sur la peau) blotch, mark; **4** (note de couleur) (petite) spot; (plus grande) patch.
■ **~ de naissance** birthmark; **~ solaire** sunspot; **~ de vin** GÉN wine stain; ANAT strawberry mark; **~s de rousseur** or **son** freckles.
IDIOMES **faire ~ d'huile** to spread like wildfire.

tâche /taʃ/ *nf* task, job; **mener une ~ à bien** to see a job through; **être à la hauteur de sa ~** to be up to the job; **les ~s ménagères** household chores.

tacher /taʃe/ [1] **I** *vtr* **1** LIT (salir) [*substance*] to stain; [*personne*] to get a stain on; **taché d'huile** oil-stained; **2** FIG (souiller) to tarnish [*réputation*]; **3** (colorer) LITER **pelage noir taché de blanc** black fur with white markings.
II *vi* [*fruit, vin, produit*] to stain.
III se tacher *vpr* **1** [*personne*] to get oneself dirty; **2** [*fruit*] to become blemished.

tâcher /taʃe/ [1] **I** *vtr* **tâchez que ce soit fini avant midi** (conseil) try and make sure it's finished before noon; (ordre) see to it that it's finished before noon.
II tâcher de *vtr ind* **~ de faire** to try to do.

tâcheron /taʃʀɔ̃/ *nm* PEJ (qui fait des tâches ingrates) drudge; (qui travaille beaucoup) hack; **un ~ de la littérature** a literary hack.

tacheter /taʃte/ [20] *vtr* to speckle, to spot [*pelage*]; to dot [*pré*].

tacite /tasit/ *adj* tacit.

taciturne /tasityʀn/ *adj* taciturn.

tacot○ /tako/ *nm* banger○ GB, crate○ US.

tact /takt/ *nm* tact; **avoir beaucoup de ~** to be very tactful; **manquer de ~** to be tactless; **avec ~** tactfully.

tactique /taktik/ **I** *adj* GÉN, MIL tactical.
II *nf* **une ~ de vente** a sales tactic; **la ~ de César/de notre entreprise est...** Caesar's/our firm's tactics are...; **la ~** (science militaire) tactics (+ *v sg*).

taie /tɛ/ *nf* **1** (enveloppe) **~ (d'oreiller)** pillowcase; **~ (de traversin)** bolstercase; **2** (sur l'œil) corneal opacity.

taillader /tajade/ [1] **I** *vtr* to slash [*poignets, rideaux*]; **~ une table** to make slashes on a table top.
II se taillader *vpr* **se ~ les poignets** to slash one's wrists; **se ~ les mains** to cut one's hands badly.

taille /taj/ *nf* **1** ▶**137**⏐ (partie du corps, de vêtement) waist, waistline; **avoir une ~ de guêpe** to be wasp-waisted, to have a very slim waist; **prendre qn par la**

Les tailles

Les tailles britanniques et américaines données dans les tableaux ci-dessous sont parfois arrondies aux tailles immédiatement supérieures: mieux vaut un vêtement un peu trop grand qu'un peu trop petit.

Les chaussures d'homme

en France	en GB et aux US
39	6½
40	7
41	7½
42	8½
43	9
44	10
45	11
46	12

Les chaussures de femme

en France	en GB	aux US
35	3	6
36	3½	6½
37	4	7
38	5	7½
39	6	8
40	7	8½
41	8	9

Les vêtements d'homme

en France	en GB et aux US
38	28
40	30
42	32
44	34
46	36
48	38
50	40
52	42
54	44
56	46

Les vêtements de femme*

en France	en GB	aux US
34	8	4
36	10	6
38	12	8
40	12	8
42	14	10
44	16	12
46	16	12
48	18	14
50	20	16

* Ces tailles sont utilisées pour les robes, chemisiers, pantalons, etc.

Les chemises d'homme

en France	en GB et aux US	en France	en GB et aux US
36	14	41	16½
37	14½	42	17
38	15	43	17½
39	15½	44	18
40	16		

L'anglais emploie le mot size à la fois pour les vêtements et pour les chaussures.

quelle taille faites-vous?	= what size are you?
quelle pointure faites-vous?	= what size are you?
faire du 85 de tour de poitrine	= to have a 34-inch bust
faire 61 de tour de taille	= to have a 24-inch waist *ou* to measure 24 inches round the waist
faire du 90 de tour de hanches	= to measure 36 inches round the hips
avez-vous une taille 40?	= have you got a size 40?
avez-vous du 7?	= have you got a size 7?
je porte du 42	= I take a size 42
je fais du 52	= my size is 52
je chausse du 40	= my shoe size is 40
je cherche un 40	= I'm looking for a shirt with a size 16 collar
une paire de chaussures en 42	= a pair of shoes size 42
une chemise taille 15	= a shirt size 15 *ou* a size 15 shirt
avez-vous ce modèle en 40?	= have you got the same thing in a 16?
avez-vous ce modèle en plus grand?	= have you got this in a larger size?
avez-vous ce modèle en plus petit?	= have you got the same thing in a smaller size?

~ to put one's arm around sb's waist; **robe à ~ haute/basse** high-/low-waisted dress; **2** (volume) size; FIG (importance) size; **de grande/petite ~** [*animal, entreprise, objet*] large/small; **entreprise de ~ moyenne** medium-sized company; **de la ~ de** the size of; **société de ~ européenne** company on a European scale; **de ~** [*problème, ambition, enjeu*] considerable; [*événement, question*] very important; **à la ~ de leurs ambitions/de l'entreprise** in keeping with their ambitions/the size of the company; **un partenaire à sa ~** a suitable partner; **l'entreprise est de ~!** it's no small undertaking!; **être de ~ à faire** to be up to *ou* capable of doing; **3** (dimension de vêtement) size; **~ 42** size 42; **'~ unique'** 'one size'; **essaie la ~ au-dessus/au-dessous** try the next size up/down; **avoir la ~ mannequin** to be a standard size; **rayon grandes ~s** outsize department; **rayon petites ~s** petite department; **4** (hauteur) height; **personne de petite/grande ~** short/tall person; **personne de ~ moyenne** person of average height; **se redresser de toute sa ~** to draw oneself up to one's full height; **5** (action de tailler) (d'arbre, buisson) pruning; (de haie) clipping, trimming; (de diamant, cristal) cutting; (de bois) carving; **6** (forme obtenue) (de diamant) cut; (de haie) shape; **7** HIST **la ~** tallage; **8** (tranchant de lame) edge.

taillé, ~e /taje/ **I** *pp* ▶ **tailler**.
II *pp adj* **1** (bâti) **~ en athlète** built like an athlete; **2** (apte) **être ~ pour faire** to be cut out to do; **3** (coupé) **cristal ~** cut glass.

taille-crayons /tajkʀɛjɔ̃/ *nm inv* pencil sharpener.

tailler /taje/ [1] **I** *vtr* **1** (couper) to cut [*rubis, cristal, marbre*]; to carve [*bois*]; to sharpen [*crayon*]; to prune [*arbre*]; to cut, to clip [*haie*]; to trim [*cheveux, barbe*]; **~ une armée en pièces** to hack an army to pieces; **elle l'a taillé en pièces** FIG she made mincemeat of him○; **bien taillé** [*moustache, haie*] neatly trimmed; [*veste*] well-cut; **taillé en pointe** [*crayon*] sharpened to a point; [*barbe*] trimmed to a point; **visage taillé à la serpe** craggy features (*pl*); **2** (découper) to cut [*steak*] (**dans** from); to carve [*sculpture*]; to cut out [*vête-*

ment]; **~ une robe dans de la soie** to make a dress out of silk; **~ un costume sur mesure** to make a suit to measure; **taillé sur mesure** [*vêtement*] made-to-measure GB, custom-made; FIG [*rôle*] tailor-made.
II *vi* **1** (faire des coupes dans) **~ dans les chairs** or **le vif** to cut into the flesh; **~ dans les programmes sociaux** FIG to make cuts in the social programmes GB; **2** (être coupé) **~ grand/petit** [*vêtement*] to be cut on the large/small side.
III se tailler *vpr* **1** (se faire) to carve out [*sth*] for oneself [*carrière, empire*]; to make [*sth*] for oneself [*belle réputation*]; **se ~ une grande part du marché** to corner a large share of the market; **se ~ un vif succès** to be a great success; **2**○ (s'enfuir) to beat it○; **3** (se couper) **se ~ la moustache** to trim one's moustache GB *ou* mustache US.
IDIOMES **ils sont tous taillés sur le même modèle** they are all exactly alike.

tailleur /tajœʀ/ *nm* **1** (tenue) (woman's) suit; **2** ▶ 374 (personne) tailor; **s'asseoir/être assis en ~** to sit down/to be sitting cross-legged.
■ **~ pour dames** ladies' tailor; **~ de pierre** stone-cutter.

taillis /taji/ *nm inv* (broussailles) undergrowth ¢; (sous-bois) coppice.

tain /tɛ̃/ *nm* silvering; **glace** or **miroir sans ~** two-way mirror.

taire /tɛʀ/ [59] **I** *vtr* **1** (ne pas dire) not to reveal [*nom, secret*]; to hush up [*vérité*]; **dire ce qu'on aurait dû ~** to say what would have been better left unsaid; **2** (cacher) LITER to keep [*sth*] to oneself [*tristesse, dépit*].
II se taire *vpr* **1** (ne pas parler) [*personne*] to be silent, to say nothing; [*nature, oiseaux*] to be silent; (ne pas dire qch) to remain silent; **se ~ sur qch** to keep quiet about sth; **2** (cesser de parler) [*personne*] to stop talking, to fall silent; [*oiseau*] to fall silent; (cesser de s'exprimer) [*journaliste, opposition*] to fall silent; **faire ~** to make [*sb*] be quiet [*élèves*]; to silence [*opposant, média*] ; to put a stop to [*rumeurs, sarcasmes*]; **faire ~ sa jalousie** to stifle one's jealousy; **fais ~ les enfants!** keep the children quiet!; **tais-toi!** (ne parle

pas) be quiet!; (ne m'en parle pas) don't talk to me about that!; **3** (s'arrêter) [*musique*] to stop; [*canon, orchestre*] to fall silent.

talc /talk/ *nm* **1** (poudre) talc, talcum powder; **2** (minéral) talc(um).

talent /talɑ̃/ *nm* **1** (aptitude) talent; **avoir du ~** to be talented, to have talent; **de ~** talented, gifted; **2** (personne douée) **chercher de nouveaux ~s** to look for new talent; **un jeune ~** a talented young person.

talentueux, -euse /talɑ̃tɥø, øz/ *adj* talented, gifted.

talion /taljɔ̃/ *nm* talion; **loi du ~** lex talionis; **appliquer la loi du ~** to demand 'an eye for an eye'.

talkie-walkie, *pl* **talkies-walkies** /tokiwoki/ *nm* walkie-talkie.

taloche○ /talɔʃ/ *nf* (gifle) clout○.

talon /talɔ̃/ *nm* **1** (de pied, chaussure) heel; **2** (de carnet, chèque) stub; **3** (aux cartes) pile.
■ **~ aiguille** stiletto heel.
IDIOMES **tourner les ~s** to turn on one's heel and walk away; **être sur les ~s de qn** to be hard ou hot on sb's heels.

talonner /talɔne/ [1] *vtr* **1** (suivre) **~ qn** to be hot on sb's heels; **2** (harceler) [*personne*] to badger [*personne*]; [*faim, inquiétude*] to torment [*personne*]; **3** SPORT to spur [sth] on [*cheval*]; (au rugby) to heel [*ballon*].

talonnette /talɔnɛt/ *nf* (de chaussures) lift (in a shoe).

talus /taly/ *nm inv* (artificiel) embankment; (naturel) bank, slope.

tamanoir /tamanwaʀ/ *nm* anteater.

tambouille○ /tɑ̃buj/ *nf* grub○.

tambour /tɑ̃buʀ/ *nm* **1** ▶392 (instrument) drum; **mener qch ~ battant** FIG to deal with sth briskly; **2** ▶374 (personne) drummer; **3** (de lave-linge, frein) drum; **4** (de porte) tambour.

tambourin /tɑ̃buʀɛ̃/ *nm* ▶392 tambourine.

tambouriner /tɑ̃buʀine/ [1] *vi* **1** (frapper) **~ à la porte/fenêtre de qn** to hammer on sb's door/window; **2** (tapoter) **~ sur la table** to drum one's fingers on the table; **la pluie tambourine sur le toit** the rain is drumming on the roof.

tamis /tami/ *nm inv* sieve; **passer au ~** to sieve, to sift.

Tamise /tamiz/ ▶260 *nprf* **la ~** the Thames.

tamiser /tamize/ [1] *vtr* to sieve, to sift [*sable, farine*]; to filter [*lumière, couleurs*]; **farine tamisée** sifted flour; **lumières tamisées** subdued lighting *C*.

tampon /tɑ̃pɔ̃/ *nm* **1** (de bureau) (marque) stamp; (objet gravé) stamp; (tissu encré) **~ (encreur)** (ink) pad; **mettre** or **apposer un ~ sur un document** to stamp a document; **2** (pour éponger, frotter) GÉN pad; MÉD swab; **3** (de wagon) buffer; **4** (pour boucher) plug.
II (-)**tampon** (*in compounds*) buffer; **solution(-)~** CHIMIE buffer (solution); **mémoire(-)~** ORDINAT buffer (storage).
■ **~ hygiénique** tampon; **~ à récurer** scouring pad.
IDIOMES **servir de ~** to act as a buffer.

tamponner /tɑ̃pɔne/ [1] *vtr* **1** (éponger) to swab [*plaie*]; to mop [*front*]; **2** (timbrer) to stamp [*document*]; **3** (heurter) to crash into [*véhicule*].

tamponneuse /tɑ̃pɔnøz/ *adj f* **auto ~** bumper car, dodgem.

tam-tam, *pl* **~s** /tamtam/ *nm* ▶392 tomtom.

tancer /tɑ̃se/ [12] *vtr* LITER to scold, to admonish SOUT; **elle s'est fait ~ vertement** or **d'importance** she was scolded sharply.

tanche /tɑ̃ʃ/ *nf* tench.

tandem /tɑ̃dɛm/ *nm* **1** (bicyclette) tandem; **2** FIG (duo) duo; **travailler en ~** to work in tandem.

tandis: **tandis que** /tɑ̃di(s)k(ə)/ *loc conj* while.

tangage /tɑ̃gaʒ/ *nm* (de navire, d'avion) pitching.

tangent, ~e¹ /tɑ̃ʒɑ̃, ɑ̃t/ *adj* **1** MATH tangent, tangential; **~ à** at a tangent to; **2**○ (de justesse) **elle passe en classe supérieure, mais c'est ~** she's moving up

a year GB ou grade US, but only by the skin of her teeth○.

tangente² /tɑ̃ʒɑ̃t/ *nf* MATH tangent.
IDIOMES **prendre la ~ ~**○ to make oneself scarce○.

tangible /tɑ̃ʒibl/ *adj* tangible.

tanguer /tɑ̃ge/ [1] *vi* **1** [*navire, avion*] to pitch; **2** [*personne*] to be unsteady on one's feet.

tanière /tanjɛʀ/ *nf* **1** (d'animal) den; **2** (retraite) lair **3** (taudis) hovel.

tank /tɑ̃k/ *nm* **1** (citerne) tank; **2** (char) tank.

tannant, -e /tanɑ̃, ɑ̃t/ *adj* **1** TECH [*produit*] tanning **2**○ (lassant) [*personne*] infuriating.

tanné, -e /tane/ **I** *pp* ▶ **tanner**.
II *pp adj* **1** [*cuir*] tanned; **2** [*visage, peau*] leathery.

tanner /tane/ [1] *vtr* **1** TECH to tan [*cuir, peaux*]; **2** (brunir) [*soleil*] to make [sth] leathery [*visage, peau*] **3**○ (lasser) to badger○ [*personne*].
IDIOMES **~ le cuir à qn** to tan sb's hide○.

tannerie /tanʀi/ *nf* **1** (établissement) tannery; **2** (métier) tanning.

tanneur, -euse /tanœʀ, øz/ ▶ **374** *nm,f* tanner.

tant /tɑ̃/ ▶ **486** **I** *adv* **1** (tellement) (modifiant un verbe so much; (modifiant un participe passé) much; **il y a ~ à faire que** there's so much to do that; **il quitta la pièce ~ il se sentait honteux** he left the room that he left the room; **vous m'en direz ~**○! you don't say!; **~ il est vrai que…** since it's a well-known fact that…; **le moment ~ attendu** the long-awaited moment; **2** (autant) **~ ses films que ses romans** both his/her films and his/her novels ou his/her films as much as his/her novels; **ce n'est pas ~ une question d'argent qu'une question de principe** it's not so much a question of money as a question of principle **n'aimer rien ~ que…** to like nothing so much as… **tu peux protester ~ que tu voudras** you can protest as much as you like; **~ bien que mal** [*réparer, organiser, diriger*] after a fashion; [*se débrouiller*] more or less; **essayer ~ bien que mal de s'adapte** to be struggling to adapt; **3** (aussi longtemps) **~ que** as long as; **je ne partirai pas ~ qu'il ne m'aura pas accordé un rendez-vous** I won't leave until he's given me an appointment; **profites-en ~ que t peux** make the most of it while you can; **~ que tu y es, balaye aussi la cuisine** while you're at it, sweep the kitchen as well; **traite-moi de menteur ~ qu tu y es**○! go ahead and call me a liar!; **4** (remplaçan un nombre) **gagner/dépenser ~ par mois** to earn/t spend so much a month; **votre lettre datée du ~** your letter of such-and-such a date.
II tant de *dét indéf* **1** (avec un nom dénombrable) s many; **et ~ d'autres** and so many others; **~ de meubles** so much furniture; **2** (avec un nom non dé nombrable) so much; **~ d'argent** so much money; **j n'ai jamais vu ~ de monde** I've never seen so man people; **~ d'humilité force le respect** such humilit commands respect.
III (dans des locutions) **~ pis** too bad; **~ pis pou toi** too bad, that's your bad luck; **~ mieux** so much the better; **~ mieux pour toi** good for you; **~ e plus** GÉN a great deal; (avec un nom dénombrable) great many; **~ et si bien que** so much so that; **il a fait ~ et si bien qu'il s'est fait renvoyer** he finall managed to get himself fired; **il avait un ~ soit pe arrogant** he's a bit arrogant; **s'il avait un ~ so peu de bon sens** if he had the slightest bit of commo sense, if he had an ounce of common sense; **si tu étai (un) ~ soit peu inquiet** if you were in the least b worried; **~ s'en faut** not by a long shot; **~ qu' faire, autant repeindre toute la pièce** we may a well repaint the whole room while we're at it; **~ qu'à faire, je préférerais que ce soit lui qui l'achèt** since somebody has to buy it, I'd rather it was him; **~ que as**; **en ~ que tel** as such; **si ~ est qu'il puisse y aller** that is if he can go at all; **~ que ça**○? (avec un nom dénombrable) that many?; (ave un nom non dénombrable ou un verbe) that much?; **je n l'aime pas ~ que ça** I don't like him/her all tha much.

Tantale /tɑ̃tal/ *npr* Tantalus; **supplice de ~** torment of Tantalus; **c'est un véritable supplice de ~** it's really tantalizing.

tante /tɑ̃t/ *nf* aunt; **~ Julie** aunt Julie.

tantinet○ /tɑ̃tinɛ/ *nm* **un ~** a trifle, a tiny bit; **un ~ de** (de whisky, sel) a dash of; (d'humour) a touch of.

tantôt /tɑ̃to/ *adv* (parfois) sometimes.

taon /tɑ̃/ *nm* horsefly.

tapage /tapaʒ/ *nm* **1** (bruit) din, racket○; **faire du ~** to make a racket○; **2** (éclat) **la nouvelle a fait du ~** the news caused a furore GB ou furor US; **3** (battage) hype; **~ médiatique** media hype.

■ **~ nocturne** disturbance of the peace at night.

tapageur, -euse /tapaʒœʀ, øz/ *adj* **1** (bruyant) [*personne*] rowdy; **2** (outrancier) [*luxe, élégance*] showy; (retentissant) [*campagne*] hyped-up; [*propos*] ostentatious.

tapante /tapɑ̃t/ *adj f* **à trois heures ~s** at three o'clock sharp ou on the dot.

tape /tap/ *nf* (amicale) pat; (plus forte) slap; **donner une petite ~ sur le dos de qn** (pour attirer l'attention) to give sb a little tap on the back.

tape-à-l'œil /tapalœj/ *adj inv* [*couleur*] loud; [*décoration, bijou, mobilier*] garish.

taper /tape/ [1] **I** *vtr* **1** (frapper) to hit [*personne, chien*]; **2** (dactylographier) to type [*lettre*]; **lettre tapée à la machine** type-written letter; **3**○ (prendre) **je peux te ~ 1 franc?** can I scrounge○ a franc off you?.

II taper sur *vtr ind* to hit [*clou*]; **~ sur l'épaule de qn** to tap sb on the shoulder; **~ sur qn**○ LIT to thump ou belt○ sb; FIG (critiquer) to badmouth○ sb; **~ sur la table** LIT to bang (one's fist) on the table; **~ sur les nerfs de qn** to get on sb's nerves; **se faire ~ sur les doigts** FIG to get one's knuckles rapped.

III *vi* **1** (frapper) **~ des mains** (de joie) to clap one's hands; **~ des pieds** (de colère) to stamp one's feet; **~ du pied** (d'impatience) to tap one's foot; **~ à la porte** to knock at the door; **~ dans un ballon** to kick a ball around; **le soleil tape**○ **aujourd'hui** FIG the sun is beating down today; **un vin qui tape**○ FIG a wine that goes to one's head; **2**○ (se servir) **~ dans ses économies** to dip into one's savings; **3** (dactylographier) **~ (à la machine)** to type.

IV se taper *vpr* **1**○ (l'un l'autre) **se ~ dessus** to knock each other about; **2** (soi-même) **je me suis tapé sur le doigt** I hit myself on the finger; **se ~ la tête contre le mur** to bang one's head against the wall; **c'est à se ~ la tête contre les murs** FIG it's enough to drive you up the wall; **3**○ (endurer) to get stuck○ with [*corvée, importun*]; **j'ai dû me ~ le trajet à pied** I had to foot it○ all the way; **je me suis tapé la route sous la pluie** I ended up having to go all the way in the rain.

IDIOMES **~ comme un sourd**○ (à la porte) to thunder on the door; (au piano) to bash○ ou thump away; **ils se tapent sur le ventre**○ they are thick as thieves; **c'est à s'en ~ le derrière par terre**○ it's hilarious, it's a riot○; **elle m'a tapé dans l'œil**○ I thought she was striking; **~ à côté** to be off target.

tapette /tapɛt/ *nf* **1**○ (langue) **faire marcher sa ~** to chatter away endlessly; **2** (pour tapis) carpet beater; **3** (pour tuer les mouches) fly swatter; **4** (piège à souris) mousetrap; **5** (petite tape) pat.

tapeur, -euse /tapœʀ, øz/ *nm,f* scrounger○.

tapinois: en tapinois /ɑ̃tapinwa/ *loc adv* furtively.

tapir¹: se tapir /tapiʀ/ [3] *vpr* [*personne, animal*] to hide; (en ramassant son corps) to crouch.

tapir² /tapiʀ/ *nm* ZOOL tapir.

tapis /tapi/ *nm inv* GÉN carpet, rug; (sur un meuble) cloth; (de salle de bains, sport) mat; **mettre qch sur le ~** FIG to bring sth up; **mettre** or **envoyer qn au ~** to throw sb.

■ **~ de bain(s)** bathmat; **~ roulant** (pour piétons) moving walkway; (pour bagages) carousel; (pour marchandises) conveyor belt; **~ vert** (sur table de conférence, de jeux) green baize; **~ volant** flying carpet.

tapisser /tapise/ [1] *vtr* **1** (poser un revêtement) to

decorate [*pièce, mur*]; to cover, to upholster [*fauteuil*]; CULIN to line [*moule*] (**de** with); **2** (servir de revêtement) [*mousse, neige*] to carpet [*sol*]; to cover [*mont, ruine*]; [*cellule, muqueuse*] to line [*organe, cavité*]; [*tentures, photos*] to cover [*mur, pièce*]; [*résidu, pâte*] to line [*fond*].

tapisserie /tapisʀi/ *nf* **1** (tenture, broderie) tapestry; **2** (papier peint) wallpaper; **3** (art, technique) tapestry work.

IDIOMES **faire ~** (au bal) to be a wallflower.

tapissier, -ière /tapisje, ɛʀ/ ▶374] *nm,f* **1** (pour meubles) upholsterer; **2** (artiste) tapestry-maker.

tapoter /tapɔte/ [1] *vtr* to tap [*table, objet*]; to pat [*joues, dos*].

taquin, ~e /takɛ̃, in/ *adj* [*personne*] teasing; **il est très ~** he's a great tease.

taquiner /takine/ [1] *vtr* [*personne*] to tease; [*histoire, douleur*] to bother.

taquinerie /takinʀi/ *nf* teasing ¢.

tarabiscoté, ~e /taʀabiskɔte/ *adj* [*motif*] over-ornate; [*écriture*] over-elaborate; [*esprit, style*] convoluted.

tarabuster○ /taʀabyste/ [1] *vtr* [*ennuis, question*] to bother; [*personne*] to badger.

taratata○ /taʀatata/ *excl* nonsense!, rubbish○! GB.

tard /taʀ/ **I** *adv* late; **plus ~** later; **au plus ~** at the latest; **~ dans la nuit** in the middle of the night; **il est un peu ~ pour changer de tactique** it's a bit late in the day to change tactics; **pas plus ~ qu'hier** only yesterday; **ce sera pour plus ~** (une autre fois) there'll be other times.

II sur le tard *loc adv* [*se marier*] late in life; **déclarant sur le ~ que** announcing rather late in the day that.

IDIOMES **mieux vaut ~ que jamais** PROV better late than never PROV; **il n'est jamais trop ~ pour bien faire** PROV it's never too late to do the right thing.

tarder /taʀde/ [1] **I** *vi* **1** (à agir) **~ à faire** (être lent) to take a long time doing; (différer) to put off ou delay doing; **trop ~ à faire qch** to wait too long to do sth; **sans ~** immediately; **sans plus ~** without further delay; **elle n'a pas tardé à faire la même chose** she lost no time in doing the same thing; **il ne tardera pas à s'en rendre compte** he'll soon realize; **ne tardez pas!** don't delay!; **2** (à arriver, se manifester) **~** (à arriver) [*saison, réaction, réponse*] to be a long time coming; [*colis*] to take a long time to come; **les enfants ne vont pas ~** (à arriver) the children won't be long; **elle tarde à revenir** she's taking a long time; **ça ne va pas ~** it won't be long; **ça n'a pas tardé** it wasn't long coming.

II *v impers* **il me tarde de la revoir/qu'elle parte** I'm longing to see her again/for her to go.

tardif, -ive /taʀdif, iv/ *adj* [*heure, floraison*] late; [*excuses, revirement*] belated.

tardivement /taʀdivmɑ̃/ *adv* [*arriver*] late; [*réagir*] rather belatedly; **ne découvrir qch que ~** to discover sth rather late in the day.

tare /taʀ/ *nf* **1** (masse) tare; **2** MÉD defect **3** (grave défaut) defect; **être accusé d'avoir toutes les ~s** to be accused of every vice in the book.

taré, ~e /taʀe/ **I** *adj* **1** MÉD [*personne, animal*] with a defect (*épith, après n*); **2**○ (fou) OFFENSIVE crazy○; **3** FIG [*société*] sick.

II *nm,f* OFFENSIVE cretin PÉJ.

targette /taʀʒɛt/ *nf* bolt.

targuer: se targuer /taʀge/ [1] *vpr* to claim (**de qch** sth; **de faire** to do), to boast (**de qch** sth); **il se targue d'avoir créé des emplois** he prides himself on having created jobs.

tarif /taʀif/ *nm* **1** (prix) GÉN rate; (de transport) fare; (de consultation) fee; **payer plein ~** GÉN to pay full price; (en train, avion, bus) to pay full fare; **~ normal/économique** POSTES = first-class/second-class rate; **~ de nuit** TÉLÉCOM night-time rate; **~ lettres** letter rate; **tu connais le ~**○, **c'est deux jours de renvoi** FIG you know the penalty—two days' suspension; **2** (document) price list.

tarification /taʀifikasjɔ̃/ *nf* (action) price setting; (résultat) tariff.

tarir /taʀiʀ/ [23] **I** *vi* **ne pas ~ sur qch/qn** to talk endlessly about sth/sb; **ne pas ~ d'éloges sur qch/qn** to be full of praise for sth/sb.
II se tarir *vpr* LIT, FIG to dry up, to run dry.

tartare /taʀtaʀ/ *adj* **1** HIST Tartar; **2** CULIN **sauce ~** tartare sauce; **steak ~** steak tartare.

tarte /taʀt/ **I**° *adj* (niais) [*personne*] daft° GB, daffy° US; [*film, chanson, chapeau, robe*] ridiculous.
II *nf* **1** CULIN tart; **2**⊕ (gifle) wallop°.
■ **~ à la crème** (idée banale) stereotype; (gag) custard pie, slapstick.
IDIOMES **c'est pas de la ~**⊕ it's no picnic°.

tartelette /taʀtəlɛt/ *nf* tart.

Tartempion° /taʀtɑ̃pjɔ̃/ *npr* **Monsieur et Madame ~** Mr and Mrs Whatnot; **demande donc à ~** go and ask what's-his-name°.

tartine /taʀtin/ *nf* **1** (pain beurré) slice of bread and butter; **peux-tu me faire une ~?** could you butter me a slice of bread?; **une ~ de confiture** a slice of bread and jam; **2**° **il en a écrit une ~** he wrote reams about it; **il y en a une ~!** there's reams of it!

tartiner /taʀtine/ [1] *vtr* to spread; **chocolat à ~** chocolate spread; **pâte à ~** sandwich spread.

tartre /taʀtʀ/ *nm* (dans une bouilloire) scale, fur GB; (sur les dents) tartar; (de vin) tartar.

tartufe /taʀtyf/ *nm* hypocrite.

tas /tɑ/ **I** *nm inv* **1** LIT heap, pile (**de** of); **en ~ dans un coin** piled in a corner; **~ de fumier** manure heap; **~ de bois** (ordonné) woodpile; (désordonné) pile of wood; **~ de ferraille** LIT scrap heap; FIG (vieille voiture)° wreck; **2**° FIG **un ~, des ~** lots (**de** of), loads° (**de** of).
II dans le tas *loc adv* **taper dans le ~** to punch people indiscriminately; **foncer dans le ~** [*personne*] to fling oneself into the crowd; [*police*] to charge the crowd.
III sur le tas *loc adv* **apprendre sur le ~** to learn on the job; **formation sur le ~** on-the-job training; **grève sur le ~** sit-down strike.

tasse /tɑs/ *nf* **1** (récipient) cup; **~ à thé** teacup; **2** (contenu) cup.
IDIOMES **boire la ~**° to swallow a mouthful of water (when swimming).

tassé, ~e /tɑse/ **I** *pp* ▶ **tasser**.
II *pp adj* [*terre*] firmly packed; [*neige*] hard packed; **bien ~** [*cigarette*] well packed; [*neige*] very hard packed; [*whisky*] stiff; **il y en a 4 kilos bien ~s**° there's a good 4 kilos of it; **il a la cinquantaine bien ~e**⊕ he's well past fifty.

tassement /tɑsmɑ̃/ *nm* (de l'emploi) contraction; **~ de vertèbres** compression of the vertebrae.

tasser /tɑse/ [1] **I** *vtr* to press down [*terre*]; to tamp down [*tabac*]; to pack down [*paille*]; to pack [*habits, gens*]; to cram [*bagages*]; **les passagers étaient tassés** the passengers were packed in tightly; **l'accident lui a tassé les vertèbres** the accident has given him/her compression of the vertebrae.
II se tasser *vpr* **1** (s'affaisser) (avec l'âge) to shrink; (volontairement) to make oneself look smaller; **2** (se serrer) [*personnes*] to squash up; **3**° (se calmer) [*conflit*] to die down; **les choses se sont tassées** things settled down.

tata° /tata/ *nf* auntie.

tâter /tɑte/ [1] **I** *vtr* **1** (palper) to feel; **~ le sol du pied** to test the ground; **2** (sonder) **~ l'opinion** to sound out public opinion.
II tâter de *vtr ind* **~ de tous les métiers** to try one's hand at all kinds of jobs; **~ de la prison** to have a taste of prison.
III se tâter° *vpr* **je me tâte** I'm thinking about it.
IDIOMES **~ le terrain** to put out feelers.

tatillon, -onne /tatijɔ̃, ɔn/ *adj* nit-picking.

tâtonnement /tɑtɔnmɑ̃/ *nm* **~s dans l'obscurité**

groping around in the dark; **les ~s des chercheurs** FIG tentative research **⊄**; **après dix années de ~s** FIG after ten years of trial and error.

tâtonner /tɑtɔne/ [1] *vi* to grope about ou around; **avancer en tâtonnant** LIT, FIG to grope one's way along; **on tâtonne** (dans des recherches) we're groping in the dark.

tâtons: à tâtons /atatɔ̃/ *loc adv* **avancer à ~** LIT, FIG to feel one's way along.

tatouage /tatwaʒ/ *nm* **1** (dessin) tattoo; **2** (procédé) tattooing.

tatouer /tatwe/ [1] *vtr* to tattoo; **se faire ~** to get tattooed; **il s'est fait ~ un aigle sur le dos** he has had an eagle tattooed on his back.

tatoueur, -euse /tatwœʀ, øz/ *nm,f* tattooist.

taudis /todi/ *nm inv* (misérable) hovel; (mal tenu)⊕ pigsty.

taule⊕ /tol/ *nf* (prison) prison, nick° GB; **faire de la ~** to do time°.

taupe /top/ *nf* **1** ZOOL mole; **2** (peau) moleskin; **en ~ moleskin** (*épith*); **3**° (femme désagréable) PÉJ **une vieille ~** an old bag° PÉJ; **4**° (espion) mole.

taupinière /topinjɛʀ/ *nf* (monticule) molehill; (galeries) (mole) tunnels (*pl*).
IDIOMES **faire une montagne d'une ~** to make a mountain out of a molehill.

taureau, ** *pl* **~x /tɔʀo/ *nm* bull.
IDIOMES **prendre le ~ par les cornes** to take the bull by the horns.

Taureau /tɔʀo/ ▶ 641 *nprm* Taurus.

taurillon /tɔʀijɔ̃/ *nm* young bull.

tauromachie /tɔʀɔmaʃi/ ▶ 329 *nf* bullfighting.

taux /to/ *nm inv* **1** GÉN rate; **~ de chômage/croissance** unemployment/growth rate; **2** MÉD (d'albumine, alcoolémie, de sucre) level; (de bactéries, spermatozoïdes) count.
■ **~ d'audience** audience ratings (*pl*); **~ de fréquentation** CIN, THÉAT audience figures (*pl*); **~ de natalité** birthrate; **~ de salaire horaire** hourly rate of pay.

tavelé, ~e /tavle/ *adj* [*peau*] spotted (**de** with); [*fruit*] blemished (**de** with).

taxation /taksasjɔ̃/ *nf* (imposition) taxation; (fixation) assessment.

taxe /taks/ *nf* **1** COMM, ÉCON tax; **les ~s sur les importations** import levies; **boutique hors ~s** duty-free shop GB ou store US; **500 francs hors ~s** 500 francs exclusive of tax; **toutes ~s comprises, TTC** inclusive of tax; **2** JUR taxation.
■ **~ d'apprentissage** ~ training levy; **~ de douane** customs duty; **~ foncière** property tax; **~ d'habitation** ~ council tax (*paid by residents to cover local services*); **~ de raccordement** connection charge; **~ à la valeur ajoutée** value added tax.

taxer /takse/ [1] *vtr* **1** COMM, ÉCON to tax; **2** (accuser) **~ qn de laxisme** to accuse sb of being lax.

taxi /taksi/ *nm* **1** (véhicule) taxi, cab US; **chauffeur de ~** taxi driver; **station de ~s** taxi rank GB, taxi stand US; **2**° (chauffeur) taxi driver.

taxidermiste /taksidɛʀmist/ ▶ 374 *nmf* taxidermist.

Tchad /tʃad/ ▶ 335 , 232 *nprm* Chad; **le lac ~** Lake Chad.

tchador /tʃadɔʀ/ *nm* chador.

tchao /tʃao/ *excl* bye°!, see you°!

Tchécoslovaquie /tʃekɔslɔvaki/ *nprf* HIST Czechoslovakia.

tchèque /tʃɛk/ ▶ 394 , 232 , 338 *adj, nm* Czech.

tchin(-tchin)° /tʃin(tʃin)/ *excl* cheers!

TD /tede/ *nmpl: abbr* ▶ **travail**.

te (**t'** *before vowel or mute h*) /t(ə)/ *pron pers* **1** (objet direct) you; **2** (objet indirect) you; **3** (pronom réfléchi) yourself; **il faut que tu ~ soignes** you must look after yourself; **va ~ laver les mains** go and wash your hands.

té /te/ *nm* (règle) T-square; **en ~** T-shaped.

technicien, -ienne /tɛknisjɛ̃, ɛn/ ▶374❘ *nm,f* **1** (professionnel) technician; ~ **supérieur** qualified technician; **2** (spécialiste) technical expert (**de** in); **c'est un très bon** ~ he's technically very good; **3** (réparateur) engineer.
■ ~ **de surface** cleaner.

technique¹ /tɛknik/ **I** *adj* technical.
II *nm* technical subjects (*pl*).

technique² /tɛknik/ *nf* **1** (méthode) technique; **il n'a pas la (bonne)** ~○ he hasn't got the knack○; **2** (maîtrise) technique; **3** ÉCON, IND technology ₵; **4** RADIO, TV **la** ~ studio production.

technocrate /tɛknɔkʀat/ *nmf* technocrat.

technologie /tɛknɔlɔʒi/ *nf* technology.

teck /tɛk/ *nm* (arbre, bois) teak; **en** ~ teak (*épith*).

teckel /tekɛl/ *nm* dachshund.

tee-shirt, *pl* ~**s** /tiʃœʀt/ *nm* T-shirt.

teigne /tɛɲ/ *nf* **1** (mite) moth; **2**○ (personne hargneuse) nasty GB ou real US piece of work○; **être méchant comme une** ~ to be a nasty GB ou real US piece of work.

teigneux○, **-euse** /tɛɲø, øz/ *adj* (hargneux) cantankerous.

teindre /tɛ̃dʀ/ [73] **I** *vtr* to dye [*cheveux, tissu, cuir*]; to stain [*bois, meuble*]; ~ **qch en vert** to dye sth green.
II se teindre *vpr* [*personne*] to dye one's hair; **se** ~ **les cheveux en roux** to dye one's hair red.

teint, ~e¹ /tɛ̃, tɛ̃t/ **I** *pp* ▶ **teindre**.
II *pp adj* [*cheveux, étoffe, cuir*] dyed; [*bois, meuble*] stained.
III *nm* **1** (peau) complexion; **joli** ~ lovely complexion; **2** (lié à la santé) **avoir le** ~ **rose** or **frais** to have a healthy glow; **avoir le** ~ **jaune** to be sallow-skinned; **avoir le** ~ **pâle** to look pale.

teinte² /tɛ̃t/ *nf* **1** (nuance de couleur) shade; **2** (couleur) colour GB; **3** (d'envie, de supériorité) **une** ~ **de** a tinge of.

teinté, ~e /tɛ̃te/ **I** *pp* ▶ **teinter**.
II *pp adj* **1** [*lunettes, verre, crème*] tinted; [*bois*] stained; ~ **jaune** yellow-tinted; **2** FIG ~ **de** [*sentiment, couleur*] tinged with.

teinter /tɛ̃te/ [1] **I** *vtr* **1** to tint [*verre*]; to stain [*bois, meuble*]; to dye [*cuir*]; **2** (nuancer) ~ **qch de** to tinge sth with.
II se teinter *vpr* LITER **se** ~ **de** to become tinged with.

teinture /tɛ̃tyʀ/ *nf* **1** (produit) (pour cheveux, tissu, cuir) dye; (pour bois) stain; ~ **d'iode** tincture of iodine; **2** (procédé) (de cheveux, tissu, cuir) dyeing; (de bois) staining; **se faire une** ~ to dye one's hair; **se faire faire une** ~ to have one's hair dyed.

teinturerie /tɛ̃tyʀʀi/ *nf* ▶374❘ **1** (boutique de nettoyage) (dry-)cleaner's; **2** (industrie) (de la teinture) dyeing; (du nettoyage) (dry-)cleaning.

teinturier, -ière /tɛ̃tyʀje, ɛʀ/ ▶374❘ *nm,f* (qui nettoie) dry-cleaner; (qui teint) dyer.

tek /tɛk/ = **teck**.

tel, telle /tɛl/ **I** *adj* **1** (pareil) such; **un** ~ **homme peut être dangereux** such a man can be dangerous, a man like that can be dangerous; **je n'ai jamais rien vu de** ~ I've never seen anything like it; **2** (pareil à) like; **3** (ainsi) **telle est la vérité** that is the truth; ~**s furent ses propos** those were his/her words; **il est honnête, du moins je le crois** ~ he's honest, at least I believe him to be so; **comme** ~, **en tant que** ~ as such; **ce n'est pas sa fille mais il la considère comme telle** she's not his daughter but he treats her as if she were; ~ **quel**, ~ **que**○ CONTROV (sans modification) as it is; **ses affaires étaient restées telles quelles** his/her things were left as they were; ~ **que** (comme) as; **si cette maison est telle que tu le dis** if the house is as you say it is; ~ **que je le connais** if I know you; ~ **que vous le voyez il a 80 ans** you wouldn't believe it to look at him but he's 80; **4** (pour exprimer l'intensité) **avec un** ~ **enthousiasme** with such enthusiasm; **il fait une telle chaleur** it is so hot; **il y avait un** ~ **bruit** there was so much noise; **de**

telle sorte or **façon** or **manière que** (accidentellement) in such a way that; (délibérément) so that; **5** (un certain) **admettons qu'il arrive** ~ **jour, à telle heure** suppose that he arrives on such and such a day, at such and such a time; **que je prenne telle ou telle décision il critique toujours** no matter what decision I make, he criticizes it; **je me moque de ce que pense telle ou telle personne** I don't care what certain people think; ~ **autre** others (*pl*); ~**s autres** certain others.
II *pron indéf* ~ **voulait la guerre**, ~ **voulait la paix** some wanted war, some wanted peace.

télé○ /tele/ **I** *adj inv* TV; **programme** ~ TV guide.
II *nf* TV; **à la** ~ on TV.

télécabine /telekabin/ *nm* cable car.

télécommande /telekɔmɑ̃d/ *nf* remote control.

télécommander /telekɔmɑ̃de/ [1] *vtr* **1** TECH to operate [sth] by remote control; **voiture télécommandée** remote-controlled car; **2** FIG (diriger) to mastermind.

télécommunication /telekɔmynikasjɔ̃/ *nf* telecommunications (+ *v sg*).

téléconférence /telekɔ̃feʀɑ̃s/ *nf* **1** (séance) (audioconférence) conference call; (vidéoconférence) teleconference; **2** (principe) video-conferencing.

télécopie /telekɔpi/ *nf* fax.

télécopier /telekɔpje/ [2] *vtr* to fax.

télécopieur /telekɔpjœʀ/ *nm* fax machine, fax.

télédiffuser /teledifyze/ [1] *vtr* to broadcast.

télé-enquêteur, -trice /teleɑ̃kɛtœʀ, tʀis/ ▶374❘ *nm,f* telemarketer.

télé-enseignement, *pl* ~**s** /teleɑ̃sɲəmɑ̃/ *nm* distance learning.

téléfilm /telefilm/ *nm* TV film, TV movie.

télégramme /telegʀam/ *nm* telegram, cable US.

télégraphier /telegʀafje/ [1] *vtr* to telegraph, to send a telegram ou cable US.

télégraphique /telegʀafik/ *adj* [*poteau, message*] telegraph; [*style*] telegraphic.

téléguidage /telegidaʒ/ *nm* radio control.

téléguider /telegide/ [1] *vtr* **1** LIT to control [sth] by radio; **voiture téléguidée** radio-controlled car; **2** FIG (diriger) to mastermind.

télématique /telematik/ **I** *adj* [*service, réseau*] viewdata GB, videotex®.
II *nf* telematics (+ *v sg*).

téléobjectif /teleɔbʒɛktif/ *nm* telephoto lens.

télépathie /telepati/ *nf* telepathy.

téléphérique /telefeʀik/ *nm* cable car, téléphérique.

téléphone /telefɔn/ *nm* (dispositif, appareil) phone; **avoir le** ~ to be on the (tele)phone GB, to have a phone; **donner un coup de** ~ to make a phone call; ~ **à touches/pièces** push-button/coin-operated telephone; ~ **à carte** cardphone.
■ ~ **arabe**○ (bouche-à-oreille) grapevine, bush telegraph; JEUX Chinese whispers (+ *v sg*); ~ **portable** transmobile phone; ~ **portatif** pocket car phone; ~ **rose** erotic chat-line; ~ **rouge** the hot-line.

téléphoner /telefɔne/ [1] **I** *vtr* ~ **qch à qn** to phone sb with sth.
II *vi* (en général) to phone; (une fois) to make a phone call; ~ **à qn** to phone sb, to call sb.
III se téléphoner *vpr* to phone each other.

téléphonique /telefɔnik/ *adj* (tele)phone (*épith*).

téléprospecteur, -trice /telepʀɔspɛktœʀ, tʀis/ ▶374❘ *nm,f* telemarketer.

téléreportage /teleʀəpɔʀtaʒ/ *nm* (activité) television reporting; (film) television report.

télescopage /telɛskɔpaʒ/ *nm* LIT collision; FIG overlap.

télescope /telɛskɔp/ *nm* telescope.

télescoper /telɛskɔpe/ [1] **I** *vtr* to collide with [*voiture*].
II se télescoper *vpr* LIT [*véhicules*] to collide; FIG [*notions, tendances*] to overlap.

téléscripteur /teleskʀiptœʀ/ *nm* teleprinter GB, teletypewriter US.

télésiège /telesjɛʒ/ *nm* chair lift.

téléski /teleski/ *nm* ski tow.

téléspectateur, -trice /telespɛktatœʀ, tʀis/ *nm,f* viewer.

télésurveillance /telesyʀvɛjɑ̃s/ *nf* electronic surveillance.

télétransmission /teletʀɑ̃smisjɔ̃/ *nf* transmission.

télévente /televɑ̃t/ *nf* telesales *pl.*

télévisé, ~e /televize/ *adj* [*programme, publicité*] television (*épith*); [*débat, retransmission*] televised.

téléviseur /televizœʀ/ *nm* television (set); **~ couleur** colour[GB] television.

télévision /televizjɔ̃/ *nf* television, TV; **travailler à la ~** to work in television.

télex /telɛks/ *nm inv* telex; **par ~** by telex.

télexer /telɛkse/ [1] *vtr* to telex.

tellement /tɛlmɑ̃/ ▶ 486 I *adv* 1 (marquant l'intensité) (modifiant un adjectif ou un adverbe) so; (modifiant un verbe ou un comparatif) so much; **pas ~** not much; **il n'aime pas ~ lire** he doesn't like reading much; **'il y avait beaucoup de monde?'—'pas ~'** 'were there many people?'—'not really'; **ce n'est pas ~ que je sois fatigué mais…** it's not so much that I'm tired but…; **cela n'a plus ~ d'importance** it doesn't really matter any more; **je n'ai plus ~ envie d'y aller** I don't really want to go any more; **il n'est pas ~ plus jeune que moi** he's not that much younger than me; **il y avait ~ de gens que je me suis perdu** there were so many people that I got lost; **2** (si nombreux) **il y en a ~ qui aimeraient le faire** so many people would like to do it; **3** (introduisant une cause) **j'ai de la peine à suivre ~ c'est compliqué** it's so complicated that I find it hard to follow.
II **tellement de** *dét indéf* **1** (avec un nom dénombrable) so many; **il y a ~ de choses à voir** there's so much to see; **2** (avec un nom non dénombrable) so much; **il a eu ~ de chance** he was so lucky; **j'ai vu ~ de monde** I saw so many people.

tellurique /tɛlyʀik/ *adj* **secousse ~** earth tremor.

téméraire /temeʀɛʀ/ *adj* [*personne, projet*] reckless; [*jugement*] rash; **courageux mais pas ~** brave but not foolhardy.

témérité /temeʀite/ *nf* (de personne, projet) recklessness; (de paroles) rashness; **avoir la ~ de faire** to have the temerity to do.

témoignage /temwaɲaʒ/ *nm* **1** (histoire personnelle) story; (compte rendu) account; **recueillir les ~s des réfugiés** to get the refugees' stories; **~s recueillis auprès de** accounts given by; **apporter son ~** to give one's own account; **selon les ~s de** according to (accounts given by); **2** (au cours d'une enquête) evidence ¢; (déposition) evidence ¢, testimony; **selon plusieurs ~s** according to several witnesses; **3** (marque) FML **~ d'amitié** (cadeau) token of friendship; (geste) expression of friendship; **~s de sympathie** expressions of sympathy; **donner des ~s de son amitié** to prove one's friendship.

témoigner /temwaɲe/ [1] I *vtr* **1** JUR to testify; **elle a témoigné l'avoir vu entrer** she testified to having seen him go in; **2** (montrer) **~ de l'affection** to show affection; **la confiance qu'elle m'a témoignée** the trust she placed in me; **les marques de sympathie qui leur ont été témoignées lors de…** the expressions of sympathy they received when…
II **témoigner de** *vtr ind* **1** (prouver) **~ de** to show; **comme en témoigne leur lettre** as their letter shows; **2** (se porter garant de) **~ du courage de qn** to vouch for sb's courage.
III *vi* **1** JUR to give evidence; **être appelé à ~** to be called to give evidence; **2** (dire) **'il était toujours poli', témoignent les voisins** neighbours[GB] say he was always polite.

témoin /temwɛ̃/ I *nm* **1** (sur les lieux) witness; **~ oculaire** or **direct** eyewitness; **être (le) ~ de** to witness; **prendre qn à ~** to call sb to witness; **2** JUR witness; **3** (à un duel) second; **4** FIG (d'une époque) **avoir été ~ de la naissance du IIIᵉ Reich** to have

witnessed the birth of the Third Reich; **5** (preuve) **ils sont cruels, ~ le massacre** they are (certainly) cruel, as evidenced by the massacre; **6** TECH (voyant) indicator ou warning light; **~ d'huile** AUT oil warning light; **7** SPORT baton.
II **(-)témoin** (*in compounds*) control **groupe(-)~** control group.
IDIOMES **Dieu** or **le Ciel m'en est ~** as God is my witness.

tempe /tɑ̃p/ ▶ 137 *nf* temple; **appuyer un pistolet sur la ~ de qn** to hold a gun to sb's head.

tempérament /tɑ̃peʀamɑ̃/ *nm* **1** (caractère) disposition; **être calme de ~** to have a calm disposition; **ce n'est pas dans mon ~ de me mettre en colère** would never lose my temper; **elle devrait aller se plaindre, mais ce n'est pas dans son ~** she should go and complain, but she's not like that; **avoir du ~** (volontaire) to have a strong character; **2** COMM **à ~** by instalments[GB].

température /tɑ̃peʀatyʀ/ *nf* **1** MÉD, PHYS temperature; **prendre la ~ de qn** to take sb's temperature; **2** (fièvre) temperature; **3** (humeur) **prendre la ~ du public** to sound out the public's mood.

tempéré, -e /tɑ̃peʀe/ *adj* GÉOG temperate.

tempérer /tɑ̃peʀe/ [14] *vtr* GÉN to temper; **~ ses ardeurs** to cool one's ardour[GB].

tempête /tɑ̃pɛt/ *nf* **1** MÉTÉO (sans pluie) gale; (avec pluie) storm; **essuyer une ~** to weather a storm; **~ de neige** snowstorm; **~ de sable** sandstorm; **2** (agitation) uproar; **après la ~ boursière** after the upheaval on the stock exchange; **~ de protestations** wave of protest *sg*; **une ~ dans un verre d'eau** a storm in a teacup GB, a tempest in a teapot US.

tempêter /tɑ̃pete/ [1] *vi* to rage (**contre** against).

temple /tɑ̃pl/ *nm* **1** RELIG (non chrétien) temple; (protestant) church; **2** FIG temple (**de** of).

tempo /tɛmpo/ *nm* **1** MUS tempo; **2** (de roman, film) pace.

temporaire /tɑ̃poʀɛʀ/ *adj* temporary; **à titre ~** [*employer, travailler*] on a temporary basis; **délivrer un permis à titre ~** to issue a temporary permit.

temporel, -elle /tɑ̃poʀɛl/ *adj* GÉN temporal; **biens ~s** worldly goods.

temporisateur, -trice /tɑ̃poʀizatœʀ, tʀis/ I *adj* temporizing (*épith*).
II *nm,f* temporizer.

temporiser /tɑ̃poʀize/ [1] *vi* to stall.

temps /tɑ̃/ *nm inv* ▶ 588 **1** MÉTÉO weather ¢; **un beau ~** fine weather; **un ~ de cochon**○ lousy○ weather; **le ~ est à la pluie** it looks like rain; **le ~ est à l'orage** there's going to be a storm; **par ~ clair** (de jour) on a clear day; (de nuit) on a clear night; **par ~ de pluie** when it rains; **2** (durée) time; **peu de ~ avant** shortly before; **dans peu de ~** shortly; **dans quelque ~** before long; (pendant) quelque temps **un certain ~** (assez courte période) for a while; (période plus longue) for some time; **pendant** or **pour un ~** for a while; **pendant ce ~(-là)** meanwhile; **en un rien de ~** in no time at all; **les trois quarts du ~** most of the time; **depuis le ~ que j'en parle!** I've been talking about it for long enough!; **depuis le ~ que ça existe, tu devrais être au courant** you should have known, it's been around for so long; **le ~ d'installation a été plus long que prévu** it took longer than expected to install; **ils sont restés le ~ de l'élection** they stayed just for the duration of the election; **il a souri le ~ de la photo** he smiled just long enough for the photo to be taken; **un an, le ~ d'écrire un roman** a year, just long enough to write a novel; **le ~ de me retourner, il avait disparu** by the time I turned round GB ou around, he had disappeared; **le ~ de ranger mes affaires et j'arrive** just let me put my things away and I'll be with you; **(j'ai) pas l'~**○! not now!; **avoir tout le ~** to have plenty of time; **avoir dix** or **cent fois le ~** to have all the time in the world; **vous avez combien de ~ pour le déjeuner?** how long do you have for lunch?; **nous avons du ~ devant nous** we have plenty of time

La température

Dans les pays anglophones, la température se mesure traditionnellement en degrés Fahrenheit, mais les degrés Celsius sont de plus en plus utilisés, surtout en Grande-Bretagne. Le bulletin météo à la télévision britannique n'utilise que les degrés Celsius.

Celsius (C)	Fahrenheit (F)	
100°	212°*	boiling point (point d'ébullition)
90°	194°	
80°	176°	
70°	158°	
60°	140°	
50°	122°	
40°	104°	
37°	98.4°	
30°	86°	
20°	68°	
10°	50°	
0°	32°	freezing point (point de congélation)
−10°	14°	
−273.15°	−459.67°	absolute zero (zéro absolu)

* *Pour la prononciation des nombres, ▶ 399 .*

65°F	= 65°F	(*sixty-five degrees Fahrenheit*)
−15°C	= −15°C	(*minus fifteen degrees Celsius*)
environ 55°	= about 55°	(*fifty-five degrees*)
presque 60°	= almost 60°	
plus de 50°	= above 50° *ou* over 50°	
moins de 60°	= below 60°	

La température des choses

quelle est la température du lait?	= what temperature is the milk?
à quelle température est-il?	= what temperature is it?
il est à une température de 53°	= it is 53°

Noter l'absence d'équivalent anglais de l'expression à une température *de*.

A est plus chaud que B	= A is hotter than B
B est moins chaud que A	= B is cooler than A
B est plus froid que A	= B is colder than A
A est à la même température que B	= A is the same temperature as B
A et B sont à la même température	= A and B are the same temperature

Noter que l'anglais n'a pas d'équivalent de la préposition à *dans ces deux derniers exemples.*

à quelle température l'eau bout-elle?	= what temperature does water boil at?
elle bout à 100°	= it boils at 100°

La température du corps

quelle est sa température?	= what is his temperature?
sa température est de 38°C	= his temperature is 38°C
il a 38°C de fièvre	= he has a temperature of 38°C
le thermomètre indique 102°F	= the thermometer shows *ou* says 102°F
il a 39,5°	= his temperature is 39.5°
la température du corps est d'environ 37°	= body temperature is about 37°

Le temps

quelle température fait-il aujourd'hui?	= what is the temperature today?
25° au-dessous de zéro	= 25° below zero
il fait 12°	= it is 12°
il fait 40 degrés	= it is 40 degrees
il fait −15°	= it is −15° (*dire* minus fifteen degrees) *ou* it is −15° (minus fifteen)
il fait plus chaud à Nice qu'à Londres	= Nice is warmer than London
il fait la même température à Nice qu'à Londres	= it's the same temperature in Nice as in London

---

plus de ~ que longer than; **ne pas prendre beaucoup de ~** not to take long; **tu as mis combien de ~?** how long did it take you?; **ça a pris** or **mis un ~ fou**○ it took ages○; **tu y as mis le ~!**, **tu en as mis du ~!** you (certainly) took your time!; **j'y mettrai le ~ qu'il faudra, mais je le ferai** however long it takes, I'll get it done; **le ~ passe vite** time flies; **faire passer le ~** to while away the time (**en faisant** doing); **j'ai perdu un ~ fou**○ I've wasted loads○ of time; **avoir du ~ à perdre** to have time on one's hands; **faire qch à ~ perdu** to do sth in one's spare time; **le ~ presse!** time is short!; **j'ai trouvé le ~ long** (the) time seemed to drag; **nous sommes dans les ~** we've still got time; **finir dans les ~** to finish in time; **3** (moment) time; **de ~ en ~, de ~ à autre** from time to time; **il était ~!** (marquant l'impatience) (and) about time too!; (marquant le soulagement) just in the nick of time!; **il est ~** it's about time; **il est grand ~** it's high time (**de faire** to do); **il n'est plus ~ de faire** it's too late to do; **en ~ utile** in time; **en ~ voulu** (à venir) in due course; (quand il aurait fallu) at the right time; **ne durer qu'un ~** to be short-lived; **4** (époque) time; **au ~ des dinosaures** in the age of the dinosaurs; **au** or **du ~ où** in the days when; **regretter le ~ où** to feel nostalgia for the days when; **le bon vieux ~** the good old days (*pl*); **c'était le bon ~!** those were the days!; **ces derniers ~** recently; **ces ~-ci** lately; **de mon ~** in my day; **dans le ~, j'étais sportif** in my day, I did a bit of sport; **dans le ~, on n'avait pas l'électricité** in those days, we didn't have electricity; **depuis le ~, les choses ont dû bien changer** since then things must have really changed; **il est loin le ~ où** the days are long gone when; **en ~ normal** usually; **en d'autres ~** at any other time; **en ~ de paix** in peacetime; **être de son ~** to move with the times; **être en retard sur son ~** to be behind the times; **avoir fait son ~** [*prisonnier, militaire*] to have

served one's time; [*fonctionnaire, diplomate*] to have put in one's time; [*personne usée*] to have outlived one's usefulness, to be past it○; [*produit à la mode, appareil, voiture*] to have had its day; **5** (phase) stage; **dans un premier ~** first; **dans un deuxième ~** subsequently; **dans un dernier ~** finally; **6** LING (de verbe) tense; **adverbe de ~** adverb of time; **7** (de travail) time; **avoir un travail à ~ partiel/plein** to have a part-/full-time job; **~ de travail quotidien** working day GB, workday US; **8** SPORT time; **il a réalisé le meilleur ~** he got the best time; **rester dans les ~** to be inside the time; **9** (de moteur) stroke; **moteur à quatre ~** four-stroke engine; **10** MUS time; **mesure à deux ~** two-four time.

■ **~ d'antenne** airtime; **~ d'attente** ORDINAT latency; **~ fort** MUS forte; FIG high point; **~ mort** ORDINAT idle time; (d'activité) slack period; **~ de positionnement** or **de recherche** ORDINAT seek time; **~ universel** Greenwich Mean Time, GMT, universal time.

IDIOMES **au ~ pour moi!** my mistake!; **le ~ perdu ne se rattrape jamais** PROV you can't make up for lost time; **par les ~ qui courent** with things as they are; **prendre le ~ comme il vient** to take things as they come; **prendre** or **se payer**○ **du bon ~** to have a whale of a time.

tenable /tənabl/ *adj* **1** (supportable) bearable; **la situation n'est pas ~** the situation is unbearable; **2** MIL (défendable) tenable; **3** (discipliné) **les élèves ne sont pas ~s aujourd'hui** the pupils are being impossible today.

tenace /tənas/ *adj* **1** [*tache, odeur, migraine*] stubborn; [*parfum*] long-lasting; [*brume, bronchite, toux*] persistent; [*rumeur, souvenir*] persistent; [*haine, croyance*] entrenched; **2** [*personne*] (obstiné) tenacious; (insistant) persistent; [*volonté*] tenacious.

ténacité /tenasite/ *nf* **1** (de personne) (obstination)

La mesure du temps

une seconde	= a second	une semaine	= a week
une minute	= a minute	un mois	= a month‡
une heure	= an hour*	une année	= a year
un jour	= a day†	un siècle	= a century

* Pour la façon de donner l'heure ▶ **298** .
† Pour les expressions utilisant les noms de jours
▶ **551** .
‡ Pour les expressions utilisant les noms de mois
▶ **382** .

Les durées
Avec des verbes

combien de temps faut-il?	= how long does it take?
il faut trois heures	= it takes three hours
il faudra une année	= it'll take a year
il a fallu un quart d'heure	= it took a quarter of an hour
ça m'a pris une demi-heure	= it took me half an hour
j'ai mis trois heures à le faire	= it took me three hours to do it
la lettre a mis un mois pour arriver	= the letter took a month to arrive

L'anglais traduit normalement passer *par* spend:
passer une année à Paris = to spend a year in Paris

Mais avec les adjectifs évaluatifs on traduira par have:
passer une bonne soirée = to have a good evening

Avec des prépositions

en deux minutes	= in two minutes
en six mois	= in six months
en un an	= in a year
en l'espace de quelques minutes	= within minutes

Noter aussi:
dans deux minutes = in two minutes

Pendant *et* pour *se traduisent par* for, *de même que* depuis *lorsqu'il exprime une durée:*

pendant une semaine	= for a week
pendant des heures et des heures	= for hours and hours
je suis ici pour deux semaines	= I'm here for two weeks
il travaille depuis un an	= he's been working for a year
depuis bientôt dix ans	= for going on ten years

Noter aussi le temps du passé utilisé avec for. *Voir d'autres exemples à l'article* for dans le dictionnaire.

il y a des années qu'ils sont mariés = they have been married for years

Noter l'ordre des mots et l'utilisation du trait d'union dans les adjectifs composés anglais qui indiquent une durée. Pour les noms anglais dénombrables (wait, delay etc.) on aura:

une attente de six semaines	= a six-week wait
un retard de cinquante minutes	= a fifty-minute delay
une journée de huit heures	= an eight-hour day

Week, month, minute, hour *etc.*, *employés comme adjectifs, ne prennent pas la marque du pluriel.*

Mais pour les noms non-dénombrables (leave, pay etc.), il y a deux traductions possibles:

quatre jours de congé	= four days' leave
	ou four days of leave
quatre semaines de salaire	= four weeks' pay
vingt-cinq ans de bonheur	= twenty-five years' happiness
	ou twenty-five years of happiness

Un point dans le temps
Dans le passé

quand est-ce que cela s'est passé? = when did it happen?

la semaine dernière	= last week
le mois dernier	= last month
l'année dernière	= last year
au cours des derniers mois	= over the last few months

Noter l'ordre des mots avec ago:

il y a deux ans	= two years ago
il y a des années	= years ago
il y aura un mois mardi	= it'll be a month ago on Tuesday
il y a huit jours hier	= a week ago yesterday
	ou a week past yesterday
il y aura huit jours demain	= a week ago tomorrow
il y a des années qu'il est mort	= he died years ago
	ou it's years since he died
un mois auparavant	= a month before
un mois plus tôt	= a month earlier
l'année d'avant	= the year before
l'année d'après	= the year after
quelques années plus tard	= a few years later
au bout de quatre jours	= after four days

Dans le futur

quand est-ce que tu le verras? = when will you see him?

la semaine prochaine	= next week
le mois prochain	= next month
l'année prochaine	= next year

Dans *se traduit souvent par* in (*comme* en; *voir ci-dessus*):

dans dix jours	= in ten days
	ou in ten days' time
dans quelques jours	= in a few days

Noter aussi:

dans un mois demain	= a month tomorrow
au cours de la semaine à venir	= this coming week
au cours des mois à venir	= over the coming months

Les fréquences

cela arrive tous les combien?	= how often does it happen?
tous les jeudis	= every Thursday
toutes les semaines	= every week
tous les deux jours	= every other day
	or every second day
le dernier jeudi du mois	= the last Thursday of the month
jour après jour	= day after day
une fois tous les trois mois	= once every three months
deux fois par an	= twice a year
trois fois par jour	= three times a day

Les salaires

combien est-ce que tu gagnes de l'heure?	= how much do you get an hour?
je gagne 70 francs de l'heure	= I get 70 francs an hour
être payé 7 000 francs par mois	= to be paid 7,000 francs a month
190 000 francs par an	= 190,000 francs a year

Mais noter:
être payé à l'heure = to be paid by the hour

---

tenacity; (insistance) persistence; **2** (de souvenir, d'illusion) persistence.

tenaille /tənɑj/ *nf* pincers (*pl*).

tenailler /tənɑje/ [1] *vtr* **il était tenaillé par le remords** he was racked with remorse; **elle était tenaillée par la faim** hunger gnawed at her.

tenancier, -ière /tənɑsje, ɛʀ/ ▶ **374** *nm,f* (de café) landlord/landlady; (d'hôtel, de casino) manager/manageress; **tenancière de maison close** madam.

tenant, ~e /tənɑ̃, ɑ̃t/ **I** *nm,f* JEUX, SPORT **~ du titre** titleholder; **~ du trophée** holder of the trophy.
II *nm* **1** (adepte) advocate; **2** (morceau) **d'un seul ~** all in one piece.

IDIOMES **les ~s et les aboutissants de qch** the ins and outs of sth.

tendance /tɑ̃dɑ̃s/ *nf* **1** (propension) tendency; **avoir ~ à faire** to tend to do; **on a trop ~ à croire que** we are too inclined to believe that; **le marché a ~ à se stabiliser** the market is becoming more stable; **2** (orientation) tendency; **toutes ~s politiques confondues** across party lines; **3** (école) trend; **la ~ dominante** the dominant trend; **4** (dynamique) trend; **~ à la baisse/hausse** downward/upward trend.

tendancieux, -ieuse /tɑ̃dɑ̃sjø, øz/ *adj* biased[GB], tendentious.

tendeur /tɑ̃dœʀ/ *nm* **1** (de tente) guy rope; **2** (de porte-bagages, galerie) elastic strap; **3** (dispositif) GÉN tightener; TECH (pour clôture) slack adjuster.

endon /tɑ̃dɔ̃/ *nm* tendon.

endre¹ /tɑ̃dʀ/ [6] **I** *vtr* **1** (étirer) to tighten [*corde, fil, câble*]; to stretch [*élastique, peau*]; to extend [*ressort*]; ~ **le cou** to crane one's neck; ~ **les bras** (allonger) to hold out one's arms; (étirer) to stretch one's arms out; **jambes et pointes de pied tendues** legs straight and toes pointed; ~ **le bras** (pour saisir, donner) to reach out; ~ **le bras à qn** (pour soutenir) to offer ou give one's arm to sb; ~ **les bras à** or **vers qn** (pour accueillir) to greet ou welcome sb with open arms; **la victoire me tend les bras** FIG victory beckons; ~ **la main** (pour saisir, donner) to reach out; (pour mendier, serrer la main à qn) to hold out one's hand; ~ **la main à qn** (pour aider) LIT to hold one's hand out to sb; FIG to lend sb a helping hand; ~ **la joue** LIT to offer one's cheek; ~ **l'autre joue** BIBLE to turn the other cheek; **2** (déployer) to spread [*toile, drap*] (**sur** over); **3** (disposer) to set [*piège*]; to put up [*fil à linge, filet*]; ~ **un piège à qn** FIG to set a trap for sb; **4** (tapisser) ~ **un mur de tissu** to hang a wall with cloth; **bureau tendu de toile de jute** office hung with hessian; **5** (présenter) ~ **qch à qn** to hold sth out to sb; ~ **une cigarette/du feu à qn** to offer sb a cigarette/a light.

II tendre à *vtr ind* **1** (viser à) ~ **à un but** to strive for a goal; **2** (avoir tendance à) ~ **à faire** to tend to do.

III *vi* **1** (s'orienter) ~ **vers** to strive for; **2** (se rapprocher) ~ **vers** to approach [*valeur, chiffre*]; to tend to [*zéro, infini*].

IV se tendre *vpr* (devenir tendu) to tighten; (devenir conflictuel) to become strained.

endre² /tɑ̃dʀ/ **I** *adj* **1** (non dur) [*roche, bois, fibre*] soft; [*chair, peau, légumes*] tender; **2** (jeune) [*pousse, herbe*] new; ~ **enfance** earliest childhood; **3** (pâle) [*rose, vert, bleu*] soft; **des chaussettes vert** ~ pale green socks; **4** (affectueux) [*personne*] loving; [*amour, sourire, paroles*] tender; [*tempérament*] gentle; **un cœur** ~ a loving heart; **poser un regard** ~ **sur qn** to look tenderly at sb; **être** ~ **avec qn** (affectueux) to be loving toward(s) sb; **ne pas être** ~ **avec qn/qch** to be hard on sb/sth; **leurs propos ne sont pas** ~ **pour le régime** they have some harsh words to say about the regime; **5** (cher) [*ami, époux*] dear.

II *nmf* soft-hearted person.

endrement /tɑ̃dʀəmɑ̃/ *adv* tenderly.

endresse /tɑ̃dʀɛs/ *nf* (donnée) tenderness; (reçue) affection; **avec une grande** ~ very tenderly; **éprouver de la** ~ **pour qn** to have tender feelings for sb; **chercher un peu de** ~ to be looking for affection.

endron /tɑ̃dʀɔ̃/ *nm* CULIN (de bœuf) plate; (de veau) flank.

endu, ~e /tɑ̃dy/ **I** *pp* ▶ **tendre¹**.

II *pp adj* [*corde*] tight.

III *adj* (crispé) [*personne, réunion*] tense; [*marché*] nervous.

enèbres /tenɛbʀ/ *nfpl* **les** ~ LIT, FIG darkness ⊄.

enèbreux, -euse /tenebʀø, øz/ *adj* LITER [*endroit*] dark; (mystérieux) obscure.

eneur /tənœʀ/ *nf* **1** (de solide) content; (de gaz, liquide) level; ~ **en sucre** sugar content; **boisson à faible** ~ **en alcool** low alcohol drink; **2** (de rapport, discours, d'acte juridique) import.

enia /tenja/ *nm* tapeworm.

enir /təniʀ/ [36] **I** *vtr* **1** (serrer) to hold; **tiens-moi ça** hold this (for me); ~ **qn par la main** to hold sb's hand; ~ **la rampe** to hold onto the banisters; **tiens! voici** here you are!; (écoute-moi) look!; **tiens! c'est pour toi** (voici un cadeau) here, it's for you; (voici une gifle) take that!; **si je le tenais!** if I could get my hands on him!; **bien** ~ to hold on to; **2** (avoir sous son contrôle) to keep [sb] under control; **il nous tient** he's got a hold on us; **3** MIL to hold; **4** (avoir attrapé) to hold; **je te tiens!** I've caught you at last! ; **pendant que je te tiens** FIG whilst I've got you; ~ **une grippe**° to have flu GB ou the flu US; **5** (posséder) to have [*renseignements*]; **de qui tenez-vous ce renseignement?** where did you get that information?; **elle tient ses**

bijoux de sa mère she inherited her jewels from her mother; **6** (avoir la charge de) to hold [*emploi*]; to run [*boutique, maison, journal*]; to be in charge of [*standard, bureau d'accueil*]; **bien** ~ **sa maison** to keep one's house spick and span; ~ **la comptabilité** to keep the books; **7** (garder) to keep; ~ **qn occupé** to keep sb busy; '~ **hors de portée des enfants**' 'keep out of reach of children'; ~ **une note** MUS to hold a note; **8** (conserver une position) ~ **sa tête droite** to hold one's head upright; ~ **les yeux baissés** to keep one's eyes lowered; **9** (maintenir en place) to hold down [*chargement*]; to hold up [*pantalon, chaussettes*]; ~ **la porte fermée avec son pied** to hold the door shut with one's foot; **10** (ne pas s'écarter de) to keep to [*trajectoire*]; **11** (résister) ~ **la mer** [*navire*] to be seaworthy; ~ **le coup** (physiquement, moralement) to hold out; ~ **le choc** [*matériel*] to withstand the impact; [*personne*] to stand the strain; **12** (contenir) to hold [*quantité, litres*]; **13** (occuper) [*objet*] to take up [*espace, volume*]; [*personne*] to hold [*rôle, position*]; **14** (considérer) ~ **qn/qch pour responsable** to hold sb/sth responsible; **je tiens mes renseignements pour exacts** I consider my information to be correct; ~ **qn pour mort** to give sb up for dead; ~ **pour certain que** to regard it as certain that.

II tenir à *vtr ind* **1** (avoir de l'attachement pour) ~ **à** to be fond of, to like; ~ **à sa réputation/à la vie** to value one's reputation/one's life; **il tient à son argent** he can't bear to be parted from his money; ~ **à son indépendance** to like one's independence; **2** (vouloir) **j'y tiens** I insist; ~ **à faire** to want to do; **je ne tiens pas à faire** I'd rather not do; ~ **à ce que qn fasse** to insist that sb should do; **je ne tiens pas à ce qu'elle y aille** I'd rather she didn't go; **je tiens beaucoup à la revoir** I'd really like to see her again; **nous tenons absolument à vous avoir à dîner bientôt** you really must come to dinner soon; **3** (être dû à) ~ **à** to be due to.

III tenir de *vtr ind* **1** (ressembler à) ~ **de** to take after; **il a de qui** ~° you can (just) see who he takes after ou where he gets it from; **de qui peut-elle** ~ **pour être si méchante?** where does she get her nastiness from?; **2** (s'apparenter à) ~ **de** to border on.

IV *vi* **1** (rester en place) [*attache, corde, étagère, barrage, soufflé*] to hold; [*timbre, colle, sparadrap*] to stick (**à** to); [*assemblage, bandage*] to stay in place; [*coiffure*] to stay tidy; [*mise en plis*] to stay in; **ces chaussures ne me tiennent pas aux pieds** these shoes won't stay on my feet; **2** (résister) ~ (**bon**) (surmonter les conditions) to hold out; (refuser de capituler) GÉN to hang on; MIL to hold out; (ne pas relâcher sa prise) [*personne*] to hang on; ~ **sans cigarettes jusqu'à la fin de la réunion** to last without cigarettes till the end of the meeting; **j'espère que ma voiture va** ~ (**bon**) I hope my car will last out; **il n'y a pas de télévision qui tienne**° there's no question of watching television; **3** (durer) **le plan tient-il toujours?** is the plan still on?; **la neige tient** the snow is settling; **les fleurs n'ont pas tenu** the flowers didn't last long; **la couleur n'a pas tenu** the colourGB has faded; **4** (rester valable) [*théorie, argument*] to hold good; [*alibi*] to stand up; **5** (être contenu) [*personnes, objets*] to fit (**dans** into); **faire** ~ **six personnes dans une voiture** to fit six people into a car; **mon article tient en trois pages** my article takes up only three pages; ~ **en hauteur/largeur/longueur** to be short enough/narrow enough/short enough (**dans** for); ~ **en hauteur dans une pièce** to fit into a room (heightwise); **ne pas** ~ **en hauteur** to be too tall (**dans** for).

V se tenir *vpr* **1** (soi-même) to hold; **se** ~ **la tête de douleur** to hold one's head in pain; **2** (l'un l'autre) **se** ~ **par le bras** to be arm in arm; **ils se tenaient par la taille** they had their arms around each other's waists; **se** ~ **par la main** to hold hands; **3** (s'accrocher) to hold on; **se** ~ **par les pieds** to hold on with one's feet; **tiens-toi** or **tenez-vous bien**° FIG prepare yourself for a shock; **4** (demeurer) **se** ~ **accroupi/**

allongé to be squatting/stretched out; **se ~ sans bouger** to stay still; **se ~ prêt** to be ready; **se ~ tranquille** (immobile) to keep still; (silencieux) to keep quiet; (dans la légalité) to behave oneself; **se ~ immobile** (debout) to stand still; **5** (se comporter) to behave; **savoir se ~** to know how to behave; **tiens-toi bien!** behave yourself!; **6** (avoir une posture) **se ~ bien/mal** to have (a) good posture/(a) bad posture; **tiens-toi droit!** (debout) stand up straight!; (assis) sit straight!; **7** (avoir lieu) [*manifestation, exposition*] to be held; **8** (être liés) [*événements*] to fit together; **9** (être cohérent) [*raisonnement, œuvre*] to hold together; **ça se tient** it makes sense; **10** (se considérer) **se ~ pour** to consider oneself to be; **tenez-vous le pour dit**○! I don't want to have to tell you again!; **11** (être fidèle) **s'en ~ à** to stand by; **12** (se limiter) **s'en ~ à** to keep to; **s'en ~ aux ordres** to stick to orders; **s'en ~ là** to leave it there; **ne pas savoir à quoi s'en ~ avec** not to know what to make of.

VI *v impers* **il ne tient qu'à toi de partir** it's up to you to decide whether to leave; **qu 'à cela ne tienne!** never mind!

VII tiens *excl* oh!; **tiens (donc), vous voilà!** oh, there you are!; **tiens, vous croyez?** do you think so?; **tiens donc!** IRON fancy that!; **tiens tiens (tiens)!** well, well!

tennis /tenis/ I ▶329⌋ *nm inv* (activité) tennis; **~ de table** table tennis.
II *nm ou f inv* (chaussure) tennis shoe.

tennisman, *pl* **tennismen** /tenisman, mɛn/ *nm* CONTROV male tennis player.

ténor /tenɔʀ/ *nm* **1** ▶98⌋ (chanteur, voix, instrument) tenor; **2** (personnalité) (de sport) star; (de parti, profession) leading light.

tensiomètre /tɑ̃sjɔmɛtʀ/ *nm* TECH tensiometer; MÉD sphygmomanometer.

tension /tɑ̃sjɔ̃/ *nf* **1** (de câble, muscle) tension; **2** MÉD **~ (artérielle)** blood pressure; **avoir de la ~** to have high blood pressure; **~ nerveuse** nervous tension; **être sous ~** to be under stress; **3** ÉLECTROTECH tension, voltage; **4** (discorde) tension; **la ~ entre les deux pays est telle que** relations between the two countries are so strained that.

tentaculaire /tɑ̃takylɛʀ/ *adj* [*ville*] sprawling (*épith*); [*entreprise, organisation*] with far-reaching interests (*après n*); [*pouvoir*] far-reaching (*épith*).

tentacule /tɑ̃takyl/ *nm* tentacle.

tentateur, -trice /tɑ̃tatœʀ, tʀis/ *nm,f* tempter/temptress.

tentation /tɑ̃tasjɔ̃/ *nf* temptation **la ~ est forte de demander plus** it's very tempting to ask for more.

tentative /tɑ̃tativ/ *nf* attempt; **~ de meurtre** GÉN murder attempt; JUR attempted murder; **faire une ~ de meurtre contre qn** to attempt to murder sb; **~ de coup d'État** attempted coup; **faire une ~ auprès de qn pour obtenir qch** to try to obtain sth from sb.

tente /tɑ̃t/ *nf* tent; **dormir sous la ~** GÉN to sleep under canvas; [*nomades*] to sleep in tents.
■ **~ à oxygène** oxygen tent.

tenter /tɑ̃te/ [1] *vtr* **1** (essayer) to attempt; **j'ai tout tenté pour l'en dissuader** I've tried everything to dissuade him/her; **~ sa chance** to try one's luck; **je vais ~ l'expérience** I'll have a go; **~ le tout pour le tout** to risk one's all; **2** (attirer) to tempt; **cela ne la tente guère** that doesn't appeal to her very much; **ça ne me tente qu'à moitié** I'm only half tempted by it; **se laisser ~ par** to let oneself be tempted by; **laisse-toi ~!** be a devil!; **3** (éprouver) to tempt; **~ le diable** to court disaster.

tenture /tɑ̃tyʀ/ *nf* **1** (grand rideau) curtain; **~s** (décoratif) draperies; **2** (tendu aux murs) fabric wall covering.

tenu, ~e[1] /təny/ I *pp* ▶ **tenir**.
II *pp adj* **1** (entretenu) **bien/mal ~** [*enfant*] well/badly cared for; [*maison*] well/badly kept; [*troupes*] well/badly turned out; **chambre bien ~/mal ~e** tidy/untidy room; **2** (contraint) **~ de faire** required to do; **~ à** bound by.

tenue[2] /təny/ *nf* **1** (vêtements) **~ (vestimentaire)** dress **C**, clothes (*pl*); **être en ~ décontractée** wear casual clothes; **~ d'hiver** GÉN winter cloth (*pl*); (de soldat, policier) winter uniform; **se mettre ~** to change; **être en petite ~** to be scantily cla **être en ~ légère** (peu vêtu) to be scantily dresse (avec vêtements légers) to be in light clothing; **mettre en grande ~** GÉN to put on ceremonial dres MIL to put on full dress uniform; **en ~ uniforme avoir une ~ impeccable** to be impeccably dresse **2** (manières) **avoir de la ~** to have good manners; **pas avoir de ~** to have bad manners; **un peu ~!** mind your manners!; **3** (posture) posture **C**; **4** (comportement) performance.
■ **~ de campagne** MIL battle ou field dress **C**; **~ de cérémonie** ceremonial dress **C**; **~ de rou** AUT roadholding **C**; **~ de travail** work(ing) cloth (*pl*); **~ de ville** smart clothes (*pl*).

ter /tɛʀ/ *adv* **1** (dans une adresse) ter; **2** (indicatio three times.

térébenthine /teʀebɑ̃tin/ *nf* **(essence de)** turpentine.

tergal® /tɛʀgal/ *nm* Terylene®.

tergiversation /tɛʀʒivɛʀsasjɔ̃/ *nf* equivocation **C**.

tergiverser /tɛʀʒivɛʀse/ [1] *vi* **1** (par indécision) dither; **2** (discuter sans résultats) to shilly-shally.

terme /tɛʀm/ I *nm* **1** (mot) term; **au sens premier ~** in the original sense of the word; **le ~ 'quot désigne** the term 'quota' designates; **en d'autr ~s** in other words; **dans tous les sens du** in every sense of the word; **c'est en ces ~s que** ministre a décrit la situation this was how the min ter described the situation; **il a décrit les résultats ces ~s** he described the results thus; **2** (fin) en **toucher à son ~** to come to an end; **arriver à** [*plan*] to come to its appointed end; [*période, contr* to expire; **mener à ~** to see [sth] through to comp tion [*projet, opération*]; **naître à ~/avant ~** to born at full term/before term; **accoucher avant ~** give birth prematurely; **enfant né avant ~** premature baby; **3** (échéance) **passé ce ~ vous pa rez des intérêts** after this date, you will pay intere **à moyen ~** [*emprunt, stratégie*] medium-te (*épith*); **4** JUR (date de paiement du loyer) due da (période de location) rental period; (montant de la lo tion) rent; **5** MATH, PHILOS term; **trouver un moyen** (équilibre) to find a happy medium; (compromis) to fi a compromise.
II **termes** *nmpl* **1** (clauses) terms; **~s l'échange** terms of trade; **2** (relations) terms; **en bo ~s** on good terms; **3** (dimension) **la question pose aussi en ~s financiers** the issue is also a nancial one.

terminaison /tɛʀminɛzɔ̃/ *nf* LING ending.

terminal, ~e[1], *mpl* **-aux** /tɛʀminal, o/ I **~** [*année*] final; **phase ~e** (d'une opération) concludi phase; (d'une maladie) terminal phase.
II *nm* terminal.

terminale[2] /tɛʀminal/ *nf* SCOL final year secondary school).

terminer /tɛʀmine/ [1] I *vtr* **1** (aller jusqu'au bout de) finish; **termine ton déjeuner** finish your lun **2** (conclure) to end; **~ son discours par une mi en garde** to end one's speech with a warning.
II *vi* to finish; **~ à la première place** to finish fir **en ~ avec** to be through with; **c'est terminé, n'irai plus jamais!** that's that, I'm never going bac **pour ~ je dirai que** in conclusion let me say that.
III **se terminer** *vpr* **1** (dans le temps) to end; **projet se termine** the project is coming to an end; **~ par** to end with; **se ~ bien/mal** [*relation, évé ment*] to end well/badly; [*film, roman*] to have a hap sad ending; **se ~ tragiquement** [*pièce*] to end trag ally; [*excursion*] to end in tragedy; **être terminé** to over; **2** (dans l'espace) **se ~ par** [*objet, mot, numé* to end in; **un morceau de bois terminé par crochet** a piece of wood with a hook at the end.

terminologie /tɛʀminɔlɔʒi/ *nf* terminology.

rminus /tɛʀminys/ *nm inv* (de train) end of the line; de bus) terminus.

rnaire /tɛʀnɛʀ/ *adj* CHIMIE, MATH ternary; MUS ompound.

rne /tɛʀn/ *adj* [*poil*] dull; [*couleur*] drab; [*blanc*] ingy; [*œil*] lifeless; [*personne, vie, événement*] dull.

rnir /tɛʀniʀ/ [3] I *vtr* **1** to tarnish [*métal*]; to fade *tissu*]; **2** to tarnish [*image, réputation*]; to detract rom [*exploit*].

I **se ternir** *vpr* to tarnish.

rrain /tɛʀɛ̃/ *nm* **1** (sol) ground ℂ, soil ℂ; (relief) round ℂ, terrain ℂ; ~s tertiaires/volcaniques ertiary/volcanic formations; **avancer sur un ~** lissant FIG to be on slippery ground; **2** (parcelle) plot f land; **~ à bâtir** building plot; **3** (étendue) land ℂ; **~ à bâtir** building land; **4** (de jeu, sport) (non amé-agé) field; (avec les installations) GÉN ground; (au golf) ourse; **sortir du ~** [*joueur*] to go off the field; *balle*] (au football) to go out of play; (au rugby) to go nto touch; **disputer un match sur ~ adverse/sur on propre ~** to play an away game/a home game; **5** (sphère d'activité) **nous ne vous suivrons pas sur e ~** we won't go along with you there; **un ~ l'entente** FIG common ground; **6** (champ de recherche) eld; **travailler sur le ~** to do fieldwork; **7** (état, ilieu) SOCIOL environment; **~ favorable** MÉD predis-osing factors (*pl*); SOCIOL favourable^GB environment; ffrir **un ~ favorable à** (à une maladie, une idéologie) o provide a fertile breeding ground for; **les jeunes ont un ~ favorable** young people are easy targets; **8** MIL (lieu d'opérations) field; (en termes de relief) errain; (en termes d'avance ou de recul) ground; **sur le ~** in the field; **occuper le ~** to hold the field; **être n ~ connu** or **familier** FIG to be on familiar terri-ory; **être sur son ~**, **avoir l'avantage du ~** LIT, FIG o be on one's own ground; **déblayer le ~** to clear he ground; **préparer le ~** FIG to pave the way; **tâter r sonder le ~** FIG to put out feelers.

~ d'atterrissage landing strip; **~ d'aviation** irfield; **~ de camping** campsite; **~ de jeu(x)** layground; **~ de manœuvre** army training round; **~ de tir** firing range; **~ de sport(s)** ports ground; **~ vague** wasteland ℂ.

rrasse /tɛʀas/ *nf* **1** (le long d'un bâtiment) terrace; **'installer à la ~ d'un café** to sit at a table outside a afé; **2** (toiture) flat roof; (grand balcon) large balcony; **3** AGRIC **culture(s) en ~s** terrace cultivation ℂ; culti-er le riz **en ~s** to grow rice on terraces.

rrassement /tɛʀasmɑ̃/ *nm* excavation; **faire des ravaux de ~** to carry out excavation work.

rrasser /tɛʀase/ [1] *vtr* **1** (jeter à terre) to knock own; **2** (priver de forces) [*maladie*] to strike down; **errassé par** (par la chaleur, le chagrin) prostrated by.

rrassier /tɛʀasje/ ▶374 *nm* building labourer.

rre /tɛʀ/ I *nf* **1** (surface du sol) ground; **sous ~** nderground; **ne frappez jamais un adversaire à ~** ever hit a man when he's down; **mettre pied à ~** *cavalier*] to dismount; **2** (matière) GÉN earth; AGRIC soil; ortir **du ~** LIT [*plante*] to come up; [*animal*] to poke ts head out of the ground; FIG **une ville nouvelle est ortie de ~** a new town has sprung up; **3** (cam-agne) land; **le retour à la ~** the movement back to he land; **4** (terrain) land ℂ; **se retirer sur ses ~s** to o and live on one's estate; **5** (région) land; **en ~ hrétienne** on Christian land; **leur pays a toujours té une ~ d'accueil** their country has always velcomed newcomers; **6** (opposé à mer) land; **aller à ~** to go ashore; **'Terre!'** 'land ho!'; **s'enfoncer à intérieur des ~s** to go deep inland; **7** (où vit l'huma-ité) earth; **il croit que la ~ entière est contre lui** e thinks the whole world is against him; **8** ART (de la **~** (glaise) clay; **une pipe en ~** a clay pipe; **un ot de** or **en ~** an earthenware pot; **9** (en électricité) arth GB, ground US; **relier qch à la ~** to earth GB ou round US sth.

I **terre à terre** *loc adj inv* [*question*] basic; conversation, personne] pedestrian.

II **par terre** *loc adv* (dehors) on the ground; dedans) on the floor; **se rouler par ~** (de rire) to fall

about laughing; **c'est à se rouler par ~**° it's hilari-ous; **se rouler par ~ de douleur** to roll on the ground with pain; **ça a fichu ·tous nos projets par ~**° it messed up all our plans°.

■ **~ d'asile** country of refuge; **~ battue** trodden earth; **sur ~ battue** [*tennis*] on a clay court; **~ de bruyère** ericaceous compost; **~ cuite** baked clay; ART **terracotta**; **~ de Sienne** sienna.

IDIOMES **avoir les pieds sur ~**° to have one's feet firmly planted on the ground; **garder les pieds sur ~**° to keep one's feet on the ground; **ne pas avoir les pieds sur ~**° to be a dreamer.

Terre /tɛʀ/ *nf* Earth; **sur la ~** on Earth.

■ **la ~ Adélie** Adelie land; **la ~ de Feu** Tierra del Fuego; **la ~ promise** the Promised Land; **la ~ Sainte** the Holy Land.

terreau, *pl* **~x** /tɛʀo/ *nm* compost; **~ de feuilles** leaf mould.

terre-neuve /tɛʀnœv/ *nm inv* Newfoundland (dog).

Terre-Neuve /tɛʀnœv/ ▶509 *nprf* GÉOG Newfound-land.

terre-plein, *pl* **terres-pleins** /tɛʀplɛ̃/ *nm* **1** (de bâti-ment) platform; **2** (de route) central reservation GB, median strip US; (de rond-point) central island; **3** MIL terreplein.

terrer: se terrer /tɛʀe/ [1] *vpr* **1** (dans son terrier) [*lapin*] to disappear into its burrow; [*renard*] to go to earth; **2** [*fugitif*] to hide; **ils se terrent chez eux** they're holed up in their house.

terrestre /tɛʀɛstʀ/ *adj* **1** GÉOG (de la planète) of the Earth (*après n*); **2** [*animaux*] land (*épith*); **3** (au sol) [*guerre, transport*] land (*épith*); **la vie/le paradis ~** life/heaven on earth.

terreur /tɛʀœʀ/ *nf* **1** (sentiment) terror; **vivre dans la ~** to live in fear; **2** (comme moyen politique) terror; **3**° (personne) **c'est la ~ du quartier** he's the terror of the neighbourhood^GB; **jouer les ~s** to be a terror.

terreux, **-euse** /tɛʀø, øz/ *adj* (semblable à la terre) earthy; **avoir le teint ~** FIG to have a grey GB ou gray US complexion.

terrible /tɛʀibl/ *adj* **1** (intense) GÉN terrible; [*soif, envie*] tremendous; **2** (épouvantable) terrible; **3**° (pé-nible) terrible; **c'est ~ de devoir faire** it's awful ou terrible having to do; **il est ~, il ne veut jamais avoir tort** it's terrible the way he never wants to admit that he's wrong; **4**° (remarquable) terrific°; **il n'est pas ~ ce film** that's not a great film.

terriblement /tɛʀibləmɑ̃/ *adv* terribly; **il a ~ grandi** he's grown an awful lot.

terrien, **-ienne** /tɛʀjɛ̃, ɛn/ *adj* **propriétaire ~** land-owner.

Terrien, **-ienne** /tɛʀjɛ̃, ɛn/ *nm,f* earthman/earth-woman.

terrier /tɛʀje/ *nm* **1** (d'une bête) GÉN hole; **un ~ de renard** a fox's earth; **2** (chien) terrier.

terrifiant, **~e** /tɛʀifjɑ̃, ɑ̃t/ *adj* **1** (faisant peur) terri-fying; **2** (hors du commun) [*bêtise, changement*] incred-ible.

terrifier /tɛʀifje/ [2] *vtr* to terrify; **s'enfuir terrifié** to flee in terror.

terrine /tɛʀin/ *nf* **1** CULIN terrine; **2** (récipient) (al-longé) terrine; (rond) earthenware bowl.

territoire /tɛʀitwaʀ/ *nm* **1** (d'un pays) territory; **sur l'ensemble du ~** throughout the country; **2** (chez les animaux) territory.

■ **~ d'outre-mer**, TOM French overseas (adminis-trative) territory.

territorial, **~e**, *mpl* **-iaux** /tɛʀitɔʀjal, o/ *adj* **1** (d'un État) territorial; **2** [*administration*] (de subdivi-sion) divisional; (de région) regional.

terroir /tɛʀwaʀ/ *nm* land; **produits/vin du ~** local products/wine; **accent du ~** regional accent.

terroriser /tɛʀɔʀize/ [1] *vtr* (user de terreur) to terror-ize; (effrayer) [*orage, mauvais rêve, adulte*] to terrify.

terrorisme /tɛʀɔʀism/ *nm* terrorism.

terroriste /tɛʀɔʀist/ *adj*, *nmf* POL terrorist.

tertiaire /tɛʀsjɛʀ/ I *adj* **1** ÉCON [*secteur, industrie*] service (*épith*); **l'activité ~** activity in the service sector; **2** (en géologie) Tertiary.

II *nm* ÉCON service sector; (en géologie) Tertiary.

tertio /tɛʀsjo/ *adv* thirdly.

tes ▶ **ton**[1].

tesson /tesɔ̃/ *nm* **~ de bouteille** piece of glass; **des ~s de bouteille** broken glass ₵.

test /tɛst/ **I** *nm* test.

II **-test** (*in compounds*) **match-~** trial match; **rencontre-~** preliminary meeting; **région-~** pilot region.

testament /tɛstamɑ̃/ *nm* JUR will; FIG legacy; **ceci est mon ~** this is my last will and testament; **l'Ancien Testament** the Old Testament.

testamentaire /tɛstamɑ̃tɛʀ/ *adj* of a will (*après n*).

tester /tɛste/ [1] *vtr* to test; **testé en laboratoire** laboratory-tested.

testicule /tɛstikyl/ *nm* testicle.

tétanos /tetanos/ ▶ **196** *nm inv* tetanus.

têtard /tɛtaʀ/ *nm* **1** ZOOL tadpole; **2** (arbre) pollard.

tête /tɛt/ ▶ **137** *nf* **1** GÉN head; **la ~ basse** (humblement) with one's head bowed; **la ~ haute** (dignement) with one's head held high; **~ baissée** [*se lancer, foncer*] headlong; **la ~ en bas** [*être suspendu, se retrouver*] upside down; **au-dessus de nos ~s** (en l'air) overhead; **sans ~** headless; **coup de ~** headbutt; **donner un coup de ~ à qn** to headbutt sb; **être tombé sur la ~**○ FIG to have gone off one's rocker; **2** (dessus du crâne) head; **se laver la ~** to wash one's hair; **j'ai la ~ toute mouillée** my hair's all wet; **3** (visage) face; **une bonne/sale ~** a nice/nasty face; **tu en fais une ~!** what a face! , why the long face?; **ne fais pas cette ~-là!** don't pull such a face!; **quelle ~ va-t-il faire?** how's he going to react?; **il (me) fait la ~** he's sulking; **ne fais pas ta mauvaise ~** don't be so difficult; **elle fait sa mauvaise ~** she's being difficult; **il a une ~ à tricher** he looks like a cheat; **tu as une ~ à faire peur, aujourd'hui!** you look dreadful today!; **4** (esprit) mind; **de ~** [*citer, réciter*] from memory; [*calculer*] in one's head; **tu n'as pas de ~!** you have a mind like a sieve!; **je n'ai pas la référence en ~** I can't recall the reference; **où avais-je la ~?** whatever was I thinking of?; **ça (ne) va pas, la ~?**○ are you out of your mind or what?; **j'avais la ~ ailleurs** I was thinking of something else; **n'avoir rien dans la ~** to be empty-headed; **c'est lui qui t'a mis ça dans la ~!** you got that idea from him!; **mets-lui ça dans la ~** drum it into him/her; **se mettre dans la ou en ~ de faire** to take it into one's head to do; **monter la ~ à Pierre contre Paul** to turn Pierre against Paul; **monter à la ~ de qn, faire tourner la ~ de qn** [*alcool, succès*] to go to sb's head; **elle t'a fait tourner la ~** she's turned your head; **il n'est pas bien dans sa ~**○ he isn't right in the head; **il a encore toute sa ~ (à lui)** he's still got all his faculties; **n'en faire qu'à sa ~** to go one's own way; **tenir ~ à qn** to stand up to sb; **sur un coup de ~** on an impulse; **5** (personne) face; **avoir ses ~s** to have one's favourites[GB]; **en ~ à ~** [*être, dîner*] alone together; **rencontrer qn en ~ à ~** to have a meeting with sb in private; **un dîner en ~ à ~** an intimate dinner for two; **6** (mesure de longueur) head; **avoir une ~ de plus que qn** to be a head taller than sb; **gagner d'une courte ~** [*personne*] to win by a narrow margin; [*cheval*] to win by a short head; **avoir une ~ d'avance sur qn** to be a short length in front of sb; **7** (unité de troupeau) head (*inv*); **8** (individu) **par ~** GÉN a head, each; (dans des statistiques) per capita; **par ~ de pipe**○ each; **9** (vie) head; **vouloir la ~ de qn** (mort) to want sb's head; (disgrâce) to be after sb's head; **risquer sa ~** to risk one's neck○; **des ~s vont tomber** FIG heads will roll; **10** (direction) **le groupe de ~** the leading group; **c'est lui la ~ pensante du mouvement** he's the brains behind the movement; **il restera à la ~ du groupe** he will stay on as head of the group; **prendre la ~ du parti** to become leader of the party; **prendre la ~ des opéra-**

tions to take charge of operations; **être à la ~ d'u** immense fortune to be the possessor of a hu fortune; **11** (premières places) top; **être en ~** (de lis classement) to be at the top; (d'élection, de cour sondage) to be in the lead; **venir en ~** to come fir **marcher en ~** to walk at the front; **marcher en d'un cortège** to head a procession; **le gouverneme** le premier ministre en ~, a décidé que... government, led by the Prime Minister, has decid that...; **des tas de gens viendront, ta femme en** heaps of people are coming, your wife to begin wit **en ~ de phrase** at the beginning of a sentence; **1** (extrémité) (de train) front; (de convoi, cortège) hea (d'arbre, de mât) top; (de vis, rivet, clou) head; **u** **place en ~ de train** a seat at the front of the trai **en ~ de file** first in line; **13** SPORT (au footba header; **faire une ~** to head the ball; **14** MIL (d'engi warhead; **15** (en électronique) (d'enregistrement, effa ment) head; (d'électrophone) cartridge; **~ de lectu** (de magnétophone, magnétoscope) head.

■ **~ d'affiche** CIN, THÉÂT top of the bill; **~ en l'a** scatterbrain; **être ~ en l'air** to be scatterbrained; **brûlée** daredevil; **~ de chapitre** chapter headin **~ à claques**○ pain○; **~ de cochon**○ = **~ d lard**, **~ d'épingle** LIT, FIG pinhead; **~ de lard** (têtu) mule; (mauvais caractère) grouch; **~ d linotte** = **~ en l'air**; **~ de liste** POL chief cand date; **~ de lit** bedhead GB, headboard; **~ de mo** (crâne) skull; (symbole de mort) death's head; (emblèm de pirates) skull and crossbones (+ *v sg*); **~ de mule** mule; **être une vraie ~ de mule** to be a stubborn as a mule; **~ d'oiseau**○ PEJ featherbrai **~ de pioche**○ = **~ de mule**; **~ de série** SPOF seeded player; **~ de série numéro deux** number tw seed; **~ de Turc**○ whipping boy.

IDIOMES **j'en mettrais ma ~ à couper** or sur **billot** I'd swear to it; **en avoir par-dessus la ~** to be fed up to the back teeth○; **se prendre la ~ deux mains**○ (pour réfléchir) to rack one's brains○ **prendre la ~**○ to be a drag○.

tête-à-queue /tɛtakø/ *nm inv* **faire un ~** to sle round GB ou around; **à la suite d'un ~** after the ca slewed around.

tête-à-tête /tɛtatɛt/ *nm inv* (d'amis, amants) tête-à tête; (de politiciens) private meeting.

tête-bêche /tɛtbɛʃ/ *adv* (pour des personnes) top-to tail; (pour des objets) head-to-tail.

tête-de-loup, *pl* **têtes-de-loup** /tɛtdəlu/ *nf* cei ing brush.

tétée /tete/ *nf* **1** (action) feeding; **2** (repas) feed.

téter /tete/ [14] **I** *vtr* [*bébé, animal*] to suck at [*sein mamelle*]; to feed from [*biberon*]; to suck [*lait*]; **~ s** **mère** to suckle, to feed.

II *vi* to suckle; **donner à ~ à** (à un bébé) to feed; (un animal) to suckle.

tétine /tetin/ *nf* **1** (de biberon) teat GB, nipple US; **2** (su cette) dummy GB, pacifier US; **3** (mamelle) teat.

téton○ /tetɔ̃/ *nm* **1** (sein) tit○, breast; **2** TECH lug.

tétraplégie /tetʀapleʒi/ *nf* quadriplegia.

têtu, ~e /tety/ *adj* stubborn.

IDIOMES **être ~ comme un âne**○ or **une mule**○ or **une bourrique**○ to be as stubborn as a mule.

texte /tɛkst/ *nm* **1** GÉN text; (livre) text; (passage) extract, text; **faire une explication de ~** to do a commentary on a text; **~s choisis de Montaigne** selected extracts from Montaigne; **en français dans le ~** in French in the original text; **'~ intégral** 'un abridged'; **2** CIN, THÉÂT (script) script; (rôle à apprendre) lines (*pl*), part; **3** ADMIN, JUR, POL (libellé) wording, text.

■ **~ de loi** (proposé) bill; (promulgué) law.

textile /tɛkstil/ **I** *adj* textile; **le secteur ~** the textile industry; **fibres ~s** fibres[GB]; **matières ~s** végé tales plant fibres[GB].

II *nm* **1** (secteur industriel) textile industry; **les ouvriers du ~** textile workers; **2** (avant tissage) fibre[GB]; (tissu) textile; **~s artificiels/synthétiques** artificial/synthetic fibres[GB].

texto○ /tɛksto/ = **textuellement**.

textuellement /tɛkstɥɛlmɑ̃/ adv [rapporter] word for word; **il m'a dit ~, 'je m'en moque'** he told me in so many words, 'I couldn't care less'.

texture /tɛkstyʀ/ nf **1** (de matériau, peinture) texture; **2** (de roman, pièce de théâtre) structure.

TGV /teʒeve/ nm (abbr = **train à grande vitesse**) TGV, high-speed train.

thé /te/ nm **1** (feuilles, infusion) tea; **~ à la bergamote** Earl Grey tea; **à l'heure du ~** at teatime; **être invité à prendre le ~** to be asked to tea; **2** (réunion) tea party.

théâtral, ~e, mpl **-aux** /teɑtʀal, o/ adj **1** THÉÂT [œuvre, langage] dramatic; [représentation] stage (épith); [saison, compagnie] theatre^GB (épith); **2** (exagéré) PEJ [geste] histrionic; [ton] melodramatic.

théâtre /teɑtʀ/ nm **1** LITTÉRAT (genre) theatre^GB; **le ~ de Racine** Racine's plays (pl); **le ~ antique** Greek classical drama; **de ~** [acteur, directeur, billet] theatre^GB (épith); [décor, costume, masque] stage (épith); FIG [gestes] histrionic; **coup de ~** LIT coup de théâtre; FIG dramatic turn of events; **2** (art dramatique) **faire du ~** (comme profession) to be an actor; (à l'école) to do drama; (en amateur) to be involved in amateur dramatics; **se destiner au ~** to intend to go on stage; **adapter une nouvelle pour le ~** to adapt a short story for the stage; **c'est du ~** FIG it's just a put-on^○; **3** (lieu) theatre^GB; **être le ~ d'émeutes** FIG to be the scene of riots; **le ~ des opérations** MIL the theatre^GB of operations.
■ **~ de Boulevard** farce; **~ de verdure** open-air theatre^GB.

théier /teje/ nm tea plant.

théière /tejɛʀ/ nf teapot.

thématique /tematik/ **I** adj thematic.
II nf themes (pl).

thème /tɛm/ nm **1** (de débat, d'émission) topic, subject; (de discours, film) theme; **~ de réflexion** topic for thought; **2** (traduction) prose; **3** MUS theme; **4** LING (radical) stem; (topique) theme.
■ **~ astral** birth chart.

théologie /teɔlɔʒi/ nf theology.

théorème /teɔʀɛm/ nm theorem.

théoricien, -ienne /teɔʀisjɛ̃, ɛn/ nm,f theoretician.

théorie /teɔʀi/ nf theory; **en ~** in theory.

théorique /teɔʀik/ adj theoretical.

thérapeute /teʀapøt/ nmf therapist.

thérapeutique /teʀapøtik/ **I** adj [effet] therapeutic; **choix ~** choice of treatment.
II nf **1** (traitement) treatment; **2** (science) therapeutics (+ v sg).

thérapie /teʀapi/ nf **1** MÉD treatment; **2** PSYCH therapy.

thermal, ~e, mpl **-aux** /tɛʀmal, o/ adj [source, eaux] thermal; **station ~e** spa.

thermalisme /tɛʀmalism/ nm **1** MÉD balneology; **2** (activité) hydrotherapy industry.

thermes /tɛʀm/ nmpl **1** (romains) thermae; **2** (établissement thermal) thermal baths.

thermique /tɛʀmik/ adj thermal.

thermo /tɛʀmo/ préf **~chimie** thermochemistry; **~formé** thermally moulded; **~gène** heat-generating; **~nucléaire** thermonuclear; **~résistant** heat-resistant.

thermocollant, ~e /tɛʀmokɔlɑ̃, ɑ̃t/ adj [tissu, ruban] iron-on (épith).

thermomètre /tɛʀmɔmɛtʀ/ nm LIT thermometer; FIG barometer; **le ~ va chuter pendant le week-end** temperatures will drop over the weekend; **le ~ des tensions internationales** the barometer of international tensions.

thermostat /tɛʀmɔsta/ nm thermostat.

thésard^○**, ~e** /tezaʀ, aʀd/ nm,f PhD student.

thésauriser /tezɔʀize/ [1] **I** vtr to hoard (up).
II vi to hoard money.

thésaurus /tezɔʀys/ nm inv **1** (de philologie, d'archéologie) lexicon; **2** (répertoire) thesaurus.

thèse /tɛz/ nf **1** UNIV (de doctorat) thesis GB, dissertation US; **2** (point de vue) thesis, argument; **roman à ~** novel with a message; **3** (supposition) theory; **avancer la ~ de l'accident** to put forward the theory that it was an accident.

Thessalonique /tesalɔnik/ ▶ 628 | npr Salonika.

thibaude /tibod/ nf carpet underlay.

thon /tɔ̃/ nm tuna.

thonier, -ière /tɔnje, ɛʀ/ **I** adj tuna (épith).
II nm tuna boat.

thoracique /tɔʀasik/ adj thoracic; **cage ~** ribcage.

thorax /tɔʀaks/ ▶ 137 | nm inv thorax.

thrombose /tʀɔ̃boz/ ▶ 196 | nf thrombosis.

Thurgovie /tyʀgɔvi/ ▶ 509 | nprf **la ~** the canton of Thurgau.

thuriféraire /tyʀifeʀɛʀ/ nm **1** (admirateur) eulogist; **2** RELIG thurifer.

thuya /tyja/ nm thuja.

thym /tɛ̃/ nm thyme.

thyroïde /tiʀɔid/ adj, nf thyroid.

tiare /tjaʀ/ nf tiara.

tibétain, ~e /tibetɛ̃, ɛn/ **I** adj Tibetan.
II ▶ 338 | nm LING Tibetan.

tibia /tibja/ nm (os) shinbone, tibia SPÉC; **un coup de pied dans les ~s** a kick in the shins.

tic /tik/ nm **1** (contraction) tic; **être plein de ~s** to be constantly twitching; **2** (geste habituel) habit; **~ de langage** verbal tic.

ticket /tikɛ/ nm (de train, quai) ticket.
■ **~ de caisse** till receipt GB, sales slip US; **~ modérateur** patient's contribution towards cost of medical treatment.

ticket-repas, pl **tickets-repas** /tikɛʀəpɑ/ nm luncheon voucher GB, meal ticket US.

ticket-restaurant®, pl **tickets-restaurant** /tikɛʀɛstɔʀɑ̃/ nm luncheon voucher GB, meal ticket US.

tic-tac /tiktak/ nm inv (also onomat) ticktock; **faire ~** to tick.

tie-break, pl **~s** /tajbʀɛk/ nm tiebreaker.

tiède /tjɛd/ **I** adj **1** LIT (désagréablement) [café, soupe] lukewarm; [bain] tepid; (agréablement) [eau, air, nuit] warm; [saison, température] mild; **2** FIG (sans enthousiasme) lukewarm.
II nmf (membre d'un parti, groupe) PEJ lukewarm ou half-hearted supporter; (adepte) PEJ half-hearted believer.
III adv **servez ~** serve slightly warm; **dépêche-toi ou tu vas manger ~** hurry up or your food will get cold; **il fait ~** (dehors) it's mild; (dedans) it's nice and warm.

tièdement /tjɛdmɑ̃/ adv FIG half-heartedly.

tiédeur /tjedœʀ/ nf **1** LIT (de saison) mildness; (d'air, de nuit, pièce) warmth; **2** FIG (de sentiment, partisan) half-heartedness.

tiédir /tjediʀ/ [3] **I** vtr to warm up [eau].
II vi **1** [liquide, air] (se réchauffer) to warm (up); (refroidir) to cool (down); **faire ~** to warm ou heat (up) [café]; **laisser ~** to allow [sth] to cool; **2** FIG [sentiment] to cool; [enthousiasme] to wane.

tien, tienne /tjɛ̃, tjɛn/ **I** adj poss **je suis tienne** I'm yours; **une tienne connaissance** LITER an acquaintance of yours.
II le tien, la tienne, les tiens, les tiennes pron poss yours; **un métier comme le ~** a job like yours; **à la tienne!** (à ta santé) cheers!; IRON good luck to you!; **les ~s** (ta famille) your family (sg); **tu as encore fait des tiennes!** you've been up to mischief again!

tiens /tjɛ̃/ ▶ tenir.

tierce¹ /tjɛʀs/ **I** adj f ▶ tiers **I**.
II nf **1** (aux cartes) three card run, tierce; **2** MUS third.

tiercé /tjɛʀse/ ▶ 329 | nm: system of betting on three placed horses; **jouer au ~** to bet on the horses.

tiers, tierce² /tjɛʀ, tjɛʀs/ **I** adj third; **un pays ~** GÉN another country; (par rapport à un groupe) a non-member country; **une tierce personne** a third party.
II nm inv **1** MATH third; **j'en suis aux deux ~** I'm two

thirds of the way through; **la ville a été détruite aux deux ~** two thirds of the town has been destroyed; **2** (personne) (inconnu) outsider; JUR third party; **s'assurer au ~** to take out third-party insurance.

■ **le Tiers État** HIST the Third Estate.

tiers-monde /tjɛʀmɔ̃d/ *nm* POL Third World.

tiers-mondisme /tjɛʀmɔ̃dism/ *nm* support for the Third World.

tiers-mondiste /tjɛʀmɔ̃dist/ **I** *adj* [*discours, politique*] in support of the Third World (*après n*).
II *nmf* supporter of the Third World.

tige /tiʒ/ *nf* **1** (de plante) GÉN stem, stalk; **2** (de botte) leg; **3** (baguette) rod; (partie allongée de clé, clou, rivet) shank; **4** (de plume) shaft.

tignasse○ /tiɲas/ *nf* mop of hair.

tigre /tigʀ/ *nm* **1** ZOOL (animal) tiger; (peau) tigerskin; **2** (personne cruelle) monster.
IDIOMES **être jaloux comme un ~** to be insanely jealous.

tigré, ~e /tigʀe/ *adj* **1** (rayé) striped; **2** (tacheté) spotted.

tigresse /tigʀɛs/ *nf* ZOOL, FIG tigress.

tillac /tijak/ *nm* deck.

tilleul /tijœl/ *nm* **1** (arbre) limetree; (bois) limewood; **2** ▶ 141 (couleur) (**vert**) **~** lime green; **3** (tisane) lime-blossom tea.

tilt /tilt/ *nm* JEUX tilt sign; **faire ~** [*machine*] to show tilt; [*personne*] to make the machine stop.
IDIOMES **ça a fait ~**○ (**dans mon esprit**) the penny dropped○; **ça a fait ~ entre nous**○ we clicked straight away.

timbale /tɛ̃bal/ *nf* **1** (gobelet) metal (tumbler); **2** ▶ 392 MUS kettledrum; **~s** timpani; **3** (moule, mets) timbale.

timbrage /tɛ̃bʀaʒ/ *nm* **1** (sur enveloppe) postmarking; **dispensé de ~** postage paid GB, post paid US; **2** (de document) stamping.

timbre /tɛ̃bʀ/ *nm* **1** (vignette, marque, instrument) stamp; (cachet de la poste) postmark; **2** (de voix, d'instrument) tone; (de voyelle) timbre; **~ chaud/riche** warm/rich tone; **voix au ~ voilé** husky voice; **voix sans ~** toneless voice; **3** (sonnette) bell; **4** MÉD patch.
■ **~ dateur** date stamp; **~ fiscal** *stamp affixed to official document*.

timbré, ~e /tɛ̃bʀe/ *adj* **voix** (**bien**) **~e** resonant voice.

timbre-poste, *pl* **timbres-poste** /tɛ̃bʀəpɔst/ *nm* postage stamp.

timbrer /tɛ̃bʀe/ [1] *vtr* to stamp, to put a stamp on.

timide /timid/ **I** *adj* [*personne, animal*] shy, timid; [*critique, réforme*] timid; [*succès, résultat*] limited.
II *nmf* shy person; **c'est un grand ~** he's terribly shy.

timidement /timidmɑ̃/ *adv* (avec timidité) shyly; (craintivement) timidly; (sans conviction) half-heartedly.

timidité /timidite/ *nf* shyness.

timing /tajmiɲ/ *nm* **1** (calendrier) schedule; **2** SPORT timing.

timon /timɔ̃/ *nm* **1** NAUT tiller; **2** (d'attelage) shaft.

timonerie /timɔnʀi/ *nf* **1** NAUT (abri) wheelhouse; (personnel) helmsmen (*pl*); **2** AUT, AVIAT steering and braking systems (*pl*).

timonier /timɔnje/ ▶ 374 *nm* NAUT helmsman.

timoré, ~e /timɔʀe/ *adj* timorous.

tinette /tinɛt/ *nf* latrine bucket.

tintamarre /tɛ̃tamaʀ/ *nm* din; **faire du ~** to make a din.

tintement /tɛ̃tmɑ̃/ *nm* (de cloche) chiming; (de clochette, grelot) tinkling; (de couverts, verres, monnaie) clinking; (de sonnette) ringing; (de clés) jingling.
■ **~ d'oreilles** MÉD ringing in the ears, tinnitus SPÉC.

tinter /tɛ̃te/ [1] *vi* [*cloche*] to chime; [*sonnette*] to ring; [*clochette, grelot*] to tinkle; [*verre, monnaie, couvert*] to clink; [*bidon*] to clang; [*clé*] to jingle; MUS [*triangle*] to ring; **faire ~** to ring [*cloche, sonnette, clochette*]; to

clink [*verre, monnaie, couvert*]; to clang [*bidon*]; to jingle [*clé*]; MUS to strike [*triangle*].

tintinnabuler /tɛ̃tinabyle/ [1] *vi* to tinkle.

tique /tik/ *nf* ZOOL tick.

tiquer○ /tike/ [1] *vi* [*personne*] to wince; **sans ~** without batting an eyelid GB ou eyelash US.

tir /tiʀ/ *nm* **1** (coups de feu) MIL fire ¢; **déclencher le ~** to open fire; **2** (discipline) MIL, SPORT shooting ¢; (avec des armes lourdes) gunnery ¢; **exercices de ~** shooting practice ¢; **3** (action, manière de tirer) MIL firing ¢; **~ de grenades/missiles** grenade/missile firing; **~ continu** continuous firing; **4** (avec ballon, boule) shot; **~ au but** (au football) shot; **5** (à la chasse) shooting; **~ aux canards** duck shooting; **6** (stand) **~ forain** rifle range.
■ **~ à l'arbalète** crossbow archery; **~ à l'arc** archery; **~ d'élite** marksmanship; **~ aux pigeons d'argile** clay pigeon shooting.

tirade /tiʀad/ *nf* **1** LITTÉRAT, THÉÂT declamation; **2** (discours) PÉJ tirade.

tirage /tiʀaʒ/ *nm* **1** (à la loterie) **~** (**au sort**) draw; **désigner par ~** (**au sort**) to draw [*nom, vainqueur*]; **2** (impression, réimpression) impression; (ensemble des exemplaires) edition; (nombre d'exemplaires) (d'un livre) run; (d'un journal) circulation; **troisième ~** third impression; **quotidien à grand ~** mass-circulation daily; **3** ORDINAT (copie papier) hard copy; **4** ART, CIN, PHOT (d'estampe, de négatif) (processus) printing ¢; (résultat) print; **5** CONSTR (de cheminée) draught GB, draft US; **6** (désaccord) friction ¢; **il y a du ~ entre eux** there's friction between them.

tiraillement /tiʀajmɑ̃/ *nm* **1** (sur une corde) pulling ¢, tugging ¢; **2** (sensation) nagging pain; **~s d'estomac** hunger pangs; **3** (friction) friction ¢.

tirailler /tiʀaje/ [1] **I** *vtr* **1** to tug (at), to pull (at) [*corde, manche, barbe*]; **2** FIG **être tiraillé entre son travail et sa famille** to be torn between one's work and one's family.
II *vi* [*soldat, tireur*] (au hasard) to fire ou shoot at random; (de temps en temps) to fire intermittently.

tirailleur /tiʀajœʀ/ *nm* skirmisher; HIST colonial infantryman.

tirant /tiʀɑ̃/ *nm* **1** (de chaussure) bootstrap; **2** (de charpente) tie beam.
■ **~ d'air** (de pont) vertical clearance; **~ d'eau** NAUT draught GB, draft US.

tire➊ /tiʀ/ *nf* (voiture) car.

tire-au-flanc○ /tiʀoflɑ̃/ *nm inv* shirker, skiver○ GB.

tire-botte, *pl* **~s** /tiʀbɔt/ *nm* bootjack.

tire-bouchon, *pl* **~s** /tiʀbuʃɔ̃/ *nm* corkscrew; **en ~** [*queue*] curly; [*pantalon*] wrinkled.

tire-bouchonner /tiʀbuʃɔne/ [1] *vi* [*manche, pantalon*] to be wrinkled.

tire-d'aile: à tire-d'aile /atiʀdɛl/ *loc adv* LIT in a flurry of wings; FIG hurriedly.

tirée○ /tiʀe/ *nf* (longue distance) long haul; (à pied) tidy walk○.

tire-larigot○: **à tire-larigot** /atiʀlaʀigo/ *loc adv* [*boire*] non-stop.

tire-ligne, *pl* **~s** /tiʀliɲ/ *nm* ruling pen.

tirelire /tiʀliʀ/ *nf* piggy bank.

tirer /tiʀe/ [1] **I** *vtr* **1** (déplacer) to pull [*véhicule*]; to pull up [*chaise*]; to pull away [*tapis*]; **~ la tête en arrière** to toss one's head back; **2** (exercer une traction) (avec une force régulière) to pull [*cheveux*]; to pull on [*corde*]; (par à-coups) to tug at; **~ qn par le bras** to pull sb's arm; **3** (tendre) **~ ses bas** to pull up one's stockings; **~ sa chemise** to straighten one's shirt; **avoir les traits tirés** to look drawn; **4** (fermer) to draw [*verrou, rideau*]; to pull down [*store*]; to close [*porte, volet*]; **5** (avec une arme) to fire off [*balle, obus, grenade*]; to fire [*missile*]; to shoot [*flèche*]; **6** SPORT (de ballon) **~ un corner/penalty** to take a corner/penalty; **7** (choisir au hasard) **~** (**au sort**) to draw [*carte, loterie, nom*]; to draw for [*partenaire*]; **~ les cartes à qn** to tell the cards for sb; **se faire ~ les cartes** to have one's fortune told with cards; **8** (prendre) to draw [*vin, électricité, argent*] (**de, sur** from); **9** (sortir) ~ **un stylo de son sac** to take a pen out of one's bag; ~ **un enfant de l'eau** to pull a child out of the water; ~ **qch de sa poche** to pull sth out of one's pocket; **10** (faire sortir) ~ **le pays de la récession** to get the country out of recession; **tire-moi de là!** get me out of this!; ~ **qn d'une maladie** to pull sb through an illness; **tu l'as tirée de son silence** you drew her out of her silence; **11** (obtenir) ~ **de qn** to get [sth] from sb [*renseignement, aveu*]; ~ **de qch** to draw [sth] from sth [*force, ressources*]; to derive [sth] from sth [*orgueil, satisfaction*]; to make [sth] out of sth [*argent*]; **tu ne tireras pas grand-chose de cette voiture** (comme argent) you won't get much for this car; (comme service) you won't get much out of this car; ~ **le maximum de la situation** to make the most of the situation; ~ **un son d'un instrument** to get a note out of an instrument; **12** (dériver) **le film est tiré du roman** the film is based on the novel; **la guillotine tire son nom de son inventeur** the guillotine gets its name from its inventor; **le mot est tiré de l'anglais** the word comes from the English; **13** (extraire) **texte tiré de Zola** text taken from Zola; **le médicament est tiré d'une plante** the drug comes from a plant; **14** (faire un tirage) to print [*livre, négatif*]; to run off [*épreuve, exemplaire*]; **journal tiré à dix mille exemplaires** newspaper with a circulation of ten thousand; **tiré à part** [*texte*] off-printed; **15** (tracer) to draw [*ligne, trait*]; ~ **un chèque** to draw a cheque GB ou check US; ~ **des plans** FIG to draw up plans; **16**○ (passer) **plus qu'une heure/semaine à** ~ only one more hour/week to go; ~ **quelques années en prison** to spend a few years in prison.

II *vi* **1** (exercer une traction) to pull; ~ **sur qch** to pull on sth; (d'un coup ou par à-coups) to tug at sth; **tire fort!** pull hard!; **2** (utiliser une arme) GÉN to shoot (**sur** at); (à feu) to fire (**sur** at); ~ **à la carabine** to shoot with a rifle; ~ **au fusil** to fire a gun; **elle lui a tiré dans la jambe** she shot him/her in the leg; **3** (au football) to shoot; (au handball, basket-ball) to take a shot; **4** (choisir au hasard) ~ (**au sort**) to draw lots; **5** (prendre) ~ **sur** to draw on; ~ **sur son compte** to draw on one's account; **6** (aspirer) **la cheminée tire bien** the chimney draws well; **7** (être imprimé) ~ **à mille exemplaires** [*périodique*] to have a circulation of one thousand; **8** (aller vers) ~ **sur le jaune/l'orangé** [*couleur*] to be yellowish/orangy; ~ **sur la cinquantaine** [*personne*] to be pushing fifty; ~ **à gauche/droite** [*voiture*] to pull to the left/right.

III se tirer *vpr* **1** (sortir) **se** ~ **de** to come through [*situation, difficultés*]; **2**◐ (partir) **se** ~ to push off○; **3** (avec une arme) **se** ~ **une balle** to shoot oneself (**dans** in); **se** ~ **dessus** (l'un l'autre) LIT to shoot at one another; **4**○ (se débrouiller) **s'en** ~ to cope, to manage; **5**○ (échapper) **s'en** ~ (à un accident) to escape; (à une maladie) to pull through; (à une punition) to get away with it○; **s'en** ~ **à bon prix** to get off lightly.

tiret /tirε/ ▶ 414 *nm* dash.

tirette /tirεt/ *nf* TECH (rigide) pull tab; (souple) cord.

tireur, -euse /tirœr, øz/ *nm,f* **1** MIL, SPORT marksman/markswoman; **être** (**un**) **bon/mauvais** ~ to be a good/poor shot; **2** (personne armée) gunman; **3** (au football) striker; (aux boules) thrower. ■ ~ **de cartes** fortune teller (*using cards*); ~ **d'élite** expert marksman.

tiroir /tirwar/ *nm* (de meuble) drawer; **finir sa carrière dans le fond d'un** ~ FIG to end one's career in a second-rate job; **à** ~**s** FIG [*pièce, roman*] episodic, à tiroirs SPÉC. IDIOMES **racler les fonds de** ~ to scrape some money together.

tiroir-caisse, *pl* **tiroirs-caisses** /tirwarkεs/ *nm* cash register.

tisane /tizan/ *nf* herbal tea, tisane.

tison /tizɔ̃/ *nm* (fire) brand.

tisonner /tizɔne/ [1] *vtr* to poke.

tisonnier /tizɔnje/ *nm* poker.

tissage /tisaʒ/ *nm* **1** (fabrication) weaving ¢; **faire du** ~ to weave; **2** (texture) weave.

tisser /tise/ [1] *vtr* **1** [*personne, machine*] to weave; **métier à** ~ weaving loom; **tissé à la main** handwoven; **récit tissé de mensonges** FIG story riddled with lies; **2** [*araignée*] to spin [*toile*].

tisserand, ~e /tisrɑ̃, ɑ̃d/ ▶ 374 *nm,f* weaver.

tissu /tisy/ *nm* **1** (étoffe) material, fabric; **2** (cellules) **le** ~ **osseux** bone tissue; **3** (ensemble) (d'intrigues) web; (de mensonges) pack, tissue; (de calomnies, d'improbabilités, inepties) string; (de contradictions) mass; ~ **social** social fabric; ~ **industriel** industrial base.

tissu-éponge, *pl* **tissus-éponges** /tisyepɔ̃ʒ/ *nm* (terry) towelling GB, terry cloth US.

tissulaire /tisylεr/ *adj* tissue (*épith*).

titan /titɑ̃/ *nm* titan; **de** ~ titanic.

titane /titan/ *nm* titanium.

titanesque /titanεsk/ *adj* titanic.

titi○ /titi/ *nm* ~ (**parisien**) urchin, scamp.

titiller /titije/ [1] *vtr* to titillate.

titrage /titraʒ/ *nm* **1** (de film, livre, chanson) titling; **2** CHIMIE (de solution) titration; **3** (de minerai) assay.

titre /titr/ ▶ 596 *nm* **1** (d'œuvre) title; (de chapitre) heading; (dans un journal) headline; **avoir pour** ~ to be entitled; **les** ~**s de l'actualité** the headlines; **2** (rang) title; ~ **mondial** world title; ~ **nobiliaire** or **de noblesse** title; **donner à qn le** ~ **de** to address sb as; **le** ~ **d'ingénieur** the status of qualified engineer; **en** ~ [*professeur, directeur*] titular; [*fournisseur*] appointed; [*maîtresse, rival*] official; **champion en** ~ title holder; ~**s universitaires** (diplômes) university qualifications; **3** (motif, qualité) **à juste** ~ quite rightly; **à plus d'un** ~ in many respects; **à** ~ **de précaution** as a precaution; **à** ~ **expérimental** by way of experiment; **à** ~ **définitif** on a permanent basis; **à** ~ **privé** in a private capacity; **à** ~ **gracieux** or **gratuit** free; **à** ~ **onéreux** for a fee; **à** ~ **indicatif** as a rough guide; **à quel** ~ **a-t-il été invité?** why was he invited?; **au même** ~ **que vous** in the same capacity as yourself; **à double** ~ on two counts; **au** ~ **de l'aide économique** in economic aid; **perçu au** ~ **de droits d'auteur** received as royalties; **4** JUR (document) deed; ~ **de propriété** title deed; **5** (en Bourse) security; **6** ÉCON item; ~ **budgétaire** budgetary item; **7** (de solution) titre GB; (de vins et spiritueux) strength; (de métal précieux) fineness. ■ ~ **de gloire** claim to fame; ~ **de transport** ticket.

titré, ~e /titre/ *adj* **1** (noble) titled; **2** CHIMIE standard.

titrer /titre/ [1] *vtr* **1** (dans un journal) **le journal du dimanche titrait...** the headlines in the Sunday paper read...; **le Temps titrait sur quatre colonnes 'la fin de la démocratie'** 'the end of democracy' announced 'le Temps' in a four-column spread; **2** CHIMIE to titrate [*solution*]; to assay [*mineral*].

titubant, ~e /titybɑ̃, ɑ̃t/ *adj* unsteady.

tituber /titybe/ [1] *vi* to stagger; **ils sont sortis du pub en titubant** they staggered out of the pub.

titulaire /titylεr/ **I** *adj* **1** GÉN permanent; UNIV [*enseignant*] tenured; **2** SPORT **joueur** ~ full member of the team.

II *nmf* **1** (membre permanent) GÉN permanent staff member; UNIV (enseignant) tenured lecturer GB ou professor US; **être** ~ **d'un poste** (d'administration) to be a permanent staff member; (d'université) to have tenure; **2** (possesseur) holder; **être** ~ **de** to hold [*diplôme, permis, chaire*]; to have [*nationalité, compte en banque, pension*].

titularisation /titylarizasjɔ̃/ *nf* (action) GÉN confirmation in a post; UNIV granting of tenure.

titulariser /titylarize/ [1] *vtr* to give permanent status to [*agent, personnel*]; UNIV to grant tenure to [*professeur*]; SPORT to make [sb] a full member of the team [*joueur*].

toast /tost/ *nm* **1** (pain grillé) toast ¢; **trois** ~**s** three

Les titres de politesse

On ne trouvera ici que quelques indications générales sur la façon de s'adresser à quelqu'un ou de parler de quelqu'un en utilisant son titre. Pour les titres militaires, ▶ 284 |, et pour les autres titres, consulter les articles du dictionnaire.

Comment s'adresser à quelqu'un

Dans la plupart des circonstances ordinaires, l'anglais n'utilise pas d'équivalent de monsieur, madame *etc.*

bonjour, madame	= good morning
bonsoir, mademoiselle	= good evening
bonjour, monsieur	= good afternoon
excusez-moi, madame	= excuse me
pardon, monsieur	
pourriez-vous me dire ...	= excuse me, could you tell me ...

Les mots Mr, Mrs, Miss *et* Ms *sont toujours utilisés avec le nom de la personne; on ne les utilise jamais seuls.*

bonjour, madame	= good morning, Mrs Smith
au revoir, mademoiselle	= goodbye, Miss Smith
bonsoir, monsieur	= good evening, Mr Smith

Attention: Ms *(dire* [mɪz] *ou* [məz]*) permet de faire référence à une femme dont on connaît le nom sans préciser sa situation de famille. Il n'y a pas d'équivalent français:*

bonjour, madame	
ou bonjour, mademoiselle	= good morning, Ms Smith

Les anglophones utilisent les prénoms beaucoup plus volontiers que les francophones. Lorsqu'en français on dit simplement bonjour*, en anglais on précise souvent* good morning, Paul *ou* good morning, Anne *etc. De même, au début d'une lettre, un anglophone écrira facilement* Dear Anne, Dear Paul *etc., bien avant que le Français n'en vienne à utiliser le prénom.*

Les mots Madam *et* Sir *ne sont utilisés que par les vendeurs des magasins, les employés de restaurants, d'hôtels etc. Ils sont toujours utilisés sans le nom propre:*

bonjour, madame	= good morning, Madam
bonne nuit, monsieur	= good night, Sir

En anglais, le titre de doctor *est utilisé pour les docteurs de toutes disciplines. Mais on ne peut l'utiliser seul, sans nom propre, que pour un docteur en médecine.*

bonsoir, docteur	= good evening, doctor (*médecin*)
bonjour, docteur	= good morning, Doctor Smith (*en médecine ou d'une autre spécialité*)

Comment parler de quelqu'un

M Dupont est arrivé	= Mr Dupont has arrived
Mme Dupont a téléphoné	= Mrs Dupont phoned *ou* Ms Dupont phoned
le rabbin Lévi est malade	= Rabbi Lévi is ill

L'anglais n'utilise pas l'article défini devant les noms de titres lorsqu'ils sont suivis du nom propre.

le roi Richard I	= King Richard I (*dire* King Richard the first)
l'inspecteur Hervet	= Inspector Hervet
le prince Charles	= Prince Charles
la princesse Anne	= Princess Anne
le pape Jean-Paul II	= Pope John-Paul II (*dire* Pope John-Paul the second)

Mais si le titre est suivi du nom du pays, du peuple, de la ville etc., l'anglais utilise l'article défini.

le roi des Belges	= the King of the Belgians
le prince de Galles	= the Prince of Wales
l'évêque de Durham	= the Bishop of Durham

---

pieces of toast; **2** (canapé) canapé; **3** (discours) toast; **porter un ~ en l'honneur de qn** to toast sb.

toboggan /tɔbɔgã/ *nm* **1** (piste glissante) slide; **2** ®(viaduc) flyover GB, overpass US; **3** TECH (pour gravats) chute; **4** SPORT (traîneau) toboggan.

toc /tɔk/ **I**◦ *nm* (faux) **c'est du ~** (ce collier) it's a fake; (ces colliers) they're fakes.
II *excl* (*also onomat*); **~! ~!** knock! knock!; **tu vois, j'avais raison, et ~**◦! you see, I was right, so there!

tocsin /tɔksɛ̃/ *nm* alarm (bell), tocsin LITTÉR; **sonner le ~** LIT, FIG to sound the alarm.

toge /tɔʒ/ *nf* UNIV gown; JUR robe; (antique) toga.

tohu-bohu◦ /tɔybɔy/ *nm inv* (confusion) confusion; (tumulte) commotion.

toi /twa/ *pron pers* **1** (sujet, objet) you; **~, ne dis rien** don't say anything; **il les voit plus souvent que ~** (que tu ne les vois) he sees them more often than you do; (qu'il ne te voit) he sees them more often than you; **ce sont des amis à ~** they're YOUR friends; **une chambre à ~** a room of your own; **c'est à ~** (appartenance) it's yours, it belongs to you; (séquence) (it's) your turn; **c'est à ~ de choisir** (ton tour) it's your turn to choose; (ta responsabilité) it's up to you to choose; **2** (pronom réfléchi) yourself; **reprends-~** pull yourself together; **3** (toi-même) yourself; **pense un peu à ~ aussi** think of yourself a little as well.

toile /twal/ *nf* **1** (tissu) cloth; **~ de lin** linen (cloth); **des vêtements de ~** (heavy) cotton clothes; **de la grosse ~** canvas; **2** (de peintre) (support) canvas; (tableau) painting; **~ de maître** master painting; **3** NAUT canvas.
■ **~ d'araignée** GÉN spider's web; (dans une maison) cobweb; **~ cirée** oilcloth; **~ de fond** THÉÂT backcloth; FIG backdrop; **~ goudronnée** tarpaulin; **~ de jute** hessian; **~ à matelas** ticking; **~ de tente** (tissu) canvas; (tente) tent.

toilettage /twaletaʒ/ *nm* **1** (d'animal) grooming; **2** FIG (de structure) cleaning up.

toilette /twalɛt/ **I** *nf* **1** (soins corporels) **faire sa ~** [*personne*] to have a wash; [*animal*] to wash itself;

savon de ~ toilet soap; **faire la ~ d'un mort** to lay out a corpse; **faire la ~ d'un chien** to groom a dog; **faire la ~ de la ville** FIG to give the town a face-lift; **2** (vêtements) outfit; **en belle** or **grande ~** all dressed up (*jamais épith*); **3** (meuble) (pour se laver) washstand; (coiffeuse) dressing table.
II toilettes *nfpl* (chez soi) toilet (*sg*) GB, bathroom (*sg*) US; (dans un lieu public) toilets, restroom (*sg*) US.

toiletter /twalete/ [1] *vtr* to groom [*chien, chat, cheval*].

toi-même /twamɛm/ *pron pers* yourself.

toise /twaz/ *nf* **1** (instrument) height gauge; **passer à la ~** to be measured; **2** ▶ 348 | (unité) toise (≈ 6 1/2 ft).

toiser /twaze/ [1] *vtr* to look [sb] up and down [*personne*].

toison /twazɔ̃/ *nf* **1** (de mouton) fleece; **2** (chevelure) mane; (poils abondants) abundant growth (of hair).
■ **la Toison d'or** the Golden Fleece.

toit /twa/ *nm* **1** LIT roof; **habiter sous les ~s** to live in a garret; **2** FIG (maison) roof; **se retrouver sans ~** to find oneself without a roof over one's head.
■ **~ ouvrant** sunroof.
IDIOMES **crier qch sur (tous) les ~s** to shout sth from the rooftops.

toiture /twatyʀ/ *nf* (structure) roof; (matériau) roofing.

tôle /tol/ *nf* **1** (matière) sheet metal; (plaque) metal sheet ou plate; **2**◦ (prison) = **taule**.
■ **~ ondulée** corrugated iron; **~ à tarte** tart tin.

tolérable /tɔleʀabl/ *adj* [*attente, douleur, situation*] bearable; [*attitude*] tolerable, acceptable.

tolérance /tɔleʀɑ̃s/ *nf* **1** (ouverture d'esprit) tolerance; (indulgence) indulgence; **être d'une grande ~ avec qn** to be very tolerant with sb; **2** (dérogation) **ce n'est pas un droit, c'est une ~** it isn't an entitlement, but it's something that is tolerated; **3** (à un médicament, au bruit) tolerance (à of).

tolérant, ~e /tɔleʀɑ̃, ɑ̃t/ *adj* tolerant.

tolérer /tɔleʀe/ [14] *vtr* to tolerate.

tôlerie /tolʀi/ *nf* (technique) sheet-metal working; (commerce) sheet-metal trade; (atelier) sheet-metal works (*pl*); (ensemble de tôles) metalwork; (de voiture) bodywork.

tôlier, -ière /tolje, ɛʀ/ **▶ 374** *nm,f* **1** IND sheet-metal worker; AUT panel beater; **2** (patron d'hôtel) hotel boss.

tollé /tɔle/ *nm* outcry, hue and cry.

TOM /tɔm/ *nm: abbr* **▶ territoire**.

tomaison /tɔmɛzɔ̃/ *nf* volume numbering.

tomate /tɔmat/ *nf* **1** (fruit) tomato; **2** (plante) tomato plant; **3** (apéritif) *pastis with a dash of grenadine*.
IDIOMES **être rouge comme une ~** (à cause du soleil) to be as red as a lobster; (à cause de la gêne) to be as red as a beetroot.

tombal, ~e, *mpl* **-aux** /tɔbal, o/ *adj* **inscription ~e** gravestone inscription

tombant, ~e /tɔbɑ̃, ɑ̃t/ *adj* [*épaules*] sloping; [*moustaches, paupières*] drooping (*épith*); [*oreilles de chien*] floppy; [*poitrine*] PEJ sagging.

tombe /tɔb/ *nf* (fosse) grave; (dalle) gravestone.

tombeau, *pl* **~x** /tɔbo/ *nm* **1** (monument) tomb; **mettre qn au ~** to lay sb in their grave; **la mise au ~** ART the Entombment; **2** (personne discrète) **c'est un ~** he/she will keep quiet; **3** (fin) death; **vivre avec qn jusqu'au ~** to live with sb till the grave.
IDIOMES **rouler à ~ ouvert**○ to drive at breakneck speed.

tombée /tɔbe/ *nf* **à la ~ du jour** at close of day LITTÉR; **(à) la ~ de la nuit** (at) nightfall.

tomber[1] /tɔbe/ [1] **I** *vtr* (+ *v avoir*) SPORT to throw [*lutteur*]; FIG to beat [*équipe*].

II *vi* (+ *v être*) **1** (faire une chute) GÉN to fall; (de sa propre hauteur) [*personne, chaise*] to fall over; [*animal*] to fall; [*arbre, mur*] to fall down; (d'une hauteur, d'un support) [*personne, vase*] to fall off; [*fruits, feuilles, bombe*] to fall; [*cheveux, dents*] to fall out; [*plâtre, revêtement*] to come off; **~ dans un trou** to fall down a hole; **j'ai fait ~ un vase** I knocked a vase over; **j'ai fait ~ le vase de l'étagère** I knocked the vase off the shelf; **le vent a fait ~ une tuile du toit** the wind blew a tile off the roof; **se laisser ~ dans un fauteuil** to flop into an armchair; **laisser ~ un gâteau sur le tapis** to drop a cake on the carpet; **le skieur s'est laissé ~ pour s'arrêter** the skier dropped to the ground to stop himself; **2** (venir d'en haut) [*pluie, neige, foudre*] to fall; [*brouillard*] to come down; [*rayon, clarté*] to fall; [*rideau de théâtre*] to fall, to drop; **il tombe des gouttes** it's spotting with rain; **qu'est-ce que ça tombe**○**!, ça tombe dru**○**!** (pluie) it's pouring down!; **la foudre est tombée sur un arbre** the lightning struck a tree; **une faible lueur tombait de la lucarne** there was a dim light coming through the skylight; **une pâle clarté tombait de la lune** the moon cast a pale light; **3** (faiblir, baisser) [*valeur, prix, température*] to fall; [*ardeur, colère*] to subside; [*fièvre*] to come down; [*vent*] to drop; [*jour*] to draw to a close; [*conversation*] to die down; **faire ~** to bring down [*prix, température*]; to dampen [*enthousiasme*]; **il est tombé bien bas** (affectivement) he's in very low spirits; (moralement) he has sunk very low; **il est tombé bien bas dans mon estime** he has gone right down in my esteem ou estimation; **je tombe de sommeil** I can't keep my eyes open; **4** (être vaincu, renversé) [*dictateur, régime, ville*] to fall; (disparaître) [*obstacle, objection*] to vanish; [*opposition*] to subside; [*préjugé*] to die out; **le roi est tombé** (aux cartes) the king has been played; **faire ~** to bring down [*régime, dictateur*]; to break down [*barrières*]; **5** (s'affaisser) [*poitrine*] to sag; [*épaules*] to slope; **6** (pendre) [*chevelure, mèche*] to fall; **~ bien/mal** [*vêtement, rideau*] to hang well/badly; **sa jupe lui tombe (jusqu')aux chevilles** her skirt comes down to her ankles; **7** (se retrouver, se placer) **~ dans la vulgarité** to lapse into vulgarity; **vous tombez dans le paradoxe** you are being paradoxical; **~ sous le coup d'une loi** JUR to fall within the provisions of a law; **la conversation est tombée sur la politique** the conversation came around to politics; **8** (devenir) to fall; **~ malade/amoureux** to fall ill/in love; **9** (être donné) [*décision*] to be announced; [*nouvelle*] to break; [*réponse*] to be

given; **~ sur les écrans** [*nouvelle*] to come through on screen; **dès que le journal tombe des presses** as soon as the newspaper comes off the press; **10** (rencontrer) **~ sur** GÉN to come across [*inconnu, détail, objet*]; to run into [*ami*]; (recevoir en partage) to get; (avoir de la chance dans ses recherches) **~ sur la bonne page** to hit on the right page; **je suis tombé sur un examinateur sévère à l'examen** I got a harsh examiner in the exam; **je suis tombé par hasard sur ce que je cherchais** I found what I was looking for by chance; **si tu prends cette rue, tu tomberas sur la place** if you follow that street, you'll come to the square; **11** (survenir) GÉN to come; **tu ne pouvais pas mieux ~!** (au bon moment) you couldn't have come at a better time!; (avoir de la chance) you couldn't have done better!; **tu tombes bien/mal, j'allais partir** you're lucky/unlucky, I was just about to leave; **il faut toujours que ça tombe sur moi** or **que ça me tombe dessus**○**!** (décision, choix) why does it always have to be me?; (mésaventure) why does it always happen to me?; **~ au milieu d'une** or **en pleine réunion** [*personne*] to walk right into a meeting; [*annonce, nouvelle*] to come right in the middle of a meeting; **12** (coïncider) [*date*] to fall on [*jour, quantième*]; **13** (abandonner) **laisser ~** to give up [*emploi, activité*]; to drop [*sujet, projet, habitude*]; **laisse ~!** (désintérêt, désabusement) forget it!; (irritation) give it a rest○! ; **laisser ~ qn** (pour se séparer) to drop sb; (pour ne plus aider) to let sb down; **14** (agresser) **~ sur qn** (physiquement) [*soldats, voyous*] to fall on sb, to lay into sb○; [*pillards, police*] to descend on sb; (critiquer) to go for sb, to lay into sb○; **15** (mourir) EUPH to die.

tomber[2] /tɔbe/ *nm* (de vêtement, tissu) hang ¢; **ce velours a un beau ~** this velvet hangs well.

tombereau, *pl* **~x** /tɔbʀo/ *nm* **1** (charrette) tip-up cart; (contenu) cartload; **2** (camion) dumper truck GB, dumptruck US; (contenu) truckload.

tombeur○ /tɔbœʀ/ *nm* **1** (séducteur) lady-killer, Casanova; **2** (vainqueur) **le ~ d'une équipe** the one who brought a team down.

tombola /tɔbɔla/ *nf* tombola GB, lottery.

tome /tɔm/ *nm* **1** (volume) volume; **2** (division) part, book.

tommette /tɔmɛt/ *nf* hexagonal floor tile.

ton[1]**, ta,** *pl* **tes** /tɔ̃, ta, te/ *adj poss*

■ Note En anglais, on ne répète pas le possessif coordonné: *ta femme et tes enfants* = your wife and children.

your; **tes parents à toi**○ your parents; **à ~ arrivée** (prochaine) when you arrive; (passée) when you arrived.

ton[2] /tɔ̃/ *nm* **1** (de la voix) (hauteur) pitch; (inflexion) tone; (qualité) tone, voice; (expression) tone (of voice); **~ grave/aigu** low/high pitch; **~ criard/rauque** shrill/husky voice; **d'un ~ dédaigneux** scornfully; **d'un ~ sec** drily; **sur un ~ solennel** in a solemn tone; **baisser le ~** LIT to lower one's voice; FIG to moderate one's tone; **eh bien, si tu le prends sur ce ~** well, if you're going to take it like that; **je le leur ai dit** or **répété sur tous les ~s** I've told them a thousand times; **2** LING tone; **langue à ~s** tone language; **3** (style) tone; **donner le ~** GÉN to set the tone; (pour une mode) to set the fashion; **être** or **se mettre dans le ~** to fit in; **de bon ~** in good taste, tasteful; **il est/serait de bon ~ de faire** it is/it would be good form to do; **4** MUS (hauteur des notes) pitch; (tonalité) key; (intervalle) tone; (instrument) pitch pipe; **5** (couleur) shade, tone; **~ sur ~** in matching tones.

tonal, ~e /tɔnal/ *adj* LING, MUS tonal; **hauteur ~e** pitch; **langue ~e** tone language.

tonalité /tɔnalite/ *nf* **1** MUS (ton) key; (échelle des sons) tonality; **2** (de voyelle) tone; **3** (qualité) (de voix) tone; (de roman, film) tone; **4** (couleurs) tonality; **5** TÉLÉCOM dialling tone GB, dial tone US.

tondeur, -euse[1] /tɔdœʀ, øz/ **▶ 374** *nm,f* **~ de chiens** dog groomer; **~ de moutons** sheep shearer.

tondeuse[2] /tɔdœz/ *nf* **1** (pour chiens) clippers (*pl*);

(pour moutons) shears (*pl*); **2** (de coiffeur) clippers (*pl*); **3** (de jardin) ~ (**à gazon**) lawnmower.

tondre /tɔ̃dʀ/ [6] *vtr* **1** LIT to shear [*mouton, laine*]; to clip [*chien, poils*]; to mow [*gazon, pelouse*]; ~ **qn** to shave sb's head; **2**○ (couper les cheveux à) ~ **qn** to cut sb's hair; **3**○ (voler) to fleece○.

tondu, ~**e** /tɔ̃dy/ **I** *adj* **1** [*mouton*] shorn; [*chien*] clipped; **2** [*cheveux*] shorn; [*crâne*] shaven GB, shaved; [*prisonnier*] with a shaven head (*après n*).
II *nm,f* skinhead.

tongs /tɔ̃g/ *nfpl* flip-flops, thongs US.

tonicité /tɔnisite/ *nf* **1** (de climat, d'air) bracing effect; **2** (de muscle) tone.

tonifiant, ~**e** /tɔnifjɑ̃, ɑ̃t/ *adj* **1** [*climat, air*] bracing; [*promenade*] invigorating; **2** (pour les muscles, la peau) [*exercice, lotion*] toning (*épith*).

tonifier /tɔnifje/ [2] *vtr* to tone up [*muscles, épiderme*]; **un climat qui tonifie** an invigorating climate.

tonique[1] /tɔnik/ **I** *adj* **1** (stimulant) [*boisson*] tonic (*épith*); FIG [*air*] invigorating; [*lecture*] stimulating; **2** (astringent) **lotion** ~ toning lotion; **3** LING tonic.
II *nm* **1** MÉD, FIG tonic; **2** (lotion) toning lotion.

tonique[2] /tɔnik/ *nf* MUS tonic.

tonitruant, ~**e** /tɔnitʀyɑ̃, ɑ̃t/ *adj* booming (*épith*).

tonitruer /tɔnitʀye/ [1] *vi* to thunder.

tonnage /tɔnaʒ/ *nm* tonnage.

tonnant, ~**e** /tɔnɑ̃, ɑ̃t/ *adj* [*voix*] booming; [*colère*] thunderous.

tonne /tɔn/ *nf* ▶ 455 tonne, metric ton; **des ~s de choses à faire**○ FIG tons ou loads○ of things to do.

tonneau, *pl* ~**x** /tɔno/ *nm* **1** (contenant, contenu) barrel; **2** (en voiture) somersault; **faire un** ~ to turn over, to somersault; **3** NAUT ton; **4** AVIAT barrel roll.
IDIOMES **du même** ~○ of the same kind.

tonnelet /tɔnlɛ/ *nm* small barrel, keg.

tonnelier /tɔnəlje/ ▶ 374 *nm* cooper.

tonnelle /tɔnɛl/ *nf* arbour GB.

tonner /tɔne/ [1] **I** *vi* **1** [*personne*] to thunder; ~ **contre** to inveigh against; **2** [*artillerie*] to thunder.
II *v impers* **il tonne** it's thundering.

tonnerre /tɔnɛʀ/ **I** *nm* **1** MÉTÉO thunder; **coup de** ~ LIT clap of thunder; FIG thunderbolt; **2** (de canons, d'artillerie) thundering; **un** ~ **d'applaudissements** thunderous applause; **3**○ (haute qualité) **du** ~ fabulous○; **ça marche du** ~ it's going fantastically well.
II *excl* blast!

tonte /tɔ̃t/ *nf* **1** (époque, action) ~ (**des moutons**) shearing; **2** (laine) fleece.

tonton○ /tɔ̃tɔ̃/ *nm* uncle; ~ **Pierre** Uncle Pierre.

tonus /tɔnys/ *nm inv* **1** (de personne) energy, dynamism; **2** (de muscle) tone, tonus.

top /tɔp/ **I**○ *adj* top.
II *nm* (signal sonore) pip, beep; **donner le** ~ **de départ** (dans une course) to give the starting signal.

topaze /tɔpaz/ **I** ▶ 141 *adj inv* (couleur) topaz-coloured GB.
II *nf* topaz.

toper /tɔpe/ [1] *vi* **topons là!** let's shake on it!, done!

topinambour /tɔpinɑ̃buʀ/ *nm* Jerusalem artichoke.

topo○ /tɔpo/ *nm* (oral) short talk; (écrit) short piece; **c'est toujours le même** ~ it's always the same old story○.

topographie /tɔpɔgʀafi/ *nf* (science, relief) topography.

toponyme /tɔpɔnim/ *nm* place name, toponym SPÉC.

toquade○ /tɔkad/ *nf* **1** (pour une activité, un objet) passion; **2** (pour une personne) crush○ (**pour** on).

toque /tɔk/ *nf* (de femme) toque; (de cuisinier) chef's hat; (de juge) hat; (de jockey) cap; ~ **en fourrure** fur cap.

toqué, ~**e**○ /tɔke/ *adj* (fou) crazy○ (**de** about).

toquer○: **se toquer** /tɔke/ [1] *vpr* **se** ~ **de qch** to go crazy about sth; **se** ~ **de qn** to fall for sb○, to become infatuated with sb.

torche /tɔʀʃ/ *nf* (flambeau) torch; ~ **vivante** human torch; **parachute en** ~ candled parachute.
■ ~ **électrique** torch GB, flashlight.

torcher○ /tɔʀʃe/ [1] *vtr* **1** (essuyer) to wipe; **2** (faire vite) to dash off○ [*article, rapport*]; (bâcler) to cobble [sth] together; **un article bien torché** a well-written article.

torchère /tɔʀʃɛʀ/ *nf* **1** (candélabre) torchère; **2** (en pétrochimie) flare stack.

torchis /tɔʀʃi/ *nm inv* cob (*for walls*).

torchon /tɔʀʃɔ̃/ *nm* **1** GÉN cloth; (pour la vaisselle) tea towel GB, dish towel US; **donner** or **passer un coup de** ~ **sur** to give [sth] a wipe [*vaisselle, meuble*]; **coup de** ~○ (épuration) purge, clean-up○; **2**○ (journal) PÉJ rag○; **3**○ (travail mal présenté) messy piece of work.
IDIOMES **le** ~ **brûle** (**entre eux**)○ it's war (between them).

tordant○, ~**e** /tɔʀdɑ̃, ɑ̃t/ *adj* hilarious.

tordre /tɔʀdʀ/ [6] **I** *vtr* **1** (tourner violemment) to twist [*bras*]; to wring [*cou*]; **2** (déformer) to bend [*clou, barre*]; **3** (contracter) **la peur lui tordait le visage** his/her face was distorted with fear; **l'angoisse lui tordait l'estomac** fear was tying his/her stomach up in knots; **4** (enrouler) to twist [*mouchoir*]; **5** (essorer) to wring out [*linge*].
II se tordre *vpr* **1** [*personne*] **se** ~ **la cheville** to twist one's ankle; **se** ~ **de douleur** to writhe in pain; **se** ~ **de rire** to double up laughing; **2** [*pare-chocs*] to bend; [*roue*] to buckle.

tordu, ~**e** /tɔʀdy/ *adj* **1** (déformé) [*nez, jambes, barre*] crooked; [*branches, ferraille*] twisted; **2** FIG [*idée*] weird, strange; [*logique, esprit*] twisted; **inventer un coup** ~○ to come up with an underhand trick.

tornade /tɔʀnad/ *nf* tornado.

torpeur /tɔʀpœʀ/ *nf* torpor.

torpille /tɔʀpij/ *nf* torpedo.

torpilleur /tɔʀpijœʀ/ *nm* **1** (bateau) torpedo boat; **2** (marin) torpedo gunner.

torréfacteur /tɔʀefaktœʀ/ *nm* **1** ▶ 374 (commerçant) coffee merchant; **2** (machine) roasting machine.

torréfier /tɔʀefje/ [2] *vtr* to roast.

torrent /tɔʀɑ̃/ *nm* LIT, FIG torrent; **des ~s de larmes** floods of tears; **pleuvoir à ~s** to rain very heavily.

torrentiel, **-ielle** /tɔʀɑ̃sjɛl/ *adj* torrential.

torride /tɔʀid/ *adj* [*climat, région*] torrid; [*soleil, été, chaleur*] scorching.

tors, **torse**[1] /tɔʀ, tɔʀs/ *adj* GÉN twisted; [*jambes*] crooked.

torsade /tɔʀsad/ *nf* **1** GÉN twist, coil; **2** (point de tricot) cable stitch; **3** ARCHIT cable moulding.

torsader /tɔʀsade/ [1] *vtr* to twist [*fils, soie*]; **bougeoir torsadé** twisted candlestick; **colonne torsadée** cable column.

torse[2] /tɔʀs/ *nm* **1** ▶ 137 GÉN chest; **se mettre** ~ **nu** to strip to the waist; **2** ANAT, ART torso.

torsion /tɔʀsjɔ̃/ *nf* **1** GÉN twisting; **2** PHYS torsion.

tort /tɔʀ/ **I** *nm* **1** (défaut de raison) **avoir** ~ to be wrong; **tu n'as pas** ~ **de les laisser tomber!** I don't blame you for dropping them!; **j'aurais tort de m'inquiéter!** it would be silly of me to worry!; **être en** ~, **être dans son** ~ to be in the wrong; **donner** ~ **à qn** [*arbitre, juge*] to blame sb; [*faits*] to prove sb wrong; **2** (faute) fault; **les ~s sont partagés** there are faults on both sides; **prendre tous les ~s à son compte** to take all the blame ou all responsibility; **reconnaître ses ~s** to acknowledge that one has done wrong; **avoir des ~s envers qn** to have wronged sb; **le jugement a été prononcé à leurs ~s** JUR the case went against them; **3** (erreur) mistake; **mon** ~, **c'est d'être trop impulsif** my trouble is that I am too impulsive; **4** (préjudice) wrong; **demander réparation d'un** ~ to demand compensation for a wrong; **faire du** or **porter** ~ **à qn/qch** to harm sb/sth.
II à tort *loc adv* [*accuser*] wrongly; **à** ~ **ou à raison** rightly or wrongly; **à** ~ **et à travers** [*dépenser*]

wildly; **parler à ~ et à travers** to talk a lot of nonsense.

torticolis /tɔʀtikɔli/ ▶ 196 | *nm inv* stiff neck.

tortillard○ /tɔʀtijaʀ/ *nm* small local train.

tortiller /tɔʀtije/ [1] I *vtr* to twist [*fibres*]; to twiddle [*mouchoir, moustache*].

II **se tortiller** *vpr* to wriggle.

IDIOMES **il n'y a pas à ~**○ there's no wriggling out of it.

tortillon /tɔʀtijɔ̃/ *nm* (de papier, tissu) twist.

tortionnaire /tɔʀsjɔnɛʀ/ *nmf* torturer.

tortue /tɔʀty/ *nf* **1** (reptile) (d'eau) turtle; (terrestre) tortoise, turtle US; **2** (personne lente) slowcoach○ GB, slowpoke○ US; **3** (papillon) tortoiseshell.

IDIOMES **avancer comme une ~** to proceed at a snail's pace.

tortueux, -euse /tɔʀtɥø, øz/ *adj* **1** LIT [*chemin, ruisseau*] winding; **2** FIG [*manœuvres*] devious; [*langage*] convoluted; [*chemin, esprit*] tortuous.

torturant, -e /tɔʀtyʀɑ̃, ɑ̃t/ *adj* agonizing.

torture /tɔʀtyʀ/ *nf* torture ¢; **sous la ~** under torture; **j'étais à la ~** FIG it was torture.

torturer /tɔʀtyʀe/ [1] I *vtr* **1** [*bourreau*] to torture [*personne*]; **2** (faire souffrir) [*pensée, sentiment*] to torment; **être torturé par la faim** to be starving; **3** (forcer le sens de) to distort [*texte*]; **style torturé** tortured style.

II **se torturer** *vpr* FIG to torment oneself; **se ~ l'esprit** (cherchant une solution) to rack one's brains.

torve /tɔʀv/ *adj* [*œil, regard*] menacing, baleful.

tôt /to/ *adv* **1** (de bonne heure) early; **~ le matin** early in the morning; **2** (bientôt, vite) soon, early; **le plus ~ serait le mieux** the sooner the better; **~ ou tard** sooner or later; **tu n'étais pas plus ~ parti qu'il est arrivé** no sooner had you left than he arrived; **j'aurai ~ fait de le réparer** it won't take me long to mend it, I'll soon have it mended; **on ne m'y reprendra pas de si ~** I won't do that again in a hurry; **tu as fini? ce n'est pas trop ~!** you've finished? about time too○!

total, ~e, *mpl* **-aux** /tɔtal, o/ I *adj* **1** (complet) complete, total; **2** (global) total.

II *nm* total; **faire le ~ des dépenses** to work out the total expenditure; **il n'a pas fermé la porte à clé, ~**○, **il s'est tout fait voler** he didn't lock the door, the upshot was that he had everything stolen.

III **au total** *loc adv* (dans un calcul) **au ~ cela fait 350 francs** altogether that comes to 350 francs.

totalement /tɔtalmɑ̃/ *adv* totally, completely.

totaliser /tɔtalize/ [1] *vtr* **1** (faire le total de) to total, to add up [*bénéfices, souscriptions*]; **2** (atteindre le total de) to have a total of [*points, buts, votes*].

totalitaire /tɔtalitɛʀ/ *adj* totalitarian.

totalitarisme /tɔtalitaʀism/ *nm* totalitarianism.

totalité /tɔtalite/ *nf* **la ~ du personnel** all the staff, the whole staff; **la ~ des dépenses** the total expenditure; **la presque ~ de ma fortune** almost all my fortune; **appréhender un problème dans sa ~** to look at a problem in its entirety; **financé en ~ par l'État** entirely ou completely state-financed; **rembourser en ~** to refund in full.

totem /tɔtɛm/ *nm* (emblème) totem.

toubib /tubib/ *nm* doctor, quack○ GB.

touchant, ~e /tuʃɑ̃, ɑ̃t/ *adj* (émouvant) moving; (attendrissant) touching; **~ de simplicité** touchingly simple.

touche /tuʃ/ *nf* **1** TECH (commande manuelle) (de clavier) key; (de machine à laver, téléviseur, vidéo) button; (d'instrument à cordes) fret; **2** ART (coup de pinceau) stroke; (style) touch; (tache de peinture) dash, touch; **3** SPORT (ligne de) **~** sideline, touchline; **sortir en ~** to go into touch; **remise en ~** (au football) throw-in; (au rugby) line-out; **mettre qn sur la ~** FIG to push sb aside FIG; **4** (en escrime) hit; **5** (à la pêche) bite; **faire une ~** to get a bite.

touche-à-tout /tuʃatu/ *adj inv* **être ~** [*bébé*] to be into everything; [*esprit curieux*] to be a jack of all trades.

toucher¹ /tuʃe/ [1] I *vtr* **1** (poser la main sur) **~ (de la main)** to touch [*objet, surface, personne*]; **~ du bois** (par superstition) to touch wood; **~ le front de qn** to feel sb's forehead; **~ qch du doigt** LIT, FIG to put one's finger on sth; **2** (être en contact avec) to be touching [*mur, plafond, fond*]; **~ le sol** [*animal, sauteur, avion*] to land; **3** (heurter) to hit [*adversaire, voiture, trottoir*]; **si tu recules encore tu vas ~ le mur** if you reverse any more, you'll hit the wall; **4** (attendrir) to touch [*personne*]; **ça me touche beaucoup** I am very touched; **5** (affecter) [*changement, crise, loi*] to affect [*personne, secteur, pays*]; [*intempérie*] to hit [*région*]; **6** (être contigu à) [*pays, maison, usine*] to be next to; **7** (encaisser) [*pension, crise, loi*] to get, to receive [*argent*]; to cash [*chèque*]; to get [*retraite*]; to win [*lot*]; **8** (joindre) **~ qn** to get hold of sb; **9** (atteindre) **~ trois millions d'auditeurs** ou **de téléspectateurs** to have an audience of three million; **~ sept millions de lecteurs** to have a readership of seven million.

II **toucher à** *vtr ind* **1** (poser la main sur) **~ à** to touch [*objets*]; **~ à tout** LIT to be into everything; FIG to be a jack of all trades; **il ne touche plus à un fusil** he won't go near a rifle anymore; **avec son air de ne pas y ~, c'est un malin**○ he looks as if butter wouldn't melt in his mouth, but he's a sly one; **2** (concerner) **~ à** to concern; **la réforme touche à l'emploi des jeunes** the reform concerns youth employment; **3** (porter atteinte à) **~ à** to infringe on [*droit, privilège*]; **4** (modifier) **~ à** to change; **on ne peut ~ aux coutumes** tradition is sacrosanct; **5** (aborder) **vous touchez à un sujet délicat** you're getting on to a delicate subject.

III **se toucher** *vpr* [*maisons, jardins*] to be next to each other.

toucher² /tuʃe/ *nm* **1** (sens) **le ~** touch, the sense of touch; **doux au ~** soft to the touch; **2** MÉD digital examination; **3** MUS (d'un pianiste) touch.

touffe /tuf/ *nf* (de cheveux, d'herbe) tuft; (de genêts, d'arbres) clump.

touffu, ~e /tufy/ *adj* **1** [*sourcils, barbe*] bushy; [*végétation, forêt*] dense; [*buisson*] thick; [*arbre*] leafy; **au poil ~** [*chien, chat*] with thick fur; **2** [*texte, discours, style*] dense.

touiller○ /tuje/ [1] *vtr* to stir [*sauce*]; to toss [*salade*].

toujours /tuʒuʀ/ *adv* **1** (exprimant la continuité, la répétition) always; **j'en rêve depuis ~** I've always dreamed about it; **de ~** [*ami*] very old; [*amitié*] long-standing; **~ plus vite** faster and faster; **des frais ~ plus importants** ever-increasing costs; **2** (encore) still; **c'est ~ aussi difficile** it's still just as hard; **3** (de toute façon) anyway; **viens ~** come anyway; **on peut ~ essayer** we can always try; **cela peut ~ servir** it might come in handy; **c'est ~ mieux que rien** it's still better than nothing; **c'est ~ ça de pris** ou **de gagné** that's something at least; **~ est-il que** the fact remains that.

toupet /tupɛ/ *nm* **1**○ (effronterie) cheek○, nerve○; **elle ne manque pas de ~!** she's got a cheek○!; **2** (de cheveux) tuft; (sur le sommet de la tête) quiff GB, forelock US; **(faux) ~** toupee.

toupie /tupi/ *nf* (jouet) top.

tour¹ /tuʀ/ *nm* **1** (mouvement rotatif) GÉN turn; (autour d'un axe) revolution; **donner un ~ de clé** to turn the key; **faire un ~ de manège** to have a go on the merry-go-round; **faire un ~ de valse** to waltz around the floor; **faire un ~ sur soi-même** [*danseur*] to spin around; [*planète*] to rotate; **un (disque) 33/45/78 ~s** an LP/a 45 ou single/a 78; **fermer qch à double ~** to double-lock sth; **à ~ de bras**○ [*frapper*] with a vengeance; [*investir, racheter*] left, right and centre○GB; **2** (mouvement autour de) **faire le ~ de qch** GÉN to go around sth; (en voiture) to drive around sth; **faire le ~ du monde** to go around the world; **la nouvelle a vite fait le ~ du village** the news spread rapidly through the village; **~ de circuit** lap; **3** ▶ 348|, 581| (pourtour) (bords) edges (*pl*); (circonférence) circumference; (mensuration) measurement; (mesure standard) size; **de 15 mètres de ~** 15 metres○GB in circumference, 15 metres○GB around; **de**

hanches hip measurement; **4** (déplacement) (à pied) walk, stroll; (à bicyclette) ride; (en voiture) drive, spin; **faire un (petit) ~** (à pied) to go for a walk ou stroll; **je suis allé faire un ~ à Paris/en ville** I went to Paris/into GB ou down US town; **faire un ~ chez des amis** to go over to some friends; **faire des ~s et des détours** LIT [*route, rivière*] to twist and turn; FIG [*personne*] to beat about the bush; **5** (examen) look; **faire le ~ d'un problème** to have a look at a problem; **faire un (rapide) ~ d'horizon** to have a quick over-all look; **faire le ~ de ses ennemis** to go through one's enemies; **on en a vite fait le ~**○ PEJ there's not much to it/her/them etc; **6** (moment d'agir) GÉN turn; (de compétition, tournoi, coupe) round; **à qui le ~?** whose turn is it?; **il perd plus souvent qu'à son ~** (il regrette) he loses more often than he would like; (je critique) he loses more often than he should; **~ à ~** (alternativement) by turns; (à la suite) in turn; **7** (consultation électorale) **~ de scrutin** ballot, round of voting; **scrutin à deux ~s** two-round ballot; **8** (manœuvre, ruse) trick; **jouer un ~ à qn** to play a trick on sb; **et le ~ est joué** (c'est fait) that's done the trick; (ce sera fait) that will do the trick; **ça te jouera des ~s** it's going to get you into trouble one of these days; **~ d'adresse** feat of skill; **~ de main** knack; **en un ~ de main** (habilement) deftly; (rapidement) in a flash; **~ de force** feat; (œuvre) tour de force; **9** (allure, aspect) turn; **~ (de phrase)** LING turn of phrase; **le ~ qu'ont pris les événements** the turn events have taken; **donner un ~ nouveau à qch** to give a new twist to sth; **10** TECH (machine-outil) lathe. ■ **~ de chant** song recital; **~ de potier** potter's wheel; **~ de rein(s)** back strain.

tour² /tuʀ/ *nf* **1** ARCHIT tower; (immeuble) tower block GB, high rise US; **2** (aux échecs) rook, castle; **3** (machine de guerre) siege-tower. ■ **~ de forage** derrick.

tourbe /tuʀb/ *nf* peat.

tourbière /tuʀbjɛʀ/ *nf* peat bog.

tourbillon /tuʀbijɔ̃/ *nm* **1** (d'air) whirlwind; (d'eau) whirlpool; **~ de poussière** whirl of dust; **2** FIG (de souvenirs) swirl; **(de réformes)** whirlwind, maelstrom; **le ~ de la vie** the merry-go-round of life.

tourbillonnement /tuʀbijɔnmɑ̃/ *nm* (de neige, feuilles) swirling, whirling; (de danseurs) twirling.

tourbillonner /tuʀbijɔne/ [1] *vi* **1** LIT [*neige, feuilles*] to swirl, to whirl; [*danseurs*] to twirl; **2** FIG [*idées, souvenirs*] to swirl around.

tourelle /tuʀɛl/ *nf* **1** ARCHIT turret; **2** (de char) turret; (de sous-marin) conning tower; **3** PHOT **~ d'objectifs** lens turret.

tourisme /tuʀism/ *nm* tourism; **l'industrie du ~** the tourist industry. ■ **~ vert** countryside holidays (*pl*) GB ou vacations (*pl*) US.

touriste /tuʀist/ *nmf* tourist; **il suit les cours en ~** HUM he goes to his lessons whenever he feels like it.

touristique /tuʀistik/ *adj* [*brochure, menu, saison*] tourist (*épith*); [*afflux*] of tourists (*épith, après n*); [*ville, région*] which attracts tourists (*épith, après n*).

tourment /tuʀmɑ̃/ *nm* LITER torment.

tourmente /tuʀmɑ̃t/ *nf* LITER **1** (tempête) storm; **2** FML (trouble) turmoil.

tourmenté, **~e** /tuʀmɑ̃te/ *adj* **1** (inquiet) [*personne, visage*] tormented; [*expression, esprit*] tortured; **2** (agité) LITER [*époque, histoire, mer, vie*] turbulent; **3** (irrégulier) [*paysage*] rugged; [*forme*] contorted; **4** (tarabiscoté) [*style*] tortured; [*parcours*] tortuous.

tourmenter /tuʀmɑ̃te/ [1] **I** *vtr* **1** (inquiéter) to worry; **2** (faire souffrir) to torment; **3** (harceler) [*créancier*] to harass [*débiteur*]. **II se tourmenter** *vpr* to worry.

tournage /tuʀnaʒ/ *nm* **1** CIN (prise de vues) shooting ₵, filming ₵; (lieu de réalisation) set; **pendant le ~** during shooting; **entre deux ~s** between two films; **2** TECH turning; **~ du bois** wood-turning.

tournant, **~e** /tuʀnɑ̃, ɑ̃t/ **I** *adj* **1** (qui pivote) [*siège, mécanisme*] swivel; [*jet*] rotating; [*porte*] revolving;

2 (qui fait des détours) [*mouvement*] turning; [*service*] mobile; **3** (qui alterne) [*grève, mesure*] staggered. **II** *nm* **1** (virage) bend; **2** (événement) turning point; **3** (charnière) turn; **au ~ du siècle** at the turn of the century; **4** (orientation) change of direction; **prendre un ~** to change tack. IDIOMES **je t'aurai au ~!** I'll get my own back!

tourné, **~e¹** /tuʀne/ *adj* **1** (orienté) **~ vers** [*regard, yeux, personne*] turned toward(s); [*activité, opération, politique*] oriented toward(s); [*ouverture, maison, passage*] facing (*épith, après n*); **~ vers le passé/l'avenir** backward-/forward-looking; **porte ~e vers la mer** gate facing the sea; **2** (fait) **bien ~** [*compliment, lettre*] nicely phrased; [*personne, taille*] shapely; **expression bien ~e** well-turned phrase; **mal ~** [*phrase*] clumsy; **3** (aigri) [*lait, sauce*] off (*jamais épith*).

tournebroche /tuʀnəbʀɔʃ/ *nm* (rotating) spit.

tourne-disque, *pl* **~s** /tuʀnədisk/ *nm* record player.

tournée² /tuʀne/ *nf* **1** (de facteur, livreur) round; (d'équipe, de chanteur, troupe) tour; **2**○ (au café) round.

tournemain: en un tournemain /ɑ̃n̆tuʀnəmɛ̃/ *loc adv* in no time.

tourner /tuʀne/ [1] **I** *vtr* **1** (faire pivoter) to turn [*volant, clé, bouton, meuble*]; **~ la tête vers** to turn to look at; **~ les yeux vers** to look at; **le bruit m'a fait ~ la tête** I looked around at the noise; **2** CIN to shoot [*film, scène*]; **3** (éluder) to get around [*difficulté, loi*]; **4** (formuler) to phrase [*lettre, compliment, critique*]; **5** TECH (façonner) to turn [*bois, pièce*]; to throw [*pot*]; **6** (transformer) **~ qn/qch en dérision** ou **ridicule** to deride ou ridicule sb/sth; **7** (orienter) to turn [*pensées, attention*] (**vers** to); to direct [*colère*] (**contre** against); **8** (envisager) **~ et retourner qch dans son esprit** to mull sth over; **~ une proposition en tous sens** to look at a proposal from every angle; **9** (remuer) to stir [*sauce*]; to toss [*salade*].

II *vi* **1** (pivoter) GÉN [*clé, disque*] to turn; [*roue*] to turn, to revolve; [*planète, hélice*] to rotate; [*porte à gonds*] to swing; [*porte à tambour*] to revolve; (rapidement) [*toupie, danseur*] to spin; **~ sur soi-même** to spin around; **faire ~** GÉN to turn; (rapidement) to spin [*roue, toupie*]; **faire ~ les tables** (en spiritisme) to do table-turning; **2** (graviter) **~ autour de** GÉN to turn around; [*planète, étoile*] to revolve around; [*avion*] to circle; **3** (aller et venir) **~ (en rond)** [*personne*] to go around and around; [*automobiliste*] to drive around and around; **~ en rond** FIG [*discussion*] to go around in circles; **il tourne dans son bureau depuis une heure** he has been pacing up and down in his office for the last hour; **4** (virer) to turn (**vers** toward(s)); **tournez à gauche** turn left; **le chemin tourne entre les arbres** the path winds between the trees; **5** (se situer) **~ autour de** [*effectifs, somme d'argent*] to be (somewhere) in the region of, to be round about○ GB, to be around; **6** (fonctionner) [*moteur, usine*] to run; **~ rond** [*moteur*] to run smoothly; [*entreprise, affaires*] to be doing well; **les affaires tournent (bien)** business is good; **faire ~** to run [*entreprise*]; **il y a quelque chose qui ne tourne pas rond dans cette histoire**○ there's something fishy○ about this business; **mon frère ne tourne pas rond**○ depuis quelque temps my brother has been acting strangely for some time; **7** (évoluer) **les choses ont bien/mal tourné pour lui** things turned out well/badly for him; **leur frère a mal tourné** their brother turned ou badly; **leur réunion a mal tourné** their meeting went badly; **~ à l'avantage de qn/au désavantage de qn** to swing in sb's favour GB/against sb; **la réunion a tourné à la bagarre/en mascarade** the meeting turned into a brawl/into a farce; **8** CIN [*réalisateur*] to shoot, to film; **~ (dans un film)** [*acteur*] to make a film GB ou movie US; **elle a tourné avec les plus grands acteurs** she's worked with top actors; **9** (faire une tournée) [*représentant, spectacle*] to tour; **10** (fermenter) [*lait, sauce, viande*] to go off; **11** (chercher à séduire) **~ autour de qn** to hang around sb.

tout

Quand *tout* fait partie d'une locution comme *à tout hasard, de toute(s) part(s), tout compte fait, tout nu, tout neuf, tout simplement* etc., la traduction sera donnée sous le terme principal.

Remarques sur l'adjectif

1 Lorsque *tout*, adjectif singulier, exprime la totalité, plusieurs traductions sont possibles mais non toujours interchangeables.

De manière générale:
on emploiera *all* lorsque le mot qualifié est non dénombrable

tout le vin	= all the wine
tout l'argent	= all the money
tout ce bruit	= all that noise
tout leur talent	= all their talent
c'est tout ce que je sais	= that's all I know

on emploiera *whole* si *tout* peut être remplacé par *entier*

tout le gâteau	= the whole cake
tout le groupe	= the whole group
tout un livre	= a whole book

Mais:
connaître tout Zola/le Japon = to know the whole of Zola/Japan

lire tout 'Les Misérables' = to read the whole of 'Les Misérables'
pendant tout mon séjour = for the whole of my stay

2 *throughout* (ou *all through*) signifie *du début à la fin, d'un bout à l'autre*. On l'emploie souvent pour insister sur la durée ou l'étendue devant un terme singulier ou pluriel qui désigne l'espace de temps ou l'événement pendant lequel un fait a lieu, ou encore le territoire sur lequel il a lieu:

pendant tout le match	= throughout the match
pendant tous ces mois	= throughout those months
la rumeur se répandit dans toute la province	= the rumour spread throughout the province
faire tout le trajet debout	= to stand throughout the journey* ou *to stand for the whole journey
il neige sur toute la France	= it's snowing throughout France *ou* it's snowing all over France

Au pluriel, *tous, toutes* se traduiront par *all* pour exprimer la totalité, par *every* pour insister sur les composants d'un ensemble, ou encore par *any* pour indiquer l'absence de discrimination. On notera que *every* et *any* sont suivis du singulier.

---

ournesol /turnəsɔl/ *nm* 1 BOT sunflower; 2 CHIMIE **papier ~** litmus paper.

ourneur, -euse /turnœr, øz/ ▶374▏ *nm,f* TECH turner; (sur machine industrielle) lathe operator.

ournevis /turnəvis/ *nm inv* screwdriver.

ournicoter° /turnikɔte/ [1] *vi* **~ autour de** to hang around.

ourniquet /turnikɛ/ *nm* 1 (barrière) turnstile; 2 (présentoir) revolving stand; 3 (d'arrosage) sprinkler; 4 (de chirurgie) tourniquet.

ournoi /turnwa/ *nm* GÉN tournament.

ournoyer /turnwaje/ [23] *vi* 1 [*feuilles, papiers*] to swirl around; [*vautours*] to wheel; [*moucherons*] to fly around in circles; 2 [*danseurs*] to whirl; **faire ~** to spin [sb] around [*personne*].

ournure /turnyr/ *nf* 1 (aspect) turn; **prendre bonne ~** to take a turn for the better; **prendre ~** [*projet*] to take shape; **cela donne à l'affaire une tout autre ~** this puts a completely different complexion on things; 2 (formulation) turn of phrase; **~ idiomatique** idiomatic expression.
■ **~ d'esprit** frame of mind.

ourte /turt/ *nf* pie; **~ à la viande** meat pie.

ourteau, *pl* **~x** /turto/ *nm* 1 CULIN, ZOOL crab; 2 AGRIC oil cake.

ourtereau, *pl* **~x** /turtəro/ I *nm* ZOOL young turtle dove.
II **tourtereaux** *nmpl* (amoureux) lovebirds.

ourterelle /turtərɛl/ *nf* turtle dove.

ourtière /turtjɛr/ *nf* pie dish.

ous ▶ **tout**.

Toussaint /tusɛ̃/ *nf* **la ~** (jour) All Saints' Day; **à la ~** (jour) on All Saints' Day; (période) at the end of October, at Halloween US.

ousser /tuse/ [1] *vi* [*personne*] to cough; [*moteur*] to splutter.

oussotement /tusɔtmɑ̃/ *nm* (de personne) (slight) cough; (de moteur) splutter.

toussoter /tusɔte/ [1] *vi* [*personne*] to have a slight cough; [*moteur*] to splutter.

tout /tu, ~e /tut/, *mpl* **tous** /tu *adj*, tus *pron*/, *fpl* **toutes** /tut/ I *pron indéf* 1 **tout** (chaque chose) everything; (n'importe quoi) anything; (l'ensemble) all; **~ est prêt** everything is ready; **~ peut arriver** anything can happen; **~ est prétexte à querelle(s)** any pretext will do to start a quarrel; **~ n'est pas perdu** all is not lost; **en ~** (au total) in all; (entièrement) in every respect; **en ~ et pour ~** all told; **~ bien compté** or **pesé** or **considéré** all in all; **~ est là** FIG that's the whole point; **c'est ~ dire** I need say no more; **et ~ et ~**○ and all that sort of thing; **ce n'est pas ~ (que) de commencer un travail, il faut le finir** it's not enough or it's all very well to start off a job, it's got to be finished; **avoir ~ d'un assassin** to look just like a murderer; 2 **tous** /tus/, **toutes** (la totalité des êtres ou choses) all; (la totalité des éléments d'une catégorie, d'un groupe) all of them/us/you; **tous ensemble** all together; **tous ne sont pas d'accord** not all of them agree; **~es tant qu'elles sont** all of them, each and every one of them; **est-ce que ça conviendra à tous?** will it suit everybody or everyone?
II *adj* 1 (exprimant la totalité) **bois ~ ton lait** drink all your milk, drink up your milk; **~ le reste** everything else; **manger ~ un pain** to eat a whole loaf; **~ Pompéi a été enseveli** the whole of Pompeii was buried; **je ne l'ai pas vu de ~ l'été** I haven't seen him all summer; **~ le problème est là** that's where the problem lies; **~ cela ne compte pas** none of that counts; **~ le monde** everybody; 2 (véritable) **c'est ~ un travail/événement** it's quite a job/an event; 3 (devant ce qui/que/dont) (l'ensemble) all; (toutes les choses) everything; (sans discrimination) anything; **~ ce dont j'ai besoin** all I need; **j'ai acheté ~ ce qui était sur la liste** I bought everything that was on the list; **il dit ~ ce qui lui passe par la tête** he says anything that comes into his head; **~ ce qu'il dit n'est pas vrai** not all of what he says is true; **être ~ ce qu'il y a de plus serviable** to be most obliging; **c'est ~ ce qu'on fait de mieux** it's the best there is; **'tu en es sûr?'—'~ ce qu'il y a de plus sûr'** 'are you sure?'—'as sure as can be'; 4 (n'importe quel) any; **à ~ âge** at any age; **à ~ moment** (n'importe quand) at any time; (sans cesse) constantly; **~e publicité est interdite** all advertising is prohibited; 5 (total) **en ~e innocence/franchise** in all innocence/honesty; **en ~e liberté** with complete freedom; **en ~e hâte** in a great hurry; **de ~e beauté** most beautiful; 6 (unique, seul) **il a souri pour ~e réponse** his

---

III **se tourner** *vpr* 1 (se diriger, par intérêt ou besoin) **se ~ vers** or **du côté de qn/qch** to turn to sb/sth; **ne pas savoir vers qui se ~/de quel côté se ~** not to know who to turn to/which way to turn; 2 (changer de position) **se ~ vers qn/qch** to turn toward(s) sb/sth; **tous les yeux se sont tournés vers elle** all eyes turned toward(s) her; 3 (faire demi-tour sur soi-même) **tourne-toi un peu plus sur la** or **à gauche** just turn a little bit more to the left; **se ~ et se retourner dans son lit** to toss and turn.

only reply was a smile, he smiled by way of a reply; **on lui donne quelques légumes pour tous gages** all that he gets in the way of wages is a few vegetables; **7 tous, toutes** (tout en soi et les autres sans distinction) all, every (+ *sg*); **en ~es choses** in all things, in everything; **~es les pages sont déchirées** all the pages are torn, every page is torn; **tous les prétextes leur sont bons** they'll use any excuse (**pour** to); **meubles tous budgets** furniture to suit every pocket; **nous irons tous les deux** both of us will go, we'll both go; **je les prends tous les quatre** I'm taking all four (of them); **8** (chaque) **tous/toutes les** every; **à tous les coins de rue** on every street corner; **tous les jours** every day; **tous les deux jours** every other day; **tous les combien?** how often?

III *adv* (*normally invariable, but agrees in gender and in number with feminine adjective beginning with consonant or h-aspirate*) **1** (très, extrêmement) very, quite; (entièrement) all; **~ doucement** very gently; **~ étonnées/~es honteuses** very surprised/ashamed; **~ enfant, elle aimait déjà dessiner** as a small child she already liked to draw; **c'est ~ naturel** it's quite natural; **des yeux ~ ronds de surprise** eyes wide with surprise; **être ~ mouillé/sale** to be all wet/dirty; **faire qch ~ seul** to do sth all by oneself; **c'est ~ autre chose, c'est une ~ autre histoire** it's a different matter altogether; **2** (devant un nom) **c'est ~ le portrait de sa mère** she's the spitting ou very image of her mother; **c'est ~ l'inverse** or **le contraire** it's the very opposite; **ça m'en a ~ l'air** it looks very much like it to me; **tu as ~ le temps d'y réfléchir** you've got plenty of time to think it over; **avec toi, c'est ~ l'un ou ~ l'autre** you see everything in black and white; **3** (tout à fait) **la ~e dernière ligne** the very last line; **~ à côté de/contre/en haut** right by/against/at the top; **il les a mangés ~ crus** he ate them raw; **j'en sais ~ autant que lui** I know just as much as he does; **maison ~ en longueur** very long and narrow house; **ils étaient ~ en sang/en sueur** they were covered in blood/bathed in sweat; **être ~ en larmes** to be in floods of tears; **la colline est ~ en fleurs** the hill is a mass of flowers; **elle est ~(e) à son travail** she's totally absorbed in her work; **4** (d'avance) **~ prêt** ready-made; **des légumes ~ épluchés** ready-peeled vegetables; **5** (en même temps) while; (bien que) although; **il lisait ~ en marchant** he was reading as he walked; **elle le défendait ~ en le sachant coupable** she defended him although she knew he was guilty; **6** (marquant une concession: quoique) **~ aussi étrange que cela paraisse** however strange it may seem; **~ malin/roi qu'il est, il...** he may be clever/a king, but he...; **7** (rien d'autre que) **je suis ~ ouïe** HUM I'm all ears; **veste ~ cuir** all leather jacket.

IV du tout *loc adv* (pas) **du ~,** (point) **du ~** not at all; **sans savoir du ~** without knowing at all

V *nm* (*pl* **~s**) **1** (ensemble) **former un ~** to make up ou form a whole; **mon ~** (charade) my whole, my all; **du ~ au ~** completely; **2 le ~** (la totalité) the whole lot, the lot; (l'essentiel) the main thing; **vendre le ~ pour 200 francs** to sell the (whole) lot for 200 francs; **le ~ est de réussir** the main ou most important thing is to succeed; **ce n'est pas le ~!** this is no good!

VI Tout- (*in compounds*) **le Tout-Paris/-Londres** the Paris/London smart set.

■ **~ à coup** suddenly; **~ d'un coup** (soudain) suddenly; (à la fois) all at once; **~ à fait** (entièrement) quite, absolutely; **être ~ à fait pour/contre** to be totally for/against; **~ à l'heure** (bientôt) in a moment; (peu avant) a little while ago, just now; **à ~ à l'heure!** see you later!; **~ de même** (quand même) all the same, even so; (indigné) **~ de même!** really!, honestly!; (vraiment) **c'est ~ de même bizarre que** it's quite strange that; **~ de suite** at once, straight away.

IDIOMES **être ~ yeux ~ oreilles** to be very attentive.

tout-à-l'égout /tutalegu/ *nm inv* main drainage.

toutefois /tutfwɑ/ *adv* however; **je viendrai demain,**

si ~ ça ne vous dérange pas I'll come tomorrow, a long as that doesn't put you out.

toute-puissance /tutpɥisãs/ *nf* (d'argent, de dictateur Dieu) omnipotence; (de pays, d'entreprise) supremacy.

toutou○ /tutu/ *nm* doggie○, dog.

tout-petit, *pl* **~s** /tup(ə)ti/ *nm* (nourrisson) baby (très jeune enfant) toddler.

tout-puissant, toute-puissante, *pl* **~s toutes-puissantes** /tupɥisã, tutpɥisãt/ *adj* al powerful; **le ~ patron** the all-powerful boss.

Tout-Puissant /tupɥisã/ *nm* RELIG **le ~** th Almighty, God Almighty.

tout-venant /tuv(ə)nã/ *nm inv* GÉN (personnes) al and sundry; **il n'a pas choisi, il a pris le ~** he di not choose, he just took whatever there was.

toux /tu/ *nf inv* cough; **une ~ grasse** a loose cough **médicament pour** or **contre la ~** cough medicine **avoir une quinte de ~** to have a coughing fit.

toxicité /tɔksisite/ *nf* toxicity.

toxicodépendance /tɔksikodepãdãs/ *nf* dru dependency.

toxicodépendant, ~e /tɔksikodepãdã, ãt/ *nm,* drug addict.

toxicologue /tɔksikɔlɔg/ ▶ 374 | *nmf* toxicologist.

toxicomane /tɔksikɔman/ *nmf* drug addict.

toxicomanie /tɔksikɔmani/ *nf* drug addiction.

toxine /tɔksin/ *nf* toxin.

toxique /tɔksik/ **I** *adj* toxic, poisonous. **II** *nm* toxin, poison.

TP /tepe/ *nmpl: abbr* ▶ **travail**.

trac○ /tʁak/ *nm* (sur scène, devant une caméra) stag fright; (avant un examen, une conférence) nerves (*pl* **avoir le ~** GÉN to feel nervous; (sur scène) to hav stage fright; **donner le ~ à qn** [*situation, pensée, per sonne*] to put the wind up sb○, to scare sb; **tout à ~** out of the blue.

traçage /tʁasaʒ/ *nm* **1** (dessin) IND, NAUT marking out CONSTR laying-out; **2** ORDINAT tracing.

traçant, ~e /tʁasã, ãt/ *adj* **1** ORDINAT **table ~** graph plotter; **2** MIL **balle ~e** tracer (bullet); **3** BO [*racine*] creeping.

tracas /tʁaka/ *nm inv* (provoqué) trouble; **donner c valoir du ~ à qn** to put sb to a lot of trouble **2** (subi) problems (*pl*); **~ quotidiens** everyda problems; **3** (inquiétude) worries (*pl*); **se faire du ~ pour** or **au sujet de qn/qch** to worry about sb/sth.

tracasser /tʁakase/ [1] **I** *vtr* to bother [*personne*]. **II se tracasser** *vpr* (s'inquiéter) to worry (**pou about).

tracasserie /tʁakasʁi/ *nf* **1** (ennui) hassle○ ¢; **2** (harcèlement) harassment ¢.

trace /tʁas/ *nf* **1** (piste) trail; **perdre la ~ d'u animal** to lose an animal's tracks; **retrouver la ~ d'un voleur** to pick up the trail of a thief; **suivre qn à la ~** LIT to track sb; FIG to follow sb's trail; **2** (em preinte) **~s** tracks; **~s de pas** footprints, foo marks; **3** (marque) (de brûlure) mark; (cicatrice) scar (de peinture) mark; (de sang, d'humidité) trace; **~s d freinage** skidmarks; **~s de doigts** fingermarks; **~ de coups** (bleus) bruises; **l'aventure avait laissé de ~s profondes en lui** the experience had marked hir deeply; **4** (indice) (d'activité) sign; (de passage, sence) trace; **des ~s d'effraction** signs of a break in; **disparaître sans laisser de ~s** to disappear with out trace; **5** (quantité infime) **des ~s de mercur** traces of mercury.

tracé /tʁase/ *nm* **1** (plan de route, ville etc) layout **2** (parcours) (de route, ligne ferroviaire) route; (de fleuve course; (de frontière, côte) line; **3** (de courbe, croquis line; **4** ORDINAT inking.

tracer /tʁase/ [12] *vtr* **1** (dessiner) to draw [*ligne, plan rectangle, portrait*]; (sur un graphique) to plot [*courbe* (écrire) to write [*caractères, mot*]; to plan the route c [*autoroute, oléoduc*]; **dessin tracé à l'encre/à la crai** ink/chalk drawing; **2** (établir) **~ un tableau pessi miste** to paint a pessimistic picture; **à 15 ans so**

avenir était déjà **tout tracé** at 15, his/her future was already mapped out; **~ les grandes lignes d'une action** to map out the main lines of action (to be taken); **3** (ouvrir) to open up [*piste, route*]; **~ le chemin à qn** FIG to show sb the way.

rachée /tʀaʃe/ *nf* windpipe.

rachée-artère, *pl* **trachées-artères** /tʀaʃeaʀtɛʀ/ *nf* windpipe, trachea.

ract /tʀakt/ *nm* pamphlet, tract.

ractation /tʀaktasjɔ̃/ *nf* negotiation.

racté, ~e /tʀakte/ *adj* [*remorque*] tractor-drawn.

racter /tʀakte/ [1] *vtr* [*véhicule*] to tow [*remorque*]; [*câble, remonte-pente*] to pull up [*funiculaire, skieur*].

racteur /tʀaktœʀ/ *nm* tractor.

raction /tʀaksjɔ̃/ *nf* **1** (mode d'entraînement) traction; **à ~ animale** drawn by animals; **2** SPORT **faire des ~s** (à la barre, aux anneaux) to do pull-ups; (au sol) to do press-ups GB ou push-ups; **3** TECH (effort mécanique) tension.
■ **~ arrière** AUT rear-wheel drive; **~ avant** AUT front-wheel drive.

radition /tʀadisjɔ̃/ *nf* **1** (coutume) tradition; **il est de ~ de** it's traditional to; **c'est la ~ que l'on fasse** or **de faire** it's traditional to do; **par ~** traditionally; **2** (légende) legend; **la ~ veut que...** legend has it that...

raditionnel, -elle /tʀadisjɔnɛl/ *adj* traditional.

raducteur, -trice /tʀadyktœʀ, tʀis/ **374│** *nm,f* translator.

raduction /tʀadyksjɔ̃/ *nf* **1** (action) translation; **la ~ de ce texte m'a pris cinq heures** it took me five hours to translate this text; **la ~ en allemand** translating into German; **2** (texte) translation; **~ en anglais** English translation; **faire des ~s** to do translation work; **3** (de sentiments, d'idées) expression.
■ **~ assistée par ordinateur** computer-aided translation.

traduire /tʀadyiʀ/ [69] **I** *vtr* **1** (dans une langue différente) to translate; **2** (exprimer) [*mot, style*] to convey; [*violence*] to be the expression of; [*hausse, instabilité*] to be the result of; **~ en actes** to put into practice; **3** JUR **~ qn en justice** to bring sb to justice.
II se traduire *vpr* **1** (être exprimé) [*joie, peur*] to show (**par** in); **2** (avoir pour résultat) [*crise, action*] to result (**par** in); [*mécontentement*] to find expression (**par** in); **se ~ par un échec** to result in failure.

traduisible /tʀadyizibl/ *adj* translatable.

trafic /tʀafik/ *nm* **1** (commerce illicite) traffic (**de** in); **~ d'armes** arms dealing; **~ de drogue** drug trafficking; **faire du ~ de qch** to traffic ou deal in sth; **2** (circulation) **~ (routier)** traffic; **~ aérien** air traffic.
IDIOMES **qu'est-ce-que c'est que ce ~°?** what's going on here?

trafiquant, ~e /tʀafikɑ̃, ɑ̃t/ *nm,f* trafficker, dealer (**de** in); **~ de drogue** drugs dealer; **~ d'armes** arms dealer, gunrunner; **petit ~** small-time dealer.

trafiquer /tʀafike/ [1] *vtr* **1** (truquer) to fiddle with [*compteur, voiture*]; **2°** (faire) PEJ **je me demande ce qu'il trafique** I wonder what he's up to.

tragédie /tʀaʒedi/ *nf* tragedy.

tragédien, -ienne /tʀaʒedjɛ̃, ɛn/ **▶374│** *nm,f* tragic actor.

tragi-comique, *pl* **~s** /tʀaʒikɔmik/ *adj* tragicomic.

tragique /tʀaʒik/ **I** *adj* tragic; **ce n'est pas ~** it's not the end of the world.
II *nm* **1** LITTÉRAT, THÉÂT (auteur) tragedian; (genre) **le ~** tragedy; (caractère) tragic elements (*pl*); **2** (gravité) tragedy; **tourner au ~** to take a tragic turn; **prendre qch au ~** to make a drama out of sth.

trahir /tʀaiʀ/ [3] **I** *vtr* **1** (manquer de fidélité à) to betray [*pays, ami, secret, confiance*]; to break [*promesse*]; **2** (révéler) to betray; **3** (rendre infidèle) [*traducteur, mots*] to misrepresent; **4** (faire défaut) [*jambes, forces*] to fail [*person*].
II se trahir *vpr* (se dévoiler) to give oneself away, to betray oneself.

trahison /tʀaizɔ̃/ *nf* **1** (manquement à un engagement) treachery ¢; **~ de qch/qn** betrayal of sth/sb; **une ~** a betrayal, an act of treachery; **2** MIL, POL treason ¢; **haute ~** high treason.

train /tʀɛ̃/ **I** *nm* **1** RAIL train; **accompagner qn au ~°** to see sb off at the station; **préférer le ~ à l'avion** to prefer train travel to flying; **2** (convoi) train; **~ de péniches** train of barges; **3** (série) series (+ *v sg*); **~ de mesures** series of measures; **4** (enchaînement) train; **le ~ des événements** the train of events; **5** (allure) pace; **accélérer/ralentir le ~** to speed up/to slow down; **aller bon** or **grand ~** (marcher vite) to walk briskly; **aller bon ~** [*rumeurs*] to be flying around; [*ventes, affaires*] to be going well; [*conversation*] to flow easily; [*équipage, voiture*] to be going quite fast; **au ~ où l'on va/vont les choses** (at) the rate we're going/things are going; **aller son ~** [*affaire*] to be getting on all right; **aller son petit ~** [*personne, affaire, négociations*] to go peacefully along; **à fond de ~°** at top speed; **6** ZOOL **~ de derrière** hindquarters (*pl*); **~ de devant** forequarters (*pl*); **7°** (de personne) backside°; **8** MIL **le ~ corps** of transport GB, transportation corps US.
II en train *loc* **1** (en forme) **être en ~** to be full of energy; **ne pas être en ~** not to have much energy; **2** (en marche) **mettre en ~** to get [sb] started ou going [*processus, travail*]; **se mettre en ~** GÉN to get going; SPORT to warm up; **3** (en cours) **être en ~ de faire** to be (busy) doing; **j'étais en ~ de dormir/lire** I was sleeping/reading.
■ **~ d'atterrissage** undercarriage; **~ électrique** electric train; (jeu avec accessoires) train set; **~ de vie** lifestyle; **réduire son ~ de vie** to live more modestly.

traînant, ~e /tʀɛnɑ̃, ɑ̃t/ *adj* shuffling; **voix ~e** drawl.

traînard°, ~e /tʀɛnaʀ, aʀd/ *nm,f* (personne lente) slowcoach° GB, slowpoke° US; (qui reste en arrière) straggler.

traînasser° /tʀɛnase/ [1] *vi* **1** (perdre son temps) to loaf° about; **2** (travailler lentement) to take ages.

traîne /tʀɛn/ *nf* **1** (de robe) train; **2** (filet) seine (net).
IDIOMES **être à la ~** [*personne, pays*] to lag behind.

traîneau, *pl* **~x** /tʀɛno/ *nm* **1** (véhicule) sleigh; **2** (d'aspirateur) cylinder; **aspirateur ~** cylinder vacuum cleaner; **3** (de pêche) seine (net).

traînée /tʀɛne/ *nf* **1** (tache allongée) streak; **~ de sang/peinture** streak of blood/paint; **2** (trace) trail.

traîner /tʀɛne/ [1] **I** *vtr* **1** (tirer) to drag [sth] (along) [*valise*]; to drag [sth] across the floor [*chaise*]; **~ qn par les pieds** to drag sb (along) by the feet; **2°** (être encombré) (en portant) to lug° [sth] around [*objet*]; (en tirant) to drag [sth] around [*objet*]; (en subissant) to drag [sb] along [*personne*]; **3** (forcer à aller) **~ qn chez le médecin** to drag sb off to the doctor's; **~ qn devant les tribunaux** to drag sb into court; **4** (supporter longtemps) **il traîne un rhume depuis deux semaines** for two weeks now he's had a cold that he can't shake off; **5** (utiliser avec lenteur) **~ les pieds** LIT, FIG to drag one's feet.
II *vi* **1** (perdre son temps) **~ dans les rues/avec des voyous** to hang around on the streets/with yobbos; **'qu'est-ce que tu as fait aujourd'hui?'—'j'ai traîné'** 'what did you do today?'—'I loafed around°'; **j'ai traîné au lit** I had a lie-in GB, I slept in; **ne traîne pas, on doit terminer à 4 heures** get a move on°, we've got to finish at four; **ne traîne pas en rentrant de l'école** don't dawdle on your way back from school; **~ (derrière)** to lag ou trail behind, to trail along in the rear; **ne traînez pas derrière!** keep up there at the back!; **2** (ne pas se terminer) [*chantier, maladie*] to drag on; [*odeur*] to linger; **faire ou laisser ~ (les choses)** to let things drag on; **un film qui traîne en longueur** a long-drawn-out film; **3** (être en contact avec) **~ par terre** [*jupe*] to trail on the ground; [*rideaux*] to trail on the floor; **~ derrière qch** to be trailing behind sth; **5** (ne pas être rangé) [*vêtements, jouets*] to be lying about ou around; **6** (être

très courant) **avec ces microbes qui traînent** with all the germs (that are) around.
III se traîner *vpr* **1** (ramper) **se ~ par terre/ jusqu'à la porte** to drag oneself along the ground/to the door; **2** (aller avec effort) **se ~ jusqu'à la cuisine** to drag oneself through to the kitchen; **3** (avancer lentement) (*voiture, escargot*) to crawl along.
IDIOMES **~ la jambe** or **la patte**○ to limp; **~ ses guêtres**○ or **ses bottes**○ to knock around○.

train(-)train○ /trɛtrɛ̃/ *nm inv* daily round.

traire /trɛr/ [58] *vtr* to milk [*vache, chèvre, brebis*]; **machine à ~** milking machine.

trait /trɛ/ I *nm* **1** (ligne) GÉN line; (fait d'un seul mouvement) stroke; (de code morse) dash; **souligner un mot d'un ~ rouge** to underline a word in red; **exposer la situation à grands ~s** to explain the situation in broad outline; **d'un ~ de plume** FIG with a stroke of the pen; **~ pour ~** [*réplique, copie*] line for line; [*reproduire*] line by line; **2** (particularité) (de chose) feature; (de personne) trait; **~ dominant** or **essentiel** main feature; **~ caractéristique** characteristic; **~ particulier** particular feature; **~ de caractère** or **personnalité** trait, characteristic; **le ~ commun entre cette méthode et l'autre** what the two methods have in common; **c'est un ~ commun entre ton fils et le mien** that's something our sons have in common; **3** LING feature; **4** (pointe verbale) **~ (mordant)** scathing remark; **diriger ses ~s contre qn** to be sarcastic at sb's expense; **5** (expression) **~ d'humour** or **d'esprit** witticism; **~ de génie** stroke of genius; **6** (rapport) **avoir ~ à** to relate to; **documents ayant ~ à la sécurité** documents relating to security; **7** (fois) **d'un (seul) ~** GÉN at one go; **lire qch d'un ~** to read sth straight through; **dire qch d'un ~** to say sth straight out; **boire qch d'un ~** to drink sth in one gulp; **boire à longs** or **grands ~s** to drink in long draughts GB ou drafts US; **8** (traction) **de ~** [*animal*] draught GB ou draft US.
II **traits** *nmpl* (visage) features; **avoir les ~s fatigués** or **tirés** to look drawn.
■ **~ d'union** LING hyphen; FIG (intermédiaire) link; **s'écrire avec un ~ d'union** to be hyphenated, to have a hyphen.
IDIOMES **tirer un ~ sur qch** to put sth firmly behind one.

traitant /trɛtɑ̃/ *adj m* **médecin ~** (généraliste) doctor, GP; (spécialiste) specialist.

traite /trɛt/ I *nf* **1** FIN draft, bill; **2** (commerce) **la ~ des Blanches** the white slave trade; **la ~ des Noirs** HIST the slave trade; **3** AGRIC milking; **la ~ des vaches** milking cows; **l'heure de la ~** milking time.
II **d'une traite** *loc adv* **d'une (seule) ~** [*réciter*] in one breath; [*boire*] in one go; **faire 500 km d'une (seule) ~** to do 500 km non-stop ou at a stretch.

traité /trɛte/ *nm* **1** JUR treaty; **le ~ de Maastricht** the Maastricht Treaty; **~ commercial** trade agreement; **2** (ouvrage) treatise (**sur, de** on).

traitement /trɛtmɑ̃/ *nm* **1** MÉD treatment ¢; **2** (salaire) salary; **3** (comportement envers) treatment; **c'est le ~ normal des prisonniers** it's the way prisoners are normally treated; **4** (manière d'aborder, de régler) handling; **il faut accélérer le ~ des demandes** applications must be dealt with ou processed more quickly; **5** ORDINAT processing ¢; **~ de l'information** data processing; **6** TECH (de minerai, d'eaux) processing ¢; (de bois, textile) treatment; **centre de ~ des eaux** water-processing plant.
■ **~ de faveur** preferential ou special treatment; **~ de texte** ORDINAT (processus) word-processing; (logiciel) word-processing package.

traiter /trɛte/ [1] I *vtr* **1** (agir envers) to treat [*personne, animal, objet*]; **la critique l'a traité durement** the critics gave him a rough ride; **2** MÉD (soigner) to treat [*malade, affection, symptôme*]; **3** (développer) to deal with [*question, sujet*]; **4** (régler) to deal with [*problème, dossier, scandale, affaire*]; **5** (soumettre à une opération) to treat [*bois, textile, aliment, sang, récoltes*]; to process [*eaux usées*]; **non traité** [*bois, aliment*] untreated; **6** ORDINAT to process [*données, information,*

image]; **7** (qualifier) **~ qn de qch** to call sb sth; **qn de menteur** to call sb a liar; **~ qn de paresseu** to call sb lazy; **elle m'a traité de tous les noms** sh called me all sorts of names.
II **traiter de** *vtr ind* **~ de** to deal with [*sujet*].
III *vi* (négocier) to negotiate, to do GB ou make a deal.
IDIOMES **~ qn comme un chien** to treat sb ver badly, to treat sb like dirt.

traiteur /trɛtœr/ **▶ 374**| *nm* caterer.

traître, traîtresse /trɛtr, trɛtrɛs/ I *adj* **1** treacher ous; **2**○ **pas un ~ mot** not a single word.
II *nm,f* traitor (**à** to); HUM traitor; **en ~** in a treacherous ou underhand way; **prendre qn en ~** t take sb by surprise.

traîtrise /trɛtriz/ *nf* **1** (acte) act of treachery, (act of) betrayal; **par ~** treacherously; **2** (de personne) treachery, treacherousness.

trajectoire /traʒɛktwar/ *nf* **1** (de projectile) trajec tory; **2** (de planète, satellite, particule) path; **3** (carrière career, path in life.

trajet /traʒɛ/ *nm* **1** (voyage) journey; (par mer) cross ing; **2** (parcours) route.

trame /tram/ *nf* **1** (de tissu) weft, woof; **2** (d'histoire de spectacle) framework; (de vie) fabric.

tramer /trame/ [1] I *vtr* **1** (tisser) to weave; **2** FIG (ourdir) to hatch.
II **se tramer** *vpr* [*complot*] to be hatched.

tramway /tramwɛ/ *nm* (voiture) tram GB, streetcar US (système) tramway GB, streetcar line US.

tranchant, ~e /trɑ̃ʃɑ̃, ɑ̃t/ I *adj* **1** LIT sharp; **2** [*personne*] forthright; [*ton*] curt.
II *nm* (de lame) sharp edge, cutting edge; **à double ~** LIT, FIG double-edged.

tranche /trɑ̃ʃ/ *nf* **1** (de pain, viande, fromage) slice; (de lard) rasher; **couper en ~s** to slice, to cut [sth] into slices; **2** (de temps) (d'opération, de travaux) phase; (dans l'emploi du temps) period, time slot; **3** (de livre, pièce de monnaie) edge.
■ **~ d'âge** age bracket; **~ d'imposition** tax bracket.
IDIOMES **s'en payer une ~**○ to have a whale of a time○, to have lots of fun.

tranché, ~e[1] /trɑ̃ʃe/ *adj* **1** [*opinion, position, réponse, catégories*] clear-cut; [*inégalités*] marked; **2** [*couleurs*] bold, distinct.

tranchée[2] /trɑ̃ʃe/ *nf* **1** MIL trench; **2** (chemin) cutting.

trancher /trɑ̃ʃe/ [1] I *vtr* **1** (couper) to slice, to cut [*pain, viande*]; to cut through, to slice through [*corde, nœud, peau*]; to cut [sth] off, to sever [*tête, membre*]; to slit [*gorge*]; **2** (régler) to settle, to resolve [*question, litige*].
II *vi* **1** (contraster) [*couleur, silhouette*] to stand out (**sur** against); **~ avec** [*joie, état, décision*] to stand out in sharp contrast to, to contrast sharply with; **2** (décider) to come to a decision; **la justice a tranché en faveur de l'accusé** the court decided in favour GB of the accused; **3** (arrêter une discussion) to break off, to stop short; **tranchons là!** let's leave it at that!

tranquille /trɑ̃kil/ *adj* **1** (calme) [*tempérament, voisins, classe*] quiet; [*allure, voix, assurance*] calm; **tiens-toi ~!** (ne bouge pas!) keep still!, stop fidgeting!; (tais-toi!) be quiet!; **2** (sans agitation) [*heure, jour*] quiet, calm; [*eau, ciel, nuit*] calm, tranquil LITTÉR; [*café, rue, vie, soirée, bonheur*] quiet; [*sommeil, vacances*] peaceful; **il s'est tenu ~ pendant quelques mois** he behaved himself for a few months; **c'est ~, ici!** it's peaceful here!; **3** (sans souci) **être ~** to be ou feel easy in one's mind; **ne pas être ~** to be ou feel uneasy, to be worried; **4** (en paix) **avoir l'esprit ~** to be easy in one's mind; **j'ai la conscience ~** my conscience is clear; **laisse ton frère ~** leave your brother alone; **je te laisse ~** I'll leave you in peace.

tranquillement /trɑ̃kilmɑ̃/ *adv* **1** (dans le calme) **elle dort ~** she's sleeping peacefully; **peut-on se voir ~?** (pour parler) could we have a quiet word?; **j'aimerais pouvoir travailler ~** I wish I could work in peace; **2** (sans bruit) quietly; **il a réussi ~ à se**

faire un nom he quietly made a name for himself; **3** (sans se presser) **nous avons marché ~** we walked along at a leisurely pace; **elle a roulé ~** she drove along unhurriedly; **je suis arrivé ~** I wandered in; **4** (sereinement) **nous étions ~ en train de discuter** we were chatting away happily; **expliquer/affirmer qch ~** to explain/to state sth calmly.

tranquillisant, **~e** /tʀɑ̃kilizɑ̃, ɑ̃t/ **I** *adj* reassuring, comforting.
II *nm* tranquillizer.

tranquilliser /tʀɑ̃kilize/ [1] *vtr* to reassure.

tranquillité /tʀɑ̃kilite/ *nf* **1** (de tempérament, personne) calmness, serenity; (d'eau, de nuit) LITER calmness, stillness; (de moment, lieu) calm, quiet; **pour une fois, j'ai pu travailler en toute ~** for once I was able to work without being disturbed; **2** (absence d'inquiétude) **~ (d'esprit)** peace of mind; **en toute ~** with complete peace of mind, with an easy mind; **3** (vie paisible) **aspirer à la ~** to long for peace and quiet; **je tiens à ma ~** I value my peace and quiet.

transaction /tʀɑ̃zaksjɔ̃/ *nf* transaction.

transalpin, **~e** /tʀɑ̃zalpɛ̃, in/ *adj* **1** (qui traverse les Alpes) transalpine; **2** (italien) Italian.

transat[1]○ /tʀɑ̃zat/ *nm* deckchair; (pour bébé) baby chair.

transat[2] /tʀɑ̃zat/ *nf* SPORT transatlantic race.

transatlantique /tʀɑ̃zatlɑ̃tik/ *adj* transatlantic.

transborder /tʀɑ̃sbɔʀde/ [1] *vtr* to transship [*marchandises*]; to transfer [*passagers*].

transbordeur /tʀɑ̃sbɔʀdœʀ/ *nm* **1** (pont) transporter bridge; **2** RAIL traverser; **3** NAUT ferry.

transcendant, **~e** /tʀɑ̃sɑ̃dɑ̃, ɑ̃t/ *adj* **1** PHILOS transcendent; **2**○ (génial) wonderful; **3** MATH transcendental.

transcender /tʀɑ̃sɑ̃de/ [1] *vtr* to transcend.

transcription /tʀɑ̃skʀipsjɔ̃/ *nf* **1** GÉN transcription; (discours transcrit) transcript; **2** JUR registration.

transcrire /tʀɑ̃skʀiʀ/ [67] *vtr* **1** GÉN, LING to transcribe [*texte, mots*]; **2** FIG to translate [*émotion, ambiance*]; **3** BIOL, MUS to transcribe.

transe /tʀɑ̃s/ *nf* trance.

transférer /tʀɑ̃sfeʀe/ [14] *vtr* **1** GÉN, ORDINAT to transfer; to relocate [*bureaux, usine*]; to transfer [*appel*]; **faire ~** to have [sth] transferred [*contrat, appels*]; **2** JUR to transfer [*biens, propriétés*]; to convey [*droit*] (**à** to); **3** PSYCH to transfer.

transfert /tʀɑ̃sfɛʀ/ *nm* **1** GÉN (de personne, pouvoirs, siège social, données, d'argent) transfer; (de bureaux, d'usine) relocation; **faire** ou **opérer un ~ de fonds** to transfer funds; **~ de technologie** technological transfer; **il a demandé son ~ dans une autre agence** he asked to be transferred to another branch; **2** JUR (de biens, propriétés) transfer; (de droit) conveyance; **3** PSYCH transference.
■ **~ d'appel** TÉLÉCOM call diversion.

transfigurer /tʀɑ̃sfigyʀe/ [1] *vtr* **1** RELIG **être transfiguré** to be transfigured; **2** (transformer) to transform; **la joie l'a transfigurée** she is transformed by happiness.

transformable /tʀɑ̃sfɔʀmabl/ *adj* [*meuble*] convertible.

transformateur /tʀɑ̃sfɔʀmatœʀ/ *nm* transformer.

transformation /tʀɑ̃sfɔʀmasjɔ̃/ *nf* **1** (modification) (de personne, pays) transformation; (de substance, d'énergie) conversion; **la maladie a opéré une profonde ~ en lui** the illness wrought a profound change in him; **2** SPORT conversion; **3** LING, MATH transformation.

transformer /tʀɑ̃sfɔʀme/ [1] **I** *vtr* **1** (modifier) to alter [*vêtement, façade*]; to change, to alter [*personne, attitude, paysage, société*]; (profondément, en mieux) to transform; **~ les mentalités** to alter people's thinking; (profondément) to transform people's thinking; **tout ~ dans le jardin** to change everything in the garden; **depuis qu'il ne boit plus, il est transformé** since he stopped drinking he's a different person; **2** (métamorphoser) **~ en** GÉN to turn into; (en améliorant)

to transform into; **~ la maison en chantier** FIG to turn the house into a building site; **~ un garage en bureau** to convert a garage into an office; **3** CHIMIE to convert [*substance*] (**en** into); **4** SPORT to convert [*essai*]; **5** MATH to transform [*figure*].
II se transformer *vpr* (délibérément) to transform oneself; (passivement) to be transformed; **se ~ en** GÉN to turn into; (radicalement, en mieux) to be transformed into.

transfrontalier, **-ière** /tʀɑ̃sfʀɔ̃talje, ɛʀ/ *adj* [*travailleur*] cross-border (*épith*).

transfuge /tʀɑ̃sfyʒ/ **I** *nmf* GÉN, POL defector.
II *nm* MIL deserter.

transfuser /tʀɑ̃sfyze/ [1] *vtr* to give a blood transfusion to; **~ du sang à** to give a blood transfusion to.

transfusion /tʀɑ̃sfyzjɔ̃/ *nf* transfusion.

transgresser /tʀɑ̃sgʀese/ [1] *vtr* to contravene [*ordre*]; to break [*loi, tabou*]; to defy [*interdiction*].

transhumance /tʀɑ̃zymɑ̃s/ *nf* transhumance, seasonal migration of livestock to summer pastures.

transi, **~e** /tʀɑ̃zi/ *adj* chilled; **~ de froid** chilled to the bone; **~ de peur** paralysed with fear; **un amoureux ~** a bashful lover.

transiger /tʀɑ̃ziʒe/ [13] *vi* to compromise.

transit /tʀɑ̃zit/ *nm* transit; **en ~** in transit.

transitaire /tʀɑ̃zitɛʀ/ **I** *adj* [*commerce*] transit (*épith*); **pays ~** transit point.
II *nmf* COMM forwarding agent.

transiter /tʀɑ̃zite/ [1] *vi* **~ par** [*marchandises, passagers*] to pass through, to go via; **les pays font ~ leur pétrole par** countries send their oil via.

transitif, **-ive** /tʀɑ̃zitif, iv/ *adj* LING, MATH transitive.

transition /tʀɑ̃zisjɔ̃/ *nf* transition (**entre** between; **vers** to); **passer sans ~ à** to move straight on to.

transitoire /tʀɑ̃zitwaʀ/ *adj* (de transition) transitional.

translucide /tʀɑ̃slysid/ *adj* translucent.

transmanche /tʀɑ̃smɑ̃ʃ/ *adj inv* cross-Channel.

transmetteur /tʀɑ̃smetœʀ/ *nm* transmitter.

transmettre /tʀɑ̃smɛtʀ/ [60] **I** *vtr* **1** (communiquer) to pass [sth] on, to convey [*information, savoir, vœux, ordre, nouvelle*] (**à** to); **envoyez votre candidature au journal qui transmettra** send your application to the newspaper which will then forward it; **transmettsleur mes amitiés** give them my regards; **2** TÉLÉCOM to transmit; **3** RADIO, TV (émettre) to broadcast; **4** (léguer) to pass [sth] on [*récit, savoir, découverte*]; to pass [sth] down, to hand [sth] down [*secret, tradition, fortune*] (**à** to); to hand [sth] on [*propriété*] (**à** to); **5** (passer) to hand over [*pouvoir*] (**à** to); **6** MÉD to transmit, to pass [sth] on [*maladie, microbe*]; **7** TECH to transmit [*vibration, chaleur*].
II se transmettre *vpr* **1** (l'un l'autre) to pass [sth] on to each other [*information*]; **2** TÉLÉCOM [*données*] to be transmitted (**par** by); **3** [*tradition, secret, culture, droit*] to be handed down, to be passed down; [*récit, savoir*] to be passed on; **4** [*maladie, microbe*] to be transmitted, to be passed on; **une maladie qui se transmet sexuellement** a sexually transmitted disease.

transmissible /tʀɑ̃smisibl/ *adj* transmissible, transmittable.

transmission /tʀɑ̃smisjɔ̃/ **I** *nf* **1** (communication) transmission, passing on; **2** PHYS, TÉLÉCOM transmission; **3** RADIO, TV broadcasting, transmission; **4** (de tradition, secret, culture) handing down, passing down; JUR (de fortune, bien, titre, d'héritage) transfer; **5** AUT transmission; **6** MÉD transmission.
II transmissions *nfpl* MIL signals.
■ **~ de pensées** thought transference.

transpalette /tʀɑ̃spalɛt/ *nm* forklift (truck).

transparaître /tʀɑ̃spaʀɛtʀ/ [73] *vi* [*forme, lumière*] to show through; [*angoisse, embarras*] to show; **laisser ~** [*visage, propos*] to betray; [*personne*] to let [sth] show [*émotions, sentiments*].

transparence /tʀɑ̃spaʀɑ̃s/ *nf* **1** LIT (de verre, diamant, tissu, cloison) transparency; (d'eau) clearness; **2** (de teint, peau) translucency; (de couleur) limpidity; **3** FIG (de personne, d'allusions, intentions) transparency; (de gestion, transaction, débat) openness; **la ~** POL openness.

transparent, **~e** /trɑ̃sparɑ̃, ɑ̃t/ I *adj* **1** [*verre, tissu, cloison*] transparent; [*eau*] clear; **2** [*teint*] translucent; [*regard, couleur*] limpid; **3** [*personne, allusion, intentions*] transparent.

II *nm* (pour rétroprojecteur) transparency.

transpercer /trɑ̃spɛrse/ [12] *vtr* **1** [*flèche, lance*] to pierce [*corps*]; [*balle*] to go through; [*personne*] (avec une épée, flèche, lance) to pierce [*corps*]; to run [sb] through [*personne*]; **~ qn du regard** to give sb a piercing look; **2** [*douleur*] to shoot through; [*froid*] to go right through.

transpiration /trɑ̃spirasjɔ̃/ *nf* **1** (phénomène) sweating, perspiration; **2** (sueur) sweat, perspiration; **3** BOT transpiration.

transpirer /trɑ̃spire/ [1] *vi* **1** LIT to sweat, to perspire; **~ à grosses gouttes** to be dripping ou streaming with sweat; **2°** (travailler dur) to sweat; **3°** (être divulgué) [*information, secret*] to leak out; [*sentiment, opinion*] to come out.

transplantation /trɑ̃splɑ̃tasjɔ̃/ *nf* **1** MÉD transplant; **~ d'organes** organ transplants (*pl*); **2** BOT transplantation.

transplanter /trɑ̃splɑ̃te/ [1] *vtr* to transplant.

transport /trɑ̃spɔr/ I *nm* transport, transportation US; **~ ferroviaire et maritime** transport by rail and sea; **~ aérien** air transport; **~ par route** GÉN road transport; (de marchandises) road haulage; **endommagé pendant le ~** damaged in transit; **au cours de mon ~ à l'hôpital** when I was being taken to hospital.

II *nmpl* **transports** **1** GÉN transport **C**, transportation **C** US; **~s en commun** public transport ou transportation US; **2** (effusion) LITER transports; **~s de joie** transports of joy.

transportable /trɑ̃spɔrtabl/ *adj* [*objet*] transportable; **il n'est pas ~** (blessé) he cannot be moved.

transporter /trɑ̃spɔrte/ [1] *vtr* **1** (déplacer) (sur soi) to carry; (avec un véhicule) to transport; **~ qch sur son dos** to carry sth on one's back; **être transporté à l'hôpital** to be taken to hospital; **2** (transférer) to carry [*pollen, virus, maladie*]; **3** (en imagination) to transport; **être transporté dans un monde féerique** to be transported to a magical world; **4** (ravir) LITER **être transporté de joie** to be beside oneself with joy.

transporteur /trɑ̃spɔrtœr/ *nm* **1** (entreprise) carrier; **~ aérien** air carrier; **~ routier** road haulier GB, road haulage contractor GB, trucking company US; **~ maritime** (de marchandises) shipping company; (de personnes) shipping line; **2** (machine) conveyor.

transposer /trɑ̃spoze/ [1] *vtr* to transpose.

transsibérien, -ienne /trɑ̃ssiberjɛ̃, ɛn/ I *adj* trans-Siberian.

II *nm* **le Transsibérien** the Trans-Siberian Railway.

transvaser /trɑ̃svaze/ [1] *vtr* to decant [*liquide*].

transversal, **~e**, *mpl* **-aux** /trɑ̃svɛrsal, o/ *adj* [*muscle, disposition*] transverse; **coupe ~e** cross-section; **poutre ~e** cross-beam; **route/rue ~e** side road/street.

transversalement /trɑ̃svɛrsalmɑ̃/ *adv* **1** GÉN crosswise; **2** AUT transversely.

trapèze /trapɛz/ *nm* **1** SPORT trapeze; **2** MATH trapezium GB, trapezoid US; **3** ANAT trapezium.

trapéziste /trapezist/ **▶ 374|** *nmf* trapeze artist.

trappe /trap/ *nf* **1** GÉN (ouverture) trap door; **2** THÉÂT trap door; **passer à la ~** FIG to be whisked off; **3** (à la chasse) trap.

trappeur /trapœr/ **▶ 374|** *nm* trapper.

trapu, **~e** /trapy/ *adj* (court et large) [*homme, silhouette*] stocky, thickset; [*bâtiment*] squat.

traque /trak/ *nf* **1** (à la chasse) tracking; **2** FIG (chasse à l'homme) hunt.

traquenard /traknar/ *nm* LIT, FIG trap.

traquer /trake/ [1] *vtr* **1** (poursuivre) to track down, to

hunt [sb] down; (importuner) [*photographe*] to houn [*vedette*]; **2** (contrôler) to monitor [*dépenses, surplus*] **3** (à la chasse) to track down, to stalk [*animal*].

traumatisant, **~e** /tromatizɑ̃, ɑ̃t/ *adj* traumatic.

traumatiser /tromatize/ [1] *vtr* to traumatize.

traumatisme /tromatism/ *nm* **1** MÉD traumatism; **crânien** cranial traumatism; **2** PSYCH, FIG trauma.

travail, *pl* **-aux** /travaj, o/ I *nm* **1** (contraire de repos work; **être en plein ~** to be busy working; **2** (tâch faite, à faire) job; (ensemble des tâches, besogne) work **C** **j'ai un ~ fou** I'm up to my eyes in work, I've got lot of work on; **les gros travaux** the heavy worl **qu'est-ce que c'est que ce ~?** what do you ca this?; **et voilà le ~!** that's that done!; **3** (fait d'exerc un emploi) work; (emploi rémunéré) work **C**, job; (lie work; **conditions de ~** working conditions; **4** ÉCO SOCIOL (activité, population active) labour[GB] **C**; **division d ~** division of labour[GB]; **5** (résultat d'un fonctionnemen (de machine, d'organe) work **C**; **le ~ musculair** muscular effort; **6** (ouvrage érudit) work (**sur** on **7** (façonnage) **le ~ de** working with ou in [*métal, boi pierre*]; **apprendre le ~ du bois/métal** to lear woodwork/metalwork; **8** (technique, exécution) worl manship; **un ~ superbe** a superb piece of workma ship; **9** PHYS work; **10** (action) (d'eau, érosion) actio (**de** of); FIG (d'imagination, inconscient) workings (*p* (**de** of); **11** (altération) (de vin) fermentation, wor ing; (de bois) warping; **12** MÉD (pendant un accouch ment) labour[GB].

II **travaux** *nmpl* **1** (en chantier) work **C**; (sur ur route) roadworks GB, roadwork **C** US; **travaux d construction** construction work **C**; **travaux d terrassement** earthworks; **'fermé pour travaux'** (s une devanture) 'closed for repairs ou alterations **'attention, travaux'** GÉN 'caution, work in progress (sur une route) 'caution, road under repair'; **2** (reche che, études) work **C** (**sur** on); **3** (débats) deliber tions; **4** (opérations de même nature) **les travaux agr coles/de la ferme** agricultural/farm work **C**; **travau de couture** needlework **C**.

■ **~ à la chaîne** assembly-line work; **~ au no** GÉN *work for which no earnings are declared*; (exerci d'un second emploi non déclaré) moonlighting; **travau dirigés, TD** UNIV practical (*sg*); **travaux forcés** J hard labour[GB] (*sg*); FIG slave labour[GB] **C**; **travau manuels** SCOL handicrafts; **travaux ménager** housework **C**; **travaux pratiques, TP** SCOL, UN practical work **C**; (en laboratoire) lab work **C**; **tra vaux publics, TP** (travail) civil engineering **C**; (o vrages) civil engineering works, public works.

travaillé, **~e** /travaje/ I *pp* ▶ **travailler**.

II *pp adj* **1** (fignolé) [*bijou*] finely-worked [*sculpture, dessin*] elaborate; [*or, argent*] wrough [*métal*] chased; [*style, article*] polished; **2** (tourmenté [*personne*] **~ par le doute** racked with doubt; **3** (no chômé) **heures ~es** (à faire) hours of work; (faites hours worked.

travailler /travaje/ [1] I *vtr* **1** (pour perfectionner) work on [*style, matière scolaire, voix, muscles*]; practise[GB] [*sport, instrument, chant*]; **2** (manipuler) work [*bois, métal*]; CULIN to knead [*pâte*]; AGRIC to worl to cultivate [*terre*]; to cultivate [*vigne*]; **3** (préoccupe **~ qn** [*affaire, idée*] to be ou prey on sb's mind, bother sb; (tourmenter) [*jalousie, douleur*] to plagu sb; **un doute me travaillait** I had a nagging doubt; **c sont ses dents qui le travaillent** (parlant d'un bébé) h is out of sorts because he's teething.

II **travailler à** *vtr ind* **~ à** to work on [*proje dissertation*]; to work toward(s) [*objectif*]; **~ à réta blir la paix** to endeavour[GB] to restore peace.

III *vi* **1** (faire un effort) [*personne, machine*] to worl [*muscles*] to work; **faire ~ son cerveau** to appl one's mind; **ton imagination travaille trop** you hav an overactive imagination; **2** (exercer un métier) work; **~ en équipes/de nuit** to work shifts/night **~ au noir** GÉN *to work without declaring one's earn ings*; (exercer un second emploi non déclaré) to moonligh **3** COMM (faire des affaires) [*commerçant, magasin, hôte* to do business; **bien ~** to do good business; **~ ave** l'étranger to do business abroad; ~ pour l'exportation to work in exports; nous travaillons surtout l'été most of our trade is in the summer; ~ à perte [*entreprise, commerce*] to run at a loss; 4 (produire un revenu) faire ~ son argent to make one's money work; 5 (œuvrer) nous voulons la paix et c'est dans ce sens que nous travaillons we want peace and we are working toward(s) it; 6 (s'entraîner) [*athlète*] to train; [*boxeur*] to train, to work out; [*musicien, danseur*] to practise^GB; 7 (se modifier) [*bois*] to warp; [*vin*] to ferment; 8 (se déformer) [*poutre*] to be in stress.

travailleur, -euse /tʀavajœʀ, øz/ I *adj* 1 (appliqué) [*élève, employé*] hardworking; 2 SOCIOL [*classes, masses*] working.

II *nm,f* worker.

travailliste /tʀavajist/ I *adj* Labour; congrès ~ Labour party congress; être ~ (membre du parti) to be a member of the Labour party; (sympathisant) to be a Labour party supporter.

II *nmf* (député) Labour MP; le candidat des ~s the Labour candidate.

travée /tʀave/ *nf* 1 (rangée) row; 2 CONSTR, TECH span.

travelling /tʀavliŋ/ *nm* CIN (méthode) tracking; (plan) tracking shot; ~ avant/arrière tracking in/out.

travers /tʀavɛʀ/ I *nm inv* 1 (petit défaut) foible, quirk; (erreur) mistake; tomber dans le ~ de la sensiblerie to lapse into sentimentality; 2 NAUT (côté) beam; 3 CULIN ~ de porc sparerib.

II à travers *loc* 1 (ponctuel) [*voir, regarder*] through; passer à ~ les mailles du filet LIT, FIG to slip through the net; 2 (dans l'espace) [*voyager, marcher*] across; voyager à ~ le monde to travel all over the world; passer or aller or couper à ~ champs to cut across the fields; 3 (dans le temps) through; voyager à ~ le temps to travel through time; à ~ l'histoire throughout history; 4 (par l'intermédiaire de) through; à ~ ces informations through this information.

III au travers *loc* (en traversant) through; passer au ~ de FIG to escape [*contrôle, inspection*]; il y a eu des licenciements, heureusement il est passé au ~ there have been redundancies, fortunately his job wasn't affected.

IV de travers *loc adv* 1 (dans une mauvaise position) askew; il a mis son chapeau de ~ he has put his hat on askew; ta veste est boutonnée de ~ your jacket is buttoned up wrongly; il a le nez de ~ he has a twisted nose; j'ai avalé de ~ LIT it went down the wrong way; regarder qn de ~ FIG to give sb filthy looks, to glare at sb; 2 (de façon inexacte) wrong, wrongly; tout va de ~ aujourd'hui everything's going wrong today; elle prend tout de ~ she takes everything the wrong way; comprendre de ~ to misunderstand.

V en travers *loc* across; un bus était en ~ de la route a bus was stuck across the road; se mettre en ~ de la route [*personnes*] to stand in the middle of the road; se mettre en ~ du chemin de qn FIG to get in sb's way; rester en ~ de la gorge de qn^○ FIG [*attitude*] to stick in sb's throat; [*propos*] to be hard to swallow.

traverse /tʀavɛʀs/ *nf* 1 RAIL sleeper GB, tie US; 2 (de fenêtre, grille, d'armoire) crosspiece, strut; (de porte) rail; 3 (rue) side street.

traversée /tʀavɛʀse/ *nf* 1 (de mer, pont, pays, d'océan) crossing; faire la ~ du Vercors à pied to cross the Vercors on foot; la ~ du désert LIT crossing the desert; FIG (d'homme politique) the wilderness years (*pl*); (entreprise) a difficult period; 2 (de ville, tunnel) évitez la ~ de Paris avoid going through Paris.

traverser /tʀavɛʀse/ I *vtr* 1 (passer d'un côté à l'autre) to cross [*route, pont, frontière*]; to cross, to go across [*ville, montagne, océan, pays, pièce*]; (passer à travers) to go through, to pass through [*ville, pays, forêt, tunnel*]; to make one's way through [*groupe, foule*]; il traversa le jardin en courant he ran across the garden GB ou yard US; ~ le lac à la nage to swim across the lake; 2 (franchir) [*rivière*] to run through, to flow through [*région, plaine*]; [*route, tunnel*] to go

through [*ville, région, montagne*]; [*pont, rivière*] to cross [*voie ferrée, ville*]; 3 (transpercer) [*humidité, pluie*] to come through [*vêtement, mur*]; la balle lui a traversé le bras the bullet went ou passed right through his/her arm; 4 (passer par une période) to go through [*crise, difficulté*]; to live through, to go through [*guerre, occupation*]; 5 FIG (se présenter de manière fugitive) [*douleur*] to shoot through; ~ l'esprit de qn to cross sb's mind.

traversin /tʀavɛʀsɛ̃/ *nm* bolster.

travesti, ~e /tʀavɛsti/ I *adj* (déguisé) in disguise; rôle ~ role played by a member of the opposite sex.

II *nm* 1 (personne) transvestite; 2 THÉÂT (acteur) actor playing a female role; (dans un cabaret) drag artist^○.

travestir /tʀavɛstiʀ/ [3] I *vtr* 1 (déguiser) to dress [sb] up [*personne*]; 2 (dénaturer) to distort [*vérité*].

II se travestir *vpr* 1 (se déguiser) to dress up; 2 (prendre l'apparence du sexe opposé) to cross-dress.

travestissement /tʀavɛstismɑ̃/ *nm* 1 (action de se déguiser) dressing-up; 2 (déguisement) fancy dress, disguise; 3 (dénaturation) distortion, travesty; 4 PSYCH transvestism, cross-dressing.

trébucher /tʀebyʃe/ [1] *vi* 1 LIT to stumble (sur on; contre against); 2 FIG [*candidat, adversaire*] to slip up; ~ sur un mot to stumble over a word.

trébuchet /tʀebyʃɛ/ *nm* 1 (piège) bird-trap; 2 (balance) assay balance.

trèfle /tʀɛfl/ *nm* 1 BOT clover; ~ à quatre feuilles four-leaf clover; 2 JEUX (carte) club; (couleur) clubs (*pl*); avoir du ~ to be holding clubs; 3^○ (argent) dough^○, bread^○; 4 (symbole de l'Irlande) shamrock.

tréfonds /tʀefɔ̃/ *nm inv* LITER le ~ de the very depths (*pl*) of.

treillage /tʀɛjaʒ/ *nm* 1 (assemblage de lattes) trellis; ~ métallique wire grille; 2 (clôture) lattice fence; 3 (pour vigne) trellis.

treille /tʀɛj/ *nf* 1 (tonnelle) (vine) arbour^GB; 2 (vigne) climbing vine.

treillis /tʀeji/ *nm inv* 1 MIL (tenue) fatigues (*pl*); 2 (de textile) canvas; 3 (assemblage de lattes) trellis; ~ métallique wire grille; 4 (de verrière, vitrail) lattice.

treize /tʀɛz/ ▶399, 298, 156 *adj inv, pron* thirteen.

treizième /tʀɛzjɛm/ ▶399, 156 *adj* thirteenth.

tréma /tʀema/ ▶414 *nm* LING diaeresis.

tremblant, ~e /tʀɑ̃blɑ̃, ɑ̃t/ *adj* 1 [*personne, animal, mains*] shaking, trembling; être tout ~ to be shaking ou trembling all over; 2 [*voix*] trembling; 3 [*image, lueur*] flickering; [*son*] tremulous, quavering.

tremble /tʀɑ̃bl/ *nm* aspen.

tremblement /tʀɑ̃bləmɑ̃/ *nm* 1 (de personne, mains) shaking ₵, trembling ₵; (de lèvres) trembling ₵; son corps était agité de ~s he/she was trembling ou shaking all over; 2 (de voix) tremor, trembling ₵; (de voix âgée) quavering ₵; (de son, note) wavering ₵; (de lueur, lumière) flickering ₵; 3 (de feuilles) quivering ₵; (de vitres) rattling ₵.

■ ~ de terre earthquake.

trembler /tʀɑ̃ble/ [1] *vi* 1 [*personne, mains, jambes*] to shake, to tremble; 2 [*voix*] (de colère, joie) to tremble, to shake; (de vieillesse) to quaver; [*son, note*] to waver; 3 [*immeuble, plancher*] to shake; la terre a encore tremblé en Californie (légèrement) there have been tremors again in California; (tremblement de terre) there has been another earthquake in California; faire ~ qch to shake sth, to make sth shake; 4 (avoir peur) to tremble; ~ pour qn to fear for sb; 5 [*lumière, flamme, image*] to flicker; 6 [*feuilles*] to quiver; (mouvement très doux) to shiver.

tremblotement /tʀɑ̃blɔtmɑ̃/ *nm* 1 (de personne, mains) trembling ₵, tremor; 2 (de voix) (émue, effrayée) tremor; (âgée) quaver; 3 (de lumière) flickering ₵.

trembloter /tʀɑ̃blɔte/ [1] *vi* 1 [*personne, mains*] to tremble slightly; 2 [*voix*] (de joie, d'émotion) to tremble; (de vieillesse) to quaver; 3 [*lumière, flamme*] to flicker.

trémolo /tʀemɔlo/ *nm* 1 (de voix) quaver; avoir des

~s dans la voix to speak in a quavering voice; **2** (d'instrument) tremolo.

trémousser: **se trémousser** /tʀemuse/ [1] *vpr* **1** (s'agiter) to fidget; **2** (danser) to wiggle around.

trempe /tʀɑ̃p/ *nf* **1** (de personne) **avoir de la ~** to be made of stern stuff; **il faudrait quelqu'un de votre ~** we need someone of your calibre[GB]; **avoir la ~ d'un dirigeant** to have the makings of a leader; **2**⁰ (coups) walloping° **₵**.

trempé, ~e /tʀɑ̃pe/ I *pp* ▶ **tremper**.

II *pp adj* **1** [*personne, vêtements*] soaked (through), drenched; [*herbe*] sodden; [*linge*] soaking wet; **être ~ de sueur** to be soaked in sweat, to be dripping with sweat; **avoir les cheveux ~s** to have dripping wet hair; **2** TECH [*acier*] tempered; [*verre*] toughened.

tremper /tʀɑ̃pe/ [1] I *vtr* **1** (beaucoup) [*pluie, personne*] to soak [*personne, vêtement*]; **2** (rapidement) to dip; **~** un biscuit dans son thé to dunk one's biscuit GB ou cookie US in one's tea; **j'ai juste trempé mes lèvres** I just had a sip; **3** (longuement) to soak [*mains, aliment*]; **4** TECH to temper [*acier, verre*].

II *vi* **1** (être dans un liquide) [*linge, légumes secs*] to soak; **faire ~ qch** to soak sth; **2** (être impliqué) **~ dans qch** to be mixed up in sth.

III **se tremper** *vpr* (dans la mer) to go for a dip; (dans un bain) to have a quick bath.

tremplin /tʀɑ̃plɛ̃/ *nm* **1** SPORT (de natation, gymnastique) springboard; (de ski) ski jump; (de ski nautique) water-ski jump; **2** FIG springboard.

trentaine /tʀɑ̃tɛn/ *nf* **avoir la ~** to be about thirty; **une ~ de passagers** about thirty passengers.

trente /tʀɑ̃t/ ▶ 399, 156 *adj inv, pron* thirty.

trente(-)et(-)un /tʀɑ̃tɛœ̃/ ▶ 399, 156 *adj inv, pron* thirty-one.

IDIOMES **être sur son trente et un**° to be dressed up to the nines.

trentenaire /tʀɑ̃tənɛʀ/ *adj* **1** (qui dure trente ans) thirty-year; **2** (qui a trente ans et plus) [*personne*] in his/her thirties (*après n*); [*arbre, construction*] around thirty years old (*après n*).

trente-six /tʀɑ̃tsis/ ▶ 399, 156 *adj inv, pron* thirty-six.

IDIOMES **voir ~ chandelles**° to see stars.

trente-trois /tʀɑ̃ttʀwa/ ▶ 399, 156 *adj inv, pron* thirty-three.

■ **~ tours** LP.

trentième /tʀɑ̃tjɛm/ ▶ 399 *adj* thirtieth.

trépan /tʀepɑ̃/ *nm* **1** TECH trepan; **2** MÉD trephine.

trépaner /tʀepane/ [1] *vtr* to trephine.

trépas† /tʀepɑ/ *nm inv* demise; **passer de vie à ~** to pass on GB, to pass away.

trépasser /tʀepase/ [1] *vi* to pass away.

trépidant, ~e /tʀepidɑ̃, ɑ̃t/ *adj* **1** [*moteur, machine*] vibrating; **2** [*allure, rythme*] pulsating; [*vie, activité*] hectic; [*histoire*] exciting.

trépidation /tʀepidasjɔ̃/ *nf* vibration.

trépied /tʀepje/ *nm* GÉN tripod; (pour chaudron) trivet.

trépigner /tʀepiɲe/ [1] *vi* (de colère, d'impatience) to stamp one's feet (**de** with); (de joie, d'excitation) to jump up and down (**de** with).

très /tʀɛ/ *adv* **1** (modifiant un adjectif) very; **~ connu** very well-known; **le dîner était ~ réussi** the dinner went (off) very well; **~ disputé** [*match*] closely contested; **~ répandu** [*pratique*] very widespread; [*opinion*] widely held; **il est ~ aimé dans l'école** he is very well liked at school; **être ~ amoureux** to be very much in love; **à un prix ~ inférieur** at a very much lower price; **la grève a été ~ suivie** the strike was very well supported; **2** (modifiant une expression adjectivale) very; **~ en avance/au courant** very early/well-informed; **~ homme d'affaires** very much a businessman; **3** (modifiant un adverbe) very; **~ tôt/bien/loin** very early/well/far; **~ volontiers** gladly; **à ~ bientôt** see you very soon; **~ franchement, je ne sais pas** quite frankly, I don't know; **'tu vas bien?'—'non, pas ~'** 'are you well?'—'no, not terribly'; **4** (dans des locutions verbales) **j'ai ~ soif** I'm

very thirsty; **elle a ~ envie de partir** she's dying° to leave.

trésor /tʀezɔʀ/ *nm* **1** (amas d'objets précieux) treasure **₵**; **découvrir un ~** to find some treasure; **chasse** or **course au ~** treasure hunt; **2** (objet précieux) treasure; **les ~s du cinéma français** the all-time greats of the French cinema; **les ~s de la mer** the riches of the sea; **3** (grande quantité) **déployer des ~s d'inventivité** to show infinite inventiveness; **4** (personne) treasure.

trésorerie /tʀezɔʀʀi/ *nf* **1** (ressources disponibles) funds (*pl*); (somme en liquide) cash **₵**; **problèmes de ~** cash flow problems; **2** (comptabilité) accounts (*pl*); **3** ADMIN **la ~** (comptabilité) government finance.

trésorier, -ière /tʀezɔʀje, ɛʀ/ *nm,f* GÉN treasurer; ADMIN paymaster.

tressaillement /tʀesajmɑ̃/ *nm* **1** (de surprise, peur) start; (de plaisir, joie, d'espoir) quiver; (de douleur) wince; **2** (tremblement) (de personne, muscle, d'animal) twitch; (de machine, sol) vibration.

tressaillir /tʀesajiʀ/ [28] *vi* **1** (de surprise, peur) to start (**de** with); (de plaisir, joie, d'espoir) to quiver; (de douleur) to wince; **2** (trembler) [*personne, animal, muscle*] to twitch; [*machine, sol, chose*] to vibrate.

tressauter /tʀesote/ [1] *vi* **1** (sursauter) to start; **2** (être secoué) [*véhicule*] to jolt; [*personne*] to be jolted; [*objets*] to jump.

tresse /tʀɛs/ *nf* **1** (de cheveux) plait, braid US; **2** (de fil, tissu, cuir) braid.

tresser /tʀese/ [1] *vtr* **1** to plait, to braid US [*cheveux*]; **2** (pour faire un cordon) to plait [*paille, fil, corde, cuir*]; (tisser) to weave [*paille, corde, objet*]; **soulier tressé** latticework shoe.

tréteau, *pl* **~x** /tʀeto/ *nm* trestle.

treuil /tʀœj/ *nm* winch.

trêve /tʀɛv/ *nf* **1** MIL truce; **2** (moment de répit) respite; **sans ~** unceasingly, without any let-up; **~ de plaisanteries/balivernes!** that's enough joking/nonsense!

tri /tʀi/ *nm* **1** (pour répartir) sorting; **faire le ~ de** to sort [*courrier*]; to sort out [*documents, vêtements*]; **2** (pour choisir) sorting out, selection; **faire le ~ de** to sort [sth] out [*photos, information*]; **faire un ~ parmi des choses/gens** to select among things/people; **opérer un ~ sévère** to be very selective; **fais le ~ dans ce qu'elle dit** don't believe everything she says.

■ **~ postal** sorting.

triage /tʀijaʒ/ *nm* **procéder au ~ de qch** to sort sth out; **gare de ~** marshalling[GB] yard.

trial[1] /tʀijal/ *nm* (épreuve) scramble.

trial[2] /tʀijal/ *nf* (moto) trial bike GB, dirt bike US.

triangle /tʀijɑ̃gl/ *nm* **1** MATH triangle; **2** (objet) triangle; **en ~** in a triangle; **3** ▶ 392 MUS triangle.

triangulaire /tʀijɑ̃gylɛʀ/ *adj* **1** (en forme de triangle) triangular; **2** (entre trois personnes, pays) three-way.

tribal, ~e, *mpl* **-aux** /tʀibal, o/ *adj* tribal.

tribord /tʀibɔʀ/ *nm* starboard.

tribu /tʀiby/ *nf* tribe; **le chef de ~** LIT the head of the tribe; HUM the Big Chief.

tribun /tʀibœ̃/ *nm* **1** HIST tribune; **2** (orateur) great orator.

tribunal, *pl* **-aux** /tʀibynal, o/ *nm* **1** JUR (lieu, magistrats) court; **porter une affaire devant les tribunaux** to bring ou take a case to court; **traîner qn devant les tribunaux** to take sb to court; **2** FIG **le ~ de l'histoire/de l'humanité** the judgment of history/of humanity.

tribune /tʀibyn/ *nf* **1** (de stade, gymnase, champ de courses) stand; **~ officielle** or **d'honneur** the VIP stand; **les ~s du public** the stands; **2** (de salle de réunion, parlement) gallery; **la ~ de la presse** the press gallery; **3** (estrade) platform; (pour une seule personne) rostrum; **monter à la ~** LIT, FIG to take the platform; **parler à la ~** to speak from the platform; **tenir la ~** to hold the floor; **4** (dans un journal) (rubrique) comments column; (lieu de débat) forum for debate; **5** ARCHIT (de chapelle, d'église) gallery.

tribut /tʀiby/ nm HIST tribute; **ils ont payé un lourd ~ à la guerre/aux accidents de la route** FIG war has/road accidents have taken a heavy toll.

tributaire /tʀibytɛʀ/ adj **1** GÉN **être ~ de qch** [pays, personne, réalisation] to depend ou be dependent on sth; **ils sont ~s les uns des autres** they're interdependent; **2** GÉOG **être ~ de qch** [fleuve] to be a tributary of sth, to flow into sth.

tricentenaire /tʀisɑ̃tnɛʀ/ adj three-hundred-year-old (épith); **être ~** to be three hundred years old.

triche○ /tʀiʃ/ nf **c'est de la ~** that's cheating.

tricher /tʀiʃe/ [1] vi **1** (agir malhonnêtement) to cheat; **~ avec les chiffres** to doctor the figures; **2** (mentir) **~ sur qch** to lie about sth; **~ sur son âge** to lie about one's age; **~ sur la qualité d'un produit** to cut corners on product quality; **~ sur le poids** to give short measure; **~ sur les prix** to overcharge.

tricherie /tʀiʃʀi/ nf **1** (action de tricher) cheating; **2** (acte trompeur) trick.

tricheur, -euse /tʀiʃœʀ, øz/ nm,f cheat.

tricolore /tʀikɔlɔʀ/ adj **1** (de trois couleurs) tricolourGB, three-colouredGB (épith); **feux ~s** traffic lights; **2** (bleu, blanc, rouge) red, white and blue; **le drapeau ~** the tricolourGB, the French flag; **3**○ (français) French; **l'équipe ~** the French team.

tricorne /tʀikɔʀn/ nm tricorne.

tricot /tʀiko/ nm **1** (activité) knitting; **faire du ~** to knit; **points de ~** knitting stitches; **2** (ouvrage) knitting ¢; **mon ~** my knitting; **j'ai commencé un ~** I've started knitting something; **3** (étoffe) knitwear; **une robe en ~** a knitted dress; **4**† (pull) sweater, jumper GB; (cardigan) cardigan.
■ **~ de corps**† vest GB, undershirt US.

tricoter /tʀikɔte/ [1] **I** vtr to knit; **~ une écharpe à qn** to knit sb a scarf, to knit a scarf for sb; **un pull tricoté (à la) main** a handknit sweater; **robe tricotée** sweater dress, knitted dress.
II vi to knit; **~ à la main** to hand-knit; **~ à la machine** to knit on a knitting machine; **aiguilles/machine à ~** knitting needles/machine.

tricycle /tʀisikl/ nm tricycle.

trident /tʀidɑ̃/ nm (objet) trident.

tridimensionnel, -elle /tʀidimɑ̃sjɔnɛl/ adj three-dimensional.

triennal, ~e, mpl **-aux** /tʀijenal, o/ adj **1** (pour trois ans) three-year (épith); **2** (tous les trois ans) [exposition, vote] three-yearly (épith), triennial; [assolement] three-yearly (épith).

trier /tʀije/ [2] vtr **1** (pour répartir) to sort [courrier]; **2** (pour choisir) to sort [sth] out [photos, information]; to select [clientèle].
IDIOMES **~ sur le volet** to handpick.

trifouiller○ /tʀifuje/ [1] vi **~ dans** to rummage through [placard, affaires]; to tinker with [appareil, moteur].

trigonométrie /tʀigɔnɔmetʀi/ nf trigonometry.

trijumeau, pl **-x** /tʀiʒymo/ **I** adj m trigeminal.
II nm trigeminal nerve.

trilingue /tʀilɛ̃g/ adj [texte, personne] trilingual.

trille /tʀij/ nm **1** MUS trill; **2** (son) **les ~s d'un oiseau** the trilling ¢ of a bird.

trillion /tʀiljɔ̃/ ▶399 | nm trillion.

trilogie /tʀilɔʒi/ nf trilogy.

trimbal(l)er○ /tʀɛ̃bale/ [1] **I** vtr to lug [sth] around [valise, objet]; to drag [sb] around [personne].
II se trimbal(l)er vpr to trail around.

trimer○ /tʀime/ [1] vi to slave away; **faire ~ qn** to keep sb slaving away.

trimestre /tʀimɛstʀ/ nm **1** SCOL, UNIV term; **2** FIN, POL, ÉCON quarter; **3** (somme reçue) quarterly income; (somme payée) quarterly payment.

trimestriel, -ielle /tʀimɛstʀijɛl/ adj **1** SCOL, UNIV **examen** or **contrôle ~** end-of-term exam; **2** [revue, numéro] quarterly; [cotisation, réunion] quarterly.

trimoteur /tʀimɔtœʀ/ **I** adj three-engined.

II nm three-engined plane.

tringle /tʀɛ̃gl/ nf **1** GÉN rail; **~ à rideaux** curtain rail, curtain rod US; **~ à vêtements** clothes rail, hanging rail; **2** TECH rod.

trinité /tʀinite/ nf (ensemble) trinity.

Trinité /tʀinite/ **I** nf RELIG **la ~** the Trinity; (fête) Trinity Sunday.
II nprf ▶232 |, 305 | (île) Trinidad; (État) **~ et Tobago** Trinidad and Tobago.
IDIOMES **à Pâques ou à la ~** when the cows come home.

trinquer /tʀɛ̃ke/ [1] vi **1** GÉN to clink glasses; **~ avec qn** LIT to clink glasses with sb; FIG to go drinking with sb; **~ à qch** to drink to sth; **trinquons à ta réussite!** let's drink to your success!; **2**○ (boire avec excès) to booze○; **3**○ (subir les conséquences de qch) to pay the price; (être puni) to take the rap○.

trio /tʀi(j)o/ nm MUS, GÉN trio.

triolet /tʀijɔlɛ/ nm **1** MUS triplet; **2** LITTÉRAT triolet.

triomphal, ~e, mpl **-aux** /tʀijɔ̃fal, o/ adj triumphant.

triomphalisme /tʀijɔ̃falism/ nm triumphalism.

triomphant, ~e /tʀijɔ̃fɑ̃, ɑ̃t/ adj triumphant.

triomphateur, -trice /tʀijɔ̃fatœʀ, tʀis/ nm,f triumphant victor.

triomphe /tʀijɔ̃f/ nm triumph; **faire un ~ à qn** to give sb a triumphal reception; **film qui remporte un ~** film which is having tremendous success; **avoir le ~ modeste** to be modest about one's success.

triompher /tʀijɔ̃fe/ [1] **I triompher de** vtr ind to triumph over [adversaire]; to overcome [résistance, crainte]; **la démocratie a triomphé du totalitarisme** democracy has triumphed over totalitarianism.
II vi **1** (réussir) [combattant] to triumph; [artiste] to have a resounding success; [mensonge, vérité] to prevail; **2** (manifester) [personne] to be triumphant ou exultant.

tripartisme /tʀipaʀtism/ nm tripartite ou three-party system.

tripatouiller○ /tʀipatuje/ [1] vtr **1** (altérer) to fiddle about○ with, to tamper with [texte]; to fiddle○, to rig [résultats électoraux]; **2** (bricoler) to fiddle with○, to tinker with [moteur, machine]; **3** (tripoter) to fiddle with○, to toy with [objet]; to paw○ [personne].

tripe /tʀip/ **I** nf **1** CULIN tripe ¢; **2**○ (sensibilité) **avoir la ~ patriotique** to be a dyed-in-the-wool patriot; **prendre** or **saisir aux ~s** to be gut-wrenching○; **chanter avec ses ~s** to sing from the heart.
II tripes○ nfpl (entrailles) guts, innards; **rendre ~s et boyaux**○ to be as sick as a dog, to spew up○.

triperie /tʀipʀi/ ▶374 | nf (boutique) tripe shop; (commerce) tripe trade.

triphasé, ~e /tʀifaze/ adj three-phase.

triplace /tʀiplas/ adj three-seater.

triple /tʀipl/ **I** adj (before n) [rôle, objectif, détonation] triple (épith); **l'avantage est ~** the advantages are threefold; **en ~ exemplaire** in triplicate; **avoir un livre/une photo en ~** to have three copies of a book/a photograph; **~ idiot**○! prize idiot○!
II nm **coûter le ~** to cost three times as much; **son salaire est le ~ du mien** he/she earns three times as much as I do.

triplé, ~e /tʀiple/ **I** nm,f (enfant) triplet.
II nm SPORT hat trick.

triplement /tʀipləmɑ̃/ **I** adv (pour trois raisons) in three respects.
II nm trebling, tripling (de of); **~ des effectifs/prix** threefold increase in staff/prices.

tripler /tʀiple/ [1] **I** vtr **1** (multiplier par trois) to treble [somme, quantité, prix]; to treble, to triple [épaisseur, dimension, volume]; **2** (refaire à nouveau) **~ une classe** SCOL to repeat a class GB ou grade US a second time.
II vi to treble, to increase threefold; **~ de** to treble in [valeur, poids, volume, taille].

triplex /tʀiplɛks/ *nm inv* **1** ®(verre de sécurité) Triplex® GB, safety glass; **2** (appartement) three-floor maisonette GB, triplex (apartment) US.

triporteur /tʀipɔʀtœʀ/ *nm* delivery tricycle.

tripot /tʀipo/ *nm* **1** (maison de jeu) gambling joint○; **2** (endroit mal famé) dive○.

tripotée○ /tʀipote/ *nf* (ribambelle) **une ~ de** hordes (*pl*) of, a whole slew of○ US.

tripoter○ /tʀipote/ [1] *vtr* **1** (caresser) PÉJ to grope○ PÉJ [*femme, fesses*]; **2** (manier) (nerveusement) to fiddle with [*objet, moustache*]; (distraitement) to finger; **cesse de te ~ le nez!** stop picking your nose!.

triptyque /tʀiptik/ *nm* **1** ART triptych; **2** LITTÉRAT, MUS trilogy; **3** ADMIN triptyque.

trique /tʀik/ *nf* (gourdin) cudgel; **battre à coups de ~** to cudgel; **recevoir un coup de ~** to be cudgelled GB.

IDIOMES **être maigre** or **sec comme un coup de ~** to be as thin as a rake, to be as skinny as a rail US.

triréacteur /tʀiʀeaktœʀ/ *nm* tri-jet.

trisaïeul, **~e** /tʀizajœl/ *nm,f* great-great-grandfather/grandmother; **~s** great-great-grandparents.

trisannuel, -elle /tʀizanɥɛl/ *adj* triennial.

trisomie /tʀizɔmi/ *nf* trisomy; **~ 21** Down's Syndrome.

trisomique /tʀizɔmik/ **I** *adj* MÉD [*enfant*] Down's syndrome (*épith*); **être ~** to have Down's syndrome.
II *nmf* Down's syndrome child.

triste /tʀist/ *adj* **1** (pas gai) [*personne, visage*] sad; [*maison, ville, région*] dreary, depressing; [*ciel, temps, journée*] gloomy; [*histoire, livre, soirée, événement*] sad, depressing; [*couleur*] drab, dreary; [*existence*] dreary; **avoir ~ mine** or **figure** [*personne*] to look pitiful; **mon gâteau a bien ~ mine** my cake is a sorry sight; **2** (déplorable) [*résultat, fin, affaire*] dreadful; [*conséquence*] sad; [*spectacle, état*] sorry; **c'est la ~ vérité** unfortunately, that's the truth of the matter; **détenir le ~ record d'alcoolisme** to hold the record for heavy drinking, a dubious achievement; **faire la ~ expérience de qch** to have learned about sth to one's sorrow; **se lamenter sur son ~ sort** to lament one's fate; **3** (méprisable) [*personnage*] unsavoury GB, disreputable; [*réputation*] dreadful; **un ~ imbécile** a despicable character; **un ~ sire** a disreputable character.

IDIOMES **~ comme la pluie** or **à mourir** desperately sad; **c'était pas ~** ○ it was quite something.

tristement /tʀistəmã/ *adv* **1** (avec tristesse) [*sourire, regarder*] sadly; [*s'habiller*] in drab colours GB; **2** (de façon regrettable) [*révélateur*] all too; **c'est ~ vrai** unfortunately, it's only too true; **une vie ~ ordinaire** a drearily ordinary life.

tristesse /tʀistɛs/ *nf* (d'histoire, événement, de personne, musique) sadness; (de lieu, maison, soirée) dreariness; (de ciel, temps, journée) gloominess; **répondre/dire avec ~** to reply/to say sadly; **c'est avec ~ que nous avons appris que** we have learned with sorrow that; **M et Mme Vernet ont la ~ de vous faire part du décès de leur fils Pierre** Mr and Mrs Vernet have to inform you of the death of their son Pierre.

triturer /tʀityʀe/ [1] *vtr* **1** (tripoter) to twist [*mouchoir*]; to fiddle with [*bouton*]; to knead [*pâte*]; **2** (broyer) to grind up.

IDIOMES **se ~ la cervelle**○ or **les méninges**○ to rack one's brains○.

trivial, **~e**, *mpl* **-iaux** /tʀivjal, o/ *adj* **1** (grossier) [*manières, humour*] coarse, crude; **2** (banal) [*objet*] ordinary, everyday (*épith*); [*style*] mundane PÉJ; **3** (simpliste) [*explication, démonstration*] simplistic; **4** MATH trivial.

trivialité /tʀivjalite/ *nf* **1** (caractère vulgaire) coarseness, crudeness; **2** (caractère banal) triteness, triviality; **3** (parole banale) platitude; **4** (chose banale) triviality.

troc /tʀɔk/ *nm* barter; **faire du ~** to barter; **faire un ~**○ to do a swap○; **économie de ~** barter economy.

troène /tʀɔɛn/ *nm* privet ¢.

troglodyte /tʀɔglɔdit/ *nm* **1** (homme) cave-dweller; **2** (oiseau) (winter) wren.

trogne○ /tʀɔɲ/ *nf* mug○, face.

trognon /tʀɔɲɔ̃/ **I**○ *adj inv* [*enfants*] sweet.
II *nm* (de pomme, poire) core; (de salade, chou) stalk.

trois /tʀwɑ/ ▶399|, 298|, 156| *adj inv, pron, nm inv* three.

IDIOMES **être haut comme ~ pommes** to be knee-high to a grasshopper; **jamais deux sans ~** bad luck comes in threes.

trois-deux /tʀwado/ *nm inv* MUS three-two time; **en ~** in three-two time.

trois-huit /tʀwaɥit/ *nmpl* system (*sg*) of three eight-hour shifts.

troisième /tʀwazjɛm/ ▶399|, 156| **I** *adj* third.
II *nf* SCOL *fourth year of secondary school, age 14–15.*
■ **le ~ âge** the elderly (+ *v pl*).

troisièmement /tʀwazjɛmmã/ *adv* thirdly.

trois-mâts /tʀwamɑ/ *nm inv* three-master.

trois-quarts /tʀwakaʀ/ **I** *adj inv* [*manches, veste*] three-quarter length.
II *nm inv* **1** (manteau) three-quarter length coat; **2** (joueur de rugby) three-quarter.
III **de trois-quarts** *loc adj* [*portrait, photo*] three-quarter length (*épith*).

trolleybus /tʀɔlebys/ *nm inv* trolley bus.

trombe /tʀɔ̃b/ *nf* **1** (cyclone) waterspout; **partir en ~** to go hurtling off; **traverser/passer en ~** to go hurtling across/past; **2** (averse) **~s d'eau** downpour ¢.

trombine○ /tʀɔ̃bin/ *nf* mug○, face.

trombone /tʀɔ̃bɔn/ *nm* **1** ▶392| (instrument) trombone; **~ à coulisse/à pistons** slide/valve trombone; **2** ▶374| (musicien) trombonist, trombone player; **3** (de bureau) paperclip.

trompe /tʀɔ̃p/ *nf* **1** ZOOL (d'éléphant) trunk; (d'insecte, de mollusque) proboscis; **2** ▶392| MUS horn.
■ **~ d'Eustache** Eustachian tube.

trompe-la-mort /tʀɔ̃plamɔʀ/ *nmf inv* daredevil.

trompe-l'œil /tʀɔ̃plœj/ *nm inv* **1** ART trompe l'oeil; **paysage/façade en ~** trompe l'oeil landscape/façade; **2** (ce qui fait illusion) smokescreen.

tromper /tʀɔ̃pe/ [1] **I** *vtr* **1** (duper) [*personne*] to deceive; **~ les électeurs** to mislead the voters; **il y a des signes** or **gestes qui ne trompent pas** there's no mistaking the signs; **~ l'ennemi** to deceive ou trick the enemy; **2** (faire des infidélités à) to be unfaithful to, to deceive [*mari, femme*]; **3** (échapper à) **~ la vigilance** or **surveillance de qn** to slip past sb's guard; **~ la défense/le gardien de but** to trick the defence GB/the goalkeeper; **4** (faire diversion à) to stave off; **~ la faim** to stave off hunger.
II **se tromper** *vpr* **1** (mentalement) to be mistaken; **se ~ sur qn** to be wrong about sb; **je me suis trompé sur leurs intentions** I misunderstood their intentions; **si je ne me trompe** if I'm not mistaken; **il ne faut pas s'y ~, qu'on ne s'y trompe pas** make no mistake about it; **2** (concrètement) to make a mistake; **se ~ de dix francs** to be ten francs out GB ou off US; **se ~ de bus** to take the wrong bus; **se ~ de jour** to get the day wrong; **se ~ de bâtiment** to get the wrong building.

tromperie /tʀɔ̃pʀi/ *nf* deceit ¢.

trompette[1] /tʀɔ̃pɛt/ ▶374| *nm* (dans un orchestre) trumpet (player); (dans l'armée) bugler; (dans une fanfare) trumpeter.

trompette[2] /tʀɔ̃pɛt/ ▶392| *nf* trumpet.

trompettiste /tʀɔ̃petist/ ▶374| *nmf* trumpet (player).

trompeur, **-euse** /tʀɔ̃pœʀ, øz/ *adj* [*promesse, chiffre*] misleading; [*distance, apparence*] deceptive.

tronc /tʀɔ̃/ *nm* **1** (fût) (d'arbre) trunk; (de colonne) shaft; **un ~ d'arbre** a tree-trunk; **2** (partie du corps) trunk, torso; **3** (dans une église) collection box.
■ **~ commun** (d'espèces, de langues) common origin; (de disciplines) (common) core curriculum.

tronche⚬ /tRɔ̃ʃ/ *nf* mug⚬, face.

tronçon /tRɔ̃sɔ̃/ *nm* section.

tronçonneuse /tRɔ̃sɔnøz/ *nf* chain saw.

trône /tRon/ *nm* throne; **monter sur le ~** to come to the throne.

trôner /tRone/ [1] *vi* **le professeur trônait au milieu de ses étudiants** the professor was holding court among his/her students; **~ sur** [*vase, photo*] to have pride of place on [*cheminée*].

tronquer /tRɔ̃ke/ [1] *vtr* to truncate [*texte, déclaration*].

trop /tRo/ ▶486 I *adv* 1 (indiquant un excès) (modifiant un adjectif ou un adverbe) too; (modifiant un verbe) too much; **j'ai ~ mangé/bu** I've had too much to eat/to drink; **j'ai ~ dormi** I've slept too long; **tu travailles ~** you work too hard; **ça c'est ~ fort**⚬! that's (just) too much!; **nous sommes ~ nombreux** there are too many of us; **nous sommes ~ peu nombreux** there are too few of us; **ce serait ~ beau!** I/you/we etc should be so lucky!; **c'est ~ bête!** how stupid!; **~ enthousiaste** overenthusiastic; **on n'est jamais ~ prudent** you can't be too careful; **tu en as ~ dit** you've already said too much; **elle en fait (un peu) ~** she overdoes it (a bit); **c'en est ~!** that's the end!; **'tu aimes la viande?'—'pas ~'** 'do you like meat?'—'not terribly' ou 'not very much'; **nous ne serons pas ~ de deux** it'll take at least two of us; **je ne le connais que ~** I know him only too well; **faire qch sans ~ y croire** to do sth without really believing in it; **~ c'est ~!** enough is enough!; **2** (employé avec valeur de superlatif) **~ mignon** too sweet ou cute⚬; **c'était ~ drôle** it was so funny; **ça ne va pas ~ mal, merci** not so bad, thanks; **je n'en sais ~ rien**⚬ I don't really know; **ça ne me dit ~ rien**⚬ I don't really feel like it; **3**⚬ (incroyable) **il est ~, lui!** he's too much⚬!; **c'est ~, ça!** that's incredible!

II trop de *dét indéf* **1** (avec nom dénombrable) too many; **il y a ~ de choses à faire** there's too much to do; **2** (avec nom non dénombrable) too much; **~ de pression** too much pressure; **~ de monde** too many people.

III de trop, **en trop** *loc adv* **il y a une assiette en ~** there's one plate too many; **j'ai dix kilos de bagages en ~** my luggage is ten kilos over the limit; **j'ai quelques kilos en ~** I'm a few kilos overweight; **si tu as du tissu en ~ tu peux faire un coussin** if you have some material left over, you can make a cushion; **il y a 12 francs de ~** there's 12 francs too much; **sa remarque était de ~** his/her remark was uncalled for; **se sentir de ~** to feel one is in the way.

IV par trop *loc adv* = **trop**.

trophée /tRofe/ *nm* trophy.

tropical, **~e**, *mpl* **-aux** /tRɔpikal, o/ *adj* tropical.

trop-perçu, *pl* **~s** /tRopεRsy/ *nm* **1** (d'argent) excess payment; **2** (d'impôts) overpayment of tax; **remboursement d'un ~** tax refund.

trop-plein, *pl* **~s** /tRoplɛ̃/ *nm* **1** (excès) excess; **avoir un ~ d'énergie** to have excess energy; **2** TECH (de lavabo, baignoire) overflow.

troquer /tRɔke/ [1] *vtr* **1** COMM to trade (**contre** for), to barter (**contre** for); **2** (échanger) **~ qch contre** or **pour qch** to exchange ou swap sth for sth.

troquet⚬ /tRɔkε/ *nm* bar.

trot /tRo/ *nm* (de cheval) trot; **au ~!** LIT trot on!; FIG at the double GB, on the double US.

trotte⚬ /tRɔt/ *nf* fair walk; **ça fait une ~** it's a fair walk, it's quite a walk.

trotter /tRɔte/ [1] *vi* **1** [*cheval, cavalier*] to trot; **2** (aller à petits pas) [*adulte, souris*] to scurry (about); [*enfant*] to toddle along; **~ dans la tête** [*pensée*] to go through one's mind; [*musique*] to go through one's head.

trotteur /tRɔtœR/ *nm* **1** (cheval) trotter; **2** (chaussure) *shoe with a low, broad heel*.

trotteuse /tRɔtøz/ *nf* (de montre, chronomètre) second hand.

trottiner /tRɔtine/ [1] *vi* **1** [*cheval*] to jog; **2** [*personne, souris*] to scurry along.

---

trop

trop adverbe modifiant un verbe se traduit par *too much*. Il se traduit par *too* lorsqu'il modifie un adjectif, un adverbe. Dans le cas d'expressions comme *avoir soif/faim/chaud* traduites par *to be* + adjectif, il se traduit par *too*:

> *j'ai trop froid, je rentre* = I'm too cold, I'm going home

Voir exemples supplémentaires et exceptions I.

trop de déterminant indéfini se traduit par *too many* lorsqu'il est suivi d'un nom dénombrable:

> *trop de livres* = too many books
> *trop d'idées* = too many ideas

et par *too much* lorsqu'il est suivi d'un nom non dénombrable:

> *trop de travail* = too much work

Attention, certains mots dénombrables français ne le sont pas en anglais et réciproquement:

> *trop de meubles* = too much furniture
> *trop de monde* = too many people

Voir exemples supplémentaires et exceptions II.

---

trottinette /tRɔtinεt/ *nf* scooter.

trottoir /tRɔtwaR/ *nm* pavement GB, sidewalk US; **le bord du ~** the kerb GB ou curb US.

■ **~ roulant** moving pavement GB, moving sidewalk US.

IDIOMES **faire le ~**⚬ to be on the game⚬ GB, to be a hooker⚬.

trou /tRu/ *nm* **1** GÉN hole; **faire son ~**⚬ [*personne*] to carve out a niche for oneself; **faire un ~ à la perceuse** to drill a hole; **2** (lacune) gap; **j'ai un ~ dans mon emploi du temps** GÉN I have a gap in my timetable; SCOL I have a free period; **3**⚬ (déficit) deficit, shortfall; **un ~ dans le budget** a budget deficit, a shortfall in the budget; **4**⚬ (petite localité) **~ (perdu)** dump⚬, god-forsaken place; **il n'est jamais sorti de son ~** he's never been out of his own backyard; **5**⚬ (prison) prison, nick⚬.

■ **~ d'air** air pocket; **~ de mémoire** memory lapse; **~ noir** black hole; **~ normand** *glass of spirits between courses to aid digestion*; **~ de serrure** keyhole; **~ du souffleur** prompt box.

IDIOMES **ne pas avoir les yeux en face des ~s**⚬ not to be able to see straight.

troublant, **~e** /tRublɑ̃, ɑ̃t/ *adj* [*problème, anecdote*] disturbing; [*coïncidence, fait*] disconcerting; [*décolleté*] that stirs desire (*après n*).

trouble /tRubl/ I *adj* **1** (pas transparent) [*eau, vin*] cloudy; [*verres, vitres*] smudgy; **2** (flou) [*image, photo*] blurred; [*contours*] vague, blurred; **3** (équivoque) [*sentiment*] confused; (louche) [*affaire, milieu*] shady.

II *adv* **je vois ~** (temporaire) my eyes are blurred; (permanent) I have blurred vision.

III *nm* **1** (insécurité) unrest; **2** (mésentente, malaise) **jeter le ~** to stir up trouble; **jeter le ~ dans les esprits** to sow confusion in people's minds; **3** (confusion) confusion; (gêne) embarrassment; **dominer son ~** to overcome one's confusion; **4** (émoi) emotion; **ressentir un ~** to feel an emotion; **5** MÉD disorder; **de légers ~s gastriques** minor gastric problems; **~s de la mémoire** memory problems.

IV **troubles** *nmpl* POL unrest ¢, disturbances; **~s ethniques** ethnic unrest.

trouble-fête /tRubləfεt/ *nmf inv* spoilsport.

troubler /tRuble/ [1] I *vtr* **1** (brouiller) to make [sth] cloudy, to cloud [*eau, vin*]; to blur [*vue, image*]; **2** (déranger) to disturb [*silence, sommeil, personne*]; to disrupt [*réunion, spectacle*]; **~ l'ordre public** [*individu*] to cause a breach of the peace; [*groupe d'insurgés*] to disturb the peace; **en ces temps troublés** in these troubled times; **3** (déconcerter) to disconcert [*accusé, candidat*]; **quelque chose me trouble** (rendre perplexe) something's bothering ou puzzling me; **4** (mettre en émoi) LITER to disturb EUPH [*personne*].

II **se troubler** *vpr* **1** (perdre contenance) [*personne,* accusé] to become flustered; **2** (devenir trouble) [*liquide*] to become cloudy, to cloud; **ma vue se troubla** my eyes became blurred.

trouée /tʀue/ *nf* **1** (ouverture) gap, opening; **2** MIL breach.

trouer /tʀue/ [1] *vtr* **1** (perforer) (d'un trou) to make a hole in; (de plusieurs trous) to make holes in; **~ un drap avec une cigarette** to make ou burn a hole in a sheet with a cigarette; **j'ai troué mes chaussures** (à la longue) I've worn holes in my shoes; **chaussettes ~es** socks with holes in them; **2** (transpercer) [*lumière, cri*] to pierce [*nuit*].

IDIOMES **~ la peau**○ **à qn** to put a bullet in sb○.

troufion○ /tʀufjɔ̃/ *nm* soldier.

trouillard○, **~e** /tʀujaʀ, aʀd/ **I** *adj* cowardly.
II *nm,f* chicken○, coward.

trouille○ /tʀuj/ *nf* fear; **avoir la ~** to be scared; **flanquer la ~ à qn** to scare sb, to give sb a fright.

troupe /tʀup/ *nf* **1** MIL troops (*pl*); **la ~** (l'armée) the army; (les simples soldats) the rank and file, the troops (*pl*); **2** THÉÂT company; (qui voyage) troupe; **3** (groupe) (d'éléphants, de cerfs) herd; (de moutons, d'oiseaux) flock; (de touristes) troop; (d'enfants) band.

troupeau, *pl* **~x** /tʀupo/ *nm* **1** (d'éléphants, de bisons, vaches, cerfs) herd; (de moutons, chèvres) flock; (d'oies) gaggle; **2** (de personnes) PEJ herd; **3** RELIG flock.

trousse /tʀus/ *nf* **1** (pochette) (little) case; **2** (contenu) kit.

■ **~ d'écolier** pencil case; **~ de maquillage** make-up bag; **~ de médecin** doctor's bag; **~ à outils** tool kit; **~ de secours** first-aid kit; **~ de toilette** toilet bag.

IDIOMES **être aux ~s**○ **de qn** to be hot on sb's heels.

trousseau, *pl* **~x** /tʀuso/ *nm* **1** (de clés) bunch; **2** (de mariée) trousseau; (d'enfant) clothes (*pl*).

trouvaille /tʀuvaj/ *nf* **1** (découverte) find; (invention) invention; **2** (idée originale) bright idea, brainwave.

trouvé, **~e** /tʀuve/ **I** *pp* ▶ **trouver**.
II *pp adj* **réplique bien ~e** neat riposte; **tout ~** [*réponse, solution, prétexte*] ready-made; [*coupable, candidat*] obvious; **vous êtes la personne toute ~e pour ce travail** you're the very person we need for the job.

trouver /tʀuve/ [1] **I** *vtr* **1** (par hasard) to find; **c'est surprenant de vous ~ ici!** I'm surprised to find you here!; **on trouve de tout ici** they have everything here; **~ qch par hasard** to come across sth; **2** (en cherchant) to find; **veuillez ~ ci-joint...** (dans une lettre) please find enclosed...; **j'ai trouvé!** I've got it!; **tu as trouvé ça tout seul?** IRON did you work that out all by yourself?; **si tu continues tu vas me ~**○! don't push your luck○!; **il va ~ à qui parler** he's going to be for it○; **~ du plaisir à faire** to get pleasure out of doing; **il ne nous reste plus qu'à ~ le financement** all we have to do now is get financial backing; **3** (voir) to find; **~ qch dans un état lamentable** to find sth in an appalling state; **ils sont tous venus me ~ après le cours** they all came to see me after the class; **je vais aller ~ le responsable du rayon** I'm going to go and see the head of the department; **4** (estimer) **~ qn gentil/pénible** to think sb is nice/tiresome; **je trouve ça bizarre/drôle** I think it's strange/funny, I find it strange/funny; **comment trouves-tu mon ami?** what do you think of my friend?, how do you like my friend?; **j'ai trouvé bon de vous prévenir** I thought it right to warn you; **~ un intérêt à qch** to find sth interesting; **elle ne me trouve que des défauts** she only sees my faults; **je me demande ce qu'elle lui trouve!** I wonder what she sees in him/her!; **elle m'a trouvé bonne mine** she thought I looked well; **je te trouve bien calme, qu'est-ce que tu as?** you're very quiet, what's the matter?; **tu trouves?** do you think so?; **5** (imaginer) to come up with [*raison, excuse, moyen, produit*]; **~ à s'occuper** to find sth to do; **~ à redire** to find fault; **~ le moyen de faire** LIT, IRON to manage to do;

il n'a rien trouvé de mieux que de le leur répéter! IRON he WOULD have to go and tell them!

II se trouver *vpr* **1** (être situé) to be; **se ~ à Rome** to be in Rome; **le sommaire se trouve page 11** the table of contents is on page 11; **se ~ confronté à de grosses difficultés** to have run into major problems; **2** (se sentir) to feel; **se ~ mal à l'aise quelque part** to feel uneasy somewhere; **se ~ bien quelque part** to be happy somewhere; **j'ai failli me ~ mal** I nearly passed out; **3** (se considérer) **il se ~ beau** he thinks he's good-looking; **4** (se procurer) to find [*raison, excuse, motif*]; **trouve-toi une occupation** find yourself something to do; **elle s'est trouvé un petit ami** she's found herself a boyfriend.

III *v impers* **il se trouve que je le connais** I happen to know him; **il se trouve qu'elle ne leur avait rien dit** as it happened, she hadn't told them anything; **ça s'est trouvé comme ça** it just happened that way; **si ça se trouve**○ **ça te plaira** you might like it.

truand /tʀyɑ̃/ *nm* **1** (membre de la pègre) gangster, mobster; **2** (escroc) crook.

trublion /tʀyblijɔ̃/ *nm* troublemaker.

truc /tʀyk/ *nm* **1**○ (procédé) knack; **avoir un ~ pour gagner de l'argent** to know a good way of making money; **ça y est, j'ai pigé le ~** that's it, I've got it; **2**○ (chose) thing; (dont on a oublié le nom) thingummy○, whatsit○; **passe-moi le ~ qui est sur la table** pass me the thingummy○ ou whatsit○ on the table; **3**○ (fait quelconque) thing; **il y a un ~ qui ne va pas** there's something wrong; **je viens juste de penser à un ~** I've just thought of something; **le vélo, c'est pas mon ~**○ cycling's not my thing; **moi, mon ~ c'est les vacances à la campagne** what I love is a holiday GB ou vacation US in the country; **4** (savoir-faire) trick; **un ~ du métier** a trick of the trade; **y a un ~**○ there's a trick to it; **5** (personne) what's-his-name/what's-her-name, thingy○.

trucage /tʀykaʒ/ *nm* **1** CIN, THÉÂT special effect; **2** (de comptes, dossier) doctoring; (d'élections) rigging, fixing.

truchement /tʀyʃmɑ̃/ *nm* (intermédiaire) LITER **par le ~ de qch** through sth; **par le ~ de qn** through the intervention of sb.

truculence /tʀykylɑ̃s/ *nf* earthiness.

truculent, **~e** /tʀykylɑ̃, ɑ̃t/ *adj* earthy.

truelle /tʀyɛl/ *nf* trowel.

truffe /tʀyf/ *nf* **1** (champignon, chocolat) truffle; **2** (de chien) nose.

truffer /tʀyfe/ [1] *vtr* **1** CULIN to stuff [sth] with truffles [*pâté, dinde*]; **2** (remplir) **il a truffé son discours de citations** he crammed his speech with quotations; **la pièce était truffée de micros** the room was full of bugging devices; **ta lettre est truffée de fautes** your letter is riddled with mistakes.

truie /tʀɥi/ *nf* sow.

truite /tʀɥit/ *nf* trout.

truquage = **trucage**.

truquer /tʀyke/ [1] *vtr* **1** (altérer) to fiddle○ [*comptes, résultats*]; to doctor [*dossier, déclaration*]; **2** JEUX to mark [*cartes*]; **3** (fausser) to fix, to rig [*enquête, élections, match*]; **un combat truqué** a rigged fight.

trust /tʀœst/ *nm* (groupement) trust; (entreprise puissante) trust, cartel; **loi anti-~** anti-trust law.

tsar /tsaʀ/ *nm* tsar, czar.

tsigane = **tzigane**.

TTC *written abbr* ▶ **taxe**.

tu /ty/ *pron pers* **1** GÉN you; **~ es en retard** you're late; **2** RELIG you, thou‡.

IDIOMES **être à ~ et à toi avec qn** to be on familiar terms with sb, to be pally○ with sb.

tuant○, **~e** /tɥɑ̃, ɑ̃t/ *adj* exhausting.

tuba /tyba/ *nm* **1** ▶ **392** MUS tuba; **2** SPORT snorkel.

tubage /tybaʒ/ *nm* **1** MÉD intubation; **2** (de forage) (well) casing.

tube /tyb/ **I** *nm* **1** (objet cylindrique) tube; (tuyau) pipe; **2** (contenant) tube; **3**○ (chanson à succès) hit; **4** (lampe) fluorescent light, lamp.

II à pleins tubes○ *loc adv* **mettre le son à pleins**

~s to turn the sound right up○; **faire passer un disque à pleins ~s** to play a record at full blast; **déconner** ◗ **à pleins ~s** (faire des erreurs) to do really stupid things; (dire des bêtises) to talk a load of rubbish○.
■ **~ cathodique** cathode ray tube; **~ digestif** digestive tract; **~ à essai** test tube; **~ au néon** fluorescent light; **~ de rouge à lèvres** lipstick.

tubercule /tybɛrkyl/ nm **1** BOT tuber; **2** ANAT tuberosity; **3** MÉD tubercle.

tuberculeux, -euse /tybɛrkylø, øz/ **I** adj [patient] tubercular.
II nm,f TB ou tuberculosis sufferer.

tuberculose /tybɛrkyloz/ ▶ 196 ⌐ nf tuberculosis, TB.

tubulaire /tybylɛr/ adj tubular.

tubulure /tybylyr/ nf **1** TECH (ensemble des tubes) tubing; (orifice) connection piece, neck; **2** (conduit) pipe.

TUC /tyk/ nmpl (abbr = **travaux d'utilité collective**) paid community service (for the young unemployed).

tué /tɥe/ nm person killed; **sept ~s, cinq blessés** seven people killed, five injured.

tuer /tɥe/ [1] **I** vtr **1** (faire périr) LIT to kill [personne, animal, plante]; FIG to kill [commerce, initiative]; **l'alcool tue** alcohol kills; **tu ne tueras point** BIBLE thou shalt not kill; **elle a été tuée d'une balle dans la tête** she was shot in the head and killed; **six personnes ont été tuées par balles** six people were shot dead; **~ qn à coups de bâton** to beat sb to death; **2**○ (épuiser) **les enfants m'ont tuée ce matin** the children have worn me out ou run me ragged○ this morning; **tu sais, quelquefois tu me tues!** I think you'll be the death of me!
II se tuer vpr **1** (trouver la mort) [personne] to be killed; **se ~ en voiture** to be killed in a car accident; **il s'est tué en tombant d'un toit** he fell to his death from a roof; **2** (se suicider) to kill oneself; **3**○ (s'épuiser) **se ~ au travail** ou **à la tâche** to work oneself to death; **se ~ à faire** to kill oneself doing; **je me tue à te le dire** I've told you a thousand times.
IDIOMES **~ le temps** to kill time.

tuerie /tyri/ nf killings (pl).

tue-tête: à tue-tête /atytɛt/ loc adv [chanter, crier] at the top of one's voice.

tueur, -euse /tɥœr, øz/ **I** adj [cellule] killer.
II nm,f **1** (assassin) killer; **2** ▶ 374 ⌐ (ouvrier d'abattoir) slaughterman/slaughterwoman.
■ **~ à gages** hired ou professional killer.

tuile /tɥil/ nf **1** CONSTR tile; **2**○ (événement fâcheux) blow; **tu parles d'une ~!** what a blow!
■ **~ aux amandes** CULIN almond biscuit.

tulipe /tylip/ nf **1** BOT tulip; **2** (lampe) tulip-shaped lamp.

tulipier /tylipje/ nm tulip tree.

tuméfier /tymefje/ [2] vtr to make [sth] swell up [partie du corps]; **avoir les paupières tuméfiées** to have swollen eyelids.

tumeur /tymœr/ nf tumour GB.

tumulte /tymylt/ nm **1** (désordre bruyant) uproar; **s'achever dans le ~** to end in uproar; **2** (agitation) turmoil.

tumultueux, -euse /tymyltɥø, øz/ adj [période, journée] turbulent; [vie, jeunesse] tempestuous; [relations, entrevue] stormy.

tumulus /tymylys/ nm inv burial mound, tumulus SPÉC.

tunique /tynik/ nf **1** (vêtement) tunic; **2** ANAT tunic, tunica SPÉC.

tunnel /tynɛl/ nm tunnel; **le ~ sous la Manche** the Channel Tunnel.
IDIOMES **voir le bout du ~** to see light at the end of the tunnel.

turban /tyrbã/ nm turban.

turbin ◗ /tyrbɛ̃/ nm daily grind○, work; **aller au ~** to go to work.

turbine /tyrbin/ nf turbine.

turboréacteur /tyrboreaktœr/ nm turbojet (engine).

turbot /tyrbo/ nm turbot.

turbulence /tyrbylãs/ nf **1** (tourbillon) turbulence ¢; **zone de ~s** area of turbulence; **2** (indiscipline) unruliness; (agitation) unrest ¢.

turbulent, ~e /tyrbylã, ãt/ adj [enfant] unruly; [classe] rowdy, unruly; [vie] tempestuous; [adolescent, région, ville] rebellious.

turc, turque /tyrk/ ▶ 338 ⌐, 394 ⌐ **I** adj Turkish; **toilettes** ou **WC à la turque** hole-in-the-ground toilet.
II nm LING Turkish.

turfiste /tœrfist/ nmf racegoer, punter○ GB.

turlupiner○ /tyrlypine/ [1] vtr [idée, problème] to bother, to bug○.

turpitude /tyrpityd/ nf **1** (caractère) turpitude SOUT, depravity; **2** (acte) base act; (parole) low remark.

turque ▶ **turc**.

Turquie /tyrki/ ▶ 232 ⌐ nprf Turkey.

turquoise /tyrkwaz/ ▶ 141 ⌐ adj inv, nf turquoise.

tutelle /tytɛl/ nf **1** JUR (d'enfant, adulte) guardianship, tutelage; **placer qn sous ~** to place sb in the care of a guardian; **2** ADMIN ~ supervision; **autorité de ~** supervision authority; **3** (en droit international) (régime de) ~ trusteeship; **territoire sous ~** trust territory; **4** (dépendance) supervision, domination.

tuteur, -trice /tytœr, tris/ **I** nm,f **1** JUR guardian; **2** ▶ 374 ⌐ SCOL, UNIV tutor.
II nm BOT stake, support.

tutoiement /tytwamã/ nm use of the form 'tu'.

tutorat /tytora/ nm **1** SCOL, UNIV tutorial system; **2** JUR system of guardianship.

tutoyer /tytwaje/ [23] **I** vtr to address [sb] using the 'tu' form; FIG to be on familiar terms with [auteurs classiques].
II se tutoyer vpr to address one another using the 'tu' form.

tutu /tyty/ nm tutu.

tuyau, pl ~x /tɥijo/ nm **1** TECH pipe; **2**○ (information) tip○; **un ~ crevé** a lousy tip.
■ **~ d'arrosage** hose; **~ de cheminée** flue; **~ d'échappement** exhaust; **~ de poêle** stovepipe.

tuyauterie /tɥijotri/ nf **1** TECH piping ¢; **2** MUS pipes (pl).

TVA /tevea/ nf (abbr = **taxe à la valeur ajoutée**) VAT.

tympan /tɛ̃pã/ nm eardrum.

type /tip/ **I** nm **1** (genre) type, kind; **les emplois de ce ~ sont rares** jobs of this kind are rare; **un climat de ~ tropical** a tropical-type climate; **2** (représentant) (classic) example; **elle est le ~ même de la femme d'affaires** she's the classic example of a business woman; **3** (modèle) type, kind; **un avion d'un ~ nouveau** a new type of plane; **4** (caractères physiques) type; **il a le ~ nordique** he is the Nordic type; **ce n'est pas mon ~** he's/she's not my type; **5**○ (homme) guy○, chap○; **quel sale ~!** what a swine○ ou bastard◗!; **c'est un chic ~** he's a really nice guy; **un brave ~** a nice chap○; **un pauvre ~** a pathetic individual.
II (-)**type** (in compounds) typical, classic; **l'intellectuel(-)~** the typical intellectual; **l'exemple(-)~** the typical example; **un cas(-)~ de schizophrénie** a classic case of schizophrenia; **le formulaire(-)~** the standard application form.

typer /tipe/ [1] vtr [auteur, dramaturge] to portray [sb] as a type [personnage]; [acteur] to play [sb] as a type [personnage].

typhoïde /tifoid/ ▶ 196 ⌐ nf typhoid fever.

typhon /tifɔ̃/ nm typhoon.

typhus /tifys/ ▶ 196 ⌐ nm inv typhus.

typique /tipik/ adj **1** (caractéristique) typical; **2** (pittoresque) CONTROV [sculpture, village] typical.

typiquement /tipikmã/ adv typically; **une famille ~ américaine** a typically American family.

typographe /tipɔgraf/ ▶ 374 ⌐ nmf typographer.

typographie /tipↄgʀafi/ *nf* typography.

typographique /tipↄgʀafik/ *adj* typographical;
erreur ~ typographical ou printer's error, misprint.

typologie /tipↄlↄʒi/ *nf* typology.

tyran /tiʀɑ̃/ *nm* tyrant; **~ domestique** domestic
tyrant.

tyrannie /tiʀani/ *nf* tyranny; **subir la ~ de qn/qch**
to be tyrannized by sb/sth.

tyrannique /tiʀanik/ *adj* tyrannical.

tyranniser /tiʀanize/ [1] *vtr* to tyrannize.

tzigane /dzigan, tsigan/ **I** *adj*, *nmf* gypsy.
II ▶ 338⌋ *nm* LING Romany.

Uu

u, U /y/ *nm inv* u, U; **en (forme de) U** U-shaped.

ubiquité /ybikɥite/ *nf* ubiquity SOUT; **je n'ai pas le don d'~!** I can't be everywhere at once!

UDF /ydeɛf/ *nf* (*abbr* = **Union pour la démocratie française**) *French political party of the centre right.*

ukrainien, -ienne /ykRɛnjɛ̃, ɛn/ ▶ 394, 338 I *adj* Ukrainian.
II *nm* LING Ukrainian.

ulcère /ylsɛR/ ▶ 196 *nm* ulcer.

ulcérer /ylseRe/ [14] *vtr* 1 (outrer) [*propos, comportement*] to sicken; 2 MÉD to ulcerate [*tissu, organe*].

ULM /yɛlɛm/ ▶ 329 *nm inv* (*abbr* = **ultraléger motorisé**) (engin) microlight; (sport) microlighting.

ultérieur, ~e /ylteRjœR/ *adj* subsequent; **une date ~e** a later date.

ultérieurement /ylteRjœRmɑ̃/ *adv* 1 (par la suite) subsequently; 2 (plus tard) later.

ultimatum /yltimatɔm/ *nm* ultimatum; **lancer un ~ à qn** to present sb with an ultimatum.

ultime /yltim/ *adj* 1 (dernier d'une série) final; 2 (suprême) ultimate; 3 LING ultimate.

ultra /yltRa/ I *adj* [*groupe*] extremist.
II *nmf* 1 POL extremist; 2 HIST ultraroyalist.

ultraconfidentiel, -ielle /yltRakɔ̃fidɑ̃sjɛl/ *adj* top secret.

ultragauche /yltRagoʃ/ *nf* POL **l'~** the radical leftists (*pl*).

ultraléger, -ère /yltRaleʒe, ɛR/ *adj* [*matériau, cigarette*] ultra light; [*équipement, tissu*] very light.

ultramoderne /yltRamɔdɛRn/ *adj* [*maison*] ultra modern; [*technique, système, matériel*] state-of-the-art (*épith*).

ultrarapide /yltRaRapid/ *adj* high-speed (*épith*).

ultrasecret, -ète /yltRasəkRɛ, ɛt/ *adj* top secret.

ultrasensible /yltRasɑ̃sibl/ *adj* [*personne*] hypersensitive; [*appareil, film*] ultrasensitive; [*problème, donnée*] highly sensitive.

ultrason /yltRasɔ̃/ *nm* ultrasound ¢.

ultraviolet /yltRavjɔlɛ/ *nm* PHYS ultraviolet ray; **séance d'~s** (en soins du corps) session on a sunbed.

ululer /ylyle/ [1] *vi* to hoot.

un, une[1] /œ̃(n), yn/ ▶ 399, 298 I *art indéf* (*pl* **des**) 1 (au singulier) a, an; **avec ~ sang-froid remarquable** with remarkable self-control; **il n'a pas dit ~ mot** he didn't say a ou one word; **il n'y avait pas ~ arbre** there wasn't a single tree; **~ chien est plus docile qu'~ chat** dogs are more docile than cats; **~ jour, je t'en parlerai** I'll tell you about it one day; 2 (au pluriel) **il y avait des mille-pattes et des scorpions** there were millipedes and scorpions; **il y a des gens qui ne comprennent jamais rien** there are some people who never understand anything; **des invités avaient déjà défait leur cravate** some guests had already loosened their ties; 3 (en emphase) **il fait ~ froid** or **~ de ces froids!** it's so cold!; **elle m'a donné une de ces gifles!** she gave me such a slap!
II *pron* (*pl* **uns, unes**) GÉN one; **(l')~ d'entre or de nous** one of us; **(l')~ des meilleurs** one of the best; **~ de ces jours** or **quatre**○ one of these days; **les ~s pensent que…** some think that…
III *adj* one, a (*devant une consonne*), an (*devant une voyelle*); **trente et une personnes ont été blessées**

un

Emploi et prononciation de *a* et *an*
On emploie *a* /ə/ devant les consonnes, les h aspirés et les semi-consonnes /j/, /w/ (dans *a university, a one-eyed man*), et *an* /ən/ devant les voyelles et h muets (*hour, honest, heir*).

un = pronom
L'emploi de *un* en corrélation avec *autre* est traité sous *autre*. Voir aussi *chose*, *comme*, ainsi que les verbes avec lesquels le pronom se substitue familièrement à un groupe nominal comme *coller* – *en coller une*, *placer* – *en placer une* etc.).

un = adjectif numéral
En général, *un*, adjectif numéral, se traduit indifféremment par *a* ou *one*:

> j'ai un garçon et deux filles
> = I have a (*ou* one) boy and two girls

En revanche *un* se traduit par *one* quand on veut insister sur le nombre. Ainsi, on dira:

> il ne reste qu'une pomme (pas deux)
> = there's only one apple left
> mais: il ne reste qu'une pomme (pas d'autres fruits)
> = there's only an apple left

> j'ai un frère et deux sœurs
> (nous sommes quatre enfants)
> = I have one brother and two sisters
> mais: j'ai un frère qui est informaticien
> (j'ai d'autres frères)
> = I have a brother who is a computer scientist

> ça coûte une livre
> = it costs a pound *ou* it costs one pound
> mais: ça coûte une livre cinquante
> = it costs one pound fifty

> cela a pris une heure
> = it took an hour *ou* it took one hour
> mais: il est une heure
> = it is one o'clock

thirty-one people were injured; **ici, il pleut ~ jour sur deux** it rains every other day here.
IV *nm,f* one; **il y en a ~ par personne** there's one each; **les deux villes n'en font plus qu'une** the two cities have merged into one; **~ à** ou **par ~** one by one.
V○ *adv* firstly, for one thing; **~, je fais ce que je veux et deux ça ne te regarde pas!** firstly, I do what I like and secondly it's none of your business!
VI *nm* 1 (nombre) one; **~, deux, trois, partez!** one, two, three, go!; 2 (valeur ordinale) **page/scène ~** page/scene one; 3 FIG **elle ne faisait qu'~ avec sa machine** she and her machine were as one.
IDIOMES **s'en jeter ~ (derrière la cravate)**○ to knock back a drink○; **il est menteur comme pas ~** he's the biggest liar; **~ pour tous et tous pour ~** all for one and one for all; ▶ **dix**.

unanime /ynanim/ *adj* unanimous (**à faire** in doing).

unanimement /ynanimmɑ̃/ *adv* 1 (en politique) unanimously; 2 FIG universally; **il est ~ célébré comme un grand écrivain** he is universally hailed as a great writer.

unanimité /ynanimite/ *nf* unanimity; **à l'~** unanimously; **il a été élu à l'~ moins deux voix** he was elected with only two votes against; **faire l'~** to have unanimous support ou backing (**parmi** from).

une² /yn/ **I** *art indéf, pron, adj* ▶ **un I, II, III, IV**.

II *nf* **la ~** the front page; **être à la ~** to be in the headlines, to be on the front page.

UNESCO /ynɛsko/ *nf* (*abbr* = **United Nations Educational, Scientific and Cultural Organization**) UNESCO.

uni, **~e** /yni/ **I** *pp* ▶ **unir**.

II *pp adj* [*communauté, famille*] close-knit; [*amis, couple*] close; [*peuple, militants*] united (**dans** in).

III *adj* **1** (d'une teinte) [*tissu, couleur*] plain; **2** (sans aspérité) [*surface*] smooth, even; [*mer*] calm.

IV *nm* **porter de l'~** to wear plain colours^{GB}.

unicellulaire /yniselylɛʀ/ *adj* unicellular.

unicité /ynisite/ *nf* uniqueness.

unidimensionnel, **-elle** /ynidimãsjɔnɛl/ *adj* unidimensional.

unidirectionnel, **-elle** /ynidiʀɛksjɔnɛl/ *adj* TÉLÉCOM [*émetteur*] unidirectional; [*récepteur*] one-way.

unième /ynjɛm/ [▶ **399**], **156**] *adj* first; **vingt et ~** twenty-first.

unification /ynifikasjɔ̃/ *nf* unification.

unifier /ynifje/ [2] **I** *vtr* **1** (rassembler) to unify [*pays, forces,*]; **2** (homogénéiser) to standardize [*procédure*].

II s'unifier *vpr* [*pays, groupes*] to unite.

uniforme /ynifɔʀm/ **I** *adj* [*paysage, maisons, mouvement*] uniform; [*augmentation, réglementation*] across-the-board (*épith*); [*existence, journées*] unchanging.

II *nm* (costume) uniform.

uniformément /ynifɔʀmemã/ *adv* uniformly.

uniformiser /ynifɔʀmize/ [1] *vtr* to standardize [*programmes, taux*]; to make [sth] uniform [*teinte*].

uniformité /ynifɔʀmite/ *nf* (de goûts, résultats, paysage) uniformity; (de vie) monotony.

unijambiste /yniʒɑ̃bist/ **I** *adj* **être ~** to have only one leg.

II *nmf* one-legged person.

unilatéral, **~e**, *mpl* **-aux** /ynilateʀal, o/ *adj* unilateral; **stationnement ~** parking on one side only.

unilingue /ynilɛ̃g/ *adj* unilingual, monolingual.

uninominal, **~e**, *mpl* **-aux** /yninɔminal, o/ *adj* POL [*scrutin*] for a single candidate (*épith, après n*).

union /ynjɔ̃/ *nf* **1** (alliance) union; **2** (association) association; **~ de consommateurs** consumers' association; **3** (mariage) union SOUT, marriage; **4** MATH union.

■ **~ douanière** customs union; **~ libre** cohabitation; **~ sacrée** united front; **~ sportive**, US sports club; **Union européenne** European Union; **Union des Républiques socialistes soviétiques** HIST Union of Soviet Socialist Republics; **Union soviétique** HIST Soviet Union.

IDIOMES **l'~ fait la force** PROV united we stand, divided we fall.

unique /ynik/ *adj* **1** (seul de son espèce) (*before n*) only; **il est l'~ témoin** he's the only witness; **2** (seul pour tous) single; **parti ~** single party; **système à parti ~** one-party system; **'prix ~'** 'all at one price'; **3** (remarquable) unique; **c'est une occasion ~ de faire** it's a unique opportunity to do; **~ au monde** [*personne, objet, fait*] unique in the world; **~ en son genre** [*personne, objet*] one of a kind (*jamais épith*); [*fait, événement*] one-off (*épith*), one-shot (*épith*) US; **4**○ (singulier) **ce type est ~!** that guy's priceless[○]!; **5** (sans frère ni sœur) **être fille** or **fils ~** to be an only child.

uniquement /ynikmã/ *adv* **1** (exclusivement) exclusively; **il pense ~ à sa famille/s'amuser** all he thinks about is his family/having fun; **en vente ~ par correspondance** available by mail order only; **2** (seulement) only; **c'était ~ pour te taquiner** it was only to tease you; **nous ne sommes pas ici ~ pour travailler** we're not here just to work; **~ dans un but commercial** purely for commercial ends.

unir /yniʀ/ [3] **I** *vtr* **1** (rassembler) to unite [*pays, territoire*] (**à** to); [*liens, intérêts, passion*] to unite, bind [sb] together [*personnes, groupes, pays*]; **des hommes unis par les mêmes idées** men brought together by

the same ideas; **2** (combiner) to combine; **méthode qui unit simplicité et efficacité** method which combines simplicity with effectiveness; **unissons nos ressources** let us combine ou pool our resources; **3** (marier) to join [sb] in matrimony SOUT.

II s'unir *vpr* **1** (se rassembler) to unite (**à, avec** with; **contre** against); **2** (se marier) to marry.

unisexe /ynisɛks/ *adj* unisex.

unisson /ynisɔ̃/ *nm* unison; **à l'~** MUS in unison; FIG in accord.

unitaire /ynitɛʀ/ *adj* **1** POL [*manifestation, campagne, stratégie*] common; **2** COMM [*prix, coût*] unit (*épith*).

unité /ynite/ *nf* **1** (cohésion) unity; **~ d'action/de lieu** THÉÂT unity of action/place; **réaliser l'~ d'un pays** to unify a country; **un film qui manque d'~** film lacking in cohesion; **2** (élément) unit; **20 francs l'~** 20 francs each; **vendre qch à l'~** to sell sth singly; **3** (dans ensemble) unit; **~ de production** production unit; **4** (étalon) unit; **~ monétaire** unit of currency; **5** MATH unit; **la colonne des ~s** the units column; **6** MIL (troupe) unit; (navire) craft; **7** TÉLÉCOM unit; **télé-carte 50 ~s** 50-unit phonecard.

■ **~ centrale** (**de traitement**) ORDINAT central processing unit, CPU; **~ de disque** ORDINAT disk drive.

univers /ynivɛʀ/ *nm inv* **1** (en astronomie) universe; **2** (humanité) whole world; **3** (monde) world; **l'~ de Kafka** Kafka's world.

universaliser /ynivɛʀsalize/ [1] *vtr* to universalize.

universalité /ynivɛʀsalite/ *nf* universality.

universel, **-elle** /ynivɛʀsɛl/ **I** *adj* [*langage, thème, méthode*] universal; [*histoire*] world (*épith*); [*remède*] all-purpose (*épith*).

II *nm* LING, PHILOS universal.

universitaire /ynivɛʀsitɛʀ/ **I** *adj* [*échange, ville, cursus*] university (*épith*); [*travail, niveau*] academic.

II *nmf* academic.

université /ynivɛʀsite/ *nf* **1** (établissement) university GB, college US; **être à l'~** to be at university GB, to be in college US; **2** (enseignement supérieur) higher education.

■ **~ d'été** UNIV summer school; POL party conference (*assembling young members and potential members*).

univoque /ynivɔk/ *adj* **1** LING univocal; **2** [*réalité, fait*] unequivocal.

uns *pron* ▶ **un II**.

Untel, **Unetelle** /œtɛl, yntɛl/ *nm,f* **Monsieur ~** Mr so-and-so; **Madame Unetelle** Mrs so-and-so.

urbain, **~e** /yʀbɛ̃, ɛn/ *adj* **1** (de la ville) urban; **vie ~e** city life; **2** FML (civil) urbane.

urbanisation /yʀbanizasjɔ̃/ *nf* urbanization.

urbanisé, **~e** /yʀbanize/ **I** *pp* ▶ **urbaniser**.

II *pp adj* [*zone*] built-up (*épith*).

urbaniser /yʀbanize/ [1] *vtr* to urbanize [*région*].

urbanisme /yʀbanism/ *nm* town planning GB, city planning US.

urbaniste /yʀbanist/ [▶ **374**] *nmf* town planner GB, city planner US.

urée /yʀe/ *nf* urea.

uretère /yʀtɛʀ/ *nm* ureter.

urètre /yʀɛtʀ/ *nm* urethra.

urgence /yʀʒɑ̃s/ *nf* **1** (caractère) urgency; **il y a ~** it's urgent; **d'~** [*agir, se réunir*] immediately; **de toute** ou **d'extrême ~** as a matter of great urgency; **transporter qn d'~ à l'hôpital** to rush sb to hospital GB ou the hospital US; **convoquer qn d'~** to summon sb urgently; **appeler qn d'~** to call sb immediately; **opérer qn d'~** to give sb emergency surgery; **mesures d'~** emergency measures; **en ~** as a matter of urgency, immediately; **2** (cas urgent) GÉN matter of urgency; MÉD emergency; **le service des ~s, les ~s** the casualty department, casualty *C*.

urgent, **~e** /yʀʒɑ̃, ɑ̃t/ *adj* urgent; **il est ~ de prendre des mesures** measures must be taken immediately.

Uri /yʀi/ [▶ **509**] *npr* **le canton d'~** the canton of Uri.

urinaire /yʀinɛʀ/ adj urinary.

urinal, pl -aux /yʀinal, o/ nm urinal.

urine /yʀin/ nf urine ¢; **une analyse des ~s** urinalysis.

uriner /yʀine/ [1] vi to urinate.

urinoir /yʀinwaʀ/ nm **1** (lieu) public urinal; **2** (cuvette) urinal.

urne /yʀn/ nf **1** (pour voter) **~ (électorale)** ballot box; **se rendre aux ~s** to go to the polls; **être appelé aux ~s** to be called upon to vote; **2** (vase) urn; **~ cinéraire** or **funéraire** funeral urn.

urologie /yʀɔlɔʒi/ nf urology.

URSS /yɛʀsɛs, yʀs/ nprf HIST (abbr = **Union des Républiques socialistes soviétiques**) USSR.

urticaire /yʀtikɛʀ/ ▶196⟩ nf hives.
IDIOMES **donner de l'~ à qn**○ to get on sb's nerves.

us /ys/ nmpl **les ~ et coutumes** the ways and customs.

US /yɛs/ nf: abbr ▶ **union**.

USA /yɛsa/ nmpl (abbr = **United States of America**) USA.

usage /yzaʒ/ nm **1** (fait d'utiliser) use; **à l'~** [rétrécir, se distendre] with use; **par l'~** [sali, encrassé] with use; **en ~** in use; **disqualifié pour ~ d'anabolisants** disqualified for using anabolic steroids; **faire ~ de** to use; **faire ~ de son autorité** to exercise one's authority; **faire bon/mauvais ~ de qch** to put sth to good/bad use; **faire de l'~** [tissu, vêtement] to last; **2** (possibilité d'utiliser) use; **'réservé à l'~ du personnel** 'for staff use only'; **à ~ privé** for private use; **à ~ externe** for external use only; **à ~s multiples** [appareil] multipurpose (épith); **il a perdu l'~ d'un œil** he's lost the use of one eye; **hors d'~** [vêtement] unwearable; [machine] out of order; **3** LING usage; **en ~** in usage; **les règles du bon ~** the rules of good usage; **4** (pratique courante) custom; **l'~ est de faire** (dans la vie courante) the custom is to do; (dans la vie professionnelle) it's usual practice to do; **comme le veut l'~** as is customary; **conformément aux ~s** in accordance with custom; **politesses d'~** customary courtesies; **précautions d'~** usual precautions.
■ **~ de faux** JUR use of false documents; **faux et ~ de faux** forgery and use of false documents.

usagé, ~e /yzaʒe/ adj **1** (usé) [vêtement] well-worn; [pneu] worn; **2** (déjà utilisé) [vêtement, seringue] used.

usager /yzaʒe/ nm (de service) user; (de langue) speaker; **~ de la route** road-user.

usant, ~e /yzɑ̃, ɑ̃t/ adj [travail, vie] exhausting, wearing; [personne] wearing, tiresome.

usé, ~e /yze/ I pp ▶ **user**.
II pp adj [vêtement, chaussure, objet, pièce] worn; [personne] worn-down; [organisme, cœur, yeux] worn-out; [sujet, plaisanterie] hackneyed; **une veste complètement ~e** a threadbare jacket; **~ jusqu'à la corde** LIT [vêtement, tapis] threadbare; [pneu] worn down to the tread; FIG [plaisanterie] hackneyed.

user /yze/ [1] I vtr [personne, temps, frottement] to wear out [vêtement, chaussure, objet]; [travail, soucis, temps] to wear down [personne]; **les piles sont usées** the batteries have run down ou out; **~ ses vêtements jusqu'à la corde** to wear one's clothes out; **~ sa santé** to ruin one's health.
II **user de** vtr ind to use [formule, termes, alcool]; to exercise [droit]; to exploit [possibilité]; to take [précautions]; **~ de diplomatie** to be diplomatic; **~ et abuser de qch** to use and abuse sth; **il faut en ~ avec modération** it should be used in moderation.

III **s'user** vpr **1** [vêtement, chaussure] to wear out; **2** [personne] **s'~ à la tâche** to wear oneself out with overwork; **s'~ la santé** to ruin one's health.

usinage /yzinaʒ/ nm **1** (fabrication avec une machine-outil) machining; **2** (fabrication industrielle) manufacture.

usine /yzin/ nf factory; **fabriqué en ~** factory-made; **c'est l'~, ici**○! FIG it's like a production line here!
■ **~ métallurgique** ironworks (pl); **~ sidérurgique** steelworks (pl).

usiner /yzine/ [1] vtr **1** (avec machine-outil) to machine; **2** (fabriquer) to manufacture.

usité, ~e /yzite/ adj commonly used (jamais épith); **peu ~** rarely used (jamais épith).

ustensile /ystɑ̃sil/ nm utensil.

usuel, -elle /yzɥɛl/ I adj [objet] everyday (épith); [mot, expression, appellation] common.
II nm (livre) reference book (not for loan).

usufruit /yzyfʀɥi/ nm JUR usufruct.

usure /yzyʀ/ nf **1** (détérioration) (de tissu, vêtement) wear and tear (**de** on); (de pneu, disque, machine) wear (**de** on); **résister à l'~** to wear well; **2** (affaiblissement) (de forces, d'énergie, adversaire) wearing down; (d'idéologie) waning; (de régime) declining power; **l'~ du pouvoir** the erosion of power; **3** (action corrosive) **~ du temps** wearing effect of time; **4** FIN, JUR usury.

usurier, -ière /yzyʀje, ɛʀ/ nm,f usurer, loan shark○.

usurpateur, -trice /yzyʀpatœʀ, tʀis/ nm,f usurper.

usurpation /yzyʀpasjɔ̃/ nf usurpation.

usurper /yzyʀpe/ [1] vtr to usurp [titre, réputation].

ut /yt/ nm MUS C.

utérin, ~e /yteʀɛ̃, in/ adj ANAT, JUR uterine.

utérus /yteʀys/ nm inv womb, uterus.

utile /ytil/ I adj **1** (d'utilité générale) useful; **2** (d'utilité ponctuelle) **être ~** [personne, livre] to be helpful; [allumette, parapluie] to come in handy; **se rendre ~** to make oneself useful; **il est ~ de signaler** it's worth pointing out; **il n'a pas jugé ~ de me prévenir** he didn't think it necessary to let me know.
II nm **joindre l'~ à l'agréable** to mix business with pleasure.

utilement /ytilmɑ̃/ adv [combattre, intervenir] effectively; [s'occuper] usefully; [compléter] nicely.

utilisable /ytilizabl/ adj usable.

utilisateur, -trice /ytilizatœʀ, tʀis/ nm,f user.

utilisation /ytilizasjɔ̃/ nf **1** (fait d'utiliser) use; **2** (utilité) use (**de** for).

utiliser /ytilize/ [1] vtr **1** (se servir) to use [méthode, outil, produit]; to make use of [compétence]; **~ au mieux** to make the most of; **bien ~** to make good use of; **2** (exploiter) to use, to exploit [personne].

utilitaire /ytilitɛʀ/ adj [conception, époque] utilitarian; [préoccupation, enseignement, rôle] practical; [objet] functional; [véhicule] commercial.

utilité /ytilite/ nf **1** (caractère utile) usefulness; **être d'une grande ~** [livre, appareil] to be very useful; [personne] to be very helpful; **d'aucune ~** of no use; **ne pas voir l'~ de faire** not to see the point in doing; **2** (utilisation) use; **je n'en ai pas l'~** I have no use for it.

utopie /ytɔpi/ nf PHILOS, POL Utopia.

utopique /ytɔpik/ adj [projet, idée] utopian.

UV /yve/ nmpl (abbr = **ultraviolets**) PHYS ultraviolet rays; **séance d'~** session on a sunbed.

uvule /yvyl/ nf uvula.

Vv

v, V /ve/ *nm inv* (lettre) v, V; **en (forme de) V** [*objet*] V-shaped; **encolure en V** V-neck; **pull en V** V-necked sweater; ▶ **vitesse**.

va /va/ ▶ **aller¹**; ▶ **vat**.

vacance /vakɑ̃s/ **I** *nf* (de charge, poste) vacancy.
II vacances *nfpl* holiday GB, vacation US; **bonnes ~s!** have a good holiday GB ou vacation US!; **grandes ~s** SCOL summer holidays GB, summer ou long vacation US.

vacancier, -ière /vakɑ̃sje, ɛʀ/ *nm,f* holidaymaker GB, vacationer US.

vacant, ~e /vakɑ̃, ɑ̃t/ *adj* vacant.

vacarme /vakaʀm/ *nm* din, racket○.

vacataire /vakatɛʀ/ **I** *adj* temporary.
II *nmf* ADMIN temporary employee; SCOL supply teacher GB, substitute teacher US.

vaccin /vaksɛ̃/ *nm* MÉD vaccine; **~ contre la grippe** flu vaccine.

vaccination /vaksinasjɔ̃/ *nf* vaccination; **~ contre la polio/variole** polio/smallpox vaccination.

vacciner /vaksine/ [1] *vtr* **1** LIT to vaccinate (**contre** against); **se faire ~** to get vaccinated; **2** (endurcir) HUM **~ qn contre** to put sb off; **plus d'affaires sentimentales, je suis vacciné○!** no more romance, I've learned my lesson!

vache /vaʃ/ **I**○ *adj* mean, nasty; **coup ~** mean ou dirty trick.
II *nf* **1** (animal) cow; **2** (cuir) cowhide; **3**○ (personne méchante) (homme) bastard●; (femme) bitch●; **faire un coup en ~ à qn** to pull a mean ou dirty trick on sb.
III○ **vache de** *loc adj* hell○ of; **on m'a offert un ~ de bouquin** I was given a hell○ of a good book.
IV○ **la vache** *excl* (admiration) wow!; (commisération) **oh la ~!** il a dû se faire mal!** God! that must have hurt!; (agacement, douleur) hell!
■ **~ à eau** water bottle; **années de ~s grasses** prosperous years; **~ à lait** AGRIC dairy cow; FIG milch cow†, money-spinner○; **~ laitière** dairy cow; **années de ~s maigres** lean years; **~ sacrée** RELIG sacred cow.
IDIOMES **parler français comme une ~ espagnole**○ to speak very bad French.

vachement○ /vaʃmɑ̃/ *adv* really; **il a ~ maigri** he lost a hell of a lot○ of weight.

vacher /vaʃe/ ▶ 374 *nm* cowman.

vachère /vaʃɛʀ/ ▶ 374 *nf* cowgirl.

vacherie○ /vaʃʀi/ *nf* **1** (attitude) meanness, nastiness; **2** (propos) nasty ou bitchy○ remark; **3** (sale coup) dirty trick; **4** (calamité) **c'est une vraie ~ ce virus** this virus is a bloody● GB ou damned○ nuisance.

vachette /vaʃɛt/ *nf* **1** (animal) young cow; **2** (cuir) calfskin.

vacillant, ~e /vasijɑ̃, ɑ̃t/ *adj* **1** (tremblant) [*jambes*] unsteady; [*personne*] unsteady on one's legs (jamais épith); [*lumière, flamme*] flickering; **2** (fragile) [*pouvoir, majorité*] shaky; [*santé, mémoire, raison*] failing.

vacillement /vasijmɑ̃/ *nm* **1** (mouvement) (de chose) swaying ¢; (de flamme) flickering ¢; **2** (irrésolution) wavering ¢; **3** (affaiblissement) faltering ¢.

vaciller /vasije/ [1] *vi* **1** (être chancelant) [*personne*] to be unsteady on one's legs; [*jambes*] to be unsteady; **2** (osciller) [*personne, objet*] to sway; [*lumière, flamme*]

to flicker; **3** (se détériorer) [*santé, mémoire, raison*] to fail; [*pouvoir, majorité*] to weaken.

vadrouille○ /vadʀuj/ *nf* stroll; **être en ~** to be wandering about; **partir en ~** to wander off.

vadrouiller○ /vadʀuje/ [1] *vi* to wander around.

va-et-vient /vaevjɛ̃/ *nm inv* **1** (allées et venues) (de personnes, véhicules) comings and goings (*pl*); (de dossiers, d'idées) to-ing and fro-ing; **faire le ~** [*personne, bateau*] to go to and fro; [*dossier*] to go back and forth; **2** ÉLECTROTECH two-way switch.

vagabond, ~e /vagabɔ̃, ɔ̃d/ **I** *adj* [*personne*] wandering (épith); [*chien*] stray (épith); [*existence, esprit, imagination*] roving (épith); [*humeur*] ever-changing.
II *nm,f* vagrant.

vagabondage /vagabɔ̃daʒ/ *nm* **1** (errance) (de personne) wandering; (de pensée) wanderings *pl*; **2** JUR vagrancy ¢.

vagabonder /vagabɔ̃de/ [1] *vi* **1** [*personne, animal*] to wander (**dans** through); **~ à travers le monde** to roam the world; **2** [*imagination*] to wander; [*pensées*] to stray.

vagin /vaʒɛ̃/ *nm* vagina.

vagir /vaʒiʀ/ [3] *vi* [*nouveau-né*] to wail.

vagissement /vaʒismɑ̃/ *nm* wail.

vague¹ /vag/ **I** *adj* (imprécis) vague; **d'un air ~** [*contempler*] vaguely; **ce sont de ~s parents** they're distant relatives.
II *nm* **il regardait dans le ~** he was staring into space; **ton regard était perdu dans le ~** you had a faraway look in your eyes; **la direction est restée dans le ~ sur la question des salaires** management has remained vague as to the question of wages.
■ **avoir du ~ à l'âme** to feel melancholic.

vague² /vag/ *nf* **1** LIT wave; **faire des ~s** [*vent*] to make ripples; FIG [*démission, scandale*] to cause a stir, to make waves; **2** FIG wave; **une ~ de violence** a wave of violence; **par ~s** [*arriver, attaquer*] in waves.
■ **~ de chaleur** heatwave; **~ de froid** cold spell.
IDIOMES **être au creux de la ~** to be at a low ebb; **pas de ~s○!** we don't want to stir up any trouble!

vaguement /vagmɑ̃/ *adv* [*évoquer, indiquer*] vaguely; [*honteux, embarrassé*] faintly; **on avait ~ décoré la pièce pour la circonstance** they had put up a few decorations for the occasion.

vaillamment /vajamɑ̃/ *adv* courageously, valiantly SOUT.

vaillance /vajɑ̃s/ *nf* courage; **avec ~** courageously.

vaillant, ~e /vajɑ̃, ɑ̃t/ *adj* **1** (courageux) courageous; **2** (vigoureux) [*personne*] strong; [*vieillard*] hale and hearty.

vain, ~e /vɛ̃, vɛn/ **I** *adj* **1** (inutile) [*effort, tentative*] vain, futile; [*regrets*] futile; [*démarche, discussion*] fruitless, futile; **avec lui, toute discussion serait ~e** talking to him would be futile; **2** (illusoire) [*promesses*] empty; [*espoirs*] vain; **3** (superficiel) [*plaisirs, mots*] vain, empty; **le pouvoir de la presse n'est pas un ~ mot** the power of the press is a very real thing; **4** (vaniteux) [*personne*] vain.
II en vain *loc adv* in vain.

vaincre /vɛ̃kʀ/ [57] **I** *vtr* to defeat [*adversaire, armée*]; to overcome [*préjugés, complexe, envie de dormir*]; to beat [*chômage, maladie*].
II *vi* to win.

vaincu, ~e /vɛ̃ky/ **I** pp ▶ **vaincre**.
II pp adj defeated; **s'avouer ~** to admit defeat.
III nm,f loser; **les ~s** MIL the defeated (+ v pl).
vainement /vɛnmɑ̃/ adv in vain.
vainqueur /vɛ̃kœʀ/ **I** adj m victorious.
II nm (de bataille) victor; (d'épreuve sportive, élections) winner (**de, devant** against); (de loterie, concours) prizewinner; (de désert, montagne) conqueror.
vaisseau, pl **~x** /vɛso/ nm **1** ANAT, BOT vessel; **2** NAUT vessel; MIL, NAUT warship; **3** ARCHIT nave.
■ **~ amiral** LIT, FIG flagship; **~ sanguin** ANAT blood vessel; **~ spatial** spaceship.
vaisselier /vɛsəlje/ nm dresser.
vaisselle /vɛsɛl/ nf **1** (pour manger) crockery, dishes (pl); **2** (à laver) dishes (pl); **laver** or **faire la ~** to do the dishes, to wash up GB, to do the washing-up GB.
val, pl **~s** or **vaux** /val, vo/ nm valley.
IDIOMES **être toujours par monts et par vaux** to be always on the move.
valable /valabl/ adj **1** (acceptable) [raison] valid; [solution] viable; [interlocuteur] recognized; **2** (non périmé) valid; **ma proposition reste ~** my offer still holds; **3**° (intéressant) [œuvre, projet] worthwhile.
valdinguer° /valdɛ̃ge/ [1] vi [personne, objet] to go flying°; **~ dans l'escalier** to go tumbling down the stairs; **envoyer ~** (faire tomber) to send [sb/sth] flying°.
valet /valɛ/ ▶374 nm **1** (serviteur) manservant; **2** JEUX jack; **~ de pique** jack of spades.
■ **~ de chambre** valet; **~ de ferme** farm hand; **~ de nuit** valet; **~ de pied** footman.
valeur /valœʀ/ nf **1** (prix) value; **prendre/perdre de la ~** to go up/to go down in value; **d'une ~ inestimable** [bijou, meuble] priceless; **avoir beaucoup de ~** to be very valuable; **n'avoir aucune ~** to have no value, to be worth nothing; **un vase de ~** a valuable vase; **les objets de ~** valuables; **mettre un terrain en ~** to develop a plot of land, to put a plot of land to good use; **2** (qualité) (de personne) worth; (d'œuvre) value, merit; (de méthode, découverte) value; **prouver sa ~** to show one's worth; **faire la ~ de qch** to give sth value; **attacher de la ~ à qch** to value sth; **sans ~** worthless; **un homme de ~** (moralement) a very estimable man; **attirer des candidats de ~** (en compétence) to attract high-quality candidates; **la ~ de l'écrivain a été reconnue** the author's talent has been recognized; **le mot garde toute sa ~** the word retains its full force; **mettre qch en ~** to emphasize, to highlight [fait, talent, qualité]; to set off [yeux, teint, tableau]; **mettre qn en ~** [couleur, maquillage] to suit sb; **se mettre en ~** [coquette] to make the best of oneself; [candidat] to show oneself to best advantage; **3** (validité) validity; **~ légale** legal validity; **avoir ~ de norme/symbole** to be the norm/a symbol; **ceci n'a pas ~ d'engagement** this does not constitute a commitment; **4** (principe moral) value; **nous n'avons pas les mêmes ~** we don't share the same values; **5** (en Bourse) security; **~s** securities, stock ¢, stocks and shares; **le marché** or **la Bourse des ~s** the stock market; **6** (en comptabilité) value; **~s disponibles** liquid assets; **7** (quantité) **ajouter la ~ de deux cuillerées à café** add the equivalent of two teaspoons; **8** MATH value; **en ~ absolue/relative** FIG in absolute/relative terms; **9** JEUX (de pion, carte) value; **10**† (courage) valour†GB.
■ **~ marchande** market value; **~ sûre** gilt-edged security GB, blue chip; FIG safe bet; **~s mobilières** securities.
valeureux, -euse /valøʀø, øz/ adj valorous†.
validation /validasjɔ̃/ nf JUR, UNIV validation; (dans les transports, dans un jeu) stamping.
valide /valid/ adj **1** [passeport, contrat] valid; **non ~** invalid; **2** [personne, population] able-bodied; [bras] good (épith); (en forme) fit; **je ne me sens pas encore bien ~** I don't feel very fit yet.
valider /valide/ [1] vtr to stamp [titre de transport];

faire ~ to have [sth] validated [bulletin de loto]; to have [sth] recognized [diplôme].
validité /validite/ nf validity.
valise /valiz/ nf (bagage) suitcase; **faire/défaire ses ~s** to pack/to unpack; **s'il n'est pas content, il n'a qu'à faire ses ~s** if he doesn't like it, he can pack his bags.
■ **~ diplomatique** diplomatic bag GB ou pouch US.
IDIOMES **avoir des ~s sous les yeux**° to have bags under one's eyes.
vallée /vale/ nf valley.
vallon /valɔ̃/ nm dale, small valley.
vallonné, ~e /valɔne/ adj [relief, paysage] undulating; [pays] hilly.
valoir /valwaʀ/ [45] **I** vtr (procurer) **~ à qn** to earn sb [châtiment, éloges, critiques]; to win sb [amitié, admiration]; to bring sb sth [ennuis]; **ça ne m'a valu que des ennuis** it brought me nothing but trouble, I got nothing but trouble out of it; **cela lui a valu d'être élu** it got him elected; **que me vaut l'honneur de ta visite?** HUM to what do I owe the honour GB (of this visit)?
II vi **1** (en termes monétaires) to be worth; **ça vaut bien 50 francs** (à peu près) it must be worth 50 francs; (largement) it's well worth 50 francs; **~ de l'or** FIG to be very valuable; **2** (qualitativement) **que vaut ce film/vin?** what's that film/wine like?; **il ne vaut pas mieux que son frère** he's no better than his brother; **le film ne vaut pas grand-chose** the film isn't very good ou isn't up to much°; **il ne vaut pas cher** he is a worthless individual ou a bad lot°; **ne rien ~** [matériau, produit, roman] to be rubbish, to be no good; [outil, traitement, méthode] to be useless; [argument] to be worthless; **il ne vaut rien comme cuisinier** he's a useless cook; **le pneu ne vaut plus rien** the tyre has had it°; **la chaleur/le climat ne me vaut rien** the heat/the climate doesn't suit me; **l'alcool ne vaut rien pour le foie** alcohol doesn't do the liver much good; **le film vaut surtout par la qualité du dialogue** the principal merit of the film is the quality of the dialogue GB; **il ne me dit rien qui vaille** I've got misgivings about him; **ça ne me dit rien qui vaille** (projet, annonce) I don't like the sound of it; **elle valait mieux que cela!** she deserved better than that!; **3** (égaler) to be as good as; **ton travail vaut bien/largement le leur** your work is just as good/every bit as good as theirs; **rien ne vaut la soie** nothing beats silk; **le frère vaut la sœur** HUM the brother is just as bad as the sister; **4** (équivaloir à) to be worth; **un ouvrier expérimenté vaut trois débutants** an experienced worker is worth three novices; **5** (mériter) to be worth; **ça vaut la peine que tu y ailles** it's worth your going; **ça en vaut la peine, ça vaut le coup**° it's worth it; **6** (être valable) [règle, critique] to apply; **la règle vaut pour tout le monde** the rule applies to everybody; **7** (avec faire) **faire ~** (faire fructifier) to put [sth] to work [argent]; to farm [terrain]; to turn [sth] to good account [bien]; (mettre en avant) to point out [mérite, nécessité]; to emphasize, to highlight [qualité, trait]; to advance [argument]; to assert [droit]; to make [sth] known [intention]; **faire ~ que** to point out that, to argue that; **se faire ~** to push oneself forward, to get oneself noticed (**auprès de qn** by sb).
III se valoir vpr [produit, œuvres] to be the same; **les deux candidats se valent** there's nothing to choose between the two candidates.
IV v impers **il vaut mieux faire, mieux vaut faire** it's better to do; **mieux vaut** or **il vaut mieux une dispute qu'un malentendu** an argument is better than a misunderstanding, rather an argument than a misunderstanding; **il vaut mieux que tu y ailles** you'd better go; **il aurait mieux valu qu'il se taise** he would have done better to keep quiet; **cela vaut mieux**° it's better like that ou that way.
valorisation /valɔʀizasjɔ̃/ nf **1** (promotion) promotion; **~ d'un produit** promotion of a product; **2** (mise en valeur) development; **3** (hausse) (de monnaie) rise; (de terrains) rise in value.

valoriser /valɔʀize/ [1] *vtr* **1** (promouvoir) to promote [*produit*]; to make [sth] attractive [*profession, études*]; **2** (mettre en valeur) to develop [*région, ressources*]; to put [sth] to good use [*diplôme, savoir-faire*]; **3** (faire fructifier) to put [sth] to work [*capital*].

valse /vals/ *nf* **1** (danse) waltz; **2** (changement fréquent) ~ **des ministres** frequent cabinet reshuffles (*pl*); ~ **des étiquettes** continual price rises (*pl*).

valse-hésitation, *pl* **valses-hésitations** /valse zitasjɔ̃/ *nf* shilly-shallying○ ¢.

valser /valse/ [1] *vi* **1** (en danse) to waltz; **l'argent valse entre leurs mains**○ they spend money hand over fist; **envoyer** ~ **qn**○ (projeter) to send sb flying; (rembarrer) to send sb packing○; **2**○ (changer) **faire** ~ **les étiquettes** to raise prices constantly; **il fait** ~ **les ministres** he keeps changing his ministers.

valseur, -euse /valsœʀ, øz/ *nm,f* waltzer.

valve /valv/ *nf* valve.

vamp /vãp/ *nf* vamp.

vampire /vãpiʀ/ *nm* **1** (revenant) vampire; **2** (personne avide) bloodsucker; **3** ZOOL vampire bat.

vampiriser /vãpiʀize/ [1] *vtr* **1** LIT to suck the lifeblood from; **2** FIG to cannibalize.

van /vã/ *nm* **1** (fourgon) (pour chevaux) horsebox GB, horse-car US; (pour marchandises) van; **2** (panier) winnowing basket.

vandale /vãdal/ *nmf* vandal.

vandalisme /vãdalism/ *nm* vandalism.

vanille /vanij/ *nf* vanilla; **à la** ~ [*glace*] vanilla (*épith*); [*crème*] vanilla-flavoured GB (*épith*).

vanillé, ~e /vanije/ *adj* [*goût*] vanilla (*épith*); [*dessert*] vanilla-flavoured GB; **sucre** ~ sugar containing vanilla.

vanité /vanite/ *nf* **1** (orgueil) vanity; **sans** ~ with all due modesty; **tirer** ~ **de qch** to pride oneself on sth; **flatter qn dans sa** ~ to flatter sb's ego; **avoir la** ~ **de croire que** to be presumptuous enough to believe that; **2** (peu de valeur) (de richesses) vanity; (d'efforts) futility; (de promesse) hollowness; (d'entreprise) uselessness; **3** ART vanitas.

vaniteux, -euse /vanitø, øz/ *adj* vain, conceited.

vanne /van/ *nf* **1** (de barrage) gate; (d'écluse, de moulin) sluice gate; **2**○ (propos) dig○; **envoyer une** ~ or **des** ~**s à qn** to have a dig at sb○. ▪ IDIOMES **ouvrir les** ~**s**○ to make funds available; **fermer les** ~**s**○ to cut funding.

vanner /vane/ [1] *vtr* **1** AGRIC to winnow; **2**○ (fatiguer) to tire [sb] out [*personne*]; **je suis vannée!** I'm tired out ou knackered➊ GB!

vannerie /vanʀi/ *nf* basket-making; **objets en** ~ wickerwork.

vantail, *pl* -**aux** /vãtaj, o/ *nm* (de porte) leaf; (de fenêtre) casement; (de volet) shutter; (d'armoire) door; **porte à double** ~ double-door.

vantard, ~e /vãtaʀ, aʀd/ *nm,f* boaster, braggart.

vantardise /vãtaʀdiz/ *nf* **1** (caractère) boastfulness; **2** (parole) boast.

vanter /vãte/ [1] *vtr* to praise, to extol; **tant vanté** much vaunted; ~ **les mérites de qn/qch** to speak highly of sb/sth.
II **se vanter** *vpr* **1** (être un vantard) to brag (**de** about); **il n'y a pas de quoi se** ~! there's nothing to brag about!; **il a cassé le vase mais il ne s'en est pas vanté** he broke the vase but he kept quiet about it; **2** (s'enorgueillir) **se** ~ **de faire** to pride oneself on doing; **3** (prétendre) **se** ~ **de faire** to make out that one does.

va-nu-pieds /vanypje/ *nmf inv* tramp, bum○.

vapeur /vapœʀ/ **I** *nf* **1** (d'eau) steam; **à** ~ [*machine, bateau*] steam (*épith*); **renverser la** ~ NAUT to go astern; FIG to backpedal; **faire cuire à la** ~ to steam; **la cuisine à la** ~ steam cooking; **2** PHYS vapour GB.
II **vapeurs** *nfpl* (émanations) fumes.

vaporeux, -euse /vapɔʀø, øz/ *adj* **1** (léger) [*vête-*

ment, matériau] diaphanous; **2** (brumeux) LITER [*paysage*] misty.

vaporisateur /vapɔʀizatœʀ/ *nm* spray.

vaporisation /vapɔʀizasjɔ̃/ *nf* **1** (d'insecticide, de parfum) spraying; **2** PHYS vaporization.

vaporiser /vapɔʀize/ [1] *vtr* (projeter) to spray.
II **se vaporiser** *vpr* PHYS to vaporize.

vaquer /vake/ [1] *vi* (s'arrêter) [*tribunal, assemblée*] to be in recess; [*cours*] to stop.
II **vaquer à** *vtr ind* ~ **à ses occupations** to attend to one's business.

varappe /vaʀap/ ▶ 329| *nf* rock-climbing.

varappeur, -euse /vaʀapœʀ, øz/ *nm,f* rock-climber.

varech /vaʀɛk/ *nm* kelp.

vareuse /vaʀøz/ *nf* **1** (dans la marine) jersey; **2** MIL uniform jacket.

variable /vaʀjabl/ **I** *adj* **1** (fluctuant) variable; **leurs sketches sont d'une durée** ~ their sketches vary in length; **2** (changeant) [*ciel, temps*] changeable; [*humeur*] unpredictable; **vent** ~ **de faible à modéré** wind varying from weak to moderate; **ils ont des opinions** ~**s** they have shifting opinions; **3** (modifiable) [*hauteur, focale*] adjustable; **4** MATH, ORDINAT [*quantité, nombre, données*] variable; **5** LING **un mot** ~ a word which inflects.
II *nf* variable.

variante /vaʀjɑ̃t/ *nf* variant.

variation /vaʀjasjɔ̃/ *nf* **1** (changement) variation; ~ **de température** variation in temperature; ~ **à la baisse/à la hausse** downward/upward movement; ~**s de l'opinion publique** changes in public opinion; **connaître de fortes** ~**s** [*prix, températures*] to fluctuate considerably; **en données corrigées des** ~**s saisonnières** according to the seasonally adjusted figures; **2** MUS variation.

varice /vaʀis/ *nf* varicose vein.

varicelle /vaʀisɛl/ ▶ 196| *nf* chicken pox.

varié, ~e /vaʀje/ *adj* **1** (diversifié) varied; **une expérience** ~**e** diverse ou varied experience; **plumage** ~ variegated plumage; **2** (multiple) [*instruments, exercices*] various; **des activités aussi** ~**es que** activities as varied as; **une population d'origines** ~**es** a population of diverse origins; **'sandwichs** ~**s'** 'a selection of sandwiches'.

varier /vaʀje/ [2] **I** *vtr* to vary; **pour** ~ **les plaisirs** just for a (pleasant) change.
II *vi* **1** (changer) to vary (**avec, en fonction de, au gré de** according to); **l'inflation varie de 4% à 6%** inflation fluctuates between 4% and 6%; **2** (changer d'opinion) **l'accusé ne varie pas** the accused is sticking to his story.
▪ IDIOMES **souvent femme varie, bien fol est qui s'y fie** PROV woman is fickle.

variété /vaʀjete/ **I** *nf* **1** (diversité) variety; **manquer de** ~ to be lacking in variety; **des menus d'une grande** ~ very varied menus; **une grande** ~ **d'articles** a wide range of items; **2** BOT variety; **3** (type) sort; **différentes** ~**s de céréales** different sorts of cereals; **une** ~ **de grippe** a strain of flu.
II **variétés** *nfpl* **spectacle de** ~**s** variety show; **la chanson de** ~**s** middle-of-the-road popular song; **les** ~**s italiennes** Italian popular music *sg*.

variole /vaʀjɔl/ ▶ 196| *nf* smallpox.

Varsovie /vaʀsɔvi/ ▶ 628| *npr* Warsaw.

vas /va/ ▶ **aller**¹.

vase¹ /vɑz/ *nm* (à fleurs, ornemental) vase.
■ ~**s communicants** PHYS connected vessels.
▪ IDIOMES **vivre/être élevé en** ~ **clos** to live/to be brought up without any contact with the outside world; **c'est la goutte d'eau qui fait déborder le** ~ it's the last straw.

vase² /vɑz/ *nf* (boue) silt, sludge.

vaseux, -euse /vazø, øz/ *adj* **1** (boueux) muddy; **2**○ (fatigué) **je me sens plutôt** ~ I'm not really with it○; **3**○ (peu cohérent) woolly.

vasistas /vazistas/ *nm inv* (à lamelles) louvre GB window; (dans une fenêtre) opening windowpane.

vasque /vask/ *nf* **1** (de fontaine) basin; **2** (coupe) bowl.

vassal, ~e, *mpl* **-aux** /vasal, o/ **I** *adj* vassal.
II *nm,f* HIST vassal; FIG slave.

vaste /vast/ *adj* **1** (de grande étendue) [*pièce, domaine, secteur, réseau*] vast; [*marché*] huge; **la salle n'est pas très ~** the room is not very large; **le ~ monde** the wide world; **2** (nombreux) [*public, choix, collection*] large; [*rassemblement*] huge; **3** (de grande envergure) [*programme, entreprise*] massive; [*campagne*] extensive; [*plaisanterie*] huge; [*débat, enquête*] wide-ranging; [*mouvement, offensive*] large-scale; [*réforme*] far-reaching; [*œuvre, sujet*] wide-ranging.

vat: à Dieu va(t) /adjøva(t)/ *loc excl* come what may.

va-t-en-guerre /vatãgɛʀ/ *nm inv* warmonger.

va-tout /vatu/ *nm inv* **jouer/tenter son ~** to stake/ to risk everything.

vaudeville /vodvil/ *nm* light comedy; **tourner au ~** to turn into a farce.

vaudou /vodu/ *adj inv, nm* voodoo.

vaurien, -ienne /voʀjɛ̃, ɛn/ *nm,f* **1** (chenapan) rascal; **2** (crapule) PEJ lout, yobbo○ GB, hoodlum○.

vautour /votuʀ/ *nm* ZOOL FIG vulture.

vautrer: se vautrer /votʀe/ [1] *vpr* **1** (s'étaler) to sprawl; **2** (s'affaler) to loll; **se ~ dans un fauteuil** to loll in an armchair; **3** (se rouler) to wallow; **se ~ dans la boue** to wallow in the mud.

vauvert: au diable vauvert /odjablǝvovɛʀ/ *loc adv* miles from anywhere.

va-vite: à la va-vite /alavavit/ *loc adv* PEJ in a rush.

veau, *pl* **~x** /vo/ *nm* **1** ZOOL calf; **2** CULIN veal; **côte de ~** veal chop; **foie/pied de ~** calf's liver/foot; **3** (cuir) calfskin.
■ **~ marin** ZOOL seal; **le ~ d'or** BIBLE the golden calf; (les richesses) Mammon.
IDIOMES **pleurer comme un ~** to cry one's eyes out; **tuer le ~ gras** to kill the fatted calf.

vecteur /vɛktœʀ/ *nm* **1** (support) vehicle; **2** MATH vector; **3** BIOL (de maladie) carrier.

vécu, ~e /veky/ **I** *pp* ▶ **vivre**.
II *pp adj* **1** (authentique) [*drame, histoire*] real-life (*épith*); **2** PHILOS (subjectif) [*durée, temps*] subjective.
III *nm* **1** (expériences) personal experiences (*pl*); **2** (réalité) real life; **c'est du ~** [*film, roman*] it's real life.

vedettariat /vǝdɛtaʀja/ *nm* stardom.

vedette /vǝdɛt/ **I** *nf* **1** (célébrité) star; **~ de cinéma** film star; **~ de la politique** famous politician; **avoir la ~** [*acteur, orateur*] to have top billing; **tenir la ~** [*acteur, événement*] to be in the limelight; **se mettre en ~** to push oneself forward; **mettre qn/qch en ~** to turn the spotlight on sb/sth; **2** NAUT launch.
II (-)**vedette** (*in compounds*) **danseur ~** star; **enfant ~** child star; **élève ~** star pupil; **mannequin ~** top model; **match ~** big match GB ou game US.
■ **~ de combat** fast attack craft; **~ de croisière** cabin cruiser; **~ lance-torpilles** motor torpedo boat GB.

végétal, ~e, *mpl* **-aux** /veʒetal, o/ **I** *adj* (propre aux plantes) [*cellule, tissu*] plant (*épith*); (venant des plantes) [*huile, teinture*] vegetable (*épith*).
II *nm* vegetable, plant.

végétalien, -ienne /veʒetaljɛ̃, ɛn/ *adj, nm,f* vegan.

végétarien, -ienne /veʒetaʀjɛ̃, ɛn/ *adj, nm,f* vegetarian; **être ~** to be a vegetarian.

végétation /veʒetasjɔ̃/ **I** *nf* BOT vegetation.
II **végétations** *nfpl* MÉD adenoids.

végéter /veʒete/ [14] *vi* [*personne*] to vegetate; [*projet*] to stagnate.

véhémence /veemãs/ *nf* vehemence; **avec ~** vehemently.

véhément, ~e /veemã, ãt/ *adj* [*personne, discours, propos*] passionate, vehement; [*orateur*] passionate.

véhicule /veikyl/ *nm* **1** (moyen de transport) vehicle;

■ **~ blindé** armoured GB vehicle; **2** (moyen d'expression) vehicle (**de** for).
■ **~ de tourisme** private car.

véhiculer /veikyle/ [1] *vtr* (transporter) to carry, to transport [*personnes, marchandises*]; (transmettre) to carry [*substance, message*]; **~ des rumeurs** to circulate ou spread rumours GB; **~ une image** to promote an image.

veille /vɛj/ *nf* **1** (jour précédent) **la ~** the day before; **la ~ au soir** the night ou evening before; **la ~ de Noël** Christmas Eve; **en cette ~ de Pâques 1951** the day before this Easter of 1951; **à la ~ de** (juste avant) on the eve of [*guerre, élections*]; **être à la ~ de faire** to be on the verge of doing; **2** (en physiologie) (état normal) waking; (état forcé) vigil; **une nuit de ~** an all-night vigil; **être en état de ~** to be awake; **ses longues heures de ~ l'ont épuisée** the many hours without sleep have worn her out; **3** (garde) watch; **des heures de ~** hours on watch.

veillée /veje/ *nf* **1** (soirée) evening; **à la ~** in the evening; **2** (auprès d'un malade) vigil.
■ **~ funèbre** or **mortuaire** wake.

veiller /veje/ [1] **I** *vtr* to watch over [*malade*]; to keep watch over [*mort*].
II *vtr ind* **~ au bon déroulement de qch** to see to it that sth goes smoothly; **~ à sa santé** to look after one's health; **~ à ce que** to make sure that, to see to it that; **~ sur un enfant** to watch over a child.
III *vi* **1** (rester éveillé) to stay up; **~ au chevet** or **auprès de qn** to sit up at sb's bedside; **2** (monter la garde) to be on watch; **3** (être vigilant) to be watchful; **heureusement, la police veille** fortunately, the police are there.
IDIOMES **~ au grain** to be on one's guard.

veilleur, -euse¹ /vɛjœʀ, øz/ ▶**374**╽ *nm,f* (guetteur) look-out; **~ de nuit** night watchman.

veilleuse² /vɛjøz/ *nf* **1** (lampe) night light; **2** (d'appareil à gaz) pilot light; **3** AUT side light GB, parking light US.

veinard○, ~e /venar, aʀd/ *nm,f* lucky devil○.

veine /vɛn/ *nf* **1** ANAT vein; **ne pas avoir de sang dans les ~s** FIG to have no guts○; **2** BOT (nervure) vein; **les ~s** (de chou, marbre) the veining ¢; (de bois) the grain ¢; **3** (mine) (de charbon) seam; (de métal) vein; **4** (inspiration) inspiration; **de** ou **dans la même ~** in the same vein; **être en ~ de générosité** to be in a generous mood; **5**○ (chance) luck; **il a de la ~** (en général) he's lucky; (cette fois) he's in luck; **il n'a pas de ~** (en général) he's unlucky; (cette fois) he's out of luck; **avoir une ~ de pendu** or **cocu**○ to have the luck of the devil○; **coup de ~** stroke of luck; **c'est bien ma ~!** that's just my luck!

veiné, ~e /vene/ *adj* [*peau, main, marbre*] veined; [*bois*] grained; **pomme ~e de rouge** apple streaked with red.

veinure /venyʀ/ *nf* (du bois) grain ¢; (du marbre) veining ¢.

vêler /vele/ [1] *vi* [*vache*] to calve.

vélin /velɛ̃/ *nm* vellum.

véliplanchiste /veliplɑ̃ʃist/ *nmf* windsurfer.

velléitaire /veleitɛʀ/ **I** *adj* weak-willed.
II *nmf* waverer.

velléité /veleite/ *nf* (désir vague) vague desire; (tentative) vague attempt; **à la moindre ~ de rébellion** at the slightest sign of rebellion.

vélo○ /velo/ *nm* **1** (bicyclette) bike○; **aller en ville en ~** to cycle into town; **2** ▶**329**╽ (sport) cycling; **faire du ~** to cycle, to go cycling.
■ **~ d'appartement** exercise bike; **~ de course** racing bike; **~ tout terrain, VTT** mountain bike.

vélocité /velosite/ *nf* (de pianiste) nimble-fingeredness; (de footballeur) speed; (d'animal) swiftness; **exercices de ~** MUS finger exercises.

vélo-cross /velokʀɔs/ *nm inv* **1** ▶**329**╽ (sport) cyclo-cross; **faire du ~** to go cyclo-cross racing; **2** (vélo) cyclo-cross bike.

vélodrome /velodʀom/ *nm* velodrome.

venir

venir de + infinitif

venir verbe auxiliaire servant à former le passé immédiat:

venir de faire	= to have just done
elle vient (tout juste) de partir	= she's (only) just left
il venait de se marier	= he'd just got married
je viens de te le dire	= I've just told you

Attention aux exceptions du genre:

vient de paraître = (pour un livre) 'just published!'
(mais pour un disque) 'new release'

venir + infinitif

La traduction de la construction dépend du temps:

j'ai demandé au plombier de venir vérifier la chaudière
= I asked the plumber to come and check the boiler
le plombier viendra vérifier la chaudière
= the plumber will come and check the boiler
le plombier vient vérifier la chaudière aujourd'hui
= the plumber is coming to check the boiler today
te rappelles-tu quel jour le plombier est venu vérifier la chaudière? = can you remember which day the plumber came to check the boiler?
il était venu vérifier la chaudière et il en a profité pour réparer le robinet de l'évier
= he had come to check the boiler and took the opportunity to mend the tap on the sink
viens voir = come and see

Cependant, pour les activités sportives, on aura:

elle a décidé de venir nager
= she has decided to come swimming
elle a décidé de venir faire du cheval
= she has decided to come riding

On pourra aussi avoir:

viens déjeuner
= come for lunch (*lunch* étant un nom)
venez nous voir un de ces jours
= come over sometime
ou (GB) come round sometime

Exemples supplémentaires et exceptions sont présentés ci-dessous aussi bien pour *venir* verbe auxiliaire I, que pour *venir* verbe intransitif II.

vélomoteur /velɔmɔtœʀ/ *nm* moped.

velours /vəluʀ/ *nm inv* (lisse) velvet; (à côtes) corduroy, cord; **rideau en** or **de ~** velvet curtain; **avoir une peau de ~** to have a velvety skin; **avoir des yeux de ~** to be doe-eyed.

IDIOMES **une main de fer dans un gant de ~** an iron fist in a velvet glove; **faire patte de ~** [*hypocrite*] to switch on the charm.

velouté, **~e** /vəlute/ I *adj* (doux) [*peau*] velvety; [*pêche*, *son*] velvety; (suave) [*sauce*, *vin*] smooth; [*regard*] mellow.
II *nm* **1** CULIN (sauce) velouté sauce; (potage) **~ de champignons** cream of mushroom soup; **2** (douceur) (au toucher) softness; (au goût) smoothness; **le ~ de sa peau** his/her velvety skin, his/her velvet skin.

velu, **~e** /vəly/ *adj* [*personne*, *animal*] hairy; [*plantes*] villous.

venaison /vənɛzɔ̃/ *nf* game; (daim) venison.

vénal, **~e**, *mpl* **-aux** /venal, o/ *adj* **1** (intéressé) [*personne*] venal; [*comportement*] mercenary; **2** COMM [*valeur*] monetary.

vendable /vɑ̃dabl/ *adj* saleable^{GB}.

vendange /vɑ̃dɑ̃ʒ/ *nf* grape harvest; **faire la ~** or **les ~s** [*vigneron*] to harvest the grapes; [*saisonnier*] to go grape-picking.

vendanger /vɑ̃dɑ̃ʒe/ [13] I *vtr* to harvest [*raisin*]; to pick the grapes from [*vigne*]; **machine à ~** mechanical grape harvester.
II *vi* AGRIC (cueillir) to harvest the grapes.

vendangeur, **-euse**¹ /vɑ̃dɑ̃ʒœʀ, øz/ *nm,f* grape-picker.

vendangeuse² /vɑ̃dɑ̃ʒøz/ *nf* **1** (machine) mechanical grape harvester; **2** BOT aster.

vendeur, **-euse** /vɑ̃dœʀ, øz/ *nm,f* **1** ▶374 (de maga-sin) shop assistant, salesclerk US, salesperson; **2** ▶374 (responsable des ventes) salesperson, salesman/saleswoman; **c'est un excellent ~** he's an excellent salesman; **3** (dans une transaction) seller; JUR vendor; **désolé mais je ne suis pas ~** sorry but I'm not selling.
■ **~ ambulant** COMM pedlar GB, peddler US; **~ de journaux** newsvendor GB, newsdealer; **~ de rêve** pedlar of dreams.

vendre /vɑ̃dʀ/ [6] I *vtr* **1** GÉN to sell; **~ à crédit** to sell on credit; **~ en gros** to wholesale, to sell [sth] wholesale; **~ au détail** to retail; **ça fait ~** it boosts sales; **~ ses charmes** to sell one's charms; **'à ~'** 'for sale'; **ma voiture n'est pas à ~** my car is not for sale; **2** (trahir) to betray, to shop° GB [*personne*, *complice*] (à to).
II **se vendre** *vpr* **se ~ à la pièce/au poids** to be sold singly/by weight; **se ~ bien/mal** to sell well/badly; **se ~** [*personne*] to sell oneself; **se ~ à l'ennemi** to sell out to the enemy.

vendredi /vɑ̃dʀədi/ ▶551 *nm* Friday; **~ saint** Good Friday.

vendu, **-e** /vɑ̃dy/ I *pp* ▶ **vendre**.
II *pp adj* (corrompu) [*juge*, *arbitre*, *fonctionnaire*] bribed; **~, l'arbitre!** the referee's a traitor!
III *nm,f* traitor; **c'est un ~!** he's sold out, he's a traitor.

vénéneux, **-euse** /venenø, øz/ *adj* poisonous.

vénérable /veneʀabl/ *adj* (respectable) [*personne*] venerable; [*arbre*, *objet*] ancient.

vénération /veneʀasjɔ̃/ *nf* veneration.

vénérer /veneʀe/ [14] *vtr* **1** RELIG to venerate; **2** (respecter) to revere [*personne*]; **~ la mémoire de qn** to venerate sb's memory.

vénerie /vɛnʀi/ *nf* hunting, venery SPÉC.

vénérien, **-ienne** /veneʀjɛ̃, ɛn/ *adj* venereal.

vengeance /vɑ̃ʒɑ̃s/ *nf* revenge; **par ~** out of revenge; **un acte de ~** an act of revenge; **mettre sa ~ à exécution** to get one's revenge; **ma ~ sera terrible!** my vengeance will be terrible!

venger /vɑ̃ʒe/ [13] I *vtr* to avenge.
II **se venger** *vpr* to get ou take one's revenge (**de qn** on sb; **se ~ sur qn/qch** to take it out on sb/sth; **se ~ de qch** to get ou take one's revenge for sth; **il l'a fait pour se ~** he did it in revenge.

vengeur, **vengeresse** /vɑ̃ʒœʀ, vɑ̃ʒʀɛs/ I *adj* [*personne*, *acte*] vengeful; [*bras*, *épée*] avenging; [*lettre*] vindictive.
II *nm,f* avenger.

véniel, **-ielle** /venjɛl/ *adj* **1** RELIG [*péché*] venial; **2** (excusable) [*faute*, *oubli*] excusable, pardonable.

venimeux, **-euse** /vənimø, øz/ *adj* venomous.

venin /vənɛ̃/ *nm* venom; **~ de serpent** snake venom; **répandre son ~ contre qn** to make venomous ou poisonous remarks about sb.

venir /vəniʀ/ [36] I *v aux* **1** (marque l'occurrence) **~ aggraver la situation** to make the situation worse; **2** (marque le mouvement) **le ballon est venu rouler sous mes pieds** the ball rolled up to my feet; **3** (marque le développement) **s'il venait à pleuvoir** if it should rain; **s'il venait à l'apprendre** if he ever got to hear about it; **il en vint à la détester** he came to hate her.
II *vi* **1** (dans l'espace) to come; **je viens** or **suis venu pour m'excuser** I've come to apologize; **il vient beaucoup de gens le samedi** lots of people come on Saturdays; **allez, viens!** come on!; **d'où viens-tu?** (reproche) where have you been?; **j'en viens** I've just been there; **je viens de sa part** he/she sent me to see you; **faire ~ qn** (demander) to send for sb, to get sb°; (en le convainquant) to get sb to come; (attirer) to attract sb [*client*]; **faire ~ le médecin** to call the doctor; **faire ~ qch** (commander) to order sth; (par la poste) to send for sth; **faire ~ ses chaussures d'Italie** to get one's shoes from Italy; **plantes venues d'ailleurs** plants from far-off places; **gens venus d'ailleurs** (de l'étranger) foreigners; (de l'extérieur) outsiders; **le nom ne me vient pas à l'esprit** the name escapes me; **les**

mots ne venaient pas he/she etc couldn't find the words; **l'inspiration ne venait pas** inspiration failed him/her etc; **l'idée lui vint que** the idea occurred to him/her that; **ça ne m'est jamais venu à l'idée** or **l'esprit** it never crossed my mind ou occurred to me; **il lui est venu une idée bizarre** he/she had a weird idea; **2** (dans le temps) **il faut prendre les choses comme elles viennent** you must take things as they come; **ça vient, ça vient**○! it's coming!, it's on its way!; **dans les jours à ~** in the next few days; **le moment venu** (au futur) when the time comes; (au passé) when the time came; **la nuit va bientôt ~** it'll soon be dark; **dans l'heure qui vient** within the hour; **les difficultés à ~** future problems; **je préfère laisser** or **voir ~ (les choses)** I'd rather wait and see how things turn out; **comment êtes-vous venu à l'enseignement?** how did you come to take up teaching?; **~ loin derrière** to trail a long way behind; **il est venu un moment où j'étais trop fatigué** I got to the point when I was too tired; **3** (marquant l'origine) **~ d'une famille protestante** to come from a Protestant family; **cette bague me vient de ma tante** my aunt left me this ring; **le succès du roman vient de son style** the novel's success is due to its style; **ça vient de ce qu'ils ne se parlent pas** it's all because they don't talk to each other; **ça me vient naturellement** or **tout seul** that's just the way I am; **4** (dans une hiérarchie) **~ après/avant** to come after/before; **5 en ~ à** to come to; **j'en viens au problème qui vous préoccupe** I now come to your problem; **en ~ à abandonner ses études** to get to the point of dropping out of college; **s'il faut en ~ là** if it gets to that point, if it comes to that; **il en était venu à la faire suivre** he even had her followed; **venons-en à l'ordre du jour** let's get down to the agenda; **où veut-il en ~ (au juste)?** what's he driving at?; **en ~ aux mains** or **aux coups** to come to blows.

vent /vɑ̃/ nm **1** MÉTÉO wind; **~ du large** seaward wind; **grand ~** gale, strong wind; **~ de côté** crosswind; **il fait** or **il y a du ~** it's windy, there's a wind blowing; **le ~ tourne** LIT, FIG the wind is turning; **coup** or **rafale de ~** gust of wind; **cheveux au ~** hair flying in the wind; **exposé à tous les ~s** exposed to all weathers; **en plein ~** LIT exposed to the wind; (dehors) in the open; **passer en coup de ~** FIG to rush through; **faire du ~** (avec un éventail) to create a breeze; HUM (en s'activant) to flap around; **2** NAUT **~ favorable, bon ~** favourable^GB wind, fair wind; **~ mauvais** unfavourable^GB wind; **avoir le ~ en poupe** LIT to sail ou run before the wind; FIG to have the wind in one's sails; **~ frais** strong breeze; **coup de ~** fresh gale; **3** (impulsion) **un ~ de liberté** a wind of freedom; **un ~ de folie soufflait dans le pays** a wave of madness swept through the country; **4** (flatulence) EUPH wind ₡.
IDIOMES **c'est du ~**! FIG it's just hot air!; **du ~**○! (partez) get lost○!; **quel bon ~ vous amène?** to what do I ou we owe the pleasure (of your visit)?; **être dans le ~** to be trendy; **avoir ~ de qch** to get wind of sth; **contre ~s et marées** [faire] come hell or high water; [avoir fait] against all odds.

Vent /vɑ̃/ ▶ 305 nprm **les îles du ~** the Windward Islands.

vente /vɑ̃t/ nf sale; **être en ~** to be for sale; **en ~ chez votre marchand de journaux** available ou for sale at your newsagent's; **en ~ libre** GÉN freely available; [médicaments] available over the counter.
■ **~ par correspondance** mail order selling; **~ au détail** retailing; **~ aux enchères** auction (sale); **~ en gros** wholesaling.

venter /vɑ̃te/ [1] v impers to blow; **il vente** the wind is blowing.

venteux, -euse /vɑ̃tø, øz/ adj [journée, mois] windy; [région, pays] windswept.

ventilateur /vɑ̃tilatœʀ/ nm GÉN fan; (aérateur) ventilator.

ventilation /vɑ̃tilasjɔ̃/ nf **1** (aération) ventilation; (système) ventilation (system); **2** (répartition) **~ du personnel** allocation of staff to different departments.

ventiler /vɑ̃tile/ [1] vtr **1** (aérer) to ventilate; **2** MÉD to ventilate [malade]; **3** (en comptabilité) to break down [dépenses, bénéfices]; **4** (diviser) to divide up [groupe, ensemble]; (répartir) to assign [personnel]; to allocate [tâches, matériaux].

ventouse /vɑ̃tuz/ nf **1** (d'adhésion) suction pad GB, suction cup US; **crochet à ~** suction hook; **faire ~** to stick; **2** (pour déboucher) plunger; **3** BOT, ZOOL sucker; (chez la grenouille) adhesive disc; **4** MÉD cupping glass; **poser des ~s à qn** to cup sb.

ventral, ~e, mpl **-aux** /vɑ̃tral, o/ adj [nageoire] ventral; **parachute ~** lap-pack parachute.

ventre /vɑ̃tʀ/ ▶ 137 nm **1** (abdomen, estomac) stomach, tummy○, belly; **s'allonger sur le ~** to lie on one's stomach, to lie face down; **rentrer son ~** to hold in one's stomach; **avoir mal au ~** to have stomach-ache; **avoir le ~ creux/plein** to have an empty/a full stomach; **le ~ de la terre** LITER the bowels (pl) of the earth LITTÉR; ▶ **affamé**; **2** (d'animal) (under)belly; **3** (utérus) womb; **4** (siège du courage) **ne rien avoir dans le ~** to have no guts○; **avoir la rage/la peur au ~** to feel sick with fury/fear; **je ne sais pas ce qu'il a dans le ~**○ I don't know what he's made of; **5** (partie renflée) (de marmite, bateau, d'avion) belly.
IDIOMES **courir ~ à terre** to run flat out; **tu as les yeux plus gros que le ~** your eyes are bigger than your stomach.

ventricule /vɑ̃tʀikyl/ nm ANAT **1** (de cœur, d'encéphale) ventricle; **2** (d'oiseau) ventriculus.

ventriloque /vɑ̃tʀilɔk/ ▶ 374 nmf ventriloquist.

ventripotent○, **~e** /vɑ̃tʀipɔtɑ̃, ɑ̃t/ adj portly, fat-bellied PÉJ.

ventru, ~e /vɑ̃tʀy/ adj [homme] paunchy, pot-bellied; [marmite, meuble] rounded; [mur] bulging.

venu, ~e^1 /vəny/ **I** pp ▶ **venir**.
II pp adj **1** (à propos) **bien ~** apt; **mal ~** badly timed; **il serait mal ~ de le leur dire** it wouldn't be a good idea to tell them; **2** (réussi) **bien ~** [œuvre, plaisanterie] clever.
III nm,f **nouveau ~** newcomer.

venue^2 /vəny/ nf visit; **les raisons de sa ~ sont obscures** it's not clear why he/she came; **~ au monde** birth; **~ du Messie** coming of the Messiah.

vêpres /vɛpʀ/ nfpl RELIG vespers.

ver /vɛʀ/ nm **1** ZOOL worm; (dans le bois) woodworm; (dans la nourriture) maggot, grub; **2** MÉD (parasite) worm.
■ **~ luisant** glowworm; **~ de sable** sandworm; **~ à soie** silkworm; **~ solitaire** tapeworm; **~ de terre** earthworm; **~ de vase** bloodworm.
IDIOMES **être nu comme un ~** to be stark naked; **tirer les ~s du nez à qn**○ to worm information out of sb.

véracité /veʀasite/ nf truthfulness, veracity SOUT.

véranda /veʀɑ̃da/ nf veranda; **sous la ~** on the veranda.

verbal, ~e, mpl **-aux** /vɛʀbal, o/ adj **1** (oral) verbal; **2** (de langage) [attaque, violence] verbal; **3** LING (de verbe) [groupe, adjectif] verbal; [catégorie, forme] verb (épith); **syntagme ~** verb phrase.

verbaliser /vɛʀbalize/ [1] **I** vtr PSYCH to verbalize [sentiments].
II vi (dresser un procès-verbal) to record an offence^GB.

verbe /vɛʀb/ nm **1** LING verb; **2** (langage) language; **avoir le ~ facile** to be quick to talk; **avoir le ~ haut** to be arrogant in one's speech; **3** RELIG **le Verbe** the Word.

verbiage /vɛʀbjaʒ/ nm verbiage, verbosity.

verdâtre /vɛʀdɑtʀ/ ▶ 141 adj PEJ greenish.

verdeur /vɛʀdœʀ/ nf **1** (truculence) rawness; **2** (vigueur) sprightliness; **3** (acidité) tartness, acidity.

verdict /vɛʀdikt/ nm **1** JUR (décision de jury) verdict; **rendre un ~** to return ou announce a verdict; **~ d'acquittement** verdict of not guilty; **2** FIG (appréciation) verdict, judgment; **un ~ sans appel** a verdict ou judgment without appeal.

verdir /vɛʀdiʀ/ [3] *vi* **1** (devenir vert) GÉN to turn green; [*cuivre*] to tarnish; **2** (pâlir) to turn pale.

verdoyant, **~e** /vɛʀdwajɑ̃, ɑ̃t/ *adj* green, verdant LITTÉR.

verdure /vɛʀdyʀ/ *nf* **1** (végétation) greenery; **2** (légumes verts) green vegetables (*pl*); **3** (couleurs) verdure LITTÉR, greenness.

véreux, **-euse** /veʀø, øz/ *adj* **1** (contenant des vers) [*fruit*] worm-eaten; **2** (malhonnête) [*politicien, avocat*] bent○, crooked; [*affaire, contrat*] shady○, dubious.

verge /vɛʀʒ/ *nf* **1** ANAT penis; **2** (pour battre) switch, birch.

vergé /vɛʀʒe/ *nm* laid paper.

verger /vɛʀʒe/ *nm* orchard.

vergeture /vɛʀʒətyʀ/ *nf* stretch mark.

verglacé, **~e** /vɛʀɡlase/ *adj* icy.

verglas /vɛʀɡla/ *nm inv* black ice.

vergogne: **sans vergogne** /sɑ̃vɛʀɡɔɲ/ **I** *loc adv* **1** (sans honte) shamelessly; **2** (sans hésitation) straight out.

II *loc adj* (sans scrupule) unscrupulous.

vergue /vɛʀɡ/ *nf* NAUT yard.

véridique /veʀidik/ *adj* [*détail, histoire, fait*] true; [*description, témoignage*] truthful; **l'anecdote est ~** the story is true.

vérifiable /veʀifjabl/ *adj* [*histoire, source, méthode*] verifiable SOUT; **être facilement ~** to be easy to check ou verify.

vérificateur, **-trice** /veʀifikatœʀ, tʀis/ ▶ **374** *nm,f* controller.

vérification /veʀifikasjɔ̃/ *nf* (d'appareil, expérience) check (**de** on); (d'alibi, de fait) verification; **une ~ d'identité** an identity check.

vérifier /veʀifje/ [2] **I** *vtr* **1** (tester) to check [*appareil, instrument*]; (contrôler) to check [*identité, adresse, norme, calcul*]; **2** (confirmer) to verify, to check [*affirmation, témoignage*]; to confirm [*hypothèse*]; to verify [*fait*].

II se vérifier *vpr* [*hypothèse, théorie*] to be borne out; **se ~ dans les faits** to be borne out by the facts.

vérin /veʀɛ̃/ *nm* (screw) jack.

véritable /veʀitabl/ *adj* **1** (authentique) [*ami*] true, genuine, real; [*sentiment, discussion*] true, real; [*artiste*] true; [*cuir*] real, genuine; [*or, argent*] real; **2** (réel) [*nom, raison, responsable*] real, actual; [*colère*] real; [*joie*] true; **3** (intensif) (*before n*) real, veritable; **la pièce est une ~ fournaise** the room is like an oven.

véritablement /veʀitabləmɑ̃/ *adv* really, actually; **c'est ~ un scandale!** it really is a scandal!

vérité /veʀite/ *nf* **1** GÉN truth; **posséder** or **détenir la ~** to know everything; **le quart d'heure** or **la minute de ~** the moment of truth; **l'épreuve de ~** the acid test; **faire la ~ sur qch** to disclose the truth about sth; **à la ~** to tell the truth; **2** (affirmation vraie) truth; **énoncer des ~s premières** to state the obvious; **toute ~ n'est pas bonne à dire** some things are better left unsaid; **3** (authenticité) (de personnage, scène, reconstitution) realism; (de sentiment, d'expression) sincerity; **4** (nature profonde) true nature.

IDIOMES **à chacun sa ~** PROV each to his own; **la ~ sort de la bouche des enfants** PROV out of the mouths of (very) babes (and sucklings).

verlan /vɛʀlɑ̃/ *nm*: *French slang formed by inverting the syllables.*

vermeil, **-eille** /vɛʀmɛj/ **I** ▶ **141** *adj* **1** (rouge vif) bright red; **teint ~** rosy complexion; **2** [*vin*] ruby.

II *nm* (argent doré) vermeil.

vermicelle /vɛʀmisɛl/ *nm* vermicelli **Ç**.

vermifuge /vɛʀmifyʒ/ **I** *adj* worm (*épith*).

II *nm* wormer.

vermillon /vɛʀmijɔ̃/ ▶ **141** **I** *adj inv* (rouge vif) bright red, vermilion.

II *nm* **1** (couleur) bright red, vermilion; **2** (sulfure de mercure) vermilion.

vermine /vɛʀmin/ *nf* **1** (parasites) vermin; **2** (personnes) scum, vermin.

vermoulu, **~e** /vɛʀmuly/ *adj* **1** [*planche, mobilier*] worm-eaten; **2** [*idéologie, institutions*] moth-eaten.

verni, **~e** /vɛʀni/ **I** *pp* ▶ **vernir**.

II *pp adj* LIT [*bois, peinture*] varnished; [*chaussures*] patent-leather (*épith*); [*faïence*] glazed.

III○ *adj* (chanceux) lucky; **il n'est pas ~** he's unlucky.

vernir /vɛʀniʀ/ [3] **I** *vtr* to varnish [*planche, meuble*]; to glaze [*faïence, poterie*]; to apply nail varnish GB ou nail polish to [*ongles*].

II se vernir *vpr* **se ~ les ongles** to varnish GB ou polish one's nails.

vernis /vɛʀni/ *nm inv* **1** (sur bois) varnish; (sur céramique) glaze; **2** (apparence) veneer; **un ~ de culture** a veneer of culture; **si on gratte le ~, on voit que...** if you scratch the surface, you'll see that...

■ **~ à ongles** nail varnish GB ou polish.

vernissage /vɛʀnisaʒ/ *nm* **1** ART preview, private view; **2** (de bois) varnishing; (de céramique) glazing.

vernissé, **~e** /vɛʀnise/ *adj* **1** [*tuiles, carreaux*] glazed; **2** [*plumes, feuilles*] glossy.

véronique /veʀɔnik/ *nf* speedwell, veronica SPÉC.

verre /vɛʀ/ *nm* **1** (matière) glass; **de** or **en ~** glass (*épith*); **travail du ~** glasswork; **des débris de ~** broken glass **Ç**; **2** (récipient) glass; **~s et couverts** glassware and cutlery; **lever son ~ à la santé de qn** to raise one's glass to sb; **3** (contenu) glass, glassful; **4** (boisson) drink; **un petit ~** a quick drink; **avoir bu un ~ de trop** to have had one too many; **boire le ~ de l'amitié** to toast one's friendship; **5** (plaque) glass; **mettre qch sous ~** to put sth under glass; **6** PHYS (lentille) lens; **~s de lunettes** spectacle lenses; **~ grossissant** magnifying glass.

■ **~ antireflet** antiglare glass; **~ de contact** contact lens; **~ correcteur** corrective lens; **~ à dents** toothglass; **~ fumé** (pour lunettes) tinted lens; (pour vitrage) tinted glass; **~ gradué** measuring jug; **~ de lampe** lamp chimney; **~ à pied** stemmed glass.

verrerie /vɛʀʀi/ *nf* **1** (fabrication) glassmaking; **2** (objets) glassware; **3** (usine) glassworks (*pl*), glass factory.

verrier, **-ière**[1] /vɛʀje, ɛʀ/ **I** *adj* glass (*épith*).

II ▶ **374** *nm* glassmaker, glass manufacturer.

verrière[2] /vɛʀjɛʀ/ *nf* **1** (toit vitré) glass roof; **2** (grand vitrage) glass wall, glassed-in wall; **3** (de cockpit) canopy.

verroterie /vɛʀɔtʀi/ *nf* glass jewellery GB ou jewelry US.

verrou /vɛʀu/ *nm* GÉN bolt; (à bouton) deadbolt; (à clé) deadlock; **~ 3 points** multilock; **mettre le ~** to shoot the bolt.

IDIOMES **être sous les ~s** to be under lock and key.

verrouillage /vɛʀujaʒ/ *nm* (action) bolting; (d'arme à feu) locking; (dispositif) locking mechanism.

■ **~ central** or **centralisé (des portes)** AUT central locking.

verrouiller /vɛʀuje/ [1] *vtr* GÉN to bolt [*fenêtre, porte*]; to lock [*portière, arme*]; to cordon off [*quartier*]; **~ une majorité parlementaire** to protect a parliamentary majority.

verrue /vɛʀy/ *nf* MÉD wart; **~ plantaire** verruca, plantar wart SPÉC.

vers[1] /vɛʀ/ *prép*

■ **Note** Lorsque *vers* indique une direction, une tendance ou une orientation, il se traduit généralement par *toward(s)*. On notera que *towards* est plus courant en anglais britannique et *toward* en anglais américain.
— Lorsque *vers* fait partie d'une expression du genre *se tourner vers, tendre vers, départ vers* etc la traduction est donnée respectivement à *tourner, tendre, départ*.
— On trouvera ci-dessous des usages particuliers de *vers*.

1 (en direction de) toward(s); **il vint ~ moi** he came toward(s) me; **il n'a même pas tourné la tête ~ elle** he didn't even look in her direction; **se déplacer**

de la gauche ~ la droite to move from left to right; **des migrations ~ le sud** migration to the south; **il habite plus ~ le nord** he lives further north; **2** (aux environs de) (lieu) near, around; (temps) about; (période) toward(s); **les rues sont toujours encombrées ~ le centre-ville** the streets are always congested around the town centre^{GB}; **~ cinq heures** about ou around five o'clock; **elle est tombée malade ~ l'âge de 25 ans** she became ill GB ou sick US when she was about 25.

vers² /vɛʀ/ **I** nm inv (ligne de poésie) line (of verse); **le troisième ~** the third line; **poème en ~** poem in verse.
II nmpl (poésie) poetry ¢.

versant /vɛʀsɑ̃/ nm side.

versatile /vɛʀsatil/ adj [personne] unpredictable, volatile.

verse: à verse /avɛʀs/ loc adv **il pleut à ~** it's pouring down.

Verseau /vɛʀso/ ▶ 641 | nprm Aquarius.

versement /vɛʀsəmɑ̃/ nm **1** (de somme) payment; **~ comptant** cash payment; **2** (échelonné) instalment^{GB}; **3** (dépôt) deposit; **faire un ~ sur son compte** to pay money into one's account.

verser /vɛʀse/ [1] **I** vtr **1** (servir) to pour [boisson]; (transvaser) to pour [liquide, sable]; (sans précautions) to tip [liquide, sable]; **~ à boire à qn** to pour sb a drink; **attention, tu verses à côté** careful, you're spilling it; **2** (payer) to pay; **on leur verse une commission** they get a commission; **3** (répandre) to shed [larme, sang]; **~ le sang** to shed blood; **~ son sang pour la patrie** (mourir) to die fighting for one's country; **4** (ajouter) to add; **~ une pièce à un dossier** to add a document to a file; **5** MIL (affecter) to assign (**dans** to).
II vi **1** (se renverser) to overturn; **2** (se laisser aller à) to lapse (**dans** into); **3** (laisser couler) [cruche] to pour.

verset /vɛʀsɛ/ nm **1** (de la Bible, du Coran) verse; **2** (prière) versicle; **3** LITTÉRAT verset.

verseur, -euse /vɛʀsœʀ, øz/ adj pouring; **flacon ~** bottle with a pouring spout.

versifier /vɛʀsifje/ [2] vtr to put [sth] into verse.

version /vɛʀsjɔ̃/ nf **1** (traduction) translation (into one's own language); **2** (interprétation) version; **la ~ officielle** the official version; **3** CIN, LITTÉRAT, MUS **en ~ espagnole** in the Spanish version; **4** IND, COMM (modèle) model, version.
■ **~ doublée** CIN dubbed version; **~ originale, vo** CIN original version.

verso /vɛʀso/ nm back; **voir au ~** see over(leaf).

vert, ~e /vɛʀ, vɛʀt/ **I** ▶ 141 | adj **1** GÉN green; [région, pays] green, verdant LITTÉR; **une banlieue ~e** a leafy suburb; **être ~ de peur** to be white with fear; **2** (non arrivé à maturité) [fruit, légume] green, unripe; [bois] green; [vin] immature; **3** (vigoureux) [vieillard] sprightly; **4** (before n) [semonce, réprimande] sharp, stiff.
II ▶ 141 | nm green; **le feu est passé au ~** the light went ou turned green.
III verts nmpl POL **les ~s** the environmentalists, the ecologists GB; **les Verts** the French Green party.
IDIOMES **en dire de ~es** to tell spicy ou risqué stories; **avoir la main ~e** to have green fingers GB ou a green thumb US; **se mettre au ~** ○ to take a break in the country.

vert-de-gris /vɛʀdəgʀi/ **I** ▶ 141 | adj inv blue-green.
II nm inv TECH verdigris.

vertébral, ~e, mpl **-aux** /vɛʀtebʀal, o/ adj vertebral.

vertèbre /vɛʀtɛbʀ/ nf vertebra; **les ~s cervicales** cervical vertebrae; **se déplacer une ~** to slip a disc.

vertébré, ~e /vɛʀtebʀe/ **I** adj vertebrate.
II nm vertebrate.

vertement /vɛʀtəmɑ̃/ adv sharply.

vertical, ~e¹, mpl **-aux** /vɛʀtikal, o/ adj **1** MATH, GÉN [axe, plan, mouvement, position, décollage] vertical;

[miroir, panneau] upright; **la station ~e** standing position; **2** (selon une hiérarchie) [intégration, organisation, croissance] vertical.

verticale² /vɛʀtikal/ nf MATH, PHYS vertical; **mettre qch à la ~** to put sth upright; **le rocher se dresse à la ~** the rock rises sheer.

verticalement /vɛʀtikalmɑ̃/ adv **1** GÉN vertically; **2** (dans les mots croisés) down.

vertige /vɛʀtiʒ/ nm **1** (sensation) dizziness, giddiness; (dû à la hauteur) vertigo; **avoir le ~** (habituellement) to suffer from vertigo; (ponctuellement) to feel dizzy ou giddy; **avoir des ~s** to have dizzy ou giddy spells; **3** (exaltation) **~ de l'amour** intoxicating effect of love.

vertigineux, -euse /vɛʀtiʒinø, øz/ adj [hauteur] dizzy, giddy; [profondeur, ascension, vitesse] breathtaking; [somme, chute, progression] staggering.

vertu /vɛʀty/ **I** nf **1** (intégrité) (moral) virtue; **2** (chasteté) virtue, honour^{GB}; **de petite ~** of easy virtue; **3** (qualité) virtue, virtue; **4** (propriété) (de plante, remède) property; (de choses abstraites) virtue.
II en **vertu de** loc prép JUR by virtue of, pursuant to; GÉN in accordance with.

vertueux, -euse /vɛʀtɥø, øz/ adj virtuous.

verve /vɛʀv/ nf eloquence; **être (très) en ~** to be in sparkling form.

verveine /vɛʀvɛn/ nf **1** BOT verbena; **2** (liqueur) (liqueur de) **~** verbena liqueur; **3** (tisane) verbena tea.

vésiculaire /vezikylɛʀ/ adj **1** MÉD of the gall bladder (après n); **2** (en forme de vésicule) vesicular.

vésicule /vezikyl/ nf **1** ANAT, BOT vesicle; **2** MÉD (cloque) blister.
■ **~ biliaire** gall bladder; **~s séminales** ANAT seminal vesicles.

vespasienne /vɛspazjɛn/ nf public urinal.

vespéral, ~e, mpl **-aux** /vɛspeʀal, o/ adj LITER evening (épith).

vessie /vesi/ nf bladder; **~ gazeuse** or **natatoire** air ou swim bladder.
IDIOMES **prendre des ~s pour des lanternes**○ to think the moon is made of green cheese; **faire prendre des ~s pour des lanternes à qn** to pull the wool over sb's eyes.

veste /vɛst/ nf jacket; **~ de survêtement** SPORT tracksuit top; **tomber la ~**○ to take off one's jacket.
IDIOMES **retourner sa ~**○ POL to change sides, to sell out; **prendre une ~**○ to come a cropper○.

vestiaire /vɛstjɛʀ/ nm **1** (salle) (dans un stade, gymnase) changing GB ou locker room; (dans un musée, un théâtre, une discothèque) cloakroom; **laisser sa fierté au ~** FIG to forget one's pride; **2** (meuble) locker.

vestibule /vɛstibyl/ nm (d'édifice) hall; (d'hôtel, de théâtre) foyer GB, lobby.

vestige /vɛstiʒ/ nm **1** (de construction, d'objet) relic; **des ~s archéologiques** archeological remains; **2** (d'époque, de civilisation) vestige.

vestimentaire /vɛstimɑ̃tɛʀ/ adj **tenue ~** way of dressing; **mode ~** fashion; **élégance ~** elegance in dress.

veston /vɛstɔ̃/ nm (man's) jacket.

vêtement /vɛtmɑ̃/ nm **1** (pièce d'habillement) item ou piece of clothing; **des ~s** clothes, clothing ¢; **~s de travail** workclothes; **ce ~ se vend très bien** this garment is selling very well; **'~s pour hommes'** 'menswear', 'men's fashions'; **~s de sport** sportswear; **2** (secteur d'activité) clothing trade, garment industry US.

vétéran /veteʀɑ̃/ nm veteran.

vétérinaire /veteʀinɛʀ/ **I** adj veterinary.
II ▶ 374 | nmf vet, veterinary surgeon GB, veterinarian US.

vétille /vetij/ nf trifle.

vêtir /vetiʀ/ [33] **I** vtr (habiller) to dress.
II se vêtir vpr to dress (oneself), to get dressed.

veto /veto/ *nm* veto; **mettre** or **opposer son ~ à qch** to veto sth.

vêtu, ~e /vɛty/ **I** *pp* ▶ **vêtir**.
II *pp adj* dressed; **être ~ de qch** to be dressed ou clad in sth, to be wearing sth.

vétuste /vetyst/ *adj* (délabré) dilapidated; (obsolète) outdated.

vétusté /vetyste/ *nf* (délabrement) dilapidation (**de** of), run-down state (**de** of); (ancienneté) (great) age (**de** of), outdated state (**de** of).

veuf, veuve /vœf, vœv/ **I** *adj* widowed; **être ~/ veuve** to be a widower/widow.
II *nm,f* widower/widow; **Mme Brun, veuve Dupont** Mrs Brun, the widow of Mr Dupont.

veule /vøl/ *adj* weak, spineless.

veuvage /vœvaʒ/ *nm* **1** (perte du conjoint) loss of one's husband/wife; **2** (état de veuf) (state of) being a widower; (état de veuve) widowhood.

veuve ▶ **veuf**.

vexant, ~e /vɛksɑ̃, ɑ̃t/ *adj* (blessant) hurtful (**pour** to); (contrariant) tiresome, vexing.

vexation /vɛksasjɔ̃/ *nf* humiliation.

vexer /vɛkse/ [1] **I** *vtr* **1** (blesser) to offend, to upset; **être vexé par qch/par qn** to be upset at sth/by sb; **2** (contrarier) to annoy.
II se vexer *vpr* to take offence^GB, to be upset.

via /vja/ *prép* **1** (en passant par) via; **2** (par l'intermédiaire de) via, through.

viabilisé, ~e /vjabilize/ *adj* [*terrain*] with all mains services (*épith, après n*).

viabilité /vjabilite/ *nf* **1** (de fœtus) viability; **2** (de régime, d'entreprise) viability; **3** (de terrain) **assurer la ~ d'un terrain** to provide a building site ou plot with services; **4** (de route) suitability for vehicles.

viable /vjabl/ *adj* **1** [*fœtus*] viable; **2** [*projet*] feasible; [*entreprise*] viable; [*situation*] bearable, tolerable.

viaduc /vjadyk/ *nm* viaduct.

viager, -ère /vjaʒe, ɛʀ/ **I** *adj* life (*épith*).
II *nm* (rente) life annuity; **acheter qch en ~** to buy sth by paying a life annuity; **vendre qch en ~** to sell sth for a life annuity.

viande /vjɑ̃d/ *nf* CULIN meat; **~ de bœuf/mouton** beef/mutton.

vibrant, ~e /vibʀɑ̃, ɑ̃t/ *adj* **1** (animé de vibrations) [*coussin, lame*] vibrating; **2** (ému) [*voix*] resonant; [*discours*] vibrant; [*hommage*] glowing; [*plaidoyer*] impassioned; [*foule*] excited, feverish; **~ d'excitation/de colère** quivering with excitement/with anger.

vibration /vibʀasjɔ̃/ *nf* vibration; **traitement par ~s** vibromassage.

vibratoire /vibʀatwaʀ/ *adj* vibratory.

vibrer /vibʀe/ [1] *vi* **1** (osciller) GÉN, PHYS [*lame, son*] to vibrate; **2** (frémir) [*voix*] to quiver (**de** with); [*cœur*] to thrill; **elle vibrait de tout son être** LITER she felt a thrill go through her; **on vibre en les écoutant** your spine tingles when you listen to them; **faire ~ la corde patriotique** to rouse people's patriotism.

vicaire /vikɛʀ/ *nm* curate.
■ **~ apostolique** vicar apostolic; **le ~ du Christ** the Vicar of Christ; **~ général** vicar general.

vice /vis/ *nm* **1** (débauche) vice; **vivre dans le ~** to lead a dissolute life; **2** (mauvaise habitude) vice; **3** (défaut physique) fault, defect.
■ **~ caché** hidden defect ou fault; **~ de construction** structural defect; **~ de fabrication** manufacturing defect; **~ de procédure** legal irregularity.

vice-amiral, *pl* **-aux** /visamiʀal, o/ ▶ **284** *nm* ~ rear-admiral.

vice-chancelier, *pl* **~s** /visʃɑ̃səlje/ ▶ **596** *nm* vice-chancellor.

vice-présidence, *pl* **~s** /vispʀezidɑ̃s/ *nf* (d'État) vice-presidency; (de comité, d'entreprise) vice-chairmanship, vice-presidency US.

vice-président, ~e, *mpl* **~s** /vispʀezidɑ̃, ɑ̃t/ *nm,f* (d'État) vice-president; (de comité, d'entreprise) vice-chair(man), vice-president US.

vice-roi, *pl* **~s** /visʀwa/ ▶ **596** *nm* viceroy.

vice(-)versa /visversa/ *adv* vice versa.

vichy /viʃi/ *nm* **1** (tissu) gingham; **2** (eau) vichy water.

vicier /visje/ [2] **I** *vtr* (altérer) to pollute [*air*]; to contaminate [*sang*].
II se vicier *vpr* [*air*] to become polluted.

vicieux, -ieuse /visjø, øz/ **I** *adj* **1** (dépravé) [*personne*] lecherous; **il faut être ~ pour aimer ça** you've got to be perverted to like that; **2** (sournois) [*personne*] sly; [*coup, attaque*] well-disguised; [*question*] trick (*épith*); [*argumentation*] deceitful; **3** (défectueux) [*locution, prononciation*] wrong; [*position*] abnormal; **un cercle ~** a vicious circle; **4** (indocile) [*cheval*] vicious.
II *nm,f* pervert.

vicinal, ~e, *mpl* **-aux** /visinal, o/ *adj* ADMIN **chemin ~** byroad.

vicissitudes /visisityd/ *nfpl* (épreuves) trials and tribulations; (changements) vicissitudes, ups and downs^○.

vicomte /vikɔ̃t/ ▶ **596** *nm* viscount.

vicomtesse /vikɔ̃tes/ ▶ **596** *nf* viscountess.

victime /viktim/ *nf* **1** (d'accident, de désastre, phénomène) victim, casualty; **être ~ d'un infarctus** to suffer a heart attack; **le joueur, ~ d'une blessure au genou**... the player, suffering from a knee injury...; **~ d'une panne, il a abandonné la course** hit by mechanical problems, he abandoned the race; **il a été ~ de son succès** his success has been his undoing; **2** JUR victim; **3** (créature offerte en sacrifice) sacrificial victim.

victoire /viktwaʀ/ *nf* GÉN victory; SPORT win, victory; **crier** or **chanter ~** to claim victory; (**remporter**) **une ~ sur soi-même** (to win) a personal battle.

victorieusement /viktɔʀjøzmɑ̃/ *adv* triumphantly.

victorieux, -ieuse /viktɔʀjø, øz/ *adj* [*pays, armée*] victorious; [*athlète, équipe*] winning (*épith*); [*débuts, tir*] successful; [*sourire*] of victory (*épith, après n*).

victuailles /viktɥaj/ *nfpl* provisions, victuals.

vidange /vidɑ̃ʒ/ *nf* **1** (de cuve, fosse, fossé) emptying; **2** AUT oil change; **faire la ~** to change the oil; **huile de ~** waste oil; **3** (tuyau d'évacuation) (de baignoire) drain; (de lave-linge) waste pipe.

vidanger /vidɑ̃ʒe/ [13] **I** *vtr* **1** to empty, to drain [*cuve, fosse*]; **2** to drain off [*liquide*].
II *vi* [*lave-linge*] to empty.

vide /vid/ **I** *adj* **1** (sans contenu) [*boîte*] empty; [*cassette, page*] blank; **les mains ~s** FIG empty-handed; **tu l'as loué ~ ou meublé?** are you renting it unfurnished or furnished?; **2** (dépeuplé, inoccupé) [*salle, rue, fauteuil*] empty; [*appartement*] empty, vacant; **3** (sans intérêt, substance, idées) [*vie, slogan, esprit*] empty; [*regard*] vacant; **j'ai la tête ~** my mind is a blank; **~ d'intérêt** devoid of any interest; **~ de sens** meaningless.
II *nm* **1** (espace) space; **sauter** or **se jeter dans le ~** LIT to jump into space; FIG to leap into the unknown ; **et au-dessous de lui, le ~** (alpiniste) and below him, a sheer drop; (acrobate) and nothing between him and the ground; **être attiré par le ~** to be drawn toward(s) the edge; **parler dans le ~** (sans auditeur) to talk to oneself; (sans sujet) to talk at random; **promettre dans le ~** FIG to make empty promises; PHYS vacuum; **emballé sous ~** vacuum packed; **faire le ~ autour de soi** FIG to drive everybody away; **j'ai besoin de faire le ~ dans ma tête** I need to forget about everything; **3** (absence à combler) vacuum, void; (absence douloureuse) void; **combler un ~** to fill a vacuum; **4** (vacuité) emptiness; **le ~ de l'existence** the emptiness of life; **5** (trou) (entre deux objets) gap, empty space; (dans un emploi du temps) gap; **combler un** or **le ~** LIT, FIG to fill a gap.
III **à vide** *loc adv* (sans contenu) empty; (sans

résultat) with no result; **la clé tourne à ~** the key is not catching; **camion à ~** truck without a load.

vidé, **~e** /vide/ **I** *pp* ▶ **vider**.
II° *pp adj* (fatigué) worn out.

vidéaste /videast/ ▶ 374┃ *nmf* video director.

vidéo /video/ *adj inv*, *nf* video.

vidéoclip /videoklip/ *nm* videoclip.

vidéoclub /videoklœb/ *nm* video store, video shop GB.

vidéoconférence /videokɔ̃ferɑ̃s/ *nf* **1** (séance) video-conference; **2** (principe) video conferencing.

vidéodisque /videodisk/ *nm* videodisc.

vide-ordures /vidɔrdyr/ *nm inv* rubbish GB ou garbage US chute.

vidéothèque /videotɛk/ *nf* (de prêt) video library; (chez soi) video collection.

vide-poches /vidpɔʃ/ *nm inv* (coupe) tidy.

vider /vide/ [1] **I** *vtr* **1** (débarrasser) to empty [*poche, boîte, pièce, verre*]; to empty, to drain [*cuve, étang, réservoir*]; (avaler) to down [*verre*]; to go through [*paquet de biscuits*]; **~ un coffre-fort** to clean out a safe; **2** (retirer) to empty [*sth*] (out) [*eau, ordures*]; **3** (rendre désert) to empty [*lieu*]; **4**° (expulser) to throw [*sb*] out°, to kick [*sb*] out° [*intrus, indésirable*]; **5** (évider) to gut [*poisson*]; to draw [*volaille*]; to core [*pomme*]; to hollow out [*tomate*]; **6** (priver) **~ qch de son sens** to deprive sth of all meaning; **7**° (épuiser) (physiquement) to wear [sb] out; (mentalement) to drain [*personne*].
II se vider *vpr* to empty; **en été, Paris se vide de ses habitants** in the summer all Parisians leave town.

videur°, **-euse** /vidœr, øz/ ▶ 374┃ *nm,f* bouncer.

vie /vi/ *nf* **1** GÉN, BIOL life; **rendre la ~ à qn** to bring sb back to life; **sans ~** lifeless; **on l'a retrouvé sans ~** they found him dead; **donner la ~ à qn** to bring sb into the world; **2** (période) life; **pour la ~** for life; **vivre sa ~** to lead one's own life; **passer sa ~ à faire** GÉN to spend one's life doing; (tout le temps) to spend all one's time doing; **à ~** [*bannir, défigurer, marquer*] for life; [*bannissement, suspension*] lifetime (*épith*); [*emprisonnement, adhésion, président*] life (*épith*); **c'est la chance de ta ~** it's the chance of a lifetime; **3** (activité) life; **la ~ d'entreprise** corporate life; **la ~ est chère** the cost of living is high; **mode de ~** lifestyle; **apprendre la ~** to learn what life is all about; **notre ~ de couple** our relationship; ▶ **château**; **4** (vitalité) life; **prendre ~** to come to life; **donner de la ~ à une fête** to liven up a party; **manquant de ~, sans ~** [*personne, lieu*] lifeless; **5** (biographie) life; **écrire la ~ de qn** to write a life of sb; **6** TECH (durabilité) life; **~ d'une pile** life of a battery.
IDIOMES **ainsi va la ~** that's the way it goes; **c'est la belle ~!** this is the life!; **avoir la ~ dure** [*préjugés*] to be ingrained; **mener la ~ dure à qn** to make life hard for sb, to give sb a hard time; **faire la ~** ° [*enfants*] to have a wild time; [*adultes*] to live it up°; **à la ~, à la mort!** till death us do part!

vieil ▶ **vieux**.

vieillard, **~e** /vjɛjar, ard/ *nm,f* old man/woman; **les ~s** old people.

vieille ▶ **vieux**.

vieillerie /vjɛjri/ *nf* (objet) old thing.

vieillesse /vjɛjɛs/ *nf* **1** (de personne) old age; (de bâtiment, d'arbre) great age; **2**° (personnes âgées) **la ~** the old (+ *v pl*).

vieilli, **~e** /vjeji/ **I** *pp* ▶ **vieillir**.
II *pp adj* **1** (usé) [*peau, tentures*] old-looking; **2** (démodé) [*équipement*] outdated; [*expression*] dated; **3** (bonifié) **vin ~ en fût** wine matured in the cask.

vieillir /vjejir/ [3] **I** *vtr* **1** (en apparence) [*coiffure, robe*] to make [sb] look older; **2** (en estimation) **ne me vieillis pas, j'ai 59 ans!** don't make me out to be any older than I am, I'm only 59!; **3** (physiquement) [*maladie, pauvreté*] to age.
II *vi* **1** (en âge) **je vieillis** I am getting old; **j'ai vieilli** I'm older; (en maturité) I have grown up; **je me sens ~** I feel my age; **pour bien ~, faites du sport** to stay young, take exercise; **je ne veux pas ~ ici** I

don't want to be here till I die; **2** (se dégrader) [*corps, bâtiment*] to show signs of age; [*personne*] to age; **il vieillit mal** (apparence) he's losing his looks; **elle vieillit bien** she looks good for her age; **3** SOCIOL **notre population vieillit** we have an ageing population; **4** (pour un vin) to mature, to age; **5** (se démoder) [*œuvre, institution*] to become outdated.
III se vieillir *vpr* **1** (en apparence) to make oneself look older; **2** (en mentant) to make oneself out to be older.

vieillissant, **~e** /vjejisɑ̃, ɑ̃t/ *adj* ageing.

vieillissement /vjejismɑ̃/ *nm* (de personne, population, peau, vin) ageing; (d'institution) stultification.

vieillot, **-otte** /vjejo, ɔt/ *adj* quaint; **cela te donne un air ~** it gives you a charming old-fashioned air.

viennois, **~e** /vjɛnwa, az/ ▶ 628┃ *adj* **1** (de ville) (en Autriche) Viennese; (en France) of Vienne; **2** CULIN [*chocolat, café, pâtisserie, pain*] Viennese; **escalope ~e** Wiener schnitzel.

viennoiserie /vjɛnwazri/ *nf* **1** (gâteau) Viennese pastry; **2** (ensemble des produits) Viennese pastries (*pl*).

vierge /vjɛrʒ/ **I** *adj* **1** [*personne*] virgin (*épith*); **2** (non utilisé) [*cassette, feuille*] blank; [*cahier, pellicule*] unused; [*casier judiciaire*] clean; [*dossier, agenda*] empty; **3** (non exploré) [*terre, domaine*] virgin; **cimes ~s** unclimbed peaks; **4** (pur) [*laine*] new; [*cire, huile d'olive*] virgin; **5** (non souillé) LITER [*neige*] virgin; [*réputation, vie*] unblemished; **~ de** free from, unsullied by; **6** (non fécondé) [*œuf, génisse*] unfertilized.
II *nf* virgin.

Vierge /vjɛrʒ/ **I** *nf* **1** RELIG **la (Sainte) ~** the (Blessed) Virgin; **Sainte ~!** Good Heavens!; **2** ART (représentation) madonna.
II ▶ 641┃ *nprf* (en astronomie, en astrologie) Virgo.

Viêt Nam /vjɛtnam/ ▶ 232┃ *nprm* Vietnam.

vietnamien, **-ienne** /vjɛtnamjɛ̃, ɛn/ ▶ 394┃, 338┃ **I** *adj* Vietnamese.
II *nm* LING Vietnamese.

vieux, (**vieil** *before vowel or mute h*), **vieille**, *mpl* **vieux** /vjø, vjɛj/ **I** *adj* old; **être ~ avant l'âge** to be old before one's time; **une institution vieille de 100 ans** a 100-year-old institution; **le ~ continent** the old world; **au bon ~ temps** in the good old days; **c'est de la vieille histoire** that's ancient history; **une vieille rivalité** a long-standing rivalry; **il est très vieille France** he's a gentleman of the old school.
II *nm,f* **1** (personne âgée) old person; **un petit ~** a little old man; **une petite vieille** a little old woman; **les ~** old people; **mes ~**° (parents) my parents; **2**° (camarade) **salut, ~!** hello, mate°! GB, hi, pal°! US; **mon pauvre ~** you poor old thing; **ça va, ma vieille?** how are you, dear?
III *adv* **vivre ~** to live to a ripe old age; **il s'habille ~** he dresses like an old man; **ta sœur fait ~** your sister looks old.
IV *nm* (objets) **le ~** old things (*pl*); **prendre un coup de ~** to age; **faire du neuf avec du ~** to revamp things.
■ **vieille fille** old maid; **vieille peau** PEJ old bag°; PEJ; **~ beau** ageing Romeo; **~ clou**° (véhicule) old crock°; **~ croûton**° PEJ old duffer°; **~ garçon** old bachelor; **~ jeu** old-fashioned; **~ rose** dusty pink, old rose; **~ schnock**° PEJ fuddy-duddy°.
IDIOMES **~ comme le monde, ~ comme Hérode** or **Mathusalem** as old as the hills; **c'est un ~ de la vieille**° (vétéran) he's an old hand.

vif, **vive¹** /vif, viv/ **I** *adj* **1** (brillant) [*couleur, lumière*] bright; **2** (animé) [*personne*] lively, vivacious; [*imagination*] vivid; **3** (agressif) [*débat, protestations*] heated; [*opposition*] fierce; **répondre d'un ton ~** to answer sharply; **sa réaction a été un peu vive** he/she reacted rather strongly; **4** (important) [*contraste*] sharp; [*intérêt, désir*] keen; [*inquiétude*] deep; [*crainte, douleur*] acute; [*préoccupation*] serious; [*déception*] bitter; [*succès*] notable; **c'est avec un ~ plaisir que** it is with great pleasure that; **5** (rapide) [*rythme, geste*]

Les villes

Les noms de villes

Toute ville peut être désignée par les expressions the town of ... *ou* the city of ...: *town s'applique en anglais britannique à toute agglomération d'une certaine importance, et en anglais américain à toute commune, même très peu peuplée. En Grande-Bretagne* city *désigne les très grandes villes, ainsi que les villes ayant une cathédrale.*

À avec les noms de villes

À *se traduit par* to *avec les verbes de mouvement (par ex.* aller, se rendre, *etc.).*

aller à Toulouse = to go to Toulouse
se rendre à La Haye = to travel to The Hague

À *se traduit par* in *avec les autres verbes (par ex.* être, habiter *etc.).*

vivre à Toulouse = to live in Toulouse

Lorsqu'une ville est une étape sur un itinéraire, à se traduira par at.

s'arrêter à Dublin = to stop at Dublin

Les noms des habitants

L'anglais est moins friand que le français de noms d'habitants des villes. Pour les villes des îles britanniques, seuls quelques-uns sont assez courants, comme Londoner, Dubliner, Liverpudlian *(de Liverpool),* Glaswegian *(de Glasgow),* Mancunian *(de Manchester) etc. Pour les villes américaines, on a* New Yorker, Philadelphian *etc. Pour les autres pays,* Parisian, Berliner, Roman *etc.*

Pour traduire un nom d'habitant de ville, il est toujours possible d'utiliser inhabitants *ou* people: *par ex., pour les* Toulousains, *on peut dire* the inhabitants of Toulouse, the people of Toulouse *etc.*

De avec les noms de villes

Les expressions françaises avec de se traduisent le plus souvent par l'emploi du nom de ville en position d'adjectif.

l'accent de Toulouse = a Toulouse accent
l'aéroport de Toulouse = Toulouse airport
les cafés de Toulouse = Toulouse cafés
l'équipe de Toulouse = the Toulouse team
les hivers de Toulouse = Toulouse winters
les hôtels de Toulouse = Toulouse hotels
la région de Toulouse = the Toulouse area
les restaurants de Toulouse = Toulouse restaurants
la route de Toulouse = the Toulouse road
les rues de Toulouse = Toulouse streets
le train de Toulouse = the Toulouse train

Mais:

je suis de Toulouse = I come from Toulouse
une lettre de Toulouse = a letter from Toulouse
le maire de Toulouse = the Mayor of Toulouse
un plan de Toulouse = a map of Toulouse

Les adjectifs dérivés

Les adjectifs dérivés des noms de villes n'ont pas toujours d'équivalent en anglais. Plusieurs cas sont possibles mais on pourra presque toujours utiliser le nom de la ville placé avant le nom qualifié:

la région bordelaise = the Bordeaux area

Pour souligner la provenance on choisira from + *le nom de la ville:*

l'équipe bordelaise = the team from Bordeaux

Pour parler de l'environnement on optera pour of + *le nom de la ville:*

les rues bordelaises = the streets of Bordeaux

Et pour situer on utilisera in + *le nom de la ville:*

mon séjour bordelais = my stay in Bordeaux

---

brisk; **à vive allure** [*conduire, rouler*] at a fast speed; [*travailler, marcher*] at a brisk pace; **avoir l'esprit ~** to be very quick; **6** (perçant, tranchant) [*froid, vent*] keen; [*arête*] sharp; **l'air est ~** the air is bracing; **cuire à feu ~** to cook over a high heat; **7** (vivant) alive; **de vive voix** in person. **II** *nm* **1** GÉN **à ~** [*chair*] bared; [*genou*] raw; [*fil électrique*] exposed; **avoir les nerfs à ~** to be on edge; **la plaie est à ~** it's an open wound; **piquer** or **blesser qn au ~** to sting ou cut sb to the quick; **(pris) sur le ~** [*croquis*] thumbnail (*épith*); [*notes*] taken on the spot (*jamais épith*); [*entretien*] live; **2** JUR **entre ~s** [*donation, partage*] inter vivos.

vigie /viʒi/ *nf* **1** NAUT (matelot) lookout; (poste) (sur le mât) crow's nest; (à la proue) lookout post; (balise) warning buoy; **2** RAIL lookout box.

vigilance /viʒilɑ̃s/ *nf* vigilance; **échapper à la ~ de qn** (de douanier, contrôleur) to escape sb's notice; (de mère, nourrice) to escape sb's attention.

vigilant, ~e /viʒilɑ̃, ɑ̃t/ *adj* [*personne*] vigilant; [*œil*] watchful.

vigile /viʒil/ *nm* **1** (veilleur de nuit) night watchman; (garde) security guard; **2** HIST watch.

vigne /viɲ/ *nf* **1** (plant) vine; **2** (terrain planté) vineyard; **3** (travail) wine growing.
■ **~ mère** stock; **~ vierge** Virginia creeper.

vigneron, -onne /viɲərɔ̃, ɔn/ ▶374 *nm,f* wine-grower.

vignette /viɲɛt/ *nf* **1** (sur un médicament) *detachable label on medicines for reimbursement by social security;* **2** AUT tax disc GB; **3** COMM label; **4** (motif) vignette.

vignoble /viɲɔbl/ *nm* vineyard; **le ~ hongrois/alsacien** the vineyards of Hungary/Alsace.

vigoureux, -euse /viguʀø, øz/ *adj* **1** (physiquement) [*personne, poignée de main*] vigorous; [*athlète, corps*] strong, powerful; [*plante*] sturdy; [*constitution, vieillard*] robust, sturdy; [*coup*] powerful; **2** (déterminé) [*résistance, mesure, style*] vigorous; [*croissance, sentiment*] strong; [*talent*] strong, robust; [*langage*] strong, force-

ful; **3** (net) [*dessin, contour*] strong, bold; [*coloris*] strong, striking.

vigueur /vigœʀ/ **I** *nf* **1** (énergie) vigour^GB; **avec ~** vigorously; **reprendre avec ~** [*lutte*] to start again with renewed vigour^GB; **2** (force musculaire) strength; **frapper avec ~** to bang; **3** (de plante) sturdiness; **4** (de trait, forme) vigour^GB.
II **en vigueur** *loc adj* [*loi, dispositif*] in force; [*régime, conditions*] current; **cesser d'être en ~** t cease to apply; **entrer en ~** to come into force.

VIH /veiaʃ/ *nm* (*abbr* = **virus immunodéficitair humain**) HIV.

vil, ~e /vil/ *adj* LITER [*personne, âme*] base LITTÉR [*action*] vile, base; [*besogne, tâche*] base LITTÉR.

vilain, ~e /vilɛ̃, ɛn/ **I** *adj* **1** (laid) [*bâtiment, pe sonne, animal*] ugly; **c'est vraiment ~ ce chapeau** that hat looks awful!; **faire ~** [*tableau, couleurs*] t look ugly; [*construction*] to be an eyesore; **2**○ (méchant) [*bête, microbe*] nasty; [*garçon, fille*] naughty **jouer un ~ tour à qn** to play a nasty trick on sb; **l discussion a tourné au ~** the discussion turne nasty○; **3** (répréhensible) [*affaire, bruits, rumeur*] nasty; [*défaut*] bad; [*mot*] dirty; **4** (inquiétant) [*tou blessure*] nasty.
II *nm,f* naughty boy/girl; **arrête de faire la ~e** stop being naughty!
III *nm* HIST villein.
IDIOMES **jeux de mains, jeux de ~s** PROV it will en in tears.

vilebrequin /vilbʀəkɛ̃/ *nm* **1** (outil) brace and bi **2** (de moteur) crankshaft.

vilenie /vileni/ *nf* LITER **1** (bassesse) baseness (**de** of **2** (action vile) vile ou base act.

villa /vila/ *nf* **1** (maison d'habitation) ≈ detached house **2** (maison de plaisance) villa; **3** (dans l'antiquité) villa.

village /vilaʒ/ *nm* village.
■ **~ de toile** tent village.

villageois, ~e /vilaʒwa, az/ **I** *adj* village (*épith*).
II *nm,f* villager.

ille /vil/ *nf* **1** (agglomération, habitants) town, (de grande importance) city; **la ~ haute/basse** the upper/lower town; **une ~ d'art** a town of artistic interest; **de ~** [*vêtements, chaussures*] town; **2** (administration) town ou city council.

■ **~ d'eau(x)** spa town; **~ franche** free city; **~ libre** semiautonomous city.

ille-dortoir, *pl* **villes-dortoirs** /vildɔrtwar/ *nf* dormitory town GB, bedroom community US.

illégiature /vilezjatyr/ *nf* (séjour) holiday GB, vacation US; **lieu de ~** holiday resort GB, vacation resort US.

in /vɛ̃/ *nm* wine; **~ rosé** rosé (wine); **~ demi-sec** medium-dry wine; **grand ~** fine wine; **~ de pays** or **de terroir** *quality wine produced in a specific region*; **ce ~ a du corps** this wine is full-bodied; **couper son ~** (en mélanger deux) to blend one's wine; (mettre de l'eau) to add water to one's wine.

■ **~ d'appellation d'origine contrôlée** appellation contrôlée wine (*with a guarantee of origin*); **~ chaud** mulled wine; **~ de coupage** blended wine; **~ cuit** *wine which has undergone heating during maturation*; **~ d'honneur** reception; **le ~ nouveau** *wine from the latest vintage*; **~ de paille** *wine made from dried grapes*.

IDIOMES **avoir le ~ gai/triste** to get happy/maudlin after one has had a few drinks; **mettre de l'eau dans son ~** to mellow; **quand le ~ est tiré, il faut le boire** PROV once you have started something, you have to see it through.

inaigre /vinɛgr/ *nm* vinegar.

IDIOMES **tourner au ~** to turn sour; **on ne prend pas les mouches avec du ~** PROV it doesn't pay to take a hard line.

inaigrer /vinegre/ [1] *vtr* to season [sth] with vinegar.

inaigrette /vinegrɛt/ *nf* vinaigrette, French dressing.

inasse /vinas/ *nf* PEJ plonk○ PÉJ GB, cheap wine.

indicatif, -ive /vɛ̃dikatif, iv/ *adj* vindictive.

indicte /vɛ̃dikt/ *nf* condemnation.

ineux, -euse /vinø, øz/ *adj* **1** ▶ 141 (couleur de vin rouge) [*teint, visage*] purplish; **2** (rappelant le vin) [*odeur*] of wine (*après n*); [*fruit*] tasting of wine; **3** (riche en alcool) [*vin*] full-bodied.

ingt /vɛ̃, vɛ̃t/ ▶ 399 , 298 , 156 I *adj inv* twenty.

II *pron* twenty; **j'ai eu ~ sur ~ à mon devoir d'histoire** ≈ I got full marks GB ou full credit US for my history paper.

ingtaine /vɛ̃tɛn/ *nf* **avoir une ~ d'années** to be about twenty; **nous étions plus d'une ~** there were more than twenty of us.

ingt-deux /vɛ̃tdø/ ▶ 399 , 298 , 156 I *adj inv*, *pron* twenty-two.

II○ *excl* look out!; **~, v'là les flics!** look out! it's the cops○!

ingtième /vɛ̃tjɛm/ ▶ 399 , 156 *adj* twentieth.

inicole /vinikɔl/ *adj* [*activité, secteur, société, région*] wine-producing (*épith*); [*cave, commerce*] wine (*épith*); [*matériel, équipement*] wine-making (*épith*).

inification /vinifikasjɔ̃/ *nf* **1** (procédé) wine production; **~ en blanc/rouge** production of white/red wine; **2** (fermentation) vinification.

inyle /vinil/ *nm* **1** (matériau) vinyl; **2** (disque) vinyl.

iol /vjɔl/ *nm* (de personne) rape; (de loi, temple) violation.

iolacé, ~e /vjɔlase/ ▶ 141 *adj* purplish.

iolation /vjɔlasjɔ̃/ *nf* **1** (de loi, territoire, traité) violation; **2** (d'accord) breach; **~ du secret professionnel** breach of confidentiality.

■ **~ de domicile** JUR forcible entry (*into a person's home*); **~ de sépulture** JUR desecration of a grave.

iolemment /vjɔlamɑ̃/ *adv* violently.

iolence /vjɔlɑ̃s/ *nf* **1** (de personne, sentiment, d'événement) violence; **~ verbale** verbal abuse; **d'une ~ insoutenable** unbearably violent; **avec ~** violently; **avec une rare ~** with extreme violence; **par la ~**

[*imposer, soumettre*] through violence; [*répondre*] with violence; **répliquer à la ~ par la ~** to meet violence with violence; **faire ~ à qn** to force sb (**pour qu'il fasse** to do); **se faire ~** to force oneself (**pour faire** to do); **2** (acte) act of violence; **~s à l'enfant** child abuse.

violent, ~e /vjɔlɑ̃, ɑ̃t/ *adj* [*personne, réaction*] violent; [*couleur*] harsh; [*poison*] powerful; [*désir*] overwhelming; **non ~** [*mouvement, moyens*] nonviolent; [*manifestation*] peaceful, nonviolent.

violenter /vjɔlɑ̃te/ [1] *vtr* (agresser) to assault sexually; (violer) to rape.

violer /vjɔle/ [1] *vtr* **1** to rape [*personne*]; **se faire ~** to be raped; **2** (profaner) to desecrate, to violate [*tombe*]; **~ l'intimité de qn** FIG to invade sb's privacy; **3** (enfreindre) to infringe, to contravene [*loi*].

violet, -ette¹ /vjɔlɛ, ɛt/ ▶ 141 I *adj* purple.

II *nm* (couleur) purple.

violette² /vjɔlɛt/ *nf* (fleur) violet.

violeur /vjɔlœr/ *nm* rapist.

violon /vjɔlɔ̃/ ▶ 392 *nm* **1** (instrument) violin; **jouer du ~** to play the violin; **2** (musicien) violin; **3**○ (prison) **au ~** in the nick○ GB ou slammer○ US ou can○ US.

■ **~ d'Ingres** hobby.

IDIOMES **accorder ses ~s** to reach an agreement; **autant pisser dans un ~**○! it's just pissing○ in the wind!; **payer les ~s du bal** to foot the bill○.

violoncelle /vjɔlɔ̃sɛl/ ▶ 392 *nm* (instrument) cello.

violoncelliste /vjɔlɔ̃selist/ ▶ 392 , 374 *nmf* cellist.

violoniste /vjɔlɔnist/ ▶ 392 , 374 *nmf* violinist.

vipère /vipɛr/ *nf* **1** ZOOL viper, adder; **2** (personne médisante) viper; **avoir** or **être une langue de ~** FIG to have a wicked tongue.

virage /viraʒ/ *nm* **1** (courbe) bend; **~ serré** sharp bend; **prendre un ~ à la corde** to hug a bend; **rater un ~** to fail to negotiate a bend; **2** (changement d'orientation) change of direction; **parti qui amorce un ~ à droite** party which takes a turn to the right ou shifts toward(s) the right; **3** SPORT (en ski) turn.

■ **~ à 180 degrés** FIG U-turn.

virée○ /vire/ *nf* (voyage) trip; (promenade) (en voiture) drive, ride, spin; (à vélo, moto) ride; **une ~ dans les bars de la ville** a tour of the bars in town.

virement /virmɑ̃/ *nm* FIN transfer.

■ **~ automatique** FIN standing order; **~ de bord** NAUT tacking.

virer /vire/ [1] I *vtr* **1** FIN to transfer [*argent, salaire*] (**sur** to); **2**○ (licencier) to fire, to sack○ GB [*employé*]; **se faire ~** to get fired; **3**○ (expulser) GÉN to throw [sb] out [*importun*]; (d'un cours) to send [sb] out [*élève*]; (du lycée) to expel [*élève*]; **4**○ (enlever) to get rid of.

II *vi* **1** (changer de direction) [*véhicule*] to turn; **~ à droite** [*véhicule, parti politique*] to turn ou shift to the right; **~ sur l'aile** to bank; **2** NAUT [*navire*] to turn; **~ de bord** or **vent devant** LIT to go about; **~ de bord** FIG to do a U-turn, to do a flip-flop US; **3** (changer de couleur) [*étoffes, solution*] to change colour GB; [*couleur*] to change; **4** PHOT [*épreuve*] to tone.

III **virer à** *vtr ind* **~ au rouge** to turn red; **~ à l'aigre** to turn sour; **~ au conservatisme** to turn conservative.

virevolter /virvɔlte/ [1] *vi* to twirl.

virginité /virʒinite/ *nf* LIT virginity.

virgule /virgyl/ *nf* **1** LING comma; **à la ~ près** down to the last comma; **2** MATH (decimal) point; **deux ~ vingt-cinq** two point two five; **s'arrêter deux chiffres après la ~** to stop at two decimal places.

viril, ~e /viril/ *adj* [*homme, force*] manly, virile; [*apparence*] masculine, virile; **il est très ~** he's very masculine; **les amitiés ~es** male friendships.

virilité /virilite/ *nf* **1** (caractéristiques physiques) masculinity, virility; **2** (aptitude à engendrer) virility; **3** (attitude masculine) manliness; **manquer de ~** to be rather unmanly.

virtualité /virtµalite/ *nf* **1** PHILOS virtuality; **2** (aptitude) potentiality.

virtuel, -elle /viʀtɥɛl/ *adj* **1** [*succès, résultat, marché*] potential; **à l'état ~** potentially; **2** PHILOS, PHYS virtual.

virtuellement /viʀtɥɛlmɑ̃/ *adv* **1** (pratiquement) virtually; **2** (en théorie) potentially.

virtuose /viʀtɥoz/ **I** *adj* virtuoso (*épith*); [*joueur*] master; **être ~ dans l'art de faire** to be a past master at doing.
II *nmf* **1** MUS virtuoso; **2** (personne douée) master.

virtuosité /viʀtɥozite/ *nf* **1** MUS virtuosity; **interpréter qch avec ~** to give a virtuoso performance of sth; **2** (habileté) brilliance.

virulence /viʀylɑ̃s/ *nf* virulence; **avec ~** virulently.
virulent, ~e /viʀylɑ̃, ɑ̃t/ *adj* virulent.

virus /viʀys/ *nm inv* **1** MÉD virus; **2** (manie) bug○, craze; **le ~ du cinéma** the film bug○; **3** ORDINAT virus.

vis /vis/ *nf inv* screw.
■ **~ cruciforme** Phillips® screw; **~ sans fin** worm, endless screw; **~ platinées** AUT contact points.
IDIOMES **serrer la ~ à qn** to tighten the screws on sb.

visa /viza/ *nm* (sur un passeport) visa; **~ de touriste** tourist visa.
■ **~ de censure** CIN (censor's) certificate.

visage /vizaʒ/ ▶ **137** *nm* LIT, FIG face; **à deux ~s** two-faced; **les deux ~s d'une politique** the two aspects of a policy; **sans ~** faceless; **à ~ découvert** openly; **faire bon ~ à qn** to give sb a warm welcome.
■ **~ pâle** HIST paleface.

vis-à-vis /vizavi/ **I** *nm inv* **1** (bâtiment) **avoir la prison pour ~** to live opposite the prison; **maison sans ~** house with an open outlook; **2** (personne) (à table, dans le train) person opposite; (voisin d'en face) person who lives opposite; **3** (position) **assis en ~** sitting opposite each other; **4** SPORT opponent; **5** (rencontre face-à-face) meeting, encounter.
II vis-à-vis de *loc prép* **1** (à l'égard de) **~ de qch** in relation to sth; **~ de qn** toward(s) sb; **~ de soi-même** with oneself; **2** (comparé à) beside.

viscéral, ~e, *mpl* **-aux** /viseʀal, o/ *adj* **1** (instinctif) [*haine, émotion*] deep-rooted; **réaction ~e** gut reaction; **2** ANAT visceral.

viscéralement /viseʀalmɑ̃/ *adv* violently, virulently.

viscère /viseʀ/ *nm* **1** ANAT internal organ; **2** (de l'abdomen) **les ~s** viscera.

visée /vize/ *nf* **1** (objectif) aim; (dessein) design; **une politique à ~ expansionniste** an expansionist policy; **avoir des ~s sur qn/qch** to have designs on sb/sth; **~s agressives sur les États voisins** aggressive intentions toward(s) neighbouring^GB states; **ils ont des ~s sur le marché européen** they are aiming at the European market; **2** (avec un instrument) GÉOG sighting; PHOT viewing; (avec une arme) aiming.

viser /vize/ [1] **I** *vtr* **1** (pointer son regard) to aim at [*cible*]; (vouloir atteindre) to aim for [*cœur, centre*]; **2** (aspirer à) to aim for [*poste, résultats*]; to aim at [*marché*]; **~ la première place** to aim to be first; **3** (concerner) [*loi, campagne*] to be aimed at; [*remarque, allusion*] to be meant or intended for; **les employés visés par la décision** the employees to whom the ruling applies; **se sentir visé** to feel one is being got at○.
II viser à *vtr ind* **~ à qch/à faire** to aim at sth/to do.
III *vi* **1** (avec un fusil, un appareil photo) to aim; **2** FIG **~ (trop) haut** to set one's sights (too) high.

viseur /vizœʀ/ *nm* **1** PHOT, CIN viewfinder; **2** (d'arme) sight.

visibilité /vizibilite/ *nf* visibility.

visible /vizibl/ *adj* **1** (perceptible) visible; **2** (manifeste) obvious; **son émotion était ~** he/she was visibly moved; **elle va beaucoup mieux, c'est ~** she's obviously a lot better; **3** (en état de recevoir) [*personne*] available; **4** (accessible au public) **les tableaux sont ~s jusqu'au 17 mai** the paintings can be seen until 17 May.

visiblement /vizibləmɑ̃/ *adv* visibly.

visière /vizjɛʀ/ *nf* **1** (de casquette) peak; **2** (sans couvre-chef) eyeshade, visor; **mettre la main en ~** to shad one's eyes with one's hand.

vision /vizjɔ̃/ *nf* **1** (faculté de voir) eyesight, vision; **~ nocturne** night vision; **2** (conception) view; **~ globale** global view; **3** (spectacle) sight; **une ~ d'horreur** a horrible sight; **4** (apparition) vision; **avoir des ~s** to see things, to have visions.

visionnaire /vizjɔnɛʀ/ *adj, nmf* visionary.

visionner /vizjɔne/ [1] *vtr* to view [*film, diapositives*].

visionneuse /vizjɔnøz/ *nf* viewer.

visite /vizit/ *nf* visit; (rapide) call; **~ de politesse** courtesy call; **rendre ~ à qn** to pay sb a call, to call on sb; **être en ~ chez qn** to be paying sb a visit; **~ accompagnée** or **guidée** guided tour; **la ~ d'une maison** (avant de l'acheter) viewing a house; **avoir de la ~** to have visitors ou company; **le médecin fai ses ~s** the doctor is making his/her (house) calls.
■ **~ de contrôle** MÉD follow-up visit; **~ médical** (contrôle) medical (examination); (bilan) checkup.

visiter /vizite/ [1] *vtr* **1** [*touriste, curieux*] to visit, to g round^GB [*musée, ville, pays*]; **faire ~ un lieu à qn** to show sb around a place; **le musée le plus visité** the museum that attracts the most visitors; **2** [*client*] to view [*appartement*]; **3** [*médecin, prêtre*] to visi [*malade, prisonnier*].

visiteur, -euse /vizitœʀ, øz/ *nm,f* visitor.

vison /vizɔ̃/ *nm* **1** (animal, fourrure) mink; **2** (manteau) mink (coat).

visqueux, -euse /viskø, øz/ *adj* **1** [*liquide, produi consistance*] viscous, viscid; **2** (poisseux) sticky gooey○.

visser /vise/ [1] *vtr* **1** (fixer avec des vis) to screw o [*serrure, boîtier*] (**dans** into; **sur** onto); **~ qch fond** to screw sth up tight; **2** (fermer) to screw [st on [*couvercle, bouchon*]; **3** (immobiliser) **être vissé su sa chaise** to be glued to one's chair.

visualisation /vizɥalizasjɔ̃/ *nf* GÉN visualization; ORI NAT display.

visualiser /vizɥalize/ [1] *vtr* **1** (mentalement) to vis alize [*image, mot*]; **2** ORDINAT to display.

visuel, -elle /vizɥɛl/ **I** *adj* visual.
II *nm,f* person with a strong visual sense.

vital, ~e, *mpl* **-aux** /vital, o/ *adj* vital.

vitalité /vitalite/ *nf* (de personne) vitality, energy; (c marché, d'économie) vitality; **elle déborde de ~** she bursting with energy.

vitamine /vitamin/ *nf* vitamin.

vitaminé, ~e /vitamine/ *adj* with added vitamir (*après n*).

vite /vit/ *adv* **1** (rapidement) quickly; **~!** quick!; **alle ~, faire ~** to be quick; **ça ira ~** (opération, trait ment) it'll soon be over; (procédure, réparation) it won take long; **faire qch ~ fait**○ to do sth quickly; **on pris un verre ~ fait**○ we had a quick drink; **2** (pe après le début) soon; **c'est une affection bénigne, ç passera ~** it's only a minor trouble, it'll soon g better; **3** (hâtivement) **j'ai parlé trop ~** (sans réfléchi I spoke too hastily; (sans tenir compte de tout) I spok too soon; **c'est ~ dit!** that's easy to say!

vitesse /vitɛs/ *nf* **1** (rapidité) speed; **~ de point** maximum speed; **il travaille à une ~!** he works s fast!; **partir à toute ~** to rush away; **la voiture es passée à toute ~** the car flashed past; **à deux ~** [*courrier, système*] two-tier (*épith*); **faire de la ~** [*automobiliste*] to drive fast; **gagner** or **prendre qn d ~** LIT, FIG to outstrip sb; **en ~** (vite) quickly; (trc vite) in a rush; **passer en ~** [*personne*] to pop in° **nous avons mangé en ~** we had a quick meal; **vous écris en ~** I'm writing you a quick note; **rang ta chambre, et en ~!** tidy up your room, and b quick about it!; (**il s'enfuit**) **de toute la ~ de se petites jambes** (he ran away) as fast as his little le would carry him; **2** TECH (engrenage, rapport) gea **boîte à cinq ~s** five-speed gearbox; **passer les ~** to change gear GB, to shift gear US; **passer la ~**

La vitesse

La vitesse des véhicules

*En anglais, on mesure couramment la vitesse des trains,
des avions et des automobiles en miles à l'heure, même
si les compteurs indiquent aussi les kilomètres.*

30 miles à l'heure valent environ 50 km/h
50 miles à l'heure valent environ 80 km/h
80 miles à l'heure valent environ 130 km/h
100 miles à l'heure valent environ 160 km/h

Noter qu'on écrit -metre *en anglais britannique, et* -meter
en anglais américain.

50 kilomètres à l'heure	=	50 kilometres an hour *ou* 50 kilometres per hour
100 km/h	=	100 kph (*dire* kilometres an hour; p *signifie* per = par)
100 miles à l'heure	=	100 mph (*dire* miles an hour), 160 km/h
à quelle vitesse la voiture roulait-elle?	=	what speed was the car going at? *ou* how fast was the car going?
elle roulait à 150 km/h	=	it was going at 150 kph
elle roulait à quatre-vingts à l'heure	=	it was going at fifty (*50 miles à l'heure*), it was going at 80 kph
la voiture faisait du combien?	=	what was the car doing?
elle faisait du 160 *(km/h)*	=	it was doing a hundred (mph), it was doing 160 kph
faire du 160 à l'heure	=	to do a hundred (mph) *ou* to do 160 kph
à une vitesse de 80 km/h	=	at a speed of 50 mph, at a speed of 80 kph

*Noter l'absence d'équivalent anglais de la préposition
française de avant le chiffre dans:*

la vitesse de la voiture était de 160 km/h	=	the speed of the car was 100 mph, the speed of the car was 160 kph
à peu près 80 km/h	=	about 50 mph, about 80 kph
presque 80 km/h	=	almost 50 mph, almost 80 kph
plus de 70 km/h	=	more than 45 mph, more than 70 kph
moins de 85 km/h	=	less than 55 mph, less than 85 kph
A va plus vite que B	=	A is faster than B
B roulait moins vite que A	=	B was going slower than A
A va aussi vite que B	=	A is as fast as B
A roulait à la même vitesse que B	=	A was going at the same speed as B
A et B vont à la même vitesse	=	A and B go at the same speed

La vitesse du son et de la lumière

le son se déplace à 330 m/s	=	sound travels at 330 metres per second (*dire* three hundred and thirty metres per second)
la vitesse de la lumière est de 300 000 km/s	=	the speed of light is 186,300

---

supérieure/inférieure to change up/down a gear;
passer à la ~ supérieure FIG to speed things up;
passer ses ~s en douceur to go smoothly through
the gears; **faire grincer les ~s** to crunch the gears;
bicyclette à trois ~s three-speed bicycle.
■ **~ de sédimentation** BIOL, MÉD sedimentation
rate.
IDIOMES **à la ~ grand V, en quatrième ~** at top
speed.

viticole /vitikɔl/ *adj* [*industrie, cave*] wine (*épith*);
[*région, pays*] wine-producing (*épith*).

viticulteur, -trice /vitikyltœʀ, tʀis/ **▶374** *nm,f*
wine-grower, viticulturalist.

viticulture /vitikyltyʀ/ *nf* wine-growing, viticulture.

vitrage /vitʀaʒ/ *nm* (surfaces vitrées) windows (*pl*);
double ~ double glazing.

vitrail, *pl* **-aux** /vitʀaj, o/ *nm* stained glass window;
l'art du ~ the art of stained glass.

vitre /vitʀ/ *nf* **1** (de fenêtre) pane, windowpane; (fenêtre) window; (panneau) pane of glass; **2** (de voiture,
train) window; **~ arrière** rear window.

vitré, ~e /vitʀe/ *adj* **1** (en vitres) glass (*épith*),
glazed (*épith*); **bureaux ~s** glass-walled offices; **toiture ~e** glass roof; **2** ANAT (de l'œil) vitreous.

vitrer /vitʀe/ [1] *vtr* to glaze [*panneau, fenêtre, serre*];
~ une porte to put windows in a door.

vitrerie /vitʀəʀi/ **▶374** *nf* **1** (magasin) glazier's; **2** (fabrication) glasswork; (industrie) glass industry.

vitreux, -euse /vitʀø, øz/ *adj* [*regard*] glazed; [*éclat*]
glassy; [*état, roche*] vitreous.

vitrier /vitʀije/ **▶374** *nm* glazier.

vitrification /vitʀifikasjɔ̃/ *nf* (de parquet) varnishing,
sealing.

vitrifier /vitʀifje/ [2] **I** *vtr* **1** (vernir) to varnish
[*parquet*]; **2** TECH (en verrerie) to vitrify; (en génie nucléaire) to vitrify.
II se vitrifier *vpr* to vitrify.

vitrine /vitʀin/ *nf* **1** (de boutique) (shop ou store)
window; **en ~** in the window; **faire les ~s** (regarder) to go window-shopping; **2** (meuble) display
cabinet GB, curio cabinet US; **3** (de musée) (show)case;
4 FIG (mise en valeur) showcase.

vitriol /vitʀijɔl/ *nm* vitriol; **discours au ~** FIG
vitriolic speech.

vitro ▶ **in vitro**.

vitupérer /vitypeʀe/ [14] *vi* to rail.

vivable /vivabl/ *adj* bearable; **pas ~** unbearable; **ce
n'est pas ~ ici** it is impossible to live here.

vivace /vivas/ *adj* **1** BOT (**plante**) **~** perennial; **2**
(durable) enduring.

vivacité /vivasite/ *nf* **1** (fougue) (de personne) vivacity; (de sentiment, passion) intensity; **2** (promptitude)
(de mouvement) vivacity; (de repartie, d'intelligence) keenness; (de réaction) swiftness; **avec ~** [*se mouvoir,
réagir*] swiftly; **3** (de souvenir, couleur, d'impression)
vividness; (de regard) spark; (de lueur) brightness.

vivant, ~e /vivɑ̃, ɑ̃t/ **I** *adj* **1** (en vie) living; **il est
~** he is alive; **un homard ~** a live lobster; **moi
~, jamais il ne l'épousera** he'll marry her over my
dead body; **2** (en chair et en os) [*exemple, symbole*]
living; **d'après le modèle ~** from life; **ta mère,
c'est un dictionnaire ~!** your mother is a walking
dictionary!; **3** (animé) [*personne, récit, style*] lively;
[*description*] vivid; **4** (vivace) **être encore ~** [*coutume, souvenir*] to be still alive.
II *nm* **les ~s** the living; **de mon ~** in my lifetime; **du ~ de mon père** while my father was alive.

vivats /viva/ *nmpl* cheers.

vive² /viv/ **I** *adj f* ▶ **vif I**.
II *nf* ZOOL weever.

vivement /vivmɑ̃/ *adv* [*encourager, réagir*] strongly;
[*inquiéter*] greatly; [*contraster*] sharply; [*émouvoir,
regretter*] deeply; [*contester, attaquer*] fiercely; [*se lever*]
swiftly; **je souhaite ~ vous rencontrer** I should
very much like to meet you; **~ dimanche!/qu'elle
s'en aille!** I can't wait for Sunday!/for her to go!

vivier /vivje/ *nm* (naturel) fishpond; (artificiel) fish-
tank.

vivifiant, ~e /vivifjɑ̃, ɑ̃t/ *adj* **1** (revigorant) invigorating; **2** (stimulant) stimulating.

vivifier /vivifje/ [2] *vtr* to invigorate .

vivisection /vivisɛksjɔ̃/ *nf* vivisection.

vivoter /vivɔte/ [1] *vi* to struggle along.

vivre /vivʀ/ [63] **I** *vtr* **1** (connaître) to live through
[*époque, période*]; to go through [*heures difficiles,
enfer*]; to experience [*amour, passion*]; **être vécu
comme un affront** to be taken as an insult; **~ sa vie**

to lead one's own life; **2** (ressentir) to cope with [*divorce, échec*].

II *vi* **1** BIOL (être vivant) to live; ~ **vieux/centenaire** to live to a great age/to be a hundred; **cesser de** ~ EUPH to pass away; **vive le président!** long live the president!; **vive la vie!** life is wonderful!; **vive moi/ nous!** three cheers for me/us!; **vive Paul!** hurray for Paul!; **2** (habiter) to live; **être facile à** ~ [*conjoint*] to be easy to live with; [*ami*] to be easy to get on with; ~ **les uns sur les autres** to live on top of each other; **3** (exister) [*personne*] to live; ~ **avec son temps** to move with the times; **se laisser** ~ to take things easy; **apprendre à** ~ **à qn**° to teach sb some manners°; **savoir** ~ (profiter de la vie) to know how to enjoy life; **4** (survivre) [*personne*] to live; **avoir de quoi** ~ to have enough to live on; ~ **de ses rentes** to have a private income; ~ **aux dépens de qn** to live off sb; **5** (durer) [*relation, mode*] to last; **avoir vécu** [*personne*] to have seen a great deal of life; (être usé) HUM to have had its day; **6** (être animé) [*ville, rue*] to be full of life.

IDIOMES **le** ~ **et le couvert** board and lodging; ~ **de l'air du temps** to live on air; ~ **sur un grand pied** to live in great style; **qui vivra verra** what will be will be.

vivres /vivʀ/ *nmpl* **1** (nourriture) food, supplies; **2** (moyens de subsistance) **couper les** ~ **à qn** to cut off sb's allowance.

vizir /viziʀ/ *nm* vizier; **le Grand** ~ the Grand Vizier.

vo /veo/ *nf: abbr* ▶ **version**.

vocable /vɔkabl/ *nm* term.

vocabulaire /vɔkabylɛʀ/ *nm* vocabulary.

vocal, ~e, *mpl* **-aux** /vɔkal, o/ *adj* vocal.

vocalement /vɔkalmã/ *adv* vocally.

vocalise /vɔkaliz/ *nf* singing exercise.

vocation /vɔkasjɔ̃/ *nf* **1** (de personne) vocation, calling; ~ **contrariée** frustrated calling; **se sentir une** ~ **de médecin** to feel that medicine is one's vocation; **il n'a pas la** ~ **de l'enseignement** he's not cut out to be a teacher; **2** (d'institution) purpose; **il assigne à l'école une double** ~ he thinks schools should serve a dual purpose; **l'association a pour** ~ **d'aider les malades** the association is intended to help the sick; **salles à** ~ **récréative** rooms intended for leisure activities; **région à** ~ **agricole** farming area.

vocifération /vɔsifeʀasjɔ̃/ *nf* clamour GB *C*.

vociférer /vɔsifeʀe/ [14] *vtr, vi* to shout (**contre** at).

vœu, *pl* ~**x** /vø/ *nm* **1** (souhait) wish; **les élèves doivent émettre des** ~**x d'orientation** pupils must indicate their preferred subject choices; **je fais des** ~**x pour que la paix revienne** I hope and pray that peace may return; **appeler qch de tous ses** ~**x** to hope and pray for sth; **former des** ~**x pour la santé de qn** to wish sb a speedy recovery; '**nos meilleurs** ~**x aux jeunes époux** ' 'our best wishes to the bride and groom'; **2** (de Nouvel An) New Year's greetings; **adresser ses** ~**x à qn** to wish sb a happy New Year; **3** (promesse) vow; **faire** ~ **de pauvreté** to take a vow of poverty; **faire** ~ **de fidélité** to vow to remain faithful.

■ ~ **pieux** wishful thinking *C*.

vogue /vɔg/ *nf* (mode) fashion, vogue; **la** ~ **des cheveux longs** the fashion for long hair; **la** ~ **des Beatles** the Beatles craze°; **en** ~ [*style, idée, personne*] fashionable; [*objet, vêtement*] in fashion (*jamais épith*).

voguer /vɔge/ [1] *vi* LITER **1** (naviguer) [*navire*] to sail; **2** FIG [*esprit, pensées*] to wander.

IDIOMES **et vogue la galère!** come what may!

voici /vwasi/ **I** *prép* ~ **un mois** a month ago; ~ **bientôt deux mois qu'elle travaille chez nous** she's been working with us for nearly two months.

II *présentatif* ~ **mes clés** here are my keys; ~ **le docteur qui arrive** here comes ou here's the doctor; '**me** ~' 'here I am'; ~ **ma fille** this is my daughter; **M. Bon que** ~ **est**... Mr Bon here is...; ~ **les résultats** here are the results, these are the results; ~ **le programme** the programme GB is as follows; **le film**

raconte l'histoire que ~ the film tells the following story; ~ **où je voulais en venir** that's the point I wanted to make; ~ **qui va vous amuser** here is ou this is something that you'll find amusing; ~ **enfin l'été** summer's here at last; ~ **venir l'hiver** here comes winter; **nous y** ~ (à la maison) here we are; (au cœur du sujet) now we're getting there.

III voici que *loc conj* LITER all of a sudden.

voie /vwa/ *nf* **1** FIG (chemin) way; **être sur la** ~ **d'un accord** to be on the way to an agreement; **montrer la** ~ **à qn** to show sb the way; **montrer la** ~ to lead the way; **ouvrir la** ~ **à** to pave the way for; **chercher sa** ~ to look for one's way in life; **s'engager dans une** ~ **dangereuse** to embark on a dangerous course; **être sur la bonne** ~ [*personne*] to be on the right track; **les travaux sont en bonne** ~ the work is progressing; **la** ~ **royale vers le pouvoir** the fast track to power; **en** ~ **de faire** in the process of doing; **en** ~ **de désintégration** disintegrating (*après n*); **par** ~**s de conséquence** consequently; **espèce en** ~ **de disparition** endangered species; **pays en** ~ **de développement** developing country; **2** (intermédiaire) channels (*pl*); **par la** ~ **du référendum** by means of a referendum; **par** ~ **de presse** through the press; **par des** ~ **détournées** by roundabout means; **par** ~ **de mer** by sea; **3** (subdivision de route) lane; (route) road; (rue) street; **route à trois** ~**s** three-lane road; ~ **à sens unique** (en ville) one-way street; **4** (rails) track; '**défense de traverser les** ~**s**' 'keep off the tracks'; **le train entre en gare** ~ **2** the train is arriving at platform 2; **5** (mode d'administration) **par** ~ **intraveineuse** intravenously; **par** ~ **buccale** or **orale** orally.

■ ~ **aérienne** air route; ~ **express** expressway; ~ **ferrée** (infrastructure) railway track GB, railroad track US; (mode de transport, ligne) railway GB, railroad US; ~ **fluviale** (inland) waterway; ~ **de garage** siding; **mettre qn sur une** ~ **de garage** FIG to shunt sb onto the sidelines; ~ **hiérarchique** ADMIN right channels (*pl*); **Voie lactée** Milky Way; ~ **maritime** sea route; ~ **navigable** waterway; ~ **privée** private road; ~ **publique** public highway; ~ **rapide** expressway; ~ **sans issue** LIT, FIG dead end; (sur panneau) no through road; ~ **souterraine** underpass; ~**s respiratoires** respiratory tract (*sg*); ~**s urinaires** urinary tract (*sg*).

voilà /vwala/ **I** *prép* ~ **un mois** a month ago; ~ **bientôt deux mois qu'elle travaille chez nous** she's been working with us for nearly two months.

II *présentatif* **voici ton parapluie et** ~ **le mien** this is your umbrella and here's mine; **voici mon fils et** ~ **ma fille** this is my son and this is my daughter; ~ **ma mère** here's ou here comes my mother; **me** ~**!** (j'arrive) I'm coming!; (je suis là) here I am!; **ah! te** ~**!** ah, there you are!; ~ **tout** that's all; ~ **où nous en étions** that's where we were up to; ~ **ce que c'est de désobéir** that's what happens if you disobey; **je n'ai pas pu venir,** ~ **tout** (ne posez pas de questions) I couldn't come, that's all there is to it; ~ **qui ne va pas arranger vos affaires** well, that won't sort things out for you; ~ **le programme** the programme GB is as follows; ~ **comment** (en introduction) this is how; (en conclusion) that's how; **seulement** ~ **je n'ai pas d'argent** the problem ou thing is I don't have any money; '**je voudrais la clé du trois**'—'~**, madame**' 'I'd like the key to number three'—'here you are, madam'; **nous y** ~ (à la maison) here we are; (au cœur du sujet) now we're getting there; **le** ~ **qui se remet à rire!** there he goes again laughing!; **te** ~ **content!** now you're happy!; **te** ~ **revenu!** you're back again!; ~ **bien les hommes!** that's men for you!; ~ **bien ta mauvaise foi!** so much for your dishonesty!

III en voilà *loc* **vous vouliez des explications? en** ~ you wanted more details! well, here you are (then); **en** ~ **pour dix francs** here's ten francs worth; **en** ~ **un mal élevé!** what a badly brought up boy!; **mon dieu! en** ~ **des histoires!** good Lord! what a fuss!; **en** ~ **assez!** that's enough!; **en** ~ **un**

qui ne recommencera pas! there's someone who won't do it again!

IV voilà que○ *loc* et **~ qu'une voiture arrive** and the next thing was a car arrived; **~ qu' il se met à rire** all of a sudden he started laughing; **et ~ qu'elle refuse** and then she had to go and refuse.

V *excl* **~! j'arrive!** (I'm) coming!, **(et) ~! ils sont partis!** there you are, they've left!; **(et) ~! il remet ça!** there he goes again!

IDIOMES **il a de l'argent, en veux-tu en ~!** he has as much money as he could wish for!

voilage /vwalaʒ/ *nm* net curtain GB, sheer curtain US.

voile[1] /vwal/ *nm* **1** (morceau d'étoffe) veil; **prendre le ~** to take the veil; **2** (étoffe) voile; **3** (masque abstrait) veil; **on jeta un ~ (pudique) sur l'affaire** a veil was drawn over the affair; **lever le ~ sur qch** to bring sth out in the open; **soulever un coin du ~ sur qch** to gain a glimpse into sth; **4** TECH (dans un liquide) cloud; (sur une radiographie) shadow; PHOT fog; **5** (écran) veil; **un ~ de larmes** a mist of tears.

■ **~ islamique** yashmak; **~ du palais** soft palate, velum.

voile[2] /vwal/ *nf* NAUT **1** (toile) sail; **faire ~ vers** to sail toward(s); **toutes ~s dehors** LIT full sail ahead, FIG using every possible means; **2** (activité) sailing; **il fait de la ~ depuis deux ans** he's been sailing for two years; **cours de ~** sailing lessons.

IDIOMES **être à ~ et à vapeur**○ to be AC/DC○; **mettre les ~s**○ to clear off○ GB, to clear out○ US.

voilé, ~e /vwale/ *adj* **1** [*personne, objet*] veiled; **~ de noir** veiled in black; [*soleil, ciel*] hazy; [*regard, yeux*] misty; [*voix*] with a catch in it (*épith, après n*); [*photo, film*] fogged; [*lune*] veiled (**de** in); **3** (obscur) [*allusion, menace, critique*] veiled; **des allusions à peine ~es** thinly veiled allusions; **4** (déformé) [*roue*] buckled; [*panneau*] warped.

voiler /vwale/ [1] **I** *vtr* **1** (dissimuler) to veil [*ciel, paysage, soleil*]; to conceal [*événement, fait*]; **2** (déformer) to buckle [*roue*]; **3** (troubler) to mist [*regard*]; **l'émotion voilait sa voix** his/her voice was choked with emotion; **4** (couvrir d'étoffe) to cover [*visage, nudité*]; to veil [*statue*].

II se voiler *vpr* **1** (se troubler) [*ciel*] to cloud over; [*soleil*] to become hazy; [*regard*] to become misty; [*voix*] to have a catch in it; **2** (avec étoffe) [*musulmane*] to wear the veil; **se ~ le visage** to veil one's face.

IDIOMES **se ~ la face** to look the other way.

voilette /vwalɛt/ *nf* veil.

voilier /vwalje/ *nm* (bateau) sailing boat GB, sailboat US; (grand navire) yacht, sailing ship.

voilure /vwalyʀ/ *nf* **1** NAUT (ensemble des voiles) sails (*pl*); (surface des voiles) sail; **une ~ de 500m²** 500m² of sail; **2** (d'avion) wing surface; (de parachute) canopy.

voir /vwaʀ/ [46] **I** *vtr* **1** (percevoir par les yeux) to see [*personne, objet*]; **je n'y vois rien** I can't see a thing; **je les ai vus comme je te vois!** I saw them as plainly as I see you standing there!; **à la ~ si triste** when you see her so sad; **à le ~, on le prendrait pour un clochard** to look at him, you'd think he was a tramp; **faire ~ qch à qn** to show sb sth; **laisser ~ qch** to show sth; **~ qch en rêve** to dream about sth; **2** (être spectateur, témoin de) [*personne*] to see [*film, incident*]; [*lieu*] to see [*événement, évolution*]; **la ville qui l'a vue naître** her native town; **le film est à ~** the film is worth seeing; **c'est beau à ~** it's beautiful to look at; **ce n'est pas beau à ~** it's not a pretty sight; **je voudrais bien t'y ~!** I'd like to see how you'd get on!; **on n'a jamais vu ça!** it's unheard of!; **on aura tout vu!** could you ever have imagined such a thing!; **voyez-moi ça!** just look at that!; (se figurer) to see; **j'ai vu le moment où il allait m'étrangler** I thought he was about to strangle me; **je vois ça d'ici** I can just imagine; **4** (juger) to see; **c'est ma façon de ~** (les choses) that's the way I see things; **c'est à toi de ~** it's up to you to decide; **~ favorablement qch** to be favourably○GB disposed toward(s) sth; **tu vas te faire ͵mal ~ de Sophie** Sophie is going to think badly of you; **5** (comprendre, déceler) to see [*moyen,*

avantage]; **je ne vois pas qui tu veux dire** I don't know who you mean; **si tu n'y vois pas d'inconvénient** if it's all right with you; **on voit bien qu'elle n'a jamais travaillé!** you can tell she's never worked!; **6** (constater, découvrir) to see; **si/pourquoi** to find out ou to see if/why; **on verra bien** well, we'll see; **'je ne paierai pas!'—'c'est ce que nous verrons.'** 'I won't pay!'—'we shall see about that!'; **c'est à ~ that** remains to be seen; **touches-y, pour ~!** (menace) you just touch it!; **7** (examiner, étudier) to see [*malade*]; to look at [*problème, dossier*]; **8** (recevoir, se rendre chez) to see [*client, médecin, ami*]; **je passerai la ~ demain** I'll call on her tomorrow; **9** (visiter) to see [*ville, monument*] ; **~ du pays** to see the world; **10** (avoir un rapport avec) **avoir quelque chose à ~ avec** to have something to do with.

II voir à *vtr ind* (veiller à) to see to; **voyez à ce que tout soit prêt** see to it ou make sure that everything is ready.

III *vi* **1** (avec les yeux) **~, y ~** to be able to see; **je** or **j'y vois à peine** I can hardly see; **je vois trouble** everything is a blur; **2** (par l'esprit) **~ clair dans qch** to have a clear understanding of sth; **~ loin** (être prévoyant) to look ahead; (être perspicace) to be far-sighted; **~ grand** to think big; **elle a vu juste** she was right; **il faut ~**○ (ça mérite réflexion) we'll have to see; **3** (rappel à l'ordre) **voyons, sois sage!** come on now, behave yourself!

IV se voir *vpr* **1** (dans la glace, en imagination) to see oneself; **il s'est vu sombrer dans la folie** he realized he was going mad; **2** (se remarquer) [*tache, défaut*] to show; **la tour se voit de loin** the tower can be seen from far away; **cela se voit tous les jours** it happens all the time ou every day; **ça ne s'est jamais vu!** it's unheard of!; **3** (se trouver) **se ~ obligé** ou **dans l'obligation de faire qch** to find oneself forced to do; **4** (se fréquenter) to see each other; **ils ne peuvent pas se ~ (en peinture)**○ they can't stand each other.

IDIOMES **ne pas ~ plus loin que le bout de son nez** to see no further than the end of one's nose; **je préfère ~ venir**○ I would rather wait and see; **on t'a vu venir**○! they/we saw you coming○!; **je te vois venir**○ I can see what you're getting at GB ou where you're coming from○; **je t'ai assez vu** I've had enough of you; **en ~ de toutes les couleurs** to go through some hard times; **j'en ai vu d'autres** I've seen worse; **en faire ~ à qn** to give sb a hard time; **qu'il aille se faire ~**○! I tell him to get lost○!; **il ferait beau ~ ça!** that would be the last straw!

voire /vwaʀ/ *adv* or even, not to say.

voirie /vwaʀi/ *nf* road, rail and waterways network.

voisin, ~e /vwazɛ̃, in/ **I** *adj* **1** (de voisinage) [*maison, ville*] neighbouring○GB (*épith*), nearby; [*rue, pays*] neighbouring○GB (*épith*); (proche) [*forêt, lac, hôpital*] nearby; (d'à côté) [*pièce, table, maison*] next (**de** to); **dans la maison ~e** in the house next door; FIG [*date, résultat, pourcentage*] close (**de** to); **les régions ~es de la Manche** the regions bordering the English Channel; **2** (similaire) [*sentiments, idées*] similar; [*espèces*] (closely) related; **~ de** [*théorie, idée*] akin to; [*espèce*] related to.

II *nm,f* neighbour○GB; **ma ~e de palier** the woman across the landing; **mon ~ de table** the man ou person next to me at table; **dire du mal du ~** FIG to speak ill of others.

voisinage /vwazinaʒ/ *nm* **1** (voisins) neighbourhood○GB, neighbours○GB (*pl*); **entretenir des rapports de bon ~** LIT, FIG to maintain neighbourly○GB relations; **2** (environs) neighbourhood○GB; **3** (proximité) proximity; **vivre dans le ~ d'une usine** to live close to a factory.

voiture /vwatyʀ/ *nf* **1** (automobile) car, automobile US; **2** (wagon) carriage GB, coach GB, car US; **en ~!** all aboard!

■ **~ à bras** hand-drawn cart; **~ à cheval** horse-drawn carriage; **~ d'enfant** pram GB, baby carriage US; **~ de poste** stage coach; **~ de tourisme** saloon (car) GB, sedan US.

IDIOMES à pied, à cheval, en ~ by whatever means of transport.

voiture-balai, *pl* **voitures-balais** /vwatyʀbalɛ/ *nf* support vehicle.

voiture-lit, *pl* **voitures-lits** /vwatyʀli/ *nf* sleeper, sleeping car US.

voix /vwa/ *nf inv* **1** (en phonétique, physiologie) voice; ~ **blanche** expressionless voice; **entendre des** ~**s** to hear voices; **à** ~ **haute** out loud; **à** ~ **basse** in a low voice; **donner de la** ~ [*chien*] to give tongue; **être/rester sans** ~ to be/to remain speechless; **à portée de** ~ within earshot; **2** (expression) voice; **la** ~ **de la sagesse/de la raison** the voice of wisdom/of reason; **c'est la** ~ **du sang qui parle** it's in the blood; **3** MUS voice; **avoir de la** ~ to have a loud voice; **poser** or **placer sa** ~ to place one's voice; **4** (opinion) voice; **faire entendre sa** ~ to make oneself heard; **5** POL vote; **avoir** ~ **délibérative** to have the right to vote; **6** LING voice.
■ ~ **off** CIN voice-over.

vol /vɔl/ **I** *nm* **1** (d'oiseau) flight; **prendre son** ~ to take wing, to fly off; **à** ~ **d'oiseau** as the crow flies; **2** (groupe) (de canards, cigognes) flight; (d'insectes) cloud; **de haut** ~ FIG [*diplomate*] high-flying; [*cambrioleur*] big-time; [*prostituée*] high-class; **3** (d'avion, de fusée) flight; **le** ~ **pour Paris** the Paris flight; **il y a trois heures de** ~ it's a three-hour flight; **avoir 1000 heures de** ~ **à son actif** to have logged 1,000 flying hours; **en (plein)** ~ in flight; **de** ~ [*conditions*] flying; [*plan, simulateur*] flight; **4** (délit) theft; (plus important) robbery; **c'est du** ~ **(manifeste)!** it's daylight robbery!; **c'est du** ~ **organisé!** it's a racket!
II au vol *loc adv* **tirer un oiseau au** ~ to shoot a bird in flight; **attraper une balle au** ~ to catch a ball in mid-air; **saisir des bribes de conversations au** ~ to catch snatches of conversation.
■ ~ **à l'arraché** bag snatching; ~ **avec effraction** burglary; ~ **à l'étalage** shoplifting; ~ **libre** SPORT hang gliding; ~ **à main armée** armed robbery; ~ **à la tire** pickpocketing; ~ **à voile** gliding.

volage /vɔlaʒ/ *adj* fickle.

volaille /vɔlaj/ *nf* **1** (ensemble) poultry; **2** (animal) fowl.

volant, ~**e** /vɔlã, ãt/ **I** *adj* **1** (qui vole) flying; **2** (mobile) [*camp, pont*] flying; [*personnel*] mobile.
II *nm* **1** (de voiture) steering wheel; **être au** ~ to be at the wheel; **reprendre le** ~ to get back behind the wheel; **donner un coup de** ~ to turn the wheel sharply; **un as du** ~ an ace driver; **la sécurité au** ~ safe driving; **2** (de vêtement) flounce, tier; **à** ~**s** flounced; **3** (réserve) margin, reserve; **4** (de badminton) shuttlecock.

volatil, ~**e**[1] /vɔlatil/ *adj* volatile.

volatile[2] /vɔlatil/ *nm* **1** (volaille) fowl; **2** (oiseau) bird.

volatiliser /vɔlatilize/ [1] **I** *vtr* CHIMIE to volatilize.
II se volatiliser *vpr* **1** CHIMIE to volatilize; **2** (disparaître) HUM to vanish into thin air, to disappear.

volcan /vɔlkã/ *nm* **1** (relief) volcano; **être assis sur un** ~ FIG to be sitting on a volcano; **2** (personne) spitfire.

volcanique /vɔlkanik/ *adj* **1** [*activité, région, roche*] volcanic; **2** [*tempérament*] explosive.

volée /vɔle/ **I** *nf* **1** (d'oiseaux) (action de voler) flight; (vol groupé) flock, flight; **une** ~ **d'étourneaux** a flock ou flight of starlings; **une** ~ **d'enfants** a swarm of children; **2** (de projectiles, coups) volley; **donner une** ~ **à qn** LIT to give sb a good thrashing; FIG to thrash sb; **3** (d'escalier) flight (of stairs); **4** (sports de raquette, volley-ball) volley; **reprendre la balle de** ~ to take the ball on the volley; **saisir la balle à la** ~ FIG to seize the opportunity.
II à toute volée *loc adv* **lancer qch à toute** ~ to hurl sth; **les cloches sonnaient à toute** ~ to bells were pealing out.
IDIOMES comme une ~ **de moineaux** like flies;

asséner une ~ **de bois vert à qn** to deliver a blistering critique of sb.

voler /vɔle/ [1] **I** *vtr* **1** (dérober) to steal (**à qn** from sb); **il s'est fait** ~ **sa voiture** he's had his car stolen; **il s'est fait** ~ **la victoire** FIG he's been robbed of his victory; **tu ne l'as pas volé!** FIG it serves you right!; **2** (léser) to rob; ~ **le client** to rip the customer off⁰; ~ **qn sur la quantité** to cheat sb over the quantity.
II *vi* to fly; ~ **au vent** to blow in the wind; ~ **en éclats** [*vitre*] to shatter; FIG [*certitude*] to be shattered; ~ **au secours de qn** to rush to sb's aid.
IDIOMES ça vole bas! that's pretty mindless stuff!

volet /vɔlɛ/ *nm* **1** (contrevent) shutter; **2** (de plan, politique, problème) constituent; **3** (de dépliant) (folding) section.

voleter /vɔlte/ [20] *vi* [*insecte, papier*] to flutter.

voleur, -**euse** /vɔlœʀ, øz/ **I** *adj* **être** ~ [*chat*] to be a thief; [*enfant*] to be light-fingered; [*commerçant*] to be dishonest.
II *nm,f* (malfaiteur) thief; (tricheur) swindler; **crier 'au** ~!' to shout 'stop thief!'; **jouer au gendarme et au** ~ to play cops and robbers.
■ ~ **de grand chemin** HIST highwayman.
IDIOMES être ~ **comme une pie** to be a real thieving magpie; **se sauver comme un** ~ to slip away like a thief in the night; **entrer/sortir comme un** ~ to slip in/out.

volière /vɔljɛʀ/ *nf* aviary.

volley(-ball) /vɔlɛ(bol)/ ▶ 329 *nm* volleyball.

volontaire /vɔlɔ̃tɛʀ/ **I** *adj* **1** (délibéré) [*départ, travail*] voluntary; [*abus*] deliberate; **ce n'était pas** ~ **de ma part** I didn't mean to; **2** (opiniâtre) [*personne, air*] determined.
II *nmf* volunteer; **se porter** ~ **pour faire** to volunteer to do.

volontairement /vɔlɔ̃tɛʀmɑ̃/ *adv* [*se priver, renoncer, partir*] voluntarily; [*dissimuler, faire mal*] deliberately.

volontariat /vɔlɔ̃taʀja/ *nm* voluntary service.

volontariste /vɔlɔ̃taʀist/ *adj* voluntarist.

volonté /vɔlɔ̃te/ **I** *nf* **1** (disposition) will; **faire preuve de bonne/mauvaise** ~ to show goodwill/ill-will; **elle y met de la mauvaise** ~ she's doing it with bad grace ou reluctantly; **aller contre la** ~ **de qn** to go against sb's wishes; **manifester la** ~ **de faire** to show one's willingness to do; ~ **de puissance** desire for power; **faire appel aux bonnes** ~**s** to appeal for volunteers; **2** (trait de caractère) willpower; **à force de** ~ by sheer willpower; **avoir une** ~ **de fer** to have an iron will.
II à volonté *loc adv* **1** (autant que l'on veut) 'vin/pain/crudités à ~' 'unlimited wine/bread/salad'; **2** (comme on veut) [*modulable*] as required.

volontiers /vɔlɔ̃tje/ *adv* **1** (avec plaisir) gladly; **j'irais** ~ **à Paris** I'd love to go to Paris; 'tu me le **prêtes?'—'~'** 'will you lend it to me?'—'certainly'; **2** (facilement) [*imaginer*] easily; [*admettre*] readily; **je le crois** ~ I'm quite ready to believe him/it.

volt /vɔlt/ *nm* volt.

volte-face /vɔlt(ə)fas/ *nf inv* **1** LIT **faire** ~ to turn around; **2** FIG volte-face, U-turn; **faire** ~ to do a U-turn.

voltige /vɔltiʒ/ *nf* **1** (au trapèze) **(haute)** ~ acrobatics (+ *v pl*); **2** AVIAT ~ **(aérienne)** aerobatics (+ *v pl*).

voltiger /vɔltiʒe/ [13] *vi* **1** (doucement) [*papiers, feuilles*] to flutter; **2** (violemment) [*classeur, objet*] to fly, to go flying.

volubile /vɔlybil/ *adj* **1** (personne) voluble; **2** BOT twining.

volubilité /vɔlybilite/ *nf* volubility.

volume /vɔlym/ *nm* **1** (grandeur) volume; **le** ~ **d'un fleuve** the volume of a river's flow; **donner du** ~ **à ses cheveux** to give one's hair body; **faire du** ~ [*colis, bagages*] to be bulky; **2** (tome) volume; **3** (intensité) volume; ~ **sonore** sound level.

volumineux, -euse /vɔlyminø, øz/ adj [*livre, dossier*] thick; [*documentation, correspondance*] voluminous; [*objet, bagages*] bulky; [*seins, fesses*] ample.

volupté /vɔlypte/ nf **1** (sensuelle) voluptuousness; **avec ~** voluptuously; **2** (intellectuelle) exquisite pleasure.

voluptueux, -euse /vɔlyptɥø, øz/ adj voluptuous.

volute /vɔlyt/ nf **1** (de colonne) volute; (de violon) scroll; **des ~s de fumée** curls of smoke; **2** ZOOL volute.

vomi○ /vɔmi/ nm vomit.

vomir /vɔmiʀ/ [3] **I** vtr **1** (recracher) [*personne*] to bring up [*repas, nourriture*]; to vomit [*bile, sang*]; **2** (projeter) to spew out [*lave, déchets*]; to belch [*feu, vapeur, fumée*]; **3** (abhorrer) to loathe.

II vi [*personne*] to be sick, to vomit; **je vais ~** I'm going to be sick; **avoir envie de ~** to feel sick; **donner envie de ~** LIT to make [sb] feel sick; FIG to make [sb] sick; **c'est à ~** FIG it makes you sick, it makes you puke●.

vomissement /vɔmismɑ̃/ nm (action) vomiting; (résultat) vomit; **être pris de ~s** to start to vomit.

vorace /vɔʀas/ adj LIT, FIG voracious.

voracité /vɔʀasite/ nf voracity, voraciousness.

vos ▶ **votre**.

votant, -e /vɔtɑ̃, ɑ̃t/ nm,f voter.

vote /vɔt/ nm **1** (action) voting, vote; **droit de ~** right to vote; **~ d'un budget** voting on a budget; **~ à main levée** vote by show of hands; **~ d'une loi** passing of a bill; **2** (opinion exprimée) vote.

voter /vɔte/ [1] **I** vtr to vote [*budget, amendement*]; to pass [*projet de loi*]; **~ les pleins pouvoirs à qn** to vote to give sb full powers.

II vi to vote; **~ (pour) Durand** to vote for Durand; **~ à bulletin secret** to vote by secret ballot; **~ contre un projet de loi** to vote a bill down; **~ blanc** to cast a blank vote.

votre, pl vos /vɔtʀ, vo/ adj poss

■ **Note** En anglais, on ne répète pas le possessif coordonné: *votre nom et votre adresse* = your name and address.

your; **c'est pour ~ bien** it's for your own good; **un de vos amis** a friend of yours; **~ gentil collègue** (collègue absent) that nice colleague of yours; (collègue présent) your kind colleague; **j'ai fait vos courses** I've done the shopping for you; **à ~ arrivée** when you arrive.

vôtre /vɔtʀ/ **I** adj poss **mes biens sont ~s** all I have is yours; **'amicalement ~'** 'best wishes'.

II le vôtre, la vôtre, les vôtres pron poss yours; **ils ont des habitudes très différentes des ~s** their habits are very different from your own; **à la ~○!** (à votre santé) cheers!; **vous avez encore fait des ~s!** you've been up to mischief again!

vouer /vwe/ [1] **I** vtr **1** (porter) **~ un sentiment à qn** to nurse a feeling for sb; **~ une reconnaissance éternelle à qn** to be ou feel eternally grateful to sb; **~ un véritable culte à qn** to worship sb; **2** (destiner) to doom; **film voué à l'échec** film doomed to failure, film bound to fail; **~ qn à la vindicte publique** to expose sb to public condemnation; **3** (consacrer) **~ sa vie/son temps à** to devote one's life/one's time to.

II se vouer vpr **1** (se consacrer) **se ~ à** to devote oneself to; **2** (se porter) **ils se vouent une haine féroce** they hate each other intensely.

IDIOMES **je ne sais plus à quel saint me ~** I don't know which way to turn.

vouloir[1] /vulwaʀ/ [48] **I** vtr **1** (exiger) **qu'est-ce qu'ils nous veulent**○ **encore?** what do they want now?; **comme le veut la loi** as the law demands; **le règlement voudrait que tu portes une cravate** you're normally required to wear a tie; **2** (désirer, souhaiter) **que veux-tu boire?** what do you want to drink?; (plus poli) what would you like to drink?; **comme tu veux** as you wish; **je voudrais un kilo de poires** I'd like a kilo of pears; **je comprends**

Le volume

Pour les mesures en litres, décilitres, hectolitres etc. voir *la capacité* ▶ **86** |. Pour la prononciation des nombres, voir *les nombres* ▶ **399** |.

Équivalences

1 cu in	= 16,38 cm³		
1 cu ft	= 1728 cu in	= 0,03 m³	
1 cu yd	= 27 cu ft	= 0,76 m³	

dire			dire
one cubic centimetre	1 cm³	= 0.061 cu in³	cubic inches
one cubic decimetre	1 dm³	= 0.035 cu ft	cubic feet
one cubic metre	1 m³	= 35.315 cu ft	cubic feet
		= 1.308 cu yd	cubic yard

Pour l'écriture, noter:

– l'anglais utilise un point là où le français a une virgule.
– on écrit -metre en anglais britannique et -meter en anglais américain.
– on peut écrire cu in ou in³, cu ft ou ft³, etc.

il y a 1 000 000 centimètres cubes dans un mètre cube	= there are a million cubic centimetres in a cubic metre
1 000 000 centimètres cubes font un mètre cube	= a million cubic centimetres make one cubic metre
quel est le volume de la caisse?	= what is the volume of the box?
elle fait 2 m³	= it is 2 cubic metres
elle a un volume de 2 m³	= its volume is 2 cubic metres
à peu près 3 m³	= about 3 cubic metres
presque 3 m³	= almost 3 cubic metres
plus de 2 m³	= more than 2 cubic metres
moins de 3 m³	= less than 3 cubic metres
le volume de A est supérieur à celui de B	= A has a greater volume than B
le volume de B est inférieur à celui de A	= B has a smaller volume than A
A et B ont le même volume	= A and B have the same volume
le volume de A est égal à celui de B	= A has the same volume as B
5 m³ de terre	= five cubic metres of soil
vendu au mètre cube	= sold by the cubic metre

Noter l'ordre des mots dans les adjectifs composés anglais, et l'utilisation du trait d'union. Noter aussi que metre, employé comme adjectif, ne prend pas la marque du pluriel.

un réservoir de 200 m³	= a 200-cubic-metre tank

On peut aussi dire a tank 200 cubic metres in volume.

---

très bien que tu ne veuilles pas répondre I can quite understand that you may not wish to reply; **il ne suffit pas de ~, il faut encore pouvoir** wishing is not enough; **il suffisait de ~** all you needed was the will to do it; **on dira ce qu'on voudra** they can say what they like; **tu veux que je te dise , c'est un escroc** I hate to say it, but he is a crook; **sans le ~** [*bousculer, révéler*] by accident; [*se retrouver*] accidentally; **il m'a fait mal sans le ~** he hurt me without meaning to; **'qu'est-ce qu'on fait ce soir?'—'comme tu veux** or **voudras'** 'what shall we do tonight?'—'whatever you like, it's up to you'; **que tu le veuilles ou non** whether you like it or not; **elle fait ce qu'elle veut de son mari** she twists her husband around her little finger; **elle fait ce qu'elle veut de ses mains** she can do anything with her hands; **je ne vous veux aucun mal** I don't wish you any harm; **tu ne veux/voudrais pas me faire croire que** you're not telling/trying to tell me that; **après ce qu'il a fait, tu voudrais que je lui fasse confiance?** do you expect me to trust him after what he's done?; **comment veux-tu que je le sache?** how should I know?; **pourquoi voudrais-tu qu'il refuse?** why should he refuse?; **que veux-tu, on n'y peut rien!** what can you do, it's hopeless!; **j'aurais voulu t'y voir**○! I'd like to have seen you in the same position!; **tu l'auras voulu!** it'll be all your own fault!;

3 (accepter) **voulez-vous fermer la fenêtre?** would you mind closing the window?; **voudriez-vous avoir l'obligeance de faire** FML would you be so kind as to do; **on voudra bien se référer aux ouvrages suivants** please refer to the following works; **voulez-vous répéter votre question, s'il vous plaît** would you repeat your question please; **veuillez patienter** (au téléphone) please hold the line; **si vous voulez bien me suivre** if you'd like to follow me; **veux-tu te taire!** will you be quiet!; **ils ont bien voulu nous prêter leur voiture** they were kind enough to lend us their car; **elle n'a pas voulu signer** she would not sign; **le moteur ne veut pas partir** the engine won't start; **elle veut bien prendre ce poste à condition d'être mieux payée** she's happy to take the job on condition that she's paid more; **je veux bien te croire** I'm quite prepared to believe you; **si l'on veut bien se rappeler que** if one remembers that; **je veux bien qu'il soit malade mais** I know he's ill, but; **'ce n'est pas cher/difficile'—'si on veut!'** 'it's not expensive/difficult'—'or so you say!'; **4** (signifier) **~ dire** to mean; **qu'est-ce que ça veut dire?** (signification) what does that mean?; (attitude) what's all this about?; **tu ne veux pas dire qu'il est médecin?** you don't mean to tell me he's a doctor?; **5** (prétendre) **comme le veut la tradition** as tradition has it; **leur théorie veut que** according to their theory; **on a voulu voir en lui un pionnier de l'architecture** people tended to see him as a pioneering architect.

II en vouloir *vtr ind* **1**° (être déterminé) **il réussira, il en veut!** he wants to get on, and he'll succeed!; **2** (garder rancune) **en ~ à qn** to bear a grudge against sb; **je leur en veux de m'avoir trompé** I hold it against them for not being honest with me; **ne m'en veux pas** please forgive me; **3** (avoir des vues sur) **en ~ à qch** to be after sth.

III se vouloir *vpr* **1** (prétendre être) [*personne*] to like to think of oneself as; [*ouvrage, théorie, méthode*] to be meant to be; **2** (chercher à être) to try to be; **3** (se reprocher) **s'en ~** to be cross with oneself; **s'en ~ de** to regret; **je m'en veux d'avoir été si dur avec elle** I really regret being so hard on her; **je m'en serais voulu de ne pas vous avoir prévenu** I would never have forgiven myself if I hadn't warned you; **il ne faut pas vous en ~** you mustn't blame yourself.

IDIOMES **~ c'est pouvoir** PROV where there's a will there's a way.

vouloir² /vulwaʀ/ *nm* PHILOS will; **bon ~** goodwill; **attendre le bon ~ de qn** to wait on sb's pleasure SOUT.

voulu, ~e /vuly/ *adj* **1** (requis) **les compétences ~es** the required skills; **avec toute la sévérité ~e** with due severity; **on n'obtient jamais les renseignements ~s** you never get the information you want; **en temps ~** in time; **au moment ~** at the right time; **2** (intentionnel) deliberate; **notre rencontre n'était pas ~e** our meeting was not planned.

vous /vu/ *pron pers* **1** (sujet) you; **je sais que ce n'est pas ~** I know it wasn't you; **c'est ~ qui avez gagné** you have won; **~ aussi, ~ avez l'air malade** you don't look very well either; **2** (dans une comparaison) **elles travaillent plus que ~** they work more than you (do); **3** (objet) **ils ~ ont trahis** they have betrayed you; **4** (après préposition) you; **après ~** after you; **ce sont des amis à ~?** are they friends of yours?; **c'est à ~** (appartenance) it's yours, it belongs to you; (séquence) it's your turn; **à ~** (dans une séquence) your turn; **à ~ de choisir** (votre tour) it's your turn to choose; (votre responsabilité) it's up to you to choose; **5** (pronom réfléchi) (singulier) yourself; (pluriel) yourselves; **allez ~ laver les mains** go and wash your hands; **6** (vous-même) yourself; (vous-mêmes) yourselves; **prenez soin de ~** look after yourself; **pensez à ~ deux** think of yourselves.

vous-même, *pl* **vous-mêmes** /vumɛm/ *pron pers* **1** (de politesse) yourself; **vous me l'avez dit ~** you told me yourself; **ne vous repliez pas sur ~** don't turn in on yourself; **2** (vous tous) **allez-y ~s** go

yourselves; **vous verrez par ~s** you'll see for yourselves.

voûte /vut/ *nf* (plafond) vault; (de porche) archway; (de tunnel) roof; (de feuillage) arch; (ouvrage) vaulting ℃.
■ **la ~ céleste** GÉN the sky; LITTÉR the heavens (*pl*); **~ crânienne** dome of the skull; **~ du palais** roof of the mouth; **~ plantaire** arch of the foot.

voûté, ~e /vute/ *adj* **1** ARCHIT vaulted, arched; **2** (courbé) [*personne*] stooping; [*dos*] bent; **il est ~** he has a stoop.

voûter /vute/ [1] **I** *vtr* (courber) to give [sb] a stoop [*personne*].
II se voûter *vpr* [*personne*] to develop a stoop; [*dos*] to become bent.

vouvoiement /vuvwamã/ *nm* using the 'vous' or polite form.

vouvoyer /vuvwaje/ [23] **I** *vtr* to address [sb] using the 'vous' form.
II se vouvoyer *vpr* to address one another using the 'vous' form.

voyage /vwajaʒ/ *nm* (dans son ensemble) trip; (déplacement) journey; **le ~ aller** the outward journey; **faire un ~ en Italie** to go on a trip ou to travel to Italy; **aimer les ~s** to love travelling^GB.
■ **~ d'études** study trip; **~ de noces** honeymoon; **~ organisé** package tour.
IDIOMES **faire le grand ~** to pass away.

voyager /vwajaʒe/ [13] *vi* to travel; **~ en train** to travel by train; **ce vin ne voyage pas bien** this wine doesn't travel well; **les bagages ont voyagé par le train** the luggage went by train; **récit qui vous fait ~ dans le temps** story that takes you on a journey through time.

voyageur, -euse /vwajaʒœʀ, øz/ **I** *adj* LITER **être d'humeur voyageuse** to have itchy feet.
II *nm,f* **1** (passager) passenger; **'réservé aux ~s munis de billets'** 'ticketholders only'; **2** (aventurier) traveller^GB; **Marco Polo fut un grand ~** Marco Polo was a great traveller^GB.
■ **~ de commerce** travelling^GB salesman.

voyagiste /vwajaʒist/ [▶374] *nmf* tour operator.

voyance /vwajãs/ *nf* clairvoyance.

voyant, ~e /vwajã, ãt/ **I** *adj* [*couleur, robe*] loud.
II *nm,f* **1** (extralucide) clairvoyant; **2** (qui y voit) sighted person.
III *nm* light; **~ d'huile** AUT oil warning light.

voyelle /vwajɛl/ *nf* vowel.

voyeur, -euse /vwajœʀ, øz/ *nm,f* voyeur.

voyou /vwaju/ *nm* lout, yobbo° GB, hoodlum° US.

vrac: en vrac /ãvʀak/ *loc adv* **1** (au détail) loose unpackaged; (en gros) in bulk; **2** (pêle-mêle) **tout mettre en ~ dans un tiroir** to throw everything haphazardly into a drawer; **jeter ses idées en ~ sur le papier** to jot down one's ideas as they come.

vrai, ~e /vʀɛ/ **I** *adj* **1** (conforme à la vérité) true; **c'est bien ~!** that's absolutely true!; **il n'en est pas moins ~ que...** it's nonetheless true that...; **il n'y a rien de ~ dans ses déclarations** there's no truth in his/her statements; **c'est bien toi qui l'as pris, pas ~?** YOU took it, didn't you?; **son film ne montre pas le ~ Napoléon** his/her film doesn't show the real Napoleon; **2** (réel) true; **une histoire ~e** a true story; **la ~e raison de mon départ** the real reason for my leaving; **3** (authentique) real, genuine [*jumeau*]; **un ~ Rembrandt** a genuine Rembrandt; **une ~e blonde** a natural blonde; **4** (intensif) real, veritable; **c'est un ~ régal** it's a real delight; **la pièce est une ~e fournaise** the room is like an oven; **ma vie est un ~ roman** my life is like something out of a novel; **5** (naturel) (*after n*) [*personnage, caractère*] true to life; [*sentiments, émotion*] true; **plus ~ que nature** [*tableau, scène*] larger than life (*après n*).
II *nm* truth; **il y a du ~ dans ce que tu dis** there's some truth in what you say; **on ne distingue plus le ~ du faux dans leur histoire** one can't tell fact from

fiction in their story; **être dans le** ~ to be in the right; **pour de** ~ for real; **à** ~ **dire, à dire** ~ to tell the truth.
III *adv* **faire** ~ to look real; **parler** ~ to speak plainly; **son discours sonne** ~ his speech has the ring of truth.

vraiment /vʀɛmɑ̃/ *adv* really.

vraisemblable /vʀɛsɑ̃blabl/ **I** *adj* (qui paraît vrai) [*excuse*] convincing, plausible; [*histoire, scénario*] plausible; (probable) likely; **il est** ~ **que** it is likely ou probable that; **peu** ~ [*excuse*] not very convincing, quite unconvincing; [*histoire*] rather implausible; **ce qui me paraît peu** ~ **c'est** what strikes me as very unlikely is.
II *nm* **nouvelles qui sont dans l'ordre du** ~ news which is within the bounds of probability; **rester dans le** ~ to keep within the bounds of credibility.

vraisemblablement /vʀɛsɑ̃blabləmɑ̃/ *adv* probably; ~ **pas** probably not; **ils ne signeront** ~ **pas ce traité** it seems unlikely that they will sign this treaty.

vraisemblance /vʀɛsɑ̃blɑ̃s/ *nf* **1** (d'hypothèse) likelihood; (de situation, d'intrigue) plausibility; (d'explication) plausibility, verisimilitude SOUT; **selon toute** ~ in all likelihood, in all probability; **2** LITTÉRAT, THÉÂT verisimilitude SOUT.

vrille /vʀij/ *nf* **1** (spirale) spiral; SPORT spiral; AVIAT tailspin, spiral; **descendre en** ~ [*avion*] to go into a spiral dive; **2** BOT tendril; **3** TECH gimlet.

vrombir /vʀɔ̃biʀ/ [3] *vi* **1** [*moteur*] to roar; (en continu) to throb; **faire** ~ **un moteur** to rev up an engine; **2** [*mouche*] to buzz.

VRP /veɛʀpe/ *nm* (*abbr* = **voyageur représentant placier**) representative, rep○.

VTT /vetete/ *nm*: *abbr* ▶ **vélo**.

vu, ~e¹ /vy/ **I** *adj* **1** (considéré) **être bien** ~ [*personne*] to be well thought of; **être mal** ~ [*personne*] not to be well thought of; **c'est bien** ~ **de faire cela** it's good form to do that; **ce serait plutôt mal** ~ it wouldn't go down well; **2** (jugé) **bien** ~!, **c'est bien** ~! good point!; **c'est tout** ~ my mind is made up; **3** (compris) ~?, **c'est bien** ~? got it○?
II *prép* in view of.
III vu que *loc conj* in view of the fact that.
IDIOMES **ni** ~ **ni connu**○! no-one will know!; **faire qch ni** ~ **ni connu**○ to do sth without anybody knowing; **pas** ~ **pas pris** it can't hurt if nobody knows; **au** ~ **et au su de tous** openly and publicly.

vue² /vy/ *nf* **1** (vision) eyesight; **les troubles de la** ~ eye trouble; **perdre/recouvrer la** ~ to lose/to regain one's sight; **don de double** ~ gift of second sight; **avoir la** ~ **basse** LIT, FIG to be short-sighted GB ou near-sighted US; **ça fatigue la** ~ it strains your eyes; **en** ~ [*personnalité*] prominent; **en** ~ **de la côte** within sight of the coast; **mettre une photo bien en** ~ to display a photo prominently; **c'est**

quelqu'un de très en ~ he's/she's very much in the public eye; **2** (regard) sight; **à première** ~ at first sight; **ne perds pas cet enfant de** ~ don't let that child out of your sight; **perdre qn de** ~ FIG to lose touch with sb; **le paysage qui s'offrait à la** ~ the landscape before us; **à** ~ [*tirer*] on sight; [*atterrir, piloter*] without instruments; FIN [*retrait*] on demand; **3** (panorama) view; **chambre avec** ~ **sur la mer** room with sea view; **avoir** ~ **sur le lac** to look out onto the lake; **d'ici, on a une** ~ **plongeante sur la vallée** from here you get a bird's-eye view of the valley; **4** (spectacle) sight; **à ma** ~, **il s'enfuit** he took to his heels when he saw me ou on seeing me; **5** (dessin, photo) view; ~ **de face/de côté** front/side view; **6** (façon de voir) view; ~s views; **une** ~ **optimiste des choses** an optimistic view of things; **7** (projet) ~s plans; (desseins) **avoir des** ~s **sur qn/qch** to have designs on sb/sth; **j'ai un terrain en** ~ (je sais lequel conviendrait) I have a plot of land in mind; (je voudrais obtenir) I've got my eye on a piece of land; **en** ~ **de qch/de faire qch** with a view to sth/to doing sth.
■ ~ **d'ensemble** overall view; **ce n'est qu'une** ~ **de l'esprit** it's entirely imaginary.
IDIOMES **à** ~ **d'œil** or **de nez**○ at a rough guess; **vouloir en mettre plein la** ~ **à qn** to try to dazzle sb.

vulcanologue /vylkanɔlɔg/ ▶ 374 *nmf* volcanologist.

vulgaire /vylgɛʀ/ **I** *adj* **1** (grossier) [*personne, propos*] vulgar, coarse; **2** (banal) ordinary; **comme un** ~ **délinquant** like a common delinquent; **c'est un** ~ **employé** he's just a lowly employee; **3** (courant) [*plante, nom*] common; **la langue** ~ the vernacular; **explication en langue** ~ explanation in simple language; **4** [*esprit, opinion*] common.
II *nm* (grossièreté) vulgarity.

vulgairement /vylgɛʀmɑ̃/ *adv* **1** (sans raffinement) [*s'habiller*] in a common way; [*s'exprimer*] coarsely; **2** (dans la langue courante) [*appeler*] commonly.

vulgarisation /vylgaʀizasjɔ̃/ *nf* popularization; **revue de** ~ **scientifique** scientific review for the general public.

vulgariser /vylgaʀize/ [1] **I** *vtr* (rendre accessible) to popularize [*science, technologie*]; to bring [sth] into general use [*expression*].
II se vulgariser *vpr* [*technologie*] to become generally accessible; [*expression*] to come into general use.

vulgarité /vylgaʀite/ *nf* **1** (grossièreté) vulgarity, coarseness; **2** (banalité) ordinariness.

vulnérabilité /vylneʀabilite/ *nf* vulnerability.

vulnérable /vylneʀabl/ *adj* vulnerable.

vulve /vylv/ *nf* vulva.

Ww

w, W /dublǝve/ *nm inv* **1** (lettre) w, W; **2 W** (*written abbr* = **watt**) **60 W** 60 W.

wagon /vagɔ̃/ *nm* **1** (pour matériel, animaux) wagon GB, car US; (pour personnes) carriage GB, car US; **2** (contenu) wagonload GB, carload US.

■ ~ **à bestiaux** cattle truck GB, cattle car US; ~ **de marchandises** goods wagon GB, freight car US.

wagon-citerne, *pl* **wagons-citernes** /vagɔ̃si tɛrn/ *nm* RAIL tanker.

wagon-lit, *pl* **wagons-lits** /vagɔ̃li/ *nm* sleeper, sleeping car US.

wagonnet /vagɔnɛ/ *nm* trolley GB, cart US.

wagon-restaurant, *pl* **wagons-restaurants** /vagɔ̃ʀɛstɔʀɑ̃/ *nm* restaurant car GB, dining car US.

wallon, -onne /walɔ̃, ɔn/ ▶338 *adj, nm* Walloon.

Wallonie /walɔni/ ▶509 *nprf* Walloon area of Belgium.

wassingue /vasɛ̃g/ *nf* floorcloth.

waters○ /watɛʀ/ *nmpl* toilets.

00tt /wat/ *nm* watt.

watt-heure, *pl* **watts-heures** /watœʀ/ *nm* watt-hour.

WC /(dublǝ)vese/ *nmpl* toilet; **aller aux** ~ to go to the toilet.

week-end, *pl* ~**s** /wikɛnd/ *nm* weekend.

whisky, *pl* **whiskies** /wiski/ *nm* (écossais) whisky, Scotch; (irlandais, américain) whiskey.

winchester /winʃɛstɛʀ/ *nf* (fusil) Winchester® rifle.

wishbone /wiʃbon/ *nm* NAUT, SPORT wishbone boom.

wisigoth, ~**e** /vizigo, ɔt/ *adj* Visigothic.

x, **X** /iks/ *nm inv* **1** (lettre) x, X; **2** MATH (inconnue) x; **il y a x temps que c'est fini** it's been over for ages; **3** (pour désigner un inconnu) **X, Monsieur X** X, Mr X; **porter plainte contre X** JUR to take an action against person or persons unknown; **4** CIN **film classé X** X-rated film GB ou movie.

xénophobe /gzenɔfɔb/ **I** *adj* xenophobic. **II** *nmf* xenophobe.

xénophobie /gzenɔfɔbi/ *nf* xenophobia.

xérès /kseʀɛs/ *nm inv* sherry.

xylographe /ksilɔgʀaf/ *nm* xylographer.

xylophone /ksilofɔn/ ▶ 392 | *nm* xylophone.

Yy

y¹, Y /igʀɛk/ *nm inv* (lettre) y, Y.

y² /i/ *pron*

■ **Note** Les expressions comme *y rester, il y a* sont traitées sous le verbe.

— Lorsque *y* met en relief un groupe exprimé, on ne le traduit pas: *tu y vas souvent, à Londres○ ?* = do you often go to London?; *je n'y comprends rien, moi, aux échecs○* = I don't understand anything about chess.

— Lorsque *y* ne remplace aucun groupe identifiable, on ne le traduit pas: *c'est plus difficile qu'il n'y paraît* = it's harder than it seems; *je n'y vois rien* = I can't see a thing.

1 (à ça) **rien n'~ fait** it's no use; **elle n'~ peut rien** there's nothing she can do about it; **j'~ viens** I'm coming to that; **tu n'~ arriveras jamais** you'll never manage; **tu ~ crois?** do you believe it?; **je vais m'~ mettre demain** I'll start tomorrow; **je n'~ comprends rien** I don't understand a thing; **il n'~ connaît rien** he knows nothing about it; **j'~ pense parfois** I sometimes think about it; **tu t'~ attendais?** were you expecting it?; **tu ~ as gagné** you got the best deal; **2** (là) there; **n'~ va pas** don't go; **j'~ suis allé hier** I went yesterday; **3** (avec le verbe avoir) **des pommes? il n'y en a plus/pas** apples? there are none left/none; **du vin? il n'y en a plus/pas** wine? there's none left/none; **il n'~ a qu'à téléphoner** just phone.

IDIOMES **~ mettre du sien** to work at it.

ya(c)k /jak/ *nm* yak.

yaourt /ˈjauʀ(t)/ *nm* yoghurt; **~ nature/aromatisé/aux fruits** natural/flavoured^{GB}/fruit yoghurt.

yaourtière /ˈjauʀtjɛʀ/ *nf* yoghurt-maker.

yéménite /ˈjemenit/ ▶ 394 , 338 *adj* Yemeni.

Yéménite /ˈjemenit/ ▶ 394 *nmf* Yemeni.

yen /ˈjɛn/ ▶ 33 *nm* yen.

yéti /ˈjeti/ *nm* yeti.

yeux *nmpl* ▶ œil.

yé-yé, *pl* **~s** /jeje/ *nm* (musique) **le ~** French version of rock 'n' roll in the 60s.

yiddish /ˈjidiʃ/ ▶ 338 *adj inv, nm* Yiddish.

yod /ˈjɔd/ *nm* LING yod.

yoga /ˈjɔga/ ▶ 329 *nm* yoga; **faire du ~** to do yoga.

yoghourt /ˈjɔguʀ(t)/ *nm* = **yaourt**.

yogi /ˈjɔgi/ *nm* yogi.

yole /ˈjɔl/ *nf* skiff.

yougoslave /ˈjugɔslav/ ▶ 394 *adj* Yugoslavian.

youpi○ /ˈjupi/ *excl* yippee!

youyou /ˈjuju/ *nm* **1** (cri) ululation SOUT; **2** (embarcation) dinghy.

yo-yo® /ˈjojo/ *nm inv* yoyo®.

Zz

Z /zɛd/ nm inv z, Z.

apper /zape/ [1] vi (à la télévision) to flick through the channels.

èbre /zɛbʀ/ nm **1** zebra; **2**° FIG bloke° GB, guy°.

ébré /zebʀe/ adj [tissu] zebra-striped; **~ de** streaked with.

ébrure /zebʀyʀ/ nf stripe.

ébu /zeby/ nm zebu.

èle /zɛl/ nm zeal, enthusiasm; **avec ~** enthusiastically, with zeal ou enthusiasm; **faire du ~** or **de l'excès de ~** to be overzealous, to overdo it.

èlé, ~e /zele/ adj enthusiastic, zealous.

èlote /zelɔt/ nm HIST Zealot.

énith /zenit/ nm LIT, FIG zenith; **à son ~** [soleil] in he ou at its zenith; [carrière] at its height; **être au ~ de qch** to be at the height of sth.

éphyr /zefiʀ/ nm LITER zephyr.

éro /zeʀo/ ▶399] **I** adj **1** (avant nom) **~ heure** midnight, twenty-four hundred (hours); **il sera exactement ~ heure vingt minutes dix secondes** the time will be twelve twenty and ten seconds; **les enfants de ~ à six ans** children from nought to six years old; **j'ai eu ~ faute dans ma dictée** I didn't make a single mistake in my dictation; **2** (après nom) zero; **niveau/croissance ~** zero level/growth.

II nm **1** (chiffre) zero, nought GB; **le prix se termine par un ~** the price ends in a nought GB ou zero; **2** (sur une échelle de valeurs) zero; **remettre un compteur à ~** to reset a counter to zero; **avoir le moral à ~** FIG to be down in the dumps°; **3** (évaluation) zero, nought GB; **avoir un ~ en latin** to get zero ou nought in Latin; **c'est beau à regarder mais question goût c'est ~**° it's nice to look at, but no marks for flavour GB; **4** (en sport) GÉN nil, nothing; (au tennis) love; **gagner trois (buts) à ~** to win three nil; **l'emporter par deux sets à ~** to win by two sets to love.

~ de conduite bad mark for behaviour GB.

DIOMES **partir de ~** to start from scratch; **tout reprendre à ~** to start all over again; **avoir la boule à ~**° to have a shaven head.

Les signes du zodiaque

	signe	personnes	date
Bélier	= Aries	Arians	Mar 21–Apr 20
Taureau	= Taurus	Taureans	Apr 21–May 20
Gémeaux	= Gemini	Geminis	May 21–Jun 21
Cancer	= Cancer	Cancerians	Jun 22–July 22
Lion	= Leo	Leos	July 23–Aug 22
Vierge	= Virgo	Virgos ou Virgoans	Aug 23–Sept 22
Balance	= Libra	Libras	Sept 23–Oct 23
Scorpion	= Scorpio	Scorpios	Oct 24–Nov 21
Sagittaire	= Sagittarius	Sagittarians	Nov 22–Dec 21
Capricorne	= Capricorn	Capricorns	Dec 22–Jan 19
Verseau	= Aquarius	Aquarians	Jan 20–Feb 18
Poissons	= Pisces	Pisceans	Feb 19–Mar 20

Dans les expressions suivantes, Lion est pris comme exemple; tous les autres signes s'utilisent de la même façon.

je suis Lion	= I'm Leo ou I'm a Leo
je suis Gémeaux	= I'm a Gemini
né sous le signe du Lion	= born under the sign of Leo ou born in Leo
les Lions/Cancers sont très généreux	= Leos/Cancerians are very generous
que dit l'horoscope pour les Lions?	= what's the horoscope for Leo?

---

este /zɛst/ nm (écorce) ¢; **un ~ de citron** the zest of a lemon; **un ~ de provocation** FIG a touch of provocation.

éta /dzeta/ nm inv zeta.

ézayer /zezeje/ [21] vi to lisp.

beline /ziblin/ nf sable; **un manteau de ~** a sable coat.

euter° /zjøte/ [1] vtr to get a load of°, take a look t.

gomar /zigɔmaʀ/ nm PEJ guy°.

goto° /zigɔto/ nm guy°; **faire le ~** to clown round.

gue° /zig/ nm guy°.

gzag /zigzag/ nm zigzag; **une route en ~** a winding road; **faire des ~s** to zigzag (parmi through); **partir en ~s** to zigzag off.

nc /zɛ̃g/ nm **1** zinc; **toiture de** or **en~** tin roofing; **2**° (comptoir) counter, bar; **3**° (avion) plane.

ngueur /zɛ̃gœʀ/ ▶374] nm roofer.

nzin /zɛ̃zɛ̃/ **I** adj inv cracked°.

I nmf (personne) lunatic, nut°.

II nm thingummy° GB, thingamajig°.

p® /zip/ nm zip GB, zipper US.

zippé, ~e /zipe/ adj [sac, blouson] zip-up (épith).

zizanie /zizani/ nf ill-feeling, discord.

zizi° /zizi/ nm willy° GB, wiener° US, penis.

zodiac® /zɔdjak/ nm NAUT inflatable dinghy.

zodiaque /zɔdjak/ nm zodiac.

zombie /zɔ̃bi/ nm zombie.

zona /zona/ ▶196] nm shingles ¢.

zonard°, **~e** /zonaʀ, aʀd/ nm,f PEJ dropout°.

zone /zon/ nf **1** (secteur) zone, area; **~ interdite** no-go area GB, off-limits area; (sur un panneau) no entry; **2** FIG (domaine) area; **~ de recherche** area of research; **3** (banlieue pauvre) **la ~** the slum belt; **de seconde ~** second-rate.

■ **~ d'activités** business park; **~ artisanale** small industrial estate GB ou park; **~ bleue** AUT restricted parking zone; **~ d'environnement protégé** environmental protection zone; **~ industrielle** industrial estate GB ou park; **~ libre** HIST unoccupied France; **~ de libre-échange** ÉCON free-trade area; **~ occupée** HIST occupied France; **~ sinistrée** ADMIN disaster area.

zoner° /zone/ [1] vi to hang about° ou around°.

zoo /zo/ nm zoo.

zoologie /zɔɔlɔʒi/ nf zoology.

zoologiste /zɔɔlɔʒist/ ▶374] nmf zoologist.

zoom /zum/ nm **1** PHOT (objectif) zoom lens; **2** CIN zoom; **un ~ avant/arrière** a zoom in/out.

zootechnicien, -ienne /zootɛknisjɛ̃, ɛn/ ▶374] nm,f animal technician.

zouave /zwav/ nm **1**° (clown) clown, comedian; **faire le ~** to play the fool GB, to clown around°; **2** (soldat) zouave.

zozo° /zozo/ nm ninny° GB, jerk°.

zozoter /zɔzɔte/ [1] vi to lisp.

zut /zyt/ excl damn°!

zygomatique /zigɔmatik/ adj, nm zygomatic.

French

correspondence

Announcing a wedding in the family

Monsieur et Madame Norbert LESOURD
Monsieur et Madame Raoul RIVIERE
Monsieur et Madame Paul AURIA

*sont heureux de vous faire part du mariage
de leurs enfants et petits-enfants*

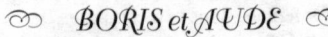 BORIS et AUDE

qui sera célébré le samedi 16 septembre 1995 à 16 heures

en l'Église Notre-Dame-des-Mariniers
à Villeneuve-lès-Avignon

33, rue de la République
74000 Annecy

86, chemin du Pont de Pierre
84000 Avignon

Invitation to a wedding

Gérard et Jacqueline Achard
12, rue Champollion
10009 Troyes

Troyes, le 5 avril 1995

Cher ami,

J'ai le plaisir de vous annoncer que nous marions notre fille Hélène le 12 juin à Paris. Vous recevrez bientôt un faire-part et une invitation pour le lunch qui suivra, mais je tenais à vous avertir dès maintenant pour que vous puissiez retenir votre journée du samedi. Le mariage aura lieu à la mairie du 6e à 14 heures et la messe sera célébrée en l'église Saint-Germain-des-Prés à 15 h 30.

Amicalement,

Jacqueline

Congratulations on a wedding

Martigues, le 18 août 1995

Chers amis,

Nous nous réjouissons pour vous du mariage de votre fille et nous vous en félicitons de tout cœur. Paul sera certainement un excellent gendre pour vous et un beau-frère apprécié par vos enfants.

Nous vous chargeons de transmettre aux futurs époux nos meilleurs vœux de bonheur et serons enchantés de venir les embrasser le jour J.

Très amicalement,

Isobelle

Announcing the birth of a baby

Pierre et Marguerite partagent avec Adrien et A
la joie de vous annoncer la naissance de

Nathalie

Le 10 juillet 1995

Monsieur et Madame Bon
24, rue Basfroi
75011 PARIS

Good wishes for the New Year

Éliane Debard
25, rue des Alouettes
38180 Seyssin

le 15 décembre 1994

Je vous présente mes meilleurs vœux de bonheur et de réussite pour la nouvelle année. Que 1995 vous apporte tout ce que vous souhaitez, à vous, à votre famille et à tous ceux qui vous sont chers.

Éliane Debard

Thanks for New Year wishes

Fanny Cogne
7, avenue Calade
10099 Troyes

le 6 janvier 1995

Je vous remercie de vos vœux. Ma famille se joint à moi pour vous adresser, à notre tour, les nôtres les plus sincères.

Fanny Cogne

Invitation to a visit

Versailles, le 26 avril 1995

Cher Charles,

A l'occasion du pont de l'Ascension, Henri et moi invitons quelques amis dans notre maison de campagne à côté de Blois. Nous serions heureux si vous pouviez être des nôtres.

Nous attendrons tous nos invités jeudi pour le déjeuner. N'oubliez pas votre équipement de golf: nous ferons un parcours si le temps le permet.

Nous vous embrassons.

Ghislaine

Invitation to a party

Paris, le 23 juin 1995

Cher Raymond,

Nous avons eu l'idée de réunir tous les copains de fac dans notre maison de Manosque le samedi 8 juillet pour arroser la thèse de Pierre. Même Albert a promis d'être là! Ce sera à la bonne franquette.

Rendez-vous aux environs de 21 heures. A bientôt.

Amicalement

Marie

Condolences: formal

Jean et Eliane Pinchon
117, boulevard Lamartine
71000 Mâcon

Mâcon, le 27 novembre 1995

Monsieur,

Nous vous adressons nos condoléances les plus sincères à l'occasion de la disparition tragique de votre épouse. Sachez qu'elle restera dans notre souvenir comme une personne exceptionnelle, et que nous partageons votre peine.

Recevez, Monsieur, l'expression de notre douloureuse sympathie.

E. Pinchon

Thanks for condolences: formal

Bordeaux, le 25 juin 1995

Madame,

Nous avons été très touchés de la sympathie que vous nous avez témoignée lors du décès de notre mère et nous vous en remercions sincèrement. Elle nous parlait souvent de vous et avait beaucoup d'estime pour vous.

Ces moments sont difficiles à traverser et les signes d'amitié sont toujours les bienvenus. Aussi nous vous prions de croire, Madame, en nos sentiments reconnaissants.

Raoul et Suzanne Dupin

Condolences: informal

Belley, le 22 avril 1995

Chère Janine,

J'ai appris par Francette la triste nouvelle du décès de Paul.

Je te présente mes condoléances les plus sincères, et t'assure que je pense beaucoup à toi en ces moments difficiles.

Crois bien, ma chère Janine, à l'expression de ma profonde sympathie.

Richard

Thanks for condolences: informal

Metz, le 18 février 1995

Très chers Paul et Lucie,

C'est vraiment gentil de nous avoir écrit ce petit mot si touchant. Nous savons très bien qu'il vous était impossible d'être avec nous le jour de l'enterrement de Jacques, mais nous vous savions proches de nous par la pensée.

Il va maintenant falloir reprendre le cours de la vie et c'est avec une amitié aussi fidèle que la vôtre que nous garderons courage.

Encore un grand merci du fond du cœur et à bientôt.

Nicole

Accepting an invitation: informal

Valence, le 29 juin 1995

Chers Marie et Pierre,

Super, l'idée de l'arrosage de thèse!
J'accepte, bien sûr, mais j'ai un dernier
rendez-vous à 20 h 15 ce jour-là, et je ne
pourrai donc pas arriver avant 22 h, le temps
de passer chez moi pour quitter ma blouse
blanche.

En attendant, bravo à Pierre, et
grosses bises.

Raymond

Invitation to a holiday together

Rueil-Malmaison, le 18 mai 1995

Chers Laurence et Alexandre

Merci beaucoup pour votre carte
de Suède. Nous avons pensé que nous
pourrions profiter de votre passage
en France pour faire ce tour de la
Corse dont nous parlons depuis si
longtemps. Nous aimerions partir le
lundi 27 juin, et rester jusqu'au
16 juillet. Qu'en pensez-vous?

Dans l'attente d'une réponse de
votre part, croyez, chers amis, à nos
sentiments les meilleurs.

Lucien

Jacqueline

Declining an invitation

Londres, le 1er mai 1995

Ma chère Ghislaine

Votre lettre m'a fait grand plaisir, et je
tiens à vous remercier d'avoir pensé à moi.
Mais je dois hélas refuser votre aimable
invitation: je m'étais précédemment engagé à
prendre part le même jour à la célébration
des noces d'or de tante Agnès et oncle Michel
à Nice.

J'espère que nous aurons très bientôt
l'occasion de nous revoir. Amicalement
à vous.

Marc

Accepting an invitation: formal

Troyes, le 17 avril 1995

Chers amis,

Je vous remercie de votre aimable
invitation au mariage de votre fille le
samedi 12 juin, que j'accepte avec joie.
J'arriverai par le train de vendredi soir,
puisqu'il n'y a plus de train le samedi.

Dans l'attente du plaisir de vous
revoir, je vous adresse mes meilleures
salutations.

Thomas Lemaître

Thanking for hospitality

Strasbourg, le 21 juin 1995

Chers madame et monsieur,

Je tiens à vous remercier de m'avoir invitée aux fiançailles d'Isolde, et je vous suis particulièrement reconnaissante de m'avoir offert de passer la nuit chez vous.

La fête a été très agréable et j'ai eu grand plaisir à vous revoir dans de si heureuses circonstances.

Encore merci pour tout. Bien à vous.

Anne

Thanking for a wedding gift

Brest, le 17 août 1995

Chère Anne

Je tenais à te remercier une fois encore pour le magnifique cadre en argent que tu nous as offert en cadeau de mariage. Nous l'avons déjà utilisé... pour exposer une photo du mariage!

Grosses bises

Isolde

Arranging an exchange visit

Dublin, le 2 avril 1995

Una et Dan Farrelly
28, Leeson Drive
Artane
Dublin 5
Irlande

      Monsieur et Madame Pierre Beaufort
      Chalet "Les Edelweiss"
      Chemin des Rousses
      74400 Chamonix

Chers Danièle et Pierre

Nous serions très heureux d'accueillir votre fils chez nous entre le 10 et le 31 juillet et d'envoyer en échange notre fils Kilian pendant le mois d'août.

Kilian a 16 ans. Il fait du français depuis 4 ans. C'est un garçon sportif: il aime la randonnée, la natation et le tennis.

Merci de nous dire assez rapidement si cette idée vous convient afin que nous puissions réserver les places d'avion.

Croyez en nos sentiments les meilleurs.

U. Farrelly

U. Farrelly

Making travel plans

Wantage, le 15 mai 1995

      Monsieur et Madame Bernard Dubois
      Villa les Etourneaux
      132 bis, Passage du Réservoir
      69140 Rillieux-la-Pape

Cher Monsieur, Chère Madame

Nous avons bien reçu votre lettre nous confirmant que vous pourriez aller chercher notre fille Lucy le 12 juillet au soir à l'aéroport. Elle s'en réjouit car elle était un peu inquiète à l'idée de prendre le bus toute seule jusqu'à la gare. Nous vous communiquerons, dès que nous l'aurons, le numéro de son vol et l'heure exacte d'arrivée.

Lucy est facilement reconnaissable: elle mesure 1 m 65 et elle a les cheveux roux. Nous nous permettrons de vous appeler le soir même afin de nous assurer qu'elle est bien arrivée.

Nous vous remercions de l'accueil que vous lui réserverez et vous prions de croire, Cher Monsieur, Chère Madame, en nos sentiments les meilleurs.

J. Smith

J. Smith

anking the host family

Nantucket, le 17 septembre 1995

Chers Monsieur et Madame Robin

Je voudrais vous remercier pour les vacances merveilleuses que j'ai passées dans votre propriété de Saint-Malo. Je n'oublierai jamais les repas où il y avait tant de bonnes choses, le bridge et les parties de pêche avec René. J'ai tant de bons souvenirs que je n'arrête pas de parler de la France à tous mes amis. J'espère que j'aurai très bientôt l'occasion de vous revoir tous.

Je vous embrasse affectueusement.

Doug

Enquiry to the tourist office

M. et Mme François Bolard
10, rue Eugène Delacroix
06200 Nice

Nice, le 24 mars 1995

Syndicat d'Initiative
de St-Gervais
74170 Saint-Gervais-les-Bains

Monsieur,

Mon mari et moi envisageons de passer nos vacances d'été à Saint-Gervais. Nous vous serions reconnaissants de bien vouloir nous faire parvenir toute la documentation dont vous disposez sur les hôtels, la station thermale ainsi que sur les activités proposées aux touristes en saison. Vous trouverez ci-joint une enveloppe timbrée pour la réponse.

Dans l'attente de vous lire, je vous prie d'agréer, Monsieur, l'expression de mes sentiments distingués.

E. Bolard

fering house exchange

Clermont, le 2 mai 1995

Pierre Clément
Résidence des Lacs d'Auvergne
Chalet n° 18
63610 Besse

Madame Perrin
2 rue de la Poste
14360 Trouville-sur-Mer

Chère Madame,

Vos amis, monsieur et madame Blanchet, nous ont dit que vous seriez heureuse de pouvoir échanger votre villa en Normandie contre notre chalet qui est au bord du lac des Corbeaux, en Auvergne. Nous serions intéressés par cette idée pour la seconde quinzaine d'août.

Si cette période vous convient, nous vous adresserons une photo et un descriptif détaillé du chalet.

Dans l'attente de vous lire, je vous adresse, Chère Madame, mes sentiments les meilleurs.

P. Clément

Responding to offer of house exchange

le 1er mai 1995

L. Dury
Chalet des Pentes
38860 les Deux-Alpes

Madame J. Lemaire
Route de Châteauroux
36200 Argenton-sur-Creuse

Madame,

J'ai bien reçu votre offre d'échanger votre ferme à la campagne et notre chalet entre le 1er et le 30 juin prochains. Nous sommes désolés, mais les dates que vous proposez ne correspondent pas à celles où nous envisageons de prendre nos vacances. Peut-être l'année prochaine cela sera-t-il possible? Nous reprendrons contact avec vous en temps voulu.

Je vous souhaite bonne chance et vous adresse, Madame, mes salutations distinguées.

L. Dury

Booking a hotel room

Bourguignon, le 22 mars 1995

Madame Solange Vernon
125 bis, Route Nationale
18340 Levet

Maison de Famille Le Repos
Chemin des Lys
06100 Grasse

Monsieur le Directeur,

J'ai bien reçu le dépliant de votre maison, ainsi que les tarifs que je vous avais demandés, et je vous en remercie.

Je souhaite réserver une chambre calme avec bains et wc, en pension complète pour la période du 27 avril au 12 mai. Je vous adresse ci-joint un chèque de 600 francs d'arrhes.

Je vous en souhaite bonne réception, et vous remerciant par avance je vous prie de croire, Monsieur le Directeur, en mes sentiments les meilleurs.

S. Vernon

P.J.: un chèque postal de 600 francs

Cancelling a hotel booking

Bourg, le 15 décembre 1995

Frédéric Brunet
5, rue du Marché
73700 Bourg-Saint-Maurice

Hôtel des Voyageurs
9, cours Gambetta
91949 Les Ulis CEDEX

Monsieur,

Je suis au regret de devoir annuler ma réservation d'une chambre pour deux personnes pour la nuit du 24 au 25 décembre, que j'avais effectuée par téléphone le 18 novembre dernier, à mon nom.

Je vous remercie de votre compréhension et vous prie d'agréer, Monsieur, l'expression de mes sentiments distingués.

F. Brunet

Letting your house

Bormes, le 4 avril 1995

Monsieur et Madame Léon Panisse
Résidence Le Bord de Mer
Rue des Pins
83230 Bormes-les-Mimosas

Monsieur Brun
8, place Colbert
69001 Lyon

Monsieur,

La maison que nous mettons en location est une villa de plain-pied, avec terrasse face à la mer et accès direct à la plage. Elle est située sur un terrain clos et boisé.

Elle se compose de deux chambres (couchage pour 6 personnes en tout), un salon-salle à manger, une kitchenette équipée, une salle de bains avec douche et un WC indépendant. Le montant de la location pour juillet est de F11 000 charges non comprises.

Souhaitant que cette offre vous convienne, je vous prie d'agréer, Monsieur, l'expression de mes sentiments distingués.

L. Panisse

Renting a holiday house

Paris, le 7 mai 1995

Monsieur C. Pernaudet
135, rue de la Gaîté-Montparnasse
75014 Paris

Agence "LES DUNES"
Promenade de l'Océan
33120 Arcachon

Messieurs,

Nous sommes à la recherche d'une location pour le mois d'août prochain dans votre région. Nous souhaitons trouver une maison pour 6/8 personnes avec un terrain clos et ombragé, même éloigné de la plage.

Pourriez-vous nous adresser le descriptif détaillé, avec si possible une photo et les tarifs de location, de ce que vous avez à nous proposer?

Dans l'attente de votre réponse, je vous prie d'agréer, Messieurs, l'expression de mes sentiments distingués.

●oking a caravan site

Sarcelles, le 14 juin 1995

Monsieur C. Bonnet
235, Bd Lénine
95200 Sarcelles

Camping-Caravaning "LES EMBRUNS"
18, allée des Capucins
22116 Moëlan-sur-Mer

Madame,

Nous souhaitons à nouveau réserver, cette année en août, l'emplacement de caravane que nous avions loué en juillet dernier et qui se trouvait dans la partie nord du camping (numéro 12/B/224).

Acceptez-vous les animaux cette année? Nous avons un tout petit chien que nous ne pouvons laisser chez nous.

Dès que nous aurons confirmation de votre part, nous vous adresserons le montant de la réservation, que vous voudrez bien nous indiquer.

Veuillez croire, Madame, en l'expression de nos sentiments distingués.

Enquiry to camp site

Fresnes, le 3 avril 1995

E. Aubin
3, bd du Maréchal Joffre
94260 Fresnes

Camping des Vagues
Bd de la Plage
44250 Saint-Brévin-les-Pins

Monsieur,

Nous avons eu votre adresse par le Syndicat d'Initiative de Saint-Brévin, et nous aimerions avoir quelques renseignements complémentaires sur votre camping.

Pourriez-vous nous préciser si les emplacements sont ombragés, si les animaux sont admis et s'il y a des commerces à proximité. Nous aimerions également connaître vos tarifs, ainsi que les délais pour réserver.

Vous remerciant par avance, je vous prie de croire, Monsieur, en mes sentiments distingués.

E. Aubin

● a neighbour

Joseph Bocquet
27, rue de Verdun
25000 Besançon

le 6 janvier 1995

M. André Delacroix
29, rue de Verdun
25000 Besançon

Monsieur,

J'ai eu la grande surprise de constater au cours de mon récent séjour dans ma villa de Besançon que vous aviez fait planter deux saules pleureurs le long du mur mitoyen qui sépare nos deux propriétés. Ces arbres n'étant pas à la distance réglementaire, et dans le souci de préserver nos bonnes relations de voisinage, je vous demande de bien vouloir les faire déplacer, et vous en remercie par avance.

Recevez mes meilleurs sentiments.

J. Bocquet

To an insurance company about a claim

Paris, le 24 mars 1995

Monsieur Ramirez
86, rue de la Convention
75015 Paris

ASSURTOURIX
123, Rue Duranton
75449 Paris CEDEX 15

Lettre recommandée
Police n° 3400510F

Messieurs,

Par la police référencée ci-dessus en date du 24 janvier 1987, j'ai fait assurer mon appartement situé rue de la Convention.

A la suite des très fortes bourrasques de la nuit dernière, les stores de la terrasse nord, ainsi que les volets, ont été arrachés et ont gravement endommagé le balcon voisin. Puis-je vous demander de m'envoyer un de vos experts le plus tôt possible, afin de constater l'étendue du sinistre et de chiffrer le montant des dommages subis?

Avec mes remerciements, je vous prie de croire, Messieurs, à l'assurance de mes sentiments distingués.

A. Ramirez

Enquiry to the tennis club

le 15 juin 1995

Madame P. Martinez
23, clos des Martyrs
13006 Marseille

CLUB DE TENNIS
DES GARRIGUES
Chemin des Bruyères
13260 Cassis

Messieurs,

Future habitante de Cassis, je souhaiterais connaître les conditions d'inscription à votre club, et savoir si vous proposez des cours particuliers ou des stages. Pratiquez-vous des tarifs familiaux? En effet, mon mari et mon fils aîné, joueurs classés, souhaitent un entraînement intensif alors que mes deux plus jeunes enfants souhaiteraient débuter.

Par avance, je vous remercie des informations que vous voudrez bien me fournir et vous prie de croire, Messieurs, en mes sentiments les meilleurs.

P. Martinez

To the telephone company

Mlle Elkabouri
27, rue Pierre et Marie Curie
88100 Epinal

le 1er mai 1995

Agence Commerciale France Télécom
88001 Epinal

Objet: demande de raccordement au réseau

Monsieur,

Je désire faire installer le téléphone dans mon nouveau domicile, 27, rue Pierre et Marie Curie. L'appartement n'est actuellement pas équipé de prise de raccordement au réseau téléphonique. J'aimerais que soient installés deux postes. Je voudrais également pouvoir disposer d'un minitel.

Je vous serais reconnaissante de bien vouloir faire le nécessaire.

Veuillez agréer, Monsieur, l'assurance de mes salutations distinguées.

F. Elkabouri

To a teacher about sick child's absence

Mours-Saint-Eusèbe, le 23 mars 1995

Madame,

Je vous demande de bien vouloir excuser l'absence de mon fils Julien DUPONT, élève de cinquième B, les 20, 21 et 22 mars dernier. Julien a dû rester alité en raison d'une double otite. Je vous adresse ci-joint un certificat médical.

Veuillez agréer, Madame, l'expression de mes sentiments distingués.

A. Dupont

To a school about admission

le 3 mars 1995

Madame H. Vannier
Lieu-dit Les Chênes Verts
1123, Route de Montluçon
18270 Culan

Monsieur le Directeur
Ecole Privée Mixte
Rue de la Gare
18200 Saint-Amand-Montrond

Monsieur,

A la rentrée scolaire prochaine, notre fils Robert fera son entrée en 6ème. Nous habitons une ferme isolée, et nous envisageons de le mettre en pension.

Avant de solliciter un rendez-vous avec vous, nous souhaiterions connaître les conditions d'admission dans votre école, ainsi que le règlement de l'internat et le montant des frais de pension et de scolarité.

Par avance, je vous remercie de votre réponse et vous prie de croire, Monsieur, en mes salutations distinguées.

H. Vannier

● a university about admission

Stephen Evans
3136 P Street NW
Washington, DC, 20007
USA

Washington, le 8 avril 1995

M. le Président de l'Université Lumière
86, rue Pasteur
69365 Lyon Cedex 07

Objet : demande de renseignements

Monsieur le Président

Je suis étudiant en latin à l'Université de
Columbia où je suis en train de terminer ma
Maîtrise (MA). Je vous serais reconnaissant de me faire savoir s'il est possible
de m'inscrire dans votre université pour y
faire un Doctorat, et de me dire quelles
sont les démarches à effectuer.

Veuillez agréer, Monsieur le Président,
l'expression de mes respectueuses salutations.

S. Evans

To the builders: asking for an estimate

le 17 mars 1995

Monsieur et Madame Yves Laplace
Villa Mon Rêve
56, rue du Bois
59600 Maubeuge
tél.: 27.09.66.46

Monsieur Berthin
Entreprise Mahieux et Cie
Zone Industrielle
Bloc Q7 T23
59600 Maubeuge

Monsieur,

**Nous souhaiterions faire construire à
l'adresse ci-dessus une piscine
chauffée et éclairée qui puisse être
utilisable dès l'été prochain.
Pourrions-nous convenir d'un rendez-
vous ici, afin que vous puissiez vous
rendre compte sur place des
caractéristiques de notre propriété?**

**Nous vous demanderons d'apporter une
documentation variée afin que nous
puissions faire notre choix. Nous
souhaiterions avoir un devis précis au
moment des vacances de Pâques.**

**Nous vous adressons, Monsieur, nos
salutations distinguées.**

Y. Laplace

● the builders: asking for work to be undertaken

Club des Sportifs
12, allée de la Plage
14800 Deauville
Tél.: 35 03 12 76

ENTREPRISE Roux
Route de Normandie
14001 Caen cedex

Deauville, le 15 mai 1995

Monsieur,

Nous avons le plaisir de vous faire savoir
que le devis que vous nous avez adressé pour
la construction d'un tennis "Clairdal"
nous convient parfaitement.

Nous souhaitons que les travaux commencent
le plus tôt possible afin que tout soit terminé, y compris l'aménagement floral, pour
le 18 juin prochain, les tournois commençant la semaine suivante.

Nous vous prions de croire, Monsieur, en nos
sentiments les meilleurs.

Monsieur Lecarré
Gérant

To the builders: complaining about delay

le 15 juin 1995

Monsieur Guy Moreau
12, rue Henri Gorjus
69004 Lyon

Entreprise Simon Associés
69006 Lyon
Lettre avec AR

Messieurs,

Lors de notre dernier rendez-vous de
chantier, je vous avais dit mon inquiétude
quant au retard qu'avaient pris les
travaux que nous vous avons confiés. Vous
m'aviez alors assuré que tout serait
terminé pour le 1er juillet.

Il est évident aujourd'hui qu'il me sera
impossible d'emménager à cette date, les
travaux de plomberie n'ayant même pas
commencé. Je vous rappelle que j'ai promis
de libérer mon logement actuel pour le 30
juin et que les frais causés par un retard
de votre part seront à votre charge.

Je vous prie d'agréer, Monsieur,
l'expression de mes sentiments
distingués.

G. Moreau

Looking for a placement in a computer company

Laurent PIGNON
14 bis, impasse des Aqueducs
69005 LYON
tél. : 78 47 98 54

Société Giudici
Z.I. des Pâquerettes
69575 DARDILLY CEDEX

Lyon, le 12 décembre 1995

à l'attention de Monsieur le Chef du Personnel

Monsieur,

Actuellement étudiant à l'Ecole d'Informatique Générale de Lyon, je dois effectuer un stage d'une durée de quatre mois dans une entreprise d'informatique afin de mettre en pratique l'enseignement qui m'est dispensé.

Connaissant bien la réputation de votre entreprise dans la région, je souhaiterais vivement pouvoir faire ce stage d'informaticien chez vous. Je me tiens à votre entière disposition si vous désirez me rencontrer.

Vous remerciant par avance de l'attention que vous voudrez bien porter à ma candidature, je vous prie, Monsieur, d'agréer l'expression de mes sentiments respectueux.

L. Pignon

p.j. : un curriculum vitae

Enquiring about jobs

Valérie Giraud
Les Flots
Route de Deauville
14360 Trouville-sur-Mer

A Monsieur le Directeur
Editions La Pensée Française
Paris

Trouville, le 27 octobre 1995

Monsieur,

Après un diplôme de sciences politiques (IEP Paris), j'ai entamé il y a quelques années une carrière de journaliste que je me suis contrainte d'abandonner pour des raisons familiales. J'aimerais dorénavant utiliser mes dons et mes compétences dans le domaine de l'édition ou de la traduction. Je parle trois des principales langues européennes, ainsi que l'indique le C.V. ci-joint, et je pense avoir de bonnes dispositions pour l'écriture.

Je suis prête à me rendre à un entretien si vous le jugez utile.

Recevez, Monsieur, l'expression de mes salutations distinguées.

V. Giraud

P.J. : un curriculum vitae

Looking for a job

Mme Lise Martin
26, boulevard Jean Jaurès
78000 Versailles
tél.: 43.20.80.20

Société Design et Déco
17, rue Henri Barbusse
75014 Paris

Versailles, le 7 novembre 1995

Monsieur,

Titulaire d'un diplôme de décoratrice d'intérieur et ayant une solide expérience dans la profession, ainsi que vous pourrez le constater à la lecture du curriculum ci-joint, je vous écris pour vous proposer mes services. Ayant élevé mes deux enfants, je cherche un emploi à plein temps, mais saurai me contenter d'un mi-temps si nécessaire.

Dans l'attente de vous lire, je vous prie d'agréer, Monsieur, l'expression de mes sentiments les meilleurs.

L. Martin

P.J.: un curriculum avec photographie
un dossier de mes réalisations antérieures

Replying to a job ad

JEAN-LUC MORIN
12, AVENUE D'ANGLETERRE
62107 CALAIS

Monsieur le Directeur
Arts et Design Gadgeteria
27, rue Victor Hugo
59001 Lille

Calais, le 14 février 1995

Monsieur,

L'annonce parue en page 2 de l'édition du 12 février du Courrier Picard concernant un poste de concepteur m'a vivement intéressé. Mon contrat à durée déterminée chez Solo and Co. touche à sa fin. Je pense posséder l'expérience et les qualifications requises pour vous donner toute satisfaction dans ce poste, comme vous pourrez le constater au vu de mon CV. Je me tiens à votre disposition pour un entretien éventuel, et vous prie d'agréer, Monsieur, l'expression de mes sentiments distingués.

J.L. Morin

P.J.: un CV avec photo

...ring a job as an au pair

le 26 mai 1995

Madame E. Dulac
...22, rue de la Mignonne
...9009 Lyon
...éléphone: 78 22 97 64

Madame,

J'ai appris par le Centre Social que votre fille de 17 ans était à la recherche d'un emploi qui lui permettrait de s'occuper de jeunes enfants. Or je cherche une jeune fille sérieuse qui puisse prendre en charge mes jumelles de cinq ans pendant le mois de juillet lorsque je serai au bureau, et qui puisse faire quelques petits travaux ménagers. Elle serait nourrie, logée, blanchie et recevrait une rémunération de 3000 F par mois.

Si cela intéresse votre fille, je lui propose de prendre contact avec moi dès que possible au numéro ci-dessus.

Je vous prie de croire, Madame, en mes sentiments les meilleurs.

E. Dulac

Applying for a job as an au pair

Sally Kendall
5, Tackley Place
Reading RG2 6RN.
England

Reading, le 17 avril 1995

Madame, Monsieur,

Vos coordonnées m'ont été communiquées par l'agence "Au Pair International", qui m'a demandé de vous écrire directement. Je suis en effet intéressée par un emploi de jeune fille au pair pour une période de six mois au moins, à partir de l'automne prochain.

J'adore les enfants, quel que soit leur âge, et j'ai une grande expérience du baby-sitting, comme vous pourrez le constater au vu du CV ci-joint.

Dans l'espoir d'une réponse favorable, je vous prie d'agréer, Madame, Monsieur, l'expression de mes respectueuses salutations.

S. Kendall

P.J.: un CV

...ing for a reference

Craig McKenzie
15 Rowan Close
Torquay
Devon
TQ2 7QJ

Torquay, le 12 janvier 1995

Monsieur,

J'ai été votre étudiant en DEA pendant l'année 1990-1991.

Je constitue actuellement un dossier pour postuler un emploi à l'Université de St Andrews et je dois fournir deux lettres de recommandation. Accepteriez-vous d'en écrire une? Si votre réponse est oui, je vous serais très reconnaissant de faire parvenir cette lettre directement à l'université.

Avec mes remerciements, et l'expression de mes sentiments respectueux.

(signature)

P.J.: description de poste
enveloppe timbrée

Thanking for a reference

JEAN-LUC MORIN
12, AVENUE D'ANGLETERRE
62107 CALAIS

le 30 mars 1995

Chère Madame,

Je tiens à vous remercier d'avoir bien voulu apporter votre soutien à ma candidature à un poste de concepteur chez Arts et Design Gadgeteria. J'ai eu un entretien avec leur directeur du personnel, et j'ai le plaisir de vous annoncer que j'ai été sélectionné. J'en suis très satisfait, d'autant plus qu'il y avait de nombreux candidats. Transmettez mon bon souvenir à mes anciens collègues.

Recevez, Chère Madame, l'expression de ma profonde gratitude.

(signature)

Accepting a job

Gabriel Maréchal
11, rue Jules Ferry
85000 La Roche-sur-Yon

M. Ramirez
Ferme modèle du Grand Pré
14260 Aunay-sur-Odon

le 3 avril 1995

Monsieur,

C'est avec le plus grand plaisir que j'ai reçu votre courrier m'informant que j'avais été choisi pour le poste de pépiniériste auquel j'étais candidat. Je vous confirme par la présente que je serai en mesure de prendre ce poste à compter du 2 mai. J'arriverai dans la soirée du 1er, et me présenterai à vous dès 7 heures le lendemain matin.

Je vous prie de croire, Monsieur, à mes sentiments les meilleurs.

G. Maréchal

Refusing a job

René Perrot
13, rue Lamartine
38590 Brézins

Entreprise Bideau
Electricité générale
Quartier des Balmes
01370 Saint-André-de-Corcy

le 28 mars 1995

Monsieur,

Je vous suis reconnaissant de m'avoir offert un emploi d'électricien dans votre entreprise. Toutefois, ma situation personnelle a changé depuis notre dernier entretien. En effet, ma femme qui travaille dans l'Education nationale vient d'être nommée en Haute-Vienne. Je me vois donc dans l'obligation de refuser votre offre.

J'espère que vous ne me tiendrez pas rigueur de ce désistement, et vous prie d'agréer l'expression de mes meilleurs sentiments.

R. Perrot

Giving a reference

🏛
UNIVERSITE DE CLERMONT-FERRAND 1
27, avenue Michelin
63567 Clermont-Ferrand Cedex 3
téléphone 73 40 60 31

Clermont-Ferrand, le 13 mars 1995

A QUI DE DROIT

Monsieur Louis Filard a été mon étudiant en classe de géométrie pendant l'année universitaire 1987–88. Bien que la classe ait été fort nombreuse, je me souviens de lui comme d'un étudiant attentif, prompt à poser des questions très souvent pertinentes, et obtenant des résultats tout à fait honorables dans ses travaux écrits. Sérieux et appliqué, il a fait montre de qualités qui laissent bien augurer de son avenir. Je ne doute pas qu'il puisse donner entièrement satisfaction dans l'emploi qu'il postule.

E. Chapier

Madame Eliane Chapier
Maître de Conférences
Faculté de Mathématiques
Université de Clermont-Ferrand

Resigning from a post

Frédéric Aubert
12, avenue de la Gare
07100 Annonay

M. Bedeau
Café-Bar des Anglais
Grand Place
07440 Alboussière

Annonay, le 12 septembre 1995

Monsieur,

Par cette lettre je vous prie de prendre note de ma décision de démissionner de mon emploi de garçon de café à dater du 12 octobre prochain. Pour des raisons familiales, je me vois en effet dans l'obligation de quitter la région.

Je vous remercie de la sympathie que vous m'avez exprimée au cours des dernières semaines, qui ont été particulièrement difficiles.

Je vous prie de croire à mes sentiments les meilleurs.

F. Aubert

...ing for a catalogue

Thomas Lavant
3, rue des Epinettes
94170 Le Perreux

> *Entreprise J. Rossi SARL*
> *Optique en gros*
> *Z.I. des Hauts Fourneaux*
> *25000 BESANÇON*

> *Le Perreux, le 12 janvier 1995*

Monsieur

> *Je vous serais reconnaissant de bien vouloir m'envoyer le catalogue des jumelles et longues-vues que vous commercialisez, avec la liste des prix.*

> *Recevez, Monsieur, l'assurance de mes salutations distinguées.*

> *T. Lavant*

Sending a catalogue

AGENCE BERNARD
S.A.R.L.
85, route de l'Hippodrome
92153 SURESNES CEDEX
tél.: 46 26 51 22   fax: 46 26 44 99

> Madame Ménard
> Résidence du Val d'Or
> Appartement 2B
> 92800 PUTEAUX

> Suresnes, le 6 février 1995

Réf. : ML-94-127

Chère Madame,

Comme chaque année, nous vous adressons un catalogue des voyages que nous proposons à des prix très avantageux aux personnes retraitées pouvant partir en dehors des périodes d'affluence. Vous y trouverez tous les détails concernant les dates, les prix, les conditions de séjour, etc.

Que vous choisissiez le Sahara ou le Cap Nord, vous serez enchantée de votre décision. De plus, nous offrons gracieusement un superbe sac de voyage à nos premiers inscrits.

Alors, à bientôt, Madame Ménard, le plaisir de vous voir et croyez en nos sentiments très dévoués.

Nicole LEFET
Responsable Commerciale

PJ: un catalogue 1995

...ing for an estimate

Monsieur et Madame Mercier
32, avenue des Marronniers
94500 Champigny sur Marne
Tél: 48 93 72 30

> le 3 juin 1995

> Cavanna & Fils
> 76, quai de la Marne
> 94170 Le Perreux

Messieurs,

Suite à notre conversation téléphonique de ce jour, nous vous confirmons notre requête.

Propriétaires d'un petit pavillon, nous souhaiterions procéder à quelques travaux d'agrandissement, et en particulier faire construire un jardin d'hiver dans le prolongement de la salle de séjour. Nous souhaiterions donc convenir d'un rendez-vous afin que vous puissiez établir un devis.

Dans l'attente de votre réponse, nous vous adressons nos sincères salutations.

C. Mercier

Sending an estimate

ENTREPRISE CAPRARA
56, rue A. Fourny
73100 Aix-les-Bains
téléphone: 79 57 88 76

> Monsieur Villeret
> 22, passage de la Gare
> 73100 Aix-les-Bains

> le 18 mai 1995

Référence: 94 AI 229 ADP

Monsieur,

A la suite de notre rendez-vous du 6 mai dernier, je vous adresse le devis que vous m'aviez demandé et qui comporte les différents aménagements dont nous avions parlé pour l'installation de votre piscine.

J'espère qu'il vous conviendra et vous remerciant de votre confiance, je vous prie d'agréer, Monsieur, l'expression de mes sentiments dévoués.

Philippe Barrault
Directeur
Commercial

Asking for discount

Société SOGEFOP
route de Pierrefeu
83170 Brignoles
téléphone : 42 27 86 13
télécopie: 42 27 00 01

Confiseries du Port
2, place du Port
13500 Martigues

Brignoles, le 14 novembre 1995

Messieurs,

Je souhaiterais offrir pour Noël à tout mon
personnel un assortiment de fruits confits.
Votre catalogue propose une présentation en
paniers de 150 grammes au prix de 46 F 50 pièce
TTC sous la réf. 18/22. Je souhaiterais pouvoir vous en commander 1580.

Etant donné l'importance de cette commande,
qui pourrait se renouveler chaque année, je
vous demande une remise de 10%.

Par avance, je vous remercie de votre réponse
et vous prie de croire, Messieurs, en mes
sentiments distingués.

Monsieur Robert Ledoux
Président-directeur
général

Accepting a discount

Société Levet
128 bis, Grande Rue
76190 Yvetot
téléphone: 35 89 27 68
télécopie: 35 89 99 99

Garage des Sapins
27, Square des Sapins
33170 Gradignan

le 16 février 1995

Référence RAD 94 35/22

Monsieur

Nous avons bien reçu votre demande de réduc
tion sur la commande du 12 janvier dernier, et
nous avons le plaisir de vous faire savoir
qu'à titre exceptionnel nous vous accordons
une remise de 2,5 %. Votre facture est donc ra
menée à 1.432.550,50 F.

Veuillez agréer, Monsieur, l'expression de
nos salutations distinguées.

R. Dormois
Directeur
Commercial

Acknowledging delivery

S. Kaoun
Société Delauney
83, avenue Charles de Gaulle
92320 Châtillon

Monsieur P. Langlois
SOTEP
76, bd de Strasbourg
77420 Champs

le 12 décembre 1995

Vos réf.: SK/CL57/94

Monsieur le Directeur,

Suite à ma commande du 23 septembre, j'ai
bien reçu les 30 bureaux Classic 57, et je
vous en remercie.

Vous trouverez ci-joint un chèque d'un montant de 10 200 francs à l'ordre de votre société qui constitue comme prévu le troisième
et dernier versement.

Veuillez agréer, Monsieur le Directeur, mes
sentiments distingués.

S. Kaoun

P.J.: un chèque bancaire de 10 200 francs

Complaining about delivery: late arrival

M. F. Lorinet
89, impasse des Cordeliers
36100 Issoudun

Société Tout pour l'Eau
92, avenue de Paris
36000 Châteauroux

le 30 mai 1995

Objet: Commande 94/3/5302/127/VG

Monsieur,

Voilà plus de deux mois que j'attends la
baignoire réf. 5302 couleur vert d'eau
que je vous ai commandée le 15 mars
dernier. Vous m'aviez assuré lors de la
commande qu'elle me serait livrée sous
trois semaines.

Je vous serais reconnaissant de me faire
savoir dans les délais les plus brefs la
date exacte où cet article me sera
livré, faute de quoi je me verrai
contraint d'annuler ma commande.

Dans l'attente de vous lire, je vous
prie de croire, Monsieur, à mes
sentiments distingués.

F. Lorinet

Complaining about delivery: wrong goods

> ### _"La Maison du Sous-Vêtement"_
>
> 15, rue Magenta
> 42000 Saint-Etienne
> Tél.: 77 42 17 82

> USINES LOIRETEXTILE
> Confection - Vente en gros
> Z.I. des Epis
> 42319 Roanne CEDEX
>
> le 12 septembre 1995

Réf: commande n° 95/08/30-ZDX

Messieurs,

J'ai bien reçu votre livraison, mais je me vois dans l'obligation de vous retourner le colis, les tailles des articles ne correspondant pas à celles indiquées sur le bon de commande.

Je vous saurais gré de bien vouloir corriger votre erreur et de me faire parvenir les articles conformes à ma commande dans les plus brefs délais.

Veuillez agréer, Messieurs, l'expression de ma considération distinguée.

> A.
> Hébert
> Gérant

Answering a complaint about delivery of wrong goods

> **LA PORTE ROUGE V.P.C.**
> Chemin des Dames
> 59339 TOURCOING CEDEX
> tél: 27 98 47 75   fax: 27 98 51 52

> Madame Guillot
> 2, place de l'Eglise
> 38250 CORRENÇON-EN-VERCORS
>
> le 15 mai 1995

Réf.: Cmde 95/fil/289

Chère cliente,

Nous avons bien reçu votre courrier du 13 mai dernier nous signalant que la livraison faite par nos services n'était pas conforme à votre commande.

En effet, la couette 240 x 220 réf. 727.372 n'étant plus disponible, nous avons pensé vous être agréable en vous adressant un article de qualité supérieure que nous vous offrons au même prix que celui que vous aviez commandé. Si toutefois vous ne souhaitez pas profiter de cette occasion exceptionnelle, vous pouvez nous retourner cet article en port dû et nous vous le rembourserons.

Nous vous prions de croire, chère cliente, en nos sentiments dévoués.

> M. Constantin
> Directeur des
> Ventes

Disputing an invoice: already paid

> B. Conrad
> Le Manoir aux Emaux
> 17108 Saintes

> Meubles Le Vieux Rustique
> Zone artisanale des Fougères
> D 939
> 17030 La Rochelle
>
> le 21 décembre 1995

Monsieur,

Par lettre du 20 décembre, vous me demandez de régler votre facture n° 721 de 47921,37 francs du 11 septembre concernant la livraison de meubles divers. Or cette facture a déjà été payée, par mandat postal daté du 7 octobre. Je vous la renvoie donc, en vous demandant de bien vouloir vérifier vos comptes.

Veuillez agréer, Monsieur, l'expression de mes salutations distinguées.

> B.Conrad

P.J.: votre facture

Answering complaint about invoice: already paid

> **IMPRIMERIE VITFAIT**
> Route de Chartreuse
> 38500 VOIRON
> Téléphone : 76.05.98.71

> Mademoiselle Estelle Dutreuil
> 8, boulevard Joseph Vallier
> 38000 Grenoble
>
> le 18 septembre 1995

Objet: commande n° 95/08/21

Mademoiselle,

Nous accusons réception de votre courrier du 12 septembre dernier concernant la facture de la commande ci-dessus. Cette facture vous a en effet été adressée en double exemplaire, ce dont nous vous prions de bien vouloir nous excuser. L'erreur est due au système informatique récemment mis en place et encore mal rodé.

Nous vous remercions de ne pas tenir compte de cette relance et vous prions d'agréer, Mademoiselle, l'expression de nos sentiments distingués.

> Louis Moulin
> Responsable du Service
> Comptable

Disputing an invoice: too high

> *"Les Amis de la Spatule"*
> Association à but non lucratif Loi 1901
> Téléphone 61 60 62 33
>
> Raoul Blanchard
> Trésorier de l'Association
> 11, rue Juliette Lamber
> 24000 Périgueux
>
> > "LA MERE LEGRAS"
> > Hôtel Restaurant
> > 6, rue Ampère
> > 24200 Sarlat
>
> > le 15 septembre 1995
>
> Madame,
>
> Je reçois votre facture n° 95/08/31/XYZ86
> correspondant au banquet des Anciens de la
> Spatule du 31 août dernier et je me permets
> d'en contester le montant.
>
> Nous étions convenus d'un prix d'environ
> 250 F par personne pour le repas, apéritifs et
> digestifs compris. Or votre facture fait
> apparaître un prix de 295 F par personne, ce
> qui ramène le prix du café (qui était en sus)
> à 45 F !
>
> Pensant qu'il s'agit d'une erreur, je vous
> demanderais de bien vouloir rectifier cette
> facture en conséquence, et vous prie
> d'agréer, Madame, l'expression de mes
> sentiments distingués.
>
> *R. Blanchard*
> R. Blanchard

Answering complaint about invoice: too high

> DUROUCHOUX SARL
> BP 52
> 95300 Pontoise
> téléphone: 33.87.29.86
>
> > Monsieur Pierre Delpuech
> > 28, Allée du Bois
> > 77300 Fontainebleau
> >
> > Pontoise, le 15 août 1995
>
> Objet: commande n° 95 EMB 127
>
> Monsieur,
>
> En réponse à votre courrier du 22 juillet 95, nou
> vous prions de bien vouloir ne pas tenir compte de "
> facture 95/999/888 qui comporte une erreur e
> votre défaveur.
>
> Vous trouverez ci-joint une facture, réf. 95/888/99
> qui correspond à votre commande.
>
> Avec toutes nos excuses, recevez, Monsieur, no
> salutations distinguées.
>
> *Boulier*
>
> P. Boulier
> Le Responsable du
> Service Comptabilité

Sending a cheque in payment

> Monsieur Linet
> Le Verger
> 14 ter, Chemin des Mouilles
> 47000 Agen
> téléphone: 58.57.39.47
>
> > Monsieur Chartier
> > Pépiniériste
> > 12, rue de la Plage
> > 34200 Sète
> >
> > Agen, le 25 février 1995
>
> Vos réf: 1994-23
>
> Monsieur,
>
> En règlement de votre facture 129-GTX-47 du
> 23 février, veuillez trouver ci-joint un
> chèque bancaire n° 9 543 395 d'un montant de
> 1257,75 F.
>
> Vous en souhaitant bonne réception, je vous
> prie d'agréer, Monsieur, l'expression de mes
> sentiments distingués.
>
> *Linet*
> C. Linet
>
> P.J.: 1 chèque de la Banque Populaire d'Agen
> et du Sud-Ouest

Acknowledging payment received

> ROBINETTERIE Durand
> 7, rue Pierre Gaultier
> 57050 METZ
> TELEPHONE: 89 57 13 24
>
> > Monsieur Dechaux
> > 21, route du Lac
> > 73100 AIX-LES-BAIN
> >
> > Le 23 juillet 1995
>
> Commande n° 12 H 889
>
> Monsieur,
>
> Par la présente, nous accusons réception d
> paiement de la facture 78900HOC par chèqu
> postal n° 0025863 du 19 juillet 1995 d'un mon
> tant de 172,89 F.
>
> Vous remerciant pour votre règlement, nou
> vous prions d'agréer, Monsieur, l'expressio
> de nos sentiments distingués.
>
> > Le Service Comptabilit

rong payment received

GARAGE SIMOUN

Place du Champ de Foire
91150 ETAMPES
téléphone: 60.14.91.49

Monsieur Dupuis
25 ter, avenue du Stade
14000 CAEN

Etampes,
le 25 octobre 1995

Réf. facture 560/94/08/25789

Monsieur,

Nous avons bien reçu votre chèque bancaire
n° 8 2563 114 du 19 octobre 1995 d'un
montant de 1500 F.

Le montant total de la facture qui vous a
été adressée étant de 1957 F 18, vous nous
êtes redevable de la somme de 457,18 F que
nous vous remercions par avance de bien
vouloir nous régler dans les plus brefs
délais.

Veuillez agréer, Monsieur, l'expression de
nos sentiments distingués.

B. Fournier
Gérant

Reminder of invoice outstanding

ENTREPRISE DE BATIMENT MAZZA

289, route Nationale
35000 Châteauroux
Tél.: 85 04 92 78

Monsieur Jean-Louis Jacquet
3, Place Albert Camus
36100 Issoudun

le 18 juillet 1995

Facture n° 95/126B72 du 22 avril 95

Monsieur,

Nous vous rappelons que notre facture n° 95/126B72 du
22 avril 95 dont le paiement était prévu au deuxième
trimestre 95 reste impayée à ce jour.

Nous vous remercions par avance de bien vouloir régulariser votre situation dans les plus brefs délais et vous
prions d'agréer, Monsieur, l'expression de nos salutations distinguées.

Luc Bayard
Agent
Comptable

---

x: business

L.C. INFORMATIQUE

12, RUE CLAUDE BERNARD
86000 POITIERS
N° de téléphone: 49 41 54 67
N° de télécopie: 49 41 22 82

TRANSMISSION PAR TELECOPIE

Date: 12 août 1995

Veuillez remettre ce document à : Jean
Briant

Numéro de télécopie : 19 44 705 82 31 54

De la part de : Stéphanie Langlois

Nombre de pages (y compris cette page) : 1

Message : Prière de me faire parvenir de
toute urgence, par Chronopost si possible,
l'original de vos billets d'avion et de
train pour que je puisse procéder à votre
remboursement.

J'aurai aussi besoin de vos notes d'hôtel
et de restaurant, mais c'est moins urgent.

Merci, et amitiés,

S. Langlois

**Si vous ne recevez pas ce document au complet, veuillez nous en
aviser le plus rapidement possible par téléphone ou télécopie.**

Fax: personal

DE: Guy Planais
Allée des Colibris
85110 Chantonnay
Télécopie: 51 72 27 32
Téléphone: 51 22 37 91

A: Jane Mella
896 Career Street
Ottawa K1N 6N5
Canada

Le 11 juin 1995

Chère Jane,

URGENT: J'aurais besoin des
coordonnées de Sun-Yun-Lee à Hong
Kong. Je n'arrive pas à les retrouver.
Ce serait gentil si tu pouvais me
refaxer dans la journée. Merci, et à
bientôt.

Guy

HEIDER Sarah Dolores

née le 27/09/52

nationalité américaine

Adresse

1123 Cedar Avenue
Evanston
Illinois 60989
Etats-Unis

Formation

PhD (Doctorat) en Littérature (La Poétique de Shakespeare et sa vision de la femme) soutenu en 1983 à Northwestern University, Evanston, Illinois.

Maîtrise de Littérature anglaise et américaine obtenue en 1977 à l'Université de Pennsylvanie, Philadelphie.

Licence d'Anglais de l'Université de Californie, Berkeley.

Expérience professionnelle

Depuis 1992   Professeur associée, Département d'anglais, Northwestern University.

1988 - 1992   Professeur assistante, spécialiste de la Renaissance, Département d'anglais, Northwestern University.

1983 - 1987   Professeur assistante, Département d'anglais, Université de Pennsylvanie, Philadelphie.

1980 - 1983   Attachée de recherche sous la direction du Professeur O'Leary (Féminisme et Poétique de Shakespeare), Northwestern University.

1979 - 1980   Attachée de recherche, Département d'études féministes, Northwestern University.

1977 - 1979   Assistante, spécialiste du théâtre de la Renaissance anglaise, Northwestern University.

Distinctions

Bourse de Recherche Wallenheimer en 1992 - 1993.

Poste de recherche doctorale Milton Wade en 1979 - 1980.

Bourse d'études de la Fondation Pankhurst/Amersham en 1977 - 1979.

Travaux de recherche et publications

Voir liste ci-jointe.

Divers

Présidente de la Commission "Renaissance Minds" (étude de l'idéologie de la période de la Renaissance anglaise).

Membre de l'UPCEO (Commission inter-universitaire pour la promotion de l'égalité des chances) depuis 1984.

Conseillère auprès des éditions Virago à Londres (collection des études sur la Renaissance) en 1989 - 1990.

Conseillère auprès des éditions Pandora, New York, en 1987.

Jacques Tessier

Spécialiste de Biologie Végétale

Docteur d'Etat

Né le 30 octobre 1943

Marié, deux enfants de 7 et 3 ans.

Adresse: 12, cours Fauriel, 42000 Saint-Etienne

Téléphone: (33) 77 24 37 12

Fax: (Université): (33) 77 19 67 23

E-mail: phyveg@ismu.univ-stet.fr

Thèse d'état soutenue en Octobre 1985 devant l'Université de Paris XII:
"Effets comparés des rayonnements Ω et r sur la croissance de _Calluna vulgaris_ et _Erica vagans_"
sous la direction de Jean-Pierre Chenu, Professeur de Biologie végétale à l'Université Paris XII.
Mention : Très Honorable à l'unanimité du jury.

EXPERIENCE PROFESSIONNELLE

Depuis 1986   Maître de Conférences de Biologie Végétale à l'Université de Saint-Etienne.

1979 - 1986   Maître-assistant de Biologie Végétale à l'Université de Brest.

1978 – 1979   Détaché à l'Université de Georgetown, U.S.A., chargé d'un projet d'étude sur le comportement des plantes dicotylédones en apesanteur pour la NASA.

1973 - 1978   Assistant de Biologie Végétale à l'Université de Caen.

1971 - 1973   Professeur agrégé de Sciences Naturelles au Lycée d'Etat de Dunkerque.

RECHERCHE ET PUBLICATIONS

Trois livres et vingt-sept articles publiés à ce jour (voir liste ci-jointe).

Principaux domaines de recherche : la croissance des plantes en fonction des conditions de lumière et d'humidité, avec un intérêt particulier pour les graminées.

CURRICULUM VITAE

Catherine Belin
18, avenue Edouard Herriot
01000 Bourg-en-Bresse
Tél.: 74 50 09 13

Nationalité française

Née le 28 mai 1976 à Vienne, Isère

FORMATION ET DIPLOMES

1987 - 1991
Collège d'enseignement général Frison-Roche, Vizille, Isère.

1991 - 1993
Lycée Carriat, Bourg-en-Bresse.
Baccalauréat série A2, mention assez bien, obtenu en juillet 1993.

EXPERIENCE PROFESSIONNELLE

Caissière dans l'hypermarché de Bourg-en-Bresse, juillet 1992.

Agent de bureau intérimaire à la Sécurité Sociale, caisse de Lons-le-Saunier, août 1992 et juillet-août 1993.

Grande expérience de garde d'enfants.

Cours particuliers de français et d'allemand de la Sixième à la Troisième.

DIVERS

Bon niveau en dactylographie (40 mots/minute environ).

Allemand courant (lu, parlé et écrit). Nombreux séjours courts en Allemagne.

Pratique du badminton et du ski de fond.

GRANTLEY Paul Alan

Adresse:
26 Countisbury Drive
BRIGHTON BN3 1RG
Grande-Bretagne
Tél.: 01273 53 49 50

Né le 22 mai 1969
Célibataire
Nationalité britannique

FORMATION

1988 – 1991

King's College, Londres: B.Sc. (Licence) en Biochimie
(2.1. = mention bien)

1987

A Levels (Deuxième partie du Baccalauréat) options: Biologie,
Chimie, Physique et Mathématiques.

1985

O Levels (Première partie du Baccalauréat) options :

Mathématiques, Physique, Biologie, Chimie, Commerce, Anglais,
Allemand et Sociologie.

1980 – 1987

Brighton College Boys' School (Lycée)

EXPERIENCE PROFESSIONNELLE

Mars 1989

une semaine comme "double" du Directeur Adjoint du Marketing chez
EAA Technology (Sources d'énergie écologiques) à Didcot près
d'Oxford.

Juillet 1988

deux semaines chez Alford & Wilston Ltd (Produits chimiques),
Warley, Midlands de l'Ouest.

CENTRES D'INTERET

Au Lycée

Capitaine de l'équipe de rugby pendant deux ans.
Membre du club d'échecs.

A l'Université

Membre de l'équipe de rugby.
Organisateur de la Semaine de Charité (1988).
Délégué aux activités sportives dans l'association des étudiants.

DIVERS

Bonne connaissance de l'outil informatique, en particulier sur
Macintosh.
Permis de conduire.
Intérêt pour les voyages : tour du monde en 1987-88, entre le
Lycée et l'Université.

Ingénieur informaticien

Hervé Maurier

né le 14 mars 1966 à Lons-le-Saunier
marié, sans enfants

25, rue Paul Doumer
54000 Nancy
Téléphone: 82 27 61 12

Formation

juin 1988	Diplôme d'Ingénieur.
1984 - 1988	Ecole Nationale de Chimie et Physique Industrielle de Metz, section Informatique.
1984	Baccalauréat série C à Lons-le-Saunier, Mention assez bien.

Expérience professionnelle

Depuis septembre 1991	Ingénieur chez SEIM Nancy, responsable de projet depuis janvier 1993, chargé de la conception des systèmes informatiques de l'E.D.F.
1989 - 1991	Ingénieur chez LID Informatique, Lunéville, emploi de cadre technico-commercial.
1988	Stage de trois mois chez Alsthom Nancy.
1987	Stage de deux mois chez Rhône-Poulenc, Strasbourg.

Divers

Président de l'antenne nancéenne des "Restos du cœur".

Anglais parlé courant : nombreux séjours de vacances aux Etats-Unis.

Pratique assidue de la spéléologie et du parapente.

Correspondance anglaise

Pour annoncer un mariage

Flat 3
2 Charwell Villas
45 Grimsby Road
Manchester M23

3rd June 1995

Dearest Suzanne,

I thought I'd write to tell you that James and I are getting married! The date we have provisionally decided on is August 5th and I do hope you will be able to make it.

The wedding is going to be here in Manchester and it should be quite grand, as my mother is doing the organizing. I only hope the weather won't let us down, as there's going to be an outdoor reception. My parents will be sending you a formal invitation, but I wanted to let you know myself.

All my love,

Julie

Invitation à un mariage

23 via Santa Croce
Florence
Italy

30 April 1995

Dear Oliver,

Kate and I are getting married soon after we return to the UK – on June 24th. We would like to invite you to the wedding. It will be at my parents' house in Hereford, probably at 2.30pm, and there will be a party afterwards, starting at about 8pm. You are welcome to stay the night as there is plenty of room, though it would help if you could let me know in advance.

Hope to see you then,

Best wishes,

Giorgio

Félicitations pour un mariage

22 Les Rosiers
Avenue des Épines
98100 Maginot
France.

22/8/95

Dear Joe,

Thanks for your letter. I was delighted to hear that you two are getting married, and I'm sure you'll be very happy together. I will do my best to come to the wedding, it'd be such a shame to miss it.

I think your plans for a small wedding sound just the thing, and I feel honoured to be invited. I wonder if you have decided where you are going for your honeymoon yet? I look forward to seeing you both soon. Sarah sends her congratulations.

Best wishes,

Eric

Pour annoncer une naissance

26 James Street
Oxford
OX4 3AA

22 May 1995

Dear Charlie,

We wanted to let you know that early this morning Julia Claire was born. She weighs 7lbs 2oz, and she and Harriet are both very well. The birth took place at home, as planned.

It would be wonderful to see you, so feel free to come and visit and meet Julia Claire whenever you want. (It might be best to give us a ring first, though.) It would be great to catch up on your news too. Give my regards to all your family, I haven't seen them for such a long time.

Looking forward to seeing you,

Nick

‥ux de bonne année

Flat 3, Alice House
44 Louis Gardens
London W5.

January 2nd 1995

Dear Arthur and Gwen,

Happy New Year! This is just a quick note to wish you all the best for 1995. I hope you had a good Christmas, and that you're both well. It seems like a long time since we last got together.

My New Year should be busy as I am trying to sell the flat. I want to buy a small house nearer my office and I'd like a change from the flat since I've been here nearly six years now. I'd very much like to see you, so why don't we get together for an evening next time you're in town? Do give me a ring so we can arrange a date.

With all good wishes from

Lance

Réponse à des vœux de bonne année

19 Wrekin Lane
Brighton
BN7 8QT

6th January 1995

My dear Renée,

Thank you so much for your letter and New Year's wishes. It was great to hear from you after all this time, and to get all your news from the past year. I'll write a "proper" reply later this month, when I've more time. I just wanted to tell you now how glad I am that we are in touch again, and to say that if you do come over in February I would love you to come and stay – I have plenty of room for you and Maurice.

All my love,

Helen

‥vitation pour un week-end

12 Castle Lane
Barcombe
Nr Lewes
Sussex BN8 6RJ
Phone: 01273 500520

3 June 1995

Dear Karen,

I heard from Sarah that you have got a job in London. Since you're now so close, why don't you come down and see me? You could come and spend a weekend in the country, it'd be a chance for a break from city life.

Barcombe is only about an hour's drive from where you live and I'd love to see you. How about next weekend or the weekend of the 25th? Give me a ring if you'd like to come.

All my love,

Lucy

Réponse à une invitation : acceptation (amis proches)

14a Ark Street
Wyrral Vale
Cardiff
CF22 9PP
Tel: 01222 556544

19 July 1995

Dearest Sarah,

It was good to hear your voice on the phone today, and I thought I'd write immediately to say thank you for inviting me to go on holiday with you. I would love to go.

The dates you suggest are fine for me. If you let me know how much the tickets cost I will send a cheque straight away. I'd love to see California, and am very excited about the trip and, of course, about seeing you.

Thanks again for suggesting it.

Love,

Eliza

Condoléances : à une relation

Larch House
Hughes Lane
Sylvan Hill
Sussex

22 June 1995

Dear Mrs Robinson,

I would like to send you my deepest sympathies on your sad loss. It came as a great shock to hear of Dr Robinson's terrible illness, and he will be greatly missed by everybody who knew him, particularly those who, like me, had the good fortune to have him as a tutor. He was an inspiring teacher and a friend I am proud to have had. I can only guess at your feelings. If there is anything I can do please do not hesitate to let me know.

With kindest regards,
Yours sincerely,

Malcolm Smith

Réponse à des condoléances : relation

55A Morford Lane
Bath
BA1 2RA

4 September 1995.

Dear Mr Bullwise,

I am most grateful for your kind letter of sympathy. Although I am saddened by Rolf's death, I am relieved that he did not suffer at all.

The funeral was beautiful. Many of Rolf's oldest friends came and their support meant a lot to me. I quite understand that you could not come over for it, but hope you will call in and see me when you are next in the country.

Yours sincerely,

Maud Allen

Condoléances à un proche

18 Giles Road
Chester CH1 1ZZ
Tel: 01224 123341

May 21st 1995

My dearest Victoria,

I was so shocked to hear of Raza's death. He seemed so well and cheerful when I saw him at Christmas time. It is a terrible loss for all of us, and he will be missed very deeply. You and the children are constantly in my thoughts.

My recent operation prevented me from coming to the funeral and I am very sorry about this. I will try to come up to see you at the beginning of July, if you feel up to it. Is there anything I can do to help?

With much love to all of you
from

Penny

Réponse à des condoléances : proche

122 Chester Street
Mold
Clwyd
CH7 1VU

15 November 1995

Dearest Rob,

Thank you very much for your kind letter of sympathy. Your support means so much to me at this time.

The whole thing has been a terrible shock, but we are now trying to pick ourselves up a little. The house does seem very empty.

With thanks and very best wishes from us all,

Love,

Elizabeth

Invitation à une soirée

> **Ms L Hedley**
> **2 Florence Drive, London SW1Z 9ZZ**
>
> _Friday 13 July 1995_
>
> Dear Alex,
>
> Would you be free to come to dinner with me when you are over in England next month? I know you'll be busy, but I would love to see you. Perhaps you could give me a ring when you get to London and we can arrange a date? Hope to see you then.
>
> Best wishes,
>
> Lena

Invitation à passer des vacances ensemble

> _Stone House_
> _Wilton Street_
> _Bingley_
>
> _Tel: 01274 364736_
>
> _20th May 1995_
>
> Dear Malek and Lea,
>
> Thanks for your postcard - great news that you'll be home in June. Will you have some leave then? Anne and I were thinking of spending a couple of weeks in Provence in July, and wondered if you'd like to come with us? We could rent a house together.
>
> If you'd like to come, let us know as soon as possible and we can sort out dates and other details. Hope you'll say yes! I'm quite happy to make all the arrangements.
>
> Lots of love from us both,
>
> Mukesh

Réponse à une invitation : refus

> c/o Oates
> Hemmingway House
> Eliot Street
> Coventry CV2 1EE
>
> March 6th 1995
>
> Dear Dr Soames,
>
> Thank you for your kind invitation to dinner on the 19th. Unfortunately, my plans have changed somewhat, and I am leaving England earlier than I had expected in order to attend a literary conference in New York. I am sorry to miss you, but perhaps I could call you next time I am in England, and we could arrange to meet.
>
> Until then, kindest regards,
>
> Michael Strong

Réponse à une invitation : acceptation

> c/o 99 Henderson Drive
> Inverness IV1 1SA
>
> 16/6/95.
>
> Dear Mrs Mayhew,
>
> It is very good of you to invite me to dinner and I shall be delighted to come on July 4th.
>
> I am as yet uncertain as to where exactly I shall be staying in the south, but I will phone you as soon as I am settled in London in order to confirm the arrangements.
>
> With renewed thanks and best wishes,
>
> Yours sincerely,
>
> Sophie Beauverie

Remerciements après une invitation

75/9A Westgate
Wakefield
Yorks

30/9/95

Dear Mr and Mrs Frankel,

It was very kind of you to invite me to William's 21st birthday party and I am especially grateful to you for letting me stay the night. I enjoyed myself very much indeed, as did everyone else as far as I could tell.

In the hurry of packing to leave, I seem to have picked up a red and white striped T-shirt. If you let me know where to send it, I'll put it in the post at once. My apologies.

Many thanks once again.

Yours,

Julia (Robertson)

Remerciements pour un cadeau de mariage

Mill House
Mill Lane
Sandwich
Kent
CT13 0LZ

June 1st 1995

Dear Len and Sally,

We would like to thank you most warmly for the lovely book of photos of Scotland that you sent us as a wedding present. It reminds us so vividly of the time we spent there and of the friends we made.

It was also good to get all your news. Do come and see us next time you are back on leave - we have plenty of room for guests.

Once again many thanks, and best wishes for your trip to New Zealand.

Kindest regards from

Pierre and Francine

Lettre à un correspondant : invitation

23 Ave Rostand
75006 Paris
France

5th June 1995

Dear Katrina,

I am writing to ask you if you would like to come and stay with my family here in Paris. We live in a pretty suburb, and my school is nearby. If you come we can go into the centre of Paris and do some sightseeing, as well as spending some time in my neighbourhood, which has a big outdoor swimming pool and a large shopping centre.

It would suit us best if you could come in August. If you say yes, my mother will write to your mother about details - it would be nice if you could stay about two weeks. I would be so happy if you could come.

Love from

Florence

À la famille d'un correspondant : renseignements

15 Durrer Place
Herne Bay
Kent CT6 2AA

Phone: (01227) 7685

29-4-95

Dear Mrs Harrison,

It was good of you to invite Jane to go to Italy with you. She really is fond of Freda and is very excited at the thought of the holiday.

The dates you suggest would suit us perfectly. Could you let me know how much spending money you think Jane will need? Also, are there any special clothes she should bring?

Yours sincerely,

Lisa Holland

a famille d'un correspondant : remerciements

97 Jasmine Close
Chelmsford
Essex
CM1 5AX

4th May 1995

Dear Mr and Mrs Newlands,

Thank you very much once again for taking me on holiday with you. I enjoyed myself very much indeed, especially seeing so many new places and trying so many delicious kinds of food.

My mum says I can invite Rachel for next year, when we shall probably go to Majorca. She will be writing to you about this.

Love from

Hazel

Au syndicat d'initiative

3 rue du Parc
56990 Lesmoines
France

4th May 1995

The Regional Tourist Office
3 Virgin Road
Canterbury
CT1A 3AA

Dear Sir/Madam,

Please send me a list of local hotels and guest houses in the medium price range. Please also send me details of local coach tours available during the last two weeks in August.

Thanking you in advance,

Yours faithfully,

Jean Lepied

ur proposer un échange de maisons

4 LONGSIDE DRIVE
KNOLEY
CAMBS
CB8 5RR
TEL: 01223 49586

May 13th 1995.

Dear Mr and Mrs Candiwell,

We found your names listed in the 1994 "Owners to Owners" handbook and would like to know if you are still taking part in the property exchange scheme.

We have a 3-bedroomed semi-detached house in a quiet village only 20 minutes' drive from Cambridge. We have two boys aged 8 and 13. If you are interested, and if three weeks in July or August would suit you, we would be happy to exchange references.

We look forward to hearing from you.

Yours sincerely,

John and Ella Valedict

John and Ella Valedict

Pour accepter un échange de maisons

Trout Villa
Burnpeat Road
Lochmahon
IZ99 9ZZ

(01463) 3456554

5/2/95

Dear Mr and Mrs Tamberley,

Further to our phone call, we would like to confirm our arrangement to exchange houses from August 2nd to August 16th inclusive. We enclose various leaflets about our area.

As we mentioned on the phone, you will be able to collect the keys from our neighbours the Brownes at 'Whitley House' (see enclosed plan).

We look forward to a mutually enjoyable exchange.

Yours sincerely,

Mr and Mrs R. Jones

Pour réserver une chambre d'hôtel

35 Prince Edward Road
Oxford OX7 3AA
Tel: 01865 322435

The Manager
Brown Fox Inn
Dawlish
Devon

23rd April 1995

Dear Sir or Madam,

I noticed your hotel listed in the "Inns of
Devon" guide for last year and wish to reserve a
double (or twin) room from August 2nd to 11th
(nine nights). I would like a quiet room at the
back of the Hotel, if one is available.

If you have a room free for this period
please let me know the price, what this covers,
and whether you require a deposit.

Yours faithfully,

Geo. Sand.

Pour annuler une réservation

35, rue Dumas
89870 Villeroy
France

16 March 1995

The Manager
The Black Bear Hotel
14 Valley Road
Dorchester

Dear Sir or Madam,

I am afraid that I must cancel my
booking for August 2nd-18th.
I would be very grateful if you could
return my £50.00 deposit at your earliest
convenience.

Yours faithfully,

Agnès Andrée.

Pour offrir une maison de vacances en location

Mrs M Henderson
333a Sisters Avenue
Battersea
London SW3 0TR
Tel: 0171-344 5657

23/4/95

Dear Mr and Mrs Suchard,

Thank you for your letter of enquiry about
our holiday home. The house is available
for the dates you mention. It has three
bedrooms, two bathrooms, a big lounge, a
dining room, a large modern kitchen and a
two-acre garden. It is five minutes' walk
from the shops. Newick is a small village
near the Sussex coast, and only one hour's
drive from London.

The rent is £250 per week; 10% (non-
refundable) of the total amount on
booking, and the balance 4 weeks before
arrival. Should you cancel the booking,
after that, the balance is returnable only
if the house is re-let. Enclosed is a photo
of the house. We look forward to hearing
from you soon.

Yours sincerely,

Margaret Henderson

Margaret Henderson

Pour louer une maison de vacances

23C TOLLWAY DRIVE
LYDDEN
KENT
CT33 9ER
(01304 399485)

4th June 1995

Dear Mr and Mrs Murchfield,

I am writing in response to the
advertisement you placed in "Home Today"
(May issue). I am very interested in renting
your Cornish cottage for any two weeks
between July 24th and August 28th. Please
would you ring me to let me know which dates
are available?

If all the dates are taken, perhaps you
could let me know whether you are likely to
be letting out the cottage next year, as this is
an area I know well and want to return to.

I look forward to hearing from you.

Yours sincerely,

Michael Settle.

...ur louer un emplacement de caravane

10 Place Saint Jean
32340 Les Marais
France

25th April 1995

Mr and Mrs F. Wilde
Peniston House
Kendal
Cumbria
England

Dear Mr and Mrs Wilde,

I found your caravan site in the Tourist
Board's brochure and would like to book in
for three nights, from July 25th to 28th.
I have a caravan with a tent extension and
will be coming with my wife and two
children. Please let me know if this is
possible, and if you require a deposit.
Would you also be good enough to send me
instructions on how to reach you from
the M6?

I look forward to hearing from you.

Yours sincerely,

John Winslow

Pour avoir des renseignements sur un camping

22 Daniel Avenue
Caldwood
Leeds LS8 7RR
Tel: 01532 9987676

3 March 1995

Dear Mr Vale,

Your campsite was recommended to me by a friend,
James Dallas, who has spent several holidays there.
I am hoping to come with my two boys aged 9 and 14
for three weeks this July.

Would you please send me details of the caravans for
hire, including mobile homes, with prices and dates
of availability for this summer. I would also appreciate some information on the area, and if you have any
brochures you could send me this would be very
helpful indeed.

Many thanks in advance.

Yours sincerely,

Frances Goodheart.

...n voisin

1025 Osage
Boston
MA 13000
U.S.A.

6.3.95

Dear Col. Mattison,

I am very grateful to you for forwarding
our mail to us and for the news about our
house (and the lodgers).

Don't worry about the garden - we knew
that it might suffer in a hard winter if we
were not there to look after it. Glad to hear
that the house is in good order and that the
lodgers are quiet. Yes, go ahead with getting
the fence replaced. I'll pay half, as I
promised.

Best wishes from us both,

Reg and Mavis Davies

À une compagnie d'assurances

Flat 2
Grant House
Pillward Avenue
Chelmsford CM1 1SS

3rd January 1995

Park-Enfield Insurance Co
22 Rare Road
Chelmsford
Essex CM3 8AA

Dear Sirs,

On 2nd January my kitchen was damaged by a
fire owing to a faulty gas cooker. Fortunately, I
was there at the time and was able to call the fire
brigade straight away, but the kitchen sustained
considerable damage, from flames and smoke.

My premium number is 277488349/YPP.
Please would you send me a claim form as soon as
possible.

Yours faithfully,

Mark Good

Pour avoir des renseignements sur un club de tennis

101 Great George St
Leeds
LS1 3TT
Tel: 0113 2567167

3 February 1995

Mr Giles Grant
Hon. Secretary
Lorley Tennis Club
Park Drive South
Leeds LS5 7ZZ

Dear Mr Grant,

I have just moved to this area and am interested in joining your tennis club. I understand that there is a waiting list for full membership and would be glad if you could let me have information on this. A telephone call would do: I tried to phone you but without success. If you require references we can provide these from the tennis club we belonged to in Edinburgh.

Yours sincerely,

Leonard Jones

Pour se faire installer le téléphone

94, avenue Beaumarchais
75011 Paris
France
Tel: (1) 45 83 35 59

24 February 1995.

British Telecom
Birmingham House
London WC18 9ZT

Dear Sirs,

I have recently purchased the house at number 48 Roedean Road, SW13 5NK, and wish to have a telephone installed as soon as possible after I take possession of the property on March 5th.

Please let me know the correct procedure for doing this and how much it will cost.

Yours faithfully,

Dr. Ellen Boe

Mot d'excuse à un professeur

23 Tollbooth Lane
Willowhurst
Sussex BN27
9UK

Tuesday 14 March

Dear Mr Jessel,

I am writing to let you know that my son Roger is unwell and will probably not be in school for the rest of the week. He has flu, and the doctor said that he should be able to go back to school sometime next week, but I will let you know if this is not the case.

Yours sincerely,

Louisa Finch

À une école pour se renseigner

3 Rue Joséphine
75018 Paris
France

2nd April 1995

Mr T Allen, BSc, DipEd.
Headmaster
Twining School
Walton
Oxon
OX44 23W

Dear Mr Allen,

I shall be moving to Walton from France this summer and am looking for a suitable school for my 11-year-old son, Pierre. Pierre is bilingual (his father is English) and has just completed his primary schooling in Paris. Your school was recommended to me by the Simpsons, whose son Bartholomew is one of your pupils.

If you have a vacancy for next term, please send me details. I shall be in Walton from 21 May, and could visit the school any time after that to discuss this with you.

Yours sincerely,

Marie-Madeleine Smith (Mrs)

une université

43 Wellington
Villas
York
YO6 93E

2.2.95

Dr T Benjamin,
Department of Fine Art
University of Brighton
Falmer Campus
Brighton
BN3 2AA

Dear Dr Benjamin,

I have been advised by Dr Kate Rellen, my MA supervisor in York, to apply to do doctoral studies in your department.

I enclose details of my current research and also my tentative Ph.D proposal, along with my up-to-date curriculum vitae, and look forward to hearing from you. I very much hope that you will agree to supervise my Ph.D. If you do, I intend to apply to the Royal Academy for funding.

Yours sincerely,

Alice Nettle

À une entreprise : demande de devis

"Pond Cottage"
Marsh Road
Cambridge
CB2 9EE

01223 456454

June 21st 1995

Shore Builders Ltd
667, Industrial Drive
Cambridge
CB12 9RR

Dear Sirs,

I have just purchased the above cottage in which several window frames are rotten. I would be glad if you could call and give me a written estimate of the cost of replacement (materials and labour). Please telephone before calling.

Yours faithfully,

T H Meadows

une entreprise pour ordonner des travaux

The Garden House
Willow Road
Hereford

Tel: 01432 566885

9th September 1995.

Ronche Building Co
33 Hangar Lane
Hereford

Dear Sirs,

I accept your estimate of £195 for replacing the rusty window frame.

Please would you phone to let me know when you will be able to do the work, as I will need to take time off to be there.
A Wednesday or Thursday afternoon would suit me best.

Yours faithfully,

R. M. Lee

À une entreprise pour se plaindre : retard

19 Colley Terrace
Bingley
Bradford

Tel: 01274 223447

4.5.95

Mr J Routledge
'Picture This'
13 High End Street
Bradford

Dear Mr Routledge,

I left a large oil portrait with you six weeks ago for framing. At the time you told me that it would be delivered to me within three weeks at the latest. Since the portrait has not yet arrived I wondered if there was some problem?

Would you please telephone to let me know what is happening, and when I can expect the delivery? I hope it will not be too long, as I am keen to see the results.

Yours sincerely,

Mrs J J Escobado

Pour demander un stage : informaticien

Rue du Lac, 989
CH-9878 Geneva
Switzerland

5th February 1995

Synapse & Bite Plc
3F Well Drive
Dolby Industrial Estate
Birmingham BH3 5FF

Dear Sirs,

As part of my advanced training relating to my current position as a junior systems trainee in Geneva, I have to work for a period of not less than two months over the summer in a computing firm in Britain or Ireland. Having heard of your firm from Mme Grenaille who worked there in 1988, I am writing to you in the hope that you will be able to offer me a placement for about eight weeks this summer.

I enclose my C.V. and a letter of recommendation.

Hoping you can help me, I remain,

Yours faithfully,

Madeleine Faure

Encls.

Candidature spontanée : enseignant

B.P. 3091
Pangaville
Panga

6th May 1995

Mrs J Allsop
Lingua School
23 Handle St
London SE3 4ZK

Dear Mrs Allsop,

My colleague Robert Martin, who used to work for you, tells me that you are planning to appoint extra staff this September. I am currently teaching French as a Foreign Language as part of the French Government's "cooperation" course in Panga which finishes in June.

You will see from my CV (enclosed) that I have appropriate qualifications and experience. I will be available for interview after the 22nd June, and may be contacted after that date at the following address:

c/o Lewis
Dexter Road
London NE2 6HQ
Tel: 0171 335 6978

Yours sincerely,

Jules Romains

Encl.

Candidature spontanée : décorateur

23 Bedford Mews
Dock Green
Cardiff
CF 23 7UU

(01222) 3445656

2nd August 1995

Marilyn Morse Ltd
Interior Design
19 Churchill Place
Cardiff C34 8MP.

Dear Sir or Madam,

I am writing in the hope that you might be able to offer me a position in your firm as an interior designer. As you will see from my enclosed CV, I have a BA in interior design and plenty of experience. I have just returned from Paris where I have lived for 5 years, and I am keen to join a small team here in Cardiff.

I would be happy to take on a part-time position until something more permanent became available. I hope you will be able to make use of my services, and should be glad to bring round a folio of my work.

Yours faithfully,

K J Dixon (Mrs)

Encls.

Réponse à une petite annonce

16 Andrew Road
Inverness IV90 OLL
Phone: 01463 34454

13th February 1995

The Personnel Manager
Dandy Industries PLC
Florence Building
Trump Estate
Bath BA55 3TT

Dear Sir or Madam,

I am interested in the post of Deputy Designer, advertised in the "Pioneer" of 13th February, and would be glad if you could send me further particulars and an application form.

I am currently nearing the end of a one-year contract with Bolney & Co, and have relevant experience and qualifications, including a BSc in Design Engineering and an MSc in Industrial Design.

Thanking you in anticipation, I remain,

Yours faithfully,

A Aziz

cherche d'une jeune fille au pair

89 Broom St
Linslade
Leighton Buzzard
Beds
LU7 7TJ

4th March 1995

Dear Julie,

Thank you for your reply to our advertisement for an au pair. Out of several applicants, I decided that I would like to offer you the job.

Could you start on the 5th June and stay until the 5th September when the boys go back to boarding school? The pay is £50 a week and you will have your own room and every second weekend free. Please let me know if you have any questions.

I look forward to receiving from you your confirmation that you accept the post.

With best wishes,

Yours sincerely,

Jean L Picard

Pour demander un emploi de jeune fille au pair

2, Rue de la Gare
54000 Nancy
France

(33) 87 65 47 92

15 April 1995

Miss D Lynch
Home from Home Agency
3435 Pine Street
Cleveland, Ohio 442233

Dear Miss Lynch,

I am seeking summer employment as an au pair. I have experience of this type of work in Britain but would now like to work in the USA. I enclose my C.V. and copies of testimonials from three British families.

I would be able to stay from the end of June to the beginning of September. Please let me know if I need a work permit, and if so, whether you can get one for me.

Yours sincerely,

Alice Demeaulnes

Encls.

---

r demander une lettre de recommandation

8 Spright Close
Kelvindale
Glasgow GL2 0DS

Tel: 0141-357 6857

23rd February 1995

Dr M Mansion
Department of Civil Engineering
University of East Anglia

Dear Dr Mansion,

As you may remember, my job here at Longiron & Co is only temporary. I have just applied for a post as Senior Engineer with Bingley & Smith in Glasgow and have taken the liberty of giving your name as a referee.

I hope you will not mind sending a reference to this company should they contact you. With luck, I should find a permanent position in the near future, and I am very grateful for your help.

With best regards,

Yours sincerely,

Helen Lee.

Remerciements pour une lettre de recommandation

The Stone House
Wallop
Cambs
CB13 9RQ

8/9/95

Dear Capt. Dominics,

I would like to thank you for writing a reference to support my recent application for the job as an assistant editor on the Art Foundation Magazine.

I expect you'll be pleased to know that I was offered the job and should be starting in three weeks' time. I am very excited about it and can't wait to start.

Many thanks once again,

Yours sincerely,

Molly (Valentine)

Pour accepter une proposition d'emploi

16 Muddy Way
Wills
Oxon
OX23 9WD
Tel: 01865 76754

Your ref : TT/99/HH   *4 July 1995*

Mr M Flynn
Mark Building
Plews Drive
London
NW4 9PP

Dear Mr Flynn,

I was delighted to receive your letter offering me the post of Senior Designer, which I hereby accept.

I confirm that I will be able to start on 31 July but not, unfortunately, before that date. Can you please inform me where and when exactly I should report on that day? I very much look forward to becoming a part of your design team.

Yours sincerely,

Nicholas Plews

Pour refuser une proposition d'emploi

4 Manchester St
London
NW6 6RR
Tel: 0181-334
5343

Your ref : 099/PLK/001   *7 July 1995*

Ms F Jamieson
Vice-President
The Nona Company
98 Percy St
YORK
YO9 6P2

Dear Ms Jamieson,

I am very grateful to you for offering me the post of Instructor. I shall have to decline this position, however, with much regret, as I have accepted a permanent post with my current firm.

I had believed that there was no possibility of my current position continuing after June, and the offer of a job, which happened only yesterday, came as a complete surprise to me. I apologize for the inconvenience to you.

Yours sincerely,

J D Salam

Recommandation : favorable

DEPT OF DESIGN

University of Hull
South Park Drive
Hull HL5 9UU
Tel: 01646 934 5768
Fax: 01646 934 5766

Your ref. DD/44/34/AW

5/3/95

Dear Sirs,

Mary O'Donnel. Date of birth 21-3-57

I am glad to be able to write most warmly in support of Ms O'Donnel's application for the post of Designer with your company.

During her studies, Ms O'Donnel proved herself to be an outstanding student. Her ideas are original and exciting, and she carries them through - her MSc thesis was an excellent piece of work. She is a pleasant, hard-working and reliable person and I can recommend her without any reservations.

Yours faithfully,

Dr A A Jamal

Lettre de démission

Editorial Office

Modern Living Magazine
22 Salisbury Road, London W3 9TT
Tel: 0171-332 4343   Fax: 0171-332 4354

To: Ms Ella Fellows   *6 June 1995*
General Editor.

Dear Ella,

I am writing to you, with great regret, to resign my post as Commissioning Editor with effect from the end of August.

As you know, I have found the recent management changes increasingly difficult to cope with. It is with great reluctance that I have come to the conclusion that I can no longer offer my best work under this management.

I wish you all the best for the future,

Yours sincerely,

Elliot Ashford-Leigh

mande de catalogue

99 South Drive
London
WC4H 2YY

7 July 1995

Hemingway & Sons
Builders Merchants
11 Boley Way
London WC12

Dear Sirs,

Thank you for sending me your catalogue of timber building materials as requested. However, the catalogue you sent is last year's and there is no current price list.

I would be glad if you would send me the up-to-date catalogue plus this year's price list.

Yours faithfully,

D Wisdom

Dr D Wisdom

Envoi de catalogue

E Hemingway

Carpet Designs
11 Allen Way
London NW4
Tel: 0171-4450034

Our ref. EH/55/4

19 February 1995

Ms J Jamal
Daniel Enterprises
144 Castle Street
Canterbury
CT1 3AA

Dear Ms Jamal,

Thank you for your interest in our products. Please find enclosed our current catalogue as well as an up-to-date price list and order form.

We would draw your attention to the discounts currently on offer on certain items and also on large orders.

Assuring you of our best attention at all times, we remain,

Yours sincerely,

Jane Penner

Jane Penner
Supplies Manager

---

mande de devis : matériau de construction

Eyer Shipyard
Old Wharf
Brighton
BN2 1AA
Tel 01273 45454
Fax 01273 45455

Our ref: TB/22/545

13 April 1995

Fankleman & Co. PLC
22 Mark Lane Estate,
Guildford,
Surrey
GU3 6AR.

Dear Sirs,

<u>Timber Supplies</u>

We would be glad if you could send us an estimate of the cost of supplying timber in the lengths and sizes specified on the enclosed list.

In general, we require large quantities for specific jobs at quite short notice and therefore need to be sure that you can supply us from current stock.

Thanking you in advance.

Yours faithfully,

G N Northwood

(Ms) G N Northwood.
General Manager, Supplies.

Encl.

Envoi d'un devis

Fairchild Interior Design Company
23 ROSE WALK
LONDON SW4
TEL: 0171-332 8989
FAX: 0171-332 8988

Job ref: 99/V/8

23 May 1995

Mr G. F. J. Price
25 Victor Street,
London,
SW4 1AA,

Dear Mr Price,

Please find enclosed our estimate for the decoration of the drawing room and hall at 25 Victor Street. As requested, we have included the cost of curtaining for both the bay windows and the hall window, in addition to the cost of sanding and polishing the drawing room floor.

The work could be carried out between the 1st and the 7th July, if this is convenient for you. Please do not hesitate to contact us if you have any queries.

We hope to have the pleasure of receiving your order.

Yours sincerely,

Marjorie Bishop *M. Bishop*

Encl.

Pour accuser réception d'une livraison

SMITH & IKE LTD
14 Adley Street
London NW11
Tel: 0181-332 4343
Fax: 0181-332 4344

Our ref: PLF/GG/3

14 February 1995

Wallis Printing
2 Shoesmith Road
London W3

Dear Sir/Madam,

We acknowledge receipt of our order (see ref. above) and would like to express our appreciation of the speed with which you managed to process it. The items were urgently required to ensure there was no interruption in our production and your cooperation made this possible.

As agreed, I am arranging for our Accounts Department to make prompt payment of your account.

Yours faithfully,

Dr J G Sing
Production Manager

Réclamation : retard de livraison

Duke & Ranger
45 High Street,
Stonebury.
SX6 0PP
Tel: 01667 98978

Your ref: 434/OP/9

9 August 1995

Do-Rite Furniture,
Block 5,
Entward Industrial Estate,
Wolverhampton.
WV6 9UP

Dear Sirs,

We are surprised not to have received delivery of the two dozen coffee tables from your "Lounge Lights" range (see our letter of 6 July) which you assured us by phone were being despatched immediately.

Our sales are being considerably hampered by the fact that the coffee tables are missing from the range and it is now over three weeks since you promised that these items would be delivered. Please phone us immediately to state exactly when they will arrive.

Yours faithfully,

Jane Malvern

Jane Malvern
Manager

Réclamation : facture déjà payée

Old Forge Pottery
4 Money Lane
Falmouth
Cornwall TR11 3TT
Tel: 01326 66758
Fax: 01326 66774

19 September 1995

Oscar Goode & Co
3 Field Place
Truro
Cornwall
TR2 6TT

Dear Mr Last,

Re: Invoice no. 4562938

I refer to your reminder of 17 September, which we were rather surprised to receive.

We settled the above invoice in the usual manner by bank transfer on 23 August and our bank has confirmed that payment was indeed made. Coming after several delays in making recent deliveries, this does cast some doubt on the efficiency of your organization.

We hope that you will be able to resolve this matter speedily.

Yours sincerely,

Rupert Grant

Rupert Grant
Accounts Manager

Réponse à une réclamation : facture déjà payée

PUSEY WESTLAND PLC
345-6 June Street
London SW13 8TT
Tel: 0181-334 5454
Fax: 0181-334 5656

6 June 1995

Our ref: 99/88/IY

Mrs E P Wells
The Round House
High St
Whitham
Oxon OX32 23R

Dear Mrs Wells,

Thank you for your letter of 22 May informing us that our invoice (see ref above) had already been settled.

We confirm that this is indeed the case and payment was made by you on 5 May. Please accept our sincere apologies for sending you a reminder in error.

Yours sincerely,

G H Founder

G H Founder
Accounts supervisor

‍clamation : facture trop élevée

The Round Place
2 Nighend High
Bristol
BS9 0UI
Tel: 0117 966900
Fax: 0117 955450

4 June 1995

Famous Gourmet
399 Old Green Road
Bristol
BS12 8TY

Dear Sirs,

Invoice no. B54/56/HP

We would be glad if you would amend your recent invoice (copy enclosed).

The quantities of the last three items are wrong, since they refer to "24 dozen" instead of the correct quantity of "14 dozen" in each case. In addition to this, our agreed discount of 4% has not been allowed.

Please check your records and issue a revised invoice, which we will then be happy to pay within the agreed time.

Yours faithfully,

M R Edwardson

M. R Edwardson
Chief Supplies Officer

Encl.

Réponse à une réclamation : facture trop élevée

TRILLING TRADERS
45-46 Staines Lane
BIRMINGHAM
BH8 9RR
Tel: 0121-222 1343
Fax: 0121-222 1465

14 March 1995

Mr T Mettyear
34 Rowland Road
London W11 7DR

Dear Mr Mettyear,

Invoice 7YY- 98776

Your letter of 7 March complaining of our failure to allow a discount on the above invoice has been referred to me by our supplies division.

I regret to inform you that we cannot agree to allow you a discount. Our letter to you of 22 February sets out our reasons. I must now press you for full payment. If, in the future, your invoices are settled promptly we will of course be glad to consider offering discounts once again.

Yours sincerely,

J Anchor

James Anchor
Deputy Managing Director

‍ur envoyer un chèque

66a Dram Villas
Sylvan Place
Edinburgh EH8 1LZ
Tel: (0131) 668 7575

5 September 1995

L. Farquharson
11 Craghill Grove
Edinburgh
EH6 44P

Dear Mr Farquharson,

Thank you for carrying out the joinery work on our window frames so quickly and efficiently.

I enclose herewith my cheque for £312.33 in full settlement of your account (invoice no.334PP). Please let me have a receipt.

Yours sincerely,

G Moreson (Mr)

Encl.

Pour accuser réception d'un paiement

Corkhill Solicitors
23 James Rise
Manchester
M14 5RT
Tel: 0161-548 6811
Fax: 0161-548 7911

10 March 1995

Ms Patricia Farnham
23 Walling Terrace
Manchester
M34 99Q

Dear Ms Farnham,

Thank you very much for your letter of 6 March and enclosed cheque.

I can confirm that we have now received payment in full for our invoice no. 5/99/UYY.

Yours sincerely,

H. Thomson

Dr Henrietta Thomson
Head of Section, Accounts

Relance pour facture impayée

ESTUARY SUPPLIES
45 Tully Street
YORK
YO3 9PO
Tel: 01904 59787
Fax: 01904 95757

Our ref: 998884/YT   9 September 1995

Ms T Blunt,
Crabbe and Long,
33-98 Grand Place,
YORK
YO8 6EF

Dear Ms Blunt,

I am writing to remind you that you have not
yet settled our invoice no. 6TT 999, a copy
of which I enclose.

We have never before had occasion to send
you a reminder, so we assume that this matter is simply an oversight on your part.
Perhaps you could arrange for payment to be
made in the next few days.

Yours sincerely,

M. Kington
Director

À un notaire pour un héritage

14 Rue Zola
75014 Paris
France

April 3rd 1995

Ms J Edgar
Loris & Jones Solicitors
18 St James Sq
London W1

Dear Ms Edgar,

Thank you for your letter of 20.3.95,
concerning the money left to me by my aunt,
Arabella Louise Edmonds. As I am now
living in Paris, I would be grateful if you
could forward the balance to my French bank.
I enclose my bank details.

Thank you for your help,

Yours sincerely,

S. Roland Williams

Encl.

À la banque à propos de frais d'agence

23 St John Rd
London EC12 4AA

5th May 1995

The Manager
Black Horse Bank
Bow Rd
London EC10 5TG

Dear Sir,

I noticed on my recent statement, that you are
charging me interest on an overdraft of £65.
I assume this is a mistake, as I have certainly had
no overdraft in the last quarter.

My account number is 0077-234-88. Please
rectify this mistake immediately, and explain to me
how this could have happened in the first place.

I look forward to your prompt reply,

Yours faithfully,

Dr J. M. Ramsbottom

Commande de livres

72 rue de la Charité
69002 Lyon

18 June 1995

Prism Books
Lower Milton St
Oxford OX6 4 DY

Dear Sirs,

I would be grateful if you could send to the
above address a copy of the recently published
book A Photographic Ethnography of Thailand
by Sean Sutton, which I have been unable to
find in France.

Please let me know what method of payment
would suit you.

Thanking you in advance.

Yours faithfully,

Jérôme Thoiron

Commande de vin

Radley House
John's Field
Kent
ME23 9JP

10 July 1995

Arthur Wine Merchants
23 Sailor's Way
London E3 4TG

Dear Sir/Madam,

I enclose my order for three dozen bottles of wine chosen from the selection in the catalogue you sent us recently. Please ensure that this order is swiftly dispatched, as the wine is needed for a family party on 16 July.

It would be helpful if you could phone and let me know when to expect the delivery, so that I can arrange to be at home.

Yours faithfully,

Ms F Allen-Johns

Encl

Commande de meubles

Rose Cottage
Maldon
Essex
CM12 9RT

9 September 1995

Mr J.J.Hassan
Sun Colours
23 Riddle Street
Chelmsford
Essex
CM2 9OD

Dear Mr Hassan,

After looking at the fabric samples you kindly sent us, and which we return herewith, we have decided to order the living room suite VV45X in the "Renaissance" pattern.

Please would you confirm receipt of this order, send details of the terms of payment, and let us know when we can expect to receive delivery.

Yours sincerely,

Julia Elscombe

Encl.

Télécopie entreprise

Swan Publishing
34 Paulton Street
London W2 9RW

FACSIMILE NUMBER: 0171-789 6544

Message for:	Charles Julien
Address:	25-30, rue Avignon, 75012 PARIS. France
Fax number:	00. 33.1 43 45 56 13
From:	Emma Wallis, Swan Publishing
Date:	May 20, 1995

Number of pages including this page: ONE

Thank you for your letter of 18 May 1995.
1. Please confirm meeting on June 6th at 10:00.
2. Two packages of brochures and two boxes of samples despatched on March 23rd. Please confirm receipt.
3. Guidelines on government policy apparently to be issued next week. Will try and get copies for discussion at June 6th meeting.
Look forward to seeing you on June 6th.

Emma Wallis

Emma Wallis,
Marketing Director

Télécopie personnelle

From:	M. Lovejoy, 140 Heriot Row, Dunedin, New Zealand
Fax:	64. 3. 1233. 5566
Date:	25-10-95

Number of pages including this page : One

Richard-

My trip finally approved for period 2-12-95 to 3-1-96. I have to spend two days in Paris first so should reach UK on 6th Dec at latest.

Delighted to meet Rev. Mark Browne and Dr Carl Hilde as you suggest, provided it can be in the week beginning the 11th. Can you make the arrangements? Thanks.

Further info on its way to you by air mail. Let me know as soon as you can.

Thanks for good wishes. Yes, lovely summer here!

All the best,

Miranda

CV : universitaire américaine

Name:	HEIDER Sarah Dolores
Address:	1123 Cedar Ave Evanston Illinois 60989 USA
Date of Birth:	9.27.52
Marital Status:	Married, 4 children (aged 8-14)

Education:

PhD degree in Shakespearean Poetics and Gender, Northwestern University, Evanston, Illinois, defended 1983

A.M. degree in English and American Literature, University of Pennsylvania, Philadelphia, completed 1977

B.A. degree (English Major), University of Berkeley, California

Professional Experience:

1992-present	Associate Professor, Department of English, Northwestern University
1988-92	Assistant Professor (Renaissance Studies), Department of English, Northwestern University
1983-87	Assistant Professor, Department of English, University of Pennsylvania
1980-83	Research Assistant to Prof D O'Leary (Feminism & Shakespearean Poetics) Northwestern University
1979-80	Research Assistant, Dept of Women's Studies Prof K. Anders (Representations of Renaissance Women), Northwestern University
1977-79	Teaching Assistant, Renaissance Drama, Northwestern University

Academic Awards and Honours:

Wallenheimer Research Fellow, 1992-3

Milton Wade Predoctoral Fellow, 1979-80

Pankhurst/Amersham Foundation Graduate Fellow, 1977-9

Isobella Sinclair Graduate Fellow, 1977-8

Research Support:	See list attached
Publications:	See list attached

Other Professional Activities & Membership of Professional Organizations:

President, Renaissance Minds Committee,1992-present

Member, UPCEO (University Professors Committee for Equal Opportunities), 1984-present

Advisor, Virago Press Renaissance series, Virago, London, 1988-1990

Advisor, Pandora Press, NY office, NY, 1987

Name:	Jacques Pierre Boyer
Address:	25 rue Paul Doumer 54500 Vandœuvre les Nancy France
Tel:(home)	82 24 37 12
Fax:(university)	82 27 41 11
E-Mail:	phyveg@ism.univ-nancy.fr
Date of Birth:	Oct 30th 1947
Nationality:	French
Marital Status:	Married, 3 children

Educational Qualifications:

Thèse d'État [Ph.D], Université de Nancy, 1977

Subject:	"Effets comparés des rayonnements π et β sur la croissance de *Calluna vulgaris* et *Erica vagans*": Très Honorable à l'unanimité du jury
Supervisor:	Jean-Pierre Mounier, Professeur de Physiologie Végétale à l'Université Paris XII

Professional Experience:

1960–65	Professeur agrégé de Sciences Naturelles, Lycée d'État de Dunkerque (Nord)
1965–70	Assistant de Physiologie Végétale à l'Université de Caen (Calvados)
1970–78	Maître-Assistant, Université de Caen (Calvados)
1978–present	Maître de Conférences à l'Université de Nancy

Current Research Interests:

Growth phenomena in ornamental plants according to conditions of humidity and light

Publications:

3 Books and 27 papers – see attached list

CV : bachelière française

NAME: Laurence BOUTON

ADDRESS: 18 Avenue Edouard Herriot
                           Bourg-en-Bresse
                           France
                           Telephone: 74 50 09 13

MARITAL STATUS: Single

EDUCATION AND QUALIFICATIONS:

1986-1993   Lycée de Brou, Bourg-en-Bresse, France
                           Baccalauréat, série A2 [this is the equivalent of A-levels in
                           French and Languages]

PREVIOUS WORK EXPERIENCE:

1991-3   Part-time: Private Tutor of English and French Language

1992 July   Camp counsellor, children's holiday camp, Nice. Duties included
                           sports and games supervision, leisure co-ordination, general
                           counselling of children aged 6-10 years

1992 March   One week exchange visit to German family in Bremen

1992 August   One month exchange visit to English family in Bournemouth

OTHER INFORMATION: Love of children (I have 3 younger brothers and 2 sisters)
                           Good spoken English and German
                           40 w.p.m Typing

INTERESTS: Classical music
                           Literature - especially modern poetry
                           Museums and exhibitions
                           Tap Dancing (participant in school competitions)

REFEREES: M. Pierre Duval
                           (Headmaster)
                           Lycée de Brou
                           Bourg-en-Bresse
                           France
                           Telephone: 74 39 84 73

                           Me Julie Huppert
                           (Lawyer)
                           44 Rue Orange
                           Bourg-en-Bresse
                           France
                           Telephone: 74 30 92 34

Name:	Paul Alan GRANTLEY
Address:	26 Countisbury Drive Brighton BN3 1RG Tel: 01273 534950
Date of Birth:	22 May 1969
Nationality:	British
Marital Status:	Single
Education:	
1980-1987	Brighton College Boys' School King John's Way Brighton
1985 (O Levels)	Maths (A), Physics (A), Biology (A), Chemistry (A), Business (B), English Lang. (B), German (B), Sociology (C)
1986 (A/O Level)	Maths (A)
1987 (A Levels)	Biology (A), Chemistry (A), Physics (B), Maths (B)
1988-1991	King's College, London B.Sc. Bio-Chemistry (2.1.)
Work Experience:	
1988, July:	2 weeks' work experience with Alford & Wilston Ltd (Chemical Company), Warley, W. Midlands
1989, March:	1 week 'shadowing' experience to Assistant Marketing Manager, EAA Technology (Environmental Energy), Didcot
Skills:	Computer Literate, particularly Macintosh software Clean driving licence
Interests:	
At School:	Captain of Rugby Team for 2 years Member of Chess club
At University:	Member of University Rugby team Organizer Charity Fun Week ('88) Student Union Sport's representative ('88)
Other:	Interest in travel - year off before University spent on round-the-world trip
Referees:	Dr J Abercrombie (Lecturer) King's College LONDON Tel: 0171-334 2938 (Ext. 2333)
	Mr Steven Jones Giffold & Partners Carley House Woolford Surrey Tel: 0181-232 3939

CV : jeune cadre français

Name:	Jean-Baptiste LENOBLE
Date of Birth:	29/7/64
Nationality:	Belgian
Permanent Address:	
(After 3/8/94)	Rue des Frontières, 33 1234 Meuseville Belgium
Telephone:	(32) (88) 123.45.67
Temporary Address:	
(Until 3/8/94)	1642 West 195th St New York NY 23456 USA
Marital Status:	Single

Education and Qualificatons:

The qualifications described below do not have exact equivalents in the British system. I enclose photocopies of my certificates with English translations.

1975-83:	Lycée Elisabeth, Meuseville, Belgium Qualification: School leaving certificate (Maths/Science option)
1983-86 1987-88	Université de Verviers: Department of Civil Engineering. Qualification: Diploma in Civil Engineering
1992-4	Masters Program in Civil Engineering, New York Harbour University. (Results pending)

Work Experience

1984-5	Summer work as volunteer at school for children with learning difficulties
1986-87	Assistant civil engineer, Verviers Region, Belgium. Work on various road projects
1988-92	Senior assistant civil engineer, Verviers Region

Other Skills & Interests

Languages: Fluent English,
Adequate spoken Dutch and German
(Native French speaker)
Clean Driving Licence
Squash: Regional finalist in University Squash team
I wish to expand my work experience in an English-speaking country given the on-going changes in the European job market.

References:	Professeur H Vandecke Département de Génie Civil Université de Verviers B-1245 Verviers Belgium	Dr Jan C Waldermaker Managing Director Waldermaker Enterprises Inc 8822 West 214th St New York NY 24568 USA

French advertisements

House/Apartment Sales

Immobilier

Ventes

VDS mais. F4, 3 ch., 100 m²
env., 2 sdb, cuis. équip.,
gar., terr. clos, Exclus.
Anse Immobilier
74 77 01 13

Urgt cède cse mutation F3
tt cft, t. b. état, ch. c. gaz
indiv., ds résid. stand.,
prest. lux., px à déb., libre
imméd. Tél.HR 72.88.63.29

Part. vd F2 + mezz. ds
mais. mitoyenne, c.c.
indiv. fuel, gar., jard.
privat., quart. calme, 800
000F ferme, libre 1/7/95.
Tél. 45 27 33 11

100 km nrd Lyon,
autoroute Tournus, mais.
bressanne, à rénov., 6 p.,
350 m² habitables,
dépendances, pré attenant
3500 m² convient pour
chevaux, px 200 000 F.
S'adres. P.LALOY, not. à
Paris 16 (1) 45 05 79 88

Sologne, belle propriété
XVᵉ, cachet, 50 ha, étgs,
bois, poss. chasse,
dépend., mais. gard.,
excel. ét., px intér. Écrire
Maisons de France, 18 bd
du Roi, 78000 Versailles

Prox. plage, vds Sanary,
villa 3/4 pers., 1 ch. +
mezz., kitch. équip., ll, lv,
park. et jard. privat. 18 U
Écr. jrnl réf. 94zx007

A saisir, Villars les
Dombes, except. terr. arb.,
hors lotissement,
constructible, 1000m²,
calme, prox. golf.
74.83.65.12.

Feyzin le Haut, près église,
suite incendie, à vdre,
épave mais. bourgeoise,
400 m² sur 6600 m² terr.
av. arbres, px 595 000F,
T.78.15.62.03

à rénov. (à rénover) needs modernization
à vdre (à vendre) for sale
c.c. (chauffage central) central heating (Note: also stands for charges comprises. See under Locations.)
ch. (chambre) bedroom
ch. c. (chauffage central) central heating
cse mutation (pour cause de mutation) because of job transfer
cuis. équip. (cuisine équipée) fully fitted kitchen
dépend. (dépendances) outbuildings
ds (dans) in
écr. (écrire à) write to
env. (environ) about
étgs (étangs) ponds
excel. ét. (excellent état) (in) excellent condition
except. (exceptionnel) exceptional
exclus. (exclusivité) sole agents
F4 (appartement quatre pièces) 3-bedroom flat
gar. (garage) garage
ha (hectare) hectare
HR (heures des repas) (at) meal times (between 12 and 2 or between 7 and 9 p.m.)
imméd. (immédiatement) (available) immediately
indiv. (individuel) individual
jard. privat. (jardin privatif) own garden
jrnl (journal) newspaper
kitch. équip. (kitchenette équipée) fully fitted kitchenette
ll (lave-linge) washing machine
lv (lave-vaisselle) dishwasher
m² (mètres carrés) square metres
mais. (maison) house
mais. gard. (maison de gardien) caretaker's house

mezz. (mezzanine) mezzanine floor
not. (notaire) notary (lawyer involved in all French property transfers)
nrd (nord) north
p. (pièce) room
p (pour) for
park. (parking) parking space
part. (particulier) private individual (i.e. not an agency)
pers. (personnes) people
poss. chasse (possibilité de chasser) hunting possible
prest. lux. (prestations luxueuses) luxuriously appointed
prox. (à proximité de) close to
px à déb. (prix à débattre) price to be discussed
px intér. (prix intéressant) attractive (i.e. low) price
quart. (quartier) neighbourhood
réf. (référence) reference (number)
résid. (résidence) apartment complex
s'adres. (s'adresser à) contact
sdb (salle de bains) bathroom
stand. (de bon standing) desirable
t. b. état (très bon état) (in) excellent condition
terr. arb. (terrain arboré) wooded land
terr. av. arb. (terrain avec arbres) wooded land
terr. clos (terrain clos) fenced plot
tt cft (tout confort) all mod cons
U (unités) units (1 unit = 10,000 francs)
urgt (urgent) urgent(ly)
vds/vd (vends) (I am) selling, for sale
XVᵉ (quinzième siècle) 15th century

...use/Apartment/Room Lets

Locations

Centr. ville Annecy, loue
mais. bourg., 8 p., récept.
...5 m2, gar., cave, jard. 300
m2, ch.c. fuel, quartier
résid., 13 500F/mens. cc,
LARAGENCE 56 32 48 79

Part. à part. ag. s'abst.,
loue F3, 2ch., sdb, ds
immeuble centre
Villeurbanne, esp. verts,
cave, b. état, 2 500F CC,
78 92 13 22 p. 249
hor. bur.

Part. loue ch. meublée
pour étudiant, 18 m2 dans
tb villa quartier univ.,
calme, av. douche, poss.
cuis., prise tél. et TV,
entrée séparée, lib. 27
sept., loyer 1 800F cc,
tél : 78 49 26 76

A LOUER Hte Loire, rég.
Chambon sur Lignon,
mais. indiv. isolée, terr.
expo. Sud, tt conft, 7 pers
maxi., juin juillet
septembre, mois, sem.,
quinz.
TEL HR 71 59 29 33

URG Dir. de Sté rech.
appart. F3 à louer, env.
Saverne, cuis. équip.,
balc., park., maxi. 3
500F/mois cc,
tél. 85 34 37 29

Cadre sup. Sophia
Antipolis ch. loc. à l'année,
mais. camp. proche Nice,
4/5 pers., calme, esp.
verts, même modeste.
Tél 67 72 63 95

. s'abst. (agences s'abstenir) no agencies (i.e.
...nly private individuals should apply)
part. (appartement) apartment, flat
. (avec) with
. état (bon état) good condition
.lc. (balcon) balcony
.dre sup. (cadre supérieur) executive
. CC (charges comprises) service charges
...ncluded (in the rent)
.ntr. ville (centre ville) city centre
. (chambre) bedroom
.c. (chauffage central) central heating
. loc. (cherche une location) seeks rented
...ccommodation
.is. équip. (cuisine équipée) fully fitted kitchen
. de Sté (directeur de société) company
...irector
(dans) in
.v. (aux environs de) in the area of, close to
.p. verts (espaces verts) green space (e.g.
...ardens, parkland)
.po. sud (exposé au sud) south facing
. (trois pièces principales) 2-bedroom
...partment
.r. (garage) garage
.r. bur. (horaires de bureau) office hours
...i.e. between 8 and 12 or between 2 and 5)
.t (heures des repas) meal times (between 12 and
... or between 7 and 9 p.m.)
.e Loire (département de la Haute Loire) the
...epartment (administrative district) of the Haute
...oire

jard. (jardin) garden
lib. (libre) free (from a certain date)
m² (mètres carrés) square metres
mais. bourg. (maison bourgeoise) substantial
family house (also conveys idea of 'comfortable')
mais. camp. (maison de campagne) house in the
country
mais. indiv. (maison individuelle) detached house
maxi (maximum) maximum
mens. (mensuels) per month
p. (pièce) room
p. 249 (poste 249) extension 249
park. (parking) parking space
part. à part (particulier à particulier) private let
pers. (personnes) people
poss. cuis. (possibilité de faire la cuisine)
cooking facilities
quartier résid. (quartier résidentiel) residential
area
quartier univ. (quartier universitaire) university
area
quinz. (quinzaine) fortnight(ly)
récept. (réception) reception room, living room
rech. (recherche) is seeking
rég. (région) region
sdb (salle de bains) bathroom
sem. (semaine) week(ly)
tb (très beau/belle) delightful
tél. (téléphone) telephone
terr. (terrain) garden or land or plot
tt conft (tout confort) all mod cons
URG (urgent) urgent(ly)

House/Apartment holiday exchanges

Échanges vacances

Échange maison ds village Landes, 4/5 pers, sdb, cuis. équip., petit jard., avec maison ou appartement Alpes sud même caract. p. 3 sem. à part du 3 juin 1995. Tél 45 20 16 38

VACANCES: éch t b maison Haute Provence (20 min. Draguignan), 6 pers., contre maison standing équiv. Sussex pour août 1995. Poss. éch. voit. Tél. 16 (1) 43 54 09 53

Échange luxueux appt Paris Avenue Foch, 2ch, 2sdb, terrasse ombragée, tv câble, a/c, parking, contre appt similaire centre Londres pour avril mai juin 1996. Tél. 16 (1) 45 27 98 12

Éch. bglw tt cft, 4/5 pers, PALAVAS LES FLOTS, contre logt équiv. Bret. sud, 14 juil/15 août. T. HR 98.72.41.68

La Ciotat, échange carav. Caravelair 4 pers. empl. ombragé ds camping 3 étoiles, prox. mer, centre com., animations, prise TV, contre standg ident. montagne ou camp. 1ère quinz. juil. Envoy. photo, descript. et propositions au jrnl, réf. EC 182

Vehicle Sales

Vente de véhicules, deux-roues, bateaux

VDS Ford Scorpio
11 cv, gris métal., août 91, ttes opts, int. cuir, TBE, 49 000 kms, sous argus, tél. dom. ap. 19 h 85 66 24 87

A vdre camping-car Ford ess., ann. 89, 3/4 pers., 120 000 kms, mot. ref. nf, intér. parf. ét., px à déb. Tél. b.57.92.13.74

VW Fourg. Diesel
92, DA, ouv s/le côté, 40 000 kms, première main, CENTRAL AUTO St Priest 78.21.80.52

Part. vd
Suzuki Dk 650
05/91, 1re m., 5 200 km, accessoires. Tél. 72.84.99.87. h.b.

Vélo femme, Peugeot 1/ course, 10 vitesses, 2 plat., vert métal., t.b.ét. occas. à saisir, 1 500F 42.51.36.10 Mme Millar

Vds dériveur 505, coqu alu., voiles terg., av. remorque. A voir Port Leucate les w.e. Prendr r.v. 67 37 90 21

---

a/c (air conditionné) air conditioning
à part (à partir de) from (a date)
appt (appartement) flat
bglw (bungalow) holiday chalet
Bret. sud (Bretagne sud) southern Brittany
camp. (campagne) country
caract. (caractéristiques) features
carav. (caravane) caravan
centre com. (centre commercial) shopping centre
ch. (chambre) bedroom
cuis. équip. (cuisine équipée) fully fitted kitchen
descript. (description) description
ds (dans) in
éch. (échange) exchange (offered for)
empl. (emplacement) site (for caravan or tent)
envoy. (envoyer) (please) send
équiv. (équivalent) equivalent
HR (heures des repas) meal times (between 12 and 2 or between 7 and 9 p.m.)
jard. (jardin) garden
jrnl (journal) newspaper
logt équiv. (logement équivalent) equivalent accommodation
min (minutes) minutes
p (pour) for
pers. (personnes) people
poss. (possibilité) possibility
prox. mer (à proximité de la mer) close to the sea
quinz. juil. (quinzaine de juillet) fortnight in July
réf. (référence) reference number
sdb (salle de bains) bathroom
sem. (semaine) week
standg équiv. (standing équivalent) comparable standard (of accommodation, fittings, etc.)
t b (très beau/belle) delightful
tél. (téléphoner) telephone
tt cft (tout confort) all mod cons
tv (télévision) television
voit. (voiture) car

1ère m. (première main) only one owner
à vdre (à vendre) for sale
alu. (aluminium) aluminium
ann. 89 (année 89) year (of manufacture) 1989
ap. (après) after
av. (avec) with
cv (chevaux) horsepower
D.A. (direction assistée) power steering
ess. (à essence) petrol engine
fourg. (fourgonnette) small van
h.b. (heures de bureau) (in) office hours (i.e. between 8 and 12 or between 2 and 5)
int.cuir. (intérieur en cuir) leather upholstery
métal. (métallisé) metallic
mot. (moteur) engine
occas. (occasion) bargain
ouv. s/le côté (ouvrant sur le côté) side door
parf. ét. (parfait état) in perfect condition
part. (particulier) private sale
pers. (personnes) people
plat. (plateaux) gear wheels
px à déb. (prix à débattre) price to be discussed
ref. nf (refait à neuf) completely reconditioned
r.v. (rendez-vous) appointment
t.b.ét., TBE (très bon état) (in) excellent condit
tél. b. (téléphoner aux heures de bureau) phone office hours (between 8 and 12 or between 2 and 5
tél. dom. (téléphoner au domicile) phone home number
terg. (tergal) Terylene
ttes opts (toutes options) all extras
vd, vds (vend, vends) for sale
w.e. (weekend) weekend

ticles for Sale

Ventes: divers

Tr. b. tap. persan, 125 x 230, frangé, fond bleu, impecc.
8 200F, à sais.
T. 25 43 18 77

Cse dble empl., vds cuisinière mixte, 60 x 60, 4 eux électr., four à gaz, t. b. ét., tél. HR 16 (1) 39.50.71.23

Cède frigo Vedette 150 l, freezer 30 l, dim. 60 x 60 x 185, peu servi, intér. impecc., T 56 32 41 76

Offr. spéc. à sais., 1 lot de lav. ling. Miele, 5 kg, b. ét. mécan., px 50% nf, à emport. ELECTROMENAGER, 152 rte de Limonest, dim. compris

---

vds sèch. linge Philips, modèle réc, état nf, 3 000 F, tél 32 21 85 91

A vdre aspirat. Hoover traîneau, rouge, silencx, tire-fil, 220 v.
tél 82.34.15.67

Vds fer à vap. Calor Pressing Plus, jam. servi, tél 58 32 14 97

A vdre chaîne hifi, dble K7, CD, 2 ampli. 25W, px à déb. T. 59.12.65.34

Suite cess. act. PME cède son outil inf.: ord. Philips P4000, disque mém. 120 millions, 3 écr., 1 impr. P2934/02, 1 log. compta. paie, gest. commerc., tt parf ét., val. ach. 270 000 F, px à déb 74.92.36.25 mat

---

URGT vds canapé 3 pl. + 2 chauff., imit. cuir fauv., parf. état 5 000 F
tél 59 45 62 71

Cse dpt, cède sal. de jard. plast. blanc, 1 tble rde 6 pers. + chaises, 2 transat. et parasol assort., 3 000 F, tél. ap. 19h
16 (1) 27 36 15 89

Cause démgnt, cède 2 paires dble ridx, 235 x 120 cm, coul. crème ; 2 paires voilages ; 1 bac fleur Riviera 1m/25cm.
Tél 52 36 47 98

---

5 x 230 (125 sur 230) 125 by 230 (centimetres)
déb. (à débattre) (price) to be discussed
emport. (à emporter) for quick sale
ais. (à saisir) bargain
dre (à vendre) for sale
apli. (amplificateurs) amplifiers
. (après) after
pirat. (aspirateur) vacuum cleaner
sort. (assortis) matching
ét. mécan. (bon état mécanique) good mechanical condition, good working order
ss. act. (cessation d'activité) going out of business, closing down
auff. (chauffeuses) easy chairs (Note: also stands for chauffage)
mpta. (comptabilité) accounts
ul. (couleur) colour
e dble empl. (pour cause de double emploi) surplus to requirements
e dpt (pour cause de départ) (as) owner leaving, moving house
le K7 (double cassette) double-cassette deck
le ridx (doubles rideaux) curtains
mgnt (déménagement) moving
iouse/premises
n. (dimensions) measurements
n. comp. (dimanches compris) including Sundays
r. (écrans) screens, monitors
ctr. (électrique) electric
iv. (fauve) fawn (colour)
go (réfrigérateur) fridge
st. commerc. (gestion commerciale) sales management
it. (imitation) imitation
pecc. (impeccable) perfect condition, as new
or. (imprimante) printer
. (informatique) computing (equipment)

intér. (intérieur) interior
jam. servi (jamais servi) never used
l (litre) litre
lav. ling. (lave-linge) washing machine
log. (logiciel) software
mat. (matin) (in the) mornings
mém. (mémoire) memory
nf (neuf) new
offr. spéc. (offre spéciale) special offer
ord. (ordinateur) computer
parf. ét. (parfait état) (in) perfect condition
pers. (personnes) people
pl. (places) seats
plast. (plastique) plastic
PME (petite et/ou moyenne entreprise) small and/or medium-sized enterprise/SME
px (prix) price
réc. (récent) recent
rte (route) road
sal. de jard. (salon de jardin) garden furniture
sèch. linge (sèche-linge) tumble dryer
silencx (silencieux) quiet
T. (téléphone) telephone
t. b. ét. (très bon état) very good condition
tap. (tapis) carpet
tble rde (table ronde) circular table
tél. HR (téléphoner aux heures des repas) phone at meal times (i.e. between 12 and 2 or between 7 and 9 p.m.)
transat (transatlantique) deckchair
tr. b. (très beau) very fine
tt (tout) all
urgt (urgent) urgent
v volt
val. ach. (valeur à l'achat) cost when new
vap. (vapeur) steam
vds (vends) for sale
W (watt) watt

Jobs

Emplois

Jne F., 23 a., diplômée Ec. Sup. Com., bil. Fr/Angl, tt txte, excel. présent. ch. empl. 1/2 tps, accept. déplcts. Ecr. jrnl Réf. OEZ98

Pr remplt cong. mater. PME ch. hot. accueil, pet. secrét., tél., tt txte, CDD 3 mois à part. 15 oct. proch., voit. indispens., ts frs payés, possib. contr. long. dur. Ecr. jrnl PU322

Centre de vac. ch. H à tt faire du 1/7/95 au 31/8/95 pr petits trvx, surveill. enfts, sér. réf. exigées, logé, nourri, blanchi + 3 500F/ms. Ecr. jrnl réf. PLM258

Etud. prépa. donne crs anglais français ts niveaux tél: 27 42 31 86

Rech. un/-e trad. spécial. bio-médical Ang/Alld et Alld/Ang. pr trad. simult congrès internat. Bruxelles du 14/6 au 17/6/95. Pdre cont. Mme Roux en écriv. au jrnal qui transmettra

J.F. nat. française, 20 ans, aimant enfts, sér. réf., souhaite trouver fam. anglophone, suivi trav. scol. poss., dispon. juil. août 95, écr. journ. ZOL150

URG fam. écossaise (avocat) rég. Glasgow, 2 enfts 3/5 ans cherche J.F. au pair, bon anglais, juil-août 95, Ecrire Mme R. Burns 5 Menzies Crescent Fintry Stirlingshire G63 0YL

Ch. f. de mén. 2x4h/sem., a.m. préfér., sér. réf. exig., Tél Mme PIERRAT 42 59 17 23

Entr. TP ch. VRP multic., départ. 42, 74, 01. Envoy. CV + photo + prétent. à BATIDUR 285 cours Lafayette 69100 Villeurbanne

Ch. cple gardiens pr propriété isolée, 250 km sud Paris, petits travx jard., logt indpt, sal. intér. sér. réf. exigées. Se présent., Château du Lac 18100 Vierzon

---

1/2 tps (mi-temps) half-time
2x4h/sem. (deux fois quatre heures par semaine) 4 hours twice a week
a. (ans) years (old)
à part. (à partir de) from (date)
accept. déplcts (accepte les déplacements) will travel
angl (anglais) English
alld (allemand) German
a.m. préfér. (l'après-midi de préférence) preferably afternoon
bil. Fr/Angl (bilingue français/anglais) bilingual French/English
CDD (contrat à durée déterminée) fixed-term contract
ch. (cherche) seeks
cong. mater. (congé de maternité) maternity leave
contr. long. dur. (contrat de longue durée) long-term contract
cple (couple) couple
crs (cours) lessons
départ. (départements) departments (French districts)
dispon. (disponible) available
Ec. Sup. Com. (École Supérieure de Commerce) Business School
ecr. (écrire à) (please) write to
empl. (emploi) job
en écriv (en écrivant) by writing
enfts (enfants) children
entr. TP (entreprise de travaux publics) civil engineering firm
envoy. (envoyer) (please) send
étud. (étudiant(e)) student
excel. présent. (excellente présentation) very smart appearance
exig. (exigé) required, essential
f. de mén. (femme de ménage) cleaning lady
fam. (famille) family
F/ms (francs par mois) francs per month
H. à tt faire (homme à tout faire) odd-job man
h/sem. (heures par semaine) hours per week
hot. accueil (hôtesse d'accueil) receptionist
indispens. (indispensable) indispensable
internat. (international) international
J.F., Jne F (jeune fille/femme) young woman

jrnl (journal) newspaper
juil. (juillet) July
logt indpt (logement indépendant) separate accommodation
ms (mois) month
nat. (nationalité) nationality
oct. (octobre) October
pdre cont. (prendre contact avec) contact
pet. secrét. (petit secrétariat) some secretarial duties
petits trvx (petits travaux) light (manual) work
PME (petite et/ou moyenne entreprise) small and/or medium-sized enterprise, SME
poss. (possible) possible
possib. (possibilité) possibility
pr (pour) for
prépa. (classe préparatoire) post-baccalaureat class for entry to Grandes Écoles
prétent. (prétentions) salary expectation
proch. (prochain) next
rech. (recherche) seeking
réf. (référence) reference (number)
rég. (région) region
remplt (remplacement) replacement
sal. intér. (salaire intéressant) attractive salary
se présent. (se présenter) apply in person
sér. réf. (sérieuses références) excellent references
surveill. enfts (surveillance d'enfants) looking after children
tél. (téléphone) telephone
trad. simult. (traduction simultanée) simultaneous translation
trad. spécial. (traducteur/-trice spécialisé/-e) technical translator
trav. scol. (travail scolaire) homework
travx jard. (travaux de jardinage) gardening
ts (tous) all
ts frs payés (tous frais payés) all expenses paid
tt txte (traitement de texte) word processing
URG. (urgent) urgent
vac. (vacances) holidays
voit. (voiture) car
VRP multic. (voyageur représentant placier multicartes) sales representative for several different companies

Petites annonces anglaises

Immobilier : ventes

For Sale: Lewes, Semi-det hse, BR 2 mins walk – 50 mins London. 1.5 baths, 4 beds, lge gdn, 2 recs, newly modernized kitchen, gch. £90,000. Tel: 01273 34790 eve/wkend.

Salcombe, Devon: Period Cott . Sea view, 2 acres gdn, 3 beds, 2 baths, lge fmly rm, wkg fireplaces, beams, fully renovated. OIRO £125,000 for quick sale. PO Box 41.

For Sale: 5 acres of land w/ Pl Permsn 3 stables/out-hses. Would make good paddock/grazing. Easy road access, 3m from Maldon. Offers: 01622 859059.

Hereford £250,000: Stunning, spacious 19th century home in 3 acres gdn and woodland. Mstr suite + 4 BR, 3 ba, huge lounge w/patio, DR, Lge mod. kit, utility rm, bsmnt. 2 miles Hereford ctr. Dble Grge. Tel: 01432 273669

Development Potential: crumbling 18th cent Cotswold farmhouse in Bexley (Oxford 5m). Needs total refurbishment. Could become beautiful 3/4 bed country hse w/lge gdn in much sought-after area. Interested? Tel 01865 27768.

£80,000   Rottingdean. Purpose built apartment. Spacious dble bedrm, lounge, kit, bath, balcony, pking avail. Quiet residential area nr shops + golf course. Brighton 2m. Owner sale, call 01273 564789

Immobilier : locations

Wanted by non-smoking professional female: room in shared hse nr city ctr, w/ 2-3 other profs/grads. Rent up to £60 p.w + bills. Will provide refs and deposit if nec. Tel: Jane 01223 432675.

For Rent: Rehabbed grnd flr apt in divided semi-det hse, 2 mins walk Balham tube. Unfurn, 2 beds, sitting rm, sml kit w/washing mach, gch, use of garden. Quiet area. £155 p.w. + bills. 2 mo sec. dep + refs. No pets. Tel: 0181 5562310 after 6pm.

Alfriston: Lakeside bungalow for six mo lease. Fully furn, 2 bed, 1 bath, gch, sml gdn, all mod cons. Slps 4-5. Nr village center. Pking. £500 pcm, bills incl. except phone. Tel: 0171 4465090

Lavender Hill: Luxury F‖ to let. 3rd flr, fully fu‖ split-level w/roof gdn ‖ spectacular view. 3 bed ‖ 1 bath, spacious loun‖ w/skylights. Gch, secur‖ entry, semi-det Georgi‖ building in quiet reside‖ tial area. BR + Clapha‖ common 5 mins wa‖ £900 pcm + bills. T‖ 0181 2243948.

To Let: Picturesque No‖ Brittany Farmhouse fo‖ mo from Jul '95. Slps 6‖ Fully modernized. Lev‖ gdn l 9089 sq yds, o‖ houses & barn. Neare‖ town 2 m, good road. T‖ 00 33 96 43 72 63

Wanted: Quiet prof. ‖ male to share small h‖ w/one other in cent‖ Chelmsford nr bus s‖ Rent £40 p.w. Cat-lo‖ pref. Tel: 01621 443228‖

---

avail (available) libre
ba (bathrooms *US*) salles de bains
baths (bathrooms *GB*) salles de bains
bed (bedroom) chambre
BR (bedroom *US*) chambre
BR (British Rail *GB*) gare
bsmnt (basement) sous-sol
cott (cottage) petite maison (rustique)
ctr (centre) centre
dble bedrm (double bedroom) chambre pour 2
  personnes
dble grge (double garage) garage pour 2 voitures
DR (dining-room) salle à manger
eve (evening) soir
fam rm (family room) séjour
fmly rm (family room) séjour
gch (gas central heating) chauffage central au gaz
gdn (garden) jardin
lge (large) grand
m (miles) miles
mins (minutes) minutes
mod kit (modern kitchen) cuisine moderne
Mstr suite (master suite *US*) grande chambre
  avec salle de bains
nr (near) à proximité de
OIRO (offers in the region of) propositions de
  l'ordre de
Pl Permsn (planning permission) permis de
  construire
receps (reception rooms) pièces principales
recs (reception rooms) pièces principales
tel (telephone) téléphone
w/ (with) avec
wkend (weekend) week-end
wkg (working) en état de marche

apt (apartment) appartement
bed (bedroom(s)) chambre(s)
BR (British Rail *GB*) gare
bus stn (bus station) gare routière
cent (century) siècle
ctr (centre) centre
dep (deposit) caution
furn (furnished) meublé
gch (gas central heating) chauffage central au g‖
grads (graduates) étudiants (après la licence)
grnd flr (ground floor) rez-de-chaussée
hse (house) maison
incl (including) comprenant
lge (large) grand
m (miles) miles
mach (machine) machine
mins (minutes) minutes
mo (months) mois
mod cons (modern conveniences) tout confort
nec (necessary) nécessaire
nr (near) près de
pcm (per calendar month) par mois
pking (parking) place de parking
pref (preferred) de préférence
prof (professional) salarié
p.w. (per week) par semaine
refs (references) références
rehabbed (rehabilitated) refait
sec. dep (security deposit) caution
semi-det (semi-detached) maison jumelée
sitting rm (sitting room) salon
slps (sleeps) peut loger
sml kit (small kitchen) petite cuisine
sq. yds (square yards) appr. mètres carrés
tel (telephone) téléphone
unfurn (unfurnished) non meublé
w/ (with) avec

anges vacances

change: Sml fam ~~o~~wned village hse nr ~~D~~jat, slps 4-5, 1 bath, ~~l~~nge, mod kit, sm gdn, ~~n~~r Seaside cott in ~~D~~evon/Cornwall for 3 wks ~~co~~mmenc. Jun 3rd 1995. ~~Te~~l: 00 33 55 25 88 99.

~~R~~om Exchange Wanted: ~~larg~~e rm in friendly non-~~smo~~kg hse w/ 3 profs in ~~ce~~ntral Oxford for similar ~~ro~~om Sept 95. Monthly ~~re~~ntal £50 p.w. Pets wel~~co~~me. Tel 01865 553389.

~~ca~~ravan Exchange ~~W~~anted: comfortable 6 ~~be~~rth caravan on N. Cor~~ni~~sh coast: running ~~w~~ater, elec, camp shop. ~~Pa~~dstow 2 m. For 3-4 ~~be~~rth caravan in S. Wales ~~ca~~mpsite for 3 wks July or ~~Au~~g 95. Tel: 0181 332 5454

Holiday Exchange: Clean, scenic, 6 pers Chalet on lively campsite in Provence (quiet town, 40 mins drive from St Tropez) offered in exch. for approx 4 pers cott on Sussex coast (pref nr. Newhaven) for 1 month beginning August 1995. Car exch poss. Tel: 00 33 96 85 04 22.

Trans-Atlantic Apartment Swap: Lux 2BR, 2ba apt in Evanston. Lake view frm balcony, prkg, fully a/c, cable, lndry, close to shops and trans to Chicago (20 mins). For 2 BR similar quality in Central Lond. No car exch. Call Sarah: 00 1 708 866 7396.

Couple Seek Bedsit Exchange: beautiful roomy dble bedsit nr Camden Lock, 5 mins tube, great clubs nrby, in exch for similar in central Edinburgh for 3 wks of Festival. Pets, smokers etc welcome. Tel 0181 223 4956

Échanges Vente de véhicules, deux-roues, bateaux

For Sale: Mini 1275GT, 1980. 1 yr MOT, tax, one owner, recon engine, sunroof. v.g.c. £1175. PX poss. Tel: 01580 86345 (eve/ wkend)

V.W Camper for Sale: 1972, 1600c elevating roof, cooker, sink, slps 4. 12 mo MOT, excellent runner. £1.100 ono. Tel: 0181 334 5687

HONDA MTX 125 R for Sale. 1990, 4000 miles, mint condition: 4 mos MOT. Steve: 01902 339586

Bicycles for Sale: One Ladies' 5-spd, 27in wheels, 19 in frame. As new £75. One Boy's 10 spd racer, suit 10-12 yrs, PX if poss, otherwise £50. Phone 01223 4459305 after 6pm.

Bargain Boat! 32 ft Kitch Motor Sailer, 5 Berth, all navigation aids, 50hp diesel. Some work needed hence price, must sell: best offer over £18000. Call Jo 01273 495869

Escort Diesel Van for Sale: 1987, E-reg, red paintwork, 60,000m vgc £2,200, no VAT. Tel 01242 584959

1600c (1600 centilitres) 1600 centilitres
ft (foot) pied
hp (horsepower) cv
in (inches) pouces
mo (months) mois
MOT (Ministry of Transport test) contrôle technique
poss (possible) possible
PX (part exchange) reprise
recon (reconditioned) remis à neuf
reg (registration) immatriculation
slps (sleeps) peut loger
spd (speed) vitesse
tel (telephone) téléphone
VAT (value added tax) TVA
vgc (very good condition) très bon état
wkend (weekend) week-end
yr(s) (year(s)) an(s)

~~a/c~~ (air conditioning *US*) ~~ai~~r conditionné
~~app~~rox (approximately) ~~a~~pproximativement
~~apt~~ (apartment) ~~ap~~partement
~~ba~~ (bathroom) salle de ~~ba~~ins
~~bat~~h (bathroom *GB*) ~~sa~~lle de bains
~~BR~~ (bedroom) ~~ch~~ambre
~~cab~~le (cable television ~~U~~S) télévision par ~~ca~~ble
~~car e~~xch. (car ~~ex~~change) échange ~~de~~ voiture
~~co~~mmenc. (commencing) à ~~pa~~rtir de
~~cot~~t (cottage) petite ~~m~~aison (rustique)
~~ele~~c (electricity) ~~él~~ectricité
~~etc~~ (et cetera) etc
~~exc~~h (exchange) ~~éc~~hange
~~fam~~ owned (family ~~ow~~ned) familial
~~frm~~ (from) à partir de
~~hse~~ (house) maison
~~large~~ rm (large room) ~~gr~~ande chambre
~~lndr~~y (laundry *US*) ~~lav~~erie

Lond (London) Londres
m (miles) miles
mod kit (modern kitchen) cuisine moderne
mos (months) mois
N. Cornish (North Cornish) au nord de la Cornouailles
non-smkg (non-smoking) non-fumeur
nr (near) à proximité de
nrby (nearby) à proximité
pers (person) personne
pref (preferred) de préférence
prkg (parking) place de parking
profs (professionals) salariés
pw (per week) par semaine
Sept (September) septembre
slps (sleeps) peut loger
trans (transport) transports en commun
wks (weeks) semaines

Ventes : divers

Carpet for Sale: Brown wool twist, excel quality and cond. 12ft x 16ft. £80 ono. 01852 345679

Electric Hob, Siemens, brown, 4 rings & small elec oven. Vgc. Offers invited. Can deliver. 01321 4659634

Hotpoint Twin tub washing machine, perf working order, bargain at £100. 01273 495068. Will Deliver.

Hoover turbo power: brand new w/guarantee, still boxed, duplicate gift. Cost £109, will accept £75. Tel. 01865 456923

Pioneer Stereo: separate units, incl. digital tuner, graphics, amp, twin cassette, deck multiplay, cd, turntable. As new £475. tel. 01223 496590.

Hotpoint Larder Fridge. Sm freezer. 3yrs old. gwo. Offers? 01432 594058.

3-Piece Suite. Brown Draylon, 3-seater settee, 2 lge armchairs. £100 ovno. Buyer collects. Tel 0181 669 4857 (eve/wkends)

Macintosh SE, nearly new, 40mb HD, 4mb RAM, w/ Imagewriter II. Still w/box & manuals. Incredible offer at £800. Tel: 0181 223 4958

Kenwood Chef Food Processor: w/attachments; mincer, dough, hood etc. Still guarant'd, hardly used. Tel: 01273 458695

Assorted Garden Tools: rake, hoe, shovel, wheelbarrow, broom. All gwo. £50 the lot, or indiv. offers accepted. Tel: 01432 458399

---

amp (amplifier) ampli(ficateur)
cd (compact disc) CD, disque compact
cond (condition) condition
elec (electric) électrique
etc (et cetera) etc
eve (evenings) soir
excel (excellent) excellent
ft (feet) pieds
guarant'd (guaranteed) garanti
gwo (good working order) bon état de marche
HD (hard disk) disque dur
incl (including) comprenant
indiv (individual) individuel
lge (large) grand
mb (megabytes) mégaoctets
ono (or nearest offer) à débattre
ovno (or very near offer) à débattre
perf (perfect) parfait
RAM (RAM) RAM
sm (small) petit
vgc (very good condition) très bon état
x (by) sur

Emplois

Female Student, 24 yrs, seeks p/t work as childminder/domestic help in Notting Hill area. Experienced, reliable, avail. mornings or afternoons, approx 15 h.p.w. Pay negotiable. 0181 339 4857.

Secretary required for temp position in dynamic small company to cover maternity leave. 60wpm typing, 90 wpm shorthand, wp experience essential, esp Wordperfect 5.1. Excellent verbal/ written communication skills. Competitive salary. Call Mrs Jones 0181 338 4958

Handyman required for summer upkeep and repairs at Sutton sports ground. 3 month contract (Jun-Aug), approx 35 hrs pw. Hourly rate £4.35. Carpentry skills essential as is prev experience. Further details from Mr Ellison 0181 3393283

French Language tuition offered. All levels in your own home, by exp native French speaker. School/ univ exams, essays, journalism, business etc. £10 ph. Tel 01902 339449

French/English translators required by French Law firm for casual contract work. Must be native French speaker w/fluent English. German an advantage. For details Tel: 0171 228 3854 ext. 6950

Au pair seeks position i family with 2-3 children i London. French femal 21yrs, non-smoker, clea drivers licence, excelle refs, good spoken En Tel: 00 33 99 30 00 44

Experienced Aupa Wanted: for 3 childre aged 2,4,7 & some lig hsewk in Shepher Bush. Must be no smoker, animal lover, d ver, 21yrs+. Appr 40hpw, own flatlet pocket money. Send CV photo to PO Box 209.

Domestic Help wante 3hrs 3 mornings pw f family home. Near b route, £5 ph. Tel 0127 49586

Agent Wanted for 5 be holiday home in Rob Hood's Bay. Duties in cleaning & gen upkee betw. lets, showing fam lies around, advice a emergency help. Sala negotiable. Suit retire person. Tel: 0181 229 48

Housesitter Wanted: f 4 bed holiday home Cornwall, for 5 mont Nov-Mar. Rent-free exch for care of 2 ac gdn, hse maintenan and bills. 6m neare town. Tel 01273 48596

---

approx (approximately) approximativement
avail (available) libre
betw (between) entre
CV (Curriculum Vitae) CV
etc (et cetera) etc
exch (exchange) échange
exp (experienced) expérimenté
gdn (garden) jardin
gen (general) général
hpw (hours per week) heures par semaine
hrs (hours) heures
hse (house) maison
hsewk (housework) ménage
m (miles) miles
Nov-Mar (November to March) de novembre à mars

ph (per hour) de l'heure
PO Box (Post Office Box) boîte postale
Prev (previous) antérieur
p/t (part time) temp partiel
pw (per week) par semaine
refs (references) références
temp (temporary) temporaire
wp (word processing traitement de texte
wpm (words per minute) mots à la minute
univ (university) université
yrs (years) ans

English–French dictionary
Dictionnaire anglais–français

Aa

a¹, A /eɪ/ n **1** (letter) a, A m; **the A to Z of cooking** la cuisine de A à Z; **2 A** MUS la m; **3 A** (place) **to get from A to B** se rendre d'un endroit à un autre; **4 a** (in house number) a; cf bis; **5 A** GB (road) **the A7** la route A7.

a² /ə, eɪ/ (avant voyelle ou 'h' muet **an** /æn, ən/) det un/ une.

AA n **1** GB AUT (abrév = **Automobile Association**) organisme m d'assistance pour les automobilistes; **2** abrév ▶ **Alcoholics Anonymous**.

aback /ə'bæk/ adv **to be taken ~** être déconcerté.

abacus /'æbəkəs/ n (pl **-cuses**) boulier m.

abandon /ə'bændən/ **I** n abandon m; **with gay ~** avec une belle désinvolture.
II vtr (leave) abandonner [person, hope]; (drop, stop) renoncer à [activity, attempt, claim]; arrêter [strike].

abandoned /ə'bændənd/ adj [person, animal] abandonné; [behaviour] dévergondé.

abandonment /ə'bændənmənt/ n GEN abandon m; (of strike) arrêt m.

abashed /ə'bæʃt/ adj décontenancé.

abate /ə'beɪt/ **I** vtr SOUT diminuer.
II vi [flood, fever] baisser; [storm, rage] diminuer.

abbess /'æbes/ n abbesse f.

abbey /'æbɪ/ n abbaye f.

abbot /'æbət/ n (père m) abbé m.

abbreviate /ə'briːvɪeɪt/ vtr abréger (**to** en).

abbreviation /ə,briːvɪ'eɪʃn/ n (short form) abréviation f.

ABC n **1** (alphabet) alphabet m; **2** (basics) **the ~ of** le b.a. ba de; **3** US TV (abrév = **American Broadcasting Company**) chaîne de télévision américaine.

abdicate /'æbdɪkeɪt/ **I** vtr renoncer à [right]; abdiquer [responsibility].
II vi abdiquer.

abdication /,æbdɪ'keɪʃn/ n (royal) abdication f; (of responsibility) renonciation f (**of** à).

abdomen /'æbdəmən/ n abdomen m.

abduct /əb'dʌkt/ vtr enlever.

abduction /əb'dʌkʃn/ n enlèvement m.

abductor /əb'dʌktə(r)/ n (kidnapper) ravisseur/-euse m/f.

aberrant /ə'berənt/ adj [behaviour, nature] aberrant; [result] anormal.

aberration /,æbə'reɪʃn/ n aberration f.

abet /ə'bet/ vtr (p prés etc **-tt-**) ▶ **aid**.

abeyance /ə'beɪəns/ n SOUT **in ~** [matter, situation] en suspens; **to hold sth in ~** garder qch vacant.

abhor /əb'hɔː(r)/ vtr (p prés etc **-rr-**) abhorrer.

abhorrence /əb'hɒrəns, US -'hɔːr-/ n horreur f.

abhorrent /əb'hɒrənt, US -'hɔːr-/ adj odieux/-ieuse.

abide /ə'baɪd/ (prét, pp abode ou ~d) **I** vtr **I can't ~ sth/doing** je ne peux pas supporter qch/de faire.
II vi **to ~ by** respecter [rule, decision].

abiding /ə'baɪdɪŋ/ adj [image, memory] inoubliable.

ability /ə'bɪlətɪ/ **I** n **1** (capability) capacité f (**to do** de faire); **to the best of one's ~** de son mieux; **2** (talent) talent m.
II abilities npl (skills) compétences fpl, SCH (of pupils) aptitudes fpl.

abject /'æbdʒekt/ adj [state] misérable; [failure] lamentable; [coward] abject; **~ poverty** misère f.

ablative /'æblətɪv/ n ablatif m.

a²
The determiner or indefinite article a or an is translated by un + masculine noun and by une + feminine noun:
   a tree   = un arbre
   a chair = une chaise

There are, however, some cases where the article is not translated:
with professions and trades:
   her mother is a teacher = sa mère est professeur
with other nouns used in apposition:
   he's a widower = il est veuf
with what a:
   what a pretty house = quelle jolie maison

For translations of a few, a little, a lot, a great many see the entries **few**, **little**, **lot**, **many**.

When expressing prices in relation to weight, the definite article le/la is used in French:
   ten francs a kilo = dix francs le kilo

In other expressions where a/an means per the French translation is usually par:
   50 kilometres an hour = 50 kilomètres par heure
   twice a day = deux fois par jour

For translations of all other expressions using the indefinite article such as to make a noise, to make a fortune, at a time etc. consult the appropriate noun entry (**noise**, **fortune**, **time** etc.).

ablaze /ə'bleɪz/ adj en feu, en flammes; **to set sth ~** mettre le feu à qch; **the house was ~** la maison flambait; **his eyes were ~ with anger** ses yeux brillaient de colère.

able /'eɪbl/ adj

■ **Note** to be able to meaning can is usually translated by the verb pouvoir: I was not able to go = je ne pouvais pas y aller; I was not able to help him = je ne pouvais pas l'aider. The main exception to this occurs when to be able to implies the acquiring of a skill, when savoir is used: he's nine and he's still not able to read = il a neuf ans et il ne sait toujours pas lire.
– For more examples and other uses, see the entry below.

1 (having ability to) **to be ~ to do** pouvoir faire; **she was ~ to play the piano at the age of four** elle savait jouer du piano à quatre ans; **2** (skilled) [lawyer, teacher etc] compétent; (gifted) [child] doué.

able: **~-bodied** adj robuste, fort; **~ rating** n matelot m breveté; **~ seaman** n matelot m de deuxième classe.

ably /'eɪblɪ/ adv [work, write] avec compétence.

abnegation /,æbnɪ'geɪʃn/ n SOUT **1** (of rights, privileges) renoncement m (**of** à); **2** (also **self-~**) abnégation f.

abnormal /æb'nɔːml/ adj anormal.

abnormality /,æbnɔː'mælətɪ/ n (feature) anomalie f.

abnormally /æb'nɔːməlɪ/ adv [high, difficult] anormalement; [behave] de façon anormale.

aboard /ə'bɔːd/ **I** adv (on ship) à bord; **to go ~** monter à bord; **all ~!** tout le monde à bord!
II prep à bord de [plane]; dans [coach, train].

abode /ə'bəʊd/ n (home) SOUT demeure f; **of no fixed ~** sans domicile fixe.

abolish /ə'bɒlɪʃ/ *vtr* abolir [*law, right*]; supprimer [*service, allowance*].

abolition /ˌæbə'lɪʃn/ *n* (of law, right) abolition *f*; (of service, allowance) suppression *f*.

abominable /ə'bɒmɪnəbl/ *adj* abominable.

abominably /ə'bɒmɪnəblɪ/ *adv* [*behave*] de manière odieuse; [*perform*] de manière abominable; [*rude*] abominablement.

abominate /ə'bɒmɪneɪt, US -mən-/ *vtr* exécrer.

aboriginal /ˌæbə'rɪdʒənl/ **I** *n* (native) indigène *mf*.
II *adj* aborigène.

Aborigine /ˌæbə'rɪdʒənɪ/ *n* aborigène *mf* (d'Australie).

abort /ə'bɔːt/ **I** *vtr* faire avorter [*fœtus*]; interrompre [*launch, plan*]; abandonner [*computer program*].
II *vi* [*mother*] avorter; FIG [*plan, launch*] échouer.

abortion /ə'bɔːʃn/ **I** *n* avortement *m*; ~ **on demand** l'avortement libre; **to have an** ~ se faire avorter.
II *noun modifier* [*law, debate*] sur l'avortement.

abortionist /ə'bɔːʃənɪst/ *n* avorteur/-euse *m/f*.

abortive /ə'bɔːtɪv/ *adj* (épith) [*attempt, project*] avorté; [*coup, raid*] manqué.

abound /ə'baʊnd/ *vi* abonder (**in, with** en).

about /ə'baʊt/

■ **Note** *about* is used after certain nouns, adjectives and verbs in English (*information about, a book about, curious about, worry about* etc). For translations, consult the appropriate entries (**information, book, curious, worry** etc).
– *about* often appears in British English as the second element of certain verb structures (*move about, jump about, lie about* etc). For translations, consult the relevant verb entries (**move, jump, lie** etc).

I *adj* **1** (expressing future intention) **to be** ~ **to do** être sur le point de faire; **2** (awake) **up and** ~ debout.
II *adv* **1** (approximately) environ, à peu près ; **it's** ~ **the same as yesterday** c'est à peu près pareil qu'hier; **at** ~ **6 pm** vers 18 h, à environ 18 h; **2** (almost) presque; **that seems** ~ **right** ça a l'air d'aller; **I've had just** ~ **enough of her!** j'en ai plus qu'assez d'elle!; **3** (in circulation) **there was no-one** ~ il n'y avait personne; **there is a lot of flu** ~ il y a beaucoup de grippes en ce moment; **4** (in the vicinity) **to be somewhere** ~ être dans les parages.
III *prep* **1** (concerning) **a book** ~ un livre sur; **what's it** ~? (of book, film etc) ça parle de quoi?; **it's** ~... il s'agit de...; **it's** ~ **my son** c'est au sujet de mon fils; ~ **your overdraft**... pour ce qui est de votre découvert...; **2** (in the nature of) **there's something weird** ~ **him** il a quelque chose de bizarre; **what I like** ~ **her is** ce que j'aime chez elle c'est; **3** (bound up with) **business is** ~ **profit** ce qui compte dans les affaires, ce sont les bénéfices; **4** (occupied with) **to know what one is** ~ savoir ce qu'on fait; **while you're** ~ **it**... tant que tu y es..., par la même occasion...; **and be quick** ~ **it!** et fais vite!; **5** (around) **to wander** ~ **the streets** errer dans les rues; **strewn** ~ **the floor** éparpillés sur le sol; **6** (in invitations, suggestions) **how** ou **what** ~ **some tea?** et si on prenait un thé?; **how** ~ **it?** ça te dit?; **7** (when soliciting opinions) **what** ~ **the legal costs?** et les frais de justice?; **what** ~ **you?** et toi?; **8** SOUT (on) **hidden** ~ **one's person** [*drugs, arms*] caché sur soi.
IDIOMS **it's** ~ **time (that)** il serait temps que (+ *subj*); ~ **time too!** ce n'est pas trop tôt○!; **that's** ~ **it** (that's all) c'est tout.

about-face, about-turn *n* GB FIG volte-face *f* inv.

above /ə'bʌv/ **I** *pron* **the** ~ (people) les personnes susnommées.
II *prep* **1** (vertically higher) au-dessus de; **the mountains** ~ **Monte Carlo** la montagne qui surplombe Monte-Carlo; ~ **it** au-dessus; **2** (north of) au nord de; **3** (upstream of) en amont de; **4** (morally) **he's** ~ **such petty behaviour** il n'est pas capable d'un comportement aussi mesquin; **they're not** ~ **cheating** ils sont tout à fait capables de tricher; **5** (in preference to) par-dessus; ~ **all others,** ~ **all else**

par-dessus tout; **6** (superior in status, rank) au-dessus de; **he thinks he's** ~ **us** il se croit supérieur à nous; **7** (greater than) au-dessus de; **to rise** ~ dépasser [*limit, average*]; **8** (beyond) ~ **suspicion** au-dessus de tout soupçon; **9** (higher in pitch) au-dessus de; **10** (over) ~ **the shouting** par-dessus les cris.
III *adj* **the** ~ **items** les articles susmentionnés FML.
IV *adv* **1** (higher up) **the apartment** ~ l'appartement du dessus; **the view from** ~ la vue d'en haut; **2** (earlier in the text) précédemment ci-dessus; **3** (more) plus; **12 and** ~ 12 ans et plus; **4** (in the sky) **to look up at the stars** ~ lever les yeux vers les étoiles.
V above all *adv phr* surtout.
IDIOMS **to get** ~ **oneself** ne plus se sentir○.

above: ~**board** *adj* régulier/-ière, correct; ~**ground** *adv* au-dessus du sol, à la surface; ~**mentioned** *adj* susmentionné FML; ~**named** *adj* susnommé.

abrasion /ə'breɪʒn/ *n* (on skin) écorchure *f*.

abrasive /ə'breɪsɪv/ *adj* [*person, manner, tone*] mordant.

abreast /ə'brest/ *adv* **1** (side by side) de front; **to be/come** ~ **of** être/venir à la hauteur de [*vehicle, person*]; **2** (in touch with) **to keep/keep sb** ~ **of** se tenir/tenir qn au courant de [*developments*].

abridge /ə'brɪdʒ/ *vtr* abréger.

abridg(e)ment /ə'brɪdʒmənt/ *n* (version) version *f* abrégée.

abroad /ə'brɔːd/ *adv* **1** [*go, live*] à l'étranger; **imported from** ~ importé de l'étranger; **2** (in circulation) **there is a new spirit** ~ il y a un nouvel état d'esprit général.

abrupt /ə'brʌpt/ *adj* **1** (sudden) [*end, change*] brusque; **to come to an** ~ **end** se terminer brusquement; **2** (curt) [*manner, person*] brusque; **3** (steep) abrupt.

abruptly /ə'brʌptlɪ/ *adv* **1** (suddenly) brusquement; **2** (curtly) avec brusquerie; **3** (steeply) à pic.

ABS *n, adj* AUT (abrév = **anti-lock braking system**) ABS.

abscess /'æbses/ *n* abcès *m*.

abscond /əb'skɒnd/ *vi* s'enfuir (**from** de; **with** avec).

abseiling /'æbseɪlɪŋ/ ▶949| *n* GB descente *f* en rappel.

absence /'æbsəns/ *n* (of person) absence *f*; (of thing) manque *m*; **in sb's** ~ en l'absence de qn; **in the** ~ **of** (failing) faute de.
IDIOMS ~ **makes the heart grow fonder** PROV l'absence attise les grandes passions.

absent **I** /'æbsənt/ *adj* **1** (not there) [*person, thing*] absent (**from** de); **2** MIL **to be** ~ **without leave** être en absence illégale; **3** (preoccupied) [*look*] absent.
II /əb'sent/ *v refl* SOUT **to** ~ **oneself** s'absenter.

absentee /ˌæbsən'tiː/ *n* GEN, SCH absent/-e *m/f*.

absenteeism /ˌæbsən'tiːɪzəm/ *n* absentéisme *m*.

absentee landlord *n* propriétaire *mf* absentéiste.

absently /'æbsəntlɪ/ *adv* d'un air absent.

absent: ~**-minded** *adj* distrait; ~**-mindedly** *adv* [*behave, speak*] distraitement; [*stare*] d'un air absent; ~**-mindedness** *n* distraction *f*.

absolute /'æbsəluːt/ **I** *n* **the** ~ l'absolu *m*.
II *adj* **1** (complete) [*monarch, minimum, majority*] ALSO MATH, PHILOS absolu; ~ **beginner** vrai débutant; **2** (emphatic) [*chaos, idiot*] véritable (*before n*); **3** PHYS, CHEM [*humidity, scale*] maximum; [*zero*] absolu; **4** JUR **decree** ~ décret *m* irrévocable; **5** LING [*ablative*] absolu.

absolutely /'æbsəluːtlɪ/ *adv* (totally) GEN absolument; [*mad*] complètement; ~ **not!** pas du tout!

absolution /ˌæbsə'luːʃn/ *n* absolution *f* (**from** de).

absolve /əb'zɒlv/ *vtr* SOUT (clear) **to** ~ **sb of sth** décharger qn de qch.

absorb /əb'zɔːb/ *vtr* LIT, FIG absorber.

absorbed /əb'zɔːbd/ *adj* absorbé (**in** ou **by** par); ~ **in one's work** plongé dans son travail; **to become** ~ **in sth** s'absorber dans qch.

absorbency /əb'zɔːbənsɪ/ *n* pouvoir *m* absorbant.

sorbent /əb'zɔ:bənt/ *n, adj* absorbant (*m*).

sorbing /əb'zɔ:bɪŋ/ *adj* passionnant.

sorption /əb'zɔ:pʃn/ *n* **1** LIT absorption *f*; **2** FIG (costs) absorption *f*; **3** (in activity, book) concentration (in sur).

stain /əb'steɪn/ *vi* s'abstenir (**from** de).

stemious /æb'sti:mɪəs/ *adj* [*person*] sobre; **you're being very ~!** tu es très raisonnable!

stention /əb'stenʃn/ *n* POL (from vote) abstention *f* (from de).

stinence /'æbstɪnəns/ *n* abstinence *f* (**from** de).

stract I /'æbstrækt/ *n* **1** (theoretical) **in the ~** dans l'abstrait; **2** (summary) résumé *m*; **3** FIN, JUR extrait *m*; **4** ART œuvre *f* abstraite.
/'æbstrækt/ *adj* abstrait.
⫻ /əb'strækt/ *vtr* **1** (summarize) tirer (**from** de); **2** (theorize) extraire (**from** de).

stracted /əb'stræktɪd/ *adj* [*gaze, expression*] distrait.

straction /əb'strækʃn/ *n* abstraction *f*; **an air of ~** un air distrait.

surd /əb'sɜ:d/ I *n* **the ~** PHILOS, THEAT l'absurde *m*.
adj ridicule; **it is ~ that** il est absurde que (+ *subj*).

surdity /əb'sɜ:dətɪ/ *n* absurdité *f*.

surdly /əb'sɜ:dlɪ/ *adv* [*expensive*] ridiculement.

undance /ə'bʌndəns/ *n* abondance *f* (**of** de); **in ~** en abondance, à profusion.

undant /ə'bʌndənt/ *adj* abondant.

undantly /ə'bʌndəntlɪ/ *adv* [*clear, obvious*] tout à fait.

use I /ə'bju:s/ *n* **1** (maltreatment) mauvais traitement *m*; (sexual) sévices *mpl* (sexuels); **2** (misuse) abus *m*; **drug ~** usage *m* des stupéfiants; **alcohol ~** abus d'alcool; **3** (insults) injures *fpl*.
/ə'bju:z/ *vtr* **1** (hurt) maltraiter; (sexually) abuser de [*woman*]; exercer des sévices sexuels sur [*child*]; **2** (misuse) abuser de [*position, power*]; **3** (insult) injurier.

usive /ə'bju:sɪv/ *adj* [*person*] grossier/-ière; (insulting) [*words*] injurieux/-ieuse.

ut /ə'bʌt/ *vi* (*p prés etc* **-tt-**) être contigu/-uë (**onto** à).

ysmal /ə'bɪzml/ *adj* épouvantable.

yss /ə'bɪs/ *n* LIT, FIG abîme *m*.

⫻ *n* (*abrév écrite* = **account**) compte *m*.

ademia /ˌækə'di:mɪə/ *n* l'université *f*.

ademic /ˌækə'demɪk/ I *n* universitaire *mf*.
adj **1** UNIV [*career, post*] universitaire; [*year*] académique; **2** (scholarly) [*achievement, reputation*] intellectuel/-elle; **not very ~** [*person*] pas très doué pour ses études; **3** (educational) [*book, publishing*] universitaire; **4** (theoretical) théorique; **that's ~** ça n'a aucun intérêt pratique; **5** ART [*painter*] académique.

ademician /əˌkædə'mɪʃn, US ˌækədə'mɪʃn/ *n* académicien/-ienne *m/f*.

ademy /ə'kædəmɪ/ *n* (place of learning) école *f*; (learned society) académie *f*.

ademy Award *n* CIN Oscar *m*.

AS /'eɪkæs/ *n* GB (*abrév* = **Advisory Conciliation and Arbitration Service**) comité *qui traite des problèmes entre employeurs et employés*.

cede /ək'si:d/ *vi* SOUT accéder (**to** à); (to treaty) adhérer (**to** à); (to throne) monter (**to** sur).

celerate /ək'seləreɪt/ *vi* **1** AUT accélérer; **to ~ away** partir en trombe (**from** de); **to ~ from 0–60 mph** monter de 0 à 100 km/h; **2** FIG [*decline, growth*] s'accélérer.

celeration /ək,selə'reɪʃn/ *n* accélération *f*.

celerator /ək'seləreɪtə(r)/ *n* accélérateur *m*.

cent I /'æksent, -sənt/ *n* accent *m*; **in** ou **with a French ~** avec l'accent français.
/æk'sent/ *vtr* LING, MUS accentuer.

cented /'æksentɪd, -sənt-/ *adj* [*speech*] avec un accent.

accentuate /æk'sentʃʊeɪt/ *vtr* GEN souligner; MUS accentuer.

accept /ək'sept/ I *vtr* (receive, resign oneself to) accepter; (tolerate) admettre; (take on) assumer.
II **accepted** *pp adj* admis; **in the ~ed sense of the word** dans le sens usuel du mot.

acceptability /ək,septə'bɪlətɪ/ *n* admissibilité *f*.

acceptable /ək'septəbl/ *adj* [*gift, money*] bienvenu; [*idea, behaviour, level*] acceptable.

acceptance /ək'septəns/ *n* (of offer, invitation, bill, policy) acceptation *f*; (of plan, proposal) approbation *f* (**of** de).

access /'ækses/ I *n* **1** (means of entry) ALSO COMPUT accès *m*; **wheelchair ~** accès pour les fauteuils roulants; **to gain ~ to sth** accéder à qch; **'No ~'** (on signs) 'accès interdit'; **2** (ability to obtain, use) accès *m* (**to** à); **open ~** libre accès; **3** JUR (right to visit) **to have ~ (to one's children)** avoir un droit de visite (auprès de ses enfants).
II *noun modifier* [*door, mode, point*] d'accès.
III *vtr* accéder à [*database, information*].

accessible /ək'sesəbl/ *adj* (easy to reach, easy to understand) accessible (**to** à); (affordable) [*price*] abordable.

accession /æk'seʃn/ *n* accession *f* (**to** à).

accessory /ək'sesərɪ/ *n* **1** accessoire *m*; (luxury item on car) extra *m*; **2** JUR complice *mf* (**to** de).

access: ~ road *n* (to building, site) route *f* d'accès; (to motorway) bretelle *f* d'accès; **~ time** *n* COMPUT temps *m* d'accès.

accident /'æksɪdənt/ I *n* **1** (mishap) accident *m* (**with** avec); **by ~** accidentellement; **car/road ~** accident de voiture/de la route; **to have an ~** avoir un accident; **to meet with an ~** être victime d'un accident; **~ and emergency service** (in hospital) service des urgences; **2** (chance) hasard *m*; **by ~** par hasard; **it was more by ~ than design** c'était accidentel plutôt que délibéré.
II *noun modifier* [*statistics*] se rapportant aux accidents; **~ victim** accidenté/-e *m/f*.

accidental /ˌæksɪ'dentl/ *adj* [*death*] accidentel/-elle; [*meeting, mistake*] fortuit.

accidentally /ˌæksɪ'dentəlɪ/ *adv* (by accident) accidentellement; (by chance) par hasard; **~ on purpose** IRON malencontreusement IRON.

accident: Accident and Emergency Unit *n* (service *m* des) urgences *fpl*; **~-prone** *adj* sujet/-ette aux accidents.

acclaim /ə'kleɪm/ I *n* (praise) louanges *fpl*; (cheering) acclamations *fpl*.
II *vtr* **1** (praise) applaudir; **~ed by the critics** encensé par la critique; **2** (cheer) acclamer; FIG **~ed as** acclamé comme; **3** (proclaim) **to ~ sb** ou **sth** proclamer qn qch.

acclimate /'æklɪmeɪt, ə'klaɪ-/ US = **acclimatize**.

acclimation /ˌæklaɪ'meɪʃn/ US = **acclimatization**.

acclimatization /ə,klaɪmətaɪ'zeɪʃn, US -tɪ'z-/ *n* LIT, FIG acclimatation *f* (**to** à).

acclimatize /ə'klaɪmətaɪz/ *vtr* acclimater (**to** à); **to get** ou **become ~d** s'acclimater.

accolade /'ækəleɪd, US -'leɪd/ *n* (from audience, in press) ovation *f*; (honour) honneur *m*; **the highest ~** la consécration suprême.

accommodate /ə'kɒmədeɪt/ *vtr* **1** (put up) loger; **2** (hold) contenir; **3** (adapt to) s'adapter à [*idiosyncrasy, view*]; **4** (satisfy) satisfaire [*need*]; **to ~ sb with sth** accorder qch à qn [*loan, credit terms*].

accommodating /ə'kɒmədeɪtɪŋ/ *adj* accommodant.

accommodation /ə,kɒmə'deɪʃn/ *n* (also **~s** US) (living quarters) logement *m*; **hotel/student ~** logement en hôtel/pour étudiants; **living ~** logement; **'~ to let'** GB 'location'; **office ~** bureaux *mpl*.

accommodation: ~ bureau GB, **~s bureau** US *n* agence *f* de logement; **~ officer** GB, **~s officer** US ▶ **1251**] *n* responsable *mf* de l'hébergement.

accompaniment /ə'kʌmpənɪmənt/ *n* accompagnement *m*; **as an ~ to sth** pour accompagner qch.

accompanist /ə'kʌmpənɪst/ *n* accompagnateur/-trice *m/f*.

accompany /ə'kʌmpənɪ/ *vtr* accompagner; **accompanied** accompagné (**by sb** par qn; **by sth** de qch; **on sth** MUS à qch).

accomplice /ə'kʌmplɪs, US ə'kɒm-/ *n* complice *mf* (**in, to** de).

accomplish /ə'kʌmplɪʃ, US ə'kɒm-/ *vtr* GEN accomplir; réaliser [*objective*].

accomplished /ə'kʌmplɪʃt, US ə'kɒm-/ *adj* très compétent.

accomplishment /ə'kʌmplɪʃmənt, US ə'kɒm-/ *n* **1** (successful feat) réussite *f*; **that's quite an ~!** c'est remarquable!; **2** (talent) talent *m*.

accord /ə'kɔːd/ **I** *n* accord *m*; **of my own ~** de moi-même; **with one ~** d'un commun accord; **to reach an ~** se mettre d'accord.
II *vtr* accorder (**sb sth** qch à qn).
III *vi* **to ~ with** concorder avec.

accordance /ə'kɔːdəns/: **in accordance with** *prep phr* **1** (in line with) [*act*] conformément à [*rules, instructions*]; [*be*] conforme à [*law, agreement*]; **2** (depending on) selon.

according /ə'kɔːdɪŋ/: **according to** *prep phr* **1** (in line with) [*act*] selon [*law, principles*]; comme prévu; **2** (as described by or in) d'après [*newspaper, person*].

accordingly /ə'kɔːdɪŋlɪ/ *adv* en conséquence.

accordion /ə'kɔːdɪən/ ▶ **1097** | *n* accordéon *m*.

accost /ə'kɒst/ *vtr* GEN aborder; (for sexual purpose) accoster.

account /ə'kaʊnt/ **I** *n* **1** (in bank, post office) compte *m* (**at, with** à); **in my/his ~** sur mon/son compte; **2** COMM (credit arrangement) compte *m*; **to charge sth to** ou **put sth on sb's ~** mettre qch sur le compte de qn; **on ~** (as part payment) d'acompte; **to settle an ~** (in shop) régler un compte; (in hotel) régler une note; **3** (in advertising) budget *m* (de publicité); **4** (bill) facture *f*; **5** (consideration) **to take sth into ~, to take ~ of sth** tenir compte de qch; **6** (description) compte-rendu *m*; (if contentious) version *f*; **by all ~s** manifestement; **by his own ~** tel qu'il le dit lui-même; **7** (impression) **to give a good ~ of oneself** faire bonne impression (**in** dans); **8** (indicating reason) **on ~ of sth** à cause de qch; **on this** ou **that ~** pour cette raison; **on no ~** sous aucun prétexte; **on my/his ~** (because of me/him) à cause de moi/lui; **9** (in matters concerning oneself) **she was worried on her own ~** elle s'inquiétait pour son (propre) sort; **to go into business on one's own ~** se mettre à son compte; **10** (importance) **it's of no ~ to them** peu leur importe.
II accounts *npl* **1** FIN (records) comptabilité *f* ⊄, comptes *mpl*; **2** (department) (service *m*) comptabilité *f*.
III *vtr* SOUT **to ~ sb a genius** considérer qn comme un génie.
■ **account for**: **~ for [sth/sb] 1** (explain) expliquer [*events, fact, behaviour*]; justifier [*expense*] (**to sb** auprès de qn); retrouver [*missing people*]; **2** (represent) représenter [*proportion, percentage*].

accountability /ə,kaʊntə'bɪlətɪ/ *n* responsabilité *f* (**to** devant).

accountable /ə'kaʊntəbl/ *adj* responsable (**to** devant; **for** de).

accountancy /ə'kaʊntənsɪ/ *n* comptabilité *f*.

accountant /ə'kaʊntənt/ ▶ **1251** | *n* comptable *mf*.

account: **~ book** *n* livre *m* de comptes; **~ holder** *n* (with bank, credit company) titulaire *mf*.

accounting /ə'kaʊntɪŋ/ *n* comptabilité *f*.

accredit /ə'kredɪt/ *vtr* (appoint) accréditer; (approve) agréer.

accreditation /ə,kredɪ'teɪʃn/ *n* accréditation *f*.

accretion /ə'kriːʃn/ *n* accumulation *f*.

accrue /ə'kruː/: **I** *vi* [*advantages*] revenir (**to** à); [*power, money*] s'accumuler.
II accrued *pp adj* [*interest*] cumulé; [*wealth*] amassé.

accumulate /ə'kjuːmjʊleɪt/ **I** *vtr* accumuler [*possessions, debts*]; amasser [*wealth*]; rassembler [*evidence*].
II *vi* s'accumuler.
III accumulated *pp adj* [*anger, tension*] accumulé.

accumulation /ə,kjuː'mjʊleɪʃn/ *n* accumulation *f*; (rubbish) entassement *m*.

accumulator /ə'kjuːmjʊleɪtə(r)/ *n* SPORT (bet) pari avec report.

accuracy /'ækjərəsɪ/ *n* (of figures, watch) justesse *f*; (map, aim) précision *f*; (of diagnosis, forecast) exactitude

accurate /'ækjərət/ *adj* [*figures, watch, informati* juste; [*reports, map*] précis; [*diagnosis, forecast*] exa [*assessment*] correct.

accurately /'ækjərətlɪ/ *adv* [*calculate*] exacteme [*report*] avec exactitude; [*estimate, assess*] préciséme

accusation /,ækjuː'zeɪʃn/ *n* accusation *f* (**of against** contre; **that** selon laquelle); **to make an** porter une accusation.

accusative /ə'kjuːzətɪv/ *n* LING accusatif *m*.

accuse /ə'kjuːz/ *vtr* accuser (**of** de; **of doing** d'av fait).

accused /ə'kjuːzd/ *n* **the ~** (one) l'accusé/-e *m*/*f*.

accuser /ə'kjuːzə(r)/ *n* accusateur/-trice *m*/*f*.

accusing /ə'kjuːzɪŋ/ *adj* accusateur/-trice.

accusingly /ə'kjuːzɪŋlɪ/ *adv* [*say*] d'un ton accusate [*point*] de façon accusatrice.

accustom /ə'kʌstəm/ *vtr* **to ~ sb to sth/to do** habituer qn à qch/à faire.

accustomed /ə'kʌstəmd/ *adj* **1 to be ~ to sth doing** avoir l'habitude de qch/de faire; **to become to sth/to doing** s'habituer à qch/à faire; **2** [*man route*] habituel/-elle.

ace /eɪs/ **I** *n* **1** (in cards) as *m*; **2** FIG (trump) carte *f* m tresse; **3** (in tennis) as *m*; **4** (expert) as *m*.
II○ *adj* (great) super○; **an ~ driver** un as du volant.
IDIOMS **to hold all the ~s** avoir tout pouvoir.

acerbic /ə'sɜːbɪk/ *adj* (all contexts) acerbe.

acetate /'æsɪteɪt/ *n* acétate *m*.

ache /eɪk/ **I** *n* (physical) douleur *f* (**in** à); **~s and pa** douleurs *fpl*.
II *vi* **1** (physically) [*person*] avoir mal; [*limb, back*] fa mal; **to ~ all over** avoir mal partout; **2** (suffer emotionally) **to ~ with** mourir de [*humiliat despair*]; **3** (yearn) brûler (**to do** de faire; **with** de).
IDIOMS **to laugh till one's sides ~** rire à se tenir côtes.

achieve /ə'tʃiːv/ *vtr* atteindre [*aim*]; atteindre [*perfection*]; arriver à [*consensus*]; obtenir [*succ result*]; réaliser [*ambition*]; **to ~ nothing** ne r accomplir.

achievement /ə'tʃiːvmənt/ *n* **1** (thing accomplish réussite *f* (**in sth** dans le domaine de qch); **2** (of attainment) performance *f*; **academic ~** le suc universitaire; **3** (fulfilment) réalisation *f* (**de** of) **sense of ~** un sentiment de satisfaction.

achiever /ə'tʃiːvə(r)/ *n* (also **high ~**) personne *f* réussit.

Achilles' heel /ə'kɪliːz hiːl/ *n* talon *m* d'Achille, po *m* faible.

aching /'eɪkɪŋ/ *adj* [*body, limbs*] douloureux/-euse; **~ void** un grand vide.

acid /'æsɪd/ **I** *n* **1** CHEM acide *m*; **2**○ (drug) acide○ *m*.
II *adj* **1** (sour) acide; **2** FIG [*tone*] aigre; [*remo* caustique.

acid: **~ drop** *n* bonbon *m* acidulé; **~ green** *n*, vert (*m*) fluo○ *inv*.

acidic /ə'sɪdɪk/ *adj* acide.

acidity /ə'sɪdətɪ/ *n* CHEM acidité *f*.

acid: **~ rain** *n* ⊄ pluies *fpl* acides; **~ rock** *n* rock *m* psychédélique; **~ stomach** *n* MED acidi gastrique; **~ test** *n* FIG épreuve *f* de vérité (**of** for pour).

acknowledge /ək'nɒlɪdʒ/ **I** *vtr* admettre [*fact*]; re naître [*error, problem, authority*]; répondre à [plause]; accuser réception de [*letter*]; citer [*sources*] **~ sb** montrer qu'on a vu qn; **she didn't even me** elle a fait semblant de ne pas me voir.
II acknowledged *pp adj* [*leader, champion, exp* incontesté; [*writer, artist*] renommé, reconnu.

acknowledgement /ək'nɒlɪdʒmənt/ **I** *n* **1** (admiss

connaissance f; (of error, guilt) aveu m; **in ~ of sth** reconnaissance de qch; **2** (confirmation of receipt) accusé m de réception; **3** (recognition of presence) signe de reconnaissance.

acknowledgements npl (in book etc) remerciements mpl.

:me /'ækmɪ/ I n **the ~ of** le summum de.

:ne /'ækni/ ▶ **1002** | n acné f.

:orn /'eikɔ:n/ n gland m.

oustic /ə'ku:stɪk/ adj GEN acoustique; [tile, materl] insonorisant.

oustic guitar ▶ **1097** | n guitare f sèche.

oustics /ə'ku:stɪks/ n **the ~ are good** acoustique est bonne.

quaint /ə'kweɪnt/ vtr **to ~ sb with sth** mettre qn courant de qch; **to be ~ed** se connaître; **to get ou ecome ~ed with sb** faire la connaissance de qn; **get ou become ~ed with sth** découvrir qch.

quaintance /ə'kweɪntəns/ n **1** (person) onnaissance f; **2** (familiarity) connaissance f (with de); **improve on ~** gagner à être connu; **to have a odding ~ with sth** avoir des notions de qch; **3** riendly relationship) amitié f; **to make sb's ~** faire la onnaissance de qn.

quiesce /ˌækwɪ'es/ vi **1** (accept) accepter; **2** (collude) ~ in sth** donner son accord tacite à qch.

quiescence /ˌækwɪ'esns/ n **1** (agreement) accord m; (collusion) connivence f.

quiescent /ˌækwɪ'esnt/ adj soumis.

quire /ə'kwaɪə(r)/ vtr acquérir [expertise]; obtenir information]; faire l'acquisition de [possessions]; prenre [meaning]; acheter [company]; contracter [habit]; ~ a taste for sth** prendre goût à qch.

quired /ə'kwaɪəd/ adj [characteristic] acquis; **it's an ~ taste** c'est quelque chose qu'il faut apprendre à imer.

quisition /ˌækwɪ'zɪʃn/ n (object, process) acquisition ; (company) achat m.

quisitive /ə'kwɪzətɪv/ adj [society] attaché aux biens le consommation; [person] rapace.

cquit /ə'kwɪt/ (p prés etc **-tt-**) I vtr JUR acquitter; **to e ~ted** être disculpé (**of** de).

I v refl **to ~ oneself well in** s'en tirer° bien à [interiew].

cquittal /ə'kwɪtl/ n JUR acquittement m.

cre /'eɪkə(r)/ ▶ **1309** | I n acre f, ~ demi-hectare m.

I acres npl **~s of** des hectares mpl de [woodland]; **~s of room**° énormément d'espace.

creage /'eɪkərɪdʒ/ n superficie f.

crid /'ækrɪd/ adj âcre.

crimonious /ˌækrɪ'məʊnɪəs/ adj acrimonieux/-ieuse.

crimony /'ækrɪmənɪ, US -məʊnɪ/ n acrimonie f.

crobat /'ækrəbæt/ n acrobate mf.

crobatic /ˌækrə'bætɪk/ adj [feat] acrobatique; [skill] d'acrobate.

crobatics /ˌækrə'bætɪks/ n (+ v pl) acrobaties fpl.

cronym /'ækrənɪm/ n acronyme m.

cross /ə'krɒs/

■ **Note** across frequently occurs as the second element in certain verb combinations (come across, run across, lean across etc). For translations, look at the appropriate verb entry (**come, run, lean** etc).

I prep **1** (from one side to the other) **to go** ou **travel ~ sth** traverser qch; **to travel ~ country** traverser la campagne; (in car) prendre les petites routes; **a journey ~ the desert** un voyage à travers le désert; **the bridge ~ the river** le pont qui traverse la rivière; **to be lying ~ the bed** être couché en travers du lit; **she leaned ~ the table** elle s'est penchée au-dessus de la table; **the scar ~ his face** la cicatrice sur sa figure; **2** (to, on the other side of) de l'autre côté de; **~ the street/desk (from me)** de l'autre côté de la rue/du bureau; **to look ~ the lake** regarder de l'autre côté du lac; **3** (all over, covering a wide range of) **~ the world** partout dans le monde, à

travers le monde; **~ the country** dans tout le pays; **scattered ~ the floor** éparpillés sur le sol.

II adv **to be two miles ~** faire deux miles de large; **to help sb ~** aider qn à traverser; **to go ~ to sb** aller vers qn; **to look ~ at sb** regarder vers qn.

III **across from** prep phr en face de.

across-the-board adj, adv à tous les niveaux.

acrylic /ə'krɪlɪk/ I n acrylique m.

II noun modifier [garment] en acrylique.

act /ækt/ I n **1** (action, deed) acte m; **an ~ of kindness** un acte de bonté; **2** JUR, POL (also **Act**) loi f; **Act of Parliament/Congress** loi votée par le Parlement/le Congrès; **3** THEAT acte m; **4** (entertainment routine) numéro m; **to put on an ~** FIG jouer la comédie; **to get in on the ~** s'y mettre.

II vtr THEAT jouer [part, role].

III vi **1** (take action) agir; **we must ~ quickly** il faut agir rapidement; **to be ~ing for the best** faire pour le mieux; **to ~ for sb, to ~ on behalf of sb** agir au nom de or pour le compte de qn; **2** (behave) agir, se comporter; **3** THEAT jouer, faire du théâtre; FIG (pretend) jouer la comédie, faire semblant; **4** (take effect) [drug] agir; **5** (serve) **to ~ as** [person, object] servir de.

IDIOMS **to be caught in the ~** être pris sur le fait or en flagrant délit; **to get one's ~ together** se prendre en main; **it's a hard ~ to follow** ça sera difficile à égaler.

■ **act out** jouer [role, part]; réaliser [fantasy].

■ **act up**° (misbehave) se tenir mal; (malfunction) être détraqué.

acting /'æktɪŋ/ I n CIN, THEAT (performance) jeu m, interprétation f; (occupation) métier m d'acteur.

II adj [director etc] intérimaire.

action /'ækʃn/ n **1 ⊄** GEN action f; (to deal with situation) mesures fpl; **to take ~** agir, prendre des mesures (**against** contre); **drastic/immediate ~** des mesures draconiennes/immédiates; **a man of ~** un homme d'action; **to put a plan into ~** mettre un projet à exécution; **to put sth out of ~** immobiliser qch; **to be out of ~** [machine] être en panne; [person] être immobilisé; **to be back in ~** être de retour; **2** (deed) acte m; **~s speak louder than words** mieux vaut agir que parler; **3** (fighting) action f, combat m; **to see (some) ~** combattre; **to go into ~** aller au combat; **killed in ~** tué au combat; **4** CIN, THEAT action f; **~!** moteur!; **5**° (excitement) **I don't want to miss out on the ~** je ne veux pas rater ce qui se passe; **that's where the ~ is** c'est là où ça bouge°; **they want a piece of the ~** (want to be involved) ils ne veulent pas être en reste; (want some of the profits) ils veulent leur part du gâteau°; **6** JUR action f, procès m; **to bring an ~ against sb** intenter une action contre qn; **7** TECH (in machine, piano) mécanisme m.

IDIOMS **~ stations!** MIL, FIG à vos postes!

action: **~ group** n groupe m de pression; **~-packed** adj [film] plein d'action; [holiday] bien rempli; **~ painting** n peinture f gestuelle; **~ replay** n GB TV répétition f d'une séquence.

activate /'æktɪveɪt/ vtr faire démarrer [machine, system]; actionner [switch]; déclencher [alarm]; activer [chemical].

active /'æktɪv/ adj **1** [person, life, member] actif/-ive; [campaign] énergique; [volcano] en activité; **to be ~ in** être un membre actif de [organization]; **to be ~ in doing** s'employer (activement) à faire; **to play an ~ role in sth** jouer un rôle déterminant dans qch; **to take an ~ interest in sth** s'intéresser activement à qch; **2** LING actif/-ive.

active duty, active service n MIL service m actif.

actively /'æktɪvlɪ/ adv activement; **to be ~ considering doing** penser sérieusement à faire.

activist /'æktɪvɪst/ n activiste mf.

activity /æk'tɪvətɪ/ n (all contexts) activité f.

activity holiday n GB ~ vacances fpl sportives.

act of God n désastre m naturel.

actor /'æktə(r)/ n acteur m, comédien m.

actress /'æktrɪs/ n actrice f, comédienne f.

actual /'æktʃʊəl/ adj **1** (real, exact) [conditions, circumstances] réel/réelle; **I don't remember the ~ words** je ne me rappelle pas les mots exacts; **in ~ fact** en fait; **it has nothing to do with the ~ problem** cela n'a rien à voir avec le problème lui-même; **2** (very) même (after n); **this is the ~ room that Shakespeare worked in** voici la pièce même où Shakespeare travaillait; **3** (as such) à proprement parler.

actuality /ˌæktʃʊ'ælətɪ/ n réalité f.

actually /'æktʃʊəlɪ/ adv **1** (contrary to expectation) en fait; **their profits have ~ risen** en fait, leurs bénéfices ont augmenté; **2** (in reality) vraiment; **yes, it ~ happened!** mais oui, c'est vraiment arrivé!; **3** (in fact) en fait; **~, I don't feel like it** à vrai dire je n'en ai pas envie; **4** (exactly) exactement; **what ~ happened?** qu'est-ce qui s'est passé exactement?; **5** (expressing indignation) carrément; **she ~ accused me of lying!** elle m'a carrément accusé de mentir!; **6** (expressing surprise) **she ~ thanked me** elle est allée jusqu'à me remercier.

actuary /'æktʃʊərɪ, US -tʃʊrɪ/ ▶ 1251 | n actuaire mf.

acumen /'ækjʊmən, ə'kju:mən/ n sagacité f; **business ~** sens m des affaires.

acupressure /'ækjʊpreʃə(r)/ n digipuncture f.

acupuncture /'ækjʊpʌŋktʃə(r)/ n acupuncture f.

acupuncturist /'ækjʊpʌŋktʃərɪst/ ▶ 1251 | n acupuncteur/-trice m/f.

acute /ə'kju:t/ adj **1** (intense) [anxiety] vif/vive; [boredom] profond; **to cause sb ~ embarrassment** beaucoup embarrasser qn; **2** MED [condition, illness] aigu/aiguë; **3** (grave) [shortage, situation] grave; **4** (keen) [mind] pénétrant.

acute: **~ accent** n LING accent m aigu; **~ angle** n angle m aigu.

acutely /ə'kju:tlɪ/ adv [suffer] vivement; [embarrassed, sensitive] excessivement.

ad /æd/ n (abrév = **advertisement**) **1** JOURN (also **small ~**) petite annonce f (for pour); **2** RADIO, TV pub° f (for pour).

AD (abrév = **Anno Domini**) ap J.-C.

adage /'ædɪdʒ/ n adage m (**that** selon lequel).

adamant /'ædəmənt/ adj catégorique (**about** sur); **he is ~ that you are wrong** il maintient que tu as tort; **to remain ~** rester inébranlable.

Adam's apple /ˌædəmz 'æpl/ n pomme f d'Adam.

adapt /ə'dæpt/ I vtr adapter (**to** à; **for** pour; **from** de). II vi s'adapter (**to** à).

adaptability /əˌdæptə'bɪlətɪ/ n (ability to change) adaptabilité f (**to** à).

adaptable /ə'dæptəbl/ adj [person, organization] souple.

adapter, adaptor /ə'dæptə(r)/ n ELEC adaptateur m.

add /æd/ vtr **1** GEN ajouter, rajouter (**onto, to** à); **to ~ that...** ajouter que...; **2** MATH (also **~ together**) additionner; **to ~ sth to** ajouter qch à [figure, total].
■ **add on**: **~ [sth] on, ~ on [sth]** ajouter.
■ **add up**: ¶ **~ up** [facts, figures] s'accorder; **it doesn't ~ up** FIG cela ne tient pas debout°; **it all ~s up!** (makes sense) je comprends tout maintenant!; **to ~ up to** [total] s'élever à [number]; ¶ **~ up [sth], ~ [sth] up** additionner [cost, numbers].

added /'ædɪd/ adj supplémentaire; **~ to which...** ajoutez à cela que...

adder /'ædə(r)/ n **1** (snake) vipère f; **2** COMPUT additionneur m.

addict /'ædɪkt/ n **1** (drug-user) toxicomane mf; **2** FIG (of TV, coffee) accro° mf (**of** de).

addicted /ə'dɪktɪd/ adj **to be ~** LIT avoir une dépendance (**to** à); FIG être accro° (**to** de).

addiction /ə'dɪkʃn/ n LIT (to alcohol, drugs) dépendance f (**to** à); FIG (to chocolate) passion f (**to** pour).

addictive /ə'dɪktɪv/ adj **1** LIT [drug, substance] qui

crée une dépendance; **2** FIG **to be ~** [chocolate power] être comme une drogue.

adding machine n machine f à calculer.

addition /ə'dɪʃn/ **I** n (to list, house) ajout m; (to tea range) adjonction f; MATH addition f.
II in addition adv phr en plus.

additional /ə'dɪʃənl/ adj supplémentaire.

additionally /ə'dɪʃənəlɪ/ adv (moreover) en out (also) en plus.

additive /'ædɪtɪv/ n additif m.

addled /'ædld/ adj [thinking] confus.

add-on /'ædɒn/ adj supplémentaire.

address /ə'dres, US 'ædres/ **I** n **1** (place of residence) adresse f; **to change (one's) ~** changer d'adresse; (speech) discours m (**to** à); **3** (as etiquette) **form of ~** (for sb) formule f pour s'adresser à qn.
II vtr **1** mettre l'adresse sur [parcel, letter]; **to ~ s to sb** adresser qch à qn; **to be wrongly ~ed** avoir un libellé incorrect; **2** (speak to) s'adresser à [group]; (aim) adresser [remark, complaint] (**to** à); **4** (tack aborder [question]; s'occuper de [problem].

address book n carnet m d'adresses.

addressee /ˌædre'si:/ n destinataire mf.

addressing /ə'dresɪŋ, US 'ædresɪŋ/ n COMP adressage m.

adenoids /'ædɪnɔɪdz, US -dən-/ npl végétations fpl (ac noïdes).

adept /ə'dept/ adj [cook, gardener] expert.

adequate /'ædɪkwət/ adj (sufficient) suffisant (**for** pou **to do** pour faire); (satisfactory) satisfaisant.

adequately /'ædɪkwətlɪ/ adv [prepared, equippe suffisamment; [describe] convenablement.

adhere /əd'hɪə(r)/ vi LIT adhérer (**to** à); **to ~ to** adhérer à [belief]; observer [policy, plan, standard].

adherence /əd'hɪərəns/ n (to belief) adhésion f (**to** (to plan, policy) observation f (**to** de).

adherent /əd'hɪərənt/ n (of cult) disciple mf; doctrine) adhérent/-e m/f; (of policy) tenant/-e m/f.

adhesion /əd'hi:ʒn/ n adhérence f.

adhesive /əd'hi:sɪv/ **I** n colle f, adhésif m.
II adj GEN collant; **~ tape** papier m collan Scotch® m; **self-~** auto-collant.

ad hoc /ˌæd 'hɒk/ adj [arrangement] improvisé; [all ance] temporaire; [committee, legislation] ad hoc in (after n); **on an ~ basis** au coup par coup.

adieu† /ə'dju:, US ə'du:/ n (pl **~s** ou **~x**) adieu n **to bid sb ~** faire ses adieux à qn.

ad infinitum /ˌæd ˌɪnfɪ'naɪtəm/ adv [continue] à n'e plus finir.

adjacent /ə'dʒeɪsnt/ adj **1** (touching) contigu/-uë; **sth** attenant à qch; **2** (nearby) voisin (**to** de).

adjective /'ædʒɪktɪv/ n adjectif m.

adjoin /ə'dʒɔɪn/ **I** vtr [room] être contigu/-uë à; [buila ing, land] être attenant à.
II adjoining pres p adj [building, land] attenant [room] voisin.

adjourn /ə'dʒɜ:n/ **I** vtr ajourner [trial] (**for** pour; unti à); **the session was ~ed** la séance a été levée.
II vi **1** (suspend proceedings) s'arrêter (**for** pour); Parlia **ment ~ed** (for break) la Chambre a interrompu le débats; (at end of debate) la Chambre a levé la séance; **2** (retire) passer (**to** à).

adjournment /ə'dʒɜ:nmənt/ n (of trial) ajournemen m; (of session) suspension f.

adjudge /ə'dʒʌdʒ/ vtr JUR **1** (decree) déclarer (**tha** que); **2** (award) adjuger [costs]; allouer, accorde [damages].

adjudicate /ə'dʒu:dɪkeɪt/ vtr juger [contest]; examine [case, claim].

adjudication /əˌdʒu:dɪ'keɪʃn/ n **1** (of contest) juge ment m; **2** JUR décision f; **under ~** en train d'être examiné.

adjudicator /ə'dʒu:dɪkeɪtə(r)/ n juge m.

adjunct /'ædʒʌŋkt/ n **1** (addition) annexe f (**of, to** de); **2** (person) subalterne mf (**of, to** de).

ljust /ə'dʒʌst/ **I** *vtr* régler [*level, position, speed*]; uster [*price, rate*]; rajuster [*clothing*]; modifier [*figres*]; **to ~** [*sth*] **upwards/downwards** revoir [qch] la hausse/baisse [*salary, sum*].
(*vi* [*person*] s'adapter (**to** à); [*seat*] être réglable.
II -adjusted *combining form* **well-~ed** [*person*] quilibré.

ljustable /ə'dʒʌstəbl/ *adj* GEN [*appliance, position, at*] réglable; [*rate*] ajustable.

ljustable spanner, adjustable wrench *n* clé à molette.

ljustment /ə'dʒʌstmənt/ *n* (of rates, charges) rajusteent *m* (**of** de); (of control, machine) réglage *m* (**of** de); nental, physical) adaptation *f* (**to** à); **to make the ~** s'adapter à [*lifestyle*].

ljutant /'ædʒʊtənt/ **▶ 1192** *n* MIL officier *m* adjoint.

(-lib /ˌæd 'lɪb/ **I** *n* (on stage) improvisation *f*; (wittism) bon mot *m*.
(*adj* [*comment*] improvisé.
(I *adv* [*speak*] en improvisant.
V *vtr, vi* (*p prés etc* **-bb-**) improviser.

(man° /'ædmæn/ *n* publicitaire *m*.

(min° /'ædmɪn/ GB *n* administration *f*.

(minister /əd'mɪnɪstə(r)/ *vtr* **1** (also **administrate**) nanage) gérer [*company, affairs, estate*]; gouverner [*tertory*]; **2** (dispense) administrer [*punishment*]; exercer *ustice*].

(ministration /ədˌmɪnɪ'streɪʃn/ *n* (of hospital, school, rritory) administration *f*; (of justice) exercice *m*; (paperork) travail *m* administratif; **the ~** US le gouvernelement.

(ministration: **~ building**, **~ block** GB *n* bâment *m* administratif; **~ costs** *n* frais *mpl* de stion.

(ministrative /əd'mɪnɪstrətɪv, US -streɪtɪv/ *adj* administratif/-ive.

(ministrator /əd'mɪnɪstreɪtə(r)/ **▶ 1251** *n* **1** COMM Iministrateur/-trice *m/f* (**for, of** de); **sales ~** recteur/-trice *m/f* des ventes; **2** (of hospital, school, eatre) administrateur *m*.

(mirable /'ædmərəbl/ *adj* admirable.

(miral /'ædmərəl/ **▶ 1192** *n* MIL, NAUT amiral *m*; eet **~** US, **~ of the fleet** GB amiral.

(miralty /'ædmərəltɪ/ *n* **1** MIL (rank of admiral) niirauté *f*; **2** GB HIST ≈ ministère *m* de la Marine.

(miration /ˌædmə'reɪʃn/ *n* admiration *f* (**for** pour); **look at sb/sth with** ou **in ~** être en admiration vant qn/qch.

(mire /əd'maɪə(r)/ *vtr* admirer; **to be ~d by sb** re admiré de qn.

(mirer /əd'maɪərə(r)/ *n* **1** admirateur/-trice *m/f*; **2** ver) soupirant *m*.

(miring /əd'maɪərɪŋ/ *adj* admiratif/-ive.

(miringly /əd'maɪərɪŋlɪ/ *adv* [*look, say*] avec admiraon.

(missible /əd'mɪsəbl/ *adj* recevable.

(mission /əd'mɪʃn/ **I** *n* **1** (entry) entrée *f*, admission **to** dans); **'no ~'** 'entrée interdite'; **2** (fee) (droit *m* entrée); **3** (confession) aveu *m*.
admissions *npl* **1** UNIV inscriptions *fpl*; **2** MED Imissions *fpl*.

(mission: **~s office** *n* UNIV service *m* d'insiptions; **~s officer** **▶ 1251** *n* UNIV agent *m* argé des inscriptions.

(mit /əd'mɪt/ *vtr* (*p prés etc* **-tt-**) **1** (accept) reconnaîe, admettre [*mistake, fact*]; **to ~ that** reconnaître ie; **to ~ to** reconnaître [*error, mistake, fact*]; **it is nnoying, I (must** ou **have to) ~** c'est embêtant, je is l'avouer; **to ~ defeat** s'avouer vaincu; **2** (conss) avouer [*crime*]; reconnaître [*guilt*]; **3** laisser trer [*person*] (**into** dans); **'dogs not ~ted'** 'entrée terdite aux chiens'; **to be ~ted to hospital** être spitalisé; **4** [*club*] admettre [*person*] (**to** à).

(mittance /əd'mɪtns/ *n* accès *m*, entrée *f*; **'no ~'** cès interdit au public'.

admittedly /əd'mɪtɪdlɪ/ *adv* il est vrai, il faut en convenir.

admonish /əd'mɒnɪʃ/ *vtr* SOUT admonester FML.

admonition /ˌædmə'nɪʃn/ *n* SOUT (reprimand) admonition *f* FML; (warning) avertissement *m*.

ad nauseam /ˌæd 'nɔːzɪæm/ *adv* [*discuss, repeat*] à n'en plus finir.

ado /ə'duː/ *n* **without more** ou **further ~** sans plus de cérémonie *f*.
IDIOMS **much ~ about nothing** beaucoup de bruit pour rien.

adolescent /ˌædə'lesnt/ **I** *n* adolescent/-e *m/f*.
II *adj* **1** (teenage) [*crisis*] d'adolescent; [*problem*] des adolescents; [*years*] de l'adolescence; **2** PEJ puéril.

adopt /ə'dɒpt/ *vtr* adopter [*child, bill, attitude*]; prendre [*tone, identity*]; choisir [*candidate*].

adopted /ə'dɒptɪd/ *adj* [*child*] adopté; [*son, daughter*] adoptif/-ive.

adoption /ə'dɒpʃn/ **I** *n* (of child, bill, identity) adoption *f*.
II *noun modifier* [*papers, process*] d'adoption.

adoption agency *n*: service officiel chargé des questions d'adoption.

adorable /ə'dɔːrəbl/ *adj* adorable.

adoration /ˌædə'reɪʃn/ *n* adoration *f*.

adore /ə'dɔː(r)/ *vtr* adorer (**to do, doing** faire).

adoring /ə'dɔːrɪŋ/ *adj* [*husband*] épris; [*fan*] passionné.

adoringly /ə'dɔːrɪŋlɪ/ *adv* avec adoration.

adorn /ə'dɔːn/ LITTER *vtr* orner [*building, room, walls*] (**with** de); parer [*body, hair*] (**with** de).

adrenalin(e) /ə'drenəlɪn/ *n* adrénaline *f*.

Adriatic (sea) /ˌeɪdrɪ'ætɪk/ **▶ 1117** *pr n* **the ~** la mer *f* Adriatique, l'Adriatique *f*.

adrift /ə'drɪft/ *adj, adv* **1** [*person, boat*] à la dérive; **2 to go ~** [*plan*] aller à vau-l'eau; **3** (loose) **to come ~** se détacher (**of, from** de).

adroit /ə'drɔɪt/ *adj* habile (**in, at** à; **in** ou **at doing** à faire).

adroitly /ə'drɔɪtlɪ/ *adv* habilement.

adspeak /'ædspiːk/ *n* jargon *m* publicitaire.

adulation /ˌædjʊ'leɪʃn, US ˌædʒʊ-/ *n* SOUT adulation *f* (**of** de); **in ~** avec adulation.

adult /'ædʌlt, ə'dʌlt/ **I** *n* adulte *mf*; **'~s only'** 'interdit aux moins de 18 ans'.
II *adj* **1** adulte; [*life*] d'adulte; **2** EUPH [*film, magazine*] pour adultes.

Adult Education *n* GB enseignement *m* pour adultes.

adulterate /ə'dʌltəreɪt/ *vtr* frelater [*wine*].

adulterous /ə'dʌltərəs/ *adj* adultère.

adultery /ə'dʌltərɪ/ *n* adultère *m* (**with** avec).

adulthood /'ædʌlthʊd/ *n* âge *m* adulte.

adult literacy *n* GB **~ classes** cours *m* d'alphabétisation pour adultes.

advance /əd'vɑːns, US -'væns/ **I** *n* **1** (forward movement) avance *f*; FIG (of civilization, in science) progrès *m*; **2** (sum of money) avance *f*, acompte *m* (**on** sur); **3** (increase) **any ~ on £100?** (at auction etc) cent livres, qui dit mieux?
II advances *npl* (sexual) avances *fpl*; (other contexts) démarches *fpl*; **to make ~s to sb** (sexually) faire des avances à qn.
III in advance *adv phr* à l'avance; **a month in ~** un mois à l'avance; **here's £30 in ~** voici 30 livres d'avance or d'acompte.
IV in advance of *adv phr* avant [*person*].
V *vtr* faire avancer [*tape, clock*]; avancer [*sum of money, theory, troops*]; faire avancer [*career*]; servir [*cause, interests*].
VI *vi* **1** (move forward) [*person*] avancer, s'avancer (**on, towards** vers); MIL [*army*] avancer (**on** sur); **2** (progress) [*civilization, knowledge*] progresser, faire des progrès; **to ~ in one's career** progresser dans sa carrière.

advance: **~ booking** *n* réservation *f* (*faite à*

l'avance); **~ booking office** *n* service *m* des réservations.

advanced /əd'vɑːnst, US -'vænst/ *adj* [*course, class*] supérieur; [*student, stage*] avancé; [*level*] élevé; [*equipment, technology*] de pointe, perfectionné; [*research*] poussé.

advanced: **~ gas-cooled reactor, AGR** *n* réacteur *m* à gaz avancé *or* poussé, AGR *m*; **Advanced Level** *n* GB SCH = **A-level**.

advancement /əd'vɑːnsmənt, US -'væns-/ *n* (of cause, minority) promotion *f*; (of science, person) avancement *m*.

advance: **~ party** *n* MIL équipe *f* d'avant-garde; **~ payment** *n* COMM avance *f*; **~ warning** *n* préavis *m*.

advantage /əd'vɑːntɪdʒ, US -'vænt-/ *n* **1** avantage *m*; **there is an ~ in doing** il y a un avantage à faire; **there is no ~ in doing** il n'est pas intéressant de faire; **2** (asset) atout *m*; **their big ~ is to have...** leur grand atout, c'est d'avoir...; **'computing experience an ~'** (in job ad) 'une expérience en informatique serait un atout'; **3** (profit) **it is to his ~ to do** il est dans son intérêt de faire; **to turn a situation to one's ~** transformer une situation à son avantage; **4** (best effect) **to show sth to (best) ~** montrer qch sous un jour avantageux; **5 to take ~ of** utiliser, profiter de [*situation, offer*]; (unfairly) exploiter [*person*]; **6** (in tennis) avantage *m*; **7** SPORT **France's three-point ~** les trois points d'avance de la France.

advantageous /ˌædvən'teɪdʒəs/ *adj* avantageux/-euse; **it would be ~** ce serait une bonne chose.

advent /'ædvent/ *n* GEN apparition *f* (**of** de); **Advent** RELIG l'Avent *m*.

adventure /əd'ventʃə(r)/ **I** *n* aventure *f*.
II *noun modifier* [*story, film*] d'aventures.

adventure playground *n* GB aire *f* de jeux (aménagée).

adventurer /əd'ventʃərə(r)/ *n* **1** (daring person) aventurier/-ière *m/f*; **2** PÉJ (schemer) aventurier *m*.

adventuress /əd'ventʃərɪs/ *n* (*pl* **~es**) aventurière *f*.

adventurous /əd'ventʃərəs/ *adj* [*person, life*] aventureux/-euse; **she doesn't have very ~ tastes** elle est très traditionnelle dans ses goûts.

adverb /'ædvɜːb/ *n* adverbe *m*.

adversary /'ædvəsərɪ, US -serɪ/ *n* adversaire *mf*.

adverse /'ædvɜːs/ *adj* [*reaction, conditions, publicity*] défavorable; [*effect, consequences*] négatif/-ive.

adversity /əd'vɜːsətɪ/ *n* adversité *f*.

advert○ /'ædvɜːt/ *n* GB (in newspaper) annonce *f*; (in small ads) petite annonce *f*; (on TV) pub○ *f*, spot *m* publicitaire.

advertise /'ædvətaɪz/ **I** *vtr* **1** (for publicity) faire de la publicité pour [*product, service*]; annoncer [*price, rate*]; **2** (for sale) mettre *or* passer une annonce pour [*car, house*]; **3** mettre *or* passer une annonce pour [*job, vacancy*]; **4** (make known) signaler [*presence*]; afficher [*weakness*]; **I wouldn't ~ the fact** à votre place, je n'en ferais pas état.
II *vi* **1** (for sales, publicity) faire de la publicité; **2** (for staff) passer une annonce.

advertisement /əd'vɜːtɪsmənt, US ˌædvər'taɪzmənt/ *n* **1** (for product, event) publicité *f* (**for** pour); **a good/bad ~ for** FIG une bonne/mauvaise publicité pour; **2** (to sell house, get job etc) annonce *f*; (in small ads) petite annonce *f*.

advertiser /'ædvətaɪzə(r)/ *n* (paying for ad) annonceur *m*.

advertising /'ædvətaɪzɪŋ/ *n* (activity, advertisements) publicité *f*.

advertising: **~ agency** *n* agence *f* de publicité; **~ agent** ▶1251 *n* publicitaire *mf*; **~ campaign** *n* campagne *f* publicitaire; **~ executive** ▶1251 *n* cadre *m* publicitaire; **~ industry** *n* publicité *f*; **~ man** ▶1251 *n* publicitaire *m*; **Advertising Standards Authority, ASA** *n* GB ADMIN, COMM bureau *m* de vérification de la publicité.

advice /əd'vaɪs/ *n* **1** ¢ (informal) conseils *mpl* (**on** sur; **about** à propos de); **my ~ is to wait** je vous

conseille d'attendre; **a word** *ou* **piece of ~** conseil; **to do sth on sb's ~** faire qch sur recommandation de qn; **it was good ~** c'était bon conseil; **if you want my ~** (opinion) si tu ve mon avis; **2** ¢ (professional) **to seek legal/medical** consulter un avocat/un médecin; **get expert** consultez un spécialiste; **3** COMM avis *m*; **~ of del ery** avis de réception.

advisability /əd,vaɪzə'bɪlətɪ/ *n* opportunité *f* doing de faire).

advisable /əd'vaɪzbl/ *adj* **it is ~ to do** (speaking o cially) il est recommandé de faire.

advise /əd'vaɪz/ **I** *vtr* **1** (give advice to) conseille donner des conseils à (**about** sur); (give information renseigner (**about** sur); **to ~ sb against doing** déconseiller à qn de faire qch; **to ~ sb of** avertir contre [*risk, danger*]; **you are ~d to...** il recommandé de...; **ill-~d** [*course of action*] malavi **2** (recommend) recommander [*rest, course of action*] SOUT (inform) aviser (**of** de).
II *vi* **to ~ on sth** (give advice) donner des conseils s qch; (inform) donner des renseignements sur qch.

advisedly /əd'vaɪzɪdlɪ/ *adv* [*say*] en tou connaissance de cause.

adviser, advisor /əd'vaɪzə(r)/ *n* (in official capac conseiller/-ère *m/f* (**to** auprès de); (unofficially) collabo teur/-trice *m/f*.

advisory /əd'vaɪzərɪ/ *adj* consultatif/-ive; **in an capacity** à titre consultatif.

advisory: **~ committee, ~ group** *n* comité consultatif; **~ service** *n* service *m* d'aide et conseil.

advocacy /'ædvəkəsɪ/ *n* plaidoyer *m* (**of** en faveur d

advocate I /'ædvəkət/ *n* **1** ▶1251 JUR avocat/-e *n* **2** (supporter) partisan *m*.
II /'ædvə,keɪt/ *vtr* recommander (**doing** de faire).

Aegean /iː'dʒiːən/ ▶1117 *pr n* **the ~** la mer Égée.

aegis /'iːdʒɪs/ *n* **under the ~ of** sous l'égide de.

aeon, eon US /'iːən/ *n* **~s ago**○ FIG il y a u éternité.

aerate /'eəreɪt/ *vtr* aérer [*soil*].

aerial /'eərɪəl/ *n* **~ camera** *n* appareil *m* de photo pour pri de vues aériennes; **~ warfare** *n* guerre *f* aérienne.

aerie /'eərɪ/ US = **eyrie**.

aerobatics /ˌeərə'bætɪks/ *n* (manoeuvres) (+ *v pl*) baties *fpl* aériennes.

aerobics /eə'rəʊbɪks/ ▶949 **I** *n* (+ *v sg*) aérobic *m*.
II *noun modifier* [*class, routine*] d'aérobic.

aerodynamics /ˌeərəʊdaɪ'næmɪks/ *n* **1** (science) (-*sg*) aérodynamique *f*; **2** (styling) (+ *v sg*) aérody misme *m*.

aerogram(me) /'eərəgræm/ *n* aérogramme *m*.

aeronautic(al) /ˌeərə'nɔːtɪk(l)/ *adj* [*skill*] aéron tique; [*magazine, college*] d'aéronautique.

aeronautic: **~(al) engineer** ▶1251 *n* ingénie *m* en aéronautique; **~(al) engineering** *n* aéron tique *f*.

aeronautics /ˌeərə'nɔːtɪks/ *n* (+ *v sg*) aéronautique

aeroplane /'eərəpleɪn/ *n* GB avion *m*.

aerosol /'eərəsɒl, US -sɔːl/ *n* **1** (spray can) bombe *f* aé sol; **2** (system) aérosol *m*.

aerospace /'eərəʊspeɪs/ **I** *n* (industry) industrie aérospatiale.
II *noun modifier* [*engineer, company*] de l'aérospatia

aesthete /'iːsθiːt/, **esthete** /'esθiːt/ US *n* esthète *mf*

aesthetic, esthetic US /iːs'θetɪk/ *adj* **1** [*ser appeal*] esthétique; **2** [*design*] harmonieux/-ieuse.

aesthetically /iːs'θetɪklɪ/, **esthetically** /es'θetɪ US *adv* [*satisfying*] esthétiquement; [*restore*] avec goû

aestheticism /iːs'θetɪsɪzəm/, **estheticis** /es'θetɪsɪzəm/ US *n* (doctrine, quality) esthétisme *m*; (ta sens *m* du beau.

aesthetics /iːs'θetɪks/, **esthetics** /es'θetɪks/ US *n* (concept) (+ *v sg*) esthétique *f*; **2** (aspects of appearan (+ *v pl*) esthétique *f*.

far /əˈfɑː(r)/ *adv* LITTÉR au loin, à distance; **from ~** de loin.

ffability /ˌæfəˈbɪlətɪ/ *n* affabilité *f*.

ffable /ˈæfəbl/ *adj* affable.

ffair /əˈfeə(r)/ **I** *n* **1** (event, incident, thing) affaire *f*; **the Haltrey ~** l'affaire Haltrey; **2** (matter) affaire *f*; **at first the conflict seemed a small ~** au début, le conflit ne paraissait pas grave; **state of ~s** situation *f*; **3** (relationship) liaison *f* (**with** avec); (casual) aventure *f*; **4** (concern) affaire *f*; **it's my ~** c'est mon affaire.
II affairs *npl* **1** POL, JOURN affaires *fpl*; **foreign ~s** affaires étrangères; **~s of state** affaires d'état; **consumer ~s** la protection du consommateur; **2** (business) affaires *fpl*.

ffect /əˈfekt/ *vtr* **1** (have effect on) avoir une incidence sur [*price, salary*]; affecter, avoir des conséquences pour [*career, future, environment*]; affecter, toucher [*region, population*]; (influence) influer sur [*decision, outcome*]; **politics ~s all of us** la politique nous concerne tous; **countries ~ed by the famine** les pays touchés par la famine; **2** (emotionally) GEN émouvoir; [*news, discovery*] affecter; **3** MED atteindre [*person*]; affecter [*health, heart, lungs*]; **4** SOUT (feign) feindre [*surprise, ignorance*]; prendre [*accent*].

ffected /əˈfektɪd/ *adj* **1** (influenced) (by event, decision) (adversely) touché (**by** par); (concerned) concerné (**by** par); **2** (emotionally) ému (**by** par); (adversely) affecté (**by** par); **3** MED [*part*] infecté (**by** par); **4** PÉJ (mannered) affecté; **5** PÉJ (feigned) affecté.

ffection /əˈfekʃn/ *n* affection *f* (**for sb** pour qn).

ffectionate /əˈfekʃənət/ *adj* [*child, animal*] affectueux/-euse; [*memory*] tendre; [*picture, account*] plein d'affection.

ffectionately /əˈfekʃənətlɪ/ *adv* affectueusement.

ffidavit /ˌæfɪˈdeɪvɪt/ *n* déclaration *f* écrite sous serment.

ffiliate /əˈfɪlɪeɪt/ **I** *vtr* affilier (**to, with** à); **~d member** adhérent/-e *m/f*.
II *vi* (combine) s'affilier (**with** à).

ffiliation /əˌfɪlɪˈeɪʃn/ *n* (process, state) affiliation *f*; (link) attaches *fpl*.

ffinity /əˈfɪnətɪ/ *n* **1** (attraction) attirance *f* (**with, for** pour); **2** (resemblance) ressemblance *f*; **3** (relationship) rapport *m* (**between** entre).

ffirm /əˈfɜːm/ *vtr* **1** (state positively) affirmer; **2** (confirm) confirmer [*support, popularity*].

ffirmative /əˈfɜːmətɪv/ **I** *n* affirmatif *m*; **in the ~** par l'affirmative.
II *adj* [*reply, nod, statement*] affirmatif/-ive.

ffix /ˈæfɪks/ *n* LING affixe *m*.
II /əˈfɪks/ *vtr* SOUT coller [*stamp*]; apposer [*signature*].

fflict /əˈflɪkt/ *vtr* [*poverty, disease*] frapper; [*grief*] accabler; [*illness*] toucher; **to be ~ed by** souffrir de [*illness*]; être affligé de [*stammer*].

ffliction /əˈflɪkʃn/ *n* (illness) affection *f*; (suffering) malheur *m*.

ffluence /ˈæfluəns/ *n* **1** (wealthiness) richesse *f*; **2** (afflux) affluence *f*.

ffluent /ˈæfluənt/ *adj* [*person, area, society*] riche.

fford /əˈfɔːd/ *vtr* **1** (have money for) **to be able to ~ sth** avoir les moyens d'acheter qch; **if I can ~ it** si j'ai les moyens; **to be able to ~ to do sth** (as necessary expense) être en mesure de faire qch; (as chosen expense) pouvoir se permettre de faire qch; **how can he ~ to buy such expensive clothes?** comment est-ce qu'il fait pour acheter des vêtements aussi chers?; **2** (spare) **to be able to ~** disposer de [*space, time*]; **3** (risk) **to be able to ~ sth/to do** se permettre qch; **he can ill ~ to wait** il ne peut guère se permettre d'attendre; **4** SOUT **to ~ sb sth** offrir qch à qn [*protection*]; fournir qch à qn [*opportunity*]; procurer qch à qn [*satisfaction*].

ffordable /əˈfɔːdəbl/ *adj* [*price*] abordable.

ffranchise /əˈfræntʃaɪz/ *vtr* affranchir.

ffront /əˈfrʌnt/ *n* offense *f*.

ffronted /əˈfrʌntɪd/ *adj* blessé.

fghan /ˈæfgæn/ **▶1100**, **1038** **I** *n* **1** (also **Afghani**) (person) Afghan/-e *m/f*; **2** (also **Afghani**) (language) pachtou *m*; **3** (coat) afghan *m*.
II *adj* (also **Afghani**) afghan.

Afghan hound *n* lévrier *m* afghan.

Afghanistan /æfˈgænɪstɑːn, -stæn/ **▶840** *pr n* Afghanistan *m*.

aficionado /əˌfɪsjəˈnɑːdəʊ, əˌfɪʃj-/ *n* (*pl* **~s**) passionné/-e *m/f*.

afield /əˈfiːld/: **far afield** *adv phr* loin; **further ~** plus loin; **from as far ~ as** d'aussi loin que.

afire /əˈfaɪə(r)/ *adj, adv* LITTÉR en feu; **to be ~ with enthusiasm** déborder d'enthousiasme.

aflame /əˈfleɪm/ *adj, adv* LITTÉR **to be ~** [*cheek*] être en feu; [*sky*] être embrasé; **to be ~ with desire** brûler de désir.

afloat /əˈfləʊt/ *adj, adv* **1** (in water) **to stay ~** [*person, object*] rester à la surface (de l'eau); [*boat*] rester à flot; FIG (financially) se maintenir à flot; **2** (at sea, on the water) sur l'eau; **a week ~** une semaine sur l'eau.

afoot /əˈfʊt/ *adj* (*après n*) **there is something ~** il se prépare quelque chose; **there are changes ~** il y a des changements dans l'air.

afraid /əˈfreɪd/ *adj* **1** (frightened) **don't be ~** n'aie pas peur; **to be ~** avoir peur (**of** de; **to do, of doing** de faire); **2** (anxious) **to be ~** craindre; **she was ~ (that) there would be an accident** elle craignait un accident; **I'm ~ it might rain** je crains qu'il (ne) pleuve; **3** (in expressions of regret) **I'm ~ I can't come** je suis désolé mais je ne peux pas venir; **'did they win?'—'I'm ~ not'** 'ont-ils gagné?'—'hélas, non'; **4** (as polite formula) **I'm ~ the house is a mess** excusez le désordre dans la maison.

afresh /əˈfreʃ/ *adv* à nouveau; **to start ~** recommencer; (in life) repartir à zéro.

Africa /ˈæfrɪkə/ *pr n* Afrique *f*; **to ~** en Afrique.

African /ˈæfrɪkən/ **I** *n* Africain/-e *m/f*.
II *adj* africain; [*elephant*] d'Afrique.

Afrikaans /ˌæfrɪˈkɑːns/ **▶1038** *n* afrikaans *m*.

Afrikaner /ˌæfrɪˈkɑːnə(r)/ **▶1100** *n* Afrikaner *mf*.

Afro-American /ˌæfrəʊəˈmerɪkən/ **I** *n* Afro-américain/-e *m/f*.
II *adj* afro-américain.

Afro-Caribbean /ˌæfrəʊˌkærɪˈbiːən/ *adj* antillais.

aft /ɑːft, US æft/ *adv* NAUT, AVIAT à l'arrière.

after /ˈɑːftə(r), US ˈæftər/

■ **Note** As both adverb and preposition, *after* is translated in most contexts by *après*: *after the meal* = après le repas; *H comes after G* = H vient après G; *day after day* = jour après jour; *just after 3 pm* = juste après 15 heures; *three weeks after* = trois semaines après.
– When *after* is used as a conjunction it is translated by *après avoir (or être) + past participle* where the two verbs have the same subject: *after I finished my book, I cooked dinner* = après avoir fini mon livre j'ai préparé le dîner; *after he had consulted Bill or after consulting Bill, he decided to accept the offer* = après avoir consulté Bill, il a décidé d'accepter l'offre.
– When the two verbs have different subjects the translation is *après que + indicative*: *I'll lend you the book after Fred has read it* = je te prêterai le livre après que Fred l'aura lu.
– For more examples and particular usages see the entry below.
– See also the usage note on time units **▶1336**.

I *adv* **1** (following time or event) après; **soon ou not long ~** peu après; **straight ~** GB, **right ~** US tout de suite après; **2** (following specific time) **the year ~** l'année suivante or d'après; **the day ~** le lendemain.
II *prep* **1** (later in time than) après; **immediately/shortly ~ the strike** aussitôt/peu après la grève; **~ that date** (in future) au-delà de cette date; (in past) après cette date; **it was ~ six o'clock** il était plus de six heures; **~ that** (cela); **the day ~ tomorrow** après-demain; **2** (given) après; **~ all we did!** après tout ce que nous avons fait!; **~ what she's been through?** malgré or après ce qu'elle a subi?; **3** (expressing contrast) après; **it's boring here ~ Paris** après

Paris, on s'ennuie ici; **4** (behind) **to chase ~ sb/sth** courir après qn/qch; **to tidy up ~ sb** ranger derrière qn; **5** (following in sequence, rank) après; **the adjective comes ~ the noun** l'adjectif vient après le nom; **~ you!** (letting someone pass ahead) après vous!; **6** (in the direction of) **to stare ~ sb** regarder qn s'éloigner; **'don't forget!'** **Mimi called ~ her** 'n'oublie pas!' lui a crié Mimi; **7** (in pursuit of) **that's the house they're ~** c'est la maison qu'ils veulent acheter; **the police are ~ him** il est recherché par la police; **he'll come ~ me** il va essayer de me retrouver; **it's me he's ~** (to settle score) c'est à moi qu'il en veut; **to be ~ sb○** (sexually) s'intéresser à qn; **8** (beyond) après; **9** (stressing continuity) **generation ~ generation** génération après génération; **year ~ year** tous les ans; **it was one disaster ~ another** on a eu catastrophe sur catastrophe; **10** (about) **to ask ~ sb** demander des nouvelles de qn; **11** (in honour or memory of) **named ~** [*street, institution*] portant le nom de; **we called her Kate ~ my mother** nous l'avons appelée Kate comme ma mère; **12** (in the manner of) **'~ Millet'** 'd'après Millet'; **13** US (past) **it's twenty ~ eleven** il est onze heures vingt.

III *conj* **1** (in sequence of events) après avoir or être (+ *pp*), après que (+ *indic*); **~ we had left we realized that** après être partis nous nous sommes rendu compte que; **2** (once) **~ you explained the situation they left** une fois que tu leur as expliqué la situation ils sont partis; **3** (in spite of the fact that) **why did he do that ~ we'd warned him?** pourquoi a-t-il fait ça alors que nous l'avions prévenu?

IV afters○ *npl* GB dessert *m*

V after all *adv, prep* après tout.

after: **~birth** *n* placenta *m*; **~care** *n* MED suivi *m* médical; **~-dinner speaker** *n* orateur/-trice *m/f* invité/-e; **~-effect** *n* MED contrecoup *m*; FIG répercussion *f*; **~life** *n* vie *f* après la mort.

aftermath /ˈɑːftəmæθ, -mɑːθ, US ˈæf-/ *n* **₵** conséquences *fpl* (of de); **in the ~ of** à la suite de [*war, scandal, election*].

afternoon /ˌɑːftəˈnuːn, US ˌæf-/ ▶812 **I** *n* après-midi *m* or *f inv*; **in the ~** (dans) l'après-midi; **at 2.30 in the ~** à 2 h 30 de l'après-midi; **in the early/late ~** en début/en fin d'après-midi; **earlier this ~** plus tôt dans l'après-midi; **the next ~** le lendemain après-midi; **the previous ~** l'après-midi d'avant.

II○ *excl* (also **good ~**) bonjour!

afternoon tea *n* thé *m* (de cinq heures).

after: **~pains** *npl* tranchées *fpl* utérines; **~-shave** *n* après-rasage *m*; **~shock** *n* secousse *f* secondaire; FIG retombées *fpl*; **~taste** *n* LIT, FIG arrière-goût *m*; **~-tax** *adj* [*profits, earnings*] après impôts.

afterthought /ˈɑːftəθɔːt, US ˈæf-/ *n* pensée *f* après coup; **as an ~** après coup, en y repensant.

afterwards /ˈɑːftəwədz, US ˈæf-/ GB, **afterward** /ˈɑːftəwəd, US ˈæf-/ US *adv* **1** (after) GEN après; (in sequence of events) ensuite; **not long ~** peu après; **directly/straight ~** aussitôt/tout de suite après; **2** (later) plus tard; **it was only ~ that** ce n'est que plus tard que; **3** (subsequently) [*regret etc*] par la suite.

again /əˈgeɪn, əˈgen/

■ **Note** When used with a verb, *again* is often translated by adding the prefix *re* to the verb in French: *to start again* = recommencer; *to marry again* = se remarier; *I'd like to read that book again* = j'aimerais relire ce livre; *she never saw them again* = elle ne les a jamais revus. You can check *re*+ verbs by consulting the French side of the dictionary.

– For other uses of *again* and for idiomatic expressions, see below.

adv encore; **sing it (once) ~!** chante-le encore (une fois)!; **yet ~ he refused** il a encore refusé; **when you are well ~** quand tu seras rétabli; **I'll never go there ~** je n'y retournerai jamais; **never ~!** jamais plus!; **not ~!** encore!; **~ and ~** à plusieurs reprises; **time and (time) ~** maintes fois; **~, you may think that** et là encore, vous pourriez penser

que; **(and) then ~, he may not** mais il se peut auss[i] qu'il ne le fasse pas.

against /əˈgeɪnst, əˈgenst/ *prep*

■ **Note** *against* is translated by *contre* when it mean[s] *physically touching* or *in opposition to*: *against the wa[ll]* = contre le mur; *he's against independence* = il e[st] contre l'indépendance; *the fight against inflation* = la lut[te] contre l'inflation.

– If you have any doubts about how to translate a fixe[d] phrase or expression beginning with *against* (*against th[e] tide, against the clock, against the grain, against the odd[s] etc*) you should consult the appropriate noun entry (*tid[e,] grain, odds* etc).

– *against* often appears in English with certain verbs (*tu[rn] against, compete against, discriminate against, stando[ff] against etc*). For translations you should consult the appr[o]priate verb entry (**turn, compete, discriminate, stan[d]** etc).

– *against* often appears in English after certain nouns a[nd] adjectives (*protection against, a law against, effectiv[e] against etc*). For translations consult the appropriate nou[n] or adjective entry (**protection, law, effective** etc). F[or] particular usages see below.

1 (physically) contre; **~ the wall** contre le mur; **2** (objecting to) **I'm ~ it** je suis contre; **20 votes ~ 2[0]** votes contre; **to be ~ the idea** s'opposer à l'idée; **to be ~ doing** être contre l'idée de faire; **3** (counter t[o]) **to go** ou **be ~** aller à l'encontre de [*tradition, policy,* *conditions, decision*] ne pas être favorable à [*person*] **4** (in opposition to) contre; **the fight ~ inflation [la]** lutte contre l'inflation; **5** (compared to) **the pound fe[ll]** **~ the dollar** la livre a baissé par rapport au dolla[r]; **the graph shows age ~ earnings** le graphiq[ue] représente la courbe des salaires en fonction de l'âg[e]; **6** (in contrast to) sur; **the blue looks pretty ~ th[e]** **yellow** le bleu est joli sur le jaune; **~ a backgroun[d]** **of** sur un fond de; **~ the light** à contre-jour; **7** (exchange for) contre, en échange de.

age /eɪdʒ/ ▶713 **I** *n* **1** (length of existence) âge *m* she's your ~ elle a ton âge; **to look one's ~** fai[re] son âge; **to be of school ~** être en âge d'aller [à] l'école; **she's twice his ~** elle a le double de son âge; **they are of an ~** ils sont du même âge; **act** ou **b[e]** **your ~!** ne fais pas l'enfant!; **men of retirement** les hommes en âge de la retraite; **to come of** **~** atteindre la majorité; **to be under ~** JUR être mineur/-e; **~ of consent** JUR âge légal (**for** pour); **[to]** **feel one's ~** se sentir vieux/vieille; **2** (latter part [of] life) **with ~** avec l'âge; **3** (era) ère *f*, époque *f* (**of** de[); **the video ~** l'ère de la vidéo; **in this day and ~** notre époque; **4○** (long time) **it's ~s since I've playe[d]** golf ça fait une éternité que je n'ai pas joué au golf; **for ~s** (long time) depuis une éternité; (for hour[s]) depuis des heures; **it takes ~s** cela prend un temp[s] fou

II *vtr* [*hairstyle, experiences etc*] vieillir [*person*].

III *vi* [*person*] vieillir; **to ~ well** bien vieillir.

age bracket, age group *n* = **age range**.

aged *adj* **1** /eɪdʒd/ (of an age) **~ between 20 and 2[5]** âgé/-e de 20 à 25 ans; **a boy ~ 12** un garçon de [12] ans; **2** /ˈeɪdʒɪd/ (old) [*person*] âgé.

ageing /ˈeɪdʒɪŋ/ **I** *n* vieillissement *m*.

II *adj* [*person, population*] vieillissant.

ageism /ˈeɪdʒɪzəm/ *n* discrimination *f* en raison [de] l'âge.

ageless /ˈeɪdʒlɪs/ *adj* **1** (of indeterminate age) sans âge; **2** (timeless) éternel/-le.

agency /ˈeɪdʒənsɪ/ *n* **1** (organization, office) agence [*f*] **through an ~** par une agence; **aid ~** organisme d'entraide; **2** GB COMM (representing firm) concessio[n]naire *m*; **3** (influence) intermédiaire *m*; **through a[n]** **outside ~** par l'intermédiaire d'un tiers.

agency: **~ fee** *n* commission *f* de gestion; **~ nurse** *n* infirmier/-ière *m/f* intérimaire.

agenda /əˈdʒendə/ *n* **1** ADMIN ordre *m* du jour; **o[n]** **the ~** à l'ordre du jour; **2** FIG (list of prioritie[s]) programme *m*; **hidden ~** programme secret; **high o[n]** **the political ~** prioritaire dans le monde politique.

Age

Note that where English says to be X years old French says avoir X ans (to have X years).

How old?

how old are you?	= quel âge as-tu?
what age is she?	= quel âge a-t-elle?

The word ans (years) is never dropped:

he is forty years old or he is forty or he is forty years of age	= il a quarante ans
she's eighty	= elle a quatre-vingts ans
the house is a hundred years old	= la maison a cent ans
a man of fifty	= un homme de cinquante ans
a child of eight and a half	= un enfant de huit ans et demi
I feel sixteen	= j'ai l'impression d'avoir seize ans
he looks sixteen	= on lui donnerait seize ans

Note the use of de after âgé and à l'âge:

a woman aged thirty	= une femme âgée de trente ans
at the age of forty	= à l'âge de quarante ans
Mrs Smith, aged forty or Mrs Smith (40)	= Mme Smith, âgée de quarante ans

Do not confuse que and de used with plus and moins:

I'm older than you	= je suis plus âgé que toi
she's younger than him	= elle est plus jeune que lui
Anne's two years younger	= Anne a deux ans de moins
Margot's older than Suzanne by five years	= Margot a cinq ans de plus que Suzanne
Robert's younger than Thomas by six years	= Robert a six ans de moins que Thomas

X-year-old

a forty-year-old	= quelqu'un de quarante ans
a sixty-year-old woman	= une femme de soixante ans
an eighty-year-old pensioner	= un retraité de quatre-vingts ans
they've got an eight-year-old and a five-year-old	= ils ont un enfant de huit ans et un autre de cinq ans

Approximate ages

Note the various ways of saying these in French:

he is about fifty	= il a environ cinquante ans or il a une cinquantaine d'années or (less formally) il a dans les cinquante ans

(Other round numbers in -aine used to express age are dizaine (10), vingtaine (20), trentaine (30), quarantaine (40), soixantaine (60) and centaine (100).)

she's just over sixty	= elle vient d'avoir soixante ans
she's just under seventy	= elle aura bientôt soixante-dix ans
she's in her sixties	= elle a entre soixante et soixante-dix ans
she's in her early sixties	= elle a entre soixante et soixante-cinq ans
she's in her late sixties	= elle va avoir soixante-dix ans or (less formally) elle va sur ses soixante-dix ans
she must be seventy	= elle doit avoir soixante-dix ans
he's in his mid-forties	= il a environ quarante-cinq ans or (less formally) il a dans les quarante-cinq ans
he's just ten	= il a tout juste dix ans
he's barely twelve	= il a à peine douze ans
games for the under twelves	= jeux pour les moins de douze ans
only for the over eighties	= seulement pour les plus de quatre-vingts ans

---

agent /'eɪdʒənt/ n **1** agent m (**for sb** de qn); **area/sole ~** agent régional/exclusif; **to go through an ~** passer par un intermédiaire; **to act as sb's ~** représenter qn; **2** POL (spy) agent m; **3** (cause, means) ALSO CHEM agent m; **cleaning ~** agent nettoyant.
IDIOMS **to be a free ~** être indépendant.

age-old adj ancestral, très vieux/vieille.

age range n tranche f d'âge.

aggravate /'ægrəveɪt/ **I** vtr (make worse) aggraver; (annoy) exaspérer.
II aggravated pp adj JUR [burglary, offence] qualifié, aggravé.

aggravating /'ægrəveɪtɪŋ/ adj **1** JUR (worsening) aggravant; **2**° (irritating) exaspérant.

aggravation /ˌægrə'veɪʃn/ n **1** ¢ (annoyance) ennuis mpl; **2** (irritation) contrariété f; **3** (worsening) aggravation f.

aggregate I /'ægrɪgət/ n **1** GEN, ECON ensemble m, total m; **in ~** dans l'ensemble; **2** SPORT score m total; **on ~** GB au total.
II /'ægrɪgət/ adj GEN, SPORT total; [data] d'ensemble.
III /'ægrɪgeɪt/ vtr rassembler [points]; regrouper [data].

aggression /ə'greʃn/ n GEN agression f; (of person) agressivité f.

aggressive /ə'gresɪv/ adj agressif/-ive.

aggressor /ə'gresə(r)/ n agresseur m.

aggrieved /ə'griːvd/ adj **1** JUR lésé; **2** (resentful) mécontent (**at** de).

aggro° /'ægrəʊ/ n GB **1** (violence) violence f; **2** (hostility) hostilité f.

aghast /ə'gɑːst, US ə'gæst/ adj horrifié (**at** par).

agile /'ædʒaɪl, US 'ædʒl/ adj agile.

agility /ə'dʒɪlətɪ/ n (physical, mental) agilité f.

agitate /'ædʒɪteɪt/ **I** vtr agiter [liquid]; troubler [person].
II vi (campaign) faire campagne (**for** pour).

agitated /'ædʒɪteɪtɪd/ adj agité, inquiet.

agitation /ˌædʒɪ'teɪʃn/ n **1** (emotional) agitation f; **2** POL (unrest) troubles mpl, agitation f; (campaigning) campagne f (**for** pour; **against** contre).

agitator /'ædʒɪteɪtə(r)/ n (person) agitateur/-trice m/f.

AGM n: abrév ▶ **Annual General Meeting**.

agnostic /æg'nɒstɪk/ n, adj agnostique (mf).

ago /ə'gəʊ/ adv **three weeks ~** il y a trois semaines; **some time/long ~** il y a quelque temps/longtemps; **how long ~?** il y a combien de temps?; **not long ~** il y a peu de temps; **as long ~ as 1986** dès 1986, déjà en 1986; **they got married forty years ~ today** cela fait quarante ans aujourd'hui qu'ils sont mariés.

agog /ə'gɒg/ adj **1** (excited) en émoi (**at** à cause de); **2** (eager) impatient (**to do** de faire).

agonize /'ægənaɪz/ vi se tourmenter (**over, about** à propos de).

agonized /'ægənaɪzd/ adj [cry] déchirant; [expression] angoissé.

agonizing /'ægənaɪzɪŋ/ adj [pain] atroce; [decision] déchirant.

agony /'ægənɪ/ n **1** (physical) douleur f atroce; **2** (mental) angoisse f; **it was ~!** HUM c'était l'horreur!

agony aunt n GB journaliste mf responsable du courrier du cœur.

agoraphobia /ˌægərə'fəʊbɪə/ n agoraphobie f.

agoraphobic /ˌægərə'fəʊbɪk/ adj agoraphobique.

agree /ə'griː/ **I** vtr (prét, pp **agreed**) **1** (concur) être d'accord (**that** sur le fait que); **2** (admit) convenir (**that** que); **I ~ it sounds unlikely** ça a l'air peu probable, j'en conviens; **it's dangerous, don't you ~?** c'est dangereux, ne crois pas?; **3** (consent) **to ~ to do** accepter de faire; **4** (settle on, arrange) se mettre d'accord sur [date, price, candidate, solution]; **to ~ to do** convenir de faire.
II vi (prét, pp **agreed**) **1** (hold same opinion) être d'accord (**with** avec; **about, on** sur; **about doing** pour faire); **'I ~!'** 'je suis bien d'accord!'; **I couldn't**

~ more! je suis entièrement d'accord!; **2** (reach mutual understanding) se mettre d'accord, tomber d'accord (**about, on** sur); **3** (consent) accepter; **to ~ to** consentir à [*plan, suggestion, terms*]; **they won't ~ to her going alone** ils ne consentiront pas à ce qu'elle y aille toute seule; **4** (hold with, approve) **to ~ with** approuver [*belief, idea, practice*]; **5** (tally) [*stories, statements, figures*] concorder (**with** avec); **6** (suit) **to ~ with sb** [*climate, weather*] être bon pour qn; [*food*] réussir à qn; **7** LING s'accorder (**with** avec; **in** en).
III agreed *pp adj* [*date, time, venue, amount, budget, rate, terms, signal*] convenu; **as ~d** comme convenu; **to be ~d on** être d'accord sur [*decision, statement, policy*]; **is that ~d?** c'est bien entendu?

agreeable /ə'griːəbl/ *adj* **1** (pleasant) [*experience, surroundings, person*] agréable; **2** SOUT (willing) **to be ~ to sth/to doing** être d'accord pour qch/pour faire.

agreeably /ə'griːəblɪ/ *adv* (pleasantly) agréablement; (amicably) aimablement.

agreement /ə'griːmənt/ *n* **1** GEN, POL, COMM accord *m* (**to do** pour faire); **to come to** ou **reach an ~** parvenir à un accord; **under an ~** en vertu d'un accord; **2** (undertaking) engagement *m* (**to do** à faire); **after an ~ by the union to end the strike** après que le syndicat s'est engagé à cesser la grève; **3** (mutual understanding) accord *m* (**about, on** sur); **to be in ~ with sb** être d'accord avec qn; **by ~ with sb** en accord avec qn; **to reach ~** se mettre d'accord; **to nod in ~** acquiescer d'un signe de tête; **4** JUR (contract) contrat *m*; **5** (consent) ~ **to** acceptation *f* de [*reform, cease-fire*]; **6** LING accord *m*.

agricultural /ˌægrɪ'kʌltʃərəl/ *adj* [*land, worker*] agricole; [*expert*] agronome; [*college*] d'agriculture.

agriculturalist /ˌægrɪ'kʌltʃərəlɪst/, **agriculturist** /ˌægrɪ'kʌltʃərɪst/ US ▶ **1251** | *n* agronome *mf*.

agricultural show *n* (rural) ~ comices *mpl* agricoles; (trade fair) foire *f* agricole.

agriculture /'ægrɪkʌltʃə(r)/ *n* agriculture *f*.

agrochemical /ˌægrəʊ'kemɪkəl/ **I** *n* substance *f* agrochimique.
II agrochemicals *npl* (+ *v sg*) (industry) agrochimie *f*.
III *adj* agrochimique.

agronomist /ə'grɒnəmɪst/ ▶ **1251** | *n* agronome *mf*.

aground /ə'graʊnd/ *adv* **to run ~** s'échouer.

ah /ɑː/ *excl* ah!; **~ well!** (resignedly) eh bien voilà!

ahead /ə'hed/

■ **Note** *ahead* is often used after verbs in English (*go ahead, plan ahead, think ahead* etc). For translations consult the appropriate verb entry (**go**, **plan**, **think** etc). For all other uses see the entry below.

I *adv* **1** (spatially) [*go on, run*] en avant; **to send sb on ~** envoyer qn en éclaireur; **to send one's luggage on ~** faire envoyer ses bagages; **a few kilometres ~** à quelques kilomètres; **2** (in time) in the months **~** pendant les mois à venir; **at least a year ~** [*apply*] au moins un an à l'avance; **who knows what lies ~?** qui sait ce que l'avenir nous réserve?; **3** FIG (in leading position) **to be ~ in the polls** être en tête dans les sondages; **to be 30 points ~** avoir 30 points d'avance; **to be 3% ~** avoir une avance de 3%; **4** FIG (more advanced) **to be ~ in** [*pupil, set*] être plus avancé en [*school subject*].
II ahead of *prep phr* **1** (in front of) devant [*person, vehicle*]; **to be three metres/seconds ~ of sb** avoir trois mètres/secondes d'avance sur qn; **~ of time** en avance; **to be ~ of one's time** être en avance sur son temps; **to arrive ~ of sb** arriver avant qn; **2** (leading) **to be ~ of sb** (in polls, ratings) avoir un avantage sur qn; **3** FIG (more advanced) **to be (way) ~ of the others** [*pupil*] être (bien) plus avancé que les autres; **to be ~ of the field** [*business*] devancer les autres.

AI *n* (*abrév* = **artificial intelligence**) IA *f*.

aid /eɪd/ **I** *n* **1** (help) aide *f*; **with the ~ of** à l'aide de [*tool etc*]; avec l'aide de [*person*]; **to come to sb's ~** venir en aide à qn; **2** (charitable support) aide *f* (**from** de; **to, for** à); **in ~ of** au profit de [*charity etc*]; (equipment) aide *f*.
II *noun modifier* [*programme etc*] d'entraide.
III *vtr* aider [*person*] (**to do** à faire); faciliter [*digestion, recovery*].
IV *vi* **1** **to ~** faciliter; **to ~ in doing sth** aider faire; **2** JUR **charged with ~ing and abetting** accusé de complicité.

aide /eɪd/ *n* aide *mf*, assistant/-e *m/f*.

Aids /eɪdz/ *n* (*abrév* = **Acquired Immune Deficiency Syndrome**) sida *m*.

ail /eɪl/ **I** *vtr* affliger [*society, economy*].
II *vi* **to be ~ing** [*person*] être souffrant; [*company*] être mal en point.

ailment /'eɪlmənt/ *n* affection *f*, maladie *f*.

aim /eɪm/ **I** *n* **1** (purpose) but *m*; **with the ~ of doing** dans le but de faire; **2** (with weapon) **to take ~ at sth/sb** viser qch/qn; **his ~ is bad** il vise mal.
II *vtr* **1** **to be ~ed at sb** [*campaign, product, remark*] viser qn; **to be ~ed at doing** [*effort, action*] viser à faire; **2** braquer [*gun*] (**at** sur); lancer [*ball, stone*] (**at** sur); tenter de donner [*blow, kick*] (**at** à); **well~ed** [*blow, kick*] bien placé.
III *vi* **1** **to ~ for sth, to ~ at sth** LIT, FIG viser qch; **to ~ at doing, to ~ to do** (try) s'efforcer de faire; (intend) avoir l'intention de faire; **to ~ high** FIG viser haut.

aimless /'eɪmlɪs/ *adj* [*person, wandering*] sans but; [*argument, gathering*] vain; [*violence*] sans objet.

ain't /eɪnt/ = **am not, is not, are not, has not, have not**.

air /eə(r)/ **I** *n* **1** (substance) air *m*; **in the open ~** en plein air, au grand air; **I need a change of ~** j'ai besoin de changer d'air; **to come up for ~** [*swimmer, animal*] remonter à la surface pour respirer; **to let the ~ out of sth** dégonfler qch; **2** (atmosphere, sky) air *m*; **he threw the ball up into the ~** il a jeté le ballon en l'air; **by ~** POST par avion; **Paris (seen) from the ~** Paris vu d'avion; **to clear the ~** LIT [*storm*] rafraîchir l'air; FIG apaiser les esprits; **3** RADIO, TV **to be/go on the ~** [*broadcaster, interviewee*] être/passer à l'antenne; **still on the ~** encore en cours de diffusion; **off the ~, she confided that...** hors antenne, elle a confié que...; **to go off the ~** [*channel*] cesser d'émettre; **4** (manner) (of person) air *m*; (aura) (of place) aspect *m*, air *m*; **with an ~ of indifference** d'un air indifférent; **an ~ of mystery surrounds the project** le projet est entouré de mystère; **5** MUS air *m*.
II *noun modifier* AVIAT [*alert, base, corridor*] aérien, -ienne; [*pollution, pressure*] atmosphérique.
III *vtr* **1** (dry) faire sécher; (freshen) aérer [*garment, room, bed*]; **that shirt hasn't been ~ed** cette chemise n'est pas complètement sèche; **2** (express) exprimer [*opinion, view*]; **to ~ one's grievances** exposer ses griefs.
IDIOMS **there was trouble in the ~** il y avait de l'orage dans l'air FIG; **there's a rumour in the ~ that...** le bruit court que...; **to put on ~s, to give oneself ~s** PÉJ se donner de grands airs; **to be up in the ~** FIG [*plans*] être très flou; **to be walking on ~** être aux anges; **to vanish into thin ~** se volatiser.

air: ~ ambulance *n* avion *m* sanitaire; **~ bag** *n* AUT airbag *m*; **~ bed** *n* GB matelas *m* pneumatique.

airborne /'eəbɔːn/ *adj* **1** BOT [*spore, seed*] porté par le vent; **2** AVIAT, MIL [*troops, division*] aéroporté; **once the plane was ~** une fois que l'avion avait décollé.

air: ~ brake *n* AUT, RAIL frein *m* à air comprimé; AVIAT aérofrein *m*; **~brush** *n* aérographe *m*; **~ bubble** *n* (in liquid, plastic, wallpaper) bulle *f* d'air; (in glass, metal etc) soufflure *f*; **~-conditioned** *adj* climatisé; **~-conditioning** *n* climatisation *f*, air *m* conditionné; **~-cooled** *adj* [*engine*] à refroidissement par air; **~craft** *n* ⊄ avion *m*, aéronef *m*; **~craft carrier** *n* porte-avions *m* *inv*; **~craft(s)man** ▶ **1192** | *n* GB soldat *m* de deuxième classe (de l'armée de l'air); **~crew** *n* équipage *m* (d'un avion); **~ cushion** n (inflatable cushion) coussin m pneumatique; (of hovercraft) coussin m d'air; **~ disaster** n catastrophe f aérienne; **~drop** n parachutage m; **~ duct** n conduit m d'air; **~fare** n tarif m d'avion; **~field** n aérodrome m, terrain m d'aviation; **~flow** n GEN, AUT, AVIAT courant m atmosphérique; (in tunnel) écoulement m d'air; **~ force** n armée f de l'air, forces fpl aériennes.

airfreight /'ɛəfreɪt/ n **1** (method of transport) transport m aérien; **2** (goods) fret m aérien; **3** (charge) tarif m aérien.

air: **~-freshener** n désodorisant m d'atmosphère; **~ gun** n fusil m or carabine f à air comprimé; **~head**○ n PÉJ évaporé/-e m/f; **~ hole** n trou m d'aération; **~ hostess** ▶ 1251 | n hôtesse f de l'air.

airing /'ɛərɪŋ/ n **1** (of linen) (drying) séchage m; (freshening) aération f; **2** FIG (mention) **to give an idea an ~** mettre une idée sur le tapis.

airing cupboard n GB placard qui contient la chaudière et où l'on range le linge.

air: **~less** adj [room] qui sent le renfermé; [evening] étouffant; **~ letter** n aérogramme m.

airlift /'ɛəlɪft/ vtr évacuer [qn] par pont aérien [evacuees]; acheminer [qch] par pont aérien [supplies].

airline /'ɛəlaɪn/ n **1** AVIAT (company) compagnie f aérienne; **2** (source of air) tuyau m d'air; (diver's) voie f d'air.

air: **~liner** n avion m de ligne; **~lock** n GEN poche f or bulle f d'air; (in spaceship) sas m.

airmail /'ɛəmeɪl/ **I** n poste f aérienne; **by ~** par avion.

II noun modifier [envelope, paper etc] par avion.

air: **~man** n GEN, MIL aviateur m; **~man basic** ▶ 1192 | n US MIL AVIAT soldat m (de l'armée de l'air américaine); **~man first class** ▶ 1192 | n US MIL AVIAT caporal m (de l'armée de l'air américaine); **~ marshal** ▶ 1192 | n GB général m de corps aérien; **~plane** n US avion m; **~ pocket** n (in pipe, enclosed space) poche f d'air; AVIAT trou m d'air; **~port** n aéroport m; **~ power** n puissance f aérienne; **~ pump** n pompe f à air, gonfleur m; **~ raid** n attaque f aérienne, raid m (aérien); **~-raid shelter** n abri m antiaérien; **~-raid siren** n sirène f d'alerte aérienne; **~-raid warning** n alerte f aérienne; **~ rifle** n carabine f à air comprimé; **~-sea rescue** n opération f de sauvetage en mer (par hélicoptère); **~ shaft** n (in mine) puits m d'aérage; **~ship** n dirigeable m; **~ show** n (flying show) meeting m aérien; (trade exhibition) salon m de l'aéronautique; **~sickness** n mal m de l'air; **~ sock** n manche f à air; **~speed** n vitesse f propre, vitesse f par rapport à l'air; **~speed indicator** n AVIAT badin m; **~stream** n GEN, METEOROL courant m atmosphérique; **~strip** n piste f (d'atterrissage or de décollage); **~ terminal** n (at airport) aérogare f; (in town: terminus) terminal m; **~tight** adj étanche à l'air; **~time** n RADIO, TV temps m d'antenne; **~-to-air** adj MIL [missile] air-air inv; [refuelling] en vol; **~-traffic controller** ▶ 1251 | n contrôleur/-euse m/f aérien/-ienne, aiguilleur m du ciel; **~ valve** n GEN soupape f d'air; (in central heating system) purgeur m d'air; **~ vent** n prise f d'air; **~ vice-marshal** n GB général m de division aérienne; **~waves** npl RADIO, TV ondes fpl.

airway /'ɛəweɪ/ n **1** AVIAT (route) voie f aérienne; (airline) compagnie f aérienne; **2** (ventilating passage) galerie f d'aérage; **3** ANAT voie f respiratoire.

air: **~worthiness** n navigabilité f; **~worthy** adj en état de navigation.

airy /'ɛərɪ/ adj **1** [room] clair/-e et spacieux/-ieuse; **2** (casual) [manner] désinvolte, insouciant.

airy-fairy○ /ˌɛərɪ'feərɪ/ adj GB [plan, person] farfelu○.

aisle /aɪl/ n **1** (in church) (side passage) bas-côté m; (centre passage) allée f centrale; **2** (passageway) (in train, plane) couloir m; (in cinema, shop) allée f.

ajar /ə'dʒɑː(r)/ adj, adv entrouvert, entrebaillé.

AK US POST abrév écrite = **Alaska**.

aka (abrév = **also known as**) alias.

akin /ə'kɪn/ adj **1** (similar) **to be ~ to** être semblable à; **to be more ~ to** ressembler davantage à; **2** (tantamount) **to be ~ to** (disapproving) équivaloir à.

AL US POST abrév écrite = **Alabama**.

alabaster /'æləbɑːstə(r), US -bæs-/ n albâtre m.

alacrity /ə'lækrɪtɪ/ n SOUT empressement m.

alarm /ə'lɑːm/ **I** n **1** (feeling) frayeur f; (concern) inquiétude f; **in ~** avec inquiétude; (stronger) apeuré; **there is no cause for ~** inutile de s'inquiéter; **2** (warning signal, device) alarme f; **smoke ~** détecteur m de fumée; **to raise the ~** LIT donner l'alarme; FIG sonner l'alarme; **3** = **alarm clock**.

II vtr (worry) inquiéter [person].

alarm bell n sonnette f d'alarme; **to set the ~s ringing** GB FIG tirer la sonnette d'alarme.

alarm: **~ call** n TELECOM réveil m par téléphone; **~ clock** n réveille-matin m, réveil m.

alarmed /ə'lɑːmd/ adj effrayé; **don't be ~!** rassurez-vous!

alarming /ə'lɑːmɪŋ/ adj alarmant.

alarmist /ə'lɑːmɪst/ n, adj alarmiste (mf).

alas /ə'læs/ excl hélas.

Albania /æl'beɪnɪə/ ▶ 840 | pr n Albanie f.

Albanian /æl'beɪnɪən/ ▶ 1100 |, 1038 | **I** n **1** (person) Albanais/-e m/f; **2** (language) albanais m.

II adj albanais.

albatross /'ælbətrɒs, US also -trɔːs/ n albatros m (also in golf).

albeit /ˌɔː'biːɪt/ conj SOUT quoique (+ subj), bien que (+ subj).

albino /æl'biːnəʊ, US -baɪ-/ n, adj albinos (inv).

albumen /'ælbjʊmɪn, US æl'bjuːmən/ n BIOL, BOT albumen m.

alchemy /'ælkəmɪ/ n CHEM, FIG alchimie f.

alcohol /'ælkəhɒl, US -hɔːl/ **I** n alcool m; **~-free** sans alcool.

II noun modifier [abuse, level, consumption] d'alcool; [poisoning] par l'alcool; **~ content** teneur f en alcool.

alcoholic /ˌælkə'hɒlɪk, US -hɔːl-/ **I** n alcoolique mf.

II adj [drink etc] alcoolisé; [person, stupor] alcoolique.

Alcoholics Anonymous, **AA** pr n Alcooliques Anonymes.

alcove /'ælkəʊv/ n renfoncement m.

alder /'ɔːldə(r)/ n (tree, wood) aulne m.

ale /eɪl/ n bière f; **brown/light/pale ~** bière brune/légère/blonde.

alert /ə'lɜːt/ **I** n alerte f; **to be on the ~ for** se méfier de [danger]; **fire/bomb ~** alerte au feu/à la bombe; **security ~** alerte de sécurité.

II adj **1** (lively) (child) éveillé; (old person) alerte; **2** (attentive) vigilant; **to be ~ to** avoir conscience de [danger, risk, fact, possibility].

III vtr **1** (contact) alerter [authorities]; **2 to ~ sb to** mettre qn en garde contre [danger]; attirer l'attention de qn sur [fact, situation].

alertness /ə'lɜːtnɪs/ n (attentiveness) vigilance f; (liveliness) vivacité f.

Aleutian Islands /ə'luːʃɪən/ ▶ 1022 | pr npl **the ~** les îles fpl Aléoutiennes.

A-level /'eɪlevl/ GB SCH **I** n **he got an ~ in history** ~ il a réussi à l'épreuve d'histoire au baccalauréat.

II A-levels npl: examen de fin de cycle secondaire, ~ baccalauréat m.

alfalfa /æl'fælfə/ n luzerne f.

alfresco /æl'freskəʊ/ adj, adv en plein air.

algae /'ældʒiː, 'ælgaɪ/ npl algues fpl.

algebra /'ældʒɪbrə/ n algèbre f.

Algeria /æl'dʒɪərɪə/ ▶ 840 | pr n Algérie f.

Algerian /æl'dʒɪərɪən/ ▶ 1100 | **I** n Algérien/-ienne m/f.

II adj algérien/-ienne.

Algiers /æl'dʒɪəz/ ▶ 1343 | pr n Alger.

ALGOL /'ælgɒl/ n (abrév = **algorithmic oriented language**) ALGOL m.

algorithm 716 **all**

---

all

As a pronoun

When *all* is used to mean *everything* it is translated by *tout*:

is that all? = c'est tout?
all is well = tout va bien

When *all* is followed by a *that* clause *all that* is translated by *tout ce qui* when it is the subject of the verb and *tout ce que* when it is the object:

all that remains to be done	=	tout ce qui reste à faire
that was all (that) he said	=	c'est tout ce qu'il a dit
after all (that) we've done	=	après tout ce que nous avons fait
we're doing all (that) we can	=	nous faisons tout ce que nous pouvons
all that you need	=	tout ce dont tu as besoin

When *all* is used to refer to a specified group of people or objects the translation reflects the number and gender of the people or objects referred to; *tous* is used for a group of people or objects of masculine or mixed or unspecified gender and *toutes* for a group of feminine gender:

we were all delighted = nous étions tous ravis
'where are the cups?' 'they're all in the kitchen' = 'où sont les tasses?' 'elles sont toutes dans la cuisine'

For more examples and particular usages see the entry *all*.

As a determiner

In French, determiners agree in gender and number with the noun they precede. So *all* is translated by *tout* + masculine singular noun:

all the time = tout le temps

by *toute* + feminine singular noun:

all the family = toute la famille

by *tous* + masculine or mixed gender plural noun:

all men = tous les hommes
all the books = tous les livres

and by *toutes* + feminine plural noun:

all women = toutes les femmes
all the chairs = toutes les chaises

For more examples and particular usages see the entry *all*.

As an adverb

When *all* is used as an adverb meaning *completely* it is generally translated by *tout*:

my coat's all dirty = mon manteau est tout sale
he was all alone = il était tout seul
they were all alone = ils étaient tout seuls
the girls were all excited = les filles étaient tout excitées

However, when the adjective that follows is in the feminine and begins with a consonant the translation is *toute/toutes*:

she was all alone = elle était toute seule
the bill is all wrong = la facture est toute fausse
the girls were all alone = les filles étaient toutes seules

For more examples and particular usages see the entry *all*. Phrases such as *all along, all but, at all, for all* and *of all* are each treated separately in the entry *all*.

---

algorithm /'ælgərɪðəm/ *n* MATH, COMPUT algorithme *m*.

alias /'eɪlɪəs/ **I** *n* faux nom *m*; **under an ~** sous un faux nom.
II *prep* alias.

alibi /'ælɪbaɪ/ *n* **1** JUR alibi *m*; **2** (excuse) excuse *f*.

alien /'eɪlɪən/ **I** *n* **1** GEN, JUR étranger/-ère *m/f* (**to** à); **2** (from space) extraterrestre *mf*.
II *adj* **to be ~ to sb/sth** être étranger/-ère à qn/qch.

alienate /'eɪlɪəneɪt/ *vtr* (estrange) éloigner [*supporters, colleagues*]; JUR aliéner (**from** de); **they ~d all their friends** ils se sont aliéné tous leurs amis.

alienation /ˌeɪlɪə'neɪʃn/ *n* **1** GEN (process) éloignement *m* (**of** de); (state) isolement *m* (**from** de); **2** JUR, POL, PSYCH aliénation *f*.

alight /ə'laɪt/ **I** *adj* **to be ~** [*fire*] être allumé; [*building*] être en feu; **to set sth ~** mettre le feu à qch.
II *vi* [*passenger*] descendre (**from** de); [*bird*] se poser (**on** sur); [*gaze*] s'arrêter (**on** sur).

align /ə'laɪn/ *vtr* aligner (**with** sur); **non-~ed** non-aligné.

alignment /ə'laɪnmənt/ *n* **1** GEN, POL alignement *m* (**with** sur); **to be in ~/out of ~** être aligné/désaligné (**with** sur); **2** COMPUT position *f*.

alike /ə'laɪk/ **I** *adj* (identical) pareil/-eille; (similar) semblable; **to look ~** se ressembler.
II *adv* [*dress, think*] de la même façon; **for young and old ~** pour les jeunes (tout) comme pour les personnes âgées.

alimentary /ˌælɪ'mentərɪ/ *adj* [*system, process*] digestif/-ive; [*rules, laws*] alimentaire; **~ canal** tube *m* digestif.

alimony /'ælɪmənɪ, US -məʊnɪ/ *n* JUR pension *f* alimentaire.

alive /ə'laɪv/ *adj* **1** LIT (living) vivant, en vie; **to keep sb/sth ~** maintenir qn/qch en vie [*person, animal*]; **to stay ~** rester en vie; **to bury sb ~** enterrer qn vivant; **to be burnt ~** être brûlé/-e vif/vive; **~ and well**, **~ and kicking** LIT, FIG bien vivant; **to be ~** [*person*] être vivant; **to come ~** [*party, place*] s'animer; [*history*] prendre vie; **3** (in existence) **to be ~** [*art, tradition*] être vivant; [*interest, faith*] être vif/vive; **to keep ~** préserver [*tradition etc*]; perpétuer [*memory*]; **it kept our hopes ~** cela nous faisait

garder espoir; **4** (teeming) **~ with** grouillant de [*insects etc*]; **5** (aware) **~ to** conscient de [*possibility etc*].

alkali /'ælkəlaɪ/ *n* alcali *m*.

alkaline /'ælkəlaɪn/ *adj* alcalin.

all /ɔːl/ **I** *pron* **1** (everything) tout; **to risk ~** tout risquer; **~ is not lost** tout n'est pas perdu; **~ was well** tout allait bien; **~ will be revealed** HUM vous saurez tout HUM; **will that be ~?** ce sera tout?; **that's ~** (all contexts) c'est tout; **500 in ~** 500 en tout; **~ in ~** somme toute; **after ~** she's been through après tout ce qu'elle a vécu; **it's not ~ (that) it should be** ça laisse à désirer; **~ because he didn't write** tout ça parce qu'il n'a pas écrit; **2** (the only thing) tout; **that's ~ I want** c'est tout ce que je veux; **she's ~ I have left** elle est tout ce qui me reste; **~ I know is that** tout ce que je sais c'est que; **that's ~ we need!** IRON il ne manquait plus que ça!; **3** (everyone) tous; **~ wish to participate** tous souhaitent participer; **thank you, one and ~** merci à (vous) tous; **'~ welcome'** 'venez nombreux'; **4** (the whole amount) **~ of our belongings** toutes nos affaires; **not ~ of the time** pas tout le temps; **5** (emphasizing entirety) **we ~ feel that** nous avons tous l'impression que; **it ~ seems so pointless** tout cela paraît si futile; **I ate it ~** j'ai tout mangé; **what's it ~ for?** (all contexts) à quoi ça sert (tout ça)?

II *det* **1** (each one of) tous/toutes; **~ those who** tous ceux qui; **in ~ three films** dans les trois films; **2** (the whole of) tout/toute; **~ his life** toute sa vie; **~ year round** toute l'année; **you are ~ the family I have!** tu es toute la famille qui me reste!; **3** (total) **in ~ honesty** en toute franchise; **4** (any) **beyond ~ expectations** au-delà de toute attente; **to deny ~ knowledge of sth** nier avoir connaissance de qch.

III *adv* **1** (emphatic: completely) tout; **~ alone** tout seul; **to be ~ wet** être tout mouillé; **~ in white** tout en blanc; **~ along the canal** tout le long du canal; **to be ~ for sth** être tout à fait pour qch; **it's ~ about...** c'est l'histoire de...; **tell me ~ about it!** raconte-moi tout!; **he's forgotten ~ about us!** il nous a complètement oubliés!; **2** (emphatic: nothing but) **to be ~ smiles** (happy) être tout souriant; (two-faced) être tout sourire; **3** SPORT **(they are) six ~** (il y a) six partout.

IV *n* **to give one's ~** tout sacrifier.

V all+ *combining form* (completely) **~-concrete** tout

en béton; **~-digital/-electronic** entièrement numérique/électronique; **~-female/-male** [*group*] composé uniquement de femmes/d'hommes.
VI all along *adv phr* [*know etc*] depuis le début, toujours.
VII all but *adv phr* pratiquement, presque.
VIII all of *adv phr* to be ~ of 50 avoir au moins 50 ans.
IX all that *adv phr* not ~ that strong pas si fort que ça; I don't know her ~ that well je ne la connais pas si bien que ça.
X all the *adv phr* ~ the more [*difficult, effective*] d'autant plus (*before adj*); to laugh ~ the more rire encore plus; ~ the better! tant mieux !
XI all too *adv phr* [*accurate, easy, widespread, often*] bien trop; she saw ~ too clearly that elle a parfaitement bien vu que.
XII and all *adv phr* **1** they moved books and ~ ils ont tout déménagé y compris les livres; **2**° GB what with the heat and ~ avec la chaleur et tout ça.
XIII at all *adv phr* not at ~! (acknowledging thanks) de rien!; (answering query) pas du tout!; it is not at ~ certain ce n'est pas du tout certain; if (it is) at ~ possible si possible; is it at ~ likely that...? y a-t-il la moindre possibilité que...? (+ *subj*); nothing at ~ rien du tout; if you knew anything at ~ about si tu avais la moindre idée de.
XIV for all *prep phr, adv phr* **1** (despite) for ~ that malgré tout, quand même; **2** (as regards) for ~ I know pour autant que je sache.
XV of all *prep phr* **1** (in rank) the easiest of ~ le plus facile; first/last of ~ pour commencer/finir; **2** (emphatic) why today of ~ days? pourquoi justement aujourd'hui?; of ~ the nerve! quel culot!
IDIOMS he's not ~ there° il n'a pas toute sa tête; it's ~ go° here! GB on s'active° ici!; it's ~ one to me ça m'est égal; it was ~ I could do not to laugh il a fallu que je me retienne pour ne pas rire; that's ~ very well, that's ~ well and good tout ça c'est bien beau.

all: **~-American** *n* GEN [*girl, boy, hero*] typiquement américain; SPORT [*record, champion*] américain; **~-around** *adj* US = **all-round**.

allay /ə'leɪ/ *vtr* SOUT dissiper [*fear, suspicion, doubt*].

all clear *n* MIL signal *m* de fin d'alerte; **to give sb the** ~ FIG donner le feu vert à qn (**to do** pour faire); [*doctor*] déclarer qn guéri.

all: **~-consuming** *adj* [*passion*] effréné; [*ambition*] démesuré; **~-day** *adj* [*event*] qui dure toute la journée.

allegation /ˌælɪ'ɡeɪʃn/ *n* GEN, JUR allégation *f* (**about** sur; **that** selon laquelle).

allege /ə'ledʒ/ I *vtr* **to** ~ **that** (claim) prétendre que (+ *conditional*); (publicly) déclarer que (+ *conditional*); **his** ~d **attempt to**... la tentative qu'il aurait faite de...; **it was** ~d **that**... il a été dit que...
II alleged *pp adj* [*attacker, crime*] présumé.

allegedly /ə'ledʒɪdlɪ/ *adv* prétendument.

allegiance /ə'li:dʒəns/ *n* GEN, JUR allégeance *f*; **to swear** ~ prêter serment m d'allégeance à.

allegory /'æliɡərɪ, US -ɡɔ:rɪ/ *n* allégorie *f* (**of** de).

all-embracing *adj* global.

allergic /ə'lɜ:dʒɪk/ *adj* allergique (**to** à) ALSO FIG.

allergist /'ælədʒɪst/ **▶ 1251** *n* allergologue *mf*.

allergy /'ælədʒɪ/ *n* allergie *f* (**to** à) ALSO FIG.

alleviate /ə'li:vɪeɪt/ *vtr* soulager [*boredom, pain*]; apaiser [*fears*]; réduire [*overcrowding, stress, unemployment*].

alley /'ælɪ/ *n* **1** (walkway) allée *f*; (for vehicles) ruelle *f*; **2** US (in tennis) couloir *m*.

alleyway /'ælɪweɪ/ *n* = **alley** 1.

all-found *adj* logé et nourri.

alliance /ə'laɪəns/ *n* GEN, POL, MIL alliance *f* (**between** entre; **with** avec).

allied /'ælaɪd/ *adj* [*group*] allié; [*trades, subjects*] connexe.

all: **~-important** *adj* essentiel/-ielle; **~-in** *adj* GB [*fee, price*] tout compris; ~ **in**° *adj* GB crevé°, épuisé°; **~-inclusive** *adj* [*fee, price*] tout compris; **~-in-one** *adj* [*garment*] d'une seule pièce; **~-in wrestling** **▶ 949** *n* SPORT catch *m*; **~-night** *adj* [*party, meeting*] qui dure toute la nuit; [*service*] ouvert toute la nuit; [*radio station*] qui émet 24 heures sur 24.

allocate /'æləkeɪt/ *vtr* affecter [*funds*] (**for, to** à); attribuer [*land*] (**to** à); accorder [*time*] (**to** à); assigner, attribuer [*tasks*] (**to** à).

allocation /ˌælə'keɪʃn/ *n* (amount) crédits *mpl*; (process) affectation *f*.

all-or-nothing *adj* [*approach, policy*] extrémiste.

allot /ə'lɒt/ *vtr* (*p prés etc* **-tt-**) attribuer [*money*] (**to** à); assigner [*task*] (**to** à); **in the** ~ted **time** dans le temps imparti.

allotment /ə'lɒtmənt/ *n* **1** GB (garden) parcelle *f* de terre (*loué pour en faire un jardin potager*); **2** (allocation) attribution *f*.

all-out /'ɔ:laʊt/ I *adj* [*strike*] total; [*attack*] en règle; [*effort*] acharné.
II all out *adv* **to go all out for success** tout faire pour réussir.

allover /'ɔ:ləʊvə(r)/ *adj* [*tan*] intégral.

all over /ˌɔ:l'əʊvə(r)/ I *adj* (finished) fini; **when it's** ~ quand tout sera fini.
II *adv* **1** (everywhere) partout; **to be trembling** ~ trembler de partout; **2**° (typically) **that's Mary** ~! c'est Mary tout craché!
III *prep* **1** partout dans [*room, town*]; ~ **China** partout en Chine; **2**° FIG (known in) **the news is** ~ **the village** la nouvelle s'est répandue dans tout le village; **3** (fawning over) **to be** ~ **sb** être aux petits soins pour qn; **they were** ~ **each other** ils n'arrêtaient pas de se bécoter°.

allow /ə'laʊ/ I *vtr* **1** (authorize) autoriser à [*person, organization*] (**to do** de faire); autoriser [*action, change*]; laisser [*choice, freedom*] (**to do** de faire); **to** ~ **sb in** autoriser qn à entrer; **she isn't** ~ed **alcohol** l'alcool lui est interdit; **2** (let) laisser; **he** ~ed **the situation to get worse** il a laissé la situation s'aggraver; **3** (enable) **to** ~ **sb/sth to do** permettre à qn/qch de faire; ~ **me!** permettez(-moi)!; **4** (allocate) prévoir; **to** ~ **two days for the job** prévoir deux jours pour faire le travail; **5** (concede) [*referee*] accorder [*goal*]; [*insurer*] agréer [*claim*]; [*supplier*] accorder, consentir [*discount*]; **6** (admit) [*club*] admettre [*non-member*]; **'no dogs** ~ed' 'interdit aux chiens'; **7** (condone) tolérer [*rudeness, swearing*].
II *v refl* **to** ~ **oneself 1** (grant) s'accorder [*drink, treat*]; **2** (allocate) prévoir; ~ **yourself two days** prévois deux jours; **3** (let) se laisser; **I** ~ed **myself to be persuaded** je me suis laissé persuader.
■ **allow for**: ~ **for** [sth] tenir compte de [*delays, wastage*].

allowable /ə'laʊəbl/ *adj* **1** (tax) déductible; **2** (permissible) GEN admissible; JUR légitime.

allowance /ə'laʊəns/ *n* **1** (grant) GEN, ADMIN allocation *f*; (from employer) indemnité *f*; **2** (tax) abattement *m* fiscal; **3** (spending money) (for child) argent *m* de poche; (for student) argent *m* (pour vivre); (from trust, guardian) rente *f*; **4** (entitlement) **your baggage** ~ **is 40 kgs** vous avez droit à 40 kg de bagages; **5** COMM (discount) rabais *m*; (in trade-in payment) reprise *f*; **6** (concession) **to make** ~(s) **for sth** tenir compte de qch; **to make** ~(s) **for sb** essayer de comprendre qn.

alloy /'ælɔɪ/ *n* alliage *m*.

alloy: ~ **steel** *n* acier *m* allié; ~ **wheel** *n* roue *f* en alliage léger.

all: ~ **points bulletin** *n* US alerte *f* générale; **~-powerful** *adj* tout-puissant; **~-purpose** *adj* [*building*] polyvalent; [*utensil*] multi-usages.

all right, alright /ˌɔ:l'raɪt/ I *adj* **1** (expressing degree of satisfaction) [*film, garment etc*] pas mal°; **she's** ~ (pleasant) elle est plutôt sympa°; (attractive) elle n'est pas mal°; (competent) son travail est correct; **'how did the interview go?'—'~'** 'comment s'est passé ton entretien?'—'ça ne s'est pas trop mal passé' or 'ça a été⁰'; **sounds ~ to me**⁰! (acceptance) pourquoi pas!; **is my hair ~?** ça va mes cheveux?; **2** (well) **to feel ~** aller bien; **3** (able to manage) **will you be ~?** est-ce que ça va aller?; **to be ~ for** avoir assez de [*money etc*]; **4** (acceptable) **is it ~ if...?** est-ce que ça va si...?; **would it be ~ to leave early?** est-ce que c'est gênant si on s'en va plus tôt?; **is that ~ with you?** ça ne te dérange pas?; **it's ~ for you** toi tu n'as pas à t'en faire; **that's (quite) ~!** ce n'est rien du tout!

II *adv* **1** [*function*] comme il faut; [*see*] bien; **she's doing ~** (doing well) tout va bien pour elle; (managing to cope) elle s'en tire correctement; **2** (without doubt) **she knows ~!** bien sûr qu'elle sait!

III *particle* d'accord; **~ ~!** point taken! ça va! j'ai compris!; **~, let's move on to...** bien, passons à...

all: **~-risk** *adj* [*policy, cover*] tous risques; **~-round** *adj* [*athlete*] complet/-ète; [*improvement*] général.

all-rounder /ˌɔːlˈraʊndə(r)/ *n* **to be a good ~** être bon en tout.

allspice /ˈɔːlspaɪs/ *n* piment *m* de la Jamaïque.

all square *adj* **to be ~** [*people*] être quitte; [*accounts*] être équilibré.

all-time /ˈɔːltaɪm/ *adj* [*record*] absolu; **the ~ greats** (people) les grands *mpl*; **~ high** record *m* absolu; **to be at an ~ low** [*person, morale*] être au plus bas; [*figures, shares*] n'avoir jamais été plus bas.

all told *adv* en tout.

allude /əˈluːd/ *vi* **to ~ to sth** faire allusion à qch.

alluring /əˈlʊərɪŋ/ *adj* séduisant.

allusion /əˈluːʒn/ *n* allusion *f* (**to** à).

all-weather *adj* [*pitch, track*] tous temps; **~ court** (terrain *m* en) quick® *m*.

ally /ˈælaɪ/ **I** *n* (*pl* **-ies**) GEN, MIL allié/-e *m/f*.
II /əˈlaɪ/ *v refl* **to ~ oneself with** s'allier avec.

almighty /ɔːlˈmaɪtɪ/ *adj* [*crash, row, explosion*] formidable.

Almighty /ɔːlˈmaɪtɪ/ *n* RELIG **the ~** le Tout-Puissant.

almond /ˈɑːmənd/ *n* **1** (nut) amande *f*; **2** (also **~ tree**) amandier *m*.

almost /ˈɔːlməʊst/

■ **Note** When *almost* is used to mean *practically* it is translated by *presque*: *we're almost ready* = nous sommes presque prêts; *it's almost dark* = il fait presque nuit; *the room was almost empty* = la salle était presque vide.
– When *almost* is used with a verb in the past tense to describe something undesirable or unpleasant that nearly happened, it is translated using the verb *faillir* followed by an infinitive: *I almost forgot* = j'ai failli oublier; *he almost fell* = il a failli tomber.

adv **1** (practically) presque; **~ any train** presque tous les trains; **we're ~ there** nous sommes presque arrivés; **2** (implying narrow escape) **he ~ died** il a failli mourir.

alms† /ɑːmz/ *npl* aumône *f*.

aloft /əˈlɒft, US əˈlɔːft/ *adv* **1** GEN [*hold, soar*] en l'air; [*seated, perched*] en haut; **from ~** d'en haut; **2** NAUT dans la mâture.

alone /əˈləʊn/ **I** *adj* (*épith*) **1** (on one's own) seul; **all ~** tout seul; **to leave sb ~** LIT laisser qn seul; (in peace) laisser qn tranquille; **leave that bike ~!** ne touche pas à ce vélo!; **2** (isolated) seul; **I feel so ~** je me sens si seul; **she is not ~ in thinking that...** elle n'est pas la seule à penser que...; **to stand ~** [*building*] être isolé; [*person*] se tenir seul; FIG être sans égal.
II *adv* **1** (on one's own) [*work, live, travel*] seul; **2** (exclusively) **for this reason ~** rien que pour cette raison; **this figure ~ shows** le chiffre à lui seul montre.
IDIOMS **to go it ~**⁰ faire cavalier seul.

along /əˈlɒŋ, US əˈlɔːŋ/

■ **Note** When *along* is used as a preposition meaning *all along* it can usually be translated by *le long de*: *there were trees along the road* = il y avait des arbres le long de la route. For particular usages see the entry below.
– *along* is often used after verbs of movement. If the addi-

tion of *along* does not change the meaning of the verb, *along* will not be translated: *as he walked along* = tout en marchant.
– However, the addition of *along* often produces a completely new meaning. This is the case in expressions like *the project is coming along, how are they getting along?*. For translations consult the appropriate verb entry (**come**, **get** etc).

I *adv* **to push/pull sth ~** pousser/tirer qch; **to be walking ~** marcher; **I'll be ~ in a second** j'arrive tout de suite.
II *prep* **1** (also **~side**) (all along) le long de; **to run ~ the beach** [*path etc*] longer la plage; **there were chairs ~ the wall** il y avait des chaises contre le mur; **2** (the length of) **to walk ~ the beach** marcher sur la plage; **to look ~ the shelves** chercher dans les rayons; **3** (at a point along) **somewhere ~ the motorway** quelque part sur l'autoroute; **halfway ~ the path** à mi-chemin; **somewhere ~ the way** LIT quelque part en chemin; FIG quelque part.
III *adv* + *prep phr* (accompanied by) **~ with** accompagné de; (at same time as) en même temps que.

alongside /əˈlɒŋsaɪd, US əlɔːŋsaɪd/ **I** *prep* **1** (all along) = **along II 1**; **2** (next to) **to draw up ~ sb** [*vehicle*] s'arrêter à la hauteur de qn; **to learn to live ~ each other** [*groups*] apprendre à coexister.
II *adv* **1** GEN à côté de; **2** NAUT **to come ~** accoster.

aloof /əˈluːf/ *adj* distant; **to remain ~ from** se tenir à l'écart de.

aloud /əˈlaʊd/ *adv* (audibly) [*say*] à haute voix; [*wonder*] tout haut.

alpaca /ælˈpækə/ *n* (all contexts) alpaga *m*.

alpha /ˈælfə/ *n* **1** (letter) alpha *m*; **2** GB UNIV (grade) **to get an ~** avoir un 20.

alphabet /ˈælfəbet/ *n* alphabet *m*.

alphabetical /ˌælfəˈbetɪkl/ *adj* alphabétique.

alphabetically /ˌælfəˈbetɪklɪ/ *adv* [*list*] par ordre alphabétique.

alpine /ˈælpaɪn/ **I** *n* plante *f* alpine.
II *adj* (also **Alpine**) GEN alpin.

Alps /ælps/ *pr npl* **the ~** les Alpes *fpl*.

already /ɔːlˈredɪ/ *adv* déjà; **it's 10 o'clock ~** il est déjà 10 heures; **he's ~ left** il est déjà parti; **I've told you twice ~!** je te l'ai déjà dit deux fois!; **it's June ~** nous sommes déjà au mois de juin.
IDIOMS **so come on ~!** US (indicating irritation) dépêche-toi à la fin!

alright = **all right**.

Alsatian /ælˈseɪʃn/ **I** *n* **1** GB (dog) berger *m* allemand; **2** (native of Alsace) Alsacien/-ienne *m/f*.
II *adj* alsacien/-ienne; **~ wines** les vins d'Alsace.

also /ˈɔːlsəʊ/ *adv* **1** (too, as well) aussi; **~ available in red** existe aussi en rouge; **it is ~ worth remembering that** il serait bon aussi de ne pas oublier que; **2** (furthermore) **~, he snores** en plus il ronfle.

altar /ˈɔːltə(r)/ *n* autel *m*.

altar: **~ boy** *n* enfant *m* de chœur; **~ cloth** *n* nappe *f* d'autel; **~ piece** *n* retable *m*.

alter /ˈɔːltə(r)/ **I** *vtr* **1** (change) changer [*opinion, lifestyle, person, rule, timetable*]; modifier [*amount, document*]; affecter [*speed, value, climate*]; transformer [*building*]; **that does not ~ the fact that** cela ne change rien au fait que; **to ~ the appearance of sth** changer l'aspect de qch; **2** retoucher [*dress, shirt etc*]; (radically) transformer.
II *vi* changer.

alteration /ˌɔːltəˈreɪʃn/ **I** *n* **1** (act of altering) (of building) transformation *f*; (of text, law, process) modification *f*; (of timetable, route, circumstances) changement *m*; **2** (result of altering) modification *f* (**to, in** de); **3** (to garment) retouche *f*; (radical) transformation *f*.
II **alterations** *npl* **1** (changes to building) transformations *fpl* (**to** à); **2** (building work) travaux *mpl*.

altercation /ˌɔːltəˈkeɪʃn/ *n* SOUT altercation *f* (**about** ou **over** à propos de).

alternate I /ɔːlˈtɜːnət/ *n* US (stand-in) remplaçant/-e *m/f*.

II /ɔːltɜːnət/ adj **1** (successive) [*chapters, layers*] en alternance; **2** (every other) **on ~ days** un jour sur deux; **3** US (other) autre; **4** BOT, MATH alterne.

III /ɔːltəneɪt/ vtr **to ~ sth and** OU **with sth** alterner qch et qch.

IV /ɔːltəneɪt/ vi [*people*] se relayer; [*colours, patterns, seasons*] alterner (**with** avec); **to ~ between hope and despair** passer de l'espoir au désespoir.

alternately /ɔːltɜːnətlɪ/ adv [*move, bring, ask*] alternativement; **they criticize and praise him ~** tantôt ils le critiquent, tantôt ils le félicitent.

alternating current n courant m alternatif.

alternative /ɔːltɜːnətɪv/ **I** n **1** (specified option) (from two) alternative f, autre possibilité f; (from several) possibilité f; **one ~ is...** une des possibilités serait...; **the ~ is to do** l'autre possibilité serait de faire; **2** (possible option) choix m; **to have no ~** ne pas avoir le choix; **I chose the expensive ~** j'ai choisi la solution chère; **as an ~ to radiotherapy, you can choose...** outre la radiothérapie, vous pouvez choisir...

II adj **1** (other) [*activity, career, date, flight, method, plan*] autre; [*accommodation, product*] de remplacement; [*solution*] de rechange; **2** (unconventional) [*comedian, bookshop*] ALSO ECOL alternatif/-ive.

alternatively /ɔːltɜːnətɪvlɪ/ adv sinon; **~, you can book by phone** vous avez aussi la possibilité de réserver par téléphone.

alternative: **~ medicine** n ⊄ médecines fpl parallèles or douces; **~ technology**, AT n technologie f alternative.

alternator /ɔːltəneɪtə(r)/ n ELEC alternateur m.

although /ɔːlðəʊ/ conj **1** (in spite of the fact that) bien que (+ subj); **~ he claims to be shy** bien qu'il prétende être timide; **they're generous, ~ poor** ils sont généreux, quoique pauvres; **2** (but, however) mais; **you don't have to attend, ~ we advise it** vous n'êtes pas obligés de venir, mais nous vous le conseillons.

altimeter /ˈæltɪmiːtə(r), US ˌælˈtɪmətər/ n altimètre m.

altitude /ˈæltɪtjuːd, US -tuːd/ n altitude f; **at ~** en altitude.

alto (pl **-tos**) /ˈæltəʊ/ n ▶1380 **1** (voice) (of female) contralto m; (of male) haute-contre f; **2** (singer) (female) contralto f; (male) haute-contre m.

altogether /ˌɔːltəˈgeðə(r)/ adv **1** (completely) complètement; **not ~ true** pas complètement vrai; **that's another matter ~** c'est une tout autre histoire; **2** (in total) en tout; **how much is that ~?** ça fait combien en tout?; **3** (all things considered) **~, it was a mistake** tout compte fait, c'était une erreur.

altruistic /ˌæltruːˈɪstɪk/ adj altruiste.

aluminium /ˌæljʊˈmɪnɪəm/ GB, **aluminum** /əˈluːmɪnəm/ US n aluminium m.

aluminium foil n papier m aluminium.

alumna /əˈlʌmnə/ n (pl **-nae**) US SCH, UNIV (of school) ancienne élève f; (of college) ancienne étudiante f.

alumnus /əˈlʌmnəs/ n (pl **-ni**) US SCH, UNIV (of school) ancien élève m; (of college) ancien étudiant m.

always /ˈɔːlweɪz/ adv toujours; **he's ~ complaining** il n'arrête pas de se plaindre.

am¹ /æm/ ▶ be.

am² /æm, eɪem/ ▶812 adv (abrév = **ante meridiem**) **three ~** trois heures (du matin).

AMA n (abrév = **American Medical Association**) US Association f médicale américaine.

amalgam /əˈmælgəm/ n (all contexts) amalgame m.

amalgamate /əˈmælgəmeɪt/ **I** vtr **1** (merge) fusionner [*companies, schools*] (**with** avec; **into** en); **2** amalgamer [*metals*] (**with** à).

II vi **1** [*company, union*] fusionner (**with** avec); **2** [*metal*] amalgamer (**with** à).

III **amalgamated** pp adj [*school, association, trade union*] unifié.

amalgamation /əˌmælgəˈmeɪʃn/ n **1** (of companies) fusion f (**with** avec; **into** en); (of styles) mélange m; **2** (of metals) amalgamation f.

amass /əˈmæs/ vtr accumuler [*data*]; amasser [*fortune*].

amateur /ˈæmətə(r)/ **I** n SPORT, GEN amateur m.

II noun modifier [*sportsperson, musician*] amateur; [*sport*] en amateur; **~ dramatics** théâtre m amateur.

amateurish /ˈæmətərɪʃ/ adj PÉJ [*work, attitude*] d'amateur.

amaze /əˈmeɪz/ vtr surprendre; (stronger) stupéfier.

amazed /əˈmeɪzd/ adj [*reaction, silence, look, person*] stupéfait; **I'm ~ (that)** ça m'étonne que (+ subj).

amazement /əˈmeɪzmənt/ n stupéfaction f; **in ~** avec stupéfaction; **to everyone's ~** à la stupéfaction générale; **to my/her etc ~** à ma/sa etc grande surprise.

amazing /əˈmeɪzɪŋ/ adj extraordinaire.

amazingly /əˈmeɪzɪŋlɪ/ adv incroyablement; **to be ~ clever** être d'une intelligence étonnante.

Amazon /ˈæməzən, US -zɒn/ ▶1214 **I** pr n **1** (river) ALSO MYTHOL Amazone m; **2** (also **amazon**) FIG (strong woman) virago f PÉJ.

II noun modifier [*basin, forest, tribe*] amazonien/-ienne.

ambassador /æmˈbæsədə(r)/ ▶937 n ambassadeur m.

ambassador-at-large n (pl **~s-at-large**) US ambassadeur m.

amber /ˈæmbə(r)/ ▶818 **I** n **1** (resin, colour) ambre m; **2** GB (traffic signal) orange m; **to change** OU **turn to ~** passer à l'orange.

II adj [*eyes, fabric*] couleur d'ambre inv; [*light*] ambré.

ambidextrous /ˌæmbɪˈdekstrəs/ adj ambidextre.

ambience /ˈæmbɪəns/ n SOUT ambiance f.

ambient /ˈæmbɪənt/ adj [*temperature, noise*] ambiant.

ambiguity /ˌæmbɪˈgjuːətɪ/ n ambiguïté f (**about** à propos de).

ambiguous /æmˈbɪgjʊəs/ adj GEN, LING ambigu/-uë.

ambiguously /æmˈbɪgjʊəslɪ/ adv de façon ambiguë.

ambition /æmˈbɪʃn/ n **1** (quality) ambition f (**to do** de faire); **2** (aim) rêve m (**to do** de faire); **it was his lifelong ~ to visit Japan** son rêve de toujours était de visiter le Japon; **3** (gen pl) (aspiration) ambition f (**to do, of doing** de faire); **political ~s** ambitions politiques.

ambitious /æmˈbɪʃəs/ adj [*person, scheme*] ambitieux/-ieuse; **to be ~ to do** avoir l'ambition de faire.

ambitiously /æmˈbɪʃəslɪ/ adv ambitieusement.

ambivalence /æmˈbɪvələns/ n ambivalence f.

ambivalent /æmˈbɪvələnt/ adj ambivalent; **to be ~ about** avoir une attitude ambivalente à propos de.

amble /ˈæmbl/ vi **1** (stroll) **to ~ off** partir tranquillement; **to ~ around the gardens** se promener tranquillement dans les jardins; **2** [*horse*] aller l'amble.

ambulance /ˈæmbjʊləns/ **I** n ambulance f.

II noun modifier [*service, station*] d'ambulances; **~ crew** équipe f d'ambulanciers/-ières.

ambulance: **~man** ▶1251 n ambulancier m; **~woman** ▶1251 n ambulancière f.

ambush /ˈæmbʊʃ/ **I** n **1** embuscade f; **to lie in ~** se tenir en embuscade.

II vtr tendre une embuscade à [*soldiers*]; **to be ~ed** être pris en embuscade.

ameba n US = **amoeba**.

amen /ɑːˈmen, eɪ-/ excl amen; **~ to that!** assurément!

amenable /əˈmiːnəbl/ adj **1** (obliging) souple; **2 ~ to** [*person*] sensible à [*reason etc*]; [*person, situation*] soumis à [*regulations*].

amend /əˈmend/ vtr **1** (alter) amender [*law*]; modifier [*document, plan*]; **2** SOUT (correct) réformer FML [*behaviour*].

amendment /əˈmendmənt/ n (to law) amendement m (**to** à); (to contract) modification f (**to** à).

amends /əˈmendz/ npl **1** (reparation) **to make ~ for** réparer [*damage, hurt*]; **to make ~ to sb** (financially) dédommager qn; **2 to make ~** (redeem oneself) se racheter.

amenity /ə'miːnɪtɪ, ə'menətɪ/ **I** n sout (pleasantness) agrément m.
II amenities npl (facilities) (of hotel, locality) équipements mpl; (of house, sports club) installations fpl.

America /ə'merɪkə/ ▶ 840 pr n Amérique f.

American /ə'merɪkən/ ▶ 1100, 1038 **I** n **1** (person) Américain/-e m/f; **2** (language) américain m.
II adj américain.

American: ~ Civil War pr n guerre f de sécession; **~ English** n américain m; **~ Indian** ▶ 1100 n Indien/-ienne m/f d'Amérique du Nord, Amérindien/-ienne m/f.

Americanism /ə'merɪkənɪzəm/ n américanisme m.

American revolution n guerre f d'Indépendance américaine.

amethyst /'æmɪθɪst/ n (gem) améthyste f; ▶ 818 (colour) violet m d'améthyste.

Amex /'eɪmeks/ n (abrév = **American Stock Exchange**) deuxième Bourse new-yorkaise.

amiable /'eɪmɪəbl/ adj [person] aimable (**to** ou **towards** avec); [mood] plaisant; [chat] amical.

amicable /'æmɪkəbl/ adj **1** (friendly) [manner, relationship] amical; **2** JUR **an ~ settlement** un arrangement à l'amiable.

amicably /'æmɪkəblɪ/ adv [behave] de façon amicale; [settle, part] à l'amiable.

amid /ə'mɪd/, **amidst** /ə'mɪdst/ prep **1** au milieu de [laughter, applause]; à la suite de [allegations, reports, rumours]; **~ growing concern** alors qu'on s'inquiète de plus en plus; **2** (surrounded by) parmi, au milieu de [fields, trees, wreckage].

amino acid /ə,miːnəʊ 'æsɪd/ n acide m aminé.

amiss /ə'mɪs/ **I** adj **there is something ~** il y a quelque chose qui ne va pas.
II adv **to take sth ~** prendre qch de travers; **a drink wouldn't come** ou **go ~!** un verre ne serait pas de refus.

ammo○ /'æməʊ/ n **¢** (abrév = **ammunition**) munitions fpl.

ammonia /ə'məʊnɪə/ n (gas) ammoniac m; (solution) ammoniaque f.

ammunition /,æmjʊ'nɪʃn/ n **¢** MIL munitions fpl; FIG armes fpl.

amnesia /æm'niːzɪə, US -ʒə/ n amnésie f.

amnesiac /æm'niːzɪæk, US -'ʒɪæk/ n, adj amnésique (mf).

amnesty /'æmnəstɪ/ n POL, JUR (pardon, period) amnistie f; **under an ~** dans le cadre de l'amnistie.

amoeba /ə'miːbə/ n amibe f.

amoebic /ə'miːbɪk/ adj [dysentery etc] amibien/-ienne.

amok /ə'mɒk/ adv **to run ~** [person, animal] être pris de folie furieuse; [imagination] se débrider.

among /ə'mʌŋ/, **amongst** /ə'mʌŋst/ prep **1** (amidst) parmi [crowd, population]; au milieu de, parmi [trees, ruins]; parmi, dans [papers, belongings]; **~ those present** parmi les personnes présentes; **to be ~ friends** être entre amis; **~ others** entre autres; **2** (affecting a particular group) chez; **unemployment ~ young people** le chômage chez les jeunes; **3** (one of) **~ the world's poorest countries** un des pays les plus pauvres du monde; **she was ~ those who survived** elle faisait partie des survivants; **to be ~ the first** être dans les premiers; **4** (between) entre; **divided ~ his heirs** partagé entre ses héritiers; **they can never agree ~ themselves** ils n'arrivent jamais à se mettre d'accord; **one bottle ~ five** une bouteille pour cinq.

amorality /eɪmə'rælɪtɪ/ n amoralité f.

amorous /'æmərəs/ adj LITTÉR ou HUM amoureux/-euse.

amorphous /ə'mɔːfəs/ adj **1** CHEM amorphe; **2** GEN [shape, collection] informe; [ideas, plans] confus.

amount /ə'maʊnt/ n **1** GEN (quantity) (of goods, food) quantité f; (of people, objects) nombre m; **a considerable ~/fair ~ of** beaucoup/pas mal de○; **a certain ~ of imagination** une certaine imagination; **I'm**

entitled to a certain **~ of respect** j'ai droit à un certain respect; **no ~ of persuasion will make him change his mind** on aura beau essayer de le persuader, rien ne le fera changer d'avis; **2** (sum of money) somme f; (bill) montant m; **the full ~** le montant total; **what is the outstanding ~?** combien reste-t-il à payer?; **~ paid (on account)** COMM acompte versé.

■ **amount to: ~ to** [sth] **1** (add up to) [cost] s'élever à; **2** (be equivalent to) équivaloir à, revenir à [confession, betrayal etc]; **it ~s to the same thing** cela revient au même; **it ~s to blackmail!** ce n'est rien d'autre que du chantage!; **not to ~ to much** [accusation, report] ne pas valoir grand-chose○.

amp /æmp/ n **1** abrév ▶ **ampere**; **2**○ (abrév = **amplifier**) ampli○ m.

amperage /'æmpərɪdʒ/ n intensité f de courant, ampérage m CONTROV.

ampere /'æmpeə(r), US 'æmpɪə(r)/ n ampère m.

ampersand /'æmpəsænd/ n esperluette f.

amphibian /æm'fɪbɪən/ n **1** ZOOL amphibie m; **2** AVIAT appareil m amphibie; **3** AUT véhicule m amphibie; **4** MIL (tank) char m amphibie.

amphibious /æm'fɪbɪəs/ adj ZOOL, MIL amphibie.

amphitheatre, amphitheater US /'æmfɪθɪətə(r)/ n **1** amphithéâtre m; **2** (natural) **~** cirque m.

ample /'æmpl/ adj **1** (plenty) [provisions, resources] largement suffisant (**for** pour); [illustration] ample; **there's ~ room** il y a largement la place; **to have ~ opportunity to do** avoir largement la possibilité de faire; **he was given ~ warning** il a été largement prévenu; **he's been given ~ opportunity to apologize** on lui a donné toutes les chances de s'excuser; **there is ~ evidence that** il est prouvé que; **2** (of generous size) [proportions, bust] généreux/-euse; [garment] large.

amplifier /'æmplɪfaɪə(r)/ n amplificateur m, ampli○ m.

amplify /'æmplɪfaɪ/ vtr **1** AUDIO, ELEC, RADIO amplifier; **2** GEN développer [account, statement, concept].

amply /'æmplɪ/ adv [compensated, fulfilled] largement; [demonstrated] amplement.

amputate /'æmpjʊteɪt/ vtr amputer; **to ~ sb's leg** amputer qn de la jambe.

amputee /,æmpjʊ'tiː/ n amputé/-e m/f.

Amsterdam /,æmstə'dæm/ ▶ 1343 pr n Amsterdam.

Amtrak /'æmtræk/ n US société de transports ferroviaires.

amuse /ə'mjuːz/ **I** vtr **1** (cause laughter) amuser; **to be ~d at** ou **by** s'amuser de; **I'm not ~d!** je ne trouve pas ça drôle!; **2** (entertain) [game, story] distraire; **3** (occupy) [activity, hobby] occuper.
II v refl **to ~ oneself 1** (entertain) se distraire; **2** (occupy) s'occuper.

amusement /ə'mjuːzmənt/ **I** n **1** (mirth) amusement m (**at** face à); **a look of ~** un air amusé; **to conceal one's ~** dissimuler son envie de rire; **2** (diversion) distraction f; **for ~** pour me/se distraire.
II amusements npl (at fairground) attractions fpl.

amusement: ~ arcade n GB salle f de jeux électroniques; **~ park** n parc m d'attractions.

amusing /ə'mjuːzɪŋ/ adj amusant.

amyl: ~ alcohol n alcool m amylique; **~ nitrate** n nitrite m amylique.

an /æn, ən/ ▶ **a²**.

anabolic steroid /,ænə'bɒlɪk 'stɪərɔɪd/ n stéroïde m anabolisant.

anachronism /ə'nækrənɪzəm/ n anachronisme m; **to be an ~** [object, custom etc] être un anachronisme.

anaemia /ə'niːmɪə/ ▶ 1002 n anémie f.

anaemic /ə'niːmɪk/ adj **1** MED anémique; **to become ~** s'anémier; **2** FIG [performance, poem] fade.

anaerobic /,æneə'rəʊbɪk/ adj anaérobie.

anaesthetic GB, **anesthetic** US /,ænɪs'θetɪk/ n, adj anesthésique (m); **to be under ~** être sous anesthésie.

aesthetist /ə'niːsθətɪst/ ▶ 1251 | n GB (médecin) anesthésiste mf.

aesthetize GB, **anesthetize** US /ə'niːsθətaɪz/ vtr anesthésier.

agram /'ænəgræm/ n anagramme f (of de).

algesic /ˌænæl'dʒiːsɪk/ n, adj analgésique (m).

alogous /ə'næləgəs/ adj analogue (to, with à).

alogy /ə'nælədʒɪ/ n analogie f; to draw an ~ faire ne analogie (between entre; with avec).

alyse GB, **analyze** US /'ænəlaɪz/ vtr 1 GEN, NG analyser; 2 GB PSYCH psychanalyser.

alysis /ə'nælɪsɪs/ n 1 GEN, LING analyse f; in the nal ou last ~ en fin de compte; 2 PSYCH psychana-/se f; to be in ~ être en analyse.

alyst /'ænəlɪst/ ▶ 1251 | n analyste mf.

alytic(al) /ˌænə'lɪtɪk(l)/ adj analytique.

archic(al) /ə'nɑːkɪk(l)/ adj anarchique.

archist /'ænəkɪst/ n, adj anarchiste (mf).

archy /'ænəkɪ/ n anarchie f.

athema /ə'næθəmə/ n (pl ~s) RELIG anathème ; FIG abomination f; history/cruelty is ~ to him il l'histoire/la cruauté en horreur.

atomical /ˌænə'tɒmɪkl/ adj anatomique.

atomy /ə'nætəmɪ/ I n 1 MED, BIOL anatomie f; 2 (of subject, event) analyse f (détaillée) (of de). noun modifier [class, lesson] d'anatomie.

NC n (abrév = **African National Congress**) ANC

cestor /'ænsestə(r)/ n LIT, FIG ancêtre mf.

cestral /æn'sestrəl/ adj ancestral.

cestry /'ænsestrɪ/ n 1 (lineage) ascendance f; 2 ncestors collectively) ancêtres mpl, aïeux mpl.

chor /'æŋkə(r)/ I n 1 NAUT ancre f; to drop ou ast ~ jeter l'ancre; to come to ~ mouiller; to be lie at ~ être ancré; to slip ~ filer par le bout; 2 point m d'ancrage; (person) soutien m. vtr 1 ancrer [ship, balloon]; arrimer [tent, roof etc] o à); 2 US RADIO, TV présenter.

chorage /'æŋkərɪdʒ/ n GEN, NAUT ancrage m.

chorman /'æŋkəmən/ ▶ 1251 | n 1 RADIO, TV pré-ntateur m; (in network, organization) pivot m; 2 SPORT layeur m.

chorwoman /'æŋkəwʊmən/ ▶ 1251 | n RADIO, TV ésentatrice f.

chovy /'æntʃəvɪ, US 'æntʃəʊvɪ/ n anchois m.

cient /'eɪnʃənt/ adj 1 (dating from BC) antique; (very) ancien/-ienne; ~ Greek LING grec ancien; ~ reece la Grèce antique; ~ history (subject) histoire ancienne; ~ monument monument m historique; ~ times dans les temps anciens; 2○ [person, car] ès vieux/vieille.

cillary /æn'sɪlərɪ, US 'ænsəlerɪ/ adj [service, staff, sk, industry, equipment, role] auxiliaire; [cost] cessoire; [road] secondaire.

d /ænd, unstressed ənd/

Note When used as a straightforward conjunction, and translated by et: to shout and sing = crier et chanter;)m and Linda = Tom et Linda; my friend and colleague = on ami et collègue.

and is sometimes used between two verbs in English to ean 'in order to' (wait and see, try and relax etc). To anslate these expressions, look under the appropriate rb entry (wait, try etc).

For examples and other uses, see the entry below.

---

nj 1 (joining words or clauses) et; cups ~ plates des sses et des assiettes; he picked up his papers and ent out il a ramassé ses papiers et il est sorti; 2 (in mbers) two hundred ~ sixty-two deux cent ixante-deux; 3 (with repetition) faster ~ faster de us en plus vite; it got worse ~ worse c'est venu de pire en pire; I waited ~ waited j'ai tendu pendant des heures; to talk on ~ on parler ndant des heures; we laughed ~ laughed! qu'est-qu'on a ri!; 4 (for emphasis) it's lovely ~ warm il it bon; come nice ~ early viens tôt; AND he

didn't even say thank you et en plus il n'a même pas dit merci; 5 (in phrases) ~ all that et tout le reste; ~ that○ GB et tout ça; ~ so on et ainsi de suite; ~ how○! et comment!; ~? et alors?; 6 (alike) summer ~ winter été comme hiver; day ~ night jour et nuit; 7 (with negative) he doesn't like singing ~ dancing il n'aime ni chanter ni danser.

Andean /æn'dɪən/ adj andin, des Andes.

Andes /'ændiːz/ pr npl the ~ les Andes fpl.

Andorra /æn'dɔːrə/ ▶ 840 | pr n Andorre f.

anecdotal /ˌænɪk'dəʊtl/ adj [memoirs, account] anecdotique; [talk, lecture] plein d'anecdotes; on the basis of ~ evidence... selon des sources non confirmées...

anemone /ə'nemənɪ/ n BOT anémone f.

anesthesiologist /ˌænɪsˌθiːzɪ'ɒlədʒɪst/ ▶ 1251 | n US (médecin) anesthésiste mf.

anesthetist /ə'niːsθətɪst/ ▶ 1251 | n US infirmier/-ière m/f anesthésiste.

anesthetize vtr US = **anaesthetize**.

anew /ə'njuː, US ə'nuː/ adv (once more) encore, de nouveau; (in a new way) à nouveau; to begin ~ recommencer.

angel /'eɪndʒl/ n LIT, FIG ange m; ~ of mercy ange de miséricorde.

IDIOMS to rush in where ~s fear to tread se lancer avec le courage de l'inconscience.

angel: ~ cake n gâteau m de Savoie (coloré en rose et blanc); ~fish n scalaire m.

angelic /æn'dʒelɪk/ adj angélique.

anger /'æŋgə(r)/ I n colère f (at devant; towards contre); in ~ sous le coup de la colère.
II vtr [decision, remark] mettre [qn] en colère [person].

angina (pectoris) /æn'dʒaɪnə ('pektərɪs)/ ▶ 1002 | n angine f de poitrine.

angle /'æŋgl/ I n 1 GEN, MATH angle m; ~ of descent angle de chute; camera ~ angle de vue; to be at an ~ to sth [table] faire un angle avec [wall]; [tower] pencher par rapport à [ground]; from every ~ sous tous les angles; seen from this ~ d'ici; at an ~ en biais; 2 (point of view) point m de vue (on sur); (perspective, slant) angle m; seen from this ~ sous cet angle; 3 (corner) angle m (of de); 4 SPORT GEN angle m; (of shot, kick) angle m de tir.
II vtr 1 (tilt) orienter [camera, light, table] (towards vers); incliner [racket, ball]; 2 SPORT (hit) jouer [qch] près des lignes [ball, shot]; 3 FIG (slant) orienter [programme].
III vi 1 (fish) pêcher (à la ligne); to ~ for salmon pêcher le saumon; 2○ FIG (try to obtain) to ~ for sth chercher à obtenir qch.

angle bracket n TECH équerre f.

Anglepoise® /'æŋglpɔɪz/ n ~ (lamp) lampe f d'architecte.

angler /'æŋglə(r)/ n pêcheur/-euse m/f (à la ligne).

anglicism /'æŋglɪsɪzəm/ n anglicisme m.

anglicize /'æŋglɪsaɪz/ vtr angliciser.

angling /'æŋglɪŋ/ ▶ 949 | n pêche f (à la ligne).

Anglo+ /'æŋgləʊ/ combining form anglo-.

Anglo-American /ˌæŋgləʊə'merɪkən/ ▶ 1100 | I n Anglo-Américain/-e m/f.
II adj anglo-américain.

Anglo-French /ˌæŋgləʊ'frentʃ/ ▶ 1100 |, 1038 | I n LING anglo-normand m.
II adj anglo-français, franco-britannique.

Anglophone /'æŋgləʊfəʊn/ n, adj anglophone (mf).

Anglo-Saxon /ˌæŋgləʊ'sæksn/ ▶ 1100 |, 1038 | I n 1 (person) Anglo-Saxon/-onne m/f; 2 (language) anglo-saxon m.
II adj anglo-saxon/-onne.

Angola /æŋ'gəʊlə/ ▶ 840 | pr n Angola m.

angrily /'æŋgrɪlɪ/ adv [react, speak] avec colère.

angry /'æŋgrɪ/ adj 1 [person, animal, reaction, tone, expression] furieux/-ieuse; [outburst, scene, words] de colère; to look ~ avoir l'air en colère; to be ~ at ou with sb être en colère contre qn; I was ~ at having to wait j'étais en colère d'avoir à attendre; to get ou **grow** ~ se fâcher; **to make sb** ~ mettre qn en colère; **2** FIG [*sea, sky*] LITTÉR menaçant; [*wound, rash*] vilain.

anguish /'æŋgwɪʃ/ *n* **1** (mental) souffrance *f*, douleur *f*; **to be in** ~ être au supplice; **2** (physical) douleur *f*.

anguished /'æŋgwɪʃt/ *adj* [*person*] angoissé; [*suffering*] aigu/-uë.

angular /'æŋgjʊlə(r)/ *adj* [*features, shape*] anguleux/-euse; [*person*] au physique anguleux; [*building*] plein d'angles.

animal /'ænɪml/ **I** *n* **1** LIT (creature, genus) animal *m*, bête *f*; **2** (brutish person) **to behave like** ~**s** [*people*] se conduire comme des brutes; **to bring out the** ~ **in sb** réveiller la bête qui est en qn; **3** FIG **she is a political** ~ elle a la politique dans le sang.
II *noun modifier* [*welfare, rights*] des animaux; [*feed*] pour animaux; [*behaviour, fat*] animal.

animal: ~ **activist** *n* militant/-e *m*/*f* pour les droits des animaux; ~ **experiment** *n* expérience *f* sur les animaux; ~ **husbandry** *n* élevage *m*; ~ **kingdom** *n* règne *m* animal; ~ **liberation front** *n* mouvement *m* pour la libération des animaux; ~ **lover** *n* ami/-e *m*/*f* des bêtes; ~ **product** *n* produit *m* d'origine animale; ~ **sanctuary** *n* refuge *m* pour animaux; ~ **testing** *n* expérimentation *f* animale.

animate I /'ænɪmət/ *adj* [*person*] vivant; [*object*] animé.
II /'ænɪmeɪt/ *vtr* animer.

animated /'ænɪmeɪtɪd/ *adj* (all contexts) animé.

animatedly /'ænɪmeɪtɪdlɪ/ *adv* avec animation.

animator /'ænɪmeɪtə(r)/ **▶ 1251** *n* (film cartoonist) animateur/-trice *m*/*f*; (director) réalisateur/-trice *m*/*f* de dessin animé.

animosity /ˌænɪ'mɒsətɪ/ *n* animosité *f* (**towards** envers).

aniseed /'ænɪsiːd/ *n* **1** (flavour) anis *m*; **2** (seed) graine *f* d'anis.

ankle /'æŋkl/ **▶ 765** *n* cheville *f*.

anklebone *n* astragale *m*.

ankle-deep *adj* **to be** ~ **in mud** avoir de la boue jusqu'aux chevilles.

ankle: ~**-length** *adj* [*dress*] descendant jusqu'aux chevilles; ~ **sock** *n* socquette *f*.

annals /'ænlz/ *npl* annales *fpl*; **to go down in the** ~ (of history) figurer dans les annales.

annex I /'æneks/ *n* (also **annexe** GB) annexe *f*.
II /ə'neks/ *vtr* annexer [*territory, land, country*] (**to** à).

annexation /ˌænɪk'seɪʃn/ *n* (action) annexion *f* (**of** de); (land annexed) territoire *m* annexé.

annihilate /ə'naɪəleɪt/ *vtr* (all contexts) anéantir.

anniversary /ˌænɪ'vɜːsərɪ/ **I** *n* anniversaire *m* (**of** de).
II *noun modifier* [*festival, reunion*] commémoratif/-ive.

anno Domini, Anno Domini /ˌænəʊ 'dɒmɪnaɪ/ *adv* après Jésus-Christ.

annotate /'ænəteɪt/ *vtr* annoter.

announce /ə'naʊns/ **I** *vtr* annoncer (**that** que).
II *vi* US annoncer sa candidature.

announcement /ə'naʊnsmənt/ *n* **1** (spoken) annonce *f* (**of** de; **that** indiquant que); **2** (written) avis *m*; (of birth, death) faire-part *m inv*.

announcer /ə'naʊnsə(r)/ *n* **1** (on TV) speaker/-erine *m*/*f*; **radio** ~ présentateur/-trice *m*/*f* de radio; **2** (at rail station) annonceur/-euse *m*/*f*.

annoy /ə'nɔɪ/ *vtr* [*person*] (by behaviour) agacer; (by opposing wishes) contrarier; [*discomfort, noise*] gêner; **what really** ~**s me is that** ce qui me contrarie, c'est que; **this man's** ~**ing me** cet homme m'embête.

annoyance /ə'nɔɪəns/ *n* **1** (crossness) agacement *m* (**at** à); contrariété *f* (**at** à); **a look of** ~ un regard agacé; **2** (nuisance) désagrément *m*.

annoyed /ə'nɔɪd/ *adj* contrarié (**at, by** par); (stronger) agacé, fâché (**at, by** par); ~ **with sb** fâché contre qn; **she was** ~ **with him for being late** elle était contrariée parce qu'il était en retard.

annoying /ə'nɔɪɪŋ/ *adj* agaçant (**to do** de faire); **the**

~ **thing is that**... ce qui est agaçant or fâcheux, c'e que...

annual /'ænjʊəl/ **I** *n* **1** (book) album *m* (annuel); (plant) plante *f* annuelle.
II *adj* annuel/-elle.

Annual General Meeting, AGM *n* assemblée *f* g nérale annuelle.

annually /'ænjʊəlɪ/ *adv* [*earn, produce*] par an; [*d inspect*] tous les ans.

annuity /ə'njuːətɪ, US -'nuː-/ *n* rente *f*.

annul /ə'nʌl/ *vtr* (*p prés etc* **-ll-**) annuler [*marriag treaty, vote*]; abroger [*law*].

annulment /ə'nʌlmənt/ *n* (of marriage) annulation (of legislation) abrogation *f*.

Annunciation /əˌnʌnsɪ'eɪʃn/ *n* Annonciation *f*.

anodyne /'ænədaɪn/ *adj* (inoffensive) inoffensif/-iv (bland) anodin.

anoint /ə'nɔɪnt/ *vtr* **1** oindre; **to** ~ **with oil** oindre **2** (appoint to office) sacrer.

anomaly /ə'nɒməlɪ/ *n* anomalie *f* (**in** dans).

anon. /ə'nɒn/ *abrév* = **anonymous**.

anonymity /ˌænə'nɪmətɪ/ *n* anonymat *m*.

anonymous /ə'nɒnɪməs/ *adj* anonyme; **to remai** ~ garder l'anonymat.

anonymously /ə'nɒnɪməslɪ/ *adv* [*complain, writ* anonymement; [*inform, donate*] de façon anonyme.

anorak /'ænəræk/ *n* anorak *m*.

anorexia /ˌænə'reksɪə/ *n* **1** (also ~ **nervosa**) and rexie *f* mentale; **2** (loss of appetite) anorexie *f*.

anorexic /ˌænə'reksɪk/ *n, adj* anorexique (*mf*).

another /ə'nʌðə(r)/

■ **Note** When *another* is used as a determiner it is trans lated by *un autre* or *une autre* according to the gende of the noun that follows: *another ticket* = un autre billet *another cup* = une autre tasse. However, when *anothe* means an *additional*, *encore* can also be used: *anothe cup of tea?* = une autre tasse de thé *or* encore une tasse de thé? For more examples and particular usages, see below.
– When *another* is used as a pronoun it is translated by *un autre* or *une autre* according to the gender of the noun it refers to: *that cake was delicious, can I have another?* = ce gâteau était délicieux, est-ce que je peux en prendre un autre?; *I see you like the peaches—have another* = je vois que tu aimes les pêches—prends-en une autre. Note that *en* is always added in French when *un/une autre* are used as pronouns. For more examples and particula usages, see **I** below.

I *det* **1** (an additional) un/-e autre, encore un/-e; **would you like** ~ **drink?** est-ce que tu veux un autre verre?; encore un verre?; **yet** ~ **letter** encore une nouvelle lettre; **that will cost you** ~ **£5** cela vous coûtera 5 livres sterling de plus; **without** ~ **word** sans rien dire de plus; **in** ~ **five weeks** dans cinq semaines; **it was** ~ **ten years before they met again** dix ans se sont écoulés avant qu'ils se rencontrent de nouveau; **and** ~ **thing,...** et de plus,...; **2** (a different) un/-e autre; ~ **time** une autre fois; **he has** ~ **job now** il a un nouveau travail maintenant; **to put it** ~ **way...** en d'autres termes...; **that's quite** ~ **matter** ça c'est une autre histoire or question; **3** (new) ~ **Garbo** une nouvelle Garbo.
II *pron* un/-e autre; **can I have** ~? est-ce que je peux en avoir un/-e autre?; ~ **of the witnesses said that** un autre témoin a dit que; **one after** ~ l'un/l'une après l'autre; **of one kind or** ~ d'une sorte ou d'une autre; **for one reason or** ~ pour une raison ou une autre; **in one way or** ~ d'une façon ou d'une autre.

answer /'ɑːnsə(r), US 'ænsər/ **I** *n* **1** (reply) réponse *f* (**to** à); **to get/give an** ~ obtenir/donner une réponse; **there's no** ~ (to door) il n'y a personne; (on phone) ça ne répond pas; **in** ~ **to sth** en réponse à qch; **I won't take no for an** ~! pas question de refuser!; **there's no** ~ **to that!** que voulez-vous répondre à ça?; **France's** ~ **to Marilyn Monroe** la version française de Marilyn Monroe; **2** (solution) (to difficulty, puzzle) solu-

tion *f* (**to** à); SCH, UNIV réponse *f* (**to** à); **the right/ wrong ~** la bonne/mauvaise réponse.
II *vtr* **1** (reply to) répondre à [*question, invitation, letter, person*]; **to ~ that**... répondre que...; **to ~ the door** aller or venir ouvrir la porte; **to ~ the telephone** répondre au téléphone; **to ~ the call** LIT, FIG répondre à l'appel; **2** GEN, JUR (respond) répondre à [*criticism, accusation, allegation*]; **to ~ a charge** répondre d'une accusation; **3** (meet) répondre à [*need, demand*]; **we saw nobody ~ing that description** nous n'avons vu personne qui réponde à cette description.
III *vi* **1** (respond) répondre; **it's not ~ing** GB TELECOM ça ne répond pas; **to ~ to the name of X** répondre au nom de X; **2** (correspond) **to ~ to** répondre or correspondre à [*description*]; **3** (account) **to ~ for sb** répondre de qn; **to ~ to sb** être responsable devant qn.
■ **answer back**: ¶ **~ back** répondre; ¶ **~** [*sb*] **back** GB répondre; **don't ~ (me) back!** comment oses-tu (me) répondre?
■ **answer for**: **~ for** [*sth*] (account for) répondre de [*action*]; **they have a lot to ~ for!** ils ont beaucoup de comptes à rendre!

answerable /'ɑːnsərəbl, US 'æns-/ *adj* **to be ~ to sb** être responsable devant qn; **to be ~ for** être responsable of [*actions*]; **they are ~ to no-one** ils n'ont de comptes à rendre à personne.

answering: **~ machine** *n* répondeur *m* (téléphonique); **~ service** *n* permanence *f* téléphonique.

answerphone /'ɑːnsəfəʊn, US 'æns-/ *n* répondeur *m* (téléphonique).

ant /ænt/ *n* fourmi *f*; **flying ~** fourmi volante.

antacid /ænt'æsɪd/ *n*, *adj* alcalin (*m*).

antagonism /æn'tægənɪzəm/ *n* antagonisme *m* (**between** entre); **~ to** ou **towards sb/sth** hostilité *f* à l'égard de qn/qch.

antagonistic /æn,tægə'nɪstɪk/ *adj* (hostile) hostile (**to, towards** à); (mutually opposed) antagoniste.

antagonize /æn'tægənaɪz/ *vtr* (annoy) contrarier (**with** avec); (stronger) éveiller l'hostilité de (**by doing** en faisant; **with** avec).

Antarctic /æn'tɑːktɪk/ **I** *pr n* **the ~** l'Antarctique *m*.
II *adj* (also **antarctic**) antarctique.

Antarctica /æn'tɑːktɪkə/ *pr n* Antarctique *m*.

Antarctic: **~ Circle** cercle *m* polaire antarctique; **~ Ocean ▶ 1117** *n* océan *m* Antarctique.

anteater /'ænti:tə(r)/ *n* fourmilier *m*.

antecedent /,æntɪ'si:dnt/ **I** *n* (precedent) antécédent *m*; (ancestor) ancêtre *m*.
II *adj* antérieur (**to** à).

antedate /,æntɪ'deɪt/ *vtr* **1** (put earlier date on) antidater [*cheque, letter*]; **2** (predate) précéder (**by** de).

antediluvian /,æntɪdɪ'lu:vɪən/ *adj* antédiluvien/ -ienne.

antelope /'æntɪləʊp/ *n* antilope *f*.

antenatal /,æntɪ'neɪtl/ GB **I** *n* examen *m* prénatal.
II *adj* prénatal.

antenatal: **~ class** *n* GB cours *m* de préparation à l'accouchement; **~ clinic** *n* GB service *m* de consultation prénatale.

antenna /æn'tenə/ *n* (*pl* **-ae** ou **-as**) antenne *f*.

anterior /æn'tɪərɪə(r)/ *adj* antérieur.

anteroom /'æntɪruːm, -rʊm/ *n* antichambre *f*.

anthem /'ænθəm/ *n* (theme tune) hymne *m*; (motet) motet *m*.

anthill /'ænthɪl/, **antheap** /'ænthiːp/ *n* fourmilière *f*.

anthologist /æn'θɒlədʒɪst/ *n* anthologiste *mf*.

anthology /æn'θɒlədʒɪ/ *n* anthologie *f*.

anthracite /'ænθrəsaɪt/ *n* anthracite *m*.

anthrax /'ænθræks/ ▶ 1002 *n* (*pl* **-thraces**) (disease) charbon *m*; (pustule) anthrax *m*.

anthropological /,ænθrəpə'lɒdʒɪkl/ *adj* anthropologique.

anthropologist /,ænθrə'pɒlədʒɪst/ ▶ 1251 *n* anthropologue *mf*, anthropologiste *mf*.

anthropology /,ænθrə'pɒlədʒɪ/ *n* anthropologie *f*.

anti /'æntɪ/ **I** *prep* contre; **to be ~** être contre.
II **anti+** *combining form* anti(-).

antiabortion /,æntɪə'bɔːʃn/ *adj* contre l'avortement.

antiabortionist /,æntɪə'bɔːʃənɪst/ *n* adversaire *mf* de l'avortement.

antiaircraft /,æntɪ'eəkrɑːft, US -kræft/ *adj* antiaérien/ -ienne.

antiapartheid /,æntɪə'pɑːteɪt, ,æntɪə'pɑːtaɪd/ *adj* anti-apartheid.

antibacterial /'æntɪbæk'tɪərɪəl/ *adj* antibactérien/ -ienne.

antiballistic missile /,æntɪbəlɪstɪk 'mɪsaɪl, US 'mɪsl/ *n* missile *m* antimissile.

antibiotic /,æntɪbaɪ'ɒtɪk/ **I** *n* antibiotique *m*; **on ~s** sous antibiotiques.
II *adj* antibiotique.

antibody /'æntɪbɒdɪ/ *n* anticorps *m*.

anticipate /æn'tɪsɪpeɪt/ **I** *vtr* **1** (expect, foresee) prévoir, s'attendre à [*problem, delay*]; **to ~ that** prévoir que; **as ~d** comme prévu; **we ~ meeting him soon** nous pensons le rencontrer bientôt; **I didn't ~ him doing** je ne m'attendais pas à ce qu'il fasse ça; **long-~d** attendu depuis si longtemps; **2** (guess in advance) anticiper [*sb's needs, result*]; **3** (preempt) devancer [*person, act*]; **4** (prefigure) préfigurer.
II *vi* anticiper.

anticipation /æn,tɪsɪ'peɪʃn/ *n* **1** (excitement) excitation *f*; (pleasure in advance) plaisir *m* anticipé; **in ~ of sth** à l'idée de qch; **she smiled in ~** elle souriait en se réjouissant d'avance; **2** (expectation) prévision *f* (**of** de); **in ~ of** en prévision de.

anticlerical /,æntɪ'klerɪkl/ *adj* anticlérical.

anticlimax /,æntɪ'klaɪmæks/ *n* déception *f*; **what an ~!** quelle déception!

anticlockwise /,æntɪ'klɒkwaɪz/ *adj*, *adv* GB dans le sens inverse des aiguilles d'une montre.

antics /'æntɪks/ *npl* (comical) pitreries *fpl*; PEJ bouffonneries *fpl*.

anticyclone /,æntɪ'saɪkləʊn/ *n* anticyclone *m*.

antidepressant /,æntɪdɪ'presnt/ *n*, *adj* antidépresseur (*m*).

antidote /'æntɪdəʊt/ *n* MED, FIG antidote *m* (**to, for** contre, à).

antiestablishment /,æntɪɪs'tæblɪʃmənt/ *adj* contestataire.

antifreeze /'æntɪfriːz/ *n* antigel *m*.

antiglare /,æntɪ'gleə(r)/ *adj* [*screen*] antireflet *inv*.

antihistamine /,æntɪ'hɪstəmɪn/ *n* antihistaminique *m*.

anti-inflation /,æntɪɪn'fleɪʃn/ *adj* (*avant n*) anti-inflation.

anti-inflationary /,æntɪɪn'fleɪʃənərɪ, US -nerɪ/ *adj* anti-inflationniste.

antilock /'æntɪlɒk/ *adj* antiblocage.

antipathy /æn'tɪpəθɪ/ *n* antipathie *f* (**for, to, towards** envers; **between** entre).

antiperspirant /,æntɪ'pɜːspɪrənt/ *n* produit *m* antitranspiration.

antipodean /æn,tɪpə'diːən/ **I** *n*: personne qui vient d'Australie ou de Nouvelle-Zélande.
II *adj* d'Australie et Nouvelle-Zélande.

Antipodes /æn'tɪpədiːz/ *npl* GB **the ~** l'Australie et la Nouvelle-Zélande.

antiquarian /,æntɪ'kweərɪən/ ▶ 1251 *n* (dealer) antiquaire *mf*; (scholar) archéologue *mf*; (collector) collectionneur/-euse *m*/*f* d'antiquités.

antiquarian bookshop *n* librairie *f* spécialisée dans le livre ancien.

antiquated /'æntɪkweɪtɪd/ *adj* [*machinery, idea*] archaïque; [*building*] vétuste.

antique /æn'tiːk/ **I** *n* **1** (piece of furniture) meuble *m* ancien or d'époque; (other object) objet *m* ancien or d'époque; **2°** PEJ (person) vieux fossile *m*.
II *adj* **1** (old) ancien/-ienne; **2** (old-style) à l'ancienne.

antique: ~ **dealer** ▶ 1251|, 1251| *n* antiquaire *mf*; ~(**s**) **fair** *n* foire *f* aux antiquités; ~ **shop** ▶ 1251| *n* magasin *m* d'antiquités.

antiquity /æn'tıkwətı/ *n* **1** (ancient times) antiquité *f*; **2** (great age) ancienneté *f*; **of great** ~ très ancien/-ienne; **3** (relic) antiquité *f*.

antiracism /ˌæntı'reɪsɪzəm/ *n* antiracisme *m*.

anti-riot /ˌæntı'raɪət/ *adj* [*police*] antiémeutes *inv*.

anti-rust /ˌæntı'rʌst/ *adj* antirouille *inv*.

anti-Semitic /ˌæntısı'mıtık/ *adj* antisémite.

anti-Semitism /ˌæntı'semıtızəm/ *n* antisémitisme *m*.

antiseptic /ˌæntı'septık/ *n*, *adj* antiseptique (*m*).

anti-skid /ˌæntı'skıd/ *adj* antidérapant.

anti-smoking /ˌæntı'sməʊkıŋ/ *adj* antitabac.

antisocial /ˌæntı'səʊʃl/ *adj* **1** ~ **behaviour** GEN comportement *m* incorrect; (criminal behaviour) comportement *m* délinquant; **2** (reclusive) sauvage.

anti-terrorist /ˌæntı'terərıst/ *adj* antiterroriste.

anti-theft /ˌæntı'θeft/ *adj* [*lock*, *device*] antivol; [*camera*] de surveillance; ~ **steering lock** antivol de direction.

antithesis /æn'tıθəsıs/ *n* (*pl* **-theses**) SOUT **1** (opposite) contraire *m* (**of** de); (in ideas) antithèse *f* (**of** de); **2** (contrast) contraste *m* (**between** entre); **3** LITERAT, PHILOS antithèse *f*.

antithetic(al) /ˌæntı'θetık(l)/ *adj* antithétique; **to be** ~ **to sth** aller à l'encontre de qch.

antitrust /ˌæntı'trʌst/ *adj* antitrust *inv*.

anti-vivisectionist /ˌæntıˌvıvı'sekʃənıst/ **I** *n* militant/-e *m/f* contre la vivisection. **II** *adj* contre la vivisection.

antlers /'æntləz/ *npl* (on stag) bois *mpl* de cerf.

antonym /'æntənım/ *n* antonyme *m*.

Antwerp /'æntwɜːp/ ▶ 1343| *pr n* Anvers.

anus /'eınəs/ *n* anus *m*.

anvil /'ænvıl/ *n* enclume *f* ALSO ANAT.

anxiety /æŋ'zaıətı/ *n* **1** (apprehension) grandes inquiétudes *fpl* (**about** à propos de; **for** pour); **she caused them great** ~ elle leur a causé beaucoup de soucis; **to be in a state of** ~ être angoissé; **2** (source of worry) souci *m*; **3** (eagerness) désir *m* ardent (**to do** de faire); **4** PSYCH anxiété *f*; ~ **attack** crise *f* d'angoisse.

anxious /'æŋkʃəs/ *adj* **1** (worried) très inquiet/-iète (**about** à propos de; **for** pour); **to be** ~ **about doing** s'inquiéter de faire; **to be very** ou **extremely** ~ être angoissé; **2** (causing worry) [*moment*, *time*] angoissant; **3** (eager) très désireux/-euse (**to do** de faire); **I am** ~ **for him to know** ou **that he should know** je tiens beaucoup à ce qu'il sache; **to be** ~ **for sth** avoir un fort désir de qch.

anxiously /'æŋkʃəslı/ *adv* **1** (worriedly) avec inquiétude; **2** (eagerly) avec impatience.

any /'enı/

■ **Note** When *any* is used as a determiner in negative sentences it is not usually translated in French: *we don't have any money* = nous n'avons pas d'argent.
– When *any* is used as a determiner in questions it is translated by *du, de l', de la* or *des* according to the gender and number of the noun that follows: *is there any soap?* = y a-t-il du savon?; *is there any flour?* = y a-t-il de la farine?; *are there any questions?* = est-ce qu'il y a des questions?
– For examples and other determiner uses see I in the entry below.
– When *any* is used as a pronoun in negative sentences and in questions it is translated by *en: we don't have any* = nous n'en avons pas; *have you got any?* = est-ce que vous en avez?
– For more examples and other pronoun uses see II below.
– For adverbial uses such as *any more, any longer, any better* etc see III below.

I *det* **1** (with negative, implied negative) **he hasn't got** ~ **money** il n'a pas d'argent; **they never receive** ~ **letters** ils ne reçoivent jamais de lettres; **they hardly**

ate ~ **cake** ils n'ont presque pas mangé de gâteau; **don't want** ~ **lunch** je ne veux pas de déjeuner; **don't need** ~ **advice** je n'ai pas besoin de conseils; **they couldn't get** ~ **information** ils n'ont pas obtenu la moindre information; **he hasn't got** ~ **common sense** il n'a aucun bon sens; **2** (in questions, conditional sentences) **is there** ~ **tea?** est-ce qu'il y a du thé?; **if you have** ~ **money** si vous avez de l'argent; **3** (no matter which) n'importe quel/quelle, tout **you can have** ~ **cup you like** vous pouvez prendre n'importe quelle tasse; ~ **information would be very useful** tout renseignement serait très utile; ~ **complaints should be addressed to Mr Cook** pour toute réclamation adressez-vous à M. Cook; **I'm ready to help in** ~ **way I can** je suis prêt à faire tout ce que je peux pour aider; **I do not wish to restrict your freedom in** ~ **way** je n'ai pas l'intention d'entraver votre liberté de quelque façon que ce soit; **he might return at** ~ **time** il peut revenir d'un moment à l'autre; **if you should want to discuss this at** ~ **time** si à un moment ou à un autre vous souhaitez discuter de cela; **come round and see me** ~ **time** passe me voir quand tu veux; **I don't buy** ~ **one brand in particular** je n'achète aucune marque en particulier.

II *pron* **1** (with negative, implied negative) **he hasn't got** ~ il n'en a pas; **there is hardly** ~ **left** il n'en reste presque pas; **she doesn't like** ~ **of them** (people) elle n'aime aucun d'entre eux/elles; (things) elle n'en aime aucun/-e; **2** (in questions, conditional sentences) **I'd like some tea, if you have** ~ je voudrais du thé, si vous en avez; **have** ~ **of you got a car?** est-ce que l'un/-e d'entre vous a une voiture?; **are** ~ **of them blue?** en a-t-il des bleus?; **3** (no matter which) n'importe lequel/laquelle; **'which colour would you like?'—'** ~ **'** 'quelle couleur veux-tu?'—'n'importe laquelle'; ~ **of those pens** n'importe lequel de ces stylos; ~ **of them could do it** n'importe qui d'entre eux/elles pourrait le faire.

III *adv* **1** (with comparatives) **is he feeling** ~ **better?** est-ce qu'il se sent mieux?; **have you got** ~ **more of these?** est-ce que vous en avez d'autres?; **do you want** ~ **more wine?** voulez-vous encore du vin?; **I don't like him** ~ **more than you do** je ne l'aime guère plus que toi; **I don't know** ~ **more than that** c'est tout ce que je sais; **he doesn't live here** ~ **more** ou longer il n'habite plus ici; **I won't put up with it** ~ **longer** ça ne peut pas continuer ainsi; **if we stay here** ~ **longer** si nous restons plus longtemps; **can't you walk** ~ **faster?** tu ne peux pas marcher plus vite?; **I can't leave** ~ **later than 6 o'clock** il faut que je parte à 6 heures au plus tard; **2**° (at all) du tout; **that doesn't help me** ~ ça ne m'aide pas du tout.

anybody /'enıbodı/ *pron* **1** (with negative, implied negative) personne; **there wasn't** ~ **in the house** il n'y avait personne dans la maison; **without** ~ **knowing** sans que personne le sache; **I didn't have** ~ **to talk to** il n'y avait personne avec qui j'aurais pu parler; **I don't like him and nor does** ~ **else** je ne l'aime pas, d'ailleurs personne ne l'aime; **hardly** ~ **came** il n'est venu presque personne; **2** (in questions, conditional sentences) quelqu'un; **is there** ~ **in the house?** est-ce qu'il y a quelqu'un dans la maison?; **if** ~ **asks, tell them I've gone out** si quelqu'un me cherche, dis que je suis sorti; **3** (no matter who) ~ **could do it** n'importe qui pourrait le faire; **but you/his boss would say yes** tout autre que toi/ton patron dirait oui; **'who shall I invite?'—'** ~ **but him'** 'qui vais-je inviter?'—'n'importe qui, sauf lui'; ~ **who wants to, can go** tous ceux qui le veulent, peuvent y aller; ~ **but you would have given it to him** n'importe qui d'autre que toi le lui aurait donné; ~ **can make a mistake** ça arrive à tout le monde de faire une erreur; ~ **would think you were deaf** c'est à croire que tu es sourd; **you can invite** ~ **(you like)** tu peux inviter qui tu veux; **4** (somebody unimportant) **we can't ask just** ~ **to do it** nous ne pouvons pas demander à n'importe qui de le faire; **5** (somebody important) ~ **who was** ~ **was at the party** tous les gens importants étaient à la soirée.

anyhow /'enihaʊ/ *adv* **1** (in any case) = **anyway**; **2** (in a careless way) n'importe comment.

anyone /'eniwʌn/ *pron* = **anybody**.

anyplace○ /'enipleis/ *adv* US = **anywhere**.

anything /'eniθiŋ/ *pron* **1** (with negative, implied negative) rien; **she didn't say/do ~** elle n'a rien dit/fait; **he didn't have ~ to do** il n'avait rien à faire; **don't believe ~ he says** ne crois pas un mot de ce qu'il dit; **2** (in questions, conditional sentences) quelque chose; **if ~ happens** ou **should happen to her** s'il lui arrive quoi que ce soit; **is there ~ to be done?** peut-on faire quelque chose?; **is there ~ in the rumour that...?** est-il vrai que...?; **3** (no matter what) tout; **~ is possible** tout est possible; **I'd do** ou **give ~ to get that job** je ferais tout pour obtenir cet emploi; **they'd do ~ for you** ils sont toujours prêts à rendre service; **she likes ~ sweet/to do with football** elle aime tout ce qui est sucré/qui a rapport au football; **to cost ~ between £50 and £100** coûter de 50 à 100 livres sterling; **he was ~ but happy/a liar** il n'était pas du tout heureux/menteur; **'was it interesting?'—'~ but!'** 'est-ce que c'était intéressant?'—'tout sauf ça'; **he wasn't annoyed, if ~, he was quite pleased** il n'était pas fâché, au contraire, il était content.

IDIOMS **~ goes** tout est permis; **as easy/funny as ~** facile/drôle comme tout; **to run/laugh/work like ~** courir/rire/travailler comme un fou○.

anytime /'enitaim/ *adv* (also **any time**) **1** (no matter when) n'importe quand; **~ after 2 pm** n'importe quand à partir de 14 heures; **~ you like** quand tu veux; **if at ~ you feel lonely...** si jamais tu te sens seul...; **at ~ of the day or night** à n'importe quelle heure du jour ou de la nuit; **2** (at any moment) à tout moment; **he could arrive ~ now** il pourrait arriver d'un moment à l'autre.

anyway /'eniwei/ *adv* **1** (in any case, besides) de toute façon; **2** (nevertheless) quand même; **I don't really like hats, but I'll try it on ~** je n'aime pas vraiment les chapeaux, mais je vais quand même l'essayer; **thanks ~** merci quand même; **3** (at least, at any rate) en tout cas; **we can't go out, not yet ~** nous ne pouvons pas sortir, pas pour l'instant en tout cas; **4** (well: as sentence adverb) **'~, we arrived at the station...'** 'bon, nous sommes arrivés à la gare...'

anywhere /'eniweə(r)/, US -hweər/ *adv* **1** (with negative, implied negative) **you can't go ~** tu ne peux aller nulle part; **there isn't ~ to sit** il n'y a pas de place pour s'asseoir; **they didn't go ~ this weekend** ils ne sont allés nulle part ce week-end; **you won't get ~ if you don't pass your exams** FIG tu n'arriveras à rien si tu ne réussis pas tes examens; **crying isn't going to get you ~** FIG ça ne t'avancera à rien de pleurer; **2** (in questions, conditional sentences) quelque part; **have you got a radio ~?** avez-vous une radio quelque part?; **did you go ~ nice?** est-ce que tu es allé dans un endroit agréable?; **we're going to Spain, if ~** si on va quelque part, ce sera en Espagne; **3** (no matter where) **~ you like** où tu veux; **~ in the world/in England** partout dans le monde/en Angleterre; **~ except** ou **but Bournemouth** partout sauf à Bournemouth; **~ she goes, he follows her** il la suit partout où elle va; **'where do you want to go?'—'~ exotic/hot'** 'où veux-tu aller?'—'dans un endroit exotique/où il fait chaud'; **~ between 50 and 100 people** entre 50 et 100 personnes.

aorta /ei'ɔːtə/ *n* (*pl* -tas, -tae) aorte *f*.

Aosta /æ'ɒstə/ *n* Aoste.

apace /ə'peis/ *adv* LITTER rapidement.

Apache /ə'pætʃi/ ▶ **1100**|, **1038**| *n* Apache *mf*.

apart /ə'pɑːt/

■ Note *apart* is used after certain verbs in English (*come apart, take apart, fall apart etc*). For translations consult the appropriate verb entry (*come, take, fall* etc).

I *adj, adv* **1** (at a distance in time or space) **the trees were planted 10 metres ~** les arbres étaient plantés à 10 mètres d'intervalle; **the houses were far ~** les maisons étaient éloignées les unes des autres;

he stood ~ (from the group) il se tenait à l'écart (du groupe); **the posts need to be placed further ~** les poteaux doivent être écartés davantage; **2** (separate from each other) séparé; **we hate being ~ (of couple)** nous détestons être séparés; **they need to be kept ~** il faut les garder séparés; **3** (leaving aside) à part; **dogs ~** à part les chiens; **4** (different) **a race/a world ~** une race/un monde à part.

II apart from *prep phr* **1** (separate from) à l'écart de; **it stands ~ from the other houses** elle est à l'écart des autres maisons; **he lives ~ from his wife** il vit séparé de sa femme; **2** (leaving aside) en dehors de, à part; **~ from working in an office, he...** en plus de travailler dans un bureau, il...; **~ from being illegal, it's also dangerous** (mis) à part que c'est illégal, c'est aussi dangereux.

apartheid /ə'pɑːtheit, -ait/ *n* apartheid *m*.

apartment /ə'pɑːtmənt/ **I** *n* (flat) appartement *m*.

II apartments *npl* (suite of rooms) appartements *mpl*.

apartment: **~ block** *n* immeuble *m*; **~ house** *n* US résidence *f*.

apathetic /ˌæpə'θetik/ *adj* (by nature) amorphe; (from illness, depression) apathique; **~ about sth/towards sb** indifférent à qch/envers qn.

apathy /'æpəθi/ *n* apathie *f*.

ape /eip/ **I** *n* grand singe *m*; **female ~** guenon *f*.

II *vtr* singer [*speech, behaviour, manners*].

Apennines /'æpənainz/ *pr npl* **the ~** les Apennins *mpl*.

aperitif /ə'perətif, US ə,perə'tiːf/ *n* apéritif *m*.

aperture /'æpətʃʊə(r)/ *n* **1** (in wall, door) ouverture *f*; (small) interstice *m*; **2** (in telescope, camera) ouverture *f*.

apex /'eipeks/ *n* (*pl* -exes, -ices) MATH, FIG sommet *m*.

aphid /'eifid/ *n* puceron *m*.

aphrodisiac /ˌæfrə'diziæk/ *n, adj* aphrodisiaque (*m*).

apiary /'eipiəri, US -ieri/ *n* rucher *m*.

apiece /ə'piːs/ *adv* **1** (for each person) chacun/-e *m/f*; **an apple ~** une pomme chacun/-e; **2** (each one) **one franc ~** un franc la pièce.

aplenty /ə'plenti/ *adv* en profusion.

apocalypse /ə'pɒkəlips/ *n* **1** BIBLE **the Apocalypse** l'Apocalypse *f*; **2** (disaster, destruction) apocalypse *f*.

apocalyptic /ə,pɒkə'liptik/ *adj* apocalyptique.

apocryphal /ə'pɒkrifl/ *adj* apocryphe.

apogee /'æpədʒiː/ *n* apogée *m*.

apolitical /ˌeipə'litikl/ *adj* apolitique.

Apollo /ə'pɒləʊ/ **I** *pr n* MYTHOL Apollon *m*.

II *n* (beautiful man) apollon *m*.

apologetic /ə,pɒlə'dʒetik/ *adj* [*gesture, letter*] d'excuse; **to be ~ about sth** s'excuser de qch; **to be ~ about doing** ou **for having done** s'excuser d'avoir fait; **to look ~** avoir l'air contrit.

apologetically /ə,pɒlə'dʒetikli/ *adv* d'un ton or d'un air contrit.

apologist /ə'pɒlədʒist/ *n* apologiste *m*; **~ for sth/sb** défenseur de qch/qn.

apologize /ə'pɒlədʒaiz/ *vi* s'excuser (**to sb** auprès de qn; **for sth** de qch; **for doing** d'avoir fait).

apology /ə'pɒlədʒi/ *n* **1** (excuse) excuses *fpl* (**for sth** pour qch; **for doing** pour avoir fait); **to make an ~** s'excuser; **to make/give one's apologies** faire/présenter ses excuses; **Mrs X sends her apologies** Mme X vous prie d'accepter ses excuses; **without ~** sans excuse; **2** (poor substitute) **an ~ for sth** un semblant de qch.

apoplectic /ˌæpə'plektik/ *adj* **1** (furious) furibond; **2†** MED [*fit, attack*] d'apoplexie.

apoplexy /'æpəpleksi/ *n* **1** (rage) accès *m* de rage; **2†** MED apoplexie *f*.

apostle /ə'pɒsl/ *n* RELIG, FIG apôtre *m* (**of** de).

apostrophe /ə'pɒstrəfi/ *n* apostrophe *f*.

apostrophize /ə'pɒstrəfaiz/ *vtr* lancer une apostrophe à.

apotheosis /ə,pɒθi'əʊsis/ *n* (*pl* -ses) SOUT apothéose *f*.

appal GB, **appall** US /ə'pɔːl/ *vtr* (GB *p prés etc* **-ll-**) (shock) scandaliser; (horrify, dismay) horrifier.

Appalachians /ˌæpə'leɪtʃɪənz/ *pr npl* **the ~** les Appalaches *fpl*.

appalled /ə'pɔːld/ *adj* (horrified, dismayed) horrifié; (shocked) scandalisé.

appalling /ə'pɔːlɪŋ/ *adj* **1** (shocking) [*crime, conditions, bigotry*] épouvantable; [*injury*] affreux/-euse; **it's ~ that** il est révoltant que (+ *subj*); **2** (very bad) [*manners, joke, taste*] exécrable; [*noise, weather*] épouvantable.

appallingly /ə'pɔːlɪŋlɪ/ *adv* [*behave, treat*] de manière épouvantable; **unemployment figures are ~ high** le taux de chômage a atteint un niveau déplorable; **furnished in ~ bad taste** meublé avec un goût exécrable.

apparatus /ˌæpə'reɪtəs, US -'rætəs/ *n* **1** (equipment) ₵ GEN équipement *m*; (in lab) instruments *mpl*; (in gym) agrès *mpl*; **2** (for specific purpose) appareil *m*.

apparent /ə'pærənt/ *adj* **1** (seeming) [*contradiction, willingness*] apparent; **2** (clear) évident; **for no ~ reason** sans raison apparente.

apparently /ə'pærəntlɪ/ *adv* apparemment.

apparition /ˌæpə'rɪʃn/ *n* apparition *f*.

appeal /ə'piːl/ **I** *n* **1** (call) appel *m* (**for** à); **an ~ for calm** un appel au calme; **2** (charity event) appel *m* (**on behalf of** en faveur de); **an ~ for** un appel au don de [*food, blankets*]; **3** SPORT contestation *f* (**against** contre; **to** auprès de); **4** JUR appel *m*; **5** (attraction) charme *m*; (interest) intérêt *m*; **to have a certain ~** avoir un certain charme; **it holds no ~ for me** ça ne m'intéresse pas.

II *vi* **1** JUR faire appel (**against** de); **to ~ to** recourir à l'arbitrage de [*tribunal, person*]; faire appel à [*high court*]; **2** SPORT **to ~ to** demander l'arbitrage de [*referee*]; **to ~ against** contester [*decision*]; **3** (call, request) **to ~ for** lancer un appel à [*order, tolerance*]; faire appel à [*witnesses*]; **to ~ to sb to do** (formal call) prier qn de faire; **to ~ to the public for help** demander de l'aide au public; **4** (attract, interest) **to ~ to sb** [*idea*] tenter qn; [*person*] plaire à qn; [*place*] attirer qn.

appeal: **~(s) court** *n* cour *f* d'appel; **~ fund** *n* fonds *m* d'aide.

appealing /ə'piːlɪŋ/ *adj* **1** (attractive) [*child, kitten*] attachant; [*plan, theory*] séduisant; [*modesty*] charmant; **2** (beseeching) suppliant.

appealingly /ə'piːlɪŋlɪ/ *adv* **1** (beseechingly) d'un air suppliant; **2** (attractively) plaisamment.

appear /ə'pɪə(r)/ *vi* **1** (become visible) apparaître; **2** (turn up) arriver; **to ~ on the scene** LIT arriver sur les lieux, FIG faire son apparition; **to ~ from nowhere** apparaître; **where did she ~ from**○? d'où est-ce qu'elle sort○? HUM; **3** (seem) **to ~ to be/to do** [*person*] avoir l'air d'être/de faire; **to ~ depressed** avoir l'air déprimé; **it ~s that** il semble que; **there ~s to be, there would ~ to be** on dirait qu'il y a; **so it ~s, so it would ~** (according to rumour) à ce qu'il paraît; (this is visibly the case) on dirait bien; **4** [*book, work, article*] paraître; **5** (perform) **to ~ on stage** paraître en scène; **to ~ on TV** passer à la télévision; **to ~ as** jouer dans le rôle de; **6** JUR (be present) comparaître (**before** devant; **for** pour); **to ~ in court** comparaître devant le tribunal; **to ~ as a witness** comparaître comme témoin; **7** (be written) [*name, score*] paraître (**on** sur; **in** dans).

appearance /ə'pɪərəns/ **I** *n* **1** (arrival) (of person, vehicle) arrivée *f*; (of development, invention) apparition *f*; **2** CIN, THEAT, TV passage *m*; **to make an ~ on television** passer à la télévision/à la scène; **cast in order of ~** THEAT distribution par ordre d'entrée en scène; CIN distribution par ordre d'apparition (à l'écran); **3** (public, sporting) apparition *f*; **this is his first ~ for Ireland** il fait ses débuts pour l'équipe d'Irlande; **to put in an ~** faire acte de présence; **4** JUR (in court) comparution *f* (**in, before** devant); **5** (look) (of person) apparence *f* (of district, object) aspect *m*; **to check one's ~** vérifier sa tenue; **6** (semblance) **to give the ~ of sth/of doing** donner l'apparence de

qch/de faire; **it had all the ~s** ou **every ~ of** cela avait tout l'air de; **7** (of book, article) parution *f*.

II appearances *npl* apparences *fpl*; **to judge** ou **go by ~s** se fier aux apparences; **for the sake of ~s, for ~s' sake** pour la forme.

appease /ə'piːz/ *vtr* apaiser.

appeasement /ə'piːzmənt/ *n* apaisement *m*; **a policy of ~** une politique de conciliation.

append /ə'pend/ *vtr* SOUT ajouter (**to** à).

appendage /ə'pendɪdʒ/ *n* appendice *m* ALSO FIG.

appendicitis /əˌpendɪ'saɪtɪs/ ▶ **1002** *n* appendicite *f*.

appendix /ə'pendɪks/ *n* (*pl* **-ixes, -ices**) **1** ANAT appendice *m*; **to have one's ~ removed** se faire opérer de l'appendicite; **2** (to printed volume) appendice *m*; (to book, report) annexe *f*.

appertain /ˌæpə'teɪn/ *vi* **to ~ to sth** se rapporter à qch.

appetite /'æpɪtaɪt/ *n* appétit *m*; **he has a good/poor ~** il a bon appétit/il n'a pas d'appétit; **the walk has given me an ~** la promenade m'a donné de l'appétit; **it'll spoil your ~** ça va te couper l'appétit.

appetite suppressant *n* coupe-faim *m inv*.

appetizer /'æpɪtaɪzə(r)/ *n* (drink) apéritif *m*; (biscuit, olive etc) amuse-gueule *m inv*; (starter) hors-d'œuvre *m*.

appetizing /'æpɪtaɪzɪŋ/ *adj* appétissant.

applaud /ə'plɔːd/ **I** *vtr* **1** (clap) applaudir [*performance*]; **2** (approve of) applaudir à [*choice, tactics*]; applaudir [*person*].

II *vi* applaudir.

applause /ə'plɔːz/ *n* ₵ applaudissements *mpl*; **there was a burst of ~** les applaudissements ont éclaté.

apple /'æpl/ **I** *n* pomme *f*; **the (Big) Apple** New York. **II** *noun modifier* [*juice, peel*] de pomme; [*tart*] aux pommes.

IDIOMS **he is the ~ of her eye** c'est la prunelle de ses yeux.

apple: **~core** *n* trognon *m* de pomme; **~ orchard** *n* pommeraie *f*; **~ tree** *n* pommier *m*.

appliance /ə'plaɪəns/ *n* appareil *m*; **electrical ~** appareil électrique; **household ~** appareil électroménager.

applicable /'æplɪkəbl, ə'plɪkəbl/ *adj* [*argument, excuse*] valable; [*law, rule*] en vigueur; **if ~** le cas échéant; **to be ~ to** s'appliquer à, concerner.

applicant /'æplɪkənt/ *n* **1** (for job, place) candidat/-e *m/f* (**for** à); **job ~** candidat/-e *m/f*; **2** (for passport, benefit, loan, visa) demandeur/-euse *m/f* (**for** de); (for citizenship) postulant/-e *m/f* (**for** à); **3** (for membership) candidat/-e *m/f*; **4** (for shares) souscripteur/-trice *m/f*; **5** JUR (for divorce, patent) demandeur/-eresse *m/f*, requérant/-e *m/f*.

application /ˌæplɪ'keɪʃn/ *n* **1** (request) (for job) candidature *f* (**for** à); (for membership, passport, loan, promotion, transfer) demande *f* (**for** de); (for shares) souscription *f* (**for** de); **to make an ~ for a job** poser sa candidature à un poste; **to make an ~ for a university place** faire une demande d'inscription à une université; **a letter of ~** une lettre de candidature; **to fill out a job ~** remplir un formulaire de candidature; **on ~** sur demande; **2** (spreading) application *f* (**to** à); **one ~ is sufficient** une (seule) couche suffit; **3** (implementation) (of law, penalty, rule) application *f*; (of theory, training) application *f*; **4** (for divorce, patent, bankruptcy) demande *f* (**for** de).

application form *n* (for loan, credit card, passport) formulaire *m* de demande; (for job) formulaire *m* de candidature; (for membership) demande *f* d'inscription.

applicator /'æplɪkeɪtə(r)/ *n* applicateur *m*.

applied /ə'plaɪd/ *adj* [*linguistics*, *maths*] appliqué.

appliqué /æ'pliːkeɪ, US ˌæplɪ'keɪ/ **I** *n* application *f*. **II** *noun modifier* [*motif, decoration*] en application.

apply /ə'plaɪ/ **I** *vtr* **1** (spread) appliquer [*make-up, paint*] (**to** sur); **2** (use) appliquer [*theory, rule, method, heat*] (**to** à); exercer [*friction, pressure*] (**to** sur); **3** (give) appliquer [*label, term*] (**to** à); **4** (affix) apposer [*sticker*] (**to** sur); appliquer [*bandage, sequins*] (**to** sur).

II *vi* **1** (request) faire une demande; **to ~ for** demander [*divorce, citizenship*]; faire une demande de

[*passport, loan, grant, visa*]; **to ~ to do** demander à faire; **2** (seek work) poser sa candidature (**for** à); **to ~ for the job of** poser sa candidature au poste de; **'~ in writing to'** 'envoyez votre candidature par lettre manuscrite à'; **'~ within'** 'adressez-vous à l'intérieur'; **3** (seek entry) (to college) faire une demande d'inscription (**to** à); (to club, society) faire une demande d'adhésion (**to** à); **to ~ to join** demander à entrer dans [*army, group*]; **4** (be valid) [*definition, term*] s'appliquer (**to** à); [*ban, rule, penalty*] être en vigueur; **5** (contact) **to ~ to** s'adresser à.
III *v refl* **to ~ oneself** s'appliquer.

appoint /ə'pɔɪnt/ **I** *vtr* **1** (name) nommer [*person*] (**to sth** à qch; **to do** pour faire; **as** comme); fixer [*date, place*]; **2** (equip) aménager.
II appointed *pp adj* [*time, place*] fixé.

appointee /əpɔɪn'tiː/ *n* candidat/-e *m/f* retenu/-e.

appointment /ə'pɔɪntmənt/ *n* **1** (meeting, consultation) rendez-vous *m* (**at** chez; **with** avec; **to do** pour faire); **business ~** rendez-vous *m* d'affaires; **by ~** sur rendez-vous; **to make an ~** prendre rendez-vous; **2** ADMIN, POL (nomination) nomination *f* (**as** comme; **to sth** à qch; **to do** pour faire); **to take up an ~** (**as sth**) prendre ses fonctions (comme qch); **3** (job) poste *m* (**as** de; **of** de); **'Appointments'** (in paper) 'Offres d'emploi'.

apportion /ə'pɔːʃn/ *vtr* répartir (**among** parmi; **between** entre).

apposite /'æpəzɪt/ *adj* pertinent.

apposition /ˌæpə'zɪʃn/ *n* apposition *f*.

appraisal /ə'preɪzl/ *n* évaluation *f*; **to make an ~ of sth** (estimation) évaluer qch.

appraise /ə'preɪz/ *vtr* **1** (examine critically) juger [*painting, information*]; **2** (evaluate) estimer [*value*]; évaluer [*performance*].

appreciable /ə'priːʃəbl/ *adj* [*time, change, quantity*] appréciable; [*difference, reduction*] sensible.

appreciably /ə'priːʃəblɪ/ *adv* sensiblement.

appreciate /ə'priːʃɪeɪt/ **I** *vtr* **1** (be grateful for) être sensible à [*honour, favour*]; être reconnaissant de [*kindness, sympathy*]; apprécier [*help, effort*]; **I'd ~ it if you could reply soon** je vous serais reconnaissant de répondre sans tarder; **I ~ being consulted** j'aime bien qu'on me consulte; **2** (realize) se rendre (bien) compte de, être conscient de; **to ~ that...** se rendre bien compte que...; **as you will ~** comme vous vous en rendrez bien compte; **3** (enjoy) apprécier [*music, art, food*].
II *vi* [*object*] prendre de la valeur; [*value*] monter.

appreciation /əˌpriːʃɪ'eɪʃn/ *n* **1** (gratitude) remerciement *m* (**for** pour); **in ~ of sth** en remerciement de qch; **to show one's ~** manifester sa gratitude; **2** (awareness) compréhension *f* (**of** de); **he has no ~ of how difficult it is to do** il ne se rend pas compte combien il est difficile de faire; **3** (enjoyment) appréciation *f* (**of** de); **4** (commentary) commentaire *m*; **5** FIN hausse *f* (**of, in** de).

appreciative /ə'priːʃətɪv/ *adj* **1** (grateful) reconnaissant (**of** de); **2** (admiring) admiratif/-ive; **3** (aware) sensible (**of** à).

apprehend /ˌæprɪ'hend/ *vtr* **1** (arrest) appréhender; **2** (comprehend) saisir.

apprehension /ˌæprɪ'henʃn/ *n* **1** (fear) (specific) crainte *f*; (vague) inquiétude *f*; **2** (arrest) arrestation *f*.

apprehensive /ˌæprɪ'hensɪv/ *adj* craintif/-ive; **to be ~** être inquiet/-iète; **to feel ~ about sth** (fearful) appréhender qch; (worried) avoir des inquiétudes au sujet de qch.

apprehensively /ˌæprɪ'hensɪvlɪ/ *adv* avec appréhension.

apprentice /ə'prentɪs/ **I** *n* **1** apprenti/-e *m/f* ALSO FIG (**to** de); **electrician's ~** apprenti/-e *m/f* électricien/-ienne.
II *noun modifier* (trainee) [*baker, mechanic*] apprenti/-e (*before n*).
III *vtr* **to be ~d to sb** être en apprentissage chez qn.

apprenticeship /ə'prentɪʃɪp/ *n* apprentissage *m* ALSO FIG; **to serve one's ~** faire son apprentissage.

apprise /ə'praɪz/ *vtr* SOUT **to ~ sb of sth** instruire qn de qch FML.

approach /ə'prəʊtʃ/ **I** *n* **1** (route of access) (to town, island) voie *f* d'accès; MIL approche *f*; **2** (advance) (of person) approche *f*, arrivée *f*; (of season, old age) approche *f*; **3** (way of dealing) approche *f*; **an original ~ to the problem** une façon originale d'aborder le problème; **we need to try a different ~** nous devons essayer une méthode différente; **4** (overture) démarche *f*; (proposal to buy etc) proposition *f*; **to make ~s to sb** GEN, COMM faire des démarches auprès de qn.
II *vtr* **1** (draw near to) s'approcher de [*person, place*]; (verge on) approcher de; **it was ~ing dawn** l'aube approchait; **it was ~ing midnight** il était presque minuit; **he is ~ing sixty** il approche (de) la soixantaine; **gales ~ing speeds of 200 km per hour** des vents qui atteignaient presque 200 km à l'heure; **2** (deal with) aborder [*problem, topic, subject*]; **3** (make overtures to) s'adresser à; (more formally) faire des démarches auprès de; (with offer of job, remuneration) solliciter (**about** au sujet de); **she was ~ed by a man in the street** elle a été abordée par un homme dans la rue; **he has been ~ed by several publishers** il a reçu des propositions de plusieurs maisons d'édition.
III *vi* [*person, car*] (s')approcher; [*event, season*] approcher.

approachable /ə'prəʊtʃəbl/ *adj* abordable, d'un abord facile.

approach: ~ lights *npl* AVIAT balises *fpl*, balisage *m*; **~ path** *n* AVIAT axe *m* d'approche; **~ road** *n* bretelle *f*, route *f* d'accès.

appropriate I /ə'prəʊprɪət/ *adj* **1** (suitable for occasion, situation) [*behaviour, choice, place*] approprié (**for** pour); [*dress, gift*] qui convient (*after n*) (**for** à); [*punishment*] juste (**for** à); [*remark*] de circonstance (*after n*); **~ to** approprié à [*needs, circumstances*]; **2** (apt) [*name, date*] bien choisi; **3** (relevant) [*authority*] compétent.
II /ə'prəʊprɪeɪt/ *vtr* **1** (for own use) GEN s'approprier; JUR affecter [*land*] (**for** à); **2** US ECON affecter [*funds*] (**for** à).

appropriately /ə'prəʊprɪətlɪ/ *adv* **1** (suitably) [*behave, dress, speak*] avec à-propos; [*dress*] convenablement; **2** (aptly) [*designed, chosen, sited*] judicieusement.

appropriation /əˌprəʊprɪ'eɪʃn/ *n* **1** JUR (removal) appropriation *f*; **2** US ECON affectation *f* (**for** à).

approval /ə'pruːvl/ *n* **1** (favourable opinion) approbation *f* (**of** de); **to win sb's ~** gagner l'approbation de qn; **2** (authorization) approbation *f*; **subject to sb's ~** soumis à l'approbation de qn; **on ~** à l'essai.

approve /ə'pruːv/ **I** *vtr* (authorize) approuver [*product, plan*]; accepter [*person*].
II *vi* (be in favour of) **to ~ of sth/sb** apprécier qch/qn; **(not) to ~ of sb doing** (ne pas) apprécier que qn fasse; **he doesn't ~ of drinking** il est contre l'alcool.

approving /ə'pruːvɪŋ/ *adj* approbateur/-trice.

approvingly /ə'pruːvɪŋlɪ/ *adv* d'un air or d'un ton approbateur.

approximate I /ə'prɒksɪmət/ *adj* approximatif/-ive; **~ to** proche de.
II /ə'prɒksɪmeɪt/ *vtr* (come close to) se rapprocher de; (resemble) ressembler à.
III /ə'prɒksɪmeɪt/ *vi* **to ~ to** (in quantity, size etc) être proche de, se rapprocher de; (in nature, quality etc) ressembler à.

approximately /ə'prɒksɪmətlɪ/ *adv* **1** (about) environ; **at ~ four o'clock** vers quatre heures; **2** [*equal, correct*] à peu près.

approximation /əˌprɒksɪ'meɪʃn/ *n* approximation *f*.

Apr *abrév écrite* = **April**.

apricot /'eɪprɪkɒt/ **▶818** **I** *n* **1** (fruit) abricot *m*; **2** (tree) abricotier *m*; **3** (colour) (couleur *f*) abricot *m*.
II *noun modifier* [*stone*] d'abricot; [*jam*] d'abricots; [*sauce*] aux abricots.
III *adj* abricot *inv*.

April /'eɪprɪl/ **▶1090** *n* avril *m*.

April: ~ **Fools' Day** *n* le premier avril; ~ **showers** *npl* ~ giboulées *fpl* de mars.

apron /'eɪprən/ *n* **1** (garment) tablier *m*; **2** (for vehicles, planes) aire *f* de stationnement.
IDIOMS **to be tied to sb's ~ strings** être pendu aux basques de qn.

apropos /ˌæprə'pəʊ/ *adv* à propos (**of** de).

apse /æps/ *n* abside *f*.

apt¹ /æpt/ *adj* **1** (suitable) [*choice, description*] heureux/-euse; [*title, style*] approprié (**to, for** à); **2** (inclined) **to be ~ to do** être enclin à faire.

apt² *abrév écrite* = **apartment**.

aptitude /'æptɪtjuːd, US -tuːd/ *n* aptitude *f*; **to have an ~ for maths** être doué pour les maths.

aptly /'æptlɪ/ *adv* [*named, described*] avec justesse; [*chosen*] bien.

aqualung /'ækwəlʌŋ/ *n* scaphandre *m* autonome.

aquamarine /ˌækwəmə'riːn/ ▶818 I *n* (gem) aigue-marine *f*; (colour) bleu-vert *m*.
II *adj* bleu-vert *inv*.

aquaplane /'ækwəpleɪn/ *vi* SPORT faire de l'aqua-plane; GB AUT faire de l'aquaplanage.

aquarium /ə'kweərɪəm/ *n* (*pl* **-iums, -ia**) aquarium *m*.

Aquarius /ə'kweərɪəs/ ▶1418 *n* Verseau *m*.

aquatic /ə'kwætɪk/ *adj* [*plant*] aquatique; [*sport*] nautique.

aqueduct /'ækwɪdʌkt/ *n* aqueduc *m*.

aquiline /'ækwɪlaɪn/ *adj* [*nose, features*] aquilin.

AR US POST *abrév écrite* = **Arkansas**.

Arab /'ærəb/ ▶1100 I *n* **1** [*person*] Arabe *mf*; **2** (horse) cheval *m* arabe; (mare) jument *f* arabe.
II *adj* arabe.

Arabia /ə'reɪbɪə/ *pr n* Arabie *f*.

Arabian /ə'reɪbɪən/ *adj* [*desert, landscape*] d'Arabie; **the ~ Sea** la mer d'Arabie.

Arabic /'ærəbɪk/ ▶1038 I *n* arabe *m*.
II *adj* arabe.

Arab-Israeli /ˌærəbɪz'reɪlɪ/ *adj* israélo-arabe.

arable /'ærəbl/ *adj* [*crop, land, sector*] arable.

Aran sweater *n* pull *m* irlandais.

arbiter /'ɑːbɪtə(r)/ *n* LIT, FIG arbitre *m* (**of** de).

arbitrary /'ɑːbɪtrərɪ, US 'ɑːrbɪtrerɪ/ *adj* arbitraire.

arbitrate /'ɑːbɪtreɪt/ I *vtr* arbitrer [*dispute, claim*].
II *vi* arbitrer, jouer le rôle d'arbitre (**between** entre).

arbitration /ˌɑːbɪ'treɪʃn/ *n* arbitrage *m*; **to go to ~** ~ aller aux prud'hommes.

arbitrator /'ɑːbɪtreɪtə(r)/ *n* (mediator) médiateur/-trice *m/f* (**between** entre); **industrial ~** (conseiller/-ère *m/f*) prud'homme *m*.

arbor *n* US = **arbour**.

arbour GB, **arbor** US /'ɑːbə(r)/ *n* charmille *f*.

arc /ɑːk/ *n* GEN, Geom arc *m*; ELEC arc *m* (électrique).

arcade /ɑː'keɪd/ *n* arcade *f*; **shopping ~** galerie *f* marchande.

arcane /ɑː'keɪn/ *adj* impénétrable, obscur.

arch /ɑːtʃ/ I *n* **1** (dome) voûte *f*; (archway) arche *f*; (for bridge) arche *f*; (triumphal) arc *m*; **2** (of foot) voûte *f* plantaire; (of eyebrows) arc *m*.
II *adj* **1** (mischievous) [*look, manner*] malicieux/-ieuse; **2** PÉJ (superior) [*person, voice, remark*] condescendant.
III *vtr* arquer; **to ~ one's back** [*person*] cambrer le dos; [*cat*] faire le dos rond.
IV **arch+** *combining form* par excellence; **~-enemy** ennemi/-e *m/f* juré/-e; **~-rival** grand rival.

archaeological GB, **archeological** US /ˌɑːkɪə'lɒdʒɪkl/ *adj* archéologique.

archaeologist GB, **archeologist** US /ˌɑːkɪ'ɒlədʒɪst/ ▶1251 *n* archéologue *mf*.

archaeology GB, **archeology** US /ˌɑːkɪ'ɒlədʒɪ/ *n* archéologie *f*.

archaic /ɑː'keɪɪk/ *adj* archaïque.

archbishop /ˌɑːtʃ'bɪʃəp/ *n* archevêque *m*.

arched /'ɑːtʃd/ *adj* GEN voûté; [*eyebrows*] arqué.

archer /'ɑːtʃə(r)/ *n* archer *m*.

archery /'ɑːtʃərɪ/ *n* tir *m* à l'arc.

archetypal /ˌɑːkɪ'taɪpl/ *adj* **the** ou **an ~ hero** l'archétype du héros.

archetype /'ɑːkɪtaɪp/ *n* archétype *m*.

archipelago /ˌɑːkɪ'peləgəʊ/ *n* archipel *m*.

architect /'ɑːkɪtekt/ ▶1251 *n* **1** (as profession) architecte *mf*; **2** FIG (of plan, policy) artisan *m*.

architectural /ˌɑːkɪ'tektʃərəl/ *adj* [*design, style*] architectural; [*student*] en architecture; [*studies*] d'architecture.

architecture /'ɑːkɪtektʃə(r)/ *n* architecture *f*.

archive /'ɑːkaɪv/ *n* archive *f*.

archly /'ɑːtʃlɪ/ *adv* **1** (mischievously) malicieusement; **2** PÉJ (condescendingly) avec condescendance.

Arctic /'ɑːktɪk/ I *pr n* **the ~** l'Arctique *m*; **to/in the ~** dans l'Arctique.
II *adj* [*climate, animal*] arctique; [*expedition*] polaire; FIG (icy) [*conditions, temperature*] glacial.

Arctic Circle *n* cercle *m* polaire arctique.

Arctic Ocean ▶1117 *n* océan *m* Arctique.

arc: **~ welder** *n* soudeur *m* à l'arc; **~ welding** *n* soudage *m* à l'arc.

ardent /'ɑːdnt/ *adj* **1** (fervent) [*revolutionary, supporter*] fervent; [*defence, opposition*] passionné; **2** (passionate) passionné.

ardently /'ɑːdntlɪ/ *adv* [*look, worship*] ardemment; [*defend, speak*] avec ardeur; [*support*] passionnément.

ardour GB, **ardor** US /'ɑːdə(r)/ *n* ardeur *f*.

arduous /'ɑːdjʊəs, US -dʒʊ-/ *adj* ardu.

arduously /'ɑːdjʊəslɪ, US -dʒʊ-/ *adv* péniblement.

are /ɑ:(r)/ ▶ **be**.

area /'eərɪə/ I *n* **1** (region) (of land) région *f*; (of sky) zone *f*; (of city) zone *f*; (district) quartier *m*; **in the London ~** dans la région de Londres; **residential ~** zone *f* résidentielle; **2** (part of building) **dining ~** zone *f* salle-à-manger; **no-smoking/smoking ~** zone *f* non-fumeurs/fumeurs; **reception ~** réception *f*; **waiting ~** salle *f* d'attente; **3** (sphere of knowledge) domaine *m*; (part of activity, business, economy) secteur *m*; **~ of interest** domaine d'intérêt; **~ of disagreement** sujet de désaccord; **4** MATH (in geometry) aire *f*; (of land) superficie *f*.
II *noun modifier* [*board, headquarters, manager, office*] régional.

area code *n* TELECOM indicatif *m* de zone.

arena /ə'riːnə/ *n* arène *f* ALSO FIG.

aren't /ɑ:nt/ (= **are not**) ▶ **be**.

Argentina /ˌɑːdʒən'tiːnə/ ▶840 *pr n* Argentine *f*.

Argentine /'ɑːdʒəntaɪn/ ▶840 I *n* **1 the ~** (Republic) l'Argentine *f*; **2** (native, inhabitant) Argentin/-e *m/f*.
II *adj* argentin.

Argentinian /ˌɑːdʒən'tɪnɪən/ ▶1100 I *n* Argentin/-e *m/f*.
II *adj* argentin.

arguable /'ɑːgjʊəbl/ *adj* discutable; **it's ~ that** on peut soutenir que.

arguably /'ɑːgjʊəblɪ/ *adv* sans doute.

argue /'ɑːgjuː/ I *vtr* **1** (debate) discuter (de), débattre (de); **to ~ the case for disarmament** exposer les raisons en faveur du désarmement; **it could be ~d that** on pourrait soutenir que; **well-~d** bien argumenté; **2** (maintain) soutenir.
II *vi* **1** (quarrel) se disputer (**with** avec); **to ~ about** ou **over money** se disputer pour des questions d'argent; **we ~d about who should pay** nous nous sommes disputés pour savoir qui devait payer; **don't ~ (with me)!** on ne discute pas!; **2** (debate) discuter, débattre; **to ~ about** discuter de, débattre de; **3** (put one's case) argumenter (**against** contre); **to ~ in favour of/against doing sth** exposer les raisons pour faire/pour ne pas faire qch; **to ~ for** ou **in favour of** parler en faveur de.

argument /'ɑːgjʊmənt/ *n* **1** (quarrel) dispute *f* (**about** à propos de); **to have an ~** se disputer; **2** (discussion) débat *m*, discussion *f* (**about** à propos de); **there is a**

lot of ~ **about this** c'est un sujet très discuté; **she won the** ~ c'est elle qui a eu le dernier mot; **it's open to** ~ c'est discutable; **one side of the** ~ une version de l'affaire; **for ~'s sake** à titre d'exemple; **3** (case) argument *m* (**for** en faveur de; **against** contre); (line of reasoning) raisonnement *m*.

argumentative /ˌɑːɡjʊ'mentətɪv/ *adj* [*person*] ergoteur/-euse.

arid /'ærɪd/ *adj* aride ALSO FIG.

aridity /ə'rɪdətɪ/ *n* aridité *f* ALSO FIG.

Aries /'eəriːz/ ▶ **1418** *n* Bélier *m*.

arise /ə'raɪz/ *vi* (*prét* **arose**, *pp* **arisen**) **1** (occur) [*problem*] survenir (**out of** du fait de); [*question*] se poser; **to** ~ **from sth** émaner de qch; **if it ~s that** s'il se trouve que; **if the need ~s** si le besoin se fait sentir; **2** (be the result of) résulter (**from** de).

aristocracy /ˌærɪ'stɒkrəsɪ/ *n* aristocratie *f*.

aristocrat /'ærɪstəkræt, US ə'rɪst-/ *n* aristocrate *mf*.

aristocratic /ˌærɪstə'krætɪk, US ə'rɪst-/ *adj* aristocratique.

arithmetic /ə'rɪθmətɪk/ *n* (subject) arithmétique *f*.

arithmetical /ˌærɪθ'metɪkl/ *adj* arithmétique.

ark /ɑːk/ *n* (boat, in synagogue) arche *f*.
IDIOMS **to be out of the** ~ être vieux/vieille comme tout.

arm /ɑːm/ ▶ **765** **I** *n* **1** ANAT, FIG bras *m*; ~ **in** ~ bras dessus bras dessous; **to give sb one's** ~ donner le bras à qn; **to take sb's** ~ prendre le bras de qn; **to have sth over/under one's** ~ avoir qch sur/sous le bras; **to fold one's ~s** croiser les bras; **within ~'s reach** à portée de la main; **2** (sleeve) manche *f*; **3** (influence) **to have a long** ~ avoir le bras long; **4** (of crane, robot, record player) bras *m*; **5** (of spectacles) branche *f*; **6** (of chair) accoudoir *m*; **7** (subsidiary) POL branche *f*; ECON branche *f*, filiale *f*; **8** (of sea) bras *m*.
II arms *npl* **1** (weapons) armes *fpl*; **to take up** ~ LIT prendre les armes; FIG s'insurger (**against** contre); **to be up in ~s** (in revolt) être en rébellion (**against** contre); (angry) être furieux/-ieuse (**against** contre); **2** armes *fpl*, armoiries *fpl*; **coat of ~s** armoiries *fpl*.
III *vtr* **1** (militarily) armer; **2** (equip) **to** ~ **sb with sth** LIT, FIG munir qn de qch.
IV *v refl* **to** ~ **oneself** MIL s'armer (**with** de).
IDIOMS **to cost an** ~ **and a leg°** coûter les yeux de la tête°; **to keep sb at** ~'s **length** tenir qn à distance; **to twist sb's** ~ faire pression sur qn; **with open ~s** à bras ouverts.

armadillo /ˌɑːmə'dɪləʊ/ *n* (*pl* ~**s**) tatou *m*.

armament /'ɑːməmənt/ MIL **I** *n* (loading of weapons) armement *m*.
II armaments *npl* (system) armements *mpl*.
III armaments *noun modifier* [*factory, firm, manufacturer*] d'armement; [*industry*] de l'armement.

armband /'ɑːmbænd/ *n* **1** (for swimmer) bracelet *m* de natation; **2** (for mourner) crêpe *m* de deuil.

armchair /'ɑːmtʃeə(r)/ **I** *n* fauteuil *m*.
II *noun modifier* PÉJ [*revolutionary, general*] de salon.

armed /ɑːmd/ *adj* [*criminal, guard*] armé (**with** de); [*raid, robbery*] à main armée; [*missile*] muni d'une tête d'ogive.

armed forces, armed services *npl* forces *fpl* armées; **to be in the** ~ être dans l'armée.

Armenia /ɑː'miːnɪə/ ▶ **840** *pr n* Arménie *f*.

Armenian /ɑː'miːnɪən/ ▶ **1100**, **1038** **I** *n* **1** (person) Arménien/-ienne *m/f*; **2** (language) arménien *m*.
II *adj* arménien/-ienne.

arm: ~**ful** *n* (*pl* ~**s**) brassée *f*; ~**hole** *n* emmanchure *f*.

armistice /'ɑːmɪstɪs/ *n* armistice *m*.

Armistice Day *n* le jour de l'armistice, le onze novembre.

armour GB, **armor** US /'ɑːmə(r)/ *n* **1** (clothing) **a suit of** ~ une armure *f* (complète); **2** (on tank, ship etc) ALSO ZOOL armure *f*; (on wire, cable) gaine *f*; FIG (against criticism) cuirasse *f*.

armour-clad /ˌɑːmə'klæd/ *adj* [*vehicle*] blindé; [*ship*] cuirassé.

armoured GB, **armored** US /'ɑːməd/ *adj* blindé.

armour: ~ **plate**, ~ **plating** *n* (on tank) blindage *m*; (on ship) cuirassage *m*; ~**-plated** *adj* = **armour-clad**.

armoury GB, **armory** US /'ɑːmərɪ/ *n* **1** MIL (store) arsenal *m*; (factory) manufacture *f* d'armes; **2** FIG (resources) arsenal *m* (**of** de).

arm: ~**pit** *n* aisselle *f*; ~**rest** *n* accoudoir *m*; ~**s control** *n* contrôle *m* des armements; ~**s dealer** *n* négociant *m* d'armes; ~**s dump** *n* dépôt *m* d'armes; ~**s factory** *n* usine *f* d'armement; ~**s limitation** *n* réduction *f* or contrôle *m* des armements; ~**s manufacturer** *n* fabricant *m* d'armes; ~**s race** *n* course *f* aux armements; ~**s treaty** *n* traité *m* sur le contrôle des armements; ~**-twisting** *n* pressions *fpl* directes; ~ **wrestling** ▶ **949** *n* bras-de-fer *m*.

army /'ɑːmɪ/ **I** *n* **1** MIL armée *f*; **in the** ~ dans l'armée; **to go into the** ~ entrer dans l'armée; **to join the** ~ s'engager; **2** FIG armée *f* (**of** de).
II *noun modifier* [*life, staff, uniform*] militaire; [*officer*] de l'armée de terre.

aroma /ə'rəʊmə/ *n* arôme *m*.

aromatherapy /əˌrəʊmə'θerəpɪ/ *n* aromathérapie *f*.

aromatic /ˌærə'mætɪk/ *adj* aromatique.

arose /ə'rəʊz/ *prét* ▶ **arise**.

around /ə'raʊnd/

■ *Note* **around** often appears as the second element of certain verb structures (*come around, look around, turn around etc*). For translations, consult the appropriate verb entry (*come, look, turn etc*).
– *go around* and *get around* generate many idiomatic expressions. For translations see the entries **go** and **get**.

I *adv* **1** (approximately) environ, à peu près; **at** ~ **3 pm** vers 15 heures; **2** (in the vicinity) **to be (somewhere)** ~ être dans les parages; **are they ~?** est-ce qu'ils sont là?; **I just happened to be** ~ je me trouvais là par hasard; **3** (in circulation) CDs **have been** ~ **for years** ça fait des années que les CD existent; **I wish I'd been** ~ **50 years ago** j'aurais aimé être là il y a 50 ans; **she's been** ~ FIG elle a roulé sa bosse°, elle a vécu; **one of the most gifted musicians** ~ un des musiciens les plus doués du moment; **4** (available) **to be** ~ être là; **there are still some strawberries** ~ on trouve encore des fraises; **5** (in all directions) **all** ~ LIT tout autour; (in general) partout; **to go all the way** ~ faire tout le tour; **the only garage for miles** ~ le seul garage à des kilomètres à la ronde; **6** (in circumference) **three metres** ~ de trois mètres de circonférence; **7** (in different, opposite direction) **a way** ~ LIT un chemin pour contourner [*obstacle*]; **there is no way** ~ **the problem** il n'y a pas moyen de contourner le problème; **to go the long way** ~ prendre le chemin le plus long; **to turn sth the other way** ~ retourner qch; **to do it the other way** ~ faire le contraire; **I didn't ask her, it was the other way** ~ ce n'est pas moi qui lui ai demandé, c'est l'inverse; **the wrong/right way** ~ dans le mauvais/bon sens; **to put one's skirt on the wrong way** ~ mettre sa jupe à l'envers; (in specific place, home) **to ask sb** (**to come**) ~ dire à qn de passer; **she's coming** ~ **today** elle passe aujourd'hui; **I'll be** ~ **in a minute** j'arrive.
II *prep* **1** (on all sides of) autour de [*fire, table, head*]; **the villages** ~ **Dublin** les villages des environs de Dublin; **2** (throughout) **clothes scattered** ~ **the room** des vêtements éparpillés partout dans la pièce; **(all)** ~ **the world** partout dans le monde; **from** ~ **the world** venant du monde entier; **doctors** ~ **the world** les médecins à travers le monde; **to go** ~ **the world** faire le tour du monde; **to walk** ~ **the town** se promener dans la ville; **3** (in the vicinity of, near) **somewhere** ~ **the house/** ~ **Paris** quelque part dans la maison/près de Paris; **I like people** ~ **the house** j'aime avoir des gens à la maison; **the people** ~ **here** les gens d'ici; **4** (at) vers; ~ **midnight/1980** vers minuit/1980; **5** (in order to circumvent) **to go** ~ éviter [*town centre*]; contourner [*obstacle*]; **6** (to the other side of) **to go** ~ **the corner**

tourner au coin; **to go ~ a bend** prendre un virage; **~ the mountain** de l'autre côté de or derrière la montagne; **7** (in sizes) **he's 90 cm ~ the chest** il fait 90 de tour de poitrine.

arousal /ə'raʊzl/ n excitation f (**of** de).

arouse /ə'raʊz/ vtr **1** (excite) éveiller [interest, attention]; exciter [anger, jealousy]; **to be ~d by sth** être excité par qch; **2** (waken) **to ~ sb from sleep** tirer qn du sommeil.

arpeggio /ɑː'pedʒɪəʊ/ n arpège m.

arrange /ə'reɪndʒ/ **I** vtr **1** (put in position) disposer [chairs, ornaments]; arranger [room, hair, clothes]; arranger, disposer [flowers]; **2** (organize) organiser [party, meeting, holiday, schedule]; fixer [date, appointment]; **to ~ sth with sb** fixer or organiser qch avec qn; **to ~ that** faire en sorte que (+ subj); **to ~ to do** s'arranger pour faire; **I'll ~ it** je ferai le nécessaire; **have you got anything ~d for this evening?** avez-vous quelque chose de prévu pour ce soir?; **3** (bring about agreement on) convenir de [loan, mortgage]; fixer [price]; **4** MUS arranger, adapter [piece].
II vi **to ~ for sth** prendre des dispositions pour qch; **to ~ for sb to do** prendre des dispositions pour que qn fasse; **to ~ with sb to do** décider avec qn de faire.

arrangement /ə'reɪndʒmənt/ n **1** (of hair, jewellery) arrangement m; (of objects, chairs) disposition f; (of ideas: on page) organisation f; (of shells, flowers) composition f; **seating ~s** disposition des invités; **2** (agreement) entente f, accord m; **by ~ with sb** par un accord avec qn; **by ~** (par) entente préalable, sur demande; **to come to an ~** s'arranger; **3** (plan) dispositions fpl; (preparations) préparatifs mpl; (measures) mesures fpl; **to make ~s to do** s'arranger pour faire; **to make ~s with sb** (for him to do) prendre des dispositions avec qn (pour qu'il fasse); **to make ~s for doing** prendre des dispositions pour faire.

array /ə'reɪ/ **I** n **1** (of goods, products) gamme f; **2** (of weaponry) panoplie f; **3** (of troops, people) déploiement m; **4** (of numbers) tableau m; **5** (clothes) habits mpl d'apparat; **6** (in electronics) réseau m.
II vtr **1** **~ed in** (dressed in) paré de; **2** JUR établir la liste des [jurors].

arrears /ə'rɪəz/ npl arriéré m; **I am in ~ with my payments** j'ai du retard dans mes paiements; **to fall into ~** s'arriérer; **rent ~** arriéré de loyer.

arrest /ə'rest/ **I** n arrestation f; **to be under ~** être en état d'arrestation; **to put sb under ~** arrêter qn.
II vtr **1** [police] arrêter; **2** (halt) arrêter [decline, development, disease].

arresting /ə'restɪŋ/ adj (attractive) saisissant.

arrival /ə'raɪvl/ n **1** (of person, transport) arrivée f; **on sb's/sth's ~** à l'arrivée de qn/qch; **2** (of new character or phenomenon) apparition f; **3** (person arriving) arrivé/-e m/f; **late ~** (in theatre) retardataire mf; **new ~** (in community) nouveau/-elle venu/-e m/f; (baby) nouveau-né m.

arrival: **~ lounge** n salon m d'arrivée; **~s board** n tableau m d'arrivée; **~ time** n heure f d'arrivée.

arrive /ə'raɪv/ vi **1** (at destination) arriver (**at** à; **from** de); **'arriving Berlin 7.25 am'** (announcement) 'arrivée à Berlin 7 heures 25'; **to ~ on the scene** LIT arriver (sur les lieux); FIG apparaître; **2** (reach) **to ~ at** parvenir à [decision, solution]; **3** (be social success) arriver.

arrogance /'ærəgəns/ n arrogance f.

arrogant /'ærəgənt/ adj arrogant.

arrogantly /'ærəgəntlɪ/ adv avec arrogance, arrogamment.

arrow /'ærəʊ/ n **1** (weapon) flèche f; **to fire an ~** décocher une flèche; **2** (symbol) flèche f.

arrow: **~head** n pointe f de flèche; **~root** n BOT marante f; CULIN arrow-root m.

arsenal /'ɑːsənl/ n LIT, FIG arsenal m.

arsenic /'ɑːsnɪk/ n arsenic m.

arson /'ɑːsn/ n incendie m criminel.

arsonist /'ɑːsənɪst/ n pyromane mf.

art /ɑːt/ **I** n **1** (creation, activity, representation) art m; **I'm bad at ~** je suis mauvais en dessin; **2** (skill) art m (**of doing** de faire).
II arts npl **1** (culture) **the ~s** les arts mpl; **2** UNIV lettres fpl; **3** **~s and crafts** GEN artisanat m; (school subject) travaux mpl manuels.

art: **~ collection** n (of paintings) collection f de tableaux; (of artworks) collection f d'œuvres d'art; **~ collector** n collectionneur/-euse m/f d'œuvres d'art; (of paintings) collectionneur/-euse m/f de tableaux; **~ college** n école f des beaux-arts; **~ dealer** ▶ 1251 | n marchand/-e m/f d'œuvres d'art; (of paintings) marchand/-e m/f de tableaux; **~ deco** n, adj art déco (m) inv.

artefact /'ɑːtɪfækt/ n objet m (fabriqué).

arterial /ɑː'tɪərɪəl/ adj (avant n) **1** ANAT artériel/-ielle; **2** **~ road** grand axe m; **~ line** RAIL grande ligne f.

artery /'ɑːtərɪ/ n **1** artère f; **2** (road) artère f; (railway) grande ligne f.

art exhibition n (paintings) exposition f de tableaux; (sculpture) exposition f de sculpture.

art form n LIT forme f d'art; **to become an ~** devenir un art.

artful /'ɑːtfl/ adj (skilful) habile; (crafty) rusé.

artfully /'ɑːtfəlɪ/ adv ingénieusement, astucieusement.

art gallery n (museum) musée m d'art; (commercial) galerie f d'art.

arthritic /ɑː'θrɪtɪk/ n, adj arthritique (mf).

arthritis /ɑː'θraɪtɪs/ ▶ 1002 | n arthrite f.

artichoke /'ɑːtɪtʃəʊk/ **I** n artichaut m.
II noun modifier [heart] d'artichaut; [salad, soup] aux artichauts.

article /'ɑːtɪkl/ **I** n **1** (object) objet m; **~ of clothing** article m vestimentaire; **2** (written) article m (**about, on** sur); **3** JUR (clause) article m; **in** ou **under Article 12** à l'article 12; **4** LING article m; **definite/indefinite/partitive ~** article défini/indéfini/partitif.
II articles npl JUR **to be in ~s** faire un stage chez un notaire.

articulate **I** /ɑː'tɪkjʊlət/ adj [speaker] qui s'exprime bien; [document, speech] bien construit.
II /ɑː'tɪkjʊleɪt/ vtr (pronounce) articuler; (express) exprimer.
III /ɑː'tɪkjʊleɪt/ vi (pronounce) articuler.

articulated lorry n GB semi-remorque m.

articulately /ɑː'tɪkjʊlətlɪ/ adv avec aisance (et clarté).

articulation /ɑːˌtɪkjʊ'leɪʃn/ n **1** (expression) articulation f; **2** (pronunciation) prononciation f; **3** ANAT articulation f.

artifact /'ɑːtɪfækt/ n = **artefact**.

artifice /'ɑːtɪfɪs/ n **1** (trick) ruse f; **2** (cunning) astuce f.

artificial /ˌɑːtɪ'fɪʃl/ adj artificiel/-ielle.

artificial intelligence, **AI** n intelligence f artificielle.

artificiality /ˌɑːtɪfɪʃɪ'æləti/ n PEJ (of person, manner) affectation f; (of situation) côté m artificiel.

artificial limb n (appareil m de) prothèse f, membre m artificiel.

artificial respiration n respiration f artificielle.

artillery /ɑː'tɪlərɪ/ n (guns, regiment) artillerie f.

artisan /ˌɑːtɪ'zæn, US 'ɑːrtɪzn/ n artisan m.

artist /'ɑːtɪst/ ▶ 1251 | n ART, THEAT artiste mf.

artiste /ɑː'tiːst/ n THEAT artiste mf.

artistic /ɑː'tɪstɪk/ adj [talent, director, activity] artistique; [temperament, person] artiste.

artistically /ɑː'tɪstɪklɪ/ adv artistiquement.

artistry /'ɑːtɪstrɪ/ n art m, talent m artistique.

artless /'ɑːtlɪs/ adj naturel/-elle.

artlessly /'ɑːtlɪslɪ/ adv [smile] avec naturel.

art nouveau /ˌɑːt 'nuːvəʊ/ n, adj modern style (m), art (m) nouveau.

art: **~ school** n école f des beaux-arts; **~s degree** n licence f ès lettres; **~s funding** n (by state) subventions *fpl* accordées aux arts; (by sponsors) mécénat *m*; **~s student** *n* étudiant/-e *m/f* en lettres; **~ student** *n* étudiant/-e *m/f* des beaux-arts; **~work** *n* travail *m* d'art.

arty° /ˈɑːtɪ/ *adj* [*person*] du genre artiste; [*district*] bohème.

Aryan /ˈeərɪən/ **I** *n* Aryen/-enne *m/f*.
II *adj* aryen/-enne.

as /æz, əz/ **I** *conj* **1** (in the manner that) comme; **~ you know** comme vous le savez; **~ usual** comme d'habitude; **~ is usual in such cases** comme c'est l'usage en pareil cas; **do ~ I say** fais ce que je te dis; **~ I see it** à mon avis; **~ I understand it** autant que je puisse en juger; **knowing you ~ I do,** it didn't surprise me je te connais tellement bien que ça ne m'a pas étonné; **the street ~ it looked in the 1930s** la rue telle qu'elle était dans les années 30; **~ often happens** comme c'est souvent le cas; **he lives abroad, ~ does his sister** il vit à l'étranger, tout comme sa sœur; **leave it ~ it is** laisse-le tel quel; **we're in enough trouble ~ it is** nous avons déjà assez d'ennuis comme ça; **~ one man to another** d'homme à homme; **~ with so many people in the 1960s, she...** comme beaucoup de personnes dans les années 60, elle...; **~ with so much in this country** comme beaucoup de choses dans ce pays; **2** (while, when) comme, alors que; (over more gradual period of time) au fur et à mesure que; **~ she grew older** au fur et à mesure qu'elle vieillissait; **~ a child, he...** (quand il était) enfant, il...; **3** (because, since) comme, puisque; **4** (although) **strange ~ it may seem** aussi curieux que cela puisse paraître; **comfortable ~ the house is,** it's still very expensive aussi confortable que soit la maison, elle reste quand même très chère; **try ~ he might, he could not forget it** il avait beau essayer, il ne pouvait pas oublier; **5 the same... ~** le/la même... que; **I've got a jacket the same ~ yours** j'ai la même veste que toi; **the same ~ always** comme d'habitude; **6** (expressing purpose) **so ~ to do** pour faire, afin de faire.
II *prep* **1** (in order to appear to be) **dressed ~ a sailor** habillé en marin; **he is portrayed ~ a victim** on le présente comme une victime; **2** (showing function, status) comme; **he works ~ a pilot** il travaille comme pilote; **a job ~ a teacher** un poste d'enseignant; **speaking ~ his closest friend, I...** en tant que son meilleur ami, je voudrais dire que je...; **my rights ~ a parent** mes droits en tant que parent; **with Lauren Bacall ~ Vivien** CIN, THEAT avec Lauren Bacall dans le rôle de Vivien; **3 to treat sb ~ an equal** traiter qn en égal; **he was quoted ~ saying that...** il aurait dit que...; **it came ~ a shock** ça a été un véritable choc.
III *adv* **1** (expressing degree, extent) **he is ~ intelligent ~ you** il est aussi intelligent que toi; **he's just ~ intelligent ~ you** il est tout aussi intelligent que toi; **she can't walk ~ fast ~** she used to elle ne peut plus marcher aussi vite qu'avant; **~ fast ~ you can** aussi vite que possible; **~ strong ~ an ox** fort comme un bœuf; **he's twice ~ strong ~ me** il est deux fois plus fort que moi; **I paid ~ much ~ she did** j'ai payé autant qu'elle; **~ much ~ possible** autant que possible; **~ little ~ possible** le moins possible; **~ soon ~ possible** dès que possible; **not nearly ~ much** beaucoup moins que; **not often** moins souvent; **the population may increase by ~ much ~ 20%** l'augmentation de la population risque d'atteindre 20%; **~ many ~ 10,000 people attended the demonstration** il n'y avait pas moins de 10 000 personnes à la manifestation; **she can play the piano ~ well ~ her sister** elle joue du piano aussi bien que sa sœur; **he has a house in Nice ~ well ~ an apartment in Paris** il a une maison à Nice ainsi qu'un appartement à Paris; **2** (expressing similarity) comme; **~ before** comme avant; **I thought ~ much!** c'est ce qu'il me semblait!
IV as against *prep phr* contre, comparé à.
V as and when *conj phr* **~ and when the passengers arrive** au fur et à mesure que les voyageurs arrivent; **~ and when the need arises** quand il le faudra, quand le besoin s'en fera sentir.
VI as for *prep phr* quant à, pour ce qui est de.
VII as from, as of *prep phr* à partir de.
VIII as if *conj phr* comme (si); **it's not ~ if she hadn't been warned!** ce n'est pas comme si elle n'avait pas été prévenue!; **he looked at me ~ if to say 'I told you so'** il m'a regardé avec l'air de dire 'je te l'avais bien dit'; **it looks ~ if we've lost** on dirait que nous avons perdu; **~ if by accident/magic** comme par hasard/magie.
IX as such *prep phr* en tant que tel.
X as to *prep phr* sur, quant à.

asbestos /æzˈbestɒs, æs-/ *n* amiante *m*.

ascend /əˈsend/ **I** *vtr* gravir [*steps, hill*].
II *vi* [*person*] monter; [*bird, soul, deity*] s'élever.

ascendancy /əˈsendənsɪ/ *n* ascendant *m*; **to gain the ~ over sb** prendre l'ascendant sur qn.

ascendant /əˈsendənt/ *n* (in astrology) ascendant *m*; **to be in the ~** [*star*] être à l'ascendant; FIG [*person*] avoir l'ascendant.

Ascension /əˈsenʃn/ *n* RELIG **the ~** l'Ascension *f*.

ascent /əˈsent/ *n* **1** (of smoke) montée *f*; (of soul, plane) ascension *f*; **2** (in cycling) montée *f*; (in mountaineering) ascension *f*.

ascertain /ˌæsəˈteɪn/ *vtr* établir (**that** que).

ascetic /əˈsetɪk/ **I** *n* ascète *mf*.
II *adj* ascétique.

ascribable /əˈskraɪbəbl/ *adj* attribuable (**to** à); (laying blame) imputable (**to** à).

---

as

When *as* is used as a preposition or a conjunction to mean *like* it is translated by *comme*:

dressed as a sailor = habillé comme un marin
as usual = comme d'habitude
as often happens = comme c'est souvent le cas

As a conjunction in time expressions, meaning *when* or *while*, *as* is translated by *comme*:

as she was coming
down the stairs = comme elle descendait l'escalier

However, where a gradual process is involved, *as* is translated by *au fur et à mesure que*:

as the day went on, he became more anxious
= au fur et à mesure que la journée
avançait il devenait plus inquiet

As a conjunction meaning *because*, *as* is translated by *comme* or *puisque*:

as he is ill, he can't go out = comme il est malade
or puisqu'il est malade,
il ne peut pas sortir

When used as an adverb in comparisons, *as ... as* is translated by *aussi ... que*:

he is as intelligent
as his brother = il est aussi intelligent que son frère

But see category number **X** in the entry **as** for *as much as* and *as many as*.

Note also the standard translation used for fixed similes:

as strong as an ox = fort comme un bœuf
as rich as Croesus = riche comme Crésus

Such similes often have a cultural equivalent rather than a direct translation. To find translations for English similes, consult the entry for the second element.

When *as* is used as a preposition to indicate a person's profession or position, it is translated by *comme*:

he works as an engineer = il travaille comme
ingénieur

Note that the article *a/an* is not translated.

When *as* is used as a preposition to mean *in my/his capacity as*, it is translated by *en tant que*:

as a teacher I believe that ... = en tant qu'enseignant
je crois que ...

For more examples, particular usages and phrases like *as for, as from, as to* etc. see the entry **as**.

ascribe /ə'skraɪb/ *vtr* **to ~ sth to sb** attribuer qch à qn [*work, phrase*]; imputer qch à qn [*accident, mistake*]; **the accident can be ~d to human error** on peut mettre l'accident sur le compte d'une erreur humaine.

aseptic /ˌeɪ'septɪk, US ə'sep-/ *adj* aseptique.

asexual /ˌeɪ'sekʃʊəl/ *adj* asexué ALSO FIG.

ash /æʃ/ **I** *n* **1** (after burning) cendre *f*; **to be burned to ~es** être réduit en cendres; **2** (tree, wood) frêne *m*. **II ashes** *npl* (remains) cendres *fpl*.

ashamed /ə'ʃeɪmd/ *adj* **to be** ou **feel ~** avoir honte (**of** de; **to do** faire); **to be ~ that** avoir honte (+ *subj*); **she was ~ to be seen with him** elle avait honte de se montrer avec lui; **you ought to be ~ of yourself** tu devrais avoir honte; **it's nothing to be ~ of** il ne faut pas en avoir honte.

ash: **~bin, ~ can** *n* US poubelle *f*; **~ blond** *adj* blond cendré *inv*.

ashen /'æʃn/ *adj* [*complexion*] terreux/-euse.

ashore /ə'ʃɔː(r)/ *adv* **1** (towards seashore) vers le rivage; (towards lake shore, river bank) vers la rive; **he was swimming ~** il nageait vers le rivage/la rive; **2** (arriving on shore) **to come/go ~** débarquer; **to swim ~** gagner le rivage/la rive à la nage; **washed ~** rejeté sur le rivage; **3** (on land) à terre; **to spend a week ~** [*sailor*] passer une semaine à terre; [*tourist*] faire une escale d'une semaine.

ash: **~tray** *n* cendrier *m*; **~ tree** *n* frêne *m*; **Ash Wednesday** *n* mercredi *m* des Cendres.

Asia /'eɪʃə, US 'eɪʒə/ ▶ **840** *pr n* Asie *f*.

Asia Minor /ˌeɪʃə'maɪnə(r), US ˌeɪʒə-/ *pr n* Asie *f* mineure.

Asian /'eɪʃn, US 'eɪʒn/ **I** *n* (from Far East) Asiatique *mf*; (in UK) personne originaire du sous-continent indien. **II** *adj* [*river, custom, politics*] asiatique.

Asiatic /ˌeɪʃɪ'ætɪk, US ˌeɪʒɪ-/ *adj* [*peoples, nations*] asiatique.

aside /ə'saɪd/ **I** *n* GEN, THEAT, CIN aparté *m*; **to say sth as** ou **in an ~** dire qch en aparté; (as digression) dire qch en passant.
II *adv* **1** (to one side) **to stand** ou **step** ou **move ~** s'écarter; **to turn ~** se détourner; **to cast** ou **throw** [*sth*] **~** mettre [qch] au rebut [*clothes, gift*]; écarter [*idea, theory*]; **to set** ou **put** ou **lay** [*sth*] **~** (save) mettre [qch] de côté; (in shop) réserver; **to brush** ou **sweep** [*sth*] **~** écarter [*objections, protests, worries*]; **to lay** ou **put a book ~** mettre un livre de côté; **to push** ou **move sb ~** écarter qn; **to take sb ~** prendre qn à part; **2** (apart) **money ~,** let's **discuss accommodation** laissons de côté la question d'argent et parlons du logement.
III aside from *prep phr* à part.

asinine /'æsɪnaɪn/ *adj* sot/sotte.

ask /ɑːsk, US æsk/ **I** *vtr* **1** (enquire as to) demander [*name, reason*]; **to ~ a question** poser une question; **to ~ sb sth** demander qch à qn; **80% of those ~ed said no** 80% des personnes interrogées ont répondu non; **I'm ~ing you how you did it** je veux savoir comment tu l'as fait; **I wasn't ~ing you** je ne t'ai rien demandé; **2** (request) demander [*permission, tolerance*]; **it's too much to ~** c'est trop demander; **to ~ to do** demander à faire; **to ~ sb to do** demander à qn de faire; **to ~ sth of** ou **from sb** demander qch à qn; **what price is she ~ing for it?** combien elle le vend?; **3** (invite) inviter [*person*]; **to ~ sb to dinner** inviter qn à [*concert, party*]; **to ~ sb to dinner** inviter qn à dîner; **to ~ sb out** inviter qn à sortir; **to ~ sb in** inviter qn à entrer; **we ~ed him along** nous l'avons invité à se joindre à nous.
II *vi* **1** (request) demander; **2** (make enquiries) se renseigner; **to ~ about sb** s'informer au sujet de qn; **I'll ~ around** je demanderai autour de moi.
III *v refl* **to ~ oneself** se demander [*reason*].
■ **ask after**: **~ after** [sb] demander des nouvelles de [*person*].
■ **ask for**: ¶ **~ for** [sth] demander [*drink, money, help, restraint*]; **he was ~ing for it°,** he **~ed for**

it°! il l'a bien cherché!; ¶ **~ for** [sb] (on telephone) demander à parler à; (from sick bed) demander à voir.

askance /ə'skæns/ *adv* **to look ~ at sb/sth** considérer qn/qch avec méfiance.

askew /ə'skjuː/ *adj, adv* de travers.

asking price *n* prix *m* demandé.

asleep /ə'sliːp/ *adj* **to be ~** dormir; **he's ~** il dort; **to fall ~** s'endormir; **they were found ~** on les a trouvés endormis; **to be half ~** (not yet awake) être à moitié endormi; (falling asleep) dormir à moitié; **to be sound** ou **fast ~** dormir à poings fermés.

asp /æsp/ *n* ZOOL aspic *m*.

asparagus /ə'spærəgəs/ **I** *n* asperge *f*.
II *noun modifier* [*sauce, soup*] aux asperges; **~ tip** pointe *f* d'asperge.

aspect /'æspekt/ *n* **1** (feature) ALSO LING aspect *m*; **2** (angle) point *m* de vue; **to examine every ~ of sth** examiner qch sous tous ses aspects; **seen from this ~** vu sous cet angle; **3** (orientation) orientation *f*; **house with a westerly ~** maison exposée à l'ouest; **4** (view) vue *f*.

aspen /'æspən/ *n* tremble *m*.

aspersions /ə'spɜːʃns, US -ʒnz/ *npl* SOUT **to cast ~ on** dénigrer [*person*]; mettre [qch] en doute [*ability, capacity*].

asphalt /'æsfælt, US -fɔːlt/ **I** *n* bitume *m*.
II *noun modifier* [*drive, playground*] bitumé.
III *vtr* bitumer.

asphyxia /əs'fɪksɪə, US æs'f-/ *n* asphyxie *f*.

asphyxiate /əs'fɪksɪeɪt, US æs'f-/ **I** *vtr* asphyxier.
II *vi* s'asphyxier.

asphyxiation /əsˌfɪksɪ'eɪʃn/ *n* asphyxie *f*; **to die of** ou **from ~** mourir asphyxié.

aspic /'æspɪk/ *n* CULIN aspic *m*; **salmon in ~** aspic de saumon.

aspirate **I** /'æspərət/ *n* LING aspirée *f*.
II /'æspərət/ *adj* aspiré.
III /'æspɪreɪt/ *vtr* aspirer.

aspiration /ˌæspɪ'reɪʃn/ *n* **1** (desire) aspiration *f* (**to** à); **to have ~s to do** aspirer à faire; **2** MED, LING aspiration *f*.

aspire /ə'spaɪə(r)/ *vi* aspirer (**to** à; **to do** à faire); **it ~s to be an exclusive restaurant** cela se veut un restaurant de luxe.

aspirin /'æspərɪn/ *n* aspirine® *f*; **two ~(s)** deux comprimés d'aspirine.

aspiring /ə'spaɪərɪŋ/ *adj* **~ authors/journalists etc** ceux qui aspirent à devenir auteurs/journalistes etc.

ass /æs/ *n* **1** (donkey) âne *m*; **2°** (fool) idiot/-e *m/f*.

assail /ə'seɪl/ *vtr* SOUT **1** (attack) attaquer; **2** (plague) assaillir; **to be ~ed by worries/doubts** être assailli par les soucis/par le doute.

assailant /ə'seɪlənt/ *n* agresseur *m*, MIL assaillant/-e *m/f*.

assassin /ə'sæsɪn, US -sn/ *n* assassin *m*.

assassinate /ə'sæsɪneɪt, US -sən-/ *vtr* assassiner.

assassination /əˌsæsɪ'neɪʃn, US -sə'neɪʃn/ *n* assassinat *m*.

assault /ə'sɔːlt/ **I** *n* **1** JUR (on person) agression *f* (**on** sur); (sexual) agression *f* sexuelle (**on** sur); **physical ~** agression *f*; **verbal ~** injures *fpl* (**on** de); **2** (attack) assaut *m* (**on** de); **air/ground ~** assaut aérien/terrestre; **to make an ~ on** monter à l'assaut de [*town*]; **3** FIG (criticism) (on theory) attaque *f* (**on** de); (on person, reputation) atteinte *f* (**on** à).
II *noun modifier* [*troops, weapon, ship*] d'assaut.
III *vtr* **1** JUR agresser; **to be indecently ~ed** être victime d'une agression sexuelle; **2** MIL assaillir; **3** FIG agresser [*ears, nerves*].

assault: **~ and battery** *n* JUR coups *mpl* et blessures *fpl*; **~ course** *n* MIL parcours *m* du combattant.

assemblage /ə'semblɪdʒ/ *n* **1** (collection) collection *f*; **2** TECH, ART assemblage *m*.

assemble /ə'sembl/ **I** *vtr* **1** (gather) rassembler; **2** (construct) assembler; **easy to ~** facile à monter.

II *vi* [*marchers, passengers, vehicles*] se rassembler; [*parliament, team, family*] se réunir.
III assembled *pp adj* [*reporters, delegates*] rassemblé; [*family, friends*] réuni.

assembler /ə'semblə(r)/ ▶1251 *n* **1** (in factory) assembleur/-euse *m/f*; **2** COMPUT assembleur *m*.

assembly /ə'sembli/ *n* **1** (of people) assemblée *f*; **2** POL (institution) assemblée *f*; **3** SCH rassemblement *m*; **4** POL (congregating) réunion *f*; **freedom of ~** liberté *f* de réunion; **5** (of components, machines) assemblage *m*; **~ instructions** instructions *fpl* de montage; **6** (device) assemblage *m*; **engine ~** bloc-moteur *m*.

assembly line *n* chaîne *f* de montage.

assent /ə'sent/ **I** *n* assentiment *m* (**to** à); **by common ~** d'un commun accord.
II *v* SOUT donner son assentiment (**to** à).

assert /ə'sɜːt/ **I** *vtr* **1** (state) affirmer (**that** que); (against opposition) soutenir (**that** que); **to ~ one's authority** affirmer son autorité; **2** (demand) revendiquer [*right, claim*].
II *v refl* **to ~ oneself** s'affirmer.

assertion /ə'sɜːʃn/ *n* (statement) déclaration *f* (**that** selon laquelle); **it was an ~ of her strength** c'était une manière d'affirmer son pouvoir.

assertive /ə'sɜːtɪv/ *adj* assuré.

assertiveness /ə'sɜːtɪvnɪs/ *n* affirmation *f* de soi; **lack of ~** manque *m* d'assurance; **I admire your ~** j'admire votre assurance.

assess /ə'ses/ **I** *vtr* **1** GEN évaluer [*ability, effect, person, problem*]; **2** (in insurance, law) estimer [*damage, value*]; **3** (for taxation) imposer [*person*]; fixer [*tax*]; **4** SCH contrôler [*pupil*].
II *vi* évaluer.

assessment /ə'sesmənt/ *n* **1** GEN appréciation *f* (**of** de); **2** (in insurance, law) estimation *f* (**of** de); **3** (for taxation) imposition *f*; **4** SCH contrôle *m*.

assessor /ə'sesə(r)/ ▶1251 *n* **1** FIN contrôleur *m*; **2** (in insurance) expert *m*; **3** JUR assesseur *m*.

asset /'æset/ **I** *n* **1** FIN bien *m*; **2** (advantage) atout *m*.
II assets *npl* (private) biens *mpl*, avoir *m* ¢; COMM, JUR actif *m* ¢; **~s and liabilities** actif et passif.

asset stripping *n* dépeçage *m*.

assiduity /ˌæsɪ'djuːɪtɪ, US -duː-/ *n* assiduité *f*.

assiduous /ə'sɪdjʊəs, US -dʒʊəs/ *adj* assidu.

assign /ə'saɪn/ *vtr* **1** (allocate) assigner [*resources*] (**to** à); **2** (delegate) **to ~ a task to sb, to ~ sb to a task** affecter qn à une tâche; **to ~ sb to do** désigner qn pour faire; **3** (attribute) attribuer [*name, value*] (**to** à); **4** (appoint) nommer (**to** à); **5** JUR (transfer) céder.

assignation /ˌæsɪg'neɪʃn/ *n* rendez-vous *m*.

assignment /ə'saɪnmənt/ *n* **1** (diplomatic, military) poste *m*; (specific duty) mission *f*; **2** (academic) devoir *m*; **3** (of duties, staff, funds) affectation *f*; **4** (of rights, contract) cession *f*.

assimilate /ə'sɪmɪleɪt/ **I** *vtr* assimiler (**to** à).
II *vi* s'assimiler (**to** à).

assimilation /ə,sɪmɪ'leɪʃn/ *n* assimilation *f* (**to** à).

assist /ə'sɪst/ **I** *vtr* **1** (help) GEN aider; (in organization) assister (**to do, in doing** à faire); **to ~ one another** s'entraider; **2** (facilitate) faciliter.
II *vi* **1** (help) aider (**in doing** à faire); **to ~ in** prendre part à [*operation, rescue*]; **2** (attend) assister (**at** à).
III -assisted *combining form* **computer-~ed** assisté par ordinateur; **government-~ed scheme** projet financé par l'État.

assistance /ə'sɪstəns/ *n* aide *f* (**to** à); (more formal) assistance *f* (**to** à); **to come to sb's ~** venir à l'aide de qn; **to give ~ to sb** prêter assistance à qn; **with the ~ of** avec l'aide de [*person*]; à l'aide de [*device*]; **can I be of ~?** puis-je aider or être utile?

assistant /ə'sɪstənt/ ▶1251 **I** *n* **1** (helper) assistant/-e *m/f*; (in hierarchy) adjoint/-e *m/f*; **2** GB SCH, UNIV (**foreign language**) **~** (in school) assistant/-e *m/f*; (in university) lecteur/-trice *m/f*.
II *noun modifier* [*editor, producer etc*] adjoint.

assistant: **~ manager** ▶1251 *n* gérant/-e *m/f*;

adjoint/-e; **~ professor** ▶1251 *n* US UNIV ≈ maître assistant *m*.

associate I /ə'səʊʃɪət/ *n* **1** (colleague, partner) associé/-e *m/f* ALSO PEJ; **an ~ in crime** un/une complice; **2** (of society) associé/-e *m/f*; (of academic body) membre *m*; **3** US UNIV ≈ DEUG *m*.
II /ə'səʊʃɪət/ *adj* [*body, member*] associé.
III /ə'səʊʃɪeɪt/ *vtr* **1** associer [*idea, memory*] (**with** à); **2 to be ~d with** [*person*] faire partie de [*movement, group*]; (of person) être mêlé à [*shady business*].
IV /ə'səʊʃɪeɪt/ *vi* **to ~ with sb** fréquenter qn.
V associated *pp adj* **1** [*idea, concept*] associé; **2** (connected) [*member*] [*benefits, expenses*] annexe; **the plan and its ~d problems** le projet et les problèmes qui en découlent.

associate: **~ company** société *f* liée; **~ director** *n* THEAT directeur/-trice *m/f* associé/-e; COMM directeur/-trice *m/f* adjoint/-e; **~ editor** ▶1251 rédacteur/-trice *m/f* associé/-e; **~ member** *n* membre *m* associé; **~ membership** *n* adhésion *f* en tant que membre associé.

association /ə,səʊsɪ'eɪʃn/ *n* **1** (club, society) association *f*; **2** (relationship) (between ideas) association *f*; (between organizations, people) relations *fpl* (**between** entre; **with** avec); (sexual) liaison *f* (**with** avec); **3** (mental evocation) (*gén pl*) souvenir *m*; **it has good/bad ~s for me** ça me rappelle de bons/mauvais souvenirs; **to have ~s with sth** évoquer qch.

assorted /ə'sɔːtɪd/ *adj* [*objects, colours etc*] varié; [*foodstuffs*] assorti; [*group*] hétérogène; **ill ~** mal assorti; **in ~ sizes** dans toutes les tailles.

assortment /ə'sɔːtmənt/ *n* GEN assortiment *m* (**of** de); (of people) mélange *m* (**of** de); **in an ~ of colours** dans différentes couleurs.

assuage /ə'sweɪdʒ/ *vtr* LITTÉR calmer.

assume /ə'sjuːm, US ə'suːm/ *vtr* **1** (suppose) supposer (**that** que); **I ~ she knows** je suppose qu'elle le sait; **it is ~d that** on suppose que; **let's ~ ou assuming that's correct** supposons que cela soit exact; **2** (take on) prendre [*control, identity, office*]; assumer [*responsibility*]; affecter [*expression, indifference*]; **under an ~d name** sous un nom d'emprunt.

assumption /ə'sʌmpʃn/ *n* **1** (supposition) supposition *f*; (belief) idée *f*; PHILOS hypothèse *f*; **the ~ that** l'idée selon laquelle; **to work on the ~ that** présumer que; **a false ~** une mauvaise hypothèse; **2** (of duty, power) prise *f* (**of** de).

Assumption /ə'sʌmpʃn/ *n* RELIG Assomption *f*.

assurance /ə'ʃɔːrəns, US ə'ʃʊərəns/ *n* **1** (guarantee) assurance *f*, garantie *f*; **to give sb an ou every ~ that** donner à qn l'assurance que; **you have my ~ that** je peux vous assurer que; **2** (self-confidence) assurance *f*; **3** GB (insurance) assurance *f*; **life ~** assurance-vie *f*.

assure /ə'ʃɔː(r), US ə'ʃʊər/ *vtr* **1** (state positively) assurer; **to ~ sb that** assurer à qn que; **to be ~d of sth** être sûr de qch; **rest ~d that** soyez assuré que; **2** (ensure) assurer; **3** GB (insure) assurer.

assured /ə'ʃɔːd, US ə'ʃʊərd/ *adj* **1** (confident) [*voice, manner*] assuré; [*person*] plein d'assurance; **2** (beyond doubt) assuré.

Assyria /ə'sɪrɪə/ ▶840 *pr n* Assyrie *f*.

asterisk /'æstərɪsk/ *n* astérisque *m*.

astern /ə'stɜːn/ *adv* NAUT à l'arrière (**of** de).

asteroid /'æstərɔɪd/ *n* astéroïde *m*.

asthma /'æsmə, US 'æzmə/ ▶1002 *n* asthme *m*; **~ sufferer** asthmatique *mf*.

asthmatic /æs'mætɪk/ *n, adj* asthmatique (*mf*).

astigmatism /ə'stɪgmətɪzəm/ *n* astigmatisme *m*.

astonish /ə'stɒnɪʃ/ *vtr* surprendre, étonner; **it ~es me that** ce qui me surprend or m'étonne c'est que.

astonished /ə'stɒnɪʃt/ *adj* surpris, étonné (**by, at** par); **to do sth** (de faire); **to be ~ that** être vraiment étonné que (+ *subj*), trouver extraordinaire que (+ *subj*).

astonishing /ə'stɒnɪʃɪŋ/ *adj* [*skill, intelligence*] étonnant; [*career, performance*] extraordinaire;

---

at

When *at* is used as a straightforward preposition it is translated by *à*:

at the airport	= à l'aéroport
at midnight	= à minuit
at the age of 50	= à l'âge de 50 ans

Remember that *à* + *le* always becomes *au* and *à* + *les* always becomes *aux* (*au bureau, aux bureaux*).

When *at* means *at the house, shop,* etc. *of* it is translated by *chez*:

at Amanda's	= chez Amanda
at the hairdresser's	= chez le coiffeur

If you have doubts about how to translate a phrase or idiom beginning with *at* (*at the top of, at home, at a guess* etc.) you should consult the appropriate noun entry (*top, home, guess* etc.). This dictionary contains usage notes on such topics as *age, the clock, length measurement, games and sports* etc. Many of these use the preposition *at*. For the index to these notes ▶ **1419**.

at also often appears in English as the second element of a phrasal verb (*look at, aim at* etc.). For translations, look at the appropriate verb entry (*look, aim* etc.).

at is used after certain nouns, adjectives and verbs in English (*surprise at, attempt at, annoyed at* etc.). For translations, consult the appropriate noun, adjective or verb entry (*surprise, attempt, annoyed* etc.).

In the entry **at**, you will find particular usages and idiomatic expressions which do not appear elsewhere in the dictionary.

[*beauty, speed, success*] incroyable; **it is ~ that** il est incroyable que (+ *subj*).

astonishingly /ə'stɒnɪʃɪŋlɪ/ *adv* incroyablement.

astonishment /ə'stɒnɪʃmənt/ *n* étonnement *m*; **to my ~** à ma grande surprise; **to look at sb/sth in ~** regarder qn/qch avec étonnement.

astound /ə'staʊnd/ *vtr* stupéfier.

astounding /ə'staʊndɪŋ/ *adj* incroyable.

astrakhan /ˌæstrə'kæn, US 'æstrəkən/ *n* astrakan *m*.

astray /ə'streɪ/ *adv* **1 to go astray** (go missing) se perdre; (go wrong) [*plan etc*] être contrarié; **2 to lead sb ~** (confuse) induire qn en erreur; (corrupt) détourner qn du droit chemin.

astride /ə'straɪd/ **I** *adv* LIT [*be, sit*] à califourchon. **II** *prep* à califourchon sur; FIG **to stand** ou **sit ~ sth** [*building, company etc*] dominer qch.

astringent /ə'strɪndʒənt/ **I** *n* astringent *m*. **II** *adj* **1** MED astringent; **2** FIG [*remark, tone*] cinglant.

astrologer /ə'strɒlədʒə(r)/ ▶ **1251** *n* astrologue *mf*.

astrological /ˌæstrə'lɒdʒɪkl/ *adj* astrologique.

astrology /ə'strɒlədʒɪ/ *n* astrologie *f*.

astronaut /'æstrənɔːt/ ▶ **1251** *n* astronaute *mf*.

astronomer /ə'strɒnəmə(r)/ ▶ **1251** *n* astronome *mf*.

astronomic /ˌæstrə'nɒmɪk/, **astronomical** /ˌæstrə'nɒmɪkl/ *adj* LIT, FIG astronomique.

astronomically /ˌæstrə'nɒmɪkəlɪ/ *adv* **prices are ~ high** les prix sont astronomiques; **~ expensive** incroyablement cher.

astronomy /ə'strɒnəmɪ/ *n* astronomie *f*.

astrophysicist /ˌæstrəʊ'fɪzɪsɪst/ ▶ **1251** *n* astrophysicien/-ienne *m/f*.

astrophysics /ˌæstrəʊ'fɪzɪks/ *n* (+ *v sg*) astrophysique *f*.

Astroturf® /'æstrəʊtɜːf/ *n* gazon *m* artificiel.

astute /ə'stjuːt, US ə'stuːt/ *adj* astucieux/-ieuse.

astutely /ə'stjuːtlɪ, US ə'stuːtlɪ/ *adv* astucieusement.

astuteness /ə'stjuːtnɪs, US -'stuː-/ *n* astuce *f*.

asylum /ə'saɪləm/ *n* asile *m*; **lunatic ~** asile de fous.

asylum-seeker *n* demandeur/-euse *m/f* d'asile.

asymmetric /ˌeɪsɪ'metrɪk/, **asymmetrical** /ˌeɪsɪ'metrɪkl/ *adj* asymétrique.

at /æt, ət/ *prep* **1** (with place, time, age etc) à; **2** (at the

---

house etc of) chez; **3** (followed by superlative) **the garden is ~ its prettiest in June** juin est le mois où le jardin est le plus beau; **I'm ~ my best in the morning** c'est le matin que je me sens le mieux; **she was ~ her best at 50** (of musician, artist etc) à 50 ans elle était au sommet de son art; **4**° (harassing) **he's been (on) ~ me to buy a new car** il n'arrête pas de me casser les pieds pour que j'achète une nouvelle voiture°.

IDIOMS **I don't know where he's ~**° je ne le comprends pas du tout; **while we're ~ it**° pendant qu'on y est°; **I've been (hard) ~ it all day** je n'ai pas arrêté de la journée.

AT *n: abrév* ▶ **alternative technology**.

atavistic /ˌætə'vɪstɪk/ *adj* atavique.

ate /eɪt/ *prét* ▶ **eat**.

atheism /'eɪθɪɪzəm/ *n* athéisme *m*.

atheist /'eɪθɪɪst/ *n, adj* athée (*mf*).

atheistic /ˌeɪθɪ'ɪstɪk/ *adj* athée.

Athens /'æθɪnz/ ▶ **1343** *pr n* Athènes.

athlete /'æθliːt/ *n* athlète *mf*.

athlete's foot /ˌæθliːts 'fʊt/ ▶ **1002** *n* mycose *f*.

athletic /æθ'letɪk/ *adj* **1** [*event, club, coach*] d'athlétisme; **2** [*person, body*] athlétique.

athletics /æθ'letɪks/ ▶ **949** **I** *n* (+ *v sg*) GB athlétisme *m*; US sports *mpl*. **II** *noun modifier* [*club*] GB d'athlétisme; US sportif/-ive.

Atlantic /ət'læntɪk/ **I** ▶ **1117** *pr n* **the ~** l'Atlantique *m*. **II** *adj* GEN de l'Atlantique; [*coast, current*] atlantique.

Atlantic Ocean *n* océan *m* Atlantique.

atlas /'ætləs/ *n* atlas *m*.

Atlas Mountains *pr npl* (montagnes *fpl* de l')Atlas *m*.

ATM *n: abrév* ▶ **automatic teller machine**.

atmosphere /'ætməsfɪə(r)/ *n* **1** (air) atmosphère *f*; **2** (mood) GEN ambiance *f*; (bad) atmosphère *f*; **there was a bit of an ~**° l'atmosphère était tendue.

atmospheric /ˌætməs'ferɪk/ **I** **atmospherics** *npl* **1** RADIO, TV (interference) parasites *mpl*, bruit *m* atmosphérique; METEOROL (disturbances) perturbations *fpl* atmosphériques; **2** (of song, film) ambiance *f*. **II** *adj* **1** [*conditions, pressure, pollution*] atmosphérique; **2** [*music*] d'ambiance; [*film*] évocateur/-trice.

atom /'ætəm/ *n* PHYS, FIG atome *m*.

atom bomb *n* bombe *f* atomique.

atomic /ə'tɒmɪk/ *adj* [*explosion, power*] nucléaire, atomique.

atomic: **~ power station** *n* centrale *f* atomique; **~ reactor** *n* réacteur *m* atomique; **~ scientist** ▶ **1251** *n* atomiste *mf*.

atomize /'ætəmaɪz/ *vtr* atomiser.

atomizer /'ætəmaɪzə(r)/ *n* atomiseur *m*.

atone /ə'təʊn/ *vi* **to ~ for** expier [*sin, crime*]; racheter [*error*].

atonement /ə'təʊnmənt/ *n* rédemption *f*.

atrocious /ə'trəʊʃəs/ *adj* (horrifying) atroce; (bad) épouvantable.

atrociously /ə'trəʊʃəslɪ/ *adv* de façon atroce.

atrocity /ə'trɒsətɪ/ *n* atrocité *f*.

atrophy /'ætrəfɪ/ **I** *n* MED atrophie *f*. **II** *vi* MED, FIG s'atrophier.

attach /ə'tætʃ/ **I** *vtr* **1** (fasten) attacher [*objet*] (**to** à); (to letter) joindre; **2** (to organization) **to be ~ed to sth** être attaché à qch; **3** (attribute) attacher (**to** à); **to ~ blame to sb for sth** reprocher qch à qn. **II** *v refl* **to ~ oneself to** LIT, FIG s'attacher à.

attaché /ə'tæʃeɪ, US ˌætə'ʃeɪ/ *n* attaché/-e *m/f*.

attaché case *n* attaché-case *m*.

attached /ə'tætʃt/ *adj* **1** (fond) **~ to sb/sth** attaché à qn/qch; **to grow ~ to sb/sth** s'attacher à qn/qch; **2** [*document*] ci-joint.

attachment /ə'tætʃmənt/ *n* **1** (affection) attachement *m*; **to form an ~ to sb** s'attacher à qn; **2** (device) accessoire *m*; **3** (placement) **to be on ~ to** GEN, MIL être en détachement à; **4** (act of fastening) fixation *f*.

attack /ə'tæk/ **I** *n* **1** GEN, MIL, SPORT attaque *f* (**on** contre); (criminal) agression *f* (**against, on** contre); (terrorist) attentat *m*; **to come under ~** MIL être attaqué (**from** par); FIG être l'objet de critiques virulentes (**from** de la part de); **to leave oneself open to ~** FIG s'exposer à la critique; **to mount** ou **launch an ~ on sth** LIT attaquer qch; FIG s'attaquer à qch; **2** MED (of chronic illness) crise *f* (**of** de); **to have an ~ of flu** attraper la grippe. **II** *vtr* **1** GEN, MED, MIL, SPORT attaquer; (criminally) agresser [*victim*]; FIG attaquer [*book, idea*]; **2** (tackle) s'attaquer à [*task, problem*].

attacker /ə'tækə(r)/ *n* GEN agresseur *m*; MIL, SPORT attaquant/-e *m/f*.

attain /ə'teɪn/ *vtr* atteindre [*position, objective, level*]; réaliser [*ambition*]; acquérir [*knowledge*]; parvenir à [*happiness*].

attainable /ə'teɪnəbl/ *adj* réalisable.

attainment /ə'teɪnmənt/ *n* **1** (achieving) (of knowledge) acquisition *f*; (of goal) réalisation *f*; **2** (success) réussite *f*.

attempt /ə'tempt/ **I** *n* **1** tentative *f* (**to do** de faire); **to make an ~ to do** ou **at doing** tenter de faire; **in an ~ to do** pour essayer de faire; **on his first ~** dès sa première tentative; **~ to escape, escape ~** tentative d'évasion; **he made no ~ to apologize** il n'a même pas tenté de s'excuser; **good ~!** bien essayé!; **2** (attack) attentat *m*; **~ on sb's life** attentat contre la vie de qn. **II** *vtr* tenter (**to do** de faire); s'attaquer à [*exam question*]; **to ~ suicide** tenter de se suicider; **~ed murder** tentative de meurtre.

attend /ə'tend/ **I** *vtr* **1** (go to) assister à [*ceremony, meeting, performance*]; aller à [*church, school*]; suivre [*class, course*]; **the event was well/poorly ~ed** beaucoup de/peu de monde assistait à l'événement; **2** (accompany) accompagner; **3** (take care of) soigner. **II** *vi* **1** (be present) être présent; **2** SOUT (pay attention) être attentif/-ive (**to** à). ■ **attend to:** **~ to** [sb/sth] s'occuper de [*person, problem*].

attendance: **~ record** *n* taux *m* de présence; **~ register** *n* SCH registre *m* des absences.

attendant /ə'tendənt/ **I** ▶ 1251 *n* (in cloakroom, museum, car park) gardien/-ienne *m/f*; (in cinema) ouvreuse *f*; (at petrol station) pompiste *mf*; (at swimming pool) surveillant/-e *m/f*; **medical ~** membre *m* du personnel médical. **II** *adj* SOUT **1** (associated) [*cost, danger, issue*] associé; [*symptom*] concomitant; **2** (attending) [*aide, bodyguard*] attaché à sa personne.

attention /ə'tenʃn/ **I** *n* **1** (notice, interest) attention *f*; **to attract ~** attirer l'attention; **to be the centre** ou **focus of ~** être le centre d'attention; **to draw ~ to sth** attirer l'attention sur qch; **to seek** ou **demand ~** [*child*] chercher à attirer l'attention; **to give one's full ~ to sth** prêter toute son attention à qch; **to pay ~** faire attention; **to bring sth to sb's ~** porter qch à l'attention de qn; **it has come to my ~ that...** j'ai appris que...; **~ please!** votre attention s'il vous plaît!; **pay ~!** écoutez!; **2** (treatment, care) GEN attention *f*; MED assistance *f*; **~ to detail** le souci du détail; **to give some ~ to sth** s'occuper de qch; **the car needs ~** il faut s'occuper de la voiture; **for the ~ of** à l'attention de; **3** MIL **to stand to** ou **at ~** être au garde-à-vous. **II** *excl* garde-à-vous!

attention-seeking I *n* besoin *m* d'attirer l'attention. **II** *adj* [*person*] cherchant à attirer l'attention.

attention span *n* **he has a very short ~** il n'arrive pas à se concentrer très longtemps.

attentive /ə'tentɪv/ *adj* (alert) attentif/-ive; (solicitous) attentionné (**to** à).

attentively /ə'tentɪvlɪ/ *adv* (alertly) attentivement; (solicitously) avec attention.

attentiveness /ə'tentɪvnɪs/ *n* **1** (concentration) attention *f*; **2** (solicitude) prévenance *f*.

attenuate /ə'tenjʊeɪt/ *vtr* modérer.

attest /ə'test/ SOUT **I** *vtr* **1** (prove) confirmer; **an ~ed fact** un fait reconnu; **2** (declare) attester (**that** que); **3** (authenticate) légaliser [*will*]. **II** *vi* **1 to ~ to** (prove) témoigner de; **2** (affirm) attester.

attic /'ætɪk/ *n* grenier *m*; **in the ~** au grenier.

Attica /'ætɪkə/ *pr n* Attique *f*.

attic: **~ room** *n* mansarde *f*; **~ window** *n* lucarne *f*.

attire† /ə'taɪə(r)/ **I** *n* vêtements *mpl*. **II** *vtr* vêtir; **~d in** vêtu de.

attitude /'ætɪtjuːd, US -tuːd/ **I** *n* **1** attitude *f* (**to, towards** GB à l'égard de); **her ~ to life/the world** sa façon de voir la vie/le monde; **2**○ (assertiveness, dynamism) **to have ~** avoir de l'allure. **II attitudes** *npl* (of social group etc) **young people's ~s towards religion** l'attitude *f* des jeunes envers la religion.

attorney /ə'tɜːnɪ/ ▶ 1251 *n* US (lawyer) avocat *m*; **power of ~** procuration *f*.

Attorney General, AG *n* (*pl* **Attorneys General**) Attorney *m* General, ministre *m* de la justice des États-Unis.

attract /ə'trækt/ *vtr* attirer; **to ~ attention** attirer l'attention; **he was very ~ed to her** elle l'attirait beaucoup.

attraction /ə'trækʃn/ *n* **1** (favourable feature) attrait *m* (**of sth** de qch; **of doing** de faire; **for** pour); **I can't see the ~ of (doing)** je ne vois pas l'intérêt de (faire); **2** (entertainment, sight) attraction *f*; **3** (instinctive allure) attirance *f* (**to** pour); **her ~ to him** son attirance pour lui; **4** PHYS attraction *f*.

attractive /ə'træktɪv/ *adj* [*person*] séduisant; [*child*] charmant; [*place, feature*] attrayant; [*offer, idea*] séduisant; [*plant*] joli.

attractively /ə'træktɪvlɪ/ *adv* [*furnished, arranged*] de manière attrayante; [*dressed*] coquettement.

attractiveness /ə'træktɪvnɪs/ *n* (of person, place) charme *m*; (of investment) attrait *m*; (of proposal) intérêt *m*.

attributable /ə'trɪbjʊtəbl/ *adj* **to be ~ to** [*change, profit, success etc*] être dû à; [*error, fall, loss etc*] être imputable à.

attribute I /'ætrɪbjuːt/ *n* GEN attribut *m*; LING épithète *f*. **II** /ə'trɪbjuːt/ *vtr* attribuer (**to** à).

attribution /ˌætrɪ'bjuːʃn/ *n* attribution *f* (**of** de; **to** à).

attributive /ə'trɪbjʊtɪv/ *adj* LING épithète.

attrition /ə'trɪʃn/ *n* (all contexts) usure *f*.

attune /ə'tjuːn, US ə'tuːn/ *vtr* **to be ~d to** (accustomed to) être habitué à; (aware of) être sensible à.

aubergine /'əʊbəʒiːn/ *n* GB aubergine *f*.

auburn /'ɔːbən/ ▶ 818 *adj* auburn *inv*.

auction /'ɔːkʃn, 'ɒkʃn/ **I** *n* enchère *f* (*gen pl*); **at ~** aux enchères; **to put sth up for ~** mettre qch aux enchères. **II** *vtr* (also **~ off**) vendre [qch] aux enchères.

auctioneer /ˌɔːkʃə'nɪə(r)/ ▶ 1251 *n* commissaire-priseur *m*.

auction: **~ house** *n* US société *f* de commissaires-priseurs; **~ room(s)** *n(pl)* salle *f* de vente aux enchères; **~ sale** *n* vente *f* aux enchères.

audacious /ɔː'deɪʃəs/ *adj* audacieux/-ieuse.

audacity /ɔː'dæsɪtɪ/ *n* audace *f*.

audible /'ɔːdəbl/ *adj* audible.

audibly /'ɔːdəblɪ/ *adv* distinctement.

audience /'ɔːdɪəns/ *n* **1** (in cinema, concert, theatre) public *m*, salle *f*; RADIO auditeurs *mpl*; TV téléspectateurs *mpl*; **2** (for books) lecteurs *mpl*; (for ideas) public *m*; **3** (meeting) audience *f* (**with sb** auprès de qn).

audience: **~ participation** *n* participation *f* du public; **~ ratings** *npl* indice *m* d'écoute; **~ research** *n* sondages *mpl* du public.

audio /'ɔːdɪəʊ/ *adj* audio *inv*.

audio: **~book** *n* livre-cassette *m*; **~ cassette** *n* audiocassette *f*.

audiotyping /'ɔːdɪəʊtaɪpɪŋ/ *n* audiotypie *f*.

audiotypist /'ɔːdɪəʊtaɪpɪst/ ▶ **1251** *n* audiotypiste *mf*.

audiovisual, **AV** /ˌɔːdɪəʊ'vɪʒʊəl/ *adj* audiovisuel/-elle.

audit /'ɔːdɪt/ **I** *n* audit *m*.
II *vtr* auditer, vérifier.

auditing /'ɔːdɪtɪŋ/ *n* audit *m*.

audition /ɔː'dɪʃn/ **I** *n* audition *f* (**for** pour); **to go for an ~** passer une audition.
II *vtr*, *vi* auditionner (**for** pour).

auditor /'ɔːdɪtə(r)/ ▶ **1251** *n* **1** commissaire *m* aux comptes; **2** US (student) auditeur/-trice *m/f*.

auditorium /ˌɔːdɪ'tɔːrɪəm/ *n* (*pl* **-iums** ou **-ia**) **1** THEAT salle *f*; **2** US (for meetings) salle *f* de conférences; SCH, UNIV amphithéâtre *m*; (concert hall) salle *f* de spectacle; (stadium) stade *m*.

auditory /'ɔːdɪtrɪ, US -tɔːrɪ/ *adj* auditif/-ive.

Aug *abrév écrite* = **August**.

augment /ɔːg'ment/ *vtr*, *vi* augmenter.

augmentation /ˌɔːgmen'teɪʃn/ *n* GEN, MUS augmentation *f*.

augur /'ɔːgə(r)/ *vi* **to ~ well/ill** être de bon/mauvais augure (**for** pour).

august /ɔː'gʌst/ *adj* SOUT imposant, auguste FML.

August /'ɔːgəst/ ▶ **1090** *n* août *m*.

auk /ɔːk/ *n* **great ~** grand pingouin *m*; **little ~** mergule *m* nain.

aunt /ɑːnt, US ænt/ *n* tante *f*; **no, Aunt** non, ma tante.

auntie, **aunty**○ /'ɑːntɪ, US 'æntɪ/ *n* tantine○ *f*, tata○ *f*.

au pair /ˌəʊ 'peə(r)/ *n* (jeune) fille *f* au pair.

aura /'ɔːrə/ *n* (*pl* **-ras** ou **-rae**) (of place) atmosphère *f*; (of person) aura *f*.

aural /'ɔːrəl, aʊrəl/ **I** *n* SCH exercice *m* de compréhension et d'expression orales; MUS = dictée *f* musicale.
II *adj* **1** GEN auditif/-ive; **2** MED auriculaire; [*test*] auditif; **3** SCH [*comprehension, test*] oral.

aurora /ɔː'rɔːrə/ *n* (*pl* **-ras** ou **-rae**) **~ australis/borealis** aurore *f* australe/boréale.

auspicious /ɔː'spɪʃəs/ *adj* prometteur/-euse.

Aussie○ /'ɒzɪ/ *n*, *adj* = **Australian**.

austere /ɒ'stɪə(r), ɔː'stɪə(r)/ *adj* austère.

austerity /ɒ'sterətɪ, ɔː'sterətɪ/ *n* austérité *f*.

Australasia /ˌɒstrə'leɪʒə, ˌɔːs-/ *pr n* Australasie *f*.

Australia /ɒ'streɪlɪə, ɔː's-/ ▶ **840** *pr n* Australie *f*.

Australian /ɒ'streɪlɪən, ɔː's-/ ▶ **1100** **I** *n* Australien/-ienne *m/f*.
II *adj* australien/-ienne.

Austria /'ɒstrɪə, 'ɔːstrɪə/ ▶ **840** *pr n* Autriche *f*.

Austrian /'ɒstrɪən, 'ɔːstrɪən/ ▶ **1100** **I** *n* Autrichien/-ienne *m/f*.
II *adj* autrichien/-ienne.

Austro-Hungarian /'ɒstrəʊ hʌŋ'geərɪən/ *adj* austro-hongrois.

autarchy /'ɔːtɑːkɪ/ *n* autocratie *f*.

authentic /ɔː'θentɪk/ *adj* authentique.

authenticate /ɔː'θentɪkeɪt/ *vtr* authentifier.

authenticity /ˌɔːθen'tɪsətɪ/ *n* authenticité *f*.

author /'ɔːθə(r)/ ▶ **1251** *n* **1** (of book, play, report) auteur *m*; **2** (by profession) écrivain *m*; **3** (of scheme) auteur *m*.

authoritarian /ɔː,θɒrɪ'teərɪən/ *adj* PEJ autoritaire.

authoritarianism /ɔː,θɒrɪ'teərɪənɪzəm/ *n* PEJ autoritarisme *m*.

authoritative /ɔː'θɒrətətɪv, US -teɪtɪv/ *adj* **1** (forceful) autoritaire; **2** (reliable) [*work*] qui fait autorité; [*source*] bien informé.

authority /ɔː'θɒrətɪ/ **I** *n* **1** (power) autorité *f* (**over** sur); **to have the ~ to do** être habilité à faire; **to be in ~** occuper un poste de responsabilité; **he will be reported to those in ~** son cas sera référé à qui de

droit; **who's in ~ here?** qui commande ici?; **to do sth on sb's ~** faire qch sous les ordres de qn; **2** (forcefulness, confidence) autorité *f*; **3** (permission) autorisation *f*; **to give sb (the) ~ to do** autoriser qn à faire; **4** (organization) autorité *f*; **5** (expert) (person) autorité *f*, expert *m* (**on** en matière de); (book , film) œuvre *f* de référence; **6** (source of information) source *f*; **I have it on good ~ that** je sais de source sûre que.
II authorities *npl* GEN, ADMIN, POL autorités *fpl*; **the school/hospital authorities** la direction de l'école/de l'hôpital.

authorization /ˌɔːθəraɪ'zeɪʃn/ *n* (authority, document) autorisation *f*; **to give** ou **grant ~ to do** accorder l'autorisation de faire.

authorize /'ɔːθəraɪz/ *vtr* autoriser (**to do** à faire); **~d** [*signature, version*] autorisé; [*dealer*] agréé.

autism /'ɔːtɪzəm/ *n* autisme *m*.

autistic /ɔː'tɪstɪk/ *adj* [*person*] autiste; [*response etc*] autistique.

auto○ /'ɔːtəʊ/ US **I** *n* auto *f*.
II *noun modifier* [*industry*] automobile; [*workers*] de l'industrie automobile.

autobiographical /ˌɔːtəʊbaɪə'græfɪkl/ *adj* autobiographique.

autobiography /ˌɔːtəʊbaɪ'ɒgrəfɪ/ *n* autobiographie *f*.

autocrat /'ɔːtəkræt/ *n* autocrate *mf*.

autocratic /ˌɔːtə'krætɪk/ *adj* autocratique.

autocue /'ɔːtəʊkjuː/ *n* TV prompteur *m*.

autograph /'ɔːtəgrɑːf, US -græf/ **I** *n* autographe *m*.
II *noun modifier* [*album, hunter*] d'autographes.
III *vtr* dédicacer [*book, record*]; signer [*memento*].

autoimmune /ˌɔːtəʊɪ'mjuːn/ *adj* [*disease*] auto-immun; [*system*] autoimmunitaire.

automate /'ɔːtəmeɪt/ *vtr* automatiser [*factory, process*].

automatic /ˌɔːtə'mætɪk/ **I** *n* **1** (washing machine) machine *f* à laver automatique; **2** (car) voiture *f* (à changement de vitesse) automatique; **3** (gun) automatique *m*; **4** (setting) **to be on ~** [*machine*] être en position automatique.
II *adj* automatique.

automatically /ˌɔːtə'mætɪklɪ/ *adv* automatiquement.

automatic pilot *n* (device) pilote *m* automatique; (system) LIT, FIG pilotage *m* automatique; **to be on ~** AVIAT être sur pilote automatique.

automatic teller machine, **ATM** *n* guichet *m* automatique.

automation /ˌɔːtə'meɪʃn/ *n* automatisation *f*; **office ~** bureautique *f*; **industrial ~** robotique *f*.

automaton /ɔː'tɒmətən, US -tɒn/ *n* (*pl* **-s**, **automata**) automate *m*.

automobile /'ɔːtəməbiːl, ˌɔːtəmə'biːl/ *n* US, GB† automobile *f*.

automotive /ˌɔːtə'məʊtɪv/ *adj* **1** [*design, industry*] automobile; **2** (self-propelling) automoteur/-trice.

autonomous /ɔː'tɒnəməs/ *adj* autonome.

autonomy /ɔː'tɒnəmɪ/ *n* autonomie *f*.

autopilot /'ɔːtəʊpaɪlət/ *n* AVIAT, FIG pilote *m* automatique, bloc *m* de pilotage.

autopsy /'ɔːtɒpsɪ/ *n* autopsie *f* ALSO FIG.

autosuggestion /ˌɔːtəʊ sə'dʒestʃən/ *n* autosuggestion *f*.

autumn /'ɔːtəm/ ▶ **1235** *n* SURTOUT GB automne *m*.

autumnal /ɔː'tʌmnəl/ *adj* d'automne.

auxiliary /ɔːg'zɪlɪərɪ/ **I** *n* (person) auxiliaire *mf*; LING auxiliaire *m*.
II *adj* [*equipment, staff*] auxiliaire.

auxiliary: **~ nurse** ▶ **1251** *n* aide-soignant/-e *m/f*; **~ verb** *n* (verbe *m*) auxiliaire *m*.

avail /ə'veɪl/ SOUT **I** *n* **to be of no ~** ne servir à rien; **to no ~**, **without ~** en vain.
II *v refl* **to ~ oneself of** profiter de [*opportunity*]; accepter [*offer*].

availability /ə,veɪlə'bɪlətɪ/ *n* (of option, service) existence *f*; (of drugs) présence *f* (sur le marché); **sub-**

available

ject to ~ (of holidays, rooms, theatre seats etc) dans la limite des places disponibles.

available /ə'veɪləbl/ *adj* disponible (**for** pour; **to** à); **to make sb** ~ **to sb** mettre qch à la disposition de qn; **to be** ~ **from** [*product*] être disponible dans [*shop*]; [*service*] être fourni par [*organization*]; **by every** ~ **means** par tous les moyens possibles; **to make oneself** ~ **for sth/sb** se libérer pour qch/qn.

avalanche /'ævəlɑ:nʃ, US -læntʃ/ *n* avalanche *f*.

avant-garde /,ævɒŋ'gɑ:d/ **I** *n* avant-garde *f*. **II** *adj* d'avant-garde.

avarice /'ævərɪs/ *n* cupidité *f*.

avaricious /,ævə'rɪʃəs/ *adj* cupide.

Ave *abrév écrite* = **Avenue**.

avenge /ə'vendʒ/ **I** *vtr* venger [*person, death, defeat*]. **II** *v refl* **to** ~ **oneself on sb** se venger de qn.

avenger /ə'vendʒə(r)/ *n* vengeur/-eresse *m/f*.

avenging /ə'vendʒɪŋ/ *adj* vengeur/-eresse.

avenue /'ævənju:, US -nu:/ *n* **1** (street, road) avenue *f*; (path, driveway) allée *f*; **2** FIG (possibility) possibilité *f*.

average /'ævərɪdʒ/ **I** *n* moyenne *f* (**of** de); **on** (**the**) ~ en moyenne; **above/below** (**the**) ~ au-dessus de/au-dessous de la moyenne; **to work out an** ~ faire une moyenne; **the law of** ~**s** la loi des probabilités; **Mr Average** Monsieur Tout-le-Monde. **II** *adj* GEN, MATH moyen/-enne; **on an** ~ **day I work seven hours** en moyenne, je travaille sept heures par jour. **III** *vtr* faire en moyenne [*distance, quantity, time*]; **we** ~**d 95 km/h** nous avons fait une moyenne de 95 km/ h.

averse /ə'vɜ:s/ *adj* opposé (**to** à); **to be** ~ **to doing** répugner à faire.

aversion /ə'vɜ:ʃn, US ə'vɜ:rʒn/ *n* aversion *f* (**to** pour); **to have an** ~ **to doing** avoir horreur de faire.

avert /ə'vɜ:t/ *vtr* **1** (avoid, prevent) éviter; **2** (turn away) **to** ~ **one's eyes/gaze from sth** détourner les yeux/ le regard de qch.

aviary /'eɪvɪərɪ, US -vɪerɪ/ *n* volière *f*.

aviation /,eɪvɪ'eɪʃn/ *n* aviation *f*.

aviation: ~ **fuel** *n* kérosène *m*; ~ **industry** *n* industrie *f* aéronautique.

aviator /'eɪvɪeɪtə(r)/ **▶ 1251** *n* aviateur/-trice *m/f*.

avid /'ævɪd/ *adj* [*collector, reader*] passionné; [*enthusiast, supporter*] fervent; **to be** ~ **for sth** être avide de qch.

avidity /ə'vɪdɪtɪ/ *n* avidité *f* (**for** de).

avidly /'ævɪdlɪ/ *adv* [*read, collect*] avec avidité; [*support*] avec ferveur.

avocado /,ævə'kɑ:dəʊ/ **I** *n* **1** (fruit) avocat *m*; **2** (plant) avocatier *m*. **II** *noun modifier* [*salad, mousse*] à l'avocat.

avoid /ə'vɔɪd/ *vtr* **1** (prevent) éviter; **to** ~ **doing** éviter de faire; **it is to be** ~**ed** c'est à éviter; **2** (keep away from) éviter [*person, location, gaze, nuisance*]; esquiver [*issue, question*].

avoidable /ə'vɔɪdəbl/ *adj* évitable.

avoidance /ə'vɔɪdəns/ *n* (of injuries, expenditure, delay) prévention *f* (**of** de); (of responsibility) refus *m* (**of** de); (of subject, problem) fuite *f* (**of** devant).

avowed /ə'vaʊd/ *adj* (admitted) avoué; (declared) déclaré.

avuncular /ə'vʌŋkjʊlə(r)/ *adj* bienveillant.

await /ə'weɪt/ *vtr* attendre; **long-**~**ed** longuement attendu; **eagerly** ~**ed** attendu avec impatience.

awake /ə'weɪk/ **I** *adj* (not yet asleep) éveillé; (after sleeping) réveillé; **wide** ~ bien réveillé; **half** ~ mal réveillé; **to lie** ~ rester au lit sans dormir; **I was still** ~ je ne dormais pas; **the noise kept me** ~ le bruit m'a empêché de dormir. **II** *vtr* (*prét* **awoke** ou **awaked** LITTÉR, *pp* **awoken** ou **awaked** LITTÉR) **1** (from sleep) réveiller; **2** FIG éveiller [*fear, suspicion*]. **III** *vi* (*prét* **awoke** ou **awaked** LITTÉR, *pp* **awoken** ou **awaked** LITTÉR) (from sleep) se réveiller; **to** ~ **from a deep sleep** sortir d'un sommeil profond.

awaken /ə'weɪkən/ (*prét* **awoke** ou **awakened** LITTÉR, *pp* **awoken** ou **awakened** LITTÉR) **I** *vtr* **1** (from sleep) réveiller; **2** (generate) faire naître [*fear, interest*]; éveiller [*suspicions*]. **II** *vi* (*prét* **awoke** ou **awakened** LITTÉR, *pp* **awoken** ou **awakened** LITTÉR) (from sleep) se réveiller.

awakening /ə'weɪkənɪŋ/ **I** *n* LIT (from sleep) réveil *m*; FIG (of emotion, interest) éveil *m* (**of** de); (of awareness) prise *f* de conscience (**to** de); **rude** ~ LIT réveil brutal; FIG rappel *m* brutal à la réalité. **II** *adj* LIT naissant; FIG naissant.

award /ə'wɔ:d/ **I** *n* **1** (prize) prix *m*; (medal, certificate) distinction *f* honorifique; **the** ~ **for the best actor** le prix du meilleur acteur; **2** (grant) bourse *f*; **3** (decision to give) (of prize, grant) attribution *f*. **II** *vtr* décerner [*prize*]; attribuer [*grant*]; accorder [*points, penalty*].

award: ~ **ceremony** *n* cérémonie *f* de remise de prix; ~ **winner** *n* lauréat/-e *m/f*; ~**-winning** *adj* [*book, film, design*] primé; [*writer, architect*] lauréat.

aware /ə'weə(r)/ *adj* **1** (conscious) conscient (**of** de); (informed) au courant (**of** de); **to become** ~ **that** prendre conscience que; **to make sb** ~ **of/that** rendre qn conscient de/que; **I'm well** ~ **of that** j'ai bien conscience de cela; **to be** ~ **that** savoir que, se rendre compte que; **as far as I'm** ~ à ma connaissance; **2** (well-informed) averti; **to be environmentally** ~ être au courant des questions d'environnement.

awareness /ə'weənɪs/ *n* conscience *f* (**of** de; **that** que); **public** ~ **of this problem has increased** l'opinion publique a de plus en plus pris conscience de ce problème.

away /ə'weɪ/

■ Note *away* often appears in English as the second element of a verb (*run away, put away, get away, give away* etc). For translations, look at the appropriate verb entry (**run, put, get, give** etc).
– *away* often appears after a verb in English to show that an action is continuous or intense. If *away* does not change the basic meaning of the verb only the verb is translated: *he was snoring away* = il ronflait. If *away* does change the basic meaning of the verb (*he's grinding away at his maths*), consult the appropriate verb entry.
– This dictionary contains Usage Notes on such topics as distance. For the index to these Notes see **▶ 1419**.

I *adj* SPORT [*goal, match, win*] à l'extérieur; **the** ~ **team** les visiteurs *mpl*. **II** *adv* **1** (not present, gone) **to be** ~ GEN, SCH être absent (**from** de); (on business trip) être en déplacement; **I'll be** ~ (**for**) **two weeks** je serai absent pendant deux semaines; **to be** ~ **on business** être en voyage d'affaires ou en déplacement; **to be** ~ **from home** ne pas être chez soi, être absent de chez soi; **I'll have to be** ~ **by 10** il faut que je sois parti avant 10 heures; **she's** ~ **in Paris** elle est à Paris; **2** (distant in space) **3 km/50 km** ~ à 3 km/50 m; **10 cm** ~ **from the edge** à 10 cm du bord; **3** (distant in time) **London is two hours** ~ Londres est à deux heures d'ici; **my birthday is two months** ~ mon anniversaire est dans deux mois; **4** (in the opposite direction) **to shuffle/crawl** ~ partir en traînant les pieds/en rampant; **5** (for emphasis) ~ **back in 1920** en 1920; ~ **over the other side of the lake** de l'autre côté du lac; **6** SPORT [*play*] à l'extérieur.

awe /ɔ:/ **I** *n* crainte *f* mêlée d'admiration; (less fearful) respect *m*; **to watch/listen in** ~ regarder/écouter impressionné; **to be in** ~ **of sb** avoir peur de qn. **II** *vtr* **to be** ~**ed by sth** être impressionné par qch.

awe-inspiring /'ɔ:ɪnspaɪərɪŋ/ *adj* impressionnant.

awesome /'ɔ:səm/ *adj* redoutable.

awful /'ɔ:fl/ *adj* **1** (bad) affreux/-euse; (stronger) exécrable; **it was** ~ **to have to...** ça a été horrible d'être obligé de...; **2** (horrifying, tragic) horrible, atroce; **3** (unwell) **I feel** ~ je ne me sens pas bien du tout; **you look** ~ tu n'as pas l'air bien du tout; **4** (guilty) ennuyé; **5**° (emphasizing) **an** ~ **lot** (**of**) énormément (de).

awfully /'ɔːflɪ/ adv extrêmement; he's ~ late il est terriblement en retard; thanks ~ mille mercis.

awkward /'ɔːkwəd/ adj **1** (not practical) [tool] peu commode; [shape, design] difficile; **2** (clumsy) maladroit; **3** (complicated, inconvenient) [arrangement, issue] compliqué, difficile; [choice] difficile; [moment, day] mal choisi; at an ~ time au mauvais moment; to make life ~ for sb compliquer la vie à qn; it's a bit ~ c'est difficile; **4** (embarrassing) [question] embarrassant; [situation] délicat; [silence] gêné; **5** (embarrassed) mal à l'aise, gené; to feel ~ about doing se sentir gêné de faire; **6** (uncooperative) [person] difficile (about à propos de); the ~ age l'âge ingrat.

awkwardly /'ɔːkwədlɪ/ adv **1** (inconveniently) ~ placed/designed mal placé/conçu; **2** (clumsily) [move, express oneself] maladroitement; [fall, land] lourdement; **3** (with embarrassment) [speak, apologize] d'un ton gêné; [behave] d'une manière embarrassée.

awkwardness /'ɔːkwədnɪs/ n **1** (clumsiness) maladresse f; **2** (delicacy) (of situation) côté m gênant; **3** (inconvenience) caractère m mal commode; **4** (embarrassment) malaise m.

awl /ɔːl/ n (for leather) alène f; (for wood etc) poinçon m.

awning /'ɔːnɪŋ/ n (on shop) banne f, auvent m; (on tent, caravan, house, restaurant) auvent m; (on market stall) bâche f.

awoke /ə'wəʊk/ prét ▶ **awake**.

awoken /ə'wəʊkən/ pp ▶ **awake**.

AWOL /'eɪwɒl/ adj, adv MIL, HUM (abrév = **absent without leave**) to be ou go ~ MIL être en absence illégale; HUM disparaître.

awry /ə'raɪ/ **I** adj de travers inv.
II adv to go ~ [plan] mal tourner; [economy] péricliter.

axe, ax US /æks/ **I** n hache f; to get the ~○ [employee] se faire virer○.
II vtr virer○ [employee]; supprimer [jobs]; abandonner [plan].
IDIOMS to have an ~ to grind servir un intérêt.

axiom /'æksɪəm/ n axiome m (that selon lequel).

axiomatic /ˌæksɪə'mætɪk/ adj axiomatique; it is ~ that... il est évident que...

axis /'æksɪs/ n (pl **axes**) GEN, MATH axe m.

axle /'æksl/ n essieu m; front/rear ~ essieu avant/arrière.

aye /aɪ/ **I** particle GB DIAL oui.
II n (in voting) the ~s les oui, les voix pour.

AZ US POST abrév écrite = **Arizona**.

Azerbaijan /ˌæzəbaɪ'dʒɑːn/ ▶ 840 | pr n Azerbaïdjan m.

Azerbaijani /ˌæzəbaɪ'dʒɑːnɪ/ ▶ 1100 |, 1038 | **I** n **1** (person) Azéri mf; **2** (language) azéri m, azerbaïdjanais m.
II adj azerbaïdjanais.

Azores /ə'zɔːz/ ▶ 1022 | pr n the ~ les Açores fpl.

AZT n (abrév = **azidothymidine**) AZT f.

Aztec /'æztek/ ▶ 1100 |, 1038 | **I** n **1** (person) Aztèque mf; **2** (language) aztèque m.
II adj aztèque.

azure /'æʒə(r), -zjə(r)/ ▶ 818 | **I** n azur m.
II adj [sea, sky, eyes] d'azur; [fabric] azur inv.

Bb

b, B /biː/ n **1** (letter) b, B m; **2 B** MUS si m; **3 b** abrév écrite = **born**.

BA n (abrév = **Bachelor of Arts**) diplôme m universitaire en lettres et sciences humaines.

baa /baː/ **I** vi (3ᵉ pers sg prés ~**s**, prét, pp ~**ed**) bêler. **II** excl bêe!

BAA n: abrév ▸ **British Airports Authority**.

babble /'bæbl/ **I** n murmure m confus. **II** vtr bafouiller [words, excuse]. **III** vi [baby] babiller; [stream] murmurer.

babe /beɪb/ n **1** LITTÉR bébé m; **a ~ in arms** LIT un enfant au berceau; FIG un jeunot○; **2**○ (woman) minette○ f; (form of address) ma belle○.

baboon /bə'buːn/ n babouin m.

baby /'beɪbɪ/ **I** n **1** (child) bébé m; **Baby Jesus** le petit Jésus; **she's the ~ of the family** c'est la petite dernière; **don't be such a ~**○! ne fais pas le bébé!; **2** (youngest) (of team, group) benjamin/-e m/f; **3**○ (pet project) **the show/project is his ~**○ il a la responsabilité du spectacle/projet; **4** (as address) chéri/-e m/f. **II** noun modifier [brother, sister, son etc] petit; [animal] bébé-; [vegetable] nain; [clothes, food] pour bébés. IDIOMS **I was left holding the ~** on m'a refilé le bébé○; **to throw the ~ out with the bathwater** jeter le bébé avec l'eau du bain.

baby: **~ bird** n oisillon m; **~ blue** ▸818 adj bleu clair inv; **~ boom** n baby boom m; **~ boomer** n personne f née pendant les années du baby boom; **~ buggy** n GB poussette f; **~ carriage** n US landau m; **~ carrier** n porte-bébé m inv (dorsal); **~-faced** adj FIG au visage innocent; **Babygro**® n grenouillère f, pyjama m de bébé.

babyish /'beɪbɪʃ/ adj enfantin; PÉJ puéril.

baby-sit /'beɪbɪsɪt/ (prét, pp **-sat**) **I** vtr garder. **II** vi faire du baby-sitting, garder des enfants.

baby: **~-sitter** n baby-sitter m/f; **~-sitting** n baby-sitting m; **~ talk** n langage m enfantin; **~ tooth** n dent f de lait; **~ walker** n trotteur m; **~wear** n vêtements mpl pour bébés; **~ wipe** n lingette f.

baccalaureate /ˌbækə'lɔːrɪət/ n **1** US UNIV (diploma) ≈ licence f; **2** SCH **European/International Baccalaureate** baccalauréat m européen/international.

bachelor /'bætʃələ(r)/ n **1** (single man) célibataire m; **2** UNIV **Bachelor of Arts/Law** ≈ diplôme m universitaire de lettres/droit.

bachelor: **~ apartment**, **~ flat** GB n garçonnière f; **~hood** n célibat m.

bacillus /bə'sɪləs/ n (pl **-li**) bacille m.

back /bæk/ ▸765 **I** n **1** ANAT, ZOOL dos m; **to be (flat) on one's ~** LIT être (à plat) sur le dos; FIG être au lit; **to turn one's ~ on sb/sth** LIT, FIG tourner le dos à qn/qch; **to do sth behind sb's ~** LIT, FIG faire qch dans le dos de qn; **I was glad to see the ~ of him** j'étais content de le voir partir; **2** (reverse side) (of page, cheque, hand, fork, envelope) dos m; (of fabric) envers m; (of medal, coin) revers m; **3** (rear-facing part) (of vehicle, head) arrière m; (of electrical appliance) face f arrière; (of shirt, coat) dos m; (of chair, sofa) dossier m; **on the ~ of the door/head** derrière la porte/tête; **the shelves are oak but the ~ is plywood** les étagères sont en chêne mais le fond est en contreplaqué; **4** (area behind building) **to be out ~**, **to be in the ~** US être dans le jardin ou la cour; **there's a small garden out ~** US round the ~ il y a un petit jardin derrière (la maison); **the steps at the ~ of the building** l'escalier à l'arrière de l'immeuble; **5** (of car, plane) arrière m; **6** (of cupboard, drawer, fridge, bus, stage) fond m; **at** ou **in the ~ of the drawer** au fond du tiroir; **those at the ~ couldn't see** ceux qui étaient derrière ne pouvaient pas voir; **7** SPORT arrière m; **left ~** arrière gauche; **8** (end) fin f; **at the ~ of the book** à la fin du livre.

II adj **1** (at the rear) [leg, paw, edge, wheel] arrière; [bedroom] du fond; [page] dernier/-ière (before n); [garden, gate] de derrière; **2** (isolated) [road] petit (before n); **~ alley** ou **lane** ruelle f; **3** FIN, COMM **~ interest/rent/tax** arriérés mpl d'intérêts/de loyer/d'impôts.

III adv **1** (after absence) **to be ~** être de retour; **I'll be ~ in five minutes** je reviens dans cinq minutes; **to arrive** ou **come ~** rentrer (from de); **he's ~ at work** il a repris le travail; **she's ~ in (the) hospital** elle est retournée à l'hôpital; **when is he due ~?** quand doit-il rentrer?; **the mini-skirt is ~** (in fashion) les mini-jupes sont de nouveau à la mode; **2** (in return) **to call** ou **phone ~** rappeler; **I'll write ~ (to him)** je lui répondrai; **to punch sb ~** rendre son coup à qn; **to smile ~ at sb** rendre son sourire à qn; **3** (backwards) [glance, jump, step, lean] en arrière; **4** (away) **we overtook him 20 km ~** nous l'avons doublé il y a 20 km; **ten lines ~** dix lignes plus haut; **ten pages ~** dix pages (avant or plus tôt); **5** (ago) **25 years ~** il y a 25 ans; **a week/five minutes ~** il y a une semaine/cinq minutes; **6** (a long time ago) **~ in April** en avril; **~ in the days when** du temps où; **it was obvious as far ~ as last year that** déjà l'année dernière il était évident que; **7** (once again) **she's ~ in power** elle a repris le pouvoir; **8** (expressing a return to a former location) **to travel to London and ~** faire l'aller-retour à Londres; **we walked there and took the train ~** nous y sommes allés à pied et nous avons pris le train pour rentrer; **9** (in a different location) **meanwhile, ~ in France, he...** pendant ce temps, en France, il...; **I'll see you ~ at the house** je te verrai à la maison.

IV back and forth adv phr **to go** ou **travel ~ and forth** (commute) [person, bus] faire la navette (between entre); **to walk** ou **go ~ and forth** (between places) faire des allées et venues (between entre); **to swing ~ and forth** [pendulum] osciller; **the film cuts** ou **moves ~ and forth between New York and Paris** le film se passe entre New York et Paris.

V vtr **1** (support) soutenir [party, person, bid, bill, strike, action]; appuyer [application]; apporter son soutien à [enterprise, project]; **2** (finance) financer [project, undertaking]; **3** (endorse) garantir [currency]; **to ~ a bill** COMM, FIN endosser ou avaliser une traite; **4** (substantiate) justifier [argument, claim] (with à l'aide de); **5** (reverse) **to ~ the car into the garage** rentrer la voiture au garage en marche arrière; **to ~ sb into sth** faire reculer qn dans qch; **6** (bet on) parier sur [horse, favourite, winner]; **7** (stiffen, line) consolider [structure]; endosser [book]; renforcer [map]; maroufler [painting]; doubler [fabric].

VI -backed combining form **1** (of furniture) **a high-/low-~ed chair** une chaise avec un dossier haut/bas; **2** (lined, stiffened) **canvas-/foam-~ed** doublé de toile/de mousse; **3** (supported) **UN-~ed** soutenu par l'ONU; **4** (financed) **government-~ed** financé par l'État. IDIOMS **to put one's ~ into it** travailler dur; **he's always on my ~**○ il est toujours sur mon dos; **to be at the ~ of sth** être à l'origine de qch; **to put sb's ~ up** offenser qn; **to live off sb's ~** vivre aux crochets de qn; **to break the ~ of a journey/task** faire le plus gros du voyage/travail.

■ **back away** reculer; **to ~ away from** LIT s'éloigner de [*person*]; FIG prendre ses distances par rapport à [*issue, problem*]; chercher à éviter [*confrontation*].

■ **back down**: **~ down** (give way) céder; **to ~ down on** OU **over** reconsidérer [*sanctions, proposal, allegations*].

■ **back off 1** (move away) reculer; **2** FIG (climb down) se montrer plus coopérant.

■ **back onto**: **~ onto** [sth] [*house*] donner sur [qch] à l'arrière.

■ **back out**: ¶ **~ out** LIT [*person*] sortir à reculons; [*car, driver*] sortir en marche arrière; **2** FIG se désister; **to ~ out of** LIT [*person*] sortir de [qch] en reculant [*room*]; [*car, driver*] sortir de [qch] en marche arrière; FIG annuler [*deal, contract*]; [*competitor*] se retirer de [*event*]; ¶ **~** [sth] **out** faire sortir [qch] en marche arrière [*vehicle*].

■ **back up**: ¶ **~ up 1** AUT reculer, faire marche arrière; **2** US (block) [*drains*] s'obstruer; [*traffic*] se bloquer; ¶ **~** [sth] **up**, **~ up** [sth] **1** (support) [*facts, evidence*] corroborer [*claims, case, theory*]; **2** COMPUT sauvegarder; ¶ **~** [sb] **up** soutenir [*person*].

backache /'bækeɪk/ n mal m de dos; **to have ~** GB, **to have a ~** US avoir mal au dos.

back bacon n CULIN bacon m maigre.

backbench /ˌbæk'bentʃ/ n (also **~es**) GB POL **1** (area of the House) banc m des députés; **2** ¢ (MPs) députés mpl.

back: **~bencher** n GB POL député m; **~biting** n médisance f; **~board** n (in basketball) panneau m; **~boiler** n chaudière f (*située derrière le foyer d'une cheminée*).

backbone /'bækbəʊn/ n **1** (spine) (of person, animal) colonne f vertébrale; (of fish) grande arête f; **2** FIG (strong feature) ossature f; **to be the ~ of** [*people, players*] constituer l'ossature de [*group, team*]; [*person, concept*] être le pilier de [*organization, project*]; **3** FIG (courage) cranᵒ m; **he has no ~** c'est une larve.

back: **~-breaking** adj éreintant; **~chat** n GB insolence f; **~cloth** n THEAT, FIG toile f de fond.

backcomb /'bækkəʊm/ vtr **to ~ one's hair** se crêper les cheveux.

back: **~ copy** n ancien numéro m; **~ cover** n GEN dos m; quatrième f de couverture.

backdate /'bækdeɪt/ vtr antidater [*cheque, letter*]; **to be ~d to 1 April** être antidaté avec effet rétroactif au 1er avril.

back door n (of car) portière f arrière; (of building) porte f de derrière.

backdrop /'bækdrɒp/ n THEAT, FIG toile f de fond.

back-end /ˌbæk'end/ n **1** (rear) arrière m; **2** COMPUT terminal m.

backer /'bækə(r)/ n **1** (supporter) allié/-e m/f; **2** FIN (of project, event) commanditaire m; (of business) bailleur m de fonds.

backfire /'bækfaɪə(r)/ vi **1** [*scheme, tactics*] avoir l'effet inverse; **to ~ on sb** se retourner contre qn; **2** [*car*] pétarader.

back: **~ flip** n saut m périlleux (en planche) arrière; **~gammon ▶ 949** n jaquet m.

background /'bækɡraʊnd/ I n **1** (of person) (social) milieu m; (personal, family) origines fpl; (professional) formation f; **to come from a poor ~** être issu d'un milieu pauvre; **a ~ in law/linguistics** une formation juridique/en linguistique; **2** (context) contexte m; **against a ~ of violence** dans un climat de violence; **what's the ~ to the situation?** qu'est-ce qui est à l'origine de la situation?; **3** (of painting, photo, scene) arrière-plan m; **in the ~** à l'arrière-plan; **against a ~ of** sur un fond or un arrière-plan de; **4** (not upfront) **in the ~** au second plan; **ill-feeling was always there in the ~** la rancune était toujours là dans l'ombre; **5** (of sound, music) **voices/music in the ~** des voix/de la musique en bruit de fond.
II noun modifier **1** [*information, knowledge*] concernant les origines de la situation; **2** [*music, lighting*] d'ambiance.

background: **~ noise** n bruit m de fond; **~ radiation** n radiation f naturelle; **~ reading** n lectures fpl complémentaires.

backhand /'bækhænd/ I n **1** SPORT revers m; **2** (writing) écriture f penchée à gauche.
II adj **1** SPORT [*volley*] de revers; **~ drive** coup m droit de dos; **2** [*writing*] penché à gauche.

back: **~handed** adj [*compliment*] équivoque; **~hander** n (bribe) pot-de-vin m.

backing /'bækɪŋ/ I n **1** (reverse layer) revêtement m intérieur; **2** FIN, FIG (support) soutien m; **3** MUS accompagnement m.
II noun modifier MUS [*singer, group*] d'accompagnement; **~ vocals** chœurs mpl, choristes mfpl.

back issue n ancien numéro m.

backlash /'bæklæʃ/ n retour m de bâton; **a ~ against sth** une réaction violente contre qch.

back: **~less** adj [*dress*] dos-nu inv; **~list** n liste f des ouvrages disponibles.

backlog /'bæklɒg/ n retard m; **I've got a huge ~ (of work)** j'ai plein de travail en retard; **a ~ of orders** une accumulation de commandes en souffrance.

back: **~ marker** n SPORT dernier/-ière m/f; **~ number** n ancien numéro m; **~pack** n sac m à dos; **~packer** n routard/-e m/f.

backpacking /'bækpækɪŋ/ n **to go ~** partir en voyage avec son sac à dos.

back: **~ passage** n ANAT rectum m; **~ pay** n rappel m de salaire; **~-pedal** vi (p prés etc -**ll-** GB, -**l-** US) LIT rétropédaler; FIG faire marche arrière; **~ pocket** n poche f arrière; **~ rest** n dossier m; **~ room** n chambre f du fond; **~ room boys** npl: experts qui travaillent dans l'ombre; **~scratcher** n gratte-dos m inv.

back seat n siège m arrière; **to take a ~** FIG s'effacer.

back: **~seat driver** n: passager qui donne sans arrêt des conseils au conducteur; **~side**ᵒ n derrière m, fesses fpl; **~space** n COMPUT retour m arrière.

backspin /'bækspɪn/ n SPORT **to put ~ on a ball** donner de l'effet à une balle.

backstage /'bæksteɪdʒ/ adv **he's ~** il est en coulisse; [*work, go*] dans les coulisses.

backstairs /'bæksteəz/ I npl escalier m de service.
II adj [*gossip, connivance*] de coulisses.

backstitch /'bækstɪtʃ/ I n point m arrière.
II vi coudre en point arrière.

back: **~stop** n SPORT (fielder) receveur m; **~ straight** n SPORT ligne f droite de retour.

backstreet /'bækstriːt/ I n petite rue f.
II noun modifier [*loanshark, abortionist*] clandestin.

back: **~stroke** n dos m crawlé; **~talk** n US = **backchat**.

back to back adv **1** (with backs touching) **to stand ~** [*two people*] se mettre dos à dos; **2** (consecutively) de suite.

back to front adj, adv (facing the wrong way) à l'envers; **you've got it all ~** FIG tu as tout compris de travers.

back: **~track** vi LIT rebrousser chemin; FIG faire marche arrière; **~ translation** n LING rétro-traduction f.

backup /'bækʌp/ I n **1** (support) soutien m; **2** MIL (reinforcements) renforts mpl; **3** (replacement) **to keep a battery as a ~** garder une batterie de secours.
II noun modifier (replacement) [*plan, system, vehicle*] de secours.

backup light n US AUT feu m de recul.

backward /'bækwəd/ I adj **1** (towards the rear) [*look, step*] en arrière; **~ roll** roulade f arrière; **~ somersault** saut m périlleux (groupé); **2** (retarded) [*child, nation, society, economy*] arriéré.
II adv US = **backwards**.
IDIOMS **she isn't ~ in coming forward** HUM elle n'hésite pas à se mettre en avant.

backward-looking adj passéiste.

backwards /'bækwədz/ *adv* **1** (in a reverse direction) [*walk, crawl*] à reculons; [*lean, step, fall*] en arrière; **to face ~** [*person*] tourner le dos; **to move ~** reculer; **to travel ~ and forwards** faire la navette (**between** entre); **to walk ~ and forwards** faire des allées et venues; ▶**bend**; **2** (starting from the end) [*count*] à rebours; [*play, wind*] à l'envers; **3** (the wrong way round) **to put sth on ~** mettre qch à l'envers; **you've got it all ~**! tu as tout mélangé!; **4** (thoroughly) **to know sth ~** connaître qch par cœur.

backwater /'bækwɔːtə(r)/ *n* **1** LIT (of pool, river) eaux *fpl* mortes; **2** FIG (isolated area) GEN village *m* tranquille; PÉJ trou○ *m* PÉJ; **cultural ~** désert *m* culturel.

backyard /ˌbæk'jɑːd/ *n* **1** GB (courtyard) arrière-cour *f*; **2** US (back garden) jardin *m* de derrière; **3** FIG **in one's ~** (in a nearby area) près de chez soi; (in nearby country) près de ses frontières.

bacon /'beɪkən/ *n* ~ lard *m*; **a rasher of ~** une tranche de bacon; **streaky/smoked ~** lard maigre/fumé; **~ and egg(s)** des œufs au bacon.
IDIOMS **to bring home the ~**○ faire bouillir la marmite○; **to save sb's ~**○ tirer qn d'affaire○.

bacon-slicer *n* coupe-jambon *m inv*.

bacteria /bæk'tɪərɪə/ *npl* bactéries *fpl*.

bacterial /bæk'tɪərɪəl/ *adj* bactérien/-ienne.

bacteriology /bækˌtɪərɪ'ɒlədʒɪ/ *n* bactériologie *f*.

bad /bæd/ **I** *n* **1** (evil) **there is good and ~ in every-one** il y a du bon et du mauvais dans chacun; **she only sees the ~ in him** elle ne voit que ses mauvais côtés; **2** (unpleasantness, unfavourableness) **the good and the ~** le bon et le mauvais.
II *adj* (*comparative* **worse**; *superlative* **worst**) **1** (poor, inferior, incompetent, unacceptable) [*book, eyesight, cook, idea*] mauvais (*before n*); [*joke*] stupide; **to have ~ hearing** ne pas très bien entendre; **to have ~ teeth/~ legs** avoir de mauvaises dents/de vilaines jambes; **to be ~ at** être mauvais en [*subject*]; **to be ~ at doing** (do badly) ne pas être doué pour faire; **not ~**○ pas mauvais, pas mal○; **2** (unfavourable) [*news, day, moment, smell, dream, result, omen, mood*] mauvais (*before n*); **it's ~ enough having to wait, but...** c'est déjà assez pénible de devoir attendre, mais...; **it looks ~** ou **things look ~** cela s'annonce mal (**for** pour); **the journey/exam wasn't ~ at all** le voyage/l'examen s'est plutôt bien passé; **it's a ~ time to buy a house** ce n'est pas le bon moment pour acheter une maison; **too ~**○! (sympathetic) pas de chance!; (hard luck) tant pis!; **3** (morally or socially unaccep-table) [*person, behaviour, reputation*] mauvais (*before n*); [*language, word*] grossier/-ière; **~ dog**! vilain!; **you ~ girl**! vilaine!; **it is ~ to do** c'est mal de faire; **it is ~ of sb to do** ce n'est pas bien de la part de qn de faire; **it is ~ that** il est regrettable que (+ *subj*); **will look~** cela fera mauvais effet; **to feel ~** avoir mauvaise conscience (**about** à propos de); **4** (severe, serious) [*accident, attack, injury, mistake*] grave; **a ~ cold** un gros rhume; **how ~ is it?** c'est grave?; **5** (harmful) **~ for** mauvais pour; **smoking is ~ for you** ou **your health** fumer est mauvais pour la santé; **it's ~ for you to eat that** tu ne devrais pas manger ça; **it's ~ for industry** c'est néfaste pour l'industrie; **it will be ~ for mothers** cela fera du tort aux mères; **6** (ill, injured) **to have a ~ back** souffrir du dos; **to have a ~ chest** être malade des poumons; **to have a ~ heart** être cardiaque; **to have a ~ leg** avoir mal à la jambe; **my back is ~ today** j'ai très mal au dos aujourd'hui; **she was very ~ in the night** elle a été très malade pendant la nuit; **to feel ~** se sentir mal; **'how are you?'—'not so ~'** 'comment vas-tu?'—'pas trop mal'; **to be in a ~ way**○ aller très mal; **7** FIN [*money, note*] faux/fausse; [*loan, debt*] douteux/-euse; **8** (rotten) [*fruit*] pourri; **to go ~** pourrir; **9**○ (good) terrible○.
III *adv*○ [*need, want*] méchamment○; **it hurts ~** ça fait sérieusement mal; **he's/she's got it ~** il/elle est vraiment mordu/-e○.
IDIOMS **to be in ~** US avoir des ennuis; **to be in ~ with sth** US être en froid avec qn; **he's ~ news** il faut se méfier de lui.

bad blood *n* **there is ~ between them** ils sont à couteaux tirés.

bad: **~ boy** *n* enfant *m* terrible; **~ breath** *n* mauvaise haleine *f*; **~ cheque** *n* chèque *m* sans provision.

baddie○, **baddy**○ /'bædɪ/ *n* méchant/-e *m/f*.

badge /bædʒ/ *n* **1** (sew-on, pin-on, adhesive) badge *m*; **2** (coat of arms) insigne *m*; **3** (symbol) symbole *m*, insigne *m* LITER; **~ of office** insigne *m* de fonction.

badger /'bædʒə(r)/ **I** *n* ZOOL blaireau *m*.
II *vtr* harceler.

badly /'bædlɪ/ *adv* (*comparative* **worse**; *superlative* **worst**) **1** (not well) [*begin, behave, sleep*] mal; [*educated, fed, made, worded*] mal; **to go ~** [*exam, interview, meeting*] mal se passer; **to do ~** [*candidate, company*] obtenir de mauvais résultats; **to take sth ~** mal prendre qch; **he didn't do too ~** il ne s'est pas mal débrouillé○; **to do ~ by sb** ne pas être correct avec qn; **please don't think ~ of me** s'il vous plaît, ne m'en veuillez pas; **2** (seriously) [*suffer*] beaucoup; [*beat*] brutalement; [*disrupt, affect*] sérieusement; [*burnt, hurt, damaged*] gravement; **~ hit** FIG durement touché; **our plans went ~ wrong** nos projets ont très mal tourné; **I was ~ mistaken** je me suis lourdement trompé; **3** (urgently) **to want/need sth ~** avoir très envie de/grand besoin de qch.

badly behaved *adj* désobéissant.

badly off *adj* (poor) pauvre; **to be ~ for space/clothes** manquer d'espace/de vêtements.

bad-mannered *adj* qui a de mauvaises manières.

badminton /'bædmɪnt(ə)n/ ▶ 949 | *n* badminton *m*.

bad-tempered *adj* (temporarily) irrité; (habitually) irritable.

baffle /'bæfl/ *vtr* rendre [qn] perplexe, confondre.

baffled /'bæfld/ *adj* perplexe (**by** devant), confondu (**by** par).

baffling /'bæflɪŋ/ *adj* déroutant.

bag /bæg/ **I** *n* (container) sac *m* (**of** de); **20 pence a ~** 20 pence le sac.
II bags *npl* **1** (baggage) bagages *mpl*; **to pack one's ~s** faire ses bagages; FIG faire ses valises; **2**○ GB (lots) **~s of** plein de [*money, time*].
III *vtr* (*p prés etc* **-gg-**) **1**○ †(save) retenir [*seat, table*]; empocher [*medal*]; **2** (put in bags) = **bag up**.
IDIOMS **a mixed ~** un mélange hétérogène; **~s I**○†, **~s me**○† GB à moi; **it's in the ~**○ c'est dans la poche○; **it's not my ~**○ US ce n'est pas mon truc○; **to have ~s under one's eyes** avoir des valises sous les yeux○.
■ **bag up**: **~ [sth] up**, **~ up [sth]** mettre [qch] en sac, ensacher.

bagel /'beɪgl/ *n* petit pain *m* (en couronne).

baggage /'bægɪdʒ/ *n* **1** (luggage) ¢ bagages *mpl*; **2** FIG (legacy) **to carry a lot of emotional ~** avoir trop de problèmes personnels.
IDIOMS **bag and ~** avec armes et bagages○.

baggage: **~ allowance** *n* franchise *f* de bagages; **~ car** *n* fourgon *m*; **~ carousel** *n* tapis *m* roulant (*pour bagages*); **~ check** *n* US bulletin *m* de consigne; **~ handler** ▶ 1251 | *n* bagagiste *mf*; **~ locker** *n* US consigne *f* automatique; **~ reclaim** *n* réception *f* des bagages.

baggy /'bægɪ/ *adj* [*garment*] large; **to go ~ at the knees** [*garment*] faire des poches aux genoux.

Baghdad /ˌbæg'dæd/ ▶ 1343 | *pr n* Bagdad.

bag: **~ lady** *n* clocharde *f*; **~ person**○ *n* clochard/-e *m/f*; **~pipes** ▶ 1097 | *n* cornemuse *f*; **~ snatcher** *n* voleur/-euse *m/f* de sacs à main.

Bahamas /bə'hɑːməz/ ▶ 840 | *pr n* **the ~** les Bahamas *fpl*.

Bahrain, **Bahrein** /bɑː'reɪn/ ▶ 840 | *pr n* Bahreïn *m*.

bail /beɪl/ **I** *n* **1** JUR caution *f*; **to be (out) on ~** être libéré sous caution; **to jump ~** ne pas comparaître (devant un tribunal); **2** SPORT (in cricket) bâtonnet *m*.

II *vtr* JUR mettre [qn] en liberté provisoire.
■ **bail out:** ¶ **~ out 1** NAUT écoper; **2** (jump from plane) sauter; ¶ **~ out** [sb/sth], **~** [sb/sth] **out 1** NAUT écoper [*water*]; vider [*boat*]; **2** (get out of trouble) tirer [qn] d'affaire [*person*]; FIN renflouer [*company*]; **3** JUR payer la caution pour [*person*].

bail bond *n* US JUR caution *f*.

bailiff /'beɪlɪf/ ▶ **1251**| *n* **1** JUR (also for evictions) huissier *m*; **2** GB (on estate) intendant/-e *m/f*.

bait /beɪt/ **I** *n* **1** LIT, FIG appât *m*; **to rise to** ou **swallow the ~** LIT, FIG mordre à l'hameçon.
II *vtr* **1** (put bait on) appâter [*trap, hook*] (**with** avec); **2** (tease) taquiner [*person*].

baize /beɪz/ *n* drap *m* de billard.

bake /beɪk/ **I** *n* (dish) **fish/vegetable ~** ~ gratin *m* de poisson/de légumes.
II *vtr* CULIN faire cuire [qch] au four [*dish, vegetable*]; faire [*bread, cake*].
III *vi* **1** (make bread) [*person*] faire du pain; (make cakes) faire de la pâtisserie; **2** (cook) [*food*] cuire; **3** (in sun) [*town, land*] cuire; [*person*] lézarder.
IV baked *pp adj* [*salmon, apple*] au four.

bake: **~d beans** *n* CULIN haricots *mpl* blancs à la sauce tomate; **~d potato** *n* CULIN pomme *f* de terre en robe des champs (au four).

baker /'beɪkə(r)/ ▶ **1251**|, **1251**| *n* **1** (who makes bread) boulanger/-ère *m/f*; (who makes bread and cakes) boulanger-pâtissier/boulangère-pâtissière *m/f*; **2** (shop) **~'s (shop)** boulangerie *f*, boulangerie-pâtisserie *f*.

bakery /'beɪkərɪ/ ▶ **1251**| *n* boulangerie *f*, boulangerie-pâtisserie *f*.

baking° /'beɪkɪŋ/ *adj* (hot) [*place, day*] brûlant; **I'm absolutely ~**! je crève° de chaud!

baking: **~ powder** *n* CULIN levure *f* chimique; **~ soda** *n* CULIN bicarbonate *m* de soude.

balaclava /ˌbælə'klɑːvə/ *n* (also **~ helmet**) cagoule *f*.

balance /'bæləns/ **I** *n* **1** (stable position) LIT, FIG équilibre *m* (**between** entre); **to lose one's ~** perdre l'équilibre; **to keep one's ~** garder son équilibre; **to catch sb off ~** FIG prendre qn au dépourvu; **to throw sb off ~** FIG perturber qn; **the right ~** le juste milieu; **the ~ of nature** l'équilibre naturel; **the ~ of power** l'équilibre des forces; **2** (scales) LIT, FIG balance *f*; **to be in the ~** FIG être dans la balance; **to hang in the ~** FIG être en jeu; **on ~** tout compte fait; **3** COMM (in account) solde *m*; **to pay the ~** verser le surplus; **4** (remainder) restant *m*.
II *vtr* **1** FIG (compensate for) (also **~ out**) compenser, équilibrer; **2** (counterbalance) contrebalancer [*weights, design, elements*]; **3** (perch) mettre [qch] en équilibre (**on** sur); **to be ~d on sth** être en équilibre sur qch; **4** (adjust) équilibrer [*diet, activity*]; **5** (weigh up, compare) peser; **to ~ sth against sth** mesurer qch en fonction de qch; **6** COMM équilibrer [*account, economy*].
III *vi* **1** LIT [*one person*] se tenir en équilibre (**on** sur); [*one thing*] tenir en équilibre (**on** sur); [*two things, persons*] s'équilibrer; **2** COMM [*books, figures, budget*] être en équilibre; **to make sth ~**, **to get sth to ~** équilibrer qch.
IV balanced *pp adj* [*person, behaviour, view, diet, budget*] équilibré; [*article, report*] objectif/-ive.

balance: **~ of payments** *n* balance *f* des paiements; **~ of power** *n* POL équilibre *m* des forces, rapport *m* de force; **~ of trade** *n* balance *f* du commerce extérieur; **~ sheet** *n* bilan *m*.

balancing act *n* LIT numéro *m* d'équilibriste; **to do a ~** FIG tenter d'atteindre un compromis.

balcony /'bælkənɪ/ *n* **1** (in house, hotel) balcon *m*; **on the ~** (seen from below) au balcon; (seen from interior) sur le balcon; **2** (of theatre) deuxième balcon *m*.

bald /bɔːld/ *adj* **1** [*man, head*] chauve; **to go ~** devenir chauve; **2** [*lawn, carpet, terrain*] pelé; **3** AUT [*tyre*] lisse; **4** (blunt) [*statement, question*] abrupt; [*fact*] brut; [*style*] dépouillé.

balding /'bɔːldɪŋ/ *adj* **he's slightly ~** il commence à perdre ses cheveux.

baldly /'bɔːldlɪ/ *adv* [*state, remark*] sans détours.

baldness /'bɔːldnɪs/ *n* (of person) calvitie *f*.

bale /beɪl/ **I** *n* balle *f*.
II *vtr* mettre [qch] en balles [*hay, cotton, paper*].

Balearic Islands /ˌbælɪˌærɪk 'aɪləndz/ ▶ **1022**| *pr npl* (also **Balearics**) (îles *fpl*) Baléares *fpl*.

baleful /'beɪlfʊl/ *adj* LITTÉR [*influence, presence*] maléfique LITER; [*glance, eye*] torve.

balk /bɔːk/ **I** *vtr* contrecarrer [*plan, intention*].
II *vi* [*person*] regarder à deux fois; **to ~ at** reculer devant [*risk, cost, prospect*]; **she ~ed at spending so much** elle rechignait à dépenser autant d'argent; **he ~ed at the idea** l'idée lui répugnait.

Balkan /'bɔːlkən/ **I Balkans** *pr npl* **the ~s** les Balkans *mpl*.
II *adj* [*state, peninsula, peoples*] balkanique.

ball /bɔːl/ **I** *n* **1** SPORT, TECH (sphere) (in tennis, golf, cricket) balle *f*; (in football, rugby) ballon *m*; (in croquet) boule *f*; (in billiards) bille *f*; (for children) balle *f*, ballon *m*; MIL, TECH balle *f*; **2** (rolled-up object) (of dough, clay) boule *f* (**of** de); (of wool, string) pelote *f* (**of** de); **to curl up into a ~** [*person, cat*] se rouler en boule; **to wind sth into a ~** pelotonner qch; **3** ANAT **the ~s of one's feet** les demi-pointes *fpl* (des pieds); **4** (dance) bal *m*.
II *vtr* (clench) serrer [*fist*].
III *vi* [*fist*] se serrer.
IDIOMS **the ~ is in your/his court** la balle est dans ton/son camp; **to be on the ~**° GEN être efficace; (old person) avoir toute sa tête; **to play ~**° coopérer (**with** avec); **to set the ~ rolling** (for conversation) lancer la conversation; (for activity) démarrer; **to have a ~**° s'amuser comme un fou/une folle°; **that's the way the ~ bounces** US c'est la vie!; **to carry the ~**° US prendre la responsabilité.

ballad /'bæləd/ *n* ballade *f*.

ball: **~ and chain** *n* LIT, FIG boulet *m*; **~-and-socket joint** *n* ANAT articulation *f* mobile.

ballast /'bæləst/ *n* **1** (in balloon, ship) lest *m*; **2** (on rail, road) ballast *m*.

ball: **~ bearing** *n* (ball) bille *f* de roulement; (bearing) roulement *m* à billes; **~boy** *n* (in tennis) ramasseur *m* de balles; **~ cock** *n* TECH robinet *m* à flotteur; **~ control** *n* contrôle *m* du ballon; **~ dress** *n* robe *f* de bal.

ballerina /ˌbælə'riːnə/ ▶ **1251**| *n* danseuse *f* de ballet, ballerine *f*.

ballet /'bæleɪ/ *n* ballet *m*.

ballet: **~ dancer** *n* danseur/-euse *m/f* de ballet; **~ dress** *n* tutu *m*; **~ shoe** *n* chausson *m* (de danse).

ballgame /'bɔːlgeɪm/ *n* **1** GEN jeu *m* de balle or ballon; **2** US match *m*.
IDIOMS **that's a whole new** ou **completely different ~**° c'est tout une autre histoire.

ball: **~ girl** *n* (in tennis) ramasseuse *f* de balles; **~ gown** *n* robe *f* de bal.

ballistic /bə'lɪstɪk/ *adj* [*missile*] balistique.

balloon /bə'luːn/ **I** *n* **1** AVIAT GEN ballon *m*; **2** (hot air) **~** montgolfière *f*; **3** (for cartoon speech) bulle *f*.
II *vi* **1** AVIAT **to go ~ing** faire de la montgolfière; **2** (also **~ out**) (swell) [*sail, skirt*] se gonfler; **3** (increase quickly) [*deficit, debt*] galoper.
IDIOMS **to go down** GB ou **go over** US **like a lead ~** tomber à plat.

balloonist /bə'luːnɪst/ *n* aéronaute *mf*.

ballot /'bælət/ **I** *n* **1** (process) scrutin *m*; **by ~** au scrutin; **2** (vote) vote *m* (à bulletins secrets) (**of** de; **on** sur); **the first/second ~** le premier/second tour de scrutin; **3** (also **~ paper**) bulletin *m* de vote.
II *vtr* consulter [qn] (par vote) (**on** sur).

ballot box *n* **1** LIT urne *f* (électorale); **2** FIG (system) urnes *fpl*; **at the ~** aux urnes.

ball: **~point (pen)** *n* stylo *m* (à) bille; **~room** *n* salle *f* de danse; **~room dancing** *n* danse *f* de salon.

balm /bɑːm/ *n* **1** (oily) baume *m*; **2** LITTÉR (peace) baume *m*; **3** BOT (also **lemon ~**) citronnelle *f*.

balmy /'bɑːmɪ/ *adj* [*air, evening, weather*] doux/douce.

balsam /'bɔːlsəm/ n **1** (oily) baume m; **2** (tree) baumier m.

Baltic /'bɔːltɪk/ **I** pr n **the ~** la Baltique.
II adj balte; **the ~ Sea** la mer f Baltique.

balustrade /ˌbælə'streɪd/ n balustrade f.

bamboo /bæm'buː/ n bambou m.

bamboozle○ /bæm'buːzl/ vtr **1** (trick) embobiner○; **to ~ sb into doing** embobiner○ qn pour qu'il fasse; **to ~ sb out of** [money]; **2** (mystify) déboussoler○, désorienter.

ban /bæn/ **I** n interdiction f (**on sth** de qch; **on doing** de faire).
II vtr (p prés etc -**nn**-) interdire [author, group, activity, book, drug]; suspendre [athlete]; **to ~ sb from** exclure qn de [sport, event]; **to ~ sb from driving** interdire à qn de conduire.

banal /bə'nɑːl, US 'beɪnl/ adj banal.

banality /bə'nælətɪ/ n banalité f.

banana /bə'nɑːnə/ **I** n **1** (fruit) banane f; **2** (also ~ palm) bananier m.
II noun modifier [yoghurt, ice cream] à la banane.

banana: **~ republic** n PÉJ république f bananière PÉJ; **~ skin** n peau f de banane.

band /bænd/ n **1** MUS (rock) groupe m (de rock); (army) clique f; (municipal) fanfare f; **2** (with common aim) groupe m (**of** de); **3** (of light, colour, land) bande f; **4** RADIO bande f; **5** GB (of age, income tax) tranche f; **6** (for binding) (for hair, hat) ruban m; (around waist) ceinture f; (around neck) col m; (around arm) brassard m; (around head) bandeau m; **7** TECH (metal) ruban m (métallique); (rubber) courroie f; **8** (ring) anneau m.
■ **band together** se réunir (**to do** pour faire).

bandage /'bændɪdʒ/ **I** n bandage m; **he has a ~ round his head** il a la tête bandée.
II vtr bander [head, limb, wound].

Band-Aid® /'bændeɪd/ n MED (plaster) pansement m (adhésif).

B and B, b and b /ˌbiː ən 'biː/ n GB abrév ▶ **bed and breakfast**.

bandit /'bændɪt/ n bandit m.

band: **~ leader** n chef m d'orchestre; **~master** n (of military band) chef m de musique; (of brass band) chef m de fanfare; **~ saw** n scie f à ruban; **~sman** n (pl **-men**) GEN, MIL musicien m; **~stand** n kiosque m (à musique).

bandwagon /'bændwægən/ n IDIOMS **to jump** ou **climb on the ~** prendre le train en marche.

bandy /'bændɪ/ **I** adj arqué.
II vtr **to ~ words with sb** avoir des mots avec qn.
■ **bandy about, bandy around**: **~** [sth] **about** ou **around** avancer [names, information, statistics].

bane /beɪn/ n fléau m (**of** de); **she/it is the ~ of my life!** elle/ça m'empoisonne la vie!

bang /bæŋ/ **I** n (noise) (of explosion) détonation f, boum m; (of door, window) claquement m.
II bangs npl US frange f.
III adv○ **~ in the middle** en plein centre; **to arrive ~ on time** arriver à l'heure pile.
IV excl (imitating gun) pan!; (imitating explosion) boum!, bang!
V vtr **1** (place noisily) **to ~ sth down on** poser bruyamment qch sur; **to ~ down the receiver** raccrocher brutalement; **2** (causing pain) **to ~ one's head** se cogner la tête (**on** contre); **3** (strike) taper sur [drum, saucepan]; **to ~ one's fist on the table** taper du poing sur la table; **4** (slam) claquer [door, window].
VI vi **1** (strike) **to ~ on** cogner à [wall, door]; **2** (make noise) [door, shutter] claquer.
IDIOMS **~ goes**○ **my holiday/my promotion** je peux dire adieu à mes vacances/mon avancement; **to go out with a ~** quitter la scène avec panache.
■ **bang in**: **~** [sth] **in, ~ in** [sth] enfoncer [nail, peg, tack] (**with** à coups de).
■ **bang into**: **~ into** [sb/sth] heurter.

banger /'bæŋə(r)/ n **1**○ (car) guimbarde○ f; **2** (firework) pétard m; **3**○ GB (sausage) saucisse f.

Bangladesh /ˌbæŋglə'deʃ/ ▶**840** pr n Bangladesh m.

bangle /'bæŋgl/ n bracelet m, jonc m.

banish /'bænɪʃ/ vtr bannir (**from** de).

banishment /'bænɪʃmənt/ n bannissement m.

banister, bannister GB /'bænɪstə(r)/ n (also **~s**) rampe f (d'escalier).

banjo /'bændʒəʊ/ ▶**1097** n (pl **-jos** ou **-joes**) banjo m.

bank /bæŋk/ **I** n **1** FIN, GAMES banque f; **it won't break the ~**○ FIG ça ne ruinera personne; **2** (border) (of river, lake) rive f; (of major river) bord m; (of canal) berge f; **3** (mound) (of earth, mud) talus m; (of snow) congère f; (by road, railway track) talus m; (by racetrack) virage m incliné; (by mineshaft) carreau m; **4** (mass) (of flowers) massif m; (of fog, mist) banc m; **5** (series) (of switches, oars, keys, floodlights) rangée f.
II vtr **1** FIN déposer [qch] à la banque [cheque, money]; **2** (border) border [track, road].
III vi FIN **to ~ with X** avoir un compte (bancaire) à la X.
IDIOMS **to be as safe as the Bank of England** être à toute épreuve.
■ **bank on**: **~ on** [sb/sth] compter sur [qn/qch] (**to do** pour faire); **~ on doing** escompter faire.
■ **bank up**: ¶ **~ up** [snow, earth] s'amonceler; ¶ **~** [sth] **up, ~ up** [sth] **1** (pile up) entasser [snow, earth]; **2** (cover with fuel) charger [fire].

bank: **~ account** n FIN compte m bancaire; **~ balance** n FIN solde m bancaire; **~book** n livret m bancaire; **~ card** n carte f bancaire; **~ charges** npl FIN frais mpl bancaires; **~ clerk** ▶**1251** n employé/-e m/f de banque.

banker /'bæŋkə(r)/ ▶**1251** n FIN (owner) banquier/-ière m/f; (executive) cadre mf de banque.

banker: **~'s draft** n FIN traite f bancaire; **~'s order** n virement m bancaire.

bank: **Bank Giro Credit, BGC** n GB FIN crédit m par virement bancaire; **~ holiday** n GB jour m férié; US jour m de fermeture des banques.

banking /'bæŋkɪŋ/ **I** n FIN **1** (business) opérations fpl bancaires; **2** (profession) la banque; **to study ~** faire des études bancaires.
II noun modifier [group, sector, system, facilities] bancaire; **~ business** affaires fpl bancaires.

banking hours n heures fpl d'ouverture des banques.

bank: **~ manager** ▶**1251** n directeur/-trice m/f d'agence bancaire; **~note** n billet m de banque; **~ raid** n hold-up m; **~ robber** n cambrioleur/-euse m/f de banque; **~ robbery** n cambriolage m de banque.

bankroll /'bæŋkrəʊl/ **I** n fonds mpl.
II○ vtr financer [person, party].

bankrupt /'bæŋkrʌpt/ **I** adj FIN [person] ruiné; [business, economy] en faillite; **~ stock** articles mpl de saisie; **to go ~** faire faillite.
II vtr mettre [qn/qch] en faillite [person, company].

bankruptcy /'bæŋkrʌpsɪ/ n FIN faillite f.

bankruptcy: **~ court** n ≈ tribunal m de commerce; **~ proceedings** npl procédure f de faillite.

bank: **~ statement** n relevé m de compte; **~ transfer** n virement m bancaire.

banner /'bænə(r)/ n **1** (in protest, festival) banderole f; **under the ~ of** sous la bannière de; **2** HIST (ensign) étendard m.

banner headline n gros titre m.

bannister n GB = **banister**.

banns /bænz/ npl RELIG bans mpl.

banquet /'bæŋkwɪt/ **I** n banquet m.
II vi banqueter.

bantam /'bæntəm/ n poule f naine; **~ cock** coq m nain; **~ hen** poule f naine.

banter /'bæntə(r)/ **I** n ¢ plaisanteries fpl.
II vi badiner (**with** avec).

baptism /'bæptɪzəm/ n **1** RELIG baptême m; **2** FIG (initiation) débuts mpl.

Baptist /'bæptɪst/ n, adj baptiste (mf).

baptize /bæp'taɪz/ vtr baptiser.

bar /bɑː(r)/ **I** n **1** (strip of metal, wood) barre f; (on cage, cell, window) barreau m; **behind ~s** derrière les barreaux; **2** (place for drinking) bar m; (counter) comptoir m; **I'll go to the ~** je vais chercher les boissons; **3** (block) (of soap, gold, chocolate) barre f; **4** (obstacle) obstacle m; **5** JUR (profession) **the ~** le barreau; **to be called to the ~** entrer au barreau; (in court) barre f; **7** SPORT barre f; **8** MUS mesure f; **9** (in electric fire) résistance f; **10** MIL GB (to medal) barrette f; US (on uniform) galon m.
II prep sauf; **all ~ one** tous sauf un seul; **~ none** sans exception.
III vtr (p prés etc **-rr-**) **1** (block) barrer [way, path]; **to ~ sb's way** barrer le passage à qn; **2** (ban) exclure [person] (**from sth** de qch); interdire [activity]; **to ~ sb from doing** interdire à qn de faire; **3** (fasten) mettre la barre à [gate, shutter].
IDIOMS **a no holds ~red contest** une lutte où tous les coups sont permis.

barb /bɑːb/ n **1** LIT barbe f; **2** FIG (remark) pique f.

Barbados /bɑː'beɪdɒs/ ▶ 840, 1022 pr n Barbade f.

barbarian /bɑː'beərɪən/ n, adj barbare (mf).

barbaric /bɑː'bærɪk/ adj barbare.

barbarism /'bɑːbərɪzəm/ n **1** (brutality, primitiveness) barbarie f; **2** LITTÉR (error) barbarisme m.

barbarity /bɑː'bærətɪ/ n **1** ₵ (brutality, primitiveness) barbarie f; **2** C (brutal act) atrocité f.

barbarous /'bɑːbərəs/ adj barbare.

barbecue /'bɑːbɪkjuː/ **I** n barbecue m.
II vtr **1** (on charcoal etc) faire [qch] au barbecue; **2** (cook in spicy sauce) faire [qch] façon barbecue.

barbed /'bɑːbd/ adj **1** [hook, arrow] à barbes; **2** [comment, criticism] acerbe; [wit] mordant.

barbed wire, **barbwire** US n (fil m de fer) barbelé m.

barber /'bɑːbə(r)/ n coiffeur m (pour hommes).

barber's shop GB, **barbershop** US ▶ 1251 n salon m de coiffure (pour hommes).

barbital /'bɑːbɪtl/ US = **barbitone**.

barbitone /'bɑːbɪtəʊn/ n GB barbital m.

barbiturate /bɑː'bɪtjʊrət/ n barbiturique m.

barbwire n US = **barbed wire**.

Barcelona /ˌbɑːsɪ'ləʊnə/ ▶ 1343 pr n Barcelone.

bar: **~ chart** n histogramme m; **~ code** n code m (à) barres; **~-coded** adj à codebarres.

bard /bɑːd/ n LITTÉR (poet) chantre m.

bare /beə(r)/ **I** adj **1** (naked) [flesh, leg, boards, wall] nu; **to sit in the sun with one's head ~** s'asseoir au soleil la tête nue ou nu-tête (inv); **with one's hands** à mains nues; **2** (empty) [cupboard, house, room] vide; **to strip sth ~** vider qch; **3** (stark) [branch, mountain, rock] nu; [earth, landscape] dénudé; **~ of** dépourvu de [leaves, flowers]; **4** (mere) **a ~ 3%/20 dollars** à peine 3%/20 dollars; **5** (absolute) strict (before n); **6** (unembellished) [facts, statistics] brut.
II vtr **to ~ one's chest** se découvrir la poitrine; **to ~ one's teeth** montrer les dents; **to ~ one's head** se découvrir; **to ~ one's soul** ouvrir son âme à.

bareback adv [ride] à cru.

bare bones /ˌbeə'bəʊnz/ npl **the ~** l'essentiel m.

barefaced /'beəfeɪst/ adj [lie] éhonté; [cheek, nerve] effronté.

barefoot /'beəfʊt/ **I** adj **to be ~** être nu-pieds.
II adv [run, walk] pieds nus.

barely /'beəlɪ/ adv **1** [audible, capable, conscious, disguised] à peine, tout juste; **to be ~ able to walk** pouvoir à peine or tout juste marcher; **~ 12 hours later** à peine 12 heures plus tard; **2** [furnished] pauvrement.

bareness /'beənɪs/ n nudité f.

bargain /'bɑːgɪn/ **I** n **1** (deal) marché m (**between**

entre); **to drive a hard ~** négocier ferme or serré; **2** (good buy) affaire f; **to get a ~** faire une affaire.
II noun modifier [price] avantageux/-euse.
III vi **1** (for deal) négocier (**with** avec); **2** (over price) marchander (**with** avec).
■ **bargain for**, **bargain on**: **~ for**, **~ on sth** s'attendre à qch; **we got more than we ~ed for** nous ne nous attendions pas à ça.

bargain basement n coin m des affaires.

bargaining /'bɑːgɪnɪŋ/ **I** n (over pay) négociations fpl.
II noun modifier [position, power, rights] de négociation.

bargaining chip n atout m dans les négociations.

barge /bɑːdʒ/ **I** n **1** péniche f; (freight only) chaland m; **2** (for ceremony) barque f d'apparat; **3** (in navy) vedette f.
II vtr (shove) bousculer [player, runner].
III vi (move roughly) **to ~ past sb** passer devant qn en le bousculant.
■ **barge in** (enter noisily) faire irruption; (interrupt) interrompre brutalement.
■ **barge into** faire irruption dans [room, house]; bousculer [person].

bargepole /'bɑːdʒpəʊl/ n: IDIOMS **I wouldn't touch him/it with a ~** je ne voudrais de lui/cela pour rien au monde.

baritone /'bærɪtəʊn/ ▶ 1380 n baryton m.

bark /bɑːk/ **I** n **1** (of tree) écorce f; **2** (of dog) aboiement m; **3** LITTÉR (boat) barque f.
II vi [dog, person] FIG aboyer (**at sb/sth** après qn/qch).
IDIOMS **his ~ is worse than his bite** il fait plus de bruit que de mal; **to be ~ing up the wrong tree** faire fausse route.

barking /'bɑːkɪŋ/ **I** n aboiements mpl.
II adj [dog] qui aboie; [cough, laugh] aboyant.
IDIOMS **to be ~ mad**○ GB être complètement fou/folle.

barley /'bɑːlɪ/ n orge f.

barley: **~corn** n grain m d'orge; **~ sugar** n sucre m d'orge; **~ water** n GB sirop m d'orgeat; **~ wine** n GB ~ bière f (très forte).

bar: **~maid** ▶ 1251 n serveuse f de bar; **~man** ▶ 1251 n (pl **~men**) barman m.

bar mitzvah /ˌbɑː 'mɪtzvə/ n **1** (also **Bar Mitzvah**) (ceremony) bar-mitsva f; **2** (boy) bar-mitsva m.

barmy○ /'bɑːmɪ/ adj GB [person] maboul○; [plan, idea, outfit] loufoque○; **to go ~** (get angry) piquer une crise○; (get excited) devenir dingue○.

barn /bɑːn/ n (for crops) grange f; (for cattle) étable f; (for horses) écurie f.

barnacle /'bɑːnəkl/ n bernacle f.

barn dance n soirée f de danses villageoises.

barn: **~ owl** n (chouette f) effraie f; **~storming** adj tonitruant; **~yard** n basse-cour f.

barometer /bə'rɒmɪtə(r)/ n MÉTÉOROL baromètre m.

barometric /ˌbærə'metrɪk/ n barométrique.

baron /'bærən/ n **1** (noble) baron m; **2** (tycoon) baron m; **drugs ~** baron m de la drogue; **media ~** magnat m des médias; **industrial ~** gros industriel m.

baroness /'bærənɪs/ n baronne f.

baronial /bə'rəʊnɪəl/ adj baronnial.

baroque /bə'rɒk, US bə'rəʊk/ n, adj baroque (m).

barrack /'bærək/ vtr GB (heckle) conspuer.

barracking /'bærəkɪŋ/ n huées fpl.

barrack room I n chambrée f.
II noun modifier PÉJ [joke] de corps de garde; [language] grossier/-ière.

barrack-room lawyer GB, **barracks lawyer** US n PÉJ chicaneur/-euse m/f.

barracks /'bærəks/ n MIL, GEN caserne f.

barrage /'bærɑːʒ, US 'bɑːrɑːʒ/ n **1** CONSTR barrage m; **2** MIL tir m de barrage; **3** FIG (of questions, criticism) barrage m; (of complaints) déluge m.

barrage balloon n ballon m de barrage.

barrel /'bærəl/ *n* **1** (container) (for beer, wine, olives etc) tonneau *m*, fût *m*; (for herring) caque *f*; (for tar) gonne *f*; (for petroleum) baril *m*; **2** (cylinder) (of cannon) tube *m*; (of firearm) canon *m*; (of pen) corps *m*.
IDIOMS **it was a ~ of laughs** ou **fun**○ IRON ce n'était pas très marrant○; **to have sb over a ~**○ avoir qn à sa merci; **he bought the farm lock, stock and ~** il a acheté la ferme et tout ce qui allait avec; **to scrape the bottom of the ~** gratter les fonds de tiroir.

barrel: **~-chested** *adj* [*person*] baraqué○; **~ organ** *n* orgue *m* de Barbarie.

barren /'bærən/ *adj* **1** [*land*] aride; **2** (unrewarding) [*effort, activity*] stérile; [*style*] sec/sèche.

barricade /ˌbærɪ'keɪd/ **I** *n* barricade *f*.
II *vtr* barricader.

barrier /'bærɪə(r)/ *n* LIT, FIG barrière *f*; (ticket) ~ RAIL guichet *m* (de quai); **language/trade** barrière *f* linguistique/douanière.

barrier: **~ cream** *n* crème *f* protectrice; **~ method** *n* MED méthode *f* de contraception locale; **~ nursing** *n* ~ traitement *m* d'isolement préventif; **~ reef** *n* barrière *f* corallienne.

barring /'bɑːrɪŋ/ *prep* à moins de.

barrister /'bærɪstə(r)/ **▶ 1251** *n* GB avocat/-e *m/f*.

barrow /'bærəʊ/ *n* **1** (for garden, building) brouette *f*; **2** GB (in market) voiture *f* de quatre saisons.

barrow boy ▶ 1251 *n* GB marchand *m* de quatre saisons.

bar: **~ school** *n* institution *f* où l'on prépare le certificat d'aptitude à la profession d'avocat; **~ stool** *n* tabouret *m* de bar; **~tender** *n* US barman/barmaid *m/f*.

barter /'bɑːtə(r)/ **I** *n* troc *m*.
II *vtr* troquer (**for** contre).
III *vi* **1** (exchange) faire du troc; **2** (haggle) marchander.

base /beɪs/ **I** *n* **1** GEN, MIL (centre of operations) base *f*; **to return to ~** MIL rentrer à sa base; **2** (bottom part) (of object, spine, mountain, structure) base *f*; (of tree, cliff, lamp) pied *m*; (of tail) point *m* d'attache; (of sculpture, statue) socle *m*; FIG (for assumption, theory) base *f*; **3** CHEM, CULIN base *f*; **4** MATH base *f*; **5** SPORT base *f*.
II *adj* (contemptible) [*act, motive, emotion*] ignoble.
III *vtr* **1** (take as foundation) fonder [*calculation, assumption, decision, research, character*] (**on** sur); **the film is ~d on a true story** le film est tiré d'une histoire vraie; **2** (have as operations centre) (*gén au passif*) baser; **to be ~d in London/Paris** [*person, company*] être basé à Londres/Paris.
IV **-based** *combining form* **computer/pupil-~d** [*method, policy*] basé sur les ordinateurs/les élèves.

base: **~ball ▶ 949** *n* base-ball *m*; **~ball boot** *n* basket *m*; **~ camp** *n* LIT, FIG camp *m* de base; **~ form** *n* LING base *f*.

Basel /'bɑːzl/, **Basle** /bɑːl/ **▶ 1343** *pr n* Bâle *m*.

base: **~ lending rate** *n* taux *m* de base bancaire; **~less** *adj* sans fondement.

baseline /'beɪslaɪn/ *n* **1** (in tennis) ligne *f* de fond; **2** FIG base *f*; **3** (in advertising) signature *f*.

basement /'beɪsmənt/ **I** *n* sous-sol *m*; **in the ~** au sous-sol.
II *noun modifier* [*flat, apartment, kitchen*] en sous-sol.

base: **~ metal** *n* métal *m* non précieux; **~ period** *n* (statistics) période *f* de base; **~ rate** *n* taux *m* de base; **~ year** *n* FIN année *f* de référence.

bash○ /bæʃ/ **I** *n* (*pl* **-es**) **1** (blow) coup *m*; **2** (accident) **I had a ~ in my car** j'ai eu un accident de voiture; **3** (attempt) tentative *f*; **to have a ~ at sth, to give sth a ~** s'essayer à qch; **4** (party) grande fête *f*; **5** US (good time) **to have a ~** bien s'amuser.
II *vtr* cogner [*person*]; rentrer dans [*tree, wall, kerb*]; **she ~ed her head on** ou **against the shelf** elle s'est cogné la tête contre l'étagère; **to ~ sb on** ou **over the head** frapper qn à la tête.
■ **bash in**: **~ [sth] in, ~ in [sth]** défoncer [*door, part of car*].

■ **bash into**: **~ into [sth]** rentrer dans.
■ **bash on** persévérer.
■ **bash out**: **~ out [sth], ~ [sth] out** expédier [*work*]; jouer [*tune*].

bashful /'bæʃfl/ *adj* timide; **to be ~ about doing** hésiter à faire.

bashfully /'bæʃfəlɪ/ *adv* timidement.

bashing○ /'bæʃɪŋ/ *n* **1** (beating, defeat) raclée○ *f*; **to take a ~** ramasser une raclée○; **2** FIG (criticism) dénigration *f* systématique.

basic /'beɪsɪk/ **I** **basics** *npl* essentiel *m*: (of knowledge, study) principes *mpl* fondamentaux; (food) denrées *fpl* de première nécessité; **to get down to ~s** aborder l'essentiel.
II *adj* **1** (fundamental) [*aim, arrangement, fact, need, quality*] essentiel/-ielle; [*belief, research, problem, principle*] fondamental; [*theme*] principal; **2** (elementary) [*education, skill, rule*] élémentaire; **3** (rudimentary) [*accommodation, meal, supplies*] de base; **the accommodation was rather ~** PÉJ le logement était un peu rudimentaire; **4** (before additions) [*pay, wage, hours*] de base; **5** CHEM basique.

basically /'beɪsɪklɪ/ *adv* **1** (fundamentally) fondamentalement; **2** (for emphasis) **~, I don't like him very much** en fait, je ne l'aime pas beaucoup; **~, life's been good** dans l'ensemble, on a eu de la chance.

basic: **~ law** *n* POL, JUR ~ Constitution *f*; **~ rate** *n* GEN taux *m* de base; (in tax) taux *m* de base d'imposition; **~ training** *n* MIL formation *f* militaire de base.

basil /'bæzl/ *n* basilic *m*.

basilica /bə'zɪlɪkə/ *n* basilique *f*.

basin /'beɪsn/ *n* **1** CULIN bol *m*; (for mixing) terrine *f*; **2** (for washing) lavabo *m*; (for washing up) cuvette *f*; **3** GEOG bassin *m*; **4** (of port, fountain) bassin *m*.

basinful /'beɪsɪnfʊl/ *n* pleine cuvette *f*.

basis /'beɪsɪs/ *n* (*pl* **-ses**) (for action, negotiation) base *f* (**for, of** de); (of discussion) cadre *m*; (of theory) point *m* de départ; (for belief, argument) fondements *mpl* (**for** de); **on the ~ of** sur la base de; **on that ~** ceci étant; **on the same ~** dans les mêmes conditions.

bask /bɑːsk, US bæsk/ *vi* **to ~ in** se prélasser à [*sunshine, warmth*]; jouir de [*approval, affection*].

basket /'bɑːskɪt, US 'bæskɪt/ *n* **1** panier *m*, corbeille *f*; (carried on back) hotte *f*; (for game, fish) bourriche *f*; **~ of currencies** FIN panier *m* de devises; **2** SPORT (in basketball) panier *m*; (in fencing) coquille *f*.

basket: **~ball ▶ 949** *n* (game) basket(-ball) *m*; (ball) ballon *m* de basket; **~ chair** *n* fauteuil *m* en osier; **~ maker ▶ 1251** *n* vannier/-ière *m/f*; **~work** *n* (craft, objects) vannerie *f*.

Basle /bɑːl/ **▶ 1343** *pr n* = **Basel**.

basque /bæsk/ *n* (on jacket etc) basques *fpl*.

Basque /bæsk, bɑːsk/ **▶ 1100**, **1038** **I** *n* **1** (person) Basque *mf*; **2** (language) basque *m*.
II *adj* basque.

bass[1] /beɪs/ **▶ 1380**, **1097** **I** *n* MUS, AUDIO basse *f*.
II *noun modifier* **1** MUS [*voice, part, line, range, solo*] de basse; [*aria*] pour basse; [*instrument*] basse; **2** AUDIO [*controls, sound, notes*] grave.

bass[2] /bæs/ *n* ZOOL (freshwater) perche *f*; (sea) ZOOL bar *m*; CULIN loup *m* (de mer).

bass /beɪs/: **~-baritone ▶ 1380** *n* baryton-basse *m*; **~ clef** *n* clé *f* de fa; **~ drum ▶ 1097** *n* grosse caisse *f*.

basset /'bæsɪt/ *n* (also **~ hound**) (chien *m*) basset *m*.

bassist /'beɪsɪst/ **▶ 1097** *n* bassiste *mf*.

bassoon /bə'suːn/ **▶ 1097** *n* basson *m*.

bastard /'bɑːstəd, US 'bæs-/ **I** *n* **1**○ (term of abuse) salaud○ *m*; **2**† (illegitimate child) bâtard/-e *m/f*.
II *adj* **1** [*child*] bâtard; **2** FIG (hybrid) bâtard, corrompu.

bastardized /'bɑːstədaɪzd, US 'bæs-/ *adj* [*language*] abâtardi; [*style of architecture*] dégradé; [*race*] dégénéré.

baste /beɪst/ vtr **1** CULIN arroser; **2** (in sewing) bâtir, faufiler.

bastion /'bæstɪən/ n LIT, FIG bastion f (**of** de).

bat /bæt/ **I** n **1** SPORT batte f; **table tennis ~** raquette f de tennis de table; **2** ZOOL chauve-souris f.
II vtr (p prés etc **-tt-**) frapper.
III vi (p prés etc **-tt-**) SPORT (be batsman) être le batteur; (handle a bat) manier la batte.
IDIOMS **to be blind as a ~** être myope comme une taupe; **to do sth off one's own ~**○ faire qch de sa propre initiative; **like a ~ out of hell**○ comme un possédé; **without ~ting an eyelid** GB ou **eye(lash)** US sans sourciller.

batch /bætʃ/ n (of loaves, cakes) fournée f; (of cement) gâchée f; (of eggs, fish) arrivage m; (of letters) tas m, liasse f; (of books, text, goods, orders) lot m; (of candidates, prisoners etc) groupe m; COMPUT lot m.

batch: **~ file** n COMPUT fichier m séquentiel; **~ mode** n COMPUT mode m différé; **~ processing** n COMPUT traitement m séquentiel.

bated /'beɪtɪd/ adj **with ~ breath** en retenant son souffle.

bath /bɑːθ, US bæθ/ **I** n **1** (wash, washing water) bain m; **2** GB (tub) baignoire f; **I was in the ~** j'étais dans mon bain; **3** US (bathroom) salle f de bains; **4** CHEM, PHOT, TECH bain m.
II baths npl **1** (for swimming) piscine f; **2** (in spa) thermes mpl; **3†** (municipal) bains mpl publics.
III vtr GB baigner.
IV vi GB prendre un bain.

bathe /beɪð/ **I** vtr laver [wound] (**in** dans; **with** à); **to ~ one's feet** prendre un bain de pieds.
II vi (swim) [person] se baigner; **2** US (take bath) prendre un bain; **3 to be ~ed in** ruisseler de [sweat]; être inondé de [light]; être baigné de [tears].

bather /'beɪðə(r)/ n baigneur/-euse m/f.

bathing /'beɪðɪŋ/ n baignade f.

bathing: **~ cap** n bonnet m de bain; **~ costume†** n costume m de bain; **~ hut** n cabine f de bain; **~ suit†** n = **bathing costume**; **~ trunks** n slip m de bain.

bath: **~ mat** n tapis m de bain; **~ oil** n huile f de bain.

bathos /'beɪθɒs/ n bathos m, chute f du sublime au trivial.

bathrobe /'bɑːθrəʊb/ n sortie f de bain.

bathroom /'bɑːθruːm, -rʊm/ n **1** (for washing) salle f de bains; **2** US (lavatory) (public) toilettes fpl; (at home) salle f de bains.

bathroom: **~ cabinet** n armoire f de toilette; **~ fittings** npl accessoires mpl de salle de bains; **~ scales** npl pèse-personne m.

bath: **~ salts** npl sels mpl de bain; **~ towel** n serviette f de bain; **~tub** n baignoire f.

baton /'bætn, 'bætɒn, US bə'tɒn/ n GB (policeman's) matraque f; MIL, MUS baguette f; SPORT (in relay race) témoin m; (used by French traffic policeman, majorette) bâton m.

baton: **~ charge** n GB charge f à la matraque; **~ round** n GB balle f en caoutchouc.

batsman /'bætsmən/ n SPORT batteur m.

battalion /bə'tælɪən/ n MIL, FIG bataillon m.

batten /'bætn/ **I** n **1** CONSTR (for door, floor) latte f; (in roofing) volige f; **2** NAUT latte f; **3** THEAT herse f.
II vtr latter [door, floor]; voliger [roof].

batter /'bætə(r)/ **I** n **1** CULIN GEN pâte f; (for frying) pâte f à frire; **fish in ~** beignets mpl de poisson.
II vtr [person] battre [person]; [storm, bombs] ravager; [waves] battre.

battered /'bætəd/ adj [kettle, hat] cabossé; [book, suit-case etc] très abimé; [person] battu; [pride] meurtri.

battering /'bætərɪŋ/ n **1** (from person) raclée○ f; **2 to take** ou **get a ~** (from bombs, storm, waves) être ravagé (**from** par); (from opponents) SPORT prendre une raclée○; (from critics) se faire descendre (**by** par); (emotionally) en prendre un coup○.

battering-ram n bélier m.

battery /'bætərɪ/ n **1** ELEC pile f; AUT batterie f; **2** MIL batterie f; **3** AGRIC (for hens) batterie f; **4** FIG (large number) (of objects, tests) batterie f; (of questions) feu m nourri; (of people) coups mpl et blessures fpl.

battery: **~ acid** n solution f acide pour piles; **~ charger** n chargeur m de batteries; **~ chicken** n poulet m d'élevage industriel; **~ controlled** adj à piles; **~ farming** n élevage m en batterie; **~ fire** n tir m par salves; **~ hen** n = **battery chicken**; **~ operated**, **~ powered** adj à piles.

battle /'bætl/ **I** n **1** MIL bataille f (**for** pour, **against** contre, **between** entre); **to die in ~** mourir au combat; **to fight a ~** combattre; **to go into ~** engager le combat; **2** FIG lutte f (**for** pour, **against** contre, **over** à propos de); **political ~** lutte f politique; **legal ~** bataille f légale; **it's a ~ of wills between them** c'est à qui l'emportera entre eux; **a ~ of words** un échange acerbe; **to fight one's own ~s** se défendre tout seul; **to fight sb's ~s** se battre pour le compte de qn.
II noun modifier MIL [formation, zone] de combat.
III vi MIL, FIG combattre (**with sb** contre qn); **to ~ for sth/to do** lutter pour qch/pour faire; **to ~ one's way through sth** vaincre qch de haute lutte.
IDIOMS **that's half the ~** c'est déjà un grand pas de fait.
■ **battle on** persévérer.
■ **battle out**: **to ~ it out** lutter avec acharnement (**for** pour).

battle-axe /'bætlæks/ n **1**○ FIG PÉJ (woman) virago○ f; **2** LIT hache f d'armes.

battle: **~ cry** n LIT, FIG cri m de ralliement; **~dress** n tenue f de campagne; **~ drill** n MIL ₵ manœuvres fpl; **~field** n LIT, FIG champ m de bataille; **~ground** n LIT champ m de bataille; FIG sujet m de discussion; **~ lines** npl MIL lignes fpl de combat; FIG stratégie f.

battlements /'bætlmənts/ npl LIT, FIG remparts mpl.

battle: **~ order** n LIT, FIG ordre m de bataille; **~-scarred** adj LIT marqué par la guerre; FIG marqué par la vie; **~ship** n cuirassé m.

batty○ /'bætɪ/ adj cinglé○, fou/folle.

bauble /'bɔːbl/ n (ornament) babiole f; PÉJ (item of jewellery) colifichet m.

Bavaria /bə'veərɪə/ pr n Bavière f.

bawdiness /'bɔːdɪnɪs/ n (of story, song) grivoiserie f; (of person) paillardise f.

bawdy /'bɔːdɪ/ adj [song] grivois; [person] paillard.

bawl /bɔːl/ vi (weep) brailler; (shout) hurler.

bay /beɪ/ **I** n **1** GEOG baie f; **2** BOT (also **~ tree**) laurier(-sauce) m; **3** (parking area) aire f de stationnement; **loading ~** aire de chargement; **4** ARCHIT (section of building) travée f; (recess) renfoncement m; (window) fenêtre f en saillie; **5** AVIAT, NAUT (compartment) soute f; **6** (horse) cheval m bai.
II adj [horse] bai.
III vi [dog] aboyer (**at** contre, après); **to ~ for sb's blood** FIG réclamer la tête de qn.
IDIOMS **to hold** ou **keep at ~** FIG tenir [qn] à distance [attacker, opponent]; stopper [famine]; enrayer [unemployment, inflation etc].

bay leaf n feuille f de laurier.

bayonet /'beɪənɪt/ n MIL, ELEC baïonnette f.

bay: **~ rum** n lotion f capillaire (au piment de la Jamaïque); **~ window** n fenêtre f en saillie.

bazaar /bə'zɑː(r)/ n bazar m.

bazooka /bə'zuːkə/ n bazooka m, lance-roquettes m inv antichar.

B & B n: abrév ▶ **bed and breakfast**.

BBC (abrév = **British Broadcasting Corporation**) BBC f.

BC (abrév = **Before Christ**) av. J.-C.

BDS n GB (abrév = **Bachelor of Dental Surgery**) diplôme m de chirurgie dentaire.

be /biː, bɪ/ vi (p prés **being**; 3ᵉ pers sg prés **is**, prét **was**, pp **been**) **1** GEN être; **it's me, it's I** c'est moi; **he's a good pupil** c'est un bon élève; **2** (in probability) **if** Henri

be (1)

The direct French equivalent of the verb *to be* in *subject + to be + predicate* sentences is *être*:

I am tired	= je suis fatigué
Caroline is French	= Caroline est française
the children are in the garden	
	= les enfants sont dans le jardin

It functions in very much the same way as *to be* does in English and it is safe to assume it will work as a translation in the great majority of cases.

Note, however, that when you are specifying a person's profession or trade, *a/an* is not translated:

she's a doctor	= elle est médecin
Claudie is still a student	= Claudie est toujours étudiante

For more information or expressions involving professions and trades consult the usage note ▶ **1251**.

For the conjugation of the verb *être* see the French verb tables.

When a noun is used in apposition to a personal pronoun, *c'est* is often used:

he's a thief	= c'est un voleur
she's a beautiful woman	= c'est une belle femme

Grammatical functions

The passive

être is used to form the passive in French just as *to be* is used in English. Note, however, that the past participle agrees in gender and number with the subject:

the rabbit was killed by a fox	= le lapin a été tué par un renard
the window had been broken	= la fenêtre avait été cassée
their books will be sold	= leurs livres seront vendus
our doors have been repainted red	= nos portes ont été repeintes en rouge

In spoken language, French native speakers find the passive cumbersome and will avoid it where possible by using the impersonal *on* where a person or people are clearly involved: *on a repeint nos portes en rouge.*

Progressive tenses

In French the idea of something happening over a period of time cannot be expressed using the verb *être* in the way that *to be* is used as an auxiliary verb in English.

The present

French uses simply the present tense where English uses the progressive form with *to be*:

I am working	= je travaille
Ben is reading a book	= Ben lit un livre

In order to accentuate duration *être en train de* is used: *je suis en train de travailler; Ben est en train de lire un livre.*

The future

French also uses the present tense where English uses the progressive form with *to be*:

we are going to London tomorrow	= nous allons à Londres demain
I'm (just) coming!	= j'arrive!
I'm (just) going!	= j'y vais!

The past

To express the distinction between *she read a newspaper* and *she was reading a newspaper* French uses the perfect and the imperfect tenses: *elle a lu un journal/elle lisait un journal*:

he wrote to his mother	= il a écrit à sa mère
he was writing to his mother	= il écrivait à sa mère

However, in order to accentuate the notion of describing an activity which went on over a period of time, the phrase *être en train de* (≈ *to be in the process of*) is often used:

'*what was he doing when you arrived?*' '*he was cooking the dinner*' = 'qu'est-ce qu'il faisait quand tu es arrivé?' 'il était en train de préparer le dîner'
she was just finishing her essay when … = elle était juste en train de finir sa dissertation quand …

The compound past

Compound past tenses in the progressive form in English are generally translated by the imperfect in French:

I've been looking for you = je te cherchais

For progressive forms + *for* and *since* (*I've been waiting for an hour, I had been waiting for an hour, I've been waiting since Monday* etc.) see the boxed notes for *for* and *since*.

Obligation

When *to be* is used as an auxiliary verb with another verb in the infinitive (*to be to do*) expressing obligation, a fixed arrangement or destiny, *devoir* is used:

she's to do it at once	= elle doit le faire tout de suite
what am I to do?	= qu'est-ce que je dois faire?
he was to arrive last Monday	= il devait arriver lundi dernier
she was never to see him again	= elle ne devait plus le revoir

In tag questions

French has no direct equivalent of tag questions like *isn't he?* or *wasn't it?* There is a general tag question *n'est-ce pas?* (literally *isn't it so?*) which will work in many cases:

their house is lovely, isn't it?
= leur maison est très belle, n'est-ce pas?
he's a doctor, isn't he? = il est médecin, n'est-ce pas?
it was a very good meal, wasn't it?
= c'était un très bon repas, n'est-ce pas?

However, *n'est-ce pas* can very rarely be used for positive tag questions and some other way will be found to express the extra meaning contained in the tag: *par hasard* (*by any chance*) can be very useful as a translation:

'*I can't find my glasses*'
'*they're not in the kitchen, are they?*'
= 'je ne trouve pas mes lunettes' 'elles ne sont pas dans la cuisine, par hasard?'
she isn't in the lounge, is she?
= elle n'est pas dans le salon, par hasard?

In cases where an opinion is being sought, *si?* meaning more or less *or is it? or was it?* etc. can be useful:

it's not broken, is it?	= ce n'est pas cassé, si?
he wasn't serious, was he?	= il n'était pas sérieux, si?

In many other cases the tag question is simply not translated at all and the speaker's intonation will convey the implied question.

In short answers

Again, there is no direct equivalent for short answers like *yes I am, no he's not* etc. Where the answer *yes* is given to contradict a negative question or statement, the most useful translation is *si*:

'*you're not going out tonight*'
'*yes I am!*' = 'tu ne sors pas ce soir' 'si'

In reply to a standard enquiry the tag will not be translated:

'*are you a doctor?*'
'*yes I am*' = 'êtes-vous médecin?' 'oui'
'*was it raining?*'
'*yes it was*' = 'est-ce qu'il pleuvait?' 'oui'

Probability

For expressions of probability and supposition (*if I were you* etc.) see the entry **be**.

Other functions

Expressing sensations and feelings

In expressing physical and mental sensations, the verb used in French is *avoir*:

to be cold	= avoir froid
to be hot	= avoir chaud
I'm cold	= j'ai froid
to be thirsty	= avoir soif
to be hungry	= avoir faim
to be ashamed	= avoir honte
my hands are cold	= j'ai froid aux mains

If, however, you are in doubt as to which verb to use in such expressions, you should consult the entry for the appropriate adjective.

☛ See next page

be (2)

Discussing health and how people are

In expressions of health and polite enquiries about how people are, *aller* is used:

how are you? = comment allez-vous?
(*more informally*) comment vas-tu?
(*very informally as a greeting*) ça va?
are you well? = vous allez bien?
how is your daughter? = comment va votre fille?
my father is better today = mon père va mieux aujourd'hui

Discussing weather and temperature

In expressions of weather and temperature *faire* is generally used:

it's cold = il fait froid
it's windy = il fait du vent

If in doubt, consult the appropriate adjective entry.

Visiting somewhere

When *to be* is used in the present perfect tense to mean *go, visit* etc., French will generally use the verbs *venir, aller* etc. rather than *être*:

I've never been to Sweden = je ne suis jamais allé en Suède

have you been to the Louvre? = est-ce que tu es déjà allé au Louvre?
or est-ce que tu as déjà visité le Louvre?

Paul has been to see us three times
= Paul est venu nous voir trois fois

Note too:

has the postman been? = est-ce que le facteur est passé?

For *here is, here are, there is, there are* see the entries **here** and **there**.

The translation for an expression or idiom containing the verb *to be* will be found in the dictionary at the entry for another word in the expression: for *to be in danger* see **danger**, for *it would be best to … see* **best** etc.

This dictionary contains usage notes on topics such as **the clock, time units, age, weight measurement, days of the week**, and **shops, trades and professions**, many of which include translations of particular uses of *to be*. For the index to these notes ▶ **1419**.

---

were here si Henri était là; **were it not that**... si ce n'était ce n'est...; **were they to know** s'ils savaient; **if I were you** à ta place; **had it not been for Frank, I'd have missed the train** sans Frank j'aurais raté le train; **3** (phrases) **so** → **it** d'accord; → **that as it may** quoi qu'il en soit; **as it were** pour ainsi dire; **even if it were so** même si c'était le cas; **I preferred it as it was** je l'aimais mieux avant; **leave it as it is** ne changez rien; **let** OU **leave him** → laisse-le tranquille.
BE *n*: *abrév* ▶ **bill of exchange**.
beach /biːtʃ/ **I** *n* plage *f*.
II *vtr* échouer [*boat*]; →**ed whale** LIT baleine *f* échouée; FIG (building, object, person) mastodonte *m*.
beach: → **ball** *n* ballon *m* de plage; → **buggy** *n* buggy *m*; → **comber** *n*: personne qui récupère les objets échoués ou oubliés sur la plage; →**head** *n* tête *f* de pont; → **hut** *n* cabine *f* de plage; →**robe** *n* serviette-cabine *f*; →**wear** *n* tenues *fpl* de plage.
beacon /'biːkən/ *n* **1** AVIAT balise *f*, phare *m*; (lighthouse) phare *m*; (lantern) fanal *m*; (signalling buoy) balise *f*; FIG (guide) phare *m*; **2** (also **radio** →) (transmitter) radiobalise *f*; **3** HIST (on hill etc) feu *m* (*pour donner l'alarme*).
bead /biːd/ *n* **1** (jewellery) perle *f*; (**string of**) →**s** collier *m*; **2** (drop) (of sweat, dew) goutte *f*, perle *f*.
beaded /'biːdɪd/ *adj* [*dress, blouse*] garni de perles.
beady-eyed /ˌbiːdɪˈraɪd/ *adj* aux yeux perçants.
beagle /'biːgl/ *n* beagle *m*.
beak /biːk/ *n* bec *m*.
beaker /'biːkə(r)/ *n* GEN gobelet *m*; CHEM vase *m* à bec.
beam /biːm/ **I** *n* **1** (of light, torch, laser) rayon *m*; (of car lights, lighthouse) ALSO PHYS faisceau *m*; **on full** GB OU **high** US → AUT en (pleins) phares; **on low** → US AUT en code; **2** (piece of wood) poutre *f*; **3** (central shaft) (of weighing scales) fléau *m*; (in mechanics) balancier *m*; **4** AVIAT, NAUT (radio or radar course) faisceau *m* de guidage; **to be off** → GB, **to be off the** → US LIT être sorti du faisceau; FIG être à côté de la plaque⁰; **5** NAUT (cross-member) traverse *f*; (greatest width) largeur *f*; **6** (smile) grand sourire *m*.
II *vtr* [*radio, satellite*] transmettre [*programme, signal*].
III *vi* LIT, FIG rayonner.
IDIOMS **to be broad in the** →⁰ être fort des hanches.
beam: → **balance** *n* balance *f* à fléau; → **compass** *n* compas *m* à verge.
beaming /'biːmɪŋ/ *adj* (all contexts) rayonnant.
bean /biːn/ *n* haricot *m*.
IDIOMS **to be full of** →**s**⁰ GB (be lively) être en pleine

forme; US (be wrong) se gourer⁰ complètement; **it's not worth a** →⁰ ça ne vaut rien.
bean: → **bag** *n* (seat) fauteuil *m* poire; (for throwing) sac *m* de haricots; → **curd** *n* fromage *m* de soja; →**feast**⁰ *n* gueuleton⁰ *m*; →**pole** *n* espalier *m*; FIG (thin person) perche *f*; →**sprout** *n* germe *m* de soja.
bear /beə(r)/ **I** *n* **1** ZOOL ours *m*; **2**⁰ PÉJ (man) ours *m* (mal léché); **3** FIN baissier *m*.
II *vtr* (*prét* **bore**, *pp* **borne**) **1** (carry) [*person, animal*] porter [*load*]; **2** (bring) [*person*] apporter [*gift, message*]; [*wind, water*] porter [*seed, sound*]; **3** (show, have) porter [*address, inscription, name*]; **he still** →**s the scars** FIG il en reste marqué; **to** → **a resemblance to** ressembler à; **to** → **no relation to** n'avoir aucun rapport avec; **to** → **witness to** témoigner de; **4** (keep) **to** → **sth in mind** tenir compte de [*suggestion, factor, information*]; **to** → **in mind that** ne pas oublier que; **5** (support) **to** → **the weight of** [*structure, platform*] supporter le poids de [*person, object*]; **6** (endure, tolerate) supporter [*illness, suspense, smell, person*]; **I can't** → **to watch** je ne veux pas voir ça; **7** FIG (accept) encourir [*cost, responsibility*]; **8** (stand up to) résister à [*scrutiny, inspection*]; **it doesn't** → **thinking about** il vaut mieux ne pas y penser; **9** (nurture) porter [*love*]; **10** (yield) donner [*fruit, blossom, crop*]; FIN [*account, investment*] rapporter [*interest*]; **to** → **fruit** [*tree*] donner des fruits; FIG [*idea, investment*] porter ses fruits; **11†** OU LITTÉR (*pp actif* **borne**, *pp passif* **born**) (give birth to) [*woman*] donner naissance à; [*animal*] mettre bas; **to** → **sb a child** donner un enfant à qn.
III *vi* (*prét* **bore**, *pp* **borne**) **1 to** → **left/right** [*person*] prendre à gauche/à droite; **to** → **east/west** [*person*] aller à l'est/à l'ouest; [*road*] obliquer vers l'est/l'ouest; **2** (weigh) **to** → **heavily/hardest on sb** [*tax, price increase*] peser lourdement/le plus durement sur qn; **to bring pressure to** → **on** exercer une pression sur [*person, system*].
IV *v refl* (*prét* **bore**, *pp* **borne**) **to** → **oneself** (behave) se comporter.
■ **bear along:** → **[sb/sth] along**, → **along [sb/sth]** entraîner.
■ **bear away:** → **[sb/sth] away**, → **away [sb/sth]** [*person*] enlever [*person*]; [*wind, water*] emporter [*person, boat*].
■ **bear down 1** GEN appuyer (fort) (**on** sur); **2** (approach) **to** → **down on** se ruer sur [*person, group*]; **3** (in childbirth) pousser.
■ **bear off** = **bear away**.
■ **bear on:** → **on [sb/sth]** avoir un effet sur; (stronger) peser sur.
■ **bear out:** ¶ → **out [sth]** confirmer [*theory, claim, story*]; ¶ → **[sb] out** appuyer.

■ **bear up**: ~ **up** [*person*] tenir le coup; [*structure*] résister.

■ **bear upon** = **bear on**.

■ **bear with**: ~ **with** [*sb*] être indulgent avec; **please ~ with me for a minute** pardonnez-moi un instant; **to ~ with it** être patient.

bearable /ˈbeərəbl/ *adj* supportable.

bear-: **~baiting** *n* combat *m* d'ours et de chiens; **~ cub** *n* ourson *m*.

beard /ˈbɪəd/ **I** *n* **1** (on man) barbe *f*; **to grow a ~** se faire pousser la barbe; **the man with the ~** l'homme qui a une barbe; **2** (tuft, barbel) (on dog, goat) barbiche *f*; (on fish) barbes *fpl*; (on bird, wheat) barbe *f*.

II *vtr* affronter.

bearded /ˈbɪədɪd/ *adj* barbu.

bearer /ˈbeərə(r)/ **I** *n* **1** (of news, gift, letter, cheque) porteur/-euse *m/f*; (of passport) titulaire *mf*.

II *noun modifier* FIN [*bond, cheque*] au porteur.

bearing /ˈbeərɪŋ/ **I** *n* **1** (posture) allure *f*; **his dignified ~** son port digne; **2** (relevance) **to have no/little ~ on sth** n'avoir aucun rapport/avoir peu de rapport avec qch; **3** NAUT relèvement *m* au compas; **to take the ship's ~s** faire le point; **4** TECH palier *m*.

II bearings *npl* **1** (orientation) **to get** ou **find one's ~s** se repérer; **to lose one's ~s** LIT être désorienté, FIG perdre le nord; **2** AUT, TECH palier *m*.

bear-: ~ **market** *n* FIN marché *m* à la baisse; ~ **pit** *n* fosse *f* aux ours; **~skin** *n* (pelt) peau *f* d'ours; (hat) bonnet *m* à poil.

beast /biːst/ *n* **1** (animal) bête *f*; **the Beast** BIBLE l'antéchrist *m*; **2**° PEJ (person) (annoying) chameau° *m*; (brutal) brute *f*; **to bring out the ~ in sb** (make lustful, brutal) réveiller la bête qui sommeille en qn.

IDIOMS it's in the nature of the ~ HUM c'est dans l'ordre des choses.

beastly° /ˈbiːstlɪ/ *adj* **1** (unpleasant) [*person, behaviour*] rosse°; [*trick*] sale (*before n*); [*weather*] moche°; **2** (bestial) bestial.

beat /biːt/ **I** *n* **1** (repeated sound) (of drum, feet) battement *m*; **to the ~ of the drum** au son du tambour; **2** MUS (rhythm) rythme *m*; (in a bar) temps *m*; (in verse) accentuation *f*; **3** (pulsation) (of heart) battement *m*, pulsation *f*; **80 ~s per minute** 80 pulsations à la minute; **4** PHYS, ELEC (pulse) battement *m*; **5** (in police force) (area) secteur *m* de surveillance; (route) ronde *f*.

II *noun modifier* LITERAT [*poet, writer, philosophy*] de la Beat Generation.

III° *adj* (tired) claqué°.

IV *vtr* (*prét* **beat**, *pp* **beaten**) **1** (strike) [*person*] battre [*person, animal, metal, ground, drum*]; [*person*] marteler [*door*] (**with** avec); [*wing*] battre [*air, ground*]; **to ~ sb with a stick/whip** donner des coups de bâton/de fouet à qn; **to ~ sth into sb** inculquer qch à qn; **he beat the dust out of the carpet** il a battu le tapis pour le dépoussiérer; **to ~ sth into shape** façonner qch; **you'll have to ~ the truth out of him** il te faudra lui arracher la vérité; **to ~ sb into submission** faire obéir qn par la manière forte; **to ~ sb black and blue** rouer qn de coups; **to ~ the hell** ° **out of sb** tabasser° qn; **to ~ time** MUS battre la mesure; **to ~ its wings** [*bird*] battre des ailes; **2** CULIN (mix vigorously) battre [*mixture, eggs*]; **to ~ sth into sth** incorporer qch à qch en battant; **3** (make escape) **to ~ one's way/a path through** se frayer un chemin/un passage à travers [*crowd, obstacles*]; **to ~ a retreat** GEN, MIL battre en retraite; ~ **it**°! fiche le camp°!; **4** (defeat) battre [*opponent, team*] (**at** à); vaincre [*inflation, drug abuse*]; surmonter [*illness*]; mettre fin à [*child abuse, rape*]; **5** (confound) **it ~s me how/why** je n'arrive pas à comprendre comment/pourquoi; **we admit to being beaten** nous nous avouons vaincus; **'~s me**°!', **'it's got me beaten'** 'ça me dépasse!'; **6** (arrive earlier) éviter [*rush, crowds*]; devancer [*person*]; **she beat me to it** elle a été plus rapide que moi; **7** (outdo) GEN, SPORT battre [*score*]; dépasser [*target*]; surclasser [*product*]; **it ~s working** c'est toujours mieux que de travailler; **you can't ~ Italian shoes** rien ne vaut les chaussures italiennes; **our prices are difficult to**

~ **nos prix sont imbattables;** ~ **that (if you can)**°! qui dit mieux!

V *vi* (*prét* **beat**, *pp* **beaten**) [*waves, rain*] battre (**against** contre); [*person*] cogner (**at, on** à); [*heart, drum, wings*] battre.

IDIOMS a rod ou **stick to ~ sb with** une arme contre qn; **if you can't ~ 'em, join 'em**° il faut savoir hurler avec les loups.

■ **beat back**: ~ [*sth*] **back**, ~ **back** [*sth*] repousser [*group, flames*].

■ **beat down**: ¶ ~ **down** [*rain, hail*] tomber à verse (**on** sur); [*sun*] taper (**on** sur); ¶ ~ [*sth*] **down**, ~ **down** [*sth*] **1** (flatten) [*rain, wind*] coucher [*crop, grass*]; **2** (break open) [*person*] enfoncer [*door*].

■ **beat in**: ~ [*sth*] **in**, ~ **in** [*sth*] défoncer [*skull*].

■ **beat off**: ~ [*sb/sth*] **off**, ~ **off** [*sb/sth*] repousser [*attack, attackers*]; chasser [*insects*].

■ **beat out**: ~ [*sth*] **out**, ~ **out** [*sth*] marteler [*metal*]; rythmer [*tune*]; battre [*rhythm*] (**on** sur); étouffer [*flames*].

■ **beat up**: ~ [*sb*] **up**, ~ **up** [*sb*] tabasser°.

beaten /ˈbiːtn/ **I** *pp* ▶ **beat**.

II *adj* battu.

IDIOMS to go off the ~ track quitter les sentiers battus.

beatify /bɪˈætɪfaɪ/ *vtr* béatifier.

beating /ˈbiːtɪŋ/ *n* **1** (punishment) LIT raclée° *f*, correction *f*; **to get a ~** recevoir une raclée°; **to take a ~** FIG [*speaker, politician*] être malmené; [*toy, car*] en voir de dures°; **2** (sound) (of drum, heart, wings) battement *m*; **3** (of metal, carpet) battage *m*.

beating-up° /ˌbiːtɪŋ ˈʌp/ *n* tabassage° *m*.

beat-up° /ˈbiːtʌp/ *adj* [*car*] déglingué°.

beau /bəʊ/ *n* (*pl* **beaux**) LITTÉR ou HUM (suitor) galant *m*.

Beaufort scale /ˌbəʊfət ˈskeɪl/ *n* échelle *f* de Beaufort.

beautician /bjuːˈtɪʃn/ ▶ **1251** *n* **1** (beauty specialist) esthéticien/-ienne *m/f*; **2** US (hairdresser) coiffeur/-euse *m/f*.

beautiful /ˈbjuːtɪfl/ *adj* [*woman, house, car, landscape*] beau/belle (*before n*); [*day, holiday, feeling, experience*] merveilleux/-euse; [*weather, goal, shot*] superbe.

■ Note the irregular form **bel** of the adjective *beau* is used before masculine nouns beginning with a vowel or a mute 'h'.

beautifully /ˈbjuːtɪfəlɪ/ *adv* **1** (perfectly) [*play, write, function*] admirablement (bien); [*written, designed etc*] admirablement; **2** (attractively) [*displayed, furnished, situated*] magnifiquement; ~ **dressed** habillé avec beaucoup de goût; **3** (emphatic) [*empty, quiet, soft, warm, accurate*] merveilleusement.

beautiful people *n* the ~ le beau monde.

beautify /ˈbjuːtɪfaɪ/ *vtr* embellir.

beauty /ˈbjuːtɪ/ **I** *n* beauté *f*; **the ~ of the system is that...** ce qu'il y a de bien dans ce système, c'est que... **II** *noun modifier* [*contest, product, treatment*] de beauté.

IDIOMS age before ~ c'est le bénéfice de l'âge; ~ **is in the eye of the beholder** PROV rien n'est laid pour celui qui aime.

beauty-: ~ **editor** *n* rédacteur/-trice *m/f* de la rubrique 'beauté'; ~ **parlour†**, ~ **shop**, ~ **salon** US ▶ **1251** *n* salon *m* de beauté; ~ **queen** *n* reine *f* de beauté.

beauty sleep *n* HUM **to need one's ~** avoir besoin de ménager sa santé.

beauty spot *n* **1** (on skin) grain *m* de beauté; (fake) mouche *f*; **2** TOURISM GEN coin *m* superbe; (official) site *m* pittoresque.

beaver /ˈbiːvə(r)/ *n* castor *m*.

■ **beaver away** travailler d'arrache-pied (**at** à).

becalmed /bɪˈkɑːmd/ *adj* encalminé.

became /bɪˈkeɪm/ *prét* ▶ **become**.

because /bɪˈkɒz, US *also* -kɔːz/ **I** *conj* parce que; **just ~ you're older doesn't mean you're right** ce n'est pas parce que tu es plus âgé que tu as raison.

II because of *prep phr* à cause de; **~ of the rain** à cause de la pluie.

beck /bek/ *n* **to be at sb's ~ and call** être à la disposition de qn.

beckon /'bekən/ **I** *vtr* faire signe à; **to ~ sb in** faire signe à qn d'entrer.
II *vi* faire signe (**to** à).

become /bɪ'kʌm/ (*prét* **became**; *pp* **become**) **I** *vtr* SOUT [*colour, dress*] aller bien à [*person*]; [*attitude, modesty*] convenir à [*person*].
II *vi* devenir; **to ~ fat** devenir gros, grossir; **to ~ law** devenir loi; **to ~ ill** tomber malade.
III *v impers* **what has ~ of your brother?** qu'est-ce que ton frère est devenu?

becoming /bɪ'kʌmɪŋ/ *adj* [*behaviour*] convenable; [*garment, hair cut*] seyant.

bed /bed/ **I** *n* **1** lit *m*; **to get into ~** se mettre au lit; **to get out of ~** sortir du lit; **to go to ~** aller au lit; **to go to ~ with** coucher avec; **to put sb to ~** mettre qn au lit; **to be in ~** être au lit, être couché; **to take to one's ~**† s'aliter; **a 40 ~ ward/hotel** une salle/un hôtel de 40 lits; **to give sb a ~ for the night** héberger qn pour une nuit; **2** (of flowers) parterre *m*; (of compost) lit *m*; (of produce) carré *m*; **3** (of sea) fond *m*; (of river) lit *m*; (in geology) couche *f*; **4 to put a newspaper to ~** boucler un journal.
II *vtr* (*p prés etc* **-dd-**) (also **~ out**) repiquer [*seedlings*]; dépoter [*plants*].
IDIOMS **to get out of ~ on the wrong side** se lever du pied gauche; **life is not a ~ of roses** tout n'est pas rose dans la vie; **you've made your ~, lie in it** PROV comme on fait son lit, on se couche PROV.
■ **bed down: ~ down** se coucher.

BEd /ˌbiː'ed/ *n* (*abrév* = **bachelor of education**) diplôme *m* universitaire de pédagogie.

bed and board *n* le gîte et le couvert *m*.

bed and breakfast, B and B /ˌbed ən 'brekfəst/ *n* (type of accommodation) chambre *f* avec petit déjeuner, ~ chambre *f* d'hôte; **to run a ~** avoir des chambres d'hôte.

bed: **~ base** *n* sommier *m*; **~ bath** *n* toilette *f* au lit; **~bug** *n* punaise *f* de lit; **~chamber**† *n* chambre *f* à coucher; **~clothes** *npl* couvertures *fpl*.

bedding /'bedɪŋ/ *n* (for humans) literie *f*; (for animals) litière *f*.

bedeck /bɪ'dek/ *vtr* orner (**with** de).

bedevil /bɪ'devl/ *vtr* (*p prés etc* **-ll-, -l-** US) (plague) tracasser [*person*]; contrarier [*plans*]; (confuse) embrouiller [*situation*].

bedfellow /'bedfeləʊ/ *n* FIG **to make strange ~s** former un tandem bizarre.

bed: **~head** *n* tête *f* de lit; **~ jacket** *n* liseuse *f*.

bedlam /'bedləm/ *n* chahut○ *m*; **it's ~ in here!** quel cirque○ ici!

bed: **~ linen** *n* draps *mpl*; **~ pad** *n* alaise *f*; **~pan** *n* MED bassin *m*.

bedraggled /bɪ'dræɡld/ *adj* [*person, clothes*] dépenaillé; [*hair*] embroussaillé.

bedridden /'bedrɪdn/ *adj* alité, cloué au lit.

bedrock /'bedrɒk/ *n* LIT substrat *m* rocheux; FIG fondement *m*.

bedroom /'bedruːm, -rʊm/ **I** *n* chambre *f* (à coucher); **a two ~ flat** GB ou **apartment** un trois pièces.
II *noun modifier* **1** [*carpet, furniture, window*] de chambre; **2** [*secrets*] intime; [*scene*] d'amour.

bedroom: **~ farce** *n* THEAT vaudeville *m*; **~ slipper** *n* pantoufle *f*; **~ suburb** *n* US banlieue-dortoir *f*.

Beds *n* GB POST *abrév écrite* = **Bedfordshire**.

bed-settee /ˌbedsə'tiː/ *n* canapé-lit *m*.

bedside /'bedsaɪd/ **I** *n* chevet *m*.
II *noun modifier* [*book, lamp, table*] de chevet.

bedside manner *n* **to have a good ~** être gentil/-ille avec les malades.

bed: **~sit**○, **~sitter** *n* GB chambre *f* meublée; **~sock** *n* chausson *m* de nuit; **~sore** *n* escarre *f*;

~spread *n* dessus *m* de lit; **~stead** *n* cadre *m* de lit.

bedtime /'bedtaɪm/ **I** *n* **it's ~** c'est l'heure d'aller se coucher.
II *noun modifier* [*story, drink*] avant de s'endormir; **~ reading** lecture *f* pour l'oreiller.

bedwetting /'bed,wetɪŋ/ *n* énurésie *f*.

bee /biː/ *n* (insect) abeille *f*.
IDIOMS **to think one is the ~'s knees**○ se prendre pour un crack○; **the birds and the ~s** HUM ≈ les cigognes et les choux HUM; **to be as busy as a ~** s'activer comme une abeille.

beech /biːtʃ/ *n* (tree) hêtre *m*; (also **~ wood**) (bois *m* de) hêtre.

beef /biːf/ *n* bœuf *m*.
■ **beef up: ~ up** [sth] étoffer [*content, resources*].

beef: **~burger** *n* hamburger *m*; **~eater** *n* gardien *m* de la Tour de Londres; **~steak** *n* steak *m* (de bœuf); **~steak tomato** *n* grosse tomate *f*; **~ stew** *n* pot-au-feu *m inv*; **~ tea** *n* bouillon *m* de bœuf.

beefy /'biːfɪ/ *adj* **1** [*flavour*] de bœuf; **2**○ [*man*] mastoc○.

bee: **~hive** *n* (for bees) ruche *f*; (hairstyle) chignon *m* en hauteur; **~keeper** ▶**1251** *n* apiculteur/-trice *m/f*.

beeline /'biːlaɪn/ *n*: IDIOMS **to make a ~ for** se diriger tout droit vers.

been /biːn, US bɪn/ *pp* ▶ **be**.

beep /biːp/ **I** *n* (of electronic device) bip *m*; (of car) coup *m* de klaxon®; RADIO top *m* sonore.
II *vtr* appeler [qn] au bip, biper.
III *vi* [*device*] faire bip or bip-bip; [*car*] klaxonner.

beeper /'biːpə(r)/ *n* bip(-bip) *m*.

beer /bɪə(r)/ **I** *n* bière *f*.
II *noun modifier* [*barrel, bottle*] de bière.

beer: **~ belly** *n* bedaine *f* (de buveur de bière); **~ bottle** *n* bouteille *f* de bière; **~ can** *n* canette *f* de bière; **~ garden** *n* GEN jardin *m* de pub; (in Germany) ≈ guinguette *f*; **~ mat** *n* dessous *m* de verre; **~swilling** *adj* PÉJ se soûlant à la bière.

bee: **~ sting** *n* piqûre *f* d'abeille; **~swax** *n* cire *f* d'abeille.

beet /biːt/ *n* betterave *f*.

beetle /'biːtl/ **I** *n* **1** ZOOL (insect) scarabée *m*; (genus) coléoptère *m*; **2**○ AUT coccinelle○ *f* (*modèle de Volkswagen*).
II *vi*○ **to ~ in** entrer précipitamment; **to ~ off** filer○.

beetroot /'biːtruːt/ *n* GB betterave *f*.
IDIOMS **to turn as red as a ~** devenir rouge comme une tomate.

befall /bɪ'fɔːl/ (*prét* **befell**, *pp* **befallen**) LITTÉR (*s'emploie uniquement à l'infinitif et à la troisième personne*) **I** *vtr* arriver à, échoir à.
II *vi* advenir.

befit /bɪ'fɪt/ *v impers* (*p prés etc* **-tt-**) SOUT convenir à.

befitting /bɪ'fɪtɪŋ/ *adj* SOUT [*modesty, honesty*] approprié.

before /bɪ'fɔː(r)/ **I** *prep* **1** (earlier than) avant; **the day ~ yesterday** avant-hier; **the day ~ the exam** la veille de l'examen; **I was there the week ~** j'y étais il y a deux semaines; **six weeks ~ then** six semaines avant or auparavant; **~ long it will be winter** ce sera bientôt l'hiver; **not ~ time!** ce n'est pas trop tôt!; **2** (in order, sequence) avant; **G comes ~ H in the alphabet** dans l'alphabet le G est avant le H; **the page ~ this one** la page précédente; **3** (in importance, priority) avant; **for him, work comes ~ everything else** pour lui le travail passe avant tout; **4** (this side of) avant; **turn left ~ the crossroads** tournez à gauche avant le carrefour; **5** ▶**812** US (in time expressions) **ten ~ six** six heures moins dix; **6** (in front of) devant; **she appeared ~ them** elle est apparue devant eux; **~ our very eyes** sous nos propres yeux; **to appear ~ a court** comparaître devant un tribu-

before

When *before* is used as a preposition in expressions of time or order of sequence or importance it is translated by *avant*:

before the meeting = avant la réunion
she left before me = elle est partie avant moi

For more examples and particular usages, see **I 1, 2, 3** in the entry *before*.

When *before* is used as a preposition meaning *in front of* (when you are talking about physical space) or *in the presence of* it is translated by *devant*:

before our eyes = devant nos yeux
he declared before
his mother that ... = il a déclaré devant sa mère que ...

When *before* is used as an adjective after a noun it is translated by *précédent/-e*:

the time before = la fois précédente

the one before is translated by *le précédent* or *la précédente*:

no, I'm not talking about that meeting but the one before = non, je ne parle pas de cette réunion-là mais de la précédente

For particular usages see **II** in the entry *before*.

When *before* is used as an adverb meaning *beforehand* it is translated by *avant* in statements about the present or future:

I'll try to talk to her before = j'essaierai de lui en parler avant
you could have told me before = tu aurais pu me le dire avant

When *before* means *previously* in statements about the past it is translated by *auparavant*:

I had met her two or three times before = je l'avais rencontrée deux ou trois fois auparavant

When *before* means *already* it is translated by *déjà*:

I've met her before = je l'ai déjà rencontrée
you've asked me
that question before = tu m'as déjà posé cette question

In negative sentences *before* is often used in English simply to reinforce the negative. In such cases it is not translated at all:

I'd never eaten snails before = je n'avais jamais mangé d'escargots
you've never told me that before = tu ne m'as jamais dit ça

For particular usages see **III** in the entry *before*.

When *before* is used as a conjunction, it is translated by *avant de* + infinitive where the two verbs have the same subject:

before he saw her he
recognized her voice = il a reconnu sa voix avant de la voir
before I cook dinner I'm going
to phone my mother = avant de préparer le dîner je vais appeler ma mère

Where the two verbs have different subjects, the translation is *avant que* + subjunctive:

Tom wants to see her
before she leaves = Tom veut la voir avant qu'elle parte

Some speakers and writers add *ne* before the verb: Tom veut la voir avant qu'elle ne parte, but this is not obligatory. For particular usages see **IV** in the entry *before*.

---

nal; **to bring a bill ~ parliament** présenter un projet de loi au parlement; **7** (confronting) face à; **these are the alternatives ~ us** voici les choix qui s'offrent à nous; **the task ~ us** la tâche qui nous attend. **II** *adj* précédent; **the day ~** la veille; **the week/year ~** la semaine/l'année précédente. **III** *adv* (at an earlier time) avant; **long ~** bien avant; **two months ~** deux mois auparavant; **have you been to India ~?** est-ce que tu es déjà allé en Inde?; **I've never been there ~** je n'y suis jamais allé; **I've never seen him ~ in my life** c'est la première fois que je le vois. **IV** *conj* **1** (in time) **~ I go, I would like to say that** avant de partir, je voudrais dire que; **~ he goes, I must remind him that** avant qu'il parte, il faut que je lui rappelle que; **it was some time ~ she was able to walk again** il lui a fallu un certain temps pour pouvoir marcher de nouveau; **oh, ~ I forget...** avant que j'oublie...; **2** (rather than) plutôt que; **he would die ~ betraying that secret** il mourrait plutôt que de révéler ce secret; **3** (or else) **get out of here ~ I call the police!** sortez d'ici ou j'appelle la police!; **4** (as necessary condition) pour que (+ *subj*); **you have to show your ticket ~ they'll let you in** il faut que tu montres ton ticket pour qu'ils te laissent entrer. IDIOMS **~ you could say Jack Robinson** en moins de deux○; **~ you know where you are...** on n'a pas le temps de dire ouf que...

beforehand /bɪ'fɔ:hænd/ *adv* **1** (ahead of time) à l'avance; **be there one hour ~** sois là une heure à l'avance; **let me know ~** prévenez-moi; **2** (earlier) auparavant, avant; **we had seen them five minutes ~** nous les avions vus cinq minutes auparavant or plus tôt.

before tax *adj* [*income*] brut; [*profit*] avant impôts.

befriend /bɪ'frend/ *vtr* (look after) prendre [qn] sous son aile; (make friends with) se lier d'amitié avec.

befuddle /bɪ'fʌdl/ *vtr* embrouiller [*mind*].

beg /beg/ **I** *vtr* (*p prés etc* **-gg-**) demander [*food, money, favour*] (from à); **to ~ sb for sth** demander qch à qn; **I ~ged his forgiveness** je lui ai demandé

de me pardonner; **to bring a bill** 'stop, I ~ (of) you!' 'arrêtez, je vous en supplie!' **II** *vi* (*p prés etc* **-gg-**) [*person*] mendier (**from** à); [*dog*] faire le beau; **to ~ for** mendier [*money, food*]; **to ~ for help** demander de l'aide; **to ~ to be forgiven** implorer le pardon. IDIOMS **these apples are going ~ging** personne ne veut de ces pommes; **to ~ the question** laisser de côté le problème de fond. ■ **beg off** s'excuser de ne pas pouvoir venir.

began /bɪ'gæn/ *prét* ▶ **begin**.

beggar /'begə(r)/ **I** *n* **1** (pauper) mendiant/-e *m/f*; **2**○ GB (man) **you lucky ~!** espèce de veinard○! **II** *vtr* ruiner [*person, company*]. IDIOMS **~s can't be choosers** PROV faute de grives on mange des merles PROV.

beggarly /'begəlɪ/ *adj* [*existence, meal*] misérable; [*wage*] dérisoire.

beggar-my-neighbour /ˌbegəmaɪ'neɪbə(r)/ ▶ 949 *n* = bataille *f*.

beg: ~ging bowl *n* sébile *f*; **~ging letter** *n* lettre *f* de sollicitation.

begin /bɪ'gɪn/ **I to begin with** *adv phr* (at first) au début, au départ; (firstly) d'abord, premièrement; **I wish I hadn't told her to ~ with** pour commencer, je n'aurais jamais dû lui en parler. **II** *vtr* (*p prés* **-nn-**; *prét* **began**; *pp* **begun**) **1** (start) commencer [*journey, list, meeting, job, game, meal*] (**with** par, avec); à [*school*]; provoquer [*debate, dispute*]; lancer [*campaign, trend*]; commencer [*tradition*]; déclencher [*war*]; fonder [*dynasty*]; **it's ~ning to rain** il commence à pleuvoir; **to ~ doing** commencer à faire; **to ~ a conversation with** engager la conversation avec; **he began life as a sailor** il a débuté comme marin; **2** (start to use) entamer [*bottle, packet*]; commencer [*page*]; **3** (come first in) marquer le commencement de [*series, collection, festival*]. **III** *vi* (*p prés* **-nn-**; *prét* **began**; *pp* **begun**) GEN commencer; [*river*] prendre sa source; **let's ~** commençons; **to ~ with** commencer par; **the week**

~ning the 25th la semaine qui commence le 25;
your problems have only just begun! tes problèmes
ne font que commencer!; **to ~ well/badly** bien/mal
commencer; **to ~ again** recommencer.

beginner /bɪˈgɪnə(r)/ n débutant/-e m/f; **~s' class**
cours m pour débutants.

beginning /bɪˈgɪnɪŋ/ I n début m, commencement m;
in ou **at the ~** au début, au départ; **at the ~ of**
September au début du mois de septembre, début
septembre; **from ~ to end** du début jusqu'à la fin; **to**
go back to the ~ reprendre au début.
II **beginnings** npl (origins) (of person, business) débuts
mpl; (of theory, movement) origines fpl.

begonia /bɪˈgəʊnɪə/ n bégonia m.

begrudge /bɪˈgrʌdʒ/ vtr = **grudge** II.

beguile /bɪˈgaɪl/ vtr **1** (entice, trick) leurrer; **to be ~d**
se laisser leurrer (**with** par); **2** (charm) captiver.

beguiling /bɪˈgaɪlɪŋ/ adj captivant.

begun /bɪˈgʌn/ pp ▶ **begin**.

behalf /bɪˈhɑːf, US -ˈhæf/ **on ~ of** GB, **in ~ of** US
prep phr [act, speak, accept award etc] au nom de,
pour; [phone, write] de la part de; [campaign, plead] en
faveur de, pour; [negotiate] pour le compte de.

behave /bɪˈheɪv/ I vi [person, group, animal] GEN se
comporter (**towards** envers); [machine, device] se
comporter; (in given circumstances) se conduire (**to-**
wards avec, envers); **he ~d badly towards her** il
s'est mal conduit envers elle.
II v refl **to ~ oneself** [person] bien se comporter;
~ yourself! tiens-toi bien!

behaviour GB, **behavior** US /bɪˈheɪvjə(r)/ n GEN
comportement m (**towards** envers); (in given set of
circumstances) conduite f; (of device, machine) fonctionnement m; **for good/bad ~** pour bonne/mauvaise
conduite.
IDIOMS **to be on one's best ~** bien se tenir.

behavioural GB, **behavioral** US /bɪˈheɪvjərəl/ adj
[change, disorder, problem] de comportement; [theory,
science] du comportement.

behaviourist GB, **behaviorist** US /bɪˈheɪvjərɪst/ n,
adj behavioriste (mf).

behead /bɪˈhed/ vtr décapiter.

beheld /bɪˈheld/ prét, pp ▶ **behold**.

behind /bɪˈhaɪnd/
■ **Note** When used as a preposition to talk about the physical position of something, behind is translated by
derrière: behind the house = derrière la maison.
– behind is sometimes used in verb combinations (fall
behind, lag behind etc). For translations, consult the appropriate verb entry (**fall**, **lag** etc).
– For adverbial uses and figurative prepositional uses see
the entry below.

I⁰ n derrière⁰ m.
II adj **to be ~ with** avoir du retard dans [studies,
work]; **to be too far ~** avoir trop de retard.
III adv [follow on, trail] derrière; [look, glance] en
arrière; **the car ~** la voiture de derrière.
IV prep **1** derrière; **~ my back** FIG derrière mon
dos; **he has three years' experience ~ him** il a
trois ans d'expérience derrière lui; **I've put all that**
~ me now j'ai oublié tout ça; **the real story ~ the**
news la véritable histoire que les médias n'ont pas révélée; **to be ~ the others** [pupil] être en retard par
rapport aux autres; **2** FIG (motivating) **the reasons ~**
his declaration les raisons qui motivent/motivaient sa
déclaration; **who is ~ this proposal?** qui est à l'origine de cette proposition?; **3** FIG (supporting) **to be (so-**
lidly) ~ sb soutenir qn (à fond).

behindhand /bɪˈhaɪndhænd/ adv **to be** ou **get ~**
with être en retard dans [work, studies].

behold /bɪˈhəʊld/ vtr (prét, pp **beheld**) LITTÉR ou
HUM voir; **it was a wonder to ~** c'était un
spectacle merveilleux.

beholder /bɪˈhəʊldə(r)/ n: IDIOMS **beauty is in the**
eye of the ~ PROV ≈ ce qu'on aime est toujours
beau PROV.

beige /beɪʒ/ **▶ 818 |** n, adj beige (m).

Beijing /beɪˈdʒɪŋ/ **▶ 1343 |** pr n Pékin, Bei-jing.

being /ˈbiːɪŋ/ n **1** (human) **~** être m (humain); **with**
my whole ~ de tout mon être; **2** (existence) **to bring**
sth into ~ faire de qch une réalité; **to come into**
~ prendre naissance.

Beirut /ˈbeɪruːt, ˌbeɪˈruːt/ **▶ 1343 |** pr n Beyrouth.

bejewelled GB, **bejeweled** US /bɪˈdʒuːəld/ adj
paré de bijoux.

belated /bɪˈleɪtɪd/ adj tardif/-ive.

belch /beltʃ/ I n renvoi m, rot m.
II vi roter⁰, avoir un renvoi.
■ **belch out:** **~** [sth] **out**, **~ out** [sth] vomir,
cracher [smoke, flames].

beleaguered /bɪˈliːgəd/ adj **1** [city, troops] assiégé; **2**
FIG [person] débordé; [company] menacé.

Belfast /ˌbelˈfɑːst/ **▶ 1343 |** pr n Belfast.

belfry /ˈbelfrɪ/ n beffroi m, clocher m.
IDIOMS **to have bats in the ~**⁰ avoir une araignée
au plafond⁰.

Belgian /ˈbeldʒən/ **▶ 1100 |** I n Belge mf.
II adj belge.

Belgium /ˈbeldʒəm/ **▶ 840 |** pr n Belgique f.

Belgrade /ˌbelˈgreɪd/ **▶ 1343 |** pr n Belgrade.

belie /bɪˈlaɪ/ vtr contredire [hopes, promises]; tromper
sur [appearances, feelings, facts].

belief /bɪˈliːf/ n **1** (conviction, opinion) conviction f
(**about** sur, à propos de); **in the ~ that** convaincu
que; **contrary to popular ~** contrairement à ce
qu'on pense généralement; **2** (confidence) confiance f,
foi f; **her ~ in democracy** sa foi ou confiance dans la
démocratie; **~ in oneself** confiance en soi; **3** RELIG
(faith) foi f; (article of faith) croyance f.

believable /bɪˈliːvəbl/ adj crédible.

believe /bɪˈliːv/ I vtr **1** croire [evidence, statement,
person]; **~ (you) me!** croyez-moi!; **~ it or not**
croyez-le ou pas; **it has to be seen to be ~d** il faut
le voir pour le croire; **I can't ~ (that) he did that** je
n'arrive pas à croire qu'il ait fait cela; **I can ~ that**
of her! ça ne m'étonne pas d'elle!; **don't you ~ it!**
n'en croyez rien!; **I don't ~ you!** ce n'est pas vrai!; **I**
can well ~ it je suis prêt à le croire; **I don't ~ a**
word of it! je n'en crois pas un mot!; **if he's to be**
~d à l'en croire; **2** (think, be of the opinion) croire, estimer; **I ~ (that) she is right, I ~ her to be right** je
crois or j'estime qu'elle a raison; **she is ~d to be a**
spy on pense que c'est une espionne; **to let sb ~**
(that) laisser croire à qn que; **I ~ so** je crois que oui;
I ~ not je crois que non.
II vi **1 to ~ in** croire à [promises, discipline, exercise
etc]; **to ~ in sb** avoir confiance en qn; **to ~ in**
doing croire or estimer qu'il est bon de faire; **2** RELIG
avoir la foi; **to ~ in God** croire en Dieu.
IDIOMS **seeing is believing** il faut le voir pour le
croire.

believer /bɪˈliːvə(r)/ n RELIG croyant/-e m/f; GEN (in
hard work, progress, liberty) adepte mf (**in** de).

belittle /bɪˈlɪtl/ vtr rabaisser [person, achievement]; déprécier [efforts]; **to feel ~d** se sentir déprécié.

belittling /bɪˈlɪtlɪŋ/ adj [comment] désobligeant.

Belize /beˈliːz/ **▶ 840 |** pr n Bélize m.

bell /bel/ n **1** (in church) cloche f; (on sheep, goat)
clochette f; (on toy, cat) grelot m; (on bicycle) sonnette f;
(for servant) clochette f; **door ~** sonnette f; **to ring**
the ~s faire sonner les cloches; **2** (warning device)
sonnerie f; **3**⁰ GB (phone call) **to give sb a ~** passer
un coup de fil à qn; **4** NAUT coup m de cloche.
IDIOMS **that name/number rings a ~** ce nom/
numéro me dit quelque chose; **to be as sound as a**
~ être en parfaite santé; **saved by the ~** sauvé par
le gong.

bell: **~-bottoms** npl pantalon m à pattes d'éléphant;
~boy ▶ 1251 | n US groom m; **~ buoy** n bouée f à
cloche.

belle /bel/ n belle f, beauté f.

bellhop ▶ 1251 | n US groom m.

belligerence /bɪˈlɪdʒərəns/ n GEN agressivité f; POL
belligérance f.

belligerent /bɪˈlɪdʒərənt/ I n POL (country) belligérant m.
II adj 1 GEN agressif/-ive ; 2 POL (at war) belligérant.

bell jar n cloche f en verre.

bellow /ˈbeləʊ/ I n (of bull) mugissement m ; (of person) hurlement m.
II vi [bull] mugir (**with** de) ; [person] hurler, beugler○.
III vtr (also **~ out**) brailler [command].

bellows /ˈbeləʊz/ npl (for fire, in forge) soufflet m ; (of organ) soufflerie f.

bell: **~-pull** n (rope) cordon m de sonnette ; **~-push** n bouton m de sonnette ; **~-ringer** n carillonneur m, sonneur f.

bell-ringing n to go **~** aller carillonner.

bell: **~-shaped** adj en forme de cloche ; **~ tower** n clocher m.

belly /ˈbeli/ n 1○ (stomach) ventre m ; (paunch) bedaine○ f ; 2 (of animal) ventre m ; 3 (abdomen) ventre m ; 4 **~ of pork** CULIN poitrine f de porc.
■ **belly out**: **~ out** [sail] se gonfler ; **~** [sth] **out** gonfler.

bellyache○ /ˈbelieɪk/ I n mal m au ventre.
II vi (p prés **-aching**) râler○ (**about** contre).

belly: **~-button** n nombril m ; **~ dancer** n danseuse f du ventre ; **~ flop**○ n (in swimming) plat m.

bellyful○ /ˈbelifʊl/ n: IDIOMS **to have a ~ of sth** en avoir sa claque○ de qch.

belong /bɪˈlɒŋ, US -ˈlɔːŋ/ vi 1 (be property of) **to ~ to** appartenir à ; **the house ~s to his mother** la maison appartient à sa mère or est à sa mère ; 2 (be member of) **to ~ to** appartenir à [family, generation, party] ; faire partie de [club, society, set] ; être inscrit à [library] ; 3 (of object) aller ; **where do these books ~?** où vont ces livres? ; **put it back where it ~s** remets-le à sa place.

belongings /bɪˈlɒŋɪŋz, US -ˈlɔːŋ-/ npl affaires fpl ; **personal ~** effets mpl personnels.

beloved /bɪˈlʌvɪd/ I n LITTÉR ou HUM bien-aimé/-e m/f.
II adj bien-aimé.

below /bɪˈləʊ/

■ **Note** When below is used as a preposition to talk about the physical position of something, it is most often translated by au-dessous de: the apartment below mine = l'appartement au-dessous du mien ; below the knee = au-dessous du genou.
– The most notable exceptions are for the expressions below the ground and below the surface, when sous is used: sous le sol, sous la surface.
– For other prepositional uses of below and for adverbial uses see the entry below.

I prep 1 (under) en dessous de ; **~ the waist** au-dessous de la taille ; **~ sea level** au-dessous du niveau de la mer ; **~ the castle** en contrebas du château ; **the valley ~ them/you etc** la vallée en contrebas ; 2 (less than) en dessous de, inférieur à ; **~ 10%** en dessous de or inférieur à 10% ; 3 (in rank) **those ~ the rank of Major** MIL les militaires qui sont au-dessous du grade de major ; 4 (south of) au sud de, au-dessous de ; (downstream from) en aval de ; 5 (unworthy of) ▶**beneath I 2**.
II adv **100 metres ~** 100 mètres plus bas ; **the village ~** le village en contrebas ; **the people/cars (down) ~** les gens/voitures en bas ; **the apartment ~** l'appartement en dessous ; **seen from ~** vu d'en bas ; **see ~** (on page) voir ci-dessous.

belt /belt/ I n 1 (for garment) also AUT, AVIAT ceinture f ; **safety** ou **seat ~** ceinture de sécurité ; 2 (area) GEN, METEOROL zone f ; **mountain/earthquake ~** zone f de montagnes/de séisme ; 3 TECH courroie f ; 4 SPORT (in boxing, judo) ceinture f ; **to be a black ~** être ceinture noire ; 5○ (blow) beigne○ f, coup m de poing ; 6 (for punishing) lanière f de cuir.
II vtr 1○ (hit) flanquer une beigne à○, gifler [person] ; 2 (as punishment) donner une correction à.
III vi **to ~ in/out etc**○ entrer/sortir etc à toute vitesse.

IDIOMS **to tighten one's ~** se serrer la ceinture ; **that remark was a bit below the ~** cette remarque était un coup bas ; **she has 15 years' experience under her ~** elle a 15 ans d'expérience à son actif.
■ **belt off**○ filer à toute vitesse.
■ **belt out**: **~ out** [sth], **~** [sth] **out** chanter [qch] à pleins poumons [song].
■ **belt up** 1○ GB (shut up) la fermer○, se taire ; **~ up!** ferme-la○! ; 2 AUT attacher sa ceinture de sécurité.

beltway /ˈbeltweɪ/ n US AUT périphérique m.

bemoan /bɪˈməʊn/ vtr SOUT déplorer.

bemused /bɪˈmjuːzd/ adj perplexe.

bench /bentʃ/ n 1 GEN, SPORT (seat) banc m ; 2 GB POL banc m ; **to be on the opposition ~es** siéger dans l'opposition ; 3 JUR (also **Bench**) (judges collectively) magistrature f (assise) ; (judge or judges in one case) Cour f ; 4 TECH (workbench) établi m.

benchmark /ˈbentʃmɑːk/ n 1 GEN point m de référence ; 2 FIN (price) prix m de référence ; 3 COMPUT test m de performance.

bend /bend/ I n 1 GEN (in road) tournant m, virage m ; (in pipe) coude m ; (in river) courbe f ; (of elbow, knee) pli m ; **there's a ~ in the road** la route fait un virage.
II **bends** ▶**1002** npl MED (+ v sg ou pl) maladie f des caissons.
III vtr (prét, pp **bent**) plier [knee, arm, leg] ; courber, pencher [head] ; courber [back] ; faire un coude à [pipe, bar] ; plier [wire] ; (by mistake) tordre [pipe, nail] ; **to ~ the rules** GEN contourner la loi (or le règlement) ; (make exception) faire une exception.
IV vi (prét, pp **bent**) 1 [road, path] tourner ; [river] (once) s'incurver ; (several times) faire des méandres ; [branch] ployer ; [nail, mudguard] se tordre ; 2 [person] se courber, se pencher ; **to ~ forward/backwards** se pencher en avant/en arrière.
IDIOMS **to drive sb (a)round the ~**○ rendre qn fou/folle ; **to ~ over backwards for sb/to do** se mettre en quatre pour qn/pour faire.
■ **bend back**: ¶ **~ back** [person] se pencher en arrière ; ¶ **to ~ sth back into shape** redresser qch.
■ **bend down**, **bend over** [person] se pencher, se courber.

beneath /bɪˈniːθ/

■ **Note** When used as a preposition (= under), beneath is translated by au-dessous de: beneath his feet = au-dessous de ses pieds. When used as an adverb (the trees beneath), beneath is translated by en dessous: the trees beneath = les arbres en dessous. For particular and figurative usages see below.

I prep 1 sous ; **~ the table** sous la table ; **the valley ~ them/you etc** la vallée en contrebas ; 2 **it is ~ you to do** c'est indigne de toi de faire.
II adv en dessous ; **the apartment ~** l'appartement en dessous ; **the valley ~** la vallée en contrebas.

Benedictine /ˌbenɪˈdɪktɪn/ I n RELIG bénédictin/-e m/f.
II adj bénédictin.

benediction /ˌbenɪˈdɪkʃn/ n bénédiction f.

benefactor /ˈbenɪfæktə(r)/ n bienfaiteur m.

beneficial /ˌbenɪˈfɪʃl/ adj [effect, influence] bénéfique ; [change] salutaire ; [outcome] favorable ; **to be ~ to the health** être bon/bonne pour la santé.

beneficiary /ˌbenɪˈfɪʃərɪ, US -ˈfɪʃɪerɪ/ n JUR bénéficiaire mf.

benefit /ˈbenɪfɪt/ I n 1 avantage m (**from** de) ; **to be of ~ to** profiter à ; **to feel the ~ of** ressentir l'effet favorable de [change, holiday] ; **to give sb the ~ of** faire profiter qn de [experience, knowledge] ; **the ~s of modern technology** les avantages de la technologie moderne ; **to have the ~ of** bénéficier de [education] ; **to be to sb's ~** être à l'avantage de qn ; **it's for your own ~** c'est pour ton propre bien ; **'salary £20,000 plus ~s'** 'salaire de 20000 livres sterling plus avantages sociaux' ; 2 (financial aid) allocation f ; **to be on ~(s)** GB toucher les allocations.
II noun modifier [concert, match] de bienfaisance ; [claim] d'allocation.

III *vtr* (*p prés etc* **-t-**) profiter à [*person*]; être avantageux/-euse pour [*group, nation*].
IV *vi* (*p prés etc* **-t-**) profiter; **to ~ from** ou **by** tirer profit de; **to ~ from** ou **by doing** gagner à faire.
IDIOMS **to give sb the ~ of the doubt** accorder à qn le bénéfice du doute.

Benelux /'benɪlʌks/ **I** *n* Bénélux *m*.
II *noun modifier* [*countries, organization*] du Bénélux.

benevolence /bɪ'nevələns/ *n* (kindness) bienveillance *f*; (generosity) générosité *f*.

benevolent /bɪ'nevələnt/ *adj* **1** [*person, smile*] bienveillant (**to, towards** envers); [*dictator*] éclairé; **2** (charitable) [*organization, fund*] de bienfaisance.

Bengal /beŋ'gɔːl/ *pr n* Bengale *m*.

benighted /bɪ'naɪtɪd/ *adj* LITTER arriéré, primitif/-ive.

benign /bɪ'naɪn/ *adj* **1** [*person, smile*] bienveillant; [*conditions*] propice; [*influence*] bénéfique; **2** MED bénin/-igne.

Benin /be'niːn/ ▶ **840** *pr n* Bénin *m*.

bent /bent/ **I** *prét, pp* ▶ **bend**.
II *n* (flair) dispositions *fpl* (**for** pour); (liking) goût *m*, penchant *m* (**for, towards** pour).
III *adj* **1** [*nail, wire, stick*] tordu; [*old person*] (stooped) courbé; **2 to be ~ on doing sth** vouloir à tout prix faire qch.

benzene /'benziːn/ *n* benzène *m*.

benzine /'benziːn/ *n* benzine *f*.

bequeath /bɪ'kwiːð/ *vtr* JUR, FIG léguer (**to** à).

bequest /bɪ'kwest/ *n* JUR, FIG legs *m* (**to** à).

berate /bɪ'reɪt/ *vtr* SOUT admonester FML, réprimander (**for** pour).

bereaved /bɪ'riːvd/ **I** *n* **the ~** (+ *v pl*) la famille endeuillée.
II *adj* [*person, family*] endeuillé, en deuil.

bereavement /bɪ'riːvmənt/ *n* (state, event, period of mourning) deuil *m*; (sorrow) chagrin *m*.

bereft /bɪ'reft/ *adj* SOUT **1 ~ of** privé de [*love, friendship*]; dépourvu de [*contents, ideas*]; **2** (forlorn) abandonné.

beret /'bereɪ, US bə'reɪ/ *n* béret *m*.

bergamot /'bɜːgəmɒt/ *n* (fruit) bergamote *f*; (tree) bergamotier *m*; (herb) monarde *f*.

Berks *n* GB POST *abrév écrite* = **Berkshire**.

Berlin /bɜː'lɪn/ ▶ **1343** *pr n* Berlin.

Berliner /bɜː'lɪnə(r)/ *n* Berlinois/-e *m/f*.

Bermuda /bə'mjuːdə/ ▶ **840** *pr n* les Bermudes *fpl*.

Bermudas /bə'mjuːdəz/, **Bermuda shorts** *npl* bermuda *m*.

berry /'berɪ/ *n* baie *f*.
IDIOMS **to be as brown as a ~** être tout bronzé.

berserk /bə'sɜːk/ *adj* fou furieux/folle furieuse; **to go ~** être pris/prise de folie furieuse.

berth /bɜːθ/ **I** *n* **1** NAUT, RAIL (for sleeping) couchette *f*; **2** NAUT (for ship) mouillage *m*; **at ~** au mouillage.
II *vtr* faire mouiller; **to be ~ed at** être mouillé à.
IDIOMS **to give sb/sth a wide ~**○ éviter qn/qch.

beseech /bɪ'siːtʃ/ *vtr* (*prét, pp* **beseeched** ou **besought**) SOUT implorer [*forgiveness*]; solliciter [*favour*]; **to ~ sb to do** supplier qn de faire.

beseeching /bɪ'siːtʃɪŋ/ *adj* SOUT implorant, suppliant.

beset /bɪ'set/ *vtr* (*prét, pp* **beset**) (*gén au passif*) assaillir (**with** de); MIL assiéger; **a country ~ by strikes** un pays en proie aux grèves.

beside /bɪ'saɪd/ *prep* **1** (next to) à côté de; **~ you** à côté de toi; **~ the sea** au bord de la mer; **2** (in comparison with) par rapport à; **my problems seem rather minor ~ yours** mes problèmes semblent assez insignifiants par rapport aux tiens ou à côté des tiens.
IDIOMS **to be ~ oneself** (with anger) être hors de soi; **to be ~ oneself** (with excitement) être surexcité; **to be ~ oneself with happiness** être fou/folle de joie.

besides /bɪ'saɪdz/ **I** *adv* **1** (moreover) d'ailleurs; **2** (in addition) en plus, aussi; **she has a car and a**

motorbike ~ elle a une voiture et en plus or aussi une moto; **and much else ~** et bien d'autres choses encore.
II *prep* (apart from) en plus de, à part; **~ John they're all teachers** à part John ils sont tous professeurs; **~ being an artist, she's also a poet** en plus d'être une artiste, elle est aussi poète; **everyone ~ me/you** tout le monde sauf moi/toi.

besiege /bɪ'siːdʒ/ *vtr* MIL assiéger; FIG assaillir.

besotted /bɪ'sɒtɪd/ *adj* follement épris (**with** de).

bespatter /bɪ'spætə(r)/ *vtr* éclabousser (**with** de).

bespectacled /bɪ'spektəkld/ *adj* à lunettes.

bespoke /bɪ'spəʊk/ *adj* GB [*suit, jacket*] (fait) sur mesure; [*tailor*] à façon.

best /best/ **I** *n* **1 the ~** le/la meilleur/-e *m/f*; **it's the ~ of his novels** c'est son meilleur roman; **we've had the ~ of the day** le beau temps est fini pour aujourd'hui; **to sound the ~** avoir le meilleur son, sonner le mieux; **the ~ of its kind** le meilleur du genre; **it's not her ~** (of book, play) ce n'est pas la meilleur/-e qu'elle ait écrit/-e; **only the ~ is good enough for me/my son** je veux ce qu'il y a de mieux pour moi/mon fils; **she is the ~ at physics/at tennis** c'est la meilleure en physique/au tennis; **who's the ~ at drawing?** qui dessine le mieux?; **it's the ~ I've got** c'est le meilleur que j'aie; **it's for the ~** (recommending course of action) c'est la meilleure solution; (of something done) c'est tant mieux; **it was not in the ~ of taste** ce n'était pas du meilleur goût; **the ~ of friends** les meilleurs amis du monde; **2** (most favourable) **the ~** mieux; **the ~ we can hope for** le mieux qu'on puisse espérer; **at ~** au mieux; **he's a difficult man at the ~ of times** déjà en temps ordinaire il est difficile à vivre; **to make the ~ of sth** s'accommoder de qch; **to get the ~** of avoir la part du lion dans [*deal, bargain*]; gagner dans [*arrangement*]; **3** (peak, apogee) **the city is at its ~ in autumn** c'est en automne que la ville est la plus belle; **Balzac at his ~** c'est Balzac dans ce qu'il a fait de meilleur; **to be at one's ~** être au mieux de sa forme; **4** (greatest personal effort) **to do one's ~** faire de son mieux or faire (tout) son possible pour faire; **is that the ~ you can do?** c'est le mieux que tu puisses faire?; **to get the ~ out of** obtenir le meilleur de [*pupil, worker*]; **to bring out the ~ in sb** [*crisis, suffering*] inciter qn à donner le meilleur de lui-même; **5** (good wishes) **all the ~!** (good luck) bonne chance!; (cheers) à ta santé!; **all the ~, Ellie** (in letter) amitiés, Ellie; **wishing you all the ~ on your retirement** meilleurs vœux de bonheur pour votre retraite.
II *adj* (*superlative of* **good**) **1** (most excellent) meilleur; **the ~ idea she's had all day** la meilleure idée qu'elle ait eue de la journée; **the ~ thing about sth/about doing** ce qu'il y a de mieux dans qch/lorsqu'on fait; **to taste ~** avoir le meilleur goût; **she looks ~ in black** c'est en noir qu'elle est le mieux; **she speaks the ~ French** c'est elle qui parle le mieux français; **my ~ dress** ma plus belle robe; **'~ before end May'** 'à consommer de préférence avant fin mai'; **2** (most competent) [*teacher, poet, actor*] meilleur; **who is the ~ swimmer?** qui nage le mieux?; **to be ~ at** être le/la meilleur/-e en [*subject*]; être le/la meilleur/-e à [*instrument, game, sport*]; **may the ~ man win!** que le meilleur gagne!; **3** (most suitable) [*tool, way, time, idea*] meilleur; **the ~ person for the job** la personne qui convient le mieux pour ce travail; **the ~ thing to do la meilleure chose à faire** ; **the ~ thing would be to do, it would be ~ to do** le mieux serait de faire.
III *adv* (*superlative of* **well**) le mieux; **to behave/fit ~** se comporter/aller le mieux; **the ~ organized person** la personne la mieux organisée; **the ~ loved woman** la femme la plus aimée; **to like sth ~** aimer qch le mieux or le plus; **~ of all** mieux que tout; **to do ~** réussir le mieux; **such advice is ~ ignored** il vaut mieux ignorer de tels conseils; **you know ~** c'est toi le meilleur juge.
IV *vtr* LITTER (in argument) avoir le dessus sur [*person*]; (in struggle) vaincre [*opponent*].

IDIOMS **it happens to the ~ of us** ça arrive à tout le monde.

best friend *n* meilleur/-e ami/-e *m/f*.

bestial /'bestɪəl, US 'bestʃəl/ *adj* LIT, FIG bestial.

bestiality /ˌbestɪˈælətɪ, US ˌbestʃɪˈ-/ *n* LIT, FIG bestialité *f*.

best man *n* témoin *m* (*de mariage*).

bestow /bɪˈstəʊ/ *vtr* SOUT GEN accorder (**on** à); conférer [*title*] (**on** à); octroyer [*gift*] (**on** à).

bestseller /ˌbestˈselə(r)/ *n* (book) bestseller *m*, livre *m* à succès; (writer) auteur *m* de bestsellers, auteur à succès.

best-selling /ˌbestˈselɪŋ/ *adj* [*product*] le/la plus vendu/-e; **the ~ novelist of 1992** le romancier qui s'est vendu le plus en 1992.

bet /bet/ I *n* **1** (gamble) pari *m*; **to place** ou **put** ou **lay a ~ on** parier ou faire un pari sur [*horse, dog*]; miser sur [*number, colour*]; **to make a ~ that** faire le pari que; **'place your ~s!'** (in roulette) 'faites vos jeux!'; **a good** ou **safe ~** FIG une valeur sûre; **2** (guess) **my ~ is that** moi je pense que; **3** (stake) GEN pari *m*; (in casino) mise *f*.
II *vtr* (*p prés etc* **-tt-**; *prét, pp* **bet** ou **~ted**) GEN parier (**on** sur); (in gambling) parier, miser; **I ~ you 100 dollars (that) I win** je te parie 100 dollars que je gagne; **~ you can/can't!** (between children) chiche!
III *vi* (*p prés etc* **-tt-**; *prét, pp* **bet** ou **~ted**) GEN parier (**on** sur) GEN parier; (in casino) miser; **to ~ on a horse/race** parier sur un cheval/dans une course; **to ~ on sth happening** parier que qch va se produire; **something will go wrong, you can ~ on it** il y a forcément quelque chose qui va aller de travers, tu peux en être sûr; **I wouldn't ~ on it!** je n'y compterais pas trop!; **you ~!** tu parles!, et comment!

beta /'biːtə, US 'beɪtə/ *n* béta *m*; **~blocker** bétabloquant *m*.

betray /bɪˈtreɪ/ *vtr* GEN trahir; tromper [*lover*]; manquer à [*promise*]; FIG révéler [*interest, nature*]; trahir [*curiosity, presence*].

betrayal /bɪˈtreɪəl/ *n* GEN trahison *f*; (of secret, plan) révélation *f*; **~ of trust** abus *m* de confiance.

betrothal‡ /bɪˈtrəʊðl/ *n* fiançailles *fpl* (**to** avec).

betrothed‡ /bɪˈtrəʊðd/ I *n* (*pl* **~**) fiancé/-e *m/f*.
II *adj* **to be ~** être fiancé.

better /'betə(r)/

■ **Note** When *better* is used as an adjective it is translated by *meilleur* or *mieux* depending on the context (see below, and note that *meilleur* is the comparative form of *bon*, *mieux* the comparative form of *bien*). The translation of the construction *to be better than* varies depending on whether *bon* or *bien* works originally with the noun collocate: *their wine is better than our wine* = leur vin est meilleur que le nôtre; *her new apartment is better than her old one* = son nouvel appartement est mieux que l'ancien; *his new film is better than his last one* = son nouveau film est mieux *or* meilleur que le précédent (both *bon* and *bien* work with the collocate in this last example). Other constructions may be translated as follows: *this is a better bag/car* = ce sac/cette voiture est mieux; *it is better to do* = il vaut mieux faire *or* il est mieux de faire.
– As an adverb, *better* can almost always be translated by *mieux*. For more examples and particular usages, see the entry below.

I *n* **1 the ~ of the two** le/la meilleur/-e *or* le/la mieux des deux; **2** (more desirable state of affairs) **to deserve/hope for ~** mériter/espérer mieux; **so much the ~, all the ~** tant mieux; **to change for the ~** s'améliorer; **3** (superior person) **one's ~s** ses supérieurs *mfpl*.
II *adj* (*comparative of* **good**) meilleur; **to get ~** GEN s'améliorer; [*ill person*] aller mieux; **the weather is no ~** le temps n'est pas meilleur ou ne s'est pas amélioré; **things are getting ~** ça va mieux; **to taste ~** être meilleur, avoir un meilleur goût; **she looks ~ in red** elle est mieux en rouge; **that's ~!** voilà qui est mieux!; **to be ~** [*patient, cold, headache*] aller

mieux; **to feel all the ~ for** se sentir mieux après [*rest, meal*]; **if it makes you feel any ~** (less worried) si ça peut te rassurer; (less sad) si ça peut te consoler; **to feel ~ about doing** (less nervous) se sentir à même de faire; (less worried, guilty) avoir moins de scrupules à faire; **they sent him to a ~ school** ils l'ont mis dans une meilleure école; **I sold the car and bought a ~ one** j'ai vendu la voiture et j'en ai acheté une mieux; **to be no ~ than a thief** être un voleur ni plus ni moins; **to be a ~ swimmer than sb** nager mieux que qn; **to be ~ at** être meilleur en [*subject, sport*]; **he's no ~ at driving than she is** il ne conduit pas mieux qu'elle; **to be ~ than nothing** être mieux que rien; **the bigger/sooner the ~** le plus grand/vite possible; **the less said about that the ~** mieux vaut ne pas parler de ça; **who ~ to play the part?** qui mieux pourrait jouer le rôle?; **fish is ~ for you than meat** le poisson est meilleur pour la santé que la viande.
III *adv* (*comparative of* **well**) mieux; **to fit/behave ~ than** aller/se comporter mieux que; **~ made/organized than** mieux fait/organisé que; **to think ~ of sb** avoir une meilleure opinion de qn; **~ behaved/educated** plus sage/cultivé; **to do ~** (in career, life) réussir mieux; (in exam, essay) faire mieux; (in health) aller mieux; **the ~ to see/hear** pour mieux voir/entendre; **it couldn't have been ~ timed** ça n'aurait pas pu mieux tomber; **the money would be ~ spent on a holiday** il vaudrait mieux garder cet argent pour les vacances; **you had ~ do, you'd do** (advising) tu ferais mieux de faire; (warning) tu as intérêt à faire; **I'd ~ go** je ferais mieux de m'en aller; **'will she come?'—'she'd ~ ○!'** 'est-ce qu'elle viendra?'—'elle a intérêt!'; **~ still,...** ou mieux,...
IV *vtr* améliorer [*one's performance, achievement*]; faire mieux que [*rival's performance, achievement*].
IDIOMS **for ~ (or) for worse** GEN advienne que pourra; (in wedding vow) pour le meilleur et pour le pire; **to get the ~ of** [*person*] triompher de [*enemy, problem*]; **his curiosity got the ~ of him** sa curiosité a pris le dessus; **to go one ~** faire encore mieux (**than** que); **to think ~ of it** changer d'avis.

better off /ˌbetərˈɒf/ I *n* **the better-off** (+ *v pl*) les riches *mpl*.
II *adj* **1** (more wealthy) plus riche (**than** que); **our better-off neighbours** nos voisins plus riches; **2** (in better situation) mieux; **you'd be ~ in hospital** tu serais mieux à l'hôpital; **you're ~ without him** tu es mieux sans lui.

betting /'betɪŋ/ *n* (activity) paris *mpl*; (odds) côte *f*; **what's the ~ that...?** quelles sont les chances que...? (+ *subj*).

betting shop *n* GB bureau *m* de PMU.

between /bɪˈtwiːn/

■ **Note** When *between* is used as a preposition expressing physical location (*between the lines*), time (*between 8 am and 11 am*), position in a range (*between 30 and 40 kilometres*), relationship (*link between, difference between*) it is translated by *entre*. For particular usages, see the entry below.

I *prep* **1** (in time, space etc) entre; **the wall ~ the two gardens** le mur entre les deux jardins; **flights ~ London and Paris** les vols entre Londres et Paris; **~ the ages of 12 and 18** entre l'âge de 12 ans et l'âge de 18 ans ou entre 12 et 18 ans; **~ now and next year** d'ici à l'année prochaine; **it costs ~ £10 and £20** cela coûte entre dix et vingt livres sterling; **it's ~ 50 and 60 kilometres away** c'est à environ 50 ou 60 kilomètres d'ici; **nothing now stands ~ us and success** rien ne peut plus faire obstacle à notre réussite maintenant; **we mustn't allow this to come ~ us** il ne faut pas que cela crée des problèmes entre nous; **2** (together, in combination) **the couples have seven children ~ them** à eux tous, les couples ont sept enfants; **they drank the whole bottle ~ (the two of) them** ils ont bu toute la bouteille à eux deux; **~ them, they collected £200** en tout, ils ont réuni 200 livres sterling.
II *adv* (also **in ~**) (in space) au milieu, entre les deux;

(in time) dans l'intervalle, entre les deux; **the two main roads and the streets (in)** ~ les deux rues principales et les petites rues situées entre elles or et les petites rues au milieu.

IDIOMS ~ **ourselves**, ~ **you and me (and the gatepost)** entre nous.

betweentimes /bɪˈtwiːntaɪmz/, **betweenwhiles** /bɪˈtwiːnwaɪlz/ US -hwaɪlz/ adv entre-temps.

betwixt /bɪˈtwɪkst/ adv ~ **and between** entre les deux.

bevel /ˈbevl/ **I** n (edge) biseau m; (larger) surface f oblique; (tool) fausse équerre f.
II vtr tailler [qch] en biseau [mirror, edge].

beverage /ˈbevərɪdʒ/ n boisson f, breuvage m.

bevy /ˈbevɪ/ n (of quails) volée f; FIG (of people) troupeau m.

beware /bɪˈweə(r)/ **I** excl prenez garde!, attention!
II vi **1** se méfier (**of** de); **to** ~ **of doing** faire attention à ne pas faire, se garder de faire FML; **2** (on sign) '~ **of pickpockets'** 'attention aux pickpockets'; '~ **of the dog'** 'attention chien méchant'.

bewilder /bɪˈwɪldə(r)/ vtr déconcerter.

bewildered /bɪˈwɪldəd/ adj [person] déconcerté (**at, by** par); [look, curiosity] perplexe.

bewildering /bɪˈwɪldərɪŋ/ adj déconcertant.

bewilderment /bɪˈwɪldəmənt/ n stupéfaction f.

bewitch /bɪˈwɪtʃ/ vtr LIT, FIG ensorceler.

beyond /bɪˈjɒnd/

■ **Note** beyond is often used with a noun to produce expressions like beyond doubt, beyond a joke, beyond the bounds of etc. For translations of these and similar expressions where beyond means outside the range of, consult the appropriate noun entry (**doubt, joke, bound** etc). See also I 3 below.

I prep **1** (in space, time) au-delà de; ~ **the city walls** au-delà des murs de la ville; **just** ~ **the tower** juste après la tour; **well** ~ **midnight** bien au-delà de minuit; ~ **the age of 10** au-delà de l'âge de 10 ans; **to go** ~ **a deadline** dépasser un délai; **2** (outside the range of) ~ **one's means** au-dessus de ses moyens; ~ **all hope** au-delà de toute espérance; ~ **one's control** hors de son contrôle; **he is** ~ **help** on ne peut rien faire pour lui; **to be wise** ~ **one's years** être très mûr pour son âge; **to be** ~ **sb's ability** [task, activity] être au-dessus des capacités de qn; **to be** ~ **sb** [activity, task, subject] dépasser qn; **it's** ~ **me how she manages** je ne sais pas comment elle s'en sort—ça me dépasse; **3** (other than) en dehors de, à part; **we know little about it** ~ **the fact that** nous savons très peu de choses là-dessus en dehors du fait que or à part que.
II adv **1** (in space) **in the room** ~ dans la pièce d'après; ~ **there was a garden** plus loin il y avait un jardin; **as far as London and** ~ jusqu'à Londres et au-delà; **2** (in time) au-delà; **up to the year 2000 and** ~ jusqu'à l'an 2000 et au-delà.
III conj à part (+ infinitive); **there was little I could do** ~ **telling him that** je ne pouvais pas faire grand-chose à part lui dire que.
IDIOMS **to be in the back of** ~ être au bout du monde.

bezique /bɪˈziːk/ ▶ 949 ◀ n bésigue m.

B film, B movie n film m de série B.

BGC n: abrév ▶ **Bank Giro Credit**.

Bhutan /buːˈtɑːn/ ▶ 840 ◀ pr n Bhoutan m.

bias /ˈbaɪəs/ **I** n (pl **-es**) **1** (prejudice) parti m pris; **to display** ~ faire preuve de parti pris; **political** ~ parti pris politique; **2** (tendency) tendance f (**in favour of, towards** pour); **an American** ~ une tendance pro-américaine; **a female** ~ un préjugé favorable envers les femmes; **3** (in sewing) biais m.
II vtr (p prés etc **-s-** ou **-ss-**) influer sur [person, decision, result]; **to** ~ **sb against/in favour of** prévenir qn contre/en faveur de.

bias binding, bias tape US n (in sewing) (ruban m de) biais m.

biased, biassed /ˈbaɪəst/ adj [decision, opinion,

person] partial; [system, report] manquant d'objectivité (**after** n); **to be** ~ [person] avoir des partis pris; **to be** ~ **against/in favour of** avoir un préjugé défavorable/favorable envers.

bib /bɪb/ n **1** (baby's) bavoir m; **2** (of apron, dungarees) bavette f.

Bible /ˈbaɪbl/ n Bible f; **it's his** ~ FIG c'est sa bible.

Bible Belt n: région du sud des États-Unis caractérisée par son fondamentalisme.

biblical /ˈbɪblɪkl/ adj biblique.

bibliographic(al) /ˌbɪblɪəˈɡræfɪk(l)/ adj bibliographique.

bibliography /ˌbɪblɪˈɒɡrəfɪ/ n bibliographie f.

bicarbonate of soda n bicarbonate m de soude.

bicentenary /ˌbaɪsenˈtiːnərɪ, US -ˈsentənerɪ/, **bicentennial** /ˌbaɪsenˈtenɪəl/ **I** n bicentenaire m.
II noun modifier [celebration, year] du bicentenaire.

biceps /ˈbaɪseps/ n (pl ~) biceps m.

bicker /ˈbɪkə(r)/ vi se chamailler (**about** au sujet de).

bickering /ˈbɪkərɪŋ/ n ¢ chamailleries fpl.

bicycle /ˈbaɪsɪkl/ **I** n bicyclette f, vélo° m; **on a/by** ~ à bicyclette; **to ride a** ~ faire de la bicyclette.
II noun modifier [pump] à bicyclette; [bell, chain, lamp] de bicyclette; [hire, repair] de bicyclettes; [race] cycliste.
III vi aller à bicyclette.

bicycle: ~ **clip** n pince f à vélo; ~ **lane** n piste f cyclable; ~ **rack** n (in yard) parc m à bicyclettes; (on car) galerie f.

bid /bɪd/ **I** n **1** (at auction) enchère f (**for** sur; **of** de); **the opening** ~ la première enchère; **to raise one's** ~ **by £200** surenchérir de 200 livres sterling; **2** (for contract) soumission f (**for** pour; **of** de); (for company) offre f (**for** pour; **of** de); **3** (attempt) tentative f (**to do** pour faire); **escape/suicide** ~ tentative f d'évasion/de suicide; **to make a** ~ **for power** tenter d'accéder au pouvoir; **4** (in bridge) (first) annonce f; (subsequent) enchère f; **it's your** ~ c'est à toi de déclarer.
II vtr (p prés **-dd-**; prét **bade** ou **bid**; pp **bidden** ou **bid**) **1** COMM, FIN offrir [money] (**for** pour); **what am I bid for this painting?** à combien est-ce que j'estime ce tableau?; **2** (say) ~ **sb good morning** dire bonjour à qn; **to** ~ **sb farewell** faire ses adieux à qn; **to** ~ **sb welcome** souhaiter la bienvenue à qn; **3** (in bridge) annoncer.
III vi (p prés **-dd-**; prét **bade** ou **bid**; pp **bidden** ou **bid**) **1** COMM, FIN (at auction) mettre une enchère, enchérir (**for** sur); (for contract) soumissionner (**for** pour); (for company) faire une offre (**for** pour); **to** ~ **against sb** (at auction) renchérir sur qn; **2** (in bridge) faire une annonce, parler.

bidden /ˈbɪdn/ pp ▶ **bid**.

bidder /ˈbɪdə(r)/ n **1** (at auction) enchérisseur/-euse m/f (**for** pour); **to go to the highest** ~ être adjugé au plus offrant; **successful** ~ adjudicataire mf; **2** COMM (for contract) soumissionnaire m (**for** pour).

bidding /ˈbɪdɪŋ/ n **1** ¢ (at auction) enchères fpl; **the** ~ **closed at £50,000** l'adjudication s'est faite à 50 000 livres sterling; **2** (command) **he did my** ~ il a fait ce que je lui ai dit; **3** ¢ (in bridge) annonces fpl.

bide‡ /baɪd/ vi: IDIOMS **to** ~ **one's time** attendre le bon moment.

bidet /ˈbiːdeɪ, US biːˈdeɪ/ n bidet m.

biennial /baɪˈenɪəl/ adj [plant] bisannuel/-elle; [event] biennal.

bier /bɪə(r)/ n (coffin) bière f; (stand) catafalque m.

bifocals /baɪˈfəʊklz/ npl verres mpl à double foyer.

big /bɪɡ/ adj **1** (tall) grand (before n); (strong) grand et fort, costaud°; EUPH (heavy) fort; **to get** ~(**ger**) (taller) grandir; (fatter) grossir; (in pregnancy) s'arrondir; **2** (in size) [bed, room, building, garden, lake, town] grand (before n); [animal, car, boat, parcel, box] gros/grosse (before n), grand (before n); **a** ~ **book** (thick) un gros livre; (large-format) un grand livre; **to have** ~ **hands** avoir de grandes mains; **3** (in age) grand (before n); **his** ~ **brother** son grand frère, son frère aîné; **4** (in extent) [family, crowd, class, party] grand (before n);

[*collection, organization, company*] gros/grosse (*before n*), grand (*before n*); [*meal*] copieux/-ieuse; **to be a ~ eater** être un gros mangeur; **5** (important) [*question, problem, decision, change, moment, event*] grand (*before n*); **it makes a ~ difference** ça fait une grande différence; **a ~ mistake** une grave erreur; **I think we're on to something ~**○ je sens qu'on est sur un gros coup○; **6** (emphatic) **you ~ baby!** espèce de bébé!; **~ bully!** espèce de grande brute!; **to be ~ in the music business**○ être très connu dans le monde de la musique; **to be in ~ trouble** être dans le pétrin○; **he gave me a ~ smile** il m'a fait un grand sourire; **the ~ moment** le grand moment; **he fell for her in a ~ way** il est tombé follement amoureux d'elle; **7**○ US (enthusiastic) **to be ~ on** être fanatique or fana○ de [*activity*]; **8** (generous) [*person*] généreux/-euse; **to have a ~ heart** être très généreux; **9** GEN, POL **the Big Four/Five** les Quatre/Cinq Grands.
IDIOMS **to be** OU **go over ~**○ faire fureur, faire un tabac○ (**in** à, en); **to have a ~ head** PÉJ avoir la grosse tête○; **to have a ~ mouth** avoir la langue trop longue○; **why can't you keep your ~ mouth shut**○? tu n'aurais pas pu la fermer○?; **to have ~ ideas, think ~**○ voir grand○; **what's the ~ idea?** qu'est-ce qui te prend?; **to make it ~**○ avoir beaucoup de succès.

bigamist /ˈbɪɡəmɪst/ *n* bigame *mf*.

bigamous /ˈbɪɡəməs/ *adj* [*person, marriage*] bigame.

bigamy /ˈbɪɡəmɪ/ *n* bigamie *f*.

big bang *n* (in astronomy) big bang *m*.

big business *n* **1** ¢ les grandes entreprises *fpl*; **2 to be ~** rapporter gros.

big: ~ cat *n* grand félin *m*; **~ dipper** *n* GB (at fair) montagnes *fpl* russes; **Big Dipper** *n* US (stars) Grande Ourse *f*, Grand Chariot *m*.

big fish○ *n*: IDIOMS **to be a ~ in a small pond** GB OU **sea** US briller dans un petit groupe.

big: ~ game *n* gros gibier *m*; **~ game hunting** chasse *f* au gros gibier; **~head** *n* PÉJ crâneur/-euse○ *m/f*; **~headed** *adj* PÉJ crâneur/-euse, prétentieux/-ieuse; **~-hearted** *adj* généreux/-euse.

bigmouth○ /ˈbɪɡmaʊθ/ *n* PÉJ **1** (indiscreet person) **he's such a ~**○! il a la langue trop longue!; **2** (loudmouth) grande gueule○ *f* PÉJ.

big name *n* (in music, art) grand nom *m*; (in film, sport) star *f*; **to be a ~** être connu (**in** dans le monde de).

big noise○ *n* gros bonnet○ *m*, huile○ *f* PÉJ.

bigot /ˈbɪɡət/ *n* **he's a ~** il est sectaire or intolérant.

bigoted /ˈbɪɡətɪd/ *adj* intolérant, sectaire.

bigotry /ˈbɪɡətrɪ/ *n* intolérance *f*, sectarisme *m*.

big: ~ screen *n* grand écran *m*; **~ shot**○ *n* gros bonnet○ *m*; **Big Smoke**○ *n* GB HUM Londres.

big time○ /ˈbɪɡtaɪm/ **I** *n* **to make** OU **hit the ~**○ percer, réussir.
II big-time *noun modifier* [*crook*] de grande envergure; **~ gambler** flambeur○ *m*.

big: ~ toe *n* gros orteil *m*; **~ top** *n* (tent) grand chapiteau *m*, FIG (circus) cirque *m*; **~wig** *n* PÉJ grosse légume○ *f*, huile○ *f* PÉJ.

bike /baɪk/ *n* (cycle) vélo *m*; (motorbike) moto *f*; **to ride a ~** (cycle) faire du vélo.

biker○ /ˈbaɪkə(r)/ *n* motard○ *m*; **~('s) jacket** veste *f* de moto.

bikini /bɪˈkiːnɪ/ *n* bikini® *m*.

bilateral /ˌbaɪˈlætərəl/ *adj* bilatéral.

bilberry /ˈbɪlbrɪ, US -berɪ/ *n* (fruit, bush) myrtille *f*.

bile /baɪl/ *n* LIT bile *f*; FIG fiel *m*.

bilge /bɪldʒ/ *n* **1** NAUT bouchain *m*; **2** (nonsense)○† inepties *fpl*.

bilingual /ˌbaɪˈlɪŋɡwəl/ *adj* bilingue.

bilingualism /ˌbaɪˈlɪŋɡwəlɪzəm/ *n* bilinguisme *m*.

bilious /ˈbɪlɪəs/ *adj* MED bilieux; FIG [*colour*] repoussant; **~ attack** crise *f* de foie.

bill /bɪl/ **I** *n* **1** COMM (in restaurant) addition *f*; (for main-

tenance, electricity etc) facture *f*; (from hotel, doctor, dentist) note *f*; **gas/telephone ~** facture *f* de gaz/de téléphone; **a ~ for £10** une note or facture de 10 livres; **2** JUR, POL (law) (also **Bill**) projet *m* de loi; **3** (poster) affiche *f*; **to top the ~** THEAT être en tête d'affiche; **'stick no ~s'** 'défense d'afficher'; **4** US (banknote) billet *m* (de banque); **5** ZOOL (beak) bec *m*.
II *vtr* **1** GEN, COMM faire une facture à [*person, company*]; **to ~ sb for sth** facturer qch à qn; **2** GEN, THEAT (advertise) **to be ~ed as…** [*event, meeting*] être annoncé comme étant…; **he is ~ed to appear as Othello** il est à l'affiche dans le rôle d'Othello.
IDIOMS **to fit the ~** OU **fill the ~** faire l'affaire; **to give sb/ sth a clean ~ of health** LIT trouver qn/qch en parfait état de santé; FIG blanchir qn/qch.

billboard /ˈbɪlbɔːd/ *n* panneau *m* d'affichage.

billet /ˈbɪlɪt/ **I** *n* MIL cantonnement *m*.
II *vtr* cantonner [*soldier, refugee*] (**on, with** chez).

bill: ~fold *n* US portefeuille *m*; **~ hook** *n* serpe *f*.

billiard /ˈbɪlɪəd/ ▶ 949 **I billiards** *n* (+ *v sg*) billard *m*.
II *noun modifier* [*ball, cue, table*] de billard.

billing /ˈbɪlɪŋ/ *n* **1 to get top ~** THEAT tenir le haut de l'affiche; **2** COMM facturation *f*.

billion /ˈbɪljən/ ▶ 1112 **I** *n* (a thousand million) milliard *m*; GB (a million million) billion *m*; **~s of**○ des tonnes○ *fpl* (**of** de).
II *adj* **a ~ people** un milliard de personnes.

billionaire /ˌbɪljəˈneə(r)/ *n* milliardaire *mf*.

bill: ~ of exchange, BE *n* COMM, FIN lettre *f* de change; **~ of fare** *n* menu *m*; **~ of rights** *n* GEN, POL déclaration *f* des droits (d'un peuple); **~ of sale** *n* acte *m* de vente.

billow /ˈbɪləʊ/ **I** *n* (of smoke, steam) tourbillons *mpl*.
II *vi* [*clouds, smoke*] s'élever en tourbillons.
■ **billow out** [*skirt, sail*] se gonfler; [*steam*] s'élever.

billposter /ˈbɪlpəʊstə(r)/, **billsticker** /ˈbɪlstɪkə(r)/ ▶ 1251 *n* colleur *m* d'affiches.

billy /ˈbɪlɪ/ *n* **1** AUSTRAL, GB (also **~can**) gamelle *f*; **2** US (truncheon) matraque *f*.

billy goat *n* bouc *m*.

bimbo○ /ˈbɪmbəʊ/ *n* PÉJ ravissante idiote *f*.

bin /bɪn/ *n* **1** GB (for rubbish) poubelle *f*; **2** (for storage) casier *m*; (for wine) casier *m* (à bouteilles).

binary /ˈbaɪnərɪ/ *adj* (all contexts) binaire.

bind /baɪnd/ **I**○ *n* corvée *f*; **what a ~!** quelle corvée!
II *vtr* (*prét, pp* **bound**) **1** (tie up) attacher [*person, hands, feet*] (**to** à); panser [*wound*]; **2 to ~ sb to do** [*law, oath*] imposer à qn de faire; **to be bound by** être tenu par [*law, oath*]; **3** (unite) (also **~ together**) unir [*people, community*]; **4** (in sewing) poser un biais sur; **5** (in bookbinding) relier [*book*]; **6** CULIN lier (**with** avec).
III *vi* (*prét, pp* **bound**) [*mixture*] lier.
IDIOMS **to be in a ~**○ être dans le pétrin○.
■ **bind over: ~** [*sb*] **over** JUR relâcher [qn] sous condition.
■ **bind up: ~ up** [*sth*], **~** [*sth*] **up** bander [*wound*]; attacher [*bundle*].

binder /ˈbaɪndə(r)/ *n* **1** (for papers) classeur *m*; **2** AGRIC lieuse *f*; **3** CONSTR, IND (for cement, paint) liant *m*.

binding /ˈbaɪndɪŋ/ **I** *n* **1** (of book) reliure *f*; **2** (in sewing) (bias) biais *m*; (for hem, seam) extrafort *m*.
II *adj* [*agreement, contract, rule*] qui lie, qui engage.

bindweed /ˈbaɪndwiːd/ *n* liseron *m*.

binge○ /bɪndʒ/ *n* (drinking) beuverie *f*; (festive eating) gueuleton○ *m*; **to go on a ~** aller faire la noce.

bingo /ˈbɪŋɡəʊ/ ▶ 949 **I** *n* bingo *m*.
II *noun modifier* [*card, game, hall*] de bingo.

bin liner *n* GB sac *m* poubelle.

binoculars /bɪˈnɒkjʊləz/ *npl* jumelles *fpl*.

biochemist /ˌbaɪəʊˈkemɪst/ ▶ 1251 *n* biochimiste *mf*.

biochemistry /ˌbaɪəʊˈkemɪstrɪ/ *n* biochimie *f*.

biodegradable /ˌbaɪəʊdɪˈɡreɪdəbl/ *adj* biodégradable.

biodiversity /ˌbaɪəʊdɪˈvɜːsətɪ/ *n* diversité *f* biologique.

bioengineering /ˌbaɪəʊˌendʒɪˈnɪərɪŋ/ *n* génie *m* biologique.

biographer /baɪˈɒɡrəfə(r)/ ▶ **1251** *n* biographe *mf*.

biographical /ˌbaɪəˈɡræfɪkl/ *adj* biographique.

biography /baɪˈɒɡrəfɪ/ *n* biographie *f*.

biological /ˌbaɪəˈlɒdʒɪkl/ *adj* biologique.

biological clock *n* horloge *f* biologique.

biologically /ˌbaɪəˈlɒdʒɪklɪ/ *adv* biologiquement.

biological: **~ powder** *n* lessive *f* avec enzyme; **~ shield** *n* bouclier *m* biologique; **~ warfare** *n* guerre *f* biologique.

biologist /baɪˈɒlədʒɪst/ ▶ **1251** *n* biologiste *mf*.

biology /baɪˈɒlədʒɪ/ *n* biologie *f*.

bionic /baɪˈɒnɪk/ *adj* bionique.

biopic○ /ˈbaɪəʊpɪk/ *n* CIN biographie *f* romancée.

biopsy /ˈbaɪɒpsɪ/ *n* biopsie *f*.

biorhythm /ˈbaɪəʊrɪðəm/ *n* biorythme *m*.

bipartisan /ˌbaɪpɑːtɪˈzæn, baɪˈpɑːtɪzn/ *adj* POL bipartisan.

bipartite /baɪˈpɑːtaɪt/ *adj* bipartite.

birch /bɜːtʃ/ I *n* **1** (tree, wood) bouleau *m*; **2** (also **~ rod**) HIST fouet *m*.
II *vtr* HIST fouetter [*offender*].

bird /bɜːd/ *n* **1** ZOOL oiseau *m*; **2**○ GB (girl) nana○ *f*.
IDIOMS **a little ~ told me**○ mon petit doigt m'a dit; **to tell sb about the ~s and the bees** expliquer à qn comment naissent les enfants; **to kill two ~s with one stone** faire d'une pierre deux coups.

bird: **~-brain**○ *n* cervelle *f* d'oiseau○; **~ call** *n* cri *m* d'oiseau.

birdie /ˈbɜːdɪ/ *n* (in golf) birdie *m*.

bird: **~like** *adj* semblable à un oiseau; **~ of paradise** *n* oiseau *m* de paradis; **~ of prey** *n* oiseau *m* de proie; **~ sanctuary** *n* réserve *f* ornithologique; **~seed** *n* ₵ graines *fpl* (pour les oiseaux); **~'s eye view** *n* vue *f* d'ensemble; **~'s nest** *n* nid *m* d'oiseau; **~'s nest soup** *n* soupe *f* aux nids d'hirondelle; **~song** *n* chant *m* des oiseaux; **~table** *n* perchoir *m*; **~watcher** *n* ornithologue *mf* amateur.

bird-watching /ˈbɜːdwɒtʃɪŋ/ *n* **to go ~** observer les oiseaux.

biro® /ˈbaɪərəʊ/ *n* GB (*pl* **~s**) stylo-bille *m*, bic® *m*.

birth /bɜːθ/ *n* GEN, LIT, FIG naissance *f* (**of** de); MED (process of giving birth) accouchement *m*; **to give ~ to** [*woman*] accoucher de; [*animal*] mettre bas; **from ~ he had lived in Paris** depuis sa naissance il vivait à Paris; **blind from ~** aveugle de naissance; **of high ~** de haute naissance; **of low ~** d'origine modeste; **of French ~** né/née français/-e.

birth: **~ certificate** *n* certificat *m* de naissance; **~ control** *n* (in society) contrôle *m* des naissances; (by couple) contraception *f*.

birthday /ˈbɜːθdeɪ/ I *n* anniversaire *m*; **to wish sb (a) happy ~** souhaiter à qn un bon or joyeux anniversaire.
II *noun modifier* [*cake, card, greetings, guest, present*] d'anniversaire.
IDIOMS **in one's ~ suit**○ HUM, EUPH en costume d'Adam or d'Ève○.

birthday party *n* (for child) goûter d'anniversaire; (for adult) soirée *f* d'anniversaire.

birth: **~ing pool** *n* MED piscine *f* d'accouchement; **~ing stool** *n* MED chaise *f* d'accouchement; **~mark** *n* tache *f* de naissance; **~place** *n* LIT lieu *m* de naissance; FIG berceau *m* (**of** de); **~rate** *n* taux *m* de natalité; **~right** *n* GEN droit *m* (acquis à la naissance); (of first-born) droit *m* d'aînesse; **~s column** *n* (in newspaper) rubrique *f* des naissances; **~ sign** *n* signe *m* du zodiaque; **~s, marriages, and deaths** *npl* (in newspaper) carnet *m* du jour; **~stone** *n* pierre *f* porte-bonheur.

biscuit /ˈbɪskɪt/ I *n* **1** GB biscuit *m*, petit gâteau *m*; **2** US pain *m* au lait.

II ▶ **818** *adj* (also **~-coloured**) de couleur bise *inv*.
IDIOMS **that takes the ~**○! ça, c'est le pompon!

biscuit barrel, **biscuit tin** *n* boîte *f* à biscuits.

bisect /baɪˈsekt/ *vtr* diviser [qch] en deux parties égales.

bisexual /baɪˈseksʃʊəl/ *n, adj* **1** [*person*] bisexuel/-elle (*m/f*); **2** BOT, ZOOL bisexué.

bishop /ˈbɪʃəp/ *n* **1** RELIG évêque *m*; **2** (in chess) fou *m*.

bistro /ˈbiːstrəʊ/ *n* ~ bistrot *m*.

bit /bɪt/ I *prét* ▶ **bite**.
II *n* **1** (of food, substance, wood) morceau *m* (**of** de); (of paper, string, garden, land) bout *m* (**of** de); **every ~ of dirt** la moindre petite saleté; **to take sth to ~s** démonter qch; **2**○ (small amount) **a ~** un peu; **would you like a ~ more?** tu en veux encore?; **a ~ of** un peu de [*time, money etc*]; **a ~ of difficulty/information** quelques difficultés/informations; **a ~ of advice** un petit conseil; **with a ~ of luck** avec un peu de chance; **to do a ~ of shopping** faire quelques courses; **it won't do a ~ of good** ça ne servira à rien; **wait a ~**! attends un peu!; **after a ~** un peu après; **quite a ~ of**, **a good ~ of** pas mal de [*time, money etc*]; **quite a ~ ou a good ~ bigger** bien plus grand; **3**○ (section) passage *m*; **listen, this ~ is brilliant!** écoute, ce passage est génial○!; **the ~ where Hamlet dies** le moment où Hamlet meurt; **4†** (coin) pièce *f*; **5** (for horse) mors *m*; **6** COMPUT bit *m*; **7** TECH (also **drill ~**) mèche *f*.
III○ **a bit** *adv phr* (rather) un peu; **a ~ deaf/cold** un peu sourd/froid; **a ~ early** un peu trop tôt; **it's asking a ~ much** c'est un peu trop demander; **she isn't a ~ like me** elle ne me ressemble pas du tout; **it's a ~ of a surprise** c'est un peu surprenant; **he's a ~ of a brute** il a un côté brute; **a ~ of a problem** un petit problème.
IDIOMS **~ by ~** petit à petit; **~s and bobs**○ affaires *fpl*; **~s and pieces** (fragments) morceaux *mpl*; (belongings) affaires *fpl*; **every ~ as good/clever** tout aussi bon/intelligent; **not a ~ of it**○! pas du tout!; **to do one's ~** faire sa part (de boulot○); **to take the ~ between one's teeth** prendre le mors aux dents.

bitch /bɪtʃ/ I *n* **1** (dog) chienne *f*; **2**♠ PEJ (woman) garce♠ *f*, salope♠ *f*; **life's a ~**○ FIG la vie n'est pas un cadeau○.
II○ *vi* **1** (gossip spitefully) dire du mal (**about** de); **2** US (complain) pester○ (**about** contre).

bitchy○ /ˈbɪtʃɪ/ *adj* [*person, comment*] malveillant.

bite /baɪt/ I *n* **1** (mouthful) bouchée *f*; **in one ~** en une bouchée; **to have ou take a ~ of sth** prendre une bouchée de qch; **2** (from insect) piqûre *f*; (from dog, snake) morsure *f*; FIG (of wind, cold) morsure *f*; (of performance, film) mordant *m*; **3** (in fishing) touche *f*; **to have a ~** LIT avoir une touche; FIG trouver amateur.
II *vtr* (*prét* **bit**; *pp* **bitten**) [*person, animal*] mordre; [*insect*] piquer; **to ~ one's nails** se ronger les ongles.
III *vi* (*prét* **bit**; *pp* **bitten**) mordre.
IDIOMS **he won't ~ you**○! il ne va pas te manger○!; **to ~ one's lip** se mordre les lèvres; **to ~ the hand that feeds you** cracher dans la soupe; **to be bitten by the DIY bug**○ attraper le virus du bricolage.
■ **bite into**: **~ into** [sth] LIT mordre dans [*fruit, sandwich etc*]; FIG avoir un effet sur [*finances*].
■ **bite off**: **~ off** [sth], **~** [sth] **off** arracher [qch] d'un coup de dent.
■ **bite through**: **~ through** [sth] percer [qch] avec ses dents.

biting /ˈbaɪtɪŋ/ *adj* [*wind*] cinglant; [*cold*] pénétrant; FIG [*comment, irony*] mordant.

bit part *n* THEAT petit rôle *m*.

bitten /ˈbɪtn/ *pp* ▶ **bite**.
IDIOMS **once ~ twice shy** PROV chat échaudé craint l'eau froide PROV.

bitter /ˈbɪtə(r)/ I *n* GB (beer) bière *f* (*légèrement amère*).
II *adj* **1** (sour) amer/-ère; **2** (resentful) [*person, memory, comment*] amer/-ère; **she felt ~ about the way they**

had treated her la façon dont ils l'avaient traitée la remplissait d'amertume; **3** (fierce) [*critic*] acerbe; [*hatred*] profond; [*attack, battle*] féroce; [*argument, feud*] violent; **they are ~ enemies** ce sont des ennemis jurés; **4** [*weather, wind*] glacial; **5** (severe) [*disappointment, truth*] cruel/-elle; [*blow*] dur. IDIOMS **it's a ~ pill to swallow** la pilule est dure à avaler; **to the ~ end** jusqu'au bout.

bitter: **~ almond** *n* amande *f* amère; **~ aloes** *n* aloès *m* médicinal; **~ lemon** *n* Schweppes® *m* (citron).

bitterly /ˈbɪtəlɪ/ *adv* [*complain, laugh, speak*] amèrement; [*disappointed*] cruellement; [*regret*] profondément; [*fight*] farouchement; [*weep*] amèrement.

bitterness /ˈbɪtənɪs/ *n* LIT, FIG amertume *f*.

bitter: **~ orange** *n* BOT, CULIN bigarade *f*; **~sweet** *adj* LIT aigre-doux/aigre-douce; FIG doux-amer/douce-amère.

bitty /ˈbɪtɪ/ *adj* [*account*] fragmentaire.

bitumen /ˈbɪtjʊmɪn, US bəˈtuːmən/ *n* bitume *m*.

bivouac /ˈbɪvʊæk/ **I** *n* bivouac *m*.
II *vi* bivouaquer.

bizarre /bɪˈzɑː(r)/ *adj* bizarre.

blab○ /blæb/ (*p prés etc* **-bb-**) **I** *vtr* (also **~ out**) aller raconter.
II *vi* **1** (reveal secret) vendre la mèche○; **2** US (talk idly) jacasser.

black /blæk/ ▶818 **I** *n* **1** (colour) noir *m*; **2** (also **Black**) (person) noir/-e *m/f*; **3** FIN **to be in the ~** être créditeur/-trice; **4** (in chess, draughts) noirs *mpl*; (in roulette) noir *m*; (snooker or pool ball) (bille *f*) noire *f*.
II *adj* **1** GEN noir; [*night*] obscur; **to paint sth ~** peindre qch en noir; **to turn ~** noircir; **2** (also **Black**) [*skin, community, culture*] noir; [*school*] pour les Noirs; **3** [*coffee*] noir; [*tea*] nature; **4** (dirty) [*face, mark, towel*] noir; **5** [*comedy, humour*] noir; **6** (gloomy) [*mood, picture, thoughts*] noir; [*despair*] profond; [*future*] sombre; [*day*] mauvais, **7** (angry) [*look*] meurtrier/-ière; [*mood*] massacrant; **8** (evil) [*deed, magic*] noir.
III *vtr* **1** (put black onto) noircir [*sb's face, hands*]; cirer [*boots*]; **2** GB (boycott) boycotter.
■ **black out**: ¶ **~ out** [*person*] s'évanouir; ¶ **~** [*sth*] **out**, **~ out** [*sth*] **1** (darken) faire le black-out dans [*house*]; faire l'obscurité sur [*stage*]; **2** (cut power) couper le courant dans [*area*].

black: **Black Africa** *pr n* GEOG Afrique *f* noire; **~ American** *n* noir/-e *m/f* américain/-e.

black and white ▶818 **I** *n* CIN, PHOT noir et blanc *m*.
II *adj* [*TV, camera film*] noir et blanc (*inv*); [*movie, photography*] (en) noir et blanc (*inv*); FIG [*matter, situation*] nettement défini.
IDIOMS **he sees everything in ~** pour lui c'est tout noir ou tout blanc.

black: **~ arts** *npl* sciences *fpl* occultes; **~ball** *vtr* blackbouler (**from** de).

black belt *n* ceinture *f* noire (**in** de).

blackberry /ˈblækbrɪ, -berɪ/ **I** *n* mûre *f*.
II *noun modifier* [*pie*] aux mûres; [*jam*] de mûres.

blackberry bush *n* BOT ronce *f*.

blackbird /ˈblækbɜːd/ *n* merle *m*.

blackboard /ˈblækbɔːd/ *n* tableau *m* (noir); **on the ~** au tableau.

black: **~ box** *n* AVIAT, COMPUT boîte *f* noire; **~bread** *n* pain *m* noir, pumpernickel *m*.

blackcurrant /ˌblækˈkʌrənt/ BOT, CULIN **I** *n* cassis *m*.
II *noun modifier* [*tart*] aux cassis; [*jam*] de cassis.

Black Death *n* peste *f* noire.

blacken /ˈblækən/ *vtr* [*actor*] se barbouiller [*qch*] de noir [*face*]; [*smoke*] noircir [*brick, wood*]; [*frost*] brûler [*plant*]; [*dirt*] salir [*towel*]; FIG ternir [*reputation, name*].

black eye /ˌblækˈaɪ/ *n* œil *m* poché, œil *m* au beurre noir○; **to give sb a ~** pocher l'œil à qn.

black: **Black Forest gateau** GB, **Black Forest**

cake US *n* CULIN Forêt-Noire *f*; **~ gold**○ *n* or *m* noir○, pétrole *m*; **~guard** *n* ‡ OU HUM canaille *f*; **~head** *n* MED point *m* noir; **~-headed gull** *n* mouette *f* rieuse; **~ ice** *n* verglas *m*.

blacking /ˈblækɪŋ/ *n* **1** GB (boycotting) boycottage *m* (**of** de); **2**† (polish) cirage *m* noir.

blackish /ˈblækɪʃ/ ▶818 *adj* tirant sur le noir, noirâtre PEJ.

blackjack /ˈblækdʒæk/ ▶949 *n* GAMES black jack *m*.

blacklist /ˈblæklɪst/ **I** *n* liste *f* noire.
II *vtr* mettre [qn] à l'index.

blackmail /ˈblækmeɪl/ **I** *n* chantage *m*.
II *vtr* faire chanter; **to ~ sb into doing** LIT faire chanter qn pour qu'il/elle fasse; FIG, HUM soudoyer qn pour qu'il/elle fasse.

black: **~mailer** *n* maître-chanteur *m*; **~ mark** *n* FIG mauvais point *m*.

black market *n* **on the ~** au marché noir.

black: **~ marketeer** *n* personne *f* qui vend au marché noir; **~ mass** *n* messe *f* noire.

blackness /ˈblæknɪs/ *n* (darkness) obscurité *f*; (dark colour) (of hair, ink) noir *m*; FIG (gloominess) caractère *m* sombre; (evilness) (of heart, thoughts) noirceur *f*.

blackout /ˈblækaʊt/ *n* **1** (power cut) panne *f* de courant; (in wartime) black-out *m*; **2** RADIO, TV interruption *f* des émissions; (in newspapers) black-out *m*; **3** (faint) étourdissement *m*; (loss of memory) trou *m* de mémoire.

black: **~ pepper** *n* poivre *m* noir; **~ pudding** *n* GB CULIN boudin *m* noir; **Black Sea** *pr n* GEOG mer *f* Noire; **~ sheep** *n* FIG brebis *f* galeuse; **Blackshirt** *n* HIST Chemise *f* noire; **~smith** ▶1251 *n* forgeron *m*.

blackspot /ˈblækspɒt/ *n* FIG point *m* noir.

black: **~ swan** *n* ZOOL cygne *m* noir; **~thorn** *n* prunellier *m*.

black tie *n* (on invitation) '~' 'tenue *f* de soirée'.

black widow (spider) *n* ZOOL veuve *f* noire.

bladder /ˈblædə(r)/ *n* ANAT vessie *f*; BOT vésicule *f*.

blade /bleɪd/ *n* **1** (of knife, sword, axe) lame *f*; (of fan, propeller, oar) pale *f*; (of turbine) aube *f*; (of windscreen wiper) balai *m*; **2** BOT (of grass) brin *m*; **3** LING (of tongue) plat *m*.

blame /bleɪm/ **I** *n* **1** (responsibility) responsabilité *f* (**for** de); **to take** OU **bear the ~** prendre ou assumer la responsabilité; **to put** OU **lay the ~ for sth on sb** attribuer la responsabilité de qch à qn; **why do I always get the ~?** pourquoi est-ce toujours moi qu'on accuse?; **2** (criticism) reproches *mpl*.
II *vtr* en vouloir à [*person, group*]; accuser [*weather, recession, system*]; **she has always ~d me** elle m'en a toujours voulu; **to ~ sb for sth** reprocher qch à qn; **to ~ sth on sb** attribuer la responsabilité de qch à qn; **to be to ~ for sth** être responsable de qch.
III *v refl* **to ~ oneself for sth** se sentir responsable de qch; **you mustn't ~ yourself** tu n'as rien à te reprocher; **you've only yourself to ~** tu ne peux t'en prendre qu'à toi-même.

blameless /ˈbleɪmlɪs/ *adj* irréprochable.

blameworthy /ˈbleɪmwɜːðɪ/ *adj* [*person*] responsable; [*conduct*] répréhensible.

blanch /blɑːntʃ, US blæntʃ/ *vtr* (all contexts) blanchir.
II *vi* SOUT [*person*] blêmir.

blancmange /bləˈmɒnʒ/ *n* blanc-manger *m*.

bland /blænd/ *adj* [*food, flavour*] fade; [*person*] terne; [*account*] insipide.

blandly /ˈblændlɪ/ *adv* platement.

blank /blæŋk/ **I** *n* **1** (empty space) blanc *m*; **to fill in the ~s** remplir les blancs; **my mind's a ~** j'ai la tête vide; **2** US (clean form) fiche *f* vierge; **3** (dummy bullet) balle *f* à blanc; **4** IND pièce *f* brute.
II *adj* **1** (without writing, pictures) [*paper, page*] blanc/blanche; [*screen*] vide; [*form, canvas*] vierge; **2** (unused) [*cassette, disk*] vierge; **3** (expressionless) **a ~ look** un air absent; **a row of ~ faces** des visages à l'air absent; **4** (uncomprehending) [*look, expression*]

ébahi; **to look ~** avoir l'air ébahi; **5** (without memory) **my mind went ~** j'ai eu un trou de mémoire; **6** (absolute) [*refusal, rejection*] catégorique.
IDIOMS **to draw a ~** faire chou blanc.
■ **blank out**: ¶ **~ out** [*person*] avoir un trou de mémoire; ¶ **~ [sth] out**, **~ out [sth]** rayer [qch] de sa mémoire.

blank cheque GB, **blank check** US *n* **1** FIN chèque *m* en blanc; **2** FIG carte *f* blanche.

blanket /'blæŋkɪt/ I *n* **1** (bedcover) couverture *f*; **electric ~** couverture chauffante; **2** (layer) (of snow, ash) couche *f*; (of cloud, fog) nappe *f*; (of smoke) nuage *m*; (of flowers, weeds) tapis *m*.
II *noun modifier* (global) [*ban, policy*] global; [*use*] excessif/-ive.
IDIOMS **to be a wet ~** être un/-e rabat-joie.

blanket: **~ box**, **~ chest** *n* GB coffre *m* à linge; **~ cover** *n* FIG couverture *f* globale; **~ coverage** *n* reportage *m* intégral; **~ stitch** *n* point *m* de feston.

blankly /'blæŋklɪ/ *adv* **1** (uncomprehendingly) d'un air ébahi; **2** (without expression) d'un air absent.

blank verse *n* vers *mpl* blancs or non rimés.

blare /bleə(r)/ *n* beuglement *m*.
■ **blare out**: ¶ **~ out** [*music, radio*] jouer à plein volume; ¶ **~ out [sth]** déverser [*music*].

blarney° /'blɑːnɪ/ *n* baratin° *m*.

blaspheme /blæs'fiːm/ *vtr, vi* blasphémer.

blasphemous /'blæsfəməs/ *adj* [*person*] blasphémateur/-trice; [*statement*] blasphématoire.

blasphemy /'blæsfəmɪ/ *n* blasphème *m*.

blast /blɑːst, US blæst/ I *n* **1** (explosion) explosion *f*; **2** (gust) rafale *f*; **3** (air current from explosion) souffle *m* (**from** de); **4** (noise) (on trumpet) sonnerie *f*; (on whistle, car horn) coup *m*; **to give a ~ on** faire sonner [*trumpet*]; donner un coup de [*whistle, carhorn*]; **he plays his records at full ~** il écoute ses disques à plein volume.
II° *excl* zut°!
III *vtr* **1** (blow up) faire sauter [*building*]; dynamiter [*rockface*]; **to ~ a hole in a wall** percer un mur à l'explosif; **2** (damage) [*wind*] endommager [*tree*]; [*frost, disease*] détruire [*crop*]; **3**° (criticize) descendre [qn/qch] en flammes°.
IV *vi* **1** (in mining) utiliser des explosifs; **to ~ through sth** faire sauter qch à l'explosif; **2** (make a noise) [*trumpets*] retentir.
■ **blast away**: **~ away** mitrailler; **to ~ away at** mitrailler [*target*].
■ **blast off** [*rocket*] décoller.
■ **blast out**: ¶ **~ out** [*music*] retentir; ¶ **~ [sth] out**, **~ out [sth]** [*radio*] cracher° [*music*].

blasted /'blɑːstɪd, US 'blæst-/ *adj* **1** (withered) flétri; **2**° (for emphasis) fichu; **some ~ idiot** une espèce d'idiot.

blast furnace *n* haut-fourneau *m*.

blasting /'blɑːstɪŋ, US 'blæst-/ *n* travail *m* à l'explosif.

blast-off /'blɑːstɒf, US 'blæst-/ *n* lancement *m*.

blatant /'bleɪtnt/ *adj* [*lie, bias, disregard*] éhonté; [*example, abuse*] flagrant; **to be ~ about** [*person*] être direct à propos de.

blatantly /'bleɪtntlɪ/ *adv* [*copy, disregard*] ouvertement; **to be ~ obvious** être l'évidence même.

blather° /'blæðə(r)/ *vi* dire n'importe quoi.

blaze /bleɪz/ I *n* **1** (fire) (in hearth) feu *m*, flambée *f*; (accidental) incendie *m*; **2** (sudden burst) (of flames) embrasement *m*; **she left in a ~ of publicity** elle est partie sous les feux des médias; **3** (on horse) liste *f*; **4** (cut in tree) encoche *f*.
II **blazes**°† *npl* **what the ~s are you up to?** qu'est-ce que tu fabriques°?; **how the ~s did he do it?** comment diable a-t-il fait ça?; **to run like ~s** courir comme un dératé/une dératée.
III *vtr* (mark) griffer [*tree*]; **to ~ a trail** LIT baliser une voie; FIG faire œuvre de pionnier.
IV *vi* **1** (also **~ away**) (burn) brûler, flamber; [*house, car*] brûler; **2** (also **~ away**) (give out light) [*lights*] briller; **3** (shoot) [*gun*] pétarader.

V blazing *pres p adj* **1** (violent) [*argument*] violent; [*heat*] accablant; [*fire*] ronflant; [*building, car*] embrasé; [*sunshine*] plein (*before n*); **2**° (furious) fou/folle de rage.

blazer /'bleɪzə(r)/ *n* blazer *m*.

bleach /bliːtʃ/ I *n* **1** (also **household ~**) (disinfectant) ~ eau *f* de javel; **2** (for hair) décolorant *m*.
II *vtr* décolorer [*hair*]; blanchir [*linen*]; faire disparaître [*colour, stain*].

bleak /bliːk/ *adj* **1** (cold, raw) [*landscape*] désolé; [*weather, season*] maussade; **2** (miserable) [*outlook, future*] sombre; [*world, surroundings*] sinistre.

bleakly /'bliːklɪ/ *adv* [*stare, say*] sombrement.

bleakness /'bliːknɪs/ *n* **1** (of weather, surroundings) sévérité *f*; **2** (of prospects, future) noirceur *f*.

bleary /'blɪərɪ/ *adj* [*eyes*] bouffi; **to be ~-eyed** avoir les yeux bouffis; **to feel ~** se sentir vaseux/-euse.

bleat /bliːt/ I *n* bêlement *m*.
II *vi* **1** [*sheep, goat*] bêler; **2** PÉJ [*person*] se lamenter.

bled /bled/ ▶ **bleed**.

bleed /bliːd/ (*prét, pp* **bled**) I *vtr* **1**† MED saigner; **2** FIG **to ~ sb for sth** soutirer qch à qn; **to ~ sb dry** saigner qn à blanc; **3** TECH purger [*radiator*].
II *vi* **1** saigner; **my finger's ~ing** j'ai le doigt qui saigne; **he was ~ing from the head** il saignait d'une blessure à la tête; **he bled to death** il est mort d'une hémorragie; **2** FIG **my heart ~s for the baby's mother** mon cœur saigne pour la mère du bébé; **3** [*colour, dye*] déteindre.

bleeding /'bliːdɪŋ/ I *n* GEN saignement *m*; (heavy) hémorragie *f*; (deliberate) saignée *f*.
II *adj* [*wound*] saignant; [*corpse*] ensanglanté; [*hand, leg*] qui saigne.

bleeding heart *n* FIG PÉJ cœur *m* sensible PÉJ.

bleep /bliːp/ I *n* **1** (signal) bip *m*, bip-bip *m*; RADIO, TV top *m*; **2** GB = **bleeper**.
II *vtr* **1** GB **to ~ sb** appeler qn (au bip), biper qn; **2** RADIO, TV censurer par un bip [*word, person*].
III *vi* émettre un signal sonore ou des signaux sonores.

bleeper /'bliːpə(r)/ *n* GB (for doctor) bip *m*.

blemish /'blemɪʃ/ I *n* GEN imperfection *f*; (on fruit) tache *f*; (pimple) bouton *m*, défaut *m* (**on** dans); (on reputation) tache *f* (**on** à).
II *vtr* tacher [*fruit*]; ternir [*beauty*]; entacher [*reputation*].

blend /blend/ I *n* **1** (fusion) (of sounds, smells) mélange *m* (**of** de); (of styles, colours, ideas) mariage *m* (**of** de); (of qualities, skills) combinaison *f* (**of** de); **2** (of coffees, teas, whiskies) mélange *m*; (of wines) coupage *m*.
II *vtr* mélanger [*foods, colours, styles*]; allier [*ideas*].
III *vi* **to ~ (together)** [*colours, tastes, styles*] se fondre ensemble; **to ~ with** [*colours, tastes, sounds*] se marier à; [*smells, visual effects*] se mêler à; [*buildings, styles, ideas*] s'accorder à.
■ **blend in**: ¶ **~ in** s'harmoniser (**with** avec); ¶ **~ in [sth]**, **~ [sth] in** incorporer.

blender /'blendə(r)/ *n* **1** (device) mixeur *m*, mixer *m*; **2** (person) (of coffee) torréfacteur *m*.

blending /'blendɪŋ/ *n* (of coffees) torréfaction *f*; (of wines) coupage *m*; (of whiskies) mélange *m*.

bless /bles/ I *vtr* **1** RELIG bénir; **God ~ you** que Dieu vous bénisse; **goodbye, God ~!** au revoir!; **2**° (affectionately) **~ her** ou **~ her heart!** c'est un ange!; **~ you!** (after sneeze) à vos souhaits!; **3**° †(in surprise) **~ me!** ou **~ my soul!** ou **well I'm ~ed!** ça alors!; **4** (favour) **to ~ sb with** doter qn de; **to be ~ed with** jouir de [*health, beauty*]; **5** (be grateful to) **~ you for answering so quickly** merci d'avoir répondu si vite.
II *v refl* **to ~ oneself** se signer.

blessed /'blesɪd/ I *n* RELIG **the ~** (+ *v pl*) les bienheureux.
II *adj* **1** (holy) [*place*] béni; **the Blessed Sacrament** le saint sacrement; **the Blessed Virgin** la Sainte Vierge; **2** (beatified) bienheureux/-euse (*before n*); **3** (welcome) [*warmth, quiet*] bienfaisant; [*relief*] heureux/-euse; **4**° (damned) fichu°.

blessedly /'blesɪdlɪ/ adv [warm, quiet] délicieusement.

blessing /'blesɪŋ/ n **1** (asset, favour) bienfait m; **it is a ~ (for him) that he is healthy** heureusement, il est en bonne santé; **dishwashers are a ~ for busy people** les lave-vaisselle sont une bénédiction pour les personnes actives; **a ~ in disguise** un bienfait caché; **2** (relief) soulagement m; **it is a ~ to know (that) he's safe** c'est un soulagement de savoir qu'il est sauf; **3** (approval) **with the ~ of sb, with sb's ~** avec la bénédiction de qn; **to give one's ~ to sth** approuver qch sans réserve; **4** RELIG bénédiction f; **to give sb one's ~** donner sa bénédiction à qn; **to say a ~ over sth** bénir qch.

blew /blu:/ prét ▶ **blow** II, III.

blight /blaɪt/ **I** n **1** BOT rouille f; **potato ~** mildiou m (de la pomme de terre); **2** FIG (on society) plaie f (**on** de); **urban ~, inner city ~** délabrement m urbain.
II vtr attaquer [crop]; FIG gâcher [childhood, chances].

blighter†○ /'blaɪtə(r)/ n GB andouille○ f; **poor ~** pauvre andouille○; **you lucky ~!** sacré veinard○!

blimey○† /'blaɪmɪ/ excl GB mince alors○!

blind /blaɪnd/ **I** n **1** (unsighted) **the ~** (+ v pl) les aveugles mpl voir note; **2** (at window) store m; **3** (front) façade f; (subterfuge) feinte f; **4** US (hide) affût m.
II adj **1** LIT [person] aveugle voir note; **to go ~** perdre la vue; **to be ~ in one eye** être borgne; **2** (unaware) [person, rage, obedience] aveugle; **to be ~ to** être insensible à [quality]; être inconscient de [danger]; **3** (from which one can't see) [corner] sans visibilité; **on my ~ side** dans mon angle mort; **4** (without looking) [tasting] en aveugle; **5** (blank) [wall, façade] aveugle.
III adv [fly] sans visibilité; [taste] en aveugle; [bake] à blanc.
IV vtr **1** LIT [injury, accident] rendre aveugle; **to be ~ed in one eye** perdre un œil; **2** (dazzle) [sun, light] éblouir; **3** (mislead) [pride, love] aveugler.
IDIOMS **it's a case of the ~ leading the ~** ils n'en savent pas plus long l'un que l'autre; **to turn a ~ eye** fermer les yeux (**to** sur).

■ Note Ce mot peut être perçu comme injurieux dans cette acception. Lui préférer *visually handicapped* ou *visually impaired*.

blind alley n LIT, FIG voie f sans issue.

blind date n rendez-vous m avec un/-e inconnu/-e.

blind drunk /ˌblaɪn'drʌŋk/ adj complètement bourré○.

blindfold /'blaɪndfəʊld/ **I** n bandeau m.
II adj (also **~ed**) aux yeux bandés; **to be ~** avoir les yeux bandés.
III adv (also **~ed**) [find way] les yeux fermés.
IV vtr bander les yeux à [person].

blinding /'blaɪndɪŋ/ adj [light] aveuglant; [headache] atroce.

blindingly /'blaɪndɪŋlɪ/ adv [shine] d'un éclat aveuglant; **to be ~ obvious** sauter aux yeux.

blindly /'blaɪndlɪ/ adv **1** FIG [obey, follow] aveuglément; **2** LIT [advance, grope] à l'aveuglette.

blind man's buff n GAMES colin-maillard m.

blindness /'blaɪndnɪs/ n **1** MED cécité f; **2** FIG aveuglement m.

blind spot n **1** (in eye) point m aveugle; **2** (in car, on hill) angle m mort; **3** FIG (point of ignorance) ignorance f ¢.

blink /blɪŋk/ **I** n battement m des paupières.
II vi [person] cligner des yeux; [light] clignoter; **without ~ing** sans ciller.
IDIOMS **on the ~**○ [television, microwave] détraqué○.
■ **blink away: to ~ away one's tears** battre des paupières pour s'arrêter de pleurer.

blinker /'blɪŋkə(r)/ n **1** AUT clignotant m; US (at crossing) (feu m) clignotant m; **2** (on horse) œillère f.

blinkered /'blɪŋkə(r)d/ adj [attitude, approach] borné.

blinking /'blɪŋkɪŋ/ n ¢ (of eye) battement m des paupières; (of light) clignotement m.

blip /blɪp/ n **1** (on screen) spot m; (on graph, line) acci-

---

dent m (d'une courbe); **2** (sound) bip m; **3** (hitch) contretemps m.

bliss /blɪs/ n **1** RELIG, LITTÉR béatitude f; **2**○ FIG délice m.

blissful /'blɪsfl/ adj **1** (wonderful) délicieux/-ieuse; **2** RELIG bienheureux/-euse.

blissfully /'blɪsfəlɪ/ adv voluptueusement; **to be ~ happy** être au comble du bonheur; **to be ~ unaware of/that** être à cent lieues de se douter de/que; **~ ignorant** dans la plus parfaite ignorance.

blister /'blɪstə(r)/ **I** n (on skin) ampoule f; (on paint) cloque f; (in glass, on metal) soufflure f.
II vtr faire peler [skin]; faire cloquer [paint].
III vi [skin, paint] cloquer; [person] peler; **my feet ~ easily** j'ai facilement des ampoules aux pieds.

blistering /'blɪstərɪŋ/ **I** n (of skin) formation f d'ampoules; (of paint) formation f de cloques.
II adj [heat] caniculaire; [sun] torride; [attack, criticism] féroce; [reply] cinglant.

blister pack n blister m, habillage m transparent.

blithe /blaɪð/ adj (nonchalant) insouciant; (cheerful) allègre.

blithely /'blaɪðlɪ/ adv (nonchalantly) avec insouciance; (cheerfully) allègrement; **~ ignorant of sth** parfaitement inconscient de qch.

blitz /blɪts/ **I** n **1** MIL AVIAT bombardement m aérien; **the Blitz** GB HIST le Blitz; **2** FIG **to have a ~ on sth** s'attaquer à qch.
II vtr LIT, FIG bombarder.

blitzkrieg /'blɪtskriːg/ n guerre f éclair inv.

blizzard /'blɪzəd/ n tempête f de neige; (in Arctic regions) blizzard m.

bloated /'bləʊtɪd/ adj **1** LIT [face, body] bouffi; [stomach] ballonné; **to feel ~** se sentir ballonné; **2** FIG [estimate] gonflé; [style] ampoulé.

blob /blɒb/ n **1** (drop) grosse goutte f; **2** (shape) forme f floue.

bloc /blɒk/ n POL bloc m; **en ~** en bloc.

block /blɒk/ **I** n **1** (slab) bloc m; **2** (building) **~ of flats** immeuble m (d'habitation); **office ~** immeuble de bureaux; **administration ~** bâtiment m administratif; **3** (group of buildings) pâté m de maisons; **to drive round the ~** faire le tour du pâté de maisons; **he lives three ~s away** il habite à trois rues d'ici; **4** (for butcher, executioner) billot m; **to put one's head on the ~** FIG donner sa tête à couper; **5** (group) (of seats, tickets) groupe m; (of shares) paquet m, tranche f; **a ~ of three lessons** trois cours d'affilée; **6** (obstruction) **to be a ~ to** être un obstacle à [reform, agreement]; **to put a ~ on** bloquer [price, sale]; entraver [initiative]; SPORT obstruction f.
II blocks npl (shoes) chaussons mpl à pointes.
III vtr **1** (obstruct) bloquer [exit, road]; boucher [drain, hole, artery]; gêner [traffic]; **to ~ sb's way** ou **path** barrer le passage à qn; **to have a ~ed nose** avoir le nez bouché; **2** (impede) faire obstacle à [advance, escape, progress]; faire opposition à [bill]; **you're ~ing my light** tu me caches la lumière; **3** FIN bloquer [assets].
■ **block in: ~ [sb/sth] in** (when parking) bloquer [car, driver].
■ **block off: ~ [sth] off, ~ off [sth]** (seal off) barrer [road, path].
■ **block out: ~ out [sth], ~ [sth] out 1** (hide) boucher [view]; cacher [light, sun]; **2** (suppress) refouler [memory, problem].
■ **block up: ~ up [sth], ~ [sth] up** boucher.

blockade /blɒ'keɪd/ **I** n MIL blocus m.
II vtr bloquer, faire le blocus de [port].

blockage /'blɒkɪdʒ/ n (in artery) obstruction f; (in pipe, drain, distribution) blocage m; (in river) engorgement m.

block: **~ and tackle** n moufle f; **~board** n latté m; **~book** vtr louer [qch] en groupe [seats]; **~-booking** n location f de groupe.

blockbuster○ /'blɒkbʌstə(r)/ **1** (book) livre m à succès, bestseller m; **2** (film) superproduction f; **3** MIL bombe f de très grande puissance.

block capital n majuscule f d'imprimerie; **in ~s** (on form) en caractères mpl or capitales fpl d'imprimerie.

block: **~head**○ n PÉJ âne○ m, imbécile○ mf; **~house** n MIL blockhaus m; US HIST (fort) fortin m; **~ letter** n = **block capital**; **~ printing** n impression f sur cliché bois; **~ release course** n cours m de formation continue; **~ vote** n vote m groupé; **~ voting** n système m du vote groupé.

bloke○ /bləʊk/ n GB type○ m, mec○ m.

blond /blɒnd/ ▶818| adj [person, hair] blond; [wood] clair.

blonde /blɒnd/ ▶818| **I** n blonde f.
II adj blond.

blood /blʌd/ n **1** BIOL sang m; **to give ~** donner son sang; **the ~ rushed to his cheeks** il a rougi; **to kill sb in cold ~** tuer qn de sang-froid; **to do ~ tests** faire des analyses de sang; **2** (breeding) sang m; **music is in her ~** elle a la musique dans le sang; **3** (anger) **his ~ is up** il est furieux; **4** (vigour) **new** ou **fresh** ou **young ~** sang m neuf.
IDIOMS **~ is thicker than water** la voix du sang est la plus forte; **he's after my ~**○! il veut ma peau○!; **it's like getting ~ out of a stone** autant essayer de faire parler un muet.

blood: **~-and-thunder** adj [novel, film] d'aventures; **~ bank** n banque f du sang; **~bath** n bain m de sang; **~ blister** n pinçon m; **~ brother** n frère m de sang; **~ cell**, **~ corpuscle** n globule m (du sang); **~ count** n numération f globulaire; **~curdling** adj à vous figer le sang dans les veines; **~ donor** n donneur/-euse m/f de sang; **~ group** n groupe m sanguin; **~hound** n limier m.

bloodless /ˈblʌdlɪs/ adj **1** (peaceful) [revolution, coup] sans effusion de sang; **2** (pale) blème; **3** (drained of blood) exsangue.

blood: **~letting** n MED saignée f; (killing) massacre m; **~ lust** n soif f de sang; **~ money** n argent m versé pour un meurtre; **~ orange** n orange f sanguine; **~ poisoning** n septicémie f.

blood pressure n MED tension f artérielle; **high ~** hypertension f; **low ~** hypotension f.

blood: **~-red** ▶818| n, adj rouge (m) sang inv; **~ relation**, **~ relative** n parent/-e m/f par le sang; **~shed** n effusion f de sang; **~shot** adj [eyes] injecté de sang; **~ sport** n sport m sanguinaire; **~stained** adj taché de sang; **~stock** n (+ v sg ou pl) bêtes fpl de race; **~stream** n courant m sanguin; **~sucker** n LIT, FIG sangsue f; **~ test** n analyse f de sang; **~thirsty** adj sanguinaire; **~ transfusion** n transfusion f sanguine; **~ type** n groupe m sanguin; **~ vessel** n vaisseau m sanguin.

bloody /ˈblʌdɪ/ **I** adj **1** (covered in blood) ensanglanté; **to have a ~ nose** avoir le nez en sang; **to give sb a ~ nose** LIT faire saigner le nez de qn; FIG faire souffrir qn; **2** (violent) [battle, deed] sanglant; [regime, tyrant] sanguinaire; **3**○ GB (expressing anger) sacré○; **4** (red) rouge sang (inv).
II○ adv GB (for emphasis) [dangerous, expensive] sacrément○; **~ awful** absolument nul○; **a ~ good film** un super○ film; **what a ~ stupid idea!** quelle idée débile○!

bloody-minded○ /ˌblʌdɪˈmaɪndɪd/ adj GB **don't be so ~** ne fais pas ta tête de mule; **he's just being ~** il fait ça pour embêter le monde.

bloom /bluːm/ **I** n **1** (flower) fleur f; **2** (flowering) floraison f; **in ~** en fleur; **to come into ~** fleurir; **3** (on skin, fruit) velouté m.
II vi (be in flower) être fleuri; (come into flower) fleurir.

bloomer /ˈbluːmə(r)/ n **1**○ †(mistake) GB bévue f; **2** GB CULIN gros pain m.

bloomers /ˈbluːməz/ npl culotte f bouffante.

blooming /ˈbluːmɪŋ/ adj **1** (healthy) [person] resplendissant (**with** de); [plant] magnifique; [friendship] florissant; **2**○ †(for emphasis) GB fichu○.

blossom /ˈblɒsəm/ **I** n **1** (flowers) fleurs fpl; **in ~** en fleur(s); **in full ~** en pleine floraison; **to come into ~** fleurir; **2** (flower) fleur f.

II vi fleurir; FIG **to ~ (out)** s'épanouir.

blot /blɒt/ **I** n GEN tache f; (of ink) pâté m; FIG ombre f.
II vtr (p prés etc **-tt-**) **1** (dry) sécher [qch] au buvard; **2** (stain) tacher; FIG ternir; **3** = **blot out**.
IDIOMS **to ~ one's copybook** se faire mal voir; **to be a ~ on the landscape** LIT gâter le paysage; FIG faire une ombre au tableau.
■ **blot out**: **~ out** [sth] [person] effacer; [mist, rain] masquer.

blotch /blɒtʃ/ **I** n (on skin) plaque f rouge; (of ink, colour) tache f.
II vtr barbouiller [paper, face].
III vi [pen] faire des taches.

blotchy /ˈblɒtʃɪ/ adj [skin] marbré; [leaf, paper] tacheté.

blotter /ˈblɒtə(r)/ n **1** (for ink) (small) tampon m buvard; (on desk) sous-main m inv; **2** US (police, commercial) registre m.

blotting paper n papier m buvard.

blotto○ /ˈblɒtəʊ/ adj cuité○.

blouse /blaʊz, US blaʊs/ ▶1260| n (woman's) chemisier m; US MIL vareuse f.

blow /bləʊ/ **I** n **1** (stroke) coup m; **killed by a ~ to the back of the head** tué d'un coup derrière la tête; **to come to ~s** en venir aux mains (**over** au sujet de); **to strike a ~ for** FIG frapper un grand coup pour [freedom, rights]; **2** FIG (shock, knock) coup m; **to be a ~** être un coup terrible (**to sth** porté à qch; **to, for sb** pour qn); **3 to give one's nose a ~** se moucher.
II vtr (prét **blew**; pp **blown**) **1** [wind] **to ~ sth out of** faire voler qch par [window]; **the wind blew the door shut** un coup de vent a fermé la porte; **to be blown off course/onto the rocks** être dévié/poussé sur les rochers par le vent; **it's ~ing a gale** il y a de la tempête; **2** faire [bubble, smoke ring]; souffler [glass]; **to ~ sb a kiss** envoyer un baiser à qn; **3 to ~ one's nose** se moucher; **4** GEN, MUS souffler dans [trumpet, whistle]; **5** [explosion] provoquer [hole] (**in** dans); **to be blown to pieces** ou **bits by** être réduit en poussière par; **6** ELEC, TECH faire sauter [fuse, gasket]; griller [lightbulb]; **7**○ (spend) claquer○ [money] (**on** dans); **8**○ (expose) faire tomber [cover]; **9**○ (make a mess of) **to ~ it** tout ficher en l'air○; **to ~ one's chances** ficher ses chances en l'air○.
III vi (prét **blew**; pp **blown**) **1** [wind] souffler; **2** (move with wind) **to ~ in the wind** [leaves, clothes] voler au vent; **3** [person] souffler (**into** dans; **on** sur); **4** (sound) [whistle] retentir; [trumpet] sonner, retentir; [foghorn] rugir; **5** (break, explode) [fuse, gasket] sauter; [bulb] griller; [tyre] éclater.
IDIOMS **to ~ a fuse**○ ou **a gasket**○ ou **one's top**○ piquer une crise○; **it really blew my mind**○ ou **blew me away**○ j'en suis resté baba○.
■ **blow around**, **blow about** GB: ¶ **~ around** voler dans tous les sens; ¶ **~ [sth] around**, **~ around [sth]** faire voler [qch] dans tous les sens.
■ **blow away**: ¶ **~ away** s'envoler○; ¶ **~ [sth] away**, **~ away [sth]** [wind] emporter [object]; ¶ **~ [sb] away**○ (kill) descendre○ [person].
■ **blow down**: ¶ **~ down** [tree, fence] tomber (à cause du vent); ¶ **~ [sth] down**, **~ down [sth]** [wind] faire tomber [tree].
■ **blow in**: ¶ **~ in 1** [snow, rain] entrer; **2** (in explosion) [door, window] être enfoncé; ¶ **~ [sth] in**, **~ in [sth] 1** [wind] faire entrer [snow, rain]; **2** [explosion] enfoncer [door, window].
■ **blow off**: ¶ **~ off** [hat] s'envoler○; ¶ **~ [sth] off**, **~ off [sth]** [wind] emporter [hat]; [explosion] emporter [limb, roof]; **to ~ the leaves off the trees** [wind] faire tomber les feuilles des arbres.
■ **blow out**: ¶ **~ out 1** [flame] s'éteindre; **2** [oil well] laisser échapper du pétrole; ¶ **~ [sth] out**, **~ out [sth] 1** (extinguish) souffler [candle]; éteindre [flames]; **2** (inflate) **to ~ one's cheeks out** gonfler les or ses joues; **to ~ itself out** [storm] tomber.
■ **blow over**: ¶ **~ over 1** (die down) [storm] tomber; [affair] être oublié; [discontent, protest] se calmer;

[*anger*] passer; **2** (topple) [*fence, tree*] tomber; **¶ ~ [sth/sth] over** [*wind*] renverser [*person, tree*].
■ **blow up**: **¶ ~ up 1** (in explosion) [*building*] sauter; [*bomb*] exploser; **2** [*storm*] se lever; **3** [*problem, affair*] éclater; **4**° (become angry) s'emporter; **5** (inflate) **it ~s up** c'est gonflable; **¶ ~ [sth/sb] up, ~ up [sb/sth]** faire sauter [*building, person*]; faire exploser [*bomb*]; **¶ ~ [sth] up, ~ up [sth]** (inflate) gonfler [*tyre*]; **2** PHOT (enlarge) agrandir; **3** (exaggerate) exagérer.

blow-by-blow *adj* [*account*] par le menu.

blow-dry /'bləʊdraɪ/ **I** *n* brushing *m*.
II *vtr* **to ~ sb's hair** faire un brushing à qn.

blowhole /'bləʊhəʊl/ *n* (of whale) évent *m*; (in ice) trou *m* d'air.

blown /bləʊn/ *pp* ▶ **blow** II, III.

blowout /'bləʊaʊt/ *n* **1** ELEC court-circuit *m*; **2** AUT (of tyre) crevaison *f*; **3** (in oil or gas well) jaillissement *m*; **4**° (meal) gueuleton° *m*.

blow: **~pipe** *n* sarbacane *f*; **~torch** /'bləʊtɔːtʃ/ *n* lampe *f* à souder.

blow-up /'bləʊʌp/ **I** *n* PHOT agrandissement *m*.
II *adj* (inflatable) [*doll, toy, dinghy*] gonflable.

blowy /'bləʊɪ/ *adj* venteux/-euse, venté.

blowzy /'blaʊzɪ/ *adj* PÉJ [*woman*] à l'aspect négligé.

blubber /'blʌbə(r)/ **I** *n* **1** (of whale) graisse *f* de baleine; **2**° FIG (of person) graisse *f*.
II° *vi* pleurer comme un veau.

blubbery /'blʌbərɪ/ *adj* adipeux/-euse.

bludgeon /'blʌdʒən/ **I** *n* matraque *f*.
II *vtr* matraquer; **to ~ sb to death** tuer qn à coups de matraque.

blue /bluː/ **I** ▶**818** | **I** *n* **1** (colour) bleu *m*; **to go** ou **turn ~** devenir bleu; **2** (sky) LITTÉR **the ~** l'azur *m* LITER; **3** GB UNIV **to be an Oxford ~** être membre d'une équipe sportive d'Oxford; **4**° GB POL **a true ~** un partisan ardent du parti Conservateur.
II blues *npl* **1** MUS **the ~s** le blues *m*; **2**° (depression) **to have the ~s** avoir le cafard°.
III *adj* **1** (in colour) bleu; FIG **~ from** ou **with the cold** bleu de froid; **2** (depressed) **to feel ~** avoir le cafard°; **3**° (smutty) [*film*] porno°; [*joke*] osé, cochon/-onne°; **4**° GB POL conservateur/-trice.
IDIOMS **to say sth out of the ~** dire qch à brûle-pourpoint; **to appear/happen out of the ~** apparaître/se passer à l'improviste; **to vanish into the ~** s'évanouir dans la nature; **black and ~** couvert de bleus; **to beat sb black and ~** battre qn comme plâtre°; **to tell sb sth until one is ~ in the face** se tuer à dire qch à qn.

blue: **Bluebeard** *pr n* Barbe-bleue *m*; **~bell** *n* BOT jacinthe *f* des bois; **~berry** *n* US BOT myrtille *f*; **~-black** ▶**818** |, *n, adj* bleu-noir (*m*) *inv*; **~ blood** *n* sang *m* bleu or noble; **~-blooded** *adj* de sang bleu or noble; **~bottle** *n* mouche *f* bleue; **~ cheese** *n* (fromage *m*) bleu *m*.

blue chip I *n* **1** FIN valeur *f* vedette; **2** GAMES (in poker) jeton *m* de grande valeur.
II *noun modifier* FIN [*company*] de premier ordre; **~ (share)** valeur *f* de premier ordre; **~ investment** placement *m* sûr or de tout repos.

blue collar *adj* **~ worker** ouvrier *m*, col *m* bleu.

blue-eyed /'bluːaɪd/ *adj* aux yeux bleus; **~ boy** GB FIG chouchou° *m*.

blue: **Blue Helmets**, **Blue Berets** *npl* MIL Casques *mpl* bleus; **~ jay** *n* geai *m* bleu; **~ jeans** *npl* jean *m*; **~ light** *n* (on emergency vehicles) gyrophare *m*.

blueness /'bluːnɪs/ *n* bleu *m* ₵.

blue pencil *n* **to go through sth with the ~** (edit) corriger qch; (censor) censurer qch.

blueprint /'bluːprɪnt/ *n* **1** ARCHIT, TECH bleu *m*; **2** FIG (plan) projet *m*, propositions *fpl* (**for** pour; **for doing** pour faire); **it's a ~ for disaster** cela mène tout droit à la catastrophe.

blue: **~ rinse** *n* rinçage *m* à reflets argentés; **~stocking** *n* PÉJ bas-bleu *m* PÉJ; **~ tit** *n* mésange *f* bleue; **~ whale** *n* baleine *f* bleue.

bluff /blʌf/ **I** *n* **1** (ruse) bluff *m*; **2** (cliff) falaise *f*.

II *adj* [*person, manner*] carré.
III *vtr* bluffer°; **to ~ sb into thinking sth** faire croire qch à qn; **to ~ one's way out of a situation** se tirer d'une situation en bluffant.
IV *vi* bluffer° (also in cards).
IDIOMS **to call sb's ~** prendre qn au mot (*sachant qu'il bluffe*); **it's time we called his ~** il est temps qu'on le mette au pied du mur; **to ~ it (out)** s'en tirer en bluffant ou au bluff.

blunder /'blʌndə(r)/ **I** *n* bourde *f*.
II *vi* **1** (make mistake) faire une bourde; **2** (move clumsily) **to ~ into the table** se cogner à la table; **to ~ about in the dark** avancer dans l'obscurité en se cognant.

blundering /'blʌndərɪŋ/ *adj* balourd.

blunt /blʌnt/ **I** *adj* **1** [*knife, scissors*] émoussé; [*pencil*] mal taillé; [*instrument*] contondant; [*needle*] épointé; **this knife is ~** ce couteau ne coupe plus; **2** (frank) [*person, manner*] abrupt; [*refusal*] catégorique; [*criticism*] direct; **to be ~ with you** pour être tout à fait franc avec toi.
II *vtr* émousser [*knife*]; épointer [*pencil, needle*]; émousser [*intelligence*]; tempérer [*enthusiasm*].

bluntly /'blʌntlɪ/ *adv* franchement.

bluntness /'blʌntnɪs/ *n* (of person) franc-parler *m*; (of manner) rudesse *f*.

blur /blɜː(r)/ **I** *n* image *f* floue; **after that it's a ~** après ça, je ne me rappelle plus rien; **her memories are just a ~** ses souvenirs sont extrêmement confus.
II *vtr* (*p prés etc* **-rr-**) brouiller.
III *vi* (*p prés etc* **-rr-**) se brouiller.

blurb /blɜːb/ *n* GEN descriptif *m* (promotionnel); (on book cover) texte *m* de présentation (*sur la couverture*); PÉJ baratin *m*.

blurred /blɜːd/ *adj* indistinct; [*image, idea*] flou; [*memory*] confus; **to have ~ vision** avoir des troubles de la vue; **to become ~** [*eyes*] se voiler.

blurt /blɜːt/ *vtr* ▶ **blurt out.**
■ **blurt out**: **~ [sth] out, ~ out [sth]** laisser échapper.

blush /blʌʃ/ **I** *n* rougeur *f*; **without a ~** sans scrupules; **to spare sb's ~es** ménager (la modestie de) qn.
II *vi* rougir (**at** devant; **with** de); **to ~ for sb** avoir honte pour qn.

blusher /'blʌʃə(r)/ *n* fard *m* à joues.

blushing /'blʌʃɪŋ/ **I** *n* rougissement *m*.
II *adj* [*person*] rougissant.

bluster /'blʌstə(r)/ **I** *n* FIG (angry) fulminations *fpl*; (boasting) fanfaronnades *fpl*.
II *vi* **1** [*wind*] souffler en bourrasques; **2** FIG [*person*] (angrily) fulminer (**at** contre); (boastfully) fanfaronner.

blustering /'blʌstərɪŋ/ **I** *n* (boasting) fanfaronnades *fpl*.
II *adj* (boastful) fanfaron/-onne; (angry) braillard.

blustery /'blʌstərɪ/ *adj* **~ wind** bourrasque *f*; **it's a ~ day** le vent souffle en bourrasques.

B movie /'biː muːvɪ/ *n* film *m* de série B.

BO° *n* (*abrév* = **body odour**) odeur *f* corporelle.

boa /'bəʊə/ *n* **1** (snake) boa *m*; **2** (feather) **~** boa *m*.

boa constrictor *n* (boa) constricteur *m*.

boar /bɔː(r)/ *n* **1** (wild) sanglier *m*; **2** (pig) verrat *m*.

board /bɔːd/ **I** *n* **1** (plank) planche *f*; **2** ADMIN conseil *m*; **~ of directors** conseil d'administration; **~ of inquiry** commission *f* d'enquête; **~ of governors** comité *m* de gestion d'une école; **3** (playing surface) tableau *m*; **4** SCH tableau *m* (noir); **5** (notice board) (for information) panneau *m* d'affichage; (to advertise) panneau *m*; **6** COMPUT, ELEC plaquette *f*; **7** (accommodation) **full ~** pension *f* complète; **half ~** demi-pension *f*; **~ and lodging, room and ~** le gîte et le couvert.
II boards *npl* **1** (floor) plancher *m*; **bare ~s** plancher nu; **2** THEAT estrade *f*; **to tread the ~s** faire du théâtre.
III *noun modifier* ADMIN [*meeting, member*] du conseil d'administration.

IV on board adv phr **to be on ~** ou **on ~ ship** être à bord; **to go on ~** embarquer, monter à bord; **to get on ~** monter dans [bus, train]; monter à bord de [plane, ship]; **to take sth on ~** LIT embarquer [cargo, passengers]; FIG prendre [qch] en compte [changes, facts]; adopter [proposal].

V vtr **1** (get on) monter à bord de [boat, plane]; monter dans [bus, train]; **2** NAUT [customs officer] arraisonner [vessel]; [pirates, marines] aborder [vessel].

VI vi être en pension (**with** chez); SCH [pupil] être interne.

IDIOMS **above ~** légal; **across the ~** à tous les niveaux; **to go by the ~** tomber à l'eau; **to sweep the ~** tout gagner, tout rafler○.

■ **board out**: **~** [sb] **out**, **~ out** [sb] mettre [qn] en pension.

■ **board up**: **~** [sth] **up**, **~ up** [sth] boucher [qch] avec des planches [window]; barricader [qch] avec des planches [house].

boarder /'bɔːdə(r)/ n **1** (lodger) pensionnaire m; **2** SCH interne mf.

board game n jeu m de société (à damier).

boarding /'bɔːdɪŋ/ n **1** AVIAT, NAUT embarquement m; **2** NAUT (by customs officer) arraisonnement m; **3** MIL abordage m.

boarding: **~ card** n carte f d'embarquement; **~ house** n pension f; **~ party** n groupe m d'abordage; **~ school** n école f privée avec internat.

board: **~room** n salle f du conseil; **~walk** n US chemin m fait de planches.

boast /bəʊst/ **I** n vantardise f; **it is his ~ that he is never late** il se vante de ne jamais être en retard; **it was an empty** ou **idle ~** c'était du bluff.

II vtr **the town ~s a beautiful church** la ville s'enorgueillit d'une belle église; **the computer ~s two disk drives** l'ordinateur est équipé de deux lecteurs de disquettes.

III vi se vanter (**about** de); **nothing to ~ about** (sth good) rien de bien extraordinaire; (sth bad) pas de quoi se vanter.

boaster /'bəʊstə(r)/ n vantard/-e m/f.

boastful /'bəʊstfl/ adj [person] vantard; **without being ~** sans se vanter.

boastfully /'bəʊstfəlɪ/ adv en se vantant.

boasting /'bəʊstɪŋ/ n vantardise f.

boat /bəʊt/ **I** n (vessel, ferry) bateau m; (sailing) voilier m; (rowing) barque f; (liner) paquebot m; **he crossed the lake in a ~** il a traversé le lac en bateau.

II noun modifier [trip] en bateau; [hire] de bateaux.

IDIOMS **to be in the same ~○** être tous dans la même galère; **to miss the ~** manquer le coche; **to push the ~ out**○ GB faire les choses en grand; **to rock the ~**○ jouer les trouble-fête○.

boater /'bəʊtə(r)/ n **1** (hat) canotier m; **2** US (person) canoteur m.

boat: **~hook** n gaffe f; **~house** n abri m à bateaux.

boating /'bəʊtɪŋ/ **I** n navigation f de plaisance; (rowing) canotage m.

II noun modifier [accident, enthusiast] de bateau; [trip] en bateau.

boatload /'bəʊtləʊd/ n (of goods) cargaison f; **~s of tourists** des bateaux pleins de touristes.

boat: **~swain** n maître m d'équipage; **~yard** n chantier m de construction de bateaux.

bob /bɒb/ **I** n **1** (haircut) coupe f au carré; **2** (nod) **a ~ of the head** un signe de tête; **3** (curtsy) petite révérence f; **4** (weight) (on plumb line) plomb m; (on pendulum) poids m; (on fishing line) bouchon m; **5** (tail) queue f écourtée; **6**○ GB (money) (pl **~**) shilling m; **to cost a ~ or two** coûter une fortune; **7** SPORT bobsleigh m.

II vtr (p prés etc **-bb-**) **1** (cut) couper [qch] au carré [hair]; couper [qch] court [tail]; **2** (nod) **to ~ one's head** faire un signe de tête; **3 to ~ a curtsy** faire une petite révérence (**to** à).

III vi (p prés etc **-bb-**) [boat, float] danser; **to ~ down** [person] se baisser subitement; **to ~ up and**

down [person, boat] s'agiter; [heads] apparaître et disparaître.

IV bobbed pp adj [hair, tail] coupé court.

bobbin /'bɒbɪn/ n bobine f; (for lace-making) fuseau m.

bobble /'bɒbl/ n pompon m; **~ hat** bonnet à pompon.

bobby○† /'bɒbɪ/ GB n agent m (de police).

bobcat /'bɒbkæt/ n lynx m roux.

bobsled /'bɒbsled/, **bobsleigh** /'bɒbsleɪ/ ▶ 949 **I** n bobsleigh m.

II vi faire du bobsleigh.

bode /bəʊd/ vi **to ~ well/ill** être de bon/mauvais augure.

bodge GB = **botch**.

bodice /'bɒdɪs/ n (of dress) corsage m.

bodily /'bɒdɪlɪ/ **I** adj [function] physiologique; [fluid] organique; [need, well-being] physique; [injury] corporel/-elle.

II adv [carry, pick up] à bras-le-corps.

bodkin /'bɒdkɪn/ n (for piercing) poinçon m.

body /'bɒdɪ/ **I** n **1** (of person, animal) corps m; **~ and soul** corps et âme; **just enough to keep ~ and soul together** juste assez pour survivre; **to sell one's ~** se prostituer; **2** (corpse) corps m, cadavre m; **3** (main section) (of car) carrosserie f; (of boat) coque f; (of aircraft) fuselage m; (of camera) boîtier m; (of violin, guitar) caisse f de résonance; (of dress) corsage m; **4** (large quantity) (of water) étendue f; (of laws) recueil m or corps m (de lois); **a large ~ of evidence** un vaste faisceau de preuves; **5** (group) (of troops, students) corps m; **the student ~** la masse des étudiants; **the main ~ of demonstrators** le gros des manifestants; **6** (organization) organisme m; **disciplinary ~** commission f disciplinaire; **7** PHYS corps m; **8** (fullness) (of wine) corps m; (of hair) volume m; **9** (garment) body m.

II noun modifier [lotion] pour le corps; [care, paint] corporel/-elle.

IDIOMS **over my dead ~!** plutôt mourir!

body blow n LIT coup m porté au corps; **to deal a ~ to** FIG porter un coup sérieux à.

body: **~builder** n culturiste mf; **~-building** n culturisme m; **~guard** n (individual) garde m du corps; (group) protection f rapprochée; **~ heat** n chaleur f corporelle; **~ language** n langage m corporel; **~ odour** GB, **~ odor** US, **BO**○ n odeur f corporelle; **~ politic** n corps m social; **~ shop** n AUT atelier m de carrosserie; **~ snatching** n vol m de cadavres; **~ stocking** n body m, justaucorps m; **~ warmer** n gilet m matelassé; **~ weight** n poids m; **~work** n carrosserie f.

boffin○ /'bɒfɪn/ n GB expert m.

bog /bɒg/ n **1** (marshy ground) marais m; **2** (also **peat ~**) tourbière f.

IDIOMS **to get ~ged down in sth** s'enliser dans qch.

bogey /'bəʊgɪ/ n **1** (evil spirit) (also **~man**) croquemitaine m; **2** (to frighten people) épouvantail m; **3** (in golf) bogey m.

boggle /'bɒgl/ vi **the mind** ou **imagination ~s at the idea** on a du mal à imaginer ça.

boggy /'bɒgɪ/ adj (swampy) marécageux/-euse; (muddy) bourbeux/-euse; (peaty) tourbeux/-euse.

bogus /'bəʊgəs/ adj [official, doctor, document] faux/ fausse (before n); [claim] bidon; [company] factice.

bohemia /bəʊ'hiːmɪə/ n (community) bohème f; (district) quartier m bohème.

bohemian /bəʊ'hiːmɪən/ adj [lifestyle] de bohème; [person] bohème inv.

boil /bɔɪl/ **I** n **1 to be on the ~** GB LIT, FIG être en ébullition; **to bring sth to the ~** porter qch à ébullition; **to go off the ~** GB [water] cesser de bouillir; **2** MED furoncle m.

II vtr **1** (also **~ up**) faire bouillir, porter [qch] à ébullition [liquid]; **2** (cook) faire bouillir, faire cuire [qch] à l'eau; **to ~ an egg** faire cuire un œuf.

III vi **1** [water, vegetables etc] bouillir; **the kettle is ~ing** l'eau bout (dans la bouilloire); **the saucepan ~ed dry** toute l'eau de la casserole s'est évaporée;

The human body

When it is clear who owns the part of the body mentioned, French tends to use the definite article, where English uses a possessive adjective:

he raised his hand	= il a levé la main
she closed her eyes	= elle a fermé les yeux

Note, for instance, the use of la *and* mon *here:*

she ran her hand over my forehead = elle a passé la main sur mon front

For expressions such as he hurt his foot *or* she brushed her teeth, *where the action involves more than the simple movement of a body part, use a reflexive verb in French:*

she has broken her leg = elle s'est cassé la jambe

(literally she has broken to herself the leg – there is no past participle agreement because the preceding reflexive pronoun se is the indirect object).

he was rubbing his hands	= il se frottait les mains
she was holding her head	= elle se tenait la tête

Note also the following:

she broke his leg	= elle lui a cassé la jambe
	(literally she broke to him the leg)
the stone split his lip	= le caillou lui a fendu la lèvre
	(literally the stone split to him the lip)

Describing people

For ways of saying how tall someone is, ▶ 1045], *of stating someone's weight,* ▶ 1392], *and of talking about the colour of hair and eyes,* ▶ 818].

Here are some ways of describing people in French:

his hair is long	= il a les cheveux longs
he has long hair	= il a les cheveux longs
a boy with long hair	= un garçon aux cheveux longs
a long-haired boy	= un garçon aux cheveux longs
the boy with long hair	= le garçon aux cheveux longs
her eyes are blue	= elle a les yeux bleus
she has blue eyes	= elle a les yeux bleus
she is blue-eyed	= elle a les yeux bleus
the girl with blue eyes	= la fille aux yeux bleus
a blue-eyed girl	= une fille aux yeux bleus
his nose is red	= il a le nez rouge
he has a red nose	= il a le nez rouge
a man with a red nose	= un homme au nez rouge
a red-nosed man	= un homme au nez rouge

When referring to a temporary state, the following phrases are useful:

his leg is broken	= il a la jambe cassée
the man with the broken leg	= l'homme à la jambe cassée

but note

a man with a broken leg = un homme avec une jambe cassée

For other expressions with body part terms, ▶ 818].

---

2 FIG [*sea*] bouillonner; [*person*] bouillir (**with** de); **to make sb's blood ~** faire sortir qn de ses gonds.
IV boiled *pp adj* **~ed chicken** poule *f* au pot; **~ed egg** œuf *m* à la coque.
■ **boil away** (evaporate) s'évaporer.
■ **boil down:** ¶ **~ down** CULIN se réaliser (par ébullition); ¶ **~ down to** FIG se ramener *or* se résumer à; ¶ **~ down** [sth], **~** [sth] **down 1** CULIN faire réduire [qch] [*sauce*]; **2** FIG réduire [*text*] (**to** à).
■ **boil over** LIT [*liquid*] déborder; FIG [*anger, tension*] déborder.
boiler /'bɔɪlə(r)/ *n* **1** (in heating system, steam generator) chaudière *f*; (for storing water) chauffe-eau *m inv*; (chicken) poule *f* (*à faire au pot*).
boiler: **~ house** *n* bâtiment *m* des chaudières; **~maker** ▶ 1251] *n* chaudronnier *m*; **~ room** *n* salle *f* des chaudières; **~ suit** *n* GB (workman's) bleu *m* de travail *or* de chauffe; (woman's) combinaison *f*.
boiling /'bɔɪlɪŋ/ *adj* **1** (at boiling point) bouillant; **2** FIG **it's ~ in here**○! il fait une chaleur infernale ici!; **3** (for cooking) (*épith*) [*fowl*] à faire au pot.
boiling: **~ hot**○ *adj* [*day*] torride; [*liquid*] bouillant○; **~ point** *n* LIT point *m* d'ébullition; FIG point *m* limite.
boisterous /'bɔɪstərəs/ *adj* **1** [*adult*] bruyant; [*child*] turbulent; [*meeting, game*] bruyant; **2** (tempestuous) [*sea*] houleux/-euse.
bold /bəʊld/ I *n* GB (in printing) (also **boldface** US) caractères *mpl* gras; **in ~** en (caractères) gras.
II *adj* **1** (daring) [*person*] intrépide; [*attempt, plan*] audacieux/-ieuse; **2** (cheeky) [*person, look*] effronté; [*behaviour*] hardi; **3** (strong) [*colour*] vif/vive; [*design*] voyant; [*handwriting*] assuré; [*outline*] net/nette; **4** (of typeface) gras/grasse.
IDIOMS **to be as ~ as brass** avoir un culot monstre○.
boldly /'bəʊldlɪ/ *adv* **1** (daringly) hardiment; (cheekily) avec effronterie; **2** [*designed*] de manière voyante; [*outlined*] nettement; **~ coloured** aux couleurs vives.
boldness /'bəʊldnɪs/ *n* **1** (intrepidity) hardiesse *f*; (cheek) effronterie *f*; **2** (of design, colour) netteté *f*.
Bolivia /bə'lɪvɪə/ ▶ 840] *pr n* Bolivie *f*.
bollard /'bɒlɑːd/ *n* **1** (on quay, ship) bollard *m*; **2** (in road) balise *f*.
Bolognese /ˌbɒlə'neɪz/ I *n* (*pl* **~**) Bolognais/-aise *m/f*.

II *adj* **~ sauce** sauce *f* bolognaise; **spaghetti ~** spaghettis *mpl* (à la) bolognaise.
boloney○ /bə'ləʊnɪ/ *n* ¢ balivernes *fpl*.
Bolshevik /'bɒlʃəvɪk, US *also* 'bəʊl-/ I *n* bolchevique *mf*.
II *adj* bolchevique.
bolshy○ GB /'bɒlʃɪ/ *adj* **1** (on one occasion) [*child*] buté; [*adult*] pas commode; **to get ~** se braquer; **2** (by temperament) **he's/she's ~** c'est un râleur○/une râleuse○.
bolster /'bəʊlstə(r)/ I *n* traversin *m*.
II *vtr* (also **~ up**) **1** (boost) renforcer [*confidence*]; **to ~ sb's ego** donner de l'assurance à qn; **2** (shore up) soutenir [*economy*]; appuyer [*argument*].
bolt /bəʊlt/ I *n* **1** (lock) verrou *m*; **2** (screw) boulon *m*; **3 ~ of lightning** coup *m* de foudre; **4** (of cloth) rouleau *m* (de tissu); **5** (for crossbow) carreau *m*; **6** (for rifle) culasse *f* mobile; **7** (in mountaineering) piton *m* à expansion; **8** (dash) départ *m* précipité; **to make a ~ for it** décamper○.
II **bolt upright** *adj phr* droit comme un i.
III *vtr* **1** (lock) verrouiller; **to be ~ed shut** être fermé au verrou; **2** CONSTR boulonner; **3** (also **~ down**) (swallow) engloutir [*food*].
IV *vi* [*horse*] s'emballer; [*rabbit, person*] détaler○; **to ~ out/off** sortir/partir à toute allure.
IDIOMS **a ~ from** OU **out of the blue** un coup de tonnerre.
bolt hole *n* GB LIT, FIG refuge *m*.
bomb /bɒm/ I *n* **1** (explosive device) bombe *f*; **2**○ GB (large amount of money) **to cost a ~** coûter un argent fou○; **3**○ (flop) fiasco *m*.
II *vtr* bombarder [*town, house*].
III○ *vi* **1** (move fast) **to ~ up the road** remonter la rue à fond de train○; **2** (fail) échouer.
■ **bomb out: we were ~ed out** nous avons été forcés de quitter notre maison à cause des bombardements.
bombard /bɒm'bɑːd/ *vtr* bombarder (**with** de).
bombardment /bɒm'bɑːdmənt/ *n* bombardement *m*.
bombastic /ˌbɒm'bæstɪk/ *adj* ampoulé, grandiloquent.
bomb: **~ attack** *n* attentat *m* à la bombe; **~ blast** *n* explosion *f*; **~ disposal** *n* déminage *m*; **~ disposal expert** ▶ 1251] *n* démineur *m*; **~ disposal squad** *n* équipe *f* de déminage.

bomber /'bɒmə(r)/ I *n* **1** MIL, AVIAT bombardier *m*; **2** (terrorist) poseur/-euse *m/f* de bombes.
II *noun modifier* [*pilot*] de bombardier; [*raid, squadron*] de bombardiers.

bomber jacket *n* blouson *m* d'aviateur.

bombing /'bɒmɪŋ/ *n* MIL bombardement *m*; (by terrorists) attentat *m* à la bombe.

bomb: **~proof** *adj* à l'épreuve des bombes; **~ scare** *n* alerte *f* à la bombe.

bombshell /'bɒmʃel/ *n* FIG bombe *f*.

bomb shelter *n* abri *m* antiaérien.

bombsite /'bɒmsaɪt/ *n* **1** LIT zone *f* touchée par une explosion; **2** FIG (mess) champ *m* de bataille.

Bomb Squad /'bɒmskwɒd/ *n* brigade *f* antiterroriste.

bona fide /ˌbəʊnə 'faɪdɪ/ *adj* [*attempt*] sincère; [*member, refugee*] vrai (*before n*); [*offer*] sérieux/-ieuse; [*contract*] de bonne foi.

bonanza /bə'nænzə/ *n* **1** (windfall) pactole *f*, filon *m*; **2** (performance, festival etc) événement *m* exceptionnel; **3** (in mining) riche filon *m*.

bond /bɒnd/ I *n* **1** (link) lien(s) *m(pl)* (**of** de; **between** entre); **to strengthen a ~** resserrer des liens; **to feel a strong ~ with sb** se sentir très proche de qn; **2** (fetter) LIT lien *m*; FIG chaîne *f* (**of** de); **3** FIN obligation *f*; **government ~** obligation d'État; **savings ~** bon *m* d'épargne; **4** (adhesion) adhérence *f*; **5** CHEM liaison *f*; **6** JUR (guarantee) engagement *m* écrit; (deposit) caution *f*; **7** (at customs) **in ~** en dépôt de douane.
II *vtr* (also **~ together**) **1** [*glue*] faire adhérer [*surfaces*]; enlier [*bricks*]; **2** [*suffering*] créer des liens entre [*people*].
III *vi* **1** GEN, PSYCH s'attacher (**with** à); **2** [*materials*] adhérer (**with** à); **3** CHEM [*atoms*] s'associer (**with** à).

bondage /'bɒndɪdʒ/ *n* LIT, FIG esclavage *m*.

bonding /'bɒndɪŋ/ *n* **1** (between mother and baby) (process) formation *f* des liens maternels; **2** (between people) (process) formation *f* du lien affectif (**between** entre); **male ~** amitié *f* virile.

bone /bəʊn/ I *n* **1** (of human, animal) os *m*; (of fish) arête *f*; **made of ~** en os; **chicken on/off the ~** poulet à l'os/désossé; **to break every ~ in one's body** se rompre les os; **2** (in corset also) baleine *f*.
II **bones** *npl* **1** (animal skeleton) ossements *mpl*; **2** (human remains) (in archeology) ossements *mpl* humains; **to lay sb's ~s to rest** enterrer la dépouille de qn.
III *vtr* CULIN désosser [*joint, chicken*]; enlever les arêtes de [*fish*].
IDIOMS **~ of contention** sujet *m* de dispute, pomme *f* de discorde; **close to the ~** (wounding) blessant; (racy) osé; **to cut sth to the ~** réduire qch au minimum; **to feel sth in one's ~s** avoir le pressentiment de qch; **to have a ~ to pick with sb** avoir un compte à régler avec qn; **to make no ~s about sth** ne pas cacher qch; **sticks and stones may break my ~s (but words will never harm me)** ≈ les chiens aboient, la caravane passe; **to work one's fingers to the ~** se crever à la tâche○.
■ **bone up on** *vi*: **~ up on** [*sth*] potasser○ [*subject*].

bone china *n* porcelaine *f* tendre or à l'os.

boned /bəʊnd/ *adj* **1** [*joint, leg, chicken*] désossé; [*fish*] sans arête; **2** [*corset, bodice*] à armature.

bone: **~ dry** *adj* complètement desséché; **~head**○ *n* abruti/-e○ *m/f*; **~ idle** *adj* flemmard○.

boneless /'bəʊnlɪs/ *adj* [*chicken breast*] sans os; [*fish*] sans arête.

bone: **~ marrow** *n* moelle *f* osseuse; **~-marrow transplant** *n* greffe *f* de moelle osseuse.

bonemeal /'bəʊnmiːl/ *n* **1** (fertilizer) engrais *m* phosphaté; **2** (feed) fourrage *m* phosphaté (*de cendres d'os*).

bonfire /'bɒnfaɪə(r)/ *n* **1** (of rubbish) feu *m* de jardin; (for celebration) feu du joie.

Bonfire Night *n* GB la soirée du 5 novembre (*fêtée avec feux de joie et feux d'artifice*).

bonkers○ /'bɒŋkəz/ *adj* dingue○.

bonnet /'bɒnɪt/ *n* **1** (hat) bonnet *m*; **2** GB AUT capot *m*.

IDIOMS **to have a bee in one's ~** avoir une idée fixe.

bonus /'bəʊnəs/ *n* **1** (payment) prime *f*; **no claims ~** GB bonus *m*; **cash ~** prime *f*; **2** (advantage) avantage *m* (**of being** d'être).

bonus point *n* bonus *m* d'un point; **five ~s** un bonus de cinq points.

bony /'bəʊnɪ/ *adj* **1** [*person, body, shoulders, face*] anguleux/-euse; [*finger, arm, knee*] osseux/-euse; **2** [*fish*] plein d'arêtes.

boo /buː/ I *n* (jeer) huée *f*.
II *excl* (to give sb a fright) hou!; (to jeer) hou! hou!
III *vtr* (3ᵉ *pers sg prés* **boos**, *prét*, *pp* **booed**) huer [*actor, speaker*]; **to be ~ed off the stage** quitter la scène sous les huées.
IV *vi* (3ᵉ *pers sg prés* **boos**, *prét*, *pp* **booed**) pousser des huées.

boob○ /buːb/ *n* **1** GB (mistake) bêtise *f*; **2** (breast) nichon○ *m*.

boo-boo○ /'buːbuː/ *n* boulette○ *f*.

booby prize *n* prix *m* de consolation (*décerné au dernier*).

booby trap I *n* **1** MIL mécanisme *m* piégé; **2** (joke) traquenard *m*.
II *vtr* (*p prés etc* **-pp-**) MIL piéger.

boogie○ /'buːgɪ/ *vi* danser.

booing /'buːɪŋ/ *n* ₵ huées *fpl*.

book /bʊk/ I *n* **1** (reading matter) livre *m*, bouquin○ *m* (**about** sur; **of** de); **history ~** livre d'histoire; **'Carlton Books'** 'Éditions *fpl* Carlton'; **2** (part) (of novel, trilogy) livre *m*, tome *m*; (of poem, epic, bible) livre *m*; **3** FIN (for recording deposits, withdrawals) livret *m* bancaire; **4** (exercise book) cahier *m*; **drawing ~** cahier de dessin; **5** (of cheques, tickets, vouchers, stamps) carnet *m*; **~ of matches** pochette *f* d'allumettes; **6** (in betting) **to keep a ~ on** prendre des paris sur; **to open** ou **start a ~ on** ouvrir les paris sur; **7** (directory) annuaire *m*; **8** (rulebook) règlement *m*; **to do things by the ~** FIG suivre le règlement; **9** (opera libretto) livret *m*.
II **books** *npl* **1** (accounts) livres *mpl* de comptes, comptabilité *f* ₵; **to keep the ~s** tenir les comptes, s'occuper de la comptabilité; **2** (records) registre *m*; **to be on the ~s of** être inscrit à [*organization*].
III *vtr* **1** (reserve) réserver [*table, room, taxi, ticket*]; faire les réservations pour [*holiday*]; engager [*babysitter, entertainer*]; **to ~ sth for sb**, **to ~ sb sth** réserver qch pour qn; **to ~ sb into a hotel** réserver une chambre dans un hôtel pour qn; **to be fully ~ed** être complet/-ète; **my Tuesday afternoons are ~ed** je suis pris le mardi après-midi; **2** (charge) [*policeman*] dresser un procès-verbal or un P.V.○ à [*motorist, offender*]; US (arrest) arrêter [*suspect*]; **he was ~ed for speeding** il a été poursuivi pour excès de vitesse; **3** GB SPORT [*referee*] donner un carton jaune à [*player*]; **to be ~ed** recevoir un carton jaune.
IV *vi* réserver; **you are advised to ~** il est conseillé de réserver.
IDIOMS **I can read her like a ~** elle ne peut rien me cacher; **his past is an open ~** il n'a rien à cacher sur son passé; **economics is a closed ~ to me** je ne connais rien à l'économie; **to throw the ~ at sb** (reprimand) passer un savon○ à qn; (accuse) n'omettre aucun chef d'accusation (*quand on arrête qn*); (punish or sentence) donner le maximum à qn; **to be in sb's good ~s** être dans les petits papiers de qn○; **to be in sb's bad ~s** ne pas avoir la cote avec qn; **in my ~**○ à mon avis.
■ **book in**: ¶ **~ in** GB (check in) se présenter à la réception; (reserve) réserver une chambre; ¶ **~ [sb] in** réserver une chambre pour.
■ **book up**: **to be ~ed up** être complet/-ète.

book: **~binder** ▶ 1251 *n* relieur/-euse *m/f*; **~binding** *n* reliure *f*; **~-burning** *n* autodafé *m*; **~case** *n* bibliothèque *f*; **~ club** *n* club *m* du livre; **~end** *n* serre-livres *m inv*; **~ fair** *n* salon *m* du livre.

bookie○ /'bʊkɪ/ *n* bookmaker *m*.

ooking /'bʊkɪŋ/ n **1** GB (reservation) réservation f; **to make a ~** faire une réservation; **2** (for performance) engagement m; **3** GB (from referee) **to get a ~** recevoir un carton jaune.

ooking: **~ clerk** ▶ 1251 n GB préposé/-e m/f aux réservations; **~ form** n GB bon m de réservation; **~ office** n GB bureau m de location.

ookish /'bʊkɪʃ/ adj [person] studieux/-ieuse.

ook: **~ jacket** n jaquette f; **~keeper** ▶ 1251 n comptable mf; **~keeping** n comptabilité f.

ooklet /'bʊklɪt/ n brochure f.

ook: **~list** n liste f de livres; **~ lover** n bibliophile mf; **~maker** ▶ 1251 n bookmaker m; **~mark** n marque-pages m, signet m; **~plate** n exlibris m; **~rest** n lutrin m; **~seller** ▶ 1251 n (person) libraire mf; (shop) librairie f; **~shelf** n (single) étagère f; (in bookcase) rayon m; **~shop** ▶ 1251 n librairie f; **~stall** n (in market) étalage m de livres; GB (station) kiosque m à journaux; **~store** ▶ 1251 n US librairie f; **~ token** n GB chèque-livre m; **~worm** n mordu/-e⁰ m/f de la lecture.

oom /buːm/ **I** n **1** (noise) (of voices, cannon, thunder) grondement m; (of waves) mugissement m; (of drum) boum m; (of explosion) détonation f; **2** (onomat) badaboum!; **3** (period of prosperity) boom m, période f de forte expansion; (in demand, prices, sales etc) explosion f (in de); **export/consumer ~** boom des exportations/ de la consommation; **property ~** boom immobilier; **4** (increase in popularity) boom m (in de); **5** NAUT (spar) bôme f; (barrage) estacade f; **6** (on crane) gui m; **7** CIN, RADIO, TV perche f.
II noun modifier [industry, town] en pleine expansion; [period, year] de croissance; [share] à la hausse.
III vi **1** (make a noise) [cannon, thunder] gronder; [bell, voice] retentir; [sea] mugir; **2** (prosper) [economy, trade] prospérer; [exports, sales] monter en flèche; [industry] être en plein essor; [hobby, sport] être en plein boom; **business is ~ing** les affaires vont bien.
■ **boom out**: ¶ **~ out** [music, sound] retentir; ¶ **~ [sth] out**, **~ out [sth]** [person] brailler [speech]; [loudspeaker] faire retentir [announcement]; [drum] faire retentir [rhythm].

boomerang /'buːməræŋ/ **I** n boomerang m; **~ effect** effet boomerang.
II vi [plan] faire boomerang.

booming /'buːmɪŋ/ adj **1** (loud) [sound] retentissant; [voice] tonitruant; **2** (flourishing) [economy] en plein essor; [demand, exports, sales] en forte progression.

boom microphone n micro m à perche.

boon /buːn/ n **1** (advantage) avantage m; **2** (asset) aide f précieuse (to à); **to be a great ~ to sb** apporter une aide précieuse à qn; **3** (stroke of luck) aubaine f (for pour).

boor /'bʊə(r), bɔː(r)/ n grossier personnage m, malotru m.

boorish /'bʊərɪʃ, bɔː-/ adj grossier/-ière.

boost /buːst/ **I** n **1** (stimulus) coup m de fouet (to à); **to give sth a ~** stimuler qch; **2** (encouragement) encouragement m; **to give sb a ~** encourager qn; **3** (publicity) publicité f; **to give sth a ~** faire du battage pour qch.
II vtr **1** (stimulate) stimuler [economy, productivity, sales]; encourager [investment, lending]; augmenter [capacity, number, pay, profit, value]; relancer [interest]; **to ~ sb's confidence** redonner confiance à qn; **to ~ morale** remonter le moral; **2** (enhance) améliorer [image, performance]; **3** (promote) faire la promotion de, promouvoir [product]; **4** ELEC, TELECOM amplifier [signal, voltage]; **5** AUT rendre [qch] plus puissant [engine]; **6** (push up) propulser [rocket].

booster /'buːstə(r)/ **I** n **1** RADIO, TELECOM amplificateur m; **2** ELEC survolteur m; **3** AUT compresseur m; **4** MED vaccin m de rappel.
II noun modifier [dose, injection] de rappel; **~ rocket** fusée d'appoint.

boot /buːt/ ▶ 1260 **I** n **1** (footwear) botte f; (for workman, soldier) brodequin m; **climbing/hiking ~** chaussure f de montagne/randonnée; **football ~** GB chaussure f

de football; **to put the ~ in** LIT rouer qn de coups de pied; FIG y aller fort; **2** GB AUT coffre m; **3**⁰ (dismissal) **to get the ~** se faire virer; **4**⁰ (kick) coup m de pied; **a ~ up the backside** un bon coup de pied au derrière ALSO FIG; **5** US (wheel clamp) sabot m de Denver.
II vtr **1**⁰ (kick) envoyer un coup de pied à [person]; donner un coup de pied dans [ball]; **2** COMPUT = **boot up**.
IDIOMS **the ~ is on the other foot** GB les rôles sont renversés; **to be/get too big for one's ~s** GB avoir/ prendre la grosse tête; **to ~** par dessus le marché; **to lick sb's ~s** lécher les bottes à qn.
■ **boot out**: **~ [sb] out**, **~ out [sb]** (from institution) renvoyer; (from company, house) mettre [qn] à la porte.
■ **boot up** COMPUT: **~ [sth] up**, **~ up [sth]** amorcer [computer].

boot: **~black** n cireur m de chaussures; **~ drive** n COMPUT unité f d'initialisation.

bootee /buː'tiː/ n **1** (knitted) chausson m; **2** (leather) bottine f.

booth /buːð, US buːθ/ n **1** (in language lab) cabine f; (in restaurant) alcôve f; (at fair) baraque f; **polling ~** isoloir m; **telephone ~** cabine f (téléphonique).

boot: **~jack** n tire-botte m; **~lace** n lacet m (de chaussure); **~legger** n US bootlegger m; **~licker** n lèche-bottes mf inv; **~maker** ▶ 1251 n bottier m; **~ polish** n cirage m; **~ scraper** n décrottoir m.

bootstrap /'buːtstræp/ n **1** (on boot) tirant m de botte; **2** COMPUT programme m d'amorce.
IDIOMS **to pull oneself up by one's ~s** se faire tout seul.

booty /'buːtɪ/ n butin m.

booze⁰ /buːz/ **I** n bibine⁰ f; (wine only) pinard⁰ m.
II vi picoler⁰.

boozer /'buːzə(r)/ n (person) poivrot/-ote⁰ m/f; (pub) GB bistro m.

booze-up⁰ /'buːzʌp/ n GB beuverie f.

boozy⁰ /'buːzɪ/ adj [meal] bien arrosé; [laughter] aviné.

bop /bɒp/ **I** n **1**⁰ (blow) coup m; **2**⁰ (dancing) **to go for a ~** aller en boîte⁰.
II⁰ vtr (p prés etc **-pp-**) cogner.
III⁰ vi (p prés etc **-pp-**) GB danser.

Bordeaux /bɔː'dəʊ/ (wine) bordeaux m.

border /'bɔːdə(r)/ ▶ 1200 **I** n **1** (frontier) frontière f; **France's ~ with Spain** la frontière entre la France et l'Espagne; **on the Swiss ~** sur la frontière suisse; **to cross the ~** passer la frontière; **to escape over** ou **across the ~** s'échapper en passant la frontière; **our allies across the ~** nos alliés de l'autre côté de la frontière; **2** (edge) (of forest) lisière f; (of estate, lake, road) bord m; **3** (decorative edge) (on crockery, paper) liseré m; (on picture, cloth) bordure f; **4** (flowerbed) platebande f; **5** (hypothetical limit) frontière f (**between** entre); **6** COMPUT (of window) bordure f.
II noun modifier [control] aux frontières; [crossing, patrol, state] frontalier/-ière; [area, post, town, zone] frontière (after n, inv); [police] des frontières; [incident] de frontière.
III vtr **1** (lie alongside) [road, land] longer [lake, forest]; [country] border [ocean]; **France ~s Italy** la France a une frontière commune avec l'Italie; **2** (surround) border; **to be ~ed by trees** être bordé d'arbres.
■ **border on**: **~ on [sth] 1** (have a frontier with) [country] avoir une frontière commune avec; [garden, land] toucher; **2** (verge on) friser.

border: **~ dispute** n différend m frontalier; **~ guard** n garde-frontière m.

borderline /'bɔːdəlaɪn/ n frontière f, limite f (**between** entre); **a ~ case** un cas limite.

border raid n incursion f armée.

bore /bɔː(r)/ **I** prét ▶ bear.
II n **1** (person) raseur⁰/-euse m/f; **2** (situation) **what a ~!** quelle barbe!; **3** (also **~hole**) trou m de forage; **4** (of gun barrel, pipe) calibre m; **12-~ shotgun** fusil m de calibre 12.

III *vtr* **1** (annoy) ennuyer; **2** (drill) percer [*hole*]; creuser [*well, tunnel*].

IV *vi* **to** ~ **into/through** forer dans/à travers; **her eyes** ~**d into me** elle me perçait de son regard.

IDIOMS **to** ~ **sb stiff** ou **to death** ou **to tears** faire mourir qn d'ennui.

bored /bɔːd/ *adj* [*person*] qui s'ennuie; [*expression, voice*] ennuyé; **to get** ou **be** ~ s'ennuyer (**with** de); **to look** ~ avoir l'air de s'ennuyer.

boredom /'bɔːdəm/ *n* **1** (feeling) ennui *m* (**with** devant); **2** (of activity, job, lifestyle) monotonie *f*.

boring /'bɔːrɪŋ/ **I** *n* (drilling) (in wood) perforation *f*; (in rock) forage *m*.
II *adj* [*person, place, activity, event*] ennuyeux/-euse; [*colour, food*] fade; **it's** ~ **being/doing** c'est assommant d'être/de faire.

born /bɔːn/ **I** *adj* [*person, animal*] né (**of** de; **to do** pour faire; **with** avec); **to be** ~ naître; **when the baby is** ~ quand le bébé sera né; ~ **a Catholic** d'origine catholique; **to be** ~ **blind** être aveugle de naissance; **to be a** ~ **leader** être un chef né; **a** ~ **liar** un parfait menteur; **to be** ~ **(out) of sth** [*idea, group*] naître de qch.
II **-born** *combining form* **London-/Irish-**~ né à Londres/en Irlande, originaire de Londres/d'Irlande.
IDIOMS **in all my** ~ **days**○ de toute ma vie; **I wasn't** ~ **yesterday**○ je ne suis pas né de la dernière pluie; **there's one** ~ **every minute**○! quel idiot/quelle idiote!

born-again /ˌbɔːnə'geɪn/ *adj* [*Christian*] régénéré.

borne /bɔːn/ *pp* ▶ **bear**.

borough /'bʌrə, US -rəʊ/ *n* arrondissement *m* urbain.

borough council *n* GB conseil *m* municipal.

borrow /'bɒrəʊ/ **I** *vtr* emprunter (**from** à).
II *vi* FIN faire un emprunt (**from** à).
IDIOMS **he/she is living on** ~**ed time** ses jours sont comptés.

borrower /'bɒrəʊə(r)/ *n* emprunteur/-euse *m/f*.

borrowing /'bɒrəʊɪŋ/ *n* **1** FIN ¢ emprunt *m*; **increase in** ~ augmentation des emprunts; ~ **costs** le coût de l'emprunt; **2** LING, LITERAT emprunt *m* (**from** à).

borstal† /'bɔːstəl/ *n* GB maison *f* de correction.

Bosnia /ˌbɒznɪə/ ▶ 840 ▏ *pr n* Bosnie *f*.

Bosnia-Herzegovina /ˌbɒznɪə ˌhɜːtsəgəʊ'viːnə/ ▶ 840 ▏ *pr n* Bosnie-Herzégovine *f*.

bosom /'bʊzəm/ *n* LITTER **1** (chest) poitrine *f*; **to hug sb to one's** ~ serrer qn contre sa poitrine; **2** (breasts) **to have a large** ~ avoir beaucoup de poitrine; **3** FIG (heart, soul) cœur *m*; **in the** ~ **of one's family** au sein de sa famille.

bosom buddy○, **bosom friend** *n* ami/-e *m/f* intime.

boss /bɒs/ *n* **1**○ (person in charge) GEN patron/-onne *m/f*; (in politics, underworld) chef *m*; **you're the** ~ IRON c'est toi le patron; **we'll show them who's** ~ on va leur montrer qui commande ici; **2** (on shield) umbo *m*; (on ceiling) bossage *m*; (on wheel) tourteau *m*.
■ **boss about**○, **boss around**○: ~ [**sb**] **about** mener [qn] par le bout du nez.

bossy○ /'bɒsɪ/ *adj* autoritaire.

bosun *n* = **boatswain**.

botanic(al) /bə'tænɪk(l)/ *adj* [*studies, drawing, term*] botanique; [*name*] latin; ~ **gardens** jardin *m* botanique.

botanist /'bɒtənɪst/ ▶ 1251 ▏ *n* botaniste *mf*.

botany /'bɒtənɪ/ *n* botanique *f*.

botany wool *n* laine *f* mérinos.

botch○ /bɒtʃ/ **I** *n* (also ~**-up**) **to make a** ~ **of sth** saboter qch.
II *vtr* bâcler.

both /bəʊθ/ **I** *adj* ~ **sides of the road** les deux côtés de la rue; ~ **her eyes/parents** ses deux yeux/parents; ~ **their faces/lives** leurs visages/vies; ~ **children came** les enfants sont venus tous les deux.
II *conj* ~ **you and I saw him** tu l'as vu comme moi; ~ **here and abroad** ici comme à l'étranger; **to show**

~ **firmness and tact** faire preuve à la fois d fermeté et de tact; ~ **Paris and London have the advantages** aussi bien Paris que Londres a ses avant ges.
III *pron* (+ *v pl*) (of things) les deux; (of people) tous l deux; **let's do** ~ faisons les deux; ~ **are youn they are** ~ **young** ils sont jeunes tous les deux.
IV **both of** *pron phr* (+ *v pl*) **let's take** ~ **of** the prenons les deux; ~ **of you are wrong** vous av tort tous les deux.

bother /'bɒðə(r)/ **I** *n* **1** (inconvenience) ennui *m*, embêt ment○ *m*; **to do sth without any** ~ faire qch sa aucune difficulté; **it's too much** ~ c'est trop c tracas; **to have the** ~ **of doing** avoir le tracas c faire; **to go to the** ~ **of doing** se donner le mal c faire; **it's no** ~ ce n'est pas un problème; **2**○ ¢ (trouble) ennuis *mpl*; **to be in a bit** ou **spot of** ~ avo des ennuis; **3** (person) casse-pieds○ *mf inv*, enquiqu neur/-euse○ *m/f*.
II○ *excl* zut alors!
III *vtr* **1** (worry) tracasser; **don't let it** ~ **you** ne tracasse pas avec ça; **to be** ~**ed by noise** être rangé par le bruit; **it** ~**s me that** cela m'ennuie qu (+ *subj*); **they won't be** ~**ing you again** ils n t'embêteront plus; **2** (inconvenience) déranger; **oh sto** ~**ing me**○! mais arrête de m'embêter à la fin○!; ~ **sb with** ennuyer qn avec [*details, problems*]; (hurt) faire souffrir.
IV *vi* **1** (take trouble) s'en faire; **please don't** ~ s'il plaît, ne te dérange pas; **why** ~? pourquoi ~ tracasser?; **I don't think I'll** ~ je ne vais pas m'emb ter avec ça; **I wouldn't** ~ ce n'est pas la peine; **~ doing** ou **to do** prendre la peine de faire; **don't** you **needn't** ~ **doing** ce n'est pas la peine de fair **to** ~ **about** se tracasser au sujet de; **I don't kno why I** ~ je ne sais pas pourquoi je me tracass **don't** ou **you needn't** ~ **coming back!** ce n'est pa la peine de revenir!; **2** (worry) **to** ~ **about** se souci de; **it's not worth** ~**ing about** ça ne vaut pas peine qu'on s'en occupe.
V bothered *pp adj* (concerned) **to be** ~**ed that** êt ennuyé que (+ *subj*); **to be** ~**ed with** s'embêter av [*detail, problem*]; **he's not** ~**ed about money** ça n l'intéresse pas d'avoir de l'argent; **I'm not** ~**ed** ça m'est égal; **you just couldn't be** ~**ed**○ **to tu up!** tu ne t'es même pas donné la peine de venir!

Botswana /bɒt'swɑːnə/ ▶ 840 ▏ *pr n* Botswana *m*.

bottle /'bɒtl/ **I** *n* **1** (container) (for drinks) bouteille *f*; (f perfume, medicine) flacon *m*; (for baby) biberon *m*; (f gas) bouteille *f*; **milk** ~ bouteille *f* de lait; **2**○ ¢ (alcohol) **to hit the** ~, **to be on the** ~ caresser bouteille○; **3**○ GB (courage) courage *m*, cran○ *m*.
II *vtr* **1** (put in bottles) embouteiller, mettre [qch] bouteilles [*milk, wine*]; **2** GB (preserve) mettre [qch] e bocal ou en conserve [*fruit*].
III bottled *pp adj* [*beer, gas*] en bouteille; ~ **water** eau *f* minérale.
■ **bottle out**○ GB se dégonfler○.
■ **bottle up**: ~ [**sth**] **up**, ~ **up** [**sth**] étouff [*anger, grief*].

bottle: ~ **bank** *n* réceptacle *m* à verre; ~ **feed** v nourrir [qn] au biberon; ~ **feeding** *n* alimentation au biberon; ~ **green** ▶ 818 ▏ *n*, *adj* vert (n bouteille *inv*.

bottleneck /'bɒtlnek/ *n* **1** (traffic jam) embouteilla *m*; **2** (narrow part of road) rétrécissement *m* de chaussée; **3** (hold-up) goulet *m* d'étranglement.

bottle: ~**-opener** *n* décapsuleur *m*; ~ **top** capsule *f* (de bouteille).

bottlewasher /'bɒtlwɒʃə(r)/ *n* **chief cook and** HUM factotum *m*.

bottom /'bɒtəm/ **I** *n* **1** (base) (of hill, pile, steps, wa pied *m*; (of page) bas *m*; (of bag, bottle, hole, river, se fond *m*; **to sink** ou **go to the** ~ [*ship*] couler; **fro the** ~ **of one's heart** du fond du cœur; **the** ~ **ha fallen** ou **dropped out of the market** le marché s'e effondré; **2** (underside) (of boat) œuvres *fpl* vives, carè *f*; (of vase, box) dessous *m*; **3** (lowest position) (of list) ba *m*; (of league) dernière place *f*; (of hierarchy) derni

rang *m*, bas *m*; **at the ~ of the heap** ou **pile** FIG au bas de l'échelle; **to be** ou **come ~ of the class** être dernier/-ière de la classe; **to hit rock ~** FIG toucher le fond; **4** (far end) (of garden, field) fond *m*; (of street) bout *m*; **5**° (buttocks) derrière° *m*; **6** FIG (root) fond *m*; **to get to the ~ of a matter** découvrir le fin fond d'une affaire.
II° **bottoms** *npl·* **pyjama ~s** pantalon *m* de pyjama; **bikini ~s** bas *m* de maillot de bain.
III *adj* **1** (lowest) [*rung, shelf*] du bas; [*sheet*] de dessous; [*apartment*] du rez-de-chaussée; [*bunk*] inférieur; [*division, half, part*] dernier/-ière; **~ of the range** bas de gamme; **2** (last) [*place, team*] dernier/-ière; [*score*] le plus bas.
IDIOMS **~s up**°! (drink up) cul sec°!; (cheers) santé!
■ **bottom out** [*recession*] atteindre son point le plus bas.

bottom drawer *n* LIT tiroir *m* du bas; FIG trousseau *m* de mariée.

bottom end *n* **1** LIT (far end) (of street) bout *m*; **2** FIG (of league, division) partie *f* inférieure; (of market) bas *m* de gamme.

bottom: ~ gear *n* GB AUT première *f*; **~less** *adj* sans fond.

bottom line *n* **1** FIN dernière ligne *f* du bilan; **2** (decisive factor) **the ~ is that** la vérité c'est que; **that's the ~** ça c'est le vrai problème.

botulism /'bɒtjʊlɪzəm/ ▶ 1002 *n* botulisme *m*.

bouffant /'buːfɑːn/ *adj* [*hair, hairstyle*] crêpé; [*sleeve*] bouffant.

bough /baʊ/ *n* branche *f*.

bought /bɔːt/ *prét, pp* ▶ **buy**.

boulder /'bəʊldə(r)/ *n* rocher *m*.

bounce /baʊns/ **I** *n* **1** (rebound of ball) rebond *m*; **2** (of mattress, material) élasticité *f*; (of hair) souplesse *f*; **3** FIG (vigour) allant *m*.
II *vtr* **1** faire rebondir [*ball*]; retransmettre [*signal*]; **2**° **to ~ a cheque** [*bank*] GB refuser d'honorer un chèque; [*person*] US faire un chèque sans provision.
III *vi* **1** [*ball, object*] rebondir (**off** sur; **over** au-dessus de); [*person*] (on trampoline, bed) faire des bonds, sauter; **to ~ up and down on sth** faire des bonds or sauter sur qch; **2** FIG (move energetically) **to ~ in/along** entrer/marcher énergiquement; **3**° [*cheque*] être sans provision.
■ **bounce back** (after illness) se remettre; (in career) faire un retour en force.

bouncer° /'baʊnsə(r)/ *n* videur *m*.

bouncy /'baʊnsɪ/ *adj* **1** [*ball*] qui rebondit bien; [*mattress*] élastique; [*walk*] sautillant; **2** [*person*] dynamique.

bound /baʊnd/ **I** *prét, pp* ▶ **bind**.
II *n* bond *m*; **in a ~, with one ~** d'un bond.
III bounds *npl* LIT, FIG limites *fpl*; **to be out of ~s** [*place*] être interdit d'accès; SPORT être hors du terrain; **to be within/beyond the ~s of sth** FIG rester dans/dépasser les limites de qch; **it's not beyond the ~s of possibility** ce n'est pas impossible; **there are no ~s to her curiosity** il n'y a pas de limites à sa curiosité.
IV *adj* **1** (certain) **to be ~ to do sth** aller sûrement faire qch; **she's ~ to know** elle le doit sûrement savoir; **it was ~ to happen** cela devait arriver; **2** (obliged) (by promise, rules, terms) tenu (**by** par; **to do** de faire); **I am ~ to say that...** je dois dire que...; **3** [*book*] relié; **leather-~** relié en cuir; **4** (heading for) **~ for** [*person, bus, train*] en route pour; [*aeroplane*] à destination de; **5** (connected) **to be ~ up with sth** être lié à qch.
V *vtr* (border) borner; **~ed by** LIT, FIG borné par.
VI *vi* bondir; **to ~ into the room** entrer dans la pièce en coup de vent.
VII -bound *combining form* **1** (heading for) **London-~** à destination de Londres; **2** (confined) **fog-/strike-~** immobilisé par le brouillard/la grève.

boundary /'baʊndrɪ/ *n* **1** GEN, GEOG limite *f* (**between** entre); **city ~** limites de la ville; **national ~**

frontières *fpl* du pays; **2** FIG (defining) limite *f*; (dividing) ligne *f*; **3** SPORT limites *fpl* du terrain.

boundless /'baʊndlɪs/ *adj* [*terrain, space*] infini; [*enthusiasm, energy, ambition*] sans bornes.

bounty /'baʊntɪ/ *n* **1** (generosity) générosité *f*; **2** (gift) don *m*; **3** (reward) prime *f*; **~ hunter** chasseur *m* de primes.

bouquet /bʊ'keɪ/ *n* bouquet *m*.

bourbon /'bɜːbən/ *n* bourbon *m*.

bourgeois /'bɔːʒwɑː, US ˌbʊər'ʒwɑː/ **I** *n* bourgeois/-e *m/f*.
II *adj* bourgeois; **a ~ woman** une bourgeoise.

bourgeoisie /ˌbɔːʒwɑː'ziː, US ˌbʊəʒwɑː'ziː/ *n* bourgeoisie *f*.

bout /baʊt/ *n* **1** (attack) (of fever, malaria) accès *m*; (of insomnia) crise *f*; **a ~ of coughing** une quinte de toux; **drinking ~** soûlerie *f*; **to have a ~ of flu** avoir une grippe; **2** SPORT combat *m*; **3** (outbreak) crise *f*; **4** (period of activity) période *f*.

boutique /buː'tiːk/ ▶ 1251 *n* boutique *f*; **fashion ~** boutique de mode.

bovine /'bəʊvaɪn/ *adj* LIT, FIG bovin.

bow[1] /bəʊ/ *n* **1** (weapon) arc *m*; **2** MUS archet *m*; **3** (knot) nœud *m*; **to tie a ~** faire un nœud.
IDIOMS **to have more than one string to one's ~** avoir plus d'une corde à son arc.

bow[2] /baʊ/ **I** *n* **1** (movement) salut *m*; **to take a ~** THEAT saluer; **2** NAUT avant *m*, proue *f*; **on the starboard ~** par tribord devant.
II *vtr* baisser [*head*]; courber [*branch*]; incliner [*tree*].
III *vi* **1** (bend forward) saluer; **to ~ to** saluer; **2** (give way) **to ~ to** s'incliner devant [*wisdom, necessity*]; **to ~ to pressure** céder à la pression; **3** (sag) [*plant, shelf*] se courber (**under** sous).
IV bowed *pp adj* [*head*] penché; [*back*] courbé.
IDIOMS **to ~ and scrape** FIG faire des courbettes (**to** devant); **to fire a shot across sb's ~s** FIG tirer un coup de semonce à qn.
■ **bow down**: ¶ **~ down** LIT se prosterner (**before** devant); FIG se soumettre (**before** devant); ¶ **~ [sth] down** [*wind*] courber [*tree*].
■ **bow out** (resign) prendre congé, tirer sa révérence°.

bowel /'baʊəl/ **I** *n* intestin *m*; **~ cancer** cancer de l'intestin.
II bowels *npl* **1** MED intestins *mpl*; **2** FIG (inner depths) profondeurs *fpl*.

bowel movement *n* selles *fpl*.

bower /'baʊə(r)/ *n* **1** (in garden) tonnelle *f*; **2** LITTÉR (chamber) boudoir *m*.

bowl /bəʊl/ **I** *n* **1** (for food) bol *m*; (large) saladier *m*; (for soup) assiette *f* creuse; (for washing) cuvette *f*; (of lavatory) cuvette *f*; **a ~(ful) of milk** un bol de lait; **2** SPORT boule *f* (en bois).
II *vtr* **1** (roll) faire rouler [*hoop, ball*]; **2** (throw) lancer [*ball*].
III *vi* **1** SPORT lancer; **to ~ to sb** lancer la balle à qn; **2** US (go bowling) aller au bowling; **3** (move fast) **to ~ along** [*vehicle*] rouler à toute vitesse.
■ **bowl over**: **~ [sb] over** **1** (knock down) renverser [*person*]; **2** (impress) stupéfier [*person*]; **to be ~ed over** être sidéré.

bowlegged /ˌbəʊ'legɪd/ *adj* [*person*] aux jambes arquées; **to be ~** avoir les jambes arquées.

bowler /'bəʊlə(r)/ *n* **1** SPORT (in cricket) lanceur *m*; (in bowls) joueur/-euse *m/f* de boules (*sur gazon*); **2** (hat) = **bowler hat**.

bowler hat *n* chapeau *m* melon.

bowling /'bəʊlɪŋ/ ▶ 949 *n* SPORT **1** (ten-pin) bowling *m*; **2** (on grass) jeu *m* de boules (*sur gazon*); **3** (in cricket) service *m*.

bowling: ~ alley *n* bowling *m*; **~ green** *n* terrain *m* de boules (*sur gazon*).

bowls /bəʊlz/ ▶ 949 *n* (+ *v sg*) jeu *m* de boules (*sur gazon*).

bow /bəʊ/: **~string** *n* corde *f* d'arc; **~ tie** *n* nœud-papillon *m*; **~ window** *n* fenêtre *f* en saillie.

box 770 **branch**

box /bɒks/ I *n* **1** (small, cardboard) boîte *f*; (larger, crate) caisse *f*; **~ of matches/of chocolates** boîte d'allumettes/de chocolats; **2** (on page) case *f*; **put a tick in the ~** cocher la case; **3** (seating area) THEAT loge *f*; SPORT tribune *f*; **4** (in stable) box *m*; **5** GB SPORT (for protection) coquille *f*; **6**° (television) **the ~** la télé; **7** SPORT (in soccer) surface *f* de réparation; **8** (in gymnastics) cheval *m* de saut; **9** POST (*also* **Box**) boîte *f* postale; (P.O.) **Box 20** BP 20; **10** (for gears) boîte *f*; **11** (slap) **a ~ on the ear** une gifle; **12** BOT buis *m*.
II *vtr* **1** (pack) mettre [qch] en caisse, encaisser; **2** (fight) boxer; **3** (strike) **to ~ sb's ears** gifler qn.
III *vi* SPORT boxer.
IV **boxed** *pp adj* [*note, information*] en encadré; **~ed set** coffret *m*; **~ed advertisement** encadré *m*.
■ **box in**: **~ in** [sth/sb], **~** [sth/sb] **in** coincer° [*runner, car*]; **to be ~ed in** [*person*] être coincé°; **to feel ~ed in** se sentir enfermé.

boxer /'bɒksə(r)/ ▶1251| *n* **1** SPORT boxeur *m*; **2** (dog) boxer *m*.

boxer shorts *npl* caleçon *m* (court).

boxing /'bɒksɪŋ/ ▶949| I *n* boxe *f*; **to take up ~** se mettre à la boxe.
II *noun modifier* [*champion, glove, match*] de boxe; **~ ring** ring *m*.

Boxing Day /'bɒksɪŋ deɪ/ *n* GB lendemain *m* de Noël.

box: **~ junction** *n* GB milieu *m* d'intersection (*délimité par des bandes jaunes*); **~ number** *n* numéro *m* de boîte postale.

box office I *n* LIT guichet *m*; FIG **to do well/badly at the ~** être bien/mal accueilli au box office.
II *noun modifier* [*failure, success*] au box office; **~ takings** recettes *fpl* des guichets; **to be a ~ attraction** attirer les foules.

box: **~ room** *n* GB petite chambre *f* (*servant de débarras*); **~wood** *n* (bois *m* de) buis *m*.

boy /bɔɪ/ I *n* **1** (young male) garçon *m*; **the ~s' toilet** les toilettes des garçons; **a ~'s bike** un vélo pour garçon; **come here ~!** viens ici, mon garçon!; **a new ~** FIG, SCH un nouveau; **there's a good ~!** voilà, c'est bien mon petit!; **look ~s and girls** regardez, les enfants; **2** (son) fils *m*; **3**° GB (man) gars° *m*; **to be one of the ~s** faire partie de la bande; **to have a drink with the ~s** boire un coup avec les copains°; **an old ~** SCH un ancien élève; (old man) un vieillard; **4** (male animal) **down ~!** doucement, mon vieux!
II° **boys** *npl* **1** (experts) gars° *mpl*; **the legal ~s** les gars° du service juridique; **2** (soldiers) gars° *mpl*.
III *noun modifier* [*detective, genius, soprano*] jeune (*before n*).
IV° *excl* **~, it's cold here!** bon sang°! ce qu'il fait froid ici!

boycott /'bɔɪkɒt/ I *n* boycottage *m*, boycott *m* (**against, of, on** de).
II *vtr* boycotter.

boy: **~friend** *n* (petit) copain *m* or ami *m*; **~hood** *n* enfance *f*.

boyish /'bɔɪɪʃ/ *adj* **1** (youthful) [*figure, looks*] d'adolescent; **2** (endearingly young) [*grin, charm*] enfantin.

BR *n*: *abrév* ▶ **British Rail**.

bra /brɑː/ ▶1260| *n* soutien-gorge *m*.

brace /breɪs/ I *n* **1** (for teeth) appareil *m* dentaire; **2** MED (for broken limb) attelle *f*; (permanent support) appareil *m* orthopédique; **3** CONSTR support *m*; **4** (pair) (of birds, animals) couple *m* (**of** de); (of pistols) paire *f* (**of** de); **5** (tool) vilebrequin *m*.
II *vtr* **1** [*person*] arc-bouter [*body, back*] (**against** contre); **to ~ one's legs/feet against sth** appuyer les jambes/pieds contre qch; **2** CONSTR renforcer, consolider [*wall, structure*].
III **braces** *npl* GB (for trousers) bretelles *fpl*.
IV *v refl* **to ~ oneself** (physically) se raidir (**for** en prévision de); FIG se préparer (**for** à; **to do** à faire).

bracelet /'breɪslɪt/ *n* **1** (jewellery) bracelet *m*; **2** (watchstrap) bracelet *m* (de montre).

bracing /'breɪsɪŋ/ *adj* vivifiant, tonifiant.

bracken /'brækən/ *n* fougère *f*.

bracket /'brækɪt/ I *n* **1** (in typography) (round) paren-

thèse *f*; (square) crochet *m*; **in ~s** entre parenthèses o crochets; **2** (support) (for shelf) équerre *f*; (for lamp applique *f*; **3** (category) tranche *f*, catégorie *f*; **age ~** tranche d'âge; **price ~** catégorie de prix.
II *vtr* **1** (put in brackets) (round) mettre [qch] entre parenthèses; (square) mettre [qch] entre crochets; **2** (put in category) accoler [*names, items*]; mettre [qn] dans le même groupe [*people*].

brackish /'brækɪʃ/ *adj* saumâtre.

bradawl /'brædɔːl/ *n* poinçon *m*.

brag /bræg/ I *n* **1** (boast) fanfaronnade *f*; **2** (card game) ~ poker *m*.
II *vi* (*p prés etc* **-gg-**) se vanter (**to** auprès de; **about** de).

bragging /'brægɪŋ/ *n* fanfaronnade *f* (**about** au sujet de).

Brahmin /'brɑːmɪn/ *n* **1** RELIG brahmane *m*; **2** FIG mandarin *m*.

braid /breɪd/ I *n* **1** (of hair) tresse *f*, natte *f*; **2** (trimming) galon *m*.
II *vtr* **1** tresser [*hair*]; **2** galonner [*cushion, uniform*].

brain /breɪn/ I *n* **1** (living organ) cerveau *m*; **2** (*also* **~s**) (substance) ~s cervelle *f*; **to blow one's ~s out**° se faire sauter la cervelle°; **3** CULIN cervelle *f*; **calves' ~s** cervelle de veau; **4** (mind) **to have a good ~** être intelligent; **to have football on the ~**° ne penser qu'au football.
II **brains** *npl* (intelligence) intelligence *f*; **to have ~s** être intelligent; **he's the ~s of the family** c'est lui le cerveau de la famille; **to use one's ~s** faire marcher ses cellules grises.
III *noun modifier* [*cell, tissue*] du cerveau, cérébral; [*tumour*] au cerveau; [*haemorrhage, fever*] cérébral.
IV° *vtr* (knock out) assommer, estourbir°.
IDIOMS **to pick sb's ~s** avoir recours aux lumières de qn.

brain: **~child** *n* grande idée *f*; **~ damage** *n* ¢ lésions *fpl* cérébrales; **~ dead** *adj* MED dans un coma dépassé; **~ death** *n* mort *f* cérébrale; **~ drain** *n* fuite *f* des cerveaux; **~less** *adj* idiot; **~ scan** *n* scanographie *f* du cerveau; **~ scanner** *n* scanographe *m*; **~storm** *n* MED, FIG coup *m* de folie; **~storming** *n* remue-méninges *m inv*; **~s trust** GB, **~ trust** US *n* brain-trust *m*, comité *m* d'experts; **~ surgeon** ▶1251| *n* neurochirurgien/-ienne *m/f*; **~ surgery** *n* neurochirurgie *f*; **~ teaser**° *n* casse-tête *m inv*.

brainwash /'breɪnwɒʃ/ *vtr* faire subir un lavage de cerveau à; **they were ~ed into thinking that...** on a fini par leur faire croire que...

brain: **~washing** *n* (of prisoners) lavage *m* de cerveau; FIG (of public) bourrage° *m* de crâne; **~wave** *n* idée *f* géniale, illumination *f*.

brainy° /'breɪnɪ/ *adj* doué.

braise /breɪz/ *vtr* braiser.

brake /breɪk/ I *n* LIT, FIG frein *m*; **to apply the ~(s)** freiner.
II *vi* LIT, FIG freiner.

brake: **~ block** *n* patin *m* de frein; **~ disc** *n* disque *m* de frein; **~ drum** *n* tambour *m* de frein; **~ fluid** *n* liquide *m* de frein; **~ light** *n* feu *m* stop; **~ lining** *n* garniture *f* de frein; **~ pad** *n* plaquette *f* de frein; **~ pedal** *n* pédale *f* de frein.

braking /'breɪkɪŋ/ *n* freinage *m*.

bramble /'bræmbl/ I *n* **1** (plant) ronce *f*; **2** GB (berry) mûre *f*.
II *noun modifier* GB [*jam, jelly*] de mûres; [*tart*] aux mûres.

bran /bræn/ *n* BOT, CULIN son *m*.

branch /brɑːntʃ, US bræntʃ/ I *n* **1** (of tree) branche *f*; FIG (of pipe, road, railway) embranchement *m*; (of river) bras *m*; (of candlestick) branche *f*; (of antlers) ramure *f*; (of family, language) rameau *m*; (of study, subject) domaine *m*; **2** COMM, ADMIN (of shop) succursale *f*; (of bank) agence *f*; (of company) filiale *f*; (of organization) division *f*, secteur *m*; (of union) section *f*.
II *vi* [*tree, river*] se ramifier; [*road, railway*] se diviser.
■ **branch off**: ¶ **~ off** [*road, river, railway*]

bifurquer; **¶ ~ off (from)** se séparer de [*road, railway*]; FIG dévier de [*topic*].
■ **branch out**: **~ out** [*business*] se diversifier; **to ~ out into** [*business, person*] se lancer dans [*new area*].

branch: **~ line** *n* ligne *f* secondaire; **~ manager** *n* (of shop) directeur *m* de succursale; (of company) directeur *m* de filiale; (of bank) directeur *m* d'agence; **~ office** *n* agence *f*.

brand /brænd/ **I** *n* **1** (make) marque *f*; **2** (type) (of humour) type *m*; (of belief) conception *f*; (of art, of music) genre *m*; **3** (for identification) (on animal) marque *f* (au fer rouge); (on prisoner) marque *f*; **4** LITTÉR (in fire) tison *m*.
II *vtr* **1** (mark) LIT marquer (au fer) [*animal*]; **2** FIG marquer [*person*]; **to ~ sb as sth** désigner qn comme qch.

branded /'brændɪd/ *adj* [*article, goods*] de marque *inv.*

brandish /'brændɪʃ/ *vtr* brandir.

brand: **~ leader** *n* leader *m* du marché; **~ name** *n* marque *f* déposée; **~-new** *adj* tout neuf/toute neuve.

brandy /'brændɪ/ *n* **1** (from grape) cognac *m*; **2** (from other fruit) eau-de-vie *f*.

brash /bræʃ/ *adj* **1** (self-confident) bravache; **2** (garish) tape-à-l'œil (*inv*); **3** (harsh) agressif/-ive.

brass /brɑːs, US bræs/ **I** *n* **1** (metal) laiton *m*, cuivre *m* jaune; **2** (fittings, objects) cuivres *mpl*; **3** MUS (also **~ section**) cuivres *mpl*; **4** (in church) plaque *f* commémorative; **5**° (money) GB pognon° *m*; **6**° (nerve) culot° *m*; **7**° MIL (+ *v pl*) **the top ~** les galonnés.
II *noun modifier* [*button, plaque*] en cuivre jaune.
IDIOMS **to get down to ~ tacks** passer aux choses sérieuses; **to be as bold as ~** avoir un drôle de culot°.

brass band *n* orchestre *m* de cuivres, fanfare *f*.

brassière† /'bræzɪə(r), US brə'zɪər/ *n* soutien-gorge *m*.

brass: **~ instrument** ▶ 1097 *n* MUS cuivre *m*; **~ neck**° *n* GB culot° *m*; **~ rubbing** *n* ART (activity) estampage *m* de plaques en laiton; (impression) estampe *f* d'une plaque en laiton.

brassy /'brɑːsɪ, US 'bræsɪ/ *adj* **1** ▶ 818 (shiny) cuivré°; **2** PÉJ [*appearance, woman*] provocant.

brat° /bræt/ *n* PÉJ marmot° *m*, môme° *mf.*

bravado /brə'vɑːdəʊ/ *n* bravade *f.*

brave /breɪv/ **I** *n* **1** (Indian) brave *m*; **2 the ~** (+ *v pl*) les courageux.
II *adj* **1** (courageous) [*person, effort*] courageux/-euse; [*smile*] brave; **be ~!** courage!; **2** (fine) LITTÉR beau/belle (*before n*).
III *vtr* braver.
IDIOMS **to put on a ~ face** faire bonne contenance.

bravely /'breɪvlɪ/ *adv* courageusement; HUM vaillamment.

bravery /'breɪvərɪ/ *n* courage *m*, bravoure *f.*

bravura /brə'vʊərə/ *n* bravoure *f.*

brawl /brɔːl/ **I** *n* bagarre *f.*
II *vi* se bagarrer (**with** avec).

brawn /brɔːn/ *n* **1** CULIN fromage *m* de tête; **2** (muscle) muscles *mpl.*

brawny /'brɔːnɪ/ *adj* musclé.

bray /breɪ/ **I** *n* (of donkey) braiment *m*; PÉJ (of person) braillement *m.*
II *vi* [*donkey*] braire; PÉJ [*person*] brailler.

brazen /'breɪzn/ *adj* éhonté.
■ **brazen out**: **~ it out** payer d'audace.

brazier /'breɪzɪə(r)/ *n* brasero *m.*

Brazil /brə'zɪl/ ▶ 840 *pr n* Brésil *m.*

Brazil nut *n* noix *f* du Brésil.

breach /briːtʃ/ **I** *n* **1** (infringement) (by breaking rule) infraction *f* (**of** à); (by failure to comply) manquement *m* (**of** à); (of copyright, privilege) violation *f*; **security ~** (of official secret) atteinte *f* à la sûreté nationale; **to be in ~ of** enfreindre [*law*]; violer [*agreement*]; **2** MIL brèche *f* ALSO FIG; **3** (in relationship) rupture *f.*

II *vtr* faire une brèche dans [*defence*]; ne pas respecter [*rule*].
IDIOMS **to step into the ~** faire un remplacement au pied levé.

breach: **~ of contract** *n* JUR rupture *f* de contrat; **~ of promise** *n* rupture *f* de mariage; **~ of the peace** *n* JUR atteinte *f* à l'ordre public; **~ of trust** *n* JUR abus *m* de confiance.

bread /bred/ **I** *n* **1** CULIN pain *m*; **a loaf/slice of ~** une miche/tranche de pain; **2**° (money) fric° *m*, argent *m*; **3** (livelihood) **to earn one's (daily) ~** gagner sa vie.
II *noun modifier* [*oven, plate*] à pain; [*sauce*] au pain.
III *vtr* CULIN paner; **~ed cutlets** côtelettes panées.
IDIOMS **to know which side one's ~ is buttered on** savoir où est son intérêt.

bread and butter **I** *n* tartine *f* de pain beurré; FIG gagne-pain *m.*
II bread-and-butter *adj* [*work*] de tous les jours.

bread: **~basket** *n* LIT corbeille *f* à pain; FIG grenier *m*; **~bin** *n* GB boîte *f* or huche *f* à pain; **~board** *n* planche *f* à pain.

breadcrumb /'bredkrʌm/ **I** *n* miette *f* de pain.
II breadcrumbs *npl* CULIN chapelure *f.*

bread: **~fruit** *n* fruit *m* de l'arbre à pain; **~knife** *n* couteau *m* à pain.

breadline /'bredlaɪn/ *n* **to be on the ~** être au seuil de l'indigence.

bread: **~ roll** *n* CULIN petit pain *m*; **~stick** *n* longuet *m.*

breadth /bretθ/ ▶ 1045 *n* **1** LIT largeur *f*; **the length and ~ of** d'un bout à l'autre de; **2** FIG (of experience, knowledge, provisions, regulations) étendue *f* (**of** de); (of mind, opinions, vision) largeur *f* (**of** de).
IDIOMS **to be** OU **come within a hair's ~ of** être à deux doigts de.

breadwinner /'bredwɪnə(r)/ *n* soutien *m* de famille.

break /breɪk/ **I** *n* **1** (fracture) fracture *f*; **2** (crack) fêlure *f*; **3** (gap) (in wall) brèche *f*; (in row, line) espace *m*; (in circuit, chain) rupture *f*; (in conversation, match) pause *f*; (in performance) entracte *m*; (in traffic) trou *m*, espace *m*; **a ~ in the clouds** une éclaircie; **a ~ in transmission** une interruption dans la retransmission; **4** RADIO, TV page *f* de publicité; **5** (pause) GEN pause *f*; SCH récréation *f*; **to take a ~** faire une pause; **to work for six hours without a ~** travailler pendant six heures sans s'arrêter; **to take** OU **have a ~ from working** ne plus travailler pendant un temps; **I often give her a ~ from looking after the kids** je m'occupe souvent des enfants pour qu'elle se repose; **6** (holiday) vacances *fpl*; **the Christmas ~** les vacances de Noël; **7** FIG (departure) rupture *f* (**with** avec); **a ~ with tradition** une rupture avec la tradition; **it's time to make a** ou **the ~ (from family)** il est temps de voler de ses propres ailes; (from job) il est temps de passer à autre chose; **8**° (opportunity) chance *f*; **her big ~ came in 1973** 1973 a été l'année de sa veine°; **he gave me a ~** il m'a donné ma chance; **9** (dawn) **at the ~ of day** au lever du jour, à l'aube *f*; **10** (escape bid) **to make a ~ for it**° (from prison) se faire la belle°; **to make a ~ for the door** se précipiter vers la porte; **11** SPORT (in tennis) break *m*; (in snooker, pool) **it's your ~** c'est à toi de casser; **to make a 50 point ~** marquer une série de 50 points.
II *vtr* (*prét* **broke**; *pp* **broken**) **1** (damage) casser [*chair, eggs, rope, stick, toy*]; casser [*plate, window*]; **to ~ a tooth/a bone** se casser une dent/un os; **to ~ one's leg** se casser la jambe; **to ~ one's neck** LIT avoir une rupture des vertèbres cervicales; FIG se casser la figure; **2** (rupture) briser [*seal*]; **the skin is not broken** il n'y a pas de plaie; **the river broke its banks** la rivière a débordé; **3** (interrupt) [*person*] rompre [*silence*]; [*shout, siren*] déchirer [*silence*]; couper [*circuit*]; rompre [*monotony, spell, ties, links*] (**with** avec); **to ~ one's silence** sortir de son silence (**on** à propos de); **we broke our journey in Milan** nous avons fait un arrêt à Milan; **4** (disobey) enfreindre [*law*]; ne pas respecter [*embargo, terms*]; violer [*treaty*]; désobéir à [*rule*]; briser [*strike*]; rompre

[*vow*]; manquer [*appointment*]; **to ~ one's word/ promise** manquer à sa parole/promesse; **5** (exceed, surpass) dépasser [*speed limit, bounds*]; battre [*record*]; franchir [*speed barrier*]; **6** (lessen the impact of) couper [*wind*]; [*branches*] freiner [*fall*]; [*hay*] amortir [*fall*]; **7** FIG (destroy) [*troops*] briser [*rebellion*]; briser [*person, resistance, will*]; **to ~ sb's spirit** saper le moral de qn; **to ~ a habit** se défaire d'une habitude; **8** (ruin) ruiner [*person*]; **9** (tame) débourrer [*young horse*]; **10** (in tennis) **to ~ sb's serve** faire le break; **11** (decipher) déchiffrer [*code*]; **12** (leave) **to ~ camp** lever le camp; **13** (announce) annoncer [*news*]; révéler [*truth*]; **to ~ the news to sb** apprendre la nouvelle à qn.

III vi (prét **broke**; pp **broken**) **1** (be damaged) [*branch, chair, egg, string*] se casser; [*plate, window*] se casser; [*arm, bone, leg*] se fracturer; [*bag*] se déchirer; **to ~ in two** se casser en deux; **the sound of ~ing glass** le bruit de verre brisé; **2** (separate) [*clouds*] se disperser; [*waves*] se briser; **3** (stop for a rest) faire une pause; **4** (change) [*good weather*] se gâter; [*heatwave*] cesser; [*day*] se lever; [*storm*] éclater; [*scandal, story*] éclater; **6** (discontinue) **to ~ with sb** rompre les relations avec qn; **to ~ with tradition** rompre avec la tradition; **7** (weaken) **their spirit never broke** leur moral n'a jamais faibli; **to ~ under torture** céder sous la torture; **8** (change tone) [*boy's voice*] muer; **in a voice ~ing with emotion** d'une voix brisée par l'émotion.

■ **break away**: ¶ ~ **away 1** (become detached) se détacher (**from** de); **to ~ away from** rompre avec [*family, organization*]; se détacher de [*herd*]; rompre [*moorings*]; **2** (escape) échapper (**from** à); **3** SPORT [*runner, cyclist*] se détacher (**from** de); ¶ ~ **away** [*sth*], ~ [*sth*] **away** enlever.

■ **break down**: ¶ ~ **down 1** (stop functioning) [*machine*] tomber en panne; **2** (collapse) FIG [*alliance*] éclater; [*negotiations*] échouer; [*communication*] cesser; [*law and order*] se dégrader; [*argument*] ne pas tenir debout; [*system*] s'effondrer; [*person*] s'effondrer, craquer; **3** (cry) fondre en larmes; **4** (be classified) se décomposer (**into** en); **5** (decompose) se décomposer (**en** into); **6** (confess) céder; ¶ ~ [*sth*] **down**, ~ **down** [*sth*] **1** (demolish) enfoncer [*door*]; démolir [*fence*]; FIG faire tomber [*barriers*]; vaincre [*resistance*]; **2** (analyse) ventiler [*cost, statistics*]; décomposer [*data, findings*] (**into** par); **3** (cause to decompose) décomposer [*compound*] (**into** en); dissoudre [*protein, starch*].

■ **break even** rentrer dans ses frais.

■ **break free**: ~ **free** [*prisoner*] s'évader; **to ~ free of** se couper de [*family*]; échapper à [*captor*].

■ **break in** ¶ **1** (enter forcibly) [*thief*] entrer (par effraction); [*police*] entrer de force; **2** (interrupt) interrompre; ¶ ~ [*sth*] **in** débourrer [*young horse*]; assouplir [*shoe*]; ¶ ~ [*sb*] **in** accoutumer [qn] au travail.

■ **break into**: ~ **into** [*sth*] **1** (enter by force) entrer dans [qch] (par effraction) [*building*]; forcer la portière de [*car*]; forcer [*safe*]; **her car was broken into** sa voiture a été cambriolée; **2** (start to use) entamer [*new packet*]; **3** (encroach on) empiéter sur [*leisure time*]; couper [*morning*]; **4** (begin to do) **to ~ into song/ cheers** se mettre à chanter/acclamer; **5** (make headway) **to ~ into a run** se mettre à courir; [*company*] s'implanter sur [*market*]; percer dans [*show business*].

■ **break off**: ¶ ~ **off 1** (snap off) [*end, mast*] se casser; [*handle, piece*] se détacher; **2** (stop speaking) s'interrompre; **3** (pause) faire une pause; ¶ ~ **off** [*sth*], ~ [*sth*] **off 1** (snap) casser; **2** (terminate) rompre [*engagement, negotiations*]; interrompre [*conversation*].

■ **break out**: ~ **out 1** (erupt) [*epidemic, fire*] se déclarer; [*fight, riot, storm*] éclater; [*rash*] apparaître; **to ~ out in a rash** [*person*] avoir une éruption de boutons; **to ~ out in a sweat** se mettre à transpirer; **2** (escape) [*prisoner*] s'évader; **to ~ out of** s'échapper de [*prison*]; sortir de [*routine*]; se libérer de [*chains*].

■ **break through**: ¶ ~ **through** [*army*] faire une percée; ¶ ~ **through** [*sth*] percer [*defences, reserve*]; franchir [*barrier*]; traverser [*mur*]; [*sun*] percer [*clouds*].

■ **break up**: ¶ ~ **up 1** (disintegrate) LIT [*wreck*] se

désagréger; FIG [*empire*] s'effondrer; [*alliance*] éclater [*family, couple*] se séparer; **2** (disperse) [*crowd*] se disperser; [*cloud, slick*] se disperser; [*meeting*] se termi∎ ner; **3** GB SCH **schools ~ up on Friday** les cours fi∎ nissent vendredi; ¶ ~ [*sth*] **up**, ~ **up** [*sth*]∎ disperser [*demonstrators*]; démanteler [*drugs ring*]; se∎ parer [*team, couple*]; désunir [*family*]; briser [*alliance*]∎ *marriage*]; démembrer [*empire*]; morceler [*land*]; [*dia∎ grams*] aérer [*text*]; mettre fin à [*party, demonstration*]

breakable /'breɪkəbl/ **I breakables** npl objets mp∎ fragiles.
II adj fragile.

breakage /'breɪkɪdʒ/ n (damage) casse f; (broken item∎ article m cassé.

breakaway /'breɪkəweɪ/ **I** n **1** (from organization) sépa∎ ration f (**from** de); (from person) rupture f (**from** avec∎ **2** SPORT échappée f.
II noun modifier POL (épith) [*faction, group, state*] sé∎ paratiste.

breakdown /'breɪkdaʊn/ **I** n **1** AUT, TECH panne∎ (**in, of** de); **in the event of a ~** en cas de panne; **he∎ had a ~** il est tombé en panne; **2** (collapse) (of commu∎ nications, negotiations) rupture f; (of alliance) éclatement m; (of plan) échec m; **3∎ MED dépression f; **to have a (nervous) ~** faire une∎ dépression (nerveuse); **4** (detailed account) (of figures statistics) ventilation f; (of argument) décomposition f; **~ of the voters according to sex/age** une réparti∎ tion de l'ensemble des électeurs par sexe/tranch∎ d'âge; **5** BIOL, CHEM décomposition f.
II noun modifier [*vehicle, truck*] de dépannage.

breaker /'breɪkə(r)/ n **1** (wave) brisant m; **2 ▶1251** (scrap merchant) casseur m; **3** (CB radio user) cibiste mf.

breaker's yard n AUT casse f.

break: **~-even** n seuil m de rentabilité; **~-even point** n point m mort.

breakfast /'brekfəst/ **I** n petit déjeuner m.
II vi prendre le petit déjeuner.

breakfast: **~ bar** n bar m de cuisine; **~ bowl ∎ assiette f creuse; **~ cereals** npl céréales fpl (pour l∎ petit déjeuner); **~ television** n télévision f à l'heur∎ du petit déjeuner.

break-in /'breɪkɪn/ n cambriolage m.

breaking /'breɪkɪŋ/ n **1** (smashing) LIT (of bone∎ fracture f; (of rope, chain) rupture f; (of glass, seal) bri∎ m; FIG (of waves) déferlement m; **2** (of promise) manque∎ ment m (**of** à); (of law, treaty) violation f (**of** de); (of contract) rupture f (**of** de); (of link, sequence, tie) rupture (**of** de); **3** (of horse) débourrage m; **4** (of voice) mue f.

breaking and entering n JUR effraction f.

breaking point n **1** TECH point m de rupture; **∎ FIG **to be at ~** être à bout.

break: **~neck** adj [*pace, speed*] fou/folle, insensé∎ **~-out** n évasion f; **~point** n SPORT balle f d∎ break; **~through** n MIL percée f; (in science, med∎ cine, career) percée f; (in negotiations, investigation) progrè∎ m; **~-up** n (of empire) démembrement m; (of alliance∎ relationship) rupture f; (of political party, family, group) écla∎ tement m; (of marriage) échec m; (of a company) morcelle∎ ment m; **~water** n brise-lames m inv.

bream /briːm/ n (pl **~**) (freshwater) brème f.

breast /brest/ **I** n **1** ANAT (woman's) sein m; (chest∎ poitrine f; **2** CULIN (of poultry) blanc m, filet m; (o∎ lamb) poitrine f; (of veal) tendron m; (of duck, pigeo∎ filet m, magret m.
II vtr affronter [*wave*]; atteindre le sommet de [*hill*].
IDIOMS **to make a clean ~ of sth** soulager sa cons∎ cience en avouant qch.

breast-feed /'brestfiːd/ vtr, vi (prét, pp **-fed**) allaiter∎ **breast-fed** nourri au sein.

breast: **~-feeding** n allaitement m maternel; **~∎ pocket** n poche f de poitrine; **~ stroke** n brasse f.

breath /breθ/ **I** n **1** (air taken into lungs) souffle m; **t∎ stop** OU **pause for ~** s'arrêter pour reprendre so∎ souffle; **to get one's ~ back** reprendre son souffle **out of ~** à bout de souffle; **to be short of ~** avoi∎ le souffle court; **to hold one's ~** LIT retenir sa resp∎

ration; FIG retenir son souffle; **2** (air in or leaving mouth) (with smell) haleine *f*; (visible) respiration *f*; **sb's hot ~** le souffle chaud de qn; **to have bad ~** avoir (une) mauvaise haleine; **I could smell alcohol on his ~** je sentais à son haleine qu'il avait bu; **3** (single act) respiration *f*; **to take a deep ~** respirer profondément or à fond; **take a deep ~!** FIG assieds-toi○!; **in a single ~** sans respirer; **in the same ~** dans la foulée; **4** (of air, wind) **a ~ of** un souffle de; **to go out for a ~ of (fresh) air** sortir prendre l'air; **sb/sth is like a ~ of fresh air** qn/qch est une vraie bouffée de fraîcheur; **5** (word) **a ~ of** un soupçon de [*scandal*].
IDIOMS **to take sb's ~ away** couper le souffle à qn; **save your ~**○ ne gaspille pas ta salive○; **to say sth under one's ~** dire qch à voix basse.

breathalyse GB, **breathalyze** US /'breθəlaɪz/ *vtr* faire subir un alcootest à [*driver*]; **to be ~d** subir un alcootest.

Breathalyzer® /'breθəlaɪzə(r)/ *n* alcootest *m*.

breathe /briːð/ **I** *vtr* **1** (inhale, respire) respirer [*air, oxygen, gas, scent*]; **to ~ one's last** rendre son dernier soupir; **2** (exhale, blow) souffler [*air, smoke, germs*] (**on** sur); cracher [*fire, vapour*]; **3** (whisper) murmurer (**to** à); **don't ~ a word!** pas un mot!; **4** (inspire with) **to ~ hope into sb** redonner de l'espoir à qn; **to ~ (some) life into sth** animer qch.
II *vi* **1** (respire) respirer; **to ~ hard** ou **heavily** souffler fort, haleter; **to ~ more easily** FIG respirer; **2** (exhale, blow) **to ~ over sb/on sth** souffler sur qn/sur qch; **3** (wine) s'aérer.
IDIOMS **to ~ down sb's neck**○ (watch closely) être sur le dos de qn○; (be close behind) être sur les talons de qn○; **to ~ fire** fulminer.
■ **breathe in**: ¶ **~ in** inspirer; ¶ **~ in** [sth], **~** [sth] **in** inhaler.
■ **breathe out**: ¶ **~ out** expirer; ¶ **~ out** [sth], **~** [sth] **out** exhaler.

breather /'briːðə(r)/ *n* **1** (from work) pause *f*; **to have** ou **take a ~** faire une pause; **2** (from pressure) répit *m*.

breathing /'briːðɪŋ/ *n* respiration *f*.

breathing apparatus *n* masque *m* à oxygène.

breathing space *n* **1** (respite) répit *m*; **to give oneself a ~** s'accorder un répit; **2** (postponement) délai *m*.

breathless /'breθlɪs/ *adj* **1** (out of breath) [*person, runner*] à bout de souffle; [*asthmatic*] haletant; **to make** ou **leave sb ~** essouffler qn; **2** (excited) [*hush, fascination*] extasié; **to be ~ with** avoir le souffle coupé par; **3** (fast) **at a ~ pace** à toute allure.

breathlessly /'breθlɪslɪ/ *adv* d'une voix haletante.

breathlessness /'breθlɪsnɪs/ *n* essoufflement *m*.

breathtaking /'breθteɪkɪŋ/ *adj* [*feat, pace, skill*] stupéfiant; [*scenery, view*] à vous couper le souffle.

breathtakingly /'breθteɪkɪŋlɪ/ *adv* **~ beautiful** d'une beauté à vous couper le souffle; **~ audacious** d'une audace stupéfiante.

breath test I *n* alcootest *m*.
II *vtr* faire subir un alcootest à [*driver*]; **to be ~ed** subir un alcootest.

bred /bred/ *prét*, *pp* ▶ **breed**.

breech /briːtʃ/ *n* **1** MED (also **~ birth**, **~ delivery**) accouchement *m* par le siège; **2** (of gun) culasse *f*.

breeches /'brɪtʃɪz/ *npl* **1** (also **knee ~**) culotte *f*; **a pair of ~** une culotte; **2** (also **riding ~**) culotte *f* (de cheval); **3**○ US pantalon *m*.

breed /briːd/ **I** *n* **1** ZOOL race *f*; **2** (type of person, thing) type *m*.
II *vtr* (*prét*, *pp* **bred**) élever [*animals*]; produire [*plants*]; FIG engendrer [*disease, unrest*]; produire [*person*].
III *vi* (*prét*, *pp* **bred**) [*animals*] se reproduire; [*organisms*] se multiplier.
IV bred *pp adj* **ill-/well-~** mal/bien élevé.

breeder /'briːdə(r)/ *n* **1** AGRIC, ZOOL (of animals) éleveur *m*; (of plants) producteur *m*; (nuclear) (also **~ reactor**) surgénérateur *m*.

breeding /'briːdɪŋ/ *n* **1** AGRIC, ZOOL reproduction *f*; **2** (good manners) bonnes manières *fpl*.

breeding ground *n* **1** ZOOL lieu *m* de reproduction (**for** de); **2** FIG foyer *m* (**for** de).

breeding: **~ period**, **~ season** *n* saison *f* de reproduction; **~ stock** *n* AGRIC ₵ reproducteurs *mpl*.

breeze /briːz/ **I** *n* brise *f*; **sea ~** brise de mer; **in the ~** dans la brise.
II *vi* **to ~ in/out** entrer/sortir d'un air dégagé; **to ~ through life** traverser la vie avec insouciance; **to ~ through an exam** réussir un examen sans difficulté.

breeze block /'briːzblɒk/ *n* GB parpaing *m*, moellon *m*.

breezily /'briːzɪlɪ/ *adv* **1** (casually) de façon désinvolte; **2** (cheerfully) jovialement; (confidently) avec assurance.

breezy /'briːzɪ/ *adj* **1** [*place*] exposé au vent; **it will be ~** il y aura de la brise; **it's a ~ morning** il y a une bonne brise ce matin; **2** (cheerful) jovial; (confident) qui a de l'aplomb; **bright and ~** enjoué.

brethren /'breðrən/ *npl* **1** HIST, RELIG, HUM frères *mpl*; **2** (in trades union) HUM camarades *mpl*.

brevity /'brevətɪ/ *n* (of event) brièveté *f*; (of speech) concision *f*.

brew /bruː/ **I** *n* **1** (beer) bière *f*; **2** (tea) thé *m*, infusion *f*; **3** (unpleasant mixture) mixture *f*.
II *vtr* brasser [*beer*]; préparer [*tea, mixture*]; FIG préparer, mijoter○ [*plot, scandal*]; **freshly ~ed coffee** café fraîchement passé.
III *vi* **1** LIT [*beer*] fermenter; [*tea*] infuser; [*brewer*] brasser; **2** FIG [*storm, crisis*] se préparer; [*quarrel, revolt*] se tramer; **there's trouble ~ing** il y a de l'orage dans l'air.

brewer /'bruːə(r)/ ▶1251 *n* brasseur *m*.

brewery /'bruːərɪ/ *n* brasserie *f*.

brewing /'bruːɪŋ/ **I** *n* brasserie *f*.
II *noun modifier* [*group, company*] qui fabrique de la bière; [*business, industry, magnate*] de la bière; [*method*] de brassage.

brew-up /'bruːʌp/ *n* GB thé *m*.

briar /'braɪə(r)/ *n* **1** (also **~ rose**) églantier *m*; **2** (heather) bruyère *f*; **3** (also **~ pipe**) pipe *f* en bruyère; **4 briars** (thorns) ronces *fpl*.

bribe /braɪb/ **I** *n* pot-de-vin *m*; **to give sb a ~** graisser la patte○ à qn.
II *vtr* **1** (large-scale) soudoyer [*police*] (**with** avec; **to do** de faire); suborner [*witness*] (**to do** de faire); acheter [*voter*]; **2** (small-scale) graisser la patte à○ [*official*].

bribery /'braɪbərɪ/ *n* corruption *f*; (de témoin) subornation *f*.

brick /brɪk/ **I** *n* **1** CONSTR brique *f*; **made of ~** en brique; **2** GB (child's toy) cube *m*.
II *noun modifier* [*wall*] de briques; [*building*] en briques.
IDIOMS **it's like banging one's head against** ou **talking to a ~ wall** autant parler à un mur; **to run up against** ou **run into a ~ wall** se heurter à un mur.
■ **brick up**: **~** [sth] **up**, **~ up** [sth] murer, boucher.

brick: **~bat** *n* FIG violente critique *f*; **~-built** *adj* en briques; **~layer** ▶1251 *n* maçon *m*; **~laying** *n* maçonnerie *f*; **~ red** ▶818 *n*, *adj* rouge (*m*) brique *inv*; **~work** *n* briquetage *m*; **~works** *n* briqueterie *f*.

bridal /'braɪdl/ *adj* [*dress etc*] de mariée; [*car, procession, bed, chamber*] des mariés; [*feast*] de noce.

bridal: **~ party** *n* (+ *v sg ou pl*) proches *mpl* de la mariée; **~ suite** *n* suite *f* nuptiale; **~ wear** *n* robes *fpl* de mariée.

bride /braɪd/ *n* **1** (jeune) mariée *f*; **his ~** (after wedding) son épouse *f*; (before wedding) sa future épouse *f*; **the ~ and (bride)groom** les (jeunes) mariés *mpl*; **2** (also **~-to-be**) future mariée *f*.

bride: **~groom** *n* jeune marié *m*; (before wedding) futur marié *m*; **~smaid** *n* demoiselle *f* d'honneur.

bridge /brɪdʒ/ **I** *n* **1** CONSTR pont *m* (**over** sur; **across** au-dessus de); **2** FIG (link) rapprochement *m*;

to build ~s établir des relations (**between** entre); **3** (intermediate stage) (transitional) passerelle *f* (**between** entre); (springboard) tremplin *m* (**to** vers); **4** (on ship) passerelle *f*; **5** (of nose) arête *f*; **6** (of spectacles) arcade *f*; **7** (on guitar, violin) chevalet *m*; **8** (for teeth) bridge *m*; **9 ▶ 949**｜ GAMES bridge *m*.
II *vtr* **1** LIT construire un pont sur [*river*]; **2** FIG **to ~ the gap between two adversaries** effectuer un rapprochement entre or rapprocher deux adversaires; **to ~ a gap in** [sth] combler un vide dans [*conversation*]; combler un trou dans [*budget*]; combler une lacune dans [*knowledge*]; **3** (span) enjamber [*two eras*].
IDIOMS **a lot of water has flowed under the ~** beaucoup d'eau a coulé sous les ponts; **it's all water under the ~** c'est du passé; **we'll cross that ~ when we come to it** on s'occupera de ce problème en temps voulu.

bridge-building *n* MIL installation *f* de ponts provisoires; FIG médiation *f* (**between** entre).

bridging loan *n* GB FIN prêt *m* relais.

bridle /'braɪdl/ **I** *n* (for horse) bride *f*; FIG frein *m*.
II *vtr* (restrain) brider [*temper*]; brider [*horse*].
III *vi* (in anger) se cabrer (**at** contre; **with** sous l'effet de).

bridle path, **bridle track**, **bridleway** *n* piste *f* cavalière.

brief /briːf/ **▶ 1260**｜ **I** *n* **1** GB (remit) attributions *fpl*; (role) tâche *f*; **it is your ~** ou **your ~ is to do** votre tâche consiste à faire; **with a ~ for** chargé de [*environment, immigration*]; **2** JUR dossier *m*; **3** GB (instructions) directives *fpl*; **designer's ~** directives du concepteur.
II briefs *npl* (undergarment) slip *m*.
III *adj* **1** (concise) [*event, summary, speech*] bref/brève; [*reply*] laconique; **to be ~** je serai bref; **in ~** en bref; **the news in ~** les brèves; **2** (short) [*skirt*] court.
IV *vtr* informer [*politician, worker*] (**on** de); donner des instructions à [*police, troops*] (**on** sur); donner des directives à [*artist, designer*] (**on** sur); confier une cause à [*lawyer*]; **to be well-~ed** être bien au courant.
IDIOMS **to hold a watching ~ on sb** tenir qn à l'œil.

briefcase /'briːfkeɪs/ *n* serviette *f*; (without handle) porte-documents *m inv*.

briefing /'briːfɪŋ/ *n* briefing *m* (**on** sur); réunion *f* d'information (**on** sur); **press ~** briefing *m* de presse.

briefly /'briːflɪ/ *adv* **1** (concisely) [*describe, speak*] brièvement; [*reply, say*] laconiquement; **2** (for short time) [*affect, look, pause*] un bref instant; [*work, meet*] brièvement; **3** (in short) en bref.

brigade /brɪ'geɪd/ *n* brigade *f*; **cavalry ~** brigade de cavalerie; **the anti-smoking ~** la brigade anti-tabac.

brigadier /ˌbrɪgə'dɪə(r)/ **▶ 1192**｜ *n* général *m* de brigade.

bright /braɪt/ **I** *adj* **1** (vivid) [*blue, red*] vif/vive; [*garment, carpet, wallpaper*] (of one colour) de couleur vive; (of several colours) aux couleurs vives; **he went ~ red** il est devenu tout rouge; **2** (clear) [*sunshine*] éclatant; [*room, day*] clair; [*weather*] radieux/-ieuse; [*sky*] lumineux/-euse; **~ spell** éclaircie *f*; **3** (shiny) [*star, eye, coin, metal*] brillant; [*jewel*] étincelant; **4** (clever) intelligent; **a ~ idea** une idée lumineuse; **5** (cheerful) [*person, mood*] joyeux/-euse; [*smile, face*] radieux/-ieuse; **to look on the ~ side** voir le bon côté des choses; **6** (promising) [*future*] brillant; **one of our ~est hopes** l'un de nos meilleurs espoirs.
II *adv* [*shine, burn*] d'un vif éclat.

brighten /'braɪtn/: ■ **brighten up**: ¶ **1** (become cheerful) [*person, mood*] s'égayer (**at** à); [*face*] s'illuminer (**at** à); [*eyes*] s'allumer (**at** à; **with** de); **2** (improve) [*situation*] s'améliorer; [*weather, sky*] s'éclaircir; ¶ **~ up** [sth], **~** [sth] **up 1** (make colourful, cheerful) égayer; **2** (illuminate) éclairer; **3** (improve) rendre [qch] plus réjouissant [*prospects*].

bright-eyed /ˌbraɪt'aɪd/ *adj* aux yeux brillants.
IDIOMS **~ and bushy-tailed** frais et dispos.

brightly /'braɪtlɪ/ *adv* **1** (vividly) [*dressed*] de couleurs vives; **~ coloured** (several colours) aux couleurs vives; (of one colour) de couleur vive; **~ painted** aux couleurs vives; **2** (of sun, fire) [*shine, burn*] d'un éclat vif; (of eyes, metal) [*shine, sparkle*] intensément; **3** (intensely) [*lit*] brillamment; **4** (cheerfully) joyeusement.

brightness /'braɪtnɪs/ *n* **1** (of colour, light, smile) éclat *m*; **2** (of room) clarté *f*; **3** (of metal, eyes) brillant *m*; **4** (cheerfulness) vivacité *f*; **5** TV luminosité *f*.

bright spark○ *n* GB petit/-e futé/-e○ *m/f*.

bright young thing *n* GB **the ~s** la jeunesse dorée.

brill /brɪl/ **I** *n* ZOOL barbue *f*, sandre *f*.
II○ *adj, excl* GB (*abrév* = **brilliant**) super○.

brilliance /'brɪlɪəns/ *n* (of light, music) éclat *m*; (of person) génie *m*.

brilliant /'brɪlɪənt/ **I** *n* (diamond) brillant *m*.
II *adj* **1** (successful) [*student, career, success*] brillant; **2** (bright) éclatant; **3** GB ○(fantastic) génial○; **we had a ~ time** c'était génial; **to be ~ at sth** être doué en qch; **to be ~ at doing** avoir le don de faire.
III *excl* super○! ALSO IRON.

brilliantly /'brɪlɪəntlɪ/ *adv* **1** (very well) brillamment; **2** (particularly) [*witty, clever*] extrêmement; **3** (very brightly) [*shine*] avec éclat; [*illuminated*] vivement; **~ coloured**, **~ colourful** aux couleurs éclatantes.

Brillo pad® /'brɪləʊ pæd/ *n* tampon *m* Jex®.

brim /brɪm/ **I** *n* bord *m*; **a hat with a wide ~** un chapeau à large bord; **to fill sth to the ~** remplir qch à ras bord; **filled to the ~ with** rempli jusqu'au bord de [*liquid, objects*].
II *vi* (*p prés etc* **-mm-**) **to ~ with** LIT [*receptacle*] être plein à ras bord de; FIG déborder de; **his eyes ~med with tears** ses yeux se remplirent de larmes.
■ **brim over** LIT, FIG déborder (**with** de).

brine /braɪn/ *n* **1** (sea water) eau *f* de mer; **2** CULIN saumure *f*.

bring /brɪŋ/ (*prét, pp* **brought**) **I** *vtr* **1** (convey, carry) apporter; **wait and see what tomorrow ~s** attends de voir ce que demain nous apportera; **to ~ sb flowers** apporter des fleurs à qn; **the case has brought him publicity** l'affaire lui a fait de la publicité; **to ~ sb wealth/fame** rendre qn riche/célèbre; **to ~ sth to** (contribute) apporter qch à [*school, work, area*]; **to ~ one's experience to sth** faire bénéficier qch de son expérience; **that ~s the total to 100** cela fait un total de 100; **to ~ a smile to sb's face** faire sourire qn; **to ~ sth into** faire entrer qch dans [*room*]; introduire qch dans [*conversation*]; **to ~ sth into existence** créer qch; **the wind brought the tree down** le vent a fait tomber l'arbre; **don't forget to ~ it home** n'oublie pas de le rapporter; **to ~ shame/disgrace on sb** attirer la honte/le déshonneur sur qn; **to ~ sth on** upon **oneself** attirer qch; **you brought it on yourself** tu l'as cherché; **2** (come with) amener [*friend, relative, dog*]; **to ~ sb with one** amener qn (**avec soi**); **to ~ sb to** amener qn à; **3** (lead, draw) **the path ~s you to the church** le chemin te conduit jusqu'à l'église; **the Games brought people to the city** les Jeux ont attiré du monde vers la ville; **I brought him to the ground** je l'ai fait tomber; **that ~s me to the question of** ceci m'amène à la question de; **to ~ sb to do sth** faire faire qch à qn; **to ~ sb/a dog into the country** faire entrer or introduire qn/un chien dans le pays; **to ~ sb into contact with sb** mettre qn en contact avec qn; **to ~ sb home** (transport home) raccompagner qn, ramener qn; (to meet family) amener qn à la maison; **4** TV, RADIO **the game will be brought to you live** le match sera retransmis en direct; **we ~ you all the latest news** on vous donne les dernières nouvelles; **5** JUR, ADMIN **to ~ a case before the court** porter une affaire devant le tribunal; **to ~ sb before the court** faire comparaître qn devant le tribunal; **to ~ a matter before the committee** soumettre une question au comité.
II *v refl* **to ~ oneself to do** se décider à faire; **I couldn't ~ myself to get up/to tell him** je n'ai pas pu me lever/le lui dire.
■ **bring about**: **~ about** [sth], **~** [sth] **about**

provoquer [*change, disaster, death*]; amener [*settlement, reconciliation*]; entraîner [*success, failure, defeat*].

■ **bring along**: ¶ ~ **along** [*sth*], ~ [*sth*] **along** apporter [*object*]; ¶ ~ **along** [*sb*], ~ [*sb*] **along** amener, venir avec [*friend, partner*].

■ **bring back**: ~ **back** [*sth*], ~ [*sth*] **back 1** (return with) rapporter [*souvenir*] (from de); **to** ~ **sb back** rapporter qch à qn; **2** (restore) redonner [*colour, shine*]; **to** ~ **sb's memory back** rendre la mémoire à qn; **3** (reintroduce) rétablir [*custom*]; restaurer [*monarchy*]; **4** (restore memory of) rappeler [*night, occasion*]; **seeing her brought it all back to me** tout m'est revenu lorsque je l'ai vue; **to** ~ **back memories** ranimer des souvenirs.

■ **bring down**: ¶ ~ **down** [*sth*], ~ [*sth*] **down 1** (cause collapse of) renverser [*government*]; **2** (reduce) réduire [*inflation, expenditure*]; faire baisser [*rate, level, price, temperature*]; diminuer [*cost of living*]; **3** (shoot down) abattre; ¶ ~ [*sb*] **down**° déprimer [*person*].

■ **bring forth**: ~ **forth** [*sth*], ~ [*sth*] **forth 1** (provoke) susciter; **2** LITTÉR (produce) produire [*object, fruit*]; faire jaillir [*water*]; donner naissance à [*child*].

■ **bring forward**: ~ **forward** [*sth*], ~ [*sth*] **forward 1** (make sooner) avancer (**by** de); **2** (propose) avancer [*proposals*]; proposer [*bill*].

■ **bring in**: ¶ ~ **in** [*sth*] rapporter [*amount, money, interest*]; introduire [*custom*]; ¶ ~ **in** [*sth*], ~ [*sth*] **in 1** (introduce) introduire [*legislation, measure*]; **2** AGRIC rentrer [*harvest*]; récolter [*wheat*]; ¶ ~ **in** [*sb*], ~ [*sb*] **in 1** (involve) faire appel à [*expert, army*] (**from** de; **as** pour être); **2** (to police station) amener [qn] (au poste).

■ **bring into**: ~ [*sb*] **into** faire participer [qn] à [*conversation, organization*].

■ **bring off**: ~ **off** [*sth*], ~ [*sth*] **off** réussir [*feat*]; conclure [*deal*]; décrocher [*victory*].

■ **bring on**: ¶ ~ **on** [*sth*], ~ [*sth*] **on** (provoke) provoquer [*attack, migraine*]; être à l'origine de [*bronchitis, rheumatism*]; ¶ ~ **on** [*sb*], ~ [*sb*] **on** (to stage, field) faire entrer [*dancer, substitute*].

■ **bring out**: ¶ ~ **out** [*sth*], ~ [*sth*] **out 1** sortir [*gun etc*]; **2** COMM sortir [*edition, new model*]; **3** (highlight) faire ressortir [*flavour, meaning*]; ¶ ~ **out** [*sb*], ~ [*sb*] **out 1** (on strike) mettre [qn] en grève [*workers*]; **2 to** ~ **sb out in spots** donner des boutons à qn.

■ **bring round**: ~ [*sb*] **round 1** (revive) faire revenir [qn] à soi; **2** (convince) convaincre.

■ **bring together**: ~ **together** [*sth/sb*], ~ [*sth/sb*] **together 1** (assemble) réunir; **2** (create bond between) rapprocher.

■ **bring up**: ¶ ~ **up** [*sth*], ~ [*sth*] **up 1** (mention) aborder, parler de; **2** (vomit) vomir, rendre; ¶ ~ **up** [*sb*], ~ [*sb*] **up** élever; **to** ~ **sb up to do** apprendre à [qn] à faire; **to be brought up as a Catholic** recevoir une éducation catholique; **well/badly brought up** bien/mal élevé.

bring and buy sale *n* GB vente *f* de charité.

brink /brɪŋk/ *n* LIT, FIG bord *m*; **on the** ~ **of doing** sur le point de faire; **on the** ~ **of disaster** à deux doigts du désastre.

brinkmanship /'brɪŋkmənʃɪp/ *n* art *m* d'aller jusqu'aux limites du possible.

brisk /brɪsk/ *adj* **1** (efficient) [*manner, tone, gesture*] vif/vive; [*person*] efficace; **2** (energetic) [*pace, trot, movements*] rapide; [*debate*] animé; **to go for a** ~ **walk/swim** faire une bonne marche/quelques longueurs; **at a** ~ **pace** à vive allure; **3** (good) [*business, trade*] florissant; **business/betting was** ~ les affaires/les paris marchaient bien; **we've been doing a** ~ **trade in suitcases** nos valises se sont bien vendues; **4** (invigorating) [*air*] vivifiant; [*wind*] vif/vive.

brisket /'brɪskɪt/ *n* CULIN poitrine *f*.

briskly /'brɪsklɪ/ *adv* **1** (efficiently) [*say*] vivement; [*work*] rapidement; [*resolve, deal with*] de façon efficace; **she moved** ~ **on to the next point** elle s'est attaquée sans tarder au point suivant; **2** (quickly) [*walk*] d'un bon pas; [*sell*] très vite.

bristle /'brɪsl/ **I** *n* **1** (single hair) (on brush, chin, animal)

poil *m*; (on pig) soie *f*; **2** (material) (on brush, mat) (real) soies *fpl*; (synthetic) poils *mpl*.

II *vi* **1** LIT [*fur*] se hérisser; [*hairs*] se dresser; **2** (react angrily) se hérisser (**at** à; **with** de).

■ **bristle with**: ~ **with** [*sth*] être hérissé de [*spikes, pins, problems*]; grouiller de [*police, soldiers*].

bristly /'brɪslɪ/ *adj* [*beard, fibres*] dru; [*surface*] couvert de poils durs.

Britain /'brɪtn/ *pr n* (also **Great** ~) Grande-Bretagne *f*.

British /'brɪtɪʃ/ ▶1100 **I** *npl* **the** ~ les Britanniques *mpl*.

II *adj* britannique; **the** ~ **embassy/ambassador** l'ambassade *f*/l'ambassadeur *m* de Grande-Bretagne.

British: ~ **Airports Authority, BAA** *n* administration *f* des aéroports britanniques; ~ **Broadcasting Corporation, BBC** *n* BBC *f*; ~ **Columbia, BC** *n* Colombie *f* britannique.

Britisher /'brɪtɪʃə(r)/ *n* US Britannique *mf*.

British: ~ **Gas** *n* GB société *f* de distribution de gaz britannique; ~ **Isles** *npl* îles *fpl* Britanniques; ~ **Rail, BR** *n* société *f* nationale des chemins de fer britanniques; ~ **Telecom, BT** *n* GB société *f* britannique de télécommunications.

Briton /'brɪtn/ *n* Britannique *mf*; HIST Breton/-onne *m*/*f*.

brittle /'brɪtl/ *adj* **1** LIT [*twig*] cassant; [*nails, hair*] fragile; **2** FIG [*relationship, confidence*] fragile; [*tone, laughter*] cassant.

brittle bones, brittle-bone disease *n* décalcification *f*.

broach /brəʊtʃ/ *vtr* aborder [*subject*]; entamer [*bottle*].

broad /brɔːd/ ▶1045 *adj* **1** (wide) large; **to have a** ~ **back** LIT, FIG avoir le dos large; **2** (extensive) [*area, expanse*] vaste; **3** (wide-ranging) [*choice, range*] grand; [*introduction, syllabus, consensus, implication*] général; [*alliance*] large; **4** (general) [*meaning, term*] large; [*base, outline, principle*] général; **5** (liberal) [*view*] large; **to have a** ~ **mind** avoir l'esprit large; **6** (unsubtle) [*wink*] bien visible; **to drop** ~ **hints about** faire des allusions évidentes à; **7** (pronounced) [*accent*] fort (before *n*); **8** (complete) **in** ~ **daylight** en plein jour; **9** (vulgar) grossier/-ière.

IDIOMS **it's as** ~ **as it's long** c'est du pareil au même°.

B road *n* GB route *f* secondaire.

broad: ~**-based** *adj* [*approach, campaign*] global; [*education*] généralisé; [*coalition*] d'origine très variée; [*consensus*] général; ~ **bean** *n* BOT, CULIN fève *f*.

broadcast /'brɔːdkɑːst, US -kæst/ **I** *n* émission *f*; **TV/radio** ~ émission télévisée/radiophonique; **news** ~ bulletin *m* d'informations.

II *vtr* (*prét, pp* ~ ou ~**ed**) **1** RADIO, TV diffuser (**to** à); **2** (tell) PÉJ raconter.

III *vi* (*prét, pp* ~ ou ~**ed**) **1** [*station, channel*] émettre (**on** sur); **2** [*person*] faire une émission; **to** ~ **on gardening** faire des émissions sur le jardinage.

IV *pp adj* (on TV) télévisé; (on radio) radiodiffusé; (on both) radiotélévisé.

broadcaster /'brɔːdkɑːstə(r), US -kæst-/ ▶1251 *n* animateur/-trice *m*/*f*; **news** ~ journaliste *mf* de radio ou télévision.

broadcasting /'brɔːdkɑːstɪŋ, US -kæst-/ **I** *n* (field) communication *f* audiovisuelle; (action) diffusion *f*; **to work in** ~ travailler dans l'audiovisuel; **children's** ~ **programmes** *mpl* pour les enfants.

II *noun modifier* [*authorities, union*] de la communication audiovisuelle; ~ **ban** interdiction *f* d'antenne.

broad-chested *adj* au torse large.

broaden /'brɔːdn/ **I** *vtr* **1** (extend) étendre [*appeal, scope*]; élargir [*horizons, knowledge*]; **travel** ~**s the mind** les voyages ouvrent l'esprit; **2** (widen) élargir [*road*].

II *vi* **1** (expand) [*appeal, horizons, scope*] s'élargir; **2** (also ~ **out**) (widen) [*river, road, pipe, smile*] s'élargir; [*skirt*] s'évaser; [*conversation*] s'étendre.

broadly /'brɔːdlɪ/ *adv* **1** (in general) [*agree, correspond*] en gros; [*similar, true*] globalement; **~ speaking** en règle générale; **2** (widely) [*smile*] largement.

broad: **~minded** *adj* [*person*] large d'esprit; [*attitude*] libéral; **~ness** *n* largeur *f*; **~sheet** *n* journal *m* de grand format; **~-shouldered** *adj* large d'épaules.

broadside /'brɔ:dsaɪd/ **I** *n* **1** (criticism) attaque *f* cinglante (**at** contre); **2** NAUT (of ship) flanc *m*; (enemy fire) bordée *f*; **to deliver a ~** lâcher une bordée. **II** *adv* (also **~ on**) par le travers.

brocade /brə'keɪd/ *n* brocart *m*.

broccoli /'brɒkəlɪ/ *n* ¢ BOT brocoli *m*; CULIN brocolis *mpl*.

brochure /'brəʊʃə(r), US brəʊ'ʃʊər/ *n* (booklet) brochure *f*; (larger) catalogue *m*; (leaflet) dépliant *m*; (for hotel) prospectus *m*.

brogue /brəʊg/ *n* **1** (shoe) richelieu *m*; **2** (accent) accent *m* du terroir.

broil /brɔɪl/ **I** *vtr* US CULIN faire griller [*meat*]. **II** *vi* CULIN, FIG griller.

broiler /'brɔɪlə(r)/ *n* **1** (also **~ chicken**) poulet *m* d'élevage; **2** US (grill) gril *m*.

broke /brəʊk/ **I** *prét* ▶ **break**. **II** *adj* (insolvent) [*person*] fauché○; [*company, Treasury*] insolvable; **to go ~** [*company*] faire faillite.

broken /'brəʊkən/ **I** *pp* ▶ **break**. **II** *adj* **1** (damaged) [*glass, window*] brisé; [*fingernail, tooth, bone, leg*] cassé; [*bottle, chair, handle, toy*] cassé; [*radio, machine*] détraqué; **2** (interrupted) [*circle, line*] brisé; [*voice*] brisé; **3** (irregular) [*coastline*] découpé; [*ground*] accidenté; **4** (depressed) [*man, woman*] brisé; [*spirit*] abattu; **5** (not honoured) [*contract, engagement, promise*] rompu; **6** (flawed) (*épith*) [*French*] mauvais (*before n*); [*sentence*] maladroit.

broken-down /ˌbrəʊkən'daʊn/ *adj* (*épith*) **1** (non-functional) [*machine*] en panne; **2** (damaged) [*wall*] délabré.

broken heart /ˌbrəʊkən 'hɑːt/ *n* cœur *m* brisé; **to die of a ~** mourir de chagrin.

broken-hearted /ˌbrəʊkən'hɑːtɪd/ *adj* [*person*] au cœur brisé; **to be ~** avoir le cœur brisé.

broken home *n* famille *f* désunie.

brokenly /'brəʊkənlɪ/ *adv* [*say*] d'une voix brisée.

broken marriage *n* foyer *m* désuni.

broker /'brəʊkə(r)/ ▶ **1251** **I** *n* FIN, COMM courtier *m*; (on stock exchange) courtier *m* en Bourse; NAUT courtier *m* maritime; **insurance ~** courtier *m* d'assurance; **real-estate ~** US agent *m* immobilier; **power ~** négociateur/-trice *m/f* influent/-e. **II** *vtr* POL négocier. **III** *vi* agir en médiateur (**between** entre).

brokerage /'brəʊkərɪdʒ/ *n* (fee, business) courtage *m*.

broking /'brəʊkɪŋ/ GB, **brokering** /'brəʊkərɪŋ/ US *n* courtage *m*.

brolly○ /'brɒlɪ/ *n* GB HUM pépin○ *m*, parapluie *m*.

bromide /'brəʊmaɪd/ *n* **1** (in pharmacy, printing) bromure *m*; **2** FIG (comment) platitude *f* (lénifiante).

bronchial /'brɒŋkɪəl/ *adj* [*infection*] des bronches; [*asthma*] bronchique; [*wheeze, cough*] bronchitique; **~ pneumonia** broncho-pneumonie *f*.

bronchitis /brɒŋ'kaɪtɪs/ ▶ **1002** *n* bronchite *f*; **to have ~** avoir une bronchite; **~ sufferer** bronchitique *mf*.

bronze /brɒnz/ **I** *n* **1** (statue, metal) bronze *m*; **2** (colour) (couleur *f* de) bronze *m*. **II** *noun modifier* [*coin, ornament*] en bronze. **III** *vtr, vi* (all contexts) bronzer.

Bronze Age *n* âge *m* du bronze.

brooch /brəʊtʃ/ *n* broche *f*.

brood /bru:d/ **I** *n* **1** ZOOL (of birds) couvée *f*, nichée *f*; (of mammals) nichée *f*; **2** HUM (of children) nichée *f*, progéniture *f* HUM. **II** *vi* **1** (ponder) broyer du noir; **to ~ about** ou **on** ou **over** ressasser, ruminer [*problem, disappointment*]; **2** ZOOL [*bird*] couver.

brooding /'bru:dɪŋ/ *adj* [*landscape*] menaçant; [*person, face*] sombre.

broody /'bru:dɪ/ *adj* **1** (depressed) mélancolique; **2 a ~ hen** une poule qui cherche à couver; **3**○ GB **to feel ~** [*woman*] désirer avoir un enfant.

brook /brʊk/ **I** *n* ruisseau *m*. **II** *vtr* SOUT tolérer [*argument, refusal*].

broom /bru:m, brʊm/ *n* **1** (for sweeping) balai *m*; **2** BOT genêt *m*. **IDIOMS a new ~ sweeps clean** PROV nouveau chef, nouvelles méthodes.

broom: **~ cupboard** *n* GB LIT cagibi○ *m*; **~ handle** *n* GB manche *m* à balai; **~stick** *n* manche *m* à balai.

Bros. *npl* COMM (*abrév écrite* = **Brothers**) Frères.

broth /brɒθ, US brɔ:θ/ *n* bouillon *m*. **IDIOMS too many cooks spoil the ~** PROV on n'arrive à rien quand tout le monde s'en mêle.

brothel /'brɒθl/ *n* maison *f* close.

brother /'brʌðə(r)/ *n* **1** (relative) frère *m*; **2** (trade unionist) camarade *m*; **3** (fellow man) frère *m*; **~s in arms** frères d'armes; **4** RELIG frère *m*.

brotherhood /'brʌðəhʊd/ *n* **1** (bond) fraternité *f*; **2** (organization) (of idealists) confrérie *f*; (trade-union) association *f*; (of monks) communauté *f*.

brother-in-law *n* (*pl* **brothers-in-law**) beau-frère *m*.

brotherly /'brʌðəlɪ/ *adj* (all contexts) fraternel/-elle.

brought /brɔ:t/ *prét, pp* ▶ **bring**.

brow /braʊ/ *n* **1** (forehead) front *m*; **2** (eyebrow) sourcil *m*; **to knit** ou **furrow one's ~s** froncer les sourcils; **3** (of hill) sommet *m*.

browbeat /'braʊbi:t/ *vtr* (*prét* **-beat**; *pp* **-beaten**) intimider; **to ~ sb into doing** forcer qn à faire; **to ~ sb into silence** réduire qn au silence.

brown /braʊn/ ▶ **818** **I** *n* (colour) (of object) marron *m*; (of hair, skin, eyes) brun *m*; **in ~** en marron. **II** *adj* **1** (in colour) [*shoes, leaves, paint, eyes*] marron *inv*; [*hair*] châtain *inv*; **to go** ou **turn ~** devenir marron; **to paint sth ~** peindre qch en marron; **to turn the water ~** rendre l'eau marron; **2** (tanned) bronzé; **to go ~** bronzer; **3** (as racial feature) basané. **III** *vtr* **1** (in cooking) faire roussir [*sauce*]; faire dorer [*meat, onions*]; **2** (tan) brunir. **IV** *vi* [*meat, potatoes*] dorer.

brown: **~ ale** *n* GB bière *f* brune; **~ bear** *n* ours *m* brun; **~ bread** *n* pain *m* complet.

browned-off○ /ˌbraʊnd'ɒf/ *adj* GB **to be ~** en avoir marre○.

brown envelope *n* enveloppe *f* kraft.

brownie /'braʊnɪ/ **I** *n* **1** US (cake) brownie *m* (*petit gâteau au chocolat et aux noix*); **2** (elf) lutin *m*. **II Brownie** *n* jeannette *f*.

brownie point○ *n* HUM bon point *m*.

brownish /'braʊnɪʃ/ ▶ **818** *adj* tirant sur le brun, brunâtre PEJ.

brown: **~out** *n* US black-out *m* partiel; **~ owl** *n* chat-huant *m*; **~ paper** *n* papier *m* kraft; **~ rice** *n* riz *m* complet; **~-skinned** *adj* basané, brun de peau; **~stone** *n* US maison *f* à façade de grès rouge; **~ sugar** *n* CULIN sucre *m* brun, cassonade *f*; **~ trout** *n* truite *f* de mer.

browse /braʊz/ **I** *n* **to have a ~ in a bookshop** flâner dans une librairie; **to have a ~ through a book** feuilleter un livre. **II** *vtr* COMPUT parcourir, survoler. **III** *vi* **1** (potter, stroll around) flâner; (look at objects in shop) regarder; **2** (graze) brouter.

bruise /bru:z/ **I** *n* (on skin) bleu *m*, ecchymose *f* SPEC (**on** sur); (on fruit) tache *f*, talure *f* (**on** sur); **covered in ~s** [*skin, limb*] couvert de bleus; **cuts and ~s** des blessures légères. **II** *vtr* **1** meurtrir [*person*]; **to ~ one's knee/arm** se meurtrir le genou/bras; **2** (damage) taler, abîmer [*fruit*]; **3** (emotionally) meurtrir, blesser. **III** *vi* [*person*] se faire facilement des bleus; [*arm, skin*] se meurtrir; [*fruit*] se taler ou s'abîmer facilement.

bruised /bru:zd/ *adj* **1** (physically) [*knee, elbow*] contusionné; [*eye, cheek, ribs*] meurtri; [*fruit*] talé, abîmé; **badly** ~ sérieusement contusionné; **2** (emotionally) [*ego, spirit*] blessé; [*heart*] meurtri, blessé.

bruiser° /'bruːzə(r)/ *n* malabar° *m*, balèze° *m*.

bruising /'bruːʒɪŋ/ I *n* contusions *fpl*, ecchymoses *fpl*. II *adj* **1** (emotionally) [*campaign, encounter*] violent; [*remark*] blessant; [*defeat*] écrasant; **2** (physically) [*game, encounter*] acharné.

brunch /brʌntʃ/ *n* brunch *m* (*petit déjeuner tardif et copieux remplaçant le déjeuner*).

Brunei /bruː'naɪ/ ▶ 840] *pr n* Brunei *m*.

brunette /bruː'net/ *n* (person) brune *f*.

brunt /brʌnt/ *n* **to bear** ou **take the ~ of** être le plus touché par [*disaster, unemployment*]; subir tout le poids de [*anger*].

brush /brʌʃ/ I *n* **1** (implement) (for hair, clothes, shoes etc) brosse *f*; (small, for sweeping up) balayette *f*; (broom) balai *m*; (for paint) pinceau *m*; (chimney sweep's) hérisson *m*; **2** (act of brushing) coup *m* de brosse; **to give one's teeth a quick ~** se brosser rapidement les dents; **3** (encounter) (confrontation with person) accrochage *m* (**with** avec); (contact with person, celebrity) contact *m* (**with** avec); **to have a ~ with the police** avoir des démêlés avec la police; **4** (light touch) frôlement *m*; **5** (vegetation or twigs) broussailles *fpl*; **6** (fox's tail) queue *f* de renard; **7** (in motor) balai *m*.
II *vtr* **1** (sweep, clean) brosser [*carpet, clothes*]; **to ~ one's hair/teeth** se brosser les cheveux/les dents; **2** (touch lightly) effleurer (**with** avec); **3** CULIN **to ~ sth with** badigeonner qch avec [*milk, egg*].
III *vi* **to ~ against** frôler; **to ~ past sb** frôler qn en passant.
IV **brushed** *pp adj* [*fabric*] gratté.
■ **brush aside**: ~ **aside** [sth/sb], ~ [sb/sth] **aside 1** (dismiss) repousser [*idea, criticism, person*]; **2** (move away) écarter.
■ **brush away**: ~ **away** [sth], ~ [sth] **away** enlever [*crumbs*]; essuyer [*tear*].
■ **brush back**: ~ **back** [sth], ~ [sth] **back** brosser [qch] en arrière.
■ **brush down**: ~ **down** [sth], ~ [sth] **down** brosser [*suit, horse*].
■ **brush off**: ~ **off** [sth/sb], ~ [sth/sb] **off** repousser [*person, offer, allegation, challenge*]; écarter [*threat, incident*].
■ **brush up**: ~ **up** [sth], ~ [sth] **up** se remettre à [*skill, subject*].

brush-off° /'brʌʃɒf/ *n* **to give sb the ~** rembarrer° qn.

brushstroke /'brʌʃstrəʊk/ *n* coup *m* de pinceau.

brushup /'brʌʃʌp/ *n* GB **to have a (wash and) ~** se rafraîchir.

brushwork *n* ART facture *f*.

brusque /bruːsk, US brʌsk/ *adj* brusque (**with** avec).

brusquely /'bruːsklɪ, US 'brʌsklɪ/ *adv* avec brusquerie.

Brussels /'brʌslz/ ▶ 1343] *pr n* Bruxelles.

Brussels sprout *n* chou *m* de Bruxelles.

brutal /'bruːtl/ *adj* [*dictator, reply*] brutal; [*murderer, régime*] cruel,-elle; [*attack*] sauvage; [*film*] violent.

brutality /bruː'tælətɪ/ *n* brutalité *f* (**of** de).

brutalize /'bruːtəlaɪz/ *vtr* **1** (make brutal) rendre [qn] brutal; **2** (treat brutally) brutaliser.

brutally /'bruːtəlɪ/ *adv* [*murder, treat*] sauvagement; [*say*] brutalement; ~ **honest** d'une honnêteté brutale.

brute /bruːt/ I *n* **1** (man) brute *f*; **2** (animal) bête *f*.
II *adj* **1** (physical) [*strength*] simple (*before n*); **by** (*sheer*) ~ **force** par la force; **2** (animal-like) bestial.

brutish /'bruːtɪʃ/ *adj* bestial.

BS *n* US UNIV (*abrév* = **Bachelor of Science**) ~ (degree) diplôme *m* universitaire de sciences; (person) diplômé,-e *m/f* en sciences.

BSc *n* GB UNIV (*abrév* = **Bachelor of Science**) diplôme *m* universitaire en sciences.

BSE *n* (*abrév* = **Bovine Spongiform Encephalopathy**) ESB *f*, encéphalopathie *f* spongiforme bovine.

B side /'biː'saɪd/ *n* (of record) face *f* B.

BST *n* (*abrév* = **British Summer Time**) heure d'été britannique.

bubble /'bʌbl/ I *n* **1** (in air, liquid, glass) bulle *f* (**in** dans); **to blow ~s** faire des bulles; **2** COMM prix *m* gonflé; **3** (germ-free chamber) chambre *f* stérile.
II *vi* **1** (form bubbles) GEN faire des bulles; [*fizzy drink*] pétiller; [*boiling liquid*] bouillonner; **2** FIG (boil) **to ~ beneath the surface** bouillonner sous la surface; **3** (be lively, happy) être très animé; **to ~ with** déborder de [*enthusiasm, ideas*]; **4** (make bubbling sound) glouglouter.
■ **bubble over** d éborder (**with** de).
■ **bubble up** [*boiling liquid*] bouillonner; [*spring water*] jaillir en bouillonnant.

bubble: ~ **bath** *n* bain *m* moussant; ~ **car** *n* GB œuf° *m* (*voiture monoplace des années 60*); ~**gum** *n* bubble-gum *m*; ~ **pack** *n* GB (for small item) blister *m*; (for pills) emballage *m* pelliculé; ~**wrap** *n* bulle-pack® *m*.

bubbling /'bʌblɪŋ/ I *n* (sound) glouglou *m*, gargouillis *m*.
II *adj* bouillonnant.

bubbly /'bʌblɪ/ I° *n* champagne *m*.
II *adj* **1** [*personality*] pétillant de vitalité; **2** [*liquid*] pétillant.

bubonic plague /bjuːˌbɒnɪk 'pleɪɡ/ ▶ 1002] *n* peste *f* bubonique.

buccaneer /ˌbʌkə'nɪə(r)/ *n* boucanier *m*.

Bucharest /ˌbjuːkə'rest/ ▶ 1343] *pr n* Bucarest.

buck /bʌk/ I *n* **1** US° (dollar) dollar *m*; **2**° (money) fric° *m*; **to make a fast** ou **quick ~** se faire du fric facile°; **3** ZOOL mâle *m*; **4** (lively horse) ruade *f*.
II *vtr* **1** (throw) [*horse*] désarçonner [*rider*]; **2** (go against) aller contre [*trend, market*].
III *vi* **1** [*horse*] ruer; **2** (oppose) **to ~ at** ou **against sth** regimber devant ou contre [*changes, rule*].
IDIOMS **to ~ up one's ideas** se secouer°; **the ~ stops here** c'est moi qui ai la responsabilité finale; **to pass the ~** refiler° la responsabilité à quelqu'un d'autre.
■ **buck up**: ¶ ~ **up 1**° (cheer up) se dérider°; ~ **up!** courage!; **2**° (hurry up) se grouiller°; ¶ ~ [sb] **up** (cheer up) remonter le moral à [*person*].

bucket /'bʌkɪt/ I *n* **1** GEN seau *m* (**of** de); **2** TECH (of scoop, dredger, waterwheel) godet *m*; (of pump) piston *m*.
II° **buckets** *npl* **to rain ~s** pleuvoir à seaux; **to cry ~s** pleurer comme une Madeleine°; **to sweat ~s** suer à grosses gouttes.
III° *vi* (also ~ **down**) pleuvoir à seaux.
IDIOMS **to kick the ~** mourir, casser sa pipe°.

bucket: ~**ful** *n* seau *m* (**of** de); ~ **seat** *n* AUT, AVIAT siège-baquet *m*; ~ **shop** *n* GB TOURISM agence *f* de voyage (*proposant des billets d'avion à prix réduit*).

bucking bronco /ˌbʌkɪŋ 'brɒŋkəʊ/ *n* cheval *m* de rodéo.

buckle /'bʌkl/ I *n* **1** (clasp) boucle *f*; **2** (dent) (in metal) gondolage *m*.
II *vtr* **1** (fasten) attacher, boucler [*belt, shoe, strap*]; ~**d** bien attaché; **to ~ sb into sth** attacher qn dans qch; **2** (damage) gondoler [*material, surface*].
III *vi* **1** (give way) LIT [*metal, surface*] se gondoler; [*wheel*] se voiler; [*pillar, wall*] se déformer; [*knees, legs*] céder, FIG [*person*] céder; **2** (fasten) [*belt, shoe, strap*] s'attacher, se boucler.
■ **buckle down** se mettre au boulot°.

buckram /'bʌkrəm/ *n* bougran *m*.

Bucks *n* GB POST *abrév écrite* = **Buckinghamshire**.

buck: ~**shot** *n* chevrotine *f*; ~**skin** *n* daim *m*; ~**teeth** *npl* PÉJ dents *fpl* de lapin PÉJ; ~**wheat** *n* sarrasin *m*, blé *m* noir.

bucolic /bjuː'kɒlɪk/ *n, adj* bucolique (*f*).

bud /bʌd/ I *n* **1** BOT (of leaf) bourgeon *m*; (of flower) bouton *m*; **in ~** [*leaf*] en bourgeon; [*flower*] en bouton; **2** BIOL bourgeon *m*.
II *vi* (*p prés etc* -**dd**-) **1** BOT (develop leaf buds) bourgeonner; (develop flower buds) boutonner; **2** (develop) [*flower, breast*] pointer.

IDIOMS **to nip sth in the ~** tuer qch dans l'œuf.

Buddha /ˈbʊdə/ pr n (god) Bouddha m.

Buddhism /ˈbʊdɪzəm/ n bouddhisme m.

Buddhist /ˈbʊdɪst/ I n bouddhiste mf.
II adj [monk, temple] bouddhiste; [art] bouddhique.

budding /ˈbʌdɪŋ/ adj 1 BOT (into leaf) bourgeonnant; (into flower) boutonnant; 2 FIG [athlete, champion] en herbe; [talent, career, romance] naissant.

buddy○ /ˈbʌdɪ/ n 1 (friend) copain m, pote○ m; 2 US (form of address) mec○ m; 3 (in Aids care) volontaire mf (attaché à un sidéen).

budge /bʌdʒ/ I vtr 1 LIT bouger; 2 FIG faire changer d'avis à.
II vi LIT bouger (from, off de); FIG changer d'avis (on sur); **she would not ~ an inch** FIG elle était inflexible.
■ **budge over**○, **budge up**○ se pousser.

budgerigar /ˈbʌdʒərɪgɑː(r)/ n perruche f.

budget /ˈbʌdʒɪt/ I n 1 (personal, commercial) budget m (for pour); **education ~** budget de l'éducation; **to go over/stay within ~** dépasser/ne pas dépasser le budget; 2 GB POL (also **Budget**) Budget m.
II noun modifier 1 [cut, deficit] budgétaire; [constraints, increase] du budget; 2 (cheap) [holiday, price] pour petits budgets; **a low-/high-~ film** un film à petit budget/à gros budget.
III vtr budgétiser [money]; US budgétiser [time].
IV vi **to ~ for** [company, government] budgétiser ses dépenses en fonction de [increase, needs]; **I hadn't ~ed for a new car** je n'avais pas prévu d'acheter une nouvelle voiture.

budget account n GB (with bank, shop) compte-crédit m.

budgetary /ˈbʌdʒɪtərɪ, US -terɪ/ adj budgétaire.

budget: **~ day** n GB POL jour m de la présentation du Budget; **~ heading** n FIN, COMM poste m budgétaire.

budgeting /ˈbʌdʒɪtɪŋ/ n **as a result of careful ~, I have paid off my debts** en gérant soigneusement mon budget, j'ai réussi à rembourser mes dettes.

budgie○ /ˈbʌdʒɪ/ n = **budgerigar**.

buff /bʌf/ I n 1○ (enthusiast) mordu/-e m/f; 2 (colour) chamois m; 3 (leather) peau m de buffle.
II adj chamois.
III vtr lustrer [shoes]; polir [fingernails, metal].

buffalo /ˈbʌfələʊ/ n (pl **-oes** or collective **~**) buffle m; US bison m.

buffer /ˈbʌfə(r)/ I n 1 FIG (protection) tampon m; 2 (for polishing) polissoir m.
II **buffers** npl RAIL (on line) butoir m; (on train) tampon m.
IDIOMS **to run into the ~s** finir en queue de poisson.

buffer: **~ state** n État m tampon; **~ zone** n zone f tampon.

buffet¹ /ˈbʊfeɪ, US bəˈfeɪ/ n buffet m.

buffet² /ˈbʌfɪt/ vtr [wind, sea] secouer; FIG [misfortune] frapper.

buffet car n GB RAIL voiture-buffet f.

buffoon /bəˈfuːn/ n bouffon/-onne m/f.

bug /bʌg/ I n 1○ (any insect) bestiole f; 2 (bedbug) punaise f; 3○ (also **stomach ~** ou **tummy ~**) ennuis mpl gastriques; 4 (germ) microbe m; 5 (fault) GEN défaut m; COMPUT bogue f, bug m; 6 (hidden microphone) micro m caché; 7○ (craze) virus m, manie f; 8○ US (enthusiast) mordu/-e m/f.
II vtr (p prés etc **-gg-**) 1 (hide microphones in) poser des micros dans [room, building]; **the room is ~ged** il y a un micro (caché) dans la pièce; 2○ (annoy) embêter○ [person].

bugaboo /ˈbʌgəbuː/ n (pl **~s**) croquemitaine m.

bugbear /ˈbʌgbeə(r)/ n (problem, annoyance) plaie○ f.

bugging /ˈbʌgɪŋ/ n pose f de micros.

bugging device n micro m d'écoute.

buggy /ˈbʌgɪ/ n 1 GB (pushchair) poussette f; 2 US (pram) landau m; 3 HIST (carriage) boghei m.

bugle /ˈbjuːgl/ ▶1097 n clairon m (instrument).

bugler /ˈbjuːglə(r)/ n clairon m (joueur).

build /bɪld/ I n carrure f; **of average ~** de carrure moyenne; **she is slender in ~** elle est mince.
II vtr (prét, pp **built**) 1 (construct) construire [factory, city, railway]; édifier [church, monument]; **to ~ an extension onto a house** agrandir une maison; 2 (assemble) construire [engine, ship]; 3 COMPUT créer [software, interface]; 4 (establish) bâtir [career, future]; établir [relations, relationship]; fonder [empire]; créer [prosperity]; former [team]; **to ~ one's hopes on sth** fonder ses espoirs sur qch; 5 GAMES former [sequence, set, word].
III vi (prét, pp **built**) 1 (construct) construire; 2 FIG (use as a foundation) **to ~ on** tirer parti de [popularity, success]; se développer à partir de [base].
■ **build in**: **~ [sth] in**, **~ in [sth]** 1 (construct) encastrer; 2 (incorporate) introduire [clause, guarantee].
■ **build up**: ¶ **~ up** [gas, deposits] s'accumuler; [traffic] s'intensifier; [business, trade] se développer; [tension, excitement] monter; ¶ **~ up [sth]**, **~ [sth] up** 1 (accumulate) accumuler; 2 (boost) établir [trust]; gonfler [morale]; **don't ~ your hopes up too high** ne te fais pas d'illusions; 3 (establish) constituer [collection]; créer [business]; constituer [army]; établir [picture, profile]; créer [database]; se faire [reputation]; ¶ **~ [sth/sb] up**, **~ up [sth/sb]** 1 (strengthen) affermir [muscles]; **to ~ oneself up** prendre des forces; 2 (promote) **they built him up to be a star** ils l'ont présenté comme si c'était une vedette.

builder /ˈbɪldə(r)/ ▶1251 n (contractor) entrepreneur m en bâtiment; (worker) ouvrier/-ière m/f du bâtiment; **a firm of ~s** une entreprise de bâtiment.

builder: **~'s labourer** ▶1251 n ouvrier/-ière m/f du bâtiment; **~'s merchant** ▶1251 n fournisseur m de matériaux de construction.

building /ˈbɪldɪŋ/ n 1 (structure) bâtiment m; (with offices, apartments) immeuble m; (palace, church) édifice m; **school ~** bâtiment m d'école; 2 (industry) bâtiment m; 3 (action) construction f.

building: **~ block** n (child's toy) cube m; (basic element) élément m de base; **~ contractor** ▶1251 n entrepreneur m en bâtiment; **~ land** n terrain m à bâtir; **~ materials** npl matériaux mpl de construction; **~ permit** n permis m de construire; **~ plot** n terrain m à bâtir; **~ site** n LIT, FIG chantier m (de construction); **~ society** n GB société f d'investissement et de crédit immobilier; **~ trade** n bâtiment m; **~ worker** ▶1251 n GB ouvrier/-ière m/f du bâtiment.

build-up /ˈbɪldʌp/ n 1 (increase) accumulation f (of de); (in traffic, pressure) intensification f (of de); (in weapons, stocks) accumulation f (of de); (in tension, excitement) accroissement m (of de); (of levels) augmentation f (of de); 2 (publicity) ∉ **the ~ to sth** les préparatifs de qch; **to give sth a good ~** faire du battage○ autour de qch.

built /bɪlt/ I prét, pp ▶ **build**.
II adj 1 (made) **he's powerfully ~** il a une puissante carrure; **he's slightly ~** il est fluet; 2 (designed) **to be ~ for** être conçu pour [efficiency, speed]; **~ to last** construit pour durer.
III **-built** combining form **Russian-~** de construction russe; **stone-~** en pierre.

built-in /ˌbɪltˈɪn/ adj 1 [wardrobe] encastré; 2 [guarantee] intégré.

built-up /ˌbɪltˈʌp/ adj [region] urbanisé; **the centre of the town has become very ~** on a beaucoup construit dans le centre de la ville; **~ area** agglomération f.

bulb /bʌlb/ n 1 ELEC ampoule f (électrique); 2 BOT bulbe m; 3 (of thermometer) réservoir m.

bulbous /ˈbʌlbəs/ adj bulbeux/-euse; **a ~ nose** un gros nez.

Bulgaria /bʌlˈgeərɪə/ ▶840 n Bulgarie f.

bulge /bʌldʒ/ I n 1 (swelling) (in clothing, carpet) bosse f; (in vase, column, pipe, tube) renflement m; (in tyre) hernie f; (in wall) bombement m; (in plaster) boursouflure f; (in cheek) gonflement *m*; **2** (in statistics) poussée *f*; **3** (in-crease) augmentation *f* (**in** de).

II *vi* [*bag, pocket*] être gonflé; [*wallet*] être bourré; [*sur-face*] se boursoufler; [*stomach*] ballonner; [*cheeks*] être gonflé; **his eyes were bulging** les yeux lui sortaient de la tête; **to be bulging with** [*bag, vehicle*] être bourré de; [*book, building*] être rempli de.

bulging /ˈbʌldʒɪŋ/ *adj* [*cheek, stomach, vein*] gonflé; [*muscle*] saillant; [*surface, wall*] bombé; [*bag*] plein à craquer⊘ (*after n*).

bulimia (nervosa) /bjuːˌlɪmɪə nɜːˈvəʊsə/ *n* boulimie *f*.

bulimic /bjuːˈlɪmɪk/ *n, adj* boulimique (*mf*).

bulk /bʌlk/ **I** *n* **1** (large size) (of package, correspondence, writings) volume *m*; (of building, vehicle) masse *f*; **2** (large body) corps *m* massif; **3** (large quantity) **in ~** [*buy, sell*] en gros; [*transport*] en vrac; **4** (majority) **the ~ of** la majeure partie de [*imports, research, applications*]; le plus gros de [*army, workforce*]; la plupart des [*workers, voters*]; **5** (dietary fibre) fibre *f*.

II *noun modifier* **1** COMM [*order, sale*] en gros; [*mail-ing*] en nombre: **2** NAUT [*cargo, shipment*] en vrac.

bulk: **~-buy** *vtr, vi* [*company*] acheter en gros; **~-buying** *n* achat *m* en gros; **~ carrier** *n* cargo *m*, vraquier *m*; **~head** *n* NAUT, AVIAT cloison *f*.

bulky /ˈbʌlkɪ/ *adj* [*person*] corpulent [*package, equip-ment, item*] volumineux/-euse; [*book*] épais/-aisse.

bull /bʊl/ **I** *n* **1** (animal) taureau *m*; **2** (large man) mâle *m*; **3** (in zodiac) **the Bull** le Taureau; **4** FIN spéculateur *m* à la hausse; **5** GB *abrév* ▶ **bull's-eye**.

II *noun modifier* [*elephant, whale*] mâle *m*.

III *adj* [*market*] à la hausse.

IV *vi* [*speculator*] spéculer à la hausse; [*shares*] être en hausse.

IDIOMS **to go at sb/sth like a ~ at a gate** foncer tête baissée sur qn/qch.

bulldog /ˈbʊldɒg/ *n* bouledogue *m*.

bulldog clip *n* pince *f* à dessin.

bulldoze /ˈbʊldəʊz/ *vtr* **1** LIT (knock down) détruire [qch] au bulldozer [*building*]; (clear) nettoyer [qch] au bulldozer [*site*]; **2** FIG (force) forcer (**into doing** à faire).

bulldozer /ˈbʊldəʊzə(r)/ *n* bulldozer *m*, bouteur *m*.

bullet /ˈbʊlɪt/ **I** *n* balle *f*.

II *noun modifier* [*wound*] par balle; [*hole, mark*] de balle.

bulletin /ˈbʊlətɪn/ *n* bulletin *m*; **news ~** bulletin d'informations; **weather ~** bulletin météorologique.

bulletin board *n* tableau *m* d'affichage; COMPUT messagerie *f*.

bulletproof /ˈbʊlɪtpruːf/ **I** *adj* [*glass, vehicle, door*] blindé; **~ vest** ou **jacket** gilet *m* pare-balles *inv*.

II *vtr* blinder [*glass, vehicle*].

bull: **~fight** *n* corrida *f*; **~fighter** ▶ **1251** *n* torero *m*; **~fighting** *n* GEN corridas *fpl*; (art) tauromachie *f*; **~frog** *n* grenouille *f* taureau; **~horn** *n* US méga-phone *m*.

bullion /ˈbʊlɪən/ *n* ¢ lingots *mpl*.

bullish /ˈbʊlɪʃ/ *adj* **1** FIN [*market, shares, stocks*] en hausse, haussier/-ière; [*trend*] à la hausse; **2** (optimistic) franchement optimiste.

bullock /ˈbʊlək/ *n* (young) bouvillon *m*; (mature) bœuf *m*.

bullring *n* (arena) arène *f*; (building) arènes *fpl*.

bull's-eye /ˈbʊlzaɪ/ *n* (on a target) mille *m*.

bully /ˈbʊlɪ/ **I** *n* **1** (child) petite brute *f*; (adult) tyran *m*; **the class ~** la terreur de la classe; **2**⊘ †(also **~ beef**) singe⊘ *m*.

II⊘ *excl* **~ for you!** tant mieux pour toi!

III *vtr* [*person, child*] maltraiter; [*country*] intimider; **to ~ sb into doing sth** forcer qn à faire qch.

bullying /ˈbʊlɪɪŋ/ **I** *n* (of person, child) mauvais traite-ments *mpl*; (of country) intimidation *f*.

II *adj* [*behaviour*] brutal; [*tactics*] d'intimidation.

bulrush /ˈbʊlrʌʃ/ *n* jonc *m* (des chaisiers).

bulwark /ˈbʊlwək/ *n* MIL, FIG rempart *m*; NAUT bastingage *m*; (breakwater) brise-lames *m inv*.

bum⊘ /bʌm/ **I** *n* **1** GB (buttocks) derrière *m*; **2** US (va-grant) clochard *m*; **3** (lazy person) fainéant/-e *m*/*f*; **4** US **to be on the ~** vivre de la manche⊘.

II *vtr* (*p prés etc* **-mm-**) (scrounge) taper⊘ [*cigarette, money*] (**off, from** à); **to ~ a ride, to ~ a lift** se faire emmener en voiture.

III *vi* (*p prés etc* **-mm-**) vivre de la manche⊘.

■ **bum around 1** (travel aimlessly) vadrouiller⊘; **2** (be lazy) traînasser.

bumbag /ˈbʌmbæg/ *n* GB (sacoche *f*) banane *f*.

bumble /ˈbʌmbl/ *vi* (also **~ on**) (mumble) marmonner.

bumblebee /ˈbʌmblbiː/ *n* bourdon *m*.

bumbler⊘ /ˈbʌmblə(r)/ *n* cafouilleur/-euse⊘ *m*/*f*.

bumbling⊘ /ˈbʌmblɪŋ/ *adj* **1** (incompetent) [*person*] empoté; [*attempt*] maladroit; **2** (mumbling) [*person*] radoteur/-euse; [*speech*] cafouilleux/-euse⊘.

bumf⊘, **bumph**⊘ /bʌmf/ *n* GB (documents) paperasse-rie⊘ *f*; (toilet paper) papier *m* hygiénique.

bump /bʌmp/ **I** *n* **1** (lump) (on body) bosse *f* (**on** à); (on road surface) bosse *f* (**on, in** sur); **2** (jolt) secousse *f*; **3** (sound of fall) bruit *m* sourd; **4** onomat boum; **to go ~** faire boum; **5**⊘ (of pregnant woman) ventre *m*.

II *vtr* **1** (knock) cogner (**against, on** contre); **to ~ one's head** se cogner la tête; **2**⊘ US (remove) **to ~ sb from** virer⊘ qn de [*list, job*]; **3**⊘ US (promote) **to ~ sb to** catapulter⊘ qn au poste de.

III *vi* **1** (knock) **to ~ against** buter contre; **2** (move jerkily) **to ~ along** [*vehicle*] brinquebaler sur [*road*]; **to ~ over** [*vehicle*] cahoter sur [*road*].

IDIOMS **to come down to earth with a ~** être ramené à la dure réalité.

■ **bump into** : ¶ **~ into** [sb/sth] (collide) rentrer dans [*person, object*]; ¶ **~ into** [sb]⊘ (meet) tomber sur⊘ qn.

■ **bump off**⊘: **~ off** [sb], **~** [sb] **off** liquider⊘.

■ **bump up**⊘: **~ up** [sth] faire grimper⊘ [*price, tax*].

bumper /ˈbʌmpə(r)/ **I** *n* **1** AUT pare-chocs *m*; **~ to ~** pare-chocs contre pare-chocs; **2** US RAIL butoir *m*.

II *adj* (*épith*) [*crop, sales, year*] record *inv*; [*edition*] exceptionnel/-elle.

bumper: **~ car** *n* auto *f* tamponneuse; **~ sticker** *n* autocollant *m*.

bumpkin /ˈbʌmpkɪn/ *n* PEJ (also **country ~**) pé-quenaud/-e⊘ *m*/*f*.

bumptious /ˈbʌmpʃəs/ *adj* fat.

bumpy /ˈbʌmpɪ/ *adj* LIT [*road surface*] accidenté; [*wall, ceiling*] irrégulier/-ière; [*flight, landing*] agité.

IDIOMS **to be in for a ~ ride** entrer dans une mauvaise passe.

bun /bʌn/ *n* **1** CULIN (roll) petit pain *m*; (cake) petit cake *m*; **2** (hairstyle) chignon *m*; **to put/wear one's hair in a ~** se faire/avoir un chignon.

bunch /bʌntʃ/ **I** *n* **1**⊘ (of people) groupe *m*; PEJ bande *f*; **a mixed ~** un groupe hétéroclite; **2** (of flowers) bouquet *m* (**of** de); **3** (of vegetables) botte *f*; (of bananas) régime *m*; **4** (of objects) **a ~ of feathers** une touffe de plumes; **a ~ of keys** un trousseau de clés; **a ~ of wires** un faisceau de fils; **5**⊘ (lot) tas⊘ *m* (**of** de); **a whole ~ of things** tout un tas⊘ de choses; **the best** ou **pick of the ~** le meilleur du lot; **6** GB (of hair) couette *f*; **7** SPORT peloton *m*.

II *vtr* mettre [qch] en bottes [*vegetables*]; mettre [qch] en bouquets [*flowers*].

bundle /ˈbʌndl/ **I** *n* **1** (collection) (of objects) ballot *m*; (of clothes, cloth) balluchon *m*; (of papers, banknotes) liasse *f*; (of books) paquet *m*; (of straw) botte *f*; **2** (baby, person) **~ of joy** petit ange *m*; IRON petit trésor *m*; **~ of nerves** boule *f* de nerfs.

II⊘ *vtr* **to ~ sb/sth into** fourrer⊘ qn/qch dans; **to ~ sb outside** ou **through the door** pousser qn dehors sans ménagement.

III⊘ *vi* **to ~ into a car** se ruer dans une voiture.

IDIOMS **I don't go a ~ on jazz** GB le jazz ne me botte pas⊘; **to make a ~**⊘ gagner un paquet⊘.

■ **bundle off**: **~** [sb] **off** faire sortir [qn] sans ména-gement; [*police*] embarquer⊘.

■ **bundle up**: ~ [sth] up, ~ up [sth] mettre [qch] en paquet [*papers*]; faire un ballot de [*clothes*]; mettre [qch] en liasse [*banknotes*].

bung /bʌŋ/ I *n* tampon *m*, bouchon *m*.
II *vtr* **1** (stop up) boucher; **2**° GB (put, throw) balancer°.
■ **bung in**° GB: ~ [sth] in, ~ in [sth] donner [qch] en prime.
■ **bung up**° GB: ~ [sth] up, ~ up [sth] boucher [*drain, nose*].

bungalow /'bʌŋgələʊ/ *n* pavillon *m* (sans étage).

bungee jumping /'bʌndʒi: dʒʌmpɪŋ/ ▶949 *n* saut *m* à l'élastique.

bungle /'bʌŋgl/ I *n* gaffe *f*.
II *vtr* rater° [*attempt, burglary*].
III *vi* rater son coup°.

bungling /'bʌŋglɪŋ/ *adj* maladroit.

bunion /'bʌnjən/ *n* MED oignon *m*.

bunk /bʌŋk/ I *n* **1** NAUT, RAIL couchette *f*; **2** GEN (also ~ **bed**) (whole unit) lits *mpl* superposés; **the top/ lower** ~ le lit du haut/du bas.
II° *vi* (also ~ **down**) dormir.
IDIOMS **to do a** ~° prendre le large°.
■ **bunk off**° s'éclipser; **to** ~ **off school** sécher l'école.

bunk bed *n* = **bunk** I 2.

bunker /'bʌŋkə(r)/ *n* **1** (shelter) (for commander) bunker *m*; (for gun) blockhaus *m*; (beneath building) abri *m*; **2** (in golf) bunker *m*; **3** (container) soute *f*.

bunny /'bʌnɪ/ *n* **1** (also ~ **rabbit**) (Jeannot) lapin *m*; **2** (also ~ **girl**) hôtesse *f* (*du club Playboy®, déguisée en lapin*).

Bunsen (**burner**) /'bʌnsn/ *n* (bec *m*) Bunsen *m*.

bunting /'bʌntɪŋ/ *n* **1** (flags) guirlandes *fpl*; **2** ZOOL bruant *m*.

buoy /bɔɪ/ I *n* GEN bouée *f*; (for marking) balise *f* (flottante).
II *vtr* **1** (also ~ **up**) (make cheerful) revigorer (**by** par); **2** (also ~ **up**) FIN stimuler [*share prices*] (**by** par); **3** (also ~ **up**) LIT (keep afloat) maintenir à flot.

buoyancy /'bɔɪənsɪ/ *n* **1** (of floating object) flottabilité *f*; (of medium) poussée *f*; **2** (cheerfulness) entrain *m*; **3** (of exports, market) fermeté *f*.

buoyancy aid *n* bouée *f*.

buoyant /'bɔɪənt/ *adj* **1** [*object*] qui flotte; **2** (cheerful) [*person*] vif/vive; [*mood, spirits*] enjoué; [*step*] allègre; **3** ECON GEN soutenu; [*economy*] en expansion.

buoyantly /'bɔɪəntlɪ/ *adv* **1** (cheerfully) [*speak*] avec enjouement; [*walk*] d'un pas allègre; **2** (lightly) [*rise, float*] vivement.

burble /'bɜ:bl/ I *n* = **burbling**.
II *vi* **1** [*stream*] glouglouter; **2** [*person*] marmonner; **to** ~ (**on**) **about sth** radoter à propos de qch.

burbling /'bɜ:blɪŋ/ I *n* **1** (of stream, voices) gargouillis *m*; **2** (rambling talk) galimatias *m*.
II *adj* [*stream, voice*] qui gargouille.

burden /'bɜ:dn/ I *n* **1** (responsibility) fardeau *m* (**to sb** pour qn); **the** ~ **of guilt/responsibility** le poids de la culpabilité/responsabilité; **the** ~ **of taxation** la pression fiscale; **to ease the** ~ **on sb** alléger le fardeau qui pèse sur qn; **the** ~ **of proof** JUR la charge de la preuve; **2** LIT (load) fardeau *m*.
II *vtr* (also ~ **down**) FIG ennuyer (**with** de); LIT encombrer (**with** de).
III *v refl* **to** ~ **oneself with sth** se charger de qch.

bureau /'bjʊərəʊ, US -'rəʊ/ *n* (*pl* ~**s** ou ~**x**) **1** (agency) agence *f*; (local office) bureau *m*; **information** ~ bureau *m* de renseignements; **2** SURTOUT US (government department) service *m*; **3** GB (writing desk) secrétaire *m*; **4** US (chest of drawers) commode *f*.

bureaucracy /bjʊə'rɒkrəsɪ/ *n* bureaucratie *f*.

bureaucrat /'bjʊərəkræt/ *n* bureaucrate *mf*.

bureaucratic /ˌbjʊərə'krætɪk/ *adj* bureaucratique.

burgeon /'bɜ:dʒən/ *vi* SOUT **1** FIG (grow) croître; (multiply) se multiplier; **2** FIG (flourish) fleurir; **3** LIT [*plant*] bourgeonner.

burgeoning /'bɜ:dʒənɪŋ/ *adj* **1** (growing) [*talent, love industry, crime*] croissant; [*population, industries*] en plein essor; **2** (flourishing) florissant; **3** [*plant*] bourgeonnant.

burger /'bɜ:gə(r)/ *n* hamburger *m*; **beef~** beefburger *m*.

burger bar *n* fast-food *m*.

burglar /'bɜ:glə(r)/ *n* cambrioleur/-euse *m/f*.

burglar alarm *n* sonnerie *f* d'alarme.

burglarize /'bɜ:gləraɪz/ *vtr* US cambrioler.

burglar-proof /'bɜ:gləpru:f/ *adj* [*house*] protégé contre les cambrioleurs; [*safe*] inviolable; [*lock*] incrochetable.

burglary /'bɜ:glərɪ/ *n* GEN cambriolage *m*; JUR vol *m* avec effraction.

burgle /'bɜ:gl/ *vtr* cambrioler.

burgundy /'bɜ:gəndɪ/ ▶1177, 818 I **Burgundy** *pr n* Bourgogne *f*; **in** ~ en Bourgogne.
II *n* (also **Burgundy**) (wine) bourgogne *m*; **2** (colour) (couleur *f*) bordeaux *m*.
III *adj* (colour) bordeaux *inv*.

burial /'berɪəl/ I *n* **1** (ceremony) enterrement *m*; **2** (of body) inhumation *f*; (of object, waste) ensevelissement *m*.
II *noun modifier* [*site*] de sépulture; [*rites*] funéraire.

burlesque /bɜ:'lesk/ I *n* **1** (piece of writing) parodie *f* (genre) (genre *m*) burlesque *m*; **2** (sham) parodie *f*; **3** US (show) burlesque *m*.
II *adj* **1** [*style, show*] burlesque; **2** (sham) caricatural.
III *vtr* parodier.

burly /'bɜ:lɪ/ *adj* [*person*] solidement charpenté [*build*] imposant.

Burma /'bɜ:mə/ ▶840 *pr n* Birmanie *f*.

burn /bɜ:n/ I *n* brûlure *f*.
II *vtr* (*prét, pp* **burned** ou **burnt** GB) **1** (damage by heat or fire) brûler [*papers, rubbish*]; incendier, faire brûler [*building*]; [*sun*] brûler; [*acid*] ronger, brûler [*alcohol, food*] brûler [*mouth*]; laisser brûler [*food*] brûler [*pan*]; **to be ~ed to the ground** ou **to ashe** être détruit par le feu; **to be ~ed alive** être brûlé vif; **to be ~ed to death** mourir carbonisé; **to** ~ **one's finger** se brûler le doigt; **2** (use) **to** ~ **coal gas** [*boiler*] marcher au charbon/au gaz.
III *vi* (*prét, pp* **burned** ou **burnt** GB) **1** (be consumed by fire) [*wood*] brûler; **2** (be turned on) [*light*] être allumé; **3** (be painful) [*blister, wound*] cuire; (from sun) brûler; **he has the kind of skin that ~s easily** il attrape facilement des coups de soleil; **his cheek were ~ing** il était rouge de honte; **4** CULIN [*toast, meat*] brûler; [*sauce*] prendre au fond; **5** FIG (be eager **to be ~ing with desire** brûler de désir.
IV *v refl* (*prét, pp* **burned** ou **burnt** GB) **to** ~ **oneself** se brûler.
IDIOMS **to** ~ **one's boats** brûler ses vaisseaux.
■ **burn away** [*candle, log*] se consumer.
■ **burn down**: ¶ ~ **down 1** [*house*] brûler complètement, être réduit en cendres; **2** [*candle, fire*] baisser ¶ ~ **down [sth]**, ~ **[sth] down** incendier, réduir [qch] en cendres [*house etc*].
■ **burn off**: ¶ ~ **off [alcohol]** s'évaporer; ¶ ~ off [sth], ~ **[sth] off** décaper [qch] au chalumeau [*paint*]; FIG dépenser [*energy*].
■ **burn out**: ¶ ~ **out** [*candle, fire*] s'éteindre; [*light bulb*] griller; [*fuse*] sauter; [*person*] (through overwork) s'user; ¶ ~ **out [sth]**, ~ **[sth] out** (destroy by fire) incendier [*building, vehicle*]; AUT, TECH grille [*clutch, motor*]; ¶ ~ **out [sb]**, ~ **[sb] out** GEN, M forcer [qn] à sortir par l'incendie.
■ **burn up**: ¶ ~ **up 1** [*fire, flames*] flamber; **2** [*satellite, meteorite*] se volatiliser; ¶ ~ **up [sth]**, ~ **[sth] up** brûler [*calories, fuel, waste*]; dépense [*energy*].

burned-out *adj* = **burnt-out**.

burner /'bɜ:nə(r)/ *n* (on gas cooker) brûleur *m*; (of lamp bec *m* (de gaz).
IDIOMS **to put sth on the back** ~ mettre qch en veilleuse.

burning /'bɜ:nɪŋ/ I *n* **1** there's a smell of ~ ça sen

le brûlé; **I can smell ~!** je sens une odeur de brûlé!; **2** (setting on fire) incendie *m*.
II *adj* **1** (on fire) en flammes, en feu; (alight) [*candle, lamp, fire*] allumé; [*ember, coal*] embrasé, ardent; FIG (very hot) brûlant; **a ~ sensation** une sensation de brûlure; **2** FIG (intense) [*fever, desire*] brûlant; [*passion*] ardent; **a ~ question** une question brûlante.

ᴜrnish /'bɜ:nɪʃ/ LITTÉR **I** *vtr* brunir.
II burnished *pp adj* [*copper, skin, leaves*] bruni.

ᴜrn: ~-out *n* surmenage *m*, épuisement *m*; **~s unit** *n* MED service *m* des grands brûlés.

ᴜrnt /bɜ:nt/ *prét, pp* ▶ **burn**.
II *adj* GEN brûlé; [*smell, taste*] de brûlé, de roussi.

ᴜrnt: ~ orange ▶ 818 | *n* orange *m* foncé; **~-out** *adj* LIT [*building, car*] calciné; FIG [*person*] usé (par le travail).

ᴜrp /bɜ:p/ **I** *n* rot *m*, renvoi *m*.
II *vtr* faire faire son rot à [*baby*].
III *vi* [*person*] roter; [*baby*] faire son rot.

ᴜrr /bɜ:(r)/ *n* **1** BOT *partie de certaines plantes qui s'accroche aux vêtements, au pelage des animaux*; **2** LING grasseyement *m*.

ᴜrrow /'bʌrəʊ/ **I** *n* terrier *m*.
II *vtr* [*animal*] creuser [*hole, tunnel*]; **to ~ one's way into sth** [*animal, person*] se creuser un chemin dans qch.
III *vi* [*animal*] creuser un terrier; **to ~ into/under sth** (in ground) creuser dans/sous qch.

ᴜrsar /'bɜ:sə(r)/ ▶ 1251 | *n* SCH, UNIV intendant/-e *m/f*.

ᴜrsary /'bɜ:sərɪ/ *n* GB SCH, UNIV **1** (grant) bourse *f* (d'études); **2** (office) bureau *m* de l'intendant.

ᴜrst /bɜ:st/ **I** *n* (of flame) jaillissement *m*, jet *m*; (of bomb, shell) éclatement *m*; (of gunfire) rafale *f*; (of activity, energy, enthusiasm) accès *m*; **a ~ of growth** une poussée; **a ~ of laughter** un éclat de rire; **a ~ of anger** un accès de colère; **a ~ of applause** un tonnerre d'applaudissements; **to put on a ~ of speed** AUT faire une pointe de vitesse.
II *vtr* (*prét, pp* **burst**) crever [*balloon, bubble, tyre*]; rompre [*blood vessel*]; **the river burst its banks** le fleuve a débordé; **a burst pipe** un tuyau qui a éclaté.
III *vi* (*prét, pp* **burst**) **1** [*balloon, bubble, tyre*] crever; [*pipe, boiler*] éclater; [*dam*] rompre; [*bomb, firework*] éclater; **to be ~ing at the seams** [*bag, room, building*] être plein à craquer; **to be ~ing to do** mourir d'envie de faire; **to be ~ing with health/pride** déborder de santé/de fierté; **2** (emerge suddenly) [*people*] surgir; [*water*] jaillir; **to ~ onto the rock scene** faire irruption dans le monde du rock.
■ **burst in: ~ in** faire irruption, entrer en trombe; **to ~ in on a meeting** interrompre brusquement une réunion.
■ **burst into: ~ into** [sth] **1** faire irruption dans [*room, meeting*]; **2 to ~ into blossom** ou **bloom** s'épanouir; **to ~ into flames** s'enflammer; **to ~ into song** se mettre à chanter; **to ~ into tears** fondre en larmes; **to ~ into laughter** éclater de rire.
■ **burst open:** ¶ **~ open** [*door*] s'ouvrir violemment; [*sack*] crever; ¶ **~ open** [sth], **~** [sth] **open** ouvrir [qch] violemment.
■ **burst out 1** (come out) **to ~ out of a room** sortir en trombe d'une pièce; **he was ~ing out of his waistcoat** il était boudiné dans son gilet; **2** (start) **to ~ out laughing** éclater de rire; **to ~ out crying** fondre en larmes; **to ~ out singing** se mettre à chanter; **3** (exclaim) s'écrier, s'exclamer.
■ **burst through: ~ through** [sth] rompre [*barricade*]; **to ~ through the door** entrer violemment ou brusquement.

ᴮurundi /bə'rʊndɪ/ ▶ 840 | *pr n* Burundi *m*.

ᴜry /'berɪ/ *vtr* **1** (after death) enterrer, inhumer [*person*]; enterrer [*animal*]; **2** [*avalanche etc*] ensevelir [*person, building, town*]; **to be buried alive** être enterré vivant; **3** (hide) enterrer, enfouir [*treasure, bone*]; **to ~ oneself in the countryside** aller s'enterrer à la campagne; **to ~ one's face in one's hands** se cacher le visage dans ses mains; **4** (suppress)

enterrer [*differences, hatred, memories*]; **5** (engross) **to be buried in** être plongé dans [*book, work*]; **6** (plunge) enfoncer [*dagger, teeth, hands*] (**in** dans).

bus /bʌs/ **I** *n* (*pl* **buses**) **1** (vehicle) autobus *m*, bus *m*; (long-distance) autocar *m*, car *m*; **by ~** [*come, go, travel*] en (auto)bus, par le bus; **on the ~** dans le bus; **2** COMPUT (also **~bar**) bus *m*.
II *noun modifier* [*depot, service, stop, ticket*] d'autobus.
III *vtr* (*p prés etc* **-ss-** GB, **-s-** US) acheminer [qn] par or en bus.

busby /'bʌzbɪ/ *n* bonnet *m* à poil (*de soldat*).

bus: ~ conductor ▶ 1251 | *n* receveur *m* d'autobus; **~ conductress** ▶ 1251 | *n* receveuse *f* d'autobus; **~ driver** ▶ 1251 | *n* conducteur/-trice *m/f* d'autobus.

bush /bʊʃ/ *n* **1** (shrub) buisson *m*; **a ~ of hair** FIG une épaisse tignasse; **2** (in Australia, Africa) **the ~** la brousse *f*.
IDIOMS **don't beat about the ~** cessez de tourner autour du pot.

bushed /bʊʃt/ *adj* (tired) crevé.

bushel /'bʊʃl/ *n* boisseau *m*; **~s of** US des quantités de.
IDIOMS **to hide one's light under a ~** être trop modeste.

bush: ~fighting *n* MIL combat *m* de brousse; **~fire** *n* feu *m* de brousse; **~ telegraph** *n* LIT téléphone *m* de brousse; FIG HUM téléphone *m* arabe.

bushy /'bʊʃɪ/ *adj* **1** [*hair, tail*] touffu; [*beard*] épais/-aisse; [*eyebrows*] broussailleux/-euse; **2** [*garden*] broussailleux/-euse.

busily /'bɪzɪlɪ/ *adv* **to be ~ doing** être occupé à faire.

business /'bɪznɪs/ **I** *n* **1** ¢ (commerce) affaires *fpl*; **to be in ~** être dans les affaires; **to go into ~** se lancer dans les affaires; **to set up in ~** s'établir à son compte; **the firm is no longer in ~** l'entreprise a fermé; **to do ~ with sb** faire des affaires avec qn; **they're in ~ together** ils sont associés; **he is a man I can do ~ with** c'est un homme avec qui je peux travailler; **to go out of ~** faire faillite; **they're back in ~** COMM ils ont repris leurs activités; **she's gone to Brussels on ~** elle est allée à Bruxelles pour affaires or en voyage d'affaires; **the recession has put them out of ~** la récession les a obligés à cesser leurs activités; **it's good/bad for ~** ça fait marcher/ ne fait pas marcher les affaires; **to talk ~** parler affaires; **are you in London for ~ or pleasure?** êtes-vous à Londres pour affaires ou pour le plaisir?; **to mix ~ with pleasure** joindre l'utile à l'agréable; **'~ as usual'** (on shop window) 'nous restons ouverts pendant les travaux'; **it is/it was ~ as usual** FIG c'est/c'était comme à l'habitude; **2** (custom, trade) **to lose ~** perdre de la clientèle; **how's ~** comment vont les affaires?; **~ is slow at the moment** les affaires marchent au ralenti en ce moment; **most of our ~ comes from tourists** la plupart de nos clients sont des touristes; **we are doing twice as much ~ as last summer** notre chiffre d'affaires a doublé par rapport à l'été dernier; **3** (trade, profession) métier *m*; **what (line of) ~ are you in?** qu'est-ce que vous faites dans la vie?; **he's in the insurance ~** il travaille dans les assurances; **4** (company, firm) affaire *f*, entreprise *f*; (shop) commerce *m*, boutique *f*; **small ~es** les petites entreprises; **a small mail-order ~** une petite affaire de vente par correspondance; **5** ¢ (important matters) questions *fpl* importantes; (duties, tasks) devoirs *mpl*, occupations *fpl*; **let's get down to ~** passons aux choses sérieuses; **can we get down to ~?** on peut s'y mettre?; **to go about one's ~** vaquer à ses occupations; **we still have some unfinished ~ to discuss** nous avons encore des choses à discuter; **he got on with the ~ of letterwriting** il s'est mis à faire la correspondance; **'any other ~'** (on agenda) 'questions diverses'; **6** (concern) **that's her ~** ça la regarde; **it's none of your ~!** ça ne te regarde pas!; **to make it one's ~ to do** se charger de faire; **mind your own ~!** occupe-toi or mêle-toi de tes affaires!; **he had no ~ telling her!** ce n'était pas à lui de le lui dire!; **7** (affair) histoire *f*, affaire *f*; **it's a bad** ou **sorry ~** c'est une triste affaire; **what a dread-**

ful ~! quelle histoire horrible!; **a nasty ~** une sale affaire; **8** (bother, nuisance) histoire f.
II *noun modifier* [*address, letter, transaction*] commercial; [*pages*] affaires; [*meeting, consortium*] d'affaires; **~ people** hommes *mpl* d'affaires; **the ~ community** le monde des affaires.
IDIOMS **now we're in ~!** maintenant nous sommes prêts!; **to be in the ~ of doing** avoir pour habitude de faire; **she can play the piano like nobody's ~**○ elle joue du piano comme personne; **to work like nobody's ~**○ travailler d'arrache-pied; **she means ~!** elle ne plaisante pas!

business: **~ activity** n activité f industrielle et commerciale; **~ analyst** ▶1251| n analyste m financier/-ière; **~ associate** n associé/-e m/f; **~ call** n (visit) visite f d'affaires; (phone call) communication f d'affaires; **~ card** n carte f de visite; **~ centre** GB, **~ center** US n centre m d'affaires; **~ class** n AVIAT classe f affaires; **~ college** n école f de commerce; **~ contact** n relation f d'affaires; **~ cycle** n cycle m économique; **~ deal** n affaire f; **~ expenses** npl frais mpl professionnels; **~ failures** npl faillites fpl d'entreprises; **~ hours** npl GEN heures fpl ouvrables; (in office) heures fpl de bureau; (of shop) heures fpl d'ouverture.

businesslike /'bɪznɪslaɪk/ adj [*person, manner*] sérieux/-ieuse; [*transaction*] régulier/-ière, sérieux/-ieuse, FIG HUM [*knife, tool*] sérieux/-ieuse.

business: **~ lunch** n déjeuner m d'affaires; **~ machine** n machine f de bureau.

businessman /'bɪznɪsmən/ ▶1251| n (pl **-men**) homme m d'affaires; **big ~** brasseur m d'affaires, affairiste m PEJ; **he's a good ~** il a le sens des affaires.

business: **~ park** n parc m d'affaires ou d'activités; **~ plan** n projet m commercial; **~ premises** npl locaux mpl commerciaux; **~ proposition** n proposition f; **~ reply envelope** n enveloppe f pré-affranchie, enveloppe-réponse f; **~ school** n école f de commerce; **~ software** n logiciel m de gestion; **~ studies** npl études fpl commerciales or de commerce; **~ suit** n costume m de ville, complet m; **~ trip** n voyage m d'affaires; **~woman** n femme f d'affaires.

bus(s)ing /'bʌsɪŋ/ n US ramassage m scolaire (*surtout pour abolir la ségrégation raciale aux États-Unis*).

busk /bʌsk/ vi GB [*musician*] jouer dans la rue; [*singer*] chanter dans la rue.

busker /'bʌskə(r)/ n GB (musician) musicien/-ienne m/f ambulant/-e; (singer) chanteur/-euse m/f ambulant/-e.

bus lane n couloir m d'autobus.

busload /'bʌsləʊd/ n car m; **a ~ of tourists** un car plein de voyageurs; **by the ~, by ~s** par cars entiers.

busman /'bʌsmən/ n employé m des autobus.
IDIOMS **a ~'s holiday** GB vacances fpl qui n'en sont pas vraiment.

bus: **~ pass** n carte f de bus; **~ route** n ligne f d'autobus; **~ shelter** n abribus® m; **~ station** n gare f routière.

bust /bʌst/ **I** n **1** (breasts) poitrine f; **2** ART buste m; **3**○ US (binge) **to go on the ~** faire la bringue○; **4**○ US (failure) (person) raté/-e m/f; (business, career) échec m; ECON effondrement m; **5**○ (police raid) rafle f; (arrest) arrestation f.
II noun modifier **~ size**, **~ measurement** tour m de poitrine.
III adj **1** (broken) fichu○; **2** (bankrupt) **to go ~** faire faillite.
IV○ vtr (prét, pp ~ ou **~ed**) **1** (break) bousiller○; **2** (break up) démanteler [*drugs ring*]; (raid) faire une descente dans [*premises*]; (arrest) épingler○ [*suspect*]; **3** (financially) ruiner [*person, firm*]; **4**○ US (demote) rétrograder [*soldier, policeman*] (**to** au rang de).
V○ vi (prét, pp ~ ou **~ed**) = **burst III**.
IDIOMS **to ~ a gut doing** se donner un mal de chien○ pour faire.

■ **bust up**○: ¶ ~ **up** [*couple*] rompre; [*friends*] se

brouiller; ¶ ~ **[sth] up**, ~ **up [sth]** flanquer [qch] en l'air○ [*party, relationship*].

buster○ /'bʌstə(r)/ n US **move over, ~!** pousse-toi de là, mon pote○!

bustle /'bʌsl/ **I** n **1** (activity) affairement m (**of** de) **hustle and ~** grande animation f; **2** HIST (on dress) faux cul○ m, tournure f.
II vi [*person, crowd*] (also ~ **about**) s'affairer; **to ~ in/out** entrer/sortir d'un air affairé.

bustling /'bʌslɪŋ/ adj [*street, shop, town*] animé [*person*] affairé.

bust-up○ /'bʌstʌp/ n engueulade○ f.

busy /'bɪzɪ/ **I** adj **1** [*person*] occupé (**with** avec; **doing** à faire); **to look ~** avoir l'air occupé; **to keep oneself/sb ~** trouver de quoi s'occuper/occuper qn; **that should keep them ~!** cela devrait les occuper!; **2** [*shop*] où il y a beaucoup de monde; [*junction, airport*] où le trafic est intense; [*road*] très fréquenté; [*street, town*] animé; [*day, week*] chargé; **were the shops ~?** est-ce qu'il y avait beaucoup de monde dans les magasins?; **3** (engaged) [*line*] occupé.
II v refl **~ oneself doing** s'occuper à faire.

busybody○ n **he's a real ~** il se mêle de tout.

but /bʌt, bət/ **I** adv (only, just) **if I had ~ known** si seulement j'avais su; **these are ~ two of the possibilities** ce ne sont que deux possibilités; **I can ~ try** je peux toujours essayer; **one can't help ~ admire her** on ne peut pas s'empêcher de l'admirer.
II prep **anything ~ that** tout, sauf ça; **anybody ~ him** n'importe qui sauf lui; **anywhere ~ Australia** n'importe où sauf en Australie; **everybody ~ Paul** tout le monde sauf Paul; **nobody ~ me knows how to do it** il n'y a que moi qui sache le faire; **he's nothing ~ a coward** ce n'est qu'un lâche; **to do nothing ~ disturb people** ne rien faire d'autre que déranger les gens; **there's nothing for it ~ to leave** il n'y a plus qu'une solution, c'est de partir; **where ~ in France?** où sinon en France?; **and whom should I meet ~ Steven!** et devine qui j'ai rencontré, Steven!; **the last ~ one** l'avant-dernier; **the next road ~ one** la deuxième rue.
III but for prep phr **~ for you, I would have died** sans toi je serais mort; **he would have gone ~ for me** si je n'avais pas été là il serait parti.
IV conj **1** (expressing contrast, contradiction) mais; **it's not an asset ~ a disadvantage** ce n'est pas un atout mais un désavantage; **I'll do it, ~ not yet** je le ferai, mais pas tout de suite; **2** (yet) mais; **cheap ~ nourishing** bon marché mais nourrissant; **3** (expressing reluctance, protest, surprise) **~ that's wonderful!** mais c'est formidable!; **~ we can't afford it!** mais c'est trop cher pour nous!; **4** (except that) **never a day passes ~ she visits him** elle ne laisse pas passer un jour sans aller le voir; **5** (in apologies) mais; **excuse me, ~** excusez-moi, mais; **6** (for emphasis) **not twice, ~ three times** pas deux mais trois fois; **7** (adding to the discussion) **~ to continue...** mais, pour continuer...; **~ first** mais tout d'abord.
IDIOMS **no ~s** (about it) il n'y a pas de 'mais' qui tienne, pas de discussion.

butane /'bju:teɪn/ n butane m.

butch○ /bʊtʃ/ adj [*woman*] INJUR hommasse○; [*man*] macho○.

butcher /'bʊtʃə(r)/ ▶1251|, ▶1251| **I** n (person) LIT, FIG boucher m; **~'s (shop)** boucherie f.
II vtr abattre [*animal*]; débiter [*meat*]; FIG massacrer.

butchery /'bʊtʃərɪ/ n **1** (trade) boucherie f; **2** (slaughter) massacre m.

butler /'bʌtlə(r)/ ▶1251| n maître m d'hôtel, majordome m.

butt /bʌt/ **I** n **1** (end) GEN bout m; (of rifle) crosse f; (of cigarette) mégot○ m; **2**○ US (buttocks) derrière○ m; **3** (barrel) (gros) tonneau m; **4** (person: target) **to be the ~ of sb's jokes** être la cible des blagues de qn; **5** (blow) (by person) coup m de tête; (by animal) coup m de corne.
II vtr [*person*] donner un coup de tête à; [*animal*] donner un coup de corne à.

■ **butt in** (on conversation) interrompre; (during meeting) intervenir; **he kept ~ing in on our conversation** il n'arrêtait pas de mettre son grain de sel○.

butter /'bʌtə(r)/ **I** n beurre m.
II vtr beurrer [bread].
IDIOMS **it's her bread and ~** c'est son gagne-pain; **~ wouldn't melt in her mouth** on lui donnerait le bon Dieu sans confession.
■ **butter up**○: **~ [sb] up, ~ up [sb]** passer de la pommade à○.

butter: **~bean** n haricot m de Lima, pois m de sept ans; **~cup** n BOT bouton d'or m; **~ dish** n beurrier m; **~fingered** adj maladroit, empoté; **~fingers** n empoté/-e m/f.

butterfly /'bʌtəflaɪ/ n **1** ZOOL (pl **-ies**) papillon m; **she's a bit of a social ~** elle papillonne en société; **2** SPORT = **butterfly stroke**.
IDIOMS **to have butterflies (in one's stomach)** avoir le trac○.

butterfly: **~ net** n filet m à papillons; **~ nut** n papillon m, écrou m à ailettes; **~ stroke** n brasse f papillon.

butter: **~milk** n babeurre m; **~ muslin** n étamine f.

butterscotch /'bʌtəskɒtʃ/ **I** n (sweet) caramel m dur; (flavour) caramel m.
II noun modifier [ice cream, sauce] au caramel.

buttock /'bʌtək/ n fesse f.

button /'bʌtn/ **I** n **1** (on coat, switch) bouton m; **to do up/undo a ~** boutonner/déboutonner un bouton; **2** US (badge) insigne m, badge m.
II vi [dress, etc] se boutonner.
IDIOMS **as bright as a ~** [child] très éveillé/-e.
■ **button up**: **~ [sth] up, ~ up [sth]** boutonner [garment].

button-down adj [collar] à pointes boutonnées; [shirt] avec col à pointes boutonnées.

buttonhole /'bʌtnhəʊl/ **I** n **1** (in sewing) boutonnière f; **2** GB (flower) fleur f (portée à la boutonnière).
II○ vtr (accost) accrocher.

button: **~hook** n tire-bouton m; **~ mushroom** n (petit) champignon m de Paris.

buttress /'bʌtrɪs/ **I** n **1** GEN contrefort m; FIG soutien m; **2** (also **flying ~**) arc-boutant m.
II vtr LIT, FIG étayer.

buxom /'bʌksəm/ adj plantureux/-euse.

buy /baɪ/ **I** n **1** (bargain) **a good/bad ~** une bonne/ mauvaise affaire; **2** (purchase) acquisition f.
II vtr (prét, pp **bought**) **1** (purchase) acheter [food, car, shares, house] (**from sb** à qn); **to ~ sth from the supermarket/from the baker's** acheter qch au supermarché/chez le boulanger; **to ~ sb sth** acheter qch à qn; **the best that money can ~** ce qui se fait de mieux; **2** (obtain with money) acheter [fame, freedom, friends]; **to ~ some time** gagner du temps; **3** (bribe) acheter [loyalty, silence, person]; **she can't be bought** elle est incorruptible; **4**○ (believe) avaler○, croire.
III v refl (prét, pp **bought**) **to ~ oneself sth** s'acheter qch.
■ **buy in** GB: **~ [sth] in, ~ in [sth]** s'approvisionner en.
■ **buy into**: **~ into [sth]** COMM acheter or acquérir une part dans.
■ **buy off**: **~ [sb] off, ~ off [sb]** acheter [person, witness].
■ **buy out**: **~ [sb] out, ~ out [sb]** COMM racheter la part de [co-owner]; **to ~ oneself out of** racheter son engagement dans [army].
■ **buy up**: **~ [sth] up, ~ up [sth]** acheter systématiquement [shares, property].

buyer /'baɪə(r)/ **▶ 1251** n acheteur/-euse m/f; **~'s market** marché m d'acheteurs, marché m où la demande est faible.

buying /'baɪɪŋ/ n achat m.

buyout /'baɪaʊt/ n COMM rachat m d'entreprise.

buzz /bʌz/ **I** n **1** (of insect, conversation) bourdonnement m; **2**○ (phone call) **to give sb a ~** passer un coup de fil à qn; **3**○ (thrill) **it gives me a ~** (from alcohol) ça me

When by is used with a passive verb it is translated by par:
he was killed by a tiger = il a été tué par un tigre
she was horrified by the news = elle a été horrifiée par la nouvelle
For particular usages, see the entry **by**.

When by is used with a present participle to mean by means of it is translated by en:
she learned French by listening to the radio = elle a appris le français en écoutant la radio
For particular usages, see the entry **by**.

When by is used with a noun to mean by means of or using it is translated by par:
by telephone = par téléphone
to hold a suitcase by the handle = tenir une valise par la poignée
Note, however:
to travel by bus/train/plane = voyager en bus/train/avion

In time expressions by is translated by avant:
it must be finished by Friday = il faut que ce soit fini avant vendredi
For particular usages, see the entry **by**.

by often appears as the second element in phrasal verbs (get by, put by, stand by etc.). For translations, consult the appropriate verb entry (**get, put, stand** etc.).

For translations of fixed phrases and expressions such as *to learn something off by heart, to deliver something by hand* etc. consult the appropriate noun entry (**heart, hand** etc.).

For all other uses of by see the entry **by**.

fait planer○; **to get a ~ out of doing** prendre son pied○ en faisant.
II vtr **1** (call) **to ~ sb** appeler qn au bip, biper; **2** [plane] raser [crowd, building]; frôler [other plane].
III vi [bee, fly] bourdonner; [buzzer] sonner; **~ if you know the answer** appuyez sur la sonnette si vous connaissez la réponse; **her head ~ed with thoughts** les idées se bousculaient dans son esprit; **the house was ~ing with activity** tout le monde s'affairait dans la maison.
■ **buzz off**○ s'en aller; **~ off!** dégage○!

buzzard /'bʌzəd/ n ZOOL buse f.

buzzer /'bʌzə(r)/ n GEN sonnerie f; (on pocket) bip m.

buzzing /'bʌzɪŋ/ **I** n (of insects) bourdonnement m; (of buzzer) vibration f.
II○ adj (lively) [town] animé; [party, atmosphere] planant○.

buzz: **~ saw** n scie f circulaire; **~word**○ n mot m à la mode.

by /baɪ/ **I** prep **1** (showing agent, result) par; **he was bitten ~ a snake** il a été mordu par un serpent; **designed ~ an architect** conçu par un architecte; **destroyed ~ fire** détruit par le feu; **~ working extra hours** en faisant des heures supplémentaires; **to begin ~ saying that** commencer par dire que; **2** (through the means of) **to travel ~ bus/train** voyager en bus/train; **~ bicycle** à bicyclette, en vélo; **to pay ~ cheque** payer par chèque; **~ candlelight** [dine] aux chandelles; [read] à la bougie; **I know her ~ sight** je la connais de vue; **I took him ~ the hand** je l'ai pris par la main; **he has two children ~ his first wife** il a deux enfants de sa première femme; **3** (according to, from evidence of) à; **~ my watch it is three o'clock** à ma montre, il est trois heures; **I could tell ~ the look on her face that she was angry** rien qu'à la regarder je savais qu'elle était fâchée; **I knew him ~ his walk** je l'ai reconnu à sa démarche; **it's all right ~ me** ça me va; **4** (via, passing through) par; **~ the back door** par la porte de derrière; **to travel ~ Rome ~ Venice and Florence** aller à Rome en passant par Venise et Florence; **5** (near, beside) à côté de, près de; **~ the bed/the window** à côté du lit/de la fenêtre; **~ the sea** au bord de la mer; **6** (past) **to go** ou **pass ~ sb** passer devant qn; **they passed us ~ in their car** ils nous ont dépassés dans leur voiture; **let us get ~** laissez-nous passer; **7** (showing authorship) de; **a film ~ Claude Chabrol** un film de Claude Chabrol; **who is it ~?** c'est de qui?; **8** (before, not later than) avant; **~ four o'clock/next Thursday** avant quatre heures/jeudi prochain; **~ this time next week** d'ici la semaine prochaine; **~ the time she had got downstairs he was gone** le temps qu'elle descende, il était parti; **he ought to be here ~ now** il devrait être déjà là; **~ now it was clear that they were going to win** à ce moment-là il était clair qu'ils allaient gagner; **9** (during) **~ day as well as ~ night** de jour comme de nuit; **~ daylight** au jour; **~ moonlight** au clair de lune; **10** (according to) **forbidden ~ law** interdit par la loi; **to play ~ the rules** jouer selon les règles; **it seems primitive ~ western standards** cela a l'air primitif selon or d'après les critères occidentaux; **11** (to the extent or degree of) **prices have risen ~ 20%** les prix ont augmenté de 20%; **he's taller than me ~ two centimetres** il fait deux centimètres de plus que moi, il est plus grand que moi de deux centimètres; **~ far** de loin; **it's better ~ far** c'est beaucoup mieux; **12** (in measurements) sur; **a room 20 metres ~ 10 metres** une pièce de 20 mètres sur 10; **13** (in multiplication, division) par; **10 multiplied ~ 5 is 50** 10 multiplié par 5 égale 50; **14** (showing rate, quantity) à; **to be paid ~ the hour** être payé à l'heure; **~ the dozen** à la douzaine; **15** (in successive degrees, units) **little ~ little** peu à peu; **day ~ day** jour après jour; **one ~ one** un par un, un à un; **16** (with regard to) de; **he is an architect ~ profession** ou **trade** il est architecte de son métier; **~ birth** de naissance; **17** (as a result of) par; **~ accident/mistake** par accident/erreur; **~ chance** par hasard; **18** (used with reflexive pronouns) **he did it all ~ himself** il l'a fait tout seul; **19** NAUT (in compass directions) quart; **south ~ south-west** sud quart sud-ouest.

II adv **1** (past) **to go ~** passer; **the people walking ~** les gens mpl qui passent/passaient, les passants mpl; **a lot of time has gone ~ since then** il s'est écoulé beaucoup de temps depuis lors; **as time goes ~** avec le temps; **2** (near) près; **he lives close ~** il

habite tout près; **3** (aside, in reserve) **to put money ~** mettre de l'argent de côté; **4** (to one's house) **come ~ for a drink** passe prendre un verre.

IDIOMS **~ and ~** bientôt, en peu de temps; **~ the ~**, **~ the bye** à propos; **but that's ~ the ~** mais ça c'est un détail, mais ça c'est autre chose.

bye /baɪ/ **I** n **1** GB SPORT **to have** ou **get a ~** gagner par défaut.
II○ excl au revoir!; **~ for now!** à bientôt!

bye-bye○ /'baɪbaɪ, bə'baɪ/ **I** excl au revoir!
II adv **to go ~** US partir; **to go ~s** GB LANG ENFANTIN aller au lit.

byelaw n = **bylaw**.

by(e)-election /'baɪlekʃn/ n GB élection f partielle.

Byelorussia /ˌbjeləʊ'rʊʃə/ ▶ 840| pr n Biélorussie f.

bygone /'baɪgɒn/ adj [days, years, scene, etc] d'antan; **a ~ age** ou **era** une époque révolue.
IDIOMS **to let ~s be ~s** enterrer le passé.

bylaw /'baɪlɔː/ n arrêté m municipal.

by-line /'baɪlaɪn/ n **1** (in newspaper) nom m de journaliste (en tête d'un article); **2** SPORT ligne f de touche.

bypass /'baɪpɑːs/ **I** n **1** AUT rocade f; **2** (pipe, channel) by-pass m inv; **3** ELEC dérivation f; **4** MED pontage m.
II vtr AUT contourner [town, city]; FIG éviter [issue, question]; contourner [law]; éviter de passer par [manager, chief].

bypass operation n MED pontage m.

by-product n BIOL, IND dérivé m; FIG effet m secondaire.

by: **~road** n petite route f, petit chemin m; **~stander** n spectateur/-trice m/f.

byte /baɪt/ n COMPUT octet m.

byway /'baɪweɪ/ n LIT petite route f, petit chemin m; FIG périphérie f.

byword /'baɪwɜːd/ n **to be a ~ for fanaticism** être synonyme de fanatisme.

by-your-leave n **without so much as a ~** sans même demander la permission.

Byzantine /baɪ'zæntaɪn, 'bɪzəntaɪn/ **I** n Byzantin/-e m/f.
II adj [art, empire] byzantin; [emperor] de Byzance.

Cc

c, C /siː/ n **1** (letter) c, C m; **2 C** MUS do m, ut m; **3** (abrév écrite = **century**) c19th, C19th XIXᵉ siècle; **4 c** (abrév écrite = **circa**) vers; c1890 vers 1890; **5 c** abrév écrite = **carat**; **6 c** US abrév écrite = **cent(s)**; **7 C** GB SCH (grade) ~ note f de 12 sur 20; **8 C** abrév = **Celsius**, **centigrade**.

CA 1 US POST abrév écrite = **California**; **2** abrév ▶**Central America**; **3** GB FIN abrév ▶**chartered accountant**.

CAA n GB abrév ▶ **Civil Aviation Authority**.

cab /kæb/ n **1** (taxi) taxi m; **2** (for driver) cabine f.

CAB 1 GB abrév ▶ **Citizens' Advice Bureau**; **2** US abrév ▶ **Civil Aeronautics Board**.

cabal /kə'bæl/ n cabale f.

cabana /kə'bɑːnə/ n US (hut) cabine f de plage.

cabaret /'kæbəreɪ, US ˌkæbə'reɪ/ n cabaret m.

cabbage /'kæbɪdʒ/ n **1** BOT, CULIN chou m; **2**° GB INJUR (person) personne réduite à l'état végétatif.

cabby° /'kæbɪ/ n chauffeur m de taxi.

cab-driver /'kæbdraɪvə(r)/ n chauffeur m de taxi.

cabin /'kæbɪn/ n **1** (hut) cabane f; (in holiday camp) chalet m; **2** NAUT cabine f; **3** AVIAT (for passengers) cabine f; (cockpit) cabine f de pilotage; **4** (in rocket) habitacle m; **5** GB (driver's compartment) cabine f.

cabin: **~ boy** n HIST mousse m; **~ crew** n AVIAT personnel m de bord; **~ cruiser** n cruiser m.

cabinet /'kæbɪnɪt/ **I** n **1** (cupboard) petit placard m; (glass-fronted) vitrine f; (decorative, on legs) cabinet m; **2** GB POL cabinet m; cf Conseil m des ministres.

II noun modifier [decision, post] ministériel/-ielle.

cabinet: **~maker** ▶**1251** n ébéniste m; **~making** n ébénisterie f; **~ meeting** n GB cf Conseil des ministres; **~ minister** n GB ministre m (faisant partie du Cabinet du premier ministre); **~ reshuffle** n GB remaniement m ministériel.

cable /'keɪbl/ **I** n **1** (rope, wire) câble m; **brake ~** câble de frein; **to lay a ~** poser un câble; **power ~** câble électrique; **2** (television) câble m; **3** (telegram) câble m.

II vtr (all contexts) câbler.

III noun modifier [channel, network] câblé.

cable: **~ car** n téléphérique m; **~gram** n câblogramme m; **~-knit** adj [sweater] à torsades; **~ railway** n funiculaire m; **~ television**, **~ TV** n télévision f par câble; **~way** n téléphérique m.

caboodle° /kə'buːdl/ n **the whole ~** tout le bazar° or bataclan°.

cab-rank, **cab stand** n station f de taxis.

cache /kæʃ/ n **1** (hoard) cache f; **2** (place) cachette f.

cachet /'kæʃeɪ, US kæ'ʃeɪ/ n cachet m.

cackle /'kækl/ **I** n (of hen) caquet m; (of person) ricanement m; **cut the ~**°! arrêtez de jacasser!

II vi [hen] caqueter; [person] (talk) caqueter; (laugh) ricaner.

cacophony /kə'kɒfənɪ/ n SOUT cacophonie f.

cactus /'kæktəs/ n (pl **-ti**) cactus m.

CAD n: abrév ▶ **computer-aided design**.

cadaver /kə'dɑːvə(r), -'deɪv-, US kə'dævər/ n SOUT cadavre m.

cadaverous /kə'dævərəs/ adj cadavérique.

CADCAM /'kædkæm/ n COMPUT (abrév = **computer-aided design and computer-aided manufacture**) CFAO f.

caddie, **caddy** /'kædɪ/ n caddie m.

caddy /'kædɪ/ n **1** US (shopping trolley) chariot m, caddie m; **2** GB (also **tea ~**) boîte f à thé; **3** SPORT = **caddie**.

cadence /'keɪdns/ n (intonation) inflexion f; (rhythm) cadence f.

cadet /kə'det/ n MIL (also **officer ~**) élève mf officier; (in police force) élève mf agent de police.

cadet: **~ corps** n MIL unité f de préparation militaire (jusqu'à 18 ans); **~ school** n école f militaire.

cadge° /kædʒ/ vtr PÉJ **to ~ sth off** ou **from sb** taper° qn de qch [sum]; taper° qch à qn [cigarette, money]; **to ~ a meal/a lift** se faire inviter/emmener en voiture.

cadger° /'kædʒə(r)/ n PÉJ GEN parasite m; (of money) tapeur/-euse° m/f; (of meals) pique-assiette° mf inv.

cadre /'kɑːdə(r), US 'kædrɪ/ n **1** (group) MIL cadre m; ADMIN, POL noyau m (d'hommes); **2** POL (person) cadre m.

CAE n COMPUT (abrév = **computer-aided engineering**) IAO f.

Caesarean, **Caesarian** /sɪ'zeərɪən/ n (also **~ section**) césarienne f.

café /'kæfeɪ, US kæ'feɪ/ n **1** GEN ~ snack-bar m (ne vendant pas de boissons alcoolisées); **pavement ~**, **sidewalk ~** café m; **2** US (restaurant) bistro m.

cafeteria /ˌkæfə'tɪərɪə/ n GEN cafétéria f; SCH cantine f; UNIV restaurant m universitaire.

caffein(e) /'kæfiːn/ n caféine f; **~-free** décaféiné.

cage /keɪdʒ/ **I** n **1** (for bird, animal) cage f; (of lift) cabine f; (in mine) cage f; **2**° (in ice-hockey) cage f (de buts).

II vtr mettre [qch] en cage [animal]; **a ~d animal** un animal en cage.

cagebird /'keɪdʒbɜːd/ n oiseau m d'appartement.

cagey, **cagy**° /'keɪdʒɪ/ adj **1** (wary) réticent/-e; **to be ~ about doing** hésiter à faire; **she's very ~ about her family** elle n'aime pas beaucoup parler de sa famille; **2** US (shrewd) astucieux/-ieuse.

cagoule /kə'guːl/ n GB K-way® m.

cahoots° /kə'huːts/ npl **to be in ~** être de mèche°.

Cain /keɪn/ pr n Caïn.

IDIOMS **to raise ~**° (make a noise) faire du boucan°.

cairn /keən/ n (of stones) cairn m.

Cairo /'kaɪrəʊ/ ▶**1343** pr n Le Caire.

cajole /kə'dʒəʊl/ vtr cajoler; **to ~ sb into doing sth** amener qn à faire qch par la cajolerie.

Cajun /'keɪdʒən/ ▶**1100**, **1038** adj acadien/-ienne.

cake /keɪk/ **I** n **1** CULIN gâteau m; (sponge) génoise f; **2** (of soap, wax) pain m; **3** (of fish, potato) croquette f.

II vi [mud, blood] former une croûte (**on** sur).

IDIOMS **it's a piece of ~**° c'est du gâteau°; **to get a** ou **one's slice** ou **share of the ~** avoir sa part du gâteau; **you can't have your ~ and eat it** on ne peut pas avoir le beurre et l'argent du beurre; ▶**hot cake**.

cake: **~ mix** n préparation f or mélange m pour gâteau; **~ pan** n US = **cake tin**; **~ shop** n ~ pâtisserie f; **~ tin** n (for baking) moule m à gâteaux; (for storing) boîte f à gâteaux.

CAL n: abrév ▶ **computer-aided learning**.

calabrese /ˌkælə'breɪzɪ/ n broccoli m.

calamine /'kæləmaɪn/ n calamine f; **~ lotion** lotion f calmante à la calamine.

calamitous /kə'læmɪtəs/ adj catastrophique, désastreux/-euse.

calamity /kə'læmətɪ/ n calamité f.

calcify /'kælsɪfaɪ/ vi se calcifier.

calcium /'kælsɪəm/ n calcium m.

calculate /'kælkjʊleɪt/ vtr **1** (work out) calculer [cost, distance, price]; **2** (estimate) évaluer [effect, probability]; **3** (intend) **to be ~d to do** avoir été conçu pour faire.

calculated /'kælkjʊleɪtɪd/ adj [crime] prémédité; [attempt, decision, insult] délibéré; [risk] calculé.

calculating /'kælkjʊleɪtɪŋ/ adj **1** (scheming) [manner, person] calculateur/-trice; **2** (shrewd) [policy] prudent.

calculating machine n machine f à calculer.

calculation /ˌkælkjʊ'leɪʃn/ n **1** (operation) calcul m; **to make** ou **do ~s** faire des calculs; **to get one's ~s wrong** se tromper dans ses calculs; **2** (scheming) préméditation f.

calculator /'kælkjʊleɪtə(r)/ n calculatrice f, calculette f.

calculus /'kælkjʊləs/ n MATH, MED calcul m.

calendar /'kælɪndə(r)/ n calendrier m.

calendar: ~ month n mois m calendaire; **~ year** n année f civile.

calf /kɑːf, US kæf/ n (pl **calves**) **1** ZOOL (cow) veau m; (deer) faon m; (buffalo) buffletin m; (elephant) éléphanteau m; (whale) baleineau m; **to be in ~** être pleine; **calves' liver** CULIN foie m de veau; **2** (leather) vachette f; **3** (part of leg) mollet m.

calf: ~ love n amour m juvénile; **~skin** n vachette f.

caliber n US = **calibre**.

calibrate /'kælɪbreɪt/ vtr étalonner [scales]; calibrer [instrument].

calibre GB, **caliber** US /'kælɪbə(r)/ n calibre m.

California /ˌkælɪ'fɔːnɪə/ **▶ 1290** pr n Californie f.

caliper n US = **calliper**.

calisthenics n = **callisthenics**.

call /kɔːl/ **I** n **1** TELECOM appel m (téléphonique) (**from** de); (**tele**)**phone ~** appel m (téléphonique); **to make a ~** appeler, téléphoner; **to make a ~ to Italy** appeler l'Italie, téléphoner en Italie; **to give sb a ~** appeler qn; **to return sb's ~** rappeler qn; **2** (cry) (human) appel m (**for** à); (animal) cri m; **to give sb a ~** appeler qn; **3** (summons) appel m; **to put out a ~ for sb** (over public address) faire appeler qn; (over radio) lancer un appel à qn; **4** (visit) visite f; **social ~** visite f de courtoisie; **to make** ou **pay a ~** LIT rendre visite (**on** à); **5** (demand) demande f (**for** de); **there were ~s for his resignation** sa démission a été réclamée; **she has many ~s on her time** elle est très sollicitée; **we don't get much ~ for that** nous n'avons guère de demande pour cela; **to have first ~ on sth** avoir la priorité sur qch; **6** (need) **there's no ~ for sth/to do** il n'y a pas de raison pour qch/de faire; **there was no ~ for her to say that** elle n'avait aucune raison or aucun besoin de dire cela; **7** (allure) appel m (**of** de); **8** SPORT décision f; **9** (for repayment) demande f de remboursement; **a ~ for capital/tenders** un appel de fonds/d'offres; **10** (duty) **to be on ~** [doctor] être de garde; [engineer] être de service; **11** RELIG (vocation) vocation f.

II vtr **1** (also **~ out**) (say loudly) appeler [name, number]; crier [answer, instructions]; annoncer [result, flight]; **to ~ the register** SCH faire l'appel; **he ~ed (out) 'Goodbye'** il a crié 'au revoir'; **2** (summon) appeler [lift]; (by shouting) appeler [person, animal]; (by phone) appeler; (by letter) convoquer; **the boss ~ed me into his office** le chef m'a fait venir dans son bureau; **the police were ~ed to the scene** la police a été appelée sur les lieux; **3** (telephone) (also **~ up**) appeler (**at** à; **from** de); **4** (give a name) appeler [person, baby, animal, place, product] (**by** par); intituler [book, film, music, play]; **5** (arrange) organiser [strike]; convoquer [meeting, rehearsal]; fixer [election]; **6** (waken) réveiller [person]; **7** (describe as) **to ~ sb stupid/a liar** traiter qn d'imbécile/de menteur/-euse; **I wouldn't ~ it spacious** je ne dirais pas que c'est spacieux; **it's not what you'd ~ an exciting film** on ne peut pas dire que ce film soit passionnant; **it's**

what you might ~ a delicate situation c'est ce qui s'appelle une situation délicate; **~ it what you will** appelle ça comme tu veux; **parapsychology or whatever they ou you ~ it°** la métapsychologie ou quelque chose dans ce goût-là°; (**let's**) **~ it £5** disons cinq livres sterling; **he hasn't a place to ~ his own** il n'a pas de chez-lui; **8** SPORT [referee] déclarer; **9** COMPUT appeler [file].

III vi **1** (also **~ out**) (cry out) [person, animal] appeler; (louder) crier; [bird] crier; **London ~ing** RADIO ici Londres; **2** (telephone) appeler; **thank you for ~ing** merci d'avoir appelé; **please ~ back in an hour** rappelez dans une heure s'il vous plaît; **who's ~ing?** qui est à l'appareil?; **3** (visit) passer; **to ~ at** passer chez [person, shop]; passer à [bank, library]; [train] s'arrêter à [town, station]; [ship] faire escale à [port]; **the London train ~ing at Reading and Slough** le train à destination de Londres desservant les gares de Reading et Slough; **4** (tossing coins) parier.

IV v refl **to ~ oneself** se faire appeler [Smith, Bob]; (claim to be) se dire, se prétendre [poet, designer]; **I am proud to ~ myself European** je suis fier d'être européen.

■ **call away: ~** [sb] **away** appeler; **to be ~ed away** être obligé de s'absenter.

■ **call back: ¶ ~ back 1** (on phone) rappeler; **2** (return) repasser; **¶ ~** [sb] **back** rappeler [person].

■ **call by** passer.

■ **call for: ~ for** [sth] **1** (shout) appeler à [help]; appeler [ambulance, doctor]; **2** (demand) demander [food, equipment]; réclamer [changes]; **3** (require) exiger [treatment, skill]; nécessiter [change, intervention]; **this ~s for a celebration!** ça se fête!; **4** (collect) passer prendre [person]; passer chercher [object].

■ **call in: ¶ ~ in 1** (visit) passer; **2** (telephone) appeler; **to ~ in sick** [employee] appeler pour dire qu'on est malade; **¶ ~ in** [sb], **~** [sb] **in** faire venir [client, patient]; faire appel à [expert, engineer]; **¶ ~ in** [sth], **~** [sth] **in** (recall) retirer [qch] du commerce [product]; demander le remboursement de [loan].

■ **call off: ~ off** [sth], **~** [sth] **off 1** LIT rappeler [dog]; **2** FIG (halt) abandonner [search]; (cancel) annuler [deal, wedding]; **to ~ off one's engagement** rompre ses fiançailles; **let's ~ the whole thing off** laissons tomber.

■ **call on: ~ on** [sb/sth] **1** (visit) (also **~ in on**) rendre visite à [relative, friend]; visiter [patient, client]; **2** (invite) demander à [speaker] (**to do** de faire); **3** (urge) demander à [person] (**to do** de faire); **4** (appeal to, resort to) s'adresser à [person]; avoir recours à [services]; faire appel à [moral quality].

■ **call out: ¶ ~ out** (cry aloud) appeler; (louder) crier; **¶ ~ out** [sb], **~** [sb] **out 1** (summon outside) appeler; **the teacher ~ed me out to the front of the class** le professeur m'a fait venir devant le reste de la classe; **2** (send for) appeler [doctor, repairman, troops]; **3** IND [union] lancer un ordre de grève à [members]; **¶ ~** [sth] **out**, **~ out** [sth] appeler [name, number].

■ **call over: ~** [sb] **over** appeler.

■ **call round** (visit) venir.

■ **call up: ¶ ~ up** appeler; **¶ ~ up** [sb/sth], **~** [sb/sth] **up 1** (on phone) appeler; **2** (summon) appeler [qn] sous les drapeaux [soldier]; invoquer [spirit]; **3** (evoke) rappeler [memory]; **4** COMPUT appeler (à l'écran), afficher [file]; **5** SPORT sélectionner [player].

CALL n: abrév **▶ computer-aided language learning**.

call: ~back facility n TELECOM rappel m automatique; **~ box** n GB cabine f téléphonique; US poste m téléphonique.

caller /'kɔːlə(r)/ n **1** TELECOM personne f qui appelle; **we've had 15 ~s today** nous avons reçu 15 appels aujourd'hui; **2** (visitor) visiteur/-euse m/f.

call girl n call-girl f.

calligrapher /kə'lɪgrəfə(r)/, **calligraphist** /kə'lɪgrəfɪst/ **▶ 1251** n calligraphe mf.

calligraphy /kə'lɪgrəfɪ/ n calligraphie f.

calling /'kɔːlɪŋ/ n (vocation) vocation f; (profession) métier m.

calliper GB, **caliper** US /'kælɪpə(r)/ **1** (leg support) appareil *m* orthopédique; **2** (for measuring) compas *m* d'épaisseur.

callisthenics /ˌkælɪs'θenɪks/ *n* (+ *v sg*) gymnastique *f* suédoise.

callous /'kæləs/ *adj* [*person*] inhumain, insensible; [*attitude, brutality, crime*] inhumain.

callously /'kæləslɪ/ *adv* [*act, speak*] durement; [*suggest*] cyniquement.

callousness /'kæləsnɪs/ *n* dureté *f*, inhumanité *f*.

call: **~-out** *n* dépannage *m*; **~-out charge** *n* frais *mpl* de déplacement.

callow /'kæləʊ/ *adj* gauche.

call: **~ sign** *n* RADIO indicatif *m*; **~-up** *n* MIL appel *m*; (of reservists) rappel *m*; **~-up papers** *npl* MIL ordre *m* d'appel.

callused /'kæləst/ *adj* calleux/-euse.

calm /kɑːm, US *also* kɑːlm/ **I** *n* **1** (of place, atmosphere) tranquillité *f*, calme *m*; **2** (of person) calme *m*; (in adversity) sang-froid *m*; **to keep one's ~** garder son sang-froid; **3** NAUT calme *m*.
II *adj* calme; **keep ~!** du calme!
III *vtr* calmer.
IDIOMS **the ~ before the storm** le calme avant la tempête.
■ **calm down**: ¶ **~ down** se calmer; ¶ **~ [sth/sb] down, ~ down [sth/sb]** calmer.

calming /'kɑːmɪŋ, US *also* 'kɑːlm-/ *adj* apaisant.

calmly /'kɑːmlɪ, US *also* 'kɑːlmlɪ/ *adv* [*act, speak*] calmement; [*sleep, smoke*] tranquillement.

calmness /'kɑːmnɪs, US *also* 'kɑːlm-/ *n* calme *m*.

Calor gas® /'kælə gæs/ *n* GB butane *m*.

calorie /'kælərɪ/ *n* calorie *f*; **low-~ diet/drink** régime/boisson à basses calories; **to be ~-conscious** faire attention aux calories.

calorific /ˌkælə'rɪfɪk/ *adj* calorifique.

calvary /'kælvərɪ/ **I** *n* calvaire *m*.
II Calvary *pr n* le Calvaire.

calve /kɑːv, US kæv/ *vi* mettre bas.

calves /kɑːvz/ *npl* ▶ **calf**.

Calvinistic /ˌkælvɪ'nɪstɪk/ *adj* calviniste.

cam /kæm/ *n* TECH came *f*.

camaraderie /ˌkæmə'rɑːdərɪ, US -'ræd-/ *n* camaraderie *f*.

camber /'kæmbə(r)/ *n* (of road) bombement *m*.

Cambodia /kæm'bəʊdɪə/ ▶ **840** *pr n* Cambodge *m*.

Cambs *n* GB POST *abrév écrite* = **Cambridgeshire**.

camcorder /'kæmkɔːdə(r)/ *n* caméscope® *m*.

came /keɪm/ *prét* ▶ **come**.

camel /'kæml/ ▶ **818** *n* **1** chameau *m*; (female) chamelle *f*; (for racing) méhari *m*; **~ train** caravane *f* de chameaux; **~ driver** chamelier *m*; **2** (colour) couleur *f* caramel.

camel hair *n* poil *m* de chameau; **~ coat** manteau *m* en poil de chameau.

camellia /kə'miːlɪə/ *n* camélia *m*.

cameo /'kæmɪəʊ/ *n* **1** camée *m*; **2** THEAT, CIN **a ~ role** un camée.

camera /'kæmərə/ *n* **1** PHOT appareil *m* photo; CIN, TV caméra *f*; **2** JUR **in ~** à huis clos.

camera: **~ crew** *n* équipe *f* de télévision; **~man** ▶ **1251** *n* cadreur *m*, cameraman *m*.

Cameroon /ˌkæmə'ruːn/ ▶ **840** *pr n* Cameroun *m*.

camisole /'kæmɪsəʊl/ *n* caraco *m*.

camomile /'kæməmaɪl/ *n* camomille *f*.

camouflage /'kæməflɑːʒ/ **I** *n* camouflage *m*.
II *vtr* camoufler (**with** avec).

camp /kæmp/ **I** *n* **1** (of tents) camp *m*; (of nomads) campement *m*; **to make** ou **pitch ~** planter son camp; **to strike ~** lever le camp; **2** FIG (group) camp *m*; **to go over to the other ~** changer de camp; **to have a foot in both ~s** avoir un pied dans chaque camp; **3**° PÉJ (mannered style) cabotinage° *m*.
II *adj* PÉJ **1** (exaggerated) [*person*] cabotin°; [*gesture, performance*] théâtral; **2** (effeminate) efféminé.

III *vi* camper; **to go ~ing** faire du camping.
IDIOMS **to ~ it up**° (overact) cabotiner°; (act effeminately) forcer dans le genre efféminé.
■ **camp out** camper.

campaign /kæm'peɪn/ **I** *n* campagne *f*.
II *vi* faire campagne (**for** pour; **against** contre).

campaigner /kæm'peɪnə(r)/ *n* GEN militant/-e *m/f* (**for** pour; **against** contre); POL candidat/-e *m/f* en campagne (électorale); **old ~** MIL vétéran *m*.

campaign: **~ literature** *n* ¢ tracts *mpl*; **~ medal** *n* médaille *f* militaire.

campaign trail *n* **on the ~** en tournée électorale.

campaign worker *n* GB POL membre *m* de l'état-major.

camp: **~ bed** *n* lit *m* de camp; **~ chair** *n* US chaise *f* pliante; **~ commandant** *n* commandant *m* de camp.

camper /'kæmpə(r)/ *n* **1** (person) campeur/-euse *m/f*; **2** (also **~ van**) camping-car *m*; **3** US (folding caravan) caravane *f* pliante.

campfire /'kæmpfaɪə(r)/ *n* feu *m* de camp.

camphor /'kæmfə(r)/ *n* camphre *m*.

camping /'kæmpɪŋ/ *n* camping *m*; **to go ~** faire du camping.

camping: **~ equipment** *n* matériel *m* de camping; **~ gas** *n* camping-gaz® *m*; **~ ground** *n* = **campsite**; **~ holiday** *n* vacances *fpl* sous la tente; **~ site** *n* = **campsite**; **~ stool** *n* GB pliant *m*; **~ stove** *n* réchaud *m*.

camp: **~site** *n* (official) terrain *m* de camping, camping *m*; **~ stool** *n* pliant *m*.

campus /'kæmpəs/ (*pl* **~es** /'kæmpəsɪz/) *n* campus *m*.

camshaft /'kæmʃɑːft, US -ʃæft/ *n* arbre *m* à cames.

can¹

can and *could* are usually translated by the verb *pouvoir*. For the conjugation of *pouvoir*, see the French verb tables.

    he can wait until tomorrow = il peut attendre jusqu'à demain
    you can go out now = vous pouvez sortir maintenant

The two notable exceptions to this are as follows:
When *can* or *could* is used to mean *know how to*, the verb *savoir* is used:

    she can speak French = elle sait parler français
    he could read at the age of four = à l'âge de quatre ans il savait lire

When *can* or *could* is used with a verb of perception such as *see, hear* or *feel* it is not translated at all:

    I can't see her = je ne la vois pas
    she couldn't feel anything = elle ne sentait rien

In requests *can* is translated by the present tense of *pouvoir* and the more polite *could* by the conditional tense of *pouvoir*:

    can you help me? = peux-tu m'aider?
    could you help me? = pourrais-tu m'aider?

For particular usages of *could* when it is not simply the preterite or conditional of *can* see **13, 15, 16** in the entry *can¹*.

See also the entry *able*.

can¹ /kæn/ *modal aux* (*prét, conditional* **could**; *nég au prés* **cannot, can't**) **1** (expressing possibility) **we ~ rent a house** nous pouvons louer une maison; **it ~ also be used to dry clothes** on peut aussi s'en servir pour sécher le linge; **you can't have forgotten!** tu ne peux pas avoir oublié!; **it cannot be explained logically** ça n'a pas d'explication logique; **it could be that...** il se peut que... (+ *subj*); **could be**° peut-être; **it could be a trap** c'est peut-être un piège, ça pourrait être un piège; **I could be wrong** je me trompe peut-être, il se peut que j'aie tort; **you could have been electrocuted!** tu aurais pu t'électrocuter!; **'did she know?'—'no, how could she?'** 'est-ce qu'elle était au courant?' —'non, comment est-ce qu'elle aurait pu l'être?'; **the**

computer couldn't ou **can't have made an error** l'ordinateur n'a pas pu faire d'erreur, il est impossible que l'ordinateur ait fait une erreur; **nothing could be simpler** il n'y a rien de plus simple; **2** (expressing permission) **you ~ turn right here** vous pouvez tourner à droite ici; **I can't leave yet** je ne peux pas partir pour le moment; **could I interrupt?** puis-je vous interrompre?; **3** (when making requests) **~ you leave us a message?** est-ce que tu peux nous laisser un message?; **~ I ask you a question?** puis-je vous poser une question?; **4** (when making an offer) **~ I give you a hand?** est-ce que je peux te donner un coup de main?; **what ~ I do for you?** (in shop) qu'y a-t-il pour votre service?; **5** (when making suggestions) **you ~ always exchange it** tu peux toujours l'échanger; **we could try and phone him** nous pourrions essayer de lui téléphoner; **6** (have skill, knowledge to) **she can't read yet** elle ne sait pas encore lire; **~ he type?** est-ce qu'il sait taper à la machine?; **7** (have ability, power to) **computers ~ process data rapidly** les ordinateurs peuvent traiter rapidement les données; **to do all one ~** faire tout ce qu'on peut ou tout son possible; **he couldn't sleep for weeks** il n'a pas pu dormir pendant des semaines; **I wish I could have been there** j'aurais aimé (pouvoir) être là; **8** (have ability, using senses, to) **~ you see it?** est-ce que tu le vois?; **I can't hear anything** je n'entends rien; **I could feel my heart beating** je sentais mon cœur battre; **9** (indicating capability, tendency) **she could be quite abrupt** elle pouvait être assez brusque; **10** (expressing likelihood, assumption) **it can't be as bad as that!** ça ne peut pas être aussi terrible que ça!; **he couldn't be more than 10 years old** (now) il ne peut pas avoir plus de 10 ans; **11** (expressing willingness to act) **we ~ take you home** nous pouvons te déposer chez toi; **I couldn't leave the children** (didn't want to) je ne voulais pas laisser les enfants; (wouldn't want to) je ne pourrais pas laisser les enfants; **12** (be in a position to) **they ~ hardly refuse** ils peuvent difficilement refuser; **I couldn't possibly accept the money** je ne peux vraiment pas accepter cet argent; **13** (expressing a reproach) **they could have warned us** ils auraient pu nous prévenir; **you could at least say sorry!** tu pourrais au moins t'excuser!; **how could you!** comment as-tu pu faire une chose pareille!; **14** (expressing surprise) **what ~ she possibly want from me?** qu'est-ce qu'elle peut bien me vouloir?; **who could it be?** qui est-ce que ça peut bien être?; **you can't** ou **cannot be serious!** tu veux rire○!; **~ you believe it!** tu te rends compte?; **15** (for emphasis) **I couldn't agree more!** je suis entièrement d'accord!; **they couldn't have been nicer** ils ont été extrêmement gentils; **you couldn't be more mistaken** tu te trompes complètement; **16** (expressing exasperation) **I was so mad I could have screamed!** j'aurais crié tellement j'étais en colère!; **I could murder him○** je le tuerais○!; **17** (expressing obligation) **she ~ ask me herself** elle peut venir me le demander elle-même; **you ~ get lost○!** va te faire fiche○!; **18** (avoiding repetition of verb) **'~ we borrow it?'—'you ~'** 'est-ce que nous pouvons l'emprunter?'—'bien sûr'; **leave as soon as you ~** partez dès que vous le pourrez; **'~ anyone give me a lift home?'—'we ~'** 'est-ce que quelqu'un peut me déposer chez moi?'—'oui, nous'.
IDIOMS **as happy/excited as ~** ou **could be** très heureux/excité; **no ~ do○** non, je ne peux pas.

can² /kæn/ **I** n (of food) boîte f; (aerosol) bombe f; (for petrol) bidon m; (of drink) cannette f.
II vtr (p prés etc **-nn-**) CULIN mettre [qch] en conserve.
III canned pp adj **1** [food] en boîte; **2**○ [laughter] enregistré.
IDIOMS **a ~ of worms** une affaire dans laquelle il vaut mieux ne pas trop fouiller; **in the ~○** CIN (of film) dans la boîte; (of negotiations) dans la poche; **to carry the ~ for sb○** porter le chapeau à la place de qn○.

Canada /ˈkænədə/ ▶840| pr n Canada m.
Canadian /kəˈneɪdɪən/ ▶1100| **I** n Canadien/-ienne.

II adj canadien/-ienne; **to speak ~ French** parler le français du Canada.

canal /kəˈnæl/ n **1** (waterway) canal m; **2** ANAT (in ear) conduit m.

canal boat, **canal barge** n péniche f.

canapé /ˈkænəpɪ, US ˌkænəˈpeɪ/ n canapé m.

Canaries /kəˈneərɪz/ ▶1022| pr npl (also **Canary Islands**) the **~** les Canaries fpl.

canary /kəˈneərɪ/ n canari m, serin m.

cancel /ˈkænsl/ (p prés etc **-ll-**, **-l-** US) **I** vtr **1** (call off) annuler; **2** (nullify) résilier [contract]; annuler [debt]; mettre une opposition à [cheque]; **3** JUR lever [order]; révoquer [decree]; **4** POST oblitérer [stamp].
II vi (from meal, function, meeting) se décommander; (after booking) annuler.
■ **cancel out**: ¶ **~ out** [arguments, figures] s'annuler; ¶ **~ out** [sth] neutraliser [emotion, effect].

cancellation /ˌkænsəˈleɪʃn/ n **1** (of event, order, booking, train, flight) annulation f; **2** (of contract, policy) résiliation f; (of debt, loan) annulation f; **3** (of order, decree) levée f.

cancer /ˈkænsə(r)/ ▶1002| n MED, FIG cancer m; **to have ~** avoir un cancer; **lung ~** cancer du poumon; **a ~ sufferer** un/-e cancéreux/-euse m/f.

Cancer /ˈkænsə(r)/ ▶1418| n **1** (in zodiac) Cancer m; **2** GEOG **tropic of ~** tropique m du Cancer.

cancerous /ˈkænsərəs/ adj cancéreux/-euse.

cancer: **~ patient** n cancéreux/-euse m/f; **~ research** n cancérologie f.

candelabra /ˌkændɪˈlɑːbrə/ n (pl **~** ou **~s**) candélabre m.

candid /ˈkændɪd/ adj franc/franche; **~ camera** caméra f invisible.

candidacy /ˈkændɪdəsɪ/, **candidature** /ˈkændɪdətʃə/ n GB candidature f.

candidate /ˈkændɪdət, US -deɪt/ n **1** POL candidat/-e m/f; **the ~ for mayor/for Oxford** le candidat à la mairie/pour Oxford; **the Conservative ~** le candidat du parti conservateur; **to stand as a ~** (in an election) se porter candidat (à une élection); **2** (for job) candidat/-e m/f, postulant/-e m/f; **to be a likely ~ (for the job)** être bien placé (pour obtenir le poste); **the successful ~** (in ad) le candidat retenu; **3** (in exam, for admission) candidat/-e m/f; **4** FIG **to be a ~ for** être candidat potentiel à.

candidature n GB = **candidacy**.

candidly /ˈkændɪdlɪ/ adv franchement.

candied /ˈkændɪd/ adj confit; **~ peel** écorce f d'orange et de citron confite.

candle /ˈkændl/ n bougie f; (in church) cierge m.
IDIOMS **to burn the ~ at both ends** brûler la chandelle par les deux bouts; **the game's not worth the ~** le jeu n'en vaut pas la chandelle; **he can't hold a ~ to his sister** il n'arrive pas à la cheville de sa sœur.

candlelight /ˈkændllaɪt/ n lueur f de bougie; **by ~** à la lueur d'une bougie ou des bougies.

candle: **~lit dinner** n dîner m aux chandelles; **Candlemas** n la Chandeleur; **~stick** n bougeoir m; (more ornate) chandelier m.

candlewick /ˈkændlwɪk/ n **~ bedspread** couvre-lit m en tuft.

candour GB, **candor** US /ˈkændə(r)/ n franchise f.

candy /ˈkændɪ/ n US **1** (sweets) bonbons mpl; **2** (sweet) bonbon m.

candy: **~ floss** n GB barbe f à papa; **~ striped** adj (pink) à rayures rose bonbon; (blue) à rayures bleu pâle.

cane /keɪn/ **I** n **1** (material) rotin m; **~ furniture** meubles en rotin; **2** (of sugar, bamboo) canne f; **3** (for walking) canne f; (for plant) tuteur m; (officer's) badine f; GB (for punishment) badine f.
II vtr **1** canner [chair]; **2** donner des coups de badine à [pupil].

cane sugar n sucre m de canne.

canine /ˈkeɪnaɪn/ **I** n **1** (tooth) canine f; **2** (animal) canidé m.

Capacity measurement
For cubic measurements, ▶ **1381** .

British liquid measurements

20 fl oz	= 0,57 ℓ *(litre)*	1 qt	= 1,13 ℓ * *(litres)*
1 pt	= 0,57 ℓ	1 gal	= 4,54 ℓ

* *There are three ways of saying* 1,13 ℓ, *and other measurements like it:* un virgule treize litres, *or (less formally)* un litre virgule treize, *or* un litre treize. *For more details on how to say numbers,* ▶ **1112** .

American liquid measurements

16 fl oz	= 0,47 ℓ	1 qt	= 0,94 ℓ
1 pt	= 0,47 ℓ	1 gal	= 3,78 ℓ

Phrases

what does the tank hold?	= combien le réservoir contient-il?
what's its capacity?	= quelle est sa contenance?
it's 200 litres	= il fait 200 litres
its capacity is 200 litres	= il fait 200 litres

my car does 28 miles to the gallon	= ma voiture fait dix litres aux cent† *or* ma voiture fait du dix litres aux cent
they use 20,000 litres a day	= ils utilisent 20 000 litres par jour

† *Note that the French calculate petrol consumption in litres per 100 km. To convert miles per gallon to litres per 100 km and vice versa simply divide the factor 280 by the known figure.*

A holds more than B	= A contient plus que B
B holds less than A	= B contient moins que A
A has a greater capacity than B	= A a une plus grande contenance que B
B has a smaller capacity than A	= B a une moins grande contenance que A
A and B have the same capacity	= A et B ont la même contenance
20 litres of wine	= 20 litres de vin
it's sold by the litre	= cela se vend au litre

Note the French construction with de, *coming after the noun it describes:*
a 200-litre tank = un réservoir de 200 litres

II *adj* **1** [*species*] canin; **2 a ~ tooth** une canine.

canister /'kænɪstə(r)/ *n* boîte *f* métallique; **a ~ of tear gas, a tear gas ~** une bombe lacrymogène.

cannabis /'kænəbɪs/ *n* cannabis *m*; **~ resin** résine *f* de cannabis.

cannibal /'kænɪbl/ *n* cannibale *mf*, anthropophage *mf*.

cannibalism /'kænɪbəlɪzəm/ *n* cannibalisme *m*, anthropophagie *f*.

cannibalize /'kænɪbəlaɪz/ *vtr* cannibaliser.

canning /'kænɪŋ/ *n* mise *f* en conserve.

cannon /'kænən/ **I** *n* (*pl* **~** ou **~s**) MIL HIST canon *m*.
II *vi* **to ~ into sb/sth** se heurter contre qn/qch.

cannonball /'kænənbɔːl/ *n* **1** (missile) boulet *m* de canon; **2** (dive) **to do a ~** faire la bombe; **3** (also **~ serve**) (in tennis) service *m* canon.

cannon fodder *n* chair *f* à canon.

cannot /'kænɒt/ ▶ **can¹**.

canoe /kə'nuː/ ▶ **949** **I** *n* GEN canoë *m*; (African) pirogue *f*; (Canadian) canoë-kayac *m*.
II *vi* faire du canoë; **they ~d down the river** ils ont descendu la rivière en canoë.

canoeing /kə'nuːɪŋ/ ▶ **949** *n* **to go ~** faire du canoë-kayac.

canoeist /kə'nuːɪst/ *n* canoéiste *mf*.

canon /'kænən/ ▶ **937** *n* **1** (rule) GEN critère *m*; (of church) canon *m*; **2** RELIG chanoine *m*; **3** LITERAT (complete works) œuvre *m*; **4** MUS canon *m*.

canonize /'kænənaɪz/ *vtr* canoniser.

canoodle◦ /kə'nuːdl/ *vi* se faire des mamours◦.

can-opener *n* ouvre-boîtes *m inv*.

canopy /'kænəpɪ/ *n* **1** (for bed) baldaquin *m*; (for throne, altar) dais *m*; (for hammock) toit *m*; **2** AVIAT (cockpit) verrière *f*; (for parachute) voilure *f*; FIG (sky, leaves) voûte *f*; **3** ECOL (forest) canopée *f*.

cant /kænt/ *n* **1** (false words) paroles *fpl* creuses; (ideas) notions *fpl* creuses; **2** (prisoners', thieves') argot *m*; (lawyers') jargon *m*; **3** (sloping surface) (of road) déclivité *f*.

can't /kɑːnt/ *abrév* = **cannot**.

cantankerous /kæn'tæŋkərəs/ *adj* acariâtre.

canteen /kæn'tiːn/ *n* **1** GB (dining room) cantine *f*; **in the ~** à la cantine; **2** MIL (flask) bidon *m*; (mess tin) gamelle *f*; **3 a ~ of cutlery** une ménagère.

canter /'kæntə(r)/ **I** *n* GEN petit galop *m*; **at a ~** au petit galop; **to go for a ~** aller faire une promenade à cheval.
II *vi* [*rider*] faire un petit galop; [*horse*] galoper.

Canterbury /'kæntəbərɪ/ ▶ **1343** *pr n* Cantorbéry; **the ~ Tales** les Contes de Cantorbéry.

cantilever /'kæntɪliːvə(r)/ *n* cantilever *m*, porte-à-faux *m inv*.

cantonal /'kæntənl, kæn'tɒnl/ *adj* cantonal.

canvas /'kænvəs/ **I** *n* **1** (fabric) toile *f*; (for tapestry) canevas *m*; **under ~** (in a tent) sous la tente; (under sail) sous voiles; **2** ART toile *f*; **3** (in boxing) tapis *m*.
II *noun modifier* [*shoes, bag, chair*] en toile.

canvass /'kænvəs/ **I** *vtr* **1** POL **to ~ voters** faire du démarchage électoral auprès des électeurs; **to ~ people for their votes** solliciter les voix des électeurs; **2** (in survey) sonder [*public*]; **to ~ views on sth** sonder l'opinion au sujet de qch; **3** COMM prospecter [*area*]; **to ~ door to door** faire du démarchage.
II *vi* **1** POL faire du démarchage électoral (**for** pour); **2** COMM faire du démarchage (**for** pour).

canvasser /'kænvəsə(r)/ *n* (for party) agent *m* électoral.

canvassing /'kænvəsɪŋ/ *n* (door to door) démarchage *m*; **~ for votes** démarchage électoral; **~ of opinion** sondage *m* d'opinion.

canyon /'kænjən/ *n* cañon *m*.

cap /kæp/ **I** *n* **1** (headgear) (peaked) casquette *f*; (of nurse) coiffe *f*; **baseball ~** casquette de baseball; **2** GB SPORT **he's got his Scottish ~** il a été sélectionné pour l'équipe écossaise; **3** (cover) (of pen, valve) capuchon *m*; (of bottle) capsule *f*; (for camera lens) bouchon *m*; **4** (of mushroom) chapeau *m*; **5** (for toy gun) amorce *f*; **6** (for tooth) couronne *f*; **7** GB (also **Dutch ~**) diaphragme *m* (contraceptif).
II *vtr* (*p prés etc* **-pp-**) **1** ADMIN imposer une limite budgétaire à [*local authority*]; plafonner [*budget*]; **2** couronner [*tooth*]; **3** GB SPORT sélectionner [qn] pour l'équipe nationale [*footballer*]; **4** (cover) couronner (**with** de).
IDIOMS **to ~ it all** pour couronner le tout; **to go to sb ~ in hand** se présenter à qn chapeau bas, aller voir qn la main tendue.

cap. /kæp/ *n* (*abrév* = **capital letter**) maj.

CAP *n*: *abrév* ▶ **Common Agricultural Policy**.

capability /ˌkeɪpə'bɪlətɪ/ *n* **1** (capacity) (of intellect, machine, system) capacité *f* (**to do** de faire); **2** (potential strength) capacité *f* (**to do** de faire); **nuclear ~** capacité nucléaire; **3** (aptitude) aptitude *f* (**for** à); **management ~** aptitude à la gestion; **within/outside my capabilities** en-deçà/au-delà de mes compétences.

capable /'keɪpəbl/ *adj* **1** (competent) compétent; **in the ~ hands of** entre les mains expertes de; **2** (able) capable (**of** de); **to be ~ of doing** (have potential to) être capable de faire; (be in danger of) risquer de faire.

capably /'keɪpəblɪ/ *adv* avec compétence.

capacious /kə'peɪʃəs/ *adj* [*pocket, car boot*] vaste.

capacity /kə'pæsətɪ/ *n* **1** (ability to hold) (of box, bottle) contenance *f*; (of barrel) capacité *f* (**of** de); (of building) capacité *f* d'accueil; (of road) capacité *f*; **seating/ storage** ~ capacité d'accueil/de stockage; **packed** ou **full to** ~ comble; **2** (of factory) capacité *f* de production; **to operate at full** ~ opérer au maximum de ses capacités; **the plant is stretched to** ~ l'usine tourne au maximum de ses capacités de production; **3** (role) **in my** ~ **as a doctor** en ma qualité de médecin; **in an advisory** ~ à titre consultatif; **4** (ability) **to have a** ~ **for** avoir de la facilité pour [*learning, maths*]; **a** ~ **for doing** une aptitude à faire; **a great** ~ **for hard work** une grande capacité de travail; **to have the** ~ **to do** avoir les moyens de faire; **the task is well within your capacities** vous êtes parfaitement capable de faire ce travail; **5** AUT cylindrée *f*; **6** ELEC capacité *f*; **7** JUR capacité *f*.

cape /keɪp/ *n* **1** (for rainwear, fashion) cape *f*; (for child, policeman) pèlerine *f*; **2** GEOG promontoire *m*, cap *m*.

cape: **Cape Coloureds** *npl* (in South Africa) métis *mpl* sud-africains; **Cape of Good Hope** *pr n* cap *m* de Bonne-Espérance; **Cape Province** *n* province *f* du Cap.

caper /ˈkeɪpə(r)/ **I** *n* **1** (playful leap) cabriole *f*; **to cut a** ~† faire des cabrioles; **2**○ (funny film) comédie *f*; **3**○ (dishonest scheme) combine○ *f*; **4** BOT, CULIN (tree) câprier *m*; (berry) câpre *f*; **5**○ GB (hassle) **what a** ~! quel bazar○!; **and all that** ~ et tout le bazar○.
II capers *npl* (antics) aventures *fpl*.
III *vi* (also ~ **about**, ~ **around**) gambader.

Cape Town ▶ 1343 │ *pr n* Le Cap.

cap: ~**ful** *n* (contenu m d'un) bouchon-mesure *m*; ~**gun** *n* pistolet *m* à amorces.

capillary /kəˈpɪlərɪ, US ˈkæpɪlərɪ/ *n, adj* capillaire (*m*).

capital /ˈkæpɪtl/ **I** *n* **1** (letter) majuscule *f*; **2** (also ~ **city**) capitale *f*; **3** ¢ GEN (wealth) capital *m*; (funds) capitaux *mpl*, capital *m*; **to make** ~ **out of sth** FIG tirer parti de qch.
II *noun modifier* [*loss, outlay, turnover*] de capital.
III *adj* **1** [*letter*] majuscule; ~ **A** A majuscule; **crazy with a** ~ **C**○ dingue avec un D majuscule or un grand D○; **2** JUR [*offence*] capital; **3** (essential) capital; **4**○ † GB (excellent) épatant.

capital: ~ **account, C/A** *n* compte *m* capital; ~ **allowances** *npl* déduction *f* fiscale pour amortissement; ~ **assets** *npl* actif *m* immobilisé; ~ **city** *n* capitale *f*; ~ **cost** *n* coût *m* d'investissement; ~ **expenditure** *n* dépenses *fpl* d'investissement; (personal) apport *m* personnel (en capital); ~ **gains tax** *n* impôt *m* sur les plus-values des capitaux; ~ **goods** *n* biens *mpl* d'équipement; ~**-intensive industry** *n* industrie *f* de capitaux; ~ **investment** *n* dépenses *fpl* d'investissement.

capitalism /ˈkæpɪtlɪzəm/ *n* capitalisme *m*.

capitalist /ˈkæpɪtəlɪst/ *n, adj* capitaliste (*m*).

capitalization /ˌkæpɪtəlaɪˈzeɪʃn, US -lɪˈz-/ *n* **1** (market value) capitalisation *f*; **2** LING emploi *m* de lettres majuscules.

capitalize /ˈkæpɪtəlaɪz/ **I** *vtr* **1** capitaliser [*assets*]; **2** LING écrire [qch] en majuscules.
II *vi* **to** ~ **on** tirer parti de [*situation, advantage*].

capital: ~ **punishment** *n* peine *f* capitale; ~ **reserves** *npl* réserves *fpl* de capitaux; ~ **spending** *n* dépenses *fpl* d'investissement; ~ **sum** *n* GEN capital *m*; (of loan) principal *m*; ~ **taxation** *n* impôt *m* sur le capital.

Capitol Hill *n* US **1** (hill) colline *f* du Capitole; **2** (congress) congrès *m* américain.

capitulate /kəˈpɪtʃʊleɪt/ *vi* GEN, MIL capituler (**to** devant).

capon /ˈkeɪpən, -ɒn/ *n* chapon *m*.

caprice /kəˈpriːs/ *n* (whim) caprice *m*.

capricious /kəˈprɪʃəs/ *adj* capricieux/-ieuse.

Capricorn /ˈkæprɪkɔːn/ ▶ 1418 │ *n* **1** (in zodiac) Capricorne *m*; **2** GEOG **tropic of** ~ tropique *m* du Capricorne.

caps (*abrév* = **capital letters**) majuscules *fpl*.

capsicum /ˈkæpsɪkəm/ *n* poivron *m*.

capsize /kæpˈsaɪz, US ˈkæpsaɪz/ **I** *vtr* faire chavirer.
II *vi* chavirer.

cap sleeve *n* mancheron *m*.

caps lock *n* (*abrév* = **capitals lock**) verr *m* maj.

capstan /ˈkæpstən/ *n* cabestan *m*.

capsule /ˈkæpsjuːl, US ˈkæpsl/ *n* capsule *f*.

Capt MIL *abrév écrite* = **Captain**.

captain /ˈkæptɪn/ ▶ 1192 │ **I** *n* GEN, MIL, SPORT capitaine *m*; US (precinct commander) (in police) commissaire *m* de quartier; (in fire service) capitaine *m* des pompiers; **naval/army** ~ capitaine de vaisseau/de l'armée de terre; ~ **of industry** FIG capitaine d'industrie.
II *vtr* être le capitaine de [*team*]; commander [*ship, platoon*].

caption /ˈkæpʃn/ **I** *n* **1** (under photo) légende *f* (**to, for** accompagnant); **2** TV, CIN (subtitle) sous-titre *m*.
II *vtr* mettre une légende à [*photo*]; sous-titrer [*film*].

captious /ˈkæpʃəs/ *adj* [*remark*] critique.

captivate /ˈkæptɪveɪt/ *vtr* captiver, fasciner; **he was** ~**d by her** elle le fascinait.

captivating /ˈkæptɪveɪtɪŋ/ *adj* fascinant.

captive /ˈkæptɪv/ **I** *n* captif/-ive *m/f*; **to hold sb** ~ garder qn en captivité; **to take sb** ~ faire qn prisonnier.
II *adj* captif/-ive; ~ **audience** public captif.

captivity /kæpˈtɪvətɪ/ *n* captivité *f*; **in** ~ en captivité.

captor /ˈkæptə(r)/ *n* (of person) geôlier/-ière *m/f*.

capture /ˈkæptʃə(r)/ **I** *n* GEN capture *f*; (of stronghold) prise *f*.
II *vtr* **1** LIT capturer [*person, animal*]; prendre [*stronghold*]; COMM s'emparer de [*market*]; **2** FIG saisir [*moment, likeness*]; rendre [*feeling, beauty*].

car /kɑː(r)/ **I** *n* **1** AUT voiture *f*; **2** RAIL wagon *m*, voiture *f*; **restaurant** ~ wagon-restaurant *m*; **3** US (also **street**~) tramway *m*.
II *noun modifier* AUT [*industry, insurance*] automobile; [*journey, chase*] en voiture; [*accident*] de voiture; ~ **allowance** indemnité *f* de déplacement.

carafe /kəˈræf/ *n* carafe *f*.

caramel /ˈkærəmel/ *n* (toffee, sugar) caramel *m*; ~ **dessert** dessert au caramel.

carat /ˈkærət/ *n* carat *m*; **18** ~ **gold** or 18 carats.

caravan /ˈkærəvæn/ **I** *n* GEN caravane *f*; (for circus, gypsies) roulotte *f*.
II *noun modifier* GB [*holiday*] en caravane; [*site, park*] pour caravanes.
III *vi* (*p prés etc* -**nn**-) **to go** ~**ning** GB faire du caravanage.

caraway /ˈkærəweɪ/ *n* (plant) carvi *m*.

carbohydrate /ˌkɑːbəˈhaɪdreɪt/ **I** *n* hydrate *m* de carbone.
II *noun modifier* **low-/high-**~ **diet** alimentation *f* pauvre/riche en hydrates de carbone.

carbolic /kɑːˈbɒlɪk/ *adj* [*soap*] phéniqué.

car bomb *n* bombe *f* dissimulée dans une voiture.

carbon /ˈkɑːbən/ **I** *n* carbone *m*.
II *noun modifier* [*atom, compound*] de carbone.

carbonate /ˈkɑːbəneɪt/ **I** *n* carbonate *m*.
II *vtr* carbonater.

carbonated /ˈkɑːbəneɪtɪd/ *adj* [*drink*] gazéifié.

carbon: ~ **copy** *n* LIT copie *f* carbone; FIG réplique *f* exacte; ~**-date** *vtr* dater [qch] au carbone 14; ~ **dating** *n* datation *f* au carbone 14; ~ **dioxide** *n* dioxyde *m* de carbone; ~ **filter** *n* filtre *m* au carbone.

carbonize /ˈkɑːbənaɪz/ *vtr* carboniser ALSO HUM.

carbon: ~ **monoxide** *n* monoxyde *m* de carbone; ~ **paper** *n* (papier *m*) carbone *m*.

car boot sale *n* GB brocante *f* (*d'objets apportés dans le coffre de sa voiture*).

carbuncle /ˈkɑːbʌŋkl/ *n* **1** MED anthrax *m*; **2** (gem) escarboucle *f*.

carburettor /ˌkɑːbəˈretə(r)/ GB, **carburetor** /ˈkɑːrbəreɪtər/ US *n* carburateur *m*.

carcass /ˈkɑːkəs/ *n* carcasse *f*.

carcinogen /kɑːˈsɪnədʒən/ n substance f cancérigène.

carcinogenic /ˌkɑːsɪnəˈdʒenɪk/ adj cancérigène.

carcinoma /ˌkɑːsɪˈnəʊmə/ n carcinome m.

card /kɑːd/ **I** n **1** (for correspondence, greetings) carte f; (for indexing) fiche f; (at races) programme m; (in golf) carte f (de parcours); **2** GAMES carte f (à jouer); **to play ~s** jouer aux cartes; **one's strongest ~** FIG sa carte maîtresse; **3**○ †GB (person) original/-e m/f.
IDIOMS **a ~ up one's sleeve** un atout dans sa manche; **it is on** GB **ou in** US **the ~s that** il est bien possible que (+ subj); **an election is on ou in the ~s** il y a de fortes chances pour qu'il y ait une élection; **to get ou be given one's ~s**○† GB être renvoyé; **to hold all the ~s** avoir tous les atouts; **to play one's ~s right** bien jouer son jeu○.

cardboard /ˈkɑːdbɔːd/ **I** n carton m.
II noun modifier [cut-out] en carton; **~ box** (boîte f en) carton m.

card: ~board city n: zone urbaine où les sans-abri logent dans des cartons; **~ catalogue, ~ catalog** US n fichier m; **~ game** n (type of game) jeu m de cartes; (single game) partie f de cartes.

cardiac /ˈkɑːdɪæk/ adj cardiaque; **~ arrest** arrêt m du cœur.

cardigan /ˈkɑːdɪɡən/ ▸ 1260 n cardigan m.

cardinal /ˈkɑːdɪnl/ **I** n RELIG cardinal m.
II adj [sin] capital; [principle] fondamental; [number] cardinal.

card index n fichier m.

cardiologist /ˌkɑːdɪˈɒlədʒɪst/ ▸ 1251 n cardiologue mf.

cardiology /ˌkɑːdɪˈɒlədʒɪ/ n cardiologie f.

cardiovascular /ˌkɑːdɪəʊˈvæskjʊlə(r)/ adj cardiovasculaire.

card: ~ key n carte f magnétique; **~phone** n téléphone m à carte; **~sharp(er)** n tricheur/-euse m/f (professionnel/-elle); **~ trick** n tour m de cartes.

care /keə(r)/ **I** n **1** (attention) attention f, soin m; **to take ~ to do** prendre soin de faire; **to take ~ not to do** faire attention de ne pas faire; **to take ~ when doing** faire attention en faisant; **to take ~ that** faire attention que (+ subj); **he took (great) ~ over ou with his work** il a fait son travail avec (le plus grand) soin; **to take ~ in doing sth** faire qch avec soin; **'take ~!'** 'fais attention!'; (expression of farewell) 'à bientôt!'; **with ~** avec soin, en faisant attention; **'handle with ~'** 'fragile'; **to exercise due ~** JUR prendre les précautions nécessaires; **2** (looking after) (of person, animal) soins mpl; (of car, plant, clothes) entretien m (of de); **to take ~ of** (deal with) GEN s'occuper de [child, client]; MED soigner [patient]; (be responsible for) s'occuper de [garden, details]; (be careful with) prendre soin de [machine, car]; (keep in good condition) entretenir [car, teeth]; (look after) garder [shop, watch]; **to take good ~ of sb/sth** prendre soin de qn/qch; **customer ~** service m auprès des clients; **to put ou leave sb/sth in sb's ~** confier qn/qch à qn; **in his/your ~** à sa/ta garde; **the pupils/patients in my ~** les élèves/malades dont j'ai la responsabilité; **in the ~ of his father** à la garde de son père; **John Smith, ~ of Mrs L. Smith** (on letter) John Smith, chez ou aux bons soins de Mme L. Smith; **to take ~ of oneself** (look after oneself) prendre soin de soi; (cope) se débrouiller tout seul; (defend oneself) se défendre; **that takes ~ of that** c'est réglé; **3** MED, PSYCH soins mpl; **~ in the community** soins en dehors du milieu hospitalier; **4** GB (for child at risk) **to be in ~** être (placé) en garde; **to take ou put a child into ~** placer un enfant sous la garde des services sociaux; **5** (worry) souci m; **without a ~ in the world** parfaitement insouciant.
II vtr **if you ~ to examine the report** si vous voulez avoir l'obligeance d'examiner le rapport; (as polite formula) **would you ~ to sit down?** voulez-vous vous asseoir?; **he has more money than he ~s to admit** il a plus d'argent qu'il ne veut bien le dire.
III vi **1** (feel concerned) **she really ~s** elle prend ça à cœur; **to ~ about** s'intéresser à [art, culture, money,

environment]; se soucier du bien-être de [pupils, the elderly]; **I don't ~!** ça m'est égal!; **what do I ~ if...?** qu'est-ce que ça peut me faire que... (+ subj)?; **as if he ~d!** comme si ça lui faisait quelque chose!; **he couldn't ~ less!** ça lui est complètement égal!; **she couldn't ~ less about...** elle se moque or se fiche○ complètement de...; **I couldn't ~ less who wins** je me moque or me fiche○ de savoir qui va gagner; **they could all have died, for all he ~d** ils auraient pu mourir tous, cela lui était égal; **I don't ~ who he marries** il peut épouser qui il veut, ça m'est égal; **I'm past caring** je m'en moque; **who ~s?** qu'est-ce que ça peut faire?; **2** (love) **to ~ about sb** aimer qn.
IDIOMS **he doesn't ~ a fig ou a damn**○ il s'en fiche○ complètement.
■ **care for:** ¶ **~ for** [sth] **1** (like) aimer; **I don't ~ for chocolate** je n'aime pas le chocolat; **would you ~ for a drink?** voulez-vous boire quelque chose?; **2** (maintain) entretenir [car, garden]; prendre soin de [skin, plant]; ¶ **~ for** [sb/sth] s'occuper de [child, animal]; soigner [patient, wounded animal].

care: ~ assistant ▸ 1251 n GB MED aide-soignant/-e m/f; **~ attendant** ▸ 1251 n GB aide f familiale.

career /kəˈrɪə(r)/ **I** n carrière f; **political ~** carrière politique; **a ~ in television/in teaching** une carrière à la télévision/dans l'enseignement; **a ~ as a journalist** une carrière de journaliste; **school ~** scolarité f.
II noun modifier [diplomat] de carrière; [soldier] de métier.
III vi **to ~ in/out** entrer/sortir à toute vitesse; **to ~ off the road** quitter la route; **to ~ out of control** s'emballer.

career break n interruption f de carrière.

career: ~ move n pas m en avant dans son évolution professionnelle; **~s adviser** GB, **~ advisor** US ▸ 1251 n conseiller/-ère m/f d'orientation; **~s guidance** n orientation f professionnelle; **~s library** n centre m d'information et d'orientation professionnelle; **~s office** n service m d'orientation professionnelle; **~s officer** n GB = **careers adviser**; **~s service** GB, **~ service** US n service m d'orientation professionnelle.

carefree /ˈkeəfriː/ adj [person, smile, life] insouciant.

careful /ˈkeəfl/ adj [person, driving] prudent; [planning, preparation] minutieux/-ieuse; [research, monitoring, examination] méticuleux/-euse; **to be ~ to do** ou **about doing** prendre soin de faire; **to be ~ that** faire attention que (+ subj); **to be ~ of sth** faire attention à qch; **to be ~ with sth** faire attention à qch; **to be ~ (when) doing** faire attention en faisant; **to be ~ what one says** faire attention à ce qu'on dit; **be ~!** (fais) attention!; **be ~ how you open it** fais attention en l'ouvrant; **you can't be too ~!** on n'est jamais trop prudent!

carefully /ˈkeəfəlɪ/ adv [go, walk, drive] prudemment; [say] avec circonspection; [open, remove, handle] prudemment, avec précaution; [write, choose words, organize, wash] soigneusement, avec soin; [listen, read, look] attentivement; **drive ~ ou ~!** soyez prudent!; **listen/think ~!** écoutez/réfléchissez bien!

careless /ˈkeəlɪs/ adj (negligent) [person] négligent, imprudent; [work] bâclé; [writing] négligé; [driving, handling] négligent; [talk] imprudent; **~ mistake** faute d'étourderie or d'inattention; **it was ~ of me to do** ça a été de la négligence de ma part de faire; **to be ~ about sth/about doing** négliger qch/de faire; **to be ~ with** ne pas prendre soin de [books, clothes]; **to be ~ of one's appearance** se négliger.

carelessly /ˈkeəlɪslɪ/ adv **1** (negligently) [do, act] avec négligence; [make, repair, write] sans soin; [drive] avec imprudence; [break, lose] par manque d'attention; [dressed, arranged] avec négligence; **2** (in carefree way) avec insouciance.

carelessness /ˈkeəlɪsnɪs/ n (negligence) négligence f.

carer /ˈkeərə(r)/ ▸ 1251 n GB (relative) personne ayant un parent handicapé ou malade à charge; (professional) aide f familiale.

caress /kə'res/ **I** n caresse f.
II vtr caresser.

caretaker /'keəteɪkə(r)/ ▶ **1251** **I** n GB (at school, club) concierge mf; (in apartments) gardien/-ienne m/f, concierge mf.
II noun modifier [administration] intérimaire; [president] par intérim.

care: **~ worker** ▶ **1251** n GB assistant/-e m/f social/-e; **~worn** adj [face] marqué par les soucis.

car ferry n ferry m.

cargo /'kɑːɡəʊ/ n (pl **~es** OU **~s**) GEN chargement m; NAUT cargaison f, chargement m.

cargo: **~ plane** n avion m cargo; **~ ship** n cargo m.

car: **~ hire** n location f de voitures; **~ hire company** n société f de location de voitures.

Caribbean /ˌkærɪ'biːən/ ▶ **1117** **I** n **1** (sea) mer f des Antilles; **2** (person) habitant/-e m/f des Caraïbes.
II noun modifier [climate, cookery] des Caraïbes; [carnival] des Antilles.

Caribbean Islands ▶ **1022** pr npl petites Antilles fpl.

caricature /'kærɪkətʃʊə(r)/ **I** n caricature f.
II vtr caricaturer.

caricaturist /'kærɪkətʃʊərɪst/ ▶ **1251** n caricaturiste mf.

caring /'keərɪŋ/ **I** n travail m social.
II noun modifier MED, SOCIOL [profession] paramédical; **~ professionals** le personnel paramédical.
III adj **1** (loving) [parent] affectueux/-euse; [environment, home] chaleureux/-euse; **2** (compassionate) [person, attitude] compréhensif/-ive; [society] humain.

carjacking /'kɑːˌdʒakɪŋ/ n vol m de voiture (avec agression du conducteur).

carload /'kɑːləʊd/ n a **~ of people** une voiture pleine de gens.

carnage /'kɑːnɪdʒ/ n carnage m ALSO FIG.

carnal /'kɑːnl/ adj [pleasure, desire] charnel/-elle.

carnation /kɑː'neɪʃn/ n œillet m.

carnation: **~ pink** ▶ **818** n rose m incarnat; **~ red** ▶ **818** n rouge m incarnat.

carnival /'kɑːnɪvl/ n **1** GB (procession) carnaval m; **2** US (funfair) fête f foraine.

carnivore /'kɑːnɪvɔː(r)/ n carnivore m.

carnivorous /kɑː'nɪvərəs/ adj carnivore.

carob /'kærəb/ n (tree) caroubier m; (pod) caroube f.

carol /'kærəl/ n chant m de Noël.

carotene /'kærətiːn/, **carotin** /'kærətɪn/ n carotène m.

carotid /kə'rɒtɪd/ **I** n carotide f.
II adj carotidien/-ienne.

carouse /kə'raʊz/ vi faire la noce.

carousel /ˌkærə'sel/ n **1** (merry-go-round) manège m; **2** (for luggage) carrousel m; **3** (for slides) carrousel m.

carp /kɑːp/ **I** n (fish) carpe f.
II○ vi maugréer (**about** contre).

car park n GB parc m de stationnement.

carpenter /'kɑːpəntə(r)/ ▶ **1251** n (joiner) menuisier m; (on building site) charpentier m.

carpentry /'kɑːpəntrɪ/ n GEN menuiserie f; (structural) charpenterie f.

carpet /'kɑːpɪt/ **I** n **1** (fitted) moquette f; (loose) tapis m; **2** FIG tapis m; **~ of flowers** tapis de fleurs.
II noun modifier [showroom] de tapis; [shampoo] pour tapis.
III vtr **1** LIT mettre de la moquette dans [room]; **to ~ the living-room floor** mettre de la moquette dans le séjour; **~ed with flowers** FIG, LITTÉR tapissé de fleurs; **2** FIG (reprimand) passer un savon à.
IDIOMS **to brush** OU **sweep sth under the ~** enterrer or étouffer qch.

carpetbagger /'kɑːpɪtbægə(r)/ n **1** US HIST carpetbagger m; **2** POL candidat m parachuté.

carpet: **~ fitter** ▶ **1251** n poseur m de moquette;

~ slipper n charentaise f; **~ sweeper** n balai m mécanique; **~ tile** n dalle f de moquette.

car: **~phone** n radiotéléphone m de voiture; **~ phone** n téléphone m de voiture.

carping /'kɑːpɪŋ/ **I** n ₵ chicaneries fpl.
II adj [criticism, person] malveillant.

car: **~ radio** n autoradio m; **~ rental** n ▶ **car hire**.

carriage /'kærɪdʒ/ n **1** (vehicle) (ceremonial) carrosse m (for transport) attelage m; **2** (of train) wagon m, voiture f; **3** ₵ (of goods, passengers) transport m; **~ free/forward** port m gratuit/dû; **~ paid** port m payé; **4** (of typewriter) chariot m; **5** (bearing) maintien m.

carriage: **~ clock** n pendulette f; **~way** n chaussée f.

carrier /'kærɪə(r)/ n **1** (transport company) transporteur m; (airline) compagnie f aérienne; **to send sth by ~** expédier qch; **2** (of disease) porteur/-euse m/f; **3** GB (also **~ bag**) sac m (en plastique).

carrier pigeon n pigeon m voyageur.

carrion /'kærɪən/ n (also **~ flesh**) charogne f.

carrot /'kærət/ n carotte f ALSO FIG.

carroty /'kærətɪ/ adj [hair] rouquin○.

carry /'kærɪ/ **I** n (range) portée f.
II vtr **1** porter [bag, shopping, load, news, message] (**in** dans; **on** sur); **to ~ sth up/down** porter qch en haut/en bas; **to ~ sth in/out** apporter/emporter qch; **to ~ a child across the road** porter un enfant pour lui faire traverser la route; **to ~ cash/a gun** avoir de l'argent liquide/un revolver sur soi; **to ~ a picture in one's mind** avoir une image toujours en tête; **to ~ sth too far** FIG pousser qch trop loin; **2** [vehicle, pipe, wire, vein] transporter; [wind, tide, current, stream] emporter; **to be carried on the wind** être porté or transporté par le vent; **his quest carried him to India** sa quête l'a amené en Inde; **3** (feature) comporter [warning, guarantee, report]; porter [symbol, label]; publier [advert]; **4** (entail) comporter [risk]; être passible de [penalty]; **to ~ conviction** être convaincant; **5** (bear, support) [bridge, road] supporter [load, traffic]; **6** (win) l'emporter dans [state, constituency]; remporter [battle, match]; **the motion was carried by 20 votes to 13** la motion l'a emporté par 20 votes contre 13; **to ~ all before one** l'emporter haut la main; **7** MED être porteur/-euse de [disease]; **8** (be pregnant with) [woman] être enceinte de [girl, twins]; [animal] porter [young]; **I am ~ing his child** je porte son enfant; **9** COMM (stock, sell) faire [item, brand]; **we ~ a wide range of** nous offrons un grand choix de; **10** (hold, bear) (permanently) porter [tail, head]; **11** MATH retenir [one, two].
III vi [sound, voice] porter; **to ~ well** porter bien.
IV v refl **to ~ oneself** se tenir.
IDIOMS **to get carried away**○ s'emballer○, se laisser emporter.

■ **carry back**: ¶ **~ back** [sth], **~** [sth] **back** rapporter [object]; ¶ **~** [sb] **back** (in memory) ramener [person] (**to** à).

■ **carry forward**: **~ forward** [sth], **~** [sth] **forward** reporter [balance, total].

■ **carry off**: ¶ **~ off** [sth] LIT emporter; FIG remporter [prize, medal]; **to ~ it off**○ (succeed) réussir, y arriver; ¶ **~ off** [sb], **~** [sb] **off** [illness, disease] emporter [person, animal]; (lead away) emmener.

■ **carry on**: ¶ **~ on 1** (continue) continuer (**doing** à faire); **to ~ on down** ou **along the road** (in car) continuer la route; (on foot) poursuivre son chemin; **to ~ on with sth** continuer or poursuivre qch; **2**○ (behave) se conduire; **3**○ (have affair) avoir une liaison; ¶ **~ on** [sth] **1** (conduct) conduire [business]; entretenir [correspondence]; mener [conversation]; **2** (continue) maintenir [tradition]; poursuivre [activity, discussion].

■ **carry out**: **~ out** [sth], **~** [sth] **out** réaliser [study]; effectuer [experiment, reform, attack, operation, repairs]; exécuter [plan, orders, punishment]; mener [investigation, campaign]; accomplir [mission]; remplir [duties]; mettre [qch] à exécution [threat]; tenir [promise].

■ **carry over**: ¶ ~ **over into** [*problem, rivalry*] s'étendre à [*personal life*]; ¶ ~ **sth over into** transférer qch dans [*private life, area of activity, adulthood*]; ¶ ~ **over** [sth], ~ [sth] **over** reporter [*debt*].

■ **carry through**: ¶ ~ **through** [sth], ~ [sth] **through** mener [qch] à bien [*reform, policy, task*]; ¶ ~ [sb] **through** [*humour*] soutenir [*person*].

carry: **~all** n US fourre-tout m inv; **~cot** n GB porte-bébé m; **~ing-on**° n (pl **carryings-on**) incartade f; **~-on**° n cirque° m; **~out** n GB (food) repas m à emporter.

car seat n siège-auto m.

carsick /'kɑːsɪk/ adj **to be ~** avoir le mal de la route.

cart /kɑːt/ **I** n (for goods) charrette f; (for passengers) carriole f.
II vtr **1**° GEN (also **~ around**, **~ about**) (drag) trimballer° [*bags, shopping*]; **2** AGRIC charrier [*hay*].
IDIOMS **to put the ~ before the horse** mettre la charrue avant les bœufs.

■ **cart off**°: ~ [sb] **off** emmener [qn] de force.

cartel /kɑː'tel/ n cartel m; **drug ~** cartel m de la drogue.

carthorse /'kɑːθɔːs/ n cheval m de trait.

cartilage /'kɑːtɪlɪdʒ/ n cartilage m.

cartload /'kɑːtləʊd/ n charretée f.

cartographer /kɑː'tɒɡrəfə(r)/ ▶1251 n cartographe mf.

cartography /kɑː'tɒɡrəfɪ/ n cartographie f.

carton /'kɑːtn/ n (small) boîte f; (of yoghurt, cream) pot m; (of juice, milk, ice cream) carton m, brique f; (of cigarettes) cartouche f; US (for house removals) carton m.

cartoon /kɑː'tuːn/ n **1** CIN dessin m animé; **2** (drawing) dessin m humoristique; (in comic) bande f dessinée; **3** ART carton m.

cartoonist /kɑː'tuːnɪst/ ▶1251 n (in newspaper) dessinateur/-trice m/f humoristique; (of strip cartoons) dessinateur/-trice m/f de bandes dessinées.

cartridge /'kɑːtrɪdʒ/ n **1** (for pen, gun) cartouche f; **2** (for video, typewriter etc) cartouche f; **3** (for camera) chargeur m.

cartridge: **~ belt** n cartouchière f; **~ paper** n ART papier m à dessin; **~ pen** n stylo m à cartouche.

cart-track /'kɑːttræk/ n chemin m charretier.

cartwheel /'kɑːtwiːl, US -hwiːl/ n **1** (in gymnastics) roue f; **to do** ou **turn a ~** faire la roue; **2** LIT roue f de charrette.

carve /kɑːv/ **I** vtr **1** (sculpt) tailler, sculpter [*wood, stone, figure*]; creuser [*channel*] (**out of, from** dans); **to ~ sth into** tailler qch en forme de; **2** (inscribe) graver (**onto** sur; **in** dans); **3** CULIN découper.
II vi découper.
■ **carve out**: ~ **out** [sth], ~ [sth] **out 1** FIG se faire [*niche, name*]; se tailler [*reputation, market*]; se construire [*career*]; **2** LIT creuser [*gorge, channel*].
■ **carve up**: ¶ ~ **up** [sth], ~ [sth] **up 1**° (divide) partager [*proceeds*]; morceler [*estate, territory*]; **2** CULIN découper; ¶ ~ **up** [sb]° **1** (with knife) taillader; **2** AUT faire une queue de poisson à.

carving /'kɑːvɪŋ/ n **1** (figure, sculpture) sculpture f; **2** (technique) (of object) sculpture f; (of motif) gravure f; **3** CULIN découpage m; **~ knife** couteau m à découper.

car: **~ wash** n lavage m automatique; **~ worker** ▶1251 n ouvrier/-ière m/f de l'industrie automobile.

cascade /kæ'skeɪd/ **I** n **1** (of water) cascade f; (of hair, silk) flot m; **2** COMPUT cascade f.
II vi tomber en cascade.

case¹ /keɪs/ **I** n **1** (instance, example) cas m; **on a ~ by ~ basis** au cas par cas; **in which ~**, **in that ~** en ce cas, dans ce cas-là; **in such** ou **these ~s** dans un cas pareil; **in 7 out of 10 ~s** 7 fois sur 10, dans 7 cas sur 10; **a ~ in point** un cas d'espèce, un exemple typique; **it's a ~ of substituting X for Y** il s'agit de substituer X à Y; **2** (state of affairs, situation) cas m; **such** ou **this being the ~** en ce cas, dans ce cas-là; **is it the ~ that...?** est-il vrai que...?; **as** ou **whatever the**

~ **may be** selon le(s) cas; **should this be the ~** ou **if this is the ~** si c'est le cas; **3** JUR **the ~ for the Crown** GB, **the ~ for the State** US l'accusation f; **the ~ for the defence** les arguments pour la défense; **to state the ~** exposer les faits; **the ~ against Foster** les faits qui sont reprochés à Foster; **the ~ is closed** JUR, FIG l'affaire ou la cause est entendue; **4** (convincing argument) arguments mpl; **to make a good ~ for sth** donner des arguments convaincants en faveur de qch; **to argue the ~ for sth** donner des arguments en faveur de qch; **there's a strong ~ for/against doing** il y a de bonnes raisons pour/pour ne pas faire; **5** (trial) affaire f, procès m; **criminal ~** affaire criminelle; **divorce/murder ~** procès en divorce/pour meurtre; **to win one's ~** gagner son procès; **his ~ comes up next week** il passe en jugement la semaine prochaine; **famous ~s** causes fpl célèbres; **6** (criminal investigation) **the Burgess ~** l'affaire Burgess; **to work** ou **be on a ~** enquêter sur une affaire; **a blackmail ~** une affaire de chantage; **the ~s of Sherlock Holmes** les enquêtes de Sherlock Holmes; **7** MED (instance of disease) cas m; (patient) malade mf; **8** (client) cas m; **9**° (person) **he's a real ~!** c'est vraiment un cas!; **a hopeless ~** un cas désespéré; **a hard ~** un dur; ▶**head case**; **10** LING cas m; **in the accusative ~** à l'accusatif.
II in any case adv phr (besides, anyway) de toute façon; (at any rate) en tout cas.
III in case conj phr au cas où (+ conditional); **in ~ it rains** au cas où il pleuvrait; **take the map just in ~** prends le plan au cas où.
IV in case of prep phr en cas de.

case² /keɪs/ **I** n **1** (suitcase) valise f; **2** (crate, chest) caisse f; **3** (display cabinet) vitrine f; **4** (for spectacles, binoculars, cartridge, weapon) étui m; (for jewels) écrin m; (of camera, watch) boîtier m; (of piano, clock) caisse f.
II° vtr (reconnoitre) **to ~ the joint** faire du repérage.

CASE /keɪs/ n (abrév = **computer-aided software engineering**) CPAO f.

case history n **1** MED antécédents mpl; **2** (study) = **case study**.

caseload /'keɪsləʊd/ n nombre m de cas à traiter; **to have a heavy ~** avoir une clientèle nombreuse.

casement window /'keɪsmənt/ n fenêtre f à battants.

case /keɪs/: **~ notes** npl dossier m; **~ study** n étude f de cas; **~ system** n LING système m casuel.

casework /'keɪswɜːk/ n **to be involved in** ou **to do ~** s'occuper des cas sociaux.

caseworker ▶1251 n ≈ assistant/-e m/f social/-e.

cash /kæʃ/ **I** n **1** (notes and coin) espèces fpl, argent m liquide; **to pay in ~** payer en espèces; **£3,000 (in) ~** 3 000 livres sterling en espèces; **to be paid ~ in hand** être payé en espèces; **I haven't got any ~ on me** je n'ai pas d'argent liquide; **2** (money in general) argent m; **3** (immediate payment) comptant m; **discount for ~** remise f pour paiement comptant; **£50 ~ in hand** ou **~ down** 50 livres sterling en liquide.
II noun modifier [*advance, book*] de caisse; [*offer, sale, discount, transaction*] au comptant; [*alternative, deposit, sum, refund, prize*] en espèces; [*price*] comptant.
III vtr encaisser [*cheque*].
■ **cash in**: ¶ ~ **in** en profiter; **to ~ in on** tirer profit de, profiter de; ¶ ~ **in** [sth], ~ [sth] **in** se faire rembourser, réaliser [*bond, policy*]; US encaisser [*check*]; encaisser [*gambling chips*].

cash: **~-and-carry** n libre-service m de vente en gros; **~ box** n caisse f; **~ card** n carte f de retrait; **~ crop** n culture f commerciale; **~ desk** n caisse f; **~ dispenser** n distributeur m automatique de billets de banque, billetterie f.

cashew /'kæʃuː/ n (also **~ nut**) cajou m.

cash flow n marge f brute d'auto-financement, MBA f.

cashier /kæ'ʃɪə(r)/ ▶1251 **I** n caissier/-ière m/f.
II vtr MIL casser [*officer*]; GEN congédier [*employee*].

cash limit n limite f budgétaire.

cashmere /ˌkæʃˈmɪə(r)/ *n* (lainage *m* en) cachemire *m*; ~ **sweater** pullover en cachemire.

cash: ~ **on delivery, COD** *n* envoi *m* contre remboursement; ~**point** *n* = **cash dispenser**; ~**point card** *n* = **cash card**; ~ **register** *n* caisse *f* enregistreuse; ~ **reserves** *npl* trésorerie *f*.

casing /ˈkeɪsɪŋ/ *n* (of bomb, machinery) revêtement *m*; (of gearbox) carter *m*; (of tyre) enveloppe *f* extérieure.

casino /kəˈsiːnəʊ/ *n* casino *m*.

cask /kɑːsk, US kæsk/ *n* fût *m*, tonneau *m*.

casket /ˈkɑːskɪt, US ˈkæskɪt/ *n* (box) coffret *m*; (coffin) cercueil *m*.

cassava /kəˈsɑːvə/ *n* BOT manioc *m*; CULIN farine *f* de manioc.

casserole /ˈkæsərəʊl/ **I** *n* CULIN **1** (container) daubière *f*, cocotte *f*; **2** GB (food) ragoût *m* cuit au four.
II *vtr* cuire [qch] à four doux.

cassette /kəˈset/ *n* cassette *f*; **to record on ~** enregistrer sur cassette; **available on ~** disponible en cassette.

cassette: ~ **deck** *n* platine *f* à cassettes; ~ **player** *n* lecteur *m* de cassettes; ~ **recorder** *n* magnétophone *m* à cassettes; ~ **tape** *n* cassette *f* audio.

cassock /ˈkæsək/ *n* soutane *f*.

cast /kɑːst, US kæst/ **I** *n* **1** CIN, THEAT, TV (list of actors) distribution *f*; (actors) acteurs *mpl*; **the members of the ~** les acteurs; ~ **of characters** (in play, novel) liste *f* des personnages; **2** (mould) moule *m*; (moulded object) moulage *m*; **3** (arrangement) ~ **of mind** tournure *f* d'esprit; **4** (in fishing) lancer *m*; **5** (squint) strabisme *m*; **to have a ~ in one eye** avoir un œil qui louche; **6** MED (also **plaster** ~) plâtre *m*; **to have one's arm in a ~** avoir un bras dans le plâtre.
II *vtr* (*prét, pp* **cast**) **1** (throw) jeter, lancer [*stone*, *net*, *fishing line*]; jeter [*dice*]; projeter [*light*, *shadow*]; **to ~ doubt on** émettre des doutes sur; **to ~ light on** éclairer; **to ~ (a) new light on** éclairer [qch] d'un jour nouveau; **to ~ a spell on** jeter un sort à [qch]; **2** (direct) jeter [*glance*, *look*] (**at** sur); **her eyes were cast downwards** elle avait les yeux baissés; **to ~ one's eyes around the room/over a letter** parcourir la pièce/une lettre des yeux; **to ~ one's mind back over sth** se remémorer qch; **if you ~ your mind back to last week** si tu te rappelles ce qui s'est passé la semaine dernière; **3** CIN, THEAT, TV distribuer les rôles de [*play, film*]; **she was cast in the role of** ou **as Blanche** elle a joué Blanche; **4** (shed) se dépouiller de [*leaves, feathers*]; **the snake ~s its skin** le serpent mue; **5** ART, TECH couler; **6** POL **to ~ one's vote** voter.

■ **cast about** GB, **cast around**: ~ **about for** chercher [*excuse*].

■ **cast down**: ~ **down** [sth], ~ [sth] **down** LIT jeter [qch] par terre [*object*]; déposer [*weapons*]; baisser [*eyes, head*]; **to be cast down** LITTÉR être abattu.

■ **cast off**: ¶ ~ **off 1** NAUT larguer les amarres; **2** (in knitting) rabattre les mailles restantes; ¶ ~ **off** [sth], ~ [sth] **off 1** (discard) ôter, enlever [*garment*]; se libérer de [*chains*]; abandonner [*lover*]; **2** NAUT larguer les amarres de; **3** (in knitting) rabattre [*stitches*].

■ **cast on**: ¶ ~ **on** monter les mailles; ¶ ~ **on** [sth] monter [*stitch*].

■ **cast out**: ~ **out** [sth/sb], ~ [sth/sb] **out** LITTÉR chasser.

castanets /ˌkæstəˈnets/ ▶ 1097 *npl* castagnettes *fpl*.

castaway /ˈkɑːstəweɪ, US ˈkæst-/ *n* naufragé/-e *m/f*.

caste /kɑːst/ *n* caste *f*; **the ~ system** le système des castes.

caster /ˈkɑːstə(r), US ˈkæstər/ *n* **1** (shaker) saupoudreuse *f*; **2** (wheel) roulette *f*.

caster sugar *n* GB sucre *m* en poudre.

casting /ˈkɑːstɪŋ, US ˈkæst-/ *n* **1** (throwing) lancement *m*; **2** (in metallurgy) coulée *f*, moulage *m*; **3** ART moulage *m*; **4** CIN, THEAT, TV distribution *f*.

casting: ~ **director** ▶ 1251 *n* directeur/-trice *m/f* de la distribution; ~ **vote** *n* voix *f* prépondérante.

cast iron I *n* fonte *f*.
II cast-iron *noun modifier* LIT [*object*] de or en fonte; FIG [*alibi*] en béton○.

castle /ˈkɑːsl, US ˈkæsl/ *n* **1** ARCHIT château *m*; **2** (in chess) tour *f*.
IDIOMS ~**s in the air** ou **in Spain** US des châteaux en Espagne.

cast-offs /ˈkɑːstɒf, US ˈkæst-/ *npl* (clothes) vêtements *mpl* dont on n'a plus besoin, vieux vêtements; **society's** ~**s** FIG les laissés *mpl* pour compte de la société.

castor /ˈkɑːstə(r), US ˈkæs-/ *n* (wheel) (also **caster**) roulette *f*.

castor oil *n* huile *f* de ricin.

castrate /kæˈstreɪt, US ˈkæstreɪt/ *vtr* castrer [*man, animal*]; FIG expurger [*book, article*].

casual /ˈkæʒʊəl/ **I** *n* (temporary worker) travailleur/-euse *m/f* temporaire; (occasional worker) travailleur/-euse *m/f* occasionnel/-elle.
II casuals *npl* (clothes) vêtements *mpl* sport.
III *adj* **1** (informal) décontracté; **to have a ~ chat** bavarder, causer○; **2** (occasional) [*acquaintance, relationship*] de passage; ~ **sex** relations *fpl* sexuelles non suivies; **3** (nonchalant) désinvolte; **4** PÉJ [*cruelty, violence*] ordinaire; [*remark, assumption*] désinvolte; **5** [*glance, onlooker*] superficiel/-ielle; **to the ~ eye it seems that** l'observateur superficiel dirait que; **6** (chance) [*encounter*] fortuit; **7** [*worker, labour*] (temporary) temporaire; (occasional) occasionnel/-elle.

casually /ˈkæʒʊəlɪ/ *adv* **1** [*inquire, remark*] d'un air détaché; [*stroll, greet*] nonchalamment; [*glance, leaf through*] superficiellement; **2** [*dressed*] simplement; **3** [*offend*] sans y penser; **4** [*employed*] temporairement.

casualness /ˈkæʒʊəlnɪs/ *n* **1** (of manner, tone, remark) désinvolture *f*; **2** (of clothes, dress) décontraction *f*.

casualty /ˈkæʒʊəltɪ/ **I** *n* **1** GEN (person) victime *f*; **2** (part of hospital) urgences *fpl*; **in ~** aux urgences; **3** FIG (person, plan) victime *f*; **to be a ~ of sth** être victime de qch.
II casualties *npl* (soldiers) pertes *fpl*; (civilians) victimes *fpl*.
III *noun modifier* [*department, nurse* GB] des urgences; [*ward* GB] d'urgence; MIL [*list*] des victimes.

cat /kæt/ **I** *n* **1** (domestic) chat *m*; (female) chatte *f*; **2** (feline) félin *m*; **3**○ PÉJ (woman) chipie *f*.
II *noun modifier* [*basket*] pour chat; [*litter, food*] pour chats; **the ~ family** les félins *mpl*.
IDIOMS **to be like a ~ on a hot tin roof** ou **on hot bricks** être sur des charbons ardents; **to fight like ~ and dog** se battre comme des chiffonniers; **to let the ~ out of the bag** vendre la mèche; **to rain ~s and dogs** pleuvoir des cordes; **to think one is the ~'s whiskers** GB ou **pajamas** US ou **meow** US se croire sorti de la cuisse de Jupiter; **when the ~'s away, the mice will play** quand le chat n'est pas là, les souris dansent; **to play ~ and mouse with sb** jouer au chat et à la souris avec qn.

CAT *n* **1** GB (*abrév* = **College of Advanced Technology**) ~ IUT; **2** COMPUT (*abrév* = **computer-assisted teaching**) enseignement *m* assisté par ordinateur; **3** COMPUT (*abrév* = **computer-assisted training**) formation *f* assistée par ordinateur.

cataclysm /ˈkætəklɪzəm/ *n* LIT, FIG cataclysme *m*.

catacombs /ˈkætəkuːmz, US -kəʊmz/ *npl* catacombes *fpl*.

Catalan /ˈkætəlæn/ ▶ 1100, 1038 *n, adj* catalan (*m*).

catalogue, catalog US /ˈkætəlɒg, US -lɔːg/ **I** *n* **1** (of goods, books etc) catalogue *m*; **2** (series) série (**of** de); **3** (also **catalog**) US UNIV brochure *f* (universitaire).
II *vtr* dresser un catalogue de.

catalyst /ˈkætəlɪst/ *n* CHEM, FIG catalyseur *m*.

catalytic /ˌkætəˈlɪtɪk/ *adj* catalytique; ~ **converter** pot *m* catalytique.

catapult /ˈkætəpʌlt/ **I** *n* **1** GB lance-pierres *m inv*; **2** MIL, AVIAT (also ~ **launcher**) catapulte *f*; **3** MIL, HIST catapulte *f*.
II *vtr* projeter; FIG **to be ~ed to** être catapulté vers [*power*].

cataract /'kætərækt/ n **1** MED cataracte f; **2** (waterfall) cataracte f.

catarrh /kə'tɑ:(r)/ n catarrhe m.

catastrophe /kə'tæstrəfɪ/ n catastrophe f.

catastrophic /ˌkætə'strɒfɪk/ adj catastrophique.

cat burglar n GB monte-en-l'air m inv.

catcall /'kætkɔ:l/ n sifflet m.

catch /kætʃ/ I n **1** (fastening) (on purse, brooch) fermoir m, fermeture f; (on window, door) fermeture f; **2** (drawback) piège m FIG; **what's the ~?** où est le piège?; **3** (break in voice) **with a ~ in his voice** d'une voix émue; **4** (act of catching) prise f; **to take a ~** GB, **to make a ~** US SPORT prendre la balle; **to play ~** jouer à la balle; **5** (haul) pêche f; (one fish) prise f; **6** (marriage partner) **a good ~** un beau parti.
II vtr (prét, pp **caught**) **1** (hold and retain) [person] attraper [ball, fish]; [container] recueillir [water, dust]; (by running) [person] attraper [person]; **I managed to ~ her in** (at home) j'ai réussi à la trouver chez elle; **2** (take by surprise) prendre, attraper; **to ~ sb doing** surprendre qn en train de faire; **to be** ou **get caught** se faire prendre; **to ~ sb in the act, to ~ sb at it°** prendre qn sur le fait; **you wouldn't ~ me smoking!** ce n'est pas moi qui fumerais!; **we got caught in the rain** nous avons été surpris par la pluie; **you've caught me at an awkward moment** vous tombez mal; **3** (be in time for) prendre [bus, train, plane]; avoir [last post]; **4** (manage to see) voir [programme]; aller voir [show]; **5** (grasp) prendre [hand, arm]; agripper [branch, rope]; captiver, éveiller [interest, imagination]; **to ~ hold of sth** attraper qch; **to ~ sb's attention** ou **eye** attirer l'attention de qn; **to ~ the chairman's eye** ADMIN obtenir la parole; **6** (hear) saisir°, comprendre; **7** (perceive) discerner [sound]; surprendre [look]; **to ~ sight of sb/sth** surprendre qn/qch; **8** (get stuck) **to ~ one's fingers in** se prendre les doigts dans [drawer, door]; **to ~ one's shirt on** accrocher sa chemise à [nail]; **to get caught in** [person] se prendre dans [net, thorns]; **9** MED attraper [disease, virus, flu]; **10** (hit, knock) heurter [object, person]; **11** (have an effect on) [light] faire briller [object]; [wind] emporter [paper, bag]; **to ~ one's breath** retenir son souffle; **12** (be affected by) **you've caught the sun** on voit bien que tu es resté au soleil; **to ~ fire** ou **light** prendre feu, s'enflammer; **to ~ the light** refléter la lumière; **13** (capture) rendre [atmosphere, spirit]; **14** SPORT ▶ **catch out**; **15** (trick) ▶ **catch out**; **16** (manage to reach) ▶ **catch up**.
III vi (prét, pp **caught**) **1** (become stuck) **to ~ on** [shirt, sleeve] s'accrocher à [nail]; [wheel] frotter contre [frame]; **2** (start to burn) [wood, fire] prendre.
IDIOMS **you'll ~ it°!** tu vas en prendre une°!
■ **catch on 1** (become popular) devenir populaire (with auprès de); **2** (understand) comprendre, saisir; **to ~ on to sth** comprendre or saisir qch.
■ **catch out: ~ [sb] out 1** (take by surprise) prendre [qn] de court; (doing something wrong) prendre [qn] sur le fait; **2** (trick) attraper, jouer un tour à; **3** (in cricket, baseball) éliminer [batsman].
■ **catch up: ¶ ~ up** (in race) regagner du terrain; (in work) rattraper son retard; **to ~ up with** rattraper; **to ~ up on** rattraper [work, sleep]; se remettre au courant de [news, gossip]; **¶ ~ [sb/sth] up 1** (manage to reach) rattraper; **2 to ~ sth up in** (tangle) prendre [qch] dans [thorns, chain]; **to get one's feet caught up in sth** se prendre les pieds dans qch; **to get caught up in** se laisser entraîner par [excitement]; se trouver pris dans [traffic]; se trouver mêlé à [scandal, argument].

catch: ~-22 situation n situation f inextricable; **~-all** adj [term] passe-partout inv; [clause] couvrant tous les cas de figure.

catcher /'kætʃə(r)/ n SPORT receveur m.

catching /'kætʃɪŋ/ adj MED, FIG contagieux/-ieuse.

catchment area n secteur m desservi.

catch: ~phrase n formule f favorite, rengaine f; **~up** n = **ketchup**; **~word** n mot m d'ordre.

catchy /'kætʃɪ/ adj [tune] entraînant; [slogan] accrocheur/-euse.

catechism /'kætəkɪzəm/ n catéchisme m.

categorical /ˌkætə'gɒrɪkl, US -'gɔ:r-/, **categoric** /ˌkætə'gɒrɪk, US -'gɔ:r-/ adj catégorique.

categorically /ˌkætə'gɒrɪklɪ, US -'gɔ:r-/ adv catégoriquement.

categorize /'kætəgəraɪz/ vtr classer (by d'après).

category /'kætəgərɪ, US -gɔ:rɪ/ n catégorie f.

cater /'keɪtə(r)/ vi **1** (supply food etc) organiser des réceptions; **2 to ~ for** GB ou **to** US (accommodate) accueillir [children, guests]; pourvoir à [needs, tastes]; (aim at) [newspaper, programme] s'adresser à; **3** (fulfil) **to ~ to** satisfaire [whim, taste].

caterer /'keɪtərə(r)/ ▶ **1251** n traiteur m.

catering /'keɪtərɪŋ/ I n (provision) approvisionnement m; (trade, industry, career) restauration f.
II noun modifier [company, staff] de restauration; **~ course** études fpl spécialisées dans la restauration.

caterpillar /'kætəpɪlə(r)/ n ZOOL, TECH chenille f.

Caterpillar® /'kætəpɪlə(r)/ n engin m à chenilles.

caterwaul /'kætəwɔ:l/ vi miauler.

caterwauling /'kætəwɔ:lɪŋ/ n ℓ miaulements mpl.

cat: ~fish n poisson-chat m; **~flap** n chattière f; **~ food** n aliments mpl pour chats; **~gut** n boyau m (de chat), catgut m.

cathedral /kə'θi:drəl/ n cathédrale f.

Catherine wheel /'kæθrɪn wi:l, US -hwi:l/ n soleil m (feu d'artifice).

catheter /'kæθɪtə(r)/ n cathéter m.

cathode /'kæθəʊd/ n sonde f, cathode f; **~-ray tube** tube m cathodique.

catholic /'kæθəlɪk/ adj éclectique.

Catholic /'kæθəlɪk/ n, adj catholique (mf).

Catholicism /kə'θɒlɪsɪzəm/ n catholicisme m.

catkin /'kætkɪn/ n chaton m.

catlike /'kætlaɪk/ adj félin.

cat litter n litière f pour chats.

catnap /'kætnæp/ I n somme m.
II vi (p prés etc **-pp-**) faire un somme, sommeiller.

cat: ~-o'-nine-tails n (pl ~) martinet m; **Catseye®** n GB plot m rétroréfléchissant; **~'s paw** n dupe f; **~suit** n combinaison-pantalon f.

catsup /'kætsəp/ n US = **ketchup**.

cattery /'kætərɪ/ n pension f pour chats.

cattiness /'kætɪnɪs/ n méchanceté f.

cattle /'kætl/ I n (+ v pl) bovins mpl.
II noun modifier [breeder, raising, rustler] de bétail.

cattle grid GB, **cattle guard** US n grille f (au sol qui empêche le passage du bétail).

cattle: ~ market n LIT marché m aux bestiaux; FIG° (for sexual encounters) lieu m de drague°; **~ shed** n étable f; **~ truck** n AUT fourgon m à bestiaux.

catty /'kætɪ/ adj méchant (about envers).

catwalk /'kætwɔ:k/ n **1** (walkway) passerelle f; **2** (at fashion show) podium m; **~ show** défilé m de mode.

Caucasian /kɔ:'keɪʒn, -'keɪzɪən/ I n **1** (white person) personne f de race blanche; **2** GEOG (inhabitant) Caucasien/-ienne m/f.
II adj **1** [race, man] blanc/blanche; **2** GEOG caucasien/-ienne.

caucus /'kɔ:kəs/ n (pl **-es**) **1** (meeting) réunion f des instances dirigeantes; **2** (faction) groupe m.

caught /kɔ:t/ prét, pp ▶ **catch**.

cauldron /'kɔ:ldrən/ n chaudron m.

cauliflower /'kɒlɪflaʊə(r), US 'kɔ:lɪ-/ n chou-fleur m; **to have a ~ ear** FIG avoir l'oreille en chou-fleur°.

cauliflower cheese n gratin m de chou-fleur.

causal /'kɔ:zl/ adj causal.

causality /kɔ:'zælətɪ/, **causation** /kɔ:'zeɪʃn/ n causalité f.

cause /kɔ:z/ I n **1** (reason) cause f, raison f (of de); **there is/he has ~ for concern/optimism** il y a a/il a des raisons de s'inquiéter/d'être optimiste; **to give sb ~ to do** donner à qn des raisons de faire; **to have ~ to do** avoir des raisons de faire; **to give ~ for concern** susciter des inquiétudes; **the immediate ~** la cause directe; **with good ~** à juste titre; **without good ~** sans motif valable; **2** (objective) cause *f*; **a lost ~** une cause perdue; **all in a good ~** pour la bonne cause; **in the ~ of equality** pour la cause de l'égalité; **3** JUR (grounds) cause *f*; **4** JUR (court action) action *f*.

II *vtr* causer, occasionner [*damage, grief, problem*]; provoquer [*chaos, delay, controversy, reaction*]; susciter [*excitement, surprise*]; entraîner [*suffering*]; amener [*dismay, confusion*]; **to ~ sb to cry/leave** faire pleurer/partir qn; **to ~ sb problems** causer des problèmes à qn; **to ~ trouble** créer des problèmes; **to ~ cancer/migraine** donner or provoquer un cancer/la migraine.

causeway /'kɔːzweɪ/ *n* chaussée *f* (*vers une île*).

caustic /'kɔːstɪk/ *adj* CHEM, FIG caustique; **~ soda** soude *f* caustique.

cauterize /'kɔːtəraɪz/ *vtr* cautériser.

caution /'kɔːʃn/ **I** *n* **1** (care) prudence *f*; **to err on the side of ~** pécher par excès de prudence; **~ should be exercised** la prudence est de mise; **2** (wariness) circonspection *f*; **3** (warning) avertissement *m*; **a word of ~** un petit conseil; **'Caution! Drive slowly!'** 'Attention! Conduire lentement!'; **4** GB JUR (given to suspect) **to be under ~** faire l'objet d'une mise en garde; **5** JUR (admonition) avertissement *m*.
II *vtr* **1** (warn) avertir (**that** que); **'he's dangerous,' she ~ed** 'il est dangereux', dit-elle à titre de mise en garde; **to ~ sb against doing** avertir qn de ne pas faire; **to ~ sb against** ou **about** mettre qn en garde contre [*danger*]; **2** JUR [*policeman*] informer [qn] de ses droits [*suspect*]; **3** JUR (admonish) réprimander; **4** SPORT donner un avertissement à [*player*].
IDIOMS **to throw** ou **cast ~ to the wind(s)** oublier toute prudence.

cautionary /'kɔːʃənərɪ, US -nerɪ/ *adj* (épith) [*look, gesture*] d'avertissement; **a ~ word** ou **comment** un avertissement; **a ~ tale** un conte moral.

cautious /'kɔːʃəs/ *adj* **1** (careful) prudent; **2** (wary) [*person, reception, response*] réservé; [*optimism*] prudent; **to be ~ about doing** ne pas aimer faire.

cautiously /'kɔːʃəslɪ/ *adv* **1** (carefully) prudemment; **2** (warily) avec circonspection; [*optimistic, confident*] raisonnablement.

cavalcade /ˌkævl'keɪd/ *n* (on horseback) cavalcade *f*; (motorized) cortège *m*.

cavalier /ˌkævə'lɪə(r)/ **I Cavalier** *pr n* GB HIST cavalier *m* (partisan de Charles Premier).
II *adj* cavalier/-ière.

cavalry /'kævlrɪ/ *n* cavalerie *f*.

cave /keɪv/ *n* grotte *f*.
■ **cave in: ~ in 1** LIT [*tunnel, roof, building*] s'effondrer; **2** FIG [*person*] céder.

caveat /'kævɪæt, US 'keɪvɪæt/ *n* mise *f* en garde.

cave: ~ dweller *n* troglodyte *m*; **~-in** *n* effondrement *m*; **~man** *n* (*pl* **-men**) homme *m* des cavernes; **~ painting** *n* peinture *f* rupestre.

caver /'keɪvə(r)/ *n* spéléologue *mf*.

cavern /'kævən/ *n* caverne *f*.

cavernous /'kævənəs/ *adj* [*groan, voice, room*] caverneux/-euse; [*mouth, yawn*] énorme; [*eyes*] cave.

caviar(e) /'kævɪɑː(r), ˌkævɪ'ɑː(r)/ *n* caviar *m*.

cavil /'kævl/ *vi* (*p prés etc* **-ll-**, **-l-** US) ergoter (**about**, **at** sur).

caving /'keɪvɪŋ/ *n* spéléologie *f*; **to go ~** faire de la spéléologie.

cavity /'kævətɪ/ *n* cavité *f*.

cavity: ~ block *n* GB moellon *m* creux; **~ wall insulation** *n* isolation *f* des murs creux.

cavort /kə'vɔːt/ *vi* (also **~ about**, **~ around**) faire des cabrioles *fpl*.

caw /kɔː/ **I** *n* **1** (noise) croassement *m*; **2** (cry) croa!
II *vi* croasser.

cayenne (**pepper**) /keɪ'en/ *n* poivre *m* de Cayenne.

CB (*abrév* = **Citizens' Band**) **I** *n* bande *f* CB.
II *noun modifier* [*equipment, radio, wavelength*] CB; **~ user** cibiste *mf*.

CBI *n* GB (*abrév* = **Confederation of British Industry**) patronat britannique; cf CNPF.

cc ▶ **1381** | *n* (*abrév* = **cubic centimetre**) cm³.

CC *n* GB *abrév* ▶ **County Council**.

CCT *n*: *abrév* ▶ **closed-circuit television**.

CD *n* **1** (*abrév* = **compact disc**) (disque *m*) compact *m*; **on ~** sur (disque) compact; **2** (*abrév* = **corps diplomatique**) CD; **3** MIL *abrév* ▶ **Civil Defence**; **4** US *abrév* ▶ **Congressional District**.

CDI *n* (*abrév* = **compact disc interactive**) CD-I *m*, disque *m* compact interactif.

CD player, CD system *n* platine *f* laser.

Cdr *n* MIL (*abrév écrite* = **Commander**) cf capitaine *m* de frégate.

CD-ROM /ˌsiːdiː'rɒm/ *n* disque *m* optique compact, CD-ROM *m*; **on ~** sur CD-ROM.

cease /siːs/ **I** *n* **without ~** sans cesse.
II *vtr* cesser; **you never ~ to amaze me!** tu m'étonneras toujours!; **to ~ fire** cesser le feu.
III *vi* cesser.

cease-fire /'siːsfaɪə(r)/ **I** *n* cessez-le-feu *m inv*.
II *noun modifier* [*agreement*] de cessez-le-feu; [*call*] au cessez-le-feu.

ceaseless /'siːslɪs/ *adj* incessant.

ceaselessly /'siːslɪslɪ/ *adv* [*labour, talk*] sans cesse; [*active, vigilant*] continuellement.

cedar /'siːdə(r)/ *n* cèdre *m*.

cede /siːd/ *vtr, vi* céder (**to** à).

cedilla /sɪ'dɪlə/ *n* cédille *f*.

ceiling /'siːlɪŋ/ *n* LIT, FIG plafond *m*; **to set a ~** fixer un plafond.
IDIOMS **to hit the ~** US sortir de ses gonds.

ceiling: ~ light *n* plafonnier *m*; **~ price** *n* COMM, ECON prix *m* plafond.

celebrate /'selɪbreɪt/ **I** *vtr* fêter [*occasion*]; (more formally) célébrer; **there's nothing/there's something to ~** il n'y a pas de quoi/il y a de quoi se réjouir; **2** RELIG célébrer [*mass, Easter*]; **3** (pay tribute to) célébrer.
II *vi* faire la fête; **let's ~!** il faut fêter ça!

celebrated /'selɪbreɪtɪd/ *adj* célèbre.

celebration /ˌselɪ'breɪʃn/ *n* **1** ¢ (action of celebrating) célébration *f*; **2** (party) fête *f*; **to have a ~** faire une fête; **3** (public festivities) **~s** cérémonies *fpl*; **4** (tribute) hommage *m* (**of** à); **5** RELIG célébration *f*.

celebratory /ˌselɪ'breɪtərɪ, US -tɔːrɪ/ *adj* [*air, mood*] de fête; **a ~ drink** un verre pour célébrer.

celebrity /sɪ'lebrətɪ/ **I** *n* célébrité *f*.
II *noun modifier* [*guest*] célèbre; [*panel*] de célébrités.

celeriac /sɪ'lerɪæk/ *n* céleri-rave *m*.

celery /'selərɪ/ *n* céleri *m*; **a stick/head of ~** une côte/un pied de céleri; **braised ~** céleris *mpl* braisés.

celestial /sɪ'lestɪəl/ *adj* céleste.

celibacy /'selɪbəsɪ/ *n* (unmarried) célibat *m*; (abstaining) chasteté *f*.

celibate /'selɪbət/ **I** *n* (unmarried) célibataire *mf*; (chaste) personne *f* chaste.
II *adj* (unmarried) célibataire; (chaste) chaste.

cell /sel/ *n* **1** (for prisoner, monk) cellule *f*; **2** BIOL, BOT cellule *f*; **3** ELEC, CHEM élément *m*; **4** POL cellule *f*.

cellar /'selə(r)/ *n* cave *f*.

cellist /'tʃelɪst/ ▶ **1251** |, **1097** | *n* violoncelliste *mf*.

cello /'tʃeləʊ/ ▶ **1097** | *n* violoncelle *m*.

cellphone /'selfəʊn/ *n* radiotéléphone *m*.

cellular /'seljʊlə(r)/ *adj* BIOL cellulaire.

cellular phone, cellular telephone *n* radiotéléphone *m*.

cellulite /'seljʊlaɪt/ *n* cellulite *f*, peau *f* d'orange○.

celluloid® /'seljʊlɔɪd/ *n* celluloïd® *m*.

cellulose /'seljʊləʊs/ *n* cellulose *f*.

Celsius /'selsɪəs/ *adj* Celsius *inv*.

Celt /kelt, US selt/ n Celte mf.

Celtic /'keltık, US 'seltık/ adj celtique, celte.

cement /sı'ment/ **I** n **1** CONSTR ciment m; (for tiles) mastic m; **2** (in dentistry) amalgame m; **3** FIG ciment m.
II vtr **1** LIT, FIG cimenter; **2** [dentist] obturer.

cement mixer n bétonnière f.

cemetery /'semətrı, US -terı/ n cimetière m.

cenotaph /'senətɑ:f, US -tæf/ n cénotaphe m.

censor /'sensə(r)/ **I** n censeur m.
II vtr censurer.

censorious /sen'sɔ:rıəs/ adj sévère (**of** envers).

censorship /'sensəʃıp/ n (all contexts) censure f.

censure /'senʃə(r)/ **I** n censure f; **vote of** ∼ vote m de censure.
II vtr critiquer.

census /'sensəs/ n recensement m; **traffic** ∼ étude f chiffrée de la circulation.

cent /sent/ ▶ 849 | n cent m; **I haven't got a** ∼ je n'ai pas un sou.

centenarian /ˌsentı'neərıən/ n, adj centenaire (mf).

centenary /sen'ti:nərı/ n centenaire m.

centennial /sen'tenıəl/ **I** n US centenaire m.
II adj (every 100 years) séculaire; (lasting 100 years) centenaire.

center n US = **centre**.

centigrade /'sentıgreıd/ adj [thermometer] Celsius; **in degrees** ∼ en degrés Celsius.

centilitre GB, **centiliter** US /'sentıli:tə(r)/ ▶ 1381 | n centilitre m.

centimetre GB, **centimeter** US /'sentımi:tə(r)/ ▶ 1045 | n centimètre m.

centipede /'sentıpi:d/ n mille-pattes m inv.

central /'sentrəl/ **I Central** pr n (also **Central Region**) (in Scotland) la région Central.
II adj **1** (in the middle) central; ∼ **London** le centre de Londres; **2** (in the town centre) situé en centre-ville; **3** (key) principal; ∼ **to** essentiel à; **4** ADMIN, POL central.

central: **Central African Republic** pr n République f centrafricaine; **Central America** pr n Amérique f centrale; **Central American** adj d'Amérique centrale; **Central Europe** pr n Europe f centrale; **Central European** adj d'Europe centrale; ∼ **heating** n chauffage m central.

centralization /ˌsentrəlaɪ'zeɪʃn, US -lɪ'z-/ n centralisation f.

centralize /'sentrəlaɪz/ vtr centraliser.

central locking n AUT verrouillage m central or centralisé.

centrally /'sentrəlı/ adv [live, work] en centre-ville; [situated] en centre-ville; [funded, managed] de façon centralisée; ∼ **heated** [flat] avec chauffage central; ∼ **planned** n planification centralisée.

central: ∼ **nervous system** n système m nerveux central; ∼ **processing unit, CPU,** ∼ **processor** n COMPUT unité f centrale; ∼ **reservation** n GB (on motorway) terre-plein m central.

centre GB, **center** US /'sentə(r)/ **I** n **1** (middle) centre m; **in the** ∼ au centre; **the** ∼ **of London** le centre de Londres; **town** ∼, **city** ∼ centre-ville m; **sweets with soft** ∼s bonbons mpl fourrés; **2** (focus) centre m; **to be at the** ∼ **of a row** être au centre d'une dispute; **the** ∼ **of attention** le centre de l'attention; **3** (seat) siège m; **4** (area) centre m; **business** ∼ quartier m des affaires; **shopping/sports/leisure** ∼ centre m commercial/sportif/de loisirs; **5** POL centre m; **to be left of** ∼ être à gauche du centre; **a** ∼**-left party** un parti du centre gauche; **6** SPORT centre m; ▶ **left**.
II noun modifier GEN central; [parting] au milieu.
III vtr, vi COMPUT, SPORT, TECH centrer; **child-centred** centré sur l'enfant.

■ **centre around, centre on**: ∼ **around** [sth] [activities, person] se concentrer sur; [people, industry] se situer autour de [town]; [life, thoughts] être centré sur [person, work]; [demands] viser [pay].

centre-fold /'sentəfəʊld/ n (pin-up) (picture) photo f de pin-up (sur double page); (model) pin-up f.

centre-forward /ˌsentə'fɔ:wəd/ n SPORT avant-centre m.

centre ground n centre m; **to occupy the** ∼ être au centre.

centre: ∼**-half** n SPORT demi-centre m; ∼ **of gravity** GB, **center of gravity** US, cg n centre m de gravité; ∼**-piece** n (of table) décoration f centrale; (of exhibition) clou m; ∼ **spread** n double page f du milieu.

centre-stage /ˌsentə'steɪdʒ/ **I** n **1** THEAT centre m de la scène; **2** FIG (prime position) **to take/occupy** ∼ devenir/être le point de mire.
II adv **to stand** ∼ se tenir au centre de la scène.

centrifugal /ˌsentrı'fju:gl, sen'trıfjʊgl/ adj centrifuge.

centrifuge /'sentrıfju:dʒ/ n centrifugeuse f.

century /'sentʃərı/ ▶ 1336 | n siècle m; **in the 20th** ∼ au XXᵉ siècle; **at the turn of the** ∼ au début du siècle; **half a** ∼ un demi-siècle; **centuries-old** séculaire.

ceramic /sı'ræmık/ **I** n céramique f.
II adj [tile, pot] en céramique; [hob] en vitrocéramique; [design, art] de la céramique.

ceramics /sı'ræmıks/ n **1** (+ v sg) (study) la céramique; **2** (+ v pl) (artefacts) céramiques fpl.

cereal /'sıərıəl/ **I** n céréale f; (for breakfast) céréales fpl; **breakfast** ∼ céréales pour le petit déjeuner.
II adj [harvest, imports] de céréales; [crop, production] céréalier/-ière.

cerebral /'serıbrəl, US sə'ri:brəl/ adj MED cérébral; FIG intellectuel/-elle.

cerebral palsy /ˌserıbrəl 'pɔ:lzı, US sə'ri:brəl/ ▶ 1002 | n paralysie f motrice centrale.

ceremonial /ˌserı'məʊnıəl/ **I** n cérémonial m; (religious) rites mpl.
II adj **1** [dress] de cérémonie; **2** (ritual) cérémoniel/-ielle; (solemn) solennel/-elle; (official) officiel/-ielle.

ceremonially /ˌserı'məʊnıəlı/ adv selon le cérémonial d'usage.

ceremoniously /ˌserı'məʊnıəslı/ adv avec cérémonie.

ceremony /'serımənı, US -məʊnı/ n **1** (event) cérémonie f; **marriage** ∼ cérémonie f du mariage; **2** ₵ (protocol) cérémonies fpl; **to stand on** ∼ faire des cérémonies.

cert° /sɜ:t/ n GB **it's a (dead)** ∼°! ça ne fait pas un pli°!

certain /'sɜ:tn/ **I** pron ∼ **of our members/friends** certains de nos adhérents/amis.
II adj **1** (sure, definite) certain, sûr (**about, of** de); **I'm** ∼ **of it** ou that j'en suis certain or sûr; **of that you can be** ∼ tu peux en être sûr; **absolutely** ∼ sûr et certain; **I'm** ∼ **that I checked** je suis sûr d'avoir vérifié; **I'm** ∼ **that he refused** je suis sûr qu'il a refusé; **she's not** ∼ **that you'll be able to do it** elle n'est pas sûre que tu sois capable de le faire; **to make** ∼ s'en assurer, vérifier; **to make** ∼ **of** s'assurer de [cooperation, support]; vérifier [facts, details]; **to make** ∼ **to do** faire bien attention de faire; **to make** ∼ **that** (ascertain) vérifier que; (ensure) faire en sorte que (+ subj); **he's** ∼ **to be there** il y sera certainement or sûrement; **the strike seems** ∼ **to continue** il est presque certain que la grève continuera; **I know for** ∼ **that** je sais de façon sûre que; **be** ∼ **to tell him that** n'oublie pas de lui dire que; **nobody knows for** ∼ personne ne sait au juste; **I can't say for** ∼ je ne sais pas au juste; **2** (assured, guaranteed) [death, defeat] certain (after n); **to be** ∼ **of doing** être sûr or certain de faire; **he's** ∼ **to agree** il sera d'accord, il n'y a aucun doute là-dessus; **the changes are** ∼ **to provoke anger** ces changements provoqueront sûrement des réactions violentes; **to my** ∼ **knowledge** à ma connaissance; **in the** ∼ **knowledge that he would fail** tout en sachant très bien qu'il allait échouer; **3** (specific) [amount, number] certain (before n); ∼ **people** certains mpl; **4** (slight) [shyness, difficulty] certain (before n); **to a** ∼ **extent** ou **degree**

dans une certaine mesure; **a ~ amount of time** un certain temps.

certainly /'sɜːtnlɪ/ *adv* (without doubt) certainement; (indicating assent) certainement, bien sûr; **~ not!** certainement pas!; **it's ~ possible that** il est tout à fait possible que (+ *subj*); **this exercise is ~ very difficult** cet exercice est vraiment très difficile; **we shall ~ attend the meeting** nous serons à la réunion sans faute; **he ~ got his revenge!** IRON c'est sûr qu'il a pris sa revanche!; **'are you annoyed?'—'I most ~ am!'** 'tu es fâché?'—'ah! ça, oui alors!'

certainty /'sɜːtnlɪ/ *n* **1** (sure thing) certitude *f* (**about** ou quant à); **for a ~** à coup sûr; **it's by no means a ~** ce n'est pas du tout sûr (**that** que + *subj*); **this candidate is a ~ for election** ce candidat est sûr d'être élu; **she is a ~ to play** elle est sûre de jouer; **2** ¢ (guarantee) certitude *f* (**of** de); **we have no ~ of success** nous ne sommes pas certains de réussir.

certifiable /ˌsɜːtɪ'faɪəbl/ *adj* **1** (mad) dont l'état justifie l'internement; **2** (verifiable) [*statement, evidence*] vérifiable.

certificate /sə'tɪfɪkət/ *n* **1** (academic) certificat *m*; (more advanced) diplôme *m*; **2** (for electrician, instructor, first-aider etc) brevet *m*; **3** (of child's proficiency in sth) brevet *m*; **4** (of safety, building standards etc) certificat *m*; **test ~, MOT** ou GB certificat *m* de contrôle technique; **5** ADMIN (of birth, death, marriage) acte *m*; **6** COMM (of authenticity, quality) certificat *m*; **7** CIN **18-~ film** film interdit aux moins de 18 ans.

certification /ˌsɜːtɪfɪ'keɪʃn/ *n* **1** JUR (of document) authentification *f*; (of ship) certification *f*; (of ownership) certificat *m*; **2** (document) certificat *m*; **3** (of mental patient) mandat *m* d'internement psychiatrique.

certified: **~ bankrupt** *n* débiteur *m* (failli); **~ public accountant, CPA** *n* US expert-comptable *m* agréé.

certify /'sɜːtɪfaɪ/ **I** *vtr* **1** (confirm) certifier, constater [*death*]; **to ~ sth a true copy** certifier qch pour copie conforme; **to ~ sb insane** certifier que qn est atteint d'aliénation mentale; **2** (authenticate) authentifier; **3** (issue certificate to) délivrer un certificat d'aptitude professionnelle à; **4** COMM garantir [*goods*].

II certified *pp adj* certifié; [*teacher*] US SCH qualifié; **to send by certified mail** US envoyer en recommandé.

certitude /'sɜːtɪtjuːd, US -tuːd/ *n* certitude *f*, conviction *f*.

cervical /'sɜːvɪkl/ *adj* cervical; **~ cancer ▶1002|** cancer *m* du col de l'utérus; **~ smear** frottis *m* vaginal.

cervix /'sɜːvɪks/ *n* col *m* de l'utérus.

cesspit /'sespɪt/, **cesspool** /'sespuːl/ *n* fosse *f* d'aisances.

Ceylon /sɪ'lɒn/ **I** *pr n* HIST Ceylan *m*.
II *noun modifier* **~ tea** thé *m* de Ceylan.

CFC *n* ECOL (*abrév* = **chlorofluorocarbon**) CFC *m*; **'contains no ~s'** 'sans CFC'.

CFE *n* GB (*abrév* = **College of Further Education**) ≈ centre *m* de formation continue.

cg 1 (*abrév* = **centigram**) cg; **2** *abrév* ▶ **centre of gravity**.

Chad /tʃæd/ **▶840|** *pr n* Tchad *m*.

chafe /tʃeɪf/ **I** *vtr* (rub) irriter; (restore circulation) frictionner.
II *vi* (rub) frotter (**on, against** sur).
IDIOMS **to ~ at the bit** ronger son frein.

chaff /tʃɑːf, tʃæf, US tʃæf/ **I** *n* AGRIC (husks) balle *f*; (fodder) menue paille *f*.
II *vtr* plaisanter (**about** sur).

chaffinch /'tʃæfɪntʃ/ *n* pinson *m*.

chagrin /'ʃægrɪn, US ʃə'griːn/ *n* dépit *m*; (**much**) **to his ~** à son grand dépit.

chain /tʃeɪn/ **I** *n* **1** (metal links) chaîne *f*; **a length of ~** une chaîne; **to put** ou **keep sb in ~s** enchaîner qn; **to keep a dog on a ~** tenir un chien à la chaîne; **2** (on lavatory) chasse *f* (d'eau); **3** (on door) chaîne *f* de sûreté; **4** COMM chaîne *f* (**of** de); **super-**

market/hotel ~ chaîne *f* de supermarchés/d'hôtels; **5** (series) (of events) série *f*; (of ideas) enchaînement *m*; **~ of causation** rapport *m* or relation *f* de cause à effet; **a link in the ~** un maillon de la chaîne; **to make** ou **form a (human) ~** faire la chaîne, faire une chaîne humaine; **6** BIOL, GEOG, PHYS chaîne *f*; **7** (measurement) = 20,12 m.

II *vtr* enchaîner [*person*]; **to ~ sb's wrists** attacher les poignets de qn avec des chaînes; **to ~ a bicycle to sth** attacher une bicyclette à qch avec une chaîne; **to be ~ed to one's desk/the kitchen sink** FIG être esclave de son travail/ses casseroles.

chain: **~ gang** *n* chaîne *f* de forçats; **~ letter** *n* (lettre *f* de) chaîne *f*; **~ mail** *n* cotte *f* de mailles; **~ of command** *n* hiérarchie *f*; **~ reaction** *n* réaction *f* en chaîne; **~ saw** *n* tronçonneuse *f*; **~-smoke** *vi* fumer comme un sapeur○, fumer sans arrêt; **~-smoker** *n* gros fumeur/grosse fumeuse *m/f*; **~ store** *n* (single shop) magasin *m* faisant partie d'une chaîne; (retail group) magasin *m* à succursales multiples.

chair /tʃeə(r)/ **I** *n* **1** (seat) (wooden) chaise *f*; (upholstered) fauteuil *m*; **to take a ~** s'asseoir; **2** (chairperson) président/-e *m/f*; **to take** ou **be in the ~** présider; **3** (professorship) chaire *f* (**of, in** de); **to hold the ~ of...** être titulaire de la chaire de...; **4** US (also **electric ~**) **to go to the ~** passer sur la chaise électrique.
II *vtr* présider [*meeting*].

chair lift *n* télésiège *m*.

chairman /'tʃeəmən/ **▶937|** *n* président/-e *m/f*; **Mr Chairman** monsieur le Président; **Madam Chairman** madame la Présidente.

■ Note L'usage moderne préfère *chairperson*.

chairmanship /'tʃeəmənʃɪp/ *n* présidence *f*.
chairperson /'tʃeəpɜːsn/ *n* président/-e *m/f*.
chairwoman /'tʃeəwʊmən/ **▶937|** *n* présidente *f*.

chalet /'ʃæleɪ/ *n* (mountain) chalet *m*; (in holiday camp) bungalow *m*.

chalice /'tʃælɪs/ *n* calice *m*.

chalk /tʃɔːk/ **I** *n* craie *f*; **a piece of ~** un bâton de craie.
II *noun modifier* **1** GEN, ART [*drawing*] à la craie; **~ mark** (on blackboard) trace *f* de craie; (in sewing) repère *m* à la craie; **2** [*cliff, landscape*] de craie.
III *vtr* **1** (write) écrire [qch] à la craie; **2** (apply chalk to) frotter [qch] avec de la craie.
IDIOMS **not by a long ~**○! loin de là○!; **white as ~** blanc comme un linge.
■ **chalk out**: **~ out** [sth], **~** [sth] **out** tracer [qch] à la craie.
■ **chalk up**: **~** [sth] **up**, **~ up** [sth] LIT, FIG marquer [*score, points*]; **~ it up to experience** la prochaine fois vous saurez.

chalkboard /'tʃɔːkbɔːd/ *n* US tableau *m* (noir).

chalky /'tʃɔːkɪ/ *adj* [*soil*] crayeux/-euse; [*hands*] couvert de craie.

challenge /'tʃælɪndʒ/ **I** *n* **1** (provocation) défi *m*; **to put out** ou **issue a ~** lancer un défi; **to take up a ~** relever un défi; **2** (situation or opportunity) (stimulating) challenge *m*; (considered difficult) épreuve *f*; **to present a ~** représenter un challenge; **to rise to** ou **meet the ~** relever le challenge; **to face a ~** affronter une épreuve; **unemployment is a ~ for us** le chômage nous met à l'épreuve; **I'm looking for a ~** je cherche un défi à relever; **the ~ of new ideas** la stimulation des idées nouvelles; **3** (contest) **to make a ~** for essayer de s'emparer de [*title*]; entrer dans la course à [*presidency*]; **leadership ~** POL tentative *f* pour s'emparer de la direction du parti; **4** (questioning) (of claim, authority) contestation *f* (**to** de); **5** SPORT attaque *f*.
II *vtr* **1** (invite to justify) défier [*person*] (**to** à; **to do** de faire); **to ~ sb to a duel** provoquer qn en duel; **2** (question) débattre [*ideas*]; contester [*statement, authority*]; [*sentry*] faire une sommation à; **3** (test) mettre à l'épreuve [*skill, person*].

challenger /'tʃælɪndʒə(r)/ *n* challenger *m* (**for** de).

challenging /'tʃælɪndʒɪŋ/ adj **1** (stimulating) [ideas, career] stimulant; [task] qui représente un challenge; [work] difficile mais motivant; [book] d'un abord difficile; **2** (confrontational) provocateur/-trice.

chamber /'tʃeɪmbə(r)/ n **1** GEN, TECH chambre f; **council ~** GB salle f de réunion; **2** GB POL **the upper/lower ~** la Chambre des lords/des communes; **3** ANAT (of heart) cavité f; (of eye) chambre f; **4** (cave) salle f; **5 chambers** npl JUR cabinet m.

chamber: **~maid** ▶ 1251 n femme f de chambre; **~ music** n musique f de chambre; **Chamber of Commerce**, **C of C** n chambre f de commerce et d'industrie; **~ orchestra** n orchestre m de chambre; **~ pot** n pot m de chambre.

chameleon /kə'miːlɪən/ n caméléon m ALSO FIG.

chamois /'ʃæmwɑː, US 'ʃæmɪ/ n (pl **~**) ZOOL chamois m.

chamois cloth US, **chamois leather** n peau f de chamois.

champ /tʃæmp/ **I** vtr mâchonner.
II vi **to ~ at the bit** [horse] piaffer d'impatience; [person] FIG ronger son frein.

champagne /ʃæm'peɪn/ n, adj champagne (m) inv.

champagne glass n (tall) flûte f à champagne; (open) coupe f à champagne.

champion /'tʃæmpɪən/ **I** n champion/-ionne m/f; **world ~** champion/-ionne m/f du monde; **~ boxer**, **boxing ~** champion m de boxe.
II vtr se faire le champion de [cause]; prendre fait et cause pour [person].

championship /'tʃæmpɪənʃɪp/ n championnat m.

chance /tʃɑːns, US tʃæns/ **I** n **1** (opportunity) occasion f; **to have** ou **get the ~ to do** avoir l'occasion de faire; **give me a ~ to explain** laisse-moi t'expliquer; **to take one's ~** saisir l'occasion; **you've missed your ~** tu as laissé passer l'occasion; **now's your ~!** c'est l'occasion ou jamais!; **I haven't had a ~ yet** je n'en ai pas encore eu l'occasion; **this is your big ~** c'est l'occasion ou jamais; **if you get a ~** si tu en as la possibilité; **when you get a** ou **the ~, can you...?** quand tu auras le temps est-ce que tu pourras...?; **2** (likelihood) chance f; **there's little ~ of sb doing** il y a peu de chances que qn fasse; **the ~s of catching the thief are slim** il y a peu de chances qu'on attrape le voleur; **there is a ~ that sb will do** il y a des chances que qn fasse; **the ~s are that** il y a de grandes chances que (+ subj); **the ~s of sb doing are poor** il y a peu de chances que qn fasse; **she has a good ~** elle a de bonnes chances; **what are his ~s of recovery?** a-t-il des chances de s'en tirer?; **any ~ of a coffee**○? est-ce que c'est possible d'avoir un café?; **3** (luck) hasard m; **a game of ~** un jeu de hasard; **by ~** par hasard; **4** (risk) risque m; **to take a ~** prendre un risque; **it's a ~ I'm willing to take** c'est un risque à prendre; **5** (possibility) chance f; **not to stand a ~** n'avoir aucune chance; **do you have his address by any ~?** auriez-vous, par hasard, son adresse?
II noun modifier [encounter, occurrence] fortuit; [discovery] accidentel/-elle.
III vtr **1** (risk) **to ~ doing** courir le risque de faire; **to ~ one's arm**, **to ~ it** tenter sa chance; **I wouldn't ~ it** je ne risquerais pas le coup; **2** (happen to do) **I ~d to see it** je l'ai vu par hasard.
IDIOMS **no ~**○! pas question○!
■ **chance upon**, **chance on**: ¶ **~ upon** [sb] rencontrer [qn] par hasard; ¶ **~ upon** [sth] trouver [qch] par hasard.

chancel /'tʃɑːnsl, US tʃænsl/ n ARCHIT chœur m.

chancellor /'tʃɑːnsələ(r), US 'tʃæns-/ n **1** (head of government) chancelier m; **2** UNIV ≈ président m.

Chancellor of the Exchequer n GB POL Chancelier m de l'Échiquier.

chancy○ /'tʃɑːnsɪ, US 'tʃænsɪ/ adj risqué.

chandelier /ˌʃændə'lɪə(r)/ n lustre m.

chandler /'tʃɑːndlə(r), US 'tʃæn-/ ▶ 1251 n (also **ship's ~**) vendeur m de matériel pour bateaux.

change /tʃeɪndʒ/ **I** n **1** (alteration) (by replacement)

changement m; (by adjustment) modification f; **the ~ in the schedule** la modification du programme; **~ of plan** changement de programme; **a ~ for the better/worse** un changement en mieux/pire; **social ~** changements sociaux; **to make a ~ in sth** changer qch; **to make ~s in** apporter des changements à [text]; faire des changements dans [room, company]; **there will have to be a ~ in your attitude** il va falloir que vous changiez d'attitude; **people opposed to ~** les personnes qui sont contre le progrès; **2** (substitution, replacement) changement m (of de); **costume ~** THEAT changement de costume; **~ of government** POL changement de gouvernement; **3** (fresh, different experience) changement m; **it makes a ~ from television/from staying at home** cela change un peu de la télévision/de rester chez soi; **that makes a nice ou refreshing ~** ça change agréablement; **she needs a ~** elle a besoin de se changer les idées; **to need a ~ of air** FIG avoir besoin de changer d'air; **for a ~** pour changer; **to ring the ~s** FIG introduire des changements; **4** (of clothes) **a ~ of clothes** des vêtements de rechange; **5** (cash) monnaie f; **small ~** petite monnaie; **she gave me 6p ~** elle m'a rendu 6 pence; **have you got ~ for £10?** pouvez-vous me changer un billet de 10 livres?; **60p in ~** 60 pence en petite monnaie; **'no ~ given'** (on machine) 'ne rend pas la monnaie'; **'exact ~ please'** 'faites l'appoint, s'il vous plaît'; **you won't get much ~ out of £20**○ tu vas payer près de 20 livres.
II vtr **1** (alter) (completely) changer; (in part) modifier; **we have ~d the look of the town** nous avons modifié l'aspect de la ville; **to ~ X into Y** transformer X en Y; **to ~ one's mind** changer d'avis (about à propos de); **to ~ one's mind about doing** abandonner l'idée de faire; **to ~ sb's mind** faire changer qn d'avis; **to ~ one's ways** changer de mode de vie; **that won't ~ anything** ça n'y changera rien; **2** (exchange for sth different) GEN changer de [clothes, name, car]; (in shop) échanger [item] (**for** pour); **can I ~ it for a size 12?** est-ce que je peux l'échanger contre une taille 12?; **if it's too big, we'll ~ it for you** s'il est trop grand, nous vous l'échangerons; **to ~ colour** changer de couleur; **hurry up and get ~d!** dépêche-toi de te changer!; **to ~ sth from X to Y** (of numbers, letters, words) remplacer X par Y; (of building, area etc) transformer X en Y; **they ~d their car for a smaller one** ils ont remplacé leur voiture par un modèle plus petit; **3** (replace with dirty, old, broken) changer; **to ~ a bed** changer les draps; **4** (exchange with sb) échanger [clothes, seats]; **to ~ places** changer de place (**with** avec); FIG (roles) intervertir les rôles; **I wouldn't ~ places with the Queen** je ne voudrais pas être à la place de la Reine; **5** (actively switch) changer de [side, job, direction, TV channel, doctor]; **to ~ hands** FIG [property, object] changer de propriétaire; **no money ~d hands** il n'y a pas eu d'échange d'argent; **6** (alter character) changer; **to ~ sb/sth into** changer qn/qch en [frog, prince]; **sugar is ~d into alcohol** le sucre se transforme en alcool; **7** (replace nappy of) changer [baby]; **8** (convert) changer [cheque, currency] (**into, for** en).
III vi **1** (alter) GEN changer; [wind] tourner; **to ~ from X (in)to Y** passer de X à Y; **2** (into different clothes) se changer; **to ~ into** passer [different garment]; **to ~ out of** ôter, enlever [garment]; **3** (from bus, train) changer; **'~ at Tours for Paris'** 'correspondance à Tours pour Paris'; **all ~!** tout le monde descend!; **4** (become transformed) se métamorphoser.
IV changed pp adj [man, woman] autre (before n).
■ **change down** GB AUT rétrograder.
■ **change over**: ¶ **~ over** (swap) [drivers] changer; **to ~ over from sth to sth** passer de qch à qch; ¶ **~ over** [sth/sb], **~** [sth/sb] **over** intervertir.
■ **change round**: ¶ **~ round** GB changer de place; ¶ **~** [sth/sb] **round**, **~ round** [sth/sb] déplacer [large objects]; changer [qn/qch] de place [workers, objects, words].
■ **change up** GB AUT passer à une vitesse supérieure.

changeable /'tʃeɪndʒəbl/ adj [condition, behaviour,

opinion, weather] changeant; [*price, rate*] variable; ~
moods sautes d'humeur.

changeless /'tʃeɪndʒlɪs/ *adj* [*law, routine*] immuable;
[*appearance*] inaltérable; [*character*] constant.

change: ~ **machine** *n* distributeur *m* de monnaie;
~ **of address** *n* changement *m* d'adresse; ~ **of
life** *n* retour *m* d'âge.

changeover /'tʃeɪndʒəʊvə(r)/ *n* **1** (time period) phase *f*
de changement; **2** (transition) passage *m* (**to** à); **3** (of
leaders) remaniement *m*; (of employees, guards) relève *f*;
4 SPORT (of ends) changement *m*; (in relay) passage *m*
du témoin.

changing /'tʃeɪndʒɪŋ/ **I** *n* changement *m*.
II *adj* [*colours, environment*] changeant; [*attitude,
world*] en évolution.

changing-room /'tʃeɪndʒɪŋ ruːm, rʊm/ *n* SPORT
vestiaire *m*; US (fitting room) cabine *f* d'essayage.

channel /'tʃænl/ **I** *n* **1** (passage for liquid) canal *m*; **2** (navigable water) chenal *m*; **3** (diplomatic, commercial) canal
m; **to do sth through the proper** ou **usual** ou **normal
~s** faire qch par la voie normale; **to go through official ~s** passer par la voie officielle; **diplomatic/
legal ~s** voie *f* diplomatique/légale; **~s of communication** un réseau de communication; **4** TV chaîne *f*;
to change ~s changer de chaîne; **to flick ~s**ᵒ
zapper; ~ **one** la première chaîne; **5** RADIO canal
m; **6** ARCHIT cannelure *f*; **7** (groove) rainure *f*.
II *vtr* (*p prés etc* **-ll-, -l-** US) **1** (carry) acheminer, canaliser [*liquid*] (**to, into** dans; **through** par l'intermédiaire de); **2** FIG (direct) concentrer, canaliser [*efforts,
energy*] (**into** dans; **into doing** pour faire); affecter
[*funds*] (**into** à); **3** (cut) creuser.

Channel /'tʃænl/ **▶ 1117**] **I** *pr n* (also **English ~**)
the ~ la Manche.
II *noun modifier* [*crossing, port*] de la Manche.

channel: ~ **ferry** *n* ferry *m* trans-Manche;
~-flickᵒ *vi* zapper; **Channel Islander** *n* habitant/
-e *m/f* des îles Anglo-Normandes; **Channel Islands
▶ 1022**] *pr npl* îles *fpl* Anglo-Normandes; **Channel
Tunnel** *pr n* tunnel *m* sous la Manche.

chant /tʃɑːnt, US tʃænt/ **I** *n* **1** GEN chant *m* scandé; **2**
MUS, RELIG mélopée *f*.
II *vtr* scander [*name, slogan*]; chanter [*psalm*]; psalmo-
dier [*liturgy, schoolwork*].
III *vi* [*crowd*] scander des slogans; MUS, RELIG
psalmodier.

chaos /'keɪɒs/ *n* **1** (on roads, at home, at work) pagaille°
f; (political) confusion *f*, désordre *m*; (economic) chaos *m*;
in a state of ~ [*house, room*] sens dessus dessous;
[*country*] en plein chaos; **to cause ~** semer la
pagaille; **2** (cosmic) chaos *m*; ~ **theory** théorie *f* du
chaos.

chaotic /keɪ'ɒtɪk/ *adj* désordonné; **it's absolutely
~**ᵒ c'est la pagaille°.

chap /tʃæp/ **I**ᵒ *n* GB GEN type° *m*; (boy) garçon *m*;
(young man) gars° *m*; **a nice ~** un chouette type; **an
old ~** un vieux; **old ~**... mon vieux...
II *vtr* (*p prés etc* **-pp-**) gercer; **~ped lips** lèvres
gercées.

chapel /'tʃæpl/ *n* chapelle *f*.

chaperone /'ʃæpərəʊn/ **I** *n* chaperon *m*.
II *vtr* chaperonner.

chaplain /'tʃæplɪn/ *n* GEN aumônier *m*; (to a person)
chapelain *m*.

chapter /'tʃæptə(r)/ *n* **1** (in book) chapitre *m*; **in ~ 3**
au chapitre 3; **2** FIG (stage) chapitre *m*; **a new ~ in**
un nouveau chapitre de.
IDIOMS **a ~ of accidents** une série d'accidents; **to
give ~ and verse** donner la référence exacte.

char /tʃɑː(r)/ **I**ᵒ *n* GB (cleaner) femme *f* de ménage.
II *vtr* (*p prés etc* **-rr-**) carboniser.
III *vi* (*p prés etc* **-rr-**) se carboniser.

character /'kærəktə(r)/ *n* **1** (personality) caractère *m*;
to have a pleasant ~ être d'un caractère agréable;
to act in/out of ~ agir de façon habituelle/surpre-
nante; **his remarks are totally in ~/out of ~** ces
remarques ne me surprennent pas/me surprennent de
sa part; **2** (reputation) réputation *f*; **a person of good**

~ une personne d'une bonne réputation; **3** LIT-
ERAT, THEAT, TV personnage *m* (**from** de); **to play
the ~ of Romeo** jouer le rôle de Roméo; **4** (person)
individu *m*; **a real ~** un sacré numéro°; **a local ~**
une figure locale; **5** COMPUT caractère *m* (also in printing).

character: ~ **actor** *n* acteur *m* de genre; ~
assassination *n* dénigrement *m*.

characteristic /ˌkærəktə'rɪstɪk/ **I** *n* (of person) trait *m*
de caractère; (of place, work) caractéristique *f*.
II *adj* caractéristique (**of** de); **it was ~ of them to
do** c'était typique de leur part de faire.

characteristically /ˌkærəktə'rɪstɪklɪ/ *adv* typiquement.

characterize /'kærəktəraɪz/ *vtr* **1** (depict) dépeindre
(**as** comme); **2** (typify) caractériser; **to be ~d by** se
caractériser par; **3** (sum up) représenter [*era, place*];
faire le portrait de [*person*].

characterless /'kærəktəlɪs/ *adj* sans caractère.

character: ~ **reference** *n* références *fpl*; ~
sketch *n* portrait *m* rapide.

charade /ʃə'rɑːd, US ʃə'reɪd/ *n* **1** (in game) charade *f*
mimée; **to play ~s** jouer aux charades; **2** PEJ (pretence) comédie *f*.

charbroiled /'tʃɑːbrɔɪld/ *adj* US = **char-grilled**.

charcoal /'tʃɑːkəʊl/ **I** *n* **1** (fuel) charbon *m* de bois; **2**
ART fusain *m*; **3** (colour) gris *m* anthracite.
II ▶ 818] *adj* (also ~ **grey**) (gris) anthracite *inv*.

charge /tʃɑːdʒ/ **I** *n* **1** (fee) frais *mpl*; **delivery/hand-
ling ~** frais de livraison/manutention; **additional
~** supplément *m*; **small** ou **token ~** participation *f*;
there's a ~ of £2 for postage il y a 2 livres de frais
de port; **there's no ~ for installation** l'installation
est gratuite; **free of ~** gratuitement; **at no extra ~**
sans supplément; **2** JUR inculpation *f*; **murder ~**
inculpation d'assassinat; **criminal ~s** poursuites *fpl*
criminelles; **to bring ~s** porter plainte; **to prefer** ou
press ~s against sth engager des poursuites contre
qch; **to drop (the) ~s** abandonner les poursuites; **3**
(accusation) accusation *f* (**of** de); **this leaves you open
to ~s of** cela laisse la porte ouverte aux accusations
de [*nepotism*]; **4** (attack) charge *f* (**against** contre); **5**
(control) **to be in ~** GEN être responsable (**of** de);
MIL commander; **the person in ~** le/la responsable;
to put sb in ~ of sth confier la charge de qch à qn
[*company, plane, project*]; **to take ~ of** assumer la
charge de; **to have ~ of** être chargé de; **the pupils
in my ~** les élèves à ma charge; **to take ~** prendre
les choses en main; **I've left Paul in ~** c'est Paul qui
sera responsable; **6** (person in one's care) (child) enfant
mf dont on s'occupe; (pupil) élève *mf*; (patient) malade
mf; **7** (explosive) charge *f*; **8** ELEC, PHYS charge *f*.
II *vtr* **1** COMM faire payer [*customer*]; prélever
[*commission*]; percevoir [*interest*] (**on** sur); **to ~ sb
for sth** faire payer qch à qn; **how much do you ~?**
vous prenez combien?; **I ~ £20 an hour** je prends 20
livres de l'heure; **interest is ~d at 2% a month**
l'intérêt perçu sera de 2% par mois; **labour is ~d at
£25 per hour** il faut compter 25 livres de l'heure pour
la main-d'œuvre; **what do you ~ for doing...?**
combien faut-il compter pour faire...?; **2** (pay on
account) **to ~ sth to** mettre qch sur [*account*]; **3**
JUR (*police*) inculper [*suspect*] (**with** de); **4** (accuse)
accuser (**with** de); **5** (rush at) charger [*enemy*]; [*bull*]
foncer sur [*person*]; **6** ELEC, PHYS charger.
III *vi* **1** (demand payment) **to ~ for** faire payer [*delivery, admission*]; **2** (rush at) **to ~ at** charger [*enemy*];
[*bull*] foncer sur [*person*]; **~!** à l'attaque!; **3** (run) se
précipiter (**into** dans; **out of** de); **to ~ across** ou
through traverser [*qch*] à toute vitesse [*room*]; **to ~
up/down** monter/descendre [*qch*] à toute vitesse
[*stairs*].

charge: ~ **account** *n* US COMM compte-client *m*;
~ **card** *n* (credit card) carte *f* de crédit; (store card)
carte *f* d'achat.

charged /tʃɑːdʒd/ *adj* **1** PHYS chargé; **2** (intense)
[*atmosphere*] très tendu; **emotionally ~** chargé
d'émotion.

charge: ~ **hand** ▶1251│ *n* sous-chef *m* d'équipe;
~ **nurse** ▶1251│ *n* infirmier/-ière *m*/f en chef.

char-grilled /'tʃɑː.grɪld/ *adj* grillé au charbon de bois.

chariot /'tʃærɪət/ *n* char *m*.

charisma /kə'rɪzmə/ *n* GEN, RELIG charisme *m*.

charismatic /,kærɪz'mætɪk/ *adj* charismatique.

charitable /'tʃærɪtəbl/ *adj* [*person, act, explanation*]
charitable (**to** envers); [*organization*] caritatif/-ive; **a
company having ~ status** ~ une association reconnue d'utilité publique; ~ **trust** fondation *f* d'utilité
publique; ~ **work** bonnes œuvres *fpl*.

charitably /'tʃærɪtəblɪ/ *adv* charitablement.

charity /'tʃærətɪ/ **I** *n* **1** (virtue) charité *f*; **out of ~** par
charité; **2** (aid, aid organizations) **to give to/collect
money for ~** donner à/collecter des fonds pour des
œuvres de bienfaisance; **to accept/refuse ~**
accepter/refuser l'aumône *f*; **3** (individual organization)
organisation *f* caritative.
II *noun modifier* [*sale, event*] au profit d'œuvres de
bienfaisance.
IDIOMS ~ **begins at home** PROV charité bien
ordonnée commence par soi-même PROV.

charity: ~ **box** *n* (in church) tronc *m*; ~ **shop** *n*
magasin *m* d'articles d'occasion (*vendus au profit d'une
œuvre de bienfaisance*); ~ **work** *n* travail *m* bénévole
(*au profit d'une œuvre de bienfaisance*).

charlady† /'tʃɑːleɪdɪ/ ▶1251│ *n* GB femme *f* de
ménage.

charm /tʃɑːm/ **I** *n* **1** (capacity to please) charme *m*; **to
turn on the ~** PÉJ se mettre à faire du charme; **2**
(jewellery) amulette *f*; ~ **bracelet** bracelet *m* à brelo-
ques; **lucky ~** porte-bonheur *m inv*; **3** (magic words)
charme *m*.
II *vtr* charmer; **he ~ed his way into Head Office** il
usa de tout son charme pour parvenir jusqu'à la direction; **the ~ed (inner) circle** les initiés *mpl*.
IDIOMS **to lead a ~ed life** être béni des dieux; **to
work like a ~** faire merveille.

charmer /'tʃɑːmə(r)/ *n* **he is a real ~** il est adorable.

charming /'tʃɑːmɪŋ/ *adj* [*person, place*] charmant;
[*child, animal*] adorable.

chart /tʃɑːt/ **I** *n* **1** (graph) graphique *m*; **temperature
~** MED feuille *f* de température; **2** (table) tableau *m*;
3 (map) carte *f*; **weather ~** carte du temps; **4** MUS
the ~s le hit-parade; **number one in the ~s**
numéro un au hit-parade.
II *vtr* **1** (on map) porter [qch] sur la carte [*feature*];
tracer [*route*]; **2** (record) enregistrer [*changes,
progress*].

charter /'tʃɑːtə(r)/ **I** *n* **1** GEN, POL charte *f*; (for
company) acte *m* constitutif; **2** (hiring) affrètement *m*;
on ~ to sous contrat d'affrètement avec.
II *vtr* affréter [*plane*].
III chartered *pp adj* [*professional*] agréé; [*corporation*] à charte.

charter: ~**ed accountant**, CA ▶1251│ *n* GB ~
expert-comptable *m*; ~**ed surveyor** ▶1251│ *n* GB
expert *m* immobilier; ~ **flight** *n* GB vol *m* charter;
~ **plane** *n* GB charter *m*.

chary /'tʃeərɪ/ *adj* méfiant; **to be ~** se méfier.

chase /tʃeɪs/ **I** *n* **1** (pursuit) poursuite *f* (**after** de); **car/
police ~** poursuite *f* en voiture/par la police; **to give
~ to sb** se lancer à la poursuite de qn; **2** (race)
course *f* (**for** à).
II *vtr* **1** (also ~ **after**) (pursue) pourchasser [*person,
animal*]; courir après [*contract, job*]; **to ~ sb/sth up**
ou **down the street** courir après qn/qch dans la rue;
2 (also ~ **after**) (make advances) courir après; **3**° (also
~ **after**) (try to win) viser [*title*]; **4** (remove) **to ~ sb/
sth from** chasser qn/qch de [*room*]; **5** (engrave) ciseler.
IDIOMS **to ~ one's (own) tail** tourner en rond.
■ **chase about**, **chase around**: ¶ ~ **about** courir
en tous sens; ¶ ~ **around**° [sth] parcourir [qch]
dans tous les sens [*building, town*]; ¶ ~ [sb] **around**
poursuivre.
■ **chase away**: ~ [sb/sth] **away**, ~ **away** [sb/
sth] LIT, FIG chasser.
■ **chase down** US = **chase up**.

■ **chase off** = **chase away**.

■ **chase up** GB: ¶ ~ **up** [sth] retrouver [*details,
statistics*]; ¶ ~ [sb] **up**, ~ **up** [sb] activer [*person*].

chaser° /'tʃeɪsə(r)/ *n* petit coup *m* entre deux verres°.

chasm /'kæzəm/ *n* gouffre *m*; (deeper) abîme *m*; FIG
abîme *m*.

chassis /'ʃæsɪ/ *n* (*pl* ~) châssis *m*.

chaste /tʃeɪst/ *adj* **1** (celibate) chaste; **2** (innocent) [*relationship*] innocent; [*kiss*] chaste; **3** (sober) [*style*] sobre.

chasten /'tʃeɪsn/ **I**† *vtr* réprimander.
II chastened *pp adj* assagi; **they were suitably
~ed** comme il se doit cela les a fait réfléchir.

chastening /'tʃeɪsnɪŋ/ *adj* humiliant.

chastise /tʃæ'staɪz/ *vtr* châtier.

chastity /'tʃæstətɪ/ *n* chasteté *f*.

chat /tʃæt/ **I** *n* conversation *f*; **to have a ~** bavarder
(**with** avec; **about** sur); **I must have a ~ with her
about her work** il faut que je lui parle de son travail.
II *vi* (*p prés etc* -**tt**) bavarder (**with, to** avec).
■ **chat up**°: ~ **up** [sb], ~ [sb] **up** GB (flirtatiously)
draguer°; (to obtain sth) baratiner°.

chat show *n* GB talk-show *m*.

chattel /'tʃætl/ *n* JUR bien *m*, possession *f*; **goods
and ~s** biens et effets.

chatter /'tʃætə(r)/ **I** *n* (of person) bavardage *m*; (of
crowd, audience) bourdonnement *m*; (of birds) GEN
gazouillis *m*; (of magpies) jacassement *m*; (of machine)
cliquetis *m*.
II *vi* (of person) **to ~ away, ~ on**) [*person*] bavarder;
[*birds*] gazouiller; [*magpies*] jacasser; [*machine*] cliqueter; **her teeth were ~ing** elle claquait des dents.

chatterbox /'tʃætəbɒks/ *n* moulin *m* à paroles°.

chatty /'tʃætɪ/ *adj* [*person*] ouvert; [*letter, style*] vivant.

chauffeur /'ʃəʊfə(r)/, US /ʃəʊ'fɜː/ ▶1251│ **I** *n* chauffeur
m; **a ~-driven car** une voiture avec chauffeur.
II *vtr* conduire.

chauvinism /'ʃəʊvɪnɪzəm/ *n* **1** GEN chauvinisme *m*;
2 (also **male ~**) machisme *m*.

chauvinist /'ʃəʊvɪnɪst/ *n, adj* **1** GEN chauvin/-e (*m/
f*); **2** (also **male ~**) macho° (*m*).

chauvinistic /,ʃəʊvɪ'nɪstɪk/ *adj* chauvin.

cheap /tʃiːp/ **I** *adj* **1** (not expensive) bon marché *inv*; **to
be ~** être bon marché, ne pas coûter cher *inv*; **it's
~ to produce** cela ne revient pas cher de le/la
produire; **it works out ~er to take the train** cela
revient moins cher de prendre le train; **the ~ seats**
les places moins chères; **it's ~ at the price** c'est une
occasion à ce prix-là; ~ **and cheerful** sans prétentions; **life is ~** la vie est sans importance; **to hold
sth ~** ne pas respecter qch; **2** PÉJ (shoddy) de
mauvaise qualité; **it's ~ and nasty** c'est de la camelote; **3** PÉJ (easy) [*joke, gimmick*] facile; **a ~ thrill**
une sensation forte; **talk is ~** bavarder est facile; **4**
PÉJ (mean) [*trick, liar*] sale (*before n*); **a ~ shot** un
coup bas.
II *adv*° [*buy, get, sell*] pour rien; **they're going ~** ils
sont au rabais.
III on the cheap *adv phr* [*buy, sell*] au rabais; **to do
things on the ~** PÉJ y aller à l'économie°.

cheapen /'tʃiːpən/ *vtr* rendre [qch] moins cher [*process*]; dévaloriser [*life, liberty*].

cheaply /'tʃiːplɪ/ *adv* [*produce, do, sell*] à bas prix;
[*available, accessible*] à un prix raisonnable; **to eat ~**
manger pour pas cher.

cheapness /'tʃiːpnɪs/ *n* **1** (low cost) bas prix *m*; **2** (of
joke, trick) bassesse *f*.

cheap rate *adj, adv* TELECOM à tarif réduit; **to cost
25 pence a minute ~** coûter 25 pence la minute au
tarif réduit.

cheat /tʃiːt/ **I** *n* tricheur/-euse *m/f*.
II *vtr* tromper [*person, company*]; **to feel ~ed** se
sentir lésé; **to ~ sb (out) of** dépouiller qn de.
III *vi* tricher; **to ~ in** tricher à [*exam, test*]; **to ~ at
cards** tricher aux cartes; **to ~ on** tromper [*person*].

check /tʃek/ **I** *n* **1** (inspection) (for quality, security)
contrôle *m* (**on** sur); **security ~** contrôle de sécurité;
to carry out ~s exercer des contrôles; **to give sth a**

~ vérifier qch; **to keep a (close) ~ on** sb/sth surveiller qn/qch (de près); **2** MED examen *m*; **eye ~** examen des yeux; **3** (restraint) frein *m* (**on** à); **to put** ou **place a ~ on** mettre un frein à [*production, growth*]; **to hold** ou **keep** sb/sth **in ~** contrôler qn/qch; **to hold oneself in ~** se maîtriser; **4** (in chess) **in ~** en échec; **to put the king in ~** faire échec au roi; **your king is in ~** échec au roi; **5** (fabric) tissu *m* à carreaux; (pattern) carreaux *mpl*; **6** US (cheque) chèque *m*; **7** US (bill) addition *f*; **to pick up the ~** payer l'addition; **8** US (receipt) ticket *m*; **9** US (tick) croix *f* (*pour cocher*).

II *noun modifier* [*fabric, garment etc*] à carreaux.

III *vtr* **1** (for security) vérifier [*vehicle, mechanism, fuse*]; contrôler [*person, product, ticket, area*]; **to ~ that/whether** vérifier que/si; **they ~ed the hotel for bombs** ils se sont assurés qu'il n'y avait pas de bombe dans l'hôtel; **2** (for accuracy, reliability) vérifier [*bill, spelling, data, signature, banknote*]; contrôler [*accounts, invoice, output, work*]; corriger [*proofs*]; **to ~ sth for defects** contrôler la qualité de qch; **to ~ that/whether** vérifier que/si; **to ~ sth against** vérifier qch par rapport à [*data, inventory*]; comparer qch avec [*signature*]; **3** (for health, progress) prendre [*temperature, blood pressure*]; tester [*reflexes*]; examiner [*eyesight*]; **to ~ that/whether** vérifier que/si; **4** (inspect) examiner [*watch, map, pocket*]; **5** (find out) vérifier [*times, details*]; **6** (curb) contrôler [*price rises, inflation*]; freiner [*increase, growth, progress*]; réduire [*abuse, emigration, influence*]; démentir [*rumour*]; déjouer [*plans*]; **7** (restrain, keep in) maîtriser [*emotions*]; retenir [*tears*]; **8** (stop) arrêter [*person, enemy, rebellion*]; **9** (in chess) faire échec à; **10** US (for safekeeping) mettre [qch] au vestiaire [*coat*]; mettre [qch] à la consigne [*baggage*]; **11** US (register) enregistrer [*baggage*]; **12** US (tick) = **check off**.

IV *vi* **1** (verify) vérifier; **to ~ with** sb demander à qn; **2** (examine) **to ~ for** dépister [*problems, disease*]; chercher [*leaks, flaws*]; **3** (register) **to ~ into** arriver à [*hotel*]; **4** US (tally) [*accounts*] être exact.

V *v refl* (restrain) **to ~ oneself** se retenir.

VI *excl* **1** (in chess) **~!** échec au roi!; **2** US (in agreement) d'accord.

VII checked *pp adj* [*fabric, garment*] à carreaux.

■ **check in**: ¶ **~ in** (at airport) enregistrer; (at hotel) remplir la fiche (**at** à); US (clock in) pointer (à l'entrée); ¶ **~** [sb/sth] **in**, **~ in** [sb/sth] **1** AVIAT, TOURISM enregistrer [*baggage, passengers*]; accueillir [*hotel guest*]; **2** US (for safekeeping) mettre [qch] à la consigne [*baggage*]; mettre [qch] au vestiaire [*coat*].

■ **check off**: **~ off** [sth], **~** [sth] **off** cocher [*items*].

■ **check on**: **~ on** [sb/sth] **1** (observe) surveiller [*person*]; **to ~ on** sb's **progress** vérifier les progrès de qn; **2** (investigate) faire une enquête sur [*person*]; **to ~ on how/whether** voir comment/si.

■ **check out**: ¶ **~ out 1** (leave) partir; **to ~ out of** quitter [*hotel*]; **2** (be correct) être correct; **3** US (clock out) pointer (à la sortie); ¶ **~ out** [sth], **~** [sth] **out 1** (investigate) vérifier [*information*]; examiner [*package, building*]; se renseigner sur [*club, scheme*]; **2** US (try) essayer; **3** US (remove) (from library) emprunter; (from cloakroom, left luggage) retirer; ¶ **~** [sb] **out**, **~ out** [sb] faire une enquête sur [*person*].

■ **check over**: ¶ **~** [sth] **over** vérifier [*document, wiring, machine*]; ¶ **~** [sb] **over** MED faire un examen médical à [*person*].

■ **check through**: **~** [sth] **through 1** vérifier [*work*]; **2** US AVIAT enregistrer [*luggage*] (**to** pour).

■ **check up**: **~ up** vérifier (**that** que); **to ~ up on** (observe) surveiller [*person*]; (investigate) faire une enquête sur [*person*]; vérifier [*story, details*].

checkbook /ˈtʃekbʊk/ *n* US carnet *m* de chèques, chéquier *m*.

checker /ˈtʃekə(r)/ ▶ 1251 **I** *n* **1** (employee) vérificateur/-trice *m/f*; **2** US (cashier) caissier/-ière *m/f*; **3** US (in fabric) carreau *m*; **4** US GAMES (piece) pion *m*.

II checkers *npl* ▶ 949 jeu *m* de dames; **to play ~s** jouer aux dames.

checkerboard /ˈtʃekəbɔːd/ *n* US damier *m*.

checkered *adj* US = **chequered**.

check-in /ˈtʃekɪn/ **I** *n* **1** (also **~ desk**) enregistrement *m*; **2** (procedure) enregistrement *m*.

II *noun modifier* [*counter*] d'enregistrement; **~ time** enregistrement *m*.

checking /ˈtʃekɪŋ/ *n* vérification *f*.

checking account *n* US compte *m* courant.

checklist /ˈtʃeklɪst/ *n* liste *f* de contrôle.

checkmate /ˈtʃekmeɪt/ **I** *n* échec *m* et mat; FIG échec *m*.

II *vtr* faire échec à [*opponent*]; FIG battre [qn] à plates coutures°.

checkout /ˈtʃekaʊt/ *n* caisse *f*; **on the ~** à la caisse.

checkout assistant, **checkout operator** *n* GB caissier/-ière *m/f*.

checkpoint /ˈtʃekpɔɪnt/ *n* poste *m* de contrôle.

checkroom /ˈtʃekruːm, -rɒm/ *n* US **1** (cloakroom) vestiaire *m*; **2** (for baggage) consigne *f*.

checkup /ˈtʃekʌp/ *n* **1** MED examen *m* médical, bilan *m* de santé; **to go for/have a ~** passer/se faire faire un examen médical; **2** (at the dentist's) visite *f* de routine.

cheddar /ˈtʃedə(r)/ *n* cheddar *m* (*fromage*).

cheek /tʃiːk/ **I** *n* **1** (of face) joue *f*; **~ to ~** joue contre joue; **2** (impudence) culot° *m*; **what a ~!** quel culot°!

II *vtr*° GB être insolent envers [*person*].

IDIOMS to turn the other ~ tendre l'autre joue.

cheekbone /ˈtʃiːkbəʊn/ *n* pommette *f*.

cheekily /ˈtʃiːkɪlɪ/ *adv* [*say*] effrontément; [*perched*] crânement.

cheeky /ˈtʃiːkɪ/ *adj* **1** (impudent) [*person*] effronté, insolent; [*question*] impoli; **2** (pert) [*grin*] espiègle, coquin.

cheer /tʃɪə(r)/ **I** *n* acclamation *f*; **to give a ~** pousser une acclamation ou un hourra; **to get a ~** être acclamé; **to give three ~s for** faire un ban à; **three ~s!** un ban!, hourra!

II cheers *excl* **1** (toast) à la vôtre°!; (to close friend) à la tienne°!; **2°** GB (thanks) merci!; **3°** GB (goodbye) salut!

III *vtr, vi* applaudir.

■ **cheer on**: **~ on** [sb], **~** [sb] **on** encourager [*person*].

■ **cheer up**: ¶ **~ up** reprendre courage; **~ up!** courage!; ¶ **~** [sb] **up** remonter le moral à [*person*]; ¶ **~ up** [sth], **~** [sth] **up** égayer [*room*].

cheerful /ˈtʃɪəfl/ *adj* [*person, smile, mood, music*] joyeux/-euse; [*news*] réjouissant; [*remark, tone*] enjoué; [*colour*] gai; [*optimism*] inébranlable; **to be ~ about** se réjouir de.

cheerfully /ˈtʃɪəfəlɪ/ *adv* (joyfully) joyeusement; (blithely) allégrement.

cheerfulness /ˈtʃɪəflnɪs/ *n* gaieté *f*.

cheerily /ˈtʃɪərɪlɪ/ *adv* joyeusement, gaiement.

cheering /ˈtʃɪərɪŋ/ **I** *n* ℂ acclamations *fpl*.

II *adj* [*message, news, words*] réconfortant, réjouissant.

cheerio /ˌtʃɪərɪˈəʊ/ *excl* salut°.

cheerleader /ˈtʃɪəliːdə(r)/ *n* majorette *f*.

cheerless /ˈtʃɪəlɪs/ *adj* [*place*] triste, morne; [*outlook*] sombre.

cheery /ˈtʃɪərɪ/ *adj* joyeux/-euse, gai.

cheese /tʃiːz/ *n* fromage *m*; **~ sandwich** sandwich au fromage.

IDIOMS they are as different as chalk and ~ c'est le jour et la nuit; **say ~!** (for photo) souriez!

■ **cheese off**°: **to be ~d off with** en avoir marre° de.

cheese: **~board** *n* (object) plateau *m* à fromage; (selection) plateau *m* de fromages; **~burger** *n* hamburger *m* au fromage; **~cake** *n* CULIN cheesecake *m*; **~cloth** *n* étamine *f*; **~ counter** *n* fromagerie *f*; **~paring** *n* économies *fpl* de bouts de chandelle.

cheesy /ˈtʃiːzɪ/ *adj* **1** [*smell*] de fromage; **2** [*grin*] large.

cheetah /ˈtʃiːtə/ *n* guépard *m*.

chef /ʃef/ ▶ **1251** | *n* chef *m* cuisinier.

chemical /'kemɪkl/ **I** *n* produit *m* chimique.
II *adj* [*process, reaction, industry, formula, warfare, waste*] chimique; [*equipment, experiment*] de chimie.

chemical engineer ▶ **1251** | *n* ingénieur *m* chimiste.

chemise /ʃə'miːz/ *n* (dress) robe-combinaison *f*; (undergarment) chemise *f*.

chemist /'kemɪst/ ▶ **1251** |, **1251** | *n* **1** GB (person) pharmacien/-ienne *m/f*; ~'s (**shop**) pharmacie *f*; **2** (scientist) chimiste *mf*.

chemistry /'kemɪstrɪ/ *n* **1** (science) chimie *f*; **2** (structure, properties) propriétés *fpl* chimiques; **3** FIG (rapport) affinités *fpl*.

chemotherapy /ˌkiːməʊ'θerəpɪ/ *n* chimiothérapie *f*.

cheque GB, **check** US /tʃek/ *n* chèque *m*; **by** ~ par chèque; **to make out** ou **write a** ~ **for £20** faire un chèque de 20 livres sterling.
IDIOMS **to give sb a blank** ~ FIG donner carte blanche à qn.

cheque: ~**book** GB, **checkbook** US *n* chéquier *m*, carnet *m* de chèques; ~ **card** *n* carte *f* de garantie bancaire.

chequer GB, **checker** US /'tʃekə(r)/ *n* **1** GAMES pion *m*; **2** (square) carreau *m*; (pattern) damier *m*.

chequered GB, **checkered** US /'tʃekəd/ *adj* **1** (patterned) à damiers; **2** FIG [*career, history*] en dents de scie.

chequers GB, **checkers** US /'tʃekəz/ ▶ **949** | *n* (+ *v sg*) dames *fpl*.

cherish /'tʃerɪʃ/ *vtr* **1** (nurture) caresser [*hope, ambition*]; chérir [*memory, idea*]; **her most** ~**ed ambition** son ambition la plus chère; **2**† (love) chérir.

cherry /'tʃerɪ/ ▶ **818** | **I** *n* **1** (fruit) cerise *f*; **2** (tree, wood) cerisier *m*.
II *adj* (also ~**red**) rouge cerise *inv*.
IDIOMS **life is not a bowl of cherries** la vie n'est pas rose.

cherry: ~ **brandy** *n* cherry *m*; ~ **orchard** *n* cerisaie *f*; ~ **tomato** *n* tomate *f* cerise; ~ **tree** *n* cerisier *m*.

cherub /'tʃerəb/ *n* (angel) chérubin *m*; (child) angelot *m*.

cherubic /tʃɪ'ruːbɪk/ *adj* [*face*] de chérubin; [*child*] angélique.

chervil /'tʃɜːvɪl/ *n* cerfeuil *m*.

chess /tʃes/ ▶ **949** | *n* échecs *mpl*; **a game of** ~ une partie d'échecs.

chess: ~**board** *n* échiquier *m*; ~**man**, ~**piece** *n* pièce *f* (de jeu d'échecs); ~ **set** *n* jeu *m* d'échecs.

chest /tʃest/ **I** *n* **1** ANAT poitrine *f*; **2** (furniture) coffre *m*; **3** (crate) caisse *f*.
II *noun modifier* [*pains*] de poitrine; [*infection, specialist*] des voies respiratoires; [*X-ray*] des poumons.
IDIOMS **to get something off one's** ~° vider son sac°; **to hold** ou **keep one's cards close to one's** ~ ne pas jouer cartes sur table.

chest: ~ **freezer** *n* congélateur *m* coffre; ~ **measurement** ▶ **1260** | *n* tour *m* de poitrine.

chestnut /'tʃesnʌt/ **I** *n* **1** (also ~ **tree**) (horse) marronnier *m* (d'Inde); (sweet) châtaignier *m*; **2** (timber) châtaignier *m*; **3** (nut) marron *m*, châtaigne *f*; **4** (horse) alezan *m*; **5** FIG (joke) **an old** ~ une plaisanterie éculée.
II *noun modifier* [*cream, puree*] de marrons; [*stuffing*] aux marrons.
III *adj* [*hair*] châtain; **a** ~ **horse** un (cheval) alezan.

chest of drawers *n* commode *f*.

chesty° /'tʃestɪ/ *adj* [*person*] fragile des bronches; [*cough*] de poitrine.

chew /tʃuː/ **I** *n* **1** (act) mâchement *m*; **2** (sweet) bonbon *m*.
II *vtr* **1** [*person*] mâcher [*food, gum*]; mordiller [*pencil etc*]; **to** ~ **a hole in sth** faire un trou dans qch (en rongeant); **2** [*animal*] ronger [*bone*]; mordiller [*carpet etc*].
III *vi* mâcher.

IDIOMS **to bite off more than one can** ~ être trop ambitieux/-ieuse.

■ **chew over**°: ~ **over** [sth], ~ [sth] **over**° cogiter sur° [*problem*].

chewing gum /'tʃuːɪŋ gʌm/ *n* chewing-gum *m*.

chewy /'tʃuːɪ/ *adj* difficile à mâcher.

chiaroscuro /kɪˌɑːrə'skʊərəʊ/ *n* clair-obscur *m*.

chic /ʃiːk/ **I** *n* chic *m*; **to have** ~ avoir du chic.
II *adj* chic *inv*.

chick /tʃɪk/ *n* **1** (fledgling) oisillon *m*; (of fowl) poussin *m*; **2**° (young woman) nana° *f*.

chicken /'tʃɪkɪn/ **I** *n* **1** (fowl) poulet *m*, poule *f*; **2** CULIN poulet *m*; **3**° (coward) poule *f* mouillée.
II *noun modifier* [*wing, stock*] de poulet; [*sandwich, soup*] au poulet.
IDIOMS **it's a** ~ **and egg situation** c'est l'histoire de l'œuf et de la poule; **to count one's** ~**s** (**before they are hatched**) vendre la peau de l'ours avant de l'avoir tué.

■ **chicken out**° se dégonfler°.

chicken: ~ **breast** *n* filet *m* de poulet; ~ **curry** *n* poulet *m* au curry; ~ **drumstick** *n* pilon *m*; ~ **farmer** ▶ **1251** | *n* éleveur *m* de volailles.

chicken feed *n* ¢ **1** AGRIC nourriture *f* pour volaille; **2**° (paltry sum) bagatelle *f*, somme *f* dérisoire.

chicken: ~ **livers** *npl* foies *mpl* de volaille; ~ **noodle soup** *n* soupe *f* de poulet au vermicelle; ~ **pox** ▶ **1002** | *n* varicelle *f*; ~ **run** *n* basse-cour *f*; ~ **wire** *n* grillage *m* (à mailles fines).

chickpea *n* pois *m* chiche.

chicory /'tʃɪkərɪ/ *n* **1** (vegetable) endive *f*; **2** (in coffee) chicorée *f*.

chief /tʃiːf/ **I** *n* **1** (leader) GEN chef *m*; **party** ~ POL dirigeant/-e *m/f* de parti; **defence** ~**s** POL responsables *mpl* de la défense; **2**° (boss) chef *m*, patron° *m*.
II *adj* **1** (primary) principal *m*; **2** (highest in rank) en chef.
III -**in-chief** *combining form* en chef.

chief: ~ **accountant** *n* chef comptable *m*; ~ **constable** *n* GB ≈ directeur *m* de police.

chief executive *n* **1** ADMIN, COMM directeur *m* général; **2** US POL Chef *m* de l'Exécutif (*le Président*).

chief inspector *n* GEN inspecteur/-trice *m/f* principal/-e; GB (of police) inspecteur *m* de police divisionnaire.

chiefly /'tʃiːflɪ/ *adv* notamment, surtout.

chief: ~ **of police** *n* ≈ préfet *m* de police; **Chief of Staff, C of S** ▶ **1192** | *n* MIL chef *m* d'état-major; (of White House) secrétaire *m* général; ~ **of state** *n* US chef *m* d'État; ~ **petty officer, CPO** ▶ **1192** | *n* premier maître *m*; **Chief Rabbi** *n* Grand Rabbin *m*; ~ **superintendent** *n* GB ≈ commissaire *m* divisionnaire.

chieftain /'tʃiːftən/ *n* chef *m* (*de clan ou de tribu*).

chiffon /'ʃɪfɒn, US ʃɪ'fɒn/ **I** *n* mousseline *f*.
II *noun modifier* [*dress, scarf*] en mousseline.

chilblain /'tʃɪlbleɪn/ *n* engelure *f*.

child /tʃaɪld/ *n* (*pl* **children**) enfant *mf*; **when I was a** ~ quand j'étais enfant; ~ **star/prodigy** enfant vedette/prodige; FIG ~ **of nature** FIG enfant de la nature.
IDIOMS **it's** ~'s **play** c'est un jeu d'enfant.

child abuse *n* GEN mauvais traitements *mpl* infligés à un enfant; (sexual) sévices *mpl* sexuels exercés sur l'enfant.

childbearing /'tʃaɪldbeərɪŋ/ *n* maternité *f*; **of** ~ **age** en âge d'avoir des enfants, nubile.

child benefit *n* GB ≈ allocations *fpl* familiales.

childbirth /'tʃaɪldbɜːθ/ *n* accouchement *m*; **in** ~ en couches.

child: ~**care** *n* (nurseries etc) structures *fpl* d'accueil pour les enfants d'âge préscolaire; (bringing up children) éducation *f* des enfants; ~**care facilities** *npl* crèche *f*; ~ **guidance** *n* GB assistance *f* sociopsychologique de l'enfance.

childhood /'tʃaɪldhʊd/ **I** *n* enfance *f*; **in** (**his**) **early** ~ dans sa prime enfance.

II *noun modifier* [*friend, memory*] d'enfance; [*illness*] infantile; [*event*] survenu dans mon/son etc enfance.

childish /'tʃaɪldɪʃ/ *adj* **1** (of child) d'enfant; **2** PÉJ (immature) puéril.

childishly /'tsaɪldɪʃlɪ/ *adv* comme un enfant.

childishness /'tʃaɪldɪʃnɪs/ *n* puérilité *f*.

childless /'tʃaɪldlɪs/ *adj* sans enfants.

childlike /'tʃaɪldlaɪk/ *adj* enfantin.

child: **~minder** ▶ **1251** *n* GB nourrice *f*; **~ molester** *n* agresseur *m* d'enfants; **~-proof** *adj* [*container, lock*] de sécurité (*à l'épreuve des enfants*).

children /'tʃɪldrən/ *pl* ▶ **child**.

children's home *n* maison *f* d'enfants.

Chile /'tʃɪlɪ/ ▶ **840** *pr n* Chili *m*.

chill /tʃɪl/ **I** *n* **1** (coldness) fraîcheur *f*; **there is a ~ in the air** le fond de l'air est frais; **2** (illness) coup *m* de froid; **to catch a ~** prendre or attraper un coup de froid; **3** FIG frisson *m*; **to send a ~ down sb's spine** donner des frissons à qn.

II *adj* **1** LIT [*wind*] frais/fraîche; **2** FIG [*reminder, words*] brutal.

III *vtr* **1** CULIN (make cool) mettre [qch] à refroidir [*dessert, soup*]; rafraîchir [*wine*]; (keep cool) réfrigérer; **2** (make cold) faire frissonner [*person*]; **3** FIG (cause to fear) faire frissonner [*person*]; **to ~ sb's ou the blood** glacer le sang à qn.

IV *vi* [*dessert*] refroidir; [*wine*] rafraîchir.

V chilled *pp adj* [*wine*] bien frais; [*food*] réfrigéré.

■ **chill out**° décompresser°; **~ out!** laisse faire!

chilli, chili /'tʃɪlɪ/ *n* **1** (pod) (also **~ pepper**) piment *m* rouge; (powder) chili *m*; **2** (also **~ con carne**) chili *m* con carne.

chilling /'tʃɪlɪŋ/ *adj* [*story, thought, look*] effrayant.

chilly /'tʃɪlɪ/ *adj* LIT, FIG froid; **it's ~** il fait froid.

chime /tʃaɪm/ **I** *n* (of clock, church bell) carillon *m*; **the ~s of the clock** (sound) le carillon de l'horloge.

II *vi* (strike) sonner; (play a tune) carillonner; **the clock ~d three** la pendule a sonné trois heures.

■ **chime in** interrompre.

chimera /kaɪ'mɪərə/ *n* LITTÉR (beast, idea) chimère *f*.

chimeric /kaɪ'merɪk/ *adj* chimérique.

chimney /'tʃɪmnɪ/ *n* (*pl* **-neys**) cheminée *f*; (in mountaineering) cheminée *f*; **in the ~ corner** au coin du feu.

chimney: **~breast** *n* manteau *m* de cheminée; **~pot** *n* mitron *m* (*sur cheminée*); **~stack** *n* cheminée *f*; **~ sweep** ▶ **1251** *n* ramoneur *m*.

chimp° /tʃɪmp/ *n* = **chimpanzee**.

chimpanzee /,tʃɪmpən'ziː, ,tʃɪmpæn'ziː/ *n* chimpanzé *m*.

chin /tʃɪn/ *n* menton *m*; **weak ~** menton fuyant.

IDIOMS **to keep one's ~ up**° tenir le coup°; **~ up!** tiens bon!; **to take it on the ~**° encaisser° bravement.

china /'tʃaɪnə/ **I** *n* ¢ porcelaine *f*; **a piece of ~** une porcelaine; **rare ~** porcelaines *fpl* rares.

II *noun modifier* [*cup, plate*] en porcelaine.

IDIOMS **like a bull in a ~ shop** comme un éléphant dans un magasin de porcelaine.

China /'tʃaɪnə/ ▶ **840** *pr n* Chine *f*.

IDIOMS **not for all the tea in ~** pour rien au monde.

china cabinet *n* vitrine *f* (*meuble*).

China: **~ Sea** *pr n* mer *f* de Chine; **~ tea** n thé *m* de Chine; **~town** n le quartier chinois.

Chinese /tʃaɪ'niːz/ ▶ **1100**, **1038** **I** *n* **1** (person) Chinois/-oise *m/f*; **2** (language) chinois *m*.

II *adj* chinois/-oise; **to eat ~** manger chinois.

Chinese: **~ cabbage** *n* US = **Chinese leaves**; **~ gooseberry** *n* kiwi *m*; **~ leaves** *npl* GB chou *m* de Chine; **~ puzzle** *n* LIT, FIG casse-tête *m inv* chinois.

chink /tʃɪŋk/ **I** *n* **1** (slit) (in wall) fente *f*; (in door, curtain) entrebâillement *m*; **2** (sound) tintement *m*.

II *vi* [*glasses, coins*] tinter.

IDIOMS **it's the ~ in his armour** c'est le défaut de sa cuirasse.

chinos /'tʃiːnəʊs/ *npl* pantalon *m* kaki.

chintz /tʃɪnts/ *n* chintz *m*.

chip /tʃɪp/ **I** *n* **1** (fragment) GEN fragment *m* (**of** de); (of wood) copeau *m*; (of glass) éclat *m*; **2** (in wood, china glass) ébréchure *f*; **3** GB CULIN (fried potato) frite *f*; **4** US (potato crisp) chips *f*; **5** COMPUT puce *f* (électronique); (in gambling) plaque *f*; (smaller) jeton *m*.

II *vtr* (*p prés etc* **-pp-**) **1** (damage) ébrécher [*glass, plate*]; écorner [*precious stone*]; écailler [*paint*]; **to ~ a tooth** se casser une dent; **2** (carve) tailler.

III *vi* (*p prés etc* **-pp-**) [*plate, glass*] s'ébrécher; [*paint*] s'écailler; [*tooth*] se casser; [*gem*] s'écorner.

IDIOMS **to have a ~ on one's shoulder** être amer/-ère; **to be a ~ off the old block** être bien le fils de son père/la fille de sa mère; **when the ~s are down** dans les moments difficiles; **he's had his ~s**° GB il est cuit°.

■ **chip away**: ¶ **~ away** [*paint, plaster*] s'écailler; **to ~ away at** tailler [*stone*]; FIG affaiblir [qch] progressivement [*authority*]; miner [*confidence*]; **~ away** [sth], **~** [sth] **away** enlever [qch] petit à petit [*plaster*].

■ **chip in** GB° **1** (in conversation) GEN interrompre; (officiously) mettre son grain de sel°; **2** (contribute money) donner un peu d'argent.

■ **chip off**: ¶ **~ off** [*paint, plaster*] s'écailler; ¶ **~ off** [sth], **~** [sth] **off** écailler [*plaster*] (**from** de).

chipboard *n* aggloméré *m*.

chipmunk /'tʃɪpmʌŋk/ *n* tamia *m*.

chip: **~ pan** *n* friteuse *f*; **~ped potatoes** *npl* frites *fpl*.

chippings /'tʃɪpɪŋz/ *npl* gravillons *mpl*; **'loose ~!'** 'danger: gravillons!'

chippy° /'tʃɪpɪ/ *n* GB marchand *m* de frites.

chip shop ▶ **1251** *n* marchand *m* de frites.

chiropodist /kɪ'rɒpədɪst/ ▶ **1251** *n* pédicure *mf*.

chiropody /kɪ'rɒpədɪ/ *n* podologie *f*.

chiropractor /'kaɪərəʊpræktə(r)/ ▶ **1251** *n* chiropraticien/-ienne *m/f*, chiropracteur *m*.

chirp /tʃɜːp/ **I** *n* pépiement *m*.

II *vi* [*bird*] pépier.

chirpy° /'tʃɜːpɪ/ *adj* pétillant.

chisel /'tʃɪzl/ **I** *n* ciseau *m*.

II *vtr* **1** (*p prés etc* **-ll-**, US **-l-**) (shape) tailler au ciseau; (finely) ciseler; **finely ~led features** traits finement ciselés; **2** US rouler° (**out of** de).

chit /tʃɪt/ *n* **1** GB (voucher) bon *m*; (bill, note, memo) note *f*; **2**° PÉJ **a ~ of a girl** une gamine.

chitchat /'tʃɪttʃæt/ *n* bavardage *m*; **to spend one's time in idle ~** perdre son temps en bavardages.

chivalrous /'ʃɪvəlrəs/ *adj* **1** (heroic) [*deeds, conduct*] chevaleresque; **2** (polite) galant.

chivalry /'ʃɪvəlrɪ/ *n* **1** ¢ (qualities, system of values) chevalerie *f*; **2** (courtesy) galanterie *f*.

chive /tʃaɪv/ *n* (*gén pl*) ciboulette *f*.

chivvy°, US **chivy**° /'tʃɪvɪ/ *vtr* harceler; **to ~ sb into doing** harceler qn jusqu'à ce qu'il fasse.

chloride /'klɔːraɪd/ *n* chlorure *m*.

chlorinate /'klɔːrɪneɪt/ *vtr* **1** CHEM chlorer; **2** (disinfect) javelliser [*water, swimming pool*].

chlorine /'klɔːriːn/ *n* chlore *m*.

chlorofluorocarbon, CFC /,klɔːrə,flʊəʊ'kɑːbən/ *n* chlorofluorocarbone *m*, CFC *m*.

chloroform /'klɒrəfɔːm/, US 'klɔːr-/ **I** *n* chloroforme *m*.

II *vtr* chloroformer.

chlorophyll /'klɒrəfɪl/ *n* chlorophylle *f*.

choc-ice /'tʃɒkaɪs/ *n* GB esquimau *m*.

chock /tʃɒk/ *n* cale *f*; **to put sth on ~s** mettre qch sur cales; **~ away!** enlevez les cales!

chock-a-block /,tʃɒkə'blɒk/ *adj* plein à craquer.

chock-full /,tʃɒk'fʊl/ *adj* archiplein (**of** de).

chocolate /'tʃɒklət/ ▶ **818** **I** *n* **1** (substance) chocolat *m*; **cooking ~** chocolat *m* de ménage; **2** (sweet) chocolat *m*; **3** (drink) chocolat *m*; **hot ~** chocolat *m* chaud; **4** (colour) chocolat *m*; **dark ~** tête-de-nègre *m*.

II noun modifier [eggs, sweets] en chocolat; [biscuit, cake, ice cream] au chocolat.

chocolate-coated adj enrobé de chocolat.

choice /tʃɔɪs/ **I** n **1** (selection) choix m; **to make a ~** faire un choix, choisir; **it was my ~ to do** c'est moi qui ai choisi de faire; **it's your ~** c'est à toi de choisir; **2 ¢** (right to select) choix m; **to have the ~** avoir le choix; **to have a free ~** être libre de choisir; **3** (option) choix m (between, of entre); **you have a ~ of three colours** tu as le choix entre trois couleurs; **to have no ~ but to do** se voir contraint de faire; **you have two ~s open to you** vous avez deux possibilités; **4** (range of options) choix m; **a wide ~** un grand choix; **a narrow ~** un choix limité; **to be spoilt for ~** avoir l'embarras du choix; **5 ¢** (preference) choix m; **a car of my ~** une voiture de mon choix; **out of** ou **from ~** par choix.
II adj **1** (quality) [example, steak] de choix; **2** (wellchosen) bien choisi.

choir /'kwaɪə(r)/ n **1** MUS (of church, school) chorale f; (professional) chœur m; (of boys at cathedral) maîtrise f; **to be** ou **sing in the ~** faire partie de la chorale; **2** ARCHIT chœur m.

choir: **~boy** n petit chanteur m, jeune choriste m; **~girl** n jeune choriste f; **~master** n chef m des chœurs; (in church) maître m de chapelle; **~ school** n GB maîtrise f, manécanterie f; **~ screen** n grille f de chœur; **~stall** n stalle f.

choke /tʃəʊk/ **I** n starter m; **to pull out/use the ~** tirer/mettre le starter.
II vtr **1** (throttle) étrangler [person]; **2** (impede breathing) [fumes, smoke] étouffer; **3** (render speechless) **~d with** [voice] étranglé par [emotion]; **4** (block) = **choke up**.
III vi s'étouffer; **to ~ on a fish bone/on a drink** s'étouffer avec une arête/en buvant; **to ~ to death** mourir étouffé; **to ~ with** étouffer de [rage].
IV choked○ pp adj **1** (angry) furieux/-ieuse (about au sujet de); **2** (upset) affecté (over, about par).
■ **choke back**: **~ back** [sth] étouffer [cough, sob]; **to ~ back one's tears** retenir ses larmes.
■ **choke off**: **~ off** [sth] stopper [lending, growth]; faire taire [opposition, protest].
■ **choke up**: **~** [sth] **up**, **~ up** [sth] (block) boucher [drain, road]; [weeds] étouffer [garden]; **~d up with traffic** embouteillé.

choker /'tʃəʊkə(r)/ n collier m ras de cou.

choking /'tʃəʊkɪŋ/ adj [gas, fumes] asphyxiant; [sensation] d'étouffement.

cholera /'kɒlərə/ ▶1002 **I** n choléra m.
II noun modifier [victim, epidemic] de choléra.

choleric /'kɒlərɪk/ adj colérique, coléreux/-euse.

cholesterol /kə'lestərɒl/ n cholestérol m.

cholesterol count, **cholesterol level** n taux m de cholestérol.

chomp /tʃɒmp/ **I** vtr mâcher bruyamment.
II vi mâcher bruyamment; **to ~ on sth** ronger qch.

choose /tʃuːz/ **I** vtr (prét **chose**; pp **chosen**) **1** (select) choisir [book, person, option] (from parmi); **to ~ sb as** choisir qn comme [adviser, friend]; élire qn [leader]; **2** (decide) décider (to do de faire).
II vi (prét **chose**; pp **chosen**) **1** (select) choisir (between entre); **there are many models to ~ from** il y a un grand choix de modèles; **there's not much to ~ from** il y a très peu de choix; **there's nothing to ~ between X and Y** il y a très peu de différence entre X et Y; **2** (prefer) vouloir; **to ~ to do** préférer faire.

choosy /'tʃuːzɪ/ adj difficile (about en ce qui concerne).

chop /tʃɒp/ **I** n **1** (blow) coup m; **2** CULIN côtelette f; **pork ~** côtelette f de porc.
II chops○ npl gueule❶ f; **to lick one's ~s** (at food) se lécher les babines; (at idea) se frotter les mains.
III vtr (p prés etc **-pp-**) **1** (cut up) couper [wood]; couper, émincer [vegetable, meat]; hacher [parsley, onion]; **to ~ sth into cubes** couper qch en cubes; **to ~ sth to pieces** ou **bits** couper qch en morceaux; **to**

~ sth finely hacher qch; **2** FIG (cut, reduce) réduire [service, deficit]; (cut out) couper [quote, footage].
IV chopped pp adj [parsley, nuts, meat] haché.
IDIOMS **~ ~**○! GB et que ça saute○!; **to ~ and change** [person] changer d'avis comme de chemise; [situation] évoluer par à-coups; **to get the ~**○ GB [person] se faire sacquer○; [scheme, service] être supprimé.
■ **chop down**: **~ down** [sth], **~** [sth] **down** abattre.
■ **chop off**: **~ off** [sth], **~** [sth] **off** couper [branch, end]; trancher [head, hand, finger].
■ **chop up**: **~ up** [sth], **~** [sth] **up** couper [wood, log]; émincer [meat, onion] (into en).

chopper /'tʃɒpə(r)/ **I** n **1** (axe) hache f; (for kitchen) hachoir m; **2**○ (helicopter) hélico○ m.
II choppers○ npl (real) dents fpl; (false) râtelier○ m, dentier m.

chopping block n billot m.
IDIOMS **to put one's head on the ~** prendre des risques.

chopping: **~ board** n planche f à découper; **~ knife** n couteau m de cuisine.

choppy /'tʃɒpɪ/ adj [sea, water] agité; [wind] instable.

chopstick /'tʃɒpstɪk/ n baguette f (chinoise).

choral /'kɔːrəl/ adj choral; **~ society** chorale f.

chord /kɔːd/ n **1** MUS accord m; **2** FIG (response) **it struck a ~ in** ou **with him/his listeners** cela a trouvé un écho en lui/chez ses auditeurs; **to strike the right ~** toucher la corde sensible; **3** (of harp) corde f.

chore /tʃɔː(r)/ n **1** (routine task) tâche f; **the (household) ~s** les tâches ménagères; **to do the ~s** faire le ménage; **2** (unpleasant task) corvée f.

choreograph /'kɒrɪəɡrɑːf, -ɡræf, US -ɡræf/ vtr LIT chorégraphier; FIG orchestrer.

choreographer /ˌkɒrɪ'ɒɡrəfə(r)/ ▶1251 n chorégraphe mf.

choreography /ˌkɒrɪ'ɒɡrəfɪ/ n chorégraphie f.

chorister /'kɒrɪstə(r)/, US 'kɔːr-/ n choriste mf.

chortle /'tʃɔːtl/ **I** n gloussement m.
II vi glousser, rire; **to ~ at** ou **about** ou **over sth** rire de qch.

chorus /'kɔːrəs/ **I** n **1** (people) (singers) chœur m; (dancers, actors) troupe f; (of town etc) chorale f; **2** (piece of music) chœur m; **3** (refrain) refrain m; (in jazz) chorus m; **to join in the ~** (one person) reprendre le refrain; (several people) reprendre le refrain en chœur; **4** (of bird song, yells) concert m; **a ~ of protest** une tempête de protestations; **in ~** en chœur; **5** THEAT chœur m.
II vtr (utter in unison) crier [qch] à l'unisson.

chorus girl n danseuse f de revue.

chose /tʃəʊz/ prét ▶ **choose**.

chosen /'tʃəʊzn/ **I** pp ▶ **choose**.
II adj élu; **the ~ few** les privilégiés; **the Chosen People** le peuple élu.

chowder /'tʃaʊdə(r)/ n: soupe épaisse à base de fruits de mer.

chow mein /ˌtʃaʊ 'meɪn/ n ¢ nouilles fpl frites.

Christ /kraɪst/ n le Christ, Jésus-Christ; **the ~ child** l'enfant m Jésus.

christen /'krɪsn/ vtr RELIG, NAUT baptiser; FIG (name, nickname) baptiser, nommer [person, pet, place]; **I was ~ed John** mon nom de baptême est John; **they ~ed the dog Max** ils ont baptisé le chien du nom de Max.

christening /'krɪsnɪŋ/ n baptême m.

Christian /'krɪstʃən/ **I** n chrétien/-ienne m/f; **to become a ~** se faire chrétien.
II adj **1** RELIG chrétien/-ienne; **2** [attitude] charitable; **a ~ burial** un enterrement convenable.

Christianity /ˌkrɪstɪ'ænətɪ/ n **1** (religion) christianisme m; **2** (fact of being a Christian) fait m d'être chrétien, qualité f de chrétien.

Christian: **~ name** n nom m de baptême; **~ Science** n science f chrétienne; **~ Scientist** n scientiste mf chrétien/-ienne.

Christmas /'krɪsməs/ **I** n (day) Noël m; (period) période f de Noël; **at ~** à Noël; **over ~** pendant la période de Noël; **Merry ~, Happy ~!** Joyeux Noël!
II noun modifier [cake, card, present] de Noël.

Christmas: ~ box n GB étrennes fpl; **~ carol** n (song) chant m de Noël; RELIG cantique m de Noël; **~ cracker** n GB diablotin m; **~ day** n jour m de Noël; **~ eve** n veille f de Noël; **~ stocking** n bas m de Noël (contenant de petits cadeaux).

Christmastime /'krɪsməstaɪm/ n période f de Noël.

chrome /krəʊm/ **I** n chrome m.
II noun modifier [article] chromé, en chrome.

chrome: ~ steel n acier m chromé; **~ yellow ▶818|** n jaune m de chrome.

chromium /'krəʊmɪəm/ n chrome m.

chromium-plated adj chromé, en chrome.

chromosome /'krəʊməsəʊm/ n chromosome m.

chronic /'krɒnɪk/ adj **1** MED [illness] chronique; **2** FIG [liar] invétéré; [problem, shortage] chronique; **3**○ GB (bad) nul/nulle○.

chronically /'krɒnɪklɪ/ adv **1** MED **to be ~ ill** souffrir d'une maladie chronique; **the ~ sick** ceux qui sont atteints d'une affection chronique; **2** FIG [jealous, underfunded] extrêmement.

chronicle /'krɒnɪkl/ **I** n (tale) chronique f; **a ~ of misfortunes** FIG une suite de mésaventures.
II vtr [person] écrire une chronique de; [book] être une chronique de.

chronological /ˌkrɒnə'lɒdʒɪkl/ adj chronologique.

chronologically /ˌkrɒnə'lɒdʒɪklɪ/ adv chronologiquement, par ordre chronologique.

chronology /krə'nɒlədʒɪ/ n chronologie f.

chrysalis /'krɪsəlɪs/ n chrysalide f.

chrysanthemum /krɪ'sænθəməm/ n chrysanthème m.

chubby /'tʃʌbɪ/ adj [child, finger] potelé; [cheek] rebondi; [face, cherub] joufflu; [adult] rondelet/-ette.

chuck /tʃʌk/ **I** n **1** (stroke) caresse f (sous le menton); **2** CULIN (also **~ steak**) macreuse f; **3** TECH mandrin m.
II vtr **1**○ (throw) balancer○, jeter (**to** à); **2**○ (get rid of) larguer○ [boyfriend, girlfriend]; **3** (stroke) **to ~ sb under the chin** caresser qn sous le menton.
■ **chuck away**○: **~ [sth] away, ~ away [sth] 1** (discard) balancer○, jeter; **2** (squander) gâcher [chance, life]; gaspiller [money].
■ **chuck down**○: **it's ~ing it down** il pleut à verse.
■ **chuck in**○: **~ [sth] in, ~ in [sth]** laisser tomber.
■ **chuck out**○: **¶ ~ [sth] out, ~ out [sth]** balancer○, jeter [rubbish]; **¶ ~ [sb] out, ~ out [sb]** vider, éjecter.

chuckle /'tʃʌkl/ **I** n gloussement m, petit rire m.
II vi glousser, rire; **to ~ at** ou **over sth** rire de qch; **to ~ with pleasure** glousser or rire de plaisir; **to ~ to oneself** rire sous cape.

chuffed○ /tʃʌft/ adj GB vachement○ content (**about, at, with** de).

chug /tʃʌg/ **I** n halètement m, teuf-teuf m.
II vi (p prés etc **-gg-**) [train] haleter, faire teuf-teuf; **the train ~ged into/out of the station** le train est entré en gare/est sorti de la gare en haletant.
■ **chug along** [train, car] avancer en haletant or en faisant teuf-teuf; [project] suivre son cours.

chum○† /tʃʌm/ n copain/copine○ m/f, pote○ m.

chummy○† /'tʃʌmɪ/ adj [person] sociable; **to be ~ with sb** être intime or très lié avec qn; **they're very ~** ils sont très copains○.

chump /tʃʌmp/ n **1**○ † idiot/-e m/f; **2** CULIN selle f d'agneau; **~ chop** tranche f de selle.

chunk /tʃʌŋk/ n **1** (piece) (of meat, fruit) morceau m; (of wood) tronçon m; (of bread) quignon m; **pineapple ~s** ananas m en morceaux; **2** (portion) (of population, text, day) partie f; **a fair ~** une bonne partie.

chunky /'tʃʌŋkɪ/ adj [sweater, jewellery] gros/grosse; [person] costaud○, trapu.

Chunnel○ /'tʃʌnl/ n GB tunnel m sous la Manche.

church /tʃɜːtʃ/ **I** n (pl **~es**) **1** (building) (Catholic, Anglican) église f; (Protestant) temple m; **2** (also **Church**) (religious body) Église f; **the Church of England** l'Église d'Angleterre; **to go into the ~** entrer dans les ordres; **3** (service) office m; (Catholic) messe f.
II noun modifier [bell, choir, clock, steeple] d'église [land] ecclésiastique; [fête] paroissial; [wedding] religieux/-ieuse.

church: ~goer n pratiquant/-e m/f; **~ hall** n salle f paroissiale; **~ school** n école f religieuse; **~ service** n GEN office m; (Catholic) messe f.

churchyard /'tʃɜːtʃjɑːd/ n cimetière m.

churlish /'tʃɜːlɪʃ/ adj (surly) revêche; (rude) grossier/-ière.

churn /tʃɜːn/ n **1** (for butter) baratte f; **2** GB (container) bidon m.
II vtr **1** to **~ butter** baratter; **2** FIG faire tourbillonner [water, air].
III vi [ideas] tourbillonner; **my stomach was ~ing** (with nausea) mon cœur se soulevait; (with nerves) j'avais l'estomac noué.
■ **churn out: ~ [sth] out, ~ out [sth]** pondre [qch] en série [novels]; produire [qch] en série [goods].
■ **churn up: ~ [sth] up, ~ up [sth]** faire des remous dans [water]; labourer [earth].

chute /ʃuːt/ n **1** (slide) toboggan m; **2** (for rubbish) vide-ordures m inv; **3** (for toboggan) piste f de toboggan; **4**○ (parachute) parachute m.

chutney /'tʃʌtnɪ/ n: condiment aigre-doux.

CI n: abrév écrite ▶ **Channel Islands**.

cicada /sɪ'kɑːdə, US -'keɪdə/ n cigale f.

CID n GB (abrév = **Criminal Investigation Department**) police f criminelle.

cider /'saɪdə(r)/ n cidre m.

cider: ~ apple n pomme f à cidre; **~ vinegar** n vinaigre m de cidre.

cigar /sɪ'gɑː(r)/ **I** n cigare m.
II noun modifier [box, case] à cigares, [smoker] de cigares; **~ cutter** coupe-cigare m.

cigarette /ˌsɪɡə'ret, US 'sɪɡərət/ **I** n cigarette f.
II noun modifier [ash, smoke] de cigarette; [case, paper] à cigarettes.

cigarette: ~ butt, ~ end n mégot m; **~ holder** n fume-cigarette m inv; **~ lighter** n (portable) briquet m; (in car) allume-cigares m inv.

cigar: ~ holder n fume-cigare m inv; **~-shaped** adj oblong/oblongue.

C-in-C /ˌsiː ɪn 'siː/ n (abrév = **Commander in Chief**) commandant m en chef.

cinch /sɪntʃ/ n **doing sth was a ~** faire qch a été facile comme bonjour; **it's a ~** c'est du gâteau○.

cinder /'sɪndə(r)/ n (glowing) braise f; (ash) cendre f; **to burn sth to a ~** réduire qch en cendres; **~ track** (piste f) cendrée f.

Cinderella /ˌsɪndə'relə/ pr n Cendrillon.

cine: ~camera n caméra f (d'amateur); **~ club** n ciné-club m; **~ film** n pellicule f cinématographique.

cinema /'sɪnəmɑː, 'sɪnəmə/ n cinéma m.

cinema: ~ complex n complexe m multisalles; **~goer** n (regular) cinéphile mf, amateur m de cinéma; (spectator) spectateur/-trice m/f.

cinematic /ˌsɪnə'mætɪk/ adj cinématographique.

cinematographer /ˌsɪnəmə'tɒɡrəfə(r)/ ▶1251| n directeur m de la photo, cameraman m.

cinematography /ˌsɪnəmə'tɒɡrəfɪ/ n technique f cinématographique.

cinnamon /'sɪnəmən/ **I** n **1** CULIN cannelle f; **2** (tree) cannelier m; **3 ▶818|** (colour) (couleur f) cannelle f.
II adj **1** CULIN [cake, cookie] à la cannelle; [stick] de cannelle; **2** (colour) cannelle inv.

cipher /'saɪfə(r)/ n **1** (code) chiffre m; **in ~** en chiffre, en code; **2** MATH zéro m; **3** (Arabic numeral) chiffre m (arabe); **4** (monogram) chiffre m.

circa /'sɜːkə/ prep environ.

circle /'sɜːkl/ **I** n **1** (shape) cercle m; (of spectators, trees,

chairs) cercle *m*; (of fabric, paper, colour) rond *m*; **to form a ~** [*objects*] former un cercle; [*people*] faire un cercle; **to sit in a ~** s'asseoir en cercle; **to go round in ~s** LIT, FIG tourner en rond; **to have ~s under one's eyes** avoir les yeux cernés; **2** (group) cercle *m*, groupe *m*; **his ~ of friends** le cercle de ses amis; **in business ~s** dans les milieux d'affaires; **literary ~s** le monde littéraire; **fashionable ~s** le beau monde; **3** THEAT balcon *m*; **in the ~** au balcon.
II *vtr* **1** (move round) [*plane*] tourner autour de [*airport*]; [*satellite*] graviter autour de [*planet*]; [*person, animal, vehicle*] faire le tour de [*building*]; tourner autour de [*person, animal*]; **2** (encircle) encercler.
III *vi* tourner en rond (**around** autour de).
IDIOMS **to come full ~** [*person*] boucler la boucle; [*situation*] revenir à son point de départ; **the wheel has come full ~** la boucle est bouclée.

circuit /'sɜːkɪt/ **I** *n* **1** (track) (for vehicles) circuit *m*; (for athletes) piste *f*; **2** (lap) tour *m*; **to do 15 ~s of the track** faire 15 tours de circuit; **3** (regular round) circuit *m*; **the tennis ~** le circuit du tennis; **4** (round trip) circuit *m*; **5** ELEC circuit *m*.
II *vtr* faire le circuit de [*course, town*].

circuit: **~ board** *n* carte *f* de circuit imprimé; **~ breaker** *n* disjoncteur *m*; **~ diagram** *n* schéma *m* de circuit; **~ judge** ▸ **1251**| *n* JUR juge *m* itinérant.

circuitous /sɜː'kjuːɪtəs/ *adj* [*route, means*] indirect; [*argument*] tortueux/-euse; [*procedure*] compliqué.

circuitry /'sɜːkɪtrɪ/ *n* ensemble *m* de circuits.

circular /'sɜːkjʊlə(r)/ **I** *n* (newsletter) circulaire *f*; (advertisement) prospectus *m*.
II *adj* [*object*] rond; [*argument*] circulaire.

circular: **~ letter** *n* circulaire *f*; **~ saw** *n* scie *f* circulaire.

circulate /'sɜːkjʊleɪt/ **I** *vtr* **1** (spread) (to limited circle) faire circuler; (widely) diffuser (**to** entre); **the report was ~d to the members** le rapport a été transmis aux membres; **2** faire circuler [*blood, water*].
II *vi* GEN circuler; **let's ~** (at party) on va aller faire connaissance.

circulation /,sɜːkjʊ'leɪʃn/ *n* **1** (of blood, air, water, fuel) circulation *f*; **2** (distribution) (of newspaper) tirage *m*; **a ~ of 2 million** un tirage de 2 millions d'exemplaires; **3** (of coins, books) circulation *f*; **4** (of document, information) circulation *f*; (to wide public) diffusion *f*; **5** (social group) **she's back in ~** elle est de nouveau dans le circuit.

circulation: **~ figures** *npl* chiffres *mpl* de tirage; **~ manager** *n* responsable *mf* du service de distribution.

circulatory /,sɜːkjʊ'leɪtərɪ, US 'sɜːkjələtəːrɪ/ *adj* circulatoire.

circumcise /'sɜːkəmsaɪz/ *vtr* circoncire [*boy*]; exciser [*girl*].

circumcision /,sɜːkəm'sɪʒn/ *n* (of boy) circoncision *f*; (of girl) excision *f*.

circumference /sə'kʌmfərəns/ *n* circonférence *f*; **to be 4 km in ~** avoir une circonférence de 4 km.

circumflex /'sɜːkəmfleks/ **I** *n* accent *m* circonflexe (**on, over** sur).
II *adj* circonflexe; **e ~** e accent circonflexe.

circumlocution /,sɜːkəmlə'kjuːʃn/ *n* circonlocution *f*, périphrase *f*.

circumnavigate /,sɜːkəm'nævɪgeɪt/ *vtr* faire le tour de [*world*]; passer [qch] au large [*cape*].

circumscribe /'sɜːkəmskraɪb/ *vtr* SOUT **1** (define) circonscrire; **2** (limit) limiter.

circumspect /'sɜːkəmspekt/ *adj* circonspect (**about** quant à); **to be ~ about doing** ne pas vouloir faire.

circumstance /'sɜːkəmstəns/ **I** *n* circonstance *f*.
II circumstances *npl* **1** (state of affairs) circonstances *fpl*; **in ou under the ~s** dans ces circonstances; **under no ~s** en aucun cas; **due to ~s beyond our control** pour des raisons indépendantes de notre volonté; **2** (conditions of life) situation *f*.

circumstantial /,sɜːkəm'stænʃl/ *adj* **1** JUR [*evidence*] indirect; **2** (detailed) circonstancié.

circumvent /,sɜːkəm'vent/ *vtr* SOUT (avoid) contourner [*law, problem*]; circonvenir [*official*].

circus /'sɜːkəs/ *n* cirque *m*.

cirrhosis /sɪ'rəʊsɪs/ ▸ **1002**| *n* cirrhose *f*.

CIS *n* (*abrév* = **Commonwealth of Independent States**) CEI *f*.

cissy *n, adj* = **sissy**.

cistern /'sɪstən/ *n* (of lavatory) réservoir *m* de chasse d'eau; (in loft or underground) citerne *f*.

citadel /'sɪtədəl/ *n* citadelle *f*.

cite /saɪt/ *vtr* **1** (quote) citer; (adduce) avancer; **2** MIL (commend) citer (**for** pour); **3** JUR citer.

citizen /'sɪtɪzn/ *n* **1** (of state) citoyen/-enne *m*/*f*; (when abroad) ressortissant/-e *m*/*f*; **2** (of town) habitant/-e *m*/*f*.

citizen: **Citizens' Advice Bureau, CAB** *n* service *m* bénévole d'assistance sur des problèmes juridiques; **~'s arrest** *n* arrestation *f* par un particulier; **~'s band, CB** *n* RADIO (bande *f*) CB *f*, citizen's band *f*; **~ship** *n* nationalité *f*.

citric /'sɪtrɪk/ *adj* citrique.

citrus /'sɪtrəs/ **I** *n* (*pl* **-ruses**) (tree) citrus *m*; (fruit) agrume *m*.
II *adj* [*colour*] acidulé; **~ trees** les citrus *mpl*.

citrus fruit *n* (individual) agrume *m*; (collectively) agrumes *mpl*.

city /'sɪtɪ/ *n* **1** (town) (grande) ville *f*; **the medieval ~** la cité médiévale; **~ life** la vie citadine; **2** GB **the City** la City (*centre des affaires à Londres*).

city: **City and Guilds certificate** *n* ~ certificat *m* d'aptitude professionnelle; **~ centre** GB, **~ center** US *n* centre-ville *m*; **~ council** *n* conseil *m* municipal; **~ councillor** *n* GB conseiller/-ère *m*/*f* municipal/-e; **~ dweller** *n* citadin/-e *m*/*f*.

city hall *n* US **1** (building) (in large town) hôtel *m* de ville; (in small town) mairie *f*; **2** ADMIN administration *f* municipale.

city: **~ manager** *n* US personne *f* chargée d'administrer une municipalité; **~ news** *n* GB rubrique *f* financière; **~ planner** ▸ **1251**| *n* urbaniste *mf*; **~scape** *n* paysage *m* urbain; **~ slicker**° *n* citadin/-e *m*/*f* branché/-e; **~ state** *n* HIST cité *f*; **~ technology college, CTC** *n* ~ collège *m* technique.

civic /'sɪvɪk/ *adj* [*administration, official*] municipal; [*pride, responsibility*] civique.

civic centre GB, **civic center** US *n* centre *m* municipal (culturel et administratif).

civics /'sɪvɪks/ *n* (+ *v sg*) instruction *f* civique.

civil /'sɪvl/ *adj* **1** (civic, not military) civil; **2** JUR [*case, court, offence*] civil; [*claim*] au civil; **3** (polite) courtois.
IDIOMS **to keep a ~ tongue in one's head** mesurer ses paroles.

civil: **Civil Aeronautics Board, CAB** *n* US administration *f* de l'aviation civile; **Civil Aviation Authority, CAA** *n* GB administration *f* de l'aviation civile; **~ defence, ~ defense** US *n* défense *f* passive; **~ disobedience** *n* résistance *f* passive; **~ engineer** ▸ **1251**| *n* ingénieur *m* des travaux publics; **~ engineering** *n* génie *m* civil.

civilian /sɪ'vɪlɪən/ **I** *n* civil/-e *m*/*f*.
II *adj* civil.

civility /sɪ'vɪlətɪ/ *n* **1** (manners) courtoisie *f*, politesse *f*; **2** (forms) civilité *f*, politesse *f*.

civilization /,sɪvəlaɪ'zeɪʃn, US -əlɪ'z-/ *n* civilisation *f*.

civilize /'sɪvəlaɪz/ *vtr* civiliser, rendre [qn/qch] plus civilisé [*manners, person*].

civilized /'sɪvəlaɪzd/ *adj* civilisé; **to become ~** se civiliser.

civil: **~ law** *n* droit *m* civil; **~ liability** *n* JUR responsabilité *f* civile; **~ liberty** *n* libertés *fpl* individuelles.

civil rights I *npl* droits *mpl* civils.
II *noun modifier* [*march, activist*] pour les droits civils.

civil: **~ servant** ▸ **1251**| *n* fonctionnaire *mf*; **~ service** *n* fonction *f* publique; **~ war** *n* guerre *f* civile; **~ wedding** *n* mariage *m* civil.

civvies° /'sɪvɪz/ *npl* **to be in ~** être en civil.

cl *n* (*abrév écrite* = **centilitre(s)**) cl.

clad /klæd/ *adj* ~ **in** habillé en, vêtu de.

cladding /'klædɪŋ/ *n* revêtement *m*.

claim /kleɪm/ I *n* **1** (demand) revendication *f*; **to make ~s** ou **lay ~ to** prétendre à [*throne*]; revendiquer [*right, land, title*]; **wage ~** revendications *fpl* salariales; **there are too many ~s on her generosity** on abuse de sa générosité; **there are many ~s on my time** je suis très pris; **to have first ~ on sth** avoir la priorité sur qch; **2** (in insurance) (against a person) réclamation *f*; (for fire, theft) demande *f* d'indemnisation; **to make** ou **put in a ~** faire une demande d'indemnisation; **3** (for welfare benefit) demande *f* d'allocation; **to make** ou **put in a ~** faire une demande d'allocation; **4** (refund request) demande *f* de remboursement; **travel ~** demande *f* de remboursement des frais de déplacement; **5** (assertion) affirmation *f* (**about** au sujet de; **by** de la part de; **of** de); **his ~ that he is innocent** ses protestations d'innocence; **her ~(s) to be able to do** ses affirmations selon lesquelles elle peut faire; **some extraordinary ~s have been made for this drug** on a affirmé des choses extraordinaires sur ce médicament; **my ~ to fame** ma prétention à la gloire; **6** (piece of land) concession *f*.

II *vtr* **1** (assert) **to ~ to be able to do** prétendre pouvoir faire; **to ~ to be innocent** prétendre être innocent; **to ~ responsibility for an attack** revendiquer un attentat; **2** (assert right to) revendiquer [*money, property*]; **3** (apply for) faire une demande de [*benefit*]; faire une demande de remboursement de [*expenses*]; **4** (cause) **the accident ~ed 50 lives** l'accident a fait 50 victimes *m* morts.

III *vi* **1** JUR **to ~ for damages** faire une demande pour dommages et intérêts; **2** (apply for benefit) faire une demande d'allocation.

■ **claim back**: ~ **back** [*sth*], ~ [*sth*] **back** se faire rembourser [*cost*]; **to ~ one's money back** se faire rembourser.

claimant /'kleɪmənt/ *n* **1** (for benefit, grant, compensation) demandeur/-euse *m/f* (**to** à); **2** (to title, estate) prétendant/-e *m/f* (**to** à).

claim form *n* déclaration *f* de sinistre.

clairvoyance /kleə'vɔɪəns/ *n* voyance *f*.

clairvoyant /kleə'vɔɪənt/ I *n* voyant/-e *m/f*, extralucide *mf*.

II *adj* [*person*] doué de seconde vue; [*powers*] de voyance.

clam /klæm/ *n* ZOOL, CULIN palourde *f*.

■ **clam up** ne plus piper mot (**on sb** à qn).

clamber /'klæmbə(r)/ *vi* grimper, se hisser (péniblement); **to ~ over/up/across** escalader.

clam chowder *n* soupe *f* aux palourdes.

clammy /'klæmɪ/ *adj* [*skin, hand*] moite (**with** de); [*surface*] collant; [*weather*] moite.

clamorous /'klæmərəs/ *adj* [*crowd*] vociférant; [*protest*] violent, bruyant; [*demand*] impérieux/-ieuse.

clamour GB, **clamor** US /'klæmə(r)/ I *n* **1** (loud shouting) clameur *f*; **2** (demands) réclamations *fpl*.

II *vi* **1** (demand) **to ~ for sth** réclamer qch; **to ~ for sb to do** réclamer à qn de faire; **2** (rush, fight) se bousculer (**for** pour avoir; **to do** pour faire); **3** (shout together) pousser des cris.

clamp /klæmp/ I *n* **1** TECH (on bench) valet *m*; (unattached) presse *f*; CHEM, MED pince *f*; **2** FIG frein *m* (**on** à); **to put a ~ on sth** freiner; **3** AUT (also **wheel~**) sabot *m* de Denver.

II *vtr* **1** TECH cramponner [*two parts*]; (at bench) fixer [qch] à l'aide d'un valet (**onto** à); **2** (clench) serrer [*jaw, teeth*]; **his jaws were ~ed shut** il serrait les mâchoires; **3** AUT (also **wheel~**) mettre un sabot de Denver à [*car*].

■ **clamp down**: ~ **down** prendre des mesures; **to ~ down on** faire de la répression contre [*crime*]; mettre un frein à [*extravagance*].

clampdown /'klæmpdaʊn/ *n* mesures *fpl* de répression (**on sb** contre qn; **on sth** de qch).

clan /klæn/ *n* LIT, FIG clan *m*.

clandestine /klæn'destɪn/ *adj* clandestin.

clang /klæŋ/ I *n* fracas *m*, bruit *m* métallique.

II *vtr* faire sonner [qch] à toute volée [*bell*].

III *vi* [*gate*] claquer avec un son métallique; [*bell*] retentir.

clanger° /'klæŋə(r)/ *n* GB boulette° *f*, gaffe *f*.

clanging /'klæŋɪŋ/ *n* bruit *m* métallique, fracas *m*.

clank /klæŋk/ I *n* bruit *m* métallique.

II *vi* [*heavy object*] cliqueter; [*chains*] s'entrechoquer.

clannish /'klænɪʃ/ *adj* PÉJ [*family, profession*] fermé [*person*] qui a l'esprit de clan.

clap /klæp/ I *n* **1** (of hands) battement *m* de mains; (round of applause) applaudissements *mpl*; (friendly slap) tape *f*; **to give sb a ~** applaudir qn; **a ~ of thunder** un coup de tonnerre.

II *vtr* (*p prés etc* **-pp-**) **1** **to ~ one's hands** battre ou taper des mains, frapper dans ses mains; **to ~ one's hand over sb's mouth** mettre or plaquer la main sur la bouche de qn; **to ~ sb on the back** taper qn dans le dos; **to ~ sth shut** fermer qch d'un coup sec; **2** (applaud) applaudir; **3**° (put) **to ~ sb in irons** mettre qn aux fers.

III *vi* (*p prés etc* **-pp-**) applaudir.

IDIOMS **to ~ eyes on** voir, poser les yeux sur.

■ **clap on**: **to ~ on one's hat** enfoncer son chapeau sur sa tête; **to ~ on the brakes**° AUT freiner brusquement, piler°.

clapboard /'klæpbɔːd/ I *n* planche *f* en clin.

II *noun modifier* [*house*] en bois.

clapped-out° /,klæpt'aʊt/ *adj* [*car*] pourri; [*machine*] mort°; [*horse*] claqué°; [*person*] (exhausted) crevé°; (passé it) fichu°, fini.

clapping /'klæpɪŋ/ *n* ¢ applaudissements *mpl*.

claptrap° /'klæptræp/ *n* ¢ âneries *fpl*.

claret /'klærət/ ▶818 I *n* **1** (wine) bordeaux *m* (rouge); **2** (colour) bordeaux *m*.

clarification /,klærɪfɪ'keɪʃn/ *n* éclaircissement *m*, clarification *f*.

clarify /'klærɪfaɪ/ I *vtr* **1** (explain) éclaircir, clarifier [*point*]; **2** CULIN clarifier [*butter, stock*]; coller [*wine*].

II *vi* [*person*] s'expliquer.

clarinet /,klærə'net/ ▶1097 *n* clarinette *f*.

clarinettist /,klærə'netɪst/ ▶1097, 1251 *n* clarinettiste *mf*.

clarity /'klærətɪ/ *n* clarté *f*.

clash /klæʃ/ I *n* **1** (confrontation) affrontement *m*; FIG (disagreement) querelle *f*; **2** (contest) affrontement *m*; **3** (contradiction) conflit *m*, incompatibilité *f*; **a ~ of cultures** un conflit de cultures; **a personality ~** un conflit de personnalités; **4** (inconvenient coincidence) **there's a ~ of meetings** les réunions ont lieu en même temps; **5** (noise) (of swords) cliquetis *m*; **a ~ of cymbals** un coup de cymbales.

II *vtr* entrechoquer [*bin lids*]; frapper [*cymbals*].

III *vi* **1** (meet and fight) [*armies, groups*] s'affronter; FIG (disagree) s'affronter; **to ~ with sb** (fight) se heurter à qn; (disagree) se quereller avec qn (**on, over** au sujet de); **2** (be in conflict) [*interests, beliefs*] être incompatibles; **3** (coincide) [*meetings*] avoir lieu en même temps (**with** que); **4** (not match) [*colours*] jurer.

clasp /klɑːsp, US klæsp/ I *n* **1** (on bracelet, bag, purse) fermoir *m*; (on belt) boucle *f*; **2** (grip) étreinte *f*.

II *vtr* **1** (hold) serrer [qch] dans la main [*purse, knife*]; **he ~ed her hand** il lui a serré la main; **2** (embrace) étreindre; **to ~ sb to one's breast** prendre qn dans ses bras.

class /klɑːs, US klæs/ I *n* **1** SOCIOL classe *f*; **2** (group of students) classe *f*; (lesson) cours *m* (**in** de); **in ~** en cours ou classe; **to give a ~** assurer un cours; **to take a ~** GB assurer un cours; US suivre un cours; **3** (year group) promotion *f*, classe *f*; **4** (category) classe *f*, catégorie *f*; **to be in a ~ of one's own** être hors catégorie; **she's in a different ~ from him** il n'y a aucune comparaison possible entre elle et lui; **he's not in the same ~ as her** il n'arrive pas à sa cheville; **5**° (elegance) classe *f*; **6** TOURISM classe *f*; **to travel first/second ~** voyager en première/deuxième classe; **a first ~ seat** une place de première classe; **7** GB UNIV ~ mention *f*; **a first-/second-~**

degree ~ licence avec mention très bien/bien; **8** BIOL, MATH classe *f*.
II *vtr* classer; **to ~ sb/sth as** assimiler qn/qch à.

class: ~ **conscious** *adj* soucieux/-ieuse des distinctions sociales; ~ **consciousness** *n* sentiment *m* de classe.

classic /'klæsɪk/ I *n* **1** (literary, sporting) classique *m*; **2**○ (hilarious example) **it was a real ~!** (of gaffe) c'était un chef-d'œuvre du genre!; (of comment, situation) c'était trop drôle!
II *adj* classique.

classical /'klæsɪkl/ *adj* GEN classique; ~ **scholar** philologue *mf*.

classically /'klæsɪklɪ/ *adv* dans un style classique.

classicism /'klæsɪsɪzəm/ *n* classicisme *m*.

classicist /'klæsɪsɪst/ *n* (student) étudiant/-e *m*/*f* en lettres classiques; (scholar) spécialiste *mf* de lettres classiques, philologue *mf*.

classics /'klæsɪks/ *n* (+ *v sg*) lettres *fpl* classiques.

classification /ˌklæsɪfɪ'keɪʃn/ *n* **1** (category) classification *f*, catégorie *f*; **2** (categorization) classement *m*.

classified /'klæsɪfaɪd/ I *n* (also ~ **ad**) petite annonce *f*.
II *adj* **1** (categorized) classifié; **2** (secret) confidentiel/-ielle.

classified: ~ **ad** *n* petite annonce *f*; ~ **section** *n* rubrique *f* des petites annonces.

classify /'klæsɪfaɪ/ *vtr* **1** (file) classer; **2** (declare secret) classer [qch] confidentiel/-ielle.

classless /'klɑːslɪs, US 'klæs-/ *adj* [society] sans classes; [accent] neutre.

class: ~ **mark** *n* cote *f*; ~**mate** *n* camarade *mf* de classe; ~**room** *n* salle *f* de classe; ~ **struggle** *n* lutte *f* des classes; ~ **system** *n* système *m* de classes; ~ **war(fare)** *n* guerre *f* des classes.

classy○ /'klɑːsɪ, US 'klæsɪ/ *adj* [person, dress] qui a de la classe; [car, hotel] de luxe; [actor, performance] de grande classe.

clatter /'klætə(r)/ I *n* cliquetis *m*; (loud) fracas *m*.
II *vi* [typewriter] cliqueter; [dishes] s'entrechoquer; [vehicle] rouler avec fracas.

clause /klɔːz/ *n* **1** LING proposition *f*; **2** JUR, POL clause *f*; (in will, act of Parliament) disposition *f*.

claustrophobia /ˌklɔːstrə'fəʊbɪə/ *n* claustrophobie *f*.

claustrophobic /ˌklɔːstrə'fəʊbɪk/ I *n* claustrophobe *mf*.
II *adj* [person] claustrophobe; [feeling] de claustrophobie; **it's ~ in here** il y a une atmosphère oppressante ici; **to get ~** avoir une sensation de claustrophobie.

clavichord /'klævɪkɔːd/ ▶ 1097 *n* clavicorde *m*.

clavicle /'klævɪkl/ *n* clavicule *f*.

claw /klɔː/ I *n* **1** ZOOL (of animal) griffe *f*; (of bird of prey) serre *f*; (of crab, lobster) pince *f*; **2**○ FIG (hand) patte○ *f*; **to get one's ~s into sb** mettre le grappin sur qn; **3** (on hammer) arrache-clou *m*, pied-de-biche *m*.
II *vtr* (scratch) griffer; **to ~ sb's eyes out** arracher les yeux de qn; FIG **he ~ed his way to the top** il est arrivé en employant tous les moyens.

■ **claw back**: ~ [sth] **back**, ~ **back** [sth] **1** FIN récupérer; **2** COMM, SPORT regagner péniblement [position].

clay /kleɪ/ I *n* **1** (for sculpture) argile *f*, terre *f* glaise; **2** (soil) argile *f*; **3** (in tennis) terre *f* battue.
II *noun modifier* **1** [pot, pipe] en terre; **2** SPORT [court] en terre battue.
IDIOMS **to have feet of** ~ avoir des pieds d'argile.

clay pigeon shooting ▶ 949 *n* ball-trap *m*, tir *m* aux pigeons d'argile.

clean /kliːn/ I *n* **to give sth a** ~ nettoyer qch.
II *adj* **1** (not dirty) [clothes, dishes, floor] propre; [air, water] pur; [syringe] désinfecté; **she keeps her house ~** elle tient sa maison propre; **my hands are ~** LIT, FIG j'ai les mains propres; ~ **and tidy** impeccable de propreté; **a ~ sheet of paper** une feuille blanche; **to rinse sth ~** rincer qch; **keep your shoes ~** ne salis pas tes chaussures; **2** (with no pollution) [fuel] propre; **3** (not obscene) [joke] anodin;

keep it ~! restons décents!; **4** (unsullied) [reputation] sans tache; [record, licence] vierge; **5** (no longer addicted) désintoxiqué; **6**○ (without illicit property) **he's ~** il n'a rien; **the room is ~** on n'a rien trouvé dans la pièce; **7** SPORT [tackle] sans faute; [hit] précis; **keep it ~** (in match) pas de bavures; **8** (neat) [lines, profile] pur; [edge] net/nette; ~ **break** MED fracture *f* simple; **to make a ~ break with the past** FIG rompre définitivement avec le passé.
III *adv* **the bullet went ~ through his shoulder** la balle lui a littéralement traversé l'épaule; **to jump ~ over the wall** sauter par-dessus le mur sans le toucher; **we're ~ out of bread** on n'a plus de pain.
IV *vtr* **1** nettoyer [room, shoes, gun]; effacer [blackboard]; **to ~ sth from** ou **off** enlever qch de [hands, car]; **to ~ed** nettoyer qch à nettoyer; **to ~ one's teeth** se brosser les dents; **2** CULIN vider [fish].
V *vi* (do housework) faire le ménage.
VI *v refl* **to ~ itself** [animal] faire sa toilette.
IDIOMS **to ~ up one's act** [person] devenir plus sérieux; **I'll have to come** ~○ il va falloir que je dise la vérité.

■ **clean down**: ~ [sth] **down**, ~ **down** [sth] nettoyer [qch] à fond.

■ **clean off**: ¶ ~ **off** [stain] partir; ¶ ~ [sth] **off**, ~ **off** [sth] enlever [stain, graffiti]; **to ~ sth off** effacer qch de [blackboard]; enlever qch de [car, wall].

■ **clean out**: ¶ ~ [sth] **out**, ~ **out** [sth] nettoyer [qch] à fond; ¶ ~ [sb/sth] **out**, ~ **out** [sb/sth] (leave empty, penniless) [thief] mettre [qch] à sac [house]; [thief, holiday] mettre [qn] à sec [person].

■ **clean up**: ¶ ~ **up 1** (remove dirt) tout nettoyer; **2** (tidy) tout remettre en ordre (**after sb** derrière qn); **3** (wash oneself) se débarbouiller; **4**○ (make profit) [dealer] faire son beurre○ (**on** avec); [gambler] rafler la mise○; ¶ ~ [sb] **up** faire la toilette de [patient]; ¶ ~ [sth] **up**, ~ **up** [sth] **1** (remove dirt) nettoyer; ~ **that rubbish up off** ou **from the floor** débarrasse le sol de ces saletés; **2** FIG (remove crime) nettoyer [street, city]; (make less obscene) expurger [comedy act].

clean-cut *adj* [image, person] soigné.

cleaner /'kliːnə(r)/ ▶ 1251 *n* **1** (person) (in workplace) agent *m* de nettoyage; (in home) (woman) femme *f* de ménage; (man) agent *m* de nettoyage; **2** (machine) nettoyeur *m*; ~ **carpet** ~ shampouineuse *f* (de tapis); **3** (detergent) produit *m* de nettoyage; **suede** ~ produit *m* pour nettoyer le daim; **4** (shop) (also **cleaner's**) pressing *m*.
IDIOMS **to take sb to the** ~**s**○ (swindle) plumer qn○; (leave penniless) nettoyer.

cleaning /'kliːnɪŋ/ *n* (domestic) ménage *m*; (commercial) nettoyage *m*, entretien *m*; **to do the** ~ faire le ménage.

cleaning: ~ **lady** ▶ 1251 *n* femme *f* de ménage; ~ **product** *n* produit *m* d'entretien.

cleanliness /'klenlɪnɪs/ *n* propreté *f*.

clean-living /ˌkliːn'lɪvɪŋ/ I *n* vie *f* saine.
II *adj* [person] aux habitudes saines.

cleanly /'kliːnlɪ/ *adv* [cut] bien, franchement; [catch, hit] avec précision; **to break off** ~ se casser net.

clean-out /'kliːnaʊt/ *n* nettoyage *m* à fond.

cleanse /klenz/ *vtr* **1** LIT nettoyer [skin, wound]; **2** FIG laver, purifier [person, mind]; nettoyer [society].

cleanser /'klenzə(r)/ *n* **1** (for face) démaquillant *m*; **2** (household) produit *m* d'entretien.

clean-shaven /ˌkliːn'ʃeɪvn/ *adj* **he's** ~ il n'a ni barbe ni moustache.

clean sheet *n* FIG (record) casier *m* vierge.

cleansing /'klenzɪŋ/ *n* nettoyage *m*.

cleansing department *n* GB ADMIN (service *m* de la) voirie *f*.

cleanup /'kliːnʌp/ *n* **to give sth a** ~○ nettoyer qch.

clear /klɪə(r)/ I *adj* **1** (transparent) [glass, liquid] transparent; [blue] limpide; [lens, varnish] incolore; **2** (distinct) [image, outline] net/nette; [writing] lisible; [sound, voice] clair; **he had a** ~ **view of the man** il voyait très bien l'homme; **3** (comprehensibly plain) [description, instruction] clair; **to make sth** ~ **to sb** faire

comprendre qch à qn; **I wish to make it ~ that** je tiens à préciser que; **is that ~?, do I make myself ~?** est-ce que c'est clair?; **to make one's views ~** exprimer clairement ses opinions; **let's get this ~** que les choses soient claires; **4** (obvious) [*need, sign*] évident; [*advantage, lead*] net/nette; [*example*] beau/belle (*before n*); [*majority*] large (*before n*); **it is ~ that** il est clair que; **5** (not confused) [*idea, memory*] clair; [*plan*] précis; **to keep a ~ head** garder les idées claires; **a ~ thinker** un esprit lucide; **I'm not ~ what to do** je ne sais pas très bien quoi faire; **6** (empty) [*road, view*] dégagé; [*table*] débarrassé; [*space*] libre; **7** (not guilty) [*conscience*] tranquille; **8** (unblemished) [*skin*] net/nette; **9** MED [*X-ray, scan*] normal; **10** (cloudless) [*sky*] sans nuage; [*day, night*] clair; **on a ~ day** par temps clair; **11** (frank) [*gaze*] franc/franche; **12** (pure) [*tone, voice*] clair; **13** CULIN [*honey*] liquide; **~ soup** consommé *m*; **14** (exempt from) **to be ~ of** être libre de [*debt*]; être exempt de [*blame*]; être lavé de [*suspicion*]; **15** (free) [*day, diary*] libre; **keep Monday ~** ne prévois rien d'autre lundi; **16** (whole) [*week, day*] entier/-ière; **17** (net) [*gain, profit*] net *inv* (*after n*).
II *adv* (away from) **to jump ~** sauter sur le côté; **jump ~ of** (jump out of) sauter hors de [*vehicle*]; (avoid) **to pull sb ~** extraire qn de [*wreckage*]; **to stay** ou **steer ~ of** éviter [*town centre*]; éviter [*alcohol, troublemakers*]; **stand ~ of the gates!** éloignez-vous des portes!; **to get ~ of** sortir de [*traffic, town*].
III *vtr* **1** (remove) abattre [*trees*]; arracher [*weeds*]; enlever [*debris, papers, mines*]; dégager [*snow*] (**from, off** de); **to ~ the streets of demonstrators** débarrasser les rues des manifestants; **2** (free from obstruction) déboucher [*drains*]; dégager [*road*]; débarrasser [*table, surface*]; déblayer [*site*]; défricher [*land*]; **to ~ the road of obstacles** dégager les obstacles de la route; **to ~ sth out of the way** (from table, seat) enlever qch; (from floor) enlever qch du passage; **to ~ the way for sth/sb** libérer le passage pour qch/qn; FIG ouvrir la voie pour [*developments*]; FIG laisser la place à [*person*]; **3** (freshen) **to ~ the air** LIT aérer; FIG apaiser les tensions; **4** (empty) vider [*desk*] (**of** de); débarrasser [*room, surface*] (**of** de); évacuer [*area, building*]; **5** (create) faire [*space*]; **to ~ a path through sth** se frayer un chemin à travers qch; **6** (disperse) dissiper [*fog, smoke*]; disperser [*crowd*]; **7** (unblock) dégager [*nose*]; **to ~ one's throat** se racler la gorge; **the fresh air will ~ your head** un peu d'air frais t'éclaircira les idées; **8** (eliminate) faire disparaître [*dandruff, spots*]; **9** COMPUT effacer [*screen*]; **10** (dispose of) liquider [*stock*]; **'reduced to ~'** 'solde'; **11** (pay off) s'acquitter de [*debt*]; **12** FIN [*bank*] compenser [*cheque*]; **13** (free from blame) innocenter [*accused*] (**of** de); **to be ~ed of suspicion** être lavé de tout soupçon; **to ~ one's name** blanchir son nom; **14** (vet) mener une enquête administrative sur [*employee*]; **15** (officially approve) approuver [*request*]; **to ~ sth with sb** obtenir l'accord de qn pour qch; **16** (jump over) franchir [*hurdle, wall*]; **17** (pass through) passer sous [*bridge*]; **to ~ customs** passer à la douane.
IV *vi* **1** (become unclouded) [*liquid, sky*] s'éclaircir; **2** (disappear) [*smoke, fog, cloud*] se dissiper; **3** (become pure) [*air*] se purifier; **4** (go away) [*rash*] disparaître; **5** FIN [*cheque*] être compensé.
IDIOMS **the coast is ~** FIG le champ est libre; **to be in the ~** (safe) être hors de danger; (free from suspicion) être lavé de tout soupçon.
■ **clear away**: ¶ **~ away** débarrasser; ¶ **~** [*sth*] **away**, **~ away** [*sth*] balayer [*leaves*]; enlever [*rubbish*]; ranger [*papers, toys*].
■ **clear off**: ¶ **~ off**○ GB (run away) filer○; (go away) ficher le camp○.
■ **clear out**: ¶ **~ out** (run away) filer○, se sauver; ¶ **~** [*sth*] **out**, **~ out** [*sth*] **1** (tidy) ranger [*room*]; faire le tri dans [*drawer*]; **2** (empty) vider [*room*]; **3** (throw away) jeter.
■ **clear up**: ¶ **~ up 1** (tidy up) faire du rangement; **2** (improve) [*weather*] s'éclaircir; [*infection*] disparaître; ¶ **~ up** [*sth*], **~** [*sth*] **up 1** (tidy) ranger [*mess, room, toys*]; ramasser [*litter*]; **2** (resolve) résoudre [*problem*];

dissiper [*misunderstanding*]; tirer [qch] au clair [*mystery*].
clearance /'klɪərəns/ *n* **1** (permission) autorisation *f*; **~ for take-off** autorisation de décoller; **to have ~ to do** être autorisé à faire; **2** (customs certificate) déclaration *f* en douane; **3** ADMIN, MIL habilitation *f* sécuritaire; **4** (removal) (of trees) abattage *m*; (of buildings) démolition *f*; (of vegetation) défrichage *m*; **5** COMM liquidation *f*; **6** (gap) **a 10 cm ~** un espace de 10 cm; **7** FIN compensation *f*.
clearance sale *n* COMM (total) liquidation *f*; (partial) soldes *mpl*.
clear-cut /ˌklɪə'kʌt/ *adj* [*plan, division*] précis; [*difference, outline*] net/nette; [*problem, rule*] clair; **the matter is not so ~** l'affaire n'est pas si simple.
clear-headed *adj* lucide.
clearing /'klɪərɪŋ/ *n* **1** (glade) clairière *f*; **2** (removal) (of obstacles) enlèvement *m*; (of road, mines, debris) déblaiement *m*; **3** (levelling) (of forest) abattage *m*; (of land) défrichage *m*; **4** FIN compensation *f*.
clearing: **~ bank** *n* GB FIN banque *f* affiliée à une chambre de compensation; **~ house** *n* FIN chambre *f* de compensation; ADMIN bureau *m* central; **~-up** *n* rangement *m*.
clearly /'klɪəlɪ/ *adv* **1** (distinctly) [*speak, hear, write*] clairement; [*audible*] nettement; [*visible*] bien; [*see*] LIT bien; FIG clairement; [*labelled*] clairement; **2** (intelligibly) [*describe*] clairement; **3** (lucidly) [*think*] clairement; **4** (obviously) manifestement.
clearness /'klɪənɪs/ *n* **1** (of glass, water) transparence *f*; **2** (of day, sky) clarté *f*; **3** (purity) (of air) pureté *f*; (of note, voice) clarté *f*; **4** (of image, writing) netteté *f*; (of memory) précision *f*; **5** (intelligibility) clarté *f*.
clear-out○ /'klɪəraʊt/ *n* GB **to have a ~** faire du rangement.
clear: **~ round** *n* parcours *m* sans faute; **~-sighted** *adj* perspicace; **~way** *n* route *f* à stationnement interdit.
cleavage /'kliːvɪdʒ/ *n* **1** (of breasts) décolleté *m*; **to show a lot of ~** avoir un décolleté plongeant; **2** (of opinion) clivage *m*, division *f*.
cleave /kliːv/ *vtr* (*prét* **clove** ou **cleaved**; *pp* **cleft** ou **cleaved**) fendre.
cleaver /'kliːvə(r)/ *n* fendoir *m*.
clef /klef/ *n* clef *f*; **in the treble ~** en clef de fa.
cleft /kleft/ **I** *n* fente *f*.
II *adj* [*chin*] marqué d'un sillon; [*palate*] fendu.
clemency /'klemənsɪ/ *n* **1** (mercy) clémence *f* (**towards** envers, à l'égard de); **2** (of weather) clémence *f*.
clement /'klemənt/ *adj* [*weather, judge*] clément.
clench /klentʃ/ *vtr* serrer; **to ~ one's fist** serrer le poing; **to ~ one's teeth** serrer les dents; **to say sth between ~ed teeth** dire qch sans desserrer les dents; **~ed-fist salute** salut *m* le poing levé.
clergy /'klɜːdʒɪ/ *n* clergé *m*.
clergyman /'klɜːdʒɪmən/ ▶1251 *n* (*pl* **-men**) ecclésiastique *m*.
cleric /'klerɪk/ *n* ecclésiastique *m*.
clerical /'klerɪkl/ *adj* (*avant n*) **1** RELIG [*matters, faction*] clérical; [*control, influence*] du clergé; **2** [*staff, worker*] de bureau; **~ work** travail *m* de bureau; **~ error** erreur *f* d'écriture (*dans les comptes*).
clerical: **~ assistant** ▶1251 *n* commis *m*; **~ collar** *n* (Catholic) col *m* romain; (Protestant) col *m* de clergyman.
clerk /klɑːk, US klɜːrk/ ▶1251 *n* **1** (in office, bank etc) employé/-e *m/f*; **booking ~** employé/-e *m/f* aux réservations; **head ~** ADMIN chef *m* de bureau; COMM premier commis *m*; **2** (in UK) (to lawyer) ~ clerc *m*; (in court) greffier/-ière *m/f*; **3** US (in hotel) réceptionniste *m/f*; (in shop) vendeur/-euse *m/f*.
clever /'klevə(r)/ *adj* **1** (intelligent) [*person*] intelligent; **to be ~ at sth/at doing** être doué pour qch/pour faire; **to be ~ with figures** être doué pour le calcul; **that wasn't very ~!** ce n'était pas malin!; **2** (ingenious) [*solution, gadget, person*] astucieux/-ieuse, futé; **how ~ of you!** félicitations!; **how ~ of you to**

find the solution je te félicite d'avoir trouvé la solution; **3** (shrewd) astucieux/-ieuse; **4** (skilful) habile, adroit; **to be ~ at doing** être habile à faire; **he's ~ with his hands** il est adroit de ses mains; **5** (persuasive) [*argument, advertisement*] astucieux/-ieuse; [*lawyer, salesperson*] malin/-igne; **6** (cunning) **to be too ~ for sb** être trop malin/-igne pour qn; **to be too ~ by half** être beaucoup trop intelligent.

cleverly /'klevəlɪ/ *adv* (intelligently) intelligemment; (astutely) astucieusement; (dextrously) adroitement.

cleverness /'klevənɪs/ *n* (intelligence) intelligence *f*; (ingenuity) ingéniosité *f*; (dexterity) adresse *f*, habileté *f*.

cliché /'kliːʃeɪ, US kliː'ʃeɪ/ *n* cliché *m*, lieu *m* commun.

clichéd /'kliːʃeɪd, US kliː'ʃeɪd/ *adj* [*expression*] rebattu; [*idea, technique*] éculé; [*art, music*] bourré○ de clichés.

click /klɪk/ **I** *n* (of metal, china) petit bruit *m* sec; (of machine) déclic *m*; (of fingers, heels, tongue) claquement *m*.
II *vtr* **to ~ one's fingers/tongue** faire claquer ses doigts/sa langue; **to ~ one's heels** claquer des talons; **to ~ sth shut** fermer qch avec un bruit sec.
III *vi* **1** [*camera, lock*] faire un déclic; [*door*] faire un petit bruit sec; **2**○ (become clear) **suddenly something ~ed** tout d'un coup ça a fait tilt○; **3** (work out perfectly) **everything ~ed for them** tout a bien marché pour eux○; **4**○ (strike a rapport) **we just ~ed** on a sympathisé du premier coup.

clicking /'klɪkɪŋ/ *n* (of machine, cameras) cliquetis *m*; **~ noise** cliquetis *m*.

client /'klaɪənt/ *n* client/-e *m*/*f*.

clientele /ˌkliːɒn'tel, US ˌklaɪən'tel/ *n* clientèle *f*.

cliff /klɪf/ *n* (by sea) falaise *f*; (inland) escarpement *m*.

cliffhanger○ /'klɪfhæŋə(r)/ *n* (film) film *m* à suspense; (story) récit *m* à suspense; (situation) situation *f* à suspense.

climactic /klaɪ'mæktɪk/ *adj* [*event, moment*] crucial.

climate /'klaɪmɪt/ *n* **1** METEOROL climat *m*; **2** FIG (surroundings) atmosphère *f*; **3** ECON, POL climat *m*.

climatic /klaɪ'mætɪk/ *adj* climatique.

climax /'klaɪmæks/ **I** *n* (of career) apogée *m*; (of war) paroxysme *m*; (of plot, speech, play) point *m* culminant; **to reach the ~** [*battle*] atteindre son paroxysme; [*contest, performance*] atteindre son point culminant; **it's a fitting ~ to a long career** c'est le couronnement d'une longue carrière.
II *vi* (reach a high point) atteindre son grand moment.

climb /klaɪm/ **I** *n* **1** (ascent) (of hill) escalade *f* (**up** de; **to** jusqu'à); (of tower) montée *f*; (of mountain, rockface) ascension *f* (**up** de; **to** jusqu'à); **it's a steep ~ to the top of the tower** il y a une montée raide jusqu'en haut de la tour; **2** (steep hill) montée *f*; **to stall on the ~** caler dans la montée; **3** AVIAT montée *f*; **4** FIG (rise) ascension *f*.
II *vtr* **1** [*car, person*] grimper [*hill*]; faire l'ascension de [*cliff, mountain*]; escalader [*lamppost, mast, wall*]; grimper à [*ladder, rope, tree*]; monter [*staircase*]; **2** [*plant*] grimper à [*trellis*].
III *vi* **1** (scale) GEN grimper (**along** le long de, **to** jusqu'à); SPORT faire de l'escalade; **to ~ down** descendre [*rockface*]; **to ~ into** monter dans [*car*]; **to ~ into bed** se mettre au lit; **to ~ over** enjamber [*log, stile*]; passer par-dessus [*fence, wall*]; escalader [*debris, rocks*]; **to ~ up** grimper à [*ladder, tree*]; monter [*steps*]; **2** (rise) [*sun*] se lever; [*aircraft*] monter; **3** (slope up) [*path, road*] monter; **4** (increase) monter.
■ **climb down** revenir sur sa décision.

climber /'klaɪmə(r)/ *n* **1** (mountaineer) grimpeur/-euse *m*/*f*, alpiniste *m*/*f*; (rock-climber) varappeur/-euse *m*/*f*; **2** (plant) plante *f* grimpante.

climbing /'klaɪmɪŋ/ ▶ **949** *n* escalade *f*.

climbing: **~ boot** *n* chaussure *f* de randonnée; **~ expedition** *n* expédition *f* en montagne; **~ frame** *n* cage *f* à poules.

clinch /klɪntʃ/ **I** *n* **1** (in boxing) corps-à-corps *m*; **2**○ (embrace) **in a ~** enlacé.
II *vtr* **1** (secure) décrocher [*victory, market, order*]; **to ~ a deal** COMM conclure une affaire; POL conclure

un accord; **2** (resolve) décider de [*argument*]; **what ~ed it was...** ce qui a été décisif c'est...

clincher○ /'klɪntʃə(r)/ *n* (act, remark) facteur *m* décisif; (argument) argument *m* décisif.

cling /klɪŋ/ (*prét, pp* **clung**) *vi* **1** (physically) **to ~ (on) to** se cramponner à; **to ~ together** se cramponner l'un à l'autre; **to ~ on to sth for dear life** se cramponner de toutes ses forces à qch; **2** (emotionally) **to ~ to** se cramponner à [*parent, beliefs, hope*]; **3** (adhere) [*leaf, moss*] coller (**to** à); [*smell*] résister.
■ **cling on** [*custom, myth*] survivre obstinément.

clingfilm /'klɪŋfɪlm/ *n* GB scellofrais® *m*.

clinging /'klɪŋɪŋ/ *adj* [*plant*] à crampons; [*person*] FIG collant.

clinic /'klɪnɪk/ *n* **1** (treatment centre) centre *m* médical; **Dr X's ~** le service du Dr X; **2** GB (nursing-home) clinique *f*; **3** (advice or teaching session) clinique *f*.

clinical /'klɪnɪkl/ *adj* **1** MED clinique; **2** (scientific) [*approach*] objectif/-ive; [*precision*] clinique; **3** (unfeeling) froid.

clinically /'klɪnɪklɪ/ *adv* **1** (medically) cliniquement; **2** (unemotionally) avec une précision clinique.

clinical: **~ psychologist** ▶ **1251** *n* psychologue *mf* clinicien/-ienne; **~ psychology** *n* psychologie *f* clinique.

clink /klɪŋk/ **I** *n* **1** (noise) tintement *m*; **2**○ (prison) taule○ *f*, trou○ *m*.
II *vtr* faire tinter [*glass, keys*]; **to ~ glasses with** trinquer avec.
III *vi* [*glass, keys*] tinter.

clip /klɪp/ **I** *n* **1** (on clipboard) pince *f*; (on earring, bow tie) clip *m*; (for hair) barrette *f*; (on pen) agrafe *f*; (jewellery) clip(s) *m*; **2** (for wire) cavalier *m*; **3** TV, CIN (excerpt) extrait *m*; **4** MIL (also **cartridge ~**) chargeur *m*.
II *vtr* (*p prés etc* **-pp-**) **1** (cut, trim) tailler [*hedge*]; couper [*nails, hair, moustache*]; tondre [*dog, sheep*]; rogner [*wing*]; **to ~ an article out of the paper** découper un article dans un journal; **2** (by hooking) accrocher [*pen, microphone*] (**to** à); (by securing) fixer [*brooch*] (**to** à); **3** GB poinçonner [*ticket*]; **4** (hit) heurter.
III *vi* (*p prés etc* **-pp-**) (by hooking) s'accrocher (**to** à); (by fastening) se fixer (**to** à).
IDIOMS **to ~ sb's wings** rogner les ailes à qn; **to give sb a ~ on the ear**○ flanquer une taloche à qn○.

clip: **~board** *n* GEN porte-bloc *m inv* à pince; COMPUT presse-papiers *m inv*; **~-clop** *n* bruit *m* de sabots; **~ frame** *n* sous-verre *m inv*.

clip-on /'klɪpɒn/ **I** clip-ons *npl* (earrings) clips *mpl*.
II *adj* [*bow tie*] agrafable; **~ microphone** microcravate *m*.

clipped /klɪpt/ *adj* [*speech*] haché.

clipper /'klɪpə(r)/ **I** *n* AVIAT, NAUT clipper *m*.
II clippers *npl* (for nails) coupe-ongles *m inv*; (for hair, hedge) tondeuse *f*.

clipping /'klɪpɪŋ/ **I** *n* (from paper) coupure *f* de presse.
II clippings *npl* (hair) cheveux *mpl* coupés; (nails) bouts *mpl* d'ongles.

clique /kliːk/ *n* clique *f* PÉJ, bande *f*.

cliquey, **cliquish** /'kliːkɪ/ *adj* [*profession, group*] fermé; [*atmosphere*] exclusif/-ive.

Cllr GB *abrév écrite* = **councillor**.

cloak /kləʊk/ **I** *n* **1** (garment) cape *f*; (long, worn by men) houppelande *f*; **2** FIG (front, cover) **to be a ~ for** servir de couverture à [*operation etc*]; **a ~ of respectability** voile *m* de respectabilité.
II *vtr* **1** (surround) **to ~ sth in** ou **with** entourer qch de [*anonymity, secrecy*]; **to ~ sth in respectability** jeter un voile de respectabilité sur qch; **~ed in** enveloppé dans [*darkness*]; enveloppé de [*ambiguity, secrecy*]; **2** (hide, disguise) masquer.

cloak-and-dagger *adj* clandestin.

cloakroom /'kləʊkrʊm/ *n* **1** (for coats) vestiaire *m*; **2** GB (lavatory) toilettes *fpl*.

cloak: **~room attendant** ▶ **1251** *n* (in hotel) préposé/-e *m*/*f* au vestiaire; GB (at toilets) préposé/-e *m*/*f* à

The clock

What time is it?

It is ...	Il est ...	say ...
4 o'clock	4 heures	
	or 4 h	quatre heures
4 o'clock in the morning		
or 4 am	4 h 00	quatre heures du matin
4 o'clock in the afternoon		
or 4 pm	16 h 00	quatre heures de l'après-midi
		or seize heures*
0400	4 h 00	quatre heures
4.02	4 h 02	quatre heures deux or
two minutes		quatre heures deux
past four	4 h 02	minutes†
4.05	4 h 05	quatre heures cinq
five past four	4 h 05	quatre heures cinq
4.10	4 h 10	quatre heures dix
ten past four	4 h 10	quatre heures dix
4.15	4 h 15	quatre heures quinze‡
a quarter past four	4 h 15	quatre heures et quart‡
4.20	4 h 20	quatre heures vingt
4.25	4 h 25	quatre heures vingt-cinq
4.30	4 h 30	quatre heures trente‡
half past four	4 h 30	quatre heures et demie§
4.35	4 h 35	quatre heures trente-cinq
twenty-five to five	4 h 35	cinq heures mois vingt-cinq
4.37	4 h 37	quatre heures trente-sept
twenty-three		
minutes to five	4 h 37	cinq heures moins vingt-trois
4.40	4 h 40	quatre heures quarante
twenty to five	4 h 40	cinq heures moins vingt
4.45	4 h 45	cinq heures moins le quart
4.50	4 h 50	quatre heures cinquante
ten to five	4 h 50	cinq heures moins dix
4.55	4 h 55	quatre heures cinquante cinq
five to five	4 h 55	cinq heures moins cinq
5 o'clock	5 h	cinq heures
16.15	16 h 15	seize heures quinze
16.25	16 h 25	seize heures vingt-cinq
8 o'clock in		
the evening	8 h du soir	huit heures du soir
8 pm	20 h 00	vingt heures
12.00	12 h 00	douze heures
noon or 12 noon	12 h 00	midi
midnight		
or 12 midnight	24 h 00	minuit

* *In timetables etc., the twenty-four hour clock is used, so that* 4 pm *is* seize heures. *In ordinary usage, one says* quatre heures (de l'après-midi).

what time is it?	=	quelle heure est-il?
my watch says five o'clock	=	il est cinq heures à ma montre
could you tell me the time?	=	pouvez-vous me donner l'heure?

it's exactly four o'clock	=	il est quatre heures juste
		or il est exactement quatre heures
it's about four	=	il est environ quatre heures
it's almost three o'clock	=	il est presque trois heures
it's just before six o'clock	=	il va être six heures
it's just after five o'clock	=	il est à peine plus de cinq heures
it's gone five	=	il est cinq heures passées

When?

French never drops the word heures: at five *is* à cinq heures *and so on.*

French always uses à, *whether or not English includes the word* at. *The only exception is when there is another preposition present, as in* vers cinq heures (*towards five o'clock*), avant cinq heures (*before five o'clock*) *etc.*

what time did it happen?	=	à quelle heure cela s'est-il passé?
what time will he come at?	=	à quelle heure va-t-il venir?
it happened at two o'clock	=	c'est arrivé à deux heures
he'll come at four	=	il viendra à quatre heures
at ten past four	=	à quatre heures dix
at half past eight	=	à huit heures et demie
at three o'clock exactly	=	à trois heures précises
at about five	=	vers cinq heures or à cinq heures environ
at five at the latest	=	à cinq heures au plus tard
a little after nine	=	un peu après neuf heures
it must be ready by ten	=	il faut que ce soit prêt avant dix heures
I'll be here until 6 pm	=	je serai là jusqu'à six heures du soir
I won't be here until 6 pm	=	je ne serai pas là avant six heures du soir
it lasts from seven till nine	=	cela dure de sept à neuf heures
closed from 1 to 2 pm	=	fermé entre treize et quatorze heures
every hour on the hour	=	toutes les heures à l'heure juste
at ten past every hour	=	toutes les heures à dix

† *This fuller form is possible in all similar cases in this list. It is used only in 'official' styles.*

‡ Quatre heures et quart *sounds less official than* quatre heures quinze (*and similarly* et demie *and* moins le quart *are the less official forms). The* demie *and* quart *forms are not used with the 24-hour clock.*

§ Demi *agrees when it follows its noun, but not when it comes before the noun to which it is hyphenated, e.g.* quatre heures et demie *but* les demi-heures *etc. Note that* midi *and* minuit *are masculine, so* midi et demi *and* minuit et demi.

---

l'entretien des toilettes; **~room ticket** *n* ticket *m* de vestiaire.

clobber⊖ /'klɒbə(r)/ **I** *n* GB attirail⊖ *m*, barda⊖ *m*.
II *vtr* **1** (hit) tabasser⊖; **2** (defeat) démolir⊖.

cloche /klɒʃ/ *n* **1** (in garden) cloche *f*; **2** (also ~ **hat**) chapeau *m* cloche.

clock /klɒk/ **▶812** **I** *n* **1** (timepiece) (large) horloge *f*; (small) pendule *f*; **to set a ~** mettre une pendule à l'heure; **to put the ~s forward/back one hour** avancer/reculer les pendules d'une heure; **he does everything by the ~** tout est minuté chez lui; **to work around the ~** travailler 24 heures sur 24; **to work against the ~** faire une course contre la montre; **2** (timer) (in computer) horloge *f* (interne); (for central heating system) horloge *f* (incorporée); **3**⊖ AUT compteur *m*; **40,000 kilometers on the ~** 40 000 kilomètres au compteur; **4** SPORT chronomètre *m*.
II *vtr* **1** (hit) flanquer un marron⊖ à qn; **2** (achieve) **to ~ 9.6 seconds in the 100 metres** faire le 100 mètres en 9,6 secondes.
IDIOMS **to turn the ~ back 200 years** revenir 200 ans en arrière.
■ **clock off** GB pointer (à la sortie).

■ **clock on** GB pointer.
■ **clock up**: ~ **up** [sth] **1** faire [*distance*]; **2** [*worker*] travailler [*hours*].

clock: ~ **face** *n* cadran *m*; ~**maker** **▶1251** *n* horloger/-ère *m/f*; ~ **radio** *n* radio-réveil *m*; ~ **tower** *n* beffroi *m*; ~**watch** *vi* regarder tout le temps l'heure; ~**wise** *adj*, *adv* dans le sens des aiguilles d'une montre.

clockwork /'klɒkwɜːk/ **I** *n* (in clock) mécanisme *m* or mouvement *m* d'horloge; (in toy) mécanisme *m*.
II *adj* [*toy*] mécanique.
IDIOMS **to be as regular as ~** être réglé comme une horloge; **to go like ~** aller comme sur des roulettes.

clod /klɒd/ *n* **1** (of earth) motte *f* (de terre); **2**⊖ (fool) plouc⊖ *m*.

clog /klɒg/ *n* sabot *m*.
IDIOMS **to pop one's ~s**⊖ casser sa pipe⊖.
■ **clog up**: ¶ ~ **up** se boucher; ¶ ~ **up** [sth], [sth] **up** boucher; **to be ~ged up with traffic** être embouteillé.

cloister /'klɔɪstə(r)/ **I** *n* cloître *m*.

II *vtr* cloîtrer; **to lead a ~ed existence** mener une vie très protégée.
clone /kləʊn/ I *n* BIOL, COMPUT, FIG clone *m*.
II *vtr* cloner.
cloning /ˈkləʊnɪŋ/ *n* clonage *m*.
close¹ /kləʊs/ I *n* 1 (road) passage *m*; 2 (of cathedral) enceinte *f*.
II *adj* 1 (with close links) [*relative*] proche; [*resemblance*] frappant; **to bear a ~ resemblance to sb/sth** ressembler beaucoup à qn/qch; **~ links with** liens *mpl* étroits avec [*country*]; liens *mpl* d'amitié avec [*group*]; **in ~ contact with** en contact permanent avec; 2 (intimate) [*friend*] proche (**to** de); **they have a ~ friendship** ils sont très bons amis; 3 (almost equal) [*contest, result*] serré; **'is it the same?'—'no but it's ~'** 'c'est le même?'—'non mais c'est proche'; 4 (careful, rigorous) [*scrutiny*] minutieux/-ieuse; [*supervision*] étroit; **to pay ~ attention to sth** faire une attention toute particulière à qch; **to keep a ~ watch ou eye on sb/sth** surveiller étroitement qn/qch; 5 (compact) [*texture*] dense; [*print, formation*] serré; 6 (stuffy) [*weather*] lourd; **it's ~** il fait lourd; 7° (secretive) **she's been very ~ about it** elle n'a rien voulu dire.
III *adv* 1 (nearby) **to live quite ~** (**by**) habiter tout près; **they look ~er than they are** ils semblent plus près qu'ils ne le sont; **how ~ is the town?** est-ce que la ville est loin?; **it's ~, I can hear it** il ne doit pas être loin, je l'entends; **the closer he came** plus il approchait; **to bring sth closer** approcher qch; **to follow ~ behind** suivre de près; **to hold sb ~** serrer qn; **~ together** serrés les uns contre les autres; 2 (close temporally) **the time is ~ when** dans peu de temps; **how ~ are they in age?** combien ont-ils de différence d'âge?; **Christmas is ~** Noël approche; 3 (almost) **that's closer to the truth** ça c'est plus proche de la vérité; **'is the answer three?'—'~!'** 'est-ce que la réponse est trois?'—'tu y es presque'.
IV **close enough** *adv phr* **that's ~ enough** (no nearer) tu es assez près; (acceptable) ça ira; **20 yachts or ~ enough** il y en a près de 20 yachts.
V **close to** *prep phr, adv phr* 1 (near) près de [*place, person, object*]; **how ~ are we to...?** à quelle distance sommes-nous de...?; 2 (on point of) au bord de [*tears, hysteria*]; **to be ~ to doing** être sur le point de faire; 3 (almost at) **closer to 30 than 40** plus proche or plus près de 40 ans que de 30; **to come closest to** s'approcher le plus de [*ideal, conception*]; **to come ~ to doing** faillir faire; **how ~ are you to completing...?** est-ce que vous êtes sur le point de finir...?; **to the time when** à peu près au moment où; **it's coming ~ to the time when we must decide** l'heure de nous décider approche; 4 (also **~ on**°) (approximately) près de, presque.
VI **close by** *prep phr, adv phr* près de [*wall, bridge*]; **the ambulance is ~ by** l'ambulance n'est pas loin.
IDIOMS (**from**) **~ to**°, (**from**) **~ up** de près; **it was a ~ call**° ou **shave**° ou **thing** je l'ai/tu l'as etc échappé belle.
close² /kləʊz/ I *n* 1 GEN, SPORT fin *f*; **to bring sth to a ~** mettre fin à qch; **to draw to a ~** tirer à sa fin; **to come to a ~** se terminer; **at the ~ of day** LITTÉR à la tombée du jour LITER; 2 FIN **~ (of trading)** clôture *f*.
II *vtr* 1 (shut) fermer; 2 (block) fermer [*border, port*]; boucher [*pipe, opening*]; barrer [*road*]; interdire l'accès à [*area of town*]; 3 (bring to an end) mettre fin à [*meeting, case*]; fermer [*account*]; **the subject is now ~d** le sujet est clos; 4 (reduce) **to ~ the gap** FIG réduire l'écart; 5 (agree) conclure [*deal, contract*].
III *vi* 1 (shut) [*airport, polls, shop*] fermer; [*door, container, eyes, mouth*] se fermer; 2 (cease to operate) [*business, mine*] fermer définitivement; 3 (end) [*meeting, play*] prendre fin; **to ~ with** se terminer par [*song*]; 4 FIN [*currency, index*] clôturer (**at** à); **the market ~d down/up** le marché a clôturé en baisse/en hausse; 5 (get smaller) se réduire; 6 (get closer) se rapprocher (**on** de).
IV **closed** *pp adj* 1 (shut) fermé; **'~d'** (sign in shop) 'fermé'; (in theatre) 'relâche'; **'~d for lunch/for repairs'** 'fermé pour le déjeuner/pour cause de répara-

tions'; **'road ~d'** 'route barrée'; **'~d to the public'** 'interdit au public'; **'~d to traffic'** 'circulation interdite'; **behind ~d doors** FIG à huis clos; 2 (restricted) [*community, meeting*] fermé; **to have a ~d mind** avoir l'esprit fermé.
■ **close down**: ¶ **~ down** [*shop, business*] fermer définitivement; ¶ **~ down** [*sth*], **~** [*sth*] **down** fermer [qch] définitivement [*business, factory*].
■ **close in** [*pursuers*] se rapprocher (**on** de); [*winter*] approcher; [*fog*] descendre (**on** sur); **the nights are closing in** les jours commencent à raccourcir.
■ **close off**: **~ off** [*sth*], **~** [*sth*] **off** fermer [qch] au public.
■ **close up**: ¶ **~ up** 1 [*flower, wound*] se refermer; [*group*] se serrer; 2 [*shopkeeper*] fermer; ¶ **~ up** [*sth*], **~** [*sth*] **up** 1 fermer [qch]; 2 boucher [*hole*].
■ **close with**: ¶ **~ with** [*sb*] 1 COMM tomber d'accord avec [*trader*]; 2 MIL engager le combat avec [*enemy*]; ¶ **~ with** [*sth*] FIN accepter [*deal*].
close /kləʊs/: **~ combat** *n* corps-à-corps *m*; **~-cropped** *adj* [*hair*] coupé ras.
closed-circuit television, **CCT** *n* télévision *f* en circuit fermé.
closedown /ˈkləʊzdaʊn/ *n* 1 COMM, IND fermeture *f* (définitive); 2 GB RADIO, TV fin *f* des émissions.
closed season /kləʊz/ *n* période *f* de fermeture de la chasse et de la pêche.
closed shop /kləʊz/ *n*: industrie employant exclusivement les membres des syndicats.
close /kləʊs/: **~-fitting** *adj* [*garment*] ajusté, près du corps; **~-knit** *adj* FIG [*family, group*] très uni.
closely /ˈkləʊslɪ/ *adv* 1 (in close proximity) [*follow, look*] LIT, FIG de près; **to work ~ together** travailler en étroite collaboration; **~ written** écrit très serré; **to be ~ packed** être entassés; 2 (not distantly) [*resemble*] beaucoup; [*identify*] tellement; [*conform*] tout à fait; [*co-ordinated*] bien; **to be ~ akin to sth** ressembler beaucoup à qch; **to be ~ related** GEN être étroitement lié (**to** à); (of people) être proches parents; 3 (rigorously) [*study, monitor*] de près; [*listen*] attentivement; [*question*] avec attention; **~ guarded secret** secret bien gardé; 4 (evenly) **~ contested** ou **fought** serré.
closeness /ˈkləʊsnɪs/ *n* 1 (emotionally) intimité *f*; 2 (in mutual understanding) bonnes relations *fpl*; **the ~ of their alliance** les liens *mpl* étroits qui les unissent; 3 (rapport) rapport *m* (**to** à); 4 (proximity) (of place) proximité *f*; (of event) approche *f*; 5 (of atmosphere) (inside) manque *m* d'air; (outside) **the ~ of the weather** le temps lourd; 6 (accuracy) (of copy) fidélité *f*.
close /kləʊs/: **~-run** *adj* très serré; **~-set** *adj* très rapproché.
closet /ˈklɒzɪt/ I *n* 1 US (cupboard) placard *m*; (for clothes) penderie *f*; **linen ~** placard *m* à linge; 2 (room) cabinet *m*.
II *noun modifier* (secret) [*alcoholic, fascist*] inavoué, qui s'en cache.
III *vtr* enfermer; **to be ~ed with sb** être en tête-à-tête avec qn.
close-up /ˈkləʊsʌp/ I *n* gros plan *m*; **in ~** en gros plan.
II **close up** /kləʊsˈʌp/ *adv* (**from**) **~** de près.
closing /ˈkləʊzɪŋ/ I *n* fermeture *f*; **Sunday ~** fermeture *f* dominicale (des magasins).
II *adj* [*minutes, months, days, words*] dernier/-ière; [*scene, pages, stage*] final; [*speech*] de clôture.
closing: **~ date** *n* date *f* limite (**for** de); **~-down sale**, **~-out sale** US *n* liquidation *f*; **~ price** *n* FIN prix *m* de clôture; **~ time** *n* heure *f* de fermeture.
closure /ˈkləʊʒə(r)/ *n* 1 (of road, lane, factory) fermeture *f*; 2 POL clôture *f*; 3 (fastening) fermeture *f*.
clot /klɒt/ I *n* 1 (in blood, milk) caillot *m*; **~ in an artery** caillot obstruant une artère; **~ on the lung/on the brain** embolie *f* pulmonaire/cérébrale; 2° GB (idiot) balourd/-e *m/f*, empoté/-e° *m/f*.
II *vtr, vi* (*p prés etc* **-tt-**) coaguler, cailler.
cloth /klɒθ, US klɔːθ/ I *n* 1 (fabric) tissu *m*; **wool ~** tissu *m* de laine; 2 (piece of fabric) (for polishing, dusting)

chiffon *m*; (for floor) serpillière *f*; (for drying dishes) torchon *m*; (for table) nappe *f*; **damp ~** (for cleaning) chiffon *m* humide; (for ironing) pattemouille *f*; **3** RELIG **a man of the ~** un ecclésiastique.

II *noun modifier* [*cover, blind*] en tissu; **hey ~ ears**○! alors, tu es sourd?; **~ cap** casquette *f* de drap.

clothe /kləʊð/ **I** *vtr* habiller, vêtir; **~d in** habillé en or vêtu de; **fully ~d** tout habillé.

II *v refl* **to ~ oneself** s'habiller, se vêtir.

clothes /kləʊðz, US kləʊz/ ▶1260 **I** *npl* **1** (garments) vêtements *mpl*; **to put on/take off one's ~** s'habiller/se déshabiller; **without any ~ on** tout nu; **2** (washing) linge *m*.

II *noun modifier* [*basket, line, peg, pin*] à linge.

clothes: **~ airer** *n* séchoir *m* à linge; **~ brush** *n* brosse *f* à habits; **~ drier** *n* (machine) sèche-linge *m inv*; (airer) séchoir *m* à linge; **~hanger** *n* cintre *m*; **~ horse** *n* LIT séchoir *m* à linge; **~ moth** *n* mite *f*; **~ shop** *n* GB magasin *m* de vêtements; **~ tree** *n* US portemanteau *m*.

clothing /ˈkləʊðɪŋ/ *n* ¢ vêtements *mpl*; **an item** ou **article of ~** un vêtement; **~ trade** habillement *m*, confection *f*.

clotted cream *n* GB ~ crème *f* fraîche épaisse.

cloud /klaʊd/ **I** *n* **1** C (in sky) nuage *m*, nuée *f* LITER; **2** ¢ METEOROL nuages *mpl*; **some patches of ~** quelques nuages; **there's a lot of ~ about** il fait un temps très nuageux; **3** (mass) (of insects, smoke, dust, gas) nuage *m*; **4** FIG (negative feature) **a ~ of gloom** un voile de tristesse; **to cast a ~ over sth** jeter une ombre sur qch; **5** (blur) (in liquid, marble, gem) nuage *m*; (in glass, on mirror) buée *f*.

II *vtr* **1** (blur) [*steam, breath*] embuer [*mirror*]; [*tears*] brouiller [*vision*]; **~ed with tears** [*eyes*] voilé or brouillé de larmes; **2** (confuse) obscurcir [*judgment*]; brouiller [*memory*]; **to ~ the issue** brouiller les cartes; **3** (blight) assombrir [*occasion*].

IDIOMS **to be living in ~-cuckoo-land** croire au père Noël; **to have one's head in the ~s** avoir la tête dans les nuages; **to be on ~ nine**○ être aux anges; **to leave under a ~** partir en état de disgrâce.

■ **cloud over** [*sky*] se couvrir (de nuages); [*face*] s'assombrir.

cloudburst *n* violente averse *f*.

cloudless /ˈklaʊdlɪs/ *adj* sans nuages, limpide.

cloudy /ˈklaʊdɪ/ *adj* **1** [*weather*] couvert; **it's ~** le temps est couvert; **2** [*liquid*] trouble; [*glass*] (misted) embué; (opaque) terni.

clout /klaʊt/ **I** *n* **1** (blow) claque *f*, coup *m*; **2** FIG (weight) influence *f* (**with** auprès de, sur); **to have** ou **carry a great deal of ~** avoir beaucoup d'influence, avoir du poids.

II○ *vtr* donner un coup or une claque à [*person*].

clove /kləʊv/ **I** *prét* ▶ **cleave**.

II *n* CULIN **1** (spice) clou *m* de girofle; **oil of ~s** essence *f* de girofle; **2** (of garlic) gousse *f*.

cloven /ˈkləʊvn/ *pp* ▶ **cleave**.

cloven foot, cloven hoof *n* (of animal) sabot *m* fendu; (of devil) pied *m* fourchu.

clover /ˈkləʊvə(r)/ *n* trèfle *m*.

IDIOMS **to be/live in ~** être/vivre comme un coq en pâte.

clown /klaʊn/ *n* **1** (in circus) clown *m*; **2** PÉJ (fool) clown *m*, pitre *m*.

■ **clown around** GB faire le clown or le pitre.

cloy /klɔɪ/ *vi* [*food*] finir par lasser; [*pleasure*] perdre son charme.

cloying /ˈklɔɪɪŋ/ *adj* mièvre, mielleux/-euse.

club /klʌb/ **I** *n* ▶949 **1** (society) (+ *v sg ou pl*) club *m*; **tennis ~** club *m* de tennis; **book ~** club *m* de livres; **to be in a ~** faire partie d'un club; **2**○ (nightclub) boîte *f* de nuit○; **3** SPORT club *m*; **football ~** club *m* de football; **4** (stick) massue *f*; (for golf) club *m*; **5** (at cards) trèfle *m*; **the ace of ~s** l'as de trèfle.

II *noun modifier* [*captain, member*] du club; [*DJ*] de boîte de nuit○.

III *vtr* (*p prés etc* **-bb-**) frapper [qn/qch] à coups de massue; **to ~ sb with sth** frapper qn avec qch.

IDIOMS **join the ~**○! tu n'es pas le seul/la seule!

■ **club together** cotiser (**for** pour; **to do** pour faire).

club: **~ car** *n* US wagon-bar *m* de première classe; **~ class** *n* classe *f* club or affaires.

club foot *n* pied *m* bot; **to have a ~** être pied-bot.

club: **~house** *n* (for changing) US vestiaire *m*; (for socializing) maison *f* de club, club-house *m*; **~ sandwich** *n* sandwich *m* mixte, club sandwich *m*; **~ soda** *n* US eau *f* de seltz.

cluck /klʌk/ **I** *n* gloussement *m*; **to give a ~** glousser.

II *vtr* **to ~ one's tongue** claquer de la langue.

III *vi* **1** [*hen*] glousser; **2** FIG **to ~ over** (fuss) s'affairer comme une mère poule autour de.

clue /kluː/ *n* **1** (in investigation) indice *m* (**to** quant à); **2** (hint) indication *f* (**to, as to** quant à); **I'll give you a ~** je vais vous mettre sur la piste; **give me a ~** aide-moi; **3**○ (notion) **I haven't (got) a ~** je n'ai aucune idée; **they haven't (got) a ~** (incompetent) ils n'(en) ont pas la moindre idée; (unsuspecting) ils ne se doutent de rien; **he hasn't (got) a ~ about history** il ne connaît rien de rien à l'histoire; **4** (to crossword) définition *f*.

clued-up○ /ˌkluːdˈʌp/ GB *adj* calé○ (**about** sur).

clueless○ /ˈkluːlɪs/ *adj* GB nul/nulle○ (**about** en).

clump /klʌmp/ **I** *n* **1** (of flowers, grass) touffe *f*; (of trees) massif *m*; (of earth) motte *f*; **2** (thud) bruit *m* sourd.

II *vtr* (also **~ together**) GEN grouper; planter [qch] en groupes [*plants*].

■ **clump about, clump around** marcher d'un pas lourd.

clumsily /ˈklʌmzɪlɪ/ *adv* [*move*] gauchement; [*painted, expressed*] de façon maladroite.

clumsiness /ˈklʌmzɪnɪs/ *n* (carelessness) maladresse *f*; (awkwardness) gaucherie *f*; (of style) lourdeur *f*; (of system) côté *m* peu pratique.

clumsy /ˈklʌmzɪ/ *adj* [*person, attempt*] maladroit; [*object*] grossier/-ière; [*animal*] pataud; [*tool*] peu maniable; [*style*] lourd; **to be ~ at tennis** ne pas être très adroit au tennis; **to be ~ with one's hands** ne pas être très adroit de ses mains.

clung /klʌŋ/ *prét, pp* ▶ **cling**.

cluster /ˈklʌstə(r)/ **I** *n* (of flowers, berries) grappe *f*; (of people, islands, insects, trees) groupe *m*; (of houses) ensemble *m*; (of ideas) ensemble *m*; (of diamonds) entourage *m*; (of stars) amas *m*.

II *vi* [*people*] se rassembler (**around** autour de); **the trees were ~ed around the church** les arbres étaient groupés tout autour de l'église.

clutch /klʌtʃ/ **I** *n* **1** AUT embrayage *m*; **to let in the ~** débrayer; **to let out the ~** embrayer; **2** (cluster) (of eggs, chicks) couvée *f*; FIG (of books, awards) ensemble *m*; (of people) groupe *m*.

II *clutches npl* **to fall into the ~es of** tomber sous les griffes ou la patte○ de.

III *vtr* tenir fermement [*object, child*]; **to ~ sb/sth** serrer qn/qch contre [*chest*].

■ **clutch at**: **~ at** [sth/sb] tenter d'attraper [*branch, rail, person*]; saisir [*arm*]; FIG s'accrocher à [*hope*]; sauter sur [*opportunity, excuse*].

clutch: **~ bag** *n* pochette *f*; **~ cable** *n* câble *m* de commande d'embrayage.

clutter /ˈklʌtə(r)/ *n* **1** (mess) fatras *m*; **in a ~** en désordre; **2** ¢ (on radar) échos *mpl* fixes or parasites.

■ **clutter up**: **~ up** [sth], **~** [sth] **up** encombrer.

cluttered /ˈklʌtəd/ *adj* encombré (**with** de).

cm (*abrév écrite* = **centimetre**) cm.

Cmdr *n* MIL *abrév écrite* = **Commander**.

CND *n* (*abrév* = **Campaign for Nuclear Disarmament**) mouvement *m* pour le désarmement nucléaire.

c/o POST (*abrév écrite* = **care of**) chez.

Co *n* **1** COMM (*abrév* = **company**) Cie; **...and co** ...et Cie; HUM et compagnie; **2** GEOG (*abrév* = **county**) comté *m*.

CO *n* **1** MIL *abrév* ▶ **commanding officer**; **2** *abrév écrite* = **Colorado**.

coach /kəʊtʃ/ **I** *n* **1** (bus) (auto)car *m*; **by ~** en (auto)-

car; **2** GB (of train) wagon *m*; **3** SPORT entraîneur/-euse *m/f*; **4** (for drama, voice) répétiteur/-trice *m/f*; **5** (tutor) professeur *m* particulier; **6** (horsedrawn) (for royalty) carrosse *m*; (for passengers) diligence *f*.
II *noun modifier* [*holiday, journey, travel*] en (auto)car.
III *vtr* **1** SPORT entraîner [*team*]; être entraîneur/-euse de [*sport*]; **2** (teach) **to ~ sb** donner des leçons particulières à qn (**in** en); **to ~ sb for an exam/for a rôle** préparer qn à un examen/pour un rôle.

coaching /'kəʊtʃɪŋ/ *n* ¢ **1** (in sport) entraînement *m*; **2** (lessons) cours *mpl* particuliers.

coach: **~man** *n* cocher *m*; **~ party** *n* GB groupe *m* voyageant en autocar; **~ station** *n* GB gare *f* routière; **~ trip** *n* excursion *f* en autocar; **~work** *n* GB carrosserie *f*.

coagulate /kəʊ'ægjʊleɪt/ *vtr, vi* coaguler.

coagulation /ˌkəʊægjʊ'leɪʃn/ *n* coagulation *f*.

coal /kəʊl/ **I** *n* **1** ¢ (mineral) charbon *m*; **2** C (piece) charbon *m*; **hot** ou **live ~s** charbons *mpl* ardents.
II *noun modifier* [*cellar, shed, shovel*] à charbon.
IDIOMS **as black as ~** noir comme du charbon; **to carry ~s to Newcastle** porter de l'eau à la rivière; **to haul sb over the ~s**○ passer un savon à qn○.

coal-burning *adj* à charbon.

coalesce /ˌkəʊə'les/ *vi* [*groups of people, ideas*] fusionner; [*substances*] se mélanger.

coal: **~face** *n* front *m* de taille or d'abattage; **~field** *n* bassin *m* houiller; **~ fire** *n* GB cheminée *f* (où brûle un feu de charbon); **~-fired** *adj* à charbon; **~ industry** *n* industrie *f* minière.

coalition /ˌkəʊə'lɪʃn/ **I** *n* **1** POL coalition *f* (**between** entre; **with** avec); **2** GEN mélange *m*.
II *noun modifier* [*government, party*] de coalition.

coal: **~ man**, **~ merchant** ▶ 1251 *n* charbonnier *m*, marchand *m* de charbon; **~mine** *n* mine *f* de charbon; **~miner** ▶ 1251 *n* mineur *m*.

coalmining /'kəʊlmaɪnɪŋ/ **I** *n* extraction *f* du charbon.
II *noun modifier* [*family, region, town*] de mineurs.

coal: **~ pit** *n* mine *f* de charbon; **~ scuttle** *n* seau *m* à charbon; **~ seam** *n* gisement *m* houiller.

coarse /kɔːs/ *adj* **1** [*texture, fibre*] grossier/-ière; [*skin*] épais/-aisse; [*hair, grass*] dru; [*sand, salt*] gros/grosse (*before n*); [*sandpaper*] à gros grains; **2** (not refined) [*laugh, manners*] grossier/-ière; [*accent*] vulgaire; **~ features** traits *mpl* grossiers; **3** (indecent) [*language, joke*] cru; **4** [*food, wine*] ordinaire.

coarse-grained *adj* (of texture) à gros grains.

coarsely /'kɔːslɪ/ *adv* [*speak*] grossièrement; **~ woven** à tissage grossier; **~ ground** à grosse mouture.

coarsen /'kɔːsn/ **I** *vtr* rendre [qch] rêche [*skin*]; rendre [qn] grossier [*person*].
II *vi* [*speech*] se dégrader; [*features*] devenir lourd.

coarseness /'kɔːsnɪs/ *n* **1** (of manners) grossièreté *f*; **2** (of sand, salt) grosseur *f*; (of cloth) grossièreté *f*.

coast /kəʊst/ **I** *n* côte *f*; **off the ~** près de la côte; **the east ~** la côte est; **from ~ to ~** dans tout le pays; **the ~ is clear** FIG la voie est libre.
II *noun modifier* [*road, path*] côtier/-ière.
III *vi* **1** (freewheel) **to ~ downhill** descendre en roue libre; **2** (travel) **to ~ along at 50 mph** rouler à une vitesse de croisière de 80 km/h; **3** NAUT caboter.

coastal /'kəʊstl/ *adj* côtier/-ière.

coaster /'kəʊstə(r)/ *n* **1** (mat) dessous-de-verre *m* *inv*; **2** (boat) caboteur *m*.

coastguard /'kəʊstgɑːd/ ▶ 1251 *n* **1** (organization) gendarmerie *f* maritime; **2** (person) garde-côte *m*.

coastguard: **~ station** *n* poste *m* de la gendarmerie maritime; **~ vessel** *n* (vedette *f*) garde-côte *m*.

coastline *n* littoral *m*.

coat /kəʊt/ ▶ 1260 **I** *n* **1** (garment) manteau *m*; (for men) pardessus *m*; (jacket) veste *f*; **2** ZOOL (of dog) poil *m*, pelage *m*; (of cat) fourrure *f*, pelage *m*; (of horse, leopard) robe *f*; **3** (layer) couche *f*.
II *vtr* **1** GEN, TECH **to ~ sth with** enduire qch de [*paint, adhesive*]; revêtir qch

de [*dust, oil*]; **2** CULIN **to ~ sth in** ou **with** enrober qch de [*breadcrumbs, chocolate, sauce*]; dorer qch à [*egg*]; **~ed with sugar** [*sweet*] glacé; [*pill*] dragéifié.

coat hanger *n* cintre *m*.

coating /'kəʊtɪŋ/ *n* (edible) enrobage *m*; IND revêtement *m*; **protective ~** enduit *m* protecteur.

coat: **~ of arms** *n* blason *m*, armoiries *fpl*; **~ of mail** *n* HIST cotte *f* de mailles; **~rack** *n* portemanteau *m*; **~room** *n* US vestiaire *m*.

coat-tails /'kəʊtteɪlz/ *npl* queue *f* d'un habit.
IDIOMS **to be always hanging on sb's ~** être toujours pendu aux basques de qn; **to ride on sb's ~** profiter des efforts de qn.

coat tree *n* US portemanteau *m*.

coax /kəʊks/ *vtr* cajoler [*person*]; attirer [qch] par la ruse [*animal*]; **to ~ sb to do** ou **into doing sth** persuader qn (gentiment) de faire qch; **to ~ sth out of sb** réussir à tirer qch de qn; **to ~ a car into starting** bichonner une voiture pour qu'elle démarre.

coaxial /kəʊ'æksɪəl/ *adj* coaxial.

coaxing /'kəʊksɪŋ/ *n* efforts *mpl* de persuasion; **no amount of ~ would make him drink it** rien ne l'amènerait à le boire.

cob /kɒb/ *n* **1** (horse) cob *m*; **2** (swan) cygne *m* mâle; **3** (of maize) épi *m* de maïs; **4** GB (nut) noisette *f*; **5** GB TECH torchis *m*.

cobble /'kɒbl/ **I cobbles** *npl* pavés *mpl*.
II *vtr* **1** paver [*road*]; **~d street** rue pavée; **2** faire [*shoes*].
■ **cobble together**: **~** [sth] **together**, **~ together** [sth] concocter [qch] à la hâte.

cobbler /'kɒblə(r)/ ▶ 1251 *n* cordonnier *m*.

cobblestones /'kɒblstəʊnz/ *npl* pavés *mpl*.

cobra /'kəʊbrə/ *n* cobra *m*; (Indian) serpent *m* à lunettes.

cobweb /'kɒbweb/ *n* toile *f* d'araignée; **that will blow away the ~s** FIG ça me/te etc rafraîchira les idées.

cobwebbed /'kɒbwebd/, **cobwebby** /'kɒbwebɪ/ *adj* couvert de toiles d'araignée.

cocaine /kəʊ'keɪn/ **I** *n* cocaïne *f*.
II *noun modifier* [*dealer, dealing*] de cocaïne; **~ addict** cocaïnomane *mf*; **~ addiction** cocaïnomanie *f*.

coccyx /'kɒksɪks/ *n* (*pl* **-yxes** ou **-yges**) coccyx *m*.

cochair /kəʊtʃeə(r)/ *n* coprésident/-e *m/f*.

cochairman /'kəʊtʃeəmən/ *n* (*pl* **-men**) coprésident *m*.

cochineal /ˌkɒtʃɪ'niːl/ *n* **1** CULIN carmin *m*; **2** ZOOL cochenille *f*.

cock /kɒk/ **I** *n* **1** (rooster) coq *m*; **2** ZOOL (male bird) (oiseau *m*) mâle *m*; **3** (of hay, straw) meulon *m*; **4** (weathervane) girouette *f*; **5** (of gun) chien *m* de fusil; **at full/half ~** au cran d'armé/de repos.
II *noun modifier* [*pheasant, sparrow*] mâle; **~ bird** mâle *m*.
III *vtr* **1** (raise) **to ~ an eyebrow** hausser les sourcils; **to ~ a leg** [*dog*] lever la patte; **to ~ an ear** dresser l'oreille; **to keep an ear ~ed** dresser l'oreille; **2** (tilt) pencher; **3** MIL armer [*gun*].
IDIOMS **to be ~ of the walk** être le roi de la basse-cour; **to go off at half ~**○ (get angry) prendre la mouche; (be hasty) être impulsif/-ive; **to live like fighting ~s** vivre comme des coqs en pâte.

cockade /kɒ'keɪd/ *n* cocarde *f*.

cock-a-doodle-doo /ˌkɒkəˌduːdl'duː/ *n* cocorico *m*; **to go ~** pousser son cocorico.

cock-a-hoop○ /ˌkɒkə'huːp/ *adj* fier/fière comme Artaban.

cock-and-bull story *n* histoire *f* abracadabrante or à dormir debout.

cockatoo /ˌkɒkə'tuː/ *n* cacatoès *m*.

cockcrow /'kɒkkrəʊ/ *n* **at ~** au chant du coq.

cocked hat *n* (two points) bicorne *m*; (three points) tricorne *m*.
IDIOMS **to knock sb/sth into a ~**○ (defeat) enfoncer○ qn/qch.

cocker (**spaniel**) /'kɒkə(r)/ n cocker m.

cockerel /'kɒkərəl/ n jeune coq m.

cockfighting /'kɒkfaɪtɪŋ/ n combats mpl de coqs.

cockily /'kɒkɪlɪ/ adv effrontément.

cockiness /'kɒkɪnɪs/ n impudence f.

cockle /'kɒkl/ n (mollusc) coque f.

cockleshell /'kɒklʃel/ n coquille f de coque.

cock: ~**pit** n AVIAT cockpit m, poste m de pilotage; NAUT, AUT cockpit m; ~**roach** n cafard m.

cocksure /,kɒk'ʃɔː(r), US ,kɒk'ʃʊər/ adj PÉJ [person, manner, attitude] présomptueux/-euse.

cocktail /'kɒkteɪl/ n **1** (drink) cocktail m; **gin** ~ cocktail à base de gin; **to have** ~**s** prendre l'apéritif; **2** (mixture) **fruit** ~ salade f de fruits; **seafood** ~ cocktail m de fruits de mer; **3** FIG (of elements, ideas, drugs) cocktail m.

cocktail: ~ **bar**, ~ **lounge** n bar m; ~ **cabinet** n GB bar m (meuble); ~ **dress** n robe f de cocktail; ~ **party** n cocktail m; ~ **shaker** n shaker m; ~ **stick** n pique f (à apéritif).

cocky /'kɒkɪ/ adj impudent.

cocoa /'kəʊkəʊ/ **I** n **1** (substance) cacao m; **2** (drink) chocolat m.
II noun modifier ~ **powder** cacao en poudre; ~ **butter** beurre m de cacao.

coconut /'kəʊkənʌt/ **I** n noix f de coco.
II noun modifier [milk, oil, butter] de coco; [ice cream] à la noix de coco.

coconut: ~ **matting** n natte f en coco; ~ **palm** n cocotier m; ~ **shy** n GB jeu m de massacre.

cocoon /kə'kuːn/ **I** n ZOOL, FIG cocon m.
II vtr envelopper douillettement; **a** ~**ed existence** une existence surprotégée.

cod /'kɒd/ **I** n **1** ZOOL (also ~**fish**) (pl ~) morue f; **2** CULIN cabillaud m.
II adj PÉJ [psychology] de cuisine; [theatre] de second ordre.

COD (abrév = **cash on delivery**, **collect on delivery** US) envoi m contre remboursement.

coddle /'kɒdl/ vtr **1** GEN dorloter; **2** CULIN ~**d eggs** œufs mpl mollets.

code /kəʊd/ **I** n **1** (laws, rules) code m; **safety** ~ règlement m de sécurité; ~ **of practice** MED déontologie f (médicale); (in advertising) code m de bonne conduite; (in banking) conditions fpl générales; ~ **of ethics** moralité f; **2** (of behaviour) code m de conduite; ~ **of conduct** code m de conduite; ~ **of honour** code m d'honneur; **3** (cipher) code m; **in** ~ en code; **4** TELECOM (**dialling**) ~ indicatif m; **5** COMPUT code m.
II vtr GEN, COMPUT coder.

codeine /'kəʊdiːn/ n codéine f.

code name n nom m de code.

codeword /'kəʊdwɜːd/ n LIT (name) nom m de code; (password) mot m de passe; FIG expression f codifiée.

codify /'kəʊdɪfaɪ, US 'kɒd-/ vtr codifier [laws].

cod-liver oil n huile f de foie de morue.

co-driver /kəʊ'draɪvə(r)/ n copilote mf.

Co Durham n: abrév écrite = **County Durham**.

coed /,kəʊ'ed/ adj: abrév = **coeducational**.

coeducational /,kəʊedʒuː'keɪʃənl/ adj mixte.

coefficient /,kəʊɪ'fɪʃnt/ n coefficient m.

coerce /kəʊ'ɜːs/ vtr exercer des pressions sur [person]; **to** ~ **sb into doing** contraindre qn à faire.

coercion /kəʊ'ɜːʃn, US -ʒn/ n coercition f.

coercive /kəʊ'ɜːsɪv/ adj coercitif/-ive.

coexist /,kəʊɪg'zɪst/ vi coexister (with avec).

C of E (abrév = **Church of England**) Église f d'Angleterre.

coffee /'kɒfɪ, US 'kɔːfɪ/ **I** n **1** (commodity, liquid) café m; **a cup of** ~ une tasse de café; **2** (cup of coffee) café m; **a black/white** ~ un café (noir)/au lait.
II noun modifier [cake, dessert] au café; [crop, drinker] de café; [cup, filter, grinder, spoon] à café.

coffee: ~ **bag** n sachet m de café moulu; ~ **bar** n café m.

coffee bean n grain m de café; **a kilo of** ~**s** un kilo de café en grains.

coffee: ~ **break** n pause(-)café f; ~**-coloured** GB, ~**-colored** US adj café-au-lait (inv); ~ **grounds** n marc m de café; ~ **house** n café m; ~ **machine** n (in café) percolateur m; (domestic) cafetière f électrique; (vending machine) machine f à café; ~ **maker**, ~ **percolator** n (electric) cafetière f électrique; (on stove) cafetière f; ~ **morning** n GB réunion entre amies pour boire le café et discuter; ~ **pot** n cafetière f; ~ **service**, ~ **set** service m à café; ~ **shop** ▶ 1251 n (merchant's) brûlerie f; (café) café m; ~ **table** n table f basse; ~**-table book** n beau livre m (sorti en grand format).

coffer /'kɒfə(r)/ n coffre m, caisse f.

coffin /'kɒfɪn/ n cercueil m.

cog /kɒg/ n TECH (tooth) dent f d'engrenage; (wheel) pignon m; **a (tiny)** ~ **in the machine** FIG un (simple) rouage de la machine.

cogency /'kəʊdʒənsɪ/ n puissance f.

cogent /'kəʊdʒənt/ adj convaincant.

cogently /'kəʊdʒəntlɪ/ adv de façon convaincante.

cogitate /'kɒdʒɪteɪt/ vi réfléchir (about, on à).

cogitation /,kɒdʒɪ'teɪʃn/ n réflexion f.

cognitive /'kɒgnɪtɪv/ adj cognitif/-ive.

cognizance /'kɒgnɪzəns/ n connaissance f.

cognoscenti /,kɒgnə'ʃentɪ/ npl connaisseurs mpl.

cohabit /kəʊ'hæbɪt/ vi cohabiter (with avec).

cohere /kəʊ'hɪə(r)/ vi être cohérent.

coherence /kəʊ'hɪərəns/ n (of thought) cohérence f; (of artistic approach) harmonie f; **to give** ~ **to sth** apporter une cohérence à qch.

coherent /kəʊ'hɪərənt/ adj [argument, plan] cohérent; **he was barely** ~ on avait peine à le comprendre.

coherently /kəʊ'hɪərəntlɪ/ adv de façon cohérente.

cohesion /kəʊ'hiːʒn/ n cohésion f.

cohesive /kəʊ'hiːsɪv/ adj [group] uni; [force] cohésif/-ive.

cohort /'kəʊhɔːt/ n cohorte f.

coil /kɔɪl/ **I** n **1** (of rope, barbed wire) rouleau m; (of electric wire) bobine f; (of smoke) volute f; (of hair) boucle f; (of snake) anneau m; **2** (contraceptive) stérilet m.
II vtr (also ~ **up**) enrouler [hair, rope, wire].
III vi [river, procession] serpenter.
IV v refl **to** ~ **itself** GEN s'enrouler; [snake] se lover.

coin /kɔɪn/ **I** n **1** pièce f (de monnaie); **a gold** ~ une pièce d'or; **a pound** ~ une pièce d'une livre; **2** ¢ (coinage) monnaie f.
II vtr **1** frapper [coins]; **she's really** ~**ing it in**○ elle fait des affaires en or○; **2** FIG forger [word, term]; **to** ~ **a phrase** comme on dit.
IDIOMS **two sides of the same** ~ les deux facettes d'un même problème; **the other side of the** ~ **is that** (sth negative) le revers de la médaille, c'est que; (sth positive) le bon côté de la chose, c'est que.

coinage /'kɔɪnɪdʒ/ n **1** ¢ (coins, currency) monnaie f; **2** (word, phrase) création f; **a recent** ~ un néologisme.

coin box n **1** (pay phone) cabine f (téléphonique) à pièces; **2** (on pay phone, in laundromat) caisse f.

coincide /,kəʊɪn'saɪd/ vi coïncider (with avec).

coincidence /kəʊ'ɪnsɪdəns/ n coïncidence f, hasard m; **it is a** ~ **that** c'est par coïncidence que; **a happy** ~ un heureux hasard; **by** ~ par hasard.

coincidental /kəʊ,ɪnsɪ'dentl/ adj fortuit.

coincidentally /kəʊ,ɪnsɪ'dentəlɪ/ adv tout à fait par hasard.

coin operated adj qui marche avec des pièces.

coke /kəʊk/ n **1** (fuel) coke m; **2**○ (cocaine) coke○ f, cocaïne f.

Col abrév écrite = **Colonel**; **Col X** (on envelope) le Colonel X.

cola /'kəʊlə/ n **1** BOT cola f, colatier m; **2** (drink) coca m.

colander /'kʌləndə(r)/ n passoire f.

cold /kəʊld/ **I** n **1** ¢ (chilliness) froid m; **to feel the** ~

être sensible au froid, être frileux/-euse; **to come in from** ou **out of the ~** LIT se mettre à l'abri du froid; FIG rentrer en grâce; **to be left out in the ~** FIG être isolé; **2 C** MED rhume *m*; **to have a ~** être enrhumé, avoir un rhume; **to catch a ~** attraper un rhume; **a bad ~** un gros rhume; **a ~ in the head** un rhume de cerveau.

II *adj* **1** (chilly) froid; FIG [*colour, light*] froid; **to be** ou **feel ~** [*person*] avoir froid; **the room was ~** il faisait froid dans la pièce; **it's** ou **the weather's ~** il fait froid; **to go ~** [*food, water*] se refroidir; **don't let the baby get ~** ne laisse pas le bébé prendre froid; **to keep sth ~** tenir [qch] au frais [*food*]; **2** (unemotional) [*manner, logic*] froid; **to be ~ to** ou **towards sb** être froid avec qn; **to leave sb ~** laisser qn froid; **3** (unconscious) **to be out ~** être sans connaissance; **to knock sb out ~** assommer qn, mettre qn KO○.

III *adv* **1**○ (without preparation) [*speak, perform*] à froid○; **2** US (thoroughly) [*learn, know*] par cœur.

IDIOMS **to have** ou **get ~ feet** avoir les jetons○; **in ~ blood** de sang-froid; **my blood runs ~** mon sang se fige; **in the ~ light of day** à tête reposée; **to be as ~ as ice** [*feet*] être gelé; [*room*] être glacial; **to pour ~ water on sth** descendre qch en flammes○.

cold-blooded /ˌkəʊldˈblʌdɪd/ *adj* **1** LIT [*animal*] à sang froid; **2** FIG [*killer*] sans pitié; [*crime*] commis de sang-froid.

cold: ~-bloodedly *adv* de sang-froid; **~ calling** *n* COMM démarchage *m* par téléphone; **~ comfort** *n* piètre consolation *f* (**for** pour); **~ cuts** *npl* assiette *f* anglaise; **~ frame** *n* châssis *m*; **~-hearted** *adj* impitoyable.

coldly /ˈkəʊldlɪ/ *adv* [*say*] froidement; [*receive, stare*] avec froideur; **~ polite** d'une politesse glaciale.

coldness /ˈkəʊldnɪs/ *n* LIT, FIG froideur *f*.

cold shoulder *n* **to give sb the ~** snober qn, battre froid à qn.

cold: ~ snap *n* brève vague *f* de froid; **~ sore** *n* bouton *m* de fièvre.

cold storage *n* (process) GEN conservation *f* par le froid; CHEM conservation *f* cryogénique.

cold store *n* chambre *f* froide or frigorifique.

cold sweat *n* sueurs *fpl* froides; **to bring sb out in a ~** donner des sueurs froides à qn.

cold: ~ table *n* buffet *m* froid; **~ tap** *n* robinet *m* d'eau froide.

cold turkey○ *n* (treatment) sevrage *m*; (reaction) réaction *f* de manque; **to go ~** s'abstenir (**on** de); **to be ~** être en manque.

Cold War *n* guerre *f* froide.

coleslaw /ˈkəʊlslɔ:/ *n* salade *f* à base de chou cru.

colic /ˈkɒlɪk/ *n* **C** coliques *fpl*.

colicky /ˈkɒlɪkɪ/ *adj* [*baby*] qui souffre de coliques.

collaborate /kəˈlæbəreɪt/ *vi* collaborer (**on, in** à; **with** avec).

collaboration /kəˌlæbəˈreɪʃn/ *n* collaboration *f* (**between** entre; **with** avec; **in** à).

collaborative /kəˈlæbərətɪv/ *adj* [*project, task*] en collaboration; [*approach*] de collaboration.

collaborator /kəˈlæbəreɪtə(r)/ *n* collaborateur/-trice *m/f*.

collage /ˈkɒlɑːʒ, US kəˈlɑːʒ/ *n* **1** ART collage *m*; **2** (film) montage *m*.

collapse /kəˈlæps/ **I** *n* **1** (of regime, system, bank, economy, market, hopes) effondrement *m* (**of, in** de); **to be on the point of ~** être sur le point de s'effondrer; **2** (of deals, talks, relationship) échec *m*; **3** (of company) faillite *f* (**of** de); **4** (of person) (physical) écroulement *m*; (mental) effondrement *m*; **to be close to ~** être sur le point de s'écrouler; **5** (of building, bridge) effondrement *m*; (of tunnel, wall) écroulement *m*; (of chair, bed) affaissement *m*; **6** MED (of lung) collapsus *m*.

II *vtr* **1** (fold) plier; **2** (combine) synthétiser.

III *vi* **1** (founder) [*regime, system, economy, hopes, plan*] s'effondrer; [*case, deal, talks*] échouer; **2** (go bankrupt) [*company*] faire faillite (**through** à cause de); **3** (slump)

[*person*] s'écrouler; **to ~ onto the bed** s'effondrer sur le lit; **to ~ and die** mourir subitement; **to ~ in tears** s'effondrer en larmes; **4** (fall down) [*building, bridge*] s'effondrer; [*tunnel, wall*] s'écrouler; [*chair*] s'affaisser (**under** sous); **5** (deflate) [*balloon*] se dégonfler; [*soufflé*] tomber; **6** MED [*lung*] se dégonfler; **7** (fold) [*bike*] se plier.

collapsible /kəˈlæpsəbl/ *adj* pliant.

collar /ˈkɒlə(r)/ **▶1260** **I** *n* **1** (on garment) col *m*; **to grab sb by the ~** prendre qn au collet; **2** (for animal) collier *m*; **3** TECH (ring) bague *f* d'arrêt.

II○ *vtr* alpaguer○ [*thief*]; (in conversation) coincer○.

IDIOMS **to get hot under the ~** se mettre en rogne○.

collar: ~bone *n* clavicule *f*; **~ size** **▶1260** *n* encolure *f*; **~ stud** *n* bouton *m* de col.

collate /kəˈleɪt/ *vtr* collationner.

collateral /kəˈlætərəl/ **I** *n* nantissement *m*; **to put up ~** offrir une garantie supplémentaire.

II *adj* **1** JUR (relative) collatéral; (subordinate) secondaire; **2** FIN **~ loan** prêt *m* nanti.

colleague /ˈkɒliːg/ *n* collègue *mf*.

collect /kəˈlekt/ **I** *adv* US TELECOM **to call sb ~** appeler qn en PCV.

II *vtr* (gather) ramasser [*wood, litter, eggs*]; rassembler [*information, documents*]; recueillir [*signatures*]; **to ~ one's wits** rassembler ses esprits; **to ~ one's strength** rassembler or ramasser ses forces; **to ~ one's thoughts** se recueillir; **2** (as hobby) collectionner, faire collection de [*stamps, coins*]; **3** (receive, contain) (intentionally) recueillir [*rain water*]; (accidentally) [*objects*] prendre, ramasser [*dust*]; **4** (obtain) percevoir [*rent*]; encaisser [*fares, money*]; recouvrer [*debt*]; toucher [*pension*]; ADMIN percevoir [*tax, fine*]; remporter [*prize*]; **to ~ money for charity** collecter de l'argent pour les bonnes œuvres; **5** (take away) ramasser [*rubbish*]; faire la levée de [*mail, post*]; **6** (pick up) aller chercher [*person*]; récupérer [*keys, book etc*]; **to ~ a suit from the cleaners** passer prendre un costume chez le teinturier.

III *vi* **1** (accumulate) [*dust, leaves*] s'accumuler; [*crowd*] se rassembler, se réunir; **2** (raise money) **to ~ for charity** faire la quête pour des bonnes œuvres.

IV collected *pp adj* **1** [*person*] calme; **2** (assembled) **the ~ed works of Dickens** les œuvres complètes de Dickens; **the ~ed poems of W. B. Yeats** la collection complète des poèmes de W. B. Yeats.

collect call *n* US TELECOM appel *m* en PCV.

collection /kəˈlekʃn/ *n* **1 ¢** (collecting) (of objects) ramassage *m*; (of old clothes, newspapers etc) collecte *f*; (of information, facts) rassemblement *m*; (of rent) encaissement *m*; (of debt) recouvrement *m*; (of tax) perception *f*; POST levée *f*; **your suit is ready for ~** votre costume est prêt; **refuse ~** ramassage *m* des ordures; **2** (set of collected items) (of coins, records etc) collection *f*; (anthology) recueil *m*; **art ~** collection *f* (de tableaux); **an odd ~ of people** un mélange curieux de gens; **spring ~** (clothes) collection de printemps; **3** (sum of money collected) GEN collecte *f* (**for** pour); (in church) quête *f*; **to make** ou **organize a ~** faire la quête, organiser une collecte.

collective /kəˈlektɪv/ **I** *n* entreprise *f* collective.

II *adj* collectif/-ive.

collective: ~ bargaining *n*: négociations entre le syndicat et le patronat; **~ farm** *n* ferme *f* collective.

collectively /kəˈlektɪvlɪ/ *adv* collectivement; **~ owned** en copropriété.

collective: ~ noun *n* LING (nom *m*) collectif *m*; **~ ownership** *n* copropriété *f*.

collector /kəˈlektə(r)/ *n* **1** (of coins etc) collectionneur/-euse *m/f*; **to be a stamp ~** collectionner les timbres; **2** (official) (of taxes) percepteur *m*; (of rent, debts) encaisseur *m*; (of funds) quêteur/-euse *m/f*.

collector's item *n* pièce *f* de collection.

college /ˈkɒlɪdʒ/ *n* **1** (place of tertiary education) établissement *m* d'enseignement supérieur; (school, part of university) collège *m*; US UNIV faculté *f*; **to go to ~**, **to be at** ou **in** US **~** faire des études supérieures; **2**

Colours

Not all English colour terms have a single exact equivalent in French: for instance, in some circumstances brown is marron, in others brun. If in doubt, look the word up in the dictionary.

Colour terms

what colour is it?	=	c'est de quelle couleur?
		or (more formally) de quelle couleur est-il?
it's green	=	il est vert *or* elle est verte
to paint sth green	=	peindre qch en vert
to dye sth green	=	teindre qch en vert
to wear green	=	porter du vert
dressed in green	=	habillé de vert

Colour nouns are all masculine in French:

I like green	=	j'aime le vert
I prefer blue	=	je préfère le bleu
red suits her	=	le rouge lui va bien
it's a pretty yellow!	=	c'est un joli jaune!
have you got it in white?	=	est-ce que vous l'avez en blanc?
a pretty shade of blue	=	un joli ton de bleu
it was a dreadful green	=	c'était un vert affreux
a range of greens	=	une gamme de verts

Most adjectives of colour agree with the noun they modify:

a blue coat	=	un manteau bleu
a blue dress	=	une robe bleue
blue clothes	=	des vêtements bleus

Some that don't agree are explained below.

Words that are not true adjectives

Some words that translate English adjectives are really nouns in French, and so don't show agreement:

a brown shoe	=	une chaussure marron
orange tablecloths	=	des nappes *fpl* orange
hazel eyes	=	des yeux *mpl* noisette

Other French words like this include: cerise (cherry-red), chocolat (chocolate-brown) and émeraude (emerald-green).

Shades of colour

Expressions like pale blue, dark green or light yellow are also invariable in French and show no agreement:

a pale blue shirt	=	une chemise bleu pâle
dark green blankets	=	des couvertures *fpl* vert foncé
a light yellow tie	=	une cravate jaune clair
bright yellow socks	=	des chaussettes *fpl* jaune vif

French can also use the colour nouns here: instead of une chemise bleu pâle you could say une chemise d'un bleu pâle; and similarly des couvertures d'un vert foncé (etc). The nouns in French are normally used to translate English adjectives of this type ending in -er and -est:

a darker blue	=	un bleu plus foncé
the dress was a darker blue	=	la robe était d'un bleu plus foncé

Similarly:

a lighter blue	=	un bleu plus clair *(etc)*

In the following examples, blue stands for most basic colour terms:

pale blue	=	bleu pâle
light blue	=	bleu clair
bright blue	=	bleu vif
dark blue	=	bleu foncé
deep blue	=	bleu profond
strong blue	=	bleu soutenu

Other types of compound in French are also invariable, and do not agree with their nouns:

a navy-blue jacket	=	une veste bleu marine

These compounds include: bleu ciel (sky-blue), vert pomme (apple-green), bleu nuit (midnight-blue), rouge sang (blood-red) etc. However, all English compounds do not translate directly into French. If in doubt, check in the dictionary.

French compounds consisting of two colour terms linked with a hyphen are also invariable:

a blue-black material	=	une étoffe bleu-noir
a greenish-blue cup	=	une tasse bleu-vert
a greeny-yellow dress	=	une robe vert-jaune

English uses the ending -ish, or sometimes -y, to show that something is approximately a certain colour, e.g. a reddish hat or a greenish paint. The French equivalent is -âtre:

blue-ish	=	bleuâtre
greenish *or* greeny	=	verdâtre
greyish	=	grisâtre
reddish	=	rougeâtre
yellowish *or* yellowy	=	jaunâtre
etc.		

Other similar French words are rosâtre, noirâtre and blanchâtre. Note however that these words are often rather negative in French. It is better not to use them if you want to be complimentary about something. Use instead tirant sur le rouge/jaune etc.

To describe a special colour, English can add -coloured to a noun such as raspberry (framboise) or flesh (chair). Note how this is said in French, where the two-word compound with couleur is invariable, and, unlike English, never has a hyphen:

a chocolate-coloured skirt	=	une jupe couleur chocolat
raspberry-coloured fabric	=	du tissu couleur framboise
flesh-coloured tights	=	un collant couleur chair

Colour verbs

English makes some colour verbs by adding -en (e.g. blacken). Similarly French has some verbs in -ir made from colour terms:

to blacken	=	noircir
to redden	=	rougir
to whiten	=	blanchir

The other French colour terms that behave like this are: bleu (bleuir), jaune (jaunir), rose (rosir) and vert (verdir). It is always safe, however, to use devenir, thus:

to turn purple	=	devenir violet

Describing people ▶ 765

Note the use of the definite article in the following:

to have black hair	=	avoir les cheveux noirs
to have blue eyes	=	avoir les yeux bleus

Note the use of à in the following:

a girl with blue eyes	=	une jeune fille aux yeux bleus
the man with black hair	=	l'homme aux cheveux noirs

Not all colours have direct equivalents in French. The following words are used for describing the colour of someone's hair (note that les cheveux is plural in French):

fair	=	blond
dark	=	brun
blonde *or* blond	=	blond
brown	=	châtain *inv*
red	=	roux
black	=	noir
grey	=	gris
white	=	blanc

Check other terms such as ginger, auburn, mousey etc. in the dictionary.

Note these nouns in French:

a fair-haired man	=	un blond
a fair-haired woman	=	une blonde
a dark-haired man	=	un brun
a dark-haired woman	=	une brune

The following words are useful for describing the colour of someone's eyes:

blue	=	bleu
light blue	=	bleu clair *inv*
light brown	=	marron clair *inv*
brown	=	marron *inv*
hazel	=	noisette *inv*
green	=	vert
grey	=	gris
greyish-green	=	gris-vert *inv*
dark	=	noir

body) (of arms, cardinals) collège *m*; (of surgeons) acadé-
nie *f*; (of midwives, nurses) association *f*.

ollege education *n* études *fpl* supérieures; **to
ave a ~** faire des études supérieures.

ollege: **~ of advanced technology, CAT** *n* GB
Institut *m* Universitaire de Technologie; **~ of agri-
ulture** *n* institut *m* agronomique; **~ of educa-
ion** *n* GB ≈ École *f* normale; **~ of further educa-
ion, CFE** *n* GB *école ouverte aux adultes et aux jeunes
our terminer un cycle d'études secondaires.*

ollide /kə'laɪd/ *vi* [*vehicle*] entrer en collision; **I ~d
with a tree** j'ai heurté un arbre; **we ~d in the corri-
lor** nous nous sommes heurtés dans le couloir.

ollie /'kɒlɪ/ *n* colley *m*.

ollier /'kɒlɪə(r)/ ▶ **1251** *n* (worker) mineur *m*.

olliery /'kɒlɪərɪ/ *n* houillère *f*.

ollision /kə'lɪʒn/ *n* **1** (crash) collision *f*; **to come into
~ with** entrer en collision avec; **2** (clash) affronte-
nent *m* (**between** entre).

ollision course *n* **the planes were on a ~** les
vions allaient se percuter; FIG **to be on a ~ with
people**] aller droit à l'affrontement.

olloquial /kə'ləʊkwɪəl/ *adj* familier/-ière; **~
English** anglais parlé.

olloquialism /kə'ləʊkwɪəlɪzəm/ *n* expression *f* fami-
ière.

olloquially /kə'ləʊkwɪəlɪ/ *adv* familièrement.

olloquium /kə'ləʊkwɪəm/ *n* (*pl* **~s** ou **-quia**)
olloque *m*.

ollude /kə'luːd/ *vi* comploter (**with** avec).

ollusion /kə'luːʒn/ *n* connivence *f*; **in ~ with** de
onnivence avec.

ologne /kə'ləʊn/ *n* eau *f* de Cologne.

olombia /kə'lɒmbɪə/ ▶ **840** *pr n* Colombie *f*.

olon /'kəʊlən/ *n* **1** ANAT côlon *m*; **2** LING deux
oints *mpl*.

olonel /'kɜːnl/ ▶ **1192** *n* colonel *m*.

olonial /kə'ləʊnɪəl/ **I** *n* colonial/-e *m/f*.
I *adj* colonial; US ARCHIT en style colonial.

olonialist /kə'ləʊnɪəlɪst/ *n, adj* colonialiste (*mf*).

olonization /ˌkɒlənaɪ'zeɪʃn, US -nɪ'z-/ *n* colonisation

olonize /'kɒlənaɪz/ *vtr* coloniser ALSO FIG.

olonizer /'kɒlənaɪzə(r)/ *n* colon *m*.

olony /'kɒlənɪ/ *n* colonie *f*.

olor US *n, vtr, vi* = **colour**.

olorado beetle /ˌkɒlə'rɑːdəʊ 'biːtl/ *n* doryphore *m*.

olor line *n* US discrimination *f* raciale.

olossal /kə'lɒsl/ *adj* colossal.

olour GB, **color** US /'kʌlə(r)/ ▶ **818** **I** *n* **1** (hue)
ouleur *f*; **what ~ is it?** de quelle couleur est-il?; **the
ky was the ~ of lead** le ciel était de la couleur du
lomb; **in ~** CIN, TV en couleur; **to give ~ to sth**
olorer qch; **to paint sth in glowing ~s** FIG brosser
n tableau brillant de qch; **'available in 12 ~s'**
existe en 12 coloris'; **2** (in writing, description) couleur *f*;
3 (dye) (for food) colorant *m*; (for hair) teinture *f*; **4** (ma-
e-up) **eye ~** fard *m* à paupières; **lip ~** rouge *m* à
èvres; **5** (pigmentation) couleur *f* de peau; **people of all
aces and ~s** des gens de toutes races et de toutes
ouleurs; **6** (complexion) couleur *f*; **to lose (one's) ~**
erdre ses couleurs; **to put ~ into sb's cheeks**
edonner des couleurs à qn; **he's getting his ~ back**
l reprend des couleurs.
I colours *npl* MIL, SPORT couleurs *fpl*; NAUT pavil-
on *m*; **racing ~s** couleurs de l'écurie; **under false
~s** FIG sous un faux jour; **to get one's football
~s** GB être sélectionné pour l'équipe de football.
II *noun modifier* **1** PHOT, TV [*photo, photography*]
en) couleur; [*copier, printer*] couleur; **~ film** (for
amera) pellicule *f* couleur; CIN film *m* en couleur; **2**
OCIOL [*prejudice, problem*] racial.
V *vtr* **1** LIT (with paints, crayons) colorier; (with
ommercial paints) peindre; (with food dye) colorer; (with
air dye) teindre; **to ~ sth blue** colorier or teindre

qch en bleu; **2** FIG (prejudice) fausser [*judgment*]; **3**
FIG (enhance) enjoliver [*account*].
V *vi* [*person*] (also **~ up**) rougir.
IDIOMS **to be off ~** ne pas être en forme; **to pass
with flying ~s** réussir haut la main; **to show one's
true ~s** se montrer sous son vrai jour.

colour: **~ bar** *n* GB discrimination *f* raciale; **~
blind** *adj* daltonien/-ienne; **~ blindness** *n* dalto-
nisme *m*.

colour code GB, **color code** US *vtr* classer [qch]
par couleurs [*files*].

coloured GB, **colored** US /'kʌləd/ **I** *n* **1** (in GB, US)
INJUR personne *f* de couleur; **2** (in South Africa) métis/
-isse *m/f*.
II coloureds *npl* (laundry) couleurs *fpl*.
III *adj* **1** LIT [*pen, paper, bead*] de couleur; [*picture*]
en couleur; [*light, glass*] coloré; **brightly ~** aux
couleurs vives; **2** (non-white) INJUR GB, US de couleur;
(in South Africa) métis/-isse.
IV -coloured *combining form* **a raspberry-~ dress**
une robe (couleur) framboise; **copper-~** couleur
cuivre; **a highly-~ account** un récit très enjolivé.

colour: **~-fast** *adj* grand teint *inv*; **~ filter** *n*
PHOT filtre *m* coloré.

colourful GB, **colorful** US /'kʌləfl/ *adj* **1** LIT aux
couleurs vives; **2** FIG [*story, life*] haut en couleur;
[*character*] pittoresque.

colourfully GB, **colorfully** US /'kʌləfəlɪ/ *adv* en
couleurs vives.

colouring GB, **coloring** US /'kʌlərɪŋ/ *n* **1** (hue) (of
plant, animal) couleurs *fpl*; (complexion) teint *m*; **2** ¢ ART
coloriage *m*; **~ book** album *m* à colorier; **3** (dye) (for
food) colorant *m*; (for hair) teinture *f*.

colourless GB, **colorless** US /'kʌləlɪs/ *adj* **1** LIT
[*liquid, gas*] incolore; **2** FIG (bland) terne.

colour: **~ scheme** *n* couleurs *fpl*, coloris *m*; **~
sense** *n* sens *m* des couleurs; **~ supplement** *n*
supplément *m* illustré; **~ television** *n* télévision *f*
(en) couleur; **~way** *n* coloris *m*.

colt /kəʊlt/ *n* ZOOL poulain *m*.

Columbus /kə'lʌmbəs/ *pr n* Christophe Colomb.

column /'kɒləm/ *n* **1** GEN, ARCHIT colonne *f*; **2** (in
newspaper) rubrique *f*; **sports/political ~** rubrique
sportive/politique; **letters ~** courrier *m* des lecteurs.

columnist /'kɒləmnɪst/ *n* journaliste *mf*.

coma /'kəʊmə/ *n* coma *m*; **in a ~** dans le coma; **to
go into a ~** entrer dans le coma.

comatose /'kəʊmətəʊs/ *adj* **1** MED comateux/-euse;
2 FIG abruti.

comb /kəʊm/ **I** *n* **1** (for hair) peigne *m*; **to run a ~
through one's hair, to give one's hair a (quick) ~**
se donner un coup de peigne; **2** (in weaving) carde *f*; **3**
(honeycomb) rayon *m*; **4** (cock's crest) crête *f*.
II *vtr* **1** to **~ sb's hair** peigner qn; **to ~ one's hair**
se peigner; **2** (search) **to ~ a place** passer un lieu au
peigne fin; **3** (in weaving) carder.
■ comb out: **~ out** [sth], **~** [sth] out démêler.
■ comb through: **~ through** [sth] passer [qch] au
peigne fin (**for sth** à la recherche de qch).

combat /'kɒmbæt/ **I** *n* combat *m*; **in ~** au combat;
close/single ~ combat rapproché/singulier.
II *noun modifier* [*aircraft, troops, zone*] de combat.
III *vtr* (*p prés etc* **-tt-**) lutter contre, combattre.

combatant /'kɒmbətənt/ *n* combattant/-e *m/f*.

combative /'kɒmbətɪv/ *adj* combatif/-ive.

combat jacket *n* veste *f* de treillis.

combination /ˌkɒmbɪ'neɪʃn/ *n* **1** (mixture) GEN combinaison *f* (**of** de); (of factors, events) conjonction *f*; **2**
(mixing) mélange *m* (**of** de); **in ~ with** en association
avec; **3** (of numbers, chemicals) combinaison *f*; **~ lock**
serrure *f* à combinaison.

combine I /'kɒmbaɪn/ *n* **1** COMM groupe *m*; **2**
AGRIC = **combine harvester**.
II *vtr* **1** /kəm'baɪn/ (pair up, link) combiner [*activities,
colours, items, elements*] (**with** avec); associer [*ideas,
aims*] (**with** à); **to ~ two companies** regrouper deux
sociétés; **to ~ fantasy with realism** allier la fantai-

sie au réalisme; **to ~ forces** [*countries, people*] (merge) s'allier; (cooperate) collaborer; **2** /kəm'baın/ CULIN mélanger (**with** avec); **3** /'kɒmbaın/ (on farm) moissonner, battre [*crops*].
III /kən'baın/ *vi* **1** (go together) [*activities, colours, elements*] se combiner; **2** (join) [*people, groups*] s'associer; [*institutions, firms*] fusionner.

combined /kəm'baınd/ *adj* **1** (joint) **~ operation** collaboration *f*; **a ~ effort** une collaboration; **2** (total) [*salary, age*] total; **3** (put together) [*effects*] combiné; [*forces*] conjoint; **~ with** combiné avec; **more than all the rest ~** plus que tous les autres réunis.

combined pill *n* pilule *f* combinée.

combine harvester *n* moissonneuse-batteuse *f*.

combustible /kəm'bʌstəbl/ *adj* combustible.

combustion /kəm'bʌstʃn/ *n* combustion *f*; **internal ~ engine** moteur *m* à combustion interne.

come /kʌm/ **I** *excl* **~ (now)!** allons!; **~, ~!** allons, allons!
II *vtr* (*prét* **came**; *pp* **come**) (travel) faire; **to ~ 100 km to see** faire 100 km pour voir.
III *vi* (*prét* **came**; *pp* **come**) **1** (arrive) [*person, day, success, fame*] venir; [*bus, letter, news, rains, winter, war*] arriver; **to ~ after sb** poursuivre qn; **to ~ by** (take) prendre [*bus, taxi, plane*]; **I came on foot/by bike** je suis venu à pied/à bicyclette; **to ~ down** descendre [*stairs, street*]; **to ~ up** monter [*stairs, street*]; **to ~ from** venir de [*airport, hospital*]; **to ~ into** entrer dans [*house, room*]; **to ~ past** [*car, person*] passer; **to ~ through** [*person*] passer par [*town centre, tunnel*]; [*water, object*] traverser [*window etc*]; **to ~ to** venir à [*school, telephone*]; **to ~ to the door** venir ouvrir; **to ~ running** arriver en courant; **when the time ~s** lorsque le moment sera venu; **the time has come to do** le moment est venu de faire; **I'm coming!** j'arrive!; **to ~ and go** aller et venir; **you can ~ and go as you please** tu es libre de tes mouvements; **fashions ~ and go** les modes vont et viennent; **~ next year** l'année prochaine; **~ Christmas/summer** à Noël/en été; **for some time to ~** encore quelque temps; **there's still the speech to ~** il y a encore le discours; **2** (approach) s'approcher; **to ~ and see/help sb** venir voir/aider qn; **to ~ to sb for** venir demander [qch] à qn [*money, advice*]; **I could see it coming** (of accident) je le voyais venir; **don't ~ any closer** ne vous approchez pas (plus); **to ~ close** ou **near to doing** faillir faire; (call, visit) [*dustman, postman*] passer; [*cleaner*] venir; **I've come to do** je viens faire; **I've come for the keys** je viens chercher les clés; **my brother is coming for me at 10 am** mon frère passe me prendre à 10 heures; **4** (attend) venir; **to ~ to** venir à [*meeting, party*]; **5** (reach) **to ~ to, to ~ up/down to** [*water*] venir jusqu'à; [*dress, curtain*] arriver à; **6** (happen) **how did you ~ to do?** comment as-tu fait pour faire?; **that's what ~s of doing** voilà ce qui arrive quand on fait; **how ~?** comment ça se fait?; **~ what may** advienne que pourra; **to take things as they ~** prendre les choses comme elles viennent; **~ to think of it** en fait, **7** (begin) **to ~ to believe/hate** finir par croire/détester; **8** (originate) **to ~ from** [*person*] être originaire de, venir de [*city, country*]; [*word, legend*] venir de [*country, language*]; [*substance*] provenir de [*raw material*]; [*coins, stamps*] provenir de [*place*]; [*smell, sound*] venir de [*place*]; **to ~ from France** [*fruit, painting*] provenir de France; [*person*] être français/-e; **9** (be available) **to ~ in** exister en [*sizes, colours*]; **to ~ with chips** être servi avec des frites; **to ~ with matching napkins** être vendu avec les serviettes assorties; **10** (tackle) **to ~ to** aborder [*problem, subject*]; **I'll ~ to that in a moment** je reviendrai sur ce point dans un moment; **11** (develop) **it ~s with practice** cela s'apprend avec la pratique; **wisdom ~s with age** la sagesse vient en vieillissant; **12** (be situated) venir; **to ~ after** suivre, venir après; **to ~ before** (in time, list, queue) précéder; (in importance) passer avant; **to ~ first/last** arriver premier/dernier; **where did you ~?** tu es arrivé combien○?; **my**

family ~s first ma famille passe avant tout; **don' let this ~ between us** on ne va pas se fâcher pou ça; **to ~ between two people** s'interposer entr deux personnes; **13** (be due) **the house ~s to m** **when they die** la maison me reviendra quand il mourront; **he had it coming (to him)**○ ça lui pendai au nez; **they got what was coming to them**○ ils on fini par avoir ce qu'ils méritaient; **14** (be a question of **when it ~s to sth/to doing** lorsqu'il s'agit de qch de faire.
IDIOMS **~ again**○? pardon?; **I don't know if I'm coming or going** je ne sais plus où j'en suis; **he's as stupid as they ~** il n'y a pas plus stupide que lui **~ to that** ou **if it ~s to that, you may be right** e fait, tu as peut-être raison; **to ~ as a shock** être un choc.

■ **come about** [*problems, reforms*] survenir; [*situa tion, change*] se produire.

■ **come across**: ¶ **~ across** [*meaning, message*] passer; [*feelings*] transparaître; **she ~s across well on TV** elle passe bien à la télé; **~ across as** donner l'impression d'être [*liar, expert*]; paraître [*enthusiastic, honest*]; ¶ **~ across** [*sth*] tomber sur [*article, exam ple*]; ¶ **~ across** [*sb*] rencontrer [*person*].

■ **come along 1** (arrive) [*bus, person*] arriver; [*oppor tunity*] se présenter; **2** (hurry up) **~ along!** dépêche toi!; **3** (attend) venir; **to ~ along to** venir à [*lecture, party*]; **4** (make progress) [*pupil*] faire des progrès; [*book, work, project*] avancer; [*painting, tennis*] progresser; [*seedling*] pousser; **your Spanish is coming along** votre espagnol a progressé.

■ **come apart 1** (accidentally) [*book, box*] se déchirer; [*toy, camera*] se casser; **the toy came apart in my hands** le jouet m'est resté dans les mains; **2** (intention ally) [*components*] se séparer; [*machine*] se démonter.

■ **come around** US = **come round**.

■ **come at**: **~ at** [*sb*] (attack) [*person*] attaquer; [*bull*] foncer sur.

■ **come away 1** (leave) partir; **to ~ away from** quitter [*cinema, match*]; sortir de [*meeting*]; **to ~ away with the feeling that** rester sur l'impression que; **2** (move away) s'éloigner; **3** (detach) se détacher (**from** de).

■ **come back 1** (return) GEN revenir (**from** de; **to** à); (to one's house) rentrer; **to ~ running back** revenir en courant; **to ~ back to** revenir à [*topic, problem*]; **to ~ back with sb** raccompagner qn; **to ~ back with** (return) revenir avec [*present, idea, flu*]; (reply) répondre par [*offer, suggestion*]; **can I ~ back to you on that?** est-ce que nous pourrions en reparler?; **it's all coming back to me now** tout me revient mainte nant; **2** (become popular) [*law, system*] être rétabli; [*trend*] revenir à la mode.

■ **come by**: ¶ **~ by** [*person*] passer; ¶ **~ by** [*sth*] trouver [*book, job, money*].

■ **come down 1** (move lower) [*person, lift, blind*] descendre; [*curtain*] tomber; **he's really come down in the world** FIG il est vraiment tombé bas; **2** (drop) [*price, inflation, temperature*] baisser (**from** de; **to** à); [*cost*] diminuer; **cars are coming down in price** le prix des voitures baisse; **3** [*snow, rain*] tomber; **4** (land) [*helicopter*] se poser; [*aircraft*] atterrir; **5** (crash) [*plane*] s'écraser; **6** (fall) [*ceiling, wall*] s'écrouler; [*hem*] se défaire; **7** FIG (be resumed) se ramener à [*problem, fact*]; **8** (catch) **to ~ down with** attraper [*flu*].

■ **come forward 1** (step forward) s'avancer; **2** (volun teer) se présenter; **to ~ forward with** présenter [*proof*]; offrir [*help, money, suggestions*].

■ **come in 1** (enter) [*person, rain*] entrer (**through** par); **2** (return) rentrer (**from** de); **3** (come inland) [*tide*] monter; **4** (arrive) venir; **we've got £2,000 a month coming in** nous avons une rentrée de 2 000 livres sterling par mois; **5** (become current) [*trend, invention*] faire son apparition; **6** RADIO **~ in, Delta Bravo!** c'est à vous, Delta Bravo!; **7** (serve a particular purpose) **where do I ~ in?** à quel moment est-ce que j'interviens?; **to ~ in useful** ou **handy** être utile; **8** (receive) **to ~ in for criticism** [*person*] être critiqué; [*plan*] faire l'objet de nombreuses critiques.

■ **come into**: ~ **into** [sth] **1** (inherit) hériter de [*money*]; entrer en possession de [*inheritance*]; **2** (be relevant) **to** ~ **into it** [*age, experience*] entrer en ligne de compte, jouer; **luck doesn't** ~ **into it** ce n'est pas une question de hasard.

■ **come off**: ¶ ~ **off 1** (become detached) (accidentally) [*button, label, handle*] se détacher; [*lid*] s'enlever; [*paint*] s'écailler; (intentionally) [*handle, panel, lid*] s'enlever; **2** (fall) [*rider*] tomber; **3** (wash, rub off) [*ink*] s'effacer; [*stain*] partir; **4** (take place) [*deal*] se réaliser; [*merger, trip*] avoir lieu; **5** (succeed) [*plan, trick*] réussir; **6** (fare) **she came off well** (in deal) elle s'en est très bien tirée; **who came off worst?** (in fight) lequel des deux a été le plus touché?; ¶ ~ **off** [sth] **1** (stop using) arrêter [*tablet, heroin*]; **2** (fall off) tomber de [*bicycle, horse*].

■ **come on 1** (follow) **I'll** ~ **on later** je vous rejoindrai plus tard; **2** (exhortation) ~ **on!** allez!; **3** (make progress) [*person, patient*] faire des progrès; [*bridge, novel*] avancer; [*plant*] pousser; **4** (begin) [*attack, headache*] commencer; [*programme*] commencer; [*rain*] se mettre à tomber; **5** (start to work) [*light*] s'allumer; [*heating, fan*] se mettre en route; **the power came on again** le courant est revenu; **6** THEAT [*actor*] entrer en scène.

■ **come out 1** (emerge) [*person, animal, vehicle*] sortir (**of** de); [*star*] apparaître; [*sun, moon*] se montrer; **he came out of it rather well** FIG il ne s'en est pas mal tiré; **2** (originate) **to** ~ **out of** [*person*] être originaire de; [*song*] venir de; [*news report*] provenir de; **the money will have to** ~ **out of your savings** il faudra prendre l'argent sur tes économies; **3** (result) **something good came out of the disaster** il est sorti quelque chose de bon du désastre; **4** (strike) faire la grève; **to** ~ **out on strike** faire la grève; **5** (fall out) [*contact lens, tooth*] tomber; [*contents*] sortir; [*cork*] s'enlever; **his hair is coming out** il commence à perdre ses cheveux; **6** (be emitted) [*water, smoke*] sortir (**through** par); **7** (wash out) [*stain*] s'en aller, partir; **8** (be published, issued) [*magazine, novel*] paraître; [*album, film, product*] sortir; **9** (become known) [*feelings*] se manifester; [*details, facts*] être révélé; [*results*] être connu; **it came out that** on a appris que; **the truth is bound to** ~ **out** la vérité finira forcément par se savoir; **10** PHOT [*photo, photocopy*] être réussi; **11** (end up) **to** ~ **out at 200 dollars** [*cost, bill*] s'élever à 200 dollars; **the jumper came out too big** le pull était trop grand; **12** (say) **to** ~ **out with** sortir [*excuse*]; raconter [*nonsense*]; **whatever will she** ~ **out with next?** qu'est-ce qu'elle va encore nous sortir○?; **to** ~ **straight out with it** le dire franchement.

■ **come over**: ¶ ~ **over 1** (drop in) venir; ~ **over for a drink** venez prendre un verre; **to** ~ **over to do** venir faire; **2** (travel) venir; **3** (convey impression) [*message*] passer; [*feelings, love*] transparaître; **to** ~ **over very well** [*person*] donner une très bonne impression; **to** ~ **over as** donner l'impression d'être [*lazy, honest*]; **4**○ (suddenly become) **to** ~ **over all embarrassed** se sentir gêné tout à coup; **to** ~ **over all faint** être pris de vertige tout d'un coup; ¶ ~ **over** [sb] [*feeling*] envahir; **what's come over you?** qu'est-ce qui te prend?

■ **come round** GB, **come around** US **1** (regain consciousness) reprendre connaissance; **2** (circulate) [*waitress*] passer; **3** (visit) venir; **4** (occur) [*event*] avoir lieu; **5** (change one's mind) changer d'avis; **to** ~ **round to my way of thinking** se rallier à mon point de vue.

■ **come through**: ¶ ~ **through 1** (survive) s'en tirer; **2** (penetrate) [*heat, ink*] traverser; [*light*] passer; **3** (arrive) **my posting has just come through** je viens de recevoir ma mutation; **4** (emerge) apparaître; ¶ ~ **through** [sth] **1** (survive) se tirer de [*crisis*]; se sortir de [*recession*]; survivre à [*operation, ordeal*]; **2** (penetrate) [*ink*] traverser; [*light*] passer au travers de.

■ **come to**: ¶ ~ **to** (regain consciousness) (from faint) reprendre connaissance; (from trance) se réveiller; ¶ ~ **to** [sth] **1** (total) [*shopping*] revenir à; [*bill, total*] s'élever à; **that** ~**s to £40** cela fait 40 livres sterling; **2** (result in) **all her plans came to nothing** aucun de

ses projets ne s'est réalisé; **I never thought it would** ~ **to this** je n'aurais jamais imaginé que les choses en arriveraient là; **it may not** ~ **to that** nous n'en arriverons peut-être pas là.

■ **come under**: ~ **under** [sth] **1** (be subjected to) **to** ~ **under scrutiny** faire l'objet d'un examen minutieux; **to** ~ **under suspicion/threat** être soupçonné/menacé; **2** (be classified under) (in library, shop) être classé dans le rayon [*reference, history*].

■ **come up 1** (arise) [*problem, issue*] être soulevé; [*name*] être mentionné; **to** ~ **up in conversation** [*subject*] être abordé dans la conversation; **2** (be due) **to** ~ **up for re-election** se représenter aux élections; **my salary** ~**s up for review in April** mon salaire sera révisé en avril; **3** (occur) [*opportunity*] se présenter; **something urgent has come up** j'ai quelque chose d'urgent à faire; **a vacancy has come up** une place s'est libérée; **4** (rise) [*sun, moon*] sortir; [*tide*] monter; [*daffodils, beans*] sortir; **5** JUR [*case, hearing*] passer au tribunal; [*person*] comparaître devant; **6 to** ~ **up against** se heurter à [*problem*]; **7** (find) **to** ~ **up with** trouver.

■ **come upon**: ~ **upon** [sth] tomber sur [*book, reference*]; trouver [*idea*].

comeback /'kʌmbæk/ **I** n **1** (of musician, actor, boxer) come-back m; (of politician) rentrée f; **to make** ou **stage a** ~ [*person*] faire un come-back ou une rentrée; [*style*] revenir à la mode; **2** (redress) recours m. **II** noun modifier [*album*] de come-back; ~ **bid** (of singer, actor) come-back m; (of politician) rentrée f.

comedian /kə'miːdɪən/ **▶ 1251** n **1** (actor) (male) comique m; (female) actrice f comique; **2** (joker) pitre m.

comedienne /kə,miːdɪ'en/ **▶ 1251** n actrice f comique.

comedown○ /'kʌmdaʊn/ n déchéance f; **it's quite a** ~ **for her to have to do** elle trouve humiliant d'avoir à faire.

comedy /'komədɪ/ n **1** (genre) comédie f; **black/light** ~ comédie f macabre/légère; **2** (play) comédie f; **3** (funny aspect) comique m.

comer /'kʌmə(r)/ n **to take on all** ~**s** se battre contre tous les challengeurs; **open to all** ~**s** ouvert à tout le monde.

comet /'kɒmɪt/ n comète f.

comeuppance○ /kʌm'ʌpəns/ n **to get one's** ~ avoir ce qu'on mérite.

comfort /'kʌmfət/ **I** n **1** (well-being) confort m; (wealth) aisance f; **to live in** ~ vivre dans l'aisance; **2** (amenity) confort m; **every modern** ~ tout le confort moderne; **home** ~**s** le confort du foyer; **3** (consolation) réconfort m, consolation f; (relief from pain) soulagement m; **it's a** ~ **to know that** il est consolant de savoir que; **to be a great** ~ **to sb** [*person*] être un grand réconfort pour qn; [*knowledge, belief*] apporter beaucoup de réconfort à qn; **to take** ~ **from** trouver un réconfort dans; **we can take** ~ **from the fact that** nous pouvons nous consoler à l'idée que; **if it's any** ~ **to you** si cela peut vous réconforter or consoler; **to be small** ~ **for sb** n'être qu'une maigre consolation pour qn. **II** vtr consoler; (stronger) réconforter. IDIOMS **it's (a bit) too close for** ~ (of where sb is, lives) ça va un peu trop près; (of fighting, war) c'est dangereusement proche, ça devient inquiétant.

comfortable /'kʌmftəbl, US -fərt-/ adj **1** [*room, chair, clothes, journey*] confortable; [*temperature*] agréable; **2** (relaxed) [*person*] à l'aise; **to make oneself** ~ (in chair) s'installer confortablement; (at ease) se mettre à son aise; **to make sb feel** ~ mettre qn à l'aise; **the patient's condition is described as** ~ l'état du malade est jugé satisfaisant; **3** (financially) [*person*] aisé; [*income*] conséquent; **4** (reassuring) [*idea, thought*] sécurisant; [*majority, lead*] confortable; **5** (happy) **I don't feel** ~ **doing** ça m'embête○ de faire; **I would feel more** ~ **about leaving if...** je partirais plus volontiers si...

comfortably /'kʌmftəblɪ, US -fərt-/ adv **1** (physically) confortablement; **2** (financially) [*live*] confortablement; ~ **off** à l'aise; **3** (easily) facilement, aisément.

comforter /'kʌmfətə(r)/ *n* **1**† (scarf) cache-nez *m inv*; **2** (person) consolateur/-trice *m/f*; **3** US (quilt) édredon *m*.

comforting /'kʌmfətɪŋ/ *adj* réconfortant.

comfort station *n* US toilettes *fpl*.

comfy○ /'kʌmfɪ/ *adj* confortable.

comic /'kɒmɪk/ ▶1251 I *n* **1** (man) comique *m*; (woman) actrice *f* comique; **2** (magazine etc) bande *f* dessinée.
II *adj* comique.

comical /'kɒmɪkl/ *adj* cocasse, comique.

comic: ~ **book** *n* bande *f* dessinée; ~ **opera** *n* opéra *m* comique.

comic relief *n* **to provide some** ~ THEAT, FIG détendre l'atmosphère.

comic strip *n* bande *f* dessinée.

coming /'kʌmɪŋ/ I *n* **1** (arrival) arrivée *f*; ~ **and going** va-et-vient *m inv*; ~**s and goings** allées et venues *fpl*; **2** (approach) (of winter, old age) approche *f*; (of new era, event) arrivée *f*; **3** RELIG avènement *m*.
II *adj* [*election, event*] prochain (*before n*); [*war, campaign*] qui se prépare (*after n*); [*months, weeks*] à venir (*after n*); **this** ~ **Monday** (ce) lundi.

comma /'kɒmə/ *n* virgule *f*.

command /kə'mɑːnd, US -'mænd/ I *n* **1** (order) ordre *m*; **to carry out/give a** ~ exécuter/donner un ordre; **2** (military control) commandement *m*; **to give sb** ~ **of sth** confier le commandement de qch à qn; **to be in** ~ commander; **to be under the** ~ **of sb** [*person*] être sous les ordres de qn; [*regiment*] être sous les ordres ou sous le commandement de qn; **I'm in** ~ **of the troops** les troupes sont sous mes ordres; ~ **of the air** maîtrise *f* du ciel; **3** (mastery) maîtrise *f*; **to have full** ~ **of one's faculties** maîtriser parfaitement ses facultés; **an excellent** ~ **of Russian** une excellente maîtrise du russe; **to be in** ~ **of the situation** avoir la situation en main; **to have sth at one's** ~ avoir qch à sa disposition; **4** COMPUT commande *f*.
II *vtr* **1** (order) ordonner à [*person*] (**to do** de faire); **to** ~ **that** ordonner que (+ *subj*); **2** (obtain as one's due) inspirer [*affection, respect*]; **to** ~ **a good price** se vendre cher; **3** (dispose of) disposer de [*funds, support, majority*]; **4** (dominate) dominer [*valley*]; **to** ~ **a view of** avoir vue sur; **5** MIL commander [*regiment*]; maîtriser [*air, sea*].
III *vi* commander.

commandant /ˌkɒmən'dænt/ *n* MIL commandant *m*.

commandeer /ˌkɒmən'dɪə(r)/ *vtr* MIL réquisitionner.

commander /kə'mɑːndə(r), US -mæn-/ ▶1192 *n* GEN chef *m*; MIL commandant *m*; MIL NAUT cf capitaine *m* de frégate; ~ **in chief** commandant en chef.

commanding /kə'mɑːndɪŋ, US -'mæn-/ *adj* **1** (authoritative) [*look, manner, voice*] impérieux/-ieuse; [*presence*] imposant; **2** (dominant) [*position*] dominant; **to have a** ~ **lead in the polls** être en tête des sondages; **3** (elevated) [*position*] surélevé.

commanding officer, CO ▶1192 *n* commandant *m*.

commandment /kə'mɑːndmənt, US -'mæn-/ *n* **1** (order) injonction *f*; **2** RELIG commandement *m*.

commando /kə'mɑːndəʊ, US -'mæn-/ *n* (*pl* **-os, -oes**) commando *m*.

command: ~ **performance** *n* GB THEAT représentation *f* de gala (*donnée en présence d'un membre de la famille royale*); ~ **post, CP** *n* MIL poste *m* de commandement.

commemorate /kə'meməreɪt/ *vtr* commémorer.

commemorative /kə'memərətɪv, US -'meməreɪt-/ *adj* commémoratif/-ive.

commend /kə'mend/ I *vtr* **1** (praise) louer (**for, on** pour); **2** (recommend) **to have much to** ~ **it** avoir de grandes qualités; **3** (entrust) confier.
II *v refl* **to** ~ **itself** être acceptable (**to** à).

commendable /kə'mendəbl/ *adj* louable; **highly** ~ très louable.

commendably /kə'mendəblɪ/ *adv* ~ **quick/restrained** avec une louable promptitude/retenue.

commendation /ˌkɒmen'deɪʃn/ *n* **1** (praise, award) éloge *m*; **2** (medal, citation) citation *f*.

commensurate /kə'menʃərət/ *adj* SOUT **1** (proportionate) proportionné (**with** à); **2** (appropriate) **to be** ~ **with** être à la mesure de.

comment /'kɒment/ I *n* **1** (remark) (public) commentaire *m* (**on** sur); (in conversation) remarque *f* (**on** sur); (written) annotation *f*; **2** ¢ (discussion) commentaires *mpl* (**about** portant sur); **without** ~ [*listen*] sans commentaire; [*occur*] sans susciter des commentaires; 'no ~' je n'ai pas de déclaration à faire'; **3** (criticism) **to be a** ~ **on** en dire long sur.
II *vtr* (orally) remarquer; (in writing) constater.
III *vi* **1** (remark) faire des commentaires *mpl*; **to** ~ **on sth/sb** faire des commentaires sur qch/qn; **2** (discuss) **to** ~ **on** commenter [*text etc*].

commentary /'kɒməntrɪ, US -terɪ/ *n* GEN, literat commentaire *m* (**on** de).

commentate /'kɒmənteɪt/ I *vtr* commenter.
II *vi* faire le commentaire; **to** ~ **on** commenter [*sporting event*].

commentator /'kɒmənteɪtə(r)/ ▶1251 *n* (sports) commentateur/-trice *m/f*; (current affairs) journaliste *mf*.

commerce /'kɒmɜːs/ *n* commerce *m*; **in** ~ dans les affaires.

commercial /kə'mɜːʃl/ I *n* annonce *f* publicitaire, publicité *f*; TV ~ annonce publicitaire à la télé; **beer** ~ annonce publicitaire pour de la bière.
II *adj* **1** [*airline, sector, radio, product*] commercial; **2** (profitable) commercial PEJ; qui se vend bien; **3** (large-scale) industriel/-ielle.

commercial: ~ **artist** *n* graphiste *mf*; ~ **break** *n* publicité *f*.

commercialism /kə'mɜːʃəlɪzəm/ *n* **1** PÉJ mercantilisme *m* PEJ; **2** (principles of commerce) esprit *m* commercial.

commercialization /kəˌmɜːʃəlaɪ'zeɪʃn, US -lɪ'z-/ *n* PÉJ commercialisation *f*.

commercialize /kə'mɜːʃəlaɪz/ *vtr* commercialiser.

commercial law *n* droit *m* commercial.

commercially /kə'mɜːʃəlɪ/ *adv* commercialement.

commercial: ~ **traveller** ▶1251 *n* voyageur *m* de commerce; ~ **vehicle** *n* véhicule *m* utilitaire.

commiserate /kə'mɪzəreɪt/ *vi* compatir (**with** avec; **about, over** à propos de).

commissar /'kɒmɪsɑː(r)/ *n* commissaire *m*.

commissariat /ˌkɒmɪ'seərɪət/ *n* **1** MIL intendance *f*; **2** POL HIST (in USSR) commissariat *m*.

commission /kə'mɪʃn/ I *n* **1** (for goods sold) commission *f*; **to get a 5%** ~ recevoir or toucher une commission de 5%; **to work on** ~ travailler à la commission; **2** (fee) commission *f*; **we charge 1%** ~ **on travellers' cheques** nous prenons 1% de commission sur les chèques de voyage; **3** (advance order) commande *f* (**for** de); **to give sb a** ~ passer une commande à qn; **to work to** ~ travailler sur commande; **4** (committee) commission *f* (**on** sur); ~ **of inquiry** commission d'enquête; **5** MIL ~ **brevet** *m*; **to get one's** ~ être nommé officier; **to resign one's** ~ démissionner; **6** (of crime, sin) perpétration *f*; **7** (operation) **in** ~ en service; **out of** ~ hors service.
II *vtr* **1** (order) commander (**from** à); **a** ~**ed portrait** un portrait sur commande; **2** (instruct) **to** ~ **sb to do** charger qn de faire; **3** MIL **a** ~**ed officer** un officier; **4** (prepare for service) armer [*ship*]; mettre [qch] en service [*plane, equipment, weapon system*].

commissionaire /kəˌmɪʃə'neə(r)/ ▶1251 *n* GB portier *m*.

commissioner /kə'mɪʃənə(r)/ *n* **1** ADMIN membre *m* d'une commission; **2** GB (in police) ≈ préfet *m* de police; **3** (in the EC Commission) membre *m* de la Commission européenne.

Commissioner for Oaths *n* GB JUR officier habilité à enregistrer les déclarations sous serment.

commit /kə'mɪt/ (*p prés etc* **-tt-**) I *vtr* **1** (perpetrate)

commettre [*crime, error*]; **to ~ adultery** commettre un adultère; **2** (engage) engager [*person*] (**to do** à faire); **3** (assign) consacrer [*money, time*] (**to** à); **4** JUR **to ~ sb for trial** mettre qn en accusation; **to ~ sb to jail/to a psychiatric hospital** faire incarcérer/interner qn; **5** (consign) SOUT confier (**to** à; **to sb's care** à la garde de qn); **to ~ sth to paper** consigner qch; **to ~ sth to memory** mémoriser qch.
II *v refl* **to ~ oneself** s'engager (**to** à); **I can't** ou **I won't ~ myself** je ne peux rien promettre (**as to** quant à).

commitment /kə'mɪtmənt/ *n* **1** (obligation) engagement *m* (**to do** à faire); **a previous ~** un engagement antérieur; **to meet one's ~s** honorer ses engagements; **to give a firm ~ that** s'engager fermement à ce que (+ *subj*); **family ~s** obligations *fpl* familiales; **2** (sense of duty) attachement *m*; **to have a strong ~ to doing** être particulièrement attaché à faire; **the job demands complete ~** ce travail exige un total don de soi.

committal /kə'mɪtl/ *n* **1** JUR (to prison) incarcération *f*; (to psychiatric hospital) internement *m*; (to court) renvoi *m* devant un tribunal; **2** (consigning) **the ~ of X to Y's care** la remise de X aux soins de Y.

committed /kə'mɪtɪd/ *adj* **1** (devoted) [*parent, teacher*] dévoué; [*Christian, Socialist*] fervent; **to be ~ to/to doing** se consacrer à/à faire; **to be politically ~** être engagé politiquement; **2** (with commitments) pris (**to doing** pour faire); **I am heavily ~** (timewise) je suis très pris; (financially) j'ai de lourds engagements.

committee /kə'mɪtɪ/ *n* GEN comité *m*; (to investigate, report) commission *f*; **in ~** en comité.

committee: **~ meeting** *n* réunion *f* du comité; **~ stage** *n*: *phase pendant laquelle une commission discute un projet de loi.*

commodious /kə'məʊdɪəs/ *adj* spacieux/-ieuse.

commodity /kə'mɒdətɪ/ *n* **1** COMM, GEN article *m*; (food) denrée *f*; **a rare ~** FIG une denrée rare; **2** (on stock market) matière *f* première.

commodore /'kɒmədɔː(r)/ ▶ 1192 *n* contre-amiral *m*.

common /'kɒmən/ **I** *n* (land) terrain *m* communal.
II commons *npl* **1** (the people) **the ~s** le peuple; **2** POL (also **Commons**) **the ~s** les Communes *fpl*.
III *adj* **1** (frequent) courant, fréquent; **in ~ use** d'un usage courant; **in ~** parlance dans le langage courant; **it is ~ for sb to do** il est courant que qn fasse; **to be ~ among** être répandu chez [*children, mammals etc*]; **2** (shared) commun (**to** à); **in ~** en commun; **for the ~ good** pour le bien commun; **it is ~ property** c'est la propriété de tous; **it is ~ knowledge** c'est de notoriété publique; **3** (ordinary) [*man*] du peuple (*after n*); **the ~ people** le peuple; **the ~ herd** PÉJ la masse; **a ~ criminal** PÉJ un criminel ordinaire; **4** PÉJ (low-class) commun; **it looks/sounds ~** ça fait commun; **5** [*courtesy, decency*] le/la plus élémentaire; **6** ZOOL, BOT commun.
IDIOMS **to be as ~ as muck** ou **dirt**○ (vulgar) être d'une vulgarité crasse○; **they are as ~ as muck**○ (widespread) on en ramasse à la pelle; **to have the ~ touch** avoir de la simplicité.

common: **Common Agricultural Policy, CAP** *n* politique *f* agricole commune; **~ cold** ▶ 1002 *n* rhume *m* de cerveau.

commoner /'kɒmənə(r)/ *n* roturier/-ière *m/f*.

common: **~ ground** *n* FIG terrain *m* d'entente; **~-law husband** *n* concubin *m*; **~-law marriage** *n* concubinage *m*; **~-law wife** *n* concubine *f*.

commonly /'kɒmənlɪ/ *adv* communément; **~ known as** communément appelé.

common market, Common Market *n* Marché *m* commun.

common: **~ noun** *n* nom *m* commun; **~-or-garden** *adj* ordinaire.

commonplace /'kɒmənpleɪs/ **I** *n* lieu *m* commun.
II *adj* (widespread) commun; (banal, trite) banal.

common room *n* salle *f* de détente.

common sense I *n* bon sens *m*, sens *m* commun.
II commonsense *adj* (also **commonsensical**) plein de bon sens.

Commonwealth /'kɒmənwelθ/ **I** *n* **1** GB POL **the (British) ~ (of Nations)** le Commonwealth; **2** GB HIST **the ~** le Commonwealth, la République de Cromwell.
II *noun modifier* [*country, Games*] du Commonwealth; [*leader*] d'un pays du Commonwealth; [*summit*] des pays du Commonwealth.

Commonwealth of Independent States *pr n* Communauté *f* des États indépendants.

commotion /kə'məʊʃn/ *n* **1** (noise) vacarme *m*, brouhaha *m*; **to make a ~** faire du vacarme; **2** (disturbance) émoi *m*, agitation *f*; **to cause a ~** causer un grand émoi; **to be in a state of ~** [*crowd*] être agité; [*town*] être en émoi.

communal /'kɒmjʊnl, kə'mjuːnl/ *adj* [*property, area, showers*] commun; [*garden*] collectif/-ive; [*facilities*] commun, collectif/-ive; **~ ownership** copropriété *f*; [*prayer*] collectif/-ive; [*life*] communautaire.

communally /'kɒmjʊnəlɪ, kə'mjuːnəlɪ/ *adv* en commun, collectivement.

commune I /'kɒmjuːn/ *n* **1** (group of people) communauté *f*; **to live in a ~** vivre en communauté; **2** ADMIN (in continental Europe) commune *f*.
II /kə'mjuːn/ *vi* **to ~ with** communier avec, être en communion avec [*nature*]; converser intimement avec [*person*].

communicable /kə'mjuːnɪkəbl/ *adj* MED contagieux/-ieuse.

communicant /kə'mjuːnɪkənt/ *n* RELIG communiant/-e *m/f*.

communicate /kə'mjuːnɪkeɪt/ **I** *vtr* **1** (convey) communiquer [*ideas, feelings*] (**to** à); transmettre [*information*] (**to** à); **his anxiety ~s itself to others** son angoisse est communicative; **2** (transmit) transmettre [*disease*].
II *vi* **1** (relate) communiquer (**by** par; **through** au moyen de; **with** avec); **2** (be in contact) communiquer (**with** avec; **by** par); **we no longer ~** nous avons perdu tout contact; **3** (connect) **to ~ with** communiquer avec.

communicating door *n* porte *f* de communication.

communication /kə,mjuːnɪ'keɪʃn/ **I** *n* **1** (of information) transmission *f*; (of ideas, feelings) communication *f*; **2** (contact) communication *f*; **the lines of ~** les voies *fpl* de communication; **to be in ~ with sb** être en communication ou en contact avec qn; **3** (message) communication *f*.
II communications *npl* communications *fpl*, liaison *f*.

communication: **~ cord** *n* GB sonnette *f* d'alarme; **~s company** *n* société *f* de communications; **~s link** *n* liaison *f*; **~s satellite** *n* satellite *m* de communication; **~s studies** *n* études *fpl* en communication.

communicative /kə'mjuːnɪkətɪv, US -keɪtɪv/ *adj* (talkative) expansif/-ive (**about** au sujet de).

communicator /kə'mjuːnɪkeɪtə(r)/ *n* **to be a good ~** avoir le sens de la communication.

communion /kə'mjuːnɪən/ *n* LITTÉR (with nature, fellow men etc) communion *f*.

Communion /kə'mjuːnɪən/ *n* (also **Holy ~**) (sainte) communion *f*, Eucharistie *f*; **to make one's First ~** faire sa première communion; **to take ~** communier.

communiqué /kə'mjuːnɪkeɪ, US kə,mjuːnə'keɪ/ *n* communiqué *m*.

Communism, communism /'kɒmjʊnɪzəm/ *n* communisme *m*.

Communist, communist /'kɒmjʊnɪst/ *n, adj* communiste (*mf*).

Communist Party, CP *n* parti *m* communiste.

community /kə'mjuːnətɪ/ **I** *n* **1** (social, cultural grouping) communauté *f*; **the student/Italian ~** la communauté estudiantine/italienne; **the business ~** le monde des affaires; **research** ~ communauté f des chercheurs; **relations between the police and the** ~ (at local level) les relations entre la police et les habitants; (at national level) les relations entre la police et le public; **sense of** ~ esprit *m* communautaire; **2** RELIG communauté f; **3** JUR communauté f.

II Community *pr n* the **(European) Community** la Communauté (Européenne).

III Community *noun modifier* communautaire, de la Communauté.

community: ~ **care** n: soins en dehors du milieu hospitalier; ~ **centre** n maison f de quartier; ~ **chest** n US fonds *m* de secours; ~ **education** n GB cours ouverts à tous organisés par la municipalité; ~ **health centre** n centre *m* médico-social; ~ **life** n vie f associative; ~ **medicine** n médecine f générale; ~ **policing** n ~ îlotage m; ~ **service** n travail *m* d'intérêt public; ~ **spirit** n esprit *m* communautaire; ~ **worker** n animateur/-trice *m/f* socio-culturel/-elle.

commute /kə'mjuːt/ **I** n US trajet *m* journalier.
II *vtr* FIN convertir; JUR commuer **(to en)**.
III *vi* **to** ~ **between Oxford and London** faire le trajet entre Oxford et Londres tous les jours; **she** ~**s to Glasgow** elle se rend à Glasgow tous les jours.

commuter /kə'mjuːtə(r)/ n navetteur/-euse *m/f*, migrant/-e *m/f* journalier/-ière.

commuter: ~ **belt** n grande banlieue f; ~ **train** n train *m* de banlieue.

Comoros /'kɒmərəʊz/ ▶840⌋ *pr n* (îles *fpl*) Comores *fpl*.

compact I /'kɒmpækt/ n **1** (agreement) (written) accord *m*, contrat *m*, convention f; (verbal) entente f; **2** (for powder) poudrier *m*.
II /kəm'pækt/ *adj* **1** (compressed) [*snow, mass*] compact, dense; [*style, sentence*] concis, ramassé; **2** (neatly constructed) compact.
III /kəm'pækt/ *vtr* comprimer [*waste, rubbish*]; tasser [*soil, snow*].

compact: ~ **disc, CD** n disque *m* compact; ~ **disc player** n platine f laser.

compactly /kəm'pæktlɪ/ *adj* ~ **built** [*person*] trapu; ~ **designed** compact.

companion /kəm'pænɪən/ n **1** (friend) compagnon/ compagne *m/f*; **to be sb's constant** ~ [*hunger, fear*] être le perpétuel compagnon de qn; **2** (also **paid** ~) dame f de compagnie; **3** (item of matching pair) pendant *m* **(to de)**; **4** (book) guide *m* **(to de)**; **5** NAUT capot *m*.

companionable /kəm'pænɪənəbl/ *adj* [*person*] sociable; [*chat, meal*] amical; [*silence*] sympathique.

companionship /kəm'pænɪənʃɪp/ n compagnie f; **I have a dog for** ~ j'ai un chien pour me tenir compagnie.

companion: ~ **volume** n pendant *m*; ~**way** n NAUT escalier *m*.

company /'kʌmpənɪ/ **I** n **1** COMM, JUR société f; **airline** ~ compagnie f aérienne; **2** MUS, THEAT troupe f, compagnie f; **theatre** ~ troupe f de théâtre, compagnie f théâtrale; **3** MIL compagnie f; **4** (companionship) compagnie f; **to keep sb** ~ tenir compagnie à qn; **to be good** ~ être d'une compagnie agréable; **I have a cat for** ~ j'ai un chat pour me tenir compagnie; **in sb's** ~ ou **in** ~ **with sb** en compagnie de qn; **to part** ~ **with** [*person*] HUM se séparer de [*person, bike*]; **on political matters they part** ~ en ce qui concerne la politique, ils divergent complètement; **to keep bad** ~ avoir de mauvaises fréquentations; **to be fit** ~ **for sb** être une fréquentation pour qn; **to keep** ~ **with sb** fréquenter qn; **5** (visitors) visiteurs *mpl*; **to have** ~ avoir du monde; **6** (society) **in** ~ en société; **in mixed** ~ quand les dames sont présentes; **Lisa and** ~ Lisa et compagnie○; **7** (similar circumstances) **you're in good** ~ tu n'es pas le seul; **8** (gathering) compagnie f; **the assembled** ~ l'assemblée; **9** NAUT équipage *m*.
II *noun modifier* GEN [*law, profits, records*] des sociétés; (of one business) [*accountant, headquarters*] de la société.

company: ~ **car** n voiture f de fonction; ~ **director** ▶1251⌋ n directeur/-trice *m/f* général/-e; ~ **doctor** n redresseur *m* d'entreprise; ~ **name** n JUR raison f sociale; ~ **pension scheme** n régime *m* de retraite de l'entreprise; ~ **policy** n ₵ politique f de l'entreprise; ~ **secretary** ▶1251⌋ n secrétaire *mf* général/-e; ~ **sergeant major, CSM** ▶1192⌋ n MIL adjudant *m* de compagnie; ~ **tax** n impôt *m* sur les sociétés.

comparability /ˌkɒmpərə'bɪlətɪ/ n **1** (comparison) comparabilité f; **2** (equivalence) harmonisation f; **pay** ~ harmonisation des salaires.

comparable /'kɒmpərəbl/ *adj* comparable **(to, with à)**.

comparative /kəm'pærətɪv/ **I** n LING comparatif *m*; **in the** ~ au comparatif.
II *adj* **1** LING comparatif/-ive; **2** (relative) relatif/-ive; **in** ~ **terms** en termes relatifs; **3** (based on comparison) [*method, study*] comparatif/-ive; [*literature, religion*] comparé.

comparatively /kəm'pærətɪvlɪ/ *adv* **1** (relatively) relativement; ~ **speaking** en termes relatifs; **2** (by comparison) comparativement.

compare /kəm'peə(r)/ **I** n **a beauty beyond** ~ une beauté incomparable; **to be brave beyond** ~ être incomparablement courageux/-euse.
II *vtr* comparer; **to** ~ **sth with** ou **to** comparer qn/qch à or avec; **to** ~ **notes with sb** FIG échanger ses impressions avec qn.
III compared with *prep phr* ~**d with sb/sth** par rapport à qn/qch.
IV *vi* être comparable **(with à)**; **to** ~ **favourably with** soutenir la comparaison avec; **how do they** ~? et si on les compare?; **how does this job** ~ **with your last one?** comment trouvez-vous cet emploi par rapport au précédent?
V *v refl* **to** ~ **oneself with** ou **to** se comparer à.

comparison /kəm'pærɪsn/ n comparaison f; **beyond** ~ sans comparaison; **to draw a** ~ **between sth and sth** comparer qch avec qch; **for** ~ à titre de comparaison; **in** ou **by** ~ **with** par rapport à.

compartment /kəm'pɑːtmənt/ n compartiment *m*.

compartmentalize /ˌkɒmpɑːt'mentəlaɪz/ *vtr* compartimenter.

compass /'kʌmpəs/ **I** n **1** GEN boussole f; NAUT compas *m*; **the points of the** ~ les points *mpl* cardinaux; **2** (extent) étendue f; (scope) portée f, rayon *m*.
II compasses *npl* **a pair of** ~**es** un compas.

compassion /kəm'pæʃn/ n compassion f **(for pour)**.

compassionate /kəm'pæʃənət/ *adj* compatissant; **on** ~ **grounds** pour raisons *fpl* personnelles; ~ **leave** n MIL permission f exceptionnelle.

compatibility /kəmˌpætə'bɪlətɪ/ n GEN, COMPUT compatibilité f.

compatible /kəm'pætəbl/ *adj* compatible **(with avec)**; **X-**~ COMPUT compatible X.

compatriot /kəm'pætrɪət, US -'peɪt-/ n compatriote *mf*.

compel /kəm'pel/ *vtr* (*p prés etc* **-ll-**) **1** (force) contraindre **(to do** à faire), obliger **(to do** de faire); **2** (win) imposer [*respect*]; retenir [*attention*].

compelling /kəm'pelɪŋ/ *adj* [*reason, argument*] convaincant; [*performance, film, speaker*] fascinant.

compellingly /kəm'pelɪŋlɪ/ *adv* [*argue*] de façon convaincante; [*speak, write*] de manière fascinante.

compendium /kəm'pendɪəm/ n (*pl* **-diums** ou **-dia**) **1** (handbook) manuel *m*; **2** GB (box of games) mallette f de jeux.

compensate /'kɒmpenseɪt/ **I** *vtr* **1** (financially) dédommager, indemniser [*person*]; **to** ~ **sb for** dédommager qn de; **2** (offset) compenser.
II *vi* compenser; **to** ~ **for** compenser [*loss, difficulty*].

compensation /ˌkɒmpen'seɪʃn/ n **1** GEN compensation f; **to be no** ~ **for sth** ne pas compenser qch; **as** ou **by way of** ~ en compensation **(for de)**; **2** JUR indemnisation f.

compère /'kɒmpeə(r)/ n GB **I** n animateur/-trice *m/f*.

II *vtr* présenter.

compete /kəm'piːt/ **I** *vi* **1** (for prominence, job, prize) rivaliser; **to ~ against** ou **with** rivaliser avec (**for** pour obtenir); **they were competing for the same job** ils se disputaient le même emploi; **I just can't ~ (with her)** je ne peux pas lui faire concurrence; **2** COMM [*companies*] se faire concurrence; **to ~ against** ou **with** faire concurrence à (**for** pour obtenir); **3** SPORT être en compétition (**against, with** avec); **to ~ in** participer à [*Olympics, race*].
II competing *pres p adj* rival.

competence /'kɒmpɪtəns/ *n* **1** (ability) compétence *f*; **to have the ~ to do** avoir la compétence voulue pour faire; **I doubt his ~ to do** je doute qu'il soit capable de faire; **2** (skill) compétences *fpl*; **her ~ as an accountant** ses compétences de comptable; **~ in word-processing** connaissances *fpl* en traitement de texte; **~ in Spanish** une bonne connaissance de l'espagnol; **3** JUR compétence *f* (**to do** pour faire); **to be within the ~ of the court** relever de la compétence du tribunal.

competent /'kɒmpɪtənt/ *adj* **1** (capable) compétent, capable; (trained) qualifié; **to be ~ to do** être compétent or qualifié pour faire, être capable de faire; **2** (adequate) [*performance*] honorable; [*knowledge*] suffisant; [*answer*] satisfaisant; **3** JUR compétent.

competently /'kɒmpɪtəntlɪ/ *adv* d'une manière compétente.

competition /ˌkɒmpə'tɪʃn/ *n* **1** ¢ GEN, COMM concurrence *f*, compétition *f* (**between** entre); **in ~ with** en concurrence or compétition avec (**for** pour); **2** C (contest) (for prize, award, job) concours *m*; (race) compétition *f*; **3** (competitors) concurrence *f*, compétition *f*.

competitive /kəm'petɪtɪv/ *adj* **1** (enjoying rivalry) [*person*] qui a l'esprit de compétition; [*environment*] compétitif/-ive; **2** COMM [*company, price, product*] compétitif/-ive; **~ edge** avantage *m* concurrentiel; **~ tender** appel *m* d'offres; **3** (decided by competition) [*sport*] de compétition; **by ~ examination** sur concours.

competitively /kəm'petɪtɪvlɪ/ *adv* [*play*] dans un esprit de compétition; [*operate*] compétitivement; **~ priced** à des prix compétitifs.

competitor /kəm'petɪtə(r)/ *n* concurrent/-e *m/f*.

compilation /ˌkɒmpɪ'leɪʃn/ *n* **1** (collection) compilation *f*; **2** (act of compiling) (of reference book) rédaction *f*; (of dossier) constitution *f*.

compile /kəm'paɪl/ *vtr* **1** (draw up) dresser [*list, catalogue*]; établir [*report*]; rédiger [*reference book, entry*]; **2** COMPUT compiler.

compiler /kəm'paɪlə(r)/ *n* compilateur/-trice *m/f*.

complacency /kəm'pleɪsnsɪ/ *n* suffisance *f*, assurance *f* excessive.

complacent /kəm'pleɪsnt/ *adj* suffisant, trop confiant; **to be ~ about** être trop confiant de [*success, future*]; **to grow ~ about** perdre sa vigilance en ce qui concerne [*danger, threat*].

complacently /kəm'pleɪsntlɪ/ *adv* avec suffisance, avec une confiance excessive.

complain /kəm'pleɪn/ *vi* GEN se plaindre (**to** à; **about** de); (officially) se plaindre (**to** auprès de), faire une réclamation (**to** à); (of illness, symptom) se plaindre (**of** de); **to ~ that** se plaindre parce que; **I can't ~** je n'ai pas à me plaindre.

complaint /kəm'pleɪnt/ *n* **1** (protest, objection) GEN plainte *f* (**about** au sujet de); (official) réclamation *f* (**about** concernant, au sujet de); **there have been ~s about the noise** on s'est plaint du bruit; **there have been ~s that the service is slow** on s'est plaint de la lenteur du service; **tiredness is a common ~** les gens se plaignent souvent de fatigue; **in case of ~**, **contact the management** en cas de réclamation, adressez-vous à la direction; **to have grounds** ou **cause for ~** avoir lieu de se plaindre; **to file a ~ against sb** déposer une plainte or porter plainte contre qn; **to make a ~** se plaindre, faire une réclamation; **I've no ~s** je n'ai rien à redire; **I've no**

~s about the service je n'ai pas à me plaindre du service; **2** MED maladie *f*.

complement /'kɒmplɪmənt/ **I** *n* GEN, MATH, LING complément *m* (**to** à); **with a full ~ of staff** avec le personnel au complet.
II *vtr* compléter; **to ~ one another** se compléter; **wine ~s cheese** le vin accompagne bien le fromage.

complementary /ˌkɒmplɪ'mentrɪ/ *adj* (all contexts) complémentaire (**to** de).

complementary medicine *n* médecine *f* parallèle.

complete /kəm'pliːt/ **I** *adj* **1** (total, utter) (*épith*) [*chaos, darkness*] complet/-ète, total; **he's a ~ fool** il est complètement idiot; **it's the ~ opposite** c'est tout à fait le contraire; **with ~ confidence** avec une confiance totale; **~ and utter** total; **it's ~ and utter rubbish** c'est complètement absurde; **2** (finished) achevé; **3** (entire, full) [*collection, works, set*] complet/-ète; **~ with** avec; **to make my happiness ~** pour que rien ne manque à mon bonheur; **4** (consummate) [*artist, star*] complet/-ète; [*gentleman*] parfait (*before n*).
II *vtr* **1** (finish) terminer [*building, course, exercise*]; achever [*task, journey*]; **half ~d** inachevé; **2** (make whole) compléter [*collection, group, phrase*]; **3** (fill in) remplir [*form*].

completely /kəm'pliːtlɪ/ *adv* complètement.

completion /kəm'pliːʃn/ *n* **1** (finishing) achèvement *m* (**of** de); **on ~** (**of the works**) à l'achèvement des travaux; **nearing ~** près d'être achevé; **2** (of house sale) signature *f* de la vente.

complex /'kɒmpleks, US kəm'pleks/ **I** *n* **1** (development) complexe *m*; **sports/leisure ~** complexe *m* sportif/de loisirs; **housing ~** complexe *m* résidentiel; **2** MED, PSYCH complexe *m*; **he's got a ~ about his weight** son poids lui donne un complexe.
II *adj* complexe.

complexion /kəm'plekʃn/ *n* **1** (skin colour) teint *m*; **to have a clear/bad ~** avoir une peau nette/à problèmes; **to have a fair/dark ~** avoir un teint clair/mat; **2** (nature) aspect *m*; **to put a new ~ on sth** présenter qch sous un jour nouveau.

complexity /kəm'pleksətɪ/ *n* complexité *f*.

compliance /kəm'plaɪəns/ *n* **1** (conformity) conformité *f* (**with** à); **in ~ with the law** conformément à la loi; **2** (yielding disposition) caractère *m* conciliant.

compliant /kəm'plaɪənt/ *adj* conciliant.

complicate /'kɒmplɪkeɪt/ *vtr* compliquer; **to ~ matters** ou **life** compliquer les choses.

complication /ˌkɒmplɪ'keɪʃn/ *n* **1** (problem) inconvénient *m*, problème *m*; **2** MED complication *f*.

complicity /kəm'plɪsətɪ/ *n* complicité *f*.

compliment /'kɒmplɪmənt/ **I** *n* compliment *m*; **to pay sb a ~** faire un compliment à qn; **to return the ~** LIT retourner le compliment; FIG répondre de la même façon.
II compliments *npl* **1** (in expressions of praise) compliments *mpl* (**to** à); **to give sb one's ~s** faire ses compliments à qn; **2** (in expressions of politeness) 'with ~s' (on transmission slip) 'avec tous nos compliments'; 'with the ~s of the author' 'avec les hommages de l'auteur'; **3** (in greetings) 'with the ~s of the season' (on Christmas cards) 'meilleurs vœux'.
III *vtr* complimenter, faire des compliments à.

complimentary /ˌkɒmplɪ'mentrɪ/ *adj* **1** (flattering) flatteur/-euse; **he wasn't very ~ about my poems** il s'est montré plutôt critique à l'égard de mes poèmes; **she was very ~ about my work** elle m'a fait des compliments sur mon travail; **2** (free) gratuit, à titre gracieux; **~ copy** exemplaire *m* donné en hommage.

compliments slip *n* carte *f* avec les compliments de l'expéditeur.

comply /kəm'plaɪ/ *vi* s'exécuter; **to ~ with** se plier à [*sb's wishes*]; accéder à [*request*]; se conformer à [*orders, regulations*]; respecter, observer [*rules*]; **failure to ~ with the rules** le non-respect des règles.

component /kəm'pəʊnənt/ *n* GEN, MATH composante *f*; AUT, TECH pièce *f*; ELEC composant *m*; CHEM constituant *m*; ~ **part** élément *m*.

compose /kəm'pəʊz/ I *vtr* **1** (write) GEN, LITERAT, MUS composer; **2** (arrange) composer [*painting*]; agencer [*elements of work*]; **3** (order) composer [*features*]; rassembler [*thoughts*]; **4** (constitute) composer; ~**d of** composé de; **5** (in printing) composer.
II *vi* (all contexts) composer.
III *v refl* **to ~ oneself** se ressaisir.

composed /kəm'pəʊzd/ *adj* [*person, features*] calme.

composer /kəm'pəʊzə(r)/ ▶1251 *n* MUS compositeur/-trice *m/f* (**of** de).

composite /'kɒmpəzɪt/ I *n* **1** (substance) composite *m*; **2** (character, photo, word) composite *m* (**of** de); **3** COMM entreprise *f* diversifiée.
II *adj* **1** CHEM, PHOT composite; **2** MATH composé; **3** COMM diversifié.

composition /ˌkɒmpə'zɪʃn/ *n* **1** (make-up) composition *f* (**of** de); **metallic in** ~ d'une composition métallique; **2** MUS, LITERAT composition *f* (**of** de); **this is my own** ~ cela est ma propre composition; **of my/her own** ~ de ma/sa composition; **3** SCH rédaction *f* (**about, on** sur); **4** ART composition *f*.

compositor /kəm'pɒzɪtə(r)/ ▶1251 *n* compositeur/-trice *m/f*.

compos mentis /ˌkɒmpɒs 'mentɪs/ *adj* **to be ~** être en possession de toutes ses facultés.

compost /'kɒmpɒst/ *n* compost *m*, terreau *m*.

composure /kəm'pəʊʒə(r)/ *n* calme *m*; **to lose/regain one's ~** perdre/retrouver son calme.

compound I /'kɒmpaʊnd/ *n* **1** (enclosure) enceinte *f*; **prison ~** enceinte *f* de prison; **workers' ~** quartier *m* de travailleurs; **2** CHEM composé *m* (**of** de); **3** (word) mot *m* composé; **4** (mixture) composé *m* (**of** de).
II /'kɒmpaʊnd/ *adj* **1** GEN, BIOL, BOT, CHEM composé; **2** LING [*tense, noun*] composé; [*sentence*] complexe; **3** MED [*fracture*] multiple; **4** FIN [*interest*] composé.
III /kəm'paʊnd/ *vtr* **1** (exacerbate) aggraver [*error, offence, problem*] (**by** par; **by doing** en faisant); **2** (combine) combiner (**with** à); ~**ed of** composé de.

comprehend /ˌkɒmprɪ'hend/ *vtr* comprendre, saisir.

comprehensible /ˌkɒmprɪ'hensəbl/ *adj* compréhensible, intelligible.

comprehension /ˌkɒmprɪ'henʃn/ *n* **1** (understanding) compréhension *f*, entendement *m*; **that is beyond my ~** cela dépasse mon entendement; **2** SCH, UNIV exercice *m* de compréhension.

comprehensive /ˌkɒmprɪ'hensɪv/ I *n* GB SCH école *f* (publique) secondaire.
II *adj* **1** (all-embracing) [*report, list*] complet/-ète, détaillé; [*knowledge*] vaste; [*planning*] global; [*coverage, training*] complet/-ète; [*measures*] d'ensemble; ~ **insurance policy** assurance *f* tous risques; **2** GB SCH **a ~ school** école *f* (publique) secondaire.

compress I /'kɒmpres/ *n* compresse *f*.
II /kəm'pres/ *vtr* **1** (condense) comprimer; ~**ed air** air comprimé; **2 to ~ one's lips** pincer les lèvres; **3** FIG (shorten) condenser [*text*]; réduire [*time*].

compression /kəm'preʃn/ *n* **1** GEN, PHYS compression *f*; **2** (condensing) (of book, chapters) réduction *f*; **3** (of data) condensation *f*, compression *f*.

compressor /kəm'presə(r)/ *n* compresseur *m*.

comprise /kəm'praɪz/ *vtr* (include) comprendre; (consist of) être composé de.

compromise /'kɒmprəmaɪz/ I *n* compromis *m*; **to come to** OU **reach a ~** arriver or aboutir à un compromis.
II *noun modifier* [*agreement, solution*] de compromis.
III *vtr* **1** (threaten) compromettre; **2** US (settle) régler [*disagreement*].
IV *vi* transiger, arriver à un compromis; **to ~ on sth** trouver un compromis sur qch.
V *v refl* **to ~ oneself** se compromettre.

compromising /'kɒmprəmaɪzɪŋ/ *adj* compromettant.

compulsion /kəm'pʌlʃn/ *n* **1** (urge) compulsion *f*; **to**

feel a ~ **to do** avoir une envie irrésistible de faire; **2** (force) force *f*; **there is no ~ on you to do** tu n'es pas obligé de faire; **to act under ~** agir sous la contrainte.

compulsive /kəm'pʌlsɪv/ *adj* **1** (inveterate) invétéré; PSYCH compulsif/-ive; ~ **eater** boulimique *mf*; **2** (fascinating) fascinant; **to be ~ viewing** être fascinant.

compulsively /kəm'pʌlsɪvlɪ/ *adv* PSYCH de façon compulsive.

compulsory /kəm'pʌlsərɪ/ *adj* [*subject, attendance, education*] obligatoire; **to be forced to take ~ redundancy** être mis au chômage d'office.

compulsory purchase *n* GB expropriation *f* (*pour cause d'utilité publique*).

compunction /kəm'pʌŋkʃn/ *n* ℂ **to have no ~ about doing** n'avoir aucun scrupule à faire.

computation /ˌkɒmpju:'teɪʃn/ *n* calcul *m*.

compute /kəm'pju:t/ *vtr* calculer.

computer /kəm'pju:tə(r)/ *n* ordinateur *m*; **by ~/on a ~** par/sur ordinateur; **to have sth on ~** avoir qch sur ordinateur; **the ~ is up/down** l'ordinateur fonctionne/est en panne.

computer: ~-**aided** *adj* assisté par ordinateur; ~-**aided design**, **CAD** *n* conception *f* assistée par ordinateur, CAO *f*; ~-**aided language learning**, **CALL** *n* apprentissage *m* des langues assisté par ordinateur; ~-**aided learning**, **CAL** *n* enseignement *m* assisté par ordinateur, EAO *m*; ~ **code** *n* code *m* informatique; ~ **dating service** *n* club *m* de rencontres (*utilisant un ordinateur*); ~ **engineer** ▶1251 *n* technicien/-ienne *m/f* en informatique; ~ **error** *n* erreur *f* informatique; ~ **game** *n* jeu *m* informatique; ~ **graphics** *n* (+ *v sg*) infographie *f*; ~ **hacker** *n* pirate *m* informatique.

computerization /kəmˌpju:təraɪ'zeɪʃn, US -rɪ'z-/ *n* (of records, accounts) mise *f* sur ordinateur; (of work, workplace) informatisation *f*.

computerize /kəm'pju:təraɪz/ *vtr* (store) mettre [qch] sur ordinateur [*records, accounts*]; (treat by computer) informatiser [*list*].

computer: ~ **keyboard** *n* clavier *m* d'ordinateur; ~ **language** *n* langage *m* de programmation; ~ **literacy** *n* notions *fpl* d'informatique; ~-**literate** *adj* ayant des notions d'informatique; ~ **operator** ▶1251 *n* opérateur/-trice *m/f* sur ordinateur; ~ **program** *n* programme *m* informatique; ~ **programmer** ▶1251 *n* programmeur/-euse *m/f*; ~ **programming** *n* programmation *f*; ~ **science** *n* informatique *f*; ~ **scientist** ▶1251 *n* informaticien/-ienne *m/f*; ~ **studies** *n* SCH, UNIV informatique *f*; ~ **virus** *n* virus *m* informatique.

computing /kəm'pju:tɪŋ/ *n* informatique *f*.

comrade /'kɒmreɪd, US -ræd/ *n* † OU POL camarade *mf*; ~-**in-arms** compagnon *m* d'armes.

con /kɒn/ I *n* escroquerie *f*, arnaque◐ *f*.
II° *vtr* (*p prés etc* -**nn**-) (swindle) rouler°, escroquer; (dupe) embobiner°, duper; **to ~ sb into doing sth**° amener qn à faire qch en abusant de sa crédulité; **to ~ sb out of sth**° obtenir qch de qn par la ruse; **I was ~ned out of £5** on m'a eu° de 5 livres sterling.

con artist *n* = **con man**.

concave /'kɒŋkeɪv/ *adj* concave.

conceal /kən'si:l/ *vtr* dissimuler (**from** à).
II **concealed** *pp adj* [*entrance, camera*] caché.

concealment /kən'si:lmənt/ *n* dissimulation *f*; **place of ~** cache *f*.

concede /kən'si:d/ I *vtr* **1** (admit) concéder [*point*]; **to ~ that** reconnaître que; **2** (surrender) accorder [*right*] (**to** à); céder [*territory*] (**to** à); **3** SPORT concéder [*point, goal*] (**to** à); **4** POL **to ~ an election** concéder la victoire électorale (**to** à).
II *vi* **1** GEN céder; **2** POL reconnaître une défaite électorale.

conceit /kən'si:t/ *n* **1** (vanity) suffisance *f*; **2** (affectation) afféterie *f* LITER.

conceited /kən'si:tɪd/ *adj* [*person*] vaniteux/-euse; [*remark*] suffisant; [*expression*] de suffisance.

conceitedly /kən'siːtɪdlɪ/ adv avec vanité.

conceivable /kən'siːvəbl/ adj concevable, imaginable; **it is ~ that** il est concevable que (+ subj).

conceivably /kən'siːvəblɪ/ adv **it might just ~ cost more than £100** il est concevable que cela coûte plus de 100 livres; **it could ~ be true** il est concevable que ce soit vrai; **I can't ~ eat all that** je ne vois pas comment je pourrai manger tout ça.

conceive /kən'siːv/ I vtr **1** concevoir [child]; **2** (develop) concevoir [hatred, idea]; **3** (believe) concevoir.
II vi **1** (become pregnant) concevoir, devenir enceinte; **2** (imagine) **to ~ of sth** imaginer or concevoir qch.

concentrate /'kɒnsntreɪt/ I n CHEM, CULIN concentré m; **tomato ~** concentré de tomates.
II vtr concentrer [effort] (**on** sur; **on doing** pour faire); employer [resources] (**on** sur; **on doing** à faire); centrer [attention] (**on** sur); **fear ~s the mind** la peur fait réfléchir.
III vi **1** (pay attention) [person] se concentrer (**on** sur); **to ~ on doing** s'appliquer à faire; **2** (focus) **to ~ on** [film, journalist] s'intéresser surtout à; **3** (congregate) se concentrer.

concentration /ˌkɒnsn'treɪʃn/ n **1** (attention) concentration f (**on** sur); **my powers of ~** mon pouvoir de concentration; **to lose one's ~** se déconcentrer; **2** (specialization) spécialisation f; **~ on sales** spécialisation dans le domaine de la vente; **3** CHEM concentration f; **high/low ~** forte/faible concentration; **4** (accumulation) concentration f.

concentration camp n camp m de concentration.

concentric /kən'sentrɪk/ adj concentrique.

concept /'kɒnsept/ n concept m.

conception /kən'sepʃn/ n MED, FIG conception f (**of** de); **you can have no ~ of** tu ne peux pas imaginer.

concern /kən'sɜːn/ I n **1** (worry) inquiétude f (**about, over** à propos de); **there is growing ~ about crime** la criminalité suscite de plus en plus d'inquiétude; **there is ~ for her safety** on s'inquiète pour sa sécurité; **to cause ~** être inquiétant; **there is no cause for ~** il n'y a pas lieu d'être inquiet; **he expressed ~ at my results/for my health** il m'a fait part de son inquiétude quant à mes résultats/ma santé; **2** (preoccupation) préoccupation f; **environmental ~s** des préoccupations écologiques; **3** (care) (for person) prévenance f; **out of ~ for him** par égard pour lui; **you have no ~ for safety** tu ne te préoccupes pas de la sécurité; **4** (company) entreprise f; **a going ~** une affaire rentable; **5** (personal business) **that's her ~** cela la regarde; **your private life is no ~ of mine** ta vie privée ne me regarde pas.
II vtr **1** (worry) inquiéter; **2** (affect, interest) concerner, intéresser; **to whom it may ~** à qui de droit; (in letter) Monsieur; **as far as the pay is ~ed** en ce qui concerne le salaire; **3** (involve) **to be ~ed with** s'occuper de [security, publicity]; **to be ~ed in** être impliqué dans [scandal]; **4** (be about) [book, programme] traiter de; [fax, letter] concerner.
III v refl **to ~ oneself with sth/with doing** s'occuper de qch/de faire.

concerned /kən'sɜːnd/ adj **1** (anxious) inquiet/-ète (**about** à propos de); **to be ~ at the news** trouver la nouvelle inquiétante; **to be ~ that sb might do** être inquiet/-iète à l'idée que qn fasse; **to be ~ for sb** se faire du souci pour qn; **2** (involved) concerné; **all (those) ~** toutes les personnes concernées.

concerning /kən'sɜːnɪŋ/ prep concernant.

concert /'kɒnsət/ I n **1** MUS concert m; **in ~ at/ with** en concert à/avec; **2** (cooperation) concert m; **in ~ de concert**, d'un commun accord.
II noun modifier [music, ticket, pianist] de concert.

concerted /kən'sɜːtɪd/ adj [action, campaign] concerté; **to make a ~ effort to do** faire un sérieux effort pour faire.

concert: **~goer** n habitué/-e m/f des concerts; **~ hall** n salle f de concert.

concertina /ˌkɒnsə'tiːnə/ ▶ 1097 I n concertina m.
II vi GB [part of vehicle] se plier en accordéon; [carriages] se télescoper.

concerto /kən'tʃeətəʊ, -'tʃɜːt-/ n concerto m.

concert: **~ performer** n concertiste mf; **~ tour** n tournée f.

concession /kən'seʃn/ n **1** (compromise) concession f (**on** sur; **to** à); **as a ~** à titre de concession; **2** (discount) réduction f; **'~s'** 'tarif réduit'; **3** (property rights) concession f; **4** (marketing rights) **to run a perfume ~** être concessionnaire de parfumerie.

concessionary /kən'seʃənərɪ/ adj [fare, price, rate] réduit.

conciliate /kən'sɪlɪeɪt/ vtr apaiser.

conciliation /kənˌsɪlɪ'eɪʃn/ n conciliation f; **~ service** commission f de conciliation.

conciliator /kən'sɪlɪeɪtə(r)/ n médiateur/-trice m/f.

conciliatory /kən'sɪlɪətərɪ, US -tɔːrɪ/ adj [gesture, mood, terms] conciliant; [measures, speech] conciliatoire.

concise /kən'saɪs/ adj **1** (succinct) concis; **2** (abridged) **A Concise History of Celtic Art** Précis m d'histoire de l'art celte.

concisely /kən'saɪslɪ/ adv avec concision.

conclude /kən'kluːd/ I vtr **1** (finish) conclure, terminer; **'finally...,' he ~d** 'enfin...,' dit-il pour conclure; **'to be ~d'** (on TV) 'suite et fin au prochain épisode'; (in magazine) 'suite et fin au prochain numéro'; **2** (settle) conclure [treaty]; **3** (deduce) conclure (**from** de).
II vi [story, event] se terminer (**with** par, sur); [speaker] conclure (**with** par); **he ~d by saying that** il a conclu en disant que.

concluding /kən'kluːdɪŋ/ adj final.

conclusion /kən'kluːʒn/ n **1** (end) fin f; **in ~** en conclusion, pour terminer; **2** (opinion, resolution) conclusion f; **to come to ou to reach a ~** arriver à une conclusion; **to draw a ~ from sth** tirer une conclusion de qch; **this leads to the ~ that** ceci nous amène à conclure que; **he jumped ou leapt to the ~ that she was dead** il en a conclu un peu trop hâtivement qu'elle était morte; **don't jump ou leap to ~s!** ne tire pas de conclusions hâtives!; **3** (outcome) conclusion f; **taken to its logical ~, this would mean that** si on va jusqu'au bout, ceci signifierait que.

conclusive /kən'kluːsɪv/ adj concluant.

concoct /kən'kɒkt/ vtr concocter.

concoction /kən'kɒkʃn/ n **1** (drink) breuvage m; (dish) mélange m; **2** FIG (style, effect) mélange m.

concord /'kɒnkɔːd/ n concorde f.

concordance /kən'kɔːdəns/ n **1** SOUT (agreement) accord m; **to be in ~ with** s'accorder avec; **2** (index) concordance f.

concourse /'kɒnkɔːs/ n (interior area) hall m.

concrete /'kɒnkriːt/ I n béton m.
II adj **1** CONSTR [block] de béton; [base] en béton; **2** FIG concret/-ète; **in ~ terms** concrètement.
■ **concrete over**: **~ over [sth]** recouvrir [qch] de béton, bétonner.

concrete: **~ jungle** n univers m de béton; **~ mixer** n bétonnière f.

concur /kən'kɜː(r)/ (p prés etc **-rr-**) I vtr convenir (**that** que).
II vi **1** (agree) être d'accord (**with** avec); **2** (act together) **to ~ in** participer à [action, measure, decision]; **to ~ with sb in condemning** se joindre à qn pour condamner; **3** (tally) [data, views] concorder (**with** avec); **4** (combine) **to ~ to do** contribuer à faire.

concurrent /kən'kʌrənt/ adj **1** (simultaneous) simultané; **2** SOUT (in agreement) **to be ~ with** [views] concorder avec.

concurrently /kən'kʌrəntlɪ/ adv simultanément.

concussion /kən'kʌʃn/ n MED commotion f cérébrale.

condemn /kən'dem/ I vtr **1** (censure) condamner (**for doing** pour avoir fait); **to ~ sth as pointless/provocative** condamner la futilité/l'aspect provocateur de qch; **to ~ sb as an opportunist** dénoncer l'opportunisme de qn; **2** JUR (sentence) **to ~ sb to death/life imprisonment** condamner qn à mort/à perpétuité;

3 (doom) **to be ~ed to do** être condamné à faire; **to ~ sb to** condamner qn à [*poverty*]; **4** (declare unsafe) déclarer [qch] inhabitable [*building*].
II condemned *pp adj* **1** [*cell*] des condamnés à mort; **~ed man/woman** condamné/-e *m/f* à mort; **2** [*building*] déclaré inhabitable.

condemnation /ˌkɒndem'neɪʃn/ *n* **1** (censure) condamnation *f*; **2** (indictment) **to be a ~ of sb/sth** remettre qn/qch en question.

condemnatory /ˌkɒndem'neɪtəri/ *adj* dénonciateur/-trice.

condensation /ˌkɒnden'seɪʃn/ *n* **1** (droplets) (on walls) condensation *f*; (on windows) buée *f*; **2** CHEM (process) condensation *f*.

condense /kən'dens/ **I** *vtr* condenser (**into** en).
II *vi* CHEM se condenser.

condensed milk *n* lait *m* concentré sucré or condensé.

condenser /kən'densə(r)/ *n* condenseur *m*.

condescend /ˌkɒndɪ'send/ **I** *vtr* (deign) **to ~ to do** condescendre à faire.
II *vi* **to ~ to sb** être condescendant envers qn.

condescending /ˌkɒndɪ'sendɪŋ/ *adj* condescendant.

condescension /ˌkɒndɪ'senʃn/ *n* condescendance *f*.

condition /kən'dɪʃn/ **I** *n* **1** (stipulation) condition *f*; **to meet** ou **satisfy the ~s** remplir les conditions; **under certain ~s** sous certaines conditions; **on ~ that** à condition que (+ *subj*); **I agree, on one ~, namely that you pay in cash** je suis d'accord, mais à une condition, que vous payiez en liquide; **2** (state) état *m*, condition *f*; **to be in good/bad ~** [*house, car etc*] être en bon/mauvais état; **he's in good ~** il est en bonne santé; **to be in a critical ~** être dans un état critique; **her ~ is serious** elle est dans un état grave; **to be in no ~ to do** ne pas être en état de faire; **3** (disease) maladie *f*; **a heart/skin ~** une maladie cardiaque/de la peau; **4** (fitness) forme *f*; **to be out of ~** ne pas être en forme; **to get one's body into ~** se mettre en forme; **5** (situation) condition *f*; **the human ~** la condition humaine.
II conditions *npl* conditions *fpl*; **to work under difficult ~s** travailler dans des conditions difficiles; **housing/living ~s** conditions de logement/de vie; **weather ~s** conditions météorologiques.
III *vtr* **1** PSYCH conditionner; **2** (treat) traiter [*hair*].

conditional /kən'dɪʃənl/ **I** *n* LING conditionnel *m*; **in the ~** au conditionnel.
II *adj* **1** conditionnel/-elle; **the offer is ~ on** ou **upon the name of the donor remaining secret** l'offre a pour condition que le nom du donateur demeure (*subj*) secret; **to make sth ~ on** ou **upon sth** faire dépendre qch de qch; **2** [*clause, sentence*] conditionnel/-elle; **in the ~ tense** au conditionnel.

conditionally /kən'dɪʃənəlɪ/ *adv* sous conditions.

conditioner /kən'dɪʃənə(r)/ *n* (for hair) après-shampooing *m*, démêlant *m*; (for laundry) assouplisseur *m*.

conditioning /kən'dɪʃənɪŋ/ **I** *n* **1** PSYCH conditionnement *m*; **2** (of hair) traitement *m*.
II *adj* [*shampoo, lotion etc*] démêlant.

condole /kən'dəʊl/ *vi* **to ~ with** présenter ses condoléances à.

condolence /kən'dəʊləns/ **I** *n* **letter of ~** lettre *f* de condoléance.
II condolences *npl* condoléances *fpl*.

condom /'kɒndɒm/ *n* préservatif *m*.

condominium /ˌkɒndə'mɪnɪəm/ *n* US **1** (also **~ unit**) appartement *m* (dans une copropriété); **2** (complex) (immeuble *m* en) copropriété *f*.

condone /kən'dəʊn/ *vtr* tolérer.

conducive /kən'djuːsɪv, US -'duː-/ *adj* **to be ~ to** être favorable à.

conduct I /'kɒndʌkt/ *n* **1** (behaviour) conduite *f* (**towards** envers); **2** (handling) conduite *f* (**of** de).
II /kən'dʌkt/ *vtr* **1** (lead) conduire [*visitor, group*]; **she ~ed us around the house** elle nous a fait faire le tour de la maison; **~ed tour** ou **visit** visite guidée; **2** (manage) mener [*life, business*]; **3** (carry out) mener [*ex-*

periment, inquiry]; faire [*poll*]; célébrer [*ceremony*]; **4** MUS diriger [*orchestra*]; **5** ELEC, PHYS conduire.
III /kən'dʌkt/ *vi* MUS diriger.
IV /kən'dʌkt/ *v refl* **to ~ oneself** se comporter.

conduction /kən'dʌkʃn/ *n* conduction *f*.

conductor /kən'dʌktə(r)/ ► **1251** *n* **1** MUS chef *m* d'orchestre; **2** (on bus) receveur *m*; RAIL chef *m* de train; **3** ELEC, PHYS conducteur *m*.

conductress /kən'dʌktrɪs/ ► **1251** *n* receveuse *f*.

conduit /'kɒndɪt, 'kɒndjuːɪt, US 'kɒndwɪt/ *n* conduit *m*.

cone /kəʊn/ *n* **1** MATH, GEN cône *m*; **paper ~** cornet *m* (en papier); **2** (also **ice-cream ~**) cornet *m*; **3** (for traffic) balise *f*.
■ **cone off**: **~** [**sth**] **off**, **~ off** [**sth**] baliser.

confection /kən'fekʃn/ *n* **1** CULIN (cake) pâtisserie *f*, gâteau *m*; (dessert) dessert *m*; **2** (combination) **a ~ of** une savante combinaison de; **3** (process) confection *f*.

confectioner /kən'fekʃənə(r)/ *n* (making sweets) confiseur/-euse *m/f*; (making cakes) pâtissier-confiseur *m*; **~'s custard** crème *f* pâtissière; **~'s** (**shop**) pâtisserie-confiserie *f*; **~'s sugar** US sucre *m* glace.

confectionery /kən'fekʃənərɪ, US -ʃənerɪ/ *n* **C** (sweets) GEN sucreries *fpl*; (high quality) confiserie *f*; (cakes) pâtisserie *f*.

confederacy /kən'fedərəsɪ/ *n* POL confédération *f*.

confederate I /kən'fedərət/ *n* **1** (in conspiracy) complice *mf*; **2** POL confédéré/-e *m/f*.
II /kən'fedərət/ *adj* POL confédéré.
III /kən'fedəreɪt/ *vi* (unite) se confédérer (**with** avec).

confederation /kənˌfedə'reɪʃn/ *n* confédération *f*.

confer /kən'fɜː(r)/ **I** *vtr* (*p prés etc* **-rr-**) conférer (**on, upon** à).
II *vi* (*p prés etc* **-rr-**) conférer (**about** de).

conference /'kɒnfərəns/ **I** *n* conférence *f*; POL congrès *m*; **peace ~** conférence pour la paix.
II *noun modifier* [*room, centre*] de conférences; **~ member** participant/-e *m/f*; **~ table** LIT table *f* de conférence; FIG table *f* de négociation.

confess /kən'fes/ **I** *vtr* **1** avouer, confesser [*crime, truth, mistake*]; avouer, reconnaître [*liking, weakness*]; **to ~ that** avouer que; **2** RELIG confesser.
II *vi* **1** (admit) avouer; **to ~ to a crime** avouer (avoir commis) un crime; **2** RELIG se confesser.

confession /kən'feʃn/ *n* **1** GEN, JUR aveu *m* (**of** de); **to make a full ~** faire des aveux complets; **2** RELIG confession *f*; **to go to ~, to make one's ~** se confesser; **to hear sb's ~** confesser qn.

confessional /kən'feʃənl/ *n* confessionnal *m*.

confessor /kən'fesə(r)/ *n* confesseur *m*.

confetti /kən'fetɪ/ *n* **C** confettis *mpl*.

confide /kən'faɪd/ **I** *vtr* confier [*secret*] (**to** à).
II *vi* **to ~ in** se confier à [*person*].

confidence /'kɒnfɪdəns/ *n* **1** (faith) confiance *f* (**in** en); **to have (every) ~ in sb/sth** avoir (pleine) confiance en qn/qch; **to put one's ~ in sb** mettre sa confiance en qn; **2** POL **vote of ~** vote *m* de confiance; **motion of no ~** motion *f* de censure; **3** (self-assurance) assurance *f*, confiance *f* en soi; **4** (certainty) assurance *f*; **I can say with ~ that** je suis sûr que; **5** (confidentiality) **to take sb into one's ~** se confier à qn; **to tell sb sth in** (**strict**) **~** dire qch à qn (tout à fait) confidentiellement; **6** (secret) confidence *f*.

confidence: ~ man, ~ trickster *n* GB escroc *m*; **~ trick** *n* escroquerie *f*.

confident /'kɒnfɪdənt/ *adj* **1** (sure) sûr, confiant; **to be ~ that** être sûr or persuadé que; **to be ~ of success** ou **of succeeding** avoir la certitude de réussir; **to feel ~ about the future** avoir confiance en l'avenir; **2** (self-assured) assuré, sûr de soi.

confidential /ˌkɒnfɪ'denʃl/ *adj* confidentiel/-ielle *m/f*; **~ secretary** secrétaire *mf* privé/-e.

confidentiality /ˌkɒnfɪdenʃɪ'ælətɪ/ *n* confidentialité *f*.

confidentially /ˌkɒnfɪ'denʃəlɪ/ *adv* confidentiellement.

confidently /'kɒnfɪdəntlɪ/ *adv* [*speak, behave*] avec assurance; [*expect, predict*] en toute confiance.

confiding /kən'faɪdɪŋ/ adj confiant.

confine /kən'faɪn/ I vtr 1 (shut up) confiner [person] (in, to dans); enfermer [animal] (in dans); **to be ~d to bed** être alité; **to be ~d to the house** être obligé de rester à la maison; **~d to barracks** MIL consigné au quartier; 2 (limit) limiter [comments etc] (**to** à); **the problem is not ~d to old people** le problème ne concerne pas uniquement les personnes âgées.
II v refl **to ~ oneself to/to doing** se contenter de/de faire.

confined /kən'faɪnd/ adj [area] confiné; [space] restreint.

confinement /kən'faɪnmənt/ n 1 (detention) (in cell) détention f (**in, to** dans); JUR réclusion f; 2 MED (labour) couches fpl; (birth) accouchement m.

confines /'kɒnfaɪnz/ npl contraintes fpl; **within the ~ of** dans le cadre de [regulations]; dans l'enceinte de [building].

confirm /kən'fɜːm/ vtr 1 (state as true, validate) confirmer; **two people were ~ed dead** on a confirmé que deux personnes ont trouvé la mort; **to ~ receipt of sth** accuser réception de qch; 2 ADMIN approuver [appointment]; 3 (justify) **to ~ sb in** conforter qn dans [belief, opinion]; 4 RELIG confirmer.

confirmation /ˌkɒnfə'meɪʃn/ n 1 (of belief, statement, news, fear) confirmation f; (of appointment, booking) confirmation f; 2 RELIG confirmation f.

confirmed /kən'fɜːmd/ adj [alcoholic, smoker, liar, habit] invétéré; [bachelor, sinner] endurci.

confiscate /'kɒnfɪskeɪt/ vtr confisquer (**from** à).

confiscation /ˌkɒnfɪ'skeɪʃn/ n confiscation f.

conflate /kən'fleɪt/ vtr regrouper.

conflict I /'kɒnflɪkt/ n conflit m; **to be in/come into ~** LIT, FIG être/entrer en conflit (**with** avec); **~ of interests** conflit d'intérêts; **to have a ~ of loyalties** être déchiré par des loyautés contradictoires.
II /kən'flɪkt/ vi (contradict) être en contradiction (**with** avec); (clash) tomber au même moment (**with** que).

conflicting /kən'flɪktɪŋ/ adj 1 (incompatible) [views, feelings] contradictoire; 2 (coinciding) **two ~ engagements** deux rendez-vous qui tombent en même temps.

confluence /'kɒnfluəns/ n (of rivers) confluent m; FIG confluence f.

conform /kən'fɔːm/ I vtr conformer (**to** à).
II vi 1 (to rules, standards) [person] se conformer (**with, to** à); [model, machine etc] être conforme (**to** à); **to ~ to type** se conformer à la norme; 2 (correspond) [ideas, beliefs] se conformer (**with, to** à); [situation] être conforme (**with, to** à).

conformist /kən'fɔːmɪst/ n, adj conformiste (mf).

conformity /kən'fɔːmətɪ/ n 1 conformité f (**to** à); **in ~ with** conformément à; 2 RELIG conformisme m.

confound /kən'faʊnd/ vtr 1 (perplex) déconcerter; 2 (discredit) donner tort à [critics].

confront /kən'frʌnt/ vtr 1 (face) affronter [danger, enemy]; faire face à [problem]; **to ~ the truth** voir la réalité en face; **to be ~ed by sth** être confronté à qch; **to be ~ed by the police** se retrouver face à la police; **the task which ~ed us** le travail qui se présentait à nous; 2 (bring together) **to ~ sb with sth/sb** mettre qn en présence de qch/qn.

confrontation /ˌkɒnfrʌn'teɪʃn/ n affrontement m.

confrontational /ˌkɒnfrʌn'teɪʃənəl/ adj provocateur/ -trice.

confuse /kən'fjuːz/ vtr 1 (bewilder) troubler [person]; **to ~ the enemy troops** semer la confusion dans les troupes ennemies; 2 (fail to distinguish) confondre (**with** avec); 3 (complicate) compliquer [argument]; **to ~ the issue** compliquer les choses.

confused /kən'fjuːzd/ adj 1 [person] troublé; [thoughts, mind] confus; **to get ~** s'embrouiller; **he was ~ about the instructions** il ne comprenait pas bien le mode d'emploi; **I'm ~ about what to do** je ne sais pas trop ce que je dois faire; 2 (muddled) [account, reasoning] confus; [memories, sounds] confus; [voices] indistinct; [impression] vague.

confusedly /kən'fjuːzɪdlɪ/ adv 1 (in bewilderment) confusément; 2 (unclearly) [speak] de façon confuse.

confusing /kən'fjuːzɪŋ/ adj déroutant, peu clair.

confusion /kən'fjuːʒn/ n confusion f; **to create ~** jeter la confusion (dans les esprits); **I was in a state of total ~** j'étais complètement embrouillé; **to avoid ~** pour éviter toute confusion; **to throw sb/sth into ~** plonger qn/qch dans la confusion.

congeal /kən'dʒiːl/ vi [fat] se figer; [blood] se coaguler.

congenial /kən'dʒiːnɪəl/ adj sympathique, agréable.

congenital /kən'dʒenɪtl/ adj 1 MED congénital; 2 FIG [fear, dislike] congénital; [liar] invétéré.

congenitally /kən'dʒenɪtəlɪ/ adv 1 MED **to be ~ deformed** avoir une malformation congénitale; 2 FIG [dishonest, lazy] congénitalement.

congested /kən'dʒestɪd/ adj 1 [road] embouteillé; [pavement, passage] encombré; [district] surpeuplé; 2 MED congestionné.

congestion /kən'dʒestʃn/ n 1 (of district) surpeuplement m; (of road) encombrement m; **traffic ~** embouteillages mpl; 2 MED congestion f.

conglomerate I /kən'glɒmərət/ n conglomérat m.
II /kən'glɒməreɪt/ vi s'agglomérer.

congratulate /kən'grætjʊleɪt/ I vtr féliciter (**on** de; **on doing** d'avoir fait); **may we ~ you on your success/engagement?** permettez-nous de vous féliciter de votre succès/à l'occasion de vos fiançailles.
II v refl **to ~ oneself** se féliciter (**on** de).

congratulations /kənˌgrætjʊ'leɪʃnz/ npl félicitations fpl; **~ on your success/on the birth of your new baby** (toutes mes or nos) félicitations pour votre succès/à l'occasion de la naissance de votre bébé; **to offer one's ~ to sb** adresser ses félicitations à qn.

congregate /'kɒŋgrɪgeɪt/ I vtr rassembler.
II vi se rassembler (**around** autour de).

congregation /ˌkɒŋgrɪ'geɪʃn/ n (+ v sg ou pl) (in church) assemblée f des fidèles; (of clergy) congrégation f.

congregational /ˌkɒŋgrɪ'geɪʃənl/ adj [prayer, singing] des fidèles; **the Congregational Church** l'Église congrégationaliste.

congress /'kɒŋgres, US 'kɒŋgrəs/ n congrès m (**on** sur).

Congress /'kɒŋgres, US 'kɒŋgrəs/ n POL Congrès m; **in ~** au Congrès.

Congressional /kən'greʃənl/ adj US [candidate] au Congrès; [committee] du Congrès.

Congressional District, CD n US circonscription f d'un membre du Congrès.

congress: **~man** n (pl **-men**) US membre m du Congrès; **~woman** n (pl **-women**) US membre m du Congrès.

conical /'kɒnɪkl/ adj conique.

conifer /'kɒnɪfə(r), 'kəʊn-/ n conifère m.

coniferous /kə'nɪfərəs, US kəʊ'n-/ adj [tree] conifère; [forest] de conifères.

conjecture /kən'dʒektʃə(r)/ I n hypothèse f; **to be a matter for ~** être hypothétique.
II vi faire des conjectures (**about** sur).

conjugal /'kɒndʒʊgl/ adj conjugal.

conjugate /'kɒndʒʊgeɪt/ I vtr conjuguer.
II vi se conjuguer [verb].

conjugation /ˌkɒndʒʊ'geɪʃn/ n conjugaison f.

conjunction /kən'dʒʌŋkʃn/ n 1 (of events) concours m; **in ~** ensemble; **in ~ with** conjointement avec; 2 LING conjonction f.

conjunctivitis /kənˌdʒʌŋktɪ'vaɪtɪs/ ▶1002 n conjonctivite f.

conjure /'kʌndʒə(r)/ vi faire des tours de prestidigitation; **a name to ~ with** FIG un nom qu'on évoque avec respect.
■ **conjure up**: **~ up** [sth] faire apparaître [qch] comme par magie; **to ~ up an image of sth** évoquer qch.

conjuring /'kʌndʒərɪŋ/ n prestidigitation f.

conjuring trick *n* tour *m* de prestidigitation.
conjuror /'kʌndʒərə(r)/ *n* prestidigitateur/-trice *m/f*.
conk /kɒŋk/: ■ **conk out**○ [*person*] s'endormir; [*car, machine*] tomber en panne.
conker○ /'kɒŋkə(r)/ *n* GB **1** marron *m*; **2 conkers** *jeu de marrons*.
con man *n* arnaqueur➌ *m*, escroc *m*.
connect /kə'nekt/ I *vtr* **1** (attach) raccorder [*end, hose*] (**to** à); accrocher [*wagon, coach*] (**to** à); **to ~ two tubes** raccorder deux tubes; **2** (link) [*road, bridge, railway*] relier [*place, road*] (**to, with** à); **I always ~ rain** with Oxford j'associe toujours la pluie à Oxford; **3** (to mains) brancher [*appliance*] (**to** à); brancher [*qch*] sur le secteur [*household*]; **4** TELECOM raccorder [*phone, subscriber*]; **to ~ sb to** passer [qn] à qn [*department*].
II *vi* **1** [*room*] communiquer (**with** avec); **2** [*service, bus*] assurer la correspondance (**with** avec).
■ **connect up**: **~ up** [sth], **~** [sth] **up** faire les branchements de [*video, computer*]; **to ~ sth up to** brancher qch sur; **to ~ two machines up** connecter deux machines.
connected /kə'nektɪd/ *adj* **1** (related) [*idea, event*] lié (**to, with** à); **everything ~ with music** tout ce qui se rapporte à la musique; **2** (in family) apparenté (**to** à); **to be well ~** (through family) être de bonne famille; (having influence) avoir des relations; **3** (linked) [*road, town*] relié (**to, with** à); [*pipe*] raccordé (**to, with** à); **4** (electrically) branché.
connecting /kə'nektɪŋ/ *adj* **1** [*flight*] de correspondance; **2** [*room*] attenant.
connection, connexion† GB /kə'nekʃn/ *n* **1** (logical link) rapport *m*; **to have no ~ with** n'avoir aucun rapport or n'avoir rien à voir avec; **to make the ~** faire le rapprochement; **in ~ with** au sujet de, à propos de; **in this ~...** à ce sujet...; **2** (personal link) lien *m* (**between** entre; **with** avec); **3** (person) (contact) relation *f*; **to have useful ~s** avoir des relations; **4** (connecting up) (to mains) branchement *m*; (of pipes, tubes) raccord *m*; (of wires) câblage *m*; **5** TELECOM (to network) raccordement *m*; (to number) mise *f* en communication (**to** avec); **bad ~** mauvaise communication *f*; **6** (in travel) correspondance *f*.
connivance /kə'naɪvəns/ *n* connivence *f*.
connive /kə'naɪv/ I *vi* **1** **to ~ at** contribuer délibérément à; **to ~ (with sb) to do sth** être de connivence or de mèche○ (avec qn) pour faire qch.
II **conniving** *pres p adj* [*person*] fourbe; **a conniving glance** un regard de connivence.
connoisseur /ˌkɒnə'sɜ:(r)/ *n* connaisseur/-euse *m/f*.
connotation /ˌkɒnə'teɪʃn/ *n* connotation *f* (**of** de).
connote /kə'nəʊt/ *vtr* **1** (summon up) évoquer; **2** LING connoter.
conquer /'kɒŋkə(r)/ I *vtr* conquérir [*territory, people*]; vaincre [*enemy, unemployment, disease*]; surmonter [*habit, fear*]; maîtriser [*skill, technology*].
II **conquering** *pres p adj* victorieux/-ieuse.
conqueror /'kɒŋkərə(r)/ *n* GEN vainqueur *m*; SPORT gagnant/-e *m/f*; MIL conquérant/-e *m/f*.
conquest /'kɒŋkwest/ *n* **1** ¢ (of country, mountain) conquête *f*; (of disease) éradication *f*; (of person) HUM conquête *f*; **2** (territory) terre *f* conquise; (person) HUM conquête *f*.
conscience /'kɒnʃəns/ *n* conscience *f*; **in all ~** en mon/son etc âme et conscience; **they have no ~** ils n'ont aucun sens moral; **the ~ of the nation** la voix de la conscience nationale; **to have a guilty** ou **bad ~** avoir mauvaise conscience; **to have a clear ~** avoir la conscience tranquille; **to do sth with a clear ~** faire qch la conscience tranquille.
conscience-stricken *adj* bourrelé de remords.
conscientious /ˌkɒnʃɪ'enʃəs/ *adj* consciencieux/-ieuse.
conscientiously /ˌkɒnʃɪ'enʃəslɪ/ *adv* consciencieusement.
conscientiousness /ˌkɒnʃɪ'enʃəsnɪs/ *n* application *f*, soin *m*.

conscientious objector, CO *n* objecteur *m* de conscience.
conscious /'kɒnʃəs/ I *n* PSYCH **the ~** le conscient.
II *adj* **1** (aware) conscient (**of** de; **that** du fait que); **politically ~** politisé; **to be environmentally ~** avoir une conscience écologique; **2** (deliberate) [*decision*] réfléchi; [*effort*] consciencieux; **3** MED conscient.
consciously /'kɒnʃəslɪ/ *adv* consciemment.
consciousness /'kɒnʃəsnɪs/ *n* **1** (awareness) conscience *f* (**of** de); (undefined) sentiment *m* (**of** de); **2** MED **to lose/regain ~** perdre/reprendre connaissance.
consciousness raising *n* sensibilisation *f*.
conscript I /'kɒnskrɪpt/ *n* appelé *m*.
II /kən'skrɪpt/ *vtr* appeler [*soldier*]; enrôler [qn] de force [*worker*].
conscription /kən'skrɪpʃn/ *n* **1** (system) conscription *f*; **2** (process) incorporation *f* (**into** dans).
consecrate /'kɒnsɪkreɪt/ *vtr* consacrer.
consecration /ˌkɒnsɪ'kreɪʃn/ *n* consécration *f*.
consecutive /kən'sekjʊtɪv/ *adj* consécutif/-ive.
consecutively /kən'sekjʊtɪvlɪ/ *adv* consécutivement.
consensus /kən'sensəs/ *n* consensus *m* (**among** au sein de; **about, as to** quant à; **for** en faveur de; **on** sur); **what's the ~?** quelle est l'opinion générale?
consent /kən'sent/ I *n* **1** (permission) (by person in authority) consentement *m*; (other) accord *m*; **age of ~** âge *m* légal; **2** (agreement) **by common** ou **mutual ~** d'un commun accord.
II *vtr* **to ~ to do** consentir à faire.
III *vi* consentir (**to** à); **to ~ to sb doing** consentir à ce que qn fasse; **~ing adults** adultes consentants.
consequence /'kɒnsɪkwəns, US -kwens/ *n* **1** (result) conséquence *f*; **as a ~ of** du fait de [*change, process*]; à la suite de [*event*]; **in ~** par conséquent; **to face the ~s** accepter les conséquences; **to suffer the ~s** subir les conséquences; **2** (importance) importance *f*; **he is a man of no ~** c'est quelqu'un sans importance; **it's of no ~ to me** cela m'est complètement indifférent.
consequent /'kɒnsɪkwənt, US -kwent/ *adj* **the strike and the ~ redundancies** la grève et les licenciements qu'elle a entraînés; **~ upon** (because of) en raison de; **to be ~ upon sth** (the result of) être la conséquence de qch.
consequently /'kɒnsɪkwentlɪ/ *adv* par conséquent.
conservation /ˌkɒnsə'veɪʃn/ I *n* **1** (of nature, natural resources) protection *f* (**of** de); **energy ~** maîtrise *f* de l'énergie; **2** (of heritage) conservation *f*; **3** PHYS conservation *f*.
II *noun modifier* [*group, measure*] de protection; **~ area** zone *f* protégée.
conservationist /ˌkɒnsə'veɪʃənɪst/ *n* défenseur *m* des ressources naturelles.
conservatism /kən'sɜ:vətɪzəm/ *n* conservatisme *m*.
conservative /kən'sɜ:vətɪv/ I *n* POL conservateur/-trice *m/f*.
II *adj* **1** POL conservateur/-trice; **2** (cautious) prudent; **at a ~ estimate** au bas mot; **3** [*taste, style*] classique.
Conservative /kən'sɜ:vətɪv/ GB POL I *n* Conservateur/-trice *m/f*.
II *adj* conservateur/-trice; **to vote ~** voter pour le parti conservateur.
conservatory /kən'sɜ:vətrɪ, US -tɔ:rɪ/ *n* **1** (for plants) jardin *m* d'hiver; **2** US MUS conservatoire *m*.
conserve /kən'sɜ:v/ I *n* (jam) confiture *f*.
II *vtr* **1** (protect) protéger [*forest*]; sauvegarder [*wild-life*]; conserver [*remains, ruins*]; **2** (save up) économiser [*resources*]; garder [*moisture*]; ménager [*energy*].
consider /kən'sɪdə(r)/ I *vtr* **1** (give thought to, study) considérer [*options, facts*]; examiner [*evidence, problem*]; étudier [*offer*]; **to ~ how** réfléchir à la façon dont; **to ~ why** examiner les raisons pour lesquelles; **to ~ whether** décider si; **the jury is ~ing its verdict** le jury délibère; **2** (take into account) prendre [qch] en considération [*risk, cost*]; songer à [*person*]; faire attention à [*person's feelings*]; **when you ~ that** quand on songe que; **all things ~ed**

tout compte fait; **3** (envisage) envisager [*course of action*]; **to ~ doing** envisager de faire; **to ~ sb for a role** penser à qn pour un rôle; **to ~ sb/sth as sth** penser à qn/qch comme qch; **4** (regard) **to ~ that** considérer or estimer que; **to ~ sb/sth favourably** voir qn/qch sous un jour favorable; **~ the matter closed** considérez que l'affaire est close; **~ it done** tiens-le pour fait.
II *vi* réfléchir.
III considered *pp adj* [*answer, view*] réfléchi; **in my ~ed opinion** selon ma conviction.
IV *v refl* **to ~ oneself (to be) a writer/genius** se prendre pour PEJ or se considérer comme un écrivain/génie.

considerable /kən'sɪdərəbl/ *adj* considérable; **to a ~ degree** ou **extent** dans une large mesure.

considerably /kən'sɪdərəblɪ/ *adv* considérablement.

considerate /kən'sɪdərət/ *adj* [*person, nature*] attentionné; [*behaviour, motorist*] courtois; **to be ~ towards sb** avoir des égards pour qn; **it was ~ of you to wait** c'est aimable à vous d'avoir attendu.

considerately /kən'sɪdərətlɪ/ *adv* [*act*] de manière attentionnée; **to behave ~ towards sb** avoir des égards pour qn.

consideration /kən‚sɪdə'reɪʃn/ *n* **1** (thought) considération *f*, réflexion *f*; **after careful ~** après mûre réflexion; **to give ~ to sth** réfléchir à qch; **to give sth careful ~** réfléchir longuement à qch; **~ is being given to…** on examine actuellement…; **to take sth into ~** prendre qch en considération; **to be under ~** [*matter*] être à l'étude; **she's under ~ for the job** on est en train d'étudier sa candidature; **2** (thoughtfulness, care) considération *f* (for envers); **out of ~** par considération; **3** (factor, thing to be considered) considération *f*; (concern) (objet *m* de) souci *m*; **safety is the overriding ~** la sécurité constitue le souci dominant; **4** (fee) **for a ~** moyennant finance.

considering /kən'sɪdərɪŋ/ **I** *prep, conj* étant donné, compte tenu de; **~ (that) he was tired** étant donné sa fatigue.
II *adv* tout compte fait.

consign /kən'saɪn/ *vtr* **1** (get rid of) reléguer (to à); **to ~ sth to the flames** livrer qch aux flammes; **2** (entrust) **to ~ sth to sb's care** confier qch aux soins de qn; **3** (send) expédier [*goods*] (to à).

consignment /kən'saɪnmənt/ *n* (sending) expédition *f*; (goods) lot *m*, livraison *f*; **for ~** à expédier.

consist /kən'sɪst/ *vi* **to ~ of** se composer de; **to ~ in résider dans; to ~ in doing** consister à faire.

consistency /kən'sɪstənsɪ/ *n* **1** (texture) consistance *f*; **2** (of view, policy) cohérence *f*; (of achievement) qualité *f* suivie.

consistent /kən'sɪstənt/ *adj* **1** [*growth, level, quality*] régulier/-ière; [*kindness, help*] constant; [*sportsman, playing*] régulier/-ière; **2** (repeated) [*attempts, demands*] répété; **3** (logical) cohérent; **4 ~ with** en accord avec [*account, belief*]; **injuries ~ with a fall** des blessures correspondant à une chute.

consistently /kən'sɪstəntlɪ/ *adv* (invariably) systématiquement, invariablement; (repeatedly) à maintes reprises.

consolation /‚kɒnsə'leɪʃn/ *n* consolation *f* (to à); **~ prize** LIT, FIG prix *m* de consolation.

console I /'kɒnsəʊl/ *n* **1** (controls) console *f*; **2** (cabinet) meuble *m* hi-fi (ou vidéo etc); **3** (table) console *f*.
II /kən'səʊl/ *vtr* console(r (for, on de; with avec).
III /kən'səʊl/ *v refl* **to ~ oneself** se consoler.

consolidate /kən'sɒlɪdeɪt/ **I** *vtr* **1** consolider [*knowledge, position*]; **2** COMM réunir [*resources*]; fusionner [*companies*].
II *vi* **1** (become stronger) s'affermir; **2** (unite) [*companies*] fusionner.

consolidation /kən‚sɒlɪ'deɪʃn/ *n* **1** (of knowledge, position) consolidation *f*; **2** (of companies) fusion *f*.

consoling /kən'səʊlɪŋ/ *adj* consolant.

consonant /'kɒnsənənt/ *n* consonne *f*.

consortium /kən'sɔːtɪəm/ *n* (*pl* **-tiums** ou **-tia**) consortium *m*.

conspicuous /kən'spɪkjʊəs/ *adj* **1** (to the eye) [*feature, sign*] visible; [*garment*] voyant; **to be ~** se remarquer (**for** à cause de); **to make oneself ~** se faire remarquer; **I feel ~** j'ai l'impression que tout le monde me regarde; **to be ~ by one's absence** IRON briller par son absence; **in a ~ position** bien en évidence; **2** (unusual) [*success*] remarquable; [*failure*] flagrant; [*lack*] total; **to be ~ for** être remarquable pour.

conspicuously /kən'spɪkjʊəslɪ/ *adv* [*placed*] bien en évidence; [*dressed*] de façon voyante; [*silent, empty*] remarquablement; **to be ~ absent** IRON briller par son absence.

conspiracy /kən'spɪrəsɪ/ *n* conspiration *f* (**against** contre; **to do** en vue de faire); **a ~ of silence** une conspiration du silence.

conspirator /kən'spɪrətə(r)/ *n* conspirateur/-trice *m/f*.

conspiratorial /kən‚spɪrə'tɔːrɪəl/ *adj* entendu.

conspire /kən'spaɪə(r)/ *vi* conspirer; **to ~ to do** [*people*] conspirer en vue de faire; [*events*] conspirer à faire.

constable /'kʌnstəbl, US 'kɒn-/ ▶937 *n* GB agent *m* (de police).

constabulary /kən'stæbjʊlərɪ, US -lerɪ/ *n* GB police *f*.

constancy /'kɒnstənsɪ/ *n* constance *f* (**to** envers).

constant /'kɒnstənt/ **I** *n* constante *f*.
II *adj* [*problem, reminder, threat*] permanent; [*care, temperature*] constant; [*disputes, questions*] incessant; [*attempts*] répété; [*companion*] éternel/-elle.

constantly /'kɒnstəntlɪ/ *adv* constamment.

constellation /‚kɒnstə'leɪʃn/ *n* constellation *f*.

consternation /‚kɒnstə'neɪʃn/ *n* consternation *f*; **in ~** frappé de consternation; **to my/his etc ~** à ma/sa etc grande consternation.

constipated /'kɒnstɪpeɪtɪd/ *adj* constipé.

constipation /‚kɒnstɪ'peɪʃn/ ▶1002 *n* constipation *f*; **to have ~** être constipé.

constituency /kən'stɪtjʊənsɪ/ *n* (district) circonscription *f* électorale; (voters) électeurs *mpl*; **~ party** GB section *f* locale du parti.

constituent /kən'stɪtjʊənt/ **I** *n* **1** POL électeur/-trice *m/f*; **2** (of character) trait *m*; (of event, work of art) élément *m*; **3** CHEM composant *m*.
II *adj* [*element, part*] constitutif/-ive; POL constituant.

constitute /'kɒnstɪtjuːt/ *vtr* **1** (represent) constituer; **2** (set up) créer.

constitution /‚kɒnstɪ'tjuːʃn, US -'tuːʃn/ *n* (all contexts) Constitution *f*.

constitutional /‚kɒnstɪ'tjuːʃənl, US -'tuː-/ **I†** *n* promenade *f*.
II *adj* **1** POL constitutionnel/-elle; **2** (innate) inné.

constitutionally /‚kɒnstɪ'tjuːʃənəlɪ, US -'tuː-/ *adv* **1** POL constitutionnellement; **2** (innately) par nature.

constrain /kən'streɪn/ *vtr* SOUT **1** (compel) contraindre (**to do** à faire); **2** (limit) entraver; **~ed** [*smile*] contraint; [*silence*] gêné; [*atmosphere*] de gêne.

constraint /kən'streɪnt/ *n* SOUT **1** (compulsion) contrainte *f*; **to put a ~ on** imposer une contrainte à; **under ~** sous la contrainte; **you are under no ~** vous n'êtes en rien obligé; **2** (uneasiness) contrainte *f*.

constrict /kən'strɪkt/ **I** *vtr* comprimer [*flow, blood vessel*]; gêner [*breathing, movement*]; **~ing clothes** vêtements serrés.
II constricted *pp adj* [*voice*] étranglé; [*breathing*] gêné; [*space*] restreint; [*life*] étriqué.

constriction /kən'strɪkʃn/ *n* **1** (constraint) contrainte *f*; **2** (of chest, throat) resserrement *m*; (of blood vessel) constriction *f*; **3** (by snake) étranglement *m*.

construct I /'kɒnstrʌkt/ *n* GEN construction *f*; PSYCH concept *m*.
II /kən'strʌkt/ *vtr* construire (**of** avec; **in** en).

construction /kən'strʌkʃn/ **I** *n* **1** (composition) construction *f*; **under ~** en construction; **2** ¢ (also **~**

industry) bâtiment *m*; **3** (interpretation) **to put the wrong ~ on sth** mal interpréter qch; **4** LING construction *f*.
II *noun modifier* [*work, toy*] de construction.

construction: **~ engineer ▶ 1251** *n* ingénieur *m* en génie civil; **~ site** *n* chantier *m*; **~ worker ▶ 1251** *n* ouvrier/-ière *m/f* du bâtiment.

constructive /kən'strʌktɪv/ *n* constructif/-ive.

constructively /kən'strʌktɪvlɪ/ *adv* de manière constructive.

construe /kən'struː/ *vtr* interpréter (**as sth** comme qch); **wrongly ~d** mal interprété.

consul /'kɒnsl/ *n* consul *m*; **the French ~** le consul de France.

consular /'kɒnsjʊlə(r), US -səl-/ *adj* consulaire.

consulate /'kɒnsjʊlət, US -səl-/ *n* consulat *m*.

consult /kən'sʌlt/ I *vtr* consulter (**about** sur).
II *vi* (also **~ together**) s'entretenir (**about** sur).

consultancy /kən'sʌltənsɪ/ I *n* **1** (also **~ firm**) cabinet-conseil *m*; **2** ¢ (advice) conseils *mpl*; **to work in ~** travailler comme consultant; **3** GB MED (job) poste *m* de spécialiste (*dans un hôpital*).
II *noun modifier* [*fees, service, work*] de conseil.

consultant /kən'sʌltənt/ **▶ 1251** I *n* **1** (expert) consultant/-e *m/f*, conseiller/-ère *m/f* (**on, in** en; **to** de); **beauty ~** esthéticienne-conseil *f*; **2** GB MED spécialiste *mf* (*attaché à un hôpital*); **~ obstetrician** chef *m* du service d'obstétrique.

consultation /ˌkɒnsl'teɪʃn/ *n* **1** (meeting) (for advice) consultation *f* (**about** sur); (for discussion) entretien *m* (**about** sur); **to have a ~** ou **~s with sb** (for advice) conférer avec qn; (for discussion) s'entretenir avec qn; **2** (process) consultation *f*; **after ~ with** après avoir consulté.

consultative /kən'sʌltətɪv/ *adj* consultatif/-ive.

consult: **~ing hours** *npl* MED heures *fpl* de consultation; **~ing room** *n* MED cabinet *m*.

consumables /kən'sjuːməblz, US -'suːm-/ *npl* consommables *mpl*.

consume /kən'sjuːm, US -'suːm-/ *vtr* **1** manger [*food*]; boire [*drink*]; **2** (use up) consommer [*fuel, food, drink*]; absorber [*time*]; **3** (destroy) [*flames*] consumer; **4** (overwhelm) **to be ~d by ou with** être dévoré par [*envy*]; brûler de [*desire*]; être rongé par [*guilt*].

consumer /kən'sjuːmə(r), US -'suːm-/ *n* GEN consommateur/-trice *m/f*; (of electricity, gas etc) abonné/-e *m/f*.

consumer: **~ advice** *n* conseils *mpl* au consommateurs; **~ durables** *npl* biens *mpl* durables; **~ goods** *npl* biens *mpl* de consommation.

consumerism /kən'sjuːmərɪzəm, US -'suːm-/ *n* consumérisme *m*.

consumerist /kən'sjuːmərɪst, US -'suːm-/ PÉJ *adj* [*society, culture*] de consommation.

consumer: **~ products** *npl* produits *mpl* de consommation; **~ protection** *n* défense *f* du consommateur; **~ society** *n* société *f* de consommation.

consuming /kən'sjuːmɪŋ, US -suːm-/ *adj* [*passion*] dévorant; [*urge, desire*] brûlant; [*hatred*] insatiable.

consummate I /kən'sʌmət/ *adj* SOUT parfait.
II /'kɒnsəmeɪt/ *vtr* SOUT consommer FML [*marriage*].

consumption /kən'sʌmpʃn/ **▶ 1002** *n* **1** (of food, fuel, goods) consommation *f*; **electricity ~** la consommation d'électricité; **unfit for human ~** impropre à la consommation; **2‡** (tuberculosis) tuberculose *f* (pulmonaire).

cont. *abrév écrite* = **continued**.

contact I /'kɒntækt/ *n* **1** (touch) LIT ou FIG contact *m* (**between** entre; **with** avec); **to be in/come in(to)/make ~** être en/entrer en/se mettre en contact; **to get in(to) ~** prendre contact; **to maintain/lose ~** garder/perdre contact; **to be in constant ~** être en rapports constants; **sporting ~s** relations *fpl* sportives; **2** (by radar, radio) contact *m*; **to make/lose ~** établir/perdre contact; **in ~** en contact; **3** (acquaintance) GEN connaissance *f*; (professional) contact *m*; (for drugs,

spy) contact *m*; **4** ELEC contact *m*; **5** MED *personne ayant approché un malade contagieux*.
II /kən'tækt, 'kɒntækt/ *vtr* contacter, se mettre en rapport avec.

contactable /kən'tæktəbl, 'kɒn-/ *adj* **she is/is not ~** on peut/ne peut pas la joindre.

contact lens *n* lentille *f* or verre *m* de contact.

contagious /kən'teɪdʒəs/ *adj* contagieux/-ieuse.

contain /kən'teɪn/ I *vtr* **1** (hold) contenir [*amount, ingredients*]; contenir, comporter [*information, mistakes*]; **2** (curb) maîtriser [*blaze*]; enrayer [*epidemic*]; limiter [*costs, problem*]; canaliser [*strike*]; **3** (within boundary) endiguer [*river*]; retenir [*flood*]; **4** (control) contenir [*joy*]; contenir [*enemy*].
II *v refl* **to ~ oneself** se contenir.

container /kən'teɪnə(r)/ *n* (for food, liquids) récipient *m*; (for plants) bac *m*; (skip, for waste) conteneur *m*; (for transporting) conteneur *m*.

container: **~ port** *n* terminal *m* à conteneurs; **~ ship** *n* porte-conteneurs *m inv*; **~ truck** *n* porte-conteneur *m*.

contaminate /kən'tæmɪneɪt/ *vtr* contaminer.

contamination /kənˌtæmɪ'neɪʃn/ *n* GEN, LING contamination *f*.

contd *abrév écrite* = **continued**.

contemplate /'kɒntəmpleɪt/ I *vtr* **1** (consider deeply) réfléchir sur, contempler; **2** (envisage) envisager (**doing** de faire); **3** (look at) contempler.
II *vi* méditer.

contemplation /ˌkɒntem'pleɪʃn/ *n* contemplation *f*.

contemplative /kən'templətɪv, 'kɒntempleɪtɪv/ *adj* songeur/-euse; RELIG contemplatif/-ive.

contemporaneous /kənˌtempə'reɪnɪəs/ *adj* contemporain (**with** de).

contemporaneously /kənˌtempə'reɪnɪəslɪ/ *adv* en même temps (**with** que).

contemporary /kən'temprərɪ, US -pərerɪ/ I *n* contemporain/-e *m/f*; **he was a ~ of mine at university** nous étions à l'université à la même époque; **our contemporaries** les gens de notre âge.
II *adj* **1** (present-day) contemporain; (up-to-date) moderne; **2** (of same period) de l'époque; **to be ~ with** [*event*] coïncider avec.

contempt /kən'tempt/ *n* mépris *m* (**for** de); **to feel ~ for sb/sth, to hold sb/sth in ~** mépriser qn/qch; **to be beneath ~** être en-dessous de tout; **~ of court** JUR outrage *m* à magistrat.

contemptible /kən'temptəbl/ *adj* méprisable.

contemptuous /kən'temptjʊəs/ *adj* méprisant; **to be ~ of sth/sb** mépriser qch/qn.

contemptuously /kən'temptjʊəslɪ/ *adv* [*smile, say, treat*] avec mépris; [*behave*] de façon méprisante.

contend /kən'tend/ I *vtr* soutenir (**that** que).
II *vi* **1** **to ~ with** affronter; **he's got a lot to ~ with** il a beaucoup de problèmes; **2** (compete) **she was ~ing with him for first place** elle lui disputait la première place.

contender /kən'tendə(r)/ *n* **1** SPORT concurrent/-e *m/f*; **to be a ~ for first place** être bien placé pour gagner; **2** (for post) candidat/-e *m/f* (**for** à).

content I *n* **1** /'kɒntent/ (relative quantity) teneur *f*; **the fat ~** la teneur en matières grasses; **low/high lead ~** faible/forte teneur en plomb; **to have a low/high fat ~** être pauvre/riche en matières grasses; **2** /'kɒntent/ (meaning) fond *m*; **form and ~** le fond et la forme; **3** /kən'tent/ (happiness) contentement *m*.
II **contents** /'kɒntents/ *npl* GEN contenu *m*; (of house, for insurance) biens *mpl* mobiliers; **he emptied the drawer of its ~s** il a vidé le tiroir de tout ce qu'il contenait; **list** ou **table of ~s** table *f* des matières.
III /kən'tent/ *adj* satisfait (**with** de); **to be ~ to do** se contenter de faire; **not ~ with doing** non content de faire; **he's ~ with what he has** il se contente de ce qu'il a; **I'm quite ~ here** je suis bien ici.
IV /kən'tent/ *v refl* **to ~ oneself with sth/with doing** se contenter de qch/de faire.

ontented /kən'tentɪd/ adj [person] content (**with** de); [feeling] de bien-être; **a ~ child** un enfant heureux.

ontentedly /kən'tentɪdlɪ/ adv de bien-être.

ontention /kən'tenʃn/ n **1** (opinion) assertion f; **it is my ~ that** je soutiens que; **2** (dispute) dispute f (**about** au sujet de); **point of ~** sujet m de dispute; **3** (competition) compétition f; **in ~** en compétition.

ontentious /kən'tenʃəs/ adj **1** [subject] controversé; [view] discutable; **2** [person, group] discuteur/-euse.

ontentment /kən'tentmənt/ n contentement m; **with ~** [sigh] de bien-être; **there was a look of ~ on his face** il avait l'air satisfait.

ontest I /'kɒntest/ n **1** (competition) concours m; **fishing ~** concours m de pêche; **sports ~** rencontre f sportive; **it's no ~** c'est couru° d'avance; **2** (struggle) lutte f; **the presidential ~** la course à la présidence.
II /kən'test/ vtr **1** (object to) contester; **2** (compete for) SPORT disputer [match]; **strongly ~ed** POL âprement disputé; **to ~ an election** POL se présenter à une élection.

ontestant /kən'testənt/ n (in competition, game) concurrent/-e m/f; (in fight) adversaire m/f; (for job, in election) candidat/-e m/f.

ontext /'kɒntekst/ n contexte m; **in ~** [study, understand] dans son contexte; **out of ~** [quote, examine] hors contexte; **to put sth into ~** replacer qch dans son contexte.

ontinent /'kɒntɪnənt/ n (land mass) continent m; **the Continent** GB l'Europe f continentale; **on the Continent** GB en Europe continentale.

ontinental /ˌkɒntɪ'nentl/ **I** n Européen/-éenne m/f du continent.
II noun modifier [vegetation, climate] continental; [universities, philosophy] d'Europe continentale; [holiday] en Europe continentale.

ontinental: **~ breakfast** n petit déjeuner m (avec café, pain, beurre et confiture); **~ quilt** GB n couette f.

ontingency /kən'tɪndʒənsɪ/ n **1** GEN imprévu m; **to provide for all contingencies** parer à toute éventualité; **2** PHILOS contingence f.

ontingency: **~ fund** n fonds m de secours; **~ plan** n plan m de réserve.

ontingent /kən'tɪndʒənt/ adj contingent; **to be ~ on** ou **upon** dépendre de.

ontinual /kən'tɪnjʊəl/ adj continuel/-elle.

ontinually /kən'tɪnjʊəlɪ/ adv continuellement.

ontinuation /kənˌtɪnjʊ'eɪʃn/ n **1** (of situation, process) continuation f; **2** (resumption) continuation f, reprise f; **3** (in book) suite f; (of route) prolongement m.

ontinue /kən'tɪnjuː/ **I** vtr **1** continuer, poursuivre [career, studies, enquiry, TV series]; **2** (resume) continuer; **'to be ~d'** (in film) 'à suivre'; **'~d overleaf'** 'suite page suivante'; **'what's more,'** she **~d** 'de plus,' reprit-elle; **3** continuer, poursuivre [journey]; **4** (preserve) maintenir.
II vi **1** [noise, debate, strike, film] se poursuivre; **2** (keep on) continuer (**doing**, to do à ou de faire); **3** [person, route] continuer; **he ~d across/down the street** il a continué de traverser/descendre la rue; **4** (in career, role) rester (**in** dans); **she will ~ as minister** elle restera ministre; **5** (in speech) poursuivre; **6** to **~ with** continuer, poursuivre [task, treatment]; **to ~ with the ironing** continuer de repasser.
III continuing pres p adj continuel/-elle.

ontinuity /ˌkɒntɪ'njuːɪtɪ/ n continuité f.

ontinuity: **~ announcer** ▶ 1251 n speaker/speakerine m/f; **~ girl** ▶ 1251 n scripte f.

ontinuous /kən'tɪnjʊəs/ adj **1** [growth, flow, decline] continu; [love, care] constant; [line, surface] ininterrompu; [noise] continu; **2** LING [tense] progressif/-ive; **in the present ~** au présent progressif.

ontinuously /kən'tɪnjʊəslɪ/ adv (without a break) sans interruption; (repeatedly) continuellement.

ontinuum /kən'tɪnjʊəm/ n (pl **-nuums** ou **-nua**) continuum m.

contort /kən'tɔːt/ **I** vtr tordre [limbs]; **to ~ one's body** se contortionner; **his features were ~ed with rage** ses traits étaient déformés par la colère.
II vi [face, features, mouth] se crisper.

contortion /kən'tɔːʃn/ n contorsion f.

contour /'kɒntʊə(r)/ n **1** (outline) contour m; **2** (also **~ line**) GEOG courbe f hypsométrique or de niveau.

contraband /'kɒntrəbænd/ n contrebande f.

contraception /ˌkɒntrə'sepʃn/ n contraception f.

contraceptive /ˌkɒntrə'septɪv/ **I** n contraceptif m.
II adj [method] contraceptif/-ive; **~ device** contraceptif m.

contract I /'kɒntrækt/ n **1** (agreement) contrat m (**for** pour; **with** avec); **employment ~, ~ of employment** contrat m de travail; **to enter into a ~ with** passer un contrat avec; **to be on a ~** être sous contrat; **to be under ~** to travailler sous contrat avec; **2** (tender) contrat m; **to win/lose a ~** remporter/perdre un contrat; **to award a ~ to** octroyer un contrat à; **to place a ~ for sth with** octroyer un contrat pour qch à; **to put work out to ~** donner un travail en sous-traitance; **3**° (for assassination) **there's a ~ out on him** un tueur a été engagé pour l'abattre.
II /'kɒntrækt/ noun modifier [labour] contractuel/-elle.
III /kən'trækt/ vtr **1** (develop) contracter [disease] (**from** par le contact avec); **2** (arrange) contracter [marriage, debt, loan]; **to be ~ed to do** être tenu par contrat de faire; **3** (tighten) contracter.
IV /kən'trækt/ vi **1** (undertake) **to ~ to do** s'engager par contrat à faire; **2** (shrink) [metal] se contracter; [support, market] diminuer; **3** MED se contracter.
■ **contract into** GB: **~ into** [sth] souscrire à.
■ **contract out** GB: **¶ ~ out** renoncer par contrat; **to ~ out of** se retirer de [scheme]; **¶ ~ out** [sth], **~** [sth] **out** donner [qch] en sous-traitance (**to** à).

contraction /kən'trækʃn/ n GEN, MED contraction f.

contract killer n tueur/-euse m/f à gages.

contractor /kən'træktə(r)/ ▶ 1251 n **1** (business) entrepreneur/-euse m/f; **2** (worker) contractuel/-elle m/f.

contractual /kən'træktʃʊəl/ adj contractuel/-elle.

contract: **~ work** n prestation f de service; **~ worker** n contractuel/-elle m/f.

contradict /ˌkɒntrə'dɪkt/ vtr, vi contredire.

contradiction /ˌkɒntrə'dɪkʃn/ n contradiction f; **in ~ with** en contradiction avec; **it's a ~ in terms** c'est une contradiction criante.

contradictory /ˌkɒntrə'dɪktərɪ/ adj contradictoire (**to** à).

contraflow /'kɒntrəfləʊ/ GB n circulation f à sens alterné.

contraindication /ˌkɒntrəɪndɪ'keɪʃn/ n contre-indication f.

contralto /kən'træltəʊ/ ▶ 1380 n (pl **-tos** ou **-ti**) (voice) contralto m; (singer) contralto f.

contraption /kən'træpʃn/ n (machine) engin° m; (device) machin° m.

contrariness /kən'treərɪnɪs/ n esprit m de contrariété.

contrariwise /'kɒntrərɪwaɪz/, US -reri/ adv **1** (conversely) inversement; **2** (in the opposite direction) en sens inverse.

contrary /'kɒntrərɪ/, US -reri/ **I** n contraire m; **quite the ~** bien au contraire; **on the ~** au contraire; **despite views/claims to the ~** contrairement à ce que certains pensent/disent; **evidence to the ~** une preuve du contraire; **unless you hear anything to the ~** sauf contrordre.
II adj [idea, view] contraire; **to be ~ to** [activity, proposal, opinion, measure] être contraire à; **2** [direction, movement] contraire (**to** à); **3** /kən'treərɪ/ [person] contrariant.
III contrary to prep phr contrairement à; **~ to popular belief/to rumours** contrairement à ce que l'on peut croire/à la rumeur; **~ to expectations** contre toute attente.

contrast I /'kɒntrɑːst/, US -træst/ n **1** (difference)

contraste *m*; **in ~ to sth**, **by ~ with sth** par contraste avec qch; **in ~ to sb** à la différence de qn; **to be a ~ to** ou **with** présenter un contraste avec; **by** ou **in ~** par contre; **2** PHOT, TV contraste *m*.
II /kən'traːst, US -'træst/ *vtr* **to ~ X with Y** faire ressortir le contraste (qui existe) entre X et Y.
III *vi* contraster (**with** avec).
IV contrasting *adj* [*examples*] opposé; [*colour, material*] contrasté; [*views, opinions*] très différents.

contravene /ˌkɒntrə'viːn/ *vtr* enfreindre.

contravention /ˌkɒntrə'venʃn/ *n* SOUT infraction *f* (**of** à); **in ~ of** en violation de [*rule, law*].

contribute /kən'trɪbjuːt/ **I** *vtr* **1** (pay) verser [*sum, percentage*] (**to** à); financer [*costs, expenses*]; **2** (to gift, charity) donner (**to** à; **towards** pour); **3** (put up) contribuer; **to ~ £5m** contribuer pour 5 millions de livres; **4** (to project, undertaking, magazine) apporter [*ideas*] (**to** à); écrire [*article, column*] (**to** pour).
II *vi* **1** (be a factor in) **to ~ to** ou **towards** contribuer à [*change, awareness, decline*]; **2** (to community life, company expansion, research) participer (**to** à); **3** (pay into) **to ~ to** cotiser à [*pension fund*]; **4** (to charity) donner (de l'argent) (**to** à); (to programme, magazine) collaborer (**to** à).

contribution /ˌkɒntrɪ'bjuːʃn/ *n* **1** (to tax, pension) contribution *f* (**towards** à); (to charity, campaign) don *m*; **to make a ~** faire un don (**to** à); **'all ~s gratefully received'** 'merci d'avance pour vos dons'; **3** (role played) **sb's ~** to le rôle que qn a joué dans [*success, undertaking*]; ce que qn a apporté à [*science, sport*]; **his outstanding ~ to politics** sa participation marquante à la vie politique; **4** (to profits, costs) contribution *f*; **5** RADIO, TV participation *f*; (to magazine) article *m*; **with ~s from** avec la collaboration de.

contributor /kən'trɪbjʊtə(r)/ *n* (to charity) donateur/-trice *m/f*; (in discussion) participant/-e *m/f*; (to magazine, book) collaborateur/-trice *m/f*.

contributory /kən'trɪbjʊtərɪ, US -tɔːrɪ/ *adj* **to be ~ to** contribuer à; **to be a ~ cause** être partiellement responsable (**of** de); **a ~ factor** in un facteur de.

con trick◦ *n* escroquerie *f*, duperie *f*.

contrite /'kɒntraɪt/ *adj* contrit.

contrivance /kən'traɪvəns/ *n* dispositif *m*, appareil *m*.

contrive /kən'traɪv/ *vtr* **1** (arrange) organiser; **to ~ to do** parvenir à faire, trouver moyen de faire; **2** (invent) fabriquer [*device*]; inventer [*plot*].

contrived /kən'traɪvd/ *adj* PEJ **1** [*incident, meeting*] non fortuit; **2** (forced) [*plot, ending*] tiré par les cheveux; [*style, effect*] étudié.

control /kən'trəʊl/ **I** *n* **1** ¢ (domination) (of animals, children, crowd, country, organization) contrôle *m* (**of** de); (of operation, project) direction *f* (**of** de); (of life, fate) maîtrise *f* (**of, over** de); (of disease, pests, social problem) lutte *f* (**of** contre); **to be in ~ of** contrôler [*territory*]; diriger [*operation, organization*]; maîtriser [*problem*]; **to have ~ over** contrôler [*territory*]; maîtriser [*fate, life*]; **to take ~ of** prendre le contrôle de [*territory*]; prendre la direction de [*organization, project*]; prendre [qch] en main [*situation*]; **to be under sb's ~** [*person*] être sous la direction de qn; [*organization, party*] être sous le contrôle de qn; **to be under ~** [*fire, problem, riot*] être maîtrisé; **everything's under ~** tout va bien; **to bring** ou **get** ou **keep [sth] under ~** maîtriser; **to be out of ~** [*crowd, riot*] être déchaîné; [*fire*] ne plus être maîtrisable; **the situation is out of ~** la situation est devenue incontrôlable; **to lose ~ of sth** perdre le contrôle de qch; **to be beyond** ou **outside sb's ~** échapper au contrôle de qn; **due to circumstances beyond our ~** pour des raisons indépendantes de notre volonté; **2** ¢ (restraint) (of self, appetite, emotion, urge) maîtrise *f*; **to have ~ over sth** maîtriser qch; **to keep ~ of oneself, to be in ~ of oneself** se maîtriser; **to lose ~ (of oneself)** perdre le contrôle (de soi); **3** ¢ (physical mastery) (of vehicle, machine, ball) contrôle *m*; (of body, process, system) maîtrise *f*; **to be in ~ of** avoir le contrôle de; **to keep/lose ~ of a car** garder/perdre le contrôle d'une voiture; **to take ~** (of plane) prendre les commandes;

his car went out of ~ il a perdu le contrôle de son véhicule; **4 C** (lever, switch) (on vehicle, equipment) commande *f*; (on TV) bouton *m* de réglage; **volume ~** TV bouton de réglage du son; **to be at the ~s** être aux commandes; **5** (regulation) contrôle *m* (**on** de); **6** (in experiment) contrôle *m*.
II *noun modifier* [*knob*] de commande; [*group*] témoin.
III *vtr* (*p prés etc* **-ll-**) **1** (dominate) dominer [*market, situation*]; contrôler [*territory*]; diriger [*traffic, project*]; s'emparer de [*mind*]; FIN être majoritaire dans [*company*]; **2** (discipline) maîtriser [*person, animal, temper, inflation, riot, fire*]; endiguer [*epidemic*]; dominer [*emotion*]; retenir [*laughter*]; commander à [*limbs*]; **3** (operate) commander [*machine, process*]; manœuvrer [*boat, vehicle*]; piloter [*plane*]; contrôler [*ball*]; **4** (regulate) régler [*speed, temperature*]; contrôler [*immigration, prices*]; **5** (check) contrôler [*quality*]; vérifier [*accounts*].
IV *v refl* (*p prés etc* **-ll-**) **to ~ oneself** se contrôler.

control column *n* AVIAT manche *m* à balai.

controlled /kən'trəʊld/ **I** *adj* LIT [*explosion, landing*] contrôlé; [*person, voice*] [*economy*] dirigé; [*performance*] maîtrisé; **electronically ~** contrôlé électroniquement; **under ~ conditions** sous contrôle.
II -controlled *combining form* **Labour-~** dominé par les Travaillistes; **computer-~** commandé par ordinateur.

controller /kən'trəʊlə(r)/ *n* **1** GEN, RADIO, directeur/-trice *m/f*; **2** FIN planificateur/-trice *m/f*.

controlling /kən'trəʊlɪŋ/ *adj* [*group, organization*] dominant; **~ interest** majorité *f* de contrôle.

control: **~ panel** *n* (for plane) tableau *m* de bord; (on machine) tableau *m* de contrôle; (on TV) (panneau *m* de) commandes *fpl*; **~ room** *n* GEN poste *m* de commande; RADIO, TV (salle *f* de) régie *f*; **~ tower** *n* tour *f* de contrôle.

controversial /ˌkɒntrə'vɜːʃl/ *adj* **1** [*decision, plan, film*] (criticized) controversé; (open to criticism) discutable; **2** [*person, group*] (much discussed) controversé; (dubious) douteux/-euse.

controversially /ˌkɒntrə'vɜːʃəlɪ/ *adv* de façon controversée.

controversy /'kɒntrəvɜːsɪ, kən'trɒvəsɪ/ *n* controverse *f*; **to be the subject of much ~** soulever de nombreuses controverses.

conundrum /kə'nʌndrəm/ *n* énigme *f*.

conurbation /ˌkɒnɜː'beɪʃn/ *n* conurbation *f*.

convalesce /ˌkɒnvə'les/ *vi* se remettre; **he's convalescing** il est en convalescence.

convalescence /ˌkɒnvə'lesns/ *n* convalescence *f*.

convalescent /ˌkɒnvə'lesnt/ **I** *n* convalescent/-e *m/f*.
II *adj* [*person*] convalescent; [*leave, home*] de convalescence.

convection /kən'vekʃn/ *n* convection *f*.

convector (heater) /kən'vektə ('hiːtə)/ *n* convecteur *m*.

convene /kən'viːn/ **I** *vtr* organiser [*meeting*]; convoquer [*group*].
II *vi* se réunir.

convener /kən'viːnə(r)/ *n* **1** (organizer) organisateur/-trice *m/f* (d'une réunion); **2** (chair) président/-e *m/f*.

convenience /kən'viːnɪəns/ *n* **1** ¢ (advantage) avantage *m* (**of doing** de faire); **the ~ of** les avantages de [*practice, method*]; la commodité de [*instant food, device, shop*]; **for (the sake of) ~** pour raison de commodité; **for his/our ~** pour sa/notre convenance; **at your ~** quand cela vous conviendra; **your earliest ~** dès que cela vous sera possible; **2** GB (toilet) toilettes *fpl*.

convenience: **~ foods** *npl* plats *mpl* (tout) préparés; **~ store** *n* épicerie *f* (*ouverte tard le soir*).

convenient /kən'viːnɪənt/ *adj* **1** (suitable) [*place, time*] commode; **now is not a very ~ time** ce n'est pas vraiment le moment maintenant; **to be ~ for sb** convenir à qn; **to be ~ for sb to do** convenir à qn de faire; **a ~ place for sth** un endroit approprié pour qch; **2** (useful, practical) pratique, commode (**that** que + *subj*; **to do** de faire); **3** (in location) [*shops, amenities*] situé tout près; [*chair, table*] à portée de main; **to be ~ for** GB, **to be ~ to** US ne pas être loin de [*station, shops*]; **4** IRON, PÉJ (expedient) [*excuse, explanation*] commode; **it's ~ for them** ça les arrange.

onveniently /kən'vi:nɪəntlɪ/ *adv* **1** [*arrange*] de façon commode; **the conference was ~ timed to coincide with** la date de la conférence était bien choisie pour coïncider avec; **~ situated, ~ located** bien situé, bien placé; **2** IRON (expediently) comme par hasard.

convenor = **convener**.

onvent /'kɒnvənt, US -vent/ *n* couvent *m*; **to enter a ~** entrer au couvent.

:onvention /kən'venʃn/ *n* **1** (meeting) (of party, profession, union) convention *f*, congrès *m*; (of society, fans) assemblée *f*; **2** ¢ (social norms) convenances *fpl*, conventions *fpl*; **to flout** ou **defy ~** braver les convenances; **3** (usual practice) convention *f*; **4** (agreement) convention *f* (**on** sur).

conventional /kən'venʃənl/ *adj* **1** (conformist) [*person*] conformiste; [*idea, role*] conventionnel/-elle; **2** (traditionally accepted) [*approach, method*] conventionnel/-elle; [*medicine, agriculture*] traditionnel/-elle; **the ~ wisdom about sth** ce qui est communément admis au sujet de qch; **3** MIL [*weapons*] conventionnel/-elle.

conventionally /kən'venʃənlɪ/ *adv* [*dress, behave*] de façon conventionnelle.

convent school *n* école *f* de religieuses.

converge /kən'vɜ:dʒ/ *vi* converger (**at** à); **to ~ on** [*people*] converger sur [*place*]; [*rays, paths*] converger vers [*point*].

convergence /kən'vɜ:dʒəns/ *n* convergence *f*.

conversant /kən'vɜ:snt/ *adj* **to be ~ with sth** être versé dans qch.

conversation /ˌkɒnvə'seɪʃn/ *n* conversation *f*; **to have** ou **hold a ~** avoir une conversation; **to make ~** faire la conversation; **in ~** en conversation.

conversational /ˌkɒnvə'seɪʃənl/ *adj* [*ability, skill, class, exercise*] de conversation.

conversationalist /ˌkɒnvə'seɪʃənəlɪst/ *n* personne *f* qui excelle dans l'art de la conversation.

converse I /'kɒnvɜ:s/ *n* **1** GEN contraire *m*; **2** MATH, PHILOS converse *f*.
II /'kɒnvɜ:s/ *adj* contraire.
III /kən'vɜ:s/ *vi* converser (**with** avec; **in** en).

conversely /'kɒnvɜ:slɪ/ *adv* inversement.

conversion /kən'vɜ:ʃn, US kən'vɜ:rʒn/ *n* **1** (transformation) transformation *f* (**from** de; **to, into** en); **2** (of currency, measurement) conversion *f* (**from** de; **into** en); **3** (of building) aménagement *m* (**to, into** en); **barn ~** grange *f* aménagée; **4** RELIG, POL conversion *f* (**from** de; **to** à); **to undergo a ~** se convertir; **5** (in rugby) transformation *f*.

conversion: **~ rate** *n* taux *m* de change; **~ table** *n* table *f* de conversion.

convert I /'kɒnvɜ:t/ *n* converti/-e *m/f* (**to** à); **to become a ~** se convertir; **to win** ou **make ~s** faire des adeptes.
II /kən'vɜ:t/ *vtr* **1** (change into sth else) transformer; **2** (modify) adapter; **3** convertir [*currency, measurement*] (**from** de; **to, into** en); **4** ARCHIT aménager [*building, loft*] (**to, into** en); **5** RELIG, POL convertir (**to** à; **from** de); **6** (in rugby) transformer [*try*].
III /kən'vɜ:t/ *vi* **1** (change) **to ~ to sth** passer à qch; **2** (be convertible) être convertible (**into** en); **3** RELIG, POL se convertir (**to** à; **from** de); **4** (in rugby) transformer.

converter /kən'vɜ:tə(r)/ *n* convertisseur *m*.

convertible /kən'vɜ:təbl/ I *n* AUT décapotable *f*.
II *adj* convertible; [*car*] décapotable.

convertor /kən'vɜ:tə(r)/ *n* = **converter**.

convex /'kɒnveks/ *adj* convexe.

convey /kən'veɪ/ *vtr* **1** (transmit) [*person*] transmettre [*message, information*] (**to** à); exprimer [*condolences, feeling, idea*] (**to** à); **to ~ to sb that/how** faire

savoir à qn que/comment; **to ~ the impression of/that** donner l'impression de/que; **2** (communicate) [*words, images*] traduire [*mood, impression*]; **3** (transport) [*vehicle*] transporter; [*pipes, network*] amener.

conveyance /kən'veɪəns/ *n* **1** (of goods, passengers) transport *m*, acheminement *m*; **2**† (vehicle) véhicule *m*.

conveyancing /kən'veɪənsɪŋ/ *n* rédaction *f* des actes de propriété.

conveyor /kən'veɪə(r)/ *n* **1** (also **~ belt**) (in factory) transporteur *m* à bande ou à courroie; (for luggage) tapis *m* roulant; **2** (of goods, persons) transporteur *m*.

convict I /'kɒnvɪkt/ *n* (imprisoned criminal) détenu/-e *m/f*; (deported criminal) bagnard *m*; **ex-~** ancien détenu; **escaped ~** détenu évadé.
II /kən'vɪkt/ *vtr* reconnaître or déclarer [qn] coupable (**of** de; **of doing** d'avoir fait); [*evidence*] condamner; **a ~ed murderer** (in prison) un condamné pour meurtre; (now released) un ancien condamné pour meurtre.

conviction /kən'vɪkʃn/ *n* **1** JUR condamnation *f* (**for** pour); **2** (belief) conviction *f* (**that** que); **to lack ~** manquer de conviction.

convince /kən'vɪns/ I *vtr* **1** (gain credibility of) convaincre [*person, jury, reader*] (**of** de; **that** que; **about** au sujet de); **2** (persuade) persuader [*voter, consumer*] (**to do** de faire); **~d** convaincu, persuadé.
II *v refl* **to ~ oneself** se convaincre.

convincing /kən'vɪnsɪŋ/ *adj* [*account, evidence, proof, theory*] convaincant; [*victory, lead, win*] indiscutable.

convincingly /kən'vɪnsɪŋlɪ/ *adv* [*argue, claim, demonstrate, portray*] de façon convaincante; [*win, beat*] de façon indiscutable.

convivial /kən'vɪvɪəl/ *adj* **1** [*atmosphere, evening*] cordial; **2** [*person*] chaleureux/-euse.

convocation /ˌkɒnvə'keɪʃn/ *n* convocation *f*.

convoke /kən'vəʊk/ *vtr* convoquer.

convoluted /'kɒnvəlu:tɪd/ *adj* **1** [*argument, style*] alambiqué; **2** [*vine, tendril*] convoluté; [*design*] vrillé.

convoy /'kɒnvɔɪ/ *n* convoi *m*; **in ~** en convoi.

convulse /kən'vʌls/ *vtr* **1** [*pain, sobs, laughter*] convulser [*person, body*]; [*joke, comic*] faire tordre de rire [*person*]; **~d with pain** convulsé de douleur; **2** [*riots, unrest*] secouer [*country*].

convulsion /kən'vʌlʃn/ *n* convulsion *f*; **to go into ~s** entrer en convulsions; **to be in ~s** FIG se tordre de rire.

convulsive /kən'vʌlsɪv/ *adj* convulsif/-ive.

convulsively /kən'vʌlsɪvlɪ/ *adv* convulsivement.

coo /ku:/ I *n* (of dove) roucoulement *m*.
II *vi* [*lover, dove*] roucouler; **to ~ over** s'extasier devant [*baby*].

cooing /'ku:ɪŋ/ *n* roucoulement *m*, roucoulade *f*.

cook /kʊk/ ▶ **1251** I *n* cuisinier/-ière *m/f*; **he's a good ~** c'est un bon cuisinier.
II *vtr* **1** CULIN faire cuire [*vegetables, pasta, eggs*]; préparer [*meal*] (**for** pour); **2**○ (falsify) trafiquer○, falsifier [*data*]; **to ~ the books** trafiquer○ la comptabilité.
III *vi* [*person*] cuisiner, faire la cuisine; [*vegetable, meat, meal*] cuire; **the carrots are ~ing** les carottes sont en train de cuire; **there's something ~ing**○ FIG il y a quelque chose qui se mijote○.
IV **cooked** *pp adj* cuit; **lightly ~ed** à peine cuit.
■ **cook up**○: **~ up** [sth] préparer [*dish, meal*]; inventer [*excuse, story*]; mijoter○ [*scheme*].

cook: **~book** *n* livre *m* de cuisine; **~-chill foods** *npl* plats *mpl* préparés; **~ed meats** *npl* ~ charcuterie *f*.

cooker /'kʊkə(r)/ *n* GB cuisinière *f*.

cookery /'kʊkərɪ/ *n* GB cuisine *f*; **~ book** livre de cuisine.

cookie /'kʊkɪ/ *n* gâteau *m* sec, biscuit *m* (sec).

cooking /'kʊkɪŋ/ *n* cuisine *f*; **to do the ~** faire la cuisine; **to be good at ~** bien cuisiner; **Chinese ~** cuisine chinoise.

cooking: **~ apple** *n* pomme *f* à cuire; **~ choco-**

late n chocolat m pâtissier; ~ **foil** n papier m aluminium; ~ **salt** n gros sel m.

cook: ~**out** n US barbecue m; ~**ware** n ustensiles mpl de cuisine.

cool /ku:l/ I n 1 (coldness) fraîcheur f; 2○ (calm) sang-froid m; **to keep one's** ~ (stay calm) garder son sang-froid; (not get angry) ne pas s'énerver; **to lose one's** ~ (get angry) s'énerver; (panic) perdre son sang-froid.
II adj 1 [day, drink, water, weather] frais/fraîche; [dress] léger/-ère; [colour] froid; **it's** ~ **today** il fait frais aujourd'hui; **to feel** ~ [surface, wine] être frais/fraîche; **I feel** ~**er now** j'ai moins chaud maintenant; **it's getting** ~, **let's go in** il commence à faire frais, rentrons; 2 (calm) [approach, handling] calme; **to stay** ~ garder son sang-froid; **to keep a** ~ **head** garder la tête froide; **keep** ~! reste calme; 3 (unemotional) [manner] détaché; [logic] froid; 4 (unfriendly) froid; **to be** ~ **with** ou **towards sb** être froid avec qn; 5 (casual) décontracté, cool○; **he's a** ~ **customer** il n'a pas froid aux yeux; 6 (for emphasis) **a** ~ **million dollars** la coquette somme d'un million de dollars○; 7○ (sophisticated) branché○; **he thinks it's** ~ **to smoke** il pense que ça fait bien de fumer; **it's not** ~ ça fait nul○; 8○ US (great) super○!
III vtr 1 (lower the temperature of) refroidir [soup, pan]; rafraîchir [wine, room]; **to** ~ **one's hands** se rafraîchir les mains; 2 FIG calmer [anger, ardour].
IV vi 1 (get colder) refroidir; 2 (subside) [passion] tiédir; [enthusiasm] faiblir; [friendship] se dégrader; **wait until tempers have** ~**ed** attends que les esprits se calment.
IDIOMS ~ **it**○! ne t'énerve pas!; **to play it** ~○ rester calme.
■ **cool down**: ¶ ~ **down** [engine, water] refroidir; FIG [person, situation] se calmer; ¶ ~ [sth] **down** refroidir [mixture]; rafraîchir [wine]; ¶ ~ [sb] **down** rafraîchir [person].
■ **cool off** (get colder) se rafraîchir; FIG (calm down) se calmer.

cool: ~ **bag** n GB sac m isotherme; ~ **box** n GB glacière f; ~**-headed** adj [person] qui garde la tête froide; [decision, approach] réfléchi.

cooling /'ku:lɪŋ/ I n refroidissement m.
II adj [drink, swim] rafraîchissant; [agent] réfrigérant; [system, tower] de refroidissement.

cooling-off period n (in industrial relations) délai m de conciliation; COMM délai m de réflexion.

coolly /'ku:lɪ/ adv 1 (lightly) [dressed] légèrement; 2 (without warmth) [greet, say] froidement; 3 (calmly) calmement; 4 (boldly) sans la moindre gêne.

coolness /'ku:lnɪs/ n 1 (coldness) fraicheur f; 2 (unfriendliness) froideur f; 3 (calmness) calme m.

coop /ku:p/ n (also **chicken** ~, **hen** ~) poulailler m.
■ **coop up**: ~ [sb/sth] **up** enfermer, cloîtrer.

co-op /'kəʊɒp/ n = **cooperative** I 1.

cooper /'ku:pə(r)/ ▶1251 n tonnelier m.

cooperate /kəʊ'ɒpəreɪt/ vi coopérer (**with** avec; **in** à; **in doing** pour faire).

cooperation /kəʊ,ɒpə'reɪʃn/ n coopération f (**on** à); **in (close)** ~ en (étroite) coopération.

cooperative /kəʊ'ɒpərətɪv/ I n 1 (organisation) coopérative f; **workers'** ~ coopérative ouvrière; 2 US (apartment house) immeuble m en copropriété.
II adj 1 (joint) conjoint; **to take** ~ **action** agir conjointement; 2 (helpful) coopératif/-ive; 3 COMM, POL [movement, society] coopératif/-ive; 4 US [apartment, building] en copropriété.

cooperatively /kəʊ'ɒpərətɪvlɪ/ adv [work] en coopération; **to act** ~ se montrer coopératif/-ive.

cooperative society n coopérative f.

co-opt /,kəʊ'ɒpt/ vtr 1 (onto committee) coopter [person] (**onto** dans); 2 (commandeer) utiliser [celebrity] (**to** pour soutenir).

coordinate I /,kəʊ'ɔ:dɪnət/ n coordonnée f.
II **coordinates** npl (clothes) ensemble m.
III **coordinating** pres p adj 1 [clothes, garment]

assorti, coordonné; 2 [committee] de coordination.
IV /,kəʊ'ɔ:dɪneɪt/ vtr coordonner (**with** avec).
V /,kəʊ'ɔ:dɪneɪt/ vi agir en coordination (**with** avec).

coordinated /,kəʊ'ɔ:dɪneɪtɪd/ adj coordonné.

coordination /,kəʊ'ɔ:dɪ'neɪʃn/ n coordination f.

coordinator /,kəʊ'ɔ:dɪneɪtə(r)/ n coordinateur/-tric m/f.

co-owner /kəʊ'əʊnə(r)/ n copropriétaire mf.

cop○ /kɒp/ I n 1 (police officer) flic m; **to play** ~**s robbers** jouer aux gendarmes et aux voleurs; 2 G (arrest) **it's a fair** ~! bien joué, je me rends○!; 3 G (use) **to be not much** ~ ne pas valoir grand-chose.
II vtr (p prés etc **-pp-**) 1 (receive) écoper de○ [punch punishment]; **to** ~ **it** trinquer○; 2 (also ~ **hold of** (catch) attraper; ~ **hold of the rope** attrape la corde.
■ **cop out**○ se dégonfler○; **to** ~ **out of doing** se défiler○ au moment de faire.

cope /kəʊp/ vi 1 (manage practically) [person] s'er sortir○, se débrouiller; [police, services, system] faire face; **to** ~ **with** [person] s'occuper de [person, corres pondence, work]; [government, police, system] faire face à [demand, disaster, inquiries]; **to learn to** ~ **alone** apprendre à se débrouiller tout seul; **it's more than I can** ~ **with** je ne m'en sors plus; **the organization can't** ~ l'organisation ne s'en sort plus ou ne peut pas faire face; 2 (manage financially) s'en sortir; **to** ~ **on £60 a week** s'en sortir avec 60 livres sterling par semaine; **to** ~ **with a loan** arriver à rembourser un prêt; 3 (manage emotionally) **to** ~ **with** supporter [bereavement, depression]; **to** ~ **with sb** supporter qn; **if you left me, I couldn't** ~ si tu me quittais, je ne pourrais pas le supporter.

Copenhagen /,kəʊpn'heɪgən/ ▶1343 pr n Copenhague.

copier /'kɒpɪə(r)/ n photocopieuse f.

co-pilot /,kəʊ'paɪlət/ n copilote mf.

copious /'kəʊpɪəs/ adj 1 (plentiful) [crop, supply, tears] abondant; ~ **notes** une quantité abondante de notes; 2 (generous) [quantity, serving] copieux/-ieuse.

copiously /'kəʊpɪəslɪ/ adv abondamment.

cop-out○ /'kɒpaʊt/ n (excuse) excuse f bidon○; (evasive act) échappatoire f.

copper /'kɒpə(r)/ ▶818 I n 1 CHEM cuivre m; 2○ (policeman) flic○ m; 3○ GB (coin) petite monnaie f ¢; **a few** ~**s** quelques sous mpl; 4 GB HIST (for washing) lessiveuse f; 5 (colour) couleur f cuivre.
II noun modifier [alloy, mine, ore] de cuivre; [bracelet, coin, pipe, wire] de ou en cuivre; [kettle, pan] en cuivre.
III adj [hair, leaf, lipstick] couleur cuivre inv.

copper: ~**-bottomed** adj sûr; ~**-coloured** GB, -**colored** US ▶818 adj [hair] cuivré; [leaf, metal] couleur cuivre inv; ~**plate** n écriture f ronde.

coppery /'kɒpərɪ/ ▶818 adj [colour] cuivré.

co-property /kəʊ'prɒpətɪ/ n copropriété f.

copse /kɒps/ n taillis m.

copulate /'kɒpjʊleɪt/ vi s'accoupler, copuler.

copy /'kɒpɪ/ I n 1 (reproduction, imitation) copie f; **certified** ~ copie f certifiée conforme; 2 (edition) (of book, newspaper, report) exemplaire m; 3 (journalist's, advertiser's text) copie f; **to be** ou **make good** ~ être un bon sujet d'article; **to file (one's)** ~ présenter sa copie.
II vtr 1 (imitate) copier [person, design] (**from** sur); 2 (duplicate) copier [document, disk]; **to** ~ **sth onto a disk** copier qch sur disquette; **to have sth copied** faire faire une copie de qch.
III vi copier (**from** sur); **to** ~ **in a test** copier à un examen.
■ **copy down**: ~ **down** [sth], ~ [sth] **down** recopier (**into** sur).
■ **copy out**: ~ **out** [sth], ~ [sth] **out** recopier.

copybook /'kɒpɪbʊk/ n cahier m d'écriture.
IDIOMS **to blot one's** ~ faire des bêtises.

copycat○ /'kɒpɪkæt/ I n PÉJ copieur/-ieuse m/f.
II adj [crime, murder] inspiré par un autre (**after** n).

copy: ~ **editor** n (on newspaper) secrétaire mf de rédaction; ~**ing machine** n photocopieuse f.

copyist /'kɒpɪıst/ n **1** (of old texts) copiste mf; **2** (forger) faussaire mf.

copyread vtr (prét, pp -**read**) US corriger (pour la publication).

copyright /'kɒpɪraɪt/ **I** n copyright m, droit m d'auteur; **to have** ou **hold the ~** détenir le copyright ou les droits; **the ~ of** ou **on sth** le copyright de qch, les droits sur qch; **to be in ~** être protégé par copyright. **II** adj [book, work] protégé par un copyright.
III vtr déposer [work].

copy: ~ **typist** ▶ **1251** n dactylo mf; ~**writer** ▶ **1251** n rédacteur/-trice m/f publicitaire.

coquetry /'kɒkɪtrı/ n coquetterie f.

coquettish /kɒ'ketʃ/ adj [person] coquet/-ette; [smile, look, manner] aguichant.

coral /'kɒrəl, US 'kɔ:rəl/ n corail m.

coral: ~ **island** n île f corallienne; ~ **pink** ▶ **818** n, adj (rouge m) corail (m) inv; ~ **reef** n récif m corallien or de corail.

cord /kɔ:d/ **I** n **1** (of dressing gown, curtains) cordon m; **sash** ~ corde f (de fenêtre à guillotine); **2** ELEC fil m, cordon m; **3**° (abrév = **corduroy**) velours m côtelé.
II npl **cords**° pantalon m en velours (côtelé).

cordial /'kɔ:dɪəl, US 'kɔ:rdʒəl/ **I** n **1** (fruit) sirop m de fruits; **2** US (liqueur) liqueur m.
II adj cordial (**to, with** avec).

cordless /'kɔ:dlıs/ adj sans fil, sans cordon; ~ **telephone** téléphone m sans fil.

cordon /'kɔ:dn/ n (all contexts) cordon m; **police** ~ cordon m de police.
■ **cordon off**: ~ **off** [sth], ~ [sth] **off** boucler [street, area]; contenir [crowd].

corduroy /'kɔ:dərɔı/ n velours m côtelé; ~**s** un pantalon m en velours (côtelé).

core /kɔ:(r)/ **I** n **1** (of apple) trognon m; **2** FIG (of problem) cœur m; **3** (inner being) **rotten to the ~** pourri jusqu'à l'os; **English to the ~** anglais jusqu'au bout des ongles; **it shook me to the ~** cela m'a remué jusqu'au fond de l'âme; **4** (nuclear) cœur m; **5** (small group) noyau m.
II vtr CULIN évider [apple].

core curriculum /ˌkɔ:kə'rıkjʊləm/ n SCH, UNIV tronc m commun.

co-respondent /ˌkɔʊrı'spɒndənt/ n JUR complice mf d'adultère.

core subject n SCH, UNIV matière f du tronc commun.

Corfu /kɔ:'fu:/ ▶ **1022** pr n Corfou f.

cork /kɔ:k/ **I** n **1** (substance) liège m; **2** (object) bouchon m.
II vtr boucher [bottle].

corkage /'kɔ:kıdʒ/ n droit m de bouchon.

corked /kɔ:kt/ adj [wine] bouchonné.

corker°† /'kɔ:kə(r)/ n GB (story) histoire f épatante°; (stroke, shot) coup m de maître.

cork: ~**screw** n tire-bouchon m; ~**screw curls** npl anglaises fpl.

corn /kɔ:n/ n **1** GB (wheat) blé m; **2** US (maize) maïs m; **3** (for sowing) grain m (de céréale); **4** MED (on foot) cor m.

corn: ~**cob** n épi m de maïs; ~ **dolly** GB n poupée f de paille.

cornea /'kɔ:nıə/ n (pl ~**s** ou -**neae**) cornée f.

corneal /'kɔ:nıəl/ adj cornéen/-éenne.

corner /'kɔ:nə(r)/ **I** n **1** LIT (in geometry) angle m; (of street, building) angle m, coin m; (of table, field, room) coin m; AUT (bend) virage m; **the house on the ~** la maison qui fait l'angle; **at the ~ of the street** au coin de la rue; **to turn** ou **go round the ~** tourner au coin de la rue; **to turn down the ~ of a page** corner une page; **just around the ~** (nearby) tout près; (around the bend) juste après le coin; **she disappeared round the ~** elle a disparu au coin de la rue;

spring is just around the ~ le printemps approche; **2** (of eye, mouth) coin m; **out of the ~ of one's eye** du coin de l'œil; **3** (place) coin m; **a remote ~ of India** une région reculée de l'Inde; **to search every ~ of the house** chercher partout dans la maison; **4** SPORT (in boxing) coin m (de repos); (in football, hockey) corner m; **to take a ~** tirer un corner.
II vtr **1** (trap) LIT acculer [animal, enemy]; FIG coincer° [person]; **2** (monopolize) accaparer [market].
III vi AUT [car] prendre un virage.
IDIOMS **to be in a tight ~** être dans une impasse; **to hold one's ~** se défendre; **to cut ~s** (financially) faire des économies; (in a procedure) simplifier les choses.

corner: ~ **cupboard** n meuble m d'angle; ~**ing** n AUT tenue f de route (dans les virages); ~ **shop** n petite épicerie f; ~**stone** n ARCHIT, FIG pierre f angulaire; ~**ways**, ~**wise** adj, adv en diagonale.

cornet /'kɔ:nıt/ n **1** (instrument) cornet m (à pistons); **2** GB (for ice cream) cornet m.

corn: ~**field** n champ m de blé; (sweetcorn) champ m de maïs; ~**flour** n farine f de maïs; ~**flower** n bleuet m, barbeau m.

cornice /'kɔ:nıs/ n (all contexts) corniche f.

Cornish pasty /'kɔ:nıʃ.pæstı/ n: petit pâté de viande et légumes.

corn: ~ **oil** n huile f de maïs; ~ **on the cob** n maïs m en épi; ~ **plaster** n pansement m pour cors; ~ **salad** n mâche f; ~ **starch** n US = **cornflour**.

cornucopia /ˌkɔ:njʊ'kəʊpıə/ n corne f d'abondance.

Cornwall /'kɔ:nwɔ:l/ ▶ **1200** pr n (comté m de) Cornouailles f.

corny° /'kɔ:nı/ adj PÉJ [joke] (old) éculé°; (feeble) faiblard°; [film, story] à la guimauve.

corollary /kə'rɒlərı, US 'kɒrəlerı/ n corollaire m (**to** de).

coronary /'kɒrənrı, US 'kɒrənerı/ n MED infarctus m.

coronary: ~ **care unit** n unité f de soins intensifs cardiologiques; ~ **thrombosis** n infarctus m du myocarde.

coronation /ˌkɒrə'neıʃn, US ˌkɔ:r-/ n couronnement m.

coroner /'kɒrənə(r), US 'kɔ:r-/ n coroner m.

coronet /'kɒrənet, US 'kɔ:r-/ n couronne f.

corp n US abrév ▶ **corporation**.

corporal /'kɔ:pərəl/ ▶ **1192** n (in infantry, air force) caporal-chef m; (in cavalry, artillery) brigadier-chef m.

corporal punishment n châtiment m corporel.

corporate /'kɔ:pərət/ adj **1** COMM [accounts, funds] appartenant à une société; [clients, employees] d'une société (or de sociétés); **2** (collective) [action] commun; [ownership] en commun; [decision] collectif/-ive.

corporate: ~ **advertising** n publicité f institutionnelle; ~ **culture** n culture f d'entreprise; ~ **identity** n image f de marque (d'une société); ~ **law** n US JUR droit m des sociétés; ~ **lawyer** n US JUR (in a firm) avocat/-e m/f d'entreprise; (business law expert) juriste mf d'entreprise; ~ **name** n raison f sociale; ~ **planning** n planification f d'entreprise; ~ **raider** n raider m (organisateur d'OPA).

corporation /ˌkɔ:pə'reıʃn/ n **1** COMM (grande) société f; **2** GB (town council) conseil m municipal.

corporation tax n GB impôt m sur les sociétés.

corps /kɔ:(r)/ n MIL corps m; ~ **de ballet** corps de ballet.

corpse /kɔ:ps/ n cadavre m.

corpus /'kɔ:pəs/ n (pl -**pora**) LING corpus m.

corpuscle /'kɔ:pʌsl/ n (blood) ~ globule m sanguin; **red/white** (blood) ~ globule m rouge/blanc.

correct /kə'rekt/ **I** adj **1** (right) [amount, answer, decision, method, order] correct, bon/bonne; [figure] exact; **that is ~** c'est exact; **the ~ time** l'heure exacte; **you are quite ~** tu as parfaitement raison; **to prove ~** s'avérer juste; **2** (proper) correct, convenable.
II vtr corriger; ~ **me if I'm wrong, but...** arrêtez-

moi si je me trompe, mais...; **I stand ~ed** je reconnais mon erreur.
III *v refl* **to ~ oneself** se reprendre.

correcting fluid *n* liquide *m* correcteur.

correction /kə'rekʃn/ *n* correction *f*; (in dictation) rectification *f*.

corrective /kə'rektɪv/ **I** *n* correctif *m*; **this is a ~ to the idea that** ceci apporte un démenti à l'idée que.
II *adj* GEN [*action, lens*] correcteur/-trice; [*measure*] de redressement; **~ surgery** chirurgie *f* réparatrice.

correctly /kə'rektlɪ/ *adv* (all contexts) correctement.

correlate /'kɒrəleɪt, US 'kɔːr-/ **I** *vtr* corréler.
II *vi* être en corrélation (**with** avec).

correlation /ˌkɒrə'leɪʃn/ *n* corrélation *f*.

correspond /ˌkɒrɪ'spɒnd, US ˌkɔːr-/ *vi* **1** (match up) concorder, correspondre (**with** à); **2** (be equivalent) être équivalent (**to** à); **3** (exchange letters) correspondre (**with** avec; **about** au sujet de).

correspondence /ˌkɒrɪ'spɒndəns, US ˌkɔːr-/ *n* (link, exchange of letters) correspondance *f*; **to be in ~ with sb** correspondre avec qn; **to enter into ~** engager une correspondance (**about** au sujet de).

correspondence: **~ column** *n* courrier *m* des lecteurs; **~ course** *n* cours *m* par correspondance.

correspondent /ˌkɒrɪ'spɒndənt, US ˌkɔːr-/ ▶ 1251 *n* **1** (journalist) journaliste *mf*; (abroad) correspondant/-e *m/f*; **political ~** commentateur/-trice *m/f* politique; **2** (letter writer) correspondant/-e *m/f*.

corresponding /ˌkɒrɪ'spɒndɪŋ, US ˌkɔːr-/ *adj* (matching) correspondant; (similar) équivalent.

correspondingly /ˌkɒrɪ'spɒndɪŋlɪ, US ˌkɔːr-/ *adv* **1** (consequently) par conséquent; **2** (proportionately) proportionnellement.

corridor /'kɒrɪdɔː(r), US 'kɔːr-/ *n* (in building, train) couloir *m*; (in international politics) corridor *m*; **the ~s of power** FIG les hautes sphères *fpl* du pouvoir.

corroborate /kə'rɒbəreɪt/ *vtr* corroborer.

corrode /kə'rəud/ **I** *vtr* LIT, FIG corroder.
II *vi* se corroder.

corrosion /kə'rəuʒn/ *n* corrosion *f*.

corrosive /kə'rəusɪv/ *adj* corrosif/-ive.

corrugated: **~ cardboard** *n* carton *m* ondulé; **~ iron** *n* tôle *f* ondulée.

corrupt /kə'rʌpt/ **I** *adj* corrompu; (character) dépravé.
II *vtr* corrompre [*person, text*]; **to ~ sb's morals** dépraver qn.
III *vi* [*lifestyle, power*] corrompre.

corruption /kə'rʌpʃn/ *n* corruption *f*; (of computer data) altération *f*.

corsage /kɔː'sɑːʒ/ *n* **1** (flowers) petit bouquet *m* de fleurs (*porté au corsage*); **2** (bodice) corsage *m*.

Corsica /'kɔːsɪkə/ ▶ 1022 , 1177 *pr n* Corse *f*.

cosh /kɒʃ/ GB **I** *n* matraque *f*.
II *vtr* matraquer.

cosignatory /ˌkəu'sɪgnətərɪ, US -tɔːrɪ/ *n* cosignataire *mf* (**to, of** de).

cosily /'kəuzɪlɪ/ *adv* [*sit, lie*] confortablement.

cosiness /'kəuzɪnɪs/ *n* **1** (of room) atmosphère *f* douillette; **2** (intimacy) intimité *f*.

cos lettuce /kɒz 'letɪs/ *n* (salade *f*) romaine *f*.

cosmetic /kɒz'metɪk/ **I** *n* produit *m* de beauté.
II *adj* **1** LIT cosmétique; **2** FIG superficiel/-ielle.

cosmetic surgery *n* chirurgie *f* esthétique.

cosmic /'kɒzmɪk/ *adj* [*ray*] cosmique; [*dust*] interstellaire; [*event, struggle*] prodigieux/-ieuse.

cosmonaut /'kɒzmənɔːt/ ▶ 1251 *n* cosmonaute *mf*.

cosmopolitan /ˌkɒzmə'pɒlɪtn/ *n, adj* cosmopolite (*mf*).

Cossack /'kɒsæk/ *n, adj* cosaque (*m*).

cosset /'kɒsɪt/ *vtr* choyer [*person*]; protéger [*industry, group*].

cost /kɒst, US kɔːst/ **I** *n* **1** (price) coût *m*, prix *m* (**of** de); (expense incurred) frais *mpl*; **at a ~ of £100** au prix de 100 livres; **at ~** au prix coûtant; **you'll bear the ~** les frais seront à votre charge; **the ~ is quite high**

ça revient assez cher; **at no extra ~** sans frais supplémentaires; **at great ~** à grands frais; **to count the ~ of** LIT estimer le coût de; FIG mesurer les conséquences de; **2** FIG prix *m*; **at all ~s** à tout prix; **he knows to his ~ that** il a appris à ses dépens que; **the ~ in human lives was great** beaucoup de vies ont été perdues; **whatever the ~** coûte que coûte.
II costs *npl* **1** JUR **to pay ~s** être condamné aux dépens; **to be awarded ~s** se voir accorder le remboursement des frais; **2** COMM frais *mpl*; **transport ~s** frais de transport; **to cut ~s** réduire les coûts.
III *vtr* **1** (*prét, pp* cost) coûter; **how much does it ~?** combien ça coûte?; **the TV will ~ £100 to repair** cela coûtera 100 livres de faire réparer la télé; **to ~ money** coûter cher; **2** (*prét, pp* cost) FIG **that decision cost him his job** cette décision lui a coûté son travail; **politeness ~s nothing** ça ne coûte rien d'être poli; **3** (*prét, pp* ~ed) COMM (also ~ **out**) calculer le prix de revient de [*product*]; calculer le coût de [*project, work*].

co-star /'kəustɑː(r)/ CIN, THEAT **I** *n* co-vedette *f*.
II *vtr* (*p prés etc* -rr-) **a film ~ring X and Y** un film avec X et Y.
III *vi* (*p prés etc* -rr-) **to ~ with sb** partager la vedette avec qn.

Costa Rica /ˌkɒstə'riːkə/ ▶ 840 *pr n* Costa Rica *m*.

cost-cutting /'kɒstkʌtɪŋ, US 'kɔːst-/ *n* réduction *f* des frais; **as a ~ exercise** pour réduire les frais.

cost: **~-effective** *adj* rentable; **~-effectiveness** *n* rentabilité *f*.

costing /'kɒstɪŋ, US 'kɔːstɪŋ/ *n* **1** (discipline) ¢ comptabilité *f* analytique or d'exploitation; **2** (process) (for project) établissement *m* des coûts; (for product) établissement *m* des coûts de production.

costly /'kɒstlɪ, US 'kɔːstlɪ/ *adj* [*scheme, exercise*] coûteux/-euse; [*error*] fâcheux/-euse; **the decision proved to be ~** la décision lui/leur etc a coûté beaucoup.

cost: **~ of living** *n* coût *m* de la vie; **~ of living allowance** *n* indemnité *f* de vie chère; **~ of living index** *n* indice *m* du coût de la vie.

cost price *n* COMM (for producer) prix *m* de revient; (for consumer) prix *m* coûtant; **at ~** au prix coûtant.

costume /'kɒstjuːm, US -tuːm/ *n* **1** (clothes) costume *m*; **in ~** costumé; **2** GB (swimsuit) (also **swimming ~**) maillot *m* de bain.

costume: **~ drama** *n* (play) pièce *f* en costume d'époque; **~ jewellery** *n* ¢ bijoux *mpl* fantaisie.

cosy GB, **cozy** US /'kəuzɪ/ *adj* **1** (comfortable) [*chair, room, atmosphere*] douillet/-ette; **to feel ~** [*person*] être confortablement installé; **it's ~ here** on est bien ici; **2** (intimate) intime; **3** FIG [*situation, belief*] rassurant.

cot /kɒt/ *n* **1** GB (for baby) lit *m* de bébé; **2** US (bed) lit *m* de camp.

cot death *n* GB mort *f* subite du nourrisson.

cottage /'kɒtɪdʒ/ *n* maisonnette *f*; (thatched) chaumière *f*; **weekend ~** maison *f* de campagne.

cottage: **~ cheese** *n* fromage *m* blanc à gros grains; **~ hospital** *n* GB ≈ polyclinique *f*; **~ industry** *n* travail *m* artisanal à domicile; **~ loaf** *n* GB miche *f* de pain; **~ pie** *n* GB hachis *m* Parmentier.

cotton /'kɒtn/ **I** *n* **1** (raw material) coton *m*; **2** (thread) fil *m* de coton.
II *noun modifier* [*clothing, fabric, field*] de coton; [*industry, town*] cotonnier/-ière.

cotton: **~ bud** *n* Coton-Tige® *m*; **~ candy** *n* US barbe *f* à papa; **~ mill** *n* filature *f* de coton; **~ reel** *n* bobine *f* de coton; **~tail** *n* US lapin *m*.

cotton wool *n* ouate *f* (de coton).
IDIOMS **to wrap sb in ~** élever qn dans du coton.

couch /kautʃ/ **I** *n* **1** (sofa) canapé *m*; **2** (doctor's) (psychoanalyst's) divan *m*.
II *vtr* formuler [*idea, response*].

couchette /kuː'ʃet/ *n* couchette *f*.

cougar /'kuːgə(r)/ *n* puma *m*.

cough /kɒf, US kɔ:f/ **I** *n* toux *f*; **to have a ~** tousser; **she has a bad ~** elle a une mauvaise toux.
II *vi* tousser.
■ **cough up**: **~ up [sth] 1** LIT cracher [*blood*]; **2**○ FIG cracher○ [*information*]; **to ~ up (the money)** cracher○.

coughing /'kɒfɪŋ, US 'kɔ:fɪŋ/ *n* toux *f*; **~ fit** accès *m* de toux; **there was a lot of ~** il y avait des gens qui toussaient.

could /kʊd/ ▶ **can**¹.

couldn't /'kʊdnt/ = **could not**.

could've /'kʊdəv/ = **could have**.

council /'kaʊnsl/ **I** *n* conseil *m*; **the Council of Europe** le Conseil de l'Europe; **in ~** en assemblée.
II *noun modifier* [*employee, workman*] municipal; [*grant*] de la municipalité.

council: **~ chamber** *n* salle *f* du conseil; **~ estate** *n* lotissement *m* de logements sociaux; **~ house** *n* habitation *f* à loyer modéré; **~ housing** *n* logements *mpl* sociaux.

councillor /'kaʊnsələ(r)/ *n* conseiller/-ère *m/f*.

council tax *n* GB ~ impôts *mpl* locaux.

counsel /'kaʊnsl/ **I** *n* **1** SOUT (advice) conseil *m*; **to keep one's own ~** être circonspect; **2** JUR avocat/-e *m/f*; **~ for the defence** avocat/-e *m/f* de la défense; **~ for the prosecution** procureur *m*.
II *vtr* **1** (advise) conseiller [*person*] (about, on sur); **2** SOUT (recommend) conseiller [*prudence*].

counselling, counseling US /'kaʊnsəlɪŋ/ **I** *n* **1** (psychological advice) aide *f* psychosociale; **2** (practical advice) assistance *f*; **careers ~** orientation *f* professionnelle; **3** SCH orientation *f* scolaire.
II *noun modifier* [*group, centre, service*] d'aide psychosociale, d'assistance.

counsellor, counselor US /'kaʊnsələ(r)/ ▶ **1251** *n* **1** (adviser) conseiller/-ère *m/f*; **2** US (in holiday camp) moniteur/-trice *m/f*.

count /kaʊnt/ ▶ **937** **I** *n* **1** (numerical record) GEN décompte *m*; POL (at election) dépouillement *m*; **at the last ~** au dernier décompte; **to lose ~** LIT ne plus savoir où on en est dans ses calculs; **I've lost ~ of the number of complaints I've received** je ne compte plus le nombre de plaintes que j'ai reçues; **2** (level) taux *m*; **cholesterol ~** taux de cholestérol; **3** (figure) chiffre *m*; **4** JUR chef *m* d'accusation; **on three ~s** pour trois chefs d'accusation; **5** (point) **on both ~s** sur les deux points; **6** (in boxing) **to be out for the ~**○ être KO ALSO FIG; **7** (also **Count**) (nobleman) comte *m*.
II *vtr* **1** (add up) compter; vérifier [*one's change*]; énumérer [*reasons, causes*]; **to ~ the votes** POL dépouiller le scrutin; GEN compter les votes; **~ing the children** en comptant les enfants; **not ~ing my sister** sans compter ma sœur; **to ~ the cost of sth** FIG faire le bilan de qch; **2** (consider) **to ~ sb as sth** considérer qn comme qch.
III *vi* **1** GEN, MATH compter; **to ~ (up) to 50** compter jusqu'à 50; **2** (be of importance) compter; **to ~ for little** compter peu; **to ~ for nothing** ne pas compter; **3** (be considered) être considéré.
IDIOMS **to ~ sheep** compter les moutons; **to ~ the pennies** regarder à la dépense; **to ~ oneself lucky** s'estimer heureux; **it's the thought that ~s** c'est l'intention qui compte; **to stand up and be ~ed** se faire entendre.
■ **count against**: **~ against [sb]** jouer contre.
■ **count in**: **~ [sb] in** (include) **~ me in!** j'en suis!
■ **count on**: **~ on [sb/sth]** compter sur [*person, event*]; **don't ~ on it!** ne comptez pas (trop) dessus!
■ **count out**: ¶ **~ out [sth]** he **~ed out the money** il a compté l'argent (pièce par pièce or billet par billet); ¶ **~ [sb] out 1** (exclude) **~ me out!** ne compte pas sur moi!; **2** SPORT **the ref ~ed him out** il est allé au tapis.
■ **count up**: **~ up [sth]** calculer [*cost, hours*]; compter [*money, boxes*].

countable /'kaʊntəbl/ *adj* LING comptable.

countdown /'kaʊntdaʊn/ *n* LIT, FIG compte *m* à rebours (**to** avant).

counter /'kaʊntə(r)/ **I** *n* **1** (service area) (in shop, snack bar) comptoir *m*; (in bank, post office) guichet *m*; (in pub, bar) bar *m*; **the girl at ou behind the ~** (in shop) la vendeuse; (in bank, post office) la caissière; **available over the ~** [*medicine*] vendu sans ordonnance; **under the ~** en sous-main; **2** (section of a shop) rayon *m*; **perfume ~** rayon parfumerie; **cheese ~** fromagerie *f*, rayon *m* fromagerie; **3** (token) jeton *m*.
II *counter to* *prep phr* [*be, go, run*] à l'encontre de; [*act, behave*] contrairement à.
III *vtr* répondre à [*accusation, threat*]; neutraliser [*effet*]; parer [*blow*]; enrayer [*inflation*].
IV *vi* (retaliate) riposter (**with sth** par qch).
V **counter+** *combining form* contre-.

counteract /ˌkaʊntə'rækt/ *vtr* contrebalancer [*influence*]; contrecarrer [*negative publicity*].

counter-attack /'kaʊntərətæk/ **I** *n* contre-attaque *f* (**against** sur).
II *vi* contre-attaquer.

counterbalance I /'kaʊntəbæləns/ *n* contrepoids *m*.
II /ˌkaʊntə'bæləns/ *vtr* contrebalancer.

counter cheque GB, **counter check** US *n* chèque-guichet *m*.

counter-claim /'kaʊntəkleɪm/ *n* rétorsion *f*.

counter clerk ▶ **1251** *n* US caissier/-ière *m/f*.

counter-clockwise /ˌkaʊntə'klɒkwaɪz/ *adj, adv* US dans le sens inverse des aiguilles d'une montre.

counter-espionage /ˌkaʊntər'espɪənɑːʒ/ *n* contre-espionnage *m*.

counterfeit /'kaʊntəfɪt/ **I** *adj* [*signature, note*] contrefait; **~ money** fausse monnaie *f*.
II *vtr* contrefaire.

counterfoil /'kaʊntəfɔɪl/ *n* talon *m*, souche *f*.

counter-inflationary /ˌkaʊntərɪnfleɪʃnrɪ, US -neri/ *adj* anti-inflationniste.

counter-insurgency /ˌkaʊntərɪn'sɜːdʒənsɪ/ *n* contre-insurrection *f*.

counter-intelligence /ˌkaʊntərɪn'telɪdʒəns/ *n* contre-espionnage *m*.

countermand /ˌkaʊntə'mɑːnd, US -'mænd/ *vtr* annuler [*order, decision*].

counter-measure /'kaʊntəmeʒə(r)/ *n* contre-mesure *f*.

counter-offensive /ˌkaʊntərə'fensɪv/ *n* contre-offensive *f* (**against** sur).

counterpane /'kaʊntəpeɪn/ *n* couvre-lit *m*.

counterpart /'kaʊntəpɑːt/ *n* (of person) homologue *mf*; (of company, institution etc) équivalent *m* (**of, to** de).

counterpoint /'kaʊntəpɔɪnt/ *n* contrepoint *m*.

counter-productive /ˌkaʊntəprə'dʌktɪv/ *adj* contre-productif/-ive.

counter-revolution /ˌkaʊntəˌrevə'luːʃn/ *n* contre-révolution *f*.

countersign /'kaʊntəsaɪn/ *vtr* contresigner.

counter staff *n* caissiers/-ières *mpl/fpl*.

counter-tenor /ˌkaʊntə'tenə(r)/ ▶ **1380** *n* (person) haute-contre *m*; (voice) haute-contre *f*.

counter-terrorism /ˌkaʊntə'terərɪzəm/ *n* contre-terrorisme *m*.

countess /'kaʊntɪs/ ▶ **937** *n* (also **Countess**) comtesse *f*.

counting /'kaʊntɪŋ/ *n* GEN calcul *m*; **the ~ of votes** le dépouillement du scrutin.

countless /'kaʊntlɪs/ *adj* **~ letters** un nombre incalculable de lettres; **on ~ occasions** je ne sais combien de fois; **~ millions of** des millions et des millions de.

countrified /'kʌntrɪfaɪd/ *adj* rustique; PEJ rustaud.

country /'kʌntrɪ/ **I** *n* **1** (nation, people) pays *m*; **to go to the ~** GB POL appeler le pays aux urnes; **2** (native land) patrie *f*; **the old ~** le pays natal; **3** (also **~side**) (out of town) campagne *f*; **in the ~** à la campagne; **open ~** rase campagne; **4** ¢ région *f*; **walking ~** une région bonne pour la marche;

Countries and continents

Most countries and all continents are used with the definite article in French:

France is a beautiful country = la France est un beau pays
I like Canada = j'aime le Canada
to visit the United States = visiter les États-Unis
to know Iran = connaître l'Iran

A very few countries do not:

to visit Israel = visiter Israël

When in doubt, check in the dictionary.

All the continent names are feminine in French. Most names of countries are feminine e.g. la France, but some are masculine e.g. le Canada.

Most names of countries are singular in French, but some are plural (usually, but not always, those that are plural in English) e.g. les États-Unis mpl (the United States), and les Philippines fpl (the Philippines). Note, however, the plural verb sont:

the Philippines is a lovely country = les Philippines sont un beau pays

In, to and from somewhere

With continent names, feminine singular names of countries and masculine singular names of countries beginning with a vowel, for in and to use en, and for from use de:

to live in Europe = vivre en Europe
to go to Europe = aller en Europe
to come from Europe = venir d'Europe
to live in France = vivre en France
to go to France = aller en France
to come from France = venir de France
to live in Afghanistan = vivre en Afghanistan
to go to Afghanistan = aller en Afghanistan
to come from Afghanistan = venir d'Afghanistan

Note that names of countries and continents that include North, South, East, or West work in the same way:

to live in North Korea = vivre en Corée du Nord
to go to North Korea = aller en Corée du Nord
to come from North Korea = venir de Corée du Nord

With masculine countries beginning with a consonant, and with plurals, use au or aux for in and to, and du or des for from:

to live in Canada = vivre au Canada
to go to Canada = aller au Canada

to come from Canada = venir du Canada
to live in the United States = vivre aux États-Unis
to go to the United States = aller aux États-Unis
to come from the United States = venir des États-Unis
to live in the Philippines = vivre aux Philippines
to go to the Philippines = aller aux Philippines
to come from the Philippines = venir des Philippines

Adjective uses: *français* or *de France* or *de la France?*

For French, the translation français is usually safe; here are some typical examples:

the French army = l'armée française
the French coast = la côte française
French cooking = la cuisine française
French currency = la monnaie française
the French Customs = la douane française
the French government = le gouvernement français
the French language = la langue française
French literature = la littérature française
French money = l'argent français
the French nation = le peuple français
French politics = la politique française
a French town = une ville française
French traditions = les traditions françaises

Some nouns, however, occur more commonly with de France (usually, but not always, their English equivalents can have of France as well as French):

the Ambassador of France
or the French Ambassador = l'ambassadeur de France
the French Embassy = l'ambassade de France
the history of France
or French history = l'histoire de France
the King of France
or the French king = le roi de France
the rivers of France = les fleuves et rivières de France
the French team = l'équipe de France

but note:

the capital of France
or the French capital = la capitale de la France

Note that many geopolitical adjectives like French can also refer to nationality, e.g. a French tourist ▶ 1100 , or to the language, e.g. a French word ▶ 1038 .

Brontë ~ le pays des Brontë; **5** (also ~ **music**) country (music) f.
II adj [road] de campagne; [scene] campagnard; ~ **life** la vie à la campagne.
IDIOMS **it's a free ~!** on est en république!, on est libre de faire ce qu'on veut!; **it's my line of ~** ça me connaît; **it's not really my line of ~** ce n'est pas vraiment mon fort.
country: ~ **and western** n musique f country et western; ~ **bumpkin** n PÉJ plouc° mf; ~ **club** n club m de loisirs; ~ **cousin** n PEJ campagnard/-e m/f; ~ **dancing** n danse f folklorique; ~ **house** n manoir m; ~ **man** n (also **fellow** ~) compatriote m; ~ **music** n country music f; ~ **seat** n domaine m.
countryside /ˈkʌntrɪsaɪd/ n campagne f; **there is some lovely ~ around here** il y a de beaux paysages par ici.
countrywide adj, adv dans tout le pays.
county /ˈkaʊntɪ/ **I** n comté m.
II adj GB [boundary, team] du comté; [accent] ~ d'aristocrate; **he's very ~** il fait très gentleman-farmer.
county: ~ **council**, **CC** n GB POL ≈ conseil m régional; ~ **court** n GB JUR ≈ tribunal m d'instance.
coup /kuː/ n (also ~ **d'état**) coup m d'État, FIG **to pull off/score a ~** réussir/faire un beau coup.
couple /ˈkʌpl/ **I** n **1** couple m; **young (married) ~** jeune couple; **2 a ~ of** (two) deux; (a few) deux ou trois; **a ~ of times** deux ou trois fois.

II vtr **1** RAIL atteler; **2** ~d **with** s'ajoutant à.
III vi [person, animal] s'accoupler.
coupon /ˈkuːpɒn/ n **1** (for goods) bon m; **petrol ~** bon d'essence; **2** (cut-out in ad) coupon m; **reply ~** coupon-réponse m; **3** (for pools) grille f de paris.
courage /ˈkʌrɪdʒ/ n courage m; **to have the ~ of one's convictions** avoir le courage de ses opinions; **to pluck up the ~ to do** trouver le courage de faire; **it takes ~** il faut du courage; **to take ~ from the fact that** trouver du réconfort dans le fait que.
courageous /kəˈreɪdʒəs/ adj courageux/-euse; **it was ~ of him** c'était courageux de sa part.
courier /ˈkʊrɪə(r)/ ▶ **1251** n **1** (also **travel ~**) accompagnateur/-trice m/f; **2** (for parcels, documents) coursier m; (for drugs) transporteur m.
course /kɔːs/ **I** n **1** (progression) (of time, event, history) cours m (**of** de); **in the ~ of** au cours de; **in (the) ~ of time** avec le temps; **in the normal ~ of events** normalement; **in ~ of restoration** en cours de restauration; **to run** ou **take its ~** suivre son cours; **in due ~** en temps utile; **2** (route) cours m; (of boat, plane) cap m; **to be on ~** AVIAT, NAUT tenir le cap; **the economy is back on ~** l'économie s'est restabilisée; **to go off ~** [ship, government] dévier de son cap; **to change ~** GEN, LIT changer de direction; AVIAT, NAUT, FIG changer de cap; ~ **of action** conduite f; **to take a ~ of action** adopter une certaine conduite; **3** SCH, UNIV cours m (**in** en; **of** de); **French ~** cours m de français; **beginners' ~** cours m pour débutants; **a ~ of study** SCH programme m scolaire; UNIV

cursus *m* universitaire; **to go on** OU **be on a ~** (aller) suivre un cours; **4** MED a **~ of treatment** un traitement; **5** SPORT (in golf, athletics) parcours *m*; (in racing) cours *m*; **to stay the ~** LIT finir la course; FIG tenir bon; **6** (part of meal) plat *m*; **the cheese ~** le plateau de fromages; **five-~ meal** repas *m* de cinq plats.
II *vi* **1** (gush) couler; **2** SPORT **to go coursing** chasser.
III of course *adv phr* bien sûr, évidemment; **of ~ I do!** (confirming suggestion) bien sûr que oui!; (refuting allegation) bien sûr que si!; **of ~ he doesn't!** bien sûr que non!; **'did you lock the door?'—'of ~ I did!'** 'tu as fermé la porte à clé?'—'mais oui, enfin!'; **'you didn't believe him?'—'of ~ not!'** 'tu ne l'as pas cru?'—'mais non, voyons!'.

course: **~ book** *n* méthode *f*; **~work** *n* SCH, UNIV devoirs *mpl* (de contrôle continu).

court /kɔːt/ **I** *n* **1** JUR cour *f*, tribunal *m*; **to go to ~** aller devant les tribunaux (**over** pour); **to take sb to ~** poursuivre qn en justice; **2** SPORT (for tennis, squash) court *m*; (for basketball) terrain *m*; **to be on ~** jouer; **3** (of sovereign) cour *f*.
II *noun modifier* JUR [*case*] judiciaire; [*ruling*] du tribunal; **~ appearance** comparution *f* en justice.
III *vtr* **1** (woo) courtiser [*woman, voters*]; **2 to ~ disaster** courir au désastre.
IV† *vi* [*couple*] se fréquenter; **he's ~ing** il a une petite amie; **in our ~ing days** avant notre mariage.
IDIOMS to get laughed out of ~ se rendre complètement ridicule; **to pay ~ to sb** faire la cour à qn.

court circular *n* bulletin *m* quotidien de la cour.

courteous /ˈkɜːtɪəs/ *adj* courtois (**to** envers).

courteously /ˈkɜːtɪəslɪ/ *adv* courtoisement.

courtesy /ˈkɜːtəsɪ/ *n* **1** courtoisie *f*; **it is only common ~** c'est la moindre des politesses; **2** (**by**) **~ of** (with permission from) avec la gracieuse permission de; (with funds from) grâce à la générosité de; (thanks to) grâce à; **a free trip ~ of the airline** un voyage gratuit offert par la compagnie aérienne.

courtesy call *n* visite *f* de courtoisie.

courthouse /ˈkɔːthaʊs/ *n* **1** JUR palais *m* de justice; **2** US ~ préfecture *f* (d'un comté).

courtier /ˈkɔːtɪə(r)/ *n* courtisan/dame de (la) cour *m/f*.

courtly /ˈkɔːtlɪ/ *adj* (polite) courtois; **~ love** amour *m* courtois.

court-martial /ˌkɔːtˈmɑːʃl/ **I** *n* (*pl* **courts-martial**) cour *f* martiale.
II *vtr* (*p prés etc* **-ll-**) faire passer [qn] en cour martiale [*soldier*]; **to be ~led** passer en cour martiale.

court: **~ of inquiry** *n* commission *f* d'enquête; **~ of law** *n* JUR cour *f* de justice; **~ order** *n* JUR décision *f* judiciaire; **~room** *n* JUR salle *f* d'audience.

courtship /ˈkɔːtʃɪp/ *n* **1** (period of courting) fréquentation *f*; **2** (act of courting) cour *f*.

courtyard *n* cour *f*.

cousin /ˈkʌzn/ *n* cousin/-e *m/f*.

cove /kəʊv/ *n* **1** (bay) anse *f*; **2**○ † (man) type○ *m*.

covenant /ˈkʌvənənt/ *n* (agreement) convention *f*; (payment agreement) engagement *m*.

Coventry /ˈkɒvəntrɪ/ *pr n*: IDIOMS **to send sb to ~** mettre qn en quarantaine.

cover /ˈkʌvə(r)/ **I** *n* **1** (protective lid, sheath) couverture *f*; (for duvet, typewriter, cushion) housse *f*; (for umbrella, blade, knife) fourreau *m*; **2** (blanket) couverture *f*; **3** (of book, magazine) couverture *f*; (of record) pochette *f*; **on the ~** (of book) sur la couverture; (of magazine) en couverture; **from ~ to ~** de la première à la dernière page; **4** (shelter) abri *m*; **take ~!** aux abris!; **under ~** à l'abri; **under ~ of darkness** à la faveur de la nuit; **5** (for spy, crime) couverture *f* (**for** pour); **to blow sb's ~**○ griller○ qn; **6** MIL couverture *f*; **air ~** couverture aérienne; **to give sb ~** couvrir qn; **7** (replacement) (for teacher, doctor) remplacement *m*; **to provide emergency ~** offrir un service d'urgence; **8**

(insurance) assurance *f* (**for** pour; **against** contre); **to give** or **provide ~ against** garantir contre.
II *vtr* **1** (conceal or protect) couvrir (**with** avec); recouvrir [*cushion, sofa, corpse*] (**with** de); **2** (coat) recouvrir [*ground, surface, person, cake*] (**with** de); **to be ~ed in glory** être couvert de gloire; **3** (be all over) [*litter, graffiti, bruises*] couvrir; **~ed in spots/litter** couvert de boutons/papiers; **4** (travel over) parcourir [*distance, area*]; (extend over) s'étendre sur [*area*]; **to ~ a lot of miles** faire beaucoup de kilomètres; **5** (deal with, include) [*article, speaker*] traiter; [*term*] englober; [*teacher*] faire; [*rule, law*] s'appliquer à; [*department*] s'occuper de; [*rep*] couvrir; **6** (report on) [*journalist*] couvrir; **~ed live on BBC1** diffusé en direct par BBC1; **7** (pay for) couvrir [*costs*]; combler [*loss*]; **£20 should ~ it** 20 livres sterling devraient suffire; **to ~ one's costs** rentrer dans ses frais; **8** (insure) assurer, couvrir [*person, possession*] (**for, against** contre; **for doing** pour faire); **9** MIL, SPORT couvrir; **I've got you ~ed!** (threat) ne bougez pas ou je tire!; **to ~ one's back** FIG se couvrir; **10** (conceal) cacher [*ignorance*]; masquer [*smell*].
III *v refl* **to ~ oneself** se protéger (**against** contre).
IV -covered: **snow-~ed** couvert de neige; **chocolate-~ed** enrobé de chocolat.
V covered *pp adj* [*market, porch*] couvert; [*dish*] à couvercle.
■ **cover for**: **~ for** [sb] (replace) remplacer [*employee*]; (conceal error) **'~ for me!'** 'trouve-moi une excuse!'
■ **cover over**: **~ over** [sth], **~** [sth] **over** couvrir [*yard, pool*] (**with** avec); recouvrir [*mark*] (**with** de).
■ **cover up**: ¶ **~ up 1** (put clothes on) se couvrir (**with** de); **2 to ~ up for** couvrir [*friend*]; **they're ~ing up for each other** ils se couvrent l'un l'autre; ¶ **~ up** [sth], **~** [sth] **up** FIG dissimuler [*mistake, truth*]; étouffer [*scandal*].

coverage /ˈkʌvərɪdʒ/ *n* **1** (in media) couverture *f*; **television/newspaper ~** couverture par la télévision/les journaux; **live ~** reportage *m* en direct; **2** (in book, programme) traitement *m*; **its ~ of the period is good/poor** il couvre bien/mal cette période.

covered: **~ market** *n* marché *m* couvert; **~ wagon** *n* chariot *m* bâché.

covering /ˈkʌvərɪŋ/ *n* **1** (for wall, floor) revêtement *m*; **2** (layer of snow, moss) couche *f*.

covering: **~ fire** *n* tir *m* de couverture; **~ letter** *n* lettre *f* d'accompagnement.

cover: **~ note** *n* (from insurance company) attestation *f* d'assurance; **~ story** *n* (in paper) article *m* annoncé en couverture.

covert I /ˈkʌvə(r)/ *n* (thicket) fourré *m*.
II /ˈkʌvət, US ˈkəʊvɜːrt/ *adj* [*operation*] secret/-ète; [*glance*] furtif/-ive; [*threat*] voilé.

covertly /ˈkʌvətlɪ, US ˈkəʊvɜːrtlɪ/ *adv* secrètement.

cover: **~-up** *n* opération *f* de camouflage; **~ version** *n* MUS version *f*.

covet /ˈkʌvɪt/ *vtr* convoiter.

covetous /ˈkʌvɪtəs/ *adj* cupide.

covetously /ˈkʌvɪtəslɪ/ *adv* avec convoitise.

cow /kaʊ/ *n* **1** (in cattle) vache *f*; (other animal) femelle *f*.
IDIOMS **till the ~s come home**○ jusqu'à la saint-glinglin○.

coward /ˈkaʊəd/ *n* lâche *mf*.

cowardice /ˈkaʊədɪs/ *n* lâcheté *f*.

cowardly /ˈkaʊədlɪ/ *adj* lâche.

cowbell *n* sonnaille *f*.

cowboy /ˈkaʊbɔɪ/ **I** *n* **1** ▶ 1251 US cowboy *m*; **to play ~s and indians** jouer aux cowboys et aux indiens; **2** (incompetent worker) PÉJ fumiste *m*.
II *noun modifier* **1** (hat, film) de cowboy; **2** PÉJ [*workman*] fumiste; [*outfit*] pas sérieux/-ieuse.

cowed /kaʊd/ *adj* apeuré.

cower /ˈkaʊə(r)/ *vi* se recroqueviller (de peur).

cow: **~herd** ▶ 1251 *n* vacher/-ère *m/f*; **~hide** *n* (leather) peau *f* de vache.

cowl /kaʊl/ n capuchon m.

cowlick○ /'kaʊlɪk/ n mèche f (de cheveux).

cowl neck /ˌkaʊl 'nek/ n col m boule.

cow: **~pat** n bouse f de vache; **~shed** n étable f.

cox /kɒks/ SPORT **I** n barreur m.
II vtr, vi barrer.

coxswain /'kɒksn/ n (on ship) ~ capitaine m en second; (in rowing) barreur m.

coy /kɔɪ/ adj **1** [smile, look] de fausse modestie; **2** (reticent) réservé (**about** à propos de).

coyly /'kɔɪlɪ/ adv avec fausse modestie; (flirtatiously) avec coquetterie.

coypu /'kɔɪpu:/ n (pl **~s** ou **~**) ragondin m.

cozy adj US = **cosy**.

CPU n COMPUT abrév ▸ **central processing unit**.

cr COMM abrév écrite = **credit** I 5.

crab /kræb/ n ZOOL, CULIN crabe m.
IDIOMS **to catch a ~** (in rowing) plonger la rame trop profond, aller à la pêche○.

crab apple n (tree) pommier m sauvage; (fruit) pomme f sauvage.

crack /kræk/ **I** n **1** (in varnish, ground) craquelure f (**in** dans); (single line in wall, cup, mirror, ground, bone) fêlure f (**in** dans); **2** (in door) entrebâillement m; (in curtains) fente f; (in rock) fissure f; **3** (drug) (also ~ **cocaine**) crack m; **4** (noise) craquement m; **5**○ (attempt) essai m, tentative f; **to have a ~ at doing** essayer de faire; **to have a ~ at** essayer de remporter [title]; essayer de battre [record]; **6** plaisanterie f (**about** à propos de); **a cheap ~** une plaisanterie facile.
II adj (tjrs épith) [player] de première; [troops, shot] d'élite.
III vtr **1** (make a crack in) fêler [mirror, bone, wall, cup]; (make fine cracks in) fendiller, faire craqueler [varnish]; **2** (break) casser [nut, egg, casing]; **to ~ a safe** fracturer un coffre-fort; **to ~ sth open** ouvrir qch; **to ~ one's head open** se fendre le crâne; **3** (solve) résoudre [problem]; déchiffrer [code]; **I've ~ed it**○ j'ai pigé○ or compris; **4** faire claquer [whip]; faire craquer [knuckles]; **to ~ sb on the head** asséner un coup sur la tête de qn; **to ~ one's head on sth** se cogner la tête sur qch; **to ~ the whip** FIG agiter le fouet; **5** (overcome) faire craquer [defences]; **6 to ~ a joke** sortir une blague○.
IV vi **1** (develop crack(s)) se fêler; [varnish] se craqueler; [skin] se crevasser; [ground] se fendre; **2** (cease to resist) [person] craquer; **to ~ under pressure** ne pas tenir le coup; **3** (make sound) [knuckles, twig] craquer; [whip] claquer; **4** [voice] se casser.
IDIOMS **not all** ou **not as good as it's ~ed up to be**○ pas aussi bon qu'on le prétend; **to get ~ing**○ s'y mettre; **go on, get ~ing**○! vas-y, remue-toi○!; **to have a fair ~ of the whip** avoir sa chance; **to give sb a fair ~ of the whip** donner sa chance à qn.
■ **crack down** prendre des mesures énergiques, sévir (**on** contre).
■ **crack up**○: ¶ ~ **up 1** (have breakdown) craquer; **2** (laugh) rire; ¶ ~ **[sb] up** faire rire qn.

crack-brained○ /'krækbreɪnd/ adj saugrenu.

crackdown /'krækdaʊn/ n mesure f sévère (**on** contre); **the ~ on drugs** l'action f anti-drogue.

cracker /'krækə(r)/ n **1** (biscuit) cracker m, biscuit m salé; **2** (for Christmas) diablotin m.

crackers○ /'krækəz/ adj GB cinglé○.

cracking /'krækɪŋ/ **I**○ adj GB [game, start] excellent; **at a ~ pace** à toute vitesse.
II○ †adv GB **a ~ good shot** un coup formidable-ment bien joué; **it was a ~ good lunch** on a formida-blement bien déjeuné.

crackle /'krækl/ **I** n (sound) crépitement m.
II vtr faire crisser [foil, paper].
III vi [twig, fire, radio] crépiter; [hot fat, burning wood] grésiller.

crackling /'kræklɪŋ/ n **1** (of fire) crépitement m; (of foil, cellophane) crissement m; (on radio) friture○ f; **2** (crisp pork) couenne f grillée.

crackpot○ n, adj cinglé/-e○ (m/f).

cradle /'kreɪdl/ **I** n **1** (for baby) berceau m ALSO FIG; **from the ~ to the grave** du berceau à la tombe; **2** (platform) nacelle f.
II vtr bercer [baby]; tenir [qch] délicatement [object].

cradlesnatcher○ /'kreɪdlsnætʃə(r)/ n **he's/she's a ~** il/elle les prend au berceau○.

craft /krɑːft, US kræft/ **I** n **1** (skill) (art-related) art m; (job-related) métier m; **2** (handiwork) artisanat m; **arts and ~s** artisanat (d'art); **3** (boat) embarcation f.
II noun modifier [exhibition, guild] artisanal.

craft: **~sman** n (manual) artisan m; (artist) artiste m; **~smanship** n (manual) dextérité f; (artistic) art m.

crafty /'krɑːftɪ, US 'kræftɪ/ adj astucieux/-ieuse.

crag /kræg/ n rocher m escarpé.

craggy /'krægɪ/ adj **1** [mountain] escarpé; **2** [features] taillé à coups de serpe.

cram /kræm/ (p prés etc **-mm-**) **I** vtr **to ~ sth into** enfoncer or fourrer○ qch dans [bag, car]; **to ~ sb into** entasser qn dans [room]; **to ~ a lot into one day** faire beaucoup de choses dans une seule journée; **to ~ three meetings into a morning** caser○ trois rendez-vous dans la matinée; **~med full** plein à craquer.
II vi SCH bachoter (**for** pour).
III v refl **to ~ oneself with** se bourrer de [sweets].

crammer○ /'kræmə(r)/ n GB (school) ~ boîte f à bac○.

cramp /kræmp/ n (pain) crampe f; **to have ~** GB ou **a ~** US avoir une crampe; **writer's ~** crampe de l'écrivain.
IDIOMS **to ~ sb's style**○ faire perdre ses moyens à qn.

cramped /kræmpt/ adj **1** [cell, house, office] exigu/-uë; **~ conditions** conditions d'exiguïté; **we're very ~ in here** nous sommes très à l'étroit ici; **2** [handwrit-ing] en pattes de mouche.

cranberry /'krænbərɪ, US -berɪ/ n canneberge f; **~ sauce** sauce f à la canneberge.

crane /kreɪn/ **I** n CONSTR grue f.
II vtr **to ~ one's neck** tendre le cou.

cranium /'kreɪnɪəm/ n (pl **~s**, **-ia**) crâne m, boîte f crânienne.

crank /kræŋk/ n **1**○ (freak) fanatique mf, fana○ mf; **2** TECH manivelle f.
■ **crank up**: ~ **up [sth]**, ~ **[sth] up** LIT remonter (à la manivelle).

cranky○ /'kræŋkɪ/ adj **1** US (grumpy) grincheux/-euse; **2** (eccentric) loufoque○; **3** [machine] déglingué○.

cranny /'krænɪ/ n petite fente f.

crap❶ /kræp/ **I** n **1** (nonsense) conneries● fpl; **2** (of film, book etc) foutaise❶ f; **3** (faeces) merde● f; **to have a ~** chier●.
II vi (p prés etc **-pp-**) chier●.

crappy❶ /'kræpɪ/ adj merdique❶, nul/nulle○.

crash /kræʃ/ **I** n **1** (noise) fracas m; **2** (accident) acci-dent m; **car** ~ accident de voiture; **train/air** ~ catastrophe f ferroviaire/aérienne; **to have a** ~ avoir un accident; **3** (of stock market) krach m.
II vtr **1** (involve in accident) **to ~ the car** avoir un acci-dent de voiture; **to ~ one's car into a bus** rentrer dans ou percuter un bus; **2**○ (gatecrash) **to ~ a party** s'introduire dans une fête sans y être invité.
III vi **1** (have accident) [car, plane] s'écraser; (collide) [vehicles, planes] se rentrer dedans, se percuter; **to ~ into sth** rentrer dans ou percuter qch; **2** [share prices] s'effondrer; **3** (move loudly) faire du boucan○; **4** (fall) **to ~ to the ground** [cup, picture] se fracasser sur le sol; [tree] s'abattre.
■ **crash out** (go to sleep) pioncer❶; (collapse) s'écrou-ler○.

crash barrier n glissière f de sécurité.

crash: **~ course** n cours m intensif; **~ diet** n régime m d'amaigrissement intensif; **~ helmet** n casque m.

crashing○ /'kræʃɪŋ/ adj **to be a ~ bore** [person] être un/une sacré/-e raseur/-euse m/f; [event] être barbant○ à mourir.

crash-land /ˌkræʃˈlænd/ I *vtr* **to ~ a plane** poser un avion en catastrophe.
II *vi* atterrir en catastrophe.

crash landing *n* atterrissage *m* en catastrophe.

crass /kræs/ *adj* GEN grossier/-ière; **~ ignorance** ignorance *f* crasse.

crate /kreɪt/ *n* **1** (for bottles, china) caisse *f*; (for fruit, vegetables) cageot *m*; **2**◦ †(car) caisse◦ *f*; (plane) zinc◦ *m*.

crater /ˈkreɪtə(r)/ *n* cratère *m*; (caused by explosion) entonnoir *m*.

cravat /krəˈvæt/ *n* foulard *m* (pour homme).

crave /kreɪv/ *vtr* **1** (also ~ **for**) avoir un besoin maladif de [*drug*]; avoir soif de [*affection*]; avoir envie de [*food*]; **2** SOUT solliciter [*permission*].

craving /ˈkreɪvɪŋ/ *n* (for drug) besoin *m* maladif (**for** de); (for fame, love) soif *f* (**for** de); (for food) envie *f* (**for** de).

crawl /krɔːl/ I *n* **1** SPORT crawl *m*; **2** (slow pace) **at a ~** au pas; **to go at a ~** [*vehicle*] rouler au pas.
II *vi* **1** [*insect, snake, person*] ramper; **to ~ in/out** entrer/sortir en rampant; **to ~ into bed** se traîner au lit; **2** (on all fours) [*baby*] marcher à quatre pattes; **3** (move slowly) [*vehicle*] rouler au pas; **to ~ along** avancer au pas; **to ~ down/up sth** descendre/monter lentement qch; **4** (pass slowly) [*time*] se traîner; **5** (seethe) **to be ~ing with** fourmiller de [*insects, tourists*]; **6**◦ (flatter) faire du lèche-bottes◦ (**to** à).
IDIOMS **to make sb's skin** or **flesh ~** donner la chair de poule à qn◦.

crayfish /ˈkreɪfɪʃ/ *n* **1** (freshwater) écrevisse *f*; **2** (spiny lobster) langouste *f*.

crayon /ˈkreɪən/ I *n* (wax) craie *f* grasse; (pencil) crayon *m* de couleur.
II *vtr* colorier.

craze /kreɪz/ I *n* vogue *f*; (passing) engouement *m*; **it's just a ~** c'est une toquade or une folie passagère; **to be the latest ~** faire fureur.
II *vi* (also ~ **over**) [*china, glaze*] se craqueler.

crazed /kreɪzd/ *adj* **1** (mad) [*animal, person*] fou/folle; **power-~** ivre de pouvoir; **2** [*china, glaze*] craquelé.

crazily /ˈkreɪzɪlɪ/ *adv* (*veer*) follement.

crazy◦ /ˈkreɪzɪ/ I *adj* **1** [*person, scheme, price, speed*] fou/folle; [*behaviour, idea*] insensé; **to go ~** devenir fou/folle; **~ with** fou/folle de [*grief*]; **2** (infatuated) **~ about** fou/folle de [*person*]; passionné de [*activity*].
II **like crazy** *adv phr* [*shout, laugh, run*] comme un fou/une folle; **they used to fight like ~** ils n'arrêtaient pas de se bagarrer.

crazy: **~ golf** ▶ 949 *n* GB mini-golf *m*; **~ paving** *n* GB pavage avec des pierres de forme irrégulière.

creak /kriːk/ I *n* (of hinge) grincement *m*; (of floorboard) craquement *m*.
II *vi* [*hinge*] grincer; [*floorboard*] craquer; **the door ~ed open** la porte s'ouvrit en grinçant.

creaking /ˈkriːkɪŋ/ I *n* = **creak** I.
II *adj* (épith) **1** LIT [*hinge, lift*] grinçant; [*floorboard*] qui craque; **2** FIG [*regime, structure*] déliquescent.

creaky /ˈkriːkɪ/ *adj* **1** [*door, hinge*] grinçant; [*leather*] qui crisse; [*joint, bone, floorboard*] qui craque; **2** FIG [*alibi, policy*] bancal◦.

cream /kriːm/ ▶ 818 I *n* (all contexts) crème *f*; **the ~ of society** FIG la fine fleur de la société; **sun/shoe ~** crème solaire/à chaussures; **orange ~** chocolat fourré à l'orange.
II *noun modifier* CULIN [*cake, bun*] à la crème.
III *adj* (colour) crème *inv*.
IV *vtr* CULIN travailler [*ingredients*]; **~ed potatoes** purée *f* de pommes de terre.
IDIOMS **to look like the cat that's got the ~** avoir l'air très content de soi.
■ **cream off**: **~ off** [sth], **~** [sth] **off** prélever [*best pupils*]; ramasser [*profits*].

cream: **~ cheese** *n* fromage *m* à tartiner; **~ cracker** *n* GB cracker *m*; **~ puff** *n* chou *m* à la crème; **~ soda** *n* soda *m* parfumé à la vanille; **~**

tea *n* GB thé *m* complet (*accompagné de scones avec de la crème fraîche et de la confiture*).

creamy /ˈkriːmɪ/ *adj* [*texture*] crémeux/-euse; [*colour*] (couleur) crème *inv*; [*complexion*] laiteux/-euse.

crease /kriːs/ I *n* (intentional) pli *m*; (accidental) faux pli *m*.
II *vtr* (crumple) froisser [*paper, cloth*].
III *vi* **1** [*cloth*] se froisser; **2 her face ~d into a smile** son visage se dérida.

creased /kriːst/ *adj* [*cloth, paper*] froissé; [*brow*] (with anxiety) inquiet.

crease-resistant /ˈkriːsrɪzɪstənt/ *adj* infroissable.

create /kriːˈeɪt/ I *vtr* GEN créer; lancer [*fashion*]; provoquer [*interest, scandal, repercussion*]; poser [*problem*]; faire [*good impression*].
II◦ *vi* GB faire une scène.

creation /kriːˈeɪʃn/ *n* (all contexts) création *f*; **job/ wealth ~** création d'emplois/de richesses.

creative /kriːˈeɪtɪv/ *adj* **1** (inventive) [*person, solution*] créatif/-ive; **2** (which creates) [*process, imagination*] créateur/-trice.

creative writing *n* (school subject) ≈ composition *f*.

creativity /ˌkriːeɪˈtɪvətɪ/ *n* créativité *f*.

creator /kriːˈeɪtə(r)/ *n* créateur/-trice *m/f* (**of** de).

creature /ˈkriːtʃə(r)/ *n* **1** (living being) créature *f*; (**the**) **poor ~!** le/la pauvre!; **2** (animal) animal *m*.

creature comforts *npl* confort *m* matériel **¢**; **to like one's ~** aimer son confort.

crèche /kreʃ, kreɪʃ/ *n* GB (nursery) crèche *f*; (in shop etc) garderie *f*; **workplace ~** crèche *f* d'entreprise.

credence /ˈkriːdns/ *n* SOUT crédit *m*; **to give ~ to sth** (believe) accorder du crédit à qch; **to lend ~ to sth** donner du crédit à qch.

credentials /krɪˈdenʃlz/ *npl* **1** (qualifications) qualifications *fpl*; **to establish one's ~ as a writer** s'affirmer comme écrivain; **2** pièce *f* d'identité.

credibility /ˌkredəˈbɪlətɪ/ *n* crédibilité *f*; **~ gap** écart *m* entre les apparences et la réalité.

credible /ˈkredəbl/ *adj* (all contexts) crédible.

credit /ˈkredɪt/ I *n* **1** (resultant praise) mérite *m* (**for** de); **to get/take the ~** se voir attribuer/s'attribuer le mérite (**for** de); **2** (subject of pride) **to be a ~ to sb/ sth** faire honneur à qn/qch; **it does you ~** c'est tout à votre honneur; **she has two medals to her ~** elle a deux médailles à son actif; **3** (recognition) **he is more intelligent than he is given ~ for** il est plus intelligent qu'on ne le croit généralement; **~ where ~ is due** il faut en convenir; **4** (credence) crédit *m*; **5** COMM crédit *m*; **on ~** à crédit; **to live on ~** vivre de crédits; **to give sb ~** faire crédit à qn; **her ~ is good** elle a une réputation de bonne payeuse; **to be £25 in ~** être créditeur de 25 livres sterling.
II **credits** *npl* CIN, TV générique *m*.
III *vtr* **1** **to ~ sb with** attribuer à qn [*achievement*]; **to ~ sb with a little intelligence** ne pas prendre qn pour un imbécile; **2** créditer [*account*] (**with** de); **to ~ sth to an account** porter qch sur un compte; **3** (believe) croire; **would you ~ it!** le croirais-tu!

creditable /ˈkredɪtəbl/ *adj* honorable.

credit: **~ account**, **C/A** *n* COMM compte *m* personnel; **~ balance** *n* solde *m* créditeur; **~ card** *n* COMM carte *f* de crédit; **~ control** *n* encadrement *m* du crédit; **~ facilities** *npl* facilités *fpl* de crédit; **~ freeze** *n* ECON gel *m* des crédits; **~ limit** *n* limite *f* de crédit; **~ line** *n* COMM ligne *f* de crédit; **~ note** *n* COMM avoir *m*.

creditor /ˈkredɪtə(r)/ *n* COMM créancier/-ière *m/f*.

credit side *n* **on the ~**... le bon côté des choses, c'est que...

credit: **~ squeeze** *n* ECON restrictions *fpl* de crédits; **~ terms** *npl* COMM conditions *fpl* de crédit; **~ transfer** *n* virement *m*.

creditworthiness /ˈkredɪtwɜːðɪnɪs/ *n* solvabilité *f*.

creditworthy /ˈkredɪtwɜːðɪ/ *adj* FIN solvable.

credulity /krɪˈdjuːlətɪ, US -ˈduː-/ *n* crédulité *f*; **to strain sb's ~** aller trop loin.

credulous /ˈkredjʊləs, US -dʒə-/ adj crédule, naïf/ naïve.

creed /kriːd/ n (religious persuasion) croyance f; (opinions) principes mpl, credo m.

creek /kriːk, US also krɪk/ n **1** GB (from sea) bras m de mer; (from river) bras m mort; **2** (stream) ruisseau m.
IDIOMS **to be up the ~ (without a paddle)**○ être mal barré○.

creep /kriːp/ I n○ **1** GB (flatterer) lèche-bottes○ mf inv; **2** (repellent person) raclure○ f.
II vi (prét, pp **crept**) **1** (furtively) **to ~ in/out** entrer/ sortir à pas de loup; **to ~ under sth** se glisser sous qch; **2** (slowly) **to ~ forward** ou **along** [vehicle] avancer lentement; [insect, cat] ramper; **3** [plant] (horizontally) ramper; (climb) grimper.
IDIOMS **to give sb the ~s**○ donner la chair de poule à qn○.
■ **creep in 1** [error] se glisser; **2** [feeling] intervenir.
■ **creep up** [inflation, unemployment] grimper; **to ~ up on sb** LIT s'approcher de qn à pas de loup; FIG prendre qn par surprise.

creeper /ˈkriːpə(r)/ n (in jungle) liane f; (climbing plant) plante f grimpante; **the ~** les plantes grimpantes.

creeping /ˈkriːpɪŋ/ adj [change, menace] insidieux/ -ieuse; [plant, animal] rampant.

creepy○ /ˈkriːpɪ/ adj [film] glaçant; [feeling] déplaisant; [person] affreux/-euse○.

creepy-crawly /ˌkriːpɪˈkrɔːlɪ/ n bestiole○ f.

cremate /krɪˈmeɪt/ vtr incinérer.

cremation /krɪˈmeɪʃn/ n (ceremony) crémation f; (practice) incinération f.

crematorium /ˌkreməˈtɔːrɪəm/ GB n crématorium m.

crepe, crêpe /kreɪp/ n (all contexts) crêpe m.

crepe: **~ bandage** n bande f Velpeau®; **~ paper** n papier m crépon; **~ soles** npl semelles fpl de crêpe.

crept /krept/ prét, pp ▶ **creep**.

crescendo /krɪˈʃendəʊ/ n MUS crescendo m inv; FIG **to reach a ~** [campaign] atteindre son apogée; [noise, protest] atteindre son paroxysme.

crescent /ˈkresnt/ n **1** (shape) croissant m; **2** rangée de maisons en arc de cercle.

crescent moon n croissant m de (la) lune.

cress /kres/ n cresson m.

crest /krest/ n **1** (ridge) crête f; **2** (coat of arms) armoiries fpl.

crested /ˈkrestɪd/ adj [bird] huppé; [stationery] armorié.
IDIOMS **to be on the ~ of a wave** être en période de réussite.

crestfallen /ˈkrestfɔːlən/ adj déconfit.

Crete /kriːt/ ▶ 1022 | pr n Crète f.

crevice /ˈkrevɪs/ n fissure f.

crew /kruː/ I prét ▶ **crow**.
II n **1** AVIAT, NAUT équipage m; **2** (rowing) équipe f; **3** CIN, TV équipe f; **4**○ PÉJ ou HUM (gang) bande f.
III vi NAUT **to ~ for sb** être l'équipier de qn.

crewcut n coupe f (de cheveux) en brosse.

crew neck sweater n pull m ras du cou.

crib /krɪb/ I n **1** (cot) lit m d'enfant; **2** GB (Nativity) crèche f; **3** (borrowing) emprunt m; **4** SCH (illicit aid) antisèche○ f; (translation) traduction f.
II vi (p prés etc **-bb-**) GEN faire des emprunts; SCH copier (**from** sur).

cribbage /ˈkrɪbɪdʒ/ n: jeu de cartes.

crick /krɪk/ I n a **~ in one's back** un tour de reins; **a ~ in one's neck** un torticolis.
II vtr **to ~ one's back** se faire un tour de reins; **to ~ one's neck** attraper un torticolis.

cricket /ˈkrɪkɪt/ ▶ 949 | n **1** ZOOL grillon m; **2** SPORT cricket m.
IDIOMS **it's not ~** ce n'est pas franc-jeu.

cricketer /ˈkrɪkɪtə(r)/ n joueur m de cricket.

crime /kraɪm/ n **1** (offence) (minor) délit m; (serious) crime m (**against** contre); **the ~ of murder/theft** meurtre/vol; **a ~ of violence** un crime violent; **2** ¢

(criminal activity) criminalité f; **3** FIG **it's a ~ to waste food** c'est un crime de gaspiller la nourriture.
II noun modifier [fiction, novel, writing] policier/-ière; [wave, rate] de criminalité.

crime: **~ of passion** n crime m passionnel; **~ prevention** n lutte f contre le crime.

criminal /ˈkrɪmɪnl/ I n criminel/-elle m/f.
II adj **1** criminel/-elle; **2** FIG **it's ~!** c'est un crime!

criminal charges npl charges fpl; **to face ~** être sous le coup d'une inculpation.

criminal: **~ inquiry** n enquête f criminelle; **Criminal Investigation Department, CID** n GB ≈ police f judiciaire; **~ justice** n justice f pénale; **~ law** n droit m pénal.

criminally insane adj dément; **to be ~** être en état de démence.

criminal: **~ offence** n délit m; **~ proceedings** npl poursuites fpl judiciaires.

criminal record n casier m judiciaire; **to have a/ no ~** avoir un casier judiciaire/vierge.

criminology /ˌkrɪmɪˈnɒlədʒɪ/ n criminologie f.

crimp /krɪmp/ vtr friser [hair]; pincer [pastry]; plisser [fabric].

crimson /ˈkrɪmzn/ ▶ 818 | I n cramoisi m.
II adj pourpre; **to go** ou **blush ~** devenir cramoisi.

cringe /krɪndʒ/ I vi **1** (physically) avoir un mouvement de recul; **2** (with embarrassment) avoir envie de rentrer sous terre; **3** (grovel) se comporter de manière servile; **4** (in disgust) **it makes me ~** ça me hérisse.
II cringing pres p adj servile.

crinkle /ˈkrɪŋkl/ I n pli m.
II vi [fabric] se froisser; [paper] se plisser.

crinkly /ˈkrɪŋklɪ/ adj [hair] frisé; [paper, material] gaufré.

cripple /ˈkrɪpl/ I n **1** (lame) INJUR impotent/-e m/f; **2** (inadequate) **emotional ~** personne f bloquée sur le plan émotionnel.
II vtr **1** (physically) estropier; **~d for life** infirme à vie; **2** FIG paralyser [country, industry]; désemparer [ship]; mettre [qch] hors d'usage [vehicle].

crippled /ˈkrɪpld/ adj **1** (physically) [person] impotent; **to be ~ with sth** être perclus de qch; **2** FIG (by debt) écrasé (**by** par); [country, industry] paralysé (**by** par); [vehicle] hors d'usage; [ship] désemparé.

crippling /ˈkrɪplɪŋ/ adj [disease] invalidant; [taxes, debts] écrasant; [strike, effect] paralysant.

crisis /ˈkraɪsɪs/ n (pl **-ses**) crise f (**in** dans; **over** à cause de); **cabinet/cash ~** crise au sein du gouvernement/de trésorerie; **midlife ~** crise des cinquante ans; **to be in ~**, **to have reached a ~** [people] être en crise; **to reach a ~** [situation] devenir critique; **at ~ level** à un niveau critique.

crisp /krɪsp/ I n GB (also **potato ~**) chip f.
II adj [batter, biscuit] croustillant; [fruit] croquant; [garment] frais/fraîche; [banknote, snow] craquant; [air] vif/vive; [morning] froid et piquant; [order, words] bref/brève; [manner] brusque.
IDIOMS **to be burnt to a ~**○ être carbonisé.

crispbread /ˈkrɪspbred/ n GB pain m grillé suédois.

crisply /ˈkrɪsplɪ/ adv [ironed] fraîchement; [speak] brusquement.

crispy /ˈkrɪspɪ/ adj croustillant.

crisscross /ˈkrɪskrɒs, US -krɔːs/ I adj en croisillons.
II adv en croisillons; **to run ~** s'entrecroiser.
III vtr sillonner.

criteria /kraɪˈtɪərɪə/ npl ▶ **criterion**.

criterion /kraɪˈtɪərɪən/ n (pl **-ia**) critère m (**for** de).

critic /ˈkrɪtɪk/ ▶ 1251 | n (reviewer) critique m; (opponent) détracteur/-trice m/f.

critical /ˈkrɪtɪkl/ adj [point, condition, remark] critique; [stage] crucial; [moment] décisif/-ive; [acclaim] de la critique; **to be ~ of sb/sth** critiquer qn/ qch; **the film was a ~ success** le film a été acclamé par la critique; **to take a ~ look at sth** examiner qch d'un œil critique.

critically /ˈkrɪtɪklɪ/ adv **1** (using judgment) [compare, *examine*] d'un œil critique; **2** (with disapproval) [*view*] sévèrement; [*speak*] avec animosité (**of, about** de); **3** (seriously) [*ill*] très gravement; **~ important** capital; **~ flawed** profondément vicié.

criticism /'krɪtɪsɪzəm/ *n* **1 C** (remark, reproach) critique *f*; **2 C** (study) étude *f* critique (**of** sur); **3 ¢** (analysis) critique *f*; **literary ~** critique *f* littéraire.

criticize /'krɪtɪsaɪz/ *vtr* **1** (find fault) critiquer; **to ~ sb for sth** reprocher qch à qn; **to ~ sb for doing** reprocher à qn de faire; **2** critiquer [*poem etc*].

croak /krəʊk/ **I** *n* (of frog) coassement *m*.
II *vtr* dire [qch] d'une voix rauque.
III *vi* **1** (frog) coasser; **2**⁰ (die) crever⁰.

Croatia /krəʊˈeɪʃə/ ▶ 840 | *pr n* Croatie *f*.

crochet /'krəʊʃeɪ, ʊs krəʊˈʃeɪ/ **I** *n* (art) crochet *m*.
II *vtr* faire [qch] au crochet; **a ~(ed) sweater** un pull au crochet.
III *vi* faire du crochet.

crock /krɒk/ *n* **1**⁰ (car) tacot⁰ *m*; (person) croulant/-e⁰ *m*/*f*; **2** (shard) tesson *m*.

crockery /'krɒkərɪ/ *n* vaisselle *f*.

crocodile /'krɒkədaɪl/ **I** *n* **1** (animal, leather) crocodile *m*; **2** GB (line) rang *m* par deux.
II *noun modifier* [*bag*] en crocodile, en croco⁰.
IDIOMS **to shed ~ tears** verser des larmes de crocodile.

croft /krɒft, ʊs krɔːft/ *n* petite ferme *f* (*en Écosse*).

crone /krəʊn/ *n* PÉJ vieille bique *f* PÉJ.

crony /'krəʊnɪ/ *n* PÉJ (petit/-e) copain/copine *m*/*f*.

crook /krʊk/ *n* (rogue) escroc *m*; (of arm) creux *m*; (shepherd's) houlette *f*; (bishop's) crosse *f*.
IDIOMS **by hook or by ~** coûte que coûte; **to ~ one's little finger** lever le petit doigt.

crooked /'krʊkɪd/ **I** *adj* **1** (with a bend) [*line*] brisé; [*limb*] tors; [*back*] difforme; [*stick, finger*] crochu; **a ~ smile** un sourire en coin; **2** (off-centre) de travers; [*house*] de guingois *inv*; **3**⁰ (dishonest) malhonnête.
II *adv* de travers.

croon /kruːn/ *vtr, vi* chantonner.

crop /krɒp/ **I** *n* **1** (type of produce) culture *f*; **a cereal ~** une culture céréalière; **2** (growing in field) (*souvent pl*) culture *f*; **the ~s will fail** les cultures seront perdues; **3** (harvest) récolte *f*; **the rice ~** la récolte de riz; **4** FIG (of medals) moisson *f*; (of students, films) cuvée *f*; **the cream of the ~** les meilleurs du lot; **5** FIG HUM (of weeds, spots) paquet⁰ *m*; **6** (haircut) coupe *f* courte; **7** (whip) cravache *f*.
II *vtr* (*p prés etc* **-pp-**) couper [qch] court [*hair*]; brouter [*grass*]; rogner [*photograph*].
■ **crop up** [*matter, problem*] surgir; [*name*] être mentionné; [*opportunity*] se présenter; **something's ~ped up** il y a un contretemps.

cropped /krɒpt/ *adj* [*hair*] coupé court; [*top*] court.

crop: **~ rotation** *n* rotation *f* des cultures; **~ spraying** *n* pulvérisation *f* de pesticides.

croquet /'krəʊkeɪ, ʊs krəʊˈkeɪ/ ▶ 949 | *n* croquet *m*.

cross /krɒs, ʊs krɔːs/ **I** *n* **1** (shape) croix *f*; **the Cross** RELIG la Croix; **to put a ~ against** cocher [*name, item*]; **'put a ~ in the box'** 'faites une croix dans la case', 'cochez la case'; **2** (hybrid) croisement *m* (**between** entre); **a ~ between X and Y** FIG un mélange de X et de Y; **3** (in sewing) **on the ~** dans le biais.
II *adj* **1** (angry) fâché; **to be ~ with sb** être fâché contre qn; **to be ~ about sth** être agacé par qch; **to get ~** se fâcher (**with** contre); **to make sb ~** mettre qn en colère, agacer qn; **2** (contrary to general direction) [*breeze*] contraire.
III *vtr* **1** (go across by moving) LIT traverser [*road, room*]; traverser, passer [*river*]; franchir [*border, line, mountains*]; (span) [*bridge*] franchir, enjamber; (have route across) [*road, railway line, river*] traverser; FIG dépasser [*limit, boundary*]; **it ~ed his mind that** il lui est venu à l'esprit or l'idée que; **to ~ the class divide** surmonter la barrière des classes; **to ~ the bounds of decency** dépasser les limites de la décence; **2** (intersect with) couper; **to ~ each other** se couper;

3 (place in shape of a cross) croiser; **to ~ one's legs/arms** croiser les jambes/bras; **4** BIOL, BOT, ZOOL croiser (**with** avec); **5** (oppose) contrarier [*person*]; **6** (draw line across) barrer [*cheque*].
IV *vi* **1** (also **~ over**) **to ~ to North America** aller en Amérique; **to ~ into Italy** passer en Italie; **2** (intersect) se croiser; [*lines*] se couper; **3** [*letters*] se croiser.
V *v refl* **to ~ oneself** faire le signe de la croix.
VI crossed *pp adj* TELECOM [*line*] brouillé.
IDIOMS **we seem to have got our wires ~ed** il semble y avoir un malentendu (quelque part); **to have a** ou **one's ~ to bear** porter sa croix.
■ **cross off**: **~ [sth/sb] off**, **~ off [sth/sb]** barrer, rayer [*name, thing*].
■ **cross out**: **~ out [sth]**, **~ [sth] out** rayer, barrer [qch].

cross: **~bar** *n* GEN barre *f*; **~-border** *adj* transfrontalier/-ière; **~bow** *n* arbalète *f*; **~bred** *n*, *adj* hybride (*m*).

crossbreed /'krɒsbriːd, ʊs krɔːs-/ **I** *n* (animal) hybride *m*; (person) INJUR métis/-isse *m*/*f*.
II *vtr* (*prét, pp* **-bred**) croiser [*animals*]; hybrider [*plants*].

cross-Channel *adj* trans-Manche.

cross-check I /'krɒstʃek, ʊs krɔːs-/ *n* revérification *f*.
II /ˌkrɒsˈtʃek, ʊs ˌkrɔːs-/ *vtr, vi* revérifier.

cross-country /ˌkrɒsˈkʌntrɪ, ʊs ˌkrɔːs-/ **I** ▶ 949 | *n* SPORT (in running) cross *m*; (in skiing) ski *m* de fond.
II *adj* **1** SPORT (running) [*race, champion*] de cross; [*runner*] de fond; (skiing) [*skiing, skier*] de fond; **2** (across fields) [*hike, run*] à travers champs; **3** (across a country) [*route*] qui traverse le pays.
III *adv* [*walk, hike*] à travers champs.

cross: **~-court** *adj* SPORT [*shot, volley*] droit croisé; **~-cultural** *adj* inter-culturel/-elle; **~current** *n* contre-courant *m*; **~-curricular** *adj* multidisciplinaire; **~-dresser** *n* travesti/-e *m*/*f*; **~-examination** *n* contre-interrogatoire *m*.

cross-examine /ˌkrɒsɪgˈzæmɪn, ʊs ˌkrɔːs-/ *vtr* JUR faire subir un contre-interrogatoire à; GEN interroger.

cross-eyed /'krɒsaɪd, ʊs krɔːs-/ *adj* [*person*] atteint de strabisme; **to be ~** loucher, avoir un strabisme.

crossfire /'krɒsfaɪə(r), ʊs krɔːs-/ *n* feux *mpl* croisés; **to be** ou **get caught in the ~** LIT, FIG être pris entre deux feux.

crossing /'krɒsɪŋ, ʊs krɔːsɪŋ/ *n* **1** (journey over water) traversée *f*; **2** (area of road) passage *m* (pour) piétons, passage *m* clouté; (level crossing) passage *m* à niveau.

crossing-out /ˌkrɒsɪŋˈaʊt, ʊs ˌkrɔːs-/ *n* (*pl* **~s-out**) rature *f*.

cross-legged /ˌkrɒsˈlegɪd, ʊs ˌkrɔːs-/ **I** *adj* assis en tailleur.
II *adv* [*sit*] en tailleur.

crossly /'krɒslɪ, ʊs krɔːslɪ/ *adv* avec humeur.

crossover /'krɒsəʊvə(r), ʊs krɔːs-/ *adj* [*straps*] croisé.

cross: **~-party** *adj* POL [*initiative*] commun à plusieurs partis; [*group*] comprenant des membres de différents partis; **~patch**⁰ *n* grognon⁰ *mf*.

cross-purposes /ˌkrɒsˈpɜːpəsɪz, ʊs ˌkrɔːs-/ *npl* **we are at ~** il y a un malentendu; (disagreement) nous sommes en désaccord; **to be at ~** se comprendre mal.

cross-question /ˌkrɒsˈkwestʃən, ʊs ˌkrɔːs-/ *vtr* faire subir un interrogatoire à [*person*].

cross-reference /ˌkrɒsˈrefrəns, ʊs ˌkrɔːs-/ **I** *n* renvoi *m* (**to** à).
II *vtr* mettre un renvoi sous [*entry, item*] (**to** à).

crossroads /'krɒsrəʊdz, ʊs krɔːs-/ *n* carrefour *m*.

cross-section /ˌkrɒsˈsekʃn, ʊs ˌkrɔːs-/ *n* **1** LIT coupe *f* transversale; **2** FIG (selection) échantillon *m* (**of** de).

cross: **~-town** *adj* ʊs qui traverse la ville; **~wind** *n* vent *m* de travers.

crosswise /'krɒswaɪz, ʊs krɔːs-/ *adj, adv* en diagonale.

crossword /'krɒswɜːd, ʊs krɔːs-/ *n* (also **~ puzzle**) mots *mpl* croisés.

crotch /krɒtʃ/ n **1** ANAT entrecuisse m; **2** (in trousers) entrejambe m.

crotchet /'krɒtʃɪt/ n GB MUS noire f.

crotchety /'krɒtʃɪtɪ/ adj grincheux/-euse.

crouch /kraʊtʃ/ vi (also ~ **down**) [person] s'accroupir; [person, animal] (in order to hide) se tapir; (for attack) se ramasser.

croupier /'kru:pɪə(r)/ ▶1251 n croupier m.

crouton /'kru:tɒn/ n croûton m.

crow /krəʊ/ I n corbeau m.
II vi **1** (exult) exulter; **it's nothing to ~ about** il n'y a pas de quoi exulter; **2** [baby] gazouiller; **3** (prét **crowed** ou **crew†**) [cock] chanter.
IDIOMS **as the ~ flies** à vol d'oiseau.

crowbar /'krəʊbɑ:(r)/ n pince-monseigneur f.

crowd /kraʊd/ I n **1** (mass of people) GEN foule f; SPORT spectateurs mpl; (audience) public m; **a ~ of 10,000** GEN une foule de 10 000 personnes; SPORT une foule de 10 000 spectateurs; **~s of people** une foule de gens; **a ~ gathered at the scene** un attroupement s'est formé sur les lieux; **we are hoping for a big ~** nous espérons que le public viendra nombreux; **2**° (group) bande f; **the usual ~** toujours la même bande.
II vtr **1** (fill) se presser sur [pavement, platform]; s'entasser sur [beach]; **tourists ~ed the bars** les bars étaient pleins de touristes; **2** (squash) entasser [people, furniture] (**into** dans); **to ~ as much as possible into a visit to Paris** voir le plus de choses possible quand on est à Paris; **3** (fill to excess) encombrer [room, house] (**with** de); **4**° (put pressure on) harceler; **don't ~ me!** arrête de me harceler!
III vi LIT **to ~ into** s'entasser dans [room, lift, vehicle]; **to ~ onto** s'entasser dans [bus, train]; **to ~ (up) against** se presser contre [barrier].
■ **crowd around, crowd round**: ¶ ~ **around** s'attrouper; ¶ ~ **around** [sth] se presser autour de.
■ **crowd in**: ~ **in** [people, animals] s'entasser; [thoughts, memories] se presser.

crowd control n contrôle m de la foule.

crowded /'kraʊdɪd/ adj **1** (place) plein de monde; (jampacked) bondé; **to be ~ with** être plein de [people, cars]; **2** (busy) [schedule] chargé.

crowd: **~-puller** n (event) grosse attraction f; **~ scene** n CIN, THEAT scène f de foule.

crowing /'krəʊɪŋ/ n **1** (of cock) cocoricos mpl; **2** (boasting) vantardises fpl.

crown /kraʊn/ I n **1** (of monarch) couronne f; **the Crown** la Couronne f; **2** (top) (of hill) crête f; (of hat) fond m; (of head) crâne m; **3** (on tooth) couronne f; **4** GB (old coin) ancienne pièce de monnaie.
II vtr **1** couronner; **to ~ sb emperor** couronner qn empereur; **2** (bring to worthy end) couronner; **to ~ it all** pour couronner le tout; **3** couronner [tooth].

crown: **~ colony** n GB POL colonie f britannique; **Crown court** n GB JUR ~ cour f d'assises; **~ed head** n POL tête f couronnée.

crowning /'kraʊnɪŋ/ I n couronnement m.
II adj [irony] suprême; [moment] grand; **~ achievement** (of artist etc) chef d'œuvre m.

crowning glory n **1** (achievement) couronnement m; **2** (hair) **her hair is her ~** sa chevelure la rend resplendissante.

crown: **~ jewels** npl joyaux mpl de la Couronne; **~ prince** n prince m héritier.

crow: **~'s feet** npl (on face) pattes-d'oie fpl; **~'s nest** n nid m de pie.

crucial /'kru:ʃl/ adj crucial; **it is ~ that** il est essentiel que (+ subj).

crucially /'kru:ʃəlɪ/ adv **~ important** d'une importance cruciale.

crucifix /'kru:sɪfɪks/ n crucifix m.

crucifixion /ˌkru:sɪ'fɪkʃn/ n crucifixion f.

crucify /'kru:sɪfaɪ/ vtr **1** (execute) crucifier; **2**° (criticize, defeat) démolir°.

crude /kru:d/ I n (oil) pétrole m brut.
II adj **1** (rough) [method] rudimentaire; [estimate]

approximatif/-ive; **2** (coarse) [person, manners] fruste; [attempt, expression] grossier/-ière; **3** (vulgar, rude) [language, joke] grossier/-ière; [person] vulgaire; **4** (unprocessed) [rubber, statistic] brut; **~ oil** pétrole m brut.

crudely /'kru:dlɪ/ adv **1** (simply) [describe, express] de manière schématique; **~ speaking,...** grosso modo...; **2** (roughly) [painted, made] grossièrement; [assembled] sommairement.

crudity /'kru:dɪtɪ/ n (vulgarity) grossièreté f.

cruel /'kru:əl/ adj cruel/-elle; [winter, climate] rigoureux/-euse; **a ~ blow** un coup très dur.
IDIOMS **you have to be ~ to be kind** qui aime bien châtie bien PROV.

cruelly /'kru:əlɪ/ adv cruellement.

cruelty /'kru:əltɪ/ n cruauté f (**to** envers).

cruet /'kru:ɪt/ n GB (also **~ stand**) service m à condiments.

cruise /kru:z/ I n croisière f; **to go on a ~** faire une croisière.
II vtr **1 to ~ the Nile/the Mediterranean** [tourist] faire une croisière sur le Nil/en Méditerranée; **2** [driver, taxi] parcourir [street, city].
III vi **1** [liner, tourist] faire une croisière (**in** en; **on** sur; **along** le long de; **around** aux abords de); **2** [plane] **to ~ at 10,000 metres** voler à une altitude de croisière de 10 000 mètres; **3** [car] **to ~ at 80 km/h** rouler à une vitesse de croisière de 80 km/h; **4**° **to ~ to victory** triompher sans peine.

cruise: **~ liner** n paquebot m; **~ missile** n missile m de croisière.

cruiser /'kru:zə(r)/ n petit bateau m de croisière.

cruising speed n vitesse f de croisière.

crumb /krʌm/ n **1** (of food) miette f; **2** (tiny amount) **a ~ of** une bribe de [information, conversation]; **a ~ of comfort** une maigre consolation.

crumble /'krʌmbl/ I vtr (also **~ up**) émietter [bread]; réduire [qch] en poussière [soil].
II vi **1** LIT [rock, façade] s'effriter; [building] se délabrer; [cliff] s'ébouler; **2** FIG [relationship, economy] se désagréger; [empire] s'écrouler; [opposition] s'effondrer.

crumbling /'krʌmblɪŋ/ adj **1** LIT [building, façade] délabré; **2** [economy, empire] prêt à s'effondrer.

crumbly /'krʌmblɪ/ adj [bread, cheese] qui s'émiette facilement; [pastry, earth] friable.

crummy° /'krʌmɪ/ adj **1** (substandard) minable°; **2** US (unwell) **to feel ~** se sentir patraque°.

crumpet /'krʌmpɪt/ n CULIN petit pain spongieux à griller.

crumple /'krʌmpl/ I vtr froisser [paper]; **to ~ sth into a ball** rouler qch en boule.
II vi **1** (crush up) [paper, garment] se froisser; **his face ~d** ses traits se sont décomposés; **the car ~s on impact** la voiture se plie sous le choc; **2** (collapse) [opposition, resistance] s'effondrer.
■ **crumple up**: ~ [sth] **up**, ~ **up** [sth] froisser.

crunch /krʌntʃ/ I n **1** (sound) (of footsteps) crissement m; (of gears, bone) craquement m; **2** US ECON (squeeze) crise f.
II vtr **1** (eat) croquer [apple, biscuit]; **2** (making noise) **she ~ed her way across the gravel** le gravier crissait sous ses pas.
IDIOMS **when** ou **if it comes to the ~** au moment crucial; **the ~ came when** le moment critique est arrivé lorsque.

crunchy /'krʌntʃɪ/ adj [vegetables, biscuits] croquant.

crusade /kru:'seɪd/ I n **1** (also **Crusade**) HIST croisade f; **2** (campaign) croisade f.
II vi (campaign) entrer en croisade.

crusader /kru:'seɪdə(r)/ n **1** HIST croisé m; **2** (campaigner) militant/-e m/f (**for** pour).

crusading /kru:'seɪdɪŋ/ adj combatif/-ive.

crush /krʌʃ/ I n **1** (crowd) bousculade f; **2** GB (drink) **orange/lemon ~** boisson f à l'orange/au citron.
II vtr **1** FIG écraser [enemy, uprising]; étouffer [protest]; anéantir [hopes]; (by ridicule) anéantir [person]; **to be ~ed by** être accablé par [sorrow, defeat]; **2**

(squash) écraser [*can, fruit, person, vehicle*] (**against** contre); broyer [*part of body*]; **to be ~ed to death** (by vehicle) se faire écraser; (by masonry) être écrasé sous les décombres; **3** (crease) chiffonner [*garment, fabric*].

crush: ~ **bar** *n* GB bar *m* (*de théâtre*); ~ **barrier** *n* GB barrière *f* de sécurité; **~ed ice** *n* glace *f* pilée; **~ed velvet** *n* velours *m* frappé.

crushing /ˈkrʌʃɪŋ/ *adj* [*defeat, weight*] écrasant; [*blow*] percutant; **a ~ setback** un revers cuisant.

crust /krʌst/ *n* croûte *f*; **the earth's ~** l'écorce *f* terrestre; **he'd share his last ~** il donnerait sa chemise.

crustacean /krʌˈsteɪʃn/ *n* crustacé *m*.

crusty /ˈkrʌsti/ *adj* **1** [*bread*] croustillant; **2** (irritable) grincheux/-euse.

crutch /krʌtʃ/ *n* **1** (prop) LIT, FIG béquille *f*; **to be on ~es** marcher avec des béquilles; **2** GB (crotch) ANAT entrecuisse *m*; (in trousers) entrejambe *m*.

crux /krʌks/ *n* **the ~ of the matter** ou **problem** le point crucial.

cry /kraɪ/ I *n* **1** (of person, bird) cri *m*; **nobody heard his cries for help** personne ne l'a entendu crier au secours; **a ~ for help** FIG un appel à l'aide; **there were cries of 'shame!'** les gens criaient au scandale; **there have been cries for reprisals** on a réclamé des représailles; **2** (of hounds) **to be in full ~** [*pack*] donner de la voix; **the press were in full ~** FIG la presse était sur la brèche.
II *vtr* **1** (shout) **'no!' he cried** 'non!' cria-t-il; **2** verser [*larmes*].
III *vi* **1** (weep) pleurer (**about** à cause de; **with** de); **he was ~ing for his mother** il réclamait sa mère en pleurant; **to ~ with laughter** rire aux larmes; **2** (call out) = **cry out**.
IDIOMS **it's a far ~ from the days when** il est loin le temps où; **this house is a far ~ from our last one** cette maison est sans comparaison avec celle que nous avions avant; **to ~ one's eyes** ou **heart out** pleurer à chaudes larmes.
■ **cry off** GB: (cancel) se décommander.
■ **cry out** (with pain, grief) pousser un cri ou des cris; (call) crier, s'écrier; **to ~ out to sb** interpeller qn; **to ~ out for** (need) avoir grand besoin de [*help, reform*].

crying /ˈkraɪɪŋ/ I *n* ¢ pleurs *mpl*.
II *adj* (blatant) [*need*] urgent; **it's a ~ shame!** c'est une honte!

crypt /krɪpt/ *n* crypte *f*.

cryptic /ˈkrɪptɪk/ *adj* (mysterious) énigmatique.

cryptically /ˈkrɪptɪklɪ/ *adv* [*say, speak*] de façon énigmatique; **~ worded** en termes sibyllins.

crystal /ˈkrɪstl/ *n* cristal *m*; (watchface) verre *m*.
IDIOMS **as clear as ~** [*sound*] cristallin; [*explanation*] clair comme de l'eau de roche.

crystal ball *n* boule *f* de cristal; **to look into one's ~** FIG essayer de deviner l'avenir.

crystal clear *adj* **1** [*water, sound*] cristallin; **2** [*explanation*] clair comme de l'eau de roche; **let me make it ~** que cela soit bien clair.

crystal gazing *n* tentatives *fpl* pour prévoir l'avenir.

crystallize /ˈkrɪstəlaɪz/ I *vtr* FIG déterminer [*attitude*]; cristalliser [*divisions*].
II *vi* **1** LIT se cristalliser; **2** FIG [*ideas*] se concrétiser.
III **crystallized** *pp adj* [*fruit, ginger*] confit.

CS gas *n* GB gaz *m* lacrymogène.

CT US POST *abrév écrite* = **Connecticut**.

cub /kʌb/ *n* ZOOL petit *m*.

Cuba /ˈkjuːbə/ ▶ 840 *pr n* Cuba *f* (*never with article*).

cubby-hole /ˈkʌbɪhəʊl/ *n* **1** (cramped space) réduit *m*; (snug room) piaule° *f*; **2** (storage space) cagibi° *m*.

cube /kjuːb/ I *n* cube *m*; **sugar ~** sucre *m*; **ice ~** glaçon *m*.
II *vtr* **1** MATH élever [qch] au cube; **2** CULIN couper [qch] en cubes.

cubic /ˈkjuːbɪk/ ▶ 1381 , 789 *adj* **1** (form) cubique; **2** (measurement) [*metre, centimetre*] cube *inv*.

cubicle /ˈkjuːbɪkl/ *n* (in changing room) cabine *f*; (in public toilets) cabinet *m*.

cubism /ˈkjuːbɪzəm/ *n* cubisme *m*.

cubist /ˈkjuːbɪst/ *n, adj* cubiste (*mf*).

cub reporter ▶ 1251 *n* journaliste *mf* stagiaire.

cuckoo /ˈkʊkuː/ *n* coucou *m*.

cuckoo clock *n* pendule *f* à coucou.

cucumber /ˈkjuːkʌmbə(r)/ *n* concombre *m*.
IDIOMS **to be as cool as a ~** être d'un calme absolu.

cud /kʌd/ *n* **to chew the ~** LIT, FIG ruminer.

cuddle /ˈkʌdl/ I *n* câlin *m*; **to give sb a ~** faire un câlin à qn.
II *vtr* câliner.
■ **cuddle up** se blottir (**against** contre).

cuddly /ˈkʌdlɪ/ *adj* (sweet) adorable; (soft) doux/douce.

cuddly toy *n* GB peluche *f*.

cue /kjuː/ *n* **1** LIT THEAT (line) réplique *f* précédente; (action) signal *m*; TV, RADIO, CIN signal *m*; **on ~** (after word) après la réplique; (after action) après le signal; FIG à point nommé; **to take one's ~ from sb** FIG faire comme qn; **2** SPORT queue *f* de billard.

cuff /kʌf/ I *n* **1** (at wrist) GEN poignet *m*; (on shirt) manchette *f*; **2** US (on trousers) revers *m*; **3** (blow) tape *f*.
II *vtr* (on head) calotter°.
IDIOMS **to speak off the ~** faire un discours au pied levé; **an off-the-~ remark** une remarque impromptu.

cuff link *n* bouton *m* de manchette.

cuisine /kwɪˈziːn/ *n* cuisine *f*; **haute ~** la grande cuisine.

cul-de-sac /ˈkʌldəsæk/ *n* (street) impasse *f*, cul-de-sac *m*; (on roadsign) voie *f* sans issue.

culinary /ˈkʌlɪnərɪ, US -nerɪ/ *adj* culinaire.

cull /kʌl/ *vtr* **1** (kill) massacrer [*seal, whale*]; **2** (gather) puiser [*information*] (**from sth** dans qch).

culminate /ˈkʌlmɪneɪt/ *vtr* aboutir (**in** à).

culmination /ˌkʌlmɪˈneɪʃn/ *n* couronnement *m* (**of** de).

culottes /kjuːˈlɒts/ *npl* jupe-culotte *f*.

culpable /ˈkʌlpəbl/ *adj* coupable (**for** de).

culpable homicide *n* JUR homicide *m* volontaire.

culprit /ˈkʌlprɪt/ *n* **1** (guilty person) coupable *mf*; **2** (main cause) principal-e responsable *mf*.

cult /kʌlt/ I *n* culte *m*; (contemporary religion) secte *f*.
II *noun modifier* **a ~ band/film** un groupe-/film-culte; **to be a ~ figure** faire l'objet d'un culte.

cultivate /ˈkʌltɪveɪt/ *vtr* **1** LIT cultiver; **2** FIG **to ~ one's image** cultiver son image; **to ~ one's mind** se cultiver l'esprit; **to ~ the right people** cultiver de bonnes relations.

cultivation /ˌkʌltɪˈveɪʃn/ *n* AGRIC culture *f*.

cultural /ˈkʌltʃərəl/ *adj* culturel/-elle.

cultural attaché ▶ 1251 *n* attaché-e *m/f* culturel/-elle.

culturally /ˈkʌltʃərəlɪ/ *adv* [*similar, different*] culturellement; **~ diverse** qui présente une variété de cultures.

culture /ˈkʌltʃə(r)/ *n* **1** ¢ (art and thought) culture *f*; **to bring ~ to the masses** mettre la culture à la portée de tous; **2** (way of life) culture *f*; **street ~** culture qui vient de la rue; **drug ~** l'univers *m* de la drogue; **3** (cultivation) culture *f*; **4** (of bacteria) culture *f* (bactérienne).

culture-bound /ˈkʌltʃəbaʊnd/ *adj* culturel/-elle.

cultured /ˈkʌltʃəd/ *adj* cultivé.

cultured pearl *n* perle *f* de culture.

culture: ~ shock *n* choc *m* culturel; **~ vulture**° *n* fana *mf* de culture°.

culvert /ˈkʌlvət/ *n* conduite *f* souterraine.

-cum- /kʌm/ *combining form* **garage~workshop** garage-atelier *m*; **gardener~handyman** jardinier-homme *m* à tout faire.

cumbersome /ˈkʌmbəsəm/ *adj* [*luggage, furniture*] encombrant; [*method, phrase*] lourd.

cummerbund /ˈkʌməbʌnd/ n large ceinture f (d'habit de soirée ou de costume hindou).

cumulative /ˈkjuːmjʊlətɪv, US -leɪtɪv/ adj cumulatif/-ive.

cunning /ˈkʌnɪŋ/ I n 1 PÉJ (of person) ruse f; (nastier) fourberie f; (of animal) ruse f; **native ~** débrouillardise f naturelle.
II adj 1 PÉJ [person] rusé; (nastier) fourbe; [animal] rusé; **he's a ~ old fox** c'est un vieux renard; 2 (clever) [trick, plot] habile; [device] astucieux/-ieuse.

cunningly /ˈkʌnɪŋlɪ/ adv [devised] astucieusement; [fashioned] ingénieusement.

cup /kʌp/ I n 1 (object, contents) tasse f; **a ~ of tea** une tasse de thé; 2 SPORT coupe f; 3 (in bra) bonnet m; 4 (of flower) corolle f.
II vtr (p prés etc **-pp-**) **to ~ sth in one's hands** prendre qch dans le creux de ses mains [butterfly, water]; **to ~ one's hands around** entourer [qch] de ses mains [insect]; mettre ses mains en paravent autour de [flame, match]; **to ~ one's hand over** couvrir [qch] de sa main [receiver]; **in one's ~ped hand** dans le creux de sa main.

cupboard /ˈkʌbəd/ n placard m.
IDIOMS **the ~ is bare** les caisses sont vides.

cupboard love n GB HUM amour m intéressé.

cupboard space n espace m de rangement.

cupful /ˈkʌpfʊl/ n tasse f (**of** de).

cupid /ˈkjuːpɪd/ n ART amour m.

Cupid /ˈkjuːpɪd/ pr n Cupidon.

cupola /ˈkjuːpələ/ n ARCHIT coupole f.

cup tie n GB match m de coupe.

cur /kɜː(r)/ n PÉJ (dog) corniaud m.

curable /ˈkjʊərəbl/ adj guérissable.

curate /ˈkjʊərət/ n vicaire m.
IDIOMS **it's like the ~'s egg** tout n'est pas mauvais.

curator /kjʊəˈreɪtə(r), US also ˈkjʊərətər/ ▶1251 n (of museum, gallery) conservateur/-trice m/f.

curb /kɜːb/ I n 1 (control) restriction f (**on** à); 2 US (sidewalk) bord m du trottoir.
II vtr 1 (control) refréner [desires]; limiter [powers, influence]; juguler [spending]; restreindre [consumption]; **to ~ one's temper** se dominer; 2 US **~ your dog!** apprenez le caniveau à votre chien!

curd cheese n fromage m blanc (lait caillé égoutté).

curdle /ˈkɜːdl/ vi [milk] se cailler; [sauce] tourner.

cure /ˈkjʊə(r)/ I n (remedy) remède m (**for** à); (for illness) traitement m (**for** pour).
II vtr 1 guérir [disease, patient] (**of** de); 2 FIG guérir [bad habit, person] (**of** de); remédier à [inflation]; 3 CULIN (dry) sécher; (salt) saler; (smoke) fumer.

cure-all /ˈkjʊərɔːl/ n panacée f (**for** contre).

curfew /ˈkɜːfjuː/ n couvre-feu m; **ten o'clock ~** couvre-feu à partir de dix heures.

curing /ˈkjʊərɪŋ/ n CULIN (drying) séchage m; (salting) salaison f; (smoking) fumage m.

curio /ˈkjʊərɪəʊ/ n curiosité f, objet m rare.

curiosity /ˌkjʊərɪˈɒsətɪ/ n 1 (desire to know, nosiness) curiosité f (**about** sur, au sujet de); **out of** (idle) **~** par (simple) curiosité; 2 (person) original/-e m/f; 3 (object) curiosité f.
IDIOMS **~ killed the cat** Prov la curiosité est un vilain défaut.

curious /ˈkjʊərɪəs/ adj 1 (interested, nosy) curieux/-ieuse; **~ to know** curieux de savoir; **to be ~ about sth** éprouver de la curiosité au sujet de qch; **I'm just ~!** j'aurais aimé savoir, c'est tout!; 2 (odd) [person, case, effect] curieux/-ieuse; [place, phenomenon] étrange.

curiously /ˈkjʊərɪəslɪ/ adv 1 (oddly) [silent, detached] étrangement; **~ shaped** d'une forme bizarre; **~ enough,...** chose assez curieuse,...; 2 [ask] avec curiosité.

curl /kɜːl/ I n 1 (of hair) boucle f; 2 (of smoke) volute f; **with a ~ of one's lip** avec une moue dédaigneuse.
II vtr 1 friser [hair]; 2 (wind, coil) **to ~ one's fingers around sth** [person] saisir qch; **to ~ itself around**

sth [snake, caterpillar] s'enrouler autour de qch; **to ~ one's lip** [person] faire une moue dédaigneuse.
III vi [hair] friser; [paper] (se) gondoler; [edges, corner, leaf] se racornir; **smoke ~ed upwards** la fumée montait en volutes.
IDIOMS **to make sb's hair ~°** (in shock) faire dresser les cheveux sur la tête de qn.
■ **curl up** [person] se pelotonner; [cat] se mettre en rond; [paper] (se) gondoler; [edges, corner, leaf] se racornir; **to ~ up in bed** se blottir dans son lit; **to ~ up into a ball** [person] se recroqueviller; [hedgehog] se mettre en boule; **to ~ up at the edges** [photo, paper] (se) gondoler.

curler /ˈkɜːlə(r)/ n (roller) bigoudi m.

curling /ˈkɜːlɪŋ/ ▶949 n SPORT curling m.

curly /ˈkɜːlɪ/ adj [hair] (tight curls) frisé; (loose curls) bouclé; [tail, eyelashes] recourbé.

curly-haired /ˌkɜːlɪˈheəd/, **curly-headed** /ˌkɜːlɪˈhedɪd/ adj (tight curls) frisé; (loose curls) bouclé.

currant /ˈkʌrənt/ I n raisin m de Corinthe.
II noun modifier **~ bun ~** brioche f aux raisins; **~ loaf ~** pain m brioché aux raisins.

currency /ˈkʌrənsɪ/ ▶849 n 1 FIN monnaie f, devise f; **the ~ of Poland** la monnaie polonaise; **to buy foreign ~** acheter des devises étrangères; **have you any German ~?** avez-vous de l'argent allemand?; **~ market** marché m monétaire; 2 (of term) fréquence f; (of idea) crédibilité f; **to gain ~** [term] devenir courant; [idea, opinion] se répandre.

current /ˈkʌrənt/ I n 1 (of electricity, water) courant m; (of air) flux m; (trend) tendance f.
II adj 1 (present) [leader, crisis, situation, policy, value] actuel/-elle; [developments, year, research] en cours; 2 (in common use) [term, word] usité; **in ~ use** usité.

current~: ~ account n GB compte m courant; **~ affairs** n (+ v sg) actualité f.

currently /ˈkʌrəntlɪ/ adv actuellement, en ce moment.

curriculum /kəˈrɪkjʊləm/ n (pl **-lums** ou **-la**) SCH programme m; **in the ~** au programme.

curriculum~: ~ development n SCH développement m des programmes; **~ vitae, CV** n curriculum vitae m, CV m.

curry /ˈkʌrɪ/ I n curry m; **chicken ~** curry de poulet.
II vtr faire un curry de [meat].
IDIOMS **to ~ favour** chercher à se faire bien voir (**with sb** de qn).

curry powder n curry m.

curse /kɜːs/ I n 1 (scourge) fléau m; 2 (swearword) juron m; 3 (spell) malédiction f; **to put a ~ on** appeler la malédiction sur.
II vtr maudire.
III vi jurer (**at** après); **to ~ and swear** jurer comme un charretier.
IV **cursed** pp adj 1 /kɜːsɪd, kɜːst/ maudit; 2 /kɜːst/ **to be ~d with** être affligé de.

cursor /ˈkɜːsə(r)/ n curseur m.

cursorily /ˈkɜːsərəlɪ/ adv rapidement.

cursory /ˈkɜːsərɪ/ adj rapide; **to give sth a ~ glance** jeter un coup d'œil rapide à qch.

curt /kɜːt/ adj sec/sèche.

curtail /kɜːˈteɪl/ vtr 1 (restrict) mettre une entrave à; 2 (cut back) réduire; 3 (cut short) écourter.

curtailment /kɜːˈteɪlmənt/ n 1 (of rights, freedom) limitation f; 2 (of expenditure, service) réduction f; 3 (of holiday) interruption f.

curtain /ˈkɜːtn/ I n 1 (drape) rideau m; 2 THEAT rideau m; **after the final ~** après la chute du rideau.
II noun modifier [hook, ring] de rideau; [rail] à rideaux.
III vtr mettre des rideaux à [room, window].
■ **curtain off: ~ [sth] off, ~ off [sth]** fermer [qch] par un rideau; **to be ~ed off from sth** être séparé de qch par un rideau.

curtain call n THEAT rappel m.

curtly /ˈkɜːtlɪ/ adv sèchement.

curtsey /ˈkɜːtsɪ/ I n (pl **-eys** or **-ies**) révérence f.
II vi (prét, pp **-seyed** or **-sied**) faire la révérence.

Currencies and money

(For how to say numbers in French, ▶ 1112)

French money

write	say
25 c	vingt-cinq centimes
1 F*	un franc
1,50† F	un franc cinquante
	or un franc cinquante centimes
2 F	deux francs
2,75 F	deux francs soixante-quinze
20 F	vingt francs
100 F	cent francs
1 000 F	mille francs
1 000 000 F	un million de francs‡

* *Note that French normally puts the abbreviation after the amount, unlike British (£1) or American ($1) English. However in some official documents amounts may be given as "FF 2 000 000, etc.".*

† *French uses a comma to separate units (e.g. 2,75 F), where English normally has a period (e.g. £5.50).*

‡ *The franc was revalued in the 1960s, when 100 old francs became 1 new franc. However, French people who were accustomed to counting in old francs still sometimes use these when referring to very large sums (e.g. the price of houses or cars), so* deux millions de francs *might very well mean* 20 000 *new francs instead of* 2 000 000 *francs.*

there are 100 centimes		
in one franc	=	il y a 100 centimes dans un franc
a hundred-franc note	=	un billet de cent francs
a twenty-franc note	=	un billet de vingt francs
a ten-franc coin	=	une pièce de dix francs
a 50-centime piece	=	une pièce de cinquante centimes

British money

write	say
1p	un penny [pɛni]
25p	vingt-cinq pence [pɛns]
	or vingt-cinq pennies [pɛni]
50p	cinquante pence *or* cinquante pennies
£1	une livre
£1.50	une livre cinquante
	or une livre cinquante pence
£2.00	deux livres

a five-pound note	=	un billet de cinq livres
a pound coin	=	une pièce d'une livre
a 50p piece	=	une pièce de cinquante pence

American money

write	say
12c	douze cents [sɛnts]
$1	un dollar
$1.50	un dollar cinquante *or* un dollar cinquante cents

a ten-dollar bill	=	un billet de dix dollars
a dollar bill	=	un billet d'un dollar
a dollar coin	=	une pièce d'un dollar

How much?

how much is it? *or*		
how much does it cost?	=	combien est-ce que cela coûte?
it's 15 francs	=	cela coûte 15 francs
the price of the book is 200 francs	=	le prix du livre est de§ 200 francs
the car costs 150,000 francs	=	la voiture coûte 150 000 francs
it costs over 500 francs	=	ça coute plus de 500 francs
just under 1,000 francs	=	un peu moins de 1 000 francs
more than 200 francs	=	plus de 200 francs
less than 200 francs	=	moins de 200 francs
it costs 100 francs a metre	=	cela coûte 100 francs le mètre

§ *The* de *is obligatory here.*

In the following examples, note the use of à *in French to introduce the amount that something costs:*

a two-franc stamp	=	un timbre à deux francs
a £10 ticket	=	un billet à 10 livres

and the use of de *to introduce the amount that something consists of:*

a £500 cheque	=	un chèque de 500 livres
a two-thousand-pound grant	=	une bourse de deux mille livres

Handling money

500 francs in cash	=	500 francs en liquide
a cheque for 500 francs	=	un chèque de 500 francs
to change a 100-franc note	=	faire la monnaie d'un billet de 100 francs
a dollar travelers' check	=	un chèque de voyage en dollars
a sterling travellers' cheque	=	un chèque de voyage en livres
a £100 travellers' cheque	=	un chèque de voyage de 100 livres
there are 6 francs to the dollar	=	le dollar vaut 6 francs

---

curvaceous /kɜ:ˈveɪʃəs/ *adj* bien faite.

curve /kɜ:v/ **I** *n* courbe *f*.
II *vtr* GEN courber.
III *vi* [*line, wall, arch*] s'incurver; [*edge*] se recourber; [*road, railway*] faire une courbe.

curved /kɜ:vd/ *adj* [*line, surface*] courbe, incurvé; [*wall, flowerbed*] courbe; [*staircase, blade*] incurvé; [*edge*] arrondi; [*arch*] cintré; [*beak*] crochu.

curvy /ˈkɜ:vɪ/ *adj* [*woman*] bien faite.

cushion /ˈkʊʃn/ **I** *n* LIT **1** coussin *m*; **2** FIG (protection, reserve) garantie *f* (**against** contre).
II *vtr* amortir.
III cushioned *pp adj* (padded) matelassé; (pampered) hyperprotégé.

cushion cover *n* housse *f* de coussin.

cushy○ /ˈkʊʃɪ/ *adj* peinard○.

custard /ˈkʌstəd/ *n* GB (creamy) ≈ crème *f* anglaise; (set, baked) flan *m*.

custard: ~ **cream** *n* GB biscuit *m* fourré; ~ **pie** *n* tarte *f* à la crème; ~ **tart** *n* tarte *f* à la crème.

custodial /kʌˈstəʊdɪəl/ *adj* ~ **sentence** peine *f* de prison.

custodian /kʌˈstəʊdɪən/ ▶ 1251 *n* (of building, collection) gardien/-ienne *m/f*; (in museum) conservateur/-trice *m/f*.

custody /ˈkʌstədɪ/ *n* **1** JUR (detention) détention *f*; **in** ~ en détention; **to take sb into** ~ arrêter qn; **2** (of child) garde *f*; **to award** ~ accorder la garde; **3** SOUT (keeping) garde *f*; **in the** ~ **of** à la garde de; **in safe** ~ en mains sûres.

custom /ˈkʌstəm/ *n* **1** (personal habit) coutume *f*, habitude *f*; **it was her** ~ **to do** elle avait l'habitude de faire; **2** (convention) coutume *f*, usage *m*; **it is the** ~ c'est la coutume; ~ **requires that** l'usage veut que (+ *subj*); **3** COMM (patronage) clientèle *f*; **they've lost a lot of** ~ ils ont perdu beaucoup de clients; **I shall take my** ~ **elsewhere** j'irai me faire servir ailleurs.

customary /ˈkʌstəmərɪ/, US -merɪ/ *adj* GEN habituel/-elle; (more formal) coutumier/-ière; **as is/was** ~ comme de coutume.

custom: ~-**built** *adj* [*house*] fait sur plans; ~ **car** *n* voiture *f* personnalisée.

customer /ˈkʌstəmə(r)/ *n* **1** COMM client/-e *m/f*; '~ **services**' 'service *m* clientèle'; **2**○ (person) type○ *m*; **a nasty** ~ un sale type○; **he's a cool** ~ il est imperturbable.

customize /ˈkʌstəmaɪz/ *vtr* personnaliser.

custom-made /ˌkʌstəmˈmeɪd/ *adj* fait sur mesure.

customs /ˈkʌstəmz/ *n* douane *f*; **at** ~ à la douane; **to go through** ~ passer à la douane.

customs: **Customs and Excise** *n* GB douane *f* (britannique); ~ **clearance** *n* dédouanement *m*; ~ **declaration** *n* déclaration *f* en douane; ~ **duties** *npl* droits *mpl* de douane; ~ **hall** *n* douane *f*; ~ **officer**, ~ **official** ▶ 1251 *n* douanier/-ière *m/f*; ~ **union** *n* union *f* douanière.

cut /kʌt/ **I** *n* **1** (incision) GEN entaille *f*; (in surgery) incision *f*; **2** (wound) coupure *f*; **3** (hairstyle) coupe *f*; **a** ~

and blow-dry une coupe-brushing; **4**° (share) part *f*; **5** (reduction) réduction *f* (**in** de); **a price ~** une baisse des prix; **a ~ in the unemployment rate** une baisse du taux de chômage; **job ~s** suppression *f* d'emplois; **to take a ~ in salary** accepter une baisse de salaire; **6** (trim) **to give [sth] a ~** couper [*hair, grass*]; **7** CULIN morceau *m*; **8** (of diamond) taille *f*; **9** (of suit, jacket) coupe *f*; **10** CIN (removal of footage) coupure *f*; (shot) plan *m* de raccord (**from** de; **to** à); **11** (in editing) coupure *f*; **12** MUS (track) morceau *m*.

II *vtr* (*p prés* **-tt-**; *prét, pp* **cut**) **1** (with knife, scissors etc) couper [*bread, fabric, wood*]; faire [*hole, slit*]; **to ~ sth out of** couper qch dans [*fabric*]; découper qch dans [*magazine*]; **to ~ sth in half** couper qch en deux; **2** (sever) couper [*rope, corn, flower*]; ouvrir [*vein*], FIG rompre [*ties*]; **3** (carve out) faire [*notch*]; creuser [*channel, tunnel*]; graver [*initials*] (**in** dans); **to ~ sth open** ouvrir qch; **4** (draw blood) couper; FIG [*remark*] blesser; **to ~ one's finger** se couper le doigt; **5** (trim) couper [*grass, hair*]; tailler [*hedge*]; **to ~ one's fringe** se couper la frange; **to have one's hair cut** se faire couper les cheveux; **6** (shape, fashion) tailler [*gem, suit, marble*]; [*locksmith*] faire [*key*]; **7** (liberate) **to ~ sb from sth** dégager qn de [*wreckage*]; **to ~ sb free** ou **loose** libérer qn (**from** de); **8** (edit) couper [*article, film*]; supprimer [*scene*]; **9** (reduce) réduire; **10** (grow) **to ~ a tooth** percer une dent; **to ~ one's teeth** faire ses dents; **11** (record) faire, graver [*album*]; **12** COMPUT couper [*paragraph*]; **~ and paste** couper-coller; **13** GAMES couper [*cards*]; **14** (intersect) [*line*] couper; **15**° (stop) **~ the cackle** arrêtez de jacasser; **~ the flattery/sarcasm!** assez de flatteries/sarcasme!; **16**° (fail to attend) sécher° [*class, lesson*]; ne pas aller à [*meeting*]; **17** (snub) ignorer, snober; **to ~ sb dead** ignorer complètement qn.

III *vi* (*p prés* **-tt-**; *prét, pp* **cut**) **1** (slice, make an incision) couper; **to ~ into** entamer [*cake, pie*]; couper [*fabric, paper*]; inciser [*flesh*]; **2** (move, go) couper; **to ~ down a sidestreet** couper par une petite rue; **to ~ in front of sb** (in a queue) passer devant qn; (in a car) faire une queue de poisson à qn; **3** CIN **to ~ from A to B** passer sans transition de A à B; **4** GAMES couper; **5** FIG **to ~ into** (impinge on) empiéter sur [*leisure time*].

IV *v refl* (*p prés* **-tt-**; *prét, pp* **cut**) **to ~ oneself** se couper.

V cut *pp adj* **1** (sliced, sawn) coupé; **2** (shaped) [*gem, stone*] taillé; **a well-cut jacket** une veste bien coupée; **3** (bleeding) [*lip*] coupé; **to have a cut finger** avoir une coupure au doigt; **4** [*hay*] fauché; [*grass, flowers*] coupé; **5** (edited) avec coupures (*after n*).

IDIOMS a ~ above supérieur; **to ~ and run** FIG fuir, partir en courant; **to ~ both ways** être à double tranchant; **to have one's work cut out** avoir du travail en perspective.

■ **cut across**: **~ across** [sth] **1** (bisect) traverser; **2** (transcend) dépasser [*class barriers, distinctions*].

■ **cut back**: **¶ ~ back** faire des économies; **¶ ~ back** [sth], **~** [sth] **back 1** (reduce) réduire [*production, spending*] (**to** à); **2** (prune) tailler.

■ **cut down**: **¶ ~ down** réduire sa consommation; **to ~ down on smoking** fumer moins; **to ~ down on alcohol** réduire sa consommation d'alcool; **¶ ~ down** [sth], **~** [sth] **down 1** (chop down) abattre; **2** (reduce) réduire; **3** (make smaller, shorter) couper; **to ~ sb down to size** rabattre le caquet à qn.

■ **cut in**: **~ in 1** (in conversation) intervenir; **to ~ in on sb** interrompre qn; **2** (in vehicle) **to ~ in in front of sb** faire une queue de poisson à qn.

■ **cut off**: **¶ ~ off** [sth], **~** [sth] **off 1** (remove) couper [*hair, piece, corner*]; enlever [*excess, crusts*]; **to ~ off one's finger** se couper le doigt; **to ~ off sb's head** couper la tête à qn; **2** (reduce) **to ~ 20 minutes off the journey** raccourcir le trajet de 20 minutes; **3** (disconnect) couper [*mains service*]; **¶ ~ off** [sth] **1** (discontinue) supprimer [*grant*]; suspendre [*aid*]; **2** (isolate) [*tide, army*]; **3** (block) bloquer [*exit*]; **¶ ~** [sb] **off 1** TELECOM couper qn; **2** (disinherit) déshériter qn; **he cut me off without a penny** il m'a déshérité; **3** (interrupt) interrompre qn; **¶ ~** [sb] **off, ~ off**

[sb] (isolate) couper; **to feel cut off** se sentir isolé; **to ~ oneself off** s'isoler.

■ **cut out**: **¶ ~ out** [*engine, fan*] s'arrêter; **¶ ~ out** [sth] (eliminate) supprimer; **¶ ~** [sth] **out, ~ out** [sth] **1** (snip out) découper (**from** dans); **2** (remove) enlever [*tumour*]; supprimer [*scene, chapter*]; éliminer [*draught, noise*]; **3**° (stop) **~ it out!** ça suffit!; **¶ ~** [sb] **out 1** (isolate) exclure qn; **to ~ sb out of one's will** déshériter qn; **2 to be cut out for teaching** être fait pour être professeur.

■ **cut short**: **¶ ~ short** [sth], **~** [sth] **short** abréger [*holiday, discussion*]; **¶ ~** [sb] **short** interrompre qn.

■ **cut through**: **~ through** [sth] [*boat*] fendre [*water*]; [*person*] éviter [*red tape*].

■ **cut up**: **~** [sth] **up, ~ up** [sth] GEN couper (**into** en) [*food*]; disséquer [*specimen*]; **to be very cut up** être très affecté (**about, by** par).

cut-and-dried *adj* [*answer, solution*] tout fait; **I like everything to be ~** j'aime que tout soit fin prêt.

cut and thrust *n* **the ~ of debate** les échanges *mpl* animés du débat.

cutback /ˈkʌtbæk/ *n* réduction *f*; **~s** in réductions dans le budget de [*defence, health, education*]; **government ~s** réductions budgétaires du gouvernement.

cute° /kjuːt/ *adj* SURTOUT US **1** (sweet, attractive) mignon/-onne; (sickly sweet) mièvre; **2** (clever) précoce; PEJ malin/-igne; **to get ~** faire le malin; **to get ~ with sb** répondre avec insolence à qn.

cut glass *n* verre *m* taillé.

cutlery /ˈkʌtləri/ *n* ₵ couverts *mpl*; **a set of ~** (for one) un couvert; (complete suite) ménagère *f*.

cutlet /ˈkʌtlɪt/ *n* côtelette *f*.

cut-off /ˈkʌtɒf/ **I** *n* (upper limit) limite *f*.

II cut-offs *npl* jean *m* coupé.

cut: **~-off date** *n* date-limite *f*; **~-off point** *n* GEN limite *f*; COMM plafond *m*.

cut-out /ˈkʌtaʊt/ *n* (outline) silhouette *f*.

cut-price /ˌkʌtˈpraɪs/ *adj, adv* à prix réduit.

cut-rate *adj* US = **cut-price**.

cutter /ˈkʌtə(r)/ *n* **1** (tool) couteau *m*, cutter *m*; **2** (ship) cotre *m*.

cut-throat /ˈkʌtθrəʊt/ **I** *n* assassin *m*.

II *adj* [*competition*] acharné; **a ~ business** un milieu très dur.

cut-throat razor *n* GB rasoir *m* (à lame), coupe-choux° *m inv*.

cutting /ˈkʌtɪŋ/ **I** *n* **1** (newspaper extract) coupure *f* (**from** de); **2** (of plant) bouture *f*; **3** (by rail track) tranchée *f*; **4** CIN montage *m*; **5** COMPUT **~ and pasting** coupé-collé *m*.

II cuttings *npl* **grass ~s** herbe *f* coupée.

III *adj* [*tone*] cassant; [*remark*] désobligeant.

cutting edge *n* **1** (blade) tranchant *m*; **2** FIG avant-garde *f*; **to be at the ~** être à l'avant-garde.

cuttingly /ˈkʌtɪŋli/ *adv* [*speak*] d'un ton cassant.

cutting room *n* CIN salle *f* de montage; **to end up on the ~ floor** être coupé au montage.

CV, cv (*abrév* = **curriculum vitae**) cv, CV.

cwt *abrév écrite* = **hundredweight**.

cyanide /ˈsaɪənaɪd/ *n* cyanure *m*.

cybernetics /ˌsaɪbəˈnetɪks/ *n* (+ *v sg*) cybernétique *f*.

cycle /ˈsaɪkl/ **I** *n* **1** (series) cycle *m*; **wash ~** cycle de lavage; **2** (bicycle) vélo *m*.

II *vtr* **to ~ 15 miles** parcourir or faire 24 km à vélo.

III *vi* aller à vélo; **to go cycling** faire du vélo; **she ~s to work** elle va au travail à vélo.

cycle: **~ clip** *n* pince *f* à vélo; **~ lane** *n* piste *f* cyclable; **~ race** *n* course *f* cycliste; **~ rack** *n* parking *m* à vélos; **~ track** *n* piste *f* cyclable.

cyclic(al) /ˈsaɪklɪk(l)/ *adj* cyclique.

cycling /ˈsaɪklɪŋ/ (▶ 949) *n* cyclisme *m*; **to do a lot of ~** GEN faire beaucoup de vélo.

cycling holiday GB *n* vacances *fpl* à vélo; **to go on a ~** faire du cyclotourisme.

cycling shorts *npl* SPORT cuissard *m*.

cyclist /'saɪklɪst/ *n* GEN cycliste *mf*; SPORT coureur/
-euse *m/f* cycliste.

cyclo-cross /'saɪkləkrɒs/ ▶ 949 *n* cyclo-cross *m*.

cyclone /'saɪkləʊn/ *n* cyclone *m*; ~ **fence** US
barrière *f* en grillage.

cygnet /'sɪgnɪt/ *n* jeune cygne *m*.

cylinder /'sɪlɪndə(r)/ *n* **1** TECH cylindre *m*; **four-~** à
quatre cylindres; **2** (of revolver) barillet *m*; **3** GB (also
hot water ~) ballon *m* d'eau chaude.
IDIOMS **to be firing on all ~s**○ être au meilleur de
sa forme.

cylindrical /sɪ'lɪndrɪkl/ *adj* cylindrique.

cymbal /'sɪmbl/ ▶ 1097 *n* cymbale *f*.

cynic /'sɪnɪk/ **I** *n* cynique *mf*.
II *adj* (all contexts) cynique.

cynical /'sɪnɪkl/ *adj* cynique (**about** en ce qui
concerne).

cynicism /'sɪnɪsɪzəm/ *n* cynisme *m*.

cypher *n, vtr* = **cipher**.

cypress (tree) /'saɪprəs/ *n* cyprès *m*.

Cyprus /'saɪprəs/ ▶ 1022, 840 *pr n* Chypre *f*.

Cyrillic /sɪ'rɪlɪk/ *adj* cyrillique.

cyst /sɪst/ *n* MED, BIOL kyste *m*.

czar, Czar /zɑ:(r)/ ▶ 937 *n* tsar *m*; **Czar Nicolas** le
tsar Nicolas.

Czech /tʃek/ ▶ 1100, 1038 **I** *n* **1** (person) Tchèque *mf*;
2 (language) tchèque *m*.
II *adj* tchèque.

Czech Republic ▶ 840 *pr n* République *f* tchèque.

Dd

d, D /diː/ *n* **1** (letter) d, D *m*; **2 D** MUS ré *m*; **3 d** *abrév écrite* = **died**.

DA *n* US JUR *abrév* ▶ **District Attorney**.

dab /dæb/ **I** *n* (of paint) touche *f*; (of butter) petit morceau *m*.
II *vtr* se tamponner [*one's eyes, mouth*]; tamponner [*wound, stain*] (**with** de); **to ~ sth on** appliquer qch par petites touches; **to ~ sth off** enlever qch en tamponnant.

dabble /'dæbl/ *vtr* **to ~ one's toes in sth** tremper ses orteils dans qch.
■ **dabble in:** **~ in** [sth] faire [qch] en amateur [*painting, writing, politics*]; flirter avec○ [*ideology*]; **to ~ in the Stock Exchange** boursicoter○.

Dacca /'dækə/ **▶ 1343** | *pr n* Dhaka.

dachshund /'dækshʊnd/ *n* teckel *m*.

dad○, **Dad** /dæd/ *n* (child speaker) papa *m*; (adult speaker) père *m*; (old man) HUM pépé○ *m*.

daddy○, **Daddy** /'dædɪ/ *n* papa *m*.

daddy-long-legs /ˌdædɪ'lɒŋlegz/ *n* (*pl* ~) GB tipule *f*; US faucheux *m*.

daffodil /'dæfədɪl/ *n* jonquille *f*.

daffodil yellow *n*, *adj* jaune (*m*) vif *inv*.

daft○ /dɑːft, US dæft/ *adj* (silly) bête.

dagger /'dægə(r)/ *n* poignard *m*.
IDIOMS **to be at ~s drawn** être à couteaux tirés (**with** avec); **to look ~s at sb** fusiller qn du regard.

Dail Éireann /ˌdɔɪl 'eɪrən/ *n* POL ~ Chambre *f* des Députés (*du parlement irlandais*).

daily /'deɪlɪ/ **I** *n* (*pl* **dailies**) **1** (newspaper) quotidien *m*; **the national dailies** les grands quotidiens; **2**○ GB (also **~ help, ~ maid**) femme *f* de ménage.
II *adj* (each day) quotidien/-ienne; (per day) [*wage, rate, intake*] journalier/-ière; **~ newspaper** (journal *m*) quotidien *m*; **on a ~ basis** tous les jours; **to be paid on a ~ basis** être payé à la journée.
III *adv* quotidiennement, tous les jours; **twice ~** deux fois par jour.

daintily /'deɪntɪlɪ/ *adv* délicatement.

dainty /'deɪntɪ/ *adj* [*porcelain, handkerchief, dish*] délicat; [*shoe, hand, foot*] mignon/-onne; [*figure*] menu.

dairy /'deərɪ/ **I** *n* **1** (on farm etc) laiterie *f*; **2** COMM (shop) crémerie *f*; (company) société *f* laitière.
II *noun modifier* [*butter*] fermier/-ière; [*cow, farm, product, cream*] laitier/-ière.

dairyman /'deərɪmæn/ *n* (on farm) ouvrier *m* de laiterie; US (farmer) éleveur *m* de vaches laitières.

dais /'deɪɪs/ *n* estrade *f*.

daisy /'deɪzɪ/ *n* (common) pâquerette *f*; (garden) marguerite *f*.
IDIOMS **to be as fresh as a ~** être frais/fraîche comme une rose; **to be pushing up (the) daisies**○ manger les pissenlits par la racine○.

daisy wheel **I** *n* COMPUT marguerite *f*.
II *noun modifier* [*printer, terminal*] à marguerite.

dale /deɪl/ *n* vallée *f*, val *m* LITER.

dally /'dælɪ/ *vi* **1** **to ~ with** FIG caresser, jouer avec [*idea*]; flirter avec [*political party*]; **2** (linger) traîner.

dam /dæm/ **I** *n* (construction) barrage *m*; (to prevent flooding) digue *f*.
II *vtr* CONSTR construire un barrage sur [*river, lake*]; (to prevent flooding) endiguer.
■ **dam up:** **~ up** [sth], **~** [sth] **up** bloquer, obstruer [*river, canal*].

damage /'dæmɪdʒ/ **I** *n* ¢ **1** (physical) (to goods, environ-

---

ment) dégâts *mpl* (**to** causés à; **from** causés par); **£300-worth of ~** pour 300 livres sterling de dégâts; **storm ~** dégâts dûs aux intempéries; **water ~** dégâts des eaux; **~ to property** dégâts matériels; **2** (medical) lésions *fpl*; **to cause ~ to** abîmer [*health, part of body*]; **brain ~** lésions *fpl* cérébrales; **3** FIG **to do sth ~** porter atteinte à [*cause, reputation, trade*]; **the ~ is done** le mal est fait.
II damages *npl* JUR dommages-intérêts *mpl*; **to be liable for ~** être civilement responsable.
III *vtr* **1** (physically) endommager [*building, machine, furniture*]; abîmer [*health, part of body*]; nuire à [*environment, crop*]; **2** FIG porter atteinte à [*reputation, relationship, negotiations*].

damaging /'dæmɪdʒɪŋ/ *adj* **1** (to reputation, career, person) préjudiciable (**to** à, pour); [*effect*] préjudiciable; [*consequences*] désastreux/-euse; **2** (to health, environment) nuisible (**to** pour).

damask /'dæmɒsk/ **I** *n* (fabric) damas *m*.
II *noun modifier* [*cloth*] damassé *inv*.

dammit○ /'dæmɪt/ *excl* zut○!; (**or**) **as near as ~**○ GB ou quelque chose dans ce goût-là.

damn /dæm/ **I**○ *n* **not to give a ~ about sb/sth** se ficher○ de qn/qch.
II○ *adj* [*object*] fichu○; **your ~ husband** ton fichu○ mari.
III○ *adv* franchement; **I should ~ well hope so!** j'espère bien!
IV○ *excl* zut○!
V *vtr* **1**○ (curse) **~ you!** tu m'énerves!; **...and ~ the consequences!** et tant pis pour le reste!; **I'll be ~ed!** ça alors!; **~ it!** merde○!, zut○!; **2** damner [*sinner*]; **to ~ sb with faint praise** déguiser le blâme sous le voile de la louange.

damnation /dæm'neɪʃn/ **I** *n* damnation *f*.
II *excl*○ zut○!

damned /dæmd/ **I** *n*, *adj* **1** RELIG damné; **2**○ **▶ damn II**.
II *adv* **▶ damn III**.

damnedest /'dæmdɪst/ *n* **1** (hardest) **to do** ou **try one's ~ (to do)** faire tout son possible (pour faire); **2** (surprising) **it was the ~ thing** c'était incroyable.

damning /'dæmɪŋ/ *adj* accablant.

damp /dæmp/ **I** *n* humidité *f*.
II *adj* GEN humide; [*skin*] moite.
III *vtr* **1** = **dampen**; **2** = **damp down**.
■ **damp down:** **~** [sth] **down**, **~ down** [sth] couvrir [*fire*]; étouffer [*flames*].

dampen /'dæmpən/ *vtr* **1** humecter [*cloth, sponge, ironing*]; **2** FIG refroidir [*enthusiasm, ardour*]; amenuiser [*hopes, resolve*]; **to ~ sb's spirits** décourager qn.

damper /'dæmpə(r)/ *n*
IDIOMS **the news put a ~ on the evening**○ la nouvelle a jeté un froid dans l'assistance.

damson /'dæmzn/ *n* (fruit) prune *f* de Damas.

dance /dɑːns, US dæns/ **I** *n* GEN danse *f*; (social occasion) soirée *f* dansante.
II *noun modifier* de danse.
III *vtr* **1** danser [*steps, dance*]; **2** (dandle) faire danser.
IV *vi* LIT, FIG danser (**with** avec); [*eyes*] briller (**with** de); **to ~ for joy** danser de joie.
IDIOMS **to ~ the night away** danser jusqu'à l'aube; **to lead sb a merry ~** donner du fil à retordre à qn. **~ about**, **~ up and down** sautiller sur place.

dance hall *n* dancing *m*.

dancer /'dɑːnsə(r), US 'dænsə(r)/ *n* danseur/-euse *m*/*f*.

dancing /'dɑːnsɪŋ, US 'dænsɪŋ/ **I ▶949** *n* danse *f*.
II *noun modifier* de danse.
III *adj* [*waves, sunbeams*] dansant.

dandle /'dændl/ *vtr* **to ~ a baby on one's knee** faire sauter un bébé sur ses genoux.

dandruff /'dændrʌf/ *n* ¢ pellicules *fpl*; **anti-~ shampoo** shampooing *m* antipelliculaire.

danger /'deɪndʒə(r)/ *n* danger *m* (**of** de; **to** pour); (from different sources) dangers *mpl*; **to be in ~** être en danger; **to be in ~ of doing** risquer de faire; **the ~ is that** le danger est que (+ *subj*); **there is a ~ that** il y a un risque que (+ *subj*); **there is a ~ that they may change their minds** ils risquent de changer d'avis; **there's no ~ of that!** ça ne risque pas○!; **out of ~** hors de danger.

danger list *n* **on the ~** MED dans un état critique.

danger money *n* prime *f* de risque.

dangerous /'deɪndʒərəs/ *adj* dangereux/-euse (**for** pour; **to do** de faire).
IDIOMS **to be on ~ ground** être sur un terrain miné.

dangerously /'deɪndʒərəslɪ/ *adv* GEN dangereusement; [*ill*] gravement; **to live ~** prendre des risques.

danger signal *n* LIT, FIG signal *m* de danger.

dangle /'dæŋgl/ **I** *vtr* balancer [*puppet, keys*]; laisser pendre [*legs*]; FIG faire miroiter [*prospect*] (**before, in front of** à).
II *vi* [*puppet, keys*] se balancer (**from** à); [*earrings*] pendiller; **with legs dangling** les jambes ballantes.

Danish /'deɪnɪʃ/ **▶1100**, **1038** **I** *n* (language) danois *m*.
II *adj* danois.

Danish pastry *n* feuilleté *m* sucré (aux fruits).

dank /dæŋk/ *adj* froid et humide.

dapper /'dæpə(r)/ *adj* soigné.

dapple /'dæpl/ **I** *vtr* tacheter.
II dappled *pp adj* [*grey, horse, sky*] pommelé; [*shade, surface*] tacheté de lumière.

dare /deə(r)/ **I** *n* défi *m*; **to do sth for a ~** faire qch pour répondre à un défi.
II *modal aux* **1** (to have the courage to) oser; **to ~ to do sth** avoir le courage de faire qch; **they don't ~** ou **daren't** GB ils n'osent pas; **~ I say it** il faut bien le dire; **I ~ say, I daresay** GB je pense; (sarcastically) certes!; **I ~ say** ou **I daresay** GB **that…** je suppose que…; **2** (expressing anger, indignation) oser (**do** faire); **they wouldn't ~!** ils n'oseraient pas!; **don't (you) ~ speak to me like that!** je t'interdis de me parler sur ce ton!; **don't you ~!** (warning) ne t'avise pas de faire ça!
III *vtr* **to ~ sb to do** défier qn de faire; **go on, I ~ you!** chiche que tu ne le fais pas○!

daredevil /'deədevl/ *n, adj* casse-cou (*mf*) *inv*.

daren't /deənt/ (= dare not) **▶ dare**.

daresay GB **▶ dare** II 1.

daring /'deərɪŋ/ **I** *n* audace *f*.
II *adj* (courageous, innovative) audacieux/-ieuse; (shocking) [*suggestion, dress*] osé.

dark /dɑːk/ **I** **the ~** le noir, l'obscurité *f*; **in the ~** dans le noir ou l'obscurité; **before/until ~** avant/jusqu'à la (tombée de la) nuit; **after ~** après la tombée de la nuit.
II *adj* **1** (lacking in light) sombre; **it is getting ~** il commence à faire noir ou nuit; **it's ~** il fait noir ou nuit; **2** (in colour) [*colour, suit*] sombre; **~ blue** bleu foncé *inv*; **3** (physically) [*hair, eyes, skin*] brun; **she's ~** elle est brune, elle a les cheveux bruns; **4** (gloomy) [*time, days, mood*] sombre; **5** (sinister) [*secret, thought*] noir (*before n*); [*threat, warning*] sombre; **the ~ side of** le côté sinistre de; **6** (evil) [*force, power*] maléfique.
IDIOMS **to be in the ~** être dans le noir; **I was completely in the ~** j'étais dans le noir le plus complet; **to leave sb in the ~** laisser qn dans l'ignorance; **to keep sb in the ~ about sth** cacher qch à qn; **a shot in the ~** (guess) un coup pour voir.

dark: **Dark Ages** *n* HIST Haut Moyen-Âge *m*; **~ chocolate** *n* chocolat *m* noir.

darken /'dɑːkən/ **I** *vtr* **1** (reduce light in) obscurcir [*sky,*

landscape]; assombrir [*house, room*]; **2** (in colour) foncer [*colour*]; brunir [*complexion*]; **3** FIG assombrir.
II *vi* **1** (lose light) s'obscurcir; **2** (in colour) foncer; [*skin*] brunir; **3** (show anger) [*eyes, face*] se rembrunir; **4** (become gloomy) s'assombrir.
III darkened *pp adj* [*room, house*] sombre.
IDIOMS **never ~ my door again!** ne remettez plus les pieds ici!

dark: **~-eyed** *adj* [*person*] aux yeux sombres or noirs; **~ glasses** *npl* lunettes *fpl* noires.

dark horse *n* **1**○ GB (enigmatic person) mystère *m*; **2** (in sports) outsider *m*.

darkly /'dɑːklɪ/ *adv* (grimly) [*mutter, hint*] sombrement.

darkness /'dɑːknɪs/ *n* (blackness) obscurité *f*; **in ~** dans l'obscurité; **as ~ fell** à la tombée de la nuit.

dark: **~room** *n* chambre *f* noire; **~-skinned** *adj* [*person*] basané.

darling /'dɑːlɪŋ/ **I** *n* **1** (term of address) (to loved one) chéri/-e *m/f*; (to child) mon chou○; (affectedly: to acquaintance) mon cher/ma chère *m/f*; **~ Rosie** ma Rosie chérie; **2** (kind, lovable person) amour *m*, ange *m*; **be a ~** sois un ange; **3** (favourite) (of circle, public) coqueluche *f*; (of family, parent, teacher) chouchou/-te *m/f*.
II *adj* **1** (expressing attachment) chéri; **2** (expressing delight) **a ~ little baby** un amour de bébé.

darn /dɑːn/ **I** *n* raccommodage *m* (**in** à).
II○ *adj* (also **darned**) sacré○ (*before n*).
III○ *adv* sacrément○; **~ good** super○.
IV○ *excl* zut○!
V *vtr* repriser, raccommoder.

darning /'dɑːnɪŋ/ *n* (all contexts) raccommodage *m*.

dart /dɑːt/ **I** *n* **1 ▶949** SPORT fléchette *f*; **to play ~s** jouer aux fléchettes; **2** (arrow) LIT, FIG flèche *f*; **3** (in garment) pince *f*.
II *vi* **to ~ in/away** entrer/filer comme une flèche.

dartboard /'dɑːtbɔːd/ *n* cible *f*.

dash /dæʃ/ **I** *n* **1** (rush) course *f* folle; **it has been a mad ~** on a dû se presser; **to make a ~ for it** (run off) s'enfuir; **to make a ~ for the train** courir pour attraper le train; **2** (small amount) (of liquid) goutte *f*; (of powder) pincée *f*; (of colour) touche *f*; **3** (flair) panache *m*; **4** (punctuation) tiret *m*; **5** (in morse code) trait *m*.
II *vtr* **1** (smash) **to ~ sb/sth against** projeter qn/qch contre [*rocks*]; **to ~ sth to the ground** lancer violemment qch par terre; **2** FIG (crush) anéantir [*hope*].
III *vi* (hurry) se précipiter (**into** dans); **to ~ out of** sortir en courant de; **I must ~!** je me sauve!
IDIOMS **to cut a ~** avoir grande allure.
■ **dash off**: ¶ **~ off** se sauver; ¶ **~ off** [*sth*], **~** [*sth*] **off** écrire [qch] en vitesse.

dashboard /'dæʃbɔːd/ *n* tableau *m* de bord.

dashing /'dæʃɪŋ/ *adj* [*person*] fringant; [*outfit*] superbe.

data /'deɪtə/ **I** *npl* GEN, COMPUT données *fpl*.
II *noun modifier* [*acquisition, analysis, base, bank, dictionary, management, structure, type*] de données.

data: **~base** *n* base *f* de données; **~base management system**, **DBMS** *n* système *m* de gestion de données, SGBD, **~ capture** *n* saisie *f* de données; **~ carrier** *n* support *m* d'information; **~ collection** *n* collecte *f* de données; **~ communications** *npl* transmission *f* de données; **~ directory** *n* répertoire *m* de données; **~ disk** *n* disque *m* enregistré; **~ entry** *n* introduction *f* de données; **~ file** *n* fichier *m* de données; **~ handling** *n* manipulation *f* de données; **~ input** *n* introduction *f* de données; **~ item** *n* donnée *f* élémentaire; **~ link** *n* liaison *f* de données; **~ processing** *n* (procedure) traitement *m* des données; (career) informatique *f*; (department) service *m* informatique; **~ protection** *n* protection *f* de l'information; **~ protection act** *n* JUR loi *f* sur l'informatique et les libertés; **~ retrieval** *n* extraction *f* de données; **~ security** *n* sécurité *f* des données; **~ storage** *n* (process) stockage *m* des données; (medium) support *m* d'information; **~ transmission**, DT *n* transmission *f* de données.

date /deɪt/ **▶854** **I** *n* **1** (day of the month) date *f*; **~ of birth** date de naissance; **what ~ is your birthday?**

Date

Where English has several ways of writing dates, such as May 10, 10 May, 10th May etc. French has only one generally accepted way: le 10 mai, (say le dix mai). However, as in English, dates in French may be written informally: 10.5.68 or 31/7/65 etc.

The general pattern in French is:

le cardinal number   month   year
le   10   mai   1901

But if the date is the first of the month, use premier, abbreviated as 1ᵉʳ:

May 1st 1901 = le 1ᵉʳ mai 1901

Note that French does not use capital letters for months, or for days of the week, ▶ **1090** and ▶ **1390**; also French does not usually abbreviate the names of the months:

Sept 10 = le 10 septembre etc.

If the day of the week is included, put it after the le:

Monday, May 1st 1901 = le lundi 1ᵉʳ mai 1901
Monday the 25th   = le lundi 25 (say le lundi vingt-cinq)

Saying and writing dates

what's the date? = quel jour sommes-nous?
it's the tenth   = nous sommes le dix
                   or (less formally) on est le dix
it's the tenth of May = nous sommes le dix mai
                        or (less formally) on est le dix mai

	Write	Say
May 1	le 1er mai	le premier mai
May 2	le 2 mai	le deux mai
May 11	le 11 mai	le onze mai
May 21	le 21 mai	le vingt et un mai
May 30	le 30 mai	le trente mai
May 6 1968	le 6 mai 1968	le six mai mille neuf cent soixante-huit*
Monday		
May 6 1968	le lundi 6 mai 1968	le lundi six mai mille neuf cent soixante-huit*
16.5.68 GB or		
5.16.68 US	16.5.68	le seize cinq soixante-huit
AD 230	230 apr. J.-C.	deux cent trente après Jésus-Christ
2500 BC	2500 av. J.-C.	deux mille cinq cents ans avant Jésus-Christ*
the 16th century	le XVIᵉ siècle†	le seizième siècle

* (i) There are two ways of saying hundreds and thousands in dates: 1968 = mille neuf cent soixante-huit
or dix-neuf cent soixante-huit

(ii) The spelling mil is used in legal French, otherwise mille is used in dates. When a round number of thousands is invoked, the words l'an are added.
1900 = mille neuf cents
2000 = l'an deux mille

† French prefers Roman numerals for centuries:
the 16th century = le XVIᵉ

Saying on

French uses only the definite article, without any word for on:

it happened on 6th March = c'est arrivé le 6 mars
                           (say le six mars)
he came on the 21st = il est arrivé le 21
                      (say le vingt et un)
see you on the 6th = on se voit le 6 (say le six))
on the 2nd of every month = le 2 de chaque mois
                            (say le deux ...)
he'll be here on the 3rd = il sera là le 3 (say le trois)

Saying in

French normally uses en for years but prefers en l'an for out-of-the-ordinary dates:

in 1968 = en 1968 (say en mille neuf cent soixante-huit or en dix-neuf cent ...)
in 1896 = en 1896 (say en mille huit cent quatre-vingt-seize or en dix-huit cent ...)
in the year 2000 = en l'an deux mille
in AD 27 = en l'an 27 (say l'an vingt-sept) de notre ère
in 132 BC = en l'an 132 (say l'an cent trente-deux) avant Jésus-Christ

With names of months, in is translated by en or au mois de:
in May 1970 = en mai mille neuf cent soixante-dix or au mois de mai mille neuf cent soixante-dix

With centuries, French uses au:
in the seventeenth century = au dix-septième siècle

The word siècle is often omitted in colloquial French:
in the eighteenth century = au dix-huitième siècle or (less formally) au dix-huitième

Note also:
in the early 12th century = au début du XIIᵉ siècle
                            (say du douzième siècle)
in the late 14th century = à or vers la fin du XIVᵉ siècle
                           (say du quatorzième siècle)

Phrases

Remember that the date in French always has the definite article, so, in combined forms, au and du are required:

from the 10th onwards = à partir du 10 (say du dix)
stay until the 14th = reste jusqu'au 14
                      (say au quatorze)
from 21st to 30th May = du 21 au 30 mai
                        (say du vingt et un au trente mai)
around 16th May = le 16 mai environ/vers le 16 mai
                  (say le seize mai) or aux environs du seize mai
                  (say du seize mai)
not until 1999 = pas avant 1999 (say mille neuf cent quatre-vingt-dix-neuf)
Shakespeare (1564–1616) = Shakespeare (1564–1616)
                          (say Shakespeare, quinze cent soixante-quatre – seize cent seize)
Shakespeare b. 1564 d.1616 = Shakespeare, né en 1564, mort en 1616 (say Shakespeare, né en quinze cent soixante-quatre, mort en seize cent seize).
                             Note that French has no abbreviations for né and mort.
in May '45 = en mai 45 (say en mai quarante-cinq)
in the 1980s = dans les années 80 (say dans les années quatre-vingts)
in the early sixties = au début des années 60 (say des années soixante)
in the late seventies = à la fin des années 70 (say des années soixante-dix)
the riots of '68 = les émeutes de 68 (say de soixante-huit)
the 14–18 war = la guerre de 14 or de 14–18 (say de quatorze or de quatorze-dix-huit)
the 1912 uprising = le soulèvement de 1912 (say de mille neuf cent douze)

---

quelle est la date de ton anniversaire?; **what's the ~ today?** on est le combien aujourd'hui?; **there's no ~ on the letter** la lettre n'est pas datée; **to set a ~** fixer une date; **at a later ~, at some future ~** plus tard; **2** (year: of event) date f; (on coin) millésime m; **3** (meeting) rendez-vous m; **to have a lunch ~** être pris à déjeuner; **to make a ~ for Monday** prendre rendez-vous pour lundi; **4** (person one is going out with) **who's your ~ for tonight?** avec qui sors-tu ce soir?; **5** (fruit) datte f.

II to date adv phr à ce jour, jusqu'ici.
III vtr **1** [person] dater; [machine] imprimer la date sur; **~d March 21st** daté du 21 mars; **a statuette ~d 1875** une statuette portant la date 1875; **2** (identify age of) dater [skeleton, building, object]; **3** (reveal age of) **that hairstyle ~s her** sa coiffure trahit son âge; **4** (go out with) sortir avec [person].
IV vi **1** (originate) **to ~ from** ou **back to** [building] dater de; [problem, custom, friendship] remonter à; **2** (become dated) se démoder.

dated /'deɪtɪd/ adj [clothes, style] démodé; [idea, convention, custom] dépassé; [expression, language] vieilli; **the film seems ~ now** le film a mal vieilli.

dateline /'deɪtlaɪn/ n (when travelling) **the international ~** la ligne de changement de date.

date stamp n (mark) cachet m, tampon m.

dating agency /'deɪtɪŋ/ n club m de rencontres.

dative /'deɪtɪv/ I n datif m; **in the ~** au datif.
II adj [case] datif/-ive; [ending, noun] au datif.

daub /dɔːb/ I n PEJ (painting) croûte○ f PEJ.
II vtr **to ~ paint on a wall** maculer un mur de peinture.

daughter /'dɔːtə(r)/ n LIT, FIG fille f.

daughter-in-law n (pl **daughters-in-law**) belle-fille f, bru f.

daunt /dɔːnt/ vtr décourager; **nothing ~ed** imperturbable.

daunting /'dɔːntɪŋ/ adj [task, prospect] décourageant; [person] intimidant; **it can be (quite) ~** c'est un pas difficile; **I'm faced with a ~ amount of work** j'ai devant moi une quantité effrayante de travail.

dawdle /'dɔːdl/ vi flâner, traînasser○; **he ~d over breakfast** il a pris son petit déjeuner en traînassant; **he ~d along the road** il a traînassé sur la route.

dawn /dɔːn/ I n **1** LIT aube f, aurore f LITER; **at ~** à l'aube; **before** ou **by ~** avant l'aube; **at the crack of ~** LIT, FIG à l'aube; **~ broke** le jour se leva; **from ~ till dusk** du matin au soir; **2** FIG (beginning) aube f; **the ~ of socialism** la naissance du socialisme.
II vi **1** (become light) [day] se lever; **the day ~ed sunny and warm** le jour s'annonçait chaud et ensoleillé; **2** (become apparent) **it ~ed on me that** je me suis rendu compte que; **it suddenly ~ed on him why** il a compris soudain pourquoi.

dawn: **~ chorus** n concert m matinal des oiseaux; **~ raid** n descente f de police très tôt le matin.

day /deɪ/ ▶1336 I n **1** (24-hour period) jour m; **one summer's ~** un jour d'été; **what ~ is it today?** quel jour sommes-nous aujourd'hui? **~ after ~**, **in ~ out** jour après jour; **every ~** tous les jours; **every other ~** tous les deux jours; **from ~ to ~** d'un jour à l'autre; **from one ~ to the next** d'un jour à l'autre; **from that ~ to this** depuis ce jour-là; **any ~ now** d'un jour à l'autre; **one ~**, **some ~** un jour; **within ~s** en quelques jours; **the ~ when** ou **that** le jour où; **it's ~s since I've seen him** ça fait des jours que je ne l'ai pas vu, je ne l'ai pas vu depuis des jours; **it's 15 years to the ~ since...** ça fait 15 ans jour pour jour que...; **to come on the wrong ~** se tromper de jour; **it had to happen today of all ~s!** il fallait que cela arrive ou que ça tombe○ aujourd'hui; **to this ~** aujourd'hui encore; **the ~ after** le lendemain; **the ~ before** la veille; **the ~ before yesterday** avant-hier; **the ~ after tomorrow** après-demain; **two ~s after/two ~s before the wedding** le surlendemain/l'avant-veille du mariage; **from that ~ onwards** dès lors; **2** (until evening) journée f; **working ~** journée de travail; **a hard ~** une journée difficile; **an enjoyable ~'s golf** une agréable journée de golf; **all ~** toute la journée; **all that ~** tout au long de cette journée; **before the ~ was out** avant la fin de la journée; **during/for the ~** pendant/pour la journée; **paid by the ~** payé à la journée; **to take all ~ doing** mettre toute une journée à faire; **pleased with their ~'s work** contents de leur journée; **we haven't got all ~!** nous n'avons pas la journée devant nous!; **it was a hot ~!** il faisait chaud; **have a nice ~!** bonne journée!; **3** (as opposed to night) jour m; **it's almost ~** il fait presque jour; **to be on ~s** être ou travailler de jour; **by ~** de jour; **4** (specific) jour m; **decision ~** le jour décisif; **the ~ of judgment** le jour du jugement dernier; **to her dying ~** jusqu'à son dernier jour; **it's not your ~ is it?** décidément c'est ton jour! IRON; **I never thought I'd see the ~** je n'aurais jamais cru; **5** (as historical period) époque f; **in those ~s** à cette époque; **in his/my ~** (at that time) de son/mon temps; (at height of success, vital-

ity) dans le temps; **his dancing ~s** sa carrière de danseur; **these ~s** ces temps-ci.
II noun modifier [job, nurse] de jour.
IDIOMS **in ~s gone by** autrefois; **it's all in a ~'s work** c'est du quotidien; **not to give sb the time of ~** ignorer qn superbement; **to pass the time of ~** bavarder; **it's one of those ~s!** il y a des jours comme ça!; **those were the ~s** c'était le bon temps; **to be a bit late in the ~** être un peu tard; **that'll be the ~!** je voudrais voir ça!; **to call it a ~** s'arrêter là; **to win the ~** avoir le dessus; **to have an off ~** ne pas être dans son assiette; **to have had its ~** avoir fait son temps; **to have seen better ~s** avoir connu des jours meilleurs; **he's 50 if he's a ~** il a 50 ans bien tassés○!; **to make a ~ of it** profiter de la journée; **to save the ~** sauver la situation; **to see the light of ~** apparaître au grand jour; **to take one ~ at a time** prendre les choses comme elles se présentent; **your ~ will come** ton heure arrivera.

day: **~boy** n GB SCH externe m; **~break** n aube f; **~care** n (for young children) service m de garderie; **~ centre** GB, **~ center** US n centre m d'accueil.

daydream /'deɪdriːm/ I n rêves mpl.
II vi rêver (**about** de; **about doing** de faire); PEJ rêvasser.

daygirl n SCH externe f.

daylight /'deɪlaɪt/ I n **1** (light) jour m, lumière f du jour; **it was still ~** il faisait encore jour; **we have two hours of ~ left** on a encore deux heures avant la tombée de la nuit; **in (the) ~** (by day) de jour; (in natural light) à la lumière du jour; **2** (dawn) lever m du jour, point m du jour.
II noun modifier de jour; **during ~ hours** pendant qu'il fait jour.

daylight robbery○ n **it's ~!** c'est de l'arnaque○!

day: **~ nursery** n garderie f; **~ pass** n forfait m pour la journée; **~ release** n formation f permanente; **~ return (-ticket)** n GB aller-retour m valable une journée; **~ school** n externat m.

daytime /'deɪtaɪm/ n journée f.

day-to-day /ˌdeɪtə'deɪ/ adj quotidien/-ienne; **on a ~ basis** au jour le jour.

day: **~-trip** n excursion f pour la journée; **~-tripper** n excursionniste mf.

daze /deɪz/ n **in a ~** (from blow) étourdi; (from drug) hébété; (from news) ahuri; (feeling vague) abruti.

dazed /deɪzd/ adj (by blow) abasourdi; (by news) ahuri.

dazzle /'dæzl/ I n (of sunlight, headlights) lumière f aveuglante.
II vtr [sun, torch] éblouir; **to ~ sb with** FIG éblouir qn par.

dazzling /'dæzlɪŋ/ adj éblouissant.

DBMS n COMPUT abrév ▶ **database management system**.

DC GEOG abrév = **District of Columbia**.

D-day /'diː deɪ/ n **1** (important day) jour m J; **2** MIL HIST le 6 juin 1944 (jour du débarquement des Alliés en Normandie).

DDP n: abrév ▶ **distributed data processing**.

DE US POST abrév écrite = **Delaware**.

dead /ded/ I n **1** **the ~** (+ v pl) (people) les morts mpl; **2** FIG (depths) **at ~ of night** en pleine nuit; **in the ~ of winter** en plein hiver.
II adj **1** (no longer living) mort; **the ~ man/woman** le mort/la morte; **a ~ body** un cadavre; **to drop (down) ~** tomber raide mort; **to play ~** faire le mort/la morte; **to shoot sb ~** abattre qn; **~ and buried** LIT, FIG mort et enterré; **they're ~ and gone** ils nous ont quittés; **to give sb up for ~** tenir qn pour mort; **I'm absolutely ~○**! (exhausted) je suis mort○!; **2** (extinct) [language] mort; [custom] désuet/-ète; [issue] dépassé; [fire] mort; **3** (dull, not lively) [place] mort; [audience] apathique; **the ~ season** la morte-saison; **4** (not functioning, idle) [battery] à plat; [capital] inactif/-ive; **the phone went ~** tout d'un coup, plus rien (sur la ligne); **5** (impervious) insensible (**to** à);

6 (numb) [*limb*] engourdi; **7** (absolute) ~ **silence** un silence de mort; **to come to a ~ stop** s'arrêter net.

III *adv* SURTOUT GB (absolutely, completely) absolument; ~ **certain** absolument sûr; ~ **level** parfaitement plat; ~ **on time** pile○ à l'heure; ~ **on six o'clock** à six heures pile○; ~ **easy**○ simple comme bonjour○; ~ **on target** parfaitement calculé; **they were ~ lucky**○! ils ont eu du pot○!; ~ **drunk**○ ivre mort; ~ **tired**○ crevé○, claqué○; **I was ~ scared**○! j'avais une trouille bleue○!; **'~ slow'** AUT 'roulez au pas'; ~ **straight** tout à fait droit; **to be ~ against** être totalement opposé à [*idea, plan*]; **to be ~ set on doing** être tout à fait décidé à faire; **to stop ~** s'arrêter net.

IDIOMS **to be ~ to the world** dormir comme une souche; **I wouldn't be seen ~ in a place like that!** pour rien au monde je ne voudrais être vu dans un endroit pareil!

deaden /'dedn/ *vtr* calmer [*pain*]; amortir [*blow*]; assourdir [*sound*].

dead end /ˌded'end/ **I** *n* LIT, FIG impasse *f*.
II dead-end *noun modifier* [*job*] sans perspectives.

deadening /'dednɪŋ/ *adj* [*effect*] LIT anesthésiant; FIG abrutissant.

deadhead /'dedhed/ **I** *n* PÉJ (stupid person) nullité *f*.
II *vtr* enlever les fleurs fanées de [*plant*].

dead heat *n* (in athletics) arrivée *f* ex-aequo; (in horseracing) dead-heat *m inv*; **it was a ~** ils ont fini ex-aequo.

deadline /'dedlaɪn/ *n* date *f* or heure *f* limite, délai *m*; **to meet a ~** respecter un délai; **to work to very tight ~s** travailler dans des délais très serrés; **the ~ for applications is the 15th** les candidatures doivent être déposées avant le 15.

deadlock /'dedlɒk/ *n* **1** (impasse) impasse *f*; **to reach (a) ~** aboutir à une impasse; **to break the ~** sortir de l'impasse; **2** (lock) verrou *m* haute sécurité.

deadlocked /'dedlɒkt/ *adj* dans l'impasse.

dead loss *n* ○PÉJ **to be a ~** être nul/nulle○.

deadly /'dedlɪ/ **I** *adj* **1** [*poison, disease, enemy*] mortel/-elle; [*hatred, weapon*] meurtrier/-ière; [*rivalry*] acharné; **2** (absolute) **in ~ earnest** avec le plus grand sérieux; **with ~ accuracy** avec la plus grande précision; **3**○ (dull, boring) [*person, event*] mortel/-elle○, rasant○.
II *adv* [*dull, boring*] terriblement; ~ **pale** pâle comme la mort; **to be ~ serious** être des plus sérieux.

dead: ~ **on arrival**, **DOA** *adj* MED mort avant d'arriver à l'hôpital; ~**pan** *adj* [*humour*] pince-sans-rire *inv*; [*expression*] de marbre.

dead ringer○ *n* **to be a ~ for sb** être le sosie de qn.

Dead Sea *pr n* mer *f* Morte.

dead set *n* GB **to make a ~ at sb** jeter son dévolu sur qn○.

dead: ~ **weight** *n* LIT poids *m* mort; FIG (burden) poids *m*; ~ **wood** *n* LIT bois *m* mort; GB FIG personnel *m* inutile.

deaf /def/ **I** *n* **the ~** (+ *v pl*) les sourds *mpl*, les malentendants *mpl* voir note.
II *adj* sourd voir note; **to go ~** devenir sourd; **to be ~ in one ear** être sourd d'une oreille; **that's his ~ ear** il n'entend pas de cette oreille; **2** FIG **to be ~ to** être sourd à; **to turn a ~ ear** to faire la sourde oreille à, rester sourd à; **to fall on ~ ears** [*request, advice*] ne pas trouver d'écho.
IDIOMS **to be as ~ as a post**○ être sourd comme un pot○.

■ Note Ce mot peut être perçu comme injurieux dans cette acception. Lui préférer *hearing-impaired*.

deaf: ~ **aid** *n* GB prothèse *f* auditive; ~**-and-dumb** *n, adj* INJUR = **deaf without speech**.

deafen /'defn/ *vtr* assourdir, rendre [qn] sourd.

deafening /'defnɪŋ/ *adj* assourdissant.

deaf-mute /ˌdef'mjuːt/ *n, adj* sourd-muet/sourde-muette (*m/f*).

deafness /'defnɪs/ *n* surdité *f*.

deaf without speech *n* (+ *v pl*) **the ~** les sourds-muets *mpl*.

deal /diːl/ **I** *n* **1** (agreement) GEN accord *m*; (in commerce, finance) affaire *f*; (with friend, criminal) marché *m*; **the pay ~** l'accord salarial; **to make a ~ with** faire un marché avec [*friend, criminal*]; négocier une affaire avec [*client, company*]; **it's a ~**! marché conclu!; **the ~'s off** le marché ne tient pas; **let's do a ~** je vous propose un marché; **a good ~** une bonne affaire; **it's all part of the ~** (part of the arrangement) ça fait partie du marché; (part of the price, package) c'est inclus dans le reste; **to be in on the ~** être dans le coup○; **2** (sale) vente *f*; **3** (special offer, bargain) **the best ~(s) in electrical goods** les meilleurs prix en électroménager; **4** (amount) **a great** OU **good ~** beaucoup (of de); **a great ~ in common** beaucoup de choses en commun; **she means a great ~ to me** je l'aime beaucoup; **it means a great ~ to me** cela compte beaucoup pour moi; **5** (treatment) **he got a raw ~** il s'est fait avoir○; **6** (in cards) donne *f*; **it's my ~** c'est à moi de donner.
II *vtr* (*prét, pp* **dealt**) **1** porter [*blow*] (**to** à); **2** distribuer [*cards*]; donner [*hand*].
III *vi* (*prét, pp* **dealt**) COMM (carry on business) [*person, firm*] être en activité; (operate on stock exchange) faire des opérations boursières; **to ~ in** être dans le commerce de [*commodity, shares*].
IDIOMS **big ~**○! IRON la belle affaire! IRON; **it's no big ~**○ (not hard) ce n'est rien du tout; **to make a big ~ out of sth** faire tout un plat○ de qch.
■ **deal out**: ~ **out** [sth], ~ [sth] **out** (mete out) administrer [*punishment, fine*].
■ **deal with**: ¶ ~ **with** [sth] **1** s'occuper de [*complaint, emergency, matter*]; faire face à [*vandalism, unemployment*]; **2** (discuss) traiter de [*issue*]; ¶ ~ **with** [sb] **1** (attend to) s'occuper de; **2** (do business with) traiter avec.

dealer /'diːlə(r)/ ▶1251 *n* **1** COMM marchand/-e *m/f*; (on a large scale) négociant/-e *m/f*; (for a specific product) concessionnaire *m*; **art ~** marchand/-e *m/f* de tableaux; **authorized ~** revendeur *m* agréé; **2** (on stock exchange) opérateur/-trice *m/f*; **3** (in drugs) revendeur/-euse *m/f* de drogue, dealer○ *m*.

dealership /'diːləʃɪp/ *n* COMM concession *f* (**for** de).

dealing /'diːlɪŋ/ **I** *n* **1** COMM vente *f*; **foreign exchange ~** opérations *fpl* de change; ~ **resumed this morning** les transactions ont repris ce matin; **share ~** transactions *fpl* boursières; **2** (trafficking) trafic *m*; **drug ~** le trafic de drogue.
II dealings *npl* GEN relations *fpl* (**with** avec); COMM relations *fpl* commerciales (**with** avec); **to have ~s with sb** traiter avec qn.

dealt /delt/ *prét, pp* ▶**deal**.

dean /diːn/ *n* doyen *m*.

dear /dɪə(r)/ **I** *n* **1** (term of address) (affectionate) mon chéri/ ma chérie *m/f*; (more formal) mon cher/ma chère *m/f*; (to woman shopper) ma petite dame○; **you poor ~** (to adult) mon pauvre/ma pauvre *m/f*; **he's a ~** il est adorable; **be a ~** sois gentil; (more affectionate) sois un amour.
II *adj* **1** (expressing attachment) [*friend, mother*] cher/chère; **she's a very ~ friend of mine** c'est une très bonne amie à moi; **he's my ~est friend** c'est mon meilleur ami; ~ **old Richard** ce bon vieux Richard; **the project is ~ to his heart** le projet lui tient vraiment à cœur; **her ~est wish** son vœu le plus cher; **2** (expressing admiration) **a ~ little house** une jolie petite maison; **a ~ old lady** une vieille dame adorable; **3** (in letter) cher/chère; **Dear Sir/Madam** Monsieur, Madame; **Dear Sirs** Messieurs; **Dear Mr Jones** Cher Monsieur; **Dear Mr and Mrs Jones** Cher Monsieur, Chère Madame; **Dear Anne and Paul** Chers Anne et Paul; **4** (expensive) cher/chère; **to get ~er** augmenter.
III *adv* FIG [*cost*] cher.

IV *excl* oh ~! (dismay, surprise) oh mon Dieu!; (less serious) aïe!, oh là là!; ~ **me, no!** certainement pas !

dearly /'dɪəlɪ/ *adv* **1** (very much) **to love sb** ~ aimer tendrement qn; **they would** ~ **love to see you fail** ils seraient ravis de te voir échouer; **I would** ~ **love to know** je payerais cher pour savoir; **2** FIG [*pay*] chèrement; ~ **bought** chèrement payé.

death /deθ/ *n* (of person) mort *f*, décès *m*; FIG anéantissement *m*; **at (the time of) his** ~ à sa mort; **a** ~ **in the family** un décès dans la famille; ~ **by drowning** mort par noyade; **to put sb to** ~ exécuter qn; **to the** ~ à mort; **to drink/work oneself to** ~ se tuer en buvant/au travail; **she fell to her** ~ elle s'est tuée en tombant; **he met his** ~ **in a skiing accident** il a trouvé la mort dans un accident de ski; **to die a violent** ~ mourir de mort violente; **'Deaths'** (newspaper column) 'Nécrologie'; **a fall would mean** ~ une chute serait fatale.

IDIOMS **to die a** OU **the** ~ [*fashion*] disparaître complètement; [*entertainer, play*] faire un bide○; **he'll be the** ~ **of me!** il me tuera!; **it's a matter of life or** ~ c'est une question de vie ou de mort; **to look like** ~ **warmed up** avoir l'air d'un cadavre ambulant; **to be at** ~**'s door** être à (l'article de) la mort; **to be worried/frightened to** ~○ être mort d'inquiétude/de peur; **to frighten sb to** ~ faire une peur bleue à qn○; **to be bored to** ~○ s'ennuyer à mourir; **I'm sick to** ~○ **of this!** j'en ai par-dessus la tête○!; **you'll catch your** ~ **(of cold)**○ tu vas attraper la crève○.

death: ~**bed** *n* lit *m* de mort; ~ **camp** *n* camp *m* de la mort; ~ **certificate** *n* JUR acte *m* de décès; ~ **duties** *npl* droits *mpl* de succession.

death knell /'deθnel/ *n* LIT, FIG glas *m*.

death list *n* liste *f* noire.

deathly /'deθlɪ/ **I** *adj* [*pallor*] cadavérique; [*calm, silence*] de mort.
II *adv* ~ **pale** d'une pâleur cadavérique; **it was** ~ **quiet** il y avait un silence de mort.

death: ~ **mask** *n* masque *m* mortuaire; ~ **penalty** *n* peine *f* de mort; ~ **rate** *n* taux *m* de mortalité; ~ **ray** *n* rayon *m* mortel; ~ **row** *n* US quartier *m* des condamnés à mort; ~ **sentence** *n* LIT, FIG condamnation *f* à mort; ~ **threat** *n* menaces *fpl* de mort.

death throes *npl* LIT, FIG agonie *f*.

death toll *n* nombre *m* de morts.

death trap *n* **to be a** ~ être très dangereux/-euse.

death: ~ **warrant** *n* ordre *m* d'exécution; ~ **wish** *n* pulsion *f* de mort.

debacle /deɪ'bɑːkl/ *n* fiasco *m*, débâcle *f*.

debar /dɪ'bɑː(r)/ *vtr* (*p prés etc* -**rr**-) exclure; **to be** ~**ed from doing** ne pas avoir le droit de faire.

debase /dɪ'beɪs/ **I** *vtr* dégrader [*emotion, ideal*]; déprécier [*currency*]; rabaisser [*person*].
II debased *pp adj* [*language*] appauvri.

debatable /dɪ'beɪtəbl/ *adj* discutable; **that's** ~! cela se discute!; **it is** ~ **whether** on peut se demander si.

debate /dɪ'beɪt/ **I** *n* (formal, about an issue) débat *m* (**on, about** sur); (informal discussion) discussion *f* (**about** à propos de); **to hold a** ~ **on** débattre de [*issue*].
II *vtr* GEN, POL (formally) débattre de [*issue, bill*]; (informally) discuter de [*question*]; **I am debating whether to leave** je me demande si je dois partir.
III *vi* **to** ~ **about sth** discuter de qch (**with** avec).

debauch /dɪ'bɔːtʃ/ *vtr* dépraver.

debauchery /dɪ'bɔːtʃərɪ/ *n* débauche *f*.

debenture: ~ **bond** *n* certificat *m* d'obligation; ~ **stock** *n* obligations *fpl* non garanties.

debilitating /dɪ'bɪlɪteɪtɪŋ/ *adj* [*disease*] débilitant.

debit /'debɪt/ FIN **I** *n* débit *m*.
II *noun modifier* [*account, balance*] débiteur/-trice; ~ **entries** sommes *fpl* inscrites au débit.
III *vtr* débiter [*account*] (**with** de).

debonair /,debə'neə(r)/ *adj* [*person*] élégant et plein d'assurance.

debrief /,diː'briːf/ *vtr* interroger; **to be** ~**ed** [*diplo-*

---

mat, agent] rendre compte (oralement) d'une mission; [*defector, freed hostage*] être interrogé.

debriefing /,diː'briːfɪŋ/ *n* **1** ¢ (of freed hostage, defector) interrogation *f*; **the soldiers will remain here for** ~ les soldats resteront ici pour rendre compte de leur mission; **2** ¢ (report) compte-rendu *m* (oral), critique *f*.

debris /'debriː, 'de-, US də'briː/ *n* (of plane) débris *mpl*; (of building) décombres *mpl*; (rubbish) déchets *mpl*.

debt /det/ **I** *n* **1** FIN dette *f* (**to** envers); **bad** ~**s** créances *fpl* douteuses; **to get into** ~ s'endetter; **to be in** ~ avoir des dettes; **she is $2,000 in** ~ elle a 2000 dollars de dettes; **to get out of** ~ acquitter ses dettes; **to pay off one's** ~**s** rembourser ses dettes; **2** (obligation) dette *f* (**to** envers); **to acknowledge one's** ~ **to sb** reconnaître qu'on doit beaucoup à qn.
II *noun modifier* FIN [*collection, recovery, relief*] des créances; [*capacity, level, ratio*] d'endettement.

debt collector *n* agent *m* de recouvrement.

debtor /'detə(r)/ FIN *n* débiteur/-trice *m/f*.

debug /,diː'bʌg/ *vtr* (*p prés etc* -**gg**-) **1** COMPUT déboguer; **2** enlever les micros cachés dans [*room*].

debunk /,diː'bʌŋk/ *vtr* démystifier [*theory*]; briser [*myth*].

debut /'deɪbjuː, US dɪ'bjuː/ **I** *n* (artistic, sporting) débuts *mpl*; **to make one's** ~ **as** (in unfamiliar activity) faire ses débuts comme [*director*]; (in particular role) débuter dans le rôle de.
II *noun modifier* [*album, concert, role*] premier/-ière.

Dec *abrév écrite* = **December**.

decade /'dekeɪd, dɪ'keɪd, US dɪ'keɪd/ *n* décennie *f*.

decadent /'dekədənt/ *adj* décadent.

decaffeinated /,diː'kæfɪneɪtɪd/ *adj* décaféiné.

decalitre GB, **decaliter** US /'dekəliːtə(r)/ ▶789 *n* décalitre *m*.

decametre GB, **decameter** US /'dekəmiːtə(r)/ ▶1045 *n* décamètre *m*.

decamp /dɪ'kæmp/ *vi* (leave) partir; **to** ~ **with sth** s'éclipser en emportant qch.

decant /dɪ'kænt/ *vtr* LIT décanter [*wine*]; transvaser [*other liquid*].

decanter /dɪ'kæntə(r)/ *n* (for wine, port) carafe *f* (à décanter); (for whisky) flacon *m* à whisky.

decapitate /dɪ'kæpɪteɪt/ *vtr* décapiter.

decathlon /dɪ'kæθlɒn/ *n* décathlon *m*.

decay /dɪ'keɪ/ **I** *n* **1** (rot) (of timber, vegetation) pourriture *f*; (of house, area) délabrement *m*; **to fall into** ~ [*building*] se délabrer; **2** (dental) carie *f*; **3** FIG (of culture) déclin *m*; (of institution, industry) déclin *m*; (of civilization) décadence *f*; **moral** ~ déchéance morale.
II *vi* **1** (rot) [*timber, vegetation, food*] pourrir; [*corpse*] se décomposer; [*tooth*] se carier; [*bone*] se détériorer; **2** (disintegrate) [*building*] se détériorer; **3** FIG (decline) [*civilization*] décliner.

deceased /dɪ'siːst/ **I** *n* **the** ~ (dead person) le défunt/la défunte; (collectively) les défunts *mpl*.
II *adj* décédé, défunt.

deceit /dɪ'siːt/ *n* malhonnêteté *f*.

deceitful /dɪ'siːtfl/ *adj* malhonnête.

deceive /dɪ'siːv/ **I** *vtr* **1** (lie to and mislead) tromper, duper [*friend*]; **to be** ~**d** (fooled) être dupe; **don't be** ~**d by his air of calm** ne te laisse pas abuser par son calme; **2** (be unfaithful to) tromper [*spouse, lover*].
II *v refl* **to** ~ **oneself** se faire des illusions.

December /dɪ'sembə(r)/ ▶1090 *n* décembre *m*.

decency /'diːsnsɪ/ *n* **1** (good manners) politesse *f*; **common** ~ la simple politesse; **you can't in all** ~... tu ne peux décemment pas...; **2** (morality) **he hasn't an ounce of** ~ il n'a pas le moindre sens moral; **3** (propriety) convenances *fpl*; (in sexual matters) décence *f*; **he has no sense of** ~ il n'a aucun sens des convenances.

decent /'diːsnt/ *adj* **1** (respectable) [*family, man, woman*] comme il faut, bien *inv*; **no** ~ **person would do a thing like that** quelqu'un de normal ne ferait jamais ça; **a** ~ **burial** un enterrement convenable; **after a** ~ **interval** après une période convenable; **to do the ~ thing** faire la chose qu'il faut/fallait; **2** (pleasant) sympathique, bien○ *inv*; **it's ~ of him** c'est très gentil à lui; **3** (adequate) [*housing, wages, level, facilities*] convenable; **4** (not shabby) [*garment*] correct; **I've nothing ~ to wear** je n'ai rien de mettable; **5** (good) [*camera, education, result*] bon/ bonne (*before n*); [*profit*] appréciable; **to make a ~ living** bien gagner sa vie; **a ~ night's sleep** une bonne nuit de sommeil; **they do a ~ fish soup** leur soupe de poisson n'est pas mauvaise; **6** (not indecent) décent, correct; **are you ~?** es-tu habillé?

decently /'di:sntlɪ/ *adv* **1** (fairly) [*paid, treated, housed*] convenablement; **2** (respectably) [*behave*] convenablement; **3** (politely) **we left as soon as we ~ could** nous sommes partis dès que nous l'avons décemment pu.

decentralize /di:'sentrəlaɪz/ *vtr* décentraliser.

decent-sized *adj* assez grand.

deception /dɪ'sepʃn/ *n* **1** ∉ (deceiving) **is she capable of such ~?** est-elle capable d'une telle duplicité?; **to obtain sth by ~** obtenir qch par fraude; **2** (trick) supercherie *f*; (to gain money, property) escroquerie *f*.

deceptive /dɪ'septɪv/ *adj* [*appearance*] trompeur/-euse.

deceptively /dɪ'septɪvlɪ/ *adv* **it's ~ easy** c'est plus difficile qu'il n'y paraît.

decide /dɪ'saɪd/ **I** *vtr* **1** (reach a decision) **to ~ to do** décider de faire; (after much thought) se décider à faire; **I ~d to do it** j'ai décidé de le faire; **I finally ~d to do it** je me suis décidé à le faire; **I ~d that I would leave** j'ai décidé de partir; **he hasn't ~d whether to resign** il n'a pas encore décidé s'il va démissionner; **2** (settle) régler [*matter*]; décider de [*fate, outcome*]; **the goal ~d the match** le but a été décisif; **3** (persuade) **to ~ sb to do** décider qn à faire. **II** *vi* décider; **let her ~** laisse-la décider or prendre la décision; **it's up to him to ~** c'est à lui de décider; **I can't ~** je n'arrive pas à me décider; **have you ~d?** as-tu pris une décision?; **to ~ against doing** décider de ne pas faire; **to ~ against** ne pas adopter [*plan, idea*]; rejeter [*candidate*]; **to ~ against sth** (choose not to buy) décider de ne pas acheter qch; **to ~ between** choisir, faire un choix entre [*applicants, books*]; **to ~ in favour of doing** décider de faire; **to ~ in favour of** choisir [*candidate, applicant*].
■ **decide on:** ¶ **~ on** [**sth**] **1** (choose) se décider pour [*hat, wallpaper*]; fixer [*date*]; **to ~ on a career in law** se diriger vers le droit; **2** (come to a decision on) décider de [*course of action, size, budget*]; ¶ **~ on** [**sb**] choisir [*member, applicant*]; sélectionner [*team*].

decided /dɪ'saɪdɪd/ *adj* **1** (appreciable) net/nette; **2** (determined) [*manner, tone*] décidé, résolu; [*views*] arrêté.

decidedly /dɪ'saɪdɪdlɪ/ *adv* (distinctly) [*smaller, better, happier*] nettement; [*unwell, violent, odd*] franchement.

decider /dɪ'saɪdə(r)/ *n* (point) point *m* décisif; (goal) but *m* décisif; **the ~** (game) la belle.

deciding /dɪ'saɪdɪŋ/ *adj* décisif/-ive.

deciduous /dɪ'sɪdjʊəs, dɪ'sɪdʒʊəs/ *adj* [*tree*] à feuilles caduques.

decigram(me) /'desɪˌgræm/ **► 1392** *n* décigramme *m*.

decilitre GB, **deciliter** US /'desɪliːtə(r)/ **► 789** *n* décilitre *m*.

decimal /'desɪml/ **I** *n* décimale *f*.
II *adj* [*system, currency*] décimal; **~ point** virgule *f*; **to calculate to two ~ places** calculer à deux décimales; **to go ~** adopter le système décimal.

decimate /'desɪmeɪt/ *vtr* LIT, FIG décimer.

decimetre GB, **decimeter** US /'desɪmiːtə(r)/ **► 1045** *n* décimètre *m*.

decipher /dɪ'saɪfə(r)/ *vtr* déchiffrer.

decision /dɪ'sɪʒn/ *n* décision *f*; **my ~ to leave** la décision que j'ai prise de partir; **to make** ou **take a ~** prendre une décision; **to reach** or **come to a ~** se décider; **the right/wrong ~** la bonne/mauvaise décision; **the judges' ~ is final** la décision du jury est sans appel.

decision-making I *n* **to be good/bad at ~** savoir/ne pas savoir prendre des décisions.

II *noun modifier* **~ skills** compétences *fpl* en matière de décision; **the ~ processes** les processus décisionnels.

decisive /dɪ'saɪsɪv/ *adj* **1** (firm) [*manner, tone*] ferme; **a more ~ leader** un dirigeant plus ferme; **2** (conclusive) [*battle, factor*] décisif/-ive; [*argument*] concluant.

decisively /dɪ'saɪsɪvlɪ/ *adv* avec fermeté.

deck /dek/ **I** *n* **1** (on ship) pont *m*; **car ~** pont des voitures; **on ~** sur le pont; **below ~(s)** sur le pont inférieur; **2** US (terrace) terrasse *f*; **3** (on bus) étage *m*; **4 ~ of cards** jeu *m* de cartes.
II *vtr* (decorate) orner [*building, table*] (**with** de); décorer [*tree*] (**with** de).
IDIOMS **all hands on ~!** tout le monde sur le pont!; **to clear the ~s** déblayer le terrain; **to hit the ~**○ tomber par terre.

deckchair *n* chaise *f* longue, transat○ *m*.

declaration /ˌdeklə'reɪʃn/ *n* déclaration *f*; **the Declaration of Independence** la Déclaration d'indépendance des États-Unis d'Amérique; **a customs ~** une déclaration en douane; **~ of intent** déclaration *f* de principe.

declare /dɪ'kleə(r)/ **I** *vtr* **1** (state firmly) déclarer (**that** que); (state openly) annoncer [*intention, support*]; **2** (proclaim) déclarer [*war*]; proclamer [*independence*]; **to ~ war on** déclarer la guerre à; **to ~ a state of emergency** déclarer l'état d'urgence; **3** (officially) déclarer [*income*]; communiquer [*dividend*].
II *vi* **1** (come out in favour) se déclarer (**for** pour); **2** US POL annoncer sa candidature (à la présidence).

declassify /ˌdiː'klæsɪfaɪ/ *vtr* rendre [qch] accessible [*document, information*].

declension /dɪ'klenʃn/ *n* déclinaison *f*.

decline /dɪ'klaɪn/ **I** *n* **1** (waning) déclin *m* (**of** de); **to be in ~** être sur le déclin; **to go into** ou **fall into ~** tomber en déclin; **2** (drop) baisse *f* (**in, of** de); **to be on the** ou **in ~** être en baisse; (of health, person) déclin *m* (**in, of** de); **to go/fall into (a) ~** dépérir.
II *vtr* décliner.
III *vi* **1** (drop) baisser (**by** de); [*support*] être en baisse; [*business*] ralentir; **2** (wane) être sur le déclin; **3** (refuse) refuser.
IV declining *pres p adj* **1** (getting fewer, less) **a declining birth rate** un taux de natalité en baisse; **declining sales** la baisse des ventes; **2** (in decline) [*industry, influence*] en déclin; **3** (getting worse) [*health*] déclinant.

declutch /ˌdiː'klʌtʃ/ *vi* GB débrayer.

decode /ˌdiː'kəʊd/ *vtr* décoder [*code, message, signal*].

decoding /ˌdiː'kəʊdɪŋ/ *n* (all contexts) décodage *m*.

décolleté /deɪ'kɒlteɪ, US -kɒl'teɪ/ *n, adj* décolleté (*m*).

decompose /ˌdiː'kəmpəʊz/ *vi* se décomposer.

decomposition /ˌdiːkɒmpə'zɪʃn/ *n* décomposition *f*.

decompression /ˌdiːkəm'preʃn/ *n* décompression *f*.

decontamination /ˌdiːkənˌtæmɪ'neɪʃn/ *n* décontamination *f*.

decor /'deɪkɔː(r), US deɪ'kɔːr/ *n* (specific style) décoration *f*, décor *m*; (of house) décoration *f*; THEAT décor *m*.

decorate /'dekəreɪt/ **I** *vtr* **1** (adorn) décorer (**with** de, avec); **2** (paint and paper) GEN refaire; (paint only) peindre; (paper only) tapisser; **the whole house needs to be ~d** il faudra refaire toute la décoration de la maison; **to ~ the kitchen** (with paint) refaire les peintures dans la cuisine; (with paper) tapisser la cuisine; **3** MIL décorer (**for** pour).
II *vi* (in house) faire des travaux de décoration.

decorating /'dekəreɪtɪŋ/ *n* (of room, house) travaux *mpl* de décoration.

decoration /ˌdekə'reɪʃn/ *n* **1** (object) décoration *f*; **to put up/take down ~s** mettre/enlever les décorations; **2** (trimming on clothes) **with embroidered ~** orné de broderies; **3** (act or result) (for festivities) décoration *f*; (by painter) travaux *mpl* de décoration; **only for ~** purement ornemental; **4** MIL décoration *f*.

decorative /'dekərətɪv, US 'dekəreɪtɪv/ *adj* [*border, frill*] décoratif/-ive; [*sculpture, design*] ornemental.

decorator /'dekəreɪtə(r)/ *n* peintre *m*, décorateur/ -trice *m/f*.

decorum /dɪˈkɔːrəm/ n with ~ en respectant les convenances; **a sense of** ~ un sens des convenances or du décorum.

decoy I /ˈdiːkɔɪ/ n (person, vehicle) leurre m; (for hunting) appeau m, leurre m.
II /dɪˈkɔɪ/ vtr attirer [qn] dans un piège.

decrease I /ˈdiːkriːs/ n GEN diminution f (**in** de); (in price) baisse f (**in** de).
II /dɪˈkriːs/ vtr diminuer, réduire.
III /dɪˈkriːs/ vi [population] diminuer; [price] baisser; [popularity, rate] baisser, diminuer.

decreasing /dɪˈkriːsɪŋ/ adj [population, proportion] décroissant; [strength] déclinant; [price] en baisse.

decreasingly /dɪˈkriːsɪŋlɪ/ adv de moins en moins.

decree /dɪˈkriː/ **I** n **1** (order) décret m; **2** (judgment) jugement m, arrêt m; ~ **absolute/nisi** (in divorce) jugement définitif/provisoire (de divorce).
II vtr **1** GEN décréter; **2** JUR ordonner.
IDIOMS **fate had** ~**d otherwise** le sort en avait décidé autrement.

decrepit /dɪˈkrepɪt/ adj [chair, table] en mauvais état; [building] délabré; [horse, old person] décrépit.

dedicate /ˈdedɪkeɪt/ vtr **1** (devote) consacrer, dédier [life, time] (**to** à); dédier [book, performance] (**to** à); **2** RELIG consacrer [church, shrine] (**to** à).

dedicated /ˈdedɪkeɪtɪd/ adj **1** (keen, devoted) [teacher, mother, fan] dévoué; [worker, secretary] zélé; [disciple] enthousiaste; [socialist] convaincu; [musician, attitude] sérieux/-ieuse; **we only want people who are really** ~ nous ne voulons que des gens sérieux; **he is** ~ **to social reform** il consacre tous ses efforts aux réformes sociales; **2** COMPUT spécialisé.

dedication /ˌdedɪˈkeɪʃn/ n **1** (devoted attitude) dévouement m (**to** à); **her** ~ **to duty** son dévouement; **2** (in a book, on music programme) dédicace f; **3** (act of dedicating) dédicace f.

deduce /dɪˈdjuːs, US -ˈduːs/ vtr déduire.

deduct /dɪˈdʌkt/ vtr prélever [subscription, tax] (**from** sur); déduire [sum, expenses] (**from** de).

deductible /dɪˈdʌktəbl/ adj COMM déductible.

deduction /dɪˈdʌkʃn/ n **1** (on wages) retenue f; (of tax) prélèvement m; (on bill) déduction f; **after** ~**s** une fois les retenues effectuées; **a** ~ **from** une déduction or une retenue or un prélèvement sur; **2** (conclusion) déduction f, conclusion f; **to make a** ~ tirer une conclusion (**from** de); **3** (reasoning) déduction f.

deed /diːd/ n **1** (action) acte m; **to do one's good** ~ **for the day** faire sa bonne action; **2** (for property) acte m de propriété.

deed: ~ **box** n coffre m à documents; ~ **of covenant** n JUR acte m de donation.

deed poll n (pl **deeds poll**) **to change one's name by** ~ changer légalement son nom.

deem /diːm/ vtr considérer; **it was** ~**ed necessary/ appropriate to do** on a jugé nécessaire/convenable de faire.

deep /diːp/ ▶ 1045 **I** n LITTÉR **the** ~ l'océan m.
II adj **1** (from top to bottom) GEN profond; [mud, snow, carpet] épais/épaisse; [container, drawer, saucepan, grass] haut; **a** ~**-pile carpet** une moquette de haute laine; **how** ~ **is the lake?** quelle est la profondeur du lac?; **the lake is 13 m** ~ le lac a 13 m de profondeur; **a hole 5 cm** ~ un trou de 5 cm; **2** (in width) [band, strip] large; **3** (from front to back) [shelf, alcove, stage] profond; **a shelf 30 cm** ~ une étagère de 30 cm de profondeur; **4** FIG (intense) GEN profond; [desire, need] grand; **to be in** ~ **trouble**° avoir de sérieux ennuis; **5** (impenetrable) GEN profond; [secret] grand; [person] réservé; **in** ~**est Wales** HUM au fin fond du pays de Galles; **you're a** ~ **one**°! tu caches bien ton jeu°!; **6** (intellectually profound) GEN profond; [knowledge] approfondi; **at a** ~**er level** plus en profondeur; **7** (dark) [colour] intense; [tan] prononcé; ~ **blue eyes** des yeux d'un bleu profond; **8** (low) [voice] profond; [note, sound] grave; **9** (involved, absorbed) ~ **in** absorbé dans [thought, entertainment]; plongé dans [book, conversation]; ~ **in debt**

endetté jusqu'au cou; **10** (long) [shot, serve] en profondeur.
III adv **1** (a long way down) [dig, bury, cut] profondément; ~ **beneath the earth's surface** à une grande profondeur sous la surface de la terre; **to sink** ~**er** s'enfoncer plus profondément; **to dig** ~**er into an affair** FIG creuser (plus loin) une affaire; **to sink** ~**er into debt** FIG s'endetter davantage; **2** (a long way in) ~ **in** ou **into** au cœur de [region]; ~ **in my heart** tout au fond de moi-même; **to be** ~ **in thought** être plongé dans ses pensées; ~ **into the night** jusque tard dans la nuit; **3** (deep down in psyche) ~ **down** ou **inside** dans mon/ton etc for intérieur; **to go** ~ [faith, loyalty] être profond; **it goes** ~**er than that** c'est plus sérieux que ça; **to run** ~ [belief, feeling, prejudice] être bien enraciné; **4** SPORT [kick, serve] en profondeur.
IDIOMS **to be in** ~°° y être jusqu'au cou°; **to be in** ~ **water** être dans de beaux draps°.

deepen /ˈdiːpən/ **I** vtr **1** (make deeper) creuser [channel, hollow]; **2** FIG (intensify) augmenter [admiration, concern, love]; **3** (make lower) rendre [qch] plus grave [voice, tone]; **4** (make darker) foncer [colour].
II vi **1** [water] devenir plus profond; [snow, mud] s'épaissir; [wrinkle] se creuser; **2** FIG (intensify) [admiration, concern, love] augmenter; [knowledge] s'approfondir; [crisis] s'aggraver; [mystery] s'épaissir; [silence] se faire plus profond; [rift] s'élargir; **3** (grow lower) [voice, pitch, tone] devenir plus grave; **4** (grow darker) [colour] foncer.
III deepening pres p adj **1** FIG (intensifying) [mystery, need, rift] croissant; [crisis] de plus en plus grave; [awareness] de plus en plus approfondi; [confusion] de plus en plus grand; [conviction] de plus en plus profond; **2** LIT [water] de plus en plus haut; [snow] de plus en plus épais/épaisse; **3** (of a voice) de plus en plus grave; **4** (becoming darker) [colour] de plus en plus foncé.

deep end /ˈdiːpend/ n grand bassin m.
IDIOMS **to go off the** ~° sortir de ses gonds°; **to jump in at the** ~ FIG prendre le taureau par les cornes; **to throw sb in at the** ~ FIG forcer qn à prendre le taureau par les cornes.

deep-felt /ˌdiːpˈfelt/ adj [admiration] sincère; [loathing] profond.

deep-freeze /ˌdiːpˈfriːz/ **I** n congélateur m.
II vtr (prét **-froze**, pp **-frozen**) congeler.

deep: ~**-fried** adj frit; ~**-frozen** adj congelé; ~**-fry** vtr faire frire; ~**-(fat)fryer** n friteuse f.

deeply /ˈdiːplɪ/ adv [felt, moving] profondément; [involved] à fond; **our most** ~ **held convictions** nos convictions les plus solides; [think] profondément; **to go** ~ **into sth** analyser qch en profondeur; [breathe, sigh, sleep] profondément; [dig, cut, thrust] profondément; [drink] à grands traits; [tanned] extrêmement.

deep: ~**-rooted** adj [anxiety, prejudice, problem] profondément enraciné; [habit] ancré; ~**-sea** adj [exploration, diver, diving] sous-marin/-e; [fisherman, fishing] hauturier/-ière; ~**-seated** adj = **deep-rooted**; ~**-set** adj (très) enfoncé; ~ **South** n US Sud m profond; ~ **space** n espace m lointain.

deer /dɪə(r)/ n (red) cerf m; (roe) chevreuil m; (fallow) daim m; (female of all species) biche f.

de-escalate /ˌdiːˈeskəleɪt/ **I** vtr faire baisser [tension, violence]; désamorcer [crisis].
II vi [tension, violence] baisser; [arms race] ralentir; [crisis] se désamorcer.

deface /dɪˈfeɪs/ vtr abîmer [wall, door]; dégrader, couvrir [qch] d'inscriptions [painting, monument]; **to** ~ **sth with** barbouiller qch de.

default /dɪˈfɔːlt/ **I** n (failure to keep up payments) non-remboursement m; (failure to pay fine, debt) non-paiement m; **the company is in** ~ la compagnie manque à ses engagements.
II vi (fail to make payments) ne pas régler ses échéances; **to** ~ **on payments** ou **on a loan** ne pas régler les échéances d'un emprunt.
III by default adv phr par défaut; **to win by** ~

gagner par forfait; **to be elected by** ~ être élu à défaut de concurrents.

IV in default of *prep phr* en l'absence de.

defeat /dɪ'fiːt/ **I** *n* **1** (getting beaten) défaite *f*; **to suffer a** ~ essuyer une défaite; **England's 3–2** ~ la défaite de l'Angleterre 2–3; **2** (of proposal, bill) rejet *m* (**of** de); **3** (personal failure) échec *m*; **an admission of** ~ un aveu d'échec; **to admit** ~ avouer son échec.

II *vtr* **1** (beat) vaincre [*enemy*]; battre [*team, opposition, candidate*]; faire subir une défaite à [*government*]; **the government was** ~**ed** le gouvernement a été mis en échec; **2** (overthrow) rejeter [*bill, proposal*]; **3** (thwart) faire échouer [*take-over bid*]; vaincre [*inflation*]; **it** ~**s the whole purpose!** ça ne sert plus à rien!

defeated /dɪ'fiːtɪd/ *adj* [*army, party*] vaincu; [*candidate, opponent*] malheureux/-euse.

defeatist /dɪ'fiːtɪst/ **I** *n* défaitiste *mf*.
II *adj* défaitiste.

defect I /'diːfekt/ *n* **1** (flaw) défaut *m*; (minor) imperfection *f*; **mechanical** ~ faute *f* mécanique; **structural** ~ vice *m* de construction; **2** (disability) **a speech** ~ un défaut d'élocution.
II /dɪ'fekt/ *vi* faire défection; **to** ~ **from** s'enfuir de [*country*]; **to** ~ **to the West** passer à l'Ouest.

defection /dɪ'fekʃn/ *n* ~ **from** défection *f* de; ~ **to** passage *m* à.

defective /dɪ'fektɪv/ *adj* (faulty) GEN défectueux/-euse; (sight etc) déficient; ~ **workmanship** malfaçons *fpl*.

defector /dɪ'fektə(r)/ *n* transfuge *mf* (**from** de).

defence GB, **defense** US /dɪ'fens/ **I** *n* **1** (act of protecting) défense *f*; **to put up a spirited** ~ se défendre vaillamment; **in** ~ **of the right to strike** pour le droit de grève; **in the** ~ **of freedom** pour défendre la liberté; **2** (means of protection) défense *f* (**against** contre); **a** ~ **against** un moyen de lutter contre [*anxiety, boredom*]; **3** (support) défense *f*; **in my own** ~ **I must say that…** je dois dire pour ma propre défense que…; **an article in** ~ **of monetarism** un article défendant le monétarisme; **4** JUR **the** ~ (representatives of the accused, case, argument) la défense; **the case for the** ~ la défense; **in her** ~ à sa décharge; **5** SPORT défense *f*; **to play in** ~ jouer en défense; **6** UNIV soutenance *f* (de thèse).
II defences *npl* GEN, MIL défenses *fpl*.
III *noun modifier* **1** MIL GEN de la défense; [*contract*] pour la défense; [*policy, forces*] de défense; [*cuts*] dans la défense; **2** JUR [*counsel, lawyer*] pour la défense; [*witness*] à décharge.

Defence Department GB, **Defense Ministry** US *n* ministère *m* de la Défense nationale.

defenceless GB, **defenseless** US /dɪ'fenslɪs/ *adj* [*person, animal*] sans défense; [*town, country*] sans défenses.

Defence minister GB, **Defense Secretary** US *n* ministre *m* de la défense nationale.

defend /dɪ'fend/ **I** *vtr* défendre [*fort, freedom, interests, client, title, belief*]; justifier [*behaviour, decision*]; **to** ~ **a thesis** soutenir une thèse.
II *vi* SPORT défendre.
III *v refl* **to** ~ **oneself** (protect oneself) LIT, FIG se défendre.
IV defending *pres p adj* [*counsel*] de la défense; **the** ~**ing champion** le tenant du titre.

defendant /dɪ'fendənt/ *n* GEN défendeur/-eresse *m/f*.

defender /dɪ'fendə(r)/ *n* GEN, SPORT défenseur *m*.

defense *n* US = **defence**.

defensive /dɪ'fensɪv/ **I** *n* GEN, SPORT, MIL défensive *f*.
II *adj* [*weapon*] défensif/-ive; [*reaction, behaviour*] de défense; **to be (very)** ~ être sur la défensive.

defer /dɪ'fɜː(r)/ **I** *vtr* (*p prés etc* -**rr**-) GEN reporter (**until** à); suspendre [*judgment*]; remettre [qch] à plus tard [*departure, journey*]; différer [*payment*].
II *vi* (*p prés etc* -**rr**-) **to** ~ **to sb** s'incliner devant qn.
III deferred *pp adj* [*departure, purchase*] différé; [*annuity, interest*] différé; [*sale*] à tempérament, à crédit.

deference /'defərəns/ *n* déférence *f*; **in** ~ **to** par déférence pour.

deferential /defə'renʃl/ *adj* déférent.

deferment /dɪ'fɜːmənt/ *n*, **deferral** /dɪ'fɜːrəl/ *n* (postponement) prorogation *f*.

defiance /dɪ'faɪəns/ *n* ¢ défi *m* (**of** à); **in** ~ **of logic/ all the evidence** contre la logique/toute évidence.

defiant /dɪ'faɪənt/ *adj* [*person*] rebelle; [*behaviour*] provocant.

defiantly /dɪ'faɪəntlɪ/ *adv* [*say*] avec défi.

deficiency /dɪ'fɪʃənsɪ/ *n* **1** (shortage) insuffisance *f* (**of**, **in** de); MED carence *f* (**of** en); **2** (weakness) **his deficiencies as a poet** ses faiblesses *fpl* en tant que poète; **3** MED défaut *m*.

deficient /dɪ'fɪʃnt/ *adj* (inadequate) insuffisant; (faulty, flawed) déficient (**in** en).

deficit /'defɪsɪt/ *n* COMM déficit *m*; **in** ~ en déficit.

defile /dɪ'faɪl/ *vtr* **1** (pollute) LIT, FIG souiller; **2** RELIG profaner.

define /dɪ'faɪn/ *vtr* **1** définir [*term, limits*] (**as** comme); **2** (pinpoint) déterminer [*problem*]; **3 to be** ~**d against** se détacher nettement sur [*sky*].

definite /'defɪnɪt/ *adj* **1** (not vague) [*plan, criteria, amount*] précis; [*impression*] net/nette; **a** ~ **answer** une réponse claire et nette; ~ **evidence** preuves *fpl* formelles; **nothing is** ~ **yet** rien n'est encore sûr; **2** (firm) [*contract, agreement, decision, intention*] ferme; [*refusal*] catégorique; **3** (obvious) [*change, improvement, increase*] net/nette; [*advantage*] certain, évident; [*smell*] très net/nette; **4 to be** ~ [*person*] (sure) être certain (**about** de); (unyielding) être formel/-elle (**about** sur).

definite article *n* LING article *m* défini.

definitely /'defɪnɪtlɪ/ *adv* **1** (certainly) sans aucun doute; **he** ~ **said he wasn't coming** il a bien dit qu'il ne viendrait pas; **she's** ~ **not there** elle n'est pas là, c'est sûr; **I'm** ~ **not going** c'est décidé, je n'y vais pas; **it's** ~ **colder today** il fait nettement plus froid aujourd'hui; **this one is** ~ **the best** celui-ci est sans conteste le meilleur; **this** ~ **isn't going to work** manifestement ça ne va pas marcher; '~**!**' 'absolument!'; **2** (categorically) [*commit oneself*] formellement.

definition /defɪ'nɪʃn/ *n* GEN, TV définition *f*.

definitive /dɪ'fɪnətɪv/ *adj* définitif/-ive.

definitively /dɪ'fɪnətɪvlɪ/ *adv* GEN définitivement; [*answer*] de manière définitive.

deflate /dɪ'fleɪt/ **I** *vtr* **1** LIT dégonfler; **2** FIG **to** ~ **sb's ego** remettre qn à sa place.
II *vi* [*tyre, balloon*] se dégonfler.

deflation /dɪ'fleɪʃn/ *n* ECON déflation *f*.

deflationary /diː'fleɪʃənərɪ, US -nerɪ/ *adj* déflationniste.

deflect /dɪ'flekt/ *vtr* **1** dévier [*missile*]; **2** FIG détourner [*blame, criticism, attention*].

deflection /dɪ'flekʃn/ *n* (of missile) déviation *f*; PHYS (of air) déflexion *f*; (of light) déviation *f*.

deform /dɪ'fɔːm/ **I** *vtr* déformer.
II deformed *pp adj* **1** MED déformé; (from birth) difforme; **2** [*metal, structure*] déformé.

defraud /dɪ'frɔːd/ *vtr* escroquer [*client, employer*]; frauder [*tax authority*]; **to** ~ **sb of sth** escroquer qch à qn.

defrost /diː'frɒst/ **I** *vtr* décongeler [*food*]; dégivrer [*refrigerator*].
II *vi* [*refrigerator*] dégivrer; [*food*] décongeler.

deft /deft/ *adj* adroit de ses mains, habile.

deftly /'deftlɪ/ *adv* adroitement.

defunct /dɪ'fʌŋkt/ *adj* [*organization, person*] défunt.

defuse /diː'fjuːz/ *vtr* désamorcer.

defy /dɪ'faɪ/ *vtr* **1** (disobey) défier [*authority, law, death, gravity, person*]; **2** (challenge) **to** ~ **sb to do** mettre qn au défi de faire; **3** (elude, resist) défier [*description, logic, analysis*].

degenerate I /dɪ'dʒenərət/ *n* dégénéré/-e *m/f*.
II /dɪ'dʒenərət/ *adj* GEN dégénéré; [*life*] dépravé.
III /dɪ'dʒenəreɪt/ *vi* dégénérer (**into** en).

degeneration /dɪ,dʒenə'reɪʃn/ *n* dégénérescence *f*.

degradation /ˌdegrəˈdeɪʃn/ n **1** (squalor) décrépitude f; **2** (debasement) déchéance f; (of culture) dégradation f.

degrade /dɪˈgreɪd/ vtr **1** (humiliate) humilier [person]; **2** (damage) dégrader [environment].

degrading /dɪˈgreɪdɪŋ/ adj [conditions, film] dégradant; [job] avilissant; [treatment] humiliant.

degree /dɪˈgriː/ n **1** GEOG, MATH, PHYS degré m; **40 ~s to the vertical** 40 degrés par rapport à la verticale; **ten ~s of latitude/longitude** 10 degrés de latitude/longitude; **30 ~s centigrade** 30 degrés centigrades; **a temperature of 104 ~s** 39 de fièvre; **2** UNIV diplôme m universitaire; **first** ou **bachelor's ~** licence f; **to get a ~** obtenir un diplôme (universitaire); **to have a ~** être diplômé; **3** (amount) degré m; **a high ~ of efficiency** beaucoup de compétence; **to such a ~ that** à un tel point que; **to a ~, to some ~** dans une certaine mesure; **to a lesser ~** dans une moindre mesure; **not in the slightest ~** pas le moins du monde; **by ~s** petit à petit; **with varying ~s of success** avec un succès variable; **4** US JUR **first ~ murder** homicide m volontaire avec préméditation.

degree: **~ ceremony** n GB UNIV cérémonie f de remise des diplômes; **~ course** n GB UNIV programme m d'études universitaires.

dehydrate /diːˈhaɪdreɪt/ vtr déshydrater.

dehydrated /ˌdiːˈhaɪdreɪtɪd/ adj GEN déshydraté; [milk] en poudre; **to become ~** se déshydrater.

dehydration /ˌdiːhaɪˈdreɪʃn/ n déshydratation f.

de-icer /ˌdiːˈaɪsə(r)/ n AUT dégivrant m.

deign /deɪn/ vtr **to ~ to do** condescendre à faire.

deity /ˈdiːɪti/ n divinité f; **the Deity** Dieu.

dejected /dɪˈdʒektɪd/ adj découragé.

delay /dɪˈleɪ/ I n **1** (of train, plane, post) retard m (**of** de; **to, on** sur); **a few minutes' ~** un délai de quelques minutes; **2** (slowness) **without (further) ~** sans (plus) tarder; **3** (time lapse) délai m (**of** de; **between** entre). II vtr **1** (postpone) différer [decision, publication]; **to ~ doing** attendre pour faire; **2** (hold up) retarder [train, arrival, post]; **flights were ~ed by up to 12 hours** les vols ont eu jusqu'à 12 heures de retard. III **delayed** pp adj [passenger] en retard; **to have a ~ed reaction** réagir après coup (**to** à). IV **delaying** pres p adj [action, tactic] dilatoire.

delayed action /dɪˈleɪd/ adj à retardement.

delegate I /ˈdelɪgət/ n délégué/-e m/f. II /ˈdelɪgeɪt/ vtr déléguer.

delete /dɪˈliːt/ vtr GEN supprimer (**from** de); (with pen) barrer; COMPUT effacer; **~ where inapplicable** rayer les mentions inutiles.

deletion /dɪˈliːʃn/ n (word, line taken out) suppression f; (word, line crossed out) rature f.

deliberate I /dɪˈlɪbərət/ adj **1** (intentional) délibéré; **it was ~** il/elle l'a fait etc exprès; **2** (measured) mesuré. II /dɪˈlɪbəreɪt/ vi délibérer (**over, about** sur).

deliberately /dɪˈlɪbərətli/ adv **1** (intentionally) [do, say] exprès; [sarcastic, provocative] délibérément; **2** (slowly and carefully) [speak] posément; [walk] délibérément.

deliberation /dɪˌlɪbəˈreɪʃn/ n **1** **after careful ~** après mûre réflexion; **2** **with ~** posément.

delicacy /ˈdelɪkəsi/ n **1** (of colour, workmanship, touch) délicatesse f; **2** (of mechanism) sensibilité f; **3** (of situation, subject) délicatesse f; **a matter of great ~** une affaire très délicate; **4** CULIN (savoury) mets m raffiné; (sweet) friandise f.

delicate /ˈdelɪkət/ adj [fabric, shade, health, mechanism, operation, situation, subject] délicat; [features] fin; [touch] léger; [china] fragile.

delicately /ˈdelɪkətli/ adv **1** [crafted, flavoured] délicatement; **2** [handle, phrase] avec délicatesse.

delicatessen /ˌdelɪkəˈtesn/ n **1** (shop) épicerie f fine; **2** US (eating-place) restaurant-traiteur m.

delicious /dɪˈlɪʃəs/ adj délicieux/-ieuse.

deliciously /dɪˈlɪʃəsli/ adv délicieusement.

delight /dɪˈlaɪt/ I n joie f, plaisir m; **to take ~ in sth/in doing** prendre un malin plaisir à qch/à faire; **a**

cry of ~ un cri de joie; **it is a ~ to do** c'est un plaisir (que) de faire; **(much) to my ~** à ma plus grande joie. II vtr ravir [person] (**with** par).

delighted /dɪˈlaɪtɪd/ adj ravi (**about, at, by, with** de; **at doing, to do** de faire); **to be ~ with sb** être très content de qn; **~ to meet you** enchanté.

delightedly /dɪˈlaɪtɪdli/ adv [announce, smile] d'un air ravi; [laugh, applaud] avec ravissement.

delightful /dɪˈlaɪtfl/ adv [warm, peaceful] agréablement; [eccentric, shy] délicieusement.

delightfully /dɪˈlaɪtfəli/ adv [warm, peaceful] agréablement; [eccentric, shy] délicieusement.

delineate /dɪˈlɪnɪeɪt/ vtr **1** déterminer [concerns, strategy, terms]; décrire [aspects, character]; **2** LIT, FIG délimiter [area, space].

delineation /dɪˌlɪnɪˈeɪʃn/ n (of problem, plan) présentation f; (of character) portrait m (psychologique).

delinquency /dɪˈlɪŋkwənsi/ n (behaviour) délinquance f.

delinquent /dɪˈlɪŋkwənt/ I n délinquant/-e m/f. II adj **1** [behaviour, child, youth] délinquant; [act] de délinquance; **2** US FIN [tax] non payé; [debtor] défaillant.

delirious /dɪˈlɪrɪəs/ adj MED, FIG délirant; **to become ~** être pris de délire.

deliriously /dɪˈlɪrɪəsli/ adv FIG follement.

delirium /dɪˈlɪrɪəm/ n MED, FIG délire m.

deliver /dɪˈlɪvə(r)/ I vtr **1** (take to address) livrer (**to** à); (to several houses) distribuer; (to an individual) apporter (**to** à); remettre [note, written message]; **'~ed to your door'** 'livraison à domicile'; **2** mettre au monde [baby, baby animal]; **3** (utter) faire [speech, sermon, reprimand]; donner [ultimatum, decision]; rendre [verdict]; réciter [lines]; **4** (hand over) céder [property] (**over to, up to** à); livrer [town] (**over to, up to** à); **5** (rescue) délivrer (**from** de). II vi [tradesman] livrer; [postman] distribuer le courrier. IDIOMS **to ~ the goods°** tenir ses engagements.

delivery /dɪˈlɪvəri/ I n **1** (of goods, milk) livraison f; (of mail) distribution f; **on ~** à la livraison; **2** (way of speaking) élocution f; **3** (of baby) accouchement m; **4** SPORT lancer m; **5** (handing over of property) remise f. II noun modifier [cost, date, note, order, service, vehicle] de livraison.

delivery: **~ address** n adresse f du destinataire; **~ man** n livreur m; **~ room** n MED salle f d'accouchement.

delta /ˈdeltə/ n (all contexts) delta m.

delude /dɪˈluːd/ I vtr tromper (**with** par). II v refl **to ~ oneself** se faire des illusions.

deluge /ˈdeljuːdʒ/ I n LIT, FIG déluge m. II vtr LIT, FIG submerger (**with** de).

delusion /dɪˈluːʒn/ n GEN illusion f; **~s of grandeur** la folie des grandeurs.

de luxe /dəˈlʌks, ˈlʊks/ adj [model, version, edition] de luxe; [accommodation] luxueux/-euse.

delve /delv/ vi **to ~ into** fouiller dans [pocket, records, past]; creuser [subject]; examiner [motive].

demand /dɪˈmɑːnd, US dɪˈmænd/ I n **1** (request) demande f; **on ~** [divorce, access] à la demande; [payable] à vue; **2** (pressure) exigence f; **I have many ~s on my time** mon temps est très pris; **3** ECON demande f (**for** de); **4** (favour) **to be in ~** être très demandé. II vtr **1** (request) demander [reform, release]; (forcefully) exiger [attention, ransom]; réclamer [inquiry]; (require) demander [skill, time] (**of sb** de qn); (more imperatively) exiger [punctuality, qualities].

demanding /dɪˈmɑːndɪŋ, US -ˈmænd-/ adj **1** [person] exigeant; **2** [work, course] ardu; [schedule] chargé.

demanning /ˌdiːˈmænɪŋ/ n GB réduction f de main-d'œuvre.

demarcation /ˌdiːmɑːˈkeɪʃn/ n **1** (physical) (action, boundary) démarcation f; **2** JUR, ADMIN délimitation f.

demarcation dispute n querelle f de compétence (*entre syndicats*).

demean /dɪˈmiːn/ v refl **to ~ oneself** s'abaisser.

demeaning /dɪˈmiːnɪŋ/ adj humiliant.

demeanour GB, **demeanor** US /dɪˈmiːnə(r)/ n (behaviour) comportement m; (bearing) maintien m.

demented /dɪˈmentɪd/ adj fou/folle.

dementia /dɪˈmenʃə/ n démence f; ▶ **senile dementia**.

demerara (**sugar**) /ˌdeməˈreərə/ n sucre m roux cristallisé.

demilitarize /ˌdiːˈmɪlɪtəraɪz/ vtr démilitariser.

demise /dɪˈmaɪz/ n **1** (of institution, movement) disparition f; (of aspirations) mort f; **2** (death) disparition f.

demisemiquaver /ˌdemɪˈsemɪkweɪvə(r)/ n GB triple croche f.

demister /ˌdiːˈmɪstə(r)/ GB n dispositif m antibuée.

demo○ /ˈdeməʊ/ **I** n (*abrév* = **demonstration**) POL manif○ f.
II noun modifier [*tape, model*] de démonstration.

demobilize /diːˈməʊbɪlaɪz/ vtr démobiliser.

democracy /dɪˈmɒkrəsɪ/ n démocratie f.

democrat /ˈdeməkræt/ n démocrate mf.

Democrat /ˈdeməkræt/ n POL Démocrate mf.

democratic /ˌdeməˈkrætɪk/ adj démocratique.

Democratic /ˌdeməˈkrætɪk/ adj US POL démocrate.

demolish /dɪˈmɒlɪʃ/ vtr **1** démolir [*building, argument, person*]; **2**○ HUM engloutir [*food*]; **3**○ battre [qn] à plates coutures [*team*].

demolition /ˌdeməˈlɪʃn/ n LIT, FIG démolition f.

demon /ˈdiːmən/ n RELIG, FIG démon m.

demonic /dɪˈmɒnɪk/ adj [*aspect, power*] diabolique; [*noise*] infernal.

demonstrable /ˈdemənstrəbl, US dɪˈmɒnstrəbl/ adj démontrable.

demonstrably /ˈdemənʃtrəblɪ, dɪˈmɒnstrəblɪ/ adv manifestement.

demonstrate /ˈdemənstreɪt/ **I** vtr **1** (illustrate, prove) démontrer [*theory, truth*]; **2** (show, reveal) manifester [*emotion, concern, support*]; montrer [*skill*]; **3** (display) faire la démonstration de [*machine, product*]; **to ~ how to do** montrer comment faire.
II vi POL manifester (**for** en faveur de; **against** contre).

demonstration /ˌdemənˈstreɪʃn/ n **1** POL manifestation f (**against** contre; **for** en faveur de); **2** (of emotion, support) manifestation f; **3** (of machine, theory) démonstration f; **to give a ~** faire une démonstration.

demonstrative /dɪˈmɒnstrətɪv/ adj démonstratif/-ive.

demonstrator /ˈdemənstreɪtə(r)/ n **1** POL manifestant/-e m/f; **2** COMM démonstrateur/-trice m/f.

demoralize /dɪˈmɒrəlaɪz, US -ˈmɔːr-/ vtr démoraliser.

demote /dɪˈməʊt/ vtr rétrograder [*person*]; ramener [qch] au deuxième plan [*idea, policy*].

demur /dɪˈmɜː(r)/ SOUT **I** n **without ~** sans objection(s).
II vi (p prés etc -**rr**-) **1** (disagree) soulever des objections (**at** contre); **2** (complain) rechigner.

demure /dɪˈmjʊə(r)/ adj [*behaviour, dress*] discret/-ète; [*girl*] sage et modeste.

den /den/ n **1** (of lion) antre m; (of fox) tanière f; **2** (room) tanière f.

denationalize /ˌdiːˈnæʃənəlaɪz/ vtr dénationaliser.

denial /dɪˈnaɪəl/ n (of accusation, rumour) démenti m; (of guilt, doctrine, rights) négation f; (of request) rejet m.

denier /ˈdenɪə(r)/ n denier m.

denigration /ˌdenɪˈɡreɪʃn/ n dénigrement m (**of** de).

denim /ˈdenɪm/ **I** n jean m; **~s** (trousers) jean m.
II noun modifier [*jacket*] en jean; **~ jeans** jean m.

Denmark /ˈdenmɑːk/ ▶ **840** pr n Danemark m.

denomination /dɪˌnɒmɪˈneɪʃn/ n **1** (name) dénomination f; **2** RELIG confession f; **3** FIN valeur f; **high ~ banknote** grosse coupure.

denote /dɪˈnəʊt/ vtr (stand for) indiquer; [*word, notice*] signifier.

denounce /dɪˈnaʊns/ vtr **1** (inform on) dénoncer (**to** à); **2** (criticize) dénoncer; **3** (accuse) accuser.

dense /dens/ adj dense.

densely /ˈdenslɪ/ adv **~ populated/wooded** très peuplé/boisé.

density /ˈdensətɪ/ n densité f.

dent /dent/ **I** n (in wood) entaille f; (in metal) bosse f.
II vtr faire une entaille dans [*wood*]; cabosser [*car*]; entamer [*pride*].

dental /ˈdentl/ **I** n LING dentale f.
II adj GEN dentaire; LING dental.

dental: **~ appointment** n rendez-vous m chez le dentiste; **~ clinic** n centre m de soins dentaires; **~ floss** n fil m dentaire; **~ plate** n dentier m; **~ surgeon** ▶ **1251** n chirurgien-dentiste m; **~ surgery** n GB (premises) cabinet m dentaire; (treatment) chirurgie f dentaire.

dentist /ˈdentɪst/ ▶ **1251** n dentiste mf.

dentistry /ˈdentɪstrɪ/ n médecine f dentaire.

denture /ˈdentʃə(r)/ **I** n (prosthesis) prothèse f dentaire.
II dentures npl dentier m (sg).

denunciation /dɪˌnʌnsɪˈeɪʃn/ n dénonciation f (**of** de).

deny /dɪˈnaɪ/ vtr **1** démentir [*rumour*]; nier [*accusation*]; **to ~ that...** nier que...; **she denies that this is true** elle nie que cela soit vrai; **to ~ doing** ou **having done** nier avoir fait; **2** (refuse) **to ~ sb sth** refuser qch à qn; **to ~ sb admittance to a building** refuser l'accès d'un bâtiment à qn; **to ~ oneself sth** se priver de qch; **3** (renounce) renier [*God*].

deodorant /diːˈəʊdərənt/ n (personal) déodorant m; (for room) déodorisant m; **roll-on/spray ~** déodorant à bille/en bombe.

deodorize /diːˈəʊdəraɪz/ vtr désodoriser.

depart /dɪˈpɑːt/ vi **1** SOUT partir (**from** de; **for** pour); **the train now ~ing from platform one** le train au départ du quai numéro un; **2** (deviate) **to ~ from** s'éloigner de [*position, truth*]; abandonner [*practice*].

departed /dɪˈpɑːtɪd/ adj EUPH (dead) défunt.

departing /dɪˈpɑːtɪŋ/ adj [*chairman*] sortant.

department /dɪˈpɑːtmənt/ n **1** COMM (section) service m; **personnel ~** service du personnel; **2** (governmental) ministère m; (administrative) service m; **social services ~** services sociaux; **3** (in store) rayon m; **electrical ~** rayon m électricité; **4** (in hospital) service m; **X ray ~** radiologie f; **5** (in university) département m; cf UFR f; **6** SCH section f (*regroupement des professeurs par matière*); **7** ADMIN, GEOG (district) département m; **8**○ (area) domaine m.

departmental /ˌdiːpɑːˈtmentl/ adj **1** POL [*colleague, meeting*] de ministère; **2** ADMIN [*head, meeting*] de service, de département.

department head n **1** ADMIN, COMM chef m de service, directeur/-trice m/f du service; **2** UNIV directeur/-trice m/f du département.

department: **~ manager** n (of business) chef m de service, directeur/-trice m/f du service; (of store) chef m de rayon; **Department of Defense, DOD** n US ministère m de la Défense; **Department of Energy, DOE** n US ministère m de l'Énergie; **Department of Health, DOH**, GB **Department of Health and Human Services** US n ministère m de la Santé; **Department of Social Security, DSS** n GB ministère m des Affaires sociales; **Department of the Environment, DOE** n GB ministère m de l'Environnement; **Department of Trade and Industry, DTI** n GB ministère m du Commerce et de l'industrie; **~ store** n grand magasin m.

departure /dɪˈpɑːtʃə(r)/ n **1** (of person, train) départ m (**from** de; **for** pour); **2** FIG (start) **a new ~ in physics** un nouveau départ en physique; **3** (from truth, regulation) entorse f (**from** à); (from policy, tradition) rupture f (**from** par rapport à); **to be a total ~ from** s'éloigner totalement de.

departure: **~ gate** n porte f de départ; **~ platform** n RAIL quai m de départ; **~s board** n tableau

French departments
The names of French departments usually have the definite article, except when used after the preposition en.

In, to and from somewhere
For in *and* to *use* dans le *or* dans les *for masculine and plural names of departments:*

to live in the Loiret	= vivre dans le Loiret
to go to the Loiret	= aller dans le Loiret
to live in the Landes	= vivre dans les Landes
to go to the Landes	= aller dans les Landes
to live in the Loir-et-Cher	= vivre dans le Loir-et-Cher
to go to the Loir-et-Cher	= aller dans le Loir-et-Cher

For in *and* to *use* en *for feminine names of departments:*

to live in Savoy	= vivre en Savoie
to go to Savoy	= aller en Savoie
to live in Seine-et-Marne	= vivre en Seine-et-Marne
to go to Seine-et-Marne	= aller en Seine-et-Marne

For from *use* du (*or* de l' *before a vowel*) *for masculine and* des *for plural names of departments:*

to come from the Loiret	= venir du Loiret
to come from the Landes	= venir des Landes
to come from the Loir-et-Cher	= venir du Loir-et-Cher

For from *use* de *without the definite article for feminine names of departments:*

to come from Savoy	= venir de Savoie
to come from Seine-et-Marne	= venir de Seine-et-Marne

Uses with nouns
Use de *with the definite article in most cases:*

a Cantal accent	= un accent du Cantal
the Var area	= la région du Var
the Creuse countryside	= les paysages de la Creuse
Loiret people	= les gens du Loiret
Yonne representatives	= les représentants de l'Yonne
Landes restaurants	= les restaurants des Landes
the Calvados team	= l'équipe du Calvados
Ardennes towns	= les villes des Ardennes

but use de *without the definite article with feminine names that include* et:

Seine-et-Marne hotels	= les hôtels de Seine-et-Marne

Some cases are undecided:

Savoy roads	= les routes de Savoie *or* de la Savoie

m des départs.

depend /dɪˈpend/ *vi* **1** (rely) **to ~ on** dépendre de, compter sur (**for** pour); **to ~ on sb/sth to do** compter sur qn/qch pour faire; **you can't ~ on the bus arriving on time** tu ne peux pas être sûr que le bus sera à l'heure; **the temperature varies ~ing on the season** la température varie suivant la saison; **2** (financially) **to ~ on sb** vivre à la charge de qn.

dependability /dɪˌpendəˈbɪlətɪ/ *n* (of equipment) fiabilité *f*.

dependable /dɪˈpendəbl/ *adj* [*person*] digne de confiance; [*machine*] fiable; [*forecast, news, source*] sûr.

dependant /dɪˈpendənt/ *n* personne *f* à charge.

dependence, **dependance** US /dɪˈpendəns/ *n* **1** (reliance) dépendance *f* (**on** vis-à-vis de); **2** (addiction) dépendance *f* (**on** à).

dependency /dɪˈpendənsɪ/ *n* **1** POL (territory) territoire *m* dépendant; **2** (reliance) dépendance *f* (**on sb** vis-à-vis de qn; **on sth** à qch).

dependent /dɪˈpendənt/ *adj* **1** (reliant) [*relative*] à charge; **to be ~ (up)on** GEN dépendre de; (financially) vivre à la charge de.

depict /dɪˈpɪkt/ *vtr* ART représenter; (in writing) dépeindre (**as** comme).

depiction /dɪˈpɪkʃn/ *n* peinture *f*, représentation *f*.

depilatory /dɪˈpɪlətrɪ, US -tɔːrɪ/ *n, adj* dépilatoire (*m*).

deplete /dɪˈpliːt/ *vtr* réduire [*reserves, numbers*].

depletion /dɪˈpliːʃn/ *n* (of resources, funds) baisse *f*.

deplorable /dɪˈplɔːrəbl/ *adj* déplorable.

deplore /dɪˈplɔː(r)/ *vtr* déplorer.

deploy /dɪˈplɔɪ/ *vtr* GEN, MIL déployer.

deployment /dɪˈplɔɪmənt/ *n* déploiement *m*.

depopulation /diːˌpɒpjʊˈleɪʃn/ *n* dépeuplement *m*.

deport /dɪˈpɔːt/ *vtr* JUR expulser (**to** vers); HIST déporter.

deportation /ˌdiːpɔːˈteɪʃn/ *n* JUR expulsion *f*; HIST déportation *f*.

deportee /ˌdiːpɔːˈtiː/ *n* déporté/-e *m/f*.

deportment /dɪˈpɔːtmənt/ *n* SOUT maintien *m*.

depose /dɪˈpəʊz/ *vtr* POL, JUR déposer.

deposit /dɪˈpɒzɪt/ **I** *n* **1** (to bank account) dépôt *m*; **on ~** en dépôt; **2** (part payment) (on house, hire purchase goods) versement *m* initial (**on** sur); (on holiday, goods) acompte *m*, arrhes *fpl* (**on** sur); **3** (to secure goods, hotel room) arrhes *fpl*, acompte *m*; **4** (paid by hirer, tenant) caution *f*; **5** (on bottle) consigne *f*; **6** GB POL cautionnement *m*; **7** (of silt, mud) dépôt *m*; (of coal, mineral) gisement *m*; **8** (sediment) dépôt *m*.
II *vtr* **1** (put down) déposer [*object*]; **2** (entrust) déposer [*money*]; **to ~ sth with sb** confier qch à qn.

deposit account *n* GB FIN compte *m* de dépôt.

depositor /dɪˈpɒzɪtə(r)/ *n* FIN déposant/-e *m/f*.

deposit slip *n* bordereau *m* de versement.

depot /ˈdepəʊ, US ˈdiːpəʊ/ *n* **1** (for storage) dépôt *m*; **2** (terminus, garage) **bus ~** dépôt *m* d'autobus; **3** US (station) (bus) gare *f* routière; (rail) gare *f* ferroviaire.

deprave /dɪˈpreɪv/ *vtr* dépraver.

depravity /dɪˈprævətɪ/ *n* dépravation *f*.

deprecating /ˈdeprɪkeɪtɪŋ/ *adj* (disapproving) désapprobateur/-trice.

deprecatingly /ˈdeprɪkeɪtɪŋlɪ/ *adv* (about oneself) avec modestie; (about sb else) avec condescendance.

deprecatory /ˌdeprɪˈkɑːtərɪ, US -tɔːrɪ/ *adj* **1** (disapproving) désapprobateur/-trice; **2** (apologetic) d'excuse.

depreciate /dɪˈpriːʃɪeɪt/ *vi* se déprécier (**against** par rapport à).

depress /dɪˈpres/ *vtr* **1** GEN déprimer; **2** COMM, FIN faire baisser [*prices*]; affaiblir [*trading*].

depressed /dɪˈprest/ *adj* **1** déprimé; **I got ~ about it** cela m'a déprimé; **2** [*region, market, industry*] en déclin; [*sales, prices*] très bas/basse.

depressing /dɪˈpresɪŋ/ *adj* déprimant.

depression /dɪˈpreʃn/ *n* **1** MED, PSYCH dépression *f*; **to suffer from ~** être dépressif/-ive; **2** (slump) récession *f*, crise *f* (**in** de); **3** (hollow) creux *m*; **4** METEOROL dépression *f*.

depressive /dɪˈpresɪv/ *n, adj* dépressif/-ive (*m/f*).

depressurize /diːˈpreʃəraɪz/ *vi* se dépressuriser.

deprivation /ˌdeprɪˈveɪʃn/ *n* **1** (poverty) (of person) privations *fpl*; (of society) dénuement *m*; **2** PSYCH carence *f* affective; **3** (of right, privilege) privation *f*.

deprive /dɪˈpraɪv/ *vtr* priver (**of** de).

deprived /dɪˈpraɪvd/ *adj* [*area, family*] démuni; [*childhood*] malheureux/-euse.

dept *abrév écrite* = **department**.

depth /depθ/ *n* **1** (measurement) (of hole, water) profondeur *f*; (of layer) épaisseur *f*; **at a ~ of 30 m** à 30 m de profondeur; **12 m in ~** profond de 12 m; **to be out of one's ~** (in water) ne plus avoir pied; FIG être complètement perdu; **in the ~s of the country-side** en pleine campagne; **2** (of colour, emotion) intensité *f*; (of crisis, recession) gravité *f*; (of ignorance) étendue *f*; (of despair) fond *m*; **3** (of knowledge) étendue *f*; (of analysis, hero, novel) profondeur *f*; **to examine sth in ~** examiner qch en détail; **4** CIN, PHOT **~ of focus** distance *f* focale; **~ of field** profondeur *f* de champ.

deputation /ˌdepjʊˈteɪʃn/ *n* délégation *f*.

depute /dɪˈpjuːt/ *vtr* SOUT charger [*person*].

deputize /ˈdepjʊtaɪz/ *vi* **to ~ for sb** remplacer qn.

deputy /ˈdepjʊtɪ/ **I** *n* **1** (aide) adjoint/-e *m/f* (**to sb** de

qn); (replacement) remplaçant/-e *m/f*; **2** (politician) député *m*; **3** US (also **~ sheriff**) shérif *m* adjoint.
II *noun modifier* [*director, editor, head, manager, mayor*] adjoint.

deputy: **~ chairman** *n* vice-président *m*; **~ leader** *n* GB POL vice-président *m*; **~ premier**, **~ prime minister** *n* POL vice-premier ministre *m*; **~ president** *n* GEN, POL vice-président *m*.

derail /dɪˈreɪl/ *vtr* faire dérailler.

derailleur gears /dəˈreɪljə(r)/ *npl* dérailleur *m*.

derailment /dɪˈreɪlmənt/ *n* déraillement *m*.

derange /dɪˈreɪndʒ/ *vtr* déranger.

deregulate /ˌdiːˈregjʊleɪt/ *vtr* FIN libérer [*prices*]; déréguler [*market*].

derelict /ˈderəlɪkt/ **I** *n* (tramp) clochard/-e *m/f*.
II *adj* (abandoned) abandonné; (ruined) en ruines.

deride /dɪˈraɪd/ *vtr* ridiculiser.

derision /dɪˈrɪʒn/ *n* ¢ moqueries *fpl*.

derisory /dɪˈraɪsərɪ/ *adj* dérisoire.

derivative /dəˈrɪvətɪv/ **I** *n* dérivé *m*.
II *adj* **1** dérivé; **2** PÉJ [*style*] sans originalité.

derive /dɪˈraɪv/ **I** *vtr* tirer [*benefit, income*] (**from** de); retirer [*satisfaction*] (**from** de).
II *vi* **to ~ from** [*power*] découler de; [*custom*] provenir de.

dermatitis /ˌdɜːməˈtaɪtɪs/ ▶ 1002 *n* dermatite *f*.

derogatory /dɪˈrɒgətrɪ, US -tɔːrɪ/ *adj* [*remark, person*] désobligeant (**about** envers); [*term*] péjoratif/-ive.

descaler /ˌdiːˈskeɪlə(r)/ GB *n* détartrant *m*.

descant /ˈdeskænt/ *n* déchant *m*.

descant recorder *n* flûte *f* à bec soprano.

descend /dɪˈsend/ **I** *vtr* descendre [*steps, slope, path*].
II *vi* **1** (go down) [*person, plane*] descendre (**from** de); **2** (fall) [*rain, darkness, mist*] tomber (**on, over** sur); **3** (be felt) [*gloom, exhaustion*] s'abattre (**on** sur); [*peace*] s'étendre (**on** sur); **4** (arrive) arriver, débarquer○; **5** (be related to) **to be ~ed from** descendre de; **6** (sink) **to ~ to doing** s'abaisser à faire.

descendant /dɪˈsendənt/ *n* descendant/-e *m/f* (**of** de).

descent /dɪˈsent/ *n* **1** (downward motion) descente *f* (**on, upon** sur); **to make one's ~** faire sa descente; **2** (extraction) descendance *f*; **to claim ~ from** prétendre descendre de; **a British citizen by ~** un citoyen britannique par filiation.

descrambler /ˌdiːˈskræmblə(r)/ *n* TELECOM, TV désembrouilleur *m*.

describe /dɪˈskraɪb/ *vtr* **1** (give details of) décrire [*person, event, object*]; **2** (characterize) qualifier; **to ~ sb as an idiot/sth as useless** qualifier qn d'idiot/qch d'inutile; **he's ~d as generous** on dit de lui qu'il est généreux; **it could be ~d as pretty** on pourrait dire que c'est joli; **3** MATH, TECH décrire.

description /dɪˈskrɪpʃn/ *n* **1** GEN description *f* (**of** de; **as** comme étant); (for police) signalement *m* (**of** de); **to be beyond ~** être indescriptible; **2** (type, kind) genre *m*; **of every ~** de toutes sortes.

descriptive /dɪˈskrɪptɪv/ *adj* descriptif/-ive.

desecrate /ˈdesɪkreɪt/ *vtr* **1** GEN défigurer; **2** RELIG profaner [*altar, shrine*].

desecration /ˌdesɪˈkreɪʃn/ *n* **1** (of area, landscape) enlaidissement *m*; **2** RELIG (of altar, shrine) profanation *f*.

desegregate /ˌdiːˈsegrɪgeɪt/ *vtr* **to ~ a school** abolir la ségrégation dans une école.

deselect /ˌdiːsɪˈlekt/ *vtr* GB **to be ~ed** perdre l'investiture du parti.

desensitize /ˌdiːˈsensɪtaɪz/ *vtr* désensibiliser (**to** à).

desert I /ˈdezət/ *n* (all contexts) désert *m*.
II /dɪˈzɜːt/ *vtr* GEN, HUM abandonner (**for** pour); déserter [*cause*]; abandonner [*post*].
III /dɪˈzɜːt/ *vi* [*soldier*] déserter; [*politician*] faire défection.

deserted /dɪˈzɜːtɪd/ *adj* **1** (empty) désert; **2** [*person*] abandonné.

deserter /dɪˈzɜːtə(r)/ *n* déserteur *m* (**from** de).

desertion /dɪˈzɜːʃn/ *n* **1** GEN, MIL désertion *f*; **2** JUR abandon *m* du domicile conjugal.

desert island *n* île *f* déserte.

deserts /dɪˈzɜːts/ *npl* **to get one's (just) ~** avoir ce qu'on mérite.

deserve /dɪˈzɜːv/ *vtr* mériter (**to do** de faire); **~s to be remembered as…** elle mérite que l'on se souvienne d'elle comme…

deservedly /dɪˈzɜːvɪdlɪ/ *adv* à juste titre.

deserving /dɪˈzɜːvɪŋ/ *adj* **1** [*winner*] méritant; [*cause*] louable; **2 to be ~ of** SOUT être digne de [*respect*].

desiccated /ˈdesɪkeɪtɪd/ *adj* **1** CULIN séché; **2** PÉJ (dried up) desséché.

design /dɪˈzaɪn/ **I** *n* **1** (idea, conception) conception *f*; **2** (planning, development) (of object, appliance) conception *f*; (of building, room) agencement *m*; (of clothing) création *f*; **3** (drawing, plan) (detailed) plan *m* (**for** de); (sketch) croquis *m* (**for** de); **4** (model, completed object) modèle *m*; **5** (art of designing) GEN design *m*; (fashion) stylisme *m*; **6** (decorative pattern) motif *m*; **a leaf ~** un motif de feuilles; **7** ART, UNIV arts *mpl* appliqués; **8** (intention) dessein *m* (**to do** de faire); **by ~** à dessein; **to have ~s on** avoir des vues *fpl* sur; **to have evil ~s on** être mal intentionné envers.
II *vtr* **1** (conceive, plan out) concevoir; **2** (intend) **to be ~ed for sth/to do** (destined for) être destiné à qch/à faire; (made for) être conçu pour qch/pour faire; **3** (draw plan for) [*draughtsman*] dessiner le patron de [*garment*]; [*designer*] créer [*costume, garment*]; dessiner [*building, appliance*].

designate I /ˈdezɪgnət, -nət/ *adj* [*president, director*] en titre.
II /ˈdezɪgneɪt/ *vtr* [*word*] désigner; **to ~ sb (as) sth** désigner qn (comme) qch; **to ~ sth (as) sth** classer qch (comme) qch; **to ~ sth for** destiner qch à.

designation /ˌdezɪgˈneɪʃn/ *n* désignation *f*; **the ~ of sth as** le classement de qch comme [*reserve, non-smoking area*].

design: **~ centre** *n* (for exhibiting) salon *m* permanent; (for planning, conception) bureau *m* d'études; **~ consultant** *n* conseiller/-ère *m/f* en aménagement.

designer /dɪˈzaɪnə(r)/ ▶ 1251 **I** *n* GEN concepteur/-trice *m/f*; (of furniture, in fashion) créateur/-trice *m/f*; (of sets) décorateur/-trice *m/f*; **costume ~** THEAT, CIN costumier/-ière *m/f*.
II *noun modifier* [*drink, cocktail, hi-fi, sunglasses*] de dernière mode; **~ clothes, ~ labels** (made to order) vêtements *mpl* de haute couture; (available in various outlets) vêtements *mpl* griffés; **~ label** griffe *f*.

design: **~ fault** *n* faute *f* de conception, vice *m* caché; **~ feature** *n* caractéristique *f* (nominale).

designing /dɪˈzaɪnɪŋ/ *adj* PÉJ intrigant.

design specification *n* spécification *f* du modèle.

desirability /dɪˌzaɪərəˈbɪlətɪ/ *n* GEN avantages *mpl*; (sexual) charmes *mpl*.

desirable /dɪˈzaɪərəbl/ *adj* **1** [*outcome, solution*] souhaitable; [*area, position*] convoité; [*job, gift*] séduisant, tentant; **~ residence, ~ property** (in ad) maison *f* de standing; **2** (sexually) désirable.

desire /dɪˈzaɪə(r)/ **I** *n* **1** GEN désir *m* (**for** de; **to do** de faire); **to have no ~ to do** n'avoir aucune envie de faire; **2** (sexual) désir *m*.
II *vtr* GEN avoir envie de, désirer; (sexually) désirer; **to ~ to do** désirer faire; **it leaves a lot to be ~d** cela laisse beaucoup à désirer.

desist /dɪˈzɪst/ *vi* cesser (**from doing** de faire).

desk /desk/ *n* **1** (furniture) bureau *m*; MUS pupitre *m*; **writing ~** secrétaire *m*; **2** SCH (pupil's) table *f*; (old-fashioned) pupitre *m*; (teacher's) bureau *m*; **3** (in public building) **reception ~** réception *f*; **information ~** bureau *m* de renseignements; **cash ~** caisse *f*; **4** (in newspaper office) **the ~** la rédaction *f*; **news ~** service *m* des informations; **5** (in organization, government office) (department) département *m*.

desk: **~bound** *adj* [*job*] sédentaire; **~ clerk** *n* US réceptionniste *mf*; **~ pad** *n* (blotter) sous-main *m*; (notebook) bloc-notes *m*.

desktop /'desktɒp/ n **1** (dessus m de) bureau m; **2** (also ~ **computer**, ~ **PC**) ordinateur m de bureau.

desktop publishing, **DTP** n micro-édition f, PAO.

desolate I /'desələt/ adj **1** (deserted) [landscape] désolé; [house] abandonné; **2** (devastated) dévasté; **3** (forlorn) [cry] désolé; [life] désespérément triste; **4** (griefstricken) affligé.
II /'desəleɪt/ vtr dévaster [town, country]; affliger [person].

desolation /,desə'leɪʃn/ n **1** (of landscape) aspect m désolé; (of person) désolation f; **2** (misery) affliction f; **3** (devastation) dévastation f.

despair /dɪ'speə(r)/ I n (emotion) désespoir m; **to be in** ~ **about** ou **over** être désespéré par; **to do sth in** ou **out of** ~ faire qch par désespoir.
II vi désespérer (**of** de; **of doing** de faire).

despairing /dɪ'speərɪŋ/ adj désespéré.

desperate /'despərət/ adj **1** [person, plea, situation] désespéré; [criminal] prêt à tout; **to be** ~ **to do** avoir très envie de faire; **to be** ~ **for** avoir désespérément besoin de [affection, help]; attendre désespérément [news]; **to do something** ~ commettre un acte de désespoir; **2°** (terrible) affreux/-euse.

desperately /'despərətlɪ/ adv **1** [plead, look, fight] désespérément; **to need sth** ~ avoir très besoin de qch; **2** [poor] terriblement; [ill] très gravement; ~ **in love** éperdument amoureux.

desperation /,despə'reɪʃn/ n désespoir m; **in** (**sheer**) ~ **she**... en désespoir de cause elle...; **her** ~ **to win** son désir intense de gagner.

despicable /dɪ'spɪkəbl, 'despɪkəbl/ adj méprisable.

despicably /dɪ'spɪkəblɪ, 'despɪkəblɪ/ adv ignoblement.

despise /dɪ'spaɪz/ vtr mépriser.

despite /dɪ'spaɪt/ prep malgré; ~ **the fact that** bien que (+ subj).

despoil /dɪ'spɔɪl/ vtr SOUT, LITTÉR dévaster.

despondency /dɪ'spɒndənsɪ/ n découragement m.

despondent /dɪ'spɒndənt/ adj découragé, abattu.

despot /'despɒt/ n despote m.

despotism /'despətɪzəm/ n despotisme m.

des res° /dez 'rez/ n (abrév = **desirable residence**) maison f de standing.

dessert /dɪ'zɜːt/ n dessert m.

dessert: ~ **apple** n pomme f à couteau; ~**spoon** n cuillère f à dessert; ~ **wine** n vin m doux.

destabilize /,diː'steɪbəlaɪz/ vtr déstabiliser.

destination /,destɪ'neɪʃn/ n destination f.

destine /'destɪn/ vtr destiner (**for** à).

destined /'destɪnd/ adj **1** (preordained) destiné (**for, to** à; **to do** à faire); **it was** ~ **to happen** cela devait arriver; **2** POST, RAIL ~ **for Paris** à destination de Paris.

destiny /'destɪnɪ/ n destin m, destinée f.

destitute /'destɪtjuːt, US -tuːt/ I n **the** ~ (+ v pl) les indigents mpl.
II adj [person, community] sans ressources; **to leave sb** ~ laisser qn dans le dénuement.

destitution /,destɪ'tjuːʃn, US -tuːt-/ n indigence f.

destroy /dɪ'strɔɪ/ vtr **1** détruire [building, landscape, evidence, hopes, career]; anéantir [person]; faire exploser [bomb, package]; **2** (kill) abattre [animal]; détruire, anéantir [population, enemy]; **3°** (defeat) écraser [opponent].

destroyer /dɪ'strɔɪə(r)/ n NAUT contre-torpilleur m.

destruct /dɪ'strʌkt/ vi s'autodétruire.

destruction /dɪ'strʌkʃn/ n (of building, population, evidence, enemy) destruction f; (of hopes, reputation) ruine f.

destructive /dɪ'strʌktɪv/ adj **1** (causing destruction) destructeur/-trice; **2** (having potential to destroy) [weapon, capacity] destructif/-ive; [urge, emotion, criticism] destructeur/-trice.

desultory /'desəltrɪ, US -tɔːrɪ/ adj [conversation] décousu; [attempt] sporadique; [friendship] épisodique.

detach /dɪ'tætʃ/ vtr détacher (**from** de); **to** ~ **oneself** se détacher (**from** de).

detachable /dɪ'tætʃəbl/ adj [coupon, section, strap] détachable; [lever, collar] amovible; PHOT [lens] mobile.

detached /dɪ'tætʃt/ adj **1** (separate) détaché; **2** [person, view, manner] détaché; [observer] indépendant.

detached: ~ **garage** n garage m indépendant; ~ **house** n maison f (individuelle); ~ **retina** n MED rétine f décollée.

detachment /dɪ'tætʃmənt/ n **1** (separation) séparation f (**from** de); **2** (emotional, intellectual) détachement m; **3** MIL détachement m.

detail /'diːteɪl, US dɪ'teɪl/ I n **1** GEN, ART détail m; **in** (**more** ou **greater**) ~ (plus) en détail; **to go into** ~**s** entrer dans les détails; **to have an eye for** ~ prêter attention aux détails; **for further** ~**s**... pour de plus amples renseignements...; **2** MIL détachement m.
II vtr **1** (list) exposer [qch] en détail [plans]; énumérer [items]; **2 to** ~ **sb to** affecter qn à.

detail drawing n épure f.

detain /dɪ'teɪn/ vtr **1** (delay) retenir; **2** (keep in custody) placer [qn] en détention; **to be** ~**ed for questioning** être placé en garde à vue pour être interrogé; **3** (in hospital) garder.

detainee /,diːteɪ'niː/ n (general) détenu/-e m/f; (political) prisonnier/-ière m/f (politique).

detect /dɪ'tekt/ vtr **1** (find) déceler [error, traces, change]; détecter [crime, leak, plane]; **2** (sense) détecter [sound]; sentir [mood].

detectable /dɪ'tektəbl/ adj discernable.

detection /dɪ'tekʃn/ n (of disease, error) détection f; **crime** ~ la lutte contre la criminalité; **to escape** ~ [criminal] ne pas être découvert; [error] ne pas être décelé.

detective /dɪ'tektɪv/ n ~ inspecteur/-trice m/f (de police); (private) détective m; **store** ~ inspecteur/-trice m/f.

detective: ~ **constable** n GB ~ enquêteur m; ~ **inspector**, **DI** n GB ~ inspecteur m principal; ~ **story** n roman m policier, polar° m; ~ **work** n enquêtes fpl ALSO FIG.

detector /dɪ'tektə(r)/ n détecteur m.

detention /dɪ'tenʃn/ n **1** (confinement) détention f; **2** (prison sentence) détention f criminelle; (awaiting trial) détention f provisoire; **3** SCH retenue f, colle° f.

deter /dɪ'tɜː(r)/ vtr (p prés etc **-rr-**) **1** (dissuade) dissuader; **a scheme to** ~ **vandalism** un projet pour décourager le vandalisme; **2** (prevent) empêcher (**from doing** de faire).

detergent /dɪ'tɜːdʒənt/ n, adj détergent (m).

deteriorate /dɪ'tɪərɪəreɪt/ vi [weather, health, situation, wood] se détériorer; [economy, sales] décliner; [work, building] se dégrader; **to** ~ **into** dégénérer en.

deterioration /dɪ,tɪərɪə'reɪʃn/ n (in weather, of building) dégradation f (**in** de); (in health, situation) détérioration f (**in** de); (in work, performance) baisse f de qualité (**in** de).

determination /dɪ,tɜːmɪ'neɪʃn/ n GEN détermination f; JUR, ADMIN décision f.

determine /dɪ'tɜːmɪn/ vtr **1** (find out) déterminer; **to** ~ **how** établir comment; **2** (decide) déterminer, fixer [price]; **to** ~ **to do** résoudre de faire; **3** (control) [factor] déterminer.

determined /dɪ'tɜːmɪnd/ adj [person] fermement décidé (**to do** à faire); [air] résolu; [attempt] ferme.

determining /dɪ'tɜːmɪnɪŋ/ adj (épith) déterminant.

deterrent /dɪ'terənt, US -'tɜː-/ I n GEN moyen m de dissuasion; MIL force f de dissuasion; **to be a** ~ **to sb** dissuader qn.
II adj [effect] dissuasif/-ive; [measure] de dissuasion.

detest /dɪ'test/ vtr détester (**doing** faire).

detonate /'detəneɪt/ I vtr faire exploser.
II vi exploser.

detonation /,detə'neɪʃn/ n détonation f, explosion f.

detonator /'detəneɪtə(r)/ n détonateur m.

detour /'diːtʊə(r), US dɪ'tʊər/ n détour m.

detoxify /,diː'tɒksɪfaɪ/ vtr désintoxiquer.

detract /dɪ'trækt/ *vi* **to ~ from** porter atteinte à [*success, value*]; nuire à, porter atteinte à [*harmony, image*]; diminuer [*pleasure*].

detractor /dɪ'træktə(r)/ *n* détracteur/-trice *m/f*.

detriment /'detrɪmənt/ *n* **to the ~ of** au détriment de; **to the great ~ of** au grand dommage de.

detrimental /,detrɪ'mentl/ *adj* nuisible (**to** à).

detritus /dɪ'traɪtəs/ *n* détritus *mpl*.

deuce /dju:s, US du:s/ *n* **1** SPORT **~!** égalité!; **2** (in cards) deux *m*.

devaluation /,di:væljʊ'eɪʃn/ *n* **1** (of currency) dévaluation *f*; (of shares) baisse *f*; **2** GEN dévalorisation *f*.

devalue /,di:'vælju:/ **I** *vtr* **1** FIN dévaluer (**against** contre); **~d by 6%** dévalué de 6%; **2** GEN (underestimate) dévaloriser.

II *vi* (currency) être dévalué (**against** par rapport à); [*property*] baisser; [*shares*] dévaloriser.

devastate /'devəsteɪt/ *vtr* ravager [*land, town*]; anéantir [*person*].

devastating /'devəsteɪtɪŋ/ *adj* **1** (stunning) LIT dévastateur/-trice; FIG ravageur/-euse; **2** (crushing) [*news, loss, criticism*] accablant; [*argument*] écrasant.

devastation /,devə'steɪʃn/ *n* LIT dévastation *f*; FIG anéantissement *m*.

develop /dɪ'veləp/ **I** *vtr* **1** (acquire) acquérir [*knowledge*]; attraper [*illness*]; prendre [*habit*]; présenter [*symptom*]; **to ~ an awareness of** prendre conscience de; **to ~ cancer** développer un cancer; **2** (evolve) élaborer [*plan, project*]; mettre au point [*technique, invention*]; exposer [*theory*]; développer [*argument*]; **3** (create) créer [*market*]; établir [*links*]; **4** (expand, build up) développer [*mind, physique, business, market*]; **5** (improve) mettre en valeur [*land, site*]; aménager [*city centre*]; **6** PHOT développer.

II *vi* **1** (evolve) [*child, society, country, plot, play*] se développer; [*intelligence*] s'épanouir; [*skills*] s'améliorer; **to ~ into** devenir; **2** (come into being) [*friendship, difficulty*] naître; [*crack, hole*] se former; [*illness*] se déclarer; **3** (progress, advance) [*friendship*] se développer; [*difficulty*] s'aggraver; [*crack, fault*] s'accentuer; [*war, illness*] s'aggraver; [*game, story*] se dérouler; **4** (in size, extent) [*town, business*] se développer.

developer /dɪ'veləpə(r)/ *n* **1** (also **property ~**) promoteur *m* (immobilier); **2** PHOT révélateur *m*; **3** PSYCH, SCH **early ~** enfant *m* précoce.

developing: **~ bath** *n* PHOT bain *m* révélateur; **~ country** *n* pays *m* en voie de développement; **~ tank** *n* PHOT cuve *f* à développement.

development /dɪ'veləpmənt/ **I** *n* **1** (creation) (of product) mise *f* au point; (of housing, industry) création *f*; **2** (evolution, growth) développement *m*; **3** (of land) mise *f* en valeur; (of site, city centre etc) aménagement *m*; **4** (land developed) housing **~** ensemble *m* d'habitation; (individual houses) lotissement *m*; **commercial ~** (ensemble *m* de) commerces et bureaux à bâtir; **5** (innovation) progrès *m*; **major ~s** des découvertes *fpl* majeures (**in** dans le domaine de); **6** (event) changement *m*; **recent ~s in Europe** les derniers événements en Europe; **to await ~s** attendre la suite des événements; **7** (of idea, theme) développement *m*.

II *noun modifier* [*area, planning*] d'aménagement; [*costs, bank*] de développement.

development company *n* groupe *m* immobilier.

deviant /'di:vɪənt/ *adj* déviant.

deviate /'di:vɪeɪt/ *vi* **1** (from norm) s'écarter (**from** de); **2** (from course) dévier (**from** de).

deviation /,di:vɪ'eɪʃn/ *n* **1** (from course, party line, policy) déviation *f* (**from** par rapport à); **2** (from norm) écart *m* (**from** par rapport à); **3** (sexual) déviance *f*.

device /dɪ'vaɪs/ *n* **1** (household) appareil *m*; **labour-saving ~** appareil *m* électroménager; **2** TECH dispositif *m*; **3** (system) système *m*; **security ~** système *m* de sécurité; **4** (also **explosive ~**, **incendiary ~**) engin *m* explosif; **5** (means) GEN moyen *m* (**for doing, to do** de or pour faire); ECON mesure *f* (**for doing, to do** pour faire); **6** LITERAT procédé *m*.

IDIOMS **to be left to one's own ~s** être laissé à soi même.

devil /'devl/ **I** *n* **1** (also **Devil**) RELIG **the ~** le Diable; **2** (evil spirit) démon *m*; **3**° (for emphasis) **we'l have a ~ of a job doing** ça va être sacrément° du de faire; **4**° (expressing affection, sympathy) **a lucky ~** un sacré veinard°.

II devilled GB, **deviled** US *adj* CULIN à la diable.

IDIOMS **be a ~**°! allez, laisse-toi tenter!; **to be caught between the ~ and the deep blue sea** être pris entre l'enclume et le marteau; **to have the luck of the ~**° GB avoir une veine de cocu°; **like the ~**° comme un fou°; **speak of the ~!** quand or parle du loup (on en voit la queue)°!

devilish /'devlɪʃ/ *adj* (all contexts) diabolique.

devilishly /'devlɪʃlɪ/ *adv* **1** (horribly) **~ cruel** d'une cruauté diabolique; **2**° FIG sacrément°.

devil-may-care /,devlmeɪ'keə(r)/ *adj* insouciant.

devilment /'devlmənt/ *n* GB malice *f*.

devil: **~'s advocate** *n* avocat *m* du diable; **~ worship** *n* satanisme *m*.

devious /'di:vɪəs/ *adj* **1** (sly) [*person, mind, plan*] retors; [*method*] détourné; **2** (winding) [*road, path*] tortueux/-euse.

deviously /'di:vɪəslɪ/ *adv* de façon retorse.

devise /dɪ'vaɪz/ *vtr* **1** (invent) concevoir [*scheme, course*]; inventer [*product, machine*]; **2** THEAT écrire [qch] en groupe.

deviser /dɪ'vaɪzə(r)/ *n* inventeur *m*.

devoid /dɪ'vɔɪd/: **devoid of** *prep phr* dépourvu de.

devolution /,di:və'lu:ʃn, US ,dev-/ *n* **1** (transfer) transfert *m* (**from** de; **to** à); **2** POL régionalisation *f*.

devolve /dɪ'vɒlv/ **I** *vtr* déléguer.

II *vi* **1** [*responsibility, duty*] incomber (**on** à); **2** JUR passer (**on, to** à).

devote /dɪ'vəʊt/ *vtr* consacrer (**to** à; **to doing** à faire); **to ~ oneself** se consacrer (**to** à; **to doing** à faire).

devoted /dɪ'vəʊtɪd/ *adj* dévoué (**to** à); [*friendship, service*] loyal; [*fan*] fervent; **they're ~ to each other** ils sont très attachés l'un à l'autre.

devotee /,devə'ti:/ *n* (of music) passionné/-e *m/f* (**of** de); (of cause) partisan/-e *m/f* (**of** de); (of person) admirateur/-trice *m/f* (**of** de); (of sect) adepte *mf*.

devotion /dɪ'vəʊʃn/ *n* (to person, work, homeland) dévouement *m* (**to** à); (to doctrine, cause) attachement *m* (**to** à); (to God) dévotion *f* (**to** à).

devour /dɪ'vaʊə(r)/ *vtr* **1** (consume) LIT, FIG dévorer [*food, book*]; consommer beaucoup de [*petrol, resources*]; **2** (destroy) dévorer.

devout /dɪ'vaʊt/ *adj* **1** [*Catholic, prayer*] fervent; [*act, person*] pieux/pieuse; **2** (sincere) ardent.

devoutly /dɪ'vaʊtlɪ/ *adv* RELIG pieusement; (sincerely) ardemment.

dew /dju:, US du:/ *n* rosée *f*.

dewy /'dju:ɪ, US 'du:-/ *adj* humide de rosée.

dewy-eyed /,dju:ɪ'aɪd, US ,du:-/ *adj* (moved) ému; (naive) ingénu.

dexterity /dek'sterətɪ/ *n* dextérité *f*.

dexterous /'dekstrəs/ *adj* [*person, movement*] adroit; [*hand*] habile; [*mind*] agile.

dexterously /'dekstrəslɪ/ *adv* [*move*] (of person) adroitement; (of animal) agilement; [*manage*] habilement.

dg *n* (*abrév écrite* = **decigram**) dg *m*.

DG *n*: *abrév* ▶ **director general**.

diabetes /,daɪə'bi:ti:z/ [▶ 1002] *n* diabète *m*.

diabetic /,daɪə'betɪk/ *n, adj* diabétique (*mf*).

diabolical /,daɪə'bɒlɪkl/ *adj* **1**° [*food*] infect; [*behaviour*] lamentable; **2** (evil) diabolique.

diabolically /,daɪə'bɒlɪklɪ/ *adv* **1**° (badly) [*perform*] de façon épouvantable; [*behave*] de façon odieuse; **2** (wickedly) de façon diabolique.

diacritic /,daɪə'krɪtɪk/ *adj* (also **diacritical**) LING diacritique.

diaeresis GB, **dieresis** US /daɪ'erəsɪs/ *n* (*pl* **-ses**) tréma *m*.

diagnose /ˈdaɪəgnəʊz, US ˌdaɪəgˈnəʊs/ vtr **1** MED diagnostiquer; **the illness was ~d as cancer** les médecins ont diagnostiqué un cancer; **2** GEN identifier.

diagnosis /ˌdaɪəgˈnəʊsɪs/ n (pl **-ses**) diagnostic m.

diagnostic /ˌdaɪəgˈnɒstɪk/ adj diagnostique.

diagnostics /ˌdaɪəgˈnɒstɪks/ n **1** MED diagnose f; **2** COMPUT (+ v pl) diagnostic m.

diagonal /daɪˈægənl/ **I** n (all contexts) diagonale f.
II adj [line, stripe] diagonal; **our street is ~ to the main road** notre rue part en biais de la rue principale.

diagonally /daɪˈægənəlɪ/ adv en diagonale.

diagram /ˈdaɪəgræm/ n GEN schéma m; MATH figure f.

dial /ˈdaɪəl/ **I** n cadran m.
II vtr (p prés etc **-ll-** GB, **-l-** US) faire; (more formal) composer [number]; appeler [person, country]; **to ~ 999 ~** (for police, ambulance) appeler police secours; (for fire brigade) appeler les pompiers.

dialect /ˈdaɪəlekt/ n dialecte m.

dialectic /ˌdaɪəˈlektɪk/ n, adj dialectique (f).

dialectics /ˌdaɪəˈlektɪks/ n (+ v sg) dialectique f.

dialling GB, **dialing** US /ˈdaɪəlɪŋ/ n **abbreviated ~** utilisation f de numéros abrégés; **direct ~** appel m direct.

dialling: **~ code** n GB indicatif m; **~ tone** n GB tonalité f.

dialogue /ˈdaɪəlɒg, US -lɔːg/ **I** n dialogue m.
II vi dialoguer (**with** avec).

dial: **~ tone** n US tonalité f; **~-up** adj [network] commuté.

dialysis /daɪˈælɪsɪs/ n (pl **-lyses**) (kidney) ~ dialyse f.

dialysis machine n rein m artificiel.

diamanté /ˌdaɪəˈmæntɪ, dɪəˈmɒnteɪ/ n (decorative trim, jewellery, material) strass m; (fabric) tissu m pailleté.

diameter /daɪˈæmɪtə(r)/ n diamètre m; **to be 2 m in ~** avoir 2 m de diamètre.

diametrically /ˌdaɪəˈmetrɪklɪ/ adv diamétralement.

diamond /ˈdaɪəmənd/ ▶ 949 **I** n **1** (stone) diamant m; **2** (shape) losange m; **3** (in cards) carreau m; **4** (in baseball) terrain m (de baseball).
II noun modifier [cutter, ring] de diamants.

diamond: **~ jubilee** n soixantième anniversaire m; **~-shaped** adj en (forme de) losange; **~ wedding** (**anniversary**) n noces fpl de diamant.

diaper /ˈdaɪəpə(r), (US) ˈdaɪpər/ US **I** n couche f (pour bébé).
II vtr changer la couche de [baby].

diaphanous /daɪˈæfənəs/ adj diaphane.

diaphragm /ˈdaɪəfræm/ n (all contexts) diaphragme m.

diarist /ˈdaɪərɪst/ n **1** (author) auteur m d'un journal (intime); **2** (journalist) chroniqueur/-euse m/f.

diarrhoea GB, **diarrhea** US /ˌdaɪəˈrɪə/ n diarrhée f.

diary /ˈdaɪərɪ/ n **1** (for appointments) agenda m; **to put sth in one's ~** noter qch dans son agenda; **2** (journal) journal m intime; **3** (in newspaper) chronique f.

diatribe /ˈdaɪətraɪb/ n diatribe f (**against** contre).

dice /daɪs/ **I** n (pl **~**) (object) dé m; (game) dés mpl; **to throw the ~** jeter le dé ou les dés; **no ~!** (refusal) pas question!; (no luck) pas de chance!
II vtr CULIN couper [qch] en dés.
IDIOMS **to ~ with death** risquer sa vie; **the ~ are loaded** les dés sont pipés.

dicey /ˈdaɪsɪ/ adj **1** (risky) risqué; **2** (uncertain, unreliable) douteux/-euse.

dichotomy /daɪˈkɒtəmɪ/ n dichotomie f.

dichromatic /ˌdaɪkrəʊˈmætɪk/ adj dichromatique.

dicky /ˈdɪkɪ/ **I** n faux plastron m.
II adj GB [heart] qui flanche; [condition] précaire.

dicta /ˈdɪktə/ pl ▶ **dictum**.

dictate I /ˈdɪkteɪt/ n (decree) ordre m.
II /dɪkˈteɪt, US ˈdɪkteɪt/ vtr **1** SCH, COMM dicter; **2** (prescribe) imposer [terms] (**to** à); déterminer [outcome]; régenter [policy]; **to ~ how** prescrire comment.

III /dɪkˈteɪt, US ˈdɪkteɪt/ vi **1** (out loud) **to ~ to one's secretary** dicter une lettre (ou un texte etc) à sa secrétaire; **2 to ~ to sb** imposer sa volonté à qn.

dictation /dɪkˈteɪʃn/ n SCH, COMM dictée f; **to take ~** écrire sous la dictée.

dictator /dɪkˈteɪtə(r), US ˈdɪkteɪtər/ n POL dictateur m; FIG tyran m.

dictatorial /ˌdɪktəˈtɔːrɪəl/ adj [person] tyrannique; [regime, powers] dictatorial.

dictatorship /dɪkˈteɪtəʃɪp, US ˈdɪkt-/ n POL dictature f; FIG tyrannie f.

diction /ˈdɪkʃn/ n (articulation) diction f; (choice of words) langage m.

dictionary /ˈdɪkʃənrɪ, US -nerɪ/ n dictionnaire m.

dictionary entry n entrée f de dictionnaire.

dictum /ˈdɪktəm/ n (pl **-ums** ou **-a**) phrase f célèbre.

did /dɪd/ prét ▶ **do**.

diddle /ˈdɪdl/ vtr (swindle) rouler, escroquer.

didn't /ˈdɪd(ə)nt/ = **did not**.

die /daɪ/ **I** n GAMES (pl **dice**) dé m à jouer.
II vtr (p prés **dying**; prét, pp **died**) **to ~ a violent death** mourir de mort violente; **to ~ a hero's death** mourir en héros.
III vi (p prés **dying**; prét, pp **died**) **1** (expire) mourir; **he was dying** il était en train de mourir; **she ~d a year ago** elle est morte il y a un an; **as she lay dying** alors qu'elle se mourait; **to be left to ~** être abandonné à la mort; **to ~ young** mourir jeune; **to ~ of** ou **from** mourir de [starvation, disease]; **2** (be killed) mourir, périr LITER (**doing** en faisant); **to ~ in action** mourir au combat; **he'd sooner** ou **rather ~ than do** il mourrait plutôt que de faire; **I'd sooner ~!** plutôt mourir!; **to ~ for** mourir pour [beliefs, person]; **3** (wither) [plant, crop] crever; **4** FIG (of boredom etc) mourir (**of** de); **5** (long) **to be dying to do** mourir d'envie de faire; **to be dying for** avoir une envie folle de; **6** (go out) [light, flame] s'éteindre; **7** (fade) [emotion, memory, fame] s'éteindre; [enthusiasm] tomber; **8** (cease functioning) [machine, engine] s'arrêter; **9** (on stage) faire un bide.
IDIOMS **never say ~!** il ne faut jamais baisser les bras!; **to ~ hard** avoir la vie dure.
■ **die down 1** (in intensity) [emotion, row] s'apaiser; [scandal, opposition, publicity] disparaître; [fighting] s'achever; [tremors, storm] se calmer; **2** (in volume) [laughter] diminuer; [applause] se calmer; **3** [plant] se flétrir.
■ **die out 1** (become extinct) disparaître; **2** (ease off) s'arrêter.

diehard /ˈdaɪhɑːd/ n **1** POL (in party) réactionnaire mf; **2** PÉJ (conservative) ultraconservateur/-trice m/f; **3** (stubborn person) irréductible mf.

dieresis US ▶ **diaeresis**.

diesel /ˈdiːzl/ n (also **~ fuel**, **~ oil**) gazole m; (also **~ car**) diesel m.

diesel: **~ engine** n (in train) motrice f Diesel; (in car) moteur m Diesel; **~ train** n train m Diesel.

diet /ˈdaɪət/ **I** n **1** (of person) alimentation f (**of** à base de); (of animal) nourriture f (**of** à base de); **2** MED (limiting food) régime m; **to go on a ~** se mettre au régime; **3** FIG cure f (**of** de); **4** HIST, POL diète f.
II vi être au régime.

dietary /ˈdaɪətrɪ, US -terɪ/ adj [habit] alimentaire; [method] diététique.

dietary: **~ fibre** GB, **~ fiber** US n fibres fpl alimentaires; **~ supplement** n complément m vitaminique.

dietician, **dietitian** /ˌdaɪəˈtɪʃn/ ▶ 1251 n diététicien/-ienne m/f.

differ /ˈdɪfə(r)/ vi **1** (be different) différer (**from** de; **in** par); **to ~ widely** être complètement différent; **2** (disagree) différer (d'opinion) (**on** sur; **from sb** de qn); **I beg to ~** permettez-moi d'être d'un avis différent.

difference /ˈdɪfrəns/ n **1** (dissimilarity) différence f (**in**, **of** de); **to tell the ~ between** faire la différence entre; **it won't make any ~** ça ne changera rien; **what ~ does it make if...?** qu'est-ce que ça change si...?; **it makes no ~ to me** cela m'est égal; **as near as makes no ~** peu s'en faut; **a vacation with a ~** des vacances pas comme les autres; **2** (disagreement) différend *m* (**between** entre; **over** à propos de; **with** avec); **a ~ of opinion** une divergence d'opinion.

different /'dɪfrənt/ *adj* **1** (dissimilar) différent (**from, to** GB, **than** US de); **they are ~ in this respect** ils diffèrent à cet égard; **it's very ~** c'est complètement différent; **2** (other) autre; **to be a ~ person** être une tout autre personne; **that's ~** c'est autre chose; **it would have been a ~ story if...** cela aurait été tout autre chose si...; **3** (distinct) différent; **4** (unusual) différent; **he has to be ~** il faut qu'il se distingue.

differential /ˌdɪfə'renʃl/ *I n* **1** (in price, rate etc) écart *m*; **pay ~s** écart des salaires; **2** MATH différentielle *f*; **3** AUT différentiel *m*.
II adj (all contexts) différentiel/-ielle.

differentiate /ˌdɪfə'renʃɪeɪt/ *I vtr* **1** (tell the difference) différencier (**from** de); **2** (make the difference) différencier (**from** de); **3** MATH calculer la différentielle de.
II vi **1** (tell the difference) faire la différence (**between** entre); **2** (show the difference) faire la distinction (**between** entre); **3** (discriminate) faire des différences (**between** entre).

differentiation /ˌdɪfərenʃɪ'eɪʃn/ *n* **1** (distinction) différenciation *f*; **2** MATH différentiation *f*.

differently /'dɪfrəntlɪ/ *adv* **1** (in another way) autrement (**from** que); **2** (in different ways) différemment (**from** de); **it affects men and women ~** cela touche les hommes et les femmes différemment.

difficult /'dɪfɪkəlt/ *adj* **1** (hard, not easy to do) difficile; **it will be ~ for me to decide** il me sera difficile de décider; **to find it ~ to do** avoir du mal à faire; **2** (complex, inaccessible) [*author, concept*] difficile; **3** (awkward) [*age, position, personality*] difficile; **~ to get on with** difficile à vivre.

difficulty /'dɪfɪkəltɪ/ *n* **1** (of task, situation) difficulté *f*; **to have ~ (in) doing** avoir du mal à faire; **I have ~ with that idea** cette idée me pose un problème; **2** (problem) difficulté *f*, problème *m*; **the difficulties of living here** les difficultés de la vie ici; **3** (trouble) **in ~** en difficulté.

diffidence /'dɪfɪdəns/ *n* manque *m* d'assurance.

diffident /'dɪfɪdənt/ *adj* [*person*] qui manque d'assurance; [*smile, gesture*] timide; **to be ~ about doing** hésiter à faire.

diffidently /'dɪfɪdəntlɪ/ *adv* d'un air or d'un ton mal assuré.

diffuse *I* /dɪ'fjuːs/ *adj* (all contexts) diffus.
II /dɪ'fjuːz/ *vtr* diffuser (**in** dans).
III /dɪ'fjuːz/ *vi* se diffuser (**into** dans).

diffuseness /dɪ'fjuːsnɪs/ *n* **1** (of argument) prolixité *f*; **2** (of organization) éparpillement *m*.

dig /dɪg/ *I n* **1** (with elbow) coup *m* de coude (**in** dans); **2**○ (jibe) pique○ *f* (**at** à); **to get in a ~ at sb** lancer une pique○ à qn; **3** (in archaeology) fouilles *fpl*; **to go on a ~** aller faire des fouilles; **4** (when gardening) coup *m* de bêche.
II **digs** *npl* GB chambre *f* (meublée) (*chez des particuliers*).
III vtr (*p prés* **-gg-**; *prét, pp* **dug**) **1** (excavate) creuser (**in** dans); **2** bêcher [*garden, plot*]; fouiller [*site*]; **3** (extract) arracher [*root crops*]; extraire [*coal, turf*] (**out of** de); **4** (embed) enfoncer [*knife, needle etc*] (**into** dans); **5**○ (like) **she really ~s that guy** ce mec la botte○.
IV vi (*p prés* **-gg-**; *prét, pp* **dug**) **1** (excavate) GEN creuser (**into** dans; **for** pour trouver); (in garden) bêcher; (in archaeology) fouiller; **2** (search) **to ~ in** ou **into** fouiller dans (**for** pour trouver) [*sb's past*]; **3 to ~ into** [*springs, thorns*] s'enfoncer dans.

■ **dig in**: **~ in** MIL, FIG se retrancher; ¶ **~ in** [sth], **~** [sth] **in** enterrer [*compost*]; enfoncer [*teeth, weapon*].

■ **dig out**: **~ out** [sth], **~** [sth] **out** déterrer [*animal*] (**of** de); arracher [*root, weed*] (**of** de); enlever [*splinter*] (**of** de); dénicher○ [*book, information*] (**of** dans).

■ **dig up**: **~ up** [sth], **~** [sth] **up** (unearth) déterre[*body, treasure*]; arracher [*roots*]; excaver [*road*]; (tur over) retourner [*soil*]; bêcher [*garden*]; FIG dénicher○ [*information*]; déterrer [*scandal*].

digest *I* /'daɪdʒest/ *n* **1** (periodical) digest *m*; **2** (summary) résumé *m*.
II /daɪ'dʒest, dɪ-/ *vtr* digérer [*food*]; assimiler [*facts*].

digestible /dɪ'dʒestəbl/ *adj* digeste.

digestion /dɪ'dʒestʃn, dɪ-/ *n* digestion *f*.

digestive /dɪ'dʒestɪv, daɪ-/ *I n* GB CULIN ~ biscuit *m* (sablé).
II adj digestif/-ive.

digestive: **~ biscuit** *n* GB ~ biscuit *m* (sablé); **~ system** *n* système *m* digestif; **~ tract** *n* appareil *m* digestif.

digger /'dɪgə(r)/ *n* (excavator) excavateur *m*.

digging /'dɪgɪŋ/ *I n* **1** (in garden) bêchage *m*; **to do some ~** bêcher; **2** CONSTR creusement *m*; **3** (in mining) forage *m* (**for** pour trouver).
II **diggings** *npl* (in archaeology) fouilles *fpl*; (from mine) déblais *mpl*.

digit /'dɪdʒɪt/ *n* **1** (number) chiffre *m*; **2** (finger) doigt *m*; (toe) orteil *m*.

digital /'dɪdʒɪtl/ *adj* **1** COMPUT [*display, recording*] numérique; [*watch*] à affichage numérique; **2** ANAT digital.

digital: **~ access lock**, **~ lock** *n* digicode® *m*; **~ audio tape**, **DAT** *n* cassette *f* audionumérique, DAT *f*; **~ computer** *n* calculateur *m* numérique.

digitizer /'dɪdʒɪtaɪzə(r)/ *n* COMPUT numériseur *m*.

dignified /'dɪgnɪfaɪd/ *adj* [*person*] digne; [*manner*] empreint de dignité.

dignify /'dɪgnɪfaɪ/ *vtr* donner du faste à [*occasion, building*].

dignitary /'dɪgnɪtərɪ/ *n* dignitaire *m*.

dignity /'dɪgnətɪ/ *n* (of person, occasion) dignité *f*; **to stand on one's ~** prendre de grands airs.

digress /daɪ'gres/ *vi* faire une digression.

digression /daɪ'greʃn/ *n* digression *f*.

dike *n* ▶ **dyke** 1.

dilapidated /dɪ'læpɪdeɪtɪd/ *adj* délabré.

dilapidation /dɪˌlæpɪ'deɪʃn/ *n* délabrement *m*.

dilate /daɪ'leɪt/ *I vtr* dilater.
II vi **1** (widen) se dilater; **2** (discuss at length) **to ~ on a subject** s'étendre sur un sujet.

dilatory /'dɪlətərɪ, US -tɔːrɪ/ *adj* SOUT **1** (slow) lent; **2** (time-wasting) dilatoire ALSO JUR.

dilemma /daɪ'lemə, dɪ-/ *n* dilemme *m* (**about, over** à propos de); **in a ~** devant un dilemme.

diligence /'dɪlɪdʒəns/ *n* zèle *m* (**in** dans; **in doing** à faire).

diligent /'dɪlɪdʒənt/ *adj* appliqué; **to be ~ in doing** sth faire qch avec application.

diligently /'dɪlɪdʒəntlɪ/ *adv* [*work*] avec zèle.

dill /dɪl/ *n* aneth *m*.

dill pickle *n* concombres *mpl* au vinaigre et à l'aneth.

dillydally○ /'dɪlɪdælɪ/ *vi* **1** (dawdle) lambiner○; **2** (be indecisive) tergiverser.

dilute /daɪ'ljuːt, US -'luːt/ *vtr* **1** LIT diluer [*liquid*] (**with** avec); éclaircir [*colour*]; **2** FIG diluer.

dilution /daɪ'ljuːʃn, US -'luːt-/ *n* LIT, FIG dilution *f* (**of** de).

dim /dɪm/ *I adj* **1** (badly lit) sombre; **2** (weak) faible; **to grow ~** s'affaiblir; **3** (hard to see) vague; **4** (vague) vague; **5**○ (stupid) bouché○; **6** (not favourable) sombre.
II vtr (*p prés etc* **-mm-**) baisser [*light*]; mettre [qch] en veilleuse [*lamp*]; US baisser [*headlights*].
III vi (*p prés etc* **-mm-**) [*lights, lamp*] baisser; [*memory*] s'estomper; [*sight*] s'affaiblir; [*colour, beauty, hope*] se ternir.
IDIOMS **to take a ~ view of sth** n'apprécier guère qch.

dime /daɪm/ *n* US (pièce *f* de) dix cents *mpl*.
IDIOMS **they're a ~ a dozen**○ on en trouve à la pelle○; **to stop on a ~**○ s'arrêter pile.

dimension /dɪ'menʃn/ n **1** (aspect) dimension f; **2** (scope) **~s** étendue f (**of** de); **3** (measurement) GEN dimension f; ARCHIT, MATH, TECH cote f.

dimensional /-dɪ'menʃənl/ combining form **three~** à trois dimensions.

dime store n US bazar m.

diminish /dɪ'mɪnɪʃ/ **I** vtr **1** (reduce) diminuer; **2** (weaken) amoindrir [influence, strength]; diminuer [emotion]; **3** (denigrate) dénigrer; **4** MUS diminuer.
II vi **1** (decrease) diminuer; **2** (weaken) [emotion] s'amenuiser; [influence, strength] s'amoindrir.

diminished /dɪ'mɪnɪʃd/ adj **1** [amount, enthusiasm, level] réduit; [awareness, support] amoindri; **2** JUR **on grounds of ~ responsibility** pour raisons de responsabilité atténuée; **3** MUS diminué.

diminution /ˌdɪmɪ'njuːʃn, US -'nuːʃn/ n (of size, quantity) diminution f; (of intensity, power) affaiblissement m.

diminutive /dɪ'mɪnjʊtɪv/ **I** n LING diminutif m.
II adj [object] minuscule; [person] tout petit.

dimly /'dɪmlɪ/ adv **1** [lit] faiblement; **2** [perceive, recall, sense] vaguement.

dimmer /'dɪmə(r)/ n (also **~ switch**) variateur m d'ambiance.

dimming /'dɪmɪŋ/ n (of lights) atténuation f; (of hope etc) ternissement m.

dimple /'dɪmpl/ n (in flesh) fossette f; (on water) ride f.

dim: **~wit**° n andouille° f; **~-witted**° adj bouché°.

din /dɪn/ n (of machine) vacarme m; (of people) chahut m.
IDIOMS **to ~ sth into sb** enfoncer qch dans la tête de qn°.

dine /daɪn/ vi dîner; ▶ **wine**.
■ **dine in** dîner à la maison.
■ **dine off, dine on**: **~ off** [sth] dîner de qch.
■ **dine out** dîner dehors; **to ~ out on** FIG resservir [story, anecdote].

diner /'daɪnə(r)/ n **1** (person) dîneur/-euse m/f; **2** US (restaurant) café-restaurant m; **3** (in train) wagon-restaurant m.

dinette /daɪ'net/ n US **1** (room) coin-repas m; **2** (also **~ set**) table f et chaises fpl de cuisine.

dingdong° /'dɪŋdɒŋ/ n **1** GB (quarrel) échange m vif de mots; **2** onomat ding dong.

dinghy /'dɪŋgɪ/ n (also **sailing ~**) dériveur m; **2** (inflatable) canot m.

dingy /'dɪndʒɪ/ adj [colour] défraîchi; [place] minable.

dining: **~ car** n wagon-restaurant m; **~ hall** n réfectoire m; **~ room** n GEN salle f à manger; (in hotel) salle f de restaurant.

dink /dɪŋk/ n SPORT amorti m.

dinky° /'dɪŋkɪ/ adj **1** GB (sweet) mignon/-onne; **2** (small) petit.

dinner /'dɪnə(r)/ n **1** (meal) (evening) dîner m; (midday) déjeuner m; **at ~** au dîner or déjeuner; **to go out to ~** dîner dehors; **to have ~** dîner; **to have chicken for ~** manger du poulet au dîner; **to give the dog its ~** donner à manger au chien; **2** (banquet) dîner m (**for** en l'honneur de).

dinner: **~ dance** n dîner-dansant m; **~ fork** n grande fourchette f; **~ hour** n GB SCH heure f du déjeuner; **~ jacket, DJ** n smoking m; **~ knife** n grand couteau m; **~ money** n GB SCH argent m pour la cantine; **~ party** n dîner m; **~ plate** n grande assiette f; **~ service, ~ set** n service m de table; **~time** n heure f du dîner; **~ware** n US vaisselle f.

dinosaur /'daɪnəsɔː(r)/ n LIT, FIG dinosaure m.

dint /dɪnt/: **by dint of** prep phr grâce à.

diocesan /daɪ'ɒsɪsn/ n, adj diocésain (m).

diocese /'daɪəsɪs/ n diocèse m.

dioxide /daɪ'ɒksaɪd/ n dioxyde m.

dip /dɪp/ **I** n **1** (bathe) baignade f; **to have a quick ~** se baigner rapidement; **2** (in ground, road) déclivité f; **3** (of plane, head) inclinaison f; **4** FIG (in prices, rate, sales) (mouvement m de) baisse f (**in** dans); **5** CULIN sauce f

froide (pour crudités); **6** (also **sheep ~**) bain m parasiticide.
II vtr (p prés etc **-pp-**) **1** (put partially) tremper (**in, into** dans); **2** (immerse) plonger [garment]; tremper [food]; baigner [sheep]; **3** GB AUT baisser [headlights]; **~ped headlights** codes mpl; **to drive with ~ped headlights** rouler en code.
III vi (p prés etc **-pp-**) **1** (move downwards) piquer; **to ~ below the horizon** [sun] disparaître derrière l'horizon; **2** (slope downwards) être en pente; **3** FIG (decrease) [price, value, speed, rate] descendre; **4** (put hand) **to ~ into one's bag for sth** chercher qch dans son sac; FIG **to ~ into one's savings** puiser dans ses économies; **5** (read a little) **to ~ into** parcourir.

Dip n: abrév écrite = **diploma**.

diphthong /'dɪfθɒŋ, US -θɔːŋ/ n diptongue f.

diploma /dɪ'pləʊmə/ n diplôme m (**in** en).

diplomacy /dɪp'ləʊməsɪ/ n GEN, POL diplomatie f.

diplomat /'dɪpləmæt/ ▶ **1251** n diplomate mf.

diplomatic /ˌdɪplə'mætɪk/ adj **1** POL diplomatique; **2** (astute) [person] diplomate; [behaviour] diplomatique; **3** (tactful) **to be ~** avoir du tact.

diplomatic bag GB, **diplomatic pouch** US n valise f diplomatique.

diplomatist /dɪ'pləʊmətɪst/ n diplomate mf.

dippy° /'dɪpɪ/ adj farfelu°.

dipstick /'dɪpstɪk/ n AUT jauge f de niveau d'huile.

dip switch n interrupteur m à positions multiples.

diptych /'dɪptɪk/ n diptyque m.

dire /'daɪə(r)/ adj **1** (terrible) [consequence] terrible; [situation] désespéré; **in ~ straits** dans une situation désespérée; **2**° (awful) affreux/-euse.

direct /daɪ'rekt, dɪ-/ **I** adj **1** (without intermediary) direct; **in ~ contact with** (touching) en contact direct avec; (communicating) directement en contact avec; **2** (without detour) direct; **to be a ~ descendant of** descendre en droite ligne de; **3** (clear) [cause, influence, reference, threat] direct; [contrast, evidence] flagrant; **to be the ~ opposite of** être tout le contraire de; **4** (straightforward) [answer, method] direct; [person] franc/franche.
II adv **1** (without intermediary) directement; **2** (without detour) directement (**from** de).
III vtr **1** (address, aim) adresser [appeal, criticism] (**at** à; **against** contre); cibler [campaign] (**at** sur); orienter [effort, resource] (**to, towards** vers); **to ~ one's attention to** concentrer son attention sur; **to ~ sb's attention to** attirer l'attention de qn sur; **2** (control) diriger [company, project]; régler [traffic]; **3** diriger [attack, light, car] (**at** vers); pointer [gun] (**at** sur); **4** CIN, RADIO, TV réaliser; THEAT mettre [qch] en scène [play]; diriger [actor, opera]; **5** (instruct) **to ~ sb to do** GEN ordonner à qn de faire; **he did it as ~ed** il l'a fait comme on le lui avait indiqué; **'to be taken as ~ed'** 'à consommer selon la prescription médicale'; **6** (show route) **to ~ sb to sth** indiquer le chemin de qch à qn.
IV vi CIN, RADIO, TV faire de la réalisation; THEAT faire de la mise en scène.

direct: **~ access** n COMPUT accès m direct; **~ access course** n unité f à accès direct; **~ current, DC** n ELEC courant m continu; **~ debit** n prélèvement m automatique; **~ discourse** n US = **direct speech**; **~ hit** n MIL coup m au but.

direction /daɪ'rekʃn, dɪ-/ ▶ **870** **I** n **1** (left, right, north, south) direction f; **in the right/wrong ~** dans la bonne/mauvaise direction; **to go in the opposite ~** aller en sens inverse; **from all ~s** de tous les côtés; **2** (taken by company, government, career) orientation f; **the right/wrong ~ for sb** la bonne/mauvaise option pour qn; **to lack ~** manquer d'objectifs; **3** CIN, RADIO, TV réalisation f; THEAT mise f en scène; MUS direction f; **4** (control) direction f; (guidance) conseils mpl.
II directions npl **1** (for route) indications fpl; **to ask for ~s** demander son chemin (**from** à); **2** (for use) instructions fpl (**as to, about** sur); **~s for use** mode m d'emploi.

directional /daɪ'rekʃnl, dɪ-/ adj directionnel/-elle.

Street directions
How do I get there?

En sortant de la gare, allez tout droit, traversez la place où attendent les taxis, puis le parking. Vous déboucherez dans la Grand-Rue. Continuez dans la même direction sur plusieurs centaines de mètres. Vous passerez trois feux rouges. Tournez à droite au troisième, et vous vous trouverez dans la rue Maginot. Prenez la troisième rue à gauche (il y a une banque qui fait l'angle) et continuez jusqu'au bout de cette rue. Vous verrez le théâtre en face de vous. Empruntez le passage à gauche du théâtre, descendez les escaliers et vous vous retrouverez dans l'avenue des Marronniers. Prenez-la sur votre gauche en marchant sur le trottoir de gauche. Vous verrez une boucherie chevaline sur la droite de la rue juste avant le deuxième carrefour. Traversez le carrefour en diagonale. Vous apercevrez une sorte de terrain vague sur votre droite après le carrefour. Le dernier magasin, juste avant le terrain vague, est celui d'un tailleur, et il y a un café dans une cour derrière. Je vous y attendrai avec la valise et toutes les instructions. Mais attention: pas un mot à qui que ce soit!

directive /daɪˈrektɪv, dɪ-/ I n ADMIN, COMPUT directive f (on relative à).
II adj directif/-ive.

directly /daɪˈrektlɪ, dɪ-/ I adv 1 (without a detour) [connect, challenge, go, refer] directement; [aim, point] droit; [move] tout droit; **to look ~ at sb** regarder qn droit dans les yeux; 2 (exactly) [above] juste; [contradict] totalement; 3 (at once) **~ after** aussitôt après; **~ before** juste avant; 4 (very soon) d'ici peu; 5 (frankly) [speak] franchement; [deny] catégoriquement.
II conj GB (as soon as) dès que.

direct mail n mailing m, publipostage m.

directness /daɪˈrektnɪs, dɪ-/ n 1 (of person, attitude) franchise f; 2 (of play, work, writing) authenticité f.

direct object n objet m direct.

director /daɪˈrektə(r), dɪ-/ n 1 ADMIN, COMM (of company, programme) (sole) directeur/-trice m/f; (one of board) administrateur/-trice m/f; 2 GEN (of project, investigation) responsable mf; 3 (of play, film) metteur m en scène; (of orchestra) chef m d'orchestre; (of choir) chef m des chœurs; 4 SCH, UNIV **~ of studies** directeur/-trice m/f des études; **~ of admissions** responsable mf du service des inscriptions.

directorate /daɪˈrektərət, dɪ-/ n (board) conseil m d'administration.

director general, DG n directeur m général.

directorial /ˌdaɪrekˈtɔːrɪəl, ˌdɪ-/ adj 1 ADMIN [duties] de directeur/-trice; 2 THEAT [debut] de metteur en scène; [style] de direction.

Director of Public Prosecutions, DPP n GB ≈ procureur m général.

directorship /daɪˈrektəʃɪp, dɪ-/ n (in organization, institution) direction f; (in company) poste m d'administrateur.

directory /daɪˈrektrɪ, dɪ-/ n 1 TELECOM annuaire m; 2 COMM répertoire m d'adresses; **street ~** répertoire m des rues; 3 COMPUT répertoire m.

directory: ~ assistance n US = **directory enquiries**; **~ enquiries** npl GB (service m des) renseignements mpl.

direct: ~ primary n US élection f primaire directe; **~ rule** n POL gouvernement m direct; **~ speech** n style m direct; **~ transfer** n virement m automatique.

dirt /dɜːt/ n 1 (mess) (on clothing, in room) saleté f; (on body, cooker) crasse f; (in carpet, engine, filter) saletés fpl; **to show the ~** être salissant; 2 (soil) terre f; (mud) boue f; 3° PÉJ (gossip) ragots mpl; 4 EUPH (obscenity) obscénités fpl; (excrement) excréments mpl.
IDIOMS **it's ~ cheap°** c'est donné.

dirtiness /ˈdɜːtɪnɪs/ n (of person etc) saleté f.

dirt track n 1 SPORT cendrée f; 2 (road) chemin m de terre battue.

dirty /ˈdɜːtɪ/ I adj 1 (messy, soiled) [face, clothing, street]

sale; [work] salissant; **to get ~** se salir; **to get** ou **make sth ~** salir qch; 2 (not sterile) [needle] qui a déjà servi; [wound] infecté; 3° (obscene) [book, joke] cochon/-onne°; [mind] mal tourné; 4° (dishonest) [contest, fighter] déloyal; [cheat] sale; [lie] grossier/-ière; 5 [colour] sale.
II° adv 1 (dishonestly) **to play** ou **fight ~** donner des coups en traître; 2 (obscenely) grossièrement.
III vtr LIT, FIG salir.
IDIOMS **to do the ~ on°** faire une crasse° à; **to give sb a ~ look°** regarder qn d'un sale œil.

dirty: ~-minded adj à l'esprit mal tourné; **~ tricks** npl POL diffamation f; **~ weekend°** n weekend m de débauche.

disability /ˌdɪsəˈbɪlətɪ/ I n MED infirmité f; **mental/physical ~** handicap m mental/physique; **partial ~** incapacité f partielle.
II noun modifier [benefit, pension] d'invalidité.

disable /dɪsˈeɪbl/ vtr 1 [accident] rendre [qn] infirme; **to be ~d by arthritis** être handicapé par l'arthrite; 2 (make useless) immobiliser [machine]; avarier [ship]; 3 MIL mettre [qch] hors d'action; 4 COMPUT désactiver.

disabled /dɪsˈeɪbld/ I n **the ~** les handicapés mpl.
II adj handicapé.

disabled: ~ access n voie f d'accès pour handicapés; **~ driver** n conducteur/-trice m/f invalide; **~ person** n invalide mf.

disabuse /ˌdɪsəˈbjuːz/ vtr SOUT détromper (of de).

disadvantage /ˌdɪsədˈvɑːntɪdʒ, US -ˈvæn-/ I n 1 (drawback) inconvénient m; 2 (position of weakness) **to be at a ~** être désavantagé; **to get sb at a ~** avoir l'avantage sur qn; 3 (discrimination) inégalité f.
II vtr désavantager.

disadvantaged /ˌdɪsədˈvɑːntɪdʒd, US -ˈvæn-/ adj défavorisé.

disadvantageous /ˌdɪsˌædvɑːnˈteɪdʒəs, US -ˈvæn-/ adj défavorable (to à).

disaffected /ˌdɪsəˈfektɪd/ adj mécontent (with de).

disagree /ˌdɪsəˈgriː/ vi 1 (differ) ne pas être d'accord (with avec; on, about sur); **we often ~** nous avons souvent des avis différents; 2 (oppose) **to ~ with** s'opposer à; 3 (conflict) être en désaccord (with avec); 4 **to ~ with sb** [food] ne pas réussir à qn; [weather] ne pas convenir à qn.

disagreeable /ˌdɪsəˈgriːəbl/ adj [person, reaction, appearance] désagréable; [remark] désobligeant.

disagreeably /ˌdɪsəˈgriːəblɪ/ adv désagréablement.

disagreement /ˌdɪsəˈgriːmənt/ n 1 (difference of opinion) désaccord m (about, on sur; as to quant à); **there is some ~ as to our aims** les avis divergent quant à nos objectifs; 2 (argument) différend m (about, over sur); 3 (inconsistency) divergence f (between entre).

disallow /ˌdɪsəˈlaʊ/ vtr 1 SPORT refuser; 2 GEN, ADMIN, JUR rejeter.

disappear /ˌdɪsəˈpɪə(r)/ vi (all contexts) disparaître; **to be fast ~ing** être en voie de disparition.

disappearance /ˌdɪsəˈpɪərəns/ n disparition f (of de).

disappoint /ˌdɪsəˈpɔɪnt/ vtr 1 (let down) décevoir [person]; 2 (upset) décevoir [hopes, dream]; contrecarrer [plan].

disappointed /ˌdɪsəˈpɔɪntɪd/ adj 1 (let down) déçu (about, at, by, with sth par qch); **I am ~ in you** tu me déçois; 2 (unfulfilled) déçu.

disappointing /ˌdɪsəˈpɔɪntɪŋ/ adj décevant.

disappointment /ˌdɪsəˈpɔɪntmənt/ n 1 (feeling) déception f; 2 (source of upset) **to be a ~ to sb** décevoir qn.

disapproval /ˌdɪsəˈpruːvl/ n désapprobation f (of de).

disapprove /ˌdɪsəˈpruːv/ vi ne pas être d'accord; **to ~ of** désapprouver [person, behaviour, lifestyle]; être contre [smoking, hunting].

disapproving /ˌdɪsəˈpruːvɪŋ/ adj [look, gesture] désapprobateur/-trice; **to be ~** être contre.

disarm /dɪsˈɑːm/ vtr, vi désarmer.

disarmament /dɪsˈɑːməmənt/ n désarmement m.

disarming /dɪs'ɑ:mɪŋ/ *adj* désarmant.

disarrange /ˌdɪsə'reɪndʒ/ *vtr* déranger [*objects*]; défaire [*clothing*].

disarray /ˌdɪsə'reɪ/ *n* **1** (confusion) confusion *f*; **in total ~** dans une confusion totale; **2** (disorder) désordre *m*.

disaster /dɪ'zɑ:stə(r), US -zæs-/ *n* GEN catastrophe *f*; (long-term) désastre *m*; **rail ~** catastrophe ferroviaire; **~ struck** le malheur a frappé.

disaster ~ **area** *n* LIT région *f* sinistrée; FIG catastrophe *f*; **~ fund** *n* fonds *m* de soutien; **~ victim** *n* sinistré/-e *m/f*.

disastrous /dɪ'zɑ:strəs, US -zæs-/ *adj* catastrophique.

disastrously /dɪ'zɑ:strəslɪ, US -zæs-/ *adv* [*end, turn out*] d'une manière désastreuse; [*fail*] lamentablement; **to go ~ wrong** tourner à la catastrophe.

disband /dɪs'bænd/ **I** *vtr* GEN dissoudre; MIL licencier.
II *vi* se disperser.

disbelief /ˌdɪsbɪ'li:f/ *n* incrédulité *f*.

disbelieve /ˌdɪsbɪ'li:v/ *vtr* ne pas croire.

disc /dɪsk/ *n* **1** GEN, MUS disque *m*; **2** ANAT disque *m* (intervertébral); **a slipped ~** une hernie discale; **3** GEN, MIL **identity ~** plaque *f* d'identité; **4** AUT **tax ~** vignette *f* (automobile).

discard /dɪs'kɑ:d/ **I** *vtr* **1** (get rid of) se débarrasser de [*possessions*]; jeter [qch] par terre [*litter*]; mettre [qch] au rebut [*furniture*]; CULIN jeter [*stalks, bones*]; **2** (drop) abandonner [*plan, policy*]; laisser tomber [*person*]; **3** (take off) enlever [*garment*]; **4** (in cards) se défausser de.
II *vi* (in cards) se défausser (d'une carte).

disc brakes *npl* AUT freins *mpl* à disques.

discern /dɪ's3:n/ *vtr* SOUT (see) discerner; (deduce) percevoir.

discernible /dɪ's3:nəbl/ *adj* perceptible.

discerning /dɪ's3:nɪŋ/ *adj* perspicace.

discharge I /'dɪstʃɑ:dʒ/ *n* **1** (release) renvoi *m* au foyer; **to get one's ~** [*soldier*] être libéré; **2** (pouring out) (of gas) émission *f*; (of liquid) écoulement *m*; MED (of pus) suppuration *f*; (of blood) perte *f*; **3** (emptying out) (of waste) déversement *m*; **4** (substance released) (waste) déchets *mpl*; MED (from eye, wound etc) sécrétions *fpl*; **5** FIN (of debt) règlement *m*; **6** ELEC décharge *f*; **7** (performance) exercice *m*; **8** (firing) décharge *f*; **9** (unloading) déchargement *m*.
II /dɪs'tʃɑ:dʒ/ *vtr* **1** (release) renvoyer [*patient*]; donner son congé à [*soldier*]; décharger [*accused*]; **to be ~d from hospital** être autorisé à quitter l'hôpital; **he has ~d himself** il a quitté l'hôpital; **to be ~d from the army** être libéré de l'armée; **2** (dismiss) renvoyer [*employee*]; **to ~ sb from his duties** démettre qn de ses fonctions; **3** (give off) émettre [*gas*]; déverser [*sewage, waste*]; **4** MED (from eye) suppurer; **5** FIN s'acquitter de [*debt*]; réhabiliter [*bankrupt*]; **6** (perform) s'acquitter de [*duty*]; remplir [*obligation*]; **7** (unload) décharger [*cargo*]; débarquer [*passengers*]; **8** (fire) décharger [*rifle*].

disciple /dɪ'saɪpl/ *n* GEN, BIBLE disciple *mf*.

disciplinarian /ˌdɪsɪplɪ'neərɪən/ *n* **to be a ~** être strict en matière de discipline.

disciplinary /'dɪsɪplɪnərɪ, US -nerɪ/ *adj* disciplinaire.

discipline /'dɪsɪplɪn/ **I** *n* **1** (controlled behaviour) discipline *f*; **2** (academic subject) discipline *f*.
II *vtr* (control) discipliner; (punish) punir.

disciplined /'dɪsɪplɪnd/ *adj* [*person, group, manner*] discipliné; [*approach*] méthodique.

disclaim /dɪs'kleɪm/ *vtr* nier.

disclaimer /dɪs'kleɪmə(r)/ *n* démenti *m*.

disclose /dɪs'kləʊz/ *vtr* laisser voir [*sight*]; révéler [*information*].

disclosure /dɪs'kləʊʒə(r)/ *n* révélation *f* (of de).

disco /'dɪskəʊ/ *n* (event) soirée *f* disco; (club) discothèque *f*.

discoloration /ˌdɪskʌlə'reɪʃn/ *n* décoloration *f*.

discomfort /dɪs'kʌmfət/ *n* **1** (physical) sensation *f* pénible; **to be in ~, to suffer ~** avoir mal; **2** (embarrassment) sentiment *m* de gêne.

disconcerting /ˌdɪskən's3:tɪŋ/ *adj* (worrying) troublant; (unnerving) déconcertant.

disconnect /ˌdɪskə'nekt/ *vtr* débrancher [*pipe, appliance*]; couper [*telephone, gas etc*]; décrocher [*carriage*].

disconnected /ˌdɪskə'nektɪd/ *adj* [*remarks*] décousu.

disconsolately /dɪs'kɒnsələtlɪ/ *adv* d'un air désespéré.

discontent /ˌdɪskən'tent/ *n* mécontentement *m*.

discontented /ˌdɪskən'tentɪd/ *adj* mécontent.

discontinue /ˌdɪskən'tɪnju:/ *vtr* supprimer [*service*]; arrêter [*production*]; cesser [*visits*]; **'~d line'** COMM 'fin de série'.

discord /'dɪskɔ:d/ *n* **1** ¢ dissensions *fpl*; **a note of ~** une note de discorde; **2** MUS discordance *f*.

discordant /dɪs'kɔ:dənt/ *adj* GEN, MUS discordant.

discount I /'dɪskaʊnt/ *n* COMM remise *f* (**on** sur); (on minor purchase) rabais *m* (**on** sur); FIN escompte *m*; **to give sb a ~** faire une remise à qn; **~ for cash** escompte de caisse (pour paiement au comptant); **at a ~** [*purchase*] au rabais; [*shares*] avec une décote.
II /dɪs'kaʊnt, US 'dɪskaʊnt/ *vtr* **1** (reject) écarter [*idea, claim, possibility*], ne pas tenir compte de [*advice, report*]; **2** /'dɪskaʊnt/ COMM solder [*goods*]; faire une remise de [*sum of money*].

discount flight *n* vol *m* à tarif réduit.

discourage /dɪs'kʌrɪdʒ/ *vtr* **1** (dishearten) décourager; **2** (deter) décourager.

discouragement /dɪs'kʌrɪdʒmənt/ *n* **1** (despondency) découragement *m*; **2** (disincentive) **it's more of a ~ than an incentive** cela décourage plutôt que cela ne motive.

discourteous /dɪs'k3:tɪəs/ *adj* peu courtois.

discover /dɪs'kʌvə(r)/ *vtr* (all contexts) découvrir.

discovery /dɪs'kʌvərɪ/ *n* GEN découverte *f*; **a voyage of ~** un voyage d'exploration.

discredit /dɪs'kredɪt/ **I** *n* discrédit *m*.
II *vtr* discréditer [*person, organization*]; mettre en doute [*report, theory*].

discreet /dɪs'kri:t/ *adj* [*behaviour, colour*] discret/-ète.

discrepancy /dɪs'krepənsɪ/ *n* divergence *f*.

discretion /dɪs'kreʃn/ *n* **1** (authority) discrétion *f*; **to use one's ~** agir à sa discrétion; **I have ~ over that decision** cette décision est à ma discrétion; **2** (tact) discrétion *f*.

discriminate /dɪs'krɪmɪneɪt/ *vi* **1** (act with prejudice) établir une discrimination (**against** envers; **in favour of** en faveur de); **2** (distinguish) **to ~ between** faire une ou la distinction entre.

discriminating /dɪs'krɪmɪneɪtɪŋ/ *adj* plein de discernement.

discrimination /dɪsˌkrɪmɪ'neɪʃn/ *n* **1** (prejudice) discrimination *f*; **2** (taste) discernement *m*; **3** (ability to differentiate) capacité *f* d'établir des distinctions.

discus /'dɪskəs/ *n* (object) disque *m*; (event) lancer *m* du disque.

discuss /dɪs'kʌs/ *vtr* (talk about) discuter de; (in writing) examiner.

discussion /dɪs'kʌʃn/ *n* GEN discussion *f*; (in public) débat *m*; (in text) analyse *f*; **under ~** en discussion; **to bring sth up for ~** soumettre qch à la discussion; **to be open to ~** être à discuter.

discussion document, discussion paper *n* avant-projet *m*.

disdain /dɪs'deɪn/ **I** *n* dédain *m* (**for** pour).
II *vtr* dédaigner; **to ~ to do** ne pas daigner faire.

disdainful /dɪs'deɪnfl/ *adj* dédaigneux/-euse.

disease /dɪ'zi:z/ *n* **1** (specific illness) maladie *f*; **2** ¢ (range of infections) maladies *fpl*.

diseased /dɪ'zi:zd/ *adj* LIT, FIG malade.

disembark /ˌdɪsɪm'bɑ:k/ *vtr, vi* débarquer.

disembodied /ˌdɪsɪm'bɒdɪd/ *adj* désincarné.

disenchanted /ˌdɪsɪn'tʃɑ:ntɪd, US -'tʃænt-/ *adj* désabusé; **to become ~ with sth** perdre ses illusions sur qch.

disenfranchise /ˌdɪsɪnˈfræntʃaɪz/ *vtr* priver [qn] du droit de vote.

disengage /ˌdɪsɪnˈgeɪdʒ/ **I** *vtr* GEN dégager (**from** de); **to ~ the clutch** AUT débrayer.
II *vi* **1** MIL cesser le combat; **2** GEN, MIL **to ~ from** se retirer de.

disentangle /ˌdɪsɪnˈtæŋgl/ *vtr* LIT, FIG démêler.

disfavour GB, **disfavor** US /dɪsˈfeɪvə(r)/ *n* désapprobation *f*; **to fall into ~** tomber en disgrâce.

disfigure /dɪsˈfɪgə(r)/, US dɪsˈfɪgjər/ *vtr* défigurer.

disgorge /dɪsˈgɔːdʒ/ *vtr* déverser [*crowd, liquid*].

disgrace /dɪsˈgreɪs/ **I** *n* (shame) honte *f*; **to bring ~ on sb** déshonorer qn; **to be in ~** (officially) être en disgrâce; **it's an absolute ~!** c'est scandaleux!
II *vtr* déshonorer [*team, family*]; **he ~d himself** il s'est mal conduit.
III disgraced *pp adj* [*leader, player*] disgracié.

disgraceful /dɪsˈgreɪsfl/ *adj* [*conduct, situation*] scandaleux/-euse.

disgruntled /dɪsˈgrʌntld/ *adj* mécontent.

disguise /dɪsˈgaɪz/ **I** *n* déguisement *m*; **in ~** déguisé.
II *vtr* déguiser [*person, voice*]; camoufler [*blemish*]; cacher [*emotion, fact*]; **there's no disguising the fact that** on ne peut pas cacher le fait que.
IDIOMS **it's a blessing in ~** c'est une bonne chose, même si ça n'en a pas l'air.

disgust /dɪsˈgʌst/ **I** *n* (physical) dégoût *m*; (moral) écœurement *m* (**at** devant); **in ~** dégoûté, écœuré.
II *vtr* (physically) dégoûter; (morally) écœurer.

disgusting /dɪsˈgʌstɪŋ/ *adj* (morally) écœurant; (physically) répugnant.

disgustingly /dɪsˈgʌstɪŋlɪ/ *adv* **to be ~ dirty/fat** être d'une saleté/obésité répugnante.

dish /dɪʃ/ **I** *n* **1** (plate) (for eating) assiette *f*; (for serving) plat *m*; **2** CULIN (food) plat *m*; **side ~** garniture *f*; **3** TV (also **satellite ~**) antenne *f* parabolique; **4°** (person) (male) beau mec° *m*, (female) belle fille *f*.
II dishes *npl* vaisselle *f*; **to do the ~es** faire la vaisselle.
■ **dish out**: **~ out** [sth] distribuer [*advice, compliments, money*]; servir [*food*].
■ **dish up**: **~ up** [sth] servir [*meal*].

dishcloth /ˈdɪʃklɒθ/ *n* (for washing) lavette *f*; (for drying) torchon *m* (à vaisselle).

dishearten /dɪsˈhɑːtn/ *vtr* décourager, démoraliser.

dishevelled /dɪˈʃevld/ *adj* [*person*] débraillé; [*hair*] décoiffé; [*clothes*] en désordre.

dishonest /dɪsˈɒnɪst/ *adj* malhonnête.

dishonesty /dɪsˈɒnɪstɪ/ *n* (lack of honesty) (financial) malhonnêteté *f*; (moral, intellectual) mauvaise foi *f*.

dishonour GB, **dishonor** US /dɪsˈɒnə(r)/ *n* déshonneur *m*; **to bring ~ on sb** déshonorer qn.

dishonourable GB, **dishonorable** US /dɪsˈɒnərəbl/ *adj* [*act*] déshonorant.

dish: **~pan** *n* US cuvette *f*; **~rag** *n* US lavette *f*; **~towel** *n* torchon *m*.

dishwasher /ˈdɪʃˌwɒʃə/ **I** *n* (machine) lave-vaisselle *m inv*; (person) plongeur/-euse *m/f*.
II *noun modifier* [*powder, salt*] pour lave-vaisselle.

dishwater /ˈdɪʃwɔːtə(r)/ *n* eau *f* de vaisselle; **as dull as ~** ennuyeux/-euse comme la pluie.

dishy° /ˈdɪʃɪ/ *adj* GB séduisant, beau/belle (*before* n).

disillusion /ˌdɪsɪˈluːʒn/ *vtr* **to ~ sb** désabuser qn.

disillusioned /ˌdɪsɪˈluːʒnd/ *adj* désabusé; **to be ~ with sth/sb** perdre ses illusions sur qch/qn.

disillusionment /ˌdɪsɪˈluːʒnmənt/ *n* désillusion *f*.

disincentive /ˌdɪsɪnˈsentɪv/ *n* démotivation *f*.

disinclined /ˌdɪsɪnˈklaɪnd/ *adj* **~ to do** peu disposé à faire.

disinfect /ˌdɪsɪnˈfekt/ *vtr* désinfecter.

disinfectant /ˌdɪsɪnˈfektənt/ *n* désinfectant *m*.

disingenuous /ˌdɪsɪnˈdʒenjʊəs/ *adj* [*comment*] peu sincère; [*smile*] faux/fausse.

disinherit /ˌdɪsɪnˈherɪt/ *vtr* déshériter.

disintegrate /dɪsˈɪntɪgreɪt/ *vi* GEN se désagréger; [*aircraft*] se désintégrer.

disinterested /dɪsˈɪntrəstɪd/ *adj* **1** (impartial) [*observer, party, stance, advice*] impartial; **2** (uninterested) USAGE CRITIQUÉ: voir note indifférent (**in** à).

■ Note Dans ce sens, utiliser de préférence *uninterested*.

disjointed /dɪsˈdʒɔɪntɪd/ *adj* [*programme, speech, report*] décousu; [*organization, effort*] incohérent.

disk /dɪsk/ *n* **1** COMPUT disque *m*; **on ~** sur disque; **2** US = **disc**.

disk: **~ directory** *n* répertoire *m* disques; **~ drive** (unit) *n* unité *f* de disque; **~ management** *n* gestion *f* disques; **~ operating system**, DOS *n* système *m* d'exploitation à disques, DOS *m*.

dislike /dɪsˈlaɪk/ **I** *n* aversion *f* (**of** pour); **to take a ~ to sb/sth** prendre qn/qch en grippe, (stronger) prendre qn/qch en aversion; **we all have our likes and ~s** chacun a ses préférences.
II *vtr* ne pas aimer (**doing** faire); **I have always ~ him** il m'a toujours été antipathique; **I ~ her intensely** je la déteste cordialement; **I don't ~ city life** je n'ai rien contre la vie urbaine.

dislocate /ˈdɪsləkeɪt, US ˈdɪsləʊkeɪt/ *vtr* **1** MED **to ~ one's shoulder** se démettre l'épaule; **2** (disrupt) désorganiser [*system*]; bouleverser [*economy, social structure*]; disperser [*population*].

dislocation /ˌdɪsləˈkeɪʃn, US ˌdɪsləʊˈkeɪʃn/ *n* (of hip, knee) luxation *f*.

dislodge /dɪsˈlɒdʒ/ *vtr* déplacer [*rock, tile, obstacle*]; déloger [*foreign body, sniper*].

disloyal /dɪsˈlɔɪəl/ *adj* déloyal (**to** envers).

dismal /ˈdɪzməl/ *adj* **1** [*place, sight*] lugubre; **2°** [*failure, attempt*] lamentable.

dismantle /dɪsˈmæntl/ *vtr* **1** (take apart) démonter [*construction*]; **2** (phase out) démanteler [*organization, service*].

dismantling /dɪsˈmæntlɪŋ/ *n* (of machine) démontage *m*; (of system) démantèlement *m*.

dismay /dɪsˈmeɪ/ *n* consternation *f* (**at** devant).

dismayed /dɪsˈmeɪd/ *adj* consterné.

dismember /dɪsˈmembə(r)/ *vtr* **1** démembrer [*corpse*]; **2** FIG démembrer [*country*]; démanteler [*organization*].

dismiss /dɪsˈmɪs/ *vtr* **1** (reject) écarter [*idea, suggestion*]; exclure [*possibility*]; **to ~ sth as insignificant** écarter qch d'emblée; **2** (put out of mind) chasser [*thought, worry*]; **3** (sack) licencier [*employee, worker*]; renvoyer [*servant*]; révoquer [*civil servant*]; démettre [qn] de ses fonctions [*director, official*]; **4** (end interview with) congédier [*person*]; (send out) [*teacher*] laisser sortir [*class*]; **5** JUR rejeter [*appeal*]; **the case was ~ed** il y a eu non-lieu.

dismissal /dɪsˈmɪsl/ *n* **1** (of employee, worker) licenciement *m*; (of servant) renvoi *m*; (of civil servant) révocation *f*; (of manager, minister) destitution *f*; **unfair ~**, **wrongful ~** licenciement abusif; **2** (of idea, threat) refus *m* de prendre qch en considération; **3** JUR (of appeal, claim) rejet *m*.

dismissive /dɪsˈmɪsɪv/ *adj* [*person, attitude*] dédaigneux/-euse; [*gesture*] de dédain; **to be ~ of** faire peu de cas de.

dismount /dɪsˈmaʊnt/ *vi* mettre pied à terre; **to ~ from** descendre de [*horse, bicycle*].

disobedient /ˌdɪsəˈbiːdɪənt/ *adj* [*child*] désobéissant.

disobey /ˌdɪsəˈbeɪ/ **I** *vtr* désobéir à [*person*]; enfreindre [*law*].
II *vi* désobéir.

disorder /dɪsˈɔːdə(r)/ *n* **1** ¢ (lack of order) désordre *m*; **to retreat in ~** MIL être mis en déroute; **2** ¢ GEN, POL (disturbances) émeutes *fpl*; **3** C MED, PSYCH (malfunction) troubles *mpl*; (disease) maladie *f*; **eating ~** troubles de l'alimentation.

disordered /dɪsˈɔːdəd/ *adj* [*life*] désordonné; MED [*mind*] déséquilibré.

disorderly /dɪsˈɔːdəlɪ/ *adj* **1** [*room*] en désordre; **2** (disorganized) désordonné; [*crowd, meeting*] turbulent.

disorderly behaviour, disorderly conduct *n* JUR perturbation *f* de l'ordre public.

disorganized /dɪsˈɔːgənaɪzd/ *adj* désorganisé.

disorientate /dɪsˈɔːrɪənteɪt/ *vtr* désorienter.

disown /dɪsˈəʊn/ *vtr* GEN désavouer; renier [*person*].

disparaging /dɪˈspærɪdʒɪŋ/ *adj* désobligeant.

disparate /ˈdɪspərət/ *adj* **1** (different) [*group*] hétérogène; **2** (incompatible) incompatible.

dispassionate /dɪsˈpæʃənət/ *adj* **1** (impartial) objectif/-ive (**about** au sujet de); **2** (unemotional) froid.

dispatch /dɪˈspætʃ/ **I** *n* **1** (report) dépêche *f*; **mentioned in ~es** MIL cité à l'ordre du jour; **2** (sending) expédition *f*; **date of ~** date d'expédition.
II *vtr* **1** (send) envoyer [*person*] (**to** à); expédier [*letter, parcel*] (**to** à); **2** HUM (consume) expédier [*plateful*]; descendre [*drink*]; **3** (complete) expédier [*work*]; régler [*problem*].

dispatch box *n* **1** valise *f* diplomatique; **2 Dispatch Box** GB POL tribune *f* (*d'où parlent les membres du gouvernement*).

dispel /dɪˈspel/ *vtr* (*p prés etc* **-ll-**) chasser [*doubt, fear*]; dissiper [*myth, notion*]; **2** SOUT dissiper [*mist*].

dispensable /dɪˈspensəbl/ *adj* **to be ~** [*thing, idea*] être superflu; [*person*] être une quantité négligeable.

dispensary /dɪˈspensərɪ/ *n* GB (in hospital) pharmacie *f*; (in chemist's) officine *f*.

dispense /dɪˈspens/ *vtr* **1** [*machine*] distribuer [*drinks, money*]; **2** SOUT exercer [*justice*]; faire [*charity*]; prodiguer [*advice*]; attribuer [*funds*]; **3** préparer [*medicine, prescription*]; **4** (exempt) dispenser.
■ **dispense with** (manage without) se passer de [*services, formalities*]; (get rid of) abandonner [*policy, regulations etc*]; (make unnecessary) rendre inutile [*resource, facility*].

dispenser /dɪˈspensə(r)/ *n* distributeur *m*.

dispensing: **~ chemist** *n* GB pharmacien/-ienne *m*/*f*; **~ optician** *n* GB opticien/-ienne *m*/*f*.

dispersal /dɪˈspɜːsl/ *n* (of fumes) dispersion *f*; (of seeds, installations) dissémination *f*.

disperse /dɪˈspɜːs/ **I** *vtr* (scatter) disperser; (distribute) disséminer; CHEM décomposer [*particle*].
II *vi* **1** [*crowd*] se disperser; **2** [*mist*] se dissiper.

dispersion /dɪˈspɜːʃn, US dɪˈspɜːrʒn/ *n* GEN dispersion *f*; (of light) décomposition *f*.

dispirited /dɪˈspɪrɪtɪd/ *adj* [*look, air*] découragé; [*mood*] abattu.

displace /dɪsˈpleɪs/ *vtr* **1** (replace) supplanter [*competitor*]; déplacer [*worker*]; **2** (expel) chasser [*person*].

displaced person /dɪsˈpleɪst/ *n* personne *f* déplacée.

displacement /dɪsˈpleɪsmənt/ *n* déplacement *m*.

display /dɪˈspleɪ/ **I** *n* **1** COMM (for sale) étalage *m*; (of larger objects) exposition *f*; **window ~** vitrine *f*; **to be on ~** être exposé; **to put sth on ~** exposer qch; **2** (for decoration, to look at) **what a lovely ~ of flowers** quel bel arrangement de fleurs; **3** (demonstration) (of art, craft) démonstration *f*; (of dance, sport) exhibition *f*; **air ~** fête *f* aéronautique; **4** (of emotion, failing, quality) démonstration *f*; (of strength) déploiement *m*; (of wealth) étalage *m*; **in a ~ of** dans un geste de [*anger, impatience*]; **5** AUT, AVIAT, COMPUT écran *m*; **6** (of advert) **full page ~** page *f* entière de publicité; **7** ZOOL parade *f*.
II *vtr* **1** GEN, COMM, COMPUT (show, set out) afficher [*information, poster*]; exposer [*object*]; **2** (reveal) faire preuve de [*intelligence, interest, skill*]; révéler [*emotion, vice, virtue*]; **3** PÉJ (flaunt) faire étalage de [*beauty, knowledge, wealth*]; exhiber [*legs, chest*].
III *vi* GEN parader [*peacock*] faire la roue.

display: **~ advertisement** *n* grande annonce *f*; **~ artist ▸ 1251** *n* COMM étalagiste *mf*; **~ cabinet**, **~ case** *n* (in house) vitrine *f*; (in museum) vitrine *f* d'exposition; **~ panel** *n* écran *m* d'affichage; **~ rack** *n* présentoir *m*; **~ window** *n* vitrine *f*.

displeased /dɪsˈpliːzd/ *adj* mécontent (**with, at** de).

displeasure /dɪsˈpleʒə(r)/ *n* mécontentement *m*.

disposable /dɪˈspəʊzəbl/ *adj* **1** (throwaway) jetable; **2** (available) disponible.

disposal /dɪˈspəʊzl/ *n* **1** (removal) (of waste product) élimination *f*; **for ~** à jeter; **2** (sale) (of company, property) vente *f*; (of deeds, securities) cession *f*; **3** (completion) exécution *f*; **4** (for use, access) **to be at sb's ~** être à la disposition de qn; **all the means at my ~** tous les moyens dont je dispose; **5** (arrangement) disposition *f*.

dispose /dɪˈspəʊz/ *vtr* **1** (arrange) disposer [*furniture, troops*]; **2** (encourage) **to ~ sb to sth/to do** disposer qn à qch/à faire.
■ **dispose of**: **~ of** [*sth/sb*] **1** se débarrasser de [*body, rival, rubbish*]; détruire [*evidence*]; désarmer [*bomb*]; **2** COMM écouler [*stock*]; (sell) vendre [*car, shares*]; **3** (deal with) expédier [*business, problem, theory*].

disposition /ˌdɪspəˈzɪʃn/ *n* **1** (temperament) tempérament *m*; **to be of a nervous ~** avoir un tempérament nerveux; **to have a cheerful ~** être d'un naturel gai; **2** (tendency) tendance *f*; **to have a ~ to do** avoir tendance à faire; **3** (arrangement) disposition *f*.

dispossessed /ˌdɪspəˈzest/ *adj* [*family*] exproprié; [*son*] déshérité.

disproportionate /ˌdɪsprəˈpɔːʃənət/ *adj* disproportionné (**to** par rapport à).

disproportionately /ˌdɪsprəˈpɔːʃənətlɪ/ *adv* [*affect*] de façon disproportionnée; **~ high** [*costs, expectations*] disproportionné.

disprove /dɪsˈpruːv/ *vtr* réfuter.

dispute /dɪˈspjuːt/ **I** *n* **1** (quarrel) (between individuals) dispute *f*; (between groups) conflit *m* (**over, about** à propos de); **to have a ~ with** se disputer avec; **2** ¢ (controversy) controverse *f* (**over, about** sur); **to be/ not to be in ~** [*fact*] être/ne pas être controversé; **beyond ~** incontestable; **without ~** sans conteste; **to be open to ~** être contestable.
II *vtr* **1** (question truth of) contester [*claim, figures*]; **I ~ that!** je m'inscris en faux!; **2** (claim possession of) se disputer [*property, title*].

disqualification /dɪsˌkwɒlɪfɪˈkeɪʃn/ *n* **1** GEN (from post) exclusion *f* (**from** de); **2** SPORT disqualification *f*; **3** GB JUR suspension *f*; **4** (also **driving ~**) AUT retrait *m* du permis de conduire.

disqualify /dɪsˈkwɒlɪfaɪ/ *vtr* **1** GEN (from post, career) exclure; **to ~ sb from doing** interdire à qn de faire; **2** SPORT [*regulation*] disqualifier; [*physical condition*] empêcher (**from doing** de faire); **3** GB AUT, JUR **to ~ sb from driving** retirer à qn son permis de conduire.

disquiet /dɪsˈkwaɪət/ SOUT *n* inquiétude *f*.

disquieting /dɪsˈkwaɪətɪŋ/ *adj* troublant.

disregard /ˌdɪsrɪˈgɑːd/ **I** *n* (for problem, feelings, person) indifférence *f* (**for sth** à qch; **for sb** envers qn); (for danger, convention, life, law, right) mépris *m* (**for** de).
II *vtr* **1** (discount) ne pas tenir compte de [*irrelevance, problem, evidence, remark*]; fermer les yeux sur [*fault*]; mépriser [*danger*]; **2** ne pas respecter [*law, instruction*].

disrepair /ˌdɪsrɪˈpeə(r)/ *n* délabrement *m*; **to fall into ~** se délabrer.

disreputable /dɪsˈrepjʊtəbl/ *adj* **1** (unsavoury) [*person*] peu recommandable; [*place*] mal famé; [*behaviour*] déshonorant; **2** (tatty) [*clothes*] miteux/-euse; **3** (discredited) [*method*] douteux/-euse.

disrepute /ˌdɪsrɪˈpjuːt/ *n* **to be held in ~** être discrédité; **to bring into ~** jeter le discrédit sur.

disrespect /ˌdɪsrɪˈspekt/ *n* manque *m* de respect (**for** envers); **to show ~ to sb** manquer de respect envers qn; **no ~ (to him/her)** avec tout le respect que je lui dois.

disrespectful /ˌdɪsrɪˈspektfl/ *adj* [*person*] irrespectueux/-euse (**to, towards** envers); [*remark, behaviour*] irrévérencieux/-ieuse.

disrupt /dɪsˈrʌpt/ *vtr* perturber [*traffic, trade, meeting*]; bouleverser [*lifestyle, schedule, routine*]; interrompre [*power supply*].

disruption /dɪsˈrʌpʃn/ n **1** ¢ (disorder) perturbations fpl (**in** dans); **to cause ~ to sth** perturber qch; **2** (disrupting) (of service, meeting) perturbation f; (of schedule) bouleversement m; ELEC interruption f.

disruptive /dɪsˈrʌptɪv/ adj perturbateur/-trice.

dissatisfaction /dɪˌsætɪsˈfækʃn/ n mécontentement m.

dissatisfied /dɪˈsætɪsfaɪd/ adj mécontent.

dissect /dɪˈsekt/ vtr **1** (cut up) disséquer [cadaver, plant]; **2** PÉJ disséquer [performance, relationship]; éplucher [book, play].

dissemble /dɪˈsembl/ vtr, vi SOUT dissimuler.

disseminate /dɪˈsemɪneɪt/ vtr diffuser [information, products]; propager [ideas, views].

dissension /dɪˈsenʃn/ n (discord) discorde f, dissensions fpl.

dissent /dɪˈsent/ **I** n ¢ GEN, POL contestation f, dissensions fpl SOUT; SPORT contestation f.
II vi GEN, JUR (disagree) contester; **to ~ from sth** contester qch.
III dissenting pres p adj GEN, POL [group, opinion, voice] contestataire.

dissertation /dɪsəˈteɪʃn/ n **1** GB UNIV mémoire m (**on** sur); **2** US UNIV thèse f (**on** sur).

disservice /dɪsˈsɜːvɪs/ n **to do a ~ to sb**, **to do sb a ~** rendre un mauvais service à qn.

dissident /ˈdɪsɪdənt/ n, adj dissident/-e (m/f).

dissimilar /dɪˈsɪmɪlə(r)/ adj dissemblable; **~ to** différent de.

dissimilarity /ˌdɪsɪmɪˈlærətɪ/ n **1** ¢ (lack of similarity) dissemblance f (**in** de; **between** entre); **2** (difference) différence f (**in** de).

dissipate /ˈdɪsɪpeɪt/ SOUT **I** vtr GEN dissiper; anéantir [hope, enthusiasm].
II vi (all contexts) se dissiper.

dissipated /ˈdɪsɪpeɪtɪd/ adj dissolu.

dissociate /dɪˈsəʊʃɪeɪt/ vtr GEN, CHEM dissocier.

dissociation /dɪˌsəʊʃɪˈeɪʃn/ n dissociation f.

dissolute /ˈdɪsəluːt/ adj [lifestyle] dissolu.

dissolve /dɪˈzɒlv/ **I** n CIN fondu m enchaîné.
II vtr **1** [acid, water] dissoudre [solid, grease]; **2** faire dissoudre [tablet, powder] (**in** dans); **3** (break up) dissoudre [assembly, parliament, partnership].
III vi **1** (liquefy) se dissoudre (**in** dans; **into** en); **2** (fade) [hope, feeling, opposition] s'évanouir; [outline, image] disparaître; **3** (collapse) **to ~ into tears** fondre en larmes; **4** (break up) [assembly] être dissous/-oute.

dissonant /ˈdɪsənənt/ adj **1** MUS dissonant; **2** SOUT [sounds etc] discordant.

dissuade /dɪˈsweɪd/ vtr dissuader.

distance /ˈdɪstəns/ ▶ 1045 **I** n LIT, FIG distance f (**between** entre; **from** de; **to** à); **at a** ou **some ~ from** à bonne distance de; **at a safe/an equal ~** à bonne/égale distance; **a long/short ~ away** loin/pas loin; **to keep sb at a ~** tenir qn à distance; **to keep one's ~** LIT, FIG garder ses distances (**from** avec); **to go the ~** SPORT, FIG tenir la distance; **from a/in the ~** de/au loin; **it's no ~** c'est tout près; **it's within walking ~** on peut y aller à pied; **he's within shouting ~** il est assez près pour pouvoir t'entendre; **at a ~ it's easy to see that I made mistakes** avec du recul je vois très bien que j'ai commis des erreurs.
II noun modifier [runner, race] de fond.
III vtr **1** créer une distance entre [two people]; **2** (outdistance) distancer [rival].
IV v refl **to ~ oneself** (dissociate oneself) se distancier (**from** de); (stand back) prendre du recul (**from** par rapport à).

distant /ˈdɪstənt/ adj **1** (remote) éloigné; **the ~ sound of sth** le bruit de qch dans le lointain; **~ from** loin de; **40 km ~ from** à 40 km de; **in the not too ~ future** dans un avenir assez proche; **2** (faint) [memory, prospect, hope, similarity] lointain; **3** (cool) [person, manner] distant.

distantly /ˈdɪstəntlɪ/ adv vaguement.

distaste /dɪsˈteɪst/ n déplaisir m; (marked) dégoût m; **~ for** répugnance f pour.

distasteful /dɪsˈteɪstfl/ adj déplaisant; (markedly) répugnant; **I find the remark ~** je trouve cette réflexion de mauvais goût.

distemper /dɪˈstempə(r)/ n **1** (in dogs) maladie f de Carré; (in horses) angine f des chevaux; **2** (paint) (on wall) badigeon m; (in art) détrempe f.

distend /dɪˈstend/ vtr distendre.

distil GB, **distill** US /dɪˈstɪl/ vtr (p prés etc **-ll-** GB) **1** (purify) distiller [liquid]; **to ~ sth from sth** extraire qch par distillation de qch; **2** (make) distiller [alcohol] (**from** à partir de).

distillation /ˌdɪstɪˈleɪʃn/ n (of liquids) distillation f; FIG condensé m.

distinct /dɪˈstɪŋkt/ adj **1** [image] (not blurred) net/nette; (easily visible) distinct; **2** (definite) [resemblance, preference, progress, impression] net/nette; [advantage] indéniable; **it's a ~ possibility** c'est fort possible; **3** (separable) distinct (**from** de); **4** (different) différent (**from** de); **as ~ from** par opposition à.

distinction /dɪˈstɪŋkʃn/ n **1** (differentiation) distinction f; **2** (difference) différence f (**between** entre); **3** (preeminence) mérite m; **of ~** réputé; **to have the ~ of doing** (have the honour) avoir le mérite de faire; (be the only one) avoir la particularité de faire; **4** (elegance) distinction f; **5** (specific honour) distinction f; **6** MUS, SCH, UNIV mention f très bien.

distinctive /dɪˈstɪŋktɪv/ adj caractéristique (**of** de).

distinctly /dɪˈstɪŋktlɪ/ adv **1** [speak, hear, see] distinctement; [remember] nettement; [say, tell] explicitement; **2** [possible, embarrassing, odd] vraiment.

distinguish /dɪˈstɪŋgwɪʃ/ **I** vtr distinguer; **to be ~ed from** se distinguer de; **to be ~ed by** se caractériser par.
II distinguishing pres p adj [factor, feature, mark] distinctif/-ive; **~ing marks** (on passport) signes mpl particuliers.

distinguishable /dɪˈstɪŋgwɪʃəbl/ adj **1 the two cars are not easily ~** il est difficile de distinguer les deux voitures; **2** (visible) visible; **3** (audible) perceptible.

distinguished /dɪˈstɪŋgwɪʃt/ adj **1** (elegant) distingué; **2** (famous) éminent.

distort /dɪˈstɔːt/ vtr **1** (misrepresent) dénaturer [statement, opinion, fact]; déformer [truth]; fausser [assessment, figures]; falsifier [history]; **2** déformer [features, sound, metal].

distortion /dɪˈstɔːʃn/ n (of truth) déformation f; (of metal) déformation f; (of sound, features, figures) distorsion f.

distract /dɪˈstrækt/ vtr distraire; **to ~ sb from doing** empêcher qn de faire; **I was ~ed by the noise** le bruit m'a empêché de me concentrer; **to ~ attention** détourner l'attention (**from** de).

distracting /dɪˈstræktɪŋ/ adj [sound, presence, flicker] gênant; **I found the noise too ~** le bruit m'empêchait de me concentrer.

distraction /dɪˈstrækʃn/ n **1** (from concentration) distraction f; **I don't want any ~s** (environmental) je ne veux pas être distrait; (human) je ne veux pas qu'on me dérange; **a moment's ~** un moment d'inattention; **2** (diversion) diversion f; **to be a ~ from** détourner l'attention de [problem, priority]; **3** (entertainment) distraction f; **4** (madness) **to drive sb to ~** rendre qn fou/folle.

distraught /dɪˈstrɔːt/ adj [person] éperdu (**with** de); **to be ~ at** ou **over sth** être bouleversé par qch.

distress /dɪˈstres/ **I** n **1** (anguish) désarroi m; **in ~** complètement bouleversé; (stronger) dans un grand désarroi; **to cause sb ~** faire de la peine à qn; **to my/his ~, they...** à mon/son grand chagrin, ils...; **2** (physical trouble) souffrance(s) f(pl); **she seems to be in ~** ça n'a pas l'air d'aller du tout; **3** (poverty) détresse f; **4** NAUT **in ~** en détresse.
II noun modifier [call, rocket, signal] de détresse.
III vtr faire de la peine à [person]; (stronger) bouleverser [person] (**to do** de faire).

IV *v refl* to ~ oneself s'inquiéter.

distressed /dɪ'strest/ *adj* (upset) [*person*] peiné (**at, by** par); (stronger) bouleversé (**at, by** par).

distressing /dɪ'stresɪŋ/ *adj* [*case, event, idea*] pénible; [*news*] navrant; [*sight*] affligeant; **it is ~ that** il est pénible que (+ *subj*).

distribute /dɪ'strɪbjuːt/ *vtr* **1** (share out) distribuer [*information, documents, supplies, money*] (**to** à; **among** entre); **2** COMM distribuer [*goods, books, films*]; **3** (spread out) répartir [*weight, load, tax burden*]; **4** (disperse) **to be ~d** [*flora, fauna, mineral deposits*] être réparti.

distribute: **~d data processing, DDP** *n* informatique *f* répartie; **~d system** *n* système *m* d'information répartie.

distribution /ˌdɪstrɪ'bjuːʃn/ *n* **1** GEN, CIN, COMM distribution *f*; **2** (spread) répartition *f*.

distributor /dɪ'strɪbjʊtə(r)/ *n* **1** COMM, CIN distributeur *m* (**for sth** de); **sole ~ for** concessionnaire *m* exclusif de; **2** AUT distributeur *m*.

district /'dɪstrɪkt/ *n* **1** (in country) région *f*; **2** (in city) quartier *m*; **3** (sector) (administrative) district *m*; US (electoral) circonscription *f* électorale; (postal) secteur *m* postal.

district attorney *n* US représentant *m* du ministère public.

district: **~ council** *n* GB ~ conseil *m* général; **~ court** *n* US cour *f* fédérale; **~ manager** *n* directeur/-trice *m/f* régional/-e; **~ nurse** *n* GB infirmière *f* visiteuse.

distrust /dɪs'trʌst/ **I** *n* méfiance *f* (**of** à l'égard de).
II *vtr* se méfier de [*person, motive, government*].

disturb /dɪ'stɜːb/ *vtr* **1** (interrupt) déranger [*person, work*]; troubler [*silence, sleep*]; **2** (upset) troubler [*person*]; (concern) inquiéter [*person*]; **to ~ the peace** JUR troubler l'ordre public; **3** (disarrange) déranger [*papers, bedclothes*]; troubler [*surface of water*]; remuer [*sediment*].

disturbance /dɪ'stɜːbəns/ *n* **1** (interruption, inconvenience) dérangement *m*; **2** (riot) troubles *mpl*; (fight) altercation *f*; **3** METEOROL perturbation *f*; **4** PSYCH trouble *m*; (more serious) perturbation *f*.

disturbed /dɪ'stɜːbd/ *adj* **1** PSYCH perturbé; **emotionally ~** qui a des troubles psychologiques; **to be mentally ~** avoir l'esprit dérangé; **2** (concerned) **I am ~ by the news** cette nouvelle m'inquiète; **3** (restless) [*sleep*] agité.

disturbing /dɪ'stɜːbɪŋ/ *adj* (unsettling) [*portrayal*] troublant; [*book, film*] perturbant; (worrying) [*report, increase*] inquiétant; (stronger) alarmant.

disuse /dɪs'juːs/ *n* (of machinery) abandon *m*; **to fall into ~** [*plant, building*] être laissé à l'abandon; [*practice, tradition*] tomber en désuétude.

disused /dɪs'juːzd/ *adj* abandonné, désaffecté.

ditch /dɪtʃ/ **I** *n* fossé *m*.
II○ *vtr* **1** (get rid of) laisser tomber [*friend, ally*]; abandonner [*system, agreement, machine*]; plaquer○ [*girlfriend, boyfriend*]; **2** US (evade) échapper à [*police*]; **3** (crash-land) **to ~ a plane** faire un amerrissage forcé; **4** US (crash) emboutir○ [*voiture*].

ditchwater /'dɪtʃwɔːtə(r)/ *n*: IDIOMS **as dull as ~** ennuyeux comme la pluie.

dither /'dɪðə(r)/ **I**○ *n* **in a ~, all of a ~** dans tous ses états.
II *vi* tergiverser (**about, over** sur).

ditto○ /'dɪtəʊ/ *adv* idem; **the food is awful and ~ the nightlife** la nourriture est affreuse la vie nocturne idem; **I'm fed up**○'**—'~'** 'j'en ai marre○'—'moi aussi'.

ditto marks *npl* guillemets *mpl* de répétition.

dive /daɪv/ **I** *n* **1** GEN, SPORT (plunge) plongeon *m*; **2** (swimming under sea) plongée *f* sous-marine; **3** (descent) (of plane, bird) piqué *m*; **to take a ~** FIG [*prices*] chuter; **4** (lunge) **to make a ~ for sth** foncer vers qch; **5**○ PÉJ (bar) tripot○ *m*.
II *vi* (prét **~d** GB, **dove** US) **1** GEN, SPORT plonger (**off, from** de; **down to** jusqu'à); **2** [*plane, bird*]

plonger; **3** (as hobby) faire de la plongée; (as job) être plongeur; **4** (throw oneself) **to ~ under the bed** plonger sous le lit; **to ~ into** s'engouffrer dans [*bar, shop*].
■ **dive for**: **~ for** [*sth*] [*diver*] pêcher [*pearls*]; **2** [*player*] plonger sur [*ball*]; **3** [*person*] foncer vers [*exit*]; **to ~ for cover** foncer à l'abri.
■ **dive in 1** LIT plonger; **2** FIG se lancer○.

dive-bomb *vtr* MIL bombarder [qch] en piqué.

diver /'daɪvə(r)/ *n* GEN plongeur/-euse *m/f*; ▶ 1251 | (deep-sea) scaphandrier *m*.

diverge /daɪ'vɜːdʒ/ *vi* [*interests, opinions, paths*] diverger; **to ~ from** s'écarter de [*truth, norm, belief*]; [*railway line, road*] se séparer de.

diverse /daɪ'vɜːs/ *adj* **1** (varied) divers; **2** (different) différent.

diversion /daɪ'vɜːʃn, US daɪ'vɜːrʒn/ *n* **1** (of watercourse, money) détournement *m*; (of traffic) déviation *f*; **2** (distraction) diversion *f* (**from** à); **3** GB (detour) déviation *f*; **4**† (entertainment) divertissement *m*.

diversionary /daɪ'vɜːʃənərɪ, US daɪ'vɜːrʒənerɪ/ *adj* [*tactic, attack*] de diversion.

divert /daɪ'vɜːt/ **I** *vtr* **1** (redirect) détourner [*water, flow*]; dévier [*traffic*]; (**onto** vers; **through** par); dérouter [*flight, plane*] (**to** sur); détourner [*resources, supplies, funds, manpower*] (**from** de; **to** au profit de); **2** (distract) détourner [*attention, efforts, conversation, person*].
II *vi* **to ~ to** se détourner sur.

divest /daɪ'vest/ SOUT *vtr* **to ~ sb of sth** (of power, rights etc) dépouiller qn de qch; (of robes, regalia) ôter qch à qn.

divide /dɪ'vaɪd/ **I** *n* **1** (split) division *f* (**between** entre); **the North-South ~** l'opposition *f* Nord-Sud; **2** (watershed) FIG démarcation *f* (**between** entre).
II *vtr* **1** (split into parts) partager [*food, money, time, work*]; diviser [*class, house, room*] (**into** en); **he ~d the pupils into boys and girls** il a séparé les garçons des filles; **2** (share) partager [*time*] (**between** entre); **3** (separate) séparer (**from** de); **4** (cause disagreement) diviser [*friends, management, group*]; **5** GB POL faire voter [*House*]; **6** MATH diviser [*number*]; **to ~ 2 into 14** diviser 14 par 2.
III *vi* **1** LIT [*road*] bifurquer; [*river, train*] se séparer en deux; [*group*] (into two) se séparer en deux; [*cell, organism*] se diviser; **2** GB POL [*House*] voter; **3** MATH être divisible.
■ **divide out**: **~** [*sth*] **out, ~ out** [*sth*] distribuer.
■ **divide up**: **~** [*sth*] **up, ~ up** [*sth*] partager (**among** entre).

dividend /'dɪvɪdend/ *n* **1** FIN (share) dividende *m*; **final ~** dividende *m* annuel; **to pay ~s** LIT, FIG rapporter; **2** FIG (bonus) avantage *m*; **peace ~** POL dividendes *mpl* de la paix.

divider /dɪ'vaɪdə(r)/ *n* (in room) cloison *f*; (in file) intercalaire *m*.

dividers /dɪ'vaɪdəz/ *npl* compas *m* à pointes sèches.

dividing /dɪ'vaɪdɪŋ/ *adj* [*wall, fence*] mitoyen/-enne.

dividing line *n* ligne *f* de démarcation.

divine /dɪ'vaɪn/ **I** *adj* divin.
II *vtr* **1** LITTÉR (intuit) deviner; **2** (dowse) découvrir [qch] par la radiesthésie.

divinely /dɪ'vaɪnlɪ/ *adv* **1** [*revealed*] divinement; **2**○ [*dance, smile*] divinement.

diving /'daɪvɪŋ/ *n* (from board) plongeon *m*; (under sea) plongée *f* sous-marine.

diving: **~ board** *n* plongeoir *m*; **~ suit** *n* scaphandre *m*.

divinity /dɪ'vɪnətɪ/ *n* (deity) divinité *f*; (theology) théologie *f*.

divisible /dɪ'vɪzəbl/ *adj* divisible (**by** par).

division /dɪ'vɪʒn/ *n* **1** (splitting) GEN, BIOL, BOT, MATH division *f* (**into** en); **2** (sharing) (of one thing) répartition *f*; (of several things) distribution *f*; **3** MIL, NAUT division *f*; ADMIN circonscription *f*; **4** COMM (branch, sector) division *f*; (department, team) service *m*; **5** (in football) division *f*; **to be in ~ one** être en

do¹

The direct French equivalent of the verb *to do* in *subject +
to do + object* sentences is *faire*:

  she's doing her homework = elle fait ses devoirs
  what are you doing? = qu'est-ce que tu fais?
  *what has he done
  with the newspaper?* = qu'est-ce qu'il a fait du journal?

faire functions in very much the same way as *to do* does
in English and it is safe to assume it will work in the great
majority of cases. For the conjugation of the verb *faire*, see
the French verb tables.

Grammatical functions

In questions

In French there is no use of an auxiliary verb in questions
equivalent to the use of *do* in English.

When the subject is a pronoun, the question is formed in
French either by inverting the subject and verb and putting
a hyphen between the two (*veux-tu?*) or by prefacing the
subject + verb by *est-ce que* (literally *is it that*):

  do you like Mozart? = aimes-tu Mozart?
  or est-ce que tu aimes Mozart?
  *did you put the glasses
  in the cupboard?* = as-tu mis les verres dans le
  placard? *or* est-ce que tu as
  mis les verres dans le placard?

When the subject is a noun there are again two
possibilities:

  did your sister ring? = est-ce que ta sœur a
  téléphoné?
  or ta sœur a-t-elle téléphoné?
  did Max find his keys? = est-ce que Max a trouvé ses
  clés?
  or Max a-t-il trouvé ses clés?

In negatives

Equally, auxiliaries are not used in negatives in French:

  I don't like Mozart = je n'aime pas Mozart
  you didn't feed the cat = tu n'as pas donné à manger
  au chat
  don't do that! = ne fais pas ça!

In emphatic uses

There is no verbal equivalent for the use of *do* in such
expressions as *I DO like your dress*. A French speaker will
find another way, according to the context, of expressing
the force of the English *do*. Here are a few
useful examples:

  I DO like your dress = j'aime beaucoup
  ta robe
  I DO hope she remembers = j'espère qu'elle
  n'oubliera pas
  I DO think you should see a doctor = je crois vraiment
  que tu devrais voir
  un médecin

When referring back to another verb

In this case the verb *to do* is not translated at all:

  I don't like him any more than you do = je ne l'aime pas
  plus que toi
  I live in Oxford and so does Lily = j'habite à Oxford et
  Lily aussi

  she gets paid more than I do = elle est payée plus que
  moi
  *I haven't written as much as
  I ought to have done* = je n'ai pas écrit autant
  que j'aurais dû
  'I love strawberries' 'so do I' = 'j'adore les fraises' 'moi
  aussi'

In polite requests

In polite requests the phrase *je vous en prie* can often be
used to render the meaning of *do*:

  do sit down = asseyez-vous, je vous en prie
  do have a piece of cake = prenez un morceau de
  gâteau, je vous en prie
  *'may I take a peach?'
  'yes, do'* = 'puis-je prendre une pêche?'
  'je vous en prie'

In imperatives

In French there is no use of an auxiliary verb in imperatives:

  don't shut the door = ne ferme pas la porte
  don't tell her anything = ne lui dis rien
  do be quiet! = tais-toi!

In tag questions

French has no direct equivalent of tag questions like
doesn't he? or *didn't it?* There is a general tag question
n'est-ce pas? (literally *isn't it so?*) which will work in many
cases:

  you like fish, don't you? = tu aimes le poisson,
  n'est-ce pas?
  he lives in London, doesn't he? = il habite à Londres,
  n'est-ce pas?

However, *n'est-ce pas* can very rarely be used for positive
tag questions and some other way will be found to express
the meaning contained in the tag: *par hasard* can often be
useful as a translation:

  Lola didn't phone, did she? = Lola n'a pas téléphoné
  par hasard?
  Paul doesn't work here, does he? = Paul ne travaille
  pas ici par hasard?

In many cases the tag is not translated at all and the
speaker's intonation will convey what is implied:

  you didn't tidy your room, did you? = tu n'as pas rangé
  (i.e. *you ought to have done*) ta chambre?

In short answers

Again, there is no direct French equivalent for short
answers like *yes I do, no he doesn't* etc. Where the answer
yes is given to contradict a negative question or statement,
the most useful translation is *si*:

  'Marion didn't say that' 'yes she did' = 'Marion n'a pas
  dit ça' 'si'
  'they don't sell vegetables at the baker's' 'yes they do' =
  'ils ne vendent pas les légumes à la boulangerie' 'si'

In response to a standard enquiry the tag will not be
translated:

  'do you like strawberries?' 'yes I do' = 'aimez-vous les
  fraises?' 'oui'

For more examples and particular usages, see the entry
do¹.

---

première division; **6** (dissent) désaccord *m* (**between**
entre); **7** (in container) compartiment *m*; **8** GB POL vote
m; **9** US UNIV faculté *f*.

divisional /dɪ'vɪʒənl/ *adj* [*commander, officer*] MIL
divisionnaire; [*championship*] SPORT de division.

divisive /dɪ'vaɪsɪv/ *adj* [*policy*] qui sème la discorde;
to be socially ~ créer des inégalités sociales.

divorce /dɪ'vɔːs/ **I** *n* LIT, FIG divorce *m* (**from** avec;
between entre); **to ask for a ~** demander le
divorce; **to file for ~, to sue for ~** JUR intenter
une action en divorce.
II *vtr* **1** LIT **to ~** divorcer de *or* d'avec [*husband,
wife*]; **2** FIG dissocier (**from** de).

divorcee /dɪ,vɔː'siː/ *n* divorcé/-e *m/f*.

divulge /daɪ'vʌldʒ/ *vtr* divulguer (**that** que; **to** à).

Dixie /'dɪksɪ/ *pr n* (also **~land**) États *mpl* du sud des
États-Unis.

DIY GB *n: abrév* ▶ **do-it-yourself**.

dizzy /'dɪzɪ/ *adj* **1** pris de vertige; **to make sb ~**
donner le vertige à qn; **to suffer from ~ spells** avoir
des vertiges; **to feel ~** avoir la tête qui tourne;
with ivre de [*delight, surprise*]; **2** [*height, spell*] vertigi-
neux/-euse; **3** (scatterbrained) écervelé.

DJ *n* **1** (*abrév* = **disc jockey**) DJ *mf*; **2** GB *abrév*
▶ **dinner jacket**.

DNA I *n* (*abrév* = **deoxyribonucleic acid**) ADN *m*.
II *noun modifier* [*testing*] de l'empreinte *f* génétique.

do¹ /duː, də/ **I** *vtr* (3ᵉ *pers sg prés* **does**; *prét* **did**; *pp*
done) **1** (be busy) faire [*washing up, ironing etc*]; **to
~ sth again** refaire qch; **she's been ~ing too**

much lately elle en fait trop ces derniers temps; **will you ~ something for me?** peux-tu me rendre un service?; **2** (make smart) **to ~ sb's hair** coiffer qn; **to ~ one's teeth** se brosser les dents; **to ~ the living room in pink** peindre le salon en rose; **3** (complete) faire [*military service, period of time*]; **4** (finish) **have you done°** complaining? tu as fini de te plaindre?; **tell him now and have done with it** dis-le lui maintenant, ce sera fait; **it's as good as done** c'est comme si c'était fait; **that's done it** (task successfully completed) ça y est; (expressing dismay) il ne manquait plus que ça; **5** (complete through study) faire [*subject, degree, homework*]; **6** (write) faire [*translation, critique*]; **7** (effect change) faire; **what have you done to your hair?** qu'est-ce que vous avez fait à vos cheveux?; **I haven't done anything with your pen!** je n'ai pas touché à ton stylo!; **that does a lot for her** ce chapeau lui va bien; **8** (hurt) faire; **to ~ sth to one's arm** se faire mal au bras; **9°** (deal with) **they don't ~ theatre tickets** ils ne vendent pas de billets de théâtre; **to ~ breakfasts** servir le petit déjeuner; **10** (cook) faire [*sausages, spaghetti etc*]; **well done** [*meat*] bien cuit; **11** (prepare) préparer [*vegetables*]; **12** (produce) monter [*play*]; faire [*film, programme*] (on sur); **13** (imitate) imiter [*celebrity, mannerism*]; **14** (travel at) faire; **to ~ 60** faire du 60 à l'heure; **15** (cover distance of) faire [*30 km etc*]; **16°** (satisfy needs of) **will this ~ you?** ça vous ira?; **17°** (cheat) **we've been done** on s'est fait avoir; **to ~ sb out of £5** refaire° qn de 5 livres sterling; **18°** (rob) **to ~ a bank** faire une casse° dans une banque; **19°** (arrest, convict) **to get done for** se faire prendre pour [*illegal parking etc*].

II *vi* (3e *pers sg prés* **does**; *prét* **did**; *pp* **done**) **1** (behave) faire; **~ as you're told** (by me) fais ce que je te dis; (by others) fais ce qu'on te dit; **2** (serve purpose) **that box will ~** cette boite fera l'affaire; **3** (be acceptable) **this really won't ~!** (as reprimand) ça ne peut pas continuer comme ça!; **4** (be sufficient) [*amount of money*] suffire; **5** (finish) finir; **6** (get on) [*person*] s'en sortir; [*business*] marcher; **7** (in health) **mother and baby are both ~ing well** la mère et l'enfant se portent bien; **the patient is ~ing well** l'état de santé du patient s'améliore rapidement.

III *v aux* (3e *pers sg prés* **does**; *prét* **did**; *pp* **done**) **1** (with questions, negatives) **own up, did you or didn't you take my pen?** avoue, est-ce que c'est toi qui as pris mon stylo ou pas?; **didn't he look wonderful!** est-ce qu'il n'était pas merveilleux!; **2** (for emphasis) **so you ~ want to go after all!** alors tu veux vraiment y aller finalement!; **I ~ wish you'd let me help you** j'aimerais tant que tu me laisses t'aider; **3** (referring back to another verb) **he said he'd tell her and he did** il a dit qu'il le lui dirait et il l'a fait; **you draw better than I ~** tu dessines mieux que moi; **4** (in requests, imperatives) **~ sit down** asseyez-vous, je vous en prie; **~ shut up!** tais-toi veux-tu!; **don't you tell me what to do!** je n'ai pas de leçons à recevoir de toi; **5** (in tag questions and responses) **he lives in France, doesn't he?** il habite en France, n'est-ce pas?; **'who wrote it?'—'I did'** 'qui l'a écrit?'—'moi'; **'shall I tell him?'—'no don't'** 'est-ce que je le lui dis?'—'non surtout pas'; **'he knows the President'—'does he?'** 'il connaît le Président'—'vraiment?'; **so/neither does he** lui aussi/non plus.

IV° *n* GB fête *f*; **his leaving ~** son pot° de départ.

IDIOMS **~ as you would be done by** ne faites pas ce que vous ne voudriez pas qu'on vous fasse; **how ~ you ~** enchanté; **it doesn't ~ to be** ce n'est pas une bonne chose d'être; **it's a poor ~°** if c'est vraiment grave si; **it was all I could ~ not to...** je me suis retenu pour ne pas...; **nothing ~ing!** (no way) pas question!; **well done!** bravo!; **what are you ~ing with yourself these days?** qu'est-ce que tu deviens?; **what are you going to ~ for money?** où vas-tu trouver l'argent?; **all the ~s and don'ts** tout ce qu'il faut/fallait faire et ne pas faire.

■ **do away with**: ¶ **~ away with** [**sth**] se débarrasser de [*procedure, custom, rule, feature*]; supprimer [*bus service etc*]; démolir [*building*]; ¶ **~ away with** [**sb**]° (kill) se débarrasser de [*person*].

■ **do in**°: **~** [**sb**] **in 1** (kill) tuer; **2** (exhaust) épuiser.

■ **do out**°: **~** [**sth**] **out, ~ out** [**sth**] faire or nettoyer à fond [*room*].

■ **do up**: ¶ **~ up** [*dress, coat*] se fermer; ¶ **~** [**sth**] **up, ~ up** [**sth**] **1** (fasten) nouer [*laces*]; remonter [*zip*]; **~ up your buttons** boutonne-toi; **2** (wrap) faire [*parcel*]; **3** (renovate) restaurer [*house, furniture*]; ¶ **~ oneself up** se faire beau/belle.

■ **do with**: **~ with** [**sth/sb**] **1** (involve) **it has something to ~ with** ça a quelque chose à voir avec; **what's it (got) to ~ with you?** en quoi est-ce que ça te regarde?; (concern) **it has nothing to ~ with you** cela ne vous concerne pas; **2** (tolerate) supporter; **I can't ~ with all these changes** je ne supporte pas tous ces changements; **3** (need) **I could ~ with a holiday** j'aurais bien besoin de partir en vacances; **4** (finish) **it's all over and done with** c'est bien fini; **have you done with my pen?** tu n'as plus besoin de mon stylo?

■ **do without**: **~ without** [**sb/sth**] se passer de [*person, advice etc*].

do² /dəʊ/ *n* MUS = **doh**.

d.o.b. *abrév écrite* = **date of birth**.

docile /ˈdəʊsaɪl, US ˈdɒsl/ *adj* docile.

dock /dɒk/ **I** *n* **1** NAUT, IND dock *m*, bassin *m*; (for repairing ship) cale *f*; **to be in ~** (for repairs) être en réparation; **2** US (wharf) appontement *m*; **3** GB JUR banc *m* des accusés; **4** US (also **loading ~**) zone *f* de chargement; **5** BOT patience *f*.
II *noun modifier* (also **~s**) NAUT, IND [*area*] des docks; [*strike*] des dockers.
III *vtr* **1** NAUT mettre [qch] à quai [*ship*]; **2** GB (reduce) faire une retenue sur [*wages*]; enlever [*marks*]; **3** [*spacecraft*] amarrer; **4** écourter [*tail*].
IV *vi* **1** NAUT (come into dock) arriver au port; (moor) accoster; **2** AEROSP s'arrimer.

docket /ˈdɒkɪt/ **I** *n* **1** COMM, ADMIN (label) étiquette *f* de reconnaissance; (customs certificate) récépissé *m* de douane; **2** US (list) GEN registre *m*.
II *vtr* COMM étiqueter [*parcel, package*].

docking /ˈdɒkɪŋ/ *n* NAUT, AEROSP amarrage *m*.

dock: ~worker *n* docker *m*; **~yard** *n* chantier *m* naval.

doctor /ˈdɒktə(r)/ ▶ **1251**, **937** **I** *n* **1** MED médecin *m*, docteur *m*; **to train as a ~** faire des études de médecine; **to be under a ~** GB être suivi par un médecin; **2** UNIV docteur *m*.
II *vtr* **1** (tamper with) frelater [*food, wine*]; falsifier [*figures*]; altérer [*document*]; **2** GB châtrer [*animal*].
IDIOMS **that's just what the ~ ordered!** c'est exactement ce qu'il me/te etc fallait!

doctorate /ˈdɒktərət/ *n* doctorat *m*.

doctor: Doctor of Philosophy, **PhD**, **DPhil** *n* **~** titulaire *mf* d'un doctorat d'État; **~'s note** *n* certificat *m* médical.

doctrine /ˈdɒktrɪn/ *n* doctrine *f*.

document /ˈdɒkjʊmənt/ **I** *n* GEN document *m*; JUR acte *m*; **travel/insurance ~s** papiers *mpl* de voyage/ d'assurance; **policy ~** POL déclaration *f* de politique générale.
II *vtr* **1** (give account of, record) décrire [*development, events*]; **this period is not well ~ed** on sait peu de choses sur cette période; **2** (support or prove with documents) documenter [*case, claim*].

documentary /ˌdɒkjʊˈmentrɪ, US -terɪ/ **I** *n* documentaire *m* (**about, on** sur).
II *adj* [*film, realism, technique, source*] documentaire; **~ evidence** JUR preuves *fpl* écrites; (in historical research) documents *mpl* de l'époque.

documentation /ˌdɒkjʊmenˈteɪʃn/ *n* ⊄ (documents) GEN documentation *f*; COMM documents *mpl*.

document: ~ case, **~ holder** *n* porte-documents *m inv*; **~ retrieval** *n* COMPUT recherche *f* documentaire; **~ wallet** *n* chemise *f* (en carton).

dodder /ˈdɒdə(r)/ *vi* tituber.

doddering /ˈdɒdərɪŋ/, **doddery** /ˈdɒdərɪ/ *adj* **1** (unsteady) branlant; **2** (senile) gâteux/-euse°.

doddle /'dɒdl/ n GB **it's a ~** c'est simple comme bonjour!

dodge /dɒdʒ/ **I** n **1** (movement) GEN mouvement m de côté; SPORT esquive f; **2**○ GB (trick) combine○ f.
II vtr esquiver [bullet, blow, difficult question]; échapper à [pursuers]; se dérober à [confrontation, accusation]; éviter de payer [tax]; éviter [person]; **to ~ the issue** éluder la question.

dodgem (car) /'dɒdʒəm/ n GB auto f tamponneuse.

dodgy /'dɒdʒɪ/ adj GB **1** (untrustworthy) [person, business, establishment, method] louche○; **2** (risky, dangerous) [decision, plan, investment] risqué; [situation, moment] délicat; [finances] précaire; [weather] instable.

doe /dəʊ/ n (deer) biche f; (rabbit) lapine f; (hare) hase f.

DOE n **1** GB abrév ▶ Department of the Environment; **2** US abrév ▶ Department of Energy.

does /dʌz/ (3e pers sg prés) ▶ **do**.

doesn't /'dʌznt/ (= does not) ▶ **do**.

dog /dɒg, US dɔːg/ **I** n **1** ZOOL chien m; (female) chienne f; **2** (male fox, wolf, etc) mâle m; **3**○ (person) **you lucky ~!** sacré veinard○!
II○ **dogs** npl the **~s** les courses fpl de lévriers.
III noun modifier [biscuit, basket] pour chien; [food] pour chiens.
IV vtr (p prés etc **-gg-**) **1 to ~ sb's footsteps** être sur les talons de qn; **2 ~ged by** poursuivi par [misfortune].
IDIOMS **it's ~ eat ~** c'est chacun pour soi, c'est la foire d'empoigne; **every ~ has its day** à chacun vient sa chance; **give a ~ a bad name (and hang him)** PROV qui veut noyer son chien l'accuse de la rage PROV; **love me, love my ~** aime-moi tel que je suis; **to go and see a man about a ~** EUPH (relieve oneself) aller se soulager; (go on unspecified business) aller voir le pape HUM; **they don't have a ~'s chance** ils n'ont pas la moindre chance or l'ombre d'une chance; **to go to the ~s**○ [company, country] aller à vau-l'eau; **it's a real ~'s breakfast**○! c'est n'importe quoi!

dog breeder ▶ 1251 n éleveur/-euse m/f de chiens.

dog collar n **1** LIT collier m de chien; **2**○ HUM (clergyman's collar) col m romain.

dog: **~ days** npl (warm weather) canicule f; FIG période f creuse; **~-eared** adj écorné; **~-end**○ n mégot○ m; **~fight** n LIT bagarre f de chiens; MIL AVIAT combat m aérien.

dogged /'dɒgɪd, US 'dɔːgɪd/ adj [attempt] obstiné; [person, persistence, refusal] tenace; [resistance] opiniâtre.

doggy: **~ bag** n: petit sac pour emporter les restes d'un repas; **~ paddle**○ n = **dog paddle**.

dog handler ▶ 1251 n maître-chien m.

doghouse /'dɒghaʊs, US 'dɔːg-/ n US niche f (à chien).
IDIOMS **to be in the ~**○ être tombé en disgrâce.

dogma /'dɒgmə, US 'dɔːgmə/ n dogme m.

dogmatic /dɒg'mætɪk, US dɔːg-/ adj dogmatique (**about** sur).

do-gooder /du:'gʊdə(r)/ n PÉJ bonne âme f.

dog: **~ paddle** n nage f à la manière d'un chien; **~sbody**○ n GB (also **general ~**) bonne f à tout faire; **~ tag**○ n US MIL plaque f d'identification (portée par le personnel militaire américain); **~-tooth check** n, adj pied-de-poule (m) inv.

doh /dəʊ/ n MUS do m, ut m.

doing /'du:ɪŋ/ **I** p prés ▶ **do**.
II n **this is her ~** c'est son ouvrage; **it's none of my ~** ce n'est pas moi qui l'ai fait; **it takes some ~!** ce n'est pas facile du tout!
III doings npl (actions) faits et gestes mpl; (events) événements mpl.

do-it-yourself /ˌdu:ɪtjə'self/, **DIY** n bricolage m.

doldrums /'dɒldrəmz/ npl FIG **to be in the ~** [person] être en pleine déprime; [economy, company] être en plein marasme.

dole /dəʊl/ n GB allocation f de chômage; **on the ~** au chômage.

■ **dole out**○: **~ out [sth], ~ [sth] out** distribuer.

doleful /'dəʊlfl/ adj dolent, triste.

dole queue n GB **1** LIT ~ file f d'attente à l'agence pour l'emploi; **2** FIG nombre m de chômeurs.

doll /dɒl, US dɔːl/ n **1** poupée f; **to play with one's ~s** jouer à la poupée; **2**○ (pretty girl) jolie nana○ f.
■ **doll up:** **~ up [sb/sth]**○, **~ [sb/sth] up**○ pomponner [person]; bichonner [room, house].

dollar /'dɒlə(r)/ ▶ 849 n dollar m.
IDIOMS **the 64 thousand ~ question** la question à mille francs.

dollar: **~ bill** n billet m d'un dollar; **~ diplomacy** n diplomatie f qui s'appuie sur le pouvoir financier; **~ sign** n symbole m du dollar.

dollop /'dɒləp/ n LIT cuillerée f; FIG bonne dose f.

dolly /'dɒlɪ, US 'dɔːlɪ/ n **1**○ (doll) poupée f; **2** (mobile platform) plate-forme f (de manutention); CIN, TV dolly m; **3** US RAIL diabolo m.

dolphin /'dɒlfɪn/ n dauphin m.

domain /də'meɪn/ n (all contexts) domaine m (**of** de).

dome /dəʊm/ n GEN dôme m; ARCHIT coupole f.

domed /dəʊmd/ adj [skyline, tower, city] à coupoles; [roof, ceiling] en dôme; [forehead, helmet] bombé.

domestic /də'mestɪk/ adj **1** POL (home) [market, affairs, flight, price] intérieur; [consumer] du pays; [crisis, issue] de politique intérieure; **2** (of house) [activity, animal] domestique; **3** (family) [life, situation, harmony] familial; [dispute] conjugal.

domestically /də'mestɪklɪ/ adv [produced, sold] à l'intérieur du pays.

domestic appliance n appareil m électroménager.

domesticate /də'mestɪkeɪt/ vtr domestiquer [animal]; **to be ~d** [person] aimer s'occuper de la maison.

domestic help n aide f ménagère.

domesticity /ˌdɒmə'stɪsətɪ, ˌdəʊ-/ n **1** (home life) vie f de famille; **2** (household duties) tâches fpl ménagères.

domiciliary /ˌdɒmɪ'sɪlɪərɪ, US -erɪ/ adj [visit, care] à domicile; [rights, information] relatif/-ive au domicile.

dominance /'dɒmɪnəns/ n **1** (domination) domination f (**of** de); BIOL, ZOOL dominance f; **2** (numerical strength) prépondérance f (**of** de).

dominant /'dɒmɪnənt/ adj GEN, BIOL dominant; MUS [chord, key] de dominante.

dominate /'dɒmɪneɪt/ **I** vtr dominer [person, region, town]; dominer dans [industry, market]; **an area ~d by factories/shops** une zone très industrielle/commerçante.
II vi [person] dominer; [issue, question] prédominer.

domineering /ˌdɒmɪ'nɪərɪŋ/ adj [person, behaviour] despotique; [ways] de despote; [tone] autoritaire.

Dominican Republic ▶ 840 pr n République f Dominicaine.

dominion /də'mɪnɪən/ n **1** (authority) domination f (**over** sur); **2** (area ruled) territoire m.

domino /'dɒmɪnəʊ/ ▶ 949 n **1** GAMES (piece) domino m; **2** HIST (cloak) domino m; (eye-mask) loup m.

don /dɒn/ n GB UNIV professeur m d'université.

donate /də'neɪt, US 'dəʊneɪt/ vtr faire don de.

donation /dəʊ'neɪʃn/ n don m (**of** de; **à** to).

done /dʌn/ **I** pp ▶ **do**.
II excl (making deal) marché conclu!
IDIOMS **it's not the ~ thing** ça ne se fait pas.

donkey /'dɒŋkɪ/ n ZOOL âne m.
IDIOMS **she could talk the hind leg off a ~!** c'est un vrai moulin à paroles○!; **I've known him for ~'s years**○ je le connais depuis des années or une éternité.

donkey: **~ jacket** n grosse veste f de travail; **~ work** n travail m pénible.

donor /'dəʊnə(r)/ n (of organ) donneur/-euse m/f; (of money) donateur/-trice m/f.

donor card n carte f de donneur d'organes.

don't /dəʊnt/ (= do not) ▶ **do**.

doodle /'du:dl/ vi gribouiller (**on** sur).

doom /du:m/ **I** n (death) mort f; (unhappy destiny) (of person) perte f; (of country, group) catastrophe f.

II *vtr* condamner [*person, project*] (**to** à); **~ed from
the start** voué à l'échec avant même de commencer.

doomsday /'du:mzdeɪ/ *n* fin *f* du monde.

doomwatch /'du:mwɒtʃ/ *n* ECOL catastrophisme *m*.

door /dɔ:(r)/ **I** *n* **1** GEN porte *f* (**to** de); **a few ~s
down** quelques maisons plus bas; **behind closed ~s**
à huis clos; **to shut** ou **close the ~ on sth** FIG
fermer la porte à qch; **to slam the ~ in sb's face**
FIG envoyer promener qn; **2** AUT, RAIL porte *f*,
portière *f*; **3** (entrance) entrée *f*.
II *noun modifier* [*handle, chime*] de porte.
IDIOMS **to be at death's ~** être à l'article de la
mort; **to get a foot in the ~** mettre un pied dans la
place; **to lay sth at sb's ~** imputer qch à qn; **to
show sb the ~** mettre qn à la porte.

door: ~ bell *n* sonnette *f*; **~man** *n* (at hotel)
portier *m*; (at cinema) contrôleur *m*; **~mat** *n* LIT, FIG
paillasson *m*; **~ plate** *n* (of doctor etc) plaque *f* (de
porte).

doorstep /'dɔ:step/ *n* **1** (step) pas *m* de porte; **2** (threshold) seuil *m*; **on the** ou **one's ~** (nearby) tout près; (un-
pleasantly close) juste à côté.

doorstop /dɔ:(r)stɒp/ *n* butoir *m* (de porte).

door-to-door /ˌdɔ:tə'dɔ:/ **I** *adj* [*canvassing*] à domicile; **~ selling** porte à porte *m inv*.
II **door to door** *adv phr* [*sell*] à domicile; **it's 90
minutes ~** le trajet prend 90 minutes de porte à
porte.

doorway /'dɔ:weɪ/ *n* **1** (frame) embrasure *f*; **2** (entrance) porte *f*, entrée *f*; **in a shop ~** à l'entrée d'une
boutique.

dope /dəʊp/ **I** *n* **1**° cannabis *m*; **2**° (fool) andouille°
f; **3**° (information) tuyaux° *mpl* (**on** sur); **4** (varnish)
enduit *m*.
II *vtr* **1** (give drug to) SPORT doper [*horse, athlete*];
GEN droguer [*person*]; **2** (put drug in) mettre un somnifère dans [*food, drink*].

dope test *n* SPORT contrôle *m* antidopage.

dopey° /'dəʊpɪ/ *adj* (not fully awake) groggy°.

dormant /'dɔ:mənt/ *adj* **1** [*emotion, talent*] latent; **to
lie ~** sommeiller; **2** [*volcano*] en repos.

dormer /'dɔ:mə(r)/ *n* (also **~ window**) lucarne *f*.

dormitory /'dɔ:mɪtrɪ, US -tɔ:rɪ/ **I** *n* **1** GB dortoir *m*; **2**
US UNIV résidence *f*, foyer *m*.
II *noun modifier* [*suburb, town*] dortoir *inv*.

dormouse /'dɔ:maʊs/ *n* (*pl* **dormice**) ZOOL
muscardin *m*.

dosage /'dəʊsɪdʒ/ *n* posologie *f*.

dose /dəʊs/ **I** *n* MED, FIG dose *f* (**of** de); **a ~ of flu**
une bonne grippe.
II *vtr* **to ~ sb with medicine** bourrer° qn de médicaments.
IDIOMS **like a ~ of salts** à la vitesse grand V.

doss° /dɒs/ *n* GB **it's a ~!** facile!
■ **doss down**° dormir.

dot /dɒt/ **I** *n* GEN point *m*; (on fabric, wallpaper) pois *m*;
'**~, ~, ~**' 'points de suspension'.
II *vtr* (*p prés etc* **-tt-**) **1** (in writing) mettre un point sur
[*letter*]; **2** CULIN parsemer (*chicken, joint*] (**with** de); **3**
(be scattered along) **the coast is ~ted with fishing
villages** il y a des ports de pêche éparpillés le long de
la côte.
IDIOMS **since the year ~**° depuis des siècles; **at
ten on the ~** à dix heures pile.

dotage /'dəʊtɪdʒ/ *n* **to be in one's ~** être dans ses
vieux jours PEJ.

dote /dəʊt/ *vi* **to ~ on sb/sth** adorer qn/qch.

dot matrix printer *n* imprimante *f* matricielle.

dotted /'dɒtɪd/ *adj* **1** [*fabric*] à pois; **2** MUS [*note*]
pointé.

dotted line *n* pointillé *m*; '**tear along ~**' 'découpez
suivant le pointillé'; **to sign on the ~** LIT signer à
l'endroit indiqué.

dotty° /'dɒtɪ/ *adj* GB farfelu°.

double /'dʌbl/ **I** *n* **1 a ~ please** (drink) un double, s'il
vous plaît; **2** (of person) sosie *m*; CIN, THEAT doublure
f; **3** GAMES (in bridge) contre *m*; (in dominoes, darts)
double *m*.
II **doubles** *npl* (in tennis) double *m*; **ladies'/mixed
~s** double dames/mixte.
III *adj* **1** (twice as much) [*portion, dose*] double (*before
n*); **2** (when spelling, giving number) **Anne is spelt** GB ou
spelled US **with a ~ 'n'** Anne s'écrit avec deux 'n';
two ~ four (244) deux cent quarante-quatre; **3** (dual,
twofold) double; **with a ~ meaning** à double sens; **4**
(intended for two people or things) [*sheet, garage etc*]
double; [*ticket, invitation*] pour deux.
IV *adv* **1** (twice) deux fois; **2** [*fold, bend*] en deux; **to
see ~** voir double.
V *vtr* **1** (increase twofold) doubler [*amount, rent, dose
etc*]; multiplier [*qch*] par deux [*number*]; **2** (also **~
over**) (fold) plier [*qch*] en deux [*blanket etc*]; **3** (in
spelling) doubler [*letter*]; **4** (in bridge) contrer.
VI *vi* **1** [*sales, prices, salaries etc*] doubler; **2 to ~ for
sb** CIN, THEAT doubler qn; **3** (serve dual purpose) **the
sofa ~s as a bed** le canapé fait aussi lit.
IDIOMS **on** ou **at the ~** FIG au plus vite; MIL au pas
redoublé; **~ or quits!** quitte ou double!
■ **double back** [*person, animal*] rebrousser chemin;
[*road etc*] former un demi-tour.
■ **double up 1** (bend one's body) se plier en deux; **to
~ up with laughter** être plié en deux de rire; **2**
(share sleeping accommodation) partager la même
chambre.

double act *n* THEAT, FIG duo *m*.

double-barrelled GB, **double-barreled** US
/ˌdʌbl'bærəld/ *adj* [*gun*] à deux coups; **~ name** GB ≈
nom à particule.

double: ~ bass ▶ 1097 *n* (instrument) contrebasse *f*;
~ bed *n* lit *m* double, grand lit; **~ bend** *n* AUT
virage *m* en S; **~ bill** *n* THEAT représentation *f* avec
deux œuvres au programme; CIN séance *f* avec deux
films à la suite; **~ bluff** *n*: fait de dire la vérité à
quelqu'un en faisant croire que c'est un mensonge; **~
boiler** *n* US ≈ bain-marie *m*.

double-book I *vtr* **to ~ a room/seat etc** réserver
la même chambre/place etc pour deux personnes.
II *vi* [*hotel, airline, company*] (as practice) surbooker.

double-breasted *adj* [*jacket*] croisé.

double check I *n* deuxième or nouveau contrôle *m*.
II **double-check** *vtr* vérifier [*qch*] à nouveau
[*detail*].

double: ~ chin *n* double menton *m*; **~ cream** *n*
GB CULIN ≈ crème *f* fraiche.

double-cross° **I** *n* trahison *f*.
II *vtr* doubler, trahir [*person*].

double cuff *n* poignet *m* mousquetaire.

double-dealing I *n* fourberie *f*.
II *adj* hypocrite, fourbe.

double-decker *n* **1** GB (bus) autobus *m* à impériale
or à deux étages; **2** (sandwich) sandwich *m* double.

double door(s) *n(pl)* porte *f* à deux battants.

double Dutch° *n* baragouinage° *m*.

double-edged *adj* LIT, FIG à double tranchant.

double entendre /ˌdu:bl ɑ:n'tɑ:ndrə/ *n* (word, phrase)
sous-entendu *m* (grivois).

double: ~ entry *n* comptabilité *f* en partie double;
~ exposure *n* PHOT (process) surimpression *f*; **~
fault** *n* double faute *f*; **~ feature** *n* CIN séance *f*
avec deux films à la suite.

double figures *npl* **to go into ~** [*inflation*] passer
la barre des 10%.

double: ~-fronted *adj* [*house*] avec une fenêtre de
part et d'autre de la porte; **~ glazing** *n* double
vitrage *m*; **~-jointed** *adj* [*person, limb, finger*]
souple; **~ knitting** (wool) *n* grosse laine *f*; **~
lock** *vtr* fermer [*qch*] à double tour.

double-park I *vtr* garer [*qch*] en double file [*vehicle*].
II *vi* se garer en double file.

double-quick I *adj* **in ~ time** en un rien de temps.
II *adv* en vitesse, le plus vite possible.

double: ~ room *n* chambre *f* pour deux personnes;
~ saucepan *n* GB ≈ bain-marie *m inv*; **~**

spacing *n* double interligne *m*; ~ **spread** *n* JOURN article *m* (or publicité *f*) sur double page.

double standard *n* **to have ~s** faire deux poids deux mesures.

double take *n* **to do a ~** avoir une réaction à retardement.

double talk *n* PÉJ langue *f* de bois.

double time *n* **1 to be paid ~** être payé double; **2** US MIL pas *m* redoublé.

double vision *n* **to have ~** voir double.

double: ~ **whammy**○ *n* double coup *m* de malchance; ~ **yellow line(s)** *n(pl)* GB AUT *marquage au sol interdisant le stationnement*.

doubling /'dʌblɪŋ/ *n* (of salary, amount, size, strength) doublement *m*; (of number, letter) (re)doublement *m*.

doubly /'dʌblɪ/ *adv* [*deprived, disappointed*] doublement; [*difficult, confident*] deux fois plus (*before n*); **I made ~ sure that** j'ai bien vérifié que.

doubt /daʊt/ **I** *n* doute *m*; **there is no ~ (that)** il ne fait aucun doute que; **there is little ~ (that)** il est presque certain que; **there is some ~ about its authenticity** son authenticité est mise en doute; **there's (some) ~ as to whether he will be able to come** on ne sait pas s'il pourra venir; **there is no ~ in my mind that I'm right** je suis convaincu d'avoir raison; **to have one's ~s about doing** hésiter à faire; **no ~ the police will want to speak to you** la police voudra sans doute vous parler; **to leave sb in no ~ about sth** ne laisser à qn aucun doute quant à qch; **to be in ~** [*outcome, project*] être incertain; [*honesty, innocence, guilt*] GEN être douteux/-euse; (on particular occasion) être mis en doute; [*person*] être dans le doute; **the election result is not in any ~** le résultat de l'élection ne fait pas l'ombre d'un doute; **if** ou **when in ~** dans le doute; **to be open to ~** [*evidence, testimony*] être sujet à caution; **without (a) ~** sans aucun doute; **to prove sth beyond (all) ~** prouver qch de façon indubitable.
II *vtr* douter de [*fact, value, ability, honesty, person*]; **I ~ it!** j'en doute!; **to ~ (if** ou **that** ou **whether)** douter que (+ *subj*).
III *vi* douter.

doubtful /'daʊtfl/ *adj* **1** (unsure) incertain; **it is ~ if** ou **that** ou **whether** il n'est pas certain que (+ *subj*); **to be ~ about doing** hésiter à faire; **to be ~ about** ou **as to** être peu convaincu par [*idea, explanation, plan*]; avoir des doutes sur [*job, object, purchase*]; **2** (questionable) [*character, past, activity, taste*] douteux/-euse.

doubtfully /'daʊtfəlɪ/ *adv* (hesitantly) d'un air ou d'un ton hésitant; (with disbelief) d'un air ou d'un ton sceptique.

doubtless /'daʊtlɪs/ *adv* sans doute.

douche /duːʃ/ **I** *n* GEN, MED douche *f*.
II *vtr* GEN, MED doucher.

dough /dəʊ/ *n* **1** CULIN pâte *f*; **pizza ~** pâte à pizza; **2**○ (money) fric○ *m*, argent *m*.

doughnut, **donut** US /'dəʊnʌt/ *n* beignet *m*.

dour /dʊə(r)/ *adj* [*person, expression*] renfrogné; [*landscape*] morne; [*mood*] maussade; [*building*] austère.

douse, **dowse** /daʊs/ *vtr* tremper [*person, room*]; éteindre [*flame*]; **to ~ sb/sth with water** tremper qn/qch.

dove **I** /dʌv/ *n* ZOOL, POL colombe *f*.
II /dəʊv/ US *prét* ▶ **dive**.

dovecot(e) /'dʌvkɒt, 'dʌvkəʊt/ *n* pigeonnier *m*.

Dover /'dəʊvə(r)/ /▶ 1343/ *pr n* Douvres; **the Straits of ~** le Pas de Calais.

dovetail /'dʌvteɪl/ **I** *vtr* **1** FIG faire concorder [*plans, policies, research, arguments*] (**with** avec); **2** CONSTR assembler [qch] à queue-d'aronde [*pieces*].
II *vi* FIG (also ~ **together**) bien cadrer ensemble.

dowdy /'daʊdɪ/ *adj* [*woman*] sans élégance; [*clothes*] vieux jeu *inv*; [*image*] vieillotte○.

down¹ /daʊn/

■ **Note** *down* often occurs as the second element in verb combinations in English (*go down, fall down, get down, keep down, put down etc*). For translations, consult the appropriate verb entry (*go, fall, get, keep, put* etc).
– When used to indicate vague direction, *down* often has no explicit translation in French: *to go down to London* = aller à Londres; *down in Brighton* = à Brighton.
– For examples and further usages, see the entry below.

I *adv* **1** (from higher to lower level) **to go** ou **come ~** descendre; **to fall ~** tomber; **to sit ~ on the floor** s'asseoir par terre; **to pull ~ a blind** baisser un store; **I'm on my way ~** je descends; **~!** (to dog) couché!; **'~'** (in crossword) 'verticalement'; **read ~ to the end of the paragraph** lire jusqu'à la fin du paragraphe; **2** (indicating position at lower level) **~ below** en bas; (when looking down from height) en contrebas; **two floors ~** deux étages plus bas; **it's on the second shelf ~** c'est au deuxième rayon en partant du haut; **~ at the bottom of the lake** tout au fond du lac; **the telephone lines are ~** les lignes téléphoniques sont coupées; **3** (from upstairs) **is Tim ~ yet?** est-ce que Tim est déjà descendu?; **4** (indicating direction) **to go ~ to London** aller à Londres; **~ in Brighton** à Brighton; **they've gone ~ to the country** ils sont allés à la campagne; **they moved ~ here from Scotland** ils ont quitté l'Écosse pour venir s'installer ici; **they live ~ south**○ ils habitent dans le sud; **5** (in a range, scale, hierarchy) **children from the age of 10 ~** les enfants de moins de dix ans; **everybody from the Prime Minister ~** tout le monde depuis le Premier Ministre; **6** (indicating loss of money etc) **bookings are ~ by a half** les réservations ont baissé de moitié; **profits are well ~ on last year's** les bénéfices sont nettement inférieurs à ceux de l'année dernière; **I'm £10 ~** il me manque 10 livres sterling; **7** (indicating reduction) **to get one's weight ~** maigrir; **to get the price ~** faire baisser le prix; **I'm ~ to my last cigarette** il ne me reste plus qu'une cigarette; **that's seven ~, three to go!** en voilà sept de faits, il n'en reste plus que trois à faire!; **8** (on list, schedule) **you're ~ to speak next** c'est toi qui es le prochain à intervenir; **I've got you ~ for next Thursday** (in appointment book) vous avez rendez-vous jeudi prochain; **9** (incapacitated) **to be ~ with the flu** avoir la grippe; **10** SPORT (behind) **to be two sets ~** [*tennis player*] avoir deux sets de retard; **11** (as deposit) **to pay £40 ~** payer 40 livres sterling comptant; **12** (downwards) **face ~** (of person) le visage face au sol.
II *prep* **1** (from higher to lower point) **to run ~ the hill** descendre la colline en courant; **did you enjoy the journey ~?** est-ce que tu as fait bon voyage?; **~ town** en ville; **2** (at lower part of) **they live ~ the road** ils habitent un peu plus loin dans la rue; **a few miles ~ the river from here** à quelques kilomètres en aval de la rivière; **3** (along) **to go ~ the street** descendre la rue; **with buttons all ~ the front** boutonné sur le devant; **he looked ~ her throat** il a regardé au fond de sa gorge; **4** (throughout) **~ the ages** ou **centuries** à travers les siècles.
III *adj* **1**○ **to feel ~** être déprimé; **2** [*escalator*] descend; [*train*] descendant; **3** COMPUT en panne.
IV○ *vtr* **1** abattre [*person*]; descendre [*plane*]; **2** descendre○ [*drink*].
IDIOMS **to have a ~ on sb** en vouloir à qn; **it's ~ to you to do it** c'est à toi de le faire; **~ with tyrants!** à bas les tyrans!

down² /daʊn/ *n* (feathers) (all contexts) duvet *m*.

down-and-out /ˌdaʊnən'aʊt/ *n* clochard/-e *m/f*.

downbeat /'daʊnbiːt/ *adj* **1** (pessimistic) [*view*] pessimiste; **2** (laidback) décontracté.

downcast /'daʊnkɑːst, US -kæst/ *adj* **1** (dejected) découragé; **2** [*eyes*] baissé.

downfall /'daʊnfɔːl/ *n* chute *f*; **drink proved to be his ~** c'est la boisson qui a causé sa perte.

downgrade /'daʊngreɪd/ *vtr* **1** (demote) rétrograder [*employee*]; **the hotel has been ~d to a guest house** l'hôtel a été déclassé et c'est maintenant une pension de famille; **2** (degrade) dévaloriser [*task*].

downhearted *adj* abattu.

downhill /ˌdaʊn'hɪl/ **I** *adj* [*path, road*] qui descend.

II adv **to go** ~ [path, person, vehicle] descendre; FIG person] être sur le déclin; **from now on it's** ~ **all the way** FIG (easy) à partir de maintenant il ne devrait plus y avoir de problèmes; (disastrous) à partir de maintenant c'est le déclin.

ownhill ski(ing) n ski m de descente.

own /daʊn/: **~-in-the-mouth**○ adj abattu; **~load** vtr COMPUT transférer; **~market** adj [products, hotel, restaurant] bas de gamme inv; [area] populaire; [newspaper, programme] grand public inv; ~ **payment** n acompte m; **~pipe** n GB gouttière f.

ownpour /daʊn.pɔ:r/ n averse f.

ownright /'daʊnraɪt/ **I** adj [insult] véritable (before n); [refusal] catégorique; [liar] fieffé (before n).
II adj [stupid, rude] carrément.

owns /daʊnz/ npl GB (hills) collines fpl.

ownside○ /'daʊnsaɪd/ **I** n GEN inconvénient m.
II downside up adj phr, adv phr US sens dessus dessous.

own's syndrome /'daʊnz sɪndrəʊm/ n trisomie f 21.

ownstairs /ˌdaʊn'steəz/ **I** n rez-de-chaussée m inv.
II adj [room] GEN en bas; (on ground-floor) du rez-de-chaussée; **the** ~ **flat** GB ou **apartment** US l'appartement du rez-de-chaussée.
II adv en bas; **to go** ou **come** ~ descendre (l'escalier).

ownstream /'daʊnstri:m/ adj, adv LIT, FIG en aval (**of** de); **to go** ~ descendre le courant.

own-to-earth /ˌdaʊntə'з:θ/ adj [person, approach] pratique; **she's very** ~ (practical) elle a les pieds sur terre; (unpretentious) elle est très simple.

owntown /'daʊntaʊn/ adj SURTOUT US du centre ville; ~ **New York** le centre de New York.

own /daʊn/: **~trodden** adj [person, country] tyrannisé; **~turn** n (in economy, career) déclin m (**in** de); (in demand, profits, spending) chute f (**in** de); ~ **under**○ adv en Australie.

ownward /'daʊnwəd/ adj [movement, glance, stroke] vers le bas.

ownwards /'daʊnwədz/ adv [look, gesture] vers le bas; **to slope** ~ être en pente (**to** vers); **read the list from the top** ~ lire la liste de haut en bas; **he was floating face** ~ il flottait le visage dans l'eau; **everybody from the boss** ~ tout le monde depuis le patron.

ownwind /ˌdaʊn'wɪnd/ adv dans le sens du vent.

owse /daʊz/ **I** vtr = **douse**.
II vi (for water) faire de la rhabdomancie; (for minerals) faire de la radiesthésie.

oz abrév écrite = **dozen**.

oze /dəʊz/ **I** n somme m.
II vi [person, cat] somnoler.
■ **doze off** (momentarily) s'assoupir; (to sleep) s'endormir.

ozen /'dʌzn/ n **1** (twelve) douzaine f; **by the** ~ à la douzaine; **2** (several) **I've told you a** ~ **times!** je te l'ai déjà dit cent fois!; **~s** des dizaines de [people, things, times].

Phil n: abrév ▶ **Doctor of Philosophy**.

PP n GB abrév ▶ **Director of Public Prosecutions**.

r n **1** abrév écrite = **Doctor**; **2** abrév écrite = **Drive**.

rab /dræb/ adj [colour, life] terne; [building] triste.

raft /drɑːft, US dræft/ **I** n **1** (of letter, speech) brouillon m; (of novel, play) ébauche f; (of contract, law) avant-projet m; **2** FIN traite f (**on** sur); **to make a** ~ **on a bank** tirer sur une banque; **3** US MIL (conscription) service m militaire; **4** US = **draught**.
I noun modifier [agreement, version] préliminaire.
II vtr **1** faire le brouillon de [letter, speech]; faire l'avant-projet de [contract, law]; **2** US (conscript) incorporer (**into** dans); **3** GB (transfer) détacher (**to** auprès de; **from** de); **4** SPORT sélectionner; **5** US (choose) **to** ~ **sb to do** charger qn de faire.
■ **draft in** GB: ~ **in** [sb], ~ [sb] **in** faire venir.

raft: ~ **board** n US MIL conseil m de révision; ~

card n US MIL ordre m d'incorporation; ~ **dodger** n US MIL insoumis m.

drafty US = **draughty**.

drag /dræg/ **I** n **1**○ (person) raseur/-euse m/f; **what a** ~! quelle barbe○!; **2** (women's clothes worn by men) vêtements mpl de travesti.
II noun modifier **1** THEAT [artist, show] de travesti; **2** AUT SPORT [race, racing] de dragsters.
III vtr (p prés etc -**gg**-) **1** (pull) tirer (**to, up to** jusqu'à; **towards** vers); **to** ~ **sth along the ground** faire traîner qch par terre; **to** ~ **sb from** arracher qn de [chair, bed]; **to** ~ **sb to** traîner qn à [place]; traîner qn chez [person]; **don't** ~ **my mother into this** ne mêle pas ma mère à ça; **2** (search) draguer [river, lake]; **3** COMPUT déplacer; **4** (trail) traîner; **to** ~ **one's feet** ou **heels** LIT traîner les pieds; FIG faire preuve de mauvaise volonté (**on** quant à).
IV vi (p prés etc -**gg**-) **1** (go slowly) [hours, days] traîner; [story, plot] traîner en longueur; **2** (trail) **to** ~ **in** [hem, belt] traîner dans [mud]; **3** (inhale) **to** ~ **on** tirer une bouffée de [cigarette].
V v refl **to** ~ **oneself to** se traîner jusqu'à.
■ **drag along**: ~ [sth] **along** traîner.
■ **drag away**: ¶ ~ [sb] **away** emmener [qn] de force; **to** ~ **sb away from** arracher qn à; ¶ ~ [oneself] **away from** [sth] partir à regret de.
■ **drag in**: ~ [sth] **in**, ~ **in** [sth] mentionner.
■ **drag on** traîner en longueur.
■ **drag out**: ¶ ~ [sth] **out** faire traîner; ¶ ~ [sth] **out of sb** arracher [qch] à qn.
■ **drag up**: ~ [sth] **up**, ~ **up** [sth] déterrer [secret].

drag lift n SPORT tire-fesses○ m inv.

dragon /'drægən/ n dragon m.

drain /dreɪn/ **I** n **1** LIT (in street) canalisation f; (in building) canalisation f d'évacuation; (pipe) descente f d'eau; (ditch) fossé m d'écoulement; **2** FIG (of people, skills, money) hémorragie f; **to be a** ~ **on sb's resources** épuiser les ressources de qn.
II vtr **1** LIT drainer [land, lake]; purger [radiator, boiler]; **2** FIG épuiser [resources]; **3** vider [glass]; boire [qch] jusqu'à la dernière goutte [drink]; **4** [river] collecter les eaux de [area, basin].
III vi **1** [liquid] s'écouler (**out of, from** de); [bath, sink] se vider; **to** ~ **into** s'écouler dans [sea, gutter]; s'infiltrer dans [soil]; **the blood** ou **colour ~ed from her face** le sang reflua de son visage; **2** [dishes, food] s'égoutter.
IDIOMS **to go down the** ~○ FIG tomber à l'eau○; **that's £100 down the** ~○ ça fait 100 livres sterling de fichues en l'air○.
■ **drain away** LIT s'écouler; FIG s'épuiser.
■ **drain off**, **drain out**: ¶ ~ **off** s'écouler; ¶ ~ [sth] **off**, ~ **off** [sth] vider [fluid, water].

drainage /'dreɪnɪdʒ/ n (of land) drainage m; (system of pipes, ditches) tout-à-l'égout m inv.

draining board n égouttoir m.

drainpipe /'dreɪnpaɪp/ n descente f.

drake /dreɪk/ n canard m (mâle).

drama /'drɑːmə/ **I** n **1** (genre) GEN théâtre m; TV, RADIO (as opposed to documentary programmes) fiction f; (acting, directing) art m dramatique; (play, dramatic event) drame m; TV, RADIO dramatique f; **to make a** ~ **out of sth** faire tout un drame de qch.
II noun modifier [school, course, student] d'art dramatique; ~ **critic** critique m dramatique; ~ **documentary** TV reportage m fiction.

dramatic /drə'mætɪk/ adj **1** [literature, art, irony, effect] dramatique; [gesture, entrance, exit] théâtral; **2** (tense, exciting) [situation, event] dramatique; **3** (sudden) [change, impact, landscape] spectaculaire.

dramatically /drə'mætɪklɪ/ adv (radically) radicalement; (causing excitement) de façon spectaculaire; LITERAT, THEAT du point de vue théâtral; [gesture, pause] de façon théâtrale.

dramatics /drə'mætɪks/ npl art m dramatique; PÉJ cinéma m PÉJ.

dramatist /'dræmətɪst/ n auteur m dramatique.

dramatization /ˌdræmətaɪ'zeɪʃn, US -tɪ'z-/ n **1** (version) version *f* théâtrale; **2** (technique) (for stage) adaptation *f* pour la scène; (for screen) adaptation *f* pour l'écran; **3** (exaggeration) dramatisation *f*.

dramatize /'dræmətaɪz/ *vtr* **1** (adapt) THEAT adapter [qch] pour la scène; CIN, TV adapter [qch] pour l'écran; RADIO adapter [qch] pour la radio; **2** (depict) dépeindre; **3** (make dramatic) donner un caractère dramatique à; PEJ dramatiser.

drank /dræŋk/ *prét* ▶ **drink**.

drape /dreɪp/ **I** *n* US (curtain) rideau *m*.
II *vtr* **to ~ sth with sth, to ~ sth over sth** draper qch de qch; **~d in sth** enveloppé dans qch.

drastic /'dræstɪk/ *adj* [*policy, measure*] draconien/-ienne; [*reduction, remedy*] drastique; [*effect*] catastrophique; [*change*] radical.

drastically /'dræstɪklɪ/ *adv* [*change, reduce*] radicalement; [*reduce, limit*] sévèrement.

draught GB, **draft** US /drɑːft, US dræft/ **I** *n* **1** (cold air) courant *m* d'air; **2** (in fireplace) tirage *m*; **3 on ~** [*beer etc*] à la pression; **4** (of liquid, air) trait *m*; **5** GB GAMES pion *m* (de jeu de dames).
II *noun modifier* [*beer, cider*] (à la) pression.
IDIOMS **to feel the ~**○ en ressentir les effets.

draughtproof GB, **draftproof** US /'drɑːftpruːf, US 'dræft-/ **I** *adj* calfeutré.
II *vtr* calfeutrer.

draughts /drɑːfts, US dræfts/ ▶ **949** *n* GB (jeu *m* de) dames *fpl*.

draughty GB, **drafty** US /'drɑːftɪ, US 'dræftɪ/ *adj* plein de courants d'air.

draw /drɔː/ **I** *n* **1** GAMES tirage *m* (au sort); **2** SPORT match *m* nul; **it was a ~** (in race) ils sont arrivés ex aequo; **3** (attraction) attraction *f*.
II *vtr* (*prét* **drew**; *pp* **drawn**) **1** LIT faire [*picture, plan*]; dessiner [*person, object*]; tracer [*line*]; **2** FIG dépeindre [*character, picture*]; faire [*comparison*]; **3** (pull) [*animal, engine*] tirer; [*machine, suction*] aspirer; **he drew the child towards him** il a attiré l'enfant vers lui; **he drew his finger along the shelf** il a passé un doigt sur l'étagère; **to ~ blood** provoquer un saignement; **4** (derive) tirer [*conclusion*] (**from** de); **I drew comfort from the fact that** cela m'a un peu réconforté de savoir que; **he drew hope from this** cela lui a donné de l'espoir; **to be drawn from** [*energy, information*] provenir de; **5** (cause to talk) faire parler [*person*] (**about, on** de); **to ~ sth from** ou **out of sb** obtenir qch de qn [*information*]; arracher qch à qn [*truth, smile*]; **6** (attract) attirer [*crowd*] (**to** vers); susciter [*reaction*]; **his speech drew great applause** son discours a soulevé des applaudissements; **to ~ sb into** mêler qn à [*conversation*]; entraîner qn dans [*argument, battle*]; **they were drawn together by their love of animals** leur amour des animaux les a rapprochés; **to ~ the enemy fire** offrir un cible au feu ennemi; **7** FIN retirer [*money*] (**from** de); tirer [*cheque*] (**on** sur); toucher [*wages, pension*]; **8** GAMES, SPORT tirer [qch] au sort [*ticket*]; **to ~ a match** faire match nul; **9** (remove) retirer [*cork*] (**from** de); sortir [*sword, knife, gun*]; tirer [*card*].
III *vi* (*prét* **drew**; *pp* **drawn**) **1** (make picture) dessiner; **2** (move) **to ~ ahead (of sth/sb)** LIT gagner du terrain (sur qch/qn); FIG prendre de l'avance (sur qch/qn); **to ~ alongside** [*boat*] accoster; **the car drew alongside the lorry** la voiture s'est mise à côté du camion; **to ~ close** ou **near** [*time*] approcher; **they drew nearer to listen** ils se sont rapprochés pour écouter; **to ~ into** [*bus*] arriver à [*station*]; **the train drew into the station** le train est entré en gare; **to ~ level** se retrouver au même niveau; **to ~ over** [*vehicle*] (stop) se ranger; (still moving) se rabattre vers le bas-côté; **to ~ round** ou **around** se rassembler; **to ~ to a halt** s'arrêter; **to ~ to a close** ou **an end** [*day, event*] toucher à sa fin; **3** (in match) faire match nul; **4** (choose at random) **to ~ for sth** tirer qch (au sort); **5** [*tea*] infuser.
IDIOMS **to be quick/slow on the ~**○ (in understanding) avoir l'esprit vif/lent; (in replying) avoir/ne pas avoir la repartie facile; [*cowboy*] dégainer/ne pas dégainer vite; **to ~ the line** fixer des limites.

■ **draw apart** se séparer.
■ **draw aside**: ¶ **~ [sth] aside, ~ aside [st** écarter; ¶ **~ [sb] aside** prendre [qn] à part.
■ **draw away**: ¶ **~ away** (move off) s'éloign (**from** de); (move ahead) prendre de l'avance (**from** sur (recoil) avoir un mouvement de recul; ¶ **~ [sth/s away, ~ away** [*sth/ sb*] retirer [*hand , foot*]; éle gner [*person, object*]; distraire [qn] de [*book, task*].
■ **draw back**: ¶ **~ back** reculer; ¶ **~ [sth] bac ~ back [sth]** ouvrir [*curtains*]; retirer [*hand, foot*]; ¶ **~ [sb] back, ~ back [sb]** faire revenir.
■ **draw down**: **~ [sth] down, ~ down [st** baisser.
■ **draw in**: ¶ **~ in 1** [*days, nights*] raccourcir; (arrive) [*bus*] arriver; [*train*] entrer en gare; ¶ **~ [** **in, ~ in [sth] 1** (in picture) ajouter; **2** tirer sur [*rop* rentrer [*stomach, claws*]; **3** (suck in) [*person*] aspir [*air*]; [*pump, machine*] aspirer [*air, liquid, gas*]; **to** **in one's breath** inspirer; **4** (attract) attirer.
■ **draw off**: ¶ **~ off** [*vehicle, train*] partir; ¶ **[sth] off, ~ off [sth]** tirer [*beer, water*]; reti [*gloves*]; MED évacuer [*fluid*].
■ **draw on**: ¶ **~ on** (approach) approcher; (pas [*time*] passer; [*evening, day, season*] (s')avancer; ¶ **on [sth]** exploiter [*skills, reserves*]; **the report ~s** **information from…** le rapport tire des informatio de…; **to ~ on one's experience** faire appel à s expérience.
■ **draw out**: ¶ **~ out 1** [*train, bus*] partir; tl **train drew out of the station** le train a quitté gare; **a car drew out in front of me** une voiture a c boîté devant moi; **2** [*day, night*] rallonger; ¶ **~ [st out, ~ out [sth] 1** GEN tirer [*handkerchief, pur knife*] (**from, out of** de); retirer [*nail, cork*] (**from, of** de); aspirer [*liquid, air*]; **2** FIN retirer [*cas money*]; **3** (cause to last longer) faire durer [*even* (unnecessarily) faire traîner; **4** obtenir [*informatio confession*]; (using force) soutirer; ¶ **~ [sb] out** fa sortir [qn] de sa coquille.
■ **draw up**: ¶ **~ up** s'arrêter; ¶ **~ up [sth], [sth] up 1** établir [*contract, programme, proposal* dresser, établir [*list, plan, report*]; **2** (pull) hiss [*bucket*]; approcher [*chair*] (**to** de); **3** tirer sur [*threa* ¶ **~ oneself up** se redresser.

drawback /'drɔːbæk/ *n* inconvénient *m*.

drawer /'drɔː(r)/ *n* **1** tiroir *m*; **2** FIN tireur/-euse *m*/*f*.

drawing /'drɔːɪŋ/ **I** *n* dessin *m*.
II *noun modifier* [*class, teacher, tools*] de dessi [*paper, pen*] à dessin.

drawing board *n* (board) planche *f* à dessin; **we have to go back to the ~** FIG il faudra to recommencer; **the project never got off the ~** le projet n'a jamais dépassé le stade de l'étude.

drawing: ~ pin *n* punaise *f*; **~ room** *n* salon *m*.

drawl /drɔːl/ **I** *n* voix *f* traînante.
II *vi* parler d'une voix traînante.

drawn /drɔːn/ **I** *pp* ▶ **draw**.
II *adj* **1** [*features*] tiré; **to look ~** avoir les tra tirés; **2** [*game, match*] nul/nulle.

dread /dred/ **I** *n* terreur *f*; **to have a ~ of sth** êt terrifié par qch; (weaker) avoir horreur de qch.
II *vtr* appréhender; (stronger) redouter; **I ~ to thir** je préfère ne pas y penser!

dreadful /'dredfl/ *adj* [*weather, person*] affreux/-eu [*day, accident*] épouvantable; [*film, book,* lamentable; **I had a ~ time trying to convince h** j'ai eu toutes les peines du monde à le convaincre; **feel ~** ne pas se sentir bien du tout; **to feel** **about sth** avoir honte de qch.

dreadfully /'dredfəlɪ/ *adv* [*disappointed, cross, short* money*] terriblement; [*suffer*] affreusement; [*beha* abominablement; **I'm ~ sorry** je suis navré.

dream /driːm/ **I** *n* rêve *m*; **I had a ~ about st** **about doing** j'ai rêvé de qch/que je faisais; **to be ir ~** être dans les nuages; **to make sb's ~ come tr** faire que le rêve de qn devienne réalité; **it work like a ~** ça a marché à merveille.
II *noun modifier* [*house, car, vacation*] de rêve.
III *vtr* (*prét, pp* **dreamt** /dremt/, **~ed**) **1** (w

asleep) rêver (**that** que); **2** (imagine) **I never dreamt (that)** je n'aurais jamais pensé que.
IV vi (prét, pp **dreamt** /dremt/, **~ed**) rêver; **he dreamt about** ou **of sth/doing** rêver de qch/qu'il faisait; **you must be ~ing if you think…** tu te fais des illusions si tu crois que…; **I wouldn't ~ of doing** il ne me viendrait jamais à l'esprit de faire.
■ **dream up**: **~ up** [sth] concevoir [idea]; imaginer [character, plot].
dreamer /ˈdriːmə(r)/ n (inattentive person) rêveur/-euse m/f; (idealist) idéaliste mf.
dreamworld /ˈdriːmwɜːld/ n monde m de rêves.
dreamy /ˈdriːmɪ/ adj **1** (distracted) rêveur/-euse; [sound, music] doux/douce; **2**° (attractive) [person] séduisant; [object] ravissant.
dreary /ˈdrɪərɪ/ adj [weather, landscape] morne; [person] ennuyeux/-euse; [life, routine] monotone.
dredge /dredʒ/ vtr **1** draguer [river]; **2** CULIN saupoudrer (**with** de).
■ **dredge up**: **~ up** [sth], **~** [sth] **up** LIT remonter qch (à la drague); FIG exhumer [incidents].
dregs /dregz/ npl (of wine) lie f; (of coffee) marc m; **the ~ of society** la lie de la société.
drench /drentʃ/ vtr (in rain, sweat) tremper (**in** de); (in perfume) asperger (**in** de); **~ed to the skin** trempé jusqu'aux os.
dress /dres/ ▶ 1260| **I** n **1** robe f; **2** ¢ tenue f; **his style of ~** son style vestimentaire.
II noun modifier [material, design] de robe.
III vtr **1** habiller [person]; **to get ~ed** s'habiller; **2** CULIN assaisonner [salad]; préparer [meat, fish]; **3** MED panser [wound].
IV vi s'habiller; **to ~ in a suit** mettre un costume.
V v refl **to ~ oneself** s'habiller.
IDIOMS **~ed to kill** habillé de façon irrésistible.
■ **dress down**: **~ down** s'habiller 'décontracté'.
■ **dress up**: ¶ **~ up** (smartly) s'habiller; (in fancy dress) se déguiser (**as** en); ¶ **~** [sb] **up**, **~ up** [sb] déguiser; ¶ **~** [sth] **up**, **~ up** [sth] agrémenter.
dress: **~ circle** n THEAT premier balcon m; **~ designer** ▶ 1251| n modéliste mf.
dresser /ˈdresə(r)/ n **1 to be a sloppy/stylish ~** s'habiller mal/avec chic; **2** (for dishes) buffet m; US (for clothes) commode-coiffeuse f.
dressing /ˈdresɪŋ/ n **1** MED pansement m; **2** (sauce) sauce f; **3** US (stuffing) farce f.
dressing: **~ gown** n robe f de chambre; **~ room** n THEAT loge f; (in house) dressing m; **~ table** n coiffeuse f.
dress: **~maker** ▶ 1251| n couturière f; **~making** n couture f; **~ rehearsal** n (répétition f) générale f.
dress sense n **to have ~** s'habiller avec goût.
dressy° /ˈdresɪ/ adj habillé.
drew /druː/ prét ▶ **draw**.
dribble /ˈdrɪbl/ **I** n **1** (of liquid) filet m; (of saliva) bave f; **2** SPORT drible m.
II vtr **1** laisser dégouliner [liquid] (**on, onto** sur); **2** SPORT dribbler.
III vi **1** [liquid] dégouliner (**on, onto** sur; **from** de); [person] baver; **2** SPORT dribbler.
dried /draɪd/ **I** prét, pp ▶ **dry**.
II adj [fruit, herb, pulse] sec/sèche; [flower, vegetable] séché; [milk, egg] en poudre.
drier /ˈdraɪə(r)/ n (clothes, hair) séchoir m; (helmet type) casque m.
drift /drɪft/ **I** n **1** (flow, movement) **the ~ of the current** le sens du courant; **the ~ of events** FIG le cours des événements; **the ~ from the land** l'exode m rural; **the slow ~ of strikers back to work** le lent retour des grévistes au travail; **2** (of snow) congère f; (of leaves, sand) tas m; (of smoke, mist) nuage m; **3** (general meaning) sens m (général); **to catch the ~ of sb's argument** comprendre où quelqu'un veut en venir.
II vi **1** (be carried by current) dériver; (by wind) [balloon] voler à la dérive; [smoke, fog] flotter; **2** (pile up) [snow] former des congères fpl; [leaves] s'amonceler; **3 to ~**

along [person] LIT flâner; FIG se laisser aller; **to ~ from job to job** passer d'un emploi à un autre.
■ **drift apart** se détacher progressivement (**from** de).
■ **drift off** (doze off) s'assoupir; (leave) s'en aller lentement.
drill /drɪl/ **I** n **1** (tool) (for wood, metal, masonry) perceuse f; (for oil) trépan m; (for mining) foreuse f; (for teeth) roulette f; **power ~** perceuse f électrique; **2** MIL exercice m; **3 fire ~** exercice m d'évacuation en cas d'incendie.
II vtr **1** GEN percer; passer la roulette à [tooth]; **2** MIL entraîner; **3 to ~ sb in sth** former (intensivement) qn à qch.
III vi **1** (in wood, metal, masonry) percer un trou (**into** dans); **to ~ for sth** faire des forages pour trouver qch; **2** MIL faire de l'exercice; **3** FIG **to ~ sth into sb** faire entrer qch dans la tête de qn.
drilling /ˈdrɪlɪŋ/ n (for oil, gas, water) forage m (**for** pour trouver); (in wood, metal, masonry) perçage m.
drink /drɪŋk/ **I** n **1** (nonalcoholic) boisson f; **to have a ~** boire quelque chose; **2** (alcoholic) verre m; **3** (act of drinking) **to take** ou **have a ~ of sth** boire une gorgée de qch; **4** ¢ (collectively) boisson f; (alcoholic) alcool m.
II vtr (prét **drank**; pp **drunk**) boire (**from** sth dans qch).
III vi (prét **drank**; pp **drunk**) **1** boire (**from, out of** dans); **don't ~ and drive** ne conduisez pas si vous avez bu; **2** (as toast) **to ~ to the bride** boire à la mariée.
IDIOMS **to drive sb to ~** pousser qn à la boisson; **I'll ~ to that!** excellente idée !
■ **drink in**: **~ in** [sth] respirer [air]; s'imbiber de [atmosphere]; [roots] absorber [water].
■ **drink up**: ¶ **~ up** finir son verre; ¶ **~ up** [sth], **~** [sth] **up** finir.
drinkable /ˈdrɪŋkəbl/ adj (safe) potable; (nice) buvable.
drink-driving n GB conduite f en état d'ivresse.
drinker /ˈdrɪŋkə(r)/ n **1** GEN buveur/-euse m/f; **2** (of alcohol) **to be a ~** boire.
drinking /ˈdrɪŋkɪŋ/ **I** n **1** (of alcohol) consommation f d'alcool; **~ and driving** l'alcool au volant.
II noun modifier [laws] sur l'alcool; [companion] de beuverie.
drinking: **~ chocolate** n GB chocolat m en poudre; **~ water** n eau f potable.
drink: **~ problem** n GB penchant m pour la boisson; **~s cupboard** n GB bar m; **~s dispenser** n GB distributeur m de boissons; **~s machine** n GB machine f à boissons; **~s party** n GB cocktail m.
drip /drɪp/ **I** n **1** goutte f (qui tombe); **the constant ~ of a tap** le bruit continuel d'un robinet qui goutte; **2** GB MED (device) goutte-à-goutte m inv; (solution) sérum m; **to be on a ~** être sous perfusion.
II vtr (p prés etc **-pp-**) [object] laisser tomber [qch] goutte à goutte [liquid]; [person] dégouliner de [sweat, blood]; **to ~ sth onto** ou **down sth** faire goutter qch sur qch.
III vi (p prés etc **-pp-**) **1** [liquid] tomber goutte à goutte; **to ~ from** ou **off** dégouliner de; **2** [tap, branches] goutter; [washing] s'égoutter; [engine] fuir; **to be ~ping with** dégouliner de [liquid]; ruisseler de [sweat].
drip-dry I adj qui se lave et s'étend sans essorage.
II vtr **'wash and ~'** 'laver et étendre sans essorer'.
drip feed /ˈdrɪp fiːd/ n alimentation f par perfusion.
dripping /ˈdrɪpɪŋ/ **I** n CULIN graisse f de rôti.
II adj [tap] qui goutte; [trees] ruisselant; [washing] trempé; **~ wet** trempé.
drive /draɪv/ **I** n **1** (in car) **to go for a ~** aller faire un tour (en voiture); **it's only five minutes' ~ from here** ce n'est qu'à cinq minutes d'ici en voiture; **it's a 40 km ~** il y a 40 km de route; **2** (campaign) campagne f (**against** contre; **for, towards** pour; **to do** pour faire); **3** (motivation) dynamisme m; **the ~ to win** la volonté de vaincre; **4** COMPUT entraînement m de disques; **5** AUT transmission f; **6** (path) allée f; **7** SPORT drive m.

II *noun modifier* AUT [*mechanism*] de transmission.
III *vtr* (*prét* **drove**; *pp* **driven**) **1** conduire [*vehicle, passenger*]; piloter [*racing car*]; transporter [*cargo, load*]; parcourir [qch] (en voiture) [*distance*]; **I ~ 15 km every day** je fais 15 km en voiture chaque jour; **to ~ sth into** rentrer qch dans [*garage, space*]; **2** (compel) pousser (**to do** à faire); **to be driven out of business** être conduit à la faillite; **3** (chase or herd) conduire; **he was driven from** ou **out of the country** il a été chassé du pays; **4** (power, propel) actionner; **the generator is driven by steam** le générateur fonctionne à la vapeur; **5** (force, push) LIT, FIG pousser [*boat, person*]; enfoncer [*nail*]; faire passer [*road*]; **6** SPORT (in golf) envoyer [*ball*]; (in tennis) envoyer [qch] d'un coup droit [*ball*].
IV *vi* (*prét* **drove**; *pp* **driven**) **1** AUT conduire; **to ~ along** rouler; **you can't ~ along the High Street** on n'a pas le droit de circuler dans la grand-rue; **to ~ to work** aller au travail en voiture; **to ~ into** entrer dans [*garage, space*]; rentrer dans [*tree, lamppost*]; **to ~ up/down a hill** monter/descendre une côte; **to ~ past** passer; **2** SPORT (in golf) driver; (in tennis) faire un drive.
V *v refl* **to ~ oneself 1** AUT conduire soi-même; **2 to ~ oneself to do** se forcer à faire; **to ~ oneself too hard** se surmener.
■ **drive away**: ¶ **~ away** démarrer; ¶ **~ away [sth/sb]**, **~ [sth/sb] away 1** AUT faire démarrer; **2** faire partir [*animals, persons*]; chasser [*fear, cares*].
■ **drive at: what are you driving at?** où veux-tu en venir?
■ **drive back**: ¶ **~ back** rentrer; **to ~ there and back** faire l'aller-retour; ¶ **~ back [sth/sb]**, **[sth/sb] back 1** (repel) repousser [*people, animals*]; **2** AUT ramener.
■ **drive off** AUT démarrer.
■ **drive on**: ¶ **~ on** (continue) poursuivre sa route; (set off again) repartir; ¶ **~ [sb] on** pousser.
■ **drive out**: **~ out [sth/sb]**, **~ [sth/sb] out** chasser.
drivel○ /'drɪvl/ *n* ℭ bêtises *fpl*.
driven /'drɪvn/ **I** *pp* ▶ **drive**.
II *adj* passionné, motivé.
III -driven *combining form* **petrol-/motor-~** à essence/moteur; **market-~** déterminé par le marché.
driver /'draɪvə(r)/ *n* **1** GEN conducteur/-trice *m/f*; (chauffeur) chauffeur *m*; **~s** (motorists) automobilistes *mfpl*; **2** (mechanical) actionneur *m*.
driver: ~'s license *n* US = **driving licence**; **~'s seat** *n* = **driving seat**.
drive: ~-through *n* US comptoir *m* de vente à l'extérieur; **~way** *n* allée *f*.
driving /'draɪvɪŋ/ **I** *n* conduite *f*; **his ~ has improved** il conduit mieux qu'avant.
II *noun modifier* [*skills, offence*] de conduite.
III *adj* [*rain*] battant; [*wind, hail*] cinglant.
driving ~ force *n* (person) force *f* agissante (**behind** de); (money, ambition, belief) moteur *m* (**behind** de); **~ instructor** ▶ 1251 *n* moniteur/-trice *m/f* d'auto-école; **~ lesson** *n* cours *m* de conduite; **~ licence** GB *n* permis *m* de conduire; **~ mirror** *n* rétroviseur *m*; **~ school** *n* auto-école *f*.
driving seat *n* place *f* du conducteur.
IDIOMS **to be in the ~** être aux commandes.
driving test *n* examen *m* du permis de conduire.
drizzle /'drɪzl/ **I** *n* bruine *f*.
II *vi* bruiner.
droll /drəʊl/ *adj* drôle.
drone /drəʊn/ **I** *n* (of engine) ronronnement *m*; (of insects) bourdonnement *m*.
II *vi* [*engine*] ronronner; [*insect*] bourdonner.
■ **drone on** PÉJ faire de longs discours rasants○.
drool /druːl/ *vi* LIT baver; ○FIG baver (d'envie); **to ~ over sth/sb** s'extasier.
droop /druːp/ **I** *n* affaissement *m*.
II *vi* [*eyelids, head*] tomber; [*branch, shoulders, wings*] s'affaisser; [*flower, plant*] commencer à se faner.
drop /drɒp/ **I** *n* **1** GEN, MED goutte *f*; **~ by ~**

goutte à goutte; **2** (decrease) GEN diminution *f* (**in** de); (in temperature) baisse *f* (**in** de); **a 5% ~ in sth** une baisse de 5% de qch; **3** (vertical distance) **there's a ~ of 100 m from the top** il y a une hauteur de 100 m du sommet; **there was a steep ~ on either side** il y avait une pente abrupte de chaque côté; **4** (delivery) (from aircraft) largage *m*; (from lorry, van) livraison *f*; (para-chute jump) saut *m* en parachute.
II *vtr* (*p prés etc* **-pp-**) **1** (allow to fall) (by accident) laisser tomber; (on purpose) mettre, lâcher; **2** (deliver) [*aircraft*] parachuter [*person, supplies, equipment*]; larguer [*bomb*]; **3** (leave) (also **~ off**) déposer [*person, object*]; **4** (lower) baisser [*level, price*]; **to ~ one's eyes** baisser les yeux; **5 to ~ a note** faire allusion à qch; **to ~ sb a note** envoyer un mot à qn; **6** (exclude) (deliberately) supprimer [*article, episode*]; écarter [*player*]; (by mistake) omettre [*figure, letter, item on list*]; ne pas prononcer [*sound*]; **7** (abandon) laisser tomber○ [*friend, school subject*]; renoncer à [*habit, idea*]; abandonner [*conversation, matter*]; retirer [*ac-cusation*]; **to ~ everything** tout laisser tomber; **can we ~ that subject, please?** on ne pourrait pas parler d'autre chose?; **8** GEN, SPORT (lose) perdre [*point, game*].
III *vi* (*p prés etc* **-pp-**) **1** (fall) [*object*] tomber; [*person*] (deliberately) se laisser tomber; (by accident) tomber; **we ~ped to the ground as the plane flew over** nous nous sommes jetés à terre quand l'avion est passé au-dessus de nous; **the plane ~ped to an altitude of 1,000 m** l'avion est descendu à une altitude de 1 000 m; **2** (fall away) **the cliff ~s into the sea** la falaise tombe dans la mer; **the road ~s steeply down the mountain** la route descend abruptement le long de la montagne; ▶ **drop away**; **3** (decrease) baisser; **to ~ (from sth) to sth** tomber (de qch) à qch; **she ~ped to third place** elle est descendue à la troisième place.
IDIOMS **to ~ a brick**○ ou **clanger**○ faire une gaffe○; **a ~ in the bucket** ou **ocean** une goutte d'eau dans la mer; **to ~ sb in it**○ mettre qn dans le pétrin○; **to be ready** ou **fit to ~** tomber de fatigue.
■ **drop away 1** (diminish) diminuer; **2** (fall steeply) descendre brusquement.
■ **drop back** (deliberately) rester en arrière; (unable to keep up) prendre du retard.
■ **drop by** passer.
■ **drop in**: ¶ **~ in** [*person*] passer; **~ [sth] in**, **~ in [sth] I'll ~ it in (to you)** later je passerai te le donner plus tard.
■ **drop off**: ¶ **~ off 1** (fall off) tomber; **2 ~ off (to sleep)** s'endormir; **3** (become smaller) diminuer; ¶ **~ [sth/sb] off**, **~ off [sth/sb]** = **drop** II 3.
■ **drop out 1** (fall out) tomber (**of** de); **2** (from race) se désister; (from project) se retirer; (from school, university) abandonner ses études; (from society) se marginaliser.
■ **drop over** = **drop round**.
■ **drop round**: ¶ **~ round** [*person*] passer; ¶ **~ [sth] round**, **~ round [sth] I'll ~ your books round** je passerai te donner tes livres.
drop: ~ goal *n* drop *m*; **~ handlebars** *npl* guidon *m* de course; **~ kick** *n* coup *m* de pied tombé.
dropout /'drɒpaʊt/ *n* (from society) marginal/-e *m/f*; (from school) étudiant/-e *m/f* qui abandonne ses études.
droppings /'drɒpɪŋz/ *npl* (of mouse, rabbit, sheep) crottes *fpl*; (of horse) crottin *m*; (of bird) fiente *f*.
drop shot *n* SPORT amorti *m*.
drop zone, dropping zone *n* (for supplies etc) zone *f* de largage; (for parachutist) zone *f* de saut.
drought /draʊt/ *n* sécheresse *f*.
drove /drəʊv/ **I** *prét* ▶ **drive**.
II *n* **~s of people** des foules *fpl* de gens.
drown /draʊn/ **I** *vtr* LIT, FIG noyer [*person, animal, food*]; couvrir [*sound*].
II *vi* se noyer.
III *v refl* **to ~ oneself** se noyer.
IDIOMS **to ~ one's sorrows** noyer son chagrin dans l'alcool.
■ **drown out**: ¶ **~ [sth] out**, **~ out [sth]** couvrir [*sound*]; ¶ **~ [sb]** out couvrir la voix de [*person*].
drowning /'draʊnɪŋ/ **I** *n* noyade *f*.

II *adj* [*person*] qui se noie.

drowse /draʊz/ *vi* (be half asleep) être à moitié endormi; (sleep lightly) somnoler.

drowsiness /'draʊzɪnɪs/ *n* somnolence *f*.

drowsy /'draʊzɪ/ *adj* à moitié endormi; **to feel ~** avoir envie de dormir.

drug /drʌg/ **I** *n* **1** MED médicament *m*; **to be on ~s** prendre des médicaments; **2** (narcotic) drogue *f*; **to be on** ou **to take ~s** GEN se droguer; SPORT se doper.
II *noun modifier* **1** (narcotic) [*problem, shipment, smuggler, trafficking*] de drogue; [*culture, use*] de la drogue; **2** MED [*company, industry*] pharmaceutique.
III *vtr* (*p prés etc* **-gg-**) **1** (sedate) [*kidnapper*] administrer des somnifères à [*victim*]; [*vet*] endormir [*animal*]; **2** (dope) mettre un somnifère dans [*drink*]; SPORT doper [*horse*].

drug: **~ abuse** *n* consommation *f* de stupéfiants; **~ addict** *n* toxicomane *mf*; **~ addiction** *n* toxicomanie *f*.

drugged /drʌgd/ *adj* [*person*] drogué; [*state*] d'abrutissement; [*drink*] additionné d'un narcotique.

drug: **~s charges** *npl* infraction *f* à la législation sur les stupéfiants; **Drug Squad** *n* GB brigade *f* des stupéfiants; **~s raid** *n* opération *f* antidrogue; **~s ring** *n* réseau *m* de trafiquants de drogue; **~store** *n* US drugstore *m*; **~-taking** *n* GEN usage *m* de stupéfiants; SPORT dopage *m*; **~ test** *n* MED SPORT contrôle *m* antidopage; **~ user** *n* toxicomane *mf*.

drum /drʌm/ **I** *n* ▶1097| **1** MUS tambour *m*; **2** IND, COMM bidon *m*; (larger) baril *m*; **3** AUT tambour *m*.
II drums *npl* batterie *f*.
III *vtr* (*p prés etc* **-mm-**) **to ~ one's fingers** tambouriner des doigts (on sur); **to ~ sth into sb** FIG enfoncer qch dans le crâne de qn○.
IV *vi* (*p prés etc* **-mm-**) **1** (beat drum) jouer du tambour; **2** (make drumming sound) [*rain*] tambouriner.
■ **drum home**: **~** [*sth*] **home** réussir à faire comprendre [*lesson, point*].
■ **drum out**: **~** [*sb*] **out** expulser [*person*].
■ **drum up**: ¶ **~ up** [*sth*] trouver [*business, custom*]; ¶ **~ up** [*sb*] racoler; **to ~ up sb's support for** obtenir le soutien de qn en faveur de.

drum kit *n* batterie *f*.

drummer /'drʌmə(r)/ ▶1251|, 1097| *n* MIL tambour *m*; (jazz or pop) batteur *m*; (classical) percussionniste *mf*.

drumstick /'drʌmstɪk/ *n* **1** MUS baguette *f* de tambour; **2** CULIN pilon *m*.

drunk /drʌŋk/ **I** *pp* ▶ **drink**.
II *n* ivrogne/-esse *m/f*.
III *adj* LIT, FIG ivre; **to get ~** s'enivrer (on de); **to get sb ~** faire boire qn.

drunkard /'drʌŋkəd/ *n* ivrogne/-esse *m/f*.

drunken /'drʌŋkən/ *adj* [*person*] ivre; [*party*] bien arrosé; [*sleep*] éthylique; [*state*] d'ivresse.

drunkenly /'drʌŋkənlɪ/ *adv* LIT [*shout, laugh*] d'une voix avinée; [*walk*] en titubant.

dry /draɪ/ **I** *adj* **1** GEN sec/sèche; **to run ~** se tarir; **to keep sth ~** tenir qch au sec; **to get ~** se sécher; **to get sth ~** (faire) sécher qch; **to wipe sth ~** essuyer qch; **on ~ land** sur la terre ferme; **a ~ day** un jour sans pluie; **2** FIG [*wit, person, remark*] pince-sans-rire *inv*; [*book, subject matter*] aride; (forbidding alcohol) [*state*] qui interdit la vente de boissons alcoolisées.
II *vtr* faire sécher [*clothes, washing*]; sécher [*meat, produce*]; **to ~ the dishes** essuyer la vaisselle; **to ~ one's hands** se sécher les mains.
III *vi* sécher.
IV *v refl* **to ~ oneself** se sécher.
IDIOMS **(as) ~ as dust** ennuyeux/-euse comme la pluie.
■ **dry off**: ¶ **~ off** [*material, object*] sécher; [*person*] se sécher; ¶ **~ off** [*sb/sth*], **~** [*sb/sth*] **off** sécher [*person, object*].
■ **dry out 1** sécher; **2**○ [*alcoholic*] se faire désintoxiquer.
■ **dry up**: ¶ **~ up 1** [*river, well*] s'assécher; **2** FIG (run out) se tarir; **3** (wipe crockery) essuyer la vaisselle;

¶ **~ up** [*sth*], **~** [*sth*] **up** assécher [*puddle, river*]; essuyer [*crockery*].

dry cell *n* pile *f* sèche.

dry-clean *vtr* nettoyer [qch] à sec; **to have sth ~ed** faire nettoyer qch (chez le teinturier).

dry: **~-cleaner's** ▶1251| *n* teinturerie *f*; **~-cleaning** *n* nettoyage *m* à sec.

dryer /'draɪə(r)/ *n* = **drier**.

dry ice *n* neige *f* carbonique.

drying-up /,draɪɪŋ'ʌp/ *n* GB **to do the ~** essuyer la vaisselle.

dryness /'draɪnɪs/ *n* sécheresse *f*; FIG causticité *f*.

dry rot *n* pourriture *f* sèche (*du bois*).

DSS *n* GB (*abrév* = **Department of Social Security**) **1** (ministry) ministère *m* des Affaires sociales; **2** (local office) *service social responsable des chômeurs*.

DT *n*: *abrév* ▶ **data transmission**.

DTI *n* GB *abrév* ▶ **Department of Trade and Industry**.

DTP *n* (*abrév* = **desktop publishing**) PAO *f*.

dual /'dju:əl, US 'du:əl/ *adj* double.

dual: **~ carriageway** *n* GB route *f* à quatre voies; **~-purpose** *adj* à double usage.

dub /dʌb/ *vtr* (*p prés etc* **-bb-**) (into foreign language) doubler (**into** en); (add soundtrack) postsynchroniser [*film*]; mixer [*sound effect*] (**onto** à).

dubbing /'dʌbɪŋ/ *n* (into foreign language) doublage *m*; (adding soundtrack) postsynchronisation *f*; (sound mixing) mixage *m*.

dubious /'dju:bɪəs, US 'du:-/ *adj* [*translation, reputation, answer*] douteux/-euse; [*motive, claim*] suspect; [*distinction*] discutable; [*person*] **to be ~ (about sth)** avoir des doutes (en ce qui concerne qch).

dubiously /'dju:bɪəslɪ, US 'du:-/ *adv* [*say*] dubitativement; [*look at*] d'un air incertain.

duchess /'dʌtʃɪs/ ▶937| *n* duchesse *f*.

duck /dʌk/ **I** *n* (*pl* **~s**, *collective* **~**) ZOOL, CULIN canard *m*; (female) cane *f*.
II *vtr* **1 to ~ one's head** baisser la tête; **2** (dodge) LIT, FIG esquiver; se dérober à [*responsibility*].
III *vi* baisser la tête; [*boxer*] esquiver un coup; **to ~ behind sth** se cacher derrière qch.
IDIOMS **he took to it like a ~ to water** il s'y est mis comme s'il avait fait ça toute sa vie; **it's like water off a ~'s back** ça ne le/la etc touche absolument pas.

duct /dʌkt/ *n* (for air, water) conduit *m*; (for wiring) canalisation *f*; MED conduit *m*.

dud○ /dʌd/ **I** *n* **to be a ~** [*banknote*] être faux/fausse; [*machine*] être détraqué; [*film*] être nul/nulle○.
II *adj* [*banknote*] faux/fausse; [*cheque*] en bois○; [*machine*] détraqué; [*person*] **to be ~**; [*book, movie*] nul/nulle○.

due /dju:, US du:/ **I** *n* dû *m*; **I must give her her ~, she**... il faut lui rendre cette justice, elle...
II dues *npl* (for membership) cotisation *f*; (for import, taxes etc) droits *mpl*.
III *adj* **1** (payable) **to be/fall ~** arriver/venir à échéance; **when ~** à l'échéance; **the rent is ~ on the 6th** le loyer doit être payé le 6; **the balance ~** le solde dû; **2** (entitled to) **they should pay him what is ~ to him** on devrait lui payer l' argent auquel il a droit; **3** (about to be paid, given) **I'm ~ some back pay** on me doit des arriérés; **we are ~ (for) a wage increase soon** nos salaires doivent bientôt être augmentés; **4** (appropriate) **with ~ solemnity** avec toute la solennité qui s'impose/s'imposait etc; **after ~ consideration** après mûre réflexion; **you will receive a letter in ~ course** vous recevrez une lettre en temps utile; **in ~ course it transpired that** à la longue il est apparu que; **5** (expected) **to be ~ to do** devoir faire; **we are ~ to leave in the evening** nous devons partir le soir; **to be ~ (in)** ou **~ to arrive** [*train, bus*] être attendu; [*person*] devoir arriver.
IV *adv* (directly) **to face ~ north** [*building*] être orienté plein nord; **to go ~ south** aller droit vers le sud.
V due to *prep phr* en raison de; **he resigned ~ to the fact that** il a démissionné parce que; **to be ~ to**

[*delay, cancellation*] être dû/due à; **~ to unforeseen circumstances** pour des raisons indépendantes de notre volonté; **it's all ~ to you** c'est uniquement grâce à toi.

duel /'dju:əl/, US 'du:əl/ *n* LIT, FIG duel *m*.

duet /dju:'et/, US du:-/ *n* (composition) duo *m* ALSO FIG.

dug /dʌg/ *prét, pp* ▶ **dig** III, IV.

duke /dju:k/, US du:k/ ▶ **937** *n* duc *m*.

dull /dʌl/ **I** *adj* **1** (uninteresting) [*person, play, book*] ennuyeux/-euse; [*life, journey*] monotone; [*music*] sans intérêt; [*food*] médiocre; [*appearance, outfit*] triste; **2** (not bright) [*eye, colour*] éteint; [*weather, day*] maussade; [*complexion*] terne; **3** (muffled) [*explosion*] sourd; **4** (not sharp) [*pain*] sourd; **5** FIN [*market*] terne.
II *vtr* ternir [*shine*]; émousser [*blade, senses, pain*].

dullness /'dʌlnɪs/ *n* (of life) ennui *m*; (of routine) monotonie *f*; (of company, conversation) manque *m* d'intérêt.

dully /'dʌlɪ/ *adv* [*say, repeat*] d'un ton morne; [*gleam*] faiblement; [*move, trail*] lourdement.

duly /'dju:lɪ/, US 'du:-/ *adv* (in proper fashion) GEN, JUR dûment; (as expected, as arranged) comme prévu.

dumb /dʌm/ *adj* **1** (handicapped) muet/muette voir note; **~ animals** les bêtes *fpl*; **to be struck ~** rester muet/muette; **2**° (stupid) [*person*] bête; [*question, idea*] idiot.

■ Note Ce mot peut être perçu comme injurieux dans cette acception. Lui préférer *speech-impaired*.

dumbfounded /dʌm'faʊndɪd/ *adj* abasourdi.

dummy /'dʌmɪ/ **I** *n* **1** (model) mannequin *m*; **2** GB (for baby) tétine *f*; **3** (in bridge) (player) mort *m*.
II *noun modifier* [*furniture, drawer*] factice; [*document*] faux/fausse; [*bullet*] à blanc; [*bomb*] d'exercice.

dummy run *n* GEN (trial) essai *m*; MIL attaque *f* simulée.

dump /dʌmp/ **I** *n* **1** (public) décharge *f* publique; (rubbish heap) tas *m* d'ordures; **2** MIL **arms/munitions ~** dépôt *m* d'armes/de munitions; **3**° PÉJ (town, village) trou° *m*; (house) baraque° *f* minable; **4** COMPUT vidage *m*; **screen ~** recopie *f* d'écran.
II *vtr* **1** jeter [*refuse*]; ensevelir [*nuclear waste*]; déverser [*waste, sewage*]; **2**° (get rid of) plaquer° [*boyfriend*]; se débarrasser de [*car, shopping*]; **3**° (put down) poser; **4** COMPUT faire un vidage de [*data*].
IDIOMS **to be down in the ~s**° avoir le cafard°.

dumper /'dʌmpə(r)/ *n* **1** (small) motobasculeur *m*; **2** (large truck) tombereau *m*, dumper *m*.

dumping /'dʌmpɪŋ/ *n* **1** déversement *m*; **'no ~'** 'interdiction de déposer des ordures'; **2** FIN dumping *m*.

dumpy /'dʌmpɪ/ *adj* (plump) boulot/-otte.

dunce /dʌns/ *n* PÉJ cancre *m* (**at, in** en).

dune /dju:n/, US du:n/ *n* dune *f*.

dung /dʌŋ/ *n* ¢ excrément *m*; (for manure) fumier *m*.

dungarees /ˌdʌŋgə'ri:z/ *npl* (fashionwear) salopette *f*; (workwear) bleu *m* de travail.

Dunkirk /dʌn'kɜ:k/ ▶ **1343** *pr n* Dunkerque.

dunno° /də'nəʊ/ = **don't know**.

duo /'dju:əʊ/, US 'du:əʊ/ *n* THEAT, MUS, FIG duo *m*.

dupe /dju:p, US du:p/ **I** *n* dupe *f*.
II *vtr* duper.

duplicate I /'dju:plɪkət, US 'du:pləkət/ *n* **1** (copy) (of document) double *m* (**of** de); (of painting, cassette) copie *f*; **in ~** en deux exemplaires; **2** (photocopy) photocopie *f*.
II /'dju:plɪkət, US 'du:pləkət/ *adj* **1** (copied) [*cheque, receipt*] en duplicata; **a ~ key/document** un double de clé/de document; **2** (in two parts) [*form, invoice*] en deux exemplaires.
III /'dju:plɪkeɪt, US 'du:pləkeɪt/ *vtr* **1** (copy) faire un double de [*document*]; copier [*painting, cassette*]; **2** (photocopy) photocopier; **3** (repeat) refaire [*qch*] inutilement [*work*]; répéter [*action, performance*].

duplicity /dju:'plɪsətɪ, US du:-/ *n* duplicité *f*.

durable /'djʊərəbl, US 'dʊərəbl/ *adj* [*material*] résistant; [*equipment*] solide; [*friendship, tradition*] durable.

duration /dju'reɪʃn, US dʊ'reɪʃn/ *n* durée *f*.

IDIOMS **for the ~**° pour une durée indéterminée.

during /'djʊərɪŋ/ *prep* pendant, au cours de.

dusk /dʌsk/ *n* (twilight) nuit *f* tombante, crépuscule *m*.

dusky /'dʌskɪ/ *adj* [*complexion*] mat.

dust /dʌst/ **I** *n* **1** (grime) poussière *f*; **thick with ~** couvert de poussière; **to allow the ~ to settle** LIT laisser retomber la poussière; FIG laisser les choses se calmer; **2** (fine powder) poudre *f*.
II *vtr* épousseter [*furniture*]; saupoudrer [*cake*] (**with** de, avec); poudrer [*face*] (**with** de, avec).
III *vi* épousseter.
IDIOMS **to bite the ~** [*person*] mordre la poussière; [*plan, idea*] tomber à l'eau.
■ **dust down**: **~** [sth] **down**, **~ down** [sth] épousseter.
■ **dust off**: **~** [sth] **off**, **~ off** [sth] épousseter [*surface*]; brosser [*crumbs, powder*] (**from** de).

dust: **~bin** *n* GB poubelle *f*; **~bin man** *n* GB éboueur *m*; **~ cover** *n* (on book) jaquette *f*; (on furniture) housse *f* (de protection).

duster /'dʌstə(r)/ *n* chiffon *m* (à poussière).

dusting /'dʌstɪŋ/ *n* (cleaning) époussetage *m*; (of snow) fine couche *f*; CULIN saupoudrage *m*.

dust: **~ jacket** *n* jaquette *f*; **~man** *n* GB éboueur *m*.

dustpan /'dʌstpæn/ *n* pelle *f* (à poussière); **a ~ and brush** une pelle (à poussière) et une balayette.

dust sheet *n* housse *f* (de protection).

dusty /'dʌstɪ/ *adj* [*house, table, road*] poussiéreux/-euse; [*climb, journey*] dans la poussière (**after** n).
IDIOMS **to give sb a ~ answer** envoyer qn sur les roses°.

Dutch /dʌtʃ/ ▶ **1100**, **1038** **I** *n* **1** (language) néerlandais *m*; **2** (people) **the ~** les Néerlandais *mpl*.
II *adj* [*culture, food, football, politics*] néerlandais; [*teacher, lesson, textbook*] de néerlandais.
IDIOMS **to go ~**° payer chacun sa part; **to go ~ with sb**° faire fifty-fifty avec qn°.

Dutch: **~ cap** *n* diaphragme *m* (*contraceptif*); **~ courage** *n* courage *m* puisé dans l'alcool; **~woman** *n* Néerlandaise *f*.

dutiable /'dju:tɪəbl, US 'du:-/ *adj* taxable; (at customs) passible de droits de douane.

dutiful /'dju:tɪfl, US 'du:-/ *adj* (obedient) [*person*] dévoué; [*smile*] poli; (conscientious) [*person*] consciencieux/-ieuse.

duty /'dju:tɪ, US 'du:tɪ/ **I** *n* **1** (obligation) devoir *m* (**to** envers); **to have a ~ to do** avoir le devoir de faire; **in the course of ~** MIL en service; GEN dans l'exercice de ses fonctions; **to feel ~ bound to do** se sentir tenu de faire; **out of a sense of ~** par devoir; **2** (task) (*gén pl*) fonction *f*; **to take up one's duties** prendre ses fonctions; **to perform** ou **carry out one's duties** remplir ses fonctions (**as** de); **3** ¢ (work) service *m*; **to be on/off ~** MIL, MED être/ne pas être de service; SCH être/ne pas être de surveillance; **to go on/off ~** commencer/finir son service; **4** (tax) taxe *f*; **customs duties** droits *mpl* de douane; **to pay ~ on sth** payer des droits de douane sur qch.
II *noun modifier* [*nurse, security guard*] (during the day) de service; (outside hours) de permanence.

duty chemist *n* pharmacien/-ienne *m/f* de garde.

duty: **~-free** *adj, adv* hors taxes *inv*; **~-free allowance** *n* quantité *f* autorisée de marchandises hors taxes; **~ roster**, **~ rota** *n* ADMIN tableau *m* de service.

duvet /'du:veɪ/ *n* GB couette *f*.

duvet cover *n* GB housse *f* de couette.

dwarf /dwɔ:f/ **I** *n, adj* (all contexts) nain/naine (*m/f*).
II *vtr* GEN faire paraître [qn/qch] tout petit; éclipser [*achievement, issue*].

dwell /dwel/ *vi* (*prét, pp* **dwelt**) demeurer LITER.
■ **dwell on**: **~ on** [sth] (talk about) s'étendre sur; (think about) s'attarder sur.

dweller /'dwelə(r)/ *n* habitant/-e *m/f*; **city** or **town ~** citadin/-e *m/f*.

dwelling /'dwelɪŋ/ *n* LITTÉR ou ADMIN habitation *f*.

dwelt /dwelt/ *prét, pp* ▶ **dwell**.

dwindle /'dwɪndl/ *vi* [*numbers, resources*] diminuer; [*interest*] tomber; [*health*] décliner.

dwindling /'dwɪndlɪŋ/ *adj* [*resources, audience, interest*] en baisse; [*strength, health*] déclinant.

dye /daɪ/ **I** *n* teinture *f*; **vegetable** ~ colorant *m* végétal.
II *vtr* teindre; **to** ~ **sth red** teindre qch en rouge.
III *vi* [*fabric*] se teindre.
IV **dyed** *pp adj* [*hair, fabric*] teint.

dyed-in-the-wool /ˌdaɪdɪnðə'wʊl/ *adj* invétéré.

dying /'daɪɪŋ/ **I** *p prés* ▶ **die**.
II *n* **1** (people) **the** ~ les agonisants *mpl*; **2** (death) mort *f*.
III *adj* **1** mourant; **to his** ~ **day** jusqu'à sa dernière heure; **with her** ~ **breath** dans son dernier souffle;

2 FIG [*art, tradition*] en voie de disparition; [*community*] moribond; **3** (final) [*moments*] dernier/-ière; **4** [*light, fire*] mourant.

dyke /daɪk/ *n* **1** (US **dike**) (to prevent flooding) digue *f*; (beside ditch) remblai *m*; **2** GB (ditch) fossé *m*.

dynamic /daɪ'næmɪk/ **I** *n, adj* dynamique (*f*).
II **dynamics** *npl* dynamique *f*.

dynamism /'daɪnəmɪzəm/ *n* dynamisme *m*.

dynamite /'daɪnəmaɪt/ *n* dynamite *f*; **political** ~ FIG une bombe politique.

dynamo /'daɪnəməʊ/ *n* **1** ELEC dynamo *f*; **2**° FIG (person) **he's a real** ~ il déborde d'énergie.

dysentery /'dɪsəntrɪ, US -terɪ/ ▶ **1002** *n* dysenterie *f*.

dyslexic /dɪs'leksɪk/ *n, adj* dyslexique (*mf*).

Ee

e, E /iː/ *n* **1** (letter) e, E *m*; **2 E** MUS mi *m*; **3 E** GEOG (*abrév* = **east**) E.

each /iːtʃ/

■ **Note** When used as a determiner *each* is translated by *chaque* when an object or person is singled out: *each document was examined* = chaque document a été examiné. *Tout/toute* and *tous les/toutes les* are also used to express *each and every*: *each passport must be checked* = chaque passeport doit être contrôlé.
– When used as a pronoun *each* (= *each one*) is almost always translated by *chacun/chacune*. For examples and exceptions see below.

I *det* [*person, group, object*] chaque *inv*; **~ time I do** chaque fois que je fais; **~ morning** chaque matin, tous les matins; **~ person will receive** chaque personne or tout le monde recevra; **~ and every day** tous les jours sans exception; **he lifted ~ box in turn,** **~ one heavier than the last** il soulevait des boîtes de plus en plus lourdes.
II *pron* chacun/-e *m/f*; **~ will receive** chacun recevra; **we ~ want something different** chacun de nous veut une chose différente; **~ of you** chacun de vous, chacun d'entre vous; **three bundles of ten notes ~** trois liasses de dix billets chacune; **I'll try a little of ~** je prendrais bien un peu de chaque; **oranges at 30p ~** des oranges à 30 pence pièce.

each other /ˌiːtʃ ˈʌðə(r)/

■ **Note** *each other* is very often translated by using a reflexive pronoun (*nous, vous, se*).
– For examples and particular usages see the entry below.

pron (also **one another**) **they know ~** ils se connaissent; **to help ~** s'entraider; **they wear ~'s clothes** ils se prêtent leurs vêtements; **to worry about ~** s'inquiéter l'un pour l'autre; **kept apart from ~** séparés l'un de l'autre.

each way /ˌiːtʃ ˈweɪ/ *adj, adv* GB **to place an ~ bet on a horse, to bet on a horse ~** jouer un cheval gagnant et placé.

eager /ˈiːɡə(r)/ *adj* [*person, acceptance*] enthousiaste; [*face*] où se lit l'enthousiasme; [*anticipation*] impatient; [*student*] plein d'enthousiasme; **~ to do** (keen) désireux/-euse de faire; (impatient) pressé de faire; **~ for sth** avide de qch; **to be ~ to please** chercher à faire plaisir; **to be ~ for sb to do** tenir vraiment à ce que qn fasse.

eager beaver○ *n* **to be an ~** être zélé.

eagerly /ˈiːɡəli/ *adv* GEN avec enthousiasme; [*listen*] avidement; [*wait*] impatiemment.

eagerness /ˈiːɡənɪs/ *n* (keenness) empressement *m* (**to do** à faire); (impatience) impatience *f* (**to do** de faire); (enthusiasm) enthousiasme *m*.

eagle /ˈiːɡl/ *n* ZOOL aigle *m*; (emblem) aigle *m*.

eagle-eyed *adj* (sharp-eyed) à l'œil *m* perçant; (vigilant) vigilant.

ear /ɪə(r)/ ▶765 **I** *n* **1** oreille *f*; **inner/middle ~** oreille *f* interne/moyenne; **to play (music) by ~** jouer de la musique à l'oreille; **to have a good ~ for languages** avoir une bonne oreille pour les langues; **2** BOT (of wheat, corn) épi *m*.
II *noun modifier* [*infection, operation*] (of one ear) de l'oreille; (of both ears) des oreilles.
IDIOMS **around one's ~s** tout autour de soi; **my ~s are burning** j'ai les oreilles qui sifflent; **to be all**

~s○ être tout ouïe; **to be out on one's ~**○ (from job) avoir été mis à la porte○; (from home) être à la rue; **to be up to one's ~s in debt** être endetté jusqu'au cou; **he's wet behind the ~s** c'est un petit jeunot; **to get a thick ~**○ recevoir une baffe○; **to have a word in sb's ~** parler à qn en privé; **to have** ou **keep one's ~ to the ground** garder l'œil ouvert; **to listen with (only) half an ~** n'écouter que d'une oreille; **to play it by ~** FIG improviser.

earache /ˈɪəreɪk/ *n* **to have ~** GB ou **an ~** avoir une otite.

eardrum *n* tympan *m*.

earl /ɜːl/ *n* comte *m*.

earlobe /ˈɪələʊb/ *n* lobe *m* de l'oreille.

early /ˈɜːlɪ/ **I** *adj* **1** (one of the first) [*attempt, role, years, novel, play*] premier/-ière; **~ man** les premiers hommes; **2** (sooner than usual) [*death*] prématuré; [*delivery, settlement*] rapide; [*vegetable, fruit*] précoce; **to have an ~ lunch/night** déjeuner/se coucher tôt; **to take ~ retirement** partir en préretraite; **at the earliest possible opportunity** le plus tôt possible; **at your earliest convenience** SOUT à votre convenance FML; **3** (in period of time) **in ~ childhood** dans la petite ou première enfance; **at an ~ age** à un très jeune âge; **to be in one's ~ thirties** avoir entre 30 et 35 ans; **to make an ~ start** partir tôt; **to take the ~ train** prendre le premier train; **at the earliest** au plus tôt; **the earliest I can manage is Monday** je ne peux rien faire avant lundi; **at an ~ hour** très tôt; **in the ~ hours** au petit matin; **in the ~ spring** au début du printemps; **in the ~ afternoon** en début d'après-midi; **an earlier attempt** une tentative précédente.
II *adv* **1** (in period of time) tôt; **it's too ~ to say** il est trop tôt pour le dire; **can you make it earlier?** (arranging time) pouvez-vous plus tôt?; **as ~ as 1983** dès 1983; **~ next year** au début de l'année prochaine; **~ in the afternoon** en début d'après-midi; **(very) ~ on** dès le début; **as I said earlier** comme je l'ai déjà dit; **2** (before expected, too soon) en avance; **I'm a bit ~** je suis un peu en avance; **to do sth two days/three weeks ~** faire qch avec deux jours/trois semaines d'avance; **to retire ~** partir en préretraite.
IDIOMS **it's ~ days yet** ce n'est que le début; **it's the ~ bird that catches the worm** PROV l'avenir appartient à ceux qui se lèvent tôt; **to be an ~ bird** être un/-e lève-tôt.

early warning *n* **to be** ou **come as an ~ of sth** être le signe avant-coureur de qch.

early warning system *n* MIL système *m* d'alerte avancée.

earmark /ˈɪəmɑːk/ **I** *n* caractéristique *f*.
II *vtr* (set aside) désigner [*money, site*] (**for** pour).

earmuffs /ˈɪəmʌfs/ *npl* cache-oreilles *m inv*.

earn /ɜːn/ *vtr* **1** (bring in) [*person*] gagner [*money*]; toucher [*salary*]; [*investment*] rapporter [*interest*]; **~ a** ou **one's living** gagner sa vie; **2** (win) **to ~ sb's respect** se faire respecter de qn; **well-~ed** bien mérité.

earned income *n* revenus *mpl* professionnels.

earner /ˈɜːnə(r)/ *n* **1** (person) salarié/-e *m/f*; **2** GB **the main (revenue) ~** la principale source de revenus; **a nice little ~**○ une belle petite source de revenus.

earnest /ˈɜːnɪst/ **I** *n* **in ~** [*speak*] sérieusement; [*begin, start*] vraiment, pour de bon; **to be in ~** être sérieux/-ieuse.

II *adj* [*person*] sérieux/-ieuse; [*intention*] ferme; [*promise, wish*] sincère; [*plea*] fervent.

earning power *n* capacité *f* de gain.

earnings /'ɜːnɪŋz/ *npl* (of person) salaire *m*, revenu *m* (from de); (of company) gains *mpl* (from de); FIN (from shares) (taux *m* de) rendement *m*; **export ~** gains *mpl* à l'exportation.

ear: **~ nose and throat department, ENT department** *n* service *m* d'oto-rhino-laryngologie, service *m* ORL; **~phones** *npl* (over ears) casque *m*; (in ears) écouteurs *mpl*; **~plug** *n* (for noise) boule *f* Quiès®; (for water) bouchon *m* d'oreille; **~ring** *n* boucle *f* d'oreille.

earshot /'ɪəʃɒt/ *n* within/out of **~** à portée de/hors de portée de voix.

earsplitting /'ɪəsplɪtɪŋ/ *adj* [*scream, shout*] strident.

earth /ɜːθ/ **I** *n* **1** (also **Earth**) (planet) Terre *f*; (soil) terre *f*; **the ~'s atmosphere** l'atmosphère terrestre; **to the ends of the ~** jusqu'au bout du monde; **to come down to ~** LIT, FIG revenir sur terre; **to go to ~** LIT, FIG se terrer; **2**○ (as intensifier) **how/ where/who on ~...?** comment/où/qui donc ou diable○...?; **nothing on ~ would persuade me to do** pour rien au monde je ne ferais; **3** GB ELEC terre *f*; **4**○ (huge amount) **to cost the ~** coûter les yeux de la tête○; **to expect the ~** demander la lune.
II *noun modifier* GB ELEC [*cable, wire*] de terre.
III *vtr* GB ELEC mettre [qch] à la terre.
IDIOMS **did the ~ move for you**○? tu as pris ton pied○?; **to look like nothing on ~** ressembler à un épouvantail; **to run sb/sth to ~** dénicher qn/qch.

earthenware /'ɜːθnweə(r)/ **I** *n* faïence *f*.
II *noun modifier* [*crockery*] en faïence.

earthly /'ɜːθlɪ/ *adj* **1** terrestre; **2** it's no **~** use ça ne sert à rien du tout; **there's no ~ reason** il n'y a aucune raison.

earth: **~quake** *n* tremblement *m* de terre; **~ science** *n* science *f* de la Terre; **~shaking**○ *adj* bouleversant; **~ tremor** *n* secousse *f* sismique; **~work** *n* (*pl* **~** ou **~s**) (embankment) rempart *m*; (excavation work) terrassement *m*; **~worm** *n* ver *m* de terre.

earthy /'ɜːθɪ/ *adj* **1** [*humour*] truculent; [*person*] naturel/-elle; [*common sense*] robuste; **2** [*taste, smell*] de terre; [*tone*] ocre.

ear: **~wax** *n* cérumen *m*; **~wig** *n* perce-oreille *m*.

ease /iːz/ **I** *n* **1** (lack of difficulty) facilité *f*; **for ~ of** pour faciliter; **2** (freedom from anxiety) **at ~** GEN à l'aise; **at ~!** MIL repos!; **to put sb at their ~** mettre qn à son aise; **to take one's ~** se détendre; **to put sb's mind at ~** rassurer qn (**about** à propos de); **3** (confidence of manner) aisance *f*; **4** (affluence) aisance *f*.
II *vtr* **1** (lessen) GEN atténuer; réduire [*congestion*]; diminuer [*burden*]; **2** (make easier) détendre [*situation*]; faciliter [*communication, transition*]; **3** (move carefully) **to ~ sth into** introduire qch délicatement dans; **to ~ sth out** sortir qch délicatement de.
III *vi* [*tension, problem, pain, pressure*] s'atténuer; [*congestion, rain, rate*] diminuer; [*situation*] se détendre; [*price*] être en légère baisse.
■ **ease off**: ¶ **~ off** [*business*] se ralentir; [*demand, congestion*] se réduire; [*traffic, rain*] diminuer; [*person*] relâcher son effort; ¶ **~ [sth] off, ~ off [sth]** ôter délicatement.
■ **ease up** [*tense person, storm, traffic*] se calmer; [*worker, team*] relâcher ses efforts; [*authorities*] relâcher la discipline; **to ~ up on sb/on sth** être moins sévère envers qn/pour qch.

easel /'iːzl/ *n* chevalet *m*.

easily /'iːzɪlɪ/ *adv* **1** (with no difficulty) facilement; **to be ~ forgotten** être facile à oublier; **2** (comfortably) [*breathe*] bien; [*talk*] à l'aise; **3** (unquestionably) de loin; **it's ~ 80 kilometres** ça fait facilement 80 kilomètres; **4** (probably) **she could ~ die** elle pourrait bien mourir.

east /iːst/ ▶**1157**│ **I** *n* est *m*.

II East *pr n* GEOG **the ~** (Orient) l'Orient *m*; (of country) l'Est *m*.
III *adj* [*side, face, coast, door*] est *inv*; [*wind*] d'est.
IV *adv* [*live, lie*] à l'est (**of** de); [*move*] vers l'est.

east: **East Africa** *pr n* Afrique *f* de l'Est; **East Berlin** *pr n* POL HIST Berlin-Est.

eastbound /'iːstbaʊnd/ *adj* [*carriageway, traffic*] en direction de l'est; **the ~ train** GB la rame direction est.

East End *pr n* quartiers *mpl* est de Londres.

Easter /'iːstə(r)/ **I** *n* (festival) Pâques *m*; **at ~** à Pâques; (in greetings) pâques *fpl*; **Happy ~** joyeuses pâques.
II *noun modifier* [*Sunday, bunny, egg*] de Pâques.

easterly /'iːstəlɪ/ **I** *n* vent *m* d'est.
II *adj* [*wind*] d'est; [*point*] à l'est; [*area*] de l'est.

eastern /'iːstən/ ▶**1157**│ *adj* **1** [*coast, border*] est; [*town, custom, accent*] de l'est; [*Europe, United States*] de l'Est; **~ France** l'est de la France; **2** (also **Eastern**) (oriental) oriental.

Eastern bloc *n* POL HIST **the ~** le bloc des pays de l'Est.

East German ▶**1100**│ POL HIST **I** *n* Allemand/-e *m/f* de l'Est.
II *adj* est-allemand.

east: **East Germany** ▶**840**│ *pr n* POL HIST Allemagne *f* de l'Est; **East Indies** *pr npl* Indes *fpl* orientales.

eastward /'iːstwəd/ ▶**1157**│ **I** *adj* [*route, movement*] vers l'est; **in an ~ direction** en direction de l'est.
II *adv* (also **~s**) vers l'est.

easy /'iːzɪ/ **I** *adj* **1** (not difficult) [*job, question, victory, life, victim*] facile; **that's ~ to fix** c'est facile à réparer; **it's not ~ to talk to him** ce n'est pas facile de lui parler; **it's an ~ walk from here** c'est facilement accessible à pied d'ici; **within ~ reach** tout près (**of** de); **to make it** ou **things easier** faciliter les choses (**for** pour); **to make life too ~ for** être trop complaisant avec [*criminal, regime*]; **to take the ~ way out** choisir la solution de facilité; **2** (relaxed) [*smile, grace*] décontracté; [*style*] plein d'aisance; **at an ~ pace** d'un pas tranquille; **to feel ~ (in one's mind) about** ne pas se faire de souci à propos de; **3**○ PÉJ (promiscuous) facile○; **4**○ **I'm ~** ça m'est égal.
II *adv* **1** (in a relaxed way) **to take it ~** on things **~** ne pas s'en faire; **stand ~!** MIL repos!; **2**○ **to go ~ on** ou **with** y aller doucement avec.
IDIOMS **as ~ as pie** ou **falling off a log** facile comme tout, simple comme bonjour; **~ on the eye** agréable à regarder; **~ come, ~ go** ça se remplace facilement; **~ does it** doucement; **he's ~ game** c'est une proie facile.

easy: **~-care** *adj* d'entretien facile; **~ chair** *n* fauteuil *m*; **~going** *adj* [*person*] accommodant; [*manner, attitude*] souple; **~ money** *n* argent *m* vite gagné; **~ terms** *n* facilités *fpl* de paiement.

eat /iːt/ **I** *vtr* (*prét* **ate**; *pp* **eaten**) (consume) GEN manger; prendre [*meal*]; **to ~ (one's) lunch/dinner** déjeuner/dîner; **she looks good enough to ~!** elle est belle à croquer○!; **to ~ sb/sth alive** [*mosquitoes*] dévorer qn/qch; **to ~ one's words** FIG ravaler ses paroles.
II *vi* (*prét* **ate**; *pp* **eaten**) manger; **to ~ from** ou **out of** manger dans; **I'll have him ~ing out of my hand** FIG j'en ferai ce que je voudrai; **we ~ at six** nous dînons à 18 heures.
■ **eat away**: ¶ **~ [sth] away, ~ away [sth]** ronger; ¶ **~ away at [sth]** ronger.
■ **eat into** **~ into [sth]** LIT faire un trou dans; FIG [*duties, interruptions*] empiéter sur; [*bills, fees*] entamer.
■ **eat out** aller au restaurant.
■ **eat up**: ¶ **~ up** finir de manger; **~ up!** finis ce que tu as dans ton assiette!; ¶ **~ [sth] up, ~ up [sth]** finir [*food*]; [*car*] dévorer [*miles*]; consommer [*petrol*]; engloutir [*savings*], FIG **to be ~en up with** être dévoré de [*curiosity, desire, envy*].

eatable /'iːtəbl/ *adj* = **edible**.

eaten /'iːtn/ *pp* ▶**eat**.

eater /ˈiːtə(r)/ n mangeur/-euse m/f; **he's a fast ~** il mange vite.

eating /ˈiːtɪŋ/ n **healthy ~ is essential** il est essentiel de manger sainement.

eating: **~ apple** n pomme f à couteau; **~ disorder** n trouble m du comportement alimentaire; **~ habits** npl habitudes fpl alimentaires.

eavesdrop /ˈiːvzdrɒp/ vi (p prés etc **-pp-**) écouter aux portes.

ebb /eb/ **I** n reflux m; **the ~ and flow** le flux et le reflux ALSO FIG.
II vi LIT descendre; FIG décliner; **to ~ and flow** monter et descendre.
IDIOMS **to be at a low ~** être au plus bas.
■ **ebb away** [strength, enthusiasm, support] décliner.

ebony /ˈebənɪ/ n **1** (wood) ébène f; **2** ▶818 (colour) noir m d'ébène.

ebullient /ɪˈbʌlɪənt, ɪˈbʊlɪənt/ adj exubérant.

EC n (abrév = **European Community**) CE f.

eccentric /ɪkˈsentrɪk/ n, adj excentrique (mf).

eccentricity /ˌeksenˈtrɪsətɪ/ n excentricité f.

ECG n (abrév = **electrocardiogram**, **electrocardiograph**) ECG m.

echo /ˈekəʊ/ **I** n (pl **~es**) écho m; **to have ~es of sth** FIG rappeler qch.
II vtr LIT répercuter; reprendre [idea, opinion]; rappeler [artist, style].
III vi retentir, résonner (**to, with** de; **around** dans).

echoing /ˈekəʊɪŋ/ adj sonore.

eclipse /ɪˈklɪps/ **I** n éclipse f (**of** de).
II vtr éclipser.

eco+ /ˈiːkəʊ-/ combining form éco+.

eco-friendly adj qui ne nuit pas à l'environnement.

ecological /ˌiːkəˈlɒdʒɪkl/ adj écologique.

ecologist /iːˈkɒlədʒɪst/ n, adj écologiste (mf).

ecology /ɪˈkɒlədʒɪ/ **I** n écologie f.
II noun modifier POL [movement, issue] écologique.

economic /ˌiːkəˈnɒmɪk, ˌek-/ adj **1** (financial) économique; **2** (profitable) [proposition, business] rentable.

economical /ˌiːkəˈnɒmɪkl, ˌek-/ adj **1** [machine, method] économique; **to be ~ on petrol** consommer peu d'essence; **2** [person] économe; **3** FIG [style, writer] concis; **to be ~ with the truth** IRON ne pas dire toute la vérité.

economically /ˌiːkəˈnɒmɪklɪ, ek-/ adv (financially) sur le plan économique; [operate] de façon économique; [write] avec concision.

economic: **~ analyst** ▶1251 n analyste mf économique; **~ and monetary union, EMU** n Union f économique et monétaire; **~ history** n histoire f de l'économie; **~ indicator** n indicateur m économique or de conjoncture; **~ management** n gestion f de l'économie.

economics /ˌiːkəˈnɒmɪks, ˌek-/ **I** n (science) (+ v sg) économie f; (subject of study) (+ v sg) sciences fpl économiques; (financial aspects) (+ v pl) aspects mpl économiques (**of** de).
II noun modifier [degree, textbook, faculty] de sciences économiques; [editor, expert] en économie.

economist /ɪˈkɒnəmɪst, ˌek-/ ▶1251 n économiste mf; **business ~** économiste mf d'entreprise.

economize /ɪˈkɒnəmaɪz/ vtr, vi économiser.

economy /ɪˈkɒnəmɪ/ n (all contexts) économie f; **the ~** l'économie du pays.

economy: **~ class** n AVIAT classe f économique; **~ drive** n campagne f de restriction; **~ pack, ~ size** n paquet m économique.

ecstasy /ˈekstəsɪ/ n **1** extase f; **2** (drug) ecstasy m.

ecstatic /ɪkˈstætɪk/ adj [person] enchanté (**about** par); [state] extatique; [reception, crowd] enthousiaste.

ecstatically /ɪkˈstætɪklɪ/ adv [applaud, welcomed] avec un enthousiasme délirant; **~ happy** radieux/-ieuse.

ectopic pregnancy /ek,tɒpɪk ˈpregnənsɪ/ n grossesse f extra-utérine.

ecu, ECU /erˈkuː/ ▶849 **I** n (abrév = **European Currency Unit**) écu m, ÉCU m; **hard ~** écu m dur.
II noun modifier [value] en écus.

Ecuador /ˈekwədɔː(r)/ ▶840 pr n Équateur m.

ecumenical /ˌiːkjuˈmenɪkl/ adj œcuménique.

eczema /ˈeksɪmə, US ɪgˈziːmə/ ▶1002 n eczéma m.

Ed.B n US UNIV (abrév = **Bachelor of Education**) diplôme m universitaire de pédagogie.

eddy /ˈedɪ/ **I** n tourbillon m.
II vi [water] faire des tourbillons; [smoke, crowd] tournoyer.

Eden /ˈiːdn/ pr n Éden m, paradis m terrestre.

edge /edʒ/ **I** n **1** (outer limit) GEN bord m; (of wood, clearing) lisière f; **on the ~ of the city** en bordure de la ville; **the film had us on the ~ of our seats** FIG le film nous a tenus en haleine; **2** (of blade) tranchant m; **with a sharp ~** bien aiguisé; **3** (of book, plank) tranche f; **4** FIG **to give an ~ to** aiguiser [appetite]; **take the ~ off** gâter [pleasure]; calmer [anger, appetite]; **there was an ~ to his voice** sa voix avait quelque chose de tendu; **to lose one's ~** [writing, style] perdre sa vivacité; [person] perdre sa vigueur; **5** (advantage) **to have the ~ over** ou on avoir l'avantage sur; **to have a slight ~** avoir une légère avance (**over** sur); **6** (touchy) **to be on ~** [person] être énervé; **that sets my teeth on ~** cela me fait grincer des dents; **7** FIG (extremity) **to live on the ~** vivre dangereusement; **the news pushed him over the ~** cette nouvelle l'a achevé.
II vtr **1** (move slowly) **to ~ sth towards** approcher qch de; **to ~ one's way along** longer la bordure de [cliff, parapet]; **2** (trim) border.
III vi (advance) **to ~ forward** avancer doucement; **to ~ closer to** se rapprocher de; **to ~ towards** s'approcher à petits pas.
■ **edge out**: ¶ **~ out** [car, driver] (of space) se dégager petit à petit (**of** de); ¶ **~ sb out of** [job] évincer qn de; **we've ~d our competitors out of the market** nous avons éliminé tous nos concurrents du marché.
■ **edge up** [prices, figure] augmenter lentement; **2 to ~ up to sb/sth** s'approcher doucement de qn/qch.

edgeways /ˈedʒweɪz/, **edgewise** /ˈedʒwaɪz/ adv [move] latéralement; [lay, put] sur le côté.
IDIOMS **I can't get a word in ~** je n'arrive pas à placer un mot.

edgily /ˈedʒɪlɪ/ adv nerveusement.

edging /ˈedʒɪŋ/ n bordure f.

edgy /ˈedʒɪ/ adj énervé, anxieux/-ieuse.

edible /ˈedɪbl/ adj [fruit, plant, mushroom, snail] comestible; [meal] mangeable.

edict /ˈiːdɪkt/ n **1** HIST édit m; **2** JUR, POL décret m.

edifice /ˈedɪfɪs/ n édifice m ALSO FIG.

edifying /ˈedɪfaɪɪŋ/ adj édifiant.

Edinburgh /ˈedɪnbərə/ ▶1343 pr n Édimbourg.

edit /ˈedɪt/ **I** n (of film) montage m; (for publication) mise f au point.
II vtr **1** (in publishing) (check) réviser; (annotate, select) éditer; (cut down) couper; **2** (in journalism) être le rédacteur/la rédactrice m/f en chef de [newspaper]; être le rédacteur/la rédactrice m/f de [page]; **3** TV, CIN monter [film, programme].
■ **edit out**: **~ out** [sth], **~** [sth] **out** CIN couper [qch] au montage; AUDIO, RADIO couper [qch].

editing /ˈedɪtɪŋ/ n **1** (tidying for publication) mise f au point; **2** (annotation, choice) édition f; **3** (of film) montage m; **4** (of newspaper) rédaction f.

edition /ɪˈdɪʃn/ n (of book, newspaper) édition f; (of news programme) édition f; (of documentary) émission f.

editor /ˈedɪtə(r)/ ▶1251 n (of newspaper) rédacteur/-trice m/f en chef (**of** de); (of book, manuscript) correcteur/-trice m/f; (of writer, works, anthology) éditeur/-trice m/f; (of dictionary) rédacteur/-trice m/f; (of film) monteur/-euse m/f.

editorial /ˌedɪˈtɔːrɪəl/ **I** n éditorial m.
II adj **1** (in journalism) [staff, office] de la rédaction; **to have ~ control** avoir la direction de la rédaction; **2**

(in publishing) [*policy, decision*] éditorial; **to have ~ control** avoir le contrôle du texte.

educate /'edʒʊkeɪt/ *vtr* **1** (teach) instruire; **2** (provide education for) assurer l'instruction de; **to ~ one's children privately** mettre ses enfants dans une école privée; **to be ~d in Paris** faire ses études à Paris; **3** (inform) informer [*public, smokers, drivers*] (**about, in** sur); éduquer [*palate, tastes, mind*].

educated /'edʒʊkeɪtɪd/ **I** *n* **the ~** (having education) les gens *mpl* instruits; (cultivated) les gens *mpl* cultivés.
II *adj* [*person*] (having an education) instruit; (cultivated) cultivé; [*taste*] raffiné; [*accent*] élégant; [*classes*] instruit.
IDIOMS **~ guess** opinion fondée (sur l'expérience).

education /ˌedʒʊ'keɪʃn/ **I** *n* **1** (training) GEN éducation *f*, instruction *f*; (in health, road safety) information *f*; **2** (formal schooling) études *fpl*; **a university** ou **college ~** des études supérieures; **to get a good ~** faire de solides études; **3** (national system) enseignement *m*; **government spending on ~** le budget de l'éducation; **4** UNIV (field of study) sciences *fpl* de l'éducation.
II *noun modifier* [*budget, spending, crisis*] de l'enseignement; [*method*] SCH, UNIV d'enseignement; [*Minister, Ministry*] ADMIN de l'éducation; **~ standards** SCH niveau *m* scolaire; UNIV niveau *m* universitaire; **the ~ system** le système éducatif.

educational /ˌedʒʊ'keɪʃənl/ *adj* **1** [*establishment, method, system*] d'enseignement; [*developments*] de l'enseignement; [*standards, supplies*] SCH scolaire; UNIV universitaire; **2** (instructive) [*game, programme, value*] éducatif/-ive; [*experience, talk*] instructif/-ive.

educationalist /ˌedʒʊ'keɪʃənəlɪst/ *n* spécialiste *mf* des sciences de l'éducation.

educationally /ˌedʒʊ'keɪʃənəlɪ/ *adv* [*useless, useful*] pédagogiquement; [*disadvantaged, privileged*] sur le plan scolaire.

educationally subnormal, ESN I *n* **the ~** les arriérés *mpl*.
II *adj* arriéré.

educational: **~ psychology** *n* psychologie *f* scolaire; **~ television**, **ETV** US télévision *f* scolaire.

education: **~ authority** *n* GB *administration locale qui gère les affaires scolaires*; **~ committee** *n* GB comité gérant les affaires scolaires d'une région.

education department *n* **1** GB (also **Department of Education and Science**) ministère *m* de l'éducation; **2** GB (in local government) service *m* chargé des affaires d'enseignement; **3** (in university) département *m* des sciences de l'éducation.

educative /'edʒʊkətɪv/ *adj* éducatif/-ive.

educator /'edʒʊkeɪtə(r)/ *n* éducateur/-trice *m/f*.

Edwardian /ed'wɔ:dɪən/ **I** *n* contemporain/-e *m/f* d'Édouard VII.
II *adj* de l'époque d'Édouard VII.

EEC I *n* (*abrév* ▶ **European Economic Community**) CEE *f*.
II *noun modifier* [*policy, directive, country*] de la CEE.

eel /i:l/ *n* anguille *f*.

eerie /'ɪərɪ/ *adj* [*silence, place*] étrange et inquiétant.

efface /ɪ'feɪs/ *vtr* effacer ALSO FIG.

effect /ɪ'fekt/ **I** *n* **1** (net result) effet *m* (**of** de; **on** sur); **to have the ~ of doing** avoir pour effet de faire; **the ~ of advertising is to increase demand** la publicité a pour effet d'accroître la demande; **the film had quite an ~ on me** ce film m'a fait forte impression; **to use sth to good ~** employer qch avec succès; **to use sth to dramatic ~** obtenir un effet spectaculaire en utilisant qch; **2** (repercussions) répercussions *fpl* (**of** de; **on** sur); **3** (power, efficacy) efficacité *f*; **of no ~** sans effet; **to little ~** sans grand résultat; **to no ~** en vain; **to take ~** [*price increases*] prendre effet; [*ruling*] entrer en vigueur; [*pills, anaesthetic*] commencer à agir; **to come into ~** JUR, ADMIN entrer en vigueur; **to put policies into ~** appliquer des directives; **with ~ from January 1** à dater du 1er janvier; **4** (theme) **the ~ of what he is saying is that** il veut dire par là que; **a note to the ~ that** un

mot pour dire que; **a remark to that ~** une remarque en ce sens; **or words to that ~** ou quelque chose de ce genre; **5** (impression) effet *m*; **the overall ~** l'effet d'ensemble; **to achieve an ~** obtenir un effet; **he paused for ~** il a fait une pause théâtrale; **she dresses like that for ~** elle s'habille comme ça pour faire de l'effet.
II effects *npl* JUR (belongings) effets *mpl*.
III in effect *adv phr* dans le fond.
IV *vtr* effectuer [*repair, sale, change*]; apporter [*improvement*]; parvenir à [*reconciliation*].

effective /ɪ'fektɪv/ *adj* **1** (successful) efficace (**against** contre; **in doing** pour faire); **2** [*legislation*] en vigueur; **to become ~** entrer en vigueur; **3** [*speech, contrast, demonstration*] percutant; **4** (actual) ECON [*rate, income*] réel/réelle; [*control*] effectif/-ive.

effectively /ɪ'fektɪvlɪ/ *adv* **1** (efficiently) efficacement; **2** (in effect) en réalité; **3** (impressively) **the statistics ~ demonstrate** les statistiques démontrent avec force.

effectiveness /ɪ'fektɪvnɪs/ *n* efficacité *f* (**of** de).

effeminate /ɪ'femɪnət/ *adj* efféminé.

effervescent /ˌefə'vesnt/ *adj* LIT effervescent; FIG exubérant.

effete /ɪ'fi:t/ *adj* PEJ [*person*] mou/molle; [*civilization*] déliquescent.

efficacious /ˌefɪ'keɪʃəs/ *adj* efficace (**in doing** pour faire).

efficacy /'efɪkəsɪ/ *n* efficacité *f* (**of** de).

efficiency /ɪ'fɪʃnsɪ/ *n* (of person, method, organization) efficacité *f* (**in doing** à faire); (of machine) rendement *m*; **to produce electricity at 50% ~** produire de l'électricité avec un rendement de 50%.

efficient /ɪ'fɪʃnt/ *adj* **1** [*person, management*] efficace (**at doing** pour ce qui est de faire); **to make ~ use of energy** faire une utilisation rationnelle de l'énergie; **2** [*machine*] économique; **to be 40% ~** avoir un rendement de 40%.

efficiently /ɪ'fɪʃntlɪ/ *adv* [*work, deal with, carry out*] de façon efficace; **the machine operates ~** la machine a un bon rendement.

effigy /'efɪdʒɪ/ *n* (all contexts) effigie *f*.

effluent /'efluənt/ **I** *n* effluent *m*.
II *noun modifier* [*treatment, management*] des effluents.

effort /'efət/ *n* **1** (energy) efforts *mpl*; **to put a lot of ~ into sth/into doing** se donner beaucoup de peine pour qch/pour faire; **to put all one's ~(s) into doing** consacrer tous ses efforts à faire; **to spare no ~** ne pas ménager ses efforts; **it's a waste of ~** c'est du travail pour rien; **to be worth the ~** en valoir la peine; **2** (difficulty) effort *m*; **it is an ~ to do** il est pénible de faire; **3** (attempt) **to make the ~** faire l'effort; **he made no ~ to apologize** il n'a fait aucun effort pour s'excuser; **his ~s at doing** ses tentatives pour faire; **to make every ~** faire tout son possible; **in an ~ to do** pour essayer de faire; **joint ~** initiative *f* commune; **this is my first ~** c'est ma toute première œuvre; **not a bad ~** pas mal; **4** (initiative) initiative *f*; **war ~** effort *m* de guerre; **5** FIG (exercise) effort *m*; **an ~ of will** un effort de volonté.

effortless /'efətlɪs/ *adj* (easy) aisé; (innate) naturel/-elle.

effortlessly /'efətlɪslɪ/ *adv* sans effort, sans peine.

effrontery /ɪ'frʌntərɪ/ *n* effronterie *f*.

effusion /ɪ'fju:ʒn/ *n* FIG (enthusiasm) débordements *mpl*; (emotional outpouring) effusion *f*; (written) épanchement *m*.

effusive /ɪ'fju:sɪv/ *adj* [*person, style*] expansif/-ive; [*thanks*] très chaleureux/-euse.

effusively /ɪ'fju:sɪvlɪ/ *adv* [*speak*] avec effusion; [*welcome, thank*] très chaleureusement.

EFL *n* (*abrév* = **English as a Foreign Language**) anglais *m* langue étrangère.
II *noun modifier* [*teacher, course*] d'anglais langue étrangère.

EFT *n*: *abrév* ▶ **electronic funds transfer**.

EFTA /'eftə/ n (abrév = **European Free Trade Association**) AELE f.

eg (abrév = **exempli gratia**) par ex.

egalitarian /ɪˌgælɪ'teərɪən/ adj [person] égalitariste; [principles, tradition] égalitaire.

egg /eg/ **I** n œuf m.
II noun modifier [sandwich] à l'œuf; [collector] d'œufs; [farm] producteur/-trice d'œufs; [noodles, sauce] aux œufs.
IDIOMS **to have ~ on one's face**○ avoir l'air fin○; **as sure as ~s is ~s** aussi vrai que deux et deux font quatre.
■ **egg on**: ~ [sb] **on** pousser FIG.

egg: ~ **box** n (pl ~es) boîte f à œufs; ~**cup** n coquetier m; ~ **custard** n flan m aux œufs; ~**head** n PÉJ grosse tête○ f; ~**nog** n (with milk) lait m de poule; (with alcohol) flip m; ~**plant** n US aubergine f; ~**-shaped** adj ovoïde; ~**shell** n coquille f d'œuf; ~ **timer** n sablier m; ~ **whisk** n fouet m à œufs; ~ **white** n blanc m d'œuf; ~ **yolk** n jaune m d'œuf.

ego /'egəʊ, 'iːgəʊ, US 'iːgəʊ/ n **1** GEN amour-propre m; **to be on an ~ trip** se faire mousser○; **2** PSYCH moi m, ego m.

egocentric /ˌegəʊ'sentrɪk, 'iːgəʊ-, US 'iːg-/ adj égocentrique.

egoism /'egəʊɪzəm, 'iːg-, US 'iːg-/ n égoïsme m.

egoist /'egəʊɪst, 'iːg-, US 'iːg-/ n égoïste mf.

egoistic(al) /ˌegəʊ'ɪstɪk(l), ˌiːg-, US ˌiːg-/ adj égoïste.

egotism /'egəʊtɪzəm, 'iːg-, US 'iːg-/ n égotisme m.

egotist /'egəʊtɪst, 'iːg-, US 'iːg-/ n égotiste mf.

Egypt /'iːdʒɪpt/ ▶ 840| pr n Égypte f.

Egyptian /ɪ'dʒɪpʃn/ ▶ 1100|, 1038| **I** n Égyptien/-ienne m/f.
II adj égyptien/-ienne.

eiderdown /'aɪdədaʊn/ n (quilt) édredon m.

eight /eɪt/ ▶ 1112| n, adj huit (m) inv; ~**-hour day** journée f de huit heures; **to work ~-hour shifts** faire les trois-huit.
IDIOMS **to be one over the ~**○ avoir un verre dans le nez○.

eighteen /eɪ'tiːn/ ▶ 1112| n, adj dix-huit (m) inv.

eighteenth /eɪ'tiːnθ/ ▶ 1112|, 854| **I** n (in order) dix-huitième mf; (of month) dix-huit m; (fraction) dix-huitième m.
II adj, adv dix-huitième.

eighth /eɪtθ/ ▶ 1112|, 854| **I** n (in order) huitième mf; (of month) huit m inv; (fraction) huitième m; MUS octave f.
II adj, adv huitième.

eighth note n US MUS croche f.

eightieth /'eɪtɪəθ/ ▶ 1112| **I** n **1** (in order) quatre-vingtième mf; **2** (fraction) quatre-vingtième m.
II adj, adv quatre-vingtième.

eighty /'eɪtɪ/ ▶ 1112|, 713| **I** n quatre-vingts m.
II adj quatre-vingts inv.

eighty-one ▶ 1112| n, adj quatre-vingt-un (m).

Éire /'eərə/ ▶ 840| pr n Éire f, République f d'Irlande.

either /'aɪðər, US 'iːðər/ **I** pron **1** (one or other) l'un/ l'une ou l'autre; **without ~ (of them)** sans l'un ni l'autre; **there was no sound from ~ of the rooms** aucun bruit ne provenait ni d'une chambre ni de l'autre; **~ or both of you can do it** vous pouvez le faire seul ou tous les deux; **2** (both) ~ **of the two is possible** les deux sont possibles; **~ of us could win** nous avons tous les deux les mêmes chances de gagner; **'which book do you want?'—'~'** 'quel livre veux-tu?'—'n'importe'.
II det **1** (one or the other) n'importe lequel/laquelle; (in the negative) **I can't see ~ child** je ne vois aucun des deux enfants; **2** (both) ~ **one of the solutions is acceptable** les deux solutions sont acceptables; **in ~ case** dans les deux cas; ~ **way, you win** vous gagnez dans les deux cas; ~ **way, it will be difficult** de toute manière, ce sera difficile; **I don't have strong views ~ way** je ne suis ni pour ni contre.

III adv non plus; **I can't do it ~** je ne peux pas le faire non plus.
IV conj **1** (as alternatives) **I was expecting him ~ Tuesday or Wednesday** je l'attendais soit mardi, soit mercredi; **it's ~ him or me** c'est lui ou moi; **2** (in the negative) **I wouldn't reward ~ Patrick or Emily** je ne donnerais de récompense ni à Patrick ni à Emily; **you're not being ~ truthful or fair** tu n'es ni honnête ni juste; **3** (as an ultimatum) ~ **you finish your work or you will be punished!** ou tu finis ton travail ou je te punis!; **put the gun down, ~ that or I call the police** pose ton arme sinon j'appelle la police.

ejaculate /ɪ'dʒækjʊleɪt/ **I** vtr (exclaim) s'exclamer.
II vi éjaculer.

ejaculation /ɪˌdʒækjʊ'leɪʃn/ n **1** exclamation f; **2** éjaculation f.

eject /ɪ'dʒekt/ **I** vtr **1** (give out) [machine, system] rejeter [waste]; [volcano] cracher [lava]; **2** AUDIO faire sortir [cassette]; **3** (throw out) expulser [troublemaker].
II vi [pilot] s'éjecter.

ejection /ɪ'dʒekʃn/ n (of gases, waste) rejet m; (of lava) éruption f; (of troublemaker) expulsion f; AVIAT éjection f.

eke /iːk/ v ■ **eke out**: ~ **out** [sth], ~ [sth] **out** faire durer [income, supplies] (**by** à force de; **by doing** en faisant); **to ~ out a living** ou **an existence** essayer de joindre les deux bouts.

elaborate **I** /ɪ'læbərət/ adj GEN compliqué; [system, network, plan] complexe; [design] travaillé; [painting, sculpture] ouvragé; [costume] recherché; [precaution, preparation] minutieux/-ieuse.
II /ɪ'læbəreɪt/ vtr élaborer [theory, scheme]; développer [point, statement, idea].
III /ɪ'læbəreɪt/ vi entrer dans les détails; **to ~ on** s'étendre sur [proposal]; développer [remark].

elaborately /ɪ'læbərətlɪ/ adv [decorated, dressed] de manière recherchée; [defined, constructed] minutieusement.

elaboration /ɪˌlæbə'reɪʃn/ n (of plan, theory) élaboration f (**of** de).

elapse /ɪ'læps/ vi s'écouler.

elastic /ɪ'læstɪk/ n, adj élastique (m).

elasticated /ɪ'læstɪkeɪtɪd/ adj [waistband, bandage] élastique.

elastic band n élastique m.

elated /ɪ'leɪtɪd/ adj transporté de joie; **I was ~ at having won** j'exultais d'avoir gagné.

elation /ɪ'leɪʃn/ n joie f, allégresse f.

Elba /'elbə/ ▶ 1022| pr n île f d'Elbe.

elbow /'elbəʊ/ **I** n (all contexts) coude m; **to lean on one's ~s** être accoudé; **at sb's ~** à portée de main; **to wear sth through at the ~s** percer or trouer qch aux coudes.
II vtr **to ~ sb aside** écarter qn du coude; **to ~ one's way through a crowd** se frayer un passage à travers la foule (en jouant des coudes).
IDIOMS **more power to your ~** GB je te souhaite bien du courage○; **out at (the) ~(s)** [person] loqueteux; [garment] miteux; **to be up to the ~s in sth** être dans qch jusqu'au cou; **to give sb the ~** se débarrasser de qn; **to rub ~s with sb**○ US fréquenter qn.

elbow grease n huile f de coude○.

elbowroom /'elbəʊruːm/ n (room to move) espace m vital; FIG marge f de manœuvre; **there isn't much ~ in this kitchen** on est un peu à l'étroit dans cette cuisine.

elder /'eldə(r)/ **I** n **1** (older person) aîné/-e m/f; (of tribe, group) ancien m; **2** BOT sureau m.
II adj aîné; **the ~ girl** l'aînée f, la fille aînée.

elderberry n baie f de sureau; ~ **wine** vin m de sureau.

elderly /'eldəlɪ/ **I** n **the ~** (+ v pl) les personnes fpl âgées.
II adj [person, population] âgé; [vehicle] vieux/vieille; **her ~ father** son vieux père.

elder statesman *n* (*pl* **-men**) (all contexts) doyen *m*.

eldest /'eldɪst/ I *n* aîné/-e *m/f*; **my ~** mon aîné/-e.
II *adj* aîné; **the ~ child** l'aîné/-e.

elect /ɪ'lekt/ I *n* **the ~** les élus *mpl*.
II *vtr* **1** (by vote) élire (**from, from among** parmi); **to be ~ed to a post** être élu à un poste; **to ~ sb (as) president** élire qn président; **2** (choose) choisir.
III *adj* (*after n*) futur; **the president ~** le président élu (*n'ayant pas encore pris ses fonctions*).

election /ɪ'lekʃn/ I *n* **1** (ballot) élection *f*, scrutin *m*; **in** OU **at the ~** aux élections; **to win/lose an ~** gagner/perdre aux élections; **2** (appointment) élection *f* (**to** à); **to stand for ~** se porter candidat aux élections.
II *noun modifier* [*manifesto*] électoral; [*day, results*] du scrutin.

electioneering /ɪ,lekʃə'nɪərɪŋ/ *n* (campaigning) campagne *f* électorale; PEJ électoralisme *m*.

elective /ɪ'lektɪv/ *adj* **1** (elected) [*office, official*] électif/-ive, élu; (empowered to elect) [*assembly, body*] électoral; **2** SCH, UNIV [*course*] facultatif/-ive.

elector /ɪ'lektə(r)/ *n* **1** (voter) électeur/-trice *m/f*; **2** US POL membre *m* du collège électoral.

electoral /ɪ'lektərəl/ *adj* électoral.

electoral: **~ register**, **~ roll** *n* listes *fpl* électorales; **~ vote** *n* US vote *m* des grands électeurs.

electorate /ɪ'lektərət/ *n* électorat *m*, électeurs *mpl*.

electric /ɪ'lektrɪk/ I○ **electrics** *npl* GB AUT circuits *mpl* électriques (d'une voiture).
II *adj* électrique ALSO FIG.

electrical /ɪ'lektrɪkl/ *adj* électrique.

electric blanket *n* couverture *f* chauffante.

electrician /ˌɪlek'trɪʃn/ ▶1251 *n* électricien/-ienne *m/f*.

electricity /ˌɪlek'trɪsəti/ I *n* LIT, FIG électricité *f*; **to turn off/on the ~** couper/rétablir le courant (électrique).
II *noun modifier* [*generator, cable*] électrique; [*bill, charges*] d'électricité.

electricity: **~ board** *n* GB compagnie *f* d'électricité; **~ supply** *n* alimentation *f* en électricité.

electric shock *n* décharge *f* électrique; **to get an ~** recevoir une décharge.

electric storm *n* orage *m*.

electrify /ɪ'lektrɪfaɪ/ *vtr* GEN électrifier; FIG électriser.

electrifying /ɪ'lektrɪfaɪɪŋ/ *adj* [*speech*] électrisant.

electro+ /ɪ'lektrəʊ/ *combining form* électro+.

electrocute /ɪ'lektrəkjuːt/ *vtr* électrocuter; **to be ~d** (accidentally) s'électrocuter.

electrocution /ɪ,lektrə'kjuːʃn/ *n* électrocution *f*.

electrode /ɪ'lektrəʊd/ *n* électrode *f*.

electrolysis /ˌɪlek'trɒləsɪs/ *n* **1** CHEM électrolyse *f*; **2** (hair removal) épilation *f* électrique.

electron /ɪ'lektrɒn/ *n* électron *m*.

electronic /ˌɪlek'trɒnɪk/ *adj* (all contexts) électronique.

electronic: **~ engineer** ▶1251 *n* électronicien/-ienne *m/f*; **~ engineering** *n* électronique *f*; **~ eye** *n* cellule *f* photoélectrique; **~ funds transfer**, **EFT** *n* transfert *m* électronique de fonds; **~ mail**, **E-mail** *n* messagerie *f* électronique.

electronics /ˌɪlek'trɒnɪks/ *n* (+ *v sg*) électronique *f*.

electroshock therapy, **electroshock treatment**, **EST** /ɪ,lektrəʊ'ʃɒk/ *n* électroconvulsivothérapie *f*, électrochocs *mpl*.

elegance /'elɪɡəns/ *n* élégance *f*.

elegant /'elɪɡənt/ *adj* [*person, clothes, gesture*] élégant; [*manners*] distingué; [*restaurant*] chic (*inv*).

elegantly /'elɪɡəntli/ *adv* [*dress, write*] avec élégance; [*dressed, furnished*] élégamment.

elegy /'elədʒi/ *n* élégie *f* (**for** à).

element /'elɪmənt/ *n* **1** (constituent) élément *m*; **the key ~ in his success** l'élément clé de son succès; **the poor salary was just one ~ in my dissatisfaction** le salaire médiocre n'expliquait que partiellement mon mécontentement; **2** (factor) facteur *m*; **the time**

~ le facteur temps; **3** (small part) part *f*; **an ~ of luck/risk** une part de chance/risque; **4** (rudiment) (of courtesy, diplomacy) élément *m*; (of grammar, mathematics etc) base *f*; **5** (constituent group) élément *m*; **6** (air, water etc) élément *m*; **the ~s** (weather) les éléments; **exposed to the ~s** exposé aux intempéries; **7** CHEM, MATH, RADIO élément *m*; **8** ELEC résistance *f*.
IDIOMS **to be in/out of one's ~** être/ne pas être dans son élément.

elementary /,elɪ'mentri/ *adj* **1** (basic, simple) élémentaire; **2** [*school*] primaire; [*teacher*] de primaire.

elephant /'elɪfənt/ *n* éléphant *m*; **baby ~** éléphanteau *m*.

elephantine /,elɪ'fæntaɪn/ *adj* [*person*] éléphantesque; [*task*] gigantesque.

elevate /'elɪveɪt/ *vtr* élever (**to** au rang de).

elevated /'elɪveɪtɪd/ *adj* GEN élevé; [*railway, canal*] surélevé.

elevated railroad *n* US métro *m* aérien.

elevation /,elɪ'veɪʃn/ *n* **1** GEN élévation *f* (**to** au rang de); **2** ARCHIT élévation *f*; **front ~** élévation de la façade; **3** (height) altitude *f*.

elevator /'elɪveɪtə(r)/ *n* **1** US (in building) ascenseur *m*; **2** (hoist) élévateur *m*; **3** US (for grain) silo *m* à grain.

eleven /ɪ'levn/ I *n* **1** onze *m inv*; **2** SPORT **the football ~** le onze; **a football ~** une équipe de football.
II *adj* onze *inv*.

eleven plus *n* ~ examen *m* d'entrée en sixième.

elevenses○ /ɪ'levnzɪz/ *n* GB pause-café *f* (*dans la matinée*).

eleventh /ɪ'levnθ/ ▶1112, 854 I *n* **1** (in order) onzième *mf*; **2** (of month) onze *m inv*; **3** (fraction) onzième *m*.
II *adj, adv* onzième.

eleventh hour *n* **at the ~** à la toute dernière minute.

elf /elf/ *n* (*pl* **elves**) lutin *m*.

elicit /ɪ'lɪsɪt/ *vtr* obtenir [*opinion*]; provoquer [*reaction, response*]; tirer [*explanation*].

eligibility /,elɪdʒə'bɪlətɪ/ *n* droit *m* (**for** à; **to do** de faire).

eligible /'elɪdʒəbl/ *adj* (qualifying) **to be ~ for** avoir droit à [*allowance, benefit, membership*]; **to be ~ for appointment** remplir les conditions pour être nommé; **to be ~ to do** être en droit de faire; **the ~ candidates** les candidats qui remplissent les conditions requises; **an ~ bachelor** un beau ou bon parti.

eliminate /ɪ'lɪmɪneɪt/ *vtr* GEN éliminer; écarter [*suspect*].

elimination /ɪ'lɪmɪneɪʃn/ *n* élimination *f*; **by a process of ~** en procédant par élimination.

élite /eɪ'liːt/ I *n* élite *f*.
II *adj* [*group, minority*] élitaire; [*restaurant, club*] réservé à l'élite; [*troop, team, squad*] d'élite.

elliptic(al) /ɪ'lɪptɪk(l)/ *adj* (all contexts) elliptique.

elm /elm/ *n* orme *m*.

elocution /,elə'kjuːʃn/ *n* élocution *f*, diction *f*.

elongate /'iːlɒŋɡeɪt, US ɪ'lɔːŋ-/ I *vtr* (lengthen) allonger; (stretch) étirer.
II *vi* s'allonger.

elope /ɪ'ləʊp/ *vi* [*couple*] s'enfuir ensemble; [*man, woman*] s'enfuir (**with** avec).

elopement /ɪ'ləʊpmənt/ *n* fugue *f* amoureuse.

eloquence /'eləkwəns/ *n* éloquence *f*.

eloquent /'eləkwənt/ *adj* [*orator, speech, gesture*] éloquent.

El Salvador /,el 'sælvədɔː(r)/ ▶840 *pr n* Salvador *m*; **in ~** au Salvador.

else /els/ I *adv* d'autre; **somebody/nothing ~** quelqu'un/rien d'autre; **something ~** autre chose; **somewhere** OU **someplace** US **~** ailleurs; **how ~ can we do it?** comment le faire autrement?; **what would you like ~?** qu'est-ce que tu voudrais d'autre?; **there's not much ~ to do** il n'y a pas grand-chose d'autre à faire; **he talks of little ~** il ne parle presque que de ça; **everyone ~ but me went to the**

football match tout le monde est allé voir le match de football sauf moi; **was anyone ~ there?** y avait-il quelqu'un d'autre?; **anyone ~ would go to bed early, but you...** à ta place n'importe qui irait se coucher tôt, mais toi, tu...; **anywhere ~ it wouldn't matter** en tout autre lieu ça n'aurait aucune importance; **he didn't see anybody ~** il n'a vu personne d'autre; **if nothing ~ he's polite** à défaut d'autre chose il est poli; **she's something ~**○! (very nice) elle est géniale!; (unusual) elle est spéciale!; **'is that you, David?'—'who ~?'** 'c'est toi, David?'—'qui veux-tu que ce soit?'

II or else conj phr sinon, ou; **eat this or ~ you'll be hungry** mange ça ou or sinon tu vas avoir faim; **stop that now, or ~...**○! arrête tout de suite, sinon...

elsewhere /ˌelsˈweə(r), US ˌelsˈhweər/ adv ailleurs; **from ~** venu/-e d'ailleurs.

ELT n: abrév ▶ **English Language Teaching**.

elucidate /ɪˈluːsɪdeɪt/ vtr élucider [mystery, problem]; expliquer [text, concept].

elude /ɪˈluːd/ vtr échapper à [pursuer, attention, memory, person]; se dérober à [police]; esquiver [blow].

elusive /ɪˈluːsɪv/ adj [person, animal, happiness] insaisissable; [prize, victory] hors d'atteinte; [scent, memory] fugace.

'em○ /əm/ = **them**.

emaciated /ɪˈmeɪʃɪeɪtɪd/ adj [person, feature] émacié; [limb, body] décharné; [animal] étique.

E-mail /ˈiːmeɪl/ n (abrév = **electronic mail**) messagerie f électronique.

emanate /ˈeməneɪt/ I vtr émettre, dégager [radiation]. II vi LIT, FIG émaner (**from** de).

emancipate /ɪˈmænsɪpeɪt/ vtr émanciper; **to become ~d** [woman] s'émanciper.

emancipation /ɪˌmænsɪˈpeɪʃn/ n émancipation f.

emasculate /ɪˈmæskjʊleɪt/ vtr LIT, FIG émasculer.

embalm /ɪmˈbɑːm, US -ˈbɑːlm/ vtr LIT, FIG embaumer.

embankment /ɪmˈbæŋkmənt/ n **1** (to carry railway, road) remblai m; **2** (to hold back water) quai m, digue f.

embargo /ɪmˈbɑːɡəʊ/ I n embargo m (**on** sur; **against** contre); **trade ~** embargo commercial; **arms ~** embargo sur les livraisons d'armes; **to impose/lift an ~** instaurer/lever un embargo. II vtr instaurer un embargo sur [trade].

embark /ɪmˈbɑːk/ I vtr NAUT embarquer. II vi **1** NAUT s'embarquer (**for** pour); **2 to ~ on** entreprendre [journey]; se lancer dans [campaign, career, relationship, process, project]; PEJ s'engager dans [dubious path]; s'embarquer dans [dubious process].

embarkation /ˌembɑːˈkeɪʃn/ n embarquement m.

embarrass /ɪmˈbærəs/ vtr plonger [qn] dans l'embarras; **to be/feel ~ed** être/se sentir gêné; **to be ~ed by** être gêné par [situation, remark]; avoir honte de [person, ignorance]; **I feel ~ed about doing** ça me gêne de faire; **to be financially ~ed** avoir des embarras d'argent.

embarrassing /ɪmˈbærəsɪŋ/ adj GEN embarrassant; **my uncle is ~** mon oncle me fait honte; **to put sb in an ~ position** mettre qn dans l'embarras.

embarrassingly /ɪmˈbærəsɪŋlɪ/ adv [behave] de façon gênante; **~ frank** d'une franchise embarrassante.

embarrassment /ɪmˈbærəsmənt/ n **1** (feeling) confusion f, gêne f (**about, at** devant); **to cause sb ~** mettre qn dans l'embarras; **to my ~** à ma grande confusion; **2** (person, action, event) **to be an ~ to sb** [person] faire honte à qn; **his past is an ~ to him** il a honte de son passé; **3** (superfluity) SOUT embarras m; **an ~ of riches** l'embarras du choix.

embassy /ˈembəsɪ/ n ambassade f.

embed /ɪmˈbed/ vtr (p prés etc **-dd-**) **1** LIT **~ded in** [sharp object, rock] enfoncé dans; [plant] ancré dans; [plaque] encastré dans; **2** FIG **to be ~ded in** être ancré dans; **3** COMPUT incorporer (**in** dans).

embellish /ɪmˈbelɪʃ/ vtr LIT, FIG embellir.

ember /ˈembə(r)/ n **the ~s** les braises fpl.

embezzle /ɪmˈbezl/ vtr détourner [funds] (**from** de).

embezzlement /ɪmˈbezlmənt/ n détournement m de fonds.

embitter /ɪmˈbɪtə(r)/ vtr aigrir, remplir [qn] d'amertume [person]; **to become ~ed** s'aigrir.

emblem /ˈembləm/ n emblème m.

emblematic /ˌembləˈmætɪk/ adj emblématique.

embodiment /ɪmˈbɒdɪmənt/ n (incarnation of quality, idea) incarnation f.

embody /ɪmˈbɒdɪ/ vtr **1** (incarnate) incarner [virtue, evil, ideal]; **to be embodied in** s'incarner dans; **2** (express) donner corps à [theory, philosophy]; **3** (legally) incorporer (**in** dans).

embolism /ˈembəlɪzəm/ n MED embolie f.

emboss /ɪmˈbɒs/ vtr gaufrer [fabric, paper]; estamper [leather]; repousser, travailler [qch] en relief [metal].

embrace /ɪmˈbreɪs/ I n étreinte f; **to hold sb in a fond ~** étreindre qn affectueusement. II vtr **1** (hug) étreindre; **2** (adopt) embrasser [religion, ideology]; épouser [cause]; s'engager dans [policy]; adopter [principle, technology, method]; **3** (include) comprendre [subject areas]; englober [cultures, beliefs]. III vi s'étreindre.

embroider /ɪmˈbrɔɪdə(r)/ I vtr LIT broder (**with** de); FIG broder sur [fact]; embellir [story, truth]. II vi broder, faire de la broderie.

embroidery /ɪmˈbrɔɪdərɪ/ I n broderie f. II noun modifier [frame, silk, thread] à broder.

embroil /ɪmˈbrɔɪl/ vtr entraîner (**in** dans).

embryo /ˈembrɪəʊ/ I n BIOL, FIG embryon m. II adj = **embryonic**.

embryonic /ˌembrɪˈɒnɪk/ adj BIOL, FIG embryonnaire.

emend /ɪˈmend/ vtr corriger.

emerald /ˈemərəld/ I n **1** (stone) émeraude f; **2** ▶ **818** (colour) émeraude m. II adj **1** [ring, necklace] d'émeraudes; **2** (colour) émeraude inv.

emerge /ɪˈmɜːdʒ/ I vi **1** [person, animal] sortir (**from** de); **2** [issue, news, problem, result] se faire jour; [trend, pattern] se dégager; [truth] apparaître; [talent] voir le jour; [evidence, message] ressortir; [new nation, ideology] naître; **to ~ victorious** ressortir vainqueur; **it ~ed that** il est apparu que. II **emerging** pres p adj [market] naissant; [democracy] qui émerge; [opportunity] qui apparaît; [writer, artist] qui devient connu.

emergence /ɪˈmɜːdʒəns/ n apparition f.

emergency /ɪˈmɜːdʒənsɪ/ I n GEN cas m d'urgence; MED urgence f; **in an ~, in case of ~** en cas d'urgence; **in times of ~** en temps de crise; **state of ~** POL état m d'urgence. II noun modifier [plan, measures, operation, repairs, aid, call, stop] d'urgence; POL [meeting, session] extraordinaire; AUT [brakes, vehicle] de secours.

emergency: **~ ambulance service** n service m ambulancier de secours d'urgence; cf SAMU; **~ case** n MED urgence f; **~ centre** GB, **~ center** US n (for refugees etc) centre m d'accueil (pour sinistrés); MED poste m de secours; AUT poste m de dépannage; **~ exit** n sortie f de secours; **~ landing** n AVIAT atterrissage m d'urgence; **~ laws** npl POL lois fpl d'exception; **~ medical service, EMS** n US service m ambulancier de secours d'urgence; cf SAMU; **~ number** n numéro m des urgences; **~ powers** npl POL ~ pleins pouvoirs mpl; **~ rations** npl vivres mpl de secours; **~ room** n US = **emergency ward**; **~ service** n MED service m de garde; AUT service m de dépannage; **~ services** npl (police) police f secours; (ambulance) service m d'aide médicale d'urgence; (fire brigade) (sapeurs-) pompiers mpl.

emergency surgery n **to undergo ~** être opéré d'urgence.

emergency: **~ ward** n salle f des urgences; **~ worker** n secouriste mf.

emergent /ɪˈmɜːdʒənt/ *adj* [*industry, nation*] jeune; [*power, artist, genre*] naissant.

emery /ˈemərɪ/ *n* émeri *m*.

emery: **~ board** *n* lime *f* à ongles; **~ paper** *n* papier-émeri *m*.

emigrant /ˈemɪgrənt/ **I** *n* (about to leave) émigrant/-e *m/f*; (settled elsewhere) émigré/-e *m/f*.
II *noun modifier* [*worker*] émigré; [*family*] d'émigrés.

emigrate /ˈemɪgreɪt/ *vi* émigrer.

emigration /ˌemɪˈgreɪʃn/ *n* émigration *f*.

eminence /ˈemɪnəns/ *n* **1** (fame) renommée; **2** (honour) distinction *f*; **3** LITTÉR (hill) éminence *f*.

eminent /ˈemɪnənt/ *adj* éminent.

eminently /ˈemɪnəntlɪ/ *adv* [*respectable*] éminemment; [*capable, suitable*] parfaitement; [*desirable*] hautement.

emirate /ˈemɪəreɪt/ *n* émirat *m*.

emissary /ˈemɪsərɪ/ *n* émissaire *m* (**to** auprès de).

emission /ɪˈmɪʃn/ *n* (all contexts) émission *f* (**from** provenant de).

emit /ɪˈmɪt/ *vtr* (discharge) émettre [*gas, heat, sound, signal*]; dégager [*smell, vapour*]; lancer [*spark*]; laisser échapper [*cry*].

Emmy /ˈemɪ/ *n*: récompense décernée par la télévision américaine.

emollient /ɪˈmɒlɪənt/ *n, adj* émollient (*m*).

emotion /ɪˈməʊʃn/ *n* émotion *f*.

emotional /ɪˈməʊʃənl/ *adj* [*development, problem*] émotif/-ive; [*reaction, state*] émotionnel/-elle; [*tie, response*] affectif/-ive; [*film*] émouvant; [*speech*] passionné; [*occasion*] chargé d'émotion; **to feel ~** se sentir ému (**about** par); **she's rather ~** elle est facilement émue; **~ health** équilibre *m* mental.

emotionally /ɪˈməʊʃənəlɪ/ *adv* [*speak, react*] avec émotion; [*drained, involved*] émotionnellement; [*immature*] sur le plan affectif; **~ charged** [*relationship*] intense; [*atmosphere*] chargée d'émotion; **~ deprived** privé d'affection; **~ disturbed** caractériel/-ielle.

emotionless /ɪˈməʊʃnlɪs/ *adj* impassible.

emotive /ɪˈməʊtɪv/ *adj* [*issue*] brûlant, qui soulève les passions; [*word*] chargé de connotations.

empathize /ˈempəθaɪz/ *vi* **to ~ with** s'identifier à [*person*].

empathy /ˈempəθɪ/ *n* empathie *f*.

emperor /ˈempərə(r)/ *n* empereur *m*.

emphasis /ˈemfəsɪs/ *n* (*pl* **-ses**) accent *m*; **the new ~ on training** l'importance récemment accordée à la formation; **to put special ~ on sth** insister sur l'importance de qch.

emphasize /ˈemfəsaɪz/ *vtr* mettre l'accent sur [*policy, need*]; mettre [qch] en valeur [*eyes*]; **to ~ that** insister sur le fait que; **to ~ the importance of sth** insister sur l'importance de qch.

emphatic /ɪmˈfætɪk/ *adj* [*statement*] catégorique; [*voice, manner*] énergique; [*tone, style*] vigoureux/-euse; **to be ~ about/that** insister sur/pour que.

emphatically /ɪmˈfætɪklɪ/ *adv* GEN énergiquement; [*insist*] avec force; **and I say this most ~** et je ne saurais trop insister là-dessus; **he is most ~ not a genius** il n'a vraiment rien d'un génie.

empire /ˈempaɪə(r)/ *n* LIT, FIG empire *m*.

empirical /ɪmˈpɪrɪkl/ *adj* empirique.

employ /ɪmˈplɔɪ/ **I** *n* SOUT **in his ~** à son service.
II *vtr* **1** employer [*person, company*] (**as** en qualité de); **2** (use) utiliser [*machine, tool*]; employer [*method, tactics, technique, expression*]; recourir à [*measures*]; **to be ~ed in doing** (busy) être en train de faire.

employable /ɪmˈplɔɪəbl/ *adj* [*person*] capable de faire un travail.

employed /ɪmˈplɔɪd/ **I** *n* **the ~** les actifs *mpl*.
II *adj* (in work) qui a un emploi; (an employee) salarié.

employee /ˌemplɔɪˈiː, ɪmˈplɔɪiː/ *n* salarié/-e *m/f*.

employer /ɪmˈplɔɪə(r)/ *n* employeur/-euse *m/f*; **~s' organizations** associations *fpl* patronales.

employment /ɪmˈplɔɪmənt/ *n* travail *m*, emploi *m*; **to take up ~** commencer un travail; **to seek/find ~**

chercher/trouver du travail; **to be in ~** avoir un emploi; **without ~** sans emploi; **people in ~** les actifs *mpl*; **conditions of ~** conditions *fpl* d'emploi; **place of ~** lieu *m* de travail.

employment: **~ agency** *n* bureau *m* de recrutement; **~ contract** *n* contrat *m* de travail; **~ exchange** *n* agence *f* pour l'emploi; **Employment Minister, Employment Secretary** *n* ministre *m* du Travail.

emporium /ɪmˈpɔːrɪəm/ *n* (*pl* **~s** ou **-ria**) SOUT ou HUM grand magasin *m*.

empower /ɪmˈpaʊə(r)/ *vtr* (legally) **to ~ sb to do** autoriser qn à faire; (politically) donner à qn le pouvoir de faire; **the police are ~ed to do** la police a pleins pouvoirs pour faire.

empress /ˈemprɪs/ *n* impératrice *f*.

emptiness /ˈemptɪnɪs/ *n* (of space, house, life) vide *m*.

empty /ˈemptɪ/ **I** *adj* **1** [*street*] désert; [*desk*] libre; [*container*] vide; [*page*] vierge; **to stand ~** être inoccupé; **2** FIG [*promise, threat*] en l'air; [*dream, rhetoric*] creux/creuse; [*gesture*] vide de sens; [*life*] vide.
II *vtr, vi* = **empty out**.
■ **empty out**: ¶ **~ out** [*building, container*] se vider; [*contents*] se répandre; ¶ **~ [sth] out, ~ out [sth]** GEN vider; verser [*liquid*].

empty: **~-handed** *adj* [*arrive, leave*] les mains vides; [*return*] bredouille *inv*; **~-headed** *adj* écervelé.

EMS *n* **1** (*abrév* = **European Monetary System**) SME *m*; **2** *abrév* ▶ **emergency medical service**.

emulate /ˈemjʊleɪt/ *vtr* SOUT **1** (imitate) imiter; (rival) rivaliser avec; **2** COMPUT émuler.

emulsify /ɪˈmʌlsɪfaɪ/ **I** *vtr* émulsionner, émulsifier.
II *vi* être émulsionné or émulsifié.

emulsion /ɪˈmʌlʃn/ *n* (all contexts) émulsion *f*.

enable /ɪˈneɪbl/ *vtr* **1** **to ~ sb to do** permettre à qn de faire; **2** (facilitate) faciliter [*growth*]; favoriser [*learning*].

enact /ɪˈnækt/ *vtr* **1** (perform) jouer; **2** JUR POL (pass) voter; (bring into effect) promulguer.

enamel /ɪˈnæml/ **I** *n* émail *m*.
II *noun modifier* [*pan*] en émail; [*ring*] en émaux.
III *vtr* émailler.
IV **enamelled, enameled** US *pp adj* [*glass, pottery*] émaillé; [*ornament*] en émaux.

enamelling, enameling US /ɪˈnæmlɪŋ/ *n* (process) émaillage *m*; (art) émaillerie *f*.

enamoured GB, **enamored** US /ɪˈnæməd/ *adj* **to be ~ of** être épris/-e or amoureux/-euse de.

enc. *abrév* = **encl.**

encampment /ɪnˈkæmpmənt/ *n* GEN campement *m*; MIL cantonnement *m*.

encapsulate /ɪnˈkæpsjʊleɪt/ *vtr* (summarize) résumer; (include) contenir.

encase /ɪnˈkeɪs/ *vtr* revêtir, recouvrir (**in** de); **~d in** pris dans [*concrete*]; serré dans [*plaster*].

encash /ɪnˈkæʃ/ *n* GB encaisser.

encephalogram /enˈkefələgræm/ *n* encéphalogramme *m*.

enchant /ɪnˈtʃɑːnt, US -tʃænt/ **I** *vtr* (all contexts) enchanter.
II **enchanted** *pp adj* [*garden, wood*] enchanté.

enchanting /ɪnˈtʃɑːntɪŋ, US -tʃænt-/ *adj* [*vision*] enchanteur/-eresse; [*smile*] ravissant.

enchantment /ɪnˈtʃɑːntmənt, US -tʃænt-/ *n* (all contexts) enchantement *m*.

encircle /ɪnˈsɜːkl/ *vtr* [*troops, police*] encercler; [*fence, wall*] entourer; [*belt, bracelet*] enserrer.

encl. I *n* (*abrév* = **enclosure**) PJ *f*.
II *adj* (*abrév* = **enclosed**) ci-joint.

enclose /ɪnˈkləʊz/ *vtr* GEN entourer (**with, by** de); (with fence, wall) clôturer (**with, by** avec); (in outer casing) enfermer (**in** dans); (in brackets) insérer (**in** dans); (in letter) joindre (**with, in** à); **please find ~d a cheque for £10** veuillez trouver ci-joint un chèque de dix livres; **a letter enclosing a cheque** une lettre accompagnée d'un chèque.

enclosed /ɪnˈkləʊzd/ *adj* [*garden, space*] clos; [*sea, harbour*] fermé; [*letter*] ci-joint.

enclosure /ɪnˈkləʊʒə(r)/ *n* **1** (space) (for animals) enclos *m*; (for race-horses) paddock *m*; (for officials) enceinte *f*; **2** (fence) clôture *f*.

encode /ɪnˈkəʊd/ *vtr* GEN coder, chiffrer; COMPUT, LING encoder.

encoder /ɪnˈkəʊdə(r)/ *n* COMPUT, LING encodeur *m*.

encompass /ɪnˈkʌmpəs/ *vtr* inclure, comprendre [*people, ideas, territories, area*].

encore /ˈɒŋkɔː(r)/ THEAT **I** *n* bis *m*; **to give** ou **play an** ~ jouer un bis; **to get an** ~ être bissé.
II *excl* ~! bis!

encounter /ɪnˈkaʊntə(r)/ **I** *n* GEN rencontre *f* (**with** avec); MIL affrontement *m*; **his frequent** ~**s with the law** ses démêlés *mpl* fréquents avec la police.
II *vtr* rencontrer [*opponent, resistance, problem*]; essuyer [*setback*]; croiser [*person*].

encourage /ɪnˈkʌrɪdʒ/ *vtr* **1** (support) encourager; (reassure) rassurer; **to** ~ **sb to do** encourager qn à faire; **these observations** ~**d him in his belief that** ces observations l'ont conforté dans l'idée que; **2** (foster) stimuler [*investment*]; favoriser [*rise, growth*].

encouragement /ɪnˈkʌrɪdʒmənt/ *n* (support) encouragement *m* (**to** pour); (inducement) incitation *f* (**to** à); **she needs no** ~ **to do** elle ne se fait pas prier pour faire; **to give** ~ **to sb, to be an** ~ **to sb** encourager qn; **without** ~ **from me** sans mon soutien.

encouraging /ɪnˈkʌrɪdʒɪŋ/ *adj* encourageant.

encroach /ɪnˈkrəʊtʃ/ *vi* **to** ~ **on** [*sea, vegetation*] gagner du terrain sur; [*person*] empiéter sur; **to** ~ **on sb's privacy** violer l'intimité de qn.

encrust /ɪnˈkrʌst/ *vtr* **to be** ~**ed with** être recouvert de [*ice*]; être incrusté de [*jewels*].

encumber /ɪnˈkʌmbə(r)/ *vtr* encombrer (**with** de).

encumbrance /ɪnˈkʌmbrəns/ *n* (hindrance) entrave *f* (**to** à); (burden) (person) charge *f* (**to** pour); (possession) embarras *m* (**to** pour).

encyclop(a)edia /ɪnˌsaɪkləˈpiːdɪə/ *n* encyclopédie *f*.

end /end/ **I** *n* **1** (final part) fin *f*; **'The End'** (of film, book etc) 'Fin'; **at the** ~ **of** à la fin de [*year, story*]; **at the** ~ **of May** fin mai; **by the** ~ **of** à la fin de [*year, journey, game*]; **to put an** ~ **to sth, to bring sth to an** ~ mettre fin à qch; **to get to the** ~ **of** arriver à la fin de [*holiday*]; arriver au bout de [*story, work*]; **to come to an** ~ se terminer; **in the** ~ I went home finalement je suis rentré chez moi; **in the** ~**, at the** ~ **of the day** (all things considered) en fin de compte; **it's the** ~ **of the line** ou **road for the project** le projet arrive en fin de course; **for days on** ~ pendant des jours et des jours; **there is no** ~ **to his talent** son talent n'a pas de limites; **no** ~ **of**° **trouble** énormément de problèmes; **that really is the** ~°! c'est vraiment le comble°!; **you really are the** ~°! tu exagères!; **2** (extremity) bout *m*, extrémité *f*; **at the** ~ **of, on the** ~ **of** au bout de; **at the** ~ **of the garden** au fond du jardin; **from one** ~ **to another** d'un bout à l'autre; **from** ~ **to** ~ de bout en bout; **to lay sth** ~ **to** ~ poser qch bout à bout; **the lower** ~ **of the street** le bas de la rue; **the third from the** ~ le/la troisième avant la fin; **to stand sth on** (its) ~ mettre qch debout; **3** (side of conversation, transaction) côté *m*; **things are fine at my** ou **this** ~ de mon côté tout va bien; **to keep one's** ~ **up** tenir bon; **there was silence at the other** ~ c'était le silence au bout du fil; **4** (of scale, spectrum) extrémité *f*; **at the lower** ~ **of the scale** au plus bas de l'échelle; **this suit is from the cheaper** ou **bottom** ~ **of the range** ce costume est un des moins chers de la gamme; **5** (aim) but *m*; **to this** ou **that** ~ dans ce but; **a means to an** ~ un moyen d'arriver à ses fins; **6** SPORT côté *m*, camp *m*; **to change** ~**s** changer de côté; **7** (scrap) (of rope, string) bout *m*; (of loaf, joint of meat) reste *m*; **8** (death) mort *f*; **to meet one's** ~ trouver la mort; **to be nearing one's** ~ sentir sa fin proche; **to come to a bad** ~ mal finir.

II *noun modifier* [*house*] du bout; [*carriage*] de queue.
III *vtr* GEN mettre fin à; rompre [*marriage*]; **to** ~ **sth with** terminer qch par; **he** ~**ed his days in hospital** il a fini ses jours à l'hôpital; **to** ~ **it all** en finir avec la vie; **the sale to** ~ **all sales** ce qu'il y a de mieux comme soldes.
IV *vi* GEN se terminer (**in, with** par); [*contract, agreement*] expirer; **where will it all** ~? comment tout cela finira-t-il?
IDIOMS **all's well that** ~**s well** tout est bien qui finit bien.

■ **end up**: finir par devenir [*president*]; finir par être [*rich*]; **to** ~ **up (by) doing** finir par faire; **to** ~ **up in Paris** se retrouver à Paris.

endanger /ɪnˈdeɪndʒə(r)/ *vtr* mettre [qch] en danger [*health, life*]; constituer une menace pour [*environment, species*]; compromettre [*reputation, career, prospects*]; ~**ed species** espèce *f* menacée.

endear /ɪnˈdɪə(r)/ **I** *vtr* **to** ~ **sb** to faire aimer qn de.
II *v refl* **to** ~ **oneself to sb** se faire aimer or apprécier de qn.

endearing /ɪnˈdɪərɪŋ/ *adj* [*person, habit*] attachant; [*remark*] touchant; [*smile*] engageant.

endearingly /ɪnˈdɪərɪŋlɪ/ *adv* [*smile*] de manière touchante; ~ **honest** d'une honnêteté touchante.

endearment /ɪnˈdɪəmənt/ *n* terme *m* d'affection; **terms of** ~ termes *mpl* d'affection.

endeavour, endeavor US /ɪnˈdevə(r)/ **I** *n* (attempt) tentative *f* (**to do** de faire); (industriousness) effort *m*.
II *vtr* **to** ~ **to do** (do one's best) faire tout son possible pour faire; (find a means) trouver un moyen de faire.

endemic /enˈdemɪk/ **I** *n* endémie *f*.
II *adj* endémique (**in, to** dans).

ending /ˈendɪŋ/ *n* GEN fin *f*, dénouement *m*; LING terminaison *f*.

endive /ˈendɪv, US -daɪv/ *n* GB (lettuce) chicorée *f*; US (chicory) endive *f*.

endless /ˈendlɪs/ *adj* (unlimited) GEN infini; [*supply, stock*] inépuisable; (interminable) interminable.

endlessly /ˈendlɪslɪ/ *adv* **1** (unlimitedly) infiniment; **2** (without stopping) [*talk, cry, argue*] sans s'arrêter; [*search, play, try*] inlassablement; **3** (to infinity) [*stretch, extend*] à perte de vue.

endo+ /ˈendəʊ/ *combining form* endo+.

endocrinology /ˌendəʊkrɪˈnɒlədʒɪ/ *n* endocrinologie *f*.

endorse /ɪnˈdɔːs/ *vtr* **1** donner son aval à [*view, policy*]; appuyer [*candidate, decision*]; approuver [*product, claim*]; endosser [*cheque, bill*]; **2** GB AUT **to have one's licence** ~**d** ~ perdre des points sur son permis de conduire.

endorsement /ɪnˈdɔːsmənt/ *n* **1** (of opinion, claim) approbation *f* (**of** de); (of candidate) appui *m* (**of** à); (of decision) sanction *f* (**of** à propos de); (of cheque) endossement *m*; **2** GB AUT **he has had two** ~**s for speeding** – il a perdu des points pour excès de vitesse.

endow /ɪnˈdaʊ/ *vtr* (with money) doter [*hospital, charity, person*] (**with** de); fonder [*academic post*].

endowment /ɪnˈdaʊmənt/ *n* **1** (action) (of hospital, school) dotation *f*; (of prize, academic post) fondation *f*; (money given) dotation *f*; **2** (talent) don *m*.

endowment insurance *n* assurance *f* à capital différé.

end: ~**paper** *n* page *f* de garde; ~ **product** *n* produit *m* fini; ~ **result** *n* résultat *m* final.

endurable /ɪnˈdjʊərəbl, US -ˈdʊə-/ *adj* supportable.

endurance /ɪnˈdjʊərəns, US -dʊə-/ *n* (physical) endurance *f*; (moral) courage *m*; (of cold) résistance *f*; **past** ou **beyond** ~ intolérable; **to provoke sb beyond** ~ pousser qn à bout.

endurance test *n* SPORT, MIL épreuve *f* d'endurance.

endure /ɪnˈdjʊə(r), US -ˈdʊər/ **I** *vtr* endurer [*personal experience, hardship*]; supporter [*behaviour, sight, person*]; subir [*attack, defeat, imprisonment*].
II *vi* durer.

enduring /ɪnˈdjʊərɪŋ, US -ˈdʊə-/ adj [influence, fame] durable; [grudge] tenace; [ability] constant; [government] stable; [charm] éternel.

end user n COMM, COMPUT utilisateur m final.

enema /ˈenɪmə/ n MED lavement m.

enemy /ˈenəmɪ/ I n (pl -mies) GEN, FIG, MIL ennemi/-e m/f; **to make enemies** se faire des ennemis; **to be one's own worst** ~ être son pire ennemi; **to go over to the** ~ passer à l'ennemi.
II noun modifier [forces, aircraft, propaganda, territory] ennemi; [agent] de l'ennemi; ~ **alien** ressortissant/-e m/f d'un pays ennemi; **killed by** ~ **action** tombé sous le feu de l'ennemi; **under** ~ **occupation** occupé par l'ennemi.

energetic /ˌenəˈdʒetɪk/ adj (full of life) GEN énergique; [exercise] vigoureux/-euse; [debate] animé.

energetically /ˌenəˈdʒetɪklɪ/ adv [work, exercise] avec vigueur; [deny] vigoureusement; [speak, promote, publicize] avec force.

energize /ˈenədʒaɪz/ vtr GEN stimuler; ELEC alimenter [qch] en courant.

energizing /ˈenədʒaɪzɪŋ/ adj [influence] stimulant.

energy /ˈenədʒɪ/ n 1 (vitality) énergie f; **it would be a waste of** ~ ce serait se donner du mal pour rien; **2** (power, fuel) énergie f; **nuclear** ~ énergie f nucléaire.

energy: ~ **efficiency** n économies fpl d'énergie; ~ **resources** npl ressources fpl énergétiques.

energy saving I n économies fpl d'énergie.
II **energy-saving** adj [device] qui permet de faire des économies d'énergie; [measure] destiné à économiser l'énergie.

enervate /ˈenəveɪt/ vtr débiliter.

enfold /ɪnˈfəʊld/ vtr envelopper.

enforce /ɪnˈfɔːs/ vtr 1 (impose) appliquer [rule, policy, decision]; faire respecter [law, court order]; faire valoir [legal rights]; imposer [silence, discipline]; exiger [payment]; faire exécuter [contract]; **2** (strengthen) renforcer [opinion, hypothesis]; appuyer [argument, theory].

enforced /ɪnˈfɔːst/ adj [abstinence, redundancy] forcé.

enforcement /ɪnˈfɔːsmənt/ n GEN application f; (of discipline) imposition f.

engage /ɪnˈɡeɪdʒ/ I vtr 1 (attract) retenir [attention]; éveiller [interest, sympathy]; séduire [imagination]; **2** (involve) **to be** ~**d in** se livrer à [activity]; **to be** ~**d in discussions/negotiations** être en discussion/négociations; **to** ~ **sb in conversation** engager la conversation avec qn; **to be otherwise** ~**d** être pris ailleurs; **to be** ~**d in doing** être en train de faire; **3** (employ) prendre [lawyer]; engager [secretary, interpreter]; **4** AUT passer [gear]; **to** ~ **the clutch** embrayer; **5** MIL engager le combat avec [enemy].
II vi SOUT **to** ~ **in** se livrer à [activity]; se lancer dans [research]; engager [dialogue, negotiations, combat].

engaged /ɪnˈɡeɪdʒd/ adj 1 (before marriage) **to be** ~ être fiancé (**to** à); **to get** ~**d** se fiancer (**to** à); **2** [WC, phone] occupé; [taxi] pris.

engaged tone n GB tonalité f 'occupé'.

engagement: ~ **book** n agenda m; ~ **ring** n bague f de fiançailles.

engaging /ɪnˈɡeɪdʒɪŋ/ adj [character] attachant; [person, laugh, tale] charmant; [smile] engageant.

engender /ɪnˈdʒendə(r)/ vtr engendrer, causer.

engine /ˈendʒɪn/ n 1 (in car, train, aeroplane, boat) moteur m; (in jet) réacteur m; (in ship) machines fpl; **jet** ~ moteur m à réaction; **2** RAIL (locomotive) locomotive f; **diesel/steam** ~ locomotive diesel/à vapeur; **to sit facing the** ~ être assis dans le sens de la marche.

engine driver ▶ 1251 n mécanicien m.

engineer /ˌendʒɪˈnɪə(r)/ ▶ 1251 I n (graduate) ingénieur m; (in factory) mécanicien m monteur m; (repairer) technicien m; (on ship) mécanicien m; US RAIL mécani-

cien m; **heating** ~ chauffagiste m; **telephone** ~ technicien m des télécommunications; ▶ **civil engineer etc**.
II vtr 1 (plot) manigancer; **2** (build) construire.

engineering /ˌendʒɪˈnɪərɪŋ/ n 1 (subject, science) GEN ingénierie f; **civil** ~ génie m civil; **2** (industry) industrie f mécanique; **light** ~ génie m léger.

engineering: ~ **company** n société f de constructions mécaniques; ~ **department** n UNIV département m d'ingénierie; ~ **factory**, ~ **works** n usine f de constructions mécaniques; ~ **industry** n industrie f mécanique; ~ **science** n UNIV ingénierie f.

engine: ~ **failure** n GEN panne f de moteur; (in jet) panne f de réacteur; ~ **oil** n huile f; ~ **room** n salle f des machines; ~ **shed** n RAIL dépôt m.

England /ˈɪŋɡlənd/ ▶ 840 pr n Angleterre f.

English /ˈɪŋɡlɪʃ/ ▶ 1100, 1038 I n 1 (language) anglais m; **the Queen's** ~ l'anglais correct; **2** (people) **the** ~ les Anglais mpl.
II adj [language, food] anglais; [lesson, teacher] d'anglais.

English: ~ **as a Foreign Language**, EFL n anglais m langue étrangère; ~ **as a Second Language**, ESL n anglais m deuxième langue.

English Channel n **the** ~ la Manche.

English: ~ **for Special Purposes**, ESP n anglais m de spécialités; ~ **Language Teaching**, ELT n enseignement m de l'anglais.

Englishman /ˈɪŋɡlɪʃmən/ n (pl -men) Anglais m.
IDIOMS **an** ~**'s home is his castle** PROV ~ charbonnier est maître dans sa maison PROV.

English: ~ **rose** n jeune fille f au teint frais; ~ **speaker** n anglophone mf; ~**-speaking** adj anglophone; ~**woman** n (pl -women) Anglaise f.

engrave /ɪnˈɡreɪv/ vtr graver.

engraving /ɪnˈɡreɪvɪŋ/ n gravure f.

engross /ɪnˈɡrəʊs/ vtr ~**ed in** absorbé ou plongé dans.

engrossing /ɪnˈɡrəʊsɪŋ/ adj absorbant.

engulf /ɪnˈɡʌlf/ vtr [sea, waves, fire] engloutir; [silence] envelopper; [panic] s'emparer de.

enhance /ɪnˈhɑːns, US -hæns/ vtr améliorer [prospects, status]; accroître [rights, power]; rehausser [public image]; mettre [qch] en valeur [appearance, qualities]; augmenter [value]; majorer [pension, salary].

enigma /ɪˈnɪɡmə/ n énigme f.

enigmatic /ˌenɪɡˈmætɪk/ adj énigmatique.

enjoy /ɪnˈdʒɔɪ/ I vtr 1 (get pleasure from) aimer; **I** ~ **looking after Paul** j'aime bien m'occuper de Paul; **he knows how to** ~ **life** il sait vivre; **I** ~**ed my day in London** j'ai passé une bonne journée à Londres; **I didn't** ~ **the party** je ne me suis pas bien amusé à la soirée; **the tourists are** ~**ing the good weather** les touristes profitent du beau temps; ~ **your meal!** bon appétit!; **2** (benefit from) jouir de.
II v refl **to** ~ **oneself** s'amuser (**doing** à faire); ~ **yourselves!** amusez-vous bien!

enjoyable /ɪnˈdʒɔɪəbl/ adj agréable.

enjoyment /ɪnˈdʒɔɪmənt/ n (pleasure) plaisir m; (of privileges, rights) jouissance f (**of** de); **to get** ~ **from chess** prendre plaisir à jouer aux échecs; **to read for** ~ lire pour le plaisir.

enlarge /ɪnˈlɑːdʒ/ I vtr agrandir [space, photograph]; développer [business]; augmenter [capacity].
II vi 1 (get bigger) [space] s'agrandir; [majority] s'accroître; **2** [pupil, pores] se dilater; [tonsils] enfler; **3 to** ~ **on** s'étendre sur [subject]; développer [idea].
III **enlarged** pp adj MED [pupil] dilaté; [tonsils, joint] enflé; [heart, liver] hypertrophié.

enlargement /ɪnˈlɑːdʒmənt/ n 1 (of space, photograph, document) agrandissement m; (of territory) élargissement m; (of business) accroissement m; (of index) augmentation f; **2** MED (of pupil) dilatation f; (of heart, liver) hypertrophie f.

enlarger /ɪnˈlɑːdʒə(r)/ n PHOT agrandisseur m.

enlighten /ɪnˈlaɪtn/ vtr éclairer (**on** sur).

enlightened /ɪn'laɪtnd/ *adj* éclairé.

enlightening /ɪn'laɪtnɪŋ/ *adj* instructif/-ive.

enlightenment /ɪn'laɪtnmənt/ *n* (edification) instruction *f*; (clarification) éclaircissement *m*; (**the Age of) the Enlightenment** le Siècle des lumières.

enlist /ɪn'lɪst/ **I** *vtr* MIL, FIG recruter; **to ~ sb's help** s'assurer l'aide de qn.
II *vi* MIL s'enrôler, s'engager.

enmesh /ɪn'meʃ/ *vtr* **to become ~ed in** s'empêtrer dans.

enmity /'enmətɪ/ *n* inimitié *f* (**towards** envers).

ennoble /ɪ'nəʊbl/ *vtr* LIT anoblir; FIG ennoblir.

enormity /ɪ'nɔːmətɪ/ *n* énormité *f*.

enormous /ɪ'nɔːməs/ *adj* GEN énorme; [*effort*] prodigieux/-ieuse; **an ~ amount of** énormément de; **an ~ number of people** un monde fou.

enormously /ɪ'nɔːməslɪ/ *adv* [*change, enjoy, vary*] énormément; [*big, long, complex, impressed*] extrêmement.

enough /ɪ'nʌf/

■ **Note** When *enough* is used as an adverb or a pronoun, it is most frequently translated by *assez*: *is the house big enough?* = est-ce que la maison est assez grande? (Note that *assez* comes before the adjective); *will there be enough?* = est-ce qu'il y en aura assez? (Note that if the sentence does not specify what it is enough of, the pronoun *en*, meaning of *it*/*of them*, must be added before the verb in French.)
– When used as a determiner, *enough* is generally translated by *assez de*: *we haven't bought enough meat* = nous n'avons pas acheté assez de viande; *there's enough meat for two meals*/*six people* = il y a assez de viande pour deux repas/six personnes; *have you got enough chairs?* = avez-vous assez de chaises?
– For more examples and particular usages, see the entry below.

adv, det, pron assez; **big ~ for us** assez grand pour nous; **big ~ to hold 50 people** assez grand pour contenir 50 personnes; **quite big ~** bien assez grand (**for** pour; **to do** pour faire); **just wide ~** juste assez large (**for** pour; **to do** pour faire); **to eat ~** manger assez; **have you had ~ to eat?** avez-vous assez mangé?; **~ money/seats** assez d'argent/de sièges; **there's more than ~ for everybody** il y en a plus qu'assez or largement assez pour tout le monde; **is there ~?** y en a-t-il assez?; **is he old ~ to vote?** a-t-il l'âge de voter?; **you're not trying hard ~** tu ne fais pas assez d'efforts; **curiously ~, I like her** aussi bizarre que cela puisse paraître, je l'aime bien; **will that be ~ (money)?** est-ce que ça suffira?; **I've had ~ of him** j'en ai assez de lui; **I've had ~ of working for one day** j'ai assez travaillé pour aujourd'hui; **I've got ~ to worry about** j'ai assez de soucis (comme ça); **I think you have said ~** je crois que vous en avez dit assez; **once was ~ for me!** une fois m'a suffi!; **that's ~ (from you)!** assez!; **~ said!** j'ai compris!; **she's a nice ~ woman** elle n'est pas désagréable; **~'s ~** ça suffit (comme ça); **and sure ~...!** et ça n'a pas manqué...!
IDIOMS **~ is as good as a feast** PROV = il ne faut pas abuser des bonnes choses.

enquire *vtr, vi* = **inquire**.

enquiry *n* = **inquiry**.

enrage /ɪn'reɪdʒ/ *vtr* mettre [qn] en rage, rendre [qn] furieux/-ieuse.

enraged /ɪn'reɪdʒd/ *adj* furieux/-ieuse.

enrich /ɪn'rɪtʃ/ *vtr* (all contexts) enrichir.

enrol, enroll US /ɪn'rəʊl/ (*p prés etc* **-ll-**) **I** *vtr* GEN inscrire; MIL enrôler.
II *vi* GEN s'inscrire; MIL s'engager (**in** dans); **to ~ on a course** s'inscrire à un cours.

enrolment, enrollment US /ɪn'rəʊlmənt/ *n* GEN inscription *f* (**in, on** à); MIL enrôlement *m*.

ensconce /ɪn'skɒns/ *vtr* **~d in** bien installé dans.

ensign /'ensən/ *n* (flag) pavillon *m*; (officer) enseigne *m*.

ensuing /ɪn'sjuːɪŋ, US -'suː-/ *adj* [*period*] qui suivit [*event*] qui s'ensuivit.

en suite /ˌɒn 'swiːt/ *adj* attenant.

ensure /ɪn'ʃɔː(r), US ɪn'ʃʊər/ *vtr* garantir; **to ~ that...** s'assurer que...

ENT *n* (*abrév* = **Ear, Nose and Throat**) ORL *f*.

entail /ɪn'teɪl/ *vtr* impliquer [*travel, action, work*]; exiger [*patience, discretion*]; entraîner [*change, expense, responsibility, study*]; nécessiter [*effort, time, journey, modification*]; **to ~ that...** impliquer que... (+ *subj*).

entangle /ɪn'tæŋgl/ *vtr* **1** LIT **to become ~d** s'enchevêtrer (**in** dans); **to be ~d in sth** être pris dans qch; **2** FIG **to be ~d with** être étroitement lié à [*ideology*]; (sexually) se compromettre avec.

entanglement /ɪn'tæŋglmənt/ *n* **1** (complicated situation) imbroglio *m*; **2** (involvement) liaison *f* (**with** avec).

enter /'entə(r)/ **I** *vtr* **1** (go into) entrer dans, pénétrer dans; **2** (commence) entrer dans [*phase, period*]; entamer [*new term, final year*]; **the country is ~ing a recession** le pays s'engage dans la récession; **3** (join) entrer dans [*profession, firm, army*]; participer à [*race, competition*]; entrer à [*institution, parliament, party, EC*]; **to ~ the war** entrer en guerre; **to ~ the Church** entrer en religion; **4** (put forward) inscrire [*competitor, candidate*] (**for** à); engager [*horse*] (**for** dans); présenter [*poem, picture*] (**for** à); **5** (record) inscrire [*figure, fact*] (**in** dans); (in diary) noter [*fact, appointment*] (**in** dans); **to ~ an item in the books** (in bookkeeping) porter un article (sur le livre de comptes); **6** FIG (come into) **to ~ sb's mind** ou **head** venir à l'idée or à l'esprit de qn; **7** COMPUT entrer [*data*].
II *vi* **1** (come in) entrer; **2** (enrol) **to ~ for** s'inscrire à [*exam*]; s'inscrire pour [*race*].
■ **enter into**: **~ into** [*sth*] **1** (embark on) entrer en [*correspondence, conversation*]; entamer [*negotiations, argument*]; se lancer dans [*explanations*]; conclure [*deal*]; passer [*agreement, contract*]; **to ~ into detail** entrer dans les détails; **to ~ into the spirit of the game** entrer dans le jeu; **2** (be part of) faire partie de [*plans*]; **that doesn't ~ into it** c'est sans rapport.
■ **enter on** = **enter upon**.
■ **enter up**: **~ up** [*sth*], **~** [*sth*] **up** inscrire [*figure, total*].
■ **enter upon**: **~ upon** [*sth*] s'engager dans.

enteritis /ˌentə'raɪtɪs/ ▶ 1002 | *n* entérite *f*.

enterprise /'entəpraɪz/ *n* **1** (undertaking) entreprise *f*; (venture) aventure *f*; **business ~** affaire *f* commerciale; **2** (initiative) esprit *m* d'initiative; **3** ECON entreprise *f*; **private ~** entreprise privée.

enterprising /'entəpraɪzɪŋ/ *adj* [*person*] entreprenant; [*plan*] audacieux/-ieuse; **it was very ~ of you** vous avez fait preuve de beaucoup d'initiative.

enterprisingly /'entəpraɪzɪŋlɪ/ *adv* de sa propre initiative.

entertain /ˌentə'teɪn/ **I** *vtr* **1** (keep amused) divertir; (make laugh) amuser; (keep occupied) distraire, occuper; **2** (play host to) recevoir; **3** entretenir [*idea*]; nourrir [*doubt, ambition, illusion*].
II *vi* recevoir.

entertainer /ˌentə'teɪnə(r)/ ▶ 1251 | *n* (comic) comique *mf*; (performer, raconteur) amuseur/-euse *m/f*.

entertaining /ˌentə'teɪnɪŋ/ **I** *adj* divertissant.
II *n* art *m* de recevoir; **they do a lot of ~** ils reçoivent beaucoup.

entertainment /ˌentə'teɪnmənt/ **I** *n* **1** ¢ divertissement *m*, distractions *fpl*; **for sb's ~** pour le divertissement de qn; **the world of ~** le monde du spectacle; **2** (event) spectacle *m*.
II *noun modifier* [*allowance, expenses*] de représentation; [*industry*] du spectacle.

enthralling /ɪn'θrɔːlɪŋ/ *adj* [*novel, performance*] captivant.

enthuse /ɪn'θjuːz, US -θuːz/ *vi* s'extasier (**about, over** devant).

enthusiasm /ɪn'θjuːzɪæzəm, US -'θuːz-/ *n* **1** ¢ enthousiasme *m* (**for** pour); **2** (hobby) passion *f*.

enthusiast /ɪn'θjuːzɪæst, US -'θuːz-/ *n* (for sport, DIY) passionné/-e *m/f*; (for music, composer) fervent/-e *m/f*.

enthusiastic /ɪnˌθjuːzɪ'æstɪk, US -ˌθuːz-/ *adj* [*crowd, response*] enthousiaste; [*discussion*] exalté; [*worker, gardener*] passionné; [*member*] fervent; **to be ~ about sth** (present or future event) être enthousiasmé par qch; (past event) parler de qch avec enthousiasme; **he's not very ~ about his work** il ne montre pas beaucoup d'enthousiasme pour son travail.

enthusiastically /ɪnˌθjuːzɪ'æstɪklɪ, US -ˌθuːz-/ *adv* avec enthousiasme.

entice /ɪn'taɪs/ *vtr* (with offer, charms, prospects) attirer; (with food, money) appâter; **to ~ sb to do** persuader qn de faire.

■ **entice away**: **~ [sb] away** détourner.

enticing /ɪn'taɪsɪŋ/ *adj* [*prospect, offer*] attrayant; [*person*] séduisant; [*food, smell*] appétissant.

entire /ɪn'taɪə(r)/ *adj* entier/-ière; **the ~ family** toute la famille, la famille (tout) entière; **throughout her ~ career** pendant toute sa carrière; **our ~ support** notre soutien absolu; **the ~ length of the street** toute la longueur de la rue; **the ~ 50,000 dollars** les 50 000 dollars dans leur totalité; **we are in ~ agreement** nous sommes entièrement d'accord.

entirely /ɪn'taɪəlɪ/ *adv* [*destroy, escape*] entièrement; [*reject*] totalement; [*innocent, different, unnecessary*] complètement; **that changes things ~** ça change tout; **not ~** pas tout à fait.

entirety /ɪn'taɪərətɪ/ *n* ensemble *m*, totalité *f*; **in its ~** dans son ensemble.

entitle /ɪn'taɪtl/ *vtr* **1** (authorize) **to ~ sb to sth** donner droit à qch à qn; **to ~ sb to do** autoriser qn à faire; **to be ~d to sth** avoir droit à qch; **to be ~d to do** avoir le droit de faire; **everyone's ~d to their own opinion** à chacun ses opinions; **2** (call) intituler [*text, music*]; donner un titre à [*work of art*]; **the poem is ~d 'Love'** le poème s'intitule 'L'amour'.

entitlement /ɪn'taɪtlmənt/ *n* droit *m* (**to sth** à qch; **to do** de faire).

entity /'entətɪ/ *n* entité *f*.

entomology /ˌentə'mɒlədʒɪ/ *n* entomologie *f*.

entrance I /'entrəns/ *n* **1** (door, act of entering) entrée *f*; **to make an ~** THEAT, FIG faire son entrée; **2** (admission) admission *f*; **to gain ~ to** être admis à or dans [*club, university*]; **to deny** ou **refuse sb ~** refuser de laisser entrer qn.

II /ɪn'trɑːns, US -'træns/ *vtr* transporter, ravir.

entrance: **~ examination** *n* GB SCH, UNIV examen *m* d'entrée; (for civil service) concours *m* d'entrée; **~ fee** *n* droit *m* d'entrée; **~ hall** *n* (in house) vestibule *m*; (in public building) hall *m*; **~ requirements** *npl* diplômes *mpl* requis; **~ ticket** *n* billet *m* d'entrée.

entrancing /ɪn'trɑːnsɪŋ, US -træns-/ *adj* ravissant.

entrant /'entrənt/ *n* (in race, competition) participant/-e *m/f*; (in exam) candidat/-e *m/f*.

entreat /ɪn'triːt/ *vtr* implorer, supplier (**to do** de faire).

entreatingly /ɪn'triːtɪŋlɪ/ *adv* [*beg, ask*] d'une voix suppliante or implorante; [*gaze*] d'un air suppliant or implorant.

entreaty /ɪn'triːtɪ/ *n* prière *f*, supplication *f*.

entrée /'ɒntreɪ/ *n* **1** CULIN GB entrée *f*; US plat *m* principal; **2** (into society) **her wealth gave her an ~ into high society** sa fortune lui a ouvert les portes de la haute société.

entrenched /ɪn'trentʃt/ *adj* **1** MIL retranché; **2** FIG [*opinion*] inébranlable; [*idea*] bien arrêté; [*tradition, rights*] bien établi.

entrepreneur /ˌɒntrəprə'nɜː(r)/ *n* entrepreneur/-euse *m/f*.

entrepreneurial /ˌɒntrəprə'nɜːrɪəl/ *adj* **to have ~ spirit/skills** avoir le sens/le don des affaires.

entrust /ɪn'trʌst/ *vtr* confier; **to ~ sb with sth**, **to ~ sth to sb** confier qch à qn.

entry /'entrɪ/ *n* **1** (door, act of entering) entrée *f*; **to gain ~ to** ou **into** s'introduire dans [*building*]; accéder à

[*computer file*]; **to force ~ to** ou **into** s'introduire de force dans; **2** (admission) GEN admission *f*; (to country) entrée *f*; **'no ~'** (on door) 'défense d'entrer'; (in one way street) 'sens interdit'; **3** (recorded item) (in dictionary, log) entrée *f*; (in encyclopedia) article *m*; (in diary) note *f*; (in register) inscription *f*; (in ledger, accounts book) écriture *f*; **to make an ~ in one's diary** écrire or noter quelque chose dans son journal; **4** (for competition) œuvre *f* présent ée à un concours; (for song contest) titre *m*; **send your ~ to...** envoyez votre réponse à...

entry: **~ fee** *n* droit *m* d'entrée; **~ form** *n* fiche *f* d'inscription; **~ permit** *n* visa *m* d'entrée; **~ phone** *n* interphone *m*; **~ requirements** *npl* diplômes *mpl* requis; **~ word** *n* US entrée *f*.

entwine /ɪn'twaɪn/ **I** *vtr* LIT entrelacer; FIG mêler (**with** à).

II *vi* LIT s'entrelacer; FIG s'entremêler.

E number *n* GB (number) numéro d'additif alimentaire (*approuvé par la CEE*); (additive) additif *m* alimentaire.

enumerate /ɪ'njuːməreɪt, US -'nuː-/ *vtr* SOUT énumérer.

enumeration /ɪˌnjuːmə'reɪʃn, US -ˌnuː-/ *n* SOUT (list) énumération *f*; (counting) dénombrement *m*.

enunciate /ɪ'nʌnsɪeɪt/ *vtr* articuler [*words, lines*]; énoncer [*truth, clause*]; exposer [*principle, policy*].

enunciation /ɪˌnʌnsɪ'eɪʃn/ *n* (of word) articulation *f*; (of facts) énonciation *f*; (of principle) exposé *m*.

envelop /ɪn'veləp/ *vtr* envelopper.

envelope /'envələʊp, 'ɒn-/ *n* enveloppe *f*; **to put sth in an ~** mettre qch sous enveloppe.

enviable /'envɪəbl/ *adj* enviable.

enviably /'envɪəblɪ/ *adv* **he was ~ slim/rich** sa minceur/richesse faisait envie.

envious /'envɪəs/ *adj* [*person*] envieux/-ieuse; [*look*] d'envie, envieux/-ieuse; **to be ~ of sb/sth** envier qn/ qch; **to make sb ~** rendre qn jaloux/-ouse.

enviously /'envɪəslɪ/ *adv* avec envie.

environment /ɪn'vaɪərənmənt/ *n* (physical, cultural) environnement *m*; (social) milieu *m*; **friendly ~** ambiance *f* amicale; **working ~** conditions *fpl* de travail.

environmental /ɪnˌvaɪərən'mentl/ *adj* [*conditions, changes*] du milieu; [*concern, issue*] lié à l'environnement, écologique; [*damage, protection, pollution*] de l'environnement; **~ effect** conséquences *fpl* sur l'environnement; **~ group** groupe *m* écologiste; **~ disaster** catastrophe *f* écologique.

environmental health *n* hygiène *f* publique.

environmentalist /ɪnˌvaɪərən'mentəlɪst/ *n* POL, ECOL écologiste *mf*.

environmentally /ɪnˌvaɪərən'mentəlɪ/ *adv* **~ safe**, **~ sound** qui ne nuit pas à l'environnement; **~ speaking** en ce qui concerne l'environnement; **~ friendly product** produit qui respecte l'environnement.

environmental: **~ scientist** *n* écologiste *mf*; **Environmental Studies** *npl* GB SCH études *fpl* géographiques et biologiques de l'environnement.

envisage /ɪn'vɪzɪdʒ/ *vtr* (anticipate) prévoir (**doing** de faire); (visualize) envisager (**doing** de faire).

envy /'envɪ/ **I** *n* (brief) envie *f*; (long-term) jalousie *f*; **out of ~** par jalousie; **in ~** par envie; **to be the ~ of sb** faire envie à qn.

II *vtr* envier; **to ~ sb sth** envier qch à qn.

enzyme /'enzaɪm/ *n* enzyme *f*.

EOC *n* GB *abrév* ▶ **Equal Opportunities Commission**.

ephemeral /ɪ'femərəl/ *adj* (all contexts) éphémère.

epic /'epɪk/ **I** *n* GEN épopée *f*; (film) film *m* à grand spectacle; (novel) roman-fleuve *m*.

II *adj* épique.

epicentre GB, **epicenter** US /'episentə(r)/ *n* épicentre *m*.

epidemic /ˌepɪ'demɪk/ **I** *n* LIT, FIG épidémie *f*.

II *adj* épidémique.

epidermis /ˌepɪ'dɜːmɪs/ *n* épiderme *m*.

epidural /ˌepɪˈdjʊərəl/ **I** n MED (anaesthetic) péridurale f.

　II adj épidural; MED [anaesthetic] péridural.

epigram /ˈepɪɡræm/ n épigramme f.

epilepsy /ˈepɪlepsɪ/ ▶ 1002 | n épilepsie f.

epileptic /ˌepɪˈleptɪk/ n, adj épileptique (mf).

Epiphany /ɪˈpɪfənɪ/ n Épiphanie f, jour m des Rois.

episode /ˈepɪsəʊd/ n (all contexts) épisode m.

episodic /ˌepɪˈsɒdɪk/ adj épisodique.

epistle /ɪˈpɪsl/ n épître f ALSO HUM.

epitaph /ˈepɪtɑːf, US -tæf/ n épitaphe f ALSO FIG.

epithet /ˈepɪθet/ n épithète f.

epitome /ɪˈpɪtəmɪ/ n (abstract) épitomé m; FIG the ~ of kindness la bonté incarnée.

epitomize /ɪˈpɪtəmaɪz/ vtr (embody) personnifier, incarner.

epoch /ˈiːpɒk, US ˈepək/ n époque f.

epoch-making adj [invention, event] marquant.

eponymous /ɪˈpɒnɪməs/ adj éponyme.

equable /ˈekwəbl/ adj [climate] tempéré; [temperament] égal.

equably /ˈekwəblɪ/ adv calmement.

equal /ˈiːkwəl/ **I** n égal/-e m/f.

　II adj 1 (same number, status, type) égal (to à); '~ work ~ pay' 'à travail égal salaire égal'; to fight for ~ pay lutter pour l'égalité des salaires; they're about ~ [candidates] ils se valent à peu près; on ~ terms [fight, compete] à armes égales; [judge, place] sur un pied d'égalité; 2 (up to) to be/feel ~ to être/ se sentir à la hauteur de; to feel ~ to doing se sentir à même de faire.

　III adv SPORT [finish] à égalité.

　IV vtr égaler.

　IDIOMS all things being ~ sauf imprévu.

equality /ɪˈkwɒlətɪ/ n égalité f; sexual ~ égalité des sexes.

equalize /ˈiːkwəlaɪz/ vtr, vi égaliser.

equalizer /ˈiːkwəlaɪzə(r)/ n 1 SPORT but m égalisateur; 2 AUDIO correcteur m de fréquence.

equally /ˈiːkwəlɪ/ adv [divide, share] en parts égales; ~ difficult/pretty tout aussi difficile/joli; ~, we might say that... de même, on pourrait dire que...

Equal Opportunities Commission, EOC n GB Commission f de l'égalité de traitement.

equal opportunity I equal opportunities npl égalité f des chances.

　II noun modifier [employer] appliquant la non-discrimination; [legislation] qui assure l'égalité d'accès.

equal: ~ **rights** npl égalité f des droits; ~s **sign** GB, ~ **sign** US n signe m égal.

equanimity /ˌekwəˈnɪmətɪ/ n sérénité f.

equate /ɪˈkweɪt/ vtr (identify) assimiler (with, to à); (compare) comparer (with, to à).

equation /ɪˈkweɪʒn/ n MATH équation f; FIG the other side of the ~ l'autre aspect du problème.

equator /ɪˈkweɪtə(r)/ n équateur m.

equatorial /ˌekwəˈtɔːrɪəl/ adj équatorial.

Equatorial Guinea pr n Guinée f équatoriale.

equestrian /ɪˈkwestrɪən/ adj [statue, portrait] équestre; [competition] hippique.

equidistant /ˌiːkwɪˈdɪstənt/ adj GEN à égale distance (from de).

equilateral /ˌiːkwɪˈlætərəl/ adj équilatéral.

equilibrium /ˌiːkwɪˈlɪbrɪəm/ n (pl **-riums** ou **-ria**) (all contexts) équilibre m; in ~ en équilibre.

equine /ˈekwaɪn/ adj [disease] équin; [species, features] chevalin.

equinox /ˈiːkwɪnɒks, ˈek-/ n équinoxe m.

equip /ɪˈkwɪp/ vtr (p prés etc **-pp-**) 1 LIT équiper (for pour); well ~ped with sth bien pourvu en qch; fully ~ped kitchen cuisine équipée; 2 FIG (psychologically) préparer; we were well ~ped to answer their questions nous étions à même de répondre à leurs questions.

equipment /ɪˈkwɪpmənt/ n IND, MIL, SPORT équipe-ment m; (office, electrical, photographic) matériel m; a piece ou item of ~ un article.

equitable /ˈekwɪtəbl/ adj équitable.

equity /ˈekwətɪ/ **I** n (fairness) équité f; FIN participation f.

　II **equities** npl FIN actions fpl ordinaires.

　III **Equity** pr n THEAT syndicat m des acteurs.

equity: ~ **capital** n FIN capital m en actions; ~ **financing** n FIN financement m par émission d'actions; ~ **market** n FIN marché m des actions.

equivalent /ɪˈkwɪvələnt/ **I** n équivalent m.

　II adj équivalent; ~ **to sth** équivalent à qch.

equivocal /ɪˈkwɪvəkl/ adj [words, attitude] équivoque [result] incertain; [behaviour, circumstances] suspect.

equivocate /ɪˈkwɪvəkeɪt/ vi user de faux-fuyants.

equivocation /ɪˌkwɪvəˈkeɪʃn/ n faux-fuyants mpl.

era /ˈɪərə/ n GEN ère f; (in politics, fashion etc) époque f.

eradicate /ɪˈrædɪkeɪt/ vtr GEN éliminer; éradiquer [disease].

eradication /ɪˌrædɪˈkeɪʃn/ n GEN élimination f; (o disease) éradication f.

erase /ɪˈreɪz, US ɪˈreɪs/ vtr 1 LIT, AUDIO, COMPUT effa cer; 2 FIG éliminer [poverty]; effacer [memory].

erase head n AUDIO, COMPUT tête f d'effacement.

eraser /ɪˈreɪzə(r), US -sər/ n (for paper) gomme f; (fo blackboard) brosse f feutrée.

eraser head n = **erase head**.

erasure /ɪˈreɪʒə(r)/ n (act) effacement m; (result) rature f.

erect /ɪˈrekt/ **I** adj [posture] droit; [tail, ears] dressé [construction] debout; [penis] en érection; with head ~ la tête haute; to hold oneself ~ se tenir droit.

　II vtr ériger [building]; monter [scaffolding, tent, sign screen]; FIG ériger [system].

erection /ɪˈrekʃn/ n 1 (of monument) érection f; (of build ing, bridge) construction f; (of tent) montage m; (of sign mise f en place; (of penis) érection f; 2 (edifice) édifice m.

ergonomics /ˌɜːɡəˈnɒmɪks/ n (+ v sg) ergonomie f.

Erie /ˈɪərɪ/ pr n Lake ~ le lac Érié.

Eritrea /ˌerɪˈtreɪə/ ▶ 840 | pr n Érythrée f.

ERM n: abrév ▶ **Exchange Rate Mechanism**.

ermine /ˈɜːmɪn/ n (animal, fur) hermine f.

erode /ɪˈrəʊd/ vtr LIT éroder; FIG saper.

erogenous /ɪˈrɒdʒənəs/ adj érogène.

erosion /ɪˈrəʊʒn/ n LIT, FIG érosion f.

erotic /ɪˈrɒtɪk/ adj érotique.

erotica /ɪˈrɒtɪkə/ npl LITERAT littérature f érotique CIN films mpl érotiques; ART art m érotique.

eroticism /ɪˈrɒtɪsɪzəm/ n érotisme m.

err /ɜː(r)/ vi 1 (make mistake) faire erreur; to ~ in one's judgment faire une erreur de jugement; 2 (stray) pécher; to ~ on the side of caution pécher par excès de prudence.

　IDIOMS to ~ is human PROV l'erreur est humaine.

errand /ˈerənd/ n commission f, course f; to go on ou to run an ~ for sb aller faire une commission pour qn; to send sb on an ~ envoyer qn faire une commission; ~ of mercy mission f de charité.

errant /ˈerənt/ adj [husband, wife] infidèle.

erratic /ɪˈrætɪk/ adj [behaviour, person, driver] imprévi sible; [performance] inégal; [moods] changeant; [move ments] désordonné; [timetable] fantaisiste; [deliveries irrégulier/-ière.

erroneous /ɪˈrəʊnɪəs/ adj erroné, faux/fausse.

erroneously /ɪˈrəʊnɪəslɪ/ adv à tort.

error /ˈerə(r)/ n (in spelling, grammar, typing) faute f MATH, COMPUT erreur f; in ~ par erreur; ~ of 10%, 10% ~ erreur de 10%; margin of ~ marge d'erreur.

　IDIOMS to see the ~ of one's ways revenir de ses erreurs.

ersatz /ˈeəzæts, ˈɜːsɑːts/ **I** n ersatz m, succédané m.

　II adj it's ~ **tobacco** c'est de l'ersatz de tabac.

erudite /'eru:daɪt/ adj [person] érudit; [book, discussion] savant.

erudition /ˌeru:'dɪʃn/ n érudition f.

erupt /ɪ'rʌpt/ vi **1** LIT entrer en éruption; MED apparaître; **2** FIG éclater.

eruption /ɪ'rʌpʃn/ n **1** (of volcano, rash) éruption f; **2** FIG (of violence, anger) explosion f; (of laughter) éclat m; (of political movement) apparition f.

escalate /'eskəleɪt/ **I** vtr intensifier [war, problem, efforts]; aggraver [inflation].
II vi [conflict, violence] s'intensifier; [prices] monter en flèche; [unemployment] augmenter rapidement.

escalation /ˌeskə'leɪʃn/ n (of violence, war) intensification f; (of prices, inflation) montée f en flèche.

escalator /'eskəleɪtə(r)/ n escalier m mécanique, escalator® m.

escapade /'eskəpeɪd, ˌeskə'peɪd/ n frasque f.

escape /ɪ'skeɪp/ **I** n **1** (of person) LIT évasion f, fuite f (from de; to vers); FIG fuite f; **to make good one's ~** réussir son évasion; **to make an** ou **one's ~** s'évader; **to have a narrow** ou **lucky ~** l'échapper belle; **2** (leak) fuite f (from de).
II vtr **1** (avoid) **to ~ death/danger** échapper à la mort/au danger; **to ~ defeat** éviter la défaite; **to ~ detection** [person] échapper aux recherches (de la police); [fault] ne pas être détecté; **we cannot ~ the fact that** on ne peut pas ignorer le fait que; **2** (elude) [name, fact] échapper à [person].
III vi **1** (get away) LIT [person] s'enfuir, s'évader; [animal] s'échapper (from de); FIG s'évader; **to ~ unharmed** s'en sortir indemne; **to ~ with one's life** s'en sortir vivant; **2** (leak) fuir.

escape: **~ chute** n AVIAT toboggan m; **~ clause** n JUR COMM clause f dérogatoire.

escapee /ɪˌskeɪ'pi:/ n évadé/-e m/f.

escape: **~ hatch** n NAUT sas m de secours; **~ road** n voie f de ralentissement d'urgence; **~ route** n (in case of fire etc) plan m d'évacuation; (for fugitives) itinéraire m d'évasion.

escapism /ɪ'skeɪpɪzəm/ n PÉJ (in literature, cinema etc) évasion f (du réel); (of person) refus m d'affronter la réalité.

escapologist /ˌeskə'pɒlədʒɪst/ ▶ 1251 n: artiste dont la spécialité est de se libérer de liens.

escarpment /ɪ'skɑ:pmənt/ n escarpement m.

eschew /ɪs'tʃu:/ vtr SOUT éviter [discussion, temptation]; rejeter [violence].

escort **I** /'eskɔ:t/ n **1** MIL, NAUT escorte f; **police ~** escorte de police; **armed ~** escorte de soldats; **to put under ~** placer sous escorte; **2** (companion) compagnon/compagne m/f; (to a dance) cavalier/-ière m/f; (in agency) hôtesse f.
II /'eskɔ:t/ noun modifier [duty, vessel] NAUT, MIL d'escorte; **~ agency** agence f d'hôtesses.
III /ɪ'skɔ:t/ vtr **1** MIL escorter; **to ~ sb in/out** faire entrer/sortir qn sous escorte; **2** (to a function) accompagner; (home) raccompagner.

Eskimo /'eskɪməʊ/ ▶ 1100, 1038 **I** n **1** (person) Esquimau/-aude m/f; **2** (language) esquimau m.
II adj esquimau/-aude.

ESL n: abrév ▶ **English as a Second Language**.

esophagus n US = **oesophagus**.

esoteric /ˌi:səʊ'terɪk, ˌe-/ adj ésotérique.

esp abrév écrite = **especially**.

ESP n **1** abrév ▶ **extrasensory perception**; **2** abrév ▶ **English for Special Purposes**.

especial /ɪ'speʃl/ adj SOUT exceptionnel/-elle; [benefit] particulier/-ière.

especially /ɪ'speʃəlɪ/ adv **1** (above all) surtout, en particulier; **him ~** lui en particulier; **~ as** d'autant plus que; **2** (on purpose) exprès, spécialement; **3** (unusually) particulièrement.

espionage /'espɪənɑ:ʒ/ n espionnage m.

espouse /ɪ'spaʊz/ vtr embrasser [cause].

espresso /e'spresəʊ/ n (pl **~s**) express m inv.

Esq GB (abrév écrite = **esquire**) (on letter) M.

essay /'eseɪ/ n SCH rédaction f (**on, about** sur); (extended) dissertation f (**on** sur); LITERAT essai m (**on** sur).

essence /'esns/ **I** n essence f; **it's the ~ of stupidity** c'est la stupidité même; **time is of the ~** la vitesse s'impose.
II in ~ adv phr essentiellement.

essential /ɪ'senʃl/ **I** n (quality) qualité f essentielle; (object) objet m indispensable.
II essentials npl **the ~s** l'essentiel m.
III adj **1** (vital) [services] de base; [role] essentiel/-ielle; [maintenance, ingredient] indispensable; **~ goods** produits de première nécessité; **it is ~** il est indispensable (**that** que (+ subj); **for sth** à qch; **to do** de faire); **2** (basic) [feature, element] essentiel/-ielle; [difference] fondamental; [reading] indispensable; [goodness, humility] intrinsèque.

essentially /ɪ'senʃəlɪ/ adv **1** (basically) essentiellement; **~, it's an old argument** en fait, c'est une vieille discussion; **2** (emphatic) (above all) avant tout; **3** (more or less) [correct, true] en gros.

est abrév écrite = **established**.

establish /ɪ'stæblɪʃ/ **I** vtr GEN établir; déterminer [cause]; fonder [company]; **to ~ that/whether** montrer que/si; **to ~ a reputation for oneself as** se faire connaître en tant que [singer, actor].
II v refl **to ~ oneself as a butcher** s'installer boucher; **to ~ oneself as a market leader** s'imposer comme leader du marché.

established /ɪ'stæblɪʃt/ adj établi; **a well ~ fact** un fait bien établi; **the ~ church** l'église d'État.

establishment /ɪ'stæblɪʃmənt/ **I** n **1** (process) instauration f; **2** (institution, organization) établissement m; **3** (shop, business) maison f.
II Establishment n GB **the Establishment** (ruling group) classe f dominante, establishment m; (social order) ordre m établi; **to become part of the Establishment** s'embourgeoiser; **the literary ~** l'establishment littéraire; **the legal ~** les institutions fpl judiciaires.

estate /ɪ'steɪt/ n **1** (stately home and park) domaine m, propriété f; **2** = **housing estate**; **3** (assets) biens mpl; **a large ~** une grande fortune; **4** GB = **estate car**.

estate: **~ agency** n GB agence f immobilière; **~ agent** n GB agent m immobilier; **~ car** n GB break m; **~ duty** n GB droits mpl de succession.

esteem /ɪ'sti:m/ n estime f; **to go up/down in sb's ~** remonter/baisser dans l'estime de qn.

esthete n US = **aesthete**.

estimate **I** /'estɪmət/ n **1** (assessment of size, quantity etc) estimation f; **the original ~** l'estimation de départ; **at a rough ~** très approximativement; **at a conservative ~** sans exagération; **2** COMM (quote) devis m; **to put in an ~** établir un devis.
II /'estɪmeɪt/ vtr évaluer [value, size, distance]; **to ~ that** estimer que.
III estimated pp adj [cost, figure] approximatif/-ive; **an ~ 300 people** environ 300 personnes.

estimated time of arrival, **ETA** n heure f d'arrivée prévue.

estimation /ˌestɪ'meɪʃn/ n **1** (esteem) estime f; **to go up/down in sb's ~** remonter/baisser dans l'estime de qn; **2** (judgment) opinion f; **in her ~** à son avis.

Estonia /ɪ'stəʊnɪə/ ▶ 840 pr n Estonie f.

estrange /ɪ'streɪndʒ/ **I** vtr brouiller (**from** avec).
II estranged pp adj **~d from sb** séparé de qn; **her ~d husband** son mari dont elle est/était séparée.

estrogen n US = **oestrogen**.

estuary /'estʃʊərɪ, US -ʊerɪ/ n estuaire m.

E Sussex n: abrév écrite = **East Sussex**.

ETA abrév ▶ **estimated time of arrival**.

et al (abrév = **et alii**) et autres; HUM et tutti quanti.

et cetera, etcetera /ɪt 'setərə, et-/ adv et cætera, et cetera.

etch /etʃ/ vtr graver [qch] à l'eau-forte; **~ed on her memory** FIG gravé dans sa mémoire.

etching /'etʃɪŋ/ n (picture) eau-forte f.

eternal /ɪ'tɜ:nl/ adj [life, salvation] éternel/-elle; [chatter, optimist] perpétuel/-elle; [recriminations] sempiternel/-elle PEJ (before n).

eternal triangle n triangle m classique, ~ ménage m à trois.

eternity /ɪ'tɜ:nətɪ/ n éternité f; **it seemed an ~ before he answered** il a mis une éternité à répondre.

ether /'i:θə(r)/ n éther m.

ethereal /ɪ'θɪərɪəl/ adj aérien/-ienne.

ethic /'eθɪk/ n éthique f.

ethical /'eθɪkl/ adj [problem, objection] moral; ~ **code** code m déontologique.

ethics /'eθɪks/ n **1** (+ v sg) PHILOS éthique f; **2** (+ v pl) (code of behaviour) moralité f; **professional** ~ déontologie f; **medical** ~ déontologie f médicale.

Ethiopia /,i:θɪ'əʊpɪə/ ▶ 840 pr n Éthiopie f.

ethnic /'eθnɪk/ adj [group, minority, music] ethnique; [clothes] inspiré du folklore (indien, africain etc).

ethnically /'eθnɪklɪ/ adv sur le plan ethnique.

ethnic cleansing n purification f ethnique.

ethnology /eθ'nɒlədʒɪ/ n ethnologie f.

ethos /'i:θɒs/ n (approach) philosophie f; **company** ~ philosophie de l'entreprise.

etiquette /'etɪket, -kət/ n **1** (social) bienséance f, étiquette f; **2** (professional, diplomatic) protocole m.

Etruscan /ɪ'trʌskən/ **I** n (person) Étrusque mf.
II adj étrusque.

etymology /,etɪ'mɒlədʒɪ/ n étymologie f.

EU (abrév = **European Union**) UE f.

eugenics /ju:'dʒenɪks/ n (+ v sg) eugénisme m.

eulogize /'ju:lədʒaɪz/ **I** vtr faire le panégyrique de.
II vi **to** ~ **over sth** faire le panégyrique de qch.

eulogy /'ju:lədʒɪ/ n GEN panégyrique m; RELIG éloge m funèbre.

eunuch /'ju:nək/ n eunuque m.

euphemism /'ju:fəmɪzəm/ n euphémisme m.

euphemistic /,ju:fə'mɪstɪk/ adj euphémique.

euphoria /ju:'fɔ:rɪə/ n euphorie f.

euphoric /ju:'fɒrɪk, US -'fɔ:r-/ adj euphorique.

Eurasian /jʊə'reɪʒn/ **I** n Eurasien/-ienne m/f.
II adj [people, region] eurasien/-ienne; [continent] eurasiatique.

EURATOM /'jʊərətɒm/ n (abrév = **European Atomic Energy Community**) EURATOM f.

eurhythmics GB, **eurythmics** US /ju:'rɪðmɪks/ n (+ v sg) gymnastique f rythmique.

Euro+ /'jʊərəʊ-/ combining form euro+.

eurobond /'jʊərəʊbɒnd/ n euro-obligation f.

eurocheque /'jʊərəʊtʃek/ n Eurochèque m; ~ **card** carte f Eurochèque.

eurocurrency /'jʊərəʊkʌrənsɪ/ n eurodevise f, euro-monnaie f; ~ **market** marché m des eurodevises.

eurodollar /'jʊərəʊdɒlə(r)/ n eurodollar m.

euromarket /'jʊərəʊmɑ:kɪt/ n marché m européen; **in the** ~ au sein du marché européen.

Euro-MP /jʊərəʊem'pi:/ n député m européen.

Europe /'jʊərəp/ ▶ 840 pr n Europe f; (EEC) le Marché commun.

European /jʊərə'pɪən/ **I** n Européen/-éenne m/f.
II adj européen/-éenne.

European: ~ **Atomic Energy Community**, **EAEC** n Communauté f Européenne de l'Énergie Atomique, CEEA; ~ **Bank for Reconstruction and Development**, **EBRD** n Banque f européenne pour la reconstruction et le développement, BERD f; ~ **Commission** n Commission f européenne; ~ **Court of Human Rights** n Cour f européenne des droits de l'homme; ~ **Court of Justice** n Cour f européenne de justice; ~ **Economic Community**, **EEC** n Communauté f économique européenne f, CEE; ~ **Free Trade Association**, **EFTA** n Association f européenne de libre-échange, AELE; ~ **Monetary System**, **EMS** système m monétaire européen, SME

m; ~ **Monetary Union** n Union f monétaire euro-péenne; ~ **Union**, **EU** Union f européenne, UE f.

eurosceptic /'jʊərəʊskeptɪk/ n GB eurosceptique mf.

eurythmics n US = **eurhythmics**.

euthanasia /,ju:θə'neɪzɪə, US -'neɪʒə/ n euthanasie f.

evacuate /ɪ'vækjʊert/ vtr évacuer.

evacuation /ɪ,vækjʊ'eɪʃn/ n évacuation f.

evacuee /ɪ,vækjʊ'i:/ n évacué/-e m/f.

evade /ɪ'veɪd/ vtr esquiver [blow]; éluder [question, problem]; fuir [responsibility]; échapper à [pursuer].

evaluate /ɪ'væljʊeɪt/ vtr GEN évaluer; mesurer [progress].

evaluation /ɪ,væljʊ'eɪʃn/ n (all contexts) évaluation f.

evangelical /,i:væn'dʒelɪkl/ adj évangélique.

evangelist /ɪ'vændʒəlɪst/ n (preacher) évangélisateur/-trice m/f.

evaporate /ɪ'væpəreɪt/ vi **1** [liquid] s'évaporer; **2** FIG [hopes, confidence] s'évaporer; [anger] se dissiper.

evaporated milk n lait m condensé non sucré.

evasion /ɪ'veɪʒn/ n **1** (of responsibility) dérobade f (of à); **tax** ~ évasion f fiscale; **2** (excuse) faux-fuyant m.

evasive /ɪ'veɪsɪv/ adj GEN évasif/-ive; [look] fuyant; **to take** ~ **action** LIT changer de cap pour éviter un accident; FIG esquiver la difficulté.

eve /i:v/ n veille f; **on the** ~ **of** à la veille de.

even[1] /'i:vn/

■ **Note** even can always be translated by même when it is used to express surprise or for emphasis. For examples and other uses, see below.

I adv **1** (showing surprise) même; **he didn't** ~ **try** il n'a même pas essayé; **without** ~ **apologizing** sans même s'excuser; **2** (emphasizing point) même; **I can't** ~ **swim, never mind dive** je ne sais même pas nager, encore moins plonger; **don't tell anyone, not** ~ **Bob** ne dis rien à personne, pas même à Bob; ~ **if/when/now** même si/quand/maintenant; **3** (with comparative) encore; ~ **colder** encore plus froid; **4** SOUT ~ **as I watched** alors même que je le regardais.

II **even so** adv phr quand même; **it was interesting** ~ **so** c'était quand même intéressant.

III **even then** adv phr (at that time) même à ce moment-là; (all the same) de toute façon.

IV **even though** conj phr bien que (+ subj).

even[2] /'i:vn/ adj [surface, voice, temper, contest] égal; [teeth, hemline] régulier/-ière; [temperature] constant; [distribution] équitable; [number] pair; **we're** ~ nous sommes quittes; **to get** ~ **with sb** rendre à qn la monnaie de sa pièce; **to be** ~ [competitors] être à égalité; **I'll give you** ~ **odds** OU **money that** il y a une chance sur deux que (+ subj).

■ **even out**: ¶ ~ **out** [differences] s'atténuer; ¶ ~ [sth] **out**, ~ **out** [sth] répartir [distribution]; réduire [inequalities].

■ **even up**: ~ [sth] **up**, ~ **up** [sth] équilibrer [contest]; **it will** ~ **things up** ce sera plus équilibré.

even-handed adj impartial.

evening /'i:vnɪŋ/ ▶ 812 **I** n **1** soir m; (with emphasis on duration) soirée f; **in the** ~ le soir; **during the** ~ pendant la soirée; **6 o'clock in the** ~ six heures du soir; **this** ~ ce soir; **later this** ~ plus tard dans la soirée; **tomorrow/yesterday** ~ demain/hier soir; **on the** ~ **of the 14th** le 14 au soir; **on Friday** ~ vendredi soir; **on the following** OU **next** ~ le lende-main soir; **the previous** ~, **the** ~ **before** la veille au soir; **every** ~ tous les soirs; **every Thursday** ~ tous les jeudis soir; **all** ~ toute la soirée; **what do you do in the** ~**s?** qu'est-ce que tu fais le soir?; **let's have an** ~ **in** passons la soirée à la maison; **to work** ~**s** travailler le soir; **to be on** ~**s** être du soir; **2** musical ~ soirée musicale.
II noun modifier [bag, shoe] habillé; [meal, newspaper, walk] du soir.

evening class n cours m du soir.

evening dress n **1** (formal clothes) tenue f de soirée; **2** (gown) robe f de soirée.

evening: ~ **performance** n représentation f en

soirée; ~ **primrose** n onagre f; ~ **shift** n équipe f du soir; ~ **star** n étoile f du berger.

evenly /'iːvnlɪ/ adv **1** [spread, apply] uniformément; [breathe] régulièrement; [divide] en parts égales; ~ **matched** de force égale; **2** (placidly) [say] posément.

event /ɪ'vent/ n **1** (incident) événement m; **unable to control** ~s incapable de contrôler la situation; **in the normal course of** ~s si tout va bien; **2** (eventuality) cas m; **in the** ~ **of** en cas de; **in the unlikely** ~ **that** au cas improbable où; **in either** ~ en tout cas; **in the** ~ GB (as things turned out) en l'occurrence; **in any** ~, **at all** ~s de toute façon; **3** (occasion) **social** ~ événement m mondain; **quite an** ~ un événement; **4** (in athletics) épreuve f; **field/track** ~ épreuve f d'athlétisme/de vitesse.

even-tempered adj d'une humeur égale.

eventful /ɪ'ventfl/ adj mouvementé.

eventing /ɪ'ventɪŋ/ n GB concours m complet.

eventual /ɪ'ventʃʊəl/ adj [aim, hope] à long terme; [outcome, decision, success] final.

eventuality /ɪˌventʃʊ'ælɪtɪ/ n éventualité f.

eventually /ɪ'ventʃʊəlɪ/ adv finalement; **to do sth** ~ finir par faire qch.

ever /'evə(r)/ **I** adv **1** (at any time) **nothing was** ~ **said** rien n'a jamais été dit; **no-one will** ~ **forget** personne ne l'oubliera jamais; **I can't say I** ~ **noticed it** je ne l'ai jamais remarqué; **rarely, if** ~ rarement sinon jamais; **hardly** ~ rarement, presque jamais; **something I would never** ~ **do** quelque chose que je ne ferais jamais de ma vie; **has he** ~ **lived abroad?** est-ce qu'il a déjà vécu à l'étranger?; **do you** ~ **make mistakes?** est-ce qu'il t'arrive de te tromper?; **if** ~ si jamais; **she's a liar if** ~ **I saw one** ou **if** ~ **there was one!** c'est une menteuse ou je ne m'y connais pas!; **2** (when making comparisons) **more beautiful than** ~ plus beau/belle que jamais; **it's windier than** ~ **today** il y a encore plus de vent aujourd'hui; **more than** ~ **before** plus que jamais; **there are more working women than** ~ **before** les femmes n'ont jamais été aussi nombreuses à travailler; **he's happier than he's** ~ **been** il n'a jamais été aussi heureux; **the worst mistake I** ~ **made** la pire erreur que j'aie jamais faite; **the last time anyone** ~ **saw him** la dernière fois qu'on l'a vu; **the first** ~ le tout premier; **3** (at all times, always) toujours; ~ **hopeful** toujours plein d'espérance; **as cheerful as** ~ toujours aussi gai; **the same as** ~ toujours le même; **they lived happily** ~ **after** ils vécurent toujours heureux; ~ **the diplomat** l'éternel diplomate; **yours** ~ (in letter) bien à toi or à vous; **4** (expressing anger, irritation) **don't (you)** ~ **do that again!** ne refais jamais ça!; **if you** ~ **speak to me like that again** si jamais tu me reparles sur ce ton; **do you** ~ **think about anyone else?** ça ne t'arrive jamais de penser à quelqu'un d'autre?; **that's the last time he** ~ **comes here!** c'est la dernière fois qu'il vient ici!; **have you** ~ **heard/seen anything like it?** as-tu jamais entendu/vu rien de pareil?; **that's all he** ~ **does!** c'est tout ce qu'il sait faire!; **5** (expressing surprise) **why** ~ **not?** GB pourquoi pas?; **who** ~ **would have guessed?** qui donc aurait deviné?; **6** GB (very) ~ **so si**; ~ **so glad** si heureux/-euse; ~ **so slightly damp** très légèrement humide; **thanks** ~ **so much!** merci mille fois!; **he's** ~ **so much better** il va beaucoup mieux; **it's** ~ **such a shame!** c'est vraiment dommage!; **7**° (in exclamations) **is he** ~ **dumb!** ce qu'il peut être bête!; **am I** ~ **glad to see you!** qu'est-ce que je suis content de te voir!; **do I** ~**!** (emphatic yes) et comment!

II ever- combining form ~**-growing** ou **-increasing** toujours croissant; ~**-present** toujours présent; ~**-changing** qui évolue sans cesse.

III as ever adv phr comme toujours.

IV ever more adv phr de plus en plus.

V ever since adv phr, conj phr depuis; ~ **since we arrived** depuis notre arrivée.

evergreen /'evəɡriːn/ **I** n **1** (tree) arbre m à feuilles persistantes; **2** (song) chanson f de toujours.

II adj (épith) **1** [tree] à feuilles persistantes; **2** (popular) [song, programme] toujours populaire.

everlasting /ˌevə'lɑːstɪŋ, US -'læst-/ adj éternel/-elle.

every /'evrɪ/

■ **Note** every is most frequently translated by tous les/toutes les + plural noun: every day = tous les jours. When every is emphasized to mean every single, it can also be translated by chaque. For examples and exceptions, see the entry below.

I det **1** (each) ~ **house in the street** toutes les maisons de la rue; ~ **time I go there** chaque fois que j'y vais; **I've read** ~ **one of his books** j'ai lu tous ses livres; **that goes for** ~ **one of you!** c'est valable pour tout le monde!; **I enjoyed** ~ **minute of it** chaque minute a été un plaisir; **he spent** ~ **last penny** il a dépensé jusqu'au dernier sou; ~ **second day** tous les deux jours; **there are three women for** ~ **ten men** il y a trois femmes pour dix hommes; **from** ~ **side** de toutes parts; **in** ~ **way** (from every point of view) à tous les égards; (using every method) par tous les moyens; **2** (emphatic) **there is** ~ **chance that** il y a toutes les chances que; ~ **right to complain** tous les droits de se plaindre; **I wish you** ~ **success** je vous souhaite beaucoup de succès; ~ **bit as much as** tout autant que; **3** (indicating frequency) ~ **day/Thursday** tous les jours/jeudis; **once** ~ **few days** tous les deux ou trois jours; ~ **20 kilometres** tous les 20 kilomètres.

II every other adj phr (alternate) ~ **other day** tous les deux jours; ~ **other Sunday** un dimanche sur deux.

IDIOMS ~ **now and then,** ~ **now and again,** ~ **so often,** ~ **once in a while** de temps en temps; ~ **man for himself!** (in fight to succeed) chacun pour soi!; (abandoning ship etc) sauve qui peut!; ~ **which way** dans tous les sens.

everybody /'evrɪbɒdɪ/ pron tout le monde; ~ **else** tous les autres; ~ **knows that** tout le monde le sait; ~ **who is anybody** tous les gens importants.

everyday /'evrɪdeɪ/ adj [activity, routine] quotidien/-ienne; [clothes] de tous les jours; **in** ~ **use** d'usage courant.

everyone /'evrɪwʌn/ pron = **everybody**.

everyplace° /'evrɪpleɪs/ adv US = **everywhere**.

everything /'evrɪθɪŋ/

■ **Note** everything is almost always translated by tout. For examples and particular usages, see below.

pron tout; **is** ~ **all right?** est-ce que tout va bien?; **don't believe** ~ **you hear** il ne faut pas croire tout ce que tu entends; ~ **else** tout le reste; **money isn't** ~ l'argent n'est pas tout; **he's got** ~ **going for him** il a tout pour lui; **she meant** ~ **to him** elle était tout pour lui; **have you got your papers and** ~**?** est-ce que vous avez vos papiers et tout le reste?

everywhere /'evrɪweə(r), US -hweər/ adv partout; ~ **else** partout ailleurs; ~ **I go** partout où je vais; **she's been** ~ elle a voyagé partout.

evict /ɪ'vɪkt/ vtr expulser (**from** de).

eviction /ɪ'vɪkʃn/ n expulsion f (**from** de).

evidence /'evɪdəns/ n **1** (proof) ¢ preuves fpl (**that** que; **of, for** de; **against** contre); **a piece of** ~ une preuve; **there is no** ~ **that** rien ne prouve que; **all the** ~ **suggests that...** tout indique que...; **the** ~ **of one's own eyes** ce qu'on a vu de ses propres yeux; **2** (testimony) témoignage m (**from** de); **convicted on the** ~ **of sb** condamné sur le témoignage de qn; **to be used in** ~ **against sb** servir de témoignage contre qn; **to give** ~ témoigner, déposer (**for sb** en faveur de qn; **against sb** contre qn); **3** (trace) trace f (**of** de); **to be (much) in** ~ être (bien) visible.

evident /'evɪdənt/ adj [anger, relief] manifeste; **it is** ~ **that** il est évident que.

evidently /'evɪdəntlɪ/ adv **1** (apparently) apparemment; **2** (patently) manifestement.

evil /'iːvl/ n **1** ¢ ~ le mal; **2** (bad thing) mal m; **the** ~**s of racism** les maux du racisme.

II *adj* [*person, forces, genius*] malfaisant; [*act, intent*] diabolique; [*spirit*] maléfique; [*smell*] nauséabond.
IDIOMS **to give sb the ~ eye** jeter le mauvais œil à qn; **the lesser of two ~s** le moindre mal; **money is the root of all ~** l'argent est la source de tous les maux; **to put off the ~ hour** ou **day** repousser le moment fatidique.

evil-smelling *adj* nauséabond.

evocative /ɪ'vɒkətɪv/ *adj* évocateur/-trice.

evoke /ɪ'vəʊk/ *vtr* **1** évoquer [*memory*]; **2** susciter [*response*].

evolution /ˌiːvə'luːʃn/ *n* évolution *f* (**from** à partir de).

evolutionary /ˌiːvə'luːʃənərɪ, US -nerɪ/ *adj* évolutionniste.

evolve /ɪ'vɒlv/ **I** *vtr* élaborer [*system, policy*].
II *vi* évoluer; **to ~ from** [*theory*] se développer à partir de; [*species*] descendre de.

ewe /juː/ *n* brebis *f*; **~ lamb** agnelle *f*.

ex /eks/ **I**○ *n* (former partner) ex○ *mf*.
II *prep* COMM **~ works/factory** [*price*] départ usine.
III **ex+** *combining form* **~-wife/-husband** ex-mari/-femme.

exacerbate /ɪg'zæsəbeɪt/ *vtr* aggraver.

exact /ɪg'zækt/ **I** *adj* GEN exact; [*moment*] précis; **it's the ~ opposite** c'est exactement le contraire; **tell me your ~ whereabouts** dis-moi où tu te trouves exactement; **those were her ~ words** voilà exactement ce qu'elle a dit; **it was in the summer, July to be ~** c'était en été, plus précisément en juillet.
II *vtr* exiger (**from** de).

exacting /ɪg'zæktɪŋ/ *adj* astreignant.

exactly /ɪg'zæktlɪ/ *adv* exactement; **my sentiments ~!** exactement!; **what ~ were you doing?** que faisais-tu au juste?; **she wasn't ~ overjoyed** IRON elle n'était pas précisément ravie.

exaggerate /ɪg'zædʒəreɪt/ **I** *vtr* GEN exagérer; (in one's own mind) s'exagérer [*problem, effect*].
II *vi* exagérer.

exaggerated /ɪg'zædʒəreɪtɪd/ *adj* exagéré; **he has an ~ sense of his own importance** il se fait une idée exagérée de son importance.

exaggeration /ɪɡˌzædʒə'reɪʃn/ *n* exagération *f*; **it's no ~ to say that…** on peut dire sans exagération que…

exalted /ɪg'zɔːltɪd/ *adj* SOUT **1** (elevated) [*rank, position*] élevé, haut; [*person*] haut placé; **2** (jubilant) exalté.

exam /ɪg'zæm/ *n* examen *m*; ▶ **examination** I 1, II.

examination /ɪɡˌzæmɪ'neɪʃn/ **I** *n* **1** examen *m* (in de); **French ~** examen *m* de français; **to take/pass an ~** passer/réussir un examen; **2** (inspection) examen *m*; on ~ après examen; **under ~** à l'examen; **to have an ~** MED passer un examen médical; **3** (of accused, witness) interrogatoire *m*.
II *noun modifier* [*question, results*] d'examen; [*candidate*] à un examen.

examination paper *n* sujets *mpl* d'examen.

examine /ɪg'zæmɪn/ *vtr* **1** (intellectually) considérer [*facts*]; examiner [*evidence*]; étudier [*question*]; **2** (visually) GEN examiner; fouiller [*luggage*]; **3** SCH, UNIV **to be ~d in maths** passer un examen en math; **4** interroger [*prisoner*].
IDIOMS **you need your head ~d**○! tu devrais te faire soigner○!

examinee /ɪɡˌzæmɪ'niː/ *n* candidat/-e *m/f*.

examiner /ɪg'zæmɪnə(r)/ *n* examinateur/-trice *m/f*.

example /ɪg'zɑːmpl, US -'zæmpl/ *n* exemple *m*; **for ~** par exemple; **to set a good ~** donner l'exemple; **he's an ~ to us all** c'est notre modèle à tous; **you're setting a bad ~** tu ne donnes pas le bon exemple; **to make an ~ of sb** punir qn pour l'exemple.

exasperate /ɪg'zæspəreɪt/ *vtr* exaspérer; **to get ~d** s'énerver.

exasperation /ɪɡˌzæspə'reɪʃn/ *n* exaspération *f*.

excavate /'ekskəveɪt/ **I** *vtr* fouiller [*site*]; creuser [*tunnel*].
II *vi* faire des fouilles.

excavation /ˌekskə'veɪʃn/ **I** *n* excavation *f*.
II excavations *npl* fouilles *fpl*.

excavator /'ekskəveɪtə(r)/ *n* (machine) excavateur *m*; (person) fouilleur/-euse *m/f*.

exceed /ɪk'siːd/ *vtr* outrepasser [*functions, authority*]; dépasser [*speed limit, credit limit*] (**by** de); **to ~ all expectations** dépasser toute attente; **do not ~ the speed limit** respecter les limitations de vitesse.

exceedingly /ɪk'siːdɪŋlɪ/ *adv* extrêmement.

excel /ɪk'sel/ **I** *vi* exceller (**at, in** en; **at** ou **in doing** à faire).
II *v refl* **to ~ oneself** se surpasser ALSO IRON.

excellence /'eksələns/ *n* excellence *f*.

Excellency /'eksələnsɪ/ *n* Excellence *f*.

excellent /'eksələnt/ **I** *adj* excellent.
II *excl* parfait!

except /ɪk'sept/

■ **Note** There are four frequently used translations for *except* when used as a preposition. By far the most frequent of these is *sauf*; the others are *excepté*, *à l'exception de* and *hormis*. Note, however, that in *what/where/who* questions, *except* is translated by *sinon*. For examples and the phrase *except for* see below.

I *prep* **everybody ~ Lisa** tout le monde sauf Lisa, tout le monde à l'exception de ou excepté or hormis Lisa; **nothing ~** rien d'autre que; **nobody ~** personne d'autre que; **~ if/when** sauf si/quand; **~ that** sauf que, si ce n'est que; **who could have done it ~ him?** qui aurait pu le faire sinon lui?
II except for *prep phr* à part, à l'exception de.
III *vtr* excepter; **~ing** à l'exception de; **present company ~ed** exception faite des personnes présentes.

exception /ɪk'sepʃn/ *n* **1** (special case) exception *f* (**for** pour); **with the (possible) ~ of** à l'exception (peut-être) de; **the only ~ being** à la seule exception de; **with some** ou **certain ~s** à quelques exceptions près; **to make an ~** faire une exception; **there can be no ~s** il n'y aura pas d'exception; **the ~ proves the rule** c'est l'exception qui confirme la règle; **2 to take ~ to** (be offended by) s'offusquer de.

exceptional /ɪk'sepʃənl/ *adj* exceptionnel/-elle.

excerpt /'eksɜːpt/ *n* extrait *m*.

excess /ɪk'ses/ **I** *n* **1** GEN excès *m* (**of** de); **to eat to ~** faire des excès de table, trop manger; **carried to ~** poussé à l'excès; **to be (far) in ~ of** dépasser (largement); **2** GB (insurance) franchise *f*.
II *adj* **~ alcohol/weight** excès *m* d'alcool/de poids; **drain off the ~ water** égoutter l'excédent d'eau.

excess baggage *n* excédent *m* de bagages.

excessive /ɪk'sesɪv/ *adj* GEN excessif/-ive.

excess: **~ luggage** *n* GB = **excess baggage**; **~ postage** *n* surtaxe *f* postale; **~ profits** *npl* superbénéfices *mpl*.

exchange /ɪks'tʃeɪndʒ/ **I** *n* **1** (swap) échange *m*; **in ~** en échange (**for** de); **2** COMM, FIN change *m*; **the rate of ~** le taux de change; **bill of ~** lettre *f* de change; **3** (discussion) discussion *f*; (in parliament) débat *m*; **a heated ~** une discussion houleuse; **4** (visit) échange *m*; **~ visit** voyage *m* d'échange; **5** TELECOM (also **telephone ~**) central *m* (téléphonique).
II *vtr* échanger (**for** contre; **with** avec); **to ~ contracts** COMM JUR signer le contrat de vente; **they ~d hostages** ils ont échangé leurs otages.

exchangeable: **~ disk** *n* COMPUT disque *m* amovible; **~ disk storage, EDS** *n* COMPUT unité *f* de disques à chargeur.

exchange: **~ control** *n* contrôle *m* des changes; **~ controls** *npl* mesures *fpl* de contrôle des changes; **~ rate** *n* taux *m* de change; **Exchange Rate Mechanism, ERM** *n* système *m* monétaire européen.

Exchequer /ɪksˈtʃekə(r)/ *pr n* GB POL the ~ l'Échiquier *m*, le ministère des finances.

excise I /ˈeksaɪz/ *n* (also **excise duty**) excise *f*, taxe *f*. II /ɪkˈsaɪz/ *vtr* **1** MED exciser; **2** (from text) supprimer.

excitable /ɪkˈsaɪtəbl/ *adj* nerveux/-euse.

excite /ɪkˈsaɪt/ *vtr* **1** GEN exciter; (fire with enthusiasm) enthousiasmer; **2** (give rise to) susciter [*interest, controversy*]; éveiller [*curiosity, suspicion*]; faire naître [*envy*].

excited /ɪkˈsaɪtɪd/ *adj* [*person, crowd, animal*] excité; [*voice, conversation*] animé; **to be ~ about sth** (enthusiastic) s'enthousiasmer pour qch; (in anticipation) être emballé° à l'idée de qch; **to get ~** s'exciter; **don't get ~!** (cross) ne t'énerve pas!

excitedly /ɪkˈsaɪtɪdlɪ/ *adv* avec animation.

excitement /ɪkˈsaɪtmənt/ *n* (emotion) excitation *f*; **what ~!** quelle émotion!; **in the ~** dans l'agitation générale; **to cause great ~** faire sensation; **he was in a state of great ~** il était tout excité.

exciting /ɪkˈsaɪtɪŋ/ *adj* GEN passionnant; **an ~ new acting talent** un acteur qui promet.

excl. *abrév* = **excluding**.

exclaim /ɪkˈskleɪm/ *vtr* s'exclamer.

exclamation /ˌekskləˈmeɪʃn/ *n* exclamation *f*.

exclamation mark, exclamation point US *n* point *m* d'exclamation.

exclude /ɪkˈskluːd/ *vtr* exclure [*person, group*] (**from** de); ne pas inclure [*name*] (**from** dans); exclure [*issue, possibility*] (**from** de).

excluding /ɪkˈskluːdɪŋ/ *prep* à l'exclusion de; **~ VAT** TVA non comprise.

exclusion /ɪkˈskluːʒn/ *n* exclusion *f* (**from** de).

exclusion zone *n* zone *f* interdite.

exclusive /ɪkˈskluːsɪv/ I *n* (report) exclusivité *f*. II *adj* **1** [*club, social circle*] fermé; [*hotel*] de luxe; [*school, district*] huppé; **2** [*story, coverage, rights*] exclusif/-ive; [*interview*] en exclusivité; **~ to Harrods** une exclusivité de Harrods; **to have ~ use of** avoir l'usage exclusif de; **to be mutually ~** s'exclure mutuellement; **~ of meals** les repas non compris.

exclusively /ɪkˈskluːsɪvlɪ/ *adv* exclusivement.

excommunicate /ˌekskəˈmjuːnɪkeɪt/ *vtr* excommunier.

excrement /ˈekskrɪmənt/ *n* excrément *m*.

excrete /ɪkˈskriːt/ *vtr* [*animal, human*] excréter; [*plant*] exsuder.

excretion /ɪkˈskriːʃn/ *n* (of animal, human) excrétion *f*; (of plant) exsudation *f*.

excruciating /ɪkˈskruːʃɪeɪtɪŋ/ *adj* **1** [*pain*] atroce; **2**° (awful) exécrable.

excruciatingly° /ɪkˈskruːʃɪeɪtɪŋlɪ/ *adv* [*boring*] mortellement; **~ funny** à mourir de rire.

excursion /ɪkˈskɜːʃn/ *n* (organized) excursion *f*; (casual) promenade *f*.

excuse I /ɪkˈskjuːs/ *n* (self-justification) excuse *f*; (pretext) prétexte *m* (**for sth** à qch; **for doing** pour faire; **to do** pour faire); **to make ~s** trouver des excuses; **to be an ~ to do** ou **for doing** servir de prétexte pour faire; **I have a good ~** j'ai une bonne excuse; **an ~ to leave early** un bon prétexte pour partir tôt; **is that the best ~ you can come up with?** c'est tout ce que tu as trouvé comme excuse?; **any ~ will do!** toutes les excuses sont bonnes!; **there's no ~ for such behaviour** ce genre de conduite est inexcusable; **that's no ~** ce n'est pas une excuse ou une raison. II /ɪkˈskjuːz/ *vtr* **1** (forgive) excuser [*person*] (**for doing** de faire, d'avoir fait); **~ me!** (bumping into sb) excusez-moi!, pardon!; (beginning an inquiry, making polite correction) excusez-moi; (making angry correction) je regrette, mais; (not hearing properly) pardon?; **may I be ~d?** GB EUPH est-ce que je peux aller aux toilettes?; **2** (justify) justifier [*intervention, procedure*]; excuser [*person*]; **3** (exempt) dispenser (**from sth** de qch; **from doing** de faire).

ex-directory /ˌeksdaɪˈrektərɪ, -dɪ-/ *adj* GB sur la liste rouge.

exec° /ɪkˈzek/ *n* US (*abrév* = **executive**) cadre *m*.

execrable /ˈeksɪkrəbl/ *adj* SOUT exécrable.

execute /ˈeksɪkjuːt/ *vtr* exécuter.

execution /ˌeksɪˈkjuːʃn/ *n* **1** (killing) exécution *f* (**by** par); **2** (of plan, task) exécution *f*; (by musician) interprétation *f*; **in the ~ of his duty** dans l'exercice *m* de ses fonctions; **3** COMPUT exécution *f*.

executioner /ˌeksɪˈkjuːʃənə(r)/ *n* bourreau *m*.

executive /ɪgˈzekjʊtɪv/ I *n* **1** (administrator) COMM cadre *m*; (in Civil Service) cadre *m* administratif; **sales ~** cadre *m* commercial; **top ~** cadre *m* supérieur; **2** (committee) exécutif *m*, comité *m* exécutif; **party/trade union ~** bureau *m* du parti/du syndicat; **3** US **the ~** le pouvoir exécutif. II *adj* **1** (administrative) [*power, committee*] exécutif/-ive; [*status*] de cadre; **2** (luxury) [*chair*] directorial.

executive: **~ council** *n* (of company) conseil *m* de direction; (of trade union, political party) commission *f* exécutive; **~ director** *n* directeur/-trice *m/f* exécutif/-ive ; **~ jet** *n* jet *m* privé; **~ producer** *n* CIN producteur *m* en chef or exécutif; **~ program** *n* COMPUT superviseur *m*; **~ secretary** *n* ADMIN secrétaire *m* exécutif; (manager's secretary) secrétaire *mf* de direction; **~ session** *n* séance *f* parlementaire à huis clos; **~ toy** *n* gadget *m* (*pour se calmer les nerfs*).

executor /ɪgˈzekjʊtə(r)/ *n* JUR exécuteur *m* testamentaire.

exemplary /ɪgˈzemplərɪ, US -lerɪ/ *adj* [*behaviour, life*] exemplaire; [*student*] modèle.

exemplify /ɪgˈzemplɪfaɪ/ *vtr* illustrer, exemplifier.

exempt /ɪgˈzempt/ I *adj* exempt (**from** de). II *vtr* exempter [*person*] (**from sth** de qch).

exemption /ɪgˈzempʃn/ *n* exemption *f* (**from** de); (from exam) dispense *f* (**from** de); **tax ~** dégrèvement *m* d'impôts.

exercise /ˈeksəsaɪz/ I *n* **1** (planned activity) opération *f*; (long-term or large-scale) stratégie *f*; **it was an academic ~** c'était pour la beauté de la chose; **public relations ~** campagne *f* de relations publiques; **an ~ in diplomacy** un exercice de diplomatie; **2** ¢ (exertion) exercice *m*; **3** (training task) exercice *m*; **maths ~** exercice de maths; **4** (of duties, rights, power) exercice *m* (**of** de); **5** MIL manœuvres *fpl*; **to go on an ~** ou **on ~s** partir en manœuvres. II *vtr* **1** (apply) faire preuve de [*caution, control, restraint*]; exercer [*power, right*]; **2** (train) exercer [*body, mind*]; faire travailler [*limb, muscles*]; promener [*dog*]; sortir [*horse*]; **3** (worry) préoccuper. III *vi* faire de l'exercice.

exercise: **~ bicycle** *n* (in gym) vélo *m* d'entraînement; (at home) vélo *m* d'appartement; **~ book** *n* cahier *m*.

exert /ɪgˈzɜːt/ I *vtr* exercer [*pressure, influence*] (**on** sur); employer [*force*]. II *v refl* **to ~ oneself** se fatiguer.

exertion /ɪgˈzɜːʃn/ *n* (physical effort) effort *m*.

ex gratia /ˌeks ˈgreɪʃə/ *adj* [*award, payment*] à titre gracieux.

exhale /eksˈheɪl/ I *vtr* [*person*] expirer; [*chimney*] dégager. II *vi* [*person*] expirer.

exhaust /ɪgˈzɔːst/ I *n* AUT **1** (pipe) pot *m* d'échappement; **2** (fumes) gaz *mpl* d'échappement. II *noun modifier* [*fumes, pipe, system*] d'échappement. III *vtr* épuiser; **~ed** épuisé.

exhaustion /ɪgˈzɔːstʃn/ *n* épuisement *m*.

exhaustive /ɪgˈzɔːstɪv/ *adj* [*bibliography, list*] exhaustif/-ive; [*analysis, description, coverage*] très détaillé; [*investigation, research*] approfondi.

exhibit /ɪgˈzɪbɪt/ I *n* **1** œuvre *f* exposée; **2** US (exhibition) exposition *f*; **a Gauguin ~** une exposition Gauguin; **3** JUR pièce *f* à conviction; **~ A** pièce à conviction numéro un. II *vtr* (display) exposer [*work of art*]; manifester [*preference, sign*].

exhibition /ˌeksɪˈbɪʃn/ I *n* **1** (of art, goods) exposition *f*; **art ~** exposition; **the Picasso ~** l'exposition

Picasso; **to be on ~** être exposé; **to make an ~ of oneself** PÉJ se donner en spectacle; **2** (of skill) démonstration *f*; **3** GB UNIV bourse *f* d'études.

II *noun modifier* [*catalogue, hall, stand*] d'exposition.

exhibition centre GB, **exhibition center** US *n* palais *m* des expositions.

exhibitionist /ˌeksɪˈbɪʃənɪst/ *n, adj* exhibitionniste (*mf*).

exhibitor /ɪɡˈzɪbɪtə(r)/ *n* exposant/-e *m*/*f*.

exhilarate /ɪɡˈzɪləreɪt/ *vtr* [*atmosphere, music, speed*] griser; **to feel ~d** être tout joyeux/toute joyeuse.

exhilarating /ɪɡˈzɪləreɪtɪŋ/ *adj* [*game*] stimulant; [*experience*] exaltant; [*music*] grisant; [*speed*] enivrant.

exhilaration /ɪɡˌzɪləˈreɪʃn/ *n* joie *f* intense.

exhume /eksˈhjuːm, US ɪɡˈzuːm/ *vtr* exhumer.

exile /ˈeksaɪl/ **I** *n* **1** (person) exilé/-e *m*/*f*; **2** (expulsion) exil *m* (**from** de); **in ~** en exil; **to go into ~** partir en exil.

II *vtr* exiler (**de** from); **to ~ for life** exiler à vie.

exist /ɪɡˈzɪst/ *vi* **1** (be) exister; **2** (survive) survivre; **3** (live) vivre; **to ~ on a diet of potatoes** ne vivre que de pommes de terre.

existence /ɪɡˈzɪstəns/ *n* existence *f* (**of** de); **the largest plane in ~** le plus grand avion qui existe; **I wasn't aware of its ~** je ne connaissais pas son existence; **to come into ~** naître.

existential /ˌeɡzɪˈstenʃl/ *adj* existentiel/-ielle.

existentialism /ˌeɡzɪˈstenʃəlɪzəm/ *n* existentialisme *m*.

existing /ɪɡˈzɪstɪŋ/ *adj* [*laws, order*] existant; [*policy, management, leadership*] actuel/-elle.

exit /ˈeksɪt/ **I** *n* sortie *f*; **'no ~'** 'interdit'; **to make a quick** ou **hasty ~** s'éclipser.

II *vi* sortir.

exit: **~ point** *n* COMPUT point *m* de sortie; **~ sign** *n* panneau *m* (de) sortie; **~ visa** *n* visa *m* de sortie.

exodus /ˈeksədəs/ *n* exode *m*.

ex officio /ˌeks əˈfɪʃɪəʊ/ *adj* [*member*] de droit.

exonerate /ɪɡˈzɒnəreɪt/ *vtr* disculper.

exorbitant /ɪɡˈzɔːbɪtənt/ *adj* exorbitant.

exorbitantly /ɪɡˈzɔːbɪtəntlɪ/ *adv* [*tax*] de façon excessive; [*expensive*] excessivement.

exorcism /ˈeksɔːsɪzəm/ *n* exorcisme *m*.

exorcist /ˈeksɔːsɪst/ *n* exorciste *mf*.

exorcize /ˈeksɔːsaɪz/ *vtr* exorciser [*demon, memory*].

exotic /ɪɡˈzɒtɪk/ *adj* exotique.

exotica /ɪɡˈzɒtɪkə/ *n* objets *mpl* exotiques.

expand /ɪkˈspænd/ **I** *vtr* **1** GEN développer; élargir [*horizon, knowledge*]; accroître [*production, workforce*]; étendre [*empire*]; gonfler [*lungs*]; **2** MATH, COMPUT développer.

II *vi* GEN se développer; [*population, production*] s'accroître; [*universe, market, economy*] être en expansion; [*metal*] se dilater; [*institution*] s'agrandir; [*chest*] se gonfler; **the company is ~ing into overseas markets** la société commence à s'implanter sur les marchés étrangers.

III **expanded** *pp adj* [*programme*] élargi.

■ **expand on**: **~ (up)on** [**sth**] s'étendre sur [*plans*].

expanding /ɪkˈspændɪŋ/ *adj* **1** (growing) [*population, sector*] en expansion; **2** [*file, bracelet*] extensible.

expanse /ɪkˈspæns/ *n* (of land, water) étendue *f*; (of flesh) étalage *m*.

expansion /ɪkˈspænʃn/ *n* GEN développement *m* (**in** de; **into** dans); (of economy) expansion *f*; (of population, borrowing) accroissement *m*; (of site) agrandissement *m*; (of sales) progression *f*; (of metal) dilatation *f*; **rate of ~** taux d'accroissement.

expansion board, **expansion card** *n* COMPUT carte *f* d'extension.

expansionist /ɪkˈspænʃənɪst/ *n, adj* ECON, POL expansionniste (*mf*).

expansion: **~ programme**, **~ scheme** *n* COMM programme *m* de développement; **~ slot** *n* COMPUT emplacement *m* libre (pour extension).

expansive /ɪkˈspænsɪv/ *adj* (effusive) [*person, mood*] expansif/-ive; (grand) [*ambitions*] grandiose.

expansively /ɪkˈspænsɪvlɪ/ *adv* (effusively) [*smile, say*] avec effusion.

expatriate /ˌeksˈpætrɪət/ *n, adj* expatrié/-e (*m*/*f*).

expect /ɪkˈspekt/ **I** *vtr* **1** (anticipate) s'attendre à [*event, victory, defeat, trouble*]; **to ~ the worst** s'attendre au pire; **what did you ~?** qu'est-ce que tu croyais?; **I ~ed as much** je m'y attendais; **you knew what to ~** tu savais à quoi t'attendre; **to ~ sb to do** s'attendre à ce que qn fasse; **she is ~ed to win** on s'attend à ce qu'elle gagne; **he is ~ed to arrive at six** on l'attend pour six heures; **to ~ that...** s'attendre à ce que... (+ *subj*); **I ~ (that) I'll lose** je m'attends à perdre; **it is only to be ~ed that he should go** c'est bien naturel qu'il y aille; **it was hardly to be ~ed that** on ne pouvait guère s'attendre à ce que (+ *subj*); **more/worse than ~ed** plus/pire que prévu; **2** (rely on) s'attendre à [*sympathy, help*] (**from** de la part de); **3** (await) attendre [*baby, guest, company*]; **~ me when you see me** GB je ne sais pas à quelle heure j'arriverai; **4** (require) demander, attendre [*commitment, hard work*] (**from** de); **I ~ you to be punctual** je vous demande d'être ponctuel; **I can't be ~ed to know everything** je ne peux pas tout savoir; **it's too much to ~** c'est trop demander; **5** GB (suppose) **I ~ so** je pense que oui; **I don't ~ so** je ne pense pas; **I ~ he's tired** il doit être fatigué.

II *vi* **1** (anticipate) **to ~ to do** s'attendre à faire; **I was ~ing to do better** je comptais faire mieux; **2** (require) **I ~ to see you there** je compte bien vous y voir; **3** (be pregnant) **to be ~ing** attendre un enfant.

expectancy /ɪkˈspektənsɪ/ *n* **to have an air of ~** avoir l'air d'attendre quelque chose; **a feeling of ~** un sentiment d'attente.

expectant /ɪkˈspektənt/ *adj* **1** [*look*] plein d'attente; **2** [*mother*] futur (*before n*).

expectantly /ɪkˈspektəntlɪ/ *adv* avec l'air d'attendre quelque chose.

expectation /ˌekspekˈteɪʃn/ *n* **1** (assumption, prediction) prévision *f*; **it is my ~ that** je m'attends à ce que (+ *subj*); **against all ~(s)** à l'encontre des prévisions générales; **2** (aspiration, hope) aspiration *f*, attente *f*; **to live up to sb's ~s** répondre à l'attente de qn; **I don't want to raise their ~s** je ne veux pas trop leur promettre; **3** (requirement, demand) exigence *f*; **to have certain ~s of** attendre or demander certaines choses de [*police, employee*].

expediency /ɪkˈspiːdɪənsɪ/ *n* **1** (appropriateness) opportunité *f*; **2** (self-interest) opportunisme *m*.

expedient /ɪkˈspiːdɪənt/ **I** *n* expédient *m*.

II *adj* **1** (appropriate) opportun; **2** (advantageous) politique.

expedite /ˈekspɪdaɪt/ *vtr* SOUT (speed up) accélérer [*operation, process*]; faciliter [*work*].

expedition /ˌekspɪˈdɪʃn/ *n* **1** (exploration) expédition *f*; **to go on an ~** partir en expédition; **2** (for leisure) **climbing ~** expédition *f* en montagne; **hunting ~** partie *f* de chasse; **sightseeing ~** visite *f* touristique; **to go on a shopping ~** aller faire des courses.

expeditionary force *n* corps *m* expéditionnaire.

expel /ɪkˈspel/ *vtr* (*p prés etc* **-ll-**) **1** expulser [*alien, diplomat*]; renvoyer [*pupil*]; **2** expulser [*air, water*].

expend /ɪkˈspend/ *vtr* consacrer [*effort, time*]; dépenser [*energy*].

expendable /ɪkˈspendəbl/ *adj* [*troops, equipment*] sacrifiable; [*worker*] licenciable à tout moment; [*goods*] non durables.

expenditure /ɪkˈspendɪtʃə(r)/ *n* **1** (amount spent) dépenses *fpl*; **defence ~** dépenses *fpl* militaires; **capital ~** dépenses *fpl* d'investissement; **public ~** dépense *f* publique; **2** (in bookkeeping) sortie *f*; **3** (output) (of energy, time, money) dépense *f*.

expense /ɪkˈspens/ **I** *n* **1** (cost) frais *mpl*; **at one's own ~** à ses propres frais; **to go to some ~** faire des frais; **to go to great ~** dépenser beaucoup d'argent (**to do** pour faire); **to put sb to ~** faire faire des frais à qn; **to spare no ~** ne pas regarder à la dépense; **2** (cause for expenditure) dépense *f*; **a wedding is a big ~** un mariage revient cher; **3 at the ~ of** (prejudicing sth) au détriment de [*health, public, safety*]; **at sb's ~** [*laugh, joke*] aux dépens de qn.

II expenses *npl* COMM frais *mpl*; **to cover sb's ~s** [*sum*] couvrir les frais de qn; **all ~s paid** tous frais payés.

expense account *n* frais *mpl* de représentation.

expensive /ɪk'spensɪv/ *adj* GEN cher/chère; (onerous) coûteux/-euse; [*taste*] de luxe; **~ to maintain** cher à entretenir.

expensively /ɪk'spensɪvlɪ/ *adv* **~ furnished** luxueusement meublé; **to be ~ dressed** porter des toilettes chères.

experience /ɪk'spɪərɪəns/ **I** *n* **1** (expertise) expérience *f*; **management ~** expérience *f* de la gestion; **from my own ~** d'après mon expérience; **in my ~** autant que je puisse dire; **to have ~ with children/computers** avoir de l'expérience avec les enfants/en informatique; **to know from ~** savoir d'expérience; **2** (incident) expérience *f*; **a new ~** une nouvelle expérience; **the ~ of a lifetime** une expérience unique.

II *vtr* connaître [*loss, problem*]; éprouver [*emotion*]; ressentir [*physical pleasure*].

experienced /ɪk'spɪərɪənst/ *adj* GEN expérimenté; [*eye*] entraîné.

experiment /ɪk'sperɪmənt/ **I** *n* expérience *f* (**in** en; **on** sur); **to conduct** OU **carry out an ~** faire OU effectuer une expérience; **as an ~** à titre d'expérience.

II *vi* expérimenter, faire des essais; **to ~ with drugs** goûter à la drogue.

experimental /ɪk,sperɪ'mentl/ *adj* expérimental; [*novelist, writing*] d'avant-garde; **~ model** prototype *m*; **on an ~ basis** à titre d'expérience.

experimentally /ɪk,sperɪ'mentəlɪ/ *adv* [*establish*] expérimentalement; [*introduce, try*] à titre d'expérience.

experimentation /ɪk,sperɪmen'teɪʃn/ *n* expériences *fpl*.

expert /'ekspɜːt/ **I** *n* spécialiste *mf* (**in** en, de), expert *m* (**in** en); **an ~ at doing** un expert dans l'art de faire; **computer ~** spécialiste *mf* en informatique; **you're the ~!** c'est toi qui t'y connais!

II *adj* [*knowledge*] spécialisé; [*opinion, advice*] autorisé; [*witness*] expert; [*eye*] exercé; **an ~ cook** un cordon bleu.

expertise /,ekspɜː'tiːz/ *n* compétences *fpl*; (very specialized) expertise *f* (**in** dans le domaine de); **to have the ~ to do** avoir les compétences requises pour faire.

expertly /'ekspɜːtlɪ/ *adv* magistralement.

expiate /'ekspɪeɪt/ *vtr* expier [*crime, sin*]; effacer [*guilt*].

expiration /,ekspɪ'reɪʃn/ *n* (end, exhalation) expiration *f*.

expiration date *n* US = **expiry date**.

expire /ɪk'spaɪə(r)/ *vi* **1** (end) [*deadline, offer*] expirer; [*period*] arriver à terme; **my passport has ~d** mon passeport est périmé; **2** (die) HUM rendre l'âme.

expiry /ɪk'spaɪərɪ/ *n* GEN expiration *f*; (of deadline, mandate) terme *m*.

expiry date *n* GB (of credit card, permit) date *f* d'expiration; (of contract) terme *m*; (of loan) date *f* d'échéance.

explain /ɪk'spleɪn/ **I** *vtr* (all contexts) expliquer (**that** que; **to** à); **I can't ~** je ne peux pas dire pourquoi; **that ~s it!** ça explique tout!

II *v refl* **to ~ oneself** s'expliquer.

■ **explain away**: **~ away** [*sth*], **~** [*sth*] **away** trouver des justifications à [*discrepancy*].

explanation /,eksplə'neɪʃn/ *n* explication *f* (**of** de; **for** à); **by way of ~, in ~** en guise d'explication; **it needs no ~** c'est clair.

explanatory /ɪk'splænətrɪ, US -tɔːrɪ/ *adj* [*leaflet, diagram*] explicatif/-ive.

expletive /ɪk'spliːtɪv, US 'eksplətɪv/ SOUT *n* (swearword) juron *m*.

explicit /ɪk'splɪsɪt/ *adj* **1** (precise) explicite; **2** (overt) GEN formel/-elle; [*aim*] avoué; **sexually ~** sexuellement explicite.

explode /ɪk'spləʊd/ **I** *vtr* faire exploser [*bomb*]; FIG pulvériser [*theory, rumour, myth*].

II *vi* **1** [*bomb*] exploser; [*boiler, building, ship*] sauter; **2** FIG [*person*] (with anger) exploser; [*affair*] éclater; [*population*] exploser; **to ~ with laughter** éclater de rire; **they ~d° onto the rock music scene** ils ont fait irruption dans le monde du rock.

exploit I /'eksplɔɪt/ *n* exploit *m*.

II /ɪk'splɔɪt/ *vtr* exploiter.

exploitation /,eksplɔɪ'teɪʃn/ *n* exploitation *f*.

exploitative /ɪk'splɔɪtətɪv/ *adj* [*system*] fondé sur l'exploitation des individus; **an ~ attitude** une mentalité d'exploiteur.

exploration /,eksplə'reɪʃn/ *n* exploration *f*; **oil ~** prospection *f* pétrolière.

exploratory /ɪk'splɔrətərɪ, US -tɔːrɪ/ *adj* [*talks*] exploratoire; [*surgery*] exploratoire/-trice.

explore /ɪk'splɔː(r)/ **I** *vtr* **1** GEN, MED explorer; **2** (investigate) étudier [*idea, opportunity*]; **to ~ ways and means of doing** explorer tous les moyens de faire; **to ~ every avenue** examiner toutes les possibilités.

II *vi* **to go exploring** [*explorer*] partir en exploration; **to ~ for oil** chercher du pétrole.

explorer /ɪk'splɔːrə(r)/ *n* explorateur/-trice *m/f*.

explosion /ɪk'spləʊʒn/ *n* **1** LIT explosion *f*; **to hear an ~** entendre une détonation; **2** FIG (of mirth, rage) explosion *f*; **pay/population ~** explosion *f* salariale/démographique.

explosive /ɪk'spləʊsɪv/ **I** *n* explosif *m*.

II *adj* GEN explosif/-ive; [*substance*] explosible.

exponent /ɪk'spəʊnənt/ *n* (of policy, theory) avocat/-e *m/f*, défenseur *m*; (of technique, art) interprète *mf*.

exponential /,ekspəʊ'nenʃl/ *adj* exponentiel/-ielle.

export I /'ekspɔːt/ *n* (process) exportation *f* (**of** de); (product) produit *m* d'exportation; **'for ~ only'** (on product) 'exportation'.

II /ɪk'spɔːt/ *vtr* (all contexts) exporter; **to ~ sth to France/Japan** exporter qch en France/au Japon.

III /ɪk'spɔːt/ *vi* exporter (**to** vers).

export: **~ agent** *n* agent *m* exportateur; **~ control** *n* contrôle *m* des exportations; **~ drive** *n* campagne *f* d'exportation; **~ duty** *n* droit *m* à l'exportation; **~ earnings** *npl* gains *mpl* à l'exportation.

exporter /ɪk'spɔːtə(r)/ *n* exportateur/-trice *m/f* (**of** de).

export: **~ finance** *n* financement *m* des exportations; **~-import company** *n* société *f* d'import-export; **~ licence** GB, **~ license** US *n* licence *f* d'exportation; **~ trade** *n* exportations *fpl*.

expose /ɪk'spəʊz/ **I** *vtr* **1** (display) exposer [*skin*]; **to ~ one's ignorance** étaler son ignorance; **2** (make public) révéler [*identity*]; dénoncer [*injustice, person, scandal*]; **3** (uncover) exposer [*inside, dirt*]; [*excavations*] mettre à jour [*fossil, remains*]; **4** (make vulnerable) **to ~ sb/sth to** exposer qn/qch à [*infection, light*]; livrer qn/qch à [*ridicule, temptation*]; **5** PHOT exposer [*film*].

II *v refl* **1 to ~ oneself** JUR commettre un outrage à la pudeur; **2 to ~ oneself to** (make oneself vulnerable) s'exposer à [*risk, danger*].

III exposed *pp adj* [*area, film*] exposé; [*beam*] apparent.

exposé /ek'spəʊzeɪ, US ,ekspə'zeɪ/ *n* (about scandal) révélations *fpl* (**of sth** sur qch).

exposition /,ekspə'zɪʃn/ *n* (of facts) présentation *f*.

expostulation /ɪk,spɒstjʊ'leɪʃn/ *n* SOUT remontrances *fpl*.

exposure /ɪk'spəʊʒə(r)/ *n* **1** (of secret, crime) révélation *f*; **to fear ~** craindre d'être démasqué; **to threaten sb with ~** menacer qn de dénonciation; **2** (to light, sun, radiation) exposition *f* (**to** à); FIG (to art, ideas, politics) contact *m* (**to** avec); **3** (to cold, weather) **to die of ~** mourir de froid; **4** (in media) couverture *f* médiatique; **5** (orientation) exposition *f*; **6** PHOT (aperture and shutter speed) temps *m* de pose; (picture) pose *f*; **a 24 ~ film** une pellicule de 24 poses.

exposure: **~ meter** *n* PHOT posemètre *m*; **~ time** *n* PHOT temps *m* de pose.

expound /ɪkˈspaʊnd/ **I** *vtr* exposer [*theory, opinion*].
II *vi* **~ on** disserter sur.

express /ɪkˈspres/ **I** *n* rapide *m*.
II *adj* **1** (rapid) [*letter, parcel*] exprès; [*delivery, train*] rapide; **2** (explicit) [*order, promise*] formel/-elle; **on the ~ condition that** à la condition expresse que (+ *subj*); **with the ~ aim** dans le but précis.
III *adv* **to send sth ~** envoyer qch en exprès.
IV *vtr* **1** (show) GEN exprimer; **2** MATH exprimer [*number, quantity*]; **to ~ sth as a percentage** exprimer qch en pourcentage; **3** (squeeze out) faire sortir [*fluid*].
V *v refl* **to ~ oneself** s'exprimer (**in** en; **through** à travers).

expression /ɪkˈspreʃn/ *n* **1** (phrase) expression *f*; **2** (look) expression *f*; **3** ₵ (utterance) expression *f*; **freedom of ~** liberté *f* d'expression; **to give ~ to** exprimer; **4** (of friendship, gratitude) témoignage *m*; **as an ~ of** en témoignage de.

expressionism /ɪkˈspreʃənɪzəm/ *n* expressionnisme *m*.

expressionless /ɪkˈspreʃnlɪs/ *adj* [*eyes, face*] inexpressif/-ive; [*tone, voice*] monocorde; [*playing*] plat.

expressive /ɪkˈspresɪv/ *adj* expressif/-ive.

expressively /ɪkˈspresɪvlɪ/ *adv* de manière significative.

expressly /ɪkˈspreslɪ/ *adv* **1** (explicitly) GEN expressément; [*forbid*] formellement; **2** (specifically) [*designed, intended*] spécialement.

expulsion /ɪkˈspʌlʃn/ *n* (of pupil) renvoi *m*; (of diplomat) expulsion *f*; (of member) exclusion *f*.

exquisite /ˈekskwɪzɪt, ɪkˈskwɪzɪt/ *adj* GEN exquis; [*setting*] charmant; [*tact, precision*] parfait; [*pleasure*] vif/ vive; **she has ~ taste** elle a un goût exquis.

exquisitely /ˈekskwɪzɪtlɪ/ *adv* [*dressed, written*] d'une façon exquise; **~ beautiful** d'une beauté exquise.

ex-serviceman /ˌeksˈsɜːvɪsmən/ *n* ancien militaire *m*.

ex-servicewoman /ˌeksˈsɜːvɪswʊmən/ *n* ancienne combattante *f*.

extant /ekˈstænt, US ˈekstənt/ *adj* existant.

extemporize /ɪkˈstempəraɪz/ *vi* improviser.

extend /ɪkˈstend/ **I** *vtr* **1** (enlarge) agrandir [*house*]; prolonger [*runway*]; élargir [*range, vocabulary*]; **2** (prolong) prolonger [*visit, visa, show*]; proroger [*loan, contract*]; **the deadline was ~ed by six months** un délai supplémentaire de six mois a été accordé; **3** (stretch) étendre; **to ~ one's hand in greeting** tendre la main; **4** (offer) SOUT présenter [*congratulations*]; accorder [*credit, loan*]; faire [*invitation*].
II *vi* **1** (stretch) (over an area) s'étendre; (from one point to another) aller; **2** (reach) **to ~ beyond** dépasser; **3** FIG (go as far as) **to ~ to doing** aller jusqu'à faire.
III extended *pp adj* [*stay*] prolongé; [*contract, leave, sentence*] de longue durée; [*area, family*] étendu; [*premises*] agrandi; [*credit*] à long terme.

extendable /ɪkˈstendəbl/ *adj* **1** (of adjustable length) [*cable*] extensible; [*ladder*] coulissant; **2** (renewable) renouvelable.

extension /ɪkˈstenʃn/ *n* **1** (extra section) (of cable, table) rallonge *f*; (of road) prolongement *m*; (of house) addition *f*; **2** (phone) poste *m* supplémentaire; (number) (numéro *m* de) poste *m*; **3** (prolongation) (of visa, loan) prorogation *f*; (of deadline) délai *m* supplémentaire; **4** (widening) (of powers, services) extension *f*; (of knowledge) élargissement *m*; (of business) développement *m*; **by ~** (logically) par extension; **5** (hair) tresse *f* artificielle.

extension: **~ ladder** *n* échelle *f* coulissante; **~ lead** *n* ELEC rallonge *f*.

extensive /ɪkˈstensɪv/ *adj* **1** (wide-ranging) [*network, programme*] vaste (*before n*); [*list*] long/longue (*before n*); [*tests*] approfondi; [*changes*] important; [*training*] complet; [*powers*] étendu; **2** (substantial) [*forest*] vaste

(*before n*); [*investment*] considérable; [*damage, loss*] grave, considérable; [*flooding*] important; [*burns*] grave; **to make ~ use of** utiliser beaucoup.

extensively /ɪkˈstensɪvlɪ/ *adv* [*correct*] considérablement; [*quote*] abondamment; [*read*] énormément.

extent /ɪkˈstent/ *n* **1** (size) (of park, problem) étendue *f*; **to its full ~** complètement; **2** (amount) (of damage) ampleur *f*; (of knowledge, influence) étendue *f*; (of involvement) importance *f*; **3** (degree) mesure *f*; **to what ~...?** dans quelle mesure...?; **to a certain/great ~** dans une certaine/large mesure; **to the ~ that** dans la mesure où; **not to any great ~** très peu.

extenuating /ɪkˈstenjʊeɪtɪŋ/ *adj* atténuant.

exterior /ɪkˈstɪərɪə(r)/ **I** *n* extérieur *m* (**of** de); **on the ~** à l'extérieur.
II *adj* GEN extérieur (**to** à); **~ decorating** peintures *fpl* extérieures; **for ~ use** (paint) pour extérieurs.

exterminate /ɪkˈstɜːmɪneɪt/ *vtr* éliminer [*vermin*]; exterminer [*people, race*].

extermination /ɪkˌstɜːmɪˈneɪʃn/ *n* (of vermin) élimination *f*; (of people, race) extermination *f*.

external /ɪkˈstɜːnl/ *adj* **1** (outer) [*appearance, reality*] extérieur (**to** à); [*surface, injury*] extérieur; **'for ~ use only'** 'usage externe'; **2** (from outside) [*examiner*] externe; [*influence, mail, call*] extérieur; **3** (foreign) extérieur; **4** COMPUT externe.

externalize /ɪkˈstɜːnəlaɪz/ *vtr* extérioriser.

externally /ɪkˈstɜːnəlɪ/ *adv* (on the outside) [*calm, healthy*] en apparence; **in good condition ~** en bon état extérieurement.

externals /ɪkˈstɜːnlz/ *npl* apparences *fpl*.

extinct /ɪkˈstɪŋkt/ *adj* [*species, animal, plant*] disparu; [*volcano, passion*] éteint; **to become ~** [*species, animal, plant*] disparaître; [*volcano*] s'éteindre.

extinction /ɪkˈstɪŋkʃn/ *n* extinction *f*.

extinguish /ɪkˈstɪŋgwɪʃ/ *vtr* GEN éteindre; anéantir [*hope*].

extinguisher /ɪkˈstɪŋgwɪʃə(r)/ *n* extincteur *m*.

extol GB, **extoll** US /ɪkˈstəʊl/ *vtr* (*p prés* **-ll-**) louer [*predecessor, rights*]; prôner [*system*]; **to ~ the virtues of** chanter les louanges de.

extort /ɪkˈstɔːt/ *vtr* extorquer [*money, promise, signature*] (**from** à); arracher [*confession*] (**from** à).

extortion /ɪkˈstɔːʃn/ *n* GEN, JUR extorsion *f*.

extortionate /ɪkˈstɔːʃənət/ *adj* exorbitant.

extra /ˈekstrə/ **I** *n* **1** (charge) supplément *m*; **there are no hidden ~s** il n'y a pas de faux frais *mpl*; **2** (feature) option *f*; **the sunroof is an ~** le toit ouvrant est en option; **the little ~s in life** (luxuries) les petits agréments *mpl* de l'existence; **3** CIN, THEAT figurant/ -e *m/f*.
II *adj* supplémentaire; **an ~ £1,000** 1 000 livres de plus; **postage is ~** les frais de port sont en supplément or en sus.
III *adv* **~ careful** encore plus prudent (que d'habitude); **you have to pay ~** il faut payer un supplément; **that model costs ~** ce modèle coûte plus cher.

extra charge *n* supplément *m*; **at no ~** sans supplément.

extract I /ˈekstrækt/ *n* (all contexts) extrait *m* (**from** de); **meat ~** extrait de viande.
II /ɪkˈstrækt/ *vtr* **1** (pull out) GEN sortir (**from** de); extraire [*tooth, bullet*] (**from** de); **2** (obtain) arracher [*confession, promise*] (**from** à); tirer [*money, energy, heat*] (**from** sth de qch); dégager [*sense*]; **3** IND extraire [*mineral, oil*] (**from** de).

extraction /ɪkˈstrækʃn/ *n* **1** (process) extraction *f*; **2** (origin) **of French ~** d'origine française.

extractor /ɪkˈstræktə(r)/ *n* GEN extracteur *m*.

extractor fan *n* ventilateur *m* d'extraction.

extra-curricular /ˌekstrəkəˈrɪkjʊlə(r)/ *adj* parascolaire.

extradite /ˈekstrədaɪt/ *vtr* extrader (**from** de; **to** vers).

extradition /ˌekstrəˈdɪʃn/ *n* extradition *f* (**from** de; **to** vers).

extra: **~-dry** adj [sherry, wine] extra-sec; [champagne] brut; **~-fast** adj ultrarapide; **~-fine** adj extra-fin.

extra-large /ˌekstra'lɑːdʒ/ adj [pullover, shirt] extra-large; [coat] de grande taille.

extramarital /ˌekstra'mærɪtl/ adj extraconjugal.

extra-mural /ˌekstra'mjʊərəl/ adj **1** GB UNIV [course, lecture] ouvert à tous et assuré par un universitaire; **2** US SCH **~ sports** matchs mpl inter-établissements.

extraneous /ɪk'streɪnɪəs/ adj (not essential) [issue, detail, information] superflu; [considerations] sans rapport avec la question.

extraordinary /ɪk'strɔːdnrɪ, US -dənerɪ/ adj (all contexts) extraordinaire; **to go to ~ lengths** se donner un mal extraordinaire; **there's nothing ~ about it** cela n'a rien d'extraordinaire; **to find it ~ that** trouver extraordinaire que (+ subj).

extrapolate /ɪk'stræpəleɪt/ vtr extrapoler (**from** de).

extrasensory perception, **ESP** n perception f extrasensorielle.

extra: **~-special** adj exceptionnel/-elle; **~-strong** adj [coffee] très serré; [paper] extra-strong; [thread] extra-solide; [disinfectant, weed killer] super-puissant.

extraterrestrial /ˌekstrətə'restrɪəl/ n, adj extraterrestre (mf).

extra time n SPORT prolongation f; **to go into** ou **play ~** jouer les prolongations.

extravagance /ɪk'strævəgəns/ n **1** ¢ (prodigality) prodigalité f; **2** C (luxury) luxe m; **3** ¢ (of behaviour, claim) extravagance f.

extravagant /ɪk'strævəgənt/ adj **1** [person] dépensier/-ière; [way of life] dispendieux/-ieuse; **to be ~ with sth** gaspiller qch; **2** (luxurious) [dish] luxueux/ -euse; **3** (exaggerated) extravagant.

extravagantly /ɪk'strævəgəntlɪ/ adv **1** [furnished] luxueusement; **2** [praise, claim] à outrance.

extravaganza /ɪkˌstrævə'gænzə/ n spectacle m somptueux.

extreme /ɪk'striːm/ I n (all contexts) extrême m; **to go from one ~ to the other** passer d'un extrême à l'autre; **~s of temperature** écarts mpl extrêmes de température; **to take/carry sth to ~s** pousser/porter qch à l'extrême; **to go to ~s** pousser les choses à l'extrême; **to be driven to ~s** être poussé à bout; **to go to any ~** ne s'arrêter devant rien; **naïve in the ~** naïf à l'extrême.
II adj [example, case, heat, edge] extrême; [view, measure, reaction] extrémiste; **fashion at its most ~** la mode poussée à l'extrême; **on the ~ right/left** à l'extrême droite/gauche; **to go to ~ lengths** ne reculer devant rien; **to be ~ in one's views** avoir des opinions extrémistes; **to have ~ difficulty doing** avoir énormément de difficulté à faire.

extremely /ɪk'striːmlɪ/ adv extrêmement; **he did ~ well** il s'est bien débrouillé.

extremism /ɪk'striːmɪzəm/ n extrémisme m.

extremity /ɪk'stremətɪ/ n **1** (of place) extrémité f (**of** de); **extremities** (of body) extrémités f; **2** (dire situation) situation f désespérée; **to do sth in ~** faire qch en dernier recours; **to be reduced to extremities** être à bout; **3** (extremeness) degré m extrême (**of** de).

extricate /'ekstrɪkeɪt/ I vtr (from trap, net) dégager (**from** de); (from situation) sortir (**from** de).
II v refl **to ~ oneself from** s'extirper de [place]; se dégager de [embrace]; se sortir de [situation].

extrovert /'ekstrəvɜːt/ n, adj extraverti/-e (m/f).

exuberance /ɪg'zjuːbərəns, US -'zuː-/ n exubérance f.

exuberant /ɪg'zjuːbərənt, US -'zuː-/ adj exubérant.

exude /ɪg'zjuːd, US -'zuːd/ vtr **1** (radiate) respirer [charm]; **2** (give off) exsuder [sap]; exhaler [smell].

exult /ɪg'zʌlt/ vi **to ~ at** ou **in sth** se réjouir de qch.

exultant /ɪg'zʌltənt/ adj GEN triomphant; [cry] de triomphe; **to be ~** exulter.

exultantly /ɪg'zʌltəntlɪ/ adv triomphalement.

ex-works /ˌeks'wɜːks/ adj [price, value] départ-usine.

---

eye /aɪ/ ▶765 I n **1** ANAT œil m; **with blue ~s** aux yeux bleus; **to lower one's ~s** baisser les yeux; **in front of** ou **before your (very) ~s** sous vos yeux; **to the untrained ~** pour un œil non exercé; **to see sth with one's own ~s** voir qch de ses propres yeux; **keep your ~s on the road!** c'est la route qu'il faut regarder!; **to keep an ~ on sth/sb** surveiller qch/qn; **under the watchful ~ of sb** sous le regard vigilant de qn; **to have one's ~ on sb/sth** (watch) surveiller qn/qch; (want) avoir envie de [house]; (lust after) loucher○ sur [person]; (aim for) viser [job]; **with an ~ to doing** en vue de faire; **to keep one ~** ou **half an ~ on sth/sb** garder un œil sur qch/qn; **to run one's ~ over sth** parcourir qch du regard; **to catch sb's ~** attirer l'attention de qn; **to close** ou **shut one's ~s** fermer les yeux; **to close** ou **shut one's ~s to sth** FIG se refuser à reconnaître qch; **to open one's ~s** ouvrir les yeux; **to open sb's ~s to sth** FIG ouvrir les yeux de qn sur qch; **to do sth with one's ~s open** FIG faire qch en toute connaissance de cause; **to go around with one's ~s shut** FIG vivre sans rien voir; **to keep an ~ out** ou **one's ~s open for sb/sth** essayer de repérer qn/qch; **as far as the ~ can see** à perte de vue; **I've got ~s in my head!** j'ai des yeux pour voir!; **use your ~s!** tu es aveugle?; **she couldn't take her ~s off him** elle ne le quittait pas des yeux; **2** (opinion) **in the ~s of the law** aux yeux de la loi; **in his ~s...** à ses yeux...; **3** (flair) **to have a good ~** avoir un bon coup d'œil; **to have an ~ for** avoir le sens de [detail, colour]; s'y connaître en [antiques]; **4** (hole in needle) chas m; (to attach hook to) œillet m; **5** (on potato) œil m; **6** (on peacock's tail) œil m, ocelle m; **7** (of storm) œil m; **the ~ of the storm** FIG l'œil de la tempête.
II noun modifier [operation] de l'œil; [muscle, tissue] de l'œil, oculaire; [ointment, lotion] pour les yeux; **~ trouble** troubles mpl oculaires.
III **-eyed** combining form **blue~d** aux yeux bleus.
IV vtr **1** (look at) regarder [person, object]; **to ~ sth with envy** regarder qch avec envie; **2**○ (ogle at) ▶ **eye up**.
IDIOMS **to be all ~s** être tout yeux; **to be up to one's ~s in** être submergé de [mail, work]; **to be up to one's ~s in debt** être endetté jusqu'au cou; **an ~ for an ~** œil pour œil; **it was one in the ~ for him** c'était bien fait pour lui IRON; **to have ~s in the back of one's head** avoir des yeux dans le dos; **to make ~s at sb** faire les yeux doux à qn; **to give sb the glad ~** faire de l'œil à qn; **to see ~ to ~ with sb (about sth)** partager le point de vue de qn (au sujet de qch).
■ **eye up**○: **~ [sb] up**, **~ up [sb]** lorgner○, reluquer○.
■ **eye up and down**: **~ [sb] up and down** (suspiciously) toiser [qn]; (appreciatively) dévorer [qn] des yeux.

eyeball /'aɪbɔːl/ n ANAT globe m oculaire; **to be ~ to ~ with sb** être nez à nez avec qn.

eye: **~ bank** n banque f des yeux; **~bath** n œillère f.

eyebrow /'aɪbraʊ/ n sourcil m; **to raise one's** ou **an ~** (in surprise) hausser les sourcils; (in disapproval) froncer les sourcils; **to raise a few ~s** provoquer quelques froncements de sourcils.

eye: **~brow pencil** n crayon m à sourcils; **~-catching** adj [design, poster] attrayant; [advertisement, headline] accrocheur/-euse.

eye contact n échange m de regards; **to make ~ with sb** croiser le regard de qn.

eyedrops /'aɪdrɒps/ npl gouttes fpl pour les yeux.

eyeful /'aɪfʊl/ n **1** (amount) **to get an ~ of** avoir [qch] plein les yeux [dust, sand]; **2**○ (good look) **to get an ~ (of sth)** se rincer l'œil○ (au spectacle de qch).

eye: **~glass** n (monocle) monocle m; **~glasses** npl US lunettes fpl (de vue); **~lash** n cil m.

eye level /'aɪ levl/ I n **at ~** à hauteur des yeux.
II **eye-level** adj [grill, shelf] à hauteur des yeux.

eye: **~lid** *n* paupière *f*; **~ make-up** *n* maquillage *m* pour les yeux; **~-opener**° *n* révélation *f*; **~-patch** *n* bandeau *m*; **~shade** *n* visière *f*; **~ shadow** *n* fard *m* à paupières; **~sight** *n* vue *f*.

eyesore /'aɪsɔː(r)/ *n* **to be an ~** choquer la vue.

eye: **~ strain** *n* fatigue *f* oculaire; **~ test** *n* examen *m* de la vue.

eyetooth /'aɪtuːθ/ *n* (*pl* **-teeth**) canine *f* supérieure. IDIOMS **I'd give my eyeteeth for that job** je donnerais n'importe quoi pour obtenir ce poste.

eye: **~wash** *n* collyre *m*; FIG (nonsense) poudre *f* aux yeux; **~witness** *n* témoin *m* oculaire.

eyrie /'eərɪ, 'aɪərɪ/ *n* aire *f*, nid *m* d'aigle.

f, F /ef/ *n* **1** (letter) f, F *m*; **2 F** MUS (note, key) fa *m*.

fa /fɑː/ *n* MUS (note) fa *m*.

FA *n* GB (*abrév* = **Football Association**) fédération *f* britannique de football; cf FFF.

FAA *n* US (*abrév* = **Federal Aviation Association**) direction *f* générale de l'aviation civile américaine.

fable /'feɪbl/ *n* fable *f*.

fabric /'fæbrɪk/ *n* (cloth) tissu *m*; (of building) structure *f*; FIG (basis) **the ~ of society** le tissu social.

fabricate /'fæbrɪkeɪt/ *vtr* **1** inventer [qch] de toutes pièces [*story, evidence*]; **2** fabriquer [*document*].

fabrication /ˌfæbrɪˈkeɪʃn/ *n* **1** (lie) fabrication *f*; **that's pure** ou **complete ~** c'est de l'invention pure et simple; **2** (of document) fabrication *f*.

fabric softener *n* (produit *m*) assouplissant *m*.

fabulous○ /'fæbjʊləs/ **I** *adj* GEN fabuleux/-euse; (wonderful) sensationnel/-elle○.

II *excl* génial!

fabulously /'fæbjʊləslɪ/ *adv* fabuleusement; **to be ~ successful** avoir un succès fou.

face /feɪs/ **I** *n* **1** (of person) visage *m*, figure *f*; (of animal) face *f*; **to slam the door/laugh in sb's ~** claquer la porte/rire au nez de qn; **I told him to his ~ that he was lazy** je lui ai dit en face qu'il était paresseux; **to be ~ up/down** [*person*] être sur le dos/ventre; **2** (expression) air *m*; **to pull** ou **make a ~** faire la grimace; **you should have seen their ~s!** tu aurais vu la tête qu'ils ont fait○!; **3** FIG (outward appearance) **to change the ~ of** changer le visage de [*industry*]; **the changing ~ of Europe** la face changeante de l'Europe; **the acceptable ~ of capitalism** le bon côté du capitalisme; **4** (dignity) **to lose ~** perdre la face; **to save ~** sauver la face; **5** (surface) (of clock, watch) cadran *m*; (of gem, dice) face *f*; (of coin) côté *m*; (of planet) surface *f*; (of cliff, mountain) face *f*; (of rock) paroi *f*; (of playing card) face *f*; (of document) recto *m*; **to disappear** ou **vanish off the ~ of the earth○** disparaître de la circulation; **~ up/down** à l'endroit/l'envers.

II *vtr* **1** (look towards) [*person*] faire face à; [*building, room*] donner sur; **to ~ north/south** [*person*] regarder au nord/sud; [*building*] être orienté au nord/sud; **facing our house, there is...** en face de notre maison, il y a...; **2** (confront) se trouver face à [*challenge, crisis*]; se voir contraint de payer [*fine*]; se trouver menacé de [*defeat, redundancy*]; être contraint de faire [*choice*]; affronter [*attacker, rival, team*]; **to be ~d with** se trouver confronté à [*problem, decision*]; **~d with the prospect of having to resign** devant la perspective d'avoir à démissionner; **to ~ sb with** confronter qn à [*truth, evidence*]; **3** (acknowledge) **~ the facts, you're finished!** regarde la réalité en face, tu es fini!; **let's ~ it, nobody's perfect** admettons-le, personne n'est parfait; **4** (tolerate prospect) **I can't ~ doing** je n'ai pas le courage de faire; **he couldn't ~ the thought of walking/eating** l'idée de marcher/manger lui était insupportable; **5** (run the risk of) risquer [*fine, suspension*]; **6** CONSTR revêtir [*façade, wall*] (**with** de); **7** (in printing) [*photo etc*] être face à [*page*].

III *vi* **1** **to ~ towards** [*person, chair*] être tourné vers; [*building, house*] être en face de; **to ~ forward** regarder devant soi; **to ~ backwards** [*person*] tourner le dos; **to be facing forward** [*person*] être de face; **2** MIL **about ~!** demi-tour!; **left ~!** à gauche!

IV in the face of *prep phr* **1** (despite) en dépit de [*difficulties*]; **2** (in confrontation with) face à, devant [*opposition, enemy, danger*].

IDIOMS **to set one's ~ against** s'élever contre.

■ **face up to:** ¶ **~ up to** [*sth*] faire face à [*problem, responsibilities*]; ¶ **~ up to** [*sb*] affronter.

faceless /'feɪslɪs/ *adj* anonyme.

face-lift /'feɪslɪft/ *n* GEN lifting *m*; FIG rénovation *f*; **to give sth a ~** rénover qch [*building*]; réaménager qch [*town-centre*].

face: **~-pack** *n* masque *m* de beauté; **~ powder** *n* poudre *f* (de riz).

face-saving /'feɪsseɪvɪŋ/ *adj* [*plan, solution*] qui permet de sauver la face (*after n*).

facet /'fæsɪt/ *n* (of gemstone, of personality) facette *f*; (of question, problem) aspect *m*.

facetious /fəˈsiːʃəs/ *adj* [*remark*] facétieux/-ieuse.

facetiousness /fəˈsiːʃəsnɪs/ *n* gouaillerie *f*.

face-to-face /ˌfeɪstəˈfeɪs/ **I** *adj* **a ~ discussion** ou **interview** ou **meeting** un face-à-face *inv*.

II face to face *adv* [*be seated*] face à face; **to come ~ with** se retrouver face à; **to meet sb ~** rencontrer qn en face-à-face; **to talk to sb ~** parler à qn en personne.

face value *n* valeur *f* nominale; FIG **to take sth at ~** prendre qch au pied de la lettre [*claim*]; prendre qch pour argent comptant [*compliment*]; **to take sb at ~** juger qn sur les apparences.

facial /'feɪʃl/ **I** *n* soin *m* (complet) du visage.

II *adj* [*hair*] du visage; [*injury*] au visage; [*angle, muscle, nerve*] facial; **~ expression** expression *f*.

facile /'fæsaɪl, US 'fæsl/ *adj* **1** (glib) spécieux/-ieuse, facile; **2** (easy) facile.

facilitate /fəˈsɪlɪteɪt/ *vtr* faciliter [*progress, talks*]; favoriser [*development*].

facility /fəˈsɪlɪtɪ/ **I** *n* **1** (building) complexe *m*, installation *f*; **manufacturing ~** complexe industriel; **computer ~** installation informatique; **2** (ease) facilité *f*; **3** (ability) talent *m*; **to have a ~ for** être doué pour; **4** (feature) fonction *f*; **a pause ~** une fonction pause; **5** ADMIN, COMM facilités *fpl*; **'fax facilities available'** 'télécopieur disponible'.

II facilities *npl* **1** (equipment) équipement *m*; **facilities for the disabled** installations *fpl* pour les handicapés; **to have cooking and washing facilities** être équipé d'une cuisine et d'une laverie; **2** (infrastructure) infrastructure *f*; **harbour facilities** installations *fpl* portuaires; **sporting facilities** infrastructure sportive; **postal facilities** service *m* postal; **3** (area) **changing facilities** vestiaire *m*; **parking facilities** (aire *f* de) parking *m*.

facing /'feɪsɪŋ/ *n* **1** ARCHIT revêtement *m*; **2** (in sewing) entoilage *m*; **3** (in fashion) revers *m*.

facsimile /fækˈsɪmɪlɪ/ *n* **1** GEN fac-similé *m*; **2** (sculpture) reproduction *f*.

fact /fækt/ *n* fait *m*; **it is a ~ that** c'est un fait que; **to know for a ~ that** savoir de source sûre que; **owing** ou **due to the ~ that** étant donné que; **in ~, as a matter of ~** en fait; **the ~ remains (that)** toujours est-il que; **~s and figures** les faits et les chiffres; **the story was presented as ~** l'histoire a été présentée comme véridique; **to be based on ~** être fondé sur des faits réels; **space travel is now a ~** les voyages dans l'espace sont désormais une réalité.

IDIOMS **to know the ~s of life** (sex) savoir comment les enfants viennent au monde; **the ~s of life** (unpalatable truths) les réalités de la vie.

fact-finding /'fæktfaɪndɪŋ/ adj [*mission, tour, trip*] d'information.

faction /'fækʃn/ n **1** (group) faction *f*; **2** (discord) dissension *f*; **3** THEAT, TV docudrame *m*.

factional /'fækʃənl/ adj [*leader, activity*] de faction; [*fighting, arguments*] entre factions.

factor /'fæktə(r)/ n GEN, MATH facteur *m*; **common ~** GEN point *m* commun; MATH facteur commun; **human ~** élément *m* humain; **protection ~** (of suntan lotion) indice *m* de protection.

factory /'fæktərɪ/ n usine *f*; **tobacco ~** manufacture *f* de tabac; **bomb ~** atelier *m* clandestin (de fabrication de bombes).

factory: **~ farming** n élevage *m* industriel; **~ floor** n (place) ateliers *mpl*; (workers) ouvriers/-ières *mpl/fpl*; **~ inspector ▶ 1251** n inspecteur/-trice *m/f* du travail; **~-made** adj fabriqué en usine; **~ ship** n navire-usine *m*; **~ unit** n unité *f* de production; **~ worker ▶ 1251** n ouvrier/-ière *m/f* (d'usine).

fact sheet n bulletin *m* d'informations.

factual /'fæktʃʊəl/ adj [*evidence*] factuel/-elle; [*account, description*] basé sur les faits; **~ error** erreur de fait; **~ programme** GB TV, RADIO reportage *m*.

factually /'fæktʃʊəlɪ/ adv [*incorrect*] dans les faits.

faculty /'fækltɪ/ n (pl **-ties**) **1** (ability) faculté *f* (**of** de; **for** de; **for doing** de faire); **critical faculties** esprit *m* critique; **2** GB UNIV faculté *f*; **3** US UNIV, SCH (staff) corps *m* enseignant.

fad /fæd/ n (craze) engouement *m* (**for** pour); (whim) (petite) manie *f*.

faddish /'fædɪʃ/, **faddy** /'fædɪ/ adj GB difficile (**about** pour).

fade /feɪd/ **I** vtr faner.
II vi **1** (get lighter) [*fabric*] se décolorer, se faner; [*colour*] passer; [*lettering, typescript*] s'effacer; **to ~ in the wash** [*garment, fabric*] se décolorer au lavage; [*colour*] passer au lavage; **2** (wither) [*flowers*] se faner; **3** (disappear) [*image, drawing*] s'estomper; [*sound*] s'affaiblir; [*smile, memory*] s'effacer; [*interest, excitement, hope*] s'évanouir; [*hearing, light*] baisser; **to ~ into the background** se fondre dans l'arrière-plan.
■ **fade away** [*sound*] s'éteindre; [*sick person*] dépérir.
■ **fade in**: ¶ **~ [sth] in** monter progressivement [*sound, voice*]; faire apparaître [qch] en fondu [*image*]; ouvrir [qch] en fondu [*scene*].
■ **fade out**: ¶ **~ out** [*speaker, scene*] disparaître en fondu; ¶ **~ [sth] out** CIN faire disparaître [qch] en fondu [*picture, scene*].

faded /'feɪdɪd/ adj [*clothing, carpet*] décoloré; [*colour, glory*] passé; [*jeans*] délavé; [*drawing*] estompé; [*photo, wallpaper*] jauni; [*flower, beauty*] fané; [*writing, lettering*] à demi effacé.

fade: **~-in** n CIN, RADIO, TV fondu *m*; **~-out** n CIN, RADIO, TV fondu *m*.

faeces, feces US /'fiːsiːz/ npl matières *fpl* fécales.

fag /fæg/ n **1**° (cigarette) clope° *f*; **2**° GB (nuisance) corvée *f*.

fag end n **1**° (cigarette) mégot° *m*; **2** (of material) restant *m*; (of day, decade, conversation) fin *f*.

faggot /'fægət/ n **1** (meatball) boulette *f* de viande; **2** (firewood) fagot *m*.

fah /fɑː/ n MUS fa *m*.

fail /feɪl/ **I** n SCH, UNIV échec *m*.
II without fail adv phr [*arrive, do*] sans faute; [*happen*] à coup sûr.
III vtr **1** SCH, UNIV échouer à [*exam, driving test*]; échouer en or être collé° en [*subject*]; coller° [*candidate, pupil*]; **2** (omit) **to ~ to do** manquer de faire; **to ~ to keep one's word** manquer à ses promesses; **it never ~s to work** ça marche à tous les coups; **to ~ to mention that...** omettre de signaler que...; **3** (be unable) **to ~ to do** ne pas réussir à faire; **one could hardly ~ to notice that...** il était évident que...; **I ~ to understand why** je n'arrive pas à comprendre pourquoi; **4** (let down) laisser tomber [*friend*]; manquer à ses engagements envers [*de-*

pendant, supporter]; [*courage*] manquer à [*person*]; [*memory*] faire défaut à [*person*].
IV vi **1** (be unsuccessful) [*exam candidate*] échouer, être collé°; [*attempt, plan*] échouer; **to ~ in one's duty** manquer or faillir à son devoir; **if all else ~s** dernier recours; **2** (weaken) [*eyesight, hearing, light*] baisser; [*health, person*] décliner; **3** (not function) [*brakes*] lâcher; [*engine*] tomber en panne; [*power, water supply*] être coupé; **4** AGRIC [*crop*] être mauvais; **5** (go bankrupt) faire faillite; **6** MED [*heart*] lâcher; **his liver ~ed** il a eu une défaillance du foie.
V failed pp adj [*actor, writer*] raté°.

failing /'feɪlɪŋ/ **I** n défaut *m*.
II pres p adj **to have ~ eyesight** avoir la vue qui baisse; **to be in ~ health** être en mauvaise santé.
III prep **~ that, ~ this** sinon.

fail-safe adj [*device, system*] à sécurité intégrée.

failure /'feɪljə(r)/ n **1** (lack of success) GEN échec *m* (**in** à); (of business) faillite *f*; **his ~ to understand the problem** son incapacité *f* à comprendre le problème; **2** (unsuccessful person) raté/-e° *m/f*; (unsuccessful venture or event) échec *m*; **he was a ~ as a teacher** comme professeur il ne valait rien; **3** (breakdown) (of engine, machine, power) panne *f*; MED (of organ) défaillance *f*; **crop ~** perte *f* de récolte; **power ~** panne de courant; **due to a mechanical ~** dû à une défaillance mécanique; **4** (omission) **~ to keep a promise** manquement *m* à une promesse; **~ to comply with the rules** non-respect *m* de la réglementation; **~ to pay** non-paiement *m*.

faint /feɪnt/ **I** n évanouissement *m*.
II adj **1** (slight) [*smell, accent, breeze*] léger/-ère; [*sound, voice, protest*] faible; [*markings*] à peine visible; [*recollection*] vague; [*chance*] minime; **I haven't the ~est idea** je n'en ai pas la moindre idée; **2** (dizzy) **to feel ~** se sentir mal, défaillir.
III vi s'évanouir (**from** sous l'effet de).

fainthearted /ˌfeɪntˈhɑːtɪd/ **I** n **the ~** (+ v pl) (cowardly) les timorés *mpl*; (over-sensitive) les natures *fpl* sensibles.
II adj [*attempt*] timide.

fainting fit /ˌfeɪntɪŋ/ n évanouissement *m*.

faintly /'feɪntlɪ/ adv [*glisten, breathe, smile*] faiblement; [*coloured, disappointed*] légèrement.

faintness /'feɪntnɪs/ n faiblesse *f*.

fair /feə(r)/ **I** n (funfair, market) foire *f*; (for charity) kermesse *f*; **book ~** GEN foire *f* du livre; (in Paris, Montreal) salon *m* du livre.
II adj **1** (just, reasonable) [*arrangement, person, trial, wage*] équitable (**to** envers); [*comment, decision, point*] juste; **it's only ~ that she should be first** ce n'est que justice qu'elle soit la première; **to give sb a ~ deal** ou **shake** US être tout à fait honnête envers qn; **that's a ~ question** c'est une question raisonnable; **a ~ sample** un échantillon représentatif; **to be ~ he did try to pay** il faut dire à sa décharge qu'il a essayé de payer; **it (just) isn't ~!** ce n'est pas juste!; **~ enough!** bon d'accord!; **2** (moderately good) [*chance, condition, performance*] assez bon/bonne; SCH passable; **3** (quite large) **a ~ number of** un bon nombre de; **to go at a ~ pace** ou **speed** aller bon train; **he's had a ~ amount of luck** il a eu pas mal de chance; **the house was a ~ size** la maison était de bonne taille; **to be a ~ way off** être à bonne distance; **4** METEOROL (fine) [*weather*] beau/belle; [*forecast*] bon/bonne; [*wind*] favorable; **5** (light-coloured) [*hair*] blond; [*complexion, skin*] clair; **6** LITTÉR (beautiful) [*lady, city*] beau/belle; **with her own ~ hands** HUM de ses belles mains; **the ~ sex** HUM le beau sexe.
III adv [*play*] franc jeu.
IDIOMS **to be ~ game for sb** être une proie rêvée pour qn; **~ and square** indiscutablement; **to win ~ and square** remporter une victoire indiscutable.

fair: **~ copy** n version *f* au propre; **~ground** n champ *m* de foire.

fairly /'feəlɪ/ adv **1** (quite, rather) assez; [*sure*] pratiquement; **2** (justly) [*obtain, win*] honnêtement; [*say*] à juste titre.

air-minded /ˌfeəˈmaɪndɪd/ *adj* impartial.

airness /ˈfeənɪs/ *n* **1** (justness) (of person) équité *f*; (of judgment) impartialité *f*; **in all ~** en toute justice; **in ~ to him, he did phone** il faut dire à sa décharge qu'il a téléphoné; **2** (lightness) (of complexion) blancheur *f*; (of hair) blondeur *f*.

air play *n* **to have a sense of ~** jouer franc jeu, être fair-play; **to ensure ~** faire respecter les règles du jeu.

fair: ~-sized *adj* assez grand; **~-skinned** *adj* à la peau claire.

fair trade *n* **1** *accords de réciprocité dans les transactions commerciales internationales*; **2** US régime *m* des prix imposés.

fairway /ˈfeəweɪ/ *n* **1** (in golf) parcours *m* normal; **2** NAUT chenal *m*.

fair-weather friend *n* PÉJ **he's a ~** dès qu'on a des ennuis, il n'est plus votre ami.

fairy /ˈfeərɪ/ *n* (magical being) fée *f*.

fairy: ~ godmother *n* bonne fée *f*; **~ lights** GB guirlande *f* électrique; **~ story** *n* conte *m* de fées.

fairy tale I *n* (story) conte *m* de fées; (lie) histoire *f* à dormir debout.
II (also **fairy-tale, fairytale**) *noun modifier* [*romance, princess*] de conte de fées.

faith /feɪθ/ *n* **1** (confidence) confiance *f*; **he has no ~ in socialism** il ne croit pas au socialisme; **I have no ~ in her** elle ne m'inspire pas confiance; **in good ~** en toute bonne foi; **2** (belief) foi *f* (**in** en); **the Muslim ~** la foi musulmane; **people of all ~s** les gens de toutes confessions.

faithful /ˈfeɪθfl/ **I** *n* **the ~** (+ *v pl*) les fidèles *mpl*.
II *adj* (all contexts) fidèle (**to** à).

faithfully /ˈfeɪθfəlɪ/ *adv* **1** (loyally, accurately) fidèlement; **2** (in letter writing) **yours ~** veuillez agréer, Monsieur/Madame, mes/nos salutations distinguées.

faithfulness /ˈfeɪθflnɪs/ *n* fidélité *f*.

faith: ~ healer *n* guérisseur *m*; **~ healing** *n* guérison *f* par la foi.

faithless /ˈfeɪθlɪs/ *adj* LITTÉR [*friend, husband*] infidèle; [*servant*] déloyal.

fake /feɪk/ **I** *n* **1** (jewel, work of art etc) faux *m*; **2** (person) imposteur *m*.
II *adj* [*fur, gem, passport*] faux/fausse; [*flower*] artificiel/-ielle; [*smile*] feint; **it's ~ wood/granite** c'est de l'imitation bois/granit.
III *vtr* **1** contrefaire [*signature, document*]; falsifier [*results*]; feindre [*emotion, illness*]; **2** US SPORT **to ~ a pass** feindre une passe.

falcon /ˈfɔːlkən, US ˈfælkən/ *n* faucon *m*.

Falklands /ˈfɔːkləndz/ **▶ 1022** *pr npl* (also **Falkland Islands**) **the ~** les îles *fpl* Malouines.

fall /fɔːl/ **▶ 1235** **I** *n* **1** LIT GEN chute *f* (**from** de); (of snow, leaves) chutes *fpl*; (of earth, soot) éboulement *m*; (of axe, hammer, dice) coup *m*; **a heavy ~ of rain** une grosse averse; **to have a ~** faire une chute, tomber; **2** (in temperature, shares, production, demand, quality, popularity) baisse *f* (**in** de); (more drastic) chute *f* (**in** de); **a ~ in value** une dépréciation; **3** (of leader, regime, town) chute *f*; (of monarchy) renversement *m*; (of seat) perte *f*; **the government's ~ from power** la chute du gouvernement; **4 ~ from grace** ou **favour** disgrâce *f*; **5** US (autumn) automne *m*; **6** (in pitch, intonation) descente *f*; **7** (in wrestling) tombé *m*; (in judo) chute *f*.
II falls *npl* chutes *fpl*.
III *vi* (*prét* **fell**; *pp* **fallen**) **1** (come down) tomber; **to ~ 10 metres** tomber de 10 mètres; **to ~ from** ou **out of** tomber de [*boat, nest, bag, hands*]; **to ~ off** ou **from** tomber de [*chair, table, roof, bike, wall*]; **to ~ on** tomber sur [*person, town*]; **to ~ in** ou **into** tomber dans [*bath, river*]; **to ~ down** tomber dans [*hole, stairs*]; **to ~ under** tomber sous [*table*]; passer sous [*bus, train*]; **to ~ through** passer à travers [*ceiling, hole*]; **to ~ through the air** tomber dans le vide; **to ~ to the floor** ou **to the ground** tomber par terre; **to ~ on the floor** tomber par terre; **2** (drop) [*quality, standard, level*] diminuer; [*temperature, price, produc-*

tion, number, attendance, morale] baisser; **to ~ (by)** baisser de; **to ~ to** descendre à; **to ~ from** descendre de; **to ~ below zero/5%** descendre au-dessous de zéro/5%; **3** (yield position) tomber; **to ~ from power** tomber; **to ~ to** tomber aux mains de [*enemy, allies*]; **the seat fell to Labour** le siège a été perdu au profit des travaillistes; **4** EUPH (die) tomber; **5** FIG (descend) [*night, silence, gaze*] tomber (**on** sur); [*blame*] retomber (**on** sur); [*shadow*] se projeter (**over** sur); **suspicion fell on her husband** les soupçons se sont portés sur son mari; **6** (occur) [*stress*] tomber (**on** sur); **Christmas ~s on a Monday** Noël tombe un lundi; **to ~ into/outside a category** rentrer/ne pas rentrer dans une catégorie; **7** (be incumbent on) **it ~s to sb to do** c'est à qn de faire; **8** (throw oneself) **to ~ into bed** se laisser tomber sur son lit; **to ~ to** ou **on one's knees** tomber à genoux; **to ~ at sb's feet/on sb's neck** se jeter aux pieds/au cou de qn.
IDIOMS **did he ~ or was he pushed?** HUM est-ce qu'il est parti de lui-même ou est-ce qu'on l'a forcé?; **the bigger you are** ou **the higher you climb, the harder you ~** plus dure sera la chute; **to stand or ~ on sth** reposer sur qch, dépendre de qch.

▪ **fall about**° GB: **to ~ about (laughing** ou **with laughter)** se tordre° de rire.

▪ **fall apart** [*bike, table*] être délabré; [*shoes*] être usé; [*car, house, hotel*] tomber en ruine; [*country*] se désagréger.

▪ **fall away 1** [*paint, plaster*] se détacher (**from** de); **2** [*ground*] descendre en pente (**to** vers); **3** [*demand, support*] diminuer.

▪ **fall back** GEN reculer; MIL se replier (**to** sur).

▪ **fall back on: ~ back on** [**sth**] avoir recours à [*savings, parents*]; **to have something to ~ back on** avoir quelque chose sur quoi se rabattre.

▪ **fall behind: ¶ ~ behind** [*country, student*] se laisser distancer; [*work, studies*] prendre du retard; **to ~ behind with** GB ou **in** US prendre du retard dans [*work, project*]; être en retard pour [*payments, rent*]; **¶ ~ behind** [**sth/sb**] se laisser devancer par.

▪ **fall down 1** LIT [*person, poster*] tomber; [*tent, scaffolding*] s'effondrer; **2** GB FIG [*argument, comparison*] faiblir; **to ~ down on** échouer à cause de [*detail, question, obstacle*].

▪ **fall for: ¶ ~ for** [**sth**] se laisser prendre à [*trick, story*]; **¶ ~ for** [**sb**] tomber amoureux/-euse de.

▪ **fall in 1** [*walls, roof*] s'écrouler, s'effondrer; **2** MIL [*soldier*] rentrer dans les rangs; [*soldiers*] former les rangs.

▪ **fall in with: ~ in with** [**sth/sb**] **1** (get involved with) faire la connaissance de [*group*]; **2** (go along with) se conformer à [*plans, action*]; **3** (be consistent with) être conforme à [*expectations*].

▪ **fall off 1** LIT [*person, hat, label*] tomber; **2** FIG [*attendance, sales, output*] diminuer; [*enthusiasm, quality*] baisser; [*support*] retomber; [*curve on graph*] décroître.

▪ **fall on: ¶ ~ on** [**sth**] se jeter sur [*food, treasure*]; **¶ ~ on** [**sb**] tomber sur [*person*].

▪ **fall open** [*book*] tomber ouvert; [*robe*] s'entrebâiller.

▪ **fall out 1** [*tooth, contact lens, page*] tomber; **his hair is ~ing out** il perd ses cheveux; **2** MIL [*soldiers*] rompre les rangs; **3**° (quarrel) se brouiller (**over** à propos de); **to ~ out with sb** GB (quarrel) se brouiller avec qn; US (have fight) se disputer avec qn; **4** GB (turn out) se passer.

▪ **fall over: ¶ ~ over** [*person*] tomber (par terre); [*object*] tomber; **¶ ~ over** [**sth**] trébucher sur [*object*]; **people were ~ing over themselves to buy shares** c'était à qui achèterait les actions.

▪ **fall through** [*plans, deal*] échouer.

▪ **fall to: ¶ ~ to** attaquer; **¶ ~ to doing** se mettre à faire.

▪ **fall upon = fall on**.

fallacious /fəˈleɪʃəs/ *adj* fallacieux/-ieuse.

fallacy /ˈfæləsɪ/ *n* (belief) erreur *f*; (argument) faux raisonnement *m*.

fallen /ˈfɔːlən/ **I** *pp* ▶ **fall**.

II *n* the ~ (+ *v pl*) les morts *mpl* au champ d'honneur.
III *pp adj* [*leaf, soldier*] mort; [*tree*] abattu.
fallibility /ˌfælə'bɪlətɪ/ *n* faillibilité *f*.
fallible /'fæləbl/ *adj* faillible.
falling-off /ˌfɔːlɪŋ'ɒf/ *n* (also **falloff**) diminution *f*.
Fallopian tube /fə'ləʊpɪən/ *n* trompe *f* de Fallope.
fall: **~out** *n* ¢ retombées *fpl*; **~out shelter** *n* abri *m* antiatomique.
fallow /'fæləʊ/ *adj* [*land*] en jachère.
fallow deer *n* daim *m*.
false /fɔːls/ *adj* faux/fausse; **to prove ~** s'avérer sans fondement; **a ~ sense of security** une fausse impression de sécurité; **to give ~ evidence** JUR faire un faux témoignage.
false: **~ alarm** *n* fausse alerte *f*; **~ bottom** *n* (in bag, box) double fond *m*; **~ economy** *n* fausse économie *f*.
falsehood /'fɔːlshʊd/ *n* (lie) mensonge *m*.
falsely /'fɔːlslɪ/ *adv* **1** (wrongly) faussement; (mistakenly) à tort; **2** [*smile, laugh*] avec affectation.
false move *n* fausse manœuvre *f*.
falseness /'fɔːlsnɪs/ *n* fausseté *f*.
false note *n* GEN couac○ *m*; (in film, novel) son *m* discordant; **to strike a ~** [*person*] faire une gaffe.
false pretences *npl* **on** OU **under ~** GEN en utilisant un subterfuge; JUR (by an action) par des moyens frauduleux.
false: **~ start** *n* faux départ *m*; **~ step** *n* faux pas *m*; **~ teeth** *npl* dentier *m*.
falsetto /fɔːl'setəʊ/ **I** *n* (voice) voix *f* de fausset; (singer) fausset *m*.
II *adj* de fausset.
falsification /ˌfɔːlsɪfɪ'keɪʃn/ *n* (of document, of figures) falsification *f*; (of the truth, of facts) déformation *f*.
falsify /'fɔːlsɪfaɪ/ *vtr* falsifier [*documents, accounts*]; déformer [*facts*].
falsity /'fɔːlsətɪ/ *n* fausseté *f*.
falter /'fɔːltə(r)/ **I** *vtr* (also **~ out**) balbutier [*word, phrase*].
II *vi* **1** [*demand, economy*] fléchir; [*person, courage*] faiblir; **2** (when speaking) [*person*] bafouiller; [*voice*] trembloter; **to speak without ~ing** parler avec assurance; **3** (when walking) [*person*] chanceler; [*footstep*] hésiter; **to walk without ~ing** marcher d'un pas assuré.
faltering /'fɔːltərɪŋ/ *adj* [*economy, demand*] en déclin; [*footsteps, voice*] hésitant.
fame /feɪm/ *n* renommée *f* (**as** en tant que); **~ and fortune** la gloire et la fortune.
famed /feɪmd/ *adj* célèbre (**for** pour; **as** en tant que).
familiar /fə'mɪlɪə(r)/ **I** *n* (animal spirit) démon *m* familier.
II *adj* GEN familier/-ière (**to** à); (customary) habituel; **her face looked ~ to me** son visage m'était familier; **that name has a ~ ring to it, that name sounds ~** ce nom me dit quelque chose; **it's a ~ story** c'est un scénario connu; **to be on ~ ground** être en terrain connu; **to be ~ with sb/sth** bien connaître qn/qch; **to make oneself ~ with sth** se familiariser avec qch.
familiarity /fəˌmɪlɪ'ærətɪ/ *n* GEN familiarité *f* (**with** avec); (of surroundings, place) caractère *m* familier.
familiarize /fə'mɪlɪəraɪz/ **I** *vtr* **to ~ sb with** familiariser qn avec [*job, procedure*]; habituer qn à [*environment, person*].
II *v refl* **to ~ oneself with** se familiariser avec [*system, work*]; s'habituer à [*person, place*].
familiarly /fə'mɪlɪəlɪ/ *adv* avec familiarité.
family /'fæməlɪ/ **I** *n* famille *f*; **to run in the ~** tenir de famille; **to be one of the ~** faire partie de la famille; **to start a ~** avoir un (premier) enfant.
II *noun modifier* [*home*] de famille; [*friend*] de la famille; **for ~ reasons** pour raisons familiales.
family: **Family Allowance** *n* GB ADMIN ≈ alloca-

tions *fpl* familiales; **~ business** *n* entreprise *f* familiale; **~ butcher** *n* boucher *m* de quartier.
family circle *n* **1** (group) cercle *m* familial; **2** U THEAT deuxième balcon *m*.
family: **~ court** *n* US JUR tribunal *m* des affaires familiales; **Family Credit** *n* GB ADMIN ≈ Complément *m* Familial; **~ man** *n* bon père *m* de famille; **~ name** *n* nom *m* de famille; **~-owned** *adj* [*business*] familial; **~ planning** *n* planning *m* familial.
family practice *n* US **to have a ~** être médecin *m* généraliste.
family: **~ room** *n* US salle *f* de jeu; **~-size(d)** *aa* familial; **~ tree** *n* arbre *m* généalogique; **~ unit** *n* SOCIOL cellule *f* familiale; **~ viewing** *n* émission pour les petits et les grands.
famine /'fæmɪn/ *n* famine *f*.
famished○ /'fæmɪʃt/ *adj* **I'm ~** je meurs de faim.
famous /'feɪməs/ *adj* GEN célèbre (**for** pour); [*school, university*] réputé (**for** pour); **a ~ victory** une grande victoire.
famously /'feɪməslɪ/ *adv* **1** (wonderfully) à merveille; **Churchill is ~ quoted as saying**... tout le monde connaît les célèbres mots de Churchill...
fan /fæn/ **I** *n* **1** (of football, jazz etc) mordu/-e○ *m/f*; (of star, actor etc) fan○ *mf*; (of politician, artist) admirateur/-trice *m/f*; SPORT (of team) supporter *m*; **I'm a ~ of American TV** j'adore la télé américaine; **2** (for cooling) GEN, AUT (mechanical) ventilateur *m*; (hand-held) éventail *m*.
II *vtr* (*p prés etc* **-nn-**) **1** (stimulate) attiser [*fire, hatred, passion*]; **2** (cool) [*breeze*] rafraîchir [*face*]; **to ~ one's face** s'éventer le visage.
III *v refl* (*p prés etc* **-nn-**) **to ~ oneself** s'éventer.
■ **fan out**: ¶ **~ out** [*police, troops*] se déployer (en éventail); [*lines, railway lines*] se diviser et partir dans toutes les directions; ¶ **~ [sth] out, ~ out [sth]** ouvrir [qch] en éventail [*cards, papers*].
fanatic /fə'nætɪk/ *n* fanatique *mf*.
fanatical /fə'nætɪkl/ *adj* fanatique.
fanaticism /fə'nætɪsɪzəm/ *n* fanatisme *m*.
fan belt *n* AUT courroie *f* de ventilateur.
fanciful /'fænsɪfl/ *adj* [*person*] fantasque; [*idea, name*] extravagant; [*explanation*] fantaisiste; [*building*] orné.
fancy /'fænsɪ/ **I** *n* **1** (liking) **to catch** OU **take sb's ~** [*object*] faire envie à qn; **he had taken her ~** (sexually) il lui avait tapé dans l'œil○; GEN il lui plaisait bien; **to take a ~ to sb** (sexually) GB s'enticher de qn; GEN s'attacher à qn; **I've taken a ~ to that car** cette voiture m'a tapé dans l'œil○; **2** (whim) caprice *m*; **as/when the ~ takes me** comme/quand ça me prend; **3** (fantasy) imagination *f*; **a flight of ~** une lubie.
II *adj* **1** (elaborate) [*lighting, equipment*] sophistiqué; [*food*] de luxe; [*paper, box*] fantaisie *inv*; ZOOL [*breed*] d'agrément; **nothing ~** (meal) rien de spécial; **2**○ PÉJ (pretentious) [*hotel, restaurant*] de luxe; [*price*] exorbitant; [*name*] tordu; [*clothes*] chic.
III *vtr* **1**○ (want) avoir (bien) envie de [*food, drink, object*]; **what do you ~ for lunch?** qu'est-ce qui te plairait pour le déjeuner?; **do you ~ going to the cinema?** ça te dirait○ d'aller au cinéma?; **I don't ~ the idea of sharing a flat** l'idée de partager un appartement ne me dit rien; **2**○ GB (feel attracted to) **she fancies him** elle s'est entichée de lui; **3** (expressing surprise) **~ her remembering my name!** figure-toi qu'elle se souvenait de mon nom!; **~ seeing you here**○! tiens donc, toi ici?; **~ that**○! pas possible○!; **4**† (believe) croire; (imagine) s'imaginer; **5** SPORT voir [qn/qch] gagnant [*athlete, horse*].
IV *v refl* ○PÉJ **he fancies himself** il ne se prend pas pour rien; **she fancies herself in that hat** elle n'arrête pas de frimer○ avec ce chapeau; **he fancies himself as James Bond** il se prend pour James Bond.
V fancied *pp adj* SPORT [*contender*] favori.
fancy dress **I** *n* ¢ GB déguisement *m*; **in ~** déguisé.
II (also **fancy-dress**) *noun modifier* [*party*] costumé; [*competition*] de déguisement.
fanfare /'fænfeə(r)/ *n* fanfare *f*.

fang /fæŋ/ *n* (of dog, wolf) croc *m*; (of snake) crochet *m* (à venin).

fan: **~ heater** *n* radiateur *m* soufflant; **~ mail** *n* ₵ lettres *fpl* envoyées par des admirateurs.

fantasize /'fæntəsaɪz/ **I** *vtr* **to ~ that** rêver que.
II *vi* fantasmer (**about** sur); **to ~ about doing** rêver de faire.

fantastic /fæn'tæstɪk/ *adj* **1**○ (wonderful) merveilleux, super○; **2** (unrealistic) invraisemblable; **3**○ (huge) [*profit*] fabuleux/-euse; [*speed, increase*] vertigineux/ -euse; **4** (magical) fantastique.

fantastically /fæn'tæstɪklɪ/ *adv* **1**○ [*wealthy*] immensément; [*expensive*] terriblement; **2**○ [*increase*] de façon vertigineuse; [*perform*] incroyablement; **3** [*coloured, portrayed*] fabuleusement.

fantasy /'fæntəsɪ/ *n* **1** GEN rêve *m*; PSYCH fantasme *m*; (untruth) idée *f* fantaisiste; **2** (genre) fantastique *m*.

FAO *n* (*abrév* = **Food and Agriculture Organization**) FAO *f*.

far /fɑː(r)/ **I** *adv* **1** (in space) loin; **have you come ~?** est-ce que vous venez de loin?; **is it ~ to York?** est-ce que York est loin d'ici?; **~ off, ~ away** au loin; **to be ~ from home** être loin de chez soi; **~ beyond the city** bien au-delà de la ville; **how ~ is it to Leeds?** combien y a-t-il (de kilomètres) jusqu'à Leeds?; **how ~ is Glasgow from London?** Glasgow est à quelle distance de Londres?; **as ~ as** jusqu'à; **2** (in time) **~ back in the past** loin dans le passé; **as ~ back as 1965** déjà en 1965; **as ~ back as he can remember** d'aussi loin qu'il s'en souvienne; **the holidays are not ~ off** c'est bientôt les vacances; **he's not ~ off 70** il n'a pas loin de 70 ans; **he worked ~ into the night** il a travaillé tard dans la nuit; **3** (to a great degree, very much) bien; **~ better** bien mieux; **~ too fast** bien trop vite; **~ too much money** bien trop d'argent; **~ more** bien plus; **~ above average** bien au-dessus de la moyenne; **4** (to what extent, to the extent that) **how ~ is it possible to...?** dans quelle mesure est-il possible de...?; **how ~ have they got?** où en sont-ils?; **as ou so ~ as we can,** as ou so **~ as possible** autant que possible, dans la mesure du possible; **as ou so ~ as we know** pour autant que nous le sachions; **as ou so ~ as I am concerned** quant à moi; **5** (to extreme degree) loin; **to go too ~** aller trop loin; **she took ou carried the joke too ~** elle a poussé la plaisanterie un peu loin; **to push sb too ~** pousser qn à bout.
II *adj* **1** (remote) **the ~ north/south (of)** l'extrême nord/sud (de); **the ~ east/west (of)** tout à fait à l'est/l'ouest (de); **2** (further away, other) autre; **at the ~ end of the room** à l'autre bout de la pièce; **on the ~ side of the wall** de l'autre côté du mur; **3** POL **the ~ right/left** l'extrême droite/gauche.
III by far *adv phr* de loin.
IV far and away *adv phr* de loin.
V far from *prep phr* loin de; **~ from satisfied** loin d'être satisfait.
VI so far *adv phr* **1** (up till now) jusqu'ici; **so ~, so good** pour l'instant tout va bien; **2** (up to a point) **they will only compromise so ~** ils sont prêts à transiger jusqu'à un certain point seulement; **you can only trust him so ~** tu ne peux pas lui faire entièrement confiance.
IDIOMS not to be ~ off ou **out** ou **wrong** ne pas être loin du compte; **~ and wide, ~ and near** partout; **~ be it from me to do** loin de moi l'idée de faire; **to be a ~ cry from** être bien loin de; **she will go ~** elle ira loin; **this wine/food won't go very ~** on ne va pas aller loin avec ce vin/ce qu'on a à manger.

faraway /'fɑːrəweɪ/ *adj* (*épith*) LIT, FIG lointain.

farce /fɑːs/ *n* THEAT, FIG farce *f*.

farcical /'fɑːsɪkl/ *adj* ridicule.

far-distant /ˌfɑːˈdɪstənt/ *adj* lointain.

fare /feə(r)/ **I** *n* **1** (cost of travelling) (on bus, underground) prix *m* du ticket; (on train, plane) prix *m* du billet; **taxi ~** prix *m* de la course; **child/adult ~** tarif *m* enfants/ adultes; **half/full ~** demi-/plein tarif *m*; **return ~** prix *m* d'un aller-retour; **~s are going up** les tarifs

augmentent; **2** (taxi passenger) client/-e *m/f* (d'un taxi); **3**† (food) nourriture *f*; **prison ~** régime *m* de prison.
II *vi* (get on) **how did you ~?** comment ça s'est passé?; **the company is faring well despite the recession** la société se porte bien malgré la récession.

far: **Far East** *pr n* Extrême-Orient *m*; **Far Eastern** *adj* [*affairs, influence, markets*] de l'Extrême-Orient.

farewell /ˌfeəˈwel/ **I** *n, excl* adieu *m*; **to say one's ~s** faire ses adieux.
II *noun modifier* [*party, speech*] d'adieu.

far-fetched /ˌfɑːˈfetʃt/ *adj* tiré par les cheveux○.

far-flung /ˌfɑːˈflʌŋ/ *adj* **1** (remote) [*country*] lointain; **2** (widely distributed) [*towns*] éloignés les uns des autres.

farm /fɑːm/ **I** *n* ferme *f*; **chicken/pig ~** élevage *m* de poulets/de porcs.
II *noun modifier* [*building, animal*] de ferme.
III *vtr* cultiver, exploiter [*land*].
IV *vi* être fermier.
V farmed *pp adj* [*fish*] élevé dans une pisciculture.
■ **farm out:** **~ out** [*sth*] sous-traiter [*work*] (**to** à).

farmer /'fɑːmə(r)/ **▶1251**] *n* (in general) fermier *m*; (in official terminology) agriculteur *m*; (arable) cultivateur *m*; **pig ~** éleveur *m* de porcs; **~'s wife** fermière *f*.

farm: **~ hand** *n* = **farm worker**; **~house** *n* (where farmer lives) habitation *f* du fermier; (house in country) ferme *f*.

farming /'fɑːmɪŋ/ **I** *n* (profession) agriculture *f*; (of land) exploitation *f*; **sheep ~** élevage *m* de moutons.
II *noun modifier* [*community*] rural; [*method*] de culture; [*subsidy*] à l'agriculture.

farm: **~ labourer** *n* = **farm worker**; **~land** *n* ₵ (for cultivation) terres *fpl* arables; **~ produce** *n* ₵ produits *mpl* de la ferme; **~ worker** **▶1251**] *n* ouvrier/-ière *m/f* agricole; **~yard** *n* cour *f* de ferme.

Faroes /'feərəʊz/ **▶1022**] *pr npl* (also **Faroe Islands**) **the ~** les îles *fpl* Féroé.

far-off /'fɑːrɒf/ *adj* (*épith*) lointain.

farrago /fəˈrɑːgəʊ/ *n* ramassis *m*.

far-reaching /ˌfɑːˈriːtʃɪŋ/ *adj* [*effect, implication*] considérable; [*change, reform*] radical; [*programme, plan, proposal*] d'une portée considérable.

farrier /'færɪə(r)/ *n* GB maréchal-ferrant *m*.

far-sighted /ˌfɑːˈsaɪtɪd/ *adj* **1** (prudent) [*person, policy*] prévoyant; **2** US MED [*person*] presbyte.

farther /'fɑːðə(r)/ (*comparative of* **far**) **I** *adv* **▶further I** 1, 2.
II *adj* **▶further II** 2.

■ Note Au sens littéral on préférera *farther* et au sens figuré *further*.

farthest /'fɑːðɪst/ *adj, adv* (*superlative of* **far**) **▶furthest**.

■ Note Au sens littéral on préférera *farthest* et au sens figuré *furthest*.

fascia /'feɪʃə/ *n* GB (dashboard) tableau *m* de bord; (over shop) panneau *m*.

fascinate /'fæsɪneɪt/ *vtr* (interest) passionner; (stronger) fasciner.

fascinated /'fæsɪneɪtɪd/ *adj* (by spectacle) captivé; (by person) fasciné; (by subject) passionné.

fascinating /'fæsɪneɪtɪŋ/ *adj* [*book, discussion*] passionnant; [*person*] fascinant.

fascination /ˌfæsɪˈneɪʃn/ *n* **1** (interest) passion *f* (**with, for** pour); **in ~** captivé; (stronger) fasciné; **2** (power) (pouvoir *m* de) fascination *f*.

fascism /'fæʃɪzəm/ *n* fascisme *m*.

fascist /'fæʃɪst/ *n, adj* fasciste (*mf*) ALSO PEJ.

fashion /'fæʃn/ **I** *n* **1** (manner) façon *f*, manière *f*; **in my own ~** à ma manière; **in the Chinese ~** à la chinoise; **after a ~** plus ou moins bien; **2** (vogue, trend) mode *f* (**for** de); **in ~** à la mode; **out of ~** démodé; **to go out of ~** se démoder, passer de mode.
II *noun modifier* [*accessory*] de mode; [*jewellery*] fantaisie *inv*.
III fashions *npl* **ladies' ~s** vêtements *mpl* pour femmes; **Paris ~s** la mode parisienne.

IV *vtr* façonner [*clay, wood*] (**into** en); fabriquer [*object*] (**out of, from** de).

fashionable /'fæʃnəbl/ *adj* [*garment, name*] à la mode (**among, with** parmi); [*resort, restaurant*] chic *inv* (**among, with** parmi); [*pastime, topic*] en vogue (**among, with** parmi); **it's no longer ~ to smoke** cela ne se fait plus de fumer.

fashionably /'fæʃnəbli/ *adv* à la mode.

fashion: **~ designer** ▶1251 | *n* GEN modéliste *mf*; (world-famous) grand couturier *m*; **~ house** *n* maison *f* de couture; **~ model** ▶1251 | *n* mannequin *m*; **~ show** *n* présentation *f* de collection.

fast /fɑːst, US fæst/ **I** *n* jeûne *m*.
II *adj* **1** (speedy) ALSO PHOT rapide; **a ~ train** un express; **a ~ time** SPORT un bon temps; **to be a ~ walker/reader** marcher/lire vite; **2** SPORT [*court, pitch, track*] rapide; **3** (ahead of time) **my watch is ~** ma montre avance; **you're five minutes ~** ta montre avance de cinq minutes; **4** (firm) (*jamais épith*) [*door, lid*] bien fermé; [*rope*] bien attaché; **to make** [*sth*] **~** amarrer [*boat*]; attacher [*rope*]; **5** (loyal) [*friend*] fidèle; [*friendship*] solide; **6** (permanent) **~ dye** grand teint *m*.
III *adv* **1** (rapidly) vite, rapidement; **how ~ can you knit/read?** est-ce que tu tricotes/lis vite?; **I need help ~** j'ai besoin d'aide tout de suite; **I ran as ~ as my legs would carry me** je me suis sauvé à toutes jambes; **2** (firmly) [*hold*] ferme; [*stuck*] bel et bien (*before pp*); [*shut*] bien; **to be ~ asleep** dormir à poings fermés.
IV *vi* (abstain from food) jeûner.
IDIOMS **to pull a ~ one on sb** rouler qn○; **to play ~ and loose** faire les quatre cents coups○.

fast: **~back** *n* GB AUT voiture *f* à l'arrière profilé; **~ breeder reactor** *n* TECH surgénérateur *m*.

fasten /'fɑːsn, US 'fæsn/ **I** *vtr* **1** (close) fermer [*lid, case*]; attacher [*belt, necklace*]; boutonner [*coat*]; boucler [*buckle*]; **2** (attach) fixer [*notice, shelf*] (**to** à; **onto** sur); attacher [*lead, rope*] (**to** à); **his eyes ~ed on me** son regard s'est fixé sur moi.
II *vi* [*box*] se fermer; [*necklace, skirt*] s'attacher.
■ **fasten down**: **~ down** [*sth*], **~** [*sth*] **down** fermer [*hatch, lid*].
■ **fasten on**: ¶ **~ on** [*lid, handle*] s'attacher; ¶ **~ on** [*sth*] attacher [*lid, handle*]; ¶ **~ on** [*sth*] FIG se mettre [qch] dans la tête [*idea*].
■ **fasten up**: **~ up** [*sth*], **~** [*sth*] **up** boutonner [*coat*].

fastener /'fɑːsnə(r), US 'fæsnə(r)/ *n* GEN attache *f*; (hook) agrafe *f*; (clasp) fermoir *m*.

fast food /ˌfɑːst 'fuːd, US ˌfæst-/ **I** *n* nourriture *f* de fast-food.
II *noun modifier* [*chain*] de restauration rapide ou de fast-food; [*industry*] de la restauration rapide or du fast-food; **a ~ restaurant** un fast-food.

fast-forward /ˌfɑːstˈfɔːwəd, US ˌfæst-/ **I** *n* AUDIO avance *f* rapide.
II *noun modifier* [*key, button*] d'avance rapide (*after n*).
III *vtr* faire avancer rapidement.

fast-growing /ˌfɑːstˈɡrəʊɪŋ, US ˌfæst-/ *adj* en pleine expansion.

fastidious /fæˈstɪdɪəs/ *adj* **1** (extremely careful) [*person*] méticuleux/-euse (**about** sur); [*work*] minutieux/-ieuse; **2** (fussy) pointilleux.

fast lane /ˈfɑːst leɪn, US ˈfæst-/ *n* AUT voie *f* de dépassement; **life in the ~** FIG la vie à cent à l'heure.

fast-talking *adj* [*salesperson*] baratineur/-euse○.

fat /fæt/ **I** *n* **1** (in diet) matières *fpl* grasses; **animal ~s** graisses *fpl* animales; **2** (on meat) gras *m*; **you can leave the ~** tu peux laisser le gras; **3** (for cooking) GEN matière *f* grasse; (from meat) graisse *f*; **4** (in body) graisse *f*; **body ~** tissu adipeux.
II *adj* **1** (overweight) [*person, animal, body, bottom, etc*] gros/grosse; (of child) [*cheek*] rebondi; [*thigh, finger*] dodu; **to get ~** grossir; **2** (full) [*wallet, envelope*] rebondi; [*file, magazine*] épais/épaisse; **3** (remunerative) [*profit, cheque*] gros/grosse.

IDIOMS the **~'s in the fire**○ ça va faire des étincelles○; **to live off the ~ of the land** vivre grassement.

fatal /'feɪtl/ *adj* [*accident, injury, blow*] mortel/-elle (**to** pour); [*flaw, mistake*] fatal; [*decision*] funeste; [*day, hour*] fatidique; **to be ~ to sb/sth** porter un coup fatal à qn/qch; **it would be ~ to do** ce serait une grave erreur de faire.

fatalist /'feɪtəlɪst/ *n* fataliste *mf*.

fatalistic /ˌfeɪtəˈlɪstɪk/ *adj* fataliste.

fatality /fəˈtælətɪ/ *n* (person killed) mort *m*; **road fatalities** accidents *mpl* mortels de la route.

fatally /'feɪtəlɪ/ *adv* **1** [*injured, wounded*] mortellement; **to be ~ ill** être condamné; **2** FIG [*flawed, compromised*] irrémédiablement.

fate /feɪt/ *n* sort *m*; **a (cruel) twist of ~** un (cruel) caprice du sort.

fated /'feɪtɪd/ *adj* **~ to do** destiné à faire; **it was ~** c'était écrit.

fateful /'feɪtfl/ *adj* [*decision*] fatal; [*day*] fatidique.

fat-free *adj* sans matières grasses.

father /'fɑːðə(r)/ **I** *n* père *m*; **to be like a ~ to sb** être un vrai père pour qn; **like ~ like son** tel père tel fils; **land of our ~s** patrie de nos pères or aïeux.
II *vtr* engendrer [*child*].

Father /'fɑːðə(r)/ ▶937 | *n* **1** RELIG (God) Père *m*; **the Our ~** le Notre Père; **God the ~** Dieu le Père; **2** (title for priest) père *m*; **~ Smith** le père Smith.

father: **Father Christmas** GB *n* le père Noël; **~ confessor** *n* RELIG confesseur *m*; FIG directeur *m* de conscience; **~ figure** *n* image *f* du père.

fatherhood /'fɑːðəhʊd/ *n* paternité *f*.

father: **~-in-law** *n* (*pl* **~s-in-law**) beau-père *m*; **~land** *n* patrie *f*.

fatherless /'fɑːðəlɪs/ *adj* sans père.

fatherly /'fɑːðəlɪ/ *adj* paternel/-elle.

fathom /'fæðəm/ **I** *n* NAUT brasse *f* anglaise (= *1,83 m*).
II *vtr* **1** NAUT sonder; **2** (also GB **~ out**) (understand) comprendre.

fatigue /fəˈtiːɡ/ **I** *n* **1** (of person) épuisement *m*; **2** TECH **metal ~** fatigue *f* du métal; **3** US MIL corvée *f*.
II **fatigues** *npl* MIL **1** (uniform) treillis *m*; **camouflage ~s** tenue *f* de camouflage; **2** (duties) corvée *f*.

fatness /'fætnɪs/ *n* corpulence *f*.

fatten /'fætn/ **I** *vtr* = **fatten up**.
II *vi* [*animal*] engraisser.
■ **fatten up**: **~** [*sb/sth*] **up**, **~ up** [*sb/sth*] engraisser [*animal*]; faire grossir [*person*].

fattening /'fætnɪŋ/ *adj* [*food, drink*] qui fait grossir (*after n*).

fatty /'fætɪ/ *adj* [*tissue, deposit*] graisseux/-euse; [*food, meat*] gras/grasse; **~ acid** acide *m* gras.

fatuous /'fætʃʊəs/ *adj* [*comment, smile*] stupide; [*activity*] futile.

faucet /'fɔːsɪt/ *n* US robinet *m*.

fault /fɔːlt/ **I** *n* **1** (flaw) défaut *m* (**in** dans); (electrical failure) panne *f*; **structural/design ~** défaut structurel/de conception; **he's always finding ~** il trouve toujours quelque chose à redire; **2** (responsibility) faute *f*; **to be sb's ~**, **to be the ~ of sb** être (de) la faute de qn; **to be sb's ~ that** être à cause de qn que; **it's my own ~** c'est de ma faute; **whose ~ was it?** à qui la faute?; **the ~ lies with him** c'est lui qui est entièrement responsable; **to be at ~** être en tort; **3** SPORT (call) faute!; **to serve a ~** faire une faute au service; **4** (in earth) faille *f*; **5** JUR faute *f*.
II *vtr* prendre [qch/qn] en défaut; **it cannot be ~ed** c'est irréprochable.

fault-finding /'fɔːltfaɪndɪŋ/ **I** *n* **1** TECH localisation *f* du défaut or de la panne; **2** (of person) habitude *f* de tout critiquer.
II *adj* [*person*] qui critique tout; [*attitude*] négatif/-ive.

faultless /'fɔːltlɪs/ *adj* [*performance, manners*] impeccable; [*taste*] irréprochable.

faulty /'fɔ:ltɪ/ *adj* [*wiring, machine*] défectueux/-euse; [*logic, argument*] erroné.

faun /fɔ:n/ *n* faune *m*.

fauna /'fɔ:nə/ *n* (*pl* **~s** ou **-ae**) faune *f*.

faux pas /ˌfəʊ 'pɑ:/ *n* (*pl* **~**) impair *m*.

favour GB, **favor** US /'feɪvə(r)/ I *n* 1 (approval) **to regard sb/sth with ~** considérer qn/qch avec bienveillance; **to win/lose ~ with sb** s'attirer/perdre les bonnes grâces de qn; **to find ~ with sb** trouver grâce aux yeux de qn; **to be out of ~ with sb** [*person*] ne plus être dans les bonnes grâces de qn; [*idea, method*] ne plus être en vogue auprès de qn; **to fall** ou **go out of ~** [*idea, method*] passer de mode; 2 (kindness) service *m*; **to do sb a ~** rendre service à qn; **they're not doing themselves any ~s** ils desservent leur (propre) cause (**by doing** en faisant); **as a (special) ~** à titre de service exceptionnel ; **to ask a ~ of sb, to ask sb a ~** demander un service à qn; **to return a ~** LIT, **to return the ~** IRON rendre la pareille (**by doing** en faisant); 3 (advantage) **to be in sb's ~** (situation) être avantageux pour qn; [*financial rates, wind*] être favorable à qn; **to have sth in one's ~** avoir qch pour soi; **the plan has a lot in its ~** le projet présente beaucoup d'avantages.
II **favours** *npl* EUPH (sexual) faveurs *fpl*.
III *vtr* 1 (prefer) être pour [*method, solution*]; préférer [*clothing, colour*]; être partisan de [*political party, course of action*]; **to ~ sb** GEN montrer une préférence pour qn; (unfairly) accorder un traitement de faveur à qn; 2 (benefit) [*plans, circumstances*] favoriser; [*law, balance of power*] privilégier.
IV **favoured** *pp adj* GEN favori/-ite; (most likely) [*date, plan, view*] privilégié.
V **in favour of** *prep phr* 1 (on the side of) en faveur de; **to be in ~ of sb/sth** être pour qn/qch; **to speak in ~ of** soutenir [*motion*]; **to speak in sb's ~** se prononcer en faveur de qn; **to come out in ~ of** exprimer son soutien à [*plan, person*]; 2 (to the advantage of) **to work in ~ of sb** avantager qn; **to decide in sb's ~** GEN donner raison à qn; JUR donner gain de cause à qn; 3 (out of preference for) [*reject*] au profit de.

favourable GB, **favorable** US /'feɪvərəbl/ *adj* GEN favorable (**to** à); (result, sign) bon/bonne (before *n*); **to have a ~ reception** être bien reçu.

favourably GB, **favorably** US /'feɪvərəblɪ/ *adv* [*speak, write*] en termes favorables; [*look on, consider*] d'un œil favorable; **to compare ~ with sth** soutenir la comparaison avec qch.

favourite GB, **favorite** US /'feɪvərɪt/ I *n* 1 préféré/-e *m/f*; **to be a great ~ with sb** avoir beaucoup de succès auprès de qn; 2 SPORT favori/-ite *m/f*.
II *adj* préféré, favori/-ite.

favouritism GB, **favoritism** US /'feɪvərɪtɪzəm/ *n* favoritisme *m*.

fawn /fɔ:n/ ▶818 I *n* 1 ZOOL faon *m*; 2 (colour) beige *m* foncé.
II *adj* beige foncé *inv*.
III *vi* **to ~ on sb** [*dog*] faire la fête à qn; [*person*] PÉJ flagorner qn.

fawning /'fɔ:nɪŋ/ *adj* servile.

fax /fæks/ I *n* (*pl* **~es**) 1 (also **~ message**) télécopie *f*, fax *m*; 2 (also **~ machine**) télécopieur *m*, fax *m*.
II *vtr* télécopier, faxer [*document*]; envoyer une télécopie ou un fax à [*person*].

fax number *n* numéro *m* de télécopie or de fax.

faze° /feɪz/ *vtr* dérouter.

FBI *n* US (abrév = **Federal Bureau of Investigation**) Police *f* judiciaire fédérale.

FCO *n* GB (abrév = **Foreign and Commonwealth Office**) ministère *m* des Affaires étrangères et du Commonwealth.

FDA *n* US (abrév = **Food and Drug Administration**) organisme gouvernemental de contrôle pharmaceutique et alimentaire.

fear /fɪə(r)/ I *n* 1 (fright) peur *f*; **he accepted out of ~** c'est la peur qui l'a fait accepter; **to live** ou **go in**

~ of one's life craindre pour sa vie; **the news struck ~ into his heart** la nouvelle l'a rempli d'effroi; 2 (apprehension) crainte *f* (**for** pour); **my ~s proved groundless** mes craintes se sont révélées injustifiées; **the future/the operation holds no ~s for her** elle n'a pas peur de l'avenir/de l'opération; 3 (possibility) **there's no ~ of him** ou **his being late** il n'y a pas de danger qu'il soit en retard.
II *vtr* craindre; **I ~ (that) she may be dead** j'ai (bien) peur or je crains qu'elle (ne) soit morte; **it is ~ed (that)** on craint que (+ *subj*); **a ruler who was greatly ~ed** un chef qui inspirait la crainte; **she's a woman to be ~ed** c'est une femme redoutable; **to ~ the worst** craindre le pire, s'attendre au pire; **I ~ not** je crains (bien) que non; **I ~ so** (to positive question) je crains bien que oui; (to negative question) j'ai bien peur que si.
III *vi* **to ~ for sth/sb** craindre pour qch/qn; **I ~ for her life** je crains pour sa vie.
IDIOMS **without ~ or favour** de façon impartiale; **in ~ and trembling** tremblant de peur.

fearful /'fɪəfl/ *adj* 1 (afraid) craintif/-ive; **to be ~ of sth/of doing** avoir peur de qch/de faire; 2 (dreadful) affreux/-euse.

fearless /'fɪəlɪs/ *adj* sans peur, intrépide.

fearsome /'fɪəsəm/ *adj* (frightening) effroyable; (formidable) redoutable.

feasibility /ˌfi:zə'bɪlətɪ/ *n* 1 (of idea, plan, proposal) faisabilité *f* (of de); **the ~ of doing** la possibilité de faire; 2 (of claim, story) vraisemblance *f* (of de).

feasible /'fi:zəbl/ *adj* 1 (possible) [*project*] réalisable; **it is ~ that** il est possible que (+ *subj*); **to be ~ to do sth** être possible de faire qch; 2 [*excuse, explanation*] plausible.

feast /fi:st/ I *n* GEN festin *m*; RELIG fête *f*; **~ day** jour *m* de fête; **wedding ~** banquet de mariage; FIG (delight for the senses) régal *m* (**to, for** pour).
II *vtr* régaler [*person*] (**on, with** de).
III *vi* se régaler (**on** de).

feat /fi:t/ *n* exploit *m*; **it was no mean ~** cela n'a pas été une mince affaire; **a ~ of engineering** une prouesse technologique.

feather /'feðə(r)/ I *n* plume *f*.
II *noun modifier* [*mattress, bed*] de plumes.

feathered /feðə(r)d/ *adj* [*garment*] à plumes.
IDIOMS **as light as a ~** léger comme une plume; **birds of a ~ (flock together)** PROV qui se ressemble s'assemble PROV; **that's a ~ in his cap** c'est un bon point pour lui; **you could have knocked me down with a ~** j'en avais le souffle coupé.

feather: **~-brained** *adj* écervelé; **~ duster** *n* plumeau *m*; **~weight** *n* poids *m* plume.

feature /'fi:tʃə(r)/ I *n* 1 (distinctive characteristic) trait *m*, caractéristique *f*; **a ~ of those times** une caractéristique de cette époque; 2 (aspect) aspect *m*, côté *m*; **to have no redeeming ~s** n'avoir rien pour soi; 3 (of face) trait *m*; **with sharp ~s** aux traits anguleux; 4 (of car, computer, product) accessoire *m*; **built-in safety ~s** équipement *m* de sécurité intégré; 5 (film) long métrage *m*; 6 (in newspaper) article *m* de fond (**on** sur); **she does a ~ in the Times** elle est chroniqueuse au 'Times'; 7 TV, RADIO reportage *m* (**on** sur); 8 LING trait *m*.
II *vtr* 1 (present) [*film, magazine*] présenter [*story, photo, star*]; [*advert, poster*] représenter [*person, scene*]; **to be ~d in** figurer dans; 2 (highlight) être équipé de [*accessory*].
III *vi* 1 (figure) figurer; 2 TV, CIN [*performer*] jouer.

feature: **~ article** *n* article *m* de fond; **~ film** *n* long métrage *m*; **~-length** *adj* long métrage *inv* (after *n*).

featureless /'fi:tʃəlɪs/ *adj* sans caractère.

Feb /feb/ *n*: abrév écrite = **February**.

February /'febrʊərɪ, US -erɪ/ ▶1090 *n* février *m*.

feckless /'feklɪs/ *adj* 1 (improvident) irresponsable; 2 (helpless) incapable; 3 (inept) maladroit.

fecund /'fi:kənd, 'fekənd/ *adj* LITTÉR fécond.

fed /fed/ *prét, pp* ▶ **feed**.

Fed /fed/ *abrév* ▶ **federal**, **federation**.

federal /'fedərəl/ **I** **Federal** *pr n* US HIST (party supporter) Fédéraliste *mf*; (soldier) nordiste *m*.
II *adj* ADMIN, POL [*court, judge, police*] fédéral; **the ~ government** US le gouvernement fédéral.
IDIOMS **to make a ~ case out of sth** US faire toute une histoire de qch○.

federalist /'fedərəlɪst/ *n, adj* fédéraliste (*mf*).

federally /'fedərəlɪ/ *adv* **1** [*elect, govern*] à un niveau fédéral; **2** US [*funded, built*] par le gouvernement fédéral.

federal: **Federal Republic of Germany** *n* République *f* fédérale d'Allemagne; **Federal Reserve Bank** *n* US banque *f* régionale des États-Unis.

federate /'fedəreɪt/ **I** *adj* fédéré.
II *vtr* fédérer.
III *vi* se fédérer.

federation /ˌfedə'reɪʃn/ *n* fédération *f*.

fed up○ /ˌfed 'ʌp/ *adj* **to be ~** en avoir marre○.

fee /fi:/ *n* **1** (for professional, artistic service) honoraires *mpl*; **school ~s** frais *mpl* de scolarité; **he charged us a ~ of $200** il nous a fait payer 200 dollars; **he will do it for a ~** il le fera s'il est payé; **2** (for admission) droit *m* d'entrée; (for membership) cotisation *f*; **registration ~** frais *mpl* d'inscription.

feeble /'fi:bl/ *adj* [*person, institution, sound, light, movement*] faible; [*argument, excuse*] peu convaincant; [*joke, attempt*] médiocre.

feeble-minded /ˌfi:bl'maɪndɪd/ *adj* imbécile; EUPH (handicapped) faible d'esprit.

feebleness /'fi:blnɪs/ *n* faiblesse *f*.

feebly /'fi:blɪ/ *adv* [*smile, wave*] faiblement; [*protest*] mollement.

feed /fi:d/ **I** *n* **1** (meal) (for animal) ration *f* de nourriture; (for baby) (breast) tétée *f*; (bottle) biberon *m*; **2** AGRIC (also **~ stuffs**) aliments *mpl* pour animaux; **3** IND, TECH (material) alimentation *f*; (mechanism) mécanisme *m* d'alimentation.
II *vtr* (*prét, pp* **fed**) **1** (supply with food) nourrir [*animal, plant, person*] (**on** de); donner à manger à [*pet*]; ravitailler [*army*]; **to ~ a baby** (on breast) donner le sein à un bébé; (on bottle) donner le biberon à un bébé; **I shall have ten to ~** je ferai la cuisine pour dix; **2** (supply) alimenter [*lake, machine*]; mettre des pièces dans [*meter*]; fournir [*information*] (**to** à); **to ~ sth into** mettre ou introduire qch dans; **3** FIG (fuel) alimenter [*ambition, prejudice*]; **4** SPORT faire passer [*ball*] (**to** à); **5** THEAT donner la réplique à [*comedian*].
III *vi* (*prét, pp* **fed**) **1** (eat) manger; **to ~ on** LIT se nourrir de; FIG être alimenté par; **2** (enter) **to ~ into** [*paper, tape*] s'introduire dans [*machine*].
IV *v refl* **to ~ oneself** [*child, invalid*] manger tout seul.
■ **feed up** GB: **~** [*sth/sb*] **up** bien nourrir [*child, invalid*]; engraisser [*animal*].

feedback /'fi:dbæk/ *n* **1** ₵ GEN (from people) remarques *fpl* (**on** sur; **from** de la part de); **I'd like some ~** j'aimerais avoir vos impressions; **we haven't had any ~** il n'y a pas eu de réactions; **2** COMPUT feed-back *m inv*; **3** AUDIO (on hifi) réaction *f* parasite.

feeder /'fi:də(r)/ *n* **1** (also **~ bib**) GB bavette *f*; **2** (also **~ road**) GB bretelle *f* de raccordement; **3** (for printer, photocopier) chargeur *m*.

feeding /'fi:dɪŋ/ *n* alimentation *f*.

feeding: **~ bottle** *n* GB biberon *m*; **~ time** *n* heure *f* de nourrir les animaux.

feel /fi:l/ **I** *n* **1** (atmosphere, impression created) atmosphère *f*; **there was a relaxed ~ about it** il régnait une atmosphère détendue; **it has the ~ of a country cottage** cela a l'allure d'une maison de campagne; **2** (sensation to the touch) sensation *f*; **to have an oily ~** être huileux au toucher; **I like the ~ of leather** j'aime le contact du cuir; **3** (act of touching, feeling) **to have a ~ of sth** tâter qch; **let me have a ~** (touch) laisse-moi toucher; (hold, weigh) laisse-moi soupeser; **4** (familiarity, understanding) **to get the ~ of** se faire à

[*controls, system*]; **to get the ~ of doing** s'habituer à faire; **5** (flair) don *m* (**for** pour); **to have a ~ for language** bien savoir manier la langue.
II *vtr* (*prét, pp* **felt**) **1** (experience) éprouver [*affection, desire, pride*]; ressentir [*hostility, obligation, effects*]; **to ~ a sense of isolation** éprouver un sentiment de solitude; **I no longer ~ anything for her** je n'éprouve plus rien pour elle; **the effects will be felt throughout the country** les effets se feront sentir dans tout le pays; **to ~ sb's loss very deeply** être très affecté par la perte de qn; **2** (believe) **to ~ (that)** estimer que; **I ~ I should warn you** je me sens dans l'obligation de vous prévenir; **I ~ he's hiding something** j'ai l'impression qu'il cache quelque chose; **I ~ deeply** ou **strongly that they are wrong** j'ai la profonde conviction qu'ils ont tort; **3** (physically) sentir [*blow, draught, heat*]; ressentir [*ache, stiffness, effects*]; **she ~s/doesn't ~ the cold** elle est/n'est pas frileuse; **4** (touch deliberately) tâter [*texture, washing, cloth*]; palper [*patient, body part, parcel*]; **to ~ the weight of sth** soupeser qch; **to ~ one's breasts for lumps** se palper les seins pour voir si on a des grosseurs; **to ~ one's way** LIT avancer à tâtons; FIG tâter le terrain; **5** (sense) avoir conscience de [*presence, tension, seriousness, irony*]; **I could ~ her frustration** je ressentais sa frustration.
III *vi* (*prét, pp* **felt**) **1** (emotionally) se sentir [*sad, happy, nervous, safe*]; être [*sure, surprised*]; avoir l'impression d'être [*trapped, betrayed*]; **to ~ afraid/ashamed** avoir peur/honte; **to ~ as if** ou **as though** avoir l'impression que; **how do you ~?** que ressens-tu?; **how do you ~ about marriage?** qu'est-ce que tu penses du mariage?; **how does it ~** ou **what does it ~ like to be a dad?** qu'est-ce que ça fait d'être papa?; ▶ **feel for**; **2** (physically) se sentir [*ill, better, tired*]; **to ~ hot/thirsty** avoir chaud/soif; **it felt as if I was floating** j'avais l'impression de flotter; **she isn't ~ing herself today** elle n'est pas dans son assiette aujourd'hui○; **3** (create certain sensation) être [*cold, smooth*]; avoir l'air [*eerie*]; **the house ~s empty** la maison fait vide; **something doesn't ~ right** il y a quelque chose qui ne va pas; **it ~s strange living alone** ça me fait tout drôle de vivre seul; **it ~s like leather** on dirait du cuir; **it ~s like (a) Sunday** on se croirait un dimanche; **the bone ~s as if it's broken** on dirait que l'os est cassé; **4** (want) **to ~ like sth** avoir envie de qch; **I ~ like a drink** je prendrais bien un verre; **I don't ~ like it** je n'en ai pas envie; **5** (touch, grope) **to ~ in** fouiller dans [*bag, pocket, drawer*]; **to ~ along** tâtonner le long de [*edge, wall*]; ▶ **feel around**, **feel for**.
IV *v refl* **to ~ oneself doing** se sentir faire; **she felt herself losing her temper** elle sentait la colère la gagner.
■ **feel about** = **feel around**.
■ **feel around**: **~ around** tâtonner; **to ~ around in** fouiller dans [*bag, drawer*]; **to ~ around for** chercher [qch] à tâtons.
■ **feel for**: ¶ **~ for** [**sth**] chercher; ¶ **~ for** [**sb**] plaindre.
■ **feel out** US: **~ out** [**sb**], **~** [**sb**] **out** tester [*person*].
■ **feel up to**: **~ up to (doing) sth** se sentir d'attaque○ ou assez bien pour (faire) qch.

feeler /'fi:lə(r)/ *n* GEN antenne *f*; (of snail) corne *f*.
IDIOMS **to put out ~s** tâter le terrain, lancer un ballon d'essai.

feelgood /'fi:lgʊd/ *adj* PÉJ faussement rassurant; **to play on the ~ factor** essayer de créer un sentiment de bien-être illusoire.

feeling /'fi:lɪŋ/ **I** *n* **1** (emotion) sentiment *m*; **it is a strange ~ to be** c'est une sensation étrange que d'être; **to put one's ~s into words** trouver des mots pour dire ce que l'on ressent; **to spare sb's ~s** ménager qn; **to hurt sb's ~s** blesser qn; **2** (opinion, belief) sentiment *m*; **I have strong ~s about it** c'est quelque chose qui me tient à cœur; **~s are running high** les esprits s'échauffent; **3** (sensitivity) sensibilité *f*; **have you no ~?** n'as-tu pas de cœur?; **to speak with great ~** parler avec beaucoup de passion; **4** (im-

feelingly

919

pression) impression *f*; **I had a ~ you'd say that** je sentais que tu allais dire ça; **I've got a bad ~ about this** j'ai le pressentiment que cela va mal se passer; **I've got a bad ~ about her** je me méfie d'elle; **5** (physical sensation) sensation *f*; **a dizzy ~** une sensation de vertige; **6** (atmosphere) ambiance *f*; **there was a general ~ of tension** l'ambiance était tendue; **7** (instinct) don *m* (**for** pour).
II *adj* [*person*] sensible; [*gesture*] sympathique.

feelingly /ˈfiːlɪŋlɪ/ *adv* [*write, speak*] avec passion; [*say*] avec compassion.

fee-paying /ˈfiːpeɪɪŋ/ **I** *n* paiement *m* des frais de scolarité.
II *adj* [*school*] payant; [*parent, pupil*] qui paie les frais de scolarité.

feet /fiːt/ *pl* ▶ **foot**.

feign /feɪn/ *vtr* SOUT feindre [*innocence, surprise*]; simuler [*illness, sleep*].

feint /feɪnt/ **I** *n* **1** SPORT, MIL feinte *f*; **2** (in printing) réglure *f* fine.
II *vi* SPORT, MIL feinter.

feisty○ /ˈfiːstɪ/ *adj* **1** (lively) fougueux/-euse; **2** US (quarrelsome) bagarreur/-euse○.

felicitous /fəˈlɪsɪtəs/ *adj* SOUT heureux/-euse.

feline /ˈfiːlaɪn/ **I** *n* félin *m*.
II *adj* LIT, FIG félin.

fell /fel/ **I** *prét* ▶ **fall**.
II *n* montagne *f* (*dans le Nord de l'Angleterre*).
III *vtr* abattre [*tree*]; assommer [*person*].
IDIOMS **in one ~ swoop** d'un seul coup.

fellow /ˈfeləʊ/ **I** *n* **1**○ (man) type○ *m*, homme *m*; **poor little ~** brave petit bonhomme; **what do you ~s think?** qu'est-ce que vous en pensez, vous autres?; **2** (of society, association) (also in titles) membre *m* (**of** de); **3** GB UNIV (lecturer) *membre du corps enseignant d'un collège universitaire*; (governor) *membre du comité de direction d'un collège universitaire*; **4** US (researcher) universitaire *mf* titulaire d'une bourse de recherche.
II *noun modifier* **her ~ lawyers/teachers** ses collègues avocats/professeurs; **he and his ~ students/sufferers** lui et les autres étudiants/malades.
fellow: ~ citizen *n* concitoyen/-enne *m/f*; **~ countryman** *n* compatriote *m*; **~ feeling** *n* (understanding) compréhension *f*; (solidarity) solidarité *f*; **~ human being, ~ man** *n* semblable *mf*.

fellowship /ˈfeləʊʃɪp/ *n* **1** (companionship) GEN camaraderie *f*; RELIG fraternité *f*; **2** (association) GEN association *f*; RELIG confrérie *f*; **3** UNIV (post) poste *m* de recherche et d'enseignement universitaire.

fellow traveller GB, **fellow traveler** US *n* LIT compagnon/compagne *m/f* de voyage; FIG POL compagnon *m* de route.

felon /ˈfelən/ *n* HIST, JUR criminel *m*.

felony /ˈfelənɪ/ *n* HIST, JUR crime *m*.

felt /felt/ **I** *prét, pp* ▶ **feel**.
II *n* (cloth) feutre *m*; (thinner) feutrine *f*.
III *noun modifier* [*cloth, cover*] en feutre; (thinner) en feutrine; **~ hat** feutre *m*.

felt-tip (pen) *n* feutre *m*.

female /ˈfiːmeɪl/ **I** *n* **1** BIOL, ZOOL femelle *f*; **2** (woman) femme *f*; PEJ bonne femme○ *f*.
II *adj* **1** BOT, ZOOL femelle; **~ rabbit** lapine *f*; **2** (relating to women) [*population, role, trait*] féminin; [*voice*] de femme; **~ student** étudiante *f*; **3** ELEC femelle.

female circumcision *n* excision *f*.

feminine /ˈfemənɪn/ **I** *n* LING féminin *m*; **in the ~** au féminin.
II *adj* GEN, LING féminin.

femininity /ˌfeməˈnɪnətɪ/ *n* féminité *f*.

feminist /ˈfemɪnɪst/ *n, adj* féministe (*mf*).

fen /fen/ *n* marais *m*.

fence /fens/ **I** *n* **1** (barrier) clôture *f*; **2** (in showjumping) obstacle *m*; (in horseracing) haie *f*; **3**○ (receiver of stolen goods) receleur/-euse *m/f*.
II *vtr* **1** (enclose) clôturer [*area, garden*]; **2**○ (sell stolen goods) fourguer○ [*stolen goods*].

III *vi* **1** SPORT faire de l'escrime; **2** (be evasive) se dérober.
IDIOMS **to mend ~s** se raccommoder (**with** avec); **to sit on the ~** ne pas prendre position.
■ **fence in**: ¶ **~ [sth] in, ~ in [sth]** entourer [qch] d'une clôture [*area, garden*]; parquer [*animals*]; ¶ **~ [sb] in** FIG étouffer.
■ **fence off**: **~ [sth] off, ~ off [sth]** clôturer [qch].

fencing /ˈfensɪŋ/ ▶ **949** *n* **1** SPORT escrime *f*; **2** (fences) enceinte *f*.

fend /fend/ *v*
■ **fend for**: **~ for oneself** se débrouiller (tout seul).
■ **fend off**: **~ off [sb/sth], ~ [sb/sth] off** repousser [*attacker*]; parer [*blow*]; écarter [*question*].

fender /ˈfendə(r)/ *n* **1** (for fire) garde-cendre *m*; **2** US AUT aile *f*.

fennel /ˈfenl/ *n* fenouil *m*.

feral /ˈfɪərəl, US ˈferəl/ *adj* sauvage.

ferment I /ˈfɜːment/ *n* (unrest) agitation *f*.
II /fəˈment/ *vtr* faire fermenter [*beer, wine*]; FIG fomenter [*trouble*].
III /fəˈment/ *vi* [*beer, yeast*] fermenter.

fermentation /ˌfɜːmenˈteɪʃn/ *n* fermentation *f*.

fern /fɜːn/ *n* fougère *f*.

ferocious /fəˈrəʊʃəs/ *adj* [*animal*] féroce; [*attack*] sauvage; [*wind*] violent; [*heat*] accablant; [*climate*] rude.

ferociously /fəˈrəʊʃəslɪ/ *adv* [*attack*] (verbally) violemment; (physically) férocement; [*bark*] avec férocité.

ferocity /fəˈrɒsətɪ/ *n* férocité *f*.

ferret /ˈferɪt/ *n* ZOOL furet *m*.
■ **ferret about** fureter, fouiller (**in** dans).
■ **ferret out**○: ¶ **~ [sth] out, ~ out [sth]** dégoter○ [*bargain*]; découvrir [*truth, information*]; ¶ **~ [sb] out** dénicher [*agent, thief*].

ferrous /ˈferəs/ *adj* ferreux/-euse.

ferry /ˈferɪ/ **I** *n* (long-distance) ferry *m*; (over short distances) bac *m*.
II *vtr* transporter [*passenger, goods*]; **to ~ sb to** emmener qn à [*school, station*].

ferryman /ˈferɪmæn/ *n* passeur *m*.

fertile /ˈfɜːtaɪl, US ˈfɜːrtl/ *adj* LIT [*land, soil*] fertile; [*human, animal, egg*] fécond; FIG [*imagination, mind, environment*] fertile.

fertility /fəˈtɪlətɪ/ **I** *n* **1** LIT (of land) fertilité *f*, fécondité *f*; (of human, animal, egg) fécondité *f*; **2** FIG (of mind, imagination) fertilité *f*.
II *noun modifier* [*symbol, rite*] de fertilité.

fertility drug *n* médicament *m* contre la stérilité.

fertilization /ˌfɜːtɪlaɪˈzeɪʃn, US -lɪˈz-/ *n* (of land) fertilisation *f*; (of animal, plant, egg) fécondation *f*.

fertilize /ˈfɜːtɪlaɪz/ *vtr* fertiliser [*land*]; féconder [*animal, plant, egg*].

fertilizer /ˈfɜːtɪlaɪzə(r)/ *n* engrais *m*.

fervent /ˈfɜːvənt/ *adj* [*admirer*] fervent; [*support*] inconditionnel.

fervently /ˈfɜːvəntlɪ/ *adv* [*declare*] avec ferveur; [*hope*] vivement.

fervour GB, **fervor** US /ˈfɜːvə(r)/ *n* ferveur *f*.

fester /ˈfestə(r)/ *vi* [*wound, sore*] suppurer; [*situation*] pourrir; [*feeling*] s'envenimer.

festival /ˈfestɪvl/ *n* GEN fête *f*; (arts event) festival *m*.

festive /ˈfestɪv/ *adj* [*occasion, person*] joyeux/-euse; **the ~ season** la saison des fêtes.

festivity /feˈstɪvətɪ/ *n* réjouissance *f*.

festoon /feˈstuːn/ **I** *n* guirlande *f*.
II *vtr* orner (**with** de).

fetch /fetʃ/ *vtr* **1** (bring) GEN aller chercher; **to ~ sth for sb** aller chercher qch pour qn; (carry back) (r)apporter qch à qn; **~ him a chair please** apportelui une chaise s'il te plaît; **~!** (to dog) rapporte!; **2** (bring financially) [*goods*] rapporter; **to ~ a good price** rapporter un bon prix; **these vases can ~ up to £600** le prix de ces vases peut atteindre 600 livres.
IDIOMS **to ~ and carry for sb** faire les quatre volontés de qn.

fetching /'fetʃɪŋ/ adj [child, habit, photo] charmant; [outfit, hat] ravissant.

fete /feɪt/ **I** n (church, village) kermesse f (paroissiale); **charity ~** fête f de bienfaisance.
II vtr fêter [celebrity, hero].

fetid, foetid /'fetɪd, US 'fiːtɪd/ adj fétide, nauséabond.

fetish /'fetɪʃ/ n **1** (object) fétiche m; **2** (obsessive interest) passion f fétichiste (**for** pour).

fetlock /'fetlɒk/ n **1** (joint) boulet m; **2** (tuft of hair) fanon m.

fetter /'fetə(r)/ **I** fetters npl LIT fers m; **the ~s of authority** FIG les entraves de l'autorité.
II vtr LIT mettre [qn] aux fers; FIG entraver l'influence de [party].

fettle /'fetl/ n IDIOMS **in fine** OU **good ~** en excellente forme.

fetus n US = **foetus**.

feud /fjuːd/ **I** n querelle f (**with** avec; **between** entre).
II vi se quereller (**with** avec; **about** au sujet de).

feudal /'fjuːdl/ adj féodal.

feuding /'fjuːdɪŋ/ adj [factions, families] en conflit.

fever /'fiːvə(r)/ n LIT, FIG fièvre f; **to have a ~** LIT avoir de la fièvre; **gold ~** la fièvre de l'or.

fevered /'fiːvəd/ adj [brow] fiévreux/-euse; [imagination] fébrile.

feverish /'fiːvərɪʃ/ adj [person, eyes] fiévreux/-euse; [dreams] délirant; [excitement, activity] fébrile.

feverishly /'fiːvərɪʃlɪ/ adv LIT fiévreusement; FIG fébrilement.

fever pitch n **to bring a crowd to ~** déchaîner une foule; **our excitement had reached ~** notre excitation était à son comble.

few /fjuː/ (comparative **fewer**; superlative **fewest**)

■ **Note** When few is used as a quantifier to indicate the smallness or insufficiency of a given number or quantity (few shops, few people, few houses) it is translated by peu de: peu de maisons, peu de gens, peu de magasins. Equally the few is translated by le peu de: the few people who knew her le peu de gens qui la connaissaient. For examples and particular usages see I 1 in the entry.
– When few is used as a quantifier in certain expressions to mean several, translations vary according to the expression: see I2 in the entry.
– When a few is used as a quantifier (a few books), it can often be translated by quelques: quelques livres; however, for expressions such as quite a few books, a good few books, see II in the entry.
– For translations of few used as a pronoun (few of us succeeded, I only need a few) see II, III in the entry.
– For translations of the few used as a noun (the few who voted for him) see III in the entry.

I quantif **1** (not many) peu de; **~ visitors/letters** peu de visiteurs/lettres; **one of my ~ pleasures** un de mes rares plaisirs; **their needs are ~** ils ont peu de besoins; **to be ~ in number** être peu nombreux; **too ~ women** trop peu de femmes; **with ~ exceptions** à quelques exceptions près; **2** (some, several) **every ~ days** tous les deux ou trois jours; **over the next ~ days/weeks** (in past) dans les jours/semaines qui ont suivi; (in future) dans les jours/semaines à venir; **these past ~ days** ces derniers jours; **the first ~ weeks** les premières semaines; **the ~ books she possessed** les quelques livres qu'elle possédait.
II **a few** quantif, pron quelques; **a ~ people/houses** quelques personnes/maisons; **I would like a ~ more** j'en voudrais quelques-uns/quelques-unes de plus; **quite a ~ people/houses** pas mal° de gens/maisons, un bon nombre de personnes/maisons; **a good ~ years** un bon nombre d'années; **a ~ of the soldiers/countries** quelques-uns or certains des soldats/pays; **a ~ of us** un certain nombre d'entre nous; **there were only a ~ of them** il n'y en avait que quelques-uns/quelques-unes; **quite a ~** ou **a good ~ of the tourists come from Germany** un bon nombre des touristes viennent d'Allemagne; **there are only a very ~ left** il n'en reste que très peu.
III pron (not many) peu; **~ of us succeeded** peu d'en-

tre nous ont réussi; **there are so ~ of them that** il y en a tellement peu que; **there are four too ~** il en manque quatre; **as ~ as four people turned up** quatre personnes seulement sont venues; **the ~ who voted for him** les rares personnes qui ont voté pour lui.
IDIOMS **they are ~ and far between** ils sont rarissimes; **to have had a ~ (too many)**° avoir bu quelques verres (de trop).

fewer /'fjuːə(r)/ (comparative of **few**) **I** adj moins de; **~ and ~ pupils** de moins en moins d'élèves.
II pron moins; **~ than 50 people** moins de 50 personnes; **no ~ than** pas moins de; **they were ~ than before** ils étaient moins nombreux qu'avant.

fewest /'fjuːɪst/ (superlative of **few**) **I** adj le moins de.
II pron le moins.

fey /feɪ/ adj **1** (clairvoyant) extralucide; **2** (whimsical) loufoque°.

fez /fez/ n (pl **~zes**) fez m.

ff (abrév écrite = **following**) et les lignes (ou pages) qui suivent.

fiancé /fɪ'ɒnseɪ, US ˌfiːɑːn'seɪ/ n fiancé m.

fiancée /fɪ'ɒnseɪ, US ˌfiːɑːn'seɪ/ n fiancée f.

fiasco /fɪ'æskəʊ/ n fiasco m.

fib° /fɪb/ **I** n bobard° m, mensonge m.
II vi (p prés etc **-bb-**) raconter des bobards°, mentir.

fibber /'fɪbə(r)/ n menteur/-euse m/f.

fibre GB, **fiber** US /'faɪbə(r)/ n **1** (strand) (of thread, wood) fibre f; **2** (material) fibre f; **3** (in diet) fibres fpl; **a high ~ diet** une alimentation riche en fibres; **4** BIOL, BOT (cell) fibre f; **5** FIG (strength) courage m.

fibre: **~glass** GB, **fiberglass** US n ∉ fibres fpl de verre; **~ optic** GB, **fiber optic** US adj [cable] à fibres optiques; [link] par fibres optiques; **~optics** GB, **fiberoptics** US n (v sg ou pl) fibres fpl optiques.

fibroid /'faɪbrɔɪd/ **I** n fibrome m.
II adj fibreux/-euse.

fibrous /'faɪbrəs/ adj fibreux/-euse.

fibula /'fɪbjʊlə/ n (pl **~s** ou **-ae**) ANAT péroné m.

fiche /fiːʃ/ n microfiche f.

fickle /'fɪkl/ adj [lover, friend] inconstant; [fate, public opinion] changeant; [weather] capricieux/-ieuse.

fickleness /'fɪklnɪs/ n (of person) inconstance f; (of behaviour) instabilité f; (of weather) caprices mpl; (of fortune, of stock market) fluctuations fpl.

fiction /'fɪkʃn/ n **1** (literary genre) le roman; **2** (books) romans mpl; **in ~** dans les romans; **3** (delusion) illusion f; **4** (untruth) histoire f; **5** (creation of the imagination) fiction f; **6** (pretence) **they keep up the ~ that** ils font croire à tout le monde que.

fictional /'fɪkʃənl/ adj [character, event] imaginaire.

fictionalize /'fɪkʃənəlaɪz/ vtr romancer.

fictitious /fɪk'tɪʃəs/ adj **1** (false) [name, address] fictif/-ive; [justification, report] fallacieux/-ieuse; **2** (imaginary) imaginaire.

fiddle /'fɪdl/ **I** n **1**° (dishonest scheme) magouille° f ∉; **tax ~** fraude f fiscale; **to be on the ~** traficoter°; **2** ▸ **1097**∣ (violin) violon m.
II vtr° (illegally) falsifier [tax return, figures].
III vi **1** (fidget) **to ~ with sth** tripoter qch; **2** (adjust) **to ~ with** tourner [knobs, controls].
IDIOMS **to be as fit as a ~** être en santé; **to ~ while Rome burns** se ficher de tout comme de l'an 40°; **to play second ~ to sb** être le sous-fifre° de qn.

■ **fiddle around with**: **~ around with [sth]** (readjust) bricoler [engine]; (fidget) jouer avec [object].

fiddly /'fɪdlɪ/ adj [job, task] délicat; [clasp, fastening] pas pratique; **~ to open** difficile à ouvrir.

fidelity /fɪ'delɪtɪ/ n GEN, TELECOM fidélité f (**of** de; **to** à).

fidget /'fɪdʒɪt/ **I** n **they're real ~s** ils n'arrêtent pas de gigoter°.
II vi (move about) ne pas tenir en place.

fidgety /'fɪdʒɪtɪ/ adj (child) remuant; (adult) agité.

fief /fiːf/, **fiefdom** /'fiːfdəm/ n fief m.

field /fiːld/ I n 1 AGRIC, GEOG, GEN champ m (of de); 2 SPORT (ground) terrain m; **football ~** terrain de football; 3 ℂ SPORT (competitors) (athletes) concurrents mpl; (horses) partants mpl; **to lead** ou **be ahead of the ~** SPORT mener le peloton; FIG être en tête; 4 (area of knowledge) domaine m (of de); 5 LING champ m sémantique; 6 (real environment) **to test sth in the ~** faire des essais de qch sur le terrain; 7 MIL **the ~ of battle** le champ de bataille; **to take the ~** se mettre en campagne; **to hold the ~** se maintenir sur ses positions; FIG [theory] dominer; 8 (range) champ m; **~ of fire** MIL secteur m de tir; 9 COMPUT, MATH, PHYS champ m.
II noun modifier 1 MIL [hospital] de campagne; 2 (in real environment) [test, study] sur le terrain.
III vtr 1 SPORT réceptionner [ball]; 2 SPORT, GEN (select) faire jouer [team, player]; présenter [candidate]; 3 (respond to) répondre à [questions].
IV vi SPORT jouer dans l'équipe de défense.
IDIOMS **to play the ~** sortir avec tout le monde.

field day n 1 SCH, UNIV sortie f (éducative); 2 US (sports day) journée f sportive.
IDIOMS **to have a ~** [press, critics] jubiler; (make money) [shopkeepers] faire d'excellentes affaires; **to have a ~ with sth** exploiter qch à fond.

fielder /ˈfiːldə(r)/ n SPORT homme m de champ, défenseur m.

field: ~ event n SPORT épreuve f sportive (de saut et de lancer); **~ hand** n US ouvrier/-ière m/f agricole; **~ hockey** ▶949 n US SPORT hockey m sur gazon; **~ label** n LING marqueur m de champ sémantique; **~ marshal, FM** ▶1192 n MIL maréchal m; **~mouse** n ZOOL mulot m; **~sman** n US SPORT = **fielder**; **~ sports** npl SPORT sports mpl de plein air; **~ trip** n SCH, UNIV (one day) sortie f éducative; (longer) voyage m d'études; **~work** n travail m de terrain; **~worker** ▶1251 n personne f qui travaille sur le terrain.

fiend /fiːnd/ n 1 (evil spirit) démon m; 2° (mischievous person) petit monstre m; 3° (fanatic) **he's a racing/football ~** c'est un fana° des courses/du football.

fiendish /ˈfiːndɪʃ/ adj 1 (cruel) [tyrant, cruelty] monstrueux/-euse [expression, glee] diabolique; 2 (ingenious) [plan, gadget] diabolique.

fiendishly /ˈfiːndɪʃlɪ/ adv 1 (wickedly) diaboliquement; 2 (extremely) extrêmement.

fierce /fɪəs/ adj [animal, expression, person] féroce; [battle, storm, hatred] violent; [determination, loyalty] farouche; [supporter] fervent; [criticism, speech] virulent; [competition] acharné; [flames, heat] intense; **he has a ~ temper** c'est un caractère explosif.

fiercely /ˈfɪəslɪ/ adv [defend, hit, oppose] avec acharnement; [fight] sauvagement; [stare] férocement; [shout, speak] violemment; [burn] avec intensité; [competitive, critical] extrêmement; [determined, loyal] farouchement.

fierceness /ˈfɪəsnɪs/ n (ferocity) (of animal) férocité f; (of person, expression, storm, battle) violence f.

fiery /ˈfaɪərɪ/ adj [person, wound, gas] enflammé; [speech, performance] passionné; [sky] embrasé; [eyes] ardent; [heat] brûlant; **~ red/orange** rouge/orange feu inv.

fiesta /fɪˈestə/ n fête f.

fife /faɪf/ ▶1097 n fifre m.

fifteen /ˌfɪfˈtiːn/ ▶1112, 812 n, adj quinze (m) inv.

fifteenth /ˌfɪfˈtiːnθ/ ▶1112, 854 I n 1 (in order) quinzième mf; 2 (of month) quinze m inv; 3 (fraction) quinzième m.
II adj, adv quinzième.

fifth /fɪfθ/ ▶1112, 854 I n 1 (in order) cinquième mf; 2 (of month) cinq m; 3 (fraction) cinquième m; 4 MUS quinte f; 5 (also **~ gear**) AUT cinquième f; 6 US (unit of measurement) ≈ 75 cl.
II adj, adv cinquième.

fifth: Fifth Amendment n US JUR cinquième amendement m; **~ columnist** n élément m subversif.

fiftieth /ˈfɪftɪəθ/ ▶1112 I n 1 (in order) cinquantième mf; 2 (fraction) cinquantième m.
II adj, adv cinquantième.

fifty /ˈfɪftɪ/ ▶1112 n, adj cinquante (m) inv.

fifty-fifty /ˌfɪftɪˈfɪftɪ/ I adj **to have a ~ chance** avoir une chance sur deux (**of doing** de faire).
II adv; **to share sth ~** partager qch moitié-moitié; **to go ~** faire moitié-moitié.

fig /fɪg/ I n (fruit) figue f.
II adj (abrév = **figurative**) figuré.

fig. n (abrév écrite = **figure**) fig.; **see ~ 3** voir fig. 3.

fight /faɪt/ I n 1 FIG (struggle) lutte f (**against** contre; **for** pour; **to do** pour faire); **to keep up the ~** continuer le combat; **to put up a ~** se défendre (**against** contre); 2 (outbreak of fighting) (between civilians) bagarre f (**between** entre; **over** pour); MIL bataille f (**between** entre; **for** pour); (between animals, in boxing) combat m (**between** entre); **to get into** ou **have a ~ with sb** se bagarrer contre or avec qn; 3 (argument) dispute f (**over** au sujet de; **with** avec); **to have a ~ with sb** se disputer avec qn; 4 (combative spirit) (physical) envie f de se battre; (psychological) envie f de lutter.
II vtr (prét, pp **fought**) 1 LIT se battre contre [person]; FIG lutter contre [disease, evil, opponent, emotion, proposal]; combattre [fire]; mener [campaign, war] (**against** contre); **to ~ one's way through** se frayer un passage dans [crowd]; 2 POL [candidate] disputer [seat, election]; 3 JUR défendre [case, cause].
III vi (prét, pp **fought**) 1 FIG (campaign) lutter; 2 LIT, MIL se battre; **to ~ for breath** suffoquer; 3 (squabble) se quereller (**over** à propos de).
IDIOMS **to ~ the good ~** se battre pour la bonne cause.
■ **fight back**: ¶ **~ back** (physically, tactically) se défendre (**against** contre); (emotionally) ne pas se laisser faire; ¶ **~ back** [sth] refréner [tears, fear, anger].
■ **fight off**: ¶ **~ off** [sth], **~** [sth] **off** LIT se libérer de [attacker]; vaincre [troops]; repousser [attack]; ¶ **~ off** [sth] FIG lutter contre [illness, despair]; rejeter [challenge, criticism, proposal].
■ **fight on** poursuivre la lutte.
■ **fight out**: **leave them to ~ it out** laissez-les régler cela entre eux.

fighter /ˈfaɪtə(r)/ n 1 (determined person) lutteur/-euse m/f; 2 (also **~ plane**) avion m de chasse.

fighter: ~ bomber n AVIAT chasseur-bombardier m; **~ pilot** ▶1251 n pilote m de chasse.

fighting /ˈfaɪtɪŋ/ I n 1 MIL combat m; **~ has broken out** la bataille a éclaté; 2 GEN bagarre f.
II adj 1 MIL [unit, force] de combat; 2 (aggressive) [talk, words] agressif/-ive.

fighting chance n **to have a ~** avoir de bonnes chances.

fighting fit adj **to be ~** être en pleine forme°.

fig leaf n BOT feuille f de figuier.

figment /ˈfɪgmənt/ n **a ~ of the/of your imagination** un produit de l'imagination/de ton imagination m.

fig tree n figuier m.

figurative /ˈfɪgərətɪv/ adj 1 LING figuré; 2 ART figuratif/-ive.

figuratively /ˈfɪgərətɪvlɪ/ adv [speak, mean] au (sens) figuré; **~ speaking,** métaphoriquement parlant,.

figure /ˈfɪgə(r), US ˈfɪgjər/ I n 1 (number, amount) chiffre m; **a four-/six-~ sum** un montant de quatre/six chiffres; **in double ~s** à deux chiffres; **to have a head for ~s, to be good with ~s** être doué pour le calcul; 2 (person) personnalité f; **well-known ~** personnalité célèbre; 3 (human form) GEN personnage m; ART figure f; **a familiar ~** un personnage familier; **reclining ~** ART figure allongée; 4 (symbol) **father ~** image f du père; **authority ~** symbole m de l'autorité; 5 (body shape) ligne f; **to lose one's ~** prendre de l'embonpoint; **to have a great ~°** avoir une silhouette sensationnelle°; 6 (geometric or other shape) figure f; 7 (diagram) figure f; **see ~ 4** voir figure 4.
II vtr 1° (suppose) **to ~ (that)** penser or se dire que; 2 LITERAT (express) symboliser.

III *vi* **1** (appear) figurer (**in** dans); **2**○ (make sense) se comprendre.
■ **figure on**○: ~ **on** [sth] s'attendre à; **to** ~ **on doing** compter faire.
■ **figure out**: ~ **out** [sth], ~ [sth] **out** trouver [*answer, reason*]; **to** ~ **out who/why** etc arriver à comprendre qui/pourquoi etc.

figurehead /'fɪgəhed, US 'fɪgjər-/ *n* **1** (symbolic leader) personnalité *f* de prestige; **2** (of ship) figure *f* de proue.

figure: ~ **of speech** *n* LITERAT, LING figure *f* de rhétorique; ~ **skater** *n* patineur/-euse *m/f* artistique; ~ **skating** ▶ 949 *n* patinage *m* artistique.

figurine /ˌfɪgəri:n, US ˌfɪgəˈri:n/ *n* figurine *f*.

Fiji /ˈfi:dʒi:/ ▶ 840, 1022 *pr n* (also ~ **Islands**) (îles *fpl*) Fidji *fpl*.

filament /ˈfɪləmənt/ *n* **1** ELEC filament *m*; **2** (of fibre) fil *m*.

filch○ /fɪltʃ/ *vtr* chiper○, voler (**from** à).

file /faɪl/ **I** *n* **1** (for papers etc) GEN dossier *m*; (cardboard) chemise *f*; (ring binder) classeur *m*; (card tray) fichier *m*; **2** (record) dossier *m* (**on** sur); **to be on** ~ être classé; **3** COMPUT fichier *m*; **4** (tool) lime *f*; **5** (line) file *f*; **in single** ~ en file indienne.
II *vtr* **1** ADMIN classer [*invoice, letter, record*] (**under** sous); **2** JUR déposer [*application, complaint*] (**with** auprès de); **to** ~ **a lawsuit** (**against sb**) intenter or faire un procès (à qn); **3** JOURN envoyer [*report*]; **4** limer [*wood, metal*]; **to** ~ **one's nails** se limer les ongles.
III *vi* **1** (walk) **they** ~**d into/out of the classroom** ils sont entrés dans/sortis de la salle l'un après l'autre; **2** JUR **to** ~ **for (a) divorce** demander le divorce.

file: ~ **cabinet** *n* US = **filing cabinet**; ~ **card** *n* US fiche *f*; ~ **clerk** *n* US = **filing clerk**; ~ **copy** *n* copie *f* de classement; ~ **manager** *n* COMPUT gestionnaire *m* de fichiers.

filial /ˈfɪlɪəl/ *adj* filial.

filibuster /ˈfɪlɪbʌstə(r)/ *n* obstruction *f* parlementaire.

filigree /ˈfɪlɪgri:/ *n* filigrane *m*.

filing /ˈfaɪlɪŋ/ *n* classement *m*.

filing: ~ **cabinet** *n* classeur *m* à tiroirs; ~ **card** *n* fiche *f*; ~ **clerk** ▶ 1251 *n* employé/-e *m/f* de bureau chargé/-e du classement; ~ **system** *n* système *m* de classement.

Filipino /ˌfɪlɪˈpi:nəʊ/ ▶ 1100 **I** *n* Philippin/-e *m/f*.
II *adj* [*culture, food*] philippin; [*embassy, captial*] des Philippines.

fill /fɪl/ **I** *n* **to eat/drink one's** ~ manger/boire tout son content; **to have had one's** ~ en avoir assez.
II *vtr* **1** (make full) remplir [*container*] (**with** de); **tears** ~**ed his eyes** ses yeux se sont remplis de larmes; **2** (occupy) [*crowd, sound*] remplir [*room, street, train*]; [*smoke, gas, light, protesters*] envahir [*building, room*]; remplir [*page, chapter, volumes, tape*] (**with** de); occuper [*time, day, hours*]; [*emotion, thought*] remplir [*heart, mind, person*] (**with** de); **3** (plug) LIT, FIG boucher [*crack, hole, void*] (**with** avec); **4** (fulfil) répondre à [*need*]; **5** (appoint for) [*company, university*] pourvoir [*post, vacancy*]; **6** (perform duties of) [*applicant*] occuper [*post, vacancy*]; **7** (put filling in) garnir [*cushion, pie, sandwich*] (**with** de); **8** [*dentist*] plomber [*tooth, cavity*]; **9** NAUT [*wind*] gonfler [*sail*].
III *vi* **1** [*bath, theatre, streets, eyes*] se remplir (**with** de); **2** NAUT [*sail*] se gonfler.
IV -**filled** *combining form* rempli de; **smoke-/book-** ~**ed room** pièce remplie de fumée/de livres.
■ **fill in**: ¶ ~ **in** [*person*] faire un remplacement; **to** ~ **in for sb** remplacer qn; ¶ ~ **in** [sth] passer [*time, hour*]; ¶ ~ **in** [sth/sb], ~ [sth/sb] **in 1** (complete) remplir [*form, section*]; **2** (plug) boucher [*hole, crack*] (**with** avec); **3** (supply) donner [*detail, name, date*]; **4** (inform) mettre [qn] au courant (**on** de); **5** (colour in) remplir [*shape, panel*].
■ **fill out**: ¶ ~ **out** [*person*] prendre du poids; [*face*] s'arrondir; ¶ ~ **out** [sth], ~ [sth] **out** remplir [*form, application*]; faire [*certificate, prescription*].
■ **fill up**: ¶ ~ **up** [*bath, theatre, bus*] se remplir

(**with** de); **to** ~ **up on sth** [*person*] se bourrer○ de [*bread, sweets*]; ¶ ~ **up** [sth], ~ [sth] **up** remplir [*kettle, box, room*] (**with** de); ¶ ~ **up** [sb], ~ [sb] **up** bourrer○ qn (**with** de).

filler /ˈfɪlə(r)/ *n* **1** (for wood) bouche-pores *m inv*; (for car body) mastic *m*; (for wall) reboucheur *m*; **2** JOURN, TV bouche-trou *m*.

fillet /ˈfɪlɪt/ **I** *n* filet *m*.
II *vtr* enlever les arêtes de, fileter [*fish*].

fillet steak *n* filet *m* de bœuf.

fill-in /ˈfɪlɪn/ *n* remplaçant/-e *m/f*.

filling /ˈfɪlɪŋ/ **I** *n* **1** CULIN (of sandwich, baked potato) garniture *f*; (stuffing for vegetable, meat, pancake) farce *f*; **pie with blackberry/meat** ~ tourte *f* fourrée aux mûres/à la viande; **2** (tooth) plombage *m*; **3** (of quilt, cushion) garnissage *m*; (of bed, mattress) garniture *f*.
II *adj* [*food, dish*] bourratif/-ive○.

filling station *n* station-service *f*.

fillip /ˈfɪlɪp/ *n* coup *m* de fouet FIG.

filly /ˈfɪlɪ/ *n* pouliche *f*.

film /fɪlm/ **I** *n* **1** CIN (movie) film *m*; **to be** ou **work in** ~**s** travailler dans le cinéma; **short** ~ court métrage *m*; **2** PHOT (for snapshots) pellicule *f*; (for movies) film *m*; **3** (layer) pellicule *f*; **4** CULIN scellofrais® *m*.
II *vtr* [*person*] filmer [*event, programme*]; enregistrer [*action, scene*].
III *vi* [*camera man, crew*] tourner.

film: ~ **archive** *n* archives *fpl* cinématographiques; ~ **award** *n* prix *m* de cinéma; ~ **buff**○ *n* mordu/-e○ *m/f* de cinéma; ~ **camera** *n* caméra *f*; ~ **club** *n* ciné-club *m*; ~ **director** ▶ 1251 *n* réalisateur/-trice *m/f*, metteur *m* en scène; ~ **festival** *n* festival *m* de cinéma; ~ **goer** *n* cinéphile *mf*; ~ **industry** *n* industrie *f* cinématographique.

filming /ˈfɪlmɪŋ/ *n* CIN tournage *m*.

film: ~ **laboratory** *n* laboratoire *m* cinématographique; ~ **library** *n* cinémathèque *f*; ~**maker** ▶ 1251 *n* cinéaste *m*; ~**making** *n* cinéma *m*; ~ **rights** *n* droits *mpl* cinématographiques; ~**set** *n* CIN plateau *m* de tournage; ~ **show** *n* présentation *f* de films; ~ **star** ▶ 1251 *n* vedette *f* de cinéma; ~ **studio** *n* studio *m* de cinéma.

filmy /ˈfɪlmɪ/ *adj* **1** (thin) [*dress*] très léger/-ère; [*fabric, screen*] transparent; [*cloud, layer*] léger/-ère; **2** (cloudy) [*glass, lens*] sale.

filter /ˈfɪltə(r)/ **I** *n* **1** AUDIO, PHOT, TECH, TELECOM filtre *m*; **sun** ~ filtre solaire; **2** GB (also ~ **lane**) voie *f* réservée aux véhicules qui tournent; **3** GB (also ~ **arrow**) flèche *f* (directionnelle).
II *vtr* filtrer [*liquid, gas*]; faire passer [*coffee*].
III *vi* **1** (also ~ **off**) ~ **to** ou ~ **off to the left** [*vehicle*] passer sur la voie de gauche pour tourner; **2** (trickle) **to** ~ **into** [*light, sound, water*] pénétrer dans [*area*].
■ **filter out**: ~ **out** [*news*] filtrer; ~ **out** [sth], ~ [sth] **out** éliminer [*applicants, impurities, light*].
■ **filter through** [*details, light, sound*] filtrer (**to** jusqu'à).

filter: ~ **cigarette** *n* cigarette *f* (à bout) filtre; ~ **coffee** *n* (cup of coffee) café *m* (filtre); (ground coffee) café *m* moulu pour filtres; ~ **paper** *n* papier-filtre *m*; ~ **tip** *n* (cigarette) filtre *m*; ~**-tipped** *adj* [*cigarette*] (à bout) filtre *inv*.

filth /fɪlθ/ *n* **1** (dirt) crasse *f*; **2** (vulgarity) obscénités *fpl*; (swearing) grossièretés *fpl*.

filthy /ˈfɪlθɪ/ *adj* **1** (dirty) crasseux/-euse; (revolting) répugnant; **that's a** ~ **habit** c'est dégoûtant; **2** (vulgar) [*language*] ordurier/-ière; [*mind*] mal tourné; **3** GB (unpleasant) [*weather*] épouvantable; [*look*] noir.

filthy rich○ *adj* plein aux as○.

fin /fɪn/ *n* **1** ZOOL (of fish, seal) nageoire *f*; (of shark) aileron *m*; **2** AEROSP empennage *m*; **3** TECH, AUT ailette *f*; **4** NAUT dérive *f*.

final /ˈfaɪnl/ **I** *n* **1** SPORT finale *f*; **2** (newspaper edition) dernière édition *f*.
II *adj* **1** (last) (*épith*) dernier/-ière [*day, question, book, meeting*]; ~ **examinations** GB UNIV examens *mpl* de

fin d'études; **US** UNIV examens *mpl* de fin de semestre; **2** (definitive) [*decision, invoice*] définitif/-ive; [*result*] final; [*judgment*] irrévocable; **she has the ~ say** c'est à elle de décider.

final approach *n* AVIAT approche *f*.

finale /fɪ'nɑːlɪ, US -næli/ *n* MUS, THEAT, GEN finale *f*.

finalist /'faɪnəlɪst/ *n* finaliste *mf*.

finality /faɪ'næləti/ *n* irrévocabilité *f*.

finalize /'faɪnəlaɪz/ *vtr* conclure [*letter, purchase, contract*]; arrêter [*plan, decision, details*]; faire la dernière mise au point de [*article, report*]; boucler [*team*]; fixer [*timetable, route*]; prononcer [*divorce*].

finally /'faɪnəli/ *adv* **1** (eventually) [*decide, accept, arrive, happen*] finalement, enfin; **2** (lastly) finalement, pour finir; **3** (definitively) [*settle, decide*] définitivement.

finals /'faɪnlz/ *npl* **1** GB UNIV examens *mpl* de fin d'études; US UNIV examens *mpl* de fin de semestre; **2** SPORT (last few games) phase *f* finale; (last game) finale *f*.

finance /'faɪnæns, fɪ'næns/ **I** *n* **1** (banking, money systems) finance *f*; **2** (funds) fonds *mpl* (**for** pour; **from** auprès de); **3** (credit) crédit *m*.
II finances *npl* (financial situation) situation *f* financière.
III *noun modifier* [*minister, ministry*] des Finances; [*committee, director, correspondent*] financier/-ière.
IV *vtr* financer [*project*].

finance company, **finance house** *n* société *f* de financement.

financial /faɪ'nænʃl, fɪ-/ *adj* financier/-ière.

financially /faɪ'nænʃəli, fɪ-/ *adv* financièrement.

financial year *n* GB exercice *m*, année *f* budgétaire.

financing /'faɪnænsɪŋ, fɪ'nænsɪŋ/ *n* financement *m*.

finch /fɪntʃ/ *n* fringillidé *m*.

find /faɪnd/ **I** *n* (discovery) GEN découverte *f*; (lucky purchase) trouvaille *f*.
II *vtr* (*prét, pp* **found**) **1** (discover by chance) trouver [*thing, person*]; **to leave sth as one found it** laisser qch dans l'état où on l'a trouvé; **to ~ sb doing** trouver qn en train de faire; **to ~ that** constater que; **2** (discover by looking) trouver, retrouver [*thing, person*]; **to ~ one's way out of** arriver à sortir de [*building, forest, city*]; **to ~ one's own way home** se débrouiller tout seul pour rentrer chez soi; **3** (discover desired thing) trouver [*job, car, seat, solution*]; avoir assez de [*time, energy, money*]; **to ~ sth for sb, to ~ sb sth** trouver qch pour qn; **to ~ oneself sth** se trouver qch; **4** (encounter) trouver [*word, term, species*]; **it is to be found in the Louvre** on peut le voir au Louvre; **5** (judge, consider) trouver (**that** que); **to ~ sb a bore** trouver qn ennuyeux; **to ~ sb/sth to be** trouver que qn/qch est; **to ~ sth easy to do** trouver qch facile à faire; **to ~ it easy to do** trouver facile de faire; **to ~ it incredible that** trouver incroyable que (+ *subj*); **6** (experience) éprouver [*pleasure, satisfaction*] (**in** dans); trouver [*comfort*] (**in** dans); **7** (reach) **to ~ its mark/its target** toucher son but/sa cible; **to ~ its way to/into** arriver dans [*bin, pocket, area*]; **8** JUR **to ~ that** conclure que; **to ~ sb guilty** déclarer qn coupable; **9** (attain) trouver [*letter, card, day*] trouver [*person*]; **the next day found him feeling ill** le lendemain il se sentait malade; **10** COMPUT rechercher.
III *vi* (*prét, pp* **found**) JUR **to ~ for/against sb** se prononcer en faveur de/contre qn.
IV *v refl* (*prét, pp* **found**) **to ~ oneself 1** (discover suddenly) se retrouver; **to ~ oneself unable to do** se sentir incapable de faire; **to ~ oneself doing** se surprendre à faire; **2** (discover one's vocation) se découvrir.
IDIOMS **to ~ one's feet** [*person*] prendre ses marques; [*company*] prendre pied; **to take sb as one ~s him/her** prendre qn comme il/elle est.
■ **find out: ~ out** (get information) se renseigner; **if he ever ~s out** si jamais il l'apprend; ¶ **~ out** [*sth*], **~** [*sth*] **out** découvrir [*fact, answer, name, cause, truth*]; ¶ **~ out who/why/where etc** trouver qui/pourquoi/où etc; ¶ **~ out that** découvrir or apprendre que; ¶ **~** [*sb*] **out** découvrir [*person*]; ¶

~ out about [*sth*] **1** (learn by chance) découvrir [*plan, affair, breakage*]; **2** (research) faire des recherches sur [*subject*].

finder /'faɪndə(r)/ *n*: IDIOMS **~s keepers (losers weepers)** celui qui le trouve le garde.

finding /'faɪndɪŋ/ *n* (conclusion) conclusion *f*.

fine /faɪn/ **I** *n* GEN amende *f*; (for traffic offence) contravention *f* (**for** pour).
II *adj* **1** (very good) [*performance, writer, example, quality*] excellent; **2** (satisfactory) [*holiday, meal, arrangement*] bien; **that's ~** très bien; **'~, thanks**' 'très bien, merci'; **'we'll go now, OK?'—'~'** 'on y va maintenant?'—'d'accord'; **that's ~ by** ou **with me** je n'y vois pas d'inconvénient; **3**◦ IRON **a ~ friend you are!** en voilà un ami!; **you're/she's etc a ~ one to talk!** c'est bien à toi/elle etc de dire ça!; **4** (nice) [*weather, morning, day*] beau/belle; **it's** ou **the weather's ~** il fait beau; **5** (delicate) [*hair, thread, line, feature, fabric, mist, layer*] fin; [*sieve, net*] à mailles fines; [*china, lace, linen, wine*] fin; **6** (small-grained) [*powder, soil*] fin; **7** (subtle) [*adjustment, detail, distinction, judgment*] subtil; **8** (refined) [*lady, clothes, manners*] beau/belle; **9** (commendable) [*person*] merveilleux/-euse; **10** (pure) [*gold, silver*] pur.
III *adv* (well) [*get along, come along, do*] très bien.
IV *vtr* GEN condamner [qn] à une amende [*offender*] (**for** pour; **for doing** pour avoir fait); (for traffic offence) donner une contravention à [*offender*].
IDIOMS **not to put too ~ a point on it** bref; **chance would be a ~ thing**◦! ça serait trop beau◦! ; **you are cutting it a bit ~** ce sera un peu juste; **there is a ~ line between X and Y** il y a une distinction subtile entre X et Y.

fine art *n* beaux-arts *mpl*.
IDIOMS **she's got cheating down to a ~** elle est passée maître dans l'art de tricher.

finely /'faɪnli/ *adv* **1** (not coarsely) [*chopped, grated*] finement; **2** (carefully) [*balanced, judged*] soigneusement; **3** (very well) [*written, painted, executed*] splendidement.

finery /'faɪnəri/ *n* parure *f*; **in all her ~** dans ses plus beaux atours.

finespun /'faɪnspʌn/ *adj* [*notion, argument*] très subtil.

finesse /fɪ'nes/ ▶ 949 **I** *n* finesse *f*.
II *vtr* (handle adroitly) manipuler adroitement [*situation, person*]; contourner [*objections*].

fine-tooth(ed) comb /ˌfaɪn'tuːθ kəʊm/ *n* peigne *m* fin.
IDIOMS **to go over** ou **through sth with a ~** passer qch au peigne fin.

fine: **~-tune** *vtr* ajuster; **~ tuning** *n* ajustement *m*.

finger /'fɪŋɡə(r)/ **I** *n* ▶ 765 **1** ANAT doigt *m*; **to point one's ~ at sb/sth** montrer qn/qch du doigt; **to run one's ~ over sth** passer les doigts sur qch; **he didn't lift** ou **raise a ~ to help** il n'a pas levé le petit doigt pour aider; **I didn't lay a ~ on her** je ne l'ai pas touchée; **to put two ~s up at sb**◦ GB, **to give sb the ~**◦ US ≈ faire un bras d'honneur à qn; **2** (of glove) doigt *m*; **3** (narrow strip) (of land) bande *f*; (of mist, smoke) volute *f*; **4** (small amount) (of whisky etc) doigt *m*.
II *vtr* toucher [*fruit, goods*]; tripoter◦ [*necklace*].
IDIOMS **to get one's ~s burnt** se brûler les doigts; **to twist** ou **wrap sb around one's little ~** mener qn par le bout du nez; **to keep one's ~s crossed** croiser les doigts (**for sb** pour qn); **to point the ~ at sb** accuser qn; **to put the ~ on sb**◦ moucharder◦ qn; **to pull one's ~ out**◦ se grouiller◦; **to slip through sb's ~s** [*opportunity*] passer sous le nez de qn; [*wanted man*] filer entre les doigts de qn.

finger: **~ biscuit** *n* CULIN ≈ boudoir *m*; **~board** *n* MUS touche *f*; **~ bowl** *n* rince-doigts *m inv*; **~ food** *n* CULIN buffet *m* froid à consommer sans couverts; **~ hole** *n* MUS trou *m* (*sur flûte, clarinette etc*).

fingering /'fɪŋɡərɪŋ/ *n* MUS doigté *m*.

finger: **~less glove** *n* mitaine *f*; **~-nail** *n* ongle *m*; **~-paint** *vi* peindre avec les doigts; **~print** *n* empreinte *f* digitale; **~printing** *n* prise *f* d'empreintes digitales.

fingertip /'fɪŋgtɪp/ *n* bout *m* du doigt.

IDIOMS **to have sth at one's ~s** connaître qch sur le bout des doigts.

fingertip control *n* contrôle *m* digital.

finicky /'fɪnɪkɪ/ *adj* [*person*] difficile (**about** pour); [*job, task*] minutieux/-ieuse.

finish /'fɪnɪʃ/ **I** *n* (*pl* **~es**) **1** (end) fin *f*; **from start to ~** du début (jusqu')à la fin; **it will be a fight to the ~** FIG la partie va être serrée; **2** SPORT arrivée *f*; **an athlete with a good ~** un athlète bon au sprint final; **3** (surface, aspect) (of clothing, wood, car) finition *f*; (of fabric, leather) apprêt *m*; **paint with a matt/silk ~** peinture mate/satinée.

II *vtr* **1** (complete) finir, terminer [*chapter, sentence, task*]; terminer, achever [*building, novel, sculpture, opera*]; **to ~ doing** finir de faire; **2** (leave) finir [*work, studies*]; **3** (consume) finir [*cigarette, drink, meal*]; **4** (put an end to) briser [*career*]; **5**° (exhaust, demoralize) achever° [*person*].

III *vi* **1** (end) [*conference, programme*] finir, se terminer; [*holidays*] se terminer; **the film ~es on Thursday** le film ne passe plus à partir de jeudi; **I'll see you when the concert ~es** je te verrai à la fin du concert; **2** (reach end of race) arriver; **the horse/the athlete failed to ~** le cheval/l'athlète n'a pas fini la course; **3** (conclude) [*speaker*] finir de parler, conclure; **4** (leave employment) **I ~ed at the bank yesterday** j'ai quitté mon travail à la banque hier.

IV finished *pp adj* **1** beautifully **~ed** [*furniture, interior etc*] avec des finitions soignées; **~ed in marble** avec des finitions en marbre; **the ~ed product** le produit fini; **2** (accomplished) [*performance*] accompli; **3** (ruined) [*person, career*] fini, fichu°.

■ **finish off**: ¶ **~** [**sth**] **off, ~ off** [**sth**] (complete) finir, terminer [*letter, meal, task*]; ¶ **~** [**sb**] **off 1** (exhaust, demoralize) achever° [*person*]; **2** (kill) achever [*person, animal*].

■ **finish up**: ¶ **~ up** [*person*] (at end of journey) se retrouver; (in situation) finir; **to ~ up (by) doing** finir par faire; ¶ **~** [**sth**] **up, ~ up** [**sth**] finir [*milk, paint, cake*].

■ **finish with**: ¶ **~ with** [**sth**] finir avec [*book, tool, pen*]; **I'm ~ed with school/politics!** j'en ai assez de l'école/de la politique!; ¶ **~ with** [**sb**] **1** (split up) rompre avec [*girlfriend, boyfriend*]; **2** (stop punishing) **you'll be sorry when I've ~ed with you!** tu vas voir ce que tu vas voir°!

finish: ~ing line GB, **~ line** US *n* SPORT, FIG ligne *f* d'arrivée; **~ing post** *n* SPORT poteau *m* d'arrivée; **~ing school** *n* SCH pension pour jeunes filles de bonne famille.

finishing touch /'fɪnɪʃɪŋ/ *n* touche *f* finale; **the ~es** la touche finale.

finite /'faɪnaɪt/ *adj* **1** GEN [*resources*] limité; **2** MATH, PHILOS, LING fini.

Finland /'fɪnlənd/ ▶ **840** *pr n* Finlande *f*.

Finn /fɪn/ ▶ **1100** *n* **1** (citizen) Finlandais/-e *m/f*; **2** (speaker) Finnois/-e *m/f*.

Finnish /'fɪnɪʃ/ ▶ **1100**, **1038** **I** *n* (language) finnois *m*. **II** *adj* finlandais.

fiord *n* = **fjord**.

fir /fɜː(r)/ *n* (also **~ tree**) sapin *m*.

fir cone *n* pomme *f* de pin.

fire /'faɪə(r)/ **I** *n* **1** (element) feu *m*; **to set ~ to sth, set sth on ~** mettre le feu à qch; **to be on ~** être en feu; **to catch ~** prendre feu; **2** (blaze) incendie *m*; **to start a ~** provoquer un incendie; **3** (for warmth) feu *m*; **4** ¢ (shots) coups *mpl* de feu; **to open ~ on sb** ouvrir le feu sur qn; **the police/passers-by came under ~** on a tiré sur la police/les passants; **to be under ~** FIG être vivement critiqué (**from** par); **to return sb's ~** riposter; **5** (verve) fougue *f*.

II *excl* **1** (raising alarm) au feu!; **2** (order to shoot) feu!

III *vtr* **1** MIL, GEN décharger [*gun, weapon*]; tirer [*shot*]; lancer [*arrow, missile*]; **to ~ questions at sb** bombarder qn de questions; **2** (inspire) **to be ~d with**

enthusiasm s'enthousiasmer; **to ~ sb's imagination** enflammer l'imagination de qn; **3** (dismiss) renvoyer, virer° [*person*]; **4** TECH cuire [*ceramics*].

IV *vi* **1** MIL, GEN tirer (**at, on** sur); **2** [*engine*] démarrer.

IDIOMS **~ away!** allez-y!; **to hang ~** MIL faire long feu; FIG [*plans, project, person*] traîner; **to play with ~** jouer avec le feu; **he'll never set the world on ~**° il ne fera jamais de miracles; ▶ **house.**

■ **fire up** **~** [**sb**] **up, ~ up** [**sb**] gonfler [qn] à bloc.

fire: ~ alarm *n* alarme *f* incendie; **~ arm** *n* arme *f* à feu; **~back** *n* plaque *f* de cheminée; **~ball** *n* boule *f* de feu; **~ bell** *n* sonnerie *f* d'alarme.

firebomb /'faɪəbɒm/ **I** *n* bombe *f* incendiaire. **II** *vtr* incendier [*building*].

fire: ~brand *n* FIG semeur *m* de discordes; **~break** *n* pare-feu *m inv*; **~ brigade** *n* pompiers *mpl*; **~ chief** *n* US chef *m* des pompiers; **~cracker** *n* pétard *m*; **~-damaged** *adj* endommagé par le feu; **~ department** *n* US pompiers *mpl*; **~ door** *n* porte *f* coupe-feu; **~ drill** *n* exercice *m* d'évacuation en cas d'incendie; **~-eater** *n* cracheur/-euse *m/f* de feu; **~ engine** *n* voiture *f* de pompiers; **~ escape** *n* escalier *m* de secours; **~ exit** *n* sortie *f* de secours; **~ extinguisher** *n* extincteur *m*; **~fighter** ▶ **1251** *n* pompier *m*; **~fighting** *n* lutte *f* contre l'incendie; **~fly** *n* luciole *f*; **~guard** *n* pare-étincelles *m inv*; **~ hazard** *n* risque *m* d'incendie; **~house** *n* US caserne *f* de pompiers; **~ hydrant** *n* bouche *f* d'incendie; **~ insurance** *n* assurance-incendie *f*; **~light** *n* lueur *f* du feu; **~lighter** *n* allume-feu *m inv*; **~man** ▶ **1251** *n* pompier *m*; **~ marshall** *n* US pompier *m* responsable de la prévention; **~place** *n* cheminée *f*; **~ plug** *n* US bouche *f* d'incendie; **~ power** *n* puissance *f* de feu; **~ practice** *n* = **fire drill**; **~proof** *adj* [*door, clothing*] ignifugé; **~ risk** *n* risque *m* d'incendie; **~ screen** *n* écran *m* de cheminée; **~ service** *n* (sapeurs-) pompiers *mpl*; **~side** *n* coin *m* du feu; **~ station** *n* caserne *f* de pompiers; **~ truck** *n* US voiture *f* de pompiers; **~warden** ▶ **1251** *n* responsable *mf* de la lutte contre l'incendie; **~wood** *n* bois *m* à brûler; **~work** *n* feu *m* d'artifice; **~works display** *n* feu *m* d'artifice.

firing /'faɪərɪŋ/ *n* **1** (of guns) tir *m*; **2** (of ceramics) cuisson *f*.

firing line *n* **to be in the ~** LIT être dans la ligne de tir; FIG (under attack) faire l'objet de violentes critiques.

firing squad *n* peloton *m* d'exécution; **to face the ~** être fusillé.

firm /fɜːm/ **I** *n* (business) entreprise *f*, société *f*; **~ of architects** cabinet *m* d'architecte.

II *adj* **1** (hard) [*mattress, fruit, handshake*] ferme; **to give sth a ~ tap/tug** taper/tirer qch d'un coup sec; **2** (steady) [*table, ladder*] solide; **3** FIG (strong) [*foundation, basis, grasp*] solide; **it's my ~ belief that** je crois fermement que; **4** (definite) [*offer, intention, refusal*] ferme; [*date*] définitif/-ive; [*evidence*] concret/-ète; **5** (resolute) [*person, stand, leadership*] ferme (**with sb** avec qn); **he needs a ~ hand** il a besoin qu'on soit ferme avec lui; **6** FIN [*dollar, market*] ferme.

III *adv* **to stand ~** tenir bon (**against** contre); **to remain** OU **hold ~** [*currency*] rester ferme (**against** par rapport à).

firmly /'fɜːmlɪ/ *adv* **1** (with authority) [*say, answer, state*] d'un ton ferme; **tell him ~ but politely...** dis-lui fermement mais poliment...; **to deal ~ with sb/sth** traiter qn/qch avec fermeté; **2** (strongly) [*believe, deny, be convinced*] fermement; **3** (tightly) [*hold, push, press*] fermement; [*attach, tie*] solidement; **we have it ~ under control** nous l'avons bien en main.

firmness /'fɜːmnɪs/ *n* **1** GEN fermeté *f*; **2** FIN stabilité *f*.

first /fɜːst/ ▶ **1112**, **854** **I** *pron* **1** (of series, group) premier/première *m/f* (**to do** à faire); **2** (of month) **the ~** (**of May**) le premier (mai); **3 First** (in titles) **Elizabeth the First** Elisabeth Première; **4** (initial moment) **the ~ I knew about his death was a letter from**

his wife c'est par une lettre de sa femme que j'ai appris qu'il était mort; **that's the ~ I've heard of it!** première nouvelle!; **5** (beginning) début *m*; **at ~** au début; **from the (very) ~** dès le début; **6** (new experience) première *f*; **a ~ for sb/sth** une première pour qn/qch; **7** AUT (gear) première *f*; ▶**gear**; **8** GB UNIV (degree) mention *f* très bien (à la licence).

II *adj* **1** (of series, group) premier/-ière (*before n*); **the ~ three pages** or **the three ~ pages** les trois premières pages; **2** (in phrases) **at ~ glance** ou **sight** à première vue; **I'll ring ~ thing tomorrow** je vous appellerai demain à la première heure; **I'll do it ~ thing** je le ferai dès que possible; **I'll do it ~ thing** je le ferai dès que possible; **he doesn't know the ~ thing about politics** il ne connaît absolument rien à la politique.

III *adv* **1** (before others) [*arrive, leave*] le premier/la première; **you go ~!** après vous!; **women and children ~** les femmes et les enfants d'abord; **to come ~** GAMES, SPORT terminer premier/première (in à); FIG [*career, family*] passer avant tout; **2** (to begin with) d'abord; **~ of all** tout d'abord; **~ she tells me one thing, then something else** elle commence par me dire une chose puis elle me dit le contraire; **there are two reasons: ~...** il y a deux raisons: d'abord...; **when we were ~ married** tout au début de notre mariage; **when he ~ arrived** quand il est arrivé; **3** (for the first time) pour la première fois; **I ~ met him in Paris** je l'ai rencontré pour la première fois à Paris; **4** (rather) plutôt.

IDIOMS **~ come ~ served** les premiers arrivés sont les premiers servis; **~ things ~** chaque chose en son temps.

first aid *n* **1** ₵ GEN premiers soins *mpl*; **2** (as skill) secourisme *m*.

first aid: ~ kit *n* trousse *f* de secours; **~ officer** *n* secouriste *mf*.

first class **I** *n* **1** RAIL première *f* (classe *f*); **2** POST tarif *m* rapide.

II **first-class** *adj* **1** TOURISM, RAIL [*compartment, hotel, ticket*] de première (classe); **2** POST [*stamp*] (au) tarif rapide; **~ mail** courrier *m* (au tarif) rapide; **3** GB UNIV [*degree*] avec mention très bien; **4** (excellent) excellent.

III *adv* **1** RAIL [*travel*] en première (classe); **2** POST [*send*] au tarif rapide.

first: ~ course *n* (of meal) entrée *f*; **~ cousin** *n* (male) cousin *m* germain; (female) cousine *f* germaine; **~ degree murder** *n* US JUR meurtre *m* avec préméditation; **~ edition** *n* édition *f* originale; **~-ever** *adj* tout premier/tout premier; **~ floor** *n* GB premier étage *m*; US rez-de-chaussée *m*; **~ form** *n* GB SCH (classe *f* de) sixième *f*; **~-generation** *adj* de la première génération; **~ grade** *n* US SCH cours *m* préparatoire; **~-hand** *adj, adv* de première main; **First Lady** *n* US POL première dame *f*; **~ light** *n* premières lueurs *fpl*.

firstly /'fɜːstlɪ/ *adv* premièrement.

first mate *n* NAUT second *m*.

first name *n* prénom *m*; **to be on ~ terms with sb** appeler qn par son prénom.

first: ~ night *n* THEAT première *f*; **~ person** *n* LING première personne *f*; **~ principle** *n* principe *m* premier; **~-rate** *adj* excellent; **~ school** *n* GB SCH école *f* préparatoire; **~-time buyer** *n* personne *f* qui achète sa première maison; **~ violin** *n* premier violon *m*.

first year *n* SCH, UNIV (group) première année *f*; (pupil) élève *mf* en première année; (student) étudiant/-e *m/f* en première année.

firth /fɜːθ/ *n* estuaire *m*.

fiscal /'fɪskl/ *adj* fiscal.

fiscal year *n* exercice *m* budgétaire or fiscal.

fish /fɪʃ/ **I** *n* (*pl ~, ~es*) poisson *m*.

II *noun modifier* [*course, bone, glue*] de poisson; [*knife, fork*] à poisson.

III *vi* **1** LIT pêcher; **to ~ for trout/cod** pêcher la truite/la morue; **2** FIG (test for response) **to ~ for**

---

information chercher à dénicher des renseignements; **to ~ for compliments** rechercher les compliments.

IDIOMS **to be neither ~ nor fowl** n'être ni chair ni poisson; **to be like a ~ out of water** ne pas se sentir dans son élément; **to drink like a ~**○ boire comme un trou; **to have other ~ to fry** avoir d'autres chats à fouetter; **there are plenty more ~ in the sea** un de perdu, dix de retrouvés.

■ **fish around** farfouiller (in dans; for pour trouver).

■ **fish out: ~ out** [sth] **1** (from bag, pocket, box) sortir [*money, pen*] (of de); **2** (from water) repêcher [*body, object*] (of de).

fish: ~ and chips *n* poisson *m* frit avec des frites; **~ and chip shop** ▶1251 *n* GB friterie *f*; **~bowl** *n* bocal *m* (à poissons); **~ cake** *n* croquette *f* de poisson.

fisherman /'fɪʃəmən/ ▶1251 *n* pêcheur *m*.

fishery /'fɪʃərɪ/ *n* (processing plant) pêcherie *f*; **~ farm** *n* centre *m* de pisciculture; **~ farming** *n* pisciculture *f*; **~ finger** *n* GB bâtonnet *m* de poisson; **~ hook** *n* hameçon *m*.

fishing /'fɪʃɪŋ/ **I** *n* pêche *f*; **to go ~** aller à la pêche. **II** *noun modifier* [*boat, fleet, port, line, net*] de pêche.

fishing: ~ ground *n* lieu *m* de pêche; **~ rod** *n* canne *f* à pêche; **~ village** *n* port *m* de pêche.

fish market *n* halle *f* aux poissons.

fishmonger /'fɪʃmʌŋgə(r)/ ▶1251 *n* GB poissonnier/-ière *m/f*; **~'s (shop)** poissonnerie *f*.

fish: ~net *adj* [*stockings*] à résille; **~ paste** *n* GB ~ beurre *m* de poisson; **~pond** *n* (ornamental) bassin *m*; (at fish farm) vivier *m*; **~ shop** GB, ~ **store** US ▶1251 *n* poissonnerie *f*; **~ slice** *n* (for frying) spatule *f*; (for serving at table) pelle *f* à poisson; **~ tank** *n* aquarium *m*.

fishy /'fɪʃɪ/ *adj* **1** LIT [*smell, taste*] de poisson; **2**○ FIG (suspect) louche○.

fission /'fɪʃn/ *n* **1** (also **nuclear ~**) PHYS fission *f*; **2** BIOL fissiparité *f*.

fissure /'fɪʃə(r)/ *n* **1** (in ground) crevasse *f*; (in wood, wall) fissure *f*; **2** ANAT scissure *f*.

fist /fɪst/ *n* poing *m*; **to shake one's ~ at sb** menacer qn du poing.

IDIOMS **to make money hand over ~** gagner des mille et des cents; **to make a good/poor ~ of doing sth** bien/mal faire qch.

fistful /'fɪstfʊl/ *n* poignée *f* (of de).

fit /fɪt/ **I** *n* **1** MED crise *f*, attaque *f*; **to have a ~** (unspecified) avoir une attaque ou une crise; **2** GEN (of rage, passion, panic) accès *m*; **~ of coughing** quinte *f* de toux; **to have sb in ~s**○ donner le fou rire à qn; **to have** ou **throw a ~**○ (be mad) piquer○ une crise; **3** (of garment) **to be a good/poor ~** être/ne pas être à la bonne taille.

II *adj* **1** [*person*] (in trim) en forme; (not ill) en bonne santé; **you're looking ~ and well!** tu as l'air en pleine forme!; **to get ~** retrouver la forme; **2** (suitable, appropriate) **to be ~ for** (worthy of) être digne de [*person, hero, king*]; (capable of) être capable de faire [*job*]; **to be ~ for nothing** n'être plus bon/bonne à rien; **~/not ~ for human consumption** propre/impropre à la consommation; **to be ~ to drive** être en état de conduire; **~ to drink** potable; **~ to live in** habitable; **I'm not ~ to be seen!** je ne suis pas présentable!; **to see** ou **think ~ to do** juger ou trouver bon de faire; **to be in no ~ state to do** ne pas être en état de faire; **3**○ (in emphatic phrases) **to laugh ~ to burst** se tordre de rire; **to cry ~ to burst** pleurer comme une madeleine.

III *vtr* (*prét* **fitted, fit** US; *pp* **fitted**) **1** (be the right size) [*garment*] être à la taille de; [*shoe*] être à la pointure de; [*key*] aller dans [*lock*]; aller dans [*envelope, space*]; **to ~ size X to Y** correspondre aux tailles X à Y; **to ~ ages 3 to 5** convenir aux enfants de 3 à 5 ans; **2** (make or find room for) **to ~ sth in** ou **into** trouver de la place pour qch dans [*room, house, car*]; **3** (install) mettre [qch] en place [*lock, door, kitchen, shower*]; **to ~ A to B, to ~ A and B together** assembler A avec B; **to ~ sth with** équiper qch de [*attachment, lock*]; **to ~ sb for** [*tailor*] prendre les mesures de qn pour [*garment, uniform*]; **to ~ sb with** [*doctor*] pourvoir qn de [*hearing aid, prosthesis*]; **4** (be compatible with) correspondre à [*description, requirements*]; aller avec [*decor*]; **the punishment should ~ the crime** la punition devrait être proportionnée à la faute; ▶ **bill**.

IV *vi* (*prét* **fitted**, **fit** US; *pp* **fitted**) **1** (be the right size) [*garment*] être à ma/ta/sa taille, aller; [*shoes*] être à ma/ta/sa pointure, aller; [*key, lid, sheet*] aller; **2** (have enough room) [*toys, books etc*] tenir (**into** dans); **will the table ~ in that corner?** y a-t-il de la place pour la table dans ce coin?; **3** (go into place) **to ~ inside one another** aller or se mettre les uns dans les autres; **to ~ into place** [*part, handle*] bien aller; [*cupboard, brick*] bien rentrer; **4** FIG (tally, correspond) **something doesn't quite ~ here** il y a quelque chose qui ne va pas ici; **to ~ with** correspondre à [*story, facts*]; **to ~ into** aller avec [*ideology, colour scheme*].

IDIOMS **by** ou **in ~s and starts** par à-coups.

■ **fit in**: ¶ **~ in 1** LIT [*key, object*] aller; **will you all ~ in?** (to car, room) est-ce qu'il y a de la place pour vous tous?; **2** FIG (be in harmony) [*person*] s'intégrer (**with** à); **I'll ~ in with your plans** j'accorderai mes projets avec les vôtres; ¶ **~ [sth/sb] in**, **~ in [sth/sb] 1** (find room for) caser [*books, objects*]; faire entrer [*key*]; **2** (find time for) caser [*game, meeting, break*]; trouver le temps pour voir [*patient, colleague*].

■ **fit out**: **~ [sth] out**, **~ out [sth]** équiper (**with** de); **to ~ sb out with** mettre [qch] à qn [*costume, garment, hearing aid*].

fitful /'fɪtfl/ *adj* [*sleep*] agité; [*wind*] changeant.

fitfully /'fɪtfəlɪ/ *adv* [*sleep, rain, shine*] par intermittence.

fitness /'fɪtnɪs/ **I** *n* **1** (physical condition) forme *f*; **2** (aptness) (of person) aptitude *f* (**for, to do** à faire).
II *noun modifier* [*club, centre, room*] de culture physique.

fitness: **~ test** *n* test *m* de condition physique; **~ training** *n* ∉ exercices *mpl* physiques.

fitted /'fɪtɪd/ *adj* [*wardrobe*] encastré; [*kitchen*] intégré.

fitted: **~ carpet** *n* moquette *f*; **~ sheet** *n* drap-housse *m*.

fitter /'fɪtə(r)/ ▶ **1251** *n* TECH monteur/-euse *m/f*.

fitting /'fɪtɪŋ/ **I** *n* **1** (standardized part) (bathroom, electrical, gas) installation *f*; **2** (for clothes, hearing aid) essayage *m*; **3** (width of shoe) largeur *f*.
II *adj* (apt, appropriate) [*description, language, site*] adéquat; [*memorial, testament*] qui convient; **a ~ tribute to her work** un hommage mérité à son œuvre.

fittingly /'fɪtɪŋlɪ/ *adv* [*named*] de façon appropriée.

fitting room *n* salon *m* d'essayage.

five /faɪv/ ▶ **1112**, **713**, **812** **I** *n* (numeral) cinq *m* *inv*.
II *adj* cinq *inv*.

IDIOMS **to take ~**○ US faire une pause.

five-a-side /ˌfaɪvə'saɪd/ *n* (also **~ football**) GB football *m* à cinq (joueurs).

fiver○ /'faɪvə(r)/ *n* GB billet *m* de cinq livres.

five spot○ *n* US billet *m* de cinq dollars.

fix /fɪks/ **I** *n* **1**○ (quandary) pétrin *m*; **to be in a ~** être dans le pétrin○; **2**○ (dose) (of drugs) shoot○ *m*; **3** (means of identification) **to take a ~ on sth** AVIAT, NAUT déterminer la position de qch; **4**○ (rigged arrangement) **it was a ~** c'était truqué.
II *vtr* **1** (establish, set) fixer [*date, venue, price, limit*]; déterminer [*chronology, position*]; **to ~ tax at 20%** établir un impôt de 20%; **nothing is ~ed yet** il n'y a encore rien d'arrêté; **2** (organize) arranger [*meeting, visit*]; préparer [*drink, meal*]; **to ~ one's hair** se donner un coup de peigne; **how are we ~ed for time/money?** qu'est-ce qu'on a comme temps/argent?○; **3** (mend) réparer [*article, equipment*]; (sort out) régler [*problem*]; **4** (attach, insert) fixer [*curtain, handle, shelf, notice*] (**on** sur; **to** à); attacher [*rope*] (**to** à); FIG faire peser [*suspicion*] (**on** sur); rejeter [*blame*] (**on** sur); **5** (concentrate) fixer [*attention*] (**on** sur); placer [*hopes*] (**on** dans); tourner [*thoughts*] (**on** vers);

to ~ one's eyes ou **gaze on sb** regarder qn fixement; **6**○ (rig, corrupt) truquer [*contest, election*]; **7** ART, BIOL, CHEM, PHOT, TECH fixer.
III fixed *pp adj* [*gaze, idea, income, order, price*] fixe; [*intervals*] régulier/-ière; [*method*] arrêté; [*desire*] tenace; [*intention*] ferme; [*proportion*] constant; [*expression*] figé; [*menu*] à prix fixe.

■ **fix on**, **fix upon**: **~ on [sb/sth]** choisir [*person, place, food, object*]; fixer [*date, venue, amount*].

■ **fix up**: ¶ **~ up [sth]**, **~ [sth] up 1** (organize) organiser [*holiday, meeting*]; décider de [*date*]; **2** (decorate) refaire [*room, house*]; ¶ **~ sb up with sth** trouver qch à qn [*accommodation, vehicle*]; faire avoir qch à qn [*ticket, meal*]; ¶ **~ sb up with sb**○ monter une baraque à qn avec qn○.

fixation /fɪk'seɪʃn/ *n* **1** GEN, PSYCH fixation *f*; **2** CHEM fixation *f*.

fixative /'fɪksətɪv/ *n* GEN, TECH produit *m* fixateur; (for hair) fixateur *m*; ART fixatif *m*; PHOT fixateur *m*.

fixed assets /fɪkst/ *npl* immobilisations *fpl*, actif *m* immobilisé.

fixedly /'fɪksɪdlɪ/ *adv* [*look, gaze*] fixement.

fixed-term contract *n* contrat *m* à durée déterminée.

fixer /'fɪksə(r)/ *n* **1**○ (schemer) magouilleur/-euse○ *m/f*; **2** PHOT fixateur *m*.

fixture /'fɪkstʃə(r)/ *n* **1** CONSTR, TECH installation *f*; **~s and fittings** équipements *mpl*; **2** SPORT rencontre *f*.

fizz /fɪz/ **I** *n* (of drink) pétillement *m*; (of match, firework) crépitement *m*.
II *vi* [*drink*] pétiller; [*match, firework*] crépiter.

■ **fizz up** mousser.

fizzle /'fɪzl/ *v*: ■ **fizzle out** [*interest, romance*] s'éteindre; [*strike, campaign, project*] faire fiasco; [*story*] se terminer en queue de poisson; [*firework*] faire long feu.

fizzy /'fɪzɪ/ *adj* gazeux/-euse.

fjord /fɪ'ɔːd/ *n* fjord *m*.

FL US *abrév écrite* = **Florida**.

flab○ /flæb/ *n* chair *f* flasque.

flabbergast /'flæbəgɑːst, US -gæst/ *vtr* sidérer.

flabby /'flæbɪ/ *adj* [*skin, muscle*] flasque; [*person*] aux chairs flasques.

flaccid /'flæsɪd/ *adj* flasque, mou/molle.

flag /flæg/ **I** *n* **1** (national symbol) drapeau *m*; **to sail under the Panamanian ~** NAUT battre pavillon panaméen; **2** (as signal) NAUT pavillon *m*; RAIL drapeau *m*; **3** (on map) drapeau *m*; **4** (stone) dalle *f*; **5** COMPUT drapeau *m*.
II *vtr* (*p prés etc* -**gg**-) **1** (mark with tab) baliser [*text*]; **2** (signal) signaler [*problem*]; **3** COMPUT signaler [qch] au moyen d'un drapeau.
III *vi* (*p prés etc* -**gg**-) [*interest*] faiblir; [*morale, strength*] baisser; [*conversation*] languir; [*athlete, campaigner*] flancher○.
IV flagging *pres p adj* [*strength*] qui baisse; [*energy, economy, industry etc*] chancelant.

IDIOMS **to fly the ~** représenter son pays (à l'étranger); **to wave the ~** faire des déclarations patriotiques.

■ **flag down**: **~ [sth] down**, **~ down [sth]** faire signe de s'arrêter à [*train*]; héler [*taxi*].

flagellation /ˌflædʒə'leɪʃn/ *n* flagellation *f*.

flageolet /ˌflædʒə'let, 'flædʒ-/ *n* flageolet *m*.

flagon /'flægən/ *n* (bottle) grosse bouteille *f*; (jug) pichet *m*.

flagpole /'flægpəʊl/ *n* mât *m* (de drapeau).

flagrant /'fleɪgrənt/ *adj* flagrant.

flagrantly /'fleɪgrəntlɪ/ *adv* [*behave, do sth*] de façon flagrante; [*artificial, dishonest etc*] manifestement.

flagship /'flægʃɪp/ **I** *n* NAUT vaisseau *m* amiral.
II *noun modifier* [*company, product*] vedette.

flag: **~stone** *n* dalle *f*; **~ stop** *n* US arrêt *m* facultatif.

flail /fleɪl/ **I** *n* fléau *m*.

II *vtr* **1** AGRIC battre [qch] au fléau [*corn*]; **2** GEN
▶**flail about**.
III *vi* ▶ **flail about**.
■ **flail about**, **flail around**: ¶ ~ **around** [*person*]
se débattre; [*arms, legs*] s'agiter; ¶ ~ **[sth] around**,
~ **around [sth]** agiter [*arms, legs*].

flair /ˈfleə(r)/ *n* **1** (talent) don; **2** (style) classe *f*.

flak /flæk/ *n* ⊄ **1** MIL tirs *mpl* des batteries antiaé-
riennes; **2**° FIG (criticism) critiques *fpl*.

flake /fleɪk/ I *n* **1** (of snow, cereal) flocon *m*; (of soap) paillette *f*; (of chocolate, cheese) copeau *m*; (of paint, rust)
écaille *f*; (of rock, flint) éclat *m*.
II *vi* (also ~ **off**) [*paint, varnish*] s'écailler; [*plaster,
stone*] s'effriter; [*skin*] peler; [*fish*] s'émietter.
■ **flake out** s'endormir comme une masse.

flak jacket GB, **flack vest** US *n* gilet *m* pare-balles.

flaky /ˈfleɪkɪ/ *adj* [*paint*] qui s'écaille; [*skin*] qui pèle;
[*plaster, rock, statue*] qui s'effrite.

flaky pastry *n* pâte *f* feuilletée.

flamboyant /flæmˈbɔɪənt/ *adj* [*person*] haut en
couleur; [*lifestyle, image*] exubérant; [*colour, clothes*]
voyant; [*gesture*] extravagant.

flame /fleɪm/ I *n* **1** flamme *f*; **in** ~**s** en flammes;
to go up in ~**s** s'enflammer; **to burst into** ~**s** s'embraser; **to be shot down in** ~**s** LIT, FIG être
descendu en flammes; **2** FIG (also ~**s**) feu *m* (**of** de);
an old ~° (person) un ancien flirt°; **3** (colour) rouge
m feu.
II *vi* [*fire, torch*] flamber.

flamenco /fləˈmeŋkəʊ/ *n* (also ~ **dancing**) flamenco
m.

flame: ~**proof** *adj* qui va au feu; ~ **retardant**
adj [*substance, chemical*] ignifuge; [*furniture, fabric*]
ignifugé; ~**thrower** *n* lance-flammes *m inv*.

flaming /ˈfleɪmɪŋ/ *adj* **1** [*vehicle, building*] en flammes;
[*torch*] allumé; **2** (*épith*) [*row*] violent.

flamingo /fləˈmɪŋgəʊ/ *n* (*pl* ~**s** ou **-oes**) flamant *m*
(rose).

flammable /ˈflæməbl/ *adj* inflammable.

flan /flæn/ *n* (savoury) quiche *f*, tarte *f*; (sweet) tarte *f*.

Flanders /ˈflɑːndəz/ *pr n* les Flandres *fpl*.

flange /flændʒ/ *n* (on wheel) boudin *m*; (on pipe) bride *f*;
(on tool) collet *m*; (on beam) aile *f*.

flank /flæŋk/ I *n* **1** (of animal, mountain) flanc *m*; **2** MIL
flanc *m*; **3** POL, SPORT aile *f*; **4** CULIN flanchet *m*.
II *vtr* flanquer [*person, door*]; border [*path, area*].

flannel /ˈflænl/ *n* **1** (wool) flanelle *f*; (cotton) pilou *m*; **2**
GB (also **face** ~) = gant *m* de toilette.

flannels /ˈflænlz/ *npl* pantalon *m* de flanelle.

flap /flæp/ I *n* **1** (on pocket, envelope, tent) rabat *m*; (on
table, bar) abattant *m*; (of trapdoor) trappe *f*; (for cat)
chatière *f*; **2** (movement) (of wings) battement *m* (**of** de);
(of sail) claquement *m* (**of** de); **3** AVIAT volet *m*; **4**°
(panic) **to get into a** ~ s'affoler; **5** LING battement
m.
II *vtr* (*p prés etc* **-pp-**) [*wind*] claquer [*sail, cloth*];
faire voleter [*paper, clothes*]; [*person*] secouer [*sheet*];
agiter [*paper, letter*] (**at sb** en direction de qn); **the
bird** ~**ped its wings** l'oiseau battait des ailes.
III *vi* (*p prés etc* **-pp-**) **1** (move) [*wing*] battre; [*sail,
flag, door*] claquer; [*paper, clothes*] voleter; **2**° (panic)
s'affoler.

flapjack /ˈflæpdʒæk/ *n* CULIN **1** GB biscuit *m* au
müesli; **2** US crêpe *f*.

flare /fleə(r)/ I *n* **1** (light signal) AVIAT (on runway)
balise *f* lumineuse; MIL (on target) fusée *f* éclairante;
NAUT (distress signal) fusée *f* (de détresse); **2** (burst of
light) (of match, lighter) lueur *f*; (of fireworks) flamboiement *m*; **3** (also **solar** ~) éruption *f* solaire.
II **flares** *npl* (trousers) pantalon *m* à pattes d'éléphant.
III *vi* **1** (burn briefly) [*firework, match*] jeter une brève
lueur; **2** (erupt) [*violence*] éclater; **3** (also ~ **out**)
(widen) [*skirt*] s'évaser; [*nostrils*] se dilater.
■ **flare up 1** (burn brightly) [*fire*] s'embraser; **2** FIG
(erupt) [*anger, violence*] éclater; [*person*] s'emporter; **3**
(recur) [*illness*] réapparaître; [*pain*] se réveiller.

flared /fleə(r)d/ *adj* [*skirt*] évasé; [*trousers*] à pattes
d'éléphant.

flash /flæʃ/ I *n* **1** (sudden light) (of torch, headlights) lueur
f soudaine; (of jewels, metal) éclat *m*; **a** ~ **of lightning**
un éclair; **2** FIG **a** ~ **of inspiration/genius** un éclair
d'inspiration/de génie; **it came to him in a** ~ **that**
l'idée lui est soudain venue que; **in** ou **like a** ~ en un
clin d'œil; **3** PHOT flash *m*; **4** (bulletin) flash *m*
(d'information); **5** (stripe) (on clothing) parement *m*; (on
car) bande *f*.
II° *adj* (posh) [*hotel*] luxueux/-euse; [*car, suit*] tape-à-
l'œil *inv*.
III *vtr* **1**° (display) [*person*] montrer [qch] rapidement
[*card, money*]; **2** (flaunt) = ~ **about**; **3** (shine) **to** ~ **a
signal/message to sb** envoyer un signal/message à
qn avec une lampe; **to** ~ **one's headlights (at)** faire
un appel de phares (à); **4** (send) FIG lancer [*look, smile*]
(**at** à); **5** (transmit) faire apparaître [*message*].
IV *vi* **1** (shine) [*light*] clignoter; [*jewels*] étinceler;
[*eyes*] lancer des éclairs; **to** ~ **on and off** clignoter; **2**
(appear suddenly) **a thought** ~**ed through my mind**
une pensée m'a traversé l'esprit; **3**° (expose oneself)
[*man*] faire l'exhibitionniste (**at** devant).
IDIOMS **to be a** ~ **in the pan** être un feu de paille;
quick as a ~ vif/vive comme l'éclair.
■ **flash about**, **flash around**: ~ **[sth] about** exhiber [*credit card*]; étaler [*money*].
■ **flash by**, **flash past** [*person, bird*] passer comme
un éclair; [*landscape*] défiler.
■ **flash up**: ~ **[sth] up**, ~ **up [sth]** afficher
[*message*] (**on** sur).

flashback /ˈflæʃbæk/ *n* **1** CIN flash-back *m* (**to** à); **2**
(memory) souvenir *m*.

flash: ~**bulb** *n* ampoule *f* de flash; ~ **card** *n* SCH
carte *f* (de support visuel); ~ **cube** *n* cube-flash *m*;
~ **flood** *n* crue *f* soudaine; ~ **gun** *n* PHOT flash
m.

flashing /ˈflæʃɪŋ/ I *n* **1** CONSTR solin *m*; **2**° (exhibition-
ism) exhibitionnisme *m*.
II *adj* [*light, sign*] clignotant.

flash light *n* lampe *f* de poche.

flashpoint /ˈflæʃpɔɪnt/ *n* **1** CHEM point *m* d'éclair; **2**
FIG (trouble spot) point *m* chaud; **3** FIG (explosive situation) point *m* critique.

flashy° /ˈflæʃɪ/ *adj* PÉJ [*driver, player*] frimeur/-euse;
[*car, dress, tie, campaign, image*] tape-à-l'œil *inv*; [*jewellery*] clinquant.

flask /flɑːsk/, US flæsk/ *n* **1** CHEM (large) flacon *m*;
(small) (round-bottomed) ballon *m*; (flat-bottomed) fiole *f*; **2**
GEN (large) bonbonne *f*; (small) bouteille *f*; (vacuum)
thermos® *f* or *m inv*; (hip) ~ flasque *f*.

flat /flæt/ I *n* **1** GB (apartment) appartement *m*; **one-
bedroom** ~ deux pièces *m inv*; **2** (level part) **the** ~
of le plat de [*hand, sword*]; **on the** ~ GB [*walk, park*]
sur le plat; **3**° (tyre) pneu *m* à plat; **4** MUS bémol *m*.
II **flats** *npl* **1** US (shoes) chaussures *fpl* plates; **2**
GEOG (marshland) marécage *m*.
III *adj* **1** (level, not rounded) GEN plat; (of flat appearance)
[*nose, face*] aplati; **squashed** ~ écrasé; **2** (deflated)
[*tyre, ball*] dégonflé; **to have a** ~ **tyre** avoir un pneu
à plat; **3** (pressed close) **her feet** ~ **on the floor** les
pieds bien à plat sur le sol; **4** (low) [*shoes, heels*] plat; **5**
(absolute) [*refusal, denial*] catégorique; **6** (standard)
[*fare, fee*] forfaitaire; [*charge*] fixe; **7** (monotonous)
[*voice, tone*] plat, monocorde; (unexciting) [*performance,
style*] plat; **8** (not fizzy) [*beer etc*] éventé; **9** (depressed) **to
feel** ~ [*person*] se sentir déprimé; **10** GB [*battery*]
ELEC usé; AUT à plat; **11** COMM, FIN (slow) [*market,
trade*] languissant; [*profits*] stagnant; **12** MUS [*note*]
bémol *inv*; (off key) [*voice, instrument*] faux/fausse.
IV *adv* **1** (horizontally) [*lay, lie*] à plat; [*fall*] de tout son
long; **to knock sb** ~ terrasser qn; **to lie** ~ [*person*]
s'étendre; [*hair*] s'aplatir; [*pleat*] être aplati; ~ **on
one's back** sur le dos; **to fall** ~ **on one's face** FIG
se casser la figure°; **2** (in close contact) **she pressed
her nose** ~ **against the window** elle a collé son nez
à la vitre; **3** (exactly) **in 10 minutes** ~ en 10 minutes
pile; **4**° (absolutely) carrément; **to turn [sth] down** ~

refuser [qch] tout net [offer, proposal]; **5** MUS [sing, play] faux.
IDIOMS **to fall ~** [performance] faire un bide○; [joke] tomber à plat; [party, evening] tourner court; [plan] tomber à l'eau.

flat: **~-bottomed** adj [boat] à fond plat; **~ broke**○ adj fauché○, à sec○.

flat-footed /ˌflætˈfʊtɪd/ adj **1** MED [person] aux pieds plats; **to be ~** avoir les pieds plats; **2**○ PÉJ (tactless) [attempt] maladroit.

flat-hunting /ˈflæthʌntɪŋ/ n GB **to go ~** chercher un appartement.

flat: **~iron** n HIST fer m à repasser (qu'on chauffe sur un fourneau); **~ jockey** ▶ 1251 n jockey m spécialisé dans les courses de plat; **~lands** npl plaine f; **~mate** n GB colocataire mf (personne avec qui on partage un appartement).

flat out○ /ˌflætˈaʊt/ **I** adj GB (also **~ tired** US) KO○, épuisé.
II adv [drive] à fond de train; [work] d'arrache-pied; **it only does 120 km per hour ~** elle ne monte qu'à 120 km à l'heure, pied au plancher.
IDIOMS **to go ~ for sth** se mettre en quatre○ pour faire qch.

flat racing n ⊄ courses fpl de plat.

flat rate /ˌflætˈreɪt/ **I** n taux m fixe.
II flat-rate noun modifier [fee, tax] forfaitaire.

flat spin /ˌflætˈspɪn/ n AVIAT vrille f à plat.
IDIOMS **to be in a ~**○ être affolé.

flatten /ˈflætn/ **I** vtr **1** (level) [rain] coucher [crops, grass]; abattre [tree, fence]; [bombing] raser [building]; **he'll ~ you**○! il va te casser la figure○!; **2** (smooth out) aplanir [surface]; aplatir [metal]; **3** (crush) écraser [animal, fruit, object]; **4** MUS baisser (le ton de) [note].
II vi = **flatten out**.
III v refl **to ~ oneself** s'aplatir (**against** contre).
■ **flatten out**: ¶ **~ out** [slope, road, ground] s'aplanir; [graph, curve, flight path] se redresser; [growth, exports, decline] se stabiliser; ¶ **~ out** [sth], **~** [sth] **out** aplanir [ground, road].

flatter /ˈflætə(r)/ **I** vtr **1** (compliment) flatter (**on** sur); **2** (enhance) [light, dress, portrait] flatter.
II v refl **to ~ oneself** se flatter (**on being** d'être).

flatterer /ˈflætərə(r)/ n flatteur/-euse m/f.

flattering /ˈflætərɪŋ/ adj [remark, portrait etc] GEN flatteur/-euse.

flattery /ˈflætərɪ/ n flatterie f.
IDIOMS **~ will get you nowhere** la flatterie ne mène à rien.

flatware /ˈflætweə(r)/ n US (cutlery) couverts mpl; (crockery) assiettes fpl.

flaunt /flɔːnt/ vtr PÉJ étaler [wealth]; faire étalage de [charms]; afficher [ability, lover]; exhiber [possession].

flautist /ˈflɔːtɪst/ ▶ 1251, 1097 n flûtiste m f.

flavour GB, **flavor** US /ˈfleɪvə(r)/ **I** n **1** CULIN goût m; (subtler) saveur f; **coffee ~** au café; **full of ~** plein de saveurs; **2** (atmosphere) (of period, place) atmosphère f; (hint) idée f.
II vtr **1** CULIN (improve taste) donner du goût à; (add specific taste) parfumer (**with** à); **2** FIG assaisonner (**with** de).
IDIOMS **to be ~ of the month**○ [thing] être en vogue; [person] être la coqueluche du moment.

flavour-enhancer GB, **flavor-enhancer** US n exhausteur m de goût.

flavouring GB, **flavoring** US /ˈfleɪvərɪŋ/ n (for sweet taste) parfum m; (for meat, fish) assaisonnement m.

flavourless GB, **flavorless** US /ˈfleɪvəlɪs/ adj insipide.

flaw /flɔː/ n GEN défaut m; (in theory) faille f.

flawed /flɔːd/ adj GEN défectueux; [character, person] vicié.

flea /fliː/ **I** n puce f.
II noun modifier [collar] antipuce; [powder] antiparasitaire.
IDIOMS **to send sb away with a ~ in their ear**○ envoyer promener○ qn.

flea: **~-bitten** adj LIT infesté de puces; FIG miteux/-euse; **~ market** n marché m aux puces; **~pit**○ n GB PÉJ cinéma m miteux.

fleck /flek/ **I** n (of colour) moucheture f; (of light) tache f; (of foam) flocon m; (of blood, paint) petite tache f; (of dust) particule f.
II vtr **~ed with** [fabric] moucheté de [colour]; [eye] piqueté de [colour]; tacheté de [paint, light].

fled /fled/ prét, pp ▶ **flee**.

fledg(e)ling /ˈfledʒlɪŋ/ **I** n ZOOL oisillon m.
II noun modifier FIG [party, group] naissant; [democracy, enterprise] jeune.

flee /fliː/ (prét, pp **fled**) vtr, vi fuir.

fleece /fliːs/ **I** n (on animal) toison f.
II○ vtr (overcharge) estamper○; (swindle) plumer○.

fleecy /ˈfliːsɪ/ adj [fabric] laineux/-euse; [clouds] flocon-neux/-euse.

fleet /fliːt/ n **1** (of ships etc) flotte f; (of small vessels) flottille f; **2** (of vehicles) (in reserve) parc m; (on road) convoi m.

fleeting /ˈfliːtɪŋ/ adj [memory, pleasure] fugace; [visit, moment] bref/brève; [glance] rapide.

Fleet Street n la presse f (londonienne).

Flemish /ˈflemɪʃ/ ▶ 1100 **I** n **1** (language) flamand m; **2 the ~** les Flamands mpl.
II adj flamand.

flesh /fleʃ/ n **1** (of human, animal) chair f; **2** (of fruit) chair f, pulpe f; **3** FIG **I'm only ~** je ne suis qu'un être humain; **one's own ~ and blood** la chair de sa chair; **in the ~** en chair et en os; **it makes my ~ creep** ça me donne la chair de poule.
IDIOMS **to demand one's pound of ~** exiger son dû impitoyablement.
■ **flesh out**: **~** [sth] **out**, **~ out** [sth] étayer [article].

flesh: **~-eating** adj carnivore; **~ wound** n blessure f superficielle.

fleshy /ˈfleʃɪ/ adj [arm, fruit, leaf] charnu.

flew /fluː/ prét ▶ **fly**.

flex /fleks/ **I** n GB (for electrical appliance) fil m.
II vtr **1** (contract) faire jouer [muscle]; **2** (bend and stretch) fléchir [limb]; plier [finger].

flexibility /ˌfleksəˈbɪlətɪ/ n souplesse f, flexibilité f.

flexible /ˈfleksəbl/ adj **1** [arrangement] flexible, souple; [plan, agenda] souple; [repayment plan] à échéances variables; **2** [person] souple (**about** en ce qui concerne); **3** [tube, wire, stem] flexible, souple.

flexible response n MIL riposte f graduée.

flexi disc /ˈfleksɪ dɪsk/ n AUDIO disque m souple.

flexitime /ˈfleksɪtaɪm/ n horaire m flexible or souple.

flick /flɪk/ **I** n **1** (with finger) chiquenaude f; (with whip, cloth) petit coup m; **2** (movement) GEN, SPORT petit coup m; **at the ~ of a switch** rien qu'en appuyant sur un bouton.
II flicks npl cinéma m.
III vtr **1** (strike) (with finger) donner une chiquenaude à; (with tail, cloth) donner un petit coup à; **to ~ sth at sb** (with finger) envoyer or lancer qch à qn d'une chiquenaude; **he ~ed his ash onto the floor** il a fait tomber sa cendre par terre; **2** (press) appuyer sur [switch]; **3** SPORT donner un petit coup à [ball].
■ **flick back**: **~** [sth] **back** rejeter [qch] en arrière [hair].
■ **flick off**: **~** [sth] **off**, **~ off** [sth] (with finger) enlever [qch] d'une chiquenaude; (with tail, cloth) enlever [qch] d'un petit geste.
■ **flick over**: **~** [sth] **over**, **~ over** [sth] feuilleter [pages].
■ **flick through**: **~ through** [sth] feuilleter [book, report]; **to ~ through the channels** TV zapper.

flicker /ˈflɪkə(r)/ **I** n **1** (unsteady light) **the ~ of a candle** la flamme vacillante d'une bougie; **2** (slight sign) (of interest, anger) lueur f (**of** de); **3** (movement) (of eyelid) clignement m; (of indicator) oscillation f.
II vi **1** (shine unsteadily) [fire, light, flame] vaciller, trembloter; [image] clignoter; **2** (move) [eye, eyelid] cligner.

III flickering *pres p adj* [*light, flame*] vacillant; [*image*] tremblant.

lick knife *n* GB couteau *m* à cran d'arrêt.

lier /ˈflaɪə(r)/ *n* **1 a powerful ~** (of bird) un oiseau au vol puissant; **2** (handbill) prospectus *m*.

light /flaɪt/ I *n* **1** AEROSP, AVIAT (journey) vol *m* (**to** vers; **from** de); **a scheduled ~** un vol régulier; **the ~ from Dublin to London** le vol Dublin-Londres; **we hope you enjoyed your ~** nous espérons que vous avez fait un bon voyage; **we took the next ~ (out)** nous avons pris l'avion suivant; **2** (course) (of bird, insect) vol *m*; (of missile, bullet) trajectoire *f*; **3** (locomotion) vol *m*; **in full ~** LIT en plein vol; FIG en plein élan; **4** (group) **a ~ of** un vol de, une volée de [*birds*]; une troupe de [*angels*]; une volée de [*arrows*]; **5** (escape) fuite *f* (**from** devant); **to take ~** prendre la fuite; **6** (set) **a ~ of steps** une volée de marches; **six ~s** (of stairs) six étages; **four ~s up** au quatrième; **a ~ of** une série de [*hurdles*]; une série de [*locks*]; un étagement de [*terraces*]; **7** (display) **~s of imagination** élans *mpl* d'imagination; **~s of rhetoric** envolées *fpl* oratoires; **a ~ of fancy** une invention.

II *noun modifier* [*simulator, plan, recorder*] de vol.

IDIOMS **to be in the top ~** être parmi les meilleurs.

light: **~ attendant ▶1251** *n* AVIAT (male) steward *m*; (female) hôtesse *f* de l'air; **~ bag** *n* bagage *m* à main; **~ deck** *n* (compartment) AVIAT poste *m* de pilotage; NAUT pont *m* d'envol; **~ engineer ▶1251** *n* mécanicien *m* navigant; **~ lieutenant ▶1192** *n* MIL capitaine *m* (de l'armée de l'air); **~ path** *n* route *f* de vol; **~-test** *vtr* essayer [qch] en vol.

flighty /ˈflaɪtɪ/ *adj* [*imagination, mind*] écervelé; [*partner*] volage.

flimsy /ˈflɪmzɪ/ *adj* [*fabric*] léger/-ère; [*structure*] peu solide; [*argument, excuse*] futile; [*evidence*] mince, piètre (*before n*).

flinch /flɪntʃ/ *vi* (psychologically) hésiter (**from doing** à faire); (physically) tressaillir; **without ~ing** sans broncher; **to ~ at** tiquer sur [*criticism, insult etc*].

fling /flɪŋ/ I *n* **1**○ (spree) bon temps *m*; **to have a ~** se payer du bon temps; **2**○ (affair) (with person) aventure *f*; (intellectual) flirt○ *m*.

II *vtr* (*prét, pp* **flung**) (throw) lancer [*ball, grenade*] (**onto** sur; **into** dans); lancer [*insult*] (**at** à); **to ~ a scarf around one's shoulders** jeter une écharpe sur ses épaules; **to ~ sb to the ground** [*person*] jeter qn à terre; [*blast*] projeter qn à terre; **I flung my arms around her neck** je me suis jeté à son cou.

III *v refl* **to ~ oneself** se jeter (**across** en travers de; **over** par dessus); **to ~ oneself off sth** sauter de [*bridge, cliff*].

■ **fling about**, **~ around**: **~** [**sth**] **around** gaspiller [*money*].

■ **fling away**: **~** [**sth**] **away** jeter qch.

■ **fling back**: **~** [**sth**] **back**, **~ back** [**sth**] renvoyer [*ball, keys*]; rejeter [qch] en arrière [*head*]; ouvrir [qch] brusquement [*door*].

■ **fling down**: **~** [**sth**] **down**, **~ down** [**sth**] jeter [qch] par terre.

■ **fling on**: **~ on** [**sth**] enfiler [qch] rapidement [*dress, coat*].

■ **fling open**: **~** [**sth**] **open**, **~ open** [**sth**] ouvrir [qch] brusquement [*door*]; ouvrir [qch] tout grand [*window*].

flint /flɪnt/ *n* **1** (rock) silex *m*; **2** (primitive tool) éclat *m* de silex; **3**† (for kindling) pierre *f* à feu; **4** (in lighter) pierre *f* à briquet.

flintlock *n* pistolet *m* à pierre.

flip /flɪp/ I *n* **1** (of finger) chiquenaude *f*; **to decide sth by the ~ of a coin** décider qch à pile ou face; **2** AVIAT, SPORT (somersault) tour *m*.

II *vtr* (*p prés etc* **-pp-**) **1** (toss) lancer [*coin*]; faire sauter [*pancake*]; **let's ~ a coin to decide** décidons à pile ou face; **2** (flick) basculer [*switch*]; **to ~ sth open** ouvrir qch rapidement.

III *vi* (*p prés etc* **-pp-**) **1** (get angry) se mettre en rogne○; **2** (go mad) perdre la boule○; **3** (get excited) devenir dingue○ (**over** de).

IDIOMS **to ~ one's lid** sortir de ses gonds○.

■ **flip over**: **¶ ~ over** [*vehicle, plane*] se retourner (complètement); **¶ ~** [**sth**] **over**, **~ over** [**sth**] retourner [*pancake, coin*]; feuilleter [*pages*].

■ **flip through**: **~ through** [**sth**] feuilleter [*book*].

flipchart *n* tableau *m* de conférence, paperboard *m*.

flip-flop /ˈflɪpflɒp/ *n* **1** (sandal) tong *f*; **2** COMPUT (device) bascule *f*; **3** US (about-face) volte-face *f inv*.

flippant /ˈflɪpənt/ *adj* (not serious) [*remark, person*] désinvolte; (lacking respect) [*tone, attitude*] cavalier/-ière.

flipper /ˈflɪpə(r)/ *n* **1** ZOOL nageoire *f*; **2** (for swimmer) palme *f*.

flipping○ /ˈflɪpɪŋ/ GB **I** *adj* fichu○.

II *adv* [*stupid, painful, cold*] drôlement○.

flip: **~ side** *n* MUS (on record) face *f* B; FIG (other side) envers *m*; **~-top** *n* capsule *f* à charnière.

flirt /flɜːt/ I *n* (person) flirteur/-euse *m/f*; PÉJ dragueur/-euse○ *m/f* PÉJ.

II *vi* flirter; **to ~ with** flirter avec [*person*]; jouer avec [*danger, image*]; caresser [*idea*].

flirtatious /ˌflɜːˈteɪʃəs/ *adj* [*person, glance, wink*] charmeur/-euse, dragueur/-euse○ PÉJ; [*laugh*] qui cherche à séduire.

flit /flɪt/ I *n* (move) **to do a ~**○ (move house) déménager à la cloche de bois○; (leave) filer à l'anglaise.

II *vi* (*p prés etc* **-tt-**) **1** (also **~ about**) [*bird, moth*] voleter; **2** (move quickly) [*person*] aller d'un pas léger; **3** (flash) **a look of panic ~ted across his face** une expression de panique lui traversa le visage.

float /fləʊt/ I *n* **1** (on net) flotteur *m*; (on line) bouchon *m*; **2** AVIAT flotteur *m*; **3** (in plumbing) flotteur *m*; **4** GB (swimmer's aid) planche *f*; US (life jacket) gilet *m* de sauvetage; **5** (carnival vehicle) char *m*; **6** (also **cash ~**) (in till) fonds *m* de caisse; **7** US (drink) *soda avec une boule de glace*.

II *vtr* **1** (person) faire flotter [*boat, logs*]; [*tide*] mettre à flot [*ship*]; **2** FIN émettre [*shares, securities, loan*]; lancer [qch] en Bourse [*company*]; laisser flotter [*currency*]; **3** (propose) lancer [*idea, suggestion*].

III *vi* **1** (on liquid, in air) flotter; **to ~ on one's back** [*swimmer*] faire la planche; **to ~ down the river** descendre la rivière; **the boat was ~ing out to sea** le bateau voguait vers le large; **to ~ up into the air** s'envoler; **2** FIG (waft) [*smoke, mist*] flotter; **to ~ across** [*cloud*] traverser lentement [*sky*]; **music ~ed out into the garden** la musique parvenait dans le jardin; **3** FIN [*currency*] flotter.

■ **float about**, **float around 1** (circulate) [*idea, rumour*] circuler; **2**○ (be nearby) **are my keys ~ing around?** mes clés sont-elles par ici?; **3**○ (aimlessly) [*person*] traîner.

■ **float away = float off**.

■ **float off**: **~** [*boat*] dériver; [*balloon*] s'envoler; [*person*] partir d'un pas léger.

floating /ˈfləʊtɪŋ/ *adj* (on water) [*bridge*] flottant; FIG (unstable) [*population*] instable.

floating: **~ assets** *npl* FIN actif *m* circulant; **~ capital** *n* FIN capital *m* disponible, fonds *mpl* de roulement; **~ rate interest** *n* FIN intérêt *m* à taux flottant ou variable; **~ restaurant** *n* bateau-restaurant *m*; **~ voter** *n* POL électeur *m* indécis.

flock /flɒk/ I *n* **1** (of sheep, goats) troupeau *m*; (of birds) volée *f*; (of people) foule *f*; **in ~s** en masse; **2** ¢ RELIG ouailles *fpl*; **3** (textile) bourre *f*; **4** (tuft) flocon *m*.

II *vi* [*animals, people*] affluer (**around** autour de; **into** dans); **to ~ together** [*people*] s'assembler; [*animals*] se rassembler.

floe /fləʊ/ *n* banquise *f*.

flog /flɒg/ *vtr* (*p prés etc* **-gg-**) **1** (beat) flageller; **2**○ GB (sell) fourguer○, vendre.

IDIOMS **to ~ sth to death**○ GB bousiller○ qch; **to ~ a joke to death**○ rabâcher une plaisanterie.

flogging /ˈflɒgɪŋ/ *n* (beating) flagellation *f*.

flood /flʌd/ I *n* **1** LIT inondation *f*; **'~!'** (on roadsign) 'attention, route inondée!'; **in ~** en crue; **2** FIG **a ~ of** un flot de [*people, light, memories*]; un déluge de [*letters, complaints*]; **to be in ~s of tears** verser des torrents de larmes.

II *vtr* **1** LIT inonder [*area*]; faire déborder [*river*]; **2** FIG [*light, mail*] inonder; **3** COMM (over-supply) inonder [*shops*] (**with** de); **4** AUT noyer [*engine*].

III *vi* **1** [*meadow, street, cellar*] être inondé; [*river*] déborder; '**road liable to ~ing**' 'chaussée inondable'; **2** FIG **to ~ into sth** [*light*] inonder qch; [*people*] envahir qch; **to ~ over sb** [*emotion*] envahir qn.

■ **flood back** [*memories*] remonter à la surface.

■ **flood in** [*light etc*] entrer à flots; FIG [*people, money*] affluer.

■ **flood out**: ¶ ~ **out** [*liquid*] jaillir à flots; ¶ ~ [*sth/sb*] **out** inonder.

flood: **~bank** *n* berge *f* inondable; **~ control** *n* prévention *f* des inondations; **~ damage** *n* dégât *m* des eaux.

floodgate /'flʌdgeɪt/ *n* LIT vanne *f*; **to open the ~s** FIG laisser entrer le flot (**to, for** de).

flood level *n* niveau *m* des eaux.

floodlight /'flʌdlaɪt/ **I** *n* projecteur *m*; **under ~s** SPORT en nocturne.

II *vtr* (*prét, pp* **floodlit**) illuminer [*building*]; éclairer [*stage*].

flood: **~mark** *n* indicateur *m* de niveau de crue; **~plain** *n* plaine *f* inondable; **~ tide** *n* marée *f* haute; **~waters** *n* eaux *fpl* d'inondation.

floor /flɔ:(r)/ **I** *n* **1** (of room) (wooden) plancher *m*, parquet *m*; (stone) sol *m*; (of car, lift) plancher *m*; **dance ~** piste *f* de danse; **on the ~** par terre; **to take the ~** [*dancer*] se lancer sur la piste de danse; **2** (of sea, tunnel, valley) fond *m*; **the forest ~** le tapis forestier; **3** (of Stock Exchange) parquet *m*; (of debating Chamber) auditoire *m*; (of factory) atelier *m*; **to hold the ~** garder la parole; **4** (storey) étage *m*; **on the first ~** GB au premier étage; US au rez-de-chaussée; **ground ~, bottom ~** GB rez-de-chaussée *m*; **six ~s up** (on the sixth storey) au sixième étage; (six storeys above this storey) six étages plus haut; **5** FIN (of prices) plancher *m* (**on** sur).

II *vtr* **1** **an oak-~ed room** une pièce avec un parquet de chêne; **2** (knock over) terrasser [*attacker, boxer*]; **3** FIG (silence) réduire [qn] au silence [*person, critic*]; (stump) [*question*] décontenancer [*candidate*].

IDIOMS **to wipe the ~ with sb** battre qn à plates coutures.

floor: **~ area** *n* superficie *f*; **~board** *n* latte *f*, planche *f* (de *plancher*); **~ cloth** *n* serpillière *f*; **~ covering** *n* revêtement *m* de sol; **~ exercises** *npl* exercices *mpl* au sol; **~ lamp** *n* US lampadaire *m*.

floor manager ► 1251 *n* **1** TV régisseur *m* de plateau; **2** COMM gérant/-e *m/f* de magasin.

floor: **~ polish** *n* encaustique *f*, cire *f*; **~ show** *n* spectacle *m* (de *cabaret*); **~ space** *n* espace *m* (au sol); **~walker** *n* US chef *m* de rayon.

flop /flɒp/ **I** *n* °(failure) fiasco° *m*.

II *vi* (*p prés etc* **-pp-**) **1** (move heavily) **to ~ down** s'effondrer; **to ~ down on** s'affaler sur [*bed, sofa*]; **2** (hang loosely) [*hair, ear*] retomber; **3°** (fail) [*play, film*] faire un four°; [*project, venture*] être un fiasco°.

■ **flop out**° US (rest) se reposer; (sleep) s'endormir.

■ **flop over**° US: ¶ ~ **over** changer d'avis; ¶ ~ **over to** [*sth*] adopter [*idea*].

floppy /'flɒpɪ/ *adj* [*ears, hair*] pendant; [*hat*] à bords tombants; [*clothes*] large; [*flesh, body*] mou/molle.

floppy disk *n* COMPUT disquette *f*.

flora /'flɔ:rə/ *n* (+ *v sg*) flore *f*.

floral /'flɔ:rəl/ *adj* [*design, fabric*] à fleurs [*arrangement, art, fragrance*] floral.

Florentine /'flɒrəntaɪn/ *adj* florentin.

florid /'flɒrɪd, US 'flɔ:r-/ *adj* **1** (ornate) [*writing, style, language*] fleuri; **2** (ruddy) [*person, face*] rougeaud.

Florida /'flɒrɪdə/ ► 1290 *pr n* Floride *f*.

florist /'flɒrɪst, US 'flɔ:rɪst/ ► 1251, 1251 *n* (person) fleuriste *mf*; **to go to the ~'s** aller chez le fleuriste.

floss /flɒs, US flɔ:s/ **I** *n* **1** (for embroidery) soie *f* floche; **2** (for teeth) fil *m* dentaire.

II *vtr* **to ~ one's teeth** utiliser du fil dentaire.

flotsam /'flɒtsəm/ *n* ¢ épave *f* flottante.

flounce /flaʊns/ **I** *n* **1** (movement) mouvement *m* vif; **2** (frill) volant *m*.

II *vi* **1 to ~ in/off** (indignantly) entrer/partir dans un mouvement d'indignation; **2** (also ~ **around, ~ about**) se démener.

flounder /'flaʊndə(r)/ **I** *n* **1** GB flet *m*; **2** US poisson *m* plat.

II *vi* **1** (also ~ **about**) [*animal, person*] se débattre (**in** dans); **2** FIG (falter) [*speaker*] bredouiller; [*economy*] stagner; [*career, company, leader*] piétiner.

flour /'flaʊə(r)/ **I** *n* farine *f*.

II *vtr* saupoudrer [qch] de farine [*cake tin, board*].

flourish /'flʌrɪʃ/ **I** *n* **1** (gesture) geste *m* théâtral; **with a ~** [*do*] de façon théâtrale; **2** (detail, touch) **with a rhetorical** ou **an emphatic ~** avec emphase; (in piece of music) **the final ~** le bouquet final; **the opening ~** le brio des premiers accords; **3** (ornamental) (in style) fioriture *f*.

II *vtr* brandir [*ticket, document*].

III *vi* [*plant, bacteria*] prospérer; [*child*] s'épanouir; [*firm, democracy*] prospérer.

flourishing /'flʌrɪʃɪŋ/ *adj* [*garden, industry*] florissant; [*business, town*] prospère.

floury /'flaʊərɪ/ *adj* [*hands*] couvert de farine; [*potato*] farineux/-euse.

flout /flaʊt/ *vtr* se moquer de [*convention, rules*].

flow /fləʊ/ **I** *n* **1** (of liquid) écoulement *m*; (of blood, electricity) circulation *f*; (of refugees, words) flot *m*; (of information) circulation *f*; **in full ~** FIG en plein discours; **traffic ~** circulation *f*; **2** GEOG (of tide) flux *m*.

II *vi* **1** (move) [*liquid, gas*] couler (**into** dans); **to ~ in/back** affluer/refluer; **to ~ downwards** tomber; **to ~ past sth** passer devant qch; **the river ~s into the sea** le fleuve se jette dans la mer; **2** (be continuous) [*conversation, words*] couler; [*wine, beer*] couler à flots; **3** (circulate) [*blood, electricity etc*] circuler (**through, round** dans); **4** (move gracefully) [*hair, dress*] flotter; [*pen*] courir (**across** sur); **5** [*tide*] monter.

flowchart /'fləʊtʃɑ:t/ *n* organigramme *m*.

flower /'flaʊə(r)/ **I** *n* **1** (bloom, plant) fleur *f*; **to be in ~** être en fleur; **in full ~** en pleine floraison; **2** FIG **the ~ of** la fine fleur de [*age, era, group*]; **in the ~ of her youth** dans la fleur de l'âge.

II *vi* LIT [*flower, tree*] fleurir; [*love, person, talent*] s'épanouir.

flower: **~ arrangement** *n* composition *f* florale; **~ arranging** *n* décoration *f* florale; **~ garden** *n* jardin *m* d'agrément.

flowering /'flaʊərɪŋ/ **I** *n* **1** BOT floraison *f* (**of** de); **2** FIG (development) épanouissement *m* (**of** de).

II *adj* [*shrub, tree*] (producing blooms) à fleurs; (in bloom) en fleurs; **early-/late-~** à floraison précoce/tardive.

flower: **~ shop** ► 1251 *n* fleuriste *m*; **~ show** *n* (large) floralies *fpl*; (amateur) exposition *f* florale.

flowery /'flaʊərɪ/ *adj* [*field*] fleuri; [*fabric*] à fleurs; [*wine*] parfumé; [*scent*] floral; [*speech, style*] fleuri.

flowing /'fləʊɪŋ/ *adj* [*style, movement*] coulant; [*rhythm*] berceur/-euse; [*line*] doux/douce; [*hair, clothes*] flottant.

flown /fləʊn/ *pp* ► **fly**.

fl oz *abrév écrite* = **fluid ounce(s)**.

flu /flu:/ ► 1002 **I** *n* grippe *f*; **to come down with ~** attraper une grippe.

II *noun modifier* [*victim, virus*] de la grippe; [*attack, epidemic*] de grippe; [*vaccine*] contre la grippe.

fluctuate /'flʌktjʊeɪt/ *vi* GEN, FIN [*rate, mood*] fluctuer (**between** entre).

flue /flu:/ *n* (of chimney) conduit *m*; (of stove, boiler) tuyau *m*.

fluency /'flu:ənsɪ/ *n* (all contexts) aisance *f*; **sb's ~ in German** l'aisance de qn à s'exprimer en allemand.

fluent /'flu:ənt/ *adj* **1** (in language) **her French is ~** elle parle couramment le français; **a ~ Greek speaker** une personne qui parle grec couramment; **in ~ English** dans un anglais parfait; **2** (eloquent) [*account, speech, speaker*] éloquent; [*writer*] qui a la plume facile; **3** (graceful) [*style*] coulant; [*movement*] fluide.

luff /flʌf/ I n 1 (down) (on clothes) peluche f; (on carpet) poussière f; (under furniture) mouton m, flocon m de poussière; (on animal) duvet m; 2° (mistake) gaffe° f; 3° US ℂ (trivia) frivolités fpl.

II vtr 1 (also ~ **up**) hérisser [feathers]; faire bouffer [cushion, hair]; 2° (get wrong) rater [cue, exam, note].

luffy /'flʌfɪ/ adj 1 [animal, down] duveteux/-euse; [fur, sweater] moelleux/-euse; [rug, sweater] moelleux/-euse; [hair] bouffant; [toy] en peluche; 2 (light) [mixture] léger/-ère; [egg white, rice] moelleux/-euse.

luid /'fluːɪd/ I n 1 GEN, BIOL liquide m; 2 CHEM, TECH fluide m.

II adj 1 GEN liquide; CHEM, TECH fluide; 2 (flexible) [arrangement, situation] vague; 3 (graceful) [movement, style, lines] fluide.

luid: ~ **assets** npl US FIN disponibilités fpl; ~ **capital** n US ℂ FIN fonds mpl de roulement; ~ **ounce** n once f liquide.

luke /fluːk/ n 1 (lucky chance) coup m de veine°; **by a (sheer) ~** (tout à fait) par hasard; 2 NAUT (of anchor) patte f (d'une ancre); (of harpoon, arrow) barbelure f; 3 ZOOL douve f; ~ **blood** ~ douve du sang.

luky, **flukey** /'fluːkɪ/ adj (lucky) [coincidence] heureux/-euse; [circumstances, goal, shot] dû au hasard; [winner] par hasard.

lummox° /'flʌməks/ vtr sidérer°.

lung /flʌŋ/ prét, pp ▶ fling.

lunk° /flʌŋk/ vtr US SCH, UNIV 1 [student] rater° [exam]; sécher sur° [subject]; 2 [teacher] coller° [class, pupil].

lunkey GB, **flunky** US /'flʌŋkɪ/ n (pl **-eys** GB, **-ies** US) 1 (servant) laquais m; 2 FIG, PÉJ larbin m PEJ.

fluorescent /flɔːˈresənt/ adj fluorescent.

fluoride /'flɔːraɪd/ US 'fluəraɪd/ n fluorure m.

fluorine /'flɔːriːn/ US 'fluər-/ n fluor m.

flurry /'flʌrɪ/ n 1 (gust) (of rain etc) rafale f; (of leaves) tourbillon m; 2 (bustle) agitation f soudaine; **a ~ of activity** un tourbillon d'activité; **a ~ of interest** un mouvement d'intérêt; 3 (of complaints, enquiries) vague f.

flush /flʌʃ/ I n 1 (blush) (on skin) rougeur f; 2 (surge) **a ~ of** un élan de [pleasure, pride]; un accès de [anger, shame]; **to be in the first ~ of youth** être de la première jeunesse; 3 (toilet device) chasse f d'eau; (sound) bruit m de la chasse d'eau; 4 GAMES (set) floche f.

II adj 1 (level) **to be ~ with** être dans l'alignement de [wall]; 2° (rich) **to feel ~** se sentir en fonds.

III vtr 1 (clean with water) **to ~ the toilet** tirer la chasse (d'eau); **to ~ (out) a pipe** nettoyer un tuyau à grande eau; 2 (colour) **to ~ sb's cheeks** empourprer les joues de qn.

IV vi 1 (redden) rougir (with de); 2 (operate) **the toilet doesn't ~** la chasse d'eau ne fonctionne pas.

■ **flush away**: ~ [sth] away, ~ **away** [sth] faire partir [waste].

■ **flush out**: ~ **out** [sb/sth] débusquer [sniper, spy]; **to ~ sb/sth out of** faire sortir qn/qch de [shelter].

flushed /flʌʃt/ adj 1 (reddened) [cheeks] rouge (with de); **to be ~** avoir les joues rouges; 2 (glowing) ~ **with** [person] rayonnant de [pride etc].

fluster /'flʌstə(r)/ I n agitation f.

II vtr énerver; **to look ~ed** avoir l'air énervé.

flute /fluːt/ ▶ **1097** I n 1 MUS flûte f; 2 ARCHIT cannelure f; 3 (glass) flûte f.

fluted /'fluːtɪd/ adj [collar] tuyauté; [glass, flan tin] cannelures; [column] cannelé.

flutist /'fluːtɪst/ ▶ **1251**, **1097** n US flûtiste mf.

flutter /'flʌtə(r)/ I n 1 (of wings, lashes) battement m; (of leaves, papers) voltigement m; (of bunting) flottement m; **heart ~** MED palpitations fpl cardiaques; 2 (stir) **a ~ of** un surcroît de [excitement]; **to be all of a ~** GB être tout en émoi; 3° GB (bet) **to have a ~ on the horses** faire un petit pari aux courses; **to have a ~ on the Stock Exchange** faire une spéculation à la Bourse; 4 ELEC (in sound) pleurage m; 5 AVIAT (fault) vibration f.

II vtr 1 (beat) **the bird ~ed its wings** l'oiseau battait

des ailes; 2 (move) agiter [fan, handkerchief]; **to ~ one's eyelashes** battre des cils.

III vi 1 (beat) [bird] battre des ailes; 2 (fly rapidly) voleter; 3 (move rapidly) [flag] flotter; [clothes, curtains, fans] s'agiter; [eyelids, lashes] battre; 4 (also ~ **down**) [leaves] tomber en voltigeant; 5 (beat irregularly) [heart] palpiter (with de); [pulse] battre faiblement.

flux /flʌks/ n 1 (uncertainty) **in (a state of) ~** dans un état de perpétuel changement; 2 PHYS, MED flux m; 3 (for metals) fondant m.

fly /flaɪ/ I n 1 ZOOL mouche f; 2 (of flag) (outer edge) bord m flottant; 3 GB HIST (carriage) fiacre m.

II **flies** npl 1 (of trousers) braguette f; 2 THEAT cintres mpl.

III° adj 1 US chic; 2 GB (clever) malin.

IV vtr (prét **flew**; pp **flown**) 1 (operate) piloter [aircraft, balloon]; faire voler [model aircraft, kite]; **the pilot flew the plane to...** le pilote a emmené l'avion jusqu'à...; 2 (transport by air) emmener [qn] par avion [person]; transporter [qch/qn] par avion [wounded, supplies]; 3 (cross by air) traverser [qch] en avion [Atlantic]; 4 (cover by air) [bird, aircraft] parcourir [distance]; **I ~ over 10,000 km a year** [passenger] je vole plus de 10 000 km par an; [pilot] je fais plus de 10 000 km par an; 5 (display) [ship] arborer [flag]; **the embassy was ~ing the German flag** le drapeau allemand flottait sur l'ambassade.

V vi (prét **flew**; pp **flown**) 1 [bird, insect, aircraft, kite] voler (**from** de; **to** à); **to ~ over** ou **across sth** survoler qch; **to ~ over(head)** passer dans le ciel; **to ~ past the window** passer devant la fenêtre (en volant); **to ~ into Gatwick** atterrir à Gatwick; **there's a mosquito ~ing around** il y a un moustique; 2 [passenger] voyager en avion, prendre l'avion; [pilot] piloter, voler; **to ~ from Orly** partir d'Orly; **to ~ from Rome to Athens** aller de Rome à Athènes en avion; **to ~ in Concorde** prendre le Concorde; **we ~ to Boston twice a day** [airline] nous avons deux vols par jour pour Boston; **to ~ out to** s'envoler pour; 3 (be propelled) [bullet, glass, sparks, insults] voler; **a splinter flew into his eye** il a reçu une écharde dans l'œil; **to ~ off** s'envoler; **to ~ open** s'ouvrir brusquement; **to go ~ing** [person] faire un vol plané; [object] valdinguer°; **to send sb ~ing** jeter qn sur le carreau°; **to ~ into a rage** FIG se mettre en colère; 4 (rush, hurry) **I must ~!** il faut que je file°!; **to ~ past/in** passer/entrer en trombe°; 5 (also ~ **past**, ~ **by**) [time, holidays] passer vite, filer°; 6 (flutter, wave) [flag, scarf, hair] flotter; **to ~ in the wind** flotter au vent.

IDIOMS **to drop like flies** tomber comme des mouches; **he wouldn't hurt a ~** il ne ferait pas de mal à une mouche; **there are no flies on her** elle n'est pas née de la dernière pluie; **to ~ in the face of** (defy) défier [authority, danger, tradition]; (contradict) être en contradiction flagrante avec [evidence]; **to let ~ (with)** LIT tirer [arrow etc]; lancer [stream of abuse]; **to let ~ at sb** s'en prendre à qn.

■ **fly away** LIT, FIG s'envoler.

■ **fly in**: ¶ ~ **in** [person] accourir en avion; ¶ ~ [sth/sb] in, ~ **in** [sth/sb] acheminer [qch] par avion [supplies].

fly: ~**away** adj [hair] indiscipliné; ~**-by-night** adj [company] douteux/-euse; [person] irresponsable; ~**-catcher** n ZOOL gobe-mouches m inv; ~**-drive** adj TOURISM avec formule avion plus voiture.

flyer /'flaɪə(r)/ n = **flier**.

fly: ~**-fishing** ▶ **949** n pêche f à la mouche; ~**-half** n SPORT demi m d'ouvertures.

flying /'flaɪɪŋ/ I n 1 (in plane) **to be afraid of ~** avoir peur de l'avion; **to take up ~** apprendre à piloter; 2 (by bird, animal) vol m; **adapted for ~** adapté au vol.

II noun modifier [lesson, instructor, school] de pilotage; [goggles, helmet, jacket] d'aviateur; [suit] de vol.

III adj 1 (able to fly) [insect, machine, trapeze] volant; 2 (in process of flying) [object, broken glass] qui vole; 3 (as if flying) **to take a ~ leap** sauter avec élan; 4 (fleeting) [visit] éclair inv.

IDIOMS **with ~ colours** [pass] haut la main.

flying: ~ **buttress** *n* arc-boutant *m*; ~ **doctor** *n* médecin *m* volant; ~ **picket** *n* piquet *m* de grève volant; ~ **squad** *n* brigade *f* volante.

flying start *n* SPORT départ *m* lancé; **to get off to a ~** FIG prendre un très bon départ.

fly: ~**leaf** *n* garde *f* volante; ~**-on-the-wall** *adj* [*film*] pris sur le vif.

flyover /'flaɪəʊvə(r)/ *n* **1** GB pont *m* routier; **2** US AVIAT défilé *m* aérien.

flypast *n* GB AVIAT défilé *m* aérien.

fly sheet *n* **1** (of tent) double-toit *m*; **2** (handbill) prospectus *m*.

fly: ~ **spray** *n* bombe *f* insecticide; ~ **swatter** *n* tapette *f* à mouches; ~**weight** *n* poids *m* mouche.

FM *n* **1** MIL *abrév* ▶ **field marshal**; **2** RADIO (*abrév* = **frequency modulation**) FM *f*.

FO *n* GB *abrév* ▶ **Foreign Office**.

foal /fəʊl/ *n* poulain *m*; **to be in ~** être pleine.

foam /fəʊm/ **I** *n* **1** (on sea) écume *f*; (on drinks, bath) mousse *f*; **2** (on animal) sueur *f*; **3** (from mouth) écume *f*; **4** (chemical) mousse *f*; **5** (made of rubber, plastic) mousse *f*.
II *noun modifier* **1** [*bath*] moussant; **2** [*rubber, mattress*] mousse.
III *vi* **1** (also ~ **up**) [*beer*] mousser; [*sea*] se couvrir d'écume; **to ~ at the mouth** LIT écumer; FIG écumer de rage; **2** (sweat) [*horse*] suer.

foam-filled *adj* en mousse.

fob /fɒb/ *n* (pocket) gousset *m*; (chain) chaîne *f*.
■ **fob off** (*p prés etc* **-bb-**): ¶ ~ [**sb**] **off**, ~ **off** [**sb**] se débarrasser de [*enquirer, customer*]; ¶ ~ **off** [**sth**] rejeter [*enquiry*]; **to ~ sth off onto sb** refiler qch à qn.

FOB *adj, adv*: *abrév* ▶ **free on board**.

focal /'fəʊkl/ *adj* focal.

focal point *n* **1** (in optics) foyer *m*; **2** (of village, building) point *m* de convergence (**of** de; **for** pour); **the room lacks a ~** cette pièce n'a pas de coin qui attire l'œil; **3** (main concern) point *m* central.

focus /'fəʊkəs/ **I** *n* (*pl* ~**es**, **foci**) **1** (focal point) foyer *m*; **in ~** au point; **to go out of ~** [*device*] se dérégler; [*image*] devenir flou; **to come into ~** se rapprocher de la mise au point; **2** (device on lens) mise *f* au point; **3** (centre of interest) centre *m*; **to become a ~ for the press** devenir le centre d'intérêt de la presse; **4** (emphasis) accent *m*.
II *vtr* (*p prés etc* **-s-** ou **-ss-**) **1** (direct) concentrer [*ray*] (**on** sur); fixer [*eyes*] (**on** sur); **2** (adjust) mettre [qch] au point, régler [*lens, camera*]; **3** (concentrate) concentrer [*mind*] (**on** sur).
III *vi* (*p prés etc* **-s-** ou **-ss-**) **1** (home in) **to ~ on** [*rays*] converger sur; [*camera*] faire le point or la mise au point sur; [*eyes, attention*] se fixer sur; **2** (concentrate) **to ~ on** [*report*] se concentrer sur.
IV **focused**, **focussed** *pp adj* [*person*] déterminé.

fodder /'fɒdə(r)/ *n* (for animals) fourrage *m*.

foe /fəʊ/ *n* LITTÉR ennemi/-e *m/f* ALSO FIG.

FoE *n*: *abrév* ▶ **Friends of the Earth**.

foetus, **fetus** US /'fiːtəs/ *n* fœtus *m*.

fog /fɒg/ **I** *n* **1** MÉTÉOROL brouillard *m*; **a patch/blanket of ~** une nappe/un manteau de brouillard; **a ~ of** un nuage épais de [*cigarette smoke*]; **2** PHOT voile *m*.
II *vtr* (*p prés etc* **-gg-**) **1** LIT (also ~ **up**) [*steam*] embuer [*glass*]; [*light*] voiler [*film*]; **2** FIG (confuse) **to ~ the issue** (unwittingly) embrouiller les choses; (deliberately) noyer le poisson.

fog bank *n* banc *m* de brume.

fogey○ /'fəʊgɪ/ *n* PÉJ vieille baderne *f* PÉJ.

foggy /'fɒgɪ/ *adj* **1** [*day, weather*] brumeux/-euse; **it will be ~ tomorrow** il y a aura du brouillard demain; **2** FIG [*idea, notion*] confus; **I haven't the foggiest idea**○ je n'en ai pas la moindre idée.

foghorn /'fɒghɔːn/ *n* NAUT corne *f* de brume; **like a ~** [*voice*] de stentor.

foglamp, **foglight** *n* AUT feu *m* de brouillard.

foible /'fɔɪbl/ *n* petite manie *f*.

foil /fɔɪl/ **I** *n* **1** (for wrapping) papier *m* d'aluminium; **silver/gold ~** papier argenté/doré; **2** SPORT fleuret *m*; **3** (deterrent) repoussoir *m*.
II *vtr* contrecarrer [*person*]; déjouer [*attempt*].

foist /fɔɪst/ *vtr* (off-load) **to ~ sth on sb** repasser qc à qn.

fold /fəʊld/ **I** *n* **1** (crease) (in fabric, paper, skin) pli *m*; **to hang in soft ~s** faire deos plis souples; **2** GÉOG repl *m*; **3** (in rock formation) plissement *m*; **4** AGRIC parc *m*.
II **-fold** *combining form* **to increase twofold/three-fold** doubler/tripler; **the problems are threefold** il a trois problèmes.
III *vtr* **1** (crease) plier [*paper, shirt, chair, umbrella*] replier [*wings*]; ~ **some newspaper around the vases** enveloppe les vases dans du papier journal; (intertwine) croiser [*arms*]; joindre [*hands*]; **he ~ed his arms across his chest** il a croisé les bras; with **her legs ~ed under her** les jambes repliées sou elle; **3** CULIN (add) incorporer (**into** à).
IV *vi* **1** [*chair*] se plier; **2** (fail) [*play*] quitter l'affiche [*company*] fermer; [*project*] échouer; [*course*] cesser.
IDIOMS **to return to the ~** rentrer au bercail.
■ **fold away**: ¶ ~ **away** [*bed, table*] se plier: ¶ ~ **away** [**sth**], ~ [**sth**] **away** plier et ranger [*clothes, linen*]; replier [*chair*].
■ **fold back**: ¶ ~ **back** [*door, shutters*] se rabattre (**against** contre): ¶ ~ **back** [**sth**], ~ [**sth**] **back** rabattre [*shutters , sheet, sleeve*].
■ **fold down**: ¶ ~ **down** [*seat, pram hood*] se rabattre; ¶ ~ [**sth**] **down**, ~ **down** [**sth**] replier [*collar, flap, sheets*]; rabattre [*seat, pram hood*].
■ **fold in**: ~ **in** [**sth**], ~ [**sth**] **in** incorporer [*sugar, flour*].
■ **fold out**: ~ **out** [**sth**], ~ [**sth**] **out** déplier [*map*].
■ **fold over**: ¶ ~ **over** se rabattre; ¶ ~ [**sth**] **over** rabattre [*flap*].
■ **fold up**: ¶ ~ **up** [*chair, pram, umbrella*] se plier; ¶ ~ [**sth**] **up**, ~ **up** [**sth**] plier [*newspaper, chair, umbrella*].

foldaway /'fəʊldəweɪ/ *adj* [*bed*] escamotable, pliant; [*table*] pliant.

folder /'fəʊldə(r)/ *n* **1** (for papers) chemise *f*; **2** (for artwork) carton *m*; **3** (brochure) prospectus *m*; **4** TECH plieuse *f*, machine *f* à plier; **5** COMPUT dossier *m*.

folding /'fəʊldɪŋ/ *adj* [*bed, bicycle, table, umbrella*] pliant; [*camera*] à soufflet; [*door*] en accordéon.

folding: ~ **seat** *n* strapontin *m*; ~ **stool** *n* (siège *m*) pliant *m*; ~ **top** *n* AUT capote *f*.

foldout *n* encart *m*.

foliage /'fəʊlɪdʒ/ *n* feuillage *m*.

folk /fəʊk/ **I** *n* **1** (people) (+ *v pl*) gens *mpl*; **old/young ~** les vieux *mpl*/jeunes *mpl*; **2** MUS (+ *v sg*) folk *m*.
II **folks** *npl* **1**○ (parents) parents *mpl*, vieux○ *mpl*; **2**○ (addressing people) **that's all, ~s**○! c'est tout, messieurs-dames○!
III *noun modifier* **1** (traditional) [*dance etc*] folklorique; **2** (modern) [*music*] folk *inv*; [*club, group*] de musique folk; **3** [*hero*] populaire.

folk: ~**lore** *n* folklore *m*; ~ **medicine** *n* médecine *f* traditionnelle; ~ **memory** *n* mémoire *f* collective; ~ **wisdom** *n* (knowledge) savoir *m* populaire.

follow /'fɒləʊ/ **I** *vtr* **1** (move after) suivre [*person, car*] (**into** dans); **to ~ sb in** entrer derrière qn; **she ~ed her father into politics** elle est entrée dans la politique comme son père; **they'll ~ us on a later flight** ils nous rejoindront par un autre vol; **2** (come after in time) suivre [*event, item on list*]; succéder à [*leader*]; ~**ed by** suivi de; **3** (be guided by) suivre [*clue, path, fashion, instinct, instructions*]; **4** (adhere to) suivre [*teachings, example*]; pratiquer [*religion*]; adhérer à [*faith, ideas*]; être le disciple de [*person, leader*]; **5** (watch closely) suivre [*stock market, serial, trial*]; **6** (understand) suivre [*explanation, reasoning, plot*]; **if you ~ my meaning** si tu vois ce que je veux dire; **7** (practise) exercer [*trade, profession*]; poursuivre [*career*]; avoir [*way of life*].
II *vi* **1** (move after) suivre; **she ~ed on her bike** elle a suivi en vélo; **to ~ in sb's footsteps** suivre les traces de qn; **2** (come after in time) suivre; **there ~ed**

a **lengthy debate** il s'ensuivit un débat interminable; **there's ice cream to ~** ensuite il y a de la glace; **the results were as ~s** les résultats ont été les suivants; **3** (be logical consequence) s'ensuivre; **it ~s that** il s'ensuit que; **it doesn't necessarily ~ that** ça ne veut pas forcément dire que; **that doesn't ~** ce n'est pas évident; **that ~s** ça me paraît logique; **4** (understand) suivre; **I don't ~** je ne suis pas.
■ **follow about, follow around**: **~** [sb] **around** suivre [qn].
■ **follow out** US: **~ out** [sth] suivre [orders, instructions, advice].
■ **follow through**: ¶ **~ through** SPORT faire un swing complet; ¶ **~ through** [sth], **~** [sth] **through** mener [qch] à terme [project]; mettre [qch] à exécution [threat]; aller jusqu'au bout de [idea, theory].
■ **follow up**: ¶ **~ up** [sth], **~** [sth] **up 1** (reinforce) confirmer [victory, success] (**with** par); consolider [good start] (**with** par); donner suite à [letter, threat] (**with** par); **to ~ up with** [boxer] enchaîner avec; **2** (act upon, pursue) suivre [story, lead]; donner suite à [complaint, offer, call, article]; examiner [suggestion]; ¶ **~ up** [sb], **~** [sb] **up** suivre [patient].

ollower /ˈfɒləʊə(r)/ n **1** (of thinker, artist) disciple m; (of political leader) partisan/-e m/f; (of teachings, tradition) adepte mf; **2** (of sport) amateur m; (of TV series) fidèle mf; (of team) supporter m; **3** (not a leader) suiveur m.

ollowing /ˈfɒləʊwɪŋ/ **I** n **1** ¢ (of theorist, religion, cult) adeptes mfpl; (of party, political figure) partisans/-anes mpl/fpl; (of soap opera, show) public m; (of sports team) supporters mpl; **2** (before list or explanation) **you will need the ~** vous aurez besoin des choses suivantes; **the ~ is a guide to…** ce qui suit est un guide sur… **II** adj (tjrs épith) **1** (next) [year, article, remark] suivant (after n); **2** (from the rear) [wind] arrière. **III** prep suite à, à la suite de [incident, allegation].

follow-on /ˌfɒləʊˈɒn/ n suite f.

follow-up /ˈfɒləʊʌp/ **I** n **1** (film, record, single, programme) suite f (**to** à); **2** (of patient, socialwork case) suivi m.
II noun modifier **1** (supplementary) [survey, work] de suivi; [interview, check] de contrôle; [discussion, article, programme, meeting] complémentaire; [letter] de rappel; **2** (of patient, ex-inmate) [visit] de contrôle.

folly /ˈfɒlɪ/ n **1** (madness) folie f; **2** ARCHIT folie f.

foment /fəʊˈment/ vtr MED, FIG fomenter.

fond /fɒnd/ adj **1** (loving) [gesture, person] affectueux/ -euse; [eyes, heart] tendre; **~ memories** de très bons souvenirs; **'with ~est love, Julie'** 'je t'embrasse affectueusement, Julie'; **2** (heartfelt) [wish, ambition] cher/chère; **3** (naive) **in the ~ hope that** bercé par la conviction que; **4** (partial) **to be ~ of sb** aimer beaucoup qn; **to be ~ of sth** aimer qch; **to be very ~ of sb/sth** adorer qn/qch; **5** (irritatingly prone) **to be ~ of doing** aimer bien faire.

fondle /ˈfɒndl/ vtr caresser.

fondness /ˈfɒndnɪs/ n **1** (love) (for person) tendresse f (**for** pour); (for thing, activity) passion f (**for** pour); **2** (irritating penchant) tendance f (**for doing** à faire).

font /fɒnt/ n **1** RELIG fonts mpl baptismaux; **2** (in printing) fonte f; **3** COMPUT police f de caractères.

food /fuːd/ **I** n **1** (sustenance) nourriture f, alimentation f; **2** ¢ (foodstuffs) aliments mpl; **frozen ~** aliments surgelés; **3** ¢ (provisions) provisions fpl; **4** (cuisine, cooking) cuisine f; **is the ~ good in Japan?** on mange bien au Japon?; **to be a lover of good ~** être gourmet; **to like one's ~** avoir bon appétit; **5** (fuel) **that's ~ for thought** ça donne à réfléchir.
II noun modifier [additive, industry, product] alimentaire; [production] d'aliments; [shop] d'alimentation.

food: Food and Drug Administration, FDA n US organisme gouvernemental de contrôle pharmaceutique et alimentaire; **~ parcel** n colis m de vivres; **~ poisoning** n intoxication f alimentaire; **~ processor** n robot m ménager; **~ science** n diététique f; **~stuff** n denrée f alimentaire.

fool /fuːl/ **I** n **1** (silly person) idiot/-e m/f (**to do** de

faire); **you stupid ~!** espèce d'idiot/-e!; **to make sb look a ~** faire passer qn pour un/-e idiot/-e; **enough to agree** assez stupide pour accepter; **she's no ~** elle n'est pas si bête; **any ~ could do that** le premier imbécile venu pourrait faire ça; **to act** ou **play the ~** faire l'imbécile, faire le pitre; **3** HIST (jester) fou m; **3** GB CULIN **fruit ~** crème f aux fruits.
II noun modifier US [politician] idiot; **that's a ~ thing to do** c'est vraiment stupide de faire ça.
III vtr tromper, duper; **don't let that ~ you!** ne t'y trompe pas!; **who are you trying to ~?** à qui veux-tu faire croire ça?; **you don't ~ me for a minute** je ne te crois pas un seul instant; **to ~ sb into believing that…** faire croire à qn que…; **to be ~ed** se laisser abuser (**by** par); **you really had me ~ed!** tu m'as vraiment fait marcher!
IDIOMS **a ~ and his money are soon parted** PROV aux idiots l'argent file entre les doigts; **you could have ~ed me!** tu m'en diras tant!
■ **fool about** GB, **fool around** GB (waste time) perdre son temps; (act stupidly) faire l'imbécile.

foolhardy /ˈfuːlhɑːdɪ/ adj téméraire.

foolish /ˈfuːlɪʃ/ adj **1** [person] bête (**to do** de faire); **2** [grin, expression] stupide; **to feel ~** se sentir ridicule; **to make sb look ~** ridiculiser qn; **3** (misguided) [decision, question, remark] idiot.

foolproof /ˈfuːlpruːf/ adj **1** [method, plan] infaillible; **2** [machine] d'utilisation très simple.

foolscap /ˈfuːlskæp/ n GB (paper) papier m ministre.

foot /fʊt/ ▶765, 1045 **I** n (pl **feet**) **1** GEN, ANAT (of person, horse) pied m; (of rabbit, cat, dog, cow) patte f; (of sock, chair) pied m; **on ~** à pied; **soft under ~** doux/ douce sous le pied; **to set ~ in** mettre les pieds dans; **from head to ~** de la tête aux pieds; **to help sb to their feet** aider qn à se lever; **her speech brought the audience to its feet** toute l'audience s'est levée pour applaudir son discours; **to get sb/sth back on their/its feet** (after setback) remettre qn/qch sur pied; **bound hand and ~** pieds et poings liés; **to wait on sb hand and ~** faire tout pour qn; **to put one's ~ down** (accelerate) appuyer sur l'accélérateur; (act firmly) mettre le holà; **2** (measurement) pied m (anglais) (= 0,3048 m); **3** (bottom) (of mountain) pied m (**of** de); **at the ~ of** au pied de [bed]; à la fin de [list, letter]; en bas de [page, stairs]; en bout de [table]; **4** (in sewing) pied m.
II vtr **to ~ the bill** payer la facture (**for** pour).
IDIOMS **not to put a ~ wrong** ne pas commettre la moindre erreur; **under sb's feet** FIG dans les pattes de qn; **rushed off one's feet** débordé; **to catch sb on the wrong ~** prendre qn au dépourvu; **to cut the ground from under sb's feet** couper l'herbe sous les pieds de qn; **to fall on one's feet** FIG retomber sur ses pieds; **to keep one's feet on the ground** avoir les pieds sur terre; **to have two left feet** être maladroit; **to put one's best ~ forward** (do one's best) faire de son mieux; (hurry) se dépêcher; **to put one's ~ in it** faire une gaffe; **to put one's feet up** se reposer, décompresser; **to stand on one's own (two) feet** se débrouiller tout seul; **to get off on the wrong/right ~** mal/bien commencer.

footage /ˈfʊtɪdʒ/ n ¢ CIN (piece of film) film m, pellicule f; **news ~** des informations filmées.

foot and mouth (disease) n fièvre f aphteuse.

football /ˈfʊtbɔːl/ ▶949 n **1** (game) GB football m; US football m américain; **2** (ball) ballon m de football.

football coupon n GB bulletin m de (participation au) loto sportif.

footballer ▶1251 n GB joueur/-euse m/f de football.

football pools npl GB **~** loto m sportif (limité aux matchs de football).

foot: ~bath n (at home) bain m de pieds; (at pool) pédiluve m; **~ brake** n AUT frein m (à pied); **~bridge** n passerelle f; **~fall** n (bruit m de) pas m; **~hills** npl contreforts mpl.

foothold /ˈfʊthəʊld/ n LIT prise f (de pied); **to gain a ~** FIG [company] prendre pied; [ideology] s'imposer; [plant, insect] se propager.

for

When *for* is used as a preposition, followed by a noun or pronoun, it is translated by *pour*:

for my sister = pour ma sœur
for the garden = pour le jardin
for me = pour moi

For particular usages see the entry **for**.

When *for* is used as a preposition indicating purpose followed by a verb it is translated by *pour* + infinitive:

for cleaning windows = pour nettoyer les vitres

When *for* is used in the construction
to be + adjective + *for* + pronoun + infinitive the translation in French is *être* + indirect pronoun + adjective + *de* + infinitive:

it's impossible for me to stay = il m'est impossible de rester

it was hard for him to understand that … = il lui était difficile de comprendre que …

it will be difficult for her to accept the changes = il lui sera difficile d'accepter les changements

For the construction *to be waiting for sb to do* see the entry **wait**. For particular usages see the entry **for**.

In time expressions

for is used in English after a verb in the progressive present perfect tense to express the time period of something that started in the past and is still going on. To express this French uses a verb in the present tense + *depuis*:

I have been waiting for three hours (and I am still waiting) = j'attends depuis trois heures
we've been together for two years (and we're still together) = nous sommes ensemble depuis deux ans

When *for* is used in English after a verb in the past perfect tense, French uses the *imperfect* + *depuis*:

I had been waiting for two hours (and was still waiting) = j'attendais depuis deux heures

for is used in English negative sentences with the present perfect tense to express the time that has elapsed since something has happened. To express this French uses the same tense as English (the perfect) + *depuis*:

I haven't seen him for ten years (and I still haven't seen him) = je ne l'ai pas vu depuis dix ans

In spoken French, there is another way of expressing this: *ça fait* or *il y a dix ans que je ne l'ai pas vu.*

When *for* is used in English in negative sentences after a verb in the past perfect tense French uses the past perfect + *depuis*:

I hadn't seen him for ten years = je ne l'avais pas vu depuis dix ans, or *(in spoken French)* ça faisait or il y avait dix ans que je ne l'avais pas vu

for is used in English after the preterite to express the time period of something that happened in the past and is no longer going on. Here French uses the present perfect + *pendant*:

last Sunday I gardened for two hours = dimanche dernier j'ai jardiné pendant deux heures

for is used in English after the present progressive tense or the future tense to express an anticipated time period in the future. Here French uses the present or the future tense + *pour*:

I'm going to Rome for six weeks
or *I will go to Rome for six weeks* = je vais à Rome pour six semaines or j'irai à Rome pour six semaines

Note, however, that when the verb *to be* is used in the future with *for* to emphasize the period of time, French uses the future + *pendant*:

I will be in Rome for six weeks = je serai à Rome pendant six semaines
he will be away for three days = il sera absent pendant trois jours

For particular usages see I **13**, **14**, **15** and **16** in the entry **for**.

for is often used in English to form a structure with nouns, adjectives and verbs (*weakness for, eager for, apply for, fend for* etc.). For translations, consult the appropriate noun, adjective or verb entry (*eager, apply, fend* etc.).

---

footing /ˈfʊtɪŋ/ n **1** (basis) **on a firm ~** sur une base solide; **on a war ~** sur le pied de guerre; **to put sth on a legal ~** légaliser qch; **to be on an equal ou even ~ with sb** être sur un pied d'égalité avec qn; **2** (grip for feet) **to lose one's ~** perdre pied.

footlights /ˈfʊtlaɪts/ npl THEAT rampe f.

footloose /ˈfʊtluːs/ adj libre comme l'air.
IDIOMS **~ and fancy free** sans attache.

foot: **~mark** n trace f (de pas); **~note** n LIT note f de bas de page; FIG (additional comment) post-scriptum m; **~ passenger** n passager m sans véhicule; **~path** n (in countryside) sentier m; (in town) trottoir m; **~print** n empreinte f (de pied); **~rest** n reposepied m.

footsore /ˈfʊtsɔː(r)/ adj **to be ~** avoir mal aux pieds.

footstep /ˈfʊtstep/ n pas m.
IDIOMS **to follow in sb's ~s** suivre les traces de qn.

foot: **~stool** n repose-pied m; **~wear** n ∉ chaussures fpl.

for /fə(r), fɔː(r)/ I prep **1** (intended to be used or belong to) pour; **who are the flowers ~?** pour qui sont les fleurs?; **to buy sth ~ sb** acheter qch pour or à qn; **~ young people** pour les jeunes; **keep some pancakes ~ us!** garde-nous des crêpes!; **not ~ me thanks** pas pour moi merci; **2** (intended to help or benefit) pour; **to do sth ~ sb** faire qch pour qn; **he cooked dinner ~ us** il nous a préparé à manger; **3** (indicating purpose) pour; **what's it ~?** c'est pour quoi faire?, ça sert à quoi?; **it's ~ removing stains** c'est pour enlever les taches; **it's not ~ cleaning windows** ce n'est pas fait pour nettoyer les vitres; **'I need it'—'what ~?'** 'j'en ai besoin'—'pourquoi?'; **what did you say that ~?** pourquoi as-tu dit cela?; **to do sth ~ a laugh** faire qch pour rigoler○; **to go ~ a swim** aller nager; **I need something ~ my cough** j'ai besoin de quelque chose contre la toux; **I sent it away ~ cleaning** je l'ai renvoyé pour qu'il soit nettoyé; **the bell rang ~ class to begin** la cloche a sonné pour indiquer le début du cours; **the idea was ~ you to work it out yourself** le but était que tu trouves (*subj*) la réponse tout seul; **4** (as member, employee of) [*work, play*] pour; (as representative) [*MP, Minister*] de; **5** (indicating cause or reason) pour; **the reason ~ doing** la raison pour laquelle on fait; **~ this reason, I'd rather...** pour cette raison je préfère...; **grounds ~ divorce** des motifs de divorce; **to jump ~ joy** sauter de joie; **imprisoned ~ murder** emprisonné pour meurtre; **she's been criticized ~ her views** on lui a reproché ses opinions; **I was unable to sleep ~ the noise** je ne pouvais pas dormir à cause du bruit; **if it weren't ~ her...** sans elle...; **she is annoyed with me ~ contradicting her** elle m'en veut parce que je l'ai contredite; **6** (indicating consequence) pour que (+ *subj*); **I haven't the patience ~ sewing** je n'ai pas la patience qu'il faut pour coudre; **there's not enough time ~ us to have a drink** nous n'avons pas le temps de prendre un verre; **7** (indicating person's attitude) pour; **to be easy ~ sb to do** être facile pour qn de faire; **the film was too earnest ~ me** le film était trop sérieux pour moi; **living in London is not ~ me** je ne suis pas

fait pour vivre à Londres; **8** (stressing particular feature) pour; **~ further information write to...** pour plus de renseignements écrivez à...; **I buy it ~ flavour** je l'achète pour le goût; **9** (considering) pour; **to be mature ~ one's age** être mûr pour son âge; **10** (towards) pour; **to have respect ~ sb** avoir du respect pour qn; **to feel sorry ~ sb** avoir de la peine pour qn; **to feel contempt ~ sb** mépriser qn; **11** (on behalf of) pour; **say hello to him ~ me** dis-lui bonjour de ma part; **I can't do it ~ you** je ne peux pas le faire à ta place; **let her answer ~ herself** laisse-la répondre elle-même; **I speak ~ everyone here** je parle au nom de toutes les personnes ici présentes; **12** (as regards) **she's a great one ~ jokes** on peut toujours compter sur elle pour raconter des blagues; **to be all right ~ money** avoir assez d'argent; **13** (taking account of past events) depuis; (stressing expected duration) pour; (stressing actual duration) pendant; **this is the best show I've seen ~ years** c'est le meilleur spectacle que j'aie vu depuis des années; **we've been together ~ 2 years** ça fait 2 ans que nous sommes ensemble; **she's off to Paris ~ the weekend** elle va à Paris pour le week-end; **will he be away ~ long?** est-ce qu'il sera absent longtemps?; **to stay ~ a year** rester un an; **to be away ~ a year** être absent pendant un an; **I was in Paris ~ 2 weeks** j'étais à Paris pendant 2 semaines; **to last ~ hours** durer des heures; **14** (indicating a deadline) pour; (in negative constructions) avant; **it will be ready ~ Saturday** ça sera prêt pour samedi; **the car won't be ready ~ another 6 weeks** la voiture ne sera pas prête avant 6 semaines; **15** (on the occasion of) pour; **invited ~ Easter** invité pour Pâques; **16** (indicating scheduled time) pour; **scheduled ~ next month** prévu pour le mois prochain; **I have an appointment ~ 4 pm** j'ai rendez-vous à 16h 00; **it's time ~ bed** c'est l'heure d'aller au lit; **17** (indicating distance) pendant; **to drive ~ miles** rouler pendant des kilomètres; **the last shop ~ 30 miles** le dernier magasin avant 50 kilomètres; **18** (indicating destination) pour; **a ticket ~ Dublin** un billet pour Dublin; **to leave ~ work** partir travailler; **to swim ~ the shore** nager vers la rive; **19** (indicating cost, value) pour; **it was sold ~ £100** ça s'est vendu (pour) 100 livres sterling; **I wouldn't do it ~ anything!** je ne le ferais pour rien au monde!; **I'll let you have it ~ £20** je vous le laisse à 20 livres sterling; **a cheque ~ £20** un chèque de 20 livres sterling; **20** (in favour of) **to be ~** être pour [*peace, divorce, reunification*]; **to be all ~ it** être tout à fait pour; **who's ~ a game of football?** qui veut jouer au football?; **21** (stressing appropriateness) **she's the person ~ the job** elle est la personne qu'il faut pour le travail; **that's ~ us to decide** c'est à nous de décider; **22** (in support of) en faveur de; **the argument ~ recycling** l'argument en faveur du recyclage; **there's no evidence ~ that** ce n'est absolument pas prouvé; **23** (indicating availability) **~ sale** à vendre; **24** (as part of ratio) pour; **one teacher ~ five pupils** un professeur pour cinq élèves; **25** (equivalent to) **T ~ Tom** T comme Tom; **what's the French ~ 'boot'?** comment dit-on 'boot' en français?; **the technical term ~ it is 'chloasma'** 'chloasme' c'est le terme technique; **26** (in explanations) **~ one thing... and ~ another...** premièrement... et deuxièmement...; **I, ~ one, agree with her** en tout cas moi, je suis d'accord avec elle; **27** (when introducing clauses) **it would be unwise ~ us to generalize** il serait imprudent pour nous de généraliser; **the best thing would be ~ them to leave** le mieux serait qu'ils s'en aillent; **there's no need ~ people to get upset** il n'y a pas de quoi s'énerver.
II *conj* SOUT car, parce que.
IDIOMS **oh ~ a nice hot bath!** je rêve d'un bon bain chaud!; **I'll be (in) ~ it if...**○ GB ça va être ma fête si...○; **that's adolescents ~ you!** que voulez-vous, c'est ça les adolescents!; **there's gratitude ~ you!** c'est comme ça qu'on me/vous etc remercie!

forage /'fɒrɪdʒ, US 'fɔːr-/ **I** *n* **1** (animal feed) fourrage *m*;

2 (search) **to go on a ~ for** aller faire provision de [*food, wood*].
II *vtr* affourager [*animals*].
III *vi* **to ~** (**about** OU **around**) **for** LIT, FIG fouiller pour trouver.

foray /'fɒreɪ, US 'fɔːreɪ/ *n* GEN, MIL incursion *f* (**into** dans); **to make a ~ into** s'essayer à [*politics, acting, sport*]; MIL faire une incursion dans [*territory*].

forbad(e) /fɔː'bæd, US fə'beɪd/ *prét* ▶ **forbid**.

forbear /fɔː'beə(r)/ *vi* (*prét* **-bore**; *pp* **-borne**) SOUT s'abstenir (**from** de; **from doing, to do** de faire).

forbid /fə'bɪd/ *vtr* (*p prés* **-dd-**; *prét* **-bad(e)**; *pp* **-bidden**) **1** (disallow) défendre, interdire; **~ sb to do** défendre or interdire à qn de faire; **~ sb sth** défendre or interdire qch à qn; **2** (prevent, preclude) interdire; **God ~!** Dieu m'en/l'en etc garde!; **God ~ she should do that!** pourvu qu'elle ne fasse pas cela!

forbidden /fə'bɪdn/ *adj* [*subject, fruit*] défendu; [*place*] interdit; **smoking is ~** il est interdit de fumer.

forbidding /fə'bɪdɪŋ/ *adj* [*edifice*] intimidant; [*landscape*] inhospitalier/-ière; [*expression*] rébarbatif/-ive.

forbore /fɔː'bɔː(r)/ *prét* ▶ **forbear**.

forborne /fɔː'bɔːn/ *pp* ▶ **forbear**.

force /fɔːs/ **I** *n* **1** (of blow, explosion, collision) force *f*; (of fall) choc *m*; **by the ~ of the blast** sous la force de l'explosion; **2** GEN, MIL force *f*; **by ~** par la force; **by ~ of arms** à la force des armes; **3** FIG force *f*; **from ~ of habit/of circumstance** par la force de l'habitude/des circonstances; **4** (influence) force *f*; **a ~ for good** une force agissant pour le bien; **a world ~** une puissance mondiale; **5** ¢ (organized group) forces *fpl*; **expeditionary ~** forces expéditionnaires; **6** (also **Force**) (police) **the ~** la police; **7** PHYS force *f*; **centrifugal ~** force centrifuge; **~ of gravity** pesanteur *f*; **8** METEOROL force *f*; **a ~ 10 gale** un vent de force 10.
II forces *npl* MIL (also **armed ~s**) **the ~s** les forces *fpl* armées.
III in force *adv phr* **1** (in large numbers, strength) en force; **2** GEN, JUR [*law, prices, ban*] en vigueur.
IV *vtr* **1** (compel, oblige) forcer (**to do** à faire); **to be ~d to do** OU **into doing** GEN être forcé de faire; **the earthquake ~d the evacuation** le tremblement de terre a provoqué l'évacuation; **2** (push) **to ~ one's way through** [sth] se frayer un chemin à travers or dans [*crowd, jungle*]; **to ~ sb up against sth** plaquer qn contre qn; **she ~d him to his knees** elle l'a forcé à se mettre à genoux; **3** (apply great pressure to) forcer [*door, window, safe*]; forcer sur [*screw*]; **to ~ an entry** JUR entrer par effraction; **4** AGRIC forcer [*plant*]; engraisser [*animal*].
V *v refl* **1** (push oneself) **to ~ oneself** se forcer (**to do** à faire); **2** (impose oneself) **I wouldn't want to ~ myself on you** je ne cherche pas à m'imposer.
IDIOMS **to ~ sb's hand** forcer la main à qn.
■ **force back**: **~ [sth] back, ~ back [sth] 1** LIT repousser [*crowd, army*]; **2** FIG réprimer [*tears*].
■ **force down**: **~ [sth] down, ~ down [sth] 1** (cause to land) forcer [qch] à se poser [*aircraft*]; **2** (eat reluctantly) se forcer à avaler [*food*]; **to ~ sth down sb**○ forcer qn à manger qch; **3** (reduce) diminuer [qch] (de force) [*prices, wages*]; réduire [qch] (de force) [*value, profits, inflation*]; **to ~ down unemployment** faire baisser le taux de chômage; **4** (squash) tasser [*contents, objects*].
■ **force in**: **~ [sth] in, ~ in [sth]** GEN faire entrer [qch] de force; (into small opening) enfoncer [qch] de force.
■ **force on**: **~ [sth] on sb** imposer [qch] à qn, forcer qn à accepter [qch]; **the decision was ~d on him** il a été forcé de prendre cette décision.
■ **force open**: **~ [sth] open, ~ open [sth]** forcer [*door, window, box, safe*].
■ **force out**: **~ [sth] out, ~ out [sth]** faire sortir [qch] par la force [*enemy, object*]; enlever [qch] de force [*cork*]; **~ one's way out (of sth)** s'échapper (de qch) par la force; **to ~ sth out of sb** arracher qch à qn [*information, apology, smile, confession*].

■ **force through**: ~ [sth] through, ~ through [sth] faire adopter [*legislation, measures*].
■ **force up**: ~ [sth] up, ~ up [sth] [*situation*] faire augmenter [*prices, demand, unemployment*]; [*company*] augmenter (de force) [*output*]; relever [*exchange rate*].

forced /fɔːst/ *adj* (all contexts) forcé.

force-feed *vtr* (*prét, pp* **-fed**) gaver [*animal, bird*] (**on, with** de); alimenter [qn] de force.

forceful /'fɔːsfl/ *adj* [*person, behaviour*] énergique; [*attack, defence, speech*] vigoureux/-euse.

forcibly /'fɔːsəblɪ/ *adv* [*restrain, repatriate*] de force.

forcing house *n* BOT forcerie *f*; FIG pépinière *f*.

ford /fɔːd/ **I** *n* gué *m*.
II *vtr* **to ~ a river** passer une rivière à gué.

fore /fɔː(r)/ **I** *n* **to the ~** en vue, en avant; FIG **to come to the ~** [*person*] se faire connaître; [*issue*] attirer l'attention; [*quality*] ressortir; [*team, party, competitor*] commencer à dominer.
II *excl* (in golf) gare!

forearm /'fɔːrɑːm/ *n* avant-bras *m inv*.

forebears /'fɔːbeəz/ *npl* SOUT aïeux *mpl*.

foreboding /fɔː'bəʊdɪŋ/ *n* pressentiment *m*; **to have ~s about** avoir de sombres pressentiments quant à.

forecast /'fɔːkɑːst, US -kæst/ **I** *n* **1** (also **weather ~**) météo⚬ *f*; bulletin *m* météorologique; **2** COMM, ECON, FIN prévisions *fpl*; **3** (in horseracing) **a** (**racing**) **~** pronostics *mpl* des courses; **4** GEN (outlook) pronostics *mpl*.
II *vtr* (*prét, pp* **-cast**) (all contexts) prévoir (**that** que); **sunshine is forecast for tomorrow** on prévoit du soleil pour demain; **investment is forecast to fall** on prévoit une chute de l'investissement.

forecaster /'fɔːkɑːstə(r), US -kæst-/ *n* **1** (of weather) spécialiste *mf* de la météorologie; **2** (economic) conjoncturiste *mf*; **3** GEN, SPORT pronostiqueur/-euse *m/f*.

forecastle, fo'c'sle /'fəʊksl/ *n* poste *m* d'équipage.

foreclose /fɔː'kləʊz/ *vtr* SOUT **1** FIN, JUR saisir [*mortgage, loan*]; **2** (remove) exclure [*possibility*].

forecourt /'fɔːkɔːt/ *n* **1** GB (of shop) parking *m*; (of garage) aire *f* de stationnement; **2** GB RAIL (of station) cour *f* de la gare; **3** (of church) ≈ parvis *m*; (of castle) avant-cour *f*.

forefathers /'fɔːfɑːðəz/ *npl* ancêtres *mpl*.

forefinger /'fɔːfɪŋgə(r)/ *n* index *m*.

forefront /'fɔːfrʌnt/ *n* **at** ou **in the ~ of** à la pointe de [*change, research, debate*]; au premier plan de [*campaign, struggle*]; **it's in the ~ of my mind** c'est ma première préoccupation.

forego *vtr* = **forgo**.

foregone /'fɔːgɒn, US -'gɔːn/ *adj* **it is/was a ~ conclusion** c'est/c'était couru d'avance.

fore: **~ground** *n* premier plan *m*; **~hand** *n* SPORT coup *m* droit; **~head** *n* front *m*.

foreign /'fɒrən, US 'fɔːr-/ *adj* **1** [*country, imports, company*] étranger/-ère; [*market*] extérieur; [*trade, travel*] à l'étranger; **2** (alien) [*concept*] étranger/-ère (**to** à).

foreign: **~ affairs** *npl* affaires *fpl* étrangères; **Foreign and Commonwealth Office, FCO** *n* GB = **foreign office**; **~ body** *n* corps *m* étranger; **~ correspondent** ▶ 1251 *n* correspondant/-e *m/f* à l'étranger.

foreigner /'fɒrənə(r)/ *n* étranger/-ère *m/f*.

foreign: **~ exchange dealer** ▶ 1251 *n* cambiste *m*, courtier/-ière *m/f* en devises; **~ exchange market** *n* marché *m* des changes; **~ legion** *n* légion *f* étrangère; **~ minister**, **~ secretary** GB *n* ministre *m* des Affaires étrangères; **Foreign Office, FO** *n* GB ministère *m* des Affaires étrangères.

foreleg /'fɔːleg/ *n* patte *f* avant; (of horse) (membre *m*) antérieur *m*.

foreman /'fɔːmən/ ▶ 1251 *n* **1** (supervisor) contremaître *m*; **2** JUR président *m* (d'un jury).

foremost /'fɔːməʊst/ **I** *adj* plus grand; **we have many problems, ~ among these are...** nous avons

beaucoup de problèmes, les premiers d'entre eux sont...
II *adv* **first and ~** avant tout.

forename /'fɔːneɪm/ *n* prénom *m*.

forensic /fə'rensɪk, US -zɪk/ **I forensics** *npl* US (public speaking) art *m* oratoire.
II *adj* **1** (in crime detection) **~ tests** expertises *fpl* médico-légales; **~ evidence** résultats *mpl* des expertises médico-légales; **2** (in debate) SOUT [*skill, eloquence*] consommé; [*attack*] dévastateur/-trice.

forensic: **~ medicine**, **~ science** *n* médecine *f* légale; **~ scientist** ▶ 1251 *n* médecin *m* de mer.

forerunner /'fɔːrʌnə(r)/ *n* **1** (predecessor) (person) précurseur *m*; (institution, invention, model) ancêtre *m*; **2** (sign) signe *m* avant-coureur.

foresee /fɔː'siː/ *vtr* (*prét* **-saw**; *pp* **-seen**) prévoir.

foreseeable /fɔː'siːəbl/ *adj* prévisible (**that** que); **for the ~ future** dans l'immédiat.

foreshadow /fɔː'ʃædəʊ/ *vtr* annoncer.

foreshore /'fɔːʃɔː(r)/ *n* laisse *f* de mer.

foresight /'fɔːsaɪt/ *n* prévoyance *f* (**to do** de faire).

foreskin /'fɔːskɪn/ *n* ANAT GEN prépuce *m*; (of horse) fourreau *m*.

forest /'fɒrɪst, US 'fɔːr-/ *n* forêt *f*.

forestall /fɔː'stɔːl/ *vtr* empêcher [*action, event, discussion*]; prévenir [*person*].

forested /'fɒrɪstɪd, US 'fɔːr-/ *adj* boisé.

forester /'fɒrɪstə(r), US 'fɔːr-/ *n* forestier/-ière *m/f*.

forest: **~ fire** *n* incendie *m* de forêt; **~ ranger** *n* US forestier *m*.

forestry /'fɒrɪstrɪ, US 'fɔːr-/ *n* (science) sylviculture *f*; (industry) exploitation *f* des forêts.

Forestry Commission *n* GB *l'office britannique des forêts*.

foretaste /'fɔːteɪst/ *n* avant-goût *m* (**of** de).

foretell /fɔː'tel/ *vtr* (*prét, pp* **-told**) prédire.

forethought /'fɔːθɔːt/ *n* prévoyance *f*.

forever /fə'revə(r)/ *adv* **1** (also **for ever**) pour toujours; **it can't go on** ou **last ~** [*situation, trend, success*] ça ne peut pas toujours durer; **~ after(wards)** pour toujours; **the desert seemed to go on ~** le désert semblait ne pas avoir de limites; **2** (persistently) **to be ~ doing sth** faire qch sans arrêt; **3**⚬ (also **for ever**) (ages) **to take ~** [*task*] prendre un temps fou⚬; [*person*] mettre un temps fou⚬ (**to do** pour faire); **to go on ~** [*pain, noise*] durer une éternité; **4** (always) toujours; **~ on the brink of doing** toujours sur le point de faire.

forevermore /fə,revə'mɔː(r)/ *adv* pour toujours.

forewarn /fɔː'wɔːn/ *vtr* avertir (**of** de; **that** que).
IDIOMS **~ed is forearmed** PROV un homme averti en vaut deux PROV.

foreword /'fɔːwɜːd/ *n* avant-propos *m inv*.

forfeit /'fɔːfɪt/ **I** *n* **1** (action, process) confiscation *f* (**of** de); **2** (sum, token) gage *m*; **3** (in game) gage *m*; **4** JUR, COMM (fine) amende *f*; (for breach of contract) dédit *m*.
II *adj* **to be ~** SOUT [*property*] être confiscable (**to** au profit de).
III *vtr* **1** (under duress) perdre [*right, liberty*]; **2** (voluntarily) renoncer à [*right*]; **3** JUR, COMM verser [*sum*].

forfeiture /'fɔːfɪtʃə(r)/ *n* (of property) confiscation *f*; (of right) déchéance *f*.

forgave /fə'geɪv/ *prét* ▶ **forgive**.

forge /fɔːdʒ/ **I** *n* forge *f*.
II *vtr* **1** forger [*metal*]; **2** (fake) contrefaire [*banknotes, signature*]; **a ~d passport** un faux passeport; **3** (alter) falsifier [*date, will*]; **4** (establish) forger [*alliance*]; établir [*identity, link*].
III *vi* **to ~ ahead** accélérer; FIG [*industry*] être en plein essor; **to ~ ahead with** aller de l'avant dans.

forger /'fɔːdʒə(r)/ *n* **1** (of documents) faussaire *m*; **2** (of artefacts) contrefacteur/-trice *m/f*; **3** (of money) faux-monnayeur *m*.

forgery /'fɔːdʒərɪ/ *n* **1** (of document) faux *m*; (of picture, banknotes) contrefaçon *f*; **2** (signature, banknote) contrefaçon *f*; (picture, document) faux *m*.

Forms of address

*Only those forms of address in frequent use are included here; titles of members of the nobility or of church dignitaries are not covered; for the use of military ranks as titles ▶ 1192]; for letter formulae (openings and closings), and ways of addressing envelopes, see the **French correspondence** section.*

Speaking to someone
Where English puts the surname after the title, French normally uses the title alone (note that when speaking to someone French does not use a capital letter for monsieur, madame and mademoiselle, unlike English Mr etc., nor for titles such as docteur).

good morning, Mr Johnson = bonjour, monsieur
good evening, Mrs Jones = bonsoir, madame
goodbye, Miss Smith = au revoir, mademoiselle

The French monsieur and madame tend to be used more often than the English Mr X or Mrs Y. Also, in English, people often say simply Good morning or Excuse me; in the equivalent situation in French, they might say Bonjour, monsieur or Pardon, madame. However, the French are slower than the British, and much slower than the Americans, to use someone's first name, so hi there, Peter! to a colleague may well be simply bonjour!, or bonjour, monsieur; bonjour, cher ami; bonjour, mon vieux etc., depending on the degree of familiarity that exists.

In both languages, other titles are also used:
hallo, Dr. Brown or hallo, Doctor = bonjour, docteur

In some cases where titles are not used in English, they are used in French, e.g. bonjour, Monsieur le directeur or bonjour, Madame la directrice to a head teacher, or bonjour, maître to a lawyer of either sex. Other titles, such as professeur (in the sense of professor), are used much less than their English equivalents in direct address. Where in English one might say Good morning, Professor, in French one would probably say Bonjour, monsieur or Bonjour, madame.

Titles of important positions are used in direct forms of address, preceded by Monsieur le or Madame le or Madame la, as in:

yes, Chair = oui, Monsieur le président
    or (to a woman) oui, Madame la présidente
yes, Minister = oui, Monsieur le ministre
    or (to a woman) oui, Madame le ministre

Note the use of Madame le when the noun in question, like ministre here, or professeur and other titles, has no feminine form, or no acceptable feminine. A woman Member of Parliament is addressed as Madame le député, a woman Senator Madame le sénateur, a woman judge Madame le juge and a woman mayor Madame le maire. Women often prefer the masculine word even when a feminine form does exist, as in Madame l'ambassadeur to a woman ambassador, Madame l'ambassadrice being reserved for the wife of an ambassador.

Speaking about someone
Mr Smith is here = monsieur Smith est là
Mrs Jones phoned = madame Jones a téléphoné
Miss Black has arrived = mademoiselle Black est arrivée
Ms Brown has left = madame Brown or (as appropriate) mademoiselle Brown est partie

(French has no equivalent of Ms.)

When the title accompanies someone's name, the definite article must be used in French:

Dr Blake has arrived = le docteur Blake est arrivé
Professor Jones spoke = le professeur Jones a parlé

This is true of all titles:

Prince Charles = le prince Charles
Princess Marie = la princesse Marie

Note that with royal etc. titles, only Iᵉʳ is spoken as an ordinal number (premier) in French; unlike English, all the others are spoken as cardinal numbers (deux, trois, and so on).

King Richard I = le roi Richard Iᵉʳ (say Richard premier)
Queen Elizabeth II = la reine Elizabeth II (Elizabeth deux)
Pope John XXIII = le pape Jean XXIII (Jean vingt-trois)

---

forget /fə'get/ (p prés **-tt-**; prét **-got**; pp **-gotten**) I vtr **1** (not remember) (**that** que; **to do** de faire; **how** comment): **~ it!** (no way) n'y compte pas!; (drop the subject) laisse tomber!; (think nothing of it) ce n'est rien!; **2** (put aside) oublier; **she'll never let me ~ it** elle n'est pas près de me le faire oublier; **3** LIT, FIG (leave behind) oublier.
II vi oublier.
■ **forget about**: **~ about** [sth/sb] (overlook) oublier.

forgetful /fə'getfl/ adj **1** (absent-minded) distrait; **to become ~** perdre un peu la mémoire; **2** (negligent) **to be ~ of one's duties** négliger ses responsabilités.

forgetfulness /fə'getflnɪs/ n **1** (absent-mindedness) distraction f, perte f de mémoire; **2** (carelessness) étourderie f.

forget-me-not n myosotis m.

forgettable /fə'getəbl/ adj [day, fact, film] peu mémorable; [actor, writer] sans grand intérêt.

forgivable /fə'gɪvəbl/ adj pardonnable.

forgive /fə'gɪv/ vtr (prét **-gave**; pp **-given**) pardonner à [person]; pardonner [act, remark]; annuler [debt]; **to ~ sb sth** pardonner qch à qn; **to ~ sb for doing** pardonner à qn d'avoir fait; **to ~ oneself** se pardonner; **he could be forgiven for believing her** on ne peut pas lui reprocher de l'avoir crue.

forgiveness /fə'gɪvnɪs/ n **1** (for action, crime) pardon m; **to be full of ~** être très indulgent; **2** (of debt) annulation f.

forgiving /fə'gɪvɪŋ/ adj [person] indulgent; [climate] clément.

forgo /fɔː'gəʊ/ vtr (prét **-went**; pp **-gone**) renoncer à.

forgot /fə'gɒt/ prét ▶ **forget**.

forgotten /fə'gɒtn/ pp ▶ **forget**.

fork /fɔːk/ I n **1** (for eating) fourchette f; **2** (tool) fourche f; **3** (in tree, in river, on bicycle) fourche f; (in railway) embranchement m; (in road) bifurcation f; **4** (in chess) fourchette f.
II vtr (all contexts) fourcher.
III vi (also **~ off**) bifurquer.
■ **fork out**° casquer° (**for** pour).
■ **fork over**: **~** [sth] **over**, **~ over** [sth] retourner à la fourche [hay, manure, garden].

forked /fɔːkt/ adj fourchu.

forked lightning n éclair m en zigzag.

fork: ~lift truck n GB (also **forklift** US) chariot m élévateur à fourche; **~ spanner** n clé f plate.

forlorn /fə'lɔːn/ adj **1** (sad) [appearance] malheureux/-euse; [landscape] morne; [sight] triste; **2** (desperate) [attempt] désespéré.

form /fɔːm/ I n **1** (kind, manifestation) (of exercise, transport, government, protest) forme f; (of entertainment, taxation, disease) sorte f; **some ~ of control is needed** un système de contrôle est nécessaire; **in the ~ of** sous forme de; **he won't touch alcohol in any ~** il évite l'alcool sous toutes ses formes; **2** (document) formulaire m; **blank ~** formulaire vierge; **3** (shape) forme f; **4** (of athlete, horse, performer) forme f; **to be in good ~** être en bonne ou pleine forme; **to return to ~** retrouver la forme; **to study the ~** étudier le tableau des performances; **true to ~, she...** fidèle à elle-même, elle...; **5** LITERAT, ART (structure) forme f; (genre) genre m; **~ and content** la forme et le fond; **6** (etiquette) **it is bad ~** cela ne se fait pas (**to do** de faire); **purely as a matter of ~** purement par politesse or pour la forme; **7** GB SCH classe f; **in the first ~** ≈ en sixième; **8** (prescribed set of words) formule f; **I agree with the ~ of words used** je suis d'accord avec la formulation; **9** LING forme *f*; **in question ~** à la forme interrogative.

II *vtr* **1** (organize or create) GEN former (**from** avec); nouer [*friendship, relationship*]; **how are stalactites ~ed?** comment se forment les stalactites?; **to ~ part of** faire partie de; **to ~ the basis of** constituer la base de; **2** (conceive) se faire [*impression, opinion*]; concevoir [*admiration*]; **3** (mould) former; **tastes ~ed by television** des goûts formés par la télévision; **4** (constitute) former [*jury, cabinet, panel*].

III *vi* (all contexts) se former.

■ **form into: ~ into** [sth] [*people*] former [*groups, teams*]; **to ~ sth into** mettre qch en [*paragraphs, circle*]; séparer [qch] en [*groups, teams, classes*].

formal /'fɔːml/ *adj* **1** (official) [*agreement, complaint, interview, invitation, reception*] officiel/-ielle; **2** (not casual) [*language*] soutenu; [*occasion*] solennel/-elle; [*manner*] cérémonieux/-ieuse; [*clothing*] habillé; (on invitation) **'dress: ~'** 'tenue de soirée'; **3** (structured) [*logic, linguistics*] formel/-elle; **4** (in recognized institution) [*training*] professionnel/-elle; [*qualification*] reconnu; **5** LIT-ERAT, ART formel/-elle.

formal: ~ dress *n* GEN tenue *f* de soirée; MIL tenue *f* de cérémonie; **~ garden** *n* jardin *m* à la française.

formalin /'fɔːməlɪn/ *n* formol *m*.

formality /fɔː'mælətɪ/ *n* **1** (legal or social convention) formalité *f*; **2** (formal nature) (of occasion, manner) solennité *f*; (of dress) caractère *m* habillé; (of room) caractère *m* cérémonieux; (of language) caractère *m* soutenu.

formalize /'fɔːməlaɪz/ *vtr* **1** GEN officialiser; **2** COMPUT formaliser.

formally /'fɔːməlɪ/ *adv* **1** (officially) officiellement; **2** (not casually) cérémonieusement.

format /'fɔːmæt/ **I** *n* **1** (general formulation) (of product, publication, passport) format *m*, présentation *f*; (of musical group) formation *f*; **2** (size, style of book or magazine) format *m*; **folio ~** format folio; **3** TV, RADIO formule *f* (**for** pour); **4** COMPUT format *m*; **in tabular ~** sous forme de tableau.

II *vtr* (p prés etc **-tt-**) COMPUT formater.

formation /fɔː'meɪʃn/ *n* **1** (creation) GEN formation *f*; (of relationship) établissement *m*; **2** (shape, arrangement) GEN, MIL, GEOG formation *f*; **a cloud ~** une masse nuageuse.

formative /'fɔːmətɪv/ *adj* **1** GEN formateur/-trice; **2** LING [*element, affix*] de formation.

formatting /'fɔːmætɪŋ/ *n* formatage *m*.

former /'fɔːmə(r)/ **I** *n* **the ~** (the first of two) le premier/la première *m/f*, celui-là/celle-là *m/f*.

II *adj* **1** (earlier) [*era, life*] antérieur; [*size, state*] initial, original; **of ~ days** ou **times** d'autrefois; **he's a shadow of his ~ self** il n'est plus que l'ombre de lui-même; **2** [*leader, husband, champion*] ancien/-ienne (*before n*); **3** (first of two) premier/-ière (*before n*).

III -former *combining form* GB SCH **fourth-~ ~** élève *mf* de troisième.

formerly /'fɔːməlɪ/ *adv* **1** (in earlier times) autrefois; **2** (no longer) anciennement; **~ Miss Martin** née Martin.

formidable /'fɔːmɪdəbl, fɔː'mɪd-/ *adj* **1** (intimidating) redoutable; **2** (awe-inspiring) impressionnant.

formless /'fɔːmlɪs/ *adj* [*mass*] informe; [*novel*] mal construit.

form: ~ of address *n* formule *f* (de politesse); **~ teacher** *n* GB SCH ≈ professeur *m* principal.

formula /'fɔːmjʊlə/ **I** *n* (*pl* **-lae** ou **~s**) **1** formule *f* (**for** doing pour faire); **2** US (for babies) (powder) lait *m* en poudre; (also **~ milk**) lait *m* reconstitué.

II Formula *noun modifier* SPORT **~ One/Two** de formule 1/2.

formulate /'fɔːmjʊleɪt/ *vtr* élaborer [*rules, principles*]; formuler [*idea, design, reply, bill, policy*].

formulation /ˌfɔːmjʊ'leɪʃn/ *n* (of idea, reply, bill) formulation *f*; (of principles, strategy) élaboration *f*.

fornication /ˌfɔːnɪ'keɪʃn/ *n* fornication *f*.

forsake /fə'seɪk/ *vtr* (*prét* **-sook**; *pp* **-saken**) SOUT abandonner.

forswear /fɔː'sweə(r)/ *vtr* (*prét* **-swore**; *pp* **-sworn**) SOUT **1** (renounce) renoncer à; **2** JUR (deny) nier.

fort /fɔːt/ *n* fort *m*.

IDIOMS **to hold** ou US **hold down the ~** s'occuper de tout.

forte /'fɔːteɪ, US fɔːrt/ *n* **1** (strong point) **to be sb's ~** être le fort de qn; **2** MUS forte *m inv*.

forth /fɔːθ/

■ **Note** *forth* often appears in English after a verb (*bring forth, set forth, sally forth*). For translations, consult the appropriate verb entry (**bring, set, sally**).
– For further uses of *forth*, see the entry below.

adv (onwards) **from this day ~** à partir d'aujourd'hui; **from that day ~** à dater de ce jour; ▶ **back, so**.

forthcoming /ˌfɔːθ'kʌmɪŋ/ *adj* **1** (happening soon) prochain (*before n*); **2** (available) (*jamais épith*) disponible; **3** (communicative) affable, ouvert; **to be ~ about sth** être disposé à parler de qch.

forthright /'fɔːθraɪt/ *adj* [*person, manner*] direct; [*reply*] sans détours; **in ~ terms** sans ambiguïté.

forthwith /fɔːθ'wɪθ, US -'wɪð/ *adv* SOUT immédiatement.

fortieth /'fɔːtɪɪθ/ ▶**1112**┃ **I** *n* **1** (in order) quarantième *mf*; **2** (fraction) quarantième *m*.

II *adj, adv* quarantième.

fortification /ˌfɔːtɪfɪ'keɪʃn/ *n* fortification *f* (**of** de).

fortify /'fɔːtɪfaɪ/ *vtr* **1** GEN fortifier (**against** contre); **to ~ oneself** se donner du courage; **2** corser [*wine*]; **fortified wine** vin *m* doux, vin *m* de liqueur.

fortitude /'fɔːtɪtjuːd, US -tuːd/ *n* détermination *f*.

fortnight /'fɔːtnaɪt/ ▶**1336**┃ *n* GB quinze jours *mpl*; **the first ~ in August** la première quinzaine d'août.

fortnightly /'fɔːtnaɪtlɪ/ GB *adj* [*meeting, visit*] qui a lieu toutes les deux semaines; [*magazine*] publié toutes les deux semaines.

Fortran /'fɔːtræn/ COMPUT *n* fortran *m*.

fortress /'fɔːtrɪs/ *n* forteresse *f*.

fortuitous /fɔː'tjuːɪtəs, US -'tuː-/ *adj* SOUT fortuit.

fortunate /'fɔːtʃənət/ *adj* heureux/-euse; **it was ~ for him that** heureusement pour lui que; **to be ~ (enough) to do** avoir la chance ou le bonheur de faire; **those less ~ than ourselves** ceux qui n'ont pas notre chance.

fortunately /'fɔːtʃənətlɪ/ *adv* heureusement.

fortune /'fɔːtʃuːn/ **I** *n* **1** (wealth) fortune *f*; **to make a ~** faire fortune; **to seek fame and ~** chercher fortune; **2** (luck) chance *f*; **to have the good ~ to do** avoir la chance ou le bonheur de faire; **by good ~** par chance; **to tell sb's ~** dire la bonne aventure à qn.

II fortunes *npl* (of team, country) destin *m*.

IDIOMS **~ favours the brave** la fortune sourit aux audacieux.

fortune: ~ cookie *n* US petit gâteau *m* sec (renfermant une prédiction); **~-teller** *n* diseur/-euse *m/f* de bonne aventure.

forty /'fɔːtɪ/ ▶**1112**┃, **713**┃, **812**┃ *n, adj* quarante (*m*) *inv*.

IDIOMS **to have ~ winks** faire un petit somme.

forum /'fɔːrəm/ *n* (*pl* **~s** ou **fora**) forum *m* (**for** de); **in an open ~** en débat ouvert.

forward /'fɔːwəd/ **I** *n* SPORT avant *m*.

II *adj* **1** (bold) effronté; **2** (towards the front) [*roll, gears*] avant *inv*; **~ pass** (in rugby) en-avant *m*; **to be too far ~** [*seat*] être trop en avant; **3** (advanced) [*season, plant*] avancé; **how far ~ are you?** où en êtes-vous?; **4** FIN [*market, price, rate*] à terme.

III *adv* **1** (ahead) **to step ~** faire un pas en avant; **to fall ~** tomber en avant; **to go** ou **walk ~** avancer; **to rush ~** se précipiter; **to move sth ~** LIT, FIG avancer qch; **a seat facing ~** une place dans le sens de la marche; **a way ~** une solution; **2** (towards the future) **to go ~ in time** voyager dans le futur; **from**

this day ~ à partir d'aujourd'hui; **3** AUDIO, VIDEO **to wind sth ~** faire défiler qch en avance rapide. **IV** *vtr* **1** (dispatch) expédier [*goods*]; (*catalogue, parcel*]; **2** (send on) faire suivre, réexpédier [*mail*].

forwarder /'fɔːwədə(r)/ *n* (of freight) transitaire *m*; (of mail) expéditeur *m*.

forwarding /'fɔːwədɪŋ/ *n* COMM transport *m*; (of mail) expédition *f*.

forwarding: **~ address** *n* nouvelle adresse *f* (pour faire suivre le courrier); **~ agent** *n* transitaire *m*; **~ charges** *npl* frais *mpl* d'expédition.

forward-looking *adj* [*company, person*] tourné vers l'avenir.

forwardness /'fɔːwədnɪs/ *n* (of child, behaviour) impertinence *f*.

forward planning *n* planification *f* à long terme.

forwards /'fɔːwədz/ *adv* = **forward** III; ▶**backwards**.

fossil /'fɒsl/ *n* (remains) fossile *m*.

fossil fuel *n* combustible *m* fossile.

fossilized /'fɒsəlaɪzd/ *adj* **1** LIT fossilisé; **2** FIG sclérosé.

foster /'fɒstə(r)/ **I** *adj* adoptif/-ive (*dans une famille de placement*). **II** *vtr* **1** (encourage) encourager [*attitude*]; promouvoir [*activity*]; **2** (cherish) entretenir; **3** (act as parent to) prendre [qn] en placement; **4** (place in care of) **to ~ sb with a family** mettre qn dans une famille.

foster: **~ family** *n* famille *f* de placement; **~ home** *n* foyer *m* de placement.

fought /fɔːt/ *prét, pp* ▶**fight**.

foul /faʊl/ **I** *n* SPORT faute *f* (**by** de; **on** sur). **II** *adj* **1** (putrid) [*conditions*] répugnant; [*smell, air*] fétide; [*water*] putride; [*taste*] infect; **2** (grim) épouvantable; **to be in a ~ mood** être d'une humeur massacrante°; **to have a ~ temper** avoir un sale caractère; **3** (evil) odieux/-ieuse; **4** (offensive) ordurier/-ière; **to have a ~ mouth** être grossier/-ière; **5** (unsporting) déloyal. **III** *adv* **to taste ~** avoir un goût infect. **IV** *vtr* **1** (pollute) polluer [*environment*]; souiller [*pavement*]; **2** (become tangled) **the propeller was ~ed by nets** des filets de pêche étaient emmêlés dans l'hélice; **3** (clog) bloquer [*mechanism*], obstruer [*channel*]; **4** SPORT commettre une faute contre. IDIOMS **to fall ~ of sb** (fall out with) se brouiller avec qn; (lose favour) s'attirer le mécontentement de qn. ◾ **foul up**°: ¶ **~ up** faire des erreurs or des bourdes°; ¶ **~ up** [sth], **~** [sth] **up 1** (bungle) ruiner [*plan*]; abîmer [*system*]; **2** (pollute) polluer.

foully /'faʊlɪ/ *adv* [*treated*] de façon scandaleuse.

foul: **~-mouthed** *adj* PÉJ grossier/-ière; **~ play** *n* (malicious act) acte *m* criminel; SPORT jeu *m* irrégulier; **~-smelling** *adj* puant; **~-tasting** *adj* infect; **~-up**° *n* cafouillage° *m*.

found /faʊnd/ **I** *prét, pp* ▶**find** II, III. **II** *vtr* **1** (establish) fonder [*base*] (**on** sur); **to be ~ed on fact** s'appuyer sur les faits; **3** TECH fondre.

foundation /faʊn'deɪʃn/ *n* **1** (base) (man-made) fondations *fpl*; (natural) base *f*; FIG (of society, belief) fondements *mpl*; **to lay the ~s for** LIT poser les fondations de; FIG jeter les fondements de; **2** FIG (truth) **without ~** sans fondement; **3** (of school, town etc) fondation *f* (**of** de); **4** FIN (trust) fondation *f*.

foundation course *n* GB UNIV année *f* de préparation à des études supérieures.

founder /'faʊndə(r)/ **I** *n* fondateur/-trice *m/f*. **II** *vi* [*ship*] sombrer (**on** sur); [*car, person*] s'embourber (**in** dans); [*marriage*] être en difficultés; [*career, talks*] être compromis (**on** par).

founder member *n* GB membre *m* fondateur.

founding /'faʊndɪŋ/ **I** *n* fondation *f*. **II** *adj* fondateur/-trice.

foundry /'faʊndrɪ/ *n* fonderie *f*.

fount /faʊnt/ *n* **1** LITTÉR source *f*; **2** (in printing) fonte *f*.

fountain /'faʊntɪn, US -tn/ *n* **1** (structure) fontaine *f*; **2** (spray) (of water) jet *m*; (of sparks, light) gerbe *f*.

fountain: **~-head** *n* LIT, FIG source *f*; **~ pen** *n* stylo *m* (à encre).

four /fɔː(r)/ ▶1112 *n, adj* quatre (*m*) *inv*. IDIOMS **on all ~s** à quatre pattes; **to the ~ winds** aux quatre vents.

four: **~-door** *adj* AUT [*model*] quatre portes; **~-engined** *adj* AVIAT quadrimoteur.

four-four time *n* MUS **in ~** à quatre-quatre.

four: **~-leaf clover** *n* trèfle *m* à quatre feuilles; **~-letter word** *n* mot *m* grossier; **~-piece band** *n* (jazz) quartette *m*; (classical) quatuor *m*; **~-poster (bed)** *n* lit *m* à baldaquin; **~some**° *n* quatuor° *m*; **~square** *adj* [*building*] cubique; [*attitude*] loyal.

four-star /'fɔːstɑː(r)/ **I** *n* GB (also **~ petrol**) super(-carburant) *m*. **II** *adj* [*hotel, restaurant*] quatre étoiles.

four-stroke /'fɔːstrəʊk/ *adj* AUT [*engine*] à quatre temps.

fourteen /ˌfɔː'tiːn/ ▶1112 *n, adj* quatorze (*m*) *inv*.

fourteenth /ˌfɔː'tiːnθ/ ▶1112, 854 **I** *n* **1** (in order) quatorzième *mf*; **2** (of month) quatorze *m inv*; **3** (fraction) quatorzième *m*. **II** *adj, adv* quatorzième.

fourth /fɔːθ/ ▶1112, 854 **I** *n* **1** (in order) quatrième *mf*; **2** (of month) quatre *m inv*; **3** (fraction) quatrième *m*; **4** MUS quarte *f*; **5** (also **~ gear**) AUT quatrième *f*. **II** *adj* quatrième. **III** *adv* [*come, finish*] quatrième, en quatrième position.

fourthly /'fɔːθlɪ/ *adv* quatrièmement.

fourth-rate /ˌfɔːθ'reɪt/ *adj* PÉJ [*job, hotel, film*] de seconde zone.

four-wheel drive (vehicle) /'fɔːˌwiːl, US -'hwiːl/ *n* quatre-quatre *m inv*, 4 x 4 *m inv*.

fowl /faʊl/ *n* GEN, CULIN (one bird) poulet *m*; (group) volaille *f*; ▶**fish**.

fox /fɒks/ **I** *n* renard *m*. **II** *vtr* dérouter.

fox: **~ cub** *n* renardeau *m*; **~ fur** *n* (skin) (peau *f* de) renard *m*; (coat) (manteau *m* en) renard *m*; **~glove** *n* digitale *f*; **~hound** *n* fox-hound *m*; **~ hunt**, **~hunting** *n* chasse *f* au renard; **~ terrier** *n* fox-terrier *m*; **~trot** *n* fox-trot *m*.

foxy /'fɒksɪ/ *adj* **1** (crafty) rusé; **2**° (sexy) sexy.

fr FIN *abrév écrite* = **franc**.

Fr RELIG *abrév écrite* = **Father**.

fracas /'fræka:, US 'freɪkəs/ *n* altercation *f*, accrochage *m*.

fraction /'frækʃn/ *n* GEN, MATH (portion) fraction *f* (**of** de); **2** (tiny amount) part *f* infime; **a ~ higher** un tout petit peu plus haut.

fractional /'frækʃənl/ *adj* **1** GEN infime; **2** MATH fractionnaire.

fractionally /'frækʃənəlɪ/ *adv* légèrement.

fracture /'fræktʃə(r)/ **I** *n* GEN, MED fracture *f*. **II** *vtr* fracturer [*bone, rock*]; FIG fissurer [*unity*]. **III** *vi* [*bone*] se fracturer; [*pipe, masonry*] se fissurer.

fragile /'frædʒaɪl, US -dʒl/ *adj* **1** (delicate) fragile; **to feel ~** (ill) se sentir patraque°; (emotionally) être fragile; **2** (tenuous) [*link*] ténu.

fragility /frə'dʒɪlətɪ/ *n* fragilité *f*.

fragment I /'frægmənt/ *n* (of shell, manuscript) fragment *m*; (of glass) morceau *m*; (of food) miette *f*. **II** /fræg'ment/ *vi* [*party, system*] se fragmenter.

fragmentary /'frægməntrɪ, US -terɪ/ *adj* **1** [*evidence, nature*] fragmentaire; **2** GEOG [*material*] détritique.

fragmented /'frægmentɪd/ *adj* [*account*] décousu; [*group*] dispersé; [*job*] morcelé; [*system*] fragmenté.

fragrance /'freɪgrəns/ *n* parfum *m*.

fragrant /'freɪgrənt/ *adj* odorant.

frail /freɪl/ *adj* [*person*] frêle; [*health, hope*] précaire.

frailty /'freɪltɪ/ *n* (of person) fragilité *f*; (of health, state) précarité *f*.

frame /freɪm/ **I** n **1** (of building, boat, roof) charpente f; (of car) châssis m; (of bicycle, racquet) cadre m; (of bed) sommier m; (of tent) armature f; **2** (of picture, window) cadre m; (of door) encadrement m; **3** (context) cadre m; **4** ANAT (skeleton) ossature f; (body) corps m; **5** (picture) CIN photogramme m; TV, PHOT image f; **6** (for weaving) métier m; **7** (in snooker) (triangle) triangle m; (single game) manche f; **8** COMPUT bloc m.
II frames npl (of spectacles) monture f.
III vtr **1** (enclose, surround) LIT, FIG encadrer [picture, face, view]; **2** (formulate in words) formuler; **3** (devise) élaborer [plan, policy]; rédiger [legislation]; **4** (mouth) articuler; **5**○ (set up) [police] monter une machination contre; [criminal] faire porter les soupçons sur.
IV -framed combining form **timber-~d** à charpente de bois.

frame of mind n état m d'esprit; **to be in the wrong ~ for sth** ne pas être d'humeur pour qch.

framer /ˈfreɪmə(r)/ | ▶ 1251 | n encadreur m.

framework /ˈfreɪmwɜːk/ n **1** LIT structure f; **2** FIG (basis) (of society, system) cadre m; (of agreement, theory) base f; (of novel, play) structure f; **legal ~** cadre juridique; **a ~ for sth** un cadre pour qch.

framing /ˈfreɪmɪŋ/ n **1** GEN encadrement m; **2** CIN cadrage m.

franc /fræŋk/ | ▶ 849 | n franc m.

France /frɑːns/ | ▶ 840 | pr n France f.

franchise /ˈfræntʃaɪz/ **I** n **1** POL droit m de vote; **universal ~** suffrage m universel; **2** COMM franchise f.
II noun modifier [business, chain] franchisé; [holder] de franchise.
III vtr US (subcontract) franchiser [product, service].

francophile /ˈfræŋkəʊfaɪl/ n, adj francophile (mf).

francophobe /ˈfræŋkəʊfəʊb/ n, adj francophobe (mf).

francophone /ˈfræŋkəfəʊn/ n, adj francophone (mf).

frank /fræŋk/ **I** adj franc/franche (**about** en ce qui concerne).
II vtr affranchir [letter, parcel]; oblitérer [stamp].

Frankfurt /ˈfræŋkfət/ | ▶ 1343 | pr n Francfort.

frankfurter /ˈfræŋkfɜːtə(r)/ n saucisse f de Francfort.

frankincense /ˈfræŋkɪnsens/ n encens m.

franking machine /ˈfræŋkɪŋ/ n machine f à affranchir.

frankly /ˈfræŋklɪ/ adv franchement.

frankness /ˈfræŋknɪs/ n franchise f.

frantic /ˈfræntɪk/ adj **1** (wild) [activity] frénétique; **2** (desperate) [effort, search] désespéré; [shout] éperdu; [person] surexcité; **to be ~ with** être fou/folle de.

frantically /ˈfræntɪklɪ/ adv **1** (wildly) frénétiquement; **2** (desperately) désespérément.

fraternal /frəˈtɜːnl/ adj fraternel/-elle.

fraternity /frəˈtɜːnətɪ/ n **1** (brotherhood) fraternité f also US Univ; **2** (sharing profession) AUSSI PÉJ confrérie f ALSO PEJ.

fraternize /ˈfrætənaɪz/ vi fraterniser; PÉJ frayer.

fraud /frɔːd/ n fraude f.

Fraud Squad n GB Service m de répression des fraudes.

fraudulence /ˈfrɔːdjʊləns/ US -dʒʊ-/ n **1** = **fraud**; **2** (of signature, figures) caractère m frauduleux.

fraudulent /ˈfrɔːdjʊlənt/ US -dʒʊ-/ adj [system, practice, dealing, use] frauduleux/-euse; [signature, cheque] falsifié; [statement] faux/fausse; [application, claim] indu; [gain, earnings] illicite.

fraught /frɔːt/ adj [situation, atmosphere] tendu; [person] accablé (**with** de); **to be ~ with** être lourd de [danger, difficulty].

fray /freɪ/ **I** n SOUT **the ~** la bataille.
II vi [material, rope] s'effilocher; [nerves] craquer○.

frayed /freɪd/ adj [material] effiloché; [nerves] à bout; **tempers were ~** les gens s'énervaient.

frazzle○ /ˈfræzl/ n **to burn sth to a ~** calciner qch; **to be worn to a ~** être lessivé○.

freak /friːk/ **I** n **1** (deformed person) LIT, FIG INJUR monstre m; **2** (strange person) original/-e m/f; **3** (unusual occurrence) aberration f; **a ~ of nature** une bizarrerie de la nature; **4**○ (enthusiast) mordu/-e○ m/f, fana○ mf.
II adj [accident, storm] exceptionnel/-elle.
■ **freak out**○: **¶ ~ out** (get angry) piquer une crise○ (get excited) se défouler; **¶ ~ [sb] out, ~ out [sb]** (upset) faire paniquer [qn].

freakish /ˈfriːkɪʃ/ adj **1** (monstrous) grotesque; **2** (surprising) exceptionnel/-elle; (unusual) bizarre.

freckle /ˈfrekl/ **I** n tache f de rousseur.
II vi [skin] se couvrir de taches de rousseur.

free /friː/ **I** n (also **~ period**) SCH = heure f de libre.
II adj **1** (unhindered, unrestricted) [person, country, election, press, translation] libre (after n); [access, choice] libre (before n); **to be ~ to do** être libre de faire; **to leave sb ~ to do** laisser qn libre de faire; **to feel ~ to do** ne pas hésiter à faire; **to break ~ of** ou **~ from** se libérer de; **to set sb ~ from** libérer qn de; **to be allowed ~ expression** pouvoir s'exprimer librement; **I oiled the hinges to allow ~ movement** j'ai graissé les gonds pour faciliter le mouvement; **2** (not captive or tied) [person, limb] libre; [animal, bird] en liberté; **one more tug and my shoe was ~** un coup de plus et ma chaussure était dégagée; **to set [sb/sth] ~** libérer [person]; rendre la liberté à [animal]; **to pull sth ~** dégager qch; **they had to cut the driver ~ (from his car)** on a dû couper la tôle de la voiture pour dégager le chauffeur; **to break ~** se libérer (de ses liens); **the boat broke ~ from** ou **of its moorings** le bateau a rompu ses amarres; **3** (devoid) **to be ~ from** ou **of sb** être libéré de qn; **~ from** ou **of pollution** dépourvu de pollution; **a day ~ from** ou **of interruptions** une journée sans interruptions; **she was ~ from** ou **of any hatred** elle n'éprouvait aucune haine; **this soup is ~ from** ou **of artificial colourings** cette soupe ne contient pas de colorants artificiels; **4** (costing nothing) gratuit; **'admission ~'** 'entrée gratuite'; **~ gift** COMM cadeau m; **you can't expect a ~ ride** FIG on n'a rien pour rien; **5** (not occupied) libre; **are you ~ for lunch on Monday?** es-tu libre lundi pour déjeuner?; **is this seat ~?** cette place est-elle libre?; **I'm trying to keep Tuesday ~** j'essaie de garder mon mardi libre; **6** (generous, lavish) **to be ~ with** être généreux/-euse avec [food]; être prodigue de [advice]; **to be very ~ with money** dépenser sans compter; **7** (familiar) familier/-ière; **8** CHEM libre; **9** LING [form] non lié; [vowel, stress] libre.
III adv **1** (at liberty) librement, en toute liberté; **to go ~** [hostage] être libéré; [criminal] circuler en toute liberté; **2** (without payment) gratuitement; **children are admitted ~** l'entrée est gratuite pour les enfants.
IV vtr **1** (from captivity) libérer; (from wreckage) dégager; **to ~ sb from** débarrasser qn de [prejudice]; décharger qn de [blame]; délivrer qn de [oppression, guilt]; soulager qn de [suffering]; **2** (make available) débloquer [money, resources]; libérer [person, hands].
V v refl **to ~ oneself from** se dégager de [chains, wreckage]; se libérer de [influence]; se débarrasser de [burden]; se décharger de [blame]; se délivrer de [guilt].
VI -free combining form **smoke/sugar-~** sans fumée/sucre; **interest-~** FIN sans intérêt.
VII for free adv phr gratuitement.
IDIOMS **to have a ~ hand** avoir carte blanche (**in** pour); **~ as a bird** ou **the air** libre comme l'air.

free agent n **to be a ~** pouvoir agir à sa guise.

free and easy adj GEN décontracté; PÉJ désinvolte.

freebie, freebee○ /ˈfriːbiː/ n (free gift) cadeau m; (newspaper) journal m gratuit; (trip) voyage m gratuit.

free: **~booter** n LIT pilleur m; FIG jouisseur/-euse m/f; **~ climbing** n escalade f libre.

freedom /ˈfriːdəm/ n **1** (liberty) liberté f (**to do** de faire); **~ of information** libre accès m à l'information; **~ of movement** (of person) liberté de mouvement; (of part, screw etc) jeu m; **to give sb his/her ~** rendre sa liberté à qn; **2** (entitlement to use) **they gave us the ~ of their house** ils nous ont laissé le plein usage de leur maison; **to give sb the ~ of a city**

nommer qn citoyen d'honneur d'une ville; **3** ~ **from** (lack of) absence *f* de; (immunity from) immunité *f* contre.

freedom fighter *n* combattant *m* de la liberté.

free: ~ **enterprise** *n* libre entreprise *f*; **~fall** *n* chute *f* libre; **Freefone**®, **Freephone**® *n* ~ numéro *m* vert®; **~-for-all** *n* mêlée *f* générale; **~hand** *adj, adv* à main levée; ~ **hit** *n* coup *m* franc; **~hold** *n* pleine propriété *f*, propriété *f* foncière perpétuelle et libre; **~holder** *n* propriétaire *mf* foncier/-ière à perpétuité; ~ **house** *n* GB pub *m* indépendant; ~ **kick** *n* coup *m* franc.

freelance /'fri:lɑ:ns, US -læns/ **I** *n* (also **freelancer**) free-lance *mf*.
II *adj* [*journalist*] free-lance.
III *adv* [*work*] en free-lance.

freeloader○ *n* parasite *m*.

freely /'fri:lɪ/ *adv* **1** (without restriction) GEN librement; [*breathe*] LIT aisément; FIG librement; (abundantly) [*spend, give*] sans compter; [*perspire*] abondamment; **to move** ~ [*part of body*] bouger aisément; [*person*] (around building, country) se déplacer librement; **to be** ~ **available** (easy to find) se trouver facilement, (accessible) être ouvert à tous; **2** (willingly) volontiers; **3** [*translate, adapt*] librement.

free: **~man of the city** *n* citoyen *m* d'honneur d'une ville; ~ **market** *n* (also ~ **economy**) économie *f* de marché; ~ **marketeer** *n* libéral/-e *m/f*, partisan *m* de l'économie de marché; **Freemason** *n* franc-maçon/-onne *m/f*; ~ **of charge** *adj* gratuit; ~ **on board**, **FOB** *adj, adv* GB franco à bord, FAB; US franco à destination; ~ **period** *n* ~ heure *f* de libre; **Freephone**® *n, adj* = **Freefone**; ~ **port** *n* port *m* franc; **~post** *n* GB (also on envelope) port *m* payé; **~-range** *adj* élevé en plein air; ~ **school** *n* école *f* privée spécialisée; ~ **speech** *n* liberté *f* d'expression.

free spirit *n* **to be a** ~ aimer sa liberté.

free: **~-standing** *adj* [*lamp, statue, heater*] sur pied; [*cooker, bath*] nonencastré; **~style** *n* (in swimming) nage *f* libre; (in skiing) figures *fpl* libres; (in wrestling) lutte *f* libre; **~thinker** *n* libre penseur/-euse *m/f*; ~ **throw** *n* (in basketball) lancer *m* franc; ~ **trade** *n* libre-échange *m*; ~ **trader** *n* partisan *m* du libre-échange; ~ **verse** *n* vers *m* libre; ~ **vote** *n* ~ vote *m* de conscience; **~way** *n* US autoroute *f*; **~wheel** *vi* LIT être ou rouler en roue libre; **~wheeling** *adj* [*person*] insouciant; [*attitude*] libre.

free will *n* libre arbitre *m*; **to do sth of one's (own)** ~ faire qch de son plein gré ou de son propre chef.

freeze /fri:z/ **I** *n* **1** METEOROL gelées *fpl*; **2** ECON, FIN (of credits, assets) gel *m* (**on** de); (of prices, wages) gel *m*, blocage *m*.
II *vtr* (*prét* **froze**; *pp* **frozen**) **1** congeler [*food*]; [*cold weather*] geler [*liquid, pipes*]; **2** ECON, FIN bloquer, geler; **3** CIN arrêter; **4** (anaesthetize) insensibiliser; **5** COMPUT figer.
III *vi* (*prét* **froze**; *pp* **frozen**) **1** (become solid) [*water, pipes*] geler; [*food*] se congeler; **2** (feel cold) geler; **to be freezing to death** mourir de froid; **3** (become motionless) se figer (**with** de); **~!** pas un geste!; **4** (become haughty) devenir glacial.
IV *v impers* METEOROL geler.
■ **freeze out**: ~ **[sb/sth] out**, ~ **out [sb/sth]** GEN tourner le dos à [*person*]; COMM supplanter [*competitor*]; éliminer [qch] du marché [*goods*].
■ **freeze over** [*lake*] geler; [*window*] se couvrir de givre.

freeze: **~-dried** *adj* lyophilisé; ~ **frame** *n* VIDEO arrêt *m* sur image.

freezer /'fri:zə(r)/ *n* congélateur *m*.

freezer compartment *n* freezer *m*.

freezing /'fri:zɪŋ/ **I** *n* **1** METEOROL below ~ en-dessous de zéro; **2** FIN, GEN gel *m*; (of prices) gel *m*, blocage *m*.
II *adj* [*room, weather*] glacial; **I'm** ~ je suis gelé; **it's** ~ **in here** on gèle ici.

freezing: ~ **cold** *adj* [*room, wind*] glacial; [*water*] glacé; ~ **fog** *n* brouillard *m* givrant; ~ **point** *n* point *m* de congélation.

freight /freɪt/ **I** *n* **1** (goods) fret *m*, marchandises *fpl*; **2** (transport system) transport *m*; **3** (cost) (frais *mpl* de) port *m*.
II *noun modifier* [*company, route, service*] de transport; [*transport, car, wagon, train, yard*] de marchandises.

freight: ~ **charges** *npl* frais *mpl* de transport; ~ **collect** *adv* US contre paiement à la livraison, port dû.

freighter /'freɪtə(r)/ *n* **1** NAUT cargo *m*; **2** AVIAT avion-cargo *m*.

freight: ~ **forward** *adv* GB contre paiement à la livraison, port dû; ~ **note** *n* lettre *f* de voiture; ~ **operator** ▶ 1251 *n* transporteur *m*; ~ **terminal** *n* aérogare *f* de fret.

French /frentʃ/ ▶ 1100, 1038 **I** *n* **1** (language) français *m*; **2** (people) **the** ~ les Français *mpl*.
II *adj* français.
IDIOMS **to take** ~ **leave** filer à l'anglaise; **pardon my** ~ HUM si vous me passez l'expression.

French bean *n* haricot *m* vert.

French Canadian ▶ 1100, 1038 **I** *n* **1** (person) Canadien/-ienne *m/f* francophone; **2** (language) français *m* du Canada.
II *adj* [*person*] canadien/-ienne *m/f* francophone; [*accent*] franco-canadien/-ienne; [*town, custom*] du Canada francophone.

French: ~ **chalk** *n* craie *f* de tailleur; ~ **doors** *npl* US porte-fenêtre *f*; ~ **dressing** *n* GB vinaigrette *f*; US sauce *f* mayonnaise; ~ **fried potatoes** *npl* pommes *fpl* frites; ~ **fries** *npl* frites *fpl*; ~ **horn** ▶ 1097 *n* cor *m* (d'harmonie); ~ **horn player** ▶ 1251 *n* corniste *mf*.

Frenchify /'frentʃɪfaɪ/ *vtr* PÉJ OU HUM franciser.

French: ~ **kiss**○ *n* patin○ *m*; ~ **knickers** *npl* culotte *f* flottante; ~ **loaf** *n* baguette *f*; **~man** *n* Français *m*; ~ **mustard** *n* moutarde *f* douce.

French pleat *n* **1** (in sewing) pli *m* plat; **2** (hairstyle) (roll) chignon *m* banane; (pleat) natte *f* africaine.

French: ~ **polish** *n* vernis *m* à l'alcool; ~ **Riviera** *n* Côte *f* d'Azur; ~ **seam** *n* couture *f* anglaise; **~-speaking** *adj* francophone; ~ **stick** *n* baguette *f*; ~ **toast** *n* pain *m* perdu; ~ **window** *n* porte-fenêtre *f*; **~woman** *n* Française *f*.

frenetic /frə'netɪk/ *adj* [*activity*] frénétique; [*lifestyle*] trépidant.

frenzied /'frenzɪd/ *adj* [*activity*] frénétique; [*passion*] déchaîné; [*attempt*] désespéré; [*mob*] (happy) en délire; (angry) déchaîné.

frenzy /'frenzɪ/ *n* frénésie *f*, délire *m*; **to be in a state of** ~ être exalté; **to drive [sb/sth] into a** ~ exciter [*crowd*]; rendre [qn] fou/folle [*person*]; **there was a** ~ **of activity** ça grouillait d'activité.

frequency /'fri:kwənsɪ/ *n* fréquence *f* (**of** de); **to occur with increasing** ~ être de plus en plus fréquent.

frequency: ~ **band** *n* bande *f* de fréquence; ~ **modulation** *n* modulation *f* de fréquence.

frequent I /'fri:kwənt/ *adj* **1** (common, usual) [*expression, use*] courant; **2** (happening often) fréquent; **to make** ~ **use of sth** se servir souvent ou fréquemment de qch; **to be in** ~ **contact with sb** être en contact régulier avec qn.
II /frɪ'kwent/ *vtr* fréquenter.

frequently /'fri:kwəntlɪ/ *adv* souvent, fréquemment.

fresco /'freskəʊ/ *n* (*pl* **-oes**) fresque *f*.

fresh /freʃ/ *adj* **1** (not old) [*foodstuff*] frais/fraîche; **to look** ~ avoir l'air frais; **to feel** ~ être frais au toucher; **to taste/smell** ~ avoir un goût frais/une odeur fraîche; **bread** ~ **from the oven** du pain frais sorti du four; **2** CULIN [*herbs, pasta, coffee*] frais/fraîche; ~ **orange juice** jus d'orange pressée; **3** (renewed, other) GEN nouveau/-elle (*before n*); [*linen*] propre; [*ammunition*] supplémentaire; **to take a** ~ **look at sth** regarder qch d'un œil neuf; **to make a** ~ **start** prendre un nouveau départ; **4** (recent) [*fingerprint, blood*] frais/fraîche; **while it is still** ~ **in your mind** tant que tu l'as tout frais à l'esprit; **5** (recently returned)

~ from ou **out of school** à peine sorti de l'école; **to be ~ from a trip abroad** être tout frais débarqué d'un voyage à l'étranger; **6** (refreshing, original) (tout) nouveau/(toute) nouvelle (*before n*); **7** (energetic, alert) **to feel** ou **be ~** être plein d'entrain; **8** (cool, refreshing) frais/fraîche; **9**° US (over-familiar) impertinent; **to be ~ with sb** être un peu familier/-ière avec qn; **10** METEOROL **a ~ breeze** une bonne brise.

IDIOMS **to be ~ out of**° être en panne de° [*supplies*].

fresh air *n* air *m* frais; **to get some ~** prendre l'air, s'oxygéner.

freshen /'freʃn/ *v*: ■ **freshen up** faire un brin de toilette.

fresh-faced /ˌfreʃ'feɪst/ *adj* au teint frais.

freshly /'freʃlɪ/ *adv* fraîchement; **~ ironed/washed** qui vient d'être repassé/lavé.

freshman /'freʃmən/ *n* **1** (also **fresher**° GB) UNIV étudiant/-e *m/f* de première année; **2** US FIG (in Congress, in firm) nouveau venu/nouvelle venue *m/f*.

freshness /'freʃnɪs/ *n* (all contexts) fraîcheur *f*.

fresh water *n* eau *f* douce.

fret /fret/ **I** *n* MUS frette *f*, touche *f*.
II *vtr* (*p prés etc* **-tt-**) chantourner [*wood, screen*].
III *vi* (*p prés etc* **-tt-**) **1** (be anxious) s'inquiéter (**over, about** pour, au sujet de); **2** [*child*] pleurer, pleurnicher.

fretful /'fretfl/ *adj* [*child*] grognon; [*adult*] énervé, agité.

fretfully /'fretfəlɪ/ *adv* [*speak*] avec énervement; **to cry ~** pleurnicher.

fret: **~saw** *n* scie *f* à découper; **~work** *n* découpure *f*.

Freudian /'frɔɪdɪən/ *n, adj* freudien/-ienne *m/f*.

Freudian slip *n* lapsus *m*.

Fri *abrév écrite* = **Friday**.

friar /'fraɪə(r)/ *n* frère *m*, moine *m*.

friction /'frɪkʃn/ *n* **1** LING, PHYS friction *f*; **2** GEN (rubbing) frottement *m*; **3** ¢ FIG (conflict) conflits *mpl* (**between** entre); **to cause ~** être cause de friction.

Friday /'fraɪdɪ/ **▶ 1390** *n* vendredi *m*.

fridge /frɪdʒ/ *n* GB frigo° *m*, réfrigérateur *m*.

fried /fraɪd/ *pp* ▶ **fry** II, III.

friend /frend/ *n* **1** (person one likes) ami/-e *m/f* (**of** de); **to make ~s** se faire des amis; **to be/make ~s with sb** être/devenir ami/-e *m/f* avec qn; **to be a good ~ to sb** GEN être un véritable ami; (in crisis) être un soutien pour qn; **Maura is a ~ of mine** Maura est une amie; **that's what ~s are for** c'est à ça que servent les amis; **2** FIG (supporter, fellow-member, ally) ami/-e *m/f*; **to have ~s in high places** avoir des amis influents; **3** FIG (familiar object) ami *m*.

IDIOMS **a ~ in need is a ~ indeed** PROV c'est dans le besoin que l'on connaît ses vrais amis PROV.

friendless /'frendlɪs/ *adj* sans amis.

friendliness /'frendlɪnɪs/ *n* gentillesse *f* (**of** de).

friendly /'frendlɪ/ **I** *n* SPORT match *m* amical.
II *adj* [*person*] amical, sympathique; [*animal*] affectueux/-euse; [*attitude, argument, match*] amical; [*smile*] (polite) aimable; (warm) amical; [*government, nation*] ami *inv* (*after n*); [*shop*] accueillant; [*agreement*] à l'amiable; **to be ~ with sb** être ami/-e *m/f* avec qn; **to get** ou **become ~ with sb** se lier d'amitié avec qn; **to be on ~ terms with sb** être en bons termes avec qn; **to be ~ to** être réceptif/-ive à [*new ideas*]; être bien disposé envers [*small firms, local groups*]; **to have a ~ relationship with sb** avoir de bonnes relations avec qn; **the people round here are very ~** les gens par ici sont très gentils; **he's very ~ with the boss** il est très copain° avec le patron.
III **-friendly** *combining form* **environment-~** qui ne nuit pas à l'environnement; **user-~** d'utilisation facile, convivial.

friendly: **~ fire** *n* MIL EUPH feu *m* allié; **Friendly Islands ▶ 1022** *pr n* Tonga *m*, îles *fpl* des Amis; **~ society** *n* GB mutuelle *f*.

friendship /'frendʃɪp/ *n* amitié *f*; **to form ~s** se faire des amis.

Friends of the Earth, **FoE** *n* Amis *mpl* de la Terre.

fries° /fraɪz/ *npl* US frites *fpl*.

frieze /friːz/ *n* frise *f*.

frigate /'frɪgɪt/ *n* frégate *f*.

fright /fraɪt/ *n* **1** (feeling of terror) peur *f*; (more sudden) frayeur *f*, effroi *m*; **to take ~** prendre peur, s'effrayer; **2** (shock) frayeur *f*, peur *f*; **to have** ou **get a ~** avoir peur; **to give sb a ~** faire peur à qn, effrayer qn; **I had the ~ of my life!** j'ai cru mourir de peur!; **3**° (person) épouvantail *m*, horreur *f*.

frighten /'fraɪtn/ *vtr* faire peur à, effrayer; **to ~ sb into doing** faire tellement peur à qn qu'il/elle finit par faire.
■ **frighten off**: **~ off** [sb], **~** [sb] **off** chasser [*intruder*]; effaroucher [*rival, buyer, bidder*].

frightened /'fraɪtnd/ *adj* apeuré; **to be ~** avoir peur (**of** de; **to do** de faire); **to be ~ that** craindre que (+ *subj*), avoir peur que (+ *subj*); **to be too ~ even to look** avoir tellement peur qu'on n'ose même pas regarder.

frightening /'fraɪtnɪŋ/ *adj* **1** LIT (scary) [*story, experience*] terrifiant; [*statistics*] effarant; **2** FIG (alarming, disturbing) effrayant.

frighteningly /'fraɪtnɪŋlɪ/ *adv* terriblement.

frightful /'fraɪtfl/ *adj* **1** (inducing horror) abominable, épouvantable; **2**° (terrible, bad) [*prospect, mistake*] terrible; [*possibility*] horrible; [*headache*] affreux/-euse; **3**° (expressing disgust) [*person*] épouvantable; [*decor*] affreux/-euse.

frightfully /'fraɪtfəlɪ/ *adv* GB terriblement; **I'm ~ sorry** je suis vraiment désolé.

frigid /'frɪdʒɪd/ *adj* **1** MED [*woman*] frigide; **2** GEOG [*zone*] glacial.

frigidity /frɪ'dʒɪdɪtɪ/ *n* **1** MED frigidité *f*; **2** FIG froideur *f*.

frill /frɪl/ **I** *n* (on dress) volant *m*; (on shirt) jabot *m*; CULIN papillotte *f*.
II **frills** *npl* **1** (on clothes, furniture) fanfreluches *fpl*; **2** (on car, appliance) options *fpl*; **3** (in writing, drawing) fioritures *fpl*.

frilled /frɪld/ *adj* [*garment, collar*] à volants.

frilly /'frɪlɪ/ *adj* [*garment*] à froufrous; [*underwear*] avec des dentelles.

fringe /frɪndʒ/ **I** *n* **1** GB (of hair) frange *f*; **2** (decorative trim) frange *f*; **3** (edge) (of forest) lisière *f*, orée *f*; (of town) abords *mpl*, périphérie *f*; **to be on the ~ of the crowd** être au bord de la foule; **4** POL (group) frange *f*, élément *m*; **5** THEAT **the ~** théâtre *m* alternatif.
II **fringes** *npl* **on the (outer) ~s of the town** à la périphérie ou aux abords de la ville; **on the ~s of society** en marge de la société.

fringe benefits *npl* **1** (pensions, life or medical cover) avantages *mpl* sociaux; **2** (of job) avantages *mpl* en nature.

fringed /frɪndʒd/ *adj* **1** [*garment*] à franges; **2** (edged) bordé (**with, by** de).

frippery /'frɪpərɪ/ *n* **1** ¢ (trivia) frivolités *fpl*; **2** (item) frivolité *f*.

Frisian /'frɪzɪən/ **▶ 1100**, **1038** *n* **1** (person) Frison/-onne *m/f*; **2** (language) frison *m*.

frisk /frɪsk/ **I** *vtr* fouiller [*person*].
II *vi* [*lamb, puppy*] gambader.

frisky /'frɪskɪ/ *adj* [*puppy*] joueur/-euse; [*horse*] nerveux/-euse, chaud.

fritter /'frɪtə(r)/ *n* beignet *m*.
■ **fritter away**: **~ away** [sth], **~** [sth] **away** gaspiller.

fritz /frɪts/: **on the fritz** *adj phr* US en panne.

frivolity /frɪ'vɒlətɪ/ *n* (all contexts) frivolité *f*.

frivolous /'frɪvələs/ *adj* **1** [*person, attitude*] frivole; **2** PÉJ [*allegation, enquiry*] pas sérieux/-ieuse.

frizz /frɪz/ *vtr* friser [*hair*].

frizzle /'frɪzl/ *vtr, vi* grésiller.

frizzy /'frɪzɪ/ *adj* [*hair*] crépu.

frock /frɒk/ ▶ 1260] *n* **1** (dress) robe *f*; **2** (of monk) bure *f*.

frog /frɒg, US frɔːg/ *n* ZOOL grenouille *f*.
IDIOMS **to have a ~ in one's throat** avoir un chat dans la gorge.

frog: **~-man** *n* homme-grenouille *m*; **~-march** *vtr* GB conduire [qn] de force; **~s' legs** *npl* cuisses *fpl* de grenouille; **~-spawn** *n* ¢ œufs *mpl* de grenouille.

frolic /'frɒlɪk/ **I** *n* **1** (fun) ébats *mpl*; **2** (film) comédie *f*; (play) farce *f*.
II *vi* LIT s'ébattre, gambader; FIG faire la fête.

from /frəm, frɒm/

■ Note When *from* is used as a straightforward preposition in English it is translated by *de* in French: *from Rome* = de Rome; *from the sea* = de la mer; *from Lisa* = de Lisa. Remember that *de* + *le* always becomes *du*: *from the office* = du bureau, and *de* + *les* always becomes *des*: *from the United States* = des États-Unis.
– *from* is often used after verbs in English (*suffer from, benefit from* etc). For translations, consult the appropriate verb entry (**suffer**, **benefit** etc).
– *from* is used after certain nouns and adjectives in English (*shelter from, exemption from, free from, safe from* etc). For translations, consult the appropriate noun or adjective entry (**shelter**, **exemption**, **free**, **safe** etc).
– This dictionary contains Usage Notes on such topics as nationalities, countries and continents, provinces and regions. Many of these use the preposition *from*. For the index to these Notes ▶ 1419].
– For examples of the above and particular usages of *from*, see the entry below.

prep **1** (indicating place of origin) **paper ~ Denmark** du papier provenant du Danemark; **a flight ~ Nice** un vol en provenance de Nice; **a friend ~ Chicago** un ami (qui vient) de Chicago; **a colleague ~ Japan** un collègue japonais; **people ~ Spain** les Espagnols; **where is he ~?** d'où est-il?, d'où vient-il?; **she comes ~ Oxford** elle vient d'Oxford; **a tunnel ~ X to Y** un tunnel qui relie X à Y; **the road ~ A to B** la route qui va de A à B; **noises ~ upstairs** du bruit venant d'en-haut; **to take sth ~ one's bag** prendre qch de son sac; **to take sth ~ the shelf** prendre qch sur l'étagère; **~ under the table** de dessous la table; **2** (expressing distance) **10 km ~ the sea** à 10 km de la mer; **it's not far ~ here** ce n'est pas loin d'ici; **the journey ~ A to B** le voyage de A à B; **3** (expressing time span) **open ~ 2 pm until 5 pm** ouvert de 14 à 17 heures; **~ June to August** du mois de juin au mois d'août; **15 years ~ now** dans 15 ans; **one month ~ now** dans un mois, d'ici un mois; **~ today** à partir d'aujourd'hui; **deaf ~ birth** sourd de naissance; **~ the age of 8** depuis l'âge de 8 ans; **~ day to day** de jour en jour; **4** (using as a basis) **a short story by Maupassant** d'après un conte de Maupassant; **to speak ~ experience** parler d'expérience; **5** (working for) **a man ~ the council** un homme qui travaille pour le conseil municipal; **a representative ~ Grunard and Co** un représentant de chez Grunard et Cie; **6** (among) **to select** ou **choose** ou **pick ~** choisir parmi; **7** (indicating a source) **a card ~ Pauline** une carte de Pauline; **a letter ~ them** une lettre de leur part; **where did it come ~?** d'où est-ce que ça vient?; **a quote ~ sb** une citation de qn; **8** (expressing extent, range) **wine ~ £5 a bottle** du vin à partir de 5 livres la bouteille; **children ~ the ages of 12 to 15** les enfants de 12 à 15 ans; **to rise ~ 10 to 17%** passer de 10 à 17%; **everything ~ paperclips to wigs** tout, des trombones aux perruques; **~ start to finish** du début à la fin; **9** (in subtraction) **10 ~ 27 leaves 17** 27 moins 10 égale 17; **10** (because of, due to) **I know ~ speaking to her that** j'ai appris en lui parlant que; **he knows her ~ work** il la connaît car ils travaillent ensemble; **11** (judging by) d'après; **the way he talks you'd think he was an expert** à l'entendre, on dirait un spécialiste.

frond /frɒnd/ *n* (of fern) fronde *f*; (of palm) feuille *f*.

front /frʌnt/ **I** *n* **1** (of house) façade *f*; (of shop) devanture *f*; (of cupboard, box) devant *m*; (of sweater) devant *m*; (of book) couverture *f*; (of card, coin, banknote) recto *m*; (of car, boat) avant *m*; (of fabric) endroit *m*; **to button at the ~** se boutonner sur le devant; **on the ~ of the envelope** au recto de l'enveloppe; **2** (of train, queue) tête *f*; (of building) devant *m*; (of auditorium) premier rang *m*; **at the ~ of the line** en tête de la file; **at the ~ of the house** sur le devant de la maison; **to sit at the ~ of the class** s'asseoir au premier rang de la classe; **I'll sit in the ~** je vais m'asseoir devant; **at the ~ of the coach** à l'avant du car; **3** MIL, POL front *m*; **4** (stomach) ventre *m*; **to spill sth down one's ~** se renverser qch sur le devant; **5** GB (promenade) front *m* de mer, bord *m* de mer; **on the sea ~** au bord de la mer; **6** METEOROL front *m*; **7** (area of activity) côté *m*; **changes on the domestic** ou **home ~** POL des changements côté politique intérieure; **8** FIG (outer appearance) façade *f*; **9**° (cover) couverture *f*.
II *adj* (*épith*) **1** (facing street) [*entrance*] côté rue; [*garden, window*] de devant; [*bedroom*] qui donne sur la rue; **2** (furthest from rear) [*wheel*] avant (*after n*); [*seat*] (in cinema) au premier rang; (in vehicle) de devant; [*leg, paw, tooth*] de devant; [*carriage*] de tête (*after n*); **3** (first) [*page*] premier/-ière (*before n*); [*racing car*] de tête; **4** (head-on) [*view*] de face (*after n*).
III in front *adv phr* **who's in ~?** qui gagne?; **I'm 30 points in ~** j'ai 30 points d'avance.
IV in front of *prep phr* (all contexts) devant.
V *vtr* **1** = **VI 1**; **2**° (lead) être à la tête de [*band*]; **3** TV présenter.
VI *vi* **1** (face) **to ~ onto** GB ou US donner sur; **2** (serve as a cover) **to ~ for** servir de couverture à.

frontage /'frʌntɪdʒ/ *n* **1** ARCHIT (of house) façade *f*; (of shop) devanture *f*; **2** (access) **with ocean/river ~** avec accès direct sur la mer/rivière.

frontal /'frʌntl/ *adj* **1** (head-on) [*assault*] de front (*after n*); **2** ANAT frontal; **3** METEOROL frontal; **4** CIN, PHOT [*lighting*] de face.

front bench /ˌfrʌnt 'bentʃ/ *n* GB POL ¢ **1** (seats) rangs *mpl* du gouvernement; **2** (also **frontbench·ers**°) députés *mpl* membres du gouvernement.

front: **~ cover** *n* couverture *f*; **~ door** *n* porte *f* d'entrée.

frontier /'frʌntɪə(r), US frʌn'tɪər/ **I** *n* LIT, FIG frontière *f*; **the ~ between France and Spain** la frontière franco-espagnole.
II *noun modifier* [*town, zone*] frontière *inv* (*after n*), frontalier/-ière.

frontier: **~ post** *n* poste *m* frontière; **~sman** *n* homme *m* de la frontière.

front line /'frʌntlaɪn/ **I** *n* **1** MIL front *m*; **2** FIG (exposed position) **to be in** GB ou **on** US **the ~** être en première ligne; **3** (in rugby) **the ~** les avants *mpl* première ligne.
II front-line *noun modifier* **1** MIL [*troops*] de front; [*positions*] de première ligne; **2** POL [*state*] frontalier/-ière avec un État en guerre.

frontman /'frʌntmən/ *n* **1** (figurehead) homme *m* de paille (**for** de); **2** (TV presenter) présentateur *m*; **3** (lead musician) leader *m*.

front: **~ matter** *n* ¢ pages *fpl* liminaires; **~ of house** *n* GB THEAT foyer *m*.

front page **I** *n* (of newspaper, book) première page *f*.
II front-page *noun modifier* [*picture, story*] à la une°; **the ~ headlines** les gros titres, la manchette.

front-runner /ˌfrʌnt'rʌnə(r)/ *n* **1** POL, GEN (favourite) favori/-ite *m/f* (**in** de); **2** SPORT *coureur qui aime se positionner en tête de course.*

front-wheel drive *n* traction *f* avant.

frost /frɒst/ *n* **1** (weather condition) gel *m*; **10° of ~** moins 10°, 10° au-dessous de zéro; **there may be ~ tonight** il pourrait geler cette nuit; **2** (one instance) gelée *f*; **3** (icy coating) givre *m* (**on** sur).
■ **frost over**, **frost up** se couvrir de givre.

frost: **~bite** *n* ¢ gelures *fpl*; **~bitten** *adj* gelé.

frosted /'frɒstɪd/ *adj* **1** [*nail varnish*] nacré; **2** [*cake*] recouvert de glaçage; **3** (opaque) [*glass*] dépoli, opaque; **4** (chilled) [*drinking glass*] givré.

frosting /'frɒstɪŋ/ *n* glaçage *m*.

frost-resistant /'frɒstrɪzɪstənt/ *adj* [*vegetable*] résistant au gel.

frosty /'frɒstɪ/ *adj* **1** [*morning*] glacial; [*windscreen*] couvert de givre; **it was a ~ night** il gelait cette nuit-là; **2** FIG [*reception*] glacial.

froth /frɒθ, US frɔ:θ/ **I** *n* **1** (on beer, champagne) mousse *f*; (on water) écume *f*; (around mouth) écume *f*; **2** ¢ (trivia) futilités *fpl*.
II *vi* écumer; **to ~ at the mouth** LIT écumer; FIG écumer de rage.

frothy /'frɒθɪ, US 'frɔ:θɪ/ *adj* **1** (foamy) [*beer, coffee, liquid*] mousseux/-euse; [*surface of sea*] écumeux/-euse; **2** (lacy) [*lingerie*] vaporeux/-euse.

frown /fraʊn/ *n* froncement *m* de sourcils.
II *vi* froncer les sourcils; **to ~ at sb** regarder qn en fronçant les sourcils.
■ **frown on, frown upon**: ~ **on** ou **upon** [*sth*] désapprouver, critiquer; **to be ~ed upon** être mal vu.

froze /frəʊz/ *prét* ▶ **freeze** II, III.

frozen /'frəʊzn/ **I** *pp* ▶ **freeze** II, III.
II *adj* **1** LIT gelé; **I'm ~** je suis gelé; **to be ~ stiff** être transi de froid; **2** FIG **to be ~ with fear** être paralysé par la peur; **to be ~ to the spot** être cloué sur place; **3** CULIN (bought) surgelé; (home-prepared) congelé; **4** FIN, ECON [*prices, assets*] bloqué, gelé.

fructify /'frʌktɪfaɪ/ *vi* fructifier.

frugal /'fru:gl/ *adj* [*person*] économe (**with** de); [*lifestyle, meal*] frugal.

frugally /'fru:gəlɪ/ *adv* [*live*] frugalement; [*stock*] avec parcimonie.

fruit /fru:t/ **I** *n* (*pl inv for collective sense*) **1** BOT (edible, inedible) fruit *m*; **a piece of ~** un fruit; **have some ~** prenez un fruit ou des fruits; **to bear ~** donner des fruits; **2** FIG fruit *m*; **to enjoy the ~(s) of one's labours** jouir des fruits de son travail.
II *vi* donner des fruits.

fruit: **~ bowl** *n* (large) coupe *f* à fruits; (individual) coupelle *f* à fruits; **~ cake** *n* CULIN cake *m*; **~ cocktail** *n* macédoine *f* de fruits; **~ drop** *n* bonbon *m* (aromatisé) aux fruits; **~ farmer** ▶ 1251 *n* producteur/-trice *m/f* de fruits; **~ farming** *n* culture *f* fruitière; **~ fly** *n* mouche *f* du vinaigre.

fruitful /'fru:tfl/ *adj* **1** [*discussion*] fructueux/-euse; [*source*] fertile; **2** LITTÉR fertile, fécond.

fruitfully /'fru:tfəlɪ/ *adv* [*teach*] avec succès; [*spend time*] de façon fructueuse.

fruitfulness /'fru:tflnɪs/ *n* **1** LITTÉR fécondité *f*; **2** (of approach) utilité *f*.

fruit gum *n* ~ pastille *f*, bonbon *m* aux fruits.

fruition /fru:'ɪʃn/ *n* **to come to ~** se réaliser; **to bring sth to ~** (effect) réaliser qch; (conclude) concrétiser qch.

fruitless /'fru:tlɪs/ *adj* [*attempt*] vain; [*discussion*] stérile.

fruit: **~ machine** *n* machine *f* à sous; **~ salad** *n* salade *f* de fruits; **~s of the forest** *npl* fruits *mpl* de la forêt; **~ tree** *n* arbre *m* fruitier.

fruity /'fru:tɪ/ *adj* **1** [*wine, fragrance*] fruité; **2** [*voice, tone*] timbré; **3** [*joke*] salé.

frump /frʌmp/ *n* PÉJ femme *f* mal fagotée.

frustrate /frʌ'streɪt, US 'frʌstreɪt/ *vtr* **1** (irk, annoy) énerver [*person*]; **2** (thwart) réduire [qch] à néant [*effort*]; contrarier [*plan*]; entraver [*attempt*].

frustrated /frʌ'streɪtɪd, US 'frʌst-/ *adj* **1** (irritated) énervé; **he became ~ at people's ignorance** l'ignorance des gens l'énervait; **2** (in aspirations) [*person*] frustré; [*desire*] inassouvi; **3** (thwarted) [*plan*] contrarié; [*effort*] réduit à néant; [*attempt*] vain (*before n*); **4** (would-be) **a ~ diplomat** un diplomate manqué; **5** (sexually) frustré.

frustrating /frʌ'streɪtɪŋ, US 'frʌst-/ *adj* **1** (irritating) énervant; **there's nothing more ~!** il n'y a rien de plus énervant!; **2** (unsatisfactory, thwarting) frustrant.

frustratingly /frʌ'streɪtɪŋlɪ, US 'frʌst-/ *adv* désespérément.

frustration /frʌ'streɪʃn/ *n* **1** (thwarted feeling) frustration *f* (**at, with** quant à); **to feel anger and ~** se sentir en colère et frustré; **in ~, he...** frustré, il...; **2** (annoying aspect) **the ~s of house-buying are endless** acheter une maison est une entreprise longue et frustrante; **3** (ruination) anéantissement *m*; **4** (sexual) frustration *f*.

fry /fraɪ/ **I** *n* **1** ZOOL fretin *m*; **2** FIG **small ~** (children) petits *mpl*, mioches○ *mpl*; (unimportant people) menu fretin *m*.
II *vtr* (*prét, pp* **fried**) CULIN faire frire.
III *vi* (*prét, pp* **fried**) CULIN frire.
IV fried *pp adj* frit; **fried fish** poisson *m* frit; **fried food** friture *f*; **fried eggs** œufs *mpl* au plat; **fried potatoes** pommes *fpl* de terre sautées.

frying pan GB *n* poêle *f* (à frire).
IDIOMS **to jump out of the ~ into the fire** tomber de Charybde en Scylla.

ft *abrév écrite* = **foot, feet**.

fuchsia /'fju:ʃə/ *n* fuchsia *m*.

fuddled /'fʌdld/ *adj* **1** (confused) [*brain*] confus, embrouillé; [*state*] de confusion; [*person*] désorienté; **2** (slightly drunk) éméché.

fuddy-duddy○ /'fʌdɪdʌdɪ/ *n* schnock○ *mf*.

fudge /fʌdʒ/ **I** *n* **1** CULIN (soft sweet) caramels *mpl* mous; **have a piece of ~** prends un caramel; **2** US CULIN (also **~ sauce**) (hot sauce) sauce *f* au chocolat; **3**○ (compromise) **it's a ~** c'est flou.
II○ *vtr* **1** (evade) esquiver [*issue*]; **2** (falsify) truquer [*figures*].

fuel /'fju:əl/ **I** *n* **1** GEN combustible *m*; (for car, plane) carburant *m*; **2** FIG **to provide ~ for** rajouter du poids à [*claims*]; attiser [*hatred*].
II *vtr* (*p prés etc* **-ll-, -l-** US) **1** (make run) alimenter [*furnace, engine*]; **to be ~led by gas** marcher au gaz; **2** (put fuel into) ravitailler [*plane*]; **3** FIG aggraver [*tension*]; attiser [*hatred*]; susciter [*speculation*].
IDIOMS **to add ~ to the flames** ou **fire** jeter de l'huile sur le feu.

fuel: **~ consumption** *n* (of plane, car) consommation *f* de carburant; (in industry) consommation *f* de combustible; **~-efficient** *adj* économique; **~ injection** *n* injection *f* (de carburant); **~ injection engine** *n* moteur *m* à injection; **~ pump** *n* pompe *f* d'alimentation; **~ saving** *n* économie *f* d'énergie; **~ tank** *n* (of car) réservoir *m*; (of plane, ship) réservoir *m* de carburant.

fuggy /'fʌgɪ/ *adj* GB (smoky) enfumé; (airless) confiné.

fugitive /'fju:dʒətɪv/ **I** *n* fugitif/-ive *m/f*; fuyard/-e *m/f*.
II *adj* **1** LITTÉR [*happiness*] éphémère, fugace; [*impression, sensation*] fugitif/-ive; **2** (in flight) [*person*] fugitif/-ive, en fuite.

fugue /fju:g/ *n* **1** MUS fugue *f*; **2** PSYCH amnésie *f* d'identité.

fulcrum /'fʊlkrəm/ *n* (*pl* **~s** ou **-cra**) LIT point *m* d'appui; FIG pivot *m*.

fulfil GB, **fulfill** US /fʊl'fɪl/ *vtr* (*p prés etc* **-ll-**) **1** (realize, carry out) réaliser [*ambition, prophecy*]; tenir [*promise*]; répondre à [*desire, need*]; **to ~ one's potential** se réaliser; **2** (satisfy) **to ~ oneself** s'épanouir; **to feel ~led** se sentir comblé; **3** (satisfy requirements of) remplir [*duty, conditions, contract*].

fulfilling /fʊl'fɪlɪŋ/ *adj* [*job, marriage*] épanouissant; [*experience*] enrichissant.

fulfilment GB, **fulfillment** US /fʊl'fɪlmənt/ *n* **1** (satisfaction) épanouissement *m*; **sexual ~** épanouissement sexuel; **personal ~** accomplissement *m* de soi; **to seek ~** rechercher la plénitude; **2** (realization) **the ~ of** la réalisation de [*ambition, need*]; l'accomplissement *m* de [*promise*]; **3** (of role, duty, obligation) accomplissement *m*; **4** (meeting requirements) **the ~ of the contract will entail...** pour remplir le contrat, il faudra...

full /fʊl/ **I** *adj* **1** (completely filled) [*box, glass, room*] plein; [*hotel, flight, car park*] complet/-ète; [*theatre*] comble; **a ~ bottle of whisky** une pleine bouteille

~ whisky; ~ **to the brim** plein à ras bord; ~ **to** ›verflowing [*bucket*] plein à déborder; [*suitcase*] plein craquer○; **I've got my hands** ~ LIT j'ai les mains .leines; FIG je suis débordé; **don't speak with your** .nouth ~ ne parle pas la bouche pleine; ~ **of** plein .e; **he's** ~ **of his holiday plans** il ne parle que de .es projets de vacances; **to be** ~ **of one's own** .mportance être plein de suffisance; **2** (also ~ **up**) *stomach*] plein; **I'm** ~○ je n'en peux plus; **3** (busy) .day, week] chargé, bien rempli; **my diary is** ~ **for** .his week mon agenda est complet pour cette .emaine; **a very** ~ **life** une vie très remplie; **4** (com- .lete) [*name, breakfast, story*] complet/-ète; [*price,* .ontrol, understanding] total; [*responsibility*] entier/ .ière; [*support*] inconditionnel/-elle; [*inquiry*] appro- .ondi; **the** ~ **extent of the damage** l'ampleur des .légâts; **the** ~ **implications of** toutes les implications .le, toute la portée de; **he has a** ~ **head of hair** il a .ous ses cheveux; **to be in** ~ **view** être parfaitement .visible; **5** (officially recognized) [*member*] à part entière; .right] plein (*before n*); **6** (maximum) [*employment,* .bloom] plein (*before n*); **at** ~ **volume** à plein volume; .at ~ **speed** à toute vitesse; **in** ~ **sunlight** en plein .soleil; **to make** ~ **use of sth, to use sth to** ~ .advantage profiter pleinement de qch; **to get** ~ .marks GB obtenir la note maximale; **7** (for emphasis) [*hour, kilo, month*] bon/bonne (*before n*); **8** (rounded) [*cheeks*] rond; [*lips*] charnu; [*figure*] fort; [*skirt, sleeve*] .ample; **9 there's a** ~ **moon** c'est la pleine lune; **10** (rich) [*flavour, tone*] riche.

II adv **1** (directly) **to hit sb** ~ **in the face** frapper qn .en plein visage; **to look sb** ~ **in the face** regarder .qn droit dans les yeux; **2** (very) **to know** ~ **well that** .savoir fort bien que; **3** (to the maximum) **with the heat-** .ing up ~ avec le chauffage à fond.

III in full adv phr [*describe, pay*] intégralement.

IDIOMS to live life to the ~ profiter pleinement de l'existence.

ull: ~-**back** n SPORT arrière m; ~ **beam** n AUT pleins phares mpl.

ull blast○ /ful'blɑːst/ adv **the TV was on** (at) ~ la .télé marchait à pleins tubes○.

ull-blooded /ful'blʌdɪd/ adj **1** (vigorous) vigoureux/ -euse; **2** (committed) pur et dur inv; **3** (pure bred) [*person*] de race pure; [*horse*] pur sang.

ull-blown /ful'bləʊn/ adj **1** MED [*disease*] déclaré; [*epidemic*] extensif/-ive; **to have** ~ **Aids** être atteint d'un sida avéré; **2** (qualified) [*doctor*] diplômé; **3** (large-scale) [*crisis, war*] à grande échelle; **4** [*rose*] épanoui.

full: ~ **board** n TOURISM pension f complète; ~-**bodied** adj [*wine*] corsé; ~-**cream milk** n GB lait m entier; ~-**dress** n GEN tenue f de cérémonie; MIL grande tenue f; ~-**face** adj, adv de face; ~-**frontal** adj [*photograph*] nu de face; ~-**grown** adj adulte.

full house n **1** THEAT **to have a** ~ faire salle comble; **2** (in poker) full m.

full-length /ful'leŋθ/ adj **1** CIN **a** ~ **film** un long métrage; **2** (head to toe) [*portrait*] en pied; ~ **window** baie f vitrée; **3** (long) [*coat, curtain*] long/longue; [*opera*] grand (*before n*).

full name n nom m et prénom m.

fullness /'fulnɪs/ n **1** (width) (of sleeve, dress) ampleur f; **2** (roundness) (of breasts) rondeur f; (of lips) épaisseur f; **3** (of flavour) richesse f.

IDIOMS in the ~ **of time** (with the passage of time) avec le temps; (eventually) en temps et lieu.

full: ~-**page** adj [*advertisement*] pleine page; ~ **pay** n traitement m intégral; ~ **price** adj, adv au prix fort.

full-scale /ful'skeɪl/ adj **1** (in proportion) [*drawing*] grandeur f nature; **2** (extensive) [*operation*] de grande envergure; [*investigation, study*] approfondi; **3** (total) [*alert*] général; [*crisis*] généralisé; **4** (complete) [*performance*] grand (*before n*).

full-size(d) /ful'saɪz(d)/ adj **1** (large) grand format inv; **2** [*violin, bike*] pour adulte.

full stop n GB (in punctuation) point m; **I'm not leav-ing,** ~**!** je ne pars pas, point final!

full time I n SPORT fin m du match.
II full-time noun modifier **1** SPORT [*score*] final; **2** (permanent) [*job, student*] à plein temps.
III adv [*study, teach, work*] à plein temps.

fully /'fulɪ/ adv **1** (completely) [*understand*] très bien; [*succeed, recover*] tout à fait; [*furnished, dressed*] entiè-rement; [*awake, developed*] complètement; [*aware*] parfaitement; **to be** ~ **qualified** avoir obtenu tous ses diplômes; **2** (to the maximum) [*open*] à fond; [*stretched*] complètement; ~ **booked** complet/-ète; **3** (comprehensively) [*study*] à fond; [*explain*] de façon détail-lée; **4** (at least) au moins.

fully-fledged /fulɪ'fledʒd/ adj **1** ZOOL [*bird*] qui a toutes ses plumes; **2** (established) [*member*] à part entière; [*lawyer*] diplômé.

fulminate /'fʌlmɪneɪt, US 'ful-/ vi fulminer, pester.

fulsome /'fulsəm/ adj SOUT [*compliments*] excessif/ -ive; [*manner*] obséquieux/-ieuse.

fumble /'fʌmbl/ **I** n SPORT échappé m.
II vtr **1** SPORT mal attraper [*ball*]; **2** (bungle) rater [*en-trance, attempt*].
III vi **to** ~ (**about**) **in one's bag for a cigarette** fouiller dans son sac pour trouver une cigarette; **to** ~ **with** manier maladroitement.
■ **fumble about** (in dark) tâtonner (**to do** pour faire); **to** ~ **about in** fouiller dans.

fume /fjuːm/ vi **1** (in anger) **to be fuming** fulminer, être furibond○; **to be fuming with anger** bouillonner de colère; **2** [*mixture, chemical*] fumer.

fumes /fjuːmz/ npl émanations fpl; **petrol** ~ GB, **gas** ~ US vapeurs fpl d'essence; **traffic** ~ fumée f des pots d'échappement.

fumigate /'fjuːmɪgeɪt/ vtr désinfecter [*qch*] par fumiga-tion.

fun /fʌn/ n plaisir m, amusement m; **to have** ~ s'amuser (**doing** en faisant; **with** avec); **we had great** ~ nous nous sommes beaucoup amusés; **it is** ~ **to do sth, doing sth is** ~ c'est amusant de faire qch; **to do sth for** ~, **to do sth for the** ~ **of it** faire qch pour s'amuser; **to do sth in** ~ pour plaisanter; **half the** ~ **of doing is...** le plus beau de faire est...; **it's not much** ~ ce n'est pas très amusant (**for** pour); **to spoil sb's** ~ gâcher le plaisir de qn; **to have a sense of** ~ avoir de l'humour; **he's** (such) ~ il est (tellement) drôle; **she is great** ~ **to be with** on s'amuse beaucoup avec elle.
IDIOMS to become a figure of ~ devenir la risée (**for** de); **to have** ~ **and games** s'amuser comme des petits fous; **to make** ~ **of** ou **poke** ~ **at** se moquer de.

function /'fʌŋkʃn/ **I** n **1** (role) (of body, organ, tool) fonc-tion f; (of person) fonction f, charge f; **to fulfil a** ~ [*person*] remplir une fonction; **in her** ~ **as...** en sa qualité de...; **the** ~ **of the heart is to do** le cœur a pour fonction de faire; **2** (reception) réception f; (cere-mony) cérémonie f (officielle); **3** COMPUT, MATH fonc-tion f.
II vi **1** (work properly) fonctionner; **2** (operate as) **to** ~ **as** [*object*] faire fonction de, servir de; [*person*] jouer le rôle de.

functional /'fʌŋkʃənl/ adj [*design*] fonctionnel/-elle; (in working order) opérationnel/-elle.

functionary /'fʌŋkʃənərɪ, US -nerɪ/ n GEN fonction-naire mf; PÉJ bureaucrate mf, rond-de-cuir m.

function: ~ **key** n touche f de fonction; ~ **room** n salle f de réception; ~ **word** n mot m grammati-cal, mot-outil m.

fund /fʌnd/ **I** n **1** (cash reserve) fonds m; **emergency/ relief** ~ caisse f de prévoyance/secours; **disaster** ~ collecte f en faveur des sinistrés; **2** FIG (store) **she's a** ~ **of wisdom** c'est un puits de sagesse.
II funds npl **1** (capital) fonds mpl, capitaux mpl; **to be in** ~**s** avoir de l'argent; **2** (credit balance) (of individual) argent m; (of company) capitaux mpl; **3** (on cheque) '**No** ~**s**', '**insufficient** ~**s** ' 'défaut de provision'.

III *vtr* **1** FIN financer [*company, project*]; **2** (convert) consolider [*debt*].

fundamental /ˌfʌndəˈmentl/ **I fundamentals** *npl* **the ~s** (of abstract ideas) les fondements *mpl* (**of** de); (of skill) les règles *fpl* de base.
II *adj* [*issue, meaning*] fondamental (**to** pour); [*error, importance*] capital; [*concern*] principal; **to be ~ to** être essentiel à.

fundamentalist /ˌfʌndəˈmentəlɪst/ *n, adj* GEN fondamentaliste (*mf*); (Islam) intégriste (*mf*).

fundamentally /ˌfʌndəˈmentəlɪ/ *adv* [*opposed, flawed*] fondamentalement; [*incompatible*] foncièrement; [*change*] radicalement.

funding /ˈfʌndɪŋ/ *n* **1** (financial aid) financement *m*; **to receive ~ from** être financé par; **self-~** autofinancé; **2** (of debt) consolidation *f*.

funding body, **funding agency** *n* organisme *m* de subvention.

fund: **~ manager** *n* FIN gestionnaire *mf* de fonds; **~-raiser** *n* (person) collecteur/-trice *m/f* de fonds; (event) collecte *f*; **~-raising** *n* collecte *f* de fonds.

funeral /ˈfjuːnərəl/ **I** *n* GEN enterrement *m*, obsèques *fpl* FML.
II *noun modifier* [*march, oration, service*] funèbre.
IDIOMS **that's your/her ~!** c'est ton/son problème○!

funeral: **~ director** ▶1251 *n* entrepreneur *m* de pompes funèbres; **~ parlour**, **~ home** US, **~ parlor** US *n* chambre *f* mortuaire (*chez un entrepreneur de pompes funèbres*).

funereal /fjuːˈnɪərɪəl/ *adj* lugubre.

fun: **~ fair** *n* fête *f* foraine; **~ fur** *n* fausse fourrure *f*.

fungal /ˈfʌŋgl/ *adj* fongique.

fungi /ˈfʌŋgaɪ, -dʒaɪ/ *pl* ▶ **fungus**.

fungus /ˈfʌŋgəs/ *n* (*pl* **-gi**) **1** BOT, MED champignon *m*; **2** (mould) moisissure *f*.

funicular /fjuːˈnɪkjʊlə(r)/ *n, adj* funiculaire (*m*).

fun-loving /ˈfʌnlʌvɪŋ/ *adj* [*person*] qui aime s'amuser.

funnel /ˈfʌnl/ **I** *n* (for liquids) entonnoir *m*; (on ship) cheminée *f*.
II *vtr* **1** LIT **to ~ sth into/through** faire passer qch dans/par; **to ~ sth out** évacuer qch; **2** FIG acheminer [*funds, aid*] (**to** vers).

funnily /ˈfʌnɪlɪ/ *adv* curieusement.

funny /ˈfʌnɪ/ *adj* **1** (amusing) drôle; (odd) bizarre; **it's ~ that she hasn't phoned** c'est drôle or bizarre qu'elle n'ait pas appelé; **to feel ~**○ se sentir tout/-e chose○.
II *adv*○ [*walk, talk, act*] bizarrement, drôlement.
IDIOMS **~ peculiar or ~ ha-ha?** drôle-bizarre ou drôle-amusant?

funny: **~ business**○ *n* ¢ magouilles○ *fpl*; **~ money**○ *n* fausse monnaie *f*.

fur /fɜː(r)/ **I** *n* ¢ **1** (on animal) poils *mpl*; (for garment) fourrure *f*; **2** GB (in kettle, pipes) tartre *m*.
II *noun modifier* [*collar, lining, coat*] de fourrure.
IDIOMS **that'll make the ~ fly!** ça va chauffer○!
■ **fur up** GB [*kettle, pipes*] s'entartrer.

furious /ˈfjʊərɪəs/ *adj* **1** (angry) furieux/-ieuse (**with, at** contre); **he's ~ about it** cela l'a rendu furieux; **I was ~ with her for coming** j'étais furieux qu'elle soit venue; **2** (violent) GEN acharné; [*storm*] déchaîné; **at a ~ rate** à un rythme effréné.
IDIOMS **the pace was fast and ~** le rythme était endiablé.

furiously /ˈfjʊərɪəslɪ/ *adv* furieusement; [*struggle*] avec acharnement.

furl /fɜːl/ *vtr* ferler [*sail*]; rouler [*flag*].

furnace /ˈfɜːnɪs/ *n* **1** (boiler) chaudière *f*; (in foundry) fourneau *m*; (for forging) four *m*; **2** FIG fournaise *f*.

furnish /ˈfɜːnɪʃ/ **I** *vtr* **1** meubler [*room, apartment*] (**with** avec); **2** fournir [*document, facts, excuse*]; **to ~ sb with sth** fournir qch à qn.
II furnished *pp adj* [*apartment*] meublé.

furnishing /ˈfɜːnɪʃɪŋ/ **I** *n* (action) ameublement *m*.

II furnishings *npl* (complete décor) ameublement *m*.
III *noun modifier* [*fabric*] d'ameublement; **~ depa** ment rayon *m* ameublement.

furniture /ˈfɜːnɪtʃə(r)/ **I** *n* ¢ mobilier *m*, meubles *m* **door ~** plaques *fpl* et poignées *fpl*; **mental** univers *m* intellectuel; **a piece of ~** un meuble.
II *noun modifier* [*shop, business, factory, maker, storer*] de meubles; [*industry*] du meuble.
IDIOMS **to be part of the ~**○ HUM faire partie meubles○.

furniture: **~ depot** *n* garde-meubles *m inv*; **polish** *n* encaustique *f*; **~ remover** ▶1251 *n* déménageur *m*; **~ store** *n* magasin *m* de meuble **~ van** *n* camion *m* de déménagement.

furore /fjʊˈrɔːrɪ/, **furor** US /ˈfjuːrɔːr/ *n* (accla enthousiasme *m*; (criticism) scandale *m*; **to cause a** (reaction, excitement) soulever les passions; (outrage) fa scandale; (acclaim) provoquer l'enthousiasme.

furrow /ˈfʌrəʊ/ **I** *n* (in earth, snow) sillon *m*; (on bre pli *m*.
II *vi* **his brow ~ed** il a plissé le front.

furry /ˈfɜːrɪ/ *adj* [*toy*] en peluche; [*kitten*] au p touffu.

further /ˈfɜːðə(r)/ **I** *adv* (*comparative of* **far**) **1** greater distance) (also **farther**) LIT, FIG plus loin; h much ~ is it? c'est encore loin?; **how much ~ ha they got to go?** est-ce qu'ils vont encore loin?; **to g ~ and ~ away** s'éloigner de plus en plus; **~ ba** forward plus en arrière/en avant; **~ away** ou plus loin; **~ on** encore plus loin; **I'll go so far but ~** j'irai jusque là mais pas plus loin; **she didn't any ~ with him than I did** elle n'est arrivée à ri de plus avec lui que moi; **we're ~ forward than w** thought on est plus avancé qu'on ne le pensait; **2** time) (also **farther**) **~ back than 1964** avant 1964 year **~ on** un an plus tard; **we must look** ahead nous devons regarder plus vers l'avenir; **haven't read ~ than page twenty** je n'ai pas lu delà de la page vingt; **3** (to a greater extent) **prices** (even) **~** les prix ont baissé encore plus; **we v** enquire **~ into the matter** nous nous renseignero davantage sur la question; **4** (furthermore) de plus, outre.
II *adj* (*comparative of* **far**) **1** (additional) **a ~ 5** people 500 personnes de plus; **~ changes** d'aut changements; **there have been ~ allegations t** il y a eu de nouvelles allégations selon lesquelles; **research** des recherches plus approfondies; **~ deta** can be obtained by writing to the manager p plus de renseignements, adressez-vous à la directio **to have no ~ use for sth** ne plus avoir besoin qch; **without ~ delay** sans plus attendre; **ther** nothing **~ to discuss** il n'y a rien d'autre à d cuter; **2** (more distant) (also **farther**) autre.
III *vtr* augmenter [*chances*]; faire avancer [*care plan*]; servir [*cause*].
IV further to *prep phr* SOUT suite à.

further education *n* GB UNIV ~ enseignement professionnel.

furthermore /ˌfɜːðəˈmɔː(r)/ *adv* de plus, en outre.

furthest /ˈfɜːðɪst/ **I** *adj* (*superlative of* **far**) le plus é gné.
II *adv* **1** (in space) (also **the ~**) le plus loin; **this p** goes **~ towards solving the problem** FIG c'est projet qui s'approche le plus de la solution problème; **2** (in time) **the ~ back I can remember 1970** je ne me rappelle rien avant 1970; **the ~ ahe** we can look is next week nous ne pouvons rien p voir au-delà de la semaine prochaine.

furtive /ˈfɜːtɪv/ *adj* [*glance, movement*] furtif/-i [*person*] agissant subrepticement; [*behaviour*] suspe [*deal, meeting*] subreptice.

furtively /ˈfɜːtɪvlɪ/ *adv* [*glance*] furtivement; [e subrepticement; [*eat, smoke*] en cachette.

fury /ˈfjʊərɪ/ *n* fureur *f*; (of storm, sea) violence *f*; **to** in a **~** être en fureur; **he flew at her in a ~** il rua sur elle dans un accès de rage.

IDIOMS to do sth like ~○ faire qch comme un fou○/
ne folle○.

se /fjuːz/ **I** n **1** ELEC fusible m; **to blow a ~** LIT
aire sauter un fusible; FIG○ piquer une crise○; **2** (for
omb) mèche f; (detonator) détonateur m.
I vtr **1** LIT munir [qch] d'un fusible [plug]; amorcer
bomb]; souder [wires]; amalgamer [metals]; **2** FIG
aire fusionner [ideas, images].
II vi **1** LIT [metals, chemicals] se fondre (ensemble);
he lights have ~d GB un fusible a sauté; **2** FIG
usionner.
V fused pp adj ELEC [plug] avec fusible incorporé.
IDIOMS to be on a short ~ être soupe au lait.
se box n boite f à fusibles.

selage /'fjuːzəlɑːʒ, -lɪdʒ/ n fuselage m.

se wire n fusible m.

sillade /ˌfjuːzəˈleɪd, US -sə-/ n MIL fusillade f; FIG
.valanche f.

sion /'fjuːʒn/ n GEN, PHYS fusion f; (of styles) mé-
ange m.

ss /fʌs/ **I** n **1** (agitation) remue-ménage m inv; (verbal)
iistoires fpl; **to make a ~** faire des histoires; **to**
nake a ~ about sth faire toute une histoire à
>ropos de qch; **to make a big ~ about nothing**
aire un tas d'histoires pour rien; **I don't see what all**
he ~ is about je ne vois pas où est le problème; **2**
angry scene) tapage m; **to kick up a ~ about sth**○
iiquer une crise○ à propos de qch; **3** (attention) **to**
nake a ~ of être aux petits soins avec or pour
person]; caresser [animal]; **she doesn't want any**
~ elle veut qu'on la reçoive simplement.
I vi **1** (worry) se faire du souci (**about** pour); **he's**
ılways ~ing over ou **about his appearance** il est
bsédé par son apparence; **2** (be agitated) s'agiter; **3**
show attention) **to ~ over sb**○ être aux petits soins
vec or pour qn.

fussily /'fʌsɪlɪ/ adv **1** (anxiously) avec maniaquerie; **2**
(ornately) de manière tarabiscotée.

fussiness /'fʌsɪnɪs/ n (of decoration) tarabiscotage m;
(choosiness) maniaquerie f.

fussing /'fʌsɪŋ/ n maniaquerie f.

fussy /'fʌsɪ/ adj **1** (difficult to please) **to be ~ about**
one's food/about details être difficile sur la nourri-
ture/maniaque sur les détails; **2** [furniture, style,
decoration] tarabiscoté; [pattern] trop chargé.

futile /'fjuːtaɪl, US -tl/ adj **1** (vain) vain; **2** (inane) futile.

futility /fjuːˈtɪlətɪ/ n inutilité f.

future /'fjuːtʃə(r)/ n **1** (on time scale) avenir m; **in the**
~ dans l'avenir; **in the near** ou **not too distant ~**
dans un proche avenir; **in ~** à l'avenir; **the train of**
the ~ le train du futur; **to see into the ~** lire l'avenir; **2** (prospects) avenir m; **3** LING (also **~ tense**)
futur m; **in the ~** au futur.
II futures npl FIN contrats mpl à terme.
III adj (épith) [generation, developments, investment,
earnings] futur; [prospects] d'avenir; [queen, prince etc]
futur (before n); **at some ~ date** à une date ultérieure.
future: ~ perfect n futur m antérieur; **~s**
market n FIN marché m de contrats à terme.

fuze n US = **fuse**.

fuzz /fʌz/ **I** n **1** (hair) tignasse f bouclée; (beard) barbiche f; (downy hair) duvet m; **2**○ (police) **the ~** les flics○
mpl.
II vtr brouiller [image, vision].
III vi (also **~ over**) [image, vision] se brouiller.

fuzziness /'fʌzɪnɪs/ n (of image) flou m; (of idea)
caractère m confus.

fuzzy /'fʌzɪ/ adj **1** [hair, beard] (curly) crépu; (downy)
duveteux/-euse; **2** (blurry) [image] flou; [idea, mind]
confus; [distinction] flou.

Gg

g, G /dʒiː/ *n* **1** (letter) g, G *m*; **2 G** MUS sol *m*; **3 g** (*abrév écrite* = **gram(s)**) g; **4 g** PHYS g *m*.

GA US POST *abrév écrite* = **Georgia**.

gab○: IDIOMS **to have the gift of the ~**○ avoir du bagou(t)○.

gabble /'gæbl/ **I** *n* charabia○ *m*.
II *vi* bredouiller.
■ **gabble away, gabble on** baragouiner○.

gable /'geɪbl/ *n* pignon *m*.

Gabon /gə'bɒn/ ▶ 840 ǀ *pr n* Gabon *m*.

gadget /'gædʒɪt/ *n* gadget *m*.

gadgetry /'gædʒɪtrɪ/ *n* ₵ gadgets *mpl*.

gaff /gæf/: IDIOMS **to blow the ~**○ GB vendre la mèche○; **to blow the ~ on sth**○ GB révéler la vérité sur [*conspiracy*].

gaffe /gæf/ *n* bévue *f*.

gaffer /'gæfə(r)/ *n* **1** GB (foreman) contremaître *m*; **2** GB (boss) patron *m*; **3** CIN, TV éclairagiste *mf*.

gag /gæg/ **I** *n* **1** LIT, FIG bâillon *m*; **to put a ~ on the press** bâillonner la presse; **2**○ (joke) blague○ *f*.
II *vtr* (*p prés etc* **-gg-**) LIT bâillonner [*hostage*]; FIG bâillonner [*media*]; museler [*journalist*].
III *vi* (*p prés etc* **-gg-**) avoir un haut-le-cœur; **he ~ged on his soup** il s'est étouffé en mangeant sa soupe.

gage /geɪdʒ/ *n, vtr* US = **gauge** I, II.

gaiety /'geɪətɪ/ *n* gaieté *f*.

gaily /'geɪlɪ/ *adv* **1** [*laugh*] de bon cœur; [*say*] joyeusement; **~ coloured** GB, **~ colored** US aux couleurs gaies; **2** (casually) [*announce, reveal*] avec désinvolture.

gain /geɪn/ **I** *n* **1** (increase) augmentation *f* (**in** de); **2** (profit) profit *m*, gain *m*; **financial ~** gain financier; **to do sth for material ~** faire qch pour l'argent; **3** (advantage) GEN gain *m*; (in status, knowledge) acquis *m*; **to make ~s** [*political party*] se renforcer.
II gains *npl* FIN gains *mpl*; **losses and ~s** pertes *fpl* et profits *mpl*; **to make ~s** [*currency, shares*] être en hausse.
III *vtr* **1** (acquire) acquérir [*experience*] (**from** de); obtenir [*advantage, information*] (**from** grâce à); gagner [*respect, support, time*]; conquérir [*freedom*]; **to ~ popularity** gagner en popularité; **we have nothing to ~** nous n'avons rien à gagner; **to ~ control of sth** prendre le contrôle de qch; **to ~ possession of sth** s'assurer la possession de qch; **to ~ ground** gagner du terrain (**on** sur); **2** (increase) **to ~ speed** prendre de la vitesse *or* de l'élan; **to ~ weight** prendre du poids; **to ~ 4 kilos** prendre 4 kilos; **to ~ 3 minutes** prendre 3 minutes d'avance; **3** (win, reach) gagner [*point, place*]; **they ~ed four seats from the Democrats** ils ont pris quatre sièges aux Démocrates; **to ~ the upper hand** prendre le dessus.
IV *vi* **1** (improve) **to ~ in prestige/popularity** gagner en prestige/en popularité; **to ~ in confidence** prendre de l'assurance; **2** (profit) **she hasn't ~ed by it** cela ne lui a rien rapporté; **do you think we'll ~ by adopting this strategy?** pensez-vous que nous y gagnerons en adoptant cette stratégie?
■ **gain on**: **~ on** [**sb/sth**] rattraper [*person, vehicle*]; **the opposition are ~ing on the government** l'opposition est en train de prendre l'avantage sur le gouvernement.

gainful /'geɪnfl/ *adj* [*employment*] rémunéré.

gainsay /ˌgeɪn'seɪ/ *vtr* (*prét, pp* **gainsaid**) SOUT réfuter [*argument*]; contredire [*person*].

gal /gæl/ *n*: *abrév écrite* = **gallon**.

galaxy /'gæləksɪ/ *n* LIT galaxie *f*; FIG pléiade *f*.

gale /geɪl/ *n* vent *m* violent; **a force 9 ~** un ve force 9; **~s of laughter** FIG éclats *mpl* de rire.

gale warning *n* avis *m* de coup de vent.

Galicia /gə'lɪsjə/ *pr n* (in Central Europe) Galicie *f*; (Spain) Galice *f*.

gall /gɔːl/ **I** *n* **1** MED bile *f*; **2** (cheek) impudence *f*.
II *vtr* exaspérer.

gallant /'gælənt/ *adj* **1** (courageous) [*soldier*] vaillan brave; [*attempt*] héroïque; **2**† (courteous) galant.

gallantry /'gæləntrɪ/ *n* **1** (courage) bravoure *f*; **2** (courtesy) galanterie *f*.

gall bladder ▶ 765 ǀ *n* vésicule *f* biliaire.

gallery /'gælərɪ/ *n* **1** (also **art ~**) (public) musée *m* (private) galerie *f*; (part of museum) galerie *f*; **2** ARCH GEN galerie *f*; (for press, public) tribune *f*; **3** THEA dernier balcon *m*.
IDIOMS **to play to the ~** chercher à épater la gale rie.

galley /'gælɪ/ *n* (ship) galère *f*; (ship's kitchen) cuisine *f* AVIAT office *m*.

Gallic /'gælɪk/ *adj* GEN français; HIST gaulois.

gallicism /'gælɪsɪzəm/ *n* gallicisme *m*.

galling /'gɔːlɪŋ/ *adj* [*remark, criticism*] vexant.

gallivant /'gælɪvænt/ *v* ■ **gallivant around, galli vant about** se balader.

gallon /'gælən/ ▶ 789 ǀ *n* gallon *m* (GB = 4.546 litres US = 3.785 litres).

gallop /'gæləp/ **I** *n* LIT, FIG galop *m*; **to go for a ~** aller faire un galop; **to break into a ~** prendre le galop; **at a ~** au galop ALSO FIG.
II *vtr, vi* **1** LIT galoper; **to ~ away** partir au galop. **2** FIG **he came ~ing down the stairs** il a descendu l'escalier à toute allure; **Japan is ~ing ahead in this field** le Japon est largement en tête dans ce domaine.

galloping /'gæləpɪŋ/ *adj* [*horse*] au galop; [*inflation, consumption*] galopant.

gallows /'gæləʊz/ *n* gibet *m*.

gallstone /'gɔːlstəʊn/ *n* calcul *m* biliaire.

galore /gə'lɔː(r)/ *adv* [*prizes, bargains, nightclubs*] à profusion; [*drinks, sandwiches*] à volonté, à gogo○.

galvanize /'gælvənaɪz/ *vtr* **1** IND galvaniser; **2** FIG galvaniser [*group, community*]; relancer [*campaign*]; **to ~ sb into doing** pousser qn à faire.

Gambia /'gæmbɪə/ ▶ 840 ǀ *pr n* the ~ la Gambie.

gambit /'gæmbɪt/ *n* **1** tactique *f*; **opening ~** tactique pour entrer en matière; **2** (in chess) gambit *m*.

gamble /'gæmbl/ **I** *n* pari *m*; **to have a ~ on sth** faire un pari sur qch; **to take a ~** faire un pari; **that's a bit of a ~** c'est un peu risqué; **his ~ paid off** il a réussi *or* gagné son pari.
II *vtr* jouer [*money*]; FIG miser (**on** sur).
III *vi* (at cards, on shares) jouer; (on horses) parier; FIG miser; **to ~ for high stakes** LIT, FIG jouer gros.
■ **gamble away**: **~ away** [**sth**], **~** [**sth**] **away** perdre [qch] au jeu.

gambler /'gæmblə(r)/ *n* joueur/-euse *m/f*; **heavy ~** flambeur *m*.

gambling /'gæmblɪŋ/ **I** *n* jeu *m* (d'argent).
II *noun modifier* [*syndicate, table, debt*] de jeu.

gambol /'gæmbl/ *vi* (*p prés etc* **-ll-**, US **-l-**) LITTÉR gambader.

Games and sports

With or without the definite article?

French normally uses the definite article with names of games and sports:

football	= le football
bridge	= le bridge
chess	= les échecs *mpl*
marbles	= les billes *fpl*
cops and robbers	= les gendarmes et les voleurs
to play football	= jouer au football
to play bridge	= jouer au bridge
to play chess	= jouer aux échecs
to play marbles	
or at marbles	= jouer aux billes
to play cops and robbers	
or at cops and robbers	= jouer aux gendarmes et aux voleurs
to like football	= aimer le football
to like chess	= aimer les échecs

But most compound nouns (e.g. saute-mouton, colin-maillard, pigeon vole) work like this:

hide-and-seek	= cache-cache *m*
to play at hide-and-seek	= jouer à cache-cache
to like hide-and-seek	= aimer jouer à cache-cache

Names of other 'official' games and sports follow the same pattern as bridge *in the following phrases:*

to play bridge with X against Y	
	= jouer au bridge avec X contre Y
to beat sb at bridge	= battre qn au bridge
to win at bridge	= gagner au bridge
to lose at bridge	= perdre au bridge

she's good at bridge	= elle joue bien au bridge
a bridge club	= un club de bridge

Players and events

a bridge player	= un joueur de bridge

but

I'm not a bridge player	= je ne joue pas au bridge
he's a good bridge player	= il joue bien au bridge
a game of bridge	= une partie de bridge
a bridge champion	= un champion de bridge
the French bridge champion	= le champion de France de bridge
a bridge championship	= un championnat de bridge
to win the French championship	= gagner le championnat de France
the rules of bridge	= les règles du bridge

Playing cards

The names of the four suits work like club *here:*

clubs	= les trèfles *mpl*
to play a club	= jouer un trèfle
a high/low club	= un gros/petit trèfle
the eight of clubs	= le huit de trèfle
the ace of clubs	= l'as de trèfle
I've no clubs left	= je n'ai plus de trèfle
have you any clubs?	= as-tu du trèfle?
clubs are trumps	= l'atout est trèfle
to call two clubs	= demander deux trèfles

Other games vocabulary can be found in the dictionary at match, game, set, trick *etc.*

---

game /geɪm/ **I** *n* **1** (activity) jeu *m*; **to play a ~** jouer à un jeu; **to play the ~** FIG jouer franc jeu; **don't play ~s with me!** (tell me the truth) ne me fais pas marcher! (don't try to be smart) n'essaie pas de jouer au plus fin avec moi!; **2** (match) (of indoor game) partie *f* (**of** de); (of football etc) match *m* (**of** de); **let's have a ~ of cowboys** on joue aux cowboys?; **3** (part of match) (in tennis) jeu *m*; (in bridge) manche *f*; **we're two ~s all** nous sommes à deux jeux partout; **~ to Hadman** jeu Hadman; **~, set and match** jeu, set et match; **grass suits my ~** je joue bien sur gazon; **to put sb off his/her ~** distraire qn; **4**○ (trick, scheme) jeu *m*; **what's your ~?** à quoi joues-tu?; **so that's his ~!** c'est donc ça sa combine○!; **5**○ (occupation) PÉJ OU HUM **the insurance ~** le domaine de l'assurance; **I've been in this ~ 10 years** je suis dans la partie depuis 10 ans; **he's new to this ~** il est nouveau dans la partie; **6** CULIN gibier *m*.
II games *npl* **1** GB SCH sport *m*; **2** (also **Games**) (sporting event) Jeux *mpl*.
III *noun modifier* **1** [*pâté, dish, stew*] de gibier; **2 games** GB [*teacher, lesson*] d'éducation physique.
IV *adj* **1** (willing to try) partant○; **he's ~ for anything** il est toujours partant○; **she's always ~ for a laugh** elle est toujours prête à rire; **OK, I'm ~** d'accord, j'en suis; **2** (plucky) courageux/-euse.
IDIOMS **that's the name of the ~** c'est la règle du jeu; **the ~'s up** tout est fichu○; **to beat sb at their own ~** battre qn à son propre jeu; **to be on the ~**○ GB faire le trottoir○; **to give the ~ away** vendre la mèche; **two can play at that ~** à bon chat, bon rat PROV.

game: ~ bird *n* gibier *m* à plumes; **~keeper** ▶ 1251 *n* garde-chasse *m*.

gamely /ˈgeɪmli/ *adv* courageusement.

game: ~ park *n* = **game reserve**; **~ plan** *n* SPORT, GEN stratégie *f*; **~ point** *n* (tennis) balle *f* de jeu; **~ reserve** *n* (for hunting) réserve *f* de chasse; (for preservation) réserve *f* naturelle (*de grands fauves*); **~ show** *n* jeu *m* télévisé.

gamesmanship /ˈgeɪmzmənʃɪp/ *n* ¢ PÉJ stratagèmes *mpl*.

game warden *n* garde-chasse *m*.

gaming: ~ laws *npl* réglementation *f* des jeux; **~ machine** *n* machine *f* à sous.

gammon /ˈgæmən/ *n* jambon *m*.

gamut /ˈgæmət/ *n* gamme *f*; **to run the ~ of sth** passer par tout l'éventail de qch.

gander /ˈgændə(r)/ *n* ZOOL jars *m*.

gang /gæŋ/ *n* **1** (of criminals) gang *m*; (of youths, friends) bande *f*; **2** (of workmen, prisoners) équipe *f*.
■ **gang together** se grouper (**to do** pour faire).
■ **gang up** se coaliser (**on, against** contre).

Ganges /ˈgændʒiːz/ ▶ 1214 *pr n* Gange *m*.

gangland /ˈgæŋlænd/ *n* ~ le Milieu.

gang leader *n* chef *m* de bande.

gangling /ˈgæŋglɪŋ/ *adj* dégingandé.

gang: ~plank *n* passerelle *f*; **~-rape** *n* viol *m* collectif.

gangrene /ˈgæŋɡriːn/ ▶ 1002 *n* gangrène *f*.

gangrenous /ˈgæŋɡrɪnəs/ *adj* gangreneux/-euse.

gangster /ˈgæŋstə(r)/ **I** *n* gangster *m*.
II *noun modifier* [*film, story, tactics*] de gangsters.

gangway /ˈgæŋweɪ/ *n* **1** (passage) allée *f*; **'Gangway!'** 'Dégagez!'; **2** NAUT passerelle *f*.

gaol *n, vtr* GB = **jail**.

gap /gæp/ *n* **1** (space) (between planks, curtains) interstice *m* (**in** entre); (in fence, wall, timetable, records, report, text, diagram) trou *m* (**in** dans); (between buildings, cars) espace *m* (**in** entre); (in hills, cloud) trouée *f* (**in** dans); **to fill a ~** LIT, FIG combler un vide; **2** (break) (in conversation) silence *m*; (of time) intervalle *m*; (in event, performance) interruption *f*; **3** (discrepancy) (in age, scores) différence *f*; (between opinions) divergence *f*; (of status) écart *m*; **a 15-year age ~** une différence d'âge de 15 ans; **to close the ~** supprimer l'écart; **4** (in knowledge, education) lacune *f* (**in** dans); **there's a ~ in my memory** j'ai un trou de mémoire; **technology ~** insuffisance *f* en matière de technologie; **5** COMM créneau *m*; **to look for a ~ in the market** chercher un créneau sur le marché; **to fill a ~ in the market** répondre à un besoin réel du marché; **6** FIN déficit *m*; **trade ~** déficit commercial.

gape /geɪp/ *vi* **1** (stare) rester bouche bée; **to ~ at sth/sb** regarder qn/qch bouche bée; **2** [*chasm*] s'ouvrir tout grand; [*wound*] être béant; [*garment*] bâiller.

gaping /'geɪpɪŋ/ adj [person] bouche bée; [beak] grand ouvert; [wound, hole] béant.

garage /'gærɑːʒ, 'gærɪdʒ, gə'rɑːʒ/ **I** n garage m.
II noun modifier [wall, door] du garage.
III vtr mettre [qch] au garage.

garage: ~ **mechanic** ▶1251 n mécanicien m; ~ **owner** n garagiste m; ~ **sale** n brocante f à domicile.

garb /gɑːb/ n costume m.

garbage /'gɑːbɪdʒ/ n ¢ **1** US ordures fpl; **2** FIG to be ~ être très mauvais.
IDIOMS ~ **in** ~ **out** COMPUT à instructions incorrectes, résultats incorrects; FIG on ne fait pas de bon pain avec du mauvais levain.

garbage: ~ **can** n US poubelle f; ~ **chute** n US vide-ordures m inv; ~ **collector**, ~ **man** ▶1251 n US éboueur m; ~ **disposal unit** n US broyeur m d'ordures; ~ **truck** n US camion m des éboueurs.

garbled /'gɑːbld/ adj [account, instructions] confus.

Garda /'gɑːdə/ ▶1037 pr n **1** GEOG Lake ~ le lac de Garde; **2** (pl -**dai**) (in Ireland) membre de la police d'Irlande du Sud.

garden /'gɑːdn/ **I** n **1** GB jardin m; **front/back** ~ jardin situé devant/derrière la maison; **2** US (flower) platebande f; (vegetable) potager m.
II gardens npl jardin m public.
III noun modifier [furniture] de jardin; [wall, fence, shed] du jardin.
IV vi jardiner, faire du jardinage.
IDIOMS to lead sb up OU US down the ~ path° mener qn en bateau°.

garden: ~ **apartment** n US appartement dans un immeuble bas entouré d'un jardin; ~ **centre** GB, ~ **center** US n jardinerie f; ~ **city** n GB cité-jardin f.

gardener /'gɑːdnə(r)/ ▶1251 n jardinier/-ière m/f; **to be a keen** ~ être un passionné de jardinage.

garden flat n GB appartement m en rez-de-jardin.

gardening /'gɑːdnɪŋ/ n jardinage m.

garden: ~ **produce** n ¢ produits mpl maraîchers; ~ **shears** npl cisailles fpl (de jardinier); ~ **suburb** n banlieue f verte; ~-**variety** adj US [writer, book] insignifiant.

gargle /'gɑːgl/ vi se gargariser (**with** avec).

gargoyle /'gɑːgɔɪl/ n gargouille f.

garish /'geərɪʃ/ adj [colour, garment] tape-à-l'œil inv; [light] cru.

garishly /'geərɪʃlɪ/ adj [dressed, decorated] de façon voyante; ~ **lit** à la lumière crue.

garland /'gɑːlənd/ **I** n guirlande f.
II vtr enguirlander (**with** de).

garlic /'gɑːlɪk/ **I** n ail m.
II noun modifier [sausage, mushrooms] à l'ail; [crouton, sauce] aillé; [salt] d'ail; ~ **butter** beurre m d'ail; ~ **bread**: pain chaud tartiné de beurre d'ail.

garlic press n presse-ail m inv.

garment /'gɑːmənt/ n vêtement m.

garnet /'gɑːnɪt/ n grenat m.

garnish /'gɑːnɪʃ/ **I** n CULIN garniture f (**of** de).
II vtr CULIN garnir (**with** de).

garret† /'gærət/ n mansarde f.

garrison /'gærɪsn/ **I** n garnison f.
II noun modifier [town, troops, life] de garnison.
III vtr [officer] placer une garnison dans [town].

garrotte GB, **garrote** US /gə'rɒt/ **I** n garrot m.
II vtr (officially) exécuter [qn] au garrot; (strangle) étrangler.

garrulous /'gærʊləs/ adj loquace.

garter /'gɑːtə(r)/ n **1** (for stocking) jarretière f; (for sock) fixe-chaussette m; **2** US (suspender) jarretelle f.
IDIOMS I'll have your guts for ~s°! j'aurai ta peau°!

garter belt n US porte-jarretelles m inv.

gas /gæs/ **I** n **1** GEN, CHEM gaz m; **to cook with** ~ cuisiner au gaz; **to turn up/turn down the** ~ augmenter/baisser le gaz; **on a low/medium** ~ à feu doux/moyen; **2** (anaesthetic) anesthésie f; **3** MIL gaz m

de combat; **4** US (petrol) essence f; **5°** US (also **pedal**) accélérateur m.
II noun modifier [industry, company] du gaz; [expansion, pipe] de gaz.
III vtr (p prés etc -**ss**-) GEN, MIL gazer.
IV° vi GB (chatter) papoter.
V v refl (p prés etc -**ss**-) **to** ~ **oneself** se suicider au gaz.
IDIOMS **to step on the** ~ appuyer sur le champignon°.
■ **gas up** US prendre de l'essence.

gas: ~ **burner** n brûleur m à gaz; ~ **chamber** n chambre f à gaz.

Gascony /'gæskənɪ/ ▶1177 pr n Gascogne f.

gas cooker n cuisinière f à gaz.

gaseous /'gæsɪəs, 'geɪsɪəs/ adj gazeux/-euse.

gas: ~ **fire** n GB (appareil m de) chauffage m à gaz; ~-**fired** adj [boiler, water heater] à gaz; [central heating] au gaz; ~ **fitter** ▶1251 n chauffagiste m.

gash /gæʃ/ **I** n GEN entaille f (**in, on** à).
II vtr entailler.

gas: ~ **heater** n (for room) (appareil m de) chauffage m à gaz; (for water) chauffe-eau m inv; ~**holder** gazomètre m; ~ **jet** n (burner) brûleur m.

gasket /'gæskɪt/ n TECH (in pump) garniture f; (in joint) joint m (d'étanchéité).

gas: ~ **lamp** n (domestic) lampe f à gaz; (in street) bec m de gaz; ~**light** n ¢ (illumination) lueur f d'une lampe à gaz; (of street lamp) lueur f d'un réverbère; ~ **lighter** n (for cooker) allume-gaz m inv; ~ **main** n canalisation f de gaz; ~ **man** ▶1251 n employé n du gaz; ~ **mask** n masque m à gaz; ~ **meter** n compteur m à gaz; ~ **oil** n gazole m.

gasoline /'gæsəliːn/ n US essence f.

gas oven n four m à gaz.

gasp /gɑːsp/ **I** n (breathing) halètement m; **to let out** OU **give a** ~ avoir le souffle coupé; **to give a** ~ **o horror** avoir le souffle coupé par l'épouvante; **at the last** ~ FIG au dernier moment.
II vi **1** (for air) haleter; **2** (show surprise) perdre le souffle; **to** ~ **in** OU **with amazement** avoir le souffle coupé par la surprise; **3°** **to be** ~**ing for a drink** mourir d'envie de boire un verre.

gas: ~ **pedal** n US accélérateur m; ~ **pipeline** n gazoduc m; ~ **ring** n GB (fixed) brûleur m à gaz; (portable) réchaud m à gaz; ~ **station** n US station service f; ~ **stove** n cuisinière f à gaz.

gassy /'gæsɪ/ adj [drink] gazeux/-euse.

gas: ~ **tank** n US AUT réservoir m; ~ **tap** n robinet m du gaz.

gastric /'gæstrɪk/ adj gastrique; ~ **flu** grippe f intestinale.

gastritis /gæ'straɪtɪs/ ▶1002 n gastrite f.

gastro-enteritis /,gæstrəʊ,entə'raɪtɪs/ ▶1002 n gastro-entérite f.

gastronomic /,gæstrə'nɒmɪk/ adj gastronomique.

gasworks n usine f à gaz.

gate /geɪt/ n **1** (of field, level crossing) barrière f; (in ground) portillon m automatique; (in town, prison, airport, garden) porte f; (of courtyard, palace) portail m; **at the** ~ à l'entrée; **2** SPORT **a** ~ **of 29,000** 29 000 spectateurs; **3** COMPUT porte f.

gatecrash° /'geɪtkræʃ/ **I** vtr (without paying) resquiller° à; (without invitation) se pointer° sans invitation à.
II vi (at concert) resquiller°; (at party) se pointer° sans invitation.

gatecrasher° /'geɪtkræʃə(r)/ n (at concert) resquilleur/-euse m/f; (at party) intrus/-e m/f.

gate: ~**house** n maison f de gardien; ~**keeper** n gardien/-ienne m/f; ~ **money** n SPORT recette f; ~**post** n poteau m d'angle; ~**way** n porte f.

gather /'gæðə(r)/ **I** n (in sewing) fronce f.
II vtr **1** LIT (pick) cueillir; (pick up) ramasser; **2** FIG recueillir [information]; rassembler [followers, strength, courage]; **the movement is** ~**ing strength** le mouvement devient plus puissant; **to** ~ **dust** LIT prendre la poussière; FIG tomber dans l'oubli; **to** ~

momentum gagner du terrain; **to ~ speed** prendre de la vitesse; **we are ~ed here today** nous sommes réunis aujourd'hui; **3** (embrace) **to ~ sb into one's arms** serrer qn dans ses bras; **4** (deduce, conclude) **to ~ that** déduire que; **I ~ (that) he was there** d'après ce que j'ai compris il était là; **I ~ from her that) he was there** d'après ce qu'elle m'a dit il était là; **as you will have ~ed** comme vous avez dû le deviner; **as far as I can ~** autant que je sache; **5** (in sewing) faire des fronces à; **~ed at the waist** froncé à la taille.

III vi [people, crowd] se rassembler; [family] se réunir; [clouds] s'amonceler; [darkness] s'épaissir.

■ **gather around** = **gather round**.

■ **gather in**: **~** [sth] **in**, **~ in** [sth] ramasser [papers, crop]; recueillir [money, contributions].

■ **gather round**: ¶ **~ round** se rassembler; **~ round!** approchez-vous!; ¶ **~ round** [sth/sb] se rassembler autour de; ¶ **~** [sth] **round oneself** s'envelopper dans.

■ **gather together**: ¶ **~ together** se réunir; ¶ **~** [sth] **together**, **~ together** [sth] rassembler [belongings, notes, followers]; recueillir [information].

■ **gather up**: **~** [sth] **up**, **~ up** [sth] ramasser.

athering /'gæðərɪŋ/ **I** n **1** (meeting) réunion f; **social/family ~** réunion entre amis/de famille; **2** (in sewing) fronces fpl.
II adj croissant.

gauche /gəʊʃ/ adj [remark] maladroit; [person, attitude] gauche.

gaudy /'gɔːdɪ/ adj tape-à-l'œil inv.

gauge /geɪdʒ/ **I** n **1** (for gun, screw) calibre m; (of metal) épaisseur f; (of needle) diamètre m; **2** RAIL écartement m (des voies); **narrow ~** voie f étroite; **3** (measuring instrument) jauge f; **fuel ~** jauge d'essence; **4** (way of judging) moyen m de jauger; **the best ~ of his experience** le meilleur moyen de jauger son expérience.
II vtr **1** (accurately) mesurer [diameter]; jauger [distance, quantity]; calibrer [screw, gun]; **2** (estimate) évaluer [mood, reaction].

Gaul /gɔːl/ n (country) Gaule f; (inhabitant) Gaulois/-e m/f.

Gaullist /'gɔːlɪst/ n, adj gaulliste (mf).

gaunt /gɔːnt/ adj [person] décharné.

gauntlet /'gɔːntlɪt/ n (for protection) gant m à crispin.
IDIOMS **to throw down the ~** FIG lancer un défi; **to pick up the ~** FIG relever le défi; **to run the ~ of criticism/danger** s'exposer au feu de la critique/au danger.

gauze /gɔːz/ **I** n (fabric) gaze f; (wire) grillage m.
II noun modifier [curtain, bandage] de gaze.

gauzy /'gɔːzɪ/ adj transparent.

gave /geɪv/ prét ▶ **give**.

gawky /'gɔːkɪ/ adj dégingandé.

gay /geɪ/ **I**° n homosexuel/-elle m/f, gay mf.
II adj **1** (homosexual) homosexuel/-elle; [club, magazine] gay; **2** (lively) gai; [laughter] joyeux/-euse; [street] animé; **3** (carefree) joyeux/-euse.

gay lib°, **gay liberation** n: mouvement pour la reconnaissance des droits des homosexuels.

Gaza strip /ˌɡɑːzə 'strɪp/ pr n bande f de Gaza.

gaze /geɪz/ **I** n regard m; **to hold sb's ~** soutenir le regard de qn.
II vi **to ~ at sb/sth** regarder qn/qch; (in wonder) contempler qn/qch.

■ **gaze about**, **gaze around** regarder autour de soi.

gazette /gə'zet/ n (newspaper title) **Gazette** Gazette f; (official journal) journal m officiel.

gazetteer /ˌɡæzə'tɪə(r)/ n index m géographique.

gazump° /gə'zʌmp/ vtr PÉJ GB en immobilier, revenir sur un accord pour vendre à plus offrant.

GB n (abrév = **Great Britain**) G.-B.

GBH n abrév ▶ **grievous bodily harm**.

GCSE n (pl **~s**) GB (abrév = **General Certificate of Secondary Education**) certificat m d'études secondaires (passé à 16 ans).

GDP n (abrév = **gross domestic product**) PIB m.

gear /gɪə(r)/ **I** n **1** (equipment) matériel m; **climbing ~** matériel d'alpinisme; **2**° (possessions) affaires fpl; **3** (clothes) fringues° fpl; **football ~** tenue f de football; **4** AUT vitesse f; **bottom** ou **first ~** première vitesse; **to be in third ~** être en troisième; **to put a car in ~** passer la vitesse; **you're not in ~** tu es au point mort; **'keep in low ~'** 'utilisez votre frein moteur'; **to get (oneself) into ~ for sth** FIG se préparer pour qch; **5** TECH roue f dentée.
II gears npl **1** AUT changement m de vitesse; **2** TECH engrenage m.
III noun modifier [box, change, lever, stick] de vitesses; **~ wheel** (on bicycle) pignon m.
IV vtr **to be ~ed to** ou **towards sb** s'adresser à qn.

■ **gear up**: ¶ **~ up** se préparer; ¶ **~** [sb] **up** préparer; **to be ~ed up** être prêt (**for** pour).

gearshift /'gɪəʃɪft/ n US (lever) levier m de vitesses.

gee° /dʒiː/ US excl (in surprise) ça alors!; (in disappointment, commiseration) mince alors!

geese /giːs/ pl ▶ **goose**.

gel /dʒel/ **I** n **1** (for bath, hair) gel m; **2** CHEM colloïde m.
II vi (p prés etc **-ll-**) CULIN prendre; FIG prendre forme.

gelatin(e) /'dʒelətiːn, -tɪn/ n (all contexts) gélatine f.

gelding /'ɡeldɪŋ/ n **1** (horse) hongre m; **2** (castration) castration f.

gelignite /'dʒelɪɡnaɪt/ n plastic m.

gem /dʒem/ n **1** LIT pierre f précieuse; **2** FIG [person] perle f; **this book is a real ~** ce livre est une vraie merveille.

Gemini /'dʒemɪnaɪ, -niː/ ▶ **1418** n Gémeaux mpl.

gen° /dʒen/ GB **I** n tuyaux° mpl; **what's the ~ on this?** qu'est-ce qu'il faut savoir là-dessus?
II adj, adv: abrév = **general**, **generally**.

■ **gen up**° GB: ¶ **~ up** se renseigner (**on** sur); ¶ **~** [sb] **up** donner tous les tuyaux à (**on** sur); **to be ~ned up on** ou **about sth** être au parfum° de qch.

Gen. abrév écrite = **General**.

gender /'dʒendə(r)/ n LING genre m; (of person, animal) sexe m.

gene /dʒiːn/ n BIOL gène m; **it's in his ~s** GEN, HUM c'est héréditaire.

genealogist /ˌdʒiːnɪ'ælədʒɪst/ ▶ **1251** n généalogiste mf.

genealogy /ˌdʒiːnɪ'ælədʒɪ/ n généalogie f.

gene pool n patrimoine m héréditaire.

general /'dʒenrəl/ ▶ **1192** **I** n **1** MIL général m; **2 the ~ and the particular** le général et le particulier.
II adj **1** (widespread) GEN général; **to be a ~ favourite** être apprécié de tous; **in ~ use** [word, term] d'usage courant; [equipment] d'utilisation courante; **2** (overall) GEN général; **do you get the ~ idea?** tu vois en gros de quoi il s'agit?; **that's the ~ idea** en gros, c'est ça l'idée; **as a ~ rule** normalement, en règle générale; **3** (miscellaneous, not specific) GEN général; [promise, assurance] vague; **to talk in ~ terms** parler en termes généraux; **a ~ discussion** une discussion d'ensemble; **to give sb a ~ idea of** donner à qn une idée d'ensemble de; **in the ~ direction of** en direction de; **4** (not specialized) [medicine, linguistics] général; [user, reader] moyen/-enne; **~ office duties** travail m de bureau; **~ assistant** employé/-e m/f de bureau; **5** (normal) général; **in the ~ way of things** en règle générale.
III in general adv phr (usually or non-specifically) en général; (overall, mostly) dans l'ensemble; **things in ~** tout.

general: **~ degree** n GB diplôme sanctionnant des études universitaires; **~ delivery** n US poste f restante; **~ election** n élections fpl législatives; **~ headquarters** n (+ v sg ou pl) quartier m général.

generality /ˌdʒenə'rælətɪ/ n **1** (remark) généralité f; **2** (majority) **the ~ of people** la plupart des gens.

generalization /ˌdʒenrəlaɪ'zeɪʃn, US -lɪ'z-/ n généralisation f (**about** sur).

generalize /'dʒenrəlaɪz/ *vtr, vi* généraliser (**about à** propos de).

general knowledge *n* culture *f* générale.

generally /'dʒenrəlɪ/ *adv* **1** (widely, usually) en général, généralement; **a ~ accepted definition** une définition couramment acceptée; **~ available** disponible pour le grand public; **it's ~ best to wait** en général, il vaut mieux attendre; **~ (speaking)**... en règle générale...; **2** (overall) **the industry ~ will be affected** l'ensemble de l'industrie sera touché; **he's ~ unwell at the moment** en ce moment il n'est vraiment pas en forme; **the quality is ~ good** dans l'ensemble la qualité est bonne; **3** (vaguely) d'une manière générale.

general: **~ manager** ▶1251⎮ *n* directeur/-trice *m/f* général/-e; **~ meeting** *n* assemblée *f* générale.

general practice *n* **1** (field of doctor's work) médecine *f* générale; **to go into ~** devenir (médecin) généraliste; **2** (health centre) cabinet *m* de médecine générale.

general: **~ practitioner**, **GP** ▶1251⎮ *n* (médecin *m*) généraliste *m*; **~ public** *n* (grand) public *m*; **~-purpose** *adj* à usages multiples; **~ science** *n* SCH la physique, la chimie et les sciences naturelles; **~ secretary** *n* secrétaire *m* général; **~ staff** *n* état-major *m*; **~ store** *n* bazar *m* (*qui fait aussi épicerie*).

generate /'dʒenəreɪt/ *vtr* **1** GEN produire; créer [*employment*]; susciter [*interest, debate, tension, ideas*]; entraîner [*loss, profit, publicity*]; **2** ELEC produire.

generating station *n* centrale *f* électrique.

generation /ˌdʒenə'reɪʃn/ *n* **1** GEN (time span) génération *f*; **the younger/older ~** la jeune/l'ancienne génération; **it's been like this for ~s** cela fait des générations qu'il en est ainsi; **2** (in product development) génération *f*; **second ~ robots** des robots de la deuxième génération; **3** (of electricity, income, traffic, data) production *f*; (of employment) création *f*.

generation gap *n* fossé *m* des générations.

generative /'dʒenərətɪv/ *adj* générateur/-trice.

generator /'dʒenəreɪtə(r)/ *n* **1** ELEC générateur *m*; (in hospital, on farm, etc) groupe *m* électrogène; **2** (of ideas) créateur *m*.

generic /dʒɪ'nerɪk/ *adj* générique.

generically /dʒɪ'nerɪklɪ/ *adv* génériquement; **~ similar** apparenté; **~ distinct** d'espèce(s) différente(s).

generosity /ˌdʒenə'rɒsətɪ/ *n* générosité *f* (**to, towards** envers); **~ of mind** ou **spirit** esprit *m* généreux.

generous /'dʒenərəs/ *adj* **1** (beneficent, lavish) généreux/-euse; **to be ~ with** ne pas être avare de [*praise, time*]; **2** (magnanimous) [*person*] magnanime; **the most ~ interpretation is that** l'interprétation la plus charitable est que; **3** (large) [*quantity, supply, funding*] libéral; [*size*] grand; [*hem*] bon/bonne.

generously /'dʒenərəslɪ/ *adv* GEN généreusement; [*sprinkle, grease*] abondamment; **~ cut** ample; **give ~!** soyez généreux!

genesis /'dʒenəsɪs/ **I** *n* (*pl* **-ses**) FIG genèse *f*. **II Genesis** *pr n* BIBLE la Genèse.

genetic /dʒɪ'netɪk/ *adj* génétique.

genetically /dʒɪ'netɪklɪ/ *adv* génétiquement; **~ engineered**, **~ manipulated** obtenu par manipulation génétique.

genetic: **~ engineering** *n* génie *m* génétique; **~ fingerprinting** *n* empreintes *fpl* génétiques.

geneticist /dʒɪ'netɪsɪst/ ▶1251⎮ *n* généticien/-ienne *m/f*.

genetic manipulation *n* ¢ manipulations *fpl* génétiques.

genetics /dʒɪ'netɪks/ *n* (+ *v sg*) génétique *f*.

genetic testing *n* ¢ tests *mpl* de dépistage génétique.

Geneva /dʒɪ'niːvə/ ▶1343⎮, 1037⎮ *pr n* Genève; **Lake ~** le lac Léman or de Genève.

genial /'dʒiːnɪəl/ *adj* (cheerful) cordial.

geniality /dʒiːnɪ'ælətɪ/ *n* cordialité *f*.

genie /'dʒiːnɪ/ *n* (*pl* **-nii** ou **-nies**) djinn *m*, génie *m*.

genital /'dʒenɪtl/ *adj* génital.

genitalia /ˌdʒenɪ'teɪlɪə/ *npl* = **genitals**.

genitals /'dʒenɪtlz/ ▶765⎮ *npl* organes *mpl* génitaux.

genitive /'dʒenətɪv/ **I** *n* génitif *m*; **in the ~** (**case**) au génitif. **II** *adj* génitif/-ive.

genius /'dʒiːnɪəs/ *n* **1** (prodigy) génie *m*; **a mathematical ~** un mathématicien de génie; **a mechanical ~** un génie de la mécanique; **2** (skill) **to have a ~ for doing** être très doué pour faire.

Genoa /'dʒenəʊə/ ▶1343⎮ *pr n* Gênes.

genocide /'dʒenəsaɪd/ *n* génocide *m*.

genotype /'dʒenəʊtaɪp/ *n* génotype *m*.

genteel /dʒen'tiːl/ *adj* **1** (refined) distingué; **2** PÉ IRON (affected) [*person*] maniéré; [*behaviour*] affecté.

gentility /dʒen'tɪlətɪ/ *n* **1**† (refinement) distinction *f*; IRON ou PÉJ (affectation) affectation *f*.

gentle /'dʒentl/ *adj* **1** (not harsh) GEN doux/douce; [*dentist, nurse*] qui a la main douce; [*hint, reminder*] discret/-ète; [*teasing, parody*] anodin/-e; **be ~ with her, she's tired** ne la brusque pas, elle est fatiguée; **the ~ sex** LITTÉR ou IRON le sexe faible; **2** (gradual) [*slope, curve*] doux/douce; [*stop*] en douceur; [*transition*] sans heurts; **3** (light) [*pressure, touch, breeze*] léger/-ère; [*exercise*] modéré; [*massage*] en douceur; [*stroll*] petit.

gentleman /'dʒentlmən/ *n* (*pl* **-men**) (man) monsieur *m*; (well-bred) gentleman *m*; (congressman) député *m*; **~ of leisure** un rentier.

gentlemanly /'dʒentlmənlɪ/ *adj* courtois.

gentlemen /'dʒentlmən/ *npl* ▶ **gentleman**.

gentleness /'dʒentlnɪs/ *n* douceur *f*.

gently /'dʒentlɪ/ *adv* **1** (not harshly) [*rock, blow, stir*] doucement; [*comb, treat, cleanse*] avec douceur; [*cook*] à feu doux; **2** (kindly) gentiment; **treat her ~** sois gentil avec elle; **to break the news ~** annoncer la nouvelle avec ménagement; **3** (lightly) [*exercise*] sans forcer; **he kissed her ~ on the cheek** il lui posa un léger baiser sur la joue; **'squeeze ~'** 'presser sans tordre'; **4** (gradually) **to slope ~ up/down** monter/descendre en pente douce; **~ does it!** doucement!

gentrification /ˌdʒentrɪfɪ'keɪʃn/ *n* PÉJ embourgeoisement *m*.

gentry /'dʒentrɪ/ *n* †ou HUM haute bourgeoisie *f*.

gents /dʒentz/ *npl* (toilets) toilettes *fpl* (*pour hommes*); (on sign) 'messieurs'.

genuine /'dʒenjuɪn/ *adj* **1** (real) [*reason, motive*] vrai; **in case of ~ emergency** s'il y a vraiment urgence; **2** (authentic) [*work of art*] authentique; [*jewel, substance*] véritable; **it's the ~ article**○ c'est du vrai○; **3** (sincere) [*person, effort, interest*] sincère; [*simplicity*] vrai; [*inability*] non feint (*after n*); [*buyer*] sérieux/-ieuse.

genuinely /'dʒenjuɪnlɪ/ *adv* (really and truly) vraiment; (in reality) réellement.

genuineness /'dʒenjuɪnnɪs/ *n* (of person) sincérité *f*; (of work of art) authenticité *f*.

genus /'dʒiːnəs/ *n* (*pl* **-nera** ou **-ses**) genre *m*.

geo- /'dʒiːəʊ/ *combining form* géo-.

geographer /dʒɪ'ɒɡrəfə(r)/ ▶1251⎮ *n* géographe *mf*.

geographic(al) /ˌdʒɪə'ɡræfɪk(l)/ *adj* géographique.

geographically /ˌdʒɪə'ɡræfɪklɪ/ *adv* géographiquement; **~ speaking** du point de vue géographique.

geographical mile *n* NAUT mille *m* marin.

geography /dʒɪ'ɒɡrəfɪ/ **I** *n* (study) géographie *f*; (layout) topographie *f*. **II** *noun modifier* [*student, teacher, lesson, book*] de géographie.

geological /dʒɪə'lɒdʒɪkl/ *adj* géologique.

geologist /dʒɪ'ɒlədʒɪst/ ▶1251⎮ *n* géologue *mf*.

geology /dʒɪ'ɒlədʒɪ/ **I** *n* géologie *f*. **II** *noun modifier* [*course, department, degree*] de géologie.

geometric(al) /ˌdʒɪə'metrɪk(l)/ *adj* géométrique.

geometry /dʒɪ'ɒmətrɪ/ **I** *n* géométrie *f*. **II** *noun modifier* [*lesson, book*] de géométrie; **~ set** nécessaire *m* de géométrie.

geopolitical /ˌdʒiːəʊpə'lɪtɪkl/ *adj* géopolitique.

Georgia /'dʒɔːdʒjə/ ▶**1290**|, **840**| *pr n* Géorgie *f*.

Georgian /'dʒɔːdʒjən/ ▶**1100**|, **1038**| I *n* **1** (person) Géorgien/-ienne *m/f*; **2** (language) géorgien *m*.
II *adj* **1** GEOG (all contexts) géorgien/-ienne; **2** GB HIST, ARCHIT, LITERAT géorgien/-ienne; **the ~ period** la période allant de 1714 à 1830.

geoscience /,dʒiːəʊ'saɪəns/ *n* ¢ sciences *fpl* de la Terre; **a ~** une des sciences de la Terre.

gerbil /'dʒɜːbɪl/ *n* gerbille *f*.

geriatric /,dʒerɪ'ætrɪk/ I *n* MED **1** personne *f* âgée; **2** PÉJ personne *f* sénile.
II *adj* **1** MED [*hospital, ward*] gériatrique; **~ care** soins *mpl* aux vieillards; **~ medicine** gériatrie *f*; **2**○ PÉJ, HUM gâteux/-euse○.

geriatrician /,dʒerɪə'trɪʃn/ ▶**1251**| *n* gériatre *mf*.

geriatrics /,dʒerɪ'ætrɪks/ *n* (+ *v sg*) gériatrie *f*.

germ /dʒɜːm/ *n* **1** (microbe) microbe *m*; **2** (seed) LIT, FIG germe *m*.

German /'dʒɜːmən/ ▶**1100**|, **1038**| I *n* **1** (person) Allemand/-e *m/f*; **2** (language) allemand *m*.
II *adj* [*custom, food etc*] allemand; [*ambassador, embassy*] d'Allemagne; [*teacher, course*] d'allemand.

germane /dʒɜː'meɪn/ *adj* [*point, remark*] approprié; **~ to** se rapporter à [*inquiry, topic*].

Germanic /dʒɜː'mænɪk/ *adj* GEN, LING germanique.

German: ~ measles ▶**1002**| *n* rubéole *f*; **~ shepherd** *n* US berger *m* allemand; **~-speaking** *adj* germanophone.

Germany /'dʒɜːmənɪ/ ▶**840**| *pr n* Allemagne *f*.

germinate /'dʒɜːmɪneɪt/ I *vtr* LIT, FIG faire germer.
II *vi* LIT, FIG germer.

germination /,dʒɜːmɪ'neɪʃn/ *n* germination *f*.

germ warfare *n* guerre *f* bactériologique.

gerrymandering /,dʒerɪ'mændərɪŋ/ *n* charcutage *m* électoral.

gerund /'dʒerənd/ *n* nom *m* verbal.

gerundive /dʒe'rʌndɪv/ I *n* adjectif *m* verbal.
II *adj* du gérondif.

gestate /dʒe'steɪt/ *vi* **1** BIOL être en gestation; **2** FIG mûrir.

gestation /dʒe'steɪʃn/ *n* **1** LIT gestation *f*; **2** FIG mûrissement *m*.

gesticulate /dʒe'stɪkjʊleɪt/ *vi* gesticuler.

gesture /'dʒestʃə(r)/ I *n* LIT, FIG geste *m* (of de); **a nice ~** un beau geste; **an empty ~** un geste qui ne signifie rien.
II *vi* faire un geste; **to ~ at** ou **towards sth** désigner qch d'un geste; **to ~ to sb** faire signe à qn.

get /get/

■ **Note** This much-used verb has no multi-purpose equivalent in French and therefore is very often translated by choosing a synonym: *to get lunch = to prepare lunch =* préparer le déjeuner.
– *get* is used in many idiomatic expressions (*to get something off one's chest etc*) and translations will be found in the appropriate entry (**chest** etc). This is also true of offensive comments (*get lost etc*) where the appropriate entry would be **lost**.
– Remember that when *get* is used to express the idea that a job is done not by you but by somebody else (*to get a room painted etc*) faire is used in French followed by an infinitive (*faire repeindre une pièce etc*).
– When *get* has the meaning of *become* and is followed by an adjective (*to get rich/drunk etc*) devenir is sometimes useful but check the appropriate entry (**rich**, **drunk** etc) as a single verb often suffices (*s'enrichir, s'enivrer etc*).
– For examples and further uses of *get* see the entry below.

I *vtr* (*p prés* **-tt-**; *prét* **got**; *pp* **got, gotten** US) **1** (receive) recevoir [*letter, grant*]; recevoir, percevoir [*salary, pension*]; TV, RADIO capter [*channel*]; **did you ~ much for it?** est-ce que tu en as tiré beaucoup d'argent?; **what did you ~ for your car?** combien as-tu revendu ta voiture?; **we ~ a lot of rain** il pleut beaucoup ici; **our garden ~s a lot of sun** notre jardin est bien ensoleillé; **we ~ a lot of tourists** nous avons beaucoup de touristes; **you ~ what you pay for** si on veut de la qualité il faut y mettre le prix; **he's ~ting help with his science** il se fait aider en sciences; **2** (inherit) **to ~ sth from sb** LIT hériter qch de qn [*article, money*]; FIG tenir qch de qn [*trait, feature*]; **3** (obtain) (by applying) obtenir [*permission, divorce, licence*]; (by contacting) trouver [*job*]; (by contacting) trouver [*plumber*]; appeler [*taxi*]; (by buying) acheter [*item*] (**from** chez); avoir [*ticket*]; **to ~ something for nothing/at a discount** avoir qch gratuitement/avec une réduction; **to ~ sb sth, to ~ sth for sb** (by buying) acheter qch à qn; **I'll ~ sth to eat at the airport** je mangerai qch à l'aéroport; **4** (subscribe to) acheter [*newspaper*]; **5** (acquire) se faire [*reputation*]; **6** (achieve) obtenir [*grade, mark, answer*]; **he got it right** (of calculation) il a obtenu le bon résultat; (of answer) il a répondu juste; **7** (fetch) chercher [*object, person, help*]; **go and ~ a chair** va chercher une chaise; **to ~ sb sth, to ~ sth for sb** aller chercher qch pour qn; **can I ~ you your coat?** est-ce que je peux vous apporter votre manteau?; **8** (manoeuvre, move) **to ~ sb/sth upstairs/downstairs** faire monter/descendre qn/qch; **I'll ~ them there somehow** je les ferai parvenir d'une façon ou d'une autre; **can you ~ between the truck and the wall?** est-ce que tu peux te glisser entre le camion et le mur?; **9** (help progress) **is this discussion ~ting us anywhere?** est-ce que cette discussion est bien utile?; **I listened to him and where has it got me?** je l'ai écouté mais à quoi ça m'a avancé?; **10** (contact) **did you ~ Harry on the phone?** tu as réussi à avoir Harry au téléphone?; **11** (deal with) **I'll ~ it** (of phone) je réponds; (of doorbell) j'y vais; **12** (prepare) préparer [*breakfast, lunch etc*]; **13** (take hold of) attraper [*person*] (**by** par); **I've got you, don't worry** je te tiens, ne t'inquiète pas; **to ~ sth from** ou **off** prendre qch sur [*shelf, table*]; **to ~ sth from** ou **out of** prendre qch dans [*drawer, cupboard*]; **14**○ (oblige to give) **to ~ sth from** ou **out of sb** faire sortir qch à qn [*money*]; FIG obtenir qch de qn [*truth*]; **15**○ (catch) GEN arrêter [*escapee*]; **got you!** GEN je t'ai eu!; (caught in act) vu!; **16** MED attraper [*disease*]; **he got measles from his sister** sa sœur lui a passé la rougeole; **17** (use as transport) prendre [*bus, train*]; **18** (have) **to have got** avoir [*object, money, friend etc*]; **I've got a headache** j'ai mal à la tête; **19** (start to have) **to ~ hold of) the idea** ou impression that se mettre dans la tête que; **20** (suffer) **to ~ a surprise** être surpris; **to ~ a shock** avoir un choc; **to ~ a bang on the head** recevoir un coup sur la tête; **21** (be given as punishment) prendre [*five years etc*]; avoir [*fine*]; **22** (hit) **to ~ sb/sth with** toucher qn/qch avec [*stone, arrow*]; **got it!** (of target) touché!; **23** (understand, hear) comprendre; **now let me ~ this right**... alors si je comprends bien...; **'where did you hear that?'—'I got it from Paul'** 'où est-ce que tu as entendu ça?'—'c'est Paul qui me l'a dit'; **~ this! he was arrested this morning** tiens-toi bien! il a été arrêté ce matin; **24**○ (annoy, affect) **what ~s me is...** ce qui m'agace c'est que...; **25** (learn, learn of) **to ~ to do**○ finir par faire; **to ~ to like sb** finir par apprécier qn; **how did you ~ to know** ou **hear of our organization?** comment avez-vous entendu parler de notre organisation?; **we got to know them last year** on a fait leur connaissance l'année dernière; **26** (have opportunity) **to ~ to do** avoir l'occasion de faire, pouvoir faire; **27** (start) **to ~ to (be)** commencer à devenir; **to ~ to doing**○ commencer à faire; **then I got to thinking that**... puis je me suis dit que...; **we'll have to ~ going** il va falloir y aller; **28** (must) **to have got to do** devoir faire [*homework, chore*]; **it's got to be done** il faut le faire; **you've got to realize that**... il faut que tu te rendes compte que...; **there's got to be a reason** il doit y avoir une raison; **29** (persuade) **to ~ sb to do** demander à qn de faire; **I got her to talk** j'ai réussi à la faire parler; **did you ~ anything out of her?** est-ce que tu as réussi à la faire parler?; **30** (have somebody do) **to ~ sth done** faire faire qch; **to ~ the car repaired** faire réparer la voiture; **to ~ one's hair cut** se faire couper les cheveux; **how**

do you ever ~ anything done? comment est-ce que tu arrives à travailler?; **31** (cause) **to ~ the car going** faire démarrer la voiture; **as hot as you can ~ it** aussi chaud que possible; **to ~ one's socks wet** mouiller ses chaussettes; **to ~ one's finger trapped** se coincer le doigt.

II *vi* (*p prés* **-tt-**; *prét* **got**; *pp* **got, gotten** US) **1** (become) devenir [*suspicious, old*]; **how lucky/stupid can you ~**! il y en a qui ont de la chance/qui sont vraiment stupides!; **it's ~ting late** il se fait tard; **how did he ~ like that?** comment est-ce qu'il en est arrivé là?; **2** (forming passive) **to ~ (oneself) killed** se faire tuer; **to ~ hurt** être blessé; **3** (become involved in) **to ~ into**○ (as hobby) se mettre à; (as job) commencer dans; FIG **to ~ into a fight** se battre; **4** (arrive) **to ~ there** arriver; **to ~ to the airport** arriver à l'aéroport; **how did your coat ~ here?** comment est-ce que ton manteau est arrivé là?; **how did you ~ here?** (by what miracle) comment est-ce que tu es arrivé là?; (by what means) comment est-ce que tu es venu?; **where did you ~ to?** où est-ce que tu étais passé?; **we've got to page 5** nous en sommes à la page 5; **5** (progress) **it got to 7 o'clock** il était 7 heures; **I'd got as far as the title** j'en étais au titre; **I'm ~ting nowhere with this essay** je n'avance pas dans cette dissertation; **now we're ~ting somewhere** il y a du progrès; **6**○ (put on) **to ~ into** mettre, enfiler○ [*pyjamas, overalls*].

IDIOMS **~ along with you**○! ne sois pas ridicule!; **~ away with you**○! arrête de raconter n'importe quoi○!; **~ him in that hat!** regarde-le avec ce chapeau!; **I'll ~ you**○ **for that** je vais te le faire payer○; **I'm ~ting there** je progresse; **he's got it bad**○ il est vraiment mordu; **I've got it** j'ai compris; **to ~ above oneself** commencer à avoir la grosse tête○; **to ~ it together**○ se ressaisir; **to tell sb where to ~ off** envoyer promener qn; **to ~ with it**○ se mettre dans le coup○; **what's got into her?** qu'est-ce qui lui a pris? ; **you've got me there!** alors là tu me poses une colle○!

■ **get about 1** (manage to move) se déplacer; **2** (travel) voyager; **he ~s about a bit** (travels) il voyage pas mal; (knows people) il connaît du monde.

■ **get across**: ¶ **~ across 1** (pass to other side) traverser; **2** [*message*] passer; ¶ **~ across** [sth] traverser [*river, road etc*]; ¶ **~** [sth] **across** (transport) **how will we ~ it across?** comment est-ce qu'on le/la fera passer de l'autre côté?; **2** (communicate) faire passer [*message*] (**to** à).

■ **get ahead 1** (make progress) progresser; **to ~ ahead of** prendre de l'avance sur [*competitor*]; **2** (go too fast) **let's not ~ ahead of ourselves** n'anticipons pas.

■ **get along 1** (progress) **how's the project ~ting along?** comment est-ce que le projet se présente?; **how are you ~ting along?** (in job, school) comment ça se passe?; (to sick or old person) comment ça va?; **2** (be suited as friends) bien s'entendre (**with** avec); **3** (go) **I must be ~ting along** il faut que j'y aille.

■ **get around**: ¶ **~ around 1** (move, spread) = **get about**; **2 to ~ around to doing**: she'll **~ around to visiting us eventually** elle va bien finir par venir nous voir; **I must ~ around to reading his article** il faut vraiment que je lise son article; **I haven't got around to it yet** je n'ai pas encore eu le temps de m'en occuper; ¶ **~ around** [sth] (circumvent) contourner [*problem, law*]; **there's no ~ting around it** il n'y a rien à faire.

■ **get at**○: **~ at** [sb/sth] **1** (reach) atteindre [*object*]; arriver jusqu'à [*person*]; FIG découvrir [*truth*]; **2** (spoil) **the ants have got at the sugar** les fourmis ont attaqué le sucre; **3** (criticize) être après [*person*]; **4** (insinuate) **what are you ~ting at?** où est-ce que tu veux en venir?

■ **get away**: **~ away 1** (leave) partir; **2** (escape) s'échapper; **3** FIG (escape unpunished) **to ~ away with a crime** échapper à la justice; **you'll never ~ away with it!** tu ne vas pas t'en tirer comme ça!; **she can ~ away with bright colours** elle peut se permettre de porter des couleurs vives.

■ **get away from**: ¶ **~ away from** [sth] **1** (leave) quitter; **I must ~ away from here!** il faut que je parte d'ici!; **'~ away from it all'** 'évadez-vous de votre quotidien'; **2** FIG (deny) **there's no ~ting away from it** on ne peut pas le nier; **3** abandonner [*practice*]; ¶ **~ away from** [sb] LIT, FIG échapper à.

■ **get back**: ¶ **~ back 1** (return) GEN rentrer; (after short time) revenir; **when we ~ back** à notre retour; **2** (move backwards) reculer; **3** (take revenge) **to ~ back at** se venger de; ¶ **~ back to** [sth] **1** (return to) rentrer à [*house, city*]; revenir à [*office, point*]; **when we ~ back to London** à notre retour à Londres; **2** (return to former condition) revenir à [*job*]; **to ~ back to sleep** se rendormir; **to ~ back to normal** redevenir normal; **3** (return to earlier stage) revenir à [*main topic, former point*]; ¶ **~ back to** [sb] (return to) revenir à; (on telephone) **I'll ~ right back to you** je vous rappelle tout de suite; ¶ **~** [sth] **back 1** (return) (personally) ramener; (by post etc) renvoyer; **2** (regain) récupérer [*lost object, loaned item*]; FIG reprendre [*strength*]; **she got her money back** elle a été remboursée; **she got her old job back** on lui a redonné son travail.

■ **get behind**: ¶ **~ behind** (delayed) prendre du retard; ¶ **~ behind** [sth] se mettre derrière.

■ **get by 1** (pass) passer; **2** (survive) s'en sortir (**on, with** avec).

■ **get down**: ¶ **~ down 1** (descend) descendre (**from, out of** de); **2** (leave table) quitter la table; **3** (lower oneself) (to floor) se coucher; (crouch) se baisser; **to ~ down to** arriver à [*lower level etc*]; atteindre [*trapped person etc*]; se mettre à [*work*]; **to ~ down to sb's level** FIG se mettre à la portée de qn; **let's ~ down to business** parlons affaires; **when you ~ right down to it** quand on regarde d'un peu plus près; **to ~ down to doing** se mettre à faire; ¶ **~ down** [sth] descendre [*slope*]; ¶ **~** [sth] **down, ~ down** [sth] **1** (from height) descendre; **2** (swallow) avaler; **3** (record) noter; ¶ **~** [sb] **down 1** (from height) faire descendre; **2**○ (depress) déprimer.

■ **get in**: ¶ **~ in 1** LIT (to building) entrer; (to vehicle) monter; **2** FIG **to ~ in** ne réussir à s'introduire dans [*project, scheme*]; **to ~ in on the deal**○ faire partie du coup; **3** (return home) rentrer; **4** (arrive at destination) arriver; **5** (penetrate) pénétrer; **6** POL [*party*] passer; [*candidate*] être élu; **7** SCH, UNIV [*applicant*] être admis; **8** (associate) **to ~ in with** se mettre bien avec [*person*]; ¶ **~ in, ~ in** [sth] **1** (buy) acheter; **2** (fit into space) **I can't ~ the drawer in** je n'arrive pas à faire rentrer le tiroir; **3** (harvest) rentrer; (plant) planter; **4** (hand in) rendre [*essay*]; **5** (include) placer; **I'll try to ~ in a bit of tennis** j'essayerai de faire un peu de tennis; ¶ **~** [sb] **in** faire entrer.

■ **get into**: ¶ **~ into** [sth] **1** (enter) entrer dans [*building*]; monter dans [*vehicle*]; **2** (be admitted) (as member) devenir membre de; (as student) être admis à; **I didn't know what I was ~ting into** FIG je ne savais pas dans quoi je m'embarquais; **3** (squeeze into) rentrer dans [*garment, size*]; ¶ **~** [sb/sth] **into** faire entrer [qn/qch] dans.

■ **get off**: ¶ **~ off 1** (from bus etc) descendre (**at** à); **2** (start on journey) partir; **3** (leave work) finir; **4**○ (escape punishment) s'en tirer (**with** avec); **5 to ~ off to a good start** prendre un bon départ; **to ~ off to sleep** s'endormir; ¶ **~ off** [sth] **1** descendre de [*wall, bus etc*]; **2** FIG s'écarter de [*subject*]; ¶ **~ off**○ [sb] (leave hold) **~ off me!** lâche-moi!; ¶ **~** [sb/sth] **off 1** (lift down) descendre [*object*]; faire descendre [*person*]; **2** (dispatch) envoyer [*letter, person*]; **3** (remove) enlever [*stain*]; **4**○ endormir [*baby*].

■ **get on**: ¶ **~ on 1** (climb aboard) monter; **2** (work) **~ on a bit faster!** travaille un peu plus vite!; **let's ~ on!** continuons!; **3** GB (like each other) bien s'entendre; **4** (fare) **how did you ~ on?** comment est-ce que ça s'est passé?; **5** (cope) **how are you ~ting on?** comment est-ce que tu t'en sors?; **6** GB (approach) **he's ~ting on for 40** il approche des quarante ans; **it's ~ting on for midnight** il est presque minuit; **7** (grow late) **time's ~ting on** le temps passe; **8** (grow old) **to be ~ting on a bit** se faire vieux/vieille; ¶ **~ on [sth]** (board) monter dans [*vehicle*]; ¶ **~ on [sth] on, ~ on [sth]** GEN mettre; monter [*tyre*].

■ **get onto**: **~ onto [sth] 1** (board) monter dans [*vehicle*]; **2** (be appointed to) être nommé à [*committee*]; **3** (start to discuss) arriver à parler de [*subject*]; **4** GB (contact) contacter.

■ **get on with**: ¶ **~ on with [sth]** (continue to do) **to ~ on with one's work** continuer à travailler; **let's ~ on with the job!** au travail!; ¶ **~ on with [sb]** GB s'entendre avec [*person*].

■ **get out**: ¶ **~ out 1** (exit) sortir (**through, by** par); **~ out and don't come back!** va-t-en et ne reviens pas!; **2** (make social outing) sortir; **3** (resign) partir; **4** (alight) descendre; **5** (be let out) [*prisoner*] être libéré; **6** (leak) être révélé; ¶ **~ [sth] out, ~ out [sth] 1** (bring out) sortir; **I couldn't ~ the words out** les mots ne voulaient pas sortir; **2** (extract) retirer [*cork*]; **3** enlever [*stain*]; **4** emprunter [*library book*]; ¶ **~ [sb] out** (release) faire libérer [*prisoner*]; **to ~ sth out of sth** (bring out) sortir qch de qch; (find and remove) récupérer qch dans qch [*stuck object*]; **I can't ~ it out of my mind** je ne peux pas l'effacer de mon esprit.

■ **get out of**: **~ out of [sth] 1** sortir de [*building, bed, meeting*]; descendre de [*vehicle*]; être libéré de [*prison*]; quitter [*organization, profession*]; échapper à [*responsibilities*]; **2** (avoid doing) s'arranger pour ne pas aller à [*appointment, meeting*]; perdre [*habit*]; **I'll try to ~ out of it** j'essaierai de me libérer; **to ~ out of doing** s'arranger pour ne pas faire; **3** (no longer do) perdre [*habit*]; **4** (gain from) **what do you ~ out of your job?** qu'est-ce que ton travail t'apporte?; **what will you ~ out of it?** qu'est-ce que vous en retirerez?

■ **get over**: ¶ **~ over** (cross) passer; ¶ **~ over [sth] 1** (cross) traverser; **2** se remettre de [*illness, shock*]; **I can't ~ over it** (in amazement) je n'en reviens pas; **she never got over him** elle ne l'a jamais oublié; **3** surmonter [*problem*]; **to ~ sth over with** en finir avec qch; ¶ **~ [sb/sth] over** faire passer [qn/qch] au-dessus de [*bridge, wall etc*]; **~ the plumber over here** faites venir le plombier.

■ **get round** GB: ¶ **~ round = get around**; ¶ **~ round [sth] = get around [sth]**; ¶ **~ round° [sb]** persuader [qn].

■ **get through**: ¶ **~ through 1** (squeeze through) passer; **2** (on phone) **to ~ through to sb** avoir qn au téléphone; **I couldn't ~ through** je n'ai pas réussi à l'avoir; **3** (communicate with) **to ~ through to** communiquer avec [*person*]; **4** [*news, supplies*] arriver; **5** [*examinee*] réussir; ¶ **~ through [sth] 1** traverser [*checkpoint, mud*]; terminer [*book, revision*]; finir [*meal, task*]; réussir à [*exam, qualifying round*]; **I thought I'd never ~ through the week** j'ai cru que je ne tiendrais pas la semaine; **2** (use) manger [*food*]; boire [*drink*]; dépenser [*money*]; **I ~ through two notebooks a week** il me faut deux carnets par semaine; ¶ **~ [sb/sth] through 1** LIT faire passer; FIG (help to endure) aider qn à tenir le coup°; **2** SCH, UNIV (help to pass) permettre à [qn] de réussir; **3** POL faire passer [*bill*].

■ **get together**: ¶ **~ together** (assemble) se réunir (**about, over** pour discuter de); ¶ **~ [sb/sth] together, ~ together [sb/sth]** GEN réunir; rassembler [*food parcels*]; former [*company, action group*].

■ **get under**: ¶ **~ under** passer en-dessous; ¶ **~ under [sth]** passer sous.

■ **get up**: ¶ **~ up 1** (from bed, chair etc) se lever (**from** de); **2** (on ledge etc) monter; **3** METEOROL [*storm*] se préparer; [*wind*] se lever; **4** **to ~ up to** (reach) arriver à; **what did you ~ up to?** FIG (sth enjoyable) qu'est-ce que tu as fait de beau?; (sth mischievous) qu'est-ce que tu as fabriqué°?; ¶ **~ up [sth] 1** arriver en haut de [*hill, ladder*]; **2** (increase) augmenter [*speed*]; **3** (muster) former [*group*]; faire [*petition*]; obtenir [*support*]; ¶ **~ [sth] up** organiser.

getaway /ˈɡetəweɪ/ *n* **to make a quick ~** décamper vite fait°; **the robbers had a ~ car** une voiture attendait les voleurs.

get: **~-together** *n* réunion *f* (entre amis); **~up**° *n*

PÉJ accoutrement *m*; **~-up-and-go** *n* dynamisme *m*; **~ well** *adj* [*card, wishes*] de prompt rétablissement.

G-force *n* force *f* de gravité.

Ghana /ˈɡɑːnə/ ▶840 *pr n* Ghana *m*.

ghastly /ˈɡɑːstlɪ, US ˈɡæstlɪ/ *adj* horrible.

gherkin /ˈɡɜːkɪn/ *n* cornichon *m*.

ghetto /ˈɡetəʊ/ *n* (*pl* ~ **ou** ~**es**) ghetto *m*.

ghetto blaster° *n* (gros) radiocassette *m* portable.

ghost /ɡəʊst/ *n* **1** (spectre) fantôme *m*; **you look as if you've seen a ~!** on dirait que tu as vu un revenant!; **2** FIG **the ~ of a smile** l'ombre *f* d'un sourire; **they haven't the ~ of a chance!** ils n'ont pas la moindre chance!

IDIOMS **to give up the ~** rendre l'âme.

ghostly /ˈɡəʊstlɪ/ *adj* spectral.

ghost: **~ story** *n* histoire *f* de fantômes; **~ town** *n* ville *f* fantôme; **~ train** *n* train *m* fantôme; **~writer** *n* nègre *m*.

ghoulish /ˈɡuːlɪʃ/ *adj* (all contexts) macabre.

GHQ *n* (*abrév* = **General Headquarters**) GQG *m*.

GI *n* (*pl* **GIs**) GI *m inv*, soldat *m* américain.

giant /ˈdʒaɪənt/ *n, adj* (all contexts) géant (*m*).

giant-killer *n* vainqueur *m* surprise.

gibber /ˈdʒɪbə(r)/ *vi* [*person*] bafouiller; [*monkey*] baragouiner.

gibberish /ˈdʒɪbərɪʃ/ *n* charabia *m*.

gibbet /ˈdʒɪbɪt/ *n* potence *f*, gibet *m*.

gibe = **jibe**.

giblets /ˈdʒɪblɪts/ *npl* abats *mpl*.

giddiness /ˈɡɪdɪnɪs/ *n* (dizziness) vertige *m*; (frivolity) légèreté *f*.

giddy /ˈɡɪdɪ/ *adj* **1** (dizzy) **to feel ~** avoir la tête qui tourne; **2** (exhilarating) [*height, speed*] vertigineux/-euse; [*success*] enivrant; **3** (frivolous) [*person*] écervelé; [*behaviour*] irréfléchi.

giddy spell *n* vertige *m*, étourdissement *m*.

gift /ɡɪft/ *n* **1** (present) cadeau *m*; **to give a ~ to sb, to give sb a ~** faire ou offrir un cadeau à qn; **to give sb a ~ of money** offrir de l'argent à qn; **they gave it to us as a ~** ils nous en ont fait cadeau; **it's for a ~** c'est pour offrir; **the ~ of life/sight** le don de la vie/la vue; **2** (donation) don *m*; **to make a ~ of sth to sb** faire don de qch à qn; **3** (talent) don *m*; **to have a ~ for** ou **of doing** avoir le don de faire.

IDIOMS **don't look a ~ horse in the mouth** PROV à cheval donné, on ne regarde pas les dents PROV.

gifted /ˈɡɪftɪd/ *adj* (talented) doué; (intellectually) surdoué.

gift: **~ shop** *n* magasin *m* de cadeaux; **~ token**, **~ voucher** *n* GB chèque-cadeau *m*.

gift wrap I /ˈɡɪftræp/ *n* papier *m* cadeau.

II **gift-wrap** /ˌɡɪftˈræp/ *vtr* (*p prés etc* **-pp-**) **would you like it ~ped?** est-ce que je vous fais un paquet-cadeau?

gig /ɡɪɡ/ *n* **1**° MUS concert *m* de rock; **2** (carriage) cabriolet *m*.

gigantic /dʒaɪˈɡæntɪk/ *adj* gigantesque.

giggle /ˈɡɪɡl/ I *n* **1** (silly) petit rire *m* bête; (nervous) petit rire *m* nerveux; **to get the ~s** attraper un fou rire; **2**° GB (joke) **to do sth for a ~**° faire qch pour rigoler.

II *vi* (stupidly) rire bêtement; (nervously) rire nerveusement.

giggly /ˈɡɪɡlɪ/ *adj* PÉJ [*person*] qui n'arrête pas de glousser; **to be in a ~ mood** se mettre à rire pour un rien.

gild /ɡɪld/ *vtr* (*prét, pp* **gilded** ou **gilt**) dorer.

gilding /ˈɡɪldɪŋ/ *n* dorure *f*.

gill¹ /ɡɪl/ *n* (of fish) branchie *f*.

IDIOMS **green about the ~s**° blanc/blanche comme un linge.

gill² /dʒɪl/ ▶789 *n* (measure) quart *m* de pinte.

gilt /ɡɪlt/ I *pp* ▶ **gild**.

II *n* dorure *f*.

III *adj* [*frame, paint*] doré.

gilt-edged /ˌɡɪlt'edʒd/ adj **1** [page] doré sur tranche; **2** [investment] en or.

gilt-edged securities, gilt-edged stock(s) n obligations fpl et titres mpl d'État.

gimlet /'ɡɪmlɪt/ n vrille f.
IDIOMS **to have eyes like ~s** avoir un regard perçant.

gimmick /'ɡɪmɪk/ n PÉJ (scheme) truc° m; (object) gadget m.

gimmicky /'ɡɪmɪkɪ/ adj PÉJ [production] plein d'effets gratuits; [clothes] fantaisiste; [idea] à la mode.

gin /dʒɪn/ n gin m.

gin: **~ and it** n GB gin-vermouth m; **~ and tonic** n gin tonic m.

ginger /'dʒɪndʒə(r)/ **I** n **1** BOT, CULIN gingembre m; **root** ou **fresh ~** gingembre frais; **2** (hair colour) roux m.
II noun modifier **1** [cake, biscuit] au gingembre; **2** [hair, beard] roux/rousse; [cat] roux/rousse.
■ **ginger up** stimuler [metabolism].

ginger: **~ ale** n: boisson gazeuse au gingembre; **~ beer** n: boisson légèrement alcoolisée à base de gingembre.

gingerbread /'dʒɪndʒəbred/ n = pain m d'épice.
IDIOMS **that takes the gilt off the ~** ça change tout.

ginger: **~ group** n GB groupe m de pression; **~-haired** adj roux/rousse.

gingerly /'dʒɪndʒəlɪ/ adv avec précaution.

gingernut, ginger snap n CULIN biscuit m au gingembre.

gingery /'dʒɪndʒərɪ/ adj [hair, beard] roux/rousse.

gingham /'ɡɪŋəm/ **I** n vichy m.
II noun modifier [garment] en vichy.

gin rummy ▶ 949 | n gin-rami m.

gipsy n = **gypsy**.

giraffe /dʒɪ'rɑːf, US dʒə'ræf/ n girafe f.

gird /ɡɜːd/ LITTER vtr ceindre LITER.
IDIOMS **to ~ (up) one's loins** FIG, HUM revêtir son armure.

girder /'ɡɜːdə(r)/ n poutre f.

girdle /'ɡɜːdl/ n **1** (corset) gaine f; **2** (belt) ceinture f.

girl /ɡɜːl/ n **1** (child) fille f; (teenager) jeune fille f; (woman) femme f; **baby ~** petite fille f, bébé m; **little ~** petite fille f, fillette f; **teenage ~** adolescente f; **young ~** jeune fille; **when I was a ~** (referring to childhood) quand j'étais petite; (to adolescence) quand j'étais jeune; **the new ~** GEN, SCH la nouvelle f; **2** (daughter) fille f; **3** (servant) bonne f; **factory ~** ouvrière f; **office ~** employée f de bureau; **sales** ou **shop ~** vendeuse f; **4** (sweetheart) (petite) amie f.

girl: **~ Friday** n aide f de bureau; **~friend** n (sweetheart) (petite) amie f; GEN amie f; **~ guide** GB, **~ scout** US n éclaireuse f.

girlie mag(azine)° n magazine m pour hommes.

girlish /'ɡɜːlɪʃ/ adj de jeune fille.

giro /'dʒaɪrəʊ/ **I** n GB FIN (system) système m de virement bancaire; (cheque) mandat m.
II noun modifier **~ payment, ~ transfer** (at bank) virement m bancaire; (at post office) virement m postal.

girth /ɡɜːθ/ n **1** (of person) tour m de taille; (of object) circonférence f.

gist /dʒɪst/ n essentiel m (**of** de).

give /ɡɪv/ n élasticité f.
II vtr (prét **gave**; pp **given**) **1** (hand over) GEN donner (**to** à); offrir [present, drink, sandwich] (**to** à); **to ~ sb sth** GEN donner qch à qn; (politely, as gift) offrir qch à qn; **~ it me!, ~ me it!** donne-moi ça!; **how much will you ~ me for it?** combien m'en donnes-tu?; **what wouldn't I ~ for...!** je donnerais cher pour...!; **2** (cause to have) **to ~ sb sth, to ~ sth to sb** donner qch à qn [headache, nightmares, advice, information]; transmettre or passer qch à qn [disease]; **to ~ sb pleasure** faire plaisir à qn; **3** (provide, produce) donner [milk, flavour, result, answer, sum]; apporter [heat, light, nutrient]; faire [total]; **she gave him two sons** elle lui donna deux fils; **4** (allow, accord) accorder [cus-

tody, grant]; laisser [qch] à qn [seat]; **to ~ sb sth** donner or accorder qch à qn [time, time period]; **to ~ sb enough room** laisser suffisamment de place à qn; **how long do you ~ their marriage?** combien de temps donnes-tu à leur mariage?; **she can sing, I'll ~ her that** elle sait chanter, je lui reconnais au moins ça; **it's original, I'll ~ you that** c'est original, je te l'accorde; **she could ~ her opponent five years** elle a au moins cinq ans de plus que son adversaire; **the polls ~ Labour a lead** les Travaillistes sont en tête dans les sondages; **I was given to understand that** on m'a laissé entendre que; **5** MED **to ~ sb sth, to ~ sth to sb** donner qch à qn [treatment, medicine]; greffer qch à qn [organ]; poser qch à qn [device]; faire qch à qn [injection, massage]; **6** TELECOM **to ~ sb sth** passer qch à qn [number, department]; **~ me the sales manager, please** passez-moi le directeur commercial, s'il vous plaît.
III vi (prét **gave**; pp **given**) **1** (contribute) donner, faire un don; **'please ~ generously'** 'merci (de vos dons)'; **2** (bend) [mattress, sofa] s'affaisser; [shelf, floorboard] fléchir; [branch] ployer; [leather, fabric] s'assouplir; **3** (yield, break) = **give way**; **4** (yield) [person, side] céder; **something has to ~** ça va finir par craquer.
IDIOMS **don't ~ me that**°! ne (me) raconte pas d'histoires!; **~ or take an inch (or two)** à quelques centimètres près; **if this is the big city, ~ me a village every time**° si c'est ça la ville, alors vive les petits villages; **'I ~ you the bride and groom!'** 'je bois à la santé des mariés!'; **I'll ~ you something to complain about**°! je vais t'apprendre à te plaindre!; **to ~ and take** faire faire des concessions; **to ~ as good as one gets** rendre coup pour coup; **to ~ it all one's got**° (y) mettre le paquet; **to ~ sb what for**° passer un savon à qn°; **what ~s?**° qu'est-ce qui se passe?
■ **give away**: ¶ **~ away** [sth], **~** [sth] **away 1** donner [item, sample]; **we're practically giving them away!** à ce prix-là, c'est donné!; **2** (reveal) révéler; **3** (lose carelessly) laisser échapper [match, goal, advantage] (**to** au bénéfice de); ¶ **~** [sb] **away, ~** [sth] **away 1** (betray) [expression, fingerprints] trahir; [person] dénoncer (**to** à); **to ~ oneself away** se trahir; **2** (in marriage) conduire [qn] à l'autel.
■ **give back**: **~** [sth] **back, ~ back** [sth] **1** (return) rendre (**to** à); ...**or we'll ~ you your money back** ...ou vous serez remboursé; **2** (yield) [echo].
■ **give in**: ¶ **~ in 1** (yield) céder (**to** à); **2** (stop trying) abandonner; **I ~ in—tell me!** je donne ma langue au chat—dis-le moi!; ¶ **~ in** [sth], **~** [sth] **in** rendre [written work]; remettre [ticket, key].
■ **give off**: **~ off** [sth] émettre [signal, scent, radiation, light]; dégager [heat, fumes, oxygen].
■ **give onto**: **~ onto** [sth] donner sur.
■ **give out**: ¶ **~ out** GEN s'épuiser; [engine, machine] tomber en panne; ¶ **~ out** [sth], **~** [sth] **out 1** (distribute) distribuer (**to** à); **2** (emit) = **give off**; **3** (announce) annoncer.
■ **give over**: ¶ **~ over**° arrêter; ¶ **~ over** [sth], **~** [sth] **over 1** affecter or réserver [place, room] (**to** à); **2** consacrer [time, life] (**to** à); **3** (hand over) remettre [qch] à; ¶ **~ oneself over to** (devote oneself) se consacrer à; (let oneself go) s'abandonner à [despair].
■ **give up**: ¶ **~ up** abandonner; **don't ~ up!** tiens bon!; **to ~ up on** laisser tomber [diet, crossword, pupil, patient]; ne plus compter sur [friend, partner]; ¶ **~ up** [sth], **~** [sth] **up 1** (renounce or sacrifice) renoncer à [vice, habit, title, claim]; sacrifier [free time]; quitter [job]; **to ~ up smoking/drinking** cesser de fumer/de boire; **2** (abandon) abandonner [search, hope, struggle, subject]; renoncer à [idea]; **to ~ up trying** abandonner; **3** (surrender) céder [seat, territory]; remettre [passport, key]; ¶ **~ up** [sb], **~** [sb] **up 1** (hand over) livrer (**to** à); **to ~ oneself up** se livrer (**to** à); **2** (drop) laisser tomber [lover]; délaisser [friend].
■ **give way 1** (collapse) GEN s'effondrer; [fence, cable] céder; **his legs gave way** ses jambes se sont dérobées sous lui; **2** GB (when driving) céder le passage (**to** à); **3** (yield) céder; **to ~ way to** faire place à.

give-and-take n ¢ concessions fpl mutuelles.

giveaway /'gɪvəweɪ/ *n* **to be a ~** être révélateur/-trice.

given /'gɪvn/ I *pp* ▶ **give**.
II *adj* **1** (specified) [*point, level, number*] donné; [*volume, length*] déterminé; **the ~ date** la date convenue; **at any ~ moment** à n'importe quel moment; **2** (prone) **to be ~ to sth/to doing** avoir tendance à qch/à faire; **I am not ~ to doing** je n'ai pas l'habitude de faire.
III *prep* **1** (in view of) étant donné (**that** que); (assuming that) à supposer que; **2** (with) avec [*training, proper care*]; **~ an opportunity I'll tell her this evening** si j'en ai l'occasion je le lui dirai ce soir; **~ the right conditions** dans de bonnes conditions.

given name *n* prénom *m*.

give way sign *n* GB panneau *m* 'cédez le passage'.

gizzard /'gɪzəd/ *n* gésier *m*.

glacier /'glæsɪə(r)/ *n* glacier *m*.

glad /glæd/ *adj* **1** (pleased) content, heureux/-euse (**about** de; **that** que; **to do** de faire); **I am ~ (that) you are able to come** je suis content que vous puissiez venir; **he was only too ~ to help me** il ne demandait qu'à m'aider; **2** (cheering) **the ~ tidings** la bonne nouvelle.
IDIOMS **to give sb the ~ eye** faire de l'œil à qn; **in one's ~ rags**○ sur son trente-et-un○; **I'll be ~ to see the back** ou **last of them**○ je serai content de les voir partir.

gladden /'glædn/ *vtr* réjouir.

glade /gleɪd/ *n* clairière *f*.

gladiator /'glædɪeɪtə(r)/ *n* gladiateur *m*.

gladiolus /ˌglædɪ'əʊləs/ *n* glaïeul *m*.

gladly /'glædlɪ/ *adv* (willingly) volontiers; (with pleasure) avec plaisir.
IDIOMS **she doesn't suffer fools ~** elle a du mal à supporter les imbéciles.

glamorize /'glæməraɪz/ *vtr* (change) embellir [*person, room*]; (describe as attractive) valoriser [*place, attitude, idea*]; peindre [qch] sous de belles couleurs [*event*].

glamorous /'glæmərəs/ *adj* [*person, image, look*] séduisant; [*older person*] élégant; [*dress*] splendide; [*occasion*] brillant; [*job*] prestigieux/-ieuse.

glamour, glamor US /'glæmə(r)/ *n* (of person) séduction *f*; (of job) prestige *m*; (of travel, cars) fascination *f*.

glance /glɑːns, US glæns/ I *n* coup *m* d'œil; **to have a ~ at** jeter un coup d'œil sur; **you can tell at a ~ that** un coup d'œil suffit pour comprendre que; **without a backward ~** sans se retourner.
II *vi* **to ~ at** jeter un coup d'œil à; **to ~ out of the window** jeter un coup d'œil par la fenêtre; **to ~ around the room** parcourir la pièce du regard.
■ **glance off**: **~ off** [sth] [*bullet, stone*] ricocher sur ou contre; [*ball*] rebondir sur ou contre; [*ray, beam*] se réfléchir sur.

glancing /'glɑːnsɪŋ, US 'glænsɪŋ/ *adj* [*blow, kick*] oblique.

gland /glænd/ *n* ANAT glande *f*; **to have swollen ~s** avoir des ganglions.

glandular fever ▶1002 *n* mononucléose *f* infectieuse.

glare /gleə(r)/ I *n* **1** (angry look) regard *m* furieux; **2** (from light, headlights etc) lumière *f* éblouissante; **in the ~ of publicity** FIG sous le feu des médias.
II *vi* [*person*] lancer un regard furieux (**at** à).

glaring /'gleərɪŋ/ *adj* **1** (obvious) flagrant; **2** (dazzling) éblouissant; **3** (angry) furieux/-ieuse.

glaringly /'gleərɪŋlɪ/ *adv* **it's ~ obvious** c'est l'évidence même.

glass /glɑːs, US glæs/ I *n* **1** (substance) verre *m*; **a piece of ~** un morceau de verre; (tiny) un éclat de verre; **2** (drinking vessel) verre *m*; **wine ~** verre à vin; **a ~ of wine** un verre de vin; **3** ¢ (also **~ware**) verrerie *f*; **4** (mirror) miroir *m*; **5** (barometer) baromètre *m*.
II *noun modifier* [*bottle, ornament, shelf*] en verre.
III **glasses** *npl* **1** (spectacles) lunettes *fpl*; **a pair of ~es** une paire de lunettes; **he wears reading ~es**

glass: **~ blowing** *n* soufflage *m* du verre; **~ case** *n* (box) vitrine *f* en verre; (dome) globe *m*; **~ cloth** *n* essuie-verres *m inv*; **~ door** *n* porte *f* vitrée; **~ eye** *n* œil *m* de verre; **~ fibre** GB, **~ fiber** US *n* fibre *f* de verre; **~ful** *n* verre *m*.

glasshouse /'glɑːshaʊs, US 'glæs-/ *n* GB serre *f*.
IDIOMS **people in glass houses shouldn't throw stones** mieux vaut balayer devant sa porte avant de critiquer.

glass: **~making** *n* fabrication *f* du verre; **~ paper** *n* papier *m* de verre; **~works** *n* verrerie *f*.

glassy /'glɑːsɪ, US 'glæsɪ/ *adj* **1** (resembling glass) [*substance*] vitreux/-euse; **2** (slippery) [*road*] (from ice) verglacé; (from rain) glissant; **3** [*waters*] (calm) lisse (comme un miroir); (clear) transparent; **4** [*eyes*] (from drink, illness) vitreux/-euse; (hostile) glacé.

glassy-eyed /ˌglɑːsɪ'aɪd, US ˌglæs-/ *adj* (from drink, illness) aux yeux vitreux; (hostile) au regard glacial.

Glaswegian /glæz'wiːdʒən/ I *n* (inhabitant) habitant/-e *m/f* de Glasgow; (native) originaire *m/f* de Glasgow.
II *adj* [*accent, speech*] de Glasgow.

glaucoma /glɔː'kəʊmə/ ▶1002 *n* glaucome *m*.

glaze /gleɪz/ I *n* **1** GEN vernis *m*; (on fabric) lustre *m*; **2** (for ceramics) glaçure *f*; (in oil painting) glacis *m*; CULIN (on pastry) dorure *f*; (of jelly) nappage *m*; (on meat) glaçage *m*; **3** US (ice) verglas *m*.
II *vtr* **1** GB vitrer [*window*]; mettre [qch] sous verre [*picture*]; **2** (coat) vernisser [*ceramics*]; vernir [*leather*]; PHOT glacer; CULIN glacer [*meat*]; dorer [*pastry*].
III *vi* (also **~ over**) [*eyes*] devenir vitreux.

glazed /gleɪzd/ *adj* [*door, window*] vitré; [*ceramics*] vernissé; [*fabric*] lustré; [*paper*] glacé; CULIN [*meat, ham*] glacé; FIG **to have a ~ look in one's eyes** avoir les yeux vitreux

glazier /'gleɪzɪə(r), US -ʒər/ ▶1251, 1251 *n* vitrier *m*.

gleam /gliːm/ I *n* (of light) lueur *f* ALSO FIG; (of sunshine) rayon *m*; (of gold, polished surface) reflet *m*; (of water) miroitement *m*.
II *vi* [*light*] luire; [*knife, leather, surface*] reluire; [*jewel*] rutiler; [*water*] miroiter; [*eyes, teeth*] briller.

gleaming /'gliːmɪŋ/ *adj* [*eyes, teeth, light*] brillant; [*leather, polished surface*] reluisant; [*water*] miroitant; [*jewel*] rutilant; [*kitchen etc*] étincelant (de propreté).

glean /gliːn/ *vtr, vi* LIT, FIG glaner.

glee /gliː/ *n* allégresse *f*; (spiteful) jubilation *f*.

gleeful /'gliːfl/ *adj* jubilant.

glib /glɪb/ *adj* PÉJ désinvolte.

glide /glaɪd/ I *n* (in skating etc) pas *m* glissé; (in air) vol *m* plané.
II *vi* GEN glisser (**on, over** sur); (in air) planer.

glider /'glaɪdə(r)/ *n* AVIAT planeur *m*.

gliding /'glaɪdɪŋ/ ▶949 *n* SPORT vol *m* à voile.

glimmer /'glɪmə(r)/ I *n* (light) faible lueur *f*; (trace) lueur *f*.
II *vi* jeter une faible lueur.

glimmering /'glɪmərɪŋ/ I *n* LIT scintillement *m*; **the ~ of an idea** l'ébauche *f* d'une idée.
II *adj* [*sea, star*] scintillant.

glimpse /glɪmps/ I *n* **1** (sighting) vision *f* fugitive (**of** de); **to catch a ~ of sth** entrevoir qch; **2** FIG (insight) aperçu *m* (**of, at** de).
II *vtr* LIT, FIG entrevoir.

glint /glɪnt/ I *n* GEN reflet *m*; (in eye) lueur *f*.
II *vi* étinceler.

glisten /'glɪsn/ *vi* [*eyes, hair, surface*] luire; [*tears*] briller; [*water*] scintiller; [*silk*] chatoyer.

glitch○ /glɪtʃ/ *n* GEN pépin○ *m*; COMPUT problème *m* technique.

glitter /'glɪtə(r)/ I *n* (substance) paillettes *fpl*; (sparkle) éclat *m*; (of frost) scintillement *m*.
II *vi* scintiller.
IDIOMS **all that ~s is not gold** PROV tout ce qui brille n'est pas or PROV.

glittering /'glɪtərɪŋ/ *adj* LIT scintillant; FIG brillant.

---

go

As an intransitive verb

go as a simple intransitive verb is translated by *aller*:

we're going to Paris	= nous allons à Paris
where are you going?	= où vas-tu?
Sasha went to London last week	= Sasha est allée à Londres la semaine dernière

Note that *aller* conjugates with *être* in compound tenses. For the conjugation of *aller* see the French verb tables. For more examples and particular usages see the entry **go**.

The verb go produces a great many phrasal verbs in English (*go up, go down, go out, go back* etc.). Many of these are translated by a single verb in French (*monter, descendre, sortir, retourner* etc.). The phrasal verbs are listed separately at the end of the entry **go**.

As an auxiliary verb

When *go* is used as an auxiliary to show intention, it is also translated by *aller*:

I'm going to buy a car tomorrow	= je vais acheter une voiture demain
I was going to talk to you about it	= j'allais t'en parler
he's not going to ask for a rise	= il ne va pas demander d'augmentation

For more examples and particular usages see **I 23** in the entry **go**. For all other uses see the entry **go**.

---

gloat /gləʊt/ *vi* jubiler (**at, over** à l'idée de).

gloating /ˈgləʊtɪŋ/ *adj* triomphant.

global /ˈgləʊbl/ *adj* (world wide) mondial; (comprehensive) global; (spherical) sphérique.

globally /ˈgləʊbəlɪ/ *adv* [*compete, produce*] à l'échelle mondiale; [*famous, influential*] dans le monde entier.

global: **~ village** *n* village *m* planétaire; **~ warming** *n* réchauffement *m* de l'atmosphère.

globe /gləʊb/ *n* **1** (world) **the ~** le globe; **2** (model) globe *m* terrestre.

globe artichoke *n* artichaut *m*.

globetrotting /ˈgləʊbtrɒtɪŋ/ **I** *n* voyages *mpl* à travers le monde. **II** *adj* voyageur/-euse.

globule /ˈglɒbjuːl/ *n* gouttelette *f* (**of** de).

gloom /gluːm/ *n* **1** LIT obscurité *f*; **2** FIG morosité *f* (**about, over** à propos de); **to cast a ~ over sb** attrister qn; **to cast a ~ over sth** assombrir qch.

gloomily /ˈgluːmɪlɪ/ *adv* [*say, do*] d'un air lugubre.

gloomy /ˈgluːmɪ/ *adj* **1** (dark) sombre; **2** (sad) [*expression, person, voice*] lugubre; [*weather*] morose; [*news, outlook*] déprimant; **to be ~ about sth** être pessimiste à propos de qch.

glorify /ˈglɔːrɪfaɪ/ *I vtr* (all contexts) glorifier. **II glorified** *pp adj* **the 'villa' was a glorified bungalow** la 'villa' n'était rien de plus qu'un simple pavillon.

glorious /ˈglɔːrɪəs/ *adj* **1** (marvellous) GEN magnifique; [*holiday, outing*] merveilleux/-euse; **2** (illustrious) glorieux/-ieuse.

gloriously /ˈglɔːrɪəslɪ/ *adv* merveilleusement.

glory /ˈglɔːrɪ/ **I** *n* **1** (honour) ALSO RELIG gloire *f*; **2** (splendour) splendeur *f*; **3** (source of pride) fierté *f*. **II** *vi* **to ~ in** être très fier/fière de.

Glos *n* GB POST *abrév écrite* = **Gloucestershire**.

gloss /glɒs/ **I** *n* **1** (lustre) (of wood, metal etc) lustre *m*; (of hair) éclat *m*; FIG (glamour) clinquant *m*; **to lose its ~** LIT, FIG perdre (de) son éclat; **to take the ~ off** FIG gâcher [*occasion*]; **2** FIG (appearance) vernis *m*; **3** (in text) glose *f*; **4** (paint) laque *f* (brillante). **II** *vtr* (explain) gloser [*word, text*].

■ **gloss over**: **~ over** [**sth**] (pass rapidly over) glisser sur; (hide) dissimuler.

glossary /ˈglɒsərɪ/ *n* glossaire *m*.

---

gloss: **~ finish** *n* brillant *m*; **~ paint** *n* laque *f* (brillante).

glossy /ˈglɒsɪ/ *adj* [*hair, fur, material*] luisant; [*wood, metal*] brillant; [*leaves*] vernissé; [*photograph*] brillant; [*brochure*] luxueux/-euse; FIG [*production, film, interior*] qui a un éclat plutôt superficiel.

glossy magazine *n* magazine *m* illustré (de luxe).

glottal stop *n* LING coup *m* de glotte.

glove /glʌv/ *n* gant *m*; **with the ~s off** FIG sans prendre de gants; **her ~d hands** ses mains gantées. IDIOMS **it fits like a ~** cela me/lui etc va comme un gant; **to be hand in ~ with sb** être de mèche avec qn○.

glove: **~ box**, **~ compartment** *n* boîte *f* à gants; **~ puppet** *n* marionnette *f* à gaine.

glow /gləʊ/ **I** *n* **1** (of coal, furnace) rougeoiement *m*; (of room, candle) lueur *f*; **2** (colour) éclat *m*; **3** (feeling) douce sensation *f*; **it gives you a warm ~** ça fait chaud au cœur.
II *vi* **1** (give off light) [*coal, metal, furnace*] rougeoyer; [*lamp, paint, cigarette*] luire; **2** (look vibrant) [*colour*] être éclatant; **her skin ~ed** elle avait un teint éblouissant; **to ~ with health** resplendir de santé; **to ~ with pride** rayonner de fierté.

glower /ˈglaʊə(r)/ *vi* lancer des regards noirs (**at** à).

glowering /ˈglaʊərɪŋ/ *adj* [*face*] courroucé; [*sky*] menaçant.

glowing /ˈgləʊɪŋ/ *adj* **1** (bright) [*ember*] rougeoyant; [*lava*] incandescent; [*face, cheeks*] (from exercise) rouge; (from pleasure) radieux/-ieuse; [*colour*] chaud; **2** (complimentary) élogieux/-ieuse.

glowworm /ˈgləʊwɜːm/ *n* ver *m* luisant.

glucose /ˈgluːkəʊs/ **I** *n* glucose *m*.
II *noun modifier* [*powder, syrup, tablets*] de glucose; [*drink*] au glucose.

glue /gluː/ **I** *n* LIT colle *f*; **to sniff ~** inhaler de la colle.
II *vtr* coller; **to ~ sth on** ou **down** coller qch.
III glued *pp adj* **to have one's eyes ~d to sb/sth** avoir les yeux fixés sur qn/qch; **to be ~d to the TV** être collé○ devant la télé; **to be ~d to the spot** être cloué sur place.

glue: **~ pen** *n* stylo *m* colle transparente; **~-sniffing** *n* inhalation *f* de colle.

glum /glʌm/ *adj* morose.

glut /glʌt/ **I** *n* GEN surabondance *f*, excès *m*.
II *vtr* (*p prés etc* **-tt-**) inonder.
III glutted *pp adj* LIT, FIG rassasié (**with** de).

glutinous /ˈgluːtənəs/ *adj* gluant.

glutton /ˈglʌtn/ *n* (greedy) glouton/-onne *m/f*; FIG **a ~ for punishment** un masochiste.

gluttony /ˈglʌtənɪ/ *n* gloutonnerie *f*.

glycerin(e) /ˈglɪsəriːn, US -rɪn/ *n* glycérine *f*.

gm *n* (*abrév écrite* = **gram**) g.

GMT *n* (*abrév* = **Greenwich Mean Time**) TU.

gnarled /nɑːld/ *adj* noueux/-euse.

gnash /næʃ/ *vtr* **to ~ one's teeth** grincer des dents.

gnat /næt/ *n* moucheron *m*.

gnaw /nɔː/ **I** *vtr* LIT ronger; FIG (torment) [*hunger, remorse*] tenailler; [*pain*] lanciner.
II *vi* **to ~ at** ou **on sth** ronger qch.

gnawing /ˈnɔːɪŋ/ *adj* [*hunger, guilt*] tenaillant; [*pain*] lancinant.

gnome /nəʊm/ *n* **1** (goblin) gnome *m*; **garden ~** petit nain *m* (en plâtre); **2**○ **~ of Zurich** banquier *m* international.

GNP *n* (*abrév* = **gross national product**) PNB *m*.

go /gəʊ/ **I** *vi* (3° *pers sg prés* **goes**; *prét* **went**; *pp* **gone**) **1** (move, travel) aller (**from** de; **to** à, en); **to ~ to Paris/to Wales/to California** aller à Paris; aller au Pays de Galles/en Californie; **to ~ to town/to the country** aller en ville/à la campagne; **they went home** ils sont rentrés chez eux; **to ~ up/down/across** monter/descendre/traverser; **I went into the room** je suis entré dans la pièce; **to ~ by bus/train** voyager en bus/train; **to ~ by** ou **past**

[*person, vehicle*] passer; **that car's going very fast!** cette voiture roule très vite!; **there he goes again!** (that's him again) le revoilà!; FIG (he's starting again) le voilà qui recommence!; **where do we ~ from here?** FIG et maintenant qu'est-ce qu'on fait?; **2** (on specific errand, activity) aller; **to ~ shopping** aller faire des courses; **to ~ on a journey/on holiday** partir en voyage/en vacances; **to ~ for a drink** aller prendre un verre; **3** (attend) aller; **to ~ to school/work** aller à l'école/au travail; **to ~ to the doctor's** aller chez le médecin; **4** (used as auxiliary with present participle) **she went running up the stairs** elle a monté l'escalier en courant; **5** (depart) partir; **6** EUPH (die) mourir, disparaître; **when I am gone** quand je ne serai plus là; **7** (disappear) partir; **the money goes on school fees** l'argent part en frais de scolarité; **the money has all gone** il ne reste plus d'argent; **I left my bike outside and now it's gone** j'ai laissé mon vélo dehors et il n'est plus là; **there goes my chance of winning!** c'en est fait de mes chances de gagner!; **8** (be sent, transmitted) **it can't ~ by post** on ne peut pas l'envoyer par la poste; **these proposals will ~ before parliament** ces propositions seront soumises au parlement; **9** (become) **to ~ red** rougir; **to ~ white** blanchir; **to ~ mad** devenir fou/folle; **10** (change over to new system) **to ~ Labour** [*country, constituency*] voter travailliste; **to ~ metric** adopter le système m étrique; **11** (be, remain) **the people went hungry** les gens n'avaient rien à manger; **we went for two days without food** nous avons passé deux jours sans rien manger; **to ~ unnoticed** passer inaperçu; **the question went unanswered** la question est restée sans réponse; **he was allowed to ~ free** il a été libéré; **12** (weaken, become impaired) **his memory is going** il perd la mémoire; **his hearing is going** il devient sourd; **my voice is going** je n'ai plus de voix; **the battery is going** la batterie est presque à plat; **13** (of time) **there are only three days to ~ before Christmas** il ne reste plus que trois jours avant Noël; **how's the time going?** quelle heure est-il?; **it's just gone seven o'clock** il est sept heures passées; **14** (be got rid of) **he'll have to ~!** il va falloir qu'on se débarrasse de lui!; **the car will have to ~** il va falloir vendre la voiture; **either she goes or I do!** c'est elle ou moi!; **six down and four to ~!** six de faits, et encore quatre à faire!; **15** (operate, function) [*vehicle, machine, clock*] marcher, fonctionner; **to set** [*sth*] **going** mettre [qch] en marche; **to get going** [*engine, machine*] se mettre en marche; FIG [*business*] démarrer; **to get the fire going** allumer le feu; **to keep going** [*person, business, machine*] se maintenir; **we have several projects going at the moment** nous avons plusieurs projets en route en ce moment; **16** (start) **let's get going!** allons-y!; **to get things going** mettre les choses en train; **here goes!, here we ~!** c'est parti!; **once he gets going, he never stops** une fois lancé, il n'arrête pas; **17** (lead) aller, conduire (**to** à); **the road goes down/goes up** la route descend/monte; **18** (extend in depth or scope) **the roots ~ very deep** les racines s'enfoncent très profondément; **these habits ~ very deep** ces habitudes sont profondément ancrées; **it's true as far as it goes** c'est vrai dans un sens; **a hundred pounds doesn't ~ far these days** on ne va pas loin avec cent livres sterling de nos jours; **this goes a long way towards explaining his attitude** ceci explique en grande partie son attitude; **you can make £5 ~ a long way** on peut faire beaucoup de choses avec 5 livres sterling; **19** (belong, be placed) aller; **the suitcases will have to ~ in the back** il va falloir mettre les valises derrière; **20** (fit) GEN rentrer; **five into four won't ~** quatre n'est pas divisible par cinq; **21** (be expressed in particular way) **I can't remember how the poem goes** je n'arrive pas à me rappeler le poème; **how does the song ~?** quel est l'air de la chanson?; **as the saying goes** comme dit le proverbe; **22** (be accepted) **what he says goes** c'est lui qui fait la loi; **it goes without saying that** il va sans dire que; **anything goes** tout est permis; **23** (be about to) **to be going to do** aller faire; **it's going to snow**

il va neiger; **24** (happen) **the party went very well** la soirée s'est très bien passée; **the way things are going** si ça continue comme ça; **how's it going○?, how are things going?** comment ça va○?; **how goes it?** HUM comment ça va○?; **25** (be on average) **it's old, as Australian towns ~** c'est une ville assez vieille pour une ville australienne; **it wasn't a bad party, as parties ~** c'était une soirée plutôt réussie par rapport à la moyenne; **26** (be sold) **the house went for over £100,000** la maison a été vendue à plus de 100 000 livres; **'going, going, gone!'** 'une fois, deux fois, trois fois, adjugé!'; **27** (be on offer) **I'll have some coffee, if there's any going** je prendrai bien un café, s'il y en a; **it's the best machine going** c'est la meilleure machine du marché; **there's a job going** il y a un poste libre; **28** (contribute) **the money will ~ towards a new roof** l'argent servira à payer un nouveau toit; **everything that goes to make a good teacher** toutes les qualités d'un bon enseignant; **29** (be given) [*award, prize*] aller (**to** à); [*estate, inheritance, title*] passer (**to** à); **the job went to a local man** le poste a été donné à un homme de la région; **30** (emphatic use) **why did he ~ and spoil it?** pourquoi est-il allé tout gâcher?; **he went and won the competition!** il s'est débrouillé pour gagner le concours!; **you've really gone and done it now!** tu peux être fier de toi! IRON; **then he had to ~ and lose his wallet** comme s'il ne manquait plus que ça, il a perdu son portefeuille; **31** (of money) (be spent, used up) **all his money goes on drink** tout son argent passe dans l'alcool; **I don't know where all my money goes** (**to**)! je ne sais pas ce que je fais de mon argent!; **32** (make sound, perform action or movement) GEN faire; [*bell, alarm*] sonner; **the cat went 'miaow'** le chat a fait 'miaou'; **wait until the bell goes** attends que la cloche sonne (*subj*); **she went like this with her fingers** elle a fait comme ça avec ses doigts; **33** (resort to, have recourse to) **to ~ to war** [*country*] entrer en guerre; [*soldier*] partir à la guerre; **to ~ to law** GB ou **to the law** US aller en justice; **34** (break, collapse etc) [*roof*] s'effondrer; [*cable, rope*] se rompre; [*light bulb*] griller; **35** (take one's turn) **you ~ next** c'est ton tour après, c'est à toi après; **you ~ first** après vous; **36** (be in harmony) **those two colours don't ~ together** ces deux couleurs ne vont pas ensemble; **37** (in takeaway) **to ~** à emporter.

II vtr (3ᵉ pers sg prés **goes**; prét **went**; pp **gone**) faire [*number of miles*]; **are you going my way?** tu vas dans la même direction que moi?

III n (pl **goes**) **1** GB (turn) tour m; (try) essai m; **whose ~ is it?** GEN à qui le tour?; (in game) à qui de jouer?; **I had to have several goes before passing** j'ai dû m'y reprendre à plusieurs fois avant de réussir; **2**○ (energy) **to be full of ~, to be all ~** être très dynamique.

IDIOMS **all systems are ~!** AÉROSP tout est paré pour le lancement!; **to have a ~ at sb** s'en prendre à qn; **to make a ~ of sth** réussir qch; **she's always on the ~** elle n'arrête jamais; **he's all ~○!** il n'arrête pas!; **we have several different projects on the ~** nous avons plusieurs projets différents en chantier; (it's) **no ~!** pas question!; **from the word ~** dès le départ; **in one ~** d'un seul coup; **to ~ one better than sb** renchérir sur qn; **that's how it goes!, that's the way it goes!** c'est la vie!; **there you ~○!** voilà!

■ **go about: ¶ ~ about 1** = **go around; 2** NAUT virer de bord; **¶ ~ about** [*sth*] **1** (undertake) s'attaquer à [*task*]; **he knows how to ~ about it** il sait s'y prendre; **2** (be busy with) **to ~ about one's business** vaquer à ses occupations.

■ **go across: ¶ ~ across** traverser; **he's gone across to the shop** il est allé au magasin en face; **¶ ~ across** [*sth*] traverser.

■ **go after: ~ after** [*sth/sb*] **1** (chase) poursuivre; **2** FIG (try hard to get) **he really went after that job** il a fait tout son possible pour avoir ce travail.

■ **go against: ~ against** [*sb/sth*] **1** (prove unfavourable to) **the vote/decision went against them** le vote/la décision leur a été défavorable; **the war is** going against them la guerre tourne à leur désavantage; **2** (conflict with) être contraire à [*rules, principles*]; **to ~ against the trend** aller à l'encontre de la tendance; **3** (resist, oppose) s'opposer à.

■ **go ahead 1** (go in front) **~ ahead, I'll follow you on** partez devant, je vous suis; **2** FIG (proceed) [*event*] avoir lieu; **~ ahead and shoot!** vas-y, tire!; **they are going ahead with the project** ils ont décidé de mettre le projet en route; **we can ~ ahead without them** nous pouvons continuer sans eux.

■ **go along 1** (move along) [*person, vehicle*] aller, avancer; **to make sth up as one goes along** FIG inventer qch au fur et à mesure; **2** (attend) aller; **I went along** j'y suis allé.

■ **go along with**: **~ along with** [*sb/sth*] être d'accord avec.

■ **go around**: ¶ **~ around 1** (move, travel about) se promener, circuler; **she goes around on a bicycle** elle circule à bicyclette; **they ~ around everywhere together** ils vont partout ensemble; **2** (circulate) [*rumour*] courir; **there isn't enough money to ~ around** il n'y a pas assez d'argent pour tout le monde; ¶ **~ around** [*sth*] faire le tour de [*house, shops*].

■ **go at**: ¶ **~ at** [*sb*] (attack) attaquer; ¶ **~ at** [*sth*] s'attaquer à.

■ **go away** [*person*] partir; **~ away and leave me alone!** va-t'en et laisse-moi tranquille!; **don't ~ away thinking that** ne va pas croire que; **this cold just won't ~ away!** je n'arrive pas à me débarrasser de ce rhume!

■ **go back 1** (return) retourner; (turn back) rebrousser chemin; (resume work) reprendre le travail; (resume classes, studies) reprendre les cours; **let's ~ back to France** retournons en France; **to ~ back to the beginning** recommencer; **to ~ back to sleep** se rendormir; **to ~ back to work** se remettre au travail; **there's no going back** FIG vous ne pouvez plus reculer; **2** (in time) remonter; **this tradition goes back a century** cette tradition est vieille d'un siècle; **we ~ back a long way** ça fait longtemps qu'on se connaît; **3** (revert) revenir (**to** à).

■ **go back on**: **~ back on** [*sth*] revenir sur [*promise, decision*].

■ **go before**: ¶ **~ before** (go in front) aller au devant; FIG (in time) se passer avant; ¶ **~ before** [*sb /sth*] comparaître devant [*court, judge*]; **the bill went before parliament** le projet de loi a été soumis au parlement.

■ **go below** GEN, NAUT descendre.

■ **go by**: ¶ **~ by** passer; **as time goes by** avec le temps; ¶ **~ by** [*sth*] **1** (judge by) juger d'après; **you mustn't ~ by what you read in the papers** il ne faut pas croire tout ce que disent les journaux; **2** (proceed by) **to ~ by the rules** suivre or observer le règlement.

■ **go down**: ¶ **~ down 1** (descend) GEN descendre; [*sun*] se coucher; **to ~ down to the pub** aller au pub; **2** (fall) tomber; (sink) couler; **the plane went down in flames** l'avion s'est écrasé en flammes; **3** (be received) **to ~ down well/badly** être bien/mal reçu; **4** (become lower) [*water level, price, temperature, standard*] baisser; [*tide*] descendre; (abate) [*storm, wind*] se calmer; (fall in price) devenir moins cher; **5** (become deflated) [*swelling*] désenfler; [*tyre*] se dégonfler; **6** GB UNIV (for holiday) terminer les cours; (permanently) quitter l'université; **7** GEN, SPORT (be defeated) perdre; (be downgraded) redescendre; **8** (be remembered) **he will ~ down as a great statesman** on se souviendra de lui comme d'un grand homme d'État; **9** (be recorded) être noté; **10** (be stricken) **to ~ down with flu/malaria** attraper la grippe/la malaria; **11**° GB (go to prison) être envoyé en prison; **12** COMPUT tomber en panne; ¶ **~ down** [*sth*] descendre dans [*mine*].

■ **go for**: ¶ **~ for** [*sb/sth*] **1**° (favour, have liking for) craquer° pour [*person*]; aimer [*style of music, literature etc*]; **2** (apply to) être valable pour, s'appliquer à; ¶ **~ for** [*sb*] **1** (attack) attaquer; **2 he has a lot going for him** il a beaucoup de choses pour lui; ¶ **~ for** [*sth*] **1** (attempt to achieve) essayer d'obtenir [*honour,*

victory]; **she's going for the world record** elle vise le record mondial; **~ for it**○! vas-y, fonce○!; **2** (choose) choisir, prendre.

■ **go forward(s)** avancer.

■ **go in 1** (enter) entrer; (go back in) rentrer; **2** MIL [*troops*] attaquer; **3** (disappear) [*sun*] se cacher.

■ **go in for**: **~ in for** [*sth*] **1** (be keen on) aimer; **2** (take up) **to ~ in for teaching** entrer dans l'enseignement; **to ~ in for politics** se lancer dans la politique; **3** (take part in) s'inscrire à [*exam, competition*].

■ **go into**: **~ into** [*sth*] **1** (enter) entrer dans; FIG (take up) se lancer dans [*business, profession*]; **2** (examine) étudier [*question*]; **3** (explain) **I won't ~ into why I did it** je n'expliquerai pas pourquoi je l'ai fait; **let's not ~ into that now** laissons cela de côté pour l'instant; **4** (be expended) **a lot of work went into this project** beaucoup de travail a été investi dans ce projet; **5** (hit) [*car, driver*] rentrer dans, heurter.

■ **go off**: ¶ **~ off 1** (explode, fire) [*bomb*] exploser; **the gun didn't ~ off** le coup n'est pas parti; **2** [*alarm clock*] sonner; [*fire alarm*] se déclencher; **3** (depart) partir, s'en aller; **he went off to work** il est parti au travail; **4** GB (go bad) [*milk, cream*] tourner; [*meat*] s'avarier; [*butter*] rancir; [*performer, athlete etc*] perdre sa forme; [*work*] se dégrader; **5**° (fall asleep) s'endormir; **6** (cease to operate) [*lights, heating*] s'éteindre; **7** (happen, take place) [*evening, organized event*] se passer; **8** THEAT quitter la scène; ¶ **~ off** [*sb/sth*] GB **I've gone off whisky** je n'aime plus tellement le whisky; **I think she's gone off the idea** je crois qu'elle a renoncé à l'idée.

■ **go off with**: **~ off with** [*sb/sth*] partir avec.

■ **go on**: ¶ **~ on 1** (happen, take place) se passer; **how long has this been going on?** depuis combien de temps est-ce que ça dure?; **a lot of stealing goes on** il y a beaucoup de vols; **2** (continue on one's way) poursuivre son chemin; **3** (continue) continuer; **the meeting went on into the afternoon** la réunion s'est prolongée jusque dans l'après-midi; **the list goes on and on** la liste est infinie; **that's enough to be going on with** ça suffit pour le moment; **here's £20 to be going on with** voici 20 livres pour te dépanner; **~ on (with you)**○! allons donc!; **4** (of time) (elapse) **as time went on, they...** avec le temps, ils...; **as the evening went on** au fur et à mesure que la soirée avançait; **5** (keep talking) **to ~ on about sth** ne pas arrêter de parler de qch; **the way she goes on, you'd think she was an expert!** à l'entendre, on croirait qu'elle est experte!; **6** (proceed) passer; **let's ~ on to the next item** passons au point suivant; **he went on to say that** puis il a dit que; **7** (go into operation) [*heating, lights*] s'allumer; **8** THEAT entrer en scène; **9** (approach) **it's going on three o'clock** il est presque trois heures; **she's four going on five** elle va sur ses cinq ans; **10** (fit) **these gloves won't ~ on** ces gants ne m'iront pas; **the lid won't ~ on properly** le couvercle ne ferme pas bien; ¶ **~ on** [*sth*] se fonder sur [*piece of evidence, information*]; **that's all we've got to ~ on** tout ce que nous savons avec certitude; **we've got nothing else to ~ on** nous n'avons pas d'autre point de départ.

■ **go on at**: **~ on at** [*sb*] s'en prendre à.

■ **go out 1** (leave, depart) sortir; **to ~ out walking** aller se promener; **to ~ out for a drink** aller prendre un verre; **she's gone out to Australia** elle est partie pour l'Australie; **2** (have relationship) **to ~ out with sb** sortir avec qn; **3** [*tide*] descendre; **4** (become unfashionable) passer de mode; (no longer be used) ne plus être utilisé; **5** (be extinguished) [*fire, light*] s'éteindre; **6** [*invitation, summons*] être envoyé; RADIO, TV (be broadcast) être diffusé; **7** (be eliminated) GEN, SPORT être éliminé; **8** (expressing sympathy) **my heart goes out to them** je les plains de tout mon cœur; **9** (disappear) **all the spirit seemed to have gone out of her** elle semblait avoir perdu tout son entrain.

■ **go over**: ¶ **~ over 1** (cross over) aller (**to** vers); **we are now going over to Washington** RADIO, TV nous passons maintenant l'antenne à Washington; **2** (be received) être reçu; **3** (switch to other side or alternative) passer (**to** à); ¶ **~ over** [*sth*] **1** (review, inspect) passer

[qch] en revue [*details, facts*]; vérifier [*accounts, figures*]; relire [*article*]; **to ~ over a house** faire le tour d'une maison; **2** (clean) **he went over the room with a duster** il a donné un coup de chiffon dans la pièce; **3** (exceed) dépasser.

■ **go round** GB: **¶ ~ round 1** (turn) tourner; **2** (call round) **to ~ round to see sb** aller voir qn; **3** (suffice) **there isn't enough food to ~ round** il n'y a pas assez de nourriture pour tout le monde; **4** (make detour) faire un détour; **we had to ~ the long way round** il a fallu qu'on prenne un chemin plus long; **¶ ~ round [sth]** (visit) faire le tour de.

■ **go through: ¶ ~ through 1** (come in) entrer; **2** (be approved) [*law, agreement*] passer; [*divorce*] être prononcé; [*business deal*] être conclu; **¶ ~ through [sth] 1** endurer, subir [*experience, ordeal*]; passer par [*stage, phase*]; **she's gone through a lot** elle a beaucoup souffert; **the country has gone through two civil wars** le pays a connu deux guerres civiles; **to ~ through a crisis** traverser une crise; **as you ~ through life** au fur et à mesure que tu vieillis; **you have to ~ through the switchboard** il faut passer par le standard; **it went through my mind that** l'idée m'a traversé l'esprit que; **2** (check, inspect) examiner; (rapidly) parcourir [*documents, files, list*]; **3** (search) fouiller; **4** (perform, rehearse) répéter [*scene*]; expliquer [*procedure*]; remplir [*formalities*]; **5** (consume, use up) dépenser [*money*]; **we went through three bottles of wine** nous avons bu trois bouteilles de vin.

■ **go through with: ~ through with [sth]** réaliser, mettre [qch] à exécution [*plan*]; **in the end they decided to ~ through with the wedding** finalement ils ont décidé que le mariage aurait lieu; **I can't ~ through with it** je ne peux pas le faire.

■ **go together 1** (harmonize) aller ensemble; **2** (entail each other) aller de pair.

■ **go under** (sink) couler; FIG [*person*] succomber; [*business, company*] faire faillite.

■ **go up: ¶ ~ up 1** (ascend, rise) monter; **to ~ up to bed** monter se coucher; **2** (rise) [*price, temperature*] monter; [*figures*] augmenter; THEAT [*curtain*] se lever (on sur); **petrol has gone up (in price)** (le prix de) l'essence a augmenté; **3** (be erected) [*building*] être construit; [*poster*] être affiché; **4** (blown up) sauter, exploser; **5** GB UNIV (start university) entrer à l'université; (start term) reprendre les cours; **6** (be upgraded) **the team has gone up to the first division** l'équipe est passée en première division; **7** (continue) **the book goes up to 1990** le livre va jusqu'en 1990; **¶ ~ up [sth] 1** (mount) monter, gravir [*hill, mountain*]; **2 to ~ up a class** SCH passer dans une classe supérieure.

■ **go with: ~ with [sth] 1** (match, suit) aller avec; **2** (accompany) aller de pair avec.

■ **go without: ~ without** s'en passer; **¶ ~ without [sth]** se passer de.

goad /gəʊd/ **I** *n* LIT, FIG aiguillon *m*.
II *vtr* **1** (prod) aiguillonner; **2** (provoke) provoquer; **to ~ sb into doing sth** pousser qn à faire qch.

go-ahead○ /ˈgəʊəhed/ *n* **to give sb the ~**○ donner le feu vert à qn; **to get the ~** recevoir le feu vert.

goal /gəʊl/ *n* GEN, SPORT but *m*; **to keep ~** ou **to play in ~** être gardien de but; **to score** ou **kick a ~** marquer un but; **to score an own ~** LIT, FIG marquer un but pour le compte de l'adversaire.

goal: ~ area *n* surface *f* de but; **~keeper ▸ 1251** *n* gardien *m* de but; **~ kick** *n* (in soccer) dégagement *m* aux six.

goalless /ˈgəʊllɪs/ *adj* **~ match** ou **draw** match *m* nul.

goalpost /ˈgəʊlpəʊst/ *n* poteau *m* de but.
IDIOMS **to move the ~s** changer les règles du jeu.

goat /gəʊt/ **I** *n* **1** ZOOL, CULIN chèvre *f*; **2**○ GB (fool) andouille○ *f*; **3**○ (lecher) vieux cochon *m*○.
II *noun modifier* [*cheese, meat, milk, stew*] de chèvre.
IDIOMS **he really gets my ~**○ il me tape sur les nerfs○; **that will separate the sheep from the ~s** cela permettra de voir ce que vaut chacun.

goatskin /ˈgəʊtskɪn/ *n* (leather) cuir *m* de chèvre; (pelt) peau *f* de chèvre.

gobble /ˈgɒbl/ **I** *n* (cry of turkey) glouglou *m*.
II *vtr* (also **~ down**) engloutir [*food*].
III *vi* **1** [*turkey*] glouglouter; **2** [*person*] se goinfrer○.
■ **gobble up** LIT, FIG: **~ [sth] up, ~ up [sth]** engloutir.

gobbledygook○ /ˈgɒbldɪguːk/ *n* charabia○ *m*.

go-between /ˈgəʊbɪtwiːn/ *n* intermédiaire *mf*.

goblet /ˈgɒblɪt/ *n* verre *m* à pied.

goblin /ˈgɒblɪn/ *n* lutin *m*.

gobsmacked○ /ˈgɒbsmækt/ *adj* GB estomaqué○.

god /gɒd/ **I** *n* LIT, FIG dieu *m*.
II God *pr n* **1** RELIG Dieu *m*; **so help me God** je le jure devant Dieu; **a man of God** un prêtre; **2** (in exclamations) (exasperated) zut○!; (surprised) ça alors○!; **God forbid**○! grands dieux, non!
III Gods○ *npl* THEAT paradis *m*, poulailler○ *m*.
IDIOMS **God helps those who help themselves** aide-toi, le ciel t'aidera; **to put the fear of God into sb** faire une peur bleue à qn; **to think one is God's gift (to women)**○ se croire irrésistible auprès des femmes.

God Almighty I *n* RELIG Dieu *m* Tout-Puissant.
II *excl* mon Dieu!
IDIOMS **he thinks he's ~** il se prend pour Dieu le père.

godchild *n* filleul-e *m/f*.

goddamn○ /ˈgɒdæm/ *adj* sacré○, fichu○.

goddaughter /ˈgɒdɔːtə(r)/ *n* filleule *f*.

goddess /ˈgɒdɪs/ *n* (divinity, woman) déesse *f*.

god: ~father *n* parrain *m*; **~-fearing** *adj* pieux/pieuse; **~-forsaken** *adj* [*country, place*] perdu.

godless /ˈgɒdlɪs/ *adj* impie.

godlike /ˈgɒdlaɪk/ *adj* divin.

godly /ˈgɒdlɪ/ *adj* pieux/pieuse.

godmother /ˈgɒdmʌðə(r)/ *n* marraine *f*.

godparent /ˈgɒdpeərənt/ *n* parrain/marraine *m/f*; **the ~s** le parrain et la marraine.

god: ~send *n* aubaine *f*; **~son** *n* filleul *m*.

goer /ˈgəʊə(r)/ **I**○ *n* GB **to be a ~** être plein d'allant.
II -goer *combining form* **theatre-~** personne *f* qui va au théâtre; (regular) amateur *m* de théâtre; **cinema-~** personne *f* qui va au cinéma; (regular) cinéphile *mf*.

goes /gəʊz/ ▸ **go**.

go: ~-getter○ *n* fonceur/-euse○ *m/f*; **~-getting**○ *adj* fonceur/-euse○.

goggle /ˈgɒgl/ *vi* [*person*] ouvrir des yeux ronds○.

goggle: ~-box *n* GB télé○ *f*; **~-eyed**○ *adj* avec des yeux ronds○.

goggles /ˈgɒglz/ *npl* (cyclist's, worker's) lunettes *fpl* protectrices; (skier's) lunettes *fpl* de ski; (for swimming) lunettes *fpl* de plongée.

go-go /ˈgəʊgəʊ/ *adj* [*dancing, girl*] de boîte○ (de nuit).

going /ˈgəʊɪŋ/ **I** *n* **1** (departure) départ *m*; **2** (progress) **that's not bad ~!, that's good ~!** c'est rapide!; **it was slow ~, the ~ was slow** (on journey) ça a été long; (at work) ça n'avançait pas vite; **the conversation was heavy ~** la conversation était laborieuse; **3** (condition of ground) état *m* du sol; **the ~ was hard** le terrain était lourd; **4** FIG (conditions) **when the ~ gets tough** quand les choses vont mal; **she finds her new job hard ~** elle trouve que son nouveau travail est difficile; **they got out while the ~ was good** ils s'en sont tirés avant qu'il ne soit trop tard.
II *adj* **1** (current) [*price*] actuel, en cours; **the ~ rate** le tarif en vigueur; **2** (operating) **~ concern** COMM affaire *f* qui marche; **they bought the business as a ~ concern** quand ils ont acheté l'entreprise elle était déjà montée; **3** (existing) **it's the best model ~** c'est le meilleur modèle sur le marché.
III -going *combining form* **theatre-~** la fréquentation des théâtres; **the theatre-~ public** les amateurs *mpl* de théâtre.

going-over○ /ˌgəʊɪŋˈəʊvə(r)/ *n* (*pl* **goings-over**) **1** (examination) (of vehicle, machine) révision *f*; (of document) vérification *f*; (cleaning) (of room, house) nettoyage *m*; **the doctor gave me a thorough ~** le médecin m'a soigneusement examiné; **2 to give sb a ~** (beat up) rouer qn de coups.

goings-on° /ˌgəʊɪŋzˈɒn/ npl (events) événements mpl; PÉJ (activities) activités fpl; (behaviour) conduite f.

go-kart /ˈgəʊkɑːt/ n kart m.

go-karting /ˈgəʊkɑːtɪŋ/ n karting m; **to go ~** faire du karting.

Golan /ˈgəʊlæn/ pr n **the ~ Heights** le (plateau m du) Golan.

gold /gəʊld/ **I** n **1** GEN, FIN or m; **to strike ~** découvrir un filon; **2** (colour) (couleur f) or m; **3** = **gold medal**.

II noun modifier [jewellery, cutlery, tooth] en or; [coin, medal, ingot, wire] d'or; [ore, deposit, alloy] d'or.

IDIOMS **as good as ~** sage comme une image; **to be worth one's weight in ~** valoir son pesant d'or.

Gold Coast n **1** HIST (Ghana) Côte-de-l'Or f; **2** (in Australia) série de stations balnéaires dans l'est de l'Australie; **3** US banlieue f huppée.

gold: **~ digger** n chercheur m d'or; **~ disc** n disque m d'or.

gold dust n LIT poudre f d'or; **to be like ~** FIG être une denrée rare.

golden /ˈgəʊldən/ adj **1** (made of gold) en or, d'or; **2** (gold coloured) doré, d'or; **~ hair** cheveux mpl dorés; **3** FIG [summer] idyllique; [voice, age, days] d'or; **a ~ opportunity** une occasion en or.

golden: **~ anniversary** n = **golden jubilee**; **~ boy** n enfant m chéri; **~-brown** ▶818 n, adj mordoré (m); **Golden Delicious** n golden f inv (pomme); **~ eagle** n aigle m royal; **Golden Fleece** n Toison f d'or; **~ girl** n enfant f chérie.

golden goose n **to kill the ~** tuer la poule aux œufs d'or.

golden: **~ handshake** n GB prime f de départ; **~ hello** n prime f d'embauche; **~ jubilee** n (wedding anniversary) noces fpl d'or; (other) jubilé m.

golden mean n (happy medium) **the ~** le juste milieu.

golden: **~ oldie** n (song) vieux succès m (de la chanson); (film) vieux succès m (du cinéma); **~ parachute** n US = **golden handshake**; **~ rule** n règle f d'or; **~ syrup** n GB ~ sirop m de sucre roux; **~ wedding** n noces fpl d'or; **~ yellow** n, adj jaune (m) d'or inv.

gold: **~ fever** n fièvre f de l'or; **~field** n terrain m aurifère; **~fish** n (pl **-fish** ou **-fishes**) poisson m rouge.

Goldilocks /ˈgəʊldɪlɒks/ pr n Boucles d'Or.

gold: **~ leaf** n feuille f d'or; **~ medal** n médaille f d'or; **~ mine** n LIT, FIG mine f d'or; **~ mining** n extraction f de l'or; **~ plate** n (coating) fine couche f d'or; (dishes) vaisselle f d'or; **~-plated** adj plaqué or inv; **~ rush** n ruée f vers l'or; **~smith** ▶1251 n orfèvre m; **~ standard** n étalon or m.

golf /gɒlf/ ▶949 **I** n golf m.

II noun modifier [ball, umbrella, equipment] de golf.

golf club n **1** (place) club m de golf; **2** (stick) crosse f de golf.

golf course n (terrain m de) golf m.

golfer /ˈgɒlfə(r)/ n joueur/-euse m/f de golf, golfeur/-euse m/f.

golfing /ˈgɒlfɪŋ/ n **to go ~** faire du golf.

golf links n = **golf course**.

gondola /ˈgɒndələ/ n **1** (boat) gondole f; **2** (under airship, balloon) nacelle f; (cable car) cabine f (de téléphérique); **3** US RAIL (also **~ car**) wagon m plat; **4** US (barge) barge f.

gone /gɒn/ **I** pp ▶ go.

II adj **1** [person] (departed) parti; (dead) disparu; **to be far ~** (ill) être très malade; (with drink) être complètement bourré°; (with drugs) planer° complètement; **to be long ~** [person] être mort depuis longtemps; [era] être révolu; **~ with the wind** autant en emporte le vent; **2** GB (pregnant) enceinte; **3** GB (past) **it's ~ six o'clock** il est six heures passées; **she's ~ eighty** elle a plus de quatre-vingts ans.

goner° /ˈgɒnə(r)/ n **to be a ~**° être fichu°.

gong /gɒŋ/ n gong m; **dinner ~** cloche f du dîner.

gonna° /ˈgɒnə/ = **going to**.

gonorrh(o)ea /ˌgɒnəˈrɪə/ ▶1002 n blennorragie f.

good /gʊd/ **I** n **1** (virtue) bien m; **to do ~** faire le bien; **to be up to no ~**° mijoter qch°; **to come to no ~** mal tourner; **2** (benefit) bien m; **for all the ~ it did me** pour le peu de bien que ça m'a fait; **she's too generous for her own ~** elle est trop généreuse et ça lui jouera des tours; **for the ~ of his health** LIT pour sa santé; **it didn't do my migraine any ~** ça n'a pas arrangé ma migraine; **no ~ can** ou **will come of it** rien de bon n'en sortira; **no ~ will come of waiting** il vaut mieux agir tout de suite; **to be all to the ~** être pour le mieux; **3** (use) **it's no ~ crying** ça ne sert à rien de pleurer; **what ~ would it do me?** à quoi cela me servirait-il?; **4** GB (profit) **to be £20 to the ~** avoir 20 livres sterling à son crédit.

II goods npl **1** (for sale) GEN articles mpl marchandise f; **stolen ~** marchandise volée; **electrical ~s** appareils mpl électro-ménagers; **~s and services** biens mpl de consommation et services; **2** GB RAIL marchandises fpl; **3** (property) affaires fpl biens mpl; **~ and chattels** biens et effets personnels **4**° **to deliver** ou **come up with the ~s** répondre à l'attente de qn; **that's the ~s!** c'est parfait!

III goods noun modifier GB RAIL [depot, station train, wagon] de marchandises.

IV adj (comparative **better**; superlative **best**) **1** (enjoyable) bon/bonne; [party] réussi; **the ~ weather** le beau temps; **to have a ~ time** bien s'amuser; **have a ~ day!** bonne journée!; **the ~ things in life** les petits plaisirs de l'existence; **the ~ life** la dolce vita; **it's ~ to see you again** je suis content de vous revoir **2** (happy) **to feel ~ about/doing** être content de/de faire; **I didn't feel very ~ about lying to him** je n'étais pas très fier de lui avoir menti; **3** (healthy) [eye, ear etc] bon/bonne; **you don't look too ~** tu as mauvaise mine; **I don't feel too ~** je ne me sens pas très bien; **4** (quality) bon/bonne; (best) [coat, china beau/belle; [degree] avec mention (after n); **I'm not ~ enough for her** je ne suis pas assez bien pour elle **nothing is too ~ for her son** rien n'est trop beau pour son fils; **5** (prestigious) (épith) [address, marriage bon/bonne; **6** (obedient) [child, dog] sage; [manners bon/bonne; **there's a ~ boy** ou **girl!** c'est bien!; **7** (favourable) bon/bonne; **the ~ thing is that** ce qui est bien c'est que; **New York is ~ for shopping** New York est un bon endroit pour faire les magasins; **8** (attractive) beau/belle; **to look ~ with** [garment, accessories] aller bien avec; **she looks ~ in blue** le bleu lui va bien; **9** (tasty) [meal] bon/bonne; **to taste ~** avoir bon goût; **to smell ~** sentir bon inv; **to look ~** avoir l'air bon; **10** (virtuous) (épith) [man, life vertueux/-euse; [Christian] bon/bonne; **the ~ guys** les bons mpl; **11** (kind) [person] gentil/-ille; **a ~ deed** une bonne action; **to do sb a ~ turn** rendre service à qn; **would you be ~ enough to do, would you be so ~ as to do** auriez-vous la gentillesse de faire **12** (pleasant) [humour, mood] bon/bonne; **to be in a ~ mood** être de bonne humeur; **to be very ~ about** se montrer très compréhensif au sujet de [mistake]; **13** (competent) bon/bonne; **she's a ~ swimmer** elle nage bien; **to be ~ at** être bon en [Latin, physics]; être bon à [badminton, chess]; **she's ~ at dancing** elle danse bien; **to be no ~ at** être nul/nulle en [tennis chemistry]; être nul/nulle à [chess, cards]; **I'm no ~ at knitting** je ne sais pas tricoter; **to be ~ with** savoir comment s'y prendre avec [children, animals] aimer [figures]; **to be ~ with one's hands** être habile de ses mains; **to be ~ with words** savoir manier la langue; **14** (beneficial) **to be ~ for** faire du bien à [person, plant]; être bon pour [health, business morale]; **exercise is ~ for you** l'exercice fait du bien; **he eats more than is ~ for him** il mange plus qu'il ne devrait; **say nothing if you know what's ~ for you** si je peux te donner un conseil, ne dis rien **15** (effective, suitable, accurate, sensible) bon/bonne; **to look ~** [design] faire de l'effet; **to keep ~ time** être très précis; **this will look ~ on your CV** GB ou

résumé US cela fera bien sur votre CV; **that's a ~ point** tout à fait; **16** (fluent) **he speaks ~ Spanish** il parle bien espagnol; **17** (fortunate) **it's a ~ job** ou **thing** (that) heureusement que; **it's a ~ job** ou **thing too!** tant mieux!; **we've never had it so ~**° les affaires n'ont jamais été aussi prospères; **it's too ~ to be true** c'est trop beau pour être vrai; **18** (serviceable) **this season ticket is ~ for two more months** cette carte d'abonnement est valable encore deux mois; **the car is ~ for another 10,000 km** la voiture fera encore 10 000 km; **it's as ~ a reason as any** c'est une raison comme une autre; **to be ~ for a loan** avoir de l'argent à prêter; **19** (substantial) (épith) [salary, size, hour] bon/bonne; **it must be worth a ~ 2,000 dollars** ça doit valoir au moins 2 000 dollars; **a ~ thick mattress** un matelas bien épais; **~ and early** de très bonne heure; **give it a ~ clean** nettoie-le bien; **we had a ~ laugh** on a bien ri; ▶**better, best.**
V as good as adv phr **1** (virtually) quasiment; **to be as ~ as new** être comme neuf/neuve; **2** (tantamount to) **it's as ~ as saying yes** c'est comme si tu disais oui; **he as ~ as called me a liar** il m'a plus ou moins traité de menteur.
VI for good adv phr pour toujours.
VII excl (expressing pleasure, satisfaction) c'est bien!; (with relief) tant mieux!; (to encourage, approve) très bien!
IDIOMS **~ for you!** (approvingly) bravo!; (sarcastically) tant mieux pour toi!; **that's a ~ one!** (of joke, excuse) elle est bonne celle-là!; **~ on you**°! GB bravo!; **~ thinking** bien vu!; **to be onto a ~ thing**°, **to have a ~ thing going**° être sur un bon filon; **you can have too much of a ~ thing** il ne faut pas abuser des bonnes choses.

good: **~ afternoon** excl (in greeting) bonjour; (in farewell) au revoir; **~-bye** n, excl au revoir; **~ evening** excl bonsoir; **~-for-nothing** n bon/bonne m/f à rien; **Good Friday** pr n RELIG Vendredi m saint; **~-hearted** adj généreux/-euse.

good-humoured GB, **good-humored** US /ˌɡʊdˈhjuːməd/ adj [crowd, discussion] détendu; [rivalry] amical; [banter] innocent; [remark, smile] plaisant; **to be ~** être de bonne humeur.

good-humouredly GB, **good-humoredly** US /ˌɡʊdˈhjuːmədlɪ/ adv [smile] plaisamment; [say] avec bonne humeur.

goodish /ˈɡʊdɪʃ/ adj assez bon/bonne.

good: **~-looking** adj beau/belle (before n); **~ looks** npl beauté f; **~ morning** excl (in greeting) bonjour; (in farewell) au revoir; **~-natured** adj [person] agréable; [animal] placide; [discussion] détendu; [remark] amical; [criticism] bien intentionné.

goodness /ˈɡʊdnɪs/ I n **1** (virtue, kindness) bonté f; **2** (nutritive value) **to be full of ~** être plein de bonnes choses; **the carrots will lose all their ~** les carottes perdront toutes leurs vertus.
II excl (also **~ gracious!**) mon Dieu!
IDIOMS **I hope to ~ that** je prie le ciel que (+ subj); **~ only knows how/when** Dieu (seul) sait comment/quand; **for ~' sake!** pour l'amour de Dieu!

good: **~-night** n, excl bonne nuit; **~-sized** adj [kitchen, room] spacieux/-ieuse; **~-tempered** adj [person] facile; [animal] placide; **~-time girl** n PÉJ (fun-loving) fêtarde° f; EUPH (prostitute) fille f de joie.

goodwill /ˌɡʊdˈwɪl/ I n **1** (helpful attitude) bonne volonté f; **2** (kindness) **to show ~ to** ou **towards sb** faire preuve de bienveillance à l'égard de qn; **in a spirit of ~** en toute amitié; **the season of ~** le temps de Noël; **3** COMM (reputation) actif m incorporel (constitué par sa réputation); (customers) clientèle f.
II noun modifier [gesture] de bonne volonté; [visite] d'amitié.

goof /ɡuːf/ I n (idiot) dingue° mf; (blunder) gaffe° f.
II vi faire une gaffe° or une bévue°.
■ **goof around**° (fool around) faire l'imbécile° mf; (laze about) glander⊃.

goon° /ɡuːn/ n (clown) cinglé°-e° mf; (thug) homme m de main.

goose /ɡuːs/ I n (pl **geese**) ZOOL, CULIN oie f; **you silly ~**°! idiot/-e!
II° vtr pincer les fesses de.
IDIOMS **to cook sb's ~**° couler° qn.

gooseberry /ˈɡʊzbərɪ, US ˈɡuːsberɪ/ n (fruit) groseille f à maquereau.
IDIOMS **to be a** ou **play ~** tenir la chandelle.

gooseberry: **~ bush** n groseillier m; **~ fool** n: purée de groseilles à maquereau à la crème.

goose: **~bumps** npl = **goose pimples**; **~flesh** n = **goose pimples**; **~ pimples** npl chair f de poule.

goose-step /ˈɡuːstep/ I n pas m de l'oie.
II vi défiler au pas de l'oie.

gore /ɡɔː(r)/ I n (blood) sang m.
II vtr encorner; **to ~ sb to death** tuer qn d'un coup de corne.

gorge /ɡɔːdʒ/ I n ANAT, GEOG gorge f.
II v refl **to ~ oneself** se gaver (on de).
IDIOMS **to make sb's ~ rise** dégoûter or écœurer qn.

gorgeous /ˈɡɔːdʒəs/ adj **1**° (lovely) [food, cake, scenery] formidable°; [kitten, baby] adorable; [weather, day, person] splendide; **2** (sumptuous) somptueux/-euse.

gorilla /ɡəˈrɪlə/ n ZOOL, FIG gorille m.

gorse /ɡɔːs/ n ¢ ajoncs mpl.

gory /ˈɡɔːrɪ/ adj [film, battle] sanglant.

gosh /ɡɒʃ/ excl ça alors°!

gosling /ˈɡɒzlɪŋ/ n oison m.

go-slow /ˌɡəʊˈsləʊ/ GB n grève f perlée.

gospel /ˈɡɒspl/ I n Évangile m; **to take sth as ~** ou **~ truth** prendre qch pour parole d'évangile.
II noun modifier MUS **~ music** gospel m; **~ singer** chanteur/-euse m/f de gospel; **~ song** gospel m.

gossamer /ˈɡɒsəmə(r)/ n (cobweb) fils mpl de la Vierge; (fabric) étoffe f très légère.

gossip /ˈɡɒsɪp/ I n **1** (news) (malicious) commérages mpl (about sur); (not malicious) nouvelles fpl (about sur); **do come for coffee and a ~** viens chez moi prendre un café et papoter; **2** (person) bavard/-e m/f.
II vi bavarder; PÉJ faire des commérages (about sur).

gossip: **~ column** n échos mpl; **~ columnist** n échotier/-ière m/f.

gossipy /ˈɡɒsɪpɪ/ adj [person] PÉJ cancanier/-ière PÉJ; [letter] plein de potins°; [style] vivant.

got /ɡɒt/ **1** prét, pp ▶**get**; **2 to have ~** avoir; **we've ~ three children** nous avons trois enfants; **I've ~ to go** il faut que j'y aille; **you've ~ to meet Flora** il faut absolument que tu fasses la connaissance de Flora.
IDIOMS **to feel ~ at**° se sentir persécuté.

gothic, Gothic /ˈɡɒθɪk/ I n gothique m.
II adj ARCHIT, LITERAT (also in printing) gothique; FIG [gloom, horror] noir.

gotta /ˈɡɒtə/ **1** = **got to**; **2** = **got a**.

gotten /ˈɡɒtn/ pp US ▶**get**.

gouge /ɡaʊdʒ/ vtr (dig) creuser (in dans).
■ **gouge out**: **~ out** [sth], **~ [sth] out** creuser [pattern]; enlever [bad bit]; **to ~ sb's eyes out** arracher les yeux de qn.

gourd /ɡʊəd/ n (container) gourde f; (fruit) calebasse f.

gout /ɡaʊt/ n ▶**1002**/ n MED goutte f.

govern /ˈɡʌvn/ I vtr **1** ADMIN, POL gouverner [country, state, city]; administrer [colony, province]; **2** (control) GEN régir [use, conduct, treatment]; **3** (determine) déterminer [decision, development]; **4** maîtriser [feelings, temper]; **5** LING régir; **6** ELEC, TECH régler.
II vi [parliament, president] gouverner; [administrator, governor] administrer.

governess /ˈɡʌvənɪs/ n (pl **~es**) gouvernante f.

governing /ˈɡʌvənɪŋ/ adj [party] au pouvoir; [factor] décisif/-ive; [class] dirigeant; **the ~ principle** l'idée directrice.

governing body n **1** GB (of school) conseil m d'établissement; (of university) conseil m d'Université; (of hospital, prison) conseil m d'administration; **2** (of sport) organisation *f* dirigeante; **3** (of trade, professional organization) comité *m* directeur.

government /ˈgʌvənmənt/ **I** *n* **1** (system) (political) gouvernement *m*; (administrative) administration *f*; **parliamentary ~** régime *m* parlementaire; **2** (body) gouvernement *m*; (the State) l'État *m*; **in ~** au pouvoir.
II *noun modifier* [*minister, official, plan, intervention*] du gouvernement; [*decree, department, majority, policy, publication*] gouvernemental; [*expenditure, borrowing*] de l'État; [*loan, funds*] public/-ique.

governmental /ˌgʌvənˈmentl/ *adj* gouvernemental.

government: ~ bond *n* FIN obligation *f* d'État; **~ corporation** *n* US régie *f* d'État; **~ employee ▶ 1251** *n* agent *m* du secteur public; **~-funded** *adj* financé par l'État; **~ official ▶ 1251** *n* fonctionnaire *mf*.

governor /ˈgʌvənə(r)/ *n* (of state, colony) gouverneur *m*; GB (of bank) gouverneur *m*; (of prison) directeur *m*; (of school) membre *m* du conseil d'établissement.

governorship /ˈgʌvənəʃɪp/ *n* (office of governor) fonctions *fpl* de gouverneur; (governing) direction *f*.

govt *n*: *abrév écrite* = **government**.

gown /gaʊn/ *n* (for evening wear) robe *f*; (of judge, academic) toge *f*; (of surgeon) blouse *f*; (of patient) chemise *f* (d'hôpital).

GP ▶ 1251 *n* (*abrév* = **general practitioner**) médecin *m* généraliste.

GPO *n* **1** GB (*abrév* = **General Post Office**) service *m* postal; **2** US (*abrév* = **Government Printing Office**) ≈ Imprimerie *f* nationale.

gr I *n*: *abrév écrite* = **gram**.
II *n, adj*: *abrév écrite* = **gross**.

grab /græb/ **I** *n* **1** (snatch) **to make a ~ at** *ou* **for** essayer d'attraper; **to be up for ~s** ˜ être bon à prendre; **2** (on excavator) pelle *f* automatique.
II *vtr* (*p prés etc* **-bb-**) **1** (seize) empoigner [*money, toy*]; saisir [*arm, person, opportunity*]; **to ~ sth from sb** arracher qch à qn; **to ~ hold of** se saisir de; **to ~ sb by the arm** saisir qn par le bras; **2** (illegally) accaparer; **3** (snatch) **to ~ some sleep** dormir un peu; **to ~ a snack** manger en vitesse; **4**○ (impress) **how does that ~ you?** qu'est-ce que tu en dis?

grace /greɪs/ **I** *n* **1** (physical charm) grâce *f*; **2** (dignity, graciousness) grâce *f*; **to do sth with** (a) **good/bad ~** faire qch de bonne/mauvaise grâce; **to have the ~ to do** avoir la bonne grâce de faire; **3** (spiritual) grâce *f*; **to fall from ~** RELIG perdre la grâce; FIG tomber en disgrâce; **4** (time allowance) **to give sb two days' ~** accorder un délai de deux jours à qn; (to debtor) accorder un délai de grâce de deux jours à qn; **5** (prayer) (before meal) bénédicité *m*; (after meal) grâces *fpl*; **6** (quality) **sb's saving ~** ce qui sauve qn; **7** (mannerism) **to have all the social ~s** avoir beaucoup de savoir-vivre.
II *vtr* **1** (decorate) orner, embellir; **2** (honour) honorer; **to ~ sb with one's presence** AUSSI IRON honorer qn de sa présence ALSO IRON.
IDIOMS **there but for the ~ of God go I** ça aurait aussi bien pu m'arriver; **to put on airs and ~s** PÉJ prendre des airs.

Grace /greɪs/ **▶ 937** *n* **1** (title of archbishop) **his/your ~** Monseigneur; **2** (title of duke) **his/your ~** Monsieur le duc; (of duchess) **her/your ~** Madame la duchesse.

graceful /ˈgreɪsfl/ *adj* **1** [*dancer, movement*] gracieux/-ieuse; [*person, building*] élégant; **2** [*apology*] élégant; **to make a ~ exit** FIG quitter discrètement les lieux.

gracefully /ˈgreɪsfəlɪ/ *adv* [*move*] avec grâce; [*concede*] gracieusement.

gracefulness /ˈgreɪsflnɪs/ *n* grâce *f*.

graceless /ˈgreɪslɪs/ *adj* [*manner*] inélégant; [*city, person*] dépourvu de charme.

gracious /ˈgreɪʃəs/ *adj* **1** (generous, dignified) [*person*] affable; **to be ~** (**to sb**) **about** ne pas en vouloir à qn pour; **to be ~ in defeat** accepter la défaite avec bonne grâce; **2** (aristocratic) (pleasant) affable; (con-

descending) condescendant; **3** (in royal title) **by ~ permission of** par la grâce de.

graciously /ˈgreɪʃəslɪ/ *adv* gracieusement; **he ~ agreed to come** IRON il a daigné venir IRON.

gradation /grəˈdeɪʃn/ *n* **1** (on a continuum) gradation *f*; **colour ~s** ART gradations *fpl* de couleurs; **~s of feeling** des degrés *mpl* d'émotion; **2** (on scale) graduation *f*.

grade /greɪd/ **I** *n* **1** COMM qualité *f*; **high-/low-~** de qualité supérieure/inférieure; **2** SCH, UNIV (mark) note *f* (in en); **to get good ~s** avoir de bonnes notes; **to get ~ A** *ou* **an A ~** ˜ avoir plus de 16 sur 20; **3** (rank) ADMIN échelon *m*; MIL rang *m*; **a top-~** civil servant un fonctionnaire de haut rang; **salary ~** échelon *m* de salaire; **4** US SCH (class) classe *f*; **she's in the eighth ~** ˜ elle est en (classe de) quatrième; **5** (also **Grade**) (level) niveau *m*; **~ IV piano** MUS niveau 4 de piano; **6** US (gradient) pente *f*.
II *vtr* **1** (categorize) (by quality) classer (**according to** selon); (by size) calibrer (**according to** selon); **2** SCH (in level of difficulty) graduer [*tasks*] (**according to** selon); **3** US (mark) noter [*work*]; **4** ART (blend) dégrader; **5** AGRIC améliorer par sélection.
III graded *pp adj* [*tests*] classé par ordre de difficulté; [*hotel*] classé NN.
IDIOMS **to make the ~** se montrer à la hauteur.

grade: ~ book *n* US carnet *m* de notes; **~ crossing** *n* US RAIL passage *m* à niveau.

grader /ˈgreɪdə(r)/ **I** *n* (of produce) (machine) calibreur *m*; (person) classeur/-euse *m/f*.
II -grader *combining form* US **eighth/ninth-~** ˜ élève de quatrième/de troisième.

grade school *n* US école *f* primaire.

gradient /ˈgreɪdɪənt/ *n* **1** (slope) pente *f*; **2** (degree of slope) inclinaison *f*; **3** MATH, PHYS gradient *m*.

grading /ˈgreɪdɪŋ/ *n* **1** (classification) GEN classification *f*; (of personnel) échelonnement *m*; **2** SCH (marking) notation *f*.

gradual /ˈgrædʒʊəl/ *adj* **1** (slow) [*change, increase*] progressif/-ive; **2** (gentle) [*slope*] doux/douce.

gradually /ˈgrædʒʊlɪ/ *adv* progressivement; **~, he...** peu à peu, il...

graduate I /ˈgrædʒʊət/ *n* UNIV diplômé/-e *m/f* (**in** en; **of, from** de); **arts ~** diplômé/-e *m/f* en lettres.
II /ˈgrædʒʊət/ *noun modifier* [*course, student*] ˜ de troisième cycle.
III /ˈgrædʒʊˌeɪt/ *vtr* **1** US (give degree to) conférer un diplôme à [*student*]; **2** TECH graduer [*container, scale*].
IV /ˈgrædʒʊˌeɪt/ *vi* **1** UNIV terminer ses études (**at** *ou* **from** à); US SCH ˜ finir le lycée; **2** (progress) **to ~** (**from sth**) **to** passer (de qch) à.
V graduated /ˈgrædʒʊˌeɪtɪd/ *pp adj* [*scale, system, tax*] proportionnel/-elle.

graduate: ~ assistant *n* US assistant/-e *m/f* (*chargé de TD*); **~ school** *n* US ˜ troisième cycle *m*; **~ teacher** *n* professeur *m* licencié; **~ training scheme** *n* GB programme *m* de formation professionnelle pour étudiants diplômés.

graduation /ˌgrædʒʊˈeɪʃn/ *n* **1** UNIV (also **~ ceremony**) (cérémonie *f* de) remise *f* des diplômes; (end of course) obtention *f* d'un diplôme; **2** (calibration) graduation *f*.

graffiti /grəˈfiːtɪ/ *n* (+ *v sg ou pl*) graffiti *mpl*.

graffiti artist *n* tagger *m*.

graft /grɑːft, US græft/ **I** *n* **1** BOT, MED greffe *f*; **skin ~** greffe de la peau; **2**○ GB (work) **hard ~** boulot○ *m* acharné.
II *vtr* BOT, MED, FIG greffer (**onto** sur).

grain /greɪn/ *n* **1** (commodity) céréales *fpl*; **2** (seed) (of rice, wheat) grain *m*; **long ~ rice** riz *m* long; **3** (of sand, salt) grain *m*; **4** FIG (of truth, comfort) brin *m*; **5** (pattern) (in wood, stone) veines *fpl*; (in leather, paper, fabric) grain *m*; **to cut along/across the ~** couper dans le fil/contre le fil; **6** PHOT grain *m*.
IDIOMS **it goes against the ~** c'est contre nature.

grainy /ˈgreɪnɪ/ *adj* **1** PHOT [*photograph*] qui a du grain; **2** (resembling wood/leather) veiné/grainé; **3** (granular) granuleux/-euse.

gram(me) /græm/ ▶ 1392 | *n* gramme *m*.

grammar /'græmə(r)/ I *n* 1 grammaire *f*; **that's bad ~** c'est grammaticalement incorrect; 2 (also **~ book**) grammaire *f*.
II *noun modifier* [*book, lesson, exercise*] de grammaire.

grammarian /grə'meəriən/ *n* grammairien/-ienne *m*/ *f*.

grammar school *n* GB ~ lycée *m* (*à recrutement sélectif*).

grammatical /grə'mætikl/ *adj* 1 LING [*error*] de grammaire; [*meaning, gender*] grammatical; 2 (correct) grammaticalement correct.

grammatically /grə'mætikli/ *adv* grammaticalement.

Grammy /'græmi/ *n* (*pl* **~s** ou **-mmies**) US MUS **to win a ~** ~ être primé aux Victoires de la musique.

gramophone† /'græməfəʊn/ *n* phonographe *m*, gramophone® *m*.

gran○ /græn/ *n* mémé○ *f*, mamie *f*.

granary /'grænəri/ I *n* (grain store) grenier *m*.
II *noun modifier* GB [*bread*] complet/-ète (*avec des grains de céréales broyés*).

grand /grænd/ I *n* GB mille livres *fpl* sterling; US mille dollars *mpl*.
II *adj* 1 (impressive) [*building, ceremony*] grandiose; [*park*] magnifique; **in ~ style** en grande pompe; **on the ~ scale** (expensively) sur un grand pied; **the ~ old man of theatre** le grand monsieur du théâtre; 2 (self-important) **she's very ~** elle joue à la grande dame PEJ; 3○ (fine) **to have a ~ time** passer un moment formidable; **'is everything all right?'—'it's ~ thanks'** 'tout va bien?'—'très bien merci'.

grandchild /'græntʃaɪld/ *n* (*pl* **-children**) (girl) petite-fille *f*; (boy) petit-fils *m*; **his grandchildren** ses petits-enfants *mpl*.

granddad○ /'grændæd/ *n* pépé○ *m*, papy○ *m*, papi *m*.

granddaddy○ /'grændædi/ *n* 1 (grandfather) pépé○ *m*, papy○ *m*, papi *m*; 2 FIG **it's the ~ of them all** HUM c'est l'ancêtre.

grand: **~daughter** *n* petite-fille *f*; **~ duchess** *n* grande-duchesse *f*; **~ duke** *n* grand-duc *m*.

grandee /græn'di:/ *n* grand personnage *m*.

grandeur /'grændʒə(r)/ *n* 1 (of scenery) majesté *f*; (of building) caractère *m* grandiose; 2 (of character) noblesse *f*; (power, status) éminence *f*.

grand: **~father** *n* grand-père *m*; **~father clock** *n* horloge *f* comtoise; **~ finale** *n* finale *m*.

grandiose /'grændiəʊs/ *adj* grandiose.

grand: **~ jury** *n* US jury qui décide s'il y a motif à inculpation; **~ larceny** *n* US vol *m* qualifié.

grandma○ /'grænma:/ *n* mémé○ *f*, mamy○ *f*, mamie○ *f*.

grand master *n* (in chess) grand maître *m*.

grandmother /'grænmʌðə(r)/ *n* grand-mère *f*.
IDIOMS **to teach one's ~ to suck eggs** apprendre à un vieux singe à faire la grimace.

Grand Old Party, GOP *n* US POL parti *m* républicain.

grandpa○ /'grænpa:/ *n* pépé○ *m*, papy○ *m*, papi○ *m*.

grandparent /'grænpeərənt/ *n* (male) grand-père *m*; (female) grand-mère *f*; **my ~s** mes grands-parents *mpl*.

grand: **~ piano** ▶ 1097 | *n* piano *m* à queue; **~ prix** *n* (*pl inv*) grand prix *m*; **~ slam** *n* GAMES, SPORT grand chelem *m*; **~son** *n* petit-fils *m*.

grandstand /'grænstænd/ *n* 1 (at stadium) tribune *f*; **to have a ~ view** ou **seat** LIT, FIG être aux premières loges; 2 (audience) public *m*.

grand total *n* total *m*; **the ~ for the repairs came to £3,000** en tout, les travaux sont revenus à 3 000 livres sterling.

grand tour *n* 1 **he took me on a ~ of the house** il m'a fait visiter toute la maison; 2 (also **the Grand Tour**) HIST le tour *m* d'Europe.

grange /greɪndʒ/ *n* GB (house) manoir *m*.

granite /'grænɪt/ *n* granit(e) *m*.

granny○ /'græni/ *n* 1 (grandmother) mémé○ *f*; 2 PEJ (fusspot, gossip) vieille mémère○.

granny flat *n* GB petit appartement *m* indépendant (*pour parent âgé*).

granola /grə'nəʊlə/ *n* US muesli *m*.

grant /gra:nt, US grænt/ I *n* (from government, local authority) subvention *f* (**for** pour; **to do** pour faire); (for study) SCH, UNIV bourse *f*; **research ~** subvention *f* de recherche.
II *vtr* 1 SOUT (allow) accorder [*permission*]; accéder à [*request*]; **permission ~ed!** permission accordée!; 2 (give) **to ~ sb sth, to ~ sth to sb** accorder qch à qn [*interview, leave, visa*]; concéder qch à qn [*citizenship*]; 3 (concede) **to ~ that** reconnaître que; **I ~ you that he's gifted** je vous accorde qu'il est doué; **~ed that, ~ing that** en admettant que (+ *subj*).
IDIOMS **to take sth for ~ed** considérer qch comme allant de soi; **he takes his mother for ~ed** il croit que sa mère est à son service.

grant aid /gra:nteɪd, US 'grænt-/ *n* Ȼ (within a country) subventions *fpl* (**for** pour); (to Third World) aide *f* au développement (**for** pour).

grant-aided /,gra:nt'eɪdɪd, US ,grænt-/ *adj* subventionné.

granted /'gra:ntɪd, US 'grænt-/ *adv* **~, it's magnificent, but very expensive** c'est magnifique, soit, mais cela coûte très cher.

grant-maintained *adj* [*school*] subventionné par l'État.

granular /'grænjʊlə(r)/ *adj* [*texture*] granuleux/-euse.

granulated *adj* [*paper*] grenelé; [*sugar*] cristallisé.

granule /'grænju:l/ *n* (of sugar, salt) grain *m*; (of instant coffee) granulé *m*.

grape /greɪp/ *n* grain *m* de raisin; **a bunch of ~s** une grappe de raisin; **I love ~s** j'adore le raisin; **to harvest the ~s** vendanger.
IDIOMS **sour ~s!** les raisins sont trop verts!

grapefruit /'greɪpfruːt/ *n* pamplemousse *m*.

grape: **~ harvest** *n* vendange *f*; **~ seed oil** *n* huile *f* de pépins de raisin; **~shot** *n* mitraille *f*.

grapevine /'greɪpvaɪn/ *n* (in vineyard) pied *m* de vigne; (in greenhouse, garden) vigne *f*.
IDIOMS **to hear sth on the ~** apprendre qch par le téléphone arabe.

graph /gra:f, US græf/ *n* graphique *m*.

graphic /'græfɪk/ I **graphics** *npl* 1 COMPUT visualisation *f* graphique; **computer ~s** infographie *f*; 2 (in film, TV) images *fpl*; (in book) illustrations *fpl*.
II *adj* 1 ART, COMPUT graphique; 2 [*account*] (of sth pleasant) vivant; (of sth unpleasant) cru.

graphic: **~ artist** ▶ 1251 | *n* graphiste *mf*; **~ arts** *npl* arts *mpl* graphiques; **~ design** *n* ART graphisme *m*; **~ designer** ▶ 1251 | *n* graphiste *mf*; **~ display** *n* COMPUT visualisation *f* graphique; **~ equalizer** *n* AUDIO égaliseur *m* graphique.

graphite /'græfaɪt/ I *n* graphite *m*.
II *noun modifier* [*fishing rod*] en fibre de carbone.

graphologist /grə'fɒlədʒɪst/ ▶ 1251 | *n* graphologue *mf*.

graphology /grə'fɒlədʒi/ *n* graphologie *f*.

graph paper *n* papier *m* millimétré.

grapple /'græpl/ *vi* **to ~ with** LIT lutter avec [*person*]; FIG se colleter avec [*problem*].

grasp /gra:sp, US græsp/ I *n* 1 (hold, grip) prise *f*; (stronger) poigne *f*; **to hold sth in one's ~** LIT tenir qch fermement; FIG tenir qch bien en main; **to take a firm ~ of sth** empoigner fermement qch; **the pen slipped from his ~** le stylo lui a glissé des doigts; **success is within their ~** FIG le succès est à leur portée; 2 (understanding) maîtrise *f*; **to have a good ~ of a subject** avoir une bonne maîtrise d'un sujet.
II *vtr* 1 LIT empoigner [*rope, hand*]; FIG saisir [*opportunity*]; **to ~ hold of** saisir; 2 (comprehend) saisir, comprendre [*concept, subject*]; suivre [*argument*]; se rendre compte de [*situation, significance*].
III *vi* **to ~ at** LIT tenter de saisir; FIG s'efforcer de comprendre [*idea*]; saisir [*excuse*].

grasping /'grɑːspɪŋ, US 'græspɪŋ/ adj cupide.

grass /grɑːs, US græs/ **I** n **1** ¢ (wild) herbe f; **a blade of ~** un brin d'herbe; **to put out to ~** LIT, FIG HUM mettre au vert; **2** ¢ (lawn) pelouse f; **keep off the ~**! défense de marcher sur les pelouses!; **3** ¢ (in tennis) gazon m; **4** BOT C graminée f; **5**○ ¢ (marijuana) herbe f; **6**○ GB (informer) mouchard○ m.
II noun modifier [slope, verge] gazonné.
IDIOMS **the ~ is greener (on the other side of the fence)** on croit toujours que c'est mieux ailleurs; **he doesn't let the ~ grow under his feet** il ne laisse pas traîner les choses.

grass: **~ court** n court m en gazon; **~ cuttings** npl herbe f coupée ¢.

grasshopper /'grɑːshɒpə(r), US 'græs-/ n ZOOL sauterelle f.
IDIOMS **kneehigh to a ~** haut comme trois pommes.

grassland /'grɑːslənd, US 'græs-/ n prairie f.

grassroots /ˌgrɑːs'ruːts, US ˌgræs-/ **I** npl **the ~** le peuple.
II adj [movement] populaire; [support] de base.

grass snake n couleuvre f.

grassy /'grɑːsɪ, US 'græsɪ/ adj herbeux/-euse.

grate /greɪt/ **I** n (fire-basket) grille f de foyer; (hearth) âtre m.
II vtr râper; **to ~ cheese over sth** parsemer qch de fromage râpé.
III vi **1** [metal object] grincer (**on** sur); **2** (annoy) agacer; **her voice ~s** sa voix m'agace; **to ~ on sb's nerves** taper sur les nerfs de qn○.

grateful /'greɪtfl/ adj [person] reconnaissant (**to** à; **for** de); [letter, kiss] de reconnaissance; **to be ~ that** être heureux/-euse que (+ subj); **let's be ~ that** estimons-nous heureux que (+ subj); **I would be ~ if you could reply** je vous serais reconnaissant de bien vouloir répondre; **with ~ thanks** avec mes or nos plus sincères remerciements.

gratefully /'greɪtfəlɪ/ adv [speak] avec reconnaissance.

grater /'greɪtə(r)/ n râpe f.

gratification /ˌgrætɪfɪ'keɪʃn/ n satisfaction f.

gratify /'grætɪfaɪ/ vtr faire plaisir à [person]; satisfaire [desire]; **to be gratified that** être très heureux que (+ subj); **it is gratifying to know that** il est agréable d'apprendre que.

grating /'greɪtɪŋ/ **I** n **1** (bars) grille f; **2** (noise) grincement m.
II adj [noise] grinçant; [voice] désagréable.

gratitude /'grætɪtjuːd, US -tuːd/ n reconnaissance f (**to, towards** envers; **for** de).

gratuitous /grə'tjuːɪtəs, US -'tuː-/ adj gratuit.

gratuity /grə'tjuːətɪ, US -'tuː-/ n (tip) pourboire m; GB (bonus) prime f.

grave /greɪv/ **I** n tombe f; **beyond the ~** après la mort; **to go to one's ~ believing that** rester convaincu jusque dans la tombe que; **to go to an early ~** avoir une fin prématurée.
II adj **1** (dangerous) [illness] grave; [risk] sérieux/-ieuse; [danger] grand (before n); **2** (solemn) sérieux/-ieuse.
IDIOMS **to dig one's own ~** creuser sa propre tombe; **to have one foot in the ~** avoir un pied dans la tombe; **to turn in one's ~** se retourner dans sa tombe.

gravedigger /'greɪvdɪgə(r)/ ▶ 1251 n fossoyeur m.

gravel /'grævl/ n ¢ **1** GEN (coarse) graviers mpl; (fine) gravillons mpl; **2** MED calculs mpl.

gravelly /'grævəlɪ/ adj [path] caillouteux/-euse; [voice] râpeux/-euse.

gravel pit n gravière f.

gravely /'greɪvlɪ/ adv **1** (extremely) [concerned] sérieusement; [displeased] extrêmement; [ill] gravement; **2** (solemnly) gravement.

graven /'greɪvn/ adj †ou LITTER gravé ALSO FIG; **~ image** BIBLE idole f.

graverobber /'greɪvˌrɒbə(r)/ n déterreur m de cadavres.

graveside /'greɪvsaɪd/ n **the mourners were gathered at the ~** tout le monde était rassemblé autour de la tombe.

gravestone /'greɪvˌstəʊn/ n pierre f tombale.

graveyard /'greɪvjɑːd/ n cimetière m.

graveyard shift○ n équipe f de nuit.

gravitas /'grævɪtæs, -tɑːs/ n envergure f.

gravitate /'grævɪteɪt/ vi **to ~ to(wards)** graviter vers.

gravity /'grævətɪ/ n **1** PHYS pesanteur f; **centre of ~** centre m de gravité; **the pull of the earth's ~** l'attraction f terrestre; **2** (of situation) gravité f; **3** (of demeanour) sérieux m.

gravy /'greɪvɪ/ n CULIN sauce f (au jus de rôti).
IDIOMS **he is on the ~ train**○ il a trouvé le filon○.

gravy boat n saucière f.

gray US = **grey**.

graze /greɪz/ **I** n écorchure f.
II vtr **1** (scrape) **to ~ one's knee** s'écorcher le genou (**on, against** sur); **2** [bullet] érafler; **3** AGRIC faire paître [animal]; utiliser comme pacage [land].
III vi AGRIC [sheep] brouter; [cow] paître.

grazing /'greɪzɪŋ/ n AGRIC pacage m; **~ land** pâturage m; **~ rights** droit m de pacage.

grease /griːs/ **I** n **1** (lubricant) graisse f; (black) cambouis m; **2** (dirt) graisse f; **3** (from hair) sébum m.
II vtr (all contexts) graisser.

grease: **~paint** n maquillage m de théâtre; **~proof paper** n papier m sulfurisé.

greaser /'griːsə(r)/ n (motorcyclist) motard○ m.

greasiness /'griːsɪnɪs/ n (of hair, surface) aspect m graisseux; (of food) aspect m huileux.

greasing /'griːsɪŋ/ n graissage m.

greasy /'griːsɪ/ adj [skin, food] gras/grasse; [overalls] graisseux/-euse.

great /greɪt/ **I** n **the ~** (+ v pl) les grands mpl.
II adj **1** (large) [height, speed, majority, object, danger, improvement] grand (before n); [number] grand (before n), important; [increase] fort (before n), important; **2** (as intensifier) [excitement, surprise, relief, success, tragedy] grand (before n); [heat] fort (before n); **a ~ deal (of)** beaucoup de; **a ~ many people** beaucoup de personnes, un grand nombre de personnes; **to have ~ difficulty doing** avoir beaucoup de mal à faire; **in ~ detail** dans les moindres détails; **the map was a ~ help** la carte a été très utile; **you're a ~ help!** IRON tu m'aides vraiment beaucoup!; **3** (remarkable) [person, name, painting, discovery] grand (before n); **4**○ (excellent) [book, party, weather] génial○, formidable○; [opportunity] formidable○; **to feel ~** se sentir en pleine forme; **you look ~!** (healthy) tu as l'air en pleine forme!; (attractive) tu es superbe!; **that dress looks ~ on you** cette robe est géniale○ sur toi; **to have a ~ time** bien s'amuser; **X is the ~est!** X est génial○!; **5**○ (talented) génial○, formidable○; **to be ~ at** être un as○ à [tennis, football]; **to be ~ with** être génial○ avec [children, animals]; **to be ~ on** être imbattable○ sur [history, architecture]; **6**○ (inveterate) [worrier, organizer] de première○; [admirer, fan] grand (before n).
III○ adv **I'm doing ~** ça marche très bien pour moi○.
IDIOMS **to cross the ~ divide** faire le grand saut.

great: **~ aunt** n grand-tante f; **Great Barrier Reef** pr n Grande Barrière f de Corail; **~ big** adj (très) grand (before n), énorme; **Great Britain** ▶ 840 pr n Grande-Bretagne f; **Great Dane** n danois m; **Greater London** pr n l'agglomération f londonienne; **~ grandchild** n (girl) arrière-petite-fille f; (garçon) arrière-petit-fils m; **~ granddaughter** n arrière-petite-fille f; **~ grandfather** n arrière-grand-père m; **~ grandmother** n arrière-grand-mère f; **~ grandson** n arrière-petit-fils m; **~-great grandchild** n (girl) arrière-arrière-petite-fille f; (boy) arrière-arrière-petit-fils m; **Great Lakes** ▶ 1037 npl Grands Lacs mpl.

greatly /'greɪtlɪ/ *adv* [*admire, regret, influence*] beaucoup, énormément; [*exceed*] de beaucoup; [*admired, surprised, distressed*] très, extrêmement; [*improved, changed*] considérablement; [*superior, inferior*] bien.

great nephew *n* petit-neveu *m*.

greatness /'greɪtnɪs/ *n* (of achievement) importance *f*; (of person) grandeur *f*.

great: **~ niece** *n* petite-nièce *f*; **Great Power** *n* POL grande puissance *f*; **~ uncle** *n* grand-oncle *m*; **Great War** *pr n* HIST Grande Guerre *f*.

Grecian /'gri:ʃn/ *adj* grec/grecque.

Greece /gri:s/ ▶840 *pr n* Grèce *f*.

greed /gri:d/ *n* **1** (for money, power) avidité *f* (**for** de); **2** (also **greediness**) (for food) gourmandise *f*.

greedy /'gri:dɪ/ *adj* **1** [*person*] (for food) gourmand; (stronger) goulu; [*look*] avide; **a ~ pig**○ un goinfre○; **2** (for money, power) avide (**for** de).

Greek /gri:k/ ▶1100, 1038 I *n* **1** (person) Grec/Grecque *m/f*; **2** (language) grec *m*.
II *adj* **1** [*food, government, island, alphabet*] grec/grecque; **2** [*teacher, lesson, dictionary*] de grec.
IDIOMS **beware of ~s bearing gifts** ne faites jamais confiance à un ennemi; **it's all ~ to me** c'est du chinois pour moi.

green /gri:n/ ▶818 I *n* **1** (colour) vert *m*; **2** (grassy area) espace *m* vert; (vegetation) verdure *f*; **3** (in bowling) boulingrin *m*; (in golf) green *m*; **4** ECOL, POL écologiste *mf*; **the Greens** les Verts.
II **greens** *npl* GB (vegetables) légumes *mpl* verts.
III *adj* **1** (in colour) vert; **to go** ou **turn ~** [*traffic lights*] passer au vert; FIG [*person*] verdir, devenir vert; **2** (with vegetation) verdoyant; **3** (not ready) [*fruit*] vert; **4**○ (naïve) naïf/naïve; **5** (inexperienced) novice; **6** ECOL, POL [*policies, candidate, issues*] écologiste; [*marketing, washing-powder*] écologique; **7** ECON [*currency*] vert; **8**○ (off-colour) patraque○.
IDIOMS **to have ~ fingers** GB ou **a ~ thumb** US avoir la main verte.

green: **~back**○ *n* US dollar *m*; **~ bean** *n* haricot *m* vert; **~ belt** *n* SPORT ceinture *f* verte.

green card *n* **1** (driving insurance) carte *f* verte (internationale); **2** US carte *f* de séjour (*permettant de travailler aux États-Unis*).

greenery /'gri:nərɪ/ *n* verdure *f*.

green-eyed monster *n* **the ~** la jalousie.

green: **~finch** *n* verdier *m*; **~fly** *n* puceron *m* (du rosier); **~gage** *n* reine-claude *f*; **~grocer** ▶1251, 1251 *n* marchand *m* de fruits et légumes.

greenhorn○ /'gri:nhɔ:n/ *n* PÉJ **1** (gullible) benêt○ *m*; **2** (new) débutant/-e *m/f*; **he's a ~** il débarque○.

green: **~house** *n* serre *f*; **~house effect** *n* effet *m* de serre.

greenish /'gri:nɪʃ/ ▶818 *adj* tirant sur le vert, verdâtre PÉJ.

Greenland /'gri:nlənd/ ▶840 *pr n* Groenland *m*.

greenness /'gri:nnɪs/ *n* **1** (of pigment) verdeur *f*; (of countryside) verdure *f*; **2** (of fruit, wood) verdeur *f*; **3** ECOL (awareness) conscience *f* écologique; **4** (inexperience) inexpérience *f*.

green: **~ onion** *n* US ciboule *f*; **~ paper** *n* GB livre *m* blanc; **~ pepper** *n* poivron *m* vert; **~room** *n* THEAT foyer *m* des artistes; **~ salad** *n* salade *f* verte; **~ tea** *n* thé *m* vert.

Greenwich Mean Time, **GMT** /ˌgrenɪtʃ 'mi:ntaɪm/ *n* temps *m* universel, TU.

greet /gri:t/ *vtr* **1** (welcome) accueillir [*person, decision*]; **2** (salute) saluer; **to ~ sb in the street** dire bonjour à qn dans la rue; **3** (receive) **to be ~ed with** ou **by** provoquer [*dismay, amusement*]; être salué par [*jeers, applause*]; **4** (confront) **an amazing sight ~ed me** une scène extraordinaire s'offrait à moi.

greeter /'gri:tə(r)/ *n* personne *f* qui accueille les clients (*dans un restaurant*).

greeting /'gri:tɪŋ/ I *n* salutation *f*; **~s!** salutations!; **to exchange ~s** se saluer; (passing) se dire bonjour.
II **greetings** *npl* Christmas **~s** vœux *mpl* de Noël; **Season's ~s** meilleurs vœux.

greetings card GB, **greeting card** US *n* carte *f* de vœux.

gregarious /grɪ'geərɪəs/ *adj* [*person*] sociable; [*animal*] grégaire.

gremlin /'gremlɪn/ *n* HUM diablotin *m*.

Grenada /grə'neɪdə/ ▶840, 1343 *pr n* (city, country) Grenade *f*.

grenade /grə'neɪd/ *n* grenade *f*.

grenadier /ˌgrenə'dɪə/ *n* MIL grenadier *m*.

grew /gru:/ *prét* ▶ **grow**.

grey GB, **gray** US /greɪ/ ▶818 I *n* **1** (colour) gris *m*; **2** (horse) cheval *m* gris.
II *adj* **1** (colour) gris; **2** (grey-haired) aux cheveux gris, grisonnant; **to go** ou **turn ~** grisonner; **3** (dull, boring) [*existence, day*] morne; [*person, town*] terne.
III *vi* grisonner; **to be ~ing at the temples** avoir les tempes grisonnantes.

grey: **~ area** *n* zone *f* floue; **~ economy** *n* économie *f* parallèle; **~-haired** *adj* aux cheveux gris; **~hound** *n* lévrier *m*; **~hound racing** ▶949 *n* course *f* de lévriers; **~hound track** *n* piste *f* de course de lévriers.

greyish GB, **grayish** US /'greɪʃ/ ▶818 *adj* tirant sur le gris, grisâtre PÉJ.

grey: **~ matter** *n* (brain) matière *f* grise; **~ seal** *n* phoque *m* gris; **~ squirrel** *n* écureuil *m* gris.

grid /grɪd/ *n* **1** (grating) grille *f*; **2** GEN, GEOG (pattern) quadrillage *m*; (of street layout) damier *m*; **3** GB (network) réseau *m*; **the national ~** le réseau électrique national; **4** (in motor racing) grille *f* de départ.

griddle /'grɪdl/ *n* (for meat) gril *m* en fonte; (for pancakes) plaque *f* en fonte.

gridiron /'grɪdaɪən/ *n* **1** CULIN gril *m*; **2** US terrain *m* de football américain.

gridlock /'grɪdlɒk/ *n* **1** LIT embouteillage *m*; **2** FIG (deadlock) impasse *f*.

grid reference *n* coordonnées *fpl*.

grief /gri:f/ *n* **1** (sorrow) chagrin *m*; **his ~ at** ou **over her death** le chagrin qu'il a ressenti à sa mort; **2**○ (trouble) **to give sb ~** ennuyer qn.
IDIOMS **to come to ~** (have an accident) avoir un accident; (fail) échouer; [*business*] péricliter.

grief-stricken /'gri:fstrɪkn/ *adj* accablé de douleur (*after n*).

grievance /'gri:vns/ *n* griefs *mpl* (**against** contre).

grievance: **~ committee** *n* commission *f* d'arbitrage; **~ procedure** *n* instance *f* prud'hommale.

grieve /gri:v/ I *vi* **to ~ for** ou **over** pleurer.
II *v impers* LITTÉR **it ~s me that** cela me fait de la peine que (+ *subj*).

grievous /'gri:vəs/ *adj* SOUT [*loss*] cruel/-elle; [*damage*] grave; **to do sb a ~ wrong** faire cruellement tort à qn.

grievous bodily harm, **GBH** *n* JUR coups *mpl* et blessures *fpl*.

grievously /'gri:vəslɪ/ *adv* [*hurt*] grièvement; [*offended*] cruellement.

grill /grɪl/ I *n* **1** GB (on cooker) gril *m*; **cook it in** ou **under the ~** faites-le griller; **2** US (barbecue) gril *m*; **3** (dish) grillade *f*; **4** (restaurant) grill *m*, restaurant *m* servant des grillades.
II *vtr* **1** CULIN faire griller; **2**○ (interrogate) mettre [qn] sur la sellette○ (**about** à propos de).
III *vi* [*steak, fish*] griller.

grille /grɪl/ *n* GEN grille *f*; (on car) calandre *f*.

grill pan *n* GB plateau *m* à poignée (*allant sous le gril*).

grim /grɪm/ *adj* **1** (depressing) [*news, town*] sinistre; [*sight, conditions*] effroyable; [*reality*] dur; **her future looks ~** son avenir a l'air sombre; **2** (unrelenting) [*struggle*] acharné; [*resolve*] terrible; **3** (unsmiling) grave; **to be ~-faced** avoir l'air grave; **4**○ (poor) [*accommodation, food*] très mauvais; **I'm feeling pretty ~** je ne me sens pas bien; **5** (black) [*humour*] macabre.

grimace /grɪ'meɪs, US 'grɪməs/ I *n* grimace *f* (**of** de).

II *vi* (involuntary) faire une grimace (**with, in** de); (pull a face) faire la grimace.

grime /graɪm/ *n* (of city) saleté *f*; (on object, person) crasse *f*.

grimly /'grɪmlɪ/ *adv* **1** (sadly) [*speak*] d'un ton grave; **2** (relentlessly) [*pursue, cling*] avec acharnement.

Grim Reaper /ˌgrɪm 'riːpə(r)/ *n* **the ~** la Faucheuse.

grimy /'grɪmɪ/ *adj* [*city*] noir; [*hands, window*] crasseux/-euse.

grin /grɪn/ **I** *n* sourire *m*; **her face broke into a ~** elle a souri.

II *vi* (*p prés etc* **-nn-**) sourire (**at** à; **with** de).

IDIOMS **to ~ and bear it** souffrir en silence.

grind /graɪnd/ **I** *n* **1**○ (hard work) boulot○ *m* or travail *m* monotone; **the daily ~**○ le boulot○ or le train-train○ quotidien; **it'll be a long hard ~**○ ça va être très dur; **2**○ US PÉJ (student) bûcheur/-euse *m/f*.

II *vtr* (*prét, pp* **ground**) **1** (crush) moudre [*corn, coffee beans*]; écraser, broyer [*grain*]; hacher [*meat*]; **to ~ sth to dust** réduire qch en poussière; **to ~ one's teeth** grincer des dents; **2** (sharpen) affûter or aiguiser [qch] (à la meule) [*knife*]; **3** (polish) polir [*lenses*]; égriser [*gems*]; **4** (turn) tourner [*handle*]; jouer de [*barrel organ*].

III *vi* (*prét, pp* **ground**) **1** (make harsh sound) [*machine*] grincer; **to ~ to a halt** GEN s'arrêter; [*vehicle*] s'arrêter avec un grincement de freins; **2**○ US (swot) bûcher○, potasser○.

■ **grind down**: **~ down** [sth], **~** [sth] **down** (crush) écraser; (pulverize) pulvériser; **to be ground down by poverty** FIG être accablé par la misère.

■ **grind on** se poursuivre inexorablement.

■ **grind out**: **~ out** [sth], **~** [sth] **out 1** (extinguish) écraser [*cigarette*]; **2** (play) **to ~ out a tune on a barrel organ** jouer un air sur un orgue de Barbarie.

grinder /'graɪndə(r)/ *n* **1** (crushing device) (industrial) broyeur *m*; (domestic) moulin *m*; **2** TECH (for sharpening) meule *f* (à aiguiser); **3** (person) rémouleur/-euse *m/f*; **4** US (sandwich) gros sandwich *m* mixte.

grinding /'graɪndɪŋ/ **I** *n* (sound) grincement *m*.

II *adj* [*noise*] grinçant; **~ poverty** misère *f* noire.

grindstone /'graɪndstəʊn/ *n* meule *f* or pierre *f* à aiguiser.

IDIOMS **to keep** OU **have one's nose to the ~** travailler sans relâche.

grip /grɪp/ **I** *n* **1** (hold) prise *f* (**on** sur); **to tighten/relax one's ~** on resserrer/relâcher sa prise sur; **she lost her ~ on the rope** elle a perdu prise et lâché la corde; **2** (control) **to take a firm ~ on the party** prendre le parti bien en main; **to lose one's ~ on reality** perdre contact avec la réalité; **to come to ~s with sth** en venir aux prises avec qch; **to get to ~s with sth** attaquer qch de front; **get a ~ on yourself!** ressaisis-toi!; **3** (ability to hold) (of tyre) adhérence *f*; **these shoes have no ~** ces chaussures n'accrochent pas au sol; **4** (clutches) **to be in the ~ of an obsession** être en proie à une obsession; **in the ~ of winter** paralysé par l'hiver; **5** (bag) sac *m* de voyage; **6** CIN accessoiriste *mf*.

II *vtr* (*p prés etc* **-pp-**) **1** (grab) agripper; (hold) serrer; **2** (adhere to) [*tyres*] adhérer à [*road*]; [*shoes*] accrocher à [*ground*]; **3** (captivate) captiver.

gripe /graɪp/ **I** *n* **1** (complaint) sujet *m* de plainte; **2** MED **to have the ~s** avoir des coliques *fpl*.

II *vi* (complain) râler○ (**about** à propos de; **that** que).

gripe water *n* GB calmant *m* (*pour coliques des nourrissons*).

griping /'graɪpɪŋ/ **I** *n*○ *C* ronchonnements *mpl*.

II *adj* MED **to have ~ pains** avoir des coliques *fpl*.

gripping /'grɪpɪŋ/ *adj* captivant.

grisly /'grɪzlɪ/ *adj* [*story, sight*] horrible; [*remains*] macabre.

grist /grɪst/ *n* **it's all ~ to the mill** tout sert.

gristle /'grɪsl/ *n* (in meat) cartilage *m*; **piece of ~** du cartilage.

grit /grɪt/ **I** *n* **1** *C* (on lens) grains *mpl* de poussière;

(sandy dirt) grains *mpl* de sable; (in wound) saletés *fpl*; GB (for roads) sable *m*; **3** (courage) cran○ *m*.

II *vtr* (*p prés etc* **-tt-**) GB sabler [*road*].

IDIOMS **to ~ one's teeth** serrer les dents.

grits /grɪts/ *npl* GB (oats) gruau *m* d'avoine; US (corn) gruau *m* de maïs.

gritter /'grɪtə(r)/ *n* GB AUT sableuse *f*.

gritty /'grɪtɪ/ *adj* **1** (sandy) plein de sable; (gravelly) graveleux/-euse; **2** (realistic, tough) [*personality*] solide et terre à terre; [*novel*] réaliste.

grizzle /'grɪzl/ *vi* GB (cry) pleurnicher.

grizzled /'grɪzld/ *adj* [*hair, beard, person*] grisonnant.

grizzly /'grɪzlɪ/ *n* (also **~ bear**) grizzli *m*.

groan /grəʊn/ **I** *n* (of pain, despair) gémissement *m*; (of disgust, protest) grognement *m*.

II *vi* **1** (in pain) gémir; (in disgust, protest) grogner; **to ~ in** OU **with pain** pousser un gémissement de douleur; **2** (creak) [*timbers*] gémir.

grocer /'grəʊsə(r)/ **▶ 1251**, **1251** *n* (person) épicier/-ière *m/f*; **~'s (shop)** épicerie *f*.

groceries /'grəʊsərɪz/ *npl* **1** (shopping) provisions *fpl*; **2** COMM épicerie *f* *C*.

grocery /'grəʊsərɪ/ **▶ 1251** *n* (also **~ shop** GB, **~ store**) épicerie *f*.

groggy /'grɒgɪ/ *adj* groggy; **to feel ~** avoir les jambes en coton○.

groin /grɔɪn/ **▶ 765** *n* **1** ANAT aine *f*; **in the ~** LIT à l'aine; EUPH dans les testicules; **2** ARCHIT arête *f*; **3** US = **groyne**.

grommet /'grɒmɪt/ *n* **1** (eyelet) œillet *m*; **2** MED diabolo *m*.

groom /gruːm/ **I** *n* **1** (bridegroom) **the ~** le jeune marié; **2** GEN palefrenier/-ière *m/f*; (for racehorse) lad *m*.

II *vtr* **1** (clean) faire la toilette de [*dog, cat*]; (professionally) toiletter [*dog, cat*]; panser [*horse*]; **to ~ oneself carefully** s'habiller et se coiffer avec soin; **2** (prepare) **to ~ sb for** préparer qn à [*exam, career*].

grooming /'gruːmɪŋ/ *n* (of horse) pansage *m*; (of dog) toilettage *m*; **personal ~** US présentation *f*, tenue *f*.

groove /gruːv/ *n* **1** LIT (on record) sillon *m*; (for sliding door) coulisse *f*; (in joinery) rainure *f*; (on head of screw) fente *f*, creux *m*; **2** (routine) **to be stuck in a ~** s'encroûter; **3** MUS rythme *m*.

grope /grəʊp/ **I** *vtr* **1** (feel) **he ~d his way past the furniture** il contourna les meubles à tâtons; **2**○ (sexually) tripoter○.

II *vi* **to ~ for sth** chercher qch à tâtons; **to ~ in the dark** FIG tâtonner.

gross /grəʊs/ **I** *n* (*pl* **~**) (twelve dozen) grosse *f*.

II *adj* **1** COMM, FIN [*income, profit*] brut; **2** (serious) GEN, JUR [*error, exaggeration*] grossier/-ière; [*ignorance*] crasse; [*abuse, inequality*] choquant; [*injustice*] flagrant; **~ negligence** JUR faute *f* lourde; **3** (coarse) [*behaviour*] vulgaire; [*language*] cru; **4**○ (revolting) dégoûtant; **5**○ (obese) obèse.

III *vtr* faire un bénéfice brut de [*x million*].

■ **gross out**○ US: **~ [sb] out** dégoûter [qn].

gross: **~ domestic product, GDP** *n* produit *m* intérieur brut, PIB *m*; **~ indecency** *n* JUR outrage *m* à la pudeur.

grossly /'grəʊslɪ/ *adv* **1** [*exaggerate*] grossièrement; [*misleading, irresponsible*] extrêmement; [*underpaid*] scandaleusement; **~ overweight** obèse; **2** (crudely) de façon grossière.

gross national product, GNP *n* produit *m* national brut, PNB *m*.

gross: **~ ton** *n* tonne *f* britannique (*1016 kilogrammes*); **~ tonnage** *n* NAUT jauge *f* brute.

grotesque /grəʊ'tesk/ *n, adj* grotesque (*m*).

grotto /'grɒtəʊ/ *n* (*pl* **~s** ou **~es**) grotte *f*.

grotty○ /'grɒtɪ/ *adj* GB GEN minable○; **to feel ~** se sentir tout chose○.

grouch /graʊtʃ/ *vi* rouspéter○ (**about sb** après qn; **about sth** contre qch).

grouchy○ /'graʊtʃɪ/ *adj* grognon.

ground /graʊnd/ I *prét, pp* ▶ **grind** II, III.
II *n* **1** (surface underfoot) sol *m*, terre *f*; **to throw sth on the ~** jeter qch par terre; **to sit on the ~** s'asseoir par terre; **to fall to the ~** tomber (par terre); **get up off the ~** lève-toi; **to get off the ~** [*plane*] décoller; FIG [*idea*] prendre FIG; **to get sth off the ~** faire démarrer qch; **to burn to the ~** brûler complètement; **to prepare the ~** FIG ouvrir la voie (**for** à); **to clear the ~** LIT, FIG déblayer le terrain; **2** (area, territory) LIT, FIG terrain *m*; **to cover a lot of ~** LIT faire beaucoup de chemin; FIG avancer beaucoup; **to go over the same ~** se répéter; **to break fresh ou new ~** innover; **on neutral ~** en terrain neutre; **to be sure of one's ~** être sûr de ce qu'on avance; **on dangerous ~** (in discussion) sur un terrain miné; (in dealings) dans une position délicate; **3** GEN, SPORT (for specific activity) terrain *m*; **4** (reason) GEN, JUR motifs *mpl*, raisons *fpl*; **5** FIG (in contest, discussion) **to gain ~** gagner du terrain (**on**, **over** sur); **to lose ~** perdre du terrain (**to** au profit de); **to give ~** céder du terrain (**to** devant; **on**, **over** au niveau de); **to make up lost ~** regagner du terrain perdu; **to hold ou stand (one's) ~** tenir bon; **to shift one's ~** FIG changer son fusil d'épaule (**on** au sujet de); **6** US ELEC terre *f*; **7** ART fond *m*.
III **grounds** *npl* **1** (of house, institution) parc *m* (**of** de); **private ~s** propriété *f* privée; **2** (reasons) **~s for** motifs de [*divorce, criticism, hope*]; **to have ~s for complaint** avoir des motifs de se plaindre; **~s for doing** motifs pour faire; **there are no ~s for supposing that** il n'y a aucun motif pour supposer que; **to give sb good ~s for doing** donner à qn de bonnes raisons de faire; **on (the) ~s of** en raison de [*cost, public interest*]; pour cause de [*adultery, negligence*]; **on (the) ~s of ill-health** pour raisons de santé; **on compassionate ~s** pour raisons personnelles; **on the ~s that** en raison du fait que.
IV **ground** *pp adj* [*coffee, pepper*] moulu.
V *vtr* **1** AVIAT immobiliser [*aircraft*]; **2** NAUT **to be ~ed** s'échouer; **3** (base) **to ~ sth on** ou **in** fonder qch sur; **4**° (keep in) priver [qn] de sortie; **5** US ELEC relier [qch] à la terre.
IDIOMS **to be thin on the ~** ne pas être légion *inv*; **to go to ~** se terrer; **to run sb/sth to ~** dénicher° qn/qch; **to run ou drive oneself into the ~** s'user au travail; **that suits me down to the ~** ça me convient parfaitement.
ground: **~ almonds** *npl* poudre *f* d'amandes; **~ beef** *n* US bœuf *m* haché; **~ control** *n* contrôle *m* au sol; **~ crew** *n* personnel *m* au sol.
ground floor SURTOUT GB *n* rez-de-chaussée *m*; **on the ~** au rez-de-chaussée.
ground: **~ forces** *npl* forces *fpl* terrestres; **~ frost** *n* givre *m*; **Groundhog Day** *n* US le 2 février (*dans la croyance populaire, jour décisif quant à la durée de l'hiver*); **~ hostess** ▶ **1251** *n* hôtesse *f* au sol.
grounding /ˈgraʊndɪŋ/ *n* **1** ¢ (preparation) bases *fpl* (**in** en, de); **to have a good ~ in sth** avoir de bonnes bases en qch; **2** AVIAT (of plane) immobilisation *f*.
ground: **~less** *adj* [*fear, rumour*] sans fondement; **~ level** *n* CONSTR rez-de-chaussée *m*; **~nut** *n* GB arachide *f*; **~nut oil** *n* GB huile *f* d'arachide; **~ rent** *n* rente *f* foncière; **~ rice** *n* semoule *f* de riz.
ground rules *npl* grands principes *mpl*; **to change the ~** modifier les règles du jeu.
ground: **~sheet** *n* tapis *m* de sol; **~ speed** *n* vitesse *f* au sol.
groundstaff /ˈgraʊndstɑːf, US -stæf/ *n* **1** (for maintenance) personnel *m* d'entretien d'un terrain de sports; **2** AVIAT personnel *m* au sol.
groundswell /ˈgraʊndswel/ *n* **1** FIG (upsurge) **a ~ of support for** une vague de soutien pour; **2** LIT, NAUT raz-de-marée *m*.
ground: **~-to-air missile** *n* missile *m* sol-air; **~ troops** *npl* troupes *fpl* terrestres; **~ wire** *n* US fil *m* de terre; **~work** *n* travail *m* préparatoire (**for** à); **~ zero** *n* point *m* zéro.
group /gruːp/ I *n* groupe *m*; **in ~s** en groupes.

II *noun modifier* [*dynamics, therapy*] de groupe.
III *vtr* (also **~ together**) grouper; **to ~ sth according to price** grouper qch en fonction du prix.
IV *vi* (also **~ together**) se grouper.
group booking *n* réservation *f* de groupe.
grouping /ˈɡruːpɪŋ/ *n* (group, alliance) groupe *m*.
group: **~ insurance** *n* assurance *f* collective; **Group of Seven** *n* groupe *m* des Sept; **~ practice** *n* MED cabinet *m* médical collectif; **~ work** *n* travail *m* en groupes.
grouse /graʊs/ I *n* (*pl* **~**) (bird, meat) tétras *m*.
II° *vi* (complain) râler° (**about** après).
grove /ɡrəʊv/ *n* bosquet *m*; **lemon ~** verger *m* de citronniers.
grovel /ˈɡrɒvl/ *vi* (*p prés etc* **-ll-**, US **-l-**) **1** FIG (humbly) ramper (**to, before** devant); **2** (crawl) **to ~ around** être à quatre pattes.
grovelling, groveling US /ˈɡrɒvlɪŋ/ *adj* obséquieux/-ieuse.
grow /ɡrəʊ/ (*prét* **grew**; *pp* **grown**) I *vtr* **1** (cultivate) cultiver; **2** (increase, allow to increase) laisser pousser [*beard, nails*]; **to ~ 5 cm** [*person*] grandir de 5 cm; [*plant*] pousser de 5 cm.
II *vi* **1** (increase physically) [*plant, hair*] pousser (**by** de); [*person*] grandir (**by** de); [*tumour*] se développer; **to let one's nails ~** laisser pousser ses ongles; **to ~ to a height of 4 metres** atteindre 4 mètres de hauteur; **2** (of something abstract) [*spending, crime, population, tension*] augmenter (**by** de); [*company, economy*] être en expansion; [*movement, opposition, support, problem*] devenir plus important; [*poverty, crisis*] s'aggraver; [*pressure, influence*] devenir plus fort; **fears are ~ing that** on craint de plus en plus que (+ *subj*); **to ~ to** atteindre [*level*]; **to ~ in** acquérir plus de [*authority, strength*]; **to ~ in popularity** devenir plus populaire; **3** (become) devenir [*hotter, stronger*]; **to ~ old** vieillir; **to ~ more and more impatient** s'impatienter de plus en plus; **to ~ to do** finir par faire; **I soon grew to like him** j'ai vite fini par l'aimer.
■ **grow apart** s'éloigner l'un de l'autre.
■ **grow into**: **~ into** [sth] **1** (become) devenir [*adult*]; **2** (fit into) s'accoutumer à [*role*]; **he'll ~ into it** (of garment) quand il aura un peu grandi il pourra le mettre.
■ **grow on**: **~ on** [sb] [*habit*] s'imposer; **it ~s on you** on finit par l'aimer.
■ **grow out of**: **~ out of** [sth] **1** (get too big for) **he's grown out of his suit** son costume est devenu trop petit pour lui; **she's grown out of discos** elle a passé l'âge des discothèques; **2** (develop from) naître de.
■ **grow together** (become close) se rapprocher.
■ **grow up 1** (grow, get bigger) [*child*] grandir; [*movement*] se développer; **to ~ up believing that** grandir dans l'idée que; **2** (become adult, mature) devenir adulte; **when I ~ up** quand je serai grand.
grow bag *n* sac *m* de culture.
grower /ˈɡrəʊə(r)/ *n* (person) (of fruit) producteur/-trice *m/f*; (of cereal crops) cultivateur/-trice *m/f*; (of flowers) horticulteur/-trice *m/f*.
growing /ˈɡrəʊɪŋ/ I *n* AGRIC culture *f*.
II *adj* **1** (physically) [*child*] en pleine croissance; [*business*] en expansion; **2** (increasing) [*number, demand*] croissant; [*pressure, optimism, opposition*] grandissant.
growing pains *npl* FIG (of firm, project) difficultés *fpl* dans le développement.
growl /ɡraʊl/ I *n* (of dog) grondement *m*; (of person) grognement *m*.
II *vi* [*dog*] gronder; [*person*] **to ~ at sb** grogner après qn.
grown /ɡrəʊn/ I *pp* ▶ **grow**.
II *adj* **a ~ man/woman** un/-e adulte.
grown-up I /ˈɡrəʊnʌp/ *n* adulte *mf*, grande personne *f*.
II /ˌɡrəʊnˈʌp/ *adj* adulte; **~ son** fils *m* adulte; **what do you want to be when you're ~?** qu'est-ce que tu veux faire quand tu seras grand?; **to be ~ for one's age** être mûr pour son âge.
growth /ɡrəʊθ/ *n* **1** (physical) (of person, plant)

croissance *f*; (of hair, nails) pousse *f*; **2** (increase) (of population, movement, idea) croissance *f* (**in, of** de); (of economy) expansion *f* (**in, of** de); (of numbers, productivity, earnings) augmentation *f* (**in** de); (of expenditure) hausse *f* (**in** de); **3** MED grosseur *f*, tumeur *f*; **4** BOT pousse *f*.

growth: **~ area** *n* secteur *m* en expansion; **~ industry** *f* en industrie *f* en expansion; **~ rate** *n* ECON taux *m* de croissance; (of person) rythme *m* de croissance; **~ ring** *n* BOT (on tree) anneau *m*.

groyne GB, **groin** US /grɔɪn/ *n* épi *m* (*pour retenir le sable*).

grub /grʌb/ *n* **1** ZOOL larve *f*; (in fruit) ver *m*; **2**◦ (food) bouffe◦ *f*.

■ **grub around**: **~ around for** fouiner pour trouver.

grubby /'grʌbɪ/ *adj* LIT malpropre; FIG infâme.

Grub Street *n*: *le monde des écrivaillons nécessiteux*.

grudge /grʌdʒ/ **I** *n* to bear **sb a ~** en vouloir à qn; **to harbour** ou **bear** ou **nurse a ~ against** garder de la rancune contre.

II *vtr* **to ~ sb their success** en vouloir à qn de sa réussite; **to ~ doing** rechigner à faire.

grudging /'grʌdʒɪŋ/ *adj* [*acceptance, admiration*] réticent; **to treat sb with ~ respect** respecter qn malgré soi; **to be ~ in one's praise** être avare de compliments.

grudgingly /'grʌdʒɪŋlɪ/ *adv* [*admit*] avec réticence.

gruel /'gru:əl/ *n* gruau *m*.

gruelling, grueling US /'gru:əlɪŋ/ *adj* exténuant.

gruesome /'gru:səm/ *adj* (gory) horrible; (horrifying) épouvantable.

gruff /grʌf/ *adj* bourru.

grumble /'grʌmbl/ **I** *n* **1** (complaint) ronchonnement *m*; **to have a ~ about** ronchonner après; **2** (of thunder) grondement *m*; (of stomach) gargouillement *m*.

II *vi* **1** [*person*] ronchonner (**at sb** après qn; **to** auprès de); **to ~ about** se plaindre de; **2** [*stomach*] gargouiller.

grumbling /'grʌmblɪŋ/ **I** *n* **1** ₵ (complaining) plaintes *fpl*; **2** (of thunder) grondement *m*; (of stomach) gargouillement *m*.

II *adj* **1** (complaining) ronchon/-onne◦; **~ appendix** appendicite *f* chronique.

grumpily /'grʌmpɪlɪ/ *adv* [*speak*] en bougonnant; [*act*] d'un air maussade.

grumpy /'grʌmpɪ/ *adj* grincheux/-euse, grognon.

grunge◦ /'grʌndʒ/ *n* (dirt) crasse *f*; (style) grunge *m*.

grunt /grʌnt/ **I** *n* grognement *m*.

II *vi* [*pig*] grogner; [*person*] grogner (**with, in** de).

G-string *n* (garment) string *m*.

Gt *abrév écrite* = **Great**.

guarantee /ˌɡærən'ti:/ **I** *n* **1** (warranty, document) garantie *f* (**against** contre); **there is a ~ on the vehicle** le véhicule est sous garantie; **this television carries a one-year ~** cette télévision est garantie un an; **2** (assurance) garantie *f* (**against** contre); **there is no ~ that** il n'est pas certain que; **3** JUR (of financial liability, sb's debts) garantie *f*; **4** (security) (cash) caution *f*; (object) gage *m*, garantie *f*; **to give** [sth] **as a ~** donner [qch] en caution [*money*]; donner [qch] en gage [*object*].

II *vtr* **1** COMM garantir (**against** contre); **it's ~d for five years** il est garanti cinq ans; **~d waterproof** garanti étanche; **2** (assure) garantir, assurer; **to ~ to do** s'engager à faire; **I can ~ that…** je peux vous garantir que…; **I can't ~ that it's true** je ne peux pas garantir que ce soit vrai; **it's a ~d bestseller** ce sera un bestseller à coup sûr; **3** JUR **to ~ a loan** se porter garant or caution d'un emprunt; **to ~ a cheque** garantir un chèque.

guarantor /ˌɡærən'tɔ:(r)/ *n* caution *f*, garant/-e *m/f*; **stand ~ for sb** se porter garant de qn.

guard /gɑ:d/ **I** *n* **1** (for person) surveillant/-e *m/f*; (for place, object) gardien/-ienne *m/f*; **2** (at prison) gardien/-ienne *m/f*; (soldier) garde *m*; **3** MIL (duty) garde *f*, surveillance *f*; **to be on ~** (duty) être de garde; **to go on/come off ~** prendre/finir son tour de garde; **to**

keep ou **stand ~** monter la garde (**over** auprès de); **the changing of the ~** GB la relève de la garde; **4** (watchfulness) **to drop one's ~** baisser la garde; **to catch sb off ~** prendre qn au dépourvu; **to be on one's ~** se méfier (**against** de); **5** (group of soldiers, police etc) **under armed ~** sous escorte armée; **6** GB RAIL chef *m* de train; **7** (for safety) (on printer) couvercle *m*; (on industrial machinery) carter *m* de protection; **8** (in Ireland) (policeman) policier *m* (irlandais).

II *vtr* **1** (protect) surveiller [*place, object*]; protéger [*person*]; **a dog ~s the house** un chien garde la maison; **the house is heavily ~ed** la maison est sous haute surveillance; **to ~ sth with one's life** protéger qch au péril de sa vie; **2** (prevent from escaping) surveiller; **3** (from discovery) garder [*secret*].

■ **guard against**: **~ against** [sth] se prémunir contre; **to ~ against doing** prendre garde à ne pas faire.

guard dog *n* chien *m* de garde.

guarded /'gɑ:dɪd/ *adj* circonspect (**about** à propos de).

guardian /'gɑ:dɪən/ *n* JUR tuteur/-trice *m/f*; GEN gardien/-ienne *m/f* (**of** de).

guardian angel *n* LIT, FIG ange *m* gardien.

guard: **~ of honour** *n* garde *f* d'honneur; **~ rail** *n* AUT glissière *f* de sécurité; (on bridge, window) garde-fou *m*; **~room** *n* salle *f* d'arrêt(s); **~'s van** *n* GB RAIL fourgon *m* à bagages.

Guatemala /ˌɡwɑːtə'mɑːlə/ ▶ **840** *pr n* Guatemala *m*.

Guatemalan /ˌɡwɑːtə'mɑːlən/ ▶ **1100** **I** *n* Guatémaltèque *mf*.

II *adj* guatémaltèque.

guava /'ɡwɑːvə, US 'ɡwɔːvə/ *n* (tree) goyavier *m*; (fruit) goyave *f*.

Guernsey /'ɡɜːnzɪ/ ▶ **1022** *pr n* GEOG Guernesey *f*.

guerrilla /ɡə'rɪlə/ *n* guérillero *m*; **urban ~s** guérilla *f* urbaine.

guerrilla: **~ war** *n* guérilla *f*; **~ warfare** *n* guérilla *f*.

guess /ges/ **I** *n* supposition *f*, conjecture *f*; **to have** ou **make a ~** essayer de deviner; **to have** ou **make a ~ at sth** essayer de deviner qch; **my ~ is that they will lose** à mon avis ils vont perdre; **at a (rough) ~ I would say that…** au hasard je dirais que…; **I'll give you three ~es!** devine un peu!; **that was a good ~!** tu as deviné juste!; **to make a wild ~** deviner au hasard; **your ~ is as good as mine** je n'en sais pas plus que toi; **it's anybody's ~!** les paris sont ouverts!

II *vtr* **1** (intuit) deviner; **to ~ that** supposer que; **to ~ sb's age** (correctly) deviner l'âge de qn; (make estimate) donner un âge à qn; **you'll never ~ what has happened!** tu ne devineras jamais ce qui vient d'arriver!; **I ~ed as much!** je m'en doutais!; **~ what!** I've won a prize! tu sais quoi◦! j'ai gagné un prix!; **~ who!** devine qui c'est!; **2** US (suppose) supposer; (believe, think) penser, croire; **'he's right, you know'—'I ~ so'** il a raison, tu sais'—'oui, je suppose'.

III *vi* **1** deviner; **to ~ at** faire des suppositions or des conjectures quant à [*plans, outcome*]; **to ~ right** deviner juste; **to ~ wrong** se tromper; **to keep sb ~ing** laisser qn dans le doute.

guess: **~timate** *n* calcul *m* approximatif; **~work** *n* conjecture *f*.

guest /ɡest/ **I** *n* **1** GEN invité/-e *m/f*; (of hotel) client/-e *m/f*; (of boarding house) pensionnaire *mf*; **~ of honour** invité/-e d'honneur; **house ~** invité/-e *m/f*; **be my ~!** je vous en prie!; **2** BIOL hôte *m*.

II *noun modifier* [*speaker*] invité; **~ book** livre *m* d'or; **~ list** liste *f* des invités; **~ star** GEN invité/-e *m/f* d'honneur; (in film credits) avec la participation de.

guest: **~house** *n* pension *f* de famille; **~ room** *n* chambre *f* d'amis; **~worker** *n* travailleur *m* immigré, travailleuse *f* immigrée.

guff◦ /ɡʌf/ *n* ₵ sottises *fpl*.

guffaw /ɡə'fɔː/ *n* gros éclat *m* de rire.

guidance /ˈgaɪdns/ *n* **ȼ** (advice) conseils *mpl* (**from** de); ~ **on legal procedures** conseils en matière de procédures légales; ~ **on how to do** conseils sur la façon de faire; **to give sb** ~ donner des conseils à qn; **to seek** ~ **on a matter** demander conseil sur une (certaine) question; **this leaflet is for your** ~ ce prospectus est pour vous, à titre d'information; **under the** ~ **of sb** sous la direction de qn.

guide /gaɪd/ **I** *n* **1** (person) guide *m*; **tour** ~ guide (touristique); **to act as a** ~ servir de guide; **2** (estimate, idea) indication *f*; **as a rough** ~ à titre d'indication; **3** GEN TOURISM (book) guide *m* (**to** de); **TV** ~ programme *m* de télé(vision); **user's** ~ manuel *m* d'utilisation; **4** (also **Girl Guide**) guide *f*.
II *vtr* **1** (steer) guider, conduire (**to** vers); **2** (influence) [*person*] guider; [*reason*] dicter; **to be** ~**d by sb's advice** suivre les conseils de qn; **3** AEROSP, MIL (télé)guider.

guide: ~ **book** *n* guide *m*; ~ **dog** *n* chien *m* d'aveugle; ~**d tour** *n* visite *f* guidée.

guideline /ˈgaɪdlaɪn/ *n* **1** (rough guide) indication *f*; **2** ADMIN, POL directive *f*; **pay** ~**s** base *f* des négociations salariales; **3** (advice) conseil *m*.

guiding /ˈgaɪdɪŋ/ *adj* ~ **force** FIG moteur *m*; ~ **principle** principe *m* directeur; ~ **light** (person) flambeau *m*.

guild /gɪld/ *n* (medieval) guilde *f*; (modern) association *f*.

guilder /ˈgɪldə(r)/ ▶ 849 | *n* florin *m*.

guile /gaɪl/ *n* **full of** ~ rusé; **without** ~ candide.

guileless /ˈgaɪlləs/ *adj* candide.

guillotine /ˈgɪləti:n/ *n* **1** (for execution) guillotine *f*; **2** (for paper) massicot *m*; **3** GB POL *système qui limite la durée des débats parlementaires*.

guilt /gɪlt/ *n* **1** (blame) GEN, JUR culpabilité *f*; **2** (feeling) sentiment *m* de culpabilité (**about sb** envers qn; **about** ou **over sth** pour qch).

guiltily /ˈgɪltɪlɪ/ *adv* [*say, look*] d'un air coupable.

guiltless /ˈgɪltlɪs/ *adj* SOUT innocent.

guilty /ˈgɪltɪ/ *adj* **1** JUR coupable; **to be found** ~/**not** ~ **of sth** être reconnu coupable/déclaré non coupable de qch; **the** ~ **party** le/la coupable *m/f*; **2** (remorseful) [*expression*] de culpabilité; [*appearance, look*] coupable; **to feel** ~ **about** se sentir coupable vis-à-vis de.

Guinea /ˈgɪnɪ/ ▶ 840 | *pr n* Guinée *f*.

guinea-fowl /ˈgɪnɪfaʊl/, **guinea-hen** /ˈgɪnɪhen/ *n* pintade *f*.

guinea-pig /ˈgɪnɪpɪg/ *n* **1** ZOOL cochon *m* d'Inde; **2** FIG cobaye *m*.

guise /gaɪz/ *n* LITTÉR **in** ou **under the** ~ **of a joke** sous (le) couvert de la plaisanterie; **in various** ~**s** sous différentes formes.

guitar /gɪˈtɑ:(r)/ ▶ 1097 | **I** *n* guitare *f*; **on the** ~ à la guitare.
II *noun modifier* [*lesson, player, string, teacher*] de guitare; ~ **case** étui *m* à guitare.

guitarist /gɪˈtɑ:rɪst/ ▶ 1251 |, 1097 | *n* guitariste *mf*.

Gulag /ˈgu:læg/ *n* Goulag *m*.

gulch /gʌltʃ/ *n* US ravin *m*.

gulf /gʌlf/ *n* **1** FIG fossé *m* (**between** qui sépare); **2** GEOG golfe *m*.

Gulf /gʌlf/ *pr n* **the** ~ la région du Golfe.

Gulf States *pr npl* **the** ~ (in Middle East) les États *mpl* du Golfe; (on US/Mexican border) *les États bordant le golfe du Mexique*.

Gulf War *pr n* guerre *f* du Golfe.

gull /gʌl/ *n* mouette *f*; (larger) goéland *m*.

gullet /ˈgʌlɪt/ *n* (throat) gosier *m*; (oesophagus) œsophage *m*.

gullibility /ˌgʌlɪˈbɪlətɪ/ *n* crédulité *f*.

gullible /ˈgʌləbl/ *adj* crédule.

gully /ˈgʌlɪ/ *n* GEOG ravin *m*.

gulp /gʌlp/ **I** *n* **1** (mouthful) (of liquid) gorgée *f*; (of air) bouffée *f*, goulée *f*; (of food) bouchée *f*; **she drained her glass in one** ~ elle a vidé son verre d'un trait; **2** (nervous) serrement *m* de gorge; (tearful) hoquet *m*.
II *vtr* engloutir [*food, drink*]; aspirer [*air*].
III *vi* avoir la gorge serrée.
■ **gulp back**: ~ **back** [sth], ~ [sth] **back** ravaler [*tears*].

gum /gʌm/ **I** *n* **1** ANAT gencive *f*; **2** (also **chewing** ~) chewing-gum *m*; **a piece of** ~ un chewing-gum; **3** (adhesive) colle *f*; **4** (resin) gomme *f*.
II *vtr* (*p prés etc* -**mm**-) coller (**to** à; **on to** sur).

gum: ~**boot** *n* GB botte *f* en caoutchouc; ~**drop** *n* boule *f* de gomme.

gumption○ /ˈgʌmpʃn/ *n* (common sense) jugeote○ *f*; (courage) cran○ *m*.

gumshoe○ *n* (private investigator) détective *m* privé; (police detective) policier *m* en civil.

gum tree *n* gommier *m*.
IDIOMS **to be up a** ~ être en position délicate.

gun /gʌn/ **I** *n* **1** (weapon) GEN arme *f* à feu; (revolver) revolver *m*; (rifle) fusil *m*; (cannon) canon *m*; **to fire a** ~ tirer; **to draw a** ~ **on sb** braquer une arme sur qn; **he's got a** ~! il est armé!; **2** (tool) pistolet *m*; **paint** ~ pistolet à peinture; **3**○ US **a hired** ~ un tueur à gages.
II *vtr* (*p prés etc* -**nn**-) **to** ~ **an engine** mettre les gaz○.
IDIOMS **to go great** ~**s**○ [*business*] marcher très fort○; [*person*] avoir la frite○; **to hold a** ~ **to sb's head** mettre le couteau sous la gorge de qn; **to jump the** ~ agir prématurément; **to stick to one's** ~**s**○ (in one's actions) s'accrocher○.
■ **gun down**: ~ [sb] **down**, ~ **down** [sb] abattre, descendre.
■ **gun for**: **to be** ~**ning for** [sb] chercher des crosses à○.

gun: ~ **barrel** *n* canon *m* de fusil; ~**boat** *n* canonnière *f*; ~**dog** *n* chien *m* de chasse; ~**fire** *n* **ȼ** (from hand-held gun) coups *mpl* de feu; (from artillery) fusillade *f*.

gunge○ /gʌndʒ/ GB *n* magma *m* répugnant.

gung ho○ /ˌgʌŋˈhəʊ/ *adj* HUM ou PÉJ (eager for war) va-t-en guerre *inv*; (overzealous) (trop) enthousiaste.

gun: ~ **laws** *npl* législation *f* sur les armes à feu; ~ **licence** *n* permis *m* de port d'armes; ~**man** *n* homme *m* armé.

gunner /ˈgʌnə(r)/ *n* GB (in navy) canonnier *m*; (in army) artilleur *m*.

gunpoint /ˈgʌnpɔɪnt/ *n* **to hold sb up at** ~ tenir qn sous la menace d'une arme.

gun: ~**powder** *n* poudre *f*; **Gunpowder Plot** *pr n* HIST Conspiration *f* des Poudres; ~**running** *n* trafic *m* d'armes; ~**shot** *n* (report) coup *m* de feu; ~**shot wound** *n* blessure *f* par balle; ~**slinger**○ *n* US bandit *m* armé; ~**smith** ▶ 1251 | *n* armurier *m*.

gunwale /ˈgʌnl/ *n* plat-bord *m*; **full to the** ~**s** plein à ras bords.

gurgle /ˈgɜ:gl/ **I** *n* (of water) gargouillement *m*; (of baby) gazouillis *m*.
II *vi* [*water*] gargouiller; [*baby*] gazouiller.

guru /ˈgʊru:, US gəˈru:/ *n* gourou *m*.

gush /gʌʃ/ **I** *n* (of liquid) jaillissement *m*.
II *vi* **1** [*liquid*] jaillir; **tears** ~**ed down her cheeks** ses joues ruisselaient de larmes; **2** FIG **to** ~ **over** s'extasier devant.
■ **gush in** [*water, oil etc*] pénétrer.

gushing /ˈgʌʃɪŋ/, **gushy** /ˈgʌʃɪ/ *adj* [*person*] hyper-expansif/-ive○; [*letter, style*] dithyrambique○.

gusset /ˈgʌsɪt/ *n* soufflet *m*.

gust /gʌst/ *n* **1** (of wind, rain, snow) rafale *f*; **a** ~ **of hot air** une bouffée d'air chaud; **2** (of anger) bouffée *f*.

gusto /ˈgʌstəʊ/ *n* **with** ~ avec enthousiasme.

gusty /ˈgʌstɪ/ *adj* [*day, weather*] de grand vent.

gut /gʌt/ **I** *n* **1**○ (abdomen, belly) bide○ *m*; **beer** ~ brioche○ *f* (*de buveur de bière*); **2** ANAT (intestine) intestin *m*; **3** (for racket, bow) boyau *m*.
II **guts**○ *npl* **1** (insides) (of human) tripes○ *fpl*; (of animal, building) entrailles *fpl*; **2** (courage) cran○ *m*.
III *noun modifier* (basic) [*feeling, reaction*] viscéral, instinctif/-ive; [*instinct*] premier/-ière (*before n*).

IV *vtr* (*p prés etc* **-tt-**) **1** CULIN vider; **2** (destroy) [*fire*] ravager; [*looters*] saccager; **3** (strip) **to ~ a house** tout refaire dans une maison.
V gutted○ *pp adj* GB abattu, découragé.

gutless /'gʌtlɪs/ *adj* mou/molle.

gutsy○ /'gʌtsɪ/ *adj* (spirited) fougueux/-euse; (brave) courageux/-euse.

gutter /'gʌtə(r)/ **I** *n* **1** (on roof) gouttière *f*; (in street) caniveau *m*; **2** FIG bas-fonds *mpl*.
II *vi* [*flame*] crépiter et vaciller.

guttering /'gʌtərɪŋ/ *n* ⊄ gouttières *fpl*.

gutter: **~ press** *n* presse *f* à sensation; **~snipe** *n* PÉJ gosse *mf* des rues.

guttural /'gʌtərəl/ *adj* guttural.

guv○ /gʌv/, **guvnor**○ /'gʌvnər/ *n* GB chef○ *m*.

guy○ /gaɪ/ *n* **1** (man) type○ *m*; **a good/bad ~** (in films etc) un bon/méchant; **hey, you ~s!** (to men, mixed group) eh! vous, les gars○!; (to women) eh! les filles○!; **2** GB effigie de Guy Fawkes qu'on brûle le 5 novembre; **3** (also **~rope**) corde *f* d'attache.

Guyana /gaɪ'ænə/ ▶ 840 *pr n* Guyana *f*.

Guy Fawkes Day /'gaɪ fɔːks deɪ/ *n* GB le 5 novembre (*anniversaire de la Conspiration des Poudres*).

guzzle○ /'gʌzl/ *vtr* engloutir.

guzzler○ /'gʌzlə(r)/ *n* goinfre○ *mf*.

gym /dʒɪm/ ▶ 949 *n* **1** (*abrév* = **gymnasium**) salle *f* de gym○, gymnase *m*; **2** (*abrév* = **gymnastics**) gym○ *f*.

gymkhana /dʒɪm'kɑːnə/ *n* jeux *mpl* à poney.

gymnasium /dʒɪm'neɪzɪəm/ *n* (*pl* **~s** ou **-ia**) gymnase *m*.

gymnast /'dʒɪmnæst/ *n* gymnaste *mf*.

gymnastic /dʒɪm'næstɪk/ *adj* de gymnastique.

gymnastics /dʒɪm'næstɪks/ ▶ 949 *npl* (all contexts) gymnastique *f*.

gym: **~ shoe** *n* (chaussure *f* de) tennis *f*; **~slip** *n* GB robe *f* chasuble (*faisant partie d'un uniforme scolaire*).

gynaecologist GB, **gynecologist** US /ˌgaɪnə'kɒlədʒɪst/ ▶ 1251 *n* gynécologue *mf*.

gynaecology GB, **gynecology** US /ˌgaɪnə'kɒlədʒɪ/ *n* gynécologie *f*.

gyp○ /dʒɪp/ **I** *n* **1** GB (pain) **my back is giving me ~** j'ai mal au dos en ce moment; **2** US (con) arnaque○ *f*.
II *vtr* US (*p prés etc* **-pp-**) **to get ~ped** se faire arnaquer○.

gypsophila /dʒɪp'sɒfɪlə/ *n* gypsophile *f*.

gypsum /'dʒɪpsəm/ *n* gypse *m*.

gypsy /'dʒɪpsɪ/ **I** *n* GEN bohémien/-ienne *m/f*; (Central European) tzigane *mf*; (Spanish) gitan/-e *m/f*.
II *noun modifier* [*camp*] de bohémiens; [*music*] tzigane.

gypsy cab○ *n* US taxi *m* clandestin.

gyrate /ˌdʒaɪ'reɪt, US 'dʒaɪreɪt/ *vi* [*dancer*] se trémousser; [*kite*] décrire des cercles.

h, H /eɪtʃ/ *n* h, H *m*.

ha /hɑ:/ I *n: abrév écrite* = **hectare**.
II *excl* ah; '~! ~!' (laughter) 'ah, ah, ah!'; (ironic) très drôle! IRON.

haberdasher /'hæbədæʃə(r)/ ▶1251 *n* 1 GB mercier/-ière *m/f*; 2 US marchand/-e *m/f* de vêtements pour hommes.

haberdashery /'hæbədæʃərɪ/ ▶1251 *n* 1 GB (in department store) rayon *m* mercerie; 2 (goods) GB mercerie *f*; 3 US magasin *m* de vêtements pour hommes.

habit /'hæbɪt/ *n* 1 (custom) GEN habitude *f*; **to have a ~ of doing, to be in the ~ of doing** avoir l'habitude de faire; **I'm not in the ~ of borrowing money** ce n'est pas dans mes habitudes d'emprunter de l'argent; **to get into/out of the ~ of doing sth** prendre/perdre l'habitude de faire qch; **to be a creature of ~** avoir ses petites habitudes; 2 (addiction) accoutumance *f*; **to kick the ~**○ (of addiction) décrocher○; (of smoking) arrêter; 3 RELIG habit *m*; 4 (for horseriding) tenue *f* d'équitation.

habitable /'hæbɪtəbl/ *adj* habitable.

habitat /'hæbɪtæt/ *n* habitat *m*.

habitation /ˌhæbɪ'teɪʃn/ *n* SOUT 1 (house) habitation *f*; 2 (being inhabited) **to show signs of ~** paraître habité; **unfit for human ~** insalubre.

habit-forming /'hæbɪtfɔːmɪŋ/ *adj* **to be ~** créer une accoutumance.

habitual /hə'bɪtʃʊəl/ *adj* [*behaviour, reaction*] habituel/-elle; [*drinker, smoker, liar*] invétéré.

habitually /hə'bɪtʃʊəlɪ/ *adv* habituellement.

hack /hæk/ I *n* 1○ PÉJ (writer) écrivaillon *m* PÉJ; 2 COMPUT = **hacker**; 3○ POL (also **party ~**) militant/-e *m/f*.
II *vtr* 1 (strike, chop) taillader [*branch, object*] (with avec, à coups de); tailler dans [*bushes*] (with à coups de); **to ~ sb (to death) with sth** frapper qn (à mort) à coups de qch; **to ~ sth/sb to pieces** tailler or mettre qch/qn en pièces; **to ~ a path** ou **one's way through sth** se tailler un chemin à travers qch; 2 COMPUT s'introduire dans [*system, database*]; 3○ (cope with) **I can't ~ it** je ne le supporte pas; **how long do you think he will ~ it?** combien de temps tu penses qu'il va tenir?
III *vi* 1 (chop) taillader (with à coups de); **to ~ through sth** tailler dans qch; 2○ COMPUT pirater○; **to ~ into** s'introduire dans [*system*].
■ **hack down: ~ down** [sth], **~** [sth] **down** abattre [*grass, bush, enemy*].
■ **hack off: ~ off** [sth], **~** [sth] **off** tailler [*piece, branch*]; trancher [*hand, head*].

hacker /'hækə(r)/ *n* COMPUT pirate○ *m* informatique.

hacking /'hækɪŋ/ *n* COMPUT piratage○ *m* informatique.

hacking cough *n* toux *f* sèche et spasmodique.

hackles /'hæklz/ *npl* (on animal) poils *mpl* du cou; **the dog's ~ began to rise** le chien se hérissait; **to make sb's ~ rise** FIG hérisser qn.

hackney cab /ˌhæknɪ'kæb/ *n* fiacre *m*.

hackneyed /'hæknɪd/ *adj* [*joke*] éculé; [*subject*] rebattu; **~ phrase, ~ expression** cliché *m*.

hack: ~ reporter *n* journaliste *mf* qui fait la rubrique des chiens écrasés; **~saw** *n* scie *f* à métaux.

had /hæd/ *prét, pp* ▶ **have**.

haddock /'hædək/ *n* (*pl* **~s** ou **~**) églefin *m*.

hadn't /'hædnt/ = **had not**.

haematoma GB, **hematoma** US /ˌhiːmə'təʊmə/ *n* (*pl* **~s** ou **-mata**) hématome *m*.

haemoglobin GB, **hemoglobin** US /ˌhiːmə'gləʊbɪn/ *n* hémoglobine *f*.

haemophilia GB, **hemophilia** US /ˌhiːmə'fɪlɪə/ ▶1002 *n* hémophilie *f*.

haemophiliac GB, **hemophiliac** US /ˌhiːmə'fɪlɪæk/ *n, adj* hémophile (*mf*).

haemorrhage GB, **hemorrhage** US /'hemərɪdʒ/ I *n* LIT, FIG hémorragie *f*.
II *vi* faire une hémorragie.

haemorrhoids GB, **hemorrhoids** US /'hemərɔɪdz/ *npl* hémorroïdes *fpl*.

hag /hæg/ *n* (witch) sorcière *f*.

haggard /'hægəd/ *adj* [*appearance, person*] exténué; [*face, expression*] défait.

haggle /'hægl/ *vi* marchander; **to ~ about** ou **over sth** discuter du prix de qch.

Hague /heɪg/ ▶1343 *pr n* **The ~** La Haye.

hail /heɪl/ I *n* LIT grêle *f*; FIG (of bullets, insults) grêle *f* (of de).
II *vtr* 1 (call, signal to) héler [*person, taxi, ship*]; 2 (praise) **to ~ sb as** acclamer qn comme; **to ~ sth as sth/as being** saluer qch comme qch/comme étant.
III *v impers* grêler.
IV *excl* Hail! Salut!
■ **hail from** SOUT être de, venir de.

hail: Hail Mary *n* 'Je vous salue Marie' *m inv*; **~stone** *n* grêlon *m*; **~storm** *n* averse *f* de grêle.

hair /heə(r)/ *n* 1 ¢ (collectively) (on head) cheveux *mpl*; (on body) poils *mpl*; (of animal) poil *m*; **a fine head of ~** une belle chevelure; **to have one's ~ done** se faire coiffer; 2 (individually) (on head) cheveu *m*; (on body) poil *m*; (animal) poil *m*; **long/short-~ed** [*person*] aux cheveux longs/courts; [*animal*] à poil long/court.
IDIOMS **by a ~, by a ~'s breadth** d'un poil○; **he didn't turn a ~** il n'a pas bronché; **he was perfect, not a ~ out of place** il était impeccable, tiré à quatre épingles; **it made my ~ stand on end** cela m'a fait dresser les cheveux sur la tête; **to get in sb's ~**○ taper sur les nerfs de qn○; **to have sb by the short ~s**○ US tenir le couteau sous la gorge de qn; **to let one's ~ down** se défouler○; **to split ~s** couper les cheveux en quatre; **to tear one's ~ out** s'arracher les cheveux; **you need a ~ of the dog (that bit you)** il te faut un petit verre pour faire passer la gueule de bois○.

hair: ~band *n* bandeau *m*; **~brush** *n* brosse *f* à cheveux; **~clip** *n* GB barrette *f*; **~ curler** *n* bigoudi *m*; **~cut** *n* coupe *f* (de cheveux); **~do**○ *n* coiffure *f*; **~dresser** ▶1251, 1251 *n* coiffeur/-euse *m/f*; **~dressing** *n* coiffure *f*; **~drier** *n* (hand-held) sèche-cheveux *m inv*; (hood) casque *m*; **~ gel** *n* gel *m* coiffant; **~grip** *n* GB pince *f* à cheveux; **~less** *adj* [*body, chin*] glabre; [*animal*] sans poils; **~line** *n* naissance *f* des cheveux; **~line crack** *n* fêlure *f*; **~line fracture** *n* MED fêlure *f*; **~net** *n* filet *m* à cheveux; **~piece** *n* postiche *m*; **~pin** *n* épingle *f* à cheveux; **~pin bend** *n* virage *m* en épingle à cheveux; **~raising** *adj* à vous faire dresser les cheveux sur la tête; **~ remover** *n* crème *f* dépilatoire; **~-slide** *n* GB barrette *f*; **~ splitting** *n* ergotage *m*; **~spray** *n* laque *f*; **~style** *n* coiffure *f*; **~ stylist** ▶1251 *n* coiffeur/-euse *m/f*; **~ transplant**

n greffe *f* de cheveux; **~ trigger** *n* détente *f* ultrasensible.

hairy /'heərɪ/ *adj* **1** [*coat, dog, chest*] poilu; BOT [*stem*] villeux/-euse; **2**○ [*adventure, moment*] atroce○.

Haiti /'heɪtɪ/ ▶840|, 1022| *pr n* Haïti *m*.

Haitian /'heɪʃn/ ▶1100|, 1038| **I** *pr n* **1** (person) Haïtien/-ienne *m/f*; **2** (language) (créole *m*) haïtien *m*.
II *adj* haïtien/-ienne.

hake /heɪk/ *n* **1** (*pl* **~** ou **~s**) ZOOL merlu *m*; **2** ¢ CULIN colin *m*.

halcyon /'hælsɪən/ *adj* [*time, period*] paradisiaque; **~ days** jours heureux.

hale /heɪl/ *adj* [*old person*] vigoureux/-euse; **to be ~ and hearty** GEN être en pleine forme.

half /hɑːf, US hæf/ ▶812| **I** *n* (*pl* **halves**) **1** (one of two parts) moitié *f*; **~ (of) the page** la moitié de la page; **to cut sth in ~** couper qch en deux; **2** (fraction) demi *m*; **four and a ~** quatre et demi; **3** SPORT (time period) mi-temps *f*; (pitch area) moitié *f* de terrain; **4** SPORT = **halfback**; **5**○ GB (half pint) demi-pinte *f*; **6** GB (half fare) demi-tarif *m*.
II *adj* **a ~ circle** un demi-cercle; **a ~-litre**, **~ litre** un demi-litre; **two and a ~ cups** deux tasses et demie.
III *pron* **1** (50%) moitié *f*; **only ~ (of the students) passed** seule la moitié (des étudiants) a réussi; **to cut sth by ~** réduire qch de moitié; **that was a meal and a ~**○! ça a été un sacré repas○!; **2** (in time) demi/-e *m/f*; **an hour and a ~** une heure et demie; **~ past two** GB, **~ two**○ deux heures et demie; **it starts at ~ past** ça commence à la demie; **the buses run at ~ past the hour** les bus passent à la demie de chaque heure; **she is ten and a ~** elle a dix ans et demi.
IV *adv* **1** à moitié; **to ~ close the window** fermer la fenêtre à moitié; **it's ~ the price** c'est moitié moins cher; **~ as much money/as many people** moitié moins d'argent/de personnes; **~ as big** moitié moins grand; **he's ~ Spanish ~ Irish** il est mi-espagnol mi-irlandais; **he was only ~ serious** il n'était qu'à moitié sérieux; **~ disappointed ~ relieved** mi-déçu mi-soulagé; **if it was ~ as easy as they say** si c'était vraiment aussi facile qu'on le dit; **I was ~ hoping that…** j'espérais presque que…; **I ~ expected it** je m'y attendais plus ou moins; **2**○ (in phrases) **not ~ old** pas jeune IRON; **he wasn't ~ surprised**○ il était drôlement○ surpris; **it doesn't ~ stink**○! ça pue drôlement○!; **not ~**○! et comment!; **not ~ bad**○ pas mauvais or mal du tout.
IDIOMS **a ~ minute** ou **second** ou **tick**○ GB ou **mo**○ une petite minute, un instant; **how the other ~ lives** comment vivent les riches; **if given ~ a chance** à la première occasion; **to have ~ a mind to do** avoir bien envie de faire; **one's better or other ~** sa (douce) moitié; **to go halves with sb** se mettre de moitié avec qn; **too clever by ~**○ un peu trop malin/-igne.

half: **~-and-half** *adj*, *adv* moitié-moitié; **~back** *n* SPORT demi *m*; **~-baked**○ *adj* bancal○; **~-board** *n* demi-pension *f*; **~-breed** *n*, *adj* INJUR métis/-isse (*m/f*); **~ brother** *n* demi-frère *m*; **~-caste** *n*, *adj* INJUR métis/-isse (*m/f*); **~ century** *n* demi-siècle *m*.

half cock *n* **at ~** LIT au cran de sûreté.
IDIOMS **to go off at ~**, **to go off half-cocked** (flop) partir en eau de boudin; (be hasty) être impulsif/-ive.

half: **~-conscious** *adj* à demi conscient; **~ crown**, **~-a-crown** *n* GB HIST demi-couronne *f*; **~-cut**○ *adj* ivre; **~ day** *n* demi-journée *f*; **~-dead**○ *adj* LIT, FIG à moitié mort; **~-dozen** *n*, *pron*, *adj* demi-douzaine (*f*); **~ fare** *n* demi-tarif *m*; **~-hearted** *adj* [*attempt, smile, participation*] peu enthousiaste; **~-heartedly** *adv* sans conviction.

half hour /ˌhɑːf'aʊə(r), US ˌhæf-/ ▶1336| *n* demi-heure *f*; **on the ~** à la demie.

half: **~-hourly** *adj*, *adv* toutes les demi-heures; **~-length** *adj* [*portrait*] en buste; **~-light** *n* LITTÉR demi-jour *m*.

half-mast /ˌhɑːf'mɑːst, US 'hæf-/ *n* **at ~** en berne.

half-moon /ˌhɑːf'muːn, US 'hæf-/ **I** *n* **1** demi-lune *f*; **2** (of fingernail) lunule *f*.
II *noun modifier* [*spectacles, shape*] en demi-lune.

half pay *n* **to be on ~** avoir un demi-salaire.

halfpenny *n* GB HIST demi-penny *m*.

half-pint /ˌhɑːf'paɪnt, US 'hæf-/ ▶789| *n* demi-pinte *f* (GB = 0.28 l, US = 0.24 l); **a ~ of milk** ~ un quart de litre de lait.

half: **~ price** *adv*, *adj* à moitié prix; **~ sister** *n* demi-sœur *f*.

half size I *n* (of shoe) demi-pointure *f*.
II *adj* [*copy*] réduit de moitié.

half: **~ slip** *n* jupon *m*; **~ smile** *n* demi-sourire *m*; **~-staff** *n* US = **half-mast**; **~-starved** *adj* à demi mort de faim; **~ term** GB SCH *n* vacances *fpl* de demi-trimestre; **~-timbered** *adj* à colombages.

half-time /ˌhɑːf'taɪm, US 'hæf-/ *n* SPORT mi-temps *f*; **at ~** à la mi-temps.

half-truth *n* demi-vérité *f*.

halfway /ˌhɑːf'weɪ, US 'hæf-/ **I** *adj* **the ~ stage** la mi-étape; **to reach the ~ mark** ou **point** être à la moitié.
II *adv* **1** (at the mid-point) à mi-chemin (**between** entre; **to** de); **I went ~** j'ai fait la moitié du chemin; **~ up** ou **down** à mi-hauteur (**stairs, tree**); **~ down the page** à mi-page; **~ across** au milieu de [*room, ocean*]; **to travel ~ across** ou **round the world for sth** faire des kilomètres et des kilomètres pour qch; **~ through (sth)** au milieu (de qch); **to be ~ through doing sth** avoir à moitié fini de faire qch; **2** FIG **to go ~ to** ou **towards** GB **sth/doing sth** être à mi-chemin de qch/de faire; **I met him ~** j'ai fait un compromis avec lui; **3**○ (in the least) [*decent, competent*] raisonnablement.

halfway house *n* **1** (compromise) compromis *m*; **2** (rehabilitation centre) centre *m* de réadaptation.

half: **~way line** *n* SPORT ligne *f* médiane; **~wit**○ *n* PÉJ abruti/-e *m/f*.

half-year /ˌhɑːf'jɪə(r), US ˌhæf-/ FIN, COMM **I** *n* semestre *m*.
II *noun modifier* [*profit, results*] semestriel/-ielle.

half-yearly *adj* [*meeting, payment*] semestriel/-ielle.

halibut /'hælɪbət/ *n* (*pl* **~** ou **~s**) flétan *m*.

halitosis /ˌhælɪ'təʊsɪs/ *n* mauvaise haleine *f*.

hall /hɔːl/ *n* **1** (in house) entrée *f*; (corridor) couloir *m*; (in hotel, airport) hall *m*; (for public events) (grande) salle *f*; **2** UNIV (residence) résidence *f* universitaire; **3** (country house) manoir *m*.

hallelujah /ˌhælɪ'luːjə/ *excl* alléluia.

hallmark /'hɔːlmɑːk/ *n* **1** GB (on metal) poinçon *m*; **2** (typical feature) caractéristique *f*.
II *vtr* poinçonner; **to be ~ed** porter un poinçon.

hallo /hə'ləʊ/ *excl* GB = **hello**.

hall: **Hall of Fame** *n* (all contexts) panthéon *m*; **~ of residence** *n* résidence *f* universitaire.

hallow /'hæləʊ/ **I** *vtr* LITTÉR sanctifier.
II **hallowed** *pp adj* **1** (venerated) [*tradition*] vénéré; **2** (sanctified) [*ground*] saint.

Halloween /ˌhæləʊ'iːn/ *n*: la veille de la Toussaint.

hallstand /'hɔːlstænd/ *n* portemanteau *m*.

hallucinate /hə'luːsɪneɪt/ *vi* avoir des hallucinations.

hallucination /həˌluːsɪ'neɪʃn/ *n* hallucination *f*.

hallucinatory /hə'luːsɪnətrɪ, US -tɔːrɪ/ *adj* [*drug*] hallucinogène; [*image*] onirique; [*effect*] hallucinatoire.

hallucinogenic /həˌluːsɪnə'dʒenɪk/ *adj* hallucinogène.

hallway /'hɔːlweɪ/ *n* entrée *f*.

halo /'heɪləʊ/ *n* (*pl* **~s** ou **~es**) **1** (around head) auréole *f*; **his ~ has become a bit tarnished** FIG son image s'est un peu ternie; **2** (in astronomy) halo *m*.

halogen /'hælədʒn/ *n* halogène *m*.

halt /hɔːlt/ **I** *n* **1** (stop) arrêt *m*; **to come to a ~** [*group, vehicle*] s'arrêter, cesser; [*negotiations*] être interrompu; **to call a ~ to sth** mettre fin à qch; **shall we call a ~?** on s'arrête?; **2** (temporary) (in activ-

ity) suspension *f* (**in** dans); (in proceedings) pause *f* (**in au**
cours de); **3** MIL (rest) halte *f*; **4** GB RAIL halte *f*.
II *excl* halte!
III *vtr* interrompre [*proceedings*]; mettre fin à [*arms
sales, experiments*]; arrêter [*inflation, offensive*].
IV *vi* [*vehicle*] s'arrêter; [*army*] faire halte.

halter /'hɔːltə(r)/ *n* **1** (for horse) licol *m*; **2** (for hanging)
corde *f* (de pendaison).

halterneck /'hɔːltənek/ *n, adj* dos (*m inv*) nu.

halting /'hɔːltɪŋ/ *adj* [*steps, attempts*] hésitant.

halve /hɑːv, US hæv/ **I** *vtr* réduire [qch] de moitié
[*number, rate*]; couper [qch] en deux [*carrot, cake*].
II *vi* [*number, rate, time*] diminuer de moitié.

halves /hɑːvz, US hævz/ *npl* ▶ **half**.

ham /hæm/ *n* **1** CULIN jambon *m*; **2** (of animal) cuisse
f; **3**○ (poor actor) cabotin/-e *m/f*; **4** (also **radio ~**)
radioamateur *m*.
IDIOMS **to ~ it up**○ jouer de façon exagérée.

ham and eggs *npl* US CULIN œufs *mpl* au jambon.

hamburger /'hæmbɜːgə(r)/ *n* **1** (patty) hamburger *m*;
2 US (ground beef) pâté *m* de viande.

ham-fisted○ GB, **ham-handed**○ US /,hæm'fɪstɪd/,
,hæm'hændɪd/ *adj* PÉJ maladroit.

hamlet /'hæmlɪt/ *n* hameau *m*.

hammer /'hæmə(r)/ **I** *n* **1** GEN, MUS marteau *m*; **to
come** ou **go under the ~** être vendu aux enchères;
2 SPORT (discipline) lancer *m* de marteau.
II *vtr* **1** LIT (beat) marteler [*metal, table, keys*]; **to ~
sth into** enfoncer qch dans [*wall, fence*]; **to ~ sth
into shape** façonner qch au marteau; **to ~ sth flat**
aplatir qch à coups de marteau; **2** FIG (insist forcefully)
to ~ sth into sb faire entrer qch dans la tête de qn;
they had Latin ~ed into them on leur a bien
inculqué le latin; **to ~ home a message** bien faire
comprendre un message; **3** (attack) critiquer; **4**○
SPORT (defeat) battre [qn] à plates coutures.
III *vi* **1** (use hammer) frapper à coups de marteau; **2**
(pound) tambouriner (**on, at** contre).
■ **hammer in**: **~ in** [sth], **~** [sth] **in** enfoncer
[qch] à coups de marteau.
■ **hammer out**: **~ out** [sth], **~** [sth] **out** (negotiate) parvenir à [qch] après maintes discussions [*agreement, policy, formula*].

hammer and sickle *n* **the ~** la faucille et le
marteau.

hammering /'hæmərɪŋ/ *n* **1** (noise) (bruit *m* de) martèlement *m* (**at** sur); **2**○ (defeat) **to take** ou **get a ~**
prendre une dérouillée○.

hammock /'hæmək/ *n* hamac *m*.

hamper /'hæmpə(r)/ **I** *n* **1** (for picnic) panier *m* à pique-
nique; **2** GB (from shop etc) *panier vendu avec une sélection de produits alimentaires de luxe*.
II *vtr* entraver [*movement, career, progress*]; handicaper [*person*].

hamster /'hæmstə(r)/ *n* hamster *m*.

hamstring /'hæmstrɪŋ/ **I** *n* (of human) tendon *m* du
jarret; (of horse) corde *f* du jarret.
II *vtr* FIG (prét, pp **-strung**) FIG paralyser.

hand /hænd/ **I** *n* **1** main *f*; **he had a pencil/
book in his ~** il avait un crayon/livre à la main;
she had a pistol/an umbrella in her ~ elle avait
un pistolet/un parapluie à la main; **to get** ou **lay one's
~s on sth** mettre la main sur qch; **to keep one's
~s off sth** ne pas toucher à [*computer, money*]; **to
keep one's ~s off sb** laisser qn tranquille; **they
were holding ~s** ils se donnaient la main; **to hold
sb's ~** LIT tenir qn par la main; FIG (give support)
[*person*] tenir la main à qn; **to do** ou **make sth by ~**
faire qch à la main; **the letter was delivered by ~**
la lettre a été remise en mains propres; **'by ~'** (on
envelope) 'par porteur'; **to have one's ~s full** LIT
avoir les mains pleines; FIG avoir assez à faire; **to
give sb a (helping) ~** donner un coup de main à qn;
~s up, or I shoot! les mains en l'air, ou je tire!; **to
be on one's ~s and knees** être à quatre pattes; **we
can always use another pair of ~s** une autre paire
de bras ne serait pas de trop; (round of applause) **to give
sb a big ~** applaudir qn très fort; (consent to marriage)

to ask for/win sb's ~ (in marriage) demander/obte-
nir la main de qn (en mariage); **to be in sb's ~s** être
entre les mains de qn; **to change ~s** changer de
mains; **I got the information first/second ~** j'ai eu
l'information de première main/par l'intermédiaire de
quelqu'un; **to fall** ou **get into sb's ~s** tomber entre
les mains de qn; **to fall** ou **get into the wrong ~s**
tomber en mauvaises mains; **in the right ~s this
information could be useful** en bonnes mains, cette
information pourrait être utile; **to be in good** ou **safe
~s** [*child, money*] être en bonnes mains; **to place** ou
put sth in sb's ~s confier qch à qn [*department,
office*]; remettre qch entre les mains de qn [*matter,
affair*]; **to play into sb's ~s** jouer le jeu de qn; **his
treatment at the ~s of his captors** la façon dont il
a été traité par ses ravisseurs; **the matter is out of
my ~s** cette affaire n'est plus de mon ressort; **to
have sth/sb on one's ~s** avoir qch/qn sur les bras;
to take sb/sth off sb's ~s débarrasser qn de qn/
qch; **to have sth to ~** avoir qch sous la main; **to be
on ~** [*person*] être disponible; **the fire extinguisher
was close to ~** ou **near at ~** l'extincteur n'était
pas loin; **to grab the first coat that comes to ~**
attraper n'importe quel manteau; **~s off**○! pas
touche○!; **2** (control) **to get out of ~** [*inflation*] déraper; [*children, fans*] devenir incontrôlable; [*demonstration, party*] dégénérer; **things are getting out of ~**
on est en train de perdre le contrôle de la situation; **to
take sth/sb in ~** prendre qch/qn en main [*situation,
person*]; **3** (writing) écriture *f*; **4** GAMES (cards dealt) jeu
m; (game) partie *f*; **to show one's ~** LIT, FIG
montrer son jeu; **5** (worker) GÉN ouvrier/-ière *m/f*;
NAUT membre *m* de l'équipage; **6** (skill) **to try one's
~ at sth** s'essayer à; **to set** ou **turn one's ~ to
sth/doing** entreprendre qch/de faire; **to keep/get
one's ~ in** garder/se faire la main; **7** (pointer) (on
clock, dial) aiguille *f*; **8** (aspect, side) **on the one ~...**,
on the other ~... d'une part... d'autre part...; **on
the other ~** (conversely) par contre.
II *vtr* **to ~ sb sth, to ~ sth to sb** donner qch à qn.
III in hand *adj phr* **1** (current) en cours; **the job/
matter in ~** le travail/l'affaire en cours; **the
preparations are well in ~** les préparatifs sont bien
avancés; **2** (to spare) **she finished the exam with 20
minutes in ~** elle a terminé l'examen avec 20
minutes d'avance; **I'll do it when I have some time
in ~** je le ferai quand j'aurai du temps devant moi.
IV out of hand *adv phr* [*reject*] d'emblée.
IDIOMS **to have a ~ in sth** prendre part à qch; **to
know sth like the back of one's ~** connaître qch
comme le dos de la main; **many ~s make light
work** plus on est nombreux plus ça va vite; **I could do
that with one ~ tied behind my back!** je pourrais
le faire les doigts dans le nez○!; **you've got to ~ it
to her/them...** il faut lui/leur faire cette justice...; **he
never does a ~'s turn** il ne remue pas le petit doigt;
to stay ou **hold one's ~** patienter; **to win ~s
down** gagner haut la main.
■ **hand back**: **~** [sth] **back, ~ back** [sth] rendre.
■ **hand down**: **~** [sth] **down, ~ down** [sth] LIT
passer [*object*]; FIG transmettre [*property, skill*].
■ **hand in**: **~** [sth] **in, ~ in** [sth] remettre [*form,
petition, ticket*] (**to** à); rendre [*homework, keys*].
■ **hand out**: **~** [sth] **out, ~ out** [sth] distribuer.
■ **hand over**: **~** [sth] **over, ~ over** [sth] TV, RADIO passer
l'antenne à [*reporter*]; passer la main à [*deputy,
successor*]; (on telephone) **I'll just ~ you over to Rosie**
je te passe Rosie; **¶ ~ over** [sth], **~** [sth] **over**
rendre [*weapon*]; céder [*territory, title, business*]; transmettre [*power*]; remettre [*keys, money*]; **¶ ~** [sb]
over, ~ over [sb] (transfer) livrer [*prisoner*]; confier
[*child, patient*].
■ **hand round**: **~** [sth] **round, ~ round** [sth]
faire circuler [*leaflets, drinks, sandwiches*].

hand: **~bag** *n* sac *m* à main; **~ baggage** *n*
bagage *m* à main.

handball /'hændbɔːl/ *n* SPORT **1** ▶ **949** SPORT
handball *m*; **2** (fault in football) faute *f* de main.

hand: **~basin** *n* lavabo *m*; **~bell** *n* clochette *f*;
~bill *n* prospectus *m*; **~book** *n* (textbook) manuel

m; (technical manual) livret *m* technique; (guide) guide *m*; **~brake** *n* AUT frein *m* à main; **~cart** *n* charrette *f* à bras; **~ cream** *n* crème *f* pour les mains.

handcuff /'hændkʌf/ **I handcuffs** *npl* menottes *fpl*.
II *vtr* passer les menottes à [*person*]; **to ~ sb to sth** attacher qn à qch avec des menottes.

hand-dryer, **hand-drier** /'hændraɪə(r)/ *n* sèche-mains *m inv*.

handful /'hændfʊl/ *n* **1** (fistful) poignée *f*; **2** (small number) (of people) poignée *f*; (of buildings, objects, works) petit nombre *m*; **3**○ (person, animal) **to be a ~** être épuisant.

hand: **~ grenade** *n* grenade *f* (à main); **~gun** *n* arme *f* de poing; **~held** *adj* [*camera*] de reportage; [*tool*] à main; [*device*] portatif/-ive; [*computer*] de poche.

handicap /'hændɪkæp/ **I** *n* GEN, SPORT handicap *m*.
II *vtr* (*p prés etc* **-pp-**) GEN, SPORT handicaper.

handicapped /'hændɪkæpt/ *adj* [*person*] handicapé; **mentally/physically ~ children** des enfants handicapés mentaux/physiques.

handicraft /'hændɪkrɑːft, US 'hændɪkræft/ *n* **1** (object) objet *m* artisanal; '**~s**' (sign on shop) 'artisanat' *m*; **2** (skill) travail *m* artisanal.

handily /'hændɪlɪ/ *adv* [*located*] bien (*before adj*).

hand in hand *adv* LIT [*run, walk*] la main dans la main; **to go ~** FIG aller de pair.

handiwork /'hændɪwɜːk/ *n* GEN ouvrage *m*; IRON œuvre *f*.

handkerchief /'hæŋkətʃɪf, -tʃiːf/ *n* mouchoir *m*.

handle /'hændl/ **I** *n* **1** (on door, drawer, bag) poignée *f*; (on bucket, cup, basket) anse *f*; (on frying pan) queue *f*; (on saucepan, cutlery, hammer, spade) manche *m*; (on wheelbarrow, pump) bras *m*; **2** FIG (hold) **to get a ~ on sb** comprendre qn.
II *vtr* **1** (touch) manipuler [*explosives, samples, food*]; manier [*gun, tool*]; **to ~ sb gently/roughly** traiter qn gentiment/rudement; **to ~ sth gently/roughly** manier qch délicatement/brutalement; **to ~ stolen goods** faire du trafic de marchandises volées; '**~ with care**' 'fragile'; **to ~ the ball** (in football) faire une faute de main; **2** (manage) manier [*horse*]; manœuvrer [*car*]; **to know how to ~ children** savoir s'y prendre avec les enfants; **he's hard to ~** il n'a pas un caractère facile; **3** (deal with) traiter [*case, negotiations*]; faire face à [*situation, crisis*]; supporter [*stress, pace*]; **4** (process) [*organization*] traiter [*money, clients, order*]; [*airport, port*] accueillir [*passengers, cargo*]; [*factory*] traiter [*waste*]; [*person*] manier [*information, money, accounts*]; [*computer*] manipuler [*graphics, information*]; [*department, official*] s'occuper de [*complaints, enquiries*]; [*agent*] s'occuper de [*sale*]; [*lawyer*] s'occuper de [*case*]; traiter [*theme*].
III *vi* AUT **the car ~s well/badly** la voiture manœuvre bien/mal.
IDIOMS to fly off the ~○ piquer une crise○; **to be too hot to ~** (of situation) être trop risqué.

handle: **~bar moustache** *n* moustache *f* en crocs; **~bars** *npl* guidon *m*.

handler /'hændlə(r)/ *n* **1** (of dog) maître-chien *m*; (of other animals) dresseur/-euse *m/f*; **2** (adviser) (of star) agent *m*; (of politician) conseiller/-ère *m/f*.

handling /'hændlɪŋ/ *n* **1** (holding, touching) (of food, waste) manipulation *f*; (of tool, weapon) maniement *m*; **old books require careful ~** les livres anciens doivent être manipulés avec soin; **2** (way of dealing) **her ~ of the theme** sa façon de traiter le thème; **the bank's ~ of the affair** la façon dont la banque a traité l'affaire; **their ~ of the economy** leur gestion de l'économie; **3** COMM (storage, shipping) manutention *f*; **4** (processing) (of data, documents) traitement *m*; (of process, business) gestion *f*; **5** (training) **dog ~** entraînement *m* des chiens.

handling charge *n* **1** COMM frais *mpl* de manutention; **2** ADMIN, FIN frais *mpl* administratifs.

hand: **~ lotion** *n* lotion *f* pour les mains; **~ luggage** *n* bagage *m* à main; **~made** *adj* fait à la

main; **~maid**, **~maiden**‡ *n* servante *f*; **~-me-down**○ *n* vieux vêtement *m*.

handout /'hændaʊt/ *n* **1** (payment) PÉJ (welfare) allocation *f*; (subsidy) subvention *f*; (charitable) don *m*; **to live off/rely on ~s** vivre de/dépendre de la charité des autres; **2** (document) document *m*; (leaflet) prospectus *m*.

hand: **~over** *n* (of property, power, territory) transfert *m*; (of prisoner, ransom) remise *f*; **~pick** *vtr* choisir [*qch*] soi-même [*produce*]; trier [qn] sur le volet [*staff*]; **~rail** *n* (on stairs) rampe *f*; (on balcony, pier) garde-fou *m*; **~-reared** *adj* [*animal*] élevé au biberon; **~set** *n* TELECOM combiné *m*; **~shake** *n* poignée *f* de main; **~ signal** *n* GEN, AUT signe *m* de la main; **~s-off** *adj* [*manager*] qui pratique la délégation du pouvoir; [*policy*] de non-intervention.

handsome /'hænsəm/ *adj* **1** (fine) [*person, town, building*] beau/belle; **2** (appreciable) [*dividend*] bon/bonne; [*sum*] beau/belle; [*reward*] généreux/-euse.

handsomely /'hænsəmlɪ/ *adv* (amply) **to pay off ~** [*investment*] être d'un bon rapport; **to be ~ rewarded** recevoir une généreuse récompense.

hand: **~s-on** *adj* [*experience, manager*] de terrain; [*control*] direct; [*approach*] pragmatique; **~spring** *n* saut *m* de mains, salto *m*; **~stand** *n* SPORT équilibre *m*; **~-to-hand** *adj*, *adv* corps à corps; **~-to-mouth** *adj* précaire; **~ towel** *n* essuie-mains *m inv*; **~-woven** *adj* tissé à la main; **~writing** *n* écriture *f*; **~written** *adj* manuscrit.

handy /'hændɪ/ *adj* **1** (useful) [*book, skill*] utile; [*tool, pocket*] pratique; **to come in ~ for sb/sth/doing** servir à qn/qch/faire; **that's ~** c'est bon à savoir; **2** (convenient) [*format, shape, size*] pratique; [*location*] bon/bonne; [*shop*] bien situé; **to keep/have sth ~** garder/avoir qch sous la main [*keys, passport*]; **3**○ (skilful) [*player*] doué (**at doing** pour faire); **to be ~ with a paintbrush** savoir se servir d'un pinceau.

handyman /'hændɪmæn/ *n* bricoleur *m*, homme *m* à tout faire.

hang /hæŋ/ **I** *n* **1** (of garment) tombant *m*; **2**○ (knack) **to get the ~ of sth**○**/of doing**○ piger○ qch/comment faire; **you're getting the ~ of it** tu as pigé○.
II *vtr* (*prét, pp* **hung**) **1** (suspend) (from projection, hook, coat-hanger) accrocher (**from** à; **by** par; **on** à); (from string, rope) suspendre (**from** à); (drape over) étendre, mettre (**over** sur); (peg up) étendre [*washing*] (**on** sur); **2** (also **~ down**) (let dangle) suspendre [*rope, line etc*] (**out of** par); laisser pendre [*arm, leg*]; **to ~ one's head in shame** baisser la tête de honte; **3** (decorate with) **to be hung with** être orné de [*flags, tapestries*]; être décoré de [*garlands*]; **4** (interior decorating) poser [*wallpaper*]; **5** CONSTR, TECH poser [*door, gate*]; **6** (*prét, pp* **hanged**) pendre [*criminal, victim*].
III *vi* (*prét, pp* **hung**) **1** (be suspended) (on hook) être accroché; (from height) être suspendu; (on washing line) être étendu; [*arm, leg*] pendre; **her arm hung over the arm of the chair** son bras pendait de l'accoudoir; **my feet ~ over the end** mes pieds dépassent; **the children were ~ing out of the window** les enfants se penchaient à la fenêtre; **2** (drape) [*curtain, garment*] tomber; **3** (float) [*fog, cloud, smoke, smell*] flotter; **4** (die) être pendu (**for** pour).
IV *v refl* (*prét, pp* **hanged**) **to ~ oneself** se pendre (**from** à).
IDIOMS ~ the expense○! au diable la dépense!; **~ed if I know**○! je n'en sais fichtre rien○!; **to let it all ~ out**○ être relax○; ▶ **sheep**.
∎ **hang around**○: ¶ (also **~ about**) (wait) attendre; (aimlessly) traîner; **to ~ around with sb** passer son temps avec qn; ¶ **~ around [sb]** (inflict oneself on) être toujours à tourner autour○ de qn.
∎ **hang back** (in fear) rester derrière; (waiting) rester; (reluctant) LIT rester à la traîne; FIG être réticent.
∎ **hang down** GEN pendre; [*hem*] être défait.
∎ **hang on**: ¶ **~ on 1**○ (wait) attendre; **2**○ (survive) tenir○; **~ on in there**○! tiens bon!; ¶ **~ on [sth] 1** (depend on) dépendre de; **2** (listen attentively) **to ~ on sb's every word** être pendu aux lèvres de qn.
∎ **hang on to**: **~ on to [sth/sb] 1** (hold) s'agripper à [*object, rail*]; agripper [*person*]; **~ on to your hat!**

LIT tiens bien ton chapeau!; FIG accroche-toi!; **2**○ FIG (retain) s'accrocher à◦ [*possession, power*].

■ **hang out**: ¶ ~ **out 1** (protrude) dépasser; **2**○ (live) crécher○; **3**○ (sit around) traîner○; ¶ ~ **out** [sth], ~ [sth] **out** étendre [*washing*]; accrocher [*sign*]; sortir [*flag*].

■ **hang over**: ~ **over** [sb/sth] [*threat, suspicion*] planer sur [*person, project*].

■ **hang together** (be consistent) se tenir.

■ **hang up**: ¶ ~ **up** (on phone) raccrocher; **to ~ up on sb** raccrocher au nez de qn; ¶ ~ **up** [sth], ~ [sth] **up 1** (on hook) accrocher; (on hanger, string) suspendre; (on line) étendre; **2** FIG, HUM **to ~ up one's skis** mettre ses skis au rancart.

hangar /ˈhæŋə(r)/ *n* hangar *m*.

hangdog /ˈhæŋdɒg/ *adj* [*expression, look*] de chien battu.

hanger /ˈhæŋə(r)/ *n* **1** (coat hanger) cintre *m*; **2** (loop) boucle *f*.

hanger-on /ˌhæŋərˈɒn/ *n* parasite *m*.

hang: **~-glider** *n* (craft) deltaplane *m*; (pilot) deltaplaniste *mf*; **~-gliding** ▶949 *n* deltaplane *m*.

hanging /ˈhæŋɪŋ/ **I** *n* **1** (strangulation) pendaison *f*; **2** (curtain) rideau *m*; (on wall) tenture *f*; **3** (suspending) (of picture) accrochage *m*; (wallpaper) pose *f*.
II *adj* JUR [*offence*] passible de pendaison.

hanging basket /ˈhæŋɪŋ/ *n* panier *m* suspendu.

hangman /ˈhæŋmən/ *n* **1** (at gallows) bourreau *m*; **2** ▶949 (game) potence *f*.

hangover /ˈhæŋəʊvə(r)/ *n* **1** (from drink) gueule *f* de bois○; **2** FIG (legacy) héritage *m* (**from** de).

hang-up○ /ˈhæŋʌp/ *n* complexe *m*, problème *m*.

hank /hæŋk/ *n* (of wool etc) écheveau *m*.

hanker /ˈhæŋkə(r)/ *vi* **to ~ after** rêver de.

hankering /ˈhæŋkərɪŋ/ *n* grande envie *f* (**for** de).

hanky, **hankie**○ /ˈhæŋkɪ/ *n* mouchoir *m*.

hanky-panky○ /ˌhæŋkɪˈpæŋkɪ/ *n* HUM (sexual) polissonneries *fpl*; (dishonest) friponneries *fpl*.

Hants *n* GB POST *abrév écrite* = **Hampshire**.

ha'penny /ˈheɪpnɪ/ *n* GB *abrév* ▶ **halfpenny**.

haphazard /hæpˈhæzəd/ *adj* peu méthodique.

haphazardly /hæpˈhæzədlɪ/ *adv* n'importe comment.

hapless /ˈhæplɪs/ *adj* LITTER pauvre, infortuné.

happen /ˈhæpən/ *vi* **1** (occur) arriver, se passer, se produire; **what's ~ing?** qu'est-ce qui se passe?; **the accident ~ed yesterday** l'accident est arrivé or s'est produit hier; **we must make sure this never ~s again** nous devons faire en sorte que cela ne se reproduise jamais; **he reacted as if nothing had ~ed** il a réagi comme si de rien n'était; **whatever ~s, don't get out of the car** quoi qu'il arrive, ne sors pas de la voiture; **it had to ~, it was bound to ~** GB ça devait arriver; **anything might ~!** il faut s'attendre à tout!; **she's the sort of person who makes things ~** elle fait bouger les choses; **2** (befall) **to ~ to sb** arriver à qn; **if anything ~s to her...** si quoi que ce soit lui arrive...; **3** (occur by chance) **there ~s to be a free parking space** il se trouve qu'il y a une place libre; **it so ~s that...** il se trouve que...; **as it ~ed, the weather that day was bad** il s'est trouvé qu'il faisait mauvais ce jour-là; **if you ~ to see her say hello** si par hasard tu la vois, salue-la de ma part; **4** (become of) devenir; **what will ~ to the children?** que deviendront les enfants?; **5** (used assertively) **he just ~s to be the best actor in Britain!** il se trouve que c'est le meilleur acteur de Grande-Bretagne!; **I ~ to think that...** je trouve que...

■ **happen on**: ~ **on** [sth] tomber sur [qch] [*object*].

happening /ˈhæpənɪŋ/ *n* (occurrence) incident *m*.

happily /ˈhæpɪlɪ/ *adv* **1** (cheerfully) [*laugh, chat, play, say*] joyeusement; **a ~ married man** un mari heureux; **they all lived ~ ever after** ils vécurent heureux jusqu'à la fin de leurs jours; **2** (luckily) heureusement; **3** (willingly) [*admit, agree, leave*] volontiers; **4** (successfully) avec bonheur.

happiness /ˈhæpɪnɪs/ *n* bonheur *m*.

happy /ˈhæpɪ/ *adj* **1** (cheerful) [*life, memory, person*] heureux/-euse (**about** de; **with sb** avec qn; **for sb** pour qn; **that** que + *subj*); **to be ~ doing** bien aimer faire; **2** (pleased) content; **to be ~ with sth** être satisfait de qch; **he's not ~ about it** il n'est pas content; **to keep sb ~** faire plaisir à qn; **3** (willing) **to be ~ to do** être heureux/-euse de faire; **he's quite ~ to leave on Monday** cela ne le dérange pas de partir lundi; **4** (in greetings) **Happy birthday!** Bon anniversaire!; **Happy Christmas!** Joyeux Noël!; **Happy New Year!** Bonne année!; **5** (fortunate) [*choice, phrase*] heureux/-euse; **he's in the ~ position of having no debts** il a la chance de ne pas avoir de dettes.
IDIOMS **to be as ~ as Larry** OU **as a sandboy** GB être heureux comme un poisson dans l'eau.

happy couple *n* **the ~** les mariés *mpl*.

happy ending *n* heureux dénouement *m*.

happy: **~-go-lucky** *adj* insouciant; **~ hour** *n*: dans un bar, période durant laquelle les boissons sont vendues à prix réduit; **~ hunting ground** *n* paradis *m*; **~ medium** *n* juste milieu *m*.

harangue /həˈræŋ/ **I** *n* (political) harangue *f*; (moral) sermon *m*.
II *vtr* (*p prés* **haranguing**) (politically) haranguer; (morally) sermonner.

harass /ˈhærəs, US həˈræs/ **I** *vtr* harceler.
II harassed *pp adj* excédé.

harassment /ˈhærəsmənt, US həˈræsmənt/ *n* harcèlement *m*; **racial ~** persécution *f* raciste.

harbinger /ˈhɑːbɪndʒə(r)/ *n* signe *m* annonciateur.

harbour GB, **harbor** US /ˈhɑːbə(r)/ **I** *n* port *m*.
II *vtr* **1** (nurse) nourrir [*emotion, suspicion, illusion*]; **2** (shelter illegally) receler [*criminal*].

hard /hɑːd/ **I** *adj* **1** (firm) dur; **to go** OU **grow** OU **become ~** durcir; **a ~ frost** une forte gelée; **frozen ~** complètement gelé; ▶ **hard lens**; **2** (difficult) [*problem, question, task*] dur, difficile; [*choice, decision*] difficile; [*bargaining, negotiations, fight*] dur, serré; **I've had a ~ day** j'ai eu une dure journée; **to be ~ to open** être dur or difficile à ouvrir; **to be ~ to please** être exigeant; **it's ~ to do** c'est dur or difficile à faire; **it was ~ for us to understand his decision** il nous était difficile de comprendre sa décision; **to find it ~ to do sth** avoir du mal à faire qch, trouver dur or difficile de faire qch; **it's ~ to accept/believe** on a du mal à accepter/croire (**that** que); **I'm not afraid of ~ work** le travail ne me fait pas peur; **it was ~ work** ou going ça a été dur or difficile; **~ work never hurt** ou killed anybody! le travail n'a jamais fait de mal à personne!; **it's too much like ~ work** c'est trop fatigant; **to be a ~ worker** être travailleur/-euse; **to do things the ~ way** se compliquer la tâche; **to find sth out** ou **learn sth the ~ way** apprendre qch à ses dépens; **3** (harsh) [*life, year*] difficile; [*blow*] FIG dur, terrible; [*winter*] rude; **to be ~ on sb** être dur envers qn; **this tax is very ~ on the unemployed** cet impôt frappe durement les chômeurs; **~ luck** ou **lines**○ GB! pas de chance!; **to fall a ~ line** adopter une attitude ferme (**on sth** à propos de qch; **with sb** envers qn); **it's a ~ life** GEN, HUM, IRON la vie est dure; **no ~ feelings!** sans rancune!; **I bear her no ~ feelings** je ne lui en veux pas; **to fall on ~ times** connaître des temps difficiles; **he's having a ~ time (of it)** il traverse une période difficile; **to give sb a ~ time**○ (make things difficult) rendre la vie impossible à qn; (tell off) passer un savon○ à qn; **4** (stern, cold) [*person, look, words*] dur, sévère; **5** (concrete) [*evidence, fact*] solide; **6** (stark) [*colour, light*] dur; **7** (strong) [*liquor*] fort; [*drug*] dur; [*pornography*] hard○ (*inv*); **to be a ~ drinker** boire des alcools forts; **8** POL **the ~ left/right** la gauche/droite (pure et) dure; **9** CHEM [*water*] dur, calcaire; **10** LING [*consonant*] dur; **11**○ (tough) [*person*] dur; **12** FIN [*currency*] dur.
II *adv* **1** (strongly, energetically) [*push, hit, cry*] fort; [*work*] dur; [*study, think*] sérieusement; [*rain*] à verse; [*snow*] abondamment; [*look, listen*] attentivement; **to be ~ hit** FIG être durement frappé (**by** par); **to try ~** (intellectually) faire beaucoup d'efforts; (physically) essayer de toutes ses forces; **no matter how ~ I try/**

work, I... j'ai beau essayer/travailler, je...; **to be ~ at it**○ ou **at work** être en plein travail; **to take sth (very)** ~ prendre (très) mal qch; **2** (with directions) **turn ~ left at the traffic lights** aux feux tournez tout de suite à gauche; **~ behind** juste derrière; ▶**heel**.

IDIOMS **to play ~ to get** se faire désirer; **to be ~ put to do** avoir du mal à faire; **to be/feel ~ done by** être/se sentir brimé.

hard and fast adj [rule, distinction, category] absolu.

hardback /'hɑ:dbæk/ **I** n livre m relié; **in ~** en édition reliée.
II noun modifier [book] cartonné, relié.

hardball /'hɑ:dbɔ:l/ ▶**949** n US SPORT baseball m.

hard: **~bitten** adj [person] endurci; **~board** n aggloméré m.

hard-boiled /,hɑ:d'bɔɪld/ adj **1** LIT [egg] dur; **2** FIG [person] endurci.

hard: **~ cash** n (argent m) liquide m; **~ copy** n COMPUT tirage m.

hard core I n **1** (of group, demonstrators) noyau m dur; **2** CONSTR remblai m.
II hard-core adj **1** (established) [supporter, opponent, protest] irréductible; **2** (extreme) [pornography, video] hard○ (inv).

hard: **~ court** n SPORT court m en dur; **~ disk** n COMPUT disque m dur; **~-drinking** adj qui boit beaucoup; **~-earned** adj [cash] durement gagné.

harden /'hɑ:dn/ **I** vtr **1** LIT GEN (faire) durcir; **2** FIG endurcir [person] (**to** à); renforcer [resolve]; durcir [attitude]; **to ~ one's heart** s'endurcir (**to** à).
II vi **1** LIT durcir; **2** FIG [voice, stance] se durcir.

hardened /'hɑ:dnd/ adj **1** LIT [glue, clay] durci; **2** FIG [criminal] endurci; [drinker, addict] invétéré; **to become ~ to** s'accoutumer à.

hard: **~-faced** adj LIT [person] aux traits durs; FIG froid; **~-fought** adj [battle] âprement mené; [election, competition] âprement disputé; **~ hat** n (helmet) GEN casque m; (for riding) bombe f; **~-headed** adj réaliste; **~-hearted** adj insensible; **~-hitting** adj [speech, criticism] musclé; [report] très critique; **~ labour** GB, **~ labor** US n travaux mpl forcés; **~ lens** n lentille f de contact rigide.

hardline adj [policy] (très) ferme; [communist, conservative, regime] intransigeant; **~ approach** jusqu'au-boutisme m.

hardliner n jusqu'au-boutiste mf; POL partisan/-e m/f de la ligne dure.

hard-luck story n **to tell** ou **give sb a ~** raconter ses malheurs à qn pour essayer de l'attendrir.

hardly /'hɑ:dlɪ/ adv **1** (only just, barely) [begin, know, see] à peine; **~ had they set off than** à peine étaient-ils partis que; **2** (not really) [expect, hope] difficilement; **it's ~ a secret!** c'est loin d'être un secret!; **it's ~ likely** c'est peu probable; **it's ~ surprising** ce n'est guère étonnant; **~!** certainement pas!; **I need ~ remind you that** inutile de vous rappeler que; **I can ~ wait!** GEN il me tarde d'y être; IRON je meurs d'envie d'y être; **I can ~ believe it!** j'ai peine à le croire!; **3** (almost not) **~ any/ever/anybody** presque pas/jamais/personne.

hardness /'hɑ:dnɪs/ n dureté f.

hard-nosed /,hɑ:d'nəʊzd/ adj (unsentimental) [person] résolu; PEJ [attitude, businessman, government] dur.

hard of hearing adj **to be ~** entendre mal.

hard porn○ n hard○ m.

hard-pressed /,hɑ:d'prest/, **hard-pushed** /,hɑ:d'pʊʃt/ adj GEN en difficulté; (for time) pressé; **to be ~ to do** avoir du mal à faire.

hard rock n MUS hard rock m, hard m.

hard sell n vente f selon des méthodes agressives; **to give sb the ~** essayer de forcer qn à acheter.

hardship /'hɑ:dʃɪp/ n **1** ¢ (difficulty) détresse f; (poverty) privations fpl; **2** C (ordeal) épreuve f.

hard: **~ shoulder** n GB bande f d'arrêt d'urgence; **~ standing** n place f de stationnement.

hard up○ /,hɑ:d'ʌp/ adj fauché○; **~ for** à court de.

hardware /'hɑ:dweə(r)/ n **1** COMPUT matériel m (informatique), hardware m; **2** MIL équipement m; **3** (household goods) articles mpl de quincaillerie.

hard: **~ware shop**, **~ware store** ▶**1251** n quincaillerie f; **~-wearing** adj résistant; **~-won** adj durement acquis; **~wood** n bois m dur, bois m de feuillu; **~-working** adj travailleur/-euse.

hardy /'hɑ:dɪ/ adj [person] robuste; [plant] résistant.

hare /heə(r)/ n ZOOL, CULIN lièvre m.

IDIOMS **to be as mad as a March ~** être complètement toqué○.

■ **hare off** GB partir en trombe○.

hare: **~brained** adj [person] écervelé; [scheme] farfelu○; **~lip** n bec-de-lièvre m.

haricot /'hærɪkəʊ/ n GB (also **~ bean**) (dried) haricot m blanc; (fresh) haricot m vert.

hark /hɑ:k/ v ■ **hark back to**: **~ back to** [sth] (recall) rappeler; (evoke) [style, song] évoquer.

harm /hɑ:m/ **I** n mal m; **to do ~ to sb**, **to do sb ~** faire du mal à qn; **to do ~ to sth** endommager qch; **I meant no ~ (by it)** je n'ai pas dit ça méchamment; **it would do no ~ to do** tu ferais ou on ferait mieux de faire; **you'll come to no ~** il ne t'arrivera rien; **no ~ done!** il n'y a pas de mal!; **where's the ~ in it?** quel mal y a-t-il à ça?; **out of ~'s way** en sûreté.
II vtr faire du mal à [person, baby]; endommager [crops, lungs]; nuire à [population, economy].

harmful /'hɑ:mfl/ adj [bacteria, chemical, ray] nocif/-ive; [behaviour, gossip, allegation] nuisible (**to** pour).

harmless /'hɑ:mlɪs/ adj **1** (not dangerous) [chemical, virus] inoffensif/-ive (**to** pour); [growth, cyst] bénin/bénigne; [rash, bite] sans danger; **2** (inoffensive) [person] inoffensif/-ive; [fun, joke] innocent.

harmonica /hɑ:'mɒnɪkə/ ▶**1097** n harmonica m.

harmonious /hɑ:'məʊnɪəs/ adj harmonieux/-ieuse.

harmonize /'hɑ:mənaɪz/ **I** vtr harmoniser.
II vi **1** [law, practice, people] s'accorder; [colour] se marier; **2** MUS jouer or chanter or être en harmonie.

harmony /'hɑ:mənɪ/ n harmonie f.

harness /'hɑ:nɪs/ **I** n (for horse, dog, person) harnais m; **I'm back in ~** j'ai repris le collier.
II vtr **1** (put harness on) harnacher; **2** (attach) atteler [animal] (**to** à); **3** (use) exploiter [power].

harp /hɑ:p/ ▶**1097** n harpe f.
■ **harp on** PEJ rabâcher○ toujours la même chose sur [issue, event].

harpist /'hɑ:pɪst/ ▶**1251** n harpiste mf.

harpoon /hɑ:'pu:n/ **I** n harpon m.
II vtr harponner.

harpsichord /'hɑ:psɪkɔ:d/ ▶**1097** n clavecin m.

harpy /'hɑ:pɪ/ n MYTHOL harpie f; PEJ mégère f PEJ.

harridan /'hærɪdən/ n PEJ mégère f PEJ.

harrow /'hærəʊ/ n AGRIC herse f.

harrowing /'hærəʊɪŋ/ adj [experience, ordeal] atroce; [film, story, image] déchirant.

harry /'hærɪ/ vtr (pursue, harass) harceler.

harsh /hɑ:ʃ/ adj **1** (severe, cruel) [punishment, measures] sévère; [regime, person] dur; [conditions] difficile; **to have ~ words for sb/sth** critiquer qn/qch; **2** (unpleasant) [light, colour] cru; [voice, sound] rude; **3** (strong) [chemical, cleaner] corrosif/-ive.

harshly /'hɑ:ʃlɪ/ adv [treat, judge, speak] durement; [punish, condemn] sévèrement.

harshness /'hɑ:ʃnɪs/ n (of punishment, law, regime) sévérité f; (of criticism) dureté f; (of climate) rigueur f; (of conditions) difficulté f; (of sound) rudesse f.

harvest /'hɑ:vɪst/ **I** n (of wheat, fruit) récolte f; (of grapes) vendange f; **to get in the ~** faire la récolte; **to reap a rich ~** FIG récolter les fruits de ses efforts; **to reap a bitter ~** FIG payer les pots cassés.
II vtr **1** LIT moissonner [corn]; récolter [vegetables]; cueillir [fruit]; **2** FIG (collect) récolter [information].
III vi faire la récolte; (of grapes) faire la vendange.

harvester /'hɑ:vɪstə(r)/ n **1** (machine) moissonneuse f; **2** (person) moissonneur/-euse m/f.

harvest festival /'hɑ:vɪst/ n fête f de la moisson.

has ▶ **have**.

has-been○ /'hæzbiːn/ n PÉJ homme fini/femme finie m/f.

hash /hæʃ/ n **1** CULIN hachis m; **2**○ (mess) **to make a ~ of sth** râter qch.

hash browns npl US pommes fpl de terre sautées.

hasn't = **has not**.

hassle /'hæsl/ **I** n complications fpl; **to cause (sb) ~** créer des complications (à qn); **it was a real ~** c'était vraiment embêtant○; **to give sb ~** embêter qn○ (**about** à propos de).
II vtr talonner (**about** à propos de); **~ d** stressé.

haste /heɪst/ n hâte f; **to act in ~** agir à la hâte; **to make ~** se dépêcher (**to do** de faire); **with undue ~** avec une hâte excessive.
IDIOMS **more ~ less speed** hâte-toi lentement.

hasten /'heɪsn/ **I** vtr accélérer [ageing, destruction]; précipiter [departure, death, decline].
II vi se hâter; **to ~ to do** s'empresser de faire.

hastily /'heɪstɪlɪ/ adv [do] à la hâte; [say] précipitamment; **too ~** avec trop de précipitation.

hasty /'heɪstɪ/ adj **1** (hurried) [talks, marriage, departure] précipité; [meal] rapide; [note, sketch] fait à la hâte; **to beat a ~ retreat** HUM se sauver; **2** (rash) [decision] inconsidéré; [judgment, conclusion] hâtif/-ive; **to be too ~ in doing** aller trop vite en besogne en faisant.

hat /hæt/ n chapeau m; **to draw the winners out of a ~** déterminer les gagnants par un tirage au sort.
IDIOMS **at the drop of a ~** pour un oui, pour un non; **old ~** dépassé; **I'll eat my ~** (**if he wins**)! je vous parie tout ce que vous voulez (qu'il ne gagnera pas)!; **to keep sth under one's ~** garder qch pour soi; **to pass the ~ around** faire la quête; **to put** ou **throw one's ~ into the ring** se porter candidat; **to take one's ~ off to sb** FIG tirer son chapeau à qn; **to talk through one's ~** parler à tort et à travers.

hat: **~band** n ruban m de chapeau; **~box** n carton m à chapeau.

hatch /hætʃ/ **I** n **1** AVIAT, AEROSP panneau m mobile; NAUT écoutille f; AUT portière f; **2** (in dining room) passe-plats m inv.
II vtr **1** (incubate) faire éclore [eggs]; **2** (plan secretly) tramer [plot, scheme].
III vi [chicks, fish eggs] éclore.
IDIOMS **down the ~!** cul sec!; ▶ **chicken**.

hatchback /'hætʃbæk/ n (car) voiture f avec hayon; (car door) hayon m.

hatchet /'hætʃɪt/ n hachette f.
IDIOMS **to bury the ~** faire la paix.

hate /heɪt/ **I** n haine f; ▶ **pet hate**.
II vtr **1** (feel antagonism towards) détester; (violently) haïr; **to ~ sb for sth/for doing** en vouloir à qn de qch/d'avoir fait; **he's someone you love to ~** c'est quelqu'un sur qui on aime bien taper○; **2** (not enjoy) avoir horreur de [sport, food, activity]; **I ~ it when** je ne supporte pas quand; **3** (regret) (in apology) **to ~ to do, to ~ doing** être désolé de faire.

hated /'heɪtɪd/ adj détesté.

hateful /'heɪtfl/ adj odieux/-ieuse (**to** avec).

hate mail n lettres fpl d'injures.

hatpin /'hætpɪn/ n épingle f à chapeau.

hatred /'heɪtrɪd/ n (of person, group, system, war) haine f (**of** de; **for** pour); (less violent) aversion f (**of** de; pour).

hat: **~ stand** GB, **~ tree** US n portemanteau m (sur pied); **~ trick** n SPORT triplé m.

haughtily /'hɔːtɪlɪ/ adv avec hauteur.

haughtiness /'hɔːtɪnɪs/ n hauteur f.

haughty /'hɔːtɪ/ adj [person] hautain; [manner] altier/-ière.

haul /hɔːl/ **I** n **1** (taken by criminals) butin m; **a £2m ~** un butin d'une valeur de 2 millions de livres; **2** (found by police, customs) saisie f; **arms/heroin ~** saisie d'armes/d'héroïne; **3** (journey) **it will be a long ~** LIT, FIG l'étape sera longue; **the long ~ from Dublin to London** le long voyage de Dublin à Londres; **4** (in transportation) courrier m; **long/**

medium/short ~ long/moyen/court courrier; **5** (of fish) pêche f.
II vtr **1** (drag) tirer; **to ~ oneself up on the roof** se hisser sur le toit; **2** (by lorry) transporter.
IDIOMS **to ~ sb over the coals** passer un savon à qn○.

haulage /'hɔːlɪdʒ/ n ₵ **1** (transport) transport m routier; **2** (cost) frais mpl de roulage ou transport.

haulier /'hɔːlɪə(r)/ GB, **hauler** /'hɔːlə(r)/ US ▶ 1251 n (owner of firm) transporteur m; (firm) société f de transports routiers; (truck driver) routier m.

haunch /hɔːntʃ/ n hanche f.

haunt /hɔːnt/ **I** n lieu m de prédilection.
II vtr LIT, FIG hanter; **he is ~ed by the fear of dying** il a la hantise de la mort.

haunted /'hɔːntɪd/ adj [house] hanté; [face, look] tourmenté.

haunting /'hɔːntɪŋ/ adj [film, book, image, music, beauty, doubt] lancinant; [memory] obsédant.

Havana /hə'vænə/ ▶ 1343 **I** pr n La Havane f.
II n (cigar) havane m.

have /hæv, həv/ **I** vtr (uses not covered in NOTE) **1** (possess) avoir; **she has (got) a dog** elle a un chien; **2** (consume) prendre; **to ~ a sandwich** manger un sandwich; **to ~ a whisky** boire un whisky; **to ~ a cigarette** fumer une cigarette; **to ~ breakfast** prendre le petit déjeuner; **to ~ dinner** dîner; **to ~ lunch** déjeuner; **I had some more cake** j'ai repris du gâteau; **3** (want) vouloir, prendre; **what will you ~?** qu'est-ce que vous prendrez ou voulez?; **she won't ~ him back** elle ne veut plus de lui; **I wouldn't ~ it any other way** ça me convient comme ça; **I wouldn't ~ him/her any other way** c'est comme ça que je l'aime; **4** (receive, get) recevoir [letter, information]; **I've had no news from him** je n'ai pas eu de nouvelles de lui; **I must ~ the information soon** il me faut l'information bientôt; **to let sb ~ sth** donner qch à qn; **5** (hold) faire [party, celebration]; tenir [meeting]; organiser [competition, ballot, exhibition]; avoir [conversation]; mener [enquiry]; **6** (exert, exhibit) avoir [effect, influence]; avoir [courage, courtesy] (**to do** de faire); **7** (spend) passer; **to ~ a nice day/ evening** passer une journée/ soirée agréable; **to ~ a good time** bien s'amuser; **to ~ a hard** ou **bad time** traverser une période difficile; **to ~ a good vacation** passer de bonnes vacances; **to ~ got** (also ~ **got**) **to ~ sth to do** avoir qch à faire; **I ~** ou **I've got letters to write** j'ai du courrier à faire; **9** (undergo, suffer) avoir; **to ~ (the) flu/a heart attack** avoir la grippe/une crise cardiaque; **to ~ toothache** avoir mal aux dents; **to ~ a shock** subir un choc; **he had his car stolen** il s'est fait voler sa voiture; **she has had her windows broken** on lui a cassé ses vitres; **they like having stories read to them** ils aiment qu'on leur lise des histoires; **to ~ an interview** avoir ou passer un entretien; **10** (cause to be done) **to ~ sth done** faire faire qch; **to ~ the house painted** faire peindre la maison; **to ~ one's hair cut** se faire couper les cheveux; **to ~ an injection** se faire faire une piqûre; **to ~ sb do sth** faire faire qch à qn; **she had him close the door** elle lui a fait fermer la porte; **they would ~ us believe that...** ils voudraient nous faire croire que...; **I would ~ you know that...** je voudrais que vous sachiez que...; **he had them laughing** il les a fait rire; **11** (cause to become) **he had his revolver ready** il avait son revolver prêt; **we'll soon ~ everything ready/clean** nous aurons bientôt fini de tout préparer/nettoyer; **if you're not careful you'll ~ that glass over** si tu ne fais pas attention tu vas renverser le verre; **she had them completely baffled** elle les a complètement déroutés; **I had it finished by 5 o'clock** je l'avais fini avant 5 heures; **12** (allow) tolérer; **I won't ~ this kind of behaviour!** je ne tolérerai pas ce comportement!; **I won't ~ it!** ça ne va pas se passer comme ça!; **I won't ~ them exploit him** je ne tolérerai pas qu'ils l'exploitent; **I won't ~ him hurt** je ne laisserai personne le blesser; **we can't ~ them staying in a hotel** on ne peut pas les laisser aller à l'hôtel;

have

When used as an auxiliary in present perfect, future perfect and past perfect tenses *have* is normally translated by *avoir*:

I have seen	= j'ai vu
I had seen	= j'avais vu

However, some verbs in French, especially verbs of movement and change of state (e.g. *aller, venir, descendre, mourir*), take *être* rather than *avoir* in these tenses:

he has left   = il est parti

In this case, remember the past participle agrees with the subject of the verb:

she has died   = elle est morte

If you are in doubt as to whether a verb conjugates with *être* or *avoir*, consult the French verb tables. Reflexive verbs (e.g. *se lever, se coucher*) always conjugate with *être*:

she has fainted = elle s'est évanouie

For translations of time expressions using *for* or *since* (*he has been in London for six months, he has been in London since June*), see the entries **for** and **since**.

For translations of time expressions using *just* (*I have just finished my essay, he has just gone*), see the entry **just¹**.

to have to meaning *must* is translated by either *devoir* or the impersonal construction *il faut que* + subjunctive:

I have to leave now = il faut que je parte maintenant
    or je dois partir maintenant

In negative sentences, *not to have to* is generally translated by *ne pas être obligé de*, e.g.

you don't have to go = tu n'es pas obligé d'y aller

For examples and particular usages see entry.

When *have* is used as a straightforward transitive verb meaning *possess*, *have* (or *have got*) can generally be translated by *avoir*, e.g.

I have (got) a car	= j'ai une voiture
she has a good memory	= elle a une bonne mémoire
they have (got) problems	= ils ont des problèmes

For examples and particular usages see entry; see also **got**.

have is also used with certain noun objects where the whole expression is equivalent to a verb:

to have dinner	= to dine
to have a try	= to try
to have a walk	= to walk

In such cases the phrase is very often translated by the equivalent verb in French (*dîner, essayer, se promener*). For translations consult the appropriate noun entry (**dinner, try, walk**).

had is used in English at the beginning of a clause to replace an expression with *if*. Such expressions are generally translated by *si* + past perfect tense, e.g.

had I taken the train, this would never have happened
= si j'avais pris le train, ce ne serait jamais arrivé
had there been a fire, we would all have been killed
= s'il y avait eu un incendie, nous serions tous morts

For examples of the above and all other uses of *have* see the entry.

---

13 (physically hold) tenir; **she had the glass in her hand** elletenait le verre dans la main; **she had him by the throat/by the arm** elle le tenait à la gorge/par le bras; **he had his hands over his eyes** il avait les mains sur les yeux; **14** (give birth to) [*woman*] avoir [*child*]; [*animal*] mettre bas, avoir [*young*]; **has she had it yet?** est-ce qu'elle a accouché?; **she's having a baby (in May)** elle va avoir un enfant (en mai); **15** (as impersonal verb) **over here, we ~ a painting by Picasso** ici vous avez un tableau de Picasso; **what we ~ here is a small group of extremists** ce à quoi nous avons affaire ici, est un petit groupe d'extrémistes; **16** (puzzle) **you ~** *ou* **you've got me there!** là tu me poses une colle°!; **17** (have at one's mercy) (also **~ got**) **I've got you/him now!** maintenant je te/le tiens!; **I'll ~ you!** je vais te montrer!

II *modal aux* **1** (must) **I ~ (got) to leave now** je dois partir maintenant, il faut que je parte maintenant; **2** (need to) **you don't ~** *ou* **you haven't got to leave so early** tu n'as pas besoin de or tu n'es pas obligé de partir si tôt; **why did this ~ to happen?** pourquoi fallait-il que ça arrive?; **something has (got) to be done** il faut faire quelque chose; **3** (for emphasis) **this has (got) to be the most difficult decision I've ever made** c'est sans doute la décision la plus difficile que j'aie jamais eu à prendre.

III *v aux* **1** GEN avoir; (with movement and reflexive verbs) être; **she has lost her bag** elle a perdu son sac; **she has already left** elle est déjà partie; **she has hurt herself** elle s'est blessée; **2** (in tag questions etc) **you've seen the film, haven't you?** tu as vu le film, n'est-ce pas?; **you haven't seen the film, ~ you?** tu n'as pas vu le film?; **you haven't seen my bag, ~ you?** tu n'as pas vu mon sac, par hasard?; **'he's already left'—'has he indeed!'** 'il est déjà parti'—'vraiment!'; **'you've never met him'—'yes I ~!'** 'tu ne l'as jamais rencontré'—'mais si!'

IV having *v aux* **1** (in time clauses) **having finished his breakfast, he went out** après avoir fini son petit déjeuner, il est sorti; **2** (because, since) **having already won twice** comme il a déjà gagné deux fois.

IDIOMS **to ~ done with sth** en finir avec qch; **this car/TV has had it**° cette voiture/télé est foutue°; **when your father finds out, you've had it**°! (in trouble) quand ton père l'apprendra, ça va être ta fête°!; **I can't do any more, I've had it**°! (tired) je n'en peux plus, je suis crevé°!; **I've had it (up to here) with...**° j'en ai marre de...°; **to ~ it in for sb**° avoir qn dans le collimateur°; **she has/doesn't ~ it in her to do** elle est capable/incapable de faire; **to ~ it out with sb** s'expliquer avec qn; **he will ~ it that il** soutient que; **I've got it!** je sais!; **the ayes/noes ~ it** les oui/non l'emportent; **the ~s and the ~-nots** les riches et les pauvres; **...and what ~ you** ...etc; **there is no milk/there are no houses to be had** on ne trouve pas de lait/de maisons.

■ **have around** US = **have over, have round**.

■ **have back**: **~ [sth] back** (have returned) **when can I ~ my car back?** quand est-ce que tu me rends ma voiture?

■ **have in**: **~ [sb] in** faire venir [*doctor, priest*].

■ **have on**: ¶ **~ [sth] on, ~ on [sth]** (be wearing) porter [*coat, skirt etc*]; **to ~ (got) nothing on** être nu; ¶ **~ [sth] on** (be busy) avoir [qch] de prévu; ¶ **~ [sb] on**° (tease) faire marcher°; ¶ **~ sth on sb** (have evidence about) avoir des preuves contre qn.

■ **have over, have round**: **~ [sb] over** inviter [*person*].

■ **have up**°: **to be had up** être jugé (**for** pour).

haven /ˈheɪvn/ *n* **1** (safe place) refuge *m* (**for** pour); **2** FIG havre *m*; **3** (harbour) port *m*.

haven't = **have not**.

haver /ˈheɪvə(r)/ *vi* (dither) vaciller.

haversack /ˈhævəsæk/ *n* GEN sac *m* à dos; MIL musette *f*.

havoc /ˈhævək/ *n* dévastation *f*; **to wreak ~ on** dévaster [*building, landscape*]; **to play ~ with** chambouler [*plans etc*]; **to cause ~** FIG tout mettre sens dessus dessous.

haw /hɔː/ *n* BOT cenelle *f*.

IDIOMS **to hum** GB *ou* **hem** US **and ~** balbutier.

Hawaii /həˈwaɪɪ/ ▶ **1022** *pr n* Hawaï *m*.

Hawaiian /həˈwaɪən/ ▶ **1100**, **1038** **I** *n* **1** (person) Hawaïen/-ïenne *m/f*; **2** (language) hawaïen *m*. **II** *adj* [*culture, landscape*] hawaïen/-ïenne.

hawk /hɔːk/ **I** *n* LIT, FIG, POL faucon *m*. **II** *vtr* GEN vendre; (door-to-door) colporter.

IDIOMS **to have eyes like a ~** avoir des yeux de lynx.

hawker /'hɔ:kə(r)/ n colporteur m.

hawkish /'hɔ:kɪʃ/ adj POL belliciste.

hawthorn /'hɔ:θɔ:n/ n (tree, flower) aubépine f.

hay /heɪ/ n foin m; **to make ~** faire les foins.
IDIOMS **to make ~ while the sun shines** saisir l'occasion au vol.

hay: **~cock** n meulon m; **~ fever** ▶ 1002 n rhume m des foins; **~ fork** n fourche f à foin; **~ loft** n grenier m à foin; **~making** n fenaison f.

haystack /'heɪstæk/ n meule f de foin.
IDIOMS **it is/was like looking for a needle in a ~** autant chercher une aiguille dans une botte de foin.

haywire° /'heɪwaɪə(r)/ adj **1** (faulty) (jamais épith) **to go ~** [plan] dérailler; [machinery, system] se détraquer; **2** US (crazy) détraqué°.

hazard /'hæzəd/ I n **1** (risk) risque m (**to** pour); **the ~s of doing** les risques qu'il y a à faire; **to be a health ~** constituer un risque pour la santé; **fire/occupational ~** risque d'incendie/du métier; **2** (chance) hasard m.
II vtr (venture) hasarder [opinion, explanation]; **to ~ a guess** hasarder une idée.

hazardous /'hæzədəs/ adj dangereux/-euse.

haze /heɪz/ n (mist) brume f; (of smoke, dust) nuage m.

hazel /'heɪzl/ I n (tree) noisetier m; (wood) bois m de noisetier.
II ▶ 818 adj [eyes] (couleur de) noisette inv.

hazelnut /'heɪzlnʌt/ n noisette f.

hazy /'heɪzɪ/ adj [weather, morning] brumeux/-euse; [sunshine] voilé; [image, outline] flou; [recollection, idea] vague; **to be ~ about sth** être dans le vague en ce qui concerne qch.

H bomb n bombe f H.

HDTV n (abrév = **high-definition television**) TVHD f.

he /hi:, hɪ/

■ Note *he* is almost always translated by *il*: *he closed the door* = *il a fermé la porte*. The emphatic form is *lui*.
– For exceptions and particular usages, see the entry below.

I pron il; **~'s seen us** il nous a vus; **here ~ is** le voici; **there ~ is** le voilà; HE **didn't take it** ce n'est pas lui qui l'a pris; **she lives in Oxford but ~ doesn't** elle habite Oxford mais lui non; **~'s a genius** c'est un génie; **~ who** celui qui; **~ and I** lui et moi.
II n **it's a ~**° (of baby) c'est un garçon; (of animal) c'est un mâle.

head /hed/ ▶ 765 I n **1** tête f; **she put her ~ round the door** elle a mis la nez à la porte; **my ~ aches** j'ai mal à la tête; **a fine ~ of hair** une belle chevelure; **to keep one's ~ down** LIT garder la tête baissée; FIG (be inconspicuous) ne pas se faire remarquer; (work hard) avoir le nez sur son travail; **from ~ to foot** ou **toe** de la tête aux pieds; **the decision was made over their ~s** la décision a été prise sans les consulter; **to stand on one's ~** faire le poirier; **~s turned at the sight of...** tout le monde s'est retourné en voyant...; **to hold a gun to sb's ~** LIT presser un pistolet contre la tête de qn; FIG tenir le couteau sous la gorge de qn; **to have a bad ~** avoir mal à la tête; **to be a ~ taller than sb** dépasser qn d'une tête; **to win by a (short) ~** [horse] gagner d'une (courte) tête; **£10 a ~** ou **per ~** 10 livres sterling par personne; **50 ~ of cattle** AGRIC 50 têtes de bétail; **2** (mind) tête f; **I can't get it into her ~ that** je n'arrive pas à lui enfoncer dans la tête que; **he has got it into his ~ that** il s'est mis dans la tête que; **he has taken it into his ~ to resign** il s'est mis en tête de démissionner; **you can put that idea out of your ~!** tu peux oublier cette idée!; **the name has gone right out of my ~** le nom m'est complètement sorti de la tête; **I can't add them up in my ~** je ne peux pas les additionner de tête; **to be over sb's ~** (too difficult) passer par-dessus la tête de qn; **use your ~**°! sers-toi de tes méninges°!; **her success has turned her ~** son succès lui a tourné la

tête; **to have a (good) ~ for figures** être doué pour le calcul; **to have no ~ for heights** avoir le vertige; **3** (leader) (of family, church, agency) chef m; (of social service, organization) responsable mf, directeur/-trice m/f; **at the ~ of** à la tête de; **~ of government/State** chef m de gouvernement/d'État; **~ of department** ADMIN chef de service; SCH professeur principal; **~ of personnel** COMM chef du personnel; **4** (of pin, nail, hammer, golf club) tête f; (of axe, spear, arrow) fer m; (of tennis racquet) tamis m; (of stick) pommeau m; (of cabbage, lettuce) pomme f; (of garlic) tête f; **5** (of tape recorder) ALSO COMPUT tête f; **6** (top end) (of bed) tête f; (of table) (haut) bout m; (of procession) tête f; (of pier, river, valley) extrémité f; **at the ~ of the stairs/list** en haut de l'escalier/de la liste; **at the ~ of the queue** en tête de la file d'attente; **7** MED (on boil, spot) tête f; **to come to a ~** LIT, MED mûrir; FIG [crisis] arriver au point critique; **to bring sth to a ~** MED faire mûrir; FIG précipiter [crisis]; amener [qch] au point critique [situation]; **8** (on beer) mousse f;.
II **heads** npl (tossing coin) face f; **'~s or tails?'** 'pile ou face?'; **~s I win/we go** face je gagne/on y va.
III noun modifier **1** [injury] à la tête; **2** (chief) [cashier, cook, gardener] en chef.
IV vtr **1** être en tête de [list, queue]; être à la tête de [firm, team]; mener [expedition, inquiry]; **2** (entitle) intituler [chapter]; **~ed writing paper** papier m à lettres à en-tête; **3** (steer) diriger [vehicle]; naviguer [boat]; **he ~ed the sheep away from the cliff** il a éloigné les moutons de la falaise; **4** SPORT **to ~ the ball** faire une tête; **he ~ed the ball into the net** il a marqué un but de la tête.
V vi **where was the train ~ed** ou **~ing?** où allait le train?; **to ~ south/north** NAUT mettre le cap au sud/au nord; **to ~ home** rentrer; **he's ~ing this way!** il se dirige par ici!; ▶ **head for**.
VI **-headed** combining form **black-~ed bird** oiseau à tête noire; **red-~ed boy** garçon (aux cheveux) roux; **two-~ed monster** monstre à deux têtes.
IDIOMS **on your own ~ be it!** à tes risques et périls!; **to go to sb's ~** monter à la tête de qn; **to go off one's ~**° perdre la boule°; **are you off your ~?** tu as perdu la boule°?; **to keep/lose one's ~** garder/perdre son sang-froid; **to be soft** ou **weak in the ~**° être faible d'esprit; **he's not right in the ~**° il a un grain°; **to laugh one's ~ off**° rire aux éclats; **to shout one's ~ off**° crier à tue-tête; **to talk one's ~ off**° ne pas arrêter de parler; **off the top of one's ~** [say, answer] sans réfléchir; **to give a horse its/sb their ~** lâcher la bride à un cheval/à qn; **to be able to do sth standing on one's ~** faire qch les doigts dans le nez°; **I can't make ~ (n)or tail of it** je n'y comprends rien, ça n'a ni queue ni tête; **if we all put our ~s together** si nous nous y mettons tous; **the leaders put their ~s together** les dirigeants se sont consultés; **two ~s are better than one** PROV deux avis valent mieux qu'un.
■ **head for:** **~ for** [sth] se diriger vers; NAUT mettre le cap sur; **to ~ for home** prendre le chemin du retour; **to ~ing for a fall** courir à l'échec.
■ **head off:** ¶ **~ off** partir (**for, towards** vers); ¶ **~ off** [sb/sth], **~** [sb/sth] **off** bloquer, barrer la route à [person]; FIG éluder [question]; éviter [quarrel].

headache /'hedeɪk/ ▶ 1002 n mal m de tête; **to have a ~** avoir mal à la tête; **to be a ~ (to sb)** FIG causer des ennuis (à qn).

head: **~band** n bandeau m; **~board** n tête f de lit; **~ boy** n GB SCH élève qui représente l'école et qui a des responsabilités; **~butt** vtr donner un coup de tête à.

head case° n **to be a ~** avoir un grain°.

head cold ▶ 1002 n rhume m de cerveau.

headcount /'hedkaʊnt/ n **to do a ~** compter (les personnes présentes).

headdress /'heddres/ n (of feathers) coiffure f; (of lace) coiffe f.

header /'hedə(r)/ n **1**° (dive) **to take a ~** piquer une tête°; **2** SPORT tête f.

head: **~first** adv LIT [*fall, plunge*] la tête la première; FIG [*rush into*] tête baissée; **~ gear** n ⊄ couvre-chef m; **~ girl** n GB SCH *élève qui représente l'école et qui a des responsabilités*.

head-hunt /'hedhʌnt/ vtr (seek to recruit) (chercher à) recruter; **she has been ~ed several times** elle a été contactée plusieurs fois par des chasseurs de tête.

head: **~-hunter** n COMM chasseur m de têtes; **~-hunting** n COMM chasse f aux têtes.

heading /'hedɪŋ/ n (of article, column) titre m; (of subject area, topic) rubrique f; (on notepaper, letter) en-tête m; **chapter ~** (quotation) tête f de chapitre; (title) titre m (de chapitre).

head: **~lamp** n (of car) phare m; (of train) fanal m; **~land** n (high) promontoire m; (flat) pointe f; **~light** n (of car) phare m; (of train) fanal m.

headline /'hedlaɪn/ n gros titre m; RADIO, TV titre m; **to hit the ~s** faire la une○; **the front-page ~** la manchette; **the news ~s** les grands titres (de l'actualité).

headlong /'hedlɒŋ/ **I** adj [*fall*] tête la première; **a ~ dash** une ruée.
II adv [*fall*] la tête la première; [*run*] à toute vitesse; **to rush ~ into sth** FIG se jeter tête baissée dans.

head: **~louse** n (pl **~lice**) pou m; **~master** ▶ 1251 , 937 n directeur m; **~mistress** ▶ 1251 , 937 n directrice f; **~ office** n siège m social.

head-on /ˌhed'ɒn/ **I** adj LIT [*crash, collision*] de front; FIG [*confrontation, approach*] direct.
II adv [*collide, crash, attack*] de front.

headphones /'hedfəʊnz/ npl casque m; **a pair of ~** un casque.

head: **~quarters** npl (+ v sg ou pl) GEN, COMM, ADMIN siège m social; MIL quartier m général; **~ rest** n GEN appui-tête m; AUT repose-tête m inv.

headroom /'hedrʊm/ n **I haven't got enough ~** le plafond est trop bas pour moi; **'max ~ 4 metres'** (on road sign) 'hauteur limitée à 4 mètres'.

head: **~scarf** n (pl **-scarves**) foulard m; **~set** n casque m; (with microphone) micro-casque m.

headstand /'hedstænd/ n **to do a ~** faire le poirier.

head start n **to have a ~** avoir une longueur d'avance (**over** sur).

head: **~stone** n (grave) pierre f tombale; **~strong** adj [*person*] têtu; [*attitude, behaviour*] obstiné; **~ teacher** ▶ 1251 n directeur/-trice m/f.

head to head n, adj **to come together in a ~** ou **in a head-to-head battle** s'affronter.

head waiter ▶ 1251 n maître m d'hôtel.

headway /'hedweɪ/ n **to make ~** LIT progresser; FIG faire des progrès.

headwind /'hedwɪnd/ n GEN vent m contraire; NAUT vent m debout.

heady /'hedɪ/ adj [*wine, mixture*] capiteux/-euse; [*perfume*] entêtant; FIG [*experience*] grisant.

heal /hiːl/ **I** vtr LIT, FIG guérir.
II vi [*wound, cut*] se cicatriser; [*fracture, scar*] guérir.

healer /'hiːlə(r)/ n guérisseur/-euse m/f; **time is a great ~** le temps apporte l'oubli.

healing /'hiːlɪŋ/ **I** n guérison f.
II adj [*power*] curatif/-ive; [*lotion*] cicatrisant; [*effect*] salutaire; **the ~ process** LIT, FIG le rétablissement.

health /helθ/ n **I** MED santé f; FIG (of economy) santé f; **in good/bad ~** en bonne/mauvaise santé; **to drink (to) sb's ~** boire à la santé de qn; **here's (to your) ~!, good ~!** à votre santé!

health: **Health Authority** n GB administration f régionale de la santé publique; **~ care** n GEN soins mpl médicaux; ADMIN services mpl médicaux; **~ centre** n GB centre m médico-social; **~ check** n visite f médicale; **~ club** n club m de remise en forme; **~ education** n ~ hygiène f publique; **~ farm** n: *établissement pour cures d'amaigrissement, de rajeunissement etc*; **~ food shop** ▶ 1251 n magasin m de produits diététiques; **~ hazard** n risque m pour la santé.

healthily /'helθɪlɪ/ adv sainement.

health: **~ inspector** ▶ 1251 n inspecteur/-trice m/f de l'hygiène; **~ insurance** n assurance f maladie; **~ officer** ▶ 1251 n inspecteur/-trice m/f de la santé; **~ resort** n (by sea) station f balnéaire; (in mountains) station f climatique; (spa town) station f thermale; **Health Secretary** n GB ministre m de la Santé.

Health Service n **1** GB services mpl de santé; **2** US UNIV infirmerie f.

health: **~ visitor** ▶ 1251 n GB infirmier/-ière m/f des services sociaux; **~ warning** n mise f en garde du ministère de la Santé.

healthy /'helθɪ/ adj [*person, animal, plant, skin, lifestyle, diet*] sain; [*air*] salutaire; [*appetite*] robuste; [*crop*] abondant; [*economy*] sain; [*profit*] excellent; [*lead*] confortable; **to have a ~ respect for** apprécier [qn] à sa juste valeur [*opponent, sb's talents*]; craindre [*teacher*].

heap /hiːp/ **I** n tas m; **to pile sth up in a ~** ou **in ~s** mettre qch en tas; **to lie in a ~** [*person*] être affalé; [*objects, bodies*] être entassés; **~s of**○ plein de [*money, food*]; un tas○ de [*work, problems*]; **we've got ~s of time** on a tout notre temps.
II vtr **1** (pile) = **heap up**; **2** FIG **to ~ sth on sb** couvrir qn de [*praise*]; accabler qn de [*work, insults*].
■ **heap up**: **~ up [sth] up, ~ up [sth]** entasser [*leaves, bodies*]; empiler [*food*].

heaped /hiːpt/ adj **a ~ spoonful** CULIN une bonne cuillerée.

hear /hɪə(r)/ (prét, pp **heard**) **I** vtr **1** entendre; **she heard a man coming up the stairs** elle a entendu un homme qui montait l'escalier; **I can ~ the train whistling** j'entends siffler le train; **to ~ her talk, you'd think (that)** à l'entendre, on croirait que; **we haven't heard the end** ou **last of it** on n'a pas fini d'en entendre parler; **to make oneself** ou **one's voice heard** LIT se faire entendre; FIG faire entendre sa voix; **2** (learn) apprendre [*news, rumour*]; **to ~ (tell) of sth** entendre parler de qch; **to ~ that** apprendre que; **to ~ it said that** entendre dire que; **I've heard so much about you** on m'a tant parlé de vous; **I've heard it all before!** je connais la chanson○!; **have you heard the one about...?** (joke) tu connais celle de...?; **have you heard?** tu es au courant?; **I ~ you want to be a doctor** il paraît que tu veux devenir médecin; **so I ~, so I've heard** c'est ce que j'ai entendu dire; **to ~ whether/why/how** savoir si/pourquoi/comment; **3** (listen to) écouter [*lecture, broadcast*]; [*judge*] entendre [*case, evidence*]; **to ~ what sb has to say** entendre ce que qn a à dire; **do you ~ (me)?** tu m'entends?; **to ~ Mass** SOUT assister à la messe.
II vi entendre; **to ~ about** entendre parler de.
IDIOMS **~! ~!** bravo!

■ **hear from**: **~ from [sb] 1** (get news) avoir des nouvelles de; **I'm waiting to ~ from the hospital** j'attends une réponse de l'hôpital; **you'll be ~ing from me!** (threat) tu auras de mes nouvelles!; **2** (on TV etc) entendre le point de vue de [*expert*]; écouter le récit de [*witness*].

■ **hear of**: **~ of [sb/sth]** entendre parler de; **that's the first I've heard of it!** première nouvelle!; **I won't ~ of it!** il n'en est pas question!

■ **hear out**: **~ out [sb], ~ [sb] out** écouter [qn] jusqu'au bout.

heard /hɜːd/ prét, pp ▶ **hear**.

hearing /'hɪərɪŋ/ **I** n **1** (sense) ouïe f, audition f; **his ~ is not very good** il n'a pas l'oreille très fine; **2** (earshot) **in my ~** en ma présence; **3** (before court) audience f; **~ of an appeal** audition f d'un appel; **closed** ou **private ~** audience à huis clos; **4** (chance to be heard) **to get a ~** se faire entendre; **to give sb/sth a ~** écouter qn/qch.
II noun modifier [*loss, test*] d'audition.

hearing: **~ aid** n prothèse f auditive; **~-impaired** adj malentendant.

hearsay /'hɪəseɪ/ n ⊄ ouï-dire m inv, on-dit m inv; **based on ~** fondé sur des ouï-dires or on-dit.

hearse /hɜːs/ n corbillard m.

heart /hɑːt/ ▶949 I *n* **1** cœur *m*; **my ~ missed a beat** mon cœur a fait un bond; **to win/steal sb's ~** gagner/prendre le cœur de qn; **to break sb's ~** briser le cœur de qn; **to break one's ~** se briser le cœur (**over sb** pour qn); **it does my ~ good to see...** cela me réchauffe le cœur de voir...; **with a heavy/light ~** le cœur lourd/léger; **to lose one's ~ to sb** tomber amoureux/-euse de qn; **to sob one's ~ out** pleurer toutes les larmes de son corps; **to know/learn sth off by ~** savoir/apprendre qch par cœur; **my ~ goes out to you** je suis avec vous de tout cœur; **from the bottom of one's ~,** from the ~ du fond du cœur; **to open one's ~ to sb** ouvrir son cœur à qn; **to take sth to ~** prendre qch à cœur; **to wish with all one's ~ that** souhaiter de tout cœur que (+ *subj*); **in my ~ (of ~s)** au fond de moi-même; **my ~ is not in sth/doing sth** je n'ai pas le cœur à qch/à faire qch; **it is close to my ~** cela me tient à cœur; **I have your interests at ~** tes intérêts me tiennent à cœur; **he's a child at ~** au fond, c'est toujours un enfant; **to have no ~** ne pas avoir de cœur; **to be all ~** avoir très bon cœur; **I didn't have the ~ to refuse** je n'ai pas eu le cœur de refuser; **have a ~!** pitié!; **to have a change of ~** changer de sentiment; (*courage*) courage *m*; **to take/lose ~** prendre/ perdre courage; **she took ~ from the fact that** elle puisait son courage dans le fait que; **to be in good ~** avoir le moral; **3** (centre) (of district) cœur *m*; **right in the ~ of London** en plein cœur de Londres; **in the ~ of the jungle** en pleine jungle; **the ~ of the matter** le fond du problème; **4** (in cards) cœur *m*; **5** (of vegetable) cœur *m*.

II noun modifier [*patient, specialist*] du cœur; [*muscle, valve*] cardiaque; [*surgery*] du cœur, cardiaque; **to have a ~ condition** être cardiaque.

IDIOMS a man after my own ~ un homme comme je les aime; **cross my ~ (and hope to die)** croix de bois, croix de fer (si je mens je vais en enfer); **his/her ~ is in the right place** il/elle a bon cœur; **home is where the ~ is** PROV où le cœur aime, là est le foyer; **to have one's ~ set on sth** vouloir à tout prix qch; **don't set your ~ on it** n'y compte pas trop.

heart: **~ache** *n* chagrin *m*; **~ attack** *n* crise *f* cardiaque, infarctus *m*; **~beat** *n* battement *m* de cœur; **~break** *n* déchirement *m*, douleur *f*; **~breaking** *adj* [*sight, story*] navrant; [*cry, appeal*] déchirant.

heartbroken /ˈhɑːtbrəʊkn/ *adj* **to be ~** avoir le cœur brisé.

heart: **~burn** *n* brûlures *fpl* d'estomac; **~ disease** *n* ⊄ maladies *fpl* cardiaques.

hearten /ˈhɑːtn/ *vtr* encourager.

heartening /ˈhɑːtnɪŋ/ *adj* encourageant.

heart: **~ failure** *n* arrêt *m* du cœur; **~felt** *adj* sincère.

hearth /hɑːθ/ *n* foyer *m*; **~ rug** petit tapis *m*.

heartily /ˈhɑːtɪlɪ/ *adv* [*greet*] chaleureusement; [*agree*] tout à fait; [*laugh, eat*] de bon cœur; [*glad*] vraiment; **I'm ~ sick of it**○ j'en ai ras le bol○.

heartiness /ˈhɑːtɪnɪs/ *n* (of person, manner) jovialité *f*.

heartland /ˈhɑːtlənd/ *n* (also **~s** *pl*) (industrial, rural centre) cœur *m*; (of region, country) centre *m*; POL fief *m*.

heartless /ˈhɑːtlɪs/ *adj* [*person*] sans cœur; [*attitude, behaviour*] sans pitié; [*treatment*] cruel.

heart: **~-lung machine** *n* cœur-poumon *m* (artificiel); **~ monitor** *n* moniteur *m* cardiaque; **~ rate** *n* rythme *m* or fréquence *f* SPEC cardiaque.

heartrending /ˈhɑːtrendɪŋ/ *adj* [*cry, appeal*] déchirant; [*sight, story*] navrant.

heart-searching /ˈhɑːtsɜːtʃɪŋ/ *n* **after much ~** après un examen de conscience approfondi.

heart: **~ surgeon** ▶1251 *n* chirurgien *m* cardiaque, cardiochirurgien *m*; **~throb**○ *n* idole *f*.

heart-to-heart /ˌhɑːttəˈhɑːt/ I *n* **to have a ~** parler à cœur ouvert (**with** avec).

II *adj, adv* à cœur ouvert.

heart: **~ transplant** *n* greffe *f* du cœur, transplanta-tion *f* cardiaque SPEC; **~ transplant patient** *n* greffé/-e *m/f* du cœur.

heart-warming *adj* qui réchauffe le cœur.

hearty /ˈhɑːtɪ/ *adj* **1** (jolly) [*welcome*] cordial; [*person*] jovial; [*laugh*] franc/franche; [*slap*] vigoureux/-euse; **2** [*appetite, meal*] solide; [*approval*] chaleureux/-euse; **he's a ~ eater** c'est un gros mangeur; **to have a ~ dislike of sth** détester cordialement qch.

heat /hiːt/ I *n* **1** GEN, PHYS, METEOROL chaleur *f*; **the plants wilted in the ~** les plantes se sont fanées à la chaleur; **in this ~** par cette chaleur; **in the ~ of** [*afternoon, summer*] au plus chaud de; FIG [*debate*] dans le feu de; **in the ~ of the moment** dans le feu de l'action; **to take the ~ off sb** soulager qn; **2** CULIN (of hotplate, gas ring) feu *m*; (of oven) température *f*; **cook at a low ~** faire cuire à feu doux; (in oven) faire cuire à basse température; **3** (heating) chauffage *m*; **4** SPORT épreuve *f* éliminatoire; (in athletics) série *f*; **5** ZOOL **to be on ou in ~** être en chaleur.

II *vtr* chauffer [*house, pool*]; faire chauffer [*food, oven*]; **~ the oven to 180°** faire chauffer le four à 180°.

III *vi* chauffer.

■ **heat up:** ¶ **~ up** [*food, drink*] chauffer; [*air*] se réchauffer; **wait until the radiator ~s up** attends que le radiateur soit chaud; ¶ **~ [sth] up, ~ up [sth]** faire chauffer [*food*]; (reheat) faire réchauffer.

heated /ˈhiːtɪd/ *adj* LIT [*water, pool*] chauffé; [*windscreen, device*] chauffant; FIG [*debate, argument*] animé; [*denial*] véhément.

heatedly /ˈhiːtɪdlɪ/ *adv* avec véhémence.

heater /ˈhiːtə(r)/ *n* appareil *m* de chauffage.

heath /hiːθ/ *n* (moor) lande *f*; (heather) bruyère *f*.

heat haze *n* brume *f* de chaleur.

heathen /ˈhiːðn/ *n, adj* (irreligious) païen/-ïenne (*m/f*); (uncivilized) barbare (*mf*).

heather /ˈheðə(r)/ *n* bruyère *f*.

heating /ˈhiːtɪŋ/ *n* chauffage *m*.

heating engineer ▶1251 *n* chauffagiste *m*.

heat: **~ loss** *n* déperdition *f* de chaleur; **~ rash** *n* éruption *f* cutanée due à la chaleur; **~-resistant** *adj* GEN résistant à la chaleur; **~ stroke** *n* coup *m* de chaleur (*avec collapsus*); **~ treatment** *n* MED thermothérapie *f*; AGRIC thermisation *f*; **~wave** *n* vague *f* de chaleur.

heave /hiːv/ I *vtr* (*prét, pp* **heaved**) (lift) hisser; (pull) traîner péniblement; (throw) lancer (**at** sur); **to ~ a sigh** pousser un soupir; **to ~ oneself up** se hisser (**onto** sur).

II *vi* (*prét, pp* **heaved**) **1** [*sea, ground*] se soulever et s'abaisser; **2** (pull) tirer de toutes ses forces; **3** (retch) avoir un haut-le-cœur; (vomit) vomir; **it made my stomach ~** ça m'a donné un haut-le-cœur.

III heaving *pres p adj* [*bosom, breast*] haletant.

heaven /ˈhevn/ *n* **1** (also **Heaven**) ciel *m*, paradis *m*; **~ and earth** ciel et terre; **~ and hell** le paradis et l'enfer; **the kingdom of ~** le royaume des cieux; **the dinner was ~** le dîner était divin; **2** (in exclamations) **~s** (above)!, **good ~s!** grands dieux!; **~ forbid she should realize!** pourvu qu'elle ne s'en rende pas compte!; **~ help us!** que Dieu nous vienne en aide!; **thank ~(s)!** Dieu soit loué!; **3** (sky) ciel *m*; **the ~s** le ciel; **the ~s opened** des trombes d'eau se sont abattues.

IDIOMS to be in seventh ~ être au septième ciel; **to move ~ and earth** remuer ciel et terre (**to do** pour faire); **to stink ou smell to high ~** puer.

heavenly /ˈhevnlɪ/ *adj, n* **1** [*choir, body*] céleste; [*peace*] divin; **Heavenly Father** père céleste; **2**○ (wonderful) divin.

heaven-sent /ˈhevnsent/ *adj* providentiel/-ielle.

heavily /ˈhevɪlɪ/ *adv* **1** [*lean, fall, move, weigh*] lourdement; [*sleep, sigh*] profondément; [*breathe*] (noisily) bruyamment; (with difficulty) péniblement; **~ built** solidement bâti; **~ underlined** souligné d'un gros trait; **2** (abundantly) [*rain*] très fort; [*snow, invest, smoke, drink, rely*] beaucoup; [*bleed*] abondamment; [*taxed,* *armed, in debt*] fortement; **to be ~ subsidized** bénéficier de beaucoup de subventions; **~ made-up** très maquillé; **to be ~ fined** avoir une forte amende; **to lose ~** (financially) perdre beaucoup; (in game) se faire écraser; **to be ~ into sth**○ s'adonner à qch.

heavy /'hevɪ/ ▸ **1392**| I○ *n* (person) grosse brute *f*.
II *adj* **1** [*person, load, bag*] lourd; MIL, IND [*machinery*] gros/grosse (*before n*), lourd; [*artillery*] lourd; **to make sth heavier** alourdir qch; **he's 5 kg heavier than me** il pèse 5 kilos de plus que moi; **2** [*fabric, coat*] lourd; [*shoes, frame*] gros/grosse (*before n*); [*line, features*] épais/épaisse; [*movement, step*] pesant, lourd; [*blow*] violent; [*perfume, accent*] fort; [*irony, responsibility, sigh*] lourd; **with a ~ heart** le cœur gros; **to be a ~ sleeper** avoir le sommeil lourd; **a ~ thud** un bruit sourd; **the interview was ~ going** l'interview a été laborieuse; **3** (abundant) [*traffic*] dense; [*gunfire*] nourri; [*bleeding*] abondant; **to be a ~ drinker/smoker** boire/fumer beaucoup; **4** (severe) [*loss, debt*] lourd; [*attack*] intense; [*sentence, fine*] sévère; [*criticism*] fort (*before n*); [*cold*] gros/grosse (*before n*); **~ fighting** de violents combats; **5** METEOROL [*rain, frost*] fort; [*fog*] épais/épaisse; [*snow*] abondant; [*sky*] chargé; **it's very ~ today** il fait très lourd aujourd'hui; **in ~ seas** par grosse mer; **6** CULIN [*meal, food*] lourd; **7** (busy) [*timetable*] chargé; **8** [*book, film, lecture*] ardu; **this book makes ~ reading** ce livre n'est pas d'une lecture facile.
III *adv* **time hung ~ on her hands** le temps lui pesait.

heavy: **~-duty** *adj* [*equipment*] à usage industriel; **~ goods vehicle, HGV** *n* poids *m* lourd; **~-handed** *adj* maladroit; **~ industry** *n* industrie *f* lourde; **~ metal** *n* MUS hard rock *m*.

heavyweight /'hevɪweɪt/ I *n* (boxer) poids *m* lourd; ○FIG (in industry) grosse légume○ *f*; (intellectual) grosse tête○ *f*.
II *noun modifier* [*boxer, title*] poids lourd; [*fabric*] lourd.

Hebrew /'hi:bru:/ ▸ **1038**| I *n* **1** (language) hébreu *m*; **2** HIST Hébreu *m*.
II *adj* [*person*] hébreu; [*calendar, alphabet*] hébraïque.

heck○ /hek/ I *n* **what the ~ is going on?** que diable se passe-t-il?; **what the ~!** je m'en fiche○!; **a ~ of a lot of** énormément de.
II *excl* zut!

heckle /'hekl/ I *vtr* (barrack) interpeller; (interrupt) interrompre grossièrement.
II *vi* chahuter.

heckler /'heklə(r)/ *n* chahuteur/-euse *m/f* (*qui interrompt un orateur*).

heckling /'heklɪŋ/ *n* **C** interpellations *fpl*, chahut *m*.

hectare /'hektɑ:(r)/ ▸ **1309**| *n* hectare *m*.

hectic /'hektɪk/ *adj* [*activity*] intense, fiévreux/-euse; [*period*] mouvementé, agité; [*day, week, schedule*] chargé, mouvementé; **at a ~ pace** très rapidement; **to have a ~ life(style)** avoir une vie trépidante.

hector /'hektə(r)/ I *vtr* haranguer.
II **hectoring** *pres p adj* dictatorial.

hedge /hedʒ/ I *n* haie *f*; FIG protection *f*.
II *vi* (equivocate) se dérober.
III **hedged** *pp adj* **~d with** bordé de; **~d about with** FIG truffé de [*problems, restrictions*].
IDIOMS **to ~ one's bets** se couvrir.

hedge: **~-clippers** *npl* cisailles *fpl* à haies; **~hog** *n* hérisson *m*; **~row** *n* haie *f*.

hedonism /'hi:dənɪzəm/ *n* hédonisme *m*.

hedonistic /ˌhi:dəˈnɪstɪk/ *adj* hédoniste, hédonistique; **a ~ existence** une vie de sybarite.

heebie-jeebies○ /ˌhi:bɪˈdʒi:bɪz/ *npl* **the ~** la frousse○, le trac○.

heed /hi:d/ I *n* **to pay ~ to** ou **take ~ of sb** tenir compte de ce que dit qn; **to pay ~ to** ou **take ~ of sth** tenir compte de qch.
II *vtr* tenir compte de.

heedless /'hi:dlɪs/ *adj* (thoughtless) irréfléchi.

heedlessly /'hɪdlɪslɪ/ *adv* à la légère, imprudemment.

heel /hi:l/ I *n* (of foot, shoe, sock) talon *m*; **to turn one's ~** tourner les talons; **at sb's ~s** sur les talons de qn; **to bring a dog to ~** rappeler un chien; **to bring [sb] to ~** FIG mettre [qn] au pas; **to come to ~** [*dog*] venir au pied; [*person*] FIG se soumettre; **to click one's ~s** claquer des talons.
II **heels** *npl* (also **high ~s**) chaussures *fpl* à (hauts) talons.
IDIOMS **to cool** ou **kick one's ~s** attendre, faire le pied de grue○; **to dig one's ~ in** se braquer○; **to go head over ~s** culbuter; **to fall/be head over ~s in love with sb** tomber/être éperdument amoureux/-euse de qn; **hard** ou **close on sb's ~s** sur les talons de qn; **to be hot on sb's ~s** talonner qn; **to follow hard on the ~s of sth** suivre de près qch; **to take to one's ~s** HUM prendre ses jambes à son cou, s'enfuir.

heel bar ▸ **1251**| *n* talon-minute *m*.

hefty /'heftɪ/ *adj* [*person*] costaud○; [*object*] pesant; [*blow*] puissant; [*portion*] imposant; [*profit, sum*] considérable.

heifer /'hefə(r)/ *n* génisse *f*.

height /haɪt/ ▸ **1045**| *n* **1** (of person) taille *f*; (of table, tower, tree) hauteur *f*; **what is your ~?** combien mesures-tu?; **to be 1 metre 60 cm in ~** [*person*] mesurer 1 mètre 60; [*object*] faire 1 mètre 60 de haut; **to draw oneself up to one's full ~** se redresser; **2** (distance from ground) (of mountain, plane) altitude *f*; **at a ~ of 200 metres** à 200 mètres d'altitude; **to fall from a ~ of 20 metres** tomber d'une hauteur de 20 mètres; **from a great ~** de très haut; **to be scared of ~s** avoir le vertige; **to rise to great ~s** FIG aller loin; **3** FIG (peak) **at the ~ of the season** en pleine saison; **at the ~ of** au plus fort de [*storm, crisis*]; **to be at the ~ of one's popularity/powers** être au sommet de sa popularité/son talent; **the violence was at its ~** la violence était à son comble; **the ~ of** le comble de [*luxury, stupidity, cheek*]; **to be the ~ of fashion** être ce que l'on fait de plus à la mode.

heighten /'haɪtn/ I *vtr* intensifier [*emotion*]; augmenter [*tension, suspense*]; accentuer [*effect*]; **to ~ sb's awareness of** rendre qn plus conscient de; **a ~ed awareness of** une conscience plus grande de.
II *vi* [*tension*] monter.

heinous /'heɪnəs/ *adj* SOUT abominable; **a ~ crime** un crime odieux.

heir /eə(r)/ *n* héritier/-ière *m/f* (**to** de); **his son and ~** son héritier; **to be ~ to** FIG hériter de.

heiress /'eərɪs/ *n* héritière *f*.

heirloom /'eəlu:m/ *n* héritage *m*; **a family ~** un objet de famille.

heist○ /haɪst/ US *n* vol *m*; (armed) hold-up *m inv*.

held /held/ *prét, pp* ▸ **hold**.

helices /'helɪsi:z, 'hi:-/ *pl* ▸ **helix**.

helicopter /'helɪkɒptə(r)/ I *n* hélicoptère *m*.
II *vtr* héliporter.

heliport /'helɪpɔ:t/ *n* héliport *m*.

helium /'hi:lɪəm/ *n* hélium *m*.

helix /'hi:lɪks/ *n* (*pl* **-lices** ou **-lixes**) hélice *f*.

hell /hel/ I *n* **1** (also **Hell**) RELIG enfer *m*; **in ~** en enfer; **2**○ FIG enfer *m*; **to make sb's life ~** rendre la vie infernale à qn; **to go through ~** en baver○; **3**○ (as intensifier) **a ~ of a shock** un choc terrible; **a ~ of a lot worse** nettement pire; **he's one ~ of a smart guy** US c'est fou ce qu'il est intelligent○; **we had a ~ of a time** (bad) on en a bavé○; (good) on s'est payé du bon temps○; **it sure as ~ wasn't me** une chose est sûre, ce n'était pas moi; **to run like ~** courir de toutes ses forces; **let's get the ~ out of here!** barrons-nous○!; **get the ~ out of here!** dégage○!; **like ~ I will/you are!** pas question!; **'it's a good film'—'like ~ it is!'** 'c'est un bon film'—'tu rigoles○!'; **why/who the ~?** pourquoi/qui bon Dieu○?; **how the ~ should I know?** comment je pourrais le savoir, bon Dieu○?; **oh, what the ~!** (too bad) tant pis!; **to ~ with it!** je laisse tomber○!
II○ *excl* bon Dieu○!; **go to ~**○! va te faire voir○!
IDIOMS **all ~**○ **broke loose** le raffut a éclaté; **come**

~ **or high water**○ coûte que coûte; **there was ~ to pay** il/elle l'a payé cher; **to catch ~**○ US prendre un savon○; **to do sth for the ~ of it**○ faire qch pour le plaisir; **to give sb ~**○ (cause to suffer) rendre la vie dure à qn; (scold) engueuler○ qn; **to raise (merry) ~**○ faire une scène (**with sb** à qn).

hell-bent /ˌhel'bent/ *adj* ~ **on doing** décidé à faire.

Hellenic /he'li:nɪk, US he'lenɪk/ *adj* [*civilization, language*] hellénique; [*people*] hellène.

hellfire /ˌhel'faɪə(r)/ *n* tourments *mpl* de l'enfer.

hell-for-leather○ *adj, adv* à toute allure.

hellish /'helɪʃ/ *adj* LIT d'enfer (*after n*); ○(awful) infernal○.

hello /hə'ləʊ/ *excl* **1** (greeting) bonjour!; (on phone) (receiving a call) allô!; (making a call) allô bonjour!; **2** (in surprise) tiens!

Hell's angel *n* ~ blouson *m* noir.

helm /helm/ *n* LIT, FIG barre *f*; **at the ~** à la barre.

helmet /'helmɪt/ *n* GEN casque *m*; HIST heaume *m*.

help /help/ **I** *n* **1** aide *f*; (in emergency) secours *m*; **with the ~ of** à l'aide de [*stick, knife*]; avec l'aide de [*person*]; **to be of ~ to sb** rendre service à qn; [*information, map*] être utile à qn; **you're a great ~!** IRON tu es vraiment d'un grand secours!; **to come to sb's ~** venir au secours de qn, venir en aide à qn; **to cry for ~** appeler au secours; **it's a ~ if you can speak the language** ça aide de parler la langue; **she needs (professional) ~** (from psychiatrist) elle devrait voir un psychiatre; **2** (also **daily ~**) (cleaning woman) femme *f* de ménage.
II *excl* au secours!
III *vtr* **1** aider (**to do** à faire); (more urgently) secourir; **to ~ each other** s'entraider; **can you ~ me with this sack?** est-ce que tu peux m'aider à porter ce sac?; **can I ~ you?** (in shop) vous désirez?; (on phone) j'écoute; **to ~ sb across/down/out** aider qn à traverser/descendre/sortir; **I ~ed him to his feet** je l'ai aidé à se lever; **to ~ sb on/off with** aider qn à mettre/enlever [*garment, boot*]; **he didn't ~ matters by writing that letter** il n'a rien arrangé en écrivant cette lettre; **2** (serve) **to ~ sb to** servir [qch] à qn [*food, wine*]; **3** (prevent) **it can't be ~ed!** on n'y peut rien!, tant pis!; **he can't ~ being stupid!** ce n'est pas de sa faute s'il est stupide!; **not if I can ~ it!** sûrement pas!; **he won't win if I can ~ it** je vais faire tout mon possible pour l'empêcher de gagner; **don't tell her any more than you can ~** ne lui dis pas plus qu'il n'en faut; **I can't ~ that** je n'y peux rien; **you can't ~ but pity him** on ne peut pas s'empêcher d'avoir pitié de lui.
IV *vi* aider; **he never ~s with the housework** il n'aide jamais à faire le ménage; **to ~ with the expenses** participer aux frais; **this map doesn't ~ much** cette carte n'est pas d'un grand secours; **every little ~s** (donating money) tous les dons sont les bienvenus; (saving) les petits ruisseaux font les grandes rivières; **would it ~ if I turned the light off?** est-ce que ce serait mieux si j'éteignais?
V *v refl* **to ~ oneself** se servir; **~ yourselves to coffee** prenez du café; **to ~ oneself to the petty cash** piquer○ (de l'argent) dans la caisse.
■ **help out:** ¶ **~ out** aider, donner un coup de main○; ¶ **~ [sb] out** aider, donner un coup de main○ à; (financially) dépanner○; (in crisis) tirer [qn] d'embarras [*person*].

helper /'helpə(r)/ *n* GEN aide *mf*, assistant/-e *m/f*; (for handicapped person) aide *f* sociale.

helpful /'helpfl/ *adj* [*tool, machine*] utile; [*person*] serviable; [*advice, suggestion*] utile; **I was only trying to be ~!** j'essayais seulement de me rendre utile!

helpfully /'helpfəlɪ/ *adv* obligeamment, gentiment.

helping /'helpɪŋ/ *n* portion *f*; **would you like another ~ of meat?** voulez-vous encore de la viande?; **he took a second ~ of strawberries** il a repris des fraises.

helping hand *n* **to give** OU **lend sb a ~** donner un coup de main à qn.

help key *n* COMPUT touche *f* d'aide.

---

her
When used as a direct object pronoun, *her* is translated by *la* (*l'* before a vowel). Note that the object pronoun normally comes before the verb in French and that in compound tenses like perfect and past perfect the past participle agrees with the pronoun:
> *I know her* = je la connais
> *I've already seen her* = je l'ai déjà vue

In imperatives, the direct object pronoun is translated by *la* and comes after the verb:
> *catch her!* = attrape-la! (*note the hyphen*)

When used as an indirect object pronoun, *her* is translated by *lui*:
> *I've given her the book* = je lui ai donné le livre
> *I've given it to her* = je le lui ai donné

In imperatives, the indirect object pronoun is translated by *lui* and comes after the verb:
> *phone her* = téléphone-lui
> *give them to her* = donne-les-lui (*note the hyphens*)

After prepositions and after the verb *to be* the translation is *elle*:
> *he did it for her* = il l'a fait pour elle
> *it's her* = c'est elle

When translating *her* as a determiner (*her house* etc.) remember that in French possessive adjectives, like most other adjectives, agree in gender and number with the noun they qualify; *her* is translated by *son* + masculine singular noun (*son chien*), *sa* + feminine singular noun (*sa maison*) BUT *son* + feminine noun beginning with a vowel or mute 'h' (*son assiette*), and *ses* + plural noun (*ses enfants*).
For *her* used with parts of the body ▶ 765.

helpless /'helplɪs/ *adj* **1** (powerless) [*person*] impuissant; (because of infirmity, disability) impotent; **~ with laughter** mort de rire○; **2** (defenceless) [*person*] sans défense; [*victim*] malheureux/-euse (*before n*); (destitute) [*orphan, family*] démuni.

helplessly /'helplɪslɪ/ *adv* [*watch*] sans pouvoir rien faire; [*struggle, try*] en vain, désespérément.

helplessness /'helplɪsnɪs/ *n* impuissance *f*; (because of infirmity, disability) impotence *f*; (of baby) vulnérabilité *f*.

helpline *n* service *m* d'assistance (téléphonique).

helter-skelter /ˌheltə'skeltə(r)/ **I** *n* GB toboggan *m* (en spirale).
II *adv* **to run ~** courir comme un dératé○ (or des dératés○).

hem /hem/ **I** *n* ourlet *m*; **to take up/let down the ~ on** raccourcir/rallonger [*garment*].
II *vtr* (*p prés etc* **-mm-**) faire un ourlet à [*garment*].
■ **hem in: ~ [sb/sth] in**, **~ in [sb/sth]** cerner; **to feel ~med in** FIG se sentir coincé.

hemisphere /'hemɪsfɪə(r)/ *n* MED, GEOG hémisphère *m*; **the western ~** JOURN le monde occidental.

hemlock /'hemlɒk/ *n* ciguë *f*.

hemp /hemp/ *n* chanvre *m*.

hen /hen/ **I** *n* poule *f*.
II *adj* femelle.

hence /hens/ *adv* SOUT **1** (from now) d'ici; **three days ~** d'ici or dans trois jours; **2** (for this reason) (*before n*) d'où; (*before adj*) donc; **3‡** (from this place) d'ici.

henceforth /ˌhens'fɔ:θ/, **henceforward** /ˌhens'fɔ:wəd/ *adv* LITTÉR (from now on) dorénavant; (from then on) dès lors.

henchman /'hentʃmən/ *n* PÉJ acolyte *m*.

hen: ~ coop *n* cage *f* à poules; **~house** *n* poulailler *m*.

henna /'henə/ *n* henné *m*.

hen party *n* soirée *f* passée entre femmes.

hen-pecked /'henpekt/ *adj* **~ husband** mari *m* mené par le bout du nez.

hepatitis /ˌhepə'taɪtɪs/ ▶ 1002 *n* hépatite *f*.

her /hɜ:(r), hə(r)/ **I** *pron* (direct object) la, l'; (indirect object) lui; **it's ~** c'est elle; **I did it for ~** je l'ai fait pour elle.

herald /'herəld/ **I** n LIT héraut m; FIG signe m avant-coureur.
II vtr (also **~ in**) annoncer.

heraldic /he'rældɪk/ adj héraldique.

heraldry /'herəldrɪ/ n (study, history) héraldique f.

herb /hɜːb/ n herbe f; **mixed ~s ~** herbes de Provence.

herbaceous border /hɜː'beɪʃəs 'bɔːdə(r)/ n bordure f de plantes herbacées.

herbal /'hɜːbl/ adj [remedy] à base de plantes.

herbalist /'hɜːbəlɪst/ ▶1251 n herboriste mf.

herb garden n: jardin de plantes aromatiques utilisées en cuisine.

herb tea, **herbal tea** n tisane f, infusion f.

herd /hɜːd/ **I** n GEN troupeau m; (of reindeer) harde f; (of people) troupeau m; **~ instinct** instinct m grégaire.
II vtr rassembler.
III vi **to ~ into sth** s'assembler dans qch.
IDIOMS **to follow the ~** FIG être un mouton de Panurge.
■ **herd together** se rassembler; (closely) se masser.

here /hɪə(r)/

■ **Note** When here is used to indicate the location of an object/point etc close to the speaker, it is generally translated by ici: come and sit here = viens t'asseoir ici.
– When the location is not so clearly defined, là is the usual translation: he's not here at the moment = il n'est pas là pour l'instant.
– Remember that voici is used to translate here is and here are when the speaker is drawing attention to an object/a place/a person etc physically close to him or her.
– For examples and particular usages, see entry below.

I adv **1** ici; **far from/near ~** loin/près d'ici; **two kilometres from ~** à deux kilomètres d'ici; **come over ~** venez par ici; **up to ~, down to ~** jusqu'ici; **I'm up ~** je suis là-haut; **~ lies** (on tombstone) ci-gît; **since you were last ~** depuis ta dernière visite ici; **~ and there** par endroits; **~ they are/she comes!** les/la voici!; **~ is my key/are my keys** voici ma clé/mes clés; **~ comes the bus** voilà le bus; **~ you are** (offering sth) tiens, tenez; **my colleague ~** mon/ma collègue; **which one? this one ~ or that one?** lequel? celui-ci ou celui-là?; **~'s what you do** voilà ce qu'il faut faire; **2** (indicating presence, arrival) **she's not ~ right now** elle n'est pas là pour le moment; **'John?'—'~ sir'** (revealing whereabouts) 'John?'—'ici Monsieur'; (during roll call) 'John?'—'présent Monsieur'; **~ we are at last** nous voilà enfin; **the train will be ~ any minute** le train va arriver d'un moment à l'autre; **we get off ~** c'est là qu'on descend; **now that summer's ~** maintenant que c'est l'été; **~'s our chance** voilà notre chance; **3**○ (emphatic) **this ~ contraption** ce truc○; **look** ou **see ~, you!** écoute-moi bien toi!
II○ excl hé!
IDIOMS **~ goes!** c'est parti!; **~'s hoping** j'espère; **~'s to our success/to you!** à notre succès/la tienne!; **~ there and everywhere** partout, par-ci par-là; **it's neither ~ nor there** (unimportant) c'est sans importance; (irrelevant) ça n'a aucun rapport.

hereabout US, **hereabouts** GB /'hɪərəbaʊt(s)/ adv par ici.

hereafter /hɪər'ɑːftə(r)/ **I** n **the ~** l'au-delà m.
II adv JUR ci-après.

here and now **I** n **the ~** (present) le présent.
II adv immédiatement.

hereby /hɪə'baɪ/ adv ADMIN, JUR **I — declare that** (in document) je déclare par la présente que.

hereditary /hɪ'redɪtrɪ, US -terɪ/ adj héréditaire.

heredity /hɪ'redətɪ/ n hérédité f.

heresy /'herəsɪ/ n (all contexts) hérésie f.

heretic /'herətɪk/ n hérétique m.

heretical /hɪ'retɪkl/ adj hérétique.

herewith /,hɪəwɪð/ adv SOUT ci-joint.

heritage /'herɪtɪdʒ/ n patrimoine m.

hermetic /hɜː'metɪk/ adj hermétique.

hermetically /hɜː'metɪklɪ/ adv hermétiquement.

hermit /'hɜːmɪt/ n ermite m.

hernia /'hɜːnɪə/ n (pl **~s** ou **~e**) hernie f.

hero /'hɪərəʊ/ n (pl **~es**) héros m; **a ~'s welcome** un accueil triomphal.

heroic /hɪ'rəʊɪk/ adj héroïque.

heroically /hɪ'rəʊɪklɪ/ adv héroïquement.

heroics /hɪ'rəʊɪks/ npl mélodrame m.

heroin /'herəʊɪn/ n héroïne f.

heroin addict n héroïnomane mf.

heroine /'herəʊɪn/ n héroïne f.

heroism /'herəʊɪzəm/ n héroïsme m.

heron /'herən/ n héron m.

hero-worship /'hɪərəʊwɜːʃɪp/ **I** n culte m du héros, adulation f.
II vtr (p prés etc **-pp-**, US **-p-**) aduler.

herpes /'hɜːpiːz/ ▶1002 n herpès m.

herring /'herɪŋ/ n hareng m.

herringbone n (design) motif m à chevrons.

hers /hɜːz/

■ **Note** In French, possessive pronouns reflect the gender and number of the noun they are standing for; hers is translated by le sien, la sienne, les siens, les siennes, according to what is being referred to.
– For examples and particular usages, see the entry below.

pron **my car is red but ~ is blue** ma voiture est rouge mais la sienne est bleue; **the green pen is ~** le stylo vert est à elle; **which house is ~?** sa maison c'est laquelle?; **I'm a friend of ~** c'est une amie à moi; **it's not ~** ce n'est pas à elle, ce n'est pas le sien ou la sienne; **the money wasn't ~ to give away** elle n'avait pas le droit de donner cet argent; **~ was not an easy task** sa tâche n'était pas facile.

herself /hɜː'self/

■ **Note** When used as a reflexive pronoun, direct and indirect, herself is translated by se (s' before a vowel): she's enjoying herself = elle s'amuse bien; she's cut herself = elle s'est coupée.
– When used in emphasis, the translation is elle or elle-même: she herself didn't know = elle ne le savait pas elle-même.
– After a preposition the translation is elle or elle-même: she can be proud of herself = elle peut être fière d'elle or d'elle-même.

pron **she's hurt ~** elle s'est blessée; **for ~** pour elle, pour elle-même; **(all) by ~** toute seule; **she's not ~ today** elle n'est pas dans son assiette aujourd'hui.

Herts n GB POST abrév écrite = **Hertfordshire**.

he's /hiːz/ = **he is, he has**.

hesitancy /'hezɪtənsɪ/ n hésitation f.

hesitant /'hezɪtənt/ adj hésitant; **to be ~ about doing** hésiter à faire; **to be ~ about** (reticent) être réticent quant à [plan, scheme].

hesitantly /'hezɪtəntlɪ/ adv [act] avec hésitation; [speak] d'un ton hésitant.

hesitate /'hezɪteɪt/ vi hésiter (**over** sur; **to do** à faire).
IDIOMS **he who ~s is lost** PROV à hésiter on n'obtient rien.

hesitation /,hezɪ'teɪʃn/ n hésitation f; **to have no ~ in doing** n'avoir aucune hésitation à faire.

hessian /'hesɪən, US 'heʃn/ n toile f de jute.

heterogeneous /,hetərə'dʒiːnɪəs/ adj hétérogène.

heterosexual /,hetərə'sekʃʊəl/ n, adj hétérosexuel/-elle (m/f).

het up○ /,het'ʌp/ adj énervé; **to get ~ about sth** s'énerver à cause de qch.

hew /hjuː/ (pp **hewn**) vtr abattre [wood, coal]; tailler [statue, canoe] (**out of** dans).

hexagon /'heksəgən, US -gɒn/ n hexagone m.

hey° /heɪ/ *excl* (call for attention) hé!, eh!; (in protest) dis donc!

heyday /'heɪdeɪ/ *n* (of movement etc) âge *m* d'or; (of person) beaux jours *mpl*; **in her ~** quand elle était à la sommet de sa gloire.

hey presto /ˌheɪ 'prestəʊ/ *excl* ô miracle!, et passez muscade!; (in narrative) comme par miracle.

hi° /haɪ/ *excl* salut°!

HI US POST *abrév écrite* = **Hawaii**.

hiatus /haɪ'eɪtəs/ *n* (*pl* **~es** *ou* **~**) (pause) temps *m* d'arrêt; (gap) lacune *f*; LING, LITERAT hiatus *m*.

hibernate /'haɪbəneɪt/ *vi* hiberner.

hibernation /ˌhaɪbə'neɪʃn/ *n* hibernation *f*.

hiccup, hiccough /'hɪkʌp/ **I** *n* **1** LIT hoquet *m*; **to have (the) ~s** avoir le hoquet; **2** FIG (setback) anicroche *f*.

II *vi* (*p prés etc* **-p-** *ou* **-pp-**) hoqueter.

hick° /hɪk/ PÉJ *n* plouc° *mf*; **~ town** trou° *m*.

hid /hɪd/ *prét* ▶ **hide**.

hidden /'hɪdn/ **I** *pp* ▶ **hide**.

II *adj* caché; **~ from view** caché, invisible.

hide /haɪd/ **I** *n* (skin) peau *f*; (leather) cuir *m*.

II *vtr* (*prét* **hid**; *pp* **hidden**) cacher (*object, person*) (**from** à); ne pas montrer (*feeling*) (**from** à).

III *vi* (*prét* **hid**; *pp* **hidden**) se cacher.

■ **hide away**: **~** [sth] **away**, **~ away** [sth] cacher.

■ **hide out** GB, **hide up** US se cacher, se planquer°.

hide: **~ and seek** GB, **~-and-go-seek** US ▶ 949 | *n* cache-cache *m inv*; **~away** *n* retraite *f*.

hidebound /'haɪdbaʊnd/ *adj* conventionnel/-elle.

hideous /'hɪdɪəs/ *adj* [*person, monster, object*] hideux/ -euse; [*noise*] affreux/-euse; [*murder*] odieux/-ieuse, atroce.

hideously /'hɪdɪəslɪ/ *adv* atrocement.

hideout *n* cachette *f*.

hiding /'haɪdɪŋ/ *n* **1 to go into ~** se cacher; **to come out of ~** sortir de sa cachette; **~ place** cachette *f*; **2** (beating) correction *f*; **to give sb a (good) ~** administrer une (bonne) correction à qn.

IDIOMS **to be on a ~ to nothing** ne pas avoir la moindre chance de réussir or de gagner.

hierarchic(al) /ˌhaɪə'rɑːkɪk(l)/ *adj* hiérarchique.

hierarchy /'haɪərɑːkɪ/ *n* hiérarchie *f*.

hieroglyph, hieroglyphic /'haɪərəglɪf, ˌhaɪərə'glɪfɪk/ *n* LIT, FIG hiéroglyphe *m*.

hi-fi /'haɪfaɪ/ *n* **1** (set of equipment) chaîne *f* hi-fi *inv*, hi-fi *f inv*; **2** (*abrév* = **high fidelity**) hi-fi *f inv*, haute-fidélité *f inv*.

higgledy-piggledy /ˌhɪgldɪ'pɪgldɪ/ *adj, adv* pêle-mêle (*inv*).

high /haɪ/ ▶ 1045 | **I** *n* **1 an all-time ~** un niveau record; **to reach a new ~** atteindre son niveau le plus élevé; **2**° **to give sb a ~** [*drug*] défoncer° qn; [*success*] monter à la tête de qn; **to be on a ~** être en pleine euphorie; **3**° US SCH = **high school**.

II *adj* **1** [*building, wall, cliff*] haut; [*table, forehead, collar*] haut (*after n*); [*cheekbones*] pommettes *fpl* saillantes; **how ~ is the cliff?** quelle est la hauteur de la falaise?; **it is 50 m ~** ça fait 50 m de haut; **I've known him since he was so ~** il n'était pas plus grand que ça quand je l'ai connu; **at ~ tide** à marée haute; **how ~ (up) are we?** (on top of building) on est à combien de mètres au-dessus du sol?; (on plane, mountain) quelle est notre altitude?; **2** [*number, ratio, price, frequency, volume*] élevé; [*wind*] violent; [*hope, expectation*] grand (*before n*); **at ~ speed** à grande vitesse; **to have a ~ temperature** avoir de la fièvre; **~ in** riche en [*fat, iron*]; **on a ~ heat** à feu vif; **to have a ~ colour** avoir le teint rougeaud; **a moment of ~ drama** un moment de grande émotion; **in ~ summer** au cœur de l'été; **feelings are running ~** les esprits s'échauffent; **3** (important) [*quality, standard, rank*] supérieur; **I have it on the ~est authority** je tiens cela des autorités les plus haut placées; **to have friends in ~ places** avoir des amis haut placés; **to be ~ up** être haut placé; **to go on to ~er things**

faire son chemin dans le monde; **4** (noble) [*ideal, principle*] noble; **5** (acute) [*pitch, sound, voice*] aigu/ -guë; [*note*] haut; **6** CULIN [*game*] faisandé; **7**° (euphoric) (on drug) défoncé°; (happy) ivre de joie; **to be ~** on être défoncé à [*drug*]; **to get ~** se défoncer°.

III *adv* **1** (to a great height) haut; **~er up** plus haut; **to climb ~er and ~er** [*person, animal*] grimper de plus en plus haut; FIG [*figures, unemployment*] augmenter de plus en plus; **don't go any ~er than £5,000** ne dépasse pas 5 000 livres sterling; **from on ~** GEN d'en haut; RELIG du Ciel; **2** (at a high level, pitch) [*set, turn on*] fort; [*sing, play*] haut; **to turn sth up ~** monter qch.

IDIOMS **it's ~ time that sb went** il est grand temps que qn y aille; **to hold one's head (up) ~** marcher la tête haute; **to search ~ and low for sth** remuer ciel et terre pour trouver qch.

high and dry *adj* **to leave sb ~** FIG laisser qn en plan°.

high: **~ beam** *n* US pleins phares *mpl*; **~born** *adj* de haute naissance; **~brow** *n, adj* intellectuel/-elle (*m/f*); **~ chair** *n* chaise *f* haute; **High Church** *n* de la Haute Église; **~-class** *adj* [*hotel, shop, car, prostitute*] de luxe; [*goods*] de première qualité; [*area*] de grand standing; **~ command** *n* haut commandement *m*; **~ commission** *n* haut-commissariat *m*; **~ commissioner** ▶ 1251 | *n* haut-commissaire *m*; **~ court** *n* cour *f* suprême; **~-definition** *adj* (à) haute définition *inv*; **~ diving** ▶ 949 | *n* plongeon *m* de haut vol; **~er education** *n* enseignement *m* supérieur; **~er mathematics** *n* (+ *v sg*) mathématiques *fpl* abstraites; **~falutin(g)**° *adj* [*language*] ampoulé; [*ideas*] prétentieux/-ieuse; **~ fashion** *n* haute couture *f*; **~-fibre** *adj* riche en fibres; **~-fidelity** *n, adj* haute-fidélité (*f*) (*inv*); **~ finance** *n* haute finance *f*; **~-flier** *n* jeune loup *m*, ambitieux/-ieuse *m/f*; **~-flown** *adj* ampoulé; **~-flying** *adj* [*aircraft*] capable de voler à haute altitude; FIG [*person*] ambitieux/-ieuse; [*career*] de haut vol; **~-frequency** *adj* (à) haute fréquence; **High German** ▶ 1038 | *n* haut allemand *m*; **~-grade** *adj* de haute qualité.

high ground *n* colline(s) *f(pl)*; **on ~** [*built*] sur une colline; [*rain*] en altitude; **to take the (moral) ~** FIG prendre une position moraliste.

high: **~-handed** *adj* despotique; **~-handedly** *adv* despotiquement; **~-heeled** *adj* à talon haut; **~ heels** *npl* hauts talons *mpl*.

high jinks° /ˌhaɪ 'dʒɪŋks/ *npl* **to get up to ~** se payer du bon temps°.

high jump ▶ 949 | *n* SPORT saut *m* en hauteur.

Highland: **~ fling** *n* danse *f* écossaise; **~ games** *npl* jeux *mpl* écossais.

highlands /'haɪləndz/ *npl* régions *fpl* montagneuses.

Highlands /'haɪləndz/ *pr npl* Highlands *mpl*, Hautes-Terres *fpl* (d'Écosse).

high: **~-level** *adj* [*talks*] à haut niveau; [*official*] de haut niveau; **~ life** *n* grande vie *f*.

highlight /'haɪlaɪt/ **I** *n* **1** ART rehaut *m*; **2** (in hair) (natural) reflet *m*; (artificial) mèche *f*; **3** FIG (of exhibition) clou *m*; (of match, show) point *m* culminant; (of week, year) point *m* fort.

II highlights *npl* SPORT, RADIO, TV résumé *m*.

III *vtr* (*prét, pp* **-lighted**) **1** ART rehausser; **2** [*sun, light*] éclairer; **3** (with fluorescent pen) surligner; **4** FIG (emphasize) mettre l'accent sur, souligner.

highlighter /'haɪlaɪtə(r)/ *n* (pen) surligneur *m*.

highly /'haɪlɪ/ *adv* [*dangerous, developed, intelligent*] extrêmement; **~ unlikely** fort peu probable; **to speak/think ~ of sb** dire/penser beaucoup de bien de qn; **to praise sb ~** chanter les louanges de qn.

highly: **~-charged** *adj* [*atmosphere*] très tendu; **~-coloured** GB, **~-colored** US *adj* aux couleurs vives; FIG enjolivé; **~-paid** *adj* très bien payé; **~-polished** *adj* d'un beau poli; **~-strung** *adj* très tendu.

high: **High Mass** n grand-messe f; **~-minded** adj [person] à l'âme noble; **~-necked** adj à col montant.

Highness /ˈhaɪnɪs/ ▶937 n His ou Her (Royal) ~ Son Altesse f.

high noon n plein midi m; **at ~** en plein midi.

high: **~-performance** adj performant; **~-pitched** adj [voice, sound] aigu/-uë; **~ point** n FIG point m culminant; **~-powered** adj [car, engine] de grande puissance; [person] dynamique; [job] de haute responsabilité.

high pressure I n METEOROL hautes pressions f.
II noun modifier TECH à haute pression; FIG [job] à haute responsabilité.

high: **~ priest** n RELIG grand prêtre m; FIG pape m (of de); **~ priestess** n RELIG, FIG grande prêtresse f (of de); **~-principled** adj [person] de haute moralité; **~-profile** adj [politician, group] bien en vue; [visit] qui fait beaucoup de bruit; **~-ranking** adj de haut rang; **~ rise** (**building**) n tour f (d'habitation); **~-risk** adj à haut risque; **~ road** n grand-route f; **~ school** n US SCH ≈ lycée m; GB SCH établissement m secondaire.

high sea n **on the ~s** en haute mer.

high: **~ season** n haute saison f; **~ society** n haute société f; **~-sounding** adj ronflant; **~-speed** adj [train] à grande vitesse; [boat] rapide; [film] ultrarapide; **~-spirited** adj plein d'entrain.

high spirits npl entrain m; **to be in ~** être plein d'entrain.

high spot n point m culminant.

high street GB (also **High Street**) n (in town) rue f principale; (in village) grand-rue f; **~ spending** dépenses fpl de consommation courante.

high: **~-street shop** ▶1251 n boutique f appartenant à une chaîne; **~ tea** n GB goûter m dînatoire.

high tech /ˌhaɪ ˈtek/ I n (interior design) high-tech m.
II° **high-tech** adj [industry] de pointe; [equipment, car] ultramoderne; [furniture] high-tech inv.

high: **~ tide** n marée f haute; **~ treason** n haute trahison f; **~ voltage** n haute tension f.

highway /ˈhaɪweɪ/ n GB route f nationale; US autoroute f; **public** ou **king's** ou **queen's ~** GB voie f publique; **~s and byways** chemins et sentiers.

highway: **Highway Code** n GB Code m de la Route; **~man** n bandit m de grand chemin; **~ patrol** n US police f de la route; **~ robbery** n LIT banditisme m.

high wire n corde f raide.

hijack /ˈhaɪdʒæk/ I n détournement m d'avion.
II vtr détourner [plane]; FIG s'approprier [theory]; récupérer [event, demonstration].

hijacker /ˈhaɪdʒækə(r)/ n (of plane) pirate m (de l'air); (of bus, truck) pirate m (de la route).

hijacking /ˈhaɪdʒækɪŋ/ n détournement m.

hike /haɪk/ I n randonnée f; **to go on** ou **for a ~** faire une randonnée.
II vi faire de la randonnée.
III vtr (also **~ up**) augmenter [rate, price].

hiker /ˈhaɪkə(r)/ n randonneur/-euse m/f.

hiking /ˈhaɪkɪŋ/ ▶949 n randonnée f.

hilarious /hɪˈleərɪəs/ adj désopilant, hilarant.

hilarity /hɪˈlærətɪ/ n hilarité f.

hill /hɪl/ n colline f; (hillside) coteau m; (incline) pente f, côte f; **over ~ and dale** LITTÉR par monts et par vaux.
IDIOMS **as old as the ~s** vieux comme Hérode; **to be over the ~** ne plus être de première jeunesse.

hillbilly /ˈhɪlbɪlɪ/ n US PÉJ péquenaud/-e° m/f PÉJ.

hillock /ˈhɪlək/ n petite colline f.

hillside /ˈhɪlsaɪd/ n **on the ~** à flanc de coteau.

hilltop /ˈhɪltɒp/ n sommet m de colline.

hilly /ˈhɪlɪ/ adj vallonné.

hilt /hɪlt/ n (of sword) poignée f; **(up) to the ~** LIT jusqu'à la garde; FIG (in debt) jusqu'au cou; **to back sb (up) to the ~** donner son appui inconditionnel à qn.

him /hɪm/

■ Note When used as a direct object pronoun, him is translated by le (l' before a vowel). Note that the object pronoun normally comes before the verb in French: I know him = je le connais; I've already seen him = je l'ai déjà vu.
– In imperatives, the direct object pronoun is translated by le and comes after the verb: catch him! = attrape-le! (note the hyphen).
– When used as an indirect object pronoun, him is translated by lui: I've given him the book = je lui ai donné le livre; I've given it to him = je le lui ai donné.
– In imperatives, the indirect object pronoun is translated by lui and comes after the verb: phone him! = téléphone-lui!; give it to him = donne-le-lui (note the hyphens).
– After prepositions and after the verb to be the translation is lui: she did it for him = elle l'a fait pour lui; it's him = c'est lui.

pron **1** (direct object) le, l'; **I like ~** je l'aime bien; **catch ~!** attrape-le!; **2** (indirect object, after prep) lui.

Himalayas /ˌhɪməˈleɪəz/ pr npl (montagnes fpl de) l'Himalaya m.

himself /hɪmˈself/

■ Note When used as a reflexive pronoun, direct and indirect, himself is translated by se (s' before a vowel): he's enjoying himself = il s'amuse bien; he's cut himself = il s'est coupé.
– When used in emphasis the translation is lui-même: he himself didn't know = il ne le savait pas lui-même.
– After a preposition, the translation is lui or lui-même: he can be proud of himself = il peut être fier de lui or de lui-même.
– For particular usages see below.

pron **he's hurt ~** il s'est blessé; **for ~** pour lui, pour lui-même; **(all) by ~** tout seul; **he's not ~ today** il n'est pas dans son assiette aujourd'hui.

hind /haɪnd/ I n (pl **~s** ou **~**) ZOOL biche f.
II adj de derrière; **~ legs** pattes fpl de derrière.

hinder /ˈhɪndə(r)/ vtr (hamper) entraver; (delay) freiner [progress, efforts]; retarder [plan].

hindquarters /ˌhaɪndˈkwɔːtəz/ npl arrière-train m.

hindrance /ˈhɪndrəns/ n entrave f; **to be a ~ to sb/sth** gêner qn/qch.

hindsight /ˈhaɪndsaɪt/ n **with (the benefit of) ~** avec du recul, rétrospectivement.

Hindu /ˌhɪnˈduː, US ˈhɪnduː/ ▶1100 I n Hindou/-e m/f.
II adj hindou.

Hinduism /ˈhɪnduːɪzəm/ n hindouisme m.

Hindustani /ˌhɪnduˈstɑːnɪ/ ▶1038 n, adj hindoustani (m), hindi (m).

hinge /hɪndʒ/ I n GEN charnière f; (lift-off) gond m; **to come off its ~s** [door] sortir de ses gonds.
II vi (p prés **hingeing**) **to ~ on** dépendre de.

hint /hɪnt/ I n allusion f (about à); FIG (of spice, flavouring, accent) pointe f; (of colour) touche f; (of smile) ébauche f; (of irony, humour) soupçon m; **~ broad** = allusion transparente; **to give a ~** faire allusion (about à); **to drop ~s** faire des allusions; **to drop ~s that** laisser entendre que; **to take a ~** ou **the ~** saisir l'allusion; **all right, I can take a ~** c'est bon, j'ai compris; **to give sb some useful ~s** donner quelques conseils utiles à qn.
II vtr **to ~ that** laisser entendre que (**to** à).
■ hint at: **~ at** [sth] faire allusion à.

hinterland /ˈhɪntəlænd/ n arrière-pays m inv.

hip /hɪp/ I n **1** ▶765 hanche f; **to break one's ~** se casser le col du fémur; **2** BOT gratte-cul m.
II° adj [person] branché.
III excl **~ hurrah!** hip hip hip hourra!

hip: **~bone** n os m iliaque; **~ flask** n flasque f.

hip measurement, **hip size** n tour m de hanches.

hippie, **hippy** /ˈhɪpɪ/ n, adj hippie (mf), hippy (mf).

hippo /ˈhɪpəʊ/ n hippopotame m.

hip pocket n poche f revolver.

Hippocratic /ˌhɪpəˈkrætɪk/ adj **~ oath** serment m d'Hippocrate.

hippopotamus /ˌhɪpə'pɒtəməs/ n (pl **-muses** ou **-mi**) hippopotame m.

hip replacement n prothèse f de la hanche.

hire /'haɪə(r)/ **I** n location f; **car ~** location de voitures; **to let sth out on ~** louer qch; **for ~** [boat, skis] à louer; [taxi] libre.
II noun modifier [car, charge, firm] de location.
III vtr louer [equipment]; engager [person].

hire purchase, **HP** n achat m à crédit; **on ~** à crédit.

his /hɪz/

■ Note In French determiners agree in gender and number with the noun they qualify. So his when used as a determiner is translated by son + masculine singular noun (son chien), by sa + feminine singular noun (sa maison) BUT by son + feminine noun beginning with a vowel or mute h (son assiette) and by ses + plural noun (ses enfants).
– When his is stressed, à lui is added after the noun: HIS house = sa maison à lui.
– For his used with parts of the body ▶ 765 .
– In French possessive pronouns reflect the gender and number of the noun they are standing for. When used as a possessive pronoun his is translated by le sien, la sienne, les siens or les siennes according to what is being referred to.
– For examples and particular usages see the entry below.

I det son/sa/ses.
II pron **all the drawings were good but ~ was the best** tous les dessins étaient bons mais le sien était le meilleur; **the blue car is ~** la voiture bleue est la sienne, la voiture bleue est à lui; **it's not ~** ce n'est pas à lui; **which house is ~?** sa maison c'est laquelle?; **I'm a colleague of ~** je suis un/-e de ses collègues; **that dog of ~** PÉJ son sale chien○; **the money was not ~ to give away** il n'avait pas le droit de donner cet argent.

Hispanic /hɪ'spænɪk/ adj (Spanish) hispanique; (Latin American) latino-américain.

hiss /hɪs/ **I** n sifflement m; (of tape) grésillement m.
II vtr siffler [person, performance, speech].
III vi [person, steam, snake] siffler; [cat] cracher; [fat, cassette] grésiller.

historian /hɪ'stɔːrɪən/ ▶ 1251 n historien/-ienne m/f; **ancient ~** spécialiste mf d'histoire de l'Antiquité.

historic /hɪ'stɒrɪk, US -'stɔːr-/ adj 1 GEN historique; LING **past ~** passé m simple; **~ present** présent m de narration.

historical /hɪ'stɒrɪkl, US -'stɔːr-/ adj historique.

historically /hɪ'stɒrɪklɪ, US -'stɔːr-/ adv historiquement; **~ speaking** d'un point de vue historique.

history /'hɪstrɪ/ **I** n 1 (past) histoire f; **French ~** histoire de France; **18th century French ~** histoire de la France au XVIIIᵉ siècle; **~ of art** histoire de l'art; **a place in ~** une place dans l'histoire; **to make ~** entrer dans l'histoire; **to go down in ~ as** entrer dans l'histoire comme; 2 (past experience) antécédents mpl; **to have a ~ of heart trouble** avoir des antécédents cardiaques; **to have a ~ of violence** avoir un passé violent; 3 (account) histoire f; 4 (tradition) tradition f.
II noun modifier [book, teacher] d'histoire.
IDIOMS **the rest is ~** tout le monde connaît la suite.

histrionic /ˌhɪstrɪ'ɒnɪk/ **I histrionics** npl cinéma○ m.
II adj PÉJ mélodramatique, théâtral.

hit /hɪt/ **I** n 1 (blow, stroke in sport) coup m; (in fencing) touche f; **to score a ~** SPORT, FIG marquer un point; 2 (success) (play, film etc) succès m; (record) tube○ m; **to be a big** ou **smash ~** avoir un succès fou; **to make a ~ with sb** faire grosse impression sur qn.
II vtr (p prés **-tt-**; prét, pp **hit**) 1 (strike) frapper [person, ball]; [head, arm] cogner contre [wall]; **to ~ one's head on sth** se cogner la tête contre qch; **his father used to ~ him** son père le battait; **to ~ a good shot** (in tennis, cricket) jouer une bonne balle; **to**

~ the brakes○ écraser le frein; 2 (strike as target) atteindre [victim, target, enemy]; 3 (collide violently with) heurter [wall]; (more violently) percuter [wall]; [vehicle] renverser [person]; 4 (affect adversely) affecter, toucher; 5 (become apparent to) **it suddenly hit me that** je me suis soudain rendu compte que; 6 (reach) arriver à [motorway]; FIG [figures, weight] atteindre [level]; 7 (come upon) rencontrer [traffic, bad weather]; 8○ (go to) **to ~ the town** sortir s'amuser; 9○ (attack) [robbers] attaquer [bank].
IDIOMS **a colour which ~s you between the eyes** une couleur criarde; **to ~ the roof**○ sauter au plafond○; **to ~ it off with sb** bien s'entendre avec qn; **not to know what has hit one**○ être sidéré.
■ **hit back**: ¶ **~ back** riposter; ¶ **~ [sb] back** rendre un coup à [qn]; ¶ **~ [sth] back** renvoyer [ball].
■ **hit out at**: **~ out at** [sth] (criticise) attaquer.
■ **hit upon**, **hit on**: **~ (up)on** [sth] avoir [idea]; découvrir [evidence, solution]; tomber sur [problem].

hit-and-miss adj [method] approximatif/-ive; [affair, undertaking] hasardeux/-euse.

hit-and-run adj [raid, attack] éclair inv; [accident] où le chauffeur a pris la fuite; **~ driver** chauffeur m en délit de fuite.

hitch /hɪtʃ/ **I** n 1 (problem) problème m, pépin○ m; **slight ~** un petit pépin○; 2 (knot) nœud m.
II vtr 1 (fasten) attacher [trailer]; atteler [horse]; accrocher [rail carriage]; 2○ (thumb) **to ~ a lift** faire du stop○.
III○ vi faire du stop○.
IDIOMS **to get ~ed** convoler en justes noces○.
■ **hitch up**: **~ up** [sth], **~ [sth] up** 1 (pull up) retrousser [skirt]; remonter [trousers, covers]; 2 = II 1.

hitchhike /'hɪtʃhaɪk/ vi faire du stop○ m; **to ~ to Paris** aller à Paris en stop○.

hitch: **~hiker** n auto-stoppeur/-euse mf/s; **~hiking** n auto-stop m.

hi-tech = **high tech**.

hither‡ /'hɪðə(r)/ adv ici; **~ and thither** de ci, de là.

hitherto /ˌhɪðə'tuː/ adv (until now) jusqu'à présent; (until then) jusqu'alors.

hit: **~ list** n liste f noire; **~ man** n tueur m (à gages); **~ parade** n palmarès m, hit-parade m; **~ single** n tube○ m.

HIV n (abrév = **human immunodeficiency virus**) (virus m) VIH m.

hive /haɪv/ **I** n 1 (beehive) ruche f; **a ~ of activity** ou **industry** FIG une vraie ruche; 2 (swarm) essaim m.
II hives npl ▶ 1002 urticaire f.
■ **hive off** (separate off) séparer; (sell off) céder.

HIV positive adj séropositif/-ive (au virus VIH).

HMI n (abrév = **His/Her Majesty's Inspector**) inspecteur m (qui se rend dans les écoles).

HMS n (abrév = **His/Her Majesty's Ship**) ~ bâtiment m de Sa Majesté; **~ Victory** le (HMS) Victoire.

HMSO n (abrév = **His/Her Majesty's Stationery Office**) service gouvernemental de publication.

HNC n GB (abrév = **Higher National Certificate**) ~ BTS m.

HND n GB (abrév = **Higher National Diploma**) diplôme supérieur d'aptitudes techniques.

hoard /hɔːd/ **I** n (of treasure) trésor m; (of provisions) provisions fpl; (of miser) magot○ m.
II vtr [person] stocker [supplies] ALSO PEJ; amasser [objects, money]; [animal] amasser [food].

hoarding /'hɔːdɪŋ/ n GB 1 (billboard) panneau m publicitaire; 2 (fence) palissade f; 3 (saving) accumulation f.

hoarfrost /'hɔːfrɒst, US -frɔːst/ n gelée f blanche, givre m.

hoarse /hɔːs/ adj [voice] rauque; **to be ~** être enroué; **to shout oneself ~** s'enrouer à force de crier.

hoary /'hɔːrɪ/ adj 1 [person] chenu, aux cheveux blancs; 2 FIG **a ~ old joke** une plaisanterie éculée.

hoax /həʊks/ **I** n (practical joke) canular m; **it was a ~** (bomb) c'était une fausse alerte à la bombe.

II *noun modifier* [*call, warning*] bidon○ *inv*.

hob /hɒb/ *n* (on stove) table *f* de cuisson; (on open fire) plaque *f* (*sur laquelle on tient la bouilloire au chaud*).

hobble /'hɒbl/ *vi* (limp) boitiller; **to ~ in/along** entrer/avancer clopin-clopant○.

hobby /'hɒbɪ/ *n* passe-temps *m inv*; **hobbies and interests** (on CV) centres *mpl* d'intérêt.

hobby horse *n* **1** (toy) *bâton emmanché d'une tête de cheval en bois*; **2** (obsession) dada *m* PÉJ; cheval *m* de bataille.

hobgoblin /'hɒbgɒblɪn/ *n* gnome *m*, lutin *m*.

hobnob○ /'hɒbnɒb/ *vi* (*p prés etc* **-bb-**) **to ~ with sb** frayer○ avec qn.

hobo /'həʊbəʊ/ *n* (*pl* **~s** ou **~es**) clochard/-e *m/f*, vagabond/-e *m/f*.

hock /hɒk/ *n* **1** (of horse etc) jarret *m*; CULIN jarret *m* (de porc); **2** (wine) vin *m* du Rhin; **3**○ (pawn) **to be in ~** être au clou○, être engagé au mont-de-piété.

hockey /'hɒkɪ/ *n* ▶ 949 | *n* GB hockey *m*; US hockey *m* sur glace; **~ stick** crosse *f* de hockey.

hocus-pocus /ˌhəʊkəs'pəʊkəs/ *n* PÉJ (trickery) supercherie *f*, tour *m* de passe-passe.

hod /hɒd/ *n* (for coal) seau *m* à charbon; (for bricks) oiseau *m*, hotte *f*.

hoe /həʊ/ **I** *n* houe *f*, binette *f*.

II *vtr* biner [*ground*]; sarcler [*plants, flowerbeds*].

hoedown /'həʊdaʊn/ *n* bal *m* (de village).

hog /hɒg/ **I** *n* **1** GB (castrated pig) porc *m* châtré; **2** US (pig) porc *m*, verrat *m*; **3**○ (person) pourceau *m*.

II○ *vtr* (*prét, pp* **-gg-**) monopoliser.

IDIOMS **to go the whole ~**○ (be extravagant) voir les choses en grand; (go to extremes) aller jusqu'au bout.

Hogmanay /'hɒgmaneɪ/ *n* GB DIAL Saint-Sylvestre *f*, réveillon *m*.

hog-tie /'hɒgtaɪ/ *vtr* lier les pattes de [*pig, cow*]; US FIG réduire [qn] à l'impuissance [*person*].

hogwash /'hɒgwɒʃ/ *n* foutaise○ *f*.

hoi polloi /ˌhɔɪ pə'lɔɪ/ *npl* PÉJ plèbe *f* PÉJ, populace *f*.

hoist /hɔɪst/ **I** *n* palan *m*; **to give sb a ~** (up) faire la courte échelle à qn.

II *vtr* hisser [*flag, sail, heavy object*].

hoity-toity○ /ˌhɔɪtɪ'tɔɪtɪ/ *adj* PÉJ prétentieux/-ieuse.

hokum○ /'həʊkəm/ *n* ¢ US (nonsense) absurdités *fpl*, niaiseries *fpl*; (sentimentality) mièvrerie *f*.

hold /həʊld/ ▶ 789 | **I** *n* **1** (grasp) prise *f*; **to get ~ of** attraper; **to keep** (a) **~ of** ou **on** tenir; **2** (possession) **to get ~ of** se procurer [*book, ticket*]; [*press*] avoir vent de [*story*]; découvrir [*information*]; **3** (contact) **to get ~ of** (by phone) joindre; (by other means) trouver; **4** (control) emprise *f* (**on, over** sur); **to have a ~ on** ou **over sb** avoir de l'emprise sur qn; **to get a ~ of oneself** se reprendre; **5** TELECOM **on ~** en attente; **to put a call on ~** mettre un appel en attente; **to put a project on ~** GEN laisser un projet en suspens; **6** (storage, area) AVIAT soute *f*; NAUT cale *f*; **7** (in wrestling) prise *f*; **8** (of spray, gel) fixation *f*.

II *vtr* (*prét, pp* **held**) **1** (clasp) tenir; **to ~ sth in one's hand** tenir qch à la main [*brush, pencil*]; (enclosed) tenir qch dans la main [*coin, sweet*]; **to ~ sb by** tenir qn par [*sleeve, leg*]; **to ~ sb** (**in one's arms**) serrer qn dans ses bras; **to ~ each other** se serrer l'un contre l'autre; **2** (maintain) **to ~ one's head still** tenir sa tête immobile; **to ~ oneself well** se tenir bien; **to ~ sth in place** maintenir qch en place; **3** (arrange) GEN organiser; avoir [*conversation*]; célébrer [*church service*]; mener [*enquiry*]; faire passer [*interview*]; **to be held** avoir lieu; **4** (have capacity for) (pouvoir) contenir [*350 people*]; **the bus ~s ten** (**people**) le bus a dix places; **5** (contain) [*drawer, cupboard, box, case*] contenir [*objects, possessions*]; **6** (support) supporter [*weight, load, crate*]; **7** (restrain) tenir [*dog*]; **there'll be no ~ing him** FIG on ne pourra plus l'arrêter; **8** (keep against will) détenir [*person*]; **to ~ sb hostage** garder qn en otage; **9** (possess) détenir, avoir [*shares, power, record*]; être titulaire de [*degree, sporting title*]; occuper [*job, position*]; avoir, être en possession de [*passport, licence*]; porter

[*title*]; avoir [*mortgage*]; [*computer*] conserver [*information*]; **10** (keep back) garder [*place, ticket*]; faire attendre [*train, flight*]; mettre [qch] en attente [*letter, order*]; **~ it**○! minute○!; **11** (believe) avoir [*opinion, belief*]; **to ~ sb/sth to be** tenir qn/qch pour; **to ~ sb liable** ou **responsible** tenir qn pour responsable; **to ~ that** [*person*] soutenir que; [*law*] dire que; **12** (defend successfully) tenir [*territory, city*]; conserver [*title, seat, lead*]; **to ~ one's own** se défendre tout seul; **13** (captivate) captiver [*audience*]; capter, retenir [*attention*]; **14** TELECOM **can you ~ the line please** ne quittez pas s'il vous plaît; **15** MUS tenir [*note*]; **16** AUT **to ~ the road** tenir la route.

III *vi* (*prét, pp* **held**) **1** (remain intact) tenir; FIG (also **~ good**) tenir; **2** (continue) [*weather*] rester beau, se maintenir; [*luck*] continuer, durer; **3** TELECOM patienter; **4** (remain steady) **~ still!** tiens-toi tranquille!

■ **hold against**: **~ sth against sb** reprocher qch à qn; **to ~ it against sb** (**that**) en vouloir à qn (parce que); **it could be held against you** [*age, sex*] ça pourrait jouer en ta défaveur.

■ **hold back**: ¶ **~ back** se retenir (**from doing** faire); ¶ **~ [sb/sth] back, ~ back [sb/sth] 1** (restrain) contenir [*water, crowd, anger*]; retenir [*hair, tears, person*]; refouler [*feelings*]; **2** (prevent progress of) entraver [*production, development*]; [*timidity, inexperience*] retenir [*person*]; **3** (withhold) différer [*payment*]; cacher [*information*]; (to protect privacy) tenir [qch] secret, ne pas divulguer.

■ **hold down**: **~ [sb/sth] down, ~ down [sb/sth] 1** (prevent from moving) maintenir [qch] en place [*carpet*]; tenir, maîtriser [*person*]; **2** (keep at certain level) limiter [*expenditure, inflation*]; limiter l'augmentation de [*wages, prices*]; **3** (not lose) garder [*job*].

■ **hold forth** PÉJ disserter, pérorer PÉJ (**about, on** sur).

■ **hold in**: **~ [sth] in, ~ in [sth]** (restrain) réprimer, contenir [*feeling*]; (pull in) rentrer [*stomach*].

■ **hold off**: ¶ **~ off** [*creditors*] accorder un délai; **I hope the rain ~s off** j'espère qu'il ne pleuvra pas; ¶ **~ [sb] off, ~ off [sb]** tenir [qn] à distance; ¶ **~ [sth] off** repousser [*attack*].

■ **hold on**: **~ on 1** (wait) GEN attendre; '**~ on**...' (on telephone) 'ne quittez pas...'; **2** (grip) tenir (**with** de, avec); '**~ on** (**tight**)!' 'tiens-toi (bien)!'; **3** (endure) tenir; ¶ **~ [sth] on** maintenir (**with** par).

■ **hold on to**: **~ on to [sb/sth] 1** (grip) s'agripper à; (to prevent from falling) agripper, retenir [*person*]; serrer [*object, purse*]; **2** (retain) conserver [*power, lead*]; garder [*shares, car*]; **to ~ on to the belief that** persister à croire que; **3** (look after) garder (**for** pour).

■ **hold out**: ¶ **~ out 1** (endure) tenir le coup, tenir bon; **to ~ out against** tenir bon devant; **to ~ out for** insister pour obtenir; **2** (remain available) durer; ¶ **~ [sth] out, ~out [sth]** tendre [*hand*]; **I don't ~ out much hope** je ne me fais guère d'illusions.

■ **hold over**: **1** (postpone) ajourner; **2** (continue to show) prolonger [*show, exhibition*].

■ **hold to**: ¶ **~ to [sth]** s'en tenir à [*belief, decision*]; ¶ **~ sb to [sth]** faire tenir [qch] à qn [*promise*]; faire honorer [qch] à qn [*contract, offer*].

■ **hold together**: ¶ **~ together 1** (not break) tenir; **2** (remain united) rester uni; ¶ **~ [sth] together 1** (keep intact) faire tenir [*machine, chair*]; maintenir ensemble [*pieces*]; **2** (unite) assurer la cohésion de.

■ **hold up**: ¶ **~ up 1** (remain intact) tenir, résister; **2** (remain valid) tenir; ¶ **~ [sb/sth] up, ~ up [sb/sth] 1** (support) soutenir [*shelf*]; tenir [*trousers*]; **2** (raise) lever; **to ~ one's hand up** lever la main; **3** (display) **to ~ sb/sth up as an example** ou **model of** présenter qn/qch comme un exemple de; **to ~ sb up to ridicule** tourner qn en ridicule, ridiculiser qn; **4** (delay) retarder [*person, flight*]; ralentir [*production, traffic*]; **5** (rob) attaquer.

■ **hold with**: not to ~ with être contre.

holdall /'həʊldɔːl/ *n* fourre-tout *m*, sac *m*.

holder /'həʊldə(r)/ *n* **1** (of passport, degree, post) titulaire *mf*; (of ticket, record) détenteur/-trice *m/f*; (of title) tenant/-e *m/f*; (of shares) porteur/-euse *m/f*; **account ~** titulaire d'un compte; **2** (stand) support *m*.

hold-up /ˈhəʊldʌp/ *n* **1** (delay) GEN retard *m*; (on road) embouteillage *m*, bouchon *m*; **2** (robbery) hold-up *m*, attaque *f* à main armée.

hole /həʊl/ **I** *n* **1** (in clothing, hedge etc) trou *m*; **2** (in wall) brèche *f*; **3** GB (in tooth) cavité *f*; **4** (in road) (pothole) nid *m* de poule; (man-made) trou *m*; **5** FIG (flaw) faille *f*; **to pick ~s in an argument** repérer les failles d'un raisonnement; **6** (of mouse) trou *m*; (of fox, rabbit) terrier *m*; **7** ECOL (in ozone layer) trou *m*; **8** (financial) trou *m*; **that holiday made a ~ in my pocket** ces vacances ont fait un trou dans mon budget; **9**○ (place) PÉJ trou *m* PÉJ; **10** (golf) trou *m*; **a nine-~ course** un parcours de neuf trous.

II *vtr* [*iceberg*] faire une brèche dans [*ship*].

IDIOMS **to get sb out of a ~** tirer qn du pétrin○.

■ **hole up** se terrer.

hole-and-corner *adj* clandestin.

holiday /ˈhɒlədeɪ/ **I** *n* **1** GB (vacation) vacances *fpl*; **on ~** en vacances; **the school ~s** les vacances scolaires; **the summer ~s** les vacances d'été, les grandes vacances; **family ~** vacances en famille; **2** GB (time off work) congé *m*; **3** (public, bank) jour *m* férié; **4** US **the ~s** les fêtes (de fin d'année).

II *vi* passer les vacances.

holiday: **~ atmosphere** *n* air *m* de fête; **~ home** *n* résidence *f* secondaire; **~ job** *n* GB (in summer) job○ *m* d'été; **~maker** *n* GB GEN vacancier/-ière *m/f*; (summer visitor) estivant/-e *m/f*; **~ resort** *n* lieu *m* de villégiature.

holier-than-thou /ˌhəʊlɪəðənˈðaʊ/ *adj* PÉJ **to be ~** se prendre pour un petit saint.

holiness /ˈhəʊlɪnɪs/ *n* sainteté *f*.

Holland /ˈhɒlənd/ ▶840 *pr n* Hollande *f*, Pays-Bas *mpl*; **in ~** en Hollande, aux Pays-Bas.

holler○ /ˈhɒlə(r)/ *vi* brailler, gueuler◐ (**at sb** après qn).

hollow /ˈhɒləʊ/ **I** *n* **1** (in tree, of hand, back) creux *m*; **2** (small valley) cuvette *f*.

II *adj* **1** (not solid) creux/creuse; **to sound ~** sonner creux; **2** (sunken) creux/creuse; **3** (booming) caverneux/-euse; **4** (insincere) [*words*] faux/fausse; [*promise*] vain; **a ~ laugh** un rire forcé; **to sound ~** sonner faux.

IDIOMS **to beat sb ~**○ battre qn à plates coutures.

■ **hollow out**: **~ [sth] out**, **~ out [sth]** creuser.

hollow: **~-cheeked** *adj* aux joues creuses; **~-eyed** *adj* aux yeux caves.

holly /ˈhɒlɪ/ *n* (tree, wood) houx *m*.

holocaust /ˈhɒləkɔːst/ *n* holocauste *m*; **the Holocaust** l'Holocauste *m*.

hologram /ˈhɒləgræm/ *n* hologramme *m*.

holograph /ˈhɒləɡrɑːf, US -ɡræf/ *n* (also **~ document**) document *m* olographe.

hols○ /hɒlz/ *n* GB (*abrév* = **holidays**) vacances *fpl*.

holster /ˈhəʊlstə(r)/ *n* étui *m* de revolver.

holy /ˈhəʊlɪ/ *adj* [*place, day, city, person*] saint; [*water*] bénit; **~ picture** image *f* pieuse; **on ~ ground** en lieu saint.

holy: **Holy Bible** *n* Sainte Bible *f*; **Holy Communion** *n* sainte communion *f*; **Holy Father** *n* Saint-Père *m*; **Holy Grail** *n* Saint-Graal *m*; **Holy Land** *n* Terre *f* Sainte; **Holy See** *n* Saint-Siège *m*; **Holy Spirit** *n* Saint-Esprit *m*; **Holy Trinity** *n* sainte Trinité *f*; **Holy Week** *n* semaine *f* sainte.

holy writ *n* Saintes Écritures *fpl*; **it's ~** c'est sacré.

homage /ˈhɒmɪdʒ/ *n* hommage *m*; **to pay ~ to** rendre hommage à.

homburg /ˈhɒmbɜːɡ/ *n* chapeau *m* mou.

home /həʊm/ **I** *n* **1** (dwelling) GEN logement *m*; (house) maison *f*; **to be far from ~** être loin de chez soi; **a ~ of one's own** un chez-soi; **to work from ~** travailler à domicile; **to set up ~ in Madrid** s'installer à Madrid; **I've made my ~ in France** je suis installé ou je vis en France; **it's ~ to me now** je m'y sens chez moi; **2** (for residential care) maison *f*; **to put sb in a ~** mettre qn dans un établissement spécia-

lisé; **3** (family base) foyer *m*; **broken ~** foyer désuni; **'good ~ wanted'** 'cherche foyer accueillant'; **to leave ~** quitter la maison; **4** (country) pays *m*; **to consider France (as) ~** considérer la France comme son pays; **5** (source) **~ of** [*country, area*] pays *m* de [*speciality*].

II *noun modifier* **1** (family) [*life*] de famille; [*background*] familial; [*comforts*] du foyer; **2** (national) [*market, affairs*] intérieur; [*news*] national; **3** SPORT [*match, win*] à domicile; [*team*] qui reçoit.

III *adv* **1** [*come, go, arrive*] (to house) à la maison, chez soi; (to country) dans son pays; **on the way ~** en rentrant chez moi/nous etc; (by boat, plane) pendant le voyage de retour; **to take sb ~** raccompagner qn à la maison; **to be ~** (around) être à la maison; (from work) être rentré; **2** (to required effect) **to push one's point ~** enfoncer le clou FIG; **to bring sth ~ to** FIG faire voir qch à; **to strike ~** FIG toucher juste.

IV **at home** *adv phr* **1** (in house) à la maison; **to live at ~** habiter chez ses parents; **2** SPORT (on own ground) [*play*] à domicile; **3** FIG (comfortable) à l'aise; **make yourself at ~** fais comme chez toi.

IDIOMS **it's nothing to write ~ about** ça n'a rien d'extraordinaire; **it's ~ from ~** GB, **it's ~ away from ~** US c'est un second chez-soi; **to be a bit too close to ~** être blessant; **to be ~ and dry** être sauvé.

■ **home in on**: **~ in on** [*sth*] se diriger sur [*target*].

home address *n* (on form) domicile *m*; (personal) adresse *f* personnelle.

homebound /ˈhəʊmbaʊnd/ *adj* SURTOUT US **1** (housebound) confiné chez soi; **2** [*traffic, car, traveller*] rentrant chez soi; [*train*] du retour.

home: **~ brew** *n* bière *f* (brassée) maison; **~ centre** GB, **~ center** US *n* maisonnerie *f*.

homecoming /ˈhəʊmkʌmɪŋ/ *n* **1** (return home) retour *m* à la maison; **2** US SPORT match de football annuel du lycée suivi d'un bal.

home: **~ computer** *n* ordinateur *m*, PC *m*; **~ cooking** *n* bonne cuisine *f* familiale; **Home Counties** *npl* GB comtés *mpl* limitrophes de Londres; **~ economics** *n* SCH cours *m* d'économie domestique.

home front *n* (during war) **the ~** l'arrière *m*; **on the ~** (in politics) pour les affaires intérieures.

home ground *n* FIG terrain *m* familier; **on one's ~** SPORT à domicile.

home: **~grown** *adj* LIT du jardin; FIG [*idea*] bien de chez soi; **~ help** *n* GB aide *f* familiale; **~land** *n* pays *m* d'origine, patrie *f*; (in S. Africa) bantoustan *m*.

homeless /ˈhəʊmlɪs/ **I** *n* **the ~** (+ *v pl*) les sans-abri *mpl inv*.

II *adj* GEN sans abri, sans logement; (after flood etc) sinistré.

home life *n* vie *f* de famille.

home: **~ loan** *n* prêt *m* immobilier; **~loving** *adj* casanier/-ière.

homely /ˈhəʊmlɪ/ *adj* **1** GB (cosy, welcoming) accueillant; **2** GB (unpretentious) [*room, cooking*] sans prétention; [*person*] simple; **3** US PÉJ (plain) [*person*] sans attraits.

home: **~made** *adj* (fait) maison; **~maker** *n* femme *f* d'intérieur; **~ movie** *n* film *m* d'amateur; **Home Office** *n* POL ministère *m* de l'Intérieur.

homeopathic /ˌhəʊmɪəˈpæθɪk/ *adj* [*medicine, clinic*] homéopathique; [*doctor*] homéopathe.

homeopathy /ˌhəʊmɪˈɒpəθɪ/ *n* homéopathie *f*.

home: **~ owner** *n* propriétaire *mf*; **~ ownership** *n* fait *m* d'être propriétaire de son logement; **~ plate** *n* SPORT marbre *m*; **~ port** *n* port *m* d'attache; **~ rule** *n* POL gouvernement *m* autonome; **~ run** *n* SPORT point *m* marqué par le batteur (*s'il réussit à toucher toutes les bases*); **Home Secretary** *n* POL Ministre *m* de l'Intérieur.

homesick /ˈhəʊmsɪk/ *adj* **to be ~** (for country) avoir le mal du pays; [*child*] s'ennuyer de ses parents.

home: **~sickness** *n* mal *m* du pays; **~ side** *n* = **home team**.

homespun /'həʊmspʌn/ adj **1** [cloth] artisanal; **2** FIG [wisdom, virtue] naturel/-elle, sans artifices.

homestead /'həʊmsted/ n **1** (house and land) domaine m; **2** (farm) ferme f; **3** US ADMIN terres fpl (acquises pour leur occupation et leur exploitation).

home: **~ team** n équipe f qui reçoit; **~ town** n ville f natale; **~ video** n vidéo f d'amateur; **~ visit** n MED visite f à domicile.

homeward /'həʊmwəd/ adv **to travel ~(s)** rentrer; **to be ~ bound** être sur le chemin de retour.

home waters npl NAUT, POL eaux fpl territoriales.

homework /'həʊmwɜːk/ n ⊄ **1** SCH devoirs mpl; **2** (research) **to do some ~ on** faire quelques recherches au sujet de.

home: **~worker** n travailleur/-euse m/f à domicile; **~working** n travail m à domicile.

homey /'həʊmɪ/ adj (cosy) accueillant; (simple) sans prétention.

homicidal /ˌhɒmɪ'saɪdl/ adj homicide.

homicide /'hɒmɪsaɪd/ n **1** (murder) homicide m; **justifiable ~** JUR homicide justifiable; **~ bureau** US brigade f criminelle; **2** (person) meurtrier/-ière m/f.

homily /'hɒmɪlɪ/ n homélie f.

homing /'həʊmɪŋ/ adj [missile] autoguidé; [system, device] d'autoguidage; **~ instinct** faculté f d'orientation; **~ pigeon** pigeon m voyageur.

hominy grits /'hɒmɪnɪ grɪts/ n US (dish) bouillie f de maïs.

homogeneity /ˌhɒmədʒɪ'niːɪtɪ/ n homogénéité f.

homogeneous /ˌhɒmə'dʒiːnɪəs, ˌhɒməʊ-/ adj homogène.

homogenize /hə'mɒdʒɪnaɪz/ vtr homogénéiser.

homogenous /hə'mɒdʒɪnəs/ adj homogène.

homograph /'hɒməgrɑːf, US -græf/ n homographe m.

homonym /'hɒmənɪm/ n homonyme m.

homophobia /ˌhɒmə'fəʊbɪə/ n intolérance f envers les homosexuels.

homosexual /ˌhɒmə'sekʃʊəl/ n, adj homosexuel/-elle (m/f).

homosexuality /ˌhɒmə,sekʃʊ'ælətɪ/ n homosexualité f.

Hon 1 (abrév écrite = **Honourable**) the **~ Anne Grey** l'honorable Anne Grey; **2** (abrév écrite = **Honorary**) honoraire.

honcho○ /'hɒntʃəʊ/ n (pl **~S**) US **he's the head ~** c'est le grand chef○.

hone /həʊn/ vtr **1** (perfect) aiguiser [technique, skill]; affûter [argument, style]; **2** (sharpen) aiguiser.

honest /'ɒnɪst/ I adj **1** (truthful) [person] intègre; [answer, account] sincère; **to be ~ about** être honnête au sujet de; **the ~ truth** la pure vérité; **2** (trustworthy) honnête; **3** (sincere) franc/franche; **to be ~ with sb** être franc avec qn; **to be ~ with oneself** être honnête avec soi-même; **be ~!** sois franc!; **to be ~,...** à dire vrai...; **4** (legal) [profit, money] honnêtement acquis; [price] juste; **by ~ means** par des moyens légitimes; **to make an ~ living** gagner honnêtement sa vie.

II excl **~**○ ou **~ to God!** parole d'honneur!

honestly /'ɒnɪstlɪ/ adv **1** (truthfully) honnêtement; **2** (legally) honnêtement; **3** (sincerely) [believe] franchement; [say] sincèrement; **quite ~,...** franchement...; **~, there's no problem** je vous assure, il n'y a aucun problème; **4**○ (in exasperation) franchement!

honest-to-goodness adj **1** (simple) simple; **2** US (authentic) véritable.

honesty /'ɒnɪstɪ/ n honnêteté f.

IDIOMS **~ is the best policy** l'honnêteté est toujours récompensée.

honey /'hʌnɪ/ n **1** (food) miel m; **clear ~** miel liquide; **2**○ (endearment) chéri/-e m/f.

honey: **~bee** n abeille f; **~bunch**○, **~bun** n US chéri/-e m/f; **~-coloured** GB, **~-colored** US ▶818 | adj (couleur de) miel inv.

honeycomb /'hʌnɪkəʊm/ n **1** (in hive) rayon m de miel; **2** (for sale) gâteau m de miel.

honeycombed /'hʌnɪkəʊmd/ adj **~ with** percé de [holes]; creusé de [passages, tunnels].

honeydew melon n melon m d'Espagne.

honeymoon /'hʌnɪmuːn/ n **1** (wedding trip) voyage m de noces; **2** FIG (also **~ period**) (calm spell) lune f de miel.

honeypot /'hʌnɪpɒt/ n: IDIOMS **like bees around a ~** comme des mouches sur un pot de miel.

honeysuckle /'hʌnɪsʌkl/ n chèvrefeuille m.

Hong Kong /ˌhɒŋ 'kɒŋ/ ▶1343 | pr n Hongkong m.

honk /hɒŋk/ I n (of horn) coup m de klaxon®; (of geese) cri m (de l'oie).

II vtr **to ~ one's horn (at sb)** klaxonner (qn).

III vi [geese] cacarder; [car horn] faire tut-tut; [driver] klaxonner.

honky-tonk /'hɒŋkɪtɒŋk/ adj [piano] bastringue○.

honor n, vtr US = **honour**.

honorable adj US = **honourable**.

honorably adv US = **honourably**.

honorary /'ɒnərərɪ, US 'ɒnəreri/ adj [doctorate] honorifique, honoris causa inv; [member] honoraire.

honorific○ /ˌɒnə'rɪfɪk/ adj honorifique.

honor roll n US **1** SCH, SPORT tableau m d'honneur; **2** MIL liste f des soldats tombés au champ d'honneur.

honor: **~ society** n US SCH club m des meilleurs élèves; **~ system** n US SCH système m de l'auto-discipline.

honour GB, **honor** US /'ɒnə(r)/ I n **1** (privilege) honneur m; **place of ~** place d'honneur; **to give sb ou do sb the ~ of doing** faire à qn l'honneur de faire; **in ~ of** en l'honneur de; **to what do I owe this ~?** SOUT ou IRON que me vaut cet honneur? SOUT ou IRON; **2** (high principles) honneur m; **to impugn sb's ~** SOUT mettre en doute l'honneur de qn; **to give one's word of ~** donner sa parole d'honneur; **3** (in titles) **Your Honour** Votre Honneur.

II **honours** npl UNIV **first/second class ~s** licence avec mention très bien/bien.

III vtr **1** (show respect for) honorer; **to feel/be ~ed** se sentir/être honoré (by par); **to ~ sb by doing** SOUT faire l'honneur à qn de faire; **our ~ed guests** nos honorables invités; **2** (fulfil, be bound by) honorer [cheque, contract, obligation]; tenir [promise, commitment]; remplir [agreement].

IDIOMS **to do the ~s** (serve food, drinks) faire les honneurs; (introduce guests) faire les présentations.

honourable GB, **honorable** US /'ɒnərəbl/ adj **1** (principled) honnête; **to do the ~ thing** faire la seule chose convenable; **2** (worthy) honorable; **3** ▶937 | (in titles) **the Honourable Mr Justice Jones** le Juge Jones; **the Honourable Gentleman** POL Monsieur le député.

honourable: **~ discharge** n libération f honorable; **~ mention** n mention f honorable.

honourably GB, **honorably** US /'ɒnərəblɪ/ adv [acquit oneself, fight, withdraw] honorablement; [behave] honorablement.

honour: **~-bound** adj tenu par l'honneur (**to do** de faire); **~s course** n: cours universitaire réservé aux meilleurs étudiants; **~s degree** n: licence réservée aux meilleurs étudiants; **Honours List** n GB liste des distinctions honorifiques conférées par le monarque.

hood /hʊd/ n **1** (head gear) (attached) capuchon m; (detached) capuche f; (balaclava) cagoule f; (for falcon) chaperon m; **2** (cover) (on cooker) hotte f; (on printer) capot m (antibruit); **3** GB (on car, pram) capote f; **4** US AUT (bonnet) capot m; **5** UNIV (part of robes) épitoge f.

hooded /'hʊdɪd/ adj **1** [garment] à capuchon; **2** [attacker] en cagoule; **3 to have ~ eyes** avoir les paupières tombantes.

hoodlum○ /'huːdləm/ n **1** (hooligan) vandale m; **2** US (crook) truand m.

hoodwink /'hʊdwɪŋk/ vtr tromper.

hoof /huːf/ n (pl **~s** ou **hooves**) sabot m (d'animal); **bought on the ~** acheté sur pied.

IDIOMS **to ~ it** aller à pinces○ ou à pied.

hoo-ha○ /'huːhɑː/ n pagaille f.

hook /hʊk/ **I** *n* **1** (for clothing, picture) crochet *m*; **2** (on fishing line) hameçon *m*; **3** (fastener) agrafe *f*; **~s and eyes** agrafes *fpl*; **4** (on pole) crosse *f*; **5** TELECOM **to take the phone off the ~** décrocher le téléphone; **6** (boxing) crochet *m*; **left ~** crochet du gauche; **7** (golf) coup *m* hooké; **8** US (bend) coude *m*, courbe *f*.
II *vtr* **1** (hang) accrocher (**on, onto** à); **2** (pull through) faire passer [*string*]; passer [*finger, stick*] (**through** dans); **3** (catch) prendre [*fish*]; FIG, HUM° mettre le grappin sur° [*spouse*].
IDIOMS **to get sb off the ~** tirer qn d'affaire.
■ **hook on** s'accrocher (**to** à).
■ **hook up**: ¶ **~ up** [*garment*] s'agrafer; ¶ **~ up** [**sth**], **~** [**sth**] **up 1** (attach) agrafer [*garment*]; accrocher [*trailer, picture*]; **2** RADIO, TV faire un duplex entre [*stations*]; **3** ELEC, TECH connecter [*appliance*].
hookah /ˈhʊkə/ *n* narguilé *m*.
hooked /hʊkt/ *adj* **1** [*nose, beak*] crochu; [*stick*] avec une crosse; **2** (addicted) **to be ~ on** se camer° à [*drugs*]; être mordu° de [*computer games*].
hook nose *n* nez *m* crochu.
hook-up /ˈhʊkʌp/ *n* **1** RADIO, TV relais *m*; **2** US (in trailer park) borne *f* de raccordement.
hooky°, **hookey** /ˈhʊkɪ/ *n* US **to play ~** faire l'école buissonnière†.
hooligan /ˈhuːlɪɡən/ *n* vandale *m*, voyou *m*; **soccer ~** hooligan *m*.
hooliganism /ˈhuːlɪɡənɪzəm/ *n* vandalisme *m*.
hoop /huːp/ *n* (ring) cerceau *m*; (in croquet) arceau *m*.
IDIOMS **to go through the ~s**, **to jump through ~s** faire des pieds et des mains.
hoopla /ˈhuːplɑː/ ▶949 *n* **1** GB (at fair) jeu *m* d'anneaux; **2**° US (fuss) pagaille *f*.
hooray /hʊˈreɪ/ *excl* hourra.
Hooray Henry *n* GB PÉJ fils *m* à papa PÉJ.
hoot /huːt/ **I** *n* **1** (noise) (of owl) (h)ululement *m*; (of train) sifflement *m*; (of ship or factory siren) mugissement *m*; (of car) coup *m* de klaxon®; (shout) rire *m* moqueur; **2**° (funny) **to be a ~** être très marrant°.
II *vtr* huer [*speaker, actor*]; **to ~ one's horn** donner un coup de klaxon® (**at sb** pour avertir qn).
III *vi* [*owl*] (h)ululer; [*train*] siffler; [*siren*] mugir; [*car*] klaxonner; [*person, crowd*] (derisively) huer; **to ~ with laughter** éclater de rire.
IDIOMS **I don't give two ~s**° ! je m'en fiche° comme de l'a quarante!
hooter /ˈhuːtə(r)/ *n* **1** (siren) sirène *f*; **2**° GB (nose) pif° *m*, nez *m*.
hoover /ˈhuːvə(r)/ *vtr* GB **to ~ a room** passer l'aspirateur dans une pièce.
Hoover® /ˈhuːvə(r)/ *n* GB aspirateur *m*.
hooves /huːvz/ *pl* ▶ **hoof**.
hop /hɒp/ **I** *n* **1** (movement) (of frog, rabbit, child) bond *m*; (of bird) sautillement *m*; **2**° (journey) **a short ~** un saut (de puce); **3**° (dance) bal *m* (populaire).
II hops *npl* (crop) houblon *m* ¢.
III *vtr* (*p prés etc* **-pp-**) **1** (jump over) franchir [qch] d'un bond [*fence*]; **2**° US (board) sauter dans [*flight, train, bus*].
IV *vi* (*p prés etc* **-pp-**) **1** (jump) [*person*] sauter; **to ~ off a wall** sauter d'un mur; **to ~ up and down with rage** trépigner de rage; **2** (on one leg) sauter à cloche-pied; **to ~ up the path** monter le sentier à cloche-pied; **3** [*animal*] sauter; [*bird*] sautiller; **a rabbit ~ped across the road** un lapin traversa la route en quelques bonds; **4** (move speedily) **to ~ into bed/off a bus** sauter dans son lit/d'un bus; **~ in!** (into car) vas-y, monte!
IDIOMS **to be ~ping mad**° être fou furieux/folle furieuse; **to catch sb on the ~**° GB prendre qn au dépourvu; **to ~ it**° GB déguerpir°; **to keep sb on the ~**° GB maintenir qn sous pression.
hope /həʊp/ **I** *n* **1** (desire, expectation) espoir *m* (**of** de); (cause for optimism) espoir *m*; **in the ~ of sth** dans l'espoir de qch; **to have high ~s of sb/sth** fonder de grands espoirs sur qn/qch; **to have ~s of doing** avoir l'espoir de faire; **there is no ~ left for them** il n'y a plus d'espoir pour eux; **to set one's ~s on**

doing espérer de tout cœur faire; **to be beyond (all) ~**, **to be without ~** être sans espoir; **to keep one's ~s high** garder espoir; **to raise sb's ~s** faire naître l'espoir chez qn; **to dash sb's ~s** anéantir l'espoir de qn; **2** (chance) chance *f*, espoir *m*; **to have no ~ of sth** n'avoir aucune chance de qch; **there is little ~ that he will come** il y a peu de chances qu'il vienne; **there is no ~ of an improvement** on ne peut pas s'attendre à une amélioration; **my last ~** mon dernier espoir; **what a ~**°!, **some ~°**! il ne faut pas rêver!; **he hasn't got a ~ in hell**° il n'a pas la moindre chance; **3** (promising person) espoir *m*.
II *vtr* espérer (**that** que); **to ~ to do** espérer faire; **it is to be ~d that** il faut espérer que (+ *indic*); **we cannot ~ to compete** nous n'avons aucune chance de rivaliser; **I only** ou **just ~ he remembers** j'espère seulement qu'il s'en souviendra; **I** (**do**) **~ so/not** j'espère (bien) que oui/que non; **hoping to hear from you** dans l'espoir d'avoir de vos nouvelles.
III *vi* espérer; **to ~ for sth** espérer avoir qch; **all we can do is ~** nous ne pouvons qu'espérer; **to ~ for the best** être optimiste.
IDIOMS **to ~ against ~** espérer en dépit de tout.
hope chest *n* US (chest) coffre *m* à trousseau; (trousseau) trousseau *m*.
hopeful /ˈhəʊpfl/ **I** *n* **young ~** jeune espoir *m*; (ambitious) ambitieux/-ieuse *m/f*.
II *adj* **1** (filled with hope) [*person, expression*] plein d'espoir; [*attitude, mood*] optimiste; **to be ~ about** être optimiste quant à; **to be ~ of doing** avoir bon espoir de faire; **2** (encouraging) [*news, sign, situation*] encourageant; [*development*] prometteur/-euse.
hopefully /ˈhəʊpfəlɪ/ *adv* **1** (with luck) avec un peu de chance; **'will he pay?'—'~'** 'c'est lui qui paiera?'—'je l'espère'; **2** (with hope) [*say*] avec optimisme.
hopeless /ˈhəʊplɪs/ *adj* **1** (desperate) [*attempt, case, grief, struggle*] désespéré; [*muddle*] inextricable; **it was ~ trying to convince her** il était impossible de la convaincre; **it's ~!** inutile!; **2**° (incompetent) nul/nulle°; **to be ~ at sth** être nul/nulle° en qch; **to be ~ at doing** être incapable de faire.
hopelessly /ˈhəʊplɪslɪ/ *adv* **1** (irretrievably) [*drunk, inadequate*] complètement; [*in love*] éperdument; **2** (despairingly) désespérément.
hopelessness /ˈhəʊplɪsnɪs/ *n* **1** (despair) désespoir *m*; **2** (futility) futilité *f* (**of doing** de faire).
hop: **~ field** *n* houblonnière *f*; **~sack** *n* US sac *m* en jute; **~scotch** ▶949 *n* marelle *f*.
horde /hɔːd/ *n* (of people) foule *f*; (of insects) nuée *f*; (of animals) horde *f*; **the ~(s)** la horde.
horizon /həˈraɪzn/ *n* **1** (skyline) horizon *m*; **on the ~** (visible) à l'horizon; (imminent) en vue; **2** (of ideas, interests) horizon *m*; **to broaden one's ~s** élargir ses horizons.
horizontal /ˌhɒrɪˈzɒntl, US ˌhɔːrɪ-/ **I** *n* horizontale *f*.
II *adj* horizontal; **~ bar** barre *f* fixe.
hormonal /hɔːˈməʊnl/ *adj* hormonal.
hormone replacement therapy, **HRT** *n* hormonothérapie *f* substitutive.
horn /hɔːn/ *n* **1** ZOOL (of animal, snail) corne *f*; (of owl) aigrette *f*; FIG (on moon, anvil) corne *f*; **2** MUS ▶1097 cor *m*; **to play the ~** jouer du cor; **for ~** pour cor; **3** (of car) klaxon® *m*, avertisseur *m* (sonore); (of ship) sirène *f*; **4** ¢ (substance) corne *f*.
IDIOMS **to draw in one's ~s** (feeling hurt) rentrer dans sa coquille; (financially) réduire son train de vie; **to lock ~s with sb** croiser le fer avec qn.
hornet /ˈhɔːnɪt/ *n* frelon *m*.
IDIOMS **to stir up a ~'s nest** donner un coup de pied dans la fourmilière.
horn: **~ of plenty** *n* corne *f* d'abondance; **~-rimmed** *adj* [*spectacles*] à monture d'écaille; [*frames*] d'écaille.
horny /ˈhɔːnɪ/ *adj* **1** (hornlike) [*claws, carapace*] corné; [*protuberance*] cornu; **2** (calloused) calleux/-euse.
horoscope /ˈhɒrəskəʊp, US ˈhɔːr-/ *n* horoscope *m*.
horrendous /hɒˈrendəs/ *adj* [*crime, conditions, acci-*

dent] épouvantable; [*problem, mistake, cost, noise*] effroyable.

horrible /'hɒrɪbl, US 'hɔːr-/ *adj* **1** (unpleasant) [*place, clothes, smell, thought*] affreux/-euse; [*weather, food, person*] épouvantable; **to be ~ to sb** être méchant avec qn; **2** (shocking) horrible.

horribly /'hɒrɪblɪ, US 'hɔːr-/ *adv* **1** [*embarrassed, rude*] terriblement; **2** [*disfigured*] horriblement.

horrid /'hɒrɪd, US 'hɔːrɪd/ *adj* (awful) affreux/-euse.

horrific /hə'rɪfɪk/ *adj* atroce.

horrified /'hɒrɪfaɪd, US 'hɔːr-/ *adj* horrifié (**at, by** par; **to do** de faire; **that** que + *subj*).

horrifying /'hɒrɪfaɪɪŋ, US 'hɔːr-/ *adj* [*experience, idea, sight*] horrifiant; [*behaviour*] effroyable.

horror /'hɒrə(r), US 'hɔːr-/ *n* **1** (feeling) horreur *f* (**at** devant); **to have a ~ of sth/of doing** avoir horreur de qch/de faire; **~ of ~s!** ô horreur!; **2**○ (person) **a little ~**○ un petit monstre○.

horror: **~ film** *n* film *m* d'épouvante; **~ story** *n* histoire *f* d'épouvante; **~-stricken**, **~-struck** *adj* frappé d'horreur.

horse /hɔːs/ *n* **1** cheval *m*; **the ~s** FIG (horseracing) les courses *fpl* (de chevaux); **2** (in gym) cheval *m* de saut; (pommel) cheval *m* d'arçons; **3** MIL ¢ cavalerie *f*.
IDIOMS **I could eat a ~** j'ai une faim de loup; **to eat like a ~** manger comme quatre; **to flog** GB ou **beat** US **a dead ~**○ perdre sa peine et son temps; **from the ~'s mouth** de source sûre; **hold your ~s**○! arrêtez!, une minute!; **it's ~s for courses** ce qui convient à l'un ne convient pas nécessairement à l'autre; **that's a ~ of a different colour** ça c'est une autre paire de manches; **wild ~s wouldn't drag it out of me** pour rien au monde je ne le révélerais.
■ **horse about**, **horse around** chahuter.

horseback /'hɔːsbæk/ *n* **on ~** à cheval.

horseback riding ▶ 949 | *n* US équitation *f*.

horse: **~box** *n* van *m*; **~ chestnut** *n* (tree) marronnier *m* (d'Inde); (fruit) marron *m* (d'Inde); **~ dealer** *n* maquignon/-onne *m/f*; **~-drawn** *adj* tiré par des chevaux; **~flesh** *n* (horses collectively) chevaux *mpl*; (meat) viande *f* de cheval; **~fly** *n* taon *m*; **~hair** *n* crin *m* (de cheval); **~man** *n* cavalier *m*; **~ manure** *n* crottin *m* de cheval; **~meat** *n* viande *f* de cheval; **~play** *n* chahut *m*.

horsepower /'hɔːspaʊə(r)/ *n* puissance *f* (en chevaux); **a 90 ~ engine** un moteur de 90 chevaux.

horse: **~ race** *n* course *f* de chevaux; **~racing** *n* courses *fpl* de chevaux, courses *fpl* hippiques; **~radish sauce** *n* sauce *f* au raifort; **~riding** ▶ 949 | *n* équitation *f*; **~shoe** *n* fer *m* à cheval; **~show** *n* concours *m* hippique; **~ trader** ▶ 1251 | *n* LIT, FIG maquignon/-onne *m/f*; **~ trials** *npl* concours *m* complet d'équitation; **~whip** *n* cravache *f*; **~woman** *n* cavalière *f*, écuyère *f*.

hors(e)y /'hɔːsɪ/ *adj* [*face*] chevalin; [*person*] passionné de chevaux.

horticultural /ˌhɔːtɪ'kʌltʃərəl/ *adj* horticole.

horticulture /'hɔːtɪkʌltʃə(r)/ *n* horticulture *f*.

horticulturist /ˌhɔːtɪ'kʌltʃərɪst/ ▶ 1251 | *n* horticulteur/-trice *m/f*.

hose /həʊz/ *n* **1** (for garden) tuyau *m* d'arrosage; (for cleaning) jet *m* d'eau; **2** (also **fire ~**) lance *f* à incendie; **3** AUT (in engine) tuyau *m*; **4** (tubing) tuyau *m*; **5** HIST (garment) haut-de-chausses *m*.

hosepipe /'həʊzpaɪp/ GB *n* **1** (for garden) tuyau *m* d'arrosage; **2** (fire hose) lance *f* à incendie.

hosiery† /'həʊzɪərɪ, US 'həʊʒərɪ/ *n* bonneterie *f*.

hospice /'hɒspɪs/ *n* (for the dying) établissement *m* de soins palliatifs.

hospitable /hɒ'spɪtəbl/ *adj* [*person, country*] hospitalier/-ière (**to** envers); [*conditions*] favorable.

hospital /'hɒspɪtl/ **I** *n* hôpital *m*; **to/from ~** GB ou **the ~** US à/de l'hôpital; **to be taken to ~ with…** être hospitalisé pour…
II *noun modifier* [*facilities, staff, treatment, ward*] hospitalier/-ière; **~ beds** lits *mpl* d'hôpital; **~ patient** patient/-e *m/f*.

hospital: **~ administrator** ▶ 1251 | *n* directeur/-trice *m/f* d'hôpital; **~ doctor** ▶ 1251 | *n* médecin *m* d'hôpital.

hospitality /ˌhɒspɪ'tælətɪ/ *n* hospitalité *f*.

hospitalize /'hɒspɪtəlaɪz/ *vtr* hospitaliser.

hospital: **~ nurse** ▶ 1251 | *n* infirmier/-ière *m/f* d'hôpital; **~ porter** ▶ 1251 | *n* GB brancardier *m*; **~ ship** *n* navire-hôpital *m*.

host /həʊst/ **I** *n* **1** (to guests, visitors) hôte *m*; **to play ~ to sb** recevoir or accueillir qn; **2** BOT, ZOOL hôte *m*; **3** RADIO, TV animateur/-trice *m/f*; **4** (multitude) foule *f* (**of**); **5** RELIG hostie *f*.
II *vtr* organiser [*function*]; RADIO, TV animer.

hostage /'hɒstɪdʒ/ *n* otage *m*; **to hold sb ~** garder qn en otage.

host country *n* pays *m* hôte or d'accueil.

hostel /'hɒstl/ *n* (for workers, refugees etc) foyer *m*; **(youth) ~** auberge *f* de jeunesse.

hostess /'həʊstɪs/ *n* **1** (to guests etc) hôtesse *f*, maîtresse *f* de maison; (on plane etc) hôtesse *f*; **2** TV animatrice *f*.

hostile /'hɒstaɪl, US -tl/ *adj* hostile (**to** à).

hostility /hɒ'stɪlətɪ/ *n* hostilité *f* (**towards sb/sth** à l'égard de qn/à qch).

hot /hɒt/ *adj* **1** (very warm) [*season, country, bath, plate, hands*] chaud; [*sun*] chaud; [*food, drink*] (bien) chaud; **it's ~ here** il fait chaud ici; **the weather is ~ in July** il fait un temps chaud au mois de juillet; **it was a ~ day** il faisait chaud ce jour-là; **to be** ou **feel ~** [*person*] avoir chaud; **to get ~** [*person*] commencer à avoir trop chaud; [*parked car*] devenir chaud; [*engine, oven*] chauffer; [*weather*] se réchauffer; **the room feels ~** il fait chaud dans cette pièce; **your forehead feels ~** tu as le front chaud; **digging is ~ work** ça donne chaud de bêcher; **when the sun is at its ~test** quand le soleil chauffe le plus; **how ~ should I have the oven?** à quelle température dois-je régler le four?; **to be ~ from the oven** sortir du four; **to go ~ and cold** (with fever) être fiévreux/-euse; (with fear) avoir des sueurs froides; **2** CULIN [*mustard, spice*] fort; [*sauce, dish*] épicé; **3** (new, fresh) [*trail, news*] tout chaud; **~ off the press** tout chaud sorti de la presse; **4** (fierce, keen) [*competition*] acharné; **5** (short) **to have a ~ temper** s'emporter facilement; **6**○ (in demand) **to be ~** avoir un succès fou; **7**○ (good) **a ~ tip** un bon tuyau○; **the ~ favourite** le grand favori; **to be ~ on sth** (knowledgeable) être calé○ en qch; (keen) être très à cheval sur qch; **8**○ (stolen) volé; **9** (bright) [*colour*] chaud; **~ pink** rose bonbon; **10** (radioactive) radioactif/-ive; **11** (close) **to be ~ on the trail of sth** être sur la piste de qch; **to set off in ~ pursuit of sb** se lancer à la poursuite de qn; **you're getting ~** (in games) tu chauffes.
IDIOMS **to be in ~ water** être dans le pétrin○; **to blow ~ and cold** être d'humeur changeante; **to get all ~ and bothered** se mettre dans tous ses états.
■ **hot up** [*match*] s'animer; [*election campaign*] s'intensifier; **things are ~ting up** ça commence à chauffer○; **the pace is ~ting up** l'allure s'accélère.

hot: **~ air**○ *n* paroles *fpl* en l'air; **~ air balloon** *n* montgolfière *f*; **~bed** *n* foyer *m* (**of** de); **~-blooded** *adj* [*reaction*] passionné.

hot cake *n* US ~ crêpe *f*.
IDIOMS **to sell like ~s** se vendre comme des petits pains.

hotchpotch /'hɒtʃpɒtʃ/ *n* GB mélange *m*, mixture *f*.

hot cross bun *n* ~ brioche *f* du vendredi saint.

hot dog *n* hot dog *m*.

hot dogging ▶ 949 | *n* ski *m* acrobatique.

hotel /həʊ'tel/ **I** *n* hôtel *m*.
II *noun modifier* [*room, manager*] d'hôtel; [*industry*] hôtelier/-ière; [*work*] dans l'hôtellerie.

hotelier /həʊ'telɪə(r)/, **hotelkeeper** /ˌhəʊtel'kiːpə(r)/ ▶ 1251 | *n* hôtelier/-ière *m/f*.

hot: **~foot** *adv* HUM, IRON [*go*] à toute vitesse or allure; **~head** *n* PÉJ tête *f* brûlée, exalté/-e *m/f*;

~-headed adj [person] impétueux/-euse; [decision] précipité.

hothouse /'hɒthaʊs/ n LIT serre f (chaude); FIG milieu m protégé.

hothousing /'hɒthaʊzɪŋ/ n SCH enseignement intensif destiné aux enfants surdoués.

hotline /'hɒtlaɪn/ n **1** ligne f ouverte, permanence f téléphonique; **2** MIL, POL téléphone m rouge.

hotly /'hɒtlɪ/ adv [say, exclaim] passionnément; [disputed, denied] violemment.

hot: **~plate** n plaque f de cuisson; **~pot** n GB ragoût m.

hot potato○ n sujet m brûlant.
　IDIOMS **to drop sb like a ~** laisser tomber qn du jour au lendemain.

hot rod n voiture f au moteur gonflé.

hot seat○ n: IDIOMS **to be in the ~** être sur la sellette.

hot: **~ shoe** n griffe f porte-flash; **~shot**○ n GEN crack○ m; PEJ gros bonnet○ m.

hot spot n **1** POL point m chaud; **2** TOURISM pays m du soleil, destination f au soleil; **3** (nightclub) boîte f de nuit.

hot spring n source f chaude.

hot stuff○ n to be ~ [person] être un crack○; **he thinks he's ~** il ne se prend pas pour rien.

hot: **~-tempered** adj colérique; **~ tub** n US ~ jacuzzi m de jardin; **~ water bottle** n bouillotte f.

hound /haʊnd/ I n **1** (in hunting) chien m de chasse; **2** HUM (dog) chien m; **3**○ (enthusiast) autograph **~** chasseur/-euse m/f d'autographes.
　II vtr (harass) harceler, traquer [person].
　■ **hound out**: **~ [sb] out** chasser (**of** de).

hound-dog○ /'haʊnddɒg/ n US chien m (de meute).

houndstooth (check) /'haʊndztuːθ/ n pied-de-poule m.

hour /aʊə(r)/ ▶ 1336 |, 812 | I n **1** (60 minutes) heure f; **an ~ ago** il y a une heure; **it's an ~** (away) **from London** c'est à une heure de Londres; **twice an ~** deux fois par heure; **£10 per ~** 10 livres sterling (de) l'heure; **to be paid by the ~** être payé à l'heure; **2** (time of day) heure f; **the bus leaves on the ~** le bus part à l'heure juste; **in the early ~s** au petit matin; **to stay out until all ~s** rentrer très tard dans la nuit; **at this ~?** à l'heure qu'il est?; **3** (point in time) heure f; **her finest ~** son heure de gloire; **in my ~ of need** dans un moment difficile.
　II **hours** npl **1** (times) heures fpl; **business** ou **opening ~s** heures fpl d'ouverture; **office ~s** heures fpl de permanence; **to keep late ~s** se coucher tard; **2** RELIG heures fpl.

hour: **~glass** n sablier m; **~ hand** n aiguille f des heures.

hourly /'aʊəlɪ/ I adj **1** (every hour) horaire; **the buses are ~** les bus partent toutes les heures; **2** (per hour) [rate] horaire; **on an ~ basis** à l'heure.
　II adv **1** (every hour) [arrive, phone] toutes les heures; **2** (per hour) **to pay sb ~** payer qn à l'heure.

house I /haʊs, pl haʊzɪz/ n **1** (home) maison f; **at my/ his ~** chez moi/lui; **to go to sb's ~** aller chez qn; **to be good around the ~** aider à la maison; **to keep ~** tenir la maison (**for** de); **2** POL (also **House**) Chambre f; **the bill before the ~** le projet de loi soumis à la Chambre; **3** COMM maison f; **on the ~** aux frais de la maison; **4** THEAT (audience) assistance f; (auditorium) salle f; (performance) séance f; **'~ full'** 'complet'; **to bring the ~ down** faire crouler la salle sous les applaudissements; **5** (also **House**) (family line) maison f; **the ~ of Windsor** la Maison des Windsor; **6** RELIG maison f; **7** GB SCH (team) maison f; **8** (music) house music f (musique de discothèque).
　II /haʊz/ vtr **1** (give lodging to) (permanently) loger; (temporarily) héberger; **badly** ou **poorly ~d** mal logé; **2** (contain) [building] abriter [books, exhibition].
　IDIOMS **to put one's ~ in order** mettre de l'ordre dans ses affaires; **to get on like a ~ on fire**○ s'entendre à merveille.

house arrest n résidence f surveillée.

houseboat /'haʊsbəʊt/ n **1** (house-shaped) habitation f flottante; **2** (barge) péniche f aménagée.

house: **~bound** adj confiné chez soi; **~breaking** n JUR cambriolage m par effraction; **~broken** adj US [pet] propre; **~ call** n visite f à domicile; **~cleaning** n US ménage m; **~ clearance sale** n vente f de mobilier à la suite d'un décès; **~coat** n déshabillé m, peignoir m; **~fly** n mouche f domestique.

houseguest /'haʊsgest/ n invité/-e m/f (pour quelques jours).

household /'haʊshəʊld/ I n maison f; (in census etc) ménage m; **head of the ~** chef m de famille.
　II noun modifier [accounts, bill] du ménage; [chore, item] ménager/-ère.

household: **~ appliance** n appareil m électroménager; **Household Cavalry** n GB cavalerie f de la Garde royale.

householder /'haʊshəʊldə(r)/ n GEN occupant/-e m/ f; (owner) propriétaire mf; (tenant) locataire mf.

household: **~ insurance** n assurance f de l'habitation; **~ linen** n linge m de maison.

household name n he's a ~ il est célèbre.

house-hunting /'haʊshʌntɪŋ/ n to go ~ se lancer à la recherche d'une maison (à acheter).

house husband n homme m au foyer.

house: **~keeper** ▶ 1251 | n (in house) gouvernante f; (in institution) responsable mf du personnel d'entretien; **~keeping** n (money) argent m du ménage; (managing of money) gestion f de l'argent du ménage; **~ lights** npl THEAT éclairage m; **~maid** ▶ 1251 | n femme f de chambre; **~martin** n hirondelle f de fenêtre; **~master** n GB SCH enseignant m responsable d'un groupe d'enfants (dans un internat britannique); **House of Commons** n Chambre f des communes; **~ officer** ▶ 1251 | n GB MED interne mf; **House of Lords** n GB Chambre f des lords, Chambre f haute; **House of Representatives** n US Chambre f des représentants; **~ painter** ▶ 1251 | n peintre m en bâtiment; **~parent** n responsable mf des enfants (dans une institution); **~ party** n réception f; **~plant** n plante f d'intérieur; **~ prices** npl prix mpl du marché immobilier; **~-proud** adj toujours en train d'astiquer; **~ sales** npl ventes fpl immobilières; **~-sit** vi garder une maison; **Houses of Congress** npl US le Sénat et la Chambre des représentants; **Houses of Parliament** n GB Parlement m Britannique; **~-to-house** adj [search] de maison en maison; **~-trained** adj US propre; **~-warming** (party) n pendaison f de crémaillère; **~wife** n (not employed outside home) femme f au foyer; (with emphasis on domestic labour) ménagère f; **~ wine** n cuvée f maison ou du patron; **~wives** npl ▶ **housewife**.

housework /'haʊswɜːk/ n travaux mpl ménagers; **to do the ~** GEN s'occuper de la maison; (clean) faire le ménage.

housing /'haʊzɪŋ/ I n (houses, flats) logements mpl.
　II noun modifier [crisis, problem] du logement; [conditions] de logement; [shortage] de logements.

housing: **~ benefit** n GB ~ allocation f logement; **~ development** n (large) cité f; (small) lotissement m; **~ estate** n GB (large) cité f; (small) lotissement m; (council-run) ~ cité f ou lotissement m HLM; **~ project** n US ~ cité f ou lotissement m HLM.

hove /həʊv/ pp, prét NAUT ▶ **heave**.

hovel /'hɒvl/ n taudis m.

hover /'hɒvə(r)/ vi **1** [bird] voleter, planer; [helicopter] faire du surplace; **to ~ around sb/sth** tourner autour de qn/qch; **2** (vacillate) vaciller; **country ~ing on the brink of war** pays au bord de la guerre.

hovercraft n (pl ~) aéroglisseur m.

how /haʊ/
　■ **Note** When how is used as a question word meaning *in what way?* or *by what means?* (how did you get here?, how will you do it?) it is almost always translated by *comment*: comment es-tu arrivé ici?; comment le feras-tu?

– When *how* is used as a conjunction meaning *the way in which* it is often translated by *comment*: *I don't know how they did it* = je ne sais pas comment ils l'ont fait; *tell me how you make a curry* = dis-moi comment on fait un curry.
– When *how* is used as a conjunction meaning *that* it is almost always translated by *que*: *he told me how he had stolen the money* = il m'a dit qu'il avait volé l'argent; *it's amazing how they survived* = c'est étonnant qu'ils aient survécu.
– For more examples and particular usages see below.

I *adv, conj* **1** (in what way, by what means) comment; **to know ~ to do** savoir faire; **I learned ~ to do it** j'ai appris à le faire; **~ do you feel about it?** qu'en penses-tu?; **2** (when enquiring) **~ are you?** comment allez-vous?; **~'s your foot?** comment va ton pied?; **~'s your brother?** comment va ton frère?; **~ did you like the party?** la fête t'a plu?; **~ are things?** comment ça va?; **~ do you do!** (greeting) enchanté!; **3** (in number, quantity etc questions) **~ much does this cost?**, **~ much is this?** combien ça coûte?; **~ much do you weigh?** combien pèses-tu?; **~ many times have you been to France?** combien de fois es-tu allé en France?; **~ many people?** combien de personnes?; **~ long will it take?** combien de temps cela va-t-il prendre?; **~ long is the rope?** de quelle longueur est cette corde?; **~ tall is the tree?** combien mesure l'arbre?; **~ big is the garden?** de quelle taille est le jardin?; **~ far is it?** c'est à quelle distance?; **~ old is she?** quel âge a-t-elle?; **4** (in exclamations) **~ wonderful!** c'est fantastique!; **~ nice you look!** que tu es beau/belle!; **~ clever of you!** comme c'est intelligent de ta part!; **~ wrong I was!** comme j'ai eu tort!; **~ it rained!** qu'est-ce qu'il a plu°!; **5°** (in whichever way) comme; **you can decorate it ~ you like** tu peux le décorer comme tu veux; **6** (why) **~ could you?** comment as-tu pu faire ça?; **7** (that) que; **you know ~ he always arrives late** tu sais qu'il arrive toujours en retard.
II° **how come** *adv phr* **'~ come?'** 'pourquoi?'; **~ come you always win?** comment ça se fait que tu gagnes toujours?
III **how's that** *adv phr* **I'll take you home, ~'s that?** je te ramènerai chez toi, ça te va?; **~'s that for an honest answer** ça c'est une réponse honnête.

howdy° /'haʊdɪ/ *excl* US salut°!

however /haʊ'evə(r)/ **I** *conj* toutefois, cependant; **~, the recession is not over yet** toutefois, la récession n'est pas encore terminée; **they can, ~, explain why** ils peuvent, cependant, expliquer pourquoi; **if, ~, you prefer to do** si, toutefois, vous préférez faire.
II *adv* **1** (no matter how) **~ hard I try, I can't** j'ai beau essayer de toutes mes forces, je n'y arrive pas; **~ difficult the task is** ou **may be, we can't give up** si difficile que soit la tâche, nous ne pouvons pas abandonner; **~ small she is** ou **may be** si petite soit-elle; **everyone, ~ poor** chacun, si pauvre soit-il; **~ much it costs** quel que soit le prix; **~ long it takes** quel que soit le temps que ça prendra; **2** (in whatever way) **~ you like** comme tu veux; **~ they travel, they will find it difficult** quelle que soit la façon dont ils voyagent, ça va être difficile; **3** (how) **~ did you guess?** comment as-tu deviné?

howl /haʊl/ **I** *n* hurlement *m*; **a ~ of pain** un hurlement de douleur; **a ~ of laughter** un éclat de rire; **~s of protest** des protestations *fpl* bruyantes.
II *vtr* hurler (**at** à).
III *vi* [*child*] hurler, pousser des hurlements; [*dog, wind*] hurler; **to ~ with rage** hurler de rage.

howling /'haʊlɪŋ/ **I** *n* **1** (of animal, wind) hurlement *m*; **2 ¢** (of baby, crowd) hurlements *mpl*.
II *adj* **1** [*child, animal*] qui hurle, hurlant; **the ~ wind** les hurlements du vent; **2°** FIG [*success*] retentissant.

hp *n* (*abrév* = **horse power**) CV *m*.

HP *n* GB *abrév* ▸ **hire purchase**.

HQ *n* MIL (*abrév* = **headquarters**) QG *m*.

hr *n* (*abrév écrite* = **hour**) h.

HRH *n* (*abrév* = **Her** ou **His Royal Highness**) Son Altesse Royale.

HRT *n*: *abrév* ▸ **hormone replacement therapy**.

HT *n, adj* (*abrév* = **high tension**) HT.

hub /hʌb/ *n* TECH moyeu *m*; FIG centre *m*.

hubbub /'hʌbʌb/ *n* (noise) brouhaha *m*; (turmoil) tohu-bohu *m*.

hubcap /'hʌbkæp/ *n* AUT enjoliveur *m*.

huckleberry /'hʌklbərɪ, US -berɪ/ *n* US myrtille *f*.

huckster /'hʌkstə(r)/ *n* **1** US (pedlar) camelot *m*; **2** PÉJ (salesman) bonimenteur *m*; PÉJ (swindler) escroc *m*.

huddle /'hʌdl/ **I** *n* **1** (of people) petit groupe *m*; (of buildings) entassement *m*; **2** (of footballers) regroupement *m* (*pour mettre au point la stratégie à adopter*).
II *vi* **he was huddling in a corner** il était blotti dans un coin; **she ~d under the bushes** elle se blottit sous les buissons; **to ~ around** se presser autour de.

hue /hjuː/ *n* **1** LITTÉR (shade) nuance *f*; (colour) couleur *f*, teinte *f*; **rose ~d** teinté de rose; **2** FIG (political) tendance *f*.

hue and cry *n* tollé *m*.

huff° /hʌf/ **I** *n* **in a ~** vexé; **to go into a ~** prendre la mouche.
II *vi* **to ~ and puff** LIT haleter; FIG faire toute une histoire.

huffiness /'hʌfɪnɪs/ *n* mauvaise humeur *f*.

hug /hʌg/ **I** *n* étreinte *f*; **to give sb a ~** serrer qn dans ses bras.
II *vtr* (*p prés etc* **-gg-**) **1** (embrace) serrer [qn] dans ses bras; **2** (keep close to) [*boat, vehicle*] raser; [*road*] longer; **to ~ the coast** serrer la côte.

huge /hjuːdʒ/ *adj* [*country, room*] immense; [*building, person, animal*] gigantesque; [*appetite, success*] énorme; [*debts, sum*] gros/grosse (*before n*).

hugely /'hjuːdʒlɪ/ *adv* **1** (emphatic) extrêmement; **2** [*increase, vary*] considérablement; [*enjoy*] énormément.

hugeness /'hjuːdʒnɪs/ *n* (of area, object) immensité *f*.

huh° /hə/ *excl* (in surprise, inquiry) hein!; (in derision, disgust) pff!

hulk /hʌlk/ *n* **1** (of ship) épave *f*; (of machine, tank) carcasse *f*; **2** FIG (bulk) masse *f* gigantesque.

hulking /'hʌlkɪŋ/ *adj* énorme.

hull /hʌl/ *n* **1** (of ship, plane) coque *f*; (of tank) carcasse *f*.
II *vtr* décortiquer [*rice, grain*]; équeuter [*strawberries*].

hullabaloo° /ˌhʌləbə'luː/ *n* (outcry) esclandre *m*; (noise) raffut° *m*.

hullo° /hʌ'ləʊ/ *excl* = **hallo**.

hum /hʌm/ **I** *n* (of insect, engine, traffic, voices) bourdonnement *m*; (of machinery) ronronnement *m*.
II *vtr* (*p prés etc* **-mm-**) fredonner [*tune*].
III *vi* (*p prés etc* **-mm-**) LIT [*person*] fredonner; [*insect, aircraft*] bourdonner; [*machine*] ronronner; FIG [*office*] bourdonner.

human /'hjuːmən/ **I** *n* humain *m*; **fellow ~** semblable *mf*.
II *adj* **1** (not animal) [*race, behaviour, body, population*] humain; [*characteristic, rights*] de l'homme; **he's only ~** il a ses faiblesses comme tout le monde; **~ being** être *m* humain; **2** (sympathetic) humain; **to lack the ~ touch** manquer de chaleur humaine.

humane /hjuː'meɪn/ *adj* **1** [*person, régime*] humain; [*act*] d'humanité; **2** [*slaughter, culling*] sans cruauté.

humanely /hjuː'meɪnlɪ/ *adv* sans cruauté.

human engineering *n* (in industry) gestion *f* des ressources humaines.

humane society *n* US société *f* américaine pour la protection des animaux, cf SPA *f*.

human interest story *n* histoire *f* vécue.

humanism /'hjuːmənɪzm/ *n* humanisme *m*.

humanist /'hjuːmənɪst/ *n, adj* humaniste (*mf*).

humanitarian /hjuːˌmænɪ'teərɪən/ **I** *n* humaniste *mf*.
II *adj* humanitaire.

humanity /hjuː'mænətɪ/ *n* **1** (the human race) humanité *f*; **2** (kindness) humanité *f*; **3 humanities** UNIV humanités *fpl*.

humanize /'hju:mənaɪz/ I *vtr* **1** GEN humaniser; **2** ART, CIN donner un visage humain à.
II **humanizing** *pres p adj* [*influence*] humanisant.

humanly /'hju:mənlɪ/ *adv* humainement.

human nature *n* nature *f* humaine; **it's ~ to…** c'est humain de…

human: **~ resource manager** ▶ 1251 *n* responsable *mf* de la gestion des ressources humaines; **~ rights** *npl* droits *mpl* de l'homme; **~ rights activist** *n* militant/-e *m/f* pour les droits de l'homme; **~ rights campaign** *n* mouvement *m* pour les droits de l'homme.

humble /'hʌmbl/ I *adj* **1** (lowly) [*origin, position*] modeste; **2** (unpretentious) AUSSI HUM [*dwelling, gift*] modeste; **3** (deferential) humble; **please accept my ~ apologies** SOUT je vous prie d'accepter mes humbles excuses FML; **4** (showing humility) humble.
II *vtr* humilier; **to ~ oneself** s'humilier.
IDIOMS **to eat ~ pie** aller à Canossa.

humbling /'hʌmblɪŋ/ *adj* humiliant, salutaire.

humbly /'hʌmblɪ/ *adv* humblement; **~ born** d'origine modeste.

humbug /'hʌmbʌg/ *n* **1**° (dishonesty) tromperie *f*; **2**° (nonsense) fumisterie° *f*; **3** GB bonbon *m* à la menthe.

humdrum /'hʌmdrʌm/ *adj* monotone.

humid /'hju:mɪd/ *adj* [*climate*] humide; [*weather*] lourd.

humidifier /hju:'mɪdɪfaɪə(r)/ *n* humidificateur *m*.

humidity /hju:'mɪdətɪ/ *n* humidité *f*.

humiliate /hju:'mɪlɪeɪt/ *vtr* humilier.

humiliating /hju:'mɪlɪeɪtɪŋ/ *adj* humiliant.

humiliation /hju:ˌmɪlɪ'eɪʃn/ *n* humiliation *f*.

humility /hju:'mɪlətɪ/ *n* humilité *f*.

humming /'hʌmɪŋ/ *n* (of insect, aircraft) bourdonnement *m*; (of machine) ronronnement *m*; (of person) fredonnement *m*.

humming bird *n* oiseau-mouche *m*, colibri *m*.

hummock /'hʌmək/ *n* (of earth) monticule *m*.

hummus /'hɒməs/ *n* hoummos *m*.

humor *n* US = **humour**.

humorist /'hju:mərɪst/ *n* humoriste *mf*.

humorless *adj* US = **humourless**.

humorous /'hju:mərəs/ *adj* **1** (amusing) humoristique; **2** (amused) plein d'humour.

humorously /'hju:mərəslɪ/ *adv* avec humour.

humour GB, **humor** US /'hju:mə(r)/ I *n* **1** (wit) humour *m*; **a good sense of ~** le sens de l'humour; **2** (mood) humeur *f*; **to be in good ~** être de bonne humeur; **to be in no ~ for arguing** ne pas être d'humeur à discuter; **when the ~ takes me** quand l'envie m'en prend.
II *vtr* amadouer [*person*]; se plier à [*request*]; ▶ **good-humoured**.

humourless GB, **humorless** US /'hju:mələs/ *adj* [*person*] qui manque d'humour; [*description, tone*] dépourvu d'humour.

hump /hʌmp/ I *n* **1** LIT (all contexts) bosse *f*; **road ~** ralentisseur *m*, dos-d'âne *m inv*.
II° *vtr* GB (lift, carry) porter, traîner.

humpback(ed) bridge *n* pont *m* en dos d'âne.

humpy /'hʌmpɪ/ *adj* [*land, field*] bosselé.

humus /'hju:məs/ *n* humus *m*.

hunch /hʌntʃ/ I *n* intuition *f*; **to have a ~ that** avoir l'intuition que.
II *vtr* **to ~ one's shoulders** rentrer les épaules.
III *vi* **to ~ over one's desk** se tenir penché à son bureau.

hunch: **~back** *n* INJUR bossu/-e *m/f*; **~backed** *adj* bossu.

hunched /hʌntʃt/ *adj* [*back*] voûté; [*shoulders*] rentré.

hundred /'hʌndrəd/ ▶ 1112 I *n* cent *m*; **two ~** deux cents; **two ~ and one** deux cent un; **a ~ to one** cent contre un; **it was a ~ to one chance** il y avait une chance sur cent; **sold in ~s** ou **by the ~** vendu par centaines; **in nineteen ~** en mille neuf cents; **in**

nineteen ~ and three en mil neuf cent trois; **~s of times** des centaines de fois.
II *adj* cent; **two ~ francs** deux cents francs; **two ~ and five francs** deux cent cinq francs; **about a ~ people** une centaine de personnes.

hundred-and-one ▶ 1112 I *n* cent un.
II *adj* LIT cent un/une; **I've a ~ things to do** FIG j'ai mille choses à faire.

hundredfold /'hʌndrədfəʊld/ *adv* **a ~** par cent; **to increase ~** centupler.

hundreds and thousands *npl* CULIN nonpareilles *fpl*.

hundredth /'hʌndrətθ/ ▶ 1112 I *n* **1** (fraction) centième *m*; **2** (in order) centième *mf*.
II *adj, adv* centième.

hundredweight ▶ 1392 *n* GB = 50,80 *kg*; US = 45,36 *kg*.

hung /hʌŋ/ I *prét, pp* ▶ **hang**.
II *adj* POL [*jury, parliament*] en suspens.

Hungarian /hʌŋ'geərɪən/ ▶ 1100, 1038 I *n* (person) Hongrois/-e *m/f*; (language) hongrois *m*.
II *adj* hongrois.

Hungary /'hʌŋgərɪ/ ▶ 840 *pr n* Hongrie *f*.

hunger /'hʌŋgə(r)/ I *n* faim *f*; FIG désir *m* ardent (**for** de).
II *vi* **to ~ for** FIG avoir faim de.

hunger strike *n* grève *f* de la faim.

hung-over° /ˌhʌŋ'əʊvə(r)/ *adj* **to be ~** avoir la gueule de bois°.

hungrily /'hʌŋgrɪlɪ/ *adv* LIT avec voracité; FIG avec avidité.

hungry /'hʌŋgrɪ/ *adj* **1** LIT **to be** ou **feel ~** avoir faim; **to make sb ~** donner faim à qn; **to go ~** (from necessity) souffrir de la faim; **I'd rather go ~!** je préfère me passer de manger!; **2** FIG avide; **~ for** assoiffé de [*success*]; **power-~** assoiffé de pouvoir.

hung-up° /ˌhʌŋ'ʌp/ *adj* **1** (tense) complexé; **2** (obsessed with) **to be ~ on sb/sth** être dingue° de qn/qch.

hunk /hʌŋk/ *n* (of bread) gros morceau *m*; (man)° beau mec° *m*.

hunker° /'hʌŋkə(r)/ I **hunkers** *npl* **to sit on one's ~s** s'accroupir; **to be on one's ~s** être accroupi.
II *vi* (also **~ down**) s'accroupir.

hunky-dory° /ˌhʌŋkɪ'dɔ:rɪ/ *adj* super°, au poil°.

hunt /hʌnt/ I *n* **1** (search) recherche *f* (**for** de); **the ~ is on for the terrorists** on recherche les terroristes; **2** (activity) chasse *f*; **lion ~** chasse au lion; **3** (fox-hunting group, area) chasse *f* à courre.
II *vtr* **1** (seek, pursue) rechercher; **to ~ sb out of** ou **off** faire sortir qn de; **2** (pursue) chasser [*game, fox*].
III *vi* **1** (for prey) chasser; **2** (search) **to ~ for sth** chercher [qch] partout [*object, person, address*]; être à la recherche de [*truth, cure*].
■ **hunt down 1** forcer [*animal*]; **2** (find) traquer [*criminal*]; persécuter [*victim, minority*].
■ **hunt up** s'enquérir de [*old friend, person*].

hunted /'hʌntɪd/ *adj* traqué.

hunter /'hʌntə(r)/ *n* **1** (person who hunts) chasseur/-euse *m/f*; (in fox-hunting) chasseur/-euse *m/f* à courre; (animal that hunts) prédateur *m* (**of** de); **2** (horse) cheval *m* de chasse; **3** (dog) chien *m* de chasse; **4** (collector) collectionneur/-euse *m/f*.

hunter-killer *n* MIL NAUT navire *m* d'un groupe de recherche et d'attaque.

hunting /'hʌntɪŋ/ I *n* chasse *f* (**of** à); **to go ~** aller à la chasse.
II *noun modifier* [*boot, knife, season*] de chasse.

hunting: **~ crop** *n* cravache *f*; **~ lodge** *n* pavillon *m* de chasse; **~ pink** *n* veste *f* de veneur.

hunt saboteur *n* GB opposant/-e *m/f* à la chasse au renard.

huntsman /'hʌntsmən/ *n* **1** (hunter) GEN chasseur *m*; (fox-hunter) chasseur *m* à courre; **2** (trainer of hounds) veneur *m*.

hunt the thimble ▶ 949 *n* cache-tampon *m inv*.

hurdle /'hɜ:dl/ I *n* ▶ 949 SPORT haie *f*; **the 100m**

~s le 100 m haies; FIG obstacle *m*; **to clear a ~** LIT franchir une haie; FIG surmonter un obstacle.
II *vi* SPORT faire de la course de haies.

hurdler /'hɜ:dlə(r)/ *n* coureur *m* de haies.

hurdling /'hɜ:dlɪŋ/ ▶ 949 *n* course *f* de haies.

hurdy-gurdy /'hɜ:dɪgɜ:dɪ/ ▶ 1097 *n* orgue *m* de Barbarie.

hurl /hɜ:l/ **I** *vtr* **1** lancer (at sur); **to be ~ed to the ground** être projeté au sol; **2** FIG **to ~ insults at sb** accabler qn d'injures.
II *v refl* **to ~ oneself** LIT se précipiter; FIG se jeter.

hurly-burly /'hɜ:lɪbɜ:lɪ/ *n* tohu-bohu *m*.

hurrah, **hurray** /hʊ'rɑ:/ *n, excl* hourra (*m*); **~ for X!** vive X!

hurricane /'hʌrɪkən, US -keɪn/ *n* ouragan *m*; **~ force wind** vent soufflant en ouragan.

hurried /'hʌrɪd/ *adj* [*note, visit, meal*] rapide; [*job, work*] fait à la va-vite; [*departure*] précipité.

hurriedly /'hʌrɪdlɪ/ *adv* [*dress, pack, write*] en toute hâte; [*leave*] précipitamment.

hurry /'hʌrɪ/ **I** *n* hâte *f*, empressement *m*; **to be in a ~** être pressé (**to do de faire**); **there's no ~** ça ne presse pas; **what's the ~?** qu'est-ce qui presse?; **to do sth in a ~** faire qch à la hâte; **I won't forget that in a ~!** je ne suis pas près d'oublier ça!
II *vtr* **1** (do hastily) terminer [qch] à la hâte [*meal, task*]; **2** (rush, bustle) bousculer [*person*]; **to ~ sb in/out** faire entrer/sortir qn en toute hâte.
III *vi* se dépêcher (**to do de faire**); **to ~ out** sortir précipitamment; **to ~ home** se dépêcher de rentrer.
■ **hurry along**: ¶ **~ along** se presser, se dépêcher; ¶ **~ along [sth]**, **~ [sth] along** faire accélérer, activer [*process*].
■ **hurry back** (to any place) se dépêcher de retourner (**to** à); (to one's home) se dépêcher de rentrer (chez soi).
■ **hurry off** se sauver.
■ **hurry up**: ¶ **~ up** se dépêcher; **~ up!** dépêche-toi!; ¶ **~ [sth] up** faire accélérer, activer [*process*].

hurt /hɜ:t/ **I** *n* blessure *f*; **his sense of ~** son sentiment d'avoir été blessé.
II *adj* peiné, blessé; **I am more angry than ~** je suis plus fâché que blessé; **she was ~ not to have been invited** elle a été peinée de ne pas avoir été invitée; **to sound** ou **look/feel ~** avoir l'air/être peiné.
III *vtr* (*prét, pp* **hurt**) **1** (injure) **to ~ oneself** se blesser, se faire mal; **to ~ one's back** se blesser or se faire mal au dos; **was anybody hurt?** y a-t-il eu des blessés?; **somebody's going to get hurt** quelqu'un va se faire mal; **it wouldn't ~ her to apologize** ça ne lui ferait pas de mal de s'excuser; **2** (cause pain to) faire mal à; **you're ~ing my arm** vous me faites mal au bras; **it ~s him to walk** il a mal quand il marche; **3** (emotionally) blesser; (offend) froisser; **to ~ sb's feelings** blesser quelqu'un; **to ~ sb's pride** blesser quelqu'un dans son amour-propre; **she's afraid of getting hurt** elle a peur de souffrir; **4** [*prices, inflation*] nuire à.
IV *vi* (*prét, pp* **hurt**) **1** (be painful) faire mal; **my throat ~s** j'ai mal à la gorge; **where does it ~?** où est-ce que vous avez mal?; **my shoes ~ mes chaussures me font mal; it ~s when I laugh** j'ai mal quand je ris; **2** (take effect) [*sanctions, taxes*] se faire sentir; **3** (emotionally) blesser; **the truth often ~s** la vérité est souvent cruelle.

hurtful /'hɜ:tfl/ *adj* blessant.

hurtle /'hɜ:tl/ *vi* **to ~ down sth** dévaler qch; **to ~ along a road** foncer sur une route; **to ~ through the air** fendre l'air; **a stone ~d through the window** une pierre vola à travers la vitre.

husband /'hʌzbənd/ **I** *n* mari *m*; ADMIN époux *m*; **to live as ~ and wife** vivre maritalement.
II *vtr* (manage prudently) bien gérer [*resources*].

husbandry /'hʌzbəndrɪ/ *n* **animal ~** élevage *m*.

hush /hʌʃ/ **I** *n* silence *m*.
II *excl* (all contexts) chut!
III *vtr* faire taire [*person*]; faire cesser [*bruit*]; calmer [*baby*].

■ **hush up**: ¶ **~ up** se taire; ¶ **~ up [sth]**, **~ [sth] up** étouffer [*affair*]; ¶ **~ up [sb]**, **~ [sb] up** faire taire [*person*].

hushed /hʌʃt/ *adj* [*conversation*] étouffé; [*room, crowd*] silencieux/-ieuse; **in ~ tones** à voix basse.

hush-hush○ /ˌhʌʃ'hʌʃ/ *adj* très confidentiel/-ielle.

hush money○ *n* **to pay sb ~** acheter le silence de qn.

husk /hʌsk/ **I** *n* (of grains) enveloppe *f* ALSO FIG.
II *vtr* décortiquer.

husky /'hʌskɪ/ **I** *n* (dog) husky *m*.
II *adj* [*voice*] enroué.

hussar /hʊ'zɑ:(r)/ *n* hussard *m*.

hustings /'hʌstɪŋz/ *n* **at/on the ~** pendant la campagne électorale.

hustle /'hʌsl/ **I** *n* **~ (and bustle)** (lively) effervescence *f*; (tiring) agitation *f*.
II *vtr* **1** (push) pousser, bousculer [*person*]; **to ~ sb into a building** pousser qn dans un bâtiment; **2** (urge) **to ~ sb (into doing)** pousser qn (à faire); **3**○ US (sell illegally) vendre illégalement; **4**○ US (obtain by dubious means) soutirer [*money*]; dégoter○ [*job*]; **5** (hurry) précipiter [*negotiations*]; bousculer [*person*].
III *vi* **1** (hurry) se dépêcher; **2**○ US (struggle, work) se démener; **3**○ US (get money dishonestly) pratiquer l'arnaque○.

hustler○ /'hʌslə(r)/ *n* US **1** (swindler) arnaqueur/-euse○ *m/f*; **2** (prostitute) prostitué/-e *m/f*.

hut /hʌt/ *n* (in garden) cabane *f*; (in shanty town) bicoque○ *f*; (on building site) baraque *f* (de chantier); (for climbers, shepherds) refuge *m*; (native type) hutte *f*, case *f*; (grass) paillote *f*; (on beach) cabine *f* (de plage).

hutch /hʌtʃ/ *n* **1** (for animals) GEN cage *f*; (for rabbits) clapier *m*; **2** FIG PEJ (house) clapier *m*; **3** US (furniture) dressoir *m*.

hyacinth /'haɪəsɪnθ/ *n* (flower) jacinthe *f*.

hybrid /'haɪbrɪd/ *n, adj* (all contexts) hybride (*m*).

hydra /'haɪdrə/ *n* (*pl* **-e** ou **~s**) hydre *f* ALSO FIG.

hydrangea /haɪ'dreɪndʒə/ *n* hortensia *m*.

hydrant /'haɪdrənt/ *n* **1** GEN prise *f* d'eau; **2** (also **fire ~**) bouche *f* d'incendie.

hydrate /'haɪdreɪt/ **I** *n* hydrate *m*.
II *vtr* hydrater.

hydraulic /haɪ'drɔ:lɪk/ *adj* (all contexts) hydraulique.

hydraulic ramp *n* AUT pont-élévateur *m*.

hydraulics /haɪ'drɔ:lɪks/ *n* (+ *v sg*) hydraulique *f*.

hydro /'haɪdrəʊ/ *n* GB établissement *m* thermal.

hydroelectric /ˌhaɪdrəʊ'lektrɪk/ *adj* hydroélectrique.

hydroelectricity /ˌhaɪdrəʊɪlek'trɪsətɪ/ *n* hydroélectricité *f*.

hydrofoil /'haɪdrəfɔɪl/ *n* **1** (craft) hydroptère *m*; **2** (foil) aile *f* portante.

hydrogen /'haɪdrədʒən/ *n* hydrogène *m*.

hydrogen: **~ bomb** *n* bombe *f* à hydrogène; **~ peroxide** *n* eau *f* oxygénée.

hydrolysis /haɪ'drɒləsɪs/ *n* hydrolyse *f*.

hydrophobia /ˌhaɪdrə'fəʊbɪə/ *n* hydrophobie *f*.

hydroplane /'haɪdrəpleɪn/ *n* (boat) hydroglisseur *m*; US (seaplane) hydravion *m*.

hydroplaning /ˌhaɪdrə'pleɪnɪŋ/ *n* aquaplanage *m*.

hydrotherapy /ˌhaɪdrəʊ'θerəpɪ/ *n* hydrothérapie *f*.

hyena /haɪ'i:nə/ *n* ZOOL hyène *f*; FIG requin *m*.

hygiene /'haɪdʒi:n/ *n* hygiène *f*; **food ~** hygiène alimentaire.

hygienic /haɪ'dʒi:nɪk/ *adj* hygiénique.

hygienist /'haɪdʒi:nɪst/ ▶ 1251 *n* hygiéniste *mf*.

hymn /hɪm/ *n* (song) cantique *m*; FIG hymne *m* (**to** à).

hymnbook /'hɪmbʊk/ *n* livre *m* de cantiques.

hype○ /haɪp/ *n* battage *m* publicitaire; **media ~** battage *m* médiatique, médiatisation *f* à outrance.

■ **hype up**: **~ up [sth]**, **~ [sth] up** doper○ [*sales, economy*]; faire du battage pour [*film, star, book*]; gonfler [*issue, story*].

hyped up○ /ˌhaɪpt'ʌp/ *adj* [*person*] surexcité.

hyper○ /'haɪpə(r)/ *adj* surexcité.

hyperactive /ˌhaɪpərˈæktɪv/ adj GEN, MED, PSYCH hyperactif/-ive.

hyperactivity /ˌhaɪpəræk'tɪvətɪ/ n hyperactivité f.

hyperbole /haɪ'pɜːbəlɪ/ n hyperbole f.

hypercritical /ˌhaɪpə'krɪtɪkl/ adj excessivement critique.

hypermarket /'haɪpəmɑːkɪt/ n GB hypermarché m.

hypersensitive /ˌhaɪpə'sensɪtɪv/ adj hypersensible.

hypertension /ˌhaɪpə'tenʃn/ n hypertension f.

hyperventilate /ˌhaɪpə'ventɪleɪt/ vi être en hyperventilation.

hyphen /'haɪfn/ n trait m d'union.

hyphenate /'haɪfəneɪt/ vtr **to be ~d** s'écrire avec un trait d'union.

hypnosis /hɪp'nəʊsɪs/ n hypnose f.

hypnotherapy /ˌhɪpnə'θerəpɪ/ n hypnothérapie f.

hypnotic /hɪp'nɒtɪk/ n, adj hypnotique (m).

hypnotism /'hɪpnətɪzəm/ n hypnotisme m.

hypnotist /'hɪpnətɪst/ n hypnotiseur m.

hypnotize /'hɪpnətaɪz/ vtr hypnotiser.

hypoallergenic /ˌhaɪpəʊælə'dʒenɪk/ adj hypoallergique.

hypochondria /ˌhaɪpə'kɒndrɪə/ n hypocondrie f.

hypochondriac /ˌhaɪpə'kɒndrɪæk/ n, adj hypocondriaque (mf).

hypocrisy /hɪ'pɒkrəsɪ/ n hypocrisie f.

hypocrite /'hɪpəkrɪt/ n hypocrite mf.

hypocritical /ˌhɪpə'krɪtɪkl/ adj hypocrite.

hypocritically /ˌhɪpə'krɪtɪklɪ/ adv hypocritement.

hypodermic /ˌhaɪpə'dɜːmɪk/ adj hypodermique.

hypotenuse /haɪ'pɒtənjuːz, US -tnuːs/ n hypoténuse f.

hypothermia /ˌhaɪpəʊ'θɜːmɪə/ n hypothermie f.

hypothesis /haɪ'pɒθəsɪs/ n (pl **-theses**) hypothèse f.

hypothesize /haɪ'pɒθəsaɪz/ vi émettre une hypothèse.

hypothetic(al) /ˌhaɪpə'θetɪk(l)/ adj hypothétique.

hysterectomy /ˌhɪstə'rektəmɪ/ n hystérectomie f.

hysteria /hɪ'stɪərɪə/ n hystérie f.

hysterical /hɪ'sterɪkl/ adj [person, behaviour] hystérique; [sob] convulsif/-ive; [demand, speech] délirant; **~ laughter** fou rire m.

hysterically /hɪ'sterɪklɪ/ adv **1** [funny] follement; **2 to sob ~** avoir une violente crise de larmes; **to laugh ~** avoir le fou rire; **to shout ~** hurler comme un/-e hystérique.

hysterics /hɪ'sterɪks/ n **1** GEN (fit) crise f de nerfs; **to go into** ou **have ~** avoir une crise de nerfs; **2** (laughter) **to be in ~** rire aux larmes.

i, I /aɪ/ *n* i, I *m*.
 IDIOMS **to dot the i's and cross the t's** mettre les points sur les i.

I /aɪ/
 ■ Note *I* is almost always translated by je which becomes j' before a vowel or mute h: *I closed the door* = j'ai fermé la porte. The emphatic form is *moi*.
 – For exceptions and particular uses see below.

 pron je, j'; **he's a student but I'm not** il est étudiant mais moi pas; **he and I went to the cinema** lui et moi sommes allés au cinéma.

IA US POST *abrév écrite* = **Iowa**.

ibex /'aɪbeks/ *n* bouquetin *m*.

ice /aɪs/ **I** *n* **1** GEN glace *f*; (on roads) verglas *m*; (in drinks) glaçons *mpl*; **to put sth on ~** LIT mettre qch à rafraîchir; FIG mettre qch en attente; **2** GB (ice cream) glace *f*; **3**◦ **¢** (diamonds) diamants *mpl*.
 II *vtr* CULIN glacer.
 III iced *pp adj* [*water*] avec des glaçons; [*tea*] glacé; [*coffee*] frappé.
 IDIOMS **to break the ~** rompre la glace; **to cut no ~ (with sb)** ne faire aucun effet (à qn); **to be treading** ou **skating on thin ~** s'aventurer sur un terrain glissant.
 ■ **ice over** [*windscreen, river*] se couvrir de glace.

ice: **~ age** *n* période *f* glaciaire; **~ axe** *n* piolet *m*.

iceberg /'aɪsbɜːg/ *n* iceberg *m*.
 IDIOMS **the tip of the ~** la partie visible de l'iceberg.

iceberg lettuce *n* laitue *f* croquante.

icebox /'aɪsbɒks/ *n* **1** GB (freezer compartment) freezer *m*; **2** US (fridge) réfrigérateur *m*.

ice: **~breaker** *n* NAUT brise-glace *m inv*; **~ bucket** *n* seau *m* à glace; **~cap** *n* calotte *f* glaciaire; **~-cold** *adj* glacé; **~ cream** *n* CULIN glace *f*; **~-cream parlour** GB, **~-cream parlor** US *n* COMM glacier *m*; **~-cream soda** *n* US *boule de glace servie dans un soda*; **~cream sundae** *n* coupe *f* glacée; **~-cube** *n* glaçon *m*; **~ dancer** ▶949 *n* danseur/-euse *m/f* sur glace; **~ floe** *n* glace *f* flottante; **~ hockey** ▶949 *n* hockey *m* sur glace.

Iceland /'aɪslənd/ ▶840 *pr n* Islande *f*.

ice: **~ pack** *n* poche *f* de glace; **~ pick** *n* CULIN pic *m* à glace; **~ rink** *n* patinoire *f*.

iceskate /'aɪsskeɪt/ ▶949 **I** *n* patin *m* à glace.
 II *vi* GEN patiner; (as a hobby) faire du patinage.

ice: **~-skating** ▶949 *n* patinage *m* sur glace; **~-tray** *n* bac *m* à glaçons.

icicle /'aɪsɪkl/ *n* stalactite *f* (de glace).

icily /'aɪsɪli/ *adv* [*stare*] de façon glaciale; [*say*] d'un ton glacial.

icing /'aɪsɪŋ/ *n* glaçage *m*.
 IDIOMS **to be the ~ on the cake** être la cerise sur le gâteau.

icing sugar *n* GB sucre *m* glace.

icon /'aɪkɒn/ *n* icône *f*; FIG (person) idole *f*; (object) symbole *m*.

iconoclast /aɪ'kɒnəklæst/ *n* iconoclaste *mf*.

iconography /ˌaɪkə'nɒgrəfi/ *n* LIT iconographie *f*.

icy /'aɪsi/ *adj* **1** [*road*] verglacé; **~ patches** plaques *fpl* de verglas; **2** (cold) [*wind*] glacial; [*hands*] glacé; **3** FIG [*look, reception*] glacial.

id /ɪd/ *n* **the ~** le ça.

I'd /aɪd/ = **I had, I should, I would.**

ID *n* **1** (*abrév* = **identification, identity**) pièce *f* d'identité; **~ card** carte *f* d'identité; **2** US POST *abrév écrite* = **Idaho**.

idea /aɪ'dɪə/ *n* **1** (thought) idée *f* (**about, on** sur); **he came up with** ou **hit on the ~ of buying a farm** l'idée lui est venue d'acheter une ferme; **to be full of ~s** avoir plein d'idées; **don't start getting ~s!** ne commence pas à te faire des idées!; **you can get** ou **put that ~ out of your head!** il n'en est pas question!; **2** (notion) conception *f* (**about, of** de); **if that's your ~ of a joke...** si c'est ça que tu appelles une plaisanterie...; **3** (impression) impression *f*; **whatever gave you that ~!** qu'est-ce qui t'a fait croire une chose pareille!; **4** (knowledge) idée *f*; **to have no ~ why/how etc** ne pas savoir pourquoi/comment etc; **to have no ~ of** ou **about** n'avoir aucune idée de [*price, time*]; **you've no ~ how pleased I was!** tu ne peux pas savoir combien j'étais content!; **5** (theory) idée *f*; **I've an ~ that he might be lying** j'ai dans l'idée qu'il ment; **6** (aim) but *m* (**behind, of** de); **7** (gist) **do you get the ~?** tu vois?; **that's the ~!** c'est ça!
 IDIOMS **the very ~!** quelle idée!

ideal /aɪ'dɪəl/ **I** *n* idéal *m* (**of** de).
 II *adj* idéal (**for** pour; **to do** pour faire).

idealism /aɪ'dɪəlɪzəm/ *n* idéalisme *m*.

idealist /aɪ'dɪəlɪst/ *n* idéaliste *mf*.

idealistic /ˌaɪdɪə'lɪstɪk/ *adj* idéaliste.

idealize /aɪ'dɪəlaɪz/ *vtr* idéaliser.

ideally /aɪ'dɪəli/ *adv* **1** (preferably) **~, the tests should be free** l'idéal serait que les examens soient gratuits; **~, we'd like to stay** l'idéal pour nous, ce serait de rester; **2** (perfectly) **~ situated** idéalement situé; **to be ~ suited** [*couple*] être parfaitement assortis; **to be ~ suited for** être parfait pour [*job*].

identical /aɪ'dentɪkl/ *adj* identique (**to, with** à); [*twin*] vrai.

identically /aɪ'dentɪkli/ *adv* de façon identique.

identifiable /aɪˌdentɪ'faɪəbl/ *adj* identifiable (**as** comme étant); **~ by sth** reconnaissable à qch.

identification /aɪˌdentɪfɪ'keɪʃn/ *n* **1** (of species, person) identification *f* (**from** à partir de); **2** (empathy) identification *f* (**with** à); **3** (proof of identity) pièce *f* d'identité.

identify /aɪ'dentɪfaɪ/ **I** *vtr* (establish identity of) identifier (**as** comme étant; **to** à); (pick out) distinguer; (consider as equivalent) **to ~ sb/sth with sb/sth** identifier qn/qch à qn/qch.
 II *vi* (empathize) **to ~ with** s'identifier à.
 III *v refl* **to ~ oneself** donner son identité.

identikit /aɪ'dentɪkɪt/ *n* (also **Identikit®, identikit picture**) portrait-robot *m*.

identity /aɪ'dentəti/ *n* identité *f*; **have you any proof of ~?** avez-vous une pièce d'identité?; **mistaken ~** erreur *f* d'identité.

identity: **~ bracelet** *n* gourmette *f*; **~ card** *n* carte *f* d'identité; **~ parade** *n* GB séance *f* d'identification.

ideogram /'ɪdɪəgræm/, **ideograph** /'ɪdɪəgrɑːf, US -græf/ *n* idéogramme *m*.

ideological /ˌaɪdɪə'lɒdʒɪkl/ *adj* idéologique.

ideologically /ˌaɪdɪə'lɒdʒɪkli/ *adv* d'un point de vue idéologique.

ideology /ˌaɪdɪ'ɒlədʒɪ/ *n* idéologie *f*.

idiocy /'ɪdɪəsɪ/ *n* (stupidity) idiotie *f*; (stupid remark) bêtise *f*.

idiom /'ɪdɪəm/ n **1** (phrase) idiome m; **2** (language) (of speakers') parler m; (of theatre, sport) langue f; (of music) style m.

idiomatic /ˌɪdɪə'mætɪk/ adj idiomatique.

idiosyncrasy /ˌɪdɪə'sɪŋkrəsɪ/ n particularité f.

idiosyncratic /ˌɪdɪəsɪŋ'krætɪk/ adj particulier/-ière.

idiot /'ɪdɪət/ n idiot/-e m/f.

idiotic /ˌɪdɪ'ɒtɪk/ adj bête.

idiotically /ˌɪdɪ'ɒtɪklɪ/ adv bêtement.

idle /'aɪdl/ I adj **1** (lazy) [person] paresseux/-euse, fainéant; **2** (vain) [boast, threat] vain; [curiosity] oiseux/-euse; [chatter] inutile; **3** (without occupation) [person] oisif/-ive; [day, hour, moment] de loisir; **4** (not functioning) [port, dock, mine] à l'arrêt; [machine] arrêté; **to lie** ou **stand** ~ [machine, factory] être à l'arrêt; [land] rester inexploité.
II vi [engine] tourner au ralenti.
IDIOMS **the devil makes work for** ~ **hands** PROV l'oisiveté est mère de tous les vices PROV.
■ **idle away**: ~ **away** [sth], ~ [sth] **away** passer [qch] à ne rien faire [day]; **to** ~ **away one's life/time** passer sa vie/son temps à ne rien faire.

idleness /'aɪdlnɪs/ n (inaction) inactivité f; (laziness) paresse f.

idler /'aɪdlə(r)/ n paresseux/-euse m/f.

idly /'aɪdlɪ/ adv (not doing anything) paresseusement; (aimlessly) [chat] pour passer le temps.

idol /'aɪdl/ n idole f.

idolatry /aɪ'dɒlətrɪ/ n idolâtrie f.

idolize /'aɪdəlaɪz/ vtr adorer [friend]; idolâtrer [star].

idyll /'ɪdɪl, US 'aɪdɪl/ n idylle f.

idyllic /ɪ'dɪlɪk, US aɪ'd-/ adj idyllique.

ie (abrév = that is) c-à-d.

if /ɪf/

■ **Note** if is almost always translated by si, except in the case of a very few usages which are shown below.

I conj **1** (in the event that, supposing that) si; **I'll help you** ~ **you pay me** je t'aiderai si tu me paies; ~ **he dies** ou ~ **he should die** s'il meurt; ~ **she is to be believed** si on l'en croit; ~ **asked, I would say that** si on me posait la question, je dirais que; ~ **you like** si tu veux; ~ **I were you, I...** (moi) à ta place, je...; ~ **it were to snow** s'il neigeait; ~ **it were not for the baby** s'il n'y avait pas le bébé; ~ **so** si c'est le cas; ~ **not** sinon; **tomorrow,** ~ **not sooner** demain au plus tard, demain ou même avant; ~ **I'm not mistaken** si je ne me trompe; **2** (whenever) si; ~ **you mention his name, she cries** il suffit de prononcer son nom pour qu'elle pleure; **3** (whether) si; **I wonder** ~ **they will come** je me demande s'ils vont venir; **4** (functioning as that) **I'm sorry** ~ **she doesn't like it but...** je suis désolé que cela ne lui plaise pas mais...; **do you mind** ~ **I smoke?** cela vous dérange si je fume?; **I don't care** ~ **he is married!** cela m'est égal qu'il soit marié!; **5** (although) si; **we'll go even** ~ **it's dangerous** nous irons même si c'est dangereux; **it's a good shop,** ~ **a little expensive** c'est un bon magasin, bien qu'un peu cher; **it was interesting,** ~ **nothing else** au moins c'était intéressant; **6** (as polite formula) ~ **you would follow me please** si vous voulez bien me suivre; **7** (expressing surprise, dismay etc) ~ **it isn't our old friend Mr Pivachon!** tiens, mais voilà notre vieil ami M. Pivachon!; **well,** ~ **she didn't try and hit him!** je vous jure, elle a essayé de le battre!; **8** (used with what) **what** ~ **he died?** et s'il mourait?; **what** ~ **I say no?** et si je dis non?; **(so) what** ~ **he** (ou **I** etc) **did?** et alors?
II **if only** conj phr ~ **only because (of)** ne serait-ce qu'à cause de; ~ **only for a moment** ne serait-ce que pour un instant; ~ **only I had known!** si (seulement) j'avais su!
IDIOMS **it's a very big** ~ c'est loin d'être sûr.

iffy° /'ɪfɪ/ adj (dubious) suspect; (undecided) incertain.

igloo /'ɪglu:/ n igloo m, iglou m.

ignite /ɪg'naɪt/ I vtr faire exploser [fuel]; enflammer [material].
II vi [petrol, gas] s'enflammer; [rubbish, timber] prendre feu.

ignition /ɪg'nɪʃn/ n AUT (system) allumage m; (starting mechanism) contact m.

ignition: ~ **key** n clé f de contact; ~ **switch** n contact m.

ignominious /ˌɪgnə'mɪnɪəs/ adj SOUT ignominieux/-ieuse.

ignoramus /ˌɪgnə'reɪməs/ n (pl **-muses**) ignare mf.

ignorance /'ɪgnərəns/ n (of person) ignorance f; **to be in** ~ **of sth** ignorer qch.
IDIOMS ~ **is bliss** l'ignorance est salvatrice.

ignorant /'ɪgnərənt/ adj [person] (of a subject) ignorant; (uneducated) inculte; [remark] d'ignorant; **to be** ~ **about** tout ignorer de [subject]; **to be** ~ **of** ignorer [possibilities].

ignorantly /'ɪgnərəntlɪ/ adv par ignorance.

ignore /ɪg'nɔː(r)/ vtr ignorer [person]; ne pas relever [criticism, mistake, remark]; ne pas tenir compte de [feeling, fact]; ne pas respecter [rule]; ne pas suivre [advice]; se désintéresser complètement de [problem]; **to** ~ **sb's very existence** faire comme si qn n'existait pas.

IL US POST abrév écrite = **Illinois**.

ilk /ɪlk/ n (sans pl) espèce f.

ill /ɪl/ I n mal m; **to wish sb** ~ souhaiter du mal à qn; **economic** ~**s** les maux de l'économie.
II adj malade; **to be** ~ **with sth** (serious illness) être atteint de qch; (less serious) souffrir de qch; **to be taken** ~, **to fall** ~ tomber malade.
III adv SOUT **1** (badly) **he is** ~ **suited to the post** il n'est guère fait pour ce poste; **to speak** ~ **of sb** dire du mal de qn; **to bode** ou **augur** ~ **for sth** LITTÉR être de mauvais augure pour qch; **2** (scarcely) **it** ~ **becomes you to criticize** il ne vous sied guère de critiquer.
IDIOMS **it's an** ~ **wind (that blows nobody any good)** PROV à quelque chose malheur est bon PROV.

I'll /aɪl/ = **I shall, I will**.

ill: ~**-advised** adj malavisé; ~**-assorted** adj mal assorti; ~ **at ease** adj gêné, mal à l'aise; ~**-bred** adj mal élevé; ~**-considered** adj [remark] irréfléchi; [measure] hâtif/-ive; ~**-disposed** adj mal disposé; ~ **effect** n conséquence f néfaste.

illegal /ɪ'liːgl/ I n US immigrant/-e m/f clandestin/-e.
II adj (unlawful) GEN clandestin; [parking] illicite; [immigrant] clandestin; SPORT irrégulier/-ière.

illegality /ˌɪlɪ'gælətɪ/ n illégalité f.

illegally /ɪ'liːgəlɪ/ adv [import, work] illégalement; [park] en infraction.

illegible /ɪ'ledʒəbl/ adj illisible.

illegibly /ɪ'ledʒəblɪ/ adv de façon illisible.

illegitimacy /ˌɪlɪ'dʒɪtɪməsɪ/ n illégitimité f.

illegitimate /ˌɪlɪ'dʒɪtɪmət/ adj illégitime.

ill: ~**-equipped** adj mal équipé; ~**-fated** adj malheureux/-euse; ~ **feeling** n ressentiment m; ~**-fitting** adj [garment, shoe] qui va mal; ~**-founded** adj sans fondement; ~**-gotten** adj mal acquis; ~ **health** n mauvaise santé f.

illicit /ɪ'lɪsɪt/ adj illicite.

illicitly /ɪ'lɪsɪtlɪ/ adv (illegally) de manière illicite; (secretly) clandestinement.

ill-informed adj mal informé.

illiteracy /ɪ'lɪtərəsɪ/ n analphabétisme m.

illiterate /ɪ'lɪtərət/ n, adj analphabète (mf).

ill: ~**-judged** adj peu judicieux/-ieuse; ~ **luck** n malchance f; ~**-mannered** adj grossier/-ière.

illness /'ɪlnɪs/ ▶ **1002** n maladie f.

illogical /ɪ'lɒdʒɪkl/ adj illogique.

illogicality /ɪˌlɒdʒɪ'kælətɪ/ n illogisme m.

illogically /ɪ'lɒdʒɪklɪ/ adv illogiquement.

ill: ~**-prepared** adj mal préparé; ~**-starred** adj LITTÉR infortuné FML; ~**-tempered** adj désagréable, déplaisant; ~**-timed** adj [arrival]

Illnesses, aches and pains

Where does it hurt?

where does it hurt? = où est-ce que ça vous fait mal? *or*
(more formally) où avez-vous mal?
his leg hurts = sa jambe lui fait mal

(*Do not confuse* faire mal à qn *with the phrase* faire du mal
à qn, *which means* to harm sb.)

he has a pain in his leg = il a mal à la jambe

Note that with avoir mal à *French uses the definite article
(*la) *with the part of the body, where English has a
possessive (*his), *hence:*

his head was aching = il avait mal à la tête

English has other ways of expressing this idea, but avoir
mal à *fits them too:*

he had toothache = il avait mal aux dents
his ears hurt = il avait mal aux oreilles

Accidents

she broke her leg = elle s'est cassé la jambe

Elle s'est cassé la jambe *means literally* she broke to
herself the leg; *because the* se *is an indirect object, the
past participle* cassé *does not agree. This is true of all
such constructions:*

she sprained her ankle = elle s'est foulé la cheville
they burned their hands = ils se sont brûlé les mains

Chronic conditions

Note that the French often use fragile (*weak*) *to express a
chronic condition:*

he has a weak heart = il a le cœur fragile
he has kidney trouble = il a les reins fragiles
he has a bad back = il a le dos fragile

Being ill

*Mostly French uses the definite article with the name of
an illness:*

to have flu = avoir la grippe
to have measles = avoir la rougeole
to have malaria = avoir la malaria

*This applies to most infectious diseases, including
childhood illnesses. However, note the exceptions ending
in* -ite (*e.g.* une hépatite, une méningite) *below.*

*When the illness affects a specific part of the body,
French uses the indefinite article:*

to have cancer = avoir un cancer
to have cancer of the liver = avoir un cancer du foie
to have pneumonia = avoir une pneumonie
to have cirrhosis = avoir une cirrhose
to have a stomach ulcer = avoir un ulcère à l'estomac

Most words in -ite (*English* -itis) *work like this:*

to have bronchitis = avoir une bronchite
to have hepatitis = avoir une hépatite

*When the illness is a generalized condition, French tends
to use* du, de la *or* des:

to have rheumatism = avoir des rhumatismes
to have emphysema = avoir de l'emphysème
to have asthma = avoir de l'asthme
to have arthritis = avoir de l'arthrite

One exception here is:

to have hay fever = avoir le rhume des foins

*When there is an adjective for such conditions, this is often
preferred in French:*

to have asthma = être asthmatique
to have epilepsy = être épileptique

*Such adjectives can be used as nouns to denote the
person with the illness, e.g.* un/une asthmatique *and*
un/une épileptique *etc.*

*French has other specific words for people with certain
illnesses:*

someone with cancer = un cancéreux/une cancéreuse

If in doubt check in the dictionary.

English with *is translated by* qui a *or* qui ont, *and this is
always safe:*

someone with malaria = quelqu'un qui a la malaria
people with Aids = les gens qui ont le Sida

Falling ill

*The above guidelines about the use of the definite and
indefinite articles in French hold good for talking about the
onset of illnesses.*

French has no general equivalent of to get. *However,
where English can use* catch, *French can use* attraper:

to catch mumps = attraper les oreillons
to catch malaria = attraper la malaria
to catch bronchitis = attraper une bronchite
to catch a cold = attraper un rhume

Similarly where English uses contract, *French uses*
contracter:

to contract Aids = contracter le Sida
to contract pneumonia = contracter une pneumonie
to contract hepatitis = contracter une hépatite

For attacks of chronic illnesses, French uses faire une
crise de:

to have a bout of malaria = faire une crise de malaria
to have an asthma attack = faire une crise d'asthme
to have an epileptic fit = faire une crise d'épilepsie

Treatment

to be treated for polio = se faire soigner contre la polio
to take sth for hay fever = prendre qch contre le rhume des foins
he's taking sth for his cough = il prend qch contre la toux
to prescribe sth for a cough = prescrire un médicament contre la toux
malaria tablets = des cachets contre la malaria
to have a cholera vaccination = se faire vacciner contre le choléra
to be vaccinated against smallpox = se faire vacciner contre la variole
to be immunized against smallpox = se faire immuniser contre la variole
to have a tetanus injection = se faire vacciner contre le tétanos
to give sb a tetanus injection = vacciner qn contre le tétanos
to be operated on for cancer = être opéré d'un cancer
to operate on sb for appendicitis = opérer qn de l'appendicite

---

inopportun; [*campaign*] malencontreux/-euse;
~-treat *vtr* maltraiter; **~ treatment** *n* mauvais
traitements *mpl.*
illuminate /ɪˈluːmɪneɪt/ *vtr* GEN éclairer; (light for
effect) illuminer; ART enluminer; **~d** [*sign*] lumi-
neux/-euse.
illuminating /ɪˈluːmɪneɪtɪŋ/ *adj* FIG éclairant.
illumination /ɪˌluːmɪˈneɪʃn/ *n* (lighting) (of building,
sign) éclairage *m*; (for effect) illumination *f*; (enlightenment) illumination *f*; ART (of manuscript) enluminure *f*.

illusion /ɪˈluːʒn/ *n* illusion *f*; **to be** ou **to labour
under the ~ that** avoir l'illusion que.
illusive /ɪˈluːsɪv/, **illusory** /ɪˈluːsərɪ/ *adj* (misleading)
trompeur/-euse; (apparent) illusoire.
illustrate /ˈɪləstreɪt/ *vtr* illustrer; **~d** [*book, poem*]
illustré; [*lecture*] support visuel.
illustration /ˌɪləˈstreɪʃn/ *n* illustration *f*.
illustrative /ˈɪləstrətɪv, US ɪˈlʌs-/ *adj* **~ material**
illustrations *fpl*; **it is ~ of...** cela illustre bien...

illustrator /'ɪləstreɪtə(r)/ ▶1251 *n* illustrateur/-trice *m/f*.

illustrious /ɪ'lʌstrɪəs/ *adj* [*person*] illustre; [*career*] glorieux/-ieuse.

ill will *n* rancune *f*.

I'm /aɪm/ = **I am**.

image /'ɪmɪdʒ/ *n* GEN image *f*; (of company, personality) image *f* de marque; **the popular ~ of life in the north** l'idée que les gens se font de la vie dans le nord; **he is the (spitting) ~ of you** c'est toi tout craché.

image: **~ builder**, **~ maker** *n* professionnel/-elle *m/f* de l'image de marque; **~-conscious** *adj* conscient de son image de marque.

imagery /'ɪmɪdʒərɪ/ *n* ¢ images *fpl*.

imaginable /ɪ'mædʒɪnəbl/ *adj* imaginable; **the funniest thing ~** la chose la plus amusante qu'on puisse imaginer.

imaginary /ɪ'mædʒɪnərɪ, US -ənerɪ/ *adj* imaginaire.

imagination /ɪˌmædʒɪ'neɪʃn/ *n* imagination *f*; **to show ~** faire preuve d'imagination; **is it my ~, or...?** je rêve, ou...?; **not by any stretch of the ~ could you say...** même en faisant un grand effort d'imagination on ne pourrait pas dire...

imaginative /ɪ'mædʒɪnətɪv, US -əneɪtɪv/ *adj* [*person, performance*] plein d'imagination; [*mind*] imaginatif/ -ive; [*solution, device*] ingénieux/-ieuse.

imaginatively /ɪ'mædʒɪnətɪvlɪ, US -əneɪtɪvlɪ/ *adv* avec imagination.

imagine /ɪ'mædʒɪn/ *vtr* **1** (visualize) (s')imaginer [*object, scene*]; **to ~ being rich/king** s'imaginer riche/roi; **just ~!**, **just ~ that!** tu t'imagines!; **just ~ my surprise** imagine un peu ma surprise; **I can't ~ him travelling alone** je ne le vois pas en train de voyager seul; **I can't ~ her liking that**, **I can't ~ (that) she liked that** je ne crois pas qu'elle ait aimé ça; **you must have ~d it** ce doit être un effet de ton imagination; **2** (suppose) (s')imaginer (**that** que); **you would ~ he'd be more careful** on aurait pu croire qu'il serait plus prudent.

imaging /'ɪmɪdʒɪŋ/ *n* imagerie *f*.

imaginings /ɪ'mædʒɪnɪŋz/ *npl* fantaisies *fpl*; **never in my worst ~** jamais dans mes rêves les plus horribles.

imbalance /ˌɪm'bæləns/ *n* déséquilibre *m*; **trade ~** ECON déséquilibre des échanges commerciaux.

imbecile /'ɪmbəsiːl, US -sl/ *n*, *adj* imbécile (*mf*).

imbecility /ˌɪmbə'sɪlətɪ/ *n* (stupidity) stupidité *f*.

imbibe /ɪm'baɪb/ **I** *vtr* SOUT **1** (drink) boire; **2** (take in) absorber [*knowledge*].
II *vi* HUM boire.

imbue /ɪm'bjuː/ *vtr* imprégner (**with** de).

IMF *n* (*abrév* = **International Monetary Fund**) FMI *m*.

imitate /'ɪmɪteɪt/ *vtr* **1** imiter; **to ~ a cock crowing** imiter le chant du coq; **2** (copy) copier [*handwriting*].

imitation /ˌɪmɪ'teɪʃn/ **I** *n* imitation *f*; **in ~ of** à l'imitation de; (fake) contrefaçon *f*.
II *adj* [*snow*] artificiel/-ielle; **~ fur** imitation *f* de fourrure; **~ gold** similor *m*; **~ jewel** faux bijou *m*; **~ leather** similicuir *m*; **~ mink** imitation *f* vison.
IDIOMS **~ is the sincerest form of flattery** l'imitation est la plus sincère des flatteries.

imitative /'ɪmɪtətɪv, US -teɪtɪv/ *adj* imitatif/-ive.

imitator /'ɪmɪteɪtə(r)/ *n* imitateur/-trice *m/f*.

immaculate /ɪ'mækjʊlət/ *adj* [*dress, manners*] impeccable; [*performance*] parfait; **the Immaculate Conception** RELIG l'Immaculée Conception *f*.

immaculately /ɪ'mækjʊlətlɪ/ *adv* de façon impeccable.

immaterial /ˌɪmə'tɪərɪəl/ *adj* **1** (unimportant) sans importance; **it's ~ (to me) whether you like it or not** peu m'importe que vous l'aimiez ou non; **2** (intangible) immatériel/-ielle.

immature /ˌɪmə'tjʊə(r), US -tʊər/ *adj* **1** (not fully grown) [*animal*] qui n'a pas atteint la maturité; [*plant*] qui n'est pas arrivé à maturité; **2** (childish) immature; **don't be so ~!** ne te conduis pas comme un enfant!

immaturity /ˌɪmə'tjʊərətɪ, US -tʊər-/ *n* **1** (of plant, animal) immaturité *f*; **2** PEJ (childishness) manque *m* de maturité.

immeasurable /ɪ'meʒərəbl/ *adj* incommensurable.

immediacy /ɪ'miːdɪəsɪ/ *n* immédiateté *f*.

immediate /ɪ'miːdɪət/ *adj* **1** (instant) [*effect, reaction*] immédiat; [*thought*] premier/-ière; **2** (urgent, current) [*concern, goal*] premier/-ière; [*problem, crisis*] urgent; **the patient is not in ~ danger** les jours du patient ne sont pas en danger; **3** (near) [*prospects*] immédiat; **his ~ family** ses proches; **in the ~ future** dans l'avenir proche; **on my ~ left** juste à ma gauche.

immediately /ɪ'miːdɪətlɪ/ **I** *adv* **1** (at once) immédiatement, tout de suite; **~ at ou to hand** sous la main; **2** (directly) [*threatened, affected*] immédiatement; **~ after/before** juste avant/après.
II *conj* GB dès que.

immemorial /ˌɪmə'mɔːrɪəl/ *adj* immémorial.

immense /ɪ'mens/ *adj* immense.

immensely /ɪ'menslɪ/ *adv* [*enjoy, help*] énormément; [*complicated, popular*] extrêmement, infiniment.

immensity /ɪ'mensətɪ/ *n* immensité *f*.

immerse /ɪ'mɜːs/ **I** *vtr* plonger (**in** dans).
II *v refl* **to ~ oneself** se plonger (**in** dans).

immersed /ɪ'mɜːst/ *adj* **1** (in liquid) immergé (**in** dans); **2** (in book, task etc) absorbé (**in** dans).

immersion /ɪ'mɜːʃn, US -ʒn/ *n* immersion *f* (**in** dans).

immersion: **~ course** *n* GB cours *m* avec immersion linguistique; **~ heater** *n* chauffe-eau *m* électrique.

immigrant /'ɪmɪgrənt/ *n, adj* (recent) immigrant/-e (*m/ f*); (established) immigré/-e (*m/f*).

immigrate /'ɪmɪgreɪt/ *vi* immigrer (**to** à, en).

immigration /ˌɪmɪ'greɪʃn/ *n* immigration *f*.

immigration: **~ authorities** *npl* services *mpl* de l'immigration; **~ control** *n* (system) contrôle *m* de l'immigration; (office) services *mpl* de l'immigration; **Immigration Service** *n* GB services *mpl* de l'immigration.

imminence /'ɪmɪnəns/ *n* imminence *f*.

imminent /'ɪmɪnənt/ *adj* imminent; **rain is ~** la pluie menace.

immobile /ɪ'məʊbaɪl, US -bl/ *adj* immobile.

immobility /ˌɪmə'bɪlətɪ/ *n* immobilité *f*.

immobilize /ɪ'məʊbɪlaɪz/ *vtr* paralyser [*traffic, organization*]; immobiliser [*engine, patient, limb*].

immoderate /ɪ'mɒdərət/ *adj* SOUT immodéré.

immodest /ɪ'mɒdɪst/ *adj* (boastful) présomptueux/ -euse; (improper) indécent.

immodesty /ɪ'mɒdɪstɪ/ *n* présomption *f*.

immoral /ɪ'mɒrəl, US ɪ'mɔː-rəl/ *adj* immoral.

immorality /ˌɪmə'rælətɪ/ *n* immoralité *f*.

immortal /ɪ'mɔːtl/ *n, adj* immortel/-elle (*m/f*).

immortality /ˌɪmɔː'tælətɪ/ *n* immortalité *f*.

immortalize /ɪ'mɔːtəlaɪz/ *vtr* immortaliser.

immovable /ɪ'muːvəbl/ **I** **immovables** *npl* JUR biens *mpl* immeubles.
II *adj* (immobile) fixe; (unchanging) [*opinion*] inébranlable; [*person*] immuable; JUR [*goods*] immeuble.

immune /ɪ'mjuːn/ *adj* **1** MED [*person*] immunisé (**to** contre); [*reaction, system*] immunitaire; **~ deficiency** déficience *f* immunitaire, immunodéficience *f*; **2** (oblivious) **~ to** insensible à; **3** (exempt) **to be ~ from** être à l'abri de [*attack, arrest*]; être exempté de [*tax*].

immunity /ɪ'mjuːnətɪ/ *n* **1** MED, ADMIN immunité *f* (**to, against** contre); **tax/legal ~** exemption *f* fiscale/ légale; **2** (to criticism) impassibilité *f* (**to** devant).

immunization /ˌɪmjʊnaɪ'zeɪʃn, US -nɪ'z-/ *n* immunisation *f* (**against** contre).

immunize /'ɪmjʊnaɪz/ *vtr* immuniser.

immunology /ˌɪmjʊ'nɒlədʒɪ/ *n* immunologie *f*.

immutable /ɪ'mjuːtəbl/ *adj* immuable.

imp /ɪmp/ *n* lutin *m*.

impact I /'ɪmpækt/ n **1** (effect) impact m (**on** sur); **2** (violent contact) (of hammer, vehicle) choc m; (of bomb, bullet) impact m; **on ~** au moment de l'impact.
II /ɪm'pækt/ vtr (affect) avoir un impact sur; (hit) percuter.
III /ɪm'pækt/ vi avoir un impact (**on** sur).

impacted /ɪm'pæktɪd/ adj **1** MED [tooth] inclus; [fracture] engrené; **2** AUT **two ~ cars** deux voitures encastrées.

impair /ɪm'peə(r)/ vtr affecter [performance]; diminuer [ability]; affaiblir [hearing, vision]; détériorer [health].

impaired /ɪm'peəd/ adj [hearing, vision] affaibli; [mobility] réduit; **his speech is ~** il a des problèmes d'élocution; ▸**visually impaired, hearing-impaired**.

impairment /ɪm'peəmənt/ n **mental/physical ~** troubles mpl mentaux/moteurs.

impale /ɪm'peɪl/ vtr empaler (**on** sur).

impalpable /ɪm'pælpəbl/ adj (intangible) impalpable; (hard to describe) indéfinissable.

impart /ɪm'pɑːt/ vtr **1** (communicate) transmettre [knowledge, enthusiasm] (**to** à); communiquer [information] (**to** à); **2** (add) donner [atmosphere].

impartial /ɪm'pɑːʃl/ adj [advice, judge] impartial; [account] objectif/-ive.

impartiality /ˌɪm,pɑːʃɪ'ælətɪ/ n impartialité f.

impassable /ɪm'pɑːsəbl, US -'pæs-/ adj [obstacle] infranchissable; [road] impraticable.

impassioned /ɪm'pæʃnd/ adj [debate] passionné; [plea] véhément.

impassive /ɪm'pæsɪv/ adj (expressionless) impassible; (unruffled) imperturbable.

impatience /ɪm'peɪʃns/ n **1** (irritation) agacement m (**with** à l'égard de; **at** devant); **my worst fault is ~** mon plus grand défaut est mon manque de patience; **2** (eagerness) impatience f (**to do** de faire).

impatient /ɪm'peɪʃnt/ adj **1** (irritable) agacé (**at** par); **to be/get ~ with sb** s'impatienter contre qn; **2** (eager) [person] impatient; [gesture, tone] d'impatience; **to be ~ to do** être impatient or avoir hâte de faire.

impatiently /ɪm'peɪʃntlɪ/ adv [wait] impatiemment; [fidget] avec impatience; [say] d'un ton agacé.

impeach /ɪm'piːtʃ/ vtr mettre [qn] en accusation.

impeccable /ɪm'pekəbl/ adj [behaviour] irréprochable; [appearance] impeccable.

impeccably /ɪm'pekəblɪ/ adv [dressed] impeccablement; [behave] de façon irréprochable.

impede /ɪm'piːd/ vtr entraver.

impediment /ɪm'pedɪmənt/ n **1** (hindrance) entrave f (**to** à); **2** (also **speech ~**) défaut m d'élocution.

impel /ɪm'pel/ vtr (p prés etc **-ll-**) **1** (drive) [emotion, idea] pousser [person] (**to do** à faire); **2** (urge) [person, speech] inciter [person] (**to** à; **to do** à faire); **to feel ~led to do** se sentir obligé de faire.

impending /ɪm'pendɪŋ/ adj (avant n) imminent.

impenetrable /ɪm'penɪtrəbl/ adj impénétrable.

imperative /ɪm'perətɪv/ I n GEN, LING impératif m.
II adj [need] urgent; [tone] impérieux/-ieuse; **it is ~ that she write** il est impératif qu'elle écrive.

imperceptible /ˌɪmpə'septəbl/ adj imperceptible.

imperfect /ɪm'pɜːfɪkt/ I n LING imparfait m.
II adj (incomplete) incomplet/-ète; (defective) [goods] défectueux/-euse; [logic] imparfait; LING **the ~ tense** l'imparfait m.

imperfection /ˌɪmpə'fekʃn/ n (in object) défectuosité f; (in person) défaut m; (state) imperfection f.

imperial /ɪm'pɪərɪəl/ adj **1** (of empire, emperor) impérial; **2** GB HIST de l'Empire; **3** GB [measure] conforme aux normes britanniques.

imperialism /ɪm'pɪərɪəlɪzəm/ n impérialisme m.

imperialist /ɪm'pɪərɪəlɪst/ n, adj impérialiste (mf).

imperil /ɪm'perɪl/ vtr (p prés etc **-ll-** GB, **-l-** US) menacer [existence]; compromettre [security, plan, scheme].

imperious /ɪm'pɪərɪəs/ adj impérieux/-ieuse.

impermeable /ɪm'pɜːmɪəbl/ adj imperméable.

impersonal /ɪm'pɜːsənl/ adj GEN, LING impersonnel/-elle.

impersonality /ɪm,pɜːsə'nælətɪ/ n (of person) froideur f; (of style, organization) impersonnalité f.

impersonate /ɪm'pɜːsəneɪt/ vtr (imitate) imiter; (pretend to be) se faire passer pour [police officer etc].

impersonation /ɪm,pɜːsə'neɪʃn/ n imitation f.

impersonator /ɪm'pɜːsəneɪtə(r)/ n imitateur/-trice m/f.

impertinence /ɪm'pɜːtɪnəns/ n impertinence f.

impertinent /ɪm'pɜːtɪnənt/ adj impertinent (**to** envers).

impertinently /ɪm'pɜːtɪnəntlɪ/ adv [act, say, reply] avec impertinence.

imperturbable /ˌɪmpə'tɜːbəbl/ adj imperturbable.

impervious /ɪm'pɜːvɪəs/ adj (to water, gas) imperméable (**to** à); FIG (to charm, suffering) indifférent (**to** à); (to demands) imperméable (**to** à).

impetuosity /ɪm,petʃʊ'ɒsətɪ/ n (of person) impétuosité f; (of action) impulsivité f.

impetuous /ɪm'petʃʊəs/ adj [person] impétueux/-euse; [action] impulsif/-ive.

impetus /'ɪmpɪtəs/ n (trigger) impulsion f; (momentum) élan m; PHYS impulsion f.

impiety /ɪm'paɪətɪ/ n GEN manque m de respect; RELIG impiété f.

impinge /ɪm'pɪndʒ/ vi **to ~ on** (restrict) empiéter sur; (affect) affecter.

impious /'ɪmpɪəs/ adj GEN irrespectueux/-euse; RELIG impie.

impish /'ɪmpɪʃ/ adj espiègle.

implacable /ɪm'plækəbl/ adj implacable.

implacably /ɪm'plækəblɪ/ adv implacablement.

implant I /'ɪmplɑːnt, US -plænt/ n implant m.
II /ɪm'plɑːnt, US -'plænt/ vtr MED, FIG implanter.

implausible /ɪm'plɔːzəbl/ adj peu plausible.

implement I /'ɪmplɪmənt/ n GEN instrument m; (tool) outil m; **farm ~s** outillage m agricole.
II /'ɪmplɪment/ vtr **1** GEN, JUR exécuter [contract, idea]; mettre [qch] en application [law]; **2** COMPUT implanter [software]; implémenter [system].

implementation /ˌɪmplɪmen'teɪʃn/ n (of contract, idea) exécution f; (of law, policy) mise f en application; COMPUT implémentation f.

implicate /'ɪmplɪkeɪt/ vtr impliquer (**in** dans).

implication /ˌɪmplɪ'keɪʃn/ n (possible consequence) implication f; (suggestion) insinuation f.

implicit /ɪm'plɪsɪt/ adj (implied) implicite (**in** dans); (absolute) [faith, trust] absolu.

implicitly /ɪm'plɪsɪtlɪ/ adv (tacitly) [assume, admit, recognize] implicitement; (absolutely) [trust, believe] sans réserve.

implied /ɪm'plaɪd/ adj implicite.

implore /ɪm'plɔː(r)/ vtr conjurer (**to do** de faire).

imploring /ɪm'plɔːrɪŋ/ adj implorant.

implosion /ɪm'pləʊʒn/ n implosion f.

imply /ɪm'plaɪ/ vtr **1** [person] (insinuate) insinuer (**that** que); (make known) laisser entendre (**that** que); **2** [argument] (mean) impliquer; **3** [term, word] (mean) laisser supposer (**that** que).

impolite /ˌɪmpə'laɪt/ adj impoli (**to** envers).

impolitely /ˌɪmpə'laɪtlɪ/ adv [behave] de manière impolie; [say] avec impolitesse.

impoliteness /ˌɪmpə'laɪtnɪs/ n impolitesse f.

import I /'ɪmpɔːt/ n **1** COMM, ECON importation f; **2** (cultural borrowing) apport m (**from** à); **3** SOUT (meaning) signification f (**in** à); **4** SOUT (importance) importance f; **of no (great) ~** de peu d'importance.
II /ɪm'pɔːt/ vtr importer (**from** de; **to** en).

importance /ɪm'pɔːtns/ n importance f; **her career is of great ~ to her** sa carrière est très importante or compte beaucoup pour elle; **it is of great ~ that** il est essentiel que (+ subj); **an event of great political ~** un événement d'une grande portée politique; **it is**

a matter of the utmost ~ c'est une question de la plus haute importance.
important /ɪmˈpɔːtnt/ *adj* important; **it is ~ that** il est important que (+ *subj*); **his children are very ~ to him** ses enfants comptent beaucoup pour lui; **he's an ~ social figure** c'est une personne en vue.
importantly /ɪmˈpɔːtntlɪ/ *adv* **1** (significantly) d'une manière importante; **and, more ~,...** et, plus important encore,...; **most ~, it means** mais surtout, cela signifie; **2** (pompously) [*announce*] d'un air important.
importation /ˌɪmpɔːˈteɪʃn/ *n* COMM importation *f*.
import duty *n* taxe *f* à l'importation.
importer /ɪmˈpɔːtə(r)/ *n* importateur/-trice *m/f*.
import-export /ˌɪmpɔːtˈekspɔːt/ *n* import-export *m*.
importing /ɪmˈpɔːtɪŋ/ **I** *n* importation *f* (**of** de).
II *adj* [*country, business*] importateur/-trice; **oil-~ country** pays *m* importateur de pétrole.
import licence GB, **import license** US *n* licence *f* d'importation.
importunate /ɪmˈpɔːtʃʊnət/ *adj* importun.
importune /ˌɪmpɔːˈtjuːn/ *vtr* importuner [*person*].
impose /ɪmˈpəʊz/ **I** *vtr* imposer [*embargo, rule*] (**on sb** à qn; **on sth** sur qch); infliger [*sanction*] (**on** à); **to ~ a fine on sb** frapper qn d'une amende; **to ~ a tax on tobacco** imposer le tabac.
II *vi* s'imposer; **to ~ on sb's kindness** abuser de la bienveillance de qn.
III *v refl* **to ~ oneself on sb** s'imposer à qn.
imposing /ɪmˈpəʊzɪŋ/ *adj* [*person*] imposant; [*sight*] impressionnant.
imposition /ˌɪmpəˈzɪʃn/ *n* **1** (exploitation) **I hope it's not too much of an ~** j'espère que je n'abuse pas de votre bienveillance; **2** (of tax) imposition *f*.
impossibility /ɪmˌpɒsəˈbɪlətɪ/ *n* impossibilité *f*; **a physical ~** une impossibilité matérielle.
impossible /ɪmˈpɒsəbl/ **I** *n* **the ~** l'impossible *m*.
II *adj* impossible; **to make it ~ for sb to do sth** mettre qn dans l'impossibilité de faire qch.
impossibly /ɪmˈpɒsəblɪ/ *adv* (appallingly) affreusement; (amazingly) incroyablement.
impostor /ɪmˈpɒstə(r)/ *n* imposteur *m*.
imposture /ɪmˈpɒstʃə(r)/ *n* imposture *f*.
impotence /ˈɪmpətəns/ *n* impuissance *f*.
impotent /ˈɪmpətənt/ *adj* impuissant.
impound /ɪmˈpaʊnd/ *vtr* emmener [qch] à la fourrière [*vehicle*]; confisquer [*goods*].
impoverish /ɪmˈpɒvərɪʃ/ *vtr* appauvrir.
impoverishment /ɪmˈpɒvərɪʃmənt/ *n* appauvrissement *m*.
impracticable /ɪmˈpræktɪkəbl/ *adj* impraticable.
impractical /ɪmˈpræktɪkl/ *adj* (unworkable) irréalisable; (unrealistic) peu réaliste; [*person*] **to be ~** manquer d'esprit pratique.
impracticality /ɪmˌpræktɪˈkælətɪ/ *n* GEN caractère *m* irréalisable; (of person) manque *m* d'esprit pratique.
imprecise /ˌɪmprɪˈsaɪs/ *adj* imprécis.
imprecision /ˌɪmprɪˈsɪʒn/ *n* imprécision *f*.
impregnable /ɪmˈpregnəbl/ *adj* imprenable.
impregnate /ˈɪmpregneɪt, US ɪmˈpreg-/ *vtr* (pervade) imprégner (**with** de); (fertilize) féconder.
impresario /ˌɪmprɪˈsɑːrɪəʊ/ *n* impresario *m*.
impress I /ˈɪmpres/ *n* SOUT empreinte *f*.
II /ɪmˈpres/ *vtr* **1** (arouse respect) impressionner (**with** par; **by doing** en faisant); **to be easily ~ed** se laisser facilement impressionner; **they were (favourably) ~ed** ça leur a fait bonne impression; **2** (emphasize) **to ~ sth (up)on sb** faire bien comprendre qch à qn; **3** (imprint) **to ~ sth on/in** marquer qch sur/faire une empreinte de qch dans.
III /ɪmˈpres/ *vi* faire bonne impression.
impression /ɪmˈpreʃn/ *n* **1** (idea) impression *f*; **to be under** ou **have the ~ that** avoir l'impression que; **2** (impact) impression *f*; **to make a good/bad ~** faire bonne/mauvaise impression (**on** sur); **to make (quite)**

an ~ faire impression or de l'effet; **3** (perception) impression *f*; **to give** ou **create an ~ of sth** l'effet de qch; **an artist's ~ of the building** le bâtiment vu par un artiste; **first ~s count** les premières impressions sont souvent les meilleures; **4** (imitation) imitation *f*; **5** (imprint) impression *f*; (from teeth) marque *f*; (of hoof) empreinte *f*.
impressionable /ɪmˈpreʃənəbl/ *adj* [*child, mind*] influençable.
impressionist /ɪmˈpreʃənɪst/ *n* **1** (also **Impressionist**) ART, MUS impressionniste *mf*; **2** (mimic) imitateur/-trice *m/f*.
impressionistic /ɪmˌpreʃəˈnɪstɪk/ *adj* impressionniste.
impressive /ɪmˈpresɪv/ *adj* [*achievement, display, result*] impressionnant; [*building, sight*] imposant; **she is very ~** elle en impose.
impressively /ɪmˈpresɪvlɪ/ *adv* de manière impressionnante.
imprint I /ˈɪmprɪnt/ *n* empreinte *f*.
II /ɪmˈprɪnt/ *vtr* **1** (fix) graver (**on** dans); **2** (print) imprimer (**on** sur).
imprison /ɪmˈprɪzn/ *vtr* emprisonner.
imprisonment /ɪmˈprɪznmənt/ *n* emprisonnement *m*.
improbability /ɪmˌprɒbəˈbɪlətɪ/ *n* **1** (of something happening) improbabilité *f*; (of something being true) invraisemblance *f*; **2** (unlikely event) improbabilité *f*.
improbable /ɪmˈprɒbəbl/ *adj* **1** (unlikely to happen) improbable; **2** (unlikely to be true) invraisemblable.
improbably /ɪmˈprɒbəblɪ/ *adv* invraisemblablement.
improper /ɪmˈprɒpə(r)/ *adj* (unseemly) malséant; (dishonest) irrégulier/-ière; (indecent) indécent; (incorrect) impropre, abusif/-ive.
improperly /ɪmˈprɒpəlɪ/ *adv* (unsuitably) de manière malséante; (dishonestly) de manière irrégulière; (indecently) indécemment; (incorrectly) improprement, abusivement; **to be ~ dressed** ne pas être habillé comme il convient.
impropriety /ˌɪmprəˈpraɪətɪ/ *n* (irregularity) irrégularité *f*; (unseemliness) inconvenance *f*; (indecency) indécence *f*.
improve /ɪmˈpruːv/ **I** *vtr* **1** (in quality) améliorer; **to ~ one's German** se perfectionner en allemand; **the new arrangements did not ~ matters** les nouveaux accords n'ont pas arrangé les choses; **to ~ one's mind** se cultiver (l'esprit); **2** (in quantity) augmenter [*wages, chances*]; accroître [*productivity*]; CONSTR aménager.
II *vi* **1** s'améliorer; **2** **to ~ on** (better) améliorer [*score*]; renchérir sur [*offer*]; **she has ~d on last year's result** elle a obtenu de meilleurs résultats que l'année dernière; **3** (increase) [*productivity*] augmenter.
improvement /ɪmˈpruːvmənt/ *n* **1** (change for the better) amélioration *f* (**in, of, to** de); **an ~ on last year's performance** une amélioration par rapport aux résultats de l'an dernier; **the new edition is an ~ on the old one** la nouvelle édition est bien meilleure que l'ancienne; **2** (progress) progrès *mpl*; **there is room for ~** on pourrait encore faire mieux; **3** (alteration) aménagement *m*; **home ~s** aménagements *mpl* du domicile.
improvident /ɪmˈprɒvɪdənt/ *adj* (heedless of the future) imprévoyant; (extravagant) prodigue.
improvisation /ˌɪmprəvaɪˈzeɪʃn, US ɪmˌprɒvəˈzeɪʃn/ *n* improvisation *f*.
improvise /ˈɪmprəvaɪz/ **I** *vtr* improviser; **an ~d table/screen** une table/un écran de fortune.
II *vi* improviser.
imprudent /ɪmˈpruːdnt/ *adj* imprudent.
impudence /ˈɪmpjʊdəns/ *n* effronterie *f*.
impudent /ˈɪmpjʊdənt/ *adj* insolent, impudent.
impulse /ˈɪmpʌls/ *n* impulsion *f*; **to have a sudden ~ to do** avoir une envie soudaine de faire; **on (an) ~** sur un coup de tête; **a generous ~** un élan de générosité.
impulse: **~ buy**, **~ purchase** *n* achat *m* d'impulsion; **~ buying** *n* ¢ achat *m* d'impulsion.
impulsion /ɪmˈpʌlʃn/ *n* envie *f* irrésistible.

impulsive /ɪmˈpʌlsɪv/ *adj* (spontaneous) spontané; (rash) [*person*] impulsif/-ive; [*remark*] irréfléchi.

impulsively /ɪmˈpʌlsɪvlɪ/ *adv* (on impulse) impulsivement; (rashly) sur un coup de tête.

impulsiveness /ɪmˈpʌlsɪvnɪs/ *n* impulsivité *f*.

impunity /ɪmˈpjuːnɪtɪ/ *n* impunité *f*.

impure /ɪmˈpjʊə(r)/ *adj* [*water, thoughts*] impur.

impurity /ɪmˈpjʊərɪtɪ/ *n* impureté *f*; **tested for impurities** pureté testée.

imputation /ˌɪmpjuːˈteɪʃn/ imputation *f* (**of** de; **to** à).

impute /ɪmˈpjuːt/ *vtr* imputer, attribuer (**to** à).

in /ɪn/

■ **Note** *in* is often used after verbs in English (*join in, tuck in, result in, write in* etc). For translations, consult the appropriate verb entry (*join, tuck, result, write* etc).
– If you have doubts about how to translate a phrase or expression beginning with *in* (*in a huff, in business, in trouble* etc) you should consult the appropriate noun entry (*huff, business, trouble* etc).
– This dictionary contains Usage Notes on such topics as age, countries, dates, islands, months, towns and cities etc. Many of these use the preposition *in*. For the index to these Notes ▶ **1419**.
– For examples of the above and particular functions and uses of *in*, see the entry below.

I *prep* **1** (expressing location or position) ~ **Paris** à Paris; ~ **Spain** en Espagne; ~ **school** à l'école; ~ **prison/town** en prison/ville; ~ **the film/newspaper** dans le film/journal; **I'm ~ here!** je suis là!; ▶ **bath, bed**; **2** (inside, within) dans; ~ **the box** dans la boîte; **there's something ~ it** il y a quelque chose dedans or à l'intérieur; **3** (expressing a subject or field) dans; ~ **insurance** dans les assurances; ▶ **course, expert**; **4** (included, involved) **to be ~ politics** faire de la politique; **to be ~ the team** faire partie de l'équipe; **to be ~ on the secret**○ être dans le secret; **I wasn't ~ on it**○ je n'étais pas dans le coup○; **5** (in expressions of time) ~ **May** en mai; ~ **1987** en 1987; ~ **the night** pendant la nuit; ~ **the twenties** dans les années 20; **at four ~ the morning** à quatre heures du matin; **day ~ day out** tous les jours (sans exception); **6** (within the space of) en; **to do sth ~ 10 minutes** faire qch en 10 minutes; **7** (expressing the future) dans; **I'll be back ~ half an hour** je serai de retour dans une demi-heure; **8** (for) depuis; **it hasn't rained ~ weeks** il n'a pas plu depuis des semaines, ça fait des semaines qu'il n'a pas plu; **9** (during, because of) dans; ~ **his hurry he forgot his keys** dans sa précipitation il a oublié ses clés; **10** (with reflexive pronouns) **it's no bad thing ~ itself** ce n'est pas une mauvaise chose en soi; **how do you feel ~ yourself?** est-ce que tu as le moral?; ▶ **itself**; **11** (present in, inherent in) **you see it ~ children** on le rencontre chez les enfants; **it's rare ~ cats** c'est rare chez les chats; **he hasn't got it ~ him to succeed** il n'est pas fait pour réussir; **there's something ~ what he says** il y a du vrai dans ce qu'il dit; **12** (expressing colour, composition) en; **available ~ several colours** disponible en plusieurs couleurs; **13** (dressed in) en; ~ **a skirt** en jupe; **dressed ~ black** habillé en noir; **14** (expressing manner or medium) ~ **German** en allemand; ~ **B flat** en si bémol; **'no,' he said ~ a whisper** 'non,' a-t-il chuchoté; **chicken ~ a white wine sauce** du poulet à la sauce au vin blanc; ~ **pencil/~ ink** au crayon/à l'encre; **15** (as regards) **rich/poor ~ minerals** riche/pauvre en minéraux; **deaf ~ one ear** sourd d'une oreille; **10 cm ~ length** 10 cm de long; **16** (by) ~ **accepting** en acceptant; ~ **doing so** en faisant cela; **17** (in superlatives) de; **the tallest tower ~ the world** la plus grande tour du monde; **18** (in measurements) **there are 100 centimetres ~ a metre** il y a 100 centimètres dans un mètre; ~ **centimetres** en centimètres; ~ **a smaller size** dans une taille plus petite; **19** (in ratios) **a gradient of 1 ~ 4** une pente de 25%; **a tax of 20 pence ~ the pound** une taxe de 20 pence par livre sterling; **to have a one ~ five chance** avoir une chance sur cinq; **20** (in approximate amounts) ~ **their**

hundreds ou **thousands** par centaines ou milliers; **to cut sth ~ three** couper qch en trois; **21** (expressing age) **she's ~ her twenties** elle a entre vingt et trente ans; **people ~ their forties** les gens qui ont entre quarante et cinquante ans; ~ **old age** avec l'âge, en vieillissant.

II in and out *prep phr* **to come ~ and out** entrer et sortir; **to weave ~ and out of** se faufiler entre [*traffic, tables*]; **to be ~ and out of prison all one's life** passer la plus grande partie de sa vie en prison.

III in that *conj phr* dans la mesure où.

IV *adv* **1** (indoors) **to come ~** entrer; **to run ~** entrer en courant; **to ask** ou **invite sb ~** faire entrer qn; **2** (at home, at work) **to be ~** être là; **I'm usually ~ by 9 am** j'arrive généralement à 9 heures; **to come ~ two days a week** venir deux jours par semaine; **to be ~ by midnight** être rentré avant minuit; ▶ **keep, stay**; **3** (in prison, in hospital) **he's ~ for murder** il a été emprisonné pour meurtre; **she's ~ for a biopsy** elle est entrée à l'hôpital pour une biopsie; **4** (arrived) **the train is ~** le train est en gare; **the ferry is ~** le ferry est à quai; **the sea** ou **tide is ~** c'est marée haute; ▶ **come, get**; **5** SPORT **the ball is ~** la balle est bonne; **6** (gathered) **the harvest is ~** la moisson est rentrée; **7** (in supply) **we don't have any ~** nous n'en avons pas en stock; **we've got some new titles ~** on a reçu quelques nouveaux titres; **to get some beer ~** aller chercher de la bière; **8** (submitted) **applications must be ~ by the 23rd** les candidatures doivent être déposées avant le 23; **the homework has to be ~ tomorrow** le devoir doit être rendu demain; ▶ **get, power, vote**.

V○ *adj* **to be ~**, **to be the ~ thing** être à la mode.

IDIOMS **to know the ~s and outs of an affair** connaître une affaire dans les moindres détails; **to have an ~ with sb** US avoir ses entrées chez qn; **to have it ~ for sb**○ avoir qn dans le collimateur○; **you're ~ for it**○ tu vas avoir des ennuis; **he's ~ for a shock/surprise** il va avoir un choc/être surpris.

in. *abrév écrite* = **inch**.

IN US POST *abrév écrite* = **Indiana**.

inability /ˌɪnəˈbɪlɪtɪ/ *n* (to drive, pay) incapacité *f* (**to do** de faire); (to help) impuissance *f* (**to do** à faire).

in absentia /ˌɪn æbˈsentɪə/ *adv* en son/leur etc absence.

inaccessible /ˌɪnækˈsesəbl/ *adj* (out of reach) inaccessible; (hard to understand) peu accessible (**to** à).

inaccuracy /ɪnˈækjərəsɪ/ *n* **1** ¢ (of report, estimate) inexactitude *f*; (of person) manque *m* d'exactitude or de précision; **2** (error) inexactitude *f*.

inaccurate /ɪnˈækjʊrət/ *adj* inexact.

inaccurately /ɪnˈækjʊrətlɪ/ *adv* inexactement.

inaction /ɪnˈækʃn/ *n* (failure to act) inaction *f*; (not being active) inactivité *f*.

inactive /ɪnˈæktɪv/ *adj* inactif/-ive.

inactivity /ˌɪnækˈtɪvɪtɪ/ *n* inactivité *f*.

inadequacy /ɪnˈædɪkwəsɪ/ *n* (insufficiency) insuffisance *f*; (defect) défaut *m*.

inadequate /ɪnˈædɪkwət/ *adj* [*funding, measures, knowledge*] insuffisant (**for** pour); [*system, facilities*] inadéquat; **to feel ~** être complexé.

inadequately /ɪnˈædɪkwətlɪ/ *adv* insuffisamment.

inadmissible /ˌɪnədˈmɪsəbl/ *adj* inadmissible; JUR [*evidence*] irrecevable.

inadvertent /ˌɪnədˈvɜːtənt/ *adj* (accidental) involontaire; (inattentive) inattentif/-ive.

inadvertently /ˌɪnədˈvɜːtntlɪ/ *adv* (unintentionally) involontairement; (unthinkingly) par mégarde.

inadvisable /ˌɪnədˈvaɪzəbl/ *adj* inopportun, à déconseiller.

inalienable /ɪnˈeɪlɪənəbl/ *adj* inaliénable.

inane /ɪˈneɪn/ *adj* [*person, conversation*] idiot; [*programme*] débile○.

inanely /ɪˈneɪnlɪ/ *adv* de façon idiote.

inanimate /ɪnˈænɪmət/ *adj* inanimé.

inanity /ɪˈnænətɪ/ *n* ineptie *f*.

inapplicable /ɪnˈæplɪkəbl/, /ˌɪnəˈplɪk-/ *adj* inapplicable.

inappropriate /ˌɪnəˈprəʊprɪət/ *adj* **1** (unsuitable) [*behaviour*] inconvenant, peu convenable; [*remark*] inopportun; **2** (incorrect) [*advice, word*] qui n'est pas approprié.

inappropriately /ˌɪnəˈprəʊprɪətlɪ/ *adv* inopportunément, mal à propos.

inapt /ɪnˈæpt/ *adj* **1** (inappropriate) inconvenant; **2** (inept) incompétent.

inarticulate /ˌɪnɑːˈtɪkjʊlət/ *adj* **1** (unable to express oneself) **to be ~** ne pas savoir s'exprimer; **2** (indistinct) [*mumble*] inintelligible; [*speech*] inintelligible; **3** (defying expression) [*rage*] inexprimable; **4** ZOOL inarticulé.

inasmuch /ˌɪnəzˈmʌtʃ/: **inasmuch as** *conj phr* (insofar as) dans la mesure où; (seeing as) vu que.

inattention /ˌɪnəˈtenʃn/ *n* inattention *f*.

inattentive /ˌɪnəˈtentɪv/ *adj* [*pupil*] inattentif/-ive; [*audience, lover*] peu attentif/-ive.

inattentively /ˌɪnəˈtentɪvlɪ/ *adv* distraitement.

inaudible /ɪnˈɔːdəbl/ *adj* [*sound*] inaudible; **he was almost ~** on l'entendait à peine.

inaugural /ɪˈnɔːgjʊrəl/ *adj* inaugural.

inaugurate /ɪˈnɔːgjʊreɪt/ *vtr* inaugurer [*exhibition*]; investir [qn] de ses fonctions [*president, official*].

inauguration /ɪˌnɔːgjʊˈreɪʃn/ *n* (of exhibition) inauguration *f*; (of president) investiture *f*.

inauspicious /ˌɪnɔːˈspɪʃəs/ *adj* (unpromising) peu propice, de mauvais augure; (unfortunate) malencontreux/-euse.

inauspiciously /ˌɪnɔːˈspɪʃəslɪ/ *adv* [*begin, start*] mal.

in-between *adj* intermédiaire.

inborn /ˈɪnbɔːn/ *adj* (innate) inné; (inherited) congénital.

inbred /ˌɪnˈbred/ *adj* (innate) inné; (produced by inbreeding) [*animal*] résultant de croisements entre animaux de même souche; [*characteristic*] résultant de croisement consanguin.

inbreeding /ɪnˈbriːdɪŋ/ *n* (in animals) croisement *m* d'animaux de même souche; (in humans) croisement *m* consanguin, consanguinité *f*.

inbuilt /ˌɪnˈbɪlt/ *adj* intrinsèque.

Inc US (*abrév écrite* = **incorporated**) SA.

incalculable /ɪnˈkælkjʊləbl/ *adj* incalculable.

incandescence /ˌɪnkænˈdesns/ *n* incandescence *f*.

incandescent /ˌɪnkænˈdesnt/ *adj* incandescent.

incapability /ɪnˌkeɪpəˈbɪlɪtɪ/ *n* GEN, JUR incapacité *f* (**to do** de faire).

incapable /ɪnˈkeɪpəbl/ *adj* incapable (**of doing** de faire); **drunk and ~** JUR en état d'ivresse publique.

incapacitate /ˌɪnkəˈpæsɪteɪt/ *vtr* [*accident, illness*] immobiliser; **severely ~d** infirme, invalide.

incapacity /ˌɪnkəˈpæsətɪ/ *n* GEN, JUR incapacité *f* (**to do** de faire).

incarcerate /ɪnˈkɑːsəreɪt/ *vtr* incarcérer.

incarnate I /ɪnˈkɑːnət/ *adj* incarné.
II /ˈɪnkɑːneɪt/ *vtr* incarner; **to be ~d in** ou **as** s'incarner en.

incarnation /ˌɪnkɑːˈneɪʃn/ *n* incarnation *f*.

incautious /ɪnˈkɔːʃəs/ *adj* imprudent, irréfléchi.

incendiary /ɪnˈsendɪərɪ, US -dɪerɪ/ **I** *n* (bomb) engin *m* incendiaire.
II *adj* incendiaire.

incendiary: **~ attack** *n* attaque *f* à la bombe incendiaire; **~ device** *n* engin *m* incendiaire.

incense I /ˈɪnsens/ *n* encens *m*.
II /ɪnˈsens/ *vtr* mettre [qn] en fureur [*person*].

incensed /ɪnˈsenst/ *adj* outré (**at** de; **by** par).

incentive /ɪnˈsentɪv/ *n* **1** (motivation) **to give sb the ~ to do** donner envie à qn de faire; **there is no ~ for people to save** rien n'incite les gens à faire des économies; **there are strong ~s to join a union** on a tout intérêt à adhérer à un syndicat; **2** FIN, COMM prime *f*; **export ~** prime à l'exportation.

incentive bonus, **incentive payment** *n* prime *f* d'encouragement.

inception /ɪnˈsepʃn/ *n* commencement *m*; **from** ou **since its ~ in 1962** depuis ses débuts en 1962.

incessant /ɪnˈsesnt/ *adj* incessant.

incessantly /ɪnˈsesntlɪ/ *adv* sans cesse.

incest /ˈɪnsest/ *n* inceste *m*.

incestuous /ɪnˈsestjʊəs, US -tʃʊəs/ *adj* incestueux/-euse.

inch /ɪntʃ/ **▶ 1045** **I** *n* (*pl* **~es**) **1** (measurement) pouce *m* (= 2,54 cm); **2** FIG (small amount) **~ by ~** petit à petit; **to come within an ~ of winning** passer à deux doigts de la victoire; **she won't give** ou **budge an ~** elle ne veut pas bouger d'un pouce.
II *vtr* **to ~ sth forward** faire avancer qch petit à petit.
III *vi* **to ~ towards sth** LIT se diriger petit à petit vers qch; FIG parvenir petit à petit à qch [*solution*].
IDIOMS **give her an ~ and she'll take a mile** ou **yard** plus on lui en donne, plus elle en veut; **I don't trust him an ~** je n'ai pas la moindre confiance en lui; **to fight every ~ of the way** lutter pied à pied.

incidence /ˈɪnsɪdəns/ *n* (occurrence) **the ~ of** la fréquence de [*thefts, deaths*]; **high/low ~ of sth** taux élevé/faible taux de qch.

incident /ˈɪnsɪdənt/ *n* incident *m*.

incidental /ˌɪnsɪˈdentl/ **I** *n* détail *m*.
II **incidentals** *npl* COMM faux-frais *mpl*.
III *adj* (minor) [*detail, remark*] secondaire; [*error*] mineur; **to be ~ to** accompagner [*activity, job*].

incidental: **~ damages** *npl* JUR dommages-intérêts *mpl* indirects; **~ expenses** *npl* faux-frais *mpl*.

incidentally /ˌɪnsɪˈdentlɪ/ *adv* (by the way) à propos; (by chance) par la même occasion.

incidental music *n* CIN musique *f* de film; THEAT musique *f* de scène.

incident room *n* GB bureau *m* des enquêteurs.

incinerate /ɪnˈsɪnəreɪt/ *vtr* incinérer.

incineration /ɪnˌsɪnəˈreɪʃn/ *n* incinération *f*.

incinerator /ɪnˈsɪnəreɪtə(r)/ *n* (industrial, domestic) incinérateur *m*; (in crematorium) four *m* crématoire.

incipient /ɪnˈsɪpɪənt/ *adj* [*disease, crisis*] à ses débuts; [*baldness*] naissant.

incise /ɪnˈsaɪz/ *vtr* (cut) inciser; (engrave) graver.

incision /ɪnˈsɪʒn/ *n* incision *f*.

incisive /ɪnˈsaɪsɪv/ *adj* [*remark, mind*] pénétrant; [*style, criticism*] incisif/-ive.

incisively /ɪnˈsaɪsɪvlɪ/ *adv* d'une manière précise.

incisor /ɪnˈsaɪzə(r)/ *n* incisive *f*.

incite /ɪnˈsaɪt/ *vtr* **to ~ violence** inciter à la violence; **to ~ sb to do** pousser ou inciter qn à faire.

incitement /ɪnˈsaɪtmənt/ *n* incitation *f* (**to** à).

incl 1 (*abrév écrite* = **including**) compris; **£20,000 ~ bonuses** 20 000 livres, primes comprises; **2** (*abrév* = **inclusive**) TTC; **£110 ~** 110 livres sterling TTC.

inclement /ɪnˈklemənt/ *adj* (all contexts) inclément.

inclination /ˌɪnklɪˈneɪʃn/ *n* **1** (tendency) tendance *f*, inclination *f*; (**to, towards** à); **by ~** par nature; **to follow one's own ~s** suivre ses penchants naturels; **2** (desire) envie *f*, désir *m* (**for** de); (liking) goût *m*; **to have an ~ to do** avoir envie de faire.

incline I /ˈɪnklaɪn/ *n* (slope) pente *f*.
II /ɪnˈklaɪn/ *vtr* **1** (tilt) incliner; **2 to be ~d to do** (have tendency) avoir tendance à faire; (have desire) avoir envie de faire; **if you feel so ~d** si l'envie vous en prend; **he was not ~d to listen** il n'était pas disposé à écouter; **to be artistically ~d** avoir un goût pour l'art; **3** SOUT (persuade) **to ~ sb to do** porter qn à faire.
III /ɪnˈklaɪn/ *vi* **1** (tend) **to ~ to** ou **towards** [*ideas, politics*] tendre vers; **to ~ towards the opinion that** avoir tendance à penser que; **2** (lean) s'incliner.

include /ɪnˈkluːd/ *vtr* inclure, comprendre; **all the ministers, Blanc ~d** tous les ministres, Blanc inclu; **breakfast is ~d in the price** le petit déjeuner est compris; **your duties ~ answering the phone** répondre au téléphone fait partie de vos fonctions; **does that ~ me?** est-ce que cela s'adresse aussi à moi?

including /ɪnˈkluːdɪŋ/ *prep* (y) compris; **~ July** y

compris juillet; **not ~ July** sans compter juillet; **up to and ~ Monday** jusqu'à lundi inclus; **~ service** service compris.

inclusion /ɪn'kluːʒn/ n inclusion f (**of** de; **in** dans).

inclusive /ɪn'kluːsɪv/ adj [charge] inclus; [price] forfaitaire; [terms] tout compris; **those aged 17–24 ~** les personnes âgées de 17 à 24 ans inclus; **the price ~ of delivery** le prix, livraison comprise.

incognito /ˌɪnkɒg'niːtəʊ, US ɪnˈkɒgnətəʊ/ **I** adj **to be ~** rester dans l'incognito; **to remain ~** garder l'incognito.
II adv [travel] incognito.

incoherence /ˌɪnkəʊ'hɪərəns/ n incohérence f.

incoherent /ˌɪnkəʊ'hɪərənt/ adj incohérent.

income /'ɪnkʌm/ n revenus mpl; **an ~ of £1,000 per month** 1000 livres sterling par mois de revenus; **to be on an ~ of £20,000 per year** gagner 20 000 livres par an; **to live within/beyond one's ~** vivre dans la limite de/au-delà de ses moyens.

income: **~ bracket**, **~ group** n tranche f de revenu; **~s policy** n politique f des revenus; **~ tax** n impôt m sur le revenu; **~ tax inspector** n inspecteur/-trice m/f des impôts.

incoming /'ɪnkʌmɪŋ/ adj [call, mail] qui vient de l'extérieur; [aircraft] qui arrive; [president, government] nouveau/-elle; [tide] montant; **this phone only takes ~ calls** ce téléphone ne peut que recevoir des appels.

incommunicado /ˌɪnkə,mjuːnɪ'kɑːdəʊ/ adj (by choice) injoignable; (involuntarily) sans contact avec l'extérieur.

incomparable /ɪn'kɒmprəbl/ adj sans pareil/-eille.

incomparably /ɪn'kɒmprəblɪ/ adv [better] infiniment; **~ beautiful** d'une beauté sans pareille.

incompatible /ˌɪnkəm'pætɪbl/ adj [person, computer, drug] incompatible; [idea, activity] inconciliable.

incompetence /ɪn'kɒmpɪtəns/, **incompetency** /ɪn'kɒmpɪtənsɪ/ n (of professional) incompétence f; (of person, child) inaptitude f; JUR incompétence f.

incompetent /ɪn'kɒmpɪtənt/ **I** n incapable mf.
II adj **1** [doctor, government] incompétent; [work, performance] mauvais; **2** JUR [person, child] incompétent; [witness] récusé; [evidence] irrecevable.

incomplete /ˌɪnkəm'pliːt/ adj **1** (unfinished) [work, building] inachevé; **2** (lacking parts) [set] incomplet/-ète; **3** (imperfect) [success] incomplet/-ète.

incompletely /ˌɪnkəm'pliːtlɪ/ adv incomplètement.

incomprehensible /ɪn,kɒmprɪ'hensəbl/ adj [reason] incompréhensible; [speech] inintelligible.

incomprehension /ɪn,kɒmprɪ'henʃn/ n incompréhension f.

inconceivable /ˌɪnkən'siːvəbl/ adj inconcevable.

inconceivably /ˌɪnkən'siːvəblɪ/ adv [tall, difficult] incroyablement.

inconclusive /ˌɪnkən'kluːsɪv/ adj [meeting] sans conclusion véritable; [election] sans résultat clair; [evidence] peu concluant.

inconclusively /ˌɪnkən'kluːsɪvlɪ/ adv [end] sans conclusion véritable; [argue] de manière peu concluante.

incongruity /ˌɪnkɒŋ'gruːətɪ/ n (of appearance) incongruité f; (of situation) absurdité f.

incongruous /ɪn'kɒŋgrʊəs/ adj [sight] déconcertant; [appearance] surprenant.

incongruously /ɪn'kɒŋgrʊəslɪ/ adv bizarrement.

inconsequential /ɪn,kɒnsɪ'kwenʃl/ adj (unimportant) sans importance; (illogical) illogique.

inconsiderate /ˌɪnkən'sɪdərət/ adj [person] peu attentif/-ive à autrui; [remark] maladroit; **to be ~ towards sb** manquer d'égards envers qn.

inconsiderately /ˌɪnkən'sɪdərətlɪ/ adv sans aucune considération.

inconsistency /ˌɪnkən'sɪstənsɪ/ n incohérence f.

inconsistent /ˌɪnkən'sɪstənt/ adj [work] inégal; [behaviour] changeant; [argument] incohérent; [attitude] inconsistant; **~ with** en contradiction avec.

inconsolable /ˌɪnkən'səʊləbl/ adj inconsolable.

inconspicuous /ˌɪnkən'spɪkjʊəs/ adj [person] qui passe inaperçu, qui ne se fait pas remarquer; [place, clothing] discret/-ète.

inconspicuously /ˌɪnkən'spɪkjʊəslɪ/ adv discrètement.

inconstancy /ɪn'kɒnstənsɪ/ n inconstance f.

inconstant /ɪn'kɒnstənt/ adj [lover] inconstant; [conditions] instable.

incontestable /ˌɪnkən'testəbl/ adj incontestable.

incontinence /ɪn'kɒntɪnəns/ n incontinence f.

incontinent /ɪn'kɒntɪnənt/ adj incontinent.

incontrovertible /ˌɪnkɒntrə'vɜːtəbl/ adj [evidence, sign] indéniable; [argument, statement] irréfutable.

incontrovertibly /ˌɪnkɒntrə'vɜːtəblɪ/ adv [true, wrong] incontestablement; [demonstrate, prove] de façon incontestable.

inconvenience /ˌɪnkən'viːnɪəns/ **I** n **1** (trouble) dérangement m; **to put sb to great ~** causer beaucoup de dérangement à qn; **2** (disadvantage) inconvénient m.
II vtr déranger.

inconvenient /ˌɪnkən'viːnɪənt/ adj **1** [location, arrangement, device] incommode; [time] inopportun; **if it's not ~** si cela ne vous/les etc dérange pas; **2** (embarrassing) gênant.

inconveniently /ˌɪnkən'viːnɪəntlɪ/ adv de façon peu pratique.

incorporate /ɪn'kɔːpəreɪt/ vtr **1** (make part of sth) incorporer (**into** dans); **2** (contain) comporter; **3** (unite) regrouper; **4** COMM, JUR **Smith and Brown Incorporated** Smith et Brown SA.

incorporation /ɪn,kɔːpə'reɪʃn/ n **1** GEN incorporation f (**into** dans); **2** JUR constitution f en société.

incorrect /ˌɪnkə'rekt/ adj incorrect (**to do** de faire); **to be ~ in doing** faire erreur en faisant.

incorrectly /ˌɪnkə'rektlɪ/ adv incorrectement.

incorrigible /ɪn'kɒrɪdʒəbl, US -'kɔːr-/ adj incorrigible.

incorruptible /ˌɪnkə'rʌptəbl/ adj incorruptible.

increase **I** /'ɪnkriːs/ n **1** (in amount) augmentation f (**in, of** de); **price ~** augmentation de prix; **a 5% ~** une augmentation de 5%; **2** (in degree) accroissement m; **to be on the ~** être en progression.
II /ɪn'kriːs/ vtr **1** GEN augmenter [sales, grant, offer, temperature] (**by** de; **to** jusqu'à); prolonger [life expectancy]; **I ~d my offer to $100** je suis monté à 100 dollars; **2** (in knitting) augmenter de [stitch].
III /ɪn'kriːs/ vi **1** [output, sales, volume] augmenter (**by** de); [appetite] grandir; [workload] s'accroître; [wind] redoubler; **to ~ in number/value** augmenter en nombre/valeur; **to ~ in volume** augmenter de volume; **to ~ in size** s'agrandir; **to ~ from... to** passer de... à; **2** (in knitting) augmenter.
IV increasing pres p adj [prices, number] croissant.
V increased pp adj [demand, probability] plus grand; [risk] accru; [attacks] plus fréquent.

increasingly /ɪn'kriːsɪŋlɪ/ adv de plus en plus.

incredible /ɪn'kredəbl/ adj **1** (unbelievable) incroyable; **2°** (wonderful) fantastique.

incredibly /ɪn'kredəblɪ/ adv (astonishingly) incroyablement; (extremely) extrêmement.

incredulity /ˌɪnkrɪ'djuːlətɪ, US -duː-/ n incrédulité f.

incredulous /ɪn'kredjʊləs, US -dʒə-/ adj incrédule.

incredulously /ɪn'kredjʊləslɪ, US -dʒə-/ adv [say] d'un ton incrédule; [look] d'un air incrédule; [listen] d'une oreille incrédule.

increment /'ɪnkrəmənt/ **I** n **1** (on salary) augmentation f (automatique); **2** COMPUT, MATH incrément m.
II vtr **1** FIN augmenter (automatique); **2** COMPUT, MATH incrémenter.

incremental /ˌɪnkrə'mentl/ adj **1** COMPUT, MATH incrémentiel/-ielle; **2** (increasing) [effect] cumulatif/-ive; [measures] progressif/-ive.

incriminate /ɪn'krɪmɪneɪt/ vtr incriminer; **to ~ sb in** impliquer qn dans [crime, activity].

incriminating /ɪn'krɪmɪneɪtɪŋ/ adj [statement, document] compromettant; [evidence] incriminant.

n-crowd○ /'ɪnkraʊd/ *n* to be in with the ~ fréquenter les gens à la mode.

ncrust *vtr* = encrust.

ncrustation /ˌɪŋkrʌ'steɪʃn/ *n* (of gems) incrustation *f*; (of salt) dépôt *m*.

ncubate /'ɪŋkjʊbeɪt/ **I** *vtr* [*hen*] couver; faire incuber [*bacteria, culture*].
II *vi* [*eggs, bacteria*] être en incubation.

ncubation /ˌɪŋkjʊ'beɪʃn/ *n* incubation *f*.

ncubator /'ɪŋkjʊbeɪtə(r)/ *n* (for child) couveuse *f*; (for eggs, bacteria) incubateur *m*.

nculcate /'ɪnkʌlkeɪt, US ɪn'kʌl-/ *vtr* to ~ sth in sb, ~ sb with sth inculquer qch à qn.

ncumbent /ɪn'kʌmbənt/ **I** *n* SOUT **1** ADMIN, POL personne *f* exerçant une charge; (minister) ministre *m*; **2** RELIG pasteur *m* (*chargé d'une paroisse*).
II *adj* **1** (morally) to be ~ on ou upon sb to do incomber à qn de faire; **2** (in office) en exercice.

ncur /ɪn'kɜ:(r)/ *vtr* (*p prés etc* **-rr-**) contracter [*debts*]; subir [*loss*]; encourir [*expense, penalty, risk, wrath*].

ncurable /ɪn'kjʊərəbl/ **I** *n* incurable *mf*.
II *adj* [*disease*] incurable; [*optimism*] incorrigible.

ncurably /ɪn'kjʊərəblɪ/ *adv* to be ~ ill souffrir d'une maladie incurable; FIG to be ~ romantic être d'un romantisme incorrigible.

ncurious /ɪn'kjʊərɪəs/ *adj* indifférent.

ncursion /ɪn'kɜ:ʃn, US -ʒn/ *n* GEN intrusion *f*; MIL incursion *f*.

ndebted /ɪn'detɪd/ *adj* **1** (grateful) to be ~ to sb (under an obligation) redevable à qn; (grateful) être reconnaissant à qn; **2** FIN endetté.

ndecency /ɪn'di:snsɪ/ *n* indécence *f*; (offence) attentat *m* à la pudeur; **gross** ~ outrage *m* à la pudeur.

ndecent /ɪn'di:snt/ *adj* (sexually) indécent; (unseemly) malséant.

ndecent: ~ **assault** *n* attentat *m* à la pudeur (**on** contre); ~ **exposure** *n* outrage *m* public à la pudeur.

ndecently /ɪn'di:sntlɪ/ *adv* [*behave, dress*] d'une manière indécente; ~ **soon** avec une rapidité malséante; ~ **early** plus tôt que nécessaire.

ndecipherable /ˌɪndɪ'saɪfrəbl/ *adj* indéchiffrable.

ndecision /ˌɪndɪ'sɪʒn/ *n* indécision *f* (**about** quant à).

ndecisive /ˌɪndɪ'saɪsɪv/ *adj* [*person, reply, result*] indécis (**about** quant à); [*battle, election*] peu concluant.

ndecisively /ˌɪndɪ'saɪsɪvlɪ/ *adv* [*speak, reply*] d'un ton indécis; [*behave*] d'une manière indécise.

ndecorous /ɪn'dekərəs/ *adj* inconvenant.

ndeed /ɪn'di:d/ *adv* **1** (certainly) en effet, effectivement; **'it's unfair'**—**'~!'** 'c'est injuste'—'en effet!'; **'~ I am!'** 'bien sûr que oui!'; **'~ you can'** ou **'you can ~'** 'bien sûr que oui'; **'he's not coming, is he?'**—**'~ he is!'** 'lui, il ne vient pas?'—'bien sûr que si!'; **2** (in fact) en fait; **she is polite,** ~ **charming** elle est polie et même charmante; **if** ~ **that is what consumers want** si c'est vraiment ce que veulent les consommateurs; **3** (for emphasis) vraiment; **that was praise** ~ c'était vraiment un compliment; **thank you very much** ~ merci mille fois; **4** IRON (expressing surprise) **'does he** ~**?'** 'ah bon?', 'vraiment?'; **a bargain** ~**!** tu parles d'une affaire!; **'why did she do it?'**—**'why** ~**?'** 'pourquoi est-ce qu'elle l'a fait?'—'ça c'est une bonne question'.

ndefatigable /ˌɪndɪ'fætɪgəbl/ *adj* inlassable.

ndefensible /ˌɪndɪ'fensəbl/ *adj* **1** (morally) inexcusable; (logically) indéfendable; **2** MIL indéfendable.

ndefinable /ˌɪndɪ'faɪnəbl/ *adj* indéfinissable.

ndefinably /ˌɪndɪ'faɪnəblɪ/ *adv* vaguement.

ndefinite /ɪn'defɪnət/ *adj* **1** (vague) vague; **2** (without limits) [*period, delay*] illimité; [*number*] indéterminé; [*ban*] pour une durée indéterminée; **3** LING the ~ **article** l'article *m* indéfini.

ndefinitely /ɪn'defɪnətlɪ/ *adv* [*continue, stay*] indéfiniment; [*postpone, ban*] pour une durée indéterminée.

ndelible /ɪn'deləbl/ *adj* [*ink, mark*] indélébile; [*impression*] ineffaçable; [*part*] indélébile.

indelibly /ɪn'deləblɪ/ *adv* **1** LIT [*marked, printed*] de manière indélébile; **2** FIG [*impressed, imprinted*] de manière ineffaçable.

indelicacy /ɪn'delɪkəsɪ/ *n* (tactlessness) indélicatesse *f*; (coarseness) grossièreté *f*.

indelicate /ɪn'delɪkət/ *adj* (tactless) indélicat; (coarse) grossier/-ière.

indemnification /ɪnˌdemnɪfɪ'keɪʃn/ *n* **1** (protection) assurance *f*; **2** (compensation) indemnisation *f* (**for** de).

indemnify /ɪn'demnɪfaɪ/ *vtr* **1** (protect) assurer (**against** contre); **2** (compensate) indemniser (**for** de).

indemnity /ɪn'demnətɪ/ *n* **1** (protection) assurance *f*; **2** (payment) indemnité *f*; **3** (exemption) décharge *f*.

indent I /'ɪndent/ *n* **1** GB COMM commande *f* (**for** de); **2** (of first line) alinéa *m*; **3** (incision) entaille *f*.
II /ɪn'dent/ *vtr* renfoncer [*line, text, word*]; faire un alinéa pour [*new paragraph*]; denteler [*edge*].
III /ɪn'dent/ *vi* GB COMM passer une commande.
IV indented *pp adj* **1** [*paragraph*] en alinéa; **2** [*coastline*] découpé; [*edge*] dentelé.

indentation /ˌɪnden'teɪʃn/ *n* **1** (dent) marque *f*; (in metal) bosse *f*; **2** (in coastline) échancrure *f*.

independence /ˌɪndɪ'pendəns/ *n* indépendance *f*.

Independence Day *n* US fête *f* de l'Indépendance.

independent /ˌɪndɪ'pendənt/ **I** *n* **1** POL candidat/-e *m/f* indépendant/-e; **2** (company) indépendant *m*, compagnie *f* indépendante.
II *adj* **1** (self-reliant) [*person*] indépendant; ~ **means, an** ~ **income** des revenus personnels; **2** POL indépendant; **3** (impartial) [*observer, inquiry*] indépendant; [*evidence, account*] objectif/-ive; **4** (unconnected) [*complaint*] indépendant; **5** (not part of an organization) indépendant; **6** (not state run) privé.

independently /ˌɪndɪ'pendntlɪ/ *adv* **1** (without help) de façon indépendante; **2** (separately) individuellement, de façon indépendante; ~ **of** indépendamment de; **3** (impartially) [*monitored*] par une autorité extérieure.

in-depth /ɪn'depθ/ **I** *adj* [*analysis, study, knowledge*] approfondi, détaillé; [*guide*] détaillé; [*interview*] en profondeur.
II in depth *adv phr* [*examine, study*] en détail.

indescribable /ˌɪndɪ'skraɪbəbl/ *adj* [*chaos, noise, smell*] indescriptible; [*pleasure, beauty*] inexprimable.

indescribably /ˌɪndɪ'skraɪbəblɪ/ *adv* ~ **beautiful/sad** d'une beauté/tristesse inexprimable; ~ **boring** incroyablement ennuyeux.

indestructible /ˌɪndɪ'strʌktəbl/ *adj* indestructible.

indeterminate /ˌɪndɪ'tɜ:mɪnət/ *adj* indéterminé.

index /'ɪndeks/ **I** *n* (*pl* ~**es** ou **-ices**) **1** (of book) index *m inv*; **thumb** ~ index à onglets; **2** (catalogue) catalogue *m*; **card** ~ fichier *m*; **3** MATH (of power) exposant *m*; (of radical) indice *m*; **4** ECON indice *m*; **cost-of-living** ~ GB, **consumer price** ~ US indice des prix à la consommation; **share** ~, **stock** ~ indice boursier; **5** PHYS indice *m*; **6** (indication) indice *m* (**of** de); **7** COMPUT index *m inv*.
II *vtr* **1** munir [qch] d'un index [*book*]; indexer [*word*]; **2** (catalogue) classer, cataloguer (**under** sous, à); **3** ECON indexer (**to** sur); **4** COMPUT indexer.

indexation /ˌɪndek'seɪʃn/ *n* indexation *f* (**to** sur).

index: ~ **card** *n* fiche *f*; ~ **finger** *n* index *m inv*; ~**-linked** *adj* indexé.

India /'ɪndɪə/ ▶ 840 *pr n* Inde *f*.

India ink *n* US encre *f* de Chine.

Indian /'ɪndɪən/ ▶ 1100 **I** *n* **1** (from India) Indien/-ienne *m/f*; **2** (American) Indien/-ienne *m/f* d'Amérique.
II *adj* (of India) [*people, culture*] indien/-ienne; [*ambassador, embassy*] de l'Inde; [*Empire*] des Indes; (American) indien/-ienne, amérindien/-ienne.

Indian: ~ **corn** *n* US maïs *m*; ~ **elephant** *n* éléphant *m* d'Asie.

Indian file *n* in ~ en file indienne, à la queue leu leu.

Indian ink *n* GB encre *f* de Chine.

Indian Ocean ▶ 1117 *pr n* the ~ l'océan *m* Indien.

Indian: ~ **summer** n été m de la Saint Martin; ~ **wrestling** n US bras m de fer.

indicate /ˈɪndɪkeɪt/ I vtr **1** (show) indiquer (**that** que; **with** de); **2** (recommend) **to be ~d** être indiqué; **3** (make known) faire savoir [intentions, feelings] (**to** à). II vi [driver] mettre son clignotant; [cyclist] faire signe.

indication /ˌɪndɪˈkeɪʃn/ n indication f, indice m; **to be an ~ of** indiquer; **it is an ~ that** c'est signe que; **to give no ~ that** [person] ne pas laisser entrevoir que; **to give no ~ of who/how** [person] ne rien dire qui permette de savoir qui/comment; [letter, speech] ne pas permettre de savoir qui/comment; **to give sb an ~ of sth** donner une idée de qch à qn; **all the ~s are that** tout porte à croire que.

indicative /ɪnˈdɪkətɪv/ I n LING indicatif m; **in the ~** à l'indicatif. II adj **1 to be ~ of** montrer; **2** LING indicatif/-ive.

indicator /ˈɪndɪkeɪtə(r)/ n **1** (pointer) aiguille f; **2** RAIL tableau m; **3** AUT clignotant m; **4** CHEM, LING, TECH indicateur m.

indices /ˈɪndɪsiːz/ npl ▶ **index**.

indict /ɪnˈdaɪt/ vtr JUR inculper.

indictable /ɪnˈdaɪtəbl/ adj passible de poursuites; ~ **offence** délit m.

indictment /ɪnˈdaɪtmənt/ n **1** JUR acte m d'accusation; **under ~ for murder** inculpé/-e de meurtre; **2** (criticism) mise f en accusation.

indie° /ˈɪndɪ/ n, adj CIN, MUS indépendant (m).

indifference /ɪnˈdɪfrəns/ n indifférence f (**to**, **towards** envers); **it is a matter of ~ to him** cela lui est indifférent.

indifferent /ɪnˈdɪfrənt/ adj **1** (uninterested) indifférent (**to**, **as to** à); (to charms) insensible (**to** à); **2** (mediocre) médiocre.

indifferently /ɪnˈdɪfrəntlɪ/ adv **1** (without caring) avec indifférence; **2** (equally) indifféremment; **3** (not well) médiocrement.

indigenous /ɪnˈdɪdʒɪnəs/ adj indigène (**to** à).

indigestible /ˌɪndɪˈdʒestəbl/ adj indigeste.

indigestion /ˌɪndɪˈdʒestʃn/ n indigestion f.

indignant /ɪnˈdɪgnənt/ adj indigné (**at** de; **about**, **over** par); **to become** ou **get ~** s'indigner (**at**, **about** de).

indignantly /ɪnˈdɪgnəntlɪ/ adv [say] avec indignation; [leave, look] d'un air indigné.

indignation /ˌɪndɪgˈneɪʃn/ n indignation f (**at** devant; **over** au sujet de).

indignity /ɪnˈdɪgnətɪ/ n indignité f.

indigo /ˈɪndɪgəʊ/ ▶ **818** I n indigo m. II adj indigo inv.

indirect /ˌɪndɪˈrekt, -daɪˈr-/ adj indirect.

indirectly /ˌɪndɪˈrektlɪ, -daɪˈr-/ adv indirectement.

indirect speech n discours m indirect.

indiscernible /ˌɪndɪˈsɜːnəbl/ adj imperceptible.

indiscreet /ˌɪndɪˈskriːt/ adj indiscret/-ète.

indiscretion /ˌɪndɪˈskreʃn/ n **1** (lack of discretion) manque m de discrétion; **2** (act) indiscrétion f.

indiscriminate /ˌɪndɪˈskrɪmɪnət/ adj (general) sans distinction; (not fussy) sans discernement; **to be ~ in** manquer de discernement dans.

indiscriminately /ˌɪndɪˈskrɪmɪnətlɪ/ adv (without distinction) sans distinction; (uncritically) sans discernement.

indispensable /ˌɪndɪˈspensəbl/ adj indispensable.

indisposed /ˌɪndɪˈspəʊzd/ adj **1** (ill) souffrant; **2** (unwilling) peu disposé (**to do** à faire).

indisputable /ˌɪndɪˈspjuːtəbl/ adj [champion] indiscuté; [fact] indiscutable; [logic] irrécusable.

indisputably /ˌɪndɪˈspjuːtəblɪ/ adv indiscutablement.

indissoluble /ˌɪndɪˈsɒljʊbl/ adj indissoluble.

indistinct /ˌɪndɪˈstɪŋkt/ adj [sound, markings] indistinct; [memory] confus; [photograph] flou.

indistinctly /ˌɪndɪˈstɪŋktlɪ/ adv indistinctement.

indistinguishable /ˌɪndɪˈstɪŋgwɪʃəbl/ adj **1** (identical) impossible à distinguer (**from** de); **2** (indiscernible) indiscernable.

individual /ˌɪndɪˈvɪdʒʊəl/ I n (person) individu m. II adj **1** (for or from one person) [effort, freedom, portion] individuel/-elle; [comfort, attitude] personnel/-elle; [tuition] particulier/-ière; **2** (separately) **each ~ article** chaque article (individuellement); **3** (idiosyncratic) particulier/-ière.

individualism /ˌɪndɪˈvɪdʒʊəlɪzəm/ n individualisme m.

individualist /ˌɪndɪˈvɪdʒʊəlɪst/ n **1** (idiosyncratic) individualiste mf; **2** (supporter of individualism) partisan/-e mf de l'individualisme.

individualistic /ˌɪndɪˌvɪdʒʊəˈlɪstɪk/ adj individualiste.

individuality /ˌɪndɪˌvɪdʒʊˈælətɪ/ n individualité f.

individually /ˌɪndɪˈvɪdʒʊəlɪ/ adv (personally, in person) individuellement; (one at a time) séparément.

indivisible /ˌɪndɪˈvɪzəbl/ adj indivisible; ~ **from** inséparable de.

Indochina /ˌɪndəʊˈtʃaɪnə/ pr n Indochine f.

indoctrinate /ɪnˈdɒktrɪneɪt/ vtr endoctriner.

indoctrination /ɪnˌdɒktrɪˈneɪʃn/ n endoctrinement m.

Indo-European /ˌɪndəʊˌjʊərəˈpɪən/ adj indo-européen/-éenne.

indolence /ˈɪndələns/ n indolence f.

indolent /ˈɪndələnt/ adj indolent.

indomitable /ɪnˈdɒmɪtəbl/ adj invincible.

Indonesia /ˌɪndəʊˈniːzjə/ ▶ **840** pr n Indonésie f.

Indonesian /ˌɪndəʊˈniːzjən/ I n ▶ **1100**, **1038** **1** (person) Indonésien/-ienne mf; **2** (language) indonésien m. II adj indonésien/-ienne.

indoor /ˈɪndɔː(r)/ adj [pool, court] couvert; [lavatory] à l'intérieur; [photography, shoes] d'intérieur.

indoors /ˌɪnˈdɔːz/ adv (in the main house) à l'intérieur; (at home) à la maison; ~ **and outdoors** dedans et dehors; **to go ~** rentrer.

indubitable /ɪnˈdjuːbɪtəbl, US -ˈduː-/ adj indubitable.

induce /ɪnˈdjuːs, US -ˈduːs/ vtr **1** (persuade) persuader (**to do** de faire); (stronger) inciter (**to** à; **to do** à faire); **2** (bring about) provoquer [emotion, response]; **drug-/stress-~d** provoqué par la drogue/le stress; **to ~ labour** MED provoquer l'accouchement.

inducement /ɪnˈdjuːsmənt, US -ˈduː-/ n **1** (reward) récompense f; (bribe) pot-de-vin m; **financial ~** avantage m pécuniaire; **2** ¢ (incentive) motivation f (**to do** pour faire); **to be an ~ to sth** encourager qch.

induction /ɪnˈdʌkʃn/ n **1** ELEC induction f; **2** (of labour) déclenchement m; **3** (inauguration) installation f; **4** US MIL incorporation f.

induction: ~ **ceremony** n cérémonie f de prise de fonctions; ~ **course** n GB stage m d'introduction.

indulge /ɪnˈdʌldʒ/ I vtr **1** (satisfy) céder à [passion, whim, desire]; **she can ~ her love of music** elle peut donner libre cours à sa passion pour la musique; **2** (humour) gâter [child]; céder à [adult]. II vi GEN se laisser tenter; EUPH (drink) boire de l'alcool; **to ~ in** se livrer à [speculation]; se complaire dans [nostalgia]; se laisser tenter par [food]. III v refl **to ~ oneself** se faire plaisir.

indulgence /ɪnˈdʌldʒəns/ n **1** (tolerance) indulgence f (**towards** envers; **for** pour); **2** (act of indulging) ~ **in food** gourmandise f; ~ **in nostalgia** abandon m à la nostalgie; **it's my one ~** c'est mon péché mignon; **3** (enjoyment) plaisir m.

indulgent /ɪnˈdʌldʒənt/ adj indulgent (**to**, **towards** pour, envers).

indulgently /ɪnˈdʌldʒəntlɪ/ adv avec indulgence.

industrial /ɪnˈdʌstrɪəl/ adj [city, area, sector, park, machinery] industriel/-ielle; [accident] du travail; [tool] à usage industriel; [worker] de l'industrie.

industrial: ~ **action** n GB (strike) grève f; ~ **arts** npl US SCH cours mpl de technologie; ~ **design** n esthétique f or conception f industrielle; ~ **designer** n concepteur/-trice mf industriel/-ielle; ~ **disease**

n maladie *f* professionnelle; **~ dispute** *n* conflit *m* social; **~ engineering** *n* génie *m* industriel; **~ estate** *n* GB zone *f* industrielle.

industrialist /ɪnˈdʌstrɪəlɪst/ *n* industriel *m*.

industrialize /ɪnˈdʌstrɪəlaɪz/ *vtr* industrialiser.

industrial: **~ relations** *npl* relations *fpl* entre les patrons et les ouvriers; **~ tribunal** *n* ~ conseil *m* des prud'hommes; **~ unrest** *n* agitation *f* ouvrière; **~ vehicle** *n* véhicule *m* utilitaire; **~ waste** *n* déchets *mpl* industriels.

industrious /ɪnˈdʌstrɪəs/ *adj* diligent.

industriously /ɪnˈdʌstrɪəslɪ/ *adv* avec diligence.

industriousness /ɪnˈdʌstrɪəsnɪs/ *n* zèle *m* au travail.

industry /ˈɪndəstrɪ/ *n* **1** industrie *f*; **the oil ~** l'industrie du pétrole; **the Shakespeare ~** FIG PÉJ le filon Shakespeare; **2** (diligence) SOUT zèle *m* (au travail).

inebriate /ɪˈniːbrɪeɪt/ *vtr* enivrer.

inedible /ɪnˈedɪbl/ *adj* [*meal*] immangeable; [*plants*] non comestible.

ineffective /ˌɪnɪˈfektɪv/ *adj* inefficace.

ineffectively /ˌɪnɪˈfektɪvlɪ/ *adv* sans succès.

ineffectiveness /ˌɪnɪˈfektɪvnɪs/ *n* inefficacité *f*.

ineffectual /ˌɪnɪˈfektʃʊəl/ *adj* [*person*] incapable; [*policy*] inefficace; [*attempt*] infructueux/-euse; [*gesture*] sans effet.

ineffectually /ˌɪnɪˈfektʃʊəlɪ/ *adv* en vain.

inefficiency /ˌɪnɪˈfɪʃnsɪ/ *n* (lack of organization) manque *m* d'organisation; (incompetence) incompétence *f*; (of machine, method) inefficacité *f*.

inefficient /ˌɪnɪˈfɪʃnt/ *adj* (disorganized) mal organisé; (incompetent) incompétent; (not effective) inefficace.

inefficiently /ˌɪnɪˈfɪʃntlɪ/ *adv* d'une manière inefficace.

ineligible /ɪnˈelɪdʒəbl/ *adj* **to be ~** (for job) ne pas remplir les conditions pour poser sa candidature (**for** à); (for election) être inéligible; (for pension, benefit) ne pas avoir droit (**for** à); **to be ~ to vote** ne pas avoir le droit de vote.

inept /ɪˈnept/ *adj* **1** (incompetent) incompétent; **2** (tactless) maladroit.

ineptitude /ɪˈneptɪtjuːd, US -tuːd/, **ineptness** /ɪˈneptnɪs/ *n* **1** (inefficiency) incompétence *f*; **2** (tactlessness) maladresse *f*.

ineptly /ɪˈneptlɪ/ *adv* **1** (inefficiently) de façon incompétente; **2** (tactlessly) maladroitement.

inequality /ˌɪnɪˈkwɒlətɪ/ *n* inégalité *f*.

ineradicable /ˌɪnɪˈrædɪkəbl/ *adj* indéracinable.

inert /ɪˈnɜːt/ *adj* GEN, CHEM inerte; [*gas*] rare.

inertia /ɪˈnɜːʃə/ *n* inertie *f*.

inescapable /ˌɪnɪˈskeɪpəbl/ *adj* indéniable.

inevitable /ɪnˈevɪtəbl/ **I** *n* **the ~** l'inévitable *m*.
II *adj* inévitable (**that** que + *subj*).

inevitably /ɪnˈevɪtəblɪ/ *adv* inévitablement.

inexact /ˌɪnɪɡˈzækt/ *adj* inexact.

inexactly /ˌɪnɪɡˈzæktlɪ/ *adv* inexactement.

inexcusable /ˌɪnɪkˈskjuːzəbl/ *adj* inexcusable (**that** que + *subj*).

inexcusably /ˌɪnɪkˈskjuːzəblɪ/ *adv* de façon inexcusable.

inexhaustible /ˌɪnɪɡˈzɔːstəbl/ *adj* inépuisable.

inexorable /ɪnˈeksərəbl/ *adj* inexorable.

inexorably /ɪnˈeksərəblɪ/ *adv* inexorablement.

inexpensive /ˌɪnɪkˈspensɪv/ *adj* pas cher/chère.

inexpensively /ˌɪnɪkˈspensɪvlɪ/ *adv* à peu de frais.

inexperience /ˌɪnɪkˈspɪərɪəns/ *n* inexpérience *f*.

inexperienced /ˌɪnɪkˈspɪərɪənst/ *adj* inexpérimenté.

inexpert /ɪnˈekspɜːt/ *adj* [*sailor*] amateur *inv*; [*repair*] maladroit; [*eye*] de néophyte.

inexpertly /ɪnˈekspɜːtlɪ/ *adv* de façon maladroite.

inexplicable /ˌɪnɪkˈsplɪkəbl/ *adj* inexplicable.

inexplicably /ˌɪnɪkˈsplɪkəblɪ/ *adv* inexplicablement.

inexpressible /ˌɪnɪkˈspresəbl/ *adj* inexprimable.

inexpressibly /ˌɪnɪkˈspresəblɪ/ *adv* au-delà de toute expression.

inexpressive /ˌɪnɪkˈspresɪv/ *adj* inexpressif/-ive.

inextricable /ɪnˈekstrɪkəbl, ˌɪnɪkˈstrɪk-/ *adj* inextricable.

inextricably /ɪnˈekstrɪkəblɪ, ˌɪnɪkˈstrɪk-/ *adv* inextricablement.

infallibility /ɪnˌfæləˈbɪlətɪ/ *n* infaillibilité *f*.

infallible /ɪnˈfæləbl/ *adj* infaillible.

infallibly /ɪnˈfæləblɪ/ *adv* infailliblement.

infamous /ˈɪnfəməs/ *adj* (notorious) [*person*] tristement célèbre; (evil) [*conduct, crime*] infâme.

infancy /ˈɪnfənsɪ/ *n* **1** (childhood) petite enfance *f*; **in early ~** dans la toute petite enfance; **in (one's) ~** en bas âge; **2** FIG débuts *mpl*; **in its ~** à ses débuts.

infant /ˈɪnfənt/ *n* **1** (baby) bébé *m*; (child) petit enfant *m*; **2** GB SCH enfant *mf* (entre 4 et 7 ans); **the ~s** les petites classes *fpl*.

infanticide /ɪnˈfæntɪsaɪd/ *n* infanticide *m*.

infantile /ˈɪnfəntaɪl/ *adj* **1** PÉJ infantile, puéril; **2** MED infantile.

infantry /ˈɪnfəntrɪ/ *n* infanterie *f*, fantassins *mpl*.

infantryman /ˈɪnfəntrɪmən/ *n* (*pl* **-men**) fantassin *m*.

infant school *n* ~ école *f* maternelle.

infatuate /ɪnˈfætʃʊeɪt/ *vtr* **~d with** entiché de; **to become ~d with** s'éprendre de [*person*]; s'engouer de or pour [*idea, object*].

infatuation /ɪnˌfætʃʊˈeɪʃn/ *n* engouement *m* (**with** pour); **a passing ~** une amourette.

infect /ɪnˈfekt/ *vtr* **1** GEN, MED contaminer [*person, blood, food*]; infecter [*wound*]; **to ~ sb/sth with sth** transmettre qch à qn/qch; **to become ~ed** [*wound*] s'infecter; [*person, blood*] être contaminé; **2** FIG (influence negatively) corrompre [*person, society*].

infection /ɪnˈfekʃn/ *n* **1** (of wound, organ) infection *f*; (of person, blood) contamination *f*; **to be exposed to ~** [*person*] être exposé à la contagion; **2** (disease) infection *f*; FIG contamination *f*.

infectious /ɪnˈfekʃəs/ *adj* [*disease*] infectieux/-ieuse; [*person*] contagieux/-ieuse; [*laughter*] communicatif/-ive.

infelicity /ˌɪnfɪˈlɪsətɪ/ *n* SOUT maladresse *f*.

infer /ɪnˈfɜː(r)/ *vtr* (*p prés etc* **-rr-**) **1** (deduce) inférer FML, déduire; **2** USAGE CRITIQUÉ (imply) suggérer.

inference /ˈɪnfərəns/ *n* **1** (act, process) déduction *f*, inférence *f*; **by ~** par déduction, par voie de conséquence; **2** (conclusion) conclusion *f*, déduction *f*; **the ~ is that** on en conclut or déduit que; **to draw an ~ from** tirer une conclusion de; **3** USAGE CRITIQUÉ (implication) suggestion *f*.

inferior /ɪnˈfɪərɪə(r)/ **I** *n* inférieur/-e *m/f*; MIL subalterne *mf*.
II *adj* **1** (poor quality) de qualité inférieure; **2** [*position*] inférieur; **to make sb feel ~** donner un sentiment d'infériorité à qn; **3** [*letter, number*] en indice.

inferiority /ɪnˌfɪərɪˈɒrətɪ, US -ˈɔːr-/ *n* infériorité *f* (**to** vis-à-vis de); **~ complex** complexe *m* d'infériorité.

infernal /ɪnˈfɜːnl/ *adj* **1**○ (damned) [*phone*] maudit○ (*before n*); (appalling) [*noise*] infernal○; **2** (of hell) infernal.

infernally /ɪnˈfɜːnəlɪ/ *adv* abominablement.

inferno /ɪnˈfɜːnəʊ/ *n* **1** (conflagration) brasier *m*; **2** (hell) enfer *m* ALSO FIG.

infertile /ɪnˈfɜːtaɪl, US -tl/ *adj* [*land*] infertile, stérile; [*person*] stérile.

infertility /ˌɪnfəˈtɪlətɪ/ *n* (of land) stérilité *f*, infertilité *f*; (of person) stérilité *f*.

infest /ɪnˈfest/ *vtr* infester (**with** de).

infestation /ˌɪnfesˈteɪʃn/ *n* infestation *f*.

infidelity /ˌɪnfɪˈdelətɪ/ *n* infidélité *f*.

infighting /ˈɪnfaɪtɪŋ/ *n* conflits *mpl* internes.

infiltrate /ˈɪnfɪltreɪt/ *vtr* infiltrer [*organization, group*].

infiltration /ˌɪnfɪlˈtreɪʃn/ *n* infiltration *f*.

infinite /ˈɪnfɪnət/ **I** *n* **the ~** l'infini *m*.
II *adj* **1** (boundless) [*patience, variety*] infini; [*wealth*] illimité; **2** MATH infini.

infinitely /'ɪnfɪnətlɪ/ *adv* infiniment.

infinitive /ɪn'fɪnətɪv/ *n* LING infinitif *m*; **in the ~** à l'infinitif.

infinity /ɪn'fɪnətɪ/ *n* GEN, MATH, PHOT infini *m*; **to ~** à l'infini; **~ of...** une infinité de...

infirm /ɪn'fɜːm/ *adj* (weak) infirme, invalide.

infirmary /ɪn'fɜːmərɪ/ *n* GEN hôpital *m*; (in school, prison) infirmerie *f*.

infirmity /ɪn'fɜːmətɪ/ *n* infirmité *f*.

in flagrante delicto /ˌɪn flæɡrænteɪ ˌdeɪ'lɪktəʊ/ *adv phr* en flagrant délit.

inflame /ɪn'fleɪm/ *vtr* enflammer [*imagination, crowd*]; exacerber [*passion*]; aggraver [*situation*]; MED enflammer.

inflammable /ɪn'flæməbl/ *adj* inflammable.

inflammation /ˌɪnflə'meɪʃn/ *n* inflammation *f*.

inflammatory /ɪn'flæmətrɪ, US -tɔːrɪ/ *adj* **1** [*speech, remarks*] incendiaire; **2** MED inflammatoire.

inflatable /ɪn'fleɪtəbl/ **I** *n* GEN objet *m* gonflable; (dinghy) canot *m* pneumatique; (toy) jouet *m* gonflable. **II** *adj* [*mattress, dinghy*] pneumatique; [*toy*] gonflable.

inflate /ɪn'fleɪt/ **I** *vtr* LIT, FIG gonfler. **II** *vi* [*tyre, toy*] se gonfler.

inflated /ɪn'fleɪtɪd/ *adj* **1** (excessive) [*price*] gonflé; [*fee, salary*] excessif/-ive; [*claim*] exagéré; [*style*] boursouflé; **an ~ ego** une très haute opinion de soi-même; **2** [*tyre*] gonflé.

inflation /ɪn'fleɪʃn/ *n* **1** ECON inflation *f*; **2** (of dinghy, tyre) gonflement *m*, gonflage *m*.

inflationary /ɪn'fleɪʃnrɪ, US -nerɪ/ *adj* ECON inflationniste.

inflect /ɪn'flekt/ **I** *vtr* **1** LING conjuguer [*verb*]; décliner [*noun, adjective*]; **2** (modulate) moduler [*voice*]. **II** *vi* [*verb*] se conjuguer; [*noun, adjective*] se décliner.

inflected /ɪn'flektɪd/ *adj* [*language*] flexionnel/-elle; [*form*] fléchi.

inflection /ɪn'flekʃn/ *n* **1** LING (of radical) flexion *f*; (of vowel) inflexion *f*; **2** (modulation) (of voice) inflexion *f*.

inflexibility /ɪnˌfleksə'bɪlətɪ/ *n* **1** (of attitude, will, rule) inflexibilité *f*; (of system, method) rigidité *f*; **2** (of material, structure) rigidité *f*.

inflexible /ɪn'fleksəbl/ *adj* **1** FIG [*person, attitude, will*] inflexible; [*system*] rigide; **2** [*material*] rigide.

inflexion *n* GB = **inflection**.

inflict /ɪn'flɪkt/ *vtr* infliger [*pain, presence, defeat*] (**on** à); causer [*damage*] (**on** à); **to ~ a wound on sb** blesser qn.

in-flight /ˌɪn'flaɪt/ *adj* en vol.

inflow /'ɪnfləʊ/ *n* (of cash, goods, people) afflux *m*; (into tank) arrivée *f*; **~ pipe** tuyau *m* d'arrivée.

influence /'ɪnfluəns/ **I** *n* **1** (force, factor affecting sth) influence *f* (**on** sur); **to be ou have an ~** avoir une influence; **to be under sb's ~** subir l'influence de qn; **under the ~ of** sous l'influence de; **to be under the ~** EUPH, HUM être éméché○; **to drive while under the ~ of alcohol** JUR conduire en état d'ébriété; **2** (power to affect sth) influence *f* (**with sb** auprès de qn; **over** sur). **II** *vtr* influencer [*person*] (**in** dans); influer sur [*decision, choice, result*]; **don't let him ~ you!** ne le laisse pas t'influencer!; **to be ~d by sb/sth** se laisser influencer par qn/qch.

influential /ˌɪnfluˈenʃl/ *adj* **1** (respected) [*theory, artist*] très suivi; [*newspaper, commentator*] très écouté; [*work*] très remarqué; **2** (key) déterminant; **3** (powerful) [*person*] influent, qui compte; **~ friends** des amis importants or en place.

influenza /ˌɪnflu'enzə/ ▶ **1002** | *n* grippe *f*.

influx /'ɪnflʌks/ *n* **1** (of people, money) afflux *m*; **2** (of liquid) arrivée *f*.

info○ /'ɪnfəʊ/ *n* renseignements *mpl*, tuyaux○ *mpl*.

inform /ɪn'fɔːm/ **I** *vtr* **1** (notify, tell) informer, avertir (**of, about** de; **that** du fait que); **to keep sb ~ed** tenir qn informé or au courant (**of, as to** de); **I ~ed him of my views** je lui ai fait part de mes vues; **I am**

pleased to ~ you that j'ai le plaisir de vous informer que; **2** (pervade) guider [*work, law*]. **II** *vi* **1** (denounce) **to ~ on** ou **against** dénoncer; **2** (give information) informer.

informal /ɪn'fɔːml/ *adj* **1** (unaffected) [*person*] sans façons; [*manner, style*] simple; **2** (casual) [*language*] familier/-ière; **~ clothes** vêtements *mpl* de tous les jours; **'dress ~'** (on invitation) 'tenue *f* de ville'; **3** (relaxed) [*mood*] décontracté; [*group*] informel/-elle; **4** (unofficial) [*announcement*] officieux/-ieuse; [*visit*] privé; [*invitation*] verbal; [*discussion, interview*] informel/-elle; **on an ~ basis** de façon informelle.

informality /ˌɪnfɔː'mælətɪ/ *n* (of person, event) simplicité *f*; (of arrangement, meeting) caractère *m* informel; (of workplace) ambiance *f* décontractée; (of language) style *m* familier.

informally /ɪn'fɔːməlɪ/ *adv* **1** (without ceremony) [*dress*] en tenue décontractée; [*speak, meet*] en toute simplicité; **2** (unofficially) [*act, discuss*] officieusement.

informant /ɪn'fɔːmənt/ *n* (source of information) informateur/-trice *m/f*; (informer) indicateur/-trice *m/f*.

information /ˌɪnfə'meɪʃn/ *n* **1** ¢ (facts, details) renseignements *mpl*, informations *fpl* (**on, about** sur); **a piece** ou **item of ~** un renseignement, une information; **my ~ is that** selon mes renseignements or informations; **'for ~'** (on document) 'à titre de renseignement'; **for your ~, I've never even met him!** au cas où tu ne le saurais pas, je ne l'ai jamais rencontré!; **2** US TELECOM (service *m* des) renseignements *mpl*; **3** COMPUT informations *fpl*.

information desk, information office *n* bureau *m* des renseignements.

information officer *n* (PR person, press officer) préposé/-e *m/f* à l'information.

information: **~ pack** *n* documentation *f*; **~ processing** *n* traitement *m* de l'information; **~ retrieval** *n* recherche *f* documentaire; **~ scientist** *n* informaticien/-ienne *m/f*; **~ service** *n* service *m* de renseignements; **~ system** *n* système *m* informatique; **~ technology, IT** *n* informatique *f*.

informative /ɪn'fɔːmətɪv/ *adj* [*lecture, book*] riche en renseignements; [*trip, day*] instructif/-ive; [*guide*] savant.

informed /ɪn'fɔːmd/ *adj* [*decision, opinion*] fondé; [*person*] averti; [*source*] informé; **well-/ill-~** bien/ mal informé or renseigné.

informer /ɪn'fɔːmə(r)/ *n* indicateur/-trice *m/f*; **to turn ~** dénoncer or vendre ses complices.

infrared /ˌɪnfrə'red/ *adj* infrarouge.

infrastructure /'ɪnfrəstrʌktʃə(r)/ *n* infrastructure *f*.

infrequent /ɪn'friːkwənt/ *adj* rare.

infrequently /ɪn'friːkwəntlɪ/ *adv* rarement.

infringe /ɪn'frɪndʒ/ **I** *vtr* enfreindre [*rule*]; ne pas respecter [*rights*]; commettre une contrefaçon de [*patent*]. **II** *vi* **to ~ on** ou **upon** empiéter sur [*rights*].

infringement /ɪn'frɪndʒmənt/ *n* (of rule) infraction *f* (**of** à); (of rights) violation *f*; (of patent) contrefaçon *f*.

infuriate /ɪn'fjʊərɪeɪt/ *vtr* exaspérer, faire rager.

infuriating /ɪn'fjʊərɪeɪtɪŋ/ *adj* exaspérant.

infuriatingly /ɪn'fjʊərɪeɪtɪŋlɪ/ *adv* [*laugh, reply*] de façon exaspérante; **~ slow** d'une lenteur exaspérante.

infuse /ɪn'fjuːz/ **I** *vtr* **1** (imbue) **to ~ sth with sth** insuffler qch à qch; **2** CULIN faire infuser. **II** *vi* infuser.

infusion /ɪn'fjuːʒn/ *n* (of cash, aid) injection *f*; CULIN infusion *f*.

ingenious /ɪn'dʒiːnɪəs/ *adj* ingénieux/-ieuse, astucieux/-ieuse.

ingeniously /ɪn'dʒiːnɪəslɪ/ *adv* ingénieusement, astucieusement.

ingenuity /ˌɪndʒɪ'njuːətɪ, US -'nuː-/ *n* ingéniosité *f*.

ingenuous /ɪn'dʒenjʊəs/ *adj* ingénu, candide.

ingenuously /ɪn'dʒenjʊəslɪ/ *adv* ingénument, candidement.

ingest /ɪnˈdʒest/ *vtr* ingérer [*food*]; assimiler [*fact*].

inglorious /ɪnˈglɔːrɪəs/ *adj* déshonorant, infamant.

ingot /ˈɪŋgət/ *n* lingot *m*.

ingrained /ɪnˈgreɪnd/ *adj* [*dirt*] bien incrusté; [*habit, hatred*] enraciné; ~ **in** ancré dans [*society*].

ingratiate /ɪnˈgreɪʃɪeɪt/ *v refl* **to** ~ **oneself** se faire bien voir (**with** de).

ingratiating /ɪnˈgreɪʃɪeɪtɪŋ/ *adj* PÉJ doucereux/-euse.

ingratitude /ɪnˈgrætɪtjuːd, US -tuːd/ *n* ingratitude *f*.

ingredient /ɪnˈgriːdɪənt/ *n* CULIN ingrédient *m*; FIG élément *m* (**of** de).

ingrowing toenail /ˌɪnˌgrəʊɪŋ ˈtəʊˌneɪl/, **ingrown toenail** /ˈɪnˌgrəʊn ˈtəʊˌneɪl/ *n* ongle *m* de pied incarné.

inhabit /ɪnˈhæbɪt/ *vtr* **1** LIT habiter [*house, region, planet*]; **2** FIG vivre dans [*fantasy world, milieu*].

inhabitable /ɪnˈhæbɪtəbl/ *adj* habitable.

inhabitant /ɪnˈhæbɪtənt/ *n* habitant/-e *m/f*.

inhalation /ˌɪnhəˈleɪʃn/ *n* inhalation *f*, aspiration *f*.

inhale /ɪnˈheɪl/ **I** *vtr* aspirer, inhaler [*vapour, fumes*]; avaler [*smoke, vomit*]; humer, respirer [*scent*].
II *vi* (breathe in) inspirer; (*smoke*) avaler la fumée.

inhaler /ɪnˈheɪlə(r)/ *n* inhalateur *m*.

inherent /ɪnˈhɪərənt, ɪnˈherənt/ *adj* ~ **in** inhérent or propre à.

inherently /ɪnˈhɪərəntlɪ, ɪnˈher-/ *adv* [*evil*] naturellement; [*difficult*] en soi; [*involve*] par sa nature.

inherit /ɪnˈherɪt/ *vtr* hériter de [*money, property*]; hériter de, succéder à [*title*]; FIG hériter de [*problem, tradition*]; **to** ~ **sth from sb** hériter qch de qn.

inheritance /ɪnˈherɪtəns/ *n* **1** (thing inherited) héritage *m* ALSO FIG; **to come into an** ~ faire un héritage; **2** (succession) succession *f*; **by** ou **through** ~ par voie de succession; **3** BIOL patrimoine *m* héréditaire.

inherited /ɪnˈherɪtɪd/ *adj* BIOL héréditaire; [*wealth*] hérité.

inheritor /ɪnˈherɪtə(r)/ *n* (all contexts) héritier/-ière *m/f*.

inhibit /ɪnˈhɪbɪt/ *vtr* **1** (restrain) inhiber [*person, reaction*]; entraver [*activity, progress*]; **to** ~ **sb from doing** (prevent) empêcher qn de faire; (discourage) dissuader qn de faire; **2** JUR (prohibit) interdire.

inhibited /ɪnˈhɪbɪtɪd/ *adj* [*person*] inhibé, refoulé; [*development*] entravé; ~ **by** [*person*] handicapé par.

inhibiting /ɪnˈhɪbɪtɪŋ/ *adj* inhibiteur/-trice.

inhibition /ˌɪnhɪˈbɪʃn, ˌɪnɪˈb-/ *n* inhibition *f*; **to get rid of one's** ~**s** se libérer de ses inhibitions.

inhospitable /ˌɪnhɒˈspɪtəbl/ *adj* inhospitalier/-ière.

in-house /ˈɪnhaʊs, -ˈhaʊs/ *adj* interne.

inhuman /ɪnˈhjuːmən/ *adj* inhumain.

inhumanity /ˌɪnhjuːˈmænətɪ/ *n* inhumanité *f* (**to** envers).

inhumation /ˌɪnhjuːˈmeɪʃn/ *n* SOUT inhumation *f*.

inimical /ɪˈnɪmɪkl/ *adj* inamical, hostile; **to be** ~ **to** aller à l'encontre de [*aim*]; être nuisible à [*unity*].

inimitable /ɪˈnɪmɪtəbl/ *adj* inimitable.

iniquitous /ɪˈnɪkwɪtəs/ *adj* inique, injuste.

iniquity /ɪˈnɪkwətɪ/ *n* iniquité *f*.

initial /ɪˈnɪʃl/ **I** *n* initiale *f*.
II *adj* [*shock, reaction*] initial, premier/-ière; [*shyness*] initial; ~ **letter** initiale *f*; **in the** ~ **stages** au début.
III *vtr* (*p prés* etc GB **-ll-**, US **-l-**) parapher or parafer.

initialize /ɪˈnɪʃəlaɪz/ *vtr* COMPUT initialiser.

initially /ɪˈnɪʃəlɪ/ *adv* au départ.

initiate **I** /ɪˈnɪʃɪət/ *n* initié/-e *m/f*.
II /ɪˈnɪʃɪeɪt/ *vtr* **1** (start up) mettre en œuvre [*project, reform*]; amorcer [*talks*]; JUR entamer, engager [*proceedings*]; **2** (admit) **to** ~ **sb into** admettre qn au sein de [*secret society*]; initier qn à [*astrology*]; **3** COMPUT lancer [*programme*]; établir [*communication*].

initiation /ɪˌnɪʃɪˈeɪʃn/ *n* **1** (of negotiations) amorce *f*; (of scheme, process) lancement *m*; **2** (into sect) admission *f* (**into** au sein de); (into knowledge) initiation *f* (**into** à); **3** (ceremony) cérémonie *f* d'initiation.

initiative /ɪˈnɪʃətɪv/ *n* **1** (quality) initiative *f*; **to have**

ou **show** ~ faire preuve d'initiative; **on one's own** ~ de son propre chef; **2** (lead) initiative *f*; **to take/lose the** ~ prendre/perdre l'initiative.

initiator /ɪˈnɪʃɪeɪtə(r)/ *n* instigateur/-trice *m/f*.

inject /ɪnˈdʒekt/ **I** *vtr* injecter [*vaccine, fuel*] (**into** dans); FIG apporter [*new ideas*] (**into** à); insuffler [*enthusiasm*] (**into** à); injecter [*cash*] (**into** dans); **to** ~ **sb with sth** faire une injection or une piqûre de qch à qn.
II *v refl* **to** ~ **oneself** se faire des piqûres (**with** de).

injection /ɪnˈdʒekʃn/ *n* MED piqûre *f*; TECH injection *f*.

in-joke /ˌɪnˈdʒəʊk/ *n* **it's an** ~ c'est une plaisanterie entre nous.

injudicious /ˌɪndʒuːˈdɪʃəs/ *adj* peu judicieux/-ieuse.

injunction /ɪnˈdʒʌŋkʃn/ *n* injonction *f*.

injure /ˈɪndʒə(r)/ *vtr* **1** MED blesser [*person*]; **to** ~ **one's hand** se blesser la main; **2** (damage) nuire à, compromettre [*health, reputation*]; blesser [*self-esteem*]; **to** ~ **sb's feelings** faire de la peine à qn.
II *v refl* **to** ~ **oneself** se blesser.

injured /ˈɪndʒəd/ **I** *n* **the** ~ (+ *v pl*) les blessés *mpl*.
II *adj* **1** MED [*person, limb, back*] blessé; **2** FIG [*pride*] blessé; [*tone*] offensé, blessé; **3** (wronged) [*wife, husband*] trompé; **the** ~ **party** JUR la partie lésée.

injurious /ɪnˈdʒʊərɪəs/ *adj* SOUT **1** (harmful) ~ **to** nuisible or préjudiciable à; **2** (abusive) [*remark*] blessant, offensant.

injury /ˈɪndʒərɪ/ *n* **1** MED blessure *f*; **head injuries** blessures à la tête; **to do sb an** ~ blesser qn; **to do oneself an** ~ HUM se faire mal; **2** (to reputation) atteinte *f* (**to** à); **3** JUR préjudice *m*, dommage *m*.

injury time *n* SPORT arrêts *mpl* de jeu.

injustice /ɪnˈdʒʌstɪs/ *n* injustice *f*; **to do sb an** ~ être or se montrer injuste envers qn.

ink /ɪŋk/ **I** *n* encre *f*; **in** ~ à l'encre.
II *vtr* encrer.
■ **ink in**: ~ **in** [sth], ~ [sth] **in** repasser [qch] à l'encre.

ink: ~**blot** *n* tache *f* d'encre, pâté *m*; ~**blot test** *n* test *m* de Rorschach; ~**jet printer** *n* imprimante *f* à jet d'encre.

inkling /ˈɪŋklɪŋ/ *n* petite idée *f*; **to have an** ~ **that** avoir l'idée que; **to have no** ~ **that** ne pas avoir la moindre idée que; **that was the first** ~ **I had that**... c'est alors que j'ai commencé à me douter que...

inky /ˈɪŋkɪ/ *adj* LIT taché d'encre; FIG [*sky*] noir comme de l'encre.

inlaid /ˌɪnˈleɪd/ **I** *prét, pp* ▶ **inlay**.
II *adj* [*jewellery*] incrusté (**with** de); [*box, furniture*] marqueté; [*sword*] damasquiné.

inland **I** /ˈɪnlənd/ *adj* **1** (not coastal) intérieur; ~ **waterways** canaux *mpl* et rivières *fpl*; **2** GB (domestic) [*mail, trade*] intérieur.
II /ˌɪnˈlænd/ *adv* [*travel, lie*] à l'intérieur des terres.

Inland Revenue *n* GB service *m* des impôts britannique.

in-laws /ˈɪnlɔːz/ *npl* (parents) beaux-parents *mpl*; (other relatives) belle-famille *f*, parents *mpl* par alliance.

inlay **I** /ˈɪnleɪ/ *n* (on brooch) incrustation *f*; (on wood) marqueterie *f*.
II /ˌɪnˈleɪ/ *vtr* incruster [*brooch*] (**with** de); marqueter [*wood*].

inlet /ˈɪnlet/ *n* **1** (of sea) bras *m* de mer, crique *f*; (of river) bras *m* de rivière; **2** (for fuel, air) arrivée *f*.

inmate /ˈɪnmeɪt/ *n* (of hospital) malade *mf*; (of mental hospital) interné/-e *m/f*; (of prison) détenu/-e *m/f*.

inn /ɪn/ *n* **1** (hotel) (small) auberge *f*; (larger) hôtellerie *f*; **2** (pub) pub *m*.

innards /ˈɪnədz/ *npl* LIT, FIG entrailles *fpl*.

innate /ɪˈneɪt/ *adj* inné, naturel/-elle.

inner /ˈɪnə(r)/ *adj* (*épith*) intérieur; **the** ~ **circle** le petit groupe.

inner city **I** *n* **the** ~ les quartiers *mpl* déshérités.
II inner-city *noun modifier* [*problems*] des quartiers déshérités; [*area*] déshérité.

inner ear *n* oreille *f* interne.

innermost /'ɪnəməʊst/ *adj* (*épith*) **sb's ~ thoughts** les pensées les plus intimes de qn; **his ~ self** ou **being** le tréfonds de son âme.

inner: **~ sanctum** *n* HUM antre *m*, saint *m* des saints; **~ tube** *n* chambre *f* à air.

inning /'ɪnɪŋ/ *n* US (in baseball) tour *m* de batte.

innings /'ɪnɪŋz/ *n* GB **1** (in cricket) (+ *v sg*) tour *m* de batte; **2** FIG **to have had a good ~** (when dead) avoir bien profité de l'existence; (when leaving) avoir fait son temps.

innkeeper /'ɪnkiːpə(r)/ *n* aubergiste *mf*.

innocence /'ɪnəsns/ *n* innocence *f*.

innocent /'ɪnəsnt/ **I** *n* innocent/-e *m*/*f*.
II *adj* **1** (not guilty) innocent (**of** de); **2** (innocuous) [*fun*] innocent, inoffensif/-ive; [*remark*] innocent, sans malice; [*error*] bénin/-igne; [*explanation*] anodin; **3** (unaware) innocent; **~ of** inconscient de [*effect*].

innocently /'ɪnəsntlɪ/ *adv* [*ask, reply, say*] innocemment; [*act, become involved*] en toute innocence.

innocuous /ɪ'nɒkjʊəs/ *adj* inoffensif/-ive.

innovate /'ɪnəveɪt/ *vi* innover.

innovation /ˌɪnə'veɪʃn/ *n* innovation *f*.

innovative /'ɪnəvətɪv/ *adj* innovateur/-trice.

innovator /'ɪnəveɪtə(r)/ *n* innovateur/-trice *m*/*f*.

innuendo /ˌɪnju:'endəʊ/ *n* (*pl* **~s** ou **~es**) (veiled slights) insinuations *fpl*; (sexual references) allusions *fpl* grivoises.

innumerable /ɪ'nju:mərəbl, US ɪ'nu:-/ *adj* innombrable, sans nombre.

inoculate /ɪ'nɒkjʊleɪt/ *vtr* vacciner (**against** contre); **to ~ sb with sth** inoculer qch à qn.

inoculation /ɪˌnɒkjʊ'leɪʃn/ *n* vaccination *f*, inoculation *f*.

inoffensive /ˌɪnə'fensɪv/ *adj* inoffensif/-ive.

inoperative /ɪn'ɒpərətɪv/ *adj* inopérant.

inopportune /ɪn'ɒpətju:n, US -tu:n/ *adj* inopportun.

inopportunely /ɪn'ɒpətju:nlɪ, US -tu:n-/ *adv* inopportunément.

inordinate /ɪn'ɔːdɪnət/ *adj* [*appetite, size, cost*] démesuré; [*desire*] immodéré; [*amount*] excessif/-ive.

inordinately /ɪn'ɔːdɪmətlɪ/ *adv* extrêmement.

in-patient /'ɪnpeɪʃnt/ *n* malade *mf* hospitalisé/-e.

input /'ɪnpʊt/ **I** *n* **1** (of money) apport *m*; (of energy) alimentation *f* (**of** en); **2** (contribution) contribution *f*; **her ~ was minimal** elle a fourni un minimum d'effort; **3** COMPUT (action) saisie *f* des données; (data) données *fpl* d'entrée or à traiter.
II *vtr* (*p prés* **-tt-**; *prét, pp* **-put** ou **-putted**) COMPUT saisir [*data*]; **to ~ data into a computer** entrer des données dans un ordinateur.

input: **~ data** *n* COMPUT données *fpl* d'entrée or à traiter; **~-output** *n* entrée-sortie *f*.

inquest /'ɪnkwest/ *n* GEN, JUR enquête *f* (**on, into** sur); **to hold an ~** mener or conduire une enquête.

inquire /ɪn'kwaɪə(r)/ **I** *vtr* demander.
II *vi* se renseigner (**about** sur); **to ~ after sb** demander des nouvelles de qn; **to ~ into** (ask for information about) se renseigner sur; (research) faire des recherches sur; ADMIN, JUR enquêter sur; **'~ within'** 's'adresser ici'.

inquiring /ɪn'kwaɪərɪŋ/ *adj* [*look, voice*] interrogateur/-trice; [*mind*] curieux/-ieuse.

inquiringly /ɪn'kwaɪərɪŋlɪ/ *adv* d'un air interrogateur.

inquiry /ɪn'kwaɪərɪ, US 'ɪŋkwərɪ/ **I** *n* **1** (request for information) demande *f* de renseignements; **to make an ~ about** ou **into** se renseigner sur; **to make inquiries** demander des renseignements (**about** sur); **'all inquiries to...'** 'pour tous renseignements, s'adresser à...'; **with reference to your ~** (by letter) en réponse à votre courrier; (by phone) suite à votre appel téléphonique; **2** ADMIN, JUR enquête *f*, investigation *f* (**into** sur); **murder ~** enquête criminelle; **to conduct an ~** mener une enquête (**into** sur); **to set up** ou **launch an ~** ouvrir une enquête; **line of ~** piste *f*.

II inquiries *npl* bureau *m* or service *m* de renseignements.

inquisition /ˌɪnkwɪ'zɪʃn/ **I** *n* enquête *f*.
II Inquisition *pr n* HIST Inquisition *f*.

inquisitive /ɪn'kwɪzətɪv/ *adj* curieux/-ieuse.

inquisitively /ɪn'kwɪzətɪvlɪ/ *adv* avec curiosité.

inquorate /ɪn'kwɔːreɪt/ *adj* **the meeting is ~** le quorum n'a pas été atteint pour cette réunion.

inroad /'ɪnrəʊd/ *n* **to make ~s into** ou **on** faire une avancée sur [*market*]; entamer [*savings*]; réduire [*lead*].

inrush /'ɪnrʌʃ/ *n* irruption *f*.

insalubrious /ˌɪnsə'lu:brɪəs/ *adj* (dirty) insalubre; (sleazy) sordide.

insane /ɪn'seɪn/ *adj* GEN [*person*] fou/folle; JUR aliéné; [*idea, desire*] fou/folle, insensé; **to go ~** perdre la raison; **to drive sb ~** rendre qn fou.

insanely /ɪn'seɪnlɪ/ *adv* [*act*] de façon insensée; **~ jealous** fou/folle de jalousie.

insanitary /ɪn'sænɪtərɪ, US -terɪ/ *adj* insalubre, malsain.

insanity /ɪn'sænətɪ/ *n* GEN folie *f*; JUR aliénation *f* mentale.

insatiable /ɪn'seɪʃəbl/ *adj* insatiable.

insatiably /ɪn'seɪʃəblɪ/ *adv* **~ curious** d'une curiosité insatiable.

inscribe /ɪn'skraɪb/ *vtr* **1** (write) inscrire (**in** dans); (engrave) graver (**on** sur); **~d with his name** gravé à son nom; **the book was ~d 'To Bruno'** le livre portait l'inscription 'À Bruno'; **2** (sign) dédicacer; **~d copy** exemplaire avec envoi.

inscription /ɪn'skrɪpʃn/ *n* GEN inscription *f*; (in book) envoi *m*.

inscrutable /ɪn'skru:təbl/ *adj* énigmatique.

insect /'ɪnsekt/ *n* insecte *m*; **~ bite** piqûre *f* d'insecte.

insecticide /ɪn'sektɪsaɪd/ *n, adj* insecticide (*m*).

insect: **~ repellent** *n* insectifuge *m*, produit *m* anti-insecte; **~ spray** *n* bombe *f* insecticide.

insecure /ˌɪnsɪ'kjʊə(r)/ *adj* **1** (lacking confidence) qui manque d'assurance; **to be ~** manquer d'assurance; **2** PSYCH inécurisé; **3** (not reliable) [*job*] précaire; [*investment*] risqué; **4** (unsafe, loose) [*screw*] qui tient mal; [*lock*] peu sûr; [*rope*] mal attaché; [*door*] qui ferme mal; [*foothold*] mal assuré; **5** (inadequately protected) peu sûr.

insecurity /ˌɪnsɪ'kjʊərətɪ/ *n* **1** (psychological) manque *m* d'assurance; **his feelings of ~** son sentiment d'insécurité; **2** (of position, situation) insécurité *f*; (of income) précarité *f*.

insemination /ɪnˌsemɪ'neɪʃn/ *n* insémination *f*.

insensibility /ɪnˌsensə'bɪlətɪ/ *n* **1** (indifference) insensibilité *f* (**to** à); **2** (to stimuli) insensibilité *f*; **3** (unconsciousness) inconscience *f*.

insensible /ɪn'sensəbl/ *adj* **1** (to plea, stimuli, criticism) insensible (**to** à); **2** (unconscious) sans connaissance; **3** (unaware) inconscient (**of, to** de).

insensitive /ɪn'sensətɪv/ *adj* [*person*] (tactless) sans tact; (unfeeling) insensible (**to** à); [*remark*] indélicat; [*attitude, policy*] peu compréhensif/-ive.

insensitivity /ɪnˌsensə'tɪvətɪ/ *n* insensibilité *f* (**to** à).

inseparable /ɪn'sepərəbl/ *adj* inséparable (**from** de).

insert I /'ɪnsɜːt/ *n* = **insertion** 2.
II /ɪn'sɜːt/ *vtr* insérer [*word, clause*] (**in** dans); introduire, insérer [*knife, finger*] (**in** dans); insérer [*advertisement, page*] (**in** dans).

insertion /ɪn'sɜːʃn/ *n* **1** (action) insertion *f*, introduction *f*; **2** JOURN (enclosed page, leaflet) encart *m*; (advertisement, amendment) insertion *f*.

in-service training *n* formation *f* continue.

inset /'ɪnset/ **I** *n* **1** (map) insert *m*; (photo) photographie *f* en médaillon; **2** (in sewing) entre-deux *m inv*.
II *vtr* (*p prés* **-tt-**; *prét, pp* **inset**) insérer.

inshore /ˌɪn'ʃɔː(r)/ **I** *adj* côtier/-ière.
II *adv* [*swim*] vers la côte; [*fish*] près de la côte.

inside I /'ɪnsaɪd/ *n* **1** (inner area or surface) intérieur *m*;

to be on the ~ [*runner*] être dans le couloir intérieur or à la corde; [*horse*] tenir la corde; [*car*] GEN être sur or dans la voie de droite; (in GB, Australia) être sur or dans la voie de gauche; **to overtake on the ~** (in Europe, US etc) doubler à droite; (in GB, Australia etc) doubler à gauche; **2** (position of trust) **sb on the ~** qn dans la place; **3**° (prison) **on the ~** en taule°.
II insides° /ın'saıdz/ *npl* (intestines) (of animal) entrailles *fpl*; (of human) intestin *m*, estomac *m*, boyaux° *mpl*.
III /ın'saıd/ *prep* (also US **~ of**) **1** (in the interior of) à l'intérieur; **~ the box** à l'intérieur de or dans la boîte; **to be ~ (the house)** être à l'intérieur (de la maison); **you'll feel better with some food ~ you** tu te sentiras mieux après avoir mangé quelque chose; **2** (within an area, organization) à l'intérieur de; **3** (under) **~ (of) an hour** en moins d'une heure; **to be ~ the world record** battre le record mondial; **~ the permitted time** dans les limites du temps imparti.
IV /'ınsaıd/ *adj* **1** (interior) [*cover, pocket, surface*] intérieur; [*toilet*] à l'intérieur; **2** (first-hand) [*information*] de première main; **the ~ story** la vérité; **3** (within an organization) **an ~ source** un informateur dans la place; **an ~ job** un coup monté de l'intérieur or par quelqu'un de la maison; **4 the ~ lane** (of road) (in Europe, US etc) la voie de droite; (in GB, Australia etc) la voie de gauche; (of athletics track) le couloir intérieur.
V /ın'saıd/ *adv* **1** (indoors) à l'intérieur; (in a container) à l'intérieur, dedans; **she's ~** elle est à l'intérieur; **to look ~** regarder à l'intérieur or dedans; **to go** ou **come** ou **step ~** entrer; **to bring sth ~** rentrer [*chairs*]; **2**° GB (in prison) en taule°.
VI inside out /'ınsaıd,aut/ *adv phr* à l'envers; **to turn sth ~ out** retourner [*bag*]; **to know sth ~ out** connaître qch à fond.
inside: **~ forward** *n* intérieur *m*, inter *m*; **~ leg** *n* entrejambes *m inv*; **~ leg measurement** *n* hauteur *f* de l'entrejambes.
insider /ın'saıdə(r)/ *n* initié/-e *m/f*.
insider: **~ dealer**, **~ trader** *n* initié *m*; **~ dealing**, **~ trading** *n* FIN délit *m* d'initié.
insidious /ın'sıdıəs/ *adj* insidieux/-ieuse.
insight /'ınsaıt/ *n* **1** (revealing glimpse) aperçu *m*, idée *f*; **a fascinating ~ into** un aperçu fascinant sur; **to give an ~ into** donner une idée de; **the book provides no new ~s** le livre n'apporte rien de nouveau (**into** sur); **to gain an ~ into sth** arriver à mieux connaître qch; **2** (intuition) perspicacité *f*, intuition *f*; **3** (understanding) compréhension *f* (**into** de).
insightful /'ınsaıtfʊl/ *adj* [*person*] perspicace; [*analysis*] pénétrant.
insignia /ın'sıgnıə/ *npl* **1** (symbols) insigne *m*; **2** (medals) insigne *m*.
insignificance /,ınsıg'nıfıkəns/ *n* insignifiance *f*; **to pale** ou **fade into ~** devenir dérisoire.
insignificant /,ınsıg'nıfıkənt/ *adj* [*cost, difference*] négligeable; [*person, detail*] insignifiant.
insincere /,ınsın'sıə(r)/ *adj* [*person, compliment*] peu sincère; **to be ~** manquer de sincérité.
insincerity /,ınsın'serətı/ *n* (of person) manque *m* de sincérité; (of smile, remark, compliment) hypocrisie *f*.
insinuate /ın'sınjʊeıt/ *vtr* insinuer (**that** que).
insinuating /ın'sınjʊeıtıŋ/ *adj* plein de sous-entendus.
insinuation /ın,sınjʊ'eıʃn/ *n* insinuation *f*; **he made all sorts of ~s about me** il a insinué toutes sortes de choses à mon propos.
insipid /ın'sıpıd/ *adj* (all contexts) fade.
insist /ın'sıst/ **I** *vtr* **1** (demand) insister (**that** pour que); (authoritatively) exiger (**that** que + *subj*); **2** (maintain forcefully) affirmer (**that** que).
II *vi* insister; **if you ~** puisque tu insistes; **to ~ on** exiger; **to ~ on doing** vouloir à tout prix faire, tenir à faire; **to ~ on sb doing** insister pour que qn fasse.
insistence /ın'sıstəns/ *n* insistance *f*; **to do sth at** ou **on sb's ~** faire qch devant l'insistance de qn; **her ~ on doing** son obstination à faire.
insistent /ın'sıstənt/ *adj* [*person, noise*] insistant; [*demand*] pressant; **to be ~** insister (**about** sur; **that** pour que + *subj*).

insistently /ın'sıstəntlı/ *adv* avec insistance.
insofar /,ınsə'fɑ:(r)/: **insofar as** *conj phr* **~ as** dans la mesure où; **~ as possible** dans la mesure du possible; **~ as I can** dans la mesure de mes moyens; **~ as X is concerned** en ce qui concerne X.
insole /'ınsəʊl/ *n* semelle *f* (intérieure).
insolence /'ınsələns/ *n* insolence *f*.
insolent /'ınsələnt/ *adj* insolent.
insolently /'ınsələntlı/ *adv* avec insolence.
insoluble /ın'sɒljʊbl/ *adj* insoluble.
insolvency /ın'sɒlvənsı/ *n* insolvabilité *f*.
insolvent /ın'sɒlvənt/ *adj* insolvable.
insomnia /ın'sɒmnıə/ *n* insomnie *f*.
insomniac /ın'sɒmnıæk/ *n* insomniaque *mf*.
insomuch /,ınsəʊ'mʌtʃ/ *adv* **~ as** (to the extent that) dans la mesure où; (seeing that) vu que.
inspect /ın'spekt/ *vtr* **1** examiner [qch] de près [*document, product*]; contrôler, vérifier [*accounts*]; inspecter [*school, factory, pitch, wiring*]; contrôler [*passport, ticket, luggage*]; **2** MIL passer [qch] en revue [*soldiers*].
inspection /ın'spekʃn/ *n* **1** (of document, picture) examen *m*, inspection *f*; (of school, machinery, wiring) inspection *f*; (of ticket, passport) contrôle *m*; **to make** ou **carry out an ~** procéder à une inspection; **on closer ~** en y regardant de plus près; **2** MIL (routine) inspection *f*; (at ceremony) revue *f*.
inspection: **~ copy** *n* spécimen *m*; **~ pit** *n* fosse *f* de visite.
inspector /ın'spektə(r)/ *n* **1** GEN inspecteur/-trice *m/f*; **2** GB (in police) inspecteur *m* de police; **3** GB SCH inspecteur/-trice *m/f*; **4** GB (on bus) contrôleur/-euse *m/f*.
inspiration /,ınspə'reıʃn/ *n* **1** (stimulus) inspiration *f* (**for** pour); **to draw one's ~ from sth** s'inspirer de qch; **she is an ~ to us all!** elle est un exemple pour nous tous!; **2** (sudden idea) inspiration *f*.
inspirational /,ınspə'reıʃənl/ *adj* **1** (inspiring) inspirateur/-trice; **2** (inspired) inspiré.
inspire /ın'spaıə(r)/ *vtr* **1** (give rise to) inspirer [*person, work, idea*]; motiver [*decision*]; **to be ~d by sth** s'inspirer de qch; **French-~d** d'inspiration française; **to ~ love in sb** inspirer de l'amour à qn; **he doesn't ~ much confidence** il n'inspire guère confiance; **2** (incite) inciter, encourager (**to do** à faire).
inspired /ın'spaıəd/ *adj* [*person, performance*] inspiré; [*idea*] lumineux/-euse; **an ~ guess** une heureuse inspiration.
inspiring /ın'spaıərıŋ/ *adj* [*person, speech*] enthousiasmant; [*thought, music*] exaltant.
instability /,ınstə'bılətı/ *n* instabilité *f*.
instal(l) /ın'stɔ:l/ **I** *vtr* LIT installer [*equipment*]; poser [*windows*]; FIG **to ~ sb in office** installer qn.
II *v refl* **to ~ oneself** s'installer.
installation /,ınstə'leıʃn/ *n* installation *f*.
installment plan *n* US contrat *m* de vente à crédit; **on the ~** à crédit.
instalment GB, **installment** US /ın'stɔ:lmənt/ *n* **1** (payment) versement *m* partiel; **monthly ~** mensualité *f*, versement *m* mensuel; **to pay an ~** faire un versement partiel; **in ~s** en plusieurs versements; **2** (of story, serial) épisode *m*; (of novel) feuilleton *m*.
instance /'ınstəns/ **I** *n* **1** (case) cas *m*; **in the first ~** en premier lieu; **2** (example) exemple *m*; **for ~** par exemple.
II *vtr* (cite) citer [qch] en exemple.
instant /'ınstənt/ **I** *n* instant *m*; **at that (very) ~** à l'instant même; **come here this ~!** viens ici tout de suite!; **the ~ we saw him** dès que nous l'avons vu.
II *adj* **1** (immediate) [*access, effect, rapport, success*] immédiat; [*solution*] instantané; **~ camera** polaroïd® *m*; **2** CULIN [*coffee, soup*] instantané; [*potato*] déshydraté; [*meal*] à préparation rapide.
instantaneous /,ınstən'teınıəs/ *adj* instantané.
instantly /'ınstəntlı/ *adv* GEN immédiatement; [*die*] sur le coup.

instant replay *n* US SPORT répétition *f* d'une séquence.

instead /ɪnˈsted/ **I** *adv* **we didn't go home, we went to the park** ~ au lieu de rentrer nous sommes allés au parc; **try camping** ~ essaie plutôt le camping; **let's take a taxi** ~ prenons plutôt un taxi; **she didn't go to London,** ~ **she decided to go to Oxford** au lieu d'aller à Londres elle a décidé d'aller à Oxford; **I was going to phone but wrote** ~ j'allais téléphoner mais finalement j'ai écrit; **her son went** ~ son fils y est allé à sa place.
II instead of *prep phr* ~ **of doing** au lieu de faire; ~ **of sth** au lieu de qch; **use oil** ~ **of butter** utilisez de l'huile à la place du beurre; ~ **of sb** à la place de qn.

instep /ˈɪnstep/ *n* cou-de-pied *m*; **to have a high** ~ avoir le pied cambré.

instigate /ˈɪnstɪɡeɪt/ *vtr* lancer [*attack*]; engager [*proceedings*].

instigation /ˌɪnstɪˈɡeɪʃn/ *n* **at the** ~ **of sb** à l'instigation de qn; **he stole the car at her** ~ c'est elle qui l'a incité à voler la voiture.

instil GB, **instill** US /ɪnˈstɪl/ *vtr* (*p prés etc* **-ll-**) inculquer [*attitude, belief*] (**in** à); donner [*confidence*] (**in** à); insuffler [*fear*] (**in** à).

instinct /ˈɪnstɪŋkt/ *n* instinct *m* (**for** de); **the** ~ **to do** l'instinct qui pousse à faire; **her** ~ **is to fight back** LIT, FIG elle se défend d'instinct; **follow your** ~(s) laisse-toi guider par ton intuition.

instinctive /ɪnˈstɪŋktɪv/ *adj* instinctif/-ive.

instinctively /ɪnˈstɪŋktɪvlɪ/ *adv* d'instinct, instinctivement.

institute /ˈɪnstɪtjuːt, US -tuːt/ **I** *n* **1** (organization) institut *m*; **2** US (course) stage *m*.
II *vtr* **1** (initiate) instituer, instaurer [*custom, prize*]; engager [*proceedings*]; **2** (found) fonder, constituer.

institution /ˌɪnstɪˈtjuːʃn, US -tuːʃn/ *n* **1** ADMIN, POL institution *f* ALSO FIG; **financial** ~ organisme *m* financier; **2** (home, hospital) établissement *m* spécialisé; (old people's home) asile *m* de vieillards; (mental hospital) hôpital *m* psychiatrique; **3** (establishment) (of rule, body, prize) institution *f*; ~ **of legal proceedings** JUR introduction *f* d'instance; **4** US = **institute I 1**.

institutional /ˌɪnstɪˈtjuːʃənl, US -tuː-/ *adj* **1** [*structure, reform*] institutionnel/-elle; [*food*] de collectivité; **to be put in** ~ **care** [*child*] être placé dans un établissement spécialisé; **2** COMM institutionnel/-elle.

institutionalize /ˌɪnstɪˈtjuːʃənəlaɪz, US -tuː-/ *vtr* **1** (place in care) placer [qn] dans un établissement spécialisé; (in mental hospital) interner; **to become** ~**d** [*patient*] être marqué par la vie réglementée d'un établissement spécialisé; **2** (establish officially) institutionnaliser, donner un caractère officiel à; ~**d** [*racism, violence*] institutionnalisé; **to become** ~**d** s'institutionnaliser.

instruct /ɪnˈstrʌkt/ *vtr* **1** (direct) **to** ~ **sb to do** donner l'ordre à qn de faire; **to be** ~**ed to do** recevoir l'ordre de faire; **2** (teach) instruire; **to** ~ **sb in** enseigner [qch] à qn [*subject*]; **to** ~ **sb how to do** enseigner à qn comment faire; **3** GB JUR **to** ~ **a solicitor** confier son/une affaire à un avocat.

instruction /ɪnˈstrʌkʃn/ **I** *n* **1** (order) instruction *f* (**to** à); **to give** ~**s to sb to do** donner l'ordre à qn de faire; **I have** ~**s to do** j'ai reçu l'ordre de faire; **to be under** ~**s to do** être chargé de faire; **2** ¢ (teaching) instruction *f*; **the language of** ~ la langue d'enseignement; **to give sb** ~ **in sth** enseigner qch à qn.
II instructions *npl* instructions *fpl*; ~**s for use** mode *m* d'emploi.

instruction: ~ **book** *n* livret *m* de l'utilisateur; ~ **manual** *n* manuel *m* d'utilisation.

instructive /ɪnˈstrʌktɪv/ *adj* instructif/-ive.

instructor /ɪnˈstrʌktə(r)/ ▶ **1251** *n* **1** (in sports, driving, flying) moniteur/-trice *m/f* (**in** de); (military) instructeur *m*; **2** US (in university) ≈ assistant/-e *m/f*; (any teacher) professeur *m*.

instructress /ɪnˈstrʌktrɪs/ *n* monitrice *f*.

instrument /ˈɪnstrʊmənt/ ▶ **1097** *n* **1** MUS instrument *m*; **to play an** ~ jouer d'un instrument; **2** AUT, AVIAT, TECH instrument *m*.

instrumental /ˌɪnstrʊˈmentl/ **I** *n* instrumental *m*.
II instrumentals *npl* partie *f* instrumentale.
III *adj* **1 to be** ~ **in sth/in doing** contribuer à qch/à faire; **2** MUS instrumental.

instrumentalist /ˌɪnstrʊˈmentəlɪst/ *n* instrumentiste *mf*.

instrument panel *n* tableau *m* de bord.

insubordination /ˌɪnsəˌbɔːdɪˈneɪʃn/ *n* insubordination *f*.

insubstantial /ˌɪnsəbˈstænʃl/ *adj* **1** (small) [*meal*] peu nourrissant; [*helping*] mesquin; **2** (flimsy) [*building*] peu solide; [*evidence*] insuffisant; **3** (unreal) insaisissable.

insufferable /ɪnˈsʌfrəbl/ *adj* [*heat, conditions*] insupportable; [*rudeness*] intolérable; **he's an** ~ **bore** il est assommant.

insufferably /ɪnˈsʌfrəblɪ/ *adv* ~ **rude** d'une impolitesse insupportable.

insufficient /ˌɪnsəˈfɪʃnt/ *adj* **there are** ~ **copies** il n'y a pas assez d'exemplaires (**to do** pour faire); **to be** ~ **for** être insuffisant pour.

insufficiently /ˌɪnsəˈfɪʃntlɪ/ *adv* (not enough) pas assez; (badly) mal.

insular /ˈɪnsjʊlə(r), US -sələr/ *adj* **1** PÉJ (narrow-minded) [*outlook*] étriqué; **to be** ~ [*person*] avoir des vues étroites; **2** GEOG insulaire.

insularity /ˌɪnsjʊˈlærətɪ, US -sʊl-/ *n* étroitesse *f* d'esprit.

insulate /ˈɪnsjʊleɪt, US -sə'l-/ *vtr* **1** (against cold, heat) isoler [*roof, room*]; calorifuger [*water tank*]; (against noise) insonoriser [*room*]; **2** ELEC isoler; **3** FIG (protect) protéger (**from** de; **against** contre); ~**d** [*wire*] isolé; [*handle*] isolant; [*tank*] calorifugé; [*room*] (against cold, heat) isolé; (against noise) insonorisé.

insulating /ˈɪnsjʊleɪtɪŋ, US -sə'l-/ *adj* isolant; ~ **tape** ruban *m* isolant.

insulation /ˌɪnsjʊˈleɪʃn, US -sə'l-/ *n* **1** (thermal) GEN isolation *f*; (of tank) calorifugeage *m*; **loft** ~ isolation du comble; **2** (acoustic) isolation *f* (acoustique), insonorisation *f*; **3** (material) isolant *m*; **4** ELEC isolation *f*.

insulator /ˈɪnsjʊleɪtə(r), US -sə'l-/ *n* **1** (substance) isolant *m*; **2** ELEC isolateur *m*.

insulin /ˈɪnsjʊlɪn, US -səl-/ *n* insuline *f*.

insult I /ˈɪnsʌlt/ *n* (remark) insulte *f*, injure *f*; (action) insulte *f*, affront *m*; **and to add** ~ **to injury...** et pour comble d'insulte...
II /ɪnˈsʌlt/ *vtr* (verbally) insulter, injurier; (by one's behaviour) insulter.

insulting /ɪnˈsʌltɪŋ/ *adj* insultant.

insultingly /ɪnˈsʌltɪŋlɪ/ *adv* de façon injurieuse.

insuperable /ɪnˈsuːpərəbl, ɪnˈsjuː-/ *adj* insurmontable.

insurance /ɪnˈʃɔːrəns, US -ˈʃʊər-/ *n* **1** ¢ (contract) assurance *f* (**against** contre; **for** pour); (policy) police *f* d'assurance; **to take out** ~ **against sth** s'assurer contre qch; **to pay the** ~ **on sth** payer l'assurance de qch; **accident/fire** ~ assurance contre les accidents/l'incendie; **travel** ~ assurance voyage; **2** (amount paid) assurance *f*; **I pay £500 in** ~ **on the car** je paie 500 livres sterling d'assurance pour la voiture; **3** (profession) **he works in** ~ il travaille dans les assurances; **4** FIG (precaution) protection *f* (**against** contre).

insurance: ~ **agent** *n* agent *m* d'assurances; ~ **broker** *n* courtier *m* en assurances; ~ **claim** *n* demande *f* d'indemnité; ~ **company** *n* compagnie *f* d'assurances; ~ **plan** *n* US régime *m* d'assurances; ~ **policy** *n* (police *f* d')assurance *f*; ~ **premium** *n* prime *f* d'assurance; ~ **scheme** *n* GB régime *m* d'assurances.

insure /ɪnˈʃɔː(r), US -ˈʃʊər/ *vtr* **1** assurer (**against** contre); **to** ~ **oneself** ou **one's life** prendre une assurance-vie; ~**d for £50** assuré pour une valeur déclarée de 50 livres; **2** (take precautions) **to ~ against delay** se garantir contre les retards; **3** US = **ensure**.

insured party *n* assuré/-e *m/f*.

insurer /ɪnˈʃɔːrə(r)/, US -ˈʃʊər-/ *n* assureur *m*.

insurgent /ɪnˈsɜːdʒənt/ *n, adj* insurgé/-e (*m/f*).

insurmountable /ˌɪnsəˈmaʊntəbl/ *adj* insurmontable.

insurrection /ˌɪnsəˈrekʃn/ *n* insurrection *f*.

intact /ɪnˈtækt/ *adj* intact; **to survive ~** rester intact.

intake /ˈɪnteɪk/ *n* **1** (consumption) consommation *f*; **2** SCH, UNIV (admissions) (+ *v sg ou pl*) admissions *fpl*; **the new ~** (at school) les nouveaux élèves *mpl*; (into training, job) les nouvelles recrues *fpl*; **3** (inhalation) **an ~ of breath** une inspiration *f*; **4** (inlet) arrivée *f*.

intangible /ɪnˈtændʒəbl/ *adj* **1** (undefinable) insaisissable; **2** JUR incorporel/-elle.

integral /ˈɪntɪɡrəl/ **I** *n* intégrale *f*.
II *adj* **1** (intrinsic) [*part, feature*] intégrant; **~ to** intrinsèque à; **2** (built-in) [*lighting, component*] incorporé; [*garage*] intégré; **3** (whole) intégral.

integrate /ˈɪntɪɡreɪt/ **I** *vtr* **1** (incorporate) intégrer [*region, company, system*] (**into** dans; **with** à); intégrer [*minority*] (**into** dans); **to be ~d with** s'intégrer à; **2** (combine) combiner [*systems*]; **3** POL (desegregate) rendre [qch] accessible à tous [*school, activity*].
II *vi* (mix) [*person*] s'intégrer (**with** à; **into** dans).

integrated /ˈɪntɪɡreɪtɪd/ *adj* [*system, service, circuit*] intégré; [*sect, ethnic group*] mixte.

integration /ˌɪntɪˈɡreɪʃn/ *n* (all contexts) intégration *f* (**with** à).

integrity /ɪnˈteɡrəti/ *n* intégrité *f*; **a man of ~** un homme d'intégrité.

intellect /ˈɪntəlekt/ *n* **1** (intelligence) intelligence *f*; **2** (person) esprit *m*.

intellectual /ˌɪntəˈlektʃʊəl/ *n, adj* intellectuel/-elle (*m/f*).

intellectualize /ˌɪntəˈlektʃʊəlaɪz/ **I** *vtr* intellectualiser [*problem*].
II *vi* philosopher, pérorer PEJ (**about** sur).

intellectually /ˌɪntəˈlektʃʊəli/ *adv* intellectuellement.

intelligence /ɪnˈtelɪdʒəns/ *n* **1** intelligence *f* (**to do** de faire); **to be of low ~** être peu intelligent; **use your ~!** réfléchis!; **that's an insult to his ~!** c'est le prendre pour un imbécile!; **2** GEN, MIL (information) renseignements *mpl*; **latest ~** informations *fpl* de dernière minute; **3** MIL (secret service) services *mpl* de renseignements; **military ~** service de renseignements de l'armée de terre.

intelligence: **~ agent** *n* agent *m* de renseignements; **Intelligence Corps** *n* GB ≈ service *m* de renseignements de l'armée; **~ quotient, IQ** *n* quotient *m* intellectuel; **Intelligence Service** *n* service *m* de renseignements; **~ test** *n* test *m* d'aptitude intellectuelle.

intelligent /ɪnˈtelɪdʒənt/ *adj* intelligent.

intelligent card *n* carte *f* à puce.

intelligently /ɪnˈtelɪdʒəntli/ *adv* intelligemment, avec intelligence.

intelligible /ɪnˈtelɪdʒəbl/ *adj* intelligible (**to** à).

intemperate /ɪnˈtempərət/ *adj* **1** [*remark*] immodéré; [*attack*] sans retenue; [*person*] intempérant; **2** [*weather*] rigoureux/-euse.

intend /ɪnˈtend/ **I** *vtr* **1** (have in mind) vouloir [*outcome*]; **as I ~ed** comme je le voulais; **sooner than I had ~ed** plus tôt que je ne voulais; **to ~ to do, to ~ doing** avoir l'intention de faire; **2** (mean) **to ~ sth as a joke** dire qch pour plaisanter; **no insult ~ed** (to one person) sans vouloir t'offenser; (to group) sans vouloir offenser personne; **it was clearly ~ed as a reference to...** c'était manifestement une allusion à...; **to be ~ed for** être destiné à [*person*]; être prévu pour [*purpose*]; **I ~ed it as a compliment** je voulais faire un compliment; **the law is ~ed to prevent...** la loi vise à empêcher...
II **intending** *pres p adj* [*applicant, traveller*] éventuel/-elle.

intended /ɪnˈtendɪd/ **I**† *n* her/his **~** son/sa futur/-e *m/f*.
II *adj* **1** (desired) [*result*] voulu; **2** (planned) [*visit, purchase*] projeté; **the ~ victim** la personne visée.

intense /ɪnˈtens/ *adj* **1** [*activity, feeling, colour, pressure*] intense; [*interest, satisfaction*] vif/vive (*before n*); **2** [*person*] sérieux/-ieuse.

intensely /ɪnˈtensli/ *adv* [*curious, problematic*] extrêmement; [*dislike, hate*] profondément.

intensifier /ɪnˈtensɪfaɪə(r)/ *n* LING intensif *m*.

intensify /ɪnˈtensɪfaɪ/ **I** *vtr* intensifier.
II *vi* s'intensifier.

intensity /ɪnˈtensəti/ *n* intensité *f* (**of** de).

intensive /ɪnˈtensɪv/ **I** *adj* (all contexts) intensif/-ive.
II **-intensive** *combining form* **energy-~** à forte consommation en énergie; **technology-~** à fort niveau technologique.

intensive care *n* **in ~** en réanimation.

intensive care unit *n* service *m* de soins intensifs.

intent /ɪnˈtent/ **I** *n* **1** (intention) intention *f*; **with ~** [*act, say*] à dessein, intentionnellement; **2** JUR **with (criminal) ~** avec une intention criminelle.
II *adj* **1** (determined) **~ on doing** résolu à faire; **2** (absorbed) absorbé (**on** par; **on doing** à faire).
IDIOMS **to all ~s and purposes** quasiment, en fait.

intention /ɪnˈtenʃn/ *n* intention *f* (**to do, of doing** de faire); **our ~ is to do** nous avons l'intention de faire; **the ~ is to do** l'objectif est de faire; **she hasn't the slightest ~ of doing** elle n'a nullement l'intention de faire; **with the best of ~s** avec les meilleures intentions du monde.

intentional /ɪnˈtenʃnl/ *adj* [*action, insult*] intentionnel/-elle; [*effect*] voulu.

intentionally /ɪnˈtenʃnəli/ *adv* [*act*] intentionnellement, exprès; [*ambiguous*] délibérément.

intently /ɪnˈtentli/ *adv* attentivement.

interact /ˌɪntərˈækt/ *vi* [*two factors, phenomena*] agir l'un sur l'autre, s'influencer mutuellement; [*people*] communiquer; COMPUT dialoguer.

interactive: **~ computing** *n* informatique *f* conversationnelle; **~ mode** *n* mode *m* conversationnel or interactif; **~ terminal** *n* terminal *m* interactif; **~ video** *n* vidéo *f* interactive.

interbreed /ˌɪntəˈbriːd/ **I** *vtr* (*prét, pp* **-bred**) croiser.
II *vi* (*prét, pp* **-bred**) se croiser.

interbreeding /ˌɪntəˈbriːdɪŋ/ *n* croisement *m*.

intercede /ˌɪntəˈsiːd/ *vi* (plead) intercéder (**with** auprès de; **on sb's behalf** en faveur de qn); (mediate) intervenir comme médiateur/-trice *m/f*.

intercept /ˌɪntəˈsept/ **I** *n* **1** TELECOM, US SPORT interception *f*; **2** MATH intersection *f*.
II *vtr* intercepter.

intercession /ˌɪntəˈseʃn/ *n* **1** (intervention) intercession *f* (**with** auprès de); **2** (mediation) médiation *f*.

interchange I /ˈɪntətʃeɪndʒ/ *n* **1** (road junction) échangeur *m*; **2** (exchange) échange *m*.
II /ˌɪntəˈtʃeɪndʒ/ *vtr* (exchange) échanger.

interchangeably /ˌɪntəˈtʃeɪndʒəbli/ *adv* de façon interchangeable.

inter-city /ˌɪntəˈsɪti/ **I** *n* GB (train) rapide *m*.
II *adj* interurbain.

intercom /ˈɪntəkɒm/ *n* interphone® *m*; **over ou on the ~** par l'interphone®.

interconnect /ˌɪntəkəˈnekt/ **I** *vtr* raccorder [*parts*].
II *vi* [*components*] se connecter; [*rooms*] communiquer; COMPUT être raccordé.

interconnecting /ˌɪntəkəˈnektɪŋ/ *adj* [*rooms*] communicant; [*cable*] de connexion.

intercourse /ˈɪntəkɔːs/ *n* (social) rapports *mpl* avec autrui; (sexual) rapports *mpl* (sexuels).

interdepartmental /ˌɪntəˌdiːpɑːˈtmentl/ *adj* UNIV entre départements; ADMIN, COMM entre services; POL interministériel/-ielle.

interdependence /ˌɪntədɪˈpendəns/ *n* interdépendance *f*.

interdisciplinary /ˌɪntəˌdɪsɪˈplɪnərɪ, US -nerɪ/ *adj* interdisciplinaire.

interest /ˈɪntrəst/ I *n* 1 ¢ (enthusiasm) intérêt *m* (in pour); **to add to the ~ of sth** ajouter un certain intérêt à qch; **of no ~ to sb** sans intérêt pour qn; **we've had a lot of ~ from Europe** beaucoup de gens en Europe nous ont manifesté leur intérêt; **to hold sb's ~** retenir l'attention de qn; **just for ~** pour le plaisir; **as a matter of ~**... juste pour savoir...; 2 (hobby) centre *m* d'intérêt; **he has wide ~s** il s'intéresse à énormément de choses; 3 (benefit) intérêt *m*; **in the ~(s) of** (to help, to promote) dans l'intérêt de [*peace, freedom, person*]; (out of concern for) par souci de [*hygiene, justice*]; **it's in your (own) ~(s) to do it** il est dans ton intérêt de faire; **I have an ~ in doing** il est de mon intérêt de faire; **to have a vested ~ in doing** avoir d'excellentes raisons de faire; **to have sb's best ~s at heart** vouloir le bien de qn; 4 (concern) GEN intérêt *m*; FIN participation *f*; **to declare one's ~s** faire état de ses participations personnelles; 5 (accrued monies) intérêts *mpl* (**on** de); **overdraft ~ charges** intérêts sur un découvert; **account paying ~** compte rémunéré; 6 COMM (share) intérêts *mpl*; **business ~s** intérêts commerciaux. II *vtr* 1 (provoke curiosity) intéresser (**in** à); **can I ~ you in buying some insurance?** est-ce qu'une assurance vous intéresserait?; **can I ~ you in our new range?** permettez-moi d'attirer votre attention sur notre nouvelle gamme; 2 (concern) [*problem, policy*] concerner.

interested /ˈɪntrəstɪd/ *adj* [*expression, onlooker*] intéressé; **to be ~ in** s'intéresser à [*subject, activity*]; **I am ~ in doing** ça m'intéresse de faire; **we're just not ~** ça ne nous intéresse pas; **to get sb ~ in** intéresser qn à [*subject*]; **the ~ parties** les intéressés.

interest group *n* groupement *m* d'intérêt.

interesting /ˈɪntrəstɪŋ/ *adj* intéressant.

interestingly /ˈɪntrəstɪŋlɪ/ *adv* 1 **~, he**... (worthy of note) chose intéressante, il...; (strangely) IRON chose curieuse, il...; **~ enough**... ce qui est très intéressant...; 2 [*speak, write*] d'une façon intéressante.

interest rate *n* FIN taux *m* d'intérêt.

interface /ˈɪntəfeɪs/ I *n* COMPUT, FIG interface *f*. II *vtr* 1 TECH connecter, relier; 2 (in sewing) entoiler.

interfacing /ˈɪntəfeɪsɪŋ/ *n* (in sewing) entoilage *m*.

interfere /ˌɪntəˈfɪə(r)/ *vi* 1 PÉJ (involve oneself) **to ~ in** se mêler de [*affairs*]; **she never ~s** elle ne se mêle jamais de ce qui ne la regarde pas; 2 (intervene) intervenir; **to ~ in** s'ingérer dans [*private life*]; 3 (touch, mess with) **to ~ with** toucher, traficoter○ [*machine*]; 4 (hinder) [*activity*] **to ~ with** empiéter sur [*family life, freedom*]; déranger [*sleep*]; 5 PHYS interférer.

interference /ˌɪntəˈfɪərəns/ *n* 1 (by government, boss) ingérence *f* (**in** dans); (by family) immixtion *f* (**in** dans); 2 (of sound waves, light waves) brouillage *m*, interférence *f*; (on radio) parasites *mpl*.

interfering /ˌɪntəˈfɪərɪŋ/ *adj* PÉJ [*person*] envahissant.

interim /ˈɪntərɪm/ I *n* **in the ~** entre-temps. II *adj* [*arrangement, bond, government*] provisoire; [*interest, payment*] intermédiaire; [*post, employee*] intérimaire; **~ profits** résultats *mpl* semestriels; **~ report** comptes *mpl* semestriels.

interior /ɪnˈtɪərɪə(r)/ I *n* 1 (inside) intérieur *m*; **a Vermeer ~** ART une scène d'intérieur de Vermeer; 2 (of country, continent) intérieur *m*; **Secretary/Department of the Interior** US POL ministre *m*/ministère *m* de l'Intérieur. II *adj* 1 [*wall, paintwork*] intérieur; 2 CIN, TV [*shot*] en intérieur; [*scene*] d'intérieur; 3 (inner) [*motive, impulse*] intérieur.

interior: **~ decorator** ▶ 1251 *n* décorateur/-trice *m/f*; **~ designer** ▶ 1251 *n* (of colours, fabrics etc) designer *m*; (of walls, space) architecte *m/f* d'intérieur.

interject /ˌɪntəˈdʒekt/ *vtr* placer [*word, comment*]; ..., **he ~ed** ..., lança-t-il.

interjection /ˌɪntəˈdʒekʃn/ *n* LING interjection *f*; (interruption) interruption *f*.

interleave /ˌɪntəˈliːv/ *vtr* intercaler.

interlink /ˌɪntəˈlɪŋk/ I *vtr* **to be ~ed** être lié (**with** à). II *vi* [*aspects, problems*] être liés.

interlock I /ˈɪntəlɒk/ *n* 1 COMPUT verrouillage *m*; 2 (knitted fabric) interlock *m*. II /ˌɪntəˈlɒk/ *vi* [*pipes*] s'emboîter; [*mechanisms*] s'enclencher; [*fingers*] s'entrelacer; [*systems*] être intimement liés.

interloper /ˈɪntələʊpə(r)/ *n* intrus/-e *m/f*.

interlude /ˈɪntəluːd/ *n* 1 (interval) GEN intervalle *m*; CIN, MUS, THEAT entracte *m*; 2 (brief entertainment) THEAT intermède *m*; MUS interlude *m*.

intermarriage /ˌɪntəˈmærɪdʒ/ *n* (within a family) intermariage *m*; (between racial groups) mariage *m* mixte; (between families, tribes) mariage *m* entre membres de familles/tribus différentes.

intermediary /ˌɪntəˈmiːdɪərɪ, US -dɪerɪ/ *n, adj* intermédiaire (*m/f*).

intermediate /ˌɪntəˈmiːdɪət/ I *n* 1 (mediator) intermédiaire *m/f*; 2 US AUT automobile *f* de taille moyenne. II *adj* 1 [*stage*] intermédiaire; 2 SCH [*exam*] de difficulté moyenne; [*course*] de niveau moyen; [*level*] moyen/-enne; 3 FIN [*credit*] à moyen terme.

interment /ɪnˈtɜːmənt/ *n* SOUT inhumation *f*.

interminably /ɪnˈtɜːmɪnəblɪ/ *adv* [*talk*] interminablement, pendant des heures; **~ long** interminable.

intermingle /ˌɪntəˈmɪŋgl/ *vi* [*patterns, themes*] s'entremêler; [*colours*] se mélanger (**with** à).

intermission /ˌɪntəˈmɪʃn/ *n* CIN, THEAT entracte *m*.

intermittent /ˌɪntəˈmɪtənt/ *adj* [*noise, activity*] intermittent; [*use*] occasionnel/-elle.

intermittently /ˌɪntəˈmɪtəntlɪ/ *adv* par intermittence.

intern I /ˈɪntɜːn/ *n* US 1 MED interne *mf*; 2 GEN stagiaire *mf*. II /ɪnˈtɜːn/ *vtr* MIL, POL interner.

internal /ɪnˈtɜːnl/ *adj* 1 (inner) [*mechanism*] interne; [*pipe*] intérieur; 2 MED [*organ, bleeding*] interne; **~ injuries** lésions *fpl* internes; **~ examination** toucher *m* vaginal; 3 (within organization) [*problem, mail, phone call*] interne; [*candidate*] interne à l'entreprise; 4 (within country) [*security, flight, trade*] intérieur; **~ revenue** revenus *mpl* fiscaux; **~ affairs** POL affaires *fpl* internes; **~ fighting** luttes *fpl* intestines.

internalize /ɪnˈtɜːnəlaɪz/ *vtr* intérioriser.

internally /ɪnˈtɜːnəlɪ/ *adv* 1 (inside) à l'intérieur; 'not to be taken ~' 'médicament à usage externe'; **to bleed ~** faire une hémorragie interne; 2 (within organization) [*recruit*] au sein de l'entreprise.

Internal Revenue Service *n* US ≈ fisc *m*.

international /ˌɪntəˈnæʃnəl/ I *n* SPORT (fixture) match *m* international; (player) international/-e *m/f*. II *adj* international.

internationally /ˌɪntəˈnæʃnəlɪ/ *adv* [*known, respected*] dans le monde entier; **~, the situation is even worse** sur le plan international, la situation est encore pire.

international: **International Monetary Fund, IMF** *n* Fonds *m* monétaire international, FMI *m*; **~ money order** *n* mandat-poste *m* international; **International Phonetic Alphabet, IPA** *n* alphabet *m* phonétique international, API *m*; **~ reply coupon** *n* coupon-réponse *m* international.

internee /ˌɪntɜːˈniː/ *n* MIL, POL interné/-e *m/f*.

internist /ɪnˈtɜːnɪst/ *n* US MED interniste *mf*.

internship /ɪnˈtɜːnʃɪp/ *n* US 1 GEN stage *m*; 2 MED internat *m*.

interpersonal /ˌɪntəˈpɜːsənl/ *adj* [*skills*] de communication; [*relations*] humain; **~ communications** communication *f*.

interplay /ˈɪntəpleɪ/ *n* interaction *f* (**of** de).

interpose /ˌɪntəˈpəʊz/ *vtr* 1 (insert) interposer (**between** entre); 2 (introduce) placer [*comment, remark*].

interpret /ɪnˈtɜːprɪt/ I *vtr* interpréter (**as** comme). II *vi* faire l'interprète.

interpretation /ɪnˌtɜːprɪˈteɪʃn/ *n* interprétation *f* (**by**

par; **of** de); **open to ~** sujet à interprétation; **to place an ~ on sth** donner une interprétation à qch.

interpreter /ɪn'tɜ:prɪtə(r)/ n **1** interprète mf; **2** (machine) traductrice f; (program) interpréteur m.

interpreting /ɪn'tɜ:prɪtɪŋ/ n (job) interprétariat m.

interrelate /ˌɪntərɪ'leɪt/ **I** vtr mettre [qch] en corrélation; **~d parts** parties interdépendantes.
II vi [events, ideas] être étroitement liés.

interrogate /ɪn'terəgeɪt/ vtr interroger.

interrogation /ɪnˌterə'geɪʃn/ **I** n interrogatoire m; **under ~** pendant mon/son etc interrogatoire.
II noun modifier [procedure, room] d'interrogatoire.

interrogative /ˌɪntə'rɒgətɪv/ **I** n LING interrogatif m; **in the ~** à la forme interrogative.
II adj GEN [look, tone] interrogateur/-trice; LING interrogatif/-ive.

interrogator /ɪn'terəgeɪtə(r)/ n interrogateur/-trice m/f.

interrupt /ˌɪntə'rʌpt/ **I** n COMPUT interruption f.
II vtr **1** (cut in) interrompre, couper la parole à [person]; **2** (disturb) déranger [person]; interrompre [meeting, lecture]; **3** (block) gêner [view]; **4** (stop) couper [supply].
III vi interrompre.

interruption /ˌɪntə'rʌpʃn/ n interruption f; **there are constant ~s** on est constamment interrompu.

intersect /ˌɪntə'sekt/ **I** vtr GEN, MATH croiser.
II vi **1** [roads, wires, ideas] se croiser; **to ~ with** croiser; **2** MATH se couper.

intersection /ˌɪntə'sekʃn/ n intersection f.

intersperse /ˌɪntə'spɜ:s/ vtr GEN parsemer (**with** de); (with music, breaks) entrecouper (**with** de); **sunshine ~d with showers** des éclaircies en alternance avec des averses.

interstate /ˌɪntə'steɪt/ **I** n (also **~ highway**) autoroute f (inter-États).
II adj US [commerce, links] entre États.

intertwine /ˌɪntə'twaɪn/ **I** vtr entrelacer.
II vi [fingers, threads] s'entrelacer; [lives, destinies, themes] se croiser.

interval /'ɪntəvl/ n **1** (in time, space) intervalle m; **at regular ~s** à intervalles réguliers; **at four-hourly ~s** toutes les quatre heures; **at 100 metre ~s** à 100 mètres d'intervalle; **bright ~s** METEOROL belles éclaircies fpl; **2** GB THEAT entracte m; SPORT (during match) pause f, mi-temps f inv; **3** MUS intervalle m.

intervene /ˌɪntə'vi:n/ vi **1** (take action) intervenir (**on behalf of** en faveur de); **2** (happen) arriver; **if nothing ~s** si rien n'arrive entre-temps; **3** (mediate) s'interposer.

intervening /ˌɪntə'vi:nɪŋ/ adj **in the ~ period** ou **hours** entre-temps; **in the ~ years** dans les années qui ont suivi.

intervention /ˌɪntə'venʃn/ n GEN, ECON intervention f (**on behalf of** en faveur de).

interventionist /ˌɪntə'venʃənɪst/ n, adj interventionniste (mf).

interview /'ɪntəvju:/ **I** n **1** (also **job ~**) entretien m; **2** JOURN interview f; **in an ~ with the Gazette** dans une interview accordée au journal la Gazette.
II vtr **1** (for job, place) faire passer un entretien à [candidate]; **2** (call to interview) convoquer [qn] pour un entretien; **3** JOURN interviewer [celebrity]; [police] interroger [suspect].
III vi [candidate] passer un entretien; [employer] faire passer des entretiens.

interviewee /ˌɪntəvjuː'iː/ n **1** (for job, place) candidat/-e m/f; **2** (on TV, radio) personne f interviewée; **3** (in survey) personne f interrogée.

interviewer /'ɪntəvjuːə(r)/ n **1** (for job, course) personne f faisant passer l'entretien; **2** (on Radio, TV, in newspaper) interviewer/-euse m/f; **3** (for survey) enquêteur/-trice m/f.

interwar /ˌɪntə'wɔ:(r)/ adj **the ~ period** ou **years** l'entre-deux-guerres.

interweave /ˌɪntə'wi:v/ (prét **-wove** /-'wəʊv/; pp

-woven /-'wəʊvn/) vtr entrelacer [fingers, threads]; mêler [themes, rhythms] (**with** à).

intestate /ɪn'testeɪt/ adj JUR intestat inv.

intestinal /ɪn'testɪnl, ˌɪntes'taɪnl/ adj intestinal; **to have ~ fortitude** US avoir quelque chose dans le ventre○.

intestine /ɪn'testɪn/ n intestin m.

intimacy /'ɪntɪməsɪ/ n **1** (closeness) intimité f; **2** EUPH (sexual relations) relations fpl (sexuelles).

intimate I /'ɪntɪmət/ n intime mf.
II /'ɪntɪmət/ adj **1** (personal) GEN intime; [belief, friendship] profond; [life] privé; **to be on ~ terms with sb** être intime avec qn; **2** [relationship] intime; **to be ~ with** EUPH avoir des relations sexuelles avec; **3** (cosy) intime; **4** (close) [bond, connection] intime; **an ~ knowledge of** une connaissance approfondie de.
III /'ɪntɪmeɪt/ vtr **1** (hint) laisser entendre [wishes]; **2** (announce) annoncer; **to ~ that** faire savoir que.

intimately /'ɪntɪmətlɪ/ adv **1** [know] intimement; [speak] de façon intime; **2** (deeply) **~ aware of** profondément conscient de; **3** [connected, related] intimement; **~ involved in** ou **with sth** mêlé de près à qch.

intimation /ˌɪntɪ'meɪʃn/ n **1** (hint) indication f; **she gave me no ~ that she was leaving** rien ne m'a laissé présager qu'elle allait partir; **he gave her an ~ that** il lui a laissé entendre que; **2** (announcement) GEN, RELIG annonce f.

intimidate /ɪn'tɪmɪdeɪt/ vtr intimider; **to ~ sb into doing** forcer qn à faire qch par des mesures d'intimidation.

intimidating /ɪn'tɪmɪdeɪtɪŋ/ adj [behaviour, experience, person] intimidant; [obstacle, sight, size] impressionnant; [prospect] redoutable.

intimidation /ɪnˌtɪmɪ'deɪʃn/ n intimidation f (**by** de la part de).

into /'ɪntə, 'ɪntuː/

■ **Note** into is used after certain nouns and verbs in English (change into, wander into etc). For translations, consult the appropriate noun or verb entry (**change, wander** etc).
– into is used in the structure verb + sb + into + doing (to bully sb into doing, to fool sb into doing). For translations of these structures see the appropriate verb entry (**bully, fool** etc).
– For translations of expressions like get into trouble, go into detail, get into debt etc you should consult the appropriate noun entry (**trouble, detail, debt** etc).

prep **1** (indicating change of location) [put, go, disappear] dans [place]; **pour the mixture ~ it** versez-y le mélange; **to move sth ~ the shade** mettre qch à l'ombre; **to go ~ town/~ the office** aller en ville/au bureau; **to get ~ bed** se mettre au lit; **to help sb ~ bed** aider qn à se mettre au lit; **2** (indicating change of form) en [new shape, foreign currency, different language]; **3** (indicating duration) **~ the 18th century** jusqu'au XVIIIᵉ siècle; **well ~ the afternoon** jusque tard dans l'après-midi; **4** (indicating a point in a process) **we were well ~ 1988 when...** l'année 1988 était bien entamée quand...; **well ~ the second half** bien après le début de la deuxième mi-temps; **to be (well) ~ one's thirties** avoir une bonne trentaine d'années; **5** (indicating direction) dans; **to speak ~ the microphone** parler dans le microphone; **6**○ (keen on) **to be ~** être fana○ de [jazz etc]; **to be ~ drugs** se droguer; **7** (indicating impact) dans; **to run ~ sth** rentrer dans qch; **to bang ~ sb/sth** heurter qn/qch; **8** MATH **8 ~ 24 goes 3 times** ou **is 3** 24 divisé par 8 égale 3.
IDIOMS **to be ~ everything** [child] toucher à tout.

intolerable /ɪn'tɒlərəbl/ adj intolérable, insupportable.

intolerably /ɪn'tɒlərəblɪ/ adv [behave] d'une façon insupportable; [painful, possessive, long] horriblement.

intolerance /ɪn'tɒlərəns/ n GEN, MED intolérance f (**of, towards** vis-à-vis de; **to** à).

intolerant /ɪn'tɒlərənt/ *adj* intolérant (**of, towards** vis-à-vis de; **with** envers).

intone /ɪn'təʊn/ *vtr* psalmodier [*prayer*]; débiter [*speech*].

intoxicate /ɪn'tɒksɪkeɪt/ *vtr* **1** (inebriate) enivrer; **2** (poison) intoxiquer; **3** FIG griser.

intoxicated /ɪn'tɒksɪkeɪtɪd/ *adj* LIT ivre; FIG grisé (**by, with** par).

intoxicating /ɪn'tɒksɪkeɪtɪŋ/ *adj* **1** LIT [*drink*] alcoolisé; [*effect, substance*] toxique; **2** FIG [*perfume*] enivrant; [*sensation*] grisant.

intoxication /ɪn,tɒksɪ'keɪʃn/ *n* LIT, FIG ivresse *f*.

intractable /ɪn'træktəbl/ *adj* [*person*] intraitable; [*opinion*] inflexible; [*illness, problem*] rebelle.

intramural /,ɪntrə'mjʊərl/ *adj* [*studies*] dispensé dans l'établissement; US SPORT interclasse (*inv*).

intransigence /ɪn'trænsɪdʒəns/ *n* intransigeance *f* (**about, over** sur; **towards** envers).

intransitive /ɪn'trænsətɪv/ *adj* intransitif/-ive.

intrauterine device, IUD *n* MED stérilet *m*.

intravenous /,ɪntrə'viːnəs/ *adj* intraveineux/-euse.

intravenous: ~ **drip** *n* perfusion *f* intraveineuse; ~ **drug user** *n* usager *m* de drogues par voie intraveineuse; ~ **injection** *n* (piqûre *f*) intraveineuse *f*.

in-tray /'ɪntreɪ/ *n* corbeille *f* arrivée.

intrepid /ɪn'trepɪd/ *adj* intrépide.

intricacy I /'ɪntrɪkəsɪ/ *n* complexité *f*.
II intricacies *npl* (of story) subtilités *fpl*; (of law) méandres *mpl*.

intricate /'ɪntrɪkət/ *adj* [*mechanism, pattern, plot, task*] compliqué; [*problem, relationship*] complexe.

intrigue I /'ɪntriːg, ɪn'triːg/ *n* **C** (plotting) intrigue *f*; **political** ~ les intrigues politiques.
II /ɪn'triːg/ *vtr* (fascinate) intriguer [*person*]; **he's ~d to know...** il est curieux de savoir...

intriguing /ɪn'triːgɪŋ/ *adj* [*person, smile*] fascinant; [*story*] curieux/-ieuse, intéressant.

intrinsic /ɪn'trɪnzɪk, -sɪk/ *adj* intrinsèque (**to** à).

introduce /,ɪntrə'djuːs, US -duːs/ *vtr* **1** (make known) présenter [*person, idea*] (**as** comme); **to** ~ **sb to** FIG initier qn à [*painting, drugs*]; **she ~d me to Mozart** elle m'a fait connaître Mozart; **introducing Abigail Bond** CIN pour la première fois à l'écran, Abigail Bond; **2** (cause to enter) introduire [*liquid, object, theme*]; **she tried to** ~ **the subject into the conversation** elle a essayé d'amener le sujet dans la conversation; **3** (establish) introduire [*law, reform*]; introduire [*word, product, change*] (**in, into** dans); **4** (preface) introduire [*talk, article*] (**with** par); TV, RADIO présenter [*programme*]; **5** (present for debate) présenter [*bill, proposal*].

introduction /,ɪntrə'dʌkʃn/ *n* **1** (making known) présentation *f*; **'our guest needs no ~'** 'il est inutile de présenter notre invité'; **letter of** ~ lettre de recommandation; **2** (insertion) introduction *f* (**into** dans); **3** (establishing of system, reform) introduction *f* (**into** dans); **this system is a recent** ~ ce système a été introduit récemment; **4** (initiation) (to art, drugs) premier contact *m* (**to** avec); **5** (preface) (to speech, article) introduction *f* (**to** de); **6** (beginner's guide) initiation *f*; **'An Introduction to French'** 'Initiation au français'; **7** POL, ADMIN (of bill, proposal) présentation *f*.

introduction agency *n* club *m* de rencontres.

introductory /,ɪntrə'dʌktərɪ/ *adj* **1** [*speech, paragraph*] préliminaire; [*course*] d'initiation; **2** COMM [*offer*] de lancement.

introspective /,ɪntrə'spektɪv/ *adj* [*person*] introspectif/-ive; [*tendency*] à l'introspection.

introvert /'ɪntrəvɜːt/ *n* introverti/-e *m/f*.

introverted /'ɪntrəvɜːtɪd/ *adj* introverti.

intrude /ɪn'truːd/ *I vtr* imposer [*opinions*].
II *vi* **1** (interfere) **to** ~ **in(to)** s'immiscer dans [*affairs*]; **2** (encroach) **to** ~ **(up)on sb's privacy** être importun; **I don't want to** ~ **on a family gathering**

je ne veux pas m'imposer dans une réunion de famille; **I don't wish to** ~ je ne veux pas vous déranger.

intruder /ɪn'truːdə(r)/ *n* (all contexts) intrus/-e *m/f*.

intruder alarm *n* sonnerie *f* d'alarme.

intrusion /ɪn'truːʒn/ *n* **1** (interruption, unwelcome arrival) intrusion *f* (**into** dans); **2** (interference) ingérence *f*, immixtion *f* (**into** dans); **it's an** ~ **into my affairs** on se mêle de mes affaires.

intrusive /ɪn'truːsɪv/ *adj* [*question, cameras*] indiscret/-ète; [*phone call, presence*] importun.

intuition /,ɪntjuː'ɪʃn, US -tuː-/ *n* intuition *f* (**about** concernant); **to have an** ~ **that** avoir l'intuition que.

intuitive /ɪn'tjuːɪtɪv, US -tuː-/ *adj* intuitif/-ive.

inundate /'ɪnʌndeɪt/ *vtr* GEN inonder; FIG submerger.

inure /ɪ'njʊə(r)/ *vtr* endurcir (**to** à).

invade /ɪn'veɪd/ *vtr* LIT, FIG envahir; **to** ~ **sb's privacy** s'immiscer dans la vie privée de qn.

invading /ɪn'veɪdɪŋ/ *adj* [*troops, army*] d'invasion; [*fans, bacteria*] envahisseur/-euse.

invalid I /'ɪnvəliːd, 'ɪnvəlɪd/ *n* (sick person) malade *mf*; (disabled person) infirme *mf*.
II /'ɪnvəliːd, 'ɪnvəlɪd/ *noun modifier* [*parent, relative*] (sick) malade; (disabled) infirme.
III /ɪn'vælɪd/ *adj* **1** (without foundation) [*argument, claim*] sans fondement; **2** (not acceptable) [*claim, passport*] pas valable; [*contract, marriage*] nul/nulle.
IV /'ɪnvəliːd, 'ɪnvəlɪd/ *vtr* ~**ed out of the army** GB réformé (pour raisons de santé).

invalidate /ɪn'vælɪdeɪt/ *vtr* infirmer [*judgment, argument*]; annuler [*claim*]; vicier [*contract*]; rendre [qch] nul et sans effet [*will*].

invaluable /ɪn'væljʊəbl/ *adj* **1** (useful) [*assistance, advice, experience*] inestimable; [*person, machine, service*] précieux/-ieuse; **2** (priceless) inestimable.

invariable /ɪn'veərɪəbl/ *adj* invariable.

invasion /ɪn'veɪʒn/ *n* invasion *f*; ~ **of** (sb's) **privacy** atteinte *f* à la vie privée (de qn).

invasive /ɪn'veɪsɪv/ *adj* [*plant*] envahissant; [*cancer*] invasif/-ive; [*treatment*] chirurgical.

inveigle /ɪn'veɪgl/ *vtr* PÉJ **to** ~ **sb into doing** convaincre qn de faire (par la ruse).

invent /ɪn'vent/ *vtr* inventer.

invention /ɪn'venʃn/ *n* invention *f*.

inventive /ɪn'ventɪv/ *adj* inventif/-ive.

inventiveness /ɪn'ventɪvnɪs/ *n* créativité *f*, esprit *m* d'invention.

inventor /ɪn'ventə(r)/ *n* inventeur/-trice *m/f*.

inventory /'ɪnvəntrɪ, US -tɔːrɪ/ *n* **1** (list) inventaire *m*; **2** US (stock) stock *m*; ~ **of fixtures** état *m* des lieux.

inverse /,ɪn'vɜːs/ *n, adj* MATH, GEN inverse (*m*).

inversion /ɪn'vɜːʃn, US ɪn'vɜːrʒn/ *n* inversion *f*.

invert /ɪn'vɜːt/ *vtr* **1** (reverse) GEN, MUS, PHOT renverser [*image, values*]; inverser [*word order*]; **it's ~ed snobbery** c'est du snobisme à rebours; **2** (upend) retourner [*object*]; **it's ~ed** c'est à l'envers.

invertebrate /ɪn'vɜːtɪbreɪt/ *n, adj* invertébré (*m*).

inverted commas /ɪnvɜːtɪd 'kɒməz/ *npl* GB guillemets *mpl*; **in** ~ entre guillemets.

invest /ɪn'vest/ *I vtr* **1** (commit) investir, placer [*money*]; consacrer [*time, energy*] (**in** à); **2** (bestow) **to** ~ **sb with** investir qn de [*right, authority, power*]; **3** POL investir [*president*].
II *vi* **1** FIN investir; **to** ~ **in shares** placer son argent en valeurs; **2** (buy) **to** ~ **in** investir dans [*equipment*]; **I** ~**ed in a carpet** je me suis acheté un tapis.

investigate /ɪn'vestɪgeɪt/ *vtr* **1** (inquire into) enquêter sur [*crime, case*]; faire une enquête sur [*person*]; vérifier [*allegation, story*]; **2** (study) examiner [*question, possibility, report*]; étudier [*subject, culture*]; COMM sonder [*market, sector*]; **3** (try out) essayer [*restaurant, club*]; **4** (find out) **it's worth investigating whether** il faudrait se renseigner pour savoir si.

investigation /ɪn,vestɪ'geɪʃn/ *n* **1** (inquiry) enquête *f* (**of, into** sur); **the crime is still under** ~ on enquête encore sur le crime; **he is under ~** il fait l'objet d'une enquête; **2** COMM, MED (study) étude *f* (**of** de); **the matter under ~** la question (actuellement) à l'étude; **3** JUR (of accounts, reports) vérification *f*.

investigative /ɪnˈvestɪgətɪv, US -geɪtɪv/ *adj* [*committee, mission, journalist, reporting*] d'investigation.

investigator /ɪnˈvestɪgeɪtə(r)/ *n* (in police) enquêteur/-trice *m/f*.

investiture /ɪnˈvestɪtʃə(r), US -tʃʊər/ *n* cérémonie *f* d'investiture.

investment /ɪnˈvestmənt/ *n* **1** FIN investissement *m*, placement *m*; **2** (commitment) **a huge emotional ~** un énorme engagement personnel; **3** MIL investissement *m*.

investment: **~ analyst** ▶1251 *n* analyste *mf* financier/-ière; **~ income** *n* revenu *m* de portefeuille de titres; **~ management** *n* gestion *f* de portefeuille; **~ manager** ▶1251 *n* gérant/-e *m/f* de portefeuille; **~ trust** *n* société *f* d'investissement.

investor /ɪnˈvestə(r)/ *n* investisseur/-euse *m/f* (**in** dans); (in shares) actionnaire *mf*; **big ~s** gros actionnaires; **private ~** petit porteur *m*.

inveterate /ɪnˈvetərət/ *adj* invétéré.

invidious /ɪnˈvɪdɪəs/ *adj* [*position*] délicat; [*choice*] difficile.

invigilate /ɪnˈvɪdʒɪleɪt/ **I** *vtr* surveiller [*examination*]. **II** *vi* être de surveillance.

invigorate /ɪnˈvɪgəreɪt/ *vtr* revigorer.

invincible /ɪnˈvɪnsəbl/ *adj* [*person, power*] invincible; [*will*] irréductible.

inviolate /ɪnˈvaɪələt/ *adj* (inviolable) [*law*] inviolable; [*group, institution*] intouchable; [*treaty*] inviolé.

invisible /ɪnˈvɪzəbl/ *adj* (all contexts) invisible.

invisible: **~ ink** *n* encre *f* sympathique; **~ mending** *n* stoppage *m*.

invisibly /ɪnˈvɪzəblɪ/ *adv* invisiblement.

invitation /ɪnvɪˈteɪʃn/ *n* **1** (request, card) invitation *f*; **an ~ to dinner** une invitation à dîner; **thank you for your kind ~** je vous remercie de votre aimable invitation; **to receive an ~ to do** être invité à faire; **2** ¢ (act of inviting) invitation *f*; **'by ~ only'** 'entrée sur invitation uniquement'; **at sb's ~** à ou sur l'invitation de qn; **3** IND (summons) offre *f*; **an urgent ~ to talks** une offre pressante de négociations; **4** FIN **an ~ to bid** ou **tender** un appel d'offres; **5** FIG (encouragement) incitation *f*; **an open ~ to burglars** une incitation manifeste pour les cambrioleurs.

invite I° /ˈɪnvaɪt/ *n* invitation *f* (**to do** à faire). **II** /ɪnˈvaɪt/ *vtr* **1** inviter [*person*]; **to ~ sb for a drink** inviter qn à prendre un verre; **why don't we ~ Tara along?** pourquoi ne pas inviter Tara à venir avec nous?; **to be ~d back** (repaying hospitality) être invité en retour; (a second time) être invité de nouveau; **to ~ sb out/in** inviter qn à sortir avec soi/à entrer; **to ~ sb over** ou **round (to one's house)** inviter qn chez soi; **to ~ sb for (an) interview** convoquer qn pour un entretien; **2** (ask for) solliciter [*comments*]; **he ~d questions from the audience** il invita l'auditoire à poser des questions; **3** (court) chercher [*trouble*]; **4** FIN **to ~ bids** ou **tenders** faire un appel d'offres.

inviting /ɪnˈvaɪtɪŋ/ *adj* [*room*] accueillant; [*smile*] engageant; [*meal*] appétissant; [*prospect*] alléchant, tentant.

invitingly /ɪnˈvaɪtɪŋlɪ/ *adv* [*smile*] d'un air engageant.

in vitro fertilization, IVF *n* fécondation *f* in vitro.

invoice /ˈɪnvɔɪs/ **I** *n* facture *f*. **II** *vtr* envoyer une facture à; **to ~ sb for sth** facturer qch à qn; **to be ~d** recevoir une facture.

invoicing /ˈɪnvɔɪsɪŋ/ *n* facturation *f*.

invoke /ɪnˈvəʊk/ *vtr* invoquer.

involuntary /ɪnˈvɒləntrɪ, US -terɪ/ *adj* involontaire; **~ repatriation** rapatriement *m* forcé.

involve /ɪnˈvɒlv/ **I** *vtr* **1** (entail) impliquer, nécessiter [*effort, travel*]; entraîner [*problems*]; **there is a lot of work/effort ~d** cela implique beaucoup de travail/d'efforts; **2** (cause to participate) GEN faire participer [*person*] (**in** à); **to be ~d in** (positive) participer à, être

engagé dans [*business, project*]; (negative) être mêlé à [*scandal, robbery*]; **to be ~d in doing** s'occuper de faire; **not to get ~d in** ou **with sth** rester à l'écart de qch; **it will ~ them in heavy expenditure** ça va les entraîner à de grosses dépenses; **3** (affect) concerner, impliquer [*person, animal, vehicle*]; **their safety is ~d** leur sécurité est en jeu; **4** (engross) [*film, book*] faire participer, prendre [*person*]; **to get ~d in** se laisser prendre par, se plonger dans [*film, book, work*]; **5** (get emotionally attached) **to get ~d with sb** devenir proche de qn; **you're too ~d to make a judgment** tu es trop concerné pour porter un jugement; **6** (make commitment) **to get ~d** s'engager. **II** *v refl* **to ~ oneself in** ou **with** prendre part à.

involved /ɪnˈvɒlvd/ *adj* **1** (complicated) [*explanation, problem*] compliqué; **2** (*après n*) [*person, group*] (implicated) impliqué; (affected) concerné; **3** (necessary) (*après n*) [*expense, effort, problems*] inhérent.

involvement /ɪnˈvɒlvmənt/ *n* **1** (participation) (in activity) participation *f* (**in** à); (commitment) (in enterprise, politics) engagement *m* (**in** dans); **2** (connections) (with group) liens *mpl*; (with person) relations *fpl*; **3** (relationship) relation *f*; **4** (engrossment) (in film, book) (vif) intérêt *m* (**in** pour).

inward /ˈɪnwəd/ **I** *adj* (inner) [*satisfaction*] personnel/-elle; [*relief, calm*] intérieur. **II** *adv* = **inwards**.

inward: **~-bound** *adj* [*journey, flight, cargo*] de retour; [*ship*] en retour; **~ investment** *n* FIN investissements *mpl* étrangers; **~-looking** *adj* [*society, person*] replié sur soi-même; [*policy*] nombriliste°.

inwardly /ˈɪnwədlɪ/ *adv* GEN intérieurement; [*know, feel*] en son for intérieur.

inwards /ˈɪnwədz/ *adv* [*fold, open, move, grow*] vers l'intérieur; [*freight, invoice*] à l'arrivée.

iodine /ˈaɪədiːn, US -daɪn/ *n* (element) iode *m*; (antiseptic) teinture *f* d'iode.

iota /aɪˈəʊtə/ *n* **1** LIT iota *m*; **2** FIG **not an** ou **one ~ of** pas un grain de [*truth etc*]; **it hasn't changed one ~** ça n'a pas changé d'un iota.

IOU *n* (*abrév* = **I owe you**) reconnaissance *f* de dette; **an ~ for £500** un reçu pour 500 livres sterling.

IPA *n* (*abrév* = **International Phonetic Alphabet**)

IQ *n* (*abrév* = **intelligence quotient**) QI *m*.

IRA *n* (*abrév* = **Irish Republican Army**) IRA *f*.

Iran /ɪˈrɑːn/ ▶840 *pr n* Iran *m*.

Iranian /ɪˈreɪnɪən/ ▶1100, 1038 **I** *n* **1** (person) Iranien/-ienne *m/f*; **2** (language) iranien *m*. **II** *adj* iranien/-ienne.

Iraq /ɪˈrɑːk/ ▶840 *pr n* Iraq *m*.

Iraqi /ɪˈrɑːkɪ/ ▶1100 **I** *n* (person) Iraquien/-ienne *m/f*. **II** *adj* iraquien/-ienne.

irate /aɪˈreɪt/ *adj* furieux/-ieuse (**about** au sujet de).

Ireland /ˈaɪələnd/ ▶840 *pr n* Irlande *f*; **the Republic of ~** la République d'Irlande.

Irish /ˈaɪrɪʃ/ ▶1038, 1100 **I** *n* **1** (language) irlandais *m*; **2** (people) **the ~** les Irlandais *mpl*. **II** *adj* irlandais.

Irish: **~ Free State** *n* État *m* libre d'Irlande; **~man** *n* Irlandais *m*; **~ Republic** ▶840 *n* République *f* d'Irlande; **~ sea** ▶1117 *n* mer *f* d'Irlande; **~woman** *n* Irlandaise *f*.

irksome /ˈɜːksəm/ *adj* agaçant.

iron /ˈaɪən, US ˈaɪərn/ **I** *n* **1** (metal) fer *m*; **old** ou **scrap ~** ferraille *f*; **~ and steel works** usine *f* sidérurgique; **a will of ~** FIG une volonté de fer; **2** (for clothes) fer *m* (à repasser); **with a cool ~** à fer doux; **to run the ~ over sth** donner un coup de fer à qch; **3** (golf) fer *m*; **a six~** un fer six; **4** (splint) attelle *f*. **II irons** *npl* fers *mpl*; **in ~s** aux fers. **III** *noun modifier* LIT [*bar, gate*] en fer; **~ sheet** tôle *f*. **IV** *adj* FIG [*constitution, grip, will*] de fer; [*rule*] draconien/-ienne. **V** *vtr* repasser [*clothes*].

Islands

In French, some names of islands always have the definite article and some never do.

Island names with definite article

These behave like the names of countries ▶ 840 |, with different constructions depending on gender and number:

Corsica	= la Corse
in Corsica	= en Corse
to Corsica	= en Corse
from Corsica	= de Corse

Note that where the English has the definite article, French normally has as well:

the Balearics	= les Baléares *fpl*
in the Balearics	= aux Baléares
to the Balearics	= aux Baléares
from the Balearics	= des Baléares

Islands without definite article

As in English, most island names have no definite article; these work like names of towns ▶ 1343 |:

Cyprus	= Chypre
in Cyprus	= à Chypre
to Cyprus	= à Chypre
from Cyprus	= de Chypre
Cyprus sherry	= le sherry de Chypre

English uses on *with the names of small islands; there is no such distinction in French:*

on St. Helena	= à Sainte-Hélène
on Naxos	= à Naxos

As with names of cities and towns, it is safest to avoid explicit genders; use l'île de ... *instead:*

Cuba is beautiful	= l'île de Cuba est belle

Names with or without *île* in them

English and French tend to work the same way in this respect:

Guernsey	= Guernesey
the island of Guernsey	= l'île de Guernesey
the Balearics	= les Baléares
the Balearic Islands	= les îles Baléares
the Orkney Isles	= les îles Orcades

Exceptions

There are some exceptions to these rules, e.g. Fiji, Jamaica. If in doubt, look up island name in the dictionary.

IDIOMS **to have a lot of ~s in the fire** avoir beaucoup d'affaires en train; **to strike while the ~ is hot** battre le fer pendant qu'il est chaud.
■ **iron out**: **~ out [sth]** LIT faire partir [qch] au fer [*creases*]; FIG aplanir [*problem, difficulty*].

Iron Curtain *n* POL HIST rideau *m* de fer; **behind the ~** au-delà du rideau de fer.

iron: **~ filings** *npl* limaille *f* de fer; **~ fist, ~ hand** *n* FIG poigne *f* de fer.

ironic(al) /aɪˈrɒnɪk(l)/ *adj* ironique.

ironically /aɪˈrɒnɪklɪ/ *adv* ironiquement; **~, she...** l'ironie, c'est qu'elle...

ironing /ˈaɪənɪŋ, US ˈaɪərn-/ *n* repassage *m*.

ironing board *n* planche *f* à repasser.

iron lung *n* poumon *m* d'acier.

ironmonger /ˈaɪənmʌŋɡə(r), US ˈaɪərn-/ ▶ 1251 | *n* quincaillier/-ière *m*/*f*; **~'s (shop)** quincaillerie *f*.

iron: **~ ore** *n* minerai *m* de fer; **~ oxide** *n* oxyde *m* de fer; **~ rations** *npl* vivres *mpl* or rations *fpl*.

irony /ˈaɪərənɪ/ *n* ironie *f*; **one of life's little ironies** une des ironies du sort.

irradiate /ɪˈreɪdɪeɪt/ *vtr* (all contexts) irradier.

irradiation /ɪˌreɪdɪˈeɪʃn/ *n* (all contexts) irradiation *f*.

irrational /ɪˈræʃnl/ *adj* [*behaviour*] irrationnel/-elle; [*fear, hostility*] sans fondement; **he's rather ~** il n'est pas très raisonnable; **she's becoming quite ~** elle déraisonne.

irrationally /ɪˈræʃənəlɪ/ *adv* [*act*] d'une façon déraisonnable or irrationnelle; [*angry, happy*] sans raison.

irreconcilable /ɪˈrekənsaɪləbl, ɪˌrekənˈsaɪləblʳ/ *adj* [*opponents*] irréconciliable (**with** avec); [*ideas*] incompatible (**with** avec); [*conflict*] inconciliable.

irrecoverable /ˌɪrɪˈkʌvərəbl/ *adj* [*object*] irrécupérable; [*loss*] irréparable; [*debt*] irrécouvrable.

irredeemable /ˌɪrɪˈdiːməbl/ *adj* **1** RELIG [*sinner*] incorrigible; **2** [*loss*] irrémédiable; **3** FIN [*shares*] irremboursable; [*loan*] non amortissable.

irregular /ɪˈreɡjʊlə(r)/ **I** *n* MIL irrégulier/-ière *m*/*f*. **II** *adj* **1** GEN, LING irrégulier/-ière; **2** US COMM [*merchandise*] de second choix.

irregularity /ɪˌreɡjʊˈlærətɪ/ *n* irrégularité *f*.

irregularly /ɪˈreɡjʊləlɪ/ *adv* irrégulièrement.

irrelevance /ɪˈreləvəns/, **irrelevancy** /ɪˈreləvənsɪ/ *n* **1** (of fact, remark, question) manque *m* d'à-propos; **~ to sth** manque *m* de rapport avec qch; **2** (unimportant thing) **to be an ~** ne pas avoir d'importance.

irrelevant /ɪˈreləvnt/ *adj* **1** (unconnected) [*remark*] hors de propos; [*facts*] hors du sujet; [*question*] sans rapport avec le sujet; **to be ~ to sth** n'avoir aucun rapport avec qch; **2** (unimportant) **the money's ~** ce n'est pas l'argent qui compte.

irreparable /ɪˈrepərəbl/ *adj* irréparable.

irreplaceable /ˌɪrɪˈpleɪsəbl/ *adj* irremplaçable.

irrepressible /ˌɪrɪˈpresəbl/ *adj* [*high spirits*] irrépressible; [*sense of humour, enthusiasm*] inextinguible; [*person*] infatigable.

irreproachable /ˌɪrɪˈprəʊtʃəbl/ *adj* irréprochable.

irresistible /ˌɪrɪˈzɪstəbl/ *adj* irrésistible.

irresolute /ɪˈrezəluːt/ *adj* irrésolu, indécis.

irrespective /ˌɪrɪˈspektɪv/: **irrespective of** *prep phr* sans tenir compte de [*age, class*]; sans distinction de [*race*]; **everyone, ~ of who they are** tous, sans exception; **~ of whether it rains** qu'il pleuve ou non.

irresponsible /ˌɪrɪˈspɒnsəbl/ *adj* irresponsable.

irresponsibly /ˌɪrɪˈspɒnsəblɪ/ *adv* de façon irresponsable.

irretrievable /ˌɪrɪˈtriːvəbl/ *adj* [*loss, harm*] irrémédiable, irréparable.

irretrievably /ˌɪrɪˈtriːvəblɪ/ *adv* irrémédiablement.

irreverent /ɪˈrevərənt/ *adj* irrévérencieux/-ieuse.

irreversible /ˌɪrɪˈvɜːsəbl/ *adj* [*process, decision*] irréversible; [*disease*] incurable.

irreversibly /ˌɪrɪˈvɜːsəblɪ/ *adv* irréversiblement.

irrevocable /ɪˈrevəkəbl/ *adj* irrévocable.

irrigation /ˌɪrɪˈɡeɪʃn/ *n* AGRIC, MED irrigation *f*.

irritability /ˌɪrɪtəˈbɪlətɪ/ *n* irritabilité *f*.

irritable /ˈɪrɪtəbl/ *adj* irritable.

irritant /ˈɪrɪtənt/ *n, adj* irritant (*m*).

irritate /ˈɪrɪteɪt/ *vtr* GEN, MED irriter.

irritating /ˈɪrɪteɪtɪŋ/ *adj* GEN, MED irritant.

is /ɪz/ *3ᵉ pers. du prés de* **be**.

-ish /ɪʃ/ *suffix* **1** ▶ 818 | greenish tirant sur le vert, verdâtre PEJ; **darkish** plutôt sombre; **earlyish** assez tôt; **2 he's thirtyish** il a dans les trente ans, il a la trentaine; **at fourish** vers quatre heures.

Islam /ˈɪzlɑːm, -læm, -ˈlɑːm/ *n* (faith) islam *m*; (Muslims) Islam *m*.

Islamic /ɪzˈlæmɪk/ *adj* islamique.

island /ˈaɪlənd/ **I** *n* **1** île *f*; (small) îlot *m*; **~ of peace** FIG îlot de paix; **2** ▶ **traffic island**. **II** *noun modifier* (of particular island) de l'île; (of islands generally) des îles.

islander /ˈaɪləndə(r)/ *n* insulaire *mf*, habitant/-e *m*/*f* d'une île (or de l'île).

island hopping *n* **to go ~** aller d'île en île.

isle /aɪl/ ▶ 1022 | *n* LITTER île *f*; **Isle of Man** île *f* de Man.

---

it

When *it* is used as a subject pronoun to refer to a specific object (or animal) *il* or *elle* is used in French according to the gender of the object referred to:

'where is the book/chair?' 'it's in the kitchen'
= 'où est le livre/la chaise?' 'il/elle est dans la cuisine'
'do you like my skirt?' 'it's lovely'
= 'est-ce que tu aimes ma jupe?' 'elle est très jolie'

However, if the object referred to is named in the same sentence, *it* is translated by *ce* (*c'* before a vowel):

it's a good film = c'est un bon film

When *it* is used as an object pronoun it is translated by *le* or *la* (*l'* before a vowel) according to the gender of the object referred to:

it's my book/my chair and I want it
= c'est mon livre/ma chaise et je le/la veux

Note that the object pronoun normally comes before the verb in French and that in compound tenses like the perfect and the past perfect, the past participle agrees with it:

I liked his shirt – did you notice it?
= j'ai aimé sa chemise – est-ce que tu l'as remarquée? *or* l'as-tu remarquée?

In imperatives only, the pronoun comes after the verb:

it's my book – give it to me
= c'est mon livre – donne-le-moi
(*note the hyphens*)

When *it* is used vaguely or impersonally followed by an adjective the translation is *ce* (*c'* before a vowel):

it's difficult = c'est difficile
it's sad = c'est triste

But when *it* is used impersonally followed by an adjective + verb the translation is *il*:

it's difficult to understand how …
= il est difficile de comprendre comment …

If in doubt consult the entry for the adjective in question.

For translations for impersonal verb uses (*it's raining, it's snowing*) consult the entry for the verb in question.

it is used in expressions of days of the week (*it's Friday*) and clock time (*it's 5 o'clock*). This dictionary contains usage notes on these and many other topics. For the index to these notes ▶ **1419**. For other impersonal and idiomatic uses see the entry **it**.

When *it* is used after a preposition in English the two words (*prep + it*) are often translated by one word in French. If the preposition would normally be translated by *de* in French (e.g. *of, about, from* etc.) the *prep + it* = *en*:

I've heard about it = j'en ai entendu parler

If the preposition would normally be translated by *à* in French (e.g. *to, in, at* etc.) the *prep + it* = *y*:

they went to it = ils y sont allés

For translations of *it* following prepositions not normally translated by *de* or *à* (e.g. *above, under, over* etc.) consult the entry for the preposition.

---

ism /'ɪzəm/ *n* PÉJ idéologie *f*.

isn't /'ɪznt/ = **is not**.

isobar /'aɪsəbɑː(r)/ *n* isobare *f*.

isolate /'aɪsəleɪt/ *vtr* (all contexts) isoler (**from** de).

isolation /ˌaɪsə'leɪʃn/ *n* isolement *m*; **in ~** dans l'isolement; **splendid ~** splendide isolement.

Isolde /ɪ'zɒldə/ *pr n* Iseult, Iseut.

isometrics /ˌaɪsəʊ'metrɪks/ *npl* exercices *mpl* musculaires isométriques.

isosceles /aɪ'sɒsəliːz/ *adj* isocèle.

Israel /'ɪzreɪl/ **▶ 840** *pr n* Israël (*never with article*); **in ~** en Israël.

Israeli /ɪz'reɪlɪ/ **▶ 1100** I *n* Israélien/-ienne *m/f*.
II *adj* israélien/-ienne.

issue /'ɪʃuː, 'ɪsjuː/ I *n* **1** (topic) problème *m*, question *f*; **to force the ~** précipiter la solution d'une question; **to make an ~ (out) of** faire une histoire de; **the point at ~** ce qui est en cause; **her beliefs are not at ~** ses croyances ne sont pas en question; **I must take ~ with you on that** je dois vous signifier mon désaccord sur ce point; **2** (allocation) (of supplies) distribution *f*; **3** (official release) (of stamps, shares) émission *f*; (of book) publication *f*; **4** (journal etc) numéro *m*; **back ~** vieux numéro *m*; **5** (flowing out) écoulement *m*; **6** (outcome) résultat *m*; **7** (offspring) descendance *f*; **without ~** sans laisser de descendance.
II *vtr* **1** (allocate) distribuer; **to ~ sb with sth** fournir qch à qn; **to be ~d with** recevoir; **2** (make public) délivrer [*declaration, ultimatum*]; émettre [*order, warning*]; **3** (release officially) émettre [*stamps, shares*]; **4** (publish) publier.
III *vi* **to ~ from** [*liquid*] s'écouler de; [*gas*] émaner de; [*shouts, laughter*] provenir de.

issuer /'ɪʃʊə(r)/ *n* FIN émetteur *m*.

it /ɪt/ *pron* **1** (in questions) **who is ~?** qui est-ce?, qui c'est○?; **~'s me** c'est moi; **where is ~?** (of object) où est-il/elle?; (of place) où est-ce?, où est-ce que c'est?, c'est où○?; **what is ~?** (of object, noise etc) qu'est-ce que c'est?, c'est quoi○?; (what's happening?) qu'est-ce qui se passe?; (what is the matter?) qu'est-ce qu'il y a?; **how was ~?** comment cela s'est-il passé?, ça s'est passé comment○?; **2** GAMES **you're ~!** c'est toi le chat!
IDIOMS **I didn't have ~ in me to refuse** je n'ai pas eu le cœur de refuser; **the worst of ~ is that** ce

qu'il y a de pire là-dedans c'est que; **that's ~!** (in triumph) voilà!, ça y est!; (in anger) ça suffit!

IT *n*: *abrév* ▶ **information technology**.

Italian /ɪ'tæljən/ **▶ 1100**, **1038** I *n* **1** (person) Italien/-ienne *m/f*; **2** (language) italien *m*.
II *adj* italien/-ienne.

italic /ɪ'tælɪk/ I **italics** *npl* italique *m*; **in ~s** en italique.
II *adj* italique.

italicize /ɪ'tælɪsaɪz/ *vtr* mettre [qch] en italique.

Italy /'ɪtəlɪ/ **▶ 840** *pr n* Italie *f*.

itch /ɪtʃ/ I *n* **1** (physical) démangeaison *f*; **to relieve an ~** soulager des démangeaisons; **2**○ (hankering) **I had an ~ to travel** l'envie de voyager me démangeait○.
II *vtr* US (scratch) gratter.
III *vi* **1** (physically) avoir des démangeaisons; **my back is ~ing** j'ai le dos qui me démange; **these socks make me ou my feet ~** ces chaussettes ou mes pieds me démangent; **2 to be ~ing for sth/to do sth** mourir○ d'envie de qch/de faire qch.

itching powder *n* poil *m* à gratter.

itchy○ /'ɪtʃɪ/ *adj* **I feel ~ all over** ça me gratte partout.
IDIOMS **to have ~ feet**○ avoir la bougeotte○.

it'd /'ɪtəd/ = **it had**, **it would**.

item /'aɪtəm/ *n* **1** GEN, COMPUT article *m*; **luxury ~** produit *m* de luxe; **an ~ of furniture** un meuble; **~s of clothing** vêtements *mpl*; **2** ADMIN POL (on agenda) point *m*; **3** (in newspaper, on news bulletin) article *m* (**about** sur); **news ~** article *m*; **the main ~** RADIO, TV le titre principal; **4** MUS morceau *m*; (in show) numéro *m*.

itemize /'aɪtəˌmaɪz/ *vtr* détailler.

itinerant /aɪ'tɪnərənt, ɪ-/ *adj* [*life, preacher*] itinérant; [*tribe*] nomade.

itinerary /aɪ'tɪnərərɪ, ɪ-, US -rerɪ/ *n* itinéraire *m*.

it'll /'ɪtl/ = **it will**.

its /ɪts/

■ **Note** In French determiners agree in number and gender with the noun they qualify. *its* is translated by *son* + *masculine noun*: *its nose* = son nez; by *sa* + *feminine noun*: *its tail* = sa queue; BUT by *son* + *feminine noun beginning with a vowel or mute h*: *its ear* = son oreille; and by *ses* + *plural noun*: *its ears* = ses oreilles.

det son/sa/ses.

it's /ɪts/ = **it is, it has**.
itself /ɪt'self/

■ **Note** When used as a reflexive pronoun, direct and indirect, *itself* is translated by *se* (*s'* before a vowel or mute h): *the cat hurt itself* = le chat s'est fait mal; *a problem presented itself* = un problème s'est présenté.
– When used for emphasis *itself* is translated by *lui-même* when standing for a masculine noun and *elle-même* when standing for a feminine noun: *the car itself was not damaged* = la voiture elle-même n'était pas endommagée.
– For examples and particular usages see the entry below.
– For uses with prepositions (*by itself etc*) see 3 below.

pron **1** (refl) se, s'; **2** (emphatic) lui-même/elle-même; **the house ~ was pretty** la maison elle-même était jolie; **in the university ~** dans l'université même or dans l'université elle-même; **he was kindness ~** c'était la bonté même or personnifiée; **3** (after preposi-

tions) **the heating comes on by ~** le chauffage se met en marche tout seul; **the house stands by ~** la maison est toute seule; **the library is a fine building in ~** la bibliothèque par elle-même est un beau bâtiment; **learning French is not difficult in ~** l'apprentissage du français n'est pas difficile en soi.

IUD *n*: *abrév* ▶ **intrauterine device**.

IV *n*: *abrév* ▶ **intravenous drip**.

I've /aɪv/ = **I have**.

IVF *n*: *abrév* ▶ **in vitro fertilization**.

ivory /'aɪvərɪ/ *n, adj* (all contexts) ivoire (*m*).

ivory: **Ivory Coast** ▶ 840⏐ *pr n* Côte *f* d'Ivoire; **~ tower** *n* FIG tour *f* d'ivoire.

ivy /'aɪvɪ/ *n* lierre *m*.

Ivy League *adj* US ~ bon chic bon genre; **the ~ colleges** les huit universités prestigieuses de la côte est américaine.

j, J /dʒeɪ/ n j, J m.

jab /dʒæb/ **I** n **1** GB MED (vaccination) vaccin m; (injection) piqûre f; **2** (poke) petit coup m; (in boxing) direct m.
II vtr to ~ sth into sth planter qch dans qch.
III vi to ~ at taper sur; (in boxing) envoyer des directs à.

jabber /'dʒæbə(r)/ **I** vtr baragouiner.
II vi (chatter) jacasser; (in foreign language) baragouiner.

jack /dʒæk/ n **1** (for car etc) cric m; **2** (in cards) valet m (of de); **3** (in bowls) cochonnet m; **4** ELEC jack m.
IDIOMS every man ~ of them jusqu'au dernier; to be (a) ~ of all trades être un/-e touche-à-tout inv; to have an I'm all right Jack attitude ne s'occuper que de sa petite personne.
■ **jack in**○ GB: ~ in [sth], ~ [sth] in plaquer○, laisser tomber [job].
■ **jack up**: ~ up [sth], ~ [sth] up **1** soulever [qch] avec un cric [vehicle]; **2**○ FIG faire grimper [price]; **3**○ US chauffer○ [crowd].

jackal /'dʒækɔ:l, US -kl/ n chacal m.

jack: **~ass** n LIT, FIG âne m; **~boot** n botte f militaire; **~daw** n choucas m.

jacket /'dʒækɪt/ ▶1260 **I** n **1** (garment) veste f; (man's) veste f, veston m; **2** (also **dust** ~) jaquette f; **3** US (of record) pochette f; **4** TECH enveloppe f isolante.
II noun modifier **1** [pocket] de veste; ~ **potato** CULIN pomme f de terre en robe des champs (au four); **2** [design] de couverture.

jack: **~hammer** n marteau-piqueur m; **~-in-the-box** n diable m à ressort.

jackknife /'dʒæknaɪf/ **I** n (knife) couteau m pliant.
II vi [lorry] se mettre en portefeuille.

jackpot /'dʒækpɒt/ n gros lot m.
IDIOMS to hit the ~ (win prize) gagner le gros lot; (have great success) faire un tabac○.

jackrabbit n lièvre m (du nord-ouest américain).

jade /dʒeɪd/ n **1** (stone) jade m; **2** ▶818 (also ~ **green**) vert m jade.

jaded /'dʒeɪdɪd/ adj **1** (exhausted) fatigué; **2** (bored) [person, palate] blasé.

jagged /'dʒægɪd/ adj [rock, cliff] déchiqueté; [knife, saw] dentelé.

jail /dʒeɪl/ **I** n prison f; to be in/go to ~ être/aller en prison; to go to ~ for 10 years faire 10 ans de prison; sentenced to 14 days in ~ condamné à 14 jours de réclusion criminelle.
II vtr emprisonner; ADMIN, JUR incarcérer.

jail: **~bird** n taulard/-e m/f; (habitual) récidiviste m/f; **~break** n évasion f; ~ **sentence** n peine f de prison.

jam /dʒæm/ **I** n **1** CULIN confiture f; **2** (congestion) (of people) foule f; (of traffic) embouteillage m; **3** (of machine, system, department) blocage m; **4**○ (difficult situation) pétrin○ m; to help sb out of a ~ tirer qn du pétrin○; **5** (also ~ **session**) MUS bœuf○ m, jam-session f.
II vtr (p prés etc **-mm-**) **1** (stuff, pile) to ~ **things into** entasser des choses dans [small space, suitcase, box]; to ~ **one's foot on the brake** freiner à bloc; **2** (fix firmly, wedge) coincer; **the key's ~med in the lock** la clé s'est coincée dans la serrure; **3** (also ~ **up**) (crowd) GEN encombrer; **cars ~med (up) the roads** les routes étaient embouteillées; **4** (also ~ **up**) (block) [dirt, malfunction, person] enrayer [mechanism]; coincer [lock, door, window, system]; **5** RADIO, TELECOM brouiller [frequency, transmission].

III vi (p prés etc **-mm-**) **1** (become stuck) [mechanism, switch] s'enrayer; [lock, door, window] se coincer, se bloquer; **2** MUS improviser.
■ **jam in**: ¶ ~ in [people] s'entasser; ¶ ~ [sth/sb] in **1** (trap, wedge) coincer; **2** (pack in) entasser.

Jamaica /dʒə'meɪkə/ ▶840 pr n la Jamaïque.

jamb /dʒæm/ n chambranle m.

James /dʒeɪmz/ pr n Jacques.

jam-full /,dʒæm'fʊl/ adj bondé; to be ~ of être bourré de.

jamjar, **jampot** n pot m à confitures.

jammy /'dʒæmɪ/ adj **1**○ GB [person] veinard○; [job] de planqué○; **2** LIT [fingers, face] plein de confiture.

jam-packed /,dʒæm'pækt/ adj bondé; to be ~ with sth être bourré de qch.

Jan abrév écrite = **January**.

jangle /'dʒæŋgl/ **I** n (of bells, pots) tintement m; (of keys) cliquetis m; (of alarm) bruit m strident.
II vtr faire tinter [bells]; faire cliqueter [keys].
III vi (make noise) [bells] tinter; [bangles] cliqueter.

jangling /'dʒæŋglɪŋ/ **I** n = **jangle I**.
II adj [noise] métallique; [alarm] strident.

janitor /'dʒænɪtə(r)/ n US, SCOT gardien m.

January /'dʒænjʊərɪ, US -jʊerɪ/ ▶1090 n janvier m.

Japan /dʒə'pæn/ ▶840 pr n Japon m.

Japanese /,dʒæpə'ni:z/ ▶1100, 1038 **I** n **1** (person) Japonais/-e m/f; **2** (language) japonais m.
II adj japonais.

jar /dʒɑ:(r)/ **I** n **1** GEN pot m; (large) bocal m; (earthenware) jarre f; **2** (jolt) LIT, FIG secousse f, choc m.
II vtr (p prés etc **-rr-**) **1** LIT, FIG ébranler, secouer; to ~ **one's shoulder** se cogner l'épaule; **2** US to ~ **sb into action** pousser qn à agir.
III vi (p prés etc **-rr-**) **1** rendre un son discordant; to ~ **on sb** ou sb's **nerves** agacer qn; **2** (rattle) [windows] trembler; **3** (clash) [colours] jurer; [note] sonner faux; [opinions] ne pas s'accorder.

jargon /'dʒɑ:gən/ n jargon m.

jasmine /'dʒæsmɪn, US 'dʒæzmən/ n jasmin m.

jaundice /'dʒɔ:ndɪs/ ▶1002 n jaunisse f.

jaundiced /'dʒɔ:ndɪst/ adj (cynical) négatif/-ive.

jaunt /dʒɔ:nt/ n balade○ f.

jaunty /'dʒɔ:ntɪ/ adj [appearance] guilleret/-ette.

javelin /'dʒævlɪn/ ▶949 n javelot m.

jaw /dʒɔ:/ ▶765 n mâchoire f.
IDIOMS his ~ dropped les bras lui en sont tombés.

jaw: **~bone** n mâchoire f; **~line** n menton m.

jay /dʒeɪ/ n geai m.

jaywalk /'dʒeɪwɔ:k/ vi traverser en dehors des passages pour piétons.

jazz /dʒæz/ n MUS jazz m.
IDIOMS and all that ~○ et tout le bataclan○.
■ **jazz up**○: ~ up [sth], ~ [sth] up **1** rajeunir [dress]; égayer [room]; ranimer [party]; **2** faire une version jazz de [tune].

jazz: ~ **band** n jazz-band m; ~ **dance** n modern-jazz m; **~man** n musicien m de jazz.

jazzy /'dʒæzɪ/ adj **1** (bright) [colour] voyant; [pattern, dress, wallpaper] bariolé; **2** [music] jazz inv.

jealous /'dʒeləs/ adj jaloux/-ouse (of de); to feel ~ être jaloux.

jealousy /'dʒeləsɪ/ n jalousie f.

jean /dʒi:n/ **I** noun modifier (made of denim) en jean.
II jeans npl jean m; a pair of ~s un jean.

jeer /dʒɪə(r)/ **I** n (from crowd) huée f; (from person) raille-rie f.
II vtr huer.
III vi se moquer; **to ~ at** se moquer de [idea]; [crowd] huer [person]; [individual] railler [person].

jeering /'dʒɪərɪŋ/ **I** n ¢ huées fpl.
II adj railleur/-euse.

jell /dʒel/ vi = **gel** II.

jellied /'dʒelɪd/ adj en aspic; **~ eels** anguilles fpl en gelée.

Jell-o® /'dʒeləʊ/ n US gelée f de fruits.

jelly /'dʒelɪ/ n **1** CULIN (savoury) gelée f; (sweet) gelée f de fruits; **2** (preserve) gelée f; **3** US (jam) confiture f.
IDIOMS **to shake like a ~** trembler comme une feuille.

jelly: **~ baby** n bonbon m; **~ bean** n bonbon m fourré à la gelée; **~fish** n (pl **~** ou **~es**) méduse f.

jeopardize /'dʒepədaɪz/ vtr compromettre [career, chance, plans]; mettre [qch] en péril [lives, troops].

jeopardy /'dʒepədɪ/ n in **~** en péril, menacé.

jerk /dʒɜːk/ **I** n **1** (jolt) GEN secousse f; (twitch) (of muscle, limb) tressaillement m, (petit) mouvement m brusque; **with a ~ of his head** d'un brusque mouve-ment de la tête; **to start off with a ~** [vehicle] dé-marrer avec un soubresaut; **2**○ PÉJ (obnoxious man) salaudᴼ m; (stupid) crétin○ m.
II vtr tirer brusquement [object].
III vi **1** (jolt) **to ~ to a halt** [vehicle] s'arrêter avec un soubresaut; **2** (twitch) [person, muscle] tressaillir.

jerkily /'dʒɜːkɪlɪ/ adv [move] par saccades; [speak] d'une voix saccadée.

jerkin /'dʒɜːkɪn/ n gilet m.

jerky /'dʒɜːkɪ/ **I** n US CULIN bœuf m séché.
II adj [movement] saccadé; [style, phrase] haché.

jerry-built /'dʒerɪbɪlt/ adj PÉJ construit à la va-vite.

jersey /'dʒɜːzɪ/ **I** n **1** (sweater) pull-over m; **football ~** maillot m de football; **2** (fabric) jersey m.
II noun modifier [garment] en jersey.

Jerusalem /dʒə'ruːsələm/ ▶ 1343 | pr n Jérusalem.

jest /dʒest/ **I** n plaisanterie f; **in ~** pour plaisanter.
II vi plaisanter.
IDIOMS **many a true word is spoken in ~** Prov plus d'une vérité est dite en plaisantant.

jester /'dʒestə(r)/ n bouffon m.

Jesuit /'dʒezjʊɪt, US 'dʒeʒəwət/ n, adj jésuite (m).

Jesus /'dʒiːzəs/ pr n Jésus; **~ Christ** Jésus-Christ.

jet /dʒet/ **I** n **1** (also **~ plane**) jet m, avion m à réac-tion; **2** (of water, flame) jet m; **3** (on hob) brûleur m; (of engine) gicleur m; **4** (stone) jais m.
II vi (p prés etc **-tt-**) **to ~ off** to s'envoler pour.

jet: **~-black** adj de jais inv; **~ engine** n moteur m à réaction, réacteur m; **~ fighter** n chasseur m à ré-action; **~-foil** n hydroglisseur m; **~ lag** n décalage m horaire; **~-powered**, **jet-propelled** adj à réac-tion; **~ propulsion** n propulsion f par réaction.

jet setter n to be a **~** faire partie du jet-set.

jet-skiing ▶ 949 | n jet-ski m.

jettison /'dʒetɪsn/ vtr **1** (from ship) jeter [qch] par-dessus bord; (from plane) larguer; **2** FIG rejeter [idea].

jetty /'dʒetɪ/ n (of stone) jetée f; (of wood) appontement m.

Jew /dʒuː/ n juif/juive m/f.

jewel /'dʒuːəl/ n **1** (gem) pierre f précieuse; (piece of jewellery) bijou m; (in watch) rubis m; **2** FIG (person) perle f; (town, object) joyau m.

jewelled GB, **jeweled** US /'dʒuːəld/ adj orné de pierres précieuses.

jeweller GB, **jeweler** US /'dʒuːələ(r)/ ▶ 1251 |, 1251 | n (person) bijoutier/-ière m/f; **~'s (shop)** bijouterie f.

jewellery GB, **jewelry** US /'dʒuːəlrɪ/ n GEN bijoux mpl; (in shop, workshop) bijouterie f; **a piece of ~** un bijou.

Jewess /'dʒuːes/ n juive f.

Jewish /'dʒuːɪʃ/ adj juif/juive.

Jewry /'dʒʊərɪ/ n communauté f juive.

Jew's harp n MUS guimbarde f.

jib /dʒɪb/ **I** n **1** NAUT foc m; **2** (of crane) flèche f.
II vi (p prés etc **-bb-**) [person] rechigner (**at** à); **to ~ at** [horse] refuser [fence].

jibe /dʒaɪb/ **I** n moquerie f.
II vi **1** (mock) **to ~ at** sb/sth se moquer de qn/qch. **2**○ US (match) coller○ (**with** avec).

jiff(y)○ /'dʒɪfɪ/ n seconde f, instant m; **in a ~** en moins de deux○.

Jiffy bag® n enveloppe f matelassée.

jig /dʒɪg/ **I** n MUS gigue f.
II vtr, vi = **jiggle**.
IDIOMS **the ~ is up**○ US c'est cuit○.

jiggle /'dʒɪgl/ **I** vtr agiter.
II vi (also **~ about**, **~ around**) gigoter; (impa-tiently) se trémousser.

jigsaw /'dʒɪgsɔː/ n **1** (also **~ puzzle**) puzzle m; **2** TECH scie f sauteuse.

jihad /dʒɪ'hɑːd/ n RELIG djihad m.

jilt /dʒɪlt/ vtr abandonner, plaquer○.

Jim Crow○ /ˌdʒɪm 'krəʊ/ n US **~ policies** politique f ségrégationniste.

jingle /'dʒɪŋgl/ **I** n **1** (of bells) tintement m; (of keys) cliquetis m; **2** (verse) ritournelle f; (for advert) refrain m publicitaire, sonal m.
II vtr faire tinter.
III vi [bells] tintinnabuler; [keys, coins] cliqueter.

jingoist /'dʒɪŋgəʊɪst/ n, adj chauvin/-e (m/f) POL.

jinx /dʒɪŋks/ **I** n **1** (curse) sort m; **to put a ~ on** jeter un sort à; **there's a ~ on me** j'ai la poisse○; **2** (un-lucky person, object) porte-malheur m inv.
II vtr porter la poisse○ à [person].

jitters /'dʒɪtəz/ npl **to have the ~** [person, stock market] être nerveux/-euse; [actor] avoir le trac.

jittery /'dʒɪtərɪ/ adj nerveux/-euse.

jive /dʒaɪv/ **I** n **1** MUS swing m; **2**○ US (talk) salades○ fpl.
II vi (dance) danser le swing.

Jnr adj: abrév écrite = **junior**.

job /dʒɒb/ **I** n **1** (employment) emploi m; (post) poste m; **to get a ~** trouver un emploi; **a teaching ~** un poste d'enseignant; **what's her ~?** qu'est-ce qu'elle fait (comme travail)?; **to have a ~ as a secretary** être employé comme secrétaire; **out of a ~** sans emploi; **2** (rôle) fonction f; **it's my ~ to do** c'est à moi de faire; **3** (duty) travail m; **she's only doing her ~** elle fait son travail; **4** (task) travail m; **to find a ~ for sb to do** trouver du travail pour qn; **5** (assign-ment) tâche f; **the ~ of building the theatre went to X** la construction du théâtre a été confiée à X; **6** (result of work) **a poor ~** du mauvais travail; **to make a good ~ of sth** faire du bon travail avec qch; **7**○ (diffi-cult activity) **a real ~**, **quite a ~** toute une affaire○ (**to do, doing** de faire); **8**○ (crime, theft) coup○ m; **9** COMPUT job○ m.
II noun modifier [advert, offer] d'emploi; [analysis] de poste; [pages] des emplois; [creation] d'emplois.
IDIOMS **(and a) good ~ too!** GB et c'est une bonne chose!; **it's a good ~ that** GB heureusement que; **~s for the boys** des planques○ pour les copains; **just the ~** tout à fait ce qu'il faut; **on the ~** (work-ing) au travail; **to learn on the ~** apprendre sur le tas○; **to fall asleep on the ~** s'endormir à la tâche; **to do the ~** FIG faire l'affaire; **to give sth up as a bad ~** GB laisser tomber qch; **to make the best of a bad ~** GB faire contre mauvaise fortune bon cœur.

Job /dʒəʊb/ pr n BIBLE Job.
IDIOMS **to be a ~'s comforter** être totalement décou-rageant; **to have the patience of ~** avoir une patience d'ange.

job action n US mouvement m de revendication.

jobber /'dʒɒbə(r)/ n US grossiste mf.

jobbing /'dʒɒbɪŋ/ adj [gardener] à la tâche.

job: **Job Centre** n GB bureau m des services natio-naux de l'emploi; **~ description** n description f de poste; **~-hunting** n chasse f à l'emploi.

jobless /'dʒɒblɪs/ **I** n **the ~** les sans-emploi mpl.

II *noun modifier* [*total*] des sans-emploi; [*rate, figures*] du chômage.

ob: ~ **lot** *n* (at auction) lot *m*; FIG ramassis *m*; ~ **satisfaction** *n* satisfaction *f* dans le travail; ~ **security** *n* sécurité *f* de l'emploi; **~-share** *adj* [*scheme*] de partage de poste; [*position*] partagé; ~ **sharing** *n* partage *m* de poste.

ockey /'dʒɒkɪ/ **I** *n* jockey *m*.
II *vi* **to** ~ **for position** LIT lutter pour la première place; FIG jouer des coudes.

ockey shorts *n* US slip *m* (d'homme).

ockstrap° /'dʒɒkstræp/ *n* suspensoir *m*.

ocular /'dʒɒkjʊlə(r)/ *adj* [*remark, mood*] badin; [*person*] enjoué.

jodhpurs /'dʒɒdpəz/ *npl* SPORT jodhpurs *mpl*.

Joe Bloggs GB, **Joe Blow** US *n* Monsieur Tout-le-Monde.

jog /dʒɒg/ **I** *n* **1** (with elbow) coup *m* de coude; **2 at a** ~ au petit trot°; **3** SPORT **to go for a** ~ aller faire un jogging; **4** US (in road) coude *m*.
II *vtr* (*p prés etc* **-gg-**) heurter; (with elbow) donner un coup de coude à; **to** ~ **sb's memory** rafraîchir la mémoire de qn.
III *vi* (*p prés etc* **-gg-**) SPORT faire du jogging.
■ **jog along** FIG [*person, business*] se maintenir.

jogger /'dʒɒgə(r)/ *n* joggeur/-euse *m/f*.

jogging /'dʒɒgɪŋ/ **▶ 949** jogging *m*.

John /dʒɒn/ *pr n* Jean.

John: ~ **Bull** *n* (Englishman) l'Anglais *m* moyen; ~ **Doe** *n* US l'homme *m* de la rue; ~ **Q Public**° *n* US l'homme *m* de la rue.

join /dʒɔɪn/ **I** *n* raccord *m*.
II *vtr* **1** (meet up with) rejoindre [*person*]; **may I** ~ **you?** (sit down) puis-je me joindre à vous?; (accompany) puis-je venir avec vous?; **2** (go to the end of) se mettre dans [*queue*]; se mettre au bout de [*row*]; ajouter son nom à [*list*]; **3** (become member of) devenir membre de [*organization, team, church*]; adhérer à [*club*]; s'inscrire à [*library*]; s'engager dans [*army*]; **to** ~ **a union** se syndiquer; ~ **the club!** FIG tu n'es pas le seul/la seule!; **4** (become part of) se joindre à [*crowd, rush*]; **5** (become employee) entrer dans [*firm*]; **to** ~ **Ford** entrer chez Ford; **6** (participate in) **▶ join in**; **7** (associate with) GEN se joindre à [*person*] (**to do, in doing** pour faire); (professionally) s'associer à [*colleague*] (**to do, in doing** pour faire); **to** ~ **forces with** (merge) s'allier à; (co-operate) collaborer avec; **8** (board) monter dans [*train*]; monter à bord de [*ship*]; **9** (attach) réunir, joindre [*ends, pieces*]; assembler [*parts*]; **10** (link) relier [*points, towns*] (**to** à); **to** ~ **hands** LIT se prendre par la main; FIG collaborer; **11** (merge with) [*road*] rejoindre [*motorway*]; [*river*] se jeter dans [*sea*].
III *vi* **1** (become member) (of party, club) adhérer; (of group, class) s'inscrire; **2** (meet) [*pieces*] se joindre; [*wires*] se raccorder; [*roads*] se rejoindre.
■ **join in**: ¶ ~ **in** participer; ¶ ~ **in** [*sth*] participer à [*talks, game*]; prendre part à [*strike, demonstration, bidding*]; **to** ~ **in the fun** se joindre à la fête.
■ **join on**: ~ [*sth*] **on,** ~ **on** [*sth*] (fasten) fixer; (add) ajouter.
■ **join up**: ¶ ~ **up 1** MIL (enlist) s'engager; **2** (meet up) [*people*] se retrouver; [*roads, tracks*] se rejoindre; ¶ ~ **up** [*sth*], ~ [*sth*] **up** relier [*characters, dots*]; assembler [*pieces*]; **~-ed-up writing** écriture *f* liée.

joiner /'dʒɔɪnə(r)/ **▶ 1251** *n* CONSTR menuisier/-ière *m/f*.

joint /dʒɔɪnt/ **I** *n* **1** ANAT articulation *f*; **to be out of** ~ [*shoulder, knee*] être déboité; **to have stiff** ou **aching** ~**s** avoir des douleurs articulaires; **2** TECH (in carpentry) assemblage *m*; (in metalwork) joint *m*; (of pipes, tubes) raccord *m*; **3** CULIN rôti *m*; **4**° PEJ (place) GEN endroit *m*; (nightclub, office, workplace) boîte° *f*; (café) boui-boui° *m*; **5**° (cannabis cigarette) joint° *m*.
II *adj* [*action*] collectif/-ive; [*programme, session*] mixte; [*measures, procedure*] commun; [*winner*] ex aequo *inv*; [*talks*] multilatéral.
IDIOMS **to have one's nose put out of** ~ être dépité.

joint: ~ **account** *n* compte *m* joint; ~ **agreement** *n* convention *f* collective; ~ **committee** *n* comité *m* mixte.

jointed /'dʒɔɪntɪd/ *adj* **1** CULIN [*chicken*] découpé; **2** (doll, puppet) articulé; **3** (rod, pole) démontable.

joint: ~ **honours** *npl* GB UNIV licence *f* combinée.

jointly /'dʒɔɪntlɪ/ *adv* [*manage, publish, own*] conjointement; **to be** ~ **owned by X et Y** être la copropriété de X et Y.

joint: ~ **management** *n* cogestion *f*; ~ **owner** *n* copropriétaire *mf*; **~-stock company** *n* société *f* par actions.

joint venture *n* **1** ECON, FIN coentreprise *f*; **2** GEN projet *m* en commun.

joist /dʒɔɪst/ *n* solive *f*.

jojoba /həʊ'həʊbə/ *n* jojoba *m*.

joke /dʒəʊk/ **I** *n* **1** (amusing story) plaisanterie *f*, blague° *f* (**about** sur); **to have a** ~ **about sth** plaisanter sur qch; **2** (laughing matter) plaisanterie *f*; **the** ~ **is on you** la plaisanterie se retourne contre toi; **this is getting beyond a** ~ la plaisanterie a assez duré; **can't you take a** ~**?** tu ne supportes pas la plaisanterie?; **it's no** ~ **doing** ce n'est pas facile de faire; **3** (prank) farce *f*; **to play a** ~ **on sb** faire une farce à qn; **4** (object of ridicule) (person) guignol *m* PEJ; (event, situation) farce *f*.
II *vi* plaisanter, blaguer°; **you must be joking!** tu veux rire!; **it's no joking matter** ça n'a rien de drôle.

joker /'dʒəʊkə(r)/ *n* **1** (who tells jokes) blagueur/-euse° *m/f*; (who plays tricks) farceur/-euse *m/f*; **2**° PEJ (person) type° *m*; **3** (in cards) joker *m*.
IDIOMS **the** ~ **in the pack** l'exception à la règle.

joking /'dʒəʊkɪŋ/ *n* Ȼ plaisanterie *f*, blague° *f*.

jokingly /'dʒəʊkɪŋlɪ/ *adv* [*say*] en plaisantant.

jollity /'dʒɒlətɪ/ *n* gaieté *f*; (of person) bonne humeur *f*.

jolly /'dʒɒlɪ/ **I** *adj* (cheerful) [*person*] enjoué; [*tune*] joyeux/-euse; **what a** ~ **time we had!** qu'est-ce qu'on s'est bien amusé!
II° *adv* GB (emphatic) drôlement.
III *vtr* **to** ~ **sb along** amadouer qn.

Jolly Roger *n* pavillon *m* noir.

jolt /dʒəʊlt/ **I** *n* **1** (jerk) secousse *f*; **2** (shock) choc *m*.
II *vtr* LIT, FIG secouer.
III *vi* [*vehicle*] cahoter.

Jordan /'dʒɔ:dn/ **▶ 840**, **1214** *pr n* **1** (country) Jordanie *f*; **2** (river) Jourdain *m*.

joss stick /'dʒɒstɪk/ *n* bâtonnet *m* d'encens.

jostle /'dʒɒsl/ **I** *vtr* bousculer [*person*].
II *vi* se bousculer (**for** pour; **to do** pour faire).

jot /dʒɒt/ **I** *n* **he doesn't care a** ~ il s'en fiche° complètement; **it doesn't matter a** ~ cela n'a pas la moindre importance.
II *vtr* (*p prés etc* **-tt-**) = **jot down**.
■ **jot down**: ~ [*sth*] **down,** ~ **down** [*sth*] noter [*ideas, names*].

jotter /'dʒɒtə(r)/ *n* GB (pad) bloc-notes *m inv*.

jottings /'dʒɒtɪŋz/ *npl* notes *fpl*.

journal /'dʒɜ:nl/ *n* **1** (diary) journal *m*; **2** (periodical) revue *f*; (newspaper) journal *m*.

journalism /'dʒɜ:nəlɪzəm/ *n* journalisme *m*.

journalist /'dʒɜ:nəlɪst/ *n* journaliste *mf*.

journey /'dʒɜ:nɪ/ **I** *n* **1** (trip) (long) voyage *m*; (short or habitual) trajet *m*; **bus** ~ trajet en bus; **to go on a** ~ partir en voyage; **to break a** ~ faire étape; **2** (distance covered) trajet *m*.
II *vi* voyager; **to** ~ **on** continuer son voyage.

jovial /'dʒəʊvɪəl/ *adj* [*person, mood*] jovial; [*remark*] enjoué; [*company*] joyeux/-euse.

jowl /dʒaʊl/ *n* (jaw) mâchoire *f*; (fleshy fold) bajoue *f*.
IDIOMS **cheek by** ~ **with sb** coude à coude avec qn.

joy /dʒɔɪ/ *n* **1** (delight) joie *f* (**at** devant); **2** (pleasure) plaisir *m*; **the** ~ **of doing** le plaisir de faire; **3**° GB (success) **I got no** ~ **out of the bank manager** mon entretien avec le directeur de banque n'a rien donné.

IDIOMS **to be full of the ~s of spring** être en pleine forme.

joyful /'dʒɔɪfl/ adj joyeux/-euse.

joyless /'dʒɔɪlɪs/ adj [marriage] malheureux/-euse; [occasion] triste; [production] terne; [existence] morne.

joyrider /'dʒɔɪraɪdə(r)/ n jeune chauffard m en voiture volée.

joyriding /'dʒɔɪraɪdɪŋ/ n rodéo m à la voiture volée.

joystick /'dʒɔɪstɪk/ n AVIAT manche m à balai; (video games) manette f.

JP n GB abrév ▶ **Justice of the Peace**.

Jr adj: abrév écrite = **junior**.

jubilant /'dʒuːbɪlənt/ adj [person] exultant; [crowd] en liesse; [expression, mood] réjoui.

jubilation /ˌdʒuːbɪ'leɪʃn/ n jubilation f (**about, at, over** devant).

jubilee /'dʒuːbɪliː/ n jubilé m.

Judaic /dʒuː'deɪɪk/ adj judaïque.

Judaism /'dʒuːdeɪɪzəm, US -dɪɪzəm/ n judaïsme m.

judder /'dʒʌdə(r)/ GB **I** n secousse f.
II vi être agité de violentes secousses.

judge /dʒʌdʒ/ **I** n **1** ▶ **937** JUR juge m; **2** (adjudicator) (at competition) membre m du jury; SPORT juge m; **3** FIG **to be a good ~ of character** savoir juger les gens; **to be no ~ of** ne pas s'y connaître en [art, wine].
II vtr **1** GEN, JUR juger [person]; **2** (adjudicate) faire partie du jury de [show, competition]; **3** (estimate) (currently) estimer [distance, age]; (in the future) prévoir [outcome, reaction]; **4** (consider) juger, estimer.
III vi juger; **judging by** ou **from…** à en juger par, d'après…
IDIOMS **to be as sober as a ~** (not drunk) ne pas être ivre du tout; (solemn) être sérieux comme un pape.

judgment, judgement /'dʒʌdʒmənt/ n **1** GEN, JUR jugement m; **to sit in ~ on** ou **over** juger [person, situation]; **2** (opinion) avis m, opinion f; **to do sth against one's better ~** faire qch en sachant que l'on fait une erreur; **3** (discernment) jugement m; **use your own ~** (in assessing) c'est à vous de juger; (in acting) faites comme bon vous semblera; **4** (punishment) punition f.

judgmental, judgemental /ˌdʒʌdʒ'mentl/ adj **don't be so ~!** ne juge pas tant les autres!

judicial /dʒuː'dɪʃl/ adj **1** [inquiry, process] judiciaire; [decision] jurisprudentiel/-ielle; **2** (wise) [mind] pondéré; **3** (impartial) [silence] réfléchi.

judiciary /dʒuː'dɪʃɪərɪ, US -ʃɪeri/ **I** n JUR **1** (system of courts) système m judiciaire; **2** (judges) magistrature f; **3** (authority) pouvoir m judiciaire.
II noun modifier [system, reforms] judiciaire.

judicious /dʒuː'dɪʃəs/ adj judicieux/-ieuse.

judo /'dʒuːdəʊ/ ▶ **949** n judo m.

jug /dʒʌg/ **I** n **1** GB (glass) carafe f; (earthenware) pichet m; (pot-bellied) cruche f; (for cream, milk, water) pot m; **2** US (earthenware) cruche f.
II vtr (p prés etc **-gg-**) CULIN cuire [qch] à l'étuvée.

jugful /'dʒʌgfʊl/ n **1** GB carafe f; **2** US cruche f.

juggernaut /'dʒʌgənɔːt/ n **1** GB (truck) poids m lourd; **2** (irresistible force) poids m écrasant.

juggle /'dʒʌgl/ **I** vtr jongler avec.
II vi jongler (**with**).

juggler /'dʒʌglə(r)/ n jongleur/-euse m/f.

jugular /'dʒʌgjʊlə(r)/ n, adj jugulaire (f).
IDIOMS **to go (straight) for the ~** frapper au point sensible.

juice /dʒuːs/ n **1** CULIN jus m; **2** BOT suc m.

juicy /'dʒuːsɪ/ adj **1** CULIN juteux/-euse; **2**○ (racy) [story] croustillant.

jukebox /'dʒuːkbɒks/ n juke-box m.

Jul abrév écrite = **July**.

julep /'dʒuːlɪp/ n (also **mint ~**) boisson f à la menthe.

July /dʒuː'laɪ/ ▶ **1090** n juillet m.

jumble /'dʒʌmbl/ **I** n **1** (of papers, objects) tas m; (of

ideas) fouillis m; (of words) fatras m; **2** GB (items for sale) bric-à-brac m, vieux objets mpl.
II vtr brouiller [ideas]; mélanger [words, letters].
■ **jumble up: ~ [sth] up, ~ up [sth]** mélanger [letters, shapes].

jumble sale n GB vente f de charité.

jumbo /'dʒʌmbəʊ/ **I** n **1** LANG ENFANTIN éléphant m; **2** = **jumbo jet**.
II noun modifier (also **~-sized**) [packet, size] géant.

jumbo jet n gros-porteur m.

jump /dʒʌmp/ **I** n **1** (leap) saut m, bond m; **to be one ~ ahead** FIG avoir une longueur d'avance (**of sb** sur qn); **2** (for horse) obstacle m; **3** (sudden increase) (in price, wages etc) bond m (**in** dans); **she's made the ~ from deputy to director** elle est passée d'un bond du poste d'adjointe à celle de directrice.
II vtr **1** (leap over) sauter [obstacle, ditch]; **2** (anticipate) **to ~ the lights** [motorist] passer au feu rouge; **to ~ the queue** passer devant tout le monde; **3** (escape) **to ~ ship** [crewman] ne pas rejoindre son bâtiment; **4** (miss) [stylus] sauter [groove]; [disease] sauter [generation]; **5**○ (attack) sauter sur [person].
III vi **1** (leap) sauter; **to ~ across** ou **over sth** franchir qch d'un bond; **to ~ up and down** [gymnast] sautiller; [child] sauter en l'air; FIG (in anger) trépigner de colère; **2** (start in surprise) [person] sursauter; **3** (rise) [prices, rate] monter en flèche; **4** (move) **the film ~s from 1800 to 1920** le film passe d'un seul coup de 1800 à 1920; **5** (welcome) **to ~ at** sauter sur [opportunity]; accepter [qch] avec enthousiasme [offer].
IDIOMS **~ to it!** et que ça saute○!
■ **jump about, jump around** sauter.
■ **jump back** [person] faire un bond en arrière; [lever, spring] reprendre sa place initiale.
■ **jump down** [person] sauter (**from** de).
■ **jump on: ¶ ~ on [sth]** (mount) sauter dans [bus, train]; sauter sur [bicycle, horse]; **~ on!** monte!; **~ on [sb]** LIT, FIG sauter sur qn.
■ **jump out** [person] sauter; **to ~ out in front of sb** surgir devant qn.
■ **jump up** [person] se lever d'un bond.

jumped-up /'dʒʌmptʌp/ adj PÉJ [clerk, waiter] prétentieux/-ieuse.

jumper /'dʒʌmpə(r)/ ▶ **1260** n **1** GB (sweater) pull m, pull-over m; **2** US (pinafore) robe f chasuble; **3** TECH barre f à mine.

jumper cables npl US AUT câbles mpl de démarrage.

jump: ~-jet n avion m à décollage vertical; **~ leads** npl câbles mpl de démarrage; **~ rope** n US corde f à sauter; **~-start** vtr démarrer [qch] avec des câbles [car]; **~ suit** n combinaison f.

jumpy○ /'dʒʌmpɪ/ adj [person] nerveux/-euse; [market] instable.

Jun abrév écrite = **June**.

junction /'dʒʌŋkʃn/ n **1** (of two roads) carrefour m; (on motorway) échangeur m; **2** RAIL (of railway lines) nœud m ferroviaire; (station) gare f de jonction; **3** TECH (point m de) raccordement m; **4** FIG SOUT fusion f.

June /dʒuːn/ ▶ **1090** n juin m.

Jungian /'jʊŋɪən/ n, adj jungien/-ienne (m/f).

jungle /'dʒʌŋgl/ n LIT, FIG jungle f.

junior /'dʒuːnɪə(r)/ **I** n **1** (younger person) cadet/-ette m/f; **2** (low-ranking worker) subalterne mf; **3** GB SCH élève mf du primaire; **4** US UNIV ≈ étudiant/-e m/f de premier cycle; (in high school) ≈ élève mf de première.
II adj **1** (low-ranking) [colleague, worker] (inferior) subalterne; (trainee) débutant; [post, rank, position] subalterne; **he's very ~** il a très peu d'expérience; **2** (young) [person] jeune; [fashion, activity] pour les jeunes; **3** SPORT [race, team] des cadets; [player, high-jumper] jeune; **4** (the younger) (also **Junior**) **Bob Mortimer ~** Bob Mortimer fils or junior.

junior: ~ college n US premier cycle m universitaire; **Junior Common Room** n GB UNIV (room) salle f des étudiants; (student body) (+ v sg ou pl) étudiants mpl; **~ doctor** n médecin m des hôpitaux; **~ high school** n US ≈ collège m; **~ minister**

secrétaire *m* d'État; **~ miss** *n* US fillettes *fpl*; **~ school** *n* GB école *f* (primaire).

juniper /'dʒuːnɪpə(r)/ *n* genièvre *m*.

junk /dʒʌŋk/ *n* **1**○ PÉJ (poor quality) (furniture, merchandise) camelote○ *f*; **clear your ~ off the table!** dégage ton bazar○ de la table!; **how can you read that ~?** comment peux-tu lire ces bêtises?; **2** (second-hand) bric-à-brac *m*; **3** (boat) jonque *f*.

junk bond *n* obligation *f* à haut rendement et à risque élevé.

junk food *n* nourriture *f* industrielle.

junkie○ /'dʒʌŋkɪ/ *n* drogué/-e *m/f*.

junk: **~ mail** *n* ⊄ prospectus *mpl*; **~ shop** *n* boutique *f* de bric-à-brac; **~yard** *n* (for scrap) dépotoir *m*; (for old cars) cimetière *f* de voitures.

junta /'dʒʌntə/ *n* junte *f*.

jurisdiction /ˌdʒʊərɪs'dɪkʃn/ *n* **1** GEN, ADMIN compétence *f* (**over** sur); **2** JUR juridiction *f* (**over** sur); **3** US (court) juridiction *f*.

jurisprudence /ˌdʒʊərɪs'pruːdns/ *n* **1** (philosophy) philosophie *f* du droit; **2** (precedents) jurisprudence *f*.

jurist /'dʒʊərɪst/ **▶ 1251** *n* juriste *mf*.

juror /'dʒʊərə(r)/ *n* juré *m*.

jury /'dʒʊərɪ/ *n* GEN, JUR jury *m*; **'members of the ~'** JUR 'mesdames et messieurs les jurés'.

jury: **~ box** *n* banc *m* des jurés; **~ duty** *n* US = **jury service**.

jury service *n* GB **to do ~** faire partie d'un jury.

just[1] /dʒʌst/ **I** *adv* **1** (very recently) **to have ~ done** venir de (juste) de faire; **2** (immediately) juste; **~ before** juste avant; **it's ~ after 10 am** il est 10 heures passées de quelques minutes; **3** (slightly) (with quantities) un peu; (indicating location or position) juste; **~ over/under 20 kg** un peu plus/moins de 20 kg; **~ after the station** juste après la gare; **4** (only, merely) juste; **~ a cup of tea** juste une tasse de thé; **~ for fun** juste pour rire; **~ two days ago** il y a juste deux jours; **~ last week** pas plus tard que la semaine dernière; **he's ~ a child** ce n'est qu'un enfant; **not ~ men** pas seulement les hommes; **5** (purposely) exprès; **he did it ~ to annoy us** il l'a fait exprès pour nous embêter; **6** (barely) tout juste; **~ on time** tout juste à l'heure; **he's ~ 20** il a tout juste 20 ans; **I (only) ~ caught the train** j'ai eu le train de justesse; **7** (simply) tout simplement; **~ tell the truth** dis la vérité, tout simplement; **she ~ won't listen** elle ne veut tout simplement pas écouter; **'~ a moment'** 'un instant'; **8** (exactly, precisely) exactement; **that's ~ what I suggested** c'est exactement ce que j'ai suggéré; **it's ~ what you were expecting** c'est bien ce à quoi tu t'attendais; **~ how do you hope to persuade him?** comment espères-tu le persuader au juste?; **it's ~ right** c'est parfait; **he likes everything to be ~ so** il aime que les choses soient parfaitement en ordre; **she looks ~ like her father** elle ressemble énormément à son père; **it's ~ like him/you to forget** c'est bien de lui/toi d'oublier; **~ so!** tout à fait; **9** (possibly, conceivably) **it might ou could ~ be true** il se peut que ce soit vrai; **10** (at this or that very moment) **to be ~ doing** être en train de faire; **to be ~ about to do** être sur le point de faire; **he was ~ leaving** il partait; **11** (positively, totally) vraiment; **that was ~ ridiculous** c'était vraiment ridicule; **12** (easily) **I can ~ imagine her as president** je n'ai aucun mal à l'imaginer présidente; **I can ~ smell the pineforests** je sens déjà l'odeur des pins; **13** (with imperatives) donc; **~ keep quiet!** tais-toi donc!; **~ look at the time!** regarde donc l'heure qu'il est!; **~ think, you could have been hurt!** mais tu te rends

compte? tu aurais pu être blessé!; **14** (in requests) **if I could ~ interrupt you** si je peux me permettre de vous interrompre; **15** (for emphasis in responses) **'that film was dreadful'—'wasn't it ~!'** 'ce film était absolument nul!'—'ah, ça oui!'; **16** (equally) **~ as big/well as...** aussi grand/bien que...

II just about *adv phr* presque; **~ about cooked/finished** presque cuit/fini; **~ about everything** à peu près tout; **I can ~ about see it** je peux tout juste le voir; **I've had ~ about enough!** j'en ai marre○!; **it's ~ about the most boring film I've seen** c'est sans doute le film le plus ennuyeux que j'aie vu.

III just now *adv phr* (at the moment) en ce moment; (a short time ago) **I saw him ~ now** je viens juste de le voir.

IV just as *conj phr* juste au moment où.

IDIOMS **~ as well!** tant mieux!; **I'd ~ as soon you didn't mention it** j'aimerais autant que tu le gardes pour toi; **take your raincoat ~ in case it rains** prends ton imperméable au cas où il pleuvrait.

just[2] /dʒʌst/ *adj* **1** (fair) [*person, society, decision, cause, comment, war*] juste; [*action, complaint, demand*] justifié; [*anger, claim, criticism, suspicion*] légitime; **it's his ~ reward** il l'a bien mérité; **as is only ~** à juste titre; **without ~ cause** sans raison valable; **2** (exact) [*account, calculation*] juste, exact; **3** JUR [*claim*] fondé; [*title, request*] valable.

justice /'dʒʌstɪs/ *n* **1** (fairness) justice *f*; **to do sb ~, to do ~ to sb** rendre justice à qn; **the portrait doesn't do her ~** le portrait ne l'avantage pas; **I couldn't do ~ to it** (refusing food) je ne pourrais pas y faire honneur; **2** (the law) justice *f*; **to bring sb to ~** traduire qn en justice; **3** (judge) GB juge *m*; US juge *m* de la Cour Suprême.

justice: **Justice Department** *n* US ministère *m* de la justice; **Justice of the Peace**, **JP** *n* juge *m* de paix.

justifiable /'dʒʌstɪfaɪəbl/ *adj* (that is justified) légitime; (that can be justified) justifiable.

justifiably /'dʒʌstɪfaɪəblɪ/ *adv* à juste titre.

justification /ˌdʒʌstɪfɪ'keɪʃn/ *n* **1** (reason) raison *f*; **to have some ~ for doing** avoir des raisons de faire; **in ~ of sth** en justification à qch; **with some ~** non sans raison; **2** (of text) justification *f*; COMPUT (moving of data) cadrage *m*.

justified /'dʒʌstɪfaɪd/ *adj* **1** GEN justifié; **to be ~ in doing** avoir raison de faire; **to feel ~ in doing** se sentir en droit de faire; **2** [*margin*] justifié; **3** COMPUT [*text, data*] cadré.

justify /'dʒʌstɪfaɪ/ *vtr* **1** GEN justifier; **2** justifier [*margins*]; **3** COMPUT cadrer [*text, data*].

justly /'dʒʌstlɪ/ *adv* **1** (equitably) avec justice; **2** (justifiably) à juste titre.

justness /'dʒʌstnɪs/ *n* **1** (aptness) justesse *f*; **2** (reasonableness) (of claim, request) caractère *m* justifié.

jut /dʒʌt/ *vi* (*p prés etc* **-tt-**) (also **~ out**) [*cape, promontory*] s'avancer en saillie (**into** dans); [*balcony*] faire saillie (**over** sur).

jute /dʒuːt/ *n* jute *m*.

juvenile /'dʒuːvənaɪl/ **I** *n* **1** SOUT (young person) jeune *mf*; JUR mineur/-e *m/f*; **2** BOT, ZOOL jeune *mf*. **II** *adj* **1** PÉJ (childish) puéril; **2** BOT, ZOOL juvénile.

juvenile: **~ crime** *n* criminalité *f* juvénile; **~ delinquency** *n* délinquance *f* juvénile; **~ delinquent** *n* jeune délinquant/-e *m/f*; **~ offender** *n* JUR délinquant/-e *m/f* mineur/-e.

juxtaposition /ˌdʒʌkstəpə'zɪʃn/ *n* juxtaposition *f*.

Kk

k, K /keɪ/ n **1** (letter) k, K m; **2 K** abrév = **kilo**; **3 K** COMPUT (abrév = **kilobyte**) K m; **4 K** (abrév = **thousand**) mille; **he earns £50 K** il gagne 50 000 livres sterling.

Kabul /'kɑːbl/ ▶1343 pr n Kaboul.

kaftan /'kæftæn/ n caftan m.

kale /keɪl/ n (also **curly ~**) chou m frisé.

kaleidoscope /kə'laɪdəskəʊp/ n LIT, FIG kaléidoscope m.

kangaroo /ˌkæŋgə'ruː/ n kangourou m.

kangaroo court n PÉJ tribunal m irrégulier.

kaolin /'keɪəlɪn/ n kaolin m.

kapok /'keɪpɒk/ n kapok m.

kaput° /kæ'pʊt/ adj kaput° inv.

karaoke /ˌkerɪ'əʊkeɪ, -kɪ/ n karaoké m.

karat /'kærət/ n US ► **carat**.

karate /kə'rɑːtɪ/ ▶949 n karaté m; **~ chop** coup de karaté.

kart /kɑːt/ n kart m.

Kashmir /kæʃ'mɪə/ pr n Cachemire m.

Kashmiri /kæʃ'mɪərɪ/ ▶1100, 1038 n **1** (person) Cachemirien/-ienne m/f; **2** (language) cachemirien m.

kayak /'kaɪæk/ n kayak m.

kazoo /kə'zuː/ n mirliton m.

KB n COMPUT (abrév = **kilobyte**) Ko m.

kebab /kɪ'bæb/ n (also **shish ~**) chiche-kebab m.

kedgeree /'kedʒərɪ, ˌkedʒə'riː/ n GB pilaf m de poisson.

keel /kiːl/ n quille f; **my finances are back on an even ~** FIG mes finances sont revenues à la normale.
■ **keel over** [boat] chavirer; [person] s'écrouler; [tree] s'abattre.

keen /kiːn/ adj **1** (eager) [admirer] fervent; [candidate] motivé; **to be ~ on** tenir à [plan, project]; être chaud° pour [idea]; **to be ~ on doing** ou **to do** tenir à faire; **to be ~ for sb to do** ou **that sb should do** tenir à ce que qn fasse; **to look ~** avoir l'air tenté ou partant°; **2** (enthusiastic) [artist, sportsplayer, supporter] enthousiaste; [student] assidu; **to be ~ on** être passionné de [activity]; avoir une passion pour [animals]; **he's ~ on my sister**° il en pince° pour ma sœur; **mad ~**° GB fana°; **3** (intense) [appetite, desire, interest] vif/vive; [admiration, sense of loss] intense; **4** (acute) [eye, intelligence] vif/vive; [sight] perçant; [hearing, sense of smell] fin; **to have a ~ eye for sth** avoir l'œil pour qch; **5** (sharp) [blade] acéré; [wit] vif/vive; [wind] pénétrant; [air] vif/vive; **6** (competitive) [price] défiant toute concurrence; [competition] intense; [demand] fort; [debate] animé.

keenly /'kiːnlɪ/ adv [interested] vivement; [awaited] ardemment; [aware] parfaitement; [feel, contest, debate] vivement.

keenness /'kiːnnɪs/ n (enthusiasm) enthousiasme m; (of senses) acuité f.

keep /kiːp/ **I** n **1** (maintenance) pension f; **to pay for one's ~** payer une pension; **to earn one's ~** gagner de quoi vivre; **2** ARCHIT donjon m.

II vtr (prét, pp **kept**) **1** (cause to remain) **to ~ sb indoors** [person] garder qn à l'intérieur; [illness] retenir qn à l'intérieur; **to ~ sth/sb clean** garder qch/qn propre; **to ~ sth warm** garder qch au chaud; **to ~ sb warm** protéger qn du froid; **to be kept clean/locked** rester propre/fermé (à clé); **to ~ sb talking/waiting** retenir/faire attendre qn; **I won't ~ you to**

your promise tu n'es pas obligé de tenir ta promesse; **to ~ an engine running** laisser un moteur en marche; **2** (detain) retenir; **I won't ~ you a minute** je n'en ai pas pour longtemps; **3** (retain) garder; **4** (have and look after) tenir [shop]; avoir [dog]; élever [chickens]; **5** (sustain) **to ~ sth going** entretenir [conversation, fire, tradition]; **I'll make you a sandwich to ~ you going** je te ferai un sandwich pour que tu tiennes le coup; **have you got enough work to ~ you going?** avez-vous assez de travail pour vous occuper?; **6** (store) mettre, ranger; **I ~ a spare key** j'ai un double de la clé; **7** (have in stock) vendre, avoir; **8** (support financially) faire vivre, entretenir [family]; avoir [servant]; **9** (maintain by writing in) tenir [accounts, diary]; **10** (conceal) **to ~ sth from sb** taire ou cacher qch à qn; **11** (prevent) **to ~ sb from doing** empêcher qn de faire; **12** (observe) tenir [promise]; garder [secret]; se rendre à [appointment]; célébrer [occasion]; observer [commandments]; **13** MUS **to ~ time** ou **the beat** battre la mesure; **14** (maintain) entretenir [car, house].

III vi (prét, pp **kept**) **1** (continue) **to ~ doing** continuer à ou de faire, ne pas arrêter de faire; **to ~ going** continuer; **~ at it!** persévérez!; **~ straight on** continuez tout droit; **'~ left'** 'tenez votre gauche'; **2** (remain) **to ~ indoors** rester à l'intérieur; **to ~ out of the rain** se protéger de la pluie; **to ~ warm** se protéger du froid; **to ~ calm** rester calme; **to ~ silent** garder le silence; **3** (stay in good condition) [food] se conserver, se garder; **4** (wait) [news, business] attendre; **5** (in health) **'how are you ~ing?'** 'comment allez-vous?'; **she's ~ing well** elle va bien.

IV v refl **to ~ oneself** subvenir à ses propres besoins; **to ~ oneself warm** se protéger du froid; **to ~ oneself healthy** rester en forme; **to ~ oneself to oneself** ne pas être sociable.

V for keeps adv phr pour de bon, pour toujours.

IDIOMS **to ~ in with sb** rester en bons termes avec qn.
■ **keep at**: ¶ **~ at** [sb] harceler [person]; ¶ **~ at it** persévérer.
■ **keep away**: ¶ **~ away** ne pas s'approcher (**from** de); ¶ **~ [sth/sb] away** empêcher [qch/qn] de s'approcher; **to ~ sb away from** empêcher qn de s'approcher de [person, fire]; tenir qn éloigné de [family].
■ **keep back**: ¶ **~ back** ne pas s'approcher (**from** de); ¶ **~ [sth/sb] back**, **~ back** [sth/sb] **1** (prevent from advancing) empêcher [qn] de s'approcher [crowd] (**from** de); faire redoubler [student]; [dam] retenir [water]; **2** (retain) garder [student]; **3** (conceal) cacher (**from** à).
■ **keep down**: ¶ **~ down** rester allongé; **~ down!** ne bougez pas!; ¶ **~ [sth] down**, **~ down** [sth] **1** (cause to remain at a low level) limiter [number, speed, inflation]; limiter l'augmentation de [prices, unemployment]; maîtriser [inflation]; **~ your voice down!** baisse la voix!; **~ the noise down!** faites moins de bruit!; **2** (retain in stomach) **he can't ~ anything down** il vomit tout ce qu'il avale; ¶ **~ [sb] down** opprimer [people].
■ **keep in**: ¶ **~ in** [car, cyclist] GB tenir sa gauche; (elsewhere) tenir sa droite; ¶ **~ [sb/sth] in 1** (cause to remain inside) empêcher [qn/qch] de sortir [person, animal]; garder [contact lenses]; **they're ~ing her in** (in hospital) ils la gardent; **2** (restrain) rentrer [stomach]; réprimer [emotions]; **3** SCH garder [qn] en retenue [pupil].
■ **keep off**: ¶ **~ off!** n'avancez pas!; ¶ **~ off** [sth] **1** (stay away from) ne pas marcher sur; **'Please ~ off**

the grass' 'Défense de marcher sur la pelouse'; **2** (refrain from) éviter [*alcohol*]; s'abstenir de parler de [*subject*]; ¶ ~ [sth] off, ~ off [sth] (prevent from touching) éloigner [*insects*]; to ~ the rain off protéger contre la pluie.

■ keep on: ¶ ~ on doing continuer à faire; to ~ on about sth ne pas arrêter de parler de qch; to ~ on at sb harceler qn (to do pour qu'il fasse); ¶ ~ [sb/sth] on garder.

■ keep out: ¶ ~ out of [sth] **1** (not enter) ne pas entrer dans [*house*]; '~ out!' 'défense d'entrer'; **2** (avoid being exposed to) rester à l'abri de [*sun, rain, danger*]; **3** (avoid getting involved in) ne pas se mêler de [*argument*]; to ~ out of sb's way, to ~ out of the way of sb (not hinder) ne pas encombrer qn; (avoid seeing) éviter qn; try to ~ out of trouble! essaie de bien te conduire!; ¶ ~ [sb/sth] out, ~ out [sb/sth] ne pas laisser entrer [*person, animal*]; to ~ the rain out empêcher la pluie d'entrer; to ~ sb out of sth (not involve in) ne pas vouloir mêler qn à qch; (not allow to enter) ne pas laisser entrer qn dans qch.

■ keep to: ¶ ~ to [sth] (stick to) LIT ne pas s'écarter de [*road, path*]; respecter, s'en tenir à [*timetable, facts*]; respecter [*law, rules*]; '~ to the left' 'tenez votre gauche'; ¶ ~ [sth] to (restrict) limiter [qch] à [*number*]; to ~ sth to oneself garder qch pour soi.

■ keep under: ~ [sb] under **1** (dominate) assujettir, soumettre; **2** (cause to remain unconscious) maintenir [qn] inconscient.

■ keep up: ¶ ~ up **1** (progress at same speed) [*car, runner, person*] suivre; [*competitors*] rester à la hauteur; [*price*] se maintenir; if the rain ~s up I'm not going s'il continue à pleuvoir je n'y vais pas; ¶ ~ [sth] up, ~ up [sth] **1** (cause to remain in position) tenir [*trousers*]; **2** (continue) continuer [*attack, studies*]; entretenir [*correspondence, friendship*]; maintenir [*membership, tradition*]; garder [*pace*]; to ~ up the pressure continuer à faire pression (for pour obtenir; on sur); to ~ up one's strength/spirits garder ses forces/le moral; ¶ ~ [sb] up [*noise, illness*] empêcher [qn] de dormir.

■ keep up with: ~ up with [sb/sth] **1** (progress at same speed as) aller aussi vite que [*person*]; suivre [*class*]; se maintenir à la hauteur de [*competitors*]; [*wages*] suivre [*inflation*]; faire face à [*demand*]; **2** (be informed about) suivre [*fashion, developments*]; **3** (remain in contact with) garder le contact avec [*friends*].

keeper /'kiːpə(r)/ *n* **1** (in zoo) gardien/-ienne *m/f*; **2** (in football) gardien/-ienne *m/f* (de but); **3** (curator) conservateur/-trice *m/f*; **4** (guard) gardien/-ienne *m/f*.

keep fit /ˌkiːp'fɪt/ *n* gymnastique *f* d'entretien.

keeping /'kiːpɪŋ/ *n* **1** (custody) in sb's ~, in the ~ of sb à la garde de qn; to put sb/sth in sb's ~ confier qn/qch à qn; **2** (conformity) in ~ with conforme à [*law, tradition*]; to be in ~ with correspondre à [*image, character*] s'harmoniser avec [*surroundings*]; to be out of ~ with ne pas correspondre à [*character, image*]; ne pas convenir à [*occasion*].

keepsake /'kiːpseɪk/ *n* souvenir *m*.

keg /keg/ *n* (for liquid) fût *m*; (for gunpowder) baril *m*.

kelp /kelp/ *n* laminaire *f*.

kelvin /'kelvɪn/ *n* degré *m* Kelvin.

kennel /'kenl/ *n* **1** GB (for dog) niche *f*; (for several dogs) chenil *m*; **2** (GB **kennels** + *v sg*) (establishment) chenil *m*.

Kenya /'kenjə/ **▶840** *pr n* Kenya *m*; in ~ au Kenya.

kept /kept/ **I** *prét, pp* ▶ **keep.**
II *adj* [*man, woman*] entretenu.

kerb /kɜːb/ *n* GB bord *m* du trottoir; to draw up at the ~ se ranger le long du trottoir; to pull away from the ~ s'éloigner du trottoir.

kernel /'kɜːnl/ *n* (of nut, fruitstone) amande *f*; (whole seed) grain *m*; FIG a ~ of truth un fond de vérité.

kerosene, kerosine /'kerəsiːn/ *n* **1** US, AUSTRAL

(paraffin) pétrole *m* (lampant); **2** (aircraft fuel) kérosène *m*.

kestrel /'kestrəl/ *n* (faucon *m*) crécerelle *f*.

ketchup /'ketʃəp/ GB *n* ketchup *m*.

kettle /'ketl/ *n* bouilloire *f*; to put the ~ on mettre l'eau à chauffer; the ~'s boiling l'eau bout.
IDIOMS a different ~ of fish une tout autre affaire.

kettledrum /'ketldrʌm/ **▶1097** *n* timbale *f*.

key /kiː/ **I** *n* **1** (locking device) clé *f*; a front-door ~ une clé de maison; a set ou bunch of ~s un jeu de clés; under lock and ~ sous clé; **2** (for clock) clé *f* (de pendule), remontoir *m*; **3** TECH clé *f*; radiator ~ clavette *f* à radiateur; **4** (on computer, piano, phone) touche *f*; (on oboe, flute) clé *f*; **5** FIG (vital clue) clé *f*, secret *m* (to de); to hold the ~ to the mystery renfermer la clé du mystère; exercise is the ~ to health l'exercice est le secret de la santé; **6** (explanatory list) (on map) légende *f*; (to abbreviations, symbols) liste *f*; (for code) clé *f*; **7** (answers) (to test, riddle) solutions *fpl*; SCH corrigé *m*; **8** MUS ton *m*, tonalité *f*; in a major ~ en majeur; to sing in/off ~ chanter juste/faux; **9** GEOG caye *m*.
II *noun modifier* [*industry, job, document, figure, role*] clé *inv*; [*difference, point*] capital.
III *vtr* **1** (type) saisir; **2** (adapt) adapter (to à).
■ key in: ~ [sth] in, ~ in [sth] saisir [*data*].

keyboard /'kiːbɔːd/ **▶1097** **I** *n* clavier *m*.
II **keyboards** *npl* MUS synthétiseur *m*.
III *vtr* saisir.

keyboarder /'kiːbɔːdə(r)/ *n* opérateur/-trice *m/f* de saisie.

keyboarding /'kiːbɔːdɪŋ/ *n* saisie *f*.

keyboard: ~ operator *n* = keyboarder; ~s player *n* joueur/-euse *m/f* de synthétiseur.

keyed-up /ˌkiːd'ʌp/ *adj* (excited) excité; (tense) tendu.

keyhole /'kiːhəʊl/ *n* trou *m* de serrure.

keyhole journalism *n* reportages *mpl* à sensation.

keying /'kiːɪŋ/ *n* saisie *f*.

key money *n* (for business) pas-de-porte *m inv*; (for apartment) reprise *f*.

keynote /'kiːnəʊt/ *n* **1** MUS tonique *f*; **2** (main theme) thème *m* principal.

keynote: ~ speaker *n* intervenant/-e *m/f* principal/-e; ~ speech *n* discours *m* programme.

key: ~-pad *n* COMPUT pavé *m* numérique; TELECOM clavier *m* numérique; ~-ring *n* porte-clés *m inv*; ~ signature *n* armature *f*; ~stroke *n* COMPUT frappe *f*; ~word *n* mot *m* clé.

kg *n* (*abrév* = **kilogram**) kg *m*.

khaki /'kɑːkɪ/ **I** *n* kaki *m*; in ~ en kaki.
II *adj* kaki *inv*.

kibbutz /kɪ'bʊts/ *n* (*pl* **~es** ou **~im**) kibboutz *m*.

kibosh○ /'kaɪbɒʃ/ *n*: IDIOMS to put the ~ on sth mettre fin à qch.

kick /kɪk/ **I** *n* **1** (of person, horse) coup *m* de pied; (of donkey, cow, goat) coup *m* de sabot; (of swimmer) battement *m* de pieds; (of footballer) tir *m*; to give sb/the door a ~ donner un coup de pied à qn/dans la porte; to aim ou take a ~ at sb/sth [*person*] lancer un coup de pied à qn/dans qch; **2**○ (thrill) to get a ~ from doing prendre plaisir à faire; **3** (of firearm) recul *m*; **4**○ (strength, zest) dynamisme *m*; this punch has quite a ~ (to it) ce punch est assez costaud○.
II *vtr* GEN (once) [*person*] donner un coup de pied à [*person*]; donner un coup de pied dans [*table, door, ball, tin can*]; [*horse*] botter; [*donkey, cow, goat*] donner un coup de sabot à [*person*]; (repeatedly) donner des coups de pied à [*person*]; donner des coups de pieds dans [*object*]; to ~ sb on the leg [*person, horse*] donner à qn un coup or des coups de pied à la jambe; [*donkey, cow*] donner à qn un coup de sabot dans la jambe; to ~ sth over a wall envoyer qch par-dessus un mur d'un coup de pied; to ~ sth away éloigner qch d'un coup de pied; to ~ a hole in sth défoncer qch d'un coup de pied; to ~ one's legs (in the air) [*baby*] pédaler; to ~ a goal marquer un but.
III *vi* **1** GEN [*person*] (once) donner un coup de pied;

(repeatedly) donner des coups de pied; [*swimmer*] faire des battements de pieds; [*dancer*] lancer la jambe; [*cow*] ruer; [*horse*] botter; **2** (recoil) [*gun*] reculer.

IDIOMS **to ~ sb when they're down** frapper un homme à terre; **to ~ the habit**○ GEN décrocher○, arrêter; (of smoking) arrêter de fumer; **I could have ~ed myself** je me serais donné des claques○; **to be alive and ~ing** être bien vivant; **to ~ over the traces** ruer dans les brancards○.

■ **kick around**, **kick about**: ¶ ~ **around**○ [*objects, clothes*] traîner○; **he's been ~ing around Europe for a year**○ il se balade○ en Europe depuis un an; ¶ ~ **[sth] around** ou **about 1** LIT donner des coups de pied dans, s'amuser avec [*ball, object*]; **2**○ discuter de, explorer [*idea*].

■ **kick against**: ~ **against** [sth] résister à [*idea*]; lutter contre [*system*].

■ **kick down**: ~ **[sth] down**, ~ **down [sth]** enfoncer [qch] d'un coup de pied or à coups de pied [*door*]; [*horse*] renverser [*fence*].

■ **kick in**: ~ **[sth] in**, ~ **in [sth]** enfoncer [qch] d'un coup de pied or à coups de pied [*door*].

■ **kick off**: ¶ ~ **off 1** SPORT donner le coup d'envoi; **2**○ (start) commencer; ¶ ~ **off [sth]**, ~ **[sth] off 1** enlever [*shoes*]; **2**○ (start) commencer; ¶ ~ **[sb] off** exclure [qn] de [*committee*].

■ **kick out**: ¶ ~ **out** [*animal*] ruer; [*person*] lancer des coups de pied; **to ~ out at sb** [*person*] lancer des coups de pied à qn; ¶ ~ **[sb] out**, ~ **out [sb]**○ virer○ [*troublemaker, employee*].

■ **kick over**: ~ **[sth] over**, ~ **over [sth]** renverser [qch] (d'un coup de pied or à coups de pied).

■ **kick up**: ~ **[sth] up**, ~ **up [sth]** soulever [*dust*]; **to ~ up a fuss**○ ou **stink**○ faire des histoires○ (about à propos de).

kick: **~back** *n* pot-de-vin *m*; **~boxing** *n* kick-boxing *m*; **~-off** *n* SPORT coup *m* d'envoi.

kick-start /'kɪkstɑːt/ **I** *n* (also **~-starter**) (on motorbike) kick *m*.
II *vtr* LIT démarrer [qch] au pied [*motorbike*]; FIG relancer.

kid /kɪd/ **I** *n* **1**○ (child) enfant *mf*, gosse○ *mf*; (youth) gamin/-e○ *m/f*; **2** (young goat) chevreau/-ette *m/f*; **3** (goatskin) chevreau *m*.
II○ *vtr* (*p prés etc* **-dd-**) **1** (tease) charrier○ (**about** à propos de); **2** (fool) faire marcher○; **to ~ sb into believing that** faire croire à qn que.
III○ *vi* (*p prés etc* **-dd-**) (tease) rigoler○; **no ~ding!** sans blague○!
IV○ *v refl* (*p prés etc* **-dd-**) **to ~ oneself** se faire des illusions.

kid glove *n* gant *m* en chevreau.
IDIOMS **to treat sb with ~s** prendre des gants avec qn.

kidnap /'kɪdnæp/ **I** *n* enlèvement *m*.
II *vtr* (*p prés etc* **-pp-**) enlever.

kidnapper /'kɪdnæpə(r)/ *n* ravisseur/-euse *m/f*.

kidnapping /'kɪdnæpɪŋ/ *n* enlèvement *m*.

kidney /'kɪdnɪ/ *n* ANAT rein *m*; CULIN rognon *m*; **to have ~ trouble** souffrir de troubles rénaux.

kidney: ~ **bean** *n* haricot *m* rouge; ~ **dialysis** *n* dialyse *f*; ~ **donor** *n* donneur/-euse *m/f* de rein; ~ **failure** *n* défaillance *f* rénale.

kidney machine *n* rein *m* artificiel; **to be on a ~** être en dialyse.

kidney: ~ **shaped** *adj* en forme de haricot; ~ **stone** *n* calcul *m* rénal.

kill /kɪl/ **I** *n* **1** (in hunting) mise *f* à mort; **to be in at the ~** LIT assister à la mise à mort; FIG assister au dénouement; **2** (prey) proie *f*.
II *vtr* **1** (cause to die) tuer; **they ~ed one another** ou **each other** ils se sont entre-tués; **~ed in action** ou **battle** tombé au champ d'honneur; **I'll do it, even if it ~s me**○! je le ferai, même si je dois y laisser ma peau○! **2**○ (make effort) **it wouldn't ~ you to turn up on time** tu pourrais faire l'effort d'arriver à l'heure; **3**○ (hurt) **my feet are ~ing me** j'ai mal aux pieds; **4** (end, stop) arrêter [*rumour*]; supprimer [*story*];

faire échouer [*idea*]; **that remark ~ed the conversation dead** cette remarque a jeté un froid dans la conversation; **5** (deaden) tuer [*smell, flavour*]; faire disparaître [*pain*]; ôter [*appetite*]; **6**○ (turn off) couper [*engine*]; éteindre [*television, light*]; **7** (spend) **to ~ time** tuer le temps (**by doing** en faisant); **I have two hours to ~** j'ai deux heures à attendre.
III *vi* tuer.
IV *v refl* **to ~ oneself** se suicider; **to ~ oneself doing** FIG se tuer à faire; **to ~ oneself laughing** être mort de rire.

■ **kill off**: ~ **off [sth]**, ~ **[sth] off** éliminer.

killer /'kɪlə(r)/ **I** *n* **1** (illness, poison) **heroin/cancer is a ~** l'héroïne/le cancer tue; **cancer is a major ~** le cancer est l'une des principales causes de mortalité; **2** (person) meurtrier *m*; (animal) tueur/-euse *m/f*.
II *noun modifier* [*disease*] mortel/-elle; [*drug*] qui tue.

killer: ~ **instinct** *n* LIT instinct *m* de tuer; FIG agressivité *f*; ~ **whale** *n* épaulard *m*.

killing /'kɪlɪŋ/ *n* (of individual) meurtre *m* (**of** de); (of animal) mise *f* à mort (**of** de).
IDIOMS **to make a ~**○ ramasser un joli paquet○.

killjoy *n* rabat-joie *mf inv*.

kiln /kɪln/ *n* four *m*.

kilo /'kiːləʊ/ **▶ 1392** *n* kilo *m*.

kilobyte /'kɪləbaɪt/ *n* kilo-octet *m*.

kilogram(me) /'kɪləgræm/ **▶ 1392** *n* kilogramme *m*.

kilometre /kɪ'lɒmɪtə(r)/ GB, **kilometer** /'kɪləmiːtə(r)/ US **▶ 1045** *n* kilomètre *m*.

kilowatt /'kɪləwɒt/ *n* kilowatt *m*.

kilt /kɪlt/ *n* kilt *m*.

kin /kɪn/ *n* ¢ parents *mpl*, famille *f*.

kind /kaɪnd/ **I** *n* **1** (sort, type) sorte *f*, genre *m*, type *m*; **this ~ of book/person** ce genre or type de livre/personne; **all ~s of people, people of all ~s** toutes sortes de personnes; **what ~ of dog is it?** qu'est-ce que c'est comme chien?; **what ~ of person is she?** comment est-elle?, quel genre de personne est-ce?; **what ~ of person does he think I am?** pour qui me prend-il?; **what ~ of (a) person would do a thing like that?** qui pourrait faire une chose pareille?; **what ~ of an answer is that?** qu'est-ce que c'est que cette réponse?; **what ~ of talk is that?** en voilà des façons de parler!; **I don't believe anything of the ~** je n'en crois rien; **a criminal of the worst ~** un criminel de la pire espèce; **they could find no food of any ~** ils n'ont pas trouvé la moindre nourriture; **this is the only one of its ~, this is one of a ~** c'est unique en son genre; **he must be some ~ of idiot** ça doit être un imbécile; **they found a fossil of some ~** ils ont trouvé une sorte de fossile; **it's some ~ of cleaning device** ce doit être un système de nettoyage; **books, toys, that ~ of thing** des livres, des jouets, ce genre de choses; **what ~ of thing(s) does he like?** qu'est-ce qu'il aime?; **that's the ~ of person she is** elle est comme ça; **I'm not that ~ of person** ce n'est pas mon genre; **they found a solution of a ~** ils ont trouvé une sorte de solution; **2** (expressing vague classification) **a ~ of** une sorte de; **a ~ of handbag/soup** une sorte de sac à main/de soupe; **a ~ of intuition** une sorte d'intuition; **I heard a ~ of rattling noise** j'ai entendu comme un cliquetis; **I felt a ~ of apprehension** j'ai ressenti une certaine appréhension; **3** (classified type) espèce *f*, genre *m*; **I know his ~** je connais les gens de son espèce.
II in kind *adv phr* **1** (in goods) en nature; **to pay in ~** payer en nature; **2** (in same way) **to repay sb in ~** rendre la pareille à qn.
III○ **kind of** *adv phr* **he's ~ of cute/forgetful** il est plutôt mignon/distrait; **they were ~ of frightened** en fait, ils avaient un peu peur; **I ~ of like him** en fait, je l'aime bien; **we ~ of thought that...** nous pensions que...; **'is it interesting?'—'~ of'** 'est-ce que c'est intéressant?'—'plutôt, oui'.
IV *adj* **1** (caring) [*person*] gentil/-ille; [*act*] bon/bonne; [*gesture, words*] gentil/-ille; **to be ~ to sb** être gentil avec qn; **'Sudso is ~ to your skin'** 'Sudso respecte votre peau'; **to be ~ to animals** bien traiter les

animaux; **life has not been ~ to him** la vie ne l'a pas épargné; **that's very ~ of you** c'est très gentil or aimable de votre part; **would you be ~ enough to pass me the salt?** auriez-vous l'amabilité de me passer le sel?; **she was ~ enough to give me a lift home** elle a eu la gentillesse de me ramener chez moi.

kindergarten /'kɪndəgɑːtn/ n jardin m d'enfants.

kind: **~-hearted** adj [person] de cœur; **~-heartedly** adv très gentiment; **~-heartedness** n bonté f.

kindle /'kɪndl/ **I** vtr allumer [fire]; mettre le feu à [wood]; FIG attiser [desire]; susciter [interest].
II vi [wood] s'enflammer, prendre feu.

kindling /'kɪndlɪŋ/ n petit bois m, bois m d'allumage.

kindly /'kaɪndlɪ/ **I** adj [person, nature] gentil/-ille; [smile, interest] bienveillant; [face] sympathique.
II adv **1** (in a kind way) avec gentillesse; **to speak ~ of sb** avoir un mot gentil pour qn; **2** (obligingly) gentiment; **would you ~ do/refrain from doing** auriez-vous l'amabilité de faire/de ne pas faire; **3** (favourably) **to look ~ on** approuver [activity]; **to think ~ of** avoir une bonne opinion de; **to take ~ to** apprécier.

kindness /'kaɪndnɪs/ n **1** ⊄ (quality) gentillesse f; **to show ~ to** ou **towards sb** témoigner de la gentillesse à l'égard de or envers qn; **an act of ~** un acte de bonté; **out of ~** par gentillesse; **2** C (instance) gentillesse f; **to do sb a ~** rendre service à qn.
IDIOMS **out of the ~ of one's heart** par pure gentillesse; **to be full of the milk of human ~** être pétri d'humanité.

kindred /'kɪndrɪd/ **I** n (+ v pl ou v sg) famille f, parents mpl.
II adj [language] apparenté; [activity] semblable.

kindred spirit n âme f sœur.

kinetic /kɪ'netɪk/ adj cinétique.

kinetics /kɪ'netɪks/ n (+ v sg) cinétique f.

king /kɪŋ/ ▶ 937 ◀ n **1** (monarch) roi m; **King Charles** le roi Charles; **to live like a ~** FIG vivre comme un coq en pâte; **2** FIG (of comedy, wines etc) roi m (**of** de); **3** (in chess, cards) roi m; (in draughts, checkers) dame f.

kingdom /'kɪŋdəm/ n **1** (monarchy) LIT, FIG royaume m; **2** BOT, ZOOL règne m.
IDIOMS **to send** ou **knock sb to ~ come** envoyer qn ad patres○ or dans l'autre monde.

kingfisher n martin-pêcheur m.

kingly /'kɪŋlɪ/ adj LIT, FIG royal, de roi.

kingpin n TECH, FIG cheville f ouvrière.

king-size(d) /'kɪŋsaɪzd/ adj [cigarette] extra-longue; [packet] géant; [portion, garden] énorme; **~ bed** grand lit m (qui fait 1,95 m de large).

kink /kɪŋk/ n **1** (in rope, tube) nœud m; **the hosepipe has a ~ in it** le tuyau d'arrosage est tordu; **2** FIG (in personality) aberration f.
II vi [rope, cable] s'entortiller.

kinky /'kɪŋkɪ/ adj **1**○ (perverse) pervers, bizarre; **2** (wavy) ondulé.

kinship /'kɪnʃɪp/ n **1** (blood relationship) parenté f; **2** FIG (empathy) affinité f (**with** avec).

kiosk /'kiːɒsk/ n **1** (stand) kiosque m; **2** GB TELECOM cabine f.

kip○ /kɪp/ GB **I** n roupillon○ m; **to get some ~** piquer un roupillon○.
II vi (p prés etc **-pp-**) (also **~ down**) se pieuter○, roupiller○.

kipper /'kɪpə(r)/ n GB hareng m fumé et salé, kipper m.

Kirghizstan /'kɜːɡɪstæn/ ▶ 840 ◀ pr n Kirghizistan m, Kirghizie f.

kirk /kɜːk/ n SCOT église f.

kiss /kɪs/ **I** n baiser m; **to give sb a ~** embrasser qn, donner un baiser à qn.
II vtr embrasser, donner un baiser à [person]; baiser [hand, ring]; **to ~ sb on** embrasser qn sur [cheek, lips]; **we ~ed each other** nous nous sommes embrassés; **to ~ sb goodnight** souhaiter bonne nuit à qn en l'embrassant; **let me ~ it better!** un petit bisou et ça ira mieux après!; **you can ~ your**

money goodbye! FIG tu peux dire adieu à ton argent!
III vi s'embrasser; **to ~ and make up** se réconcilier; **to ~ and tell** avoir une liaison et le faire savoir publiquement.

kiss of death n coup m fatal; **to be the ~** porter le coup fatal.

kiss of life n GB bouche-à-bouche m inv; **to give sb the ~** faire le bouche à bouche à qn.

kissogram /'kɪsəɡræm/ n: service par lequel une personne en tenue légère est employée pour aller embrasser et présenter des vœux à quelqu'un.

kit /kɪt/ n **1** (implements) trousse f; **2** ⊄ (gear, clothes) affaires fpl; **football/tennis ~** affaires de football/de tennis; **3** (parts for assembly) kit m; **to come in ~ form** être vendu en kit; **4** MIL paquetage m.
■ **kit out** GB: **~ out [sb/sth]**, **~ [sb/sth] out** équiper (**with** de).

kit: **~bag** n (for sport) sac m de sport; (for travel) sac m de voyage; MIL (soldier's) sac m de soldat; **~car** n voiture f en kit.

kitchen /'kɪtʃɪn/ n cuisine f.
IDIOMS **if you can't stand the heat get out of the ~** si tu trouves la situation insupportable, tu n'es pas obligé de rester.

kitchenette /ˌkɪtʃɪ'net/ n kitchenette f.

kitchen: **~ foil** n papier m d'aluminium; **~ garden** n jardin m potager; **~ paper** n essuie-tout m inv, sopalin® m; **~ roll** n essuie-tout m inv; **~ scales** npl balance f de cuisine.

kitchen sink n évier m.
IDIOMS **to take everything but the ~** tout emporter sauf les meubles.

kitchen: **~ sink drama** n GB théâtre m naturaliste; **~ unit** n élément m de cuisine; **~ware** n ⊄ (implements) ustensiles mpl de cuisine; (crockery) vaisselle f; **~ waste** n ⊄ déchets mpl domestiques.

kite /kaɪt/ n **1** (toy) cerf-volant m; **to fly a ~** LIT faire voler un cerf-volant; FIG lancer un ballon d'essai; **2** (bird) milan m.

kitemark /'kaɪtmɑːk/ n GB label m de qualité.

kitsch /kɪtʃ/ n, adj kitsch (m).

kitten /'kɪtn/ n chaton m; FIG **to have ~s**○ piquer une crise○.

kitty /'kɪtɪ/ n **1**○ (cat) minet m, minou○ m; **2** (of money) cagnotte f.

kiwi /'kiːwiː/ n ZOOL kiwi m.

kiwi fruit n kiwi m.

kleptomania /ˌkleptə'meɪnɪə/ n kleptomanie f.

kleptomaniac /ˌkleptə'meɪnɪæk/ n, adj kleptomane (mf).

km (abrév écrite = **kilometre**) km.

kmh (abrév écrite = **kilometres per hour**) km/h.

knack /næk/ n **1** (dexterity) tour m de main (**of doing** pour faire); **to get the ~** attraper le tour de main; **to lose the ~** perdre la main; **2** (talent) don m (**of** ou **for doing** de faire).

knapsack /'næpsæk/ n sac m à dos.

knave /neɪv/ n **1** (in cards) valet m; **2**‡ (rogue) coquin‡ m.

knead /niːd/ vtr pétrir [dough]; masser [flesh].

knee /niː/ **I** ▶ 765 ◀ n ANAT genou m; **to be on/fall to one's ~s** être/tomber à genoux; **on (one's) hands and ~s** à quatre pattes; **to go down on bended ~ to sb** se mettre à genoux devant qn.
II vtr donner un coup de genou à [person].
IDIOMS **to bring** ou **force sb/sth to his/its ~s** mettre qn/qch à genoux; **to go weak at the ~s** avoir les jambes qui flageolent.

knee-breeches n knickers mpl.

kneecap /'niːkæp/ **I** n rotule f.
II vtr briser les rotules à [person].

knee-deep /ˌniː'diːp/ adj **the water was ~** l'eau arrivait aux genoux; **to be ~ in paperwork** FIG être dans les papiers jusqu'au cou.

knee: **~-high** adj à hauteur des genoux; **~-jerk** adj [*reaction, response*] automatique.

kneel /niːl/ vi (also **~ down**) (prét, pp **kneeled**, **knelt**) GEN se mettre à genoux; (in prayer) s'agenouiller; **~ing** à genoux; (in prayer) agenouillé.

knee: **~-length** adj [*skirt*] qui s'arrête au genou; [*boots*] haut; [*socks*] long/longue; **~-pad** n genouillère f.

knell /nel/ n glas m; **to sound the death ~ for sth** sonner le glas de qch.

knelt /nelt/ prét, pp ▶ **kneel**.

knew /njuː, US nuː/ prét ▶ **know**.

knickerbocker glory n coupe f glacée.

knickerbockers /ˈnɪkəbɒkəz/ npl knickers mpl.

knickers /ˈnɪkəz/ [▶ **1260**] npl GB petite culotte f.

knick-knack /ˈnɪknæk/ n bibelot m.

knife /naɪf/ I n (pl **knives**) couteau m.
II vtr donner un coup de couteau à [*person*] (**in** dans); **to be ~d** recevoir un coup de couteau.
IDIOMS **to have one's ~ into sb**⚬ en avoir après qn⚬; **to put the ~ in** critiquer; **to twist the ~ in the wound** remuer le couteau dans la plaie.

knife-edge n FIG **to be on a ~** [*negotiations*] ne tenir qu'à un fil; **to be (living) on a ~** [*person*] être au bord de l'abîme.

knife-point n **at ~** sous la menace d'un couteau.

knife sharpener n aiguisoir m.

knifing /ˈnaɪfɪŋ/ n attaque f au couteau.

knight /naɪt/ I n **1** GEN, HIST chevalier m; **2** (in chess) cavalier m.
II vtr GB anoblir [*person*] (**for** pour).

knighthood /ˈnaɪthʊd/ n (title) titre m de chevalier; (chivalry) chevalerie f.

knit /nɪt/ I n (garment) tricot m; **cotton ~** tricot en coton.
II vtr (prét, pp **knitted**, **knit**) tricoter; **to ~ sb sth** tricoter qch pour qn.
III vi (prét, pp **knitted**, **knit**) **1** (with wool) tricoter; **~ted** en tricot; **2** (join together) [*broken bones*] se souder.
IDIOMS **to ~ one's brows** froncer les sourcils.
■ **knit together**: ¶ **~ together** [*bones*] se souder; ¶ **~ [sth] together**, **~ together [sth]** LIT tricoter [qch] ensemble [*strands*]; FIG entrelacer [*themes*]; unir [*community*].

knitter /ˈnɪtə(r)/ n tricoteur/-euse m/f.

knitting /ˈnɪtɪŋ/ I n tricot m.
II noun modifier [*bag*] à tricot; [*machine, needle, wool*] à tricoter.

knitwear /ˈnɪtweə(r)/ n ⊄ tricots mpl.

knives /naɪvz/ pl ▶ **knife**.

knob /nɒb/ n **1** (of door, drawer) bouton m; (of cane) pommeau m; (on bannister, furniture) boule f; **2** (control button) bouton m; **3** (of butter etc) noix f.

knobbly /ˈnɒblɪ/, GB, **knobby** /ˈnɒbɪ/ US adj [*fingers*] noueux/-euse; [*knees*] saillant.

knock /nɒk/ I n **1** (blow) coup m (**on** sur; **with** de); **a ~ at the door** un coup à la porte; **I'll give you a ~ at 7.30** je frapperai à ta porte à 7 h 30; **2** onomat **~! ~!** toc! toc!; **3** FIG (setback) coup m; **to take a ~** en prendre un coup; **to take the ~s** encaisser⚬ (les coups).
II vtr **1** (strike) cogner [*object*]; **to ~ one's head on sth** se cogner la tête contre qch; **to ~ sb on the arm** donner un coup sur le bras de qn; **to ~ sth against** projeter qch contre qch; **to ~ sb unconscious** ou **silly**⚬ assommer qn; **to ~ a hole in sth** faire un trou dans qch; **2** (cause to move) **to ~ sth off** ou **out of sth** faire tomber qch de qch; **to ~ sb/sth over sth** envoyer qn/qch par-dessus qch; **to ~ a nail into sth** enfoncer un clou dans qch; **to ~ sb off his feet** [*blast, wave*] soulever qn; **to ~ sb flat** étendre qn par terre; **3** (criticize) critiquer [*method, achievement*]; dénigrer [*person*].
III vi **1** (make sound) [*branch, engine, object*] cogner (**on, against** contre); [*person*] frapper (**at, on** à); **2** (col-

lide) **to ~ into** ou **against sth** heurter qch; **to ~ into each other** se heurter.
IDIOMS **his knees were ~ing** ses genoux s'entrechoquaient de peur; **to ~ sth on the head**⚬ mettre fin à qch; **to be ~ing on a bit**⚬ commencer à se faire vieux.
■ **knock about**⚬, **knock around**⚬: ¶ **~ about** traîner; **to ~ about with sb** fréquenter qn; ¶ **~ about [sth]** [*object*] traîner dans [*house*].
■ **knock back**: ¶ **~ back [sth]**, **~ [sth] back 1** (return) [*player*] renvoyer [*ball*]; **2**⚬ (swallow) descendre⚬ [*drink*]; **3**⚬ (reject) rejeter [*offer*]; refuser [*invitation*]; ¶ **~ [sb] back** (surprise) [*news*] secouer [*person*].
■ **knock down**: **~ [sb/sth] down**, **~ down [sb/sth] 1** (cause to fall) (deliberately) [*aggressor*] jeter [qn] à terre [*victim, opponent*]; défoncer [*door*]; démolir [*building*]; (accidentally) renverser [*person, object*]; abattre [*fence*]; **2** (reduce) [*buyer*] faire baisser [*price*]; [*seller*] baisser [*price*]; **3** (allocate) [*auctioneer*] adjuger [*lot*].
■ **knock in**: **~ [sth] in**, **~ in [sth]** planter [*nail, peg*].
■ **knock off**: ¶ **~ off**⚬ [*worker*] arrêter de travailler; ¶ **~ [sb/sth] off**, **~ off [sb/sth] 1** (cause to fall) [*person, blow, force*] faire tomber [*person, object*]; **2**⚬ (reduce) **I'll ~ £10 off for you** je vous ferai une réduction de 10 livres; **3**⚬ (steal) subtiliser [*car, object*]; **4**⚬ (stop) **~ it off!** ça suffit!
■ **knock out**: ¶ **~ [sb/sth] out**, **~ out [sb/sth] 1** (dislodge) casser [*tooth*]; arracher [*nail, support*]; [*person, blow*] vider [*contents*]; **2** (make unconscious) [*person, blow*] assommer; [*drug*] endormir; [*boxer*] mettre [qn] au tapis [*opponent*]; **3** (destroy) faire sauter [*tank*]; mettre [qch] hors service [*factory*]; **4** SPORT (eliminate) éliminer [*opponent, team*]; **5** (straighten) redresser [*dent, metal*]; **6**⚬ (overwhelm) émerveiller [*person*]; ¶ **~ oneself out** s'assommer.
■ **knock over**: **~ [sb/sth] over**, **~ over [sb/sth]** renverser.
■ **knock together**: ¶ **~ together** [*knees, objects*] s'entrechoquer; ¶ **~ [sth] together**, **~ together [sth]**⚬ **1** (create) bricoler [*furniture*]; confectionner [*meal*]; **2** (bang together) cogner l'un contre l'autre.
■ **knock up**: ¶ **~ up** (in tennis) faire des balles (**with** avec); ¶ **~ [sth] up**, **~ up [sth] 1**⚬ (make) bricoler [*furniture*]; confectionner [*meal, outfit*]; **2**⚬ SPORT (competitor) totaliser [*points*]; réaliser [*score*]; ¶ **~ [sb] up**, **~ up [sb]** (awaken) réveiller [*person*].

knockabout /ˈnɒkəbaʊt/ I n **1** SPORT échange m de balles; **2** US NAUT dériveur m.
II adj [*comedy, comedian*] loufoque.

knockdown /ˈnɒkdaʊn/ adj [*price*] sacrifié.

knocker /ˈnɒkə(r)/ n heurtoir m.

knocking /ˈnɒkɪŋ/ n GEN coups mpl; (in engine) cognement m.

knocking-off time⚬ /ˌnɒkɪŋˈɒftaɪm/ n heure f de la sortie.

knock: **~-kneed** adj cagneux/-euse; **~-on effect** n implications fpl.

knock-out /ˈnɒkaʊt/ I n **1** (in boxing) knock-out m; **2**⚬ (show etc) réussite f.
II adj **1** SPORT [*competition*] avec tours éliminatoires; **2**⚬ (incapacitating) [*pills, injection*] sédatif/-ive.

knoll /nəʊl/ n butte f.

knot /nɒt/ I n **1** (tied part) nœud m; **to tie sth in a ~** nouer qch; **2** (tangle) nœud m; **to comb the ~s out of one's hair** se démêler les cheveux avec un peigne; **3** (in wood) nœud m; **4** (group) petit groupe m (of de); **5** (tense feeling) **to have a ~ in one's stomach** avoir l'estomac noué; **6** NAUT nœud m.
II vtr (p prés etc **-tt-**) nouer (**together** ensemble); **to ~ one's tie** faire un nœud à sa cravate.
IDIOMS **at a rate of ~s** à toute allure; **to get tied up in ~s** s'embrouiller; **to tie the ~** se marier.

knotty /ˈnɒtɪ/ adj [*wood*] noueux/-euse; [*problem*] épineux/-euse.

know /nəʊ/ I vtr (prét **knew** /njuː/; pp **known** /nəʊn/) **1** (have knowledge of) connaître [*person, place, name, opinion, result, value, rules, situation, system,* *way*]; savoir, connaître [*answer, language, reason, truth, words*]; **he ~s everything** il sait tout; **to ~ sb by name/sight** connaître qn de nom/vue; **to ~ sth by heart** savoir or connaître qch par cœur; **to ~ how to do** savoir faire; (stressing method) savoir comment faire; **to ~ that**... savoir que...; **to ~ for certain** ou **for sure that** savoir avec certitude que; **I wasn't to ~ that**... je ne pouvais pas savoir que...; **you ~ what children are** tu sais comment sont les enfants; **to ~ sb/sth as** connaître qn/qch sous le nom de; **Virginia known as Ginny to her friends** Virginia ou Ginny pour ses amis; **to let it be known** ou **to make it known that** faire savoir que; **to have known sb/sth to do** avoir déjà vu qn/qch faire; **it has been known to snow here** il est arrivé qu'il neige ici; **if I ~ him** tel que je le connais; **he is known to the police** il est connu de la police; **I ~ all about redundancy!** je sais ce que c'est que le chômage!; **as you well ~** comme tu le sais bien; **(do) you ~ something?**, **do you ~ what?** tu sais quoi?; **there's no ~ing whether** on ne peut pas savoir si; **to ~ one's way home** connaître le chemin pour rentrer chez soi; **to ~ one's way around a town** connaître une ville; **to ~ one's way around an engine** savoir se débrouiller avec les moteurs; **I ~ that for a fact** j'en suis absolument sûr; **I ~ what!** j'ai une idée!; **he ~s all about it** il est au courant; **2** (feel certain) être sûr; **I knew it!** j'en étais sûr!; **I don't ~ that I want to go really** je ne suis pas vraiment sûr d'avoir envie d'y aller; **3** (realize) se rendre compte; **you don't ~ how pleased I am** tu ne peux pas savoir comme je suis content; **don't I ~ it!** ne m'en parle pas!; **4** (recognize) reconnaître (**by** à; **from** de); **only their parents ~ one from the other** il n'y a que leurs parents qui sachent les distinguer; **she ~s a bargain when she sees one** elle sait repérer les bonnes affaires; **5** (acknowledge) **to be known for sth/for doing** être connu pour qch/pour faire; **6** (experience) connaître.

II *vi* (*prét* **knew**; *pp* **known**) **1** (have knowledge) savoir; **as you ~** comme vous le savez; **I wouldn't ~** je ne saurais dire; **to ~ about** (have information) être au courant de [*event*]; (have skill) s'y connaître en [*computing, engines*]; **to ~ of** (from experience) connaître; (from information) avoir entendu parler de; **not that I ~ of** pas que je sache; **to let sb ~ of** ou **about** tenir qn au courant de; **we'll let you ~** nous vous tiendrons au courant; **how should I ~**°! comment veux-tu que je sache!; **if you must ~** si tu veux tout savoir; **you ~ better than to argue with him** tu as mieux à faire que de te disputer avec lui; **you ought to have known better** tu n'aurais pas dû; **he says he came home early but I ~ better** il dit qu'il est rentré tôt mais je n'en crois rien; **they don't ~ any better** ils n'en savent pas plus; **2** (feel certain) **'he won't win'—'oh I don't ~'** 'il ne va pas gagner'—'oh je n'en suis pas si sûr'; **'I'll take the morning off'—'I don't ~ about that!'** 'je vais prendre ma matinée'—'c'est ce que vous croyez°!'; **I don't ~ about you but**... je ne sais pas ce que tu en penses, mais...

IDIOMS it takes one to ~ one qui se ressemble s'assemble; **not to ~ what to do with oneself** ne pas savoir quoi faire de son temps; **not to ~ where** ou **which way to turn** FIG ne pas savoir à quel saint se vouer; **not to ~ where to put oneself** ne pas savoir où se mettre; **not to ~ whether one is coming or going** ne plus savoir ce qu'on fait; **to be in the ~**° être bien informé; **to be in the ~ about sth**° être au courant de qch.

know: **~-all**° *n* GB je-sais-tout *mf inv*; **~-how**° *n* savoir-faire *m inv*.

knowing /ˈnəʊɪŋ/ *adj* [*look, smile*] entendu.

knowingly /ˈnəʊɪŋlɪ/ *adv* (intentionally) délibérément; (with understanding) d'un air entendu.

know-it-all° *n* US = **know-all**.

knowledge /ˈnɒlɪdʒ/ *n* **1** (awareness) connaissance *f*; **to bring sth to sb's ~** porter qch à la connaissance de qn; **to my ~** à ma connaissance; **with the full ~ of sb** au vu et au su de qn; **to have ~ of** avoir connaissance de; **he has no ~ of what happened** il ne sait pas ce qui s'est passé; **to my certain ~ he**... je sais de façon certaine qu'il...; **without sb's ~** à l'insu de qn; **2** (factual wisdom) GEN connaissances *fpl*; (of specific field) connaissance *f*; **technical ~** connaissances techniques; **~ of Monet's work** la connaissance des œuvres de Monet.

knowledgeable /ˈnɒlɪdʒəbl/ *adj* [*person*] savant; [*article*] bien documenté; **to be ~ about** s'y connaître en [*subject*].

knowledgeably /ˈnɒlɪdʒəblɪ/ *adv* en connaissance de cause.

known /nəʊn/ **I** *pp* ▶ **know**. **II** *adj* [*authority, danger*] reconnu; [*celebrity, cure*] connu; [*quantity*] défini.

knuckle /ˈnʌkl/ *n* **1** (of person) jointure *f*, articulation *f*; **to crack one's ~s** faire craquer ses doigts; **to rap sb on** ou **over the ~s** LIT, FIG taper sur les doigts de qn; **2** (on animal) jarret *m*; **3** CULIN (of lamb, mutton) manche *m* de gigot; (of pork, veal) jarret *m*.
■ **knuckle down**° (work seriously).
■ **knuckle under**° se soumettre, céder.

knuckle: **~bone** *n* articulation *f*, jointure *f*; **~-duster** *n* coup-de-poing *m* américain.

koala (bear) /kəʊˈɑːlə/ *n* koala *m*.

kohl /kəʊl/ *n* khôl *m*.

kookie°, **kooky**° /ˈkuːkɪ/ *adj* US dingue°.

Koran /kəˈrɑːn/ *n* Coran *m*.

Korea /kəˈrɪə/ **▶ 840** *pr n* Corée *f*.

Korean /kəˈrɪən/ **▶ 1100**, **1038** **I** *n* **1** (person) Coréen/-éenne *m/f*; **2** (language) coréen *m*. **II** *adj* coréen/-éenne; **the ~ War** la guerre de Corée.

korma /ˈkɔːmə/ *n*: sorte de curry à la crème et à la noix de coco.

kosher /ˈkəʊʃə(r)/ *adj* **1** RELIG casher; **2**° FIG (legitimate) **it's ~** c'est réglo°; **there's something not quite ~ about it** il y a quelque chose de pas très catholique° là-dedans.

kowtow /ˌkaʊˈtaʊ/ *vi* PEJ courber l'échine; **to ~ to sb** faire des courbettes à qn PEJ.

kph (*abrév écrite* = **kilometres per hour**) km/h.

KS US POST *abrév écrite* = **Kansas**.

Kt *n*: *abrév* = **knight**.

kudos° /ˈkjuːdɒs/ *n* prestige *m*.

kumquat /ˈkʌmkwɒt/ *n* kumquat *m*.

Kurdish /ˈkɜːdɪʃ/ **▶ 1038** **I** *n* (language) kurde *m*. **II** *adj* kurde.

Kurdistan /ˌkɜːdɪˈstæn/ *pr n* Kurdistan *m*.

Kuwaiti /kʊˈweɪtɪ/ **▶ 1100** **I** *n* Kuweitien/-ienne *m/f*. **II** *adj* kuweitien/-ienne.

kW (*abrév écrite* = **kilowatt**) kW.

kWh *n* (*abrév* = **kilowatt-hour**) kWh.

KY US POST *abrév écrite* = **Kentucky**.

LI

l, L /el/ n **1** (letter) l, L m; **2** L (abrév écrite = **litre(s)** GB, **liter(s)** US) l; **3** L GB AUT (abrév écrite = **Learner**) élève m conducteur accompagné; **4** L US RAIL **the L** le métro aérien; **5** L abrév écrite = **Lake**; **6** L abrév écrite = **left**; **7** l (abrév écrite = **line**) (in poetry) V; (in prose) l; **8** L (abrév écrite = **large**) L.

LA 1 US (abrév = **Los Angeles**) LA; **2** US POST abrév écrite = **Louisiana**.

lab /læb/ n labo° m.

Lab. GB POL abrév écrite = **Labour (Party)**.

lab coat n blouse f blanche.

label /'leɪbl/ **I** n **1** LIT (on clothing, jar) étiquette f; (on diagram) légende f; **2** FIG étiquette f; **3** MUS (also **record ~**) label m; **4** COMPUT label m; **5** LING (in grammar) étiquette f; (in dictionary) marqueur m.
II vtr (p prés etc -**ll**-, US -**l**-) **1** LIT (stick label on) étiqueter [clothing, jar]; mettre des légendes sur [diagram]; **2** FIG (pigeon-hole) classer, étiqueter PEJ [person, work] (**as** comme); **3** LING étiqueter.

labelling /'leɪblɪŋ/ n étiquetage m.

labor n US = **labour**.

laboratory /lə'bɒrətrɪ, US 'læbrətɔːrɪ/ n laboratoire m.

laboratory: **~ assistant** n laborantin/-e m/f; **~ technician** n technicien/-ienne m/f de laboratoire.

labor: **Labor Day** n US fête f du travail; **Labor Department** n US ministère m du travail.

laborious /lə'bɔːrɪəs/ adj laborieux/-ieuse.

labor union n US syndicat m.

labour GB, **labor** US /'leɪbə(r)/ **I** n **1** GEN (work) travail m, labeur m LITER; **to withdraw one's ~** se mettre en grève; **2** IND (workforce) GEN main-d'œuvre f; **3** MED accouchement m; **to go into** ou **begin ~** commencer à avoir des contractions.
II noun modifier IND [costs] de la main-d'œuvre; [dispute, relations] ouvriers-patronat inv; [market] du travail; [shortage] de main-d'œuvre; [leader] syndical.
III vi **1** (work, try hard) travailler (dur) (**at** à; **on** sur; **to do** pour faire); **2** (have difficulties) peiner (**to do** à faire); **to ~ up** monter avec peine or péniblement; **to be ~ing under the illusion** ou **misapprehension that** s'imaginer que.
IDIOMS **a ~ of love** une tâche demandant beaucoup de passion; **to ~ the point** insister lourdement.

Labour /'leɪbə(r)/ **I** pr n GB (+ v pl) le parti travailliste.
II adj GB [supporter, view, manifesto] du parti travailliste; [MP, vote] travailliste.

labour camp n camp m de travaux forcés, bagne m.

laboured GB, **labored** US /'leɪbəd/ adj **1** (difficult) [movement] pénible; [breathing] difficile; **2** (showing effort) [joke, humour, speech] lourd.

labourer GB, **laborer** US /'leɪbərə(r)/ ▶1251 n ouvrier/-ière m/f du bâtiment.

labour: **~ exchange**† n GB Bourse f du Travail; **~ force** n main-d'œuvre f.

labour-intensive adj IND **to be ~** nécessiter une main-d'œuvre importante.

labour: **~ law** n législation f or droit m du travail; **Labour Party** n GB parti m travailliste.

labour-saving adj [equipment, feature, system] qui facilite le travail; **~ device** appareil m ménager.

labour ward n (ward) salles fpl d'accouchement.

labrador /'læbrədɔː(r)/ n ZOOL labrador m.

laburnum /lə'bɜːnəm/ n cytise m, faux ébénier m.

labyrinth /'læbərɪnθ/ n MYTHOL, FIG labyrinthe m, dédale m.

lace /leɪs/ **I** n **1** ¢ (fabric) dentelle f; **2** ¢ (on shoe, boot, dress) lacet m; (on tent) cordon m.
II noun modifier [curtain, dress] en dentelle.
III vtr **1** (tie) lacer [shoes, corset]; attacher [tent flap]; **2** (add substance to) **to ~ a drink with sth** mettre qch dans une boisson.
■ **lace up**: **~** [sth] **up**, **~ up** [sth] lacer [shoes, corset]; attacher [tent flap].

lacerate /'læsəreɪt/ vtr lacérer.

laceration /,læsə'reɪʃn/ n GEN, MED lacération f.

lace-up (shoe) n chaussure f à lacet.

lack /læk/ **I** n manque m (**of** de); **for** ou **through ~ of** par manque de.
II vtr manque de [confidence, humour, funds].
III vi **to be ~ing** manquer (**in** de).

lackadaisical /,lækə'deɪzɪkl/ adj [person, attitude] nonchalant.

lackey /'lækɪ/ n laquais m ALSO FIG, PEJ.

lacklustre GB, **lackluster** US /'læklʌstə(r)/ adj [person, performance, style] terne.

laconic /lə'kɒnɪk/ adj laconique.

lacquer /'lækə(r)/ **I** n **1** (for hair) laque f; **2** (varnish) laque f; **3** ART (ware) laques mpl.
II vtr **1** laquer [surface]; **2** GB mettre de la laque sur [hair].

lactate I /læ'kteɪt/ n lactate m.
II /'læk'teɪt/ vi produire du lait.

lactation /læk'teɪʃn/ n lactation f.

lactic /'læktɪk/ adj lactique; **~ acid** acide m lactique.

lactose /'læktəʊs/ n lactose m.

lacy /'leɪsɪ/ adj en or de dentelle.

lad° /læd/ n **1** (boy) garçon m; **2** (in racing stables) lad m; (in riding stables) palefrenier m.

ladder /'lædə(r)/ **I** n **1** (for climbing) échelle f ALSO FIG; **to work one's way up the ~** FIG gravir les échelons; **2** GB (in stockings) échelle f, maille f filée.
II vtr filer [stocking].
III vi [stocking] filer.

ladderproof adj GB [stockings] indémaillable.

laddish° /'lædɪʃ/ adj PEJ macho° inv.

laden /'leɪdn/ adj [lorry, cart] en pleine charge; **~ with** LIT chargé de [supplies, fruit]; FIG LITTÉR accablé de [remorse, guilt].

ladle /'leɪdl/ **I** n **1** CULIN louche f; **2** IND cuillère f de coulée.
II vtr servir [qch] à la louche [soup, sauce].
■ **ladle out**: **~** [sth] **out**, **~ out** [sth] **1** LIT = **ladle II**; **2** FIG se répandre en [compliments]; prodiguer [money, advice].

lady /'leɪdɪ/ (pl **ladies**) **I** n **1** (woman) dame f; **ladies and gentlemen** mesdames et messieurs; **behave yourself, young ~!** (to child) sois sage, ma petite!; **a little old ~** une petite vieille; **she's a real ~** FIG elle est très distinguée; **the ~ of the house** la maîtresse de maison; **2** (aristocrat) aristocrate f; **3** ▶937 (in titles) **Lady Churchill** Lady Churchill.
II Ladies npl (on toilets) 'Dames'; **where's the Ladies?** où sont les toilettes?

lady: **~bird** n coccinelle f; **~-in-waiting** n dame f d'honneur; **~-killer°** n tombeur° m; **~like** adj [behaviour] distingué; **~ mayoress** ▶937 n GB titre officiel de la femme du lord-maire.

Ladyship /'leɪdɪʃɪp/ ▶937 *n* her/your ~ Madame (la baronne or la comtesse etc).

lady's maid *n* femme *f* de chambre.

lag /læg/ I *n* **1** (time period) (lapse) décalage *m*; (delay) retard *m*; **2**° (criminal) old ~ repris *m* de justice. II *vtr* (*p prés etc* **-gg-**) calorifuger [*pipe, tank*]; isoler [*roof*].
■ **lag behind**: ¶ ~ **behind** [*person, prices*] être à la traîne; ¶ ~ **behind** [**sb/sth**] traîner derrière [*person*]; FIG être en retard sur [*rival, product*].

lager /'lɑːgə(r)/ *n* bière *f* blonde.

lager lout *n* GB PÉJ voyou° *m* (*qui se soûle à la bière*).

lagging /'lægɪŋ/ *n* (material) isolant *m*.

lagoon /lə'guːn/ *n* lagune *f*.

lah, la /lɑː/ *n* MUS la *m*.

laid /leɪd/ *prét, pp* ▶ **lay**.

laidback° /,leɪd'bæk/ *adj* décontracté.

lain /leɪn/ *pp* ▶ **lie** III 2, 3, 4, 5.

lair /leə(r)/ *n* repaire *m* ALSO FIG.

laird /leəd/ *n* SCOT propriétaire *m* foncier, laird *m*.

lake /leɪk/ *n* lac *m*.
IDIOMS **go and jump in the ~**°! va te faire voir ailleurs°!

lakeside /'leɪksaɪd/ I *n* **by the ~** au bord du lac. II *noun modifier* [*café, scenery*] de bord de lac.

lama /'lɑːmə/ *n* lama *m*.

lamb /læm/ I *n* **1** (animal) agneau *m*; **leg of ~** gigot *m* d'agneau; **2** (term of endearment) ange *m*. II *noun modifier* CULIN [*chops, stew*] d'agneau. III *vi* [*ewe*] mettre bas; [*farmer*] aider les brebis à mettre bas.

lambast(e) /læm'beɪst/ *vtr* SOUT **1** (beat) rosser; **2** (censure) vilipender [*person, organization*].

lambskin /'læmskɪn/ I *n* peau *f* d'agneau. II *noun modifier* [*garment, rug*] en agneau.

lamb: **~'s tails** *npl* BOT chatons *mpl*; **~'s wool** *n* laine *f* d'agneau, lambswool *m*.

lame /leɪm/ *adj* LIT, FIG [*person, animal, excuse*] boiteux/-euse; **to be ~** LIT [*person, animal*] boiter.

lame duck I *n* canard *m* boiteux. II *noun modifier* US POL ~ **president/government** président/gouvernement vaincu aux élections.

lamely /'leɪmlɪ/ *adv* (say) sans conviction.

lament /lə'ment/ I *n* **1** (expression of grief) lamentation *f*, pleurs *mpl* (**for** pour); **2** LITERAT (song) complainte *f* (**for** pour); (poem) élégie *f* (**for** à). II *vtr* **1** (grieve over) pleurer [*wife, loss, death*]; se lamenter sur [*fate, misfortune*]; **2** (complain about) déplorer [*lack, weakness*]; **to ~ that** déplorer que (+ *subj*).

lamentable /'læməntəbl/ *adj* déplorable.

lamentably /'læməntəblɪ/ *adv* lamentablement.

lamentation /,læmən'teɪʃn/ *n* (expression of grief) lamentation *f*.

laminate I /'læmɪnət/ *n* (plastic) stratifié *m*; (metal) laminé *m*. II /'læmɪneɪt/ *vtr* laminer [*metal*].

laminated /'læmɪneɪtɪd/ *adj* [*plastic, surface*] stratifié; [*metal*] laminé; [*wood*] contreplaqué; [*glass*] feuilleté; [*card, cover*] plastifié.

lamp /læmp/ *n* lampe *f*.

lamp bracket *n* applique *f*.

lampoon /læm'puːn/ I *n* satire *f*. II *vtr* railler [*person, institution*].

lamppost /'læmppəʊst/ *n* réverbère *m*.
IDIOMS **between you, me and the ~** entre nous.

lampshade /'læmpʃeɪd/ *n* abat-jour *m*.

lance /lɑːns, US læns/ I *n* **1** (weapon) lance *f*; **2** MED lancette *f*. II *vtr* MED percer [*boil, abscess*].

lance corporal ▶1192 *n* GB soldat *m* de première classe.

lancet /'lɑːnsɪt, US 'læn-/ *n* MED lancette *f*.

land /lænd/ I *n* **1** (terrain, property) terrain *m*; (very large) terres *fpl*; **the lie** GB OU **lay** US **of the ~** LIT le relief du terrain; **to get the lie** GB OU **lay** US **of the ~** FIG savoir de quoi il retourne; **private/public ~** propriété *f* privée/publique; **2** AGRIC (farmland) terre *f*; **to work the ~** travailler la terre; **3** (countryside) campagne *f*; **4** (country) pays *m*; **5** (not sea) terre *f*; **to reach ~** toucher terre; **by ~** par voie de terre. II *noun modifier* [*clearance, drainage, prices*] du terrain; [*purchase, sale*] de terrain; [*deal, tax*] foncier/-ière; [*law*] agraire; [*battle, forces, animal*] terrestre. III *vtr* **1** AVIAT [*pilot*] poser [*aircraft*]; faire atterrir [*space capsule*]; **2** (in fishing) prendre [*fish*]; **3**° FIG (secure) décrocher° [*job, contract, prize*]; **4**° (leave with problem) **he ~ed me with washing the car** il m'a refilé° la voiture à laver; **to be ~ed with sb/sth** se retrouver avec qn/qch sur les bras; **now you've really ~ed her in it!** tu l'as vraiment fichue° dans de beaux draps!; **5**° (deliver) flanquer° [*blow, punch*]. IV *vi* **1** AVIAT [*aircraft, passenger*] atterrir; **as the plane came in to ~** alors que l'avion se préparait à atterrir; **2** NAUT [*passenger*] débarquer; [*ship*] accoster; **3** SPORT, GEN [*person, animal, object*] atterrir; [*ball*] toucher le sol; **most of the paint ~ed on me** presque toute la peinture m'est tombée dessus; **the punch ~ed on his chin** le coup de poing l'a touché au menton. V *v refl* **to ~ oneself in** se mettre dans [*situation*]; **to ~ oneself with**° se retrouver avec [*task, problem*].
IDIOMS **to find out how the ~ lies** savoir de quoi il retourne.
■ **land up**°: ¶ ~ **up** (end up) **to ~ up in the river** finir dans la rivière ; **to ~ up with the bill** se retrouver avec la facture; ¶ ~ **up doing** finir par faire.

land: **~ agent** ▶1251 *n* (on estate) régisseur *m*; (broker) expert *m* foncier; **~ army** *n* GB HIST corps de femmes employées aux travaux agricoles pendant la guerre.

landed /'lændɪd/ *adj* [*class*] de propriétaires terriens; [*property, estates*] foncier/-ière.

landfall /'lændfɔːl/ *n* NAUT (land reached or sighted) escale *f*; **to make ~** [*boat, person*] accoster; [*hurricane*] atteindre la terre.

land: **~fill site** *n* site *m* d'enfouissement des déchets; **~form** *n* relief *m* (du sol).

landing /'lændɪŋ/ *n* **1** (at turn of stairs) palier *m*; (storey) étage *m*; **2** (from boat) (of people) débarquement *m*; (of cargo) déchargement *m*; (from plane) (by parachute) parachutage *m*; (on runway) largage *m*; **3** AVIAT atterrissage *m* (**on** sur); **4** SPORT, GEN (of animal, athlete) réception *f*; (of parachutist, bird) atterrissage *m*.

landing: **~ beacon** *n* balise *f* d'atterrissage; **~ card** *n* AVIAT, NAUT carte *f* de débarquement; **~ craft** *n* péniche *f* de débarquement; **~ gear** *n* train *m* d'atterrissage; **~ lights** *npl* (on plane) phares *mpl* d'atterrissage; (on airfield) balises *fpl* d'atterrissage; **~**

Lakes

Normally, English Lake X *becomes* le lac X *in French (note the small* l *at* lac):

Lake Michigan	= le lac Michigan
Lake Victoria	= le lac Victoria

But when a lake shares its name with a town, English Lake X *becomes* le lac de X *in French*:

Lake Annecy	= le lac d'Annecy
Lake Constance	= le lac de Constance
Lake Como	= le lac de Côme

Sometimes English can drop the word Lake *but it is always safe to keep the word* lac *in French*:

Trasimeno	= le lac Trasimène
Balaton	= le lac Balaton

Loch *and* Lough *in names are normally not translated (note the use of the definite article and the small* l *in French)*:

Loch Ness	= le loch Ness
Lough Erne	= le lough Erne

Languages

Note that names of languages in French are always written with a small letter, not a capital as in English; also, French almost always uses the definite article with languages, while English does not. In the examples below the name of any language may be substituted for French *and* français:

French is easy = le français est facile
I like French = j'aime le français
to learn French = apprendre le français

However, the article is never used after en:

say it in French = dis-le en français
a book in French = un livre en français
to translate sth into French = traduire qch en français

and it may be omitted with parler:

to speak French = parler français *or* parler le français

When French *means in French or of the French, it is translated by* français:

a French expression = une expression française
the French language = la langue française
a French proverb = un proverbe français
a French word = un mot français

and when you want to make it clear you mean in French and not from France, use en français:

a French book = un livre en français
a French broadcast = une émission en français

When French *means relating to French or about French it is translated by* de français:

a French class = une classe de français
a French course = un cours de français
a French dictionary = un dictionnaire de français
a French teacher = un professeur de français

but

a French-English dictionary = un dictionnaire français-anglais

See the dictionary entry for -speaking *and* speaker *for expressions like* Japanese-speaking *or* German speaker. *French has special words for some of these expressions:*

English-speaking = anglophone
a French speaker = un/une francophone

Note also that language adjectives like French *can also refer to nationality e.g.* a French tourist, ▶ **1100**, *or to the country e.g.* a French town, ▶ **840**.

---

party *n* MIL commando *m* de débarquement; **~ stage** *n* débarcadère *m*.

land: **~lady** *n* (owner of property) propriétaire *f*; (living-in) logeuse *f*; (of pub) patronne *f*; **~locked** *adj* sans débouché sur la mer; **~lord** *n* (owner of property) propriétaire *m*; (living in) logeur *m*; (of pub) patron *m*; **~lubber** *n* HUM OU PÉJ marin *m* d'eau douce.

landmark /'lændmɑːk/ **I** *n* point *m* de repère; FIG étape *f* importante.
II *noun modifier* [*reform, speech, victory*] décisif/-ive.

land: **~mass** *n* masse *f* terrestre; **~ mine** *n* MIL mine *f* terrestre; **~owner** *n* propriétaire *mf* foncier/-ière; **~ reform** *n* réforme *f* agraire; **~ registry** *n* cadastre *m*.

landscape /'lænskeɪp/ **I** *n* paysage *m*.
II *noun modifier* [*gardening*] paysagiste; [*architecture, art, design*] paysager/-ère.
III *vtr* aménager [*grounds*].

landscape: **~ architect** ▶ **1251** *n* architecte *mf* paysagiste; **~ gardener** ▶ **1251** *n* jardinier/-ière *m*/ *f* paysagiste.

landscaping /'lænskeɪpɪŋ/ *n* aménagement *m*.

landslide /'lændslaɪd/ **I** *n* **1** LIT glissement *m* de terrain; **2** FIG POL victoire *f* écrasante.
II *noun modifier* POL [*victory, majority*] écrasant.

land: **~slip** *n* glissement *m* de terrain; **~ surveyor** ▶ **1251** *n* géomètre *m*; **~ yacht** *n* char *m* à voile.

lane /leɪn/ *n* **1** (narrow road) (in country) chemin *m*, petite route *f*; (in town) ruelle *f*; **2** (of road) voie *f*, file *f*; AVIAT, NAUT, SPORT couloir *m*; '**get in ~**' GB 'mettez-vous sur la bonne file'.

lane: **~ closure** *n* fermeture *f* de voie; **~ discipline** *n* respect *m* du marquage au sol; **~ markings** *n* marquage *m* au sol.

language /'læŋgwɪdʒ/ *n* **1** (system) langage *m*; (of a particular nation) langue *f*; GEN, COMPUT langage *m*; **formal/legal ~** langage formel/juridique; **spoken ~** langue parlée; **bad** ou **strong** ou **foul ~** langage grossier; **mind your ~**! sois poli!; **don't use that ~ with me!** ne me parle pas de cette façon!

language: **~ barrier** *n* obstacle *m* or barrière *f* de la langue; **~ laboratory**, **~ lab** *n* laboratoire *m* de langues.

languid /'læŋgwɪd/ *adj* languissant.

languidly /'læŋgwɪdlɪ/ *adv* avec langueur.

languish /'læŋgwɪʃ/ *vi* **1** (remain neglected) [*person*] languir; [*object*] traîner; **2** (lose strength) dépérir.

languor /'læŋgə(r)/ *n* langueur *f*.

lank /læŋk/ *adj* [*hair*] plat.

lanky /'læŋkɪ/ *adj* (grand et) maigre.

lanolin /'lænəlɪn/ *n* lanoline *f*.

lantern /'læntən/ *n* lanterne *f*.

lantern jawed *adj* aux joues creuses.

lanyard /'lænjəd/ *n* NAUT (rope) ride *f* de hauban.

Laos /'lɑːɒs, laʊs/ ▶ **840** *pr n* Laos *m*.

lap /læp/ **I** *n* **1** (area of body) genoux *mpl*; **in one's ~** sur les genoux; **2** SPORT (of track) tour *m* de piste; (of racecourse) tour *m* de circuit; **a ten-~ race** une course en dix tours; **to be on the last ~** LIT faire le dernier tour; FIG en être à la dernière étape; **3** (part of journey) étape *f*.
II *vtr* (*p prés etc* **-pp-**) **1** SPORT avoir un tour d'avance sur [*person*]; **2** (drink) laper [*water*].
III *vi* (*p prés etc* **-pp-**) (splash) [*water*] clapoter.
IDIOMS **in the ~ of the gods** entre les mains des dieux; **in the ~ of luxury** dans le plus grand luxe; **to drop a problem in sb's ~** se décharger d'un problème sur qn; **to fall into sb's ~** tomber tout cuit dans le bec de qn○.
■ **lap up**: **~ [sth] up**, **~ up [sth] 1** LIT laper [*milk, water*]; **2** FIG boire [qch] comme du petit lait [*compliment, flattery*].

lap: **~ and shoulder belt** *n* AUT, AVIAT ceinture *f* trois points; **~ belt** *n* AUT, AVIAT ceinture *f* ventrale.

lapdog *n* **1** LIT chien *m* de salon; **2** (person) PÉJ **he's her ~** elle le mène par le bout du nez.

lapel /lə'pel/ *n* revers *m*.

Lapland /'læplænd/ ▶ **840** *pr n* Laponie *f*.

lapping /'læpɪŋ/ *n* (sound) clapotis *m*.

lapse /læps/ **I** *n* **1** (slip) défaillance *f*; **a ~ of memory** un trou de mémoire; **a ~ in concentration** un relâchement de l'attention; **2** (moral error) écart *m* de conduite; **3** (interval) intervalle *m*, laps *m* de temps.
II *vi* **1** (drift) **to ~ into** se mettre à parler [*slang, jargon, German*]; tomber dans [*coma*]; **to ~ into bad habits** prendre de mauvaises habitudes; **2** (expire) [*right, patent, law*] tomber en désuétude; [*contract, policy, membership*] expirer; **3** (slip, slide) [*standard*] baisser; **to ~ from** manquer à [*virtue, principle*].
III *lapsed pp adj* [*patent, policy*] caduc/caduque; [*contract*] périmé; [*Catholic*] qui n'est plus pratiquant.

laptop /'læptɒp/ *n* (also **~ computer**) COMPUT portable *m*.

lapwing /'læpwɪŋ/ *n* vanneau *m*.

larceny /'lɑːsənɪ/ *n* vol *m*.

larch /lɑːtʃ/ *n* mélèze *m*.

lard /lɑːd/ **I** *n* saindoux *m*.
II *vtr* **1** CULIN larder [*meat*]; **2** FIG (embellish) **to ~ sth with** truffer qch de [*quotations, allusions*].

larder /'lɑːdə(r)/ *n* garde-manger *m inv*.

large /lɑːdʒ/ ▶ 1260 | I adj 1 (big) [area, car, feet, house] grand (before n); [appetite, piece, nose] gros/grosse (before n); 2 (substantial) [amount] important, gros/grosse (before n); [part] gros/grosse (before n); [number, quantity] grand (before n); [population] fort (before n), important; [crowd, family] nombreux/-euse (after n); 3 (fat) [person] gros/grosse (before n).
II **at large** adj phr 1 (free) [prisoner] en liberté; 2 (in general) [society, population] en général, dans son ensemble.
IDIOMS **by and ~** en général; **~r than life** exubérant; **as ~ as life** bien vivant.

large intestine n gros intestin m.

largely /ˈlɑːdʒlɪ/ adv [ignored, obsolete, responsible] en grande partie; **they are ~ children** pour la plupart ce sont des enfants.

largeness /ˈlɑːdʒnɪs/ n (of body, object) grandeur f; (of quantity, sum) importance f.

large-scale adj à grande échelle.

largish /ˈlɑːdʒɪʃ/ adj [amount, sum] assez important; [crowd, house, town] assez grand (before n).

lark /lɑːk/ n 1 ZOOL alouette f; 2° (fun) rigolade° f.
IDIOMS **to be up with the ~** se lever au chant du coq.
■ **lark about** GB faire l'idiot.

larkspur /ˈlɑːkspɜː(r)/ n pied m d'alouette, delphinium m.

larva /ˈlɑːvə/ n (pl **-vae**) larve f.

laryngitis /ˌlærɪnˈdʒaɪtɪs/ ▶ 1002 | n laryngite f.

larynx /ˈlærɪŋks/ n larynx m.

lasagne /ləˈzænjə/ n lasagnes fpl.

lascivious /ləˈsɪvɪəs/ adj lascif/-ive.

laser /ˈleɪzə(r)/ I n laser m.
II noun modifier [beam, disc] laser inv; [guided] par laser; [printer] à laser; [surgery, treatment] au laser.

lash /læʃ/ I n 1 ANAT (eyelash) cil m; 2 (whipstroke) coup m de fouet; 3 (whip) lanière f.
II vtr 1 LIT (whip) fouetter; [rain] cingler [windows]; [storm] balayer [region]; [waves] fouetter [shore]; 2 (criticize) **to ~ sb with one's tongue** faire des remarques cinglantes à qn; 3 (secure) attacher (**to** à).
■ **lash out 1** (hit out) [person] devenir violent, se démener; [cat] donner un coup de patte; **to ~ out at** [person] frapper; [tiger] donner un coup de patte à; **2** (verbally) **to ~ out at** ou **against sb/sth** invectiver qn/qch; 3 (spend freely) **to ~ out on sth** faire une folie et acheter qch.

lass /læs/ n GB DIAL jeune fille f.

lasso /læˈsuː/ I n (pl **-oes**) lasso m.
II vtr attraper [qch] au lasso.

last /lɑːst, US læst/ ▶ 1336 | I n 1 (for shoes) forme f; 2 (end of life) **to the ~** jusqu'au bout.
II pron (final) **the ~** le dernier/la dernière m/f (**to** à faire); **he poured out the ~ of the whisky** il a versé ce qui restait de whisky; **the ~ of the guests** les derniers invités; **that was the ~ I saw of her** c'est la dernière fois que je l'ai vue; **I thought we'd seen the ~ of him!** je croyais qu'on en avait fini avec lui!; **you haven't heard the ~ of this!** l'affaire n'en restera pas là!; **the ~ I heard...** aux dernières nouvelles...; **the ~ but one** l'avant-dernier/-ière; **the night before ~** (evening) avant-hier soir; (night) la nuit d'avant-hier; **the week before ~** il y a deux semaines.
III adj 1 (final) [hope, novel, time] dernier/-ière (before n); **the ~ person to do** la dernière personne à faire; **for the ~ time, will you be quiet!** c'est la dernière fois que je vous le dis, taisez-vous!; **your ~ name please?** votre nom de famille s'il vous plaît?; **in my ~ job** là où je travaillais avant; **every ~ one of them** tous jusqu'au dernier; **the ~ building but one** l'avant-dernier bâtiment; **his name is ~ but two on the list** son nom est le troisième à partir de la fin de la liste; **the ~ few children** les deux ou trois derniers enfants; 2 (describing past time) dernier/-ière; **~ week/year** la semaine/l'année dernière; **~ Christmas** à Noël l'an dernier; **in** ou **over the ~ ten years** durant ces dix dernières années; **Anne has**

been in Cambridge for the ~ eight months Anne est à Cambridge depuis huit mois; **~ night** (evening) hier soir; (night-time) la nuit dernière; **3** (most unlikely) dernier/-ière; **he's the ~ person I'd ask!** c'est la dernière personne à qui je m'adresserais!; **the ~ thing they want is publicity!** la publicité, c'est vraiment ce qu'ils souhaitent le moins!; **the ~ thing I need is guests for the weekend** il ne me manquait plus que des invités pour le week-end IRON.
IV adv 1 (in final position) **to come in ~** [runner, racing car] arriver en dernier; **to be placed ~** être classé dernier/-ière; **the girls left ~** les filles sont parties les dernières; **to leave sth till ~** s'occuper de qch en dernier (lieu); **~ of all** en dernier lieu; 2 (most recently) **she was ~ in Canada in 1976** la dernière fois qu'elle est allée au Canada, c'était en 1976.
V vtr **a loaf ~s me two days** un pain me fait deux jours; **we have enough food to ~ (us) three days** nous avons assez de provisions pour trois jours.
VI vi 1 (extend in time) durer; **it won't ~!** ça ne durera pas longtemps!; **it's too good to ~!** c'est trop beau pour que ça dure!; **he won't ~ long in this place** il ne tiendra pas longtemps ici; **that beer won't ~** cette bière n'a pas fait long feu°; 2 (maintain condition) [fabric] faire de l'usage; [perishables] se conserver.
■ **last out**: ¶ **~ out 1** (not run out) [money] suffire; [supplies] durer; 2 (persist) [person] tenir; ¶ **~ out** [sth] tenir jusqu'à la fin de [siege].

last-ditch adj [attempt, stand] désespéré, ultime.

lasting /ˈlɑːstɪŋ, US ˈlæstɪŋ/ adj [effect, impression, contribution] durable; [relationship] sérieux/-ieuse; [damage] irréparable.

lastly /ˈlɑːstlɪ, US ˈlæstlɪ/ adv enfin, finalement.

last: **~-minute** adj [arrival, rains, publication, implementation] de dernière minute; **~ post** n (each evening) retraite f au clairon; **~ rites** npl RELIG derniers sacrements mpl; **Last Supper** n Cène f.

latch /lætʃ/ n (fastening) loquet m; (spring lock) serrure f (de sûreté); **to put the door on the ~** bloquer le verrou en position ouverte.
■ **latch on**°: ¶ **~ on** (understand) saisir°; ¶ **~ on to** [sth/sb] 1 (seize on) LIT s'accrocher à [object, person]; (exploit) exploiter [idea]; reprendre [weakness]; 2 (realize) se rendre compte de [truth, fact].

latch: **~key** n clé f plate; **~key child**, **~key kid°** n GB enfant m/f laissé/-e à lui-/elle-même.

late /leɪt/ I adj 1 (after expected time) [arrival, rains, publication, implementation] tardif/-ive; **in case of ~ delivery** en cas de retard de livraison; **to have a ~ lunch** déjeuner plus tard que d'habitude; **to be ~ (for sth)** être en retard (pour qch); **to make sb ~** retarder qn; **to be ~ with the rent** payer son loyer avec du retard; **dinner will be a bit ~** le dîner sera retardé; **to be more than three days ~** avoir plus de trois jours de retard; 2 (towards end of day, season etc) [hour, supper, date, pregnancy] tardif/-ive; **to take a ~ holiday** GB ou **vacation** US prendre des vacances en fin de saison; **to have a ~ night** (aller) se coucher tard; **in ~r life** plus tard dans la vie; **to be in one's ~ fifties** approcher de la soixantaine; **to be a ~ starter** commencer tard; **at this ~ stage** à ce stade avancé; **in ~ January** (à la) fin janvier; **in the ~ 50's** à la fin des années 50; **~ Victorian** de la fin de l'époque victorienne; **it will be ~ afternoon when I arrive** j'arriverai en fin d'après-midi; **the ~st appointment is at 4 pm** le dernier rendez-vous est à 16 h; **in one of her ~r films** dans un de ses derniers films; **in a ~r novel** dans un roman postérieur; **her ~r experiments** ses expériences ultérieures; 3 (deceased) **the ~ President** feu le Président FML; **my ~ husband** mon pauvre mari.
II adv 1 (after expected time) [arrive, start, finish] en retard; **to be running ~** [person] être en retard; [train, bus] avoir du retard; **to start three months ~** commencer avec trois mois de retard; 2 (towards end of time period) [get up, open, close] tard; **~ last night/in the evening** tard hier soir/dans la soirée;

~ last week à la fin de la semaine dernière; **~r on** plus tard; **it's a bit ~ (in the day) to do** FIG c'est un peu tard pour faire; **too ~!** trop tard!; **don't leave it too ~!** n'attendez pas trop (longtemps)!; **to leave no ~r than 6 am** partir au plus tard à 6 h; **to marry ~** se marier sur le tard; **he left for Italy six months ~r** il est parti pour l'Italie six mois après; **see you ~r!** à tout à l'heure!; **3** ADMIN (formerly) **Miss Stewart, ~ of 48 Temple Rd** Mlle Stewart, autrefois domiciliée au 48 Temple Rd.

III of late adv phr dernièrement, ces jours-ci.

latecomer /ˈleɪtkʌmə(r)/ n (to event) retardataire mf.

late developer n **to be a ~** [child] être lent; [adult] HUM être un peu en retard.

lately /ˈleɪtlɪ/ adv ces derniers temps.

lateness /ˈleɪtnɪs/ n (of person, train etc) retard m.

late-night adj [film] dernier/-ière (before n); [session] en nocturne; **it's ~ shopping on Thursdays** les magasins restent ouverts tard le jeudi.

latent /ˈleɪtnt/ adj latent.

lateral /ˈlætərəl/ adj latéral.

late riser n lève-tard mf inv.

latest /ˈleɪtɪst/ **I** superlative adj ▶ **late**.
II adj (most recent) dernier/-ière.
III pron **1** (news etc) **have you heard the ~?** est-ce que tu connais la dernière°?; **what's the ~ on her condition?** quoi de neuf sur son état de santé?; **2** (most recent) **the ~ in modern technology** la technologie moderne.
IV at the latest adv phr au plus tard.

latex /ˈleɪteks/ n latex m.

lath /lɑːθ, US læθ/ n latte f.

lathe /leɪð/ n tour m.

lather /ˈlɑːðə(r), ˈlæðə(r), US ˈlæð-/ n **1** (of soap) mousse f; **2** (frothy sweat) écume f; **he was in a real ~°** FIG il était dans tous ses états°.

Latin /ˈlætɪn, US ˈlætn/ ▶ **1038** **I** n **1** (language) latin m; **2** (hispanic) Latin/-e m/f.
II adj latin.

Latin America pr n GEOG Amérique f latine.

Latin American I n Latino-Américain/-e m/f.
II adj latino-américain.

Latino /læˈtiːnəʊ/ n US Latino-Américain/-e m/f.

latitude /ˈlætɪtjuːd, US -tuːd/ n GEOG, GEN latitude f.

latrine /ləˈtriːn/ n latrines fpl.

latter /ˈlætə(r)/ **I** n **the ~** ce dernier/cette dernière m/f.
II adj (of several) dernier/-ière; (of two) deuxième; **the former or the ~ explanation** la première ou la deuxième explication; **in the ~ part of the evening** vers la fin de la soirée.

latterday /ˌlætəˈdeɪ/ adj [crusader, pilgrim] des temps modernes; [invention, technique] d'aujourd'hui.

latterly /ˈlætəlɪ/ adv **1** (recently) dernièrement; **2** (in later times) (pendant) les dernières années.

lattice /ˈlætɪs/ n (screen) treillis m; (fence, plant support) treillage m.

lattice: ~ window n fenêtre f à croisillons de plomb; **~ work** n treillis m.

Latvia /ˈlætvɪə/ ▶ **840** pr n Lettonie f.

laudable /ˈlɔːdəbl/ adj louable.

laudatory /ˈlɔːdətərɪ, US -tɔːrɪ/ adj élogieux/-ieuse.

laugh /lɑːf, US læf/ **I** n **1** (amused noise) rire m; **she gave a loud ~** elle a ri bruyamment; **with a ~** en riant; **to like a good ~** aimer bien rire; **to get** ou **raise a ~** faire rire; **2°** (source of amusement) **to do sth for a ~** faire qch pour rigoler°; **their brother is a real ~** leur frère est très drôle ou marrant°; **let's go to the party, it will be a ~°** allons à la fête, on va bien s'amuser; **the script isn't exactly full of ~s** le scénario n'est pas ce qu'on peut appeler hilarant.
II vi rire (**about, over** de); **to make sb ~** faire rire qn; **to ~ out loud** rire aux éclats, rire tout haut; **to ~ to oneself** rire en soi-même, rire tout bas; **to ~ at sb/sth** rire de qn/qch; **the children ~ed at the clown** le clown a fait rire les enfants; **we're ~ing**

with you not at you on ne rit pas méchamment; **he ~ed nervously** il a eu un rire nerveux; **I don't know whether to ~ or cry!** je ne sais pas si je dois rire ou bien pleurer!; **he's afraid of being ~ed at** il a peur qu'on se moque de lui; **he doesn't have much to ~ at** ou **about these days** ce n'est pas drôle pour lui en ce moment.

IDIOMS **we're ~ing°** (in good position) on n'a plus à s'en faire; **he who ~s last ~s longest** PROV rira bien qui rira le dernier, PROV; **~ and the world ~s with you** celui qui rit s'entoure d'amis; **you'll be ~ing on the other side of your face** tu riras jaune, ça va t'ôter l'envie de rire; **to be ~ing all the way to the bank** remplir ses poches; **to have the last ~ over sb** l'emporter finalement sur qn; **she had the last ~ finalement** c'est elle qui a bien ri; **to ~ in sb's face** rire au nez de qn; **to ~ oneself sick** ou **silly** se tordre de rire.

■ **laugh off: ~** [sth] **off, ~ off** [sth] écarter [qch] par une plaisanterie [rumour, accusation]; choisir de rire de [criticism, insult]; **she ~ed the matter off** elle a tourné la chose en plaisanterie.

laughable /ˈlɑːfəbl, US ˈlæf-/ adj ridicule.

laughing /ˈlɑːfɪŋ, US ˈlæfɪŋ/ adj [person] qui rit; [eyes, face, expression] rieur/rieuse; **it's no ~ matter** il n'y a pas de quoi rire.

laughing gas n gaz m hilarant.

laughingly /ˈlɑːfɪŋlɪ, US ˈlæf-/ adv [say, explain] en riant; **it is ~ called a hotel** cela porte pompeusement le nom d'hôtel.

laughing stock n risée f.

laughter /ˈlɑːftə(r), US ˈlæf-/ n ₵ rires mpl; **to roar ou howl with ~** hurler de rire; **a fit of ~** un fou rire.

laughter line GB, **laugh line** US n ~ ride f d'expression.

launch /lɔːntʃ/ **I** n **1** NAUT (also **motor ~**) (for patrolling) vedette f; (for pleasure) bateau m de plaisance; **2** (setting in motion) (of new boat, rocket) lancement m; (of lifeboat) mise f à l'eau; (of campaign, product) lancement m.
II vtr mettre [qch] à l'eau [dinghy, lifeboat]; lancer [new ship, missile, rocket] (**against,** at sur); **air-/sea-~ed** lancé du ciel/depuis la mer; (start) lancer [attack, campaign, career, company, product]; ouvrir [investigation]; mettre [qch] en action [plan].
III vi **to ~ (forth) into** se lancer dans [description, story]; attaquer [chorus, song]; **to ~ oneself at sb/ sth** se lancer sur qn/qch.

launcher /ˈlɔːntʃə(r)/ n lanceur m.

launch: ~ pad, ~ing pad n (for rocket) aire f de lancement; FIG tremplin m (**for** pour); **~ party** n réception f (pour le lancement d'un produit); **~ vehicle** n lanceur m.

launder /ˈlɔːndə(r)/ vtr LIT laver [clothes, linen]; FIG blanchir [money, profits].

launderette /ˌlɔːnˈdret, ˌlɔːnˈdəˈret/ GB, **laundromat** /ˈlɔːndrəmæt/ US n laverie f automatique.

laundering /ˈlɔːndərɪŋ/ n LIT, FIG blanchissage m.

laundrette n GB = **launderette**.

laundromat n US = **launderette**.

laundry /ˈlɔːndrɪ/ n **1** (place) (commercial) blanchisserie f; (in hotel, house) laverie f; **2** (linen) linge m; **to do the ~** faire la lessive; **~ basket** panier m à linge.

laureate /ˈlɒrɪət, US ˈlɔː-/ n, adj lauréat/-e (m/f).

laurel /ˈlɒrəl, US ˈlɔːrəl/ n LIT, FIG laurier m.
IDIOMS **to look to one's ~s** veiller à la concurrence; **to rest on one's ~s** se reposer ou s'endormir sur ses lauriers.

lav° /læv/ n GB (abrév = **lavatory**) toilettes fpl.

lava /ˈlɑːvə/ n lave f.

lavatorial /ˌlævəˈtɔːrɪəl/ adj [humour] scatologique.

lavatory /ˈlævətrɪ, US -tɔːrɪ/ n toilettes fpl.

lavatory: ~ attendant ▶ **1251** n employé/-e m/f à l'entretien des toilettes; **~ paper** n papier m hygiénique.

lavender /ˈlævəndə(r)/ ▶ **818** n, adj lavande (f).

lavender blue ▶ **818** n, adj bleu (m) lavande inv.

lavish /'lævɪʃ/ **I** adj [party, home, lifestyle] somptueux/ -euse; **to be ~ with sth** être généreux avec qch. **II** vtr prodiguer [money, affection] (**on** à); **to ~ praise on sth/sb** se répandre en louanges sur qch/qn.

lavishly /'lævɪʃlɪ/ adv [decorated, furnished] luxueusement; [spend] sans compter; [entertain] généreusement.

law /lɔː/ n **1** ¢ (body of rules) loi f; **to be against the ~** être contraire à la loi FML, être interdit; **the ~ of the land** la législation du pays; **under Italian ~** d'après la loi italienne; **by ~** conformément à la loi; **it's required by ~** c'est obligatoire légalement; **the bill became ~ yesterday** le projet de loi a été adopté hier; **court of ~** cour f de justice; **to take the ~ into one's own hands** faire justice soi-même; **2** JUR (rule) loi f; **a ~ against sth** une loi interdisant qch; **the ~s on sth** les lois sur qch; **there ought to be a ~ against it** ça devrait être interdit; **3** (scientific principle) loi f; **4**⁰ (police) police f; **5** (academic subject) droit m; **to study ~** faire son droit. IDIOMS **to be a ~ unto oneself** être un peu original; **to lay down the ~** dicter or imposer sa loi.

law: **~-abiding** adj respectueux/-euse des lois; **~ and order** n ordre m public; **~breaker** n personne f qui enfreint la loi; **~-breaking** n violation(s) f(pl) de la loi; **~ court** n tribunal m; **~ enforcement agency** n US organisme m responsable du maintien de l'ordre; **~ enforcement officer** n US personne f responsable du maintien de l'ordre; **~ faculty** n faculté f de droit.

lawful /'lɔːfl/ adj [custody, owner, strike, excuse] légal; [conduct] licite; [wife, husband] légitime.

lawfully /'lɔːfəlɪ/ adv légalement.

lawfulness /'lɔːflnɪs/ n légalité f.

lawgiver /'lɔːgɪvə(r)/ n législateur/-trice m/f.

lawless /'lɔːlɪs/ adj [period, society] anarchique; [area, town] tombé dans l'anarchie.

lawlessness /'lɔːlɪsnɪs/ n anarchie f.

law: **Law Lord** n GB juge m (siégeant à la Chambre des Lords); **~man** n US policier m.

lawn /lɔːn/ n pelouse f.

lawn: **~mower** n tondeuse f (à gazon); **~ tennis** ▶ 949 | n GEN tennis m; (on grass) tennis m sur gazon.

law: **~ school** n faculté f de droit; **~suit** n procès m.

lawyer /'lɔːjə(r)/ ▶ 1251 | n (who practises law) avocat/-e m/f; (expert in law) juriste m/f.

lax /læks/ adj [government] laxiste; [security] relâché.

laxative /'læksətɪv/ **I** n laxatif m. **II** adj laxatif/-ive.

laxity /'læksətɪ/, **laxness** /'læksnɪs/ n laxisme m.

lay /leɪ/ **I** prét ▶ **lie** III 2, 3, 4, 5. **II** adj **1** GEN [helper, worker] non initié; **~ person** profane mf; **2** RELIG [preacher, member, reader] laïque; [brother, sister] lai. **III** vtr (prét, pp **laid**) **1** LIT (place) poser [object, card] (**in** dans; **on** sur); (spread out) étaler [rug, covering, newspaper] (**on** sur); (arrange) disposer (**on** sur); déposer [wreath]; **he laid his hand on my forehead** il a posé sa main sur mon front; **she laid the baby in the cot** elle a couché le bébé dans le berceau; **to ~ hands on sth** FIG (find) mettre la main sur qch; **to ~ hands on sb** RELIG imposer les mains à qn; **2** (set for meal) **to ~ the table** (**for**) mettre la table (pour); **to ~ an extra place** ajouter un couvert; **3** (prepare) préparer [plan, trail]; poser [basis, foundation]; tendre [trap]; **4** (fix in place) poser [carpet, tiles, paving, turf, cable, mine]; construire [railway, road, sewer]; **5** ZOOL pondre [egg]; **6** FIG (attribute) porter [charge, accusation]; déposer [complaint]; jeter [curse, spell] (**on** à); **to ~ stress** ou **emphasis on sth** mettre l'accent sur qch; **7** (bet) vtr **to ~ a bet** ou **money on sth** parier sur qch. **IV** vi (prét, pp **laid**) [bird] pondre. IDIOMS **to ~ it on the line** ne pas mâcher ses mots; **to ~ a finger** ou **hand on sb** (beat) lever la main sur qn; **to ~ it on a bit thick** forcer un peu la dose⁰.
■ **lay about**: **~ about** [sb] rouer [qn] de coups.
■ **lay aside**: **~ aside** [sth], **~** [sth] **aside** (for

another activity) poser [book, sewing, toy]; (after one stage in process) mettre [qch] de côté [part-finished dish, model]; abandonner [studies, cares]; renoncer à [responsibility, principle, doubt].
■ **lay before**: **~** [sth] **before sb** soumettre [qch] à qn [law, bill]; exposer [qch] à qn [case, facts].
■ **lay by**: **~ by** [sth], **~** [sth] **by** mettre [qch] de côté.
■ **lay down**: **~ down** [sth], **~** [sth] **down 1** LIT coucher [object, baby, patient]; étaler [rug, garment, cards]; poser [book, implement, suitcase]; déposer [weapon, arms]; **2** FIG **to ~ down one's life for sb/ sth** sacrifier sa vie pour qn/qch; **3** (establish) établir [rule, procedure, plan]; poser [condition]; **it is laid down that...** il est stipulé que...
■ **lay in**: **~ in** [sth] faire provision de.
■ **lay into**: **~ into** [sb] **1** LIT bourrer [qn] de coups; **2**⁰ FIG (abuse) **she laid into me** elle m'est tombée dessus⁰.
■ **lay off**: ¶ (stop) ⁰ arrêter; ¶ **~ off** [sb], **lay** [sb] **off** (sack) (temporarily) mettre [qn] en chômage technique; (permanently) licencier; ¶ **~ off** [sb] (leave alone)⁰ laisser [qn] tranquille.
■ **lay on**: **~ on** [sth], **~** [sth] **on 1** (apply) appliquer [paint, plaster]; **2** GB (install) installer [gas, electricity]; **3** (supply) prévoir [meal, transport]; organiser [entertainment, excursion].
■ **lay open**: **~** [sth] **open** exposer (**to** à); **to ~ oneself open to sth** s'exposer à qch.
■ **lay out**: ¶ **~** [sth] **out**, **~** [sth] **out 1** LIT (spread out) disposer [goods, food]; (unfold) étaler [map, garment, fabric]; **2** (design) concevoir [building, book, advertisement]; mettre [qch] en page [letter, illustrations]; monter [page]; dessiner [town, garden]; **3** (explain) exposer [reasons, demands, facts]; **4**⁰ (spend) débourser [sum]; ¶ **~ out** [sb], **~** [sb] **out 1** (prepare for burial) faire la toilette mortuaire de [person]; **2**⁰ (knock unconscious) mettre [qn] KO⁰.
■ **lay up**: ¶ **~ up** [sth], **~** [sth] **up** (store away) LIT faire provision de [food, supplies]; FIG s'attirer [trouble]; ¶ **~** [sb] **up** (confine to bed) **to be laid up** être alité.

lay: **~about**⁰ n PÉJ fainéant/-e⁰ m/f; **~-by** n GB aire f de repos.

layer /'leɪə(r)/ **I** n couche f; **~ of clothing** épaisseur f de vêtements. **II** vtr **1** (in hairdressing) couper [qch] en dégradé; **2** (arrange in layers) disposer [qch] en couches.

laying /'leɪɪŋ/ n (of floor, stone, cable, mines) pose f; (of railway) construction f; (of egg) ponte f.

layman /'leɪmən/ n GEN profane m; RELIG laïc m.

lay-off /'leɪɒf/ n (permanent) licenciement m; (temporary) mise f en chômage technique.

layout /'leɪaʊt/ n (of page, book, computer screen) mise f en page; (of advertisement, article) présentation f; (of building) agencement m; (of rooms, cards) disposition f; (of town, estate, engine) plan m; (of garden, park) dessin m.

layout artist ▶ 1251 | n maquettiste m/f.

laze /leɪz/ vi (also **about**, **~ around**) paresser; **to ~ in bed** traîner⁰ au lit.

lazily /'leɪzɪlɪ/ adv [move, wonder etc] nonchalamment; (relaxedly) [lie, float] mollement; [flow, bob] doucement.

laziness /'leɪzɪnɪs/ n paresse f.

lazy /'leɪzɪ/ adj [person] paresseux/-euse; [smile] nonchalant; [yawn] indolent; [day, holiday] paisible; [movement, pace] lent.

lazy: **~bones** n paresseux/-euse m/f; **~ eye** n amblyopie f; **~ Susan** n plateau m tournant.

lb abrév écrite = **pound**.

LCD n (abrév = **liquid crystal display**) affichage m à cristaux liquides, LCD SPEC.

LDS n (abrév = **Licentiate of Dental Surgery**) diplômé en chirurgie dentaire.

LEA n (abrév = **Local Education Authority**) GB administration locale qui gère les affaires scolaires.

lead[1] /liːd/ **I** n **1** (winning position) **to be in the ~**, **to have the ~** être en tête; **to go into the ~**, **to take the ~** passer en tête; **2** (amount by which one is winning) avance *f* (**over** sur); **to have a ~ of three points** avoir trois points d'avance; **to increase one's ~** creuser l'écart (**by** de); **3** (initiative) **to take the ~** prendre l'initiative; **to take the ~ in doing** être le premier/la première à faire; **to follow sb's ~** suivre l'exemple de qn; **4** (clue) piste *f*; **5** THEAT, CIN (rôle) rôle *m* principal; **6** (in newspaper) **to be the ~** être à la une°; **7** ELEC (wire) fil *m*; **8** GB (for dog) laisse *f*.

II *noun modifier* [*guitarist, guitar*] premier/-ière (*before n*); [*role, singer*] principal.

III *vtr* (*prét, pp* **led**) **1** (guide, escort) mener, conduire [*person*] (**to sth** à qch; **to sb** auprès de qn; **out of** hors de; **through** à travers); **to ~ sb away** éloigner qn (**from** de); **to ~ sb across the road** faire traverser la rue à qn; **2** (bring) [*path, sign, smell*] mener [*person*] (**to** à); **to ~ sb to do** amener qn à faire; **he led me to expect that…** d'après ce qu'il m'avait dit je m'attendais à ce que (+ *subj*); **everything ~s me to conclude that** tout me porte à conclure que; **to be easily led** être très influençable; **this ~s me to my main point** ceci m'amène à mon sujet principal; **3** (be leader of) mener [*army, team, attack, strike, procession*]; diriger [*orchestra, research*]; **to ~ a congregation in prayer** entonner les prières; **4** SPORT, COMM (be ahead of) avoir une avance sur [*rival, team*]; **to ~ the world** être au premier rang mondial; **to ~ the field** (in commerce, research) être le plus avancé; (in race) mener, être en tête; **to ~ the market** être le leader du marché; **5** (conduct, have) mener [*active life*]; **to ~ a life of luxury** vivre dans le luxe.

IV *vi* (*prét, pp* **led**) **1** (go, be directed) **to ~ to** [*path*] mener à; [*door*] s'ouvrir sur; [*exit, trapdoor*] donner accès à; **2** (result in) **to ~ to** entraîner [*complication, discovery, accident, response*]; **it was bound to ~ to trouble** ça devait mal finir; **one thing led to another, and we…** de fil en aiguille, nous…; **3** (be ahead) [*runner, car, company*] être en tête; [*team, side*] mener; **to ~ by 15 seconds** avoir 15 secondes d'avance; **4** (go first) (in walk, procession) aller devant; (in action, discussion) prendre l'initiative; **5** (in dancing) conduire; **6** (in newspaper) **to ~ with** mettre [qch] à la une° [*story, headline*]; **7** (in boxing) **to ~ with one's left/right** attaquer de gauche/de droite.

IDIOMS **to ~ the way** (go first) passer devant; (guide others) montrer le chemin; (be ahead, winning) être en tête; **to ~ the way in space research** être le numéro un dans le domaine de la recherche spatiale.

■ **lead on**: **~ [sb] on 1** (give false hope) mener [qn] en bateau° [*client, investor*]; **2** (sexually) provoquer.

■ **lead up to**: **~ up to [sth] 1** (precede) précéder; **2** (culminate in) se terminer par [*argument, outburst*]; **3** (introduce) amener [*topic*].

lead² /led/ *n* **1** (metal) plomb *m*; **red ~** minium *m*; **2**° FIG (bullets) pruneaux° *mpl*; **3** (also **black ~**) (graphite) mine *f* de plomb; (in pencil) mine *f*; **4** (of window) (baguette *f* de) plomb *m*; **~s** (of windows) plombure *f* ⊄; **5** GB (for roofing) couverture *f* de plomb ⊄.

IDIOMS **to fill ou pump sb full of ~**° cribler qn de balles°; **to get the ~ out** US (stop loafing) se bouger; (speed up) se grouiller°; **to go over** US ou **down** GB **like a ~ balloon**° tomber à plat°.

lead /led/: **~ed petrol** GB, **~ed gasoline** US *n* essence *f* au plomb; **~ed window** *n* fenêtre *f* à petits carreaux.

leaden /'ledn/ *adj* **1** (made of lead) de plomb, en plomb; **2** (lead coloured) [*sky, clouds*] de plomb; [*complexion*] grisâtre; **3** FIG [*silence*] de mort; [*atmosphere*] écrasant; [*footsteps, pace*] lourd; [*performance*] raide.

leader /'li:də(r)/ *n* **1** (chief) (of nation) chef *m* d'État, dirigeant/-e *m/f*; (of gang, group, team) chef *m*; (of council, club, association) président/-e *m/f*; (of party, opposition) leader *m*; (of trade union) secrétaire *mf*; (of army, troops) commandant/-e *m/f*; (of expedition) responsable *mf*; (of strike, movement) meneur/-euse *m/f*; (of project, operation) directeur/-trice *m/f*; **2** (one in front) (in race or competition) premier/-ière *m/f*; (of procession, line of walkers) chef *m* de file; (horse) cheval *m* de tête; (in market, field) leader *m*; **3** (in newspaper) éditorial *m*.

leadership /'li:dəʃɪp/ *n* **1** (of party, union etc) dirigeants

mpl, direction *f*; **during her ~** pendant son mandat; **under the ~ of** sous la direction de; **2** (quality) qualités *fpl* de leader.

leadership contest, **leadership election** *n* POL élection *f* à la direction du parti.

lead-free *adj* sans plomb.

lead-in *n* préambule *m*.

leading /'li:dɪŋ/ *adj* **1** (top) [*lawyer, politician etc*] éminent, important; [*company, bank*] important; [*brand*] dominant; [*position*] de premier plan; **2** (main) [*role*] THEAT principal; GEN majeur; **3** SPORT (in race) [*driver, car*] en tête de course; (in league) [*club, team*] en tête du classement; **4** (at the front) [*aircraft, car*] de tête.

leading article *n* éditorial *m*.

leading edge I *n* **1** AVIAT bord *m* d'attaque; **2** FIG **at the ~ of** à la pointe de [*technology*]. **II leading-edge** *noun modifier* [*technology*] de pointe.

leading: **~ lady** *n* THEAT, CIN actrice *f* principale; **~ light** *n* membre *m* très actif (**in** de); **~ man** *n* acteur *m* principal; **~ question** *n* question *f* qui suggère la réponse.

lead /led/: **~ pencil** *n* crayon *m* à papier; **~ shot** *n* grenaille *f* de plomb.

lead story /li:d/ *n* histoire *f* à la une°.

leaf /li:f/ *n* (*pl* **leaves**) **1** (of plant) feuille *f*; **to come into ~** se couvrir de feuilles; **2** (of paper) feuille *f*; (of book) page *f*; **3** (of gold, silver) feuille *f*; **4** (of table) (sliding, removable) rallonge *f*; (hinged) abattant *m*.

IDIOMS **to shake like a ~** trembler comme une feuille; **to take a ~ out of sb's book** s'inspirer de qn; **to turn over a new ~** tourner la page.

■ **leaf through**: **~ through [sth]** feuilleter [*pages, papers, book*].

leaflet /'li:flɪt/ **I** *n* GEN dépliant *m*; (advertising) prospectus *m*; (polemic) tract *m*; **information ~** notice *f* explicative. **II** *vtr* **to ~ a town/an area** couvrir une ville/un quartier de prospectus ou de tracts.

leaf vegetable *n* légume *m* dont on consomme la feuille.

leafy /'li:fɪ/ *adj* [*tree, wood*] touffu; [*suburb, area*] vert.

league /li:g/ *n* **1** (alliance) GEN, POL ligue *f*; **to be in ~ with** être allié avec; **2** GB SPORT (competition) championnat *m*; (association of clubs) ligue *f*; **3** FIG (class) niveau *m*; **they're not in the same ~** ils ne sont pas comparables; **to be in the big ~** être dans le peloton de tête.

IDIOMS **to be ~s ahead of sth/sb** être bien meilleur que qch/qn.

league table *n* GB classement *m*.

leak /li:k/ **I** *n* **1** (crack) (in container, roof) fuite *f*; (in ship) voie *f* d'eau; **to spring a ~** [*pipe, tank*] se mettre à fuir; **2** (escape) fuite *f*; **3** JOURN (disclosure) fuite *f* (**about** au sujet de). **II** *vtr* **1** (disclose) divulguer [*information, document*]; **2** (expel) répandre [*oil, effluent*]; dégager [*fumes*]. **III** *vi* **1** (have crack) [*container, pipe, roof*] fuir; [*boat*] faire eau; **2** (seep) [*liquid, gas*] échapper (**from, out of** de); **to ~ into** se répandre dans [*sea, soil*].

IDIOMS **to take a ~**° aller se soulager°.

■ **leak out** [*information, news, secret*] être divulgué; [*water, gas*] se répandre.

leakage /'li:kɪdʒ/ *n* **1** (leaking) fuite *f*; **2** (of information, secrets) fuite *f*; **3** COMM (natural loss) perte *f*.

leaky /'li:kɪ/ *adj* [*container, pipe*] qui fuit; [*boat*] qui prend l'eau.

lean /li:n/ **I** *adj* [*person, body, face*] mince; [*meat*] maigre; FIG (difficult) [*year, times*] difficile. **II** *vtr* (*prét, pp* **leaned** ou **leant**) appuyer (**against** contre); **to ~ one's head out of the window** se pencher par la fenêtre; **to ~ one's elbows on sth** s'accouder à qch. **III** *vi* (*prét, pp* **leaned** ou **leant**) [*wall, building*] pencher; [*bicycle, ladder*] être appuyé contre qch; **to ~ against sth** [*person*] s'appuyer contre qch.

IDIOMS **to have a ~ time of it** manger de la vache enragée○.

■ **lean across**: ¶ **~ across** [*person*] se pencher; ¶ **~ across** [*sth*] se pencher par-dessus [*desk* , *table*].

■ **lean back** se pencher en arrière.

■ **lean forward** se pencher en avant.

■ **lean on**: ¶ **~ on** [*sth/sb*] LIT s'appuyer sur [*stick, person*]; s'accouder à [*windowsill*]; ¶ **~ on** [*sb*] **1** LIT s'appuyer sur [*person*]; **2** FIG (depend on) compter sur [*person*]; **3** FIG (pressurize) faire pression sur [*person*].

■ **lean out**: **~ out** se pencher au dehors; **to ~ out of** [*sth*] se pencher par [*window*].

■ **lean over**: ¶ **~ over** [*person*] GEN se pencher; ¶ **~ over** [*sth*] se pencher par-dessus [qch].

leaning /'li:nɪŋ/ *adj* [*tree, tower, post*] penché.

leanings /'li:nɪŋz/ *npl* (gift, predisposition) dispositions *fpl*; (tendencies) tendances *fpl*.

leant /lent/ *prét, pp* ▶ **lean.**

lean-to /'li:ntu:/ *n* appentis *m*.

leap /li:p/ **I** *n* **1** LIT, GEN saut *m*, bond *m*; SPORT saut *m*; **in** ou **at one ~** d'un bond; **2** FIG (big step) bond *m* (en avant); **a ~ of the imagination** un grand effort de l'imagination; **3** (in price, demand) bond *m* (**in** dans).

II *vtr* (*prét, pp* **leapt, leaped**) franchir [qch] d'un bond [*hedge, chasm*]; **to ~ three metres** sauter trois mètres.

III *vi* (*prét, pp* **leapt, leaped**) **1** [*person, animal*] bondir, sauter; **to ~ to one's feet** se lever d'un bond; **to ~ across** ou **over sth** franchir qch d'un bond; **to ~ out of bed** sauter du lit; **2** FIG [*heart*] bondir (**with** de); **to ~ to sb's defence** FIG bondir au secours de qn; **3** (increase) [*price, profit, stock market*] grimper (**by** de).

IDIOMS **look before you ~** PROV il faut réfléchir avant d'agir; **to come on in ~s and bounds** faire des progrès à pas de géant.

■ **leap about, leap around** sautiller.

■ **leap at**: **~ at** [*sth*] sauter sur [*chance, offer*].

■ **leap in** (with answer, retort) se lancer.

■ **leap out** ¶ LIT surgir (**from behind** de derrière); ¶ **~ out at** [*sb*] LIT surgir devant [*passer-by*]; FIG sauter aux yeux de.

■ **leap up 1** (jump to one's feet) bondir sur ses pieds; **to ~ up at sb** bondir sur qn; **2** [*price, rate*] grimper.

leapfrog /'li:pfrɒg/ **I** *n* saute-mouton *m*.

II *vtr* (*p prés etc* **-gg-**) sauter par-dessus [*obstacle*].

leapt /lept/ *pp, prét* ▶ **leap.**

leap year *n* année *f* bissextile.

learn /lɜ:n/ **I** *vtr* (*prét, pp* **learned** ou **learnt**) **1** (through study, practice) apprendre [*language, facts, trade*]; acquérir [*skills*] (**from** de); **to ~ (how) to do** apprendre à faire; **to ~ to live with sth** finir par se faire à qch; **2** (discover) **to ~ that** apprendre que.

II *vi* (*prét, pp* **learned** ou **learnt**) apprendre (**that** que); **to ~ about sth** apprendre qch; **to ~ from one's mistakes** tirer la leçon de ses erreurs; **it's been a ~ing experience** ça a été une expérience pleine d'enseignements; **you'll ~!** un jour tu comprendras!

IDIOMS **(you) live and ~** c'est une bonne leçon.

learned *adj* **1** /'lɜ:nɪd/ (erudite) [*person, book*] érudit; [*remark, speech*] savant; [*journal*] spécialisé; [*society*] savant; **my ~ friend** JUR mon distingué confrère; **2** /lɜ:nd/ (*behaviour, response*] acquis.

learner /'lɜ:nə(r)/ *n* apprenant/-e *m/f*; **he's only a ~** ce n'est qu'un débutant; **to be a quick/slow ~** apprendre/ne pas apprendre vite.

learner driver *n* GB personne *f* qui apprend à conduire.

learning /'lɜ:nɪŋ/ *n* **1** (erudition) érudition *f*; **2** (process) apprentissage *m*.

IDIOMS **a little ~ is a dangerous thing** PROV il est dangereux de jouer aux experts.

learning: **~ difficulties** *npl* (of schoolchildren) difficultés *fpl* scolaires; (of adults) difficultés *fpl* d'apprentissage; **~ disability** *n* US SCH difficultés *fpl* scolaires.

learnt /lɜ:nt/ *prét, pp* ▶ **learn.**

lease /li:s/ **I** *n* bail *m*.

II *vtr* louer [qch] à bail [*house*]; louer [*car*].

IDIOMS **to give sb a new ~ of** GB ou **on life** [*operation, drug*] redonner vie à qn; [*news, experience*] redonner des forces à qn; **to give a new ~ of life to** donner un second souffle à [*party, company, movement*].

leasehold /'li:shəʊld/ **I** *n* (tenure) bail *m*.

II *adj* [*property*] loué à bail.

leaseholder *n* locataire *mf* à bail.

leash /li:ʃ/ *n* (for dog) laisse *f*; **to keep sb on a tight ~** FIG tenir la bride haute à qn; **to be straining at the ~** FIG [*person*] brûler d'impatience.

leasing /'li:sɪŋ/ **I** *n* (by company) crédit-bail *m*; (by individual) location *f* avec option d'achat.

II *noun modifier* [*company, scheme*] de leasing.

least /li:st/ (*superlative of* **little**)

■ **Note** When *the least* is used as a quantifier followed by a noun to mean the *smallest quantity* of it is translated by *le moins de*: *to have the least food* = avoir le moins de nourriture.

– But when *the least* is used as a quantifier to mean *the slightest* it is translated by *le* or *la moindre*: *I haven't the least idea* = je n'en ai pas la moindre idée.

– For examples of these and particular usages see I below.

– For translations of *least* as a pronoun or adverb see II and III below.

– The phrase *at least* is usually translated by *au moins*.

– For examples and exceptions see IV below.

– For the phrase *in the least* see V below.

I *quantif* **(the) ~** (le) moins de; (in negative constructions) (le ou la) moindre; **they have the ~ food** ce sont eux qui ont le moins de nourriture or le moins à manger; **they haven't the ~ chance of winning** ils n'ont pas la moindre chance de gagner; **I haven't the ~ idea** je n'en ai pas la moindre idée; **the ~ thing annoys him** la moindre chose l'agace; **he wasn't the ~ bit jealous** il n'était pas jaloux du tout.

II *pron* le moins; **we have the ~** c'est nous qui en avons le moins; **it was the ~ I could do!** c'est la moindre des choses!; **the ~ he could have done was phone the police** il aurait au moins pu appeler la police; **that's the ~ of our problems!** c'est le cadet de nos soucis!; **that's the ~ of it** ce n'est pas tout; **she was surprised, to say the ~ (of it)** le moins qu'on puisse dire, c'est qu'elle était surprise.

III *adv* **1** (with adjective or noun) **the ~** le/la moins; (with plural noun) les moins; **the ~ wealthy families** les familles les moins riches; **2** (with verbs) le moins *inv*; **I like that one (the) ~** c'est celui-là que j'aime le moins; **those ~ able to cope** ceux qui ont le plus de mal à se débrouiller; **nobody liked it, John ~ of all** ou **~ of all** John personne ne l'aimait, John encore moins que les autres.

IV at least *adv phr* (at the minimum) au moins; (qualifying statement) du moins; **at ~ 50 people** au moins 50 personnes; **she's at ~ 40** elle a au moins 40 ans; **he's at ~ as qualified as she is** il est au moins aussi qualifié qu'elle; **they could at ~ have phoned!** ils auraient au moins pu téléphoner!; **he's gone to bed—at ~ I think so** il est allé se coucher—du moins, je pense; **such people are at the very ~ guilty of negligence** de telles personnes sont au moins coupables de négligence.

V in the least *adv phr* **I'm not worried in the ~, I'm not in the ~ (bit) worried** je ne suis pas inquiet le moins du monde; **I'm not hungry in the ~, I'm not in the ~ (bit) hungry** je n'ai absolument pas faim; **it doesn't matter in the ~** ça n'a pas la moindre importance.

IDIOMS **last but not ~, last but by no means ~** enfin et surtout.

leather /'leðə(r)/ **I** *n* **1** (material) cuir *m*; **2** (also **wash ~**) peau *f* de chamois.

II leathers *npl* vêtements *mpl* en cuir.

III *noun modifier* [*garment, object*] de cuir, en cuir.

IDIOMS **to go hell for ~**° aller à un train d'enfer°.

leatherette /ˌleðəˈret/ n similicuir m.

leathery /ˈleðərɪ/ adj [skin] tanné; [meat] coriace.

leave /liːv/ **I** n **1** (also **~ of absence**) (time off) GEN congé m; MIL permission f; **to take three days' ~** prendre trois jours de congé; **2** (permission) autorisation f; **to give sb ~ to do** donner à qn l'autorisation de faire; **by** ou **with your ~** avec votre permission; **3** (departure) **to take ~ of sb** prendre congé de qn; **he took his ~** il a pris congé.
II vtr (prét, pp **left**) **1** (depart from) GEN partir de [house, station etc]; (more permanently) quitter [country, city etc]; (by going out) sortir de [room, building]; **he left home early** il est parti tôt de chez lui; **to ~ school** (permanently) quitter l'école; **to ~ the road/table** quitter la route/table; **to ~ the track** [train] dérailler; **to ~ the ground** [plane] décoller; **to ~ one's seat** se lever; **I left him cleaning his car** quand je suis parti, il nettoyait sa voiture; **the smile left her face** FIG son sourire s'est effacé; **2** (leave behind) (forgetfully) laisser [person]; oublier [object]; (deliberately) quitter [partner]; laisser [key, instructions, name, tip] (for pour; with à); (permanently) abandonner [animal, family]; **to ~ sb sth** laisser qch à qn; **to ~ sb/sth in sb's care** confier qn/qch à qn; **3** (let remain) laisser [food, drink, gap]; **you ~ me no choice** ou **alternative but to...** vous ne me laissez pas d'autre choix que de...; **he left us in no doubt as to** ou **about his feelings** il ne nous a laissé aucun doute quant à ses sentiments; **to ~ sth lying around** laisser traîner qch; **to ~ sth tidy** laisser qch en ordre; **there are/we have five minutes left** il reste/il nous reste cinq minutes; **he was left short of money** il ne lui restait plus beaucoup d'argent; **the accident left him an orphan/a cripple** l'accident a fait de lui un orphelin/un invalide; **the attack left her with a scar** elle garde une cicatrice de l'agression; **where does that ~ me?** qu'est-ce que je vais devenir?; **4** (allow to do) **to ~ sth to sb** laisser [qch] à qn [job, task]; **to ~ it (up) to sb to do** laisser à qn le soin de faire; **to ~ the decision (up) to sb** laisser à qn le soin de décider; **~ him to sleep** laisse-le dormir; **to ~ sb to it** (to do something) laisser qn se débrouiller; (to be alone) laisser qn tranquille; **to ~ sb to himself, to ~ sb be**° laisser qn tranquille; **to ~ it to** ou **with me** je m'en occupe; **5** (result in) [oil, wine] faire [stain]; [cup, plate etc] laisser [stain, mark]; faire [hole, dent]; **6** (postpone) laisser [task, homework]; **~ it till tomorrow/the end** laisse ça pour demain/la fin; **7** (stop and agree) **to ~ it that** convenir que; **to ~ it at that** en rester là; **8** JUR (bequeath) léguer (**to sb** à qn); **9** (pass) **to ~ sth on one's left/right** passer qch à gauche/à droite.
III vi (prét, pp **left**) partir (for pour).
IV v refl (prét, pp **left**) **to ~ oneself (with)** se réserver [time, money].

■ **leave about, leave around: ~** [sth] **around** (carelessly) laisser traîner [books, toys]; (deliberately) disposer [cushions, books].

■ **leave aside: ~** [sth] **aside, ~ aside** [sth] laisser [qch] de côté; **leaving aside the question of...** (not mentioning) sans parler du problème de...

■ **leave behind: ~** [sb/sth] **behind 1** (go faster than) distancer [person, competitor]; **to be** ou **get left behind** (physically) [person] se faire distancer; (intellectually) ne pas suivre, être largué°; (in business) [country, company] se laisser distancer; **2** (move away from) [vehicle, plane] s'éloigner de [coast, country, ground]; [traveller] laisser derrière soi [town, country]; [person] quitter [family, husband]; FIG en finir avec [past, problems]; **3** (fail to bring) oublier, laisser [object, child, animal]; **4** (cause to remain) laisser [chaos, problems, bitterness] [earthquake, storm, flood] faire [damage].

■ **leave go, leave hold** USAGE CRITIQUÉ lâcher; **to ~ go** ou **hold of sb/sth** lâcher qn/qch.

■ **leave off: ¶ ~ off** [rain] cesser; [person] s'interrompre; **to carry on** ou **continue where one left off** reprendre là où on en était; **¶ ~ off doing** (stop) arrêter de faire; **¶ ~** [sth] **off 1** (not put on) ne pas mettre [coat, lid, blanket]; (not put back on) ne pas

remettre [coat, lid, blanket]; **2** (not switch on) ne pas allumer [light, TV]; ne pas brancher [iron, kettle]; (leave switched off) laisser [qch] éteint [light, central heating, TV]; laisser [qch] débranché [iron, kettle]; **3** (omit) omettre, oublier [name, item, letter].

■ **leave on: ~** [sth] **on 1** (not remove) garder [coat, hat]; laisser [lid, blanket, bandage]; **2** (not switch off) laisser [qch] allumé [light, TV, central heating]; laisser [qch] branché [iron]; laisser [qch] ouvert [gas, tap].

■ **leave out: ~** [sb/sth] **out, ~ out** [sb/sth] **1** (fail to include) (accidentally) oublier [word, fact, ingredient, person]; (deliberately) omettre [name, fact, reference]; ne pas mettre [ingredient, object]; (from social group, activity) tenir [qn] à l'écart; **to feel left out** se sentir tenu à l'écart; **to ~ sth out of** omettre qch de [text]; **to ~ sb out of** exclure qn de [group]; **2** (let remain outdoors) laisser [qch] dehors.

■ **leave over: ~** [sth] **over 1** (cause to remain) laisser [food, drink]; **there is/we have some money left over** il reste/il nous reste de l'argent; **2** (postpone) remettre [qch] à plus tard.

leaven /ˈlevn/ vtr CULIN faire lever; FIG relever (**with** de).

leaves /liːvz/ npl ▶ **leaf**.

leaving /ˈliːvɪŋ/ **I** n départ m.
II noun modifier [party, present] d'adieu.

Lebanon /ˈlebənən/ ▶ **840** pr n (also **the ~**) (le) Liban m.

lecher /ˈletʃə(r)/ n PÉJ coureur m de jupons.

lecherous /ˈletʃərəs/ adj lubrique.

lectern /ˈlektɜːn/ n (in church) lutrin m; (for lecture notes) pupitre m.

lecture /ˈlektʃə(r)/ **I** n **1** (public talk) conférence f (on sur); GB UNIV cours m magistral (on sur); **to give a ~** (public talk) donner une conférence (**to** à); GB UNIV faire un cours (**to** à); **2** (scolding) **he gave me a ~** il m'a fait la leçon.
II vtr **1** GB UNIV donner un cours à; **2** (scold) faire la leçon à.
III vi **1** GB UNIV (on specific subject) faire un cours (**to** à; **on** sur); **she ~s in mathematics** elle enseigne les mathématiques (à l'université); **2** (give public talk) donner une conférence (**on** sur).

lecture: ~ hall n US amphithéâtre m; **~ notes** npl GB UNIV notes fpl de cours.

lecturer /ˈlektʃərə(r)/ ▶ **1251** n **1** (speaker) conférencier/-ière m/f; **2** GB UNIV enseignant/-e m/f (du supérieur); **junior ~** ≈ assistant/-e m/f; **senior ~** ≈ maître m de conférences; **she's a maths ~** elle enseigne les maths (à l'université); **3** US UNIV ~ chargé m de cours.

lecture: ~ room n GB UNIV salle f de conférences; **~ship** n GB UNIV poste m d'enseignant à l'université; **~ theatre** n GB UNIV amphithéâtre m.

led /led/ prét, pp ▶ **lead¹**.

ledge /ledʒ/ n **1** (shelf) rebord m; **2** (on mountain) saillie f (rocheuse); (tiny) aspérité f; (in climbing) vire f.

ledger /ˈledʒə(r)/ n (in book-keeping) registre m (de comptabilité), grand livre m.

lee /liː/ **I** n côté m sous le vent; **in the ~ of** à l'abri de.
II adj sous le vent.

leech /liːtʃ/ n sangsue f; **to cling to sb like a ~** coller° qn comme une sangsue.

leek /liːk/ n poireau m.

leer /lɪə(r)/ PÉJ **I** n (cunning) regard m sournois; (lustful) regard m libidineux.
II vi **to ~ at sb/sth** lorgner° qn/qch.

lees /liːz/ npl (wine sediment) lie f.

leeway /ˈliːweɪ/ n NAUT, AVIAT dérive f; FIG liberté f de manœuvre.

left /left/ **I** prét, pp ▶ **leave**.
II ▶ **870** n **1** (side or direction) gauche f; **on the ~** sur la gauche; **on your ~** sur votre gauche; **to the ~** vers la gauche; **keep (to the) ~** AUT tenez votre ou restez à gauche; **2** POL **the ~** la gauche; **on the ~** à gauche; **3** SPORT (poing m) gauche m.

Length measurement (1)

Note that French has a comma where English has a decimal point.

1 in	= 2,54 cm*	(*centimètres*)
1 ft	= 30,48 cm	
1 yd	= 91,44 cm	
1 furlong	= 201,17 m	(*mètres*)
1 ml	= 1,61 km	(*kilomètres*)

* *There are three ways of saying 2,54 cm, and other measurements like it:* deux virgule cinquante-quatre centimètres, *or* (*less formally*) deux centimètres virgule cinquante-quatre, *or* deux centimètres cinquante-quatre. *For more details on how to say numbers,* ▶ 1112 |.

Length

how long is the rope?	= de quelle longueur est la corde?
it's ten metres long	= elle fait dix mètres
a rope about six metres long	= une corde d'environ six mètres de* long
A is longer than B	= A est plus long que B
B is shorter than A	= B est plus court que A
A is as long as B	= A est aussi long que B
A is the same length as B	= A a la même longueur que B
A and B are the same length	= A et B ont la même longueur *or* A et B sont de* la même longueur
it's three metres too short	= il est trop court de trois mètres
it's three metres too long	= il est trop long de trois mètres
six metres of silk	= six mètres de soie
ten metres of rope	= dix mètres de corde
sold by the metre	= vendu au mètre

Note the French construction with de, coming after the noun it describes:

a six-foot-long python	= un python de six pieds de* long
an avenue four kilometres long	= une avenue de quatre kilomètres de* long

* *The de is obligatory in these constructions.*

Height
People

how tall is he?	= quelle est sa taille? *or* combien est-ce qu'il mesure?
he's six feet tall	= il fait un mètre quatre-vingts *or* il mesure un mètre quatre-vingts
he's 1m 50	= il fait 1,50 m (*say* un mètre cinquante)

he's about five feet	= il fait à peu près un mètre cinquante
A is taller than B	= A est plus grand que B
B is smaller than A	= B est plus petit que A
A is as tall as B	= A est aussi grand que B
A is the same height as B	= A a la même taille que B
A and B are the same height	
	= A et B ont la même taille *or* A et B sont de* la même taille

Note the French construction with de, coming after the noun it describes:

a six-foot-tall athlete	= un athlète d'un mètre quatre-vingts
a footballer over six feet in height	
	= un footballeur de plus d'un mètre quatre-vingts

Things

how high is the tower?	= quelle est la hauteur de la tour?
it's 50 metres	= elle fait 50 mètres *or* elle mesure 50 mètres
about 25 metres high	= environ 25 mètres de* haut
it's 100 metres high	= elle fait cent mètres de* haut *or* elle fait cent mètres de hauteur
at a height of two metres	= à une hauteur de deux mètres *or* à deux mètres de hauteur
A is higher than B	= A est plus haut que B
B is lower than A	= B est moins haut que A
A is as high as B	= A est aussi haut que B
A is the same height as B	= A a la même hauteur que B
A and B are the same height	= A et B ont la même hauteur *or* A et B sont de* la même hauteur

Note the French construction with de, coming after the noun it describes:

a 100-metre-high tower	= une tour de 100 mètres de* haut
a mountain over 4,000 metres in height	
	= une montagne de plus de quatre mille mètres
how high is the plane?	
	= à quelle hauteur *or* à quelle altitude est l'avion?
what height is the plane flying at?	
	= à quelle altitude l'avion vole-t-il?
the plane is flying at 5,000 metres	
	= l'avion vole à une altitude de cinq mille mètres *or* à cinq mille mètres d'altitude*

* *The de is obligatory in these constructions.*

☞ See next page

III *adj* gauche.
IV *adv* à gauche.
IDIOMS **~, right and centre** (everywhere) partout.
left: **~-hand** *adj* de gauche; **~-hand drive**, **lhd** *adj* [*car*] avec la conduite à gauche; **~-handed** *adj* [*person*] gaucher/-ère.
leftie○ /'lefti/ *n* AUSSI PÉJ gauchiste *mf*.
leftist /'leftist/ POL **I** *n* homme/femme *m/f* de gauche.
II *adj* de gauche.
left: **~-luggage** (**office**) *n* GB consigne *f*; **~-over** *adj* restant; **~-overs** *npl* restes *mpl*.
left wing POL **I** *n* the **~** la gauche.
II **left-wing** *adj* de gauche.
left-winger *n* POL homme/femme *m/f* de gauche.
leg /leg/ **I** *n* **1** ▶ 765| (of person) jambe *f*; (of animal) GEN patte *f*; (of horse) jambe *f*; **to stand on one ~** se tenir debout sur une jambe; **2** (of furniture) pied *m*; **3** CULIN (of lamb) gigot *m*; (of veal) cuisseau *m*; (of poultry, pork, frog) cuisse *f*; (of venison) cuissot *m*; **4** (of trousers) jambe *f*; **to be too long in the ~** [*trousers*] avoir les jambes trop longues; **5** (of journey, race) étape *f*.
II○ *vtr* (*p prés etc* **-gg-**) **to ~ it** (walk) marcher, aller à pied; (walk fast) galoper○; (run away) cavaler○.
III **-legged** *combining form* **three-~ged** [*furniture*] à trois pieds; **four-~ged** [*animal*] à quatre pattes; **long-~ged** [*person*] à jambes longues.
IDIOMS **she doesn't have a ~ to stand on** elle n'a rien sur quoi s'appuyer; **to be on its last ~s** [*machine, car*] avoir fait son temps; [*regime*] n'en avoir plus pour longtemps; [*company*] être au bord de la faillite; **he is on his last ~s** il n'en a plus pour longtemps; **to cost an arm and a ~** coûter les yeux

de la tête; **to give sb a ~ up** faire la courte échelle à qn; FIG dépanner qn○; **to pull sb's ~** faire marcher qn.
legacy /'legəsi/ *n* **1** JUR legs *m*; **2** FIG the **~ of** l'héritage *m* de [*era, artist*]; les séquelles *fpl* de [*war*].
legal /'li:gl/ *adj* **1** (relating to the law) [*document, matter, system, profession*] juridique; [*process, status*] légal; [*costs*] de justice; **to take ~ advice** consulter un avocat; **2** (lawful) [*act, age, heir, right, separation*] légal; [*owner, claim*] légitime.
legal action *n* poursuite *f* judiciaire; **to bring a** OU **take ~ against sb** intenter un procès à qn.
legal: **~ aid** *n* JUR aide *f* juridique; **~ eagle**○ *n* as *m* du barreau○; **~ holiday** *n* US jour *m* férié.
legality /li:'gæləti/ *n* légalité *f*.
legalization /ˌli:gəlaɪ'zeɪʃn, US -lɪ'z-/ *n* légalisation *f*.
legalize /'li:gəlaɪz/ *vtr* légaliser.
legally /'li:gəli/ *adv* **1** [*liable, valid, void*] juridiquement; **~ represented** représenté par un avocat; **to be ~ entitled to do** avoir le droit de faire; **this contract is ~ binding** ce contrat vous engage; **2** (lawfully) [*act*] légalement.
legal: **~ practitioner** *n* juriste *mf*; **~ proceedings** *npl* poursuites *fpl* judiciaires; **~ tender** *n* monnaie *f* légale.
legate /'legit/ *n* légat *m*.
legend /'ledʒənd/ *n* légende *f* (**of** de); **~ has it that** selon la légende; **~ has it that** selon la légende; **to become a ~ in one's own lifetime** passer dans la légende de son vivant.
legendary /'ledʒəndrɪ, US -derɪ/ *adj* légendaire.

Length measurement (2)

Distance

what's the distance from A to B?	= quelle distance y a-t-il entre A et B?
how far is it from Paris to Nice?	= combien y a-t-il de kilomètres de Paris à Nice?
how far away is the school from the church?	= à quelle distance l'école est-elle de l'église?
it's two kilometres	= il y a deux kilomètres
it's about two kilometres	= il y a environ deux kilomètres
at a distance of five kilometres	= à une distance de cinq kilomètres or à cinq kilomètres de distance
C is nearer B than A is	= C est plus près de B que A
A is nearer to B than to C	= A est plus près de B que de C
it's further than from B to C	= c'est plus loin que de B à C
A is as far away as B	= A est aussi loin que B
A and B are the same distance away	= A et B sont à la même distance

Note the French construction with de, coming after the noun it describes:

a ten-kilometre walk = une promenade de dix kilomètres

Width/breadth

In the following examples, **broad** may replace **wide** and **breadth** may replace **width**, but the French remains **large** and **largeur**.

what width is the river?	= de* quelle largeur est la rivière?
how wide is it?	= combien fait-elle de* large?
about seven metres wide	= environ sept mètres de* large
it's seven metres wide	= elle fait sept mètres de* large or de* largeur
A is wider than B	= A est plus large que B
B is narrower than A	= B est plus étroit que A
A is as wide as B	= A est aussi large que B
A is the same width as B	= A a la même largeur que B
A and B are the same width	= A et B ont la même largeur or A et B sont de* la même largeur

Note the French construction with de, coming after the noun it describes:

a ditch two metres wide	= un fossé de deux mètres de* large
a piece of cloth two metres in width	= une pièce de tissu de deux mètres de* largeur
a river 50 metres wide	= une rivière de 50 mètres de* largeur

* *The de is obligatory in these constructions.*

Depth

what depth is the river?	= de* quelle profondeur est la rivière?
how deep is it?	= combien fait-elle de* profondeur?
about ten metres deep	= environ dix mètres de* profondeur
it's four metres deep	= elle fait quatre mètres de* profondeur
at a depth of ten metres	= à dix mètres de* profondeur or à une profondeur de* dix mètres
A is deeper than B	= A est plus profond que B
B is shallower than A	= B est moins profond que A

(note that French has no word for shallow)

A is as deep as B	= A est aussi profond que B
A is the same depth as B	= A a la même profondeur que B
A and B are the same depth	= A et B ont la même profondeur

Note the French construction with de, coming after the noun it describes:

a well 20 metres deep = un puits de vingt mètres de* profondeur

* *The de is obligatory in these constructions.*

---

leggings /'legɪnz/ npl GEN cuissardes *fpl*; (for baby) collant *m*; (for woman) caleçon *m*.

leggy /'legɪ/ adj [*person*] aux longues jambes.

legibility /ˌledʒə'bɪlətɪ/ n lisibilité *f*.

legible /'ledʒəbl/ adj lisible.

legion /'liːdʒən/ **I** n MIL légion *f*; FIG multitude *f*.
II adj (*jamais épith*) légion (*inv*).

legionnaire /ˌliːdʒə'neə(r)/ n MIL légionnaire *m*.

legionnaire's disease ▶ 1002 | n maladie *f* du légionnaire.

legislate /'ledʒɪsleɪt/ vi légiférer (**on** sur); **to ~ against** faire des lois contre.

legislation /ˌledʒɪs'leɪʃn/ n législation *f*; **a piece of ~** une loi; **to introduce ~** faire adopter des lois.

legislative /'ledʒɪslətɪv/, US -leɪtɪv/ adj législatif/-ive.

legislator /'ledʒɪsleɪtə(r)/ n JUR, POL législateur/-trice *m/f*.

legislature /'ledʒɪsleɪtʃə(r)/ n JUR, POL législature *f*.

legitimacy /lɪ'dʒɪtɪməsɪ/ n légitimité *f*.

legitimate /lɪ'dʒɪtɪmət/ adj **1** (justifiable) [*action, question, request, target*] légitime; [*excuse*] valable; **2** (lawful) [*business, organization*] régulier/-ière; [*act, child, claim, heir, owner*] légitime.

legitimately /lɪ'dʒɪtɪmətlɪ/ adv **1** (justifiably) légitimement; **2** (legally) légalement.

legitimize /lɪ'dʒɪtɪmaɪz/ vtr **1** (legalize) légaliser; **2** (justify) justifier.

legless /'leglɪs/ adj LIT sans jambes; °GB (drunk) HUM soûl comme un cochon°.

leg: **~-pulling** n mise *f* en boîte°; **~room** n place *f* pour les jambes; **~ warmer** n jambière *f*.

legwork /'legwɜːk/ n déplacements *mpl*; **to do the ~** déblayer le terrain° FIG.

Leics GB POST abrév écrite = **Leicestershire**.

leisure /'leʒə(r), US 'liːʒə(r)/ **I** n ¢ (spare time) loisir(s) *m(pl)*; (activities) loisirs *mpl*; **to do sth at (one's) ~** prendre son temps pour faire qch.
II noun modifier [*centre, facilities*] de loisirs; **~ industry** industrie *f* des loisirs.

leisured /'leʒəd, US 'liːʒəd/ adj **1** privilégié; **the ~ classes** les classes *fpl* privilégiées, les nantis *mpl*; **2** (tjrs épith) = **leisurely**.

leisurely /'leʒəlɪ, US 'liː-/ adj [*person*] calme; [*walk, breakfast*] tranquille; **at a ~ pace** sans se presser.

leisure: **~ time** n loisirs *mpl*, temps *m* libre; **~ wear** n ¢ vêtements *mpl* de sport.

lemming /'lemɪŋ/ n lemming *m*.

lemon /'lemən/ ▶ 818 | **I** n **1** (fruit) citron *m*; (colour) jaune *m* citron; **2**° HUM **to look a ~** avoir l'air tout bête; **3**° US PEJ (film, book etc) navet° *m*.
II adj (colour) jaune citron *inv*.

lemonade /ˌlemə'neɪd/ n (fizzy) limonade *f*; (still) citronnade *f*; US (fresh) citron *m* pressé.

lemon: **~ cheese**, **~ curd** n GB crème *f* de citron; **~ juice** n jus *m* de citron; GB (drink) citron *m* pressé; **~ sole** n GB limande-sole *f*; **~ squash** n GB = sirop *m* de citron; **~ tea** n thé *m* au citron; **~ tree** n citronnier *m*; **~ yellow** ▶ 818 | n, adj jaune (*m*) citron *inv*.

lend /lend/ **I** vtr (*prét, pp* **lent**) prêter [*object, money*];

conférer [*quality, credibility*] (**to** à); prêter [*support*];
to ~ sb sth prêter qch à qn; **to ~ a hand** prêter
une main; **to ~ one's name to** prêter son nom à; **it doesn't
~ weight to sth** donner du poids à qch; **it doesn't
~ itself to...** il ne se prête pas à...
II *vi* (*prét, pp* **lent**) COMM prêter (**to** à); **to ~ at
15%** prêter à 15%.

lender /'lendə(r)/ *n* prêteur/-euse *m/f*.

lending /'lendɪŋ/ **I** *n* prêt *m*.
II *noun modifier* [*bank, library, scheme*] de prêt; [*agreement, rate*] d'emprunt.

length /leŋθ/ ▶1045 **I** *n* **1** longueur *f*; **to be 15 cm/
50 km in ~** faire 15 cm/50 km de long; **X is twice
the ~ of Y** X est deux fois plus long que Y; **along
the whole ~ of** sur toute la longueur de; **to cycle
the (whole) ~ of Italy** faire l'Italie d'un bout à l'autre à bicyclette; **there was a ladder running the
(whole) ~ of her stocking** son bas était filé sur
toute sa hauteur; **2** (duration) (of book, list, syllable)
longueur *f*; (of event, activity, prison sentence) durée *f*; **a
film three hours in ~** un film de trois heures or qui
dure trois heures; **a considerable ~ of time** un
temps considérable; **he can't concentrate for any ~
of time** il n'arrive pas à se concentrer pendant (très)
longtemps; **3** (piece) (of string, carpet, wood) morceau *m*;
(of fabric) ~ métrage *m*; (of piping, track) tronçon *m*;
dress/skirt ~ hauteur *f* de robe/de jupe; **4** SPORT
longueur *f*.
II lengths *npl* **to go to great ~s to do sth** se
donner beaucoup de mal pour faire qch; **to be willing
to go to any ~s** être prêt à faire n'importe quoi; **to
go to the ~s of doing** aller jusqu'à faire.
III at length *adv phr* (for a long time) longuement; (at
last) finalement.
IV -length *combining form* **shoulder-~** hair des
cheveux qui arrivent aux épaules; **floor-~** curtains
des rideaux qui descendent jusqu'au sol; ▶**full-
length**.

lengthen /'leŋθən/ **I** *vtr* rallonger [*garment*] (**by** de,
par); prolonger [*wall, shelf*] (**by** de, par); prolonger
[*stay, visit*]; LING allonger [*vowel, syllable*].
II *vi* [*queue, list, shadow*] s'allonger; [*skirts, trousers*]
devenir plus long; [*days, nights*] rallonger.

lengthily /'leŋθɪlɪ/ *adv* longuement.

lengthwise /'leŋθwaɪz/, **lengthways** /'leŋθweɪz/ GB
adv [*cut, fold, place*] dans le sens de la longueur;
[*place, lay*] en long.

lengthy /'leŋθɪ/ *adj* long/longue.

lenience /'liːnɪəns/, **leniency** /'liːnɪənsɪ/ *n* (of person)
indulgence *f* (**with** pour; **towards** envers); (of punishment) légèreté *f*.

lenient /'liːnɪənt/ *adj* [*person, treatment*] indulgent
(**with** pour; **towards** envers); [*punishment*] léger/-ère.

lens /lenz/ *n* **1** (in optical instruments) lentille *f*; (in
spectacles) verre *m*; (in camera) objectif *m*; (contact)
lentille *f*; **2** ANAT cristallin *m*.

lens: **~ cap** *n* bouchon *m* d'objectif; **~ hood** *n*
parasoleil *m*.

lent /lent/ *prét, pp* ▶**lend**.

Lent /lent/ *n* carême *m*.

lentil /'lentl/ **I** *n* BOT, CULIN lentille *f*.
II *noun modifier* [*soup*] aux lentilles.

Leo /'liːəʊ/ ▶1418 *pr n* **1** (star) Lion *m*; **2** (name) Léon *m*.

leopard /'lepəd/ *n* léopard *m*.
IDIOMS **a ~ cannot change his spots** PROV
chassez le naturel, il revient au galop PROV.

leopardskin /'lepədskɪn/ **I** *n* peau *f* de léopard.
II *noun modifier* [*garment, rug*] en peau de léopard.

leotard /'liːətɑːd/ *n* justaucorps *m inv*.

leper /'lepə(r)/ *n* MED, FIG lépreux/-euse *m/f*.

leprosy /'leprəsɪ/ *n* lèpre *f*.

leprous /'leprəs/ *adj* [*person*] lépreux/-euse.

lesbian /'lezbɪən/ **I** *n* lesbienne *f*.
II *adj* lesbien/-ienne.

lesion /'liːʒn/ *n* lésion *f*.

less /les/ (*comparative of* **little**) **I** *quantif* moins

less

When *less* is used as a quantifier (*less money*) it is
translated by *moins de*: *moins d'argent*. For examples
and particular usages, see **I** in the entry **less**.

When *less* is used as a pronoun (*you should have taken
less*), it is translated by *moins*: *tu aurais dû en prendre
moins*.

less than is usually translated by *moins que* and *even
less* by *encore moins*. For examples and particular
usages of these see **II** in the entry **less**.

When *less* is used as an adverb followed by a verb, an
adjective, or another adverb (*to eat less, less interesting,
less often*) it is translated by *moins*: *manger moins, moins
intéressant, moins souvent*. For examples and particular
usages see **III** in the entry **less**.

For *less* used as a preposition (*less 10%*) see **IV** in the
entry **less**. For the phrase *less and less* see **V** in the
entry **less**.

de; **~ beer** moins de bière; **I have ~ money than
him** j'ai moins d'argent que lui; **of ~ importance** de
moindre importance; **to grow ~** diminuer.
II *pron* moins; **I have ~ than you** j'en ai moins que
toi; **even ~** encore moins; **~ than half** moins de la
moitié; **in ~ than three hours** en moins de trois
heures; **13 is ~ than 18** 13 est plus petit que 18; **a
sum of not ~ than £1,000** une somme qui s'élève au
moins à 1 000 livres sterling; **he was ~ than helpful**
il était loin d'être serviable; **it's an improvement,
but ~ of one than I had hoped** c'est un progrès,
mais pas au point que j'aurais espéré; **she's nothing
~ than a liar** elle n'est rien de moins qu'une
menteuse; **it's nothing ~ than a scandal!** c'est un
véritable scandale!; **they let me have it for ~** ils me
l'ont laissé pour moins; **he's ~ of a fool than you
think** il est moins bête que tu ne le penses; **they will
think all the ~ of her for it** ça va la faire descendre
dans leur estime; **£100 and not a penny ~!** cent
livres et pas un centime de moins!; **the ~ said about
it the better** moins on en parle, mieux ça vaut;
people have been shot for ~! il y en a qui ont été
tués pour moins que ça!
III *adv* moins; **I liked it ~ than you did** je l'ai
moins aimé que toi; **I dislike him no ~ than you** je
ne l'aime pas plus que toi; **it matters ~ than it did
before** cela a moins d'importance qu'avant; **she is no
~ qualified than you** elle n'est pas moins qualifiée
que toi; **it's ~ a village than a town** c'est plutôt une
ville qu'un village; **the more I see him, the ~ I like
him** plus je le vois, moins je l'aime; **no ~ than 85%**
au moins 85%; **they live in Kensington, no ~!** ils
habitent à Kensington, rien que ça!; **no ~ a person
than the emperor** l'empereur en personne; **he was
~ offended than shocked** il était plus choqué
qu'offensé.
IV *prep* moins; **~ 15% discount** moins 15% de
remise; **~ tax** avant impôts.
V less and less *adv phr* de moins en moins.

lessee /le'siː/ *n* JUR preneur/-euse *m/f* à bail.

lessen /'lesn/ **I** *vtr* GEN diminuer, réduire [*cost,
production*]; atténuer [*impact, pain*].
II *vi* diminuer.

lessening /'lesnɪŋ/ *n* diminution *f*.

lesser /'lesə(r)/ **I** *adj* GEN moindre; [*life form*] peu
évolué; **to a ~ degree** ou **extent** à un moindre
degré; **~ being** ou **mortal** être inférieur; **the ~
works of an artist** les œuvres mineures d'un artiste.
II *adv* moins.

lesson /'lesn/ *n* **1** cours *m*, leçon *f*; **Spanish ~** cours
d'espagnol; **driving ~** leçon de conduite; **to give
~s** donner des cours (**in** de); **to take/have ~s** prendre/suivre des cours (**in** de); **we have ~s from 9 to
12** nous avons cours de 9 heures à midi; **2** RELIG
leçon *f*; **to read the ~** lire la leçon; **3** FIG leçon *f*;
let that be a ~ to you! que cela te serve de leçon!;
I'm going to teach him a ~! je vais lui donner une

let¹

When *let* is used in English with another verb in order to make a suggestion (*let's do it at once*), the first person plural *-ons* of the appropriate verb can generally be used to express this in French: *faisons-le tout de suite*. (Note that the verb alone translates *let us do* and no pronoun appears in French.)

In the spoken language, however, which is the usual context for such suggestions, French speakers will use the much more colloquial *on + present tense* or *si on + imperfect tense*:

let's do it at once = on le fait tout de suite?
or si on le faisait tout de suite?

let's go to the
cinema tonight = si on allait au cinéma ce soir?
let's go! = allons-y! *or* on y va!

These translations can also be used for negative suggestions:

let's not take *or* don't let's take the bus – let's walk
= on ne prend pas le bus, on y va à pied
or ne prenons pas le bus, allons-y à pied

For more examples and particular usages see I 1 in the entry *let¹*.

When *let* is used in English with another verb to express defiance or a command (*just let him try!*) the French uses the structure *que + present subjunctive*:

just let him try! = qu'il essaie!
don't let me see you here again! = que je ne te revoie plus ici!

For more examples and particular usages see I 1 in the entry *let¹*.

When *let* is used to mean *allow*, it is generally translated by the verb *laisser*. For examples and particular usages see I 2 in the entry *let¹*.

For translations of expressions such as *let fly, let loose, let slip* etc., consult the entry for the second word (*fly, loose, slip* etc.).

bonne leçon!; **that'll teach you a ~!** cela t'apprendra!

lessor /leˈsɔː(r)/ *n* JUR bailleur/-eresse *m/f*.

lest /lest/ *conj* SOUT (for fear that) de peur de (+ *infinitive*), de crainte de (+ *infinitive*), de crainte que (+ *ne + subj*); (in case that) au cas où; '**~ we forget**' ~ 'In memoriam'.

let¹ /let/ **I** *vtr* (*p prés* **-tt-**; *prét, pp* let) **1** (when making suggestion, expressing command) **~'s go** allons-y; **~'s go for a swim** allons nager; **~'s begin by doing** commençons par faire; **~'s get out of here!** sortons d'ici!; **~'s not** ou **don't ~'s** GB **talk about that!** n'en parlons pas!; **~'s see if...** voyons si...; **~'s pretend that...** faisons comme si...; **~'s face it** soyons honnêtes; **~ me see, ~'s see...** voyons...; **~ me think about it** laisse-moi réfléchir; **it's more complex than, ~'s say, a computer** c'est plus compliqué que, disons, un ordinateur; **~ there be no doubt about it!** qu'il n'y ait aucun doute là-dessus!; **~ the festivities begin!** que la fête commence!; **never ~ it be said that** qu'il ne soit pas dit que; **just ~ him try it!** qu'il essaie!; **if he wants tea, ~ him make it himself!** s'il veut du thé, qu'il le fasse lui-même!; **~ me tell you...** crois-moi, croyez-moi...; **2** (allow) **to ~ sb do sth** laisser qn faire qch; **~ me explain** laisse-moi t'expliquer; **she let herself be intimidated** elle s'est laissée intimider; **don't ~ it get you down** ne te laisse pas abattre; **she wanted to go but they wouldn't ~ her** elle voulait y aller mais ils ne l'ont pas laissée faire; **I won't ~ them talk to me like that!** je ne permets pas qu'on me parle sur ce ton!; **don't ~ me forget to do** rappelle-moi de faire; **~ me see, ~ me have a look** fais voir, fais-moi voir; **~ me introduce you to...** laissez-moi vous présenter à...; **to ~ sth fall** laisser tomber qch; **to ~ one's hair grow** se laisser pousser les cheveux; **to ~ sb through** laisser passer qn; **to ~ sb on/off the bus** laisser qn monter dans/descendre de l'autobus;

can you ~ me off here? pouvez-vous me déposer ici?; to ~ the air out of dégonfler [*tyre, balloon*].
II let alone *conj phr* à plus forte raison.

■ **let down**: ¶ **~ [sb] down 1** (disappoint) laisser tomber [qn]; **it has never let me down** [*technique, machine*] ça a toujours marché; **to feel let down** être déçu; **2** (embarrass) faire honte à [qn]; ¶ **~ [sth] down, ~ down [sth] 1** GB (deflate) dégonfler [*tyre*]; **2** (lower) faire descendre [*bucket*]; baisser [*window*]; **3** (lengthen) rallonger [*garment*]; **4** détacher [*hair*].

■ **let go** ¶ LIT lâcher prise; **to ~ go of sb/sth** LIT lâcher qn/qch; FIG se détacher de qn/qch; ¶ **~ [sb] go, ~ go [sb] 1** (free) relâcher [*prisoner*]; **2** lâcher [*person, arm*]; **3** EUPH licencier [*employee*]; **4 to ~ oneself go** se laisser aller; ¶ **~ [sth] go, ~ go [sth] 1** lâcher [*rope, bar*]; **2** FIG **to ~ it go** (not to react) laisser passer; (stop fretting about) ne plus y penser.

■ **let in**: ¶ **~ in [sth], ~ [sth] in** [*roof, window*] laisser passer [*rain*]; [*shoes*] prendre [*water*]; [*curtains*] laisser passer [*light*]; ¶ **~ [sb] in, ~ in [sb] 1** (show in) faire entrer; (admit) laisser entrer; **I let myself in** suis entré avec ma clé; **2 to ~ oneself in for** aller au devant de [*trouble, disappointment*]; **I had no idea what I was ~ting myself in for** je n'avais aucune idée de là où je mettais les pieds°; **3 to ~ sb in on, to ~ sb into** mettre qn au courant de [*secret, joke*].

■ **let off**: ¶ **~ off [sth]** tirer [*fireworks*]; faire exploser [*bomb*]; faire partir [*gun*]; ¶ **~ [sb] off 1** GB SCH laisser sortir [*pupils*]; **2** (excuse) **to ~ sb off** dispenser qn de [*homework*]; **3** (leave unpunished) ne pas punir [*culprit*]; **to be ~ off with** s'en tirer avec [*fine, caution*]; **to ~ sb off lightly** laisser qn s'en tirer à bon compte.

■ **let on 1** (reveal) dire (**to sb** à qn); **don't ~ on that you speak German** ne dis pas que tu parles allemand; **2** GB (pretend) **to ~ on that** faire croire que.

■ **let out**: ¶ **~ out** US [*movie, school*] finir (**at** à); ¶ **~ out [sth]** laisser échapper [*cry, sigh*]; **to ~ out a roar** beugler; **2** GB (reveal) révéler (**that** que); ¶ **~ [sth] out, ~ out [sth] 1** (release) faire sortir [*animal*]; FIG donner libre cours à [*grief, anger*]; **2** élargir [*skirt, jacket*]; rallonger [*waistband*]; ¶ **~ [sb] out 1** (set free) laisser sortir [*prisoner*] (**of** de); faire sortir [*pupils, employees*] (**of** de); **2** (show out) reconduire [qn] à la porte; **I'll ~ myself out** ne vous dérangez pas, je peux sortir tout seul.

■ **let through**: ¶ **~ [sb] through, ~ through [sb] 1** (in crowd) laisser passer; **2** SCH, UNIV accorder un examen à; ¶ **~ [sth] through, ~ through [sth]** laisser passer [*error, faulty product*].

■ **let up** [*rain, wind*] se calmer; [*pressure*] s'arrêter; [*heat*] diminuer; **the rain never once let up** il a plu sans arrêt; **he never ~s up** (works hard) il travaille sans relâche; (talks) il n'arrête pas de parler.

let² /let/ **I** *n* **1** GB (lease) bail *m*; **2** SPORT let *m*, balle *f* let; **to serve a ~** jouer un let.
II *vtr* (*p prés* **-tt-**; *prét, pp* let) (also GB **~ out**) (lease) louer (**to** à); '**to ~**' 'à louer'.

letdown /ˈletdaʊn/ *n* déception *f*.

lethal /ˈliːθl/ *adj* [*substance, gas, dose*] mortel/-elle; [*disease, blow*] fatal; [*weapon*] meurtrier/-ière; [*machine, stretch of road*] très dangereux/-euse; **a ~ mixture** (drink) FIG, HUM un mélange redoutable.

lethargic /lɪˈθɑːdʒɪk/ *adj* LIT léthargique; FIG (lazy) apathique; **to feel ~** se sentir engourdi.

lethargy /ˈleθədʒɪ/ *n* léthargie *f*.

let's /lets/ = **let us**.

letter /ˈletə(r)/ **I** *n* **1** lettre *f* (**to** pour; **from** de); **to inform sb by ~** informer qn par lettre; **he receives a lot of ~s** il reçoit beaucoup de courrier; **~s to the editor** (in newspaper) courrier des lecteurs; **the ~s of Henry James** la correspondance de Henry James; **2** (of alphabet) lettre *f*; (character) caractère *m*.
II letters *npl* (literature) belles-lettres *fpl*; **a man/woman of ~s** un homme/une femme de lettres.
IDIOMS **the ~ of the law** la lettre de la loi; **to follow instructions to the ~** suivre des instructions à la lettre.

letter: ~ **bomb** *n* lettre *f* piégée; ~ **box** *n* boîte *f* à lettres; ~**head** *n* en-tête *m*.

lettering /'letərɪŋ/ *n* caractères *mpl*.

letter: ~ **post** *n* tarif *m* lettre; ~ **rack** *n* porte-lettres *m inv*; ~**s page** *n* (in newspaper) courrier *m* des lecteurs.

letting /'letɪŋ/ *n* GB location *f*.

lettuce /'letɪs/ *n* salade *f*, laitue *f*.

letup /'letʌp/ *n* GEN accalmie *f*; (respite) pause *f*.

leuk(a)emia /luː'kiːmɪə/ ▶1002 *n* leucémie *f*; **to have** ~ être atteint de leucémie.

level /'levl/ **I** *n* **1** GEN, SCH niveau *m*; **an intermediate** ~ **textbook** un manuel pour le niveau intermédiaire; **to be on the same** ~ **as sb** être du même niveau que qn; **to talk to sb on their** ~ parler à qn d'égal à égal; **on a** ~ **with the first floor** à la hauteur du premier étage; **on the same** ~ au même niveau or à la même hauteur; **at waist-/knee-**~ à la hauteur de la taille/des genoux; **at street** ~ au niveau de la rue; **that is on a** ~ **with blackmail** FIG ça revient à faire du chantage; **on a purely practical** ~ sur un plan strictement pratique; **to be reduced to the same** ~ être mis sur le même plan que; **the** ~ **of training** la qualité de la formation; **2** (degree) (of pollution, noise) niveau *m*; (of unemployment) taux *m*; (of spending) montant *m*; (of satisfaction, anxiety) degré *m*; **glucose** ~**s** taux de glucose; **3** (position in hierarchy) échelon *m*; **at local** ~ à l'échelon local; **at a lower** ~ à un échelon inférieur.
II *adj* **1** (not at an angle) [*shelf, floor*] droit; [*surface*] plan; [*table*] horizontal; **2** (not bumpy) [*ground, surface, land*] plat; **3** CULIN [*teaspoonful*] ras; **4** (equally high) **to be** ~ [*shoulders, windows*] être à la même hauteur; [*floor, building*] être au même niveau; ~ **with the ground** au ras du sol; **5** FIG (in achievement, rank) **to be** ~ [*competitors*] être à égalité; **6** FIG (even) [*tone*] égal; **to remain** ~ [*figures*] rester stable.
III *adv* **to draw** ~ arriver à la même hauteur (**with** que).
IV *vtr* (*p prés etc* **-ll-** GB, **-l-** US) **1** raser [*village, area*]; **2** (aim) braquer [*gun, weapon*] (**at** sur); lancer [*accusation*] (**at** contre); adresser [*criticism*] (**at** à).
IDIOMS **to be** ~**-pegging** être à égalité; **to be on the** ~ (trustworthy) être réglo○; **to** ~ **with sb**○ être honnête avec qn; **to keep a** ~ **head** garder son sang-froid; **to try one's** ~ **best to do** faire tout son possible pour faire.

■ **level off**: ~ **off 1** [*path*] continuer sur terrain plat; FIG [*prices, curve*] se stabiliser; **2** [*plane, pilot*] amorcer le vol en palier.

■ **level out** [*terrain*] s'aplanir; FIG se stabiliser.

level: ~ **crossing** *n* passage *m* à niveau; ~**-headed** *adj* sensé.

levelling /'levəlɪŋ/ **I** *n* **1** (making smooth) nivellement *m*; **2** (demolition) démolition *f*.
II *noun modifier* [*effect*] de nivellement.

lever /'liːvə(r), US 'levər/ **I** *n* AUT, TECH levier *m*; (small) manette *f*.
II *vtr* LIT **to** ~ **sth up/off** soulever/enlever qch à l'aide d'un levier; **to** ~ **sth open** utiliser un levier pour ouvrir qch.

leverage /'liːvərɪdʒ, US 'levərɪdʒ/ *n* **1** ECON, POL force *f* d'appui (**on, over** sur); **2** PHYS puissance *f* de levier.

leveret /'levərɪt/ *n* levraut *m*.

levitate /'levɪteɪt/ **I** *vtr* faire léviter.
II *vi* léviter.

levity /'levətɪ/ *n* désinvolture *f*.

levy /'levɪ/ **I** *n* (tax) taxe *f*, impôt *m*; (act of collecting) perception *f*; **import** ~ taxe à l'importation.
II *vtr* prélever [*tax, duty*]; imposer [*fine*].

lewd /ljuːd, US 'luːd/ *adj* [*joke, gesture, remark*] obscène; [*person, expression*] lubrique.

lewdness /'ljuːdnɪs, US 'luːd-/ *n* (of joke, remark) obscénité *f*; (of person, behaviour) lubricité *f*.

lexical /'leksɪkl/ *adj* lexical.

lexicographer /ˌleksɪ'kɒɡrəfə(r)/ ▶1251 *n* lexicographe *mf*.

lexicography /ˌleksɪ'kɒɡrəfɪ/ *n* lexicographie *f*.

lexicon /'leksɪkən, US -kɒn/ *n* GEN, LING lexique *m*.

liability /ˌlaɪə'bɪlətɪ/ **I** *n* **1** JUR responsabilité *f*; ~ **for tax** assujettissement *m* à l'impôt; **2** FIG (drawback) handicap *m*.
II liabilities *npl* passif *m*, dettes *fpl*.

liable /'laɪəbl/ *adj* **1** (likely) **to be** ~ **to do** risquer de faire; **it's** ~ **to rain** il risque de pleuvoir, il se peut qu'il pleuve; **2** (prone) **to be** ~ **to** être susceptible à; **she is** ~ **to colds** elle est sujette aux rhumes; **the contract is** ~ **to changes** le contrat peut faire l'objet de modifications; **3** (legally subject) **to be** ~ **to** être passible de [*fine, prosecution*]; **to be** ~ **for** ou **to tax** [*person, company*] être imposable; [*goods*] être soumis à l'impôt; ~ **for military service** astreint au service militaire; **to be** ~ **for sb's debts** répondre des dettes de qn; ~ **for damages** tenu de payer des dommages et intérêts.

liaise /lɪ'eɪz/ *vi* travailler en liaison (**with** avec).

liaison /lɪ'eɪzn, US 'lɪəzɒn/ *n* liaison *f*.

liaison officer *n* MIL officier *m* de liaison; ADMIN responsable *mf* de la communication.

liar /'laɪə(r)/ *n* menteur/-euse *m/f*.

Lib Dem○ *n, adj* GB POL *abrév* = **Liberal Democrat**.

libel /'laɪbl/ **I** *n* **1** (crime) diffamation *f*; **to sue sb for** ~ intenter un procès en diffamation à qn; **2** (article, statement) écrit *m* diffamatoire; **3** (slander) calomnie *f*.
II *noun modifier* [*action, case, suit*] en diffamation; [*damages*] pour diffamation; [*laws*] sur la diffamation.
III *vtr* (*p prés etc* **-ll-**, US **-l-**) diffamer.

libellous GB, **libelous** US /'laɪbələs/ *adj* diffamatoire.

liberal /'lɪbərəl/ **I** *n* GEN, POL libéral/-e *m/f*; gauchisant/-e *m/f* PÉJ.
II *adj* **1** [*person, institution*] GEN, POL, RELIG libéral; PÉJ bien intentionné; **2** (generous) [*amount, offer*] généreux/-euse; [*person*] prodigue (**with** de); **to make** ~ **use of sth** faire amplement usage de qch; **3** [*interpretation*] libre.

Liberal /'lɪbərəl/ *n, adj* POL libéral/-e (*m/f*).

Liberal Democrat *n* GB POL libéral-démocrate *mf*; **the** ~**s** les libéraux-démocrates.

liberalism /'lɪbərəlɪzəm/ *n* GEN, POL, ECON libéralisme *m*.

liberality /ˌlɪbə'rælɪtɪ/ *n* **1** (generosity) libéralité *f*; **2** (open-mindedness) libéralisme *m*.

liberalize /'lɪbərəlaɪz/ *vtr* libéraliser.

liberally /'lɪbərəlɪ/ *adv* **1** (generously) libéralement; **2** (tolerantly) de façon libérale; **3** [*interpret*] librement.

liberal-minded *adj* large d'esprit.

liberate /'lɪbəreɪt/ **I** *vtr* libérer (**from** de).
II liberated *pp adj* [*lifestyle, woman*] libéré.
III liberating *pres p adj* libérateur/-trice.

liberation /ˌlɪbə'reɪʃn/ *n* GEN, POL libération *f* (**from** de); **women's** ~ libération de la femme.

liberator /'lɪbəreɪtə(r)/ *n* libérateur/-trice *m/f*.

Liberia /laɪ'bɪərɪə/ ▶840 *pr n* Liberia *m*.

liberty /'lɪbətɪ/ *n* GEN, POL liberté *f*; **civil liberties** droits *mpl* civils; **to be at** ~ être en liberté; **to be at** ~ **to do** être libre de faire; **I am not at** ~ **to say** SOUT je n'ai pas le droit de vous le dire; **to take the** ~ **of doing** prendre la liberté de faire.
IDIOMS **it's** ~ **hall here!** chacun fait comme il veut ici!

libido /lɪ'biːdəʊ, 'lɪbɪdəʊ/ *n* (*pl* **-os**) libido *f*.

Libra /'liːbrə/ ▶1418 *n* Balance *f*.

librarian /laɪ'breərɪən/ ▶1251 *n* bibliothécaire *mf*.

library /'laɪbrərɪ, US -brerɪ/ **I** *n* bibliothèque *f*; **public** ~ bibliothèque municipale; **photo(graphic)** ~ photothèque *f*.
II *noun modifier* [*book, card, ticket*] de bibliothèque.

libretto /lɪ'bretəʊ/ *n* (*pl* **-tti** ou **-ttos**) livret *m*, libretto *m*.

Libya /'lɪbɪə/ ▶840 *pr n* Libye *f*.

lice /laɪs/ *pl* ▶ **louse**.

licence GB, **license** US /ˈlaɪsns/ n **1** (for trading) licence f (**to do** de faire); **sold under ~** (**from**) vendu sous licence (de); **2** (to drive, carry gun, fish) permis m (**to do** pour faire); (for TV) redevance f; **to lose one's** (**driving**) **~** se faire retirer son permis (de conduire); **to be married by special ~** se marier avec dispense; **artistic ~** liberté f de l'artiste; **this law is a ~ to harass the innocent** FIG cette loi laisse le champ libre pour harceler les innocents; **a ~ to print money** un pactole.

licence: **~ fee** n GB redevance f; **~ number** n (of car) numéro m minéralogique or d'immatriculation; **~ plate** GB, **licence tag** US n plaque f minéralogique or d'immatriculation.

license /ˈlaɪsns/ **I** n US = **licence**.
II vtr **1** (authorize) autoriser (**to do** à faire); **2** obtenir un permis pour [gun]; faire immatriculer [vehicle].

licensed /ˈlaɪsnst/ adj **1** [restaurant, café, club] qui a une licence de débit de boissons; **2** [dealer, firm, taxi] agréé; [pilot] breveté; [vehicle] en règle; **to be ~ to carry a gun** avoir un permis de port d'armes.

licensee /ˌlaɪsənˈsiː/ n (of pub etc) titulaire mf d'une licence de débit de boissons.

licensing: **~ hours** npl GB heures fpl d'ouverture des débits de boissons; **~ laws** npl GB lois fpl réglementant la vente des boissons alcoolisées.

licentious /laɪˈsenʃəs/ adj SOUT licencieux/-ieuse.

lichen /ˈlaɪkən/ n lichen m.

lick /lɪk/ **I** n **1** coup m de langue; **to give sth a ~** lécher qch; **2** FIG **a ~ of paint** un petit coup de peinture; **3** MUS (in jazz) chorus m.
II vtr **1** lécher; **the cat was ~ing its paws** le chat se léchait les pattes; **to ~ sth clean** [animal] nettoyer qch à coups de langue; **to ~ one's chops** OU **lips** LIT se lécher les babines; FIG (at prospect) se délecter (**at** à); **to ~ sb's boots** lécher les bottes de or à qn; **2** (beat in game) écraser [team, opponent]; (beat physically) battre [person]; **to get ~ed** (in game) se faire écraser; **I think we've got the problem ~ed** je crois que nous avons réussi à venir à bout de ce problème.
IDIOMS **at a fair** OU **good ~** à toute allure; **to ~ one's wounds** panser ses blessures.

licorice n US = **liquorice**.

lid /lɪd/ n **1** (cover) couvercle m; **2** (eyelid) paupière f.
IDIOMS **to blow the ~ off sth** lever le voile sur qch; **to flip one's ~** éclater; **to keep the ~ on sth** contrôler qch; **that really puts the (tin) ~ on it**! ça, c'est vraiment le pompon!

lido /ˈliːdəʊ/ n (pl **-os**) (beach) plage f (aménagée); GB (pool) piscine f (en plein air).

lie /laɪ/ **I** n mensonge m; **to tell a ~** mentir; **to give the ~ to sth/sb** démentir qch/qn.
II vtr (p prés **lying**; prét, pp **lied**) mentir; **he ~d his way into the job** il a obtenu le poste grâce à des mensonges.
III vi **1** (p prés **lying**; prét, pp **lied**) (tell falsehood) mentir (**to sb** à qn; **about** à propos de); **he ~d about her** il a menti à son propos; **2** (p prés **lying**, prét **lay**, pp **lain** also for 3, 4, 5) (in horizontal position) [person, animal] (action) s'allonger; (state) être allongé; [objects] être couché; **to ~ on one's back/on one's front** OU **face down** être allongé or s'allonger sur le dos/ventre; **to ~ in bed all morning** rester au lit toute la matinée; **don't ~ in the sun too long** ne restez pas allongé trop longtemps au soleil; **~ still** ne bougez pas; **he lay dead** il gisait mort; **here ~s John Brown** ci-gît John Brown; **3** (be situated) être; (remain) rester; **their unhappy past lay behind them** leur passé malheureux était derrière eux; **that's where our future ~s** c'est là qu'est notre avenir; **to ~ before sb** [life, career] s'ouvrir devant qn; **what ~s ahead?** qu'est-ce qui nous attend?; **the toys lay all over the floor** le sol était couvert de jouets; **his clothes lay where he'd left them** ses vêtements étaient restés là où il les avais laissés; **4** (can be found) résider; **their interests ~ elsewhere** leurs intérêts résident ailleurs; **to ~ in** [cause, secret, talent] résider

dans; [popularity, strength, fault] venir de; **to ~ in doing** [solution, cure] consister à faire; **to ~ behind** (be hidden) se cacher derrière; (instigate) être à l'origine de; **the responsibility ~ with them** c'est eux qui sont responsables; **5** LIT, FIG (as covering) [snow] tenir; **the snow lay thick** il y avait une épaisse couche de neige; **to ~ over** [atmosphere] recouvrir [place, gathering].
IDIOMS **to ~ low** garder un profil bas; **to live a ~** vivre dans le mensonge; **to take it lying down** se laisser faire.
■ **lie about** = **lie around**.
■ **lie around**: ¶ **~ around** [person, object] traîner; **to leave sth lying around** laisser traîner qch; ¶ **~ around** [sth] traîner dans [house].
■ **lie back** (horizontally) s'allonger (**on** sur); **she lay back on the pillow** elle s'est adossée à l'oreiller.
■ **lie down** (briefly) s'allonger; (for longer period) se coucher.
■ **lie in** (in bed) faire la grasse matinée.
■ **lie up 1** (stay in bed) garder le lit; **2** (hide) se cacher.

Liechtenstein /ˈlɪktənstaɪn/ ▶840 pr n Liechtenstein m.

lie detector n détecteur m de mensonge.

lie-down /ˈlaɪdaʊn/ n **to have a ~** aller s'allonger.

lie-in /ˈlaɪɪn/ n **to have a ~** faire la grasse matinée.

lieu /ljuː/ **I in lieu** adv phr: **one week's holiday in ~** une semaine de vacances pour compenser.
II in lieu of prep phr à la place de.

lieutenant, **Lt** /lefˈtenənt, US luːˈt-/ ▶1192 n (GB army, US police) lieutenant m; (GB, US navy) lieutenant m de vaisseau.

lieutenant: **~ colonel** n lieutenant-colonel m; **~ Governor** n gouverneur m adjoint.

life /laɪf/ (pl **lives**) **I** n **1** (as opposed to death) vie f; **a matter of ~ and death** une question de vie ou de mort; **to have a love of ~** aimer la vie; **to bring sb back to ~** GEN rendre la vie à qn; MED ranimer qn; **plant ~** la vie végétale; **to take one's own ~** se donner la mort; **to take ~ as it comes** prendre la vie comme elle vient; **~ must go on** la vie continue; **that's ~**! c'est la vie!; **run for your ~**! sauve qui peut!; **2** (period from birth to death) vie f; **throughout one's ~** pendant toute sa vie; **the first time in my ~** la première fois de ma vie; **a day in the ~ of** une journée de la vie de; **a job for ~** un emploi à vie; **a friend for ~** un ami pour la vie; **in later ~** plus tard dans sa vie; **early in ~** très tôt; **in adult ~** à l'âge adulte; **at my time of ~** à mon âge; **for the rest of one's ~** pour le restant de ses jours; **the ~ and times of X** la vie et l'époque de X; **to write a ~ of sb** écrire une biographie de qn; **3** (animation) vie f, vitalité f; **full of ~** plein de vie; **there's not much ~ in this town** cette ville n'est pas très vivante; **to come to ~** [person] reprendre conscience; FIG sortir de sa réserve; [fictional character] prendre vie; [party] s'animer; **to bring a subject to ~** traiter un sujet de manière très vivante; **put a bit of ~ into it** mettezy un peu de tonus; **4** (social activity, lifestyle) vie f; **private ~** vie privée; **his way of ~** son mode de vie; **a ~ of crime** une vie de criminel; **to live the good** ou **high ~** mener la grande vie; **it's no ~ for a child** ce n'est pas une vie pour un enfant; **5** (human being(s)) **without loss of ~** sans perte de vies humaines; **the ship sank with the loss of 500 lives** le naufrage du navire a fait 500 morts; **6** (useful duration) (of machine, vehicle, product) durée f; **7** JUR **to do** ou **serve ~** être emprisonné à vie; **to sentence sb to ~** condamner qn à perpétuité; **to get ~** se faire condamner à perpette; **8** ART **from ~** [draw, paint] d'après nature.
II noun modifier [member, peer, membership] à vie.
IDIOMS **anything for a quiet ~** tout ce que tu voudras mais laisse-moi tranquille; **for dear ~** de toutes mes/ses etc forces; **he couldn't for the ~ of him see why** il n'arrivait absolument pas à comprendre pourquoi; **not on your ~**! jamais de la vie!; **this is the ~**! c'est la belle vie!; **to frighten the ~ out of sb** faire mourir qn de peur; **to have the**

time of one's ~ s'amuser comme un fou/une folle;
to take one's ~ in one's hands risquer sa vie.
life: **~-and-death** adj [decision, issue] crucial;
~belt n bouée f de sauvetage; **~ blood** n FIG
force f vitale; **~boat** n canot m de sauvetage;
~buoy n bouée f de sauvetage; **~ drawing** n
ART dessin m d'après modèle; **~ expectancy** n
BIOL espérance f de vie; (of product) durée f probable;
~ force n LITTÉR force f vitale; **~ form** n être m
vivant; **~guard** ▶ 1251 n surveillant/-e m/f de
baignade; **~ imprisonment** n réclusion f à perpétuité; **~ insurance** n assurance-vie f; **~jacket** n
gilet m de sauvetage.
lifeless /'laɪflɪs/ adj inanimé; FIG [performance] peu
vivant; [voice] éteint.
lifelike /'laɪflaɪk/ adj très ressemblant.
lifeline /'laɪflaɪn/ n (on boat) bouée f de sauvetage;
(safety line) corde f de sécurité; (in climbing) assurance f.
lifelong /'laɪflɒŋ/ adj [friendship, fear] de toute une
vie; **to have had a ~ ambition to do** avoir toujours
rêvé de faire.
life: **~ mask** n ART masque m, empreinte f du
visage; **~ preserver** n = **lifejacket, lifebuoy**.
lifesaver /'laɪfseɪvə(r)/ n (lifeguard) sauveteur m.
lifesaving /'laɪfseɪvɪŋ/ **I** n GEN sauvetage m; MED
secourisme m.
II noun modifier [course] (swimming) de sauvetage;
MED de secourisme.
life: **~ sentence** n JUR condamnation f à perpétuité; **~-size** adj grandeur nature inv; **~ span** n
durée f de vie; **~ story** n vie f; **~style** n style m
de vie.
life-support machine n appareil m de respiration
artificielle; **to be on a ~** être sous assistance respiratoire.
lifetime /'laɪftaɪm/ n vie f; **the work of a ~** l'œuvre
d'une vie; **in her ~** de son vivant; **the chance of a
~** la chance de ma/ta etc vie; **to seem like a ~**
sembler une éternité.
life vest n US = **lifejacket**.
lift /lɪft/ **I** n **1** GB (elevator) (for people) ascenseur m; (for
goods) monte-charge m inv; **2** (ride) **she asked me for
a ~** elle m'a demandé de la conduire; **can I give you
a ~?** je peux te déposer quelque part?; **to give ~s
to hitchhikers** prendre des auto-stoppeurs; **don't
accept ~s from strangers** ne monte jamais dans la
voiture d'un inconnu; **3**° (boost) **to give sb a ~**
remonter le moral à qn; **4** SPORT (in weightlifting) essai
m.
II vtr **1** soulever [object, person]; lever [one's arm,
head] (from de); FIG lever [siege, ban, sanctions]; **to
~ sth off a ledge** soulever qch d'un rebord; **to ~
sth out of the box** sortir qch de la boîte ; **to ~ sth
over the wall** faire passer qch par-dessus le mur; **she
~ed the spoon to her lips** elle a porté la cuillère à
sa bouche; **I feel as if a great weight has been ~ed
from my mind** je me sens soulagé d'un grand poids; **2**
(boost) **to ~ sb's spirits** remonter le moral à qn; **3**°
(steal) piquer°, voler [file, keys, ideas] (from dans);
copier [article, passage] (from sur); **4** SPORT lifter
[ball]; **to ~ weights** faire des haltères; **5 to have
one's face ~ed** se faire faire un lifting.
III vi [lid] se soulever; [bad mood, headache] disparaître; [fog] se dissiper.
IDIOMS **not to ~ a finger** ne pas lever le petit doigt.
■ **lift down**: **¶ ~ [sb/sth] down**, **~ down [sb/sth]**
descendre [object].
■ **lift off**: **¶ ~ off** [rocket] décoller; [top, cover] s'enlever; **¶ ~ [sth] off**, **~ off [sth]** enlever [cover, lid].
■ **lift up**: **¶ ~ up** [lid, curtain] se soulever; **¶ ~
[sb/sth] up**, **~ up [sb/sth]** soulever [book, suitcase,
lid]; lever [head, veil, eyes]; relever [jumper, coat].
liftboy n GB liftier m.
lifting /'lɪftɪŋ/ n (of ban, siege) levée f.
lift-off /'lɪftɒf/ n (of rocket) lancement m.
ligament /'lɪɡəmənt/ n ligament m.
light /laɪt/ ▶ 1392 **I** n **1** (brightness) lumière f; **by the
~ of** à la lumière de [fire]; à la clarté de [moon]; **in**

the ~ **of day** LIT, FIG au grand jour; **to cast** ou
throw ou **shed ~ on** LIT projeter de la lumière sur;
FIG éclaircir; **to hold sth up to the ~** tenir qch à la
lumière; **against the ~** à contre-jour; **with the ~
behind her** le dos tourné à la lumière; **2** (in building,
machine, oven) lumière f; (in street) réverbère m; (on ship)
feu m; **to put** ou **turn a ~ on/off** allumer/éteindre
une lumière; **3** (part of gauge, indicator, dashboard) voyant
m (lumineux); **4** AUT (headlight) phare m; (rearlight) feu
m arrière; (inside car) veilleuse f; **5** (flame) **to put a ~
to** allumer [fire, gas]; **to set ~ to** mettre le feu à;
have you got a ~? (for cigarette) tu as du feu?; **6** FIG
(aspect) jour m; **to see sth in a different ~** voir qch
sous un jour différent; **looking at it in that ~**... vu
sous cet angle...; **to appear in a bad ~** apparaître
sous un jour défavorable; **to review sth in the ~ of** compte tenu
de; **to review sth in the ~ of** réexaminer qch à la
lumière de [evidence, experience]; **7** FIG (exposure) **to
bring to ~** découvrir [fact, evidence, truth]; **to come
to** ou **be brought to ~** être découvert.
II lights npl **1** (traffic) **~s** feu m, feux mpl; **the
~s are red** le feu est au rouge; **to stop at the ~s**
s'arrêter au feu; **to shoot**° ou **jump**° **the ~s** griller°
un feu rouge; **2** (decorative display) illuminations fpl.
III adj **1** (bright) [evening, room] clair; **to get** ou **grow
~er** [sky] s'éclaircir; **while it's still ~** pendant qu'il
fait encore jour; **2** [colour, fabric, wood, skin] clair;
[hair] blond; **~ blue** bleu clair inv; **3** (not heavy)
[material, substance, snow, wind, clothing, meal] léger/
-ère; [rain] fin; [drinker] modéré; [damage, sentence]
léger/-ère; **to be a ~ sleeper** avoir le sommeil léger;
she is 2 kg ~er elle pèse 2 kg de moins; **4** (delicate)
[knock, footsteps] léger/-ère; [movement] délicat; **to be
~ on one's feet** avoir la démarche légère; **5** (not
tiring) [work] peu fatigant; [exercise] léger/-ère; **~
duties** petits travaux mpl; **to make ~ work of sth**
faire qch sans peine; **6** [music, verse] léger/-ère; **a bit
of ~ relief** un peu de divertissement; **some ~ reading** quelque chose de facile à lire; **it is no ~ matter**
c'est une chose sérieuse; **to make ~ of** traiter [qch]
à la légère [rumour, problem]; ne pas attacher
d'importance à [injury].
IV vtr (prét, pp **lit** ou **lighted**) **1** allumer [candle,
oven, cigarette]; enflammer [wood, paper]; tirer [fire-
work]; craquer [match]; **to ~ a fire** faire un or du
feu; **to ~ the fire** allumer le feu; **2** (illuminate) éclairer.
V vi (prét, pp **lit**) [fire] prendre; [gas, match] s'allumer.
IDIOMS **the ~ of sb's life** le rayon de soleil de qn;
many hands make ~ work PROV à plusieurs la
besogne va vite; **to go out like a ~** s'endormir tout
de suite; **to see the ~** comprendre.
■ **light on**: **~ on** [sth] [eyes, person] tomber sur.
■ **light up**: **¶ ~ up 1** (light cigarette) allumer une
cigarette (or une pipe etc); **2** [lamp] s'allumer; FIG
[face] s'éclairer; [eyes] briller de joie; **¶ ~ up [sth]**,
~ [sth] up 1 allumer [cigarette, pipe]; **2** (illuminate)
illuminer.
light bulb n ampoule f.
lighten /'laɪtn/ **I** vtr **1** éclairer [room, surroundings];
éclaircir [colour, hair, wood, skin]; FIG détendre [atmo-
sphere]; **2** alléger [burden, pressure].
II vi **1** [sky, colour, hair] s'éclaircir; FIG [atmosphere]
se détendre; **2** [burden, pressure, workload] s'alléger.
light entertainment n variétés fpl.
lighter /'laɪtə(r)/ n **1** (for smokers) GEN briquet m; (for
gas cooker) allume-gaz m inv; **2** NAUT allège f.
lighter fuel n (gas) gaz m à briquet; (liquid) essence f à
briquet.
light: **~-fingered** adj (thieving) chapardeur/-euse;
(skilful) [thief] adroit; **~-footed** adj agile, au pied
léger LITER; **~-headed** adj [person] étourdi;
~-hearted adj (happy) enjoué; (not serious) humoristique; **~house** n phare m; **~ industry** n industrie f légère.
lighting /'laɪtɪŋ/ n GEN, THEAT éclairage m.
lightly /'laɪtlɪ/ adv **1** (delicately) GEN légèrement;
[move, run] avec légèreté; (frivolously) [take decision] à

like¹

When *like* is used as a preposition (*like a child, do it like this*) it can generally be translated by *comme*.

Note however that *be like* and *look like* meaning *resemble* are translated by *ressembler à*:

> she's like her father
> or she looks like her father = elle ressemble à son père

like is used after certain other verbs in English to express particular kinds of resemblance (*taste like, feel like, smell like* etc.). For translations, consult the appropriate verb entry.

When *like* is used as a conjunction it is translated by *comme*:

> songs like my mother sings = des chansons comme celles que chante ma mère

When *like* is used to introduce an illustrative example (*big cities like London*) it can be translated by either *comme* or *tel/telle/tels/telles que: les grandes villes comme Londres* or *les grandes villes telles que Londres*.

For particular usages of *like* as a preposition or conjunction and for noun and adverb uses, see the entry *like¹*.

---

la légère; **to sleep ~** avoir le sommeil léger; **2** (with little punishment) **to get off ~** s'en tirer à bon compte.

lightness /'laɪtnɪs/ *n* **1** (brightness) clarté *f*; **2** (in weight) légèreté *f*.

lightning /'laɪtnɪŋ/ **I** *n* ⊄ éclairs *mpl*; **a flash of ~** un éclair; **struck by ~** frappé par la foudre.
II *adj* [*raid, visit*] éclair (*inv*).
IDIOMS **as quick as ~** en un rien de temps; **like greased ~**, **like a streak of ~** en quatrième vitesse.

lightning: ~ conductor GB, **~ rod** *n* paratonnerre *m*; **~ strike** *n* grève *f* surprise.

light: ~ opera *n* opérette *f*; **~ pen** *n* (for computer screen) crayon *m* optique; **~ railway** *n* transport *m* urbain sur rail; **~-sensitive** *adj* photosensible; **~ switch** *n* interrupteur *m*.

lightweight /'laɪtweɪt/ **I** *n* SPORT poids *m* léger; FIG PÉJ personne *f* médiocre.
II *adj* GEN léger/-ère; SPORT [*champion, title*] des poids légers; FIG PÉJ médiocre.

light year *n* année-lumière *f*; **it was ~s ago** ça fait des siècles.

like¹ /laɪk/ **I** *prep* **1** (in the same manner as) comme; **to act ~ a professional** agir comme un professionnel or en professionnel; **~ the liar that she is, she...** en bonne menteuse, elle...; **stop behaving ~ an idiot!** arrête de faire l'idiot!; **it happened ~ this** voilà comment cela s'est passé; **when I see things ~ that** quand je vois des choses pareilles; **I'm sorry to disturb you ~ this** je suis désolé de vous déranger comme ça; **2** (similar to, resembling) comme; **to be ~ sb/sth** être comme qn/qch; **you know what she's ~!** tu sais comment elle est!; **it was just ~ a fairytale!** on aurait dit un conte de fée!; **what's it ~?** c'est comment?; **so this is what it feels ~ to be poor** maintenant je sais (or on sait etc) ce que c'est d'être pauvre!; **there's nothing ~ a nice warm bath!** rien ne vaut un bon bain chaud!; **I've never seen anything ~ it!** je n'ai jamais rien vu de pareil!; **that's more ~ it!** voilà qui est mieux!; **I don't earn anything ~ as much as she does** je suis loin de gagner autant qu'elle; **what was the weather ~?** quel temps faisait-il?; **3** (typical of) **it's not ~ her to be late** ça ne lui ressemble pas or ce n'est pas son genre d'être en retard; **it's just ~ him to be so spiteful!** c'est bien lui d'être si méchant!; **just ~ a man!** c'est typiquement masculin!; **4** (expressing probability) **it looks ~ rain** on dirait qu'il va pleuvoir; **it looks ~ the war will be a long one** il y a des chances pour que la guerre dure; **you seem ~ an intelligent man** tu as l'air intelligent; **5** (close to) **it cost something**

~ £20 cela a coûté dans les 20 livres or environ 20 livres; **with something ~ enthusiasm** avec un semblant d'enthousiasme.
II *adj* SOUT pareil/-eille, semblable, du même genre.
III *conj* **1** (in the same way as) comme; **~ I said, I wasn't there**° comme je vous l'ai déjà dit, je n'étais pas là; **~ they used to** comme ils le faisaient autrefois; **2**° (as if) comme si; **he acts ~ he owns the place** il se conduit comme s'il était chez lui.
IV *adv* (akin to, near) **it's nothing ~ as nice as...** c'est loin d'être aussi beau que...; **'the figures are 10% more than last year'—'20%, more ~**°**!'** 'les chiffres sont de 10% supérieurs à l'année dernière'—'20%, plutôt!'
V *n* **fires, floods and the ~** des incendies, des inondations et autres catastrophes de ce genre; **I've never seen the ~ (of it)** je n'ai jamais vu une chose pareille; **the ~(s) of Al Capone** des gens comme Al Capone; **she won't even speak to the ~s of us**°**!** elle refuse même de parler à des gens comme nous!
VI -like *combining form* **bird-~** qui fait penser à un oiseau; **child-~** enfantin; **king-~** royal.
IDIOMS **~ enough, (as) ~ as not** probablement; **~ father ~ son** PROV tel père tel fils PROV.

like² /laɪk/ *vtr* **1** aimer bien [*person*]; aimer (bien) [*artist, food, music, style*]; **to ~ A better than B** préférer A à B, aimer mieux A que B; **to ~ A best** préférer A; **to be well ~d** être apprécié; **to want to be ~d** vouloir plaire; **2 how do you ~ your tea?** comment aimes-tu boire ton thé?; **what I ~ about him/this car is...** ce que j'aime (bien) chez lui/dans cette voiture, c'est...; **she didn't ~ the look of the hotel** l'hôtel ne lui disait rien; **I don't ~ the look of that man** cet homme a une tête qui ne me revient pas; **I don't ~ the look of her, call the doctor** elle a une drôle de mine, appelle le médecin; **I don't ~ the sound of that** ça ne me dit rien qui vaille; **if you ~ that sort of thing** à condition d'aimer ce genre de choses; **I ~ cheese but it doesn't ~ me**° j'aime le fromage mais ça ne me réussit pas; **this plant ~s sunlight** cette plante se plaît au soleil; **I ~ doing, I ~ to do** j'aime (bien) faire; **I ~ to see people doing** j'aime (bien) que les gens fassent; **how do you ~ living in London?** ça te plaît de vivre à Londres?; **the boss won't ~ it if you're late** le patron ne sera pas content si tu arrives en retard; **she doesn't ~ to be kept waiting** elle n'aime pas qu'on la fasse attendre; **I ~ it!** ça me plaît!; **~ it or not we all pay tax** que ça nous plaise ou non nous payons tous des impôts; **3** (wish) vouloir, aimer; **I would** ou **should ~ a ticket** je voudrais un billet; **I would** ou **should ~ to do** je voudrais or j'aimerais faire; **would you ~ to come to dinner?** voudriez-vous venir dîner?; **I wouldn't ~ to think I'd upset her** j'espère bien que je ne lui ai pas fait de peine; **we'd ~ her to do** nous voudrions or aimerions qu'elle fasse; **would you ~ me to come?** voulez-vous que je vienne?; **if you ~** si tu veux; **you can do what you ~** tu peux faire ce que tu veux; **say what you ~, I think it's a good idea** tu peux dire ce que tu veux, je pense que c'est une bonne idée; **sit (any)where you ~** asseyez-vous où vous voulez; **4** (think important) **to ~ to do** tenir à faire.

likeable /'laɪkəbl/ *adj* [*person*] sympathique; [*novel, music*] agréable.

likelihood /'laɪklɪhʊd/ *n* probabilité *f*, chances *fpl*; **in all ~** selon toute probabilité; **the ~ is that she got lost** il est probable qu'elle se soit perdue; **there is no ~ of peace** il n'y a aucune chance de paix.

likely /'laɪklɪ/ **I** *adj* **1** (probable) probable, [*explanation*] plausible; **to be ~ to fail** risquer d'échouer; **to be ~ to become president** avoir de fortes chances de devenir président; **the man most ~ to win** l'homme qui a le plus de chances de gagner; **it is** ou **seems ~ that** il est probable que; **it is not** ou **hardly ~ that** il y a peu de chances que (+ *subj*); **he looks ~ to fail** il échouera probablement; **a ~ story!** IRON à d'autres**°**!; **2** (promising) [*person, candidate*] prometteur/-euse; **3** (potential) [*client, candidate*] potentiel/-ielle.

II adv (probably) probablement; **as ~ as not** probablement; **not ~**°! GB que tu crois°!

like-minded /laɪk'maɪndɪd/ adj du même avis.

liken /'laɪkən/ vtr comparer (**to** à).

likeness /'laɪknɪs/ n **1** (similarity) ressemblance f (**between** entre); **family ~** air m de famille; **to be a good ~** [picture] être ressemblant; **2** (form) **to assume** ou **take on the ~ of** se métamorphoser en.

likewise /'laɪkwaɪz/ adv (similarly) également, de même; (also) aussi, de même; **to do ~** faire de même.

liking /'laɪkɪŋ/ n **to have a ~ for** aimer; **to take a ~ to sb** se prendre d'affection pour qn; **you should find this more to your ~** ceci devrait vous plaire davantage; **he's too smart for my ~** il est trop malin à mon goût.

lilac /'laɪlək/ **I** n lilas m. **II** ▶818 adj (colour) lilas inv.

Lilo® /'laɪləʊ/ n matelas m pneumatique.

lilt /lɪlt/ n (of tune) cadence f; (of accent) intonation f.

lilting /'lɪltɪŋ/ adj mélodieux/-ieuse.

lily /'lɪlɪ/ n lys m inv.

lily: **~-livered** adj poltron/-onne; **~ of the valley** n muguet m; **~ pond** n bassin m aux nénuphars.

limb /lɪm/ n **1** ANAT membre m; **2** (of tree) branche f (maîtresse). **IDIOMS to be out on a ~** se retrouver isolé; **to go out on a ~** se mouiller°; **to risk life and ~** risquer sa vie; **to tear sb ~ from ~** mettre qn en pièces.

limber /'lɪmbə(r)/ adj LITTÉR souple. ■ **limber up** s'échauffer.

limbo /'lɪmbəʊ/ n **1** ¢ RELIG, FIG les limbes mpl; **2** (dance) limbo m.

lime /laɪm/ n **1** (calcium) chaux f; **2** (fruit) citron m vert; (tree) tilleul m.

lime: **~ green** ▶818 n, adj citron (m) vert inv; **~ juice** n jus m de citron vert.

limelight /'laɪmlaɪt/ n vedette f; **to be in the ~** tenir la vedette.

limerick /'lɪmərɪk/ n limerick m (poème humoristique en cinq lignes).

limestone n calcaire m.

limit /'lɪmɪt/ **I** n **1** (boundary) LIT, FIG limite f; **there will be no ~ to the violence** la violence ne connaîtra pas de limites; **within the ~s of what we can do** dans la limite de ce que l'on peut faire; **to be off ~s** MIL être interdit d'accès; **the garden is off ~s** l'accès au jardin est interdit; **to push sb to the ~** pousser qn à bout; **2** (legal restriction) limitation f (on sur); **speed ~** limitation de vitesse; **to be over the ~** (of alcohol) avoir trop d'alcool dans le sang. **II** vtr limiter; **places are ~ed to 60** le nombre de places est limité à 60; **to ~ oneself to** se limiter à.

limitation /ˌlɪmɪ'teɪʃn/ n **1** (restriction) restriction f (on à); **2** (shortcoming) limite f; **to know one's (own) ~s** connaître ses propres limites.

limited /'lɪmɪtɪd/ adj **1** [resources, vocabulary, intelligence, space] limité; **2** COMM **Nolan Computers Limited** Nolan Computers SA.

limited: **~ company** n GB société f anonyme; **~ edition** n (book, lithograph) tirage m limité; (recording) production f limitée.

limitless /'lɪmɪtlɪs/ adj illimité.

limousine /'lɪməzi:n, ˌlɪmə'zi:n/ n limousine f.

limp /lɪmp/ **I** n **to have a ~** boiter. **II** adj [material, gesture, handshake, style] mou/molle; **I felt his body go ~** j'ai senti tous les muscles de son corps se relâcher. **III** vi **to ~ along** boiter; **to ~ in/away** entrer/s'éloigner en boitant.

limpid /'lɪmpɪd/ adj limpide.

limply /'lɪmplɪ/ adv mollement.

limpness /'lɪmpnɪs/ n (of body) mollesse f.

limp-wristed /ˌlɪmp'rɪstɪd/ adj PÉJ efféminé.

linchpin /'lɪntʃpɪn/ n (essential element) **the ~ of** [person] le pilier de; [principle] la base de.

Lincs GB POST abrév écrite = **Lincolnshire**.

linctus /'lɪŋktəs/ n sirop m (contre la toux).

linden (tree) /'lɪndən/ n LITTÉR tilleul m.

line /laɪn/ **I** n **1** GEN, SPORT ligne f; (shorter, thicker) trait m; ART trait m; **a straight/curved ~** une ligne droite/courbe; **to put a ~ through sth** barrer qch; **the ~ AB** (in geometry) la droite AB; **2** (of people, cars) file f; (of trees) rangée f; **in straight ~s** [plant, arrange] en lignes droites; **to be in ~** [buildings] être dans l'alignement; **put the desks in ~** alignez les bureaux; **3** FIG **to be in ~ for promotion** avoir des chances d'être promu; **you're next in ~** ça va être ton tour; **in ~ for** bien placé pour obtenir; **4** (queue) file f; **to stand in** ou **wait in ~** faire la queue; **to form a ~** [people] faire la queue; **please form a ~** mettez-vous en file s'il vous plaît; **5** (on face) ride f; **6** ARCHIT (outline shape) ligne f (of de); **7** (boundary) frontière f; **there's a fine ~ between knowledge and pedantry** de la culture à la pédanterie il n'y a qu'un pas; **8** (rope) corde f; (for fishing) ligne f; **to put the washing on the ~** étendre le linge; **9** (cable) ELEC ligne f (électrique); **10** TELECOM (connection) ligne f; **to be on the ~ to sb** être en ligne avec qn; **to get off the ~**° raccrocher; **at the other end of the ~** au bout du fil; **the ~ is dead** il n'y a pas de tonalité; **the ~ went dead** la ligne a été coupée; **11** (rail route) ligne f (**between** entre); (rails) voie f; (shipping company, airline) compagnie f; **12** (in genealogy) lignée f; **the male ~** la lignée par les hommes; **the Tudor ~** la maison des Tudor; **to trace one's ~ back to sb** retracer son ascendance jusqu'à qn; **she is second in ~ to the throne** elle est la deuxième dans l'ordre de succession au trône; **13** (in prose) ligne f; (in poetry) vers m; (of music) ligne f; **100 ~s** 100 lignes; **to start a new ~** aller à la ligne; **a ~ from** une citation de [poem etc]; **he has all the best ~s** il a les meilleures répliques; **to learn one's ~s** THEAT apprendre son texte; **14** (conformity) **to fall into ~ with** s'aligner sur; **to bring sb into ~** ramener qn dans le rang; **to bring regional laws into ~ with federal laws** harmoniser les lois régionales et les lois fédérales; **to keep sb in ~** tenir qn en main; **our prices are out of ~ with those of our competitors** nos prix ne s'accordent pas avec ceux de nos concurrents; **you're way out of ~**°! franchement, tu exagères!; **15**° (piece of information) **to have a ~ on sth** avoir des informations sur qch; **don't give me that ~!** ne me raconte pas ces histoires!; **16**° (stance) **the official ~** la position officielle; **something along these ~s** quelque chose dans le même genre; **to be on the right ~s** être sur la bonne voie; **to take a firm ~ with sb** se montrer ferme avec qn; **I don't know what ~ to take** je ne sais pas quelle ligne de conduite adopter; **17** (type of product) gamme f; **18** MIL **enemy ~s** lignes fpl ennemies; **19** (equator) **the ~** la ligne; **20**° (of cocaine) ligne° f (**of** de).

II in line with prep phr en accord avec [policy, trend]; **to increase in ~ with** augmenter proportionnellement à; **to vary in ~ with** varier parallèlement à.

III vtr doubler [garment] (**with** avec); tapisser [box, shelf] (**with** de); [spectators] border [route].

IDIOMS all along the ~, right down the ~ sur toute la ligne; **somewhere along the ~** (at point in time) à un certain moment; (at stage) quelque part.

■ **line up**: ¶ **~ up 1** (side by side) se mettre en rang; (one behind the other) se mettre en file; **2** (take sides) **to ~ up against sb** se regrouper contre qn; ¶ **~ up [sb], ~ [sb] up** (in row) faire s'aligner; ¶ **~ [sth] up, ~ up [sth] 1** (align) aligner (**with** sur); **2** (organize) sélectionner [team]; **to have sb/sth ~d up** avoir qn/qch en vue [work, candidate]; **what have you got ~d up for us tonight?** qu'est-ce que tu nous as prévu pour ce soir°?

lineage /'lɪnɪdʒ/ n lignage m.

linear /'lɪnɪə(r)/ adj linéaire.

lined /laɪnd/ adj [face] ridé; [paper] ligné; [curtains] doublé.

line: **~ drawing** n dessin m au trait; **~man** n US

SPORT *au football américain, joueur qui se place sur la ligne*; **~ management** *n* (system) direction *f* hiérarchique; **~ manager** *n* responsable opérationnel/-elle *m/f*.

linen /'lɪnɪn/ **I** *n* **1** (fabric) lin *m*; **2** (household) linge *m* de maison; (underwear) linge *m* de corps.
II *noun modifier* [*jacket, sheet*] en lin, de lin.
IDIOMS **to wash one's dirty ~ in public** laver son linge sale en public.

linen: **~ basket** *n* panier *m* à linge sale; **~ cupboard** GB, **~ closet** US *n* armoire *f* à linge.

line: **~ of argument** *n* raisonnement *m*; **~ of attack** *n* FIG plan *m* d'action.

line of duty *n* **killed in the ~** [*policeman*] mort en service (commandé); [*soldier*] mort au combat.

line: **~ of enquiry** *n* (in investigation) piste *f*; (in research) ligne *f* de recherche; **~ of fire** *n* ligne *f* de tir; **~ of work** *n* métier *m*; **~-out** *n* (rugby) remise *f* en touche.

liner /'laɪnə(r)/ *n* paquebot *m* de grande ligne.

linesman /'laɪnzmən/ *n* GB (in tennis) juge *m* de ligne; (in football, hockey) juge *m* de touche.

line-spacing *n* interlignage *m*.

line-up /'laɪnʌp/ *n* **1** SPORT équipe *f*; (personnel, pop group) groupe *m*; **2** (identification) séance *f* d'identification (*de suspects*).

linger /'lɪŋgə(r)/ *vi* **1** [*person*] s'attarder; [*gaze*] s'attarder (**on** sur); **to ~ for a few weeks (before dying)** vivre encore quelques semaines; **2** [*memory, smell*] persister; **3** [*doubt, suspicion*] subsister.
■ **linger on** [*memory*] persister.
■ **linger over**: **~ over** [*sth*] savourer [*meal*].

lingerie /'lænʒəriː, US ˌlɑːndʒəˈreɪ/ *n* ¢ lingerie *f*.

lingering /'lɪŋgərɪŋ/ *adj* [*look*] prolongé; [*death*] lent; **some ~ doubts remain** il subsiste encore quelques doutes.

lingo° /'lɪŋgəʊ/ *n* baragouin° *m*.

linguist /'lɪŋgwɪst/ *n* linguiste *mf*.

linguistic /lɪŋˈgwɪstɪk/ *adj* linguistique.

linguistics /lɪŋˈgwɪstɪks/ **I** *n* (+ *v sg*) linguistique *f*.
II *noun modifier* [*course, lecturer*] de linguistique.

liniment /'lɪnɪmənt/ *n* (ointment) pommade *f*.

lining /'laɪnɪŋ/ *n* doublure *f*.
IDIOMS **every cloud has a silver ~** à quelque chose malheur est bon.

link /lɪŋk/ **I** *n* **1** (in chain) maillon *m*; FIG **the weak ~** le point faible; **2** (connection by rail, road) liaison *f*; **3** (connection between facts, events) rapport *m* (**between** entre); (between people) lien *m* (**with** avec); **4** (economic or trading tie) relation *f* (**with** avec; **between** entre); (historical or friendly tie) lien *m* (**with** avec; **between** entre); **5** TELECOM, RADIO, COMPUT liaison *f*.
II *vtr* **1** (connect physically) [*road, cable*] relier [*places, objects*]; **to ~ A to B** ou **A and B** relier A à B; **to ~ arms** [*people*] se donner le bras; **to ~ arms with sb** prendre qn par le bras; **2** (relate, establish connection between) **to ~ sth to** ou **with** lier qch à [*inflation*]; établir un lien entre qch et [*fact, crime, illness*]; **his name has been ~ed with** son nom a été associé à [*deed, name*]; **3** COMPUT connecter [*terminals*]; **to ~ sth to** ou **with** connecter qch à [*mainframe, terminal*]; **4** TV, RADIO établir une liaison entre [*places*] (**by** par).
III linked *pp adj* **1** [*circles, symbols*] entrelacé; **2** FIG [*issues, problems*] lié; **they are romantically ~ed** il y a quelque chose entre eux.
■ **link up**: **~ up** [*firms*] s'associer; **to ~ up with** s'associer avec [*college, firm*].

linkage /'lɪŋkɪdʒ/ *n* **1** (connection) lien *m* (**between** entre); **2** (of issues in international relations) association *f* (**between** entre); **3** (in genetics) linkage *m*.

link: **~man** *n* présentateur *m*; **~ road** *n* GB route *f* de raccordement.

links /lɪŋks/ *n* golf *m*, terrain *m* de golf.

link-up /'lɪŋkʌp/ *n* **1** TV, RADIO liaison *f*; **2** COMM association *f* (**between** entre; **with** avec).

lino /'laɪnəʊ/ *n* lino *m*.

lino cut, **lino print** *n* gravure *f* sur linoléum.

linseed oil /'lɪnsiːd ɔɪl/ *n* huile *f* de lin.

lint /lɪnt/ *n* **1** (bandage) tissu *m* ouaté; **2** (fluff) peluches *fpl*.

lintel /'lɪntl/ *n* linteau *m*.

lion /'laɪən/ *n* lion *m*; **the ~'s den** LIT, FIG l'antre du lion; **literary ~** célébrité *f* littéraire.
IDIOMS **to take the ~'s share** se tailler la part du lion.

lion cub *n* lionceau *m*.

lioness /'laɪənes/ *n* lionne *f*.

lionize /'laɪənaɪz/ *vtr* aduler.

lip /lɪp/ **I** *n* **1** ANAT lèvre *f*; **to read sb's ~s** lire sur les lèvres de qn; **my ~s are sealed!** bouche cousue°!; **2** (of bowl, crater) bord *m*; (of jug) bec *m*; **3**° (cheek) insolence *f*.
II *noun modifier* [*gloss, pencil*] à lèvres.
III -lipped *combining form* **thin-/thick-~ped** aux lèvres minces/charnues.
IDIOMS **to keep a stiff upper ~** rester flegmatique.

liposuction /'laɪpəʊsʌkʃn, 'lɪpəʊ-/ *n* liposuccion *f*.

lip: **~-read** *vi* (*prét, pp* **-read** /-red/) lire sur les lèvres de quelqu'un; **~reading** *n* lecture *f* sur les lèvres; **~salve** *n* baume *m* pour les lèvres.

lip service *n* PÉJ **to pay ~ to feminism** se dire féministe pour la forme.

lipstick *n* rouge *m* à lèvres.

liquefy /'lɪkwɪfaɪ/ **I** *vtr* liquéfier.
II *vi* se liquéfier.

liqueur /lɪˈkjʊə(r), US -'kɜːr/ *n* liqueur *f*.

liqueur glass *n* verre *m* à liqueur.

liquid /'lɪkwɪd/ **I** *n* (substance) liquide *m*; **drink plenty of ~s** buvez beaucoup.
II *adj* [*substance, nitrogen*] liquide; [*gaze*] clair.

liquid assets *npl* liquidités *fpl*.

liquidate /'lɪkwɪdeɪt/ *vtr* (all contexts) liquider.

liquidation /ˌlɪkwɪˈdeɪʃn/ *n* liquidation *f*.

liquidator /'lɪkwɪdeɪtə(r)/ *n* liquidateur/-trice *m/f*.

liquidity /lɪˈkwɪdəti/ *n* liquidité *f*.

liquidize /'lɪkwɪdaɪz/ *vtr* GB CULIN passer [qch] au mixeur.

liquidizer /'lɪkwɪdaɪzə(r)/ *n* GB CULIN mixeur *m*.

liquid: **~ lunch** *n* HUM alcool *m* en fait de déjeuner; **~ measure** *n* mesure *f* de capacité des liquides.

liquor /'lɪkə(r)/ *n* (alcohol) alcool *m*.

liquorice, **licorice** US /'lɪkərɪs/ **I** *n* **1** (plant) réglisse *f*; **2** (substance) réglisse *m*.
II *noun modifier* [*root, stick*] de réglisse.

liquor store *n* US magasin *m* de vins et spiritueux.

lira /'lɪərə/ **▶ 849** *n* (*pl* **lire**) lire *f*.

Lisbon /'lɪzbən/ **▶ 1343** *pr n* Lisbonne.

lisle /laɪl/ **I** *n* fil *m* d'Écosse.
II *noun modifier* **~ stockings** bas *mpl* de fil.

lisp /lɪsp/ **I** *n* zézaiement *m*; **to have a ~** zézayer.
II *vi* zézayer, zozoter°.

lissom /'lɪsəm/ *adj* svelte.

list /lɪst/ **I** *n* **1** (catalogue) liste *f* (**of** de); **to be at the top of the ~** LIT arriver en tête de liste; FIG être en tête des priorités; **to be low on one's ~ of priorities** ne pas figurer en tête de ses priorités; **2** NAUT (leaning) bande *f*.
II *vtr* **1** GEN faire la liste de [*objets, people*]; **to be ~ed under** être classé à; **to be ~ed among** figurer parmi; **to be ~ed in a directory** être repris dans un répertoire; **2** COMPUT lister; **3** **to be ~ed on the Stock Exchange** être coté en Bourse.
III *vi* NAUT donner de la bande.
IV listed *pp adj* GB [*building*] classé.

listen /'lɪsn/ **I** *n* **have a ~ to this**°! écoute un peu ça!
II *vi* **1** (to words, music, sounds) écouter; **to ~ at the door** écouter aux portes; **to ~ to sb/sth** écouter qn/qch; **2** (pay heed) écouter; **sorry, I wasn't ~ing** excusez-moi, je n'écoutais pas; **~, can you come**

tomorrow? écoute, est-ce que tu peux venir demain?; **to ~ to reason** écouter la voix de la raison; **3** (wait) **to ~ (out) for** guetter [*sound*].

■ **listen in** écouter (indiscrètement); **to ~ in on** ou **to sth** écouter qch indiscrètement.

listener /ˈlɪsnə(r)/ *n* **1** (personal) **to be a good ~** savoir écouter; **a ready ~** une oreille attentive; **2** RADIO auditeur/-trice *m/f*.

listening /ˈlɪsnɪŋ/ *n* **it makes interesting ~** c'est intéressant à écouter; **'easy ~'** MUS 'variétés' *fpl*.

listeria /lɪˈstɪərɪə/ *n* (bacteria) listéria *f*; (illness) listériose *f*.

listeriosis /lɪˌstɪərɪˈəʊsɪs/ *n* MED listériose *f*.

listing /ˈlɪstɪŋ/ **I** *n* **1** GEN inscription *f* (**in** dans); **Stock Exchange ~** liste *f* des sociétés cotées en Bourse; **2** COMPUT listing *m*.
II listings *npl* pages *fpl* d'informations.

listless /ˈlɪstlɪs/ *adj* [*person*] apathique.

listlessly /ˈlɪstlɪslɪ/ *adv* [*speak*] sans enthousiasme; [*move*] mollement.

list price *n* prix *m* au catalogue.

lit /lɪt/ **I** *prét*, *pp* ▶ **light IV**, **V**.
II° (*abrév* = **literature**) littérature *f*.

litany /ˈlɪtənɪ/ *n* **1** RELIG litanies *fpl*; **2** FIG (of complaints etc) litanie *f*.

literacy /ˈlɪtərəsɪ/ **I** *n* (in a population) taux *m* d'alphabétisation; **our goal is 100% adult ~** notre but est que 100% des adultes soient alphabétisés.
II *noun modifier* [*campaign*, *level*] d'alphabétisation.

literal /ˈlɪtərəl/ *adj* **1** [*meaning*] littéral; **2** [*translation*] mot à mot; **3** [*rendering*] GEN fidèle; PÉJ sans imagination PÉJ.

literally /ˈlɪtərəlɪ/ *adv* **1** [*mean*] littéralement; [*translate*] mot à mot; **to take sth ~** prendre qch au pied de la lettre; **2** (without exaggeration) bel et bien.

literary /ˈlɪtərərɪ, US ˈlɪtərerɪ/ *adj* littéraire.

literary: **~ critic** *n* critique *m* littéraire; **~ criticism** *n* critique *f* littéraire; **~ theory** *n* théorie *f* littéraire.

literate /ˈlɪtərət/ *adj* **1** (able to read and write) **to be ~** savoir lire et écrire; **2** (cultured) [*person*] cultivé; [*work*, *film*] érudit.

literati /ˌlɪtəˈrɑːtɪ/ *npl* gens *mpl* de lettres.

literature /ˈlɪtrətʃə(r), US -tʃʊər/ **I** *n* **1** (literary writings) littérature *f*; **a work of ~** une œuvre littéraire; **2** (pamphlets, brochures etc) documentation *f*.
II *noun modifier* [*course*] de littérature.

lithe /laɪð/ *adj* leste.

lithograph /ˈlɪθəɡrɑːf, US -ɡræf/ **I** *n* lithographie *f*.
II *vtr* lithographier.

lithographer /lɪˈθɒɡrəfə(r)/ **▶ 1251** *n* lithographe *mf*.

lithography /lɪˈθɒɡrəfɪ/ *n* lithographie *f*.

Lithuania /ˌlɪθjuːˈeɪnɪə/ **▶ 840** *pr n* Lituanie *f*.

litigation /ˌlɪtɪˈɡeɪʃn/ *n* ¢ litiges *mpl*; **to come to ~** être porté devant les tribunaux.

litigious /lɪˈtɪdʒəs/ *adj* [*person*] procédurier/-ière.

litmus: **~ paper** *n* papier *m* de tournesol; **~ test** *n* CHEM réaction *f* au (papier de) tournesol; FIG test *m* décisif.

litre, liter US /ˈliːtə(r)/ **▶ 789** **I** *n* litre *m*.
II *noun modifier* [*jug*, *measure*] d'un litre.

litter /ˈlɪtə(r)/ **I** *n* **1** (rubbish) détritus *mpl*; (more substantial) ordures *fpl*; (paper) papiers *mpl*; **'no ~'** 'défense de déposer des ordures'; **2** (random collection) fouillis *m* (**of** de); **3** (of animal) (young) portée *f*; **to have a ~** mettre bas; **4** (for casualty) brancard *m*; (for dignitary) litière *f*; **5** (for pet tray) litière *f*.
II *vtr* [*leaves*, *books*] joncher [*ground*]; **to ~ the house with sth** [*person*] semer qch dans toute la maison; **to be ~ed with corpses** [*ground*] être jonché de cadavres.

litter: **~ bin** *n* poubelle *f*; **~bug** *n* PÉJ *personne qui jette des détritus par terre*; **~ lout** *n* GB = **litter-bug**; **~ tray** *n* bac *m* à litière.

---

little[1] /ˈlɪtl/ (*comparative* **less**; *superlative* **least**)

■ **Note** When *little* is used as a quantifier (*little hope*, *little damage*) it is translated by *peu de*: peu d'espoir, peu de dégâts.
– For examples and particular usages see **I** below.
– When *a little* is used as a pronoun (*give me a little*) it is translated by *un peu*: donne-m'en un peu.
– When *little* is used alone as a pronoun (*there's little I can do*) it is very often translated by *pas grand-chose*: je ne peux pas faire grand-chose.
– For examples of these and other uses of *little* as a pronoun (*to do as little as possible etc*) see **II** below.
– For uses of *little* and *a little* as adverbs see the entry below.
– Note that *less* and *least* are treated as separate entries in the dictionary.

I *quantif* **~ chance** peu de chances; **there's so ~ time** il y a si peu de temps; **too ~ money** trop peu or pas assez d'argent; **~ or no influence** presque pas d'influence; **I have ~ time for cheats** je ne supporte pas les tricheurs; **I see ~ of Paul these days** je ne vois pas beaucoup Paul en ce moment.
II *pron* **save a ~ for me** gardes-en un peu pour moi; **I only ate a ~** je n'en ai mangé qu'un peu; **I did what ~ I could** j'ai fait le peu que j'ai pu; **he remembers very ~** il ne se souvient pas bien; **there's ~ I can do** je ne peux pas faire grand-chose; **age has ~ to do with it** l'âge n'a pas grand-chose à voir là-dedans; **to do as ~ as possible** faire le moins possible; **~ of note** rien de bien particulier; **~ or nothing** quasiment rien.
III *adv* **1** (not much) peu; **I go there very ~** j'y vais très peu; **the next results were ~ better** les résultats suivants étaient à peine meilleurs; **~ more than an hour ago** il y a à peine plus d'une heure; **it's ~ short of madness** cela frise la folie; **a ~-known novel** un roman peu connu; **2** (not at all) **~ did she realize** elle ne s'est pas du tout rendu compte; **~ did they know that** ils étaient bien loin de se douter que.
IV a little (**bit**) *adv phr* (slightly) un peu; **a ~ (bit) anxious** un peu inquiet; **a ~ less/more** un peu moins/plus; **stay a ~ longer** reste encore un peu.
V as little as *adv phr* **for as ~ as 10 dollars a day** pour seulement 10 dollars par jour; **as ~ as £60** juste 60 livres sterling.

little[2] /ˈlɪtl/ *adj* **1** (small) [*house, smile, voice*] petit (*before n*); **poor ~ thing** pauvre petit/-e *m/f*; **she's a nice ~ thing** elle est adorable; **2** (young) [*sister, boy*] petit (*before n*); **when I was ~** quand j'étais petit; **3** (in a small way) [*farmer, businessman*] petit (*before n*); **4** (expressing scorn) **a poky ~ flat** un petit appartement minable; **a nasty ~ boy** un méchant petit garçon; **5** (short) [*snooze*] petit (*before n*); **a ~ holiday** quelques jours de vacances; **a ~ break** une petite pause.
IDIOMS **~ by ~** petit à petit; **to make ~ of** (not understand) ne pas comprendre grand-chose à [*speech*].

■ **Note** Pour le comparatif et le superlatif on préférera les formes *smaller* et *smallest* à *littler* et *littlest*.

little finger *n* petit doigt *m*, auriculaire *m*.
IDIOMS **to wrap** ou **twist sb around one's ~** mener qn par le bout du nez.

liturgy /ˈlɪtədʒɪ/ *n* liturgie *f*.

live[1] /lɪv/ **I** *vtr* (conduct) vivre [*life*]; **to ~ a normal/peaceful life** vivre normalement/paisiblement; **to ~ a life of luxury** vivre dans le luxe; **to ~ the life of a recluse** vivre en reclus.
II *vi* **1** (dwell) [*animal*] vivre; [*person*] GEN vivre, habiter (**with** avec); (have one's address) habiter; **they ~ at number 7** ils habitent au numéro 7; **to ~ together** vivre ou habiter ensemble; **to ~ in** vivre dans, habiter [*house, apartment*]; **not fit to ~ in** insalubre; **easy to ~ with** facile à vivre; **it's a nice place to ~** il fait bon y vivre; **have you found anywhere to ~ yet?** avez-vous trouvé à vous loger?; **he ~s in jeans** il est toujours en jean; **2** (lead one's life) vivre; **to ~ in poverty** vivre dans la pauvreté; **we ~ in the computer age** nous vivons à l'ère de l'informatique; **to ~ for** ne vivre que pour [*sport, work*]; **to ~ through sth** vivre [*experience*]; **3** (remain

alive) GEN, FIG vivre; (survive) survivre; **to ~ to be eighty** vivre jusqu'à l'âge de quatre-vingts ans; **to be still living** être encore en vie; **as long as I ~**... tant que je vivrai...; **I don't think he'll ~** je ne pense pas qu'il survive; **to ~ through the night** passer la nuit; **I'll ~!** HUM je n'en mourrai pas!; **nothing left to ~ for** plus de raison de vivre; **to ~ to regret sth** en venir à regretter qch; **long ~ democracy!** vive la démocratie!; **4** (subsist) vivre; **to ~ by one's wits** vivre d'expédients; **to ~ on** ou **off** vivre de [*fruit, charity*]; vivre sur [*wage, capital*]; **that's not enough to ~ on** ça ne suffit pas pour vivre; **to ~ on junk food** ne manger que des cochonneries○; **5** (put up with) **to ~ with** accepter [*situation*]; supporter [*décor*]; **to ~ with the fact that** admettre que; **6** (experience life) vivre; **come on! ~ a little!** allez viens! laisse-toi vivre!; **you haven't ~d until you've been to...** tu n'as rien vu tant que tu n'es pas allé à...

IDIOMS **~ and let ~** il faut être tolérant; **to ~ it up**○ faire la fête○; **we ~ and learn** on en apprend tous les jours; **to ~ sth down** faire oublier qch.
■ **live in** [*caretaker*] avoir un logement de fonction; [*nanny, maid*] être logé et nourri.
■ **live on** [*reputation, tradition*] se perpétuer.
■ **live out**: ¶ **~ out** [*nanny*] ne pas être logé; [*teacher*] vivre en ville; ¶ **~ out** [*sth*] **1** (survive) passer [*winter*]; **2** (spend) **to ~ out one's days somewhere** finir ses jours quelque part; **3** (enact) vivre [*fantasies*].
■ **live up to** [*person*] répondre à [*expectations*]; être à la hauteur de [*reputation*]; [*product*] ne pas démentir [*advertising*].

live² /laɪv/ **I** *adj* **1** (not dead) [*animal*] vivant; [*birth*] d'un enfant viable; **real ~** en chair et en os; **2** RADIO, TV [*broadcast*] en direct; [*performance*] sur scène; [*theatre*] vivant; [*album*] enregistré sur scène; **before a ~ audience** devant un public; **3** (burning) [*coal*] ardent; **4** (capable of exploding) [*ammunition*] réel/réelle; (unexploded) [*shell*] nonexplosé; **5** ELEC sous tension.
II *adv* RADIO, TV [*appear, broadcast*] en direct.

lived-in○ /'lɪvdɪn/ *adj* **to have that ~ look** donner une impression de confort.

live-in /'lɪvɪn/ *adj* [*maid, nanny*] qui est logé et nourri; **to have a ~ lover** vivre en concubinage.

livelihood /'laɪvlɪhʊd/ *n* gagne-pain *m*; **to lose one's ~** perdre ses moyens d'existence.

liveliness /'laɪvlɪnɪs/ *n* (of place, person) gaieté *f*; (of style) vivacité *f*.

lively /'laɪvlɪ/ *adj* **1** (vivacious) [*person*] plein d'entrain; [*place, atmosphere, conversation*] animé; [*account*] vivant; [*interest, mind*] vif/vive; [*campaign*] percutant; **2** (fast) [*pace*] vif/vive; [*music, dance*] entraînant.
IDIOMS **look ~**○! réveillez-vous!

liven /'laɪvn/ *v* ■ **liven up**: ¶ **~ up** s'animer; ¶ **~ up** [*sth*] **~** [*sth*] **up** égayer [*person*]; animer [*event*].

liver /'lɪvə(r)/ *n* CULIN, MED foie *m*.

live rail /laɪv/ *n* rail *m* conducteur.

liver paste, **liver pâté** *n* pâté *m* de foie.

Liverpudlian /ˌlɪvə'pʌdlɪən/ *n* (living there) habitant/-e *m/f* de Liverpool; (born there) natif/-ive *m/f* de Liverpool.

liver: **~ salts** *npl* sels *mpl* pour le foie; **~ spot** *n* tache *f* de vieillesse; **~wurst** *n* US **~** pâté *m* de foie.

livery /'lɪvərɪ/ *n* **1** (uniform) livrée *f*; **2** (boarding horses) **at ~** en pension.

lives /laɪvz/ *npl* ▶ **life**.

live /laɪv/: **~stock** *n* bétail *m*; **~ wire** *n* FIG boute-en-train *m inv*.

livid /'lɪvɪd/ *adj* **1**○ (furious) furieux/-ieuse; **2** [*face, scar*] livide; **~ with rage** blème de rage.

living /'lɪvɪŋ/ **I** *n* **1** (livelihood) vie *f*; **to work for a ~** travailler pour gagner sa vie; **what do you do for a ~?** qu'est-ce que vous faites dans la vie?; **2** (lifestyle) vie *f*; **loose ~** une vie de débauche; **3** RELIG (incumbency) cure *f*; **4 the ~** (+ *v pl*) les vivants *mpl*.
II *adj* vivant; **to be ~ proof of** être la preuve vivante de; **a ~ hell** un véritable enfer; **within ~**

memory de mémoire d'homme; **there wasn't a ~ soul** il n'y avait pas âme qui vive.
IDIOMS **to be still in the land of the ~** être encore de ce monde.

living: **~ conditions** *npl* conditions *fpl* de vie; **~ dead** *npl* morts-vivants *mpl*; **~ death** *n* FIG enfer *m*, calvaire *m*; **~ expenses** *npl* frais *mpl* de subsistance; **~ quarters** *npl* quartiers *mpl*; **~ room** *n* salle *f* de séjour, salon *m*; **~ standards** *npl* niveau *m* de vie; **~ wage** *n* salaire *m* adéquat.

lizard /'lɪzəd/ *n* lézard *m*.

llama /'lɑːmə/ *n* lama *m*.

LLB *n* (*abrév écrite* = **Bachelor of Laws**) ≈ licence *f* en droit.

LLD *n* (*abrév écrite* = **Doctor of Laws**) ≈ doctorat *m* en droit.

load /ləʊd/ **I** *n* **1** (sth carried) charge *f*; (on vehicle, animal) chargement *m*; (on ship, plane) cargaison *f*; FIG fardeau *m*; **to take a ~ off sb's mind** soulager qn (d'un grand poids); **a bus-~ of children** un autobus plein d'enfants; **2** TECH (weight) charge *f* (**on** sur); **3** (shipment, batch) (of sand, gravel) cargaison *f*; **four ~s of washing** quatre machines de linge; **4** ELEC charge *f*; **5** FIG (amount of work) travail *m*; **to lighten/spread the ~** alléger/répartir le travail; **6**○ (a lot) **a ~** ou **a whole ~ of people** des tas○ de gens; **that's a ~ of nonsense**○ c'est de la blague○.
II○ **loads** *npl* **~s of** (plus plural nouns) des tas○ de; **~s of times** plein de or des tas○ de fois; **we've got ~s of time** nous avons tout notre temps; **we had ~s to drink** on n'a pas arrêté de boire; **~s of energy** de l'énergie à revendre; **~s of champagne** du champagne en quantité; **~s of work** un travail fou○; **~s of money** énormément d'argent.
III *vtr* **1** GEN charger [*vehicle, gun, washing machine*] (**with** de); mettre un film dans [*camera*]; **2** COMPUT charger [*program*]; **3** FIG (inundate) **to ~ sb with** combler or couvrir qn de [*presents, honours*].
IV *vi* charger.
IDIOMS **get a ~ of this**○! (listen) écoute un peu ça○!; **get a ~ of that**○! (look) vise un peu ça○!; **the dice are ~ed against him** tout est contre lui.
■ **load down**: **~** [sb] **down** charger qn (**with** de); **to be ~ed down with sth** plier sous le poids de qch.

load-bearing *adj* [*wall*] porteur/-euse.

loaded /'ləʊdɪd/ *adj* **1** (full, laden) [*tray, lorry, gun*] chargé (**with** de); FIG **~ with meaning** plein de sens; **2** (weighed down) [*person*] chargé (**with** de); FIG **to be ~ with honours** être couvert d'honneurs; **3**○ FIG (rich) plein aux as○, bourré de fric○; **4** (leading) [*question*] tendancieux/-ieuse; **5**○ US (drunk) bourré○.

loading /'ləʊdɪŋ/ *n* (of vehicle) chargement *m*.

loading bay *n* aire *f* or zone *f* de chargement.

loaf /ləʊf/ *n* (*pl* **loaves**) pain *m*; **a ~ of bread** un pain.
IDIOMS **half a ~ is better than none** PROV faute de grives on mange des merles; **use your ~**○! fais marcher tes méninges○!
■ **loaf about**, **loaf around** traînasser.

loafer /'ləʊfə(r)/ *n* **1** (shoe) mocassin *m*; **2** (idler) flemmard/-e○ *m/f*.

loam /ləʊm/ *n* terreau *m*.

loan /ləʊn/ **I** *n* **1** GEN (when borrowing) emprunt *m*; (when lending) prêt *m*; **to have the ~ of sth** emprunter qch; **to be on ~** [*museum object*] être prêté (**to** à); **the book is already on ~** le livre a déjà été emprunté.
II *vtr* prêter (also **~ out**) prêter [*object, money*].

loan: **~ account** *n* COMM compte *m* de prêt; **~ agreement** *n* contrat *m* de prêt; **~ facility** *n* facilité *f* de crédit; **~ shark**○ *n* PÉJ usurier/-ière *m/f*.

loath /ləʊθ/ *adj* **to be ~ to do** répugner à faire.

loathe /ləʊð/ *vtr* détester (**doing** faire).

loathing /'ləʊðɪŋ/ *n* répugnance *f* (**for** pour).

loathsome /'ləʊðsəm/ *adj* répugnant.

loaves /ləʊvz/ *npl* ▶ **loaf**.

lob /lɒb/ **I** *n* SPORT lob *m*.
II *vtr* (*p prés etc* **-bb-**) **1** GEN lancer; **2** SPORT lober.

lobby /'lɒbɪ/ I n **1** (of hotel) hall m; (of theatre) lobby m; **2** GB POL (also **division ~**) (where MPs vote) vestibule où les députés se répartissent pour voter; **3** (also **~ group**) lobby m.
II vtr [group] faire pression sur [group] (**about** à propos de); POL appuyer [bill].
III vi faire pression (**for** pour obtenir).
lobbying /'lɒbɪɪŋ/ n lobbying m.
lobbyist /'lɒbɪɪst/ n membre m d'un groupe de pression, lobbyiste mf.
lobe /ləʊb/ n ANAT, BOT lobe m.
lobelia /lə'biːljə/ n lobélie f.
lobster /'lɒbstə(r)/ I n CULIN, ZOOL homard m.
II noun modifier [salad, soup] au homard.
lobster pot n casier m à homards.
local /'ləʊkl/ I n **1** (person) **is he a ~?** il est du coin?; **the ~s** les gens mpl du coin; **2** (pub) pub m du coin.
II adj **1** (neighbourhood) [library, shop] du quartier; (of the town) [newspaper] local; **3** (regional) [radio, news] régional; [speciality] du pays; [tradition] local; [business] de la région; **4** (of a country) [currency, time] local.
local: **~ anaesthetic** n anesthésique m local; **~ authority** n GB ADMIN (+ v sg ou pl) autorités fpl locales; **~ call** n TELECOM communication f téléphonique locale; **~ colour** GB, **~ color** US n couleur f locale.
locale /ləʊ'kɑːl, US -'kæl/ n endroit m.
Local Education Authority, LEA n GB administration locale qui gère les affaires scolaires.
local: **~ election** n élection f locale; **~ government** n administration f locale.
locality /ləʊ'kælətɪ/ n **1** (neighbourhood) voisinage m; **2** (place) endroit m.
localize /'ləʊkəlaɪz/ I vtr localiser [problem]; restreindre [damage].
II **localized** pp adj localisé.
locate /ləʊ'keɪt, US 'ləʊkeɪt/ vtr **1** (find) retrouver [object]; localiser [fault]; **2** (position) situer [site]; **to be ~d in London** se trouver à Londres.
location /ləʊ'keɪʃn/ n GEN endroit m; (in house particulars) **a central ~** un emplacement central; **to know the ~ of sth** savoir où se trouve qch; CIN **on ~** en extérieur.
loch /lɒk, lɒx/ n loch m, lac m.
lock /lɒk/ I n **1** (with key) serrure f; (with bolt) verrou m; **under ~ and key** sous clé; **2** (of hair) mèche f; **curly ~s** cheveux mpl bouclés; **3** NAUT écluse f; **4** (in wrestling) clé f; **5** AUT **to have a good ~** [car] bien braquer; **to turn the wheel full ~** braquer le volant à fond; **6** COMPUT verrouillage m.
II vtr **1** (close securely) (with key) fermer [qch] à clé; (with bolt) verrouiller; **to ~ sth into a drawer** enfermer qch dans un tiroir; **2** COMPUT verrouiller [file]; **~ed in combat** aux prises; **to ~ horns** FIG se disputer violemment.
III vi **1** (close securely) [door, drawer] fermer à clé; **2** (seize up) [steering wheel] bloquer.
■ **lock away**: **~ [sth] away** mettre [qch] sous clé.
■ **lock in**: **~ [sb] in** enfermer [person]; **to ~ oneself in** s'enfermer.
■ **lock out**: **~ [sb] out** (on purpose) fermer la porte à clé pour empêcher qn d'entrer; (by mistake) laisser qn dehors sans clé; **to get ~ed out** se retrouver sans clé à la porte.
■ **lock together** [components, pieces] s'emboîter.
■ **lock up**: ¶ **~ up** fermer; ¶ **~ [sth] up**, ¶ **~ up [sth]** fermer [qch] à clé [house]; immobiliser [capital]; ¶ **~ [sb] up**, **~ up [sb]** enfermer [hostage]; mettre [qn] sous les verrous [killer].
locker /'lɒkə(r)/ n casier m, vestiaire m.
locker room n vestiaire m.
locket /'lɒkɪt/ n médaillon m.
lock gate n porte f d'écluse.
locking /'lɒkɪŋ/ I n GEN, COMPUT verrouillage m.
II adj [petrol cap] antivol.
lock: **~jaw** n tétanos m; **~ keeper** n éclusier/-ière

m/f; **~-out** n lock-out m inv, grève f patronale; **~smith** n serrurier m; **~-up garage** n GB box m.
loco /'ləʊkəʊ/ I° n GB RAIL loco° f.
II° adj fou/folle.
locomotive /ˌləʊkə'məʊtɪv/ n locomotive f.
locum /'ləʊkəm/ n GB remplaçant/-e m/f.
locust /'ləʊkəst/ n locuste f, sauterelle f.
lodge /lɒdʒ/ I n **1** (small house) pavillon m; (for gatekeeper) loge f (du gardien); (in castle) conciergerie f; **porter's ~** UNIV loge du concierge; **2** (Masonic) loge f.
II vtr **1** (accommodate) loger [person]; **2** JUR **to ~ an appeal** faire appel; **to ~ a complaint** porter plainte; **to ~ a protest** protester.
III vi **1** (reside) loger (**with** chez); **2** (stick) [bullet] se loger; [small object] se coincer; **3** (in memory) s'incruster.
lodger /'lɒdʒə(r)/ n (room only) locataire mf; (with meals) pensionnaire mf.
lodging /'lɒdʒɪŋ/ I n logement m; **board and ~** le gîte et le couvert.
II **lodgings** npl logement m; **to take ~s** prendre une chambre (**with** chez).
loft /lɒft, US lɔːft/ n **1** (attic) grenier m; **2** US (apartment) loft m; **3** ARCHIT **organ ~** tribune d'orgue.
loft conversion n aménagement m de grenier.
loftily /'lɒftɪlɪ, US 'lɔːftɪlɪ/ adv avec hauteur.
lofty /'lɒftɪ, US 'lɔːftɪ/ adj **1** [building, peak] haut; [manner] hautain; [ideals] noble.
log /lɒg, US lɔːg/ I n **1** (of wood) rondin m; (for burning) bûche f; **2** (written record) registre m; **3** (of ship) journal m de bord; (of plane) carnet m de vol; **4** COMPUT carnet m d'exploitation; **5** MATH logarithme m.
II vtr (p prés etc **-gg-**) **1** (record) noter; **2** (clock up) (also **~ up**) avoir à son actif [miles]; **3** [car, train] rouler à [speed]; [plane] voler à [speed]; [ship] filer à [knots].
IDIOMS **to sleep like a ~** dormir comme une souche.
■ **log in, log on** COMPUT ouvrir une session, se connecter.
■ **log off, log out** COMPUT clore une session, se déconnecter.
logarithm /'lɒgərɪðəm, US 'lɔːg-/ n logarithme m.
log book n **1** (of car) ~ carte f grise; **2** (of ship) journal m de bord; (of plane) carnet m de vol; **3** (written record) registre m.
log: **~ cabin** n cabane f en rondins; **~ fire** n feu m de bois.
logger /'lɒgə(r)/ n bûcheron m.
loggerheads /'lɒgəhedz/ npl **to be at ~** être en désaccord (**with** avec).
logging /'lɒgɪŋ/ n abattage m (des arbres).
logic /'lɒdʒɪk/ n GEN, PHILOS, COMPUT logique f.
logical /'lɒdʒɪkl/ adj logique.
logically /'lɒdʒɪklɪ/ adv logiquement.
logistic /lə'dʒɪstɪk/ adj logistique.
logistically /lə'dʒɪstɪklɪ/ adv d'un point de vue logistique.
logistics /lə'dʒɪstɪks/ n (+ v sg ou pl) logistique f.
log jam n LIT embouteillage m (de bois de flottage); FIG blocage m.
logo /'ləʊgəʊ/ n logo m.
log: **~rolling** n US POL trafic m de faveurs; **~ tables** npl tables fpl de logarithmes.
loin /lɔɪn/ I n CULIN GB ~ côtes fpl premières; US ~ filet m.
II **loins**† npl ANAT reins mpl; **to gird up one's ~s** LIT ceindre les reins; FIG s'armer de courage.
loin: **~ chop** n côte f première; **~cloth** n pagne m.
loiter /'lɔɪtə(r)/ vi (idly) traîner; (pleasurably) flâner; (suspiciously) rôder.
loll /lɒl/ vi [person] se prélasser; [part of body] tomber; [tongue] pendre.
■ **loll about** traîner sans rien faire.
lollipop /'lɒlɪpɒp/ n sucette f.

lollop /'lɒləp/ *vi* galoper (maladroitement).

lolly /'lɒlɪ/ *n* GB **1**○ (money) fric○ *m*; **2** (sweet) sucette *f*; **ice** ~ glace *f* à l'eau (*sur un bâton*).

London /'lʌndən/ ▶ 1343 **I** *pr n* Londres; **in/to** ~ à Londres; **inner** ~ Londres intra-muros; **outer** ~ la banlieue de Londres.
II *noun modifier* [*accent, train*] de Londres.

Londoner /'lʌndənə(r)/ *n* Londonien/-ienne *m/f*.

lone /ləʊn/ *adj* LITTÉR (only one) seul.

loneliness /'ləʊnlɪnɪs/ *n* (of person) solitude *f*; (of position) isolement *m*.

lonely /'ləʊnlɪ/ *adj* [*person*] solitaire; [*place*] isolé; [*decision*] que l'on prend seul.

lonely: ~ **hearts' club** club *m* de rencontres; ~ **hearts' column** *n* petites annonces *fpl* (*de rencontre*).

lone parent *n* parent *m* isolé.

loner /'ləʊnə(r)/ *n* solitaire *mf*.

lonesome /'ləʊnsəm/ *adj* US solitaire.

long /lɒŋ, US lɔ:ŋ/ ▶ 1045 **I** *adj* **1** (lengthy, protracted) [*process, wait, journey, vowel*] long/longue; [*delay*] important; [*bath, sigh*] grand (*before n*); **to be 20 minutes** ~ durer 20 minutes; **how** ~ **is the interval?** combien de temps dure l'entracte?; **is an hour** ~ **enough?** est-ce qu'une heure suffira?; **it's been a** ~ **day** la journée a été longue; **to get** ~**er** [*days*] s'allonger; **to take a** ~ **hard look at sth** réfléchir sérieusement à qch; **to work** ~ **hours** faire de longues journées; **a friend of** ~ **standing** un ami de longue date; **2** (in expressions of time) **she's been away a** ~ **time** elle est restée longtemps absente; **it's been a** ~ **time since I saw you** ça fait longtemps que je ne t'ai pas vu; **you've been a** ~ **time getting here** tu as mis longtemps pour arriver; **they've taken a** ~ **time to decide** il leur a fallu du temps pour se décider; **that's a** ~ **time** c'est long; **I've been a teacher for a** ~ **time** je suis professeur depuis longtemps; **she hasn't been well for a** ~ **time** ça fait longtemps qu'elle est malade; **for a** ~ **time I didn't believe her** pendant longtemps je ne l'ai pas crue; **a** ~ **time ago** il y a longtemps; **to take a** ~ **time** [*person*] être lent; [*task*] prendre longtemps; **3** (in measuring) [*dress, hair, queue*] long/longue; [*grass*] haut; [*detour*] grand; **20 m** ~ de 20 m de long; **to be 20 m** ~ avoir 20 m de long; **to get** ~ [*grass, hair*] pousser; [*list, queue*] s'allonger; **she's growing her hair** ~ elle se laisse pousser les cheveux; **to make sth** ~**er** allonger [*sleeve*]; augmenter la longueur de [*shelf*]; **4** (in expressions of distance) **a** ~ **way** loin; **January is a** ~ **way off** janvier est loin; **don't fall, it's a** ~ **way down** ne tombe pas, c'est haut; **a** ~ **way down the list** loin sur la liste; **a** ~ **way out** (at sea) loin au large; (in calculations) loin du compte; **we've come a** ~ **way** nous avons fait beaucoup de chemin; **to go a** ~ **way** [*person*] (be successful) aller loin; **to make sth go a** ~ **way** faire durer qch; **to go a** ~ **way towards doing** contribuer largement à faire; **to have a** ~ **way to go** FIG [*worker, planner*] avoir encore beaucoup d'efforts à faire; **by a** ~ **way** de loin; **to take the** ~ **way round** faire un long détour.
II *adv* **1** (a long time) longtemps; **to be** ~ (doing sth) en avoir pour longtemps; **how** ~ **will you be in the meeting?** cette réunion va te prendre combien de temps?; **not very** ~ pas très longtemps; **don't be** ~ dépêche-toi; **how** ~ **will it be before we know?** dans combien de temps le saura-t-on?; **it won't be** ~ **before...** dans peu de temps...; **I've been here** ~**er than anyone else** je suis ici depuis plus longtemps que personne; **I can't stand it a day** ~**er** je ne le supporterai pas un jour de plus; **I can't stand it any** ~**er** j'en ai assez; **the** ~**er we stayed the hotter it grew** plus le temps passait et plus il faisait chaud; **it's not that** ~ **since...** il ne s'est pas passé tellement de temps depuis...; **it wasn't** ~ **before...** il n'a pas fallu longtemps pour que...; **has he been gone** ~? est-ce qu'il y a longtemps qu'il est parti?; **I haven't got** ~ je n'ai pas beaucoup de temps; ~ **enough** assez longtemps; **just** ~ **enough to...** juste le temps de...; **that doesn't give us** ~ ça ne nous laisse pas beau-

coup de temps; **this won't take** ~ ça ne prendra pas longtemps; ~**er than expected** plus longtemps que prévu; **how** ~ **did it take him?** il lui a fallu combien de temps?; ~**er than he thought** plus de temps qu'il ne pensait; **three days at the** ~**est** trois jours tout au plus; **before** ~ (in past) peu après; (in future) dans peu de temps; **before much** ~**er** sous peu; **not for** ~ pas longtemps; **will you be gone for** ~? seras-tu longtemps absent?; ~ **after** longtemps après; **not** ~ **after** peu après; **it's** ~ **past your bedtime** tu devrais être couché depuis longtemps; ~ **ago** il y a longtemps; ~ **before** bien avant; **not** ~ **before lunch** peu de temps avant le déjeuner; ~ **since** depuis longtemps; **he's no** ~ **head** il n'est plus chef; **5 minutes, no** ~**er!** 5 minutes, pas plus!; **2** (for a long time) (*avant pp*) depuis longtemps; **those days are** ~ **gone** ce temps-là n'est plus; **3** (throughout) (*après n*) **all day** ~ toute la journée.
III as long as, so long as *conj phr* **1** (in time) aussi longtemps que; **(for) as** ~ **as you like** aussi longtemps que tu veux; **as** ~ **as I live** toute ma vie; **2** (provided that) du moment que (+ *indic*), pourvu que (+ *subj*).
IV *vi* **to** ~ **for sth/sb** avoir très envie de qch/de voir qn; **to** ~ **to do** (be impatient) être très impatient de faire; (desire sth elusive) rêver de faire.
IDIOMS ~ **time no see**○! HUM ça fait une paye○ qu'on ne s'est pas vus!; **she's not** ~ **for this world** elle ne fera pas de vieux os; **so** ~○! salut!; **why all the** ~ **faces?** vous en faites une tête○!; **to pull a** ~ **face** faire triste mine; **to have a** ~ **memory** être rancunier/-ière.

long: ~**-awaited** *adj* longtemps attendu; ~**boat** *n* chaloupe *f*; ~**-delayed** *adj* longuement différé.

long-distance I *adj* [*runner*] de fond; [*telephone call*] (within the country) interurbain; (abroad) international; ~ **lorry driver** GB routier *m*.
II *adv* de loin; (from abroad) de l'étranger.

long: ~**-drawn-out** *adj* interminable; ~**ed-for** *adj* tant attendu; ~**-established** *adj* fondé il y a longtemps.

longevity /lɒn'dʒevətɪ/ *n* (of person) longévité *f*.

long-haired *adj* [*person*] aux cheveux longs; [*animal*] à poil long.

longhand /'lɒŋhænd/ *n* **in** ~ écrit à la main.

long-haul *adj* AVIAT long-courrier *inv*.

longing /'lɒŋɪŋ, US 'lɔ:ŋɪŋ/ **I** *n* grand désir *m* (**for** de; **to do** de faire); (stronger) convoitise *f* (**for** envers); (nostalgic) nostalgie *f* (**for** de).
II *adj* [*look*] (greedy) plein de convoitise.

longingly /'lɒŋɪŋlɪ, US 'lɔ:ŋ-/ *adv* (greedily) avec convoitise; (nostalgically) avec nostalgie.

longish /'lɒŋɪʃ, US 'lɔ:ŋɪʃ/ *adj* assez long/longue; **a** ~ **time** pas mal de temps.

longitude /'lɒndʒɪtju:d, US -tu:d/ *n* longitude *f*; **at a** ~ **of 52°** par 52° de longitude.

long: ~ **johns**○ *npl* caleçon *m* long; ~ **jump** ▶ 949 *n* GB saut *m* en longueur; ~**-lasting** *adj* qui dure longtemps; ~**-life** [*milk*] longue conservation *inv*; [*battery*] longue durée *inv*; ~**-limbed** *adj* aux membres longs; ~**-line** *adj* long/longue; ~**-lived** *adj* [*tradition*] persistant; ~**-lost** *adj* [*relative*] perdu de vue depuis longtemps; ~**-range** *adj* [*missile*] (à) longue portée; [*forecast*] à long terme; ~**-running** *adj* [*play, dispute*] qui dure depuis longtemps; ~**shoreman** *n* US docker *m*.

long shot *n* (risky attempt) **it's a** ~ c'est risqué; (guess) **this is a** ~ je dis ça à tout hasard.

long: ~**-sighted** *adj* MED presbyte; ~**-sleeved** *adj* à manches longues; ~**-standing** *adj* de longue date; ~**-suffering** *adj* qui supporte tout sans se plaindre; ~**-tailed** *adj* à longue queue.

long term I *n* **in the** ~ à long terme.
II long-term *adj, adv* à long terme.

long: ~**-time** *adj* de longue date; ~**-wave** *n* grandes ondes *fpl*; ~**-ways** *adv* dans le sens de la longueur; ~**-winded** *adj* verbeux/-euse.

loo○ /lu:/ *n* GB vécés○ *mpl*, toilettes *fpl*.

loofah /ˈluːfə/ n loufa m.

look /lʊk/ **I** n **1** (glance) coup m d'œil; **to have** ou **take a ~ at sth** jeter un coup d'œil à or sur qch; **to have** ou **take a good ~ at** FIG examiner [qch] soigneusement; LIT regarder [qch] de près; **I didn't get a good ~** je n'ai pas bien vu; **to have a ~ inside/behind sth** regarder à l'intérieur de/derrière qch; **to have a ~ round** faire un tour de [house, town]; **to have a ~ round the shops** faire le tour des magasins; **to have a ~ through** (scan) chercher dans [archives, files]; parcourir [essay, report]; **I took one ~ at him and knew that he was ill** j'ai tout de suite vu qu'il était malade; **let's have a ~ at that grazed knee** voyons ce genou écorché; **to take a long hard ~ at sth** étudier sérieusement qch; **2** (search) **to have a (good) ~** (bien) chercher; **3** (expression) regard m; **a ~ of sadness/anger** un regard triste/rempli de colère; **to give sb a pitying ~** regarder qn avec pitié; **he got some odd** ou **funny ~s** on l'a regardé d'un drôle d'air; **I don't like the ~ on his face** je n'aime pas son air; **from the ~ on his face...** à son expression...; **4** (appearance) (of person) air m; (of building, scenery) aspect m; **to have a dated ~** ne pas faire très moderne; **she has a ~ of her father** elle a quelque chose de son père; **to have the ~ of a military man** avoir l'allure d'un militaire; **I like the ~ of it** ça a l'air bien; **I like the ~ of him** il a l'air sympaᵒ; **I don't like the ~ of him** il ne m'inspire pas confiance; **I don't like the ~ of the weather** ciel n'annonce rien de bon; **I don't like the ~ of that rash** ces rougeurs m'inquiètent; **by the ~ of him...** à le voir...; **5** (style) lookᵒ m.

II looks npl **he's got the ~s** il a le physique; **~s aren't everything** il n'y a pas que la beauté qui compte; **to keep one's ~s** rester beau/belle; **he's losing his ~s** il n'est pas aussi beau qu'autrefois; **you can't go by ~s alone** il ne faut pas se fier aux apparences.

III vtr **1** (gaze, stare) regarder; **to ~ sb in the eye/in the face** regarder qn dans les yeux/en face; **to ~ sb up and down** (appraisingly) regarder qn de haut en bas; **~ who it is!** regarde qui voilà!; **2** (appear) **to ~ one's age** faire son âge; **she's 40 but she doesn't ~ it** elle a 40 ans mais elle ne les fait pas; **he ~s about 50** il doit avoir la cinquantaine; **to ~ one's best** être à son avantage; **she still ~s the same** elle n'a pas changé; **to ~ a fool** avoir l'air ridicule; **it won't ~ good** ça sera mal vu; **he doesn't ~ himself** il n'a pas l'air dans son assiette.

IV vi **1** regarder (into dans; over par-dessus); **to ~ and see who's at the door** regarder qui est à la porte; **to ~ away** détourner le regard or les yeux; **to ~ out of the window** regarder par la fenêtre; **to ~ the other way** LIT regarder ailleurs; FIG fermer les yeux; **to ~ up and down the street** regarder partout dans la rue; **I didn't know where to ~** FIG je ne savais plus où me mettre; (in shop) **I'm just ~ing** je ne fais que regarder; **2** (search) chercher, regarder; **to ~ down** parcourir [list]; **3** (appear, seem) avoir l'air, paraître; **you ~ cold** tu as l'air d'avoir froid; **he ~s young for his age** il fait jeune pour son âge; **that makes you ~ younger** ça te rajeunit; **how do I ~?** comment me trouves-tu?; **you ~ well** tu as bonne mine; **you ~ good in that hat** ce chapeau te va bien; **you ~ good enough to eat!** tu es mignon/une croquerᵒ!; **the picture will ~ good in the study** le tableau ira bien dans le bureau; **it doesn't ~ right** ça ne va pas; **how does it ~ to you?** qu'est-ce que tu en penses?; **it ~s OK to me** ça m'a l'air d'aller; **things are ~ing good** les choses se présentent bien; **it ~s to me as if** ou **likeᵒ...** j'ai l'impression que...; **it ~s as if it will snow** on dirait qu'il va neiger; **it ~s likely that** il semble probable que (+ subj); **it ~s certain that** il semble certain que (+ indic); **to ~ like sb/sth** ressembler à qn/qch; **that photograph doesn't ~ like you** on ne te reconnaît pas du tout sur cette photo; **what does the house ~ like?** comment est la maison?; **it ~s like being fun** cela promet d'être amusant; **you ~ like being the only man there** il y a de fortes chances pour que tu sois le seul homme présent; **it ~s like rain** on dirait qu'il va pleuvoir; **it certainly ~s like it** ça en a tout l'air; **it ~s like cancer to me** je pense que c'est un cancer; **4** (listen) écoute; **~ here** écoute-moi bien; **5** (be oriented) **to ~ north** [house, room] être orienté au nord.

V **-looking** combining form **distinguished-~ing** [person] à l'air distingué; **sinister-~ing** [place] à l'aspect sinistre; **he's not bad-~ing** il n'est pas mal.

IDIOMS **if ~s could kill...** il/elle etc m'a fusillé du regard.

■ **look after**: ¶ **~ after [sb/sth] 1** (care for) soigner [patient]; garder [child]; s'occuper de [customer, plant]; entretenir [car]; prendre soin de [belongings]; **2** (be responsible for) s'occuper de [finances, shop]; surveiller [class, luggage]; **to ~ after sb's interests** veiller aux intérêts de qn; ¶ **~ after oneself 1** (cope) se débrouiller tout seul; **2** (be careful) **safe journey, and ~ after yourself** bon voyage, fais bien attention à toi!

■ **look ahead** LIT regarder devant soi; FIG regarder vers l'avenir.

■ **look around**: ¶ **~ around 1** (glance around) regarder autour de soi; **2** (search) chercher; **to ~ around for sb/sth** chercher qn/qch; **3** (visit, examine) (in town) faire un tour; ¶ **~ around [sth]** visiter [church, town]; **to ~ around the shops** faire les magasins.

■ **look at**: **~ at [sth] 1** GEN regarder; (briefly) jeter un coup d'œil sur; **~ at the state of you!** regarde un peu de quoi tu as l'air!; **you'd never guess, to ~ at her** à la voir on ne devinerait jamais; **he's not much to ~ at** il ne paie pas de mine; **2** (examine) vérifier [equipment]; examiner [patient]; jeter un coup d'œil à [car, plumbing]; étudier [problem, options]; **3** (see, view) voir [life, situation]; envisager [problem]; **try and ~ at it my way** essaie de voir les choses de mon point de vue; **that's how I ~ at it** c'est comme ça que je vois les choses; **you can't be too careful, ~ at Tom!** il faut être très prudent, regarde ce qui est arrivé à Tom!; **4** (talk about) **you're ~ing at about 3,000 dollars** ça va vous coûter aux alentours de 3 000 dollars.

■ **look back**: **~ back 1** (turn around) se retourner (at pour regarder); **2** (reminisce) **let's ~ back to 1964** revenons à l'année 1964; **if we ~ back to the 19th century** si l'on considère le dix-neuvième siècle; **she's never ~ed back** tout s'est très bien passé pour elle; **to ~ back on** se tourner sur [past]; repenser à [experience]; **~ing back on it** rétrospectivement.

■ **look down**: ¶ **~ down** (with modesty, shame) baisser les yeux; (from a height) regarder en bas; ¶ **~ down on [sb/sth] 1** LIT regarder [qch] d'en haut; **2** FIG mépriser; **3** (loom above) dominer.

■ **look for**: ¶ **~ for [sb/sth]** (search for) chercher qn/qch; ¶ **~ for [sth]** (expect) attendre [commitment, co-operation, result, reward] (**from** de).

■ **look forward**: **to ~ forward to [sth]** attendre [qch] avec impatience; **she's ~ing forward to going on holiday** elle a hâte de partir en vacances; **I'm not ~ing forward to the interview** la perspective de l'entretien ne me réjouit pas; **I ~ forward to hearing from you** (to a friend) j'espère avoir bientôt de tes nouvelles; (formal) dans l'attente de votre réponse.

■ **look in** (pay a visit) passer.

■ **look into**: **~ into [sth]** examiner, étudier [matter, possibility, problem]; examiner [accounts]; enquêter sur [death, disappearance].

■ **look on**: ¶ **~ on** (watch) regarder; (be present) assister; ¶ **~ on [sb/sth]** considérer [person, event] (**as** comme; **with** avec).

■ **look onto**: **~ onto [sth]** [house] donner sur [street].

■ **look out**: ¶ **~ out** (take care) faire attention (**for** à); (be wary) se méfier (**for** de); **~ out!** attention!; ¶ **~ out for [sb/sth]** guetter [person]; être à l'affût de [bargain, new talent]; être à la recherche de [apartment]; guetter l'apparition de [symptoms]; repérer [examples]; ¶ **~ out for [oneself]** se débrouiller tout seul; ¶ **~ out over [sth]** [window] donner sur [sea].

■ **look over**: ¶ **~ [sb] over** passer [qn] en revue; ¶

~ [sth] over examiner [*car, animal*]; ¶ **~ over 1** (read) (in detail) examiner; (rapidly) parcourir; **2** (visit) visiter [*factory, gardens*].

■ **look round** ¶ **1** (look behind one) se retourner; **2** (look about) regarder autour de soi; **3** (try to find) **we're ~ing round for a new house** nous cherchons une nouvelle maison; ¶ **~ round [sth]** visiter [*town*].

■ **look through**: ¶ **~ through [sth] 1** (read) consulter [*archive, files*]; parcourir [*essay, report, notes*]; (scan idly) feuilleter [*magazine*]; **2** (search) fouiller dans [*belongings, briefcase*]; ¶ **~ through [sb]** faire semblant de ne pas voir [*person*].

■ **look to**: ¶ **~ to [sb/sth] 1** (rely on) compter sur qn/qch; **2** (turn to) se tourner vers [*future, friends*]; ¶ **~ to [sth]** (pay attention) veiller à [*interests*]; ¶ **~ to do** (expect) espérer faire.

■ **look up**: ¶ **~ up 1** (raise one's eyes) lever les yeux (**from** de); **2** (raise one's head) lever la tête; **to ~ up at the clouds** regarder les nuages; **3** (improve) [*business*] aller mieux; [*situation*] s'améliorer; [*property market*] reprendre; **things are ~ing up for us** les choses s'arrangent pour nous; ¶ **~ [sb/sth] up, ~ up [sb/sth] 1** (check in book) chercher [*phone number, price*] (**in** dans); **2** (visit) passer voir [*acquaintance*]; ¶ **~ up to [sb]** admirer [*person*].

look: **~-alike** n sosie m; **~ed-for** adj (tjrs épith) [*result*] attendu; [*benefit*] escompté.

look-in /'lʊkɪn/ n GB **to get a ~** avoir sa chance; **to give sb a ~** donner sa chance à qn.

looking-glass n LITTÉR miroir m.

look-out /'lʊkaʊt/ I n **1 to be on the ~ for** rechercher [*stolen vehicle*]; être à l'affût de [*bargain, new talent*]; guetter [*visitor*]; **2** (sentry) (on ship) vigie f; (in army) guetteur m; **3** (place) poste m d'observation; **4**° GB (private concern) **that's his ~** c'est son affaire. **II** *noun modifier* [*tower*] d'observation; **to be on ~ duty** (on ship) être de quart; (in army) faire le guet.

loom /luːm/ I n métier m à tisser. **II** vi **1** (also **~ up**) surgir (**out of** de; **over** au-dessus de); **2** [*war, crisis*] menacer; [*exam, interview*] être imminent; **to ~ large** [*exam, issue*] peser lourd. **III looming** pres p adj **1** FIG [*crisis*] qui menace; [*deadline*] qui approche dangereusement; **2** LIT [*spire, cliff*] menaçant.

loony° /'luːnɪ/ I n (pl **-ies**) **1** (eccentric) farfelu/-e m/f; **2** (crazy) dingue° mf; INJUR (mentally ill) taré/-e° m/f OFFENSIVE. **II** adj farfelu°.

loony-bin° n asile m de fous.

loop /luːp/ I n **1** boucle f; **2** AVIAT **to ~ the ~** faire un looping; **3** COMPUT boucle f. **II** vtr nouer. **III** vi [*road, path*] faire une boucle. **IDIOMS to throw sb for a ~** US sidérer qn.

loophole /'luːphəʊl/ n FIG lacune f.

loopy° /'luːpɪ/ adj loufoque°.

loose /luːs/ I n **on the ~** qui s'est échappé; **a gang of hooligans on the ~ in the town** une bande de voyous qui rôdent dans les rues de la ville; **he is still on the ~** il est toujours en liberté. **II** adj **1** LIT (not firm or tight) [*knot, screw*] desserré; [*handle*] branlant; [*component*] mal fixé; [*button*] qui se décout; [*thread*] décousu; [*tooth*] qui se déchausse; **to come ~** [*knot, screw*] se desserrer; [*handle*] être branlant; [*tooth*] se déchausser; **to hang ~** [*hair*] être dénoué; [*rope*] pendre; **~ connection** ELEC faux contact; **2** (free) **to break ~** [*animal*] s'échapper (**from** de); **to cut sb ~** détacher qn; **to let** ou **set** ou **turn ~** libérer [*animal, prisoner*]; **3** COMM (not packed) [*tea, sweets*] en vrac; (as individual item) au détail; **just put the apples in the bag ~** mettez donc les pommes à même le sac; **~ change** petite monnaie; **4** (that has come apart) [*page*] volant; [*fragment*] détaché; **to come ~** [*pages*] se détacher; '**~ chippings**' GB, '**~ gravel**' US (roadsign) 'attention gravillons'; **5** (not tight) [*jacket, trousers*] ample; [*collar*] lâche; [*skin*] flasque; **6** (not compacted) [*soil*] meuble; [*link, weave*] lâche; **to have ~ bowels** avoir la diarrhée; **7** (not strict or exact) [*translation, interpretation*] assez libre;

[*wording*] imprécis; [*connection, guideline*] vague; [*style*] relâché; **8** (dissolute) [*morals*] dissolu; **~ living** (vie f de) débauche f. **IDIOMS to be at a ~ end** GB, **to be at ~ ends** US ne pas trop savoir quoi faire.

loose: **~-box** n GB box m; **~ cover** n GB housse ; (de fauteuil); **~-fitting** adj ample; **~-leaf** adj à feuilles mobiles.

loose-limbed adj souple.

loosely /'luːslɪ/ adv **1** LIT (not tightly) [*fasten, wrap*] sans serrer; (not firmly) [*fix*] pas solidement; **his clothes hung ~ on him** il flottait dans ses vêtements; **2** FIG [*connected*] de façon souple; [*structured*] assez librement; **3** FIG (imprecisely) [*translate*] assez librement; **the film is ~ based on the novel** le film est une adaptation assez libre du roman; **~ termed Marxist** qualifié grossièrement de marxiste.

loosely knit adj [*group, structure*] peu uni.

loosen /'luːsn/ I vtr **1** (make less tight) desserrer [*belt, strap, collar*]; dégager [*nail, post*]; relâcher [*rope, control*]; dénouer [*hair*]; **to ~ one's grip** ou **hold on sth** LIT relâcher sa prise sur qch; FIG relâcher son emprise sur qch; **2 to ~ the bowels** MED avoir une action laxative. **II** vi (become less tight) [*fastening, grip*] se desserrer. ■ **loosen up**°: **~ up** FIG [*person*] se détendre, se dégeler°.

looseness /'luːsnɪs/ n (of clothing) ampleur f; FIG (of translation, argument) manque m de rigueur.

loot /luːt/ I n **1** (stolen goods) butin m; **2**° (money) fric° m. **II** vtr piller. **III** vi se livrer au pillage.

looter /'luːtə(r)/ n pillard/-e m/f.

looting /'luːtɪŋ/ n pillage m.

lop /lɒp/ (p prés etc **-pp-**) vtr élaguer [*branch*]; **she ~ped 10 seconds off the record** elle a retranché 10 secondes du record.

lope /ləʊp/ vi **to ~ off** partir à grandes enjambées.

lop-eared /'lɒpɪəd/ adj aux oreilles pendantes.

lopsided /ˌlɒp'saɪdɪd/ adj **1** [*object, smile*] de travers; **2** FIG [*argument, view*] irrationnel/-elle.

lord /lɔːd/ ▶937 n **1** (ruler) seigneur m (**of** de); **2** (peer) lord m; **the (House of) Lords** la Chambre des Lords; **my Lord** (to noble) Monsieur le comte/duc etc. **IDIOMS to ~ it over sb**° regarder qn de haut.

Lord /lɔːd/ n **1** RELIG Seigneur m; **the year of our ~** l'an de grâce; **2**° (in exclamations) **good ~!** grand Dieu!; **~ knows where/why** Dieu sait où/pourquoi.

Lord: **~ Chancellor** n Lord m Chancelier; cf ministre m de la Justice; **~ Chief Justice** n: le plus haut magistrat de la Haute Cour de Justice en Grande-Bretagne.

lordly /'lɔːdlɪ/ adj **1** (proud) [*manner*] hautain; **2** (like a lord) [*bearing*] princier/-ière.

Lord Mayor ▶937 n lord-maire m (titre des maires des grandes villes de Grande-Bretagne).

lordship /'lɔːdʃɪp/ ▶937 n (also **Lordship**) (title) **your/his ~** (of noble) Monsieur; (of judge) Monsieur le Juge.

Lord's Prayer n Notre Père m.

lore /lɔː(r)/ n (of a people) traditions fpl.

lorry /'lɒrɪ, US 'lɔːrɪ/ n (pl **-ies**) GB camion m; **heavy ~** poids m lourd; **army ~** camion militaire. **IDIOMS it fell off the back of a ~**° EUPH c'est de la marchandise récupérée.

lorry: **~ driver** ▶1251 n GB GEN routier m, chauffeur m de poids lourd; **~ load** n GB chargement m, camion m.

lose /luːz/ I vtr (prét, pp **lost**) **1** (mislay) perdre [*object, person*]; **to ~ one's way** LIT se perdre; FIG s'égarer; **2** (not have any longer) perdre; **to ~ interest in sth** se désintéresser de qch; **to ~ touch** (with person, reality) perdre contact; **to ~ the use of** perdre l'usage de [*limb, muscle*]; **to ~ one's life** mourir; **many lives were lost** il y a eu de nombreuses victimes; **200 jobs will be lost** 200 emplois vont être supprimés; **to ~**

one's figure s'épaissir; **he's losing his looks** il n'est plus aussi beau qu'autrefois; **nothing to** ~○ rien à perdre; **I've got too much to** ~ c'est trop risqué; **3** (miss, waste) manquer [*chance*]; perdre [*time*]; **there's no time to** ~ il n'y a pas de temps à perdre; **this allusion was not lost on him** cette allusion ne lui a pas échappé; **4** (be defeated in) GEN, JUR, POL, SPORT perdre [*war, race, bet, election*]; avoir le dessous dans [*argument*]; perdre en [*appeal*]; **5** (lose sight of) perdre [*qch*] de vue [*moving object*]; FIG **you've lost me there**○! je ne vous suis plus!; **6** (shake off, get rid of) se débarrasser de [*habit*]; semer○ [*pursuer*]; supprimer [*job*]; **7** (go slow) [*clock*] retarder de [*minutes, seconds*]; **8** (cause to forfeit) **to** ~ **sb sth** faire perdre qch à qn.
II *vi* (*prét, pp* **lost**) **1** (be defeated) se faire battre (**to** par); **2** (be worse off, deteriorate) perdre; **they lost on the house** ils ont vendu la maison à perte; **3** [*clock, watch*] retarder.
III *v refl* (*prét, pp* **lost**) **to** ~ **oneself in** se plonger dans [*book*]; se perdre dans [*contemplation*].
■ **lose out** être perdant; **to** ~ **out on** perdre dans [*deal*].
loser /'luːzə(r)/ *n* GEN, SPORT perdant/-e *m/f*; **to be a good/bad** ~ être bon/mauvais perdant.
losing /'luːzɪŋ/ *adj* **1** GEN, SPORT [*team*] perdant; **2** COMM [*concern*] déficitaire.
IDIOMS **it's a** ~ **battle** c'est une bataille perdue d'avance; **to be on a** ~ **streak** ne pas être en veine○.
loss /lɒs, US lɔːs/ *n* **1** GEN, COMM, POL perte *f* (**of** de); **there was heavy** ~ **of life** il y a eu de nombreuses victimes; ~ **of income** ou **earnings** manque *m* à gagner; ~ **of sound/vision** TV interruption *f* du son/ de l'image; **the** ~ **of 300 jobs** la suppression de 300 emplois; **a sense of** ~ un sentiment de vide; **to make a** ~ COMM enregistrer une perte; **2 to be at a** ~ (puzzled) être perplexe; (helpless) être perdu; **to be at a** ~ **as to what to do** ne pas savoir du tout quoi faire; **I'm at a** ~ **to explain it** je suis dans l'impossibilité de l'expliquer; **he was at a** ~ **for words** les mots lui manquaient; **she's never at a** ~ **for words** elle a toujours quelque chose à dire.
IDIOMS **to cut one's** ~**es** arrêter les dégâts○; **it's his/their** ~ tant pis pour lui/eux; **their** ~ **is our gain** autant de gagné pour nous.
loss: ~ **adjuster** *n* COMM expert *m* en assurances; ~ **leader** *n* article *m* promotionnel (*vendu à perte*); ~**-making** *adj* [*product*] vendu à perte; [*company*] travaillant à perte.
lost /lɒst, US lɔːst/ **I** *prét, pp* ▶ **lose**.
II *adj* **1** [*person, animal*] perdu; **we're** ~ nous sommes perdus; **to get** ~ [*person, animal*] se perdre; [*object*] s'égarer; **get** ~○! fiche le camp○!; **2** (wasted, vanished) [*opportunity*] manqué; [*innocence*] perdu; [*civilisation*] disparu; **to give sb/sth up for** ~ considérer qn/qch comme perdu; **to be** ~ **on sb** passer audessus de la tête de qn; **3** (mystified) [*person, look*] perdu; **to be** ~ **for words** être interloqué; **4 to be** ~ **in** être plongé dans [*book, thought*]; **5** (doomed) LITTÉR ou HUM perdu; **a** ~ **cause** une cause perdue.
lost: ~ **and found** *n* objets *mpl* trouvés; ~ **property** GB *n* objets *mpl* trouvés.
lot¹ /lɒt/ **I** *pron* **1** (great deal) **a** ~ beaucoup; **we bought a** ~ nous avons acheté beaucoup de choses; **he spent a** ~ il a beaucoup dépensé, il a dépensé beaucoup d'argent; **to get a** ~ **out of** tirer beaucoup de [*book*]; **there's not a** ~ **to tell** il n'y a pas grandchose à raconter; **he knows a** ~ **about sport** il s'y connaît beaucoup en sport; **you've taken (rather) a** ~ **on** tu en fais (un peu) trop; **I'd give a** ~ **to**... je donnerais cher pour...; **it says a** ~ **about her** ça en dit long sur elle; **that has a** ~ **to do with it** c'est très lié; **an awful** ~ énormément; **quite a** ~ beaucoup, pas mal○; **to mean quite a** ~ **to sb** avoir beaucoup d'importance pour qn; **such a** ~ tellement; **2**○ (entire amount or selection) **the** ~ (le) tout; **I'll write you a cheque for the** ~ je vous ferai un chèque pour le tout; **the nicest dress of the** ~ la plus belle robe de toutes; **heartburn, cramps, the** ~! des brûlu-

res d'estomac, des crampes, bref tout!; **3**○ (specific group of people) **she's the nicest of the** ~ c'est la plus gentille (de tous/toutes); **that** ~ PÉJ ces gens-là PÉJ; **you** ~ vous, vous autres; **my** ~ **can't even spell properly** les miens ne savent même pas écrire correctement; **they're not a bad** ~ ils ne sont pas méchants; **the best of a bad** ~○ le moins pire○.
II *quantif* **1** (great deal) **a** ~ **of** beaucoup de; **a** ~ **of money/time** beaucoup d'argent/de temps; **not a** ~ **of people know that** il n'y a pas beaucoup de personnes ou gens qui savent ça; **I see a** ~ **of him** je le vois beaucoup; **an awful**○ ~ **of** énormément de; **quite a** ~ **of** beaucoup ou pas mal○ de; **quite a** ~ **of our support**... une bonne part de notre soutien...; **what a** ~ **of people!** que de monde!; **2**○ (entire group) **I'd sack the** ~ **of them!** je les mettrais tous à la porte!
III lots *quantif, pron* ~**s** (**and** ~**s**) **of** des tas○ de (+ *pl nouns only*); beaucoup de (+ *any nouns*); ~**s of things** des tas○ de choses; ...**and** ~**s more** ...et beaucoup d'autres choses.
IV lots *adv* ~**s better** beaucoup ou vachement○ mieux.
V a lot *adv phr* beaucoup; **a** ~ **better** beaucoup mieux; **a** ~ **worse** bien pire; **they talk a** ~ **about justice** ils parlent beaucoup de justice; **you find this a** ~ **on** on rencontre beaucoup ce problème; **the situation has improved a** ~ la situation s'est beaucoup améliorée; **this happens quite a** ~ cela arrive très souvent; **an awful** ~ **cheaper** beaucoup moins cher; **it would help an awful**○ ~ ça aiderait beaucoup; **he travels abroad such a** ~ il voyage beaucoup à l'étranger.
lot² /lɒt/ *n* **1** (destiny) sort *m*; (quality of life) condition *f*; **to be the** ~ **of many** être le lot de beaucoup de gens; **to throw in one's** ~ **with sb** allier son destin à celui de qn; **2** US parcelle *f* (de terrain); **vacant** ~ terrain *m* vague; **used car** ~ garage *m* vendant des voitures d'occasion; **3** (at auction) lot *m*; **4** (decisionmaking process) tirage *m* au sort; **to draw ou cast** ~**s** tirer au sort; **5** CIN studio *m*; **6** (batch) of students, tourists) fournée *f*.
lotion /'ləʊʃn/ *n* lotion *f*.
lottery /'lɒtəri/ *n* LIT, FIG loterie *f*.
lotto /'lɒtəʊ/ ▶ **949** *n* loto *m*.
loud /laʊd/ **I** *adj* **1** (noisy) [*bang, music, voice*] fort; [*crash, scream*] grand; [*comment, laugh*] bruyant; [*applause*] vif/vive; [*whisper*] audible; **2** (emphatic) [*objection*] vif/vive; **3** (vulgar) PÉJ [*colour, pattern*] criard; [*person, behaviour*] exubérant.
II *adv* fort; **out** ~ à voix haute; ~ **and clear** clairement.
IDIOMS **for crying out** ~○! pour l'amour de Dieu!
loudhailer /ˌlaʊdˈheɪlə(r)/ *n* GB mégaphone *m*.

lot¹

When *a lot* is used as a pronoun (*they eat a lot, he spends a lot*), it is translated by *beaucoup*: **ils mangent beaucoup**, **il dépense beaucoup**. For particular usages, see **I 1** in the entry **lot**¹.

When *a lot* is used to mean *much* in negative expressions (*they didn't have a lot*) it is translated by *pas grand-chose*: **ils n'avaient pas grand-chose**. For particular usages, see **I 1** in the entry **lot**¹.

When *the lot* is used as a pronoun (*they took the lot*), it is usually translated by *tout*: **ils ont tout pris**. For particular usages, see **I 2** in the entry **lot**¹.

When *a lot of* is used as a quantifier (*a lot of money*) it is translated by *beaucoup de*. For particular usages, see **II 1** in the entry **lot**¹. For translations of *lots* of see **III** in the entry **lot**¹.

When *a lot* is used as an adverb (*a lot stronger, he's changed a lot*) it is translated by *beaucoup*: **beaucoup plus fort**, **il a beaucoup changé**. For particular usages, see **V** in the entry **lot**¹.

loudly /'laʊdlɪ/ adv [knock, talk, sing] bruyamment; [play music, scream] fort; [protest] vivement.

loud: **~mouth**○ n grande gueule❶ f; **~mouthed**○ adj fort en gueule❶.

loudness /'laʊdnɪs/ n intensité f.

loudspeaker n (for announcements) haut-parleur m; (for hi-fi) enceinte f.

lounge /laʊndʒ/ I n 1 (in house, hotel) salon m; 2 (in airport) **departure ~** salle f d'embarquement; 3 US (also **cocktail ~**) bar m.
II vi (sprawl) s'avachir (**on** sur).
■ **lounge about**, **lounge around** paresser PEJ.

lounge: **~ bar** n GB grande salle f de pub; **~ lizard**○ n salonnard○ m; **~ suit** n GB costume m.

louse /laʊs/ n 1 (pl **lice**) (insect) pou m; 2❶ (pl **~s**) PEJ salaud❶ m.
■ **louse up**❶: **~** [sth] up, **~** up [sth] bousiller.

lousy /'laʊzɪ/ I adj ○[book, holiday] mauvais; [meal, working conditions] infect○; [salary] minable○; **to feel ~** être mal fichu○; **a ~ trick** un sale tour.
II❶ adv US **to do ~** se débrouiller comme un manche○.

lout /laʊt/ n (rude-mannered) malotru○ m.

loutish /'laʊtɪʃ/ adj [person] grossier/-ière; [behaviour] de voyou.

louvred GB, **louvered** US /'luːvəd/ adj à lamelles.

lovable /'lʌvəbl/ adj [person] sympathique; [child] adorable.

love /lʌv/ I n 1 (affection, devotion) amour m; **to do sth for the ~ of it** faire qch par goût; **for the ~ of God!** pour l'amour de Dieu!; **to be/fall in ~** être/ tomber amoureux/-euse (**with** de); **he's in ~ with the sound of his own voice** il s'écoute parler; **to make ~** (have sex) faire l'amour; 2 (in polite formulas) **give my ~ to Jo** transmets mes amitiés à Jo; **~ to Don** baisers à Don; **Andy sends his ~** Andy t'embrasse; **with ~ from Bob**, **~ Bob** affectueusement, Bob; 3 (object of affection) amour m; **be a ~**○ GB sois gentil; 4 GB (term of address) (to adult) mon amour m, mon chéri/ma chérie m/f; (to child) mon chéri/ma chérie m/f; 5 (in tennis) zéro m.
II noun modifier [letter, song, story] d'amour.
III vtr 1 (feel affection for) aimer; **to ~ sb very much** adorer qn; **to ~ each other** s'aimer; 2 (appreciate) aimer beaucoup (**to do** faire); (accepting invitation) **'I'd ~ to!'** 'avec plaisir!'; 3○ (in exaggerated speech) adorer; **she'll ~ that!** IRON elle sera vraiment ravie! IRON.
IDIOMS **~ at first sight** le coup de foudre; **there's no ~ lost between them** ils/elles se détestent cordialement.

love affair n liaison f (**with** avec; **between** entre).

love: **~ child** n EUPH enfant mf de l'amour; **~-hate relationship** n relation f oscillant entre l'amour et la haine.

loveless /'lʌvlɪs/ adj [marriage] sans amour.

love-life n vie f amoureuse.

loveliness /'lʌvlɪnɪs/ n beauté f.

lovely /'lʌvlɪ/ adj 1 (beautiful) [colour, garden, woman] beau/belle, joli (before n); **you look ~** tu es ravissante; **the hat will look ~ with it** le chapeau ira très bien avec; 2 (pleasant) [letter, person] charmant; [meal, smell] délicieux/-ieuse; [idea, surprise] bon/bonne (before n); [weekend outing] excellent; [present, weather] magnifique; **it's ~ to do** c'est tellement agréable de faire; **to smell ~** sentir bon; **to taste ~** être délicieux/-ieuse; 3 (emphatic) **~ and hot/fresh** bien chaud/frais.

love: **~making** n rapports mpl (sexuels); **~ match** n union f parfaite.

lover /'lʌvə(r)/ n 1 amant m; **to take a ~** prendre un amant; 2 (person in love) amoureux/-euse m/f; 3 (enthusiast) amateur m (**of** de); **jazz ~** amateur de jazz.

love: **~ seat** n confident m; **~sick** adj languissant d'amour.

lovey-dovey○ /ˌlʌvɪ'dʌvɪ/ adj GB **to get all ~** se mettre à roucouler○.

loving /'lʌvɪŋ/ I adj [mother, husband, look, smile] tendre; [kiss] amoureux/-euse; [care] affectueux/-euse (in letter-writing) **your ~ son** ton fils qui t'aime.
II **-loving** combining form **football-/music-~** amateur de football/de musique.

lovingly /'lʌvɪŋlɪ/ adv (all contexts) avec amour.

low /ləʊ/ I n 1 METEOROL dépression f; 2 FIG (low point) **to be at** ou **have hit an all-time ~** être au plus bas.
II adj 1 (close to the ground) [branch, building, chair, cloud] bas/basse; **on ~ ground** [flood] dans les basses terres; [built] dans une dépression; 2 (nearly depleted) [reservoir, stocks, level] bas/basse; [battery] faible; **the fire was getting ~** le feu baissait; **to be ~ on staff** manquer de personnel; **I'm getting ~ on petrol** je n'ai plus beaucoup d'essence; **to be ~ in sugar** contenir peu de sucre; 3 (minimal) [price, wage] bas/basse; [capacity, speed] réduit; [number, rate] faible; [pressure, temperature] bas/basse; **on a ~ heat** à feu doux; **the temperature was in the ~ twenties** il faisait dans les vingt degrés; 4 (inferior) [mark, standard] mauvais; 5 (depressed) déprimé; 6 (deep) [tone, voice] bas/basse; **in a ~ voice** tout bas; 7 (vulgar) [humour] peu relevé; (base) [behaviour] ignoble; 8 NAUT **~ tide** marée f basse.
III adv 1 (near the ground) [aim] bas; [bend] très bas; **to fly ~** voler à basse altitude; **I wouldn't sink** ou **stoop so ~** FIG je ne m'abaisserais pas à ce point-là; 2 (near the bottom) **very ~** (**down**) **on the list** FIG tout à fait secondaire; 3 (at a reduced level) [speak] bas; **to turn sth down ~** baisser [heating, light]; **stocks are running ~** les stocks sont en baisse; **to rate sb pretty ~** ne pas tenir qn en grande estime; 4 [sing] bas.
IV vi [cow] meugler.
IDIOMS **to be the ~est of the ~** être le dernier des derniers; **to be laid ~ by** être cloué au lit par.

low-alcohol adj peu alcoolisé.

lowbrow /'ləʊbraʊ/ PEJ I n personne f peu intellectuelle.
II adj [person] peu intellectuel/-elle.

low: **~-budget** adj à petit budget; **~-calorie** adj [diet] hypocalorique; [food] à faible teneur en calories; **~-cost** adj économique, bon marché; **Low Countries** pr npl Pays-Bas mpl; **~-cut** adj décolleté; **~-down**○ n tuyau○ m.

lower[1] /'ləʊə(r)/ I vi LITTÉR (frown) prendre un air comminatoire (**at** avec).
II **lowering** pres p adj [sky] menaçant.

lower[2] /'ləʊə(r)/ I adj (comparative of **low**) inférieur; **in the ~ back** au bas du dos.
II vtr 1 (bring down) baisser [barrier, curtain, flag]; abaisser [ceiling]; **to ~ sb/sth** (let down) descendre qn/qch (**into** dans; **onto** sur); 2 (reduce) baisser [light, prices, standards]; réduire [pressure, temperature]; diminuer [resistance]; abaisser [age limit]; **to ~ one's voice** baisser la voix; **to ~ one's guard** FIG relâcher sa vigilance; 3 (abolish) abolir [trade barrier]; 4 NAUT affaler [sail]; mettre [qch] à la mer [lifeboat].
III v refl **to ~ oneself** 1 (demean oneself) s'abaisser; 2 (sit carefully) **to ~ oneself into** entrer lentement dans [bath]; s'asseoir précautionneusement dans [chair].

lower case /'ləʊə(r)/ n bas m de casse, minuscules fpl.

lower class /'ləʊə(r)/ I n (pl **~es**) **the ~(es)** la classe ouvrière.
II **lower-class** adj GEN de la classe ouvrière; [accent, district] populaire.

lowering /'ləʊərɪŋ/ n GEN baisse f; (of age limit) abaissement m; (of resistance) diminution f; (of flag, sail) abaissement m; (of trade barriers) abolition f.

lower middle class /'ləʊə(r)/ I n (pl **~es**) **the ~(es)** la petite bourgeoisie.
II adj petit-bourgeois/petite-bourgeoise.

lower sixth /'ləʊə(r)/ n GB SCH ~ classe f de première; **to be in the ~** ≈ être en première.

lowest common denominator n MATH, FIG plus petit dénominateur m commun.

low: **~-fat** *adj* [*diet*] sans matières grasses; [*cheese*] allégé; [*milk*] écrémé; **~-flying** *adj* volant à faible altitude; **~-frequency** *adj* [*sonar, sound*] (à) basse fréquence (*after n*); **~-grade** *adj* [*product*] de qualité inférieure; [*official*] de grade inférieur; **~-heeled** *adj* plat, à talons plats; **~-income** *adj* [*family*] à faible revenu; [*bracket*] des bas salaires; **~-key** *adj* [*approach*] discret/-ète; [*meeting, talks*] informel/-elle.

lowland /'ləʊlənd/ **I** *n* (*also* **~s**) basses-terres *fpl*.
II *noun modifier* [*area*] à faible altitude.

low-level *adj* [*bombing*] à basse altitude; [*talks*] informel/-elle; [*radiation*] faible.

low-life I *n* ○(person) (*pl* **~s**) crapule *f*.
II *noun modifier* [*character, scene*] des bas-fonds; [*friend, contact*] du milieu.

low: **~-lying** *adj* à basse altitude; **~-necked** *adj* décolleté.

lowness /'ləʊnɪs/ *n* **1** (of bridge, ceiling) faible hauteur *f*; **2** METEOROL, PHYS the **~ of the temperature/ pressure** la basse température/pression.

low-paid I *n* the **~** (+ *v pl*) les petits salaires *mpl*.
II *adj* [*job*] faiblement rémunéré; [*worker*] peu rémunéré.

low: **~-priced** *adj* COMM à bas prix; **~-profile** *adj* (discreet) discret/-ète; **~-quality** *adj* de qualité inférieure; **~-rise** *adj* [*building*] bas/basse (*after n*); **~-risk** *adj* [*investment*] à risque limité; [*borrower*] fiable; **~-scoring** *adj* SPORT [*match*] avec peu de points de marqués; **~ season** *n* TOURISM basse saison *f*; **~-slung** *adj* [*chassis*] surbaissé; **~-tar** *adj* à faible teneur en goudrons; **~-tech** *adj* (de type) traditionnel; **~ tide** *n* marée *f* basse.

low voltage I *n* basse tension *f*.
II low-voltage *adj* de basse tension.

loyal /'lɔɪəl/ *adj* [*friend*] loyal (**to** envers); [*customer*] fidèle (**to** à).

loyalist /'lɔɪəlɪst/ *n, adj* loyaliste (*mf*).

loyally /'lɔɪəlɪ/ *adv* [*serve*] fidèlement; [*speak*] avec dévouement.

loyalty /'lɔɪəltɪ/ *n* loyauté *f* (**to, towards** envers); **to have divided loyalties** se sentir écartelé.

lozenge /'lɒzɪndʒ/ *n* pastille *f*.

LP *n* (*abrév* = **long-playing record**) (disque *m*) 33 tours *m*.

L-plate /'el pleɪt/ *n* GB AUT plaque *f* d'élève conducteur débutant accompagné.

LSE *n* GB (*abrév* = **London School of Economics**) faculté des Sciences économiques de l'Université de Londres.

L-shaped *adj* en (forme de) L.

Lt *abrév écrite* ▶ **lieutenant**.

Ltd GB (*abrév écrite* = **limited** (**liability**)) cf SARL.

lubricant /'lu:brɪkənt/ *n* lubrifiant *m*.

lubricate /'lu:brɪkeɪt/ *vtr* GEN lubrifier.

lucid /'lu:sɪd/ *adj* **1** (clear) clair; **2** (sane) [*person*] lucide; [*moment*] de lucidité.

lucidity /lu:'sɪdətɪ/ *n* **1** (clarity) clarté *f*; **2** (sanity) lucidité *f*.

luck /lʌk/ *n* **1** (good or bad) **good ~** chance *f*; **bad ~** malchance *f*; **to bring sb good/bad ~** porter bonheur/malheur à qn; **it's good ~** ça porte chance; **it is bad ~ that** ce n'est pas de chance que (+ *subj*); **to try one's ~** tenter sa chance; **as ~ would have it**... le hasard a voulu que... (+ *subj*); **bad** ou **hard ~!** pas de chance!; **just my ~!** c'est bien ma chance!; **good ~!** bonne chance!; **better ~ next time!** tu auras plus de chance la prochaine fois!; **to be down on one's ~** être dans une mauvaise passe; **2** (good luck) chance *f*; **with a bit of ~**... avec un peu de chance...; **our ~ ran out** notre chance a tourné; **to wear sth for ~** porter qch comme porte-bonheur; **by a stroke of ~** par un coup de chance; **any ~?** ça donne quelque chose?; **to be in/out of ~** avoir de la/ ne pas avoir de chance.
IDIOMS **it's the ~ of the draw** c'est une question de chance; **one for ~** un/une de plus tant qu'on y est; **my ~'s in!** c'est mon jour de chance!; **no such ~!**

hélas non!; **once more for ~** encore une fois à tout hasard; **you'll have to take pot ~** (at meal) ce sera à la fortune du pot.
■ **luck out** US avoir de la veine○.

luckily /'lʌkɪlɪ/ *adv* heureusement (**for** pour).

luckless /'lʌklɪs/ *adj* LITTÉR [*person*] infortuné.

lucky /'lʌkɪ/ *adj* **1** (fortunate) **to be ~ to do/to be** avoir la chance de faire/d'être; **to be ~ to get out alive** avoir eu la chance de s'en tirer vivant; **you'll be ~ to get a taxi** tu auras bien de la chance si tu trouves un taxi; **it was ~ for me** j'ai eu de la chance; **to be ~ enough to do** avoir la chance de faire; **I'm not ~** je n'ai jamais de chance; **~ you○!** veinard/-e○ *m/f*!; **I/you etc should be so ~○!** GB IRON ça serait trop beau!; **you should think** ou **count yourself ~** tu peux te considérer heureux/-euse; **to have a ~ escape** l'échapper belle; **2** (bringing good luck) [*charm, colour, number*] porte-bonheur *inv*; **it's my ~ day!** c'est mon jour de chance!
IDIOMS **to strike it ~** décrocher le gros lot○; **to thank one's ~ stars** remercier le ciel.

lucrative /'lu:krətɪv/ *adj* lucratif/-ive.

lucre○† /'lu:kə(r)/ *n* fric○ *m*.

ludicrous /'lu:dɪkrəs/ *adj* grotesque.

ludo /'lu:dəʊ/ ▶ **949** *n* GB jeu *m* des petits chevaux.

lug /lʌg/ **I** *n* **1** TECH patte *f*; **2**○ = **lughole**.
II *vtr* (*p prés etc* **-gg-**) traîner.

luggage /'lʌgɪdʒ/ *n ¢* bagages *mpl*.

luggage: **~ handler** ▶ **1251** *n* bagagiste *mf*; **~ rack** *n* compartiment *m* à bagages; **~ van** *n* GB fourgon *m* à bagages.

lughole○ /'lʌgəʊl/ *n* GB esgourde○ *f*.

lukewarm /,lu:k'wɔ:m/ *adj* tiède.

lull /lʌl/ **I** *n* (in storm, fighting) accalmie *f*; (in conversation) pause *f*; (in trading) ralentissement *m*.
II *vtr* apaiser [*person*]; **he ~ed them into thinking that**... il leur a fait croire que...; **to be ~ed into a false sense of security** se laisser aller à un sentiment de sécurité trompeur.

lullaby /'lʌləbaɪ/ *n* berceuse *f*.

lumbar /'lʌmbə(r)/ *adj* lombaire.

lumber /'lʌmbə(r)/ **I** *n* US (wood) bois *m* de construction.
II *vtr* ○GB **to be ~ed with sb/sth** se retrouver avec qn/qch sur les bras; **to be ~ed with a chore** se taper une corvée.
III *vi* **1** (*also* **~ along**) avancer d'un pas lourd; [*vehicle*] avancer péniblement; **to ~ away** ou **off** [*person*] s'éloigner d'un pas lourd; **2** US (cut timber) débiter le bois.

lumbering /'lʌmbərɪŋ/ *adj* [*animal, person*] au pas lourd (*after n*); FIG [*bureaucracy*] pesant.

lumber: **~jack** ▶ **1251** *n* bûcheron/-onne *m/f*; **~jack shirt** *n* chemise *f* épaisse à carreaux; **~ mill** *n* scierie *f*.

luminary /'lu:mɪnərɪ, US -nerɪ/ *n* FIG (person) sommité *f*.

luminous /'lu:mɪnəs/ *adj* lumineux/-euse.

lump /lʌmp/ **I** *n* **1** morceau *m*; (of soil, clay) motte *f*; (in sauce) grumeau *m*; **in one ~** FIG en bloc; **2** (on body) (from knock) bosse *f* (**on** sur); (tumour) grosseur *f* (**in, on** à); **3**○ (idle person) (man) balourd○ *m*; (woman) dondon○ *f*.
II *vtr* **to ~ X together with Y** regrouper X et Y; PÉJ mettre X et Y dans le même panier○.
IDIOMS **to have a ~ in one's throat** avoir la gorge serrée; **I'll/he'll have to ~ it○** il va falloir faire avec/ qu'il fasse avec○; **like it or ~ it○** que ça te/lui etc chante ou pas.

lump: **~ sugar** *n* sucre *m* en morceaux; **~ sum** *n* COMM (complete payment) versement *m* unique.

lumpy /'lʌmpɪ/ *adj* [*sauce*] grumeleux/-euse; [*mattress, pillow, soil*] défoncé.

lunacy /'lu:nəsɪ/ *n* FIG folie *f*.

lunar /'lu:nə(r)/ *adj* [*landscape, module, orbit*] lunaire; [*eclipse*] de lune; [*landing*] sur la lune.

lunatic /'lu:nətɪk/ **I** *n* FIG fou/folle *m/f*.
II *adj* FIG [*person*] fou/folle; [*plan, idea*] démentiel/-ielle.
lunatic: ~ **asylum** *n* asile *m* d'aliénés†; ~ **fringe** *n* PÉJ les jusqu'au-boutistes *mfpl*.

lunch /lʌntʃ/ **I** *n* déjeuner *m*; **to have** ~ déjeuner; **to take sb out for** ~ emmener qn déjeuner au restaurant; **she's gone to** ~ elle est partie déjeuner; ~!, **time for** ~! à table!; **to close for** ~ fermer le midi; **to do good** ~**es** servir de bons repas le midi.
II *vi* déjeuner (**on, off** de).
IDIOMS **out to** ~○ dingue○; **there's no such thing as a free** ~ on ne fait jamais rien pour rien.
lunch: ~**box** *n* boîte *f* à sandwichs; ~**break** *n* pause-déjeuner *f*.

luncheon /'lʌntʃən/ *n* SOUT déjeuner *m*.

luncheon: ~ **meat** *n* ~ viande *f* en conserve; ~ **voucher**, **LV** *n* ticket-repas *m*, ticket-restaurant® *m*.

lunch: ~ **hour** *n* heure *f* du déjeuner; ~**time** *n* heure *f* du déjeuner.

lung /lʌŋ/ **I** *n* poumon *m*.
II *noun modifier* [*disease*] pulmonaire; [*transplant, cancer*] du poumon.

lunge /lʌndʒ/ **I** *n* brusque mouvement *m* vers l'avant; **a desperate** ~ **for the ball** un bond désespéré vers la balle.
II *vtr* faire tourner [qch] à la longe [*horse*].
III *vi* GEN bondir.

lurch /lɜ:tʃ/ **I** *n* **to give a** ~ [*vehicle*] faire une embardée.
II *vi* LIT [*person, vehicle*] tanguer; **to** ~ **forward** tressauter; **to** ~ **to a halt** faire une embardée et s'arrêter.
IDIOMS **to leave sb in the** ~ abandonner qn.

lurcher /'lɜ:tʃə(r)/ *n* GB chien *m* de chasse (*croisé entre un collie et un lévrier*).

lure /lʊə(r)/ **I** *n* **1** (*attraction*) attrait *m* (**of** de); **2** (in hunting) leurre *m*.
II *vtr* attirer (**into** dans; **with** avec); **they** ~**d him out of his house** ils ont réussi à le faire sortir de chez lui par la ruse; **to** ~ **sb away from her studies** détourner qn de ses études.

lurid /'lʊərɪd/ *adj* [*colour*] criard; [*detail*] épouvantable.

lurk /lɜ:k/ **I** *vi* **1** he was ~**ing in the bushes** il était tapi dans les buissons; **2** FIG [*danger*] menacer.

II lurking *pres p adj* [*doubt*] persistant.

luscious /'lʌʃəs/ *adj* [*food*] succulent; [*woman*]○ pulpeux/-euse.

lush /lʌʃ/ **I**○ *n* poivrot/-ote○ *m/f*.
II *adj* [*vegetation*] luxuriant; [*surroundings*] luxueux/-euse.

lust /lʌst/ **I** *n* GEN désir *m* (**for** de); (deadly sin) luxure *f*; **the** ~ **for power** la soif du pouvoir.
II *vi* **to** ~ **for** ou **after sb/sth** convoiter qn/qch.

lustre GB, **luster** US /'lʌstə(r)/ *n* éclat *m*.

lustreware GB, **lusterware** US /'lʌstəweə(r)/ *n* poterie *f* à reflet métallique.

lusty /'lʌstɪ/ *adj* vigoureux/-euse.

lute /lu:t/ ▶ 1097 | *n* luth *m*.

Luxembourg /'lʌksəmbɜ:g/ ▶ 840 | *pr n* Luxembourg *m*.

luxuriate /lʌg'zjʊərɪeɪt/ *vi* **to** ~ **in** s'abandonner avec délices à [*warmth, bath*]; savourer [*attention*].

luxurious /lʌg'zjʊərɪəs/ *adj* [*apartment, lifestyle*] de luxe (*never after v*); **his apartment is** ~ son appartement est luxueux.

luxuriously /lʌg'zjʊərɪəslɪ/ *adv* [*decorate*] luxueusement; [*yawn, stretch*] voluptueusement.

luxury /'lʌkʃərɪ/ **I** *n* (all contexts) luxe *m*.
II *noun modifier* [*product, holiday*] de luxe.

LV *n* (*abrév* = **luncheon voucher**) ticket-repas *m*.

LW *n* RADIO (*abrév* = **long wave**) GO *fpl*.

lychee /'laɪtʃi:, ˌlaɪ'tʃi:/ *n* litchi *m*.

lychgate /'lɪtʃgeɪt/ *n* porche *m* d'entrée du cimetière.

lying /'laɪɪŋ/ *n* ¢ mensonges *mpl*.

lymph /lɪmf/ *n* lymphe *f*.

lynch /lɪntʃ/ *vtr* lyncher.

lynch mob *n* lyncheurs *mpl*.

Lyons /'li:ɔ:ŋ/ ▶ 1343 | *pr n* Lyon.

lyric /'lɪrɪk/ **I** *n* LITERAT poème *m* lyrique.
II lyrics *npl* (of song) paroles *fpl* (*d'une chanson*).
III *adj* lyrique.

lyrical /'lɪrɪkl/ *adj* (all contexts) lyrique; **to wax** ~ (**about** ou **over sth**) disserter avec lyrisme (sur qch).

lyricism /'lɪrɪsɪzəm/ *n* (all contexts) lyrisme *m*.

lyric-writer ▶ 1251 | *n* parolier/-ière *m/f*.

m, M /em/ *n* **1** (letter) m, M *m*; **2 m** (*abrév écrite* = **metre(s)** GB, **meter(s)** US) m; **3 M** (*abrév* = **motorway**) autoroute *f*; the M3 l'autoroute M3; **4 m** *abrév écrite* = **mile(s)**; **5 m** *abrév écrite* = **million**.

MA *n* **1** (*abrév* = **Master of Arts**) diplôme *m* supérieur de lettres; **2** US POST *abrév écrite* = **Massachusetts**.

ma'am /mæm, mɑːm/ *n* (*abrév* = **madam**) GEN madame *f*, mademoiselle *f*; (to Queen) madame *f*.

mac○ /mæk/ *n* GB (*abrév* = **mackintosh**) imper○ *m*.

macaroni /ˌmækəˈrəʊnɪ/ *n ¢* macaronis *mpl*.

macaroni cheese *n* gratin *m* de macaronis.

macaroon /ˌmækəˈruːn/ *n* macaron *m*.

mace /meɪs/ *n* **1** (spice) macis *m*; **2** (ceremonial staff) masse *f*.

Macedonia /ˌmæsɪˈdəʊnɪə/ *pr n* Macédoine *f*.

macerate /ˈmæsəreɪt/ *vi* macérer.

machete /məˈtʃetɪ, US məˈʃetɪ/ *n* machette *f*.

machination /ˌmækɪˈneɪʃn/ *n* machination *f*.

machine /məˈʃiːn/ I *n* **1** (piece of equipment) machine *f* (for doing à faire); sewing ~ machine à coudre; **to operate a** ~ faire fonctionner une machine; **by** ~ à la machine; **2** FIG (apparatus) machine *f*; **publicity** ~ machine publicitaire.
II *vtr* IND usiner.

machine: **~-assisted translation**, **MAT** *n* traduction *f* assistée par ordinateur, TAO *f*; **~ gun** *n* mitrailleuse *f*; **~ intelligence** *n* intelligence *f* artificielle; **~ operator** *n* IND opérateur/-trice *m/f*; **~-readable** *adj* COMPUT [*data, text*] directement exploitable; [*passport*] vérifiable par ordinateur.

machinery /məˈʃiːnərɪ/ *n ¢* **1** (equipment) machines *fpl*; (working parts) mécanisme *m*, rouages *mpl*; **a piece of** ~ une machine; **heavy** ~ machines *fpl* lourdes; **2** FIG (apparatus) dispositifs *mpl*; **the** ~ **to settle industrial disputes** le système mis en place pour régler les conflits sociaux; **the** ~ **of justice** les rouages de la justice.

machine: **~-stitch** *vtr* piquer à la machine; **~ translation**, **MT** *n* traduction *f* automatique.

machinist /məˈʃiːnɪst/ ▶1251 *n* opérateur/-trice *m/f*.

machismo /məˈtʃɪzməʊ, -ˈkɪzməʊ/ *n* machisme *m*.

macho /ˈmætʃəʊ/ *adj* PÉJ macho; (manly) viril.

mackerel /ˈmækrəl/ *n* maquereau *m*.

mackintosh, **macintosh** /ˈmækɪntɒʃ/ *n* imperméable *m*.

macro /ˈmækrəʊ/ I *n* COMPUT macro *f*.
II **macro+** *combining form* macro-.

macrocosm /ˈmækrəʊkɒzəm/ *n* macrocosme *m*.

mad /mæd/ *adj* **1** [*person*] fou/folle (with de); [*dog, bull*] enragé; **to go** ~ devenir fou/folle; **2** (foolish) [*idea, scheme*] insensé; **it is** ~ **to do** ou **doing** c'est fou○ or de la folie de faire; **they are** ~ **to do** c'est de la folie de leur part de faire; **to go** ~○ (spend money) faire des folies; **3**○ (angry) (*jamais épith*) très en colère, furieux/-ieuse; **to be** ~ **at** ou **with sb** être très en colère contre qn; **to get** ~ **at** ou **with sb** se mettre en colère contre qn; **to be** ~ **about sth** être en colère à cause de qch; **to go** ~ être fou de rage; **to make sb** ~ exaspérer qn; **to drive sb** ~ rendre qn fou; **4**○ (enthusiastic) ~ **about** ou **on** fou de○ [*person, hobby*]; **to be movie-**~ être un passionné ou un mordu○ de cinéma; **5** (frantic) [*panic*] infernal; **to be** ~ **for blood** être assoiffé de sang ou de vengeance; ~ **for food** affamé; **the audience went** ~ le public

s'est déchaîné; **to be in a** ~ **rush** être très pressé; **it was a** ~ **scramble to do** ça a été la panique○ pour faire; **we made a** ~ **dash for the bus** on a couru comme des fous pour attraper le bus.
IDIOMS **to work like** ~ travailler comme un fou/une folle.

Madagascar /ˌmædəˈɡæskə/ ▶840 *pr n* Madagascar *m*.

madam /ˈmædəm/ **1** (also **Madam**) (form of address) madame *f*; **Madam Chairman** Madame la Présidente; **Dear Madam** Madame; **2**○ GB (young woman) (stuck up) pimbêche○ *f*; (cheeky) insolente *f*.

mad: **~cap** *adj* (*épith*) [*person, idea*] insensé; ~ **cow disease** *n* maladie *f* de la vache folle.

madden /ˈmædn/ *vtr* [*attitude*] exaspérer; [*pain, heat, insects*] rendre [qn] fou; **it** ~**s me to do/that** ça m'exaspère de faire/que (+ *subj*).

maddening /ˈmædnɪŋ/ *adj* [*person*] énervant; [*delay, situation*] exaspérant; **it's** ~ **to** c'est exaspérant de.

made /meɪd/ I *prét, pp* ▶ **make**.
II *adj* **to be** ~ avoir réussi; **a** ~ **man** un homme qui a réussi.
III **-made** *combining form* Italian-~ fabriqué en Italie.
IDIOMS **he's got it** ~○ (sure to succeed) sa réussite est assurée; (has succeeded) il n'a plus à s'en faire.

Madeira /məˈdɪərə/ ▶1022 *pr n* **1** (island) Madère; **2** (wine) madère *m*.

made-to-measure *adj* [*garment*] fait sur mesure.

made-up /ˌmeɪdˈʌp/ *adj* **1** (wearing make-up) maquillé; **2** [*story*] fabriqué; **3** [*road*] goudronné; **4** [*garment*] de prêt-à-porter.

madhouse○ /ˈmædhaʊs/ *n* (bedlam) maison *f* de fous.

madly /ˈmædlɪ/ *adv* **1** (frantically) frénétiquement; **2** (extremely) follement; ~ **in love (with sb)** follement or éperdument amoureux (de qn).

madman○ /ˈmædmən/ *n* fou○ *m*, malade○ *m*.

madness /ˈmædnɪs/ *n* folie *f*; **it is** ~ **to do** c'est de la folie de faire.

madwoman○ /ˈmædwʊmən/ *n* folle○ *f*, malade○ *f*.

MAFF *n* GB (*abrév* = **Ministry of Agriculture, Fisheries and Food**) ministère *m* de l'Agriculture, de la pêche et de l'alimentation.

mafia /ˈmæfɪə, US ˈmɑː-/ *n* **the Mafia** la Mafia; FIG **the** ~ la mafia.

mag○ /mæg/ *n*: *abrév* ▶ **magazine** 1.

magazine /ˌmæɡəˈziːn/ *n* **1** (periodical) revue *f*; (mainly photos) magazine *m*; **computer** ~ revue d'informatique; **monthly** ~ revue mensuelle; **fashion** ~ magazine de mode; **women's** ~ journal *m* féminin; **2** (on radio, TV) magazine *m*; **3** (of gun, camera) magasin *m*.

maggot /ˈmæɡət/ *n* (in fruit) ver *m*; (for fishing) asticot *m*.

magic /ˈmædʒɪk/ I *n* **1** (supernatural power) magie *f*; **to do sth by** ~ faire qch par magie; **as if by** ~ comme par enchantement; **it works like** ~! c'est miraculeux!; **2** (enchantment) magie *f* (of de).
II *adj* magique; **the Magic Flute** la Flûte enchantée.

magical /ˈmædʒɪkl/ *adj* **1** (supernatural) magique; **2** (enchanting) [*moment*] magique; [*week, stay*] merveilleux/-euse.

magic carpet *n* tapis *m* volant.

magician /məˈdʒɪʃn/ *n* (wizard) magicien *m*; (entertainer) illusionniste *m*.

magisterial /ˌmædʒɪ'stɪərɪəl/ *adj* **1** (authoritative) magistral; **2** JUR [*office, duties*] de magistrat.

magistrate /'mædʒɪstreɪt/ ▶ 1251 | *n* magistrat *m* (*non professionnel*); **to appear before (the) ~s** comparaître devant les magistrats.

magistrates' court, Magistrates' Court *n* ~ tribunal *m* de police.

magna cum laude /ˌmægnə kʊm 'laʊdeɪ/ *adv* US UNIV **to graduate** ~ obtenir son diplôme avec mention très bien.

magnanimity /ˌmægnə'nɪmətɪ/ *n* magnanimité *f*.

magnanimous /mæg'nænɪməs/ *adj* magnanime.

magnate /'mægneɪt/ *n* magnat *m*; **oil ~** magnat du pétrole.

magnesia /mæg'ni:ʃə/ *n* magnésie *f*.

magnesium /mæg'ni:zɪəm/ *n* magnésium *m*.

magnet /'mægnɪt/ *n* LIT aimant *m*; FIG pôle *m* d'attraction (**for** pour).

magnetic /mæg'netɪk/ *adj* **1** [*block, rod*] aimanté; [*force, properties*] magnétique; **2** [*appeal, smile*] irrésistible.

magnetically /mæg'netɪklɪ/ *adv* **1** LIT par magnétisme; **2** FIG irrésistiblement.

magnetic: **~ compass** *n* boussole *f*; **~ tape** *n* bande *f* magnétique.

magnetism /'mægnɪtɪzəm/ *n* LIT, FIG magnétisme *m*.

magnetize /'mægnɪtaɪz/ *vtr* **1** LIT aimanter; **2** FIG magnétiser.

magnification /ˌmægnɪfɪ'keɪʃn/ *n* grossissement *m*.

magnificence /mæg'nɪfɪsns/ *n* splendeur *f*.

magnificent /mæg'nɪfɪsnt/ *adj* magnifique.

magnificently /mæg'nɪfɪsntlɪ/ *adv* [*play, perform*] magnifiquement; [*dressed, decorated*] superbement.

magnify /'mægnɪfaɪ/ *vtr* **1** LIT grossir; **2** (exaggerate) exagérer.

magnifying glass *n* loupe *f*.

magnitude /'mægnɪtju:d, US -tu:d/ *n* **1** (of problem, disaster) ampleur *f*; **of the first ~** de la première importance; **2** (in astronomy) magnitude *f*.

magnolia /mæg'nəʊlɪə/ ▶ 818 | *n* **1** BOT (also **~ tree**) magnolia *m*; **2** (colour) crème *m*.

magnum opus /ˌmægnəm 'əʊpəs/ *n* œuvre *f* maîtresse.

magpie /'mægpaɪ/ *n* ZOOL pie *f*.

mahogany /mə'hɒgənɪ/ ▶ 818 | **I** *n* (wood, tree, colour) acajou *m*.

II *noun modifier* [*table, chest*] d'acajou, en acajou.

maid /meɪd/ *n* (in house) bonne *f*; (in hotel) femme *f* de chambre; **~ of honour** demoiselle *f* d'honneur.

maiden /'meɪdn/ **I** *n* LITTÉR jeune fille *f*.

II *adj* [*flight, voyage, speech*] inaugural.

maiden name *n* nom *m* de jeune fille.

maidservant /'meɪdsɜ:vənt/ *n* servante *f*.

mail /meɪl/ **I** *n* **1** (postal service) poste *f*; **by ~** par la poste; **2** (correspondence) courrier *m*; **3** MIL HIST **a coat of ~** une cotte de mailles.

II *vtr* envoyer, expédier [*letter, parcel*] (**to** à).

mail: **~bag** *n* (for transport) sac *m* postal; (of postman) sacoche *f* (du facteur); (correspondence) courrier *m*; **~ bomb** *n* colis *m* piégé; **~box** *n* SURTOUT US (for posting) boîte *f* aux lettres; (for delivery) boîte *f* à lettres; **~ car** *n* US wagon-poste *m*; **~ carrier** *n* US préposé/-e *m/f*; **~ coach** *n* RAIL wagon-poste *m*; **~ delivery** *n* distribution *f* du courrier.

mailing /'meɪlɪŋ/ *n* **1** (dispatch) envoi *m* (par la poste); **2** (for advertising) publipostage *m*, mailing *m*.

mailing: **~ address** *n* adresse *f* postale; **~ house** *n* (company) société *f* de routage; (department) service *m* du courrier; **~ list** *n* COMM fichier-clientèle *m*; THEAT liste *f* d'abonnés.

mailman /'meɪlmən/ ▶ 1251 | *n* US (*pl* **-men**) facteur *m*.

mail order /'meɪl ɔ:də(r)/ **I** *n* **to buy (by) ~** acheter par correspondance; **available by ~** disponible sur commande.

II *noun modifier* [*business, goods*] de vente *f* par correspondance.

mail: **~ room** *n* (service *m* du) courrier *m*; **~ shot** *n* publipostage *m*; **~ slot** *n* boîte *f* à lettres; **~ train** *n* train *m* postal; **~ van** *n* (in train) wagon-poste *m*; (delivery vehicle) camionnette *f* de la poste.

maim /meɪm/ *vtr* estropier.

main /meɪn/ **I** *n* **1** (pipe, conduit) (for water, gas, electricity) canalisation *f*; (for sewage) égout *m* (collecteur); **2** (network) **the ~s** (of water, gas, electricity) le réseau de distribution; (of sewage) le réseau d'évacuation; **to turn sth on/off at the ~s** mettre/couper qch (au compteur); **to work** ou **run off the ~s** fonctionner sur secteur.

II mains *noun modifier* [*gas*] de ville; [*electricity*] du secteur; [*water*] courant; [*radio, appliance*] sur secteur; [*plug, lead, voltage*] de secteur.

III *adj* principal; **the ~ thing is to...** le principal, c'est de...; **that's the ~ thing!** c'est le principal! IDIOMS **in the ~** dans l'ensemble.

main chance *n*: IDIOMS **to have an eye for** ou **to the ~** ne jamais perdre de vue ses intérêts.

main: **~ course** *n* plat *m* principal; **~ deck** *n* pont *m* supérieur.

mainframe /'meɪnfreɪm/ **I** *n* (also **~ computer, ~ processor**) ordinateur *m* central.

II *noun modifier* [*system, network*] informatiquement centralisé.

mainland /'meɪnlənd/ *n* territoire *m* continental; **on the ~** sur le continent; **the Chinese ~** la Chine continentale.

main line I /ˌmeɪn 'laɪn/ *n* RAIL grande ligne *f*.

II /'meɪnˌlaɪn/ *noun modifier* [*station, terminus, train*] de grande ligne.

III° mainline /'meɪnlaɪn/ *vi* ARGOT DES DROGUÉS se piquer.

mainly /'meɪnlɪ/ *adv* surtout, essentiellement.

main: **~ man**° *n* US copain *m*, pote° *m*; **~mast** *n* grand mât *m*; **~ memory** *n* COMPUT mémoire *f* centrale; **~ office** *n* (of company, organization, newspaper) siège *m* (social); **~ road** *n* (country) route *f* principale; (in town) grande rue *f*; **~sail** *n* grand-voile *f*.

mainspring /'meɪnsprɪŋ/ *n* **1** FIG (of action, plot) ressort *m* (**of** de); (of life) raison *f* d'être (**of** de); **2** (of watch) ressort *m* principal.

mainstream /'meɪnstri:m/ **I** *n* courant *m* dominant.

II *adj* **1** (conventional) traditionnel/-elle; **2** MUS **~ jazz** jazz mainstream.

maintain /meɪn'teɪn/ *vtr* **1** (keep steady) maintenir [*temperature, standards*]; **2** (support) subvenir aux besoins de [*family*]; garder [*army*]; entretenir [*lifestyle*]; **3** (look after) entretenir; **4** (assert) continuer à affirmer [*innocence*]; **to ~ that** soutenir que.

maintenance /'meɪntənəns/ **I** *n* **1** (upkeep) entretien *m* (**of** de); **2** (of standards etc) maintien *m* (**of** de); **3** GB JUR (alimony) pension *f* alimentaire.

II *noun modifier* [*contract, crew, fees*] d'entretien; **~ man** ouvrier *m* chargé de l'entretien.

maintenance: **~ grant** *n* (for student) bourse *f* (d'études); **~ order** *n* GB ordonnance *f* de versement de pension alimentaire.

maisonette /ˌmeɪzə'net/ *n* duplex *m*.

maize /meɪz/ *n* maïs *m*.

Maj *n*: *abrév écrite* = **Major**.

majestic /mə'dʒestɪk/ *adj* majestueux/-euse.

majesty /'mædʒəstɪ/ **I** *n* **1** (of building, ceremony) majesté *f*; **2** (royal authority) majesté *f*.

II *n* **Majesty** (in titles) Her/His **~** sa Majesté; **Her/His ~'s government** le gouvernement britannique.

major /'meɪdʒə(r)/ **I** *n* **1** MIL commandant *m*; **2** US UNIV (subject) matière *f* principale; (student) **I'm a physics ~** ma matière principale est la physique; **3** JUR majeur/-e *m/f*; **4** MUS ton *m* majeur.

II *adj* **1** (important) [*championship, event*] important; [*difference, role*] majeur; [*influence, significance*] capital; **a ~ operation, ~ surgery** MED une grosse opération; **2** (main) principal; **3** MUS majeur.

III *vi* US UNIV **to ~ in** se spécialiser en.

Majorca /mə'jɔːkə, mə'dʒɔːkə/ [▶ **1022**] *pr n* Majorque *f*; **in ~** à Majorque.

major-general /ˌmeɪdʒə'dʒenrəl/ *n* général *m* de division.

majority /mə'dʒɒrətɪ, US -'dʒɔːr-/ **I** *n* **1** (greater part) (+ *v sg ou pl* GB) majorité *f* (**of** de); **the vast ~** la grande majorité; **to be in a** ou **the ~** être en majorité; **2** POL majorité *f*; **by a ~ of 50** à une majorité de 50; **a three to one ~** une majorité de trois contre un; **a working ~** une majorité suffisante; **3** JUR majorité *f*.

II *noun modifier* [*government, rule*] majoritaire; [*support, view*] de la majorité; [*verdict*] rendu à la majorité; [*decision*] pris à la majorité.

make /meɪk/ **I** *n* (brand) marque *f*; **what ~ is your car?** de quelle marque est ta voiture?

II *vtr* (*prét, pp* **made**) **1** (create) faire [*cake, film, noise*]; **to ~ a rule** établir une règle; **to ~ sth from** faire qch avec; **wine is made from grapes** le vin se fait avec du raisin; **to ~ sth for sb, to ~ sb sth** faire qch pour qn; **to be made for sb** être fait pour qn; **to ~ room/the time for sth** trouver de la place/du temps pour qch; **to ~ sth out of** faire qch en; **it's made (out) of gold** c'est en or; **let's see what he's made of** voyons de quoi il est fait; **to ~ a house into apartments** transformer une maison en appartements; **made in France/by Macron** fabriqué en France/par Macron; **God made man** Dieu a créé l'homme; **to ~ the bed** faire le lit; **2** (cause to be or become, render) se faire [*friends, enemies*]; **to ~ sb happy** rendre qn heureux; **to ~ sb hungry** donner faim à qn; **to ~ oneself available** se rendre disponible; **to ~ oneself understood** se faire comprendre; **to ~ sth bigger/better/worse** agrandir/améliorer/aggraver qch; **to ~ passing exams easier, to ~ it easier to pass exams** faciliter les examens; **to ~ it possible to do** [*person*] faire en sorte qu'il soit possible de faire; **3** (cause to do) **to ~ sb cry** faire pleurer qn; **I made her smile** je l'ai fait sourire; **to ~ sb do sth** faire faire qch à qn; **I made her lose patience** je lui ai fait perdre patience; **it ~s me look fat** ça me grossit; **to ~ sth happen** faire que qch se produise; **to ~ the story end happily** faire en sorte que l'histoire se termine bien; **to ~ sth work** [*person*] réussir à faire marcher qch [*machine*]; **to ~ sth grow** [*person*] réussir à faire pousser qch; [*chemical, product*] faire pousser qch; **it ~s her voice sound funny** cela lui donne une drôle de voix; **4** (force, compel) **to ~ sb do** obliger ou forcer qn à faire; **to ~ sb wait/talk** faire attendre/parler qn; **5** (turn into) **to ~ sb sth, to ~ sth of sb** faire de qn qch; **we made him treasurer** on l'a fait trésorier; **we made Tom treasurer** on a choisi Tom comme trésorier; **to ~ sb one's assistant** faire de qn son adjoint; **it'll ~ a man of you** ça fera de toi un homme; **he'll never ~ a teacher** il ne fera jamais un bon professeur; **to ~ sb a good husband** être un bon mari pour qn; **to ~ sth, to ~ sth of sth** faire de qch qch; **to ~ a habit/an issue of sth** faire de qch une habitude/une affaire; **it's been made into a film** on en a fait ou tiré un film; **to ~ too much of sth** faire tout un plat de qch○; **that will ~ a good shelter** cela fera un bon abri; **6** (add up to, amount to) faire; **three and three ~ six** trois et trois font six; **that ~s ten altogether** ça fait dix en tout; **7** (earn) gagner [*salary, amount*]; **to ~ a living** gagner sa vie; **to ~ a profit** réaliser des bénéfices; **to ~ a loss** subir des pertes; **8** (reach, achieve) arriver jusqu'à [*place, position*]; atteindre [*ranking, level*]; faire [*speed, distance*]; **we'll never ~ it** nous n'y arriverons jamais; **to ~ the first team/the charts** entrer dans la première équipe/au hit-parade; **to ~ the front page** faire la une; **to ~ six spades** (in bridge) faire six piques; **9** (estimate, say) **I ~ it five o'clock** il est cinq heures à ma montre; **what time do you ~ it?** quelle heure as-tu?; **let's ~ it five dollars** disons cinq dollars; **can we ~ it a bit later?** peut-on dire un peu plus tard?; **what do you ~ of it?** qu'en dis-tu?; **I can't ~ anything of it** je n'y comprends rien; **10**

(cause success of) assurer la réussite de [*holiday, meal, day*]; **it really ~s the room** [*feature, colour*] ça rend bien; **it really made my day** ça m'a rendu heureux pour la journée; **to ~ or break** décider de l'avenir de; **11** ELEC fermer [*circuit*]; **12** GAMES (shuffle) battre [*cards*]; **to ~ a trick** (win) faire une levée.

IDIOMS **to be as clever as they ~ them** être malin comme pas un○; **to be on the ~**○ (for profit) avoir les dents longues; (for sex) être en chasse○; **to ~ it**○ (in career, life) y arriver; (to party, meeting) réussir à venir; (be on time for train etc) y être; **I can't ~ it** je ne peux pas y aller.

■ **make after: ~ after** [*sb*] poursuivre.

■ **make do** faire avec; **to ~ do with** se contenter de qch.

■ **make for: ¶ ~ for** [*sth*] **1** (head for) se diriger vers; **2** (help create) permettre, assurer; **¶ ~ for** [*sb*] **1** (attack) se jeter sur; **2** (approach) se diriger vers.

■ **make good: ¶ ~ good** réussir; **¶ ~ good** [*sth*] **1** réparer [*damage, omission*]; rattraper [*lost time*]; combler [*deficit*]; **2** tenir [*promise*].

■ **make off** filer○; **to ~ off with** se tirer○ avec.

■ **make out: ¶ ~ out 1** (manage) s'en tirer○; **2**○ US (grope) se peloter○; **3** (claim) affirmer (**that** que); **¶ ~ out** [*sth*], **~** [*sth*] **out 1** (see, distinguish) distinguer; **2** (claim) **to ~ sth out to be** prétendre que qch est; **3** (understand, work out) comprendre (**if** si); **I can't ~ him out** je n'arrive pas à le comprendre; **4** (write out) faire, rédiger; **to ~ out a cheque to sb** faire un chèque à qn; **it is made out to X** il est à l'ordre de X; **5** (expound) **to ~ out a case for** argumenter en faveur de; **¶ ~ oneself out to be** prétendre être [*rich, brilliant*]; faire semblant d'être [*stupid, incompetent*].

■ **make over: ~ over** [*sth*], **~** [*sth*] **over 1** (transform) transformer (**into** en); **2** (transfer) céder (**to** à).

■ **make towards: ~ towards** [*sth/sb*] se diriger vers.

■ **make up: ¶ ~ up 1** (put make-up on) se maquiller; **2** (after quarrel) se réconcilier (**with** avec); **3** (compensate for) **to ~ up for** rattraper [*lost time, lost sleep*]; combler [*deficit*]; compenser [*personal loss*]; **4** **to ~ up to**○ faire de la lèche à○; **¶ ~ up** [*sth*], **~** [*sth*] **up 1** (invent) inventer; **2** (prepare) faire [*parcel, garment, bed*]; préparer [*prescription*]; **3** (constitute) faire; **to be made up of** être fait ou composé de; **to ~ up 10% of** constituer 10% de; **4** (compensate for) rattraper [*loss, time*]; combler [*deficit*]; **5** (put make-up on) maquiller; **to ~ oneself up** se maquiller; **6** **to ~ it up** (make friends) se réconcilier (**with** avec); **to ~ it up to sb** (when at fault) se faire pardonner; (when not at fault) trouver quelque chose pour compenser.

make-believe I /'meɪkbɪliːv/ *n* fantaisie *f*; **it's only ~** ce n'est qu'une histoire imaginaire; **the land of ~** le pays des contes de fées. **II make believe** /ˌmeɪk bɪ'liːv/ *vtr* **to ~ that** imaginer que.

make: ~-do-and-mend *vi* faire avec; **~fast** *n* point m d'amarrage; **~over** *n* transformation *f*.

maker /'meɪkə(r)/ *n* (of clothes, food, appliance) fabricant *m*; (of cars, aircraft) constructeur *m*; **the ~'s label** la marque du fabricant; ▶ **coffee maker**. IDIOMS **to (go to) meet one's Maker** rendre l'âme.

makeshift /'meɪkʃɪft/ *adj* improvisé.

make-up /'meɪkʌp/ *n* **1** GEN, THEAT maquillage *m*; **to wear ~** se maquiller; **to put on one's ~** se maquiller; **2** (character) caractère *m*; **to be part of sb's ~** faire partie du caractère de qn; **3** (of whole, committee) composition *f*; **4** (in printing) mise *f* en page.

make-up: ~ artist [▶ **1251**] *n* maquilleur/-euse *m/f*; **~ bag** *n* trousse *f* de maquillage; **~ remover** *n* démaquillant *m*.

making /'meɪkɪŋ/ *n* **1** (of film, programme) réalisation *f*; (of industrial product) fabrication *f*; (of clothes) confection *f*; **problems of sb's own ~** des problèmes du propre fait de qn; **a disaster is in the ~** une catastrophe est en train de se produire; **2** (of person, personality) **to be the ~ of sb** (past events) être ce qui a fait de qn ce qu'il/elle est; **this contract will be the ~ of her** ce contrat sera le point de départ de sa carrière.

IDIOMS **to have all the ~s of** avoir tout pour faire.

maladjusted /ˌmælə'dʒʌstɪd/ adj PSYCH inadapté.

maladministration /ˌmælədˌmɪnɪ'streɪʃn/ n ℭ **1** ADMIN mauvaise gestion f; **2** JUR malversations fpl.

Malagasy /ˌmælə'gæsɪ/ ▶**1100**, **1038**⎮ I n (pl **-ies**) **1** (native of Madagascar) Malgache mf; **2** (language) malgache m.
II adj malgache.

malaria /mə'leərɪə/ ▶**1002**⎮ n paludisme m; **a ~ attack** une crise de paludisme; **anti-~ tablet** cachet m antipaludique.

Malawi /mə'lɑ:wɪ/ ▶**840**⎮ pr n Malawi m.

Malaya /mə'leɪə/ ▶**840**⎮ pr n Malaisie f.

Malaysia /mə'leɪzɪə/ ▶**840**⎮ pr n Malaisie f.

Malaysian /mə'leɪzɪən/ ▶**1100**⎮ I n (inhabitant) Malaisien/-ienne mf.
II adj malaisien/-ienne.

male /meɪl/ I n **1** BIOL, ZOOL mâle m; **in the ~** chez le mâle; **2** (man) homme m; HUM mâle m.
II adj **1** BIOL, ZOOL mâle; **2** (of men) [population, role, trait] masculin; [company] des hommes; **a ~ voice** une voix d'homme; **the ~ body** le corps de l'homme; **~ singer** chanteur m; **~ student** étudiant m; **3** ELEC mâle.

male: **~ chauvinism** n machisme m; **~ chauvinist** n phallocrate m.

male-dominated /ˌmeɪl'dɒmɪneɪtɪd/ adj **1** (run by men) dominé par les hommes; **2** (mainly masculine) où les hommes dominent.

male: **~ menopause** n retour m d'âge masculin; **~ model** n mannequin m homme or masculin; **~ voice choir** n chœur m d'hommes.

malevolence /mə'levələns/ n malveillance f.

malevolent /mə'levələnt/ adj malveillant.

malformation /ˌmælfɔ:'meɪʃn/ n malformation f.

malformed /ˌmæl'fɔ:md/ adj [limb, nose] difforme; [heart, kidney, leaf, shoot] malformé.

malfunction /ˌmæl'fʌŋkʃn/ I n **1** (poor operation) mauvais fonctionnement m; **2** (breakdown) défaillance f; **a computer ~** une défaillance de l'ordinateur.
II vi mal fonctionner.

Mali /'mɑ:lɪ/ ▶**840**⎮ pr n Mali m.

malice /'mælɪs/ n (spite) méchanceté f (**towards** à); **there's no ~ in him** il n'est pas méchant; **with ~ aforethought** JUR avec préméditation.

malicious /mə'lɪʃəs/ adj [comment, person] malveillant; [act] méchant; [allegation] calomnieux/-ieuse; **with ~ intent** JUR avec l'intention de nuire.

malign /mə'laɪn/ I adj nuisible.
II vtr calomnier; **much-~ed** tant décrié.

malignancy /mə'lɪgnənsɪ/ n **1** MED malignité f; **2** GEN malveillance f.

malignant /mə'lɪgnənt/ adj **1** [criticism, look] malveillant; [person] malfaisant; [nature] cruel/-elle; **2** MED malin/-igne.

mall /mæl, mɔ:l/ n **1** (shopping arcade) (in town) galerie f marchande; (in suburbs) US centre m commercial; **2** US (street) rue f piétonne.

mallard /'mælɑ:d, US 'mælərd/ n (pl ~ ou ~**s**) colvert m.

malleable /'mælɪəbl/ adj malléable.

mallet /'mælɪt/ n SPORT, TECH maillet m.

malnutrition /ˌmælnju:'trɪʃn, US -nu:-/ n GEN sous-alimentation f; MED SPÉC malnutrition f.

malpractice /ˌmæl'præktɪs/ n ℭ **1** ADMIN, JUR malversations fpl; **electoral ~** fraude f électorale; **professional ~** faute f professionnelle; **2** US MED erreur f médicale.

malt /mɔ:lt/ n **1** (grain) malt m; **2** (whisky) whisky m pur malt; **3** US (drink) lait m malté, milk-shake m.

Malta /'mɔ:ltə/ ▶**1022**⎮ pr n Malte f.

Maltese /ˌmɔ:l'ti:z/ ▶**1100**, **1038**⎮ I n **1** (person) Maltais/-e mf; **2** (language) maltais m.
II adj maltais.

maltreat /ˌmæl'tri:t/ vtr maltraiter.

maltreatment /ˌmæl'tri:tmənt/ n mauvais traitement m.

malt: **~ vinegar** n vinaigre m de malt; **~ whisky** n whisky m pur malt.

mammal /'mæml/ n mammifère m.

mammary /'mæmərɪ/ adj mammaire.

mammograph /'mæməgrɑ:f, US -græf/ n mammographie f.

mammoth /'mæməθ/ I n ZOOL mammouth m.
II adj [project, task] gigantesque; [organization, structure] géant.

man /mæn/ I n (pl **men**) **1** (adult male) homme m; **middle-aged ~** homme d'âge mûr; **as one ~ to another** entre hommes; **he's not a ~ to do** ce n'est pas le genre d'homme à faire; **a blind ~** un aveugle; **an old ~** un vieillard; **a single ~** un célibataire; **a ladies' ~** un homme à femmes; **a beer ~** un buveur de bière; **a ~ of God** un homme de Dieu; **they've arrested the right ~** on a arrêté le vrai coupable; **he's your ~** c'est l'homme qu'il te faut; **~ of the match** héros m du match; **good ~!** (well done) bravo mon gars!; **2** (husband, partner) homme m; **he is the right ~ for her** c'est l'homme qu'il lui fallait; **~ and wife** mari et femme; **to live as ~ and wife** vivre maritalement; **3** (person) homme m; **no ~ could have done more** personne n'aurait pu faire davantage; **as good as the next ~** aussi bien que n'importe qui; **the common ~** l'homme du commun; **4** (person of courage) homme m; **be a ~** sois un homme; **to make a ~ of sb** faire un homme de qn; **5** (mankind) (also **Man**) l'humanité f; **6** SPORT (team member) joueur m; **7** (piece) (in chess) pièce f; (in draughts) pion m.
II **men** npl MIL (subordinates) hommes mpl.
III vtr (p prés etc **-nn-**) **1** GEN tenir [switchboard, desk]; **will the telephone be ~ned?** est-ce qu'il y aura quelqu'un pour répondre au téléphone?; **2** MIL armer [qch] en hommes [ship]; assigner des hommes à [barricade, gun].
IV **manned** pp adj [flight, spacecraft, base] habité; **fully ~ned** (of ship) avec un équipage complet.
IDIOMS **every ~ for himself** chacun pour soi; **to a ~** sans exception; **as one ~** comme un seul homme; **to sort out the men from the boys** séparer les hommes des mauviettes○; **he took it like a ~** il a pris ça en homme; **to be a ~'s ~** aimer être entre hommes; **to be one's own ~** être son propre maître.

manage /'mænɪdʒ/ I vtr **1** (succeed) **to ~ to do** réussir à faire, se débrouiller○ pour faire; **he ~d to offend everybody** IRON il a réussi à froisser tout le monde; **2** (find possible) **she ~d a smile** elle a réussi à sourire; **I can ~ a few words in Italian** j'arrive à dire quelques mots en italien; **can you ~ lunch on Friday?** est-ce que tu seras libre pour déjeuner vendredi?; **3** (administer) diriger, administrer [project, finances]; diriger [organization]; gérer [business, shop, hotel, estate]; **4** (organize) gérer [money, time]; **5** (handle) savoir s'y prendre avec [person, animal]; manier [tool, boat]; **they ~d the situation very badly** ils s'y sont très mal pris.
II vi se débrouiller○; **can you ~?** tu y arrives?

manageable /'mænɪdʒəbl/ adj [size, car] maniable; [problem] maîtrisable; [boat] facile à manœuvrer; [person, animal] docile; [level] raisonnable.

management /'mænɪdʒmənt/ I n **1** (control) gestion f; **her skilful ~ of the situation** sa façon adroite de gérer la situation; **2** (managers collectively) direction f; **top ~** la haute direction, les cadres mpl dirigeants; **~ and unions** la direction et les syndicats, les partenaires mpl sociaux; **'under new ~'** 'changement de direction'.
II noun modifier [committee, studies] de gestion; [career] dans le management; [job] de cadre; [staff] d'encadrement; **the ~ team** l'équipe dirigeante.

management: **~ accounting** n comptabilité f analytique; **~ buyout**, **MBO** n rachat m d'une entreprise par ses cadres; **~ consultancy** n cabinet m de conseil; **~ consultant** ▶**1251**⎮ n conseiller m en gestion or en management.

manager /'mænɪdʒə(r)/ n (of firm, bank) directeur/-trice m/f; (of shop) gérant/-e m/f; (of farm) exploitant/-e m/f; (of project) chef m, directeur/-trice m/f; (in show business) directeur/-trice m/f artistique; SPORT manager m; **to be a good ~** GEN être un bon gestionnaire; (of household) savoir bien gérer le budget domestique.

manageress /ˌmænɪdʒə'res/ n (of firm, bank) directrice f; (of shop) gérante f.

managerial /ˌmænɪ'dʒɪərɪəl/ adj [experience] en gestion; [decision] de la direction; **~ staff** les cadres mpl; **at ~ level** au niveau des cadres.

managing: **~ director** n directeur/-trice m/f général-e; **~ editor** n directeur/-trice m/f de la rédaction.

Manchu /mænˈtʃuː/ [▶ 1100], 1038] n 1 (person) Mandchou/-e m/f; 2 (language) mandchou m.

Manchuria /mænˈtʃʊərɪə/ pr n Mandchourie f.

mandarin /'mændərɪn/ n 1 (fruit) mandarine f; (tree) mandarinier m; 2 (person) mandarin m ALSO PEJ.

mandate /'mændeɪt/ n 1 (authority) GEN autorité f; POL mandat m; **to have a ~ to do** POL avoir reçu mandat de faire; **this gives us a clear ~ to proceed** ceci nous donne toute latitude pour poursuivre; 2 HIST territoire m sous mandat; 3 FIN, JUR (document) procuration f, mandat m.

mandatory /'mændətərɪ, US -tɔːrɪ/ adj obligatoire.

mandible /'mændɪbl/ n (of vertebrate) mâchoire f inférieure; (of bird, insect) mandibule f.

mandolin /ˌmændə'lɪn/ [▶ 1097] n mandoline f.

mandrake /'mændreɪk/ n mandragore f.

mane /meɪn/ n LIT, FIG crinière f.

maneuver US n, vtr, vi = **manoeuvre**.

man Friday /ˌmæn 'fraɪdeɪ/ n (helper) factotum m.

mange /meɪndʒ/ n gale f.

manger /'meɪndʒə(r)/ n mangeoire f.

mangle /'mæŋgl/ I n essoreuse f à rouleaux.
II vtr mutiler [body]; broyer [vehicle]; FIG massacrer [work, music].

mango /'mæŋgəʊ/ n (fruit) mangue f; (tree) manguier m.

mangrove /'mæŋgrəʊv/ n palétuvier m, manglier m.

mangy /'meɪndʒɪ/ adj LIT galeux/-euse; FIG [rug] élimé; [hotel] miteux/-euse.

manhandle /'mænhændl/ vtr 1 (treat roughly) malmener, maltraiter; 2 (move by manpower) manutentionner.

man: **~hole** n (in road) regard m, bouche f d'égout; (of boiler, tank) regard m; **~hood** n (state) âge m d'homme; (masculinity) masculinité f; **~-hour** n IND heure f de main-d'œuvre; **~hunt** n chasse f à l'homme.

mania /'meɪnɪə/ n PSYCH manie f; **to have a ~ for doing** avoir la manie de faire.

maniac /'meɪnɪæk/ n 1 PSYCH maniaque mf; 2° FIG fou/folle m/f.

maniacal /mə'naɪəkl/ adj PSYCH maniaque; FIG dément.

manic /'mænɪk/ adj 1 (manic-depressive) maniaco-dépressif/-ive; (obsessive) obsessionnel/-elle; 2 FIG frénétique.

manic depression n psychose f maniaco-dépressive.

manicure /'mænɪkjʊə(r)/ I n manucure f.
II vtr manucurer [person]; **to ~ one's nails** se faire les ongles.

manicure set n trousse f de manucure.

manicurist /'mænɪkjʊərɪst/ [▶ 1251] n manucure mf.

manifest /'mænɪfest/ I n NAUT, AVIAT manifeste m.
II adj manifeste, évident.
III vtr manifester; **to ~ itself** se manifester.

manifestation /ˌmænɪfe'steɪʃn/ n manifestation f.

manifesto /ˌmænɪ'festəʊ/ n manifeste m, programme m.

manipulate /mə'nɪpjʊleɪt/ vtr 1 (handle, control) manipuler, manœuvrer [machine]; 2 PEJ manipuler [person, situation]; jouer sur [emotions]; **she ~d him**

into accepting the offer elle l'a manipulé pour qu'il accepte la proposition; **to ~ sb's emotions** jouer sur les émotions de qn; 3 (falsify) PEJ falsifier [data]; 4 MED (in physiotherapy) manipuler.

manipulation /məˌnɪpjʊ'leɪʃn/ n 1 (of machine) manipulation f, manœuvre f; 2 (of person, situation) PEJ manipulation f; 3 (of data) PEJ falsification f; 4 MED manipulation f.

manipulative /mə'nɪpjʊlətɪv/ adj manipulateur/-trice.

mankind /ˌmæn'kaɪnd/ n humanité f.

manly /'mænlɪ/ adj viril.

man-made /ˌmæn'meɪd/ adj [fibre, fabric] synthétique; [pond] artificiel/-ielle; [environment] façonné par l'homme; [catastrophe] d'origine humaine.

manna /'mænə/ n BIBLE, FIG manne f.

manner /'mænə(r)/ I n 1 (way, method) manière f, façon f; **in this ~** de cette manière or façon; **the ~ in which they were treated** la manière or la façon dont on les a traités; **to do sth in such a ~ that** faire qch de telle sorte que (+ subj); **in a ~ of speaking** pour ainsi dire; **in ou after the ~ of** à la manière de; 2 (way of behaving) attitude f; **she has a bad ~** elle a une attitude déplaisante; **something in his ~ disturbed her** quelque chose dans son comportement la troublait; **to have a good telephone ~** savoir parler au téléphone; 3 LITTER (sort, kind) sorte f, genre m; **what ~ of man is he?** quel genre d'homme est-ce?; **by no ~ of means** pas du tout.
II **manners** npl 1 (social behaviour) manières fpl; **to have good/bad ~s** avoir de bonnes/mauvaises manières; **it's bad ~s to do** il est mal élevé de faire; **he has no ~s** il n'a aucun savoir-vivre; (child) il ne sait pas se tenir; **to have the ~s to do** avoir la politesse de faire; **road ~s** politesse f au volant; 2 (social habits) mœurs fpl; **comedy of ~s** comédie f de mœurs.
III **-mannered** combining form **ill/well-~ed** mal/bien élevé; **mild-~ed** doux/douce, aux manières douces.

mannerism /'mænərɪzəm/ n (habit) particularité f; PEJ (quirk) manie f PEJ.

manning /'mænɪŋ/ n 1 MIL armement m; 2 IND effectifs mpl.

mannish /'mænɪʃ/ adj masculin, PEJ hommasse°.

manoeuvrable GB, **maneuverable** US /mə'nuːvrəbl/ adj maniable.

manoeuvre GB, **maneuver** US /mə'nuːvə(r)/ I n LIT, FIG manœuvre f; **on ~s** MIL en manœuvres; **some room for ~** FIG une marge de manœuvre.
II vtr 1 LIT manœuvrer [vehicle, object]; **to ~ sth in/out** faire entrer/sortir qch en manœuvrant; **to ~ sth into position** manœuvrer qch pour le mettre en position; 2 FIG manœuvrer [person]; faire dévier [discussion] (to vers); **to ~ sb into doing** manœuvrer qn pour qu'il fasse.
III vi manœuvrer.

manoeuvring GB, **maneuvering** US /mə'nuːvərɪŋ/ n ℃ manigances fpl.

man-of-war /ˌmænəv'wɔː(r)/ n (ship) navire m de guerre.

manor /'mænə(r)/ n (also **~ house**) manoir m; HIST (estate) domaine m seigneurial; **Lord/Lady of the ~** châtelain/châtelaine m/f.

manpower /'mænpaʊə(r)/ n 1 GEN main-d'œuvre f; MIL hommes mpl; 2 (physical force) force f; **by sheer ~** à la force des poignets.

manse /mæns/ n presbytère m (de pasteur).

manservant /'mænsɜːvənt/ n valet m.

mansion /'mænʃn/ n (in countryside) demeure f; (in town) hôtel m particulier.

man: **~-sized** adj [tissues] grand modèle inv; **~slaughter** n JUR homicide m involontaire.

mantelpiece /'mæntlpiːs/ n (manteau m de) cheminée f.

mantis /'mæntɪs/ n (also **praying ~**) mante f (religieuse).

man-to-man /ˌmæntəˈmæn/ *adj* d'homme à homme.

manual /ˈmænjʊəl/ **I** *n* **1** (book) manuel *m*; **2** MUS clavier *m*.
II *adj* [*labour, worker*] manuel/-elle; [*gearbox, typewriter*] mécanique.

manufacture /ˌmænjʊˈfæktʃə(r)/ **I** *n* (of materials, tools) fabrication *f*; (of food products, arms) production *f*; **car ~** construction *f* automobile.
II *vtr* LIT fabriquer; FIG PÉJ fabriquer (de toutes pièces) [*excuse*].
III manufactured *pp adj* **~d goods** biens manufacturés.

manufacturer /ˌmænjʊˈfæktʃərə(r)/ *n* GEN fabricant *m* (of de); **car ~** constructeur *m* automobile.

manufacturing /ˌmænjʊˈfæktʃərɪŋ/ **I** *n* **1** ECON (sector) industrie *f* de transformation; **the importance of ~** l'importance de la production industrielle; **2** (making) GEN fabrication *f*; (of cars, heavy machinery) construction *f*.
II *noun modifier* [*output, workforce*] industriel/-ielle; [*capacity, costs, engineer*] de production; [*process*] de fabrication; **~ plant** usine *f*.

manufacturing base *n* tissu *m* industriel, base *f* industrielle.

manure /məˈnjʊə(r)/ *n* fumier *m*; **liquid ~** purin *m*; **horse ~** crottin *m* de cheval.

manuscript /ˈmænjʊskrɪpt/ *n* manuscrit *m*; **in ~** (not yet printed) sous forme de manuscrit.

Manx /mæŋks/ ▶ 1038 *n* **1** (language) mannois *m*; **2** (people) **the ~** les habitants *mpl* de l'île de Man.

many /ˈmenɪ/ (*comparative* **more**; *superlative* **most**) **I** *quantif* beaucoup de, un grand nombre de; **~ times** de nombreuses fois, bien des fois; **for ~ years** pendant de nombreuses années; **in ~ ways** à bien des égards; **his ~ friends** ses nombreux amis; **the ~ advantages of city life** les nombreux avantages de la vie citadine; **how ~ people/times?** combien de personnes/fois?; **there are too ~ people** il y a trop de monde; **for a great ~ years** pendant de nombreuses années; **a good ~ people attended** de nombreuses personnes sont venues; **like so ~ other women** comme tant d'autres femmes; **I have as ~ books as you (do)** j'ai autant de livres que toi; **five exams in as ~ days** cinq examens en autant de jours; **~ a man would be glad of such an opportunity** plus d'un homme se réjouirait d'une telle occasion; **~'s the time I've been there** j'y suis allé maintes fois.
II *pron* beaucoup; **not ~** pas beaucoup; **too ~** trop; **how ~?** combien?; **as ~ as you like** autant que tu veux; **I didn't know there were so ~** je ne savais pas qu'il y en avait autant; **we don't need ~ more** il ne nous en faut pas beaucoup plus; **~ of them were killed** beaucoup d'entre eux ont été tués; **there were too ~ of them** ils étaient trop nombreux; **a good ~ of the houses were damaged** bon nombre de maisons ont été endommagées; **one too ~** un de trop; **you've set one place too ~** tu as mis un couvert de trop; **to have had one too ~**° avoir bu un coup de trop°.

many: **~-coloured** LITTÉR *adj* multicolore; **~-sided** *adj* [*personality, phenomenon*] à multiples facettes.

map /mæp/ **I** *n* (of region) carte *f* (of de); (of town, underground) plan *m* (of de); (of town, underground) plan *m* (of de); **weather ~** carte météo(rologique); **street ~** plan des rues; **the political ~ of Europe** FIG le paysage politique de l'Europe.
II *vtr* **1** faire la carte de [*region, planet*]; faire le plan de [*town*]; **2** COMPUT faire une projection de.
IDIOMS **to put sb/sth on the ~** mettre qn/qch en vedette.
■ **map out:** **~ out** [sth], **~** [sth] **out** élaborer, mettre [qch] au point [*plans, strategy*]; planifier [*schedule*]; tracer [*sb's future*].

maple /ˈmeɪpl/ *n* **1** (tree) érable *m*; **2** (wood) bois *m* d'érable.

mapping /ˈmæpɪŋ/ *n* **1** GEOG, BIOL cartographie *f*; **2** COMPUT projection *f* topographique.

mar /mɑː(r)/ *vtr* (*p prés etc* **-rr-**) (*souvent au passif*) gâcher.

Mar *abrév écrite* = **March**.

marathon /ˈmærəθən, US -θɒn/ **I** *n* (all contexts) marathon *m*.
II *noun modifier* **1** SPORT **~ runner** marathonien/-ienne *m/f*; **2** (massive) -marathon *inv*; **a ~ session** une séance-marathon.

marauding /məˈrɔːdɪŋ/ *adj* en maraude.

marble /ˈmɑːbl/ *n* **1** (stone, sculpture) marbre *m*; **2** GAMES bille *f*; **to play** OU **shoot** US **~s** jouer aux billes.
IDIOMS **to lose one's ~s**° perdre la boule°; **she still has all her ~s**° elle garde toute sa tête.

march /mɑːtʃ/ **I** *n* **1** MIL marche *f*; **a 40 km ~** une marche de 40 km; **to be on the ~** LIT être en marche; FIG [*prices*] être en hausse; **quick/slow ~** marche au pas accéléré/au pas de parade; **2** (demonstration) marche *f* (**against** contre; **for** pour); **peace ~** marche *f* pacifiste; **3** MUS marche *f*; **4** FIG **the ~ of time** la marche du temps.
II *vtr* **she ~ed him into the office** elle l'a emmené d'autorité dans le bureau.
III *vi* **1** MIL marcher au pas; **to ~ on Rome** marcher sur Rome; **to ~ (for) 40 km** faire une marche de 40 km; **forward ~!** en avant, marche!; **2** (in protest) manifester (**against** contre; **for** pour); **3** (walk briskly) marcher d'un pas vif; (angrily) marcher l'air furieux; **he ~ed out of the room** il est sorti l'air furieux; **she ~ed up to his desk** elle s'est dirigée droit vers son bureau.
IDIOMS **to give sb their ~ing orders** renvoyer qn avec perte et fracas.

March /mɑːtʃ/ ▶ 1090 *n* mars *m*.
IDIOMS **to be as mad as a ~ hare** être complètement fou.

marcher /ˈmɑːtʃə(r)/ *n* (in demonstration) manifestant/-e *m/f*; (in procession, band) marcheur/-euse *m/f*.

marchioness /ˌmɑːʃəˈnes/ *n* marquise *f*.

march-past /ˈmɑːtʃpɑːst/ *n* défilé *m*.

mare /meə(r)/ *n* (horse) jument *f*; (donkey) ânesse *f*.

margarine /ˌmɑːdʒəˈriːn/ *n* margarine *f*.

marge° /mɑːdʒ/ GB *abrév* = **margarine**.

margin /ˈmɑːdʒɪn/ *n* **1** (on paper) marge *f*; **in the ~** dans la marge; **left ~** marge à gauche; **2** (of wood, field) lisière *f*; (of river) bord *m*; **3** marge *f* (**of** de); **by a narrow ~** de peu, de justesse; **to lose by a small ~** perdre de peu; **4** FIG (fringe) (*souvent pl*) marge *f*; **at** OU **on the ~(s) of** en marge de; **5** (allowance) marge *f*; **~ of** OU **for error** marge d'erreur; **safety ~** marge de sécurité; **6** (also **profit ~**) marge *f* bénéficiaire.

marginal /ˈmɑːdʒɪnl/ *adj* **1** (minor or peripheral) marginal; **2** GB POL disputé; **3** [*note*] en marge.

marginalize /ˈmɑːdʒɪnəlaɪz/ *vtr* marginaliser.

marginally /ˈmɑːdʒɪnəlɪ/ *adv* très légèrement.

marigold /ˈmærɪɡəʊld/ *n* BOT souci *m*.

marijuana /ˌmærjuˈɑːnə/ *n* marijuana *f*.

marinade /ˌmærɪˈneɪd/ **I** *n* marinade *f*.
II *vtr* (also **marinate**) faire mariner (**in** dans).

marine /məˈriːn/ **I** *n* **1** (soldier) fusilier *m* marin; **the Marines** les marines *mpl*; **2** (navy) **the merchant ~** la marine marchande.
II *adj* [*mammal, biology*] marin; [*explorer, life*] sous-marin; [*insurance, law, transport*] maritime.
IDIOMS **tell it to the ~s!** raconte ça à d'autres!

marine: **Marine Corps** *n* corps *m* des marines américains; **~ engineer** ▶ 1251 *n* ingénieur *m* du génie maritime.

marital /ˈmærɪtl/ *adj* conjugal; **~ status** ADMIN situation *f* de famille.

maritime /ˈmærɪtaɪm/ *adj* (all contexts) maritime.

marjoram /ˈmɑːdʒərəm/ *n* BOT, CULIN marjolaine *f*.

mark /mɑːk/ **I** *n* **1** (stain, animal marking) tache *f*; (from injury) marque *f*; **to make one's ~** LIT signer d'une croix; FIG faire ses preuves; **2** (lasting impression) **to leave one's ~ on sth** [*person*] marquer qch de son

influence [*company*]; [*recession*] marquer qch [*country*]; **3** (symbol) **as a ~ of** en signe de [*esteem*]; **4** SCH, UNIV note *f*; **he gets no ~s for effort** FIG pour l'effort, il mérite zéro; **5** (number on scale) **the 3-mile ~** la borne de trois miles; **unemployment has reached the two million ~** le chômage a atteint la barre des deux millions; **the high-tide ~** le maximum de la marée haute; **at gas ~ 7** à thermostat 7; **6** SPORT (starting line) marque *f*; **on your ~s!** à vos marques!; **to get off the ~** prendre le départ; **he's very quick/a bit slow off the ~** FIG il a l'esprit vif/un peu lent; **you were quick off the ~!** FIG tu n'as pas perdu de temps!; **7** (target) (in archery etc) but *m*; **to find its ~** [*arrow*] atteindre son but; FIG [*remark*] mettre dans le mille; **to be (way) off the ~, to be wide of the ~** FIG être à côté de la plaque○; **8** SPORT (in rugby) arrêt *m* de volée; **9** (also **Mark**) (model in series) Mark; **Jaguar Mark II** Jaguar Mark II; **10** ▶849 (also **Deutschmark**) deutschmark *m*.
II *vtr* **1** (make visible impression on) (stain) tacher [*clothes*]; [*bruise, scar*] marquer [*skin*]; (with pen) marquer [*map, belongings*]; **to ~ sb for life** (physically) défigurer qn à vie; (mentally) marquer qn à vie; **2** (indicate, label) [*person*] marquer [*name, price*] (**on** sur); [*arrow, sign, label*] indiquer [*position, road*]; FIG [*event*] marquer [*end, change*]; **to ~ the occasion with** marquer l'occasion par [*firework display, party*]; **X ~s the spot** l'endroit est indiqué par une croix; **to ~ one's place** (in book) marquer la page; **3** (characterize) caractériser; **4** SCH, UNIV corriger; **to ~ sb absent** noter qn absent; **5** (pay attention to) noter (bien); **he'll not live long, ~ my words!** tu verras, il ne vivra pas longtemps!; **6** SPORT marquer.
III *vi* **1** SCH, UNIV faire des corrections; **2** (stain) se tacher; **3** SPORT marquer.
IV mark you *conj phr* n'empêche que (+ *indic*).
IDIOMS **to be an easy ~** être une poire○; **to ~ time** MIL marquer le pas; **I'm ~ing time working as a waitress until I go to France** FIG je travaille comme serveuse en attendant d'aller en France.
■ **mark down**: ¶ **~** [*sth*] **down, ~ down** [*sth*] démarquer [*product*]; ¶ **~** [*sb*] **down** baisser les notes de [*person*].
■ **mark out**: **~** [*sb*] **out, ~ out** [*sb*] **1** (distinguish) distinguer (**from** de); **2** (select) désigner (**for** pour).
■ **mark up**: ¶ **~** [*sth*] **up, ~ up** [*sth*] [*company*] majorer le prix de [*item*] (**by** de); [*shopkeeper*] augmenter le prix de [*item*] (**by** de); ¶ **~** [*sb*] **up** SCH, UNIV remonter les notes de [*person*].

marked /mɑːkt/ *adj* **1** (noticeable) GEN marqué, net/nette (*before n*); [*accent*] prononcé; **2** (in danger) **he's a ~ man** on en veut à sa vie.

marker /ˈmɑːkə(r)/ *n* **1** (pen) marqueur *m*; **2** (tag) repère *m*; **3** (scorekeeper) marqueur/-euse *m/f*; **4** SCH, UNIV examinateur/-trice *m/f*; **5** SPORT marqueur/-euse *m/f*.

market /ˈmɑːkɪt/ **I** *n* **1** ECON marché *m*; **the job ~** le marché du travail; **cars at the upper** ou **top end of the ~** les voitures haut de gamme; **to come onto the ~** arriver sur le marché; **to be in the ~ for** chercher (à acquérir); **2** COMM (potential customers) marché *m* (**for** pour); **domestic/French ~** marché intérieur/français; **a poor/steady ~ for** une demande faible/stable de; **the teenage ~** les adolescents; **a gap in the ~** un créneau, un besoin du marché; **3** (place) marché *m*; **fish ~** halle *f* aux poissons; **to go to the ~** aller au marché; **4** (stock market) Bourse *f*; **to play the ~** spéculer.
II *noun modifier* [*share*] de marché; [*conditions, rates*] du marché.
III *vtr* **1** (sell) commercialiser, vendre; **2** (promote) lancer ou mettre [qch] sur le marché.

market: **~ analyst** *n* analyste *mf* de marché; **~ capitalization** *n* capitalisation *f* boursière; **~ day** *n* jour *m* du marché; **~ economy** *n* économie *f* de marché; **~ forces** *npl* forces *fpl* du marché; **~ gardener** ▶1251 *n* maraîcher/-ère *m/f*; **~ gardening** *n* culture *f* maraîchère.

marketing /ˈmɑːkɪtɪŋ/ *n* **1** (process, theory) marketing

m, mercatique *f*; **2** (department) service *m* de marketing.

marketing: **~ agreement** *n* accord *m* de commercialisation; **~ campaign** *n* campagne *f* de vente; **~ man** *n* commercial *m*; **~ process** *n* processus *m* de commercialisation; **~ strategy** *n* stratégie *f* commerciale.

market: **~ leader** *n* (product) produit *m* vedette; (company) leader *m* du marché; **~-led** *adj* GEN déterminé par le marché; [*economy*] de marché; **~ opportunity** *n* créneau *m*; **~place** *n* (square) place *f* du marché; ECON, FIN marché *m*; **~ price** *n* prix *m* du marché; **~ research** *n* étude *f* de marché; **~ researcher** ▶1251 *n* chargé/-e *m/f* d'études de marketing; **~ square** *n* place *f* du marché; **~ stall** *n* étal *m*; **~ town** *n* bourg *m*; **~ trader** *n* vendeur/-euse *m/f* sur un marché; **~ value** *n* valeur *f* marchande ou d'échange.

marking /ˈmɑːkɪŋ/ *n* **1** (on animal) tache *f*; (on aircraft) marque *f*; **road ~s** signalisation *f* horizontale; **2** GB SCH, UNIV (process) ¢ corrections *fpl*; (marks given) notation *f*; **3** SPORT marquage *m*.

mark: **~sman** *n* MIL, SPORT tireur *m* d'élite; **~smanship** *n* MIL, SPORT adresse *f* au tir; **~-up** *n* (retailer's margin) marge *f*; (increase) augmentation *f*.

marmalade /ˈmɑːməleɪd/ *n* confiture *f* ou marmelade *f* d'oranges.

marmalade cat *n* chat/chatte *m/f* roux/rousse.

marmoset /ˈmɑːməzet/ *n* ouistiti *m*.

marmot /ˈmɑːmət/ *n* marmotte *f*.

maroon /məˈruːn/ ▶818 **I** *n* **1** (colour) bordeaux *m*; **2** GB (rocket) fusée *f* de détresse.
II *vtr* **to be ~ed on an island** être bloqué sur une île; **the ~ed sailors** les naufragés.

marquee /mɑːˈkiː/ *n* **1** GB (tent) grande tente *f*; (of circus) chapiteau *m*; **2** US (canopy) (grand) auvent *m*.

marquess /ˈmɑːkwɪs/ *n* marquis *m*.

marquetry /ˈmɑːkɪtrɪ/ *n* marqueterie *f*.

marquis /ˈmɑːkwɪs/ *n* marquis *m*.

marriage /ˈmærɪdʒ/ **I** *n* **1** (ceremony, contract) mariage *m* (**to** avec); **broken ~** mariage brisé; **proposal of ~** proposition *f* de mariage; **by ~** par alliance; **2** FIG (alliance) mariage *m*; **3** (in cards) mariage *m*.
II *noun modifier* [*guidance*] conjugal; [*contract, vows*] de mariage.

marriage: **~ bureau** *n* agence *f* matrimoniale; **~ ceremony** *n* cérémonie *f* nuptiale; **~ certificate** *n* extrait *m* d'acte de mariage; **~ guidance counsellor** *n* conseiller/-ère *m/f* conjugal/-e; **~ of convenience** *n* mariage *m* de convenance.

married /ˈmærɪd/ *adj* [*person*] marié (**to** à); [*life*] conjugal; **~ couple** couple *m*.

marrow /ˈmærəʊ/ *n* **1** ANAT moelle *f*; **frozen to the ~** gelé jusqu'à la moelle; **2** GB BOT courge *f*; **baby ~** GB courgette *f*.

marrowbone /ˈmærəʊbəʊn/ *n* os *m* à moelle.

marry /ˈmærɪ/ **I** *vtr* **1** LIT [*priest*] marier [*couple*]; se marier avec, épouser [*fiancé(e)*]; **to get married** se marier (**to** avec); **will you ~ me?** veux-tu m'épouser?; **2** FIG marier [*ideas, colours*]; **to be married to one's job** HUM ne vivre que pour son travail.
II *vi* se marier; **to ~ into a family** entrer dans une famille par le mariage; **to ~ for love** faire un mariage d'amour; **to ~ into money** épouser un homme ou une femme riche; **to ~ beneath oneself** se mésallier.
■ **marry off**: **~ off** [*sb*], **~** [*sb*] **off** marier (**to** à, avec).

marsh /mɑːʃ/ *n* (also **marshland**) (terrain) marécage *m*; (region) marais *m*.

marshal /ˈmɑːʃl/ **I** *n* **1** MIL maréchal *m*; **2** GB JUR *avocat accompagnant un juge itinérant*; **3** (at rally, ceremony) membre *m* du service d'ordre; **4** US JUR ~ huissier *m* de justice; **5** US HIST (sheriff) marshal *m*; **6** US (in fire service) capitaine *m* des pompiers.
II (*p prés* **-ll-** GB, **-l-** US) *vtr* **1** GEN, MIL rassembler

[*troops*]; diriger [*crowd*]; RAIL trier [*wagons*]; FIG rassembler [*facts*]; **2** (guide) conduire [*person*].

marshalling yard *n* GB RAIL gare *f* de triage.

marsh: **~ fever** ▶ 1002 *n* paludisme *m*; **~ harrier** *n* busard *m* des roseaux; **~mallow** *n* CULIN pâte *f* de guimauve.

marten /'mɑːtɪn, US -tn/ *n* martre *f*.

martial /'mɑːʃl/ *adj* [*music, art, law*] martial; [*spirit*] guerrier/-ière.

martinet /ˌmɑːtɪ'net, US -tn'et/ *n* **to be a ~** être stricte en matière de discipline.

martyr /'mɑːtə(r)/ **I** *n* RELIG, FIG martyr/-e *m/f*; **a ~ to the cause** un martyr de la cause; **to play the ~** jouer les martyrs.
II *vtr* LIT, FIG martyriser.

martyrdom /'mɑːtədəm/ *n* martyre *m*.

marvel /'mɑːvl/ **I** *n* merveille *f*; **it was a ~ to behold** c'était merveilleux à voir; **to work ~s** faire des merveilles; **he's a ~ of patience** il est merveilleusement patient.
II *vtr* (*p prés etc* GB **-ll-**, US **-l-**) **to ~ that** s'étonner de ce que (+ *subj*).
III *vi* s'étonner (**at** de), être émerveillé (**at** par).

marvellous GB, **marvelous** US /'mɑːvələs/ *adj* [*weather, holiday*] merveilleux/-euse; **but that's ~!** mais c'est formidable!

marvellously GB, **marvelously** US /'mɑːvələslɪ/ *adv* [*sing, get on*] à merveille; [*clever, painted*] merveilleusement.

marzipan /'mɑːzɪpæn, ˌmɑːzɪ'pæn/ *n* pâte *f* d'amandes.

mascot /'mæskət, -skɒt/ *n* mascotte *f*; **lucky ~** portebonheur *m inv*.

masculine /'mæskjʊlɪn/ *n, adj* masculin (*m*).

masculinity /ˌmæskjʊ'lɪnɪtɪ/ *n* masculinité *f*.

mash /mæʃ/ **I** *n* **1** AGRIC pâtée *f*; **2** (in brewing) trempe *f*; **3**○ GB CULIN purée *f* (de pommes de terre).
II *vtr* **1** (also **~ up**) écraser [*fruit*]; **to ~ potatoes** faire de la purée; **2** (in brewing) brasser.

MASH /mæʃ/ *n* US (*abrév* = **mobile army surgical hospital**) unité *f* médicale de campagne.

mask /mɑːsk, US mæsk/ **I** *n* GEN masque *m*; (for eyes only) loup *m*.
II *vtr* masquer [*face*]; dissimuler [*truth, emotions*]; masquer [*taste*].

mask: **~ed ball** *n* bal *m* masqué; **~ing tape** *n* ruban *m* adhésif.

masochist /'mæsəkɪst/ *n, adj* masochiste (*mf*).

mason /'meɪsn/ ▶ 1251 *n* **1** CONSTR maçon *m*; **2 Mason** (also **Free~**) franc-maçon *m*.

masonic /mə'sɒnɪk/ *adj* maçonnique.

masonry /'meɪsənrɪ/ *n* maçonnerie *f*.

masquerade /ˌmɑːskə'reɪd, US ˌmæsk-/ **I** *n* **1** (ball) bal *m* masqué; **2** FIG (pretence) mascarade *f*.
II *vi* **to ~ as sb** se faire passer pour qn.

mass /mæs/ **I** *n* **1** (vast body) masse *f* (**of** de); (cluster) amas *m* (**of** de); **2** (amount) (of people) foule *f* (**of** de); (of details) quantité *f* (**of** de); **3** RELIG messe *f*; **4** PHYS, ART masse *f*.
II masses *npl* **1** (the people) **the ~es** GEN la foule; (working class) les masses *fpl*; **2**○ GB (lots) **~es of work** beaucoup ou plein○ de travail; **~es of people** une foule de gens; **to have ~es of time** avoir largement le temps.
III *noun modifier* **1** (large scale) [*audience*] de masse; [*destruction, exodus, protest, unemployment*] massif/ -ive; [*sackings*] en masse; **~ meeting** rassemblement *m* de masse; **2** (of the people) [*movement, tourism*] de masse; **to have ~ appeal** avoir un succès de masse.
IV *vi* [*troops*] se regrouper; [*bees*] se masser; [*clouds*] s'amonceler.

massacre /'mæsəkə(r)/ **I** *n* LIT, FIG massacre *m*.
II *vtr* **1** LIT massacrer; **2** FIG massacrer [*tune*]; démolir○ [*team*].

massage /'mæsɑːʒ, US mə'sɑːʒ/ **I** *n* massage *m*.

II *vtr* masser [*person*]; FIG tricher sur [*figures*]; flatter [*ego*].

mass: **~ cult**○ *n* US culture *f* de masse; **~-energy** *n* masse-énergie *f*; **~ grave** *n* charnier *m*, fosse *f* commune; **~ hysteria** *n* hystérie *f* collective.

massive /'mæsɪv/ *adj* [*object, amount, error*] énorme; [*explosion*] retentissant; [*majority*] écrasant; [*campaign, task*] de grande envergure; [*increase, cut*] massif/-ive; [*haemorrhage*] grave.

massively /'mæsɪvlɪ/ *adv* [*reduce, increase*] énormément; [*overrated*] considérablement.

mass: **~ market** *n* marché *m* grand public; **~-marketing** *n* commercialisation *f* massive; **~ media** *n* (+ *v sg* ou *pl*) (mass) médias *mpl*; **~ murder** *n* massacre *m*; **~ murderer** *n* auteur *m* d'un massacre; **~-produce** *vtr* fabriquer [qch] en série; **~ production** *n* fabrication *f* en série; **~ screening** *n* MED dépistage *m* systématique.

mast /mɑːst, US mæst/ *n* **1** (on ship, for flags) mât *m*; RADIO, TV pylône *m*; **the ~s of a ship** la mâture *f* d'un navire; **2** ₵ AGRIC glands *mpl* et faines *fpl*.
IDIOMS **to nail one's colours to the ~** afficher ses opinions (une fois pour toutes).

master /'mɑːstə(r), US 'mæs-/ **I** *n* **1** (man in charge) maître *m*; **the ~ of the house** le maître de maison; **to be ~ in one's own house** être maître chez soi; **2** (person in control) maître/-esse *m/f*; **to be one's own ~** être son propre maître; **3** (person who excels) maître *m*; **a ~ of** un maître de [*violin, narrative*]; un/-e expert/-e en [*tactics, public relations*]; **to be a ~ at doing** être maître dans l'art de faire; **4** (also **Master**) ART maître *m*; **5** SCH (primary) instituteur *m*; (secondary) professeur *m*; (headmaster) proviseur *m*; **6** GB UNIV (of college) principal *m*; **7** (also **~ copy**) original *m*; **8** UNIV (graduate) ~ titulaire *m/f* d'une maîtrise; **~'s (degree)** maîtrise *f* (**in** en, de); **9** NAUT capitaine *m*; **10** (title of young man) monsieur *m*; **Master Ian Todd** (on envelope) Monsieur Ian Todd.
II *noun modifier* [*architect, chef*] maître (*before n*); [*smuggler, spy*] professionnel/-elle.
III *vtr* **1** (learn) maîtriser [*subject*]; posséder [*skill*]; **2** (control) dominer [*feelings*]; surmonter [*phobia*].

master: **~ bedroom** *n* chambre *f* principale; **~ builder** ▶ 1251 *n* maître *m* d'œuvre; **~ copy** *n* original *m*; **~ disk** *n* COMPUT disque *m* d'exploitation.

master key *n* passe-partout *m inv*.

masterly /'mɑːstəlɪ, US 'mæs-/ *adj* [*technique, writing*] magistral.

mastermind /'mɑːstəmaɪnd/ **I** *n* cerveau *m* (**of, behind** de).
II *vtr* échafauder [*crime*]; organiser [*event*].

master: **Master of Arts** *n* ~ maîtrise *f* de lettres; **~ of ceremonies** *n* (presenting entertainment) animateur/-trice *m/f*; (at formal occasion) maître *m* des cérémonies; **Master of Science** *n* ~ maîtrise *f* de sciences; **~piece** *n* chef-d'œuvre *m* ALSO FIG; **~ plan** *n* plan *m* d'ensemble; **~ race** *n* race *f* supérieure; **~stroke** *n* (piece of skill) coup *m* de maître; (idea) idée *f* de génie; **~ tape** *n* bande *f* mère.

mastery /'mɑːstərɪ, US 'mæs-/ *n* **1** (competence) maîtrise *f* (**of** de); **2** (control) domination *f*, maîtrise *f*; **to have ~ over sb/sth** dominer qn/qch.

masticate /'mæstɪkeɪt/ *vi* mastiquer, mâcher.

mat /mæt/ **I** *n* **1** (on floor) (petit) tapis *m*; (for wiping feet) paillasson *m*; **exercise ~** tapis; **2** (on table) (heatproof) dessous-de-plat *m inv*; (ornamental) napperon *m*; **place ~ set** *m* de table.
II *adj* = **matt**.
III *vi* (*p prés etc* **-tt-**) [*hair*] s'emmêler; [*wool*] se feutrer; [*fibres*] s'enchevêtrer.

MAT *n* (*abrév* = **machine-assisted translation**) TAO *f*.

match /mætʃ/ **I** *n* **1** SPORT match *m*; **2** (for lighting fire) allumette *f*; **to put a ~ to sth** mettre le feu à qch; **3** (equal) **to be a ~ for sb** être un adversaire à la mesure de qn; **to be no ~ for sb** être trop faible pour qn; **to meet one's ~** trouver quelqu'un à sa

auteur; **to be more than a ~ for sb** surpasser qn;
4 (thing that harmonizes) **to be a good ~ for sth**
shoes, curtains, colour] aller très bien avec qch; **to be**
an exact ~ with correspondre parfaitement à; **5**
marriage) union *f*, mariage *m*; **to make a good ~**
épouser un bon parti.

II *vtr* **1** (correspond to) [*colour, bag*] être assorti à;
[*blood type*] correspondre à; [*product, supply*] répondre
à [*demand*]; [*word*] correspondre à [*definition*]; **2**
(equal) égaler [*record, achievements*]; **the government**
will ~ your donation le gouvernement donnera la
même somme que vous; **his wit cannot be ~ed** il a
une intelligence hors pair; **she more than ~ed him**
in aggression elle le valait bien sur le plan de
l'agressivité; **he is to be ~ed against the**
champion on a organisé une rencontre entre lui et le
champion; **there's nobody to ~ him** (disparagingly) il
n'y en a pas deux comme lui; **3** (find a match for) **to ~**
trainees with companies mettre en rapport des
stagiaires avec des sociétés.

II *vi* [*colours, clothes, curtains*] être assortis/-ies;
[*components*] aller ensemble; **that button doesn't ~**
ce bouton n'est pas identique aux autres; **with gloves**
to ~ avec des gants assortis.

■ **match up:** ¶ **~ up** [*pieces, bits*] aller ensemble; ¶
~ up [sth], ~ [sth] up ajuster [*pieces*]; **to ~ up to**
être à la hauteur de [*expectation*].

matchbox /'mætʃbɒks/ *n* boîte *f* d'allumettes.

matchmaker /'mætʃmeɪkə(r)/ *n* (for couples) marieur/
-euse *m/f*; (for business) intermédiaire *mf*.

match point *n* balle *f* de match; **at ~** à la balle de
match.

matchstick /'mætʃstɪk/ **I** *n* (bois *m* d') allumette *f*.

II *noun modifier* [*man, figure*] stylisé, filiforme.

mate /meɪt/ **I** *n* **1**° GB (friend) copain° *m*; (at work,
school) camarade *mf*; **2** ZOOL (male) mâle *m*; (female)
femelle *f*; **3** (assistant) aide *mf*; **builder's ~** aide-
maçon *m*; **4** (in chess) mat *m*.

II *vtr* **1** accoupler [*animal*] (**with** à or avec); **2** (in
chess) faire mat.

III *vi* [*animal*] s'accoupler (**with** à, avec).

material /mə'tɪərɪəl/ **I** *n* **1** (data) documentation *f*,
documents *mpl*; **teaching ~** matériel *m* pédagogique;
reference ~ ouvrages *mpl* de référence; **2** (subject
matter) contenu *m*; **3** THEAT, TV (script) texte *m*; (show)
spectacle *m*; **she writes all her own ~** elle écrit ses
textes elle-même; MUS elle est auteur-compositrice; **4**
(substance) GEN matière *f*, substance *f*; CONSTR, TECH
matériau *m*; **packing ~** matériaux *mpl* d'emballage;
waste ~ déchets *mpl*; **5** (fabric) tissu *m*, étoffe *f*; **6**
(personal potential) étoffe *f*; **she is star ~** elle a l'étoffe
d'une vedette; **to be university ~** être capable d'entreprendre des études universitaires.

II materials *npl* (equipment) matériel *m*; **art ~s**, **art-**
ist's ~s fournitures *fpl* de dessin; **cleaning ~s**
produits *mpl* d'entretien.

III *adj* **1** (significant, relevant) [*assistance, benefit,*
change, damage, evidence] matériel-ielle; [*question*]
important; [*fact*] pertinent; **to be ~ to sth** se
rapporter à qch; **2** (concrete) [*comfort, gains, posses-*
sions, success] matériel/-ielle; **in ~ terms** sur le plan
matériel; **to do sth for ~ gain** faire qch par intérêt.

materialist /mə'tɪərɪəlɪst/ *n, adj* matérialiste (*mf*).

materialistic /mə,tɪərɪə'lɪstɪk/ *adj* matérialiste.

materialize /mə'tɪərɪəlaɪz/ *vi* **1** (happen) [*hope, offer,*
plan, threat] se concrétiser; [*event, situation*] se réaliser; [*idea*] prendre forme; **the strike failed to ~** la
grève n'a pas eu lieu; **2** (appear) [*person, object*] surgir;
[*spirit*] se matérialiser; **I waited, but he failed to ~**
HUM j'ai attendu, mais il ne s'est pas montré.

materially /mə'tɪərɪəlɪ/ *adv* **1** (considerably) sensiblement; **2** (physically) matériellement.

maternal /mə'tɜːnl/ *adj* maternel/-elle (**towards**
avec).

maternity /mə'tɜːnətɪ/ **I** *n* maternité *f*.

II *noun modifier* [*clothes*] de grossesse; [*leave, benefit*]
de maternité.

maternity: **~ department** *n* (in store) rayon *m*

future maman; **~ hospital** *n* maternité *f*; **~ unit**
n service *m* d'obstétrique; **~ ward** *n* maternité *f*.

matey° /'meɪtɪ/ *adj* GB copain° (**with** avec).

math° /mæθ/ *n* US = **maths**°.

mathematical /,mæθə'mætɪkl/ *adj* mathématique;
it's a ~ impossibility c'est mathématiquement
impossible.

mathematician /,mæθəmə'tɪʃn/ ▶ **1251** *n* mathémati-
cien/-ienne *m/f*.

mathematics /,mæθə'mætɪks/ *n* (subject) (+ *v sg*)
mathématiques *fpl*; (operations) (+ *v sg* ou *v pl*) calculs
mpl.

maths° /mæθs/ GB **I** *n* (+ *v sg*) maths° *fpl*.

II *noun modifier* [*class, teacher*] de maths.

matinée /'mætɪneɪ, 'mætneɪ, US ,mætn'eɪ/ **I** *n* CIN,
THEAT matinée *f*.

II *noun modifier* [*performance*] en matinée.

mating /'meɪtɪŋ/ *n* accouplement *m*.

mating: **~ call** *n* chant *m* nuptial; **~ season** *n*
saison *f* des amours.

matriarchal /,meɪtrɪ'ɑːkl/ *adj* matriarcal.

matrices /'meɪtrɪsiːz/ *pl* ▶ **matrix**.

matriculate /mə'trɪkjʊleɪt/ **I** *vtr* inscrire [*student*].

II *vi* (enrol) (student) s'inscrire.

matrimony /'mætrɪmənɪ, US -məʊnɪ/ *n* mariage *m*;
united in holy ~ unis dans le sacrement du mariage.

matrix /'meɪtrɪks/ *n* (*pl* -**trices**) matrice *f*.

matron /'meɪtrən/ *n* **1** GB (nurse) (in hospital) infirmière
f en chef; (in school) infirmière *f* (*chargée également de*
l'intendance); **2** (of nursing home) directrice *f*; **3** US
(warder) gardienne *f*; **4** (woman) PÉJ matrone *f* PÉJ.

matronly /'meɪtrənlɪ/ *adj* [*duties, manner*] de mère de
famille, de matrone; [*figure*] fort, corpulent.

matron-of-honour GB, **matron-of-honor** US *n*
dame *f* d'honneur.

matt GB, **matte** US /mæt/ *adj* [*paint*] mat; [*photo-*
graph] sur papier mat.

matter /'mætə(r)/ **I** *n* **1** (affair) (of specified nature)
affaire *f*; (requiring solution) problème *m*; (on agenda)
point *m*; **business ~s** affaires *fpl*; **the ~ in hand**
l'affaire en question; **it will be no easy ~** cela ne
sera pas (une affaire) facile; **important ~s to**
discuss des choses importantes à discuter; **~s aris-**
ing (in meeting) points non inscrits à l'ordre du jour;
private ~ affaire privée; **a ~ for the police** un
problème qui relève de la police; **that's another ~**
c'est une autre histoire; **it's no small ~** ce n'est pas
une broutille; **to let the ~ drop** en rester là; **to take**
the ~ further aller plus loin; **the fact of the ~ is**
that la vérité est que; **I know nothing of the ~** je
ne suis au courant de rien; **2** (question) question *f*; **it's**
a ~ of urgency c'est urgent; **a ~ of life and death**
une question de vie ou de mort; **it will just be a ~ of**
months ce ne sera qu'une question de mois; **a ~ of**
a few days l'affaire de quelques jours; **it's only a ~**
of time before they separate ils vont se séparer, ce
n'est plus qu'une question de temps; **3** (trouble) **is**
anything the ~? y a-t-il un problème?; **what's the**
~? qu'est-ce qu'il y a?; **there's nothing the ~ with**
me je n'ai rien; **what's the ~ with Louise?** qu'est-
ce qu'elle a Louise?; **4** (substance) matière *f*; **vegetable**
~ matière végétale; **colouring ~** colorant *m*; **5** (on
paper) **printed ~** imprimés *mpl*; **advertising ~**
publicité *f*; **reading ~** lecture *f*; **6** (content of book,
speech etc) contenu *m*; **subject ~** contenu *m*; **~ and**
style le fond et la forme; **7** MED (pus) pus *m*.

II *vi* être important; **to ~ to sb** [*behaviour, action*]
avoir de l'importance pour qn; [*person*] compter pour
qn; **it ~s little to me where you go** peu m'importe
où tu vas; **it doesn't ~ whether** peu importe que (+
subj); **it doesn't ~** ça n'a aucune importance, ça ne
fait rien; **does it really ~?** qu'est-ce que ça peut
faire?

IDIOMS as a ~ of course automatiquement; **as a**
~ of fact en fait; **for that ~** d'ailleurs; **no ~!** peu
importe!; **no ~ how late it is** peu importe l'heure;
that's the end of the ~ c'est mon/son etc dernier

may¹

When *may* (or *may have*) is used with another verb in English to convey *possibility*, French will generally use the adverb *peut-être* (= perhaps) with the equivalent verb:

it may rain	=	il pleuvra peut-être
we may never know what happened	=	nous ne saurons peut-être jamais ce qui s'est passé
he may have got lost	=	il s'est peut-être perdu

Alternatively, and more formally, the construction *il se peut que* + subjunctive may be used: *il se peut qu'il pleuve*; *il se peut que nous ne sachions jamais*. For particular usages, see **1** in the entry **may**.

peut-être is also used in French to convey *concession*:

he may be slow but he's not stupid	=	il est peut-être lent mais il n'est pas bête
you may think I'm crazy but …	=	tu penses peut-être que je suis fou mais …

When *may* is used to convey *permission*, the French equivalent is *pouvoir*:

you may close the door = vous pouvez fermer la porte

Note that the polite question *may I …?* is translated by *puis-je …?*:

may I make a suggestion? = puis-je faire une suggestion?

For particular usages, see **2** in the entry **may**.

When *may* is used in rather formal English to convey purpose in the construction *in order that* + *may* the French equivalent is *pour que* + subjunctive:

in order that he may know = pour qu'il sache

When *may* is used with another verb to express a wish the French uses *que* + subjunctive:

may they be happy!	=	qu'ils soient heureux!
long may it last!	=	que ça dure!

When *may well* + *verb* is used to convey likelihood the French uses *il est fort possible que* + subjunctive:

he may well have gone elsewhere = il est fort possible qu'il soit allé ailleurs

But note:

that may well be but … = c'est possible mais …

In the phrase *may as well*, *may* is used interchangeably with *might*, which is more frequently used. For translations see the entry *well¹* II 2.

---

mot; **to make ~s worse** pour ne rien arranger; **to take ~s into one's own hands** prendre les choses en main.

Matterhorn /'mætəhɔːn/ *pr n* **the ~** le (mont) Cervin.

matter-of-fact *adj* [*voice, tone*] détaché; [*person*] terre à terre.

Matthew /'mæθjuː/ *pr n* Mathieu; BIBLE Matthieu.

mattress /'mætrɪs/ *n* matelas *m*.

maturation /ˌmætjʊˈreɪʃn/ *n* (of tree, body) maturation *f*; (of whisky, wine) vieillissement *m*; (of cheese) affinage *m*.

mature /məˈtjʊə(r), US -ˈtʊər/ **I** *adj* **1** [*plant, animal*] adulte; **~ garden** beau jardin (*planté depuis quelques années*); **2** (psychologically) [*person*] mûr; [*attitude, reader*] adulte; **her most ~ novel** son roman le plus achevé; **after ~ consideration** après mûre réflexion; **3** [*hard cheese*] fort; [*soft cheese*] affiné; [*whisky*] vieux; **4** FIN [*policy*] arrivé à échéance. **II** *vi* **1** (physically) [*person, animal*] devenir adulte; [*plant*] atteindre la taille adulte; **2** (psychologically) [*person*] mûrir; **3** [*idea*] mûrir; **4** [*wine*] vieillir; [*cheese*] s'affiner; **5** FIN [*policy*] arriver à échéance.

mature student *n* GB personne *f* qui reprend des études (*après un temps au foyer ou dans la vie active*).

maturity /məˈtjʊərəti, US -ˈtʊə-/ *n* GEN maturité *f*;

FIN échéance *f*; **to reach ~** [*person*] atteindre l'âg adulte; [*tree*] arriver à maturité.

maudlin /'mɔːdlɪn/ *adj* [*song*] larmoyant; [*person*] mé lancolique.

maul /mɔːl/ **I** *n* **1** (hammer) masse *f*; **2** (in rugby) mau *m*. **II** *vtr* **1** (attack) [*animal*] mutiler; (fatally) déchiqueter **2** (manhandle) malmener; **3** (sexually) tripoter [*woman*]; **4** FIG [*critics*] démolir.

Maundy Thursday *n* jeudi *m* saint.

Mauritius /məˈrɪʃəs/ ▶840, 1022 *pr n* l'île Maurice.

mausoleum /ˌmɔːsəˈliːəm/ *n* **1** (tomb) mausolée *m*; **2** (big house) PÉJ grande baraque○ *f*.

mauve /məʊv/ ▶818 *n, adj* mauve (*m*).

maverick /'mævərɪk/ *n, adj* nonconformiste (*mf*).

mawkish /'mɔːkɪʃ/ *adj* PÉJ **1** (sentimental) mièvre; **2** (insipid) fade.

maxi /'mæksi/ *n* **1** (also **~ dress**) robe *f* maxi; **2** (also **~ skirt**) jupe *f* maxi.

maxim /'mæksɪm/ *n* maxime *f*.

maxima /'mæksɪmə/ *pl* ▶ **maximum**.

maximization /ˌmæksɪmaɪˈzeɪʃn/ *n* maximalisation *f*.

maximize /'mæksɪmaɪz/ *vtr* GEN maximiser [*profit, sales*]; COMPUT agrandir.

maximum /'mæksɪməm/ **I** *n* (*pl* **-imums**, **-ima**) maximum *m*; **to hold a ~ of 300** contenir 300 personnes au maximum. **II** *adj* [*price*] maximum; [*temperature*] maximal; [*speed*] maximum, maximal; [*load*] limite. **III** *adv* au maximum.

maximum security prison *n* prison *f* de haute surveillance.

may¹ /meɪ/ *modal aux* **1** (possibility) **he ~ come** il se peut qu'il vienne, il viendra peut-être; **'are you going to accept?'—'I ~'** 'tu vas accepter?'—'peut-être'; **this medicine ~ cause drowsiness** ce médicament peut provoquer des réactions de somnolence; **they're afraid she ~ die** ils ont peur qu'elle (ne) meure; **even if I invite him he ~ not come** même si je l'invite il risque de ne pas venir; **that's as ~ be, but…** peut-être bien, mais…; **come what ~** advienne que pourra; **be that as it ~** quoi qu'il en soit; **2** (permission) **~ I come in?** puis-je entrer?; **I'll sit down, if I ~** je vais m'asseoir si vous le permettez; **if I ~ say so** si je puis me permettre; **and who are you, ~ I ask?** IRON qui êtes-vous au juste?; ▶ **well¹** II 2.

may² /meɪ/ *n* (hawthorn) aubépine *f*.

May /meɪ/ ▶ 1090 *n* (month) mai *m*.

maybe /'meɪbi/ **I** *adv* peut-être; **~ they'll arrive early** peut-être arriveront-ils tôt; **~ three weeks ago** il y a peut-être trois semaines. **II** *n* **'is that a yes?'—'it's a ~'** 'c'est oui?'—'c'est peut-être'.

May: **~ beetle**, **~ bug** *n* hanneton *m*; **~day** *n* RADIO mayday *m*; **~ Day** *n* premier mai *m*, fête *f* du travail.

mayhem /'meɪhem/ *n* **1** (chaos) désordre *m*; (violence) grabuge○ *m*; **to create ~** semer la pagaille○; **2** JUR (crime *m* de) mutilation *f*.

mayn't /'meɪənt/ = **may not**.

mayor /meə(r), US 'meɪər/ ▶ 937 *n* maire *m*.

mayoress /'meərɪs, US 'meɪərɪs/ ▶ 937 *n* (wife of mayor) femme *f* du maire; (lady mayor) mairesse *f*.

May: **maypole** *n* mât *m* (de fête) (*à l'occasion du premier mai*); **~ queen** *n* reine *f* du premier mai.

maze /meɪz/ *n* (puzzle) labyrinthe *m*; FIG (of streets, corridors) dédale *m*; (of pipes) enchevêtrement *m*.

Mb *n* COMPUT (*abrév* = **megabyte**) Mo.

MBA *n* UNIV (*abrév* = **Master of Business Administration**) ≈ maîtrise *f* de gestion.

MBE *n* GB (*abrév* = **Member of the Order of the British Empire**) membre *m* de l'ordre de l'empire britannique.

MBO *n*: *abrév* ▶ **management buyout**.

MC *n* **1** (*abrév* = **Master of Ceremonies**) (in cabaret)

animateur *m*; (at banquet) maître *m* de cérémonie; **2**
MUS (rapper) MC *m*; **3** US POL *abrév écrite* =
Member of Congress.

IcCoy /mə'kɔɪ/ *n*: IDIOMS **it's the real ~** c'est de
l'authentique.

ID *n* **1** MED, UNIV (*abrév* = **Doctor of Medicine**)
docteur *m* en médecine; **2** US POST *abrév écrite* =
Maryland; **3** (*abrév* = **Managing Director**)
directeur *m* général.

ne¹ /miː, mɪ/

■ **Note** When used as a direct or indirect object pronoun
me is translated by *me* (or *m'* before a vowel): *she knows
me* = elle me connaît; *he loves me* = il m'aime.
– Note that the object pronoun normally comes before the
verb in French and that in compound tenses like the
present perfect and past perfect, the past participle of the
verb agrees with the direct object pronoun: *he's seen me*
(female speaker) = il m'a vue.
– In imperatives the translation for both the direct and the
indirect object pronoun is *moi* and comes after the verb:
kiss me! = embrasse-moi!; *give it to me!* = donne-le-moi!
(note the hyphens).
– After prepositions and the verb *to be* the translation is
moi: *she did it for me* = elle l'a fait pour moi; *it's me* = c'est
moi.
– For particular expressions see below.

pron me; (*before vowel*) m'; **it's for ~** c'est pour moi;
poor little ~○ pauvre de moi; **if you were ~** à ma
place.

ne² /miː/ *n* MUS mi *m*.

ME *n* **1** MED *abrév* ▶ **myalgic encephalomyelitis**;
2 US POST *abrév écrite* = **Maine**; **3** LING *abrév*
▶ **Middle English**; **4** US MED *abrév* ▶ **medical
examiner**.

mead /miːd/ *n* hydromel *m*.

meadow /'medəʊ/ *n* **1** (field) pré *m*; **2** ¢ (also
~land) prés *mpl*, prairies *fpl*; **3** (also **water ~**)
prairie *f* inondable.

meadowsweet *n* reine-des-prés *f*.

meagre GB, **meager** US /'miːgə(r)/ *adj* [*income, sum,
meal*] maigre (*before n*); [*living*] chiche; [*response,
returns*] piètre (*before n*).

meal /miːl/ *n* **1** (food) repas *m*; **to enjoy one's ~**
bien manger; **to go out for a ~** aller (manger) au
restaurant; **2** (from grain) farine *f*.
IDIOMS **don't make a ~ of it**○! n'en fais pas tout un
plat○!

meal ticket *n* **1** (voucher) ticket-repas *m*; **2**○ FIG (quality, qualification) gagne-pain *m inv*; (person) **I'm just a ~
for you!** pour toi je ne suis qu'un portefeuille!

mean /miːn/ **I** *n* **1** GEN, MATH moyenne *f*; **above the
~** au-dessus de la moyenne; **2** FIG (middle point)
milieu *m*.
II *adj* **1** (average) [*weight, age*] moyen/-enne; **2** (ungenerous) [*person*] avare, radin○; [*attitude, nature*] mesquin;
[*examiner*] sévère; **he's ~ with his time** il est avare
de son temps; **he's ~ with money** il est près de ses
sous; **3** (unkind) [*person*] méchant (**to** avec); **a ~ trick**
un sale tour; **4** (vicious) [*animal, person, expression*]
méchant; **that dog has got a ~ streak** ce chien a la
méchanceté en lui; **5** (tough) [*city*] implacable; [*street*]
hostile; **6**○ (skilful) [*artist, cook, cocktail*] formidable, du
tonnerre○ (*after n*); **7** (small) **that's no ~ feat!** ce
n'est pas un mince exploit!; **8** (lowly) LITTÉR [*dwelling*] misérable; [*birth*] bas/basse; [*origin*] modeste; **9**○
US (off colour) **to feel ~** ne pas être dans son
assiette○.
III *vtr* (*prét, pp* **meant**) **1** (signify) [*word, phrase,
symbol*] signifier, vouloir dire; [*sign*] vouloir dire; **the
term ~s nothing to him** le terme ne lui dit rien; **2 ~**
(intend) **to ~ to do** avoir l'intention de faire; **to ~
sb to do** GB, **to ~ for sb to do** US vouloir que qn
fasse; **to be meant for sb** [*question, bomb*] être
destiné à qn; **I meant it as a joke** c'était une blague
de ma part; **she meant no offence** elle n'y entendait
pas malice; **he doesn't ~ you any harm** il ne te
veut aucun mal; **what do you ~ by opening my
letters?** qu'est-ce qui te prend d'ouvrir mon courrier?;

to ~ well avoir de bonnes intentions; **she ~s business** elle ne plaisante pas; **he ~s what he says** (he
is sincere) il est sérieux; (he is menacing) il ne plaisante
pas; **I didn't ~ to do it** je ne l'ai pas fait exprès;
without ~ing to par inadvertance; **3** (entail) [*strike,
law*] entraîner [*shortages, changes*]; **4** (intend to say)
vouloir dire; **what do you ~ by that remark?**
qu'est-ce que tu veux dire par là?; **do you ~ me?**
c'est de moi que tu parles?; **I ~ to say**○, **who wants
a car that won't start?** non mais, qui voudrait d'une
voiture qui ne démarre pas?; **I know what you ~** je
comprends; **5** (be of value) **a promise ~s nothing**
une promesse ne veut pas dire grand-chose; **money
~s a lot to him** l'argent compte beaucoup pour lui;
your friendship ~s a lot to me ton amitié est très
importante pour moi; **6** (be destined) **to be meant to
do** être destiné à faire; **it was meant to be** ou
happen cela devait arriver; **they were meant for
each other** ils étaient faits l'un pour l'autre; **7** (be
supposed to be) **he's meant to be** il est censé être.

meander /mɪ'ændə(r)/ *vi* **1** (wind) [*river, road*]
serpenter; **~ing path** sentier sinueux; **2** (wander)
[*person*] flâner; [*thoughts*] vagabonder.

meaning /'miːnɪŋ/ *n* **1** (sense) (of word, remark) sens *m*;
(of symbol, film, dream) signification *f*; **a word with two
~s** un mot à double sens; **what is the ~ of this?**
qu'est-ce que cela signifie?; **yes, I get your ~**○ oui, je
vois ce que tu veux dire; **2** (purpose) sens *m*; **my life
no longer has any ~** ma vie n'a plus aucun sens; **to
give new ~ to** donner un sens nouveau à [*life,
work*]; **full of ~** lourd de sens.

meaningful /'miːnɪŋfl/ *adj* **1** (significant) [*word, statement, result*] significatif/-ive; **2** (profound) [*relationship,
comment, lyric*] sérieux/-ieuse; [*experience*] riche; [*insight*] poussé; **3** (eloquent) [*look, smile*] entendu;
[*gesture*] significatif/-ive; **4** (constructive) [*talk*] cons-
tructif/-ive; [*work*] utile; [*process, input*] positif/-ive.

meaningless /'miːnɪŋlɪs/ *adj* **1** (having no sense)
[*claim, phrase*] dépourvu de sens; [*code, figure*]
incompréhensible; **2** (worthless) [*chatter, role, title*]
insignifiant; [*action, remark*] sans importance; [*effort*]
inutile; **a ~ exercise** une opération inutile; **3** (pointless) [*act, sacrifice, violence*] insensé; **my life is ~** ma
vie n'a pas de sens.

meanness /'miːnnɪs/ *n* **1** (stinginess) (of person) avarice
f; (of portion) maigreur *f*; **2** (nastiness) méchanceté *f* (**to**
envers); **towards** à l'égard de); **3** (humbleness) LITTÉR
pauvreté *f*.

means /miːnz/ **I** *n* (*pl* **~**) (way) moyen *m* (**of doing**
de faire); **whatever ~ possible** tous les moyens; **a
~ of** un moyen de [*communication, transport*]; **by ~
of** au moyen de; **yes, by all ~** oui, certainement; **if
you wish to leave, then by all ~ do** si vous voulez
partir, cela ne tient qu'à vous; **it is by no ~ certain**
c'est loin d'être sûr.
II *npl* (resources) moyens *mpl*, revenus *mpl*; **of moderate ~** [*person, family*] aux revenus modestes; **to live
within one's ~** vivre selon ses moyens; **a man of
~** un homme riche or fortuné.
IDIOMS **by fair ~ or foul** par tous les moyens; **a ~
to an end** un moyen d'arriver à ses fins.

mean-spirited *adj* petit, mesquin.

means test I *n* enquête *f* sur les ressources.
II means-test *vtr* soumettre [qn] à un examen de
ressources.

meant /ment/ *prét, pp* ▶ **mean** III.

meantime /'miːntaɪm/ *adv* **for the ~** pour le
moment; **(in the)** ~ pendant ce temps.

meanwhile /'miːnwaɪl/ **I** *adv* **1** (during this time)
pendant ce temps; **2** (until then) en attendant; **3** (since
then) entre-temps; **4** (by way of contrast) au même
moment.
II in the meanwhile *adv phr* = **meanwhile I**.

measles /'miːzlz/ ▶ **1002** *n* (+ *v sg*) rougeole *f*.

measly○ /'miːzlɪ/ *adj* [*amount*] misérable; [*gift, result*]
minable○.

measurable /'meʒərəbl/ *adj* **1** (perceptible) [*difference*] notable; **2** (quantifiable) [*change*] mesurable; [*phenomena*] quantifiable.

measure /'meʒə(r)/ ▶1045⎜, ▶1309⎜, 789⎜, 1381⎜, 1392⎜, 1260⎜ **I** *n* **1** (unit) unité *f* de mesure; **weights and ~s** les poids *mpl* et mesures *fpl*; **liquid ~** mesure *f* de capacité pour les liquides; **it's made to ~** (garment) c'est fait sur mesure, c'est du sur mesure; **2** (of alcohol) mesure *f*; **he gave me short ~** il a triché sur la quantité; **3** (device for measuring) instrument *m* de mesure; **4** (qualified amount, extent) **a ~ of success** un certain succès; **a small ~ of support** un soutien limité; **a good** ou **wide ~ of autonomy** une grande autonomie; **in large ~** dans une large mesure; **in full ~** [*feel, possess, contribute*] pleinement; **5** (way of estimating) (of price rises) mesure *f*; (of success, anger) mesure *f*, indication *f*; (of efficiency, performance) critère *m*; **to be the ~ of** donner la mesure de; **to give some ~ of** donner une idée de [*delight, talent*]; **to use sth as a ~ of** utiliser qch pour mesurer [*effects, impact*]; **this is a ~ of how dangerous it is** ceci montre à quel point c'est dangereux; **beyond ~** [*change*] énormément; [*beautiful*] extrêmement; **it has improved beyond ~** il y a eu d'énormes progrès; **to take the ~ of sb** jauger qn; **I have the ~ of them** je sais ce qu'ils valent; **6** (action, step) mesure *f*; **to take ~s** prendre des mesures; **safety ~** mesure de sécurité; **as a precautionary ~** par mesure de précaution; **as a preventive ~** à titre préventif; **as a temporary ~** provisoirement. **II** *vtr* **1** (assess size) mesurer [*length, rate, person*]; **to ~ sth in** mesurer qch en [*metres*]; **to get oneself ~d for** faire prendre ses mesures pour; **2** (have measurement of) mesurer; **to ~ four by five metres** mesurer quatre mètres sur cinq; **a tremor measuring 5.2 on the Richter scale** une secousse de 5,2 sur l'échelle de Richter; **3** (assess) mesurer [*performance, ability*] (**against** à); **4** (compare) **to ~ sth against** comparer qch à [*achievement*].
IDIOMS **for good ~** pour faire bonne mesure; **to do things by half-~s** se contenter de demi-mesures.
■ **measure off**: **~ off** [*sth*] mesurer [*fabric*].
■ **measure out**: **~ out** [*sth*] mesurer [*land, flour, liquid*]; doser [*medicine*]; compter [*drops*].
■ **measure up**: ¶ **~ up** [*person*] avoir les qualités requises; **to ~ up to** être à la hauteur de [*expectations*]; soutenir la comparaison avec [*achievement*]; ¶ **~ up** [*sth*] mesurer [*room etc*].

measured /'meʒəd/ *adj* [*tone*] mesuré; [*comment*] circonspect.

measurement /'meʒəmənt/ ▶1309⎜, 1260⎜ *n* **1** (of room, object) dimension *f*; **2** (of person) **to take sb's ~s** prendre les mensurations de qn; **chest ~** tour *m* de poitrine; **leg ~** longueur *f* de jambe.

measuring: **~ jug** *n* verre *m* gradué; **~ spoon** *n* cuillère-mesure *f*.

meat /mi:t/ *n* (flesh) viande *f*; **red ~** viande rouge; **crab ~** chair *f* de crabe; **~ and two veg**° viande garnie de deux légumes.
IDIOMS **political scandals are ~ and drink to them** ils se repaissent de scandales politiques; **to be strong ~** être choquant; **one man's ~ is another man's poison** PROV le malheur des uns fait le bonheur des autres PROV.

meatball /'mi:tbɔ:l/ *n* **1** CULIN (*gén pl*) boulette *f* de viande; **2**° US (person) andouille° *f*.

meat-eater /'mi:ti:tə(r)/ *n* **1** (animal) carnivore *m*; **2** (person) **they're not great ~s** ils ne mangent pas beaucoup de viande.

meat: **~ hook** *n* croc *m* de boucherie; **~ loaf** *n* pain *m* de viande; **~ pie** *n* ~ pâté *m* en croûte.

meaty /'mi:tɪ/ *adj* **1** (with meat) [*stew, sauce*] riche en viande; [*chop*] beau/belle; [*flavour, smell*] de viande; **2** FIG [*role, story*] riche.

Mecca /'mekə/ ▶1343⎜ *pr n* La Mecque; **a ~ for** FIG la Mecque des [*tourists, scholars*].

mechanic /mɪ'kænɪk/ ▶1251⎜ *n* mécanicien/-ienne *m/f*.

mechanical /mɪ'kænɪkl/ *adj* mécanique.

mechanical: **~ drawing** *n* US TECH dessin *m* industriel; **~ engineering** *n* construction *f* mécanique.

mechanics /mɪ'kænɪks/ *npl* **1** (subject) (+ *v sg*) mécanique *f*; **2** (workings) (+ *v pl*) LIT, FIG mécanisme *m*; **the ~ of** le mécanisme de [*engine, pump*]; les mécanismes de [*management, law*]; **the ~ of doing** la méthode pour faire.

mechanism /'mekənɪzəm/ *n* **1** TECH, BIOL, PSYCH, PHILOS mécanisme *m*; **2** (procedure) mécanisme *m* (**o** de); **legal ~s** procédures *fpl* légales.

mechanization /ˌmekənaɪ'zeɪʃn, US -nɪ'z-/ *n* mécanisation *f*.

medal /'medl/ *n* médaille *f*; **gold/silver ~** médaille d'or/d'argent.

medallion /mɪ'dælɪən/ *n* (all contexts) médaillon *m*.

medallist GB, **medalist** US /'medəlɪst/ *n* médaillé/-e *m/f*; **gold/silver ~** médaillé/-e *m/f* d'or/d'argent.

Medal of Honor *n* US MIL Médaille *f* d'honneur (*la plus haute décoration militaire des États-Unis*).

meddle /'medl/ *vi* PÉJ **stop meddling!** mêle-toi de tes affaires!; **to ~ in** s'immiscer dans [*affairs*]; **to ~ with** toucher à [*property*].

media /'mi:dɪə/ **I** *n* (+ *v pl ou sg*) **the ~** les médias *pl*; **news ~** presse *f* d'information; **in the ~** dans les médias. **II** *noun modifier* [*advertising*] dans les médias; [*analyst, interest*] des médias; [*coverage, image*] médiatique; [*consultant*] de médias; [*sales*] par les médias; [*person*] qui travaille dans les médias.

median /'mi:dɪən/ **I** *n* **1** (in maths, statistics) médiane *f*; **2** (also **~ strip**) US AUT terre-plein *m* central. **II** *adj* **1** (in statistics) [*price, income, sum*] moyen/-enne; **2** (in maths) [*point, line*] médian; [*value*] moyen/-enne.

media studies *npl* communication *f* et journalisme *m*.

mediate /'mi:dɪeɪt/ **I** *vtr* négocier [*settlement, peace*]. **II** *vi* arbitrer; **to ~ in/between** servir de médiateur dans/entre.

mediator /'mi:dɪeɪtə(r)/ *n* médiateur/-trice *m/f*.

medic° /'medɪk/ *n* **1** (doctor) toubib° *m*, médecin *m*; **2** (student) étudiant/-e *m/f* en médecine; **3** MIL infirmier/-ière *m/f* militaire.

Medicaid /'medɪkeɪd/ *n* US assistance *f* médicale aux économiquement faibles.

medical /'medɪkl/ **I** *n* (in school, army, for job) visite *f* médicale; (private) examen *m* médical. **II** *adj* médical; **on ~ grounds** pour raisons de santé.

medical advice *n* conseils *mpl* d'un médecin; **to seek ~** consulter un médecin; **against ~** contre l'avis du médecin.

medical: **~ board** *n* MIL commission *f* médicale; **~ care** *n* ₵ GEN soins *mpl* médicaux; ADMIN assistance *f* médicale; **~ check-up** *n* bilan *m* de santé; **~ doctor** ▶1251⎜ *n* docteur *m* en médecine; **~ emergency** *n* urgence *f*; **~ examination** *n* = **medical** I; **~ examiner** *n* US JUR médecin *m* légiste; **~ history** *n* (background) antécédents *mpl* médicaux; (notes) dossier *m* médical; **~ insurance** *n* assurance-maladie *f*.

medically /'medɪklɪ/ *adv* **~ fit/unfit** en bonne/mauvaise santé; **a ~ qualified person** une personne ayant une formation médicale.

medical officer, MO *n* MIL médecin *m* militaire; IND médecin *m* du travail.

medical profession *n* **the ~** (doctors collectively) le corps médical; (occupation) la médecine.

medical: **Medical Research Council** *n* GB *institut national britannique de la recherche médicale*; **~ school** *n* faculté *f* de médecine; **~ student** *n* étudiant/-e *m/f* en médecine.

Medicare /'medɪkeə(r)/ *n* US assistance *f* médicale aux personnes âgées.

medicated /'medɪkeɪtɪd/ *adj* [*bandage*] médical; [*shampoo*] traitant.

medication /ˌmedɪ'keɪʃn/ *n* **1** ₵ (drug treatment) médicaments *mpl*; **to be on ~** prendre des médicaments;

to put sb on/take sb off ~ prescrire/supprimer des médicaments à qn; **2 C** (medicine) médicament *m*.

medicinal /mɪˈdɪsɪnl/ *adj* [*property, use*] thérapeutique; [*herb*] médicinal; ~ **drugs** médicaments *mpl*; **I drink brandy for** ~ **purposes** HUM je bois du cognac à des fins thérapeutiques.

medicine /ˈmedsn, US ˈmedɪsn/ *n* **1 ₵** médecine *f*; **to study** ~ étudier la médecine; **doctor of** ~ docteur *m* en médecine; **2 C** (drug) médicament *m* (**for** pour); **the best** ~ LIT, FIG le meilleur remède.

IDIOMS **to give sb a taste of their own** ~ rendre à qn la monnaie de sa pièce; **to take one's** ~ **like a man** avaler la pilule○.

medicine: ~ **ball** *n* médecine-ball *m*; ~ **bottle** *n* fiole *f*; ~ **cabinet**, ~ **cupboard** *n* armoire *f* à pharmacie; ~ **man** *n* sorcier *m* guérisseur.

medico○ /ˈmedɪkəʊ/ **I** *n* = **medic**.
II medico+ *combining form* médico-.

medieval /ˌmedɪˈiːvl, US ˌmiːd-, *also* mɪˈdiːvl/ *adj* médiéval; FIG (primitive) moyenâgeux/-euse PEJ.

mediocre /ˌmiːdɪˈəʊkə(r)/ *adj* médiocre.

mediocrity /ˌmiːdɪˈɒkrətɪ/ *n* **1** (state) médiocrité *f*; **2** (person) médiocre *mf*.

meditate /ˈmedɪteɪt/ *vtr, vi* méditer.

meditative /ˈmedɪtətɪv, US -teɪt-/ *adj* [*person, expression*] méditatif/-ive; [*music, experience*] contemplatif/-ive; [*calm*] recueilli.

Mediterranean /ˌmedɪtəˈreɪnɪən/ ▶1117 **I** *pr n* **1** (also ~ **sea**) **the** ~ la (mer) Méditerranée; **2** (region) **the** ~ les pays méditerranéens; **3** (native) méditerranéen/-éenne *m/f*.
II *adj* méditerranéen/-éenne.

medium /ˈmiːdɪəm/ ▶1260 **I** *n* **1** (*pl* **-iums** ou **-ia**) CIN, RADIO, THEAT, TV moyen *m* d'expression; **advertising** ~ support *m* publicitaire; **through the** ~ **of** par l'intermédiaire de; **2** (*pl* **-ia**) ART (technique) technique *f*; (material) matériel *m*; **3** (mid-point) milieu *m*; **to find** ou **strike a happy** ~ trouver le juste milieu; **4** (*pl* **-iums**) BIOL, BOT milieu *m*; **5** (*pl* **-iums**) (spiritualist) médium *m*.
II *adj* **1** [*size, temperature*] moyen/-enne; **in the** ~ **term** à moyen terme; **2** RADIO [*wave*] moyen/-enne; **on** ~ **wave** sur les ondes moyennes.

medium: ~**-dry** *adj* [*drink*] demi-sec; ~**-fine** *adj* [*pen*] à pointe moyenne; [*tip, point*] moyen/-enne; ~**-length** *adj* [*book, film, article*] de longueur moyenne; [*hair, skirt*] mi-long/mi-longue; ~**-range** *adj* [*missile*] à moyenne portée; ~**-rare** *adj* [*meat*] à point; ~**-sized** *adj* de taille moyenne.

medlar /ˈmedlə(r)/ *n* **1** (fruit) nèfle *f*; **2** (tree) néflier *m*.

medley /ˈmedlɪ/ *n* **1** MUS pot-pourri *m* (**of** de); **2** (in swimming) ~ **relay** relais *m* quatre nages; **3** (mixture) (of people, groups) mélange *m*.

meek /miːk/ *adj* docile.

meet /miːt/ **I** *n* **1** SPORT rencontre *f* (sportive); **track** ~ US rencontre *f* d'athlétisme; **2** GB (in hunting) rendez-vous *m* de chasseurs.
II *vtr* (*prét, pp* **met**) **1** (encounter) rencontrer [*person, team, enemy*]; **to** ~ **one's death** trouver la mort; **2** (make acquaintance of) faire la connaissance de [*person*]; **Paul,** ~ **Frances** (as introduction) Paul, je vous présente Frances; **3** (await) attendre; (fetch) chercher; **she went to** ~ **them** elle est allée les attendre ou chercher; **to** ~ **sb off** GB ou **at** US **the plane** attendre qn à l'aéroport; **4** (come into contact with) rencontrer; **his eyes met hers** son regard a rencontré le sien; **an incredible sight met her eyes** un spectacle incroyable s'est offert à ses yeux; **5** (fulfil) satisfaire [*order*]; répondre à, satisfaire à [*criteria, standards, needs*]; payer [*bills, costs*]; couvrir [*debts, overheads*]; compenser [*loss*]; faire face à [*obligations, commitments*]; remplir [*conditions*]; **6** (rise to) se montrer à la hauteur de [*challenge*]; **7** (respond to) répondre à [*criticism*].
III *vi* (*prét, pp* **met**) **1** (come together) [*people, teams*] se rencontrer; [*committee, parliament*] se réunir; [*cars*] se croiser; **the two trains met head-on** les deux trains se sont heurtés de front; **to** ~ **again** [*people*]

se revoir; **goodbye, till we** ~ **again!** au revoir! à la prochaine fois!; **2** (make acquaintance) [*people*] faire connaissance; **3** (come into contact) [*lips, roads*] se rencontrer; **their eyes met** leurs regards se croisèrent.

IDIOMS **there's more to this than** ~**s the eye** ce n'est pas aussi clair que cela en a l'air; **to make ends** ~ joindre les deux bouts.

■ **meet up** se retrouver; **to** ~ **up with**○ retrouver [*friend*].

■ **meet with**: ¶ ~ **with** [sb] rencontrer [*person, delegation*]; ¶ ~ **with** [sth] rencontrer [*success, suspicion*]; être accueilli avec [*approval*]; subir [*failure*]; **he met with an accident** il lui est arrivé un accident; **to** ~ **with no response** ne susciter aucune réaction; **to be met with** être accueilli par [*silence, shouts*]; se heurter à [*disapproval*]; susciter [*anger*].

meeting /ˈmiːtɪŋ/ *n* **1** (official assembly) réunion *f*; **to call a** ~ convoquer une réunion; **in a** ~ en réunion; **2** (coming together) rencontre *f*; **a** ~ **of minds** FIG une profonde entente; **3** GB SPORT rencontre *f* (sportive).

meeting: ~**-place** *n* (lieu *m* de) rendez-vous *m*; ~ **point** *n* point *m* de rencontre.

mega /ˈmegə/ **mega+** *combining form* méga-.

megabyte /ˈmegəbaɪt/ *n* COMPUT mégaoctet *m*.

megalith /ˈmegəlɪθ/ *n* mégalithe *m*.

megalomaniac /ˌmegələˈmeɪnɪæk/ *n, adj* mégalomane (*mf*).

megaphone /ˈmegəfəʊn/ *n* porte-voix *m inv*.

megaton /ˈmegətʌn/ *n* mégatonne *f*.

melancholy /ˈmelənkəlɪ/ **I** *n* mélancolie *f*.
II *adj* [*person*] mélancolique; [*music, occasion*] triste.

Melanesia /ˌmeləˈniːzɪə/ ▶840 *pr n* Mélanésie *f*.

Melba: ~ **sauce** *n* coulis *m* de framboises; ~ **toast** *n* ~ toast *m* très mince.

mellow /ˈmeləʊ/ **I** *adj* **1** [*wine*] moelleux/-euse; [*flavour*] suave; [*tone*] mélodieux/-ieuse; [*colour, light, sound*] doux/douce; [*fruit*] fondant; **2** (weathered) [*stone*] patiné par l'âge; **3** (calm) **to get** ou **grow** ~ **with age** s'assagir avec l'âge; **4** (relaxed) [*person*] détendu; [*atmosphere*] serein.
II *vtr* **1** (calm) [*experience*] assagir [*person*]; [*music, wine*] détendre [*person*]; **2** (ripen) faire mûrir [*fruit*]; donner du moelleux à [*wine*].
III *vi* **1** (calm down) [*person, behaviour*] s'assagir; **2** (tone down) [*attitude*] s'adoucir; **3** (ripen) [*fruit*] mûrir; [*taste*] prendre du moelleux.

melodic /mɪˈlɒdɪk/ *adj* GEN mélodieux/-ieuse; MUS mélodique.

melodrama /ˈmelədrɑːmə/ *n* mélodrame *m* ALSO FIG.

melodramatic /ˌmelədrəˈmætɪk/ *adj* mélodramatique; **you're being** ~! tu dramatises les choses!

melody /ˈmelədɪ/ *n* mélodie *f*.

melon /ˈmelən/ *n* (fruit) melon *m*.

melt /melt/ **I** *n* **1** (thaw) dégel *m*, fonte *f* des neiges; **2** US CULIN sandwich *m* recouvert de fromage fondu.
II *vtr* LIT [*heat, sun, person*] faire fondre [*snow, plastic, butter*]; FIG attendrir [*heart*].
III *vi* **1** LIT fondre; **to** ~ **in your mouth** fondre dans la bouche; **2** FIG (soften) [*heart, person*] fondre (**with** de); **3** (merge) **to** ~ **into** se fondre dans [*crowd*].

■ **melt away** **1** LIT [*snow, ice*] fondre complètement; **2** FIG [*fear, confidence*] se dissiper; [*crowd, people*] se disperser; [*money*] fondre.

■ **melt down**: ~ **down** [sth], ~ [sth] **down** fondre [*metal*].

meltdown /ˈmeltdaʊn/ *n* **1** (of reactor) fusion *f* du cœur d'un réacteur; **in** ~ en fusion; **2**○ FIN (crash) chute *f* des actions, krach *m* boursier.

melting point *n* point *m* de fusion.

melting pot *n* (of people, nationalities) melting-pot *m*.
IDIOMS **to be in the** ~ être remis en question.

member /ˈmembə(r)/ *n* **1** (of group, commission) membre *m*; **to be a** ~ **of** faire partie de [*group*]; être membre de [*club, committee*]; ~ **of staff** GEN employé/-e *m/f*; (in school) professeur *m*; ~ **of the**

opposite sex personne *f* de l'autre sexe; '**~s only**' 'réservé aux membres'; **~ of the public** (in street) passant/-e *m/f*; (in theatre, cinema) spectateur/-trice *m/f*; **an ordinary ~ of the public** un simple citoyen; **like any other ~ of the public** comme tout le monde; **2** (also **Member**) POL (of parliament) député *m*; **3** CONSTR pièce *f*; **cross ~** traverse *f*; **4** MATH (of set) élément *m*; **5** (limb) membre *m*.

II *noun modifier* [*nation, state*] membre.

Member of Congress, MC *n* US POL membre *m* du Congrès.

Member of Parliament, MP ▶ 937 | *n* GB POL député *m* (**for** de).

Member of the European Parliament, MEP *n* député *m* au Parlement européen.

membership /ˈmembəʃɪp/ *n* **1** adhésion *f* (**of** à); EC **~** adhésion à la CE; **full/group ~** adhésion à part entière/en groupe; **to resign one's ~** rendre sa carte de membre; **~ of** GB OU **in** US **the club is open to all** le club est ouvert à tous; **to take out joint ~ of** GB OU **in** US **the club** adhérer en couple au club; **2** (fee) cotisation *f*; **3** (people belonging) (+ *v sg* ou *pl*) membres *mpl*; **it has a ~ of 200** il y a 200 membres; **~ is declining** le nombre des membres décroît.

membrane /ˈmembreɪn/ *n* (all contexts) membrane *f*.

memento /mɪˈmentəʊ/ *n* (*pl* **~s** ou **~es**) souvenir *m* (**of** de); **as a ~** en souvenir.

memo /ˈmeməʊ/ *n* (*abrév* = **memorandum**) ADMIN note *f* de service.

memo board *n* tableau *m* d'affichage.

memoirs /ˈmemwɑː(r)z/ *npl* mémoires *mpl*.

memo pad *n* bloc-notes *m*.

memorabilia /ˌmemərəˈbɪlɪə/ *npl* souvenirs *mpl*.

memorable /ˈmemərəbl/ *adj* [*event*] mémorable; [*person, quality*] inoubliable.

memorandum /ˌmeməˈrændəm/ *n* (*pl* **memoranda**) **1** ADMIN note *f* de service (**to** à l'attention de; **from** de la part de); **2** POL mémorandum *m*.

memorial /məˈmɔːrɪəl/ **I** *n* **1** (monument) mémorial *m* (**to** à); **2** (reminder) **as a ~ to** à la mémoire de; **3** (document) mémoire *m*.

II *adj* commémoratif/-ive; **~ service** messe *f* commémorative.

Memorial Day *n* US *jour de commémoration des soldats américains morts à la guerre*.

memorize /ˈmeməraɪz/ *vtr* apprendre [*qch*] par cœur.

memory /ˈmeməri/ *n* **1** (faculty) mémoire *f*; **to have a good ~** avoir bonne mémoire; **to have a bad ~** ne pas avoir de mémoire; **from ~** de mémoire; **to have a good ~ for faces** être physionomiste; **if my ~ serves me right** si je me souviens bien; **to have a long ~** être rancunier/-ière; **2** (recollection) (*souvent pl*) souvenir *m*; **3** (period of time) **in living** ou **recent ~** de mémoire d'homme; **4** (posthumous fame) souvenir *m*; **their ~ lives on** leur souvenir est toujours vivant; **to keep sb's ~ alive** maintenir le souvenir de qn en vie; **5** (commemoration) **in (loving) ~ of** à la mémoire de; **6** COMPUT mémoire *f*.

IDIOMS **to take a trip down ~ lane** se pencher sur ses souvenirs.

memory bank *n* bloc *m* mémoire.

men /men/ *pl* ▶ **man**.

menace /ˈmenəs/ **I** *n* **1** (threat) menace *f*; **with ~s** JUR par des menaces; **2** (danger) **a ~ to other motorists** un danger public; **3**° (nuisance) **he's a real ~** c'est une vraie plaie.

II *vtr* menacer (**with** de, avec).

mend /mend/ **I** *n* **1** (in fabric) (stitched) raccommodage *m*; (darned) reprise *f*; (patched) rapiéçage *m*; **2** FIG **to be on the ~** [*person*] être en voie de guérison; [*economy*] reprendre; [*weather, situation*] s'améliorer.

II *vtr* **1** (repair) réparer [*object, road*]; **2** (in sewing) (stitch) raccommoder; (darn) repriser; (add patch) rapiécer; **3** (improve) **to ~ relations with** améliorer les relations avec; **that won't ~ matters** ça n'arrangera pas les choses.

III *vi* [*injury*] guérir; [*person*] se rétablir.

IDIOMS **to ~ one's ways** s'amender.

mending /ˈmendɪŋ/ *n* raccommodage *m*.

menfolk /ˈmenfəʊk/ *npl* hommes *mpl*.

menial /ˈmiːnɪəl/ *adj* [*job*] subalterne; [*attitude*] servile; **~ tasks** basses besognes.

meningitis /ˌmenɪnˈdʒaɪtɪs/ ▶ 1002 | *n* méningite *f*.

menopause /ˈmenəpɔːz/ *n* ménopause *f*.

Menorca /mɪˈnɔːkə/ ▶ 1022 | *pr n* Minorque *f*.

men's room /ˈmenzruːm, -rʊm/ *n* US toilettes *fpl* pour hommes.

menstruate /ˈmenstrʊeɪt/ *vi* avoir ses règles.

menswear /ˈmenzweə(r)/ *n* prêt-à-porter *m* pour hommes.

mental /ˈmentl/ *adj* **1** MED [*handicap, illness, patient*] mental; [*hospital, institution*] psychiatrique; [*ward*] de psychiatrie; **2** (of the mind) [*ability, effort, energy*] intellectuel/-elle; [*process, age*] mental; **3** (in one's head) [*arithmetic, picture*] mental; **to make a ~ note to do** se dire qu'il faut faire; **4**° (mad) fou/folle, malade°.

mental: ~ block *n* blocage *m* psychologique; **~ health** *n* (of person) santé *f* mentale; ADMIN psychiatrie *f*; **~ home** *n* clinique *f* psychiatrique.

mentality /menˈtælətɪ/ *n* mentalité *f*.

mentally /ˈmentəlɪ/ *adv* **1** MED **~ handicapped** handicapé mental; **~ retarded** retardé; **the ~ ill** les malades mentaux; **to be ~ deranged** avoir l'esprit dérangé; **2** (regarding the mind) **~ exhausted** surmené intellectuellement; **to be ~ alert** avoir l'esprit alerte; **~ slow** lent d'esprit; **3** (inwardly) [*resolve*] dans son for intérieur; [*calculate*] mentalement.

mentholated /ˈmenθəleɪtɪd/ *adj* au menthol.

mention /ˈmenʃn/ **I** *n* **1** (reference) mention *f* (**of** de); **the mere ~ of my name** la seule évocation de mon nom; **to make no ~ of** [*report, person*] ne pas faire mention de; **it got a ~ on the radio** on en a parlé à la radio; **2** (acknowledgement) mention *f*; **honourable ~** GEN mention honorable; MIL citation *f*.

II *vtr* **1** (allude to) faire mention de [*person, topic, fact*]; **please don't ~ my name** ne mentionnez pas mon nom; **she never ~s her work** elle ne parle jamais de son travail; **to ~ sb/sth to sb** parler de qn/qch à qn; **to ~ that...** dire (en passant) que...; **I hardly need to ~ that...** inutile de signaler que...; **not to ~** sans parler de; **without ~ing any names** sans nommer personne; **too numerous to ~** trop nombreux pour être cités; **to be ~ed in a will** figurer sur un testament; **just ~ my name** (as introduction) dis-leur que tu viens de ma part; **don't ~ it!** je vous en or je t'en prie!; **2** (acknowledge) citer [*name*]; mentionner [*service*].

menu /ˈmenjuː/ *n* (all contexts) menu *m*.

MEP *n* (*abrév* = **Member of the European Parliament**) député *m* au Parlement européen.

mercantile /ˈmɜːkəntaɪl, US -tiːl, -tɪl/ *adj* [*ship, nation*] marchand; [*law*] commercial; [*system, theory*] mercantile.

mercenary /ˈmɜːsɪnərɪ, US -nerɪ/ **I** *n* mercenaire *mf*.

II *adj* [*action, person*] intéressé; [*business interest*] mercantile.

merchandise /ˈmɜːtʃəndaɪz/ **I** *n* marchandise(s) *f(pl)*.

II *vtr* (also **merchandize**) **1** (buy and sell) faire le commerce de; **2** (promote) assurer la promotion de.

merchant /ˈmɜːtʃənt/ **I** *n* GEN négociant *m*; (selling small quantities) marchand *m*; (retailer) détaillant *m*; **speed ~**° fou/folle *m/f* du volant.

II *noun modifier* [*ship*] marchand; [*sailor*] de la marine marchande.

merchant: ~ bank *n* GB banque *f* d'affaires; **~ banker** ▶ 1251 | *n* GB (executive) cadre *m* d'une banque d'affaires; (owner) banquier *m* d'affaires; **~man** *n* NAUT navire *m* marchand; **~ navy** GB, **~ marine** US *n* marine *f* marchande.

merciful /ˈmɜːsɪfl/ *adj* **1** (kind) [*person, sentence*] clément (**to, towards** envers); [*act*] charitable; [*God*] miséricordieux/-ieuse; **2** (fortunate) [*occurrence*] heureux/-euse; **a ~ release** une délivrance.

mercifully /ˈmɜːsɪfəlɪ/ adv **1** (compassionately) avec clémence; **2** (fortunately) par bonheur, par chance.

merciless /ˈmɜːsɪlɪs/ adj [ruler, criticism] impitoyable (**to, towards** envers); [heat] implacable.

mercurial /mɜːˈkjʊərɪəl/ adj **1** CHEM [compound, poisoning] au mercure; **2** (quick-witted) [person] vif/vive; (changeable) [temperament, person] lunatique.

mercury /ˈmɜːkjʊrɪ/ **I** n mercure m.
II Mercury pr n **1** (planet) Mercure f; **2** MYTHOL Mercure m.

mercy /ˈmɜːsɪ/ n **1** (clemency) clémence f; **to show ~ to sb** se montrer clément à l'égard de qn; **to have ~ on sb** avoir pitié de qn; **to beg for ~** demander grâce; **an act of ~** un acte de compassion; **a mission of ~** une mission humanitaire; **2** (power) merci f; **at the ~ of** à la merci de; **to throw oneself on sb's ~** s'en remettre au bon vouloir de qn; **3** (fortunate event) **it's a ~ that** c'est une chance que (+ subj).
IDIOMS **let's be grateful for small mercies** sachons apprécier notre chance.

mercy killing n **1** ⊄ euthanasie f; **2** (act) C acte m d'euthanasie.

mere /mɪə(r)/ adj **1** (simple) [coincidence, nonsense] pur (before n); [fiction, formality] simple (before n); **he's a ~ child** ce n'est qu'un enfant; **a ~ nothing** trois fois rien; **he's a ~ nobody** c'est quelqu'un d'insignifiant; **2** (least) [sight, idea] simple, seul; **the ~ mention of her name** la simple évocation de son nom; **the ~ sight of her** sa seule vue; **the ~ presence of asbestos...** le seul fait qu'il y ait de l'amiante...; **3** (bare) seulement; **the beach is a ~ 2 km from here** la plage n'est qu'à 2 km d'ici; **to last a ~ 20 minutes** durer tout juste 20 minutes.

merely /ˈmɪəlɪ/ adv simplement, seulement; **his accusations ~ damaged his reputation** ses accusations n'ont fait que nuire à sa réputation; **it is not enough ~ to do** il ne suffit pas de faire.

merge /mɜːdʒ/ **I** vtr **1** (join) **to ~ sth with sth** fusionner qch avec qch [company, group]; **2** (blend) mélanger [colour, design].
II vi **1** (also **~ together**) [companies, departments] fusionner; [roads, rivers] se rejoindre; **to ~ with** fusionner avec [company, department]; rejoindre [river, road]; **2** (blend) [colours, sounds] se confondre; **to ~ into** se fondre avec [colour, sky, trees].

merger /ˈmɜːdʒə(r)/ n **1** (of companies) fusion f; **2** (process of merging) fusionnement m.

meridian /məˈrɪdɪən/ **I** n LIT méridien m; FIG (peak) apogée m.
II noun modifier [time] méridien/-ienne.

merit /ˈmerɪt/ **I** n (of idea) valeur f; (of person) mérite m; **to judge sb on their own ~s/sth on its own ~s** juger qn selon son mérite/qch selon ses qualités propres; **there's little ~ in his work** son œuvre a peu de valeur; **certificate of ~** accessit m.
II vtr mériter.

merit: **~ award** n récompense f honorifique; **~ list** n tableau m d'honneur; **~ mark, ~ point** n SCH bon point m.

meritorious /ˌmerɪˈtɔːrɪəs/ adj méritoire.

mermaid /ˈmɜːmeɪd/ n sirène f.

merman /ˈmɜːmæn/ n (pl **-men**) triton m.

merrily /ˈmerɪlɪ/ adv **1** (happily) joyeusement; **2** (unconcernedly) avec insouciance.

merriment /ˈmerɪmənt/ n (fun) joie f; (laughter) hilarité f.

merry /ˈmerɪ/ adj **1** (happy) joyeux/-euse, gai; **~ Christmas!** joyeux Noël!; **2**° (tipsy) éméché; **3** ‡ ou HUM (also **merrie**) **~ England** l'Angleterre du bon vieux temps; **the ~ month of May** le joli mois de mai.
IDIOMS **the more the merrier!** PROV plus on est de fous, plus on rit PROV; **to give sb ~ hell**° passer un bon savon à qn°; **to make ~** faire la noce.

merry: **~-go-round** n LIT manège m; FIG tourbillon m; **~maker** n noceur/-euse° m/f.

mesh /meʃ/ **I** n **1** (of string) filet m; (of metal) grillage

m; **2** (net) mailles fpl; **3** TECH engrenure f; **in ~** engrené.
II vi **1** (also **~ together**) [branches] s'enchevêtrer; **2** (also **~ together**) [ideas] concorder; **to ~ with** être en accord avec; **3** TECH [cogs] s'engrener; **to ~ with** s'emboîter dans.

mesmerize /ˈmezməraɪz/ **I** vtr hypnotiser.
II mesmerized pp adj fasciné, médusé.

mess /mes/ **I** n **1** (untidy or dirty state) désordre m; **what a ~!** quel désordre!, quelle pagaille°!; **to make a ~** [person] mettre du désordre; **in a ~** en désordre; **to tidy** ou **clear up the ~** mettre de l'ordre; **this report is a ~!** ce rapport est fait n'importe comment!; **my hair is a ~** je suis complètement décoiffée; **you look a ~!** GB, **you look like a ~!** US tu es dans un bel état!; **to make a ~ on the carpet** salir la moquette; **2** FIG (muddled state) **my life is a ~** ma vie est un désastre; **to be in a terrible ~** [economy] être dans une situation catastrophique; **to make a ~ of the job** massacrer° le travail; **how did we get into this ~?** comment a-t-on fait pour en arriver là?; **this is a fine ~ we're in** nous voilà dans de beaux draps!; **3**° (pitiful state) **his face was a ~** il avait le visage amoché; **he's a ~**° (psychologically) il est dans un sale état; **4** (excrement) saletés fpl; **to make a ~** [dog] faire ses saletés; **dog ~**° crotte° f de chien; **5** MIL cantine f; **officers' ~** (in the army) mess m; (in the navy) carré m des officiers; **6**° US portion f.
II° vi (meddle) **to ~ with** toucher à [drugs]; **don't ~ with him** évite-le.
■ **mess about**°, **mess around**°: ¶ **~ around 1** (act the fool) faire l'imbécile; **to ~ around with** jouer avec [chemicals, matches]; toucher à [drugs]; [potter] **to ~ around in the garden** s'amuser dans le jardin; **3** (sexually) **he ~es around** c'est un coureur; ¶ **~ [sb] around**° faire tourner qn en bourrique°.
■ **mess up**°: ¶ **~ up** US faire l'imbécile; ¶ **~ [sth] up, ~ up [sth] 1** (muddle up) semer la pagaille dans [papers]; mettre du désordre dans [kitchen]; (dirty) salir [napkin, sheets]; **2** (ruin) bricoler [exam, work]; gâcher [chances]; ¶ **~ [sb] up** [drugs, alcohol] détruire [person]; [experience] faire perdre les pédales° à qn.

message /ˈmesɪdʒ/ n **1** (communication) message m ALSO COMPUT (**about** au sujet de); **a telephone ~** un message téléphonique; **to send sb a ~ that** envoyer un message à qn pour lui dire que; **to receive a ~ that** recevoir un message selon lequel; **2** (meaning) GEN, RELIG, POL message m; **to get one's ~ across** (be understood) se faire comprendre; (convince people) faire passer son message; **to get the ~**° comprendre; **his ~ isn't getting through** son message ne passe pas.

messaging /ˈmesɪdʒɪŋ/ n COMPUT messagerie f électronique.

mess dress n MIL grand uniforme m.

messenger /ˈmesɪndʒə(r)/ n GEN messager/-ère m/f; (for hotel, company) garçon m de courses, coursier/-ière m/f.

messenger boy ▶ **1251** n garçon m de courses, coursier m.

messiah /mɪˈsaɪə/ n messie m; **the Messiah** le Messie.

Messrs /ˈmesəz/ n (abrév écrite = **messieurs**) MM.

messy /ˈmesɪ/ adj **1** (untidy) [house] en désordre; [appearance] négligé; [handwriting] peu soigné; **2** (dirty) [activity] salissant; **he's a ~ eater** il mange salement; **3** (confused) [lawsuit] pénible; [business] sale (before n).

mestizo /meˈstiːzəʊ/ n (pl **-zoes** ou **-zos**) métis/métisse m/f (d'ascendants européen et amérindien).

met /met/ prét, pp ▶ **meet**.

metabolic /ˌmetəˈbɒlɪk/ adj [disease, needs, stress] du métabolisme.

metabolism /mɪˈtæbəlɪzəm/ n métabolisme m.

metal /ˈmetl/ **I** n métal m.
II noun modifier [coin, container] en métal.

metal: **~ detector** n détecteur m de métaux; **~ fatigue** n fatigue f du métal.

metallic /mɪˈtælɪk/ adj **1** [substance] métallique; **2**

[*paint, finish*] métallisé; **3** (resembling metal) [*sound, appearance*] métallique; [*taste*] de métal.

metallurgist /mɪˈtælədʒɪst, US ˈmetlɜːrdʒɪst/ ▶1251 *n* métallurgiste *m*.

metallurgy /mɪˈtælədʒɪ, US ˈmetlɜːrdʒɪ/ *n* métallurgie *f*.

metal: ~ **polish** *n* produit *m* à astiquer les métaux; ~**work** *n* ferronnerie *f*.

metamorphose /ˌmetəˈmɔːfəʊz/ **I** *vtr* métamorphoser (**into** en).
II *vi* se métamorphoser (**into** en).

metamorphosis /ˌmetəˈmɔːfəsɪs/ *n* (*pl* **-phoses**) métamorphose *f* (**into** en).

metaphor /ˈmetəfə(r)/ *n* métaphore *f*; **to mix one's** ~**s** faire des métaphores incohérentes.

metaphoric(al) /ˌmetəˈfɒrɪk(l)/ *adj* métaphorique.

metaphorically /ˌmetəˈfɒrɪklɪ/ *adv* métaphoriquement; ~ **speaking** pour employer une métaphore.

metaphysical /ˌmetəˈfɪzɪkl/ *adj* **1** PHILOS métaphysique; **2** (abstract) abstrait.

mete /miːt/ *v* ■ **mete out**: ~ [sth] **out**, ~ **out** [sth] infliger [*punishment*]; rendre [*justice*].

meteor /ˈmiːtɪə(r)/ *n* météore *m*.

meteoric /ˌmiːtɪˈɒrɪk, US -ˈɔːr-/ *adj* LIT météorique; FIG [*rise*] fulgurant.

meteorite /ˈmiːtɪəraɪt/ *n* météorite *f*.

meteorological /ˌmiːtɪərəˈlɒdʒɪkl/ *adj* météorologique.

Meteorological Office *n*: météorologie nationale britannique.

meteorologist /ˌmiːtɪəˈrɒlədʒɪst/ ▶1251 *n* météorologue *mf*.

meteorology /ˌmiːtɪəˈrɒlədʒɪ/ *n* météorologie *f*.

meter /ˈmiːtə(r)/ **I** *n* **1** (measuring device) compteur *m*; **gas** ~ compteur de gaz; **to read the** ~ relever le compteur; **2** (also **parking** ~) parcmètre *m*; **3** US = **metre**.
II *vtr* **1** mesurer [*electricity, gas, pressure*]; **2** affranchir [qch] à la machine [*letter*].

meter reader *n* releveur *m* de compteur.

methane /ˈmiːθeɪn/ *n* méthane *m*.

method /ˈmeθəd/ *n* **1** (of teaching, contraception, training) méthode *f* (**for doing** pour faire); (of payment, treatment) mode *m* (**of** de); ~ **of transport** moyen *m* de transport; **production** ~**s** modes de production; **2** (orderliness) méthode *f*; **a man of** ~ un homme méthodique.

method: ~ **acting** *n* méthode *f* Stanislavski, jeu *m* 'Actor's Studio'; ~ **actor** *n* adepte *mf* de 'l'Actor's Studio'.

methodical /mɪˈθɒdɪkl/ *adj* méthodique.

Methodist /ˈmeθədɪst/ *n*, *adj* méthodiste (*mf*).

methodology /ˌmeθəˈdɒlədʒɪ/ *n* méthodologie *f*.

methyl /ˈmeθɪl/ *n* méthyle *m*.

methylated /ˈmeθəleɪtɪd/ *adj* méthylique.

methylated spirit(s) *n* (+ *v sg*) alcool *m* à brûler.

meticulous /mɪˈtɪkjʊləs/ *adj* méticuleux/-euse; ~ **about** méticuleux/-euse dans [*work*]; **to be** ~ **about doing** faire très attention à faire.

métier /ˈmetɪeɪ/ *n* vocation *f*.

Met Office *n* GB *abrév* ▶ **Meteorological Office**.

metre /ˈmiːtə(r)/ ▶1045 *n* **1** GB (measurement) mètre *m*; **2** LITERAT mètre *m*; **3** MUS mesure *f*.

metric /ˈmetrɪk/ *adj* métrique; **to go** ~° adopter le système métrique.

metricate /ˈmetrɪkeɪt/ *vtr* faire passer [qch] au système métrique.

metrics /ˈmetrɪks/ *n* (+ *v sg*) métrique *f*.

metronome /ˈmetrənəʊm/ *n* métronome *m*.

metropolis /məˈtrɒpəlɪs/ *n* métropole *f*.

metropolitan /ˌmetrəˈpɒlɪtən/ *adj* **1** (of city) [*area, population*] urbain; [*buildings, traffic, values*] des grandes villes; ~ **New York** l'agglomération de New York; **2** (home territory) ~ **France** la France métropolitaine; **3** RELIG métropolitain.

metropolitan: ~ **district** *n* GB ADMIN circonscrip-

tion *f* administrative (d'une conurbation); **Metropolitan police** *n* GB police *f* de Londres.

mettle /ˈmetl/ *n* courage *m*; **to be on one's** ~ être sur la sellette; **to put sb on his** ~ amener qn à montrer de quoi il est capable.

mew /mjuː/ **I** *n* **1** (of cat) miaulement *m*; **2** (seagull) mouette *f*.
II *vi* miauler.

mews /mjuːz/ *n* GB **1** (+ *v sg*) (street) ruelle *f*; (yard) cour *f*; **2** (+ *v pl*) (stables) écuries *fpl*.

Mexican /ˈmeksɪkən/ ▶1100 **I** *n* (person) Mexicain/-e *m/f*.
II *adj* mexicain.

Mexican: ~ **jumping bean** *n* pois *m* sauteur; ~ **stand off** *n* US impasse *f*; ~ **wave** *n* ola *f* (*mouvement de vague engendré par les spectateurs qui se lèvent successivement autour du terrain*).

Mexico /ˈmeksɪkəʊ/ ▶840 *pr n* Mexique *m*.

Mexico City ▶1343 *pr n* Mexico.

mezzanine /ˈmezəniːn/ *n* **1** GEN mezzanine *f*; **2** THEAT US corbeille *f*; GB premier dessous *m*.

MF *n* (*abrév* = **medium frequency**) FM *f*.

Mgr (*abrév écrite* = **Monseigneur**, **Monsignor**) Mgr.

mi /miː/ *n* mi *m*.

MI US POST *abrév écrite* = **Michigan**.

MI5 *n* (*abrév* = **Military Intelligence Section Five**) service *m* britannique de contre-espionnage.

MI6 *n* (*abrév* = **Military Intelligence Section Six**) service *m* britannique de surveillance du territoire; cf DST.

miaow /miːˈaʊ/ **I** *n* miaou *m*.
II *vi* miauler.

miasma /mɪˈæzmə/ *n* miasmes *mpl*.

mice /maɪs/ *pl* ▶ **mouse**.

Michaelmas /ˈmɪklməs/ *pr n* la Saint-Michel.

Michaelmas: ~ **daisy** *n* GB aster *m*; ~ **Term** *n* GB UNIV premier trimestre *m*.

Michelangelo /ˌmaɪklˈændʒələʊ/ *pr n* GB Michel-Ange.

mickey /ˈmɪkɪ/ *n* GB IDIOMS **are you taking the** ~ **out of me?** tu te paies ma tête?

micro /ˈmaɪkrəʊ/ **I** *n* COMPUT micro *m*.
II **micro** + *combining form* micro-.

microbe /ˈmaɪkrəʊb/ *n* microbe *m*.

microchip /ˈmaɪkrəʊtʃɪp/ **I** *n* puce *f*, circuit *m* intégré.
II *noun modifier* [*industry, technology*] du circuit intégré; [*factory*] de circuits intégrés.

microcomputing /ˌmaɪkrəʊkəmˈpjuːtɪŋ/ *n* micro-informatique *f*.

microcosm /ˈmaɪkrəkɒzəm/ *n* microcosme *m*.

microfilm /ˈmaɪkrəʊfɪlm/ **I** *n* microfilm *m*.
II *vtr* microfilmer.

microlighting /ˈmaɪkrəˌlaɪtɪŋ/ ▶949 *n* ULM *m*, ultra léger *m* motorisé.

micromesh /ˈmaɪkrəʊmeʃ/ *adj* ~ **tights** GB, ~ **pantyhose** US collant *m* mousse.

microphone /ˈmaɪkrəfəʊn/ *n* microphone *m*.

microphysics /ˈmaɪkrəʊfɪzɪks/ *n* (+ *v sg*) microphysique *f*.

microprocessing /ˌmaɪkrəʊˈprəʊsesɪŋ/ *n* micro-informatique *f*.

microscope /ˈmaɪkrəskəʊp/ *n* microscope *m*; **under the** ~ LIT, FIG au microscope.

microscopic /ˌmaɪkrəˈskɒpɪk/ *adj* **1** (minute) microscopique; **2** (using a microscope) au microscope.

microsurgery /ˌmaɪkrəʊˈsɜːdʒərɪ/ *n* microchirurgie *f*.

microsurgical /ˌmaɪkrəʊˈsɜːdʒɪkl/ *adj* [*technique, procedure*] de microchirurgie; [*specialist, knowledge*] en microchirurgie.

microwave /ˈmaɪkrəweɪv/ **I** *n* **1** (wave) micro-onde *f*; **2** (oven) four *m* à micro-ondes.
II *noun modifier* [*transmitter*] à micro-ondes; [*cookery*] au four à micro-ondes.
III *vtr* passer [qch] au four à micro-ondes.

mid+ /mɪd/ *combining form* in the ~-20th century au milieu du vingtième siècle; ~-afternoon milieu *m* de l'après-midi; (in) ~-May (à la) mi-mai; he's in his ~-forties il a environ quarante-cinq ans.

midair /ˌmɪd'eə(r)/ I *adj* [*collision*] en plein vol.
II in midair *adv phr* (in mid-flight) en plein vol; (in the air) en l'air; to leave sth in ~ FIG laisser qch en suspens.

midday /ˌmɪd'deɪ/ ▶ 812 I *n* midi *m*.
II *noun modifier* [*sun, meal*] de midi.

middle /'mɪdl/ I *n* 1 milieu *m*; in the ~ of au milieu de; to be caught in the ~ être pris entre deux feux; I was in the ~ of a book when… j'étais plongé dans un livre quand…; in the ~ of May à la mi-mai; right in the ~ of en plein milieu de; to be in the ~ of doing être en train de faire; to split [sth] down the ~ partager [qch] en deux [*bill, work*]; diviser [qch] en deux [*group, opinion*]; 2 ° (waist) taille *f*.
II *adj* [*door, shelf*] du milieu; [*price*] modéré; [*size, difficulty*] moyen/-enne; in ~ life au milieu de ma/ta etc vie; to be in one's ~ thirties GB avoir environ 35 ans; there must be a ~ course ou way il doit y avoir un juste milieu; to steer ou take ou follow a ~ course adopter une position intermédiaire.
IDIOMS in the ~ of nowhere dans un trou perdu.

middle: ~ age *n* âge *m* mûr; ~-aged *adj* [*person*] d'âge mûr; FIG [*outlook, view*] vieux jeu *inv*.
Middle Ages *n* the ~ le Moyen Âge; the early/late ~ le bas/haut Moyen Âge.

middle: ~-age spread *n* embonpoint *m* dû à l'âge; **Middle America** *n* (social group) *Américains aisés et aux idées conservatrices*; ~brow *adj* [*book, person*] sans prétentions intellectuelles.

middle class I *n* classe *f* moyenne.
II middle-class *adj* [*person*] de la classe moyenne; [*attitude, view*] bourgeois.

middle distance I *n* 1 ART, PHOT, CIN second plan *m*; 2 GEN in the ~ au loin; to gaze into the ~ regarder dans le vague.
II middle-distance *adj* SPORT [*event, athlete*] de demi-fond.

Middle East I *pr n* Moyen-Orient *m*.
II *noun modifier* [*affairs*] du Moyen-Orient; [*talks*] sur le Moyen-Orient.

middle: ~-eastern *adj* [*nation, politics*] du Moyen-Orient; **Middle English** *n* moyen anglais *m*; ~ finger ▶ 765 I *n* majeur *m*.

middle ground *n* GEN juste milieu *m*; (in argument) terrain *m* d'entente; POL the ~ les modérés *mpl*.

middle: ~-income *adj* [*person, family, country*] aux revenus moyens; ~man *n* GEN, COMM intermédiaire *m*; ~ manager *n* cadre *m* moyen; ~-of-the-road *adj* (banal) très ordinaire; (with wide appeal) populaire; [*policy*] GEN modéré; PÉJ tiède; ~-ranking *adj* d'un rang intermédiaire; ~ school *n* GB école pour élèves entre 9 et 13 ans; US école pour élèves entre 12 et 14 ans; ~-size(d) *adj* de taille moyenne; ~ weight *n* poids *m* moyen.

middling /'mɪdlɪŋ/ *adj* [*ability*] moyen/-enne.
IDIOMS fair to ~ pas trop mal.

Middx GB POST *abrév écrite* = **Middlesex**.

midfield /ˌmɪd'fiːld/ *n* milieu *m* du terrain.

mid-flight /ˌmɪd'flaɪt/ I *adj* en plein vol.
II in mid-flight *adv phr* en plein vol.

midge /mɪdʒ/ *n* moucheron *m*.

midget /'mɪdʒɪt/ I *n* nain/-e *m/f*.
II *adj* miniature; ~ submarine MIL sous-marin *m* de poche.

Midlands /'mɪdləndz/ *pr n* (+ *v sg*) the ~s la région *f* des Midlands (*au centre de l'Angleterre*).

midlife /'mɪdlaɪf/ I *n* âge *m* mûr.
II *noun modifier* [*crisis, problems*] de la cinquantaine.

midnight /'mɪdnaɪt/ ▶ 812 *n* minuit *m*.
IDIOMS to burn the ~ oil travailler jusqu'à l'aube.

mid-range /ˌmɪd'reɪndʒ/ I *n* to be in the ~ [*product, hotel*] être en milieu de gamme.

II *noun modifier* [*car, hotel*] de milieu de gamme.

midriff /'mɪdrɪf/ *n* ventre *m*.

mid-season /ˌmɪd'siːzn/ *adj* de milieu de saison.

midshipman /'mɪdʃɪpmən/ *n* (*pl* -men) 1 GB (officer) aspirant *m* (*de la Marine*); 2 US (trainee) élève *m* de l'École navale.

midst /mɪdst/ *n* in the ~ of au beau milieu de; in the ~ of change/war en plein changement/pleine guerre; in our ~ parmi nous.

midstream /ˌmɪd'striːm/ *n* in midstream *adv phr* (in river) au milieu du courant; FIG (in speech) en plein milieu d'une phrase.

midsummer /ˌmɪd'sʌmə(r)/ I *n* (high summer) milieu *m* de l'été; (solstice) solstice *m* d'été.
II *noun modifier* [*heat, days*] de plein été.

Midsummer('s) Day *n* la Saint-Jean.

mid-term /ˌmɪd'tɜːm/ I *n* in ~ POL au milieu de son/leur etc mandat; SCH au milieu du trimestre; (of pregnancy) au milieu de ma/sa etc grossesse.
II *noun modifier* POL [*crisis, reshuffle*] de milieu de mandat; SCH [*report, test*] de milieu de trimestre.

midtown /'mɪdtaʊn/ *n* US centre-ville *m*.

midway /ˌmɪd'weɪ/ I *n* US attractions *fpl* foraines.
II *adj* [*post, position*] de mi-course; [*stage, point*] de mi-parcours.
III *adv* ~ between/along à mi-chemin entre/le long de; ~ through au milieu de.

midweek /ˌmɪd'wiːk/ I *adj* de milieu de semaine.
II *adv* en milieu de semaine.

midwife /'mɪdwaɪf/ ▶ 1251 *n* (*pl* -wives) sage-femme *f*; male ~ homme *m* sage-femme.

midwifery /'mɪdwɪfərɪ, US -waɪf-/ *n* profession *f* de sage-femme.

midwinter /ˌmɪd'wɪntə(r)/ I *n* 1 (season) milieu *m* de l'hiver; 2 (solstice) solstice *m* d'hiver.
II *noun modifier* [*day, weather*] de plein hiver.

miffed /mɪft/ *adj* to be ou feel ~ être vexé.

might¹ /maɪt/ *modal aux* (*nég* **might not**, **mightn't**) 1 (indicating possibility) she ~ be right elle a peut-être raison; they ~ not go peut-être qu'ils n'iront pas; 'will you come?'—'I ~' 'tu viendras?'—'peut-être'; you ~ finish the painting before tonight il se peut que tu finisses de peindre avant ce soir; they ~ have got lost ils se sont peut-être perdus; you ~ have guessed that… vous aurez peut-être deviné que…; the plane ~ have landed by now il se peut que l'avion ait déjà atterri; I ~ (well) lose my job je risque de perdre mon travail; it ~ well improve the standard ça pourrait bien améliorer le niveau; try as I ~, I can't do it j'ai beau essayer, je n'y arrive pas; however unlikely that ~ be si improbable que cela puisse paraître; 2 (indicating unrealized possibility) I ~ have been killed! j'aurais pu être tué!; he was thinking about what ~ have been il pensait à ce qui se serait passé si les choses avaient été différentes; if they had acted quickly he ~ well be alive s'ils avaient agi plus vite il serait peut-être encore en vie; 3 (*prét de* may) (in sequence of tenses, in reported speech) I said I ~ go into town j'ai dit que j'irais peut-être en ville; I thought it ~ rain j'ai pensé qu'il risquait de pleuvoir; she asked if she ~ leave elle demanda si elle pouvait partir; 4 SOUT (when making requests) ~ I make a suggestion? puis-je me permettre de faire une suggestion?; ~ I ask who's calling? c'est de la part de qui s'il vous plaît?; and who, ~ I ask, are you?, and who ~ you be? (aggressive) on peut savoir qui vous êtes?; 5 (when making suggestions) it ~ be a good idea to do ce serait peut-être une bonne idée de faire; you ~ try making some enquiries tu devrais essayer de te renseigner; we ~ go out for a meal later nous pourrions aller manger au restaurant plus tard; you ~ like to drop in later tu veux peut-être passer plus tard; 6 (when making statement, argument) one ~ argue ou it ~ be argued that on pourrait dire ou faire valoir que; as you ou one ~ expect comme de bien entendu; as you ~ imagine comme vous pouvez le deviner; 7 (expressing reproach, irritation) I ~ have

might¹

Although usage shows that *may* and *might* are interchangeable in many contexts, *might* indicates a more remote possibility than *may*. French generally translates this element of possibility using *peut-être* with the appropriate verb tense:

it might snow = il va peut-être neiger

(It is also possible to translate this more formally using *il se peut que* + subjunctive: *il se peut qu'il neige*). For particular examples see **might¹** 1.

It is possible to translate *might* differently depending on the nature of the context and the speaker's point of view:

he might not come = il risque de ne pas venir

implies that this is not a desirable outcome for the speaker;

he might not come = il pourrait ne pas venir
or il se peut qu'il ne vienne pas

however, is neutral in tone. Where there is the idea of a possibility in the past which has not in fact occurred (see **might¹** 2), French uses the past conditional of the verb (which is often *pouvoir*):

it might have been serious
(but wasn't in fact) = ça aurait pu être grave

This is also the case where something which could have taken place did not, thus causing annoyance:

you might have said thanks! = tu aurais pu dire merci! (see **might¹** 7).

Might, as the past tense of *may*, will automatically occur in instances of reported speech:

he said you might be hurt = il a dit que tu serais peut-être blessé

For more examples see the entry **might¹** and bear in mind the rules for the agreement of tenses.

Where there is a choice between *may* and *might* in making requests, *might* is more formal and even rather dated. French uses inversion (*je peux* = *puis-je?*) in this context and *puis-je me permettre de …?* (= *might I …?*) is extremely formal.

Might can be used to polite effect – to soften direct statements: *you might imagine that …* or to offer advice tactfully: *it might be wise to …*. In both cases, French uses the conditional tense of the verb: *on pourrait penser que …*; *ce serait peut-être une bonne idée de …*. The use of *well* in phrases such as *he might well be right* etc. implies a greater degree of likelihood.

For translations of *might well*, *may well*, see II 2 in the entry **well¹**. For translations of the phrase *might as well* (*we might as well go home*), see **well¹** II 2.

---

known ou **guessed!** j'aurais dû m'en douter!; **he ~ at least apologize!** il pourrait au moins s'excuser!; **you ~ have warned me!** tu aurais pu me prévenir!; **8** (in concessives) **they ~ not be fast but they're reliable** ils ne sont peut-être pas rapides mais on peut au moins compter sur eux; ▶ **well¹** II 2.

might² /maɪt/ n **1** (power) puissance f; **2** (physical strength) force f; **with all his ~** de toutes ses forces.

mightn't /'maɪtn̩t/ = **might not**.

mighty /'maɪtɪ/ **I** n **the ~** les puissants.
II adj **1** (powerful) puissant; **2** (large) imposant; **3**○ (huge, terrific) énorme.
III○ adv (emphatic) vachement○, très.
IDIOMS how are the ~ fallen! comme tombent les puissants!; **high and ~** hautain.

migrant /'maɪgrənt/ **I** n (person) migrant/-e m/f; (bird) oiseau m migrateur; (animal) animal m migrateur.
II adj [labour] saisonnier/-ière; [bird, animal] migrateur/-trice.

migrate /maɪ'greɪt, US 'maɪgreɪt/ vi **1** [person] émigrer; **2** [bird, animal] migrer.

migration /maɪ'greɪʃn/ n migration f.

migratory /'maɪgrətrɪ, maɪ'greɪtərɪ, US 'maɪgrətɔːrɪ/ adj [animal] migrateur/-trice; [journey, behaviour] migratoire.

mike○ /maɪk/ n (microphone) micro○ m.

mild /maɪld/ **I** n (GB (also **~ ale**) bière f anglaise brune (légère).
II adj **1** (moderate) [amusement, surprise] léger/-ère; [interest, irritation] modéré; **2** (not cold) [weather, winter] doux/douce; [climate] tempéré; **a ~ spell** une période de beau temps; **3** (in flavour) [beer, taste, tobacco] léger/-ère; [cheese] doux/douce; [curry] peu épicé; **4** [soap, detergent, cream] doux/douce; **5** [case, infection] bénin/-igne; [attack, sedative] léger/-ère; **a ~ heart attack** une petite crise cardiaque; **6** (gentle) [person, voice] doux/douce.

mildew /'mɪldjuː, US -duː/ n **1** (on plant) mildiou m; **2** (mould) moisissure f.

mildly /'maɪldlɪ/ adv **1** (moderately) légèrement; **to put it ~** pour dire les choses avec modération; **that's putting it ~** c'est un euphémisme; **2** (gently) [speak] avec douceur; [rebuke] légèrement.

mildness /'maɪldnɪs/ n (of weather, product) douceur f; (of taste) légèreté f; (of protest) modération f.

mile /maɪl/ ▶ **1045J**, **1185J** **I** n **1** LIT mile m (= 1609 mètres); **it's 50 ~s away** ≈ c'est à 80 kilomètres d'ici; **2** FIG **to walk for ~s** marcher pendant des kilomètres; **it's ~s away!** c'est au bout du monde; **to be**

~s away (daydreaming) être complètement ailleurs; **~s from anywhere** loin de tout; **not a million ~s from here** pas très loin d'ici; **you could smell it a ~ off** on pouvait le sentir à cent lieues à la ronde; **to stand out a ~** sauter aux yeux; **I'd run a ~** je prendrais mes jambes à mon cou.
II○ **miles** npl (as intensifier) beaucoup; **~s better** bien meilleur; **to be ~s out** [estimate, figure] être complètement faux; [person] être très loin du compte.
IDIOMS a miss is as good as a ~ PROV rater, même de peu, c'est rater.

mileage /'maɪlɪdʒ/ n **1** nombre m de miles; **what's the ~ for the trip?** ≈ combien de kilomètres fait l'ensemble du voyage?; **2** (done by car) kilométrage m; **3** (miles per gallon) consommation f; **4** FIG (use) **he's had plenty of ~ out of that coat** ce manteau lui a beaucoup servi; **the press got maximum ~ out of the story** la presse a exploité l'histoire au maximum; **5** = **mileage allowance**.

mileage: **~ allowance** n ≈ indemnité f kilométrique; **~ indicator** n ≈ compteur m kilométrique; **~ post** n borne f (milliaire).

milestone /'maɪlstəʊn/ n **1** LIT borne f (milliaire); **2** FIG étape f importante.

militant /'mɪlɪtənt/ **I** n (activist) agitateur/-trice m/f; (armed) partisan/-e m/f de la lutte armée.
II adj militant.

militarism /'mɪlɪtərɪzəm/ n PÉJ militarisme m.

militarize /'mɪlɪtəraɪz/ vtr militariser; **~d zone** zone f militarisée.

military /'mɪlɪtrɪ, US -terɪ/ **I** n **the ~** (army) l'armée f; (soldiers) les militaires mpl.
II adj militaire.

military: **~ academy** n école f militaire; **~ policeman**, **MP** n membre m de la police militaire.

military service n service m militaire; **to be called up for ~** être appelé sous les drapeaux.

militate /'mɪlɪteɪt/ vi **to ~ against sth** compromettre qch; **to ~ for** militer en faveur de.

militia /mɪ'lɪʃə/ n **1** (citizen army) milice f; **2** US (liable for draft) **the ~** la réserve.

milk /mɪlk/ **I** n lait m; **baby ~** lait m pour bébé; **condensed ~** lait concentré sucré; **powdered/evaporated ~** lait en poudre/concentré; **full cream ~** lait entier; **long-life ~** lait longue conservation; **skimmed ~** lait écrémé; **breast ~** lait maternel; **cleansing ~** lait démaquillant.
II vtr **1** LIT traire; **2** FIG (exploit) (for money) pomper (**for** de); **to ~ sb dry** saigner qn à blanc.

III *vi* [*cow, goat*] donner du lait; [*farmer*] faire la traite.
IDIOMS **it's no good crying over spilt ~** PROV il est trop tard pour pleurer.

milk: **~-and-water** *adj* insipide; **~ chocolate** *n* chocolat *m* au lait; **~ diet** *n* régime *m* lacté; **~ float** *n* GB camionnette *f* de laitier; **~ jug** *n* pot *m* à lait; **~man ▶1251┃** *n* laitier *m*; **~ products** *npl* produits *mpl* laitiers; **~ pudding** *n* dessert *m* à base de lait; **~ run**○ *n* AVIAT vol *m* de routine; **~ tooth** *n* dent *f* de lait; **~ train** *n* premier train *m* du matin; **~ truck** *n* US camionnette *f* de laitier.

milky /ˈmɪlkɪ/ *adj* **1** (containing milk) [*drink*] au lait; [*diet*] lacté; **2** [*skin, liquid, colour*] laiteux/-euse.

Milky Way *pr n* Voie *f* lactée.

mill /mɪl/ **I** *n* **1** (building) (for flour) moulin *m*; **water ~** moulin à eau; **2** (factory) fabrique *f*; **steel ~** aciérie *f*; **3** (for pepper) moulin *m*; **4** FIG (routine) routine *f* ardue; **5** US FIG usine *f*; **diploma ~** usine à diplômes.
II *vtr* moudre [*flour, pepper*]; fabriquer [*steel*]; broyer [*paper*]; filer [*cotton*]; tisser [*textiles*]; moleter [*screw*]; fraiser [*nut, bolt*]; denteler [*coin*].
IDIOMS **there'll be trouble at t'mill**○ HUM on va avoir des ennuis; **to go through the ~** en voir de toutes les couleurs○; **to put sb through the ~** mettre qn à rude épreuve.
■ **mill around**, **mill about** grouiller.

millennium /mɪˈlenɪəm/ *n* (*pl* **-niums** ou **-nia**) **1** millénaire *m*; **2** RELIG, FIG millénium *m*.

miller /ˈmɪlə(r)/ **▶1251┃** *n* **1** (person) AGRIC meunier/ -ière *m/f*; IND fraiseur/-euse *m/f*; **2** (machine) fraiseuse *f*.

millet /ˈmɪlɪt/ *n* **1** (grass) (European) millet *m* des roseaux; (Indian) millet *m* commun; **2** (seed) millet *m*.

milligram(me) /ˈmɪlɪɡræm/ **▶1392┃** *n* milligramme *m*.

millimetre GB, **millimeter** US /ˈmɪlɪmiːtə(r)/ **▶1045┃** *n* millimètre *m*.

milliner /ˈmɪlɪnə(r)/ **▶1251┃** *n* modiste *f*.

milling /ˈmɪlɪŋ/ **I** *n* (of corn) mouture *f*; (of paper) broyage *m*; (of cloth) tissage *m*; (of metal) fraisage *m*; (on coin) dentelage *m*.
II *adj* [*crowd*] grouillant.

million /ˈmɪljən/ **▶1112┃** **I** *n* million *m*; **thanks a ~!** merci mille fois!; IRON merci quand même○!; **to have ~s** être riche à millions.
II millions *npl* des millions (**of** de); **the starving ~s** les masses *fpl* affamées.
III *adj* **a ~ people/pounds** un million de personnes/de livres.
IDIOMS **to feel like a ~ dollars**○ se sentir des ailes; **to look like a ~ dollars**○ être superbe; **to be one in a ~**○ être un oiseau rare○; **a chance in a ~** (slim) une chance sur un million; (exceptional) une chance unique.

millipede /ˈmɪlɪpiːd/ *n* mille-pattes *m inv*.

mill pond *n* bassin *m* de retenue (d'un moulin).

millstone /ˈmɪlstəʊn/ *n* meule *f*.
IDIOMS **to be a ~ round one's neck** être un boulet au pied.

mill: **~stream** *n* bief *m* de moulin; **~wheel** *n* roue *f* de moulin.

milometer /maɪˈlɒmɪtə(r)/ *n* GB ≈ compteur *m* kilométrique; **to turn back the ~** trafiquer le compteur.

mime /maɪm/ **I** *n* **1** (art) mime *m*; **2** (performance) pantomime *f*; **3** (performer) mime *mf*.
II *vtr*, *vi* mimer.

mime artist ▶1251┃ *n* mime *mf*.

mimic /ˈmɪmɪk/ **I** *n* imitateur/-trice *m/f*.
II *vtr* (*p prés etc* **-ck-**) **1** GEN imiter; (to ridicule) parodier; **2** (simulate) simuler; ZOOL imiter [*colouring*]; **3** PÉJ (copy) singer PÉJ.

mimicry /ˈmɪmɪkrɪ/ *n* GEN imitation *f*; ZOOL mimétisme *m*.

mince /mɪns/ **I** *n* GB CULIN viande *f* hachée; **beef ~** bœuf *m* haché.
II *vtr* hacher [*meat*].

III *vi* PÉJ (walk) marcher en se trémoussant.
IDIOMS **not to ~ matters** ou **one's words** ne pas mâcher ses mots.

mincemeat /ˈmɪnsmiːt/ *n* GB CULIN garniture composée de fruits secs et d'épices.
IDIOMS **to make ~ of sb** ne faire qu'une bouchée de qn.

mince pie *n*: tartelette garnie d'une pâte de fruits secs.

mincer /ˈmɪnsə(r)/ *n* hachoir *m*; **to put sth through the ~** passer qch au hachoir.

mincing /ˈmɪnsɪŋ/ *adj* affecté.

mind /maɪnd/ **I** *n* **1** (centre of thought, feelings) esprit *m*; **peace of ~** tranquillité d'esprit; **it's all in the ~** c'est tout dans la tête○; **to cross sb's ~** venir à l'esprit de qn; **at the back of my ~** j'avais des doutes au fond de moi j'avais des doutes; **that's a load** ou **weight off my ~** ça me soulage beaucoup; **to feel easy in one's ~ about sth** se sentir rassuré quant à qch; **to have something on one's ~** être préoccupé; **to set sb's ~ at rest** rassurer qn; **nothing could be further from my ~** loin de moi cette pensée; **2** (brain) intelligence *f*; **with the ~ of a two-year-old** avec l'intelligence d'un enfant de deux ans; **to have a very good ~** être très intelligent; **he has a fine legal ~** c'est un brillant juriste; **it's a case of ~ over matter** c'est la victoire de l'esprit sur la matière; **3** (way of thinking) esprit *m*; **to have a logical ~** avoir l'esprit logique; **the criminal ~** l'esprit criminel; **4** (opinion) avis *m*; **to be of one ~** être du même avis; **to my ~** à mon avis; **to make up one's ~ about/ to do** se décider à propos de/à faire; **my ~'s made up** je suis décidé; **to change one's ~ about sth** changer d'avis sur qch; **to keep an open ~ about sth** ne pas avoir de préjugés sur qch; **to know one's own ~** avoir des idées bien à soi; **to speak one's ~** dire ce qu'on a à dire; **5** (attention) esprit *m*; **to concentrate** ou **keep one's ~ on sth** se concentrer sur; **to give** ou **put one's ~ to sth** accorder son attention à qch; **to take sb's ~ off sth** distraire qn de qch; **6** (memory) esprit *m*; **I can't get him out of my ~** je n'arrive pas à l'oublier; **try to put it out of your ~** essaie de ne plus y penser; **my ~'s a blank** j'ai un trou de mémoire; **it went right** ou **clean** ou **completely out of my ~** cela m'est complètement sorti de la tête; **to bring sth to ~** rappeler qch; **7** (sanity) raison *f*; **his ~ is going** il n'a plus toute sa raison; **are you out of your ~?** tu es fou/folle○?; **8** (person as intellectual) esprit *m*.
II in mind *adv phr* **I bought it with you in ~** je l'ai acheté en pensant à toi; **I have something in ~ for this evening** j'ai une idée pour ce soir; **with the future in ~** en prévision de l'avenir; **with this in ~,...** avec cette idée en tête,...; **to have it in ~ to do sth** avoir l'intention de faire qch; **to put sb in ~ of sb/sth** rappeler qn/qch à qn.
III *vtr* **1** (pay attention to) faire attention à [*hazard*]; surveiller [*manners, language*]; **don't ~ me** GEN ne faites pas attention à moi; IRON ne vous gênez pas!; **~ how you go** GB faites bien attention à vous; **it's a secret, ~**○ c'est un secret, n'oublie pas; **~ you**○, **it won't be easy** remarque, ce ne sera pas facile; **2** (object to) **I don't ~ the cold** le froid ne me dérange pas; **I don't ~ cats, but I prefer dogs** je n'ai rien contre les chats, mais je préfère les chiens; **'today or tomorrow?'—'I don't ~'** 'aujourd'hui ou demain?'—'ça m'est égal'; **will they ~ us being late?** est-ce qu'ils seront fâchés si nous sommes en retard?; **would you ~ keeping my seat for me?** est-ce que ça vous ennuierait de garder ma place?; **if you don't ~ my asking...** si ce n'est pas une question indiscrète...; **'like a cigarette?'—'don't ~ if I do'**○ 'une cigarette?'—'c'est pas de refus'○; **I wouldn't ~ a glass of wine** je prendrais volontiers un verre de vin; **if you don't ~** si cela ne vous fait rien ALSO IRON; **3** (care) se soucier de; **do you ~!** IRON non mais!; **never ~** (don't worry) ne t'en fais pas; (it doesn't matter) peu importe; **he can't afford an apartment, never ~ a big house** il ne peut pas se permettre un

appartement encore moins une grande maison; **4** (look after) s'occuper de [*animal, children*]; tenir [*shop*].
IDIOMS **great ~s think alike** les grands esprits se rencontrent; **to read sb's ~** lire dans les pensées de qn; **if you've a ~ to** si le cœur vous en dit; **to see sth in one's ~'s eye** imaginer qch; **I gave him a piece of my ~**○! je lui ai dit ma façon de penser!; **to have a good ~** ou **half a ~ to do** GB avoir bien envie de faire; **to have a ~ of one's own** savoir ce qu'on veut.
■ **mind out** faire attention; **~ out of the way**○! dégage○!

mind: **~bending** *adj* [*drug*] psychotrope; [*problem*] très complexe; **~-blowing**○ *adj* époustouflant○; **~-boggling**○ *adj* stupéfiant.

minded /'maɪndɪd/ **I** *adj* SOUT **if you're so ~** si ça vous dit.
II -minded *combining form* **1** (with certain talent) **to be mechanically-/business-~** avoir le sens de la mécanique/des affaires; **2** (with certain attitude) **to be small-/open-~** avoir l'esprit étroit/ouvert; **3** (with certain trait) **to be feeble-~** être simplet/-ette.

minder /'maɪndə(r)/ *n* GB **1**○ (bodyguard) garde *m* du corps; **2** (also **child ~**) nourrice *f*.

mindful /'maɪndfl/ *adj* **~ of** soucieux/-ieuse de.

mindless /'maɪndlɪs/ *adj* PÉJ (stupid) [*person, programme*] bête; [*work*] abrutissant; [*vandalism*] gratuit; [*task*] machinal.

mindreader /'maɪndriːdə(r)/ *n* télépathe *mf*; **you must be a ~** HUM mais tu lis dans mes pensées.

mine¹ /maɪn/

■ **Note** In French, pronouns reflect the gender and number of the noun they are standing for. So *mine* is translated by *le mien, la mienne, les miens, les miennes*, according to what is being referred to: *the blue car is mine* = la voiture bleue est la mienne; *his children are older than mine* = ses enfants sont plus âgés que les miens.
– For examples and particular usages, see the entry below.

pron **his car is red but ~ is blue** sa voiture est rouge mais la mienne est bleue; **which (glass) is ~?** lequel (de ces verres) est le mien?; **~'s a whisky**○ un whisky pour moi; **she's a friend of ~** c'est une amie à moi; **it's not ~** ce n'est pas à moi; **that brother of ~** GEN mon frère; PÉJ mon imbécile de frère○.

mine² /maɪn/ **I** *n* **1** LIT, FIG mine *f*; **to work in** ou **down the ~s** travailler dans les mines; **to have a ~ of experience to draw on** pouvoir s'appuyer sur son expérience; **a ~ of information** une mine de renseignements; **2** (explosive) mine *f*; **to lay a ~** (on land) poser une mine; (in sea) mouiller une mine.
II *vtr* **1** extraire [*gems, mineral*]; exploiter [*area*]; **2** MIL miner [*area*].
III *vi* exploiter un gisement; **to ~ for** extraire [*gems, mineral*].

minefield /'maɪnfiːld/ *n* LIT champ *m* de mines; FIG terrain *m* miné; **a political ~** une poudrière politique.

miner /'maɪnə(r)/ ▶ 1251 *n* mineur *m*.

mineral /'mɪnərəl/ *n* **1** (substance, class) minéral *m*; (for extraction) minerai *m*; **2** GB (drink) eau *f* minérale.
II *adj* GEN minéral; **~ ore** minerai *m*.

mineralogy /ˌmɪnə'rælədʒɪ/ *n* minéralogie *f*.

mineral: **~ oil** *n* pétrole *m*; US (paraffin) huile *f* minérale; **~ rights** *npl* concession *f* d'exploitation minière; **~ water** *n* eau *f* minérale.

mine /maɪn/: **~sweeper** *n* dragueur *m* de mines; **~worker** ▶ 1251 *n* mineur *m*.

mingle /'mɪŋgl/ **I** *vtr* mêler [*quality, feeling*] (**with** à); mélanger [*sand, colour, taste*] (**with** avec).
II *vi* **1 to ~ with** se mêler à [*crowd, guests*]; fréquenter [*social group*]; **2** [*sounds*] se confondre (**with** à); [*smells, feelings*] se mêler (**with** à).

mini /'mɪnɪ/ **I** *n* mini-jupe *f*.
II mini+ *combining form* mini-.

miniature /'mɪnətʃə(r), US 'mɪnɪətʃʊər/ **I** *n* (all contexts) miniature *f*.

II *adj* GEN miniature; [*breed, dog, horse*] nain.

miniature: **~ golf** ▶ 949 *n* mini-golf *m*; **~ railway** *n* petit train *m*.

minibudget /ˌmɪnɪ'bʌdʒɪt/ *n* GB POL budget *m* provisoire.

minicab /'mɪnɪkæb/ *n* GB taxi *m* (non agréé).

minicourse /'mɪnɪkɔːs/ *n* US UNIV stage *m*.

minim /'mɪnɪm/ *n* **1** MUS GB blanche *f*; **2** (liquid measure) goutte *f*.

minima /'mɪnɪmə/ *pl* ▶ **minimum**.

minimal /'mɪnɪml/ *adj* **1** (very small) minime; **2** (minimum) minimal.

minimalist /'mɪnɪməlɪst/ *n, adj* minimaliste (*mf*).

minimally /'mɪnɪməlɪ/ *adv* très légèrement.

minimarket /'mɪnɪmaːkɪt/, **minimart** /'mɪnɪmaːt/ *n* supérette *f*.

minimize /'mɪnɪmaɪz/ *vtr* **1** (reduce) réduire [qch] au maximum [*cost, risk*]; **2** (play down) minimiser [*incident*]; **3** COMPUT réduire.

minimum /'mɪnɪməm/ **I** *n* minimum *m* (**of** de); **to keep to a/to the ~** maintenir à un/au minimum; **to reduce to a** ou **to the ~** réduire au maximum; **the bare** ou **absolute ~** le strict minimum.
II *adj* minimum, minimal.

mining /'maɪnɪŋ/ **I** *n* **1** exploitation *f* minière; **2** MIL (on land) pose *f* de mines; (at sea) mouillage *m* de mines.
II *noun modifier* [*area, industry, town*] minier/-ière; [*family, union*] de mineurs; [*accident*] de mine.

mining: **~ engineer** ▶ 1251 *n* ingénieur *m* des mines; **~ engineering** *n* génie *m* minier.

minister /'mɪnɪstə(r)/ ▶ 937 **I** *n* **1** GB POL ministre *m*; **~ of** ou **for Defence, Defence ~** ministre de la Défense; **2** RELIG ministre *m* (du culte).
II *vi* (care for) SOUT **to ~ to** donner des soins à [*person*]; **to ~ to sb's needs** pourvoir aux besoins de qn.

ministering angel *n* ange *m* de dévouement.

minister of state *n* GB POL ministre *m* délégué; **Minister of State for Education** ministre délégué auprès du ministre de l'Éducation.

ministry /'mɪnɪstrɪ/ *n* **1** GB POL (department, building) ministère *m*; **Ministry of Transport** ministère des Transports; **2** RELIG **the ~** le ministère.

mink /mɪŋk/ *n* (animal, fur, coat) vison *m*.
II *noun modifier* [*coat*] de vison.

minnow /'mɪnəʊ/ *n* **1** (fish) vairon *m*; **2** FIG menu fretin *m*.

minor /'maɪnə(r)/ *n* JUR mineur/-e *m/f*.
II *adj* **1** [*change, repair, role*] mineur; **~ road** route secondaire; **2** (not serious) [*injury, burn, fracture*] léger/-ère; [*operation, surgery*] mineur; **3** MUS mineur; **C ~** Do mineur; **in a ~ key** en mineur.
III *vi* US UNIV **to ~ in sth** prendre qch en matière secondaire.

Minorca /mɪ'nɔːkə/ ▶ 1022 *pr n* Minorque *f*.

minority /maɪ'nɒrətɪ, US -'nɔːr-/ **I** *n* **1** GEN minorité *f* (**of** de); **to be in the ~** être en minorité; **vocal ~** minorité agissante; **to be in a ~ of one** être le seul/la seule à penser cela; **2** US POL opposition *f*.
II *noun modifier* minoritaire.

minority: **~ leader** *n* US POL chef *m* de l'opposition; **~ president** *n* US POL président dont le parti n'a pas la majorité au Congrès; **~ rule** *n* gouvernement *m* par la minorité.

minor: **~ league** US SPORT *n* division *f* secondaire; **~ offence** GB, **~ offense** US *n* délit *m* mineur.

minster /'mɪnstə(r)/ *n* (cathedral) cathédrale *f*; (large church) église *f* abbatiale.

minstrel /'mɪnstrəl/ *n* ménestrel *m*.

mint /mɪnt/ **I** *n* **1** BOT, CULIN menthe *f*; **2** (sweet) bonbon *m* à la menthe; **after-dinner ~** chocolat *m* à la menthe; **3** (for coins) hôtel *m* des Monnaies; **the Royal Mint** GB l'hôtel de la Monnaie (*à Londres*); **4**○ (vast sum) fortune *f*.

II *noun modifier* [*sauce, tea*] à la menthe; [*essence, flower, leaf*] de menthe.
III *adj* (new) **in ~ condition** à l'état neuf.
IV *vtr* **1** frapper [*coin*]; **2** forger [*word, expression*].

mint: **~-flavoured** *adj* parfumé à la menthe; **~ green** *n, adj* couleur (*f*) menthe à l'eau *inv*.

minuet /ˌmɪnjʊ'et/ *n* menuet *m*.

minus /'maɪnəs/ **I** *n* **1** MATH moins *m*; **two ~es make a plus** moins par moins égale plus; **2** (drawback) inconvénient *m*.
II *adj* **1** [*sign, symbol, button*] moins; [*number, quantity, value*] négatif/-ive; **2** [*factor, point*] négatif/-ive; **on the ~ side**... pour ce qui est des inconvénients...
III *prep* **1** MATH moins; **what is 20 ~ 8?** combien font 20 moins 8?; **it is ~ 15** (degrees) il fait moins 15 (degrés); **2** HUM (without) sans; **he woke up ~ his passport** quand il s'est réveillé il n'avait plus son passeport.

minuscule /'mɪnəskju:l/ *n, adj* (letter) minuscule (*f*).

minute¹ /'mɪnɪt/ ▶**1336**, **812**] **I** *n* **1** (unit of time, short moment) minute *f*; **five ~s past ten** dix heures cinq; **it's five ~s'** walk away c'est à cinq minutes à pied; **we arrived at eight o'clock to the ~** nous sommes arrivés à huit heures pile; **without a ~ to spare** au tout dernier moment; **just a ~ please** une minute, s'il vous plaît; **she won't be a ~** elle sera là dans un instant; **it won't take a ~** ce ne sera pas long; **2** (exact instant) **the ~ I heard the news** dès que j'ai entendu la nouvelle; **at that very ~** à cet instant précis; **any ~ now** d'une minute à l'autre; **stop it this ~!** arrêtez immédiatement!; **I was just this ~ going to phone you** j'allais t'appeler à l'instant; **he's at this ~ starting his speech** il est tout juste en train de commencer son discours; **to put sth off to the last ~** repousser qch au dernier moment; **he's always up to the ~ with the news** il est toujours au courant des dernières nouvelles.
II **~s** *npl* ADMIN compte-rendu *m*; **to take the ~s** rédiger le compte-rendu.
III *vtr* inscrire [*qch*] au procès-verbal.

minute² /maɪ'nju:t, US -'nu:t/ *adj* [*particle*] minuscule; [*quantity*] infime; [*risk, variation*] minime.

minute hand *n* aiguille *f* des minutes.

minutely /maɪ'nju:tlɪ, US -'nu:tlɪ/ *adv* [*describe, examine*] minutieusement; [*vary, differ*] de manière infime.

minutiae /maɪ'nju:ʃiː, US mɪ'nu:ʃiː/ *npl* menus détails *mpl*.

miracle /'mɪrəkl/ **I** *n* miracle *m*; **to work** ou **perform ~s** faire des miracles; **a ~ of** un prodige de [*efficiency etc*].
II *noun modifier* [*cure, drug*] miracle; [*recovery*] miraculeux.

miraculous /mɪ'rækjʊləs/ *adj* **1** [*cure, escape, recovery*] miraculeux/-euse; **2** [*speed, efficiency*] prodigieux/-ieuse.

mirror /'mɪrə(r)/ **I** *n* GEN miroir *m*, glace *f*; AUT rétroviseur *m*; FIG reflet *m*.
II *vtr* LIT, FIG refléter; **to be ~ed in** se refléter dans.

mirror image *n* FIG image *f* inversée.

mirth /mɜ:θ/ *n* (laughter) hilarité *f*; (joy) joie *f*.

mirthless /'mɜ:θlɪs/ *adj* SOUT [*laugh*] forcé; [*account*] dépourvu d'humour; [*occasion*] triste.

misadventure /ˌmɪsəd'ventʃə(r)/ *n* SOUT mésaventure *f*; **verdict of death by ~** GB JUR verdict de mort accidentelle.

misapprehension /ˌmɪsæprɪ'henʃn/ *n* malentendu *m*, erreur *f*; **to be (labouring) under a ~** se tromper.

misappropriate /ˌmɪsə'prəʊprɪeɪt/ *vtr* détourner [*funds*].

misbehave /ˌmɪsbɪ'heɪv/ **I** *vi* [*child*] se tenir mal; [*adult*] se conduire mal.
II *v refl* **to ~ oneself** = **misbehave**.

misbehaviour, **misbehavior** US /ˌmɪsbɪ'heɪvɪə(r)/ *n* GEN mauvais comportement *m*; SCH mauvaise conduite *f*.

miscalculation /ˌmɪskælkjʊ'leɪʃn/ *n* LIT erreur *f* de calcul; FIG mauvais calcul *m*.

miscarriage /'mɪskærɪdʒ, ˌmɪs'kærɪdʒ/ *n* **1** MED fausse couche *f*; **2** JUR **a ~ of justice** une grave erreur judiciaire.

miscarry /ˌmɪs'kærɪ/ *vi* **1** MED [*woman*] faire une fausse couche; [*animal*] avorter; **2** [*plan, attack, strategy*] échouer.

miscellaneous /ˌmɪsə'leɪnɪəs/ *adj* divers.

miscellany /mɪ'selənɪ, US 'mɪsəleɪnɪ/ *n* (of people, things) collection *f* disparate (**of** de); LITERAT (anthology) morceaux *mpl* choisis; TV, RADIO choix *m*.

mischief /'mɪstʃɪf/ *n* (playfulness) espièglerie *f*; (witty) malice *f*; (done by children) bêtises *fpl*; **to get into ~** faire des bêtises; **he's up to ~** il prépare quelque chose; **it keeps them out of ~** ça les occupe.

mischievous /'mɪstʃɪvəs/ *adj* [*child, comedy, humour*] espiègle; [*smile, eyes*] malicieux/-ieuse.

misconceived /ˌmɪskən'siːvd/ *adj* [*idea, argument*] mal fondé; [*agreement, project*] mal conçu.

misconception /ˌmɪskən'sepʃn/ *n* idée *f* fausse; **it is a popular ~ that** on croit souvent à tort que.

misconduct /ˌmɪs'kɒndʌkt/ *n* (moral) inconduite *f*; **professional ~** faute professionnelle.

misconstrue /ˌmɪskən'struː/ *vtr* SOUT mal interpréter.

miscount /ˌmɪs'kaʊnt/ **I** *n* POL **to make a ~** faire une erreur dans le compte des suffrages exprimés.
II *vtr, vi* GEN, POL mal compter.

misdeed /ˌmɪs'diːd/ *n* méfait *m*.

misdemeanour, **misdemeanor** US /ˌmɪsdɪ'miːnə(r)/ *n* JUR délit *m*.

misdirect /ˌmɪsdaɪ'rekt, -dɪ'rekt/ *vtr* **1** mal orienter; **to ~ sb to** diriger qn par erreur vers; **2** (address wrongly) mal libeller l'adresse de [*letter, parcel*]; **the letter was ~ed to our old address** la lettre a été envoyée par erreur à notre ancienne adresse.

miser /'maɪzə(r)/ *n* avare *mf*.

miserable /'mɪzrəbl/ *adj* **1** (gloomy) [*person, event, expression*] malheureux/-euse; [*thoughts*] noir; [*weather*] sale (*before n*); **to feel ~** avoir le cafard; **2** (pathetic) [*quantity*] misérable; [*wage*] de misère; [*attempt, failure, performance, result*] lamentable; **3** (depressing) [*life*] de misère; [*dwelling*] misérable.

miserably /'mɪzrəblɪ/ *adv* **1** (unhappily) [*speak*] d'un ton malheureux; [*stare*] d'un air malheureux; **he was ~ cold** il avait horriblement froid; **2** (pathetically) [*fail, perform*] lamentablement; **a ~ low wage** un salaire de misère.

miserly /'maɪzəlɪ/ *adj* [*person*] avare; [*habits*] mesquin; [*allowance, amount*] maigre.

misery /'mɪzərɪ/ *n* **1** (unhappiness) souffrance *f*; (gloom) abattement *m*; **to make sb's life a ~** faire de la vie de qn un enfer; **to put sb out of their ~** EUPH (kill) abréger les souffrances de qn EUPH; **to put an animal out of its ~** EUPH achever un animal; **2** (misfortune) **the miseries of unemployment** le chômage et son cortège de misères; **3°** GB (child) pleurnicheur/-euse *m/f*; (adult) rabat-joie *mf inv*.

misfire /ˌmɪs'faɪə(r)/ *vi* LIT [*gun, rocket*] faire long feu; [*engine*] avoir des ratés; FIG [*plan, joke*] tomber à plat.

misfit /'mɪsfɪt/ *n* (at work, in a group) marginal/-e *m/f*; **social ~** inadapté/-e *m/f* social/-e.

misfortune /ˌmɪs'fɔːtʃuːn/ *n* (unfortunate event) malheur *m*; (bad luck) malchance *f*; **to have the ~ to do** avoir la malchance de faire.

misgiving /mɪs'gɪvɪŋ/ *n* crainte *f*; **to have ~s about sth** avoir des craintes quant à qch; **to have ~s about sb** avoir des doutes au sujet de qn; **not without ~(s)** non sans appréhension.

misguided /ˌmɪs'gaɪdɪd/ *adj* [*strategy, attempt*] peu judicieux/-ieuse; [*politicians, teacher*] malavisé.

mishandle /ˌmɪs'hændl/ *vtr* **1** (inefficiently) mal conduire [*operation, meeting*]; ne pas savoir comment s'y prendre avec [*person*]; **2** (roughly) manier [*qch*] sans précaution [*object*]; malmener [*person, animal*].

mishap /'mɪshæp/ *n* incident *m*; **a slight ~** un incident sans importance; **without ~** sans incident.

mishear /ˌmɪs'hɪə(r)/ *vtr* (*prét*, *pp* **-heard**) mal entendre.

mishmash○ /'mɪʃmæʃ/ *n* méli-mélo○ *m*; **a ~ of** un ramassis de.

misinform /ˌmɪsɪn'fɔːm/ *vtr* mal renseigner.

misinformation /ˌmɪsɪnfə'meɪʃn/ *n* (intentional) désinformation *f*; (unintentional) renseignements *mpl* inexacts (**about** sur).

misinterpret /ˌmɪsɪn'tɜːprɪt/ *vtr* mal interpréter.

misinterpretation /ˌmɪsɪntɜːprɪ'teɪʃn/ *n* interprétation *f* erronée.

misjudge /ˌmɪs'dʒʌdʒ/ *vtr* mal évaluer [*speed, distance, public feeling*]; mal calculer [*shot*]; mal juger [*person, character*].

miskick GB /ˌmɪs'kɪk/ **I** *vtr* mal envoyer [*ball*]; rater [*penalty*].
II *vi* rater son tir.

mislay /ˌmɪs'leɪ/ *vtr* (*prét*, *pp* **-laid**) égarer.

mislead /ˌmɪs'liːd/ *vtr* (*prét*, *pp* **-led**) (deliberately) tromper; (unintentionally) induire [qn] en erreur.

misleading /ˌmɪs'liːdɪŋ/ *adj* [*impression, title, information*] trompeur/-euse; [*claim, statement, advertising*] mensonger/-ère.

mismanage /ˌmɪs'mænɪdʒ/ *vtr* (administratively) mal diriger; (financially) mal gérer.

mismanagement /ˌmɪs'mænɪdʒmənt/ *n* (of economy, funds) mauvaise gestion *f*; (of company, project) mauvaise direction *f*.

mismatch /'mɪsmætʃ/ *n* (of styles, colours) discordance *f* (**between** de); (of concepts, perceptions) disparité *f* (**between** de).

misname /ˌmɪs'neɪm/ *vtr* (incorrectly) appeler à tort; (unsuitably) mal nommer.

misnomer /ˌmɪs'nəʊmə(r)/ *n* appellation *f* impropre.

misogynist /mɪ'sɒdʒɪnɪst/ *n* misogyne *mf*.

misplace /ˌmɪs'pleɪs/ **I** *vtr* **1** (mislay) égarer; **2** (put in wrong place) mal ranger.
II misplaced *pp adj* [*fears, criticisms*] déplacé; [*money, passport*] égaré.

misprint /'mɪsprɪnt/ *n* coquille *f*, faute *f* typographique.

mispronounce /ˌmɪsprə'naʊns/ *vtr* mal prononcer.

mispronunciation /ˌmɪsprəˌnʌnsɪ'eɪʃn/ *n* (act) prononciation *f* incorrecte (**of** de); (instance) erreur *f* de prononciation.

misquote /ˌmɪs'kwəʊt/ *vtr* déformer les propos de [*person*]; déformer [*text*]; citer incorrectement [*price*].

misread /ˌmɪs'riːd/ *vtr* (*prét*, *pp* **-read** /-'red/) **1** (read wrongly) mal lire [*sentence, map*]; mal relever [*meter*]; **2** (misinterpret) mal interpréter [*actions*].

misrepresent /ˌmɪsˌreprɪ'zent/ *vtr* présenter [qn] sous un faux jour [*person*]; déformer [*views, intentions, facts*]; **to ~ sb as sth** présenter qn à tort comme qch.

misrepresentation /ˌmɪsˌreprɪzen'teɪʃn/ *n* (of facts, opinions) déformation *f*.

miss /mɪs/ **I** *n* **1** (failure to score) (in game) coup *m* manqué ou raté; **the first shot was a ~** le premier coup a manqué; **2 to give [sth] a ~**○ ne pas aller à [*film, lecture*]; se passer de [*dish, drink, meal*]; **3** (failure) échec *m*.
II Miss ▶937 (woman's title) Mademoiselle *f*; (written abbreviation) Mlle; (mode of address) mademoiselle *f*.
III *vtr* **1** (fail to hit or reach) manquer [*target*]; passer à côté de [*record*]; **the stone just ~ed my head** la pierre m'a frôlé la tête; **he just ~ed the other car/a pedestrian** il a failli emboutir l'autre voiture/renverser un piéton; **2** (fail to catch or take) rater [*bus, plane, event, meeting*]; laisser passer [*chance, opportunity*]; **I ~ed the train by five minutes** j'ai raté le train de cinq minutes; **it's wonderful, don't ~ it!** c'est génial, à ne pas rater!; **3** (fail to see) rater; **the shop's easy to ~** la boutique peut facilement se rater; **4** (fail to hear or understand) ne pas saisir [*joke, remark*]; **he doesn't ~ a thing** rien ne lui échappe;

you've ~ed the whole point! tu n'as rien compris!; **5** (omit) sauter [*line, class*]; **6** (fail to attend) manquer [*school*]; **7** (avoid) échapper à [*death, injury*]; éviter [*traffic, bad weather, rush hour*]; **he just ~ed being caught** il a failli être pris; **how she ~ed being run over I'll never know!** comment elle n'a pas été renversée je ne le saurai jamais!; **8** (notice absence of) remarquer la disparition de; **oh, is it mine? I hadn't ~ed it** c'est le mien? je n'avais pas remarqué qu'il avait disparu; **keep it, I won't ~ it** garde-le, je n'en aurai pas besoin; **9** (regret absence of) **I ~ you** tu me manques; **he ~ed Paris** Paris lui manquait; **I'll ~ coming to the office** le bureau va me manquer; **she'll be greatly** ou **sadly ~ed** son absence sera très regrettée; **he won't be ~ed**○! bon débarras!
IV *vi* **1** GAMES, MIL, SPORT rater son coup; **2** AUT [*engine*] avoir des ratés.
IDIOMS **to ~ the boat** ou **bus**○ rater le coche.
■ **miss out**: ¶ **~ out** être lésé; ¶ **~ out on** [sth] laisser passer; ¶ **~ out** [sb/sth], **~ [sb/sth] out** sauter [*line, verse*]; omettre [*fact, point, person*].

misshapen /ˌmɪs'ʃeɪpən/ *adj* [*leg*] difforme; [*object*] déformé.

missile /'mɪsaɪl, US 'mɪsl/ **I** *n* MIL missile *m*; GEN (rock, bottle) projectile *m*.
II *noun modifier* [*attack, base, site*] de missiles; **~ launcher** lance-missiles *m inv*.

missing /'mɪsɪŋ/ *adj* **the ~ jewels/child** les bijoux disparus/l'enfant disparu; **there are two books ~** il manque deux livres; **the ~ link** le chaînon manquant; **to be ~** manquer; **the book was ~ from its usual place** le livre n'était pas à sa place habituelle; **to go ~** [*person, object*] disparaître; **to report sb ~** signaler la disparition de qn; **~ presumed dead** porté disparu, présumé mort.

missing in action, MIA *adj* MIL porté disparu.

mission /'mɪʃn/ **I** *n* (all contexts) mission *f*; **our ~ was to do** nous avions pour mission de faire; **to be on a ~** être en mission.
II *noun modifier* [*hospital, school*] géré par une mission.

missionary /'mɪʃnrɪ, US -nerɪ/ ▶1251 *n* RELIG missionnaire *mf*.

misspelling /ˌmɪs'spelɪŋ/ *n* faute *f* d'orthographe.

misspent /ˌmɪs'spent/ *adj* **a ~ youth** une folle jeunesse.

mist /mɪst/ **I** *n* GEN brume *f*; (from breath, on window) buée *f*; (of tears) voile *m*.
II *vtr* vaporiser [*plant*].
IDIOMS **in the ~s of time** dans la nuit des temps.
■ **mist over** [*lens, mirror*] s'embuer; [*landscape*] s'embrumer.
■ **mist up** [*lens, window*] s'embuer.

mistake /mɪ'steɪk/ **I** *n* (error) GEN erreur *f*; (in spelling, typing) faute *f*; **to make a stupid ~** faire une bêtise; **to make a ~ about sb/sth** se tromper sur le compte de qn/sur qch; **it was a ~ to leave my umbrella at home** j'ai eu tort de laisser mon parapluie à la maison; **by ~** par erreur; **she took my keys in ~ for hers** elle a pris mes clés au lieu des siennes; **we all make ~s** des erreurs, on en fait tous; **there is no ~** il n'y a pas d'erreur possible; **you'll be punished, make no ~ about it** ou **that!** tu seras puni, fais-moi confiance!; **there must be some ~** il doit y avoir erreur; **my ~!** mea culpa!; **...and no ~** ...il n'y a pas de doute; **to learn by one's ~s** tirer la leçon de ses erreurs.
II *vtr* (*prét* **-took**, *pp* **-taken**) **1** (confuse) **to ~ sth for sth else** prendre qch pour qch d'autre; **to ~ sb for sb else** confondre qn avec qn d'autre; **there's no mistaking that voice** il est impossible de ne pas reconnaître cette voix; **2** (misinterpret) mal interpréter [*meaning*].

mistaken /mɪ'steɪkən/ **I** *pp* ▶ **mistake**.
II *adj* **1 to be ~** avoir tort; **he was ~ in thinking it was over** il avait tort de croire que c'était fini; **unless I'm very much ~** si je ne me trompe; **to do sth in the ~ belief that** faire qch croyant à tort que;

it's a case of ~ identity JUR il y a erreur sur la personne; **2** [*enthusiasm, generosity*] mal placé.

mistakenly /mɪˈsteɪkənlɪ/ *adv* à tort.

mister /ˈmɪstə(r)/ *n*: *forme complète de* **Mr**, *assez rare*.

mistletoe /ˈmɪsltəʊ/ *n* gui *m*.

mistook /mɪˈstʊk/ *prét* ▶ **mistake**.

mistranslate /ˌmɪstrænsˈleɪt/ *vtr* mal traduire.

mistranslation /ˌmɪstrænsˈleɪʃn/ *n* erreur *f* de traduction.

mistreat /ˌmɪsˈtriːt/ *vtr* maltraiter.

mistreatment /ˌmɪsˈtriːtmənt/ *n* mauvais traitement *m*.

mistress /ˈmɪstrɪs/ *n* **1** maîtresse *f*; **2**† GB (teacher) professeur *m*.

mistrust /ˌmɪsˈtrʌst/ **I** *n* méfiance *f* (**of, towards** à l'égard de).
II *vtr* se méfier de.

misty /ˈmɪstɪ/ *adj* [*conditions, morning*] brumeux/-euse; [*hills, view*] embrumé; [*lens, window*] embué; [*photo*] flou.

misty-eyed /ˈmɪstɪˌaɪd/ *adj* [*look*] tendre; **he goes all ~ about it** il est tout ému quand il en parle.

misunderstand /ˌmɪsʌndəˈstænd/ **I** *vtr* (*prét, pp* **-stood**) mal comprendre; (completely) ne pas comprendre; **don't ~ me** (to clarify oneself) comprends-moi bien.
II misunderstood *pp adj* **to feel misunderstood** se sentir incompris; **much misunderstood** souvent mal compris.

misunderstanding /ˌmɪsʌndəˈstændɪŋ/ *n* malentendu *m*.

misuse I /ˌmɪsˈjuːs/ *n* (of equipment) mauvais usage *m*; (of word) usage *m* impropre; (of talents) mauvais emploi *m*; **~ of funds** détournement *m* de fonds.
II /ˌmɪsˈjuːz/ *vtr* faire mauvais usage de [*equipment*]; mal employer [*word, resources*]; abuser de [*authority*].

mite /maɪt/ *n* **1** (child) **poor little ~!** pauvre petit!; **2** (animal) acarien *m*.

miter *n* US = **mitre**.

mitigate /ˈmɪtɪgeɪt/ *vtr* atténuer [*effects, distress, sentence*]; réduire [*risks*]; minimiser [*loss*]; **mitigating circumstances ou factors** JUR circonstances *fpl* atténuantes.

mitre GB, **miter** US /ˈmaɪtə(r)/ *n* (of bishop) mitre *f*.

mitt /mɪt/ *n* **1** (mitten) moufle *f*; **2**○ (hand) main *f*; **3** SPORT gant *m* de baseball.

mitten /ˈmɪtn/ *n* moufle *f*.

mix /mɪks/ **I** *n* **1** GEN, CULIN mélange *m*; **a cake ~** une préparation pour gâteau; **2** MUS mixage *m*, mix *m*.
II *vtr* **1** (combine) mélanger [*colours, ingredients*] (**with** avec; **and** à); combiner [*styles, methods, systems*] (**with** avec; **and** à); **to ~ sth into** (add to) incorporer qch à; **to ~ and match** assortir; **2** (make) préparer [*drink*]; malaxer [*cement, paste*]; **3** MUS mixer.
III *vi* **1** (combine) (also **~ together**) se mélanger (**with** avec, à); **2** (socialize) être sociable; **to ~ with** fréquenter.
■ **mix in**: **~** [sth] **in**, **~ in** [sth] incorporer [*ingredient, substance*] (**with** à).
■ **mix up**: **~** [sth] **up**, **~up** [sth] **1** (confuse) confondre; **to get two things ~ed up** confondre deux choses; **2** (jumble up) mélanger, mêler [*papers, photos*]; **3** (involve) **to ~ sb up in** impliquer qn dans; **to get ~ed up in** se trouver mêlé à.

mixed /mɪkst/ *adj* **1** (varied) [*collection, programme, diet*] varié; [*nuts, sweets*] assorti; [*salad*] composé; [*group, community*] (socially, in age) mélangé; (racially) d'origines diverses; **of ~ blood** de sang mêlé; **2** (for both sexes) [*school, team, sauna*] mixte; **in ~ company** en présence d'hommes et de femmes; **3** (contrasting) [*reaction, feelings, reception*] mitigé.

mixed: **~ ability** *adj* SCH [*class, teaching*] sans groupes de niveau; **~ bag** *n* FIG mélange *m*.

mixed blessing *n* **to be a ~** avoir ses avantages et ses inconvénients.

mixed: **~ doubles** *n* double *m* mixte; **~ economy** *n* économie *f* mixte; **~ grill** *n* assortiment *m* de grillades; **~ marriage** *n* mariage *m* mixte; **~ media** *adj* multimédia; **~ metaphor** *n* métaphore *f* incohérente.

mixed race *n* race *f* mêlée; **of ~** métis/-isse.

mixed: **~-up**○ *adj* [*person*] perturbé; [*emotions*] confus; **~ vegetables** *npl* macédoine *f* de légumes.

mixer /ˈmɪksə(r)/ *n* **1** CULIN (electric) batteur *m* électrique; **2** (drink) boisson *f* nonalcoolisée (*à ajouter à une boisson alcoolisée*); **3** (for cement) bétonnière *f*; **4** MUS (engineer) ingénieur *m* du son; (device) mélangeur *m* de son; **5** (sociable person) **to be a good/bad ~** être très/peu sociable.

mixing /ˈmɪksɪŋ/ *n* **1** (combining) (of people, objects, ingredients) mélange *m*; (of cement) malaxage *m*; **2** MUS mixage *m*.

mixing: **~ bowl** *n* bol *m* à mixer, saladier *m*; **~ desk** *n* MUS console *f* de mixage.

mixture /ˈmɪkstʃə(r)/ *n* mélange *m* (**of** de).

mix-up /ˈmɪksʌp/ *n* confusion *f* (**over** sur).

mm (*abrév écrite* = **millimetre(s)**) mm.

MN US POST *abrév écrite* = **Minnesota**.

MO 1 MIL *abrév* ▶ **Medical Officer**; **2** US POST *abrév écrite* = **Missouri**; **3** *abrév* ▶ **money order**.

moan /məʊn/ **I** *n* **1** (of person, wind) gémissement *m*; **2**○ (complaint) plainte *f* (**about** au sujet de).
II *vi* **1** (wail) gémir (**with** de); **2**○ (complain) râler○ (**about** contre).

moat /məʊt/ *n* douve *f*.

mob /mɒb/ **I** *n* **1** (crowd) foule *f* (**of** de); (gang) gang *m*; **the Mob** la Mafia; **2**○ (group) clique○ *f* ALSO PEJ; **and all that ~** et toute la clique○; **3** (masses) PÉJ **the ~** la populace *f*.
II *noun modifier* **1** (Mafia) [*boss, leader*] de la Mafia; **2** [*violence, hysteria*] de la foule.
III *vtr* (*p prés etc* **-bb-**) assaillir [*person*]; envahir [*place*].

mobile /ˈməʊbaɪl, US -bl, *also* -biːl/ **I** *n* GEN, ART mobile *m*.
II *adj* **1** (moveable) GEN mobile; [*canteen, classroom*] ambulant; [*communications, phone*] sans fil; **2** (expressive) [*features*] mobile; **3 to be ~** (able to walk) pouvoir marcher; (able to travel) pouvoir se déplacer.

mobile: **~ library** *n* GB bibliobus *m*; **~ shop** *n* commerce *m* ambulant.

mobility /məʊˈbɪlətɪ/ *n* (ability to move) mobilité *f*; (agility) agilité *f*; **social ~** mobilité *f*.

mobility allowance *n* GB *allocation de transport pour personnes à mobilité réduite*.

mobilization /ˌməʊbɪlaɪˈzeɪʃn, US -lɪˈz-/ *n* GEN, MIL mobilisation *f*.

mobilize /ˈməʊbɪlaɪz/ *vtr, vi* GEN, MIL mobiliser (**against** contre); **to ~ the support of sb** essayer de trouver le soutien auprès de qn.

mocha /ˈmɒkə, US ˈməʊkə/ *n* **1** (coffee) moka *m*; **2** (flavour) arôme *m* de café et de chocolat.

mock /mɒk/ **I** *n* GB SCH examen *m* blanc.
II *adj* (before *n*) **1** (imitation) [*suede, ivory*] faux/fausse; **~ leather** similicuir *m*; **2** (feigned) simulé; **in ~ terror** en feignant la terreur.
III *vtr* se moquer de.
IV *vi* se moquer.

mockery /ˈmɒkərɪ/ *n* **1** (ridicule) moquerie *f*; **to make a ~ of** tourner [qn/qch] en dérision [*person, process, report, work*]; bafouer [*law, rule*]; **2** (travesty) parodie *f*.

mock-heroic /ˌmɒkhɪˈrəʊɪk/ *adj* héroï-comique.

mocking /ˈmɒkɪŋ/ **I** *n* ₵ moqueries *fpl*.
II *adj* moqueur/-euse.

mock: **~ orange** *n* BOT seringa *m*; **~-up** *n* maquette *f*.

MoD *n* GB (*abrév* = **Ministry of Defence**) ministère *m* de la Défense.

mod con /ˌmɒd ˈkɒn/ *n* GB (*abrév* = **modern convenience**) confort *m* (moderne); **'all ~s'** (in advert) 'tout confort'.

mode /məʊd/ *n* **1** (style) mode *m*; ~ **of dress** tenue *f*; ~ **of expression** façon *f* de s'exprimer; ~ **of leadership** façon *f* de diriger; **2** (method) ~ **of funding** type *m* de financement; ~ **of production** méthode *f* de production; ~ **of transport** moyen *m* de transport; **3** (state) (of equipment) mode *m*; (of person) humeur *f*.

model /'mɒdl/ **I** *n* **1** (scale representation) maquette *f* (**of** de); **2** (version of car, appliance, garment) modèle *m*; **computer** ~ modèle informatique; **3** (person) (for artist) modèle *m*; (showing clothes) mannequin *m*; **4** (example, thing to be copied) modèle *m* (**of** de).
II *adj* **1** [*railway, soldier, village*] miniature; [*aeroplane, boat, car*] modèle réduit; **2** (pilot) [*hospital, prison*] modèle; **3** (perfect) [*husband, student*] modèle.
III *vtr* (*p prés etc* **-ll-, -l-** US) **1** to ~ **sth on sth** modeler qch sur qch; **2** présenter [*garment, design*]; **3** modeler [*clay, figure*] (**in** en).
IV *vi* (*p prés etc* **-ll-, -l-** US) **1** [*artist's model*] poser; **2** [*fashion model*] travailler comme mannequin; **3** [*sculptor, artist*] **to ~ in** modeler en [*clay, wax*].
V modelled, modeled US *pp adj* **1** [*clothes*] présenté (**by** par); **2** ~**led on sth** modelé sur qch.
VI *v refl* **to ~ oneself on sb** se modeler sur qn.

modelling, modeling US /'mɒdəlɪŋ/ *n* **1** (of clothes) **to take up ~** devenir mannequin; **have you done any ~?** as-tu déjà travaillé comme mannequin?; **2** (for artist) **to do some ~** poser comme modèle; **3** (with clay etc) modelage *m*; **4** COMPUT modélisation *f*.

modelling clay *n* pâte *f* à modeler.

moderate I /'mɒdərət/ *adj* **1** (not extreme) ALSO POL modéré (**in** dans); **2** (of average extent) moyen/-enne.
II /'mɒdəreɪt/ *vtr* GEN, POL modérer.
III /'mɒdəreɪt/ *vi* se modérer; [*wind, storm*] s'apaiser; [*rain*] se calmer.

moderate: ~ **breeze** *n* jolie brise *f*; ~ **gale** *n* grand frais *m*.

moderately /'mɒdərətlɪ/ *adv* **1** (averagely) moyennement, assez; ~ **priced** de milieu de gamme; ~ **sized** de taille moyenne; **2** (restrainedly) avec modération.

moderating /'mɒdəreɪtɪŋ/ *adj* [*influence, role*] modérateur/-trice.

moderation /,mɒdə'reɪʃn/ *n* modération *f* (**in** dans); **in ~** avec modération.

modern /'mɒdn/ **I** *n* moderne *mf*.
II *adj* GEN moderne; **all ~ conveniences** tout confort (moderne); [*world*] contemporain; ~ **China** la Chine d'aujourd'hui.

modern-day *adj* des temps modernes.

modernism /'mɒdənɪzəm/ *n* (also **Modernism**) modernisme *m*.

modernity /mɒ'dɜːnətɪ/ *n* modernité *f*.

modernization /,mɒdɜːnaɪ'zeɪʃn, US -nɪ'z-/ *n* modernisation *f*.

modernize /'mɒdənaɪz/ **I** *vtr* moderniser.
II *vi* se moderniser.

modern language I modern languages *npl* langues *fpl* vivantes.
II *noun modifier* (also ~**s**) [*student*] en langues vivantes; [*lecturer, teacher*] de langues vivantes.

modest /'mɒdɪst/ *adj* **1** (unassuming) modeste (**about** au sujet de); **he's just being ~!** il fait le modeste!; **2** (moderate) [*gift, aim*] modeste; [*sum, salary*] modique; **3** (demure) [*dress*] décent; [*person*] pudique.

modestly /'mɒdɪstlɪ/ *adv* (unassumingly) avec modestie; (demurely) décemment; (moderately) **he has been ~ successful** il a remporté un succès modeste.

modesty /'mɒdɪstɪ/ *n* **1** (humility) modestie *f*; **2** (demureness) (of person) pudeur *f*; (of dress) décence *f*; **3** (smallness) modicité *f*.

modicum /'mɒdɪkəm/ *n* minimum *m* (**of** de).

modification /,mɒdɪfɪ'keɪʃn/ *n* modification *f*; **we accept it without further ~s** nous l'acceptons tel quel.

modifier /'mɒdɪfaɪə(r)/ *n* LING modificateur *m*.

modify /'mɒdɪfaɪ/ *vtr* **1** (alter) GEN, LING modifier; **2** (moderate) modérer [*demand, statement, policy*]; atténuer [*punishment*] (**to** en).

modular /'mɒdjʊlə(r), US -dʒʊ-/ *adj* (all contexts) modulaire.

modulation /,mɒdjʊ'leɪʃn, US -dʒʊ-/ *n* (all contexts) modulation *f*.

module /'mɒdjuːl, US -dʒʊ-/ *n* (all contexts) module *m*.

modus operandi /,məʊdəs ,ɒpə'rændi/ *n* manière *f* de procéder.

mogul /'məʊgl/ *n* **1** (magnate) magnat *m*; **2** (in skiing) bosse *f*.

Mohammed /məʊ'hæmed/ *pr n* Mahomet.

Mohammedan /məʊ'hæmɪdən/ **I** *n* Mahométan/-e *m/f*.
II *adj* mahométan.

Mohammedanism /məʊ'hæmɪdənɪzəm/ *n* mahométisme *m*.

mohican /məʊ'hiːkən/ *n* **1** (hairstyle) iroquois *m*; **2** ▶ **1100** | **Mohican** (person) Mohican *m*.

moist /mɔɪst/ *adj* [*soil*] humide; [*cake*] moelleux/-euse; [*hands*] (with sweat) moite; [*skin*] bien hydraté.

moisten /'mɔɪsn/ *vtr* GEN humecter; CULIN mouiller légèrement.

moisture /'mɔɪstʃə(r)/ *n* (of soil, in walls) humidité *f*; (on glass) buée *f*; (in skin) hydratation *f*; (sweat) moiteur *f*.

moisturize /'mɔɪstʃəraɪz/ **I** *vtr* hydrater [*skin*].
II moisturizing *pres p adj* hydratant.

moisturizer /'mɔɪstʃəraɪzə(r)/ *n* (lotion) lait *m* hydratant; (cream) crème *f* hydratante.

molar /'məʊlə(r)/ *n, adj* molaire (*f*).

molasses /mə'læsɪz/ *n* (+ *v sg*) mélasse *f*.

mold *n, vtr* US ▶ **mould**.

mole /məʊl/ *n* **1** ZOOL taupe *f*; **2** (spy) taupe *f*; **3** (on skin) grain *m* de beauté; **4** (breakwater) môle *m*.

molecular /mə'lekjʊlə(r)/ *adj* moléculaire.

molecule /'mɒlɪkjuːl/ *n* molécule *f*.

molehill /'məʊlhɪl/ *n* taupinière *f*.
IDIOMS **to make a mountain out of a ~** faire une montagne d'une taupinière.

moleskin /'məʊlskɪn/ *n* (fur) (peau *f* de) taupe *f*; (cotton) moleskine *f*.

molest /mə'lest/ *vtr* (sexually assault) agresser [qn] sexuellement.

molester *n* ▶ **child molester**.

mollify /'mɒlɪfaɪ/ *vtr* apaiser, calmer.

mollusc, mollusk US /'mɒləsk/ *n* mollusque *m*.

mollycoddle /'mɒlɪkɒdl/ *vtr* dorloter.

molt *n, vi* US = **moult**.

molten /'məʊltən/ *adj* (*épith*) en fusion.

moment /'məʊmənt/ *n* **1** (instant) instant *m*; **it will only take you a ~** tu en as pour un instant; **just for a ~ I thought you were Paul** l'espace d'un instant j'ai cru que tu étais Paul; **at any ~** à tout instant; **I don't believe that for one ~** je ne le crois pas du tout; **and not a ~ too soon!** il était temps!; **the car hasn't given me a ~'s trouble** la voiture ne m'a pas créé le moindre ennui; **2** (point in time) moment *m*; **at the right ~** au bon moment; **to choose one's ~** choisir le bon moment; **phone me the ~ (that) he arrives** appelle-moi dès qu'il arrivera; **at this ~ in time** à l'heure actuelle; **I've only this ~ arrived** je viens tout juste d'arriver; **at this ~ in time** à l'heure actuelle; **3** (good patch) **the film had its ~s** le film avait ses bons moments; **he has his ~s** il a ses bons côtés; **4** (importance) LITTER importance *f*.

momentarily /'məʊməntrəlɪ, US ,məʊmən'terəlɪ/ *adv* **1** (for an instant) momentanément; **2** US (very soon) dans un instant; (at any moment) d'un moment à l'autre.

momentary /'məʊməntrɪ, US -terɪ/ *adj* **1** (temporary) momentané; **a ~ silence** un moment de silence; **2** (fleeting) GEN passager/-ère; [*glimpse*] rapide.

momentous /mə'mentəs, məʊ'm-/ *adj* capital.

momentum /mə'mentəm, məʊ'm-/ *n* LIT, FIG élan *m*; PHYS vitesse *f*.

Mon *abrév écrite* = **Monday**.

Mona Lisa /,məʊnə 'liːzə/ *pr n* **the ~** la Joconde.

monarch /'mɒnək/ *n* monarque *m*.

monarchy /'mɒnəkɪ/ *n* monarchie *f*.

monastery /'mɒnəstrɪ, US -terɪ/ n monastère m.

monastic /mə'næstɪk/ adj **1** RELIG monastique; **2** (ascetic) monacal.

Monday /'mʌndeɪ, -dɪ/ ▶1390 n lundi m.

monetarism /'mʌnɪtərɪzəm/ n monétarisme m.

monetary /'mʌnɪtrɪ, US -terɪ/ adj monétaire.

money /'mʌnɪ/ I n argent m; **to make ~** (person) gagner de l'argent; (business, project) rapporter de l'argent; **to get one's ~ back** (in shop) être remboursé; (after loan, resale) rentrer dans ses frais; (after risky venture, with difficulty) récupérer son argent; **there's no ~ in it** ça ne rapporte pas; **to raise ~** GEN trouver des capitaux; (for charity) collecter des fonds; **to pay good ~** payer en bel et bon argent; **to earn good ~** bien gagner sa vie; **to make one's ~ in business** faire (sa) fortune dans les affaires; **there's a lot of ~ (to be made) in computing** l'informatique, ça peut rapporter.
II **monies, moneys** npl (funds) fonds mpl; (sums) sommes fpl.
III noun modifier [matters, problems, worries] d'argent.
IDIOMS **not for love nor ~** pour rien au monde; **for my ~...** à mon avis...; **it's ~ for jam, it's ~ for old rope** c'est de l'argent facile; **~ talks** avec l'argent on obtient ce qu'on veut; **to be in the ~** être en fonds; **to be made of ~** être cousu d'or; **to get one's ~'s worth, to get a good run for one's ~** en avoir pour son argent; **to have ~ to burn** avoir de l'argent à ne savoir qu'en faire; **to put one's ~ where one's mouth is** sortir son portefeuille; **to throw good ~ after bad** investir en pure perte; **your ~ or your life!** la bourse ou la vie!

money: **~ belt** n ceinture f porte-monnaie; **~box** n tirelire f; **~-grubbing** adj PÉJ rapace FIG; **~lender** ▶1251 n prêteur/-euse m/f; **~maker** n (product) article m qui rapporte beaucoup; (activity) activité f lucrative; **~making** adj [scheme] pour faire fortune; **~man** n financier m; **~ market** n marché m monétaire; **~ order, MO** n mandat m postal; **~ rate** n taux m du loyer de l'argent; **~ spinner** n GB mine f d'or FIG; **~ supply** n masse f monétaire.

mongrel /'mʌŋgrl/ n (chien m) bâtard m.

monitor /'mɒnɪtə(r)/ I n **1** GEN, TECH dispositif m de surveillance; (security TV) écran m de contrôle; **2** MED, AUDIO, COMPUT moniteur m; **~ program** moniteur m; **3** RADIO permanencier m.
II vtr GEN, TECH, MED surveiller; SCH suivre [student, progress]; RADIO être à l'écoute de.

monitoring /'mɒnɪtərɪŋ/ I n **1** TECH, MED (by person) surveillance f; (by device) monitoring m; **careful ~ for problems** contrôle m systématique des problèmes éventuels; **2** GB SCH suivi m; **3** RADIO service m d'écoute.
II noun modifier [device, equipment] de surveillance.

monk /mʌŋk/ n moine m.

monkey /'mʌŋkɪ/ n **1** ZOOL singe m; **2**° (rascal) galopin° m.
IDIOMS **I don't give a ~'s about it**° je m'en fous complètement°; **to make a ~ out of sb**° se payer la tête de qn°.

monkey: **~ business**° n Œ (fooling) bêtises fpl; (cheating) grenouillage° m; **~ nut**° n GB cacahuète f; **~ tricks** npl = **monkey business**; **~ wrench** n clé f à molette.

monkfish /'mʌŋkfɪʃ/ n (pl ~) lotte f.

mono /'mɒnəʊ/ I n AUDIO monophonie f; **in ~** en mono.
II adj AUDIO mono inv.
III **mono+** combining form mono-.

monochrome /'mɒnəkrəʊm/ I n **1** (technique) **in ~** ART, PHOT en monochrome; CIN, TV en noir et blanc; **2** (print) monochrome m.
II adj **1** CIN, TV [film] en noir et blanc; ART, COMPUT, PHOT monochrome; **2** FIG (dull) monotone.

monogamy /mə'nɒgəmɪ/ n monogamie f.

monogram /'mɒnəgræm/ n monogramme m.

monograph /'mɒnəgrɑːf, US -græf/ n monographie f.

monolith /'mɒnəlɪθ/ n monolithe m.

monologue, monolog US /'mɒnəlɒg/ n monologue m.

monomania /ˌmɒnə'meɪnɪə/ n monomanie f.

monoplane /'mɒnəpleɪn/ n monoplan m.

monopolize /mə'nɒpəlaɪz/ vtr ECON détenir le monopole de; FIG monopoliser.

monopoly /mə'nɒpəlɪ/ n ECON, FIG monopole m.

monoski /'mɒnəski:/ I n monoski m.
II vi faire du monoski.

monosodium glutamate /ˌmɒnəʊˌsəʊdɪəm 'gluːtəmeɪt/ n glutamate m (de sodium).

monosyllable /'mɒnəsɪləbl/ n monosyllabe m.

monotonous /mə'nɒtənəs/ adj monotone.

monotony /mə'nɒtənɪ/ n monotonie f.

monsoon /mɒn'suːn/ n mousson f.

monster /'mɒnstə(r)/ I n LIT, FIG monstre m; **sea ~** monstre marin.
II noun modifier géant.

monstrosity /mɒn'strɒsɪtɪ/ n (eyesore) horreur f; (of act) monstruosité f.

monstrous /'mɒnstrəs/ adj **1** (odious) GEN monstrueux/-euse; [building] hideux/-euse; **it is ~ that** il est scandaleux que (+ subj); **2** (huge) énorme.

montage /mɒn'tɑːʒ/ n ART, CIN montage m; PHOT photomontage m.

month /mʌnθ/ ▶1090, ▶1336 n mois m; **in two ~s, in two ~s' time** dans deux mois; **the ~ before last** pas le mois dernier, celui d'avant; **the ~ after next** pas le mois prochain, celui d'après; **every other ~** tous les deux mois; **in the ~ of June** au mois de juin; **at the end of the ~** à la fin du mois; ADMIN, COMM fin courant; **what day of the ~ is today?** nous le combien aujourd'hui?; **a ~'s rent** un mois de loyer; **six ~s' pay** six mois de salaire; **your salary for the ~ beginning May 15** votre salaire du 15 mai au 15 juin.
IDIOMS **it's her time of the ~** EUPH elle est indisposée.

monthly /'mʌnθlɪ/ I n (journal) mensuel m.
II adj mensuel/-elle; **~ instalment** mensualité f.
III adv [pay, earn] au mois; [happen, visit, publish] tous les mois.

monument /'mɒnjʊmənt/ n LIT, FIG monument m; **the building is a ~ to his art** le bâtiment témoigne de son art.

monumental /ˌmɒnjʊ'mentl/ adj (all contexts) monumental.

monumentally /ˌmɒnjʊ'mentəlɪ/ adv [boring] mortellement; **~ ignorant** d'une ignorance monumentale.

moo /muː/ vi meugler.

mooch /muːtʃ/ I n US tapeur/-euse° m/f.
II vtr US (cadge) **to ~ sth from** ou **off sb** taper° qch à qn.
III vi GB **to ~ along** ou **about** traîner.

mood /muːd/ n **1** (frame of mind) humeur f; **in a good/bad ~** de bonne/mauvaise humeur; **to be in the ~ for doing** ou **to do** avoir envie de faire; **to be in a relaxed ~** être détendu; **when he's in the ~** quand l'envie l'en prend; **when** ou **as the ~ takes him** selon son humeur; **I'm not in the ~ for joking** ou jokes je ne suis pas d'humeur à plaisanter; **'are you coming to the beach?'—'no, I'm not in the ~'** 'tu viens à la plage?'—'non, ça ne me dit rien'; **2** (bad temper) saute f d'humeur; **to be in a ~** être de mauvaise humeur; **3** (atmosphere) (in room, meeting) ambiance f; (of place, era, artwork) atmosphère f; (of group, party) état m d'esprit; **the general ~ was one of despair** le sentiment général était au désespoir; **4** LING mode m; **in the subjunctive ~** au subjonctif.

moodily /'muːdɪlɪ/ adv [say] d'un ton maussade; [look, sit, stare] d'un air morose.

moody /'muːdɪ/ adj **1** (unpredictable) d'humeur changeante, lunatique; **2** (sulky) de mauvaise humeur.

moon /muːn/ I n GEN lune f; **the ~** (of the earth) la

The months of the year

Don't use capitals for the names of the months in French, and note that there are no common abbreviations in French as there are in English (Jan, Feb and so on). The French only abbreviate in printed calendars etc.

January	= janvier	July	= juillet
February	= février	August	= août
March	= mars	September	= septembre
April	= avril	October	= octobre
May	= mai	November	= novembre
June	= juin	December	= décembre

Which month?

(*May in this note stands for any month; they all work the same way; for more information on dates in French* ▶ 854 |.)

what month is it?	= quel mois sommes-nous? *or* (*very informally*) on est quel mois?
it was May	= nous étions en mai
what month was he born?	= de quel mois est-il?

When?

in May	= en mai *or* au mois de mai
they're getting married this May	= ils se marient en mai
that May	= cette année-là en mai
next May	= en mai prochain
in May next year	= l'an prochain en mai
last May	= l'année dernière en mai
the May after next	= dans deux ans en mai
the May before last	= il y a deux ans en mai

which part of the month?

at the beginning of May	= au début de mai
in early May	= début mai
at the end of May	= à la fin de mai
in late May	= fin mai
in mid-May	= à la mi-mai
for the whole of May	= pendant tout le mois de mai
throughout May	= tout au long du mois de mai

Regular events

every May	= tous les ans en mai
every other May	= tous les deux ans en mai
most Mays	= presque tous les ans en mai

Uses with other nouns

one May morning	= par un matin de mai
one May night	= par une nuit de mai *or* (*if evening*) par un soir de mai

For other uses, it is always safe to use du mois de:

May classes	= les cours du mois de mai
May flights	= les vols du mois de mai
the May sales	= les soldes du mois de mai

Uses with adjectives

the warmest May	= le mois de mai le plus chaud
a rainy May	= un mois de mai pluvieux
a lovely May	= un beau mois de mai

Lune; **there will be a ~ tonight** il y aura clair de lune cette nuit.
II *vi* (daydream) rêvasser (**over sth/sb** à qch/qn).
IDIOMS **to be over the ~** être aux anges; **once in a blue ~** tous les trente-six du mois°; **the man in the ~** le visage de la Lune.
■ **moon about**°, **moon around**° musarder.

moon: ~beam *n* rayon *m* de lune; **~ buggy** *n* jeep *f* lunaire; **~-faced** *adj* aux joues rondes.

moonlight /'muːnlaɪt/ **I** *n* clair *m* de lune.
II *vi* travailler au noir.
IDIOMS **to do a ~ flit**° GB filer de nuit sans payer.

moonlit /'muːnlɪt/ *adj* [*sky, evening*] éclairé par la lune; **a ~ night** une nuit de lune.

moonshine /'muːnʃaɪn/ *n* **1** (nonsense) fadaises° *fpl*; **2** US (liquor) alcool *m* de contrebande.

moor /mɔː(r), US mʊər/ **I** *n* lande *f*; **on the ~s** sur la lande.
II *vtr* NAUT amarrer.
III *vi* NAUT mouiller.

moorhen /'mɔːhen, US 'mʊər-/ *n* GB poule *f* d'eau.

mooring /'mɔːrɪŋ, US 'mʊər-/ **I** *n* mouillage *m*; **a boat at its ~s** un bateau amarré.
II moorings *npl* amarres *fpl*.

Moorish /'mʊərɪʃ/ *adj* mauresque.

moorland /'mɔːlənd, US 'mʊər-/ *n* lande *f*.

moose /muːs/ *n* (*pl* ~) (Canadian) orignal *m*; (European) élan *m*.

moot point *n* **that is a ~** c'est difficile à dire.

mop /mɒp/ **I** *n* **1** (for floors) (of cotton) balai *m* à franges; (of sponge) balai *m* éponge; (for dishes) lavette *f*; **2** (hair) crinière° *f*.
II *vtr* (*p prés etc* **-pp-**) **1** (wash) laver [qch] à grande eau; **2** (wipe) **to ~ one's face/brow** s'éponger le visage/le front.
■ **mop down: ~** [*sth*] **down, ~ down** [*sth*] laver [qch] à grande eau [*floor, deck*].
■ **mop up:** ¶ **~ up** éponger; ¶ **~ up** [*sth*], **~** [*sth*] **up 1** LIT éponger; **2** FIG balayer [*resistance, rebels*]; engloutir [*savings, profits, surplus*].

mope /məʊp/ *vi* (brood) se morfondre.
■ **mope about**, **mope around** traîner (comme une âme en peine).

moped /'məʊped/ *n* vélomoteur *m*.

moral /'mɒrəl, US 'mɔːrəl/ **I** *n* morale *f*; **to draw a ~ from sth** tirer une leçon de qch.
II morals *npl* **1** (habits) mœurs *fpl*; **2** (morality) moralité *f*; **to have no ~s** être sans moralité.
III *adj* (all contexts) moral; **to take the ~ high ground** prendre une position moraliste.

morale /mə'rɑːl, US -'ræl/ *n* moral *m*.

morale-booster *n* **his comment was a ~** sa remarque m'a/leur a etc remonté le moral.

moral fibre GB, **moral fiber** US /,mɒrəl 'faɪbə(r), US ,mɔːr-/ *n* force *f* morale.

moralist /'mɒrəlɪst, US 'mɔːrəlɪst/ *n* moraliste *mf*.

moralistic /,mɒrə'lɪstɪk, US ,mɔːr-/ *adj* moralisateur/-trice.

morality /mə'rælətɪ/ *n* moralité *f*.

moralize /'mɒrəlaɪz, US 'mɔːr-/ *vi* moraliser.

morally /'mɒrəlɪ, US 'mɔːr-/ *adv* moralement; **~ wrong** contraire à la morale.

moral: ~ majority *n* majorité *f* bien-pensante; **~ philosopher** *n* PHILOS moraliste *mf*; **~ philosophy** *n* morale *f*.

morass /mə'ræs/ *n* LIT, FIG bourbier *m*.

moratorium /,mɒrə'tɔːrɪəm/ *n* (*pl* **-toria**) moratoire *m* (**on** sur).

morbid /'mɔːbɪd/ *adj* (all contexts) morbide.

morbidly /'mɔːbɪdlɪ/ *adv* de façon malsaine.

more /mɔː(r)/

■ **Note** When used to modify an adjective or an adverb to form the comparative *more* is very often translated by *plus*: *more expensive* = plus cher/chère; *more beautiful* = plus beau/belle; *more easily* = plus facilement; *more regularly* = plus régulièrement. For examples and further uses see I1 below.
– When used as a quantifier to indicate a greater amount or quantity of something *more* is very often translated by *plus de*: *more money/cars/people* = plus d'argent/de voitures/de gens. For examples and further uses see II1 below.

I *adv* **1** (comparative) **it's ~ serious than we thought** c'est plus grave que nous ne pensions; **the ~ intelligent (child) of the two** (l'enfant) le plus intelligent des deux; **he's no ~ honest than his sister** il n'est pas plus honnête que sa sœur; **2** (to a greater extent) plus, davantage; **you must work/rest ~** il faut que tu travailles/te reposes davantage; **he sleeps ~ than I do** il dort plus que moi; **the ~ you think about it, the harder it will seem** plus tu y penseras, plus ça te paraîtra dur; **he is (all) the ~ angry**

because il est d'autant plus en colère que; **3** (longer) **I don't work there any ~** je n'y travaille plus; **4** (again) **once ~** une fois de plus; **5** (rather) **~ surprised than angry** plus étonné que fâché.

II *quantif* **~ cars than people** plus de voitures que de gens; **~ cars than expected** plus de voitures que prévu; **some ~ books** quelques livres de plus; **a little/lot ~ wine** un peu/beaucoup plus de vin; **~ bread** encore un peu de pain; **there's no ~ bread** il n'y a plus de pain; **have some ~ beer!** reprenez de la bière; **have you any ~ questions?** avez-vous d'autres questions?; **nothing ~** rien de plus; **something ~** autre chose.

III *pron* **1** (larger amount or number) plus; **it costs ~ than the other one** il/elle coûte plus cher que l'autre; **he eats ~ than you** il mange plus que toi; **the children take up ~ of my time** les enfants prennent une plus grande partie de mon temps; **many were disappointed, ~ were angry** beaucoup de gens ont été déçus, un plus grand nombre étaient fâchés; **we'd like to see ~ of you** nous voudrions te voir plus souvent; **2** (additional amount) davantage; (additional number) plus; **I need ~ of them** il m'en faut plus; **I need ~ of it** il m'en faut davantage; **several/a few ~ (of them)** plusieurs/quelques autres; **I can't tell you any ~** je ne peux pas t'en dire plus; **I have nothing ~ to say** je n'ai rien à ajouter; **in Mexico, of which ~ later...** au Mexique, dont nous reparlerons plus tard...; **let's** ou **we'll say no ~ about it** n'en parlons plus.

IV more and more *det phr, adv phr* de plus en plus; **~ and ~ work** de plus en plus de travail; **to sleep ~ and ~** dormir de plus en plus; **~ and ~ regularly** de plus en plus régulièrement.

V more or less *adv phr* plus ou moins.

VI more so *adv phr* encore plus; **in York, and even ~ so in Oxford** à York et encore plus à Oxford; **he is just as active as her, if not ~ so** ou **or even ~ so** il est aussi actif qu'elle, si ce n'est plus; **they are all disappointed, none ~ so than Mr Lowe** ils sont tous déçus, en particulier M. Lowe; **no ~ so than usual** pas plus que d'habitude.

VII more than *adv phr, prep phr* **1** (greater amount or number) plus de; **~ than 20 people** plus de 20 personnes; **~ than half** plus de la moitié; **~ than enough** plus qu'assez; **2** (extremely) **~ than generous** plus que généreux; **the cheque ~ than covered the cost** le chèque a amplement couvert les frais.

IDIOMS **she's nothing ~ (nor less) than a thief, she's a thief, neither ~ nor less** c'est une voleuse, ni plus ni moins; **he's nothing** ou **no** ou **not much ~ than a servant** ce n'est qu'un serviteur; **and what is ~...** et qui plus est...; **there's ~ where that came from** ce n'est qu'un début.

moreish○ /'mɔːrɪʃ/ *adj* GB **to be ~** avoir un petit goût de revenez-y.

moreover /mɔːˈrəʊvə(r)/ *adv* de plus, qui plus est.

morgue /mɔːg/ *n* morgue *f*.

MORI /ˈmɒrɪ/ *n* (*abrév* = **Market and Opinion Research Institute**) *institut de sondage britannique*.

morning /ˈmɔːnɪŋ/ ▶812 **I** *n* matin *m*; (with emphasis on duration) matinée *f*; **at 3 o'clock in the ~** à 3 heures du matin; **on Monday ~s** le lundi matin; (on) **Monday ~** lundi matin; **later this ~** plus tard dans la matinée; **the previous ~** la veille au matin; **the following ~, the ~ after, the next ~** le lendemain matin; **early** ou **first thing in the ~** (dawn) tôt le matin; **I'll do it first thing in the ~** je le ferai dès demain matin; **to be on ~s** être du matin.

II *noun modifier* du matin; **that early ~ feeling** la torpeur matinale.

III *excl* (also **good ~**) bonjour!

IDIOMS **the ~ after the night before** un lendemain de cuite○.

morning: **~-after pill** *n* pilule *f* du lendemain; **~ coffee** *n* pause-café *f*; **~ dress** *n* habit *m*; **~ sickness** *n* nausées *fpl* du matin.

Moroccan /məˈrɒkən/ ▶1100 **I** *n* Marocain/-e *m/f*.

II *adj* marocain.

morocco (leather) /məˈrɒkəʊ/ **I** *n* maroquin *m*.

II *noun modifier* [*binding, shoes*] en maroquin.

Morocco /məˈrɒkəʊ/ ▶840 *pr n* Maroc *m*.

moronic /məˈrɒnɪk/ *adj* débile.

morris dance *n*: *danse folklorique anglaise*.

Morse (code) /mɔːs/ **I** *n* morse *m*; **in ~** en morse.

II *noun modifier* [*signal*] en morse.

morsel /ˈmɔːsl/ *n* (of food) morceau *m*; (of sense, self-respect) once *f*.

mortal /ˈmɔːtl/ **I** *n* mortel/-elle *m/f*.

II *adj* [*enemy, danger, sin*] mortel/-elle; [*injury, blow*] fatal.

mortal combat *n* lutte *f* à mort.

mortality /mɔːˈtælətɪ/ *n* mortalité *f*.

mortally /ˈmɔːtəlɪ/ *adv* (all contexts) mortellement.

mortar /ˈmɔːtə(r)/ *n* mortier *m*.

mortgage /ˈmɔːgɪdʒ/ **I** *n* emprunt-logement *m* (**on** pour); **to raise/take out a ~** obtenir/faire un emprunt-logement.

II *noun modifier* [*agreement, deed*] hypothécaire.

III *vtr* hypothéquer (**for** pour).

mortgage: **~ broker** ▶1251 *n* courtier *m* en prêts hypothécaires; **~ rate** *n* taux *m* de l'emprunt-logement; **~ relief** *n*: *dégrèvement fiscal pour emprunt-logement*; **~ repayment** *n* mensualité *f* de remboursement.

mortician /mɔːˈtɪʃn/ ▶1251 *n* US entrepreneur *m* de pompes funèbres.

mortification /ˌmɔːtɪfɪˈkeɪʃn/ *n* (all contexts) mortification *f*.

mortify /ˈmɔːtɪfaɪ/ **I** *vtr* mortifier.

II mortifying *pres p adj* mortifiant.

mortuary /ˈmɔːtʃərɪ, US ˈmɔːtʃʊerɪ/ **I** *n* morgue *f*.

II *adj* mortuaire.

mosaic /məʊˈzeɪɪk/ **I** *n* LIT, FIG mosaïque *f*.

II *noun modifier* [*floor, pattern*] en mosaïque.

Moscow /ˈmɒskəʊ/ ▶1343 *pr n* Moscou.

Moses /ˈməʊzɪz/ *pr n* Moïse; **Holy ~**○! grand Dieu!

Moslem /ˈmɒzləm/ **I** *n* Musulman/-e *m/f*.

II *adj* musulman.

mosque /mɒsk/ *n* mosquée *f*.

mosquito /məˈskiːtəʊ, mɒs-/ *n* moustique *m*.

mosquito: **~ bite** *n* piqûre *f* de moustique; **~ net** *n* moustiquaire *f*; **~ repellent** *n* antimoustique *m*.

moss /mɒs, US mɔːs/ *n* BOT mousse *f*.

IDIOMS **a rolling stone gathers no ~** PROV pierre qui roule n'amasse pas mousse PROV.

mossy /ˈmɒsɪ, US ˈmɔːsɪ/ *adj* moussu.

most /məʊst/

■ **Note** When used to form the superlative of adjectives *most* is translated by *le plus* or *la plus* depending on the gender of the noun and by *les plus* with plural noun: *the most beautiful woman in the room* = la plus belle femme de la pièce; *the most expensive hotel in Paris* = l'hôtel le plus cher de Paris; *the most difficult problems* = les problèmes les plus difficiles. For examples and further uses see the entry below.

I *det* **1** (the majority of, nearly all) la plupart de; **~ people** la plupart des gens; **2** (superlative: more than all the others) le plus de; **she got the ~ votes/money** c'est elle qui a obtenu le plus de voix/d'argent.

II *pron* **1** (the greatest number) la plupart (**of** de); (the largest part) la plus grande partie (**of** de); **~ of the time** la plupart du temps; **~ of us** la plupart d'entre nous; **~ of the money** la plus grande partie de l'argent; **for ~ of the day** pendant la plus grande partie de la journée; **~ of the bread** presque tout le pain; **~ agreed** la plupart étaient d'accord; **2** (the maximum) **the ~ you can expect is...** tout ce que tu peux espérer c'est...; **the ~ I can do is...** tout ce que je peux faire, c'est..., le mieux que je puisse faire, c'est...; **3** (more than all the others) le plus; **John has got the ~** c'est John qui en a le plus.

III *adv* **1** (used to form superlative) **the ~ beautiful château in France** le plus beau château de France; **~ easily** le plus facilement; **2** (very) très, extrême-

ment; **~ encouraging** très or extrêmement encourageant; **~ probably** très vraisemblablement; **3** (more than all the rest) le plus; **what ~ annoyed him** ou **what annoyed him ~ (of all) was** ce qui l'ennuyait le plus c'était que; **those who will suffer ~** ceux qui souffriront le plus; **4**° US (almost) presque; **~ everyone** presque tout le monde.
IV at (the) most *adv phr* au maximum , au plus.
V for the most part *adv phr* (most of them) pour la plupart; (most of the time) la plupart du temps; (basically) essentiellement, surtout; **for the ~ part, they...** pour la plupart, ils...; **for the ~ part he works in his office** il travaille la plupart du temps, il travaille dans son bureau; **his experience is, for the ~ part, in publishing** son expérience est surtout or essentiellement dans l'édition.
VI most of all *adv phr* par-dessus tout.
IDIOMS **to make the ~ of** tirer le meilleur parti de [*situation, resources, looks, rest, abilities, space*]; profiter de [*holiday, opportunity, good weather*].

mostly /ˈməʊstlɪ/ *adv* **1** (chiefly) surtout, essentiellement; (most of them) pour la plupart; **he composes ~ for the piano** il compose surtout pour le piano; **200 people, ~ Belgians** 200 personnes, des Belges pour la plupart; **2** (most of the time) la plupart du temps; **~ we travelled by train** la plupart du temps, nous avons pris le train.

MOT /ˌeməʊˈtiː/ GB AUT (*abrév* = **Ministry of Transport**) **I** *n* (also **~ test**, **~ inspection**) contrôle *m* technique des véhicules; **to pass the ~** obtenir le certificat de contrôle; **'~ until June'** 'certificat de contrôle valable jusqu'à juin'.
II *noun modifier* [*certificate, centre*] de contrôle technique.
III *vtr* effectuer le contrôle technique de [*car*].

moth /mɒθ, US mɔːθ/ *n* GEN papillon *m* de nuit; (in clothes) mite *f*.

mothball /ˈmɒθbɔːl, US ˈmɔːθ-/ **I** *n* boule *f* de naphtaline; **to put sth in/take sth out of ~s** FIG mettre qch au/sortir qch du placard FIG.
II *vtr* mettre [qch] en sommeil.

moth-eaten /ˈmɒθiːtn, US ˈmɔːθ-/ *adj* (shabby) miteux/-euse; (damaged by moths) mité.

mother /ˈmʌðə(r)/ **I** *n* **1** (parent) mère *f*; **2** (form of address) mère *f* FML, maman *f*.
II Mother *pr n* RELIG Mère *f*; **Reverend Mother** révérende Mère.
III *vtr* LIT materner; FIG dorloter ALSO PEJ.
IDIOMS **every ~'s son (of them)** tous sans exception; **to learn sth at one's ~'s knee** apprendre qch dans sa plus tendre enfance.

motherhood /ˈmʌðəhʊd/ *n* maternité *f*; **the responsibilities of ~** les responsabilités incombant à une mère de famille; **to combine ~ with a career** combiner les enfants et le travail.

mothering /ˈmʌðərɪŋ/ *n* ¢ (motherly care) soins *mpl* maternels; (being a mother) fait *m* d'être mère.

Mothering Sunday *n* GB fête *f* des Mères.

mother: **~-in-law** *n* (*pl* **mothers-in-law**) belle-mère *f*; **~land** *n* patrie *f*.

motherless /ˈmʌðəlɪs/ *adj* [*child*] orphelin de mère; [*animal*] sans mère.

motherly /ˈmʌðəlɪ/ *adj* maternel/-elle.

mother-of-pearl /ˌmʌðərəvˈpɜːl/ **I** *n* nacre *f*.
II *noun modifier* [*necklace, box*] de or en nacre.

mother: **~'s boy** *n* fils *m* à maman°; **Mother's Day** *n* fête *f* des Mères; **~'s help** GB, **~'s helper** US *n* aide *f* maternelle; **~-to-be** *n* future mère *f*, future maman *f*; **~ tongue** *n* langue *f* maternelle.

motif /məʊˈtiːf/ *n* (in art, music) motif *m*; (in literature) thème *m*.

motion /ˈməʊʃn/ **I** *n* **1** (movement) mouvement *m*; **to set sth in ~** LIT mettre qch en marche; FIG mettre qch en route [*plan*]; déclencher [*chain of events*]; **to set the wheels in ~** FIG mettre les choses en route; **2** (gesture) (of hands) geste *m*; (of head, body) mouvement *m*; **3** ADMIN, POL motion *f*; **to table/second the ~**

déposer/appuyer la motion; **to carry/defeat the ~** adopter/rejeter la motion; **4** MED selles *fpl*.
II *vtr* **to ~ sb to approach** faire signe à qn de s'approcher.
III *vi* faire signe (**to** à).
IDIOMS **to go through the ~s** agir machinalement **to go through the ~s of doing** faire mine de faire.

motionless /ˈməʊʃnlɪs/ *adj* [*cloud*] immobile; [*sit, stand*] sans bouger.

motion picture I *n* film *m*.
II *noun modifier* [*industry*] du cinéma; [*director*] de cinéma.

motion sickness *n* mal *m* des transports.

motivate /ˈməʊtɪveɪt/ **I** *vtr* motiver [*person, décision*]; **to ~ sb to do** inciter or pousser qn à faire.
II motivating *pres p adj* [*force, factor*] motivant.

motivated /ˈməʊtɪveɪtɪd/ *adj* **1** [*person, pupil*] motivé; **2 politically/racially ~** [*act*] politique/raciste.

motivation /ˌməʊtɪˈveɪʃn/ *n* (all contexts) motivation *f* (**for** de; **for doing, to do** pour faire).

motive /ˈməʊtɪv/ **I** *n* **1** GEN motif *m* (**for, behind** de); **sb's ~ in** ou **for doing** le motif qui pousse qn à faire; **2** JUR mobile *m* (**for** de).
II *adj* [*force, power*] moteur/-trice.

motley /ˈmɒtlɪ/ *adj* [*crowd, gathering*] bigarré; [*collection*] hétéroclite.

motor /ˈməʊtə(r)/ **I** *n* (engine) moteur *m*.
II *noun modifier* **1** AUT [*industry, insurance, racing, vehicle*] automobile; [*show*] de l'automobile; **2** MED [*activity, area of brain, disorder, function, nerve*] moteur/-trice; **3** [*mower*] à moteur.
III *vi* **1**† (travel by car) voyager en voiture; **2**° (go fast) tracer°.

motorail /ˈməʊtəreɪl/ *n* GB train *m* auto-couchettes.

motor: **~bike** *n* moto *f*; **~boat** *n* canot *m* automobile; **~cade** *n* cortège *m* (de véhicules); **~ car**† *n* automobile† *f*; **~ court**, **~ inn** *n* US = **motor lodge**; **~cycle** *n* motocyclette *f*; **~cycle escort** *n* escorte *f* de motards; **~cycle messenger** *n* coursier/-ière *m/f* à moto; **~cycling** ▶ 949 *n* motocyclisme *m*; **~cyclist** *n* motocycliste *mf*; **~ home** *n* auto-caravane *f*.

motoring /ˈməʊtərɪŋ/ **I**† *n* promenade *f* en voiture.
II *noun modifier* [*organization, correspondent, magazine*] automobile; [*accident*] de voiture; [*holiday*] en voiture; [*offence*] de conduite.

motorist /ˈməʊtərɪst/ *n* automobiliste *mf*.

motorize /ˈməʊtəraɪz/ **I** *vtr* motoriser [*vehicle, troops, police*]; équiper [qch] d'un moteur [*system, device*].
II motorized *pp adj* [*transport, vehicle, regiment*] motorisé; [*camera, device*] équipé d'un moteur.

motor: **~ launch** *n* vedette *f*; **~ lodge** *n* US motel *m*; **~man** ▶ 1251 *n* US machiniste *m*; **~ mechanic** ▶ 1251 *n* mécanicien/-ienne *m/f* auto(mobile); **~mouth**° *n* moulin à paroles°; **~ oil** *n* huile *f* de graissage; **~ scooter** *n* scooter *m*.

motorway /ˈməʊtəweɪ/ GB **I** *n* autoroute *f*.
II *noun modifier* [*markings, police, service station*] de l'autoroute; [*traffic, system, junction*] autoroutier/-ière; [*crash*] sur l'autoroute; [*driving*] sur autoroute.

mottled /ˈmɒtld/ *adj* [*skin, paper*] marbré; [*hands*] tacheté.

motto /ˈmɒtəʊ/ *n* devise *f*.

mould GB, **mold** US /məʊld/ **I** *n* **1** (cast, container) moule *m*; FIG moule *m*; **2** (fungi) moisissure *f*; **3** (soil) terreau *m*.
II *vtr* LIT modeler [*plastic, clay*] (**into sth** pour en faire qch); modeler [*sculpture, shape*] (**out of, from, in** en); FIG façonner (**into** pour en faire).
III *vi* **to ~ to sth**, **to ~ round sth** mouler qch; **to be ~ed to sb's body** [*dress*] mouler (le corps de) qn.

moulder GB, **molder** US /ˈməʊldə(r)/ *vi* (also **~ away**) LIT [*ruins*] tomber en poussière; [*corpse, refuse*] se décomposer; FIG pourrir.

moulding GB, **molding** US /ˈməʊldɪŋ/ *n* **1** (of clay, model) moulage *m*; **2** (of opinion, character) modelage *m*; **3** (trim) moulure *f*.

mouldy GB, **moldy** US /'məʊldɪ/ *adj* moisi; **to go ~** moisir.

moult GB, **molt** US /məʊlt/ **I** *n* mue *f*.
II *vi* [*cat, dog*] perdre ses poils; [*bird*] muer.

mound /maʊnd/ *n* (hillock) tertre *m*; (heap) monceau *m* (**of** de).

mount /maʊnt/ **I** *n* **1** (mountain) mont *m*; **2** (horse) monture *f*; **3** (surround) (for jewel, lens) monture *f*; (for picture) carton *m* de montage.
II *vtr* **1** (ascend) gravir [*stairs*]; monter sur [*platform, scaffold, horse, bicycle*]; **2** (fix into place) monter [*jewel, picture*] (**on** sur); coller [*stamp*]; monter [*exhibit, specimen*]; installer [*engine*]; **3** (set up, hold) monter [*campaign*]; organiser [*demonstration*]; **4** ZOOL monter.
III *vi* GEN monter (**to** jusqu'à); [*number, toll*] augmenter; [*concern*] grandir; (on horse) se mettre en selle.
IV mounting *pres p adj* croissant.

mountain /'maʊntɪn, US -ntn/ **I** *n* LIT, FIG montagne *f*; **in the ~s** à la montagne; **meat/butter ~** ECON excédents *mpl* de viande/de beurre.
II *noun modifier* [*road, stream, scenery*] de montagne; [*air*] de la montagne; [*tribe*] des montagnes.

mountain: **~ bike** *n* vélo *m* tout-terrain, VTT *m*; **~ climbing ▶ 949 |** *n* alpinisme *m*.

mountaineer /ˌmaʊntɪ'nɪə(r), US -ntn'ɪər/ **▶ 1251|** *n* (climber) alpiniste *mf*; US montagnard/-e *m/f*.

mountaineering /ˌmaʊntɪ'nɪərɪŋ, US -ntn'ɪərɪŋ/ **▶ 949|** *n* alpinisme *m*.

mountainous /'maʊntɪnəs, US -ntnəs/ *adj* LIT montagneux/-euse; FIG gigantesque.

mountain: **~ range** *n* chaîne *f* de montagnes; **~ top** *n* cime *f*.

mounted police *n* (+ *v pl*) police *f* montée.

mourn /mɔːn/ **I** *vtr* pleurer.
II *vi* porter le deuil; **to ~ for sth/sb** pleurer qch/qn.

mournful /'mɔːnfl/ *adj* mélancolique.

mourning /'mɔːnɪŋ/ *n* **1** (state, clothes) deuil *m*; **to be in deep ~** être en grand deuil; **to go into/come out of ~** prendre/quitter le deuil; **2** (wailing) lamentations *fpl*.

mouse /maʊs/ *n* (*pl* **mice**) LIT, FIG, COMPUT souris *f*.

mouse: **~hole** *n* trou *m* de souris; **~trap** *n* souricière *f*.

mousey /'maʊsɪ/ *adj* **1** (colour) châtain terne *inv*; **2** (timid) PÉJ effacé; [*colour*] de souris.

moustache /mə'stɑːʃ/, **mustache** US /'mʌstæʃ/ *n* moustache *f*.

mousy *adj* = **mousey**.

mouth /maʊθ/ **I** *n* **1** (of human, horse) bouche *f*; (of other animal) gueule *f*; **with my/his etc ~ open** GEN la bouche ouverte; (in surprise, admiration) bouche bée *inv*; **2** (of cave, tunnel) entrée *f*; (of river) embouchure *f*; (of geyser, volcano) bouche *f*; (of valley) débouché *m*; (of jar, bottle, decanter) goulot *m*; (of bag, sack) ouverture *f*.
II *vtr* **1** articuler silencieusement; **2** débiter [*platitudes, rhetoric*].
IDIOMS **by word of ~** de bouche à oreille; **don't put words in my ~** ne me fais pas dire ce que je n'ai pas dit; **his heart was in his ~** son cœur battait la chamade; **to be down in the ~** être tout triste; **to leave a bad** ou **nasty taste in one's** ou **the ~** FIG laisser un arrière-goût amer; **to take the words right out of sb's ~** ôter les mots de la bouche de qn; **wash your ~ out!** ne dis pas de gros mots!

mouthful /'maʊθfʊl/ *n* **1** (of food) bouchée *f*; (of liquid) gorgée *f*; **2**° (word) mot *m* long d'un kilomètre°; (name) nom *m* à coucher dehors°; **3**° **to give sb a ~** passer une engueulade° à qn.

mouth organ ▶ 1097| *n* harmonica *m*.

mouthpiece /'maʊθpiːs/ *n* **1** (of musical instrument) embouchure *f*; (of microphone) microphone *m*; (of pipe, snorkel) embout *m*; **2** (person) porte-parole *m* (**of, for** de); (newspaper) organe *m* (**of** de).

mouth: **~-to-mouth** *adj* [*technique, method*] du bouche-à-bouche *inv*; **~-to-mouth resuscitation** *n* bouche-à-bouche *m inv*; **~wash** *n* eau *f* dentifrice; **~-watering** *adj* appétissant.

movable /'muːvəbl/ *adj* GEN mobile; JUR mobilier/-ière.

move /muːv/ **I** *n* **1** (movement) GEN mouvement *m*; (gesture) geste *m*; **to watch sb's every ~** surveiller chacun des gestes de qn; **2** (transfer) (of residence) déménagement *m*; (of company) transfert *m*; **to make the ~ to London** [*family*] s'installer à Londres; [*firm*] être transféré à Londres; [*employee*] être muté à Londres; **she made the ~ from sales to management** elle est passée des ventes à la direction; **3** GAMES coup *m*; **white has the first ~** les blancs jouent en premier; **it's your ~** c'est ton tour; **4** (step, act) manœuvre *f*; **a good/bad ~** une bonne/mauvaise idée; **to make the first ~** faire le premier pas; **they have made no ~(s) to allay public anxiety** ils n'ont rien fait pour rassurer l'opinion publique; **in a ~ to counter opposition attacks**... pour tenter de parer aux attaques de l'opposition...
II on the move *adj phr* **to be on the ~** [*army*] être en mouvement; [*train*] être en marche; **to be always on the ~** [*diplomat, family*] être tout le temps en train de déménager; [*nomad, traveller*] être toujours sur les routes.
III *vtr* **1** (change position of) GEN déplacer; transporter [*patient, army*]; (to clear a space) enlever [*object*]; **~ your head, I can't see!** pousse ta tête, je ne vois rien!; **to ~ sth into** transporter qch dans [*room, garden*]; **to ~ sth upstairs/downstairs** monter/descendre qch; **to ~ sth further away/closer** éloigner/rapprocher qch; **2** (set in motion) [*person*] bouger [*limb, head*]; [*wind, mechanism*] faire bouger [*leaf, wheel*]; **3** (to new location or job) muter [*staff*]; transférer [*office*]; **4** (to new house, site) déménager; **to ~ house** déménager; **5** (affect) émouvoir; **6** (motivate) **to ~ sb to do** amener qn à faire; **7** (propose) proposer; **to ~ that the matter be put to the vote** proposer que la question soit soumise au vote; **8** (sell) vendre.
IV *vi* **1** (stir) GEN bouger; [*lips*] remuer; **will you please ~!** veux-tu te pousser?; **2** (travel) [*vehicle*] rouler; [*person*] avancer; [*procession, army*] être en marche; **we must get things moving** FIG nous devons faire avancer les choses; **things are starting to ~ on the job front** les choses commencent à avancer côté travail; **go on, get moving!** allez, avance!; **to ~ back** reculer; **to ~ forward** s'avancer; **to ~ away** s'éloigner; **3**° (proceed quickly) **that car's really moving!** t'as vu comme elle va vite cette voiture°!; **4** (change home, location) déménager; **to ~ to the countryside/to Japan** s'installer à la campagne/au Japon; **5** (change job) être muté; **6** (act) agir; **to ~ to do** intervenir pour faire; **7** GAMES [*player*] jouer; [*piece*] se déplacer; **8** COMM (sell) se vendre.
IDIOMS **let's make a ~**° si on bougeait°?; **it's time I made a ~**° il est temps de partir; **to get a ~ on**° se dépêcher; **to ~ with the times** vivre avec son temps.
■ **move about**, **move around**: ¶ **~ about 1** (to different position) [*person*] remuer; [*object*] bouger; **2** (to different home) déménager; ¶ **~ [sb/sth] about** déplacer; **they ~ him around a lot between branches** on le fait souvent changer de succursale.
■ **move along**: ¶ **~ along 1** (stop loitering) circuler; (proceed) avancer; (squeeze up) se pousser; **2** FIG (progress) **things are moving along nicely** les choses se mettent en place; ¶ **~ [sb/sth] along** faire circuler [*loiterers, crowd*]; faire avancer [*herd, group*].
■ **move away**: ¶ **~ away** (by moving house) déménager; (by leaving scene) partir; **to ~ away from** quitter; ¶ **~ [sb/sth] away**, **~ away [sb/sth]** faire reculer [*crowd*]; déplacer [*obstruction*].
■ **move down**: ¶ **~ down** descendre; ¶ **~ [sb] down**, **~ down [sb]** GB SCH faire repasser [qn] au niveau inférieur; GEN faire redescendre; ¶ **~ [sth] down**, **~ down [sth]** (to lower shelf etc) mettre [qch] plus bas.

■ **move in**: ¶ ~ **in 1** (to house) emménager; **to ~ in with** s'installer avec [*friend, relative*]; aller vivre avec [*lover*]; **2** (advance, attack) s'avancer; **to ~ in on** [*police, attackers, demolition men*] s'avancer sur; [*corporate raider, racketeer*] lancer une opération sur; **3** (intervene) [*company, government*] intervenir; ¶ ~ [sb] **in**, ~ **in** [sb] **1** (place in housing) installer; **2** (change residence) **a friend helped to ~ me in** un ami m'a aidé à emménager.

■ **move off** [*procession*] partir; [*vehicle*] se mettre en route; [*troops*] se mettre en marche.

■ **move on**: ¶ ~ **on 1** [*person, traveller*] se mettre en route; [*vehicle*] repartir; [*time*] passer; **to ~ on to** passer à [*next item*]; **let's ~ on** passons au point suivant; **2** (keep moving) circuler; **3** (develop) **things have ~d on since** depuis, les choses ont changé; ¶ ~ [sth] **on**, ~ **on** [sth] GB faire avancer; ¶ ~ [sb] **on**, ~ **on** [sb] GB faire circuler.

■ **move out**: ¶ ~ **out** (of house) déménager; [*soldiers, tanks*] quitter les lieux; **to ~ out of** quitter; ¶ ~ [sb/sth] **out**, ~ **out** [sb/sth] évacuer [*residents*]; enlever [*object*].

■ **move over**: ¶ ~ **over 1** se pousser; **2** FIG céder la place (**for sb** à qn); ¶ ~ [sb/sth] **over** déplacer [*person, object*].

■ **move up**: ¶ ~ **up 1** (make room) se pousser; **2** (be promoted) être promu; **to ~ up to the first division** passer en première division; ¶ ~ [sb] **up**, ~ **up** [sb] **1** GB SCH faire passer [qn] au niveau supérieur; **2** SPORT faire monter; ¶ ~ [sth] **up** mettre [qch] plus haut.

moveable *adj* = **movable**.

movement /'muːvmənt/ *n* **1** GEN, ECON, MUS mouvement *m*; (of hand, arm) geste *m*; **to watch sb's ~s** surveiller les faits et gestes de qn; **an upward/ downward ~ in prices** une augmentation/diminution des prix; **a ~ towards liberalization** une évolution vers la libéralisation; **a ~ away from marriage** une tendance à rejeter le mariage; **2** (transporting) acheminement *m*; **3** (circulation) circulation *f*.

movie /'muːvɪ/ **I** *n* SURTOUT US film *m*. **II movies** *npl* **the ~s** le cinéma.

movie: ~ **camera** *n* caméra *f*; ~ **director** ▶ 1251 *n* réalisateur/-trice *m/f* de cinéma; ~ **film** *n* pellicule *f* cinématographique; ~**goer** *n* spectateur/ -trice *m/f* de cinéma; ~ **star** *n* vedette *f* de cinéma; ~ **theater** *n* US cinéma *m*.

moving /'muːvɪŋ/ *adj* **1** [*vehicle*] en marche; [*parts, target*] mobile; [*staircase, walkway*] roulant; **2** (emotional) [*scene, speech*] émouvant; **3** FIG **to be the ~ force** ou **spirit behind sth** être l'âme de qch.

mow /məʊ/ *vtr* (*pp* ~**ed**, **mown**) tondre [*grass, lawn*]; couper [*hay*].

■ **mow down**: ~ **down** [sb], ~ [sb] **down** faucher.

mower /'məʊə(r)/ *n* (machine) tondeuse *f* à gazon; (person) faucheur/-euse *m/f*.

mown /məʊn/ *pp* ▶ **mow**.

MP *n* **1** GB (*abrév* = **Member of Parliament**) député *m*; **2** *abrév* ▶ **military policeman**.

mpg *n* (*abrév* = **miles per gallon**) miles *mpl* au gallon.

mph *n* (*abrév* = **miles per hour**) miles *mpl* à l'heure.

MPhil *n* UNIV (*abrév* = **Master of Philosophy**) diplôme *m* supérieur de lettres et sciences humaines.

Mr /'mɪstə(r)/ ▶ 937 *n* (*pl* **Messrs**) M., Monsieur; ~ **Right** le Prince Charmant; ~ **President** Monsieur le Président.

Mrs /'mɪsɪz/ ▶ 937 *n* Mme, Madame.

Ms /mɪz, məz/ ▶ 937 *n* ~ Mme.

■ Note *Ms* est l'équivalent féminin de *Mr* (M.) et permet de s'adresser à une femme dont on connaît le nom sans préciser sa situation de famille: Ms Brown.

MS *n* **1** *abrév écrite* = **manuscript**; **2** *abrév* ▶ **multiple sclerosis**; **3** US POST *abrév écrite* = **Mississippi**.

MSc *n* UNIV (*abrév* = **Master of Science**) diplôme *m* supérieur en sciences.

MT *n* **1** *abrév* ▶ **machine translation**; **2** US POST *abrév écrite* = **Montana**.

much /mʌtʃ/

■ Note When *much* is used as an adverb, it is translated by *beaucoup*: *it's much longer* = c'est beaucoup plus long; *she doesn't talk much* = elle ne parle pas beaucoup.
– For particular usages, see I below.
– When *much* is used as a pronoun, it is usually translated by *beaucoup*: *there is much to learn* = il y a beaucoup à apprendre. However, in negative sentences *grand-chose* is also used: *I didn't learn much* = je n'ai pas beaucoup appris *or* je n'ai pas appris grand-chose.
– When *much* is used as a quantifier, it is translated by *beaucoup de*: *they don't have much money* = ils n'ont pas beaucoup d'argent.
– For particular usages see III below.

I *adv* **1** (to a considerable degree) beaucoup; ~ **smaller** beaucoup plus petit; **the film is ~ better** le film est bien meilleur; **it's ~ better organized** c'est beaucoup mieux organisé; **she doesn't worry ~ about it** ça ne l'inquiète pas beaucoup; **we'd ~ rather stay here** nous préférerions de beaucoup rester ici; **they are ~ to be pitied** ils sont bien à plaindre; **~ loved by her friends** très aimée de ses amis; **your comments would be ~ appreciated** tous vos commentaires seront les bienvenus; **he's not ~ good at doing** il n'est pas très doué pour faire; **does it hurt ~?** est-ce que ça fait très mal?; **she's ~ the best teacher here** elle est de loin le meilleur professeur ici; **~ to my surprise** à ma grande surprise; **2** (often) beaucoup, souvent; **we don't go out ~** nous ne sortons pas beaucoup; **do you go to concerts ~?** est-ce que tu vas souvent au concert?; **3** (nearly) plus ou moins, à peu près; **it's ~ the same** c'est à peu près pareil (**as** que); **it's pretty ~ like driving a car** c'est plus ou moins la même chose que de conduire une voiture; **in ~ the same way** à peu près de la même façon (**as** que); **~ the same is true of China** la situation est à peu près la même en Chine; **4** (specifying degree to which something is true) **too ~** trop; **very ~** (a lot) beaucoup; (absolutely) tout à fait; **he misses you very ~** tu lui manques beaucoup; **it's very ~ the norm** c'est tout à fait la norme; **I feel very ~ the foreigner** je me sens tout à fait étranger; **so ~** tellement; **as ~ as you** (**do**) je les aime autant que toi; **they hated each other as ~ as ever** ils se détestaient toujours autant; **I thought as ~** ça ne m'étonne pas, je m'en doutais; **however ~** même si; **you'll have to accept the decision however ~ you disagree** il va falloir que tu acceptes la décision même si tu n'es pas d'accord; **5** (emphatic: setting up a contrast) **the discovery wasn't so ~ shocking as depressing** la découverte était moins choquante que déprimante.

II *pron* **1** (a great deal) beaucoup; (in negative sentences) grand-chose; **do you have ~ left?** est-ce qu'il vous en reste beaucoup?; **we didn't eat ~** nous n'avons pas mangé grand-chose; **there isn't ~ to do** il n'y a pas grand-chose à faire; **he doesn't have ~ to complain about** il n'a pas à se plaindre; **it leaves ~ to be desired** ça laisse (vraiment) à désirer; **there's ~ to be said for it** ça présente des avantages; **~ of une grande partie de; ~ of the difficulty lies in...** une grande partie de la difficulté réside dans...; **I don't see ~ of them now** je ne les vois plus beaucoup maintenant; **to make ~ of sth** (focus on) insister sur qch; (understand) comprendre qch; **2** (expressing a relative amount, degree) **so ~** tellement, tant; **we'd eaten so ~ that** nous avions tellement mangé que; **so ~ of her work is gloomy** une si grande partie de son œuvre est sombre; **so ~ of the time, it's a question of patience** la plupart du temps c'est une question de patience; **too ~** trop; **it costs too ~** c'est trop cher; **it's too ~!** LIT c'est trop!; (in protest) c'en est trop!; **she was too ~ of an egotist to do** elle était trop égoïste pour faire; **the heat was too ~ for them** ils n'ont pas pu supporter la chaleur; **he was**

too **~ for his opponent** il était trop fort pour son adversaire; **he's read this ~ already** il a déjà lu tout ça; **I'll say this ~ for him, he's honest** il a au moins ça pour lui, il est honnête; **this ~ is certain, we'll have no choice** une chose est certaine, nous n'aurons pas le choix; **twice as ~** deux fois plus; **if we had half as ~ as you** si nous avions la moitié de ce que tu as; **as ~ as possible** autant que possible; **it can cost as ~ as £50** ça peut coûter jusqu'à 50 livres sterling; **it was as ~ as I could do not to laugh** il a fallu que je me retienne pour ne pas rire; **as ~ as to say…** d'un air de dire…; **how ~?** combien?; **tell them how ~ you won** dis-leur combien tu as gagné; **do you know how ~ this means to me?** est-ce que tu sais à quel point or combien c'est important pour moi?; **3** (focusing on limitations, inadequacy) **it's not** ou **nothing ~** ce n'est pas grand-chose; **it's not up to ~** GB ça ne vaut pas grand-chose; **he's not ~ to look at** il n'est pas très beau; **she doesn't think ~ of him** elle n'a pas très bonne opinion de lui; **I'm not ~ of a reader** je n'aime pas beaucoup lire; **it wasn't ~ of a life** ce n'était pas une vie; **I'm not ~ of a one for cooking** la cuisine ce n'est pas mon fort°.

III *quantif* beaucoup de; **I haven't got (very) ~ time** je n'ai pas beaucoup de temps; **she didn't speak ~ English** elle ne connaissait que quelques mots d'anglais; **to spend too ~ money** dépenser trop d'argent; **we don't have too ~ time** nous n'avons pas beaucoup de temps; **don't use so ~ salt** ne mets pas tant de sel; **we paid twice as ~ money** nous avons payé deux fois plus d'argent; **how ~ time have we got left?** combien de temps nous reste-t-il?

IV **much+** *combining form* **~-loved/-respected** très apprécié/respecté; **~-maligned** tant décrié; **~-needed** indispensable.

V *much* as *conj phr* bien que (+ *subj*); **~ as we regret our decision we have no choice** bien que nous regrettions or nous avons beau regretter notre décision, nous n'avons pas le choix.

VI *much less* *conj phr* encore moins; **I've never seen him ~ less spoken to him** je n'ai jamais eu l'occasion de le voir encore moins de lui parler.

VII *so much as* *adv phr* without **so ~ as saying goodbye/as an apology** sans même dire au revoir/s'excuser; **if you so ~ as move** si tu fais le moindre mouvement.

IDIOMS **there isn't ~ in** GB ou **to** US **it** (in contest, competition) ils se suivent de près; **there isn't ~ in it for us** (to our advantage) ça ne va pas nous apporter grand-chose; **she's late again? that's a bit ~!** elle est encore en retard? elle exagère!; **they're ~ of a muchness** il n'y a pas beaucoup de différence entre eux.

muck /mʌk/ *n* **1** LIT saletés *fpl*; (mud) boue *f*; (manure) fumier *m*; **dog ~** crotte *f* de chien; **2**° FIG (book, film, dish) saleté *f*; **it's ~** c'est dégoûtant.
■ **muck about**°, **muck around**°: ¶ **~ about** (fool about) faire l'imbécile; (do nothing) traîner; **to ~ about with** traficoter° [*appliance*]; toucher à [*object*]; ¶ **~ [sb] about** se ficher de°.
■ **muck in** (share task) mettre la main à la pâte°; (share accommodation) partager le gîte et le couvert.
■ **muck out**: **~ out** [sth] nettoyer [*cowshed, stable*].
■ **muck up**: **~ up** [sth] **1** (spoil) chambouler° [*plans*]; cochonner° [*task*]; louper° [*exam, interview, opportunity*]; **2** salir [*clothes, carpet*].

muckraking /ˈmʌkreɪkɪŋ/ **I** *n* course *f* au scandale.
II *adj* [*story*] infâme; [*campaign*] de diffamation.

mucus /ˈmjuːkəs/ *n* mucus *m*, mucosités *fpl*.

mud /mʌd/ *n* boue *f*.
IDIOMS **his name is ~** on l'exècre, il est très mal vu; **it's as clear as ~**°! c'est d'un clair°!; **to drag sb's name in** ou **through the ~** traîner qn dans la boue.

muddle /ˈmʌdl/ **I** *n* **1** (mess) ¢ (of papers) pagaille° *f*; (of string) embrouillamini *m*; FIG (in administration) confusion *f*; **2** (mix-up) malentendu *m* (**over** à propos de); **3** (mental confusion) **to be in a ~** avoir les idées embrouillées; **to get into a ~** s'embrouiller.
II *vtr* = **muddle up**.

■ **muddle along** vivoter°.
■ **muddle through** se débrouiller.
■ **muddle up**: ¶ **~ [sth] up, ~ up [sth]** (disorder) semer la pagaille° dans; ¶ **~ [sb] up** embrouiller les idées de; **to get sth ~d up** s'embrouiller dans qch [*dates, names*]; **I got you ~d up with Martin** je t'ai confondu avec Martin.

muddled /ˈmʌdld/ *adj* confus.

muddle-headed /ˌmʌdlˈhedɪd/ *adj* [*plan*] confus; [*person*] aux idées confuses.

muddy /ˈmʌdɪ/ **I** *adj* [*hand*] couvert de boue; [*shoe, garment*] crotté; [*road, water, coffee*] boueux/-euse; [*pink*] sale; [*green, yellow*] terne; [*complexion*] terreux/-euse.
II *vtr* couvrir [qch] de boue [*hands*]; crotter [*shoes, clothes*]; troubler [*water*].
IDIOMS **to ~ the waters** brouiller les pistes.

mud: **~ flat** *n* laisse *f*; **~guard** *n* garde-boue *m inv*; **~ hut** *n* hutte *f* de terre; **~pack** *n* masque *m* de beauté à l'argile; **~ pie** *n* pâté *m* de boue; **~slide** *n* éboulement *m* de terrain; **~-slinging** *n* dénigrement *m*.

muff /mʌf/ **I** *n* (mitten) manchon *m*.
II° *vtr* louper° [*shot*]; rater° [*chance*]; se tromper dans [*lines*].

muffle /ˈmʌfl/ *vtr* **1** (wrap up) emmitoufler (**in** dans); **2** assourdir [*bell, drum*]; étouffer [*voice, laughter*].

muffler /ˈmʌflə(r)/ *n* **1** cache-nez *m inv*; **2** US AUT silencieux *m*.

mug /mʌg/ **I** *n* **1** (for tea, coffee) grande tasse *f*; (for beer) chope *f*; **2** (contents) (also **~ful**) grande tasse *f* (**of** de); **3**° (face) gueule° *f*; **4** GB (fool) poire° *f*; **it's a ~'s game** c'est un attrape-nigaud.
II *vtr* (*p prés etc* **-gg-**) agresser; **to be ~ged** se faire agresser.
■ **mug up**° GB: **~ up** [sth] potasser° [*subject*].

mugger /ˈmʌgə(r)/ *n* agresseur *m*.

mugging /ˈmʌgɪŋ/ *n* **1** (attack) agression *f*; **2** ¢ (crime) agressions *fpl*.

muggy /ˈmʌgɪ/ *adj* [*room, day*] étouffant; [*weather*] lourd.

Muhammad /məˈhæmɪd/ *pr n* Mahomet.

mujaheddin, mujahedeen /ˌmuːdʒəˈdiːn/ *npl* **the ~** les Moudjahidin *mpl*.

mulatto /mjuːˈlætəʊ, US məˈl-/ **I** *n* mulâtre/-esse *m/f*.
II *adj* mulâtre.

mulberry /ˈmʌlbrɪ, US -berɪ/ *n* (tree) mûrier *m*; (fruit) mûre *f*.

mule /mjuːl/ *n* (animal) mulet *m*; (stubborn person)° tête *f* de mule; (slipper) mule *f*.

mulish /ˈmjuːlɪʃ/ *adj* entêté.

mull /mʌl/ *vtr* CULIN chauffer et épicer [*wine*].
■ **mull over**: **~ over** [sth], **~** [sth] **over** retourner [qch] dans sa tête.

mullet /ˈmʌlɪt/ *n* (red) rouget *m*; (grey) mulet *m*.

mullioned /ˈmʌlɪənd/ *adj* [*windows*] à meneaux.

multi+ /ˈmʌltɪ/ *combining form* multi-.

multi-access /ˌmʌltɪˈækses/ *n* COMPUT accès *m* multiple.

multicellular /ˌmʌltɪˈseljʊlə(r)/ *adj* pluricellulaire.

multichannel /ˌmʌltɪˈtʃænl/ *adj* [*television*] à canaux multiples; [*reception*] de plusieurs chaînes.

multicultural /ˌmʌltɪˈkʌltʃərəl/ *adj* multiculturel/-elle.

multidisciplinary /ˌmʌltɪdɪsɪˈplɪnərɪ, US -nerɪ/ *adj* SCH, UNIV pluridisciplinaire.

multi-faceted /ˌmʌltɪˈfæsɪtɪd/ *adj* **1** [*career, personality*] à multiples facettes; **2** [*gemstone*] facetté.

multi-function /ˌmʌltɪˈfʌŋkʃn/ *adj* [*watch, calculator, computer*] multifonctions *inv*.

multigym /ˈmʌltɪdʒɪm/ *n* appareil *m* de musculation.

multilateral /ˌmʌltɪˈlætərəl/ *adj* POL multilatéral; MATH à plusieurs côtés.

multilevel /ˌmʌltɪˈlevl/ *adj* **1** [*parking, access, analysis*] à plusieurs niveaux; [*building, complex*] de plusieurs étages; **2** COMPUT multiniveaux *inv*.

multilingual /ˌmʌltɪ'lɪŋgwəl/ adj plurilingue.

multimedia /ˌmʌltɪ'miːdɪə/ adj (all contexts) multimédia inv.

multi-million /ˌmʌltɪ'mɪljən/ adj de plusieurs millions.

multinational /ˌmʌltɪ'næʃənl/ I n (also ~ company) multinationale f.
II adj [company, force, agreement] multinational.

multi-party /ˌmʌltɪ'pɑːtɪ/ adj POL [government, system] pluripartite.

multiple /'mʌltɪpl/ I n 1 MATH multiple m (of de); **sold in ~s of six** vendus par six; **2** GB (chain of shops) magasin m à succursales multiples; **3** FIN action f multiple.
II adj (all contexts) multiple.

multiple: ~ **choice** adj [test, question] à choix multiple; ~ **entry visa** n visa m valable pour plusieurs entrées; ~ **occupancy** n: occupation d'une maison par plusieurs personnes; ~ **ownership** n multipropriété f; ~ **pile-up** n carambolage m; ~ **sclerosis, MS** n sclérose f en plaques; ~ **store** n GB magasin m à succursales multiples.

multiplex /'mʌltɪpleks/ I n 1 TELECOM multiplex m; **2** US CIN complexe m multi-salles.
II adj TELECOM multiplex inv.
III vtr TELECOM multiplexer.

multiplication /ˌmʌltɪplɪ'keɪʃn/ n GEN, MATH multiplication f; **to do ~** faire des multiplications.

multiplier /'mʌltɪplaɪə(r)/ n (all contexts) multiplicateur m.

multiply /'mʌltɪplaɪ/ I vtr (all contexts) multiplier (by par).
II vi 1 MATH multiplier; **2** GEN, BIOL (increase) se multiplier.

multiply handicapped /ˌmʌltɪplɪ 'hændɪkæpt/ adj polyhandicapé.

multiprocessing /ˌmʌltɪ'prəʊsesɪŋ/ n COMPUT multitraitement m.

multipurpose /ˌmʌltɪ'pɜːpəs/ adj [tool, gadget] à usages multiples; [area, organization] polyvalent.

multistorey /ˌmʌltɪ'stɔːrɪ/ adj GB [carpark] à niveaux multiples; [building] à étages.

multitrack /ˈmʌltɪtræk/ adj AUDIO multipiste inv.

multitude /'mʌltɪtjuːd, US -tuːd/ n multitude f.
IDIOMS **to hide** ou **cover a ~ of sins** HUM (servir à) camoufler pas mal de choses.

multiuser /ˌmʌltɪ'juːzə(r)/ adj COMPUT [computer] à utilisateurs multiples; [system, installation] multiposte inv.

mum° /mʌm/ n GB maman f.
IDIOMS ~'s **the word** motus et bouche cousue; **to keep ~** ne pas piper mot.

mumble /'mʌmbl/ I n marmonnement m.
II vtr, vi marmonner.

mumbo jumbo° /ˌmʌmbəʊ 'dʒʌmbəʊ/ n PÉJ (speech, writing) charabia° m; (ritual) cérémonial m.

mummify /'mʌmɪfaɪ/ vtr momifier.

mummy /'mʌmɪ/ n 1° GB maman f; **2** (embalmed body) momie f.

mummy's boy n GB PÉJ fils m à maman.

mumps /mʌmps/ ▶1002 n (+ v sg) oreillons mpl.

munch /mʌntʃ/ vtr [person] mâcher; [animal] mâchonner; **to ~ one's way through** dévorer.

mundane /mʌn'deɪn/ adj terre-à-terre, quelconque.

municipal /mjuː'nɪsɪpl/ adj municipal.

municipal court n US JUR tribunal m d'instance.

municipality /mjuːˌnɪsɪ'pælətɪ/ n municipalité f.

munitions /mjuː'nɪʃnz/ I npl MIL munitions fpl.
II noun modifier [factory, industry] de munitions.

mural /'mjʊərəl/ I n peinture f murale; (in cave) peinture f rupestre.
II adj [art, decoration] mural.

murder /'mɜːdə(r)/ I n 1 meurtre m; **attempted ~** tentative f de meurtre or d'assassinat; **2**° **it's ~ in town today!** c'est infernal en ville aujourd'hui°!
II noun modifier [inquiry, investigation] sur un meur-

tre; [scene, weapon] du crime; [squad, trial] criminel/-elle; [story, mystery] policier/-ière; ~ **suspect** meurtrier/-ière m/f présumé/-e; ~ **hunt** chasse f à l'assassin; ~ **victim** victime f (d'un meurtre).
III vtr 1 (kill) assassiner (with avec); **2**° **I could ~ her**°! je l'étranglerais volontiers!; **3**° massacrer° [language, piece of music]; **4**° (defeat) écraser°.
IV **murdered** pp adj **the ~ed man/woman** la victime.
IDIOMS **to get away with ~** [dishonest person] exercer ses talents en toute impunité; **that child gets away with ~!** on lui passe tout à cet enfant!; **to yell blue ~** GB [child] crier comme un putois.

murder: ~ **case** n (for police) affaire f d'homicide; (for court) procès m en homicide; ~ **charge** n inculpation f de meurtre.

murderer /'mɜːdərə(r)/ n assassin m, meurtrier m.

murderess /'mɜːdərɪs/ n meurtrière f.

murderous /'mɜːdərəs/ adj 1 (deadly) [regime, expression, look] assassin; [deeds, tendencies, thoughts] meurtrier/-ière; [intent] de meurtre; **2**° [heat, conditions, pressure] infernal; [route, conditions] meurtrier/-ière.

murky /'mɜːkɪ/ adj 1 [water, colour] glauque; [weather] maussade; [distance] opaque; **2** [past] trouble.

murmur /'mɜːmə(r)/ I n GEN murmure m (of de); (of traffic) bourdonnement m (of de).
II vtr, vi (all contexts) murmurer.

murmuring /'mɜːmərɪŋ/ I n murmure m.
II **murmurings** npl (complaints) murmures mpl (about contre); (rumours) rumeurs fpl.
III adj [stream] murmurant.

muscle /'mʌsl/ I n 1 (in arm, leg etc) muscle m; (tissue) muscles mpl; **without moving a ~** sans bouger; **don't move a ~!** ne bouge pas!; **2** FIG puissance f; **we have the ~ to compete with them** nous sommes assez forts pour leur faire concurrence; **to give ~ to** donner du poids à.
II noun modifier [exercise, relaxant] pour les muscles; [fatigue, injury, tissue] musculaire.
III vtr **to ~ one's way into sth** essayer de s'imposer dans [discussion].
■ **muscle in**° s'imposer (on dans).

muscle strain n élongation f.

muscular /'mʌskjʊlə(r)/ adj [disease, tissue] musculaire; [body, limbs] musclé; [attitude, pose] musclé; **to have a ~ build** être tout en muscles.

muscular dystrophy ▶1002 n dystrophie f musculaire.

museum /mjuː'zɪəm/ I n musée m.
II noun modifier [curator, collection] de musée.

mushroom /'mʌʃrʊm, -ruːm/ ▶818 I n BOT, CULIN champignon m; (colour) beige m rosé.
II noun modifier CULIN [soup] aux champignons.
III vi [towns, groups] proliférer; [demand, profits] s'accroître rapidement.

mushroom: ~ **cloud** n champignon m atomique; ~ **growth** n croissance f rapide.

mushrooming /'mʌʃruːmɪŋ, -rʊmɪŋ/ I n 1 (activity) **to go ~** aller aux champignons; **2** (spread) prolifération f.
II adj [demand] croissant; [trade] florissant.

mushy° /'mʌʃɪ/ adj 1 (pulpy) [texture] pâteux/-euse; [vegetables] en bouillie; **2** (sentimental) [film, story] à l'eau de rose.

music /'mjuːzɪk/ I n 1 (art, composition) musique f; **to set sth to ~** mettre qch en musique; **2** (printed) partition f.
II noun modifier [exam, lesson, teacher, festival] de musique; [critic, practice] musical.
IDIOMS **to face the ~** affronter l'orage; **to be ~ to sb's ears** être doux à l'oreille de qn.

musical /'mjuːzɪkl/ I n (also ~ **comedy**) comédie f musicale.
II adj 1 [person] (gifted) musicien/-ienne; (interested) mélomane; **2** [voice, laughter] mélodieux/-ieuse; [accompaniment, director, score] musical.

Musical instruments

Playing an instrument
Note the use of de with jouer:

to play the piano	= jouer du piano
to play the clarinet	= jouer de la clarinette

but

to learn the piano	= apprendre le piano

Players
English -ist is often French -iste; the gender reflects the sex of the player.

a violinist	= un or une violoniste
a pianist	= un or une pianiste

A phrase with joueur/joueuse de X is usually safe.

a piccolo player	= un joueur or une joueuse de piccolo
a horn player	= un joueur or une joueuse de cor

But note the French when these words are used with good and bad like this:

he's a good pianist	= il joue bien du piano
he's not a good pianist	= il ne joue pas bien du piano
he's a bad pianist	= il joue mal du piano

As in English, the name of the instrument is often used to refer to its player:

she's a first violin	= elle est premier violon

Music

a piano piece	= un morceau pour piano
a piano arrangement	= un arrangement pour piano
a piano sonata	= une sonate pour piano
a concerto for piano and orchestra	= un concerto pour piano et orchestre
the piano part	= la partie pour piano

Use with another noun
De is usually correct:

to take piano lessons	= prendre des leçons de piano
a violin maker	= un fabricant de violons
a violin solo	= un solo de violon
a piano teacher	= un professeur de piano

but note the à here:

a violin case	= un étui à violon

---

musical: ~ **box** n GB boîte f à musique; ~ **instrument** n instrument m de musique.

music: ~ **box** n boîte f à musique; ~ **case** n porte-musique m inv; ~ **centre** n GB chaîne f compacte stéréo.

musician /mju:ˈzɪʃn/ ▶ 1251 ⌡ n musicien/-ienne m/f.

music lover n mélomane mf.

musicology /ˌmju:zɪˈkɒlədʒɪ/ n musicologie f.

music: ~ **stand** n pupitre m à musique; ~ **stool** n tabouret m de piano; ~ **video** n clip m (vidéo).

musing /ˈmju:zɪŋ/ **I** musings npl songeries fpl. **II** adj [stare, way] songeur/-euse.

musk /mʌsk/ n musc m.

musket /ˈmʌskɪt/ n mousquet m.

musketeer /ˌmʌskɪˈtɪə(r)/ n mousquetaire m.

musky /ˈmʌskɪ/ adj musqué.

Muslim /ˈmʊzlɪm, US ˈmʌzləm/ = **Moslem**.

muslin /ˈmʌzlɪn/ **I** n (cloth) mousseline f; CULIN étamine f.
II noun modifier [apron, curtain] en mousseline.

mussel /ˈmʌsl/ n moule f.

mussel bed n parc m à moules.

must /mʌst, məst/

■ **Note** When must indicates obligation or necessity, French tends to use either the verb devoir or the impersonal construction il faut que + subjunctive: I must go = je dois partir, il faut que je parte. For examples and particular usages see I 1 and I 3 below. See also have II 1 and the related usage note.
– When must expresses assumption or probability, the verb devoir is always used: it must strike you as odd that = ça doit te sembler bizarre que (+ subj). See I 7 below for further examples.
– For the conjugation of devoir, see the French verb tables.

I modal aux (nég **must not**, **mustn't**) **1** (indicating obligation, prohibition) you ~ **check your rearview mirror** il faut regarder dans le rétroviseur; **the feeding bottles ~ be sterilized** les biberons doivent être stérilisés; **they said she ~ be consulted first** ils ont dit qu'il fallait d'abord la consulter; **you mustn't mention this to anyone** il ne faut en parler à personne, tu ne dois en parler à personne; **all visitors ~ leave the premises** tous les visiteurs doivent quitter les lieux; **the loan ~ be repaid in one year** le prêt est remboursable en un an; **withdrawals ~ not exceed £200** les retraits ne doivent pas dépasser 200 livres sterling; **it ~ eventually have an effect** ça doit finir par avoir un effet; **2** (indicating requirement, condition) **candidates ~ be EC nationals** les candidats doivent être ressortissants d'un des pays de la CE; **to gain a licence you ~ spend 40 hours in the** **air** pour obtenir son brevet il faut avoir 40 heures de vol; **3** (stressing importance, necessity) **you ~ be patient** il faut que tu sois patient, tu dois être patient; **tell her she mustn't worry** dis-lui de ne pas s'inquiéter; **we ~ never forget** il ne faut jamais oublier; **I ~ ask you not to smoke** je dois vous demander de ne pas fumer; **I feel I ~ tell you that...** je pense devoir te dire que...; **it ~ be said that** il faut dire que; **I ~ apologize for being late** je vous demande d'excuser mon retard; **I ~ say I was impressed** je dois avouer que j'ai été impressionné; **that was pretty rude I ~ say!** je dois dire que c'était assez impoli!; **very nice, I ~ say!** IRON très gentil vraiment! IRON; **4** (expressing intention) **I ~ check the reference** je dois vérifier la référence, il faut que je vérifie la référence; **5** (indicating irritation) **well, come in if you ~** bon, entre si tu y tiens; **why ~ she always be so cynical?** pourquoi faut-il toujours qu'elle soit si cynique?; **he's ill, if you ~ know** il est malade si tu veux vraiment le savoir; **~ you make such a mess?** est-ce que tu as vraiment besoin de mettre le désordre?; **6** (in invitations, suggestions) **we really ~ get together soon** il faudrait vraiment qu'on se voie bientôt; **you ~ meet Flora Brown** il faut absolument que tu fasses la connaissance de Flora Brown; **7** (expressing assumption, probability) **it ~ be difficult living there** ça doit être difficile de vivre là-bas; **there ~ be some mistake!** il doit y avoir une erreur!; **what ~ people think?** qu'est-ce que les gens doivent penser?; **viewers ~ have been surprised** les téléspectateurs ont dû être surpris; **we thought he ~ be shy** nous pensions qu'il devait être timide; **they ~ really detest each other** ils doivent vraiment se détester; **anyone who believes her ~ be naïve** il faut vraiment être naïf pour la croire; **you ~ be out of your mind!** tu es fou!; **8** (expressing strong interest, desire) **this I ~ see!** il faut que je voie ça!; **we simply ~ get away from this town!** il faut à tout prix que nous quittions cette ville!
II n **it's a ~** c'est indispensable; **this film is a ~** ce film est à voir or à ne pas rater; **a visit to the Louvre is a ~** une visite au Louvre s'impose.

mustache n US = **moustache**.

mustard /ˈmʌstəd/ ▶ 818 ⌡ **I** n **1** (plant, condiment) moutarde f; **2** (colour) (jaune m) moutarde m.
II noun modifier [powder, seed] de moutarde; [pot, spoon] à moutarde.
IDIOMS **to be as keen as ~** déborder d'enthousiasme.

muster /ˈmʌstə(r)/ **I** n MIL rassemblement m.
II vtr (also ~ **up**) (summon) rassembler [energy, troops]; rallier [support]; préparer [argument].
III vi GEN, MIL se rassembler.
IDIOMS **to pass ~** être acceptable.

mustn't /'mʌsnt/ abrév = **must not**.

musty /'mʌstɪ/ adj **1** [room] qui sent le renfermé; [book, clothing] qui a une odeur de moisi; **to smell ~** sentir le moisi ou le renfermé; **2** FIG [ideas] vieux jeu.

mutant /'mju:tənt/ n, adj mutant/-e (m/f).

mutate /mju:'teɪt, US 'mju:teɪt/ **I** vtr faire subir une mutation à.
II vi [cell, organism] subir une mutation; [alien, monster] se métamorphoser (**into** en).

mutation /mju:'teɪʃn/ n **1** GEN, BIOL mutation f; **2** LING altération f.

mute /mju:t/ **I** n MUS sourdine f.
II adj muet/-ette.

muted /'mju:tɪd/ adj **1** (subdued) [response] tiède; [celebration, pleasure] mitigé; [criticism] voilé; [colour] sourd; [sound] assourdi; **2** MUS [trumpet] bouché.

mutilate /'mju:tɪleɪt/ vtr mutiler.

mutilation /ˌmju:tɪ'leɪʃn/ n **1** (of body, property) mutilation f; **2** (injury) blessure f.

mutinous /'mju:tɪnəs/ adj GEN rebelle; [soldier, sailor] mutiné.

mutiny /'mju:tɪnɪ/ n mutinerie f.

mutter /'mʌtə(r)/ **I** n marmonnement m.
II vtr, vi marmonner.

mutton /'mʌtn/ n CULIN mouton m.
II noun modifier [stew, pie] de mouton.
IDIOMS **as dead as ~** mort et bien mort; **~ dressed as lamb** habillé trop jeune pour son âge.

mutton chops npl (whiskers) (favoris mpl en) côtelettes fpl.

mutual /'mju:tʃʊəl/ adj (reciprocal) réciproque; (common) commun; [society, consent] mutuel/-elle; **by ~ agreement** d'un commun accord; **it is to their ~ advantage** c'est dans leur intérêt à tous deux.

mutual aid, **mutual assistance** n entraide f.

mutually /'mju:tʃʊəlɪ/ adv mutuellement; **~ acceptable** acceptable pour les deux parties; **~ agreed** fixé d'un commun accord.

Muzak® /'mju:zæk/ n PÉJ musique f d'ambiance (enregistrée).

muzzle /'mʌzl/ **I** n (snout) museau m; (worn by animal) muselière f; (of gun) canon m; (of canon) bouche f.
II vtr museler.

MW n RADIO (abrév = **medium wave**) ondes fpl moyennes.

my /maɪ/

■ **Note** In French, determiners agree in gender and number with the noun that follows. So my is translated by mon + masculine singular noun (mon chien), ma + feminine singular noun (ma maison) BUT by mon + feminine noun beginning with a vowel or mute h (mon assiette) and by mes + plural noun (mes enfants).
– When my is stressed, à moi is added after the noun: MY house = ma maison à moi.
– For my used with parts of the body see the Usage Note ▶ 765 |.

I det **1** GEN mon/ma/mes; **2** (used emphatically) MY **house** ma maison à moi.
II excl **~ ~!** ça alors!

myalgic encephalomyelitis, **ME** /maɪˌældʒɪk enˌsefələʊˌmaɪə'laɪtɪs/ ▶ 1002| n encéphalomyélite f myalgique.

myopia /maɪ'əʊpɪə/ n MED myopie f ALSO FIG.

myopic /maɪ'ɒpɪk/ adj **1** [vision] myope; **2** FIG [policy] myope; [view] étroit.

myself /maɪ'self, mə'self/

■ **Note** When used as a reflexive pronoun, direct and indirect, myself is translated by me which is always placed before the verb: I've hurt myself = je me suis fait mal.
– When used as an emphatic the translation is moi-même: I did it myself = je l'ai fait moi-même.
– When used after a preposition myself is translated by moi or moi-même: I did it for myself = je l'ai fait pour moi or moi-même.
– For particular usages see below.

pron **1** (refl) me, (before vowel) m'; **2** (emphatic) moi-même; **I saw it ~** je l'ai vu moi-même; **for ~** pour moi, pour moi-même; **(all) by ~** tout seul; **3** (expressions) **I'm not much of a dog-lover ~** personnellement je n'aime pas trop les chiens; **I'm not ~ today** je ne suis pas dans mon assiette aujourd'hui.

mysterious /mɪ'stɪərɪəs/ adj mystérieux/-ieuse; **to be ~ about** faire grand mystère de.

mysteriously /mɪ'stɪərɪəslɪ/ adv [die, disappear, appear] mystérieusement; [say, smile, signal] d'un air mystérieux.

mystery /'mɪstərɪ/ **I** n **1** mystère m; **it's a ~ to me how** je n'arrive pas à comprendre comment; **it's a ~ how** on ne sait pas comment; **there is no ~ about her success** son succès n'a rien de mystérieux; **2** (book) roman m policier; **3** RELIG mystère m.
II noun modifier [death, illness, voice] mystérieux/-ieuse; [guest, visitor] mystère; [prize, tour] surprise; **the ~ man/woman** l'inconnu/-e.

mystery: **~ play** n mystère m; **~ tour** n voyage m surprise.

mystic(al) /'mɪstɪk(l)/ adj GEN mystique.

mysticism /'mɪstɪsɪzəm/ n mysticisme m.

mystification /ˌmɪstɪfɪ'keɪʃn/ n **1** (of issue, process) mystification f; **2** (of person) perplexité f; **in some ~, he...** quelque peu perplexe, il...

mystify /'mɪstɪfaɪ/ vtr laisser [qn] perplexe; **I am completely mystified** je suis tout à fait perplexe.

mystifying /'mɪstɪfaɪɪŋ/ adj intrigant.

myth /mɪθ/ n (fallacy) mythe m; (mythology) mythologie f.

mythic(al) /'mɪθɪk(l)/ adj mythique.

mythological /ˌmɪθə'lɒdʒɪkl/ adj mythologique.

mythology /mɪ'θɒlədʒɪ/ n mythologie f.

Nn

n, N /en/ *n* **1** (letter) n, N *m*; **for the nth time** pour la énième fois; **2** N GEOG (*abrév écrite* = **north**) N.

n/a, N/A (*abrév* = **not applicable**) s/o.

NA *n: abrév* ▶ **North America**.

nab /næb/ *vtr* (*p prés etc* **-bb-**) (catch) pincer○ [*wrongdoer*]; coincer○ [*passer-by*]; (steal) piquer○.

nadir /'neɪdɪə(r)/ *n* LIT nadir *m*; FIG point *m* le plus bas.

naff○ /næf/ *adj* GB ringard○.

nag /næg/ **I** *vtr* (*p prés etc* **-gg-**) **1** (pester) enquiquiner○ (**about** au sujet de); **2** (niggle) lanciner.
II *vi* (*p prés etc* **-gg-**) **1** (moan) faire des remarques continuelles; **to ~ at sb** enquiquiner○ qn; **2** (niggle) **to ~ (away) at sb** travailler qn.
III nagging *pres p adj* **1** (complaining) PÉJ his **~ging wife** sa mégère de femme PEJ; **2** (niggling) [*pain, doubt, suspicion*] tenace; [*problem*] obsédant.

nail /neɪl/ **I** *n* **1** ANAT ongle *m*; **to bite one's ~s** se ronger les ongles; **2** TECH clou *m*.
II *vtr* **1** (attach with nails) clouer; **2**○ (pin down) coincer [*wrongdoer*]; démasquer [*liar*]; **3**○ (expose) démentir [*rumour*]; démolir [*myth*].
IDIOMS **to hit the ~ on the head** mettre le doigt dessus; **cash on the ~** argent *m* comptant; **to be as hard** ou **as tough as ~s** être sans cœur; **to fight tooth and ~** se battre avec acharnement.
▪ **nail down**: ¶ ~ **down** [sth], ~ [sth] **down 1** clouer; **2** FIG (define) définir; ¶ ~ [sb] **down** coincer○ [*person*]; **to ~ sb down to a time** obtenir de qn qu'il fixe (*subj*) une heure.
▪ **nail up**: ~ **up** [sth], ~ [sth] **up** GEN clouer; (board up) condamner (*avec des planches*).

nail-biting /'neɪlbaɪtɪŋ/ **I** *n* habitude *f* de se ronger les ongles.
II *adj* [*match, finish*] palpitant; [*wait*] angoissant.

nail: **~brush** *n* brosse *f* à ongles; **~ clippers** *npl* coupe-ongles *m inv*; **~ file** *n* lime *f* à ongles; **~ polish** *n* vernis *m* à ongles; **~ polish remover** *n* dissolvant *m*; **~ scissors** *npl* ciseaux *mpl* à ongles; **~ varnish** *n* vernis *m* à ongles.

naïve /naɪ'iːv/ *adj* GEN, ART naïf/-ïve.

naïvely /naɪ'iːvlɪ/ *adv* [*believe, say, behave*] naïvement; [*draw, write*] dans un style naïf.

naked /'neɪkɪd/ *adj* **1** **to the waist** torse nu; **2** [*flame, light bulb, sword*] nu; **3** [*truth*] tout nu; [*facts*] brut; [*emotion*] non déguisé.

name /neɪm/ **I** *n* **1** (title) GEN nom *m*; (of book, film) titre *m*; **first ~** prénom *m*; **my ~ is Louis** je m'appelle Louis; **what ~ shall I say?** (on phone) c'est de la part de qui?; (in person) qui dois-je annoncer?; **he goes by the ~ of Max** il s'appelle Max; **I know it by another ~** je le connais sous un autre nom; **I only know the company by ~** je ne connais la société que de nom; **he's president in ~ only** il n'a de président que le nom; **to be party leader in all** ou **everything but ~** être chef du parti en pratique, sinon en titre; **to take** ou **get one's ~ from** porter le nom de; **to put one's ~ down for** s'inscrire à; **2** (reputation) réputation *f*; **3** (insult) **to call sb ~s** injurier qn; **he called me all sorts of ~s** il m'a traité de tous les noms.
II *vtr* **1** (call) appeler [*person, area*]; baptiser [*boat, planet*]; **they ~d her after** GB ou **for** US **her mother** ils l'ont appelée comme sa mère; **we'll ~ him Martin after Martin Luther King** on l'appellera Martin en souvenir de Martin Luther King; **a boy ~d Joe** un

garçon nommé Joe; **the product is ~d after its inventor** le produit porte le nom de son inventeur; **2** (cite) citer; **~ three American States** citez trois États américains; **illnesses? you ~ it, I've had it!** des maladies? je les ai toutes eues!; **3** (reveal identity of) citer [*names*]; révéler [*sources*]; révéler l'identité de [*suspect*]; **to ~ ~s** donner des noms; **naming no ~s** sans vouloir dénoncer personne; **to be ~d as a suspect** être désigné comme suspect; **4** (appoint) nommer [*captain*]; donner la composition de [*team*]; désigner [*heir*]; nommer [*successor*]; **5** (state) indiquer [*place, time*]; fixer [*price, terms*].
IDIOMS **that's the ~ of the game** c'est la règle du jeu; **to see one's ~ in lights** devenir célèbre.

name: **~ day** *n* RELIG fête *f*; **~-drop** *vi* PÉJ citer des gens célèbres (*qu'on prétend connaître*).

nameless /'neɪmlɪs/ *adj* [*person*] anonyme; [*fear, dread*] inexprimable.

namely /'neɪmlɪ/ *adv* à savoir.

name: **~ plate** *n* plaque *f*; **~sake** *n* homonyme *m*; **~ tag** *n* étiquette *f* (*sur laquelle est marqué le nom du propriétaire*); **~ tape** *n* nom *m* tissé.

Namibia /nə'mɪbɪə/ ▶ 840 *pr n* Namibie *f*.

nanny /'nænɪ/ *n* GB (nurse) bonne *f* d'enfants; (grandmother)○ mamie *f*.

nanny goat *n* chèvre *f*.

nap /næp/ **I** *n* **1** (snooze) petit somme *m*; **afternoon ~** sieste *f*; **2** (pile) poil *m*; (direction of cut) sens *m*; **against the ~** à rebrousse-poil.
II *vi* (*p prés etc* **-pp-**) sommeiller.
IDIOMS **to catch sb ~ping**○ prendre qn au dépourvu.

napalm /'neɪpɑːm/ *n* napalm *m*.

nape /neɪp/ *n* nuque *f*; **the ~ of the neck** la nuque.

napkin /'næpkɪn/ *n* (serviette) serviette *f* (de table); **~ ring** rond *m* de serviette.

nappy /'næpɪ/ *n* GB couche *f* (de bébé).

nappy: **~ liner** *n* lange *m* fin; **~ rash** *n* GB érythème *m* fessier.

narcotic /nɑː'kɒtɪk/ **I** *n* (soporific) LIT, FIG narcotique *m*; (illegal drug) stupéfiant *m*.
II *adj* LIT, FIG narcotique.

narcotics agent *n* US agent *m* de la brigade des stupéfiants.

narked○ /nɑːkt/ *adj* en rogne○, en boule○.

narration /nə'reɪʃn/ *n* récit *m*, narration *f*.

narrative /'nærətɪv/ **I** *n* (account) récit *m*; (storytelling) narration *f*.
II *noun modifier* [*prose, poem*] narratif/-ive; [*skill, talent*] de conteur.

narrator /nə'reɪtə(r)/ *n* LITERAT narrateur/-trice *m/f*; MUS récitant/-e *m/f*.

narrow /'nærəʊ/ ▶ 1045 **I narrows** *npl* goulet *m*.
II *adj* **1** (in breadth, size, shape) étroit; **to grow** ou **become ~** [*road, river*] se rétrécir; [*valley*] se resserrer; **2** (in scope) [*range, choice*] restreint; [*issue, field, boundaries, group, sense, definition*] étroit; [*vision, life, interests, understanding*] limité; [*views, version*] étriqué PÉJ; **3** (in degree) [*majority, margin*] faible; **to have a ~ lead** avoir une légère avance; **to win a ~ victory** gagner de justesse; **to have a ~ escape** ou **a ~ squeak**○ GB l'échapper belle.
III *vtr* **1** (limit) GEN limiter (**to** à); restreindre [*sense, definition*] (**to** à); **2** (reduce) réduire (**from** de; **to** à); **Elliott has ~ed the gap** (in race, poll) Elliott a réduit

Nationalities

Words like French can also refer to the language
(e.g. a French textbook, ▶ 1038) and to the country
(e.g. French history ▶ 840).

Note the different use of capital letters in English and
French; adjectives never have capitals in French:

a French student = un étudiant français/une étudiante
française
a French nurse = une infirmière française/un infirmier
français
a French tourist = un touriste français/une touriste
française

Nouns have capitals in French when they mean a person
of a specific nationality:

a Frenchman = un Français
a Frenchwoman = une Française
French people *or* the French = les Français *mpl*
a Chinese man = un Chinois
a Chinese woman = une Chinoise
Chinese people *or* the Chinese = les Chinois *mpl*

English sometimes has a special word for a person of a
specific nationality; in French, the same word can almost
always be either an adjective (no capitals) or a noun
(with capitals):

Danish = danois
a Dane = un Danois, une Danoise
the Danes = les Danois *mpl*

Note the alternatives using either adjective (il/elle est ...
etc.) or noun (c'est ...) in French:

he is French = il est français
or c'est un Français
she is French = elle est française
or c'est une Française
they are French = *(men or mixed)* ils sont français
or ce sont des Français
(women) elles sont françaises
or ce sont des Françaises

When the subject is a noun, like the teacher *or* Paul *below,*
the adjective construction is normally used in French:

the teacher is French = le professeur est français
Paul is French = Paul est français
Anne is French = Anne est française
Paul and Anne are French = Paul et Anne sont français

Other ways of expressing someone's nationality or
origins are:

he's of French extraction = il est d'origine française
she was born in Germany = elle est née en Allemagne
he is a Spanish citizen = il est espagnol
a Belgian national = un ressortissant belge
she comes from Nepal = elle vient du Népal

---

l'écart; **3** (reduce breadth of) rétrécir [*road, path,
arteries*]; **to ~ one's eyes** plisser les yeux.
IV *vi* **1** LIT GEN se rétrécir; [*valley, arteries*] se
resserrer; **2** FIG [*gap, deficit, margin, lead*] se réduire
(**to** à); [*choice*] se limiter (**to** à).
IDIOMS **the straight and ~** le droit chemin.
■ **narrow down** ¶ [*investigation, search*] se limiter
(**to** à); [*field of contestants, suspects*] se réduire (**to** à); ¶
~ [sth] down, ~ down [sth] réduire [*numbers, list,
choice*] (**to** à); limiter [*investigation, research*] (**to** à).
narrow boat *n* GB péniche *f*.
narrowly /ˈnærəʊlɪ/ *adv* (barely) de justesse; (strictly)
strictement.
narrow-minded /ˌnærəʊˈmaɪndɪd/ *adj* PÉJ borné.
nasal /ˈneɪzl/ **I** *n* LING nasale *f*.
II *adj* LING nasal; GEN nasillard.
nasal spray *n* nébuliseur *m* (*pour le nez*).
nastily /ˈnɑːstɪlɪ/ *adv* [*behave, speak, laugh*] d'une
façon désagréable; **to say sth ~** dire qch d'un ton
sarcastique.
nastiness /ˈnɑːstɪnɪs/ *n* GEN méchanceté *f*; (of food,
medicine) mauvais goût *m*.
nasturtium /nəˈstɜːʃəm/ *n* capucine *f*.
nasty /ˈnɑːstɪ/ **I**○ *n* (in food, water, air) saleté *f*; **video
~** film *m* d'épouvante en vidéo.
II *adj* **1** (unpleasant) [*crime, experience, sight, taste,
surprise, suspicion*] horrible; [*feeling, task*] désagréable; [*habit, weather, smell, taste*] mauvais; [*expression, look*] méchant; [*rumour*] inquiétant; [*stain*] gros/
grosse; [*affair, business*] sale (*before n*); **I got a ~
fright** j'ai vraiment eu un choc; **things could get ~**
les choses pourraient mal tourner; **to turn ~**
[*person, dog*] devenir méchant; [*weather*] se gâter; **to
be a ~ piece of work**○ GB être un sale type○/une
sale bonne femme○; **2** (unkind) [*person*] désagréable;
[*trick*] sale (*before n*), vilain; [*gossip, remark, letter*]
méchant; **you've got a ~ mind** tu vois toujours le
mal partout; **to be ~ to** être dur envers; **3** (serious)
[*cut, bruise*] vilain (*before n*); [*bump, crack, fall, accident*] grave; [*cold*] mauvais (*before n*); **4** (ugly) affreux/
-euse; **5** (tricky) [*problem, question*] difficile; [*bend*]
dangereux/-euse.
nation /ˈneɪʃn/ *n* POL (entity) nation *f*; (people) peuple
m.
national /ˈnæʃnl/ **I** *n* **1** (citizen) ressortissant/-e *m/f*;
2○ GB (newspaper) **the ~s** les grands quotidiens *mpl*.
II *adj* national; **the ~ press** *ou* **newspapers** GB les
grands quotidiens *mpl*; **~ affairs** les affaires du pays.

national: **~ anthem** *n* hymne *m* national; **National Curriculum** *n* GB programme *m* scolaire
national; **~ debt** *n* dette *f* publique; **National
Front, NF** *n* GB *parti britannique d'extrême droite*;
~ grid *n* ELEC réseau *m* national haute-tension.
National Health *n* GB **to get sth on the ~** ≈ se
faire rembourser qch par la Sécurité Sociale.
national: **National Health Service, NHS** *n* GB
services *mpl* de santé britanniques, ≈ Sécurité *f*
Sociale; **National Insurance, NI** *n* GB securité *f*
sociale britannique; **National Insurance number**
n numéro *m* de sécurité sociale.
nationalism /ˈnæʃnəlɪzəm/ *n* nationalisme *m*.
nationality /ˌnæʃəˈnælɪtɪ/ *n* nationalité *f*.
nationalization /ˌnæʃnəlaɪˈzeɪʃn, US -lɪˈz-/ *n* nationalisation *f*.
nationalize /ˈnæʃnəlaɪz/ *vtr* nationaliser [*industry*].
nationally /ˈnæʃnəlɪ/ *adv* **1** (at national level) à l'échelon national; **2** (nationwide) [*broadcast, enforce, employ,
distribute*] sur l'ensemble du pays; [*known, respected,
available*] dans tout le pays.
national: **~ monument** *n* monument *m* historique; **National Savings Bank** *n* GB ≈ Caisse *f*
d'Épargne; **~ service** *n* GB HIST service *m* militaire; **National Trust, NT** *n* GB commission *f*
nationale des sites et monuments historiques.
nation-state *n* État-nation *m*.
nationwide /ˌneɪʃnˈwaɪd/ **I** *adj* [*appeal, coverage,
scheme, strike*] sur l'ensemble du territoire; [*campaign*]
national; [*survey, poll*] à l'échelle nationale.
II *adv* [*broadcast, travel, compete*] dans tout le pays.
native /ˈneɪtɪv/ **I** *n* (person) autochtone *mf*; BOT, ZOOL
espèce *f* indigène; **to be a ~ of** [*person, plant*] être
originaire de; **to speak a language like a ~** parler
une langue comme si c'était sa langue maternelle.
II *adj* **1** (original) [*land*] natal; [*tongue*] maternel/-elle;
~ German speaker personne *f* de langue maternelle
allemande; **~ English speaker** anglophone *mf*; **2**
BOT, ZOOL indigène; **to go ~** HUM adopter les
coutumes locales; **3** [*cunning*] inné; [*wit*] naturel/-elle.
Native American *n*, *adj* amérindien/-ienne (*m/f*).
native speaker *n* locuteur natif/locutrice native
m/f; **'we require a ~ of English'** 'recherchons
personne de langue maternelle anglaise'.
Nativity /nəˈtɪvɪtɪ/ *n* RELIG, ART nativité *f*.
Nato, NATO *n* (*abrév* = **North Atlantic Treaty
Organization**) OTAN *f*.

natter° /ˈnætə(r)/ GB **I** n causette° f (**about** sur).
II vi (also ~ **on**) papoter.

natty° /ˈnætɪ/ adj (smart) chic inv; (clever) astucieux/-ieuse.

natural /ˈnætʃrəl/ **I** n **1**° (person) **as an actress, she's a ~** c'est une actrice née; **2** MUS (sign) bécarre m; (note) note f naturelle.
II adj **1** naturel/-elle, normal; **it's only ~** c'est tout à fait naturel; **to die of ~ causes** mourir de mort naturelle; **2** (innate) [gift, emotion, trait] inné; [artist, professional] né; [affinity] naturel/-elle; **a ~ advantage** un atout; **3** (unaffected) simple, naturel/-elle; **4** MUS naturel/-elle.

natural childbirth n accouchement m sans douleur.

naturalist /ˈnætʃrəlɪst/ n, adj naturaliste (mf).

naturalization /ˌnætʃrəlaɪˈzeɪʃn, US -lɪˈz-/ n **1** ADMIN naturalisation f; **2** BOT, ZOOL acclimatation f.

naturalize /ˈnætʃrəlaɪz/ **I** vtr **1** ADMIN naturaliser [person]; **to be ~d** se faire naturaliser; **2** BOT, ZOOL acclimater.
II vi BOT, ZOOL s'acclimater.

natural justice n principes d'égalité s'appliquant au règlement de disputes.

naturally /ˈnætʃrəlɪ/ adv **1** (obviously, of course) naturellement, bien entendu; **~ enough, she refused** naturellement, elle a refusé; **2** (by nature) de nature; **her hair is ~ blonde** elle a des cheveux blond naturel; **I was doing what comes ~** j'ai fait ce qui me semblait naturel; **politeness comes ~ to him** il est d'un naturel poli; **3** (unaffectedly) avec naturel; **4** (in natural world) à l'état naturel.

nature /ˈneɪtʃə(r)/ **I** n **1** (the natural world) nature f; **let ~ take its course** laissez faire la nature; **~ versus nurture** l'inné et l'acquis; **to obey a call of ~** EUPH aller se soulager°; **2** (character, temperament) nature f, naturel m; **it's not in her ~ to be aggressive** elle n'est pas agressive de nature; **3** (kind, sort) nature f, sorte f; **matters of a medical ~** des choses d'ordre médical; **her letter was something in the ~ of a confession** sa lettre tenait de la confession; **'~ of contents'** 'désignation du contenu'; **4** (essential character) nature f, essence f; **it is in the ~ of things** il est dans l'ordre des choses.
II -natured combining form **sweet-/pleasant-~d** d'un naturel doux/agréable.

nature: **~ conservancy** n protection f de la nature; **~ reserve** n réserve f naturelle; **~ trail** n sentier m écologique.

naturist /ˈneɪtʃərɪst/ n, adj naturiste (mf).

naughtily /ˈnɔːtɪlɪ/ adv (disobediently) **to behave ~** être vilain; (suggestively) **she winked at him ~** HUM elle lui a fait un clin d'œil coquin.

naughtiness /ˈnɔːtɪnɪs/ n **1** (of child, pet) mauvaise conduite f; **2** (of joke, suggestion) grivoiserie f.

naughty /ˈnɔːtɪ/ adj **1** (disobedient) [child] vilain; **a ~ word** un gros mot; **2** (suggestive) coquin; **the ~ nineties** ≈ la Belle Époque.

nausea /ˈnɔːsɪə, US ˈnɔːʒə/ n nausée f.

nauseate /ˈnɔːzɪeɪt, US ˈnɔːz-/ vtr LIT, FIG écœurer.

nauseating /ˈnɔːzɪeɪtɪŋ, US ˈnɔːz-/ adj écœurant.

nauseatingly /ˈnɔːzɪeɪtɪŋlɪ, US ˈnɔːz-/ adv **~ sweet/rich** d'une douceur/richesse écœurante.

nauseous /ˈnɔːsɪəs, US ˈnɔːʃəs/ adj [taste, smell] écœurant; **to feel ~** avoir la nausée.

nautical /ˈnɔːtɪkl/ adj [instrument, almanac, term, mile] nautique; [rules] de navigation; [theme] marin.

naval /ˈneɪvl/ adj naval; [officer, recruit, uniform, affairs] de la marine; [traditions, strength, building] maritime.

naval: **~ base**, **~ station** n base f navale; **~ dockyard** n chantier m naval; **~ stores** npl (depot) entrepôt m maritime; (supplies) fournitures fpl maritimes.

nave /neɪv/ n ARCHIT nef f.

navel /ˈneɪvl/ n nombril m.

navigable /ˈnævɪɡəbl/ adj [river] navigable.

navigate /ˈnævɪɡeɪt/ **I** vtr **1** (sail) parcourir [seas]; **2** (guide) piloter [plane, ship]; **3** (steer) piloter [plane]; gouverner [ship]; **to ~ one's way through** retrouver son chemin dans [streets].
II vi NAUT, AVIAT naviguer; AUT (in a rally) faire le copilote; (on a journey) tenir la carte; (without a map) retrouver son chemin.

navigation /ˌnævɪˈɡeɪʃn/ n navigation f.

navigational /ˌnævɪˈɡeɪʃənl/ adj [instruments] de navigation; [science] de la navigation.

navigation laws npl code m maritime.

navigator /ˈnævɪɡeɪtə(r)/ n AVIAT, NAUT navigateur/-trice m/f; AUT copilote mf.

navy /ˈneɪvɪ/ **I** n **1** (fleet) flotte f; (fighting force) marine f; **2** (also ~ **blue**) bleu m marine.
II adj ▶818 **1** (also ~ **blue**) bleu marine inv; **2** MIL, NAUT [life, uniform, wife] de marin.

nay /neɪ/ ‡ ou LITTER **I** n (negative vote) non m.
II adv et même.

Nazi /ˈnɑːtsɪ/ n, adj nazi/-e (m/f).

NBC n US TV (abrév = **National Broadcasting Company**) chaîne nationale de la télévision américaine.

NC 1 COMM (abrév = **no charge**) gratuit; **2** US POST abrév écrite = **North Carolina**.

NCO n MIL (abrév = **noncommissioned officer**) sous-officier m.

ND US POST abrév écrite = **North Dakota**.

NE 1 ▶1157 (abrév = **northeast**) NE m; **2** abrév écrite = **Nebraska**.

near /nɪə(r)/ **I** adv **1** (nearby) **to live quite ~** habiter tout près; **to move** ou **draw ~er** s'approcher davantage (**to** de); **to bring sth ~er** approcher qch; **2** (close in time) **the time is ~ when**... dans peu de temps,...; **how ~ are they in age?** combien ont-ils de différence d'âge?; **3** (nearly) **as ~ perfect as it could be** aussi proche de la perfection que possible; **nowhere ~ finished** loin d'être fini.
II near enough adv phr **1** (approximately) à peu près; **2** (sufficiently close) **that's ~ enough** (not any closer) tu es assez près; (acceptable as quantity) ça ira.
III prep **1** (in space) près de; **2** (in time) **~er the time** quand la date approchera; **it's getting ~ Christmas** Noël approche; **on** or **~ the 12th** autour du 12; **3** (in degree) proche de; **~ the beginning of the article** presque au début de l'article; **he's no ~er (making) a decision** il n'est pas plus décidé; **she's nowhere ~ finishing** elle est loin d'avoir fini; **£400? it cost ~er £600** 400 livres sterling? je dirais plutôt 600; **nobody comes anywhere ~ her** FIG personne ne lui arrive à la cheville.
IV near to prep prep **1** (in space) près de; **~ to where** près de l'endroit où; **how ~ are we to Dijon?** à quelle distance sommes-nous de Dijon?; **2** (on point of) au bord de [tears, hysteria, collapse]; **to be ~ to doing** être sur le point de faire; **how ~ are you to completing...?** est-ce que vous êtes sur le point de finir...?; **3** (in degree) **to come ~est to** s'approcher le plus de; **to come ~ to doing** faillir faire.
V adj **1** (close in distance, time) proche; **2** (in degree) **he's the ~est thing to an accountant we've got** c'est lui qui a le plus de connaissances en comptabilité parmi nos employés; **it's the ~est thing** (to article, colour required) c'est ça le plus approchant; **3** (short) **the ~est route** le chemin le plus court.
VI near + combining form presque; **a ~-catastrophic blunder** une gaffe presque catastrophique.
VII vtr LIT, FIG (draw close to) approcher de; **to ~ completion** toucher à sa fin; **to ~ retirement** partir bientôt à la retraite.

nearby /nɪəˈbaɪ/ **I** adj [person] qui se trouve/trouvait etc à proximité; [town, village] d'à côté; **they drove to a ~ garage** ils ont conduit jusqu'au garage le plus proche.
II adv à proximité; **~, there's a village** tout près il y a un village.

Near East pr n Proche-Orient m.

nearly /'nɪəlɪ/ adv **1** (almost) presque; **have you ~ finished?** as-tu bientôt fini?; **he ~ laughed** il a réprimé un rire; **I very ~ gave up** j'ai bien failli abandonner; **2** (used with negatives) **not ~** loin d'être; **not ~ as talented as** loin d'être aussi doué que.

nearly new adj [clothes] d'occasion.

near miss n risque m de collision; **to have a ~** [planes] frôler la collision; [cars] faillir se percuter.

nearness /'nɪənɪs/ n GEN proximité f; (of event) approche f.

nearside /'nɪəsaɪd/ **I** n GB côté m gauche; (elsewhere) côté m droit.
II noun modifier GB [lane] gauche; (elsewhere) [lane] droit.

near: **~-sighted** adj myope; **~-sightedness** n myopie f.

neat /niːt/ **I** adj **1** (tidy) [person] (in habits) ordonné; (in appearance) soigné; [room, house, desk] bien rangé; [garden, handwriting] soigné; **in ~ piles** en piles régulières; **2** (adroit) [explanation, solution] habile; [formula, slogan] bien trouvé; [summary] concis; **that's a ~ way of doing it!** c'est astucieux!; **3** (trim) [figure] bien fait; [features] régulier/-ière; **4**° US (very good) [plan, party, car] super°; [sum of money] joli; **5** [alcohol, spirits] sans eau.
II adv sec, sans eau.
IDIOMS **to be as ~ as a new pin** être propre comme un sou neuf.

neaten /'niːtn/ vtr arranger [tie, skirt]; ranger [pile of paper].

neatly /'niːtlɪ/ adv **1** (tidily) GEN avec soin; [write] proprement; **his hair was ~ combed** ses cheveux étaient impeccablement peignés; **2** (perfectly) GEN parfaitement; [link] habilement; **~ put!** bien or joliment dit!; **the case is designed to fit ~ into your pocket** l'étui est conçu pour rentrer facilement dans la poche.

neatness /'niːtnɪs/ n **1** (tidiness, orderliness) (of person, garden) aspect m soigné; (in habits) méticulosité f; (of room, house) propreté f; (of handwriting) netteté f; **extra marks are given for** ~ on tiendra compte de la présentation dans la notation; **2** (of figure, features) finesse f; (of explanation, solution) habileté f.

necessarily /ˌnesəˈserəlɪ, ˈnesəsərəlɪ/ adv (definitely) forcément; (of necessity) nécessairement.

necessary /'nesəsərɪ, US -serɪ/ **I** n **1**° (money) fric° m; **2** (needed thing) **to do the ~** faire le nécessaire.
II adj (required, essential, inevitable) GEN nécessaire; [qualification] requis; **if ~, as ~** si besoin est; **'no experience ~'** 'aucune expérience requise'; **to become ~** devenir urgent; **to find it ~ to do** éprouver le besoin de faire; **it is ~ for him to do** il faut qu'il fasse; **it is ~ that she should do** il faut vraiment qu'elle fasse.

necessitate /nɪ'sesɪteɪt/ vtr nécessiter; **the job would ~ your moving** le travail t'obligerait à déménager.

necessity /nɪ'sesɪtɪ/ n **1** (need) nécessité f; **from** ou **out of ~** par nécessité; **the ~ for** le besoin de; **of ~** nécessairement; **2** (essential item) **the necessities of life** les produits mpl de première nécessité; **to be a ~** être indispensable; **3** (essential measure) impératif m; **to be an absolute ~** être indispensable; **4**† (poverty) besoin m.

neck /nek/ **I** n ▶765 **1** (of person) cou m; (of horse, donkey) encolure f; **to fling one's arms around sb's ~** sauter au cou de qn; **the back of the ~** la nuque; **2** (collar) col m; (neckline) encolure f; **with a high ~** à or avec un col montant; **with a low ~** décolleté; **3** CULIN (also **best end of ~**) collet m; **4** (of bottle, vase, womb) col m.
II° vi se bécoter°.
IDIOMS **to be a pain in the ~**° être casse-pieds°; **to be ~ and ~** LIT, FIG être à égalité; **to get** ou **catch it in the ~**° en prendre pour son grade°; **to risk one's ~**° risquer sa peau°; **to stick one's ~ out**° prendre des risques; **in this ~ of the woods**° par ici; **to be dead from the ~ up**° être abruti.

necking° /'nekɪŋ/ n ₵ papouilles° fpl.

neck: **~lace** n collier m; (longer) sautoir m; **~line** n encolure f; **~tie** n US cravate f.

nectar /'nektə(r)/ n (all contexts) nectar m.

nectarine /'nektərɪn/ n (fruit) nectarine f, brugnon m; (tree) brugnonier m.

need /niːd/

■ Note When **need** is used as a verb meaning to require or to want it is generally translated by avoir besoin de in French: I need help = j'ai besoin d'aide.
– When **need** is used as a verb to mean must or have to it can generally be translated by devoir + infinitive or by il faut que + subjunctive: I need to leave = je dois partir, il faut que je parte.
– When **need** is used as a modal auxiliary in the negative to say that there is no obligation it is generally translated by ne pas être obligé de + infinitive: you needn't finish it today = tu n'es pas obligé de le finir aujourd'hui.
– When **needn't** is used as a modal auxiliary to say that something is not worthwhile or necessary it is generally translated by ce n'est pas la peine de + infinitive or ce n'est pas la peine que + subjunctive: I needn't have hurried = ce n'était pas la peine de me dépêcher or ce n'était pas la peine que je me dépêche.
– For examples of the above and further uses of need, see the entry below.

I modal aux **1** (must, have to) **'I waited'—'you needn't have'** 'j'ai attendu'—'ce n'était pas la peine'; **~ he reply?** est-ce qu'il faut qu'il réponde?, est-ce qu'il doit répondre?; **~ I say more?** tu vois ce que je veux dire?; **I hardly ~ say that...** inutile de dire que...; **did you ~ to be so unpleasant to him?** est-ce que tu avais besoin d'être si désagréable avec lui?; **'previous applicants ~ not apply'** 'les candidats ayant déjà répondu à l'annonce sont priés de ne pas se représenter'; **2** (be logically inevitable) **~ that be true?** est-ce que c'est forcément vrai?; **they needn't have died** leur mort aurait pu être évitée.
II vtr **1** (require) **to ~ sth** avoir besoin de qch; **my shoes ~ to be polished, my shoes ~ polishing** mes chaussures ont besoin d'être cirées; **I ~ you to hold the ladder** j'ai besoin de toi pour tenir l'échelle; **more money is ~ed** nous avons besoin de plus d'argent; **everything you ~** tout ce qu'il vous faut; **I gave it a much-~ed clean** je l'ai nettoyé, il en avait grand besoin; **this job ~s a lot of concentration** ce travail demande beaucoup de concentration; **to raise the money ~ed for the deposit** réunir l'argent nécessaire pour la caution; **they ~ to have things explained to them** il faut tout leur expliquer; **you don't ~ me to tell you that...** vous n'êtes pas sans savoir que...; **everything you ~ to know about computers** tout ce que vous devez savoir sur les ordinateurs; **that's all I ~!** il ne me manquait plus que ça; **2** (have to) **you'll ~ to work hard** il va falloir que tu travailles dur; **something ~ed to be done** il fallait faire quelque chose; **it ~ only be said that** il suffit de dire que; **nobody ~ know** que cela reste entre nous; **nobody ~ know that I did it** personne ne doit savoir que c'est moi qui l'ai fait.
III n **1** (necessity) nécessité f (for de); **I can't see the ~ for it** je n'en vois pas la nécessité; **without the ~ for an inquiry** sans qu'une enquête soit nécessaire; **to feel the ~ to do** éprouver le besoin de faire; **there's no ~ to wait** inutile d'attendre; **there's no ~ for panic** ça ne sert à rien de s'affoler; **there's no ~ to worry** ce n'est pas la peine de s'inquiéter; **if ~ be** s'il le faut; **if the ~ arises** si le besoin s'en fait sentir; **there's no ~, I've done it** inutile, c'est fait; **2** (want, requirement) besoin m (for de); **to satisfy a ~** répondre à un besoin; **to meet sb's ~s** répondre aux besoins de qn; **a list of your ~s** une liste de ce dont vous avez besoin; **my ~s are few** j'ai peu de besoins; **energy ~s** besoins mpl en énergie; **3** (adversity, distress) **to help sb in times of ~** aider qn à faire face à l'adversité; **she was there in my hour of ~** elle était là quand j'ai eu besoin d'elle; **your ~ is greater than mine** tu en as plus besoin que moi; **4** (poverty) besoin m; **to be in ~** être dans le besoin.

needful /'niːdfl/ I *n* **to do the ~** faire le nécessaire.
II *adj* SOUT nécessaire.

needle /'niːdl/ I *n* LIT (all contexts) aiguille *f*.
II *vtr* (annoy) harceler.
IDIOMS **as sharp as a ~** rusé comme un singe; **to have pins and ~s** avoir des fourmis.

needless /'niːdlɪs/ *adj* [*anxiety, delay, suffering*] inutile; [*intrusion, intervention*] inopportun.

needlessly /'niːdlɪslɪ/ *adv* pour rien.

needlework *n* couture *f*.

needs /niːdz/ *adv* **~ must†** il faut bien.

need-to-know *adj* **we operate on a ~ basis, we have a ~ policy** nous avons pour principe de ne divulguer les informations qu'aux personnes strictement concernées.

needy /'niːdɪ/ I *n* **the ~** (+ *v pl*) les indigents *mpl*.
II *adj* [*person*] nécessiteux/-euse; [*sector, area*] sans ressources.

negate /nɪ'geɪt/ *vtr* (cancel out) réduire [qch] à néant; (deny) nier; (contradict) contredire; LING mettre [qch] à la forme négative.

negation /nɪ'geɪʃn/ *n* GEN, LING négation *f*; (denial) réfutation *f*.

negative /'negətɪv/ I *n* **1** (refusal) réponse *f* négative; **to answer** OU **reply in the ~** répondre par la négative; **2** PHOT, ELEC négatif *m*; **3** LING négation *f*; **in the ~** à la forme négative.
II *adj* **1** GEN (negating, unpleasant, pessimistic) négatif/-ive; [*effect, influence*] néfaste; **2** PHOT en négatif.

negatively /'negətɪvlɪ/ *adv* [*react, respond*] négativement; [*affect, influence*] de façon néfaste.

neglect /nɪ'glekt/ I *n* **1** (lack of care) (of person) négligence *f*, (of building, garden equipment) manque *m* d'entretien; (of health, appearance) manque *m* de soin; **to fall into ~** être laissé à l'abandon; **2** (lack of interest) indifférence *f* (**of** à l'égard de).
II *vtr* **1** (fail to care for) ne pas s'occuper de [*person, dog, plant*]; ne pas entretenir [*garden, house*]; négliger [*health, appearance*]; **2** (ignore) négliger [*problem, friend, artist, subject, work*]; se désintéresser de [*industry, economy, sector*]; ne pas tenir compte de [*needs, wishes*]; ignorer [*offer, opportunity*]; **3** (fail) **to ~ to do** négliger de faire; **to ~ to mention** omettre de mentionner.
III *v refl* **to ~ oneself** se laisser aller.

neglected /nɪ'glektɪd/ *adj* GEN négligé; [*garden, building*] mal entretenu; **to feel ~** se sentir délaissé.

neglectful /nɪ'glektfl/ *adj* négligent.

negligence /'neglɪdʒəns/ *n* GEN négligence *f*.

negligent /'neglɪdʒənt/ *adj* [*person, procedure*] négligent; [*air, manner*] nonchalant.

negligible /'neglɪdʒəbl/ *adj* négligeable.

negotiable /nɪ'gəʊʃəbl/ *adj* **1** FIN, COMM négociable; **'not ~'** [*cheque*] 'non à ordre'; **2** [*road, pass*] praticable; [*obstacle*] franchissable.

negotiate /nɪ'gəʊʃɪeɪt/ I *vtr* **1** (discuss) GEN, FIN négocier (**with** avec); **'to be ~d'** 'à négocier'; **2** (manoeuvre around) négocier [*bend, turn*]; franchir [*obstacle*]; **3** résoudre [*problem*]; surmonter [*difficulty*].
II *vi* négocier (**with** avec; **for** pour obtenir).
III **negotiated** *pp adj* [*settlement, peace, solution*] négocié.

negotiating /nɪ'gəʊʃɪeɪtɪŋ/ *adj* **1** [*ploy, position*] de négociation; [*rights*] à la négociation; **the ~ table** la table des négociations; **2** [*team, committee*] qui conduit les négociations.

negotiation /nɪ,gəʊʃɪ'eɪʃn/ *n* négociation *f*; **to be under ~** être en cours de négociations; **to be open for ~** être négociable; **to be up for ~** être à négocier.

negotiator /nɪ'gəʊʃɪeɪtə(r)/ *n* négociateur/-trice *m/f*.

Negro /'niːgrəʊ/ I *n* (*pl* **-es**) INJUR nègre *m*.
II *adj* [*descent, race*] noir, nègre.

neigh /neɪ/ *vi* hennir.

neighbour, **neighbor** US /'neɪbə(r)/ I *n* **1** voisin/-e *m/f*; **next-door-~** voisin/-e *m/f* d'à côté; **England's**

nearest ~ is France le pays le plus proche de l'Angleterre est la France; **2** RELIG, LITTÉR prochain *m*.
II *vi* **to ~ on sth** [*building*] avoisiner qch; [*country*] border qch.

neighbourhood GB, **neighborhood** US /'neɪbəhʊd/ I *n* **1** (district) quartier *m*; **2** (vicinity) **in the ~** dans le voisinage.
II *noun modifier* [*facility, shop, office*] du quartier.

neighbourhood: **~ television** *n* télévision *f* locale; **~ watch** (**scheme**) *n* surveillance *f* par les gens du quartier.

neighbouring GB, **neighboring** US /'neɪbərɪŋ/ *adj* voisin.

neighbourly GB, **neighborly** US /'neɪbəlɪ/ *adj* [*person, act*] gentil/-ille; [*relations*] de bon voisinage.

neither /'naɪðə(r), 'niːð-/

■ **Note** When used as co-ordinating conjunctions *neither…nor* are translated by *ni…ni*: she speaks neither English nor French = elle ne parle ni anglais ni français; he is neither intelligent nor kind = il n'est ni intelligent ni gentil; neither tea, nor milk = ni (le) thé, ni (le) lait. Note that the preceding verb is negated by *ne*.
– For examples and further uses see the entry **neither** I1.
– When used as a conjunction to show agreement or similarity with a negative statement, *neither* is translated by *non plus*: 'I don't like him'—'neither do I' = 'je ne l'aime pas'—'moi non plus'; 'he's not Spanish'—'neither is John' = 'il n'est pas espagnol'—'John non plus'; 'I can't sleep'—'neither can I' = 'je n'arrive pas à dormir'—'moi non plus'.
– When used to give additional information to a negative statement *neither* can often be translated by *non plus* preceded by a negative verb: she hasn't written, neither has she telephoned = elle n'a pas écrit, et elle n'a pas téléphoné non plus; I don't wish to insult you, but neither do I wish to lose money = je ne veux pas vous offenser, mais je ne souhaite pas non plus perdre de l'argent.
– For examples and further uses see the entry **neither** I2.

I *conj* **1** (not either) ni…ni; **I have ~ the time nor the money** je n'ai ni le temps ni l'argent; **I've seen ~ him nor her** je ne les ai vus ni l'un ni l'autre; **2** (nor) **he doesn't have the time, ~ does he have the money** il n'a pas le temps, ni l'argent non plus; **you don't have to tell him, ~ should you** tu n'es pas obligé de le lui dire, tu ferais même mieux d'éviter.
II *det* aucun des deux; **~ book is suitable** aucun des deux livres ne convient; **~ girl replied** aucune des deux filles n'a répondu.
III *pron* ni l'un/-e, ni l'autre *m/f*; **~ of them came** ni l'un ni l'autre n'est venu; **'which one is responsible?'—'~'** 'lequel des deux est responsable?'—'ni l'un ni l'autre'.

nem con /,nem'kɒn/ *adv* (*abrév* = **nemine contradicente**) à l'unanimité.

neo+ /niːəʊ/ *combining form* néo-.

neologism /niː'ɒlədʒɪzəm/ *n* néologisme *m*.

neon /'niːɒn/ I *n* néon *m*.
II *noun modifier* [*light, lighting, sign*] au néon; [*atom*] de néon.

nephew /'nevjuː, 'nef-/ *n* neveu *m*.

nephritis /nɪ'fraɪtɪs/ **▶ 1002** / *n* néphrite *f*.

nerve /nɜːv/ I *n* **1** ANAT nerf *m*; BOT nervure *f*; **2** (courage) courage *m*; (confidence) assurance *f*; **to keep one's ~** conserver son sang-froid; **to recover one's ~** retrouver son assurance; **3**° (cheek) culot° *m*.
II **nerves** *npl* (nervousness) nerfs *mpl*; (stage fright) trac° *m*; **to have an attack of ~s** faire une crise de nerfs; **it's only ~s!** c'est nerveux!; **his ~s were on edge** il était sur les nerfs; **to calm sb's ~s** calmer qn.
III *vtr* **to ~ oneself to do** s'armer de courage pour faire.
IDIOMS **to touch** OU **hit a raw ~** toucher un point sensible; **to strain every ~ to do** s'évertuer à faire.

nerve racking, **nerve wracking** *adj* angoissant.

nerviness /'nɜːvɪnɪs/ *n* GB nervosité *f*; US aplomb *m*.

nervous /'nɜːvəs/ *adj* **1** [*person*] (fearful) timide; (anxious) angoissé; (highly strung) nerveux/-euse; [*smile, laugh, habit*] nerveux/-euse; **to be ~ of** GB ou **around** us avoir peur de [*strangers, animals*]; **to be ~ of** GB ou **about** us redouter [*change, disagreement*]; **to be ~ about doing** avoir peur de faire; **to feel ~** (apprehensive) GEN être angoissé; (before performance) avoir le trac⊙; (afraid) avoir peur; (ill at ease) se sentir mal à l'aise; **she makes me feel ~** (intimidates me) elle me met mal à l'aise; (puts my nerves on edge) elle me rend nerveux/-euse; **2** ANAT, MED nerveux/-euse; **3** FIN instable.

nervous: **~ breakdown** *n* dépression *f* nerveuse; **~ energy** *n* énergie *f*.

nervously /'nɜːvəslɪ/ *adv* nerveusement.

nervousness /'nɜːvəsnɪs/ *n* **1** (of person) (shyness) timidité *f*; (fear) peur *f*; (anxiety) inquiétude *f*; (stage fright) trac⊙ *m*; (physical embarrassment) agitation *f*; (tenseness) nervosité *f*; **2** FIN instabilité *f*.

nervous: **~ system** *n* système *m* nerveux; **~ wreck**⊙ *n* boule *f* de nerfs⊙.

nervy⊙ /'nɜːvɪ/ *adj* GB (anxious) nerveux/-euse; us (cheeky) gonflé⊙.

nest /nest/ **I** *n* **1** (of animal) nid *m*; (group of baby birds, mice) nichée *f* (**of** de); **2** (of criminals, traitors) nid *m*; (of boxes, bowls) série *f*; **~ of tables** tables *fpl* gigognes.
II *vi* [*bird*] faire son nid; [*pans*] s'emboîter.
IDIOMS **to feather one's** (**own**) **~** se remplir les poches.

nested /'nestɪd/ *adj* COMPUT imbriqué.

nest egg *n* magot⊙ *m*.

nesting /'nestɪŋ/ **I** *n* ZOOL construction *f* de nid; COMPUT imbrication *f*.
II *noun modifier* [*place*] propice à la construction des nids; [*habit, season*] de construction des nids.

nestle /'nesl/ **I** *vtr* **to ~ one's head** appuyer sa tête (**on** sur; **against** contre); **to ~ a baby in one's arms** tenir un bébé dans ses bras.
II *vi* **1** [*person, animal*] se blottir (**against** contre; **under** sous); **2** [*village, house, object*] être niché.
■ **nestle down** s'installer confortablement.
■ **nestle up** se blottir (**against, to** contre).

nestling /'neslɪŋ/ *n* oisillon *m*.

net /net/ **I** *n* **1** LIT filet *m*; **2** SPORT (in tennis) filet *m*; **to come** (**up**) **to the ~** monter au filet; (in football) filets *mpl*; **3** FIG piège *m*; **to slip through the ~** passer à travers les mailles du filet; **4** TELECOM réseau *m*; **5** (fabric) voile *m*, tulle *m*.
II *adj* (also **nett**) **1** GEN, FIN, COMM net/nette; [*loss*] sec/sèche; **~ of tax** net après impôt; **terms strictly ~** prix nets; **2** GEN [*result, effect, increase*] net/nette.
III *vtr* (*p prés etc* **-tt-**) **1** (catch) prendre [qch] au filet; **2** COMM, FIN [*person*] faire un bénéfice de; [*sale, export, deal*] rapporter; **3** (in football) marquer [*goal*]; gagner [*trophy*].
IDIOMS **to cast one's ~ wide** ratisser large.

net: **~ball** *n*: *sport d'équipe proche du basket joué par les femmes*; **~ cord** *n* SPORT (in tennis) (shot) net *m*; (cord) corde *f* (du filet); **~ curtain** *n* voilage *m*.

Netherlands /'neðələndz/ ▶840│ **I** *pr n* **the ~** les Pays-Bas *mpl*, la Hollande.
II *adj* [*tradition, climate*] hollandais, des Pays-Bas.

netting /'netɪŋ/ *n* **1** (of rope) filet *m*; (of metal, plastic) grillage *m*; (fabric) voile *m*, tulle *m*.

nettle /'netl/ **I** *n* (also **stinging ~**) ortie *f*.
II *vtr* agacer.
IDIOMS **to grasp** ou **seize the ~** prendre le taureau par les cornes.

net ton ▶1392│ *n* us tonne *f* courte.

network /'netwɜːk/ **I** *n* (all contexts) réseau *m* (**of** de).
II *vtr* TV, RADIO diffuser; COMPUT interconnecter.
III *vi* tisser un réseau de relations.
IV networked *pp adj* [*computer, workstation*] interconnecté.

networking /'netwɜːkɪŋ/ *n* **1** COMM constitution *f* de réseaux; **2** COMPUT interconnexion *f*; **3** (establishing

contacts) **~ is important** c'est important d'avoir des contacts.

network television *n* us chaîne *f* nationale.

neuralgia /njʊəˈrældʒə, us ˌnʊ-/ ▶1002│ *n* névralgie *f*.

neuritis /njʊəˈraɪtɪs, us ˌnʊ-/ ▶1002│ *n* névrite *f*.

neurologist /njʊəˈrɒlədʒɪst, us ˌnʊ-/ ▶1251│ *n* neurologue *mf*.

neurosis /njʊəˈrəʊsɪs, us nʊ-/ *n* (*pl* **-oses**) névrose *f*; FIG **to have a ~ about sth** avoir une idée fixe à propos de qch.

neurosurgeon /ˌnjʊərəʊˈsɜːdʒn, us ˌnʊ-/ ▶1251│ *n* neurochirurgien *m*.

neurotic /njʊəˈrɒtɪk, us nʊ-/ **I** *n* névrosé/-e *m/f*.
II *adj* névrosé; **to be ~ about sth/about doing** être complètement maniaque en ce qui concerne qch/quand il s'agit de faire.

neurotically /njʊəˈrɒtɪklɪ, us nʊ-/ *adv* de façon obsessionnelle.

neuter /'njuːtə(r), us 'nuː-/ **I** *n* LING neutre *m*.
II *adj* neutre.
III *vtr* châtrer.

neutral /'njuːtrəl, us 'nuː-/ **I** *n* **1** MIL, POL neutre *mf*; **2** AUT point *m* mort; **in/into ~** au point mort.
II *adj* (all contexts) neutre (**about** en ce qui concerne); **to have a ~ policy** pratiquer une politique de neutralité; **to have a ~ effect on sth** ne pas avoir d'effet sur qch.

neutrality /njuːˈtrælətɪ, us nuː-/ *n* **1** CHEM, POL (status) neutralité *f*; **2** POL, GEN (attitude) attitude *f* de neutralité (**towards** vis-à-vis).

neutralize /'njuːtrəlaɪz, us 'nuː-/ *vtr* AUSSI EUPH neutraliser ALSO EUPH.

neutron /'njuːtrɒn, us 'nuː-/ **I** *n* neutron *m*.
II *noun modifier* [*bomb, star*] à neutrons.

never /'nevə(r)/

■ **Note** When *never* is used to modify a verb (*she never wears a hat, I've never seen him*) it is translated *ne...jamais* in French; *ne* comes before the verb, and before the auxiliary in compound tenses, and *jamais* comes after the verb or auxiliary: *elle ne porte jamais de chapeau, je ne l'ai jamais vu*.
– When *never* is used without a verb, it is translated by *jamais* alone: '*admit it!*'—'*never!*' = 'avoue-le!'—'jamais'.
– For examples and particular usages, see the entry below.

adv **1** (not ever) **I ~ go to London** je ne vais jamais à Londres; **she ~ says anything** elle ne dit jamais rien; **I've ~ known him to be late** ce n'est pas le genre à être en retard; **~ have I seen such poverty** je n'ai jamais vu une telle pauvreté; **it's now or ~** c'est le moment ou jamais; **~ again** plus jamais; **he ~ ever drinks alcohol** il ne boit absolument jamais d'alcool; **~ one to refuse a free meal, he agreed** il a accepté parce qu'il ne dit jamais non à un repas gratuit; **~ a day passes but he phones me** pas un jour ne passe sans qu'il me téléphone; **2** (as an emphatic negative) **he ~ said a word** il n'a rien dit; **I ~ knew that** je ne le savais pas; **he ~ so much as apologized** il ne s'est même pas excusé; **she mustn't catch you crying! that would ~ do** il ne faut surtout pas qu'elle te voie pleurer; ▶**fear, mind**; **3** (expressing surprise, shock) **you're ~ 40!** GB ce n'est pas possible, tu n'as pas 40 ans!; **you've ~ gone and broken it have you**⊙! GB ne me dis pas que tu l'as cassé!; **~!** pas possible!; **well I ~** (**did**) **!** ça par exemple!

never-ending /ˌnevərˈendɪŋ/ *adj* interminable.

nevermore /ˌnevəˈmɔː(r)/ *adv* plus jamais.

never-never⊙ /ˌnevəˈnevə(r)/ *n* GB **to buy sth on the ~** acheter qch à crédit.

never-never land *n* pays *m* imaginaire.

nevertheless /ˌnevəðəˈles/ *adv* **1** (all the same) quand même; **thanks ~** merci quand même; **2** (nonetheless) pourtant, néanmoins; **so strong yet ~ so gentle** si fort et pourtant si doux; **3** (however) pourtant, néanmoins; **he did ~ say that...** il a pourtant or néanmoins dit que...

new /nju:, US nu:/ *adj* (recent, different, not known, seen, owned etc before) nouveau/-elle; (brand new) neuf/neuve; **I bought a ~ computer** (to replace old one) j'ai acheté un nouvel ordinateur; (a brand new model) j'ai acheté un ordinateur neuf; **the area is ~ to me** la région m'est inconnue; **the subject is ~ to me** je ne connais rien au sujet; **as good as ~** LIT, FIG comme neuf; **'as ~'** (in advertisement) 'état neuf'; **I feel like a ~ man** je suis transformé; **someone/something ~** quelqu'un/quelque chose d'autre; **could I have a ~ plate? this one is dirty** est-ce que je pourrais avoir une autre assiette? celle-ci est sale; **to be ~ to** ne pas être habitué à [*job, way of life*]; **we're ~ to the area** nous sommes nouveaux venus dans la région.

New Age I *n* New Age *m*.
II *noun modifier* [*music, ideas, sect*] New Age *inv*.

new blood *n* sang *m* frais.

newborn /'nju:bɔ:n, US 'nu:-/ *adj* nouveau-né/-née; **~ baby** nouveau-né/-née *m/f*.

new: **New Caledonia** ▶ 1022 *pr n* Nouvelle-Calédonie *f*; **~comer** *n* (in place, job, club) nouveau venu/nouvelle venue *m/f*; (in sport, theatre, cinema) nouveau/-elle *m/f*; **~fangled** *adj* PÉJ moderne; **~found** *adj* tout nouveau/toute nouvelle.

Newfoundland /nju:'faʊndlənd, US nu:-/ *pr n* GEOG Terre-Neuve *f*; **to/in ~** à Terre-Neuve.

New Guinea ▶ 840 *pr n* Nouvelle-Guinée *f*.

newish /'nju:ɪʃ, US 'nu:-/ *adj* assez neuf/neuve.

new look I *n* nouveau style *m*.
II new-look *adj* [*product*] nouvelle version *inv*; [*car, team*] nouveau/-elle (*before n*); [*edition, show*] remanié.

newly /'nju:lɪ, US 'nu:-/ *adv* (recently) GEN nouvellement; [*washed*] fraîchement; (differently) différemment.

newlyweds /'nju:lɪwedz, US 'nu:-/ *npl* jeunes mariés *mpl*.

news /nju:z, US nu:z/ *n* **1** (political, public, personal) nouvelle(s) *f(pl)*; **an item ou piece of ~** GEN une nouvelle; (in newspaper) une information; **a sad bit of ~** une triste nouvelle; **have you heard the ~?** tu connais la nouvelle?; **the latest ~ is that all is quiet** aux dernières nouvelles tout était calme; **the ~ that she had resigned** la nouvelle selon laquelle elle aurait démissionné; **~ is just coming in of an explosion** on vient d'apprendre qu'une explosion s'est produite; **here now with ~ of today's sport is X** et voici maintenant, pour nous parler du sport aujourd'hui, X; **these events are not ~** ces événements n'ont rien de nouveau; **to be in the ~, to make (the) ~** défrayer la chronique; **she's always in the ~** on parle beaucoup d'elle dans les médias; **have I got ~ for you**○! j'ai une nouvelle à t'apprendre!; **tell me all your ~**! raconte-moi ce que tu deviens!; **that's ~ to me**○! ça, c'est du nouveau○!; **2** RADIO, TV (programme) **the ~** les informations *fpl*, le journal *m*; **to see sth/sb on the ~** voir qch/qn aux informations; **3** (in newspaper) **'financial ~'** 'chronique *f* financière'; **'Home News'** 'les informations *fpl* nationales'.
IDIOMS **no ~ is good ~** pas de nouvelles, bonnes nouvelles.

news: **~ agency** *n* agence *f* de presse; **~agent** ▶ 1251 *n* GB marchand de journaux; **~agent's** *n* GB magasin *m* de journaux; **~ bulletin** GB, **~cast** US *n* RADIO, TV bulletin *m* d'information; **~caster** ▶ 1251 *n* présentateur/-trice *m/f* des informations; **~ conference** *n* conférence *f* de presse; **~dealer** ▶ 1251 *n* US marchand *m* de journaux; **~ desk** *n* (at newspaper) (salle *f* de) rédaction *f*; **~ editor** ▶ 1251 *n* rédacteur/-trice *m/f*; **~ headlines** *npl* TV titres *mpl* de l'actualité; **~ item** *n* sujet *m* d'actualité; **~letter** *n* bulletin *m*; **~man** ▶ 1251 *n* journaliste *m*.

newspaper /'nju:speɪpə(r), US 'nu:z-/ **I** *n* (item) journal *m*; (substance) papier *m* journal.
II *noun modifier* [*article, cutting, photograph*] de presse; [*archives*] du journal, de la rédaction.

newspaper: **~man** ▶ 1251 *n* journaliste *m*; **~**

office *n* bureau *m* de rédaction; **~woman** ▶ 1251 *n* journaliste *f*.

newspeak /'nju:spi:k, US 'nu:-/ *n* PÉJ jargon *m* administratif PÉJ.

news: **~print** *n* (paper) papier *m* journal; (ink) encre *f* d'imprimerie; **~reader** ▶ 1251 *n* GB présentateur/-trice *m/f* des informations; **~reel** *n* CIN HIST actualités *fpl*; **~room** *n* (salle *f* de) rédaction *f*; **~ service** *n* (agency) agence *f* de presse; (service provided by media) service *m* d'information; **~ sheet** *n* bulletin *m*; **~stand** *n* kiosque *m* à journaux; **~ value** *n* valeur *f* médiatique; **~worthy** *adj* médiatique.

newsy /'nju:zɪ, US 'nu:-/ *adj* [*letter*] plein de nouvelles.

New Testament, **NT** *pr n* Nouveau Testament *m*.

new wave *n*, *adj* nouvelle vague (*f*).

New Year *n* **1** (January 1st) nouvel an *m*; **closed for** ou US **~'s** COMM fermé pour les fêtes du nouvel an; **to see in the ~** fêter la Saint-Sylvestre; **Happy ~!** bonne année!; **2** (next year) (whole) l'année *f* prochaine; (the beginning) la nouvelle année.

New Year: **~ Honours list** *n* GB liste *f* des décorés du 1er janvier; **~ resolution** *n* résolution *f* pour la nouvelle année; **~'s day** GB, **~'s** US *n* le jour *m* de l'an; **~'s Eve** *n* la Saint-Sylvestre.

New Zealand /nju:'zi:lənd, US nu:-/ **I** ▶ 840 *pr n* Nouvelle-Zélande *f*.
II *adj* néo-zélandais.

next /nekst/

■ **Note** When *next* is used as an adjective it is generally translated by *prochain* when referring to something which is still to come or happen and by *suivant* when referring to something which has passed or happened: *I'll be 40 next year* = j'aurai 40 ans l'année prochaine; *the next year, he went to Spain* = l'année suivante il est allé en Espagne.
– For examples and further usages see the entry below.
– See also the usage note on time units ▶ 1336.

I *pron* **after this train the ~ is at noon** le train suivant est à midi; **he's happy one minute, sad the ~** il passe facilement du rire aux larmes; **I hope my ~ will be a boy** j'espère que mon prochain enfant sera un garçon; **from one minute to the ~** d'un instant à l'autre; **to survive from one day to the ~** survivre au jour le jour; **the ~ to speak was Emily** ensuite, c'est Emily qui a parlé; **the week/month after ~** dans deux semaines/mois.
II *adj* **1** (in list, order or series) (following) suivant; (still to come) prochain; **get the ~ train** prenez le prochain train; **he got on the ~ train** il a pris le train suivant; **what's ~ on the list?** qu'est-ce qu'on doit faire maintenant?; **the ~ thing to do is** ce qu'il faut faire maintenant c'est; **'~!'** 'au suivant!'; **'who's ~?'** 'c'est à qui le tour?'; **'you're ~'** 'c'est à vous'; **you're ~ in line** la prochaine fois c'est ton tour; **you're ~** but one plus qu'une personne et c'est à toi; **~ to last** avant-dernier/-ière; **the ~ size (up)** la taille au-dessus; **2** (in expressions of time) (in the future) prochain; (in the past) suivant; **~ Thursday, Thursday ~** jeudi prochain; **I'll phone in the ~ few days** je téléphonerai d'ici quelques jours; **he's due to arrive in the ~ 10 minutes** il devrait arriver d'ici 10 minutes; **this time ~ week** dans une semaine; **the ~ week she was late** la semaine suivante elle était en retard; **the ~ day** le lendemain; **the ~ day but one** le surlendemain; **the ~ moment** l'instant d'après; **(the) ~ thing I knew, the police were at the door** la police était à la porte avant que j'aie eu le temps de comprendre ce qui se passait; **3** (adjacent) [*room, street*] voisin; [*building, house*] voisin, d'à côté.
III *adv* **1** (afterwards) ensuite, après; **what happened ~?** que s'est-il passé ensuite?; **what word comes ~?** quel mot vient après?; **whatever ~!** et quoi encore!; **2** (now) ~, **I'd like to say**... je voudrais dire maintenant...; **what shall we do ~?** qu'est-ce qu'on fait maintenant?; **3** (on a future occasion) **when I ~ go there** la prochaine fois que j'irai; **they ~ met in 1981** ils se sont ensuite revus en 1981; **4** (nearest in order) **the ~ tallest is Patrick** ensuite c'est Patrick qui est le plus grand; **after 65, 50 is the ~ best**

score c'est 65 le meilleur score, ensuite c'est 50; **the ~ best thing would be to...** à défaut, le mieux serait de...

IV next to *adv phr* presque; **~ to impossible** presque impossible; **to get sth for ~ to nothing** avoir qch pour quasiment rien; **in ~ to no time it was over** en un rien de temps c'était fini.

V next to *prep phr* à côté de; **two seats ~ to each other** deux sièges l'un à côté de l'autre; **to wear silk ~ to the skin** porter de la soie à même la peau; **~ to Picasso, my favourite painter is Chagall** après Picasso c'est Chagall mon peintre préféré.

IDIOMS **he's as honest as the ~ man** OU **person** il est aussi honnête que n'importe qui.

next door I *n* (people) les voisins *mpl*; **~'s cat** le chat des voisins; **~'s garden** le jardin d'à côté.
II *adj* (also **next-door**) d'à côté; **the girl ~** LIT la fille d'à côté; FIG une fille très simple.
III *adv* [*live, move in*] à côté.

next-door neighbour *n* voisin/-e *m/f* (d'à côté); **we're ~s** nous habitons à côté l'un de l'autre.

next of kin *n* **to be sb's ~** être le parent le plus proche de qn.

nexus /'neksəs/ *n* (*pl* **~** ou **-uses**) (link) connexion *f*; (network) réseau *m*.

NF *n* **1** GB POL *abrév* ▶ **National Front**; **2** FIN (also **N/F**) (*abrév* = **no funds**) défaut *m* de provision.

NH US POST *abrév écrite* = **New Hampshire**.

NHS I *n* GB (*abrév* = **National Health Service**) services *mpl* de santé britanniques; **on the ~ ~** remboursé par la sécurité sociale.
II *noun modifier* [*hospital, bed*] conventionné; [*treatment*] remboursé par la sécurité sociale.

NI *n* **1** GB *abrév* ▶ **National Insurance**; **2** GEOG (*abrév écrite* = **Northern Ireland**) Irlande *f* du Nord.

nib /nɪb/ *n* plume *f*.

nibble /'nɪbl/ I *n* **1** (snack food) (*gén pl*) amuse-gueule *m inv*; **2** (action) mordillement *m*; **to have** ou **take a ~ at** grignoter; **3** (small meal) collation *f*.
II *vtr* (eat) **1** [*rodent, person*] grignoter; [*sheep, goat*] brouter; **2** (playfully) mordiller [*ear, neck*].
III *vi* **1** LIT [*animal*] mordiller; [*person*] grignoter; **to ~ at** [*mouse, rabbit*] grignoter; [*sheep, goat*] brouter; [*fish*] mordre à [*bait*]; [*person*] manger [qch] du bout des dents; **2** FIG **to ~ at** considérer [*idea, proposal*].

Nicaragua /ˌnɪkəˈrægjʊə/ ▶ **840** *pr n* Nicaragua *m*.

nice /naɪs/ *adj* **1** (enjoyable) agréable; **it would be ~ to do** ce serait bien de faire; **did you have a ~ time?** tu t'es bien amusé?; **~ weather isn't it?** beau temps, n'est-ce pas?; **a ~ cool drink** une boisson bien fraîche; **it's ~ and sunny** il fait beau; **to have a ~ long chat** bien bavarder; **~ work if you can get it!** HUM il y en a qui ont de la veine○!; **~ to have met you** ravi d'avoir fait votre connaissance; **have a ~ day!** bonne journée!; **2** (attractive) GEN beau/belle; [*place*] agréable; **you look very ~** tu es très chic; **3** (tasty) bon/bonne; **to taste ~** avoir bon goût; **4** (kind) sympathique; **to be ~** être gentil avec; **he says really ~ things about you** il dit beaucoup de bien de toi; **5** [*behaviour, neighbourhood, school*] comme il faut *inv*; **it is not ~ to do** ce n'est pas bien de faire; **that's not very ~!** ça ne se fait pas!; **6** (used ironically) **~ friends you've got!** ils sont bien tes amis!; **a ~ mess you've got us into!** tu nous as fichus dans un beau pétrin○!; **that's a ~ way to talk to your father!** en voilà une façon de parler à ton père!; **this is a ~ state of affairs!** c'est du propre!; **7** SOUT (subtle) subtil.
IDIOMS **~ one!** (in admiration) bravo!; IRON il ne manquait plus que ça!

nice-looking /ˌnaɪsˈlʊkɪŋ/ *adj* beau/belle.

nicely /'naɪslɪ/ *adv* **1** (kindly) gentiment; **2** (attractively) agréablement; **she sings very ~** elle chante très bien; **3** (satisfactorily) bien; **to be ~ chilled** être juste frais/fraîche comme il faut; **that will do ~** cela fera l'affaire; **4** (politely) [*eat, speak*] convenablement; [*ask, explain*] poliment.

niceness /'naɪsnɪs/ *n* (kindness) gentillesse *f*; (subtlety) subtilité *f*.

nicety /'naɪsətɪ/ *n* subtilité *f*; **the social niceties** les raffinements *mpl* mondains.

niche /nɪtʃ, niːʃ/ *n* (role) place *f*; (recess) niche *f*; COMM créneau *m*; ECOL niche *f* écologique.

niche market *n* marché *m* spécialisé.

nick /nɪk/ I *n* **1** (notch) encoche *f* (**in** dans); **2**○ GB **to be in good/bad** [*object*] être en bon/mauvais état; [*person*] être ou ne pas être en forme; **3**○ GB (jail) taule *f*; (police station) poste *m*.
II *vtr* **1** (cut) faire une entaille dans; **2**○ GB (steal) piquer○; (arrest) pincer○; **3**○ US (strike) donner un coup léger à.
III *v refl* **to ~ oneself** s'écorcher.
IDIOMS **just in the ~ of time** juste à temps.

nickel /'nɪkl/ *n* **1** US (coin) pièce *f* de cinq cents; **2** (metal) nickel *m*.

nickel-and-dime○ *adj* US qui ne vaut pas un clou○.

nickelodeon /ˌnɪkəˈləʊdɪən/ *n* US (juke box) juke-box *m*.

nickname /'nɪkneɪm/ I *n* surnom *m*.
II *vtr* surnommer.

nicotine /'nɪkətiːn/ I *n* nicotine *f*.
II *noun modifier* [*addiction, poisoning, chewing gum*] à la nicotine; [*stain*] de nicotine.

niece /niːs/ *n* nièce *f*.

nifty○ /'nɪftɪ/ *adj* (skilful) habile; (attractive) chouette○.

Nigeria /naɪˈdʒɪərɪə/ ▶ **840** *pr n* Nigeria *m*.

niggardly /'nɪgədlɪ/ *adj* **1** [*person*] avare; **2** [*portion, amount*] mesquin.

niggle○ /'nɪgl/ I *n* (complaint) remarque *f*; **I've a ~ at the back of my mind** il y a quelque chose qui me travaille.
II *vtr* (irritate) tracasser.
III *vi* (complain) se plaindre sans arrêt (**about, over** de; **that** que).

niggling /'nɪglɪŋ/ I *n* chicanerie *f*.
II *adj* [*person*] tatillon/-onne; [*doubt, worry*] insidieux/-ieuse.

night /naɪt/ ▶ **1336** *n* **1** (period of darkness) nuit *f*; (before going to bed) soir *m*; **at ~** la nuit; **all ~ long** toute la nuit; **Moscow by ~** Moscou la nuit; **eight o'clock at ~** huit heures du soir; **late at ~** tard le soir; **he arrived last ~** il est arrivé hier soir; **I slept badly last ~** j'ai mal dormi la nuit dernière; **he arrived the ~ before last** il est arrivé avant-hier soir; **she had arrived the ~ before** elle était arrivée la veille au soir; **on Tuesday ~s** le mardi soir; **to sit up all ~ reading** passer toute la nuit à lire; **to have a good/bad ~** bien/mal dormir; **to have a late ~** se coucher tard; **to get an early ~** se coucher tôt; **to stay out all ~** ne pas rentrer de la nuit; **2** (evening) soir *m*; (evening as a whole) soirée *f*; **it's his ~ out** c'est son soir de sortie; **to take a ~ off** se libérer une soirée; **it's my ~ off** ce soir je suis libre; **a ~ to remember** une soirée mémorable; **to make a ~ of it** faire la fête○; **3** (darkness) nuit *f*.

nightcap /'naɪtkæp/ *n* **1** (hat) bonnet *m* de nuit; **2** (drink) **to have a ~** boire quelque chose (avant d'aller se coucher).

nightclub *n* boîte *f* de nuit.

nightclubbing *n* **to go ~** aller en boîte○.

nightdress *n* chemise *f* de nuit.

nightie○ /'naɪtɪ/ *n* chemise *f* de nuit.

nightingale /'naɪtɪŋgeɪl, US -tng-/ *n* rossignol *m*.

night: ~life /'naɪtlaɪf/ *n* vie *f* nocturne; **~-light** *n* veilleuse *f*.

nightly /'naɪtlɪ/ *adj* GEN de tous les soirs; [*revels, visitor, disturbance*] LITTER nocturne.

nightmare /'naɪtmeə(r)/ *n* cauchemar *m*; **to have a ~** faire un cauchemar.

night: ~marish *adj* cauchemardesque; **~ owl** *n* couche-tard *mf inv*; **~ porter** *n* portier *m* de nuit; **~ school** *n* cours *mpl* du soir; **~ shelter** *n* asile *m* de nuit.

night shift *n* **1** (period) **to be/work on the ~** être/travailler de nuit; **2** (workers) équipe *f* de nuit.

nightshirt *n* chemise *f* de nuit (d'homme).

night: **~ spot**° *n* boîte *f* de nuit°; **~stand** *n* US table *f* de nuit; **~stick** *n* US matraque *f*.

night-time /ˈnaɪttaɪm/ **I** *n* nuit *f*; **at ~** la nuit. **II** *noun modifier* nocturne.

night: **~ vision** *n* vision *f* nocturne; **~ watchman** ▶ 1251 | *n* veilleur *m* de nuit; **~wear** *n* vêtements *mpl* de nuit.

nil /nɪl/ *n* **1 to be ~** [*courage, enthusiasm*] être à zéro; [*progress*] être zéro; **2** SPORT zéro *m*; **3** (on forms) néant *m*.

Nile /naɪl/ ▶ 1214 | *pr n* Nil *m*.

nimble /ˈnɪmbl/ *adj* [*person*] agile (**at doing** pour faire; **with** de); [*fingers*] habile; [*mind*] vif/vive.

nincompoop° /ˈnɪŋkəmpuːp/ *n* nigaud/-e *m/f*.

nine /naɪn/ ▶ 1112 | *n, adj* neuf (*m*) *inv*. IDIOMS **a ~ day(s') wonder** la merveille d'un jour; **to be dressed up to the ~s**° être sur son trente et un°.

ninepin /ˈnaɪnpɪn/ *n* quille *f*. IDIOMS **to go down** ou **fall like ~s** tomber comme des mouches.

nineteen /ˌnaɪnˈtiːn/ ▶ 1112 | *n, adj* dix-neuf (*m*) *inv*. IDIOMS **to talk ~ to the dozen** parler à n'en plus finir.

nineteenth /ˌnaɪnˈtiːnθ/ ▶ 1112 |, 854 | **I** *n* **1** (in order) dix-neuvième *mf*; **2** (of month) dix-neuf *m inv*; **3** (fraction) dix-neuvième *m*. **II** *adj, adv* dix-neuvième.

ninetieth /ˈnaɪntɪəθ/ ▶ 1112 | **I** *n* **1** (in order) quatre-vingt-dixième *mf*; **2** (fraction) quatre-vingt-dixième *m*. **II** *adj, adv* quatre-vingt-dixième.

nine-to-five /ˌnaɪntəˈfaɪv/ **I** *adj* [*job, routine*] de bureau. **II nine to five** *adv* [*work*] de neuf à cinq.

ninety /ˈnaɪntɪ/ ▶ 1112 | *n, adj* quatre-vingt-dix (*m*) *inv*.

nip /nɪp/ *n* **1** (pinch) pincement *m*; (bite) morsure *f*; FIG **there's a ~ in the air** il fait frisquet°. **II** *vtr* (*p prés etc* **-pp-**) (pinch) pincer; (bite) donner un petit coup de dent à; (playfully) mordiller. **III** *vi* **1** (bite) [*animal*] mordre; (playfully) mordiller; [*bird*] donner un petit coup de bec à; **2**° GB (go) **to ~ into a shop** entrer rapidement dans un magasin; **to ~ in front of sb** passer devant qn; **to ~ over to France** faire un saut en France. IDIOMS **to ~ sth in the bud** étouffer qch dans l'œuf; **~ and tuck**° (cosmetic surgery) chirurgie *f* esthétique; (neck and neck) US au coude à coude. ■ **nip along** aller à bonne allure. ■ **nip off**: ¶ **~ off** [*person*] se sauver; ¶ **~ off** [*sth*], **~** [*sth*] **off** couper [*flower*]; pincer [*bud*].

nipple /ˈnɪpl/ *n* **1** ANAT mamelon *m*; **2** TECH graisseur *m*.

nippy° /ˈnɪpɪ/ *adj* **1** (cold) [*air*] piquant; **it's a bit ~** il fait frisquet°; **2** GB (quick) [*person*] vif/vive; [*car*] rapide; **be ~ about it!** fais vite!

nit /nɪt/ *n* (egg) lente *f*; (larva) larve *f* de pou.

nit-pick *vi* chercher la petite bête°.

nitrate /ˈnaɪtreɪt/ *n* **1** CHEM nitrate *m*; **2** (fertilizer) engrais *m* azoté.

nitric /ˈnaɪtrɪk/ *adj* nitrique.

nitrogen /ˈnaɪtrədʒən/ *n* azote *m*.

nitty-gritty° /ˌnɪtɪˈɡrɪtɪ/ *n* **the ~** la réalité pure et dure; **to get down to the ~** passer aux choses sérieuses.

nitwit° /ˈnɪtwɪt/ *n* imbécile *mf*.

NJ *abrév écrite* US POST = **New Jersey**.

NM *abrév écrite* US POST = **New Mexico**.

no /nəʊ/ **I** *particle* non. **II** *det* **1** (none, not any) **to have ~ money/shoes** ne pas avoir d'argent/de chaussures; **~ intelligent man would have done that** aucun homme intelligent n'aurait fait cela; **~ two people would agree on this** il

n'y a pas deux personnes qui seraient d'accord là-dessus; **of ~ interest** sans intérêt; **there's ~ chocolate like Belgian chocolate** il n'y a pas de meilleur chocolat que le chocolat belge; **2** (with gerund) **there's ~ knowing what will happen** (il est) impossible de savoir ce qui va arriver; **there's ~ denying that...** (il est) inutile de nier que...; **3** (prohibiting) **~ smoking** défense de fumer; **~ parking** stationnement interdit; **~ talking!** silence!; **~ job losses!** non aux licenciements!; **4** (for emphasis) **he's ~ expert** ce n'est certes pas un expert; **this is ~ time to cry** ce n'est pas le moment de pleurer; **at ~ time did I say that...** je n'ai jamais dit que...; **5** (hardly any) **in ~ time** en un rien de temps; **it was ~ distance** ce n'était pas loin. **III** *n* GEN non *m inv*; (vote against) non *m inv*. **IV** *adv* **it's ~ further/easier than** ce n'est pas plus loin/facile que; **I ~ longer work there** je n'y travaille plus; **~ later than Wednesday** pas plus tard que mercredi; **it's ~ different from driving a car** c'est exactement comme conduire une voiture; **~ fewer than 50 people** pas moins de 50 personnes; **they need ~ less than three weeks** ils ont besoin d'au moins trois semaines.

no., No. (*abrév écrite* = **number**) n°.

Noah /ˈnəʊə/ *pr n* Noé; **~'s Ark** l'arche *f* de Noé.

nobility /nəʊˈbɪlətɪ/ *n* noblesse *f*.

noble /ˈnəʊbl/ **I** *n* noble *m*. **II** *adj* noble.

noble: **~man** *n* noble *m*; **~-minded** *adj* au grand cœur; **~ savage** *n* bon sauvage *m*.

nobly /ˈnəʊblɪ/ *adv* GEN noblement; (selflessly) généreusement; **~ born** de haute naissance.

nobody /ˈnəʊbədɪ/

> ■ **Note** When *nobody* is used as a pronoun it is almost always translated by *personne*.
> – When the pronoun *nobody* is the subject or object of a verb, the French requires *ne* before the verb (or auxiliary): *nobody likes him* = personne ne l'aime; *I heard nobody* = je n'ai entendu personne.
> – For examples and particular usages, see the entry below.

I *pron* (also **no-one**) personne; **~ saw her** personne ne l'a vue; **there was ~ in the car** il n'y avait personne dans la voiture; **~ but me** personne sauf moi. **II** *n* **to be a ~** être insignifiant; **I knew her when she was still a ~** je la connaissais alors qu'elle n'était encore qu'une inconnue. IDIOMS **to work like ~'s business**° GB travailler comme un fou/une folle; **he's ~'s fool** on ne la lui fait pas°.

nocturnal /nɒkˈtɜːnl/ *adj* (all contexts) nocturne.

nod /nɒd/ **I** *n* signe *m* de (la) tête; **she gave him a ~** GEN elle lui a fait un signe de (la) tête; (as greeting) elle l'a salué d'un signe de tête; (indicating assent) elle a fait oui de la tête. **II** *vtr* (*p prés etc* **-dd-**) **to ~ one's head** GEN faire un signe de tête; (to indicate assent) hocher la tête; **he ~ded his assent/approval** il a hoché la tête en signe d'assentiment/d'approbation. **III** *vi* (*p prés etc* **-dd-**) **1** GEN faire un signe de tête (**to** à); (in assent) faire oui de la tête; **2** (sway) [*flowers, treetops*] onduler; **3** (be drowsy) sommeiller. IDIOMS **to give sb/sth the ~**° GB donner le feu vert à qn/qch; **on the ~**° GB sans discussion; **a ~ is as good as a wink** (to a blind man) ne t'en fais pas°, on a compris. ■ **nod off** s'endormir.

no-go° /ˌnəʊˈɡəʊ/ *adj* **it's (a) ~** ça ne sert à rien.

no: **~-go area** *n* quartier *m* chaud (*où la police etc ne s'aventure plus*); **~-hoper**° *n* raté/-e° *m/f*.

noise /nɔɪz/ *n* GEN bruit *m*; (shouting) tapage *m*; **background ~** bruit de fond; **a rattling ~** un cliquetis. IDIOMS **to be a big ~** (in sth)° être une grosse légume (de qch)°; **to make a ~ about sth** se plaindre de qch; **she made ~s about leaving** elle a laissé entendre qu'elle voulait partir; **to make polite**

~s dire des choses polies; **to make the right ~s** dire ce qui convient.

noise: **~less** adj silencieux/-ieuse; **~ level** n niveau m sonore; **~ nuisance**, **~ pollution** n nuisances fpl sonores.

noisily /'nɔɪzɪli/ adv bruyamment.

noisy /'nɔɪzɪ/ adj [person, place] bruyant; [meeting, protest] tumultueux/-euse.

nomad /'nəʊmæd/ n nomade mf.

nominal /'nɒmɪnl/ adj GEN nominal; [fee, sum] minimal; [fine, penalty] symbolique.

nominally /'nɒmɪnəlɪ/ adv (in name) nominalement; (in theory) théoriquement.

nominate /'nɒmɪneɪt/ vtr **1** (propose) proposer; **to ~ sb for a prize** sélectionner qn pour un prix; **2** (appoint) nommer; **to ~ sb (as) chairman** nommer qn président; **to ~ sb to do** désigner qn pour faire.

nomination /ˌnɒmɪ'neɪʃn/ n (as candidate) proposition f de candidat; (for award) sélection f; (appointment) nomination f (**to** à).

nominative /'nɒmɪnətɪv/ n, adj nominatif (m).

nominee /ˌnɒmɪ'ni:/ n candidat/-e mf désigné/-e.

non+ /nɒn-/ combining form (+ noun) non-; (+ adj) non.

nonacademic /ˌnɒnækə'demɪk/ adj [course] pré-professionnel/-elle; [staff] non enseignant.

nonaddictive /ˌnɒnə'dɪktɪv/ adj qui ne crée pas de dépendance.

nonalcoholic /ˌnɒnælkə'hɒlɪk/ adj non alcoolisé.

nonattendance /ˌnɒnə'tendəns/ n absence f.

nonbeliever /ˌnɒnbɪ'li:və(r)/ n non-croyant/-e mf.

non-budgetary /ˌnɒn'bʌdʒɪtrɪ/ adj extrabudgétaire.

nonchalant /'nɒnʃələnt/ adj nonchalant.

nonclassified /ˌnɒn'klæsɪfaɪd/ adj [information] non confidentiel/-ielle.

noncombustible /ˌnɒnkəm'bʌstəbl/ adj incombustible.

non-commercial /ˌnɒnkə'mɜ:ʃl/ adj [event, activity] à but non lucratif.

noncommissioned officer n MIL sous-officier m.

noncommittal /ˌnɒnkə'mɪtl/ adj [person, reply] évasif/-ive (**about** au sujet de).

noncompliance /ˌnɒnkəm'plaɪəns/ n (with standards) (of substance, machine) non-conformité f (**with** à); (with orders) (of person) non-obéissance f (**with** à).

non compos mentis /ˌnɒn ˌkɒmpəs 'mentɪs/ adj phr **to be ~** JUR être en état de démence (au moment des faits); GEN ne pas avoir toutes ses facultés.

nonconformist /ˌnɒnkən'fɔ:mɪst/ **I** n nonconformiste mf.
II adj non conformiste.

noncooperation /ˌnɒnkəʊˌɒpə'reɪʃn/ n refus m de coopération.

nondenominational /ˌnɒndɪˌnɒmɪ'neɪʃənl/ adj [church] œcuménique; [school] laïque.

nondescript /'nɒndɪskrɪpt/ adj [person, clothes] insignifiant; [building] quelconque; [colour] indéfinissable; [performance, book] sans intérêt.

none /nʌn/ **I** pron **1** (not any) aucun/-e mf; **~ of them** aucun d'entre eux; **'have you any pens?'—'~ at all'** 'as-tu des stylos?'—'pas un seul'; **he saw three dogs, ~ of which had a tail** il a vu trois chiens, dont aucun n'avait de queue; **~ of the wine/milk** pas une goutte de vin/lait; **~ of the bread** pas une miette de pain; **~ of the cheese** pas un morceau de fromage; **'is there any money left?'—'~ at all'** 'est-ce qu'il reste de l'argent?'—'pas du tout'; **'did you have any difficulty?'—'~ whatsoever** OU **at all'** 'as-tu eu des difficultés?'—'aucune'; **we have ~** nous n'en avons pas; **there's ~ left** il n'y en a plus; **~ of it was true** il n'y avait rien de vrai; **he was having ~ of it** il ne voulait rien entendre; **2** (nobody, not one person) personne; **~ can sing so well as her** personne ne chante aussi bien qu'elle; **there's ~ better than** il n'y en a pas de meilleur que; **~ but**

him personne sauf lui; **it was ~ other than** ce n'était autre que; **3** (on form, questionnaire) néant m.
II adv (not, not at all) **it was ~ too easy** c'était loin d'être facile; **I was ~ too sure** je n'étais pas trop sûr; **he was ~ the worse for the experience** il ne se portait pas plus mal après cette expérience; **the play is long, but ~ the worse for that** la pièce est longue mais ce n'est pas un défaut.

non-EC adj [country] hors CEE; [national] non ressortissant de la CEE.

nonentity /nɒ'nentətɪ/ n PÉJ (person) personne f insignifiante.

nonessentials /ˌnɒnɪ'senʃlz/ npl (objects) accessoires mpl; (details) accessoire m sg; **forget the ~** oublie l'accessoire.

nonetheless /ˌnʌnðə'les/ adv ▶ **nevertheless**.

nonexistent /ˌnɒnɪg'zɪstənt/ adj inexistant.

non-family /ˌnɒn'fæmɪlɪ/ adj en dehors de la famille.

nonfat /nɒn'fæt/ adj sans matières grasses.

nonfiction /nɒn'fɪkʃn/ n œuvres fpl non fictionnelles.

nonflammable /nɒn'flæməbl/ adj ininflammable.

non-fulfilment /ˌnɒnfʊl'fɪlmənt/ n (of contract, obligation) inexécution f; (of desire) inaccomplissement m.

non-infectious /ˌnɒnɪn'fekʃəs/ adj intransmissible.

noniron /ˌnɒn'aɪən, US -'aɪərn/ adj infroissable.

nonjudgmental /ˌnɒndʒʌdʒ'mentl/ adj neutre.

non-league /ˌnɒn'li:g/ adj SPORT hors division.

no-no /'nəʊnəʊ/ n **that's a ~** ça ne se fait pas.

no-nonsense /ˌnəʊ'nɒnsəns/ adj [manner, look, tone, attitude, policy] direct; [person] franc/franche.

nonpartisan /ˌnɒnpɑ:tɪ'zæn/ adj impartial.

nonparty /ˌnɒn'pɑ:tɪ/ adj [issue, decision] non partisan; [person] non affilié au parti.

nonperson /ˌnɒn'pɜ:sn/ n **1** PÉJ (insignificant person) être m falot; **2** POL **officially, he's a ~** officiellement, il n'a jamais existé.

nonplussed /ˌnɒn'plʌst/ adj perplexe.

nonprofessional /ˌnɒnprə'feʃənl/ n, adj amateur (m).

non-profitmaking /ˌnɒn'prɒfɪtmeɪkɪŋ/ adj [organization] à but non lucratif.

non-redeemable /ˌnɒnrɪ'di:məbl/ adj FIN perpétuel/-elle.

nonrefillable /ˌnɒnri:'fɪləbl/ adj [lighter, pen] non rechargeable; [can, bottle] non réutilisable.

nonreligious /ˌnɒnrɪ'lɪdʒəs/ adj laïque.

nonresident /ˌnɒn'rezɪdənt/ **I** n non-résident/-e mf.
II adj **1** [guest] de passage; [student, visitor] non résident; [caretaker] de jour; **2** (also **non-residential**) [job, course] sans hébergement; **3** COMPUT [routine] qui ne réside pas en permanence en mémoire centrale.

nonreturnable /ˌnɒnrɪ'tɜ:nəbl/ adj [bottle] non consigné.

nonsegregated /ˌnɒn'segrɪgeɪtɪd/ adj [area] sans ségrégation; [society] non ségrégationniste.

nonsense /'nɒnsns, US -sens/ n (foolishness) absurdités fpl; **it's a ~ that** c'est absurde que; **to make (a) ~ of** être en totale contradiction avec; **what's all this ~ about leaving work?** qu'est-ce que c'est que ces histoires de quitter le travail?; **there's no ~ about him** il ne permet pas de fantaisie.

nonsensical /nɒn'sensɪkl/ adj (stupid) absurde.

non sequitur /ˌnɒn 'sekwɪtə(r)/ n **1** GEN **to be a ~** être illogique; **2** (in philosophy) illogisme m.

nonskid /ˌnɒn'skɪd/, **nonslip** /ˌnɒn'slɪp/ n antidérapant m.

non-specialized /ˌnɒn'speʃəlaɪzd/ adj généraliste.

nonstarter /ˌnɒn'stɑ:tə(r)/ n FIG **to be a ~** [person] être hors-course; [plan, idea] être voué à l'échec.

nonstick /ˌnɒn'stɪk/ adj antiadhésif/-ive.

nonstop /ˌnɒn'stɒp/ **I** adj [flight] sans escale; [journey] sans arrêt; [train] direct; [talk, work, pressure, noise] incessant; [service, show] permanent; [coverage] non-stop inv.
II adv GEN sans arrêt; [fly] sans escale.

non-taxable /ˌnɒn'tæksəbl/ *adj* non imposable.

non-union /ˌnɒn'juːnɪən/ *adj* non syndiqué.

non-white, **non-White** /ˌnɒn'waɪt/ *n* personne *f* de couleur.

noodles /'nuːdlz/ *npl* CULIN nouilles *fpl*.

nook /nʊk/ *n* coin *m*.
IDIOMS **every ~ and cranny** tous les coins et recoins.

noon /nuːn/ *n* midi *m*; **at 12 ~** à midi; **at high ~** en plein midi.
IDIOMS **morning, ~ and night** du matin au soir.

no-one /'nəʊwʌn/ *pron* = **nobody** I.

noose /nuːs/ *n* (loop) nœud *m* coulant; (for hanging) corde *f*; **the hangman's ~** la corde de la potence.
IDIOMS **to put one's head in a ~** se jeter dans la gueule du loup.

nor /nɔː(r), nə(r)/

■ **Note** If you want to know how to translate *nor* when used in combination with *neither* look at the entry **neither**.
– When used as a conjunction to show agreement or similarity with a negative statement, *nor* is very often translated by *non plus*: *'I don't like him'—'nor do I'* = 'je ne l'aime pas'—'moi non plus'; *'he's not Spanish'—'nor is John'* = 'il n'est pas espagnol'—'John non plus'; *'I can't sleep'—'nor can I'* = 'je n'arrive pas à dormir'—'moi non plus'.
– When used to give additional information to a negative statement *nor* can very often be translated by *non plus* preceded by a negative verb: *she hasn't written, nor has she telephoned* = elle n'a pas écrit, et elle n'a pas téléphoné non plus; *I do not wish to insult you, (but) nor do I wish to lose money* = je ne veux pas vous offenser, mais je ne souhaite pas non plus perdre de l'argent.
– For examples and further uses of *nor* see the entry below.

conj **you don't have to tell him, ~ should you** tu n'es pas obligé de le lui dire, et même tu ne devrais pas; **he was not a cruel man, ~ a mean one** il n'était ni cruel, ni méchant.

norm /nɔːm/ *n* norme *f* (**for** pour; **to do** de faire).

normal /'nɔːml/ **I** *n* GEN, MATH normale *f*; **above/below ~** au-dessus/en dessous de la norme. **II** *adj* GEN, MATH, PSYCH normal; [*place, time*] habituel/-elle; **as ~** comme d'habitude; **in the ~ course of events** si tout va bien; **in ~ circumstances** en temps normal.

normality /nɔː'mælɪtɪ/ *n* normalité *f*.

normally /'nɔːməlɪ/ *adv* normalement.

Norman /'nɔːmən/ **I** *n* **1** GEN, HIST Normand/-e *m/f*; **2** (also **~ French**) LING normand *m*. **II** *adj* **1** GEN, HIST [*landscape, village*] normand; [*produce*] de Normandie; **2** ARCHIT roman.

Norse /nɔːs/ *adj* [*mythology, saga*] nordique.

north /nɔːθ/ **▶1157**| **I** *n* (compass direction) nord *m*; **true ~** le nord géographique. **II North** *pr n* POL, GEOG (part of world, country) **the North** le Nord; **the far North** le Grand Nord. **III** *adj* GEN nord *inv*; [*wind*] du nord; **in/from ~ London** dans le/du nord de Londres. **IV** *adv* [*move*] vers le nord; [*lie, live*] au nord (**of** de); **to go ~ of sth** passer au nord de qch.

north: **North Africa ▶840**| *n* Afrique *f* du Nord; **North America ▶840**| *n* Amérique *f* du Nord.

Northants *n* GB POST *abrév écrite* = **Northamptonshire**.

northbound *adj* en direction du nord.

Northd *n* GB POST *abrév écrite* **▶Northumberland**.

northeast /ˌnɔːθ'iːst/ **▶1157**| **I** *n* nord-est *m*. **II** *adj* [*coast, side*] nord-est *inv*; [*wind*] de nord-est. **III** *adv* [*move*] vers le nord-est; [*lie, live*] au nord-est.

northeasterly /ˌnɔːθ'iːstəlɪ/ **I** *n* vent *m* de nord-est. **II** *adj* [*wind*] de nord-est; [*point*] au nord-est.

northeastern /ˌnɔːθ'iːstən/ **▶1157**| *adj* [*coast*] nord-est *inv*; [*town, accent*] du nord-est.

northerly /'nɔːðəlɪ/ **I** *n* vent *m* du nord. **II** *adj* [*wind, area*] du nord; [*point*] au nord.

northern /'nɔːðən/ **▶1157**| *adj* [*coast*] nord *inv*; [*town, accent*] du nord; [*latitude*] boréal; [*hemisphere*] Nord *inv*; **~ England** le nord de l'Angleterre.

northerner /'nɔːðənə(r)/ *n* **~s** les gens *mpl* du Nord.

northern: **Northern Ireland ▶840**| *n* Irlande *f* du Nord; **Northern Lights** *npl* aurore *f* boréale.

North Pole *n* pôle *m* Nord.

North Sea ▶1117| *n* **the ~** la mer du Nord.

North Star *n* étoile *f* polaire.

northward /'nɔːθwəd/ **▶1157**| **I** *adj* [*side*] nord *inv*; [*wall, slope*] du côté nord; [*journey*] vers le nord. **II** *adv* (also **~s**) vers le nord.

northwest /ˌnɔːθ'west/ **▶1157**| **I** *n* nord-ouest *m*. **II** *adj* [*coast*] nord-ouest *inv*; [*wind*] de nord-ouest. **III** *adv* [*move*] vers le nord-ouest; [*lie, live*] au nord-ouest.

northwesterly /ˌnɔːθ'westəlɪ/ **I** *n* vent *m* de nord-ouest, noroît *m*. **II** *adj* [*wind*] de nord-ouest; [*point*] au nord-ouest.

northwestern /ˌnɔːθ'westən/ *adj* [*coast*] nord-ouest *inv*; [*town, accent*] du nord-ouest.

Norway /'nɔːweɪ/ **▶840**| *pr n* Norvège *f*.

Norwegian /nɔː'wiːdʒən/ **▶1100**|, **1038**| **I** *n* **1** (person) Norvégien/-ienne *m/f*; **2** (language) norvégien *m*. **II** *adj* norvégien/-ienne.

nose /nəʊz/ **I ▶765**| *n* **1** ANAT nez *m*; **to speak through one's ~** parler du nez; **2** (of plane, boat) nez *m*; (of car) avant *m*; **to travel ~ to tail** rouler à touche-touche; **3** (sense of smell) GEN odorat *m*; (of wine or perfume expert) nez *m*; (of dog) flair *m*; **4** (smell of wine) bouquet *m*; **5** FIG (instinct) **to have a ~ for sth** avoir du flair pour qch; **to follow one's ~** se fier à son instinct. **II** *vtr* (manœuvre) **to ~ sth in/out** faire entrer/sortir qch avec précaution [*boat, vehicle*]. **III** *vi* **to ~ in/out of sth** [*boat, vehicle*] entrer dans/sortir de qch avec prudence; **the car ~d into the traffic** la voiture s'est faufilée dans la circulation.
IDIOMS **to hit sb on the ~** US taper qch dans le mille; **to lead sb by the ~** mener qn par le bout du nez; **to look down one's ~ at sb/sth** prendre qn/qch de haut; **to pay through the ~ for sth** payer le prix fort pour qch; **to poke** ou **stick one's ~ into sth**○ fourrer○ son nez dans qch; **to turn one's ~ up at sth** faire le dégoûté/la dégoûtée devant qch; **(right) under sb's ~** sous le nez de qn; **with one's ~ in the air** d'un air supérieur.
■ **nose about**, **nose around** fouiner (**in** dans).
■ **nose out**: ¶ **~ out** [*vehicle*] déboîter prudemment; [*boat*] sortir avec prudence; ¶ **~ out [sth]**, **~ [sth] out** LIT dépister [*animal*]; FIG dénicher [*facts, secret*].

nosebleed *n* saignement *m* de nez.

nose-dive /'nəʊzdaɪv/ **I** *n* AVIAT piqué *m*; FIG **to go into** ou **take a ~** [*currency, rate*] chuter. **II** *vi* [*plane*] descendre en piqué; [*demand, prices, sales*] chuter.

nosey○ *adj* = **nosy**.

no-show *n*: personne ayant fait une réservation qui ne se présente pas à l'hôtel, l'aéroport etc.

nosily /'nəʊzɪlɪ/ *adv* indiscrètement.

nostalgia /nɒ'stældʒə/ *n* nostalgie *f*.

nostalgic /nɒ'stældʒɪk/ *adj* nostalgique; **to feel ~ for** avoir la nostalgie de.

nostril /'nɒstrɪl/ *n* (of person) narine *f*; (of horse) naseau *m*.

nosy○ /'nəʊzɪ/ *adj* fouineur/-euse○.

not /nɒt/ **I** *adv* ne...pas; **she isn't at home** (voir note ci-dessous) elle n'est pas chez elle; **we won't need a car** nous n'aurons pas besoin d'une voiture; **has he ~ seen it?** il ne l'a pas vu alors?; **I hope ~** j'espère que non; **certainly ~** sûrement pas; **~ only** ou **just** non seulement; **whether it rains or ~** qu'il pleuve ou non; **why ~?** pourquoi pas?; **they live in caves, ~ in houses** ils habitent non pas dans des maisons, mais dans des grottes; **he's ~ so much aggressive as assertive** il est plutôt sûr de lui qu'agressif; **a ~** ou

---

not

When *not* is used without a verb before an adjective, an adverb, a verb or a noun it is translated by *pas*:

it's a cat not a dog	= c'est un chat pas un chien
not at all	= pas du tout
not bad	= pas mal

For examples and particular usages see the entry **not**.

When *not* is used to make the verb *be* negative (*it's not a cat*) it is translated by *ne ... pas* in French; *ne* comes before the verb or the auxiliary in compound tenses and *pas* comes after the verb or auxiliary: ce n'est pas un chat.

she hasn't been ill = elle n'a pas été malade.

When *not* is used with the auxiliary *do* to make a verb negative (*he doesn't like oranges*) do + *not* is translated by *ne ... pas* in French: il n'aime pas les oranges.

When *not* is used in the present perfect tense (*I haven't seen him, she hasn't arrived yet*), ne ... pas is again used in French on either side of the appropriate auxiliary (*avoir* or *être*): je ne l'ai pas vu, elle n'est pas encore arrivée.

When *not* is used with *will* to make a verb negative (*will not, won't*), ne ... pas is used with the *future tense* in French:

she won't come by car = elle ne viendra pas en voiture

When used with a verb in the infinitive *ne pas* are placed together before the verb:

he decided not to go = il a décidé de ne pas y aller
you were wrong not to tell her = tu as eu tort de ne pas le lui dire

When *not* is used in question tags the whole tag can usually be translated by the French *n'est-ce pas*, e.g.

she bought it, didn't she? = elle l'a acheté, n'est-ce pas?

For usages not covered in this note see the entry **not**.

~ an (entirely) unexpected response une réponse prévisible; **~ three hours from here** à moins de trois heures d'ici; **hadn't we better leave?** est-ce qu'on ne ferait pas mieux de partir?; **~ everyone likes it** tout le monde ne l'aime pas; **it's ~ every day that** ce n'est pas tous les jours que; **~ a sound was heard** on n'entendait pas un bruit.
II not at all *adv phr* GEN pas du tout; (responding to thanks) de rien.
III not that *conj phr* **~ that I know of** pas (autant) que je sache; **if she refuses, ~ that she will**... si elle refuse, je ne dis pas qu'elle le fera...

■ Note Dans la langue parlée ou familière, *not* utilisé avec un auxiliaire ou un modal prend parfois la forme *n't* qui est alors accolée au verbe (eg *you can't go, he hasn't finished*).

notable /'nəʊtəbl/ *adj* [*person*] remarquable; [*event, success, difference*] notable.

notably /'nəʊtəblɪ/ *adv* (in particular) notamment; (markedly) remarquablement; **most ~** plus or tout particulièrement.

notary /'nəʊtərɪ/ ▶1251 *n* notaire *m*.

notation /nəʊ'teɪʃn/ *n* notation *f*.

notch /nɒtʃ/ **I** *n* (in plank) entaille *f*; (in fabric, belt) cran *m*; (in lid, as record) encoche *f*; **to go up a ~** [*opinion*] monter d'un cran.
II *vtr* (mark) encocher [*stick*]; cranter [*fabric*].
■ **notch up**○: **~ up** [sth] remporter [*point, prize*].

note /nəʊt/ **I** *n* **1** GEN note *f*; (short letter) mot *m*; **to make a ~ of** noter [*date, address*]; **to take ~ of** LIT, FIG prendre note de; **2** FIG **to hit the right ~** trouver le ton juste; **to strike** ou **hit a wrong ~** commettre un impair; **on a less serious ~** en passant à un registre moins sérieux; **3** MUS (sound, symbol) note *f*; (piano key) touche *f*; **4** (banknote) billet *m*.
II of note *adj phr* [*person*] éminent, réputé; [*development, contribution*] digne d'intérêt.
III *vtr* GEN noter; (pay attention to) prendre bonne note de.

IV noted *pp adj* [*intellectual, criminal*] célèbre; **to be ~d for** être réputé pour [*tact, wit*].
IDIOMS **to compare ~s** échanger ses impressions (with sb).
■ **note down**: **~ down** [sth], **~** [sth] **down** noter.

note: **~book** *n* GEN carnet *m*; COMPUT agenda *m* électronique; **~pad** *n* bloc-notes *m*; **~paper** *n* papier *m* à lettres; **~worthy** *adj* remarquable.

not guilty *adj* JUR [*person*] non coupable; [*verdict*] d'acquittement.

nothing /'nʌθɪŋ/ ▶1111 **I** *pron* rien; (as object of verb) ne...rien; (as subject of verb) rien...ne; **I knew ~ about it** je n'en savais rien; **we can do ~ (about it)** nous n'y pouvons rien; **next to ~** presque rien; **~ much** pas grand-chose; **~ more** rien de plus; **is there ~ more you can do?** vous ne pouvez rien faire de plus?; **she's just a friend, ~ more or less** c'est une amie, c'est tout; **~ else** rien d'autre; **if ~ else it will be a change for us** au moins ça nous changera les idées; **I had ~ to do with it!** je n'y étais pour rien!; **it's ~ to do with us** ça ne nous regarde pas; **to come to ~** n'aboutir à rien; **to stop at ~** ne reculer devant rien (**to do** pour faire); **to have ~ on** (no clothes) être nu; (no engagements, plans) n'avoir rien de prévu; **you've got ~ on me**○! (to incriminate) vous n'avez rien contre moi!; **he's got ~ on you**○! (to rival) il ne t'arrive pas à la cheville○!; **we were talking about ~ much** nous parlions de tout et de rien; **he means** ou **is ~ to me** il n'est rien pour moi; **it meant ~ to him** ça lui était complètement égal (**that, whether** que + *subj*); **the names meant ~ to him** les noms ne lui disaient rien; **he cares ~ for convention** il se moque des conventions; **to think ~ of doing** (consider normal) trouver tout à fait normal de faire; (not baulk at) ne pas hésiter à faire; **think ~ of it!** ce n'est rien!; **there's really ~ to it** c'est tout ce qu'il y a de plus facile; **it costs next to ~** ça ne coûte presque rien; **for ~** (for free) gratuitement; (pointlessly) pour rien; **it's money for ~** c'est de l'argent vite gagné; **it seems easy but it's ~ of the kind** cela paraît facile mais il n'en est rien; **you'll do ~ of the sort!** tu n'en feras rien!; **there's ~ like it!** il n'y a rien de tel ou de mieux!; **I can think of ~ worse than** je ne peux rien imaginer de pire que; **to say ~ of** sans parler de; **you get ~ out of it** ça ne rapporte rien; **there's ~ in it for me** ça n'a aucun intérêt pour moi; **there's ~ in it** (in gossip, rumour) il n'y a rien de vrai là-dedans; (in magazine, booklet) c'est sans intérêt.
II *adv* **it is ~ like as difficult as** c'est loin d'être aussi difficile que; **she is** or **looks ~ like her sister** elle ne ressemble pas du tout à sa sœur ; **it's ~ short of brilliant** c'est tout à fait génial; **~ short of a miracle can save them** il n'y a qu'un miracle qui puisse les sauver; **I'm ~ if not stubborn!** le moins qu'on puisse dire c'est que je suis têtu!
III *adj* **to be ~ without sb/sth** ne rien être sans qn/qch.
IV *n* néant *m*; **it's a mere ~ compared to** ce n'est pratiquement rien par rapport à; ▶ **sweet**.
V nothing but *adv phr* **he's ~ but a coward** ce n'est qu'un lâche; **they've done ~ but moan** ils n'ont fait que râler○; **it's caused me ~ but trouble** ça ne m'a valu que des ennuis; **she has ~ but praise for them** elle ne tarit pas d'éloges sur eux.
VI nothing less than *adv phr* **it's ~ less than a betrayal** c'est une véritable trahison; **~ less than real saffron will do** il n'y a que du vrai safran qui fera l'affaire.
VII nothing more than *adv phr* **it's ~ more than a strategy to do** ce n'est qu'une stratégie pour faire; **the stories are ~ more than gossip** ces histoires ne sont rien d'autre que des ragots; **they'd like ~ more than to do** ils ne demandent pas mieux que de faire.

notice /'nəʊtɪs/ **I** *n* **1** (written sign) pancarte *f*; (advertisement) annonce *f*; (announcing birth, marriage, death) avis *m*; (review of a play) compte-rendu *m*; **2** (attention) attention *f*; **to take ~** faire attention (**of** à); **it was**

beneath her ~ ça ne méritait pas son attention; **it has come to my ~ that** il m'a été signalé que; **3** (notification) préavis *m*; **one month's ~** un mois de préavis; **to do sth at short ~** faire qch au pied levé; **to give sb ~ of sth** avertir or prévenir qn de qch; **until further ~** jusqu'à nouvel ordre; **I'm sorry it's such short ~** je suis désolé de vous prévenir si tard; **to give in** ou **hand in one's ~** donner sa démission; [*domestic servant*] donner ses huit jours; **to give sb (their) ~** congédier qn; **to get one's ~** recevoir son congé.
II *vtr* remarquer [*absence, mark*]; **I ~ that** je vois que; **to get oneself ~d** se faire remarquer; **I can't say I ~d** je n'ai pas fait attention.

noticeable /ˈnəʊtɪsəbl/ *adj* visible.

noticeably /ˈnəʊtɪsəblɪ/ *adv* [*increase, improve*] sensiblement; [*better, colder*] nettement.

notice: **~board** *n* panneau *m* d'affichage; **~ to pay** *n* avis *m* de paiement.

notification /ˌnəʊtɪfɪˈkeɪʃn/ *n* GEN notification *f*; (in newspaper) avis *m*; **to receive ~ that** être avisé que.

notify /ˈnəʊtɪfaɪ/ *vtr* **1** GB (give notice of) notifier; **to ~ sb of** ou **about** aviser qn de [*result, incident*]; avertir qn de [*intention*]; **2** (announce formally) **to ~ sb of** informer qn de [*birth, death*].

notion /ˈnəʊʃn/ *n* **1** (idea) idée *f*; **I never had any ~ of asking her** il ne m'est jamais venu à l'idée de lui demander; **2** (vague understanding) notion *f*; **some ~ of** quelques notions de; **3** (whim, desire) idée *f*; **he had** ou **took a sudden ~ to go for a swim** il a eu l'envie soudaine d'aller nager.

notorious /nəʊˈtɔːrɪəs/ *adj* [*criminal, organization*] notoire; [*district, venue*] mal famé; [*example, case*] tristement célèbre; **~ for/as sth** [*person, place*] connu pour/comme qch.

notoriously /nəʊˈtɔːrɪəslɪ/ *adv* notoirement; **they're ~ unreliable** il est bien connu qu'on ne peut pas compter sur eux.

Notts *n* GB POST *abrév écrite* = **Nottinghamshire**.

notwithstanding /ˌnɒtwɪθˈstændɪŋ/ **I** *adv* SOUT néanmoins.
II *prep* (in spite of) en dépit de; (excepted) exception faite de; JUR nonobstant.

nought /nɔːt/ *n* zéro *m*.

noughts and crosses ▶ 949 *n* (+ *v sg*) (jeu *m* de) morpion *m*.

noun /naʊn/ *n* nom *m*, substantif *m*.

nourish /ˈnʌrɪʃ/ *vtr* nourrir (**with** avec; **on** de).

nourishment /ˈnʌrɪʃmənt/ *n* (food) nourriture *f*.

Nov *abrév écrite* = **November**.

novel /ˈnɒvl/ **I** *n* roman *m*.
II *adj* original.

novelette /ˌnɒvəˈlet/ *n* PÉJ (over-sentimental) roman *m* à l'eau de rose.

novelist /ˈnɒvəlɪst/ ▶ 1251 *n* romancier/-ière *m/f*.

novelty /ˈnɒvltɪ/ **I** *n* **1** nouveauté *f* (**of doing** de faire); **to be a ~ to sb** avoir l'attrait de la nouveauté pour qn; **2** (trinket) babiole *f*.
II *noun modifier* [*key ring, mug*] fantaisie.

November /nəʊˈvembə(r)/ ▶ 1090 *n* novembre *m*.

novice /ˈnɒvɪs/ *n* débutant/-e *m/f*; RELIG novice *mf*.

now /naʊ/ **I** *conj* **~ (that)** maintenant que.
II *adv* **1** (at the present moment) maintenant; **I'm doing it ~** je suis en train de le faire; **~ is the best time to do** c'est le meilleur moment pour faire; **right ~** tout de suite; **it's a week ~ since she left** cela fait une semaine (maintenant) qu'elle est partie; **any time** ou **moment ~** d'un moment à l'autre; **I'll be more careful ~** je serai plus prudent dorénavant; **~ fast, ~ slowly** tantôt vite, tantôt lentement; **(every) ~ and then** ou **again** de temps en temps; **~ for the next question** passons à la question suivante; **2** (with preposition) **you should have phoned him before ~** tu aurais dû lui téléphoner avant; **before** ou **until ~** jusqu'à présent; **he should be finished by ~** il devrait avoir déjà fini; **between ~ and next Friday** d'ici vendredi prochain; **between ~ and then** d'ici

---

nothing

When *nothing* is used alone as a reply to a question in English, it is translated by *rien*:

> 'what are you doing?' 'nothing' = 'que fais-tu?' 'rien'

nothing as a pronoun when it is the subject of a verb is translated by *rien ne* in French:

nothing changes	= rien ne change
nothing has changed	= rien n'a changé

nothing as a pronoun when it is the object of a verb is translated by *ne rien*; *ne* comes before the verb, and before the auxiliary in compound tenses, and *rien* comes after the verb or auxiliary:

I see nothing	= je ne vois rien
I saw nothing	= je n'ai rien vu

When *ne rien* is used with an infinitive the two words are not separated:

> *I prefer to say nothing* = je préfère ne rien dire

For examples and particular usages, see **I** in the entry **nothing**.

For translations of *nothing* as an adverb (*it's nothing like as difficult*) and for the phrases *nothing but, nothing less than, nothing more than*, see **II, V, VI** and **VII** respectively in the entry **nothing**.

---

là; **from ~ on(wards)** dorénavant; **that's enough for ~** ça suffit pour le moment; **good-bye for ~** à bientôt; **3** (in the past) **it was ~ 4 pm** il était alors 16 heures; **by ~ it was too late** à ce moment-là, il était trop tard; **4** (without temporal force) **~ there's a man I can trust!** ah! voilà un homme en qui on peut avoir confiance!; **~ Paul would never do a thing like that** Paul, lui, ne ferait jamais une chose pareille; **careful ~!** attention!; **~ let's see** voyons donc; **~! ~!, come ~!** allons!; **there ~, what did I tell you?** eh bien, qu'est-ce que je t'avais dit?; **~ then, let's get down to work** bon, reprenons le travail.

nowadays /ˈnaʊədeɪz/ *adv* (these days) de nos jours, aujourd'hui; (at present, now) actuellement, maintenant.

nowhere /ˈnəʊweə(r)/ **I** *adv* nulle part; **I've got ~ else to go** je n'ai nulle part où aller; **~ else will you find a better bargain** vous ne trouverez pas de meilleure affaire ailleurs; **there's ~ to sit down** il n'y a pas d'endroit pour s'asseoir; **~ is this custom more widespread than in China** c'est en Chine que cette coutume est la plus répandue; **this company/this team is going ~** l'entreprise/l'équipe stagne; **£10 goes ~ these days** avec 10 livres sterling on ne va pas loin de nos jours; **all this talk is getting us ~** tout ce bavardage ne nous avance à rien; **flattery will get you ~!** tu n'arriveras à rien en me flattant.
II nowhere near *adv phr, prep phr* loin de; **~ near sufficient** loin d'être suffisant.

noxious /ˈnɒkʃəs/ *adj* nocif/-ive.

nozzle /ˈnɒzl/ *n* (of hose, pipe) ajutage *m*; (of bellows) bec *m*; (of hoover) suceur *m*; (for icing) douille *f*.

nr *abrév écrite* = **near**.

NSPCC *n* GB (*abrév* = **National Society for the Prevention of Cruelty to Children**) société pour la protection de l'enfance.

NT *abrév* ▶ **New Testament**.

nth /enθ/ *adj* MATH, FIG énième; **to the ~ power** ou **degree** à la puissance n.

nub /nʌb/ *n* (of problem) fond *m*; **the ~ of the matter** le cœur du sujet.

nubile /ˈnjuːbaɪl, US ˈnuːbl/ *adj* (attractive) désirable.

nuclear /ˈnjuːklɪə(r), US ˈnuː-/ *adj* nucléaire.

nuclear: **~ bomb** *n* bombe *f* atomique; **~ deterrent** *n* force *f* de dissuasion nucléaire; **~ energy** *n* énergie *f* nucléaire or atomique; **~-free zone** *n* GB zone *f* où les expériences nucléaires sont interdites; **~ physics** *n* (+ *v sg*) physique *f* nucléaire.

nuclear power *n* **1** (energy) = **nuclear energy**; **2** (country) puissance *f* nucléaire.

Numbers (1)

Cardinal numbers in French

0	zéro*
1	un†
2	deux
3	trois
4	quatre
5	cinq
6	six
7	sept
8	huit
9	neuf
10	dix
11	onze
12	douze
13	treize
14	quatorze
15	quinze
16	seize
17	dix-sept
18	dix-huit
19	dix-neuf
20	vingt
21	vingt et un
22	vingt-deux
30	trente
31	trente et un
32	trente-deux
40	quarante
50	cinquante
60	soixante
70	soixante-dix; septante (in Belgium, Canada, Switzerland etc.)
71	soixante et onze septante et un (etc)
72	soixante-douze
73	soixante-treize
74	soixante-quatorze
75	soixante-quinze
76	soixante-seize
77	soixante-dix-sept
78	soixante-dix-huit
79	soixante-dix-neuf
80	quatre-vingts‡
81	quatre-vingt-un§
82	quatre-vingt-deux
90	quatre-vingt-dix nonante (in Belgium, Canada, Switzerland etc.)
91	quatre-vingt-onze nonante et un
92	quatre-vingt-douze nonante-deux (etc)
99	quatre-vingt-dix-neuf
101	cent un†
102	cent deux
110	cent dix
111	cent onze
112	cent douze
187	cent quatre-vingt-sept
200	deux cents
250	deux cent‖ cinquante
300	trois cents
1 000‖	mille
1 001	mille un†
1 002	mille deux
1 020	mille vingt
1 200	mille** deux cents
2 000	deux mille††
10 000	dix mille
10 200	dix mille deux cents
100 000	cent mille
102 000	cent deux mille
1 000 000	un million‡‡
1 264 932	un million deux cent soixante-quatre mille neuf cent trente-deux
1 000 000 000	un milliard‡‡
1 000 000 000 000	un billion‡‡

Use of en

Note the use of en *in the following examples:*

there are six	=	il y en a six
I've got a hundred	=	j'en ai cent

En must be used when the thing you are talking about is not expressed (*the French says literally* there are of them are six, I of them have a hundred *etc.*). *However,* en *is not needed when the object is specified:*

there are six apples	=	il y a six pommes

Approximate numbers

When you want to say about ..., *remember the French ending* -aine:

about ten	=	une dizaine
about ten books	=	une dizaine de livres
about fifteen	=	une quinzaine
about fifteen people	=	une quinzaine de personnes
about twenty	=	une vingtaine
about twenty hours	=	une vingtaine d'heures

Similarly une trentaine, une quarantaine, une cinquantaine, une soixantaine *and* une centaine (*and* une douzaine *means* a dozen). *For other numbers, use* environ (about):

about thirty-five	=	environ trente-cinq
about thirty-five francs	=	environ trente-cinq francs
about four thousand	=	environ quatre mille
about four thousand pages	=	environ quatre mille pages

Environ can be used with any number: environ dix, environ quinze *etc.* are as good as une dizaine, une quinzaine *etc.*

Note the use of centaines *and* milliers *to express approximate quantities:*

hundreds of books	=	des centaines de livres
I've got hundreds	=	j'en ai des centaines
hundreds and hundreds of fish	=	des centaines et des centaines de poissons
I've got thousands	=	j'en ai des milliers
thousands of books	=	des milliers de livres
thousands and thousands	=	des milliers et des milliers
millions and millions	=	des millions et des millions

---

* *In English 0 may be called* nought, zero *or even* nothing; *French is always* zéro; a nought = un zéro.

† *Note that* one *is* une *in French when it agrees with a feminine noun, so* un crayon *but* une table, une des tables, vingt et une tables, combien de tables? – il y en a une seule *etc.*

‡ *Also* huitante *in Switzerland. Note that when 80 is used as a page number it has no* s, *e.g. page eighty = page* quatre-vingt.

§ *Note that* vingt *has no* s *when it is in the middle of a number. The only exception to this rule is when* quatre-vingts *is followed by* millions, milliards *or* billions, *e.g.* quatre-vingts millions, quatre-vingts billions *etc.*

¶ *Note that* cent *does not take an* s *when it is in the middle of a number. The only exception to this rule is when it is followed by* millions, milliards *or* billions, *e.g.* trois cents millions, six cents billions *etc. It has a normal plural when it modifies other nouns, e.g. 200 inhabitants =* deux cents habitants.

‖ *Note that figures in French are set out differently; where English would have a comma, French has simply a space. It is also possible in French to use a full stop (period) here, e.g.* 1.000. *French, like English, writes dates without any separation between thousands and hundreds, e.g.* in 1995 = *en* 1995.

** *When such a figure refers to a date, the spelling* mil *is preferred to* mille, *i.e.* en 1200 = en mil deux cents. *Note however the exceptions: when the year is a round number of thousands, the spelling is always* mille, *so* en l'an mille, en l'an deux mille *etc.*

†† *Mille is invariable; it never takes an* s.

‡‡ *Note that the French words* million, milliard *and* billion *are nouns, and when written out in full they take* de *before another noun, e.g. a* million inhabitants *is* un million d'habitants, a billion francs *is* un billion de francs. *However, when written in figures,* 1,000,000 inhabitants *is* 1 000 000 habitants, *but is still spoken as* un million d'habitants. *When* million *etc. is part of a complex number,* de *is not used before the nouns, e.g.* 6,000,210 people = *six* millions deux cent dix personnes.

☛ See next page

Numbers (2)

Phrases

numbers up to ten	=	les nombres jusqu'à dix
to count up to ten	=	compter jusqu'à dix
almost ten	=	presque dix
less than ten	=	moins de dix
more than ten	=	plus de dix
all ten of them	=	tous les dix
all ten boys	=	les dix garçons

Note the French word order:

my last ten pounds	=	mes dix dernières livres
the next twelve weeks	=	les douze prochaines semaines
the other two	=	les deux autres
the last four	=	les quatre derniers

Calculations in French

		say
10 + 3 = 13		dix et trois font *ou* égalent treize
10 − 3 = 7		trois ôté de dix il reste sept *or* dix moins trois égale sept
10 × 3 = 30		dix fois trois égale trente
30 : 3 = 10		(30 ÷ 3 = 10) trente divisé par trois égale dix

Note how the French division sign differs from the English.

5^2	cinq au carré
5^3	cinq puissance trois
5^4	cinq puissance quatre
5^{100}	cinq puissance cent
5^n	cinq puissance n
$\sqrt{12}$	racine carrée de douze
$\sqrt{25} = 5$	racine carrée de vingt-cinq égale cinq
B > A	B est plus grand que A
A < B	A est plus petit que B

Decimals in French

Note that French uses a comma where English has a decimal point.

	say
0,25	zéro virgule vingt-cinq
0,05	zéro virgule zéro cinq
0,75	zéro virgule soixante-quinze
3,45	trois virgule quarante-cinq
8,195	huit virgule cent quatre-vingt-quinze
9,1567	neuf virgule quinze cent soixante-sept *or* neuf virgule mille cinq cent soixante-sept
9,3456	neuf virgule trois mille quatre cent cinquante-six

Percentages in French

	say
25%	vingt-cinq pour cent
50%	cinquante pour cent
100%	cent pour cent
200%	deux cents pour cent
365%	trois cent soixante-cinq pour cent
4,25%	quatre virgule vingt-cinq pour cent

Ordinal numbers in French§

1st	1er‡	premier *(feminine* première*)*
2nd	2^e	second *or* deuxième
3rd	3^e	troisième
4th	4^e	quatrième
5th	5^e	cinquième
6th	6^e	sixième
7th	7^e	septième
8th	8^e	huitième
9th	9^e	neuvième
10th	10^e	dixième
11th	11^e	onzième
12th	12^e	douzième
13th	13^e	treizième
14th	14^e	quatorzième
15th	15^e	quinzième
16th	16^e	seizième
17th	17^e	dix-septième
18th	18^e	dix-huitième
19th	19^e	dix-neuvième
20th	20^e	vingtième
21st	21^e	vingt et unième
22nd	22^e	vingt-deuxième
23rd	23^e	vingt-troisième
24th	24^e	vingt-quatrième
25th	25^e	vingt-cinquième
30th	30^e	trentième
31st	31^e	trente et unième
40th	40^e	quarantième
50th	50^e	cinquantième
60th	60^e	soixantième
70th	70^e	soixante-dixième septantième *(in Belgium, Canada, Switzerland etc.)*
71st	71^e	soixante et onzième septante et unième *(etc.)*
72nd	72^e	soixante-douzième
73rd	73^e	soixante-treizième
74th	74^e	soixante-quatorzième
75th	75^e	soixante-quinzième
76th	76^e	soixante-seizième
77th	77^e	soixante-dix-septième
78th	78^e	soixante-dix-huitième
79th	79^e	soixante-dix-neuvième
80th	80^e	quatre-vingtième¶
81st	81^e	quatre-vingt-unième
90th	90^e	quatre-vingt-dixième nonantième *(in Belgium, Canada, Switzerland etc.)*
91st	91^e	quatre-vingt-onzième nonante et unième *(etc.)*
99th	99^e	quatre-vingt-dix-neuvième
100th	100^e	centième
101st	101^e	cent et unième
102nd	102^e	cent-deuxième
196th	196^e	cent quatre-vingt-seizième
200th	200^e	deux centième
300th	300^e	trois centième
400th	400^e	quatre centième
1,000th	$1\,000^e$	millième
2,000th	$2\,000^e$	deux millième
1,000,000th	$1\,000\,000^e$	millionième

Like English, French makes nouns by adding the definite article:

the first	=	le premier *(or* la première, *or* les premiers *mpl or* les premières *fpl)*
the second	=	le second *(or* la seconde *etc.)*
the first three	=	les trois premiers *or* les trois premières

Note the French word order in:

the third richest country in the world = le troisième pays le plus riche du monde

Fractions in French

	say
½	un demi*
⅓	un tiers
¼	un quart
⅕	un cinquième
⅙	un sixième
⅐	un septième
⅛	un huitième
⅑	un neuvième
¹⁄₁₀	un dixième
¹⁄₁₁	un onzième
¹⁄₁₂	un douzième *(etc.)*
⅔	deux tiers†
⅖	deux cinquièmes
²⁄₁₀	deux dixièmes *(etc.)*
¾	trois quarts
⅗	trois cinquièmes
³⁄₁₀	trois dixièmes *(etc.)*
1½	un et demi
1⅓	un (et) un tiers
1¼	un et quart
1⅕	un (et) un cinquième
1⅙	un (et) un sixième
1⅐	un (et) un septième *(etc.)*
5⅔	cinq (et) deux tiers
5¾	cinq (et) trois quarts
5⅘	cinq (et) quatre cinquièmes

45/100ths of a second = quarante-cinq centièmes de seconde

---

* *Note that half, when not a fraction, is translated by the noun* moitié *or the adjective* demi; *see the dictionary entry.*

† *Note the use of* les *and* d'entre *when these fractions are used about a group of people or things:* two-thirds of them = les deux tiers d'entre eux.

‡ *This is the masculine form; the feminine is* 1re *and the plural* 1ers (m) *or* 1res (f). *All the other abbreviations of ordinal numbers are invariable.*

§ *All the ordinal numbers in French behave like ordinary adjectives and take normal plural endings where appropriate.*

¶ *Also* huitantième *in Switzerland.*

nuclear: ~ **power station** n centrale f nucléaire;
~ **shelter** n abri m antiatomique.

nucleus /'njuːklɪəs, US 'nuː-/ n (pl **-clei**) noyau m.

nude /njuːd, US nuːd/ I n ART nu/-e m/f; **in the ~**
nu.
II adj [person] nu.

nudge /nʌdʒ/ I n coup m de coude, poussée f.
II vtr (push) pousser du coude; (accidentally) heurter;
(brush against) frôler.

nudist /'njuːdɪst, US 'nuː-/ n nudiste mf.

nudity /'njuːdətɪ, US 'nuː-/ n nudité f.

nugget /'nʌgɪt/ n pépite f.

nuisance /'njuːsns, US 'nuː-/ n GEN embêtement m;
JUR nuisance f; **to be a ~** [thing] être gênant;
[person] être pénible; **to make a ~ of oneself** embêter tout le monde; **the ~ is that**... l'ennui c'est
que...; **what a ~!** que c'est agaçant!; **I'm sorry to be
such a ~** excusez-moi de vous déranger tout le
temps.

nuisance call n TELECOM appel m anonyme.

null /nʌl/ adj JUR ~ **and void** nul et non avenu.

nullify /'nʌlɪfaɪ/ vtr invalider, annuler.

numb /nʌm/ I adj **1** [limb, face] (due to cold, pressure)
engourdi (**with** par); (due to anaesthetic) insensible; **to
go ~** s'engourdir; **2** FIG [person] hébété (**with** par).
II vtr [cold] engourdir; [anaesthetic] insensibiliser; **to
~ the pain** endormir la douleur.

number /'nʌmbə(r)/ ▶ 1112 I n **1** GEN, LING nombre
m; (written figure) chiffre m; **a three-figure ~** un
nombre à trois chiffres; **2** (of bus, house, page, telephone)
numéro m; **a wrong ~** un faux numéro; **there's no
reply at that ~** ce numéro ne répond pas; **to be ~
three on the list** être troisième sur la liste; **3** (amount,
quantity) nombre m; **a ~ of people/times** un certain
nombre de personnes/fois; **for a ~ of reasons** pour
plusieurs raisons; **large ~s of people** beaucoup de
gens; **on a ~ of occasions** plusieurs fois; **they were
sixteen in ~** ils étaient (au nombre de) seize; **one of
our ~** un des nôtres; **in equal ~s** en nombre égal;
any ~ of times maintes fois; **4** (issue) (of magazine,
periodical) numéro m; **the May ~** le numéro de mai;
5 MUS, THEAT (act) numéro m; (song) chanson f; **6** ◦
(object of admiration) **a little black ~** (dress) une petite
robe noire; **that car is a neat little ~** elle est
chouette◦, cette voiture.
II **numbers** npl (in company, school) effectifs mpl; (of
crowd, army) nombre m; **to win by force** or **weight of
~s** gagner parce que l'on est plus nombreux; **to
make up the ~s** pour compléter le nombre.
III vtr **1** (allocate number to) numéroter; **2** (amount to)
compter; **the regiment ~ed 1,000 men** le régiment
comptait 1000 hommes; **3** (include) compter (**among**
parmi).
IV vi (comprise in number) **a crowd ~ing in the thousands** une foule de plusieurs milliers de personnes; **to
~ among the great musicians** compter parmi les
plus grands musiciens.
IDIOMS **your ~'s up**◦! ton compte est bon!; **to do
sth by the ~s** US ou **by ~s** faire qch mécaniquement; **his days are ~ed** ses jours sont comptés.

numbering /'nʌmbərɪŋ/ n (action) numérotage m; (sequence of numbers) numérotation f.

number one n **1** (most important) numéro un m (**in**
de); **2**◦ (oneself) **to look after** ou **look out for** ou **take
care of ~** penser avant tout à son propre intérêt.

numberplate n GB plaque f minéralogique or
d'immatriculation.

numeracy /'njuːmərəsɪ, US 'nuː-/ n aptitude f au
calcul; **to improve pupils' standards of ~** améliorer le niveau des élèves en calcul.

numeral /'njuːmərəl, US 'nuː-/ n chiffre m, nombre m.

numerate /'njuːmərət, US 'nuː-/ adj **to be ~** savoir
compter.

numerical /njuː'merɪkl, US 'nuː-/ adj numérique.

numerous /'njuːmərəs, US 'nuː-/ adj nombreux/-euse.

nun /nʌn/ n religieuse f, bonne sœur f; **to become a
~** entrer au couvent.

nurse /nɜːs/ ▶ 1251 I n **1** MED infirmier/-ière m/f;
male ~ infirmier m; **2** = **nursemaid**.
II vtr **1** MED soigner [person, cold]; **2** (clasp) serrer
[object]; **to ~ a baby in one's arms** bercer un bébé
dans ses bras; **to ~ one's drink** faire durer sa
boisson; **3** (suckle) allaiter [baby]; **4** (foster) nourrir
[grievance, hope].
III vi **1** (be a nurse) être infirmier/-ière; **2** (feed) [baby]
téter.

nursemaid n nurse f, bonne f d'enfants.

nursery /'nɜːsərɪ/ n **1** (also **day ~**) GEN crèche f; (in
hotel, shop) garderie f; **2** (room) chambre f d'enfants; **3**
(for plants) pépinière f.

nursery: ~ **rhyme** n comptine f; ~ **school** n
école f maternelle; ~ **slope** n GB piste f pour débutants.

nurse's aide ▶ 1251 n US aide-soignant/-e m/f.

nursing /'nɜːsɪŋ/ ▶ 1251 I n (profession) profession f
d'infirmier/-ière; (care) soins mpl.
II adj **1** [mother] qui allaite; **2** MED [staff] infirmier/
-ière; [methods, practice] de soins.

nursing auxiliary n GB aide-soignant/-e m/f.

nursing home n **1** (old people's) maison f de retraite;
(convalescent) maison f de repos; **2** GB (small private hospital) clinique f; (maternity) clinique f obstétricale.

nurture /'nɜːtʃə(r)/ SOUT I n ₵ soins mpl.
II vtr **1** LIT élever [child]; soigner [plant]; **2** FIG
nourrir [hope, feeling, talent].
IDIOMS **the nature ~ debate** la question de l'inné et
de l'acquis.

nut /nʌt/ n **1** CULIN (walnut) noix f; (hazel) noisette f;
(almond) amande f; (peanut) cacahuète f; **2** TECH écrou
m.
IDIOMS **he's a hard** ou **tough ~ to crack** il est dur à
convaincre; **to be ~s about sb/sth**◦ être fou/folle
de qn/qch; **the ~s and bolts** les détails pratiques (**of**
de).

nut: ~**cracker(s)** n(pl) casse-noisettes m inv; ~
cutlet n côtelette f végétarienne (à base de noisettes);
~**meg** n (spice) noix f de muscade.

nutrient /'njuːtrɪənt, US 'nuː-/ n substance f nutritive.

nutrition /njuː'trɪʃn, US 'nuː-/ n (process) nutrition f,
alimentation f; (science) diététique f.

nutritional /njuː'trɪʃənl, US nuː-/ adj [value] nutritif/
-ive; [composition, information] nutritionnel/-elle.

nutritious /njuː'trɪʃəs, US nuː-/ adj nourrissant.

nutshell /'nʌtʃel/ n **1** LIT coquille f de noix or
noisette; **2** FIG **in a ~** en un mot; **to put sth in a ~**
résumer qch en un mot.

nuzzle /'nʌzl/ I vtr frotter son nez contre.
II vi = **nuzzle up**.
■ **nuzzle up: to ~ up against** ou **to sb** se blottir
contre qn.

NV US POST abrév écrite = **Nevada**.

NY US POST abrév écrite = **New York**.

NYC US abrév écrite = **New York City**.

nylon /'naɪlɒn/ n nylon® m.

nylons /'naɪlɒnz/ npl bas mpl nylon.

nymph /nɪmf/ n nymphe f.

nymphomaniac /ˌnɪmfəˈmeɪnɪæk/ n, adj nymphomane (f).

NZ abrév écrite = **New Zealand**.

Oo

o, O /əʊ/ *n* **1** (letter) o, O *m*; **2 O** (spoken number) zéro.

o' /ə/ *prep* (abrév = **of**) de.

oaf /əʊf/ *n* (clumsy) balourd/-e *m/f*; (loutish) mufle *m*.

oak /əʊk/ **I** *n* chêne *m*.
II *noun modifier* [*table*] de ou en chêne.
IDIOMS **great ~s from little acorns grow** PROV les petits ruisseaux font les grandes rivières PROV.

OAP *n* GB **1** (abrév = **old age pensioner**) retraité/-e *m/f*; **2** (abrév = **old age pension**) retraite *f* de la sécurité sociale.

oar /ɔː(r)/ *n* rame *f*; (person) rameur/-euse *m/f*.

OAS *n* US (abrév = **Organization of American States**) Organisation *f* des États américains.

oasis /əʊˈeɪsɪs/ *n* (*pl* **oases**) (in desert) oasis *f*; FIG (of peace) havre *m*.

oat /əʊt/ *n* **~s** avoine *f*.
IDIOMS **to sow one's wild ~s** jeter sa gourme.

oatcake /ˈəʊtkeɪk/ *n* galette *f* d'avoine.

oath /əʊθ/ *n* **1** JUR serment *m*; **under ~, on ~** GB sous serment; **to take the ~** prêter serment; **to swear** ou **take an ~** prêter serment (**to do** de faire; **that** que); **to administer the ~ to sb, to put sb under ~** faire prêter serment à qn; **2** (swearword) juron *m*.

oatmeal /ˈəʊtmiːl/ **I** *n* ¢ **1** (cereal) farine *f* d'avoine; **2** US (porridge) bouillie *f* d'avoine; **3** (colour) grège *m*.
II ▶ **818** *adj* grège.

obdurate /ˈɒbdjʊrət, US -dər-/ *adj* **1** (stubborn) obstiné, entêté; **2** (hardhearted) endurci.

OBE *n* GB (abrév = **Officer of the (Order of the) British Empire**) officier *m* de l'ordre de l'empire britannique.

obedience /əˈbiːdɪəns/ *n* GEN obéissance *f* (**to** à); RELIG obédience *f*; **in ~ to** conformément à.

obedient /əˈbiːdɪənt/ *adj* obéissant.

obediently /əˈbiːdɪəntlɪ/ *adv* docilement.

obelisk /ˈɒbəlɪsk/ *n* ARCHIT obélisque *m*.

obese /əʊˈbiːs/ *adj* obèse.

obesity /əʊˈbiːsətɪ/ *n* obésité *f*.

obey /əˈbeɪ/ **I** *vtr* GEN obéir à; se conformer à [*instructions*]; JUR obtempérer à [*summons, order*].
II *vi* obéir.

obituary /əˈbɪtʃʊərɪ, US -tʃʊerɪ/ **I** *n* (also **~ notice**) nécrologie *f*.
II *noun modifier* [*column, page*] nécrologique.

object I /ˈɒbdʒɪkt/ *n* **1** (item) objet *m*; **2** (goal) but *m* (**of** de); **with the ~ of doing** dans le but de faire; **3** (focus) **to be the ~ of** être l'objet de; **4** LING complément *m* d'objet.
II /əbˈdʒekt/ *vtr* objecter (**that** que).
III /əbˈdʒekt/ *vi* soulever des objections; '**I ~!**' 'je proteste!'; **to ~ to** s'opposer à [*plan, law*]; se plaindre de [*noise*]; récuser [*witness, juror*]; **to ~ strongly to** s'opposer catégoriquement à; **to ~ to sb on grounds of sex/age** objecter à qn son sexe/âge; **to ~ to sb('s) doing** s'opposer à ce que qn fasse; **do you ~ to my** ou **me smoking?** est-ce que cela vous ennuie que je fume?
IDIOMS **money is no ~** l'argent n'est pas un problème.

objection /əbˈdʒekʃn/ *n* objection *f* (**to** à; **from** de la part de); **I've no ~(s)** je n'y vois pas d'inconvénient; **I've no ~ to them coming** cela ne me dérange pas qu'ils viennent; **to make ~ to** JUR marquer son opposition à [*argument, statement*].

objectionable /əbˈdʒekʃənəbl/ *adj* [*remark*] désobligeant; [*behaviour*] choquant; [*person*] insupportable.

objective /əbˈdʒektɪv/ **I** *n* GEN objectif *m*; LING accusatif *m*.
II *adj* (unbiased) objectif/-ive, impartial (**about** en ce qui concerne); LING accusatif/-ive.

objectively /əbˈdʒektɪvlɪ/ *adv* objectivement.

objectivity /ˌɒbdʒekˈtɪvətɪ/ *n* objectivité *f*.

object lesson *n* démonstration *f* (**in** de).

objector /əbˈdʒektə(r)/ *n* opposant/-e *m/f*.

obligation /ˌɒblɪˈɡeɪʃn/ *n* **1** (duty) devoir *m* (**towards, to** envers); **to be under (an) ~ to do** être obligé de faire; **2** (commitment) (contractual) obligation *f* (**to** envers; **to do** de faire); (personal) engagement *m* (**to** envers); **3** (debt) (financial) dette *f*; (of gratitude) dette *f* de reconnaissance; **to be under ~ to sb for sth** être redevable à qn de qch.

obligatory /əˈblɪɡətrɪ, US -tɔːrɪ/ *adj* (compulsory) obligatoire (**to do** de faire); (customary) de rigueur.

oblige /əˈblaɪdʒ/ *vtr* **1** (compel) obliger (**to do** à faire); **2** (be helpful) rendre service à; **could you ~ me with a lift?** auriez-vous l'amabilité de me déposer?; **anything to ~!** à votre service!; **3** (be grateful) **to be ~d to sb** être reconnaissant à qn (**for** de; **for doing** d'avoir fait); **I would be ~d if you'd stop smoking** je vous saurais gré de ne pas fumer; **much ~d!** merci beaucoup!

obliging /əˈblaɪdʒɪŋ/ *adj* serviable; **it is ~ of them** c'est aimable de leur part (**to do** de faire).

oblique /əˈbliːk/ **I** *n* (in printing) oblique *f*.
II *adj* GEN oblique; [*reference, compliment*] indirect.

obliquely /əˈbliːklɪ/ *adv* [*drawn*] obliquement, de biais; [*answer, refer*] indirectement.

obliterate /əˈblɪtəreɪt/ *vtr* **1** (destroy) anéantir [*landmark, city*]; (remove) effacer [*trace, word*]; **2** (cover) masquer [*sun, view*]; **3** (erase from mind) effacer [*memory*].

obliteration /əˌblɪtəˈreɪʃn/ *n* (of mark, memory) effacement *m*; (of city) anéantissement *m*.

oblivion /əˈblɪvɪən/ *n* **1** (obscurity) oubli *m*; **2** (unconsciousness) néant *m*.

oblivious /əˈblɪvɪəs/ *adj* **1** (unaware) inconscient; **to be ~ of** ou **to** ne pas être conscient de; **2** (forgetful) oublieux/-ieuse (**of** de).

oblong /ˈɒblɒŋ, US -lɔːŋ/ **I** *n* rectangle *m*.
II *adj* [*table, building*] oblong/-ongue, rectangulaire.

obnoxious /əbˈnɒkʃəs/ *adj* [*person, behaviour*] odieux/-ieuse, exécrable; [*smell*] nauséabond.

oboe /ˈəʊbəʊ/ ▶ **1097** *n* hautbois *m*.

obscene /əbˈsiːn/ *adj* **1** [*film, publication, remark*] obscène; **2** [*wealth*] indécent; [*war*] monstrueux/-euse.

obscenely /əbˈsiːnlɪ/ *adv* [*leer, suggest*] de manière obscène; **to be ~ rich** être tellement riche que c'en est indécent.

obscenity /əbˈsenətɪ/ *n* obscénité *f*.

obscure /əbˈskjʊə(r)/ **I** *adj* GEN obscur; (indistinct) vague.
II *vtr* GEN obscurcir; cacher [*view*]; **to ~ the issue** embrouiller la question.

obscurity /əbˈskjʊərətɪ/ *n* obscurité *f*.

obsequious /əbˈsiːkwɪəs/ *adj* obséquieux/-ieuse.

observable /əbˈzɜːvəbl/ *adj* (discernible) observable; (noteworthy) notable.

observance /əbˈzɜːvəns/ *n* **1** (of law, right) respect *m* (of de); (of sabbath) observance *f* (of de); **2** (ceremony) observance *f*.

observant /əb'zɜ:vənt/ *adj* observateur/-trice.

observation /ˌɒbzə'veɪʃn/ *n* **1** GEN, MED observation *f* (of de); (in hospital) être en observation; **to keep sb/sth under ~** GEN surveiller qn/qch; **2** (remark) remarque *f*; (critical) observation *f*; **to make the ~ that** faire observer que.

observation: **~ car** *n* wagon *m* panoramique; **~ tower** *n* mirador *m*.

observatory /əb'zɜ:vətrɪ, US -tɔ:rɪ/ *n* observatoire *m*.

observe /əb'zɜ:v/ *vtr* **1** (see, notice) observer (**that** que); **2** (watch) [*doctor, police*] surveiller; [*scientist, researcher*] observer; **3** (remark) faire observer (**that** que); **4** (adhere to) observer [*law, custom, festival*].

observer /əb'zɜ:və(r)/ *n* GEN observateur/-trice *m/f* (**of** de); (commentator) spécialiste *mf*.

obsess /əb'ses/ *vtr* obséder.

obsession /əb'seʃn/ *n* obsession *f*; **she has an ~ with tidiness** elle a la manie de l'ordre; **sailing is an ~ with him** sa passion pour la voile tient de l'obsession.

obsessive /əb'sesɪv/ *adj* [*person*] maniaque; [*neurosis*] obsessionnel/-elle; [*thought, memory*] obsédant; **his ~ fear of illness** sa hantise de la maladie.

obsessively /əb'sesɪvlɪ/ *adv* **~ clean** d'une propreté maniaque; **to be ~ interested in sth** s'intéresser à qch au point d'en être obsédé.

obsolescence /ˌɒbsə'lesns/ *n* GEN désuétude *f*; ECON obsolescence *f*; **built-in ~, planned ~** obsolescence planifiée.

obsolete /'ɒbsəli:t/ *adj* [*technology*] dépassé; [*custom, idea*] démodé; [*word*] désuet.

obstacle /'ɒbstəkl/ *n* LIT, FIG obstacle *m*; **to be an ~ to sth, to put an ~ in the way of sth** faire obstacle à qch; **to put an ~ in sb's way** faire obstacle à qn.

obstacle: **~ course** *n* MIL parcours *m* du combattant; FIG course *f* d'obstacles; **~ race** *n* course *f* d'obstacles.

obstetric /əb'stetrɪk/ **I obstetrics** *n* (+ *v sg*) obstétrique *f*.
II *adj* [*service, technique*] obstétrical.

obstetrician /ˌɒbstə'trɪʃn/ ▶1251 *n* obstétricien/-ienne *m/f*.

obstinacy /'ɒbstɪnəsɪ/ *n* (of person) entêtement *m* (**in doing** à faire); (of cough, illnesss) persistance *f*.

obstinate /'ɒbstɪnət/ *adj* [*person*] têtu (**about** en ce qui concerne); [*behaviour, silence, effort*] obstiné; [*resistance*] acharné; [*illness, cough*] persistant; [*fever, stain*] rebelle.

obstreperous /əb'strepərəs/ *adj* [*drunk, child*] tapageur/-euse; [*crowd*] tumultueux/-euse.

obstruct /əb'strʌkt/ *vtr* **1** (block) cacher [*view*]; bloquer [*road*]; MED obstruer (**with** de); **2** (impede) gêner [*traffic, person, progress*]; faire obstacle à [*plan*]; faire obstruction à [*player*]; entraver le cours de [*justice*]; **to ~ the police** gêner la police dans l'exercice de ses fonctions.

obstruction /əb'strʌkʃn/ *n* **1** ¢ (act, state) (of road) encombrement *m*; (of pipe, artery) engorgement *m*; POL obstruction *f*; **2** (blockage) (to traffic, progress) obstacle *m*; (in pipe) bouchon *m*; MED obstruction *f*; **3** SPORT obstruction *f*.

obstructive /əb'strʌktɪv/ *adj* **1** [*policy, tactics*] obstructionniste; [*person*] peu coopératif/-ive; [*behaviour*] récalcitrant; **2** MED qui obstrue, obstruant.

obtain /əb'teɪn/ **I** *vtr* obtenir [*information, permission, degree, visa, prize*]; (for oneself) se procurer [*money, goods*]; acquérir [*experience*]; **to ~ sth for sb** procurer qch à qn; **our products may be ~ed from any supermarket** vous trouverez nos produits dans tous les supermarchés.
II *vi* SOUT [*situation*] avoir cours; [*rule*] être de rigueur.

obtainable /əb'teɪnəbl/ *adj* **~ in all good bookstores** disponible dans toutes les bonnes librairies;

petrol is easily ~ on peut se procurer de l'essence facilement.

obtrude /əb'tru:d/ *vi* **1** SOUT (impinge) **to ~ on** empiéter sur; **2** SOUT (become apparent) transparaître; **3** (stick out) sortir.

obtrusive /əb'tru:sɪv/ *adj* **1** (conspicuous) [*decor*] choquant; [*stain*] visible; [*noise*] gênant; **2** (indiscreet) [*person, behaviour*] importun.

obtuse /əb'tju:s, US -'tu:s-/ *adj* **1** [*person*] obtus; [*remark*] stupide; **he's being deliberately ~** il joue les abrutis○; **2** MATH obtus.

obverse /'ɒbvɜ:s/ *adj* **1** (contrary) [*argument*] contraire; **2** (of coin) **the ~ side** ou **face** l'avers *m*.

obviate /'ɒbvɪeɪt/ *vtr* SOUT obvier à [*difficulty*]; éviter [*delay, requirement*]; écarter [*danger*].

obvious /'ɒbvɪəs/ **I** *n* **to state the ~** enfoncer les portes ouvertes.
II *adj* **1** (evident) évident (**to** pour); **it's ~ that** il est évident que; **her anxiety was ~** il était évident qu'elle était inquiète; **she is the ~ choice for the job** c'est la personne qu'il nous faut pour ce poste; **it was the ~ solution to choose** la solution s'imposait d'elle-même; **the ~ thing to do** la chose à faire; **for ~ reasons** pour des raisons évidentes; **2** (unsubtle) [*lie*] flagrant; [*joke*] lourd; **she was too ~ about it** elle a un peu trop manqué de finesse.

obviously /'ɒbvɪəslɪ/ **I** *adv* manifestement; **she ~ needs help** il est évident qu'elle a besoin d'aide; **he's ~ lying** il est clair qu'il ment; **he was ~ in pain** il souffrait visiblement; **'hasn't he heard of them?'—'~ not'** IRON 'n'en a-t-il pas entendu parler?'—'on dirait que non'.
II *excl* (indicating assent) bien sûr!, évidemment!

occasion /ə'keɪʒn/ **I** *n* **1** (particular time) occasion *f*; **on that ~** à cette occasion, cette fois-là; **on one ~** une fois; **on a previous ~** précédemment; **on ~** à l'occasion; **on the ~ of** à l'occasion de; **when the ~ demands it** lorsque les circonstances l'exigent; **to rise to the ~** se montrer à la hauteur des circonstances; **2** SOUT (opportunity) occasion *f*; **to have ~ to do** avoir l'occasion de faire; **it's no ~ for laughter** ce n'est pas le moment de rire; **should the ~ arise** si l'occasion se présente; **3** (event, function) occasion *f*, événement *m*; **on special ~s** dans les grandes occasions; **for the ~** pour l'occasion; **the wedding was quite an ~** le mariage a été un événement; **state ~** cérémonie *f* officielle; **4** SOUT (cause) raison *f*; **there is no ~ for alarm** il n'y a pas lieu de s'inquiéter.
II *vtr* SOUT occasionner, provoquer.

occasional /ə'keɪʒənl/ *adj* **1** [*event*] qui a lieu de temps en temps; **the ~ letter** une lettre de temps en temps; **~ showers** METEOROL averses *fpl* intermittentes; **2** SOUT [*poem, music*] de circonstance.

occasionally /ə'keɪʒənəlɪ/ *adv* de temps à autre; **very ~** très rarement, presque jamais.

occlude /ə'klu:d/ *vtr* occlure.

occult I /ɒ'kʌlt, US ə'kʌlt/ *n* **the ~** (+ *v sg*) les sciences *fpl* occultes.
II /ɒ'kʌlt/ *adj* [*powers, arts, literature*] occulte.

occupancy /'ɒkjʊpənsɪ/ *n* occupation *f*; **sole ~ of a house** occupation d'une maison par une seule personne; **a change of ~** un changement d'occupant/-e *m/f*; **available for immediate ~** libre immédiatement.

occupant /'ɒkjʊpənt/ *n* **1** (of building, bed) occupant/-e *m/f*; **2** (of vehicle) passager/-ère *m/f*; **3** (of post) titulaire *mf*.

occupation /ˌɒkjʊ'peɪʃn/ *n* **1** (of house) **to be in ~** être installé; **ready for ~** prêt à être habité; **to take up ~** s'installer (**of** dans); **2** MIL, POL occupation *f* (**de** of); **to come under ~** être envahi; **3** (job) (trade) métier *m*; (profession) profession *f*; **4** (leisure activity) occupation *f*.

occupational /ˌɒkjʊ'peɪʃənl/ *adj* [*accident*] du travail; [*activity*] professionnel/-elle; [*risk*] du métier; [*safety*] au travail.

occupational: **~ hazard** *n* risque *m* professionnel; **~ health** *n* médecine *f* du travail; **~**

pension *n* GB retraite *f* professionnelle; **~ psychologist** ▶ 1251 *n* psychologue *mf* du travail; **~ therapist** ▶ 1251 *n* ergothérapeute *mf*; **~ therapy** *n* ergothérapie *f*.

occupier /'ɒkjʊpaɪə(r)/ *n* occupant/-e *m/f*.

occupy /'ɒkjʊpaɪ/ *vtr* **1** (inhabit) occuper [*premises*]; **2** (fill) occuper [*bed, seat, room*]; **3** (take over) occuper [*country, building*]; **4** (take up) prendre [*time*] [*activity*] durer [*afternoon*]; occuper [*area, surface*]; **5** (keep busy) occuper [*person, mind*]; capter [*attention*]; **I'm fully occupied with the garden** le jardin prend tout mon temps; **to keep oneself occupied** s'occuper (**by doing** en faisant); **6** (hold) remplir [*post*].

occur /ə'kɜː(r)/ *vi* (*p prés etc* **-rr-**) **1** (happen) [*change, delay, fault*] se produire; [*epidemic*] se déclarer; [*symptom*] apparaître; [*opportunity*] se présenter; [*sale, visit*] s'effectuer; **2** (be present) [*disease, infection*] se produire; [*species, toxin, misprint*] se trouver; [*phrase*] se rencontrer; **3** (suggest itself) **the idea ~red to me that** l'idée m'est venue à l'esprit que; **it ~s to me that she's wrong** il me semble qu'elle a tort; **it didn't ~ to me to do** il ne m'est pas venu à l'idée de faire.

occurrence /ə'kʌrəns/ *n* **1** (event) fait *m*; **to be a rare ~** se produire rarement; **2** (instance) occurrence *f*; **3** (of disease, phenomenon) cas *m*.

ocean /'əʊʃn/ **I** *n* LIT océan *m*.
II oceans° *npl* **~s of** plein de° [*food, space, time, work etc*].
III *noun modifier* [*voyage, wave*] océanique; **~ bed** fond *m* de l'océan.

ocean-going /'əʊʃngəʊɪŋ/ *adj* [*vessel, ship*] de haute mer.

ochre GB, **ocher** US /'əʊkə(r)/ ▶ 818 *n, adj* (colour) ocre (*mf*) *inv*.

o'clock /ə'klɒk/ ▶ 812 *adv* **at one ~** à une heure; **it's two ~/12 ~ midday** il est deux heures/midi; **the 10 ~ screening** la séance de 10 heures.

Oct *abrév écrite* = **October**.

octagon /'ɒktəgən, US -gɒn/ *n* octogone *m*.

octane /'ɒkteɪn/ *n* octane *m*.

octave /'ɒktɪv/ *n* MUS octave *f*; LITERAT huitain *m*.

octavo /ɒk'teɪvəʊ/ *n, noun modifier* in-octavo (*m*).

octet /ɒk'tet/ *n* MUS octuor *m*; COMPUT octet *m*; LITERAT huitain *m*.

October /ɒk'təʊbə(r)/ ▶ 1090 *n* octobre *m*.

octogenarian /ˌɒktədʒɪ'neərɪən/ *n, adj* octogénaire (*mf*).

octopus /'ɒktəpəs/ *n* **1** ZOOL pieuvre *f*; CULIN poulpe *m*; **2** GB (elastic straps) fixe-bagages *m inv*.

oculist /'ɒkjʊlɪst/ *n* ophtalmologiste *mf*.

OD° /əʊdiː/ **I** *n* = **overdose I**.
II *vi* (3ᵉ *pers sg prés* **OD's**; *p prés* **OD'ing**; *prét, pp* **OD'd, OD'ed**) **to ~ on** LIT prendre une dose mortelle de [*tablets*]; prendre une overdose de [*drugs*]; FIG se gaver de [*chocolate*]; s'abrutir de [*television*].

odd /ɒd/ **I** *adj* **1** (strange, unusual) [*person, object, occurrence*] bizarre; **there is something ~ about** il y a quelque chose de bizarre dans [*appearance, statement*]; **it is ~ how...** c'est bizarre de voir comme...; **to be an ~ couple** former un drôle de couple; **that's ~** (c'est) bizarre; **he's a bit ~** il est un peu loufoque°; **2** (occasional) **I have the ~ drink** il m'arrive de boire un verre; **to write the ~ article** écrire un article de temps en temps; **except for the ~ tree** à part un arbre ou deux; **3** [*socks, gloves*] dépareillés; **4** (miscellaneous) **there were some ~ bits of cloth left** il restait encore quelques bouts de tissu; **a few ~ coins** un reste de monnaie; **5** MATH [*number*] impair; **6** (different) **spot the ~ man** ou **one out** trouvez l'intrus; **to feel the ~ one out** ne pas se sentir à sa place.
II -odd *combining form* (approximately) **there were sixty-~ people** il y avait soixante et quelques personnes; **twenty-~ years later** une vingtaine d'années plus tard.

Oceans and seas

Note that the words océan *and* mer *do not have capitals in French.*

the Atlantic Ocean	= l'océan Atlantique
the Pacific Ocean	= l'océan Pacifique
the Indian Ocean	= l'océan Indien
the Caspian Sea	= la mer Caspienne
the Baltic Sea	= la mer Baltique

As in English, French often drops the words océan *or* mer. *When this happens, oceans have masculine gender (from the masculine word* océan*) and seas have feminine gender (from the feminine* mer*):*

the Pacific	= le Pacifique
the Baltic	= la Baltique

but

the Aegean	= la mer Égée

If in doubt, look up the name in the dictionary.

Use with other nouns

Here are some useful patterns, using Pacifique *as a typical name:*

the Pacific coast	= la côte du Pacifique
a Pacific crossing	= une traversée du Pacifique
a Pacific cruise	= une croisière dans le Pacifique
Pacific currents	= les courants du Pacifique
Pacific fish	= les poissons du Pacifique
the Pacific islands	= les îles du Pacifique

---

odd: **~ball**° *n* farfelu/-e° *m/f*; **~ bod**° *n* GB drôle de mec°/nana° *m/f*.

oddity /'ɒdɪtɪ/ *n* (odd thing) bizarrerie *f*; (person) excentrique *mf*.

odd job *n* (for money) petit boulot *m*; **to do ~s around the house** bricoler dans la maison.

odd-jobman *n* homme *m* à tout faire.

odds /ɒdz/ *npl* **1** (in betting) cote *f* (**on** sur); **what are the ~?** quelle est la cote?; **the ~ are 20 to 1** la cote est 20 contre 1; **the ~ on X are short/long** X est bien/mal coté; **2** (chance, likelihood) chances *fpl*; **the ~ are against/in favour of sth** qch est improbable/probable; **the ~ are against it** il y a peu de chances; **the ~ against/in favour of sth happening** les chances que qch n'arrive pas/arrive; **the ~ are in our favour** (in venture) nous avons toutes les chances de réussir; **to win against the ~** gagner contre toute attente; **to shorten/lengthen the ~ on sth** rendre qch plus/moins probable.
IDIOMS **it makes no ~** GB ça n'a pas d'importance; **to pay over the ~ for sth** payer le prix fort pour qch; **at ~** (in dispute) être en conflit; (inconsistent) en contradiction.

odds and ends, **odds and sods**° GB *npl* broco-les° *fpl*.

odds-on /ˌɒdz'ɒn/ *adj* **1**° (likely) **it is ~ that** il y a de fortes chances que (+ *subj*); **he has an ~ chance of doing** il a de fortes chances de faire; **2** (in betting) **to be the ~ favourite** être le grand favori.

odious /'əʊdɪəs/ *adj* odieux/-ieuse.

odium /'əʊdɪəm/ *n* réprobation *f* générale.

odometer /ɒ'dɒmɪtə(r)/ *n* AUT odomètre *m*.

odour GB, **odor** US /'əʊdə(r)/ *n* odeur *f*.

odourless GB, **odorless** US /'əʊdəlɪs/ *adj* [*gas*] inodore; [*cosmetic*] non parfumé.

odyssey /'ɒdɪsɪ/ *n* odyssée *f*; **the Odyssey** l'Odyssée *f*.

OECD *n* (*abrév* = **Organization for Economic Cooperation and Development**) OCDE *f*.

oedema GB, **edema** US /ɪ'diːmə/ *n* œdème *m*.

o'er /ɔː(r)/ LITTÉR = **over¹**.

oesophagus GB, **esophagus** US /ɪ'sɒfəgəs/ *n* œsophage *m*.

oestrogen GB, **estrogen** US /'iːstrədʒən/ *n* œstrogène *m*.

of /ɒv, əv/ *prep* **1** (in most uses) de; **the leg ~ the table** le pied de la table; **2** (made of) **a ring (made) ~ gold** une bague en or; **a will ~ iron** FIG une volonté

of

In almost all its uses the preposition *of* is translated by *de*. Exceptions to this are substances (*made of gold*), uses with a personal pronoun (*that's kind of you*), proportions (*some of us, of the 12 of us …*) and time expressions (*of an evening*). For translations of these, see the entry *of*. Remember that *de* + *le* always becomes *du* and that *de* + *les* always becomes *des*.

To find translations for phrases beginning with *of* (*of course, of all, of interest, of late, of old*) you should consult the appropriate noun etc. entry (**course, all, interest, late, old** etc.).

of also often appears as the second element of a verb (*consist of, deprive of, die of, think of*). For translations, consult the appropriate verb entry.

of is used after certain nouns, pronouns and adjectives in English (*a member of, a game of, some of, most of, afraid of, capable of, ashamed of*). For translations, consult the appropriate noun, pronoun or adjective entry.

When *of it* or *of them* are used for something already referred to they are translated by *en*:

there's a lot of it = il y en a beaucoup
there are several of them = il y en a plusieurs

Note, however, the following expressions used when referring to people:

there are six of them = ils sont six
there were several of them = ils étaient plusieurs

For particular usages see the entry *of*.

This dictionary contains usage notes on such topics as **age, capacity measurement, dates, illnesses, length measurement, quantities, towns and cities**, and **weight measurement**, many of which use *of*. For the index to these notes ► **1419**.

de fer; **3** (indicating an agent) **that's kind ~ you** c'est très gentil de votre part or à vous; **4** (indicating a proportion) **some ~ us** quelques-uns d'entre nous; **of the twelve ~ us**… sur les douze (que nous sommes/étions)…; **5** GB (in expressions of time) **I like to play golf ~ an afternoon** j'aime jouer au golf l'après-midi.

off /ɒf, US ɔːf/

■ Note *off* is often found as the second element in verb combinations (*fall off, run off* etc) and in offensive interjections (*clear off* etc). For translations consult the appropriate verb entry (**fall, run, clear** etc).
– *off* is used in certain expressions such as *off limits, off colour* etc and translations for these will be found under the noun entry (**limit, colour** etc).
– For other uses of *off* see the entry below.

I ○ *n* (**from**) **the ~** (dès) le départ; **just before the ~** (of race) juste avant le départ.

II *adv* **1** (leaving) **to be ~** partir, s'en aller; **it's time you were ~** il est temps que tu partes; **I'm ~** GEN je m'en vais; (to avoid sb) je ne suis pas là; **to be ~ to a good start** avoir pris un bon départ; **he's ~ again talking about his exploits!** FIG et voilà c'est reparti, il raconte encore ses exploits!; **2** (at a distance) **to be 30 metres ~** être à 30 mètres; **some way ~** assez loin; **3** (ahead in time) **Easter is a month ~** Pâques est dans un mois; **the exam is still several months ~** l'examen n'aura pas lieu avant plusieurs mois; **4** THEAT **trumpet sound ~** on entend une trompette dans les coulisses.

III *adj* **1** (free) **Tuesday's my day ~** je ne travaille pas le mardi; **to have the morning ~** avoir la matinée libre; **2** (turned off) **to be ~** [*water, gas*] (at mains) être coupé; [*tap*] être fermé; [*light, TV*] être éteint; **3** (cancelled) **to be ~** [*match, party*] être annulé; **our engagement's ~** nous avons rompu nos fiançailles; **the 'coq au vin' is ~** (from menu) il n'y a plus de 'coq au vin'; **4** (removed) **the lid is ~** il n'y a pas de couvercle; **with her make-up ~** sans maquillage; **to have one's leg ~**○ se faire couper la jambe; **25%**

~ COMM 25% de remise; **5**○ (bad) **to be ~** [*food*] être avarié; [*milk*] avoir tourné.

IV off and on *adv phr* par périodes.

V *prep* **1** (away from in distance) **~ the west coast** au large de la côte ouest; **three metres ~ the ground** à trois mètres (au-dessus) du sol; **2** (away from in time) **to be a long way ~ doing** être encore loin de faire; **3** (also **just ~**) juste à côté de [*kitchen etc*]; **just ~ the path** à quelques mètres du sentier; **4** (astray from) **it is ~ the point** là n'est pas la question; **to be ~ centre** être mal centré; **5** (detached from) **to be ~ its hinges** être sorti de ses gonds; **there's a button ~** [*cuff etc*] il manque un bouton à; **6**○ (no longer interested in) **to be ~ one's food** ne pas avoir d'appétit; **I'm ~ her at the moment!** il ne faut pas me parler d'elle en ce moment!; **7**○ (also **~ of**) **to borrow sth ~ a neighbour** emprunter qch à un voisin; **to eat ~ a tray** manger sur un plateau.
IDIOMS **how are we ~**○ **for…?** qu'est-ce qu'il nous reste comme…? [*flour etc*]; **~ with her head!** qu'on lui coupe la tête!; **that's a bit ~**○ GB ça c'est un peu fort○; **to feel a bit ~**○(**-colour**) GB ne pas être dans son assiette○; **to have an ~ day** ne pas être dans un de ses bons jours.

offal /ˈɒfl, US ˈɔːfl/ *n* abats *mpl*.

off-: **~beat** *adj* MUS [*rhythm*] à temps faible; FIG [*humour*] cocasse; **~-centre** GB, **~-center** US *adj* décentré.

off-chance /ˈɒftʃɑːns, US -tʃæns/ *n* chance *f*; **there's just an ~ that** il y a une chance pour que (+ *subj*); **just on the ~** au cas où.

off-: **~-color** *adj* US [*story, joke*] indécent; **~-colour**○ *adj* GB (unwell) patraque○.

offence GB, **offense** US /əˈfens/ *n* **1** JUR infraction *f*; **it is an ~ to do** il est illégal de faire; **2** (insult) offense *f*; **to cause** ou **give ~ to sb** offenser qn; **to take ~ (at)** s'offenser (de); **no ~ intended, but…** je ne voudrais pas te vexer, mais…; **no ~ taken** il n'y a pas de mal; **3** (attack) atteinte *f* (**against** à); **4** MIL offensive *f*; **5** US SPORT **the ~** les attaquants *mpl*.

offend /əˈfend/ **I** *vtr* **1** (hurt) blesser, offenser [*person*]; [*behaviour, remark*]; **to get ~ed** se vexer; **2** (displease) outrager [*sense of justice*]; **to ~ the eye** [*building etc*] choquer la vue.
II *vi* JUR commettre une infraction (**against** à); **to ~ again** récidiver.
III offending *pres p adj* (responsible) [*object*] en cause; [*person*] responsable.
■ **offend against**: **~ against** [*sth*] **1** enfreindre [*law*]; **2** (violate) offenser [*good taste*]; être un outrage à [*common sense*].

offender /əˈfendə(r)/ *n* **1** JUR (against the law) délinquant/-e *m/f*; (against regulations) contrevenant/-e *m/f* (**against** à); **2** (culprit) coupable *mf*; **the worst ~** le/la plus à blâmer.

offense *n* US ► **offence**.

offensive /əˈfensɪv/ **I** *n* **1** MIL, POL, SPORT offensive *f* (**against** contre); **to go on the ~** passer à l'offensive; **to be on the ~** être passé à l'attaque; **2** COMM (campaign) campagne *f*.
II *adj* **1** (insulting) [*remark*] injurieux/-ieuse (**to** pour); [*behaviour*] insultant; **2** (vulgar) [*language*] grossier/-ière; [*behaviour, gesture*] choquant; **3** (revolting) [*smell*] repoussant; [*behaviour, idea*] répugnant; **4** MIL, SPORT, [*action, play*] offensif/-ive.

offer /ˈɒfə(r), US ˈɔːf-/ **I** *n* **1** (proposition) GEN, FIN offre *f* (**to do** de faire); **job ~** offre d'emploi; **an ~ of marriage** une proposition de mariage; **that's my final** ou **best ~** c'est mon dernier mot; **to be open to ~s** être ouvert à toute proposition; **the house is under ~** il y a une promesse d'achat sur cette maison; **or near(est) ~** (in property ad) à débattre; **~s in the region of £80,000** prix 80000 livres, à débattre; **2** COMM (promotion) promotion *f*; **to be on special ~** être en promotion; **3** (available) **the goods/cases on ~ were dear** les marchandises/valises en vente étaient chères; **there's a lot/nothing on ~** il y a beaucoup/peu de choix; **what's on ~ in the catalogue?** qu'est-ce qu'on propose dans le catalogue?

II *vtr* **1** (proffer) donner [*advice, explanation, information, friendship*]; offrir [*cigarette, help, job, reward, suggestion, support*]; émettre [*opinion*]; faire [*reduction*]; proposer [*service*]; accorder [*discount*]; **to ~ sb sth, to ~ sth to sb** offrir qch à qn; **to ~ to do** se proposer pour faire; **she has a lot to ~ the company** elle peut beaucoup apporter à la société; **he had little to ~ in the way of news** il n'avait pas beaucoup de nouvelles à apporter; **2** (provide) offrir [*facilities, advantages, guarantee, resistance*]; donner [*insight*]; **3** (possess) posséder [*language*]; avoir [*experience*]; **4** (sell) offrir [*goods*]; **the radios were being ~ed at bargain prices** les radios étaient vendues à prix réduit; **to ~ sth for sale** mettre qch en vente; **5** (present) présenter.
III *vi* (volunteer) se proposer.
IV *v refl* **to ~ oneself** se proposer (**for** pour); **to ~ itself** [*opportunity*] se présenter.
■ **offer up**: **~** [**sth**] **up, ~ up** [**sth**] offrir [*prayer*]; faire l'offrande de [*animal, sacrifice*].

offering /ˈɒfərɪŋ, US ˈɔːf-/ *n* **1** (act of giving) offre *f*; **2** (gift) cadeau *m*; **the band's latest ~** IRON, PÉJ le dernier album du groupe; **3** RELIG collecte; **4** (sacrifice) offrande *f*.

offer price *n* COMM prix *m* de vente.

offertory /ˈɒfətrɪ, US ˈɔːfətəːrɪ/ *n* RELIG offertoire *m*.

offhand /ˌɒfˈhænd, US ˌɔːf-/ **I** *adj* (impolite) désinvolte.
II *adv* **~, I don't know** comme ça au pied levé je ne sais pas.

office /ˈɒfɪs, US ˈɔːf-/ **I** *n* **1** (place) bureau *m*; **the accounts ~** le service comptable; **lawyer's ~** cabinet *m* de notaire; **2** (function) fonction *f*, charge *f*; **public ~** fonctions *fpl* officielles; **to perform the ~ of** remplir les fonctions de; **to hold ~** [*president, mayor*] être en fonction; [*minister*] avoir un portefeuille; [*political party*] être au pouvoir; **to take ~** [*president, mayor*] entrer en fonction; [*political party*] arriver au pouvoir; **to go out of ~** [*president, mayor*] quitter ses fonctions; [*minister*] perdre son portefeuille; [*political party*] perdre le pouvoir; **to stand** GB US **to run** US **for ~** être candidat aux élections; **to rise to high ~** être promu à un poste élevé; **3** RELIG office *m* (**for** de).
II **offices** *npl* **1** SOUT (services) offices *mpl*, aide *f*; **2** GB (of property) **'the usual ~s'** 'cuisine *f* et dépendances *fpl*'; (in smaller house) 'cuisine *f* et salle *f* de bains'.

office automation *n* bureautique *f*.

office: **~ block, ~ building** *n* GB immeuble *m* de bureaux; **~ junior** *n* employé/-e *m/f* de bureau; **~ politics** *n* intrigues *fpl* de bureau.

officer /ˈɒfɪsə(r), US ˈɔːf-/ *n* **1** MIL, NAUT officier *m*; **2** (official) (in a company) responsable *mf*; (in government) fonctionnaire *mf*; (in committee, union, club) membre *m* du comité directeur; **3** (also **police ~**) policier *m*.

office worker ▶ **1251** / *n* employé/-e *m/f* de bureau.

official /əˈfɪʃl/ **I** *n* POL, ADMIN fonctionnaire *mf*; (of party, trade union) officiel/-ielle *m/f*; (of police, customs) agent *m*; (at town hall) employé/-e *m/f*.
II *adj* GEN officiel/-ielle; [*biography*] autorisé.

officialdom /əˈfɪʃldəm/ *n* bureaucratie *f*.

Official Secrets Act *n* GB loi *f* relative aux secrets d'État; **to have signed the ~** être astreint au secret.

officiate /əˈfɪʃɪeɪt/ *vi* [*official*] présider; [*priest*] officier; [*referee, umpire*] arbitrer.

officious /əˈfɪʃəs/ *adj* PÉJ trop empressé, zélé.

offing /ˈɒfɪŋ/: **in the offing** *adv phr* [*storm, war*] imminent; [*deal, wedding*] en perspective.

off: **~-key** *adj* MUS faux/fausse; **~-licence** *n* GB magasin *m* de vins et de spiritueux; **~-limits** *adj* interdit; **~-line** *adj* COMPUT [*equipment, system*] autonome; [*processing*] en différé; [*storage*] non connecté.

off-load /ˌɒfˈləʊd, US ˌɔːf-/ *vtr* **1** FIG (get rid of) écouler [*goods, stock*]; se dégager de [*investments*]; **to ~ the blame onto sb** rejeter la responsabilité sur qn; **2** COMPUT décharger.

off-peak /ˌɒfˈpiːk, US ˌɔːf-/ **I** *adj* [*electricity*] au tarif de

nuit; [*travel*] en période creuse; **~ call** TELECOM appel *m* au tarif réduit.
II *adv* TELECOM [*call, cost*] aux heures de tarif réduit.

offprint /ˈɒfprɪnt, US ˈɔːf-/ *n* tiré *m* or tirage *m* à part.

off-putting /ˌɒfˈpʊtɪŋ, US ˌɔːf-/ *adj* [*manner*] peu engageant; **it was very ~** c'était déroutant.

off-screen /ˌɒfˈskriːn, US ˌɔːf-/ **I** *adj* CIN [*action*] horschamp; [*voice*] off *inv*; [*relationship*] dans la vie.
II *adv* en privé.

off-season /ˌɒfˈsiːzn, US ˈɔːf-/ *adj* [*cruise*] hors saison; [*losses, deficit*] de basse saison.

offset /ˈɒfset, US ˈɔːf-/ *vtr* (*p prés* **-tt-**; *prét, pp* **offset**) compenser (**by** par); **to ~ sth against sth** mettre qch et qch en balance.

offset printing *n* offset *m*.

offshoot /ˈɒfʃuːt, US ˈɔːf-/ *n* (of tree, organization) ramification *f*; (of plant) rejeton *m*; (of idea, decision) conséquence *f*.

offshore /ˌɒfˈʃɔː(r), US ˌɔːf-/ **I** *adj* **1** NAUT [*waters*] du large; [*fishing*] au large; **~ wind** brise *f* de terre; **2** FIN [*funds*] hors-lieu *inv*; **3** [*oil rig*] offshore.
II *adv* **1** NAUT **to invest ~** faire des investissements horslieu; **2** (in oil industry) [*work*] en mer, offshore.

offside /ˌɒfˈsaɪd, US ˌɔːf-/ **I** *n* GB AUT côté *m* conducteur.
II *adj* **1** GB AUT [*lane*] GEN de gauche; GB de droite; **the ~ rear wheel** la roue arrière côté conducteur; **2** SPORT [*position*] hors jeu.

off: **~spring** *n* (*pl* **~**) progéniture *f* ALSO HUM; **~stage** *adj, adv* THEAT dans les coulisses; **~-the-cuff** *adj* [*remark, speech*] impromptu; **~-the-peg** *adj* [*garment*] de prêt-à-porter.

off-the-shelf *adj* **1** COMM [*goods*] disponible en magasin; **2** COMPUT [*software*] fixe.

off-the-shoulder *adj* **an ~ dress** une robe qui dégage les épaules.

off: **~-the-wall**° *adj* loufoque°; **~-white** *adj* blanc cassé *inv*.

often /ˈɒfn, ˈɒftən, US ˈɔːfn/ *adv* souvent; **as ~ as not**, **more ~ than not** le plus souvent; **how ~ do you meet?** vous vous voyez tous les combien?; **how ~ do the planes depart?** les avions partent tous les combien?; **it cannot be said too ~ that** on ne répétera jamais assez que; **once too ~** une fois de trop; **every so ~** (in time) de temps en temps; (in distance, space) ça et là.

ogle° /ˈəʊgl/ *vtr* reluquer°.

ogre /ˈəʊgə(r)/ *n* **1** (giant) ogre *m*; **2** FIG (man) monstre *m*; (woman) dragon° *m*; **3** (grim vision) spectre *m*.

oh /əʊ/ *excl* oh!; **~ dear!** (sympathetic) oh là là!; (dismayed, cross) mon Dieu!; **~ (really)?** (interested) ah bon?; (sceptical) tiens donc!; **~ really!** (cross) ah c'est pas possible°!; **~ by the way** ah au fait; **~ no it isn't!** mais non!; **~ yes?** (pleased) ah bon?; (sceptical) tiens donc!; **~ for some sun!** oh si seulement il faisait beau!

OH US POST *abrév écrite* = **Ohio**.

OHMS GB (*abrév écrite* = **On Her/His Majesty's Service**) au service de sa majesté (*formule apparaissant sur le courrier officiel de l'administration*).

oil /ɔɪl/ **I** *n* **1** (for fuel) pétrole *m*; (for lubrication) huile *f*; **crude ~** pétrole brut; **engine ~** huile de moteur; **heating ~** fioul *m*, mazout *m*; **to check the ~** AUT vérifier le niveau d'huile; **to change the ~** AUT faire la vidange; **to strike ~** LIT découvrir du pétrole; FIG découvrir une mine d'or; **2** (for cooking) huile *f*; **corn/sunflower ~** huile de maïs/tournesol; **an ~ and vinegar dressing** une vinaigrette; **3** ART (medium, picture) huile *f* ¢; **to work in ~s** peindre à l'huile; **4** ART (picture) huile *f*; **5** (medicinal, beauty) huile *f*; **~ of cloves** essence *f* de girofle.
II *noun modifier* [*deposit, exporter, producer*] de pétrole; [*prices*] du pétrole; [*company, crisis, industry, reserves*] pétrolier/-ière.
III *vtr* huiler.
IDIOMS **to ~ the wheels** mettre de l'huile dans les

rouages; **to pour ~ on troubled waters** apaiser les esprits.

oil: **~-burning** adj [stove, boiler] à mazout; **~can** n (applicator) burette f (d'huile); (container) bidon m (d'huile); **~ change** n vidange f; **~cloth** n toile f cirée.

oiler /ˈɔɪlə(r)/ n **1** (ship) pétrolier m; **2** (worker) pétrolier m; **3**◇ (oilcan) burette f.

oil: **~ field** n champ m pétrolifère; **~ filter** n filtre m à huile; **~-fired** adj [furnace, heating] au fuel or fioul; **~ gauge** n jauge f de niveau d'huile; **~ heater** n poêle m à mazout; **~ lamp** n lampe f à pétrole; **~ man** n pétrolier m; **~ paint** n couleur f à l'huile; **~ painting** n peinture f à l'huile; **~ pan** n US carter m; **~ pipeline** n oléoduc m; **~ pollution** n pollution f aux hydrocarbures; **~ pressure** n pression f d'huile; **~-producing** adj [country] producteur/-trice de pétrole; **~ refinery** n raffinerie f de pétrole; **~ rig** n (offshore) plate-forme f pétrolière; (on land) tour f de forage; **~seed rape** n colza m.

oilskin /ˈɔɪlskɪn/ GB **I** n (fabric) toile f huilée.
II oilskins npl ciré m.

oil: **~ slick** n marée f noire; **~ spill** n déversement m accidentel d'hydrocarbures; **~ stove** n poêle m à mazout; **~ tank** n (domestic) cuve f à mazout; (industrial) réserve f de stockage de pétrole; **~ tanker** n pétrolier m; **~ well** n puits m de pétrole.

oily /ˈɔɪlɪ/ adj **1** (saturated) [cloth, food, hair] gras/grasse; [hand] plein de graisse; **2** (in consistency) [dressing] huileux/-euse; [lotion] gras/grasse; **3** PÉJ [person, manner] onctueux/-euse.

ointment /ˈɔɪntmənt/ n pommade f.
IDIOMS **the fly in the ~** (thing) le hic◇.

o.i.r.o. GB (abrév écrite = **offers in the region of**) **~ £75,000** 75 000 livres à débattre.

OK 1 = **okay**; **2** US POST abrév écrite = **Oklahoma**.

okay, OK◇ /ˌəʊˈkeɪ/ **I** n accord m; **to give sth the ~** donner le feu vert à qch.
II adj **1** it's ~ **by me/him** ça ne me/le dérange pas; **is it ~ if …?** est-ce que ça va si …?; **to be ~ for** avoir assez de [time, money]; **he's ~** il est sympa◇; **to feel ~** aller bien; **'how was the meeting?'—'~'** 'comment as-tu trouvé la réunion?'—'ça s'est bien passé'; **2** (acceptable) **that's ~ for men, but…** les hommes peuvent se le permettre, mais…; **it's ~ to call him by his nickname** tu peux l'appeler par son petit nom; **3** (in agreement, confirmation) [reply, signal] d'accord.
III adv [cope, work out] (assez) bien.
IV particle **1** (giving agreement) d'accord; **2** (seeking consensus) d'accord?; **3** (seeking information) bon d'accord; **~, whose idea was this?** bon d'accord, qui a eu cette idée?; **4** (introducing topic) bien; **~, let's move on to…** bien, passons à…
V vtr approuver [change, plan].

old /əʊld/ ▶713| **I** n **1** (old people) **the ~** (+ v pl) les personnes fpl âgées; **2** (in days) **of ~** (au temps) jadis; **I know him of ~** je le connais depuis longtemps.
II adj **1** (not young) vieux/vieille, âgé; **an ~ man** un vieil homme, un vieillard; **~ people** les vieux; **to get ~** vieillir; **~ before one's time** vieux avant l'âge; **~ Mr Salter or young Mr Salter?** M Salter père ou fils?; **2** (of a particular age) **how ~ are you?** quel âge as-tu?; **to know how ~ sth is** connaître l'âge de qch; **a six-year-~ boy** un garçon (âgé) de six ans; **a week ~** [bread etc] vieux d'une semaine; **to be as ~ as sb** avoir le même âge que qn; **she is 10 years ~er than him** elle a 10 ans de plus que lui; **my ~er brother** mon frère aîné; **the ~er children play here** les grands jouent ici; **I'll tell you when you're ~er** je te le dirai quand tu seras plus grand; **I'm the ~est** c'est moi l'aîné/-e; **to be ~ enough to do** être en âge de faire; **you're ~ enough to know better** à ton âge tu devrais avoir plus de bon sens; **that dress is too ~ for you** cette robe fait trop vieux pour toi; **to be ~ for one's age** être mûr pour son âge; **3** (not new) [object, song, tradition, family]

vieux/vieille; [excuse] classique; [joke] rebattu; **an ~ firm** une maison établie depuis longtemps; **4** (former, previous) [address, school, job, admirer, system] ancien/-ienne (before n); **in the ~ days** autrefois; **just like ~ times** comme au bon vieux temps; **5**◇ (as term of affection) vieux/vieille; **good ~ British weather!** IRON ce sacré◇ climat anglais!; **6**◇ (as intensifier) **a right ~ mess** une sacrée pagaille◇; **any ~ how** n'importe comment; **any ~ doctor** n'importe quel docteur.

■ Note The irregular form vieil of the adjective vieux/vieille is used before masculine nouns beginning with a vowel or a mute 'h'.

old age n vieillesse f.

old: **~-age pension** n GB retraite f de la sécurité sociale; **~-age pensioner, OAP** n GB retraité/-e m/f.

old boy n **1** (ex-pupil) ancien élève m; **2**◇ (old man) vieux m; **3**◇ †(dear chap) (mon) vieux m.

old country n mère f patrie.

olden /ˈəʊldən/ adj **the ~ days** l'ancien temps.

old-established adj établi depuis longtemps.

olde-worlde /ˌəʊldˈwɜːld/ adj HUM ou PÉJ pseudo-ancien/-ienne.

old-fashioned /ˌəʊldˈfæʃnd/ adj **1** [person, ways, manners] vieux jeu inv; [idea, attitude, garment, machine] à l'ancienne, démodé PÉJ; **2 ~ look** (reproving) regard m réprobateur; (quizzical) regard m perplexe.

old: **~ favourite** n (song, film) succès m de toujours; (book, play) classique m; **~ flame** n ancien flirt m.

old girl n **1** (ex-pupil) ancienne élève f; **2**◇ (old lady) (petite) vieille f.

Old Glory n drapeau m des États-Unis.

old hand n vieux routier m; **to be an ~ at sth/at doing** s'y connaître en qch/à faire.

old hat◇ adj **to be ~** être dépassé.

oldie◇ /ˈəʊldɪ/ n **1** (film, song) vieux succès m; **2** (person) ancien/-ienne m/f.

old lady n **1** (elderly woman) vieille dame f; **2**◇ **my ~** (wife) la bourgeoise◇; (mother) ma maternelle◇.

old maid n PÉJ vieille fille f PÉJ.

old man n **1** (elderly man) vieil homme m, vieillard m; **2**◇ **my ~** (husband) mon homme◇; (father) mon paternel◇; **3**◇ †(dear chap) (mon) vieux◇; **4**◇ (boss) **the ~** le patron◇, le singe◇.

old: **~ master** n (work) tableau m de maître ancien; **~ people's home** n maison f de retraite; **~ soldier** n (former soldier) ancien combattant m; **~ stager**◇ n GB ancien/-ienne m/f; **~ style** adj à l'ancienne (after n); **Old Testament** n Ancien Testament m; **~-time** adj du temps jadis; **~-time dancing** n danses fpl de salon; **~ timer**◇ n ancien/-ienne m/f; **~ wives' tale** n conte m de bonne femme.

old woman n **1** (elderly lady) vieille femme f, vieille f; **2** PÉJ (man) **to have the ~ manies de petite vieille**; **3**◇ **my ~** (wife) la bourgeoise◇; (mother) ma maternelle◇.

old-world adj [cottage, charm, courtesy] d'autrefois.

oleander /ˌəʊlɪˈændə(r)/ n laurier-rose m.

olive /ˈɒlɪv/ **I** n **1** (fruit) olive f; **green/black ~** olive verte/noire; **2** (also **~ tree**) olivier m; **3** (colour) vert m olive.
II adj [dress, eyes] vert olive inv; [complexion] olivâtre.
IDIOMS **to hold out** ou **extend an ~ branch to** FIG tendre la main à.

olive: **~ green** ▶818| n, adj vert (m) olive inv; **~ grove** n oliveraie f; **~ oil** n huile f d'olive; **~-skinned** adj au teint olivâtre.

Olympic /əˈlɪmpɪk/ adj olympique; **the ~ Games** les jeux Olympiques.

ombudsman /ˈɒmbʊdzmən/ n ADMIN médiateur m.

omelette /ˈɒmlɪt/ n omelette f.

omen /ˈəʊmən/ n présage m.

ominous /ˈɒmɪnəs/ adj [presence, cloud] menaçant; [development, news] inquiétant; [sign] de mauvais augure.

omission /əˈmɪʃn/ n **1** GEN, JUR omission f; **2** (from list, team) absence f.

omit /əˈmɪt/ vtr (p prés etc **-tt-**) omettre (**from** de; **to do** de faire).

omnibus /ˈɒmnɪbəs/ **I** n **1** (also **~ edition**) GB TV rediffusion des épisodes de la semaine; **2** (also **~ volume**) recueil m; **3**† (bus) omnibus† m.
II adj US de portée générale.

omnipotent /ɒmˈnɪpətənt/ adj omnipotent.

on /ɒn/

■ Note When on is used as a straightforward preposition expressing position (on the beach, on the table) it is generally translated by sur: sur la plage, sur la table; on it is translated by dessus: there's a table over there, put the key on it = il y a une table là-bas, mets la clé dessus.
– on is often used in verb combinations in English (depend on, rely on etc). For translations, consult the appropriate verb entry (depend, rely etc).
– If you have doubts about how to translate a phrase or expression beginning with on (on demand, on impulse, on top etc) consult the appropriate noun or other entry (demand, impulse, top etc).
– This dictionary contains Usage Notes on such topics as dates, islands, rivers etc. Many of these use the preposition on. For the index to these notes ▶ 1419|.
– For examples of the above and further uses of on, see the entry below.

I prep **1** (position) sur [table, coast, motorway etc]; **~ top of the piano** sur le piano; **~ the floor** par terre; **there's a stain ~ it** il y a une tache dessus; **to live ~ Park Avenue** habiter Park Avenue; **a studio ~ Avenue Montaigne** un studio Avenue Montaigne; **the paintings ~ the wall** les tableaux qui sont au mur; **2** (indicating attachment, contact) **to hang sth ~ a nail** accrocher qch à un clou; **~ a string** au bout d'une ficelle; **3** (on or about one's person) **I've got no small change ~ me** je n'ai pas de monnaie sur moi; **a girl with sandals ~ her feet** une fille avec des sandales aux pieds; **to have a smile ~ one's face** sourire; **4** (about, on the subject of) sur; **a programme ~ Africa** une émission sur l'Afrique; **have you heard him ~ electoral reform?** est-ce que tu l'as entendu parler de la réforme électorale?; **we're ~ fractions** nous en sommes aux fractions; **5** (employed, active) **to be ~** faire partie de [team]; être membre de [board, committee]; **to be ~ the Gazette** travailler pour la Gazette; **a job ~ the railways** un travail dans les chemins de fer; **there's a bouncer ~ the door** il y a un videur à la porte; **6** (in expressions of time) **~ 22 February** le 22 février; **~ or about the 23rd** vers le 23; **~ sunny days** quand il fait beau; **7** (immediately after) **~ his arrival** à son arrivée; **~ hearing the truth she...** quand elle a appris la vérité, elle...; **8** (taking, using) **to be ~ steroids** prendre des stéroïdes; **to be ~ drugs** se droguer; **to be ~ 40 (cigarettes) a day** fumer 40 cigarettes par jour; **9** (powered by) **to run ~ batteries** fonctionner sur piles; **to run ~ electricity** marcher à l'électricité; **10** (indicating support) sur; **to stand ~ one leg** se tenir sur un pied; **11** (indicating a medium) **~ TV** à la télé; **I heard it ~ the news** j'ai entendu ça aux informations; **~ video** en vidéo; **with Lou Luciano ~ drums** avec Lou Luciano à la batterie; **12** (income, amount of money) **to be ~ £20,000 a year** gagner 20 000 livres sterling par an; **to be ~ a low income** avoir un bas salaire; **13** (paid for by, at the expense of) **this round is ~ me** c'est ma tournée; **have a beer ~ me** je te paye une bière; **14** (in scoring) **to be ~ 25 points** avoir 25 points; **15** (indicating means of transport) **to travel ~ the bus** voyager en bus; **~ the plane** dans l'avion; **to be ~ one's bike** être à vélo; **to leave ~ the first train** prendre le premier train.
II adj **1** (taking place, happening) **is the match still ~?** est-ce que le match aura lieu quand même?; **the engagement is back ~ again** ils sont à nouveau fiancés; **while the meeting is ~** pendant la réunion; **there's a war ~** il y a une guerre; **I've got nothing**

~ tonight je n'ai rien de prévu pour ce soir; **I've got a lot ~** je suis très occupé; **2** (being performed) **the news is ~ in 10 minutes** les informations sont dans 10 minutes; **what's ~?** (on TV) qu'est-ce qu'il y a à la télé?; (at the cinema, at the theatre) qu'est-ce qu'on joue?; **there's nothing ~** il n'y a rien de bien; **3** (functional, live) **to be ~** il y a du courant; [hand-brake] être serré; [dishwasher, radio] marcher; [tap] être ouvert; **the power is ~** il y a du courant; **the power is back ~** le courant est rétabli; **in the '~' position** en position 'allumé'; **4** GB (permissible) **it's just** ou **simply not ~** (out of the question) c'est hors de question; (not the done thing) ça ne se fait pas; (unacceptable) c'est inadmissible; **5** (attached, in place) **to be ~** [lid] être mis; **not properly ~** mal mis; **once the roof is ~** une fois le toit construit.
III adv **1** (on or about one's person) **to have a hat ~** porter un chapeau; **to have nothing ~** être nu; **~ with your coats!** allez, mettez vos manteaux!; **to have make-up ~** être maquillé; **with slippers ~** en pantoufles; **2** (ahead in time) **20 years ~ he was still the same** 20 ans plus tard, il n'avait pas changé; **a few years ~ from now** dans quelques années; **from that day ~** à partir de ce jour-là; **to be well ~ in years** ne plus être tout jeune; **3** (further) **to walk ~** continuer à marcher; **to go to Paris then ~ to Marseilles** aller à Paris et de là à Marseille; **a little further ~** un peu plus loin; **4** (on stage) **I'm ~ after the juggler** je passe juste après le jongleur; **to come ~** entrer en scène.
IV on and off adv phr (also **off and on**) **to see sb ~ and off** voir qn de temps en temps; **she's been working at the novel ~ and off for years** ça fait des années que son roman est en chantier; **to flash ~ and off** clignoter.
V on and on adv phr **to go ~ and ~** [speaker] parler pendant des heures; [speech] durer des heures; **to go ~ and ~ about** ne pas arrêter de parler de; **the list goes ~ and ~** la liste n'en finit pas.
IDIOMS **you're ~** d'accord; **to be always ~ at sb** être toujours sur le dos de qn; **what's he ~ about?** GB qu'est-ce qu'il raconte?; **he's been ~ to me about the lost files** GB il m'a contacté à propos des dossiers perdus.

once /wʌns/ **I** n **I've only been there the ~** je n'y suis allé qu'une seule fois; **just this ~** pour cette fois; **for ~** pour une fois.
II adv **1** (one time) une fois; **~ before** une fois déjà; **I will tell you ~ only** je ne te le dirai qu'une seule fois; **if I've told you ~ I've told you a hundred times** je te l'ai dit mille fois; **~ and for all** une bonne fois pour toutes; **never ~ did he offer to help** il ne s'est pas une seule fois proposé pour aider; **~ too often** une fois de trop; **~ a day** une fois par jour; **(every) ~ in a while** de temps en temps; **it was a ~-in-a-lifetime experience** c'était une expérience unique; **if ~ you forget the code** si jamais vous oubliez le code; **~ a thief, always a thief** qui a volé, volera; **2** (formerly) autrefois; **she was ~ very famous** (autrefois) elle était très célèbre; **I'm not as young as I ~ was** je ne suis plus très jeune; **~ upon a time there was** il était une fois.
III at once adv phr **1** (immediately) tout de suite; **all at ~** tout d'un coup; **2** (simultaneously) à la fois.
IV conj une fois que; **~ you've signed, it's too late to...** une fois qu'on a signé, il est trop tard pour...; **~ he had eaten he...** après avoir mangé il...

once-over° /ˈwʌnsəʊvə(r)/ n **1** (quick look) **to give sth the ~** jeter un rapide coup d'œil à qch; **to give sb the ~** GEN évaluer qn au premier coup d'œil; [doctor] faire un rapide bilan de santé à qn; **2** (quick clean) **to give sth a quick ~** (with duster) donner un coup de chiffon à qch.

oncoming /ˈɒnkʌmɪŋ/ adj [car, vehicle] venant en sens inverse; **'beware of ~ traffic'** 'circulation dans les deux sens'.

one /wʌn/ ▶ 1112|, 713|, 812|

■ Note When one is used as a personal pronoun it is translated by on when it is the subject of the verb: one never

knows = on ne sait jamais. When *one* is the object of the verb or comes after a preposition it is usually translated by *vous*: *it can make one ill* = cela peut vous rendre malade.
– For more examples and all other uses, see the entry below.

I *det* **1** (single) un/une; **to raise ~ hand** lever la main; **no ~ person can do it alone** personne ne peut faire cela tout seul; **2** (unique, sole) seul; **she's the ~ person who can help** c'est la seule personne qui puisse nous aider; **the ~ and only Edith Piaf** l'incomparable Edith Piaf; **she's ~ fine artist** US c'est une très grande artiste; **3** (same) même; **at ~ and the same time** en même temps; **~ and the same thing** exactement la même chose; **to be of ~ mind** être d'accord; **it's all ~ to me** ça m'est égal; **4** (for emphasis) **~ Simon Richard** un certain Simon Richard.

II *pron* **1** (indefinite) un/une *m/f*; **can you lend me ~?** tu peux m'en prêter un/une?; **every ~ of them** tous/toutes sans exception (+ *v pl*); **she's ~ of us** elle est des nôtres; **2** (impersonal) (as subject) on; (as object) vous; **~ would like to think that…** on aimerait penser que…; **it can make ~ ill** cela peut vous rendre malade; **3** (referring to specific person) **the advice of ~ who knows** les conseils de quelqu'un qui s'y connaît; **I'm not ~ for doing** ce n'est pas mon genre de faire; **she's a clever ~** elle est intelligente; **you're a ~**° toi alors!; **I for ~ think that…** pour ma part je crois que…; **4** (demonstrative) **the grey ~** le gris/la grise; **this ~** celui-ci/celle-ci; **which ~?** lequel/laquelle?; **that's the ~** c'est celui-là/celle-là; **he's the ~ who** c'est lui qui; **5** (in knitting) **knit ~, purl ~** une maille à l'endroit, une maille à l'envers; **6** (in currency) **~-fifty** (in sterling) une livre cinquante; (in dollars) un dollar cinquante; **7**° (drink) **he's had ~ too many** il a bu un coup° de trop; **8**° (joke) **have you heard the ~ about…?** est-ce que tu connais l'histoire de…?; **9**° (blow) **to land** ou **sock sb ~** en coller à qn°; **10**° (question, problem) **that's a tricky ~** c'est une question difficile.

III *n* **1** (number) un *m*; (referring to feminine) une *f*; **to throw a ~** (on dice) faire un un; **~ o'clock** une heure; **to arrive in ~s and twos** arriver par petits groupes; **2** (person) **her loved ~s** ceux qui lui sont/étaient chers; **the little ~s** les petits.

IV **as one** *adv phr* [*rise*] comme un seul homme; [*shout, reply*] tous ensemble.

V **one by one** *adv phr* [*pick up, wash*] un par un/une par une.

IDIOMS **to down a drink in ~** boire un verre cul sec°; **you've got it in ~** tu as trouvé tout de suite; **to be ~ up on sb**° avoir un avantage sur qn; **to go ~ better than sb** faire mieux que qn; **to have a thousand** ou **million and ~ things to do** avoir un tas de choses à faire.

one another

■ **Note** *one another* is very often translated by using a reflexive pronoun (*nous*, *vous*, *se*, *s'*).
– For examples and particular usages see the entry below.

pron **they love ~** ils s'aiment; **to help ~** s'aider mutuellement; **we often use ~'s cars** souvent nous échangeons nos voitures; **to worry about ~** s'inquiéter l'un pour l'autre.

one: ~-armed *adj* manchot; **~-armed bandit** *n* machine *f* à sous.

one-dimensional /ˌwʌndɪˈmenʃənl/ *adj* **1** GEN, MATH unidimensionnel/-elle; **2** FIG **to be ~** [*character*] LITERAT manquer d'épaisseur.

one: ~-eyed *adj* borgne; **~-for-one** *adj* = **one-to-one** I 2; **~-handed** *adv* [*catch, hold*] d'une seule main; **~-horse town**° *n* PÉJ bled° *m*; **~-legged** *adj* unijambiste; **~-liner** *n* bon mot *m*.

one-man /ˌwʌnˈmæn/ *adj* **1** (for one person) **it's a ~ outfit** ou **operation** il est tout seul; **she's a ~ woman** elle est fidèle en amour; **2** SPORT [*bobsled*] monoplace.

one-man band *n* LIT homme-orchestre *m*; FIG **to be a ~** faire tout soi-même.

one: ~-off *adj* GB [*experiment, order, deal, design*] unique; [*event, decision, offer, payment*] exceptionnel/-elle; [*example*] peu courant; [*issue, magazine*] spécial; **~-parent family** *n* famille *f* monoparentale.

one-piece /ˈwʌnpiːs/ *adj* GEN, TECH d'une seule pièce; **~ swimsuit** maillot *m* de bain une pièce.

one-room flat, **one-room apartment** *n* studio *m*.

onerous /ˈɒnərəs/ *adj* [*task*] lourd; JUR [*terms*] dur.

one's /wʌnz/

■ **Note** In French determiners agree in gender and number with the noun they qualify. So when *one's* is used as a determiner it is translated by *son* + masculine singular noun (*son argent*), by *sa* + feminine noun (*sa voiture*) BUT by *son* + feminine noun beginning with a vowel or mute h (*son assiette*) and by *ses* + plural noun (*ses enfants*).
– When *one's* is stressed, *à soi* is added after the noun.
– When *one's* is used as a reflexive pronoun it is translated by *se* (or *s'* before a vowel or mute h): *to brush one's teeth* = se brosser les dents; ▶ **765**.
– For examples and particular usages see the entry below.

I = **one is**, **one has**.
II *det* son/sa/ses; **~ books/friends** ses livres/amis; **to wash ~ hands** se laver les mains; **to do ~ best** faire de son mieux; **it upsets ~ concentration** ça perturbe la concentration; **a house of ~ own** une maison à soi.

oneself /wʌnˈself/

■ **Note** When used as a reflexive pronoun, direct and indirect, *oneself* is translated by *se* (or *s'* before a vowel): *to hurt oneself* = se blesser; *to enjoy oneself* = s'amuser.
– When used in emphasis the translation is *soi-même*: *to do something oneself* = faire quelque chose soi-même.
– After a preposition, the translation is *soi*.
– For particular usages see the entry below.

pron **1** (refl) se, s'; **to wash/cut ~** se laver/couper; **2** (for emphasis) soi-même; **3** (after prep) soi; **sure of ~** sûr de soi; **to have the house all to ~** avoir la maison pour soi tout seul/toute seule; **to talk to ~** parler tout seul/toute seule; (**all**) **by ~** tout seul/toute seule.

one-shot *adj* US = **one-off**.

one-sided /ˌwʌnˈsaɪdɪd/ *adj* **1** (biased) [*account*] partial; **2** (unequal) [*decision*] unilatéral; [*contest*] inégal; [*deal*] inéquitable.

one: ~-size *adj* [*garment*] taille unique; **~-time** *adj* ancien/-ienne (*before n*).

one-to-one /ˌwʌntəˈwʌn/ **I** *adj* **1** (private) **~ meeting** tête-à-tête *m inv*; **~ session** GEN, PSYCH face *m* à face; **~ tuition** cours *mpl* particuliers; **2** MATH biunivoque; **3** SPORT [*contest*] à deux (*after n*); [*marking*] individuel/-elle. **II** *adv* [*discuss*] en tête à tête.

one-upmanship /ˌwʌnˈʌpmənʃɪp/ *n* art *m* de paraître supérieur aux autres.

one-way /ˌwʌnˈweɪ/ **I** *adj* **1** [*traffic*] à sens unique; **~ street** ou **system** sens *m* unique; **2** (single) **~ ticket** aller *m* simple; **3** [*process, conversation*] à sens unique; [*friendship*] non partagé; [*transaction*] unilatéral; **4** ELEC, TELECOM [*circuit*] unidirectionnel/-elle. **II** *adv* **it costs £10 ~** l'aller simple coûte 10 livres sterling.

one-woman /ˌwʌnˈwʊmən/ *adj* **it's a ~ outfit**° elle est toute seule; **he's a ~ man** il est fidèle en amour.

ongoing /ˈɒnɡəʊɪŋ/ *adj* [*process*] continu; [*battle, saga*] continuel/-elle.

onion /ˈʌnɪən/ *n* oignon *m*.
IDIOMS **to know one's ~s**° GB connaître son affaire.

onionskin *n* (paper) papier *m* pelure.

on-line /ˌɒnˈlaɪn/ *adj* COMPUT [*access*] direct; [*mode*] connecté; [*data processing*] en direct; [*storage*] en ligne.

onlooker /ˈɒnlʊkə(r)/ *n* spectateur/-trice *m/f*.

only /ˈəʊnlɪ/ **I** *conj* (but) mais; **I'd come ~ I'm working tonight** je viendrais bien mais ce soir je travaille; **it's like a mouse ~ bigger** c'est comme une souris mais en plus gros.

II *adj* **1** (sole) seul; **~ child** enfant unique; **the ~ one left** le seul/la seule *m/f* qui reste; **one and ~ seul; the ~ thing is, I'm broke**○ le seul problème, c'est que je suis fauché○; **2** (best, preferred) **skiing is the ~ sport for me** pour moi, aucun sport ne vaut le ski.

III *adv* **1** (exclusively) **~ in Italy can one...** il n'y a qu'en Italie que l'on peut...; **I'll go but ~ if you'll go too** je n'irai que si tu y vas aussi; **~ Annie saw her** Annie est la seule à l'avoir vue; **~ time will tell** seul l'avenir nous le dira; **'men ~'** 'réservé aux hommes'; **'for external use ~'** 'usage externe'; **2** (nothing more than) **it's ~ fair to let him explain** ce n'est que justice de le laisser s'expliquer; **it's ~ polite** c'est la moindre des politesses; **3** (in expressions of time) **~ yesterday** pas plus tard qu'hier; **it seems like ~ yesterday** j'ai l'impression que c'était hier; **I saw him ~ recently** je l'ai vu très récemment; **4** (merely) **you ~ had to ask** tu n'avais qu'à demander; **he ~ grazed his knees** il s'est juste égratigné les genoux; **~ half the money** juste la moitié de l'argent; **~ twenty people turned up** seules vingt personnes sont venues; **you've ~ got to look around you** il suffit de regarder autour de soi; **I was ~ joking!** je plaisantais!; **5** (just) **I ~ hope she'll realize** j'espère simplement qu'elle s'en rendra compte; **I can ~ think that Claire did it** la seule explication qui me vienne à l'esprit c'est que c'est Claire qui l'a fait; **open up, it's ~ me** ouvre, c'est moi; **I got home ~ to find (that) I'd been burgled** quand je suis rentré à la maison j'ai découvert que j'avais été cambriolé.

IV only just *adv phr* **1** (very recently) **to have ~ just done** venir juste de faire; **2** (barely) **it's ~ just tolerable** c'est à peine tolérable; **~ just wide enough** juste assez large; **I caught the bus, but ~ just** j'ai eu le bus mais de justesse.

V only too *adv phr* **I remember it ~ too well** je m'en souviens trop bien; **they were ~ too pleased to help** ils étaient trop contents de se rendre utiles.

IDIOMS goodness ou **God** ou **Heaven ~ knows!** Dieu seul le sait!

o.n.o. GB (*abrév écrite* = **or nearest offer**) à débattre.

on-off *adj* [*button, control*] marche-arrêt.

onrush /ˈɒnrʌʃ/ *n* (of water) torrent *m*; (of people) ruée *f*; (of pain) accès *m*.

on-screen /ˌɒnˈskriːn/ *adj* CIN, COMPUT sur l'écran.

onset /ˈɒnset/ *n* début *m* (**of** de).

onshore /ˈɒnʃɔː(r)/ *adj* [*work*] à terre; [*wind*] du large.

onside /ˌɒnˈsaɪd/ *adj, adv* SPORT en jeu.

on-site /ˌɒnˈsaɪt/ *adj* sur place.

onslaught /ˈɒnslɔːt/ *n* attaque *f* (**on** contre).

onstage /ˌɒnˈsteɪdʒ/ *adj, adv* sur scène.

on-the-job *adj* [*training*] sur le lieu de travail.

on-the-spot I *adj* [*team, reporting*] sur place; [*investigation*] sur les lieux; [*advice, quotation*] immédiat.

II on the spot *adv phr* [*decide etc*] GEN sur place.

onto /ˈɒntuː/ *prep* (also **on to**) sur.

IDIOMS to be ~ something○ être sur une piste; **I think I'm ~ something big**○ je suis sur un gros coup○; **the police are ~ him**○ la police est après lui.

onus /ˈəʊnəs/ *n* obligation *f*; **the ~ is on sb to do sth** il incombe à qn de faire qch; **to put the ~ on sb to do sth** obliger qn à faire qch.

onward /ˈɒnwəd/ **I** *adj* **~ flight** correspondance *f* (**to** à destination de); **the ~ march of progress** la marche inéluctable du progrès.

II *adv* = **onwards**.

onwards /ˈɒnwədz/ *adv* **1** (forwards) **the journey ~ to Tokyo** le voyage jusqu'à Tokyo; **to go ~ and upwards** gravir les échelons de la hiérarchie; **2** (in

time phrases) **from tomorrow ~** à partir de demain; **from now ~** à partir d'aujourd'hui; **from that day ~** à dater de ce jour.

oodles○ /ˈuːdlz/ *n* des masses○ *fpl*.

ooh /uː/ *excl* oh!; **~s and ahs** des oh et des ah.

oomph○ /ʊmf/ *n* punch○ *m*, dynamisme *m*.

oops○ /uːps, ʊps/ *excl* oh là là!

ooze /uːz/ **I** *n* (silt) vase *f*.

II *vtr* **1 the wound ~d blood** du sang suintait de la blessure; **to ~ butter** déborder de beurre; **2** FIG [*person*] rayonner de [*charm*].

III *vi* **to ~ with** déborder de [*butter, cream*]; rayonner de [*charm*].

■ **ooze out** s'écouler.

op○ /ɒp/ *n* MED, COMPUT *abrév* = **operation** 2, 5.

opal /ˈəʊpl/ *n* opale *f*.

opaque /əʊˈpeɪk/ *adj* LIT, FIG opaque.

Opec, OPEC /ˈəʊpek/ *n* (*abrév* = **Organization of Petroleum Exporting Countries**) OPEP *f*.

open /ˈəʊpən/ **I** *n* **1** (outside) **in the ~** dehors, en plein air; **2** (exposed position) **in/into the ~** en terrain découvert; FIG **out in the ~** étalé en plein jour; **to bring sth out into the ~** mettre qch au grand jour; **3** (also **Open**) SPORT (tournoi *m*) open *m*.

II *adj* **1** (not closed) [*door, box, book, eyes, shirt, wound, flower*] ouvert; [*arms, legs*] écarté; (to the public) [*bank, bridge, meeting*] ouvert; **to get sth ~** ouvrir qch; **to burst** ou **fly ~** s'ouvrir brusquement; **the book lay ~** le livre était ouvert; **the door was partly** ou **half ~** la porte était entrouverte; **~ for business** ouvert au public; **in ~ court** en audience publique; **2** (not obstructed) **to be ~** [*road*] être ouvert (à la circulation); [*canal, harbour*] être ouvert (à la navigation); [*telephone line, frequency*] être libre; **the ~ air** le plein air; **~ country** la rase campagne; **~ ground** un terrain vague; **the ~ road** la grand-route; **the ~ sea** la haute mer; **the (wide) ~ spaces** les (grands) espaces libres; **an ~ view** une vue dégagée (**of** de); **3** (not covered) [*car, carriage*] découvert, décapoté; [*mine, sewer*] à ciel ouvert; **an ~ fire** un feu (de cheminée); **4** (susceptible) **~ to** exposé à [*air, wind, elements*]; **to ~ to attack** exposé à l'attaque; **to be ~ to** prêter le flanc à [*criticism*]; **I'm ~ to offers** je suis ouvert à toute proposition; **to be ~ to persuasion** être prêt à se laisser convaincre; **to lay oneself ~ to criticism** s'exposer (ouvertement) à la critique; **it is ~ to question whether** on peut douter que (+ *subj*); **5** (accessible) (*jamais épith*) [*job, position*] libre, vacant; [*access, competition*] ouvert à tous; [*meeting, session*] public/-ique; **there are several courses of action ~ to us** nous avons le choix entre plusieurs lignes de conduite; **6** (candid) [*person, discussion, declaration, statement*] franc/franche (**about** à propos de); **7** (blatant) [*hostility, contempt*] non dissimulé; [*disagreement, disrespect*] manifeste; **8** (undecided) **to leave the date ~** laisser la date en suspens; **the election is (wide) ~** l'issue de l'élection est indécise; **to keep an ~ mind about sth** réserver son jugement sur qch; **~ ticket** (for traveller) billet *m* ouvert; **she kept my job ~** elle m'a gardé mon travail; **I have an ~ invitation to visit him** je suis invité chez lui quand je veux; **9** (with spaces) [*weave*] ajouré; **10** SPORT [*contest*] open; **11** MUS [*string*] à vide; **12** LING ouvert.

III *vtr* **1** (cause not to be closed) GEN ouvrir; **to ~ a door slightly** ou **a little** entrouvrir une porte; **to ~ one's mind (to sth)** s'ouvrir (à qch); **2** (begin) entamer [*discussions, meeting*]; ouvrir [*account, enquiry, show, shop*]; **to ~ fire** ouvrir le feu; **3** (inaugurate) inaugurer [*shop, bridge*]; ouvrir [*exhibition*]; **4** (make wider) ▶ **open up**.

IV *vi* **1** (become open) [*door, flower, curtain*] s'ouvrir; **his eyes ~ed** il a ouvert les yeux; **to ~ into** ou **onto sth** [*door, window*] donner sur qch; **~ wide!** (at dentist's) ouvrez grand!; **to ~ slightly** ou **a little** [*window, door*] s'entrouvrir; **2** COMM (operate) [*shop, bar*] ouvrir; **3** (begin) [*meeting, discussion, play*] commencer (**with** par); **to ~ by doing** [*person*] commencer par faire; **4** (have first performance) [*film*] sortir (sur les écrans); [*exhibition*] ouvrir; **the play**

~s on the 25th la première de la pièce aura lieu le 25; **5** (be first speaker) [*person*] ouvrir le débat; **6** (become wider) ▶ **open up**; **7** FIN [*shares*] débuter.

■ **open out**: ¶ ~ **out** [*river, path, view*] s'élargir; [*countryside*] s'étendre; **to ~ out into** [*passage*] déboucher sur [*room*]; [*stream*] se jeter dans [*pool*]; ¶ ~ [*sth*] **out**, ~ **out** [*sth*] déplier [*map*].

■ **open up**: ¶ ~ **up 1** (unlock a building) ouvrir; **I'll ~ up for you** je t'ouvre; **2** (appear) [*gap*] se creuser; [*crack*] LIT, FIG se former; **3** (speak freely) se confier; **to ~ up to sb about sth** s'ouvrir à qn de qch; **4** (develop) [*opportunities, market*] s'ouvrir; **5** COMM (start up) [*shop, branch*] ouvrir; ¶ ~ [*sth*] **up**, ~ **up** [*sth*] **1** (make open) ouvrir [*parcel, suitcase, wound*]; **2** (make wider) creuser [*gap*]; **to ~ up a lead** [*athlete*] creuser l'écart; **3** (unlock) ouvrir [*building*]; **4** (start up) ouvrir [*shop*]; **5** (make accessible) ouvrir [*area, road*]; exploiter [*forest, desert*], FIG ouvrir [*possibilities, career*].

open: ~**-air** *adj* [*pool, market, stage*] en plein air; ~**cast mining** *n* GB exploitation *f* minière à ciel ouvert; ~ **competition** *n* concours *m*; ~ **day** *n* journée *f* portes ouvertes; ~**-door** *adj* ECON, POL [*policy*] de la porte ouverte; ~**-ended** *adj* [*strategy*] flexible; [*contract*] modifiable; [*debate, question*] ouvert; [*relationship, situation*] flou; [*stay*] de durée indéterminée; [*period*] indéterminé.

opener /'əʊpnə(r)/ **I** *n* **1** TV, THEAT (first act) premier numéro *m*; (first episode) premier épisode *m*; **2** GAMES (in bridge) (bid) ouverture *f*; (player) ouvreur/-euse *m/f*; **3** (for bottles) décapsuleur *m*; (for cans) ouvre-boîte *m*.

II for openers○ *adv phr* pour commencer.

open: ~**-face(d) sandwich** *n* US canapé *m*; ~ **government** *n* POL politique *f* de transparence; ~**-handed** *adj* généreux/-euse; ~**-hearted** *adj* chaleureux/-euse; ~**-heart surgery** *n* MED (operation) opération *f* à cœur ouvert.

open house *n* **1** it's always ~ **at the Batemans'** les Bateman sont très hospitaliers; **2** US (open day) journée *f* portes ouvertes.

opening /'əʊpnɪŋ/ **I** *n* **1** (start) (of book, film, piece of music) début *m*; **2** (official act of opening) (of exhibition, shop) ouverture *f*; (of play, film) première *f*; **3** (gap) (in wall, garment, forest) trouée *f*; **4** (opportunity) GEN occasion *f* (**to do** de faire); COMM (in market etc) débouché *m*, marché *m* (**for** pour); (for employment) (in company) poste *m* (disponible); (in field) possibilité *f* de travail; **5** GAMES ouverture *f*.

II *adj* [*scene, move*] premier/-ière (*before n*); [*remarks, speech, statement*] préliminaire; FIN [*price, offer, bid*] de départ; [*share price*] d'ouverture.

opening: ~ **balance** *n* FIN (of individual) solde *m* initial; (of company) solde *m* en début d'exercice; ~ **ceremony** *n* (cérémonie *f* d')inauguration *f*; ~ **hours** *n* COMM heures *fpl* d'ouverture.

open market *n* ECON marché *m* libre.

open-minded /ˌəʊpən'maɪndɪd/ *adj* **to be ~** avoir l'esprit ouvert; **to be ~ about** n'avoir aucun préjugé sur.

open: ~**-mouthed** *adj* bouche bée *inv*; ~**-necked** *n* [*shirt*] à col ouvert.

openness /'əʊpənnɪs/ *n* **1** (candour) (of person) franchise *f*; (of manner) caractère *m* franc; (of government, atmosphere) transparence *f*; **2** (receptiveness) ouverture *f* d'esprit (**to** en ce qui concerne).

open: ~**-plan** *adj* [*office*] paysagé; ~ **scholarship** *n* UNIV bourse *f* décernée par un concours ouvert à tous; ~ **season** *n* (in hunting) saison *f* de la chasse; ~ **secret** *n* secret *m* de Polichinelle; **Open University**, **OU** GB UNIV *n*: *système d'enseignement universitaire par correspondance ouvert à tous*; ~ **verdict** *n* JUR verdict *m* constatant l'impossibilité de déterminer les causes d'un décès.

opera /'ɒprə/ *n* opéra *m*.

operable /'ɒprəbl/ *adj* **1** [*plan*] réalisable; [*machine*] en état de marche; [*system*] capable de fonctionner; **2** MED [*tumour*] opérable.

opera: ~ **glasses** *n* jumelles *fpl* de théâtre; ~ **house** *n* opéra *m*.

operate /'ɒpəreɪt/ **I** *vtr* **1** (run) faire marcher [*appliance, vehicle*]; **2** (enforce) pratiquer [*policy, system*]; mettre [qch] en vigueur [*ban*]; **3** (manage) gérer [*service, radio station*]; exploiter [*mine, racket*]; [*bank*] avoir [*pension plan*].

II *vi* **1** (do business) opérer; **they ~ out of London** ils ont Londres comme base d'opérations; [*captain*] marcher; **2** (take effect) agir; **3** FIG (work) [*factor, law*] jouer (**in favour of** en faveur de; **against** contre); **5** (run) [*service*] fonctionner; **6** MED opérer; **to ~ on** opérer [*person*]; **to ~ on sb's leg/on sb for appendicitis** opérer qn à la jambe/qn de l'appendicite.

operatic /ˌɒpə'rætɪk/ *adj* [*voice*] de chanteur/-euse d'opéra; [*composer*] d'opéras.

operating /'ɒpəreɪtɪŋ/ *adj* [*costs*] d'exploitation.

operating: ~ **instructions** *npl* mode *m* d'emploi; ~ **room** *n* US salle *f* d'opération; ~ **system** *n* système *m* d'exploitation; ~ **table** *n* table *f* d'opération; ~ **theatre** *n* GB salle *f* d'opération.

operation /ˌɒpə'reɪʃn/ *n* **1** (working) fonctionnement *m*; **2** MED opération *f*; **to have an ~** subir une opération; **to have a major/minor ~** subir une grosse/petite opération; **to have a heart ~** se faire opérer du cœur; **3** (use) (of machinery) utilisation *f*; (of plant, mine) exploitation *f*; (of law, scheme) mise *f* en vigueur; **to be in ~** [*plan*] être en vigueur; [*oil rig, mine*] être en exploitation; [*machine*] fonctionner; **out of ~** hors service; **4** (undertaking) opération *f*; **a big ~** une grosse opération; **5** (business) **their European ~ is expanding** ils étendent leurs activités en Europe; **6** COMPUT, FIN opération *f*.

operational /ˌɒpə'reɪʃənl/ *adj* **1** GEN, MIL (ready to operate) opérationnel/-elle; **2** [*budget, costs, manager*] d'exploitation.

operations: ~ **research** *n* US recherche *f* opérationnelle; ~ **room** *n* MIL salle *f* d'opérations; (police) centre *m* d'opérations.

operative /'ɒpərətɪv, US -reɪt-/ **I** *n* (worker) employé/-e *m/f*; (secret agent) agent *m*.

II *adj* **1** (effective) [*rule, law, system*] en vigueur; **2** (important) **X being the ~ word** X étant le mot qui compte.

operator /'ɒpəreɪtə(r)/ ▶ **1251** *n* **1** TELECOM standardiste *mf*; **2** COMPUT, RADIO, TECH opérateur *m*; **3** TOURISM compagnie *f* de voyages organisés; **4** COMM (of business) entrepreneur *m*; **he's a smooth** ou **shrewd ~** PEJ il sait s'y prendre.

operetta /ˌɒpə'retə/ *n* opérette *f*.

ophthalmic /ɒf'θælmɪk/ *adj* GB [*nerve*] ophtalmique; [*surgeon, clinic, research*] ophtalmologique.

opiate /'əʊpɪət/ *n* (from opium) opiacé *m*; (narcotic) narcotique *m*.

opinion /ə'pɪnɪən/ *n* **1** (belief, view) opinion *f* (**about** de), avis *m* (**about, on** sur); **conflicting ~s** avis contradictoires; **informed ~** les gens bien informés; **to be of the ~ that** estimer que; **if you want my honest ~** si vous voulez savoir ce que je pense honnêtement; **that's a matter of ~** chacun ses opinions; **in the experts' ~** d'après les experts; **2** (evaluation) opinion *f* (**of** de); **high/low ~ of sb/sth** bonne/mauvaise opinion de qn/qch; **to get a second ~** GEN demander un autre avis; MED consulter un autre médecin; **3** ¢ (range of views) opinions *fpl*; **a difference of ~** une divergence d'opinions; **~ is divided** les opinions sont partagées.

opinionated /ə'pɪnɪəneɪtɪd/ *adj* [*person*] qui a des avis sur tout; [*tone*] dogmatique.

opinion poll *n* sondage *m* d'opinion.

opium /'əʊpɪəm/ *n* LIT, FIG opium *m*.

opponent /ə'pəʊnənt/ *n* GEN adversaire *mf*; (of regime) opposant/-e *m/f* (**of** à).

opportune /'ɒpətjuːn, US -tuːn/ *adj* [*moment*] opportun.

opportunist /ˌɒpə'tjuːnɪst, US -'tuːn-/ *n, adj* opportuniste (*mf*).

opportunity /ˌɒpə'tjuːnətɪ, US -'tuːn-/ *n* **1** (occasion) occasion *f* (**for** de); **an ~ for discussion** une occasion de or pour discuter; **to give sb every ~** donner à qn toutes les chances (**to do** de faire); **I should like to take this ~ to say** j'aimerais profiter de cette occasion pour dire; **at the earliest** ~ à la première occasion; **2** (possibility) possibilité *f*; **training opportunities** possibilités de formation.

IDIOMS **~ knocks!** la chance frappe à la porte!

oppose /ə'pəʊz/ **I** *vtr* GEN, POL s'opposer à [*plan, bill*]; faire opposition à [*bail*]; **to be ~d to/to doing** être contre/contre l'idée de.
II as opposed to *prep phr* par opposition à.
III opposing *pres p adj* [*party, team*] adverse; [*army*] ennemi; [*view, style*] opposé.

opposite /'ɒpəzɪt/ **I** *n* contraire *m* (**to, of** de); **the exact ~** tout le contraire; **it does the ~ of what one expects** cela fait l'inverse de ce à quoi on pourrait s'attendre.
II *adj* **1** (facing) [*direction, side, pole*] opposé ALSO MATH; [*building*] d'en face; [*page*] ci-contre; **at ~ ends of** aux deux bouts de [*table, street*]; **2** (different) [*viewpoint, camp*] opposé; [*effect, approach*] inverse; [*sex*] autre.
III *adv* [*live, stand*] en face; **directly ~** juste en face.
IV *prep* GEN en face de [*building, park, person*]; NAUT devant [*port*].

opposite number *n* GEN, POL homologue *m*; SPORT adversaire *mf*.

opposition /,ɒpə'zɪʃn/ **I** *n* **1** GEN opposition *f* (**to** à); **to put up ~ against** faire opposition à; **2** (*also* **Opposition**) POL opposition *f*; **3** SPORT **the ~** l'adversaire *m*.
II *noun modifier* POL [*politician, debate, party etc*] de l'opposition.

oppress /ə'pres/ *vtr* **1** (subjugate) opprimer; **2** [*anxiety, responsibility*] accabler.

oppression /ə'preʃn/ *n* oppression *f*.

oppressive /ə'presɪv/ *adj* **1** [*law*] oppressif/-ive; **2** [*heat*] oppressant.

oppressively /ə'presɪvlɪ/ *adv* [*govern, rule*] de façon oppressive; **it's ~ hot** il fait une chaleur accablante.

oppressor /ə'presə(r)/ *n* oppresseur *m*.

opt /ɒpt/ *vi* **~ for sth** opter pour qch; **to ~ to do/not to do** choisir de faire/de ne pas faire.
■ **opt out** [*person, country*] décider de ne pas participer (**of** à); [*school, hospital*] choisir d'assurer sa propre gestion.

optic /'ɒptɪk/ *adj* [*nerve, disc, fibre*] optique.

optical /'ɒptɪkl/ *adj* (all contexts) optique.

optical: **~ illusion** *n* illusion *f* d'optique; **~ wand** *n* crayon-lecteur *m* optique.

optician /ɒp'tɪʃn/ ▶ **1251** *n* (selling glasses) opticien/-ienne *m/f*; (eye specialist) GB optométriste *mf*.

optics /'ɒptɪks/ *n* (+ *v sg*) optique *f*.

optimism /'ɒptɪmɪzəm/ *n* optimisme *m*.

optimist /'ɒptɪmɪst/ *n* optimiste *mf*.

optimistic /,ɒptɪ'mɪstɪk/ *adj* optimiste (**about** quant à); **wildly/cautiously ~** exagérément/raisonnablement optimiste; **to be ~ that sth will happen** avoir bon espoir que qch arrivera.

optimize /'ɒptɪmaɪz/ *vtr* optimiser.

optimum /'ɒptɪməm/ *n, adj* optimum (*m*).

option /'ɒpʃn/ *n* **1** GEN, COMPUT option *f* (**to do** de faire); **soft/safe ~** solution *f* facile/la plus sûre; **zero ~** option zéro; **it's the only ~ for us** nous n'avons pas d'autre possibilité; **the only ~ open to me** la seule possibilité que j'aie; **to keep one's ~s open** ne pas s'engager; **2** (possibility of choosing) choix *m*; **to have the ~ of doing sth** pouvoir choisir de faire qch; **I had little ~** je n'avais guère le choix; **3** COMM, FIN option *f* (**on** sur; **to do** pour faire); **to take up an ~** lever une option; **to have first ~** avoir priorité d'option.

optional /'ɒpʃənl/ *adj* [*activity, subject*] facultatif/-ive; [*colour, size*] au choix; **~ extras** accessoires *mpl* en option.

opulent /'ɒpjʊlənt/ *adj* [*lifestyle*] opulent; [*hotel, furnishings*] somptueux/-euse.

opus /'əʊpəs/ *n* (*pl* **~es** ou **opera**) opus *m*.

or /ɔ:(r)/

■ **Note** In most uses *or* is translated by *ou*. There are two exceptions to this:
– When used to link alternatives after a negative verb (*I can't come today or tomorrow*). For translations see 3 below.
– When used to indicate consequence (*be careful or you'll cut yourself*) or explanation (*it can't be serious or she'd have called us*) the translation is *sinon*: fais attention sinon tu vas te couper; ça ne peut pas être grave sinon elle nous aurait appelés. See 6 and 7 below.

conj **1** (linking two or more alternatives) ou; **with ~ without sugar?** avec ou sans sucre?; **any brothers ~ sisters?** tu as des frères et sœurs?; **either here ~ at Dave's** soit ici soit chez Dave; **whether he likes it ~ not** que cela lui plaise ou non; **rain ~ no rain** qu'il pleuve ou non; **car ~ no car, you've got to get to work** voiture ou pas, il faut que tu ailles travailler; **2** (linking alternatives in the negative) **not today ~ tomorrow** ni aujourd'hui ni demain; **I couldn't eat ~ sleep** je ne pouvais ni manger ni dormir; **she doesn't drink ~ smoke** elle ne boit pas et ne fume pas non plus; **3** (indicating approximation, vagueness) ou; **once ~ twice a week** une ou deux fois par semaine; **someone ~ other** quelqu'un; **in a week ~ so** dans huit jours environ; **4** (introducing qualification, correction, explanation) ou; **~ rather** ou plutôt; **~ should I say** ou bien devrais-je dire; **5** (indicating consequence: otherwise) sinon, autrement; **be careful ~ you'll cut yourself** fais attention sinon tu vas te couper; **do as you're told—~ else**○! fais ce qu'on te dit—sinon (gare○ à toi)!

OR US POST *abrév écrite* = **Oregon**.

oracle /'ɒrəkl, US 'ɔ:r-/ *n* **1** GEN, HIST, RELIG oracle *m*; **2 Oracle**® GB TV cf Antiope *f*.

oral /'ɔ:rəl/ **I** *n* oral *m*.
II *adj* **1** GEN oral; [*contraceptive, medicine*] par voie orale; [*hygiene*] buccal; [*history*] transmis oralement; [*evidence*] verbal.

orally /'ɔ:rəlɪ/ *adv* (verbally) oralement; (by mouth) par voie orale.

orange /'ɒrɪndʒ, US 'ɔ:r-/ ▶ **818** **I** *n* **1** (fruit) orange *f*; **2** (colour) orange *m*.
II *noun modifier* [*drink, pudding, sauce*] à l'orange; [*jam*] d'orange.
III *adj* (colour) orange *inv*.

orange: **~ blossom** *n* fleur *f* d'oranger; **~ grove** *n* orangeraie *f*; **~ juice** *n* jus *m* d'orange; **~ peel** *n* GEN écorce *f* d'orange; CULIN zeste *m* d'orange; **~ squash** *n* GB ~ sirop *m* d'orange; **~ tree** *n* oranger *m*.

oration /ɒ'reɪʃn/ *n* SOUT harangue *f*.

oratory /'ɒrətrɪ, US 'ɔ:rətɔ:rɪ/ *n* (art) art *m* oratoire; (talent) éloquence *f*.

orb /ɔ:b/ *n* LITTÉR (all contexts) globe *m*.

orbit /'ɔ:bɪt/ **I** *n* orbite *f*.
II *vtr* décrire une orbite autour de.
III *vi* [*spacecraft*] orbiter.

orbital road /'ɔ:bɪtl rəʊd/ *n* rocade *f*.

orchard /'ɔ:tʃəd/ *n* verger *m*.

orchestra /'ɔ:kɪstrə/ *n* orchestre *m*; **chamber ~** orchestre de chambre.

orchestral /ɔ:'kestrəl/ *adj* [*concert, music*] orchestral; [*instrument*] d'orchestre.

orchestra: **~ pit** *n* fosse *f* d'orchestre; **~ seats** US, **~ stalls** GB *n* fauteuils *mpl* d'orchestre.

orchestrate /'ɔ:kɪstreɪt/ *vtr* LIT, FIG orchestrer.

orchid /'ɔ:kɪd/ *n* orchidée *f*.

ordain /ɔ:'deɪn/ *vtr* **1** (decree) décréter (**that** que); **2** RELIG ordonner.

ordeal /ɔ:'di:l, 'ɔ:di:l/ *n* GEN épreuve *f*.

order /'ɔ:də(r)/ **I** *n* **1** (logical arrangement) ordre *m*; **to set** ou **put one's life in ~** remettre de l'ordre dans sa vie; **2** (sequence) ordre *m*; **in alphabetical ~** dans l'ordre alphabétique; **to do things in ~** procéder par

ordre; **in the right/wrong ~** dans le bon/mauvais ordre; **to be out of ~** [*files, records*] être déclassé; **3** (discipline, control) ordre *m*; **to restore ~** rétablir l'ordre; **to keep ~** [*teacher*] maintenir la discipline; **4** (established state) ordre *m*; **the existing ~** l'ordre actuel; **5** (command) ordre *m* (**to do** de faire) ALSO JUR; **to have** OU **to be under ~s to do** avoir (l')ordre de faire; **I'm not taking ~s from you** je ne suis pas à vos ordres; **until further ~s** jusqu'à nouvel ordre; **6** (in shop, restaurant) commande *f*; **a rush/repeat ~** une commande urgente/renouvelée; **the books are on ~** les livres ont été commandés; **made to ~** fait sur commande; **7** (operational state) **in good ~** en bon état; **in working ~** en état de marche; **to be out of ~** [*phone line*] être en dérangement; [*lift, machine*] être en panne; **8** (in public debate) **~! ~!** un peu de silence, s'il vous plaît!; **to call sb to ~** rappeler qn à l'ordre; **out of ~** contraire à la procédure; **9** (all right) **in ~** [*documents*] en règle; **that is perfectly in ~** aucune objection; **that remark was way out of ~** cette remarque était tout à fait déplacée; **I hear that congratulations are in ~!** il paraît que les félicitations sont à l'ordre du jour!; **economy is the ~ of the day** l'austérité est de mise; **10** RELIG ordre *m*; **11** (rank, scale) **craftsmen of the highest ~** des artisans de premier ordre; **talent of this ~** un tel talent; **the lower ~s** les classes inférieures; **of the ~ of 15%** GB, **in the ~ of 15%** US de l'ordre de 15%; **12** FIN **pay to the ~ of** (on cheque, draft) payer à l'ordre de; **13** GB (honorary association, title) ordre *m*.
II orders *npl* RELIG ordres *mpl*; **to take Holy ~s** entrer dans les ordres.
III in order that *conj phr* (with the same subject) afin de (+ *infinitive*), pour (+ *infinitive*); (with different subjects) afin que (+ *subj*), pour que (+ *subj*); **I've come in ~ that I might help you** je suis venu pour t'aider; **he brought the proofs in ~ that I might check them** il a apporté les épreuves pour que je puisse les vérifier.
IV in order to *prep phr* pour (+ *infinitive*), afin de (+ *infinitive*); **in ~ to talk to him** pour lui parler.
V *vtr* **1** (command) ordonner [*inquiry, retrial*]; **to ~ sb to do** ordonner à qn de faire; **to ~ the building to be demolished** ordonner la démolition du bâtiment; **the soldiers were ~ed to disembark** les soldats ont reçu l'ordre de débarquer; **2** commander [*goods, meal*]; réserver [*taxi*] (**for** pour); **3** (put in order) classer [*files, cards*]; mettre [qch] dans l'ordre [*names, dates*]; **to ~ one's affairs** s'organiser.
VI *vi* [*diner, customer*] commander.
VII ordered *pp adj* [*series*] ordonné.
■ **order about, order around: ~** [sb] **around** donner des ordres à.
■ **order off** SPORT: **~** [sb] **off** expulser [*player*].
order book *n* carnet *m* de commandes.
ordered /ˈɔːdəd/ *adj* **1** [*list*] méthodique; [*structure*] régulier/-ière; **an ~ whole** un ensemble ordonné; **in ~ ranks** en rangs réguliers; **2** MATH [*set*] ordonné.
order form *n* bon *m* or bulletin *m* de commande.
orderly /ˈɔːdəlɪ/ **I** *n* **1** MIL planton *m*; **2** MED aide-soignant/-e *m/f*.
II *adj* **1** (well-regulated) [*queue, line*] ordonné; [*arrangement, pattern*] régulier/-ière; [*file, row, rank*] régulier/-ière; [*mind, system*] méthodique; [*lifestyle, society*] bien réglé; **2** (calm) [*crowd, demonstration, debate*] calme; **in an ~ fashion** ou **manner** [*leave etc*] dans le calme.
orderly officer *n* MIL officier *m* de service.
ordinal /ˈɔːdɪnl, US -dənl/ *n, adj* ordinal (*m*).
ordinarily /ˈɔːdənrəlɪ, US ˌɔːdn'erəlɪ/ *adv* (normally) d'ordinaire.
ordinary /ˈɔːdənrɪ, US 'ɔːrdəneri/ **I** *n* (normal) **to be out of the ~** sortir de l'ordinaire.
II *adj* **1** (normal) [*clothes*] de tous les jours (*after n*); [*citizen, life, family*] ordinaire; **to be just ~ people** n'être que des gens bien ordinaires; **this is no ~ case** c'est un cas inhabituel; **in the ~ way** normalement; **2** (average) [*consumer, family*] moyen/-enne; **3** PÉJ (uninspiring) **very ~** très quelconque.

ordination /ˌɔːdɪˈneɪʃn, US -dnˈeɪʃn/ *n* ordination *f*.
ordnance /ˈɔːdnəns/ *n* ₵ (supplies) matériel *m* (militaire).
ordnance: Ordnance Survey, OS *n* GB *institut géographique national de Grande-Bretagne*; **Ordnance Survey map** *n* ~ carte *f* d'état-major.
ore /ɔː(r)/ *n* minerai *m*; **iron ~** minerai de fer.
oregano /ˌɒrɪˈgɑːnəʊ/ *n* origan *m*.
organ /ˈɔːgən/ **I** *n* **1** BOT, ANAT organe *m*; **donor ~, transplant ~** (sought) don *m* d'organe; (transplanted) transplant *m*; **male ~** membre *m* viril; **2** MUS (also **pipe ~**) orgue *m*; **on the ~** à l'orgue; **to play the ~** jouer de l'orgue; (as job) tenir l'orgue; **3** FIG (publication, organization) organe *m* (**of** de).
II *noun modifier* MUS [*music, composition*] pour orgue.
organ donor *n* MED donneur/-euse *m/f* d'organes.
organic /ɔːˈgænɪk/ *adj* **1** GEN, BIOL organique; [*produce, farming*] biologique; [*fertilizer*] naturel/-elle; **2** (integrated) [*society, whole*] intégré.
organic chemistry *n* chimie *f* organique.
organism /ˈɔːgənɪzəm/ *n* (all contexts) organisme *m*.
organist /ˈɔːgənɪst/ [▶ 1251] *n* organiste *mf*.
organization /ˌɔːgənaɪˈzeɪʃn, US -nɪˈz-/ *n* **1** (group) GEN organisation *f*; (bureaucratic) organisme *m*; (voluntary) association *f*; **human rights ~** association de défense des droits de l'homme; **2** (arrangement) organisation *f* (**of** de).
organizational /ˌɔːgənaɪˈzeɪʃənl, US -nɪˈz-/ *adj* [*ability, role*] d'organisateur/-trice; [*problem*] d'organisation.
organize /ˈɔːgənaɪz/ **I** *vtr* organiser [*event, day, time*]; ranger [*books, papers*]; **to ~ sth into chapters** répartir qch en chapitres; **I'll ~ the drinks** je m'occuperai des boissons; **to ~ a babysitter** trouver une baby-sitter; **to get (oneself) ~d** s'organiser.
II *vi* (unionize) se syndiquer.
organized: ~ crime *n* grand banditisme *m*; **~ labour** *n* main-d'œuvre *f* syndiquée.
organizer /ˈɔːgənaɪzə(r)/ *n* **1** (person) organisateur/-trice *m/f* (**of** de); **union ~, labour ~** militant/-e *m/f* syndicaliste; **2** (also **personal ~**) (agenda *m*) organiseur *m*; **electronic ~** agenda électronique; **3** (container) **desk ~** (pot *m*) range-tout *m inv*.
organizing /ˈɔːgənaɪzɪŋ/ **I** *n* organisation *f*; **she did all the ~** c'est elle qui a tout organisé.
II *adj* [*group, committee*] organisateur/-trice.
organ: ~ loft *n* tribune *f* d'orgue; **~ stop** *n* MUS (register) jeu *m* d'orgues; (knob) registre *m* d'orgues; **~ transplant** *n* MED transplantation *f* d'organe.
orgasm /ˈɔːgæzəm/ *n* orgasme *m*.
orgy /ˈɔːdʒɪ/ *n* (all contexts) orgie *f*.
orient /ˈɔːrɪənt/ **I** *n* **the Orient** l'Orient *m*.
II *vtr* FIG orienter [*person, society*] (**towards** en faveur de).
III *v refl* **to ~ oneself** FIG s'adapter (**to, in** à); LIT s'orienter.
oriental /ˌɔːrɪˈentl/ **I** **Oriental** *n* Oriental/-e *m/f*.
II *adj* GEN oriental; [*appearance, eyes*] d'Oriental; [*carpet*] d'Orient.
orientate /ˈɔːrɪənteɪt/ *vtr, v refl* = **orient** II, III.
-orientated /-ˈɔːrɪənteɪtɪd/ *combining form* = **-oriented**.
orientation /ˌɔːrɪənˈteɪʃn/ **I** *n* **1** (beginning of studies) cours *m* d'introduction; **2** (inclination) (political, intellectual) orientation *f*; (sexual) tendance *f*.
II *noun modifier* [*week*] d'introduction.
-oriented /-ˈɔːrɪəntɪd/ *combining form* **family-~** orienté vers la famille.
orienteering /ˌɔːrɪənˈtɪərɪŋ/ *n* course *f* d'orientation.
origin /ˈɒrɪdʒɪn/ *n* **1** (of person, custom, idea etc) origine *f*; **the problem has its ~(s) in...** le problème provient de...; **2** (of goods) provenance *f*; **country of ~** pays d'origine.
original /əˈrɪdʒənl/ **I** *n* (genuine article) original *m*; **to read sth in the ~** lire qch dans le texte original.
II *adj* **1** (initial) [*inhabitant, owner*] premier/-ière; [*ver-*

sion] original; [*question, site, strategy*] originel/-elle; [*member*] originaire; **2** (not copied) [*manuscript, painting*] original; [*invoice, receipt*] d'origine; **3** (creative) [*design, suggestion*] original; **he's ~** il est créatif; **an ~ thinker** un esprit novateur; **4** (eccentric) original.

original cost *n* COMM, ECON prix *m* d'achat.

originality /ə,rɪdʒə'nælətɪ/ *n* originalité *f*.

originally /ə'rɪdʒənəlɪ/ *adv* **1** (initially) au départ; **2** (in the first place) à l'origine; **I am** ou **come from France ~** je suis originaire de France.

originate /ə'rɪdʒɪneɪt/ *vi* [*custom, style, tradition*] voir le jour; [*fire*] se déclarer; **to ~ from** [*goods*] provenir de; [*proposal*] émaner de.

originator /ə'rɪdʒɪneɪtə(r)/ *n* **1** (of idea, rumour) auteur *m*; **2** (of invention, system) créateur/-trice *m/f*.

Orkney /'ɔ:knɪ/ ▶ 1022 *pr npl* (also **~ Islands**) (îles *fpl*) Orcades; **in/on ~** dans les Orcades.

ornament /'ɔ:nəmənt/ *n* **1** C (trinket) bibelot *m*; **2** ¢ (ornamentation) ornement *m*.

ornamental /,ɔ:nə'mentl/ *adj* [*plant*] ornemental; [*garden, lake*] d'agrément; [*motif, artwork*] décoratif/-ive.

ornate /ɔ:'neɪt/ *adj* GEN richement orné; [*style*] très fleuri.

ornithologist /,ɔ:nɪ'θɒlədʒɪst/ ▶ 1251 *n* ornithologue *mf*.

ornithology /,ɔ:nɪ'θɒlədʒɪ/ *n* ornithologie *f*.

orphan /'ɔ:fn/ **I** *n* orphelin/-e *m/f*.
II *adj* orphelin.

orphanage /'ɔ:fənɪdʒ/ *n* orphelinat *m*.

orthodontist /,ɔ:θə'dɒntɪst/ ▶ 1251 *n* orthodontiste *mf*.

orthodox /'ɔ:θədɒks/ *adj* GEN, RELIG orthodoxe; **Greek Orthodox church** église orthodoxe grecque.

orthopaedic, **orthopedic** US /,ɔ:θə'pi:dɪk/ *adj* orthopédique; **~ surgeon** chirugien *m* orthopédiste.

orthopaedics, **orthopedics** US /,ɔ:θə'pi:dɪks/ *n* (+ *v sg*) orthopédie *f*.

OS 1 *abrév* ▶ **outsize**; **2** GB GEOG *abrév* ▶ **Ordnance Survey**.

oscillate /'ɒsɪleɪt/ *vi* GEN, PHYS, TECH osciller.

osmosis /ɒz'məʊsɪs/ *n* osmose *f*; **by ~** par osmose.

ossify /'ɒsɪfaɪ/ *vi* FIG se scléroser.

ostensible /ɒ'stensəbl/ *adj* apparent.

ostensibly /ɒ'stensəblɪ/ *adv* (supposedly) soi-disant.

ostentatious /,ɒsten'teɪʃəs/ *adj* [*house, surroundings*] tape-à-l'œil.

ostentatiously /,ɒsten'teɪʃəslɪ/ *adv* avec ostentation.

osteopath /'ɒstɪəpæθ/ ▶ 1251 *n* ostéopathe *mf*.

osteopathy /,ɒstɪ'ɒpəθɪ/ *n* ostéopathie *f*.

osteoporosis /,ɒstɪəʊpə'rəʊsɪs/ ▶ 1002 *n* ostéoporose *f*.

ostracism /'ɒstrəsɪzəm/ *n* ostracisme *m*.

ostracize /'ɒstrəsaɪz/ *vtr* ostraciser.

ostrich /'ɒstrɪtʃ/ **I** *n* ZOOL, FIG autruche *f*.
II *noun modifier* [*feather, egg*] d'autruche.

other /'ʌðə(r)/ **I** *adj* **1** (what is left, the rest) autre; **the ~ one** l'autre; **the ~ 25** les 25 autres; **2** (alternative, additional) autre; **I only have one ~ shirt** je n'ai qu'une seule autre chemise; **3** (alternate) **every ~ year** tous les deux ans; **every ~ Saturday** un samedi sur deux; **4** (different, not the same) autre; **~ people** les autres; **I wouldn't have him any ~ way** je ne voudrais pas qu'il change; **some ~ time perhaps** une autre fois peut-être; **at all ~ times** en dehors de ces heures-là; **the '~ woman'** (mistress) la maîtresse; **5** (opposite) autre; **he was going the ~ way** il allait dans la direction opposée; **6** (recent) **the ~ day** l'autre jour; **7** (in lists) **she will visit Japan, among ~ places** entre autres, elle ira au Japon.
II *other than* *prep phr* **1** (except) **~ than that** à part ça; **there's nobody here ~ than Carole** il n'y a personne ici à part Carole; **we can't get home ~ than by car** nous ne pouvons pas rentrer autrement qu'en voiture; **I have no choice ~ than to fire her** je n'ai pas d'autre solution que de la renvoyer; **2** (any-

thing but) **he could scarcely be ~ than relieved** il aurait difficilement pu être autre chose que soulagé.
III *pron* **the ~s** les autres; **~s** (as subject) d'autres; (as object) les autres; **one after the ~** l'un après l'autre; **one or ~ of them** un d'entre eux; **somebody** ou **someone or ~** quelqu'un; **some book or ~** un livre, je ne sais plus lequel; **somehow or ~** d'une manière ou d'une autre; **Bob something or ~** Bob quelque chose.
IDIOMS **my ~ half**° ma moitié° *f*.

otherwise /'ʌðəwaɪz/ **I** *adv* **1** (differently, in other ways) **to do ~** faire autrement; **improve or ~ change sth** améliorer ou modifier qch d'une manière ou d'une autre; **no woman, married or ~** aucune femme, mariée ou non; **unless we are told ~** à moins qu'on ne nous dise le contraire; **I know ~** je sais que ce n'est pas le cas; **William ~ known as Bill** William, qu'on connaît aussi sous le nom de Bill; **2** (in other respects) à part cela, par ailleurs; **less damage than might ~ have been the case** moins de dégâts qu'on aurait pu s'y attendre.
II *conj* (or else, in other circumstances) sinon; **it's quite safe, ~ I wouldn't do it** ce n'est pas dangereux du tout, sinon je ne le ferais pas.

otherworldly /,ʌðə'wɜ:ldlɪ/ *adj* **to be ~** ne pas avoir les pieds sur terre.

OTT *adj*: *abrév* ▶ **over-the-top**.

otter /'ɒtə(r)/ *n* loutre *f*; **sea ~** loutre marine.

OU *n* GB UNIV *abrév* ▶ **Open University**.

ouch /aʊtʃ/ *excl* aïe.

ought /ɔ:t/

■ **Note** In virtually all cases, *ought* is translated by the conditional tense of *devoir*: *you ought to go now* = tu devrais partir maintenant; *they ought to arrive tomorrow* ils devraient arriver demain.
– The past *ought to have done/seen etc* is translated by the past conditional of *devoir*: *he ought to have been more polite* = il aurait dû être plus poli. For further examples, including negative sentences, see the entry below.
– The French verb *devoir* is irregular. For its conjugation see the French verb tables.

modal aux **1** (expressing probability, expectation) **that ~ to fix it** ça devrait arranger les choses; **2** (making polite but firm suggestion) **oughtn't we to ask?** ne croyez-vous pas que nous devrions demander?; **3** (indicating moral obligation) **someone ~ to have accompanied her** quelqu'un aurait dû l'accompagner; **4** (when prefacing important point) **you ~ to know that** il vaudrait mieux que tu saches que.

ounce /aʊns/ ▶ 1392, 789 *n* **1** (weight) once *f* (= *28,35 g*); **2** GB (fluid) = *0,028 l*; US = *0,035 l*; **3** FIG once *f*.

our /'aʊə(r), ɑ:(r)/

■ **Note** In French, determiners agree in gender and number with the noun they qualify. So *our* is translated by *notre* + masculine or feminine singular noun (notre chien, notre maison) and *nos* + plural noun (nos enfants).
– When *our* is stressed, *à nous* is added after the noun: OUR house = notre maison à nous.
– For *our* used with parts of the body ▶ 765.

det notre/nos.

ours /'aʊəz/

■ **Note** In French, pronouns reflect the number and gender of the noun they are standing for. Thus *ours* is translated by *le nôtre*, *la nôtre* or *les nôtres* according to what is being referred to: *the blue car is ours* = la voiture bleue est la nôtre; *their children are older than ours* = leurs enfants sont plus âgés que les nôtres.

pron le nôtre/la nôtre/les nôtres; **which tickets are ~?** lesquels de ces billets sont les nôtres?; **a friend of ~** un ami à nous; **~ is not an easy task** SOUT notre tâche n'est pas facile.

ourselves /aʊə'selvz, ɑ:-/

■ **Note** When used as a reflexive pronoun, direct and indirect, *ourselves* is translated by *nous* in standard French: *we've hurt ourselves* = nous nous sommes fait mal. However, if the more informal *on* is used to translate *we*, the

translation of ourselves will be *se* (or *s'* before a vowel): on s'est fait mal.
– When used as an emphatic the translation is *nous-mêmes*: *we did it ourselves* = nous l'avons fait nous-mêmes.
– When used after a preposition *ourselves* is translated by *nous* or *nous-mêmes*.

pron 1 (refl) nous; **2** (emphatic) nous-mêmes; **3** (after prep) **for** ~ pour nous, pour nous-mêmes; (all) **by** ~ tout seuls/toutes seules.

oust /aʊst/ *vtr* évincer [*person*] **(from** de; **as** comme); forcer [qn] à démissionner [*government*].

out /aʊt/

■ Note *out* is used after many verbs in English to alter or reinforce the meaning of the verb (*hold out, wipe out, filter out etc*). Very often in French, a verb alone will be used to translate these combinations. For translations you should consult the appropriate verb entry (*hold, wipe, filter* etc).
– When *out* is used as an adverb meaning *outside*, it often adds little to the sense of the phrase: *they're out in the garden* = *they're in the garden*. In such cases *out* will not usually be translated: *ils sont dans le jardin*.
– *out* is used as an adverb to mean *absent* or *not at home*. In this case *she's out* really means *she's gone out* and the French translation is *elle est sortie*.
– For the phrase *out of* see III in the entry below.
– For examples of the above and other uses, see the entry below.

I *vtr* révéler l'homosexualité de [*person*].
II *adv* **1** (outside) dehors; **to stand** ~ **in the rain** rester (dehors) sous la pluie; **to be** ~ **in the garden** être dans le jardin; ~ **there** dehors; ~ **here** ici; **to tear a page** ~ arracher une page; **2** (from within) **to go** ou **walk** ~ sortir; **to pull/take sth** ~ retirer/sortir qch; **I couldn't find my way** ~ je ne trouvais pas la sortie; **3** (at a distance) ~ **in China** en Chine; **two days** ~ **from port** à deux jours du port; **when the tide is** ~ à marée basse; **further** ~ plus loin; **4** (in the world at large) **there are a lot of people** ~ **there looking for work** il y a beaucoup de gens qui cherchent du travail en ce moment; **5** (absent) **to be** ~ GEN être sorti; [*strikers*] être en grève; **6** (for social activity) **to invite sb** ~ **to dinner** inviter qn au restaurant; **a day** ~ une sortie pour la journée; **7** (published, now public) **to be** ~ [*book, exam results*] être publié; **my secret is** ~ mon secret est révélé; **8** (in bloom) **to be** ~ [*tree, shrub*] être en fleurs; **to be fully** ~ [*flower*] être épanoui; **9** (shining) **to be** ~ [*sun, moon, stars*] briller; **10** (extinguished) **to be** ~ [*fire, light*] être éteint; **lights** ~ extinction des feux; **11** SPORT, GAMES **to be** ~ [*player*] être éliminé; **'~!'** (of ball) 'out!'; **12** (unconscious) **to be** ~ **(cold)**○ GEN être dans les pommes○; [*boxer*] être K.O.; **13** (over, finished) **before the week is** ~ avant la fin de la semaine; **14** GB (incorrect) **to be** ~ **in one's calculations** s'être trompé dans ses calculs; **my watch is two minutes** ~ (slow) ma montre retarde de deux minutes; (fast) ma montre avance de deux minutes; **15**○ (not possible) exclu; **no, that option is** ~ non, cette solution est exclue; **16**○ (actively in search of) **to be** ~ **to do sth** être bien décidé à faire qch; **he's just** ~ **for what he can get** PÉJ c'est l'intérêt qui le guide; **he's** ~ **to get you** il t'en veut à mort; (killer) il veut ta peau○; **17**○ (not in fashion) passé de mode.
III out of *prep phr* **1** (from) **to go** ou **walk** ou **come** ~ sortir; **get** ~ **of here!** sors d'ici!; **to jump** ~ **of the window** sauter par la fenêtre; **to take sth** ~ **of a box** retirer qch d'une boîte; **to take sth** ~ **of one's bag** prendre qch dans son sac; **2** (expressing ratio) sur; **two** ~ **of every three** deux sur trois; **3** (part of whole) ~ **of a book** tiré d'un livre; **4** JUR **to be** ~ [*jury*] être en délibération; **5** (beyond defined limits) hors de [*reach, sight*]; en dehors de [*city*]; **6** (free from confinement) ~ **of hospital** sorti de l'hôpital; **7** (sheltered) à l'abri de [*sun*]; **8** (lacking) **to be (right)** ~ **of** ne plus avoir de [*item*]; **9** (made from) en [*wood, metal*]; **10** (due to) par [*respect*].
IDIOMS **I want** ~○! je ne marche plus avec vous/eux etc○; **come on,** ~ **with it**○! allez, dis ce que tu as à

dire!; **to be** ~ **and about** (after illness) être à nouveau sur pied; **to be** ~ **of it**○ être dans les vapes○; **to feel** ~ **of it** se sentir exclu; **you're well** ~ **of it** c'est mieux comme ça.

out-and-out /ˌaʊtənˈaʊt/ *adj* [*villain, liar*] fieffé; [*supporter*] pur et dur; [*success, failure*] total.

outback /ˈaʊtbæk/ *n* **the** ~ la brousse (australienne).

outbid /ˌaʊtˈbɪd/ *vtr* (*p prés* **-dd-**; *prét, pp* **outbid**) surenchérir sur.

outboard motor /ˈaʊtbɔːdˈməʊtə(r)/ *n* moteur *m* hors-bord.

outbreak /ˈaʊtbreɪk/ *n* (of war, unrest) déclenchement *m*; (of violence, spots) éruption *f*; (of disease) déclaration *f*; **at the** ~ **of war** quand la guerre a éclaté.

outbuilding /ˈaʊtbɪldɪŋ/ *n* dépendance *f*.

outburst /ˈaʊtbɜːst/ *n* (of laughter) éclat *m*; (of anger) accès *m*; FIG (of trouble) éruption *f*.

outcast /ˈaʊtkɑːst/ us -kæst/ *n* exclu/-e *m/f*.

outclass /ˌaʊtˈklɑːs/ us -ˈklæs/ *vtr* dominer.

outcome /ˈaʊtkʌm/ *n* résultat *m*.

outcrop /ˈaʊtkrɒp/ *n* affleurement *m*.

outcry /ˈaʊtkraɪ/ *n* tollé *m* (**about, against** contre).

outdated /ˌaʊtˈdeɪtɪd/ *adj* GEN dépassé; [*clothing*] démodé.

outdistance /ˌaʊtˈdɪstəns/ *vtr* LIT, FIG distancer.

outdo /ˌaʊtˈduː/ *vtr* (*prét* **outdid**; *pp* **outdone**) surpasser.

outdoor /ˈaʊtdɔː(r)/ *adj* [*life, activity, sport*] de plein air; [*restaurant, cinema*] en plein air; [*shoes*] de marche; **to be an** ~ **type** être sportif.

outdoors /ˌaʊtˈdɔːz/ **I** *n* **the great** ~ (+ *v sg*) la pleine nature.
II *adv* GEN dehors; [*live*] en plein air.

outer /ˈaʊtə(r)/ *adj* **1** (furthest) [*limit*] extrême; **2** (outside) GEN extérieur; [*clothing*] de dessus.

outer: ~ **space** *n* espace *m* extra-atmosphérique or extérieur; ~ **suburbs** *npl* grande banlieue *f*.

outfit /ˈaʊtfɪt/ *n* **1** (set of clothes) tenue *f*; **2**○ (company) boîte○ *f*.

outfitter /ˈaʊtfɪtə(r)/ *n* **ladies'/men's** ~ spécialiste *mf* de confection pour femmes/hommes.

outflank /ˌaʊtˈflæŋk/ *vtr* MIL, FIG déborder.

outflow /ˈaʊtfləʊ/ *n* (of money) sortie *f*.

outgoing /ˈaʊtɡəʊɪŋ/ *adj* **1** (sociable) ouvert et sociable; **2** (departing) [*government*] sortant; [*mail*] en partance; [*tide*] descendant; TELECOM ~ **call** appel téléphonique.

outgoings /ˈaʊtɡəʊɪŋz/ *npl* GB sorties *fpl* (de fonds).

outgrow /aʊtˈɡrəʊ/ *vtr* (*prét* **outgrew**; *pp* **outgrown**) **1** (grow too big for) devenir trop grand pour; **2** (grow too old for) se lasser de [qch] avec le temps; **he'll** ~ **it** ça lui passera; **3** (grow taller than) devenir plus grand que.

outhouse /ˈaʊthaʊs/ *n* (separate) dépendance *f*; (adjoining) appentis *m*.

outlandish /aʊtˈlændɪʃ/ *adj* bizarre.

outlast /ˌaʊtˈlɑːst/ us -læst/ *vtr* durer plus longtemps que.

outlaw /ˈaʊtlɔː/ **I** *n* hors-la-loi *m inv*.
II *vtr* déclarer illégal [*practice, organization*].

outlay /ˈaʊtleɪ/ *n* dépenses *fpl* (**on** en); **capital** ~ frais *mpl* d'établissement; **initial** ~ mise *f* de fonds initiale.

outlet /ˈaʊtlet/ *n* **1** LIT (for gas, air, water) tuyau *m* de sortie; **2** COMM (market) débouché *m*; **retail** ~, **sales** ~ point *m* de vente; **3** FIG (for emotion, talent) exutoire *m*; **4** US Elec prise *f* de courant.

outline /ˈaʊtlaɪn/ **I** *n* **1** (of object) contour *m*; **2** (of plan, policy) grandes lignes *fpl*; (of essay) plan *m*.
II *vtr* **1** (give summary of) exposer brièvement [*aims, plan, reasons*]; **2** (draw round) dessiner le contour de [*eye, picture*] (**in, with** en); **to be ~ed against the sky** se découper sur le ciel.

outline agreement *n* accord-cadre *m*.

outlive /ˌaʊt'lɪv/ *vtr* survivre à [*person*]; **it has ~d its usefulness** il/elle a fait son temps.

outlook /'aʊtlʊk/ *n* **1** (attitude) conception *f*, vue *f*; **to be conservative in ~** avoir une vue conservatrice des choses; **2** (prospects) perspectives *fpl*; **3 the ~ for tomorrow is rain** demain on prévoit un temps pluvieux; **4** (from window) vue *f* (**over, onto** sur).

outlying /'aʊtlaɪɪŋ/ *adj* (away from city centre) excentré; (remote) isolé.

outmanoeuvre GB, **outmaneuver** US /ˌaʊtmə'nuːvə(r)/ *vtr* déjouer les plans de.

outmoded /ˌaʊt'məʊdɪd/ *adj* dépassé.

outnumber /ˌaʊt'nʌmbə(r)/ *vtr* être plus nombreux que; **~ed two to one** deux fois moins nombreux.

out of bounds *adj, adv* **1 to be ~** [*area*] être interdit (**to** à); **2** SPORT **to be ~** être hors jeu.

out-of-date *adj* [*ticket, passport*] périmé; [*clothing*] démodé; [*theory, concept*] dépassé.

out-of-pocket *adj* **1 ~ expenses** frais *mpl* complémentaires; **2 to be out of pocket** être perdant.

out-of-the-way **I** *adj* [*places*] à l'écart.
II out of the way *adv phr* **get out of the way!** pousse-toi!

outpatient /'aʊtpeɪʃnt/ *n* malade *mf* externe; **~s' department** service *m* de consultation.

outpost /'aʊtpəʊst/ *n* MIL, GEN avant-poste *m*; **the last ~** le dernier bastion.

output /'aʊtpʊt/ **I** *n* **1** GEN (yield) rendement *m*; (of factory) production *f*; **2** COMPUT (données *fpl* de) sortie *f*; **computer ~** sortie *f* d'ordinateur.
II *noun modifier* COMPUT [*data, equipment*] de sortie.
III *vtr* (*p prés* **-tt-**; *prét, pp* **-put** ou **-putted**) [*computer*] sortir [*data*].

outrage /'aʊtreɪdʒ/ **I** *n* **1** (anger) indignation *f* (**at** devant); **2** (horrifying act) attentat *m*; **3** (scandal) (against decency) outrage *m*; **it's an ~ that** c'est un scandale que (+ *subj*).
II *vtr* scandaliser [*public*].
III outraged *pp adj* outragé (**by** par).

outrageous /aʊt'reɪdʒəs/ *adj* **1** (disgraceful) scandaleux/-euse; **2** (unconventional) [*person, outfit*] incroyable; [*remark*] outrancier/-ière.

outré /'uːtreɪ, US uː'treɪ/ *adj* outrancier/-ière.

outrider /'aʊtraɪdə(r)/ *n* (also **motorcycle ~**) motard *m* (*d'une escorte*).

outright /'aʊtraɪt/ **I** *adj* **1** (absolute) [*control, defiance, majority*] absolu; [*ban, rejection*] catégorique; **2** (obvious) [*favourite, victory, winner*] incontesté; **3** (unreserved) [*disbelief, hostility*] pur et simple.
II *adv* **1** (completely) GEN catégoriquement; [*killed*] sur le coup; **to own one's house ~** être pleinement propriétaire; **2** (openly) franchement.

outrun /ˌaʊt'rʌn/ *vtr* (*p prés* **-nn-**; *prét, pp* **-ran**) **1** LIT distancer; **2** FIG (exceed) dépasser.

outsell /ˌaʊt'sel/ *vtr* [*product*] se vendre mieux que.

outset /'aʊtset/ *n* **at the ~** au début; **from the ~** dès le début.

outside /aʊt'saɪd, 'aʊtsaɪd/ **I** *n* **1** extérieur *m*; **on the ~** à l'extérieur; **on the ~ of** (on surface itself) sur l'extérieur de [*box, file*]; **2** (maximum) **at the ~** au maximum.
II *adj* **1** (outdoor) [*temperature*] extérieur; [*broadcast*] enregistré hors studio; **2** (outer) [*edge, world, wall*] extérieur; **3** TELECOM [*line*] extérieur; [*call*] de l'extérieur; **4** (leisure) **~ interests** centres *mpl* d'intérêt personnels; **5** (from elsewhere) [*help*] de l'extérieur; [*opinion, influence*] extérieur; **6 ~ lane** (in GB) voie *f* de droite; (in US, Europe) voie *f* de gauche; (on athletics track) couloir *m* extérieur; **7** (faint) **an ~ chance** une faible chance.
III *adv* dehors.
IV *prep* (also **~ of**) **1** (not within) en dehors de [*city*]; de l'autre côté de [*boundary*]; à l'extérieur de [*prison*]; **2** (in front of) devant [*house*]; **3** (over) **to wear a shirt ~ one's trousers** porter une chemise sur son pantalon; **4** FIG (beyond) **~ office hours** en dehors des heures de bureau.

outsider /ˌaʊt'saɪdə(r)/ *n* **1** (in community) étranger/-ère *m/f*; (to organization, company) personne *f* de l'extérieur; **2** (unlikely to win) outsider *m*.

outsize /'aʊtsaɪz/ **I** *n* (large garment) grandes tailles *fpl*.
II *adj* GEN (also **~d**) énorme.

outskirts /'aʊtskɜːts/ *npl* (of town) périphérie *f*.

outsmart /ˌaʊt'smaːt/ *vtr* se montrer plus futé que.

outspoken /ˌaʊt'spəʊkən/ *adj* **to be ~** parler sans détour.

outspread /ˌaʊt'spred/ *adj* [*arms*] grand ouvert; [*wings*] déployé; [*fingers*] écarté.

outstanding /ˌaʊt'stændɪŋ/ *adj* **1** (praiseworthy) remarquable; **2** (striking) frappant; **3** (unresolved) [*issue*] en suspens; [*work*] inachevé; [*account*] impayé; [*interest*] échu; **~ debts** créances *fpl* à recouvrer.

outstandingly /ˌaʊt'stændɪŋlɪ/ *adv* remarquablement; **~ good** remarquable.

outstay /ˌaʊt'steɪ/ *vtr* **to ~ one's welcome** s'éterniser.

outstretched /ˌaʊt'stretʃt/ *adj* [*hand, arm, fingers*] tendu; [*wings*] déployé; [*legs*] allongé.

outstrip /ˌaʊt'strɪp/ *vtr* (*p prés etc* **-pp-**) dépasser [*person*]; excéder [*production, demand*].

out-tray /'aʊttreɪ/ *n* corbeille *f* départ.

outvote /ˌaʊt'vəʊt/ *vtr* **to be ~d** être battu aux voix.

outward /'aʊtwəd/ **I** *adj* [*appearance, sign*] extérieur; [*calm*] apparent; **~ journey** aller *m*.
II *adv* = **outwards**.

outwardly /'aʊtwədlɪ/ *adv* (apparently) en apparence.

outwards /'aʊtwədz/ *adv* (also **outward**) [*open, turn*] vers l'extérieur.

outweigh /ˌaʊt'weɪ/ *vtr* l'emporter sur.

outwit /ˌaʊt'wɪt/ *vtr* (*p prés etc* **-tt-**) GEN être plus futé que; déjouer la surveillance de [*guard*]; déjouer les manœuvres de [*opponent*].

outworker /'aʊtwɜːkə(r)/ *n* GB travailleur/-euse *m/f* à domicile.

outworn /ˌaʊt'wɔːn/ *adj* (outmoded) désuet/-ète.

oval /'əʊvl/ **I** *n* ovale *m*.
II *adj* (also **~-shaped**) ovale.

ovary /'əʊvərɪ/ *n* ANAT, BOT ovaire *m*.

ovation /əʊ'veɪʃn/ *n* ovation *f*; **to give sb a standing ~** se lever pour ovationner qn.

oven /'ʌvn/ *n* four *m*; **cook in a slow ~** faites cuire à four doux.

oven: **~ cleaner** *n* nettoyant *m* pour four; **~ glove** *n* manique *f*; **~proof** *adj* qui va au four; **~-ready** *adj* prêt à cuire.

over¹ /'əʊvə(r)/

■ **Note** *over* is used after many verbs in English (*change over, fall over, lean over* etc). For translations, consult the appropriate verb entry (**change**, **fall**, **lean** etc).
– *over* is often used with another preposition in English (*to, in, on*) without altering the meaning. In this case *over* is usually not translated in French: *to be over in France* = être en France; *to swim over to sb* = nager vers qn.
– *over* is often used with nouns in English when talking about superiority (*control over* etc) or when giving the cause of something (*concern over, worries over* etc). For translations, consult the appropriate noun entry (**control**, **concern**, **worry** etc).
– *over* is often used as a prefix in verb combinations (*overeat*), adjective combinations (*overconfident*) and noun combinations (*overcoat*). These combinations are treated as headwords in the dictionary.
– For particular usages see the entry below.

I *prep* **1** (across the top of) par-dessus; **he jumped ~ it** il a sauté par-dessus; **a bridge ~ the Thames** un pont sur la Tamise; **2** (from or on the other side of) **the house ~ the road** la maison d'en face; **it's just ~ the road** c'est juste de l'autre côté de la rue; **~ here/there** par ici/là; **come ~ here!** viens (par) ici!; **~ there** (above) au-dessus de; **they live ~ the shop** ils habitent au-dessus de la boutique; **4** (covering, surrounding) GEN sur; **to wear a sweater ~ one's shirt** porter un pull par-dessus sa chemise; **shutters ~ the**

windows des volets aux fenêtres; **5** (physically higher than) **the water came ~ my ankles** j'avais de l'eau jusqu'aux chevilles; **6** (more than) plus de; **children ~ six** les enfants de plus de six ans; **temperatures ~ 40°** des températures supérieures à 40°; **7** (in the course of) **~ the weekend** pendant le week-end; **~ a period of** sur une période de; **~ the last few days** au cours de ces derniers jours; **~ the years** avec le temps; **~ Christmas** à Noël; **to stay with sb ~ Easter** passer les vacances de Pâques chez qn; **8** (recovered from) **to be ~** s'être remis de [*illness, operation*]; **to be ~ the worst** avoir passé le pire; **9** (by means of) **~ the phone** par téléphone; **~ the radio** à la radio; **10** (everywhere) **all ~ the house** partout dans la maison; **to show sb ~ a house** faire visiter une maison à qn.

II over and above *prep phr* **~ and above that** en plus de cela; **~ and above the minimum requirement** au-delà du minimum requis.

III *adj, adv* **1** (use with verbs not covered in NOTE) **~ you go!** allez hop!; **2** (finished) **to be ~** [*term, meeting*] être terminé; [*war*] être fini; **to get sth ~ with** en finir avec qch; **3** (more) **children of six and ~** les enfants de plus de six ans; **4** (remaining) **there's one ~** il en reste un; **there's nothing ~** il ne reste rien; **5** (to one's house, country) **to invite ou ask sb ~** inviter qn; **we had them ~ on Sunday** ils sont venus dimanche; **when you're next ~ this way** la prochaine fois que tu passes dans le coin; **6** RADIO, TV **~ to you** à vous; **now ~ to Tim for the weather** laissons la place à Tim pour la météo; **now ~ to our Paris studios** nous passons l'antenne à nos studios de Paris; **7** (showing repetition) **five times ~** cinq fois de suite; **to start all ~ again** recommencer à zéro; **I had to do it ~** US j'ai dû recommencer; **I've told you ~ and ~ (again)**... je t'ai dit je ne sais combien de fois...; **8** GB (excessively) **I'm not ~ keen** je ne suis pas très enthousiaste.

overact /ˌəʊvərˈækt/ *vi* en faire trop.

overactive /ˌəʊvərˈæktɪv/ *adj* [*imagination*] débordant.

overall /ˈəʊvərɔːl/ **I** *n* GB (coat-type) blouse *f*; (child's) tablier *m*.
II overalls *npl* GB combinaison *f*; US salopette *f*.
III /ˌəʊvərˈɔːl/ *adj* [*cost*] global; [*improvement, increase, trend*] général; [*control, impression, effect*] d'ensemble; [*majority*] absolu; [*winner*] au classement général.
IV *adv* **1** (in total) en tout; **2** (in general) dans l'ensemble.

overarm /ˈəʊvərɑːm/ *adj, adv* SPORT par le haut.

overate /ˌəʊvərˈeɪt/ *prét* ▶ **overeat**.

overawe /ˌəʊvərˈɔː/ *vtr* intimider.

overbalance /ˌəʊvəˈbæləns/ *vi* [*person*] perdre l'équilibre; [*pile of objects*] s'écrouler.

overbearing /ˌəʊvəˈbeərɪŋ/ *adj* dominateur-trice.

overblown /ˌəʊvəˈbləʊn/ *adj* [*style*] ampoulé.

overboard /ˈəʊvəbɔːd/ *adv* à l'eau; **man ~!** un homme à la mer!; **to go ~** FIG aller trop loin.

overbook /ˌəʊvəˈbʊk/ *vtr, vi* surréserver.

overburden /ˌəʊvəˈbɜːdn/ *vtr* (with work) surcharger (**with** de); (with responsibility, debt, guilt) accabler.

overcapacity /ˌəʊvəkəˈpæsəti/ *n* surcapacité *f*.

overcast /ˌəʊvəˈkɑːst, US -ˈkæst/ *adj* METEOROL couvert.

overcharge /ˌəʊvəˈtʃɑːdʒ/ **I** *vtr* faire payer trop cher à; **they ~d him by £10** ils lui ont fait payer 10 livres de trop.
II *vi* pratiquer des prix trop élevés.

overcoat /ˈəʊvəkəʊt/ *n* pardessus *m*.

overcome /ˌəʊvəˈkʌm/ **I** *vtr* (*prét* **-came**; *pp* **-come**) **1** (defeat) battre [*opponent*]; vaincre [*enemy*]; maîtriser [*nerves*]; surmonter [*dislike, fear*]; **2** (overwhelm) **to be overcome by smoke** être suffoqué par la fumée; **to be overcome with despair** succomber au désespoir; **to be quite overcome** être bouleversé.
II *vi* (*prét* **-came**, *pp* **-come**) triompher.

overcompensate /ˌəʊvəˈkɒmpenseɪt/ *vi* **to ~ for sth** trop compenser qch (**by doing** en faisant).

overconfident /ˌəʊvəˈkɒnfɪdənt/ *adj* trop sûr de soi.

overcook /ˌəʊvəˈkʊk/ *vtr* trop cuire.

overcrowded /ˌəʊvəˈkraʊdɪd/ *adj* [*train, room*] (with people) bondé (**with** de); [*road*] surencombré; [*institution, city*] surpeuplé (**with** de); [*class*] surchargé.

overcrowding /ˌəʊvəˈkraʊdɪŋ/ *n* (in city, institution) surpeuplement *m*; (in transport) surencombrement *m*; **~ in classrooms** les classes surchargées.

overdo /ˌəʊvəˈduː/ *vtr* (*prét* **overdid**; *pp* **overdone**) **1** (exaggerate) **to ~ it** exagérer; (when describing) forcer la note○; (when performing) forcer la note○; (when working) en faire trop○; **2** (use too much of) avoir la main lourde○ sur [*salt, makeup*]; **3** (overcook) faire trop cuire [*meat*].

overdone /ˌəʊvəˈdʌn/ *adj* (exaggerated) exagéré; (overcooked) trop cuit.

overdose /ˈəʊvədəʊs/ **I** *n* **1** (large dose) surdose *f*, dose *f* excessive; **2** (lethal dose) (of medicine) dose *f* mortelle; (of drugs) overdose *f*; **to take an ~** absorber une dose excessive de médicaments.
II *vi* (on medicine) prendre une dose mortelle de médicaments; (on drugs) faire une overdose.

overdraft /ˈəʊvədrɑːft, US -dræft/ *n* découvert *m*; **to have an ~** être à découvert.

overdraw /ˌəʊvəˈdrɔː/ **I** *vtr* (*prét* **overdrew**; *pp* **overdrawn**) faire un découvert sur [*account*].
II *vi* être à découvert.

overdressed /ˌəʊvəˈdrest/ *adj* trop habillé.

overdrive /ˈəʊvədraɪv/ *n* **1** AUT vitesse *f* surmultipliée; **2** FIG **to go into ~** s'activer intensivement.

overdue /ˌəʊvəˈdjuː, US -ˈduː/ *adj* [*baby, work*] en retard (**by** de); [*bill*] impayé; [*cheque*] présenté tardivement; **this measure is long ~** cette mesure aurait dû être prise il y a longtemps; **the book is ~** ce livre aurait déjà dû être rendu.

overeat /ˌəʊvərˈiːt/ *vi* (*prét* **overate**; *pp* **overeaten**) manger à l'excès.

overemphasize /ˌəʊvərˈemfəsaɪz/ *vtr* accorder trop d'importance à [*aspect, fact*]; exagérer [*importance*].

overenthusiastic /ˌəʊvərɪnˌθjuːziˈæstɪk, US -ˌθuː-/ *adj* trop enthousiaste.

overestimate /ˌəʊvərˈestɪmeɪt/ *vtr* surestimer.

overexcited /ˌəʊvərɪkˈsaɪtɪd/ *adj* surexcité.

overexert /ˌəʊvərɪɡˈzɜːt/ *v refl* **to ~ oneself** se surmener.

overexposure /ˌəʊvərɪkˈspəʊʒə(r)/ *n* **1** PHOT surexposition *f*; **2** CIN, TV médiatisation *f* excessive.

overfeed /ˌəʊvəˈfiːd/ *vtr* (*prét, pp* **-fed**) suralimenter [*child, pet*]; donner trop d'engrais à [*plant*].

overflow I /ˈəʊvəfləʊ/ *n* **1** (surplus) **the ~ of students** les étudiants en surnombre; **2** (from bath, sink) trop-plein *m*; (from dam) déversoir *m*; **3** COMM dépassement *m* de capacité.
II /ˌəʊvəˈfləʊ/ *vtr* [*river*] inonder [*banks*].
III /ˌəʊvəˈfləʊ/ *vi* déborder (**into** dans; **with** de); **to be full to ~ing** [*room*] être plein à craquer.
IV overflowing /ˌəʊvəˈfləʊɪŋ/ *pres p adj* [*school*] saturé; [*prison*] surpeuplé.

overgenerous /ˌəʊvəˈdʒenərəs/ *adj* trop généreux/-euse (**with** avec); [*amount*] excessif/-ive.

overgrown /ˌəʊvəˈɡrəʊn/ *adj* [*garden*] envahi par la végétation; **to behave like an ~ schoolboy** se conduire comme un collégien.

overhang I /ˈəʊvəhæŋ/ *n* (of cliff) surplomb *m*; (of roof) avancée *f*.
II /ˌəʊvəˈhæŋ/ *vtr* surplomber.

overhanging /ˌəʊvəˈhæŋɪŋ/ *adj* [*ledge, cliff*] surplomb; [*tree, branch*] qui surplombe.

overhaul I /ˈəʊvəhɔːl/ *n* (of machine) révision *f*; FIG (of system) restructuration *f*.
II /ˌəʊvəˈhɔːl/ *vtr* réviser [*car, machine*]; restructurer [*system*].

overhead /ˈəʊvəhed/ **I overheads** *npl* COMM frais *mpl* généraux.
II *adj* [*cable, railway*] aérien/-ienne.
III /ˌəʊvəˈhed/ *adv* **1** (in the sky) dans le ciel; **2** (above sb's head) au-dessus de ma/sa etc tête.

overhead: ~ **light** n plafonnier m; ~ **locker** n AVIAT compartiment m à bagages; ~ **projector** n rétroprojecteur m.

overhear /ˌəʊvəˈhɪə(r)/ vtr (p prés, pp **-heard**) entendre par hasard; **I overheard a conversation between**... j'ai surpris une conversation entre...

overheat /ˌəʊvəˈhiːt/ **I** vtr CULIN faire trop chauffer.
II vi [car, equipment] chauffer; [oven] chauffer trop; [economy] être en surchauffe.

overindulge /ˌəʊvərɪnˈdʌldʒ/ **I** vtr gâter [child].
II vi faire des excès.

overindulgence /ˌəʊvərɪnˈdʌldʒəns/ n **1** (excess) abus m (**in** de); **2** (laxity) trop grande indulgence f (**of, towards** envers).

overjoyed /ˌəʊvəˈdʒɔɪd/ adj [person] fou/folle de joie (**at** devant).

overkill /ˈəʊvəkɪl/ n (excess publicity) matraquage m.

overland /ˈəʊvəlænd/ **I** adj [route] terrestre; [journey] par route.
II adv par route.

overlap /ˈəʊvəlæp/ n chevauchement m (**between** de); (undesirable) empiétement m.
II /ˌəʊvəˈlæp/ vi (p prés etc **-pp-**) **1** FIG [theories] se chevaucher; [duties] se recouvrir partiellement; [visits, holidays] coïncider en partie; **2** LIT [materials, edges] se recouvrir partiellement; [one edge] dépasser; [roof tiles] s'imbriquer.

overlay /ˌəʊvəˈleɪ/ vtr (prét, pp **-laid**) recouvrir (**with** de).

overleaf /ˌəʊvəˈliːf/ adv au verso.

overload **I** /ˈəʊvələʊd/ n FIG surcharge f.
II /ˌəʊvəˈləʊd/ vtr surcharger (**with** de).

overlook /ˌəʊvəˈlʊk/ vtr **1** (have a view of) [building, window] donner sur; **2** (miss) ne pas voir [detail, error]; **to ~ the fact that** négliger le fait que; **3** (ignore) laisser passer [behaviour]; ignorer [effect, fact, need, problem].

overly /ˈəʊvəlɪ/ adv trop, excessivement.

overmanned /ˌəʊvəˈmænd/ adj en sureffectif.

overmanning /ˌəʊvəˈmænɪŋ/ n sureffectif m, effectif m pléthorique.

overmuch /ˌəʊvəˈmʌtʃ/ adv trop.

overnight /ˈəʊvənaɪt/ **I** adj **1** (night-time) [journey, train] de nuit; [stay] d'une nuit; [guest] pour la nuit; [stop] pour une nuit; **2** FIG (rapid) [success] immédiat.
II /ˌəʊvəˈnaɪt/ adv **1** (during the night) dans la nuit; (for the night) pour la nuit; **to stay ~** passer la nuit; **2** FIG (rapidly) du jour au lendemain.

overnight bag n petit sac m de voyage.

overpass /ˈəʊvəpɑːs, US -pæs/ n (for cars) toboggan m.

overpay /ˌəʊvəˈpeɪ/ vtr (prét, pp **-paid**) **I was overpaid by £500** on m'a versé 500 livres de trop; **they are overpaid** ils sont trop bien payés.

overplay /ˌəʊvəˈpleɪ/ vtr (exaggerate) exagérer.
IDIOMS **to ~ one's hand** aller trop loin.

overpopulated /ˌəʊvəˈpɒpjʊleɪtɪd/ adj surpeuplé.

overpower /ˌəʊvəˈpaʊə(r)/ vtr **1** LIT maîtriser [thief]; vaincre [army]; **2** FIG [smell, smoke] accabler.

overpowering /ˌəʊvəˈpaʊərɪŋ/ adj [person] intimidant; [personality] écrasant; [desire, urge] irrésistible; [heat] accablant; [smell] irrespirable.

overpriced /ˌəʊvəˈpraɪst/ adj **it's ~** c'est trop cher pour ce que c'est.

overproduction /ˌəʊvəprəˈdʌkʃn/ n surproduction f.

overqualified /ˌəʊvəˈkwɒlɪfaɪd/ adj surqualifié.

overrate /ˌəʊvəˈreɪt/ vtr surestimer.

overrated /ˌəʊvəˈreɪtɪd/ adj [person, work] surfait; **his films are ~** ses films sont loin d'être aussi bien qu'on le dit.

overreach /ˌəʊvəˈriːtʃ/ v refl **to ~ oneself** se fixer des objectifs trop ambitieux.

overreact /ˌəʊvərɪˈækt/ vi réagir de façon excessive.

override /ˌəʊvəˈraɪd/ vtr (prét **-rode**; pp **-ridden**) **1** (take precedence over) l'emporter sur [consideration]; **2** (quash) passer outre à [decision].

overriding /ˌəʊvəˈraɪdɪŋ/ adj [importance] primordial; [priority] numéro un.

overripe /ˌəʊvəˈraɪp/ adj [fruit] trop mûr, blet/blette; [cheese] trop fait.

overrule /ˌəʊvəˈruːl/ vtr **to be ~d** [decision] être annulé; **I was ~d** mon avis n'a pas prévalu.

overrun /ˈəʊvərʌn/ **I** n FIN dépassement m (**of** de); **cost ~** dépassement m du budget, surcoût m.
II /ˌəʊvəˈrʌn/ vtr (p prés **-nn-**; prét **overran**; pp **overrun**) **1** (invade) envahir [country, site]; **2** (exceed) dépasser [time, budget].
III vi **the lecture overran by an hour** la conférence a duré une heure de plus que prévu.

overseas /ˌəʊvəˈsiːz/ **I** adj **1** (from abroad) [student, investor] étranger/-ère; **2** (in or to other countries) [travel, investment] à l'étranger; [trade, market] extérieur.
II adv (abroad) [work, retire] à l'étranger; (across the sea) outre-mer.

oversee /ˌəʊvəˈsiː/ vtr (prét **-saw**; pp **-seen**) superviser.

oversell /ˌəʊvəˈsel/ vtr (prét, pp **-sold**) trop vanter [idea, plan].

oversensitive /ˌəʊvəˈsensɪtɪv/ adj [personne] trop susceptible.

oversexed○ /ˌəʊvəˈsekst/ adj **to be ~** être un/une obsédé/-e sexuel/-elle.

overshadow /ˌəʊvəˈʃædəʊ/ vtr éclipser [achievement].

overshoe /ˈəʊvəʃuː/ n (rubber) caoutchouc m.

overshoot /ˌəʊvəˈʃuːt/ vtr (prét, pp **-shot**) dépasser.
IDIOMS **to ~ the mark** se planter○.

oversight /ˈəʊvəsaɪt/ n erreur f; (viewed critically) négligence f; **due to an ~** par inadvertance.

oversimplification /ˌəʊvəˌsɪmplɪfɪˈkeɪʃn/ n simplification f excessive.

oversimplify /ˌəʊvəˈsɪmplɪfaɪ/ **I** vtr simplifier [qch] à l'excès.
II oversimplified pp adj simpliste, trop simple.

oversize(d) /ˈəʊvəsaɪzd/ adj GEN énorme.

oversleep /ˌəʊvəˈsliːp/ vi (prét, pp **-slept**) se réveiller trop tard; **I overslept** je ne me suis pas réveillé.

overspend /ˌəʊvəˈspend/ vi (prét, pp **-spent**) trop dépenser.

overspending /ˌəʊvəˈspendɪŋ/ n **ℂ** GEN dépense f excessive; FIN, ADMIN dépassement m budgétaire.

overspill /ˈəʊvəspɪl/ **I** n excédent m de population.
II noun modifier **an ~ (housing) development** une cité de relogement; **~ population** population f excédentaire.

overstaffed /ˌəʊvəˈstɑːft, US -ˈstæft/ adj **to be ~** avoir du personnel en surnombre.

overstaffing /ˌəʊvəˈstɑːfɪŋ, US -ˈstæfɪŋ/ n **is a problem** les sureffectifs sont un problème.

overstate /ˌəʊvəˈsteɪt/ vtr GEN exagérer; **to ~ the case** exagérer; **its importance cannot be ~d** son importance ne saurait être trop soulignée.

overstatement /ˌəʊvəˈsteɪtmənt/ n exagération f.

overstay /ˌəʊvəˈsteɪ/ vtr **to ~ one's visa** dépasser la limite de validité de son visa; **to ~ one's time** ne pas rentrer à temps.

overstep /ˌəʊvəˈstep/ vtr (p prés etc **-pp-**) dépasser [bounds]; **to ~ the mark** aller trop loin.

overstretched /ˌəʊvəˈstretʃt/ adj [budget] excessivement serré; [resources] surexploité; **she is ~** elle a beaucoup trop à faire.

oversubscribed /ˌəʊvəsəbˈskraɪbd/ adj [offer, tickets] en excès de demandes; [share issue] sursouscrit.

overt /ˈəʊvɜːt, US əʊˈvɜːrt/ adj déclaré.

overtake /ˌəʊvəˈteɪk/ (prét **-took**; pp **-taken**) **I** vtr **1** (pass) [vehicle, person] dépasser; **2** FIG [disaster] frapper [project, country]; [storm] surprendre [person]; **to be overtaken by events** être pris de vitesse.
II vi GB dépasser; **'no overtaking'** 'dépassement interdit'.

overtax /ˌəʊvəˈtæks/ **I** vtr **1 to ~ one's brain** se surmener; **to ~ one's heart** fatiguer son cœur; **2** FIN surimposer [taxpayer].

II *v refl* to ~ **oneself** se surmener.

over-the-counter /ˌəʊvəðə'kaʊntə(r)/ **I** *adj* (*épith*) [*medicines*] vendu sans ordonnance.

II *adv* to **sell sth over the counter** vendre qch sans ordonnance.

over-the-top° /ˌəʊvəðə'tɒp/, **OTT** *adj* **1** (*épith*) outrancier/-ière; **2** (*après v*) to **go over the top** aller trop loin.

overthrow /'əʊvəθrəʊ/ **I** *n* renversement *m*.

II /ˌəʊvə'θrəʊ/ *vtr* (*prét* **-threw**; *pp* **-thrown**) renverser [*government, system*].

overtime /'əʊvətaɪm/ **I** *n* (time, money) heures *fpl* supplémentaires.

II *adv* to **work** ~ [*person*] faire des heures supplémentaires.

overtired /ˌəʊvə'taɪəd/ *adj* GEN épuisé; (baby, child) énervé.

overtly /'əʊvɜ:tlɪ, US əʊ'vɜ:tlɪ/ *adv* ouvertement.

overtone /'əʊvətəʊn/ *n* (nuance) sous-entendu *m*, connotation *f*.

overture /'əʊvətjʊə(r)/ *n* **1** MUS ouverture *f* (**to** de); **2** (approach) (*gén pl*) (social) ouverture *f* (**to** à); (business) proposition *f*.

overturn /ˌəʊvə'tɜ:n/ **I** *vtr* **1** (roll over) renverser [*car, chair*]; faire chavirer [*boat*]; **2** (reverse) faire annuler [*decision, sentence*]; casser [*judgment, ruling*]; faire basculer [*majority*].

II *vi* [*car, chair*] se renverser; [*boat*] chavirer.

overvalue /ˌəʊvə'vælju:/ *vtr* FIN surévaluer [*currency, property*].

overview /'əʊvəvju:/ *n* vue *f* d'ensemble (**of** de).

overweening /ˌəʊvə'wi:nɪŋ/ *adj* démesuré.

overweight /ˌəʊvə'weɪt/ *adj* **1** [*person*] trop gros/grosse; to **be** ~ avoir des kilos en trop; **2** [*suitcase*] to **be** ~ être trop lourd; **my case is 10 kilos** ~ j'ai un excédent de bagages de 10 kilos.

overwhelm /ˌəʊvə'welm, US -hwelm/ **I** *vtr* **1** LIT [*wave, avalanche*] submerger; [*enemy*] écraser; **2** FIG [*shame*] accabler; [*grandeur*] impressionner.

II **overwhelmed** *pp adj* (with letters, offers, phone calls, kindness) submergé (**with, by** de); (with shame, unhappiness, work) accablé (**with, by** de); (by sight, experience) ébloui (**by** par); to **be quite** ~**ed** (with emotion) être très ému.

overwhelming /ˌəʊvə'welmɪŋ, US -hwelm-/ *adj* [*defeat, victory, majority, argument, evidence*] écrasant; [*desire*] irrésistible; [*heat, sorrow*] accablant; [*concern, impression*] dominant; [*support*] massif/-ive; [*conviction*] absolu.

overwhelmingly /ˌəʊvə'welmɪŋlɪ, US -hwelm-/ *adv* [*generous*] extraordinairement; [*vote, accept, reject*] à une écrasante majorité; ~ **Protestant** presque exclusivement protestant.

overwork /ˌəʊvəwɜ:k/ **I** *n* surmenage *m*.

II /ˌəʊvə'wɜ:k/ *vtr* surmener [*employee, heart*].

III *vi* se surmener.

overworked /ˌəʊvə'wɜ:kt/ *adj* [*employee*] surmené; [*excuse, word*] éculé.

overwrite /ˌəʊvə'raɪt/ *vtr* (*prét* **-wrote**; *pp* **-written**) COMPUT remplacer [*data, memory*].

overwrought /ˌəʊvə'rɔ:t/ *adj* à bout de nerfs.

ow /aʊ/ *excl* aïe!

owe /əʊ/ *vtr* **1** (be indebted for) devoir [*money, invention, life, success*]; to ~ **sth to sb** devoir qch à qn [*failure, artistic style, money*]; **can I** ~ **it to you?** (borrowing money) est-ce que je peux te le rendre plus tard?; **my mother, to whom I** ~ **so much** ma mère, à qui je dois tant; **I** ~ **you one**° ou **a favour** je te revaudrai ça; **he** ~**s me one**° il me doit bien ça; **2** (be morally bound to give) devoir [*duty, loyalty, explanation*]; **I** ~ **you an apology** je te dois des excuses; **I** ~ **it to yourself to try everything** tu te dois de tout essayer; **he thinks the world** ~**s him a living** il s'imagine que tout lui est dû.

owing /'əʊɪŋ/ **I** *adj* (*après n, après v*) à payer, dû (**for** pour); **£20 is still** ~ il y a encore 20 livres à payer.

II **owing to** *prep phr* en raison de.

owl /aʊl/ *n* hibou *m*; (with tufted ears) chouette *f*.

own /əʊn/ **I** *adj* propre; **her** ~ **car/house/business** sa propre voiture/maison/affaire; **he has his** ~ **ideas about it** il a son idée là-dessus; **he has his** ~ **problems** il a assez de problèmes comme ça; **he's very nice in his** ~ **way** il est très gentil à sa manière; **the house has its** ~ **garage/garden** c'est une maison avec garage/jardin (privatif); **she does her** ~ **cooking** c'est elle qui se fait à manger; **he makes his** ~ **decisions** il prend ses décisions tout seul.

II *pron* **my** ~ le mien, la mienne; **his/her** ~ le sien, la sienne; **they have problems of their** ~ ils ont assez de problèmes comme ça; **when you have children of your** ~ quand tu auras des enfants; **he has a room of his** ~ il a sa propre chambre; **a house of our (very)** ~ une maison (bien) à nous; **my time's not my** ~ je n'ai pas une minute à moi.

III *vtr* **1** (possess) avoir [*car, house, dog*]; **she** ~**s three shops** elle est propriétaire de trois magasins; **who** ~**s that house?** à qui est cette maison?; **he walks around as if he** ~**s the place** il se conduit comme s'il était chez lui; **2** (admit) reconnaître, avouer.

IV *vi* to ~ **to misgivings** avouer son appréhension.

IDIOMS to **come into one's** ~ s'épanouir FIG; to **do one's** ~ **thing** être indépendant; **each to his** ~ chacun son goût°; to **get one's** ~ **back** se venger (**on sb** de qn); to **hold one's** ~ bien se défendre; **on one's** ~ tout seul; to **get sb on their** ~ voir qn en privé.

■ **own up** avouer; to ~ **up to the murder** avouer avoir commis le meurtre.

owner /'əʊnə(r)/ *n* propriétaire *mf*; **car** ~ automobiliste *mf*; **home** ~ propriétaire *mf*; **previous** ~ ancien/-ienne propriétaire; **proud** ~ heureux/-euse propriétaire; **rightful** ~ possesseur *m* légitime.

owner: ~**-driver** *n* conducteur/-trice *m/f* propriétaire; ~**-occupied** *adj* occupé par le propriétaire; ~**-occupier** *n* propriétaire *mf* occupant/-e.

ownership /'əʊnəʃɪp/ *n* propriété *f*; (of land) possession *f*; **joint** ~ copropriété *f*; to **be in private** ~ appartenir à une personne privée; **share** ~ participation *f* dans le capital d'une société; to **take into public** ~ nationaliser; **'under new** ~**'** 'changement de propriétaire'; **home** ~ **is increasing** le nombre de personnes propriétaires de leur logement augmente; to **provide proof of** ~ prouver qu'on est propriétaire.

ox /ɒks/ *n* (*pl* ~**en**) bœuf *m*.

IDIOMS **as strong as an** ~ fort comme un bœuf.

oxblood *adj* [*shoes, polish*] rouge foncé *m inv*.

Oxbridge /'ɒksbrɪdʒ/ *n* universités *fpl* d'Oxford et de Cambridge.

ox cart *n* char *m* à bœufs.

oxen /'ɒksn/ *pl* ▶ **ox**.

oxfords /'ɒksfədz/ *npl* chaussures *fpl* d'homme (*basses, à lacets et bouts renforcés*).

oxidize /'ɒksɪdaɪz/ **I** *vtr* oxyder.

II *vi* s'oxyder.

Oxon /'ɒksən/ **1** GB POST *abrév écrite* = **Oxfordshire**; **2** GB UNIV (*abrév écrite* = **Oxoniensis**) d'Oxford.

oxygen /'ɒksɪdʒən/ **I** *n* oxygène *m*.

II *noun modifier* [*bottle, supply, tank*] d'oxygène; [*mask, tent*] à oxygène.

oyster /'ɔɪstə(r)/ **I** *n* (fish) huître *f*.

II *noun modifier* [*knife*] à huîtres; [*sauce*] aux huîtres; [*shell*] d'huître.

IDIOMS **the world's your** ~ le monde est à toi.

oyster: ~ **bed** *n* banc *m* d'huîtres; ~ **cracker** *n* US petit biscuit *m* salé; ~ **farm** *n* parc *m* à huîtres.

oz *abrév écrite* = **ounce(s)**.

ozone /'əʊzəʊn/ *n* **1** CHEM ozone *m*; **2**° (sea air) air *m* pur marin.

ozone: ~ **depletion** *n* destruction *f* de la couche d'ozone; ~ **layer** *n* couche *f* d'ozone.

Pp

p, P /piː/ *n* **1** (letter) p, P *m*; **2 p** GB (*abrév* = **penny, pence**) (nouveau) penny *m*, (nouveaux) pence *mpl*. IDIOMS **to mind one's p's and q's** veiller aux convenances.

p.a. (*abrév écrite* = **per annum**) par an.

PA 1 (*abrév* = **personal assistant**) secrétaire *mf* de direction; **2** US POST *abrév écrite* = **Pennsylvania**.

pace /peɪs/ **I** *n* (short stride, unit of measurement) pas *m*; (rate of movement) (of person walking, of life) rythme *m*; **at a fast/slow ~** vite/lentement; **to quicken one's ~** presser le pas; **to keep ~ with developments** rester à la page; **I can't stand the ~** LIT, FIG je n'arrive pas à suivre; **to step up/slow the ~** accélérer/ralentir le rythme; **to set the ~** FIG donner le ton.
II *vtr* arpenter [*cage, room*].
III *vi* **to ~ up and down** (impatiently) faire les cent pas; **to ~ up and down sth** arpenter qch.
IDIOMS **to put sb through their ~s** mettre qn à l'épreuve.

pacemaker /ˈpeɪsmeɪkə(r)/ *n* **1** MED stimulateur *m* cardiaque; **2** (athlete) lièvre *m*.

pacesetter /ˈpeɪssetə(r)/ *n* (athlete) lièvre *m*; (leader, inspiration) locomotive *f*.

pacific /pəˈsɪfɪk/ *adj* pacifique.

Pacific /pəˈsɪfɪk/ ▶ 1117 | *pr n* **the ~** le Pacifique.

Pacific: **~ Ocean** *n* océan *m* Pacifique; **~ Standard Time, PST** *n* heure *f* du Pacifique.

pacifier /ˈpæsɪfaɪə(r)/ *n* US (for baby) tétine *f*, sucette *f*.

pacifist /ˈpæsɪfɪst/ *n, adj* pacifiste (*mf*).

pacify /ˈpæsɪfaɪ/ *vtr* apaiser [*person*].

pack /pæk/ **I** *n* **1** US (container) (box) paquet *m*; (large box) boîte *f*; (bag) sachet *m*; **2** (group) meute *f*; **3** (in rugby) pack *m*; **4** (of scouts) section *f*; **5** (backpack) sac *m* à dos; (carried by animal) ballot *m*.
II -**pack** *combining form* **a four-~** (of cassettes) un lot de quatre; (of beer) un pack de quatre.
III *vtr* **1** (stow) (in suitcase) mettre [qch] dans une valise [*clothes*]; (in box, crate) emballer [*ornaments, books*]; **2** (put things into) emballer [*box, crate*]; **to ~ one's suitcase** faire sa valise; **to ~ one's bags** LIT, FIG faire ses valises; **3** (package commercially) conditionner [*fruit, meat, goods*]; **4** (cram into) [*crowd*] remplir complètement [*church, theatre*]; **to be ~ed with** être bondé de [*people*]; être plein de [*ideas*]; **5** (press firmly) tasser [*snow, earth*].
IV *vi* **1** (get ready for departure) [*person*] faire ses valises; **2** (crowd) **to ~ into** s'entasser dans [*place*].
IDIOMS **a ~ of lies** un tissu de mensonges; **to send sb ~ing** envoyer promener qn.
■ **pack in**: **~ [sth] in, ~ in [sth] 1** (cram in) entasser [*people*]; **2**○ (give up) plaquer○ [*job, boyfriend*]; **~ it in!** arrête!, ça suffit!
■ **pack off**: **~ [sb] off, ~ off [sb]** expédier.
■ **pack up**: **¶ ~ up 1** (prepare to go) [*person*] faire ses valises○; **2**○ (break down) [*TV, machine*] se détraquer○; [*car*] tomber en panne; [*heart, liver*] lâcher○; **¶ ~ [sth] up, ~ up [sth]** (put away) ranger [*books*]; (in boxes, crates) emballer [*books, objects*].

package /ˈpækɪdʒ/ **I** *n* **1** (parcel) paquet *m*, colis *m*; **2** (collection) (of reforms, measures, proposals) ensemble *m* (**of** de); **part of the ~** compris dans le prix; **3** COMPUT progiciel *m*.
II *vtr* **1** (put into packaging) emballer [*goods, object*];

2 (design image for) concevoir un conditionnement pour [*product*]; présenter [*policy, proposal*].

package: **~ deal** *n* offre *f* globale; **~ holiday** GB, **~ tour** *n* voyage *m* organisé.

packaging /ˈpækɪdʒɪŋ/ *n* **1** COMM (materials) emballage *m*; **2** (promotion) (of product) conditionnement *m*; (of policy, film, singer) image *f* publique.

packed /pækt/ *adj* (crowded) comble; **~ with** plein de; **I'm ~** j'ai fait mes valises.

packed lunch *n* panier-repas *m*.

packer /ˈpækə(r)/ *n* IND (person) emballeur/-euse *m/f*; (machine) emballeuse *f*.

packet /ˈpækɪt/ **I** *n* (box) paquet *m*; (bag) sachet *m*; (parcel) paquet *m*; (for drinks) brique *f*.
II *noun modifier* [*soup*] en sachet; [*drink*] en brique.
IDIOMS **to cost a ~**○ coûter un argent fou○.

pack ice *n* pack *m*, banquise *f*.

packing /ˈpækɪŋ/ *n* **1** COMM emballage *m*; **2 to do one's ~** faire ses valises; **3** TECH garniture *f* d'étanchéité; ▶ **postage**.

packing: **~ case** *n* caisse *f* d'emballage; **~ density** *n* COMPUT densité *f* d'enregistrement.

pact /pækt/ *n* GEN, POL pacte *m*; **to make a ~ to do** se mettre d'accord pour faire.

pad /pæd/ **I** *n* **1** (of paper) bloc *m*; **2** (to prevent chafing) protection *f*; (to absorb liquid) tampon *m*; (to give shape) rembourrage *m*; **3** (sticky part on object, plant) ventouse *f*; **4** (of paw) coussinet *m*; (of finger) pulpe *f*; **5** (sanitary towel) serviette *f* hygiénique; **6** SPORT (in general) protection *f*; (for leg) jambière *f*; **7** (also **launch ~**) rampe *f* de lancement.
II *vtr* (*p prés etc* -**dd-**) **1** (put padding in, on) rembourrer [*chair, shoulders, jacket*] (**with** avec); capitonner [*walls, floor, large surface*]; **to ~ a wound with cotton wool** mettre un tampon de coton sur une plaie; **2** (make longer) = **pad out**.
III *vi* (*p prés etc* -**dd-**) **to ~ along/around** avancer/aller et venir à pas feutrés.
■ **pad out**: **~ out [sth], ~ [sth] out 1** FIG étoffer, délayer PEJ [*essay, speech*] (**with** à l'aide de); allonger [*meal, dish*] (**with** avec); **2** LIT rembourrer [*garment*].

padded: **~ cell** *n* cellule *f* capitonnée; **~ envelope** *n* enveloppe *f* matelassée.

padding /ˈpædɪŋ/ *n* **1** (stuffing) rembourrage *m*; (on large surface) capitonnage *m*; **2** (in speech, essay) remplissage *m*.

paddle /ˈpædl/ **I** *n* **1** (oar) pagaie *f*; **2** US SPORT raquette *f* de ping-pong®; **3 to go for a ~** faire trempette *f*.
II *vtr* **1** (row) **to ~ a canoe** pagayer; **2** (dip) agiter [*feet, fingers*] (**in** dans); **3** US donner une fessée à.
III *vi* **1** (row) pagayer; **2** (wade) patauger; **3** [*duck, swan*] barboter.

paddling pool *n* (public) pataugeoire *f*; (inflatable) piscine *f* gonflable.

paddock /ˈpædək/ *n* (field) paddock *m*.

paddy: **~ field** *n* rizière *f*; **~ wagon**○ *n* US panier *m* à salade○.

padlock /ˈpædlɒk/ **I** *n* GEN cadenas *m*; (for bicycle) antivol *m*.
II *vtr* cadenasser [*door, gate*]; mettre un antivol à [*bicycle*].

paediatric *adj* = **pediatric**.

pagan /ˈpeɪɡən/ *n, adj* païen/païenne (*m/f*).

page /peɪdʒ/ **I** n **1** (in book) page f; **on ~ two** à la page deux; **2** COMPUT page-écran f; **3** (attendant) groom m; US coursier m; HIST page m.
II vtr (on pager) rechercher; (over loudspeaker) faire appeler; **'paging Mr Jones'** 'on demande M. Jones'.

pageant /'pædʒənt/ n (play) reconstitution f historique; (carnival) fête f à thème historique.

pageantry /'pædʒəntrɪ/ n pompe f.

page: ~boy n (bride's attendant) garçon m d'honneur; **~ break** n COMPUT fin f de page; **~ number** n numéro m de page; **~ proof** n tierce f.

pager /'peɪdʒə(r)/ n TELECOM récepteur m d'appel.

page: ~ reference n page f; **~ set-up** n COMPUT mise f en page; **~ three** n GB page f des pin-up.

paging /'peɪdʒɪŋ/ n COMPUT pagination f.

paid /peɪd/ **I** prét, pp ▶ **pay**.
II adj [job] rémunéré; [holiday] payé; **~ assassin** tueur m à gages.
IDIOMS **to put ~ to sth** GB mettre un terme à qch.

paid: ~-up adj GB [payment, instalment] à jour; [share, capital] remboursé; **~-up member** n GB adhérent/-e m/f.

pail /peɪl/ n seau m (of de).

pain /peɪn/ **I** n **1** GEN, MED douleur f; **to feel ~, to be in ~** souffrir; **he's caused me a lot of ~** il m'a fait beaucoup souffrir; **period ~s** règles fpl douloureuses; **where is the ~?** où avez-vous mal?; **2**○ (annoying person, thing) **she can be a real ~** elle peut être très enquiquinante○; **it's a real ~** c'est très enquiquinant○; **he's a ~ in the neck**○ il est casse-pieds○; **3 on ~ of death** sous peine de mort.
II pains npl **to be at ~s to do sth** prendre grand soin de faire qch; **to take great ~s over** ou **with sth** se donner beaucoup de mal pour faire qch.
III vtr **1** (hurt) **my leg ~s me a little** ma jambe me fait un peu mal; **2** SOUT (grieve) chagriner.
IV pained pp adj **with a ~ed expression** d'un air affligé.

painful /'peɪnfl/ adj **1** (injury, swelling etc) douloureux/-euse; FIG [lesson, progress, memory, reminder, task] pénible; [blow] dur; **2**○ (bad) lamentable.

painfully /'peɪnfəlɪ/ adv **1** (excruciatingly) **his arm is ~ swollen** son bras est enflé et lui fait mal; **to be ~ shy** être d'une timidité maladive; **I am ~ aware of that** je n'en ai que trop conscience; **2** FIG **progress has been ~ slow** les progrès ont été terriblement lents.

painkiller n analgésique m.

painless /'peɪnlɪs/ adj **1** [operation, injection] indolore; [death] sans souffrance; **2** (trouble-free) sans peine.

painlessly /'peɪnlɪslɪ/ adv LIT sans douleur; (easily) sans trop de mal.

painstaking /'peɪnzteɪkɪŋ/ adj minutieux/-ieuse.

paint /peɪnt/ **I** n GEN, ART peinture f; **'wet ~'** 'peinture fraîche'.
II paints npl ART couleurs fpl.
III vtr **1** LIT peindre [wall, subject]; peindre le portrait de [person]; **to ~ sth on** appliquer [varnish, undercoat]; **to ~ sth out** peindre par-dessus qch; **to ~ one's nails** se vernir les ongles; **2** FIG (depict) dépeindre; **3** MED badigeonner [cut, wound] (**with** de).
IV vi peindre.
IDIOMS **to ~ the town red** faire la noce.

paint: ~box n boîte f de couleurs; **~brush** n pinceau m.

painter /'peɪntə(r)/ ▶ **1251** **1** n **1** (artist, workman) peintre m; **2** NAUT amarre f.

painting /'peɪntɪŋ/ n **1** ¢ (activity, art form) peinture f; **2** (work of art) tableau m; (unframed) toile f; (of person) portrait m; **3** ¢ (decorating) peintures fpl.

paint: ~pot n pot m de peinture; **~ remover** n (for removing stains) solvant m; **~ roller** n rouleau m à peinture; **~ spray** n bombe f de peinture; **~ stripper** n (chemical) décapant m; (tool) racloir m; **~ tray** n bac m à peinture; **~work** n ¢ GEN peintures fpl; (on car) peinture f.

pair /peə(r)/ **I** n **1** (two matching items) paire f; **to be one of a ~** faire partie d'une paire; **to work in ~s** travailler en groupes de deux; **these gloves are not a ~** ces gants sont dépareillés; **2** (two people, animals etc) (sexually attached) couple m; (grouped together) paire f; **a coach and ~** une voiture à deux chevaux.
II pairs noun modifier SPORT [competition, final] pour équipes de deux.
III vtr ranger par deux [gloves, socks]; **to ~ Paul with Julie** mettre Paul avec Julie; **to ~ each name with a photograph** associer chaque nom à une photo.
■ **pair off** (as a couple) se mettre ensemble; (for temporary purposes) se mettre par deux.
■ **pair up** [dancers, lovers] former un couple; [competitors] faire équipe.

paisley /'peɪzlɪ/ n tissu m à motifs cachemire.

pajamas npl US = **pyjamas**.

Pakistani /ˌpɑːkɪ'stɑːnɪ, ˌpækɪ-/ ▶ **1100** **I** n Pakistanais/-e m/f.
II adj pakistanais.

pal○ /pæl/ n copain○/copine○ m/f.

PAL /pæl/ n TV (abrév = **phase alternative line**) PAL m.

palace /'pælɪs/ n (of monarch) palais m; (of bishop) évêché m.

palatable /'pælətəbl/ n [food] savoureux; [solution, law] acceptable.

palate /'pælət/ n palais m; **too sweet for my ~** trop sucré à mon goût.

palatial /pə'leɪʃl/ adj immense.

palaver○ /pə'lɑːvə(r), US '-læv-/ n **1** (bother) bazar○ m; **2** (talks) discussion f.

pale /peɪl/ **I** adj [colour, complexion] pâle; [light, dawn] blafard; **to turn** ou **go ~** pâlir.
II vi LIT pâlir; FIG **to ~ into insignificance** devenir dérisoire.
IDIOMS **to be beyond the ~** [remark, behaviour] être inadmissible; [person] être infréquentable.

Palestine Liberation Organization, PLO n Organisation f de Libération de la Palestine.

palette /'pælɪt/ n (object, colours) palette f.

palette knife n **1** ART couteau m à palette; **2** CULIN palette f.

paling /'peɪlɪŋ/ **I** n (stake) palis m.
II palings npl (fence) palissade f.

palisade /ˌpælɪ'seɪd/ **I** n (fence) palissade f.
II palisades npl US muraille f de falaises à pic.

pall /pɔːl/ **I** n **1** (coffin-cloth) drap m mortuaire; (coffin) cercueil m; **2** FIG (of smoke, dust) nuage m; (of gloom, mystery, silence) manteau m.
II vi **it never ~s** on ne s'en lasse jamais.

pallet /'pælɪt/ n (for loading) palette f.

palliative /'pælɪətɪv/ adj **I** n GEN, MED palliatif m.
II adj GEN, MED palliatif/-ive m/f.

pallid /'pælɪd/ adj [skin, light] blafard.

pallor /'pælə(r)/ n pâleur f.

palm /pɑːm/ **I** n **1** (of hand) paume f; **in the ~ of one's hand** dans le creux de la main; **he read my ~** il m'a lu les lignes de la main; **2** BOT (plant) (also **~ tree**) palmier m; (branch) branche f de palmier; (leaf) palme f; **3** RELIG rameau m.
II vtr escamoter [card, coin]; subtiliser [money].
IDIOMS **you have him in the ~ of your hand!** tu pourrais lui faire faire tout ce que tu veux!
■ **palm off**○: **~ [sth] off, ~ off [sth]** faire passer qch (**as** pour); **to ~ sth off on sb, to ~ sb off with sth** refiler○ qch à qn.

palmistry /'pɑːmɪstrɪ/ n chiromancie f.

Palm Sunday n dimanche m des Rameaux.

palmy /'pɑːmɪ/ adj **in the ~ days of sth** aux beaux jours de qch.

palpable /'pælpəbl/ adj [fear, tension] palpable; [lie, error, nonsense] manifeste.

palpitate /'pælpɪteɪt/ vi (all contexts) palpiter (**with** de).

paltry /'pɔːltrɪ/ adj [sum] dérisoire; [excuse] piètre.

pampas /'pæmpəs, US -əz/ n (+ v sg) pampa f.

pamper /'pæmpə(r)/ **I** *vtr* choyer [*person, pet*].
II *v refl* **to ~ oneself** se bichonner○.

pamphlet /'pæmflɪt/ *n* GEN brochure *f*; (political) tract *m*; HIST (satirical) pamphlet *m*.

pan /pæn/ **I** *n* **1** CULIN (saucepan) casserole *f*; **heat up a ~ of water** faites bouillir de l'eau dans une casserole; **2** (on scales) plateau *m*; **3** (in lavatory) cuvette *f*.
II *vtr* (*p prés etc* **-nn-**) **1**○ (criticize) éreinter; **2** CIN, PHOT, TV faire un panoramique de.
III *vi* **1** PHOT (*p prés etc* **-nn-**) [*camera*] faire un panoramique; **2** (prospect) **to ~ for** chercher [*gold*].
IV Pan+ *combining form* **Pan-American** panaméricain/-aine; **Pan-African** panafricain/-aine.
■ **pan out** (turn out) marcher; (turn out well) s'arranger.

pancake /'pænkeɪk/ *n* **1** CULIN crêpe *f*; **2** THEAT (makeup) fond *m* de teint.
IDIOMS **as flat as a ~**○ plat comme une galette.

pancake: **~ day** *n* mardi *m* gras; **~ filling** *n* garniture *f* pour crêpes.

panda car○ *n* GB voiture *f* pie.

pandemonium /ˌpændɪ'məʊnɪəm/ *n* tohu-bohu *m*.

pander /'pændə(r)/ *vi* **to ~ to** céder aux exigences de [*person*]; flatter [*whim*].

pane /peɪn/ *n* vitre *f*, carreau *m*; **a ~ of glass** une vitre, un carreau.

panel /'pænl/ **I** *n* **1** (of experts, judges) commission *f*; TV, RADIO (on discussion programme) invités *mpl*; (on quiz show) jury *m*; **to be on a ~** (of experts) être membre d'un comité; TV, RADIO faire partie d'un jury; **2** ARCHIT, CONSTR (section of wall) panneau *m*; **3** AUT, TECH (section) panneau *m*; (of instruments, switches) tableau *m*.
II *vtr* (*p prés etc* **-ll-**, **-l-** US) recouvrir [qch] de panneaux.
III panelled, **paneled** US *pp adj* [*fencing*] en panneaux; [*wall, ceiling*] lambrissé; [*bath*] cloisonné.

panel: **~ beater** ▶ 1251 *n* tôlier *m*; **~ discussion** *n* RADIO, TV débat *m*; **~ game** *n* RADIO jeu *m* radiophonique; TV jeu *m* télévisé.

panelling, **paneling** US /'pænəlɪŋ/ *n* lambris *m*.

panellist, **panelist** US /'pænəlɪst/ *n* RADIO, TV invité/-e *m/f*.

panel truck *n* US camionnette *f*.

pan-fry /'pænfraɪ/ *vtr* faire sauter.

pang /pæŋ/ *n* **1** (emotional) serrement *m* de cœur; **a ~ of jealousy** une pointe de jalousie; **~s of conscience** ou **guilt** remords *mpl* de conscience; **2** (physical) **~s of hunger** crampes *fpl* d'estomac; **birth ~s** FIG difficultés *fpl* initiales.

panhandler○ /'pænhændlə(r)/ *n* US mendiant/-e *m/f*.

panic /'pænɪk/ **I** *n* affolement *m*; **to get into a ~** s'affoler (**about** à cause de); **to throw sb into a ~** affoler qn.
II *noun modifier* [*decision*] pris dans un moment de panique; [*reaction*] de panique.
III *vtr* (*p prés etc* **-ck-**) affoler [*person, animal*]; semer la panique dans [*crowd*]; **to be ~ked into doing** se laisser affoler et faire.
IV *vi* (*p prés etc* **-ck-**) s'affoler; **don't ~!** pas de panique!

panic: **~ button** *n* signal *m* d'alarme; **~ buying** *n* ¢ achats *mpl* par crainte de la pénurie.

panicky /'pænɪkɪ/ *adj* affolé.

panic: **~ measure** *n* POL, ECON disposition *f* précipitée; **~ selling** *n* ¢ FIN mouvements *mpl* de panique chez les petits porteurs.

pannier /'pænɪə(r)/ *n* (on bike) sacoche *f*; (on mule) panier *m* de bât.

pan scourer, **pan scrubber** *n* tampon *m* à récurer.

pansy /'pænzɪ/ *n* BOT pensée *f*.

pant /pænt/ **I** *n* halètement *m*.
II *vtr* = **pant out**.
III *vi* haleter; **to be ~ing for breath** être tout essoufflé.

■ **pant out**: **~ out** [sth], **~** [sth] **out** dire [qch] d'une voix haletante.

panther /'pænθə(r)/ *n* **1** (leopard) panthère *f*; **2** US (puma) puma *m*.

panties /'pæntɪz/ ▶ 1260 *npl* slip *m* (de femme).

pantomime /'pæntəmaɪm/ *n* **1** GB THEAT spectacle *m* pour enfants (*à Noël*); **2** (mime) mime *m*.

pantry /'pæntrɪ/ *n* **1** (larder) garde-manger *m inv*; **2** (butler's etc) office *m*.

pants /pænts/ ▶ 1260 *npl* **1** US (trousers) pantalon *m*; GB (underwear) slip *m*.
IDIOMS **to bore the ~ off sb**○ faire mourir d'ennui qn; **to scare the ~ off sb**○ flanquer la trouille à qn○; **to catch sb with his/her ~ down**○ prendre qn au dépourvu; **to fly by the seat of one's ~** [*pilot*] naviguer à l'instinct.

pantsuit /'pæntsuːt, -sjuːt/ *n* US tailleur-pantalon *m*.

panty: **~ girdle** *n* gaine-culotte *f*; **~ hose** *n* ¢ collant *m*; **~-liner** *n* protège-slip *m*.

papacy /'peɪpəsɪ/ *n* papauté *f*.

papal /'peɪpl/ *adj* papal, pontifical.

paper /'peɪpə(r)/ **I** *n* **1** (substance) (for writing etc) papier *m*; **to put sth down on ~** mettre qch par écrit; **it's a good idea on ~** FIG c'est une bonne idée en théorie; **this contract isn't worth the ~ it's written on** ce contrat ne vaut absolument rien; **2** (also **wall~**) papier *m* peint; **3** (newspaper) journal *m*; **4** (scholarly article) article *m* (**on** sur); (lecture) communication *f* (**on** sur); (report) exposé *m* (**on** sur); **5** (examination) épreuve *f* (**on** de); **6** FIN effet *f* de commerce; **7** (government publication) livre *m*.
II papers *npl* ADMIN papiers *mpl*.
III *noun modifier* **1** LIT [*bag, hat, handkerchief, napkin*] en papier; [*plate, cup*] en carton; [*industry*] du papier; [*manufacture*] de papier; **2** FIG [*loss, profit*] théorique; [*promise, agreement*] sans valeur.
IV *vtr* (also **wall~**) tapisser [*room, wall*].
V *vi* **to ~ over the existing wallpaper** recouvrir le papier actuel; **to ~ over one's differences** passer sur ses différences.
IDIOMS **to ~ over the cracks** passer les problèmes.

paperback /'peɪpəbæk/ **I** *n* livre *m* de poche.
II *noun modifier* [*edition, version*] de poche.

paper: **~ bank** *n* conteneur *m* de récupération de vieux papiers; **~ boy** *n* livreur *m* de journaux; **~ chain** *n* guirlande *f* de papier; **~ chase** *n* jeu *m* de piste; **~clip** *n* trombone *m*; **~ currency** *n* monnaie *f* de papier; **~ fastener** *n* attache *f* parisienne; **~ feed tray** *n* COMPUT bac *m* d'alimentation en papier; **~ knife** *n* coupe-papier *m inv*.

paperless /'peɪpəlɪs/ *adj* COMPUT [*office*] électronique; [*system*] informatisé.

paper: **~ mill** *n* papeterie *f*; **~ qualifications** *npl* diplômes *mpl*.

paper round *n* **he has** ou **does a ~** il livre des journaux.

paper: **~ shop** *n* marchand *m* de journaux; **~ shredder** *n* déchiqueteuse *f* à papier; **~ tape** *n* COMPUT bande *f* perforée; **~ thin** *adj* mince comme du papier à cigarette; **~ towel** *n* essuie-tout *m inv*; **~weight** *n* presse-papier *m inv*; **~work** *n* (administration) travail *m* administratif; (documentation) documents *mpl*.

papery /'peɪpərɪ/ *adj* [*texture, leaves*] mince comme du papier; [*skin*] parcheminé.

Papua New Guinea /ˌpæpʊə njuː 'gɪniː, US nuː-/ ▶ 840 *pr n* Papouasie-Nouvelle-Guinée *f*.

par /pɑː(r)/ *n* **1** GEN **to be on a ~ with** [*performance*] être comparable à; [*person*] être l'égal de; **to be up to ~** être à la hauteur; **to be below** ou **under ~** [*performance*] être en dessous de la moyenne; [*person*] ne pas se sentir en forme; **2** (in golf) par *m*; **3** ECON, FIN pair *m*.
IDIOMS **to be ~ for the course** être typique.

para /'pærə/ *n* **1** *abrév écrite* = **paragraph**; **2**○ GB MIL (*abrév* = **paratrooper**) para○ *m*.

parable /ˈpærəbl/ n parabole f.

parachute /ˈpærəʃuːt/ I n parachute m.
II vtr parachuter.
III vi descendre en parachute.

parachute: ~ **drop** n parachutage m; ~ **jump** n saut m en parachute.

parachuting /ˈpærəʃuːtɪŋ/ ▶949 n to go ~ faire du parachutisme.

parade /pəˈreɪd/ I n 1 (procession) parade f; 2 MIL (march) défilé m; (review) prise f d'armes; (in barracks) appel m; **to be on** ~ être à l'exercice; 3 (display) (of designs) défilé m; (of ideas) souvent péj étalage m; 4 GB (row) **a** ~ **of shops** une rangée de magasins.
II vtr 1 (display) faire étalage de; 2 (claim) **to** ~ **sth as sth** présenter qch comme qch.
III vi 1 (march) défiler (**through** dans) ; **to** ~ **up and down** [soldier, model] défiler; [child, person] parader.

parade ground n champ m de manœuvres.

paradise /ˈpærədaɪs/ n paradis m; **in** ~ au paradis.

paradox /ˈpærədɒks/ n paradoxe m.

paradoxical /ˌpærəˈdɒksɪkl/ adj paradoxal.

paraffin /ˈpærəfɪn/ I n 1 GB (fuel) pétrole m; 2 (also ~ **wax**) paraffine f.
II noun modifier GB [lamp, heater] à pétrole.

paragliding /ˈpærəˌglaɪdɪŋ/ ▶949 n parapente m.

paragon /ˈpærəgən, US -gɒn/ n modèle m (**of** de).

paragraph /ˈpærəgrɑːf, US -græf/ I n 1 (section) paragraphe m; **new** ~ (in dictation) à la ligne; 2 (article) entrefilet m.

parallel /ˈpærəlel/ I n 1 MATH parallèle f; 2 (comparison) parallèle m; **to be on a** ~ **with sth** être comparable à qch; **without** ~ sans pareil; 3 GEOG parallèle m.
II adj 1 COMPUT, MATH parallèle; 2 (similar) analogue (**to, with** à); 3 (simultaneous) parallèle.
III adv ~ **to,** ~ **with** parallèlement à.
IV vtr (p prés GB **-ll-,** US **-l-**) (equal) égaler; (find a comparison) trouver un équivalent à.

parallel: ~ **processing** n COMPUT traitement m en parallèle; ~ **turn** n SPORT virage m parallèle.

paralyse GB, **paralyze** US /ˈpærəlaɪz/ vtr MED, FIG paralyser.

paralysis /pəˈræləsɪs/ n MED, FIG paralysie f.

paralytic /ˌpærəˈlɪtɪk/ adj 1 MED [person] paralytique; [arm, leg] paralysé; 2° GB (drunk) complètement bourré°.

paramedic /ˌpærəˈmedɪk/ ▶1251 n auxiliaire mf médical/-e.

parameter /pəˈræmɪtə(r)/ n paramètre m; **within the** ~**s of** FIG dans les limites de.

paramilitary /ˌpærəˈmɪlɪtrɪ, US -terɪ/ I n membre m d'une organisation paramilitaire.
II adj paramilitaire.

paramount /ˈpærəmaʊnt/ adj [consideration, goal] suprême; **to be** ~, **to be of** ~ **importance** être d'une importance capitale.

paranoid /ˈpærənɔɪd/ I n paranoïaque mf.
II adj 1 PSYCH paranoïde; 2 (suspicious) paranoïaque (**about** au sujet de); **to be** ~ **about being burgled** avoir une peur maladive d'être cambriolé.

parapet /ˈpærəpɪt/ n ARCHIT, MIL parapet m.

paraphernalia /ˌpærəfəˈneɪlɪə/ n (+ v sg) 1 (articles, accessories) attirail m; 2 GB (rigmarole) comédie° f.

paraphrase /ˈpærəfreɪz/ I n paraphrase f.
II vtr paraphraser.

paraplegic /ˌpærəˈpliːdʒɪk/ I n paraplégique mf.
II adj [person] paraplégique; [games] pour les paraplégiques.

parascending /ˈpærəsendɪŋ/ n GB parachutisme m ascensionnel.

parasite /ˈpærəsaɪt/ n LIT, FIG parasite m.

paratrooper /ˈpærətruːpə(r)/ n parachutiste m.

parboil /ˈpɑːbɔɪl/ vtr faire cuire [qch] à demi.

parcel /ˈpɑːsl/ n 1 GEN, FIN paquet m; 2° (of people, problems) tas° m.

IDIOMS **to be part and** ~ **of** faire partie intégrante de.
■ **parcel out:** ~ **out** [sth], ~ [sth] **out** répartir.
■ **parcel up:** ~ **up** [sth], ~ [sth] **up** emballer.

parcel: ~ **bomb** n colis m piégé; ~ **office** n (bureau m des) messageries fpl; ~ **post** n service m de colis postaux; ~**s service** n société f d'expédition des colis postaux.

parched /pɑːtʃt/ adj 1 [earth] desséché; 2 **to be** ~° mourir de soif.

parchment /ˈpɑːtʃmənt/ n (document) parchemin m; (paper) papier-parchemin m.

pardon /ˈpɑːdn/ I n 1 GEN pardon m; **to beg sb's** ~ demander pardon à qn; 2 JUR (also **free** ~) grâce f.
II excl (what?) pardon?; (sorry!) pardon!
III vtr GEN pardonner; JUR grâcier [criminal].

pare /peə(r)/ vtr peler [apple]; rogner [nails].
IDIOMS **to** ~ **sth to the bone** réduire qch au minimum vital.
■ **pare off:** ~ [sth] **off,** ~ **off** [sth] peler [rind, peel]; réduire [amount, percentage].

pared-down /ˌpeəd ˈdaʊn/ adj [budget] réduit; [version] abrégé; [prose, plot] dépouillé.

parent /ˈpeərənt/ n 1 (of child) parent m; **as a** ~ en ma/votre etc qualité de parent; 2 COMM (company) maison f mère; (organization) organisation f mère.

parentage /ˈpeərəntɪdʒ/ n ascendance f.

parental /pəˈrentl/ adj parental FML, des parents.

parent: ~ **company** n maison f mère; ~**-governor** n GB SCH membre du conseil d'établissement et représentant des parents d'élèves.

parenthesis /pəˈrenθəsɪs/ n (pl **-eses**) parenthèse f.

parenthood /ˈpeərənthʊd/ n (fatherhood) paternité f; (motherhood) maternité f.

parenting /ˈpeərəntɪŋ/ n éducation f des enfants.

parent: ~ **organization** n organisation f mère; ~ **power** n SCH pouvoir m décisionnel des parents d'élèves; ~**s' evening** n SCH réunion f pour les parents d'élèves; ~**-teacher association** n ▶ PTA.

parer /ˈpeərə(r)/ n épluche-légumes m inv.

parings /ˈpeərɪŋz/ npl 1 (of fruit) épluchures fpl; 2 (of nails) rognures fpl.

Paris /ˈpærɪs/ ▶1343 I pr n Paris.
II noun modifier [fashion, metro, restaurant] parisien/-ienne.

parish /ˈpærɪʃ/ I n 1 RELIG paroisse f; 2 GB (administrative) commune f.
II noun modifier [church, hall, meeting, register] paroissial.

parishioner /pəˈrɪʃənə(r)/ n paroissien/-ienne m/f.

parish priest n (Protestant) pasteur m; (Catholic) curé m.

Parisian /pəˈrɪzɪən/ I n Parisien/-ienne m/f.
II adj parisien/-ienne.

parity /ˈpærɪtɪ/ n (equality) parité f (**with** avec).

park /pɑːk/ I n 1 (public garden) jardin m public; 2 (estate) parc m also Comm, IND; 3 GB (pitch) terrain m; US (stadium) stade m; 4 (on automatic gearbox) position f parking.
II vtr 1 AUT garer; 2° (deposit) laisser.
III vi [driver] se garer.
IV **parked** pp adj en stationnement.
V v refl **to** ~ **oneself** s'installer.

park-and-ride n GB parking situé à l'entrée d'une ville avec service de transport menant au centre.

parking /ˈpɑːkɪŋ/ I n 1 (action) stationnement m; '**No** ~' 'stationnement interdit'; 2 (space for cars) place f de stationnement.
II noun modifier [area, bay, charge, permit, problem, regulations, restrictions] de stationnement; [facilities] pour le stationnement.

parking: ~ **attendant** ▶1251 n gardien/-ienne m/f de parking; ~ **light** n AUT feu m de position; ~ **lot** n US parking m; ~ **meter** n parcmètre m; ~ **offence** GB, ~ **offense** US n infraction f aux règles de stationnement; **~ place**, **~ space** n place f; **~ ticket** n (from machine) ticket m de stationnement; (fine) contravention f, PV○.

ark: **~land** n parc m boisé; **~ ranger**, **~ warden ▶1251|** n (on estate) garde m forestier; (in game reserve) garde-chasse m.

arliament /'pɑːləmənt/ **I** n POL parlement m.
II Parliament pr n GB **1** (institution) Parlement m; **to get into Parliament** se faire élire député; **2** (parliamentary session) session f parlementaire.

arliamentarian /ˌpɑːləmenˈteərɪən/ n **1** (member) parlementaire m; **2** (expert in procedure) expert m des procédures parlementaires.

arliamentary /ˌpɑːləˈmentrɪ, US -terɪ/ adj parlementaire.

arliamentary: **~ election** n élections fpl législatives; **~ privilege** n immunité f parlementaire; **~ secretary** n GB député m attaché ministériel.

arlour GB, **parlor** US /'pɑːlə(r)/ n **1**† (in house) petit salon m; **2** (in convent) parloir m.

arochial /pəˈrəʊkɪəl/ adj **1** PÉJ [interest, view] de clocher; **2** US (of parish) paroissial.

arody /'pærədɪ/ **I** n (all contexts) parodie f.
II vtr parodier [person, style].

arole /pəˈrəʊl/ **I** n **1** JUR liberté f conditionnelle; **2** MIL parole f (d'honneur).
II vtr JUR mettre [qn] en liberté conditionnelle.

aroxysm /'pærəksɪzəm/ n crise f (**of** de).

arquet /'pɑːkeɪ, US pɑːrˈkeɪ/ **I** n (floor) parquet m; US THEAT parterre m.
II vtr parqueter.

arrot /'pærət/ **I** n ZOOL, PÉJ (person) perroquet m.
II vtr PÉJ répéter comme un perroquet.
IDIOMS **as sick as a ~**○ en rage.

arry /'pærɪ/ **I** n **1** SPORT parade f; **2** (verbal) riposte f.
II vtr **1** SPORT parer; **2** éluder [question].
III vi (in fencing, boxing) parer.

parse /pɑːz/ vtr LING, COMPUT faire l'analyse grammaticale de.

parsimonious /ˌpɑːsɪˈməʊnɪəs/ adj SOUT parcimonieux/-ieuse FML.

parsley /'pɑːslɪ/ n persil m.

parsnip /'pɑːsnɪp/ n panais m.

parson /'pɑːsn/ n pasteur m.

part /pɑːt/ **I** n **1** (of whole) GEN partie f; (of country) région f; **in** ou **around these ~s** dans la région; **~ of the reason is**... c'est en partie parce que...; **to be (a) ~ of** faire partie de; **the early ~ of my life** ma jeunesse; **it's all ~ of being young** il faut bien que jeunesse se passe; **that's the best/hardest ~** c'est ça le meilleur/le plus dur; **that's the ~ I don't understand** voilà ce que je ne comprends pas; **to be good in ~s** GB avoir de bons passages; **for the most ~** dans l'ensemble; **my ~ of the world** mon pays; **what are you doing in this ~ of the world?** qu'est-ce que tu fais par ici?; **2** TECH (component) pièce f; **spare ~s** pièces détachées; **3** TV (of serial, programme) partie f; **a two-~ series** une série en deux épisodes; **4** (share, role) rôle m (in dans); **to do one's ~** jouer son rôle; **I want no ~ in it, I don't want any ~ of it** je ne veux pas m'en mêler; **to take ~** participer (in à); **they took no further ~ in it** ils n'ont rien fait de plus; **5** THEAT, TV, CIN rôle n (of de); **6** (equal measure) mesure f; **mix X and Y in equal ~s** mélangez une quantité égale de X et Y; **in a concentration of 30,000 ~s per million** dans une concentration de 3%; **7** MUS (for instrument, voice) partie f; (score) partition f; **8** (behalf) **on the ~ of** de la part de; **for my ~** pour ma part; **to take sb's ~** prendre le parti de qn; **9** US (in hair) raie f.
II adv (partly) en partie; **it was ~ fear, ~ greed** c'était à la fois de la crainte et de la cupidité.
III vtr **1** (separate) séparer [two people]; écarter [legs]; entrouvrir [lips, curtains]; fendre [crowd, ocean, waves]; **2** (make parting in) **to ~ one's hair** se faire une raie.
IV vi **1** (split up) se séparer; **we ~ed friends** nous

sommes quittés bons amis; **to ~ from sb** quitter qn; **2** [crowd, clouds] (divide) s'ouvrir; [rope, cable] se rompre.
IDIOMS **a man of (many) ~s** un homme qui a plusieurs cordes à son arc; **to look the ~** avoir la tête de l'emploi; **to take sth in good ~** prendre qch en bonne part.
■ **part with**: **~ with** [sth] se défaire de [money]; se séparer de [object].

partake /pɑːˈteɪk/ vi SOUT **1 to ~ of** prendre [food, drink]; tenir de [quality]; **2 to ~ in** participer à.

part exchange n GB reprise f; **to take sth in ~** reprendre qch.

partial /'pɑːʃl/ adj **1** (not complete) partiel/-ielle; **2** (biased) partial; **3** (fond) **to be ~ to** avoir un faible pour.

partiality /ˌpɑːʃɪˈælətɪ/ n **1** (bias) partialité f; **2** (liking) **~ to** ou **for** penchant m pour.

partially /'pɑːʃəlɪ/ adv **1** (incompletely) partiellement; **2** (with bias) avec partialité.

partially sighted I n **the ~** (+ v pl) les malvoyants mpl.
II adj malvoyant.

participant /pɑːˈtɪsɪpənt/ n participant/-e m/f (**in** à).

participate /pɑːˈtɪsɪpeɪt/ vi participer (**in** à).

participation /pɑːˌtɪsɪˈpeɪʃn/ n participation f (**in** à).

participle /'pɑːtɪsɪpl/ n participe m.

particle /'pɑːtɪkl/ n (all contexts) particule f.

particular /pəˈtɪkjʊlə(r)/ **I** n **1** détail m; **in every ~** dans tous les détails; **in one ~** sur un point précis; **in several ~s** à plus d'un titre; **2 in ~** en particulier; **are you looking for anything in ~?** vous cherchez quelque chose de précis?
II particulars npl (information) détails mpl; (from person) (name, address etc) coordonnées fpl; (for missing person, suspect) signalement m; ADMIN (for vehicle, stolen goods etc) description f; **for further ~s please phone**... pour plus amples renseignements veuillez téléphoner à...
III adj **1** (specific) particulier/-ière; **this ~ colour doesn't really suit me** cette couleur-là ne me va pas très bien; **is there any ~ colour you would prefer?** est-ce que vous désirez une couleur en particulier?; **no ~ time has been arranged** on n'a pas fixé d'heure précise; **2** (special, exceptional) particulier/-ière; **to take ~ care over sth** faire qch avec un soin tout particulier; **he is a ~ friend of mine** c'est un de mes meilleurs amis; **3** (fussy) méticuleux/-euse; **to be ~ about** être exigeant sur [cleanliness, punctuality]; faire attention à [appearance]; être difficile pour [food]; **'any special time?'—'no, I'm not ~'** 'y a-t-il une heure spéciale qui vous convient?'—'non, je n'ai pas de préférence'.

particularize /pəˈtɪkjʊləraɪz/ vtr, vi préciser.

particularly /pəˈtɪkjʊləlɪ/ adv **1** (in particular) en particulier; **2** (especially) spécialement.

parting /'pɑːtɪŋ/ **I** n **1** (division) séparation f; **the ~ of the ways** la croisée des chemins; **2** GB (in hair) raie f.
II adj [gift, words] d'adieu ALSO IRON; **~ shot** flèche f du Parthe.

partisan /'pɑːtɪzæn, ˌpɑːtɪˈzæn, US 'pɑːrtɪzn/ **I** n MIL, GEN partisan m.
II adj **1** (biased) partisan; **2** MIL de partisans.

partition /pɑːˈtɪʃn/ **I** n **1** (in room, house) cloison f; **2** POL (of country) partition f; **3** JUR (of property) morcellement m.
II vtr **1** = **partition off**; **2** POL diviser; **3** JUR morceler.
■ **partition off**: **~ off** [sth], **~** [sth] **off** cloisonner [area, room].

partitive /'pɑːtɪtɪv/ adj partitif/-ive.

partly /'pɑːtlɪ/ adv en partie.

partner /'pɑːtnə(r)/ **I** n **1** COMM, JUR associé/-e m/f (**in** dans); **active ~** associé-gérant m; **business ~** associé/-e m/f; **general ~** commandité m; **limited ~** commanditaire m; **2** ECON, POL, SPORT partenaire

m; **3** (married) époux/-se *m/f*; (unmarried) partenaire *mf*;
4 (workmate) collègue *mf*.

II *vtr* être le collègue de [*workmate*]; être le partenaire
de [*dancer*]; faire équipe avec [*player*].

IDIOMS **to be ~s in crime** être complices.

partnership /'pɑːtnəʃɪp/ *n* **1** JUR association *f*; **to go
into ~ with** s'associer à; **to take sb into ~** prendre qn pour associé/-e *m/f*; **general ~** ~ société *f* en
nom collectif; **professional ~, non-trading ~** association professionnelle; **2** (alliance) partenariat *m*; **3**
(pairing) association *f*; **a working ~** une équipe.

part: **~ of speech** *n* partie *f* du discours; **~
owner** *n* copropriétaire *mf*; **~ payment** *n* règlement *m* partiel.

partridge /'pɑːtrɪdʒ/ *n* perdrix *f*.

part song *n* chant *m* polyphonique.

part-time /ˌpɑːt'taɪm/ **I** *n* temps *m* partiel.
II *adj, adv* [*work, worker*] à temps partiel.

partway /ˌpɑːt'weɪ/ *adv* **~ through the evening** à
un moment de la soirée; **~ down the page** vers le
bas de la page; **to be ~ through doing** être en train
de faire.

party /'pɑːtɪ/ **I** *n* **1** (social event) fête *f*; (in evening)
soirée *f*; (formal) réception *f*; **birthday ~** (fête d')anni-
versaire *m*; **children's ~** goûter *m* d'enfants; **leaving
~** pot *m* de départ; **2** (group) groupe *m*; MIL détachement *m*; **rescue ~** équipe *f* de secouristes; **3** POL
parti *m*; **4** JUR (individual, group) partie *f*; **5** SOUT **to
be a ~ to** être complice de.
II *noun modifier* **1** [*spirit*] de fête; [*game*] de société;
2 POL [*member, policy*] du parti.
III ○ *vi* faire la fête.

party: **~ dress** *n* (formal) robe *f* de soirée; **~goer**
n fêtard/-e ○ *m/f*; **~ hat** *n* chapeau *m* en papier.

party line *n* **1** POL, FIG **the ~** la ligne du parti; **2**
TELECOM ligne *f* commune.

party piece *n* **to do one's ~**○ faire son numéro○.

party: **~ political broadcast** *n* *émission dans
laquelle un parti expose sa politique*; **~ politics** *n*
PÉJ politique *f* politicienne; **~ wall** *n* mur *m*
mitoyen.

pass /pɑːs, US pæs/ **I** *n* **1** (to enter, leave) laisser-passer
m inv; (for journalists) coupe-file *m*; (to be absent) permission *f* ALSO MIL; (of safe conduct) sauf-conduit *m*; **2**
(travel document) carte *f* d'abonnement; **3** SCH, UNIV
(success) moyenne *f* (**in** en); **to get a ~** être reçu; **4**
SPORT (in ball games) passe *f*; (in fencing) botte *f*; **5**
GEOG (in mountains) col *m*; **6** AVIAT **to make a ~
over sth** survoler qch.
II *vtr* **1** (go past) (to far side) passer [*checkpoint,
customs*]; franchir [*lips*]; (alongside and beyond) passer
devant [*building, area*]; dépasser [*level, understanding,
expectation, vehicle*]; **to ~ sb in the street** croiser qn
dans la rue; **2** (hand over) (directly) passer; (indirectly)
faire passer; **3** (move) passer ALSO SPORT; **4** (spend)
passer [*time*] (**doing** à faire); **5** (succeed in) [*person*] réussir; [*car, machine etc*] passer [qch] (avec succès); **6**
(declare satisfactory) admettre [*candidate*]; approuver [*invoice*]; **to ~ sth** (as being) **safe** juger qch sans
danger; **7** adopter [*bill, motion*]; **8** (pronounce)
prononcer; **to ~ a remark about sb/sth** faire une
remarque sur qn/qch; **9** MED **to ~ water** uriner; **to
~ blood** avoir du sang dans les urines.
III *vi* **1** (go past, be transferred, accepted) passer ALSO
SPORT, GAMES; [*letter, knowing look*] être échangé; ·
to ~ through sth traverser qch; **~ down the bus
please** avancez dans le fond s'il vous plaît; **let the
remark ~** laissez couler; **I'm afraid I must ~** on
that one FIG (in discussion) je cède mon tour de parole;
she ~es for 40 on lui donnerait 40 ans; **2** LITTÉR
(happen) se passer; **3** (in exam) réussir.
IDIOMS **to come to such a ~ that** arriver à un tel
point que; **to make a ~ at sb** faire du plat○ à qn; **to
~ the word** passer la consigne.

■ **pass along**: **~** [sth] **along, ~ along** [sth] faire
passer.

■ **pass around, pass round**: **~** [sth] **around, ~**

around [sth] faire circuler [*document, photos*]; fair
passer [*food, plates etc*].

■ **pass away** EUPH décéder.

■ **pass by**: [*procession*] défiler; [*person*] passer; **lif
seems to have ~ed me by** j'ai le sentiment d'êtr
passé à côté de la vie.

■ **pass down**: **~** [sth] **down, ~ down** [sth] trans
mettre (**from** de; **to** à).

■ **pass off**: ¶ **~ off 1** (take place) [*demonstration*] s
dérouler; [*fête*] se passer; **2** (disappear) se dissiper; ·
~ [sb/sth] **off, ~ off** [sb/sth] faire passer (**a**
pour).

■ **pass on**: ¶ **~ on** poursuivre; **to ~ on to sth**
passer à qch; **~** [sth] **on, ~ on** [sth] transmettr
[*good wishes, condolences, message, title*]; passer [*book
clothes, cold*] (**to** à); répercuter [*costs*].

■ **pass out**: ¶ **~ out 1** (faint) perdre connaissance
(fall drunk) tomber ivre mort; **2** MIL (complete training)
sortir avec ses diplômes (**of, from** de); ¶ **~** [sth] **out
~ out** [sth] distribuer [*leaflets*].

■ **pass over**: ¶ **~ over**† = **pass away**; ¶ **~** [sb]
over délaisser; **he was ~ed over in favour o**
another candidate on lui a préféré un autre candidat
¶ **~ over** [sth] ne pas tenir compte de.

■ **pass through**: **~ through** [sth] traverser; **I'm
just ~ing through** je suis de passage.

■ **pass up**○: **~ up** [sth] laisser passer.

passable /'pɑːsəbl, US 'pæs-/ *adj* **1** (acceptable) GEN
passable; [*knowledge, performance*] assez bon/bonne
only ~ moyen/-enne sans plus; **2** (traversable) [*road*]
praticable; [*river*] franchissable.

passage /'pæsɪdʒ/ *n* **1** (also **~way**) (indoors) corridor
m; (outdoors) passage *m*; **2** ANAT conduit *m*; **nasal
~s** fosses *fpl* nasales; **3** MUS, LITERAT passage *m*;
selected ~s LITERAT morceaux *mpl* choisis; **4**
(movement) passage *m*; **~ of arms** passe *f* d'armes; **5**
(journey) traversée *f*; **the bill had a stormy ~
through parliament** FIG la discussion de ce projet de
loi au parlement a été mouvementée.

pass: **~book** *n* FIN livret *m* (bancaire); **~ degree**
n UNIV diplôme *m* avec mention passable.

passé /'pæseɪ, US pæ'seɪ/ *adj* PÉJ démodé.

passenger /'pæsɪndʒə(r)/ *n* **1** (in car, plane, ship) passa-
ger/-ère *m/f*; (in train, bus, tube) voyageur/-euse *m/f*; **2**
GB PÉJ parasite *m*.

passenger: **~ compartment** *n* GB AUT habitacle
m; **~ ferry** *n* ferry *m*; **~ plane** *n* avion *m* de
ligne; **~ service** *n* ligne *f*; **~ train** *n* train *m* de
voyageurs.

passe-partout /ˌpæspɑː'tuː, ˌpɑːs-/ *n* (key) passe-
partout *m inv*; (frame) sous-verre *m inv*.

passerby /ˌpɑːsə'baɪ/ *n* passant/-e *m/f*.

passing /'pɑːsɪŋ, US 'pæs-/ **I** *n* **1** (movement) passage
m; **with the ~ of time** avec le temps; **2** (end) fin *f*; **3**
EUPH (death) disparition *f* EUPH.
II *adj* **1** (going by) [*motorist, policeman*] qui passe;
with each ~ day de jour en jour; **2** [*whim*] passa-
ger/-ère; **3** (cursory) [*reference*] en passant *inv*; **4** (vague)
[*resemblance*] vague (**before** n).

passing: **~ place** *n* aire *f* de croisement; **~ shot**
n (in tennis) tir *m* passant.

passion /'pæʃn/ *n* **1** (love, feeling) passion *f*; **2** (anger)
colère *f*; **3 Passion** RELIG Passion *f*.

passionate /'pæʃənət/ *adj* [*kiss, person, nature,
speech*] passionné; [*advocate, belief, plea*] fervent; [*relationship*] passionnel/-elle.

passionately /'pæʃənətlɪ/ *adv* [*love, kiss*] passionnément; [*write, defend*] avec passion; [*believe, want*]
ardemment; [*oppose*] farouchement; **to be ~ fond of
sb/sth** adorer qn/qch.

Passion Sunday *n* dimanche *m* d'avant les
Rameaux.

passive /'pæsɪv/ **I** *n* LING **the ~** le passif, la voix
passive.
II *adj* (all contexts) passif/-ive.

passively /'pæsɪvlɪ/ *adv* **1** [*gaze, stare*] d'un air passif;
[*wait, react*] passivement; **2** LING au passif.

ass: **~key** n passe m; **~ mark** n SCH, UNIV
moyenne f.

assover /'pɑːsəʊvə(r), US 'pæs-/ n Pâque f juive.

assport /'pɑːspɔːt, US 'pæs-/ n passeport m ALSO
IG; **visitor's ~** GB passeport temporaire.

assport holder n détenteur/-trice m/f d'un passe-
▸ort.

ass: **~-through** n US passe-plat m; **~word** n (all
ontexts) mot m de passe.

ast /pɑːst, US pæst/

> Note For a full set of translations for past used in
> clocktime consult the Usage Note ▶ 812].

I n **1** GEN passé m; **in the ~** dans le passé; **she has**
▸ **~** elle a un passé chargé; **2** LING (also **~ tense**)
▸assé m; **in the ~** au passé.

I adj **1** (preceding) dernier/-ière; **2** (former) [times,
▸chievements, problems, experience] passé; [president,
▸ncumbent] ancien/-ienne; [government] précédent; **in
times ~** autrefois, jadis; **3** (finished) **summer is ~**
▸été est fini; **that's all ~** c'est du passé.

II prep **1** (moving) **to walk** ou **go ~ sb/sth** passer
▸evant qn/qch; **to drive ~ sth** passer devant qch (en
▸oiture); **2** (in time) **it's ~ 6** il est 6 heures passées;
twenty ~ two deux heures vingt; **half ~ two** deux
▸eures et demie; **he is ~ 70** il a 70 ans passés; **3**
(beyond in position) après; **~ the church** après l'église;
4 (beyond a certain level) **the temperature soared ~**
40°C la température est montée brutalement à plus de
▸0°C; **he didn't get ~ the first chapter** il n'est pas
▸llé plus loin que le premier chapitre; **he didn't get
~ the first interview** il n'a pas passé la barrière du
▸remier entretien; **5** (beyond scope of) **to be ~ under-**
standing dépasser l'entendement; **to be ~ caring** ne
▸lus s'en faire; **he is ~ playing football** ce n'est plus
▸e son âge de jouer au foot.

V adv **1** (onwards) **to go** ou **walk ~** passer; **2** (ago)
two years ~ il y a deux ans.

IDIOMS **to be ~ it°** avoir passé l'âge; **to be ~ its
▸est** [food] être un peu avancé; [wine] être un peu
▸venté; **I wouldn't put it ~ him to do** je ne pense
▸as que ça le gênerait de faire.

asta /'pæstə/ n ¢ pâtes fpl (alimentaires).

aste /peɪst/ I n **1** (glue) colle f; **2** (mixture) pâte f; **3**
▸ULIN (fish, meat) pâté m; (vegetable) purée f; **4** (in jewel-
▸ry) strass m.

I vtr **1** (stick) coller ALSO COMPUT; **2** (coat in glue)
▸ncoller; **3°** (defeat) battre [qn] à plates coutures°.

paste up: **~ [sth] up**, **~ up [sth]** afficher
▸notice, poster]; faire une maquette de [article, page].

asteboard /'peɪstbɔːd/ n carton m.

astel /'pæstl, US pæ'stel/ I n (medium, stick) pastel m;
▸drawing) dessin m au pastel.

I noun modifier [colour, green, pink, shade] pastel;
▸drawing] au pastel.

asteurize /'pɑːstʃəraɪz, US 'pæst-/ vtr pasteuriser.

ast historic n LING passé m simple.

astime /'pɑːstaɪm, US 'pæs-/ n passe-temps m inv.

asting° /'peɪstɪŋ/ n (defeat) gamelle° f; (criticism) **to
▸ake a ~** se faire descendre en flammes.

ast master n **to be a ~ at doing** avoir l'art de
▸aire.

astor /'pɑːstə(r), US 'pæs-/ ▶ 1251] n pasteur m.

astoral /'pɑːstərəl, US 'pæs-/ I n pastorale f.

I adj **1** ART, LITERAT, RELIG pastoral; **2** GB SCH,
▸NIV [role, work] de conseiller/-ère; **he looks after
▸tudents' ~ needs** il s'occupe du bien-être des étu-
▸iants.

ast perfect n LING plus-que-parfait m.

astrami /pæ'strɑːmɪ/ n bœuf m fumé.

astry /'peɪstrɪ/ n **1** (mixture) pâte f; **to roll out ~**
▸taler une pâte; **2** (cake) pâtisserie f.

astry: **~ case** n fond m de tarte; **~ cook** n pâ-
▸issier/-ière m/f; **~ shell** n = **pastry case**.

ast tense n LING passé m.

asture /'pɑːstʃə(r), US 'pæs-/ n (land) pré m, pâturage
▸n; (grass) herbe f.

IDIOMS **to leave for ~s new** partir vers de
nouveaux horizons; **to put sb out to ~** mettre qn au
vert.

pasty I /'pæstɪ/ n GB CULIN petit pâté en croûte.
II /'peɪstɪ/ adj **1** [skin] terreux/-euse; **2** [mixture]
pâteux/-euse.

pat /pæt/ I n **1** (gentle tap) petite tape f; **2** (of butter) noix
f; (larger) morceau m.
II adj **1** (glib) tout prêt; **2** (apt) pertinent.
III vtr (p prés etc **-tt-**) tapoter [ball, hand]; caresser
[dog]; **to ~ one's hair into place** arranger ses
cheveux.
IDIOMS **to have sth off** GB ou **down** US **~** connaître qch par cœur; **to get a ~ on the back** se faire féliciter; **to stand ~** US demeurer inflexible.

patch /pætʃ/ I n (pl **~es**) **1** (in clothes) pièce f; (on
tyre, airbed) rustine® f; (on eye) bandeau m; **2** (small
area) (of snow, ice) plaque f; (of colour, damp, rust, sunlight)
tache f; (of fog) nappe f; (of oil) flaque f; (of blue sky)
coin m; **in ~es** par endroits; **3** (area of ground) GEN
zone f; (for planting) carré m; **a ~ of grass** un coin
d'herbe; **4** GB° (territory) (of gangster, salesman) territoire m; (of policeman, official) secteur m; **5°** (period)
période f.
II vtr **1** rapiécer [hole, trousers]; réparer [tyre]; **2**
COMPUT corriger.
IDIOMS **the film isn't a ~ on the book** le film est
loin de valoir le livre.
■ **patch together**: **~ [sth] together** rafistoler°
[fragments]; concocter [deal, report].
■ **patch up**: **~ ~ up [sth]**, **~ [sth] up** soigner
[person]; rapiécer [hole, trousers]; réparer [ceiling,
tyre]; FIG rafistoler° [marriage]; ¶ **~ up [sth]** résoudre [differences, quarrel].

patch: **~ pocket** n poche f plaquée; **~ test** n
MED test m cutané; **~work** n LIT, FIG patchwork
m.

patchy /'pætʃɪ/ adj [colour, essay, quality] inégal;
[knowledge] incomplet/-ète; **~ cloud** nuages mpl
épars; **~ fog** nappes fpl de brouillard.

patent /'pætnt, 'peɪtnt, US 'pætnt/ I n (document) brevet
m (**for, on** pour); **to hold/take out a ~** détenir/obte-
nir un brevet; **to come out of ~** ou **off ~** tomber
dans le domaine public; **~ pending** en cours de
brevetage m.
II adj **1** (obvious) manifeste; **2** JUR (licensed) breveté.
III vtr JUR faire breveter.

patent leather n cuir m verni.

patently /'peɪtntlɪ, US 'pæt-/ adv manifestement.

patent: **~ medicine** n: médicament de marque déposée; **Patent Office** GB, **Patent and Trademark
Office** US n ~ Institut m national de la propriété
industrielle.

paternal /pə'tɜːnl/ adj (all contexts) paternel/-elle.

paternity /pə'tɜːnətɪ/ n paternité f.

paternity: **~ leave** n congé m de paternité; **~
suit** n action f en recherche de paternité.

path /pɑːθ, US pæθ/ n **1** (track) (also **~way**) chemin
m; (narrower) sentier m; (in garden) allée f; **2** (course) (of
projectile, vehicle) trajectoire f; (of planet, river, sun) cours
m; (of hurricane) passage m; **to stand in sb's ~** LIT,
FIG barrer le chemin à qn; **3** (option) voie f; **4** (means)
(difficult) chemin m (**to** de); (easy) route f (**to** de); **5**
(abrév = **pathology**) pathologie f.

pathetic /pə'θetɪk/ adj **1** (full of pathos) pathétique; **2**
PÉJ (inadequate) misérable; **3°** PÉJ (contemptible)
lamentable.

pathetically /pə'θetɪklɪ/ adv **1** [vulnerable] pathétiquement; [grateful] éperdument; **2°** PÉJ de façon
lamentable.

pathetic fallacy n ~ sophisme m sentimental.

pathological /ˌpæθə'lɒdʒɪkl/ adj **1** [fear, hatred]
pathologique; **he's a ~ liar°** c'est pathologique chez
lui, il ment sans arrêt°; **2** [journal] médical; [re-
search] des causes pathologiques.

pathologically /ˌpæθə'lɒdʒɪklɪ/ adv **he's ~ jealous**
sa jalousie est pathologique.

pathologist /pəˈθɒlədʒɪst/ ▶1251 *n* (doing post-mortems) médecin *m* légiste; (specialist in pathology) pathologiste *mf*.

pathology /pəˈθɒlədʒɪ/ *n* pathologie *f*.

patience /ˈpeɪʃns/ *n* **1** patience *f* (**with** avec); **2** ▶949 (game) réussite *f*.

patient /ˈpeɪʃnt/ **I** *n* patient/-e *m/f*; **heart** ~ patient souffrant d'une maladie cardiaque.
II *adj* patient (**with** avec).

patiently /ˈpeɪʃntlɪ/ *adv* avec patience, patiemment.

patio /ˈpætɪəʊ/ *n* **1** (terrace) terrasse *f*; **2** (courtyard) patio *m*.

patio: ~ **doors** *npl* porte-fenêtre *f*; ~ **furniture** *n* meubles *mpl* de jardin; ~ **garden** *n* patio *m*.

patriarch /ˈpeɪtrɪɑːk, US ˈpæt-/ *n* patriarche *m*.

patriot /ˈpætrɪət, US ˈpeɪt-/ *n* patriote *mf*.

patriotic /ˌpætrɪˈɒtɪk, US ˈpeɪt-/ *adj* [*mood, song*] patrio-tique; [*person*] patriote.

patriotism /ˈpætrɪətɪzəm, US ˈpeɪt-/ *n* patriotisme *m*.

patrol /pəˈtrəʊl/ **I** *n* (all contexts) patrouille *f*; **to carry out a** ~ faire une ronde.
II *noun modifier* [*helicopter, vehicle*] de patrouille.
III *vtr, vi* (*p prés etc* -**ll-**) patrouiller.

patrol: ~ **boat**, ~ **vessel** *n* patrouilleur *m*; ~ **car** *n* voiture *f* de police.

patrolman /pəˈtrəʊlmən/ ▶1251 *n* **1** US (policeman) agent *m* de police; **2** GB AUT *agent d'un service d'assistance routière privé*.

patrol wagon *n* US fourgon *m* cellulaire.

patron /ˈpeɪtrən/ *n* **1** (supporter) (of artist) mécène *m*; (of person) protecteur/-trice *m/f*; (of charity) bienfaiteur/-trice *m/f*; **to be** ~ **of an organization** parrainer une organisation; **2** (client) client/-e *m/f* (**of** de).

patronage /ˈpætrənɪdʒ/ *n* **1** (support) patronage *m*; ~ **of the arts** mécénat *m*; **2** POL (right to appoint) droit *m* de présentation; **political** ~ copinage *m* PÉJ.

patronize /ˈpætrənaɪz/ *vtr* **1** PÉJ traiter [qn] avec condescendance; **don't** ~ **me!** ne prends pas cet air supérieur avec moi!; **2** COMM fréquenter [*restaurant, cinema*]; se fournir chez [*shop*]; **3** (support) protéger [*charity, the arts*].

patronizing /ˈpætrənaɪzɪŋ/ *adj* PÉJ condescendant.

patron saint *n* saint/-e *m/f* patron/-onne (**of** de).

patter /ˈpætə(r)/ **I** *n* **1** (of rain) crépitement *m*; ~ **of footsteps** bruit *m* de pas rapides et légers; **we'll soon be hearing the** ~ **of tiny feet** HUM la maison retentira bientôt de rires enfantins; **2** (of salesman etc) baratin *m*.
II *vi* [*child, mouse*] trottiner; [*rain, hailstones*] crépiter.

pattern /ˈpætn/ **I** *n* **1** (design) dessin *m*, motif *m*; **2** (regular way of happening) ~ **of behaviour, behaviour** ~ mode *m* de comportement; **working** ~**s in industry** l'organisation *f* du travail dans l'industrie; **the current** ~ **of events** la situation actuelle; **a clear** ~ **emerges from these statistics** une tendance nette ressort de ces statistiques; **he could detect a** ~ **in the plot** il arrivait à discerner une logique dans l'intrigue; **to follow a set** ~ se dérouler toujours de la même façon; **traffic** ~ distribution *f* de la circula-tion; **weather** ~**s** tendances *fpl* climatiques; **3** (model) modèle *m* ALSO LING; **4** (in dressmaking) patron *m*; (in knitting) modèle *m*; **5** (style of manufacture) style *m*; **6** (sample) échantillon *m*.
II *vtr* (model) modeler (**on, after** sur).

patterned /ˈpætnd/ *adj* [*fabric etc*] à motifs.

patty /ˈpætɪ/ *n* **1** US (in hamburger etc) steak *m* haché; **2** (pie) petit feuilleté *m*.

paunch /pɔːntʃ/ *n* (of person) ventre *m*.

pauper /ˈpɔːpə(r)/ *n* indigent/-e *m/f*.

pause /pɔːz/ **I** *n* **1** (brief silence) silence *m*; **2** (break) pause *f* (**in** dans; **for** pour); **3** (stoppage) interruption *f*; **4** MUS point *m* d'orgue.
II *vi* **1** (stop speaking) marquer une pause; **2** (stop) s'arrêter; **to** ~ **in** interrompre [*activity*]; **to** ~ **for thought** faire une pause pour réfléchir; **3** (hesitate) hé-siter.

■ **pause over**: ~ **over** [**sth**] s'arrêter sur.

pave /peɪv/ *vtr* paver (**with** de).
IDIOMS **to** ~ **the way for sth** ouvrir la voie à qch.

pavement /ˈpeɪvmənt/ *n* **1** GB (footpath) trottoir *m*; **2** US (roadway) chaussée *f*; (road surface) revêtement *m* (de la chaussée); **3** (paved area) surface *f* pavée; **4** (material) dallage *m*.

pavement café *n* GB ~ café *m* avec terrasse.

pavilion /pəˈvɪlɪən/ *n* (all contexts) pavillon *m*.

paving /ˈpeɪvɪŋ/ *n* ¢ dalles *fpl*.

paving slab, **paving stone** *n* dalle *f*.

pavlova /ˈpævləvə, pævˈləʊvə/ *n* GB *gâteau meringué aux fruits*.

paw /pɔː/ **I** *n* (of animal) patte *f*; PÉJ (hand) patte° *f*.
II *vtr* **1** [*animal*] donner des coups de patte à; **to** ~ **the ground** [*horse*] piaffer; [*bull*] frapper le sol du sabot; **2** PÉJ [*person*] peloter°.

pawn /pɔːn/ **I** *n* **1** (in chess) pion *m* ALSO FIG; **2** COMM gage *m*; **to be in** ~ être au mont-de-piété.
II *vtr* mettre [qch] au mont-de-piété.

pawn: ~**broker** ▶1251 *n* prêteur/-euse *m/f* sur gages; ~**shop** *n* mont-de-piété *m*.

pay /peɪ/ **I** *n* GEN salaire *m*; (to soldier) solde *f*; ADMIN traitement *m*; **back** ~ rappel *m* de salaire; **extra** ~ prime *f* de salaire; **to be in the** ~ **of sb** PÉJ être à la solde de qn; ~ **and allowances** rémunération princi-pale et indemnités; **the** ~ **is good** c'est bien payé.
II *noun modifier* [*agreement, claim, negotiations, deal*] salarial; [*rise, cut*] de salaire; [*freeze, structure, policy*] des salaires.
III *vtr* (*prét, pp* **paid**) **1** (for goods, services) GEN payer; verser [*down payment*]; **to** ~ **cash** payer comptant; **to** ~ **£100 on account** verser un acompte de 100 livres; **to** ~ **sth into** verser qch sur [*account*]; **to** ~ **high/low wages** payer bien/mal; **all expenses paid** tous frais payés; **2** FIN (accrue) rapporter [*interest*]; **to** ~ **dividends** FIG finir par rapporter; **3** (give) **to** ~ **attention/heed to** faire/prêter attention à; **to** ~ **a tribute to sb** rendre hommage à qn; **to** ~ **sb a compliment** faire des compliments à qn; **to** ~ **sb a visit** rendre visite à qn; **4** (benefit) **it would** ~ **him to** ~ **her etc to do** FIG il/elle etc y gagnerait à faire; **it doesn't** ~ **to do** cela ne sert à rien de faire.
IV *vi* (*prét, pp* **paid**) **1** GEN payer; **to** ~ **for sth** payer qch ALSO FIG; **I'll make you** ~ **for this!** FIG tu me le paieras!; **they're paying for him to go to college** ils lui paient ses études; **'** ~ **on entry'** 'paie-ment à l'entrée'; **you have to** ~ **to get in** l'entrée est payante; **'** ~ **and display'** (in carpark) 'payez et laissez le ticket en évidence'; ~ **on demand** (on cheque) payer à vue; **to** ~ **one's own way** payer sa part; **the work doesn't** ~ **very well** le travail est mal payé; **2** (bring gain) [*business*] rapporter; [*activity, quality*] payer; **to** ~ **handsomely** rapporter gros; **to** ~ **for itself** [*business, purchase*] s'amortir; **to make sth** ~ rentabiliser qch.
IDIOMS **there'll be hell**° OU **the devil to** ~ ça va barder°; **to** ~ **a visit** EUPH aller au petit coin°.

■ **pay back**: ¶ ~ [**sb**] **back** rembourser; **I'll** ~ **him back for the trick he played on me** je lui revaudrai le tour qu'il m'a joué; ¶ ~ [**sth**] **back**, ~ **back** [**sth**] rembourser.

■ **pay down**: ~ [**sth**] **down** verser un acompte de.

■ **pay in**: ~ [**sth**] **in**, ~ **in** [**sth**] déposer.

■ **pay off**: ¶ ~ **off** FIG être payant; ¶ ~ [**sb**] **off** ~ **off** [**sb**] **1** (dismiss) congédier [*worker*]; **2**° (buy silence) acheter le silence de; ¶ ~ [**sth**] **off**, ~ [**sth**] **off** rembourser.

■ **pay out**: ~ **out** [**sth**] **1** (hand over) débourser (**for** pour); **he paid out £300 for his new washing machine** il a payé 300 livres sa nouvelle machine à laver; **2** (release) laisser filer [*rope*].

■ **pay up**°: ~ **up** payer.

payable /ˈpeɪəbl/ *adj* **1** (which will be paid) à payer; **to make a cheque** ~ **to** faire un chèque à l'ordre de; **2** (requiring payment) **to be** ~ être payable; ~ **on demand** payable à vue; **3** (may be paid) payable; (profitable) rentable.

pay: **~-as-you-earn**, **PAYE** *n* GB (tax) prélèvement *m* de l'impôt à la source; **~back** *n* (of debt) remboursement *m*; **~ cheque** GB, **~ check** US *n* chèque *m* de paie; **~day** *n* (for wages) jour *m* de paie; (in Stock Exchange) séance *f* de liquidation; **~desk** *n* caisse *f*.

PAYE *n* GB *abrév* ▶ **pay-as-you-earn**.

payee /peɪˈiː/ *n* bénéficiaire *mf*.

payer /ˈpeɪə(r)/ *n* GEN payeur/-euse *m*|*f*.

pay gate *n* tourniquet *m*.

paying /ˈpeɪɪŋ/ *adj* [*proposition*] rentable.

paying: **~ guest** *n* hôte *m* payant; **~-in slip** GB, **~-in deposit slip** US *n* bordereau *m* de versement.

payload /ˈpeɪləʊd/ *n* **1** (of aircraft, ship) passagers et fret *mpl*; **2** (of bomb) charge *f* explosive.

paymaster /ˈpeɪmɑːstə(r)/, US -mæstər/ *n* **1** GEN caissier *m*; NAUT commissaire *m*; MIL trésorier *m*; **2** PÉJ (employer) commandataire *m*.

payment /ˈpeɪmənt/ *n* GEN paiement *m*; (in settlement) règlement *m*; (into account, of instalments) versement *m*; (to creditor) remboursement *m*; FIG (for help) récompense *f* ALSO IRON; **cash ~** (not credit) paiement comptant; (not cheque) paiement en liquide; **~ in full is now requested** un règlement complet est désormais exigé; **in monthly ~s of £30** en mensualités de 30 livres sterling; **~ on** (instalment) traite de [*television, washing machine etc*]; **on ~ of £30** moyennant 30 livres sterling; **Social Security ~s** prestations *fpl* de la Sécurité sociale.

pay: **~off** *n* (reward) récompense *f*; FIG bouquet *m*; **~-packet** *n* enveloppe *f* de paie; FIG paie *f*; **~ phone** *n* téléphone *m* public.

payroll /ˈpeɪrəʊl/ *n* (list) fichier *m* des salaires; (sum of money) paie *f* (de tous les employés); (employees collectively) ensemble *m* du personnel; **to be on a company's ~** être employé par une entreprise; **to take sb off the ~** licencier qn; **a ~ of 500 workers** un effectif de 500 ouvriers.

payslip *n* bulletin *m* de salaire.

pc *n* **1** (also **PC**) *abrév* ▶ **personal computer**; **2** *abrév* ▶ **per cent**; **3** *abrév* ▶ **postcard**; **4** (also **PC**) *abrév* ▶ **politically correct**.

PC *n* GB *abrév* ▶ **Police Constable**.

pd (*abrév* = **paid**) payé.

PD *n* US *abrév* ▶ **Police Department**.

PDQ machine *n* TPV *m*, terminal *m* point de vente.

PE *n*: *abrév* ▶ **physical education**.

pea /piː/ *n* **1** BOT pois *m*; **2** CULIN (also **green ~**) petit pois *m*.

peace /piːs/ **I** *n* (all contexts) paix *f*; **to be at ~** (free from war) être en paix; (dead) avoir trouvé la paix; **to keep the ~** (between countries, individuals) maintenir la paix; (in town) [*police*] maintenir l'ordre public; [*citizen*] ne pas troubler l'ordre public; **I need a bit of ~ and quiet** j'ai besoin d'un peu de calme; **to find ~ of mind** trouver la paix.
II *noun modifier* [*plan, talks*] de paix; [*campaign, march, moves*] pour la paix.
IDIOMS **to hold one's ~** rester muet; **to make one's ~ with sb** faire la paix avec qn.

peaceable /ˈpiːsəbl/ *adj* [*person*] pacifique.

peace: **~ campaigner** *n* militant/-e *m*|*f* pacifiste; **Peace Corps** *n* US ADMIN *organisation composée de volontaires pour l'aide aux pays en voie de développement*; **~ envoy** *n* négociateur/-trice *m*|*f* de paix.

peaceful /ˈpiːsfl/ *adj* **1** (tranquil) paisible; **2** (without conflict) pacifique.

peacefully /ˈpiːsfəli/ *adv* **1** (without disturbance) [*sleep*] paisiblement; [*situated*] à un endroit paisible; **2** (without violence) pacifiquement.

peacekeeping /ˈpiːskiːpɪŋ/ *n* MIL, POL maintien *m* de la paix.
II *noun modifier* [*force, troops*] de maintien de la paix.

peace: **~-loving** *adj* pacifique; **~maker** *n* POL artisan *m* de la paix; (in family) conciliateur *m*; **~**

offering *n* gage *m* de réconciliation; **~ pipe** *n* calumet *m* de la paix.

peacetime /ˈpiːstaɪm/ **I** *n* temps *m* de paix.
II *noun modifier* [*army, alliance, training*] en temps de paix; [*planning, government*] de temps de paix.

peach /piːtʃ/ **I** *n* **1** (fruit, colour) pêche *f*; (tree) pêcher *m*; **2**○ **~ of a game**○ un match formidable.
II *noun modifier* [*jam, yoghurt*] aux pêches; [*stone*] de pêche.

peacock /ˈpiːkɒk/ *n* paon *m*.

peacock: **~ blue** ▶818 *n, adj* bleu (*m*) canard *inv*; **~ butterfly** *n* paon *m* de jour.

peak /piːk/ **I** *n* **1** (of mountain) pic *m* (**of** de); **2** (of cap) visière *f*; **3** (of inflation, demand, price) maximum *m* (**in** dans; **of** de); (on a graph) sommet *m*; **4** (high point) (of career, empire, creativity) apogée *m* (**of** de); (of fitness, form) meilleur *m* (**of** de); **in the ~ of condition** en excellente santé; **to be past its** OU **one's ~** avoir fait son temps; **5** (busiest time) GEN heure *f* de pointe; TELECOM heures *fpl* rouges.
II *noun modifier* [*figure, level, price, risk*] maximum; [*fitness, form, performance*] meilleur.
III *vi* LIT, FIG culminer (**at** à); **to ~ too early** [*runner*] se lancer trop tôt; [*prodigy*] s'épanouir trop tôt; (in career) réussir trop tôt.
■ **peak out**○ [*athlete, prowess, skill, luck*] commencer à décliner; [*inflation, rate*] commencer à décroître.

peak demand *n* GEN demande *f* record; ELEC période *f* de consommation de pointe.

peaked /piːkt/ *adj* **1** [*cap, hat*] à visière; [*roof*] pointu; **2** US = **peaky**.

peak: **~ period** *n* période *f* de pointe; **~ rate** *n* TELECOM tarif *m* rouge; **~ season** *n* haute saison *f*; **~ time** *n* (on TV) heures *fpl* de grande écoute; (for switchboard, traffic) heures *fpl* de pointe.

peaky○ /ˈpiːkɪ/ *adj* pâlot/-otte.

peal /piːl/ *n* (of bells) carillonnement *m*; (of doorbell) sonnerie *f*; (of thunder) grondement *m*; (of organ) retentissement *m*; **~s of laughter** éclats *mpl* de rire.
■ **peal out** [*bells*] carillonner; [*thunder*] gronder; [*organ*] retentir; [*laughter*] éclater.

peanut /ˈpiːnʌt/ **I** *n* (nut) cacahuète *f*; (plant) arachide *f*.
II peanuts○ *npl* clopinettes○ *fpl*.

peanut: **~ butter** *n* beurre *m* de cacahuètes; **~ oil** *n* huile *f* d'arachide.

pear /peə(r)/ *n* (fruit) poire *f*; (tree) poirier *m*.

pearl /pɜːl/ ▶818 **I** *n* **1** LIT, FIG perle *f* (**of** de); (city, building) joyau *m*; **~s of wisdom** trésors *mpl* de sagesse; **2** (colour) (couleur *f*) perle *f*.
II *noun modifier* [*necklace, brooch etc*] de perles; [*button*] en nacre.

pearl: **~ barley** *n* orge *m* perlé; **~ diver** *n* pêcheur/-euse *m*|*f* de perles; **~ grey** ▶818 *n, adj* gris (*m*) perle *inv*.

pearly /ˈpɜːlɪ/ *adj* nacré.

Pearly Gates *npl* **the ~** HUM les portes *fpl* du Paradis.

peasant /ˈpeznt/ **I** *n* AUSSI PÉJ paysan/-anne *m*|*f*.
II *noun modifier* [*class, custom, cuisine, craft, life*] paysan/-anne; [*costume*] de paysan/-anne.

peat /piːt/ *n* (substance) tourbe *f*.

pebble /ˈpebl/ *n* caillou *m*; (on beach) galet *m*.

pebbledash /ˈpebldæʃ/ *n* crépi *m*, mouchetis *m*.

pecan /ˈpiːkən, pɪˈkæn, US pɪˈkɑːn/ *n* **1** (nut) noix *f* de pecan; **2** (tree) pacanier *m*.

peck /pek/ **I** *n* **1** (from bird) coup *m* de bec; **2**○ (kiss) bise *f*.
II *vtr* [*bird*] picorer [*food*]; donner un coup de bec à [*person, animal*]; **to ~ a hole in sth** faire un trou dans qch à (force de) coups de bec.
III *vi* **1** (with beak) **to ~ at** picorer [*food*]; donner des coups de bec contre [*window, tree*]; **2**○ FIG **to ~ at one's food** chipoter.
■ **peck out**: **~** [*sth*] **out**, **~ out** [*sth*] arracher [qch] à coups de bec [*kernel, seeds*].

pecking order *n* LIT, FIG ordre *m* hiérarchique.

peckish○ /'pekɪʃ/ adj GB **to be** ou **feel** ~ avoir un petit creux○.

pectoral /'pektərəl/ **I pectorals** npl (also **pecs**○) pectoraux mpl.
II adj pectoral.

peculiar /pɪ'kju:lɪə(r)/ adj **1** (odd) bizarre; **to feel** ~ se sentir bizarre; **funny** ~○ HUM bizarre; **2** (exceptional) [situation, circumstances] particulier/-ière; **3** (exclusive to) particulier/-ière; **to be** ~ **to** [feature, trait] être particulier/-ière à or propre à.

peculiarity /pɪˌkju:lɪ'ærətɪ/ n **1** (feature) particularité f; **2** (strangeness) bizarrerie f.

peculiarly /pɪ'kju:lɪəlɪ/ adv **1** (strangely) de façon étrange; **2** (particularly) particulièrement.

pecuniary /pɪ'kju:nɪərɪ, US -ɪerɪ/ adj pécuniaire.

pedagogic(al) /ˌpedə'gɒdʒɪkl/ adj pédagogique.

pedal /'pedl/ **I** n (all contexts) pédale f.
II vtr (p prés etc **-ll-** GB, **-l-** US) **to** ~ **a bicycle** pédaler.
III vi (p prés etc **-ll-** GB, **-l-** US) **1** (use pedal) pédaler; **to** ~ **hard** pédaler dur; **2** (cycle) **to** ~ **down/through** descendre/traverser à vélo.

pedal: ~ **bin** n GB poubelle f à pédale; ~ **boat** n pédalo® m; ~ **cycle** n bicyclette f; ~ **pushers** npl (pantalon m) corsaire m.

pedantic /pɪ'dæntɪk/ adj pédant.

pedantry /'pedntrɪ/ n pédantisme m.

peddle /'pedl/ vtr colporter [wares, ideas]; **to** ~ **drugs** faire du trafic de drogue (à petite échelle).

peddler /'pedlə(r)/ n **1** (street vendor) colporteur m; **2** **drug** ~ trafiquant m.

pedestal /'pedɪstl/ n (of statue, ornament) socle m, piédestal m; (of washbasin) colonne f.
IDIOMS **to put sb on a** ~ mettre qn sur un piédestal; **to knock sb off their** ~ détrôner qn.

pedestrian /pɪ'destrɪən/ **I** n piéton m.
II noun modifier [street, area] piétonnier/-ière, piéton/-onne.
III adj (humdrum) terre à terre inv.

pedestrian: ~ **crossing** n passage m pour piétons; ~ **precinct** n GB zone f piétonne.

pediatric /ˌpi:dɪ'ætrɪk/ adj [ward] de pédiatrie; [illness] infantile; ~ **nursing** puériculture f.

pediatrician /ˌpi:dɪə'trɪʃn/ n ▶ 1251 n pédiatre mf.

pediatrics /ˌpi:dɪ'ætrɪks/ n (+ v sg) pédiatrie f.

pedicure /'pedɪkjʊə(r)/ n **to have a** ~ se faire soigner les pieds.

pedigree /'pedɪgri:/ **I** n **1** (ancestry) (of animal) pedigree m; (of person, family) (line) ascendance f; (tree, chart) arbre m généalogique; (background) origines fpl; **2** (pure-bred animal) animal m avec pedigree; (pure-bred person, artist) antécédents mpl.
II noun modifier [animal] de pure race.

pediment /'pedɪmənt/ n fronton m.

pedlar /'pedlar/ n = **peddler** 1.

pee○ /pi:/ n pipi○ m; **to have** ou **do a** ~ faire pipi○.

peek /pi:k/ **I** n **to have a** ~ **at** jeter un coup d'œil furtif à.
II vi jeter un coup d'œil furtif (**at** à, sur).

peekaboo /ˌpi:kə'bu:/ excl coucou!

peel /pi:l/ **I** n (before peeling) peau f; (after peeling) épluchures fpl.
II vtr éplucher [carrot etc]; décortiquer [prawn]; écorcer [stick].
III vi [skin] peler; [fruit, vegetable] s'éplucher.
■ **peel off**: ¶ ~ **off** [label] se détacher (**from** de); [paint] s'écailler; [paper] se décoller; ¶ ~ **off** [sth], ~ [sth] **off** enlever [clothing, label, leaves].

peeler /'pi:lə(r)/ n (manual) économe m; (electric) éplucheur m électrique; **potato** ~ épluche-légumes m inv.

peeling /'pi:lɪŋ/ **I peelings** npl épluchures fpl.
II adj [walls, paint] qui s'écaille; [skin] qui pèle.

peep /pi:p/ **I** n **1** (look) (quick) coup m d'œil; **to have a** ~ **at sth** jeter un coup d'œil à qch; (furtively) regarder

qch à la dérobée; **2** (noise) (of chick) pépiement m **there wasn't a** ~ **out of him** il n'a pas pipé mot.
II vi **1** (look) jeter un coup d'œil (**over** par-dessus; **through** par); **to** ~ **at sth/sb** GEN jeter un coup d'œil à qch/qn; (furtively) regarder qch/qn furtivement; **2** (make noise) [chick] pépier.
■ **peep out** [person, animal] se montrer, apparaître; [gun, hanky] dépasser (**of** de).

peep: ~ **hole** /'pi:phəʊl/ n GEN trou m; (in door) judas m; **Peeping Tom**○ n voyeur m.

peer /pɪə(r)/ **I** n **1** (equal) (in status) pair m also GB POL; (in profession) collègue m/f; **2** (contemporary) (adult) personne f de la même génération; (teenager) adolescent/-e m/f du même âge; (child) enfant mf du même âge; **3** (person of equal merit) égal/-e m/f.
II vi **to** ~ **at** regarder (fixement); **to** ~ **shortsightedly at sth** regarder qch avec des yeux de myope.

peerage /'pɪərɪdʒ/ n **1** GB POL pairie f; **to be given a** ~ être anobli; **2** (book) nobiliaire m.

peer group n **1** (of same status) pairs mpl; **2** (contemporary) (adults) personnes fpl de la même génération; (children) enfants mpl du même âge.

peer group pressure n pression f du groupe.

peerless /'pɪəlɪs/ adj hors pair inv.

peeved○ /pi:vd/ adj [person, expression] irrité.

peevish /'pi:vɪʃ/ adj grognon/-onne.

peg /peg/ **I** n **1** (to hang garment) patère f; **2** GB (also **clothes** ~) pince f à linge; **3** (to mark place) piquet m; **4** (in carpentry, music) cheville f; **5** ECON indice m; **6** (barrel stop) fausset m.
II vtr (p prés etc **-gg-**) **1** (fasten cloth) **to** ~ **sth on** ou **onto a line** accrocher qch sur une corde avec des pinces; **to** ~ **sth down** ou **in place** fixer qch avec des piquets; **2** (fasten wood) cheviller (**to** à; **together** ensemble); **3** ECON indexer (**to** sur); **to** ~ **sth at 10%** indexer qch à 10%; **4** US (characterize) cataloguer.
IDIOMS **to be a square** ~ (**in a round hole**) ne pas être dans son élément; **to take** ou **bring sb down a** ~ (**or two**)○ remettre qn à sa place.
■ **peg away**○ travailler ferme, bosser○ (**at** sur).

pegboard /'pegbɔ:d/ n panneau m alvéolé.

pejorative /pɪ'dʒɒrətɪv, US -'dʒɔ:r-/ adj péjoratif/-ive.

Pekin(g)ese /ˌpi:kɪ'ni:z/ ▶ 1038 n pékinois m.

Peking /ˌpi:'kɪŋ/ ▶ 1343 pr n Pékin.

pelican /'pelɪkən/ n pélican m.

pelican crossing n GB passage m pour piétons.

pellet /'pelɪt/ **I** n **1** (of paper, wax, mud) boulette f; **2** (of shot) plomb m; **3** AGRIC granulé m.

pell-mell /ˌpel'mel/ adv pêle-mêle.

pelmet /'pelmɪt/ n cantonnière f.

pelt /pelt/ **I** n (fur) fourrure f; (hide) peau f.
II at full pelt adv phr à toute vitesse.
III vtr bombarder; **to** ~ **sb with sth** lancer une volée de qch à qn.
IV vi **1** (also ~ **down**) tomber à verse; **the** ~**ing rain** la pluie battante; **2**○ (run) courir à toutes jambes; **to** ~ **down the road** descendre la rue à toutes jambes.

pelvis /'pelvɪs/ ▶ 765 n bassin m, pelvis m SPEC.

pen /pen/ **I** n **1** (for writing) stylo m; **to run one's** ~ **through sth** barrer qch; **to put** ~ **to paper** (write) écrire, prendre la plume; (give signature) signer; **2** (for animals) parc m, enclos m; **3** ZOOL cygne m femelle; **4**○ US (prison) taule○ f, prison f.
II vtr (p prés etc **-nn-**) **1** (write) écrire; **2** (also ~ **in**) enfermer, parquer.

penal /'pi:nl/ n [reform, law, code, system] pénal; [colony, institution] pénitentiaire; ~ **servitude** HIST travaux mpl forcés.

penalize /'pi:nəlaɪz/ vtr pénaliser.

penalty /'penltɪ/ n **1** JUR, GEN (punishment) peine f, pénalité f; (fine) amende f; **on** ~ **of** sous peine de; **2** FIG (unpleasant result) prix m (**for** de); **3** SPORT (in soccer) penalty m; (in rugby) pénalité f; **to take a** ~ tirer un penalty; **4** GAMES amende f.

penalty: ~ **area** n SPORT surface f de réparation; ~ **clause** n COMM, JUR clause f pénale; ~ **goal**

(in rugby) but *m* sur pénalité; **~ kick** *n* (in rugby) coup *m* de pied de pénalité; (in soccer) penalty *m*.

penance /'penəns/ *n* GEN, RELIG pénitence *f*.

pence /pens/ *npl* GB ▶ **penny**.

penchant /'pɑːnʃɑːn, US 'pentʃənt/ *n* penchant *m*; **to have a ~ for doing** avoir tendance *f* à faire.

pencil /'pensl/ **I** *n* crayon *m*; **in ~** au crayon.
II *vtr* (*p prés etc* -ll- GB, -l- US) écrire [qch] au crayon.
■ **pencil in**: **~** [sth] **in**, **~ in** [sth] LIT écrire [qch] au crayon; **let's ~ in the second of May** disons le deux mai pour l'instant.

pencil: **~ case** *n* trousse *f* (à crayons); **~ pusher**○ *n* US PÉJ gratte-papier *m inv* PÉJ; **~ sharpener** *n* taille-crayon *m*.

pendant /'pendənt/ *n* **1** (necklace) pendentif *m*; **2** (bauble) pendeloque *f*.

pending /'pendɪŋ/ **I** *adj* **1** JUR [*case, charge*] en instance; GEN [*matter*] en souffrance; **patent ~** modèle *m* déposé; **2** (imminent) imminent.
II *prep* en attendant.

pending tray *n* corbeille *f* des affaires en souffrance.

pendulum /'pendjʊləm, US -dʒʊləm/ *n* pendule *m*, balancier *m*.

penetrate /'penɪtreɪt/ **I** *vtr* **1** (enter into or through) pénétrer [*protective layer, territory, surface*]; percer [*cloud, silence, defences*]; traverser [*wall*]; **2** FIG (permeate) pénétrer [*market, mind, ideas*]; [*spy*] infiltrer [*organization*]; **3** (understand) percer [*disguise, mystery*].
II *vi* **1** (enter) pénétrer (**into** dans; **as far as** jusqu'à); **2** [*sound*] parvenir (**to** à); **nothing I say seems to ~** j'ai l'impression de parler à un mur.

penetrating /'penɪtreɪtɪŋ/ *adj* **1** (invasive) [*cold, eyes, wind*] pénétrant; [*sound, voice*] perçant; **2** (perceptive) [*analysis, question*] pénétrant.

penetratingly /'penɪtreɪtɪŋlɪ/ *adv* **1** (loudly) d'une voix pénétrante; **2** (perceptively) avec pénétration.

penetration /,penɪ'treɪʃn/ *n* **1** (entering) pénétration *f*; (by spies) infiltration *f*; **2** (insight) perspicacité *f*.

pen friend *n* correspondant/-e *m/f*.

penguin /'peŋgwɪn/ *n* pingouin *m*, manchot *m*.

penicillin /,penɪ'sɪlɪn/ *n* pénicilline *f*.

peninsula /pə'nɪnsjʊlə, US -nsələ/ *n* péninsule *f*.

penis /'piːnɪs/ *n* pénis *m*.

penitence /'penɪtəns/ *n* GEN, RELIG pénitence *f*.

penitent /'penɪtənt/ *n, adj* pénitent/-e (*m/f*).

penitentiary /,penɪ'tenʃərɪ/ *n* US prison *f*.

pen: **~-knife** *n* canif *m*; **~manship** *n* calligraphie *f*; **~ name** *n* pseudonyme *m*, nom *m* de plume.

pennant /'penənt/ *n* **1** (flag) (on boat) flamme *f*; (in competition, procession, on car) fanion *m*; **2** US SPORT championnat *m*.

penniless /'penɪlɪs/ *adj* sans le sou, sans ressources.

penny /'penɪ/ *n* **1** (*pl* **pennies**) (small amount of money) **~ centime** *m*; **when he died she didn't get a ~** quand il est mort elle n'a pas eu un sou; **not to have a ~ to one's name** être sans le sou; **2** GB (*pl* **pence** ou **pennies**) (unit of currency) penny *m*; **a five pence** ou **five p piece** une pièce de cinq pence; **a 25 pence** ou **25p stamp** un timbre-poste à 25 pence; **3** US (*pl* **pennies**) cent *m*.
IDIOMS **a ~ for your thoughts** ou **for them**○ à quoi penses-tu?; **a pretty ~**○ une jolie somme; **in for a ~ in for a pound** lorsque le vin est tiré, il faut le boire; **take care of the pennies and the pounds will take care of themselves** PROV il n'y a pas de petites économies; **the ~ dropped**○ ça a fait tilt○; **they are ten a ~** on les ramasse à la pelle○; **to spend a ~**○ GB EUPH aller au petit coin EUPH; **to turn up like a bad ~** revenir continuellement.

■ Note Le pluriel de *penny* est *pence* pour une somme spécifique: *10 pence, 24 pence*. À l'oral et à l'écrit on utilise souvent l'abréviation *p*: *47p, 1p*. Le pluriel de *penny* est *pennies* pour les pièces en tant qu'objets comptables: *a bag of pennies*.

penny: **~-farthing** *n* grand bi *m*; **~-pinching** *adj* grippe-sou *inv*; **~ whistle** *n* flûteau *m*.

pen: **~ pal**○ *n* correspondant/-e *m/f*; **~ pusher**○ *n* PÉJ gratte-papier○ *m inv* PÉJ.

pension /'penʃn/ *n* **1** (from state) pension *f*; **to be** ou **live on a ~** être pensionné; **old age ~** pension *f* de retraite; **2** (from employer) retraite *f*; **company ~** retraite *f* de société; **3** (hotel) pension *f*.

pensionable /'penʃənəbl/ *adj* [*post, service*] donnant droit à la retraite; [*employee*] ayant droit à la retraite.

pensioner /'penʃənə(r)/ *n* retraité/-e *m/f*.

pension: **~ fund** *n* fonds *m* d'assurance-vieillesse; **~ plan**, **~ scheme** *n* plan *m* de retraite; **~ rights** *npl* droit *m* à une retraite complémentaire.

pensive /'pensɪv/ *adj* songeur/-euse, pensif/-ive.

pentagon /'pentəgən, US -gɒn/ *n* **1** MATH pentagone *m*; **2 Pentagon** US POL **the ~** le Pentagone *m*.

pentathlon /pen'tæθlən, -lɒn/ *n* pentathlon *m*.

Pentecost /'pentɪkɒst, US -kɔːst/ *n* Pentecôte *f*.

penthouse /'penthaʊs/ **I** *n* **1** (flat) appartement *m* de grand standing (*construit au dernier étage d'un immeuble*); **2** (roof) auvent *m*.
II *noun modifier* [*accommodation, suite*] de grand standing.

pent-up /pent'ʌp/ *adj* [*energy, frustration*] contenu; [*feelings*] réprimé.

penultimate /pen'ʌltɪmət/ *adj* avant-dernier/-ière.

penury /'penjʊrɪ/ *n* indigence *f*.

peony /'piːənɪ/ *n* pivoine *f*.

people /'piːpl/ **I** *n* (nation) peuple *m*, peuplade *f*; **the English-speaking ~s** les anglophones *mpl*.
II *npl* **1** (in general) gens *mpl*; (specified or counted) personnes *fpl*; **old ~** les personnes âgées; **they're nice ~** ce sont des gens sympathiques; **there were a lot of ~** il y avait beaucoup de monde; **other ~ say that...** d'autres disent que...; **other ~'s property** la propriété des autres; **he likes helping ~** il aime aider les autres; **you shouldn't do that in front of ~** tu ne devrais pas faire ça en public; **~ in general** le grand public; **what do you ~ want?** que voulez-vous?; **you of all ~!** je n'aurais jamais pensé ça de toi!; **you of all ~ should know that...** tu devrais savoir encore mieux que les autres que...; **2** (inhabitants) (of town) habitants *mpl*; (of a country) peuple *m*; **3** (citizens, subjects) **the ~** le peuple; **a man of the ~** un homme du peuple; **4**○ (experts) gens○ *mpl*; **the tax ~** les gens○ des impôts; **5**○ (relations) famille *f*; (parents) parents *mpl*.

■ Note *gens* est masculin pluriel and never countable (you CANNOT say '*trois gens*'). When used with *gens*, some adjectives such as *vieux, bon, mauvais, petit, vilain* placed before *gens* take the feminine form: *les vieilles gens*.

people: **~ mover** *n* US tapis *m* roulant; **~'s democracy** *n* démocratie *f* populaire; **People's Republic of China** ▶ 840 *pr n* République *f* populaire de Chine.

pep /pep/ *v* ■ **pep up**: ¶ **~ up** [*person*] retrouver des forces; [*business*] reprendre; ¶ **~ [sb/sth] up**, **~ up [sb/sth]** remettre [qn] d'aplomb [*person*]; animer [*party, team*].

pepper /'pepə(r)/ **I** *n* **1** (spice) poivre *m*; **black/white ~** poivre noir/blanc; **2** (vegetable) poivron *m*.
II *vtr* **1** LIT poivrer [*food*]; **2** FIG **to be ~ed with** être parsemé de [*swearwords, criticisms*]; **3** (fire at) cribler (**with** de).

pepper: **~-and-salt** *adj* [*hair*] poivre et sel; [*material*] chiné noir et blanc; **~corn** *n* grain *m* de poivre; **~ mill** *n* moulin *m* à poivre.

peppermint /'pepəmɪnt/ **I** *n* **1** (sweet) pastille *f* de menthe; **2** (plant) menthe *f* poivrée.
II *noun modifier* (also **~-flavoured**) à la menthe.

pepper pot, **pepper shaker** *n* poivrier *m*.

peppery /'pepərɪ/ *adj* **1** (spicy) poivré; **2** (irritable) irascible.

pep: **~ pill**° *n* excitant *m*; **~ talk**° *n* laïus° *m* d'encouragement.

peptic /'peptɪk/ *adj* GEN digestif/-ive; **~ ulcer** ulcère *m* de l'estomac.

per /pɜː(r)/ *prep* **1** (for each) par; **~ head** par tête or personne; **~ annum** par an; **80 km ~ hour** 80 km à l'heure; **£5 ~ hour** 5 livres (de) l'heure; **revolutions ~ minute** tours-minute; **as ~ usual**° comme d'habitude; **2** (by means of) **~ post** par la poste; **3** COMM **as ~ invoice** suivant facture; **as ~ your instructions** conformément à vos instructions.

per capita *adj, adv* par habitant.

perceive /pə'siːv/ **I** *vtr* percevoir; **to ~ oneself as (being) sth** se percevoir comme qch.
II perceived *pp adj* [*need, success*] perçu/-e comme tel/telle.

per cent, pc /pə'sent/ **I** *n* pour-cent *m*.
II *adv* pour cent.

percentage /pə'sentɪdʒ/ **I** *n* pourcentage *m*; **to get a ~ on** toucher un pourcentage sur [*sale*].
II *noun modifier* [*increase, decrease, change*] en pourcentage.

perceptible /pə'septəbl/ *adj* perceptible (**to** à).

perceptibly /pə'septəblɪ/ *adv* sensiblement.

perception /pə'sepʃn/ *n* **1** PHILOS, PSYCH perception *f*; **2** (view) **my ~ of him** l'idée que je me fais de lui; **the popular ~ of** l'idée que les gens se font de; **3** (also **perceptiveness**) (of person) perspicacité *f*; (of essay, novel) finesse *f*; **4** COMM, FIN perception *f*.

perceptive /pə'septɪv/ *adj* **1** [*person*] perspicace; [*study*] pertinent; [*comedy*] spirituel/-elle; **2** PSYCH perceptif/-ive.

perceptively /pə'septɪvlɪ/ *adv* avec perspicacité.

perch /pɜːtʃ/ **I** *n* **1** (for bird) perchoir *m*; **2** FIG (vantage point) position *f* élevée; **3** (fish) perche *f*.
II *vtr* percher.
III *vi* se percher (**on** sur).
IDIOMS **to knock sb off their ~**° détrôner qn.

percolate /'pɜːkəleɪt/ **I** *vtr* **~d coffee** café fait dans une cafetière à pression.
II *vi* (also **~ through**) [*coffee*] passer; [*water*] passer, filtrer; [*information*] filtrer (**into, to** jusqu'à).

percolator /'pɜːkəleɪtə(r)/ *n* cafetière *f* à pression.

percussion /pə'kʌʃn/ *n* ₵ MUS percussions *fpl*.

percussionist /pə'kʌʃənɪst/ *n* percussionniste *mf*.

peremptory /pə'remptərɪ, US 'perəmptɔːrɪ/ *adj* péremptoire.

perennial /pə'renɪəl/ **I** *n* plante *f* vivace; **hardy ~** plante *f* vivace.
II *adj* **1** (recurring) perpétuel/-elle; **2** BOT [*plant*] vivace.

perfect I /'pɜːfɪkt/ *n* LING parfait *m*; **in the ~** au parfait.
II /'pɜːfɪkt/ *adj* **1** (flawless) GEN parfait (**for** pour); [*choice, holiday, moment, name, opportunity, place, partner, solution*] idéal (**for** pour); [*hostess*] exemplaire; **that screw will be ~ for the job** cette vis fera parfaitement l'affaire; **that jacket is a ~ fit** cette veste va parfaitement; **to do sth with ~ timing** faire qch au bon moment; **2** (total) [*stranger, fool*] parfait (*before n*); [*pest*] véritable (*before n*); **3** LING **the ~ tense** le parfait.
III /pə'fekt/ *vtr* perfectionner.

perfection /pə'fekʃn/ *n* perfection *f* (**of** de); **to ~** à la perfection.

perfectionist /pə'fekʃənɪst/ *n, adj* perfectionniste (*mf*).

perfective /pə'fektɪv/ *n* LING (verb) verbe *m* perfectif.

perfectly /'pɜːfɪktlɪ/ *adv* **1** (totally) GEN tout à fait; **to be ~ entitled to do** avoir parfaitement le droit de faire; **2** (very well) [*fit, illustrate*] parfaitement.

perfidious /pə'fɪdɪəs/ *adj* perfide.

perforate /'pɜːfəreɪt/ *vtr* perforer.

perform /pə'fɔːm/ **I** *vtr* **1** (carry out) exécuter [*task*]; accomplir [*duties*]; procéder à [*operation*]; **2** (for

entertainment) jouer [*play*]; chanter [*song*]; exécuter [*dance, trick*]; **3** (enact) célébrer [*ceremony*].
II *vi* **1** [*actor, musician*] jouer; **2** (conduct oneself) **to ~ well/badly** [*team*] bien/mal jouer; [*interviewee*] faire bonne/mauvaise impression; [*exam candidate*] avoir de bons/de mauvais résultats; **3** COMM, FIN [*company, department*] avoir de bons résultats; **sterling ~ed badly** la livre sterling a baissé.

performance /pə'fɔːməns/ *n* **1** (rendition) interprétation *f* (**of** de); **2** (concert, show, play) représentation *f* (**of** de); **to put on a ~** monter un spectacle; **3** (of team, sportsman) performance *f* (**in** à); **4** ₵ (economic, political record) performances *fpl*; **5** (of duties) exercice *m* (**of** de); (of task) célébration *f* (**of** de); (of task) exécution *f* (**of** de); **6** ₵ AUT (of car, engine) performances *fpl*; **7**° (outburst) scène *f*; (elaborate procedure) affaire *f*; **8** ART art *m* vivant.

performance: **~ artist** ▶ 1251 *n* artiste *mf* de performances; **~ indicators** *npl* tableau *m* de bord.

performer /pə'fɔːmə(r)/ *n* **1** (artist) artiste *mf*; **2** (achiever) **the car is a good ~ on hilly terrain** la voiture se comporte bien en terrain vallonné.

performing /pə'fɔːmɪŋ/ *adj* [*seal, elephant*] savant.

performing arts *npl* arts *mpl* scéniques.

perfume /'pɜːfjuːm, US pər'fjuːm/ **I** *n* parfum *m*.
II *vtr* parfumer.

perfunctory /pə'fʌŋktərɪ, US -tɔːrɪ/ *adj* [*search, greeting*] pour la forme; [*kiss, nod*] sans conviction; [*investigation*] sommaire.

perhaps /pə'hæps/ *adv* peut-être; **~ she's forgotten** elle a peut-être oublié.

peril /'perəl/ *n* péril *m*, danger *m*.

perilous /'perələs/ *adj* périlleux/-euse.

perilously /'perələslɪ/ *adv* dangereusement; **he came ~ close to doing** il a failli faire.

perimeter /pə'rɪmɪtə(r)/ *n* périmètre *m*; **on the ~ of** aux abords de [*park, site*].

perimeter fence *n* clôture *f* grillagée.

perineum /ˌperɪ'niːəm/ *n* (*pl* **-nea**) périnée *m*.

period /'pɪərɪəd/ **I** *n* **1** GEN, ART, GEOG, HIST période *f*; (longer) époque *f*; **trial ~** période d'essai; **bright ~s** METEOROL éclaircies *fpl*; **rainy ~s** Meteorol averses *fpl*; **over a two-year ~** en deux ans; **for a long ~** pendant longtemps; **2** US (full stop) LIT, FIG point *m*; **3** (menstruation) règles *fpl*; **4** SCH (lesson) cours *m*, leçon *f*; **a double ~ of French** deux cours de français à la suite; **to have a free ~** avoir une heure de libre; **5** SPORT période *f* de jeu.
II *noun modifier* (of a certain era) [*costume, furniture, instrument*] d'époque; (reproduction) [*costume, instrument*] caractéristique de l'époque; [*furniture*] de style (ancien).

periodic /ˌpɪərɪ'ɒdɪk/ *adj* périodique.

periodical /ˌpɪərɪ'ɒdɪkl/ *n, adj* périodique (*m*).

periodically /ˌpɪərɪ'ɒdɪklɪ/ *adv* périodiquement.

periodic: **~ law** *n* principe *m* de classification périodique des éléments chimiques; **~ table** *n* tableau *m* de classification périodique des éléments.

period: **~ of office** *n* POL, ADMIN mandat *m*; **~ pains** *npl* règles *fpl* douloureuses; **~ piece** *n* curiosité *f* d'époque.

peripheral /pə'rɪfərəl/ *adj* [*equipment, vision, suburb*] périphérique; [*issue, investment*] annexe; **to be ~ to** être secondaire par rapport à.

periphery /pə'rɪfərɪ/ *n* **1** (edge) périphérie *f*; **2** FIG (fringes) **to be on the ~ of** être dans la mouvance de [*party*]; **to remain on the ~ of** rester à l'écart de [*event, movement*].

periscope /'perɪskəʊp/ *n* périscope *m*.

perish /'perɪʃ/ *vi* **1** LITTÉR (die) périr (**from** de); **to do sth or ~ in the attempt** HUM faire qch coûte que coûte; **~ the thought!** le Ciel nous en préserve!; **2** (rot) [*food*] se gâter; [*rubber*] se détériorer.

perishable /'perɪʃəbl/ *adj* périssable.

perished° /'perɪʃt/ *adj* **to be ~** [*person*] être gelé°.

peritonitis /ˌperɪtə'naɪtɪs/ ▶ 1002 *n* péritonite *f*.

periwinkle /'perɪwɪŋkl/ n **1** BOT pervenche f; **2** ZOOL bigorneau m; **3** ▶818 (also ~ **blue**) bleu m pervenche.

perjure /'pɜːdʒə(r)/ v refl **to ~ oneself** JUR faire un faux témoignage; (morally) se parjurer.

perjury /'pɜːdʒərɪ/ n JUR faux témoignage m.

perk° /pɜːk/ n GEN avantage m; (benefit in kind) avantage m en nature.
■ **perk up**: ¶ ~ **up** [person] se ragaillardir; [business, life, plant] reprendre; [weather] s'adoucir; ¶ ~ [sth] **up**, ~ **up** [sth] revigorer [person, plant, business]; égayer [dress].

perky /'pɜːkɪ/ adj guilleret/-ette.

perm /pɜːm/ I n permanente f; **to have a ~** se faire faire une permanente.
II vtr **to ~ sb's hair** faire une permanente à qn.

permanence /'pɜːmənəns/ n permanence f.

permanent /'pɜːmənənt/ I n US permanente f.
II adj [job, disability, exhibition, address] permanent; [premises, closure] définitif/-ive; [contract] à durée indéterminée; [staff] ayant un contrat à durée indéterminée.

permanently /'pɜːmənəntlɪ/ adv (constantly) [happy, tired] en permanence; (definitively) [employed, disabled] de façon permanente; [appointed] à titre définitif; [close, emigrate, settle] définitivement.

permanent secretary (of state) n GB POL ADMIN directeur/-trice m/f de cabinet.

permeate /'pɜːmɪeɪt/ I vtr **1** [liquid, gas] s'infiltrer dans; [odour] pénétrer dans; **2** FIG [ideas] imprégner.
II **permeated** pp adj **to be ~d with** être imprégné de ALSO FIG.

permissible /pə'mɪsɪbl/ adj [level, conduct] admissible; [error] acceptable; **to tell sb what is ~** dire à qn ce qui est permis.

permission /pə'mɪʃn/ n GEN permission f; (official) autorisation f; **to have ~ to do** avoir la permission or l'autorisation de faire; **to get ~ to do** obtenir la permission or l'autorisation de faire; **written ~ to do** l'autorisation écrite de faire; **by kind ~ of** avec l'aimable autorisation de.

permissive /pə'mɪsɪv/ adj **1** (morally lax) permissif/-ive; **2** (liberal) [view, law] libéral.

permit I /'pɜːmɪt/ n **1** (document) permis m; (official permission) autorisation f; **to apply for a ~** faire une demande de permis; **work ~** permis m de travail; **2** US AUT permis m (de conduire).
II /pə'mɪt/ vtr (p prés etc **-tt-**) **1** (allow) permettre [action, measure]; **smoking is not ~ted** il est interdit de fumer; **to ~ sb to do** permettre à qn de faire; **to ~ oneself** se permettre [smile, drink]; **2** (allow formally, officially) autoriser.
III /pə'mɪt/ vi (p prés etc **-tt-**) permettre; **weather ~ting** si le temps le permet; **time ~ting** à condition d'en avoir le temps.

permutation /ˌpɜːmjuː'teɪʃn/ n permutation f.

pernicious /pə'nɪʃəs/ adj pernicieux/-ieuse.

pernickety° GB /pə'nɪkətɪ/ adj **1** (detail-conscious) pointilleux/-euse (**about** sur); **2** (choosy) PÉJ tatillon/-onne (**about** quant à).

peroxide /pə'rɒksaɪd/ n **1** CHEM peroxyde m; **2** (also **hydrogen ~**) eau f oxygénée.

peroxide blonde n PÉJ blonde f décolorée.

perpendicular /ˌpɜːpən'dɪkjʊlə(r)/ I n GEN, MATH verticale f (**to** à).
II adj [line] perpendiculaire; **a ~ cliff face** un à-pic.

perpetrate /'pɜːpɪtreɪt/ vtr perpétrer [deed, fraud]; monter [hoax].

perpetrator /'pɜːpɪtreɪtə(r)/ n auteur m (**of** de).

perpetual /pə'petʃʊəl/ adj [meetings, longing, turmoil] perpétuel/-elle; [darkness, stench] permanent; [banter] éternel/-elle.

perpetually /pə'petʃʊəlɪ/ adv perpétuellement.

perpetuate /pə'petjʊeɪt/ vtr perpétuer.

perpetuity /ˌpɜːpɪ'tjuːətɪ, US -'tuː-/ n perpétuité f.

perplexed /pə'plekst/ adj perplexe; **to be ~ as to why/how** se demander pourquoi/comment.

perplexing /pə'pleksɪŋ/ adj [behaviour] curieux/-ieuse; [situation] confus; [question] difficile.

perquisite /'pɜːkwɪzɪt/ n avantage m.

per se /ˌpɜː 'seɪ/ adv en soi.

persecute /'pɜːsɪkjuːt/ vtr persécuter (**for** pour; **for doing** pour avoir fait).

persecution /ˌpɜːsɪ'kjuːʃn/ n persécution f.

persecution complex n délire m de persécution.

perseverance /ˌpɜːsɪ'vɪərəns/ n persévérance f.

persevere /ˌpɜːsɪ'vɪə(r)/ vi persévérer (**with, at** dans).

Persian /'pɜːʃn/ ▶1100, 1038 I n **1** (person) (ancient) Perse mf; (from 7th century on) Persan/-e m/f; **2** (language) persan m.
II adj (ancient) perse; (from 7th century on) persan.

Persian: ~ **cat** n chat m persan; ~ **Gulf** ▶1117 pr n Golfe m persique; ~ **lamb** n astrakan m.

persimmon /pɜː'sɪmən/ n (tree) plaqueminier m; (fruit) kaki m.

persist /pə'sɪst/ vi persister (**in** dans; **in doing** à faire).

persistence /pə'sɪstəns/ n GEN persévérance f; PÉJ persistance f (**in** à faire).

persistent /pə'sɪstənt/ adj **1** (persevering) persévérant; (obstinate) obstiné PÉJ (**in** dans); **2** (continual) [rain, denial] persistant; [inquiries, noise, pressure] continuel/-elle; [illness, fears, idea] tenace.

persistently /pə'sɪstəntlɪ/ adv continuellement.

persistent offender n JUR récidiviste mf.

person /'pɜːsn/ n **1** (human being) (pl **people**, **persons** SOUT) personne f; **the average ~ cannot afford** une personne ordinaire ne peut pas se permettre; **to do sth in ~** faire qch en personne; **he's not the kind of ~ who would do such a thing** ce n'est pas le genre à faire ça; **single ~** célibataire mf; **the ~ concerned** l'interessé/-e m/f; **there's no such ~** cette personne n'a jamais existé; **the very ~ I was looking for!** c'est justement toi que je cherchais!; **2** (type) **I didn't know he was a horsey ~°!** je ne savais pas que c'était un passionné de cheval!; **what's she like as a ~?** en tant que femme, elle est comment?; **he's a very discreet ~** il est très discret; **3** (body) **with drugs concealed about his ~** avec de la drogue cachée sur lui; **offences against the ~** JUR atteintes à la personne f; **4** LING personne f; **the first ~ singular** la première personne du singulier.

persona /pɜː'səʊnə/ n THEAT, PSYCH personnage m.

personable /'pɜːsənəbl/ adj qui présente bien.

personage /'pɜːsənɪdʒ/ n personnalité f.

personal /'pɜːsnl/ I n US petite annonce f personnelle.
II adj [opinion, life, problem, attack, call, matter] personnel/-elle; [safety, freedom, choice, income, profit, insurance] individuel/-elle; [service] personnalisé; **don't be so ~!** ne fais pas d'allusions personnelles!; **the discussion became rather ~** la discussion a pris un ton personnel; **on ou at a ~ level** sur le plan personnel; **to take care of one's ~ appearance** prendre soin de son apparence; **to make a ~ appearance** venir en personne (**at** à); **he paid them a ~ visit** il leur a rendu visite en personne; ~ **belongings** ou **effects** ou **possessions** effets mpl personnels; ~ **hygiene** hygiène f intime; **my ~ best is 10 seconds** mon meilleur temps est de 10 secondes; **as a ~ favour to you** pour te faire plaisir.

personal: ~ **ad** n petite annonce f personnelle; ~ **assistant** ▶1251 n (secretary) (also **PA**) secrétaire mf de direction; (assistant) assistant/-e m/f; ~ **column** n petites annonces fpl personnelles; ~ **computer**, **PC** n ordinateur m (personnel); ~ **details** npl GEN renseignements mpl d'ordre personnel; (more intimate) détails mpl intimes; (on application form) état civil m et coordonnées fpl; ~ **injury** n JUR préjudices m individuels.

personality /ˌpɜːsə'nælətɪ/ n **1** (character) personnalité f; **2** (person) personnalité f; **a TV ~** une vedette de la télévision.

personalize /ˈpɜːsənəlaɪz/ vtr **1** personnaliser [*stationery, clothing*]; **2** ramener [qch] à un plan personnel [*issue, dispute*].

personal loan n FIN (borrowed) emprunt m (à titre personnel); (given by bank etc) prêt m personnel.

personally /ˈpɜːsənəlɪ/ adv personnellement; **to take sth ~** se sentir visé personnellement par qch.

personal: **~ organizer** n ~ agenda m; **~ pension plan**, **~ pension scheme** n plan m de retraite; **~ pronoun** n LING pronom m personnel; **~ property** n ⊄ JUR biens mpl personnels; **~ stereo** n AUDIO baladeur m.

personification /pəˌsɒnɪfɪˈkeɪʃn/ n **1** (embodiment) incarnation f (**of** de); **2** LITERAT personnification f.

personify /pəˈsɒnɪfaɪ/ vtr **1** incarner [*ideal*]; **2** LITERAT personnifier.

personnel /ˌpɜːsəˈnel/ n **1** GEN, MIL (staff, troops) personnel m; **2** ADMIN (also **Personnel**) service m du personnel.

personnel: **~ carrier** n véhicule m de transport de troupes; **~ department** n service m du personnel; **~ manager** ▶ 1251 n directeur/-trice m/f du personnel; **~ officer** ▶ 1251 n responsable m/f du personnel.

person-to-person adj TELECOM avec préavis.

perspective /pəˈspektɪv/ n GEN, ART perspective f; **from one's (own) ~** de son (propre) point de vue; **to keep things in ~** garder un sens de la mesure; **to put things into ~** relativiser les choses.

perspex® /ˈpɜːspeks/ n plexiglas® m.

perspiration /ˌpɜːspɪˈreɪʃn/ n **1** (sweat) sueur f; **2** (sweating) transpiration f.

perspire /pəˈspaɪə(r)/ vi transpirer.

persuade /pəˈsweɪd/ vtr **1** (influence) persuader [*person*]; **to ~ sb to do** persuader qn de faire; **2** (convince intellectually) convaincre (**of** de); **to ~ oneself** réussir à se convaincre (**that** que).

persuasion /pəˈsweɪʒn/ n **1** ⊄ (persuading, persuasiveness) persuasion f; **no amount of ~ will make her change her mind** on aura beau essayer de la persuader, rien ne la fera changer d'avis; **to be open to ~** être prêt à se laisser convaincre; **2** RELIG confession f; **3** (political view) conviction f; **4** (kind, sort) sorte f.

persuasive /pəˈsweɪsɪv/ adj [*person*] persuasif/-ive; [*argument, evidence*] convaincant.

persuasively /pəˈsweɪsɪvlɪ/ adv [*speak*] d'un ton persuasif; [*demonstrate*] d'une manière convaincante.

pert /pɜːt/ adj [*person, manner*] espiègle; [*hat, nose*] coquin.

pertain /pəˈteɪn/ vi **to ~ to** JUR dépendre de; GEN se rapporter à.

pertinent /ˈpɜːtɪnənt, US -tənənt/ adj [*question, point*] pertinent; **to be ~ to** avoir rapport à; **to be ~ to do** être approprié de faire.

perturb /pəˈtɜːb/ vtr perturber; **to be ~ed by** [*person*] être troublé par; (more deeply) être alarmé par.

perturbing /pəˈtɜːbɪŋ/ adj troublant; (more deeply) alarmant.

Peru /pəˈruː/ ▶ 840 pr n Pérou m.

peruse /pəˈruːz/ vtr SOUT parcourir [*paper*].

pervade /pəˈveɪd/ vtr imprégner.

pervasive /pəˈveɪsɪv/ adj [*smell*] pénétrant; [*feeling*] envahissant.

perverse /pəˈvɜːs/ adj **1** (twisted) [*person*] retors; [*desire*] pervers; **2** (contrary) [*refusal, attempt, attitude*] illogique; [*effect*] contraire; **to take a ~ pleasure in doing** prendre un malin plaisir à faire.

perversely /pəˈvɜːslɪ/ adv avec un malin plaisir.

perversion /pəˈvɜːʃn, US -ʒn/ n **1** (deviation) perversion f (**of** de); **2** (wrong interpretation) (of facts, justice) travestissement m (**of** de).

perversity /pəˈvɜːsətɪ/ n (corruptness) (of person) mauvais esprit m; (of action) malignité f.

pervert I /ˈpɜːvɜːt/ n pervers/-e mf.
II /pəˈvɜːt/ vtr **1** (corrupt) corrompre; **2** (misrepresent) travestir [*truth*]; dénaturer [*meaning*]; fausser [*values*];

to ~ the course of justice JUR entraver l'action de la justice.

perverted /pəˈvɜːtɪd/ adj **1** (sexually deviant) pervers; **2** (distorted) [*idea*] tordu; [*act*] vicieux/-ieuse.

pessimism /ˈpesɪmɪzəm/ n pessimisme m.

pessimist /ˈpesɪmɪst/ n pessimiste mf.

pessimistic /ˌpesɪˈmɪstɪk/ adj pessimiste.

pest /pest/ n **1** AGRIC (animal) animal m nuisible; (insect) insecte m nuisible; **2**° (person) GEN enquiquineur/-euse° m/f; (little boy) garnement m; (little girl) chipie° f.

pest control n (of insects) désinsectisation f; (of rats) dératisation f.

pester /ˈpestə(r)/ vtr **1** (annoy) harceler; **stop ~ing me!** fiche-moi la paix°!; **2** (harass sexually) harceler, poursuivre [qn] de ses assiduités.

pesticide /ˈpestɪsaɪd/ n pesticide m.

pestilential /ˌpestɪˈlenʃl/ adj **1** HUM (annoying) satané° (before n); **2** (unhealthy) SOUT pestilentiel/-ielle.

pestle /ˈpesl/ n pilon m.

pet /pet/ **I** n **1** (animal) animal m de compagnie; 'no ~s' 'les animaux domestiques ne sont pas acceptés'; **2** (favourite) chouchou/chouchoute° m/f; **3** (sweet person) chou° m.
II adj (favourite) [*charity, theory*] favori/-ite; **~ dog** chien.
III vtr (p prés etc **-tt-**) **1** (spoil) chouchouter°; **2** (caress) caresser.

petal /ˈpetl/ n pétale m.

peter /ˈpiːtə(r)/ v ■ **peter out** [*conversation*] tarir; [*meeting*] tourner court; [*plan*] tomber à l'eau; [*supplies*] s'épuiser.

Peter /ˈpiːtə(r)/ pr n Pierre.
IDIOMS to rob ~ to pay Paul déshabiller Pierre pour habiller Paul.

pet: **~ food** n aliments mpl pour chiens et chats; **~ hate** GB n bête f noire.

petite /pəˈtiːt/ adj [*woman*] menue; [*size*] petite.

petition /pəˈtɪʃn/ **I** n **1** (document) pétition f (**to** à); **a ~ calling for** une pétition réclamant; **2** (formal request) pétition f; **3** JUR demande f; **a ~ for divorce** une demande de divorce.
II vtr adresser une pétition à [*person, body*].
III vi **1** GEN faire une pétition; **2** JUR **to ~ for divorce** demander le divorce.

petitioner /pəˈtɪʃnə(r)/ n **1** (signatory) pétitionnaire mf; **2** JUR GEN requérant/-ante m/f; (in divorce) demandeur/-deresse m/f.

pet: **~ name** n petit nom m; **~ project** n enfant m chéri FIG.

petrified /ˈpetrɪfaɪd/ adj (all contexts) pétrifié.

petrify /ˈpetrɪfaɪ/ vi [*substance*] se pétrifier; [*civilisation, system*] se fossiliser.

petrifying /ˈpetrɪfaɪɪŋ/ adj (terrifying) terrifiant.

petrochemical /ˌpetrəʊˈkemɪkl/ n produit m pétrochimique.

petrodollar /ˈpetrəʊdɒlə(r)/ n pétrodollar m.

petrol /ˈpetrəl/ GB **I** n essence f; **to fill up with ~** faire le plein (d'essence); **to run on ~** fonctionner à l'essence; **to run out of ~** [*car*] tomber en panne d'essence; [*garage*] ne plus avoir d'essence.
II noun modifier [*prices, rationing*] d'essence; [*tax*] sur l'essence.

petrol: **~ bomb** n GB cocktail m Molotov; **~ can** n GB bidon m à essence; **~ cap** n GB bouchon m de réservoir (d'essence); **~ engine** n GB moteur m à essence.

petroleum /pəˈtrəʊlɪəm/ **I** n pétrole m.
II noun modifier [*product, industry, engineer*] pétrolier/-ière.

petroleum jelly n vaseline® f.

petrol: **~ gauge** n GB jauge f d'essence; **~ pump** n GB (at garage, in engine) pompe f à essence; **~ station** n GB station f d'essence; **~ tank** n GB réservoir m d'essence; **~ tanker** n GB (ship) pétrolier m; (lorry) camion-citerne m.

pet: ~ **shop** GB, ~ **store** US *n* animalerie *f*; ~ **subject** *n* sujet *m* favori, dada *m*.

petticoat /'petɪkəʊt/ *n* (full slip) combinaison *m*; (half slip) jupon *m*.

pettifogging /'petɪfɒɡɪŋ/ *adj* PÉJ pointilleux/-euse.

pettiness /'petɪnɪs/ *n* mesquinerie *f*.

petting /'petɪŋ/ *n* caresses *fpl*, pelotage° *m*.

pettish /'petɪʃ/ *adj* grincheux/-euse.

petty /'petɪ/ *adj* [*person, squabble*] mesquin; [*detail*] insignifiant; [*regulation*] tracassier/-ière; [*snobbery*] étroit.

petty: ~ **cash**, **p/c** *n* petite caisse *f*; ~ **crime** *n* petite délinquance *f*; ~ **expenses** *npl* menues dépenses *fpl*; ~**minded** *adj* mesquin; ~ **officer** *n* NAUT ~ maître *m*; ~ **official** *n* PÉJ petit fonctionnaire *m*; ~ **theft** *n* JUR larcin *m*.

petulant /'petjʊlənt/, US -tʃʊ-/ *adj* irascible.

petulantly /'petʊləntlɪ, US -tʃʊ-/ *adv* avec humeur.

pew /pju:/ *n* banc *m* (d'église).

pewter /'pju:tə(r)/ *n* **1** (metal) étain *m*; **2** (colour) (gris *m*) anthracite *m inv*.

PG *n* CIN (*abrév* = **Parental Guidance**) *tous publics avec accord parental suggéré.*

PGCE *n* (*abrév* = **postgraduate certificate in education**) diplôme *m* de spécialisation dans l'enseignement.

phallus /'fæləs/ *n* (*pl* **-luses** ou **-li**) phallus *m*.

phantom /'fæntəm/ *n* **1** (ghost) fantôme *m*; **2** AVIAT Phantom *m*.

pharaoh /'feərəʊ/ *n* (also **Pharaoh**) pharaon *m*; (title) Pharaon *m*.

pharmaceutical /ˌfɑ:mə'sju:tɪkl, US -'su:-/ *adj* pharmaceutique.

pharmaceuticals /ˌfɑ:mə'sju:tɪklz, US -'su:-/ **I** *npl* produits *mpl* pharmaceutiques.
II *noun modifier* [*industry, factory*] pharmaceutique.

pharmacist /'fɑ:məsɪst/ ▶ **1251**, **1251** *n* (person) pharmacien/-ienne *m/f*.

pharmacology /ˌfɑ:mə'kɒlədʒɪ/ *n* pharmacologie *f*.

pharmacy /'fɑ:məsɪ/ ▶ **1251** *n* **1** (shop) pharmacie *f*; **2** (also **pharmaceutics**) pharmaceutique *f*.

phase /feɪz/ **I** *n* (all contexts) phase *f*; **it's just a ~** (she's going through) ça lui passera; **to be out of ~** ELEC être déphasé; FIG ne pas être en harmonie.
II *vtr* échelonner [*changes*] (**over** sur).
■ **phase out**: ~ **out** [*sth*] supprimer [qch] peu à peu.

PhD *n* (*abrév* = **Doctor of Philosophy**) doctorat *m*.

pheasant /'feznt/ *n* faisan/-e *m/f*.

phenix *n* US = **phoenix**.

phenomena /fə'nɒmɪnə/ *pl* ▶ **phenomenon**.

phenomenal /fə'nɒmɪnl/ *adj* phénoménal.

phenomenally /fə'nɒmɪnəlɪ/ *adv* [*grow, increase*] de manière phénoménale; [*stupid, successful*] extraordinairement.

phenomenon /fə'nɒmɪnən/ *n* (*pl* **-na**) phénomène *m*.

phew /fju:/ *excl* (in relief) ouf; (when too hot) pff; (in surprise) oh.

phial /'faɪəl/ *n* fiole *f*.

Phi Beta Kappa /ˌfaɪ bi:tə 'kæpə/ *n* US UNIV (group) *association d'anciens étudiants d'élite.*

Philadelphia lawyer /ˌfɪlə'delfɪə/ *n* US PÉJ avocat *m* retors.

philanderer /fɪ'lændərə(r)/ *n* coureur *m* de jupons°.

philanthropist /fɪ'lænθrəpɪst/ *n* philanthrope *mf*.

philatelist /fɪ'lætəlɪst/ *n* philatéliste *mf*.

philharmonic /ˌfɪlɑ:'mɒnɪk/ *adj* philharmonique.

philistine /'fɪlɪstaɪn/ **I** *n* béotien/-ienne *m/f*.
II *adj* [*attitude, article*] béotien/-ienne; [*public*] de béotiens.

Phillips screwdriver /'fɪlɪps/ *n* tournevis *m* cruciforme.

philology /fɪ'lɒlədʒɪ/ *n* philologie *f*.

philosopher /fɪ'lɒsəfə(r)/ ▶ **1251** *n* LIT, FIG philosophe *mf*.

philosophic(al) /ˌfɪlə'sɒfɪk(l)/ *adj* **1** [*knowledge, question, treatise*] philosophique; **2** FIG (calm, stoical) philosophe (**about** à propos de).

philosophically /ˌfɪlə'sɒfɪklɪ/ *adv* philosophiquement; **he took it all very ~** FIG il a pris tout ça avec philosophie.

philosophize /fɪ'lɒsəfaɪz/ *vi* philosopher (**about** sur).

philosophy /fɪ'lɒsəfɪ/ *n* philosophie *f*.

phlebitis /flɪ'baɪtɪs/ ▶ **1002** *n* phlébite *f*.

phlegm /flem/ *n* **1** MED mucosité *f*; **2** (calm) flegme *m*.

phlegmatic /fleg'mætɪk/ *adj* flegmatique (**about** au sujet de).

phobia /'fəʊbɪə/ *n* phobie *f*.

phobic /'fəʊbɪk/ *adj* phobique.

phoenix /'fi:nɪks/ *n* phénix *m*.

phone /fəʊn/ **I** *n* téléphone *m*; **to be on the ~** (be talking) être au téléphone (**to sb** avec qn); (be subscriber) avoir le téléphone.
II *vtr* passer un coup de fil à°, téléphoner à [*person, company*]; **to ~ France** téléphoner en France.
III *vi* téléphoner; **to ~ for a taxi** appeler un taxi.
■ **phone in** téléphoner; **she ~d in sick** elle a téléphoné au bureau pour dire qu'elle était malade.
■ **phone up**: ~ **up** [sb], ~ [sb] **up** téléphoner à, appeler [*person, organization*].

phone: ~ **book** *n* annuaire *m* (du téléphone); ~ **booth**, ~ **box** *n* cabine *f* téléphonique; ~ **call** *n* GEN coup *m* de fil°; ADMIN communication *f* (téléphonique); ~ **card** *n* GB télécarte *f*; ~**-in** *n* émission *f* à ligne ouverte; ~ **link** *n* liaison *f* téléphonique.

phoneme /'fəʊni:m/ *n* phonème *m*.

phone: ~ **number** *n* numéro *m* de téléphone; ~ **tapping** *n* ¢ écoutes *fpl* téléphoniques.

phonetic /fə'netɪk/ *adj* phonétique.

phonetics /fə'netɪks/ *n* phonétique *f*.

phoney° /'fəʊnɪ/ PÉJ **I** *n* (affected person) poseur/-euse *m/f*; (impostor) charlatan *m*; (forgery, fake) faux *m*.
II *adj* [*address, accent, jewel*] faux/fausse (*before n*); [*company, excuse*] bidon°; [*emotion*] simulé.

phoney war *n* HIST **the ~** la drôle de guerre.

phonology /fə'nɒlədʒɪ/ *n* phonologie *f*.

phooey /'fu:ɪ/ *excl* peuh!, pfft!

phosphate /'fɒsfeɪt/ **I** *n* CHEM phosphate *m*.
II phosphates *npl* AGRIC phosphates *mpl*, engrais *mpl* phosphatés.

phosphorescent /ˌfɒsfə'resnt/ *adj* phosphorescent.

phosphorus /'fɒsfərəs/ *n* phosphore *m*.

photo /'fəʊtəʊ/ **I** *n* photo *f*; ▶ **photograph**.
II photo+ *combining form* photo-.

photo: ~ **album** *n* album *m* de photos; ~ **booth** *n* photomaton® *m*; ~**call** *n* GB séance *f* de photos.

photocell /'fəʊtəʊsel/ *n* cellule *f* photo-électrique.

photocopier /'fəʊtəʊkɒpɪə(r)/ *n* photocopieuse *f*.

photocopy /'fəʊtəʊkɒpɪ/ **I** *n* photocopie *f*.
II *vtr* photocopier.

photoengraving /ˌfəʊtəʊɪn'greɪvɪŋ/ *n* photogravure *f*.

photo finish *n* (picture) photo-finish *f*; (result) arrivée *f* départagée au photo-finish.

Photofit® /'fəʊtəʊfɪt/ *n* GB portrait-robot *m*.

photoflash *n* ampoule *f* de flash.

photogenic /ˌfəʊtəʊ'dʒenɪk/ *adj* photogénique.

photograph /'fəʊtəɡrɑ:f, US -ɡræf/ **I** *n* photo *f*; **in the ~** sur la photo; **to take a ~ of sb/sth** prendre qn/qch en photo.
II *vtr* photographier, prendre [qn/qch] en photo.
III *vi* **to ~ well** [*person*] être photogénique.

photograph album *n* album *m* de photos.

photographer /fə'tɒɡrəfə(r)/ ▶ **1251** *n* photographe *mf*.

photographic /ˌfəʊtə'ɡræfɪk/ *adj* [*image, reproduction, equipment*] photographique; [*studio*] de photo;

[*shop, agency, exhibition*] de photos; **to have a ~ memory** avoir une mémoire visuelle exceptionnelle.

photographically /ˌfəʊtəˈɡræfɪklɪ/ *adv* en termes de photographie.

photographic library *n* photothèque *f*.

photography /fəˈtɒɡrəfɪ/ *n* photographie *f*.

photojournalist /ˌfəʊtəʊˈdʒɜːnəlɪst/ ▶ **1251** *n* photo-journaliste *mf*.

photo-offset /ˌfəʊtəʊˈɒfset/ *n* offset *m*.

photo opportunity *n* séance *f* de photos.

photorealism /ˌfəʊtəʊˈrɪəlɪzəm/ *n* hyperréalisme *m*.

photosensitive /ˌfəʊtəʊˈsensətɪv/ *adj* photosensible.

photo session *n* séance *f* de photos.

photoset /ˈfəʊtəʊset/ *vtr* (*p prés* **-tt-**; *prét, pp* **-set**) photocomposer.

Photostat® /ˈfəʊtəstæt/ *n* photocopie *f*.

photosynthesis /ˌfəʊtəʊˈsɪnθəsɪs/ *n* photosynthèse *f*.

phrasal verb *n* verbe *m* à particule.

phrase /freɪz/ **I** *n* **1** (expression) GEN expression *f*, LING locution *f*; **2** LING (part of clause) syntagme *m*; **noun ~** syntagme nominal; **3** MUS phrase *f*.
II *vtr* **1** (formulate) exprimer [*idea*]; formuler [*question, speech*]; **2** MUS phraser.

phrase: **~book** *n* manuel *m* de conversation; **~ marker** *n* marqueur *m* syntagmatique.

phrasing /ˈfreɪzɪŋ/ *n* **1** GEN formulation *f*; **2** MUS phrasé *m*.

phut○ /fʌt/ *adv* **to go ~** [*car*] rendre l'âme; [*plan*] tomber à l'eau○.

phylogenesis /ˌfaɪləʊˈdʒenəsɪs/, **phylogeny** /faɪˈlɒdʒɪnɪ/ *n* phylogénie *f*.

physical /ˈfɪzɪkl/ **I**○ *n* bilan *m* de santé; **to have a ~** se faire faire un bilan de santé.
II *adj* **1** (of the body) [*strength, pain etc*] physique; **~ abuse** sévices *mpl*; **it's a ~ impossibility** c'est physiquement impossible; **she's very ~** (demonstrative) elle est très démonstrative; **did he get ~?** (become violent) est-ce qu'il en est venu aux mains?; **2** [*chemistry, science, property*] physique.

physical: **~ education, PE** *n* éducation *f* physique; **~ examination** *n* examen *m* médical; **~ fitness** *n* forme *f* physique; **~ geography** *n* géographie *f* physique.

physically /ˈfɪzɪklɪ/ *adv* physiquement.

physically handicapped *adj* **to be ~** être handi-capé/-e *m/f* physique.

physical: **~ sciences** *npl* sciences *fpl* physiques; **~ therapist** ▶ **1251** *n* US MED kinésithérapeute *mf*; **~ therapy** *n* US MED kinésithérapie *f*; **~ training, PT** *n* éducation *f* physique.

physician /fɪˈzɪʃn/ ▶ **1251** *n* GB†, US médecin *m*; GB spécialiste *mf*.

physicist /ˈfɪzɪsɪst/ ▶ **1251** *n* physicien/-ienne *m/f*.

physics /ˈfɪzɪks/ *n* (+ *v sg*) physique *f*.

physio○ /ˈfɪzɪəʊ/ ▶ **1251** *n* GB **1** (*abrév* = **physiotherapist**) kinési○ *mf*, kinésithérapeute *mf*; **2** (*abrév* = **physiotherapy**) kinési○ *f*, kinésithérapie *f*.

physiological /ˌfɪzɪəˈlɒdʒɪkl/ *adj* physiologique.

physiologist /ˌfɪzɪˈɒlədʒɪst/ ▶ **1251** *n* physiologiste *mf*.

physiology /ˌfɪzɪˈɒlədʒɪ/ *n* physiologie *f*.

physiotherapist /ˌfɪzɪəʊˈθerəpɪst/ ▶ **1251** *n* kinési-thérapeute *mf*.

physiotherapy /ˌfɪzɪəʊˈθerəpɪ/ *n* kinésithérapie *f*.

physique /fɪˈziːk/ *n* physique *m*.

pianist /ˈpɪənɪst/ ▶ **1251**, **1097** *n* pianiste *mf*.

piano /pɪˈænəʊ/ ▶ **1097** **I** *n* piano *m*.
II *noun modifier* [*lesson, teacher*] de piano; [*concerto, music*] pour piano.

piano: **~ accordion** ▶ **1097** *n* accordéon *m* à clavier; **~ bar** *n* piano-bar *m*.

pianola® /pɪəˈnəʊlə/ ▶ **1097** *n* (also **piano organ**) piano *m* mécanique.

piano stool *n* tabouret *m* (de piano).

piazza /pɪˈætsə/ *n* **1** (public square) place *f*; **2** US (ver-anda) véranda *f*.

piccalilli /ˌpɪkəˈlɪlɪ/ *n* ₵ pickles *mpl* à la moutarde.

pick /pɪk/ **I** *n* **1** (tool) GEN pioche *f*, pic *m*; (of climber) piolet *m*; (of mason) smille *f*; **to dig with a ~** creuser à la pioche; **2** (choice) choix *m*; **to have one's ~ of** avoir le choix parmi; **take your ~** choisis; **3** (best) meilleur/-e *m/f*; **the ~ of the crop** (fruit) les meilleurs fruits; **the ~ of the bunch** le/la etc meilleur/-e etc du lot.
II *vtr* **1** (choose, select) GEN choisir (**from** parmi); SPORT sélectionner [*player*] (**from** parmi); former [*team*]; **you ~ed the wrong person** tu as choisi la mauvaise personne; **to ~ a fight** (physically) chercher à se bagarrer○ (**with** avec); **to ~ a fight** ou **a quarrel** chercher querelle (**with** à); **2** (navigate) **to ~ one's way through** avancer avec précaution parmi [*rubble, litter*]; **3** (pluck, gather) cueillir [*fruit, flowers*]; **4** (poke at) gratter [*spot, scab*]; **to ~ sth from** ou **off** enlever qch de; **to ~ one's nose** mettre les doigts dans son nez; **to ~ one's teeth** se curer les dents; **to ~ a lock** crocheter une serrure; **to ~ sb's pocket** faire les poches de qn.
III *vi* choisir; **to ~ and choose** faire le/la difficile (**among, between** pour choisir parmi).

■ **pick at**: **~ at** [*sth*] **1** [*person*] manger [qch] du bout des dents [*food*]; gratter [*spot, scab*]; **2** [*bird*] picorer [*crumbs*].

■ **pick off**: ¶ **~** [*sb*] **off, ~ off** [*sb*] (kill) abattre; ¶ **~** [*sth*] **off, ~ off** [*sth*] enlever [qch]; ¶ **~** [*sth*] **off** sth cueillir [qch] sur qch [*apple, cherry*]; **to ~ sth off the floor** ramasser qch qui était par terre.

■ **pick on**: **~ on** [*sb*] harceler.

■ **pick out**: **~** [*sb/sth*] **out, ~ out** [*sb/sth*] **1** (select) GEN choisir; (single out) repérer; **to ~ out three winners** sélectionner trois gagnants (**from** parmi); **2** (make out) distinguer [*landmark*]; saisir [*words*]; reconnaître [*person in photo*]; repérer [*person in crowd*]; **3** (highlight) [*torch etc*] révéler; **to be ~ed out in red** [*pattern*] être mis en valeur en rouge.

■ **pick over**: **~** [*sth*] **over, ~ over** [*sth*] LIT trier; FIG analyser.

■ **pick up**: ¶ **~ up 1** (improve) [*trade, market*] reprendre; [*weather, performance, health*] s'améliorer; [*ill person*] se rétablir; **2** (resume) reprendre; **to pick up (from) where one left off** reprendre là où on s'est arrêté; ¶ **~** [*sb/sth*] **up, ~ up** [*sb/sth*] **1** (lift, take hold of) (to tidy) ramasser; (to examine) prendre; (after fall) relever; (for cuddle) prendre [qn] dans ses bras; **to ~ sth up in** ou **with one's left hand** prendre qch de sa main gauche; **to ~ up the telephone** décrocher le téléphone; **to ~ up the bill** régler l'addition; **2** (collect) prendre [*passenger, cargo*]; (passer) prendre [*ticket, keys*]; **could you ~ me up?** est-ce que tu peux venir me chercher?; ¶ **~** [*sth*] **up, ~ up** [*sth*] **1** (buy) prendre, acheter; dénicher [*bargain*]; **2** (learn, acquire) apprendre [*language*]; prendre [*habit, accent*]; développer [*skill*]; **you'll soon ~ it up** tu t'y mettras vite; **3** (catch) attraper [*illness*]; **4** (notice, register) [*person*] repérer [*error*]; [*person, machine*] détecter [*defect*]; **5** (detect) trouver [*trail, scent*]; [*radar*] détecter la présence de [*aircraft, person, object*]; RADIO, TELE-COM capter [*signal*]; **6** (gain, earn) gagner [*point, size*]; acquérir [*reputation*]; **to ~ up speed** prendre de la vitesse; **7** (resume) reprendre [*conversation, career*]; **you'll soon ~ up your French again** ton français te reviendra vite; ¶ **~** [*sb*] **up, ~ up** [*sb*] **1** (rescue) recueillir [*person*]; **2** (arrest) arrêter [*suspect*]; **3** (meet) PÉJ ramasser [*partner, prostitute*]; **4** (find fault with) faire des remarques à [*person*] (**on** sur); ¶ **~ oneself up** (get up) se relever; (recover) se reprendre.

pickaxe GB, **pickax** US /ˈpɪkæks/ *n* pioche *f*.

picker /ˈpɪkə(r)/ *n* cueilleur/-euse *m/f*.

picket /ˈpɪkɪt/ **I** *n* **1** (in strike) (group of people) piquet *m* (de grève); (one person) gréviste *mf* (*qui fait partie d'un piquet*); **to be on a ~** faire partie d'un piquet de grève; **2** MIL (detachment) détachement *m*; (one soldier) factionnaire *m*; **3** (stake) piquet *m*, pieu *m*.
II *vtr* **1** (to stop work) installer un piquet de grève aux

portes de [*factory*]; (to protest) former un cordon de protestation devant [*meeting place, embassy*]; **2** (fence in) clôturer, palissader.

picket duty *n* **to be on ~** IND faire partie d'un piquet de grève; MIL être (de service) de guet.

picket: **~ fence** *n* palissade *f*; **~ line** *n* (in strike) (cordon *m* de) piquet *m* de grève; (in protest) cordon *m* de protestation.

picking /ˈpɪkɪŋ/ **I** *n* (of crop) cueillette *f*.
II pickings *npl* (rewards) gains *mpl*.

pickle /ˈpɪkl/ **I** *n* **1** ₵ (preserved food) conserves *fpl* au vinaigre; **2 C** (gherkin) cornichon *m*; **~s** pickles *mpl*; **3** ₵ (brine) saumure *f*; (vinegar) vinaigre *m*.
II *vtr* conserver [qch] dans du vinaigre or dans de la saumure.
IDIOMS **to be in a ~** HUM être dans le pétrin○.

pickled /ˈpɪkld/ *adj* **1** CULIN au vinaigre; **2**○ GB (drunk) bourré○.

pick: **~-me-up** *n* remontant *m*; **~pocket** *n* voleur *m* à la tire.

pickup /ˈpɪkʌp/ *n* **1** (also **~ arm**) lecteur *m*; **2** (on electric guitar) capteur *m*; **3** RADIO, TV (reception) réception *f*; **4** (collection) (of goods) ramassage *m*; (passenger) passager/-ère *m/f* ramassé/-e en route; **5** ₵ AUT (acceleration) reprises *fpl*; **6** (in business, economy) reprise *f* (**in** de); **7** = **pickup truck**.

pickup○: **~ point** *n* (for passengers) point *m* de ramassage; (for goods) point *m* de chargement; **~ truck**, **~ van** GB *n* pick-up *m inv*.

picky○ /ˈpɪki/ *adj* difficile (**about** pour ce qui est de).

picnic /ˈpɪknɪk/ **I** *n* pique-nique *m*.
II *noun modifier* [*basket, hamper*] à pique-nique.
IDIOMS **it's no ~!** ce n'est pas une partie de plaisir!

picnic lunch *n* pique-nique *m*.

pictogram /ˈpɪktəgræm/ *n* **1** (symbol) pictogramme *m*; **2** (chart) carte *f* thématique.

pictorial /pɪkˈtɔːrɪəl/ *adj* **1** (in pictures) [*magazine*] illustré; [*record, information*] graphique; [*technique*] artistique; **2** (resembling pictures) [*language, description*] imagé.

picture /ˈpɪktʃə(r)/ **I** *n* **1** (visual depiction) (painting) peinture *f*, tableau *m*; (drawing) dessin *m*; (in book) GEN illustration *f*; (in child's book) image *f*; (in mind) image *f*; **to paint a ~ of sb/sth** peindre qn/qch; **to paint sb's ~** faire le portrait de qn; **2** FIG (description) description *f*; **to paint a ~ of sb/sth** dépeindre qn/qch; **to give** OU **present a clear ~ of sth** dépeindre qch avec clarté; **3** PHOT photo *f*, photographie *f*; **to take a ~ (of)** prendre une photo (de); **4** FIG (overview) situation *f*; **to get the ~** comprendre la situation; **to be in the ~** être au courant; **5** CIN (film) film *m*; **to make a ~** faire un film; **6** TV image *f*.
II pictures○ *npl* **the ~s** le cinéma.
III *vtr* **1** (form mental image of) s'imaginer; **2** (show in picture form) **to be ~d** être représenté; **the vase (~d above) is...** le vase (voir photo ci-dessus) est...
IDIOMS **to be the ~ of health** respirer la santé; **to look a ~** être ravissant; **her face was a ~!** son expression en disait long!

picture: **~ book** *n* livre *m* d'images; **~ card** *n* GAMES figure *f* (*carte*); **~ desk** *n* (of newspaper) service *m* photo; **~ editor** ▶ 1251 *n* (of newspaper) directeur/-trice *m/f* du service photo; **~ frame** *n* cadre *m*; **~ framing** *n* encadrement *m*; **~ gallery** *n* galerie *f* de peinture; **~ hook** *n* crochet *m* (à tableaux); **~ postcard** *n* carte *f* postale; **~ rail** *n* cimaise *f*.

picturesque /ˌpɪktʃəˈresk/ *adj* pittoresque.

piddle○ /ˈpɪdl/ *vi* (urinate) faire pipi○.

piddling○ /ˈpɪdlɪŋ/ *adj* insignifiant.

pidgin /ˈpɪdʒɪn/ *n* **1** (also **~ English**) pidgin *m*; **2** (also **~ French**) GEN petit nègre *m*; (French with Arab) sabir *m*; **3** PÉJ charabia *m*.

pie /paɪ/ *n* **1** (savoury) GEN tourte *f*; **meat ~** tourte à la viande; **pork ~** pâté *m* de porc en croûte; **2** (sweet) tarte *f* (*recouverte de pâte*).
IDIOMS **it's all ~ in the sky** c'est de l'utopie; **as**

easy as ~ simple comme bonjour; **to have a finger in every ~** être mêlé à tout; **as nice as ~** GEN gentil/-ille comme tout, PÉJ tout sucre tout miel.

piebald /ˈpaɪbɔːld/ *n* cheval *m* pie.

piece /piːs/ *n* **1** GEN morceau *m*; (of string, ribbon) bout *m*; **2** (unit) **a ~ of furniture** un meuble; **a ~ of luggage** une valise; **a ~ of advice** un conseil; **a ~ of information** un renseignement; **a ~ of legislation** une loi; **a ~ of work** GEN un travail; (referring to book etc) une œuvre; **a ~ of luck** un coup dde chance; **to be paid by the ~** être payé à la pièce; **3** (of jigsaw, machine, model) pièce *f*; **in ~s** en pièces (détachées); **to come in ~s** [*furniture*] être livré en kit; **to take sth to ~s** démonter qch; **4** (broken fragment) morceau *m*; **to fall to ~s** [*object*] tomber en morceaux; FIG [*argument*] s'effondrer; **to go to ~s** FIG (from shock) s'effondrer; (emotionally) craquer○; (in interview) paniquer complètement; **5** (artistic work) (of music) morceau *m*; (sculpture) sculpture *f*; (painting) peinture *f*; (article) article *m* (**on** sur); (play) pièce *f*; (in book) passage *m*; **6** (instance) **a ~ of** un exemple de [*propaganda*]; **a wonderful ~ of running/acting** une très belle course/interprétation; **7** (coin) pièce *f*; **a 50p ~** une pièce de 50 pence; **8** GAMES (in chess) pièce *f*; (in draughts) pion *m*; **9** MIL (gun) fusil *m*; (cannon) pièce *f* (d'artillerie); **10**○ (gun) flingue○ *m*, pistolet *m*.
IDIOMS **to be (all) of a ~ with** s'accorder avec; **to be still in one ~** LIT être intact; FIG être sain et sauf; **to give sb a ~ of one's mind** dire ses quatre vérités à qn.
■ **piece together**: **~ [sth] together**, **~ together [sth]** reconstituer [*vase, garment, letter*]; assembler [*puzzle*]; FIG reconstituer [*facts, evidence*].

piecemeal /ˈpiːsmiːl/ **I** *adj* [*approach, reforms*] fragmentaire; [*description*] décousu; [*research, construction, development*] (random) fragmentaire; (at different times) irrégulier/-ière.
II *adv* petit à petit.

piecework /ˈpiːswɜːk/ *n* **to be on ~** être payé à la pièce.

pie: **~ chart** *n* diagramme *m* circulaire sectorisé, camembert○ *m*; **~ crust** *n* croûte *f*; **~ dish** *n* tourtière *f*; **~-eyed**○ *adj* rond○, soûl○.

pier /pɪə(r)/ *n* **1** (at seaside) jetée *f* (sur pilotis) (*où les gens viennent se promener*); **2** (part of harbour) (built of stone) digue *f*; (landing stage) embarcadère *f*; **3** CONSTR (of bridge, dam, foundations) pile *f*; (pillar in church, of gateway) pilier *m*; (wall between openings) trumeau *m*.

pierce /pɪəs/ *vtr* **1** (make hole in) percer; (penetrate) transpercer [*armour, skin*]; **2** FIG (penetrate) [*cry, light*] percer; [*wind*] transpercer; **3** MIL pénétrer [*enemy lines*].

piercing /ˈpɪəsɪŋ/ *adj* [*noise*] perçant; [*light*] intense; [*wind*] glacial, pénétrant.

piety /ˈpaɪəti/ *n* (religiousness) piété *f*.

piffling○ /ˈpɪflɪŋ/ *adj* GB insignifiant.

pig /pɪg/ *n* **1** (animal) porc *m*, cochon *m*; **2**○ (greedy) goinfre○ *m*; (dirty) cochon/-onne○ *m/f*; (nasty) sale type○ *m*; **to make a ~ of oneself** manger comme un goinfre○; **3**○ PÉJ **the ~s** les flics○ *mpl*.
IDIOMS **to buy a ~ in a poke** acheter chat en poche; **~s might fly!** le jour où les poules auront des dents!; **in a ~'s eye**○! US mon œil○!; **to make a ~'s ear of sth** bousiller○ qch.
■ **pig out**○ se goinfrer○, s'empiffrer○ (**on** de).

pigeon /ˈpɪdʒɪn/ *n* pigeon *m*.
IDIOMS **to put** OU **set the cat among the ~s** jeter or lancer un pavé dans la mare.

pigeon: **~-breasted**, **~-chested** *adj* à la poitrine bombée; **~ fancier** *n* colombophile *mf*.

pigeonhole /ˈpɪdʒɪnhəʊl/ GB **I** *n* casier *m*.
II *vtr* étiqueter, cataloguer.

pigeon: **~ house**, **~ loft** *n* pigeonnier *m*; **~ racing** *n* ₵ courses *fpl* de pigeons voyageurs.

pigeon-toed *adj* **to be ~** marcher les pieds en dedans.

pig farming *n* élevage *m* de porcs.

piggery /'pɪgərɪ/ n (pigsty) porcherie f.

piggy /'pɪgɪ/ n LANG ENFANTIN cochon m.
IDIOMS **to be ~ in the middle** se trouver entre deux chaises.

piggyback /'pɪgɪbæk/ I n (also **~ ride**) **to give sb a ~** porter qn sur son dos or sur ses épaules.
II adv [ride, carry] sur le dos.

piggy bank n tirelire f (en forme de cochon).

pigheaded /ˌpɪg'hedɪd/ adj PÉJ entêté, obstiné.

pig iron n métal m en gueuse.

piglet /'pɪglɪt/ n porcelet m, petit cochon m.

pigment /'pɪgmənt/ n BIOL, ART pigment m.

pigmentation /ˌpɪgmən'teɪʃn/ n pigmentation f.

pig: **~pen** n US = **pigsty**; **~skin** n peau f de porc; **~sty** n (pl **-sties**) LIT, FIG porcherie f; **~tail** n (hair) natte f.

pike /paɪk/ n **1** HIST (spear) pique f; **2** (fish) brochet m.

pikestaff /'paɪkstɑːf, US -stæf/ n: IDIOMS **it's as plain as a ~** ça se voit comme le nez au milieu de la figure.

pilchard /'pɪltʃəd/ n pilchard m.

pile /paɪl/ I n **1** (untidy heap) tas m (**of** de); (stack) pile f (**of** de); **in a ~** en tas or en pile; **2** (of fabric, carpet) poil m; **3**° (large amount) **a ~** ou **~s of** un tas° or des tas° de; **to have ~s of money** avoir plein d'argent°; **4** CONSTR pilier m; **5** ELEC pile f; **6** LITTÉR ou HUM (building) édifice m.
II **piles** npl MED hémorroïdes fpl.
III vtr (in a heap) entasser (**on** sur; **into** dans); **a plate ~d high with cakes** une assiette avec une montagne de gâteaux.
IV vi° **to ~ into** (board) s'engouffrer dans [vehicle]; (crash) rentrer dans [vehicle].
IDIOMS **to make one's ~**° faire fortune.
■ **pile in**°: **the bus came and we all ~d in** le bus est arrivé et nous y sommes montés en nous serrant.
■ **pile on**°: **to ~ on the charm** jouer à fond sur la séduction; **to ~ it on** mettre le paquet°.
■ **pile up**: ¶ **~ up** [leaves, snow, rubbish] s'entasser; [money] s'amasser; [debts, problems, work] s'accumuler; ¶ **~ [sth] up**, **~ up [sth]** (in a heap) entasser; (in a stack) empiler.

pile: **~ driver** n sonnette f de battage; **~ fabric** n (velvet) velours m; (other) fourrure f synthétique; **~up** n AUT carambolage m.

pilfer /'pɪlfə(r)/ I vtr dérober (**from** dans).
II vi commettre des larcins.

pilgrim /'pɪlgrɪm/ n pèlerin m (**to** de).

pilgrimage /'pɪlgrɪmɪdʒ/ n RELIG, FIG pèlerinage m; **to go on** ou **make a ~** faire un pèlerinage (**to** à).

pill /pɪl/ n MED (for general use) comprimé m, cachet m; **to be on the ~** (contraceptive) prendre la pilule.
IDIOMS **it was a bitter ~ to swallow** la pilule était amère; **to sugar** ou **sweeten the ~** dorer la pilule°.

pillage /'pɪlɪdʒ/ I n pillage m.
II vtr, vi piller.

pillar /'pɪlə(r)/ n **1** ARCHIT pilier m; FIG (of smoke, fire etc) colonne f; **a ~ of salt** BIBLE une statue de sel; **2** FIG (of institution, society) pilier m (**of** de); **to be a ~ of strength to sb** être d'un grand soutien à qn.
IDIOMS **to be sent from ~ to post**° (for information, papers) se faire renvoyer de service en service°.

pillar box n GB boîte f aux lettres.

pillbox /'pɪlbɒks/ n **1** (for pills) boîte f à pilules; **2** (also **~ hat**) toque f.

pillion /'pɪlɪən/ I n (also **~ seat**) siège m de passager.
II noun modifier [passenger] arrière inv.
III adv **to ride ~** monter en croupe.

pillory /'pɪlərɪ/ I n HIST pilori m.
II vtr LIT, FIG mettre [qn] au pilori (**for** pour).

pillow /'pɪləʊ/ n oreiller m.

pillow: **~case** n taie f d'oreiller; **~ talk** n ₵ confidences fpl sur l'oreiller.

pilot /'paɪlət/ **▶ 1251** I n **1** AVIAT, AEROSP, NAUT pilote m; **2** RADIO, TV (programme) émission f pilote

(for pour); **3** (also **~ light**) (gas) veilleuse f; (electric) voyant m lumineux.
II noun modifier **1** COMM, IND [course, project, study] pilote; RADIO, TV [programme, series] expérimental; **2** AVIAT [instruction, training] des pilotes; [error] de pilotage.
III vtr **1** AVIAT, NAUT (navigate) piloter; **to ~ sb through** FIG guider qn à travers [crowd, streets]; **to ~ a bill through parliament** assurer le passage d'un projet de loi au parlement; **2** (test) mettre [qch] au banc d'essai [course, system].

pilot: **~ boat** n bateau-pilote m; **~ burner** n (gas) veilleuse f; (electric) voyant m lumineux; **~ scheme** n projet-pilote m; **~'s licence** n brevet m de pilote.

pimp /pɪmp/ I n proxénète m.
II vi faire du proxénétisme.

pimple /'pɪmpl/ n bouton m.

pimply /'pɪmplɪ/ adj boutonneux/-euse ALSO PÉJ.

pin /pɪn/ I n **1** (for sewing, fastening cloth or paper) épingle f; **2** ELEC (of plug) fiche f; **two-/three-~ plug** à deux/trois fiches; **3** TECH (to attach wood or metal) goujon m; (machine part) goupille f; **4** MED (in surgery) broche f; **5** (brooch) barrette f; **6** (in bowling) quille f; **7** (in golf) drapeau m (de trou).
II **pins**° npl quilles° fpl, jambes fpl.
III vtr (p prés etc **-nn-**) **1** (attach with pins) épingler [dress, hem, curtain]; **to ~ sth on(to)** (with drawing pin) fixer qch avec une punaise sur [board, wall]; **to ~ sth with** attacher qch avec [brooch, grip, pin]; **2** (trap, press) coincer [person, part of body]; **to ~ sb against** ou **to** coincer qn contre [wall, sofa, floor]; **her arms were ~ned to her sides** elle avait les bras plaqués au corps; **3**° (attribute, attach) **to ~ sth on sb** imputer qch à qn [blame, crime]; **4** MIL, SPORT coincer, bloquer.
IDIOMS **for two ~s I would do** pour un peu je ferais; **to ~ one's ears back**° ouvrir grand les oreilles°; **you could have heard a ~ drop** on aurait entendu voler une mouche.
■ **pin down**: ¶ **~ down** [sb], **~ [sb] down 1** (physically) immobiliser (**to** à); **2** FIG coincer; **to ~ sb down to a definite date** arriver à soutirer une date fixe à qn; **to ~ sb down to doing** obliger qn à s'engager à faire; ¶ **~ down** [sth], **~ [sth] down 1** LIT accrocher [piece of paper, cloth]; épingler [sheet]; **2** FIG (define) identifier [concept, feeling]; **I can't ~ it down** je n'arrive pas à mettre le doigt dessus.
■ **pin up**: **~ up** [sth], **~ [sth] up** accrocher [poster, notice] (**on** à); remonter [hair].

PIN /pɪn/ n (also **~ number**) (abrév = **personal identification number**) code m confidentiel (pour carte bancaire).

pinafore /'pɪnəfɔː(r)/ n (apron) tablier m; (overall) blouse f.

pinball ▶ 949 n flipper m.

pincer /'pɪnsə(r)/ I n ZOOL pince f.
II **pincers** npl (tool) tenailles fpl.

pinch /pɪntʃ/ I n **1** pincement m; **to give sb a ~ on the cheek** pincer la joue de qn; **2** (of salt, spice) pincée f; (of snuff) prise f.
II vtr **1** pincer; **2** [shoe] serrer; **3**° (steal) faucher (**from** à); **4** (remove) **to ~ out** ou **off** enlever [bud, tip].
III vi [shoe] serrer.
IDIOMS **at** GB ou **on** US **a ~** à la rigueur; **to feel the ~** avoir de la peine à joindre les deux bouts; **to ~ and scrape** rogner sur tout.

pinched /pɪntʃt/ adj **to look ~** avoir les traits tirés.

pincushion /'pɪnkʊʃn/ n pelote f à épingles.

pine /paɪn/ I n pin m; **stripped ~** pin décapé.
II noun modifier [furniture] en pin.
III vi languir (**for** après; **to do** de faire).
■ **pine away** se laisser dépérir.

pineapple /'paɪnæpl/ n (fruit, plant) ananas m.

pine: **~cone** n pomme f de pin; **~ kernel** n pignon m de pin; **~-needle** n aiguille f de pin.

ping /pɪŋ/ I n (of bell) tintement m; (of bullet) claquement m.

II *vi* [*bell*] tinter; [*bullet*] claquer.

ping-pong® /'pɪŋpɒŋ/ ► 949 *n* ping-pong® *m*.

pinhead /'pɪnhed/ *n* **1** LIT tête *f* d'épingle; **2**○ PÉJ abruti-e○ *m/f*.

pinion /'pɪnɪən/ **I** *n* TECH pignon *m*.
II *vtr* **to ~ sb against** plaquer qn contre [*wall, door*]; **to ~ sb's arms** tenir les bras de qn.

pink /pɪŋk/ ► 818 **I** *n* **1** (colour) rose *m*; **2** BOT œillet *m* mignardise.
II *adj* **1** (rosy) rose; **to go** ou **turn ~** rosir; (blush) rougir (**with** de); **2** (leftwing) gauchisant.
IDIOMS **to be in the ~** être en pleine forme.

pinking shears, **pinking scissors** *npl* ciseaux *mpl* cranteurs.

pin money *n* argent *m* de poche.

pinnacle /'pɪnəkl/ *n* ARCHIT pinacle *m*; (of rock) cime *f* (**of** de); FIG apogée *m* (**of** de).

pinpoint /'pɪnpɔɪnt/ **I** *n* tête *f* d'épingle; **a ~ of light** un point lumineux.
II *vtr* **1** (identify, pick out) indiquer [*problem, risk, causes*]; **2** (place exactly) indiquer [*location, position, site*]; déterminer [*time, exact moment*].

pinprick /'pɪnprɪk/ *n* **1** LIT coup *m* d'épingle; (feeling caused) sensation *f* de piqûre; **2** FIG (of jealousy, remorse) pointe *f*.

pinstripe /'pɪnstraɪp/ **I pinstripes** *npl* (suit) costume *m* à fines rayures.
II *noun modifier* (also **pinstriped**) [*fabric, suit*] à fines rayures.

pint /paɪnt/ ► 789 *n* **1** pinte *f* (GB = *0.57 l*, US = *0.47 l*); **a ~ of milk** ≈ un demi-litre de lait; **2**○ GB **to go for a ~** ≈ aller boire une bière.

pint: **~ glass**, **~ pot** *n* ≈ chope *f* (d'un demi-litre); **~-size(d)** *adj* petit.

pinup /'pɪnʌp/ *n* **1** (woman) pin-up *f*; (man) photo *f* d'homme à moitié nu; **2** (poster of star) affiche *f* de vedette; (star) idole *f*.

pioneer /ˌpaɪə'nɪə(r)/ **I** *n* pionnier *m* (**of, in** de).
II *noun modifier* [*research*] novateur/-trice; **a ~ astronaut** un des premiers astronautes.
III *vtr* **to ~ the use of** être le premier à utiliser.
IV pioneering *pres p adj* [*scientist, scheme*] innovateur/-trice.

pious /'paɪəs/ *adj* pieux/pieuse; PÉJ plein de componction.

pip /pɪp/ **I** *n* **1** (seed) pépin *m*; **2** GB TELECOM **the ~s** tonalité *f* (*indiquant qu'il faut introduire à nouveau de l'argent*); **3** RADIO top *m* (*signal pour indiquer l'heure*); **4** (on card, dice, domino) point *m*.
IDIOMS **to be ~ped at** ou **to the post** se faire souffler la victoire; **to give sb the ~**○† énerver qn.

pipe /paɪp/ ► 1097 **I** *n* **1** (for gas, water etc) (in building) tuyau *m*; (underground) conduite *f*; **2** (smoker's) pipe *f*; **3** MUS (on organ) tuyau *m* (d'orgue); (flute) chalumeau *m*.
II pipes *npl* MUS cornemuse *f*.
III *vtr* **1** (carry) **to ~ water into a house** alimenter un four en eau; **oil is ~d across/to** le pétrole est transporté par canalisation à travers/jusqu'à; **2** (transmit) diffuser [*music*] (**to** dans); **3** (in sewing) passepoiler [*cushion, collar*]; **4** CULIN **to ~ icing onto a cake** décorer un gâteau; **5** NAUT siffler [*order*]; **to ~ sb aboard** accueillir qn à bord au son du sifflet.
IV *vi* siffler.
■ **pipe down**○ (quieten down) faire moins de bruit.
■ **pipe up** [*voice*] se faire entendre; **'it's me!' she ~d up** 'c'est moi!' dit-elle d'une petite voix.

pipe: **~-clay** *n* terre *f* de pipe; **~-cleaner** *n* cure-pipe *m*; **~d music** *n* musique *f* d'ambiance; **~-dream** *n* chimère *f*.

pipeline /'paɪplaɪn/ *n* TECH oléoduc *m*; **to be in the ~** FIG être en cours.

pipe: **~ of peace** *n* calumet *m* de la paix; **~ organ** *n* MUS orgue *m*.

piper /'paɪpə(r)/ ► 1251, 1097 *n* (bag-pipe player) joueur/-euse *m/f* de cornemuse; (flute-player) joueur/-euse *m/f* de chalumeau.

IDIOMS **he who pays the ~ calls the tune** PROV l'argent c'est le pouvoir.

pipe: **~-smoker** *n* fumeur/-euse *m/f* de pipe; **~ tobacco** *n* tabac *m* à pipe.

piping /'paɪpɪŋ/ **I** *n* **1** ¢ (pipes) tuyauterie *f*; **2** (in sewing) passepoil *m*; **3** CULIN décoration *f* (en sucre).
II *adj* [*voice, tone*] flûté.

piping hot *adj* fumant.

piquant /'piːkənt/ *adj* piquant.

pique /piːk/ **I** *n* dépit *m*; **in a fit of ~** dans un accès de dépit.
II *vtr* **1** (hurt) froisser; **2** (arouse) piquer [*interest*].

piqued /piːkt/ *adj* vexé (**at, by** par); **to do** de faire).

piracy /'paɪərəsɪ/ *n* **1** NAUT piraterie *f*; **2** (of tapes, software) duplication *f* pirate (**of** de).

pirate /'paɪərət/ **I** *n* **1** NAUT pirate *m*; **2** (copy of tape etc) contrefaçon *f*; **3** (also **~ station**) station *f* pirate; **4** (entrepreneur) pirate *m*; **5** (copier) contrefacteur *m*.
II *noun modifier* [*video, tape*] pirate; [*ship*] de pirates.
III *vtr* pirater [*tape, video, software*].

pirate radio *n* radio *f* pirate.

Pisces /'paɪsiːz/ ► 1418 *n* Poissons *mpl*.

pistachio /pɪ'stɑːʃɪəʊ, US -æʃɪəʊ/ *n* (*pl* **~s**) **1** (nut, flavour) pistache *f*; **2** (tree) pistachier *m*.

pistol /'pɪstl/ *n* pistolet *m*.

piston /'pɪstən/ *n* piston *m*.

piston: **~ engine** *n* moteur *m* à pistons; **~ pin** *n* axe *m* de piston; **~ rod** *n* tige *f* de piston.

pit /pɪt/ **I** *n* **1** (for storage, weapons, bodies) ALSO AUT fosse *f*; (trap) trappe *f*; (at racetrack) stand *m*; **gravel ~** carrière *f* de gravier; **the ~ of the stomach** le creux du ventre; **2** (mine) mine *f*; **to go down the ~** aller travailler à la mine; **3** THEAT parterre *m*; **orchestra ~** fosse *f* d'orchestre; **4** US (in peach, olive) noyau *m*.
II *vtr* (*p prés etc* **-tt-**) **1** (in struggle) **to ~ sb against** opposer qn à [*opponent*]; **2** (mark) marquer [*surface, stone*]; **3** US dénoyauter [*peach, olive*].
III *v refl* **to ~ oneself against sb** se mesurer à qn.
IDIOMS **it's the ~s**○! c'est l'enfer!

pitapat /ˌpɪtə'pæt/ *n* **to go ~** faire toc-toc.

pit bull terrier *n* pit bull *m*.

pitch /pɪtʃ/ **I** *n* **1** SPORT terrain *m*; **football ~** terrain de foot(ball); **2** (sound level) GEN (of note, voice) hauteur *f*; MUS ton *m*; **absolute ~**, **perfect ~** oreille *f* absolue; **3** (degree) degré *m*; (highest point) comble *m*; **excitement was at full ~** l'excitation était à son comble; **4** (sales talk) GEN, COMM boniment *m*; **5** CONSTR, NAUT (tar) brai *m*; **6** (for street trader) emplacement *m*.
II *vtr* **1** (throw) jeter [*object*] (**into** dans); SPORT lancer; **to be ~ed forward** [*person*] être projeté vers l'avant; **2** (aim) adapter [*campaign, speech*] (**at** à); (set) fixer [*price*]; **programme ~ed at young people** émission qui vise un public jeune; **the exam was ~ed at a high level** l'examen a été ajusté à un haut niveau; **3** MUS [*singer*] trouver [*note*]; [*player*] donner [*note*]; **to ~ one's voice higher/lower** hausser/baisser le ton de la voix; **4** (erect) planter [*tent*]; **to ~ camp** établir un camp.
III *vi* **1** (be thrown) [*rider, passenger*] être projeté; **to ~ and roll** ou **toss** NAUT tanguer; **2** US (in baseball) lancer (la balle).
■ **pitch in**○ (set to work) s'atteler à la tâche; (start to eat) attaquer○; (join in) y mettre du sien○; (help) donner un coup de main○.
■ **pitch into**: ¶ **~ into** [*sth*] (attack) attaquer [*opponent, speaker*]; attaquer [*work, meal*]; ¶ **~ [sb] into** propulser [qn] dans [*situation*].
■ **pitch out**○: **~ out** [*sb/sth*], **~ [sb/sth] out** éjecter [*person*] (**from** de).

pitch: **~-and-putt** *n* mini-golf *m*; **~-black**, **~ dark** *adj* tout noir; **~ed battle** *n* LIT, FIG bataille *f* rangée.

pitcher /'pɪtʃə(r)/ *n* **1** (jug) cruche *f*; **2** US SPORT lanceur *m*.

pitchfork /'pɪtʃfɔːk/ **I** *n* fourche *f*.

II *vtr* **1** AGRIC ramasser à la fourche; **2** FIG **to ~ sb into** parachuter qn dans [*situation*].

piteous /'pɪtɪəs/ *adj* [*sight, story*] pitoyable; [*state*] piteux/-euse.

pitfall /'pɪtfɔːl/ *n* FIG écueil *m* (**of** de).

pith /pɪθ/ *n* (of fruit) peau *f* blanche; (of stem) moelle *f*; FIG essence *f* (**of** de).

pit head *n* carreau *m* de mine.

pithy /'pɪθɪ/ *adj* [*remark, style, writing*] (concise) concis; (incisive) piquant.

pitiable /'pɪtɪəbl/ *adj* [*existence, sight*] pitoyable; [*salary*] misérable; [*attempt, excuse*] lamentable.

pitiful /'pɪtɪfl/ *adj* [*cry, sight*] pitoyable; [*income*] misérable; [*attempt, excuse, state*] lamentable; [*amount*] ridicule.

pitifully /'pɪtɪfʊlɪ/ *adv* [*thin*] à faire peur; [*cry, suffer*] pitoyablement; [*poor, small*] lamentablement.

pitiless /'pɪtɪlɪs/ *adj* impitoyable.

pittance /'pɪtns/ *n* **to live on/earn a ~** vivre avec/gagner trois fois rien.

pitted /'pɪtɪd/ *adj* **1** [*surface*] rongé; [*face, skin*] grêlé (**with** de); **2** [*olive*] dénoyauté.

pitter-patter /'pɪtəpætə(r)/ *n* = **pitapat**.

pituitary /pɪ'tjuːɪtərɪ, US -tu:əterɪ/ *adj* pituitaire; **~ gland** hypophyse *f*.

pit worker ▸ **1251** *n* mineur *m* de fond.

pity /'pɪtɪ/ **I** *n* **1** (compassion) pitié *f* (**for** pour); **out of ~** par pitié; **to feel ~** avoir de la pitié; **2** (shame) dommage *m*; **what a ~!** quel dommage!; **I'm not rich, more's the ~** je ne suis pas riche, c'est bien dommage.

II *vtr* avoir pitié de; **he's to be pitied** il faut avoir pitié de lui; **it's the police I ~, not the criminals** c'est la police que je plains, pas les criminels.

pityingly /'pɪtɪɪŋlɪ/ *adv* **1** (compassionately) avec pitié; **2** (scornfully) avec mépris.

pivot /'pɪvət/ **I** *n* MIL, TECH, FIG pivot *m*.

II *vtr* faire pivoter [*lever*]; orienter [*lamp*].

III *vi* [*lamp, device*] pivoter (**on** sur); FIG [*outcome, success*] reposer (**on** sur).

pivotal /'pɪvətl/ *adj* [*role, decision*] essentiel/-ielle; [*moment*] crucial.

pixie /'pɪksɪ/ *n* lutin *m*.

pizza /'piːtsə/ **I** *n* pizza *f*.

II *noun modifier* [*base, oven, pan*] à pizza.

pizza parlour GB, **pizza parlor** US *n* pizzeria *f*.

pizzazz° /pɪ'zæz/ *n* panache *m*.

placard /'plækɑːd/ *n* (at protest march) pancarte *f*; (on wall) affiche *f*.

placate /plə'keɪt, US 'pleɪkeɪt/ *vtr* apaiser, calmer.

placatory /plə'keɪtərɪ, US 'pleɪkətɔ:rɪ/ *adj* apaisant.

place /pleɪs/ **I** *n* **1** (location, position) endroit *m*; **from ~ to ~** d'un endroit à l'autre; **same time, same ~** même heure, même endroit; **in ~s** [*hilly, damaged, worn*] par endroits; **in several ~s** (in region) dans plusieurs endroits; (on body) à plusieurs endroits; **~ of birth/work** lieu *m* de naissance/travail; **~ of residence** domicile *m*; **this is the ~ for me!** c'est le rêve ici!; **to be in the right ~ at the right time** être là où il faut quand il le faut; **I can't be in two ~s at once!** je ne peux pas être partout à la fois!; **in Oxford, of all ~s!** à Oxford, figure-toi!; **to lose/find one's ~** (in book) perdre/retrouver sa page; (in paragraph, speech) perdre/retrouver le fil; **he had no ~ to go**° SURTOUT US il n'avait nulle part où aller; **some ~**° SURTOUT US quelque part; **2** (town, hotel etc) endroit *m*; **a good ~ to eat** une bonne adresse (pour manger); **a little ~ called...** un petit village du nom de...; **in a ~ like Kent** dans une région comme le Kent; **to be seen in all the right ~s** se montrer dans les lieux qui comptent; **all over the ~** (everywhere) partout; FIG° [*speech, lecture*] complètement décousu; [*hair*] en bataille; **3** (home) **David's ~** chez David; **a ~ by the sea** une maison au bord de la mer; **a ~ of one's own** un endroit à soi; **your ~ or mine?** chez toi ou chez moi?; **4** (seat, space) (on bus, at

table, in queue) place *f*; (setting) couvert *m*; **to keep a ~** garder une place (**for** pour); **please take your ~s** veuillez prendre place; **to lay** ou **set a ~ for sb** mettre un couvert pour qn; **5** (on team, with firm) place *f* (**on** dans); (on committee, board) siège *m* (**on** au sein de); **a ~ as** une place comme [*au pair, cook, cleaner*]; **6** GB UNIV place *f* (**at** à); **to get a ~ on** obtenir une place dans [*course*]; **she has a ~ on a carpentry course** elle a été acceptée pour suivre des cours de menuiserie; **7** (in competition, race) place *f*; **to finish in first ~** terminer premier/-ière or à la première place; **to take second ~** FIG (in importance) passer au deuxième plan; **in the first ~** FIG (firstly) en premier lieu; (at the outset) pour commencer; **8** (in order, correct position) **everything is in its ~** tout est bien à sa place; **to hold sth in ~** maintenir qch en place; **in ~** [*law, system, scheme*] en place; **to put sb in his/her ~** remettre qn à sa place; **to know one's ~** rester à sa place; **9** (role) **it's not my ~ to do** ce n'est pas à moi de faire; **to take sb's ~** prendre la place de qn; **to have no ~ in** n'avoir aucune place dans [*organization, philosophy*]; **10** (situation) **in my/his ~** à ma/sa place; **to change ~s with sb** changer de place avec qn; **11** (moment) moment *m*; **in ~s** [*funny, boring, silly*] par moments.

II **out of place** *adj phr* déplacé; **to look out of ~** [*building, person*] détonner; **to feel out of ~** ne pas se sentir à l'aise.

III **in place of** *prep phr* à la place de [*person, object*].

IV *vtr* **1** (put) placer, mettre [*object*]; mettre [*advertisement*]; **to ~ sth back on** remettre qch sur [*shelf, table*]; **to ~ an order for sth** passer une commande pour qch; **to ~ emphasis on sth** mettre l'accent sur qch; **to ~ one's trust in** placer sa confiance en; **to ~ sb at risk** faire courir des risques à qn; **2** (locate) placer; **to be awkwardly ~d** être mal placé; **he is not well ~d to judge** il est mal placé pour juger; **3** (rank) (in competition) classer; (in exam) GB classer; **to be ~d third** [*horse, athlete*] arriver troisième; **4** (identify) situer [*person*]; reconnaître [*accent*]; **I can't ~ his face** je ne le reconnais pas; **5** ADMIN (send, appoint) placer [*student, trainee*] (**in** dans); (find home for) placer [*child*]; **to ~ sb in charge of a project** confier la direction d'un projet à qn.

IDIOMS **that young man is really going ~s**° voilà un jeune homme qui ira loin; **to have friends in high ~s** avoir des amis haut placés; **to fall** ou **fit into ~** devenir clair; ▸ **take place**.

placebo /plə'si:bəʊ/ *n* **1** MED placebo *m*; **2** FIG os *m* à ronger.

place mat *n* set *m* de table.

placement /'pleɪsmənt/ *n* **1** GB (also **work ~**) (trainee post) stage *m*; **to get a ~** trouver un stage; **2** (in accommodation, employment) (of child, unemployed person) placement *m* (**in** dans); **3** FIN placement *m*.

place-name /'pleɪsneɪm/ *n* nom *m* de lieu.

placid /'plæsɪd/ *adj* [*person, animal, nature, smile*] placide.

placing /'pleɪsɪŋ/ *n* **1** (position) (in race, contest, league) classement *m*, place *f*; **2** (of ball, players) (positioning) positionnement *m*; (location) position *f*; **3** FIN placement *m*.

plagiarism /'pleɪdʒərɪzəm/ *n* plagiat *m*.

plagiarize /'pleɪdʒəraɪz/ *vtr, vi* plagier.

plague /pleɪg/ **I** *n* **1** MED (bubonic) peste *f*; (epidemic) épidémie *f*; FIG (of ants, rats, locusts etc) invasion *f*; **what a ~ that boy is!** quelle plaie ce garçon!

II *vtr* **1** (beset) **to be ~d by** ou **with** être en proie à [*doubts, remorse, difficulties*]; **he's ~d by ill health** il a sans arrêt des ennuis de santé; **2** (harass) harceler.

IDIOMS **to avoid sb/sth like the ~** fuir qn/qch comme la peste.

plaice /pleɪs/ *n* (*pl* **~**) plie *f*, carrelet *m*.

plaid /plæd/ **I** *n* (fabric) tissu *m* écossais; (pattern) motif *m* écossais.

II *noun modifier* [*scarf, shirt, design*] écossais.

plain /pleɪn/ **I** *n* plaine *f*.

II *adj* **1** (simple) [*dress, food, language*] simple; [*build-*

ing, furniture] sobre; **a ~ man** un homme simple; **2** [*background, fabric*] uni; [*envelope*] sans inscription; [*paper*] (unlined) non réglé; (unheaded) libre; **under ~ cover** POST sous pli discret; **3** EUPH (unattractive) [*woman*] quelconque; **she's rather ~** elle n'a rien d'une beauté; **4** (obvious) évident, clair; **it's ~ to see** ça saute aux yeux; **to make it ~ to sb that** faire comprendre clairement à qn que; **5** (direct) [*answer, language*] franc/franche; **~ speaking** franchise *f*; **in ~ English, this means that...** en clair, ceci veut dire que...; **6** (*tjrs épith*) (downright) [*common sense*] simple (*before n*); [*ignorance, laziness*] pur et simple (*after n*); **7** [*yoghurt, crisps, rice*] nature *inv*; **8** (in knitting) [*stitch, row*] à l'endroit.
III *adv* [*stupid, wrong*] tout bonnement.
IDIOMS **to be as ~ as day** être clair comme l'eau de roche; **to be ~ sailing** [*project, task etc*] marcher comme sur des roulettes.

plain chocolate *n* chocolat *m* à croquer.

plain clothes I *npl* **to wear ~, to be in ~** être en civil.
II plain-clothes *adj* [*policeman etc*] en civil.

plain flour *n* CULIN farine *f* (*sans levure*).

plainly /'pleɪnlɪ/ *adv* **1** (obviously) manifestement; **2** (distinctly) [*hear*] distinctement; [*see, remember, state*] clairement; **3** (frankly) [*speak*] franchement; **4** [*dress, eat*] simplement; [*furnished*] sobrement.

plainness /'pleɪnnɪs/ *n* **1** (of decor, dress) sobriété *f*; (of food, language) simplicité *f*; **2** (unattractiveness) manque *m* de beauté.

plain: **~song** *n* plain-chant *m*; **~-spoken** *adj* direct.

plaintiff /'pleɪntɪf/ *n* JUR plaignant/-e *m/f*.

plaintive /'pleɪntɪv/ *adj* plaintif/-ive.

plait /plæt/ **I** *n* natte *f*; **to wear ~s** avoir des nattes.
II *vtr* tresser [*hair, rope*]; **to ~ one's hair** se faire des nattes.

plan /plæn/ **I** *n* **1** (scheme, course of action) plan *m*; **the ~ is to leave very early** nous avons prévu de partir très tôt; **to go according to ~** se passer comme prévu; **2** (definite aim) projet *m* (**for** de; **to do** pour faire); **to have a ~ to do** projeter de faire; **3** (outline, map) ALSO ARCHIT, CONSTR, TECH plan *m*.
II plans *npl* **1** (arrangements) projets *mpl*; **what are your ~s for the future?** quels sont vos projets d'avenir?; **to make ~s for sth** (organize arrangements) organiser qch; (envisage) projeter qch; **I have no particular ~s** (for tonight) je n'ai rien de prévu; (for the future) je n'ai pas de projets bien déterminés; **but Paul had other ~s** mais Paul avait prévu autre chose; **2** ARCHIT, CONSTR **the ~s** les plans *mpl*.
III *vtr* (*p prés etc* **-nn-**) **1** (prepare, organize) planifier [*future, economy*]; organiser, préparer [*timetable, meeting, expedition*]; préparer [*retirement*]; organiser [*day*]; faire un plan de [*career*]; faire le plan de [*essay, book*]; préméditer [*crime*]; **he ~ned it so he could leave early** il s'est organisé pour pouvoir partir tôt; **to ~ a family** planifier les naissances; **2** (intend, propose) projeter [*visit, trip*]; prévoir [*new development, factory*]; **to ~ to do** projeter de faire; **3** ARCHIT, CONSTR (design) concevoir [*kitchen, garden, city centre*].
IV *vi* (*p prés* **-nn-**) prévoir; **to ~ on doing/on sth** (expect) s'attendre à faire/à qch; (intend) compter faire/ sur qch.
■ **plan ahead** (vaguely) faire des projets; (look, think ahead) prévoir.

plane /pleɪn/ **I** *n* **1** AVIAT avion *m*; **2** (in geometry) plan *m*; (face of cube, pyramid) face *f*; **3** TECH (tool) rabot *m*; **4** BOT (also **~ tree**) platane *m*.
II *adj* (flat) plan, uni.
III *vtr* raboter [*wood, edge*]; **to ~ sth smooth** lisser qch au rabot.
IV *vi* [*bird, aircraft, glider*] planer.

planet /'plænɪt/ *n* planète *f*.

plank /plæŋk/ **I** *n* planche *f*; FIG (of policy, argument) point *m*; **to walk the ~** NAUT HIST être exécuté par noyade.

IDIOMS **to be as thick as two (short) ~s**⊙ en tenir une couche⊙.

planner /'plænə(r)/ *n* GEN planificateur/-trice *m/f*; (in town planning) urbaniste *mf*.

planning /'plænɪŋ/ **I** *n* **1** (of industry, economy, work) planification *f*; (of holiday, party) organisation *f*; **2** ARCHIT (in town) urbanisme *m*; (out of town) aménagement *m* du territoire.
II *noun modifier* GEN, ADMIN [*decision*] prévisionnel/ -elle; ARCHIT [*department, authorities*] de l'urbanisme; **at the ~ stage** à l'état de projet.

planning application *n* demande *f* de permis de construire.

planning board *n* **1** (in town-planning) commission *f* d'urbanisme; **2** ECON commission *f* de planification.

planning: **~ committee** *n* = **planning board** 1; **~ permission** *n* permis *m* de construire.

plant /plɑːnt, US plænt/ **I** *n* **1** BOT plante *f*; **2** IND (factory) usine *f*; (power station) centrale *f*; **3** ¢ IND (buildings and machinery) installations *fpl* industrielles et commerciales; (fixed machinery) installations *fpl*; (movable machinery) matériel *m*.
II *vtr* **1** planter [*seed, bulb, tree*]; **to ~ a field with wheat** semer un champ de blé; **2** (illicitly) placer [*bomb, spy*]; **to ~ a weapon on sb** placer une arme sur qn pour l'incriminer; **3** (place) **to ~ a kiss on sb** planter un baiser sur qch; **to ~ an idea in sb's mind** mettre une idée dans la tête de qn.
III *v refl* **to ~ oneself between/in front of** se planter entre/devant.
■ **plant out**: **~ [sth] out, ~ out [sth]** repiquer [*seedlings*].

plantation /plæn'teɪʃn/ *n* (all contexts) plantation *f*.

planter /'plɑːntə(r), US 'plænt-/ *n* (person) planteur/ -euse *m/f*; (machine) planteuse *f*.

plant: **~ food** *n* engrais *m*; **~ hire** *n* GB location *f* de machines.

planting /'plɑːntɪŋ, US 'plænt-/ *n* plantation *f*.

plant: **~ kingdom** *n* règne *m* végétal; **~ life** *n* flore *f*.

plaque /plɑːk, US plæk/ *n* **1** (on wall, monument) plaque *f*; **2** (dental) **~** plaque *f* dentaire.

plasma /'plæzmə/ *n* MED, PHYS plasma *m*.

plaster /'plɑːstə(r), US 'plæs-/ **I** *n* **1** CONSTR, MED, ART plâtre *m*; **2** GB (bandage) sparadrap *m*; **a (piece of)** ~ un pansement.
II *vtr* **1** CONSTR **to ~ the walls of a house** faire les plâtres d'une maison; **2** (cover) (with posters, pictures) couvrir (**with** de).
■ **plaster down**: **~ down [sth], ~ [sth] down** plaquer [*hair*].
■ **plaster over**: **~ over [sth]** CONSTR boucher [*crack, hole*].

plaster: **~board** *n* placoplâtre® *m*; **~ cast** *n* MED plâtre *m*; ART (mould) moulage *m*; (sculpture) plâtre *m*.

plastered⊙ /'plɑːstəd, US 'plæst-/ *adj* (drunk) beurré⊙.

plasterer /'plɑːstərə(r), US 'plæst-/ ▶1251 *n* plâtrier *m*.

plastic /'plæstɪk/ **I** *n* plastique *m*.
II plastics *npl* (matières *fpl*) plastiques *mpl*.
III *adj* **1** [*bag*] en plastique; **2** ART plastique.

plastic: **~ bomb** *n* bombe *f* au plastic; **~ bullet** *n* balle *f* (de) plastique; **~ foam** *n* polystyrène *m* expansé.

Plasticine® /'plæstɪsiːn/ *n* pâte *f* à modeler.

plastic: **~ money**⊙ *n* cartes *fpl* de crédit; **~ surgeon** ▶1251 *n* chirurgien *m* esthétique; **~ surgery** *n* (cosmetic) chirurgie *f* esthétique; MED chirurgie *f* plastique.

plate /pleɪt/ **I** *n* **1** (dish) (for eating) assiette *f*; (for serving) plat *m*; **to hand** ou **present sth to sb on a ~** LIT, GB FIG apporter or présenter qch à qn sur un plateau; **2** (dishful) assiette *f*; **3** (sheet of metal) plaque *f*, tôle *f*; **4** (name plaque) plaque *f*; **5** (registration plaque) plaque *f* minéralogique; **6** ¢ (silverware) GEN argenterie *f*; RELIG trésor *m*; **7** (metal coating) plaqué *m*; **8**

(illustration) planche *f*; **9** PHOT plaque *f*; **10** (in dentistry) dentier *m*; **11** GEOG, ZOOL plaque *f*; **12** SPORT (trophy) plaque *f*; (competition) coupe *f*; **13** MED plaque *f*.

II *vtr* plaquer [*bracelet, candlestick*] (**with** avec, de).

III -plated *combining form* gold/silver-~d plaqué or/argent.

IDIOMS **to have a lot on one's ~** avoir beaucoup à faire.

plateau /ˈplætəʊ, US plæˈtəʊ/ *n* (*pl* ~**s** or ~**x**) **1** GEOG plateau *m*; **2** FIG palier *m*.

plate glass I *n* verre *m* à vitre.

II *noun modifier* [*window, door*] en verre à vitre.

platelet /ˈpleɪtlɪt/ *n* plaquette *f*.

plate: **~-rack** *n* (for draining) égouttoir *m*; **~ warmer** *n* chauffe-assiettes *m inv*.

platform /ˈplætfɔːm/ *n* **1** (stage) (for performance) estrade *f*; (at public meeting) tribune *f*; **to provide a ~ for sb/sth** offrir une tribune à qn/qch; **2** (in oil industry, in scaffolding, on vehicle, for guns) plate-forme *f*; (on weighing machine) plateau *m*; **3** POL plate-forme *f* électorale; **4** RAIL quai *m*.

platform: **~ scales** *n* bascule *f*; **~ shoes** *npl* chaussures *fpl* à plateforme; **~ ticket** *n* GB RAIL ticket *m* de quai.

platinum /ˈplætɪnəm/ **I** *n* platine *m*.

II *noun modifier* [*ring, jewellery*] de or en platine.

platinum blonde *n* blonde *f* platine or platinée.

platitude /ˈplætɪtjuːd, US -tuːd/ *n* platitude *f*.

Platonic /pləˈtɒnɪk/ *adj* **1** (also **platonic**) [*love, relationship*] platonique; **2** PHILOS platonicien/-ienne.

platoon /pləˈtuːn/ *n* (+ *v sg ou pl*) MIL (of soldiers, police, firemen) section *f*; (in cavalry, armoured corps) peloton *m*; FIG régiment *m*.

platter /ˈplætə(r)/ *n* **1** (dish) plat *m*; **2** CULIN **seafood ~** assiette *f* de fruits de mer.

platypus /ˈplætɪpəs/ *n* ornithorynque *m*.

plausible /ˈplɔːzəbl/ *adj* [*story, plot, alibi*] plausible, vraisemblable; [*person*] convaincant.

plausibly /ˈplɔːzəblɪ/ *adv* avec vraisemblance.

play /pleɪ/ ▶ **949**, **1097** **I** *n* **1** THEAT pièce *f* (**about** sur); **a radio ~** une pièce radiophonique; **2** (amusement, recreation) **the sound of children at ~** le bruit d'enfants en train de jouer; **to learn through ~** apprendre par le jeu; **3** SPORT, GAMES **~ starts at 11** la partie commence à 11 heures; **the ball is out of ~/in** ~ la balle est hors jeu/en jeu; **there was some fine ~ from the Danish team** l'équipe danoise a bien joué; **4** FIG (movement, interaction) jeu *m*; **to come into ~** entrer en jeu; **it has brought new factors into ~** cela a introduit de nouveaux éléments; **a ~ on words** un jeu de mots.

II *vtr* **1** jouer à [*game, match, cards*]; jouer [*card*]; **to ~ a club** jouer du trèfle; **to ~ goal** (in football) être gardien de but; **to ~ the ball to sb** (in basketball) passer la balle à qn; **to ~ hide and seek** jouer à cache-cache; **to ~ a joke on sb** jouer un tour à qn; **2** MUS jouer de [*instrument*]; jouer [*tune, symphony, chord*]; **they're ~ing the jazz club on Saturday** ils jouent au club de jazz samedi; **3** (act out) THEAT interpréter, jouer [*role*]; **4** AUDIO mettre [*tape, video, CD*]; **~ me the record** mets-moi le disque; **to ~ music** écouter de la musique; **let me ~ the tape for you** je vais vous faire entendre la cassette; **5** FIN **to ~ the stock market** boursicoter○.

III *vi* **1** (children) jouer (**with** avec); **2** FIG **to ~ at being an artist** jouer à l'artiste; **what does he think he's ~ing at?** GB○ qu'est-ce qu'il fabrique○?; **3** SPORT, GAMES jouer; **do you ~?** est-ce que tu sais jouer?; **to ~ fair** jouer franc-jeu; **to ~ into the net** envoyer la balle dans le filet; **4** MUS [*musician, band, orchestra*] jouer (**for** pour); **to ~ to large audiences** jouer devant un grand public; **5** CIN, THEAT [*play*] se jouer; [*film*] passer; [*actor*] jouer; **she's ~ing opposite him in 'Macbeth'** elle lui donne la réplique dans 'Macbeth'; **6** [*fountain, water*] couler; MUS [*record*] jouer; **I could hear music ~ing** j'entendais de la musique.

IDIOMS **to ~ for time** essayer de gagner du temps; **all work and no ~ (makes Jack a dull boy)** PROV il n'y a pas que le travail dans la vie; **to make great ~ of sth** accorder beaucoup d'importance à qch.

■ **play along**: **to ~ along with sb** MUS accompagner qn; FIG entrer dans le jeu de qn.

■ **play around**○ (act the fool) faire l'imbécile; **to ~ around with** trafiquer [*figures*]; **how much money do we have to ~ around with?** combien d'argent avons-nous à notre disposition?

■ **play back**: **~ [sth] back, ~ back [sth]** repasser [*song, film, video*].

■ **play down**: **~ down [sth]** minimiser.

■ **play off**: **to ~ sb off against sb** monter qn contre qn (pour en tirer avantage).

■ **play on**: ¶ **~ on** [*musicians, footballers*] continuer à jouer; ¶ **~ on** [*sth*] exploiter [*fears, prejudices*].

■ **play out**: **~ out** [*sth*] vivre [*fantasy*]; **the drama which is being ~ed out in India** le drame qui se déroule en Inde.

■ **play up**: ¶ **~ up**○ [*computer, person*] commencer à faire des siennes○; ¶ **~ up** [*sth*] mettre l'accent sur [*dangers, advantages*].

■ **play upon** = **play on**.

play: **~-acting** *n* comédie *f*, simagrées *fpl*; **~ area** *n* (outside) aire *f* de jeu; (inside) coin-jeu *m*; **~bill** *n* THEAT affiche *f*; **~boy** *n* playboy *m*; **~-by-play** *n* US SPORT commentaire *m* suivi.

player /ˈpleɪə(r)/ *n* SPORT, MUS joueur/-euse *m/f*; THEAT comédien/-ienne *m/f*; FIG (in negotiations, crisis) protagoniste *mf*; **tennis ~** joueur/-euse *m/f* de tennis.

playful /ˈpleɪfl/ *adj* [*remark*] taquin; [*child, kitten*] joueur/-euse.

playfully /ˈpleɪfəlɪ/ *adv* avec espièglerie.

play: **~ground** *n* (in school) cour *f* de récréation; FIG (for the rich) lieu *m* de divertissement; **~group** *n* ~ halte-garderie *f*; **~house** *n* théâtre *m*.

playing /ˈpleɪɪŋ/ *n* MUS, THEAT interprétation *f*; SPORT jeu *m*.

playing: **~ card** *n* carte *f* à jouer; **~ field** *n* terrain *m* de sport.

play: **~mate** *n* camarade *mf* de jeu; **~-off** *n* GB (at end of match) prolongation *f*; US match *m* crucial; **~pen** *n* parc *m* (pour bébé); **~room** *n* salle *f* de jeux; **~school** *n* ~ halte-garderie *f*; **~thing** *n* LIT, FIG jouet *m*; **~wright** *n* auteur *m* dramatique.

plaza /ˈplɑːzə, US ˈplæzə/ *n* **1** (public square) place *f*; **shopping ~** centre *m* commercial; **2** US (services point) aire *f* de service; (toll point) péage *m*.

plc, PLC (*abrév* = **public limited company**) GB SA.

plea /pliː/ *n* **1** (for tolerance, mercy etc) appel *m* (**for** à); (for money, food) demande *f* (**for** de); **to make a ~ for aid** lancer un appel à l'aide; **2** JUR **to make** ou **enter a ~ of guilty/not guilty** plaider coupable/non coupable; **3** (excuse) excuse *f*; **on the ~ that** sous prétexte que.

plead /pliːd/ **I** *vtr* (*prét, pp* **pleaded**, US **pled**) **1** (beg) supplier; **2** (argue) plaider; **to ~ sb's case** JUR, FIG plaider la cause de qn; **3** (give as excuse) **to ~ ignorance** plaider l'ignorance.

II *vi* (*prét, pp* **pleaded**, US **pled**) **1** (beg) supplier; (more fervently) implorer; **2** JUR plaider.

pleading /ˈpliːdɪŋ/ **I** *n* **1** ¢ (requests) supplications *fpl*; **2** JUR (presentation of a case) plaidoirie *f*.

II *adj* [*voice, look*] suppliant.

pleasant /ˈpleznt/ *adj* [*taste, voice, place etc*] agréable; [*person*] agréable, aimable (**to** avec); **it makes a ~ change from work!** ça change du travail!

pleasantly /ˈplezntlɪ/ *adv* [*say, smile, behave*] aimablement; **~ surprised** agréablement surpris; **it was ~ warm** il faisait bon.

pleasantry /ˈplezntrɪ/ **I** *n* SOUT (joke) plaisanterie *f*.

II pleasantries *npl* (polite remarks) civilités *fpl*; **to exchange pleasantries** bavarder aimablement.

please /pliːz/ **I** *adv* GEN s'il vous plaît; (to close friend) s'il te plaît; **~ be seated** SOUT veuillez vous asseoir

FML; '~ **do not smoke'** 'prière de ne pas fumer'; ~, **come in** entrez, je vous en prie; **'may I?'—'~ do'** 'je peux?'—'oui, je vous en prie'; ~ **tell me if you need anything** n'hésitez pas à me dire si vous avez besoin de quelque chose; ~ **don't!** pas ça, s'il vous plaît!; **he married a countess, if you ~!** il a épousé une comtesse, rien que ça! **II** *vtr* faire plaisir à [*person*]; **she is hard to ~** elle est difficile à contenter; **you're easily ~d!** ce n'est pas dur de te faire plaisir!; **there's no pleasing him** il n'est jamais satisfait. **III** *vi* plaire; **we aim to ~** vous satisfaire est notre priorité; **do as you ~** fais comme tu veux. **IV** *v refl* **to ~ oneself** faire comme on veut.

pleased /pliːzd/ *adj* content (**that** que + *subj*; **about, at** de; **with** de; **for sb** pour qn); **to look ~ with oneself** avoir l'air content de soi; **I am ~ to announce that...** j'ai le plaisir d'annoncer que...; **I'm ~ to hear it!** quelle bonne nouvelle!; **~ to meet you** enchanté.

pleasing /ˈpliːzɪŋ/ *adj* [*appearance, shape, colour, voice*] agréable; [*manner, smile, personality*] avenant; [*effect, result*] heureux/-euse.

pleasingly /ˈpliːzɪŋlɪ/ *adv* agréablement.

pleasurable /ˈplɛʒərəbl/ *adj* agréable.

pleasure /ˈplɛʒə(r)/ *n* **1** ¢ (enjoyment) plaisir *m* (**of** de; **of doing** de faire); **to take all the ~ out of** enlever tout le plaisir de; **to do sth for ~** faire qch par plaisir; **it gives me no ~ to do** il ne m'est pas agréable de faire; **2** C (enjoyable activity, experience) plaisir *m* (**of** de); **it is/was a ~ to do** c'est/c'était agréable de faire; **to mix business and ~** joindre l'utile à l'agréable; **are you in Paris for business or ~?** êtes-vous à Paris pour affaires ou pour le plaisir?; **3** (in polite formulae) **it gives me great ~ to do** c'est avec plaisir que je fais; **I look forward to the ~ of meeting you** (some day) j'espère avoir un jour le plaisir de vous rencontrer; **my ~** (replying to request for help) avec plaisir; (replying to thanks) je vous en prie; **what an unexpected ~!** GEN quelle excellente surprise!; IRON ça! par exemple!; **'Mr and Mrs Moor request the ~ of your company at their daughter's wedding'** 'M. et Mme Moor vous prient d'assister à la cérémonie de mariage de leur fille'; **at one's ~** à son gré.

pleasure: **~ boat** *n* bateau *m* de plaisance; **~ craft** *n* ¢ bateaux *mpl* de plaisance; **~ cruise** *n* croisière *f*.

pleat /pliːt/ **I** *n* pli *m*. **II** *vtr* plisser. **III pleated** *pp adj* [*skirt*] plissé; [*trousers*] à plis.

plebeian /plɪˈbiːən/ *n*, *adj* PÉJ plébéien/-ienne (*m/f*).

pled /plɛd/ US *pp* ▶ **plead**.

pledge /plɛdʒ/ **I** *n* **1** (promise) promesse *f*; **to give** ou **make a ~ to do** prendre l'engagement de faire; **2** (deposited as security) (to creditor, pawnbroker) gage *m*; **as a ~ of her friendship** FIG en gage or en témoignage de son amitié; **3** (money promised to charity) promesse *f* de don. **II** *vtr* **1** (promise) promettre [*allegiance, aid, support*] (**to** à); **to ~** (**oneself**) **to do, to ~ that one will do** s'engager à faire; **the treaty ~s the signatories to** do le traité engage les signataires à faire; **to be ~d to secrecy** être tenu au secret; **to ~ one's word** donner sa parole; **2** (to creditor, pawnbroker) mettre [qch] en gage.

plenary /ˈpliːnərɪ, US -erɪ/ *adj* (*before n*) [*session*] plénier/-ière; [*powers*] plein (*épith*); [*authority*] absolu.

plenipotentiary /ˌplɛnɪpəˈtɛnʃərɪ, US -erɪ/ *adj* [*powers*] plein; [*authority, ambassador*] plénipotentiaire.

plentiful /ˈplɛntɪfl/ *adj* [*diet, food, harvest*] abondant; **a ~ supply of** une abondance de.

plenty /ˈplɛntɪ/ **I** *quantif* **1** (a lot, quite enough) **to have ~ of** avoir beaucoup de [*time, money, friends*]; **there is ~ of time/money** on a tout le temps/l'argent qu'il faut; **there's ~ more where that came from**⊙! (of food, joke etc) profites-en, j'en ai toute une réserve!;

that's ~ c'est bien assez; **£10 will be ~** 10 livres sterling suffiront largement; **2 ¢** (abundance) **a time of ~** une époque prospère; **in ~** en abondance. **II**⊙ *adv* **that's ~ big enough!** c'est bien assez grand!; **he cried ~** US il a beaucoup pleuré.

pleurisy /ˈplʊərəsɪ/ ▶ **1002** *n* pleurésie *f*.

pliable /ˈplaɪəbl/ *adj* [*twig, plastic*] flexible; [*person*] malléable.

pliers /ˈplaɪəz/ *npl* pinces *fpl*; **a pair of ~** des pinces.

plight /plaɪt/ *n* **1** (dilemma) situation *f* désespérée; **2** (suffering) détresse *f*; **the ~ of the homeless** la détresse des sans-abri.

plimsoll /ˈplɪmsəl/ *n* GB chaussure *f* de tennis.

plinth /plɪnθ/ *n* ARCHIT plinthe *f*; (of statue) socle *m*.

PLO *n* (*abrév* = **Palestine Liberation Organization**) OLP *f*.

plod /plɒd/ *vi* (*p prés etc* **-dd-**) (walk) marcher péniblement.

■ **plod along** LIT, FIG avancer d'un pas lent.
■ **plod away** travailler ferme, bosser⊙.
■ **plod on** LIT continuer à marcher; FIG persévérer.
■ **plod through**: **~ through** [sth] FIG faire [qch] laborieusement.

plodder /ˈplɒdə(r)/ *n* bûcheur/-euse⊙ *m/f*.

plodding /ˈplɒdɪŋ/ *adj* [*step*] lourd; FIG laborieux/-ieuse.

plonk /plɒŋk/ **I** *n* **1** (sound) plouf⊙ *m*, son *m* creux; **2**⊙ (wine) vin *m* ordinaire, pinard⊙ *m*. **II**⊙ *vtr* planter [*plate, bottle*] (**on** sur).

■ **plonk down**⊙: ¶ **~** [sth] **down** poser [*box, sack*] (**on** sur); **to ~ oneself down on** s'installer sur [*sofa*]; ¶ **~ down** [sth] US (pay) allonger⊙, payer [*sum*].

plop /plɒp/ **I** *n* floc *m*. **II** *vi* (*p prés etc* **-pp-**) faire floc.

plot /plɒt/ **I** *n* **1** (conspiracy) complot *m*; **2** CIN, LITERAT (of novel, film, play) intrigue *f*; **the ~ thickens** l'histoire se corse; **3** AGRIC (allotment) **~ of land** parcelle *f* de terre; **a vegetable ~** un carré de légumes; **4** CONSTR (site) terrain *m* à bâtir. **II** *vtr* (*p prés etc* **-tt-**) **1** (plan) comploter [*murder, attack, return*]; fomenter [*revolution*]; **2** (chart) relever [qch] sur une carte [*course*]; tracer [qch] sur une carte [*progress*]; **we ~ted our position on the map** nous avons pointé notre position sur la carte; **3** MATH (on graph) tracer [qch] point par point [*curve, graph*]; reporter [*figures, points*]; **to ~ the progress of sth** tracer la courbe de progression de qch; **4** LITERAT (invent) inventer [*episode, story, destiny*]. **III** *vi* (conspire) conspirer (**against** contre).

plotter /ˈplɒtə(r)/ *n* **1** (schemer) conspirateur/-trice *m/f*; **2** COMPUT traceur *m* (de courbes).

plotting /ˈplɒtɪŋ/ *n* ¢ (scheming) complots *mpl*; **to be accused of ~** être accusé d'avoir tramé un complot.

plough GB, **plow** US /plaʊ/ **I** *n* AGRIC charrue *f*. **II Plough** *pr n* **the Plough** le Grand Chariot *m*. **III** *vtr* **1** AGRIC labourer [*land, field*]; creuser [*furrow*]; **2** (invest) **to ~ money into** investir beaucoup d'argent dans [*project, company*]. **IV** *vi* AGRIC labourer.

■ **plough back**: **~** [sth] **back, ~ back** [sth] réinvestir [*profits, money*] (**into** dans).
■ **plough into**: **~ into** [sth] **1** [*vehicle*] percuter [*tree, wall*]; **the car ~ed into the crowd** la voiture a foncé dans la foule; **2** US se lancer à corps perdu dans [*work*].
■ **plough through**: **~ through** [sth] FIG [*person*] ramer⊙ sur [*book, task*]; [*walker, vehicle*] avancer péniblement dans [*mud, snow*].
■ **plough up**: **~** [sth] **up, ~ up** [sth] AGRIC mettre [qch] en labour [*field*]; FIG [*car, person*] défoncer [*ground*].

ploughing GB, **plowing** US /ˈplaʊɪŋ/ *n* labourage *m*.

plough: **~man** GB, **plow-man** US ▶ **1251** *n* laboureur *m*; **~man's lunch** *n* GB plat servi dans les pubs composé de fromage, de pain et de salade.

plow *n, vtr, vi* US = **plough**.

ploy /plɔɪ/ *n* stratagème *m* (**to do** pour faire).

pluck /plʌk/ **I** *n* (courage) courage *m*, cran° *m*.
II *vtr* **1** cueillir [*flower, fruit*]; **to ~ sth from sb's grasp** arracher qch à qn; **2** CULIN plumer [*chicken*]; **3** MUS pincer [*strings*]; pincer les cordes de [*guitar*]; **4** **to ~ one's eyebrows** s'épiler les sourcils.
IDIOMS **to ~ up one's courage** prendre son courage à deux mains.
■ **pluck at**: **to ~ at sb's sleeve/arm** tirer qn par la manche/le bras.
■ **pluck off**: **~ off** [sth], **~** [sth] **off** arracher.
■ **pluck out**: **~ out** [sth], **~** [sth] **out** arracher.

pluckily /'plʌkɪlɪ/ *adv* vaillamment.

plucky /'plʌkɪ/ *adj* courageux/-euse.

plug /plʌg/ **I** *n* **1** ELEC (on appliance) prise *f* (de courant); (connecting device) (on computer, for phone) fiche *f*; **to pull out the ~** débrancher la prise; **to pull the ~ on**° retirer son soutien à [*scheme, project*]; **a mains ~** une prise secteur; **2** (in bath, sink, barrel) bonde *f*; **to pull out the ~** retirer la bonde; **3** CONSTR (for screw) cheville *f*; **4** (stopper) bonde *f*; (for leak) bouchon *m*; (for medical purpose) tampon *m*; **5** AUT (also **spark ~**) bougie *f*; **6** (in advertising) **to give sth a ~** faire de la publicité pour qch.
II *vtr* (*p prés etc* -**gg**-) **1** (block) colmater [*leak*] (**with** avec); boucher [*hole*] (**with** avec); **2**° (promote) faire de la publicité pour [*book, show, product*]; **3** ELEC **to ~ sth into** brancher qch à.
III *vi* (*p prés etc* -**gg**-) **to ~ into** se brancher à [*TV, computer*]; FIG se mettre au courant de [*public opinion, mood*].
■ **plug away**° s'acharner (**at** sur).
■ **plug in**: **¶ ~ in** se brancher; **¶ ~** [sth] **in**, **~ in** [sth] brancher [*appliance*].
■ **plug up**: **~ up** [sth], **~** [sth] **up** boucher [*hole, gap*] (**with** avec).

plughole /'plʌghəʊl/ *n* GB bonde *f*; **to go down the ~** [*ring etc*] tomber dans le trou de l'évier; FIG° s'en aller à vau-l'eau.

plug-in *adj* [*appliance*] enfichable.

plum /plʌm/ **▶818** **I** *n* BOT (fruit) prune *f*; (tree) prunier *m*.
II *noun modifier* CULIN [*tart*] aux prunes; [*jam*] de prunes.
III *adj* **1** (also **~-coloured**) prune *inv*; **2**° (good) **to get a ~ job/part** décrocher un boulot/rôle en or°.

plumage /'pluːmɪdʒ/ *n* plumage *m*.

plumb /plʌm/ **I** *n* (also **~ line**) CONSTR fil *m* à plomb; NAUT sonde *f*; **2 to be out of ~** ou **off ~** ne pas être d'aplomb.
II *adv* **1**° US [*crazy, wrong*] complètement; **2**° (precisely) **~ in the middle** en plein milieu.
III *vtr* sonder [*sea, depths*]; **to ~ the depths of** FIG toucher le fond de [*despair, misery*].

plumber /'plʌmə(r)/ *n* plombier *m*.

plumbing /'plʌmɪŋ/ *n* plomberie *f*.

plume /pluːm/ *n* (feather) plume *f*; (of several feathers) panache *m*; FIG (of steam, smoke etc) panache *m* (**of** de).

plumed /pluːmd/ *adj* [*horse, helmet*] empanaché *m*; [*hat*] à plumes.

plummet /'plʌmɪt/ *vi* [*bird, aircraft*] tomber à pic; FIG [*prices, profits, sales*] s'effondrer; [*temperature, popularity*] baisser brusquement.

plummy° /'plʌmɪ/ *adj* GB [*voice*] maniéré; [*accent*] affecté.

plump /plʌmp/ *adj* [*person, arm, leg*] potelé; [*cheek, face*] rond, plein.
■ **plump down**° [*person*] s'asseoir (lourdement) (**into** dans; **onto** sur).
■ **plump for**°: **~ for** [sth] opter pour.
■ **plump up**: **~ up** [sth] redonner du volume à [*cushion*].

plumpness /'plʌmpnɪs/ *n* (of person) embonpoint *m*; (of arms, legs etc) rondeur *f*.

plunder /'plʌndə(r)/ **I** *n* **1** (act) pillage *m*; **2** (booty) butin *m*.
II *vtr* piller.
III *vi* se livrer au pillage.

plunge /plʌndʒ/ **I** *n* **1** (from height) plongeon *m*; **to take a ~** (dive) piquer une tête; **2** FIN (of share prices etc) chute *f* libre.
II *vtr* plonger (**into** dans); **to be ~d into** être plongé dans [*darkness, crisis, strike*]; être submergé de [*debt*].
III *vi* [*road, cliff, waterfall*] plonger; [*bird, plane*] piquer; [*person*] (dive) plonger; (fall) tomber (**from** de); FIG [*rate, value*] chuter; **to ~ into** FIG se lancer dans [*activity, career*]; sombrer dans [*chaos*].
IDIOMS **to take the ~** se jeter à l'eau.
■ **plunge in** [*swimmer*] plonger; FIG (impetuously) lancer.

plunger /'plʌndʒə(r)/ *n* (for sink) ventouse *f*.

plunging /'plʌndʒɪŋ/ *adj* **~ neckline** décolleté *m* plongeant.

pluperfect /ˌpluː'pɜːfɪkt/ LING **I** *n* plus-que-parfait *m*.
II *noun modifier* [*tense*] au plus-que-parfait; [*form*] du plus-que-parfait.

plural /'plʊərəl/ **I** *n* LING pluriel *m*; **in the ~** au pluriel.
II *adj* LING [*noun, adjective*] au pluriel; [*form, ending*] du pluriel.

pluralism /'plʊərəlɪzəm/ *n* pluralisme *m*.

plus /plʌs/ **I** *n* MATH plus *m*; FIG (advantage) avantage *m*.
II *adj* MATH, ELEC positif/-ive; **~ factor**, **~ point** FIG atout *m*; **the ~ side** le côté positif; **the 65-~ age group** les personnes qui ont 65 ans et plus.
III *prep* MATH plus; **15 ~ 12** 15 plus 12.
IV *conj* et; **bedroom ~ bathroom** chambre et salle de bains.

plus-fours /ˌplʌs'fɔːz/ *npl* culotte *f* de golf.

plush /plʌʃ/ **I** *n* (textile) peluche *f*.
II° *adj* [*room, hotel*] somptueux/-euse; [*area*] riche.

plus sign *n* MATH signe *m* plus.

Pluto /'pluːtəʊ/ *pr n* **1** MYTHOL Pluton *m*; **2** (planet) Pluton *f*.

plutonium /pluː'təʊnɪəm/ *n* plutonium *m*.

ply /plaɪ/ **I** *n* épaisseur *f*; **two ~ wool** laine deux fils; **three ~ wood** contreplaqué trois plis.
II *vtr* **1** vendre [*wares*]; **to ~ one's trade** exercer son métier; **2†** manier [*pen, oars*]; **3 to ~ sb with** assaillir qn de [*questions*]; **to ~ sb with food/drink** ne cesser de remplir l'assiette/le verre de qn.
III *vi* [*boat, bus*] faire la navette (**between** entre).

plywood /'plaɪwʊd/ *n* contreplaqué *m*.

pm /ˌpiː'em/ **▶812** *adv* (*abrév* = **post meridiem**) **two pm** deux heures de l'après-midi; **nine pm** neuf heures du soir.

PM *n* GB *abrév* ▶ **Prime Minister**.

PMS *n* (*abrév* = **premenstrual syndrome**) SPM *m*.

PMT *n* (*abrév* = **premenstrual tension**) SPM *m*.

pneumatic /nju:'mætɪk, US nu:-/ *adj* pneumatique.

pneumatic drill *n* marteau *m* piqueur.

pneumonia /nju:'məʊnɪə, US nu:-/ **▶1002** *n* pneumonie *f*.

PO 1 *abrév* ▶ **post office**; **2** *abrév* ▶ **postal order**.

poach /pəʊtʃ/ **I** *vtr* **1** chasser [qch] illégalement [*game*]; FIG (steal) débaucher [*staff, players*] (**from** de); s'approprier [*idea*] (**from** de); **2** CULIN faire pocher.
II *vi* (hunt) LIT braconner; **to ~ on sb's territory** FIG empiéter sur le territoire de qn.
III *poached pp adj* CULIN [*egg, fish*] poché.

poacher /'pəʊtʃə(r)/ *n* **1** (hunter) braconnier *m*; **2** (for eggs) pocheuse *f*.

poaching /'pəʊtʃɪŋ/ *n* (of game) braconnage *m*.

PO Box (*abrév écrite* = **Post Office Box**) **~ 20** BP 20.

pocket /'pɒkɪt/ **I** *n* **1** poche *f*; **to go through sb's ~s** faire les poches de qn; **he paid for it out of his own ~** il l'a payé de sa poche; **prices to suit every ~** FIG des prix à la portée de tout le monde; **2** (in billiards) bourse *f*.

Points of the compass
abbreviated as

north	= nord	N
south	= sud	S
east	= est	E
west	= ouest	O

nord, sud, est, ouest is the normal order in French as well as English.

northeast	= nord-est	NE
northwest	= nord-ouest	NO
north-northeast	= nord-nord-est	NNE
east-northeast	= est-nord-est	ENE

Where?
Compass points in French are not normally written with a capital letter. However, when they refer to a specific region in phrases such as I love the North *or* he lives in the North, *and it is clear where this* North *is, without any further specification such as* of France *or* of Europe, *then they are written with a capital letter, as they often are in English, too. In the following examples,* north *and* nord *stand for any compass point word.*

I love the North	= j'aime le Nord
to live in the North	= vivre dans le Nord

Normally, however, these words do not take a capital letter:

in the north of Scotland = dans le nord de l'Écosse

Take care to distinguish this from

to the north of Scotland *(i.e. further north than Scotland)*	
	= au nord de l'Écosse
in the south of Spain	= dans le sud de l'Espagne*
it is north of the hill	= c'est au nord de la colline
a few kilometres north	= à quelques kilomètres au nord
due north of here	= droit au nord

* *Note that the south of France is more usually referred to as* le Midi.

There is another set of words in French for north, south *etc., some of which are more common than others:*

(north)	septentrion *(rarely used)*	septentrional(e)
(south)	midi	méridional(e)
(east)	orient	oriental(e)
(west)	occident	occidental(e)

Translating northern etc.

a northern town	= une ville du Nord
a northern accent	= l'accent du Nord
the most northerly outpost	= l'avant-poste le plus au nord

Regions of countries and continents work like this:

northern Europe	= l'Europe du Nord
the northern parts of Japan	= le nord du Japon
eastern France	= l'est de la France

For names of countries and continents which include these compass point words, such as North America *or* South Korea, *see the dictionary entry.*

Where to?
French has fewer ways of expressing this than English has; vers le *is usually safe:*

to go north	= aller vers le nord
to head towards the north	= se diriger vers le nord
to go northwards	= aller vers le nord
to go in a northerly direction	= aller vers le nord
a northbound ship	= un bateau qui se dirige vers le nord

With some verbs, such as face, *the French expression changes:*

the windows face north	= les fenêtres donnent au nord
a north-facing slope	= une pente orientée au nord

If in doubt, check in the dictionary.

Where from?
The usual way of expressing from the *is* du:

it comes from the north	= cela vient du nord
from the north of Germany	= du nord de l'Allemagne

Note also these expressions relating to the direction of the wind:

the north wind	= le vent de nord
a northerly wind	= un vent du nord
prevailing north winds	= des vents dominants du nord
the wind is in the north	= le vent est au nord
the wind is coming from the north	= le vent vient du nord

Compass point words used as adjectives
The French words nord, sud, est *and* ouest *are really nouns, so they when they are used as adjectives they are invariable.*

the north coast	= la côte nord
the north door	= la porte nord
the north face *(of a mountain)*	= la face nord
the north side	= le côté nord
the north wall	= le mur nord

Nautical bearings
The preposition by *is translated by* quart *in expressions like the following:*

north by northwest	= nord quart nord-ouest
southeast by south	= sud-est quart sud

II *noun modifier* [*flask, diary, dictionary, edition*] de poche.
III *vtr* LIT, FIG empocher.
IDIOMS **to be in ~** GB être en fonds; **to be out of ~** GB en être de sa poche; **to have sb in one's ~** avoir qn dans sa poche; **to live in each other's ~s** être tout le temps l'un sur l'autre; **to ~ one's pride** ravaler sa fierté.

pocketbook /'pɒkɪtbʊk/ *n* **1** (wallet) portefeuille *m*; **2** US (also **pocket book**) livre *m* de poche; **3** US (handbag) sac *m* à main.

pocketful /'pɒkɪtfʊl/ *n* poche *f* pleine (**of** de).

pocket: **~-handkerchief** *n* pochette *f*; **~knife** *n* couteau *m* de poche; **~ money** *n* argent *m* de poche; **~-size(d)** *adj* [*book, map, edition etc*] de poche; FIG (tiny) tout petit.

pockmarked *adj* [*skin, face*] grêlé.

pod /pɒd/ *n* (of peas, beans) (intact) gousse *f*; (empty) cosse *f*; (of vanilla) gousse *f*.

podgy° /'pɒdʒɪ/ *adj* grassouillet/-ette.

podium /'pəʊdɪəm/ *n* (*pl* **-iums, -ia**) (for speaker, conductor) estrade *f*; (for winner) podium *m*.

poem /'pəʊɪm/ *n* poème *m*.

poet /'pəʊɪt/ *n* poète *m*.

poetic /pəʊ'etɪk/ *adj* poétique.

poetically /pəʊ'etɪklɪ/ *adv* avec poésie.

poetic: **~ justice** *n* justice *f* immanente; **~ licence** GB, **~ license** US *n* licence *f* poétique.

poetry /'pəʊɪtrɪ/ *n* poésie *f*; **to write/read ~** écrire/lire des poèmes; **a collection of ~** un recueil de poèmes.

po-faced° /'pəʊfeɪst/ *adj* GB **to look/be ~** avoir l'air pincé.

pogo-stick /'pəʊgəʊstɪk/ *n* GAMES échasse *f* à ressort.

poignant /'pɔɪnjənt/ *adj* poignant.

point /pɔɪnt/ **I** *n* **1** (of knife, needle, pencil etc) pointe *f*; **2** (location, position on scale) point *m*; (less specific) endroit *m*; **embarkation ~** lieu *m* d'embarquement; **~ of entry** (into country) point d'arrivée; (of bullet into body) point d'impact; (into atmosphere) point d'entrée; **~ of no return** point de non-retour; **3** (extent, degree) point *m*; **I've got to the ~ where I can't take any more** j'en suis arrivé au point où je n'en peux plus; **up to a ~** jusqu'à un certain point; **4** (moment) (precise) moment *m*; (stage) stade *m*; **to be on the ~ of doing** être sur le point de faire; **at this ~ he broke down** à ce moment-là il a fondu en larmes; **at some ~ in the future** plus tard; **at one ~** à un moment donné; **when it came to the ~ of deciding** quand il a fallu décider; **at this ~ in time** dans l'état actuel des choses; **5** (question, idea) point *m*; **to take up** ou **return to sb's ~** revenir sur un point soulevé par qn; **this**

proves my ~ cela confirme ce que je viens de dire; **to make a** ~ faire une remarque (**about** sur); **to make the** ~ **that** faire remarquer que; **you've made your** ~, **please let me speak** vous vous êtes exprimé, laissez-moi parler; **to make a** ~ **of doing sth** (as matter of pride) mettre un point d'honneur à faire qch; (do deliberately) faire qch exprès; **to raise a** ~ **about sth** soulever la question de qch; **my** ~ **was that** ce que je voulais dire, c'était que; **that's a good** ~ c'est une remarque judicieuse; **I take your** ~ (agreeing) je suis d'accord avec vous; **I take your** ~, **but** je vois bien où vous voulez en venir, mais; **all right,** ~ **taken!** très bien, j'en prends note; **good** ~! très juste!; **you've got a** ~ **there** vous n'avez pas tort; **in** ~ **of fact** en fait; **6** (central idea) point *m* essentiel; **to come straight to the** ~ aller droit au fait; **to keep** ou **stick to the** ~ rester dans le sujet; **to miss the** ~ ne pas comprendre; **what she said was short and to the** ~ ce qu'elle a dit était bref et pertinent; **that's beside the** ~ là n'est pas la question; **to get the** ~ comprendre; **that's not the** ~ il ne s'agit pas de cela; **7** (purpose) objet *m*; **what's the** ~ **of doing...?** à quoi bon faire...?; **there's no** ~ **in doing** ça ne sert à rien de faire; **I don't see the** ~ **of doing** je ne vois pas l'intérêt de faire; **8** (feature, characteristic) point *m*, côté *m*; **her strong** ~ son point fort; **9** SPORT, FIN (in scoring) point *m*; **to win by 4** ~s gagner à 4 points près; **to win on** ~s (in boxing) remporter une victoire aux points; **match** ~ (in tennis) balle *f* de match; **10** (dot) point *m*; (decimal point) virgule *f*; (diacritic) signe *m* diacritique; MATH point *m*; **11** GEOG (headland) pointe *f*.
II points *npl* **1** GB RAIL aiguillages *mpl*, aiguilles *fpl*; **2** AUT électrodes *fpl*; **3** (in ballet) **to dance on** ~(s) faire des pointes *fpl*.
III *vtr* **1** (aim, direct) **to** ~ **sth at sb** braquer qch sur qn [*camera, gun*]; **to** ~ **one's finger at sb** montrer qn du doigt; **to** ~ **the finger at sb** (accuse) accuser qn; **to** ~ **sth towards** (of car, boat) diriger qch vers; **to** ~ **sb in the right direction** LIT, FIG mettre qn dans la bonne direction; **2** (show) **to** ~ **the way to** LIT (person, signpost) indiquer la direction de; **to** ~ **the way to a fairer system** ouvrir la voie à un système plus équitable; **3** (in ballet, gym) **to** ~ **one's toes** faire des pointes; **4** CONSTR jointoyer [*wall*].
IV *vi* **1** (indicate) indiquer ou montrer (du doigt); **to** ~ **at sb/sth** montrer qn/qch du doigt; **2** [*signpost, arrow*] indiquer; **to** ~ **at sb** ou **in sb's direction** [*gun, camera*] être braqué sur qn; **everything** ~s **in that direction** tout semble indiquer que c'est ainsi; **to** ~ **to sth as evidence of success** citer qch comme preuve d'une réussite.

■ **point out**: ¶ ~ **out** [*sth/sb*], ~ [*sth/sb*] **out** (show) montrer (**to** à); ¶ ~ **out** [*sth*] faire remarquer [*fact, discrepancy*]; **as he** ~ed **out** comme il l'a fait remarquer.
■ **point up**: ~ **up** [*sth*] souligner [*contrast, need*].
point-blank /ˌpɔɪntˈblæŋk/ *adv* **1** LIT [*shoot*] à bout portant; **2** FIG [*refuse, deny*] catégoriquement; [*ask, reply*] de but en blanc.
point duty *n* GB **to be on** ~ être affecté à la circulation.
pointed /ˈpɔɪntɪd/ *adj* **1** (sharp) [*hat, stick, chin*] pointu; [*window*] en pointe; [*arch*] en ogive; **2** FIG [*remark*] qui vise quelqu'un.
pointedly /ˈpɔɪntɪdlɪ/ *adv* [*ignore, look*] ostensiblement.
pointer /ˈpɔɪntə(r)/ *n* **1** (piece of information) indication *f*; **2** (dog breed) pointer *m*; **3** (for teaching) baguette *f*; **4** (on projector screen) flèche *f*; **5** COMPUT pointeur *m*.
pointillism /ˈpɔɪntɪlɪzəm, ˈpwæntiːlɪzm/ *n* pointillisme *m*.
pointing /ˈpɔɪntɪŋ/ *n* CONSTR jointoiement *m*.
pointless /ˈpɔɪntlɪs/ *adj* [*request, activity*] absurde; [*gesture*] inutile; [*attempt*] vain; **it's** ~ **to do/for me to do** ça ne sert à rien de faire/que je fasse.
pointlessly /ˈpɔɪntlɪslɪ/ *adv* pour rien.
pointlessness /ˈpɔɪntlɪsnɪs/ *n* absurdité *f*.
point: ~ **of contact** *n* contact *m*; ~ **of**

departure *n* point *m* de départ; ~ **of order** *n* question *f* relative à la procédure; ~ **of reference** *n* point *m* de référence; ~ **of sale** *n* point *m* de vente; ~**-of-sale advertising** *n* publicité *f* sur les lieux de vente, PLV *f*; ~ **of view** *n* point *m* de vue; ~(**s**) **system** *n* système *m* de points.
poise /pɔɪz/ **I** *n* **1** (confidence) assurance *f*; **2** (physical elegance) aisance *f*.
II *vtr* tenir [*javelin, spade*].
poised /pɔɪzd/ *adj* **1** (self-possessed) [*person*] plein d'assurance; [*manner*] posé; **2** (elegant) plein d'aisance; **3** (suspended) [*pen, knife, hand*] en suspens; **4** (balanced) **to be** ~ **on** se tenir sur [*rock, platform, cliff*]; **5** (on the point of) **to be** ~ **to do** être sur le point de faire.
poison /ˈpɔɪzn/ **I** *n* LIT, FIG poison *m*.
II *vtr* **1** (give poison to) [*person*] empoisonner [*person, animal*] (**with** avec); [*lead, fumes*] intoxiquer; **2** (make poisonous) mettre du poison dans [*foodstuffs, water*]; ECOL (contaminate) empoisonner [*environment, air, rivers*] (**with** avec); FIG (damage) empoisonner [*relationship, life*]; corrompre [*mind*].
poisoner /ˈpɔɪzənər/ *n* empoisonneur/-euse *m/f*.
poison gas *n* gaz *m* asphyxiant or toxique.
poisoning /ˈpɔɪzənɪŋ/ *n* empoisonnement *m*.
poisonous /ˈpɔɪzənəs/ *adj* **1** (noxious) [*chemicals, gas*] toxique; [*plant, mushroom, berry*] vénéneux/-euse; ZOOL [*snake, insect, bite*] venimeux/-euse; **2** FIG (vicious) [*rumour, propaganda*] pernicieux/-ieuse; [*person*] malveillant.
poison-pen letter *n* lettre *f* anonyme pleine de venin.
poke /pəʊk/ **I** *n* (prod) coup *m*.
II *vtr* **1** (jab, prod) pousser [qn] du bout du doigt [*person*]; donner un coup dans [*pile, substance*]; tisonner [*fire*] **he** ~d **his food with his fork** il inspecta le contenu de son assiette avec sa fourchette; **2** (push, put) **to** ~ **sth into** enfoncer qch dans [*hole, pot*]; **to** ~ **one's finger into a hole/pot** mettre le doigt dans un trou/pot; **to** ~ **one's head round the door/out of the window** passer la tête par la porte/par la fenêtre; **3** (pierce) **to** ~ **a hole in sth** faire un trou dans qch (**with** avec).
IDIOMS **it's better than a** ~ **in the eye** (**with a sharp stick**) c'est mieux que rien.
■ **poke around**, **poke about** GB fouiner, farfouiller (**in** dans).
■ **poke at**: ~ **at** [*sb/sth*] (with finger) pousser [qn] du bout du doigt [*person*]; enfoncer son doigt dans [*pile of objects, cake*]; tâter du bout du doigt [*vegetables, fruit*]; (with stick) piquer dans [*pile of objects*]; chipoter dans [*food*].
■ **poke out**: ¶ ~ **out** [*elbow, toe, blade, spring*] dépasser; [*flower*] poindre; ¶ **to** ~ **out** [*sth*], ~ [*sth*] **out** sortir [*head, nose, tongue*]; **to** ~ **sb's eye out** crever l'œil de qn.
poker /ˈpəʊkə(r)/ ▶ 949 ▮ *n* **1** (for fire) tisonnier *m*; **2** (cardgame) poker *m*.
IDIOMS (**as**) **stiff as a** ~ raide comme la justice.
poker-faced /ˈpəʊkəfeɪst/ *adj* [*person*] au visage impénétrable.
poky /ˈpəʊkɪ/ *adj* (small) [*room*] minuscule.
Poland /ˈpəʊlənd/ ▶ 840 ▮ *pr n* Pologne *f*.
polar /ˈpəʊlə(r)/ *adj* GEOG, ELEC [*icecap, lights, bear, region*] polaire; [*attraction*] (one) du pôle; (both) des pôles.
polarity /pəˈlærətɪ/ *n* **1** ELEC, PHYS polarité *f*; **2** FIG opposition *f*.
polarize /ˈpəʊləraɪz/ **I** *vtr* **1** ELEC, PHYS polariser; **2** (divide) diviser [*opinion*].
II *vi* (divide) [*opinions*] diverger.
pole /pəʊl/ *n* **1** (stick) GEN perche *f*; (for tent, flag) mât *m*; (in show jumping) barre *f*; (for skiing) bâton *m*; (piste marker) piquet *m*; **2** GEOG, PHYS pôle *m*; **to be at the opposite** ~ **from** FIG être aux antipodes de; **3** (in fishing) canne *f* à pêche.
IDIOMS **to be** ~s **apart** [*people*] être complètement différents; [*theories, methods, opinions*] être diamétralement opposés.

Pole /pəʊl/ ► 1100 *n* Polonais/-e *m/f*.

polecat /ˈpəʊlkæt/ *n* **1** (ferret) putois *m*; **2** US (skunk) mouf(f)ette *f*.

polemic /pəˈlemɪk/ *n* polémique *f* (**about** sur).

polemical /pəˈlemɪkl/ *adj* polémique.

pole: ~ **position** *n* pole position *f*; ~ **star** *n* étoile *f* polaire; ~ **vault** *n* saut *m* à la perche.

police /pəˈliːs/ I *n* **1** (+ *v pl*) (official body) **the ~** la police; **2** ¢ (individuals) policiers *mpl*.
II *vtr* **1** (keep order) maintenir l'ordre dans [*area*]; **2** (patrol) surveiller [*area, frontier*]; organiser le service d'ordre pour [*demonstration, match*]; **3** (monitor) contrôler l'application de [*measures*].

police: ~ **chief** *n* commissaire *m* divisionnaire; ~ **college** *n* centre *m* de formation de la police; ~ **constable**, **PC** *n* agent *m* de police; ~ **court** *n* tribunal de police et correctionnel; ~ **custody** *n* garde *f* à vue; **Police Department**, **PD** *n* US services *mpl* de police (d'une ville); ~ **escort** *n* escorte *f* policière; ~ **force** *n* police *f*; ~ **headquarters** *npl* administration *f* centrale de la police; ~**man** *n* agent *m* de police; ~ **officer** *n* policier *m*; ~ **record** *n* casier *m* judiciaire; ~ **state** *n* PÉJ État *m* policier; ~ **station** *n* poste *m* de police; (larger) commissariat *m*; ~ **van** *n* fourgon *m* cellulaire; ~**woman** *n* femme *f* policier.

police work *n* **1** ¢ (detection) investigations *fpl* policières; **2** (profession) métier *m* de policier.

policing /pəˈliːsɪŋ/ *n* **1** (maintaining law and order) maintien *m* de l'ordre; **2** (patrolling) surveillance *f*; **3** (of demonstration, match) organisation *f* du service d'ordre; **4** (of measures, regulations) contrôle *m* de l'application.

policy /ˈpɒləsɪ/ I *n* **1** (plan, rule) politique *f* (**on** sur); **it is our ~ to do** nous avons pour politique de faire; **to follow** ou **follow a ~ of doing** avoir pour politique de faire; **it is our ~ that** notre politique est de; **our company has a no-smoking ~** notre société a mis en place des mesures de restriction du tabagisme; **2** (in insurance) (type of cover) contrat *m*; (document) police *f*.
II *noun modifier* [*decision, statement*] de principe; [*discussion, matter, meeting, paper*] de politique générale.

policy: ~**holder** *n* assuré/-e *m/f*; ~**-making** *n* ¢ décisions *fpl*; ~ **unit** *n* comité *m* de conseillers politiques.

polio /ˈpəʊlɪəʊ/, **poliomyelitis** /ˌpəʊlɪəʊˌmaɪəˈlaɪtɪs/ ► 1002 *n* poliomyélite *f*.

polish /ˈpɒlɪʃ/ I *n* **1** (substance) (for wood, floor) cire *f*; (for shoes) cirage *m*; (for brass, silver) pâte *f* à polir; (for car) lustre *m*; **2** (shiny surface) éclat *m*; **3** FIG (elegance) (of manner, performance) brio *m*; (of person) chic *m*.
II *vtr* **1** LIT cirer [*shoes, furniture*]; astiquer [*leather, car, glass, brass*]; polir [*stone*]; **2** FIG (refine) soigner [*performance, image*]; affiner [*style*].
III *vi* cirer.
■ **polish off**○: ~ **off** [sth], ~ [sth] **off** (eat, finish) expédier○ [*food, job*].
■ **polish up**: ~ **up** [sth], ~ [sth] **up 1** LIT astiquer [*glass, car, silver*]; cirer [*wood, floor*]; **2**○ (perfect) parfaire [*Spanish, piano playing*]; perfectionner [*sporting skill*]; **to ~ up one's act** fignoler○ son numéro.

Polish /ˈpəʊlɪʃ/ ► 1100, 1038 I *n* (language) polonais *m*.
II *adj* polonais.

polished /ˈpɒlɪʃt/ *adj* **1** LIT [*surface, wood*] poli; [*floor, shoes*] ciré; [*silver, brass*] astiqué; **2** FIG (refined) [*manner*] raffiné; **3** (accomplished) (bien) rodé.

polite /pəˈlaɪt/ *adj* poli (**to** avec, envers FML); **to be ~ about sth** faire des commentaires polis sur qch; **to make ~ conversation** échanger des politesses; **in ~ company** ou **society** en bonne société; **to keep a ~ distance** rester à une distance respectueuse; **to use the ~ form** LING utiliser le vouvoiement.

politely /pəˈlaɪtlɪ/ *adv* poliment.

politeness /pəˈlaɪtnɪs/ *n* politesse *f*.

politic /ˈpɒlɪtɪk/ *adj* SOUT (wise) avisé; ► **body politic**.

political /pəˈlɪtɪkl/ *adj* politique.

political: ~ **analyst**, ~ **commentator** ► 1251 *n* commentateur/-trice *m/f* politique; ~ **football** *n* enjeu *m* politique.

politically /pəˈlɪtɪklɪ/ *adv* [*motivated, biased*] politiquement; ~ (**speaking**)... du point de vue politique...

politically: ~ **correct**, **PC** *adj* politiquement correct; ~**-sensitive** *adj* [*issue, problem*] délicat sur le plan politique.

political: ~ **prisoner** *n* prisonnier/-ière *m/f* politique; ~ **science** *n* sciences *fpl* politiques.

politician /ˌpɒlɪˈtɪʃn/ ► 1251 *n* homme/femme *m/f* politique.

politicize /pəˈlɪtɪsaɪz/ *vtr* politiser.

politics /ˈpɒlɪtɪks/ *n* **1** (+ *v sg*) (political life, affairs) politique *f*; **2** (+ *v sg*) SCH, UNIV sciences *fpl* politiques; **3** (+ *v pl*) (political views) opinions *fpl* politiques.

polka dot *n* pois *m*.

poll /pəʊl/ I *n* **1** (vote casting) scrutin *m*, vote *m*; (election) élections *fpl*; (number of votes cast) voix *fpl*; **the result of the ~** les résultats du scrutin; **to go to the ~s** se rendre aux urnes; **a heavy defeat at the ~s** une lourde défaite aux élections; **2** (list of voters) liste *f* électorale; (list of taxpayers) liste *f* de contribuables; **3** (survey) sondage *m* (**on** sur); **a ~ of teachers** un sondage effectué auprès des enseignants.
II *vtr* **1** (obtain in election) obtenir [*votes*]; **2** (canvass) interroger [*group*]; **3** COMPUT interroger.
III *vi* (obtain votes) **to ~ badly/well** recueillir peu de/ beaucoup de voix.

pollen /ˈpɒlən/ *n* pollen *m*.

pollen: ~ **count** *n* taux *m* de pollen dans l'atmosphère; ~ **sac** *n* sac *m* pollinique.

polling /ˈpəʊlɪŋ/ *n* **1** (voting) vote *m*; (election) élections *fpl*; (turnout) participation *f* électorale; **2** COMPUT interrogation *f*.

polling: ~ **booth** *n* isoloir *m*; ~ **day** *n* jour *m* des élections; ~ **place** *n* US = **polling station**; ~ **station** *n* bureau *m* de vote.

pollster /ˈpəʊlstə(r)/ *n* (person) sondeur *m*; (organization) institut *m* de sondage.

poll tax *n* GB ≈ impôts *mpl* locaux.

■ Note Le terme officiel était **community charge**. Il a été remplacé par **council tax** en avril 1993.

pollutant /pəˈluːtənt/ *n* polluant *m*.

pollute /pəˈluːt/ *vtr* **1** ECOL polluer (**with** avec); **2** FIG (morally) corrompre; (physically) souiller.

polluter /pəˈluːtə(r)/ *n* pollueur/-euse *m/f*.

pollution /pəˈluːʃn/ *n* **1** ECOL pollution *f* (**of** de); **2** FIG (moral) corruption *f*.

polo /ˈpəʊləʊ/ *n* **1** ► 949 SPORT polo *m*; **2** GB (sweater) col *m* roulé.

polo neck *n* GB (collar, sweater) col *m* roulé.

poltergeist /ˈpɒltəgaɪst/ *n* esprit *m* frappeur.

poly /ˈpɒlɪ/ I○ *n* GB *abrév* ► **polytechnic**.
II **poly+** *combining form* poly-.

polyanthus /ˌpɒlɪˈænθəs/ *n* (*pl* ~ ou **-thuses**) primevère *f*.

polychrome /ˈpɒlɪkrəʊm/ *adj* polychrome.

polycotton /ˌpɒlɪˈkɒtn/ *n* polyester *m* et coton *m*.

polyester /ˌpɒlɪˈestə(r)/ *n* polyester *m*.

polygamy /pəˈlɪɡəmɪ/ *n* polygamie *f*.

polyglot /ˈpɒlɪɡlɒt/ *n, adj* polyglotte (*mf*).

polymath /ˈpɒlɪmæθ/ *n* esprit *m* universel.

polymer /ˈpɒlɪmə(r)/ *n* polymère *m*.

polyp /ˈpɒlɪp/ *n* MED, ZOOL polype *m*.

polystyrene /ˌpɒlɪˈstaɪriːn/ *n* polystyrène *m*.

polystyrene cement *n* colle *f* polystyrène.

polytechnic /ˌpɒlɪˈteknɪk/ *n* GB établissement *m* d'enseignement supérieur.

polythene /ˈpɒlɪθiːn/ *n* GB polyéthylène *m*.

polyunsaturates /ˌpɒlɪʌnˈsætʃəraɪts/ *npl* acides *mpl* gras polyinsaturés; **high in ~** riche en acides gras polyinsaturés.

polyurethane /ˌpɒlɪˈjʊərəθeɪn/ n, noun modifier polyuréthane (m).

pomade /pəˈmɑːd/ n brillantine f.

pomander /pəˈmændə(r)/ n diffuseur m de parfum.

pomegranate /ˈpɒmɪgrænɪt/ n (fruit) grenade f; (tree) grenadier m.

pomp /pɒmp/ n pompe f; **with great ~** en grande pompe; **~ and circumstance** grand apparat.

pompom, pompon /ˈpɒmpɒm/ n pompon m.

pomposity /pɒmˈpɒsətɪ/ n air m or ton m pompeux.

pompous /ˈpɒmpəs/ adj [person] plein de suffisance; [air, speech, style] pompeux/-euse.

pompously /ˈpɒmpəslɪ/ adv de manière pompeuse.

pond /pɒnd/ n (large) étang m; (smaller) mare f; (in garden) bassin m.

ponder /ˈpɒndə(r)/ I vtr considérer [options]; réfléchir à [past events].
II vi réfléchir (on à); (more deeply) méditer (on sur).

ponderous /ˈpɒndərəs/ adj [movement] lourd; [tone] pesant.

pong○ /pɒŋ/ GB I n puanteur f; **what a ~!** ça pue○!
II vi puer○.

pontiff /ˈpɒntɪf/ n pontife m.

pontifical /pɒnˈtɪfɪkl/ adj **1** RELIG pontifical; **2** PÉJ [manner, tone] pontifiant.

pontificate I /pɒnˈtɪfɪkət/ n pontificat m.
II /pɒnˈtɪfɪkeɪt/ vi pontifier (about, on sur).

pontoon /pɒnˈtuːn/ n **1** (pier) ponton m; **2** AVIAT (float) flotteur m; **3** ▶ 949 | GB GAMES vingt-et-un m.

pony /ˈpəʊnɪ/ n poney m.

ponytail /ˈpəʊnɪteɪl/ n queue f de cheval.

pooch○ /puːtʃ/ n clebs○ m, chien m.

poodle /ˈpuːdl/ n caniche m.

poof○ /pʊf/, **poofter**○ /ˈpʊftə(r)/ n GB INJUR (homosexual) homosexuel m.

pooh /puː/ I n GB LANG ENFANTIN caca○ m BABY TALK.
II excl (expressing disgust) berk○!; (expressing scorn) peuh!

pooh-pooh /ˌpuːˈpuː/ vtr faire peu de cas de [idea].

pool /puːl/ I n **1** (pond) étang m; (artificial) bassin m; (still spot in river) plan m d'eau; (underground: of oil, gas) nappe f; **2** (also **swimming** ~) piscine f; **3** (puddle) flaque f; **a ~ of blood** une mare de sang; **a ~ of light** une flaque de lumière; **4** (kitty, in cards) mises fpl; GEN cagnotte f; **5** (common supply) (of money, resources) pool m; (of ideas, experience) réservoir m; (of labour) réserve f; (of teachers, players, candidates) liste f; **6** SPORT (billiards) billard m américain; ▶ **gene pool**.
II **pools** npl GB (also **football** ~s) ≈ loto m sportif.
III vtr mettre [qch] en commun [money, resources, information].

pool: **~ attendant** ▶ 1251 | n surveillant/-e m/f de baignade; **~ liner** n revêtement m de piscine; **~ party** n réception f au bord de la piscine; **~ room** n salle f de billard américain; **~side** adj au bord de la piscine; **~ table** n table f de billard américain.

pooped○ /puːpt/ adj **to be ~ (out)** être crevé○.

poor /pɔː(r), US pʊər/ adj **1** (not wealthy) [person, country] pauvre (never before n) (in en); **to become** ou **get ~er** s'appauvrir; **2** (inferior) GEN mauvais; [school, work] faible; [soil] pauvre; [appetite] petit; [chance, attendance] faible; **to be ~ at** [person] être faible en [maths, French]; **I'm a ~ traveller** je supporte mal les voyages; **3** (deserving pity) pauvre; **~ you!** pauvre de toi!; **4** (sorry, pathetic) [attempt, creature] pauvre; [excuse] piètre (before n).
IDIOMS **as ~ as a church mouse** pauvre comme Job.

poorly /ˈpɔːlɪ, US ˈpʊərlɪ/ I adj malade, souffrant.
II adv **1** (not richly) [live, dress, dressed] pauvrement; **2** (badly) [written, managed, lit, paid, argued] mal.

poorness /ˈpɔːnɪs, US ˈpʊərnɪs/ n (of land, diet) pauvreté f; (of education, pay) médiocrité f; (of eyesight, hearing) défaillance f.

poor relation n LIT, FIG parent m pauvre.

pop /pɒp/ I n **1** (sound) (aussi onomat) pan m; **to go ~** faire pan; **2**○ (drink) soda m; **3** (popular music) musique f pop; **4**○ US (dad) (also **~s**) papa m.
II noun modifier [concert, group, music, song, video] pop; [record, singer, star] de pop.
III vtr (p prés etc **-pp-**) **1**○ (burst) faire éclater [balloon, bubble]; **2** (remove) faire sauter [cork]; **3**○ (put) **to ~ sth in(to)** mettre qch dans [oven, cupboard, mouth]; **to ~ one's head through the window** passer la tête par la fenêtre; **4**○ (take) prendre [pills].
IV vi (p prés etc **-pp-**) **1** (go bang) [balloon] éclater; [cork, buttons] sauter; **2** [ears] se déboucher brusquement; **her eyes were ~ping out of her head** les yeux lui sortaient de la tête; **3**○ (go) **to ~ into town/the bank** faire un saut○ en ville/à la banque.
IDIOMS **to ~ the question** faire sa demande en mariage.
■ **pop back**○ GB repasser.
■ **pop in**○ GB passer.
■ **pop off** GB **1** (leave) filer○; **2** (die) crever○.
■ **pop out** GB sortir.
■ **pop round**, **pop over** GB passer.
■ **pop up**○ [head] surgir; [missing person] refaire surface○.

pope /pəʊp/ n pape m; **Pope Paul VI** le Pape Paul VI.

poplar /ˈpɒplə(r)/ n peuplier m.

poplin /ˈpɒplɪn/ n popeline f.

popover /ˈpɒpəʊvə(r)/ n US CULIN chausson m.

poppet○ /ˈpɒpɪt/ n GB **my (little) ~** ma puce; **she's a real ~** c'est un amour.

poppy /ˈpɒpɪ/ n BOT pavot m; **wild ~** coquelicot m.

Poppy Day○ n GB anniversaire m de l'armistice (de 1918).

Popsicle® /ˈpɒpsɪkl/ n US glace f à l'eau (en bâtonnet).

pop sock n mi-bas m.

populace /ˈpɒpjʊləs/ n population f.

popular /ˈpɒpjʊlə(r)/ adj **1** (generally liked) [actor, politician] populaire (with, among parmi); [profession, hobby, sport] répandu (with, among chez); [food, dish] prisé (with, among par); [product, resort, colour, design] en vogue (with, among chez); **John is very ~** John a beaucoup d'amis; **Smith was a ~ choice as chairman** le choix de Smith comme président a été très apprécié; **she's ~ with the boys** elle a du succès auprès des garçons; **I'm not very ~ with my husband at the moment** je n'ai pas tellement la cote○ auprès de mon mari en ce moment; **2** (of or for the people) [music, song] populaire; [entertainment, TV programme] grand public inv; [science, history etc] de vulgarisation; [enthusiasm, interest, support] du public; [discontent, uprising] du peuple; [movement, press] populaire; **contrary to ~ belief** contrairement à ce qu'on pense généralement; **the ~ view** ou **perception of sth** l'opinion générale sur qch; **by ~ demand** ou **request** à la demande générale.

popularity /ˌpɒpjʊˈlærətɪ/ n popularité f (of de; with auprès de).

popularization /ˌpɒpjʊləraɪˈzeɪʃn, US -rɪˈz-/ n popularisation f; (of ideas, science) vulgarisation f.

popularize /ˈpɒpjʊləraɪz/ vtr **1** (make fashionable) généraliser; **2** (make accessible) vulgariser.

popularly /ˈpɒpjʊləlɪ/ adv généralement.

populate /ˈpɒpjʊleɪt/ vtr peupler (with de).

population /ˌpɒpjʊˈleɪʃn/ I n population f.
II noun modifier [increase, decrease, explosion, figure] démographique; **~ control** contrôle m des naissances.

populist /ˈpɒpjʊlɪst/ n, adj populiste (mf).

populous /ˈpɒpjʊləs/ adj populeux/-euse.

pop: **~-up book** n livre m avec découpes en relief, livre m animé; **~-up toaster** grille-pain m vertical.

porcelain /ˈpɔːsəlɪn/ n porcelaine f.

porch /pɔːtʃ/ n **1** (of house, church) porche m; **2** US (veranda) véranda f.

porcupine /ˈpɔːkjʊpaɪn/ n porc-épic m.

pore /pɔː(r)/ n pore m.

■ **pore over**: ~ **over** [sth] être plongé dans [book]; étudier soigneusement [map, details].

pork /pɔːk/ n (viande f de) porc m; **a leg of ~** un jambon.

pork: ~ **butcher** n charcutier/-ière m/f; ~ **chop** n côte f de porc; ~ **sausage** n saucisse f; ~ **scratchings** npl GB grattons mpl.

porn○ /pɔːn/ n (abrév = **pornography**) porno○ m.

pornographic /ˌpɔːnəˈɡræfɪk/ adj pornographique.

pornography /pɔːˈnɒɡrəfi/ n pornographie f.

porous /ˈpɔːrəs/ adj [rock, wood, substance] poreux/-euse.

porpoise /ˈpɔːpəs/ n ZOOL marsouin m.

porridge /ˈpɒrɪdʒ, US ˈpɔːr-/ n porridge m (bouillie de flocons d'avoine).

port /pɔːt/ I n 1 (harbour) port m; **in** ~ au port; **the ship left** ~ le bateau a appareillé; ~ **of call** NAUT escale f; FIG (stop) arrêt m; 2 (drink) porto m; 3 AVIAT, NAUT (window) = **porthole**; 4 MIL NAUT (gunport) sabord m; 5 AVIAT, NAUT (left) bâbord m; 6 TECH (in engine) orifice m; 7 COMPUT port m.
II noun modifier (harbour) [area, authorities, facilities, security] portuaire.
III vtr COMPUT transporter [qch] (d'un système à l'autre).
IDIOMS **any** ~ **in a storm** nécessité fait loi.

portable /ˈpɔːtəbl/ I n portable m.
II adj GEN, COMPUT portable.

Portakabin® /ˈpɔːtəkæbɪn/ n GEN bâtiment m préfabriqué; (on building site) baraque f (de chantier).

portcullis /ˌpɔːtˈkʌlɪs/ n herse f (de forteresse).

portentous /pɔːˈtentəs/ adj LITTÉR 1 (ominous) sinistre; 2 (significant) très important, capital; 3 (solemn) grave; 4 (pompous) pompeux/-euse.

portentously /pɔːˈtentəslɪ/ adv LITTÉR 1 (ominously) [say, announce] d'un ton solennel; 2 (pompously) [say, announce] d'un ton pompeux.

porter /ˈpɔːtə(r)/ **▶ 1251** n 1 (in station, airport, hotel) porteur m; (in hospital) brancardier m; (in market) débardeur m; 2 GB (at entrance) (of hotel) portier m; (of apartment block) gardien/-ienne m/f; (of school) concierge mf; 3 US RAIL (steward) employé m des wagons-lits.

portfolio /pɔːtˈfəʊliəʊ/ n 1 (case) porte-documents m inv; (for drawings) carton m (à dessins); 2 ART, PHOT (sample) portfolio m; 3 POL (post) portefeuille m (ministériel); 4 FIN (of investments) portefeuille m.

porthole /ˈpɔːthəʊl/ n hublot m.

portico /ˈpɔːtɪkəʊ/ n portique m.

portion /ˈpɔːʃn/ n 1 (part, segment) (of house, machine, document, country) partie f (**of** de); 2 (share) (of money, food) part f (**of** de); (of responsibility, blame) part f (**of** de); 3 (at meal) portion f; 4 LITTÉR (fate) destin m.

portly /ˈpɔːtlɪ/ adj corpulent.

portrait /ˈpɔːtreɪt, -trɪt/ n portrait m.

portray /pɔːˈtreɪ/ vtr 1 (depict) décrire [place, era, event]; présenter [person, group, situation]; 2 CIN, THEAT [actor] interpréter [character]; 3 ART [artist] peindre [person]; [picture, artist] représenter [scene].

portrayal /pɔːˈtreɪəl/ n 1 (by actor) interprétation f (**of** de); 2 (by author, filmmaker) portrait m.

Portugal /ˈpɔːtʃʊɡl/ **▶ 840** pr n Portugal m.

Portuguese /ˌpɔːtjʊˈɡiːz/ **▶ 1100**, **1038** I n 1 (person) Portugais/-e m/f; **the** ~ les Portugais mpl; 2 (language) portugais m.
II adj [course] portugais.

pose /pəʊz/ I n 1 (for portrait, photo) pose f; 2 PÉJ (posture) pose f; **to strike a** ~ [dancer, model] prendre une pose; **to strike an aggressive** ~ prendre un air agressif.
II vtr (present) poser [problem] (**for** pour); présenter [challenge] (**to** à); représenter [threat, risk] (**to** pour); soulever [question] (**about** de).
III vi 1 [artist's model] poser; 2 (masquerade) **to** ~ **as** se faire passer pour; 3 PÉJ (posture) frimer.

poser○ /ˈpəʊzə(r)/ n 1 (person) frimeur/-euse m/f; 2 (puzzle) colle○ f.

poseur /pəʊˈzɜː(r)/ n frimeur/-euse m/f.

posh○ /pɒʃ/ adj 1 (high-class) [person] huppé○; [house, resort, area, clothes, car] chic inv; [voice] distingué; [party] mondain; 2 PÉJ [school, district] de rupins○; **to talk** ~○ parler comme les gens de la haute○.

position /pəˈzɪʃn/ I n 1 (situation, state) situation f; **in a strong** ~ en position de force; **to be in a** ~ **to do** être en mesure de faire; **to be in a good/in no** ~ **to do** être bien/mal placé pour faire; **to be** ou **find oneself in the happy/unhappy** ~ **of doing** avoir la chance/malchance de faire; **if I were in your** ~ si j'étais à ta place; 2 (attitude, stance) position f; **the official** ~ la position officielle; 3 (place, location) position f; **to be in** ~ (in place) être en place; (ready) être prêt; **to get into** ~ se mettre en place; **the house is in a good** ~ la maison est bien située; 4 (posture) position f; **to be in a sitting** ~ être assis; 5 (of lever, switch) position f; 6 (ranking) place f, rang m; (in sport, competition) position f; 7 SPORT poste m; **what** ~ **does he play?** quel est son poste?; 8 (job) poste m; **to hold** ou **occupy a senior** ~ occuper un poste responsable; 9 (place in society, army) position f; 10 (counter) guichet m; '~ **closed**' 'guichet fermé'.
II vtr 1 (station) poster [policemen, soldiers]; 2 (situate) disposer [object]; 3 (get correct angle) orienter [telescope, lamp, aerial].
III v refl **to** ~ **oneself** prendre position.

positive /ˈpɒzətɪv/ I n 1 LING (degré m) affirmatif m; 2 PHOT positif m; 3 MATH nombre m positif; 4 ELEC (pôle m) positif m.
II adj 1 (affirmative) [answer] positif/-ive; 2 (optimistic) [message, person, response, tone] positif/-ive; **to be** ~ **about** être enthousiaste à propos de [idea, proposal]; **to think** ~ voir les choses de façon positive; 3 (constructive) [contribution, effect, progress] positif/-ive; [advantage, good] réel/réelle; 4 (pleasant) [experience, feeling] positif/-ive; 5 (sure) [identification, proof] formel/-elle; [fact] indéniable; **to be** ~ être sûr (**about** de; **that** que); '~!' 'certain!'; 6 (forceful) [action, measure] catégorique; 7 MED [reaction, result, test] positif/-ive; 8 CHEM, ELEC, MATH, PHOT, PHYS positif/-ive; 9 (épith) (extreme) [pleasure] pur (before n); [disgrace, outrage, genius] véritable (before n).

positive discrimination n mesures fpl antidiscriminatoires.

positively /ˈpɒzətɪvlɪ/ adv 1 (constructively) [contribute, criticize] de façon constructive; 2 (favourably) [react, refer, speak] favorablement; 3 (actively) [participate, prepare, promote] activement; 4 (definitely) [identify, prove] formellement; 5 (absolutely) [disgraceful, beautiful, dangerous, idiotic] vraiment; [refuse, forbid] catégoriquement.

positive vetting n enquête f administrative.

posse /ˈpɒsɪ/ n détachement m.

possess /pəˈzes/ I vtr 1 (have) posséder [property, weapon, proof, charm]; avoir [power, advantage]; (illegally) détenir [arms, drugs]; **to be** ~**ed of** SOUT avoir [charm, feature]; 2 (take control of) [anger, fury] s'emparer de [person]; [devil] posséder [person]; **to be** ~**ed by** être obsédé par [idea, illusion]; **what** ~**ed you to do that?** qu'est-ce qui t'a pris de faire ça?
II possessed pp adj (by demon) possédé.

possession /pəˈzeʃn/ I n 1 (state of having) possession f (**of** de); **to be in** ~ **of** être en possession de; **to have** ~ **of sth** posséder qch; 2 JUR (illegal) détention f (**of** de); 3 JUR (of property) jouissance f (**of** de); **to take** ~ **of** prendre possession de [premises, property]; **to be in** ~ occuper les lieux; 4 SPORT **to be in** ou **have** ~ contrôler le ballon; 5 (by demon) possession f (**by** par); 6 (colonial) possession f.
II possessions npl (belongings) biens mpl.
IDIOMS ~ **is nine-tenths of the law** PROV possession vaut titre PROV.

possessive /pəˈzesɪv/ I n LING possessif m.
II adj GEN, LING [person, behaviour] possessif/-ive (**towards** à l'égard de; **with** avec).

possessor /pə'zesə(r)/ *n* possesseur *m*.

possibility /ˌpɒsə'bɪlətɪ/ **I** *n* **1** (chance, prospect) possibilité *f*; **there is a definite ~ that he'll come** il y a de très grandes chances qu'il vienne; **there is no ~ of changing the text** il est impossible de changer le texte; **within the bounds of ~** dans la limite du possible; **2** (eventuality) éventualité *f*; **the ~ of a refusal/of failure** l'éventualité d'un refus/d'un échec; **the collapse of the company is now a ~** l'effondrement de la société est à présent de l'ordre du possible.
II possibilities *npl* (potential) **the idea has possibilities** l'idée a un fort potentiel.

possible /'pɒsəbl/ **I** *n* Ⓒ **1** (possibility) possible *m*; **2** (potential candidate) (for job) candidat *m* possible; (for team) joueur/-euse *m/f* possible.
II *adj* possible; **he did as much as ~** il a fait tout son possible; **as far as ~** dans la mesure du possible; **as quickly as ~** le plus vite possible; **of what ~ interest/benefit can it be to you?** quel intérêt/avantage cela peut-il bien avoir pour toi?

possibly /'pɒsəblɪ/ *adv* **1** (maybe) peut-être; **2** (for emphasis) **how could they ~ understand?** comment donc pourraient-ils comprendre?; **what can he ~ do to you?** qu'est-ce que tu veux qu'il te fasse?; **we can't ~ afford it** nous n'en avons absolument pas les moyens; **I'll do everything I ~ can** je ferai (absolument) tout mon possible.

possum○ /'pɒsəm/ *n* opossum *m*; **to play ~** faire le mort.

post /pəʊst/ **I** *n* **1** ADMIN (job) poste *m* (**as** comme; **of** de); **to hold a ~** occuper un poste; **2** GB POST (system) poste *f*; (letters) courrier *m*; (delivery) distribution *f*; **by return of ~** par retour du courrier; **it was lost in the ~** cela s'est égaré dans le courrier; **to catch the ~** ne pas manquer la levée; **3** (duty, station) GEN, MIL poste *m*; **at one's ~** à son poste; **4** (pole) GEN, SPORT poteau *m*; **to be the first past the ~** SPORT être le premier à l'arrivée; FIG POL obtenir la majorité.
II *post-* *combining form* post-; **in ~-1992 Europe** dans l'Europe d'après 1992.
III *vtr* **1** GB (send by post) poster or expédier (par la poste); (put in letterbox) mettre [qch] à la poste; **2** (stick up) afficher [*notice, poster*]; annoncer [*details, results*]; **3** GEN, MIL (send abroad) affecter (**to** à); **4** (station) GEN, MIL poster [*guard, sentry*].
IDIOMS **to keep sb ~ed (about sth)** tenir qn au courant (de qch).
■ **post on** GB: **~ on** [sth], **~** [sth] **on** faire suivre.

postage /'pəʊstɪdʒ/ *n* affranchissement *m*; **including ~ and packing** frais *mpl* d'expédition inclus; **~ extra** affranchissement en supplément; **~ free** franc de port.

postage: **~ meter** *n* US machine *f* à affranchir; **~ stamp** *n* timbre-poste *m*.

postal /'pəʊstl/ *adj* [*charges, district*] postal; [*application*] par la poste.

postal order, **PO** *n* GB mandat *m* (**for** de).

postal service *n* **1** (institution) Service *m* des Postes; **2** (service) POST distribution *f* du courrier; (of company) service *m* de ventes par correspondance.

postal vote *n* GB vote *m* par correspondance.

postbag /'pəʊstbæg/ *n* GB **1** LIT sac *m* postal; **2** (mail) courrier *m*.

post: **~box** *n* GB boîte *f* aux lettres; **~card**, **pc** *n* carte *f* postale; **~ code** *n* GB code *m* postal.

postdate /ˌpəʊst'deɪt/ *vtr* postdater.

poster /'pəʊstə(r)/ *n* (for information) affiche *f*; (decorative) poster *m*.

posterior /pɒ'stɪərɪə(r)/ **I** *n* HUM (buttocks) derrière *m*.
II *adj* SOUT postérieur (**to** à).

posterity /pɒ'sterətɪ/ *n* postérité *f*.

poster paint *n* gouache *f*.

postgraduate /ˌpəʊst'grædʒʊət/ **I** *n* ≈ étudiant/-e *m/f* de troisième cycle.
II *adj* ≈ de troisième cycle.

posthumous /'pɒstjʊməs, US 'pɒstʃəməs/ *adj* posthume.

posthumously /'pɒstjʊməslɪ, US 'pɒstʃəməslɪ/ *adv* [*publish*] après la mort de l'auteur; [*award*] à titre posthume.

posting /'pəʊstɪŋ/ *n* **1** (job) affectation *f* (**to** à); **2** GB POST envoi *m*; **proof of ~** justificatif *m* d'expédition.

postman /'pəʊstmən/ ▶1251 *n* facteur *m*.

postmark /'pəʊstmɑːk/ **I** *n* cachet *m* de la poste.
II *vtr* timbrer.

post: **~master** ▶1251 *n* receveur *m* des Postes; **Postmaster General** *n* ministre *m* des Postes et Télécommunications; **~mistress** ▶1251 *n* receveuse *f* des Postes.

postmodernist /ˌpəʊst'mɒdənɪst/ *n, adj* postmoderniste (*mf*).

post-mortem /ˌpəʊst'mɔːtəm/ *n* MED autopsie *f*; FIG analyse *f* rétrospective.

post-natal /ˌpəʊst'neɪtl/ *adj* post-natal.

post: **~ office**, **PO** *n* poste *f*; **Post Office Box**, **PO Box** *n* boîte *f* postale.

post-operative /ˌpəʊst'ɒpərətɪv, US -reɪt-/ *adj* MED postopératoire.

postpone /pə'spəʊn/ *vtr* reporter, remettre (**until** à; **for** de).

postponement /pə'spəʊnmənt/ *n* report *m*, renvoi *m* (**until** à).

postscript /'pəʊsskrɪpt/ *n* (at end of letter) post-scriptum *m inv* (**to** à); (to book, document) postface *f* (**to** à); FIG suite *f* (**to** à).

post-tax /ˌpəʊst'tæks/ *adj, adv* après paiement des impôts.

postulate /'pɒstjʊleɪt, US -tʃʊ-/ *vtr* poser comme postulat; **to ~ that** postuler que.

posture /'pɒstʃə(r)/ **I** *n* **1** (pose) posture *f*; FIG (stance) position *f*; **2** (bearing) maintien *m*; **to have good/bad ~** se tenir bien/mal.
II *vi* PÉJ poser, prendre des poses.

posturing /'pɒstʃərɪŋ/ *n* PÉJ affectation *f*.

post-viral (fatigue) syndrome ▶1002 *n* encéphalomyélite *f* myalgique.

postwar /ˌpəʊst'wɔː(r)/ *adj* d'après-guerre.

posy /'pəʊzɪ/ *n* petit bouquet *m* (de fleurs).

pot /pɒt/ **I** *n* **1** (container) pot *m*; **a ~ of tea for two** deux thés; **to make a ~ of tea/coffee** faire du thé/du café; **~s and pans** casseroles; **2** (piece of pottery) poterie *f*; **3**○ (hashish) hasch○ *m*; **4** (for infant) pot *m*.
II *vtr* (**-tt-**) **1** mettre [qch] en pot [*jam*]; **2** (in billiards) blouser [*ball*]; **3** (also **~ up**) mettre [qch] en pot [*plant*].
III potted *pp adj* **1** CULIN **~ted meat** GB terrine *f* de viande; **~ted shrimps** crevettes *fpl* conservées (*dans du beurre*); **2** [*palm, plant*] en pot; **3** (condensed) [*biography, history*] bref/brève.
IDIOMS **to go to ~**○ (person) se laisser aller; (thing) aller à vau-l'eau; **to have ~s of money**○ GB avoir un tas○ d'argent; **a watched ~ never boils** PROV quand on est impatient chaque seconde semble durer une éternité; **to take ~ luck** (for meal) GB manger à la fortune du pot; (for hotel room etc) prendre ce que l'on trouve.

potash /'pɒtæʃ/ *n* potasse *f*.

potassium /pə'tæsɪəm/ *n* potassium *m*.

potato /pə'teɪtəʊ/ *n* (*pl* **-es**) BOT CULIN pomme *f* de terre.

potato: **~ crisps** GB, **~ chips** US *npl* chips *fpl*; **~ masher** *n* presse-purée *m inv*; **~ peeler** *n* épluche-légumes *m inv*.

pot: **~ bellied** *adj* [*person*] bedonnant○; [*stove*] renflé; **~ belly** *n* bedaine *f*; **~boiler** *n* PÉJ œuvre *f* alimentaire.

potency /'pəʊtnsɪ/ *n* **1** (of drug, remedy, image, voice) puissance *f*; (of drink) force *f*; **2** (sexual) virilité *f*.

potent /'pəʊtnt/ *adj* **1** [*argument, force, symbol, drug*] puissant; [*drink, mixture*] fort; **2** (sexually) viril.

potentate /'pəʊtnteɪt/ *n* potentat *m*.

potential /pə'tenʃl/ **I** n potentiel m (**as** en tant que; **for** de); **the ~ to do** les qualités fpl nécessaires pour faire; **to fulfil one's ~** montrer de quoi on est capable.
II adj [buyer, danger, energy, market, value, victim] potentiel/-ielle; [champion, rival] en puissance; [investor] éventuel/-elle; **to be a ~ success** avoir toutes les qualités pour réussir.

potentially /pə'tenʃəli/ adv potentiellement.

pot: **~hole** n (in road) fondrière f, nid m de poule; **~holer** n GB spéléologue mf; **~holing** ▶ 949 | n GB spéléologie f; **~hook** n crémaillère f.

potion /'pəʊʃn/ n potion f.

pot: **~pie** n US tourte f à la viande; **~ plant** n plante f d'appartement; **~ roast** n rôti m (cuit dans une cocotte).

potshot /'pɒtʃɒt/ n **to take a ~ at sth** tirer à vue sur qch.

potter /'pɒtə(r)/ ▶ 1251 | n potier m.
■ **potter about**, **potter around** GB (do odd jobs) bricoler○; (go about daily chores) suivre son petit train-train○; (pass time idly) traîner.

potter's wheel n tour m de potier.

pottery /'pɒtəri/ n **1** (craft, subject) poterie f; **2** ¢ (ware) poteries fpl; **3** (factory, workshop) poterie f.

pot: **~ting compost** n terreau m; **~ting shed** n abri m de jardin.

potty○ /'pɒti/ **I** n LANG ENFANTIN pot m (d'enfant).
II adj GB **1** (crazy) dingue○; [idea] farfelu○; **2** (enthusiastic) **to be ~ about sb/sth** être toqué○ de qn/qch.

potty-train /'pɒtɪtreɪn/ vtr **to ~ a child** apprendre à un enfant à aller sur le pot.

pouch /paʊtʃ/ n **1** (bag) petit sac m; (for tobacco) blague f (à tabac); (for ammunition) étui m (à munitions); (for cartridges) giberne f; (for mail) sac m postal; (for money) bourse f; (of clothes, skin) poche f; **2** ZOOL (of marsupials) poche f ventrale; (of rodents) abajoue f.

pouf(fe) /pu:f/ n (cushion) pouf m.

poultice /'pəʊltɪs/ n cataplasme m.

poultry /'pəʊltrɪ/ n ¢ (birds) volailles fpl; (meat) volaille f.

poultry: **~ farm** n (ferme f d')élevage m de volailles; **~ farming** n élevage m de volailles; **~man** ▶ 1251 | n US volailleur m.

pounce /paʊns/ **I** n bond m.
II vi bondir; **to ~ on** [animal] bondir sur [prey, object]; [person] se jeter sur [victim].

pound /paʊnd/ **I** n **1** ▶ 1392 | (weight measurement) livre f (de 453,6g); **two ~s of apples** ~ un kilo de pommes; **pears are 80 pence a** ou **per ~** ~ les poires sont à 80 pence la livre; **~ for ~ chicken is better value than pork** tout comparé le poulet revient moins cher que le porc; **2** (unit of currency) ▶ 849 | livre f; **I'll match your donation ~ for ~** je donnerai exactement la même somme que toi; **3** (compound) (for dogs, cars) fourrière f.
II vtr **1** CULIN (crush) piler [spices, grain, salt]; aplatir [meat]; **to ~ sth to** réduire qch en [powder, paste, pieces]; **2** (beat) [waves] battre [shore]; **to ~ sth with one's fists** frapper sur qch avec ses poings [door, table]; **3** (bombard) [artillery] pilonner [city]; **4** (tread heavily) **to ~ the streets** battre le pavé.
III vi **1** (knock loudly) **to ~ on** marteler [door, wall]; **2** (beat) [heart] battre ; **to ~ on** [waves] battre contre [beach, rocks]; **3** (run noisily) **to ~ up/down the stairs** monter/descendre l'escalier d'un pas lourd; **4** (throb) **my head is ~ing** j'ai des élancements dans la tête.
■ **pound away**: **~ away at** [sth] **1** (strike hard) taper à tour de bras sur [piano, typewriter]; **2** (work doggedly) travailler d'arrache-pied sur.

pounding /'paʊndɪŋ/ n (sound) (of waves, drums, heart) battement m; (of fists, hooves) martèlement m; (of guns) pilonnage m.

pour /pɔ:(r)/ **I** vtr **1** verser [liquid]; couler [cement, metal, wax]; **2** (also **~ out**) (serve) servir [drink]; **can I ~ you some more coffee?** puis-je vous resservir

du café?; **to ~ oneself a drink** se servir un verre; **3** (supply freely) **to ~ money into sth** investir des sommes énormes dans qch; **to ~ one's energies into one's work** mettre toute son énergie dans son travail.
II vi **1** (flow) [liquid] couler (à flots); **to ~ into** [water, liquid] couler dans; [smoke, fumes] se répandre dans; [light] inonder [room]; **to ~ out of** ou **from** [smoke, fumes] s'échapper de; [water] ruisseler de; **tears ~ed down her face** les larmes ruisselaient sur son visage; **water ~ed down the walls** l'eau coulait le long des murs; **light ~ed through the window** la lumière entrait à flots par la fenêtre; **relief ~ed over me** j'ai été envahi par une sensation de soulagement; **2** FIG **to ~ into** [people] affluer dans; **to ~ from** ou **out of** [people, cars] sortir en grand nombre de; [supplies, money] sortir en masse de; **to ~ across** ou **over** [border, bridge] traverser [qch] en grand nombre; **3** (serve tea, coffee) **shall I ~?** je vous sers?; **4** [jug, teapot] verser.
III **pouring** pres p adj [rain] battant.
IV v impers **it's ~ing (with rain)** il pleut à verse.
IDIOMS **to ~ cold water on** se montrer peu enthousiaste pour.
■ **pour away**: **~ away** [sth], **~** [sth] **away** vider.
■ **pour down** pleuvoir à verse.
■ **pour in**: **~ in** [people] affluer; [letters, money, requests] pleuvoir; [water] entrer à flots.
■ **pour off**: **~ off** [sth], **~** [sth] **off** vider.
■ **pour out**: ¶ **~ out** [liquid, smoke] se déverser; [people] sortir en grand nombre. ¶ **~ out** [sth], **~** [sth] **out** **1** verser, servir [coffee, wine etc]; **2** FIG donner libre cours à [ideas, feelings, troubles] (**to sb** devant qn); rejeter [fumes, sewage]; **to ~ out one's troubles** ou **heart to sb** s'épancher auprès de qn.

pout /paʊt/ **I** n moue f.
II vi faire la moue.

poverty /'pɒvətɪ/ n **1** (lack of money) pauvreté f; (more severe) misère f; **2** (of imagination, resources) pauvreté f.

poverty: **~ line** n, **~ level** n seuil m de pauvreté; **~-stricken** adj misérable.

POW n (abrév = **prisoner of war**) prisonnier/-ière m/f de guerre.

powder /'paʊdə(r)/ **I** n GEN poudre f; (snow) poudreuse f; **in ~ form** en poudre.
II vtr **to ~ one's face** se poudrer le visage.
III **powdered** pp adj [egg, milk, coffee] en poudre.
IDIOMS **to keep one's ~ dry** être paré; **to ~ one's nose** EUPH HUM se refaire une beauté EUPH HUM.

powder: **~ blue** ▶ 818 | n, adj bleu (m) pastel inv; **~ compact** n poudrier m; **~ keg** n FIG poudrière f FIG; **~ puff** n houppette f; **~ room** n EUPH toilettes fpl pour dames.

powdery /'paʊdərɪ/ adj **1** (in consistency) [snow] poudreux/-euse; [stone] friable; **2** (covered with powder) couvert de poudre.

power /'paʊə(r)/ **I** n **1** GEN, POL (control) pouvoir m; **to be in/come to ~** être/accéder au pouvoir; **to be in sb's ~** être à la merci de qn; **2** (strength) puissance f; **3** (influence) influence f (**over** sur); **4** (capability) pouvoir m; **to do everything in one's ~** faire tout ce qui est en son pouvoir (**to do** pour faire); **to lose the ~ of speech** perdre l'usage de la parole; **to be at the height of one's ~s** GEN avoir atteint la plénitude de ses moyens; [artist] être au sommet de son art; **5** ¢ (also **~s**) (authority) attributions fpl; **police ~s** les attributions de la police; **6** (physical force) (of person, explosion) force f; (of storm) violence f; **7** PHYS, TECH GEN énergie f; (current) courant m; **to switch on the ~** mettre le courant; **8** (of vehicle, plane) puissance f; **to be running at full/half ~** fonctionner à plein/mi-régime; **9** (magnification) puissance f; **10** MATH **8 to the ~ of 3** 8 puissance 3; **11** (country) puissance f.
II noun modifier TECH, ELEC [drill, circuit, cable] électrique; [steering, brakes] assisté; [mower] à moteur; [shovel] mécanique.
III vtr faire marcher [engine]; propulser [plane, boat]; **~ed by** propulsé par [engine]; alimenté par [electricity, gas, generator].

IDIOMS **to do sb a ~ of good** faire à qn un bien fou; **the ~s of darkness** les puissances des ténèbres; **the ~s that be** les autorités.

power: **~-assisted** *adj* [*steering*] assisté; **~ base** *n* base *f* politique; **~boat** *n* hors-bord *m inv*; **~ broker** *n*: celui/celle qui détient les clés du pouvoir; **~ cut** *n* coupure *f* de courant; **~ dressing** *n* tenue *f* vestimentaire qui en impose (*portée par les femmes cadres au travail*).

powerful /'paʊǝfl/ *adj* [*person, arms, engine, computer, description*] puissant; [*bomb*] de forte puissance; [*smell, emotion, impression, light, voice, government*] fort; [*blow*] bon/bonne; [*argument, evidence*] solide; [*portrayal*] saisissant; [*performance*] magistral.

powerfully /'paʊǝfǝlɪ/ *adv* [*influenced, affected*] fortement; [*portrayed*] d'une manière saisissante; [*argue*] avec force; [*smell*] fortement (**of** de); **to be ~ built** avoir une forte carrure.

powerhouse /'paʊǝhaʊs/ *n* **1** LIT centrale *f* électrique; **2**° FIG (of ideas etc) laboratoire *m*; **3** FIG (person) locomotive *f*.

powerless /'paʊǝlɪs/ *adj* impuissant (**against** face à); **to be ~ to do** ne pas pouvoir faire.

power: **~ line** *n* ligne *f* à haute tension; **~ of attorney** *n* procuration *f*; **~ plant** US = **power station**; **~ play** *n* US FIG coup *m* de force; **~ point** *n* prise *f* (de courant); **~ politics** *npl* (using military force) politique *f* de la force armée; (using coercion) politique *f* d'intimidation; **~ sharing** *n* partage *m* du pouvoir; **~ station** *n* centrale *f* (électrique).

powwow /'paʊwaʊ/ *n* **1** (meeting) assemblée *f* (d'Indiens d'Amérique); **2**° FIG discussion *f* importante.

pp 1 (on document) (*abrév* = **per procurationem**) po; **2** (*abrév* = **pages**) pp.

p & p *n* (*abrév* = **postage and packing**) frais *mpl* d'expédition.

PR *n* **1** *abrév* ▶ **public relations**; **2** *abrév* ▶ **proportional representation**.

practicability /ˌpræktɪkǝ'bɪlǝtɪ/ *n* faisabilité *f*.

practicable /'præktɪkǝbl/ *adj* [*proposal, plan*] réalisable.

practical /'præktɪkl/ **I** *n* (exam) épreuve *f* pratique; (lesson) travaux *mpl* pratiques.
II *adj* **1** (concrete, not theoretical) pratique; **in ~ terms** en pratique; **2** [*person*] (sensible) pratique; (with hands) adroit; **3** (functional) [*clothes, furniture, equipment*] pratique; **4** (viable) [*plan etc*] réalisable.

practicality /ˌpræktɪ'kælǝtɪ/ **I** *n* **1** (of person) esprit *m* pratique; (of clothes, equipment) facilité *f* d'utilisation; **2** (of scheme, idea, project) aspect *m* pratique.
II practicalities *npl* détails *mpl* pratiques.

practical joke *n* farce *f*.

practically /'præktɪklɪ/ *adv* **1** (almost, virtually) pratiquement; **2** (in a practical way) d'une manière pratique.

practice /'præktɪs/ **I** *n* **1** ₡ (exercises) exercices *mpl*; (experience) entraînement *m*; **to have had ~ in** ou **at sth/in** ou **at doing** avoir l'expérience en qch/pour ce qui est de faire; **to be in ~** (for sport) être bien entraîné; (for music) être bien exercé; **to be out of ~** être rouillé°; **2** (meeting) (for sport) entraînement *m*; (for music, drama) répétition *f*; **3** (procedure) pratique *f*, usage *m*; **it's standard ~ to do** il est d'usage de faire; **business ~** usage en affaires; **4** ₡ (habit) habitude *f*; **as is my usual ~** comme je le fais d'habitude; **5** (custom) coutume *f*; **6** (business of doctor, lawyer) cabinet *m*; **to be in ~** exercer; **to set up in** ou **go into ~** s'établir en tant que médecin ou juriste; **7** ₡ (as opposed to theory) pratique *f*; **in ~** en pratique.
II *noun modifier* [*game, match*] d'essai; [*flight*] d'entraînement.
III *vtr, vi* US = **practise**.

IDIOMS **~ makes perfect** PROV c'est en forgeant qu'on devient forgeron PROV.

practise GB, **practice** US /'præktɪs/ **I** *vtr* **1** (work at) travailler [*song, speech, French*]; s'exercer à [*movement, shot*]; réviser [*technique*]; répéter [*play*]; **to ~**

the piano travailler le piano; **to ~ doing** ou **how to do** s'entraîner à faire; **2** (use) pratiquer [*restraint, kindness*]; utiliser [*method*]; **3** (follow a profession) exercer; **4** (observe) pratiquer [*custom, religion*].
II *vi* **1** (train) (at piano, violin) s'exercer; (for sports) s'entraîner; (for play, concert) répéter; **2** (follow a profession) exercer; **to ~ as** exercer la profession de [*doctor, lawyer*].

IDIOMS **to ~ what one preaches** prêcher d'exemple.

practised GB, **practiced** US /'præktɪst/ *adj* [*player, lawyer, cheat*] expérimenté; [*eye, ear, movement*] expert; **to be ~ in/in doing** être fort dans/pour faire.

practising GB, **practicing** US /'præktɪsɪŋ/ *adj* [*Christian, Muslim*] pratiquant; [*doctor, lawyer*] en exercice; [*homosexual*] actif/-ive.

practitioner /præk'tɪʃǝnǝ(r)/ *n* praticien/-ienne *m/f*; **dental ~** dentiste *mf*.

pragmatic /præg'mætɪk/ *adj* pragmatique.

pragmatics /præg'mætɪks/ *n* (+ *v sg*) **1** LING pragmatique *f*; **2** (of scheme, situation) détails *mpl* pratiques.

pragmatism /'prægmǝtɪzǝm/ *n* pragmatisme *m*.

pragmatist /'prægmǝtɪst/ *n* GEN, LING pragmatiste *mf*.

prairie /'preǝrɪ/ *n* plaine *f* (herbeuse), prairie *f*.

prairie wolf *n* US coyote *m*.

praise /preɪz/ **I** *n* GEN éloges *mpl*, louanges *fpl*; **in ~ of sb** à la louange de qn; **in ~ of sth** louant qch; **to be highly ~d** être couvert d'éloges; **that's ~ indeed coming from her** venant d'elle c'est un compliment.
II *vtr* **1** GEN faire l'éloge de [*person, book, achievement*] (**as** en tant que); **to ~ sb for sth/for doing** féliciter qn pour qch/d'avoir fait; **to ~ sb/sth to the skies** porter qn/qch aux nues; **2** RELIG louer [*God*].

praiseworthy /'preɪzwɜːðɪ/ *adj* digne d'éloges.

pram /præm/ *n* GB landau *m*.

prance /prɑːns, US præns/ *vi* [*horse*] caracoler; [*person*] sautiller; **to ~ in/out** [*person*] entrer/sortir allègrement.

prank /præŋk/ *n* farce *f*.

prattle /'prætl/ **I** *n* bavardage *m*; (of children) babillage *m*.
II *vi* bavarder; [*children*] babiller; **to ~ on about sth** parler de qch à n'en plus finir.

prawn /prɔːn/ **I** *n* crevette *f* rose, bouquet *m*.
II *noun modifier* [*salad, sandwich*] aux crevettes; **~ cocktail** salade *f* de crevettes.

pray /preɪ/ **I** ‡ ou IRON *adv* je vous prie.
II *vtr* prier (**that** pour que + *subj*).
III *vi* GEN, RELIG prier (**for** pour).

prayer /'preǝ(r)/ **I** *n* RELIG prière *f*; FIG (hope) souhait *m*; **to say one's ~s** faire sa prière; **his ~s were answered** LIT, FIG sa prière a été exaucée.
II prayers *npl* (informal) prière *f*; (formal) office *m*.
IDIOMS **on a wing and a ~**° Dieu sait comment.

prayer: **~ beads** *npl* chapelet *m*; **~ book** *n* livre *m* de prières; **~ shawl** *n* taled *m*; **~ wheel** *n* moulin *m* à prière.

preach /priːtʃ/ **I** *vi* RELIG prêcher (**to** à); FIG PEJ sermonner.
II *vtr* RELIG prêcher (**to** à); FIG prêcher, prôner [*tolerance, virtue, pacifism*].
IDIOMS **to practise what one ~es** conformer ses actes à ses paroles; **to ~ to the converted** prêcher les convertis.

preacher /'priːtʃǝ(r)/ *n* pasteur *m*.

preamble /priː'æmbl/ *n* préambule *m* (**to** à).

prearrange /ˌpriːǝ'reɪndʒ/ *vtr* fixer [qch] à l'avance.

precarious /prɪ'keǝrɪǝs/ *adj* précaire.

precast /ˌpriː'kɑːst, US -'kæst/ *adj* [*concrete*] précoulé.

precaution /prɪ'kɔːʃn/ *n* précaution *f* (**against** contre).

precautionary /prɪ'kɔːʃǝnǝrɪ, US -nerɪ/ *adj* préventif/-ive.

precede /prɪ'siːd/ *vtr* précéder.

precedence /'presɪdəns/ n **1** (in importance) priorité f (**over** sur); **2** (in rank) préséance f (**over** sur).

precedent /'presɪdənt/ n précédent m.

preceding /prɪ'si:dɪŋ/ adj précédent.

precept /'pri:sept/ n précepte m.

preceptor /pri:'septə(r)/ n US UNIV ≈ moniteur/-trice m/f.

precinct /'pri:sɪŋkt/ n **1** GB (also **shopping ~**) quartier m commerçant; **2** GB (also **pedestrian ~**) zone f piétonne; **3** US ADMIN circonscription f.

precious /'preʃəs/ **I** n (as endearment) mon trésor.
II adj **1** (valuable) précieux/-ieuse; **2** (held dear) [person] cher/chère (**to** à) ALSO IRON; **3** PÉJ (affected) [person, style] précieux/-ieuse, affecté.
III adv (very) **~ little time** fort peu de temps; **~ few cars** fort peu de voitures.

precipice /'presɪpɪs/ n LIT, FIG précipice m.

precipitate I /prɪ'sɪpɪteɪt/ n CHEM précipité m.
II /prɪ'sɪpɪtət/ adj (hasty) [action] précipité.

precipitately /prɪ'sɪpɪtətlɪ/ adv SOUT précipitamment.

precipitation /prɪ,sɪpɪ'teɪʃn/ n **1** CHEM précipitation f; **2** ₵ METEOROL précipitations fpl.

precipitous /prɪ'sɪpɪtəs/ adj **1** SOUT (steep) [cliff] à pic inv; [road] escarpé; [steps] raide; **2** (hasty) = **precipitate II**.

précis /'preɪsi:, US preɪ'si:/ **I** n résumé m.
II vtr faire un résumé de [text, speech].

precise /prɪ'saɪs/ adj **1** (exact) [sum, measurement] précis; **2** (meticulous) [person, mind] méticuleux/-euse.

precisely /prɪ'saɪslɪ/ adv **1** (exactly) exactement, précisément; **at ten o'clock ~** à dix heures précises; **2** (accurately) [describe, record] avec précision.

precision /prɪ'sɪʒn/ n précision f.

preclude /prɪ'klu:d/ vtr exclure [possibility]; empêcher [action].

precocious /prɪ'kəʊʃəs/ adj GEN précoce.

precociousness /prɪ'kəʊʃəsnɪs/, **precocity** /prɪ'kɒsətɪ/ n précocité f.

preconceived /,pri:kən'si:vd/ adj préconçu.

preconception /,pri:kən'sepʃn/ n opinion f préconçue.

precondition /,pri:kən'dɪʃn/ **I** n condition f requise.
II vtr PSYCH conditionner.

precook /,pri:'kʊk/ vtr précuire.

precursor /,pri:'kɜ:sə(r)/ n (person) précurseur m; (sign) signe m avant-coureur; (prelude) prélude m (**to, of** à); (earlier form) ancêtre m.

predate /,pri:'deɪt/ vtr **1** (put earlier date) antidater [cheque, document]; **2** (exist before) [discovery, building] être antérieur à.

predator /'predətə(r)/ n LIT, FIG prédateur m.

predatory /'predətrɪ, US -tɔ:rɪ/ adj prédateur/-trice.

predecessor /'pri:dɪsesə(r), US 'predə-/ n prédécesseur m.

predestination /,pri:destɪ'neɪʃn/ n prédestination f.

predestine /,pri:'destɪn/ vtr prédestiner.

predetermine /,pri:dɪ'tɜ:mɪn/ vtr **1** (fix beforehand) déterminer d'avance; **2** RELIG, PHILOS prédéterminer.

predicament /prɪ'dɪkəmənt/ n situation f difficile.

predicate I /'predɪkət/ n LING, PHILOS prédicat m.
II /'predɪkət/ adj LING, PHILOS prédicatif/-ive.
III /'predɪkeɪt/ vtr **1** GEN (assert) avancer [theory]; **to ~ that** poser que; **2** PHILOS (affirm) affirmer (**of** de); **3** (base) fonder (**on** sur).

predicative /prɪ'dɪkətɪv, US 'predɪkeɪtɪv/ adj LING prédicatif/-ive.

predict /prɪ'dɪkt/ vtr prédire.

predictable /prɪ'dɪktəbl/ adj prévisible.

predictably /prɪ'dɪktəblɪ/ adv [boring, late] comme prévu; **~, he came** comme on pouvait s'y attendre, il est venu.

prediction /prɪ'dɪkʃn/ n prédiction f (**that** selon laquelle).

predigested /,pri:daɪ'dʒestɪd/ adj prédigéré.

predilection /,pri:dɪ'lekʃn, US ,predl'ek-/ n prédilection f.

predispose /,pri:dɪ'spəʊz/ vtr prédisposer.

predisposition /,pri:dɪspə'zɪʃn/ n prédisposition f.

predominance /prɪ'dɒmɪnəns/ n prédominance f (**of** de; **over** sur).

predominant /prɪ'dɒmɪnənt/ adj prédominant.

predominantly /prɪ'dɒmɪnəntlɪ/ adv [represent, feature] principalement; [Muslim, female] essentiellement; **the flowers were ~ pink** la plupart des fleurs étaient roses.

predominate /prɪ'dɒmɪneɪt/ vi prédominer.

pre-eminence /,pri:'emɪnəns/ n GEN suprématie f; SPORT supériorité f.

pre-eminent /,pri:'emɪnənt/ adj **1** (distinguished) [celebrity, scientist] éminent; **2** (leading) [nation, cult, company] dominant.

pre-eminently /,pri:'emɪnəntlɪ/ adv **1** (highly) [successful, distinguished] particulièrement; **2** (above all) [religious, political] avant tout.

pre-empt /,pri:'empt/ vtr **1** (anticipate) anticiper [question, decision, move]; devancer [person]; **2** (thwart) contrecarrer [action, plan].

pre-emptive /,pri:'emptɪv/ adj [strike, move, attack] préventif/-ive.

preen /pri:n/ **I** vi [bird] se lisser les plumes.
II v refl **to ~ oneself** [bird] se lisser les plumes; [person] PÉJ se pomponner.

pre-exist /,pri:ɪg'zɪst/ **I** vtr préexister à.
II vi [situation] préexister; [person, soul] avoir une vie antérieure.
III **pre-existing** pres p adj préexistant.

prefab /'pri:fæb, US ,pri:'fæb/ n (bâtiment m) préfabriqué m.

prefabricate /,pri:'fæbrɪkeɪt/ vtr préfabriquer.

preface /'prefɪs/ **I** n (to book) préface f; (to speech) préambule m.
II vtr préfacer [livre]; **to ~ sth with sth** faire précéder qch de qch.

prefatory /'prefətrɪ, US -tɔ:rɪ/ adj [comments] préliminaire; [pages, notes] liminaire.

prefect /'pri:fekt/ n **1** GB SCH élève chargé de la surveillance; **2** POL préfet m.

prefecture /'pri:fektjʊə(r), US -tʃər/ n préfecture f.

prefer /prɪ'fɜ:(r)/ **I** vtr **1** (like better) préférer, aimer mieux; **I ~ painting to drawing** je préfère la peinture au dessin; **to ~ it if** aimer mieux que (+ subj); **2** JUR **to ~ charges** porter plainte; **3** (promote) élever [clergyman].
II **preferred** pp adj (tjrs épith) [method, option, solution] préféré; [creditor, candidate] prioritaire.

preferable /'prefrəbl/ adj préférable (**to** à).

preferably /'prefrəblɪ/ adv de préférence.

preference /'prefrəns/ n préférence f (**for** pour); **in ~ to** de préférence à; **in ~ to doing** plutôt que de faire.

preference share n GB FIN action f privilégiée.

preferential /,prefə'renʃl/ adj (all contexts) préférentiel/-ielle.

preferment /prɪ'fɜ:mənt/ n ADMIN élévation f.

prefigure /,pri:'fɪgə(r), US -gjər/ vtr **1** (be an early sign of) [event] préfigurer; [person] être le précurseur de; **2** (imagine beforehand) imaginer d'avance.

prefix /'pri:fɪks/ **I** n (pl **-es**) LING préfixe m.
II vtr préfixer [word]; **to ~ X to Y** faire précéder Y de X.

pregnancy /'pregnənsɪ/ n (of woman) grossesse f; (of animal) gestation f.

pregnant /'pregnənt/ n **1** MED [woman] enceinte; [animal] pleine; **to get sb ~○** faire un enfant à qn○; **2** FIG [pause] éloquent; **~ with meaning/danger** lourd de sens/danger.

preheat /,pri:'hi:t/ vtr préchauffer [oven].

prehistoric /,pri:hɪ'stɒrɪk, US -tɔ:rɪk/ adj préhistorique ALSO FIG.

prehistory /ˌpriːˈhɪstrɪ/ n **1** HIST préhistoire f; **2** ¢ FIG (beginnings) débuts mpl.

pre-ignition /ˌpriːɪɡˈnɪʃn/ n autoallumage m.

prejudge /ˌpriːˈdʒʌdʒ/ vtr juger [qn] d'avance [person]; préjuger [issue].

prejudice /ˈpredʒʊdɪs/ I n **1** C préjugé m; **2** ¢ préjugés mpl; **racial/political ~** préjugés raciaux/en matière de politique; **3** (harm) GEN, JUR préjudice m.
II vtr **1** (bias) influencer; **to ~ sb against/in favour of** prévenir qn contre/en faveur de; **2** (harm, jeopardize) porter préjudice à [claim, case]; léser [person]; compromettre [chances].

prejudiced /ˈpredʒʊdɪst/ adj [person] plein de préjugés; [judgment, account] partial; [opinion] préconçu.

prejudicial /ˌpredʒʊˈdɪʃl/ adj SOUT préjudiciable.

prelate /ˈprelət/ n prélat m.

prelim /ˈpriːlɪm/ n (gén pl) **1** GB UNIV examen m de passage en deuxième année; **2** GB SCH ≈ bac m blanc.

preliminary /prɪˈlɪmɪnərɪ, US -nerɪ/ I n **1 as a ~ to** en prélude à; **2** SPORT épreuve f éliminatoire.
II **preliminaries** npl préliminaires mpl (**to** à).
III adj [comment, data, test] préliminaire; [heat, round] éliminatoire; JUR [hearing, inquiry, ruling] préliminaire; **~ to** préalable à.

prelude /ˈpreljuːd/ n GEN, MUS prélude m (**to** à).

premarital /ˌpriːˈmærɪtl/ adj avant le mariage.

premature /ˈpremətʃə(r), US ˌpriːməˈtʊər/ adj GEN, MED prématuré; [ejaculation, menopause] précoce; **to be born two weeks ~** naître deux semaines avant terme.

prematurely /ˈpremətʃʊəlɪ, US ˌpriːməˈtʊərlɪ/ adv prématurément.

premedication /ˌpriːmedɪˈkeɪʃn/ n (also **premed**) MED prémédication f.

premeditate /ˌpriːˈmedɪteɪt/ vtr préméditer.

premenstrual: **~ syndrome, PMS** n SPÉC syndrome m prémenstruel; **~ tension, PMT** n syndrome m prémenstruel.

premier /ˈpremɪə(r), US ˈpriːmɪər/ I n **1** (prime minister) premier ministre m; **2** (head of government) chef m du gouvernement.
II adj premier/-ière.

première /ˈpremɪeə(r), US prɪˈmɪər/ I n première f.
II vtr donner [qch] en première [film, play].
III vi [film] passer en première.

premiership /ˈpremɪəʃɪp, US prɪˈmɪərʃɪp/ n POL fonction f de premier ministre or de chef du gouvernement; (period of office) ministère m.

premise /ˈpremɪs/ I n GB (also **premiss** GB) prémisse f; **on the ~ that** en supposant que (+ subj).
II **premises** npl locaux mpl; **on the ~s** sur place; **off the ~s** à l'extérieur; **to leave the ~s** quitter les lieux.

premium /ˈpriːmɪəm/ n **1** GEN (extra payment) supplément m; **2** (Stock Exchange) prime f d'émission; **3** (in insurance) prime f (d'assurance); **4** COMM (payment for lease) reprise f; **5** FIG **to be at a ~** valoir de l'or; **to put** OU **place** OU **set a (high) ~ on sth** mettre qch au (tout) premier plan.

premium bond GB n obligation f à lots.

prenatal /ˌpriːˈneɪtl/ adj SURTOUT US prénatal.

preoccupation /ˌpriːɒkjʊˈpeɪʃn/ n préoccupation f; **to have a ~ with** se préoccuper de; **his ~ with** son obsession pour.

preoccupied /ˌpriːˈɒkjʊpaɪd/ adj préoccupé.

preoccupy /ˌpriːˈɒkjʊpaɪ/ vtr (prét, pp **-pied**) préoccuper.

preoperative /ˌpriːˈɒpərətɪv, US -reɪt-/ adj préopératoire.

preordained /ˌpriːɔːˈdeɪnd/ adj **1** GEN [decree, order] prescrit d'avance; **2** RELIG, PHILOS [outcome] prédestiné; [pattern] préétabli.

prep○ /prep/ n **1** GB SCH ¢ (homework) devoirs mpl; (study period) étude f; **2** US SCH élève mf d'un lycée privé.

prepack /ˌpriːˈpæk/, **prepackage** /ˌpriːˈpækɪdʒ/ vtr pré-emballer.

prepaid /ˌpriːˈpeɪd/ adj GEN payé d'avance; **carriage ~** port payé; **~ envelope** enveloppe f affranchie pour la réponse.

preparation /ˌprepəˈreɪʃn/ n **1** (of meal, report, lecture, event) préparation f; **~s** préparatifs mpl; **in ~ for sth** en vue de qch; **2** (physical, psychological) préparation f (**for** pour); (sporting) entraînement (**for** pour); **3** (substance) préparation f; **4** ¢ GB (homework) devoirs mpl.

preparatory /prɪˈpærətrɪ, US -tɔːrɪ/ adj [training, course, drawing] préparatoire; [meeting, report, investigations] préliminaire; **~ to sth/to doing** en vue de qch/de faire.

preparatory school n **1** GB école f primaire privée; **2** US lycée m privé.

prepare /prɪˈpeə(r)/ I vtr (plan) préparer [food, room, class, speech, report]; préparer [surprise]; **to ~ to do** se préparer à faire; **to ~ sb for** préparer qn à [exam, situation, shock].
II vi **to ~ for** se préparer à [trip, talks, exam, election, storm, war]; se préparer pour [party, ceremony, game].
III v refl **to ~ oneself** se préparer.

prepared /prɪˈpeəd/ adj **1** (willing) **to be ~ to do** être prêt à faire; **2** (ready) **to be ~ for** [event, conflict, change] être prêt à; **to be well-/ill-~** (with materials) être bien/mal équipé; **to come ~** venir bien préparé; **to be ~ for the worst** s'attendre au pire; **I really wasn't ~ for this!** je ne m'attendais pas du tout à ça!; **3** (ready-made) [speech, response] préparé d'avance; [meal] tout prêt.

preparedness /prɪˈpeədnɪs/ n **1 ~ for** préparation f en cas de; **a state of ~** MIL un état d'alerte; **2** (willingness) **her ~ to address major issues** son empressement à aborder des problèmes importants.

prepay /ˌpriːˈpeɪ/ vtr payer [qch] d'avance.

prepayment /ˌpriːˈpeɪmənt/ n paiement m d'avance.

preponderantly /prɪˈpɒndərəntlɪ/ adv principalement.

preponderate /prɪˈpɒndəreɪt/ vi prédominer.

preposition /ˌprepəˈzɪʃn/ n préposition f.

prepositional /ˌprepəˈzɪʃənl/ adj prépositionnel/-elle; **~ phrase** (used as preposition) locution f prépositive; (introduced by preposition) syntagme m prépositionnel.

prepossessing /ˌpriːpəˈzesɪŋ/ adj avenant.

preposterous /prɪˈpɒstərəs/ adj grotesque.

preposterously /prɪˈpɒstərəslɪ/ adv ridiculement.

preppy○, **preppie**○ /ˈprepɪ/ US I n SCH (student) élève mf d'une école privée; (alumnus) ancien élève/ ancienne élève m/f d'une école privée.
II adj ≈ BCBG○ inv.

preprogrammed /ˌpriːˈprəʊɡræmd, US -ɡrəmd/ adj GEN programmé; COMPUT préprogrammé.

prep school /ˈprepskuːl/ n GB école f primaire privée; US lycée m privé.

prerecord /ˌpriːrɪˈkɔːd/ I vtr TV, RADIO enregistrer [qch] à l'avance.
II **prerecorded** pp adj [broadcast] préenregistré, en différé inv.

prerequisite /ˌpriːˈrekwɪzɪt/ I n **1** GEN préalable m (**of** de; **for** à); **2** US UNIV unité f de valeur.
II adj [condition] préalable.

prerogative /prɪˈrɒɡətɪv/ n (official) prérogative f; (personal) droit m.

presage /ˈpresɪdʒ/ SOUT I n présage m (**of** de).
II vtr laisser présager [disaster].

preschool /ˌpriːˈskuːl/ I n US (kindergarten) école f maternelle; **in ~** à l'école maternelle.
II adj [child] d'âge préscolaire inv; [years] préscolaire.

prescribe /prɪˈskraɪb/ I vtr **1** MED FIG prescrire (**for sb** à qn; **for sth** pour qch); **2** (lay down) imposer [rule].
II **prescribed** pp adj **1** MED, FIG prescrit; **2** (set) [rule] imposé; SCH, UNIV [book] inscrit au programme.

prescription /prɪˈskrɪpʃn/ I n 1 MED ordonnance f; **repeat ~** ordonnance renouvelable; 2 FIG (formula) recette f; (set of rules) prescription f.
II noun modifier MED [glasses, lenses] correcteur/-trice; **~ drug** préparation médicinale.

prescription charges npl GB MED frais mpl d'ordonnance.

prescriptive /prɪˈskrɪptɪv/ adj GEN, LING normatif/-ive; JUR prescriptible.

presence /ˈprezns/ n (all contexts) présence f; **signed in the ~ of X** JUR signé par-devant X; **your ~ is requested at** vous êtes prié d'assister à; **a heavy police ~** (in streets) une forte présence policière; (at match, demonstration) un important service d'ordre.
IDIOMS **to make one's ~ felt** ne pas passer inaperçu.

presence of mind n présence f d'esprit.

present I /ˈpreznt/ n 1 (gift) cadeau m; **to give sb sth as a ~** offrir qch à qn; 2 (the ~) (now) le présent; **for the ~** pour le moment, pour l'instant; 3 LING (also **~ tense**) présent m; **in the ~** au présent.
II /ˈpreznt/ adj 1 (attending) présent; **to be ~ at** assister à; **~ company excepted** à l'exception des personnes ici présentes; **all ~ and correct!** tous présents à l'appel!; 2 (current) actuel/-elle; **up to the ~ day** jusqu'à ce jour; **at the ~ time** ou **moment** actuellement; **the ~ writer feels that** l'auteur (de cet article) pense que; 3 LING présent.
III **at present** adv phr (at this moment) en ce moment; (nowadays) actuellement, à présent.
IV /prɪˈzent/ vtr 1 (raise) présenter [problem, challenge, risk]; offrir [chance, opportunity]; 2 (proffer, show) présenter; **to be ~ed with a choice** se trouver face à un choix; **to be ~ed with a huge bill** se retrouver avec une énorme facture; 3 (submit for consideration) présenter [plan, figures, petition]; fournir [evidence]; 4 (formally give) remettre [prize, certificate]; présenter [apologies, respects, compliments]; **may I ~ my son Piers?** permettez-moi de vous présenter mon fils Piers; 5 (portray) présenter [person, situation] (**as** comme étant); **to ~ sth in a different light** présenter qch sous un jour différent; 6 TV, RADIO, THEAT présenter [programme, show]; donner [production, play, concert]; 7 MIL présenter [arms].
V vi MED [patient, baby] se présenter; [symptom, condition] apparaître.
VI v refl 1 **to ~ oneself** se présenter; **to learn how to ~ oneself** apprendre à mettre en avant ses qualités; 2 **to ~ itself** [opportunity, thought] se présenter.
IDIOMS **there is no time like the ~** il ne faut jamais remettre au lendemain ce que l'on peut faire le jour même.

presentable /prɪˈzentəbl/ adj présentable.

presentation /ˌprezənˈteɪʃn/ n 1 (of plan, report, bill, idea, person etc) présentation f; 2 (by salesman, colleague, executive etc) exposé m; 3 (of gift, award) remise f (**of** de); **the chairman will make the ~** le président remettra le prix; **there will be a ~ at 5.30** il y aura une cérémonie à 17 h 30; 4 (portrayal) GEN, THEAT représentation f; 5 MED (of baby) présentation f.

presentation : **~ box** n coffret-cadeau m; **~ copy** n hommage m (de l'auteur ou de l'éditeur); **~ pack** n présentoir m.

presentation skills npl **to have good ~** avoir le sens de la communication.

present-day /ˌprezntˈdeɪ/ adj actuel/-elle.

presenter /prɪˈzentə(r)/ ▶ 1251 n TV, RADIO présentateur/-trice m/f.

presently /ˈprezntlɪ/ adv (currently) à présent; (soon afterwards, in past) peu de temps après; (soon, in future) bientôt.

present perfect n passé m composé.

preservation /ˌprezəˈveɪʃn/ n (of building, wildlife, tradition, peace, dignity) préservation f (**of** de); (of food) conservation f (**of** de); (of life) protection f (**of** de).

preservation order n **to put a ~ on sth** classer qch.

preservative /prɪˈzɜːvətɪv/ I n (for food) agent m de conservation; (for wood) revêtement m (protecteur).
II adj [mixture, product, effect] de conservation.

preserve /prɪˈzɜːv/ I n 1 CULIN (also **~s**) confiture f; (pickle) conserve f; 2 (territory) LIT, FIG chasse f gardée (**of** de).
II vtr 1 (rescue, save from destruction) préserver [land, building, tradition] (**for** pour); entretenir [wood, leather, painting]; 2 (maintain) préserver [peace, standards, rights]; maintenir [order]; 3 (keep, hold onto) garder [humour, dignity, health]; 4 CULIN (stop rotting) conserver; (make into jam) faire de la confiture de.
III **preserved** pp adj [food] en conserve; [site, castle] protégé; **~d on film** conservé sur la pellicule.

preserving pan n bassine f à confiture.

preset /ˌpriːˈset/ vtr (prét, pp ~) régler (à l'avance) [timer, cooker]; programmer [magnétoscope].

preshrunk /ˌpriːˈʃrʌŋk/ adj [fabric] irrétrécissable.

preside /prɪˈzaɪd/ vi présider; **to ~ at sth** présider qch; **to ~ over** présider [conference, committee]; présider à [activity, change].

presidency /ˈprezɪdənsɪ/ n présidence f.

president /ˈprezɪdənt/ ▶ 937 n 1 GEN, POL président/-e m/f; **to run for ~** être candidat/-e à la présidence; 2 US COMM président-directeur m général.

presidential /ˌprezɪˈdenʃl/ adj [election, government, term] présidentiel/-ielle; [race, candidate] à la présidence; [adviser, office, policy] du président.

pre-soak /ˌpriːˈsəʊk/ vtr faire tremper [washing].

press /pres/ I n 1 **the ~, the Press** la presse f; **to get a good/bad ~** LIT, FIG avoir bonne/mauvaise presse; 2 (also **printing ~**) presse f; **to go to ~** être mis sous presse; **at** ou **in (the) ~** sous presse; 3 (publishing house) maison f d'éditon; (print works) imprimerie f; **the Starlight Press** les Éditions Starlight; 4 (device for flattening) presse f; 5 (act of pushing) pression f; **to give sth a ~** appuyer sur qch; 6 (with iron) repassage m; **to give sth a ~** repasser qch; 7 (crowd) foule f (**of** de).
II noun modifier [acclaim, freedom, criticism] de la presse; [campaign, photo, photographer] de presse; [announcement, advertising] par voie de presse; **~ story, ~ report** reportage m.
III vtr 1 (push) appuyer sur; **to ~ sth in** enfoncer qch; **~ the pedal right down** appuie à fond sur la pédale; **~ the switch down** pousse l'interrupteur vers le bas; **to ~ sth into** enfoncer qch dans [clay, mud, ground, pillow]; **to ~ sth into sb's hand** glisser qch dans la main de qn; 2 (apply) **to ~ one's nose against sth** coller son nez contre qch; **to ~ one's hands to one's ears** se plaquer les mains contre les oreilles; **to ~ one's knees together** serrer les genoux; 3 (squeeze) presser [fruit, flower]; serrer [arm, hand, person]; **to ~ sb to one** presser qn contre soi; 4 (iron) repasser [clothes]; 5 (urge) faire pression sur [person]; insister sur [point]; mettre [qch] en avant [matter, issue]; défendre [qch] avec insistance [case]; **to ~ sb to do** presser qn de faire; **to ~ sb into doing** forcer qn à faire; **I must ~ you for an answer** je dois avoir une réponse; **when ~ed, he admitted that...** quand on a insisté, il a reconnu que...; **to ~ a point** insister; 6 TECH former [shape, object]; presser [record, CD]; emboutir [steel, metal, car body].
IV vi 1 (push with hand, foot, object) **to ~ down** appuyer; 2 [crowd, person] se presser (**against** contre; **around** autour de; **forward** vers l'avant).
V v refl **to ~ oneself against** se plaquer contre [wall]; se presser contre [person].
■ **press ahead** aller de l'avant; **to ~ ahead with** [sth] faire avancer [reform, plan, negotiations].
■ **press for**: **~ for** [sth] faire pression pour obtenir [change, support, release]; **to be ~ed for sth** ne pas avoir beaucoup de qch.
■ **press on**: ¶ **~ on** 1 (on journey) continuer; **to ~ on regardless** continuer malgré tout; 2 (move on) FIG passer à la suite; **to ~ on with** faire avancer [reform, plan]; passer à [next item]; ¶ **~** [sth] **on sb** forcer qn à prendre.

press: ~ **agency** n agence f de presse; ~ **agent** ▶ 1251 | n attaché /-e m/f de presse; **Press Association** n GB agence f de presse britannique; ~ **attaché** n = **press agent**; ~ **baron** n magnat m de la presse; ~ **card** n carte f de presse; ~ **conference** n conférence f de presse; ~ **corps** n ¢ journalistes mpl; ~ **cutting** n coupure f de presse; ~ **gallery** n tribune f de la presse.

press-gang /'presgæŋ/ vtr HIST racoler; **to ~ sb into doing** FIG forcer qn à faire.

pressing /'presɪŋ/ **I** n **1** (of olives) pression f; **2** (of records) pressage m.
II adj **1** (urgent) urgent; **2** (insistent) [invitation] pressant; [anxiety] oppressant.

press lord n magnat m de la presse.

pressman /'presmən/ ▶ 1251 | n **1** (printer) imprimeur/ -euse m/f; **2** GB (journalist) journaliste m.

press: ~ **officer** n = **press agent**; ~ **pass** n coupe-file m; ~ **release** n communiqué m de presse; **~room** n (for printing) salle f des presses; (for press conferences) salle f de presse; ~ **run** n tirage m; ~ **secretary** n = **press agent**; **~-stud** n GB (bouton-) pression m; **~-up** n pompe° f.

pressure /'preʃə(r)/ **I** n **1** GEN, FIG, TECH, METEOROL pression f; **to put ~ on sb** faire pression sur qn; **to do sth under ~** faire qch sous la contrainte; **she has come under a lot of ~ to do** on exerce de fortes pressions sur elle pour l'amener à faire; **due to ~ of work** pour cause d'emploi du temps chargé; **financial ~s** contraintes financières; **the ~s of modern life** le stress de la vie moderne; **2** (volume) (of traffic, tourists, visitors) flux m.
II vtr = **pressurize**.

pressure: **~-cook** vtr cuire [qch] à la cocotte-minute®; ~ **cooker** n cocotte-minute f®; ~ **gauge** n manomètre m; ~ **group** n groupe m de pression; ~ **point** n point m de compression.

pressurize /'preʃəraɪz/ vtr **1** LIT pressuriser; **2** FIG faire pression sur [person]; **to be ~d into doing** être contraint de faire.

presswoman /'preswʌmən/ ▶ 1251 | n journaliste f.

prestige /pre'stiːʒ/ **I** n prestige m.
II noun modifier [car, site] de prestige; [housing, hotel] de grand standing.

prestigious /pre'stɪdʒəs/ adj prestigieux/-ieuse.

presumably /prɪ'zjuːməblɪ, US -'zuːm-/ adv sans doute.

presume /prɪ'zjuːm, US -'zuːm/ **I** vtr **1** (suppose) supposer, présumer; **I ~d him to be honest** je le croyais honnête; **'does he know?'—'I ~ so'** 'le sait-il?'—'probablement'; **2** (presuppose) présupposer; **3** (dare) **to ~ to do** se permettre de faire.
II vi **to ~ upon** abuser de [person, kindness]; **I hope I'm not presuming** j'espère que je ne m'avance pas trop.

presumption /prɪ'zʌmpʃn/ n **1** (supposition) supposition f (that que); **on the ~ that** en supposant que; **to make a ~** supposer; **2** (basis) arguments mpl; **3** (impudence) audace f.

presumptive /prɪ'zʌmptɪv/ adj GEN par présomption.

presumptuous /prɪ'zʌmptʃʊəs/ adj audacieux/-ieuse.

presuppose /ˌpriːsə'pəʊz/ vtr présupposer (that que).

pre-tax /ˌpriː'tæks/ adj avant impôts inv.

pretence GB, **pretense** US /prɪ'tens/ n **1** (false show) faux-semblant m; **to make a ~ of sth** feindre qch; **to make a ~ of doing** faire semblant de faire; **to make no ~ of sth** ne pas se donner la peine de feindre qch; **on** ou **under the ~ of doing** sous prétexte de faire; **to keep up the ~ of doing** entretenir l'illusion de faire; **2** (sham) simulacre m (of de); (of illness) simulation f (of de).

pretend /prɪ'tend/ **I**° adj LANG ENFANTIN [gun, car] imaginaire; [jewels] faux/fausse (before n); **it's only ~!** c'est pour rire!
II vtr **1** (feign) simuler; **to ~ that** faire comme si; **to ~ to do** faire semblant de faire; **a thief ~ing to be**

a policeman un voleur se faisant passer pour un policier; **2** (claim) **to ~ to understand** avoir la prétention de comprendre; **to ~ to be** prétendre être.
III vi **1** (feign) faire semblant; **2** (maintain deception) jouer la comédie; **I was only ~ing** c'était pour rire.
IV pretended pp adj [emotion, ignorance] simulé.

pretender /prɪ'tendə(r)/ n prétendant/-e m/f (to à).

pretense n US = **pretence**.

pretension /prɪ'tenʃn/ n prétention f; **to have ~s to sth** prétendre à qch.

pretentious /prɪ'tenʃəs/ adj prétentieux/-ieuse.

preterite /'pretərət/ n prétérit.

pretext /'priːtekst/ n prétexte m.

prettily /'prɪtɪlɪ/ adv [arrange, dress, decorate, perform, talk] joliment; [blush, smile] de façon charmante; [apologize, thank] gentiment.

pretty /'prɪtɪ/ **I** adj **1** (attractive) joli; **it was not a ~ sight** ce n'était pas beau à voir; **2** PÉJ (trite) joli.
II° adv (very) vraiment; (fairly) assez; (almost) pratiquement; ~ **good** pas mal du tout; ~ **well all** pratiquement tout; **'how are you?' '~ well'** 'comment ça va?' 'très bien'.
IDIOMS ~ **as a picture** ravissant; **I'm not just a ~ face**° HUM j'ai aussi quelque chose dans la tête; **this is a ~ mess** ou **a ~ state of affairs** IRON voilà du beau travail IRON; **that must have cost you a ~ penny**° ça a dû te coûter cher; **to be sitting ~**° se la couler douce°; **things have come to a ~ pass when...** ça commence à ne plus aller du tout quand...
■ **pretty up** ~ [sth] **up**, ~ **up** [sth] enjoliver.

pretty: ~ **boy**° n PÉJ minet° m PEJ; **~-pretty** adj PÉJ trop coquet/-ette.

prevail /prɪ'veɪl/ vi **1** (win) prévaloir (against contre); **2** (be usual) prédominer.
■ **prevail upon**: ~ **upon** [sb] persuader.

prevailing /prɪ'veɪlɪŋ/ adj GEN [attitude, style] qui prévaut; [rate] en vigueur; [wind] dominant.

prevalence /'prevələns/ n **1** (widespread nature) fréquence f; **2** (superior position) prédominance f.

prevalent /'prevələnt/ adj **1** (widespread) répandu; **2** (ruling) qui prévaut.

prevaricate /prɪ'værɪkeɪt/ vi SOUT se dérober.

prevent /prɪ'vent/ vtr prévenir [fire, illness, violence]; éviter [conflict, disaster, damage]; faire obstacle à [marriage]; **to ~ the outbreak of war** empêcher le déclenchement d'une guerre.

preventable /prɪ'ventəbl/ adj évitable.

preventative /prɪ'ventətɪv/ adj = **preventive**.

prevention /prɪ'venʃn/ n prévention f; **accident ~** GEN prévention f des accidents; (on road) prévention f routière; **crime ~** lutte f contre la délinquance.
IDIOMS ~ **is better than cure** PROV mieux vaut prévenir que guérir PROV.

preventive /prɪ'ventɪv/ adj préventif/-ive.

preview /'priːvjuː/ **I** n (of film, play) avant-première f; (of exhibition) vernissage m; (of match, programme) présentation f (of de).
II vtr présenter [match, programme].

previous /'priːvɪəs/ **I** adj **1** (before) [day, meeting, manager] GEN précédent; (further back in time) antérieur; **on a ~ occasion** (une fois) déjà; **on ~ occasions** à plusieurs reprises; **he has no ~ convictions** JUR a un casier judiciaire vierge; **to have a ~ engagement** être déjà pris; **'~ experience essential'** 'expérience préalable indispensable'; **2**° (hasty) [decision] hâtif/-ive; [action] prématuré.
II previous to prep phr avant.

previously /'priːvɪəslɪ/ adv (before) auparavant, avant; (already) déjà.

prewar /ˌpriː'wɔː(r)/ adj d'avant-guerre inv.

prewash /ˌpriː'wɒʃ/ n prélavage m.

prey /preɪ/ n LIT, FIG proie f.
■ **prey on**: ¶ ~ **on** [sth] **1** (hunt) chasser; **2** FIG (worry) **to ~ on sb's mind** préoccuper qn; **3** (exploit) exploiter [fears, worries]; ¶ ~ **on** [sb] [conman] choisir ses victimes parmi; [mugger, rapist] s'attaquer à.

price /praɪs/ I n **1** GEN, COMM, LIT, FIG (cost) prix m; **the ~ per kilo** le prix du kilo; **'we pay top ~s for...'** 'nous payons le prix fort pour...'; **cars have gone up in ~** les voitures ont augmenté; **what sort of ~ did you have to pay?** à peu près combien est-ce que tu as eu à payer?; **to pay a high ~ for sth** LIT, FIG payer qch cher; **that's a small ~ to pay for sth** FIG ce n'est pas un gros sacrifice pour obtenir qch; **2** GEN, COMM, LIT, FIG (value) valeur f; **beyond** ou **above ~** (d'une valeur) inestimable; **to put a ~ on** LIT évaluer [object, antique]; **to put** ou **set a high ~ on** attacher beaucoup de prix à [loyalty, hard work]; **what ~ all his good intentions now!** qu'en est-il maintenant de ses bonnes intentions! II vtr **1** (fix, determine the price of) fixer le prix de (**at** à); **a dress ~d at £30** une robe à 30 livres; **a moderately-~d hotel** un hôtel aux tarifs raisonnables; **2** (evaluate the worth of) estimer la valeur de; **3** (mark the price of) marquer le prix de. IDIOMS **to put a ~ on sb's head** mettre à prix la tête de qn. ■ **price out**: ~ **oneself** ou **one's goods out of the market** perdre un marché en pratiquant des prix trop élevés.

price: ~ **bracket** n = **price range**; ~ **control** n contrôle m des prix; ~ **cut**, ~ **cutting** n baisse f du prix; ~ **fixing** n détermination f illégale des prix; ~ **freeze** n blocage m des prix; ~ **index** n indice m des prix; ~ **label** n étiquette f.

priceless /ˈpraɪslɪs/ adj **1** (extremely valuable) inestimable; **2**○ (amusing) impayable○.

price list n (in shop, catalogue) liste f des prix; (in bar, restaurant) tarif m.

price range n fourchette f; **that's out of my ~** cela n'est pas dans mes prix.

price: ~ **restrictions** n contrôle m des prix; ~ **ring** n cartel m de vendeurs; ~ **rise** n hausse f des prix; ~ **tag** n (label) étiquette f; FIG (cost) coût m; ~ **ticket** n étiquette f; ~ **war** n guerre f des prix.

prick /prɪk/ I n (of needle etc) (feeling) piqûre f; (hole) trou m (d'épingle); **to give sth a ~** piquer qch. II vtr **1** (cause pain) piquer; **to ~ one's finger** se piquer le doigt; **his conscience ~ed him** FIG il avait mauvaise conscience; **2** (pierce) percer [paper, plastic, hole]; crever [bubble, balloon]; CULIN piquer [potato etc]; **3** = **prick up**. III vi **1** [eyes] piquer; [skin] picoter; **2** [thorn] piquer. IDIOMS **to kick against the ~s** s'obstiner pour rien. ■ **prick out**: ~ **out** [sth], ~ [sth] **out** repiquer [seedlings]; ART piquer [design, outline]. ■ **prick up**: ~ **up** [dog's ears] se dresser; **to ~ up its** ou **one's ears** [dog] dresser les oreilles; [person] dresser l'oreille.

prickle /ˈprɪkl/ I n (of hedgehog, plant) piquant m. II vtr [clothes, jumper] gratter. III vi [hairs] se hérisser (**with** de).

prickly /ˈprɪklɪ/ adj **1** [bush, leaf] épineux/-euse; [animal] armé de piquants; [thorn] piquant; **2** (itchy) qui gratte; **3**○ (touchy) irritable (**about** à propos de).

pride /praɪd/ I n **1** (source of satisfaction) fierté f (**in sb/sth** éprouvée pour qn/qch); **to take ~ in** être fier/fière de [ability, achievement]; soigner [appearance, work]; **to be sb's ~ and joy** être la (grande) fierté de qn; **2** (self-respect) amour-propre m; PÉJ orgueil m; **family ~** honneur m familial; **national ~** sentiment m de fierté nationale; **3** (of lions) troupe f. II v refl **to ~ oneself on sth/on doing** être fier/fière de qch/de faire. IDIOMS **to have ~ of place** être mis en vedette; ~ **comes before a fall** PROV péché d'orgueil ne va pas sans danger.

priest /priːst/ n prêtre m; **parish ~** curé m.

priesthood /ˈpriːsthʊd/ n (calling) prêtrise f; (clergy) clergé m; **to enter the ~** entrer dans les ordres.

prig /prɪg/ n bégueule mf.

prim /prɪm/ adj (also ~ **and proper**) [person, manner, appearance] guindé; [expression] pincé; [voice] affecté; [clothing] très convenable.

prima ballerina /ˌpriːmə ˌbælə'riːnə/ n danseuse f étoile.

primacy /ˈpraɪməsɪ/ n GEN primauté f; (of party, power) suprématie f; RELIG primatie f.

primaeval adj = **primeval**.

prima facie /ˌpraɪmə 'feɪʃiː/ I adj JUR, GEN légitime (à première vue). II adv JUR, GEN de prime abord.

primal /ˈpraɪml/ adj [quality, myth, feeling] primitif/-ive; [stage, cause, origins] premier/-ière.

primarily /ˈpraɪmərəlɪ, US praɪ'merəlɪ/ adv (chiefly) essentiellement; (originally) à l'origine.

primary /ˈpraɪmərɪ, US -merɪ/ I n **1** US POL (also ~ **election**) primaire f; **2** SCH ▶ **primary school**. II adj **1** (main) GEN principal; [sense, meaning, stage] premier/-ière; **of ~ importance** de première importance; **2** SCH [teaching, education] primaire; [post] dans l'enseignement primaire; **3** ECON [industry, products] de base.

primary: ~ **colour** n couleur f primaire; ~ **health care** n soins mpl de premier recours; ~ **school** n école f primaire; ~ **sector** n ECON secteur m primaire; ~ (**school**) **teacher** ▶ **1251** n SURTOUT GB instituteur/-trice m/f.

primate /ˈpraɪmeɪt/ n **1** ZOOL (mammal) primate m; **2** RELIG (also **Primate**) primat m (**of** de).

prime /praɪm/ I n **1** (peak period) **in one's ~** (professionally) à son apogée; (physically) dans la fleur de l'âge; **in its ~** à son apogée; **to be past its ~** avoir connu des jours meilleurs; **2** MATH (also ~ **number**) nombre m premier. II adj **1** (chief) GEN principal; [importance] primordial; **2** COMM (good quality) [site] de premier ordre; [meat, cuts] de premier choix; [foodstuffs] d'une parfaite fraîcheur; **in ~ condition** [machine] en parfait état; [livestock] en parfaite condition; **of ~ quality** de première qualité; **3** (épith) (classic) [example, instance] excellent; **4** MATH premier/-ière. III vtr **1** (brief) préparer; **to ~ sb about** mettre qn au courant de; **to ~ sb to say** souffler à qn de dire; **2** (apply primer to) appliquer un apprêt sur; **3** MIL, TECH amorcer.

prime: ~ **cost** n prix m de revient; ~ **minister**, **PM** ▶ **937** n Premier ministre m; ~**-ministerial** adj de Premier ministre.

prime mover n **1** (person) promoteur/-trice m/f; (instinct) moteur m principal; **2** PHYS, TECH force f motrice.

primer /ˈpraɪmə(r)/ n **1** (paint) apprêt m; **2** (for detonating) amorce f.

prime time I n heures fpl de grande écoute. II **prime-time** noun modifier [advertising, programme] passant aux heures de grande écoute.

primeval /praɪ'miːvl/ adj primitif/-ive.

primitive /ˈprɪmɪtɪv/ I n ART primitif m. II adj (all contexts) primitif/-ive.

primly /ˈprɪmlɪ/ adv **1** (starchily) [behave, smile] d'une manière guindée; [say, reply] d'un ton guindé; **2** (demurely) [behave, sit] très sagement.

primordial /praɪ'mɔːdɪəl/ adj primitif/-ive.

primrose /ˈprɪmrəʊz/ n primevère f (jaune). IDIOMS **the ~ path** le chemin de la facilité.

prince /prɪns/ ▶ **937** n prince m ALSO FIG.

princely /ˈprɪnslɪ/ adj [amount, style] princier/-ière; [life, rôle] de prince.

princess /prɪn'ses/ ▶ **937** n princesse f.

principal /ˈprɪnsəpl/ I n **1** ▶ **937** (of senior school) proviseur m; (of junior school, college) directeur/-trice m/f; **2** THEAT acteur/-trice m/f principal/-e; **3** MUS chef m de pupitre; **4** (client) mandant m; **5** FIN capital m; (debt before interest) principal m. II adj **1** (main) principal; **2** [violin, clarinet] premier/-ière (before n); [dancer] étoile; **3** LING [clause] principal; **the ~ parts of a verb** les temps primitifs d'un verbe.

principality /ˌprɪnsə'pælɪtɪ/ n principauté f.

principally /ˈprɪnsəplɪ/ adv principalement.

principle /'prɪnsəpl/ *n* (all contexts) principe *m*; **to have high ~s** avoir beaucoup de principes; **in ~** en principe; **on ~** par principe; **to make it a ~ to do** avoir pour principe de faire; **to get back to first ~s** repartir sur des bases concrètes.

principled /'prɪnsəpld/ *adj* [*decision*] de principe; [*person*] de principes; **to be ~** avoir des principes.

print /prɪnt/ **I** *n* **1** Ɔ (typeface) caractères *mpl*; **the ~ is very small** c'est écrit très petit; **the small** ou **fine ~** FIG les détails; **don't forget to read the small ~** n'oubliez pas de lire tous les détails; **2** (published form) **in ~** disponible en librairie; **out of ~** épuisé; **to go into ~** être publié; **to put** ou **get sth into ~** publier qch; **to see sth in ~** voir qch noir sur blanc; **to see oneself in ~** se voir publié; **'at the time of going to ~'** 'à l'heure où nous mettons sous presse'; **3** ART (etching) estampe *f*; (engraving) gravure *f*; **4** PHOT épreuve *f*; **5** CIN copie *f*; **6** (of finger, hand, foot) empreinte *f*; (of tyre) trace *f*; **7** (fabric) tissu *m* imprimé; **8** (handwriting) script *m*.
II *noun modifier* [*curtains, dress*] en tissu imprimé.
III *vtr* **1** (on press) imprimer also Art; **2** (publish) publier; **3** PHOT tirer [*copy*]; faire développer [*photos*]; **4** (write) écrire [qch] en script.
IV *vi* **1** (write) écrire en script; **2** (on press) imprimer.
V **printed** *pp adj* imprimé; **'~ed matter'** POST 'imprimés' *mpl*; **~ed notepaper** papier *m* à lettres à entête.
▪ **print off**: **~ off** [sth], **~** [sth] **off** tirer [*copies*].
▪ **print out**: **~ out** [sth], **~** [sth] **out** GEN, COMPUT imprimer.

printer /'prɪntə(r)/ *n* (person, firm) imprimeur *m*; (machine) imprimante *f*.

printing /'prɪntɪŋ/ *n* (technique) imprimerie *f*; (result) impression *f*; (print run) tirage *m*.

printing: **~ business**, **~ house**, **~industry** *n* imprimerie *f*; **~ press** *n* presse *f* (typographique); **~ works** *n* imprimerie *f*.

print: **~ journalism** *n* (journalisme *m* de) presse *f* écrite; **~out** *n* sortie *f* sur imprimante; (perforated) listing *m*; **~ run** *n* tirage *m*; **~ shop** *n* (workshop) imprimerie *f*; (art shop) boutique *f* d'art.

prior /'praɪə(r)/ **I** *n* RELIG prieur *m*.
II *adj* **1** (previous) préalable; **~ notice** préavis *m*; **2** (more important) prioritaire.
III **prior to** *prep phr* avant.

priority /praɪ'ɒrətɪ, US -'ɔːr-/ *n* (all contexts) priorité *f*; **the main** ou **highest ~** la priorité absolue; **to get one's priorities right/wrong** définir correctement/ mal définir l'ordre de ses priorités.
II *noun modifier* [*case, debt, expense, mail*] prioritaire; [*call*] de priorité; [*appointment*] en priorité.

priory /'praɪərɪ/ *n* prieuré *m*.

prise /praɪz/ *v* ▪ **prise apart**: **~** [sth] **apart** séparer [*layers, people*]; ouvrir [qch] de force [*lips, teeth*].
▪ **prise away**: **to ~ sb away from** FIG arracher qn à [*TV, work*].
▪ **prise off**: **~** [sth] **off** enlever [qch] en forçant.
▪ **prise open**: **~** [sth] **open**, **~ open** [sth] ouvrir [qch] en forçant.
▪ **prise out**: **~** [sth] **out** LIT retirer (**of, from** de); **to ~ sth out of sb** FIG arracher qch à qn; **to ~ sb out of** LIT arracher qn de.
▪ **prise up**: **~** [sth] **up** soulever [qch] en forçant.

prism /'prɪzəm/ *n* prisme *m*.

prison /'prɪzn/ **I** *n* prison *f*; **to put sb in ~** emprisonner qn; **to have been in ~** avoir fait de la prison.
II *noun modifier* [*administration, authorities, regulation*] pénitentiaire; [*population, reform*] pénal; [*cell, governor, visitor, guard, yard*] de prison; [*chapel, kitchen*] de la prison; [*conditions*] de détention.

prison camp *n* camp *m* de prisonniers.

prisoner /'prɪznə(r)/ *n* GEN, FIG prisonnier/-ière *m/f*; (in jail) détenu/-e *m/f*; **they took me ~** ils m'ont fait prisonnier; **~ of conscience** prisonnier/-ière *m/f* d'opinion.

prison: **~ issue** *adj* fourni par la prison; **~ officer** ▶1251 *n* GB (officially) surveillant/-e *m/f* de

prison; GEN gardien/-ienne *m/f* de prison; **~ sentence**, **~ term** *n* peine *f* de prison; **~ service** *n* administration *f* pénitentiaire; **~ van** *n* fourgon *m* cellulaire.

prissy /'prɪsɪ/ *adj* [*person*] collet monté *inv*; [*style*] surchargé.

pristine /'prɪstiːn, 'prɪstaɪn/ *adj* immaculé.

privacy /'prɪvəsɪ, 'praɪ-/ *n* **1** (private life) vie *f* privée; **to invade sb's ~** s'immiscer dans la vie privée de qn; **2** (solitude) intimité *f*.

private /'praɪvɪt/ **I** ▶1192 *n* simple soldat *m*.
II *adj* **1** (not for general public) privé; **room with ~ bath** chambre avec salle de bains particulière; **the funeral will be ~** l'enterrement aura lieu dans la plus stricte intimité; **2** (personal, not associated with company) [*letter, phone call, capacity*] personnel/-elle; [*sale*] de particulier à particulier; **~ life** vie privée; **the ~ citizen** le (simple) particulier; **3** (not public, not state-run) GEN privé; [*housing, accommodation, landlord, lesson*] particulier/-ière; **~ industry** le (secteur) privé; **4** [*talk, meeting, matter*] privé; [*reason, opinion, thought*] personnel/-elle; **to come to a ~ understanding** s'arranger à l'amiable; **to keep sth ~** préserver l'intimité de qch; **a ~ joke** une plaisanterie pour initiés; **5** [*place*] tranquille; **6** (secretive) renfermé (sur soi-même).
III **in private** *adv phr* en privé.
IDIOMS **to go ~** GB MED se faire soigner dans le (secteur) privé.

private: **~ company** *n* société *f* privée; **~ enterprise** *n* entreprise *f* privée; **~ eye**○ *n* détective *m* privé; **~ hotel** *n* ~ pension *f* de famille; **~ investor** *n* petit porteur *m*.

privately /'praɪvɪtlɪ/ *adv* **1** (in private) en privé; (out of public sector) dans le privé; **~ managed** à gestion privée; **~ funded**, **~ financed** à financement privé; **2** (in one's heart) [*believe, doubt*] en mon/son etc for intérieur.

private parts *npl* EUPH parties *fpl* génitales.

private practice *n* GB MED cabinet *m* privé; **to work** ou **be in ~** travailler hors des services de santé de l'État.

private secretary *n* GEN secrétaire *mf* particulier/ -ière; POL conseiller/-ère *mf* particulier/-ière.

private treaty *n* **by ~** de gré à gré.

private view *n* ART vernissage *m*.

privatization /ˌpraɪvətaɪ'zeɪʃn, US -tɪ'z-/ *n* privatisation *f*.

privatize /'praɪvɪtaɪz/ *vtr* privatiser.

privilege /'prɪvəlɪdʒ/ *n* **1** (honour, advantage) privilège *m*; **tax ~s** avantages *mpl* fiscaux; **2** (prerogative) apanage *m*; **3** US FIN option *f*.

privileged /'prɪvəlɪdʒd/ *adj* [*minority, life, position*] privilégié; [*information*] confidentiel/-ielle.

prize /praɪz/ **I** *n* **1** (award) prix *m*; (in lottery) lot *m*; **first ~** premier prix *m*; (in lottery) gros lot; **2** LITTÉR (valued object) trésor *m*; (reward for effort) récompense *f*.
II *noun modifier* **1** [*vegetable, bull etc*] (for competitions) de concours; (prize-winning) primé; [*pupil*] hors-pair *inv*; **a ~ example of** un parfait exemple de; **2** [*possession*] précieux/-ieuse.
III *vtr* **1** priser [*independence, possession*]; **2** = **prise**.
IV **prized** *pp adj* [*possession, asset*] précieux/-ieuse; **to be ~d for sth** être prisé pour qch.
IDIOMS **no ~s for guessing who was there!** il n'est pas difficile de deviner qui était là!

prize: **~ day** *n* jour *m* de la distribution des prix; **~ draw** *n* (for charity) tombola *f*; (for advertising) tirage *m* au sort; **~ fighter** *n* boxeur *m* professionnel; **~-giving** *n* remise *f* des prix; **~ money** *n* (for one prize) argent *m* du prix; (total amount given out) montant *m* total des prix; **~winner** *n* (in lottery etc) gagnant/-e *m/f*; (of literary award) lauréat/-e *m/f*; **~-winning** *adj* primé.

pro /prəʊ/ **I** *n* **1**○ (professional) pro○ *mf*; **2** (advantage) **the ~s and cons** le pour et le contre; **the ~s and cons of sth** les avantages et les inconvénients de qch.
II○ *prep* (in favour of) pour.

III pro- *combining form* **to be ~-democracy** être pour la démocratie; **to be a ~-abortionist** être partisan/-e de l'avortement.

PRO *n* **1** *abrév* ▶ **public relations officer**; **2** *abrév* ▶ **Public Records Office**.

probability /ˌprɒbəˈbɪlətɪ/ *n* **1** (likelihood) (of desirable event) chances *fpl*; (of unwelcome event) risques *mpl*; **in all ~** selon toute probabilité; **2** (likely result) probabilité *f* ALSO MATH.

probable /ˈprɒbəbl/ *adj* probable.

probably /ˈprɒbəblɪ/ *adv* probablement.

probate /ˈprəʊbeɪt/ *n* JUR (process) homologation *f*; **to grant ~ (of a will)** homologuer un testament.

probation /prəˈbeɪʃn, US prəʊ-/ *n* **1** JUR (for adult) sursis *m* avec mise à l'épreuve; (for juvenile) mise *f* en liberté surveillée; **2** (trial period) période *f* d'essai.

probationary /prəˈbeɪʃnrɪ, US prəʊˈbeɪʃənərɪ/ *adj* **1** (trial) [*period, year*] d'essai; **2** (training) [*month, period*] probatoire.

probationary teacher *n* GB SCH ~ professeur *m* en stage pratique.

probationer /prəˈbeɪʃənə(r), US prəʊ-/ *n* (trainee) stagiaire *mf*; (employee on trial) employé/-e *m/f* engagé/-e à l'essai.

probation: **~ officer** ▶ **1251** *n* JUR (for juveniles) délégué/-e *m/f* à la liberté surveillée; (for adults) agent *m* de probation; **~ order** *n* JUR ordonnance *f* de probation; **~ service** *n* JUR comité *m* de probation.

probe /prəʊb/ I *n* **1** (investigation) enquête *f*; **2** (instrument) sonde *f*; (operation) sondage *m*; **3** (in space) sonde *f*.
II *vtr* **1** (investigate) enquêter sur [*affair, mystery*]; **2** [*dentist*] examiner [qch] avec une sonde [*tooth*]; **3** MED, TECH sonder [*ground, wound*] (**with** avec); **4** AÉROSP explorer [*space*]; **5** (explore) explorer [qch] avec soin [*hole, surface*].
III *vi* faire des recherches.
■ **probe into**: **~ into** [sth] enquêter sur [*suspicious activity*]; regarder [qch] de plus près, fouiller dans PÉJ [*private affairs*]; sonder [*mind*]; scruter [*thoughts*].

probing /ˈprəʊbɪŋ/ I *n* LIT exploration *f*; (questions) questions *fpl*.
II *adj* [*look*] inquisiteur/-trice; [*question*] pénétrant; [*study, examination*] très poussé.

problem /ˈprɒbləm/ I *n* GEN, MATH problème *m*; **to have a drink ~** avoir un problème d'alcoolisme; **to cause** OU **present a ~** poser un problème; **to be a ~ to sb** poser des problèmes à qn.
II *noun modifier* PSYCH, SOCIOL [*child*] difficile; [*family*] à problèmes; [*group*] qui pose des problèmes.

problematic(al) /ˌprɒbləˈmætɪk(l)/ *adj* problématique.

problem: **~ case** *n* SOCIOL cas *m* social; **~ page** *n* courrier *m* du cœur.

procedural /prəˈsiːdʒərəl/ *adj* [*detail, error*] de procédure.

procedure /prəˈsiːdʒə(r)/ *n* (all contexts) procédure *f*.

proceed /prəˈsiːd, prəʊ-/ I *vtr* **to ~ to do** entreprendre de faire; **'so...,' he ~ed** 'alors...,' a-t-il continué.
II *vi* **1** (act) (set about) procéder; (continue) poursuivre; **to ~ with** poursuivre [*idea, plan, sale*]; procéder à [*election*]; **to ~ to** passer à [*item, problem*]; **let us ~** (begin) commençons; (continue) poursuivons; **2** (be in progress) [*project, work*] avancer; [*interview, talks, trial*] se poursuivre; (take place) [*work, interview, talks*] se dérouler; **everything is ~ing according to plan** tout se passe comme prévu; **3** (move along) [*person, road*] continuer; [*vehicle*] avancer; **4** SOUT (issue) **to ~ from** provenir de.

proceeding /prəˈsiːdɪŋ/ I *n* (procedure) procédure *f*.
II **proceedings** *npl* **1** GEN (meeting) réunion *f*; (ceremony) cérémonie *f*; (discussion) débats *mpl*; **to direct ~s** diriger les opérations; **2** JUR poursuites *fpl*; **extradition ~s** procédure *f* d'extradition; **to take** OU **institute ~s** engager des poursuites; **to start**

divorce ~s intenter un procès en divorce; **3** (report) GEN rapport *m*; (of conference, society) actes *mpl*.

proceeds /ˈprəʊsiːdz/ *npl* (of deal) produit *m*; (of event) recette *f*.

process I /ˈprəʊses, US ˈprɒses/ *n* GEN, COMPUT processus *m* (**of** de); **the ~ of doing** le processus consistant à faire; **to begin the ~ of doing** entreprendre de faire; **to be in the ~ of doing** être en train de faire; **in the ~ of doing this, he...** pendant qu'il faisait cela, il...; **in the ~** en même temps; **it's a long** OU **slow ~** cela prend du temps; **2** (method) procédé *m*.
II /ˈprəʊses, US ˈprɒses/ *vtr* **1** GEN, ADMIN, COMPUT traiter; **2** IND transformer [*raw materials, food product*]; traiter [*chemical, waste*]; **3** PHOT développer [*film*]; **4** CULIN (mix) mixer; (chop) hacher.
III /prəˈsɛs/ *vi* **1** RELIG faire des processions; **2** SOUT (move) **to ~ down/along** défiler dans/le long de [*road*].
IV **processed** /ˈprəʊsest/ *pp adj* [*food*] qui a subi un traitement; [*meat, peas*] en conserve; [*steel*] traité.

processing /ˈprəʊsesɪŋ, US ˈprɒ-/ *n* **1** GEN traitement *m*; **2** IND (of raw material, food product) transformation *f*; (of chemical waste) traitement *m*; **the food ~ industry** l'industrie alimentaire; **3** PHOT développement *m*.

procession /prəˈseʃn/ *n* (of demonstration, carnival) défilé *m*; (formal) cortège *m*; RELIG procession *f*.

processor /ˈprəʊsesə(r), US ˈprɒ-/ *n* **1** COMPUT unité *f* centrale; **2** = **food processor**.

pro-choice /prəʊˈtʃɔɪs/ *adj* favorable à l'avortement.

proclaim /prəˈkleɪm/ *vtr* (all contexts) proclamer.

proclamation /ˌprɒkləˈmeɪʃn/ *n* proclamation *f*.

proclivity /prəˈklɪvətɪ/ *n* propension *f*; **sexual proclivities** tendances *fpl* sexuelles.

procrastinate /prəˈkræstɪneɪt/ *vi* atermoyer.

procrastination /prəʊˌkræstɪˈneɪʃn/ *n* ₵ atermoiements *mpl*.
IDIOMS **~ is the thief of time** ≈ ne remettez pas à demain ce que vous pouvez faire aujourd'hui.

procreate /ˈprəʊkrɪeɪt/ I *vtr* procréer [*children, young*].
II *vi* se reproduire.

procreation /ˌprəʊkrɪˈeɪʃn/ *n* (human) procréation *f*; (animal) reproduction *f*.

procure /prəˈkjʊə(r)/ I *vtr* (obtain) procurer ALSO JUR; **to ~ sth for sb** (directly) procurer qch à qn; (indirectly) faire obtenir qch à qn.
II *vi* JUR (in prostitution) faire du proxénétisme.

procurement /prəˈkjʊəmənt/ *n* GEN obtention *f*; MIL, COMM acquisition *f*.

procurer /prəˈkjʊərə(r)/ *n* COMM acheteur/-euse *m/f*; JUR proxénète *m*.

prod /prɒd/ I *n* **1** LIT (poke) petit coup *m*; **to give sth/sb a ~** (with implement) donner un petit coup à qch/qn; (with finger) toucher qch/qn; **2**° FIG (reminder) **to give sb a ~** secouer° qn; **he/she needs a ~ to do** il faut le/la pousser pour qu'il/elle fasse.
II *vtr* (*p prés etc* **-dd-**) (also **~ at**) **1** (poke) (with foot, instrument, stick) donner des petits coups à; (with finger) toucher; (with fork) piquer; **stop ~ding me!** arrête de me bousculer!; **2**° (remind) pousser; **to ~ sb into doing** pousser qn à faire; **3** (interrogate) interroger.

prodding /ˈprɒdɪŋ/ *n* **1** (reminding) **after a bit of ~ he agreed** il a fallu insister pour qu'il donne son accord; **she needs a bit of ~** elle a besoin d'être poussée; **2** ₵ (interrogation) questions *fpl*.

prodigal /ˈprɒdɪgl/ *adj* LITTÉR [*expenditure, generosity*] extravagant; [*government, body, son*] prodigue; **to be ~ with** OU **of** être prodigue de.

prodigiously /prəˈdɪdʒəslɪ/ *adv* GEN prodigieusement; [*eat, drink*] énormément.

prodigy /ˈprɒdɪdʒɪ/ *n* (all contexts) prodige *m*.

produce I /ˈprɒdjuːs, US -duːs/ *n* ₵ produits *mpl*.
II /prəˈdjuːs, US -ˈduːs/ *vtr* **1** (cause) GEN, BIOL produire [*result, effect, plant*]; provoquer [*reaction, change*]; **2** AGRIC, IND [*region, farmer, company*] produire (**from** à partir de); [*worker, machine*] fabri-

quer; **3** (generate, create) produire [*heat, sound, energy*]; rapporter [*gains, profits, returns*]; **4** (present) produire [*passport, report*]; fournir [*evidence, argument, example*]; **to ~ sth from** sortir qch de [*pocket, bag*]; CIN, MUS, RADIO, TV produire [*show, film*]; GB THEAT mettre en scène [*play*]; **well-~d** bien réalisé; **6** (put together) préparer [*meal*]; mettre au point [*argument, timetable, package, solution*]; éditer [*brochure, guide*]; **a well-~d brochure** une brochure bien faite.

producer /prə'dju:sə(r), US -'du:s-/ ▶ 1251 ⊥ *n* **1** (of produce, food) producteur *m*; (of machinery, goods) fabricant *m*; **2** CIN, RADIO, TV producteur/-trice *m/f*; GB THEAT metteur *m* en scène.

producer goods *npl* biens *mpl* d'équipement.

producing /prə'dju:sɪŋ, US -'du:s-/ I *adj* producteur/-trice.
II **-producing** *combining form* producteur/-trice de; **oil-~ countries** pays producteurs de pétrole.

product /'prɒdʌkt/ I *n* COMM, MATH produit *m*; **consumer ~s** produits de consommation; **the end ~** le résultat final.
II *noun modifier* [*design, launch, development, testing*] d'un produit; **~ range** gamme *f* de produits; **~ designer** créateur/-trice *m/f* de produit.

production /prə'dʌkʃn/ I *n* **1** AGRIC, IND (of crop, foodstuffs, metal) production *f* (**of** de); (of machinery, furniture, cars) fabrication (**of** de); **to go into** ou **be in ~** être fabriqué; **to be in full ~** tourner à plein rendement; **to take land out of ~** cesser l'exploitation d'une terre; **2** (output) production *f* ALSO BIOL, PHYS; **3** (presentation) (of document, ticket, report) présentation *f* (**of** de); (of evidence) production *f*; **4** CIN, MUS production *f* (**of** de); THEAT mise *f* en scène (**of** de); **X's ~ of 'Le Cid'** 'Le Cid', mis en scène par X; **to work in TV ~** être producteur/-trice à la télévision; **to put on a ~ of** THEAT mettre en scène [*play*].
II *noun modifier* [*costs, difficulties, levels, methods, company, quota, unit*] de production; [*control, department, manager*] de la production.

production line *n* chaîne *f* de fabrication.

productive /prə'dʌktɪv/ *adj* **1** (efficient) [*factory, land*] productif/-ive; [*system, method, use*] efficace; **2** (constructive) [*discussion*] fructueux/-euse; [*day, phase, period*] productif/-ive; **3** ECON productif/-ive; **4** (resulting in) **to be ~ of** être générateur/-trice de.

productively /prə'dʌktɪvlɪ/ *adv* [*work*] de façon profitable; [*cultivate*] de façon rentable; [*spend time*] utilement.

productivity /ˌprɒdʌk'tɪvətɪ/ I *n* productivité *f*.
II *noun modifier* [*agreement, bonus, drive, gains, growth*] de productivité.

product: **~ liability** *n* responsabilité *f* de produits; **~ licence** *n* autorisation *f* de mise sur le marché; **~ manager** ▶ 1251 ⊥ *n* chef *m* de produit.

profane /prə'feɪm, US prəʊ'feɪn/ I *adj* **1** (blasphemous) impie; **2** (secular) profane.
II *vtr* profaner [*shrine, tradition, honour*].

profanity /prə'fænətɪ, US prəʊ-/ *n* SOUT **1** (behaviour) impiété *f*; **2** (oath) blasphème *m*.

profess /prə'fes/ *vtr* **1** (claim) prétendre (**to do** de faire; **that** que); **2** (declare openly) faire profession de [*opinion, religion*].

professed /prə'fest/ *adj* GEN (genuine) déclaré; (pretended) soi-disant; RELIG profès/-esse.

professedly /prə'fesɪdlɪ/ *adv* SOUT (avowedly) de son/leur etc propre aveu; (with notion of insincerity) soi-disant.

profession /prə'feʃn/ *n* **1** (occupation, group) profession *f*; **by ~** de profession; **the ~s** les professions libérales; **to enter a ~** embrasser une profession; **the legal ~** le corps judiciaire; **2** (statement) déclaration *f*.

professional /prə'feʃnl/ I *n* **1** (not amateur) professionnel/-elle *m/f*; **2** (in small ad) salarié/-e *m/f*.
II *adj* (all contexts) GEN professionnel/-elle; [*diplomat, soldier*] de carrière; **~ career** carrière *f*; **he needs**

~ help il devrait consulter un spécialiste; **they are ~ people** ils exercent une profession libérale; **to turn ~** [*actor, singer*] devenir professionnel/-elle; [*footballer, athlete*] passer professionnel/-elle.

professional: **~ fee** *n* honoraire *m*; **~ foul** *n* SPORT faute *f* délibérée.

professionalism /prə'feʃnəlɪzəm/ *n* (of person, organization) professionnalisme *m* ALSO SPORT; (of performance, piece of work) (haute) qualité *f*.

professionally /prə'feʃnəlɪ/ *adv* **1** (expertly) [*designed*] par un professionnel; **~ qualified** diplômé; **he is ~ trained** il a reçu une formation professionnelle; **2** (from an expert standpoint) d'un point de vue professionnel; **3** (in work situation) dans un cadre professionnel; **he is known ~ as Tim Jones** dans le métier, il est connu sous le nom de Tim Jones; **4** [*play sport*] en professionnel/-elle; **he sings/dances ~** il est chanteur/danseur professionnel; **5** (to a high standard) de manière professionnelle.

professional school *n* US UNIV (business school) école *f* de commerce; (law school) faculté *f* de droit; (medical school) faculté *f* de médecine.

professor /prə'fesə(r)/ ▶ 937 ⊥ *n* UNIV (chair holder) professeur *m* d'Université; US UNIV (teacher) professeur *m*.

professorial /ˌprɒfɪ'sɔ:rɪəl/ *adj* **1** UNIV [*duties, post, salary*] de professeur (d'Université); US professoral; **2** (imposing) imposant.

professorship /prə'fesəʃɪp/ *n* (chair) chaire *f*; US poste *m* de professeur.

proffer /'prɒfə(r)/ *vtr* SOUT (hold out) tendre; FIG (offer) offrir.

proficiency /prə'fɪʃnsɪ/ *n* (practical) compétence *f* (**in**, **at** en; **in doing** à faire); (academic) niveau *m* (**in** en).

proficient /prə'fɪʃnt/ *adj* compétent; **she is a highly ~ musician** c'est une très bonne musicienne.

profile /'prəʊfaɪl/ I *n* **1** (of face) profil *m* ALSO FIG; **in ~** de profil; **to have/maintain a high ~** FIG occuper/rester sur le devant de la scène; **he enjoys a high ~ in the literary world** il est très en vue dans le monde littéraire; **to raise one's ~** se rendre plus connu; **2** (of body, mountain) silhouette *f*; **3** (by journalist) portrait *m* (**of** de); **4** (graph, table, list) profil *m*.
II *vtr* dresser le portrait de [*person*].
III **profiled** *pp adj* (silhouetted) **to be ~d** se profiler.

profit /'prɒfɪt/ I *n* **1** COMM bénéfice *m*, profit *m*; **gross/net ~** bénéfice brut/net; **to operate at a ~** être rentable; **there isn't much ~ in that line of business** ce genre de métier ne rapporte pas gros; **2** FIG (benefit) profit *m*.
II *vtr* LITTÉR profiter à.
III *vi* **to ~ by** ou **from sth** tirer profit de qch.

profitability /ˌprɒfɪtə'bɪlətɪ/ *n* rentabilité *f*.

profitable /'prɒfɪtəbl/ *adj* COMM rentable; FIG fructueux/-euse; **to make ~ use of sth** mettre qch à profit.

profitably /'prɒfɪtəblɪ/ *adv* **1** FIN [*sell, trade*] à profit; [*invest*] avec profit; **2** (usefully) utilement.

profiteer /ˌprɒfɪ'tɪə(r)/ PÉJ I *n* profiteur/-euse *m/f*.
II *vi* faire des bénéfices excessifs.

profiteering /ˌprɒfɪ'tɪərɪŋ/ PÉJ I *n* réalisation *f* de bénéfices excessifs.
II *adj* profiteur/-euse.

profit: **~-making organization** *n* organisation *f* à but lucratif; **~ margin** *n* marge *f* bénéficiaire; **~ sharing** *n* intéressement *m* des salariés aux bénéfices; **~ squeeze** *n* FIN contraction *f* des marges bénéficiaires; **~ taking** *n* prise *f* de bénéfices.

profligate /'prɒflɪgət/ *adj* SOUT **1** (extravagant) [*government, body*] extrêmement prodigue; [*spending*] excessif/-ive; **2** (dissolute) débauché.

profound /prə'faʊnd/ *adj* profond.

profoundly /prə'faʊndlɪ/ *adv* **1** (very) profondément; **2** (wisely) avec profondeur.

profuse /prə'fju:s/ *adj* [*praise, thanks*] profus; [*growth, bleeding*] abondant.

profusely /prə'fju:slɪ/ *adv* [*sweat, bleed*] abondamment; [*bloom*] à profusion; [*thank*] avec effusion; **to apologize** ~ se confondre en excuses.

prognosis /prɒgˈnəʊsɪs/ *n* **1** MED pronostic *m* (**on**, **about** sur); **2** (prediction) pronostics *mpl* (**for** sur).

prognosticate /prɒgˈnɒstɪkeɪt/ *vtr* pronostiquer.

program /ˈprəʊgræm, US -grəm/ **I** *n* **1** COMPUT programme *m*; **to run a** ~ lancer un programme; **2** US RADIO, TV émission *f*.

II *vtr, vi* (*p prés etc* **-mm-** GB, **-m-** US) GEN, COMPUT programmer (**to do** pour faire).

programer *n* US = **programmer**.

programing *n* US = **programming**.

programme GB, **program** US /ˈprəʊgræm, US -grəm/ **I** *n* **1** TV, RADIO (single broadcast) émission *f* (**about** sur); (schedule of broadcasting) programme *m*; **2** (schedule) programme *m*; **3** MUS, THEAT programme *m*.

II *vtr* (set) programmer [*machine*] (**to do** pour faire).

programme: ~ **music** *n* MUS musique *f* à programme; ~ **note** *n* commentaire *m* de programme.

programmer GB, **programer** US /ˈprəʊgræmə(r), US -grəm-/ ▶ **1251**] *n* programmeur/-euse *m*/*f*.

programming, **programing** US /ˈprəʊgræmɪŋ, US -grəm-/ *n* (all contexts) programmation *f*.

progress I /ˈprəʊgres, US ˈprɒgres/ *n* **1** (advances) progrès *m*; **to make slow/steady** ~ progresser lentement/régulièrement; **the patient is making** ~ l'état de santé du malade s'améliore; **2** (course, evolution) (of person, vehicle, inquiry, event) progression *f*; (of talks, dispute, disease, career) évolution *f*; **to make (slow/ steady)** ~ progresser (lentement/régulièrement); **to be in** ~ [*discussions, meeting, exam, work*] être en cours.

II /prəˈgres/ *vi* **1** (develop, improve) [*person, work, studies*] progresser; **to** ~ **towards democracy** s'acheminer vers la démocratie; **2** (follow course) [*person, vehicle, discussion*] progresser.

progression /prəˈgreʃn/ *n* **1** (development) (evolution) évolution *f*; (improvement) progression *f*; **2** (series) suite *f* also MATH; **3** MUS progression *f*.

progressive /prəˈgresɪv/ **I** *n* progressiste *mf*.

II *adj* **1** (gradual) [*increase, change*] progressif/-ive; [*illness*] évolutif/-ive; **to show a** ~ **improvement** s'améliorer progressivement; **2** (radical) [*person, art, idea, policy*] progressiste; [*school*] parallèle; [*age, period*] progressif/-ive; **3** LING progressif/-ive.

progressively /prəˈgresɪvlɪ/ *adv* progressivement.

progress report *n* (on construction work) rapport *m* sur l'état des travaux; (on project) rapport *m* sur l'état du projet; (on patient) bulletin *m* de santé; (on pupil) bulletin *m* scolaire.

prohibit /prəˈhɪbɪt, US prəʊ-/ *vtr* (forbid) interdire; **to** ~ **sb from doing** interdire à qn de faire; **'smoking** ~**ed'** 'défense de fumer'.

prohibition /ˌprəʊhɪˈbɪʃn, US ˌprəʊəˈbɪʃn/ **I** *n* interdiction *f* (**on, against** de).

II Prohibition *pr n* **the Prohibition** US HIST la prohibition.

prohibitive /prəˈhɪbətɪv, US prəʊ-/ *adj* [*cost, price*] prohibitif/-ive.

prohibitively /prəˈhɪbɪtɪvlɪ, US prəʊ-/ *adv* **prices are** ~ **high** les prix sont prohibitifs.

project I /ˈprɒdʒekt/ *n* **1** (scheme) projet *m* (**to do** pour faire); **2** SCH dossier *m* (**on** sur); UNIV mémoire *m* (**on** sur); **research** ~ programme *m* de recherches; **3** US (state housing) (large) ≈ cité *f* HLM; (small) ≈ lotissement *m* HLM.

II /ˈprɒdʒekt/ *noun modifier* [*budget, funds*] d'un projet; ~ **manager** GEN directeur/-trice *m*/*f* de projet; CONSTR maître *m* d'œuvre; ~ **outline** avant-projet *m*.

III /prəˈdʒekt/ *vtr* **1** (throw, send) projeter [*object*]; envoyer [*missile*]; faire porter [*voice*]; donner [*image*]; **2** (transfer) projeter [*guilt, doubts, anxiety*]; **3** (estimate) prévoir; **4** CIN, PHYS, MATH projeter; **5** GEOG faire la projection de.

IV /prəˈdʒekt/ *vi* **1** GEN (stick out) faire saillie (**from** sur); **to** ~ **over** surplomber; **2** THEAT [*actor*] passer la rampe.

V projected *pp adj* [*figure, deficit*] prévu.

VI /prəˈdʒekt/ *v refl* **to** ~ **oneself 1** (make an impression) faire impression; **to** ~ **oneself as being** donner l'impression d'être; **2 to** ~ **oneself into the future** se projeter dans l'avenir.

projectile /prəˈdʒektaɪl, US -tl/ *n* projectile *m*.

projecting /prəˈdʒektɪŋ/ *adj* saillant.

projection /prəˈdʒekʃn/ *n* **1** (of object, thoughts, emotions) projection *f* also CIN, MATH, GEOG; **2** (estimate) prévision *f*.

projection room *n* cabine *f* de projection.

projector /prəˈdʒektə(r)/ *n* projecteur *m*.

proletarian /ˌprəʊlɪˈteərɪən/ **I** *n* prolétaire *mf*.

II *adj* POL, ECON prolétarien/-ienne; GEN ouvrier/ -ière.

pro-life /ˌprəʊˈlaɪf/ *adj* contre l'avortement.

proliferate /prəˈlɪfəreɪt, US prəʊ-/ *vi* proliférer.

prolific /prəˈlɪfɪk/ *adj* (productive) [*writer, plant, parent*] prolifique; [*decade*] fécond; [*growth*] rapide.

prologue /ˈprəʊlɒg, US -lɔːg/ *n* LITERAT prologue *m* (**to** de); FIG prélude *m* (**to** à).

prolong /prəˈlɒŋ, US -ˈlɔːŋ/ *vtr* prolonger.

prom○ /prɒm/ *n* **1** GB concert *m*; **2** US (at high school) bal *m* de lycéens; (college) bal *m* d'étudiants; **3** GB (at seaside) front *m* de mer.

promenade /ˌprɒməˈnɑːd, US -ˈneɪd/ **I** *n* **1** (path) promenade *f*; (by sea) front *m* de mer; **2** (dance) promenade *f*.

II *vtr* SOUT promener [*virtues etc*].

III *vi* SOUT se promener.

promenade concerts *npl* GB série *f* annuelle de concerts.

prominence /ˈprɒmɪnəns/ *n* (of person, issue) importance *f*; (of object, feature) proéminence *f*; **to rise to** ~ devenir connu.

prominent /ˈprɒmɪnənt/ *adj* **1** [*figure, campaigner*] très en vue; [*artist, intellectual, industrialist*] éminent; **to play a** ~ **part** ou **role in sth** jouer un rôle de premier plan dans qch; **2** [*position, place, feature*] proéminent; [*peak, ridge, cheekbone*] saillant; [*marking*] bien visible; [*eye*] exorbité.

prominently /ˈprɒmɪnəntlɪ/ *adv* [*displayed*] en évidence; **to feature** ou **figure** ~ **in sth** jouer un rôle important dans qch.

promiscuity /ˌprɒmɪˈskjuːɪtɪ/ *n* (sexual) vagabondage *m* sexuel.

promiscuous /prəˈmɪskjʊəs/ *adj* PÉJ [*person*] aux mœurs légères; ~ **behaviour** mœurs légères.

promise /ˈprɒmɪs/ **I** *n* **1** (undertaking) promesse *f*; **to break one's** ~ manquer à sa promesse; **they held him to his** ~ ils lui ont fait tenir sa promesse; **2** ¢ (hope) espoir *m*; **3** ¢ (likelihood of success) **she shows great** ~ elle promet beaucoup.

II *vtr* **1** (pledge) **to** ~ **sb sth** promettre qch à qn; **as** ~**d** comme promis; **2** (give prospect of) annoncer; **it** ~**s to be a fine day** la journée s'annonce belle; **3** (assure) assurer; **it won't be easy, I** ~ **you** cela ne sera pas facile, je te l'assure.

III *vi* **1** (give pledge) promettre; **do you** ~? c'est promis?; **2** FIG **to** ~ **well** [*young talent, candidate*] être très prometteur; [*result, situation, event*] s'annoncer bien; **this doesn't** ~ **well for the future** cela ne présage rien de bon pour le futur.

promising /ˈprɒmɪsɪŋ/ *adj* [*situation, result, future*] prometteur/-euse; [*artist, candidate*] qui promet; **the future looks more** ~ l'avenir s'annonce meilleur; **'I've been shortlisted for the job'—'that's** ~**'** 'je suis sur la liste des candidats retenus'—'c'est bon signe'.

promisingly /ˈprɒmɪsɪŋlɪ/ *adv* d'une façon prometteuse.

promo○ *n* (d'un produit) vidéo *f* publicitaire; (d'un artiste) vidéo *f* de présentation.

promontory /ˈprɒmɪntrɪ, US -tɔːrɪ/ *n* promontoire *m*.

promote /prə'məʊt/ I *vtr* **1** (in rank) promouvoir (**to à**); **2** (advertise) faire de la publicité pour; (market) promouvoir; **to ~ a candidate** mettre un candidat en avant; **3** (encourage) promouvoir; **4** GB (in football) **to be ~d from the fourth to the third division** passer de quatrième en troisième division; **5** US SCH **to be ~d** être admis dans la classe supérieure.
II *vtr* **to ~ oneself** se mettre en avant.

promoter /prə'məʊtə(r)/ *n* (all contexts) promoteur/ -trice *m/f*.

promotion /prə'məʊʃn/ *n* **1** (of employee) promotion *f*; **to gain ~** être promu; **to apply for ~** demander une promotion; **to be in line for ~** avoir des chances d'être promu; **2** COMM promotion *f* (**of** de); **3** (encouragement) promotion *f* (**of** de); **4** US SCH admission *f* dans la classe supérieure.

promotional /prə'məʊʃənl/ *adj* COMM promotionnel/ -elle; **the ~ ladder** les échelons *mpl*.

promotional video *n* (d'un produit) vidéo *f* publicitaire; (d'un artiste) vidéo *f* de présentation.

promotion: **~ prospects** *npl* (long-term) perspectives *fpl* d'avenir; (immediate) possibilités *fpl* d'avenir; **~s manager** ▶ 1251 *n* directeur/-trice *m/f* de la publicité.

prompt /prɒmpt/ I *n* **1** COMPUT message *m* guide-opérateur; **2** COMM délai *m* de paiement.
II *adj* rapide; **to be ~ to do** être prompt à faire.
III *adv* pile; **at six o'clock ~** à six heures pile.
IV *vtr* **1** (cause) provoquer [*reaction, decision*]; susciter [*concern, accusation, comment, warning*]; **to ~ sb to do sth** inciter qn à faire qch; **2** (encourage to talk) **'and then what?' she ~ed** 'et puis quoi?' demanda-t-elle; **3** GEN, THEAT (remind) souffler à [*person*].
V *vi* GEN, THEAT souffler.

prompt box *n* THEAT trou *m* du souffleur.

prompter /'prɒmptə(r)/ *n* **1** THEAT souffleur/-euse *m/f*; **2** US TV téléprompteur *m*.

prompting /'prɒmptɪŋ/ *n* encouragement *m*; **without any ~** de mon/son etc plein gré.

promptly /'prɒmptlɪ/ *adv* **1** (immediately) immédiatement; **2** (without delay) rapidement; **3** (punctually) à l'heure; **~ at six o'clock** à six heures précises.

promptness /'prɒmptnɪs/ *n* (speed) rapidité *f* (**in doing** à faire); (punctuality) ponctualité *f*.

prompt note *n* COMM rappel *m* de paiement.

promulgate /'prɒmlgeɪt/ *vtr* (promote) répandre; (proclaim) promulguer.

prone /prəʊn/ I *adj* **1** (liable) **to be ~ to** être sujet/ -ette à [*migraines, colds*]; être enclin à [*depression, violence*]; **2** (prostrate) **to lie ~** (sleeping, sunbathing) être allongé sur le ventre; (injured) être allongé face contre terre.
II **-prone** *combining form* **accident-~** sujet/-ette aux accidents.

prong /prɒŋ, US prɔːŋ/ *n* (on fork) dent *f*.

-pronged /prɒŋd, US prɔːŋd/ *combining form* **1 two/ three ~ attack** attaque *f* sur deux/trois fronts; **2** [*fork, spear*] **two/three ~** à deux/trois dents.

pronoun /'prəʊnaʊn/ *n* pronom *m*.

pronounce /prə'naʊns/ I *vtr* **1** LING prononcer [*letter, word*]; **2** GEN prononcer [*judgment, sentence*]; rendre [*verdict*]; émettre [*opinion*]; **to ~ sb dead** déclarer qn mort.
II *vi* JUR prononcer; **to ~ for/against sb** rendre un jugement favorable/défavorable à qn.
III *v refl* **to ~ oneself satisfied/bored** se déclarer satisfait/ennuyé.
■ **pronounce on**: **~ on [sth]** se prononcer sur [*case, matter*]; affirmer [*existence, truth*].

pronounceable /prə'naʊnsəbl/ *adj* prononçable.

pronounced /prə'naʊnst/ *adj* **1** (noticeable) [*accent, limp, tendency*] prononcé; [*change, difference, increase*] marqué; **2** (strongly felt) [*idea, opinion*] arrêté.

pronouncement /prə'naʊnsmənt/ *n* (statement) déclaration *f*; (verdict) verdict *m*.

pronunciation /prə.nʌnsɪ'eɪʃn/ *n* prononciation *f*.

proof /pruːf/ I *n* **1** (evidence) preuve *f* ALSO MATH; **to**

have ~ that pouvoir prouver que; **there is no ~ that** rien ne prouve que; **to produce sth as ~** produire qch à titre de preuve; **to be ~ of sb's worth** prouver la valeur de qn; **~ of identity** pièce *f* d'identité; **2** (in printing) épreuve *f*; **to read sth in ~** lire qch sur épreuves; **3** PHOT épreuve *f*; **4** (of alcohol) niveau *m* étalon; **to be 70° ou 70% ~** ~ titrer 40° d'alcool.
II *adj* **to be ~ against** être à l'épreuve de [*heat, infection*]; être à l'abri de [*temptation, charms*].
III **- proof** *combining form* (resistant to) **vandal-~** protégé contre les vandales; **earthquake-~** anti-sismique.
IV *vtr* **1** imperméabiliser [*fabric*]; insonoriser [*room, house*]; **2** = **proofread**.

proof: **~ of delivery** *n* reçu *m* de livraison; **~ of ownership** *n* titre *m* de propriété; **~ of postage** *n* certificat *m* d'expédition; **~ of purchase** *n* justificatif *m* d'achat.

proofread /'pruːfriːd/ I *vtr* (*prét, pp* **-read** /red/) **1** (check copy) corriger; **2** (check proofs) corriger les épreuves de.
II *vi* (*prét, pp* **-read** /red/) **1** (check copy) corriger; **2** (check proofs) corriger des épreuves.

proof: **~reader** ▶ 1251 *n* correcteur/-trice *m/f*; **~reading** *n* correction *f* d'épreuves; **~ spirit** *n* GB alcool *m* à 57,1°; US alcool *m* à 50°.

prop /prɒp/ I *n* **1** CONSTR, TECH étai *m*; **2** (supportive person) soutien *m* (**for** pour); **3** THEAT (*abrév* = **property**) accessoire *m*; **4** (in rugby) pilier *m*.
II *vtr* (*p prés etc* **-pp-**) **1** (support) étayer; **I ~ed his head on a pillow** je lui ai soutenu la tête avec un oreiller; **2** (lean) **to ~ sb/sth against sth** appuyer qn/qch contre qch.
III *v refl* (*p prés etc* **-pp-**) **to ~ oneself against sth** s'appuyer à qch.
■ **prop up**: **~ [sth] up, ~ up [sth]** LIT étayer; FIG soutenir.

propaganda /.prɒpə'gændə/ I *n* propagande *f*.
II *noun modifier* [*campaign, exercise, film, war*] de propagande.

propagate /'prɒpəgeɪt/ I *vtr* LIT, FIG propager.
II *vi* se propager.

propagator /'prɒpəgeɪtə(r)/ *n* (tray) germoir *m*.

propel /prə'pel/ *vtr* (*p prés etc* **-ll-**) **1** (power) propulser [*vehicle, ship*]; **2** (push) pousser [*person*]; (more violently) propulser [*person*].

propellant /prə'pelənt/ *n* **1** (in aerosol) gaz *m* propulseur; **2** (in rocket) propergol *m*; **3** (in gun) poudre *f* propulsive.

propeller /prə'pelə(r)/ *n* AVIAT, NAUT hélice *f*.

propeller shaft *n* AUT arbre *m* de transmission; NAUT arbre *m* porte-hélice; AVIAT arbre *m* de propulsion.

propelling pencil *n* GB portemine *m*.

propensity /prə'pensətɪ/ *n* propension *f* (**to, for** à).

proper /'prɒpə(r)/ *adj* **1** (right) [*term, spelling*] correct; [*order, manner, tool, choice, response*] bon/bonne; [*sense*] propre; [*precautions*] nécessaire; [*clothing*] qu'il faut; **it's only ~ for her to keep the money** il est tout naturel qu'elle garde l'argent; **everything is in the ~ place** tout est à sa place; **to go through the ~ channels** passer par la filière officielle; **in the ~ way** correctement; **2** (adequate) [*funding, recognition*] convenable; [*education, training*] bon/bonne; [*care, control*] requis; **we have no ~ tennis courts** nous n'avons pas de courts de tennis convenables; **it has ~ facilities** c'est bien équipé; **3** (fitting) **~ to** SOUT convenant à [*position, status*]; **I did as I thought ~**, j'ai agi comme je l'ai jugé bon; **4** (respectably correct) [*person*] correct; [*upbringing*] convenable; **5** (real, full) [*doctor, holiday, job*] vrai (*before n*); **he did a ~ job of repairing the car** il a bien réparé la voiture; **6°** (complete) **I felt a ~ fool!** je me suis senti complètement stupide!; **7** (actual) (*après n*) **in the village ~** dans le village même; **the competition ~** le concours proprement dit.

IDIOMS **to beat sb good and ~** FIG battre qn haut la main.

properly /ˈprɒpəlɪ/ adv **1** (correctly) correctement; **~ speaking** à proprement parler; **behave ~!** tiens-toi comme il faut!; **2** (fully) complètement; **read the letter ~** lis la lettre correctement; **~ prepared for the interview** bien préparé pour l'entretien; **I didn't have time to thank you ~** je n'ai pas eu le temps de vous remercier; **3** (adequately) convenablement; **4** (suitably) [*dressed*] correctement.

proper name, **proper noun** n LING nom m propre.

property /ˈprɒpətɪ/ **I** n **1** (belongings) propriété f, bien(s) m(pl); **government ~** propriété f de l'État; **that is not your ~** cela ne vous appartient pas; **2** ¢ (real estate) biens mpl immobiliers; **to invest in ~** investir dans l'immobilier; **~ was damaged** il y a eu des dégâts matériels; **3** (house) propriété f; **the ~ is detached** c'est une maison indépendante; **4** CHEM, PHYS, JUR propriété f.
II properties npl **1** FIN immobilier m; **2** THEAT accessoires mpl.
III noun modifier (real estate) [*company, development, group, law, speculator, value*] immobilier/-ière; [*market, prices*] de l'immobilier.
IDIOMS **to be hot ~** être demandé.

property: **~ dealer** n marchand m de biens; **~ developer** n promoteur m immobilier; **~ insurance** n assurance f des biens; **~ owner** n propriétaire mf; **~ sales** npl vente f immobilière; **~ speculation** n spéculation f foncière; **~ tax** n impôt m foncier.

prophecy /ˈprɒfəsɪ/ n prophétie f.

prophesy /ˈprɒfəsaɪ/ **I** vtr prophétiser (**that** que).
II vi faire des prophéties (**about** sur).

prophet /ˈprɒfɪt/ n prophète m.

prophetic /prəˈfetɪk/ adj prophétique.

prophylactic /ˌprɒfɪˈlæktɪk/ **I** n **1** MED (treatment) traitement m prophylactique; (measure) mesure f prophylactique; **2** (condom) préservatif m.
II adj prophylactique.

propitiate /prəˈpɪʃɪeɪt/ vtr se concilier [*person, gods*].

propitious /prəˈpɪʃəs/ adj SOUT propice (**for** à).

propitiously /prəˈpɪʃəslɪ/ adv SOUT [*start*] sous de bons auspices; [*arrive*] fort à propos; [*disposed*] favorablement.

proponent /prəˈpəʊnənt/ n partisan/-e mf (**of** de).

proportion /prəˈpɔːʃn/ **I** n **1** (part, quantity) (of group, population etc) proportion f (**of** de); (of income, profit, work etc) part f (**of** de); **2** (ratio) ALSO MATH proportion f; **productivity increases in ~ to the incentives offered** l'augmentation de la productivité est directement proportionnelle aux primes de rendement; **tax should be in ~ to income** les contributions devraient être en fonction des revenus; **3** (harmony, symmetry) **out of/in ~** hors de proportion; **4** FIG (perspective) **to get sth out of all ~** faire tout un drame de qch; **to be out of all ~** être tout à fait disproportionné (**to** par rapport à); **you've got to have a sense of ~** il faut avoir le sens de la mesure.
II proportions npl LIT, FIG dimensions fpl.
III -proportioned combining form **well-/badly-~ed** bien/mal proportionné.

proportional /prəˈpɔːʃənl/ adj proportionnel/-elle.

proportionally /prəˈpɔːʃənəlɪ/ adv proportionnellement.

proportional representation, **PR** n représentation f proportionnelle.

proportionate /prəˈpɔːʃənət/ adj proportionnel/-elle.

proportionately /prəˈpɔːʃənətlɪ/ adv [*larger, higher*] proportionnellement; [*distribute*] en proportion.

proposal /prəˈpəʊzl/ n **1** (suggestion) proposition f (**for** sth de qch); **2** (offer of marriage) demande f en mariage; **3** (insurance) (also **~ form**) proposition f d'assurance.

propose /prəˈpəʊz/ **I** vtr (nominate, intend, suggest) proposer; présenter [*motion*].
II vi faire sa demande en mariage (**to** à).

III proposed pp adj [*action, reform*] envisagé.

proposer /prəˈpəʊzə(r)/ n **1** (of motion) auteur m; **2** (of candidate) personne proposant un candidat à un poste; **3** (of member) parrain/marraine mf.

proposition /ˌprɒpəˈzɪʃn/ **I** n **1** (suggestion) proposition f ALSO MATH; **2** (assertion) assertion f; **3** (enterprise) affaire f.
II vtr faire une proposition à [*person*].

propound /prəˈpaʊnd/ vtr avancer.

proprietary /prəˈpraɪətrɪ, US -terɪ/ adj **1** [*rights, duties*] du propriétaire; [*manner, attitude*] de propriétaire; **2** COMM [*information*] qui est la propriété de la compagnie; [*system*] breveté.

proprietary: **~ brand** n marque f déposée; **~ medicine** n spécialité f pharmaceutique.

proprietor /prəˈpraɪətə(r)/ n propriétaire mf (**of** de).

propriety /prəˈpraɪətɪ/ n **1** (politeness) correction f; **2** (morality) décence f.

propulsion /prəˈpʌlʃn/ n propulsion f.

pro rata /ˌprəʊ ˈrɑːtə/ **I** adj **on a ~ basis** en rapport, au prorata.
II adv [*increase*] dans la même proportion; **salary £15,000 ~** salaire 15000 livres sterling au prorata des heures travaillées.

prosaic /prəˈzeɪɪk/ adj prosaïque.

proscenium /prəˈsiːnɪəm/ n THEAT avant-scène f.

proscribe /prəˈskraɪb, US prəʊ-/ vtr proscrire.

prose /prəʊz/ n **1** (not verse) prose f; **2** GB (translation) thème m.

prosecute /ˈprɒsɪkjuːt/ **I** vtr **1** JUR poursuivre [qn] en justice; **to ~ sb for doing** poursuivre qn pour avoir fait; **2** (pursue) poursuivre.
II vi engager des poursuites.

prosecuting: **~ attorney** n US (lawyer) avocat/-e mf de la partie civile; (public official) procureur m; **~ lawyer** n avocat/-e mf de l'accusation.

prosecution /ˌprɒsɪˈkjuːʃn/ n **1** JUR (accusation) poursuites fpl (judiciaires); **the ~ process** la procédure d'inculpation; **2** JUR (party) **the ~** (private individual) le/les plaignant/-s; (state, Crown) le ministère public; **3** (of war, research) poursuite f (**of** de).

prosecutor /ˈprɒsɪkjuːtə(r)/ n JUR **1** (instituting prosecution) **to be the ~** être chargé de poursuites; **2** (in court) procureur m; **3** US (prosecuting attorney) avocat/-e mf de la partie civile; (public official) procureur m.

prospect I /ˈprɒspekt/ n **1** (hope) (of change, improvement) espoir m; (of success) chance f; **a bleak/gloomy ~** une perspective triste/sombre; **2** (outlook) perspective f; **to be in ~** être à prévoir; **3** (good option) (for job) recrue f potentielle; (for sports team) espoir m; **4** COMM (likely client) client/-e mf potentiel/-ielle; **5** (view) LITTÉR vue f.
II prospects npl perspectives fpl; **she has good career ~s** elle a de bonnes perspectives de carrière; **to have no ~s** [*person*] ne pas avoir d'avenir; [*job*] être sans avenir.
III /prəˈspekt, US ˈprɒspekt/ vtr prospecter [*land, region*].
IV /prəˈspekt, US ˈprɒspekt/ vi prospecter; **to ~ for** chercher.

prospecting /prəˈspektɪŋ/ **I** n prospection f.
II noun modifier [*rights, licence*] de prospection.

prospective /prəˈspektɪv/ adj [*buyer, candidate*] potentiel/-ielle; [*son-in-law, mother-in-law*] futur.

prospector /prəˈspektə(r), US ˈprɒspektər/ n prospecteur/-trice mf; **gold ~** chercheur/-euse mf d'or.

prospectus /prəˈspektəs/ n GEN brochure f; (for shares, funding) prospectus m d'émission; **university ~, college ~** livret m de l'étudiant.

prosper /ˈprɒspə(r)/ vi prospérer.

prosperity /prɒˈsperɪtɪ/ n prospérité f.

prosperous /ˈprɒspərəs/ adj [*person, farm, country*] prospère; [*appearance*] de prospérité.

prostate /ˈprɒsteɪt/ n (also **~ gland**) prostate f.

prostitute /ˈprɒstɪtjuːt, US -tuːt/ **I** n (woman) prostituée f; **male ~** prostitué m.

II *vtr* prostituer [*person, talent*].

prostitution /ˌprɒstɪˈtjuːʃn/, US -tuːt-/ *n* prostitution *f*.

prostrate I /ˈprɒstreɪt/ *adj* **1** (on stomach) allongé à plat ventre; **2** FIG (incapacitated) prostré; **~ with grief** accablé de chagrin.
II /prɒˈstreɪt/, US ˈprɒstreɪt/ *vtr* **to be ~d by** être abattu par.
III /prɒˈstreɪt/, US ˈprɒstreɪt/ *v refl* **to ~ oneself** se prosterner (**before** devant).

prostration /prɒˈstreɪʃn/ *n* (from illness, overwork) prostration *f*.

protagonist /prəˈtægənɪst/ *n* **1** LITERAT, CIN protagoniste *mf*; **2** (advocate) partisan/-e *m/f* (**of** de); (participant) participant/-e *m/f*.

protect /prəˈtekt/ **I** *vtr* **1** (keep safe) protéger; **2** (defend) défendre [*consumer, interests, privilege*]; (**against** contre); préserver [*privacy*]; protéger [*investment, standards, economy*].
II *v refl* **to ~ oneself** (against threat) se protéger; (against attack) se défendre.

protection /prəˈtekʃn/ *n* **1** (safeguard) LIT, FIG protection *f*; **to give** ou **offer sb ~ against sth** protéger qn contre qch; **for his own ~** (moral) pour son bien; (physical) pour le protéger; **2** ECON (also **trade ~**) protectionnisme *m*; **3** (extortion) **to pay sb ~** payer un impôt à qn (*pour être protégé*) IRON; **to buy ~** acheter sa tranquillité (*à un racketteur*); **4** COMPUT protection *f*; **data ~** protection *f* de données; **5** (protective clothing) **head ~** casque *m*; **eye ~** lunettes *fpl*.

protection factor *n* (of sun cream) indice *m* de protection.

protectionist /prəˈtekʃənɪst/ *n, adj* protectionniste *mf*.

protection: **~ money** *n* EUPH argent versé à un racketteur; **~ racket** *n* racket *m*.

protective /prəˈtektɪv/ **I** *n* US (condom) préservatif *m*.
II *adj* **1** (providing security) [*clothing, layer*] protecteur/-trice; [*measure*] de protection; **2** (caring) protecteur/-trice; **to be ~ of** veiller jalousement sur [*possessions*]; protéger [*discovery, research*]; **3** ECON [*tarif, system*] protectionniste.

protective custody *n* JUR **to place sb in ~** détenir qn pour sa (propre) protection.

protector /prəˈtektə(r)/ *n* **1** (defender) GEN protecteur/-trice *m/f*; (of rights) défenseur *m*; **2** (pads etc) **ear ~s** casque *m* antibruit; **elbow ~** protège-coude *m*.

protein /ˈprəʊtiːn/ *n* protéine *f*; **high-~** riche en protéines.

protest I /ˈprəʊtest/ *n* **1** ¢ (disapproval) protestation *f*; **in ~** en signe de protestation; **without ~** sans protester; **I followed him under ~** je l'ai suivi contre mon gré; **2** ¢ (complaint) réclamation *f*; **as a ~ against** ou **at sth** pour protester contre qch; **to lodge a ~** faire une réclamation; **3** (demonstration) manifestation *f*.
II /ˈprəʊtest/ *noun modifier* [*march, movement, song*] de protestation.
III /prəˈtest/ *vtr* **1** (declare) affirmer [*truth*]; **to ~ one's innocence** protester de son innocence; **2** (complain) **'that's unfair!' they ~ed** 'c'est injuste!' s'écrièrent-ils; **to ~ that** protester que; **3** US (complain about) protester contre (**to** auprès de).
IV /prəˈtest/ *vi* **1** (complain) protester; **2** (demonstrate) manifester.

Protestant /ˈprɒtɪstənt/ **I** *n* protestant/-e *m/f*.
II *adj* protestant; **the ~ Church** l'Église protestante; (in official names) l'Église Réformée.

protestation /ˌprɒtɪˈsteɪʃn/ *n* protestation *f*; **in ~** pour protester.

protester /prəˈtestə(r)/ *n* manifestant/-e *m/f*.

protocol /ˌprəʊtəˈkɒl/, US -kɔːl/ *n* GEN, POL, COMPUT protocole *m*.

prototype /ˈprəʊtətaɪp/ **I** *n* prototype *m* (**of** de).
II *noun modifier* [*vehicle, aircraft*] prototype.

protrude /prəˈtruːd/, US prəʊ-/ *vi* GEN dépasser.

protruding /prəˈtruːdɪŋ/, US prəʊ-/ *adj* [*rock*] en saillie; [*nail*] qui dépasse; [*eyes*] globuleux/-euse; [*ears*] dé-

collé; [*ribs*] saillant; [*chin*] en avant; **to have ~ teeth** avoir les dents qui avancent.

protrusion /prəˈtruːʒn/, US prəʊ-/ *n* SOUT (on rocks) saillie *f*; (part of building) avancée *f*; (on skin) protubérance *f*.

proud /praʊd/ *adj* **1** (satisfied, self-respecting) GEN fier/fière; [*owner*] heureux/-euse; **2** (great) [*day, moment*] grand; **3** GB **fill the hole ~** bouchez le trou en laissant une protubérance.
IDIOMS **to do sb ~** (entertain) traiter qn royalement; (praise) faire honneur à qn; **to do oneself ~** ne rien se refuser.

proudly /ˈpraʊdlɪ/ *adv* [*display, show*] avec fierté; [*move, speak*] fièrement; **Disney Studios ~ present** CIN les studios Disney ont le plaisir de présenter.

provable /ˈpruːvəbl/ *adj* démontrable.

prove /pruːv/ **I** *vtr* **1** (show) GEN prouver; (by demonstration) démontrer; **to ~ a point** montrer qu'on a raison; **2** JUR authentifier [*will*]; **3** CULIN faire lever [*dough*].
II *vi* **1** (turn out) s'avérer; **it ~d otherwise** il en est allé autrement; **if I ~ to be mistaken** s'il arrive que j'ai tort; **2** CULIN [*dough*] lever.
III *v refl* **to ~ oneself** faire ses preuves; **to ~ oneself (to be)** se révéler.

proven /ˈpruːvn/ *adj* éprouvé.

proverb /ˈprɒvɜːb/ *n* proverbe *m*.

proverbial /prəˈvɜːbɪəl/ *adj* **1** [*wisdom, saying*] proverbial; **2** (widely known) légendaire.

proverbially /prəˈvɜːbɪəlɪ/ *adv* **he is ~ stupid/mean** il est d'une stupidité/avarice légendaire.

provide /prəˈvaɪd/ **I** *vtr* **1** (supply) fournir [*opportunity, evidence, jobs, meals*] (**for** à); apporter [*answer, support, understanding*] (**for** à); donner [*satisfaction*] (**for** à); assurer [*service, food, access, training, shelter*] (**for** à); **to ~ an incentive to do** être un encouragement à faire; **please use the bin ~d** veuillez utiliser la poubelle mise à votre disposition; **2** JUR, ADMIN (stipulate) prévoir; **except as ~d** sauf indication contraire.
II *vi* pourvoir aux besoins.
■ **provide against**: **~ against** [sth] parer à.
■ **provide for**: ¶ **~ for** [sth] **1** (account for) envisager; **2** JUR prévoir; ¶ **~ for** [sb] subvenir aux besoins de; **to be well ~d for** être à l'abri du besoin.

provided /prəˈvaɪdɪd/, **providing** /prəˈvaɪdɪŋ/ *conj* (also **~ that**) à condition que (+ *subj*); **~ always that** JUR, ADMIN sous réserve que.

providence /ˈprɒvɪdəns/ *n* (fate) providence *f*.

provident /ˈprɒvɪdənt/ *adj* prévoyant.

providential /ˌprɒvɪˈdenʃl/ *adj* SOUT providentiel/-ielle.

provider /prəˈvaɪdə(r)/ *n* **1** (in family) **to be a good ~** bien subvenir aux besoins de sa famille; **2** COMM pourvoyeur/-euse *m/f*.

providing /prəˈvaɪdɪŋ/ *conj* = **provided**.

province /ˈprɒvɪns/ *n* **1** (region) province *f*; **in the ~s** en province; **2** FIG (field, area) domaine *m*.

provincial /prəˈvɪnʃl/ **I** *n* (from provinces) provincial/-e *m/f* ALSO PEJ.
II *adj* **1** [*doctor, newspaper, capital*] de province; [*life*] provincial; [*tour*] en province; **2** PÉJ (narrow) provincial.

proving ground *n* terrain *m* d'essai.

provision /prəˈvɪʒn/ **I** *n* **1** (of housing, information, facility, equipment) mise *f* à disposition; (of food) approvisionnement *m*; (of service) prestation *f*; **health care ~** services *mpl* pour la santé; **to be responsible for the ~ of transport** être responsable d'assurer le transport; **2** (for future) dispositions *fpl*; **3** JUR, ADMIN (of agreement) clause *f*; (of bill, act) disposition *f*; **~ to the contrary** stipulation *f* du contraire; **to make ~ for** prévoir; **under the ~s of** aux termes de; **with the ~ that** à la condition que; **within the ~s of the treaty** dans le cadre du traité.
II provisions *npl* (food) provisions *fpl*.

provisional /prəˈvɪʒənl/ *adj* provisoire.

French provinces and regions

Both traditional pre-Revolution regions and modern administrative regions usually take the definite article as in l'Alsace, la Champagne etc.:

I like Alsace	= j'aime l'Alsace
Champagne is beautiful	= la Champagne est belle

For names which have a compound form, such as Midi-Pyrénées or Rhône-Alpes, it is safer to include the words la région:

do you know Midi-Pyrénées?	= connaissez-vous la région Midi-Pyrénées?

In, to and from somewhere

There are certain general principles regarding names of French provinces and regions. However, usage is sometimes uncertain; doubtful items should be checked in the dictionary.

For in and to, with feminine names and with masculine ones beginning with a vowel, use en without the definite article:

to live in Burgundy	= vivre en Bourgogne
to go to Burgundy	= aller en Bourgogne
to live in Anjou	= vivre en Anjou
to go to Anjou	= aller en Anjou

For in and to with masculine names beginning with a consonant, use dans le:

to live in the Berry	= vivre dans le Berry
to go to the Berry	= aller dans le Berry

For from with feminine names and with masculine ones beginning with a vowel, use de without the definite article:

to come from Burgundy	= venir de Bourgogne
to come from Anjou	= venir d'Anjou

For from with masculine names beginning with a consonant, use du:

to come from the Berry	= venir du Berry

Regional adjectives

Related adjectives and nouns exist for most of the names of provinces and regions. Here is a list of the commonest:

Alsace	alsacien(ne)
Anjou	angevin(e)
Aquitaine	aquitain(e)
Auvergne	auvergnat(e)
Béarn	béarnais(e)
Berry	berrichon(ne)
Bourbonnais	bourbonnais(e)
Bourgogne	bourguignon(ne)
Bresse	bressan(e)
Bretagne	breton(ne)
Cévennes	cévenol(e)
Champagne	champenois(e)
Charente	charentais(e)
Corse	corse
Dauphiné	dauphinois(e)
Flandre	flamand(e)
Franche-Comté	franc-comtois(e)
Jura	jurassien(ne)
Languedoc	languedocien(ne)
Limousin	limousin(e)
Lorraine	lorrain(e)
Normandie	normand(e)
Périgord	périgourdin(e)
Picardie	picard(e)
Poitou	poitevin(e)
Provence	provençal(e)
Savoie	savoyard(e)
Touraine	tourangeau(-elle)
Vendée	vendéen(ne)
Vosges	vosgien(ne)

These adjectives mean of X, as in the following (where alsacien stands for any of them):

an Alsace accent	= un accent alsacien
Alsace costume	= le costume alsacien
the Alsace countryside	= les paysages alsaciens
Alsace traditions	= les traditions alsaciennes
Alsace villages	= les villages alsaciens

These words can also be used as nouns, meaning a person from X; in this case they are written with a capital letter:

a person from Alsace	= un Alsacien
an Alsace woman	= une Alsacienne
the people of Alsace	= les Alsaciens *mpl*

---

provisional driving licence *n* GB ~ permis *m* de conduire d'élève conducteur.

Provisional IRA *n* faction *f* dure de l'IRA.

provisionally /prə'vɪʒnəlɪ/ *adv* provisoirement.

proviso /prə'vaɪzəʊ/ *n* GEN condition *f*.

provisory /prə'vaɪzərɪ/ *adj* conditionnel/-elle.

provocation /ˌprɒvə'keɪʃn/ *n* provocation *f*.

provocative /prə'vɒkətɪv/ *adj* **1** (causing controversy) provocant; **to be ~** faire de la provocation; **2** (sexually) provocant; **3** (challenging) [*book, film*] qui fait réfléchir.

provoke /prə'vəʊk/ *vtr* **1** (annoy) provoquer; **to ~ sb to do** ou **into doing sth** pousser qn à faire qch; **2** (cause) susciter [*anger, complaints*]; provoquer [*laughter, reaction, crisis*].

provost /'prɒvəst/ *n* **1** GB UNIV, SCH principal *m*; **2** US UNIV doyen *m*; **3** (in Scotland) maire *m*; **4** RELIG prévôt *m*.

prow /praʊ/ *n* proue *f*.

prowess /'praʊɪs/ *n* **1** ¢ (skill) prouesses *fpl*; **2** (bravery) vaillance *f*.

prowl /praʊl/ **I** *n* **to be on the ~** rôder (**for** en quête de); **to go on the ~** [*animal*] partir en quête d'une proie; FIG faire une virée.
II *vtr* **to ~ the streets at night** rôder dans les rues la nuit.
III *vi* (also **~ around**, **~ about** GB) [*animal, person*] GEN rôder; (restlessly) [*person*] faire les cent pas; [*animal*] (in cage) tourner.

proximity /prɒk'sɪmətɪ/ *n* proximité *f*.

proxy /'prɒksɪ/ *n* **1** (person) mandataire *mf*; **to be sb's ~** avoir procuration pour qn; **2** (authority) GEN, POL, FIN procuration *f*; **by ~** par procuration.

prude /pruːd/ *n* bégueule *mf*.

prudent /'pruːdnt/ *adj* prudent.

prudently /'pruːdntlɪ/ *adv* (with caution) avec circonspection; (wisely) prudemment.

prudish /'pruːdɪʃ/ *adj* pudibond.

prune /pruːn/ **I** *n* CULIN pruneau *m*.
II *vtr* LIT (also **~ back**) (cut back) tailler; (thin out) élaguer; FIG élaguer [*essay, article*]; réduire [*budget, expenditure*].

pruning /'pruːnɪŋ/ *n* (of bush, tree) taille *f*.

prurient /'prʊərɪənt/ *adj* SOUT lubrique.

pry /praɪ/ **I** *n* US levier *m*.
II *vtr* US LIT **to ~ sth open** ouvrir qch en faisant levier; **to ~ the lid off a jar** forcer le couvercle d'un pot; **2** FIG **to ~ sth out of sb** soutirer qch à qn.
III *vi* **to ~ into** mettre son nez dans [*business*].

prying /'praɪɪŋ/ *adj* curieux/-ieuse, indiscret/-ète.

PS (*abrév* = **postscriptum**) PS *m*.

psalm /sɑːm/ *n* psaume *m*.

pseud○ /sjuːd, US 'suːd/ *n, adj* prétentieux/-ieuse (*m/f*).

pseudo+ /'sjuːdəʊ, US 'suːdəʊ/ *combining form* pseudo-.

pseudonym /'sjuːdənɪm, US 'suːd-/ *n* pseudonyme *m*.

PST *abrév* ▶ **Pacific Standard Time**.

PSV GB *abrév* ▶ **public service vehicle**.

psych /saɪk/ *v* ■ **psych out**○: **~ [sb/sth] out**, **~ out [sb/sth]**○ **1** (unnerve) déstabiliser; **2** US (outguess) deviner.
■ **psych up**○: **to ~ oneself up** se préparer (psychologiquement) (**for** pour).

psychiatric /ˌsaɪkɪ'ætrɪk/ *adj* [*hospital, care, nurse,* _treatment, help]_ psychiatrique; [_illness, disorder]_ mental; [_patient]_ d'un hôpital psychiatrique.

psychiatrist /saɪˈkaɪətrɪst, US sɪ-/ ▶ **1251** _n_ psychiatre _mf_.

psychiatry /saɪˈkaɪətrɪ, US sɪ-/ _n_ psychiatrie _f_.

psychic /ˈsaɪkɪk/ **I** _n_ médium _m_, voyant/-e _m/f_.
II _adj_ **1** (paranormal) parapsychologique; (telepathic) télépathe; **to have ~ powers** avoir des dons de voyance; **2** (psychological) psychologique.

psychical /ˈsaɪkɪkl/ _adj_ = **psychic** II.

psychic: **~ research** _n_ parapsychologie _f_; **~ surgery** _n_ opération _f_ à main nue.

psycho+ /ˈsaɪkəʊ/ _combining form_ psycho.

psychoanalyse GB, **psychoanalyze** US /ˌsaɪkəʊˈænəlaɪz/ _vtr_ psychanalyser.

psychoanalysis /ˌsaɪkəʊəˈnæləsɪs/ _n_ psychanalyse _f_; **to undergo ~** se faire psychanalyser.

psychoanalyst /ˌsaɪkəʊˈænəlɪst/ ▶ **1251** _n_ psychanalyste _mf_.

psychological /ˌsaɪkəˈlɒdʒɪkl/ _adj_ (all contexts) psychologique.

psychologist /saɪˈkɒlədʒɪst/ ▶ **1251** _n_ psychologue _mf_.

psychology /saɪˈkɒlədʒɪ/ _n_ (all contexts) psychologie _f_.

psychopath /ˈsaɪkəʊpæθ/ _n_ psychopathe _mf_.

psychopathic /ˌsaɪkəʊˈpæθɪk/ _adj_ [_personality_] psychopathique.

psychosis /saɪˈkəʊsɪs/ _n_ psychose _f_.

psychotherapist /ˌsaɪkəʊˈθerəpɪst/ ▶ **1251** _n_ psychothérapeute _mf_.

psychotic /saɪˈkɒtɪk/ _n, adj_ psychotique (_mf_).

pt _n_: _abrév écrite_ = **pint**.

PT _n_: _abrév_ ▶ **physical training**.

PTA _n_ (_abrév_ = **Parent-Teacher Association**) association _f_ des parents d'élèves et des professeurs.

PTO (_abrév_ = **please turn over**) TSVP.

puberty /ˈpjuːbətɪ/ _n_ puberté _f_.

public /ˈpʌblɪk/ **I** _n_ **the ~** le public; **the theatregoing ~** les amateurs _mpl_ de théâtre.
II _adj_ [_health, property, park, inquiry_] public/-ique; [_disquiet, enthusiasm, indifference, support_] général; [_library, amenity_] municipal; [_duty, spirit_] civique; **to be in the ~ eye** être exposé à l'opinion publique; **she has decided to go ~ (with her story)** elle a décidé de rendre son histoire publique; **the company is going ~** la société va être cotée en Bourse; **it is ~ knowledge that** il est de notoriété publique que; **let's go somewhere less ~** allons dans un endroit plus discret; **at ~ expense** aux frais du contribuable.
III in public _adv phr_ en public.

public address (system) _n_ (système _m_ de) sonorisation _f_.

publican /ˈpʌblɪkən/ ▶ **1251** _n_ GB patron/-onne _m/f_ de pub.

public assistance _n_ US aide _f_ sociale.

publication /ˌpʌblɪˈkeɪʃn/ _n_ publication _f_; **to accept sth for ~** accepter de publier qch; **on the day of ~** le jour de la sortie; **'not for ~'** 'confidentiel'.

publications list _n_ liste _f_ de titres.

public: **~ company** _n_ société _f_ anonyme par actions; **~ convenience** _n_ GB toilettes _fpl_; **~ corporation** _n_ GB organisme _m_ public; **~ examination** _n_ examen _m_ ouvert à tous; **~ gallery** _n_ tribune _f_ réservée au public; **~ holiday** _n_ GB jour _m_ férié.

public house _n_ **1** GB pub _m_; **2** US auberge _f_.

publicist /ˈpʌblɪsɪst/ _n_ (advertiser) agent _m_ de publicité; (press agent) attaché/-e _m/f_ de presse.

publicity /pʌˈblɪsətɪ/ **I** _n_ **1** (media attention) **to attract ~** attirer l'attention des médias; **to take place in a blaze of ~** avoir lieu sous les feux des médias; **to receive bad** ou **adverse ~** faire l'objet de critiques dans les médias; **2** (advertising) publicité _f_; **advance ~** promotion _f_; **3 ¢** (advertising material) (brochures) brochures _fpl_ publicitaires; (posters) affiches _fpl_ publicitaires; (films) films _mpl_ publicitaires.

II _noun modifier_ [_bureau, launch_] de publicité.

publicity: **~ agency** _n_ agence _f_ de publicité; **~ agent** ▶ **1251** _n_ attaché/-e _m/f_ de presse; **~ campaign**, **~ drive** _n_ (to sell product) campagne _f_ publicitaire; (to raise social issue) campagne _f_ de sensibilisation; **~ stunt** _n_ coup _m_ publicitaire.

publicize /ˈpʌblɪsaɪz/ _vtr_ **1** (raise awareness of) attirer l'attention du public sur; **well-~d**, **much-~d** [_event_] dont on parle beaucoup dans les médias; [_scandal, controversy_] qui fait ou qui a fait la une de tous les journaux; **2** (make public) rendre [qch] public; **3** (advertise) faire de la publicité pour; **well-~d, much-~d** annoncé à grand renfort de publicité.

publicly /ˈpʌblɪklɪ/ _adv_ publiquement; **~ owned** (state-owned) public; (floated on market) à actionnaires multiples; **~-funded** réalisé à l'aide de fonds publics.

public ownership _n_ **to be in ~, to be taken into ~** être nationalisé; **to bring [sth] under** ou **into ~** nationaliser [_industry_].

public: **~ prosecutor** _n_ procureur _m_ général; **~ purse** _n_ Trésor _m_ public; **Public Records Office**, **PRO** _npl_ Archives _fpl_ nationales.

public relations, **PR I** _n_ relations _fpl_ publiques.
II _noun modifier_ [_manager, department_] des relations publiques; [_consultant, expert_] en relations publiques; [_firm_] de relations publiques.

public: **~ relations officer**, **PRO** _n_ responsable _mf_ des relations publiques; **~ restroom** _n_ US toilettes _fpl_; **~ school** _n_ GB école _f_ privée; US école _f_ publique; **~ sector** _n_ secteur _m_ public; **~ servant** _n_ fonctionnaire _mf_.

public service _n_ **1** C (transport, education etc) service _m_ public; **2 ¢** (public administration, civil service) fonction _f_ publique.

public: **~ service broadcasting** _n_ **¢** chaînes _fpl_ de télévision et radios _fpl_ publiques; **~ service corporation** _n_ US service _m_ public non étatisé; **~ service vehicle**, **PSV** _n_ véhicule _m_ de transport en commun.

public speaking _n_ **the art of ~** l'art de parler en public.

public-spirited _adj_ à l'esprit civique; **it was ~ of you to do** tu as fait preuve de civisme en faisant.

public: **~ transport** _n_ transports _mpl_ en commun; **~ utilities** _npl_ équipements _mpl_ collectifs; **~ utility** _n_ service _m_ public.

publish /ˈpʌblɪʃ/ **I** _vtr_ **1** (print commercially) publier [_book, letter, guide_]; éditer [_newspaper, magazine_]; **who ~es Amis?** qui est-ce qui édite Amis?; **to be ~ed weekly** paraître toutes les semaines; **2** (make public) publier; **3** [_scholar, academic_] publier.
II _vi_ [_scholar, academic_] faire une publication ou des publications.

publisher /ˈpʌblɪʃə(r)/ ▶ **1251** _n_ (person) éditeur/-trice _m/f_; (company) maison _f_ d'édition; **newspaper ~** (person) patron _m_ de presse; (company) maison _f_ de presse.

publishing /ˈpʌblɪʃɪŋ/ **I** _n_ édition _f_.
II _noun modifier_ [_group, empire_] de presse.

publishing house _n_ maison _f_ d'édition.

puce /pjuːs/ ▶ **818** _adj_ rouge-brun _inv_; [_curtains, silk_] cramoisi.

puck /pʌk/ _n_ **1** (in ice-hockey) palet _m_; **2** (sprite) lutin _m_.

pucker /ˈpʌkə(r)/ _vi_ [_fabric, face, mouth_] se plisser; [_skirt_] goder; [_seam, cloth_] froncer.

pudding /ˈpʊdɪŋ/ _n_ **1** (cooked dish) pudding _m_; **steak-and-kidney ~** pain _m_ de viande au bœuf et aux rognons; **2** GB (dessert) dessert _m_; **3** GB (sausage) **black/white ~** boudin _m_ noir/blanc; **4** PÉJ (fat person) patapouf○ _mf_; (slow person) empoté○/-e PÉJ.
IDIOMS **the proof of the ~ is in the eating** PROV la qualité se révèle à l'usage.

pudding: **~ basin**, **~ bowl** _n_ jatte _f_; **~ rice** _n_ riz _m_ à grains ronds.

puddle /ˈpʌdl/ _n_ flaque _f_.

Puerto Rico /ˌpwɜːtəʊ ˈriːkə/ ▶ **840** _pr n_ Porto Rico _f_.

puff /pʌf/ **I** n **1** (of air, smoke, steam) bouffée f; (of breath) souffle m; **to disappear in a ~ of smoke** LIT disparaître dans un nuage de fumée; FIG partir en fumée; **~s of cloud** quelques petits nuages; **2**° GB (breath) souffle m; **3** CULIN feuilleté m; **4**° (favourable review) article m élogieux; (favourable publicity) battage° m.
II vtr **1** tirer sur [pipe]; **to ~ smoke** lancer des bouffées de fumée; **2**° (praise) faire du battage° autour de.
III vi **1** souffler; **smoke ~ed from the chimney** des bouffées de fumée s'échappaient de la cheminée; **to ~ (away) at** tirer des bouffées de [cigarette]; **to ~ along** [train] avancer en lançant des bouffées de fumée; **2** (pant) souffler; **she came ~ing and blowing up the hill** elle s'essoufflait en montant la côte.
■ **puff out**: ¶ ~ **out** [sails] se gonfler; [sleeve, skirt] bouffer; ¶ ~ **out** [sth], ~ [sth] **out 1** (swell) gonfler [sails]; **to ~ out one's cheeks** gonfler ses joues; **to ~ out one's chest** bomber le torse; **the bird ~ed out its feathers** l'oiseau a hérissé ses plumes; **2** (give out) **to ~ out smoke** lancer des bouffées de fumée.
■ **puff up**: ¶ ~ **up** [feathers] se hérisser; [eyes] bouffir; [rice] gonfler; ¶ ~ **up** [sth], ~ [sth] **up** hérisser [feathers, fur]; **to be ~ed up with pride** être rempli d'orgueil.
puffed /pʌft/ adj **1**° (breathless) essoufflé; **2** [sleeve] bouffant.
puffiness /'pʌfɪnɪs/ n (of face, eyes) boursouflure f.
puff pastry n pâte f feuilletée.
puffy /'pʌfɪ/ adj bouffi.
pug /pʌg/ n (also **~dog**) carlin m.
pugnacious /pʌg'neɪʃəs/ adj combatif/-ive.
pull /pʊl/ **I** n **1** (tug) coup m; **to give sth a ~** tirer sur qch; **2** (attraction) LIT force f; FIG attrait m (of de); **3**° (influence) influence f (over, with sur); **4**° (swig) lampée° f; **5**° (on cigarette etc) bouffée f; **6** SPORT (in rowing) coup m d'aviron; (in golf) coup m hooké; **it was a hard ~ to the summit** cela a été très dur d'arriver jusqu'au sommet; **7** (snag) in sweater maille f tirée.
II vtr **1** (tug) tirer [chain, curtain, hair, tail]; tirer sur [cord, rope]; **to ~ the sheets over one's head** se cacher la tête sous les draps; **to ~ a sweater over one's head** (put on) enfiler un pull-over; (take off) retirer un pull-over; **2** (tug, move) (towards oneself) tirer (**towards** vers); (by dragging) tirer (**along** le long de); (to show sth) entraîner [qn] par le bras [person]; **to ~ sb/sth through** faire passer qn/qch par [hole, window]; **3** (draw) GEN tirer; [vehicle] tracter; **4** (remove) **to ~ sth off** [child, cat] faire tomber qch de; **he ~ed her attacker off her** il a fait lâcher prise à son assaillant; **to ~ sth out of** tirer qch de [pocket, drawer]; **to ~ sb out of** retirer qn de [wreckage]; sortir qn de [river]; **5**° sortir [gun, knife]; **to ~ a gun on sb** menacer qn avec un pistolet; **6** (operate) appuyer sur [trigger]; tirer [lever]; **7** MED se faire une élongation à [muscle]; **8** (steer, guide) **to ~ a boat into the bank** amener une barque jusqu'à la berge; **to ~ a plane out of a dive** redresser un avion; **9** SPORT [golfer, batsman] hooker; **to ~ one's punches** LIT retenir ses coups; FIG **he didn't ~ his punches** il n'a pas mâché ses mots; **10**° GB tirer [pint of beer]; **11**° (attract) attirer; **12** (make) **to ~ a face** faire la grimace.
III vi **1** (tug) tirer (**at , on** sur); **2** (move, resist restraint) tirer (**at, on** sur); **to ~ ahead of sb** [athlete, rally driver] prendre de l'avance sur qn; [company] avoir de l'avance sur; **3** SPORT [golfer, batsman] hooker; (row) ramer.
IDIOMS **~ the other one, (it's got bells on)**°! à d'autres (mais pas à moi)°!
■ **pull along**: ¶ ~ [sth] **along**, ~ **along** [sth] tirer; ¶ ~ [sb] **along** tirer qn par le bras.
■ **pull apart**: ¶ ~ **apart** se séparer; ¶ ~ [sb/sth] **apart 1** (dismantle) démonter; **2** (destroy) [child] mettre en pièces; [animal] déchiqueter; **3** FIG (disparage) descendre [qch] en flammes; **4** (separate) séparer.
■ **pull away**: ¶ ~ **away 1** (move away, leave) [car] démarrer; [person] s'écarter; **2** (become detached, increase

lead) se détacher; ¶ ~ **away from** [sb/sth] s'éloigner de [person, kerb]; ¶ ~ [sb/sth] **away** éloigner [person]; retirer [hand]; **to ~ sth away from sb** arracher qch à qn; **to ~ sb/sth away from** éloigner qn/qch de [danger]; écarter qn/qch de [window, wall etc].
■ **pull back**: ¶ ~ **back 1** [troops] se retirer (**from** de); **2** [car, person] reculer; **3** (close the gap) rattraper mon/son etc retard; ¶ ~ [sb/sth] **back**, ~ **back** [sb/sth] (restrain) retenir; (tug back) ~ **the rope back hard** tire fort sur la corde.
■ **pull down**: ¶ ~ [sth] **down**, ~ **down** [sth] (demolish) démolir; (lower) baisser [blind, trousers]; réduire [inflation]; baisser [prices]; ¶ ~ [sb/sth] **down**, ~ **down** [sb/sth] LIT tirer (**onto** sur); FIG entraîner.
■ **pull in**: ¶ ~ **in** [car, bus, driver] s'arrêter; **to ~ in to the kerb** s'arrêter le long du trottoir; ¶ ~ [sb] **in**, ~ **in** [sb] [police] appréhender [person]; **2** [exhibition, show] attirer [crowds, tourists]; ¶ ~ [sth] **in**, ~ **in** [sth] **1** (retract) rentrer; **2**° (earn) réunir [money]; **3** arrêter [car].
■ **pull off**: ¶ ~ **off** [lid] s'enlever; [handle] être amovible; ¶ ~ **off** [sth] (leave) quitter [road]; ¶ ~ **off** [sth], ~ [sth] **off 1** (remove) ôter [coat, sweater]; enlever [shoes, socks, lid, wrapping, sticker]; **2**° (clinch) réussir [raid, robbery]; conclure [deal]; réaliser [coup, feat]; décrocher [win, victory].
■ **pull out**: ¶ ~ **out 1** (emerge) [car, truck] déboîter; **just as the train was ~ing out** au moment où le train partait; **to ~ out of** (withdraw) se retirer (**of** de); **3** (come away) [drawer] s'enlever; [component, section] se détacher; ¶ ~ [sth] **out, ~ out** [sth] **1** extraire [tooth]; enlever [splinter]; arracher [weeds]; **2** (from pocket) sortir; **3** (withdraw) retirer [troops].
■ **pull over**: ¶ ~ **over** [motorist, car] s'arrêter (sur le côté); ¶ ~ [sb/sth] **over** [police] forcer [qn/qch] à se ranger sur le côté.
■ **pull through**: ¶ ~ **through** [accident victim] s'en tirer; ¶ ~ [sb/sth] **through** faire passer.
■ **pull together**: ¶ ~ **together** faire un effort; ¶ ~ [sth] **together**: ~ **the two pieces together** mettez les deux morceaux l'un contre l'autre; **to ~ oneself together** se ressaisir.
■ **pull up**: ¶ ~ **up 1** (stop) s'arrêter; **2** (regain lost ground) rattraper son retard; ¶ ~ **up** [sth], ~ **up** [sth] **1** (uproot) arracher; **2** (lift) lever; **to ~ up one's trousers/socks** remonter son pantalon/ses chaussettes; **to ~ up a chair** prendre une chaise; **3** (stop) arrêter [horse]; ¶ ~ [sb] **up 1** (lift) hisser; **2** (reprimand) réprimander; **3** (stop) arrêter [driver]; disqualifier [athlete].
pull-down menu n COMPUT menu m déroulant.
pulley /'pʊli/ n poulie f.
pull-in /'pʊlɪn/ n GB **1**° (café) routier m; **2** (lay-by) aire f de stationnement (en bordure de la chaussée).
pulling power n pouvoir m d'attraction.
Pullman /'pʊlmən/ n **1** (train) pullman m; (carriage) voiture f pullman; **2** US (suitcase) valise f.
pull-off /'pʊlɒf/ adj détachable.
pull-out /'pʊlaʊt/ **I** n **1** (in book etc) encart m; **2** (withdrawal) retrait m.
II adj [supplement] détachable; [map, diagram] horstexte inv.
pullover /'pʊləʊvə(r)/ n pull-over m.
pulmonary /'pʌlmənərɪ, US -nerɪ/ adj pulmonaire.
pulp /pʌlp/ **I** n **1** (soft centre) pulpe f; (crushed mass) pâte f; **to beat sb to a ~**° réduire qn en bouillie°; **2**° PÉJ (trashy books) littérature f de gare PÉJ.
II noun modifier [novel, literature] de gare; [magazine] à sensation.
III vtr **1** (crush) écraser [fruit, vegetable]; réduire [qch] en pâte [wood, cloth]; mettre [qch] au pilon [newspapers, books]; **2**° FIG (in fight) écrabouiller°.
pulpit /'pʊlpɪt/ n (in church) chaire f.
pulsate /pʌl'seɪt, US 'pʌlseɪt/ **I** vi [vein, heart] palpiter; [blood] circuler.

II pulsating *pres p adj* **1** LIT (beating) [*heart, vein*] qui palpite; [*beat, rhythm*] entraînant; **2** FIG (exciting) palpitant.

pulse /pʌls/ **I** *n* **1** ANAT, MED pouls *m*; **his ~ raced** son cœur battait très vite; **to take/feel sb's ~** prendre/tâter le pouls de qn; **to have one's finger on the ~ of sth** FIG être à l'écoute de qch; **2** (beat, vibration) (of music) rythme *m*; (of drums) battement *m* rythmique; **3** AUDIO, ELEC, PHYS impulsion *f*; **4** BOT, CULIN graine *f* de légumineuse.

II *vi* [*blood*] circuler; [*heart*] battre fort.

pulse rate *n* pouls *m*.

pulverize /'pʌlvəraɪz/ *vtr* LIT, FIG pulvériser.

pumice /'pʌmɪs/ *n* (also **~ stone**) pierre *f* ponce.

pummel /'pʌml/ *vtr* (*p prés etc* **-ll-** GB, **-l-** US) marteler.

pump /pʌmp/ **I** *n* **1** TECH pompe *f*; **bicycle ~** pompe à bicyclette; **to prime the ~** LIT amorcer la pompe; FIG réamorcer la pompe; **2** (plimsoll) chaussure *f* de sport; (flat shoe) GB ballerine *f*; (shoe with heel) US chaussure *f* à talon.

II *vtr* **1** (push) pomper (**out of** de); **to ~ air into a tyre** injecter de l'air dans un pneu; **to ~ sewage into the sea** déverser les eaux usées dans la mer; **the boiler ~s water to the radiators** la chaudière distribue l'eau dans les radiateurs; **to ~ bullets** cracher des balles; **to ~ sb full of drugs**⚬ gaver qn de médicaments; **to ~ iron**⚬ faire de la gonflette⚬; **2** actionner [*handle, lever*]; **3** (shake) **to ~ sb's hand** donner une poignée de main vigoureuse à qn; **4**⚬ (question) cuisiner⚬ [*person*] (**about** à propos de); **5** MED **to ~ sb's stomach** faire un lavage d'estomac à qn.

III *vi* **1** (function) [*machine, piston*] fonctionner; **2** (flow) gicler (**from, out of** de); **3** (beat) battre violemment.

■ **pump out**: **~ out** [*sth*], **~** [*sth*] **out 1** (pour out) débiter [*music, propaganda*]; cracher [*fumes*]; déverser [*sewage*]; **2** (empty) pomper [*qch*] à sec; **to ~ sb's stomach out** faire un lavage d'estomac à qn.

■ **pump up**: **~ up** [*sth*], **~** [*sth*] **up 1** (inflate) gonfler; **2**⚬ monter [*volume*].

pump attendant ▶ **1251** *n* pompiste *mf*.

pumpkin /'pʌmpkɪn/ *n* citrouille *f*.

pun /pʌn/ **I** *n* jeu *m* de mots, calembour *m* (**on** sur).

II *vi* (*p prés etc* **-nn-**) faire des jeux de mots, faire des calembours.

punch /pʌntʃ/ **I** *n* **1** (blow) coup *m* de poing; **2** FIG (forcefulness) (of person) punch⚬ *m*; (of style, performance) énergie *f*; **it lacks ~** ça manque de nerf⚬; **3** (tool) (for leather) alène *f*; (for metal) perçoir *m*; COMPUT perforateur *m*; **ticket ~** pince *f* à composter; **4** (drink) punch *m*.

II *vtr* **1** (hit) **to ~ sb in the face** donner un coup de poing dans la figure de qn; **to ~ sb on the nose** donner un coup de poing dans le nez de qn; **2** COMPUT, TELECOM perforer [*cards, tape*]; appuyer sur [*key*]; **3** (make hole in) (manually) poinçonner; (in machine) composter [*ticket*].

III *vi* cogner, donner des coups de poing.

IDIOMS **to pack a ~**⚬ [*boxer*] avoir du punch; [*cocktail*] être corsé; [*book, film*] avoir un fort impact; **to pull no ~es** LIT, FIG ne pas y aller de main morte.

■ **punch in**: **~ in** [*sth*], **~** [*sth*] **in** COMPUT introduire [*data*].

■ **punch out**: **~ out** [*sth*], **~** [*sth*] **out** (shape) découper qch à l'emporte-pièce; **to ~ out a number on the phone** composer un numéro au téléphone.

Punch /pʌntʃ/ *pr n* Polichinelle.

IDIOMS **to be as pleased as ~** être ravi.

Punch-and-Judy show *n* **~** (spectacle *m* de) guignol *m*.

punch: **~bag** *n* GB SPORT sac *m* de sable; **~ ball** *n* punching-ball *m*; **~ card** *n* carte *f* perforée; **~-drunk** *adj* (in boxing) abruti par les coups; FIG (from tiredness) abruti de fatigue; **~ line** *n* chute *f* (*d'une histoire drôle*); **~-up**⚬ *n* GB bagarre⚬ *f*.

punchy⚬ /'pʌntʃɪ/ *adj* [*person, style*] énergique; [*article*] percutant.

punctilious /pʌŋk'tɪlɪəs/ *adj* SOUT scrupuleux/-euse.

punctual /'pʌŋktʃʊəl/ *adj* [*person, delivery*] ponctuel/-elle; **to be ~ for sth** être à l'heure pour qch.

punctuality /ˌpʌŋktʃʊ'ælətɪ/ *n* ponctualité *f*.

punctually /'pʌŋktʃʊəlɪ/ *adv* [*start, arrive, leave*] à l'heure; **to arrive ~ at 10** arriver ponctuellement à 10 heures.

punctuate /'pʌŋktʃʊeɪt/ *vtr, vi* ponctuer.

punctuation /ˌpʌŋktʃʊ'eɪʃn/ *n* ponctuation *f*.

punctuation mark *n* signe *m* de ponctuation.

puncture /'pʌŋktʃə(r)/ **I** *n* (in tyre, balloon, airbed) crevaison *f*; (in skin) piqûre *f*; **we had a ~ on the way** on a crevé en chemin.

II *vtr* **1** (perforate) crever [*tyre, balloon, airbed*]; ponctionner [*organ*]; **to ~ a lung** MED se perforer un poumon; **2** FIG démolir [*myth*]; **to ~ sb's pride** ou **ego** décontenancer qn.

III *vi* [*tyre, balloon*] crever.

puncture: **~ (repair) kit** *n* boîte *f* de rustines®; **~-proof** *adj* increvable.

pundit /'pʌndɪt/ *n* (expert) expert/-e *m/f*.

pungency /'pʌndʒənsɪ/ *n* (of sauce, dish) goût *m* piquant; (of smoke, smell) âcreté *f*; (of speech, satire) mordant *m*.

pungent /'pʌndʒənt/ *adj* [*flavour*] relevé; [*smell*, *gas, smoke*] âcre; [*speech, satire*] mordant, virulent.

punish /'pʌnɪʃ/ *vtr* **1** punir; **2**⚬ (treat roughly) malmener [*opponent*]; fatiguer [*car, horse*].

punishable /'pʌnɪʃəbl/ *adj* [*offence*] punissable.

punishing /'pʌnɪʃɪŋ/ **I** *n* punition *f*; **to take a ~**⚬ prendre une raclée⚬.

II *adj* [*schedule, pace*] éprouvant; [*defeat*] cuisant.

punishment /'pʌnɪʃmənt/ *n* **1** punition *f*; (stronger) châtiment *m*; **as ~ for** en punition de; **2**⚬ (rough treatment) **to take a lot of ~** être mis à rude épreuve.

punitive /'pjuːnətɪv/ *adj* [*measure, action*] punitif/-ive; [*taxation*] très sévère; **~ damages** JUR dommages et intérêts à valeur répressive.

punnet /'pʌnɪt/ *n* GB barquette *f*.

punt /pʌnt/ **I** *n* **1** (boat) barque *f* (*à fond plat*); **2** (Irish pound) livre *f* irlandaise.

II *vi* **1** (travel by punt) **to go ~ing** faire une promenade en barque; **2** (bet) miser.

punter⚬ /'pʌntə(r)/ *n* GB **1** (at races) parieur *m*; (at casino) joueur/-euse *m/f*; **2** (average client) client/-e *m/f*.

puny /'pjuːnɪ/ *adj* [*person, body*] chétif/-ive; [*effort*] piteux/-euse.

pup /pʌp/ **I** *n* (dog) chiot *m*; (seal, otter etc) petit *m*.

II *vi* (*p prés etc* **-pp-**) [*bitch, seal*] mettre bas.

IDIOMS **to be sold a ~**⚬ se faire avoir⚬.

pupil /'pjuːpɪl/ *n* **1** SCH élève *mf*; **2** ANAT pupille *f*.

puppet /'pʌpɪt/ **I** *n* LIT, FIG marionnette *f*.

II *noun modifier* [*government, state*] fantoche.

puppy /'pʌpɪ/ *n* chiot *m*.

puppy: **~ fat** *n* ⊄ rondeurs *fpl* de l'enfance; **~ love** *n* amour *m* d'adolescent/-e.

purchase /'pɜːtʃəs/ **I** *n* **1** COMM achat *m*; **2** (grip) prise *f*; **to get** ou **gain (a) ~ on** [*climber*] trouver une prise sur; [*vehicle*] adhérer à.

II *vtr* **1** COMM acheter; **2** FIG acquérir [*liberty*].

purchaser /'pɜːtʃəsə(r)/ *n* acheteur/-euse *m/f*.

purchasing /'pɜːtʃəsɪŋ/ *n* achat *m*.

purchasing power *n* pouvoir *m* d'achat.

purdah /'pɜːdə/ *n*: isolement des femmes conformément à certaines religions; **to go into ~** FIG s'isoler.

pure /pjʊə(r)/ *adj* (all contexts) pur; **~ new wool** laine *f* vierge; **by ~ accident** de façon purement accidentelle; **~ research** recherche *f* fondamentale.

purebred /'pjʊəbred/ **I** *n* (horse) pur-sang *m inv*.

II *adj* de race, pur-sang *inv*.

puree /'pjʊəreɪ, US pjʊə'reɪ/ **I** *n* purée *f*.

II *vtr* écraser; **~d vegetables** purée de légumes.

purely /'pjʊəlɪ/ *adv* purement; **~ to be polite** uniquement pour être poli.

purgatorial /ˌpɜːgə'tɔːrɪəl/ *adj* du purgatoire; FIG infernal.

purgatory /'pɜːgətrɪ, US -tɔːrɪ/ n purgatoire m.

purge /pɜːdʒ/ I n (all contexts) purge f.
II vtr 1 GEN, MED purger; 2 POL purger [country, party]; éliminer [extremists, dissidents etc]; 3 RELIG expier [sin]; purger LITER [mind, heart].

purification /ˌpjʊərɪfɪ'keɪʃn/ n 1 (of water, air, chemicals) épuration f; 2 RELIG purification f.

purifier /'pjʊərɪfaɪə(r)/ n (for water) épurateur m; (for air) purificateur m.

purify /'pjʊərɪfaɪ/ vtr GEN, TECH épurer; RELIG purifier.

purist /'pjʊərɪst/ n, adj puriste (mf).

puritan /'pjʊərɪtən/ n, adj FIG puritain/-e (mf).

purity /'pjʊərətɪ/ n pureté f.

purl /pɜːl/ I n maille f à l'envers.
II vtr tricoter [qch] à l'envers [row, stitch].

purple /'pɜːpl/ ▶818 | I n 1 (colour) violet m; 2 RELIG **the ~** (rank) la pourpre; (bishops) GB évêques mpl anglicans.
II adj (bluish) violet/-ette; (reddish) pourpre; **to turn ~** (in anger) devenir rouge de colère.

purple passage, purple patch n LITERAT PÉJ passage m ampoulé.

purplish /'pɜːplɪʃ/ ▶818 | adj violacé.

purport SOUT I /'pɜːpɔːt/ n sens m.
II /pə'pɔːt/ vtr **to ~ to do** prétendre faire.

purpose /'pɜːpəs/ I n 1 (aim) but m; **for the ~ of doing** dans le but de faire; **for cooking ~s** pour la cuisine; **for our ~s, we can assume that...** dans l'optique qui nous intéresse, nous pouvons considérer que...; **for the ~s of this book** pour (les besoins de) ce livre; **for all practical ~s** en pratique; **unknown** usage m inconnu; **put it in the bin provided for the ~** mets-le dans la poubelle prévue à cet effet; **to some** ou **good ~** utilement; **to no ~** inutilement; **to the ~** SOUT à propos; 2 (determination) (also **strength of ~**) résolution f; **to have a sense of ~** savoir ce que l'on veut.
II **on ~** adv phr exprès.

purpose-built /ˌpɜːpəs'bɪlt/ adj GB conçu pour un usage déterminé; **a ~ apartment** ≈ un appartement indépendant.

purposeful /'pɜːpəsfl/ adj résolu.

purposely /'pɜːpəslɪ/ adv exprès, intentionnellement.

purpose-made /ˌpɜːpəs'meɪd/ adj GB fait spécialement (**for** pour).

purr /pɜː(r)/ I n (of cat, engine) ronronnement m.
II vi [cat, engine] ronronner.

purse /pɜːs/ n 1 (for money) porte-monnaie m inv; US (handbag) sac m à main; 2 FIG (resources) moyens mpl; 3 (prize) prix m.
IDIOMS **to hold the ~-strings** tenir les cordons de la bourse; **to ~ one's lips** faire une moue désapprobatrice.

purser /'pɜːsə(r)/ ▶1251 | n commissaire m de bord.

purse snatcher n US voleur/-euse m/f de sacs à main.

pursue /pə'sjuː, US -'suː-/ vtr poursuivre [person, aim, ambition, studies]; mener [policy]; se livrer à [occupation, interest]; **to ~ a career** faire carrière (**in** dans); **to ~ a line of inquiry** suivre une piste.

pursuer /pə'sjuːə(r), US -'suː-/ n poursuivant/-e m/f.

pursuit /pə'sjuːt, US -'suː-/ n 1 ¢ (following) poursuite f; **in ~ of** à la poursuite de; **the ~ of happiness** la recherche du bonheur; **in close** ou **hot ~** à vos/ses etc trousses; 2 (hobby) passe-temps m; **artistic ~s** activités fpl artistiques.

push /pʊʃ/ I n 1 LIT (shove, press) poussée f; **to give sb/sth a ~** pousser qn/qch; **the car won't start—we need a ~** la voiture ne veut pas démarrer—il faut la pousser; **at the ~ of a button** en appuyant sur un bouton; 2 (campaign, drive) campagne f; 3 FIG (stimulus) impulsion f; **to give sth/sb a ~** encourager qch/qn; **this gave me the ~ I needed** c'est ça qui m'a décidé à faire quelque chose; **to give sth a ~ in the right direction** faire avancer qch

dans la bonne direction; 4 MIL poussée f; **the big ~** la grande offensive; 5 (spirit, drive) esprit m battant.
II vtr 1 (move, shove, press) GEN pousser; appuyer sur [button, switch, bell]; **to ~ sb/sth away** repousser qn/qch; **she ~ed him down the stairs** elle l'a poussé dans l'escalier; **to ~ one's finger into** enfoncer son doigt dans; **to ~ sth into sb's hand** mettre qch de force dans la main de qn; **to ~ sb/sth out of the way** écarter qn/qch; **to ~ sb aside** écarter qn; **to ~ one's way through sth** se frayer un chemin à travers qch; **to ~ sth off the road** enlever qch de la chaussée; **to ~ the door open, to ~ the door shut** pousser la porte; **to ~ sb too far** FIG pousser qn à bout; **to be ~ed** (under pressure) être à la bourre○; **to be ~ed for sth** (short of) être à court de qch; 2○ (promote) faire la promotion de [product]; promouvoir [policy, theory]; 3○ (sell) vendre [drugs].
III vi pousser; **to ~ against** s'appuyer contre; **to ~ at sth** repousser qch; **to ~ past sb** bousculer qn; **to ~ through** se frayer un chemin à travers.
IV v refl **to ~ oneself upright** se redresser; **to ~ oneself through a gap** passer par un trou; (drive oneself) se pousser (**to do** à faire).
IDIOMS **at a ~**○ GB s'il le faut; **if it comes to the ~** si on en vient à cette extrémité; **to be ~ing 50** friser la cinquantaine; **to give sb the ~**○ GB (fire) virer qn○; (break up with) larguer qn○; **to ~ one's luck, to ~ it**○ forcer sa chance; **that's ~ing it a bit**○! (cutting it fine) c'est un peu juste ou risqué!

■ **push ahead** (with plans) persévérer (**with** dans); (on journey) continuer.

■ **push around**○: **~ [sb] around** FIG bousculer.

■ **push back: ~ [sth] back, ~ back [sth]** repousser [forest, frontier, date, enemy]; pousser [object, furniture].

■ **push down: ¶ ~ [sth] down, ~ down [sth]** faire chuter; **¶ ~ down [sb], ~ [sb] down** faire tomber.

■ **push for: ~ for [sth]** faire pression en faveur de.

■ **push forward: ¶ ~ forward** (with plans) persévérer (**with** dans); (on journey) continuer; **¶ ~ [sth] forward, ~ forward [sth]** faire valoir; **to ~ oneself forward** se mettre en avant.

■ **push in: ¶ ~ in** s'introduire dans la file; **¶ ~ [sth] in, ~ in [sth]** enfoncer [button, door, window].

■ **push off** 1○ GB filer○; 2 NAUT pousser.

■ **push on** = **push ahead**.

■ **push over: ¶ ~ over**○ (move over) se pousser; **~ over [sth/sb], ~ [sth/sb] over** renverser [person, table, car].

■ **push through: ~ [sth] through, ~ through [sth]** faire voter [bill, legislation]; faire passer [deal]; **to ~ through a passport application** accélérer l'obtention d'un passeport.

■ **push up: ~ up [sth], ~ [sth] up** faire monter.

push-button /'pʊʃbʌtn/ I **push button** n bouton-poussoir m.
II adj [control, tuning, selection] par bouton-poussoir; [telephone] à touches; [radio] à boutons-poussoirs; [dialling] au clavier.

push: ~cart n charrette f à bras; **~chair** n GB poussette f.

pusher○ /'pʊʃə(r)/ n (also **drug ~**) revendeur/-euse m/f de drogue.

pushiness /'pʊʃɪnɪs/ n (ambition) arrivisme m; (tenacity) obstination f.

pushing /'pʊʃɪŋ/ n bousculade f.

Pushkin /'pʊʃkɪn/ pr n Pouchkine.

push: ~over n (easy to do, beat) jeu m d'enfant; **~pin** n US punaise f; **~rod** n poussoir m.

push-start I /'pʊʃstɑːt/ n **to give sth a ~** pousser qch pour le/la faire démarrer.
II /ˌpʊʃ'stɑːt/ vtr pousser [qch] pour le/la faire démarrer [vehicle].

push-up /'pʊʃʌp/ n SPORT pompe○ f.

pushy○ /'pʊʃɪ/ adj (ambitious) arriviste; **she's very ~** (assertive) elle s'impose.

puss○ /pʊs/ n 1 (cat) minet○ m; 2 US (mouth) gueule○ f.

pussy cat *n* **1** LANG ENFANTIN minou *m* BABY
TALK; **2**○ FIG **he's a real ~** il est très conciliant.

pussyfoot○ /'pʊsɪfʊt/ *vi* (also **~ around**) tourner
autour du pot○.

pussyfooting /'pʊsɪfʊtɪŋ/ **I** *n* ¢ tergiversations *fpl*.
II *adj* [*attitude, behaviour*] timoré.

put /pʊt/ **I** *vtr* (*p prés* **-tt-**; *prét, pp* **put**) **1** (place)
mettre [*object, person*]; **to ~ more sugar in one's
tea** ajouter du sucre dans son thé; **to ~ more soap
in the bathroom** remettre du savon dans la salle de
bains; **2** (cause to go or undergo) **to ~ sth through**
glisser qch dans [*letterbox*]; passer qch par [*window*];
to ~ one's head through the window passer la
tête par la fenêtre; **to ~ one's fist through the
window** casser la fenêtre d'un coup de poing; **to ~
sth through a test** faire passer un test à qch; **to ~
sth through a process** faire suivre un processus à
qch; **to ~ sb through** envoyer qn à [*university,
college*]; faire passer qn par [*suffering, ordeal*]; faire
passer [qch] à qn [*test*]; faire suivre [qch] à qn [*course*];
after all you've put me through après tout ce que tu
m'as fait subir; **to ~ one's hand to** porter la main à
[*mouth*]; **to ~ sb to washing sth** faire laver qch à
qn; **3** (devote, invest) **to ~ money/energy into sth**
investir de l'argent/son énergie dans qch; **to ~ a lot
into** s'engager à fond pour [*work, project*]; sacrifier
beaucoup à [*marriage*]; **4** (add) **to ~ sth towards**
mettre qch pour; **~ it towards some new clothes**
dépense-le en nouveaux vêtements; **to ~ tax/duty
on sth** taxer/imposer qch; **to ~ a penny on income
tax** GB augmenter l'impôt sur le revenu d'un pour-
cent; **5** (express) **how would you ~ that in French?**
comment dirait-on ça en français?; **to ~ it bluntly**
pour parler franchement; **let me ~ it another way**
laissez-moi m'exprimer différemment; **that was very
well put** c'était très bien tourné; **to ~ one's feelings into words** trouver les mots pour exprimer ses
sentiments; **6** (offer for consideration) présenter [*point of
view, proposal*]; **to ~ sth to** soumettre qch à [*meeting, conference, board*]; **to ~ sth to the vote** mettre
qch au vote; **7** (rate, rank) placer; **I ~ a sense of
humour first** pour moi le plus important c'est le sens
de l'humour; **to ~ safety first** faire passer la sécurité avant tout; **8** (estimate) **to ~ sth at** évaluer qch à
[*sum*]; **I'd ~ him at about 40** je lui donnerais à peu
près 40 ans; **9** SPORT lancer [*shot*].
II *v refl* (*p prés* **-tt-**; *prét, pp* **put**) **to ~ oneself in a
strong position/in sb's place** se mettre dans une posi-
tion de force/à la place de qn.
IDIOMS **I wouldn't ~ it past him!** je ne pense pas
que ça le gênerait!; **to ~ one over** OU **across** GB **on
sb**○ faire marcher qn○.

■ **put about**: **~ about** NAUT virer de bord; ¶
~ [sth] about, ~ about [sth] 1 (spread) faire circuler; **it is being put about that** le bruit court que; **2**
NAUT faire virer de bord.

■ **put across**: **~ across [sth], ~ [sth] across**
communiquer [*idea, message, case*]; mettre [qch] en
valeur [*personality*]; **to ~ oneself across** se mettre
en valeur.

■ **put aside**: **~ aside [sth], ~ [sth] aside** mettre
[qch] de côté.

■ **put away**: ¶ **~ away [sth], ~ [sth] away 1**
(tidy away) ranger; **2** (save) mettre [qch] de côté; **3**○
avaler [*food*]; descendre○ [*drink*]; **~ away [sb]**○,
~ [sb] away○ (in mental hospital) enfermer; (in prison)
boucler○.

■ **put back**: **~ back [sth], ~ [sth] back 1** (return,
restore) remettre; **to ~ sth back where it belongs**
remettre qch à sa place; **2** (postpone) remettre [*meeting,
departure*] (**to** à; **until** jusqu'à); repousser [*date*]; **3**
retarder [*clock, watch*]; **4** (delay) retarder (**by** de); **5**○
(knock back) descendre○.

■ **put by** GB: **~ [sth] by, ~ by [sth]** mettre [qch]
de côté.

■ **put down**: ¶ **~ down** [*aircraft*] atterrir; ¶ **~
[sth] down, ~ down [sth] 1** poser [*object, plane*];
mettre [*rat poison etc*]; **2** (suppress) réprimer; **3** (write
down) mettre (par écrit); **4** (ascribe) **to ~ sth down to**
mettre qch sur le compte de; **to ~ sth down to the**

fact that imputer qch au fait que; **5** (charge) **to ~ sth
down to** mettre qch sur; **6** (destroy) (by injection)
piquer; (by other method) abattre [*animal*]; **7** (deposit)
~ down a deposit verser des arrhes; **to ~ £50
down on sth** verser 50 livres d'arrhes sur qch; **8**
(store) mettre [qch] en cave [*wine*]; affiner [*cheese*]; **9**
(put on agenda) inscrire [qch] à l'ordre du jour; ¶ **~
[sb] down, ~ down [sb] 1** déposer [*passenger*]; **2**
(humiliate) rabaisser; **3** SCH (into lower group) faire
descendre (**from** de; **to, into** à); **4** (classify, count in) **to
~ sb down as** considérer qn comme [*possibility,
candidate, fool*]; **to ~ sb down for** (note as wanting or
offering) compter [qch] pour qn [*contribution*]; (put on
waiting list) inscrire qn sur la liste d'attente pour; **to
~ sb down for £10** compter 10 livres pour qn; **to
~ sb down for three tickets** réserver trois billets
pour qn.

■ **put forward**: ¶ **~ forward [sth], ~ [sth]
forward 1** (propose) avancer [*idea, theory, name*];
soumettre [*plan, suggestion*]; émettre [*opinion*]; **2** (in
time) avancer [*meeting, date, clock*] (**by** de; **to** à); ¶ **~
[sb] forward, ~ forward [sb]** présenter la candidature de (**for** pour); ¶ **~ sb forward as** présenter qn
comme.

■ **put in**: ¶ **~ in 1** [*ship*] faire escale (**at** à; **to** dans;
for pour); **2** (apply) **to ~ in for** postuler pour [*job,
promotion, rise*]; demander [*transfer, overtime*]; ¶ **~
in [sth], ~ [sth] in 1** (fit, install) installer; **2** (make)
faire [*request, claim, offer*]; **to ~ in an application
for** déposer une demande de [*visa etc*]; poser sa candidature pour [*job*]; **to ~ in a protest** protester; **to
~ in an appearance** faire une apparition; **3** passer
[*time, hours, days*]; contribuer pour [*sum, amount*]; **to
~ in a lot of time doing** consacrer beaucoup de
temps à faire; **to ~ in a good day's work** avoir une
bonne journée de travail; **to ~ in a lot of work** se
donner beaucoup de mal; **4** (insert) mettre [*paragraph,
reference*]; **5** (elect) élire; ¶ **~ [sb] in for** présenter
[qn] pour [*exam*]; poser la candidature de [qn] pour
[*promotion, job*]; recommander [qn] pour [*prize,
award*].

■ **put off**: ¶ **~ off** NAUT partir; **to ~ off from**
s'éloigner de [*quay, jetty*]; ¶ **~ off [sth], ~ [sth] off
1** (delay, defer) remettre [qch] (à plus tard); **2** (turn off)
éteindre [*light, radio*]; couper [*heating*]; ¶ **~ off [sb],
~ [sb] off 1** (fob off, postpone seeing) décommander
[*guest*]; dissuader [*person*]; **to be easily put off** se décourager facilement; **2** (repel) [*appearance, smell*] dégoûter; [*manner, person*] déconcerter; **3** GB (distract)
distraire; **4** (drop off) déposer [*passenger*].

■ **put on**: ¶ **~ on [sth], ~ [sth] on 1** mettre [*garment, make-up*]; **2** (switch on) allumer [*light, heating*];
mettre [*record, tape, music*]; **to ~ the kettle on**
mettre de l'eau à chauffer; **to ~ the brakes on** freiner; **3** prendre [*weight, kilo*]; rajouter [*extra duty, tax*];
4 (produce) monter [*play, exhibition*]; **5** (adopt) prendre
[*accent, expression*]; **he's ~ting it on** il fait semblant;
6 (offer) ajouter [*train, bus service*]; proposer [*meal*]; **7**
avancer [*clock*]; **8** (bet) parier; ¶ **~ [sb] on 1** TELE-
COM passer; **I'll ~ him on** je vous le passe; **2**○ US
faire marcher○; **3** (recommend) **to ~ sb on to sth**
indiquer qch à qn; **who put you on to me?** qui vous
a envoyé à moi?; **4** (put on track of) **to ~ sb on to**
mettre qn sur la piste de○.

■ **put out**: ¶ **~ out** NAUT partir; ¶ **~ out [sth],
~ [sth] out 1** (extend) tendre [*hand*]; **to ~ out
one's tongue** tirer la langue; **2** (extinguish) éteindre; **3**
sortir [*bin, garbage*]; faire sortir [*cat*]; **4** (issue) diffuser [*report, warning, statement*]; **5** (arrange) mettre
[*food, dishes, towels etc*]; **6** (sprout) [*plant*] déployer
[*buds, shoots*]; **7** (distort) fausser [*figure, estimate,
result*]; **8** (dislocate) se démettre [*shoulder*]; **9** (subcontract) confier [qch] en sous-traitance (**to** à); ¶ **~ [sb]
out 1** (inconvenience) déranger; **to ~ oneself out for
sb** se donner beaucoup de mal pour qn; **2** (annoy)
contrarier; **3** (evict) expulser.

■ **put over = put across**.

■ **put through**: **~ [sth/ sb] through, ~ through
[sth/sb] 1** (implement) faire passer; **2** TELECOM
passer.

■ **put together**: ~ **[sb/sth] together**, ~ **together [sb/sth] 1** (assemble) assembler; **to ~ sth together again**, **to ~ sth back together** reconstituer qch; **smarter than all the rest put together** plus intelligent que tous les autres réunis; **2** (place together) mettre ensemble; **3** (form) former; **4** (edit) constituer [*file, portfolio, anthology*]; rédiger [*newsletter, leaflet*]; établir [*list*]; faire [*film, programme, video*]; **5** improviser [*meal*]; **6** (present) constituer [*case*]; construire [*argument, essay*].

■ **put up**: ¶ ~ **up 1** (stay) **to ~ up at sb's** se faire héberger par qn; **to ~ up in a hotel** descendre à l'hôtel; **2 to ~ up with** (tolerate) supporter; ¶ ~ **up [sth]** opposer [*resistance*]; **to ~ up a fight** ou **struggle** combattre; **to ~ up a good performance** SPORT bien se défendre; ¶ ~ **[sth] up**, ~ **up [sth] 1** hisser [*flag, sail*]; relever [*hair*]; **to ~ up one's hand** lever la main; ~ **your hands up!** (in class) levez le doigt!; **2** (post up) mettre [*sign, plaque*]; afficher [*list*]; **3** (erect) dresser [*fence, barrier, tent*]; construire [*building*]; **4** (increase) augmenter [*rent, prices, tax*]; faire monter [*temperature, pressure*]; **5** (provide) fournir [*money*]; **6** (present) soumettre [*proposal, argument*]; **7** AEROSP placer [qch] en orbite [*satellite, probe*]; ¶ ~ **[sb] up**, ~ **up [sb] 1** (lodge) héberger; **2** (propose) présenter [*candidate*]; **to ~ sb up for** proposer qn comme [*leader, chairman*]; proposer qn pour [*promotion, position*]; **3** (promote) faire passer [qn] au niveau supérieur; **4** (incite) **to ~ sb up to sth/to doing** pousser qn à qch/à faire.

■ **put upon**: ~ **upon [sb]** abuser de [*person*]; **to be put upon** se faire marcher sur les pieds.

put: ~**-down** *n* remarque *f* humiliante; ~**-out**° *adj* vexé.

putt /pʌt/ **I** *n* putt *m*.
II *vtr, vi* putter.

putty /'pʌti/ **I** *n* mastic *m*.
II *vtr* mastiquer.

put: ~**-up job**° *n* coup *m* monté; ~**-you-up**° *n* GB canapé-lit *m*.

puzzle /'pʌzl/ **I** *n* (mystery) mystère *m*; GAMES casse-tête *m inv*.
II *vtr* [*question, attitude*] déconcerter [*person*].
III *vi* **to ~ over sth** réfléchir à qch.
■ **puzzle out**: ~ **out [sth]**, ~ **[sth] out** deviner.

puzzle book *n* livre *m* de jeux.

puzzled /'pʌzld/ *adj* [*person, smile*] perplexe; **to be ~ as to why** se demander pourquoi.

puzzling /'pʌzlɪŋ/ *adj* curieux/-ieuse.

pygmy /'pɪgmi/ *n* pygmée *mf*.

pyjama GB, **pajama** US /pə'dʒɑːmə/ **I** *noun modifier* [*cord, jacket, trousers*] de pyjama.
II pyjamas *npl* pyjama *m*; **a pair of ~s** un pyjama.

pylon /'paɪlən, -lɒn/ *n* ELEC, AVIAT pylône *m*.

pyramid /'pɪrəmɪd/ *n* pyramide *f*.

pyramid selling *n* vente *f* en cascade.

pyre /'paɪə(r)/ *n* bûcher *m*.

pyromaniac /ˌpaɪrəʊ'meɪnɪæk/ *n* pyromane *mf*.

pyrotechnics /ˌpaɪrə'tekniks/ *n* **1** (science) pyrotechnie *f*; **2** (display) feu *m* d'artifice ALSO FIG.

Qq

q, Q /kjuː/ n q, Q m.

Q and A n (abrév = **question and answer**) questions-réponses fpl.

Qatar /kæˈtɑː/ ▶840 pr n Qatar m.

QC n GB JUR (abrév = **Queen's Counsel**) titre conféré à un avocat éminent.

QED (abrév = **quod erat demonstrandum**) CQFD.

qty n: abrév écrite = **quantity**.

quack /kwæk/ I n **1** (impostor) charlatan m; **2**○ GB (doctor) toubib○ m; **3** onomat coin-coin m inv. II vi onomat cancaner.

quad /kwɒd/ n **1** abrév ▶ **quadrangle**; **2** abrév ▶ **quadruplet**.

quadrangle /ˈkwɒdræŋgl/ n **1** MATH quadrilatère m; **2** ARCHIT cour f carrée.

quadraphonics /ˌkwɒdrəˈfɒnɪks/ n (+ v sg) quadriphonie f.

quadratic equation n équation f du second degré.

quadrilateral /ˌkwɒdrɪˈlætərəl/ I n quadrilatère m. II adj quadrilatéral.

quadriplegic /ˌkwɒdrɪˈpliːdʒɪk/ adj tétraplégique.

quadruple I /ˈkwɒdrʊpl, US kwɒˈdruːpl/ n, adj quadruple (m). II /kwɒˈdruːpl/ vtr, vi quadrupler.

quadruplet /ˈkwɒdrʊplət, US kwɒˈdruːp-/ n quadruplé/-e m/f; **a set of ~s** des quadruplés.

quadruplicate /kwɒˈdruːplɪkət/ n **in ~** en quatre exemplaires.

quagmire /ˈkwɒgmaɪə(r), ˈkwæg-/ n bourbier m.

quail /kweɪl/ I n (pl **~s** ou collective **~**) (bird) caille f. II vi trembler.

quaint /kweɪnt/ adj **1** (pretty) pittoresque; **2** (old-world) d'un charme suranné; (slightly ridiculous) au charme vieillot; **3** (odd) bizarre; (unusual) original.

quake /kweɪk/ I n (earthquake) tremblement m de terre. II vi (earth, person) trembler.

qualification /ˌkwɒlɪfɪˈkeɪʃn/ n **1** (diploma, degree etc) diplôme m (**in** en); (experience, skills) qualification f; **to have the (necessary** ou **right) ~s for sth** (on paper) avoir les titres requis pour qch; (in experience, skills) avoir les qualifications pour qch; **2** GB (graduation) **my first job after ~** mon premier travail après avoir reçu mon diplôme; **3** (restriction) restriction f; **my only ~ is (that)** ma seule réserve est que; **4** ADMIN (eligibility) droit m; **5** LING qualification f.

qualified /ˈkwɒlɪfaɪd/ adj **1** (for job) (having diploma) diplômé; (having experience, skills) qualifié; **to be ~ for sth** (on paper) avoir les titres requis pour qch; (by experience, skills) être qualifié pour qch; **2** (competent) (having authority) qualifié; (having knowledge) compétent; **3** (modified) nuancé, mitigé.

qualifier /ˈkwɒlɪfaɪə(r)/ n **1** SPORT (contestant) qualifié/-e m/f; (match) éliminatoire m; **2** LING qualificatif m.

qualify /ˈkwɒlɪfaɪ/ I vtr **1** (make competent) **to ~ sb for a job** (degree, diploma) habiliter qn à exercer un emploi; (experience, skills) rendre qn apte à exercer un emploi; **2** ADMIN **to ~ sb for sth** donner droit à qch à qn; **to ~ sb to do** donner à qn le droit de faire; **3** GEN (give authority to) **to ~ sb to do** autoriser qn à faire; **4** (modify) nuancer [acceptance, approval, opinion]; préciser [statement, remark]; **5** LING qualifier. II vi **1** (obtain diploma, degree etc) obtenir son diplôme (**as** de, en); (have experience, skill) avoir les connaissances requises (**for** pour); **to ~ to do** avoir les connaissances requises pour faire; **while she was ~ing as an engineer** pendant qu'elle faisait ses études d'ingénieur; **2** ADMIN remplir les conditions (requises); **to ~ for** avoir droit à; **to ~ to do** avoir le droit de faire; **3** (meet standard) **he hardly qualifies as a poet** ce n'est pas vraiment ce que l'on peut appeler un poète; **4** SPORT se qualifier.

qualifying /ˈkwɒlɪfaɪɪŋ/ adj **1** GEN, SPORT de qualification; **~ period** (until trained) (periode f de) stage m; (until eligible) période f d'attente; **2** LING qualificatif/-ive.

qualitative /ˈkwɒlɪtətɪv, US -teɪt-/ adj qualitatif/-ive.

quality /ˈkwɒlətɪ/ I n (all contexts) qualité f. II noun modifier [car, workmanship, press] de qualité.

quality control I n contrôle m de qualité. II noun modifier [procedure] de contrôle de qualité.

quality controller ▶1251 n contrôleur/-euse m/f chargé/-e du contrôle de la qualité.

qualm /kwɑːm/ n scrupule m.

quandary /ˈkwɒndərɪ/ n embarras m; (serious) dilemme m.

quango /ˈkwæŋgəʊ/ n (pl **~s**) GB organisme m autonome d'État.

quantifiable /ˌkwɒntɪˈfaɪəbl/ adj facile à évaluer.

quantify /ˈkwɒntɪfaɪ/ vtr GEN évaluer avec précision; MATH, PHYS quantifier.

quantitative /ˈkwɒntɪtətɪv, US -teɪt-/ adj GEN quantitatif/-ive.

quantity /ˈkwɒntətɪ/ ▶1185 I n GEN, LITERAT quantité f; **in ~** en grande quantité; **unknown ~** MATH, FIG inconnue f. II noun modifier [purchase, sale] en grande quantité; [production] en série.

quantity: **~ surveying** n métrage m; **~ surveyor** ▶1251 n métreur m.

quantum /ˈkwɒntəm/ I n (pl **-ta**) quantum m. II noun modifier [mechanics, theory] quantique.

quantum leap n PHYS saut m quantique; FIG bond m prodigieux.

quarantine /ˈkwɒrəntiːn, US ˈkwɔːr-/ I n quarantaine f. II noun modifier [hospital, period] de quarantaine. III vtr mettre [qn/qch] en quarantaine.

quarrel /ˈkwɒrəl, US ˈkwɔːrəl/ I n **1** (argument) dispute f (**between** entre; **over** au sujet de); **while she was disputer; 2** (feud) brouille f (**about, over** au sujet de); **to have a ~ with sb** être brouillé avec qn; **3** (difference of opinion) différend m; **to have no ~ with sb/sth** ne rien avoir contre qn/à redire à qch. II vi (p prés etc **-ll-**, US **-l-**) **1** (argue) se disputer; **2** (sever relations) se brouiller; **3** (dispute) **to ~ with** contester [claim, idea]; se plaindre de [price, verdict].

quarrelling, quarreling US /ˈkwɒrəlɪŋ, US ˈkwɔː-/ ∉ disputes fpl.

quarrelsome /ˈkwɒrəlsəm, US ˈkwɔː-/ adj [person, nature] querelleur/-euse; [remark] agressif/-ive.

quarry /ˈkwɒrɪ, US ˈkwɔːrɪ/ I n **1** (in ground) carrière f; **2** (prey) proie f; (in hunting) gibier m ALSO FIG. II vtr (also **~ out**) extraire [stone]. III vi **to ~ for** extraire [stone, gravel].

quarry tile n carreau m de terre cuite.

quart /kwɔːt/ ▶789 n **~** litre m (GB = 1.136 litres, US = 0.946 litres).

quarter /ˈkwɔːtə(r)/ ▶812, 849, 1392 I n **1** (one

Quantities

Note the use of **en** *(of it or of them) in the following examples. This word must be included when the thing you are talking about is not expressed (the French says literally there is of it a lot, there is of it two kilos, I have of them a lot etc.). However,* **en** *is not needed when the commodity is specified e.g. there is a lot of butter =* il y a beaucoup de beurre.

how much is there?	= combien y en a-t-il?
there's a lot	= il y en a beaucoup
there's not much	= il n'y en a pas beaucoup
there's two kilos	= il y en a deux kilos
how much sugar have you?	= combien de sucre as-tu?
I've got a lot	= j'en ai beaucoup
I haven't got (very) much	= je n'en ai pas beaucoup*
I've got two kilos	= j'en ai deux kilos
how many are there?	= combien y en a-t-il?
there are a lot	= il y en a beaucoup
there aren't many	= il n'y en a pas beaucoup
there are twenty	= il y en a vingt
how many apples have you?	= combien de pommes as-tu? *or* tu as combien de pommes?
I've got a lot	= j'en ai beaucoup
I haven't many	= je n'en ai pas beaucoup
I've got twenty	= j'en ai vingt
A has got more than B	= A en a plus que B
A has got more money than B	= A a d'argent que B
much more than	= beaucoup plus que
a little more than	= un peu plus que
A has got more apples than B	= A a plus de pommes que B
many more apples than B	= beaucoup plus de pommes que B
a few more apples than B	= quelques pommes de plus que B
a few more people than yesterday	= quelques personnes de plus qu'hier
B has got less than A	= B en a moins que A
B has got less money than A	= B a moins d'argent que A

much less than	= beaucoup moins que
a little less than	= un peu moins que
B has got fewer than A	= B en a moins que A
B has got fewer apples than A	= B a moins de pommes que A
many fewer than	= beaucoup moins que

Relative quantities

how many are there to the kilo?	= combien y en a-t-il au kilo?
there are ten to the kilo	= il y en a dix au kilo
you can count six to the kilo	= il faut en compter six au kilo
how many do you get for ten francs?	= combien peut-on en avoir pour dix francs?
you get five for ten francs	= il y en a cinq pour dix francs
how much does it cost a litre?	= combien coûte le litre?
it costs £5 a litre	= ça coûte cinq livres le litre
how much do apples cost a kilo?	= combien coûte le kilo de pommes?
apples cost ten francs a kilo	= les pommes coûtent dix francs le kilo
how much does it cost a metre?	= combien coûte le mètre?
how much does your car do to the gallon?	= combien consomme votre voiture?
it does 28 miles to the gallon	= elle fait dix litres aux cent

(Note that the French calculate petrol consumption in litres per 100 km. To convert mpg to litres per 100 km and vice versa, simply divide 280 by the known figure.)

how many glasses do you get to the bottle?	= combien y a-t-il de verres par bouteille?
you get six glasses to the bottle	= il y a six verres par bouteille

* *Never use* très *with* beaucoup.

---

fourth) quart *m*; **~ of an hour** quart *m* d'heure; **2** GEN, FIN (three months) trimestre *m*; **3** (district) quartier *m*; **4** (group) milieu *m*; **don't expect help from that ~** n'attends aucune aide de ce côté-là; **5** (mercy) LITTÉR **to get no ~ from sb** ne recevoir aucune pitié de la part de qn; **to give no ~** ne pas faire de quartier; **6** US (25 cents) vingt-cinq cents *mpl*; **7** US (measurement) = 12,7 kg.
II quarters *npl* MIL quartiers *mpl*, GEN logement *m*; **to take up ~s** se loger (**in** dans).
III *pron* **1** (25%) quart *m*; **only a ~ passed** seul le quart a réussi; **2** (in time phrases) **at (a) ~ to 11** GB, **at a ~ of 11** US à onze heures moins le quart; **an hour and a ~** une heure et quart; **3** (in age) **she's ten and a ~** elle a dix ans et trois mois.
IV *adj* **a ~ share in the company** un quart des actions de l'entreprise; **a ~ century** un quart de siècle.
V *adv* **a ~ full** au quart plein; **a ~ as big** quatre fois moins grand; **~ the price** quatre fois moins cher.
VI at close quarters *adv phr* de près; **to fight at close ~s** lutter au corps à corps.
VII *vtr* **1** (divide into four) couper [qch] en quatre [*cake, apple*]; **2** (accommodate) cantonner [*troops*]; loger [*people*]; abriter [*livestock*].
quarter: **~back** *n* US quarterback *m* (*joueur qui dirige l'attaque*); **~deck** *n* NAUT (on ship) plage *f* arrière; **~final** *n* quart *m* de finale.
quarterly /ˈkwɔːtəlɪ/ **I** *adj* trimestriel/-ielle.
II *adv* tous les trois mois.
quarter: **~master** ▶ 1192 | *n* (in army) intendant *m*; (in navy) maître *m* de timonerie; **~note** *n* US MUS noire *f*; **~staff** *n* MIL HIST bâton *m*.

quartet /kwɔːˈtet/ *n* GEN, MUS quatuor *m*; **jazz ~** quartette *m*.
quarto /ˈkwɔːtəʊ/ *n, noun modifier* (*pl* **-tos**) in-quarto (*m*).
quartz /kwɔːts/ **I** *n* quartz *m*.
II *noun modifier* [*crystal*] de quartz; [*clock*] à quartz.
quash /kwɒʃ/ *vtr* rejeter [*proposal*]; réprimer [*rebellion*].
quasi+ /ˈkweɪzaɪ, ˈkwɑːzɪ/ (*combining form*) quasi (+ *adj*), quasi- (+ *noun*).
quatercentenary /ˌkwætəsənˈtiːnərɪ, US -ˈsentənerɪ/ *n* quatrième centenaire *m*.
quaternary /kwəˈtɜːnərɪ/ **I** *n* **1** MATH quatre *m*; (set) ensemble *m* de quatre; **2 the Quaternary** (in geology) le quaternaire.
II *adj* quaternaire.
quaver /ˈkweɪvə(r)/ **I** *n* **1** MUS GB croche *f*; **2** (trembling) tremblement *m* (**in** dans).
II *vi* trembloter.
quay /kiː/ *n* quai *m*; **on the ~** sur le quai.
queasiness /ˈkwiːzɪnɪs/ *n* nausée *f*.
queasy /ˈkwiːzɪ/ *adj* **1** LIT **to be ou feel ~** avoir mal au cœur; **2** FIG [*conscience*] mauvais; **to feel ~ about** se sentir mal à l'aise en ce qui concerne.
Quebec /kwɪˈbek/ ▶ 1343 | **I** *pr n* **1** (town) Québec *m*; **in ~** à Québec; **2** (province) Québec *m*; **in ~** au Québec.
II *noun modifier* [*people, culture*] québécois.
queen /kwiːn/ **I** *n* ▶ 937 | **1** LIT, FIG reine *f*; **2** ZOOL reine *f*; **3** (in chess) reine *f*; (in cards) dame *f*.
II *vtr* (in chess) damer [*pawn*].
IDIOMS to ~ it over sb prendre de grands airs avec qn.

queen bee *n* **1** ZOOL reine *f* des abeilles; **2** FIG **she thinks she's (the) ~** elle se prend pour la reine.

queenly /'kwi:nlɪ/ *adj* de reine.

queen: **~ mother** *n* Reine mère *f*; **Queen's Counsel, QC** *n* GB JUR avocat *m* éminent *(qui tient son titre de la Reine)*.

Queen's English *n* **to speak the ~** parler un anglais correct.

Queen's evidence *n* **to turn ~** GB JUR dénoncer ses complices contre promesse de pardon.

Queensland /'kwi:nzlənd/ *pr n* Queensland *m*.

Queen's Regulations *npl* GB MIL code *m* militaire.

queer /kwɪə(r)/ *adj* **1** (strange) étrange, bizarre; **2** (suspicious) louche, suspect; **3**† GB (ill) patraque○; **4**○ INJUR (homosexual) pédé◑ OFFENSIVE, homosexuel/-elle.
IDIOMS **to ~ sb's pitch** contrecarrer les plans de qn.

queerly /'kwɪəlɪ/ *adv* singulièrement.

quell /kwel/ *vtr* étouffer [*anger, anxiety, revolt*]; **to ~ sb with a look** faire taire qn du regard.

quench /kwentʃ/ *vtr* **1** étancher [*thirst*]; étouffer [*desire*]; **2** LITTÉR éteindre [*flame*]; **3** TECH tremper [*metal*].

querulous /'kwerʊləs/ *adj* grincheux/-euse.

query /'kwɪərɪ/ **I** *n* **1** (request for information) question *f* (**about** au sujet de); **a ~ from sb** une question venant de qn; **queries from customers** demandes *fpl* de renseignement venant des clients; **2** (expression of doubt) question *f* (**about** à propos de); **3** COMPUT interrogation *f*; **4** (question mark) point *m* d'interrogation.
II *vtr* mettre en doute; **to ~ whether** demander si; **nobody dares to ~ that…** personne n'ose douter de fait que…; **to ~ sb's ability** mettre en doute les capacités de qn; **some may ~ my interpretation of the data** il se peut que certains doutent de mon interprétation des données.

quest /kwest/ *n* quête *f*; **the ~ for sb/sth** la recherche de qn/qch; **his ~ to do** son désir de faire.

question /'kwestʃən/ **I** *n* **1** (request for information) question *f* (**about** sur); (in exam) question *f*; **to ask sb a ~** poser une question à qn; **in reply to a ~ from Mr John Molloy** en réponse à une question posée par M. John Molloy; **to do sth without ~** faire qch sans poser de question; **what a ~!** en voilà une question!; **a ~ from the floor** (in parliament) une question provenant de l'assemblée; **2** (practical issue) problème *m*; (ethical issue) question *f*; **the Palestinian ~** la question palestinienne; **the ~ of pollution** le problème de la pollution; **it's a ~ of doing** il s'agit de faire; **the ~ of where to live** le problème de savoir où habiter; **the ~ arises as to who is going to pay the bill** la question se pose, à savoir qui va payer la note; **that's another ~** c'est une autre affaire; **the ~ is whether** il s'agit ici de savoir si; **there was never any ~ of you paying** il n'a jamais été question que tu paies; **the person in ~** la personne en question; **it's out of the ~ for him to leave** il est hors de question qu'il parte; **3** (uncertainty) doute *m*; **to call sth into ~** mettre qch en doute; **to prove beyond ~ that** prouver sans l'ombre d'un doute que; **it's open to ~** cela se discute; **his honesty was never in ~** on n'a jamais douté de son honnêteté.
II *vtr* **1** (interrogate) questionner [*suspect, politician*]; **2** (cast doubt upon) (on one occasion) mettre en doute [*tactics, methods*]; (over longer period) douter de [*tactics, methods*]; **to ~ whether** douter que (+ *subj*).

questionable /'kwestʃənəbl/ *adj* (debatable) [*motive, decision*] discutable; (dubious) [*evidence, taste*] douteux/-euse; **it is ~ whether** il est douteux que (+ *subj*).

questioner /'kwestʃənə(r)/ *n* interrogateur/-trice *m/f*.

questioning /'kwestʃənɪŋ/ **I** *n* **1** (of person) interrogation *f*; (relentless) interrogatoire *m*; **to bring sb in for ~** amener qn pour interrogatoire; **he is wanted for ~ in connection with the explosion** la police le recherche suite à l'explosion; **under ~** [*admit*]

pendant un interrogatoire; **a line of ~** une série de questions; **2** (of criteria) remise *f* en question (**of** de).
II *adj* **1** [*look, tone*] interrogateur/-trice; **2** [*techniques*] d'interrogation; (by official) d'interrogatoire.

question mark *n* **1** (in punctuation) point *m* d'interrogation; **2** (doubt) **there is a ~ about his honesty** on s'interroge quant à son honnêteté; **there is a ~ about his suitability for the job** on se demande s'il est apte à occuper ce poste; **there is a ~ hanging over his future** l'incertitude plane sur son avenir.

question master *n* animateur/-trice *m/f* de jeu.

questionnaire /ˌkwestʃə'neə(r)/ *n* questionnaire *m* (**on** sur; **to do** pour faire).

question tag *n* LING queue *f* de phrase interrogative, tag○ *m*.

queue /kju:/ **I** *n* GB (of people) queue *f*, file *f* (d'attente); (of vehicles) file *f*; **to stand in a ~** faire la queue; **to join the ~** [*person*] se mettre à la queue; [*car*] se mettre dans la file; **go to the back of the ~!** à la queue!; **to jump the ~**○ passer avant son tour.
II *vi* GB (also **~ up**) [*people*] faire la queue (**for** pour); [*taxis*] attendre en ligne; **to ~ up to do sth** FIG se précipiter pour faire qch.

queue-jump *vi* GB resquiller, passer avant son tour.

quibble /'kwɪbl/ **I** *n* chicane *f* (**about, over** sur).
II *vi* chicaner (**about, over** sur).

quick /kwɪk/ **I** *n* ANAT, MED chair *f* vive; **to the ~ [*bite nails*]** jusqu'au sang.
II *adj* **1** (speedy) [*pace, reply, profit, meal*] rapide; [*storm, shower*] bref/brève; **to make a ~ phone call** passer un coup de téléphone rapide; **to have a ~ coffee** prendre un café en vitesse; **to have a ~ wash** faire une toilette rapide; **she's a ~ worker** elle travaille vite; **the ~est way to…** le meilleur moyen de…; **we're hoping for a ~ sale** nous espérons que cela se vendra rapidement; **we had a ~ chat about our plans** nous avons rapidement discuté de nos projets; **to make a ~ recovery** se rétablir vite; **to pay a ~ visit to sb** faire une petite visite à qn; **be ~ (about it)!** dépêche-toi!; **2** (clever) [*child, student*] vif/vive d'esprit; **to be ~ at** être bon/bonne en [*arithmetic*]; **3** (prompt) **to be a ~ learner** apprendre vite; **to be (too) ~ to condemn** condamner (trop) facilement; **she was ~ to see the advantages** elle a tout de suite vu les avantages; **4** (lively) **a ~ temper** un tempérament vif; **to have a ~ temper** s'emporter facilement.
III *adv* **~!** vite!; **~ as a flash** avec la rapidité de l'éclair.
IDIOMS **a ~ one = quickie 1, 2**; **the ~ and the dead** les vivants et les morts; **to cut sb sting sb to the ~** piquer qn au vif; **to make a ~ buck**○ gagner de l'argent facile; **to make a ~ killing**○ faire fortune rapidement.

quick-assembly *adj* facile à monter.

quicken /'kwɪkən/ **I** *vtr* accélérer [*pace*]; FIG stimuler [*interest*].
II *vi* **1** [*pace*] s'accélérer; FIG [*anger*] s'intensifier; **2** [*fœtus*] bouger.

quick fire /'kwɪkfaɪə/ **I** *n* LIT tir *m* rapide.
II *quick-fire noun modifier* [*question, sketch*] rapide.

quick-freeze *vtr* (*prét* **-froze**, *pp* **-frozen**) surgeler.

quickie○ /'kwɪkɪ/ *n* **1** (drink) pot○ *m* en vitesse; **2** (question) question *f* rapide; **3** US CIN *film fait rapidement*.

quicklime *n* chaux *f* vive.

quickly /'kwɪklɪ/ *adv* [*arrive, resolve*] (rapidly) vite, rapidement; (without delay) sans tarder; (**come**) **~!** (viens) vite!; **I acted ~ on his advice** je me suis dépêché de suivre ses conseils; **I ~ changed the subject** je me suis empressé de changer de sujet.

quick march *n* MIL ~ pas *m* cadencé; **~!** (as order) ~ pas cadencé marche!

quickness /'kwɪknɪs/ *n* **1** (speed) (of person, movement) rapidité *f*; **~ to respond/react** promptitude *f* à répondre/réagir; **2** (nimbleness) (of person, movements) vivacité *f*; **3** (liveliness of mind) vivacité *f* d'esprit.

quick: **~sand** *n* ¢ LIT sables *mpl* mouvants; FIG bourbier *m*; **~-setting** *adj* à prise rapide; **~silver**

n CHEM mercure *m*; **~-tempered** *adj* coléreux/ -euse; **~ time** *n* US marche *f* rapide; **~ trick** *n* (in bridge) levée *f* assurée; **~-witted** *adj* [*person*] à l'esprit vif; [*reaction*] vif/vive.

quid○ /kwɪd/ *n* GB (*pl* **~**) livre *f* (sterling).

quid pro quo /ˌkwɪd prəʊ ˈkwəʊ/ *n* contrepartie *f*.

quiescent /kwaɪˈesnt, kwɪˈesnt/ *adj* SOUT [*person*] passif/-ive; [*mood, state*] tranquille; [*soul, spirit*] en repos.

quiet /ˈkwaɪət/ **I** *n* **1** (silence) silence *m*; **~ please!** silence, s'il vous plaît!; **2** (peace) tranquillité *f*; **3**○ (secret) **to do sth on the ~** faire qch discrètement.
II *adj* **1** (silent) [*church, person, room*] silencieux/ -ieuse; **to keep ~** garder le silence; **to go ~** [*person, assembly*] se taire; **to keep sb ~** faire taire [*dog, child*]; **be ~** (stop talking) tais-toi; (make no noise) ne fais pas de bruit; **2** (not noisy) [*voice*] bas/basse; [*engine*] silencieux/-ieuse; [*music*] doux/douce; [*cough, laugh*] discret/-ète; **in a ~ voice** à voix basse; **to keep the children ~** [*activity*] tenir les enfants tranquilles; **3** (discreet) [*diplomacy*] discret/-ète; [*deal*] en privé; [*confidence*] serein; [*despair*] voilé; [*colour*] sobre; **to have a ~ word with sb** prendre qn à part pour lui parler; **4** (calm) [*village, holiday, night, life*] tranquille; **the stock market is ~** la Bourse est calme; **5** (for few people) [*meal*] intime; [*wedding*] célébré dans l'intimité; **6** (docile) [*pony*] paisible; **7** (secret) **to keep** [sth] **~** ne pas divulguer [*plans*]; garder [qch] secret/-ète [*engagement*].
III *vtr* US = **quieten**.

quieten /ˈkwaɪətn/ *vtr* **1** (calm) calmer [*person, animal*]; **2** (allay) dissiper [*doubts*]; **3** (silence) faire taire [*critics, children*].
■ **quieten down**: ¶ **~ down 1** (become calm) [*person, activity*] se calmer; **2** (fall silent) se taire; ¶ **~ down** [sb/sth], **~** [sb/sth] **down 1** (calm) calmer; **2** (silence) faire taire.

quietly /ˈkwaɪətlɪ/ *adv* **1** (not noisily) [*move*] sans bruit; [*cough, speak, play*] doucement; **2** (silently) [*play, read, sit*] en silence; **3** (discreetly) [*pleased etc*] modérément; **to be ~ confident that** avoir la conviction intime que; **4** (simply) [*live*] simplement; [*get married*] dans l'intimité; **5** (calmly) calmement; **6** (soberly) [*dress*] de façon discrète.

quietness /ˈkwaɪətnɪs/ *n* **1** (silence) silence *m*; **2** (lowness) (of voice) faiblesse *f*; **3** (of place) tranquillité *f*.

quiff /kwɪf/ *n* GB (on forehead) toupet *m*; (on top of head) houppe *f*.

quill /kwɪl/ *n* **1** (feather) penne *f*; (stem of feather) tuyau *m* de plume; **2** (on porcupine) piquant *m*; **3** (also **~ pen**) (for writing) plume *f* d'oie.

quilt /kwɪlt/ **I** *n* **1** GB (duvet) couette *f*; **2** (bed cover) dessus *m* de lit.
II *vtr* matelasser.

quilting /ˈkwɪltɪŋ/ *n* (technique) matelassage *m*; (fabric) matelassure *f*.

quince /kwɪns/ *n* (fruit) coing *m*; (tree) cognassier *m*.

quincentenary /ˌkwɪnsenˈtiːnərɪ, US -ˈsentənerɪ/ *n* cinq centième anniversaire *m*.

quinine /kwɪˈniːn, US ˈkwaɪnaɪn/ *n* quinine *f*.

quintessential /ˌkwɪntɪˈsenʃl/ *adj* [*quality*] fondamental; **the ~ Renaissance man** l'homme de la Renaissance par excellence.

quintet /kwɪnˈtet/ *n* MUS quintette *m*.

quintuple I /ˈkwɪntjʊpl, US kwɪnˈtuːpl/ *adj* quintuple.
II /kwɪnˈtjʊpl/ *vtr* quintupler.

quintuplet /ˈkwɪntjuːplet, US kwɪnˈtuːplɪt/ *n* quintuplé/-e *m/f*.

quip /kwɪp/ *n* trait *m* d'esprit.

quire /ˈkwaɪə(r)/ *n* (in printing) (4 sheets) cahier *m*; (24 or 25 sheets) main *f*.

quirk /kwɜːk/ *n* (of person) excentricité *f*; (of fate, nature) caprice *m*.

quisling /ˈkwɪzlɪŋ/ *n* PÉJ collaborateur/-trice *m/f* PÉJ.

quit /kwɪt/ **I** *vtr* (*p prés* **-tt-**; *prét, pp* **quit** ou **quitted**) (leave) démissionner de, laisser tomber○ [*job*]; quitter [*place, person, profession*].

II *vi* (*p prés* **-tt-**; *prét, pp* **quit** ou **quitted**) **1** (give up) arrêter; **to ~ whilst one is ahead** GEN s'arrêter avant que les choses se gâtent; (in career) partir au summum de la gloire; **2** (resign) [*person*] démissionner.

quite /kwaɪt/ *adv* **1** (completely) [*new, ready, understand*] tout à fait; [*alone, empty, exhausted, ridiculous*] complètement; [*impossible*] totalement; [*justified*] entièrement; [*extraordinary*] vraiment; **I ~ agree** je suis tout à fait d'accord; **you're ~ right** vous avez entièrement raison; **it's ~ all right** (in reply to apology) c'est sans importance; **it's ~ out of the question** il n'en est pas du tout question; **I can ~ believe it** je veux bien le croire; **are you ~ sure?** en êtes-vous certain?; **to be ~ aware that** être tout à fait conscient du fait que; **~ clearly** [*see*] très clairement; **it's ~ clear** c'est parfaitement clair; **and right too!** à juste titre!; **that's ~ enough!** ça suffit!; **2** (exactly) **not ~** pas exactement; **not ~ so much** un petit peu moins; **not ~ as many** pas tout à fait autant; **I don't ~ know** je ne sais pas du tout; **nobody knew ~ what he meant** personne ne savait exactement ce qu'il voulait dire; **that's not ~ all** (giving account of sth) et ce n'est pas tout; **3** (definitely) **it was ~ the best answer** c'était de loin la meilleure réponse; **he's ~ the stupidest man!** il est vraiment stupide!; **~ simply** tout simplement; **4** (rather) [*big, easily, often*] assez; **it's ~ small** ce n'est pas très grand; **it's ~ warm today** il fait bon aujourd'hui; **it's ~ likely that** il est très probable que; **I ~ like Chinese food** j'aime assez la cuisine chinoise; **~ a few** un bon nombre de [*people, examples*]; **~ a lot of money** pas mal d'argent; **~ a lot of opposition** une opposition assez forte; **I've thought about it ~ a bit** j'y ai pas mal réfléchi; **5** (as intensifier) **~ a difference** une différence considérable; **that will be ~ a change for you** ça va te faire un grand changement; **she's ~ a woman!** quelle femme!; **to be ~ something** [*house, car*] valoir le coup d'œil○; **6** (expressing agreement) **~ (so)** c'est sûr.

quits○ /kwɪts/ *adj* **to be ~** être quitte (**with sb** envers qn); **to call it ~** en rester là.

quiver /ˈkwɪvə(r)/ **I** *n* **1** (trembling) (of voice, part of body) tremblement *m*; (of leaves) frémissement *m*; (of excitement) frémissement *m*; **2** (for arrows) carquois *m*.
II *vi* [*voice, lip, animal*] trembler (**with** de); [*leaves*] frémir; [*wings*] battre; [*flame*] vaciller.

quixotic /kwɪkˈsɒtɪk/ *adj* (unrealistic) chimérique.

quiz /kwɪz/ **I** *n* (*pl* **~zes**) **1** (game) jeu *m* de questions-réponses, quiz *m*; (written, in magazine) questionnaire *m* (**about** sur); **2** US SCH interrogation *f*.
II *vtr* (*p prés etc* **-zz-**) questionner (**about** au sujet de).

quiz game, quiz show *n* jeu *m* de questions-réponses.

quizzical /ˈkwɪzɪkl/ *adj* interrogateur/-trice.

quoit /kɔɪt, US kwɔɪt/ *n* palet *m*.

quorum /ˈkwɔːrəm/ *n* quorum *m*; **the ~ is ten** le quorum est fixé à dix; **to have a ~** avoir atteint le quorum.

quota /ˈkwəʊtə/ *n* **1** GEN, COMM (prescribed number) quota *m* (**of, for** de); **this year's ~** le quota fixé pour cette année; **2** (share) part *f* (**of** de); (officially allocated) quote-part *f*.

quotation /kwəʊˈteɪʃn/ *n* **1** (phrase, passage cited) citation *f*; **2** (estimate) devis *m*; **3** FIN cours *m*, cote *f*.

quotation marks *npl* guillemets *mpl*; **in ~** entre guillemets.

quote /kwəʊt/ **I** *n* **1** (quotation) citation *f* (**from** de); **2** (statement to journalist) déclaration *f*; **3** (estimate) devis *m*; **4** FIN cote *f*.
II quotes *npl* = **quotation marks**.
III *vtr* **1** (repeat, recall) citer [*person, passage, proverb*]; rapporter [*words*]; rappeler [*reference number*]; **don't ~ me on this, but...** ne répète pas ce que je dis, mais...; **she was ~d as saying that...** elle aurait dit que...; **2** COMM (state) indiquer [*price, figure*]; **they ~d us £200** dans leur devis, ils ont demandé £200;

3 (on stock exchange) coter [*share, price*] (**at** à) ; **~d company** société *f* cotée en Bourse; **4** (in betting) **to ~ odds of** proposer une cote de; **to be ~d 6 to 1** être coté entre 6 et 1.

IV *vi* (from text, author) faire des citations; **to ~ from Keats** citer Keats; **~ ... unquote** (in dictation) ouvrez les guillemets ... fermez les guillemets; (in lecture, speech) je cite ... fin de citation; **on ~ 'business' unquote** soi-disant pour affaires.

quotient /'kwəʊʃnt/ *n* **1** MATH quotient *m*; **2** GEN niveau *m*.

r, **R** /ɑ:(r)/ n **1** (letter) r, R m; **the three R's** l'écriture, la lecture et le calcul; **2 R** abrév écrite = **right**; **3 R** GB abrév = **Regina**.

rabbi /'ræbaɪ/ n rabbin m.

rabbit /'ræbɪt/ n (male) lapin m; (female) lapine f; (fur, meat) lapin m; **wild** ~ lapin de garenne.

IDIOMS **to pull a** ~ **out of a hat** FIG faire un coup de théâtre.

■ **rabbit on**○ GB parler sans cesse (**about** de).

Rabbit® /'ræbɪt/ pr n TELECOM ≈ Bibop® m.

rabbit: ~ **burrow**, ~ **hole** n terrier m de lapin; ~ **hutch** n clapier m; ~ **warren** n LIT garenne f; FIG (maze) labyrinthe m.

rabble /'ræbl/ n PÉJ (crowd) foule f; (populace) **the** ~ la populace PÉJ; **~-rousing** incitation f à la violence.

rabid /'ræbɪd, US 'reɪbɪd/ adj **1** (with rabies) enragé; **2** (fanatical) fanatique.

rabies /'reɪbi:z/ ▶ 1002 | I n rage f.

II noun modifier [injection, legislation] antirabique; [virus] de la rage.

RAC n GB (abrév = **Royal Automobile Club**) organisme m d'assistance pour les automobilistes.

raccoon /rə'ku:n, US ræ-/ n (pl **~s** ou **~**) raton m laveur.

race /reɪs/ I n **1** SPORT course f; **to have a** ~ faire la course; **to run a** ~ courir (**with** contre); **boat** ~ course nautique; **a** ~ **against the clock** ou **against time** LIT, FIG une course contre la montre; **2** FIG (contest) course f (**for** à; **to do** pour faire); **the** ~ **to reach the moon** la course à la lune; **presidential** ~ course à la présidence; **3** SOCIOL race f; **4** BOT, ZOOL espèce f.

II noun modifier [attack, equality, law] racial.

III vtr **1** (compete with) faire la course avec [person, car, horse] (**to** jusqu'à); **2** (enter for race) faire courir [horse, dog]; courir en [car, boat]; courir sur [Formula One]; faire voler [qch] en compétition [pigeon]; **3** (rev) faire ronfler [engine].

IV vi **1** (compete in race) courir (**at** à; **to** vers; **for** pour atteindre); **to** ~ **around the track** faire le tour de la piste; **2** (rush) ~ **in/away** entrer/partir en courant; **to** ~ **after sb/sth** courir après qn/qch; **to** ~ **through** faire [qch] rapidement [task]; **3** [pulse] battre précipitamment; [engine] s'emballer; **my mind started to** ~ je me suis mis à imaginer toutes sortes de choses; **4** (hurry) se dépêcher (**to do** de faire).

■ **race by** [time, person] passer à toute allure.

race: ~ **card** n programme m des courses; **~goer** n turfiste mf; **~horse** n cheval m de course; ~ **meeting** n GB réunion f de courses.

racer /'reɪsə(r)/ n (bike) vélo m de course; (motorbike) moto f de course; (car) voiture f de course; (runner, cyclist etc) coureur/-euse m/f.

race: ~ **relations** npl relations fpl inter-raciales; **~track** n (for horses) champ m de courses; (for cars) circuit m; (for dogs, cycles) piste f; **~way** n US (for cars) circuit m; (for dogs, harness racing) piste f.

racial /'reɪʃl/ adj (all contexts) racial.

racialist /'reɪʃəlɪst/ n, adj raciste (mf).

racing /'reɪsɪŋ/ I n **1** (for horses) hippisme m; **did you see the** ~? as-tu vu les courses (de chevaux)?; **2** (with vehicle, dogs) course f.

II noun modifier [car, yacht] de course; [fan, commentator] des courses; [stable] de courses.

racing: ~ **cyclist** n coureur/-euse m/f cycliste; ~

driver n coureur/-euse m/f automobile; ~ **pigeon** n pigeon m de compétition.

racist /'reɪsɪst/ n, adj raciste (mf).

rack /ræk/ I n **1** (for plates) égouttoir m; (in dishwasher) panier m; (on train) compartiment m à bagages; (for clothes) portant m; (for cakes) grille f (à gâteau); (for bottles) casier m; (for newspapers) porte-revues m inv; (shelving) étagère f; ▶ **roof rack**; **2** (torture) chevalet m; **3** CULIN ~ **of lamb** carré m d'agneau.

II vtr FIG (torment) [pain, guilt, fear] torturer.

IDIOMS **to** ~ **one's brains** se creuser la cervelle○; ▶ **ruin**.

racket /'rækɪt/ n **1** SPORT raquette f; **2**○ (noise) vacarme m, raffut○ m; **to make a** ~ faire du vacarme, faire du raffut; **3** (swindle) escroquerie f; **4** (illegal activity) trafic m; **in on the** ~○ dans le coup○.

racketeering /ˌrækə'tɪərɪŋ/ n racket m.

racking /'rækɪŋ/ adj [pain] atroce; [sobs] déchirant.

racoon n = **raccoon**.

racquet n = **racket** 1.

racquetball /'rækɪtbɔ:l/ ▶ 949 | n US ≈ squash m.

racy /'reɪsɪ/ adj [account, style] plein de verve; (risqué) osé.

radar /'reɪdɑ:(r)/ n, noun modifier radar (m).

radar trap n contrôle-radar m inv; **to get caught in a** ~ se faire piéger par un radar.

raddled /'rædld/ adj [features] marqué par la vie.

radial /'reɪdɪəl/ I n (also ~ **tyre**) pneu m radial.

II adj [lines, roads] rayonnant.

radiance /'reɪdɪəns/, **radiancy** /'reɪdɪənsɪ/ n LIT, FIG éclat m.

radiant /'reɪdɪənt/ I n **1** (on electric fire) résistance f chauffante; **2** (of meteors) point m radiant.

II adj **1** FIG [person, beauty, smile] radieux/-ieuse; ~ **with** rayonnant de [joy, health]; **2** (shining) éclatant; **3** PHYS radiant.

radiantly /'reɪdɪəntlɪ/ adv [shine] d'un vif éclat; [smile] d'un air radieux.

radiate /'reɪdɪeɪt/ I vtr **1** rayonner de [health, happiness]; déborder de [confidence]; **2** PHYS émettre [heat].

II vi **1 to** ~ **from** [confidence, happiness] émaner de; [roads] rayonner (à partir) de; **2** PHYS [heat] rayonner; [light] irradier.

radiation /ˌreɪdɪ'eɪʃn/ I n **1** (medical, nuclear) radiation f; (rays) radiations fpl; **a low level of** ~ un faible niveau de radiations; **2** PHYS rayonnement m.

II noun modifier [levels] de radiation; [effects] des radiations; [leak] de radiations.

radiation: ~ **exposure** n irradiation f; ~ **sickness** n maladie f des rayons; ~ **therapy** n radiothérapie f.

radiator /'reɪdɪeɪtə(r)/ n GEN, AUT radiateur m; **to turn up/down a** ~ monter/baisser le chauffage.

radical /'rædɪkl/ n, adj (all contexts) radical/-e (m/f).

radii /'reɪdɪaɪ/ pl ▶ **radius**.

radio /'reɪdɪəʊ/ I n (pl **~s**) **1** AUDIO radio f; **she was on the** ~ **this morning** elle est passée à la radio ce matin; **2** TELECOM radio f.

II noun modifier [contact, equipment, link, operator, signal] radio inv; [mast, programme] de radio.

III vtr (3ᵉ pers sg prés **~s**; prét, pp **~ed**) **to** ~ **sb for sth** appeler qn par radio pour demander qch; **to** ~ **sth** (**to sb**) communiquer qch par radio (à qn).

IV vi (3ᵉ pers sg prés **~s**; prét, pp **~ed**) **to** ~ **for help** appeler au secours par radio.

radio: **~active** adj radioactif/-ive; **~ alarm**
(**clock**) n radio-réveil m; **~ announcer** n speaker/
-erine m/f; **~ broadcast** n émission f de radio, émission f radiophonique; **~ cab** n radio-taxi m; **~ car**
n voiture-radio f; **~carbon dating** n datation f au
carbone quatorze; **~ cassette** (**recorder**) n radiocassette f; **~ communication** n contact m radio
inv; **~-controlled** adj [toy, boat] télécommandé;
[taxi] radioguidé; **~ frequency** n radiofréquence f.

radiographer /ˌreɪdɪˈɒɡrəfə(r)/ ▶ **1251** n manipula-
teur/-trice m/f radiographe.

radiography /ˌreɪdɪˈɒɡrəfɪ/ n radiographie f.

radio: **~ ham**○ n radio-amateur m; **~ interview**
n entretien m radiophonique.

radiologist /ˌreɪdɪˈɒlədʒɪst/ ▶ **1251** n radiologue mf.

radio: **~ microphone**, **~ mike**○ n micro m sans
fil; **~ station** n (channel) station f de radio; (installation) station f émettrice; **~telephone** n radiotéléphone m; **~therapy** n radiothérapie f.

radish /ˈrædɪʃ/ n radis m.

radius /ˈreɪdɪəs/ n (pl **-dii** ou **-diuses**) **1** GEN,
MATH rayon m; **within a 10 km ~ of here** dans un
rayon de 10 km; **2** ANAT radius m.

RAF n GB MIL abrév ▶ **Royal Air Force**.

raffish /ˈræfɪʃ/ adj libertin.

raffle /ˈræfl/ **I** n tombola f; **in a ~** à une tombola.
II vtr (also **~ off**) mettre [qch] en tombola.

raft /rɑːft, US ræft/ n radeau m.

rafter /ˈrɑːftə(r), US ˈræftə(r)/ n CONSTR chevron m.

rag /ræɡ/ **I** n **1** (cloth) chiffon m; **a bit of ~** un
chiffon; **2**○ (local newspaper) canard○ m.
II rags npl (old clothes) loques fpl.
III○ vtr (p prés etc **-gg-**) taquiner.
IDIOMS **it's like a red ~ to a bull** ça a le don de
l'exciter; **to go from ~s to riches** connaître une
ascension spectaculaire; **to lose one's ~**○ GB sortir
de ses gonds○.

ragamuffin† /ˈræɡəmʌfɪn/ n va-nu-pieds mf inv.

rag: **~-and-bone man**† n GB chiffonnier m;
~bag n FIG ramassis m.

rage /reɪdʒ/ **I** n **1** (anger) rage f, colère f; **to fly into a
~** entrer dans une colère noire; **2**○ (fashion) **to be
(all) the ~** faire fureur.
II vi **1** [storm, battle] faire rage; [controversy] se déchaîner (**over, about** à propos de); **2** [person] tempêter (**at, against** contre); **3**○ (party) faire la fête.

ragged /ˈræɡɪd/ adj **1** [garment] en loques; [cuff,
collar] effiloché; [person] dépenaillé; **2** (uneven) irrégu-
lier/-ière; **3** (motley) [group] disparate; **4** (in quality)
[performance] inégal.
IDIOMS **to run sb ~**○ épuiser qn.

raging /ˈreɪdʒɪŋ/ adj **1** [passion, argument] violent;
[thirst, pain] atroce; **a ~ toothache** une rage de
dents; **2** [blizzard, sea] déchaîné; **there was a ~
storm** la tempête faisait rage.

ragtag○ /ˈræɡtæɡ/ adj PÉJ [group] désordonné.
IDIOMS **the ~ and bobtail**○ la canaille.

rag trade○ n the **~** la confection.

rag week n GB UNIV semaine f du carnaval étudiant
(au profit d'institutions caritatives).

raid /reɪd/ **I** n MIL, FIN raid m (**on** sur); (on bank) hold-
up m (**on de**); (on home) cambriolage m (**on de, dans**);
(by police, customs) rafle f (**on dans**).
II vtr **1** (attack) [military] faire un raid sur; attaquer
[bank]; cambrioler [house]; [police] faire une rafle
dans; **2** FIG casser [piggybank]; faire une razzia○ sur
[fridge]; **3** FIN [company] entamer [reserves].

raider /ˈreɪdə(r)/ n (thief) pillard m; (corporate) raider m;
(soldier) (membre m d'un) commando m.

rail /reɪl/ **I** n **1** (in fence) barreau m; (on balcony) balustrade f; (on tower) garde-fou m; (handrail) rampe f; (on
ship) bastingage m; **2** (for display) (in shop) présentoir m;
3 (for curtains) tringle f; **4** (for vehicle) rail m; FIG **to go
off the ~s** dérailler○.
II rails npl (on racetrack) corde f; **to come up on the
~s** tenir la corde.
III noun modifier [network, traffic, transport] ferro-

viaire; [journey, travel] en train; **~ strike** grève f des
cheminots.

rail: **~car** n autorail m; **~card** n GB carte f
d'abonnement; **~head** n tête f de ligne.

railing /ˈreɪlɪŋ/ n **1** (also **~s**) (in park, stadium) grille f;
2 (on wall) main courante f; (on tower) garde-fou m; (on
balcony) balustrade f.

railroad /ˈreɪlrəʊd/ **I** n US RAIL **1** (network) chemin m
de fer; **2** (also **~ track**) voie f ferrée; **3** (company)
compagnie f des chemins de fer.
II○ vtr (push) **to ~ sb into doing** forcer qn à faire;
to ~ the bill through tout faire pour faire adopter le
projet de loi.

railroad car n US wagon m.

railway /ˈreɪlweɪ/ GB RAIL **I** n **1** (network) chemin m
de fer; **to use the ~s** voyager en train; **2** (also **~
line**) ligne f; **light ~** ligne locale; **3** (line) voie f
ferrée; **4** (company) compagnie f des chemins de fer.
II noun modifier [bridge] de chemin de fer; [museum]
des chemins de fer; [link, tunnel, accident] ferroviaire.

railway: **~ carriage** n GB wagon m; **~ embankment** n remblai m; **~ engine** n GB locomotive f;
~ junction n gare f de raccordement; **~ line** n
GB (route) ligne f de chemin de fer; (tracks) voie f
ferrée; **~man** ▶ **1251** GB n cheminot m; **~
station** n GB gare f.

rain /reɪn/ **I** n METEOROL pluie f; **the ~ stopped** il s'est
arrêté de pleuvoir; **steady/driving/pouring ~** pluie
régulière/battante/diluvienne; **in the ~** sous la pluie;
it looks like ~ le temps est à la pluie.
II rains npl saison f des pluies.
III vtr **to ~ blows on sb** rouer qn de coups.
IV v impers **1** METEOROL pleuvoir; **it's ~ing** (**hard**) il
pleut (à verse); **2** FIG = **rain down**.
IDIOMS **come ~ or shine** qu'il pleuve ou qu'il vente;
it never ~s but it pours un malheur n'arrive jamais
seul; **to be** (**as**) **right as ~** GB [person] se porter
comme un charme.
■ **rain down** [blows, ash, insults] pleuvoir.
■ **rain off** GB, **rain out** US: **to be ~ed off**
(cancelled) être annulé pour cause de pluie; (stopped)
être interrompu par la pluie.

rainbow /ˈreɪnbəʊ/ n LIT, FIG arc-en-ciel m.
IDIOMS **at the ~'s end** du domaine du rêve.

rain check n US SPORT billet pour un autre match si
le premier est annulé pour cause de pluie.
IDIOMS **to take a ~ on sth** reporter qch.

rain: **~coat** n imperméable m; **~drop** n goutte f
de pluie.

rainfall /ˈreɪnfɔːl/ n niveau m de précipitations;
heavy/low ~ fortes/faibles précipitations.

rain: **~ forest** n forêt f tropicale; **~storm** n
trombe f d'eau.

rainy /ˈreɪnɪ/ adj [afternoon, climate] pluvieux/-ieuse;
~ season saison f des pluies.
IDIOMS **to keep** ou **save something for a ~ day**
mettre de l'argent de côté.

raise /reɪz/ **I** n **1** US (pay rise) augmentation f; **2**
GAMES (in poker) mise f supérieure.
II vtr **1** (lift) lever [baton, barrier, curtain]; hisser
[flag]; soulever [box, lid]; élever [standard]; renflouer
[sunken ship]; **to ~ one's hand/head** lever la main/
tête; **he ~d the glass to his lips** il a porté le verre à
ses lèvres; **to ~ a glass to sb** lever son verre à
l'honneur de qn; **I've never ~d a hand to my children** je n'ai jamais levé la main sur mes enfants;
nobody ~d an eyebrow at my suggestion FIG ma
suggestion n'a fait sourciller personne; **2** (place upright)
dresser [mast]; redresser [patient]; **3** (increase)
augmenter [price, offer, salary, volume] (**from** de; **to**
à); élever [standard]; reculer [age limit]; **to raise sb's
awareness of** sensibiliser qn à; **to ~ one's voice** (to
be heard) parler plus fort; (in anger) élever la voix; **to
~ the temperature** LIT, FIG faire monter la température; **4** (cause) faire naître [doubts, fears]; soulever
[dust]; provoquer [protests]; **to ~ a cheer** [speech] déclencher des hourras; **to ~ a smile** [joke] faire
sourire; **5** (mention) soulever; **6** (bring up) élever [child,

family]; **to be ~d (as) a Catholic** être élevé dans la religion catholique; **7** (breed) élever [*livestock*]; **8** (find) trouver [*capital*]; **9** (form) lever [*army*]; former [*team*]; **10** (collect) lever [*tax*]; obtenir [*support*]; [*person*] collecter [*money*]; **the money ~d from the concert** la recette du concert; **11** (erect) élever [*monument*] (**to sb** en l'honneur de qn); **12** (end) lever [*ban*]; **13** (contact) contacter [*person*]; **14** (give) **to ~ the alarm** FIG donner l'alarme; **15** (improve) **to ~ the tone** hausser le ton; **to ~ sb's spirits** remonter le moral à qn; **16** (increase the stake) **I'll ~ you 200 dollars!** 200 dollars de mieux!; **to ~ the bidding** (in gambling) monter la mise; (at auction) monter l'enchère; **17** MATH élever [*number*].

III *v refl* **to ~ oneself** se redresser.

raised /reɪzd/ *adj* [*platform, jetty*] surélevé; **I heard ~ voices** j'ai entendu des éclats de voix.

raisin /ˈreɪzn/ *n* raisin *m* sec.

Raj /rɑːdʒ/ *n* GB HIST empire *m* britannique aux Indes.

rake /reɪk/ **I** *n* **1** (tool) râteau *m*; (in casino) râteau *m* de croupier; **2†** (libertine) débauché *m*.

II *vtr* **1** (in gardening) ratisser; **2** (scan) balayer.

III *vi* **to ~ among** ou **through** fouiller dans.

■ **rake in**○: **~ in** [*sth*] amasser [*money*]; **he's raking it in**○! il brasse l'argent à la pelle○!

■ **rake over**: **~ over** [*sth*] ratisser [*soil*].

■ **rake up**: **~ up** [*sth*], **~** [*sth*] **up 1** LIT ramasser [*qch*] avec un râteau [*leaves*]; **2** FIG ressusciter [*grievance*]; remuer [*past*].

rake-off○ /ˈreɪkɒf/ *n* (legal) commission *f*; (illicit) ristourne *f* illicite.

rakish /ˈreɪkɪʃ/ *adj* **1†** (dissolute) débauché; **2** (jaunty) désinvolte.

rally /ˈrælɪ/ **I** *n* **1** (meeting) rassemblement *m*; **2** (race) rallye *m*; **3** (in tennis) échange *m*; **4** (recovery) GEN amélioration *f* (**in** dans); FIN reprise *f*.

II *vtr* rassembler [*support, troops*]; rallier [*opinion*].

III *vi* **1** (come together) [*people*] se rallier (**to** à); **to ~ to the defence of sb** se porter au secours de qn; **2** (recover) [*dollar*] remonter; [*patient*] se rétablir; [*sportsperson*] se ressaisir.

■ **rally round**, **rally around**: ¶ **~ round** [*supporters*] se rallier; ¶ **~ round** [**sb**] soutenir [*person*].

rallying: **~ call**, **~ cry** *n* LIT, FIG cri *m* de ralliement; **~ point** *n* LIT, FIG point *m* de ralliement.

ram /ræm/ **I** *n* bélier *m*.

II *vtr* (*p prés etc* **-mm-**) **1** (crash into) rentrer dans, heurter; **2** (push) enfoncer; **~med down** enfoncé.

III *vi* (*p prés etc* **-mm-**) **to ~ into sth** [*vehicle*] rentrer dans qch, heurter qch.

■ **ram home**: **~** [*sth*] **home**, **~ home** [*sth*] LIT placer [*ball, fist*]; FIG faire clairement comprendre [*message, point*].

RAM /ræm/ *n* (*abrév* = **random access memory**) RAM *f*.

ramble /ˈræmbl/ **I** *n* randonnée *f*, balade *f*.

II *vi* (walk) faire une randonnée, faire une balade.

■ **ramble on** discourir (**about** sur).

rambler /ˈræmblə(r)/ *n* randonneur/-euse *m/f*.

rambling /ˈræmblɪŋ/ **I** *n* randonnée *f*.

II *adj* **1** [*house*] plein de coins et de recoins; **2** [*talk, article*] décousu; **3** [*plant*] grimpant.

ramification /ˌræmɪfɪˈkeɪʃn/ *n* ramification *f*.

ramify /ˈræmɪfaɪ/ *vi* se ramifier.

ramp /ræmp/ *n* GEN rampe *f*; GB (in roadworks) dénivellation *f*; AUT, TECH pont *m* de graissage; AVIAT passerelle *f*; US AUT (on, off highway) bretelle *f*; **hydraulic ~** pont *m* élévateur.

rampage I /ˈræmpeɪdʒ/ *n* **to be** ou **go on the ~** tout saccager.

II /ræmˈpeɪdʒ/ *vi* se déchaîner (**through** dans).

rampant /ˈræmpənt/ *adj* [*crime, disease*] endémique.

rampart /ˈræmpɑːt/ *n* LIT, FIG rempart *m*.

ramshackle /ˈræmʃækl/ *adj* LIT, FIG délabré.

ran /ræn/ *prét* ▶ **run**.

ranch /rɑːntʃ, US ræntʃ/ *n* ranch *m*.

rancher /ˈrɑːntʃə(r), US ˈræntʃə(r)/ *n* propriétaire *mf* de ranch.

rancid /ˈrænsɪd/ *adj* rance; **to go ~** rancir.

rancorous /ˈræŋkərəs/ *adj* rancunier/-ière.

rancour GB, **rancor** US /ˈræŋkə(r)/ *n* rancœur *f*.

rand /rænd/ ▶ **849** *n* rand *m*.

random /ˈrændəm/ *adj* (fait) au hasard.

rang /ræŋ/ *prét* ▶ **ring**.

range /reɪndʒ/ **I** *n* **1** (choice) (of prices, products) gamme *f*; (of activities, options) éventail *m*, choix *m*; (of people, abilities, beliefs, emotions) variété *f*; (of benefits, salaries) éventail *m*; (of issues, assumptions) série *f*; **a top of the ~ computer** un ordinateur haut de gamme; **age ~** tranche *f* d'âge; **price/salary ~** éventail de prix/des salaires; **in the £50–£100 ~** entre 50 et 100 livres sterling; **to have a wide ~ of interests** s'intéresser à beaucoup de choses; **a wide ~ of views** des vues très diverses; **2** (scope) (of influence, knowledge) étendue *f*; (of investigation, research) domaine *m*; **3** (of radar, weapon, transmitter) portée *f* (**of** de); **to be out of ~** être hors de portée; **4** AEROSP, AUT, AVIAT autonomie *f*; **5** US (prairie) prairie *f*; **on the ~** dans les pâturages; **6** (of mountains) chaîne *f*; **7** (stove) (wood etc) fourneau *m*; (gas, electric) cuisinière *f*; **8** (firing area) (for weapons) champ *m* de tir; (for missiles) zone *f* de tir; **9** (of actor) répertoire *m*; **10** MUS tessiture *f*.

II *vtr* **1** (set) opposer (**against** à); **2** (draw up) aligner, ranger [*forces*].

III *vi* **1** (extend) aller (**from** de; **to** à); (vary) varier; **to ~ over sth** couvrir qch; **2** (roam, wander) vagabonder.

ranger /ˈreɪndʒə(r)/ *n* **1** (in forest) garde-forestier *m*; **2** US, MIL ranger *m*.

rangy /ˈreɪndʒɪ/ *adj* élancé.

rank /ræŋk/ ▶ **1192** **I** *n* **1** (in military, police) grade *m*; (in company, politics) rang *m*; (social status) rang *m*; **to pull ~** abuser de son rang; **2** (line) (of people) rang *m*; (of objects) rangée *f*; **to break ~s** LIT [*soldiers*] rompre les rangs; FIG [*politician*] se rebeller; **to close ~s** LIT, FIG serrer les rangs; **3** (for taxis) station *f*; **taxi ~** station de taxis.

II ranks *npl* MIL, POL, IND rangs *mpl*; **to rise through the ~s** sortir du rang.

III *adj* **1** (absolute) [*outsider, beginner*] complet/-ète; [*favouritism, stupidity*] flagrant; **2** (foul) [*odour*] fétide; **3** (exuberant) [*ivy, weeds*] envahissant.

IV *vtr* **1** (classify) [*person*] classer [*player, novel, restaurant*] (**among** parmi); **above** au-dessus de; **below** au-dessous de; **2** US (be senior to) commander [*person*].

V *vi* **1** (rate) se classer (**among** parmi); **to ~ as a great composer** être considéré comme un grand compositeur; **to ~ above/alongside sb** occuper un rang supérieur/égal à qn; **this has to ~ as one of the worst films I've ever seen** c'est un des films les pires que j'aie jamais vus; **that doesn't ~ very high on my list** cela ne figure pas très haut dans ma liste; **2** US MIL (be most senior) commander.

rank and file /ˌræŋk ən ˈfaɪl/ *n* base *f*.

II rank-and-file *noun modifier* [*opinion*] de la base; [*member*] de base.

ranking /ˈræŋkɪŋ/ **I** *n* SPORT classement *m*.

II -ranking *combining form* **high/low-~** de haut/ bas rang.

rankle /ˈræŋkl/ *vi* **to ~ with sb** rester en travers de la gorge de qn○; **but it still ~s** mais ça laisse toujours un goût saumâtre.

ransack /ˈrænsæk, US rænˈsæk/ *vtr* fouiller [*drawer*] (**for** pour trouver); mettre [qch] à sac [*house*].

ransom /ˈrænsəm/ *n* rançon *f*; **to hold sb to** GB ou **for** US **~** LIT garder qn en otage; FIG tenir qn en otage.

IDIOMS **a king's ~** une somme fabuleuse.

rant /rænt/ *vi* déclamer; **to ~ and rave** tempêter (**at** contre); **to ~ on** divaguer (**about** sur).

ranting /ˈræntɪŋ/ *n* (*also* **~s**) rodomontades *fpl*.

rap /ræp/ **I** *n* **1** (tap) coup *m* sec; **2** MUS rap *m*; **3**○ (conversation) conversation *f*; **4**○ (accusation) accusation *f*; **to beat the ~** s'en tirer à bon compte.

Military ranks and titles

The following list gives the principal ranks in the French services.

The Navy = La marine nationale
amiral
vice-amiral d'escadre
vice-amiral
contre-amiral
capitaine de vaisseau
capitaine de frégate
capitaine de corvette
lieutenant de vaisseau
enseigne de vaisseau
  (1re et 2e classe)
aspirant
major
maître principal
premier maître
maître
second maître
quartier-maître (1re et 2e classe)
matelot

The Army = L'armée de terre
général d'armée
général de corps d'armée
général de division
général de brigade
colonel
lieutenant-colonel
commandant
capitaine
lieutenant
sous-lieutenant
aspirant
major
adjudant-chef

adjudant
sergent-chef
  or maréchal des logis-chef (*cavalry*)
sergent
  or maréchal des logis (*cavalry*)
caporal-chef
  or brigadier-chef (*cavalry*)
caporal
  or brigadier (*cavalry*)
soldat
  or cavalier (*cavalry*)

The Air Force = L'armée de l'air
général d'armée aérienne
général de corps aérien
général de division aérienne
général de brigade aérienne
colonel
lieutenant-colonel
commandant
capitaine
lieutenant
sous-lieutenant
aspirant
major
adjudant-chef
adjudant
sergent-chef
sergent
caporal-chef
caporal
aviateur

Speaking about someone
he's a colonel   =   il est colonel
to be promoted
to colonel   =   être promu colonel

he has the rank of colonel	=	il a le rang de colonel
she's a lieutenant in the Army	=	elle est lieutenant dans l'armée de terre
he's just a private	=	il est simple soldat
Colonel Smith has arrived	=	le colonel Smith est arrivé

Speaking to someone
In the armée de terre, *the* mon *is used to superior officers from lieutenant upwards, except for major. Mon is never prefixed to ranks in the marine nationale or the* armée de l'air *and never used to personnel of inferior rank in any of the three services.*

Service personnel to superior officers

yes, sir	=	oui, mon colonel (*or* mon capitaine, mon lieutenant etc.)
yes, ma'am	=	oui, colonel (*or* capitaine, lieutenant etc.)

Service personnel to someone of lower rank

yes, sergeant = oui, sergent

II *vtr* (*p prés etc* **-pp-**) (tap) frapper sur.
III *vi* (*p prés etc* **-pp-**) **1** (tap) donner des coups secs (**on** sur); **2** MUS faire du rap; **3**° US (talk) parler.

rapacious /rə'peɪʃəs/ *adj* rapace.

rape /reɪp/ **I** *n* **1** (attack) viol *m*; **2** AGRIC colza *m*.
II *vtr* violer.

rape(seed) oil *n* huile *f* de colza.

rapid /'ræpɪd/ *adj* GEN rapide; **in ~ succession** coup sur coup.

rapid: **~ deployment force** *n* MIL force *f* d'intervention rapide; **~ eye movement, REM** *n* mouvements *mpl* oculaires rapides.

rapidity /rə'pɪdətɪ/ *n* rapidité *f*.

rapidly /'ræpɪdlɪ/ *adv* rapidement.

rapids /'ræpɪdz/ *npl* rapides *mpl*.

rapid transit *n* US transport *m* public.

rapist /'reɪpɪst/ *n* violeur *m*.

rapper /'ræpə(r)/ *n* **1** MUS rappeur/-euse *m/f*; **2** US (door-knocker) heurtoir *m*.

rapport /ræ'pɔː(r), US -'pɔːrt/ *n* bons rapports *mpl*; **in ~ with** en harmonie avec.

rapt /ræpt/ *adj* GEN absorbé; [*smile*] extasié.

rapture /'ræptʃə(r)/ *n* ravissement *m*; **to go into ~s over** ou **about sth** s'extasier sur qch.

rapturous /'ræptʃərəs/ *adj* [*delight*] extasié; [*welcome*] enthousiaste; [*applause*] frénétique.

rare /reə(r)/ *adj* **1** (uncommon) rare; **2** [*steak*] saignant; **3** [*atmosphere, air*] raréfié.

rarebit /'reəbɪt/ *n* ▶ **Welsh rarebit**.

rarefied /'reərɪfaɪd/ *adj* LIT raréfié; FIG étouffant.

rarely /'reəlɪ/ *adv* rarement.

raring /'reərɪŋ/ *adj* **to be ~ to do** être très impatient de faire; **to be ~ to go** piaffer d'impatience.

rarity /'reərətɪ/ *n* **1** (collector's item) pièce *f* rare; **2** (rare occurrence) phénomène *m* rare; **to be a ~** être rare; **3** (rareness) rareté *f*.

rascal /'rɑːskl, US 'ræskl/ *n* **1** (used affectionately) coquin/-e *m/f*; **2**† (villain) voyou *m*.

rash /ræʃ/ **I** *n* **1** (skin) rougeurs *fpl*; **2** FIG vague *f*.
II *adj* [*person, decision*] irréfléchi; **it was ~ to do** il n'était pas raisonnable de faire.

rasher /'ræʃə(r)/ *n* tranche *f*.

rashly /'ræʃlɪ/ *adv* sans réfléchir.

rashness /'ræʃnɪs/ *n* inconséquence *f*.

rasp /rɑːsp, US ræsp/ **I** *n* **1** (of saw, voice) grincement *m*; **2** (file) râpe *f*.
II *vtr* (rub) râper.
III *vi* [*saw*] grincer.
IV **rasping** *pres p adj* [*voice, sound*] râpeux/-euse.

raspberry /'rɑːzbrɪ, US 'ræzberɪ/ **I** *n* **1** (fruit) framboise *f*; **2** (noise) **to blow a ~** faire un bruit de dérision.
II *noun modifier* [*ice cream, tart*] à la framboise; [*jam*] de framboise.

Rastafarian /ˌræstə'feərɪən/ *n* rasta *mf*, rastafari *mf*.

rat /ræt/ **I** *n* **1** ZOOL rat *m*; **2**° (person) **you ~**! canaille°!; **3** US (informer) mouchard/-e° *m/f*.
II° *vi* (*p prés etc* **-tt-**) **to ~ on** moucharder°, dénoncer [*person*]; se dédire de [*deal*].
III rats *excl* mince alors°!
IDIOMS to look like a drowned ~ être trempé comme une soupe°; **to smell a ~** flairer quelque chose de louche.

ratcatcher /'rætkætʃə(r)/ *n* HIST chasseur *m* de rats.

ratchet /'rætʃɪt/ *n* (toothed rack) crémaillère *f*.

rate /reɪt/ **I** *n* **1** (speed) rythme *m*; **at this ~** ou **at the ~ we're going we'll never be able to afford a car** FIG à ce train-là nous n'aurons jamais les moyens d'acheter une voiture; **at a terrific ~** à toute vitesse; **2** (level) taux *m*; **the interest ~** le taux d'intérêt; **3** (charge) tarif *m*; **at a reduced ~** à tarif réduit; **hourly ~** salaire *m* horaire; **4** (in foreign exchange) cours *m*.
II rates *npl* GB (taxation) impôts *mpl* locaux; **business ~s** ≈ taxe *f* professionnelle.
III *vtr* **1** (classify) **I ~ his new novel very highly**

j'admire beaucoup son nouveau roman; **how do you ~ this restaurant?** que pensez-vous de ce restaurant?; **to ~ sb as a great composer** considérer qn comme un grand compositeur; **to ~ sb among** classer qn parmi; **highly ~d** très coté; **2** (deserve) mériter [*medal, round of applause*]; **3** (value) estimer [*honesty, friendship, person*].
IV *vi* (rank) **she ~s among the best sopranos in Europe** elle compte parmi les meilleures sopranos européennes.
V *v refl* **how do you ~ yourself as a driver?** comment vous jugez-vous en tant que conducteur?; **she doesn't ~ herself very highly** elle n'a pas une très haute opinion d'elle-même.
IDIOMS at any ~ en tout cas.
rateable GB, **ratable** US /'reɪtəbl/ *adj* [*property*] imposable; **~ value** valeur *f* locative imposable.
rate-cap /'reɪtkæp/ *vtr* (*p prés etc* **-pp-**) GB POL, ECON imposer un plafond aux impôts locaux.
rate: **~-capping** *n* GB plafonnement *m* des impôts locaux; **~-payer** *n* GB contribuable *mf*.
rather /'rɑːðə(r)/ *adv* **1** (somewhat) plutôt; **I ~ like him** je le trouve plutôt sympathique; **it's ~ like an apple** ça ressemble un peu à une pomme; **it's ~ a pity** c'est assez dommage; **it's ~ too/more difficult** c'est un peu trop/plus difficile; **2** (preferably) **~ than sth/do** plutôt que qch/de faire; **I would (much) ~ do** je préférerais de loin (faire) (de que faire); **I'd ~ die!** plutôt mourir!; **I'd ~ not** j'aimerais mieux pas; **3** (more exactly) plutôt; **a tree, or ~ a bush** un arbre, ou plutôt un buisson; **practical ~ than decorative** pratique plutôt que décoratif.
ratification /ˌrætɪfɪ'keɪʃn/ *n* ratification *f*.
ratify /'rætɪfaɪ/ *vtr* ratifier.
rating /'reɪtɪŋ/ **I** *n* **1** (score) cote *f*; **2** FIN (status) cote *f*; **share ~** cote *f* en Bourse; **3** GB (in taxation) (valuation) valeur *f* imposable; **4** MIL NAUT ~ matelot *m*.
II ratings *npl* TV Radio indice *m* d'écoute, audimat® *m*.
rating system *n* GB répartition *f* des impôts locaux.
ratio /'reɪʃɪəʊ/ *n* GEN proportion *f*, rapport *m*; MATH raison *f*; **the pupil to teacher ~** le nombre d'élèves par enseignant; **the ~ of men to women is two to five** la proportion d'hommes est de deux pour cinq femmes; **in** ou **by a ~ of 60:40** dans une proportion de 60 à 40.
ration /'ræʃn/ **I** *n* LIT ration *f*; FIG (of problems) compte *m*.
II *noun modifier* [*book, card*] de rationnement.
III *vtr* rationner [*food etc*] (**to** à); limiter la ration de [*person*] (**to** à).
rational /'ræʃnl/ *adj* [*approach, argument*] rationnel/-elle; [*person*] sensé; **it is ~ to do** il est logique de faire; **~ being** être *m* doué de raison.
rationale /ˌræʃə'nɑːl, US -'næl/ *n* (*sans pl*) **1** (reasons) raisons *fpl* (**for** pour; **for doing** de faire); **2** (logic) logique *f* (**behind** de).
rationalist /'ræʃnəlɪst/ *n, adj* rationaliste (*mf*).
rationalization /ˌræʃnəlaɪ'zeɪʃn/ *n* **1** (justification) justification *f* (**for** de); **2** GB, ECON rationalisation *f*.
rationalize /'ræʃnəlaɪz/ *vtr* **1** (justify) justifier; **2** GB ECON rationaliser.
rationally /'ræʃnəlɪ/ *adv* rationnellement.
rationing /'ræʃnɪŋ/ *n* rationnement *m*.
rat: **~ poison** *n* mort-aux-rats *f inv*; **~ race** *n* PÉJ foire *f* d'empoigne.
rattan /ræ'tæn/ *n* (tree, material) rotin *m*.
rat-tat-tat /ˌrættæt'tæt/ *n* toc-toc *m*.
rattle /'rætl/ **I** *n* **1** (noise) (of bottles, cutlery, chains) cliquetis *m*; (of window, engine) vibration *f*; (of car bodywork) bruit *m* de ferraille; (of rattlesnake) bruit *m* de crécelle; (of gun) crépitement *m*; **2** (of baby) hochet *m*; (of sports fan) crécelle *f*; **3** (snake's tail) cascabelle *f*.
II *vtr* **1** (shake) [*person*] faire s'entrechoquer [*bottles, cutlery, chains*]; [*wind*] faire vibrer [*window*]; [*person*] s'acharner sur [*handle*]; **2°** (annoy) énerver [*person*].
III *vi* [*bottles, cutlery, chains*] s'entrechoquer;

[*window*] vibrer; **the car ~d along** la voiture avançait dans un bruit de ferraille.
IDIOMS to shake sb until his/her etc teeth ~ secouer qn comme un prunier.
rattlesnake /'rætlsneɪk/ *n* serpent *m* à sonnette, crotale *m*.
rattling /'rætlɪŋ/ **I** *n* = **rattle I 1**.
II *adj* (vibrating) [*chain, window*] bruyant.
rat trap *n* piège *m* à rats, ratière *f*.
ratty° /'rætɪ/ *adj* **1** GB (grumpy) grincheux/-euse; **2** US (shabby) miteux/-euse; **3** US (tangled) [*hair*] emmêlé.
raucous /'rɔːkəs/ *adj* [*laugh*] éraillé; [*person*] bruyant.
raucously /'rɔːkəslɪ/ *adv* [*call*] d'une voix éraillée.
raunchy° /'rɔːntʃɪ/ *adj* **1** (earthy) [*performer, voice, song*] torride; **2** (bawdy) paillard.
ravage /'rævɪdʒ/ **I** *ravages* *npl* ravages *mpl* (**of** de).
II *vtr* ravager.
rave /reɪv/ **I°** *n* GB (party) bringue° *f* (branchée°).
II° *adj* **a ~ review** une critique dithyrambique.
III *vi* (enthusiastically) s'emballer (**about** au sujet de); (angrily) tempêter; (when fevered) délirer.
raven /'reɪvn/ *n* grand corbeau *m*.
raven-haired /ˌreɪvn'heəd/ *adj* aux cheveux de jais.
ravenous /'rævənəs/ *adj* [*animal*] vorace; [*appetite*] féroce; **to be ~** avoir une faim de loup.
ravenously /'rævənəslɪ/ *adv* avec voracité.
rave-up° /'reɪvʌp/ *n* GB fête *f*.
ravine /rə'viːn/ *n* ravin *m*.
raving /'reɪvɪŋ/ **I** *ravings* *npl* divagations *fpl*.
II *adj* **1** (fanatical) enragé; **a ~ lunatic** un fou furieux/ une folle furieuse; **2** (tremendous) [*success*] éclatant.
IDIOMS (stark) ~ mad° complètement fou.
ravioli /ˌrævɪ'əʊlɪ/ *n* ravioli *mpl*.
ravish /'rævɪʃ/ *vtr* LITTÉR (delight) ravir.
ravishing /'rævɪʃɪŋ/ *adj* ravissant.
raw /rɔː/ *adj* **1** [*food*] cru; [*rubber, sugar*] brut; [*data*] brut; [*sewage*] non traité; **2** (without skin) [*patch*] à vif; **3** (cold) [*weather*] froid et humide; [*air*] cru; [*wind*] pénétrant; **4** (inexperienced) inexpérimenté; **5** (realistic) [*description*] cru; **6** (undisguised) [*emotion*] à l'état brut; [*energy*] sauvage; **7** US (vulgar) obscène.
IDIOMS in the ~° GB (naked) nu; **life in the ~** la vie dans le vif; **to give sb a ~ deal°** traiter qn de façon injuste; **to touch a ~ nerve** toucher un point sensible.
raw: **~hide** *n* (leather) cuir *m* brut; **~ material** *n* LIT, FIG matière *f* première.
ray /reɪ/ *n* **1** (beam) rayon *m*; **~ gun** pistolet *m* à rayons; **a ~ of** FIG une lueur de [*hope etc*]; **2** (fish) raie *f*.
rayon /'reɪɒn/ *n* rayonne *f*.
raze /reɪz/ *vtr* raser.
razor /'reɪzə(r)/ *n* rasoir *m*.
IDIOMS to live on a ~('s) edge être au bord de l'abîme.
razor: **~ blade** *n* lame *f* de rasoir; **~ burn** *n* feu *m* du rasoir; **~-sharp** *adj* LIT tranchant comme un rasoir; FIG acéré; **~ wire** *n* feuillard *m*.
razzle° /'ræzl/ *n* GB **to go on the ~°** faire la fête°.
razzledazzle° /ˌræzl'dæzl/ *n* éclat *m* (trompeur).
razzmatazz° /ˌræzmə'tæz/ *n* folklore° *m*, cirque° *m*.
R & B *n* (*abrév* = **rhythm and blues**) rhythm and blues *m*.
RC *n, adj: abrév* ▶ **Roman Catholic**.
Rd *n: abrév écrite* = **road**.
R&D *n: abrév* ▶ **research and development**.
RDA *n* (*abrév* = **recommended daily amount**) AQR *mpl*.
re¹ /reɪ/ *n* ré *m*.
re² /riː/ *prep* (*abrév* = **with reference to**) (in letter head) 'objet:'; (about) au sujet de; **~ your letter...** suite à votre lettre...
RE *n* GB SCH (*abrév* = **Religious Education**) éducation *f* religieuse.
reach /riːtʃ/ **I** *n* portée *f*; **beyond** ou **out of ~** hors

de portée; **within (arm's)** ~ à portée de (la) main; **within easy** ~ **of** à proximité de [*shops, facility*]; **within** ~ **for sb** à la portée de qn.

II reaches *npl* **the upper/lower** ~**es** (of society) les échelons *mpl* les plus hauts/les plus bas; (of river) la partie supérieure/inférieure.

III *vtr* **1** (arrive at) [*person, train, river*] atteindre [*place, person*]; [*sound, news, letter*] parvenir à [*person, place*]; **to** ~ **land** toucher terre; **the message took three days to** ~ **Paris** le message a mis trois jours pour arriver jusqu'à Paris; **easily** ~**ed by bus** facilement accessible par le bus; **2** (attain) atteindre [*age, level*]; **matters** ~**ed a point where**... les choses en sont arrivées à un point où...; **to** ~ **the finals** parvenir en finale; **3** (come to) arriver à [*decision, understanding, conclusion*]; **to** ~ **a verdict** JUR rendre un verdict; **4** (by stretching) atteindre [*object, shelf, switch*]; **5** (contact) joindre; **6** (make impact on) toucher [*audience, market*]; **7** (in height, length) arriver à [*floor, ceiling*].

IV *vi* **1** (stretch) **to** ~ **up/down** lever/baisser le bras; **to** ~ **across** étendre le bras; **to** ~ **for one's gun** étendre le bras pour saisir son arme; ~ **for the sky!** les mains en l'air!; **2** (extend) **to** ~ **(up/down) to** arriver jusqu'à.

■ **reach out** LIT étendre le bras; **to** ~ **out for** chercher [*affection, success*]; **to** ~ **out to** (help) aider; (make contact) établir un contact avec.

react /rɪˈækt/ *vi* GEN, CHEM réagir (**to** à; **against** contre; **with** avec; **on** sur).

reaction /rɪˈækʃn/ *n* GEN, CHEM réaction *f*.

reactionary /rɪˈækʃənɪ, US -ənerɪ/ *n, adj* réactionnaire (*mf*).

reactivate /rɪˈæktɪveɪt/ *vtr* remettre [qch] en fonction.

reactor /rɪˈæktə(r)/ *n* CHEM réacteur *m*.

read I /riːd/ *n* **to have a** ~ **of**° lire [*article, magazine*]; **to be an easy** ~ être facile à lire.

II /riːd/ *vtr* (*prét, pp* **read** /red/) **1** (in text etc) lire [*book, map, music, sign*]; **to** ~ **sth to oneself** lire qch; **I can** ~ **German** je lis l'allemand; **2** (say) **the card** ~**s 'Happy Birthday Dad'** sur la carte il est écrit 'bon anniversaire Papa'; **3** (decipher) lire [*braille, handwriting*]; **4** (interpret) reconnaître [*signs*]; interpréter [*intentions, reactions*]; voir [*situation*]; **to** ~ **sb's thoughts** ou **mind** lire dans les pensées de qn; **to** ~ **sb's mood** connaître les humeurs de qn; **to** ~ **a remark as** considérer une remarque comme; **the book can be read as a satire** le livre peut se lire comme une satire; **don't** ~ **too much into his reply** ne va pas imaginer des choses qu'il n'a pas dites; **5** UNIV faire des études de [*history etc*]; **6** (take a recording) relever [*meter*]; lire [*dial*]; **7** RADIO, TELECOM recevoir [*person*]; **I can** ~ **you loud and clear** je vous reçois cinq sur cinq.

III /riːd/ *vi* (*prét, pp* **read** /red/) **1** (look at or articulate text) lire (**to sb** à qn); **to** ~ **about sth** lire quelque chose sur qch; **to** ~ **from sth** lire qch à qn; **2** GB UNIV **to** ~ **for a degree** ~ préparer une licence (**in** de); **3** (create an impression) **the document** ~**s well/badly** le document se lit bien/mal; **the translation** ~**s like the original** la traduction est aussi bonne que l'original.

IDIOMS **to take sth as read** considérer qch comme lu; **to** ~ **between the lines** lire entre les lignes.

■ **read back**: ~ [sth] **back** relire [*message, sentence*].

■ **read on** continuer à lire.

■ **read out**: ~ [sth] **out**, ~ **out** [sth] lire [qch] à haute voix.

■ **read over, read through**: ~ **over** ou **through** [sth], ~ [sth] **over** ou **through** lire; (reread) relire.

■ **read up**: **to** ~ **up on sth/sb** étudier qch/qn à fond.

readable /ˈriːdəbl/ *adj* **1** (legible) lisible; **2** (enjoyable) agréable à lire.

reader /ˈriːdə(r)/ *n* **1** GEN lecteur/-trice *m/f*; **he's a slow** ~ il lit lentement; **2** (anthology) recueil *m* de textes; **3** GB UNIV chargé/-e *m/f* de cours; US UNIV directeur/-trice *m/f* d'études.

readership /ˈriːdəʃɪp/ *n* lecteurs *mpl*.

read head *n* COMPUT tête *f* de lecture.

readily /ˈredɪlɪ/ *adv* **1** (willingly) [*accept, reply, give*] sans hésiter; **2** (easily) facilement.

readiness /ˈredɪnɪs/ *n* **1** (preparedness) niveau *m* de préparation; **in** ~ **for sth** en prévision de qch; **to be in a state of** ~ être (fin) prêt; **2** (willingness) empressement *m* (**to do** à faire).

reading /ˈriːdɪŋ/ *n* **1** (skill, pastime) lecture *f*; ~ **and writing** la lecture et l'écriture; **his** ~ **is poor** il lit mal; **her novels make light/heavy** ~ ses romans sont faciles/difficiles à lire; **2** (measurement) (on meter) relevé *m* (**on** de); (on instrument) indication *f* (**on** de); **3** (interpretation) interprétation *f* (**of** de); **4** (spoken extract) lecture *f* (**from** de); **5** GB POL (of bill) lecture *f* (**of** de).

reading: ~ **age** *n* SCH niveau *m* de lecture; ~ **glass** *n* loupe *f*; ~ **glasses** *npl* lunettes *fpl* (pour lire); ~ **lamp** *n* (by bed) lampe *f* de chevet; (on desk) lampe *f* de bureau; ~ **list** *n* SCH, UNIV liste *f* d'ouvrages recommandés; ~ **matter** *n* lecture *¢ f*; ~ **room** *n* salle *f* de lecture.

readjust /ˌriːəˈdʒʌst/ **I** *vtr* rajuster [*hat*]; régler [qch] de nouveau [*TV, lens*]; remettre [qch] à l'heure [*watch*]; réajuster [*salary*].
II *vi* se réadapter (**to** à).

read-only memory, ROM *n* COMPUT mémoire *f* morte; ~**-out** *n* COMPUT extraction *f*.

readvertise /ˌriːˈædvətaɪz/ *vtr* refaire paraître une annonce pour [*post, sale, item*].

ready /ˈredɪ/ **I** *n* **to have) a gun/pen at the** ~ (être) prêt à tirer/écrire.
II° **readies** *npl* argent *m*.
III *adj* **1** (prepared) prêt (**for** pour); ~ **to do** prêt à faire; **to get** ~ se préparer; **to get sth** ~ préparer qch; ~ **when you are** quand tu veux; ~, **steady, go** SPORT à vos marques, prêts, partez!; **I'm** ~, **willing and able** je suis à votre service; ~ **and waiting** fin prêt; **2** (willing) prêt (**to do** à faire); **more than** ~ **to do** plus que disposé à faire; **to be** ~ **for** avoir besoin de [*meal, vacation*]; **3** (quick) [*answer*] tout prêt; [*wit*] vif/vive; [*smile*] facile; **to be** ~ **with one's criticism** être prompt à critiquer; **4** (available) [*market, supply*] à portée de main; [*access*] direct; ~ **cash**°, ~ **money**° (argent *m*) liquide *m*.
IV *vtr* préparer [*ship, car*] (**for sth** à qch).

ready-made /ˌredɪˈmeɪd/ *adj* [*suit*] de prêt-à-porter; [*curtains*] prêt à poser; [*furniture*] déjà monté; [*excuse, phrase*] tout fait.

ready: ~**-to-serve** *adj* [*food*] cuisiné; ~**-to-wear** *adj* [*garment*] prêt-à-porter.

reaffirm /ˌriːəˈfɜːm/ *vtr* réaffirmer.

reafforestation GB, **reforestation** US /ˌriːəˌfɒrɪˈsteɪʃn, US ˌriːəˌfɔːrəˈsteɪʃn/ *n* reboisement *m*.

real /rɪəl/ **I** *n* réel *m*.
II *adj* **1** (not imaginary) véritable, réel/réelle; **in** ~ **life** dans la réalité; **the** ~ **world** le monde réel, la réalité; **in** ~ **terms** en réalité; **2** (not artificial) [*diamond, flower, leather*] vrai (*before n*), authentique; **the** ~ **thing, the** ~ **McCoy**° de l'authentique, du vrai de vrai°; **this time it's the** ~ **thing** cette fois c'est pour de vrai°; **3** (true, proper) [*holiday, rest*] véritable, vrai (*before n*); **he knows the** ~ **you** il connaît ta vraie personnalité; **the** ~ **Africa** l'Afrique profonde; **4** (for emphasis) [*charmer, pleasure*] vrai (*before n*); **it's a** ~ **shame** c'est vraiment dommage; **5** FIN, COMM [*cost, value*] réel/réelle; **6** MATH réel/réelle.
IDIOMS **for** ~° pour de vrai°.

real estate *n* **1** JUR, COMM (property) biens *mpl* immobiliers; **2** US (profession) immobilier *m*.

real estate: ~ **agent** *n* US agent *m* immobilier; ~ **developer** *n* US promoteur *m*; ~ **office** *n* US agence *f* immobilière.

realign /ˌriːəˈlaɪn/ **I** *vtr* remettre [qch] dans l'alignement [*objects*]; FIG redéfinir [*views*].
II *vi* POL former de nouvelles alliances.

realignment /ˌriːəˈlaɪnmənt/ *n* (of view) redéfinition *f*; POL, FIN réalignement *m*.

realism /'ri:əlızəm/ *n* réalisme *m*.

realist /'ri:əlıst/ *n, adj* réaliste (*mf*).

realistic /ˌrıə'lıstık/ *adj* réaliste.

realistically /ˌrıə'lıstıklı/ *adv* [*look at, think, describe*] de façon réaliste; **~,...** en réalité,...

reality /rı'ælətı/ *n* réalité *f* (**of** de); **to be out of touch with ~** vivre hors des réalités.

realization /ˌrıəlaı'zeıʃn, US -lı'z-/ *n* **1** (awareness) prise *f* de conscience (**of** de; **that** du fait que); **to come to the ~ that** se rendre compte que; **2** (achievement) réalisation *f* (**of** de).

realize /'rıəlaız/ *vtr* **1** (know) se rendre compte de [*error, significance, fact*]; **to ~ that** se rendre compte que; **to ~ how/what** comprendre comment/ce que; **more/less than people ~** plus/moins que les gens n'en ont conscience; **to come to ~ sth** prendre conscience de qch; **to make sb ~ sth** faire comprendre qch à qn; **I didn't ~!** je ne le savais pas!; **I ~ that!** oui, je sais bien!; **2** (make real) réaliser [*idea, dream, goal, design*]; **my worst fears were ~d** ce que je craignais le plus est arrivé; **to ~ one's potential** développer ses capacités; **3** FIN (liquidate) réaliser [*assets*]; **4** COMM [*sale*] rapporter [*sum*]; [*person, vendor*] faire [*sum*] (**on** en vendant).

reallocate /ri:'ælə,keıt/ *vtr* réattribuer.

really /'rıəlı/ **I** *adv* **1** (for emphasis) vraiment, réellement; **they ~ enjoyed the film** le film leur a vraiment plu; **you ~ must taste it** il faut absolument que tu y goûtes; **2** (very) [*cheap, hot*] très, vraiment; **3** (in actual fact) en fait, réellement; **what I ~ mean is that...** en fait, ce que je veux dire c'est que...; **he's a good teacher ~** en fait, c'est un bon professeur; **ghosts don't ~ exist** les fantômes n'existent pas; **I'll tell you what ~ happened** je vais te dire ce qui s'est réellement passé; **4** (seriously) vraiment; **I ~ don't know** je ne sais vraiment pas; **do you ~ think he'll apologize?** tu penses vraiment qu'il s'excusera?; **~?** (expressing disbelief) c'est vrai?; **does she ~?** c'est vrai?

II *excl* (also **well ~**) (annoyed) franchement!

realm /relm/ *n* (kingdom) royaume *m*; FIG domaine *m*.

real tennis ▶ 949 *n* jeu *m* de paume.

realty /'ri:əltı/ *n* US biens *mpl* immobiliers.

ream /ri:m/ *n* (of paper) rame *f* (de papier); **she wrote ~s about it** FIG elle en a écrit toute une tartine°.

reanimate /ˌri:'ænı,meıt/ *vtr* ranimer.

reap /ri:p/ **I** *vtr* **1** AGRIC recueillir [*crop*]; **2** FIG récolter [*benefits*]; **to ~ the rewards of one's efforts** recueillir le fruit de ses efforts.

II *vi* moissonner.

reaper /'ri:pə(r)/ *n* (machine) moissonneuse *f*; (person) moissonneur/-euse *m/f*.

reappear /ˌri:ə'pıə(r)/ *vi* reparaître.

reappearance /ˌri:ə'pıərəns/ *n* réapparition *f*.

reapply /ˌri:ə'plaı/ *vi* reposer sa candidature (**for** à).

reappoint /ˌri:ə'pɔınt/ *vtr* renommer (**to** à).

reappraise /ˌri:ə'preız/ *vtr* réexaminer [*question, policy*]; réévaluer [*writer, work*].

rear /rıə(r)/ **I** *n* **1** (of building, car, room etc) arrière *m*; **at the ~ of the house** derrière la maison; (of procession, train) queue *f*; MIL (of unit, convoy) arrière-garde *f*, arrières *mpl*; (of column) queue *f*; **to bring up the ~** fermer la marche; **2** EUPH (of person) derrière° *m*.

II *adj* **1** [*entrance, garden*] de derrière; **2** AUT [*light, seat, suspension*] arrière *inv*.

III *vtr* élever [*child, animals*]; cultiver [*plants*].

IV *vi* (also **~ up**) [*horse*] se cabrer; [*snake*] se dresser.

rear: ~ admiral *n* contre-amiral *m*; **~-drive** *adj* à traction *f* arrière.

rear end /ˌrıər 'end/ **I** *n* **1** (of vehicle) arrière *m*; **2** EUPH° (of person) derrière *m*.

II° **rear-end** *vtr* US emboutir° l'arrière de [*car*].

rearguard /'rıəgɑ:d/ *n* MIL, FIG arrière-garde *f*.

rearguard action *n* combat *m* d'arrière-garde.

rearm /ˌri:'ɑ:m/ *vtr, vi* réarmer.

rearmament /ˌri:'ɑ:məmənt/ *n* réarmement *m*.

rearmost /'rıəməʊst/ *adj* GEN tout/-e dernier/-ière; [*carriage*] de queue.

rearrange /ˌri:ə'reındʒ/ *vtr* réarranger [*hair*]; redisposer [*furniture*]; réaménager [*room*]; modifier [*plans*].

rear: ~-view mirror *n* rétroviseur *m*; **~ wheel** *n* AUT roue *f* arrière *inv*; **~-wheel drive** *n* AUT traction *f* arrière *inv*; **~ window** *n* AUT vitre *f* arrière *inv*.

reason /'ri:zn/ **I** *n* **1** (cause) raison *f* (**for, behind** de); **for no (good) ~,** sans raison valable; **if you are late for any ~** si tu es en retard, pour une raison ou pour une autre; **I have ~ to believe that...** j'ai des raisons de croire que...; **by ~ of** SOUT en raison de; **for that ~ I can't do it** c'est pour cette raison que je ne peux pas le faire; **the ~ why...** la raison pour laquelle...; **I'll tell you the ~ why...** je vais te dire pourquoi...; **give me one ~ why I should!** et pourquoi donc devrais-je le faire?; **what was his ~ for resigning?** pour quelle raison a-t-il démissionné?; **the ~ is that...** la raison en est que...; **the ~ given is that...** la raison invoquée est que...; **to have every** ou **good ~ for doing** ou **to do** avoir tout lieu de faire; **there was no ~ for you to worry** tu n'avais aucune raison de t'inquiéter; **all the more ~ to insist on it** raison de plus pour insister; **she was angry, and with good ~** elle était fâchée, et à juste titre; **2** (common sense) raison *f*; **to lose one's ~** perdre la raison; **to listen to** ou **see ~** entendre raison; **it stands to ~ that** il va sans dire que; **within ~** dans la limite du raisonnable.

II *vtr* **1** (argue) soutenir; **2** (conclude) déduire.

III *vi* **to ~ with sb** raisonner qn.

IV reasoned *pp adj* raisonné.

reasonable /'ri:znəbl/ *adj* **1** (sensible) raisonnable; **2** (understanding) compréhensif/-ive (**about** au sujet de); **3** (justified) raisonnable; **it is ~ for sb to do** il est légitime que qn fasse; **beyond ~ doubt** JUR sans aucun doute possible; **4** (moderately good) convenable; **there is a ~ chance that** il est fort possible que.

reasonableness /'ri:znəblnıs/ *n* (of remark, argument) bien-fondé *m*.

reasonably /'ri:znəblı/ *adv* **1** (legitimately) légitimement; (sensibly) raisonnablement; **2** (rather) assez.

reasoning /'ri:znıŋ/ *n* raisonnement *m*.

reassemble /ˌri:ə'sembl/ **I** *vtr* **1** rassembler [*troops, pupils*]; **2** TECH remonter [*unit, engine etc*].

II *vi* [*people*] se rassembler.

reassert /ˌri:ə'sɜ:t/ *vtr* réaffirmer [*authority, claim*].

reassess /ˌri:ə'ses/ *vtr* GEN réexaminer, reconsidérer [*problem, situation*]; recalculer [*tax liability*].

reassessment /ˌri:ə'sesmənt/ *n* (of situation) réexamen *m*; (of tax) nouveau calcul *m*.

reassurance /ˌri:ə'ʃɔ:rəns, US -'ʃʊər-/ *n* **1** (comfort) réconfort *m*; **2** (official guarantee) garantie *f*.

reassure /ˌri:ə'ʃɔ:(r), US -'ʃʊər-/ *vtr* rassurer [*person*] (**about** sur).

reassuring /ˌri:ə'ʃɔ:rıŋ, US -'ʃʊər-/ *adj* rassurant.

reassuringly /ˌri:ə'ʃɔ:rıŋlı, US -'ʃʊər-/ *adv* d'une manière rassurante.

reawaken /ˌri:ə'weıkən/ **I** *vtr* **1** SOUT réveiller à nouveau [*person*]; **2** FIG faire renaître [*interest*].

II *vi* SOUT [*person*] se réveiller de nouveau.

reawakening /ˌri:ə'weıkənıŋ/ *n* SOUT réveil *m*.

rebate /'ri:beıt/ *n* (refund) remboursement *m*; (discount) remise *f*.

rebel **I** /'rebl/ *n, noun modifier* rebelle (*mf*).

II /rı'bel/ *vi* (*p prés etc* **-ll-**) LIT, FIG se rebeller.

rebellion /rı'beljən/ *n* rébellion *f*, révolte *f*.

rebellious /rı'beljəs/ *adj* [*nation, child*] rebelle, insoumis; [*school, class*] indiscipliné.

rebirth /ˌri:'bɜ:θ/ *n* LIT, FIG renaissance *f*.

reboot /ˌri:'bu:t/ *vtr* COMPUT réinitialiser, réamorcer.

reborn /ˌri:'bɔ:n/ *adj* RELIG **to be ~** renaître; FIG **to be ~ as sth** réapparaître sous la forme de qch.

rebound **I** /'ri:baʊnd/ *n* (of ball) rebond *m*; (in basket-

ball) panier *m*; **to marry sb on the ~** épouser qn sous le coup d'une déception amoureuse.
II /rɪ'baʊnd/ *vi* LIT (bounce) rebondir; **to ~ on** FIG se retourner contre.

rebuff /rɪ'bʌf/ **I** *n* rebuffade *f*.
II *vtr* rabrouer [*person*]; repousser [*suggestion, advances*].

rebuild /ˌriː'bɪld/ *vtr* (*prét, pp* **rebuilt** /ˌriː'bɪlt/) reconstruire.

rebuilding /ˌriː'bɪldɪŋ/ *n* reconstruction *f*.

rebuke /rɪ'bjuːk/ **I** *n* réprimande *f*.
II *vtr* réprimander (**for** pour).

rebut /rɪ'bʌt/ *vtr* (*p prés etc* **-tt-**) réfuter.

rebuttal /rɪ'bʌtl/ *n* réfutation *f*.

recalcitrant /rɪ'kælsɪtrənt/ *adj* SOUT récalcitrant.

recalculate /ˌriː'kælkjʊˌleɪt/ *vtr* recalculer.

recall **I** /'riːkɔːl/ *n* **1** (memory) mémoire *f*; **to have total ~ of sth** se souvenir de qch dans les moindres détails; **2** GEN, MIL, COMPUT (summons) rappel *m*.
II /rɪ'kɔːl/ *vtr* **1** (remember) se souvenir de; **I ~ seeing/what happened** je me souviens d'avoir vu/de ce qui est arrivé; **as I ~** si je m'en souviens bien; **2** (remind of) rappeler; **3** (summon back) GEN rappeler; convoquer [*parliament*].

recant /rɪ'kænt/ **I** *vtr* abjurer [*heresy*]; désavouer [*opinion*]; rétracter [*statement*].
II *vi* GEN se rétracter; RELIG abjurer.

recap **I○** *n* /'riːkæp/ *abrév* ▶ **recapitulation.**
II○ *vtr* (*p prés etc* **-pp-**) /'riːkæp/ *abrév* ▶ **recapitulate.**

recapitulate /ˌriːkə'pɪtʃʊleɪt/ *vtr, vi* récapituler.

recapitulation /ˌriːkəpɪtʃʊ'leɪʃn/ *n* récapitulation *f*.

recapture /ˌriː'kæptʃə(r)/ **I** *n* (of prisoner, animal) capture *f*; (of town, position) reprise *f*.
II *vtr* LIT recapturer [*prisoner, animal*]; MIL reprendre [*town, position*]; POL reconquérir [*seat*]; FIG retrouver [*feeling*]; recréer [*period, atmosphere*].

recast /ˌriː'kɑːst, US -'kæst/ *vtr* (*prét, pp* **recast**) reformuler [*sentence*]; remanier [*text, plan*].

recede **I** /rɪ'siːd/ *vi* **1** LIT, GEN s'éloigner; [*tide*] descendre; FIG [*hope, memory, prospect*] s'estomper; [*threat*] s'éloigner; [*prices*] baisser; **2** (go bald) [*person*] se dégarnir.
II receding /rɪ'siːdɪŋ/ *pres p adj* [*chin, forehead*] fuyant; **he has a receding hairline** son front se dégarnit.

receipt /rɪ'siːt/ **I** *n* **1** COMM (in writing) reçu *m*, récépissé *m* (**for** pour); (from till) ticket *m* de caisse; (for rent) quittance *f*; POST (on sending) reçu *m*; (on delivery) accusé *m* de réception (**for** pour); **2** (of goods, letters) réception *f*; **to be in ~ of** recevoir [*income, benefits*].
II receipts *npl* COMM (takings) recette *f* (**from** de).

receive /rɪ'siːv/ **I** *vtr* **1** (get) recevoir [*letter, money, treatment, education*]; receler [*stolen goods*]; **he ~d a 30-year sentence** JUR il a été condamné à 30 ans de prison; **'~d with thanks'** COMM 'pour acquit'; **2** (meet) accueillir, recevoir [*visitor, proposal, play*] (**with** avec); **to be well** ou **positively ~d** être bien reçu; **to be ~d into** être reçu ou admis dans [*church, order*]; **3** RADIO, TV capter, recevoir.
II received *pp adj* [*ideas, opinions*] reçu.

received: **Received Pronunciation, RP** *n* GB prononciation *f* standard (de l'anglais); **Received Standard** *n* US = **Received Pronunciation**; **~ wisdom** *n* opinion *f* générale.

receiver /rɪ'siːvə(r)/ *n* **1** (telephone) combiné *m*; **2** RADIO, TV (equipment) (poste *m*) récepteur *m*; **3** GB FIN JUR (also **Official Receiver**) administrateur *m* judiciaire.

receivership /rɪ'siːvəʃɪp/ *n* GB FIN JUR **to go into ~** être placé sous administration judiciaire.

receiving /rɪ'siːvɪŋ/ *n* GB JUR recel *m*.
IDIOMS **to be on the ~ end of** faire les frais de [*criticism, hostility*]; recevoir [*blow, punch*].

recent /'riːsnt/ *adj* [*event, change, arrival, film*] récent; [*acquaintance, development*] nouveau/-elle; **in ~**

times récemment; **in ~ years/weeks** au cours des dernières années/semaines.

recently /'riːsntlɪ/ *adv* récemment, dernièrement; **as ~ as Monday** pas plus tard que lundi; **until ~** jusqu'à ces derniers temps.

receptacle /rɪ'septəkl/ *n* récipient *m*.

reception /rɪ'sepʃn/ *n* **1** (also **~ desk**) réception *f*; **2** (gathering) réception *f* (**for sb** en l'honneur de qn; **for sth** à l'occasion de qch); **3** (public response) accueil *m* (**for** de); **they gave us a great ~** [*fans, audience*] ils nous ont fait un accueil formidable; **4** RADIO, TV réception *f* (**on** sur).

reception: **~ area** *n* réception *f*; **~ camp**, **~ centre** *n* centre *m* d'accueil (**for** pour); **~ class** *n* GB SCH = cours *m* préparatoire; **~ committee** *n* comité *m* d'accueil ALSO FIG.

receptionist /rɪ'sepʃənɪst/ *n* [▶ **1251**] *n* réceptionniste *mf*.

reception room *n* **1** (in house) (grande) pièce *f*, pièce *f* de réception; **2** (in hotel) salle *f* de réception, salon *m*.

receptive /rɪ'septɪv/ *adj* réceptif/-ive (**to** à).

recess /rɪ'ses, US 'riːses/ *n* **1** JUR, POL vacances *fpl*; **2** US (break) (in school) récréation *f*; (during meeting) pause *f*; **3** CONSTR (for door, window) embrasure *f*; (alcove) alcôve *f*, niche *f*, recoin *m*.
II recesses *npl* LIT, FIG recoins *mpl* (**of** de).
III *vtr* US (interrupt) suspendre [*meeting, hearing*].
IV *vi* US JUR, POL suspendre les séances.

recession /rɪ'seʃn/ *n* ECON récession *f*.

recessive /rɪ'sesɪv/ *adj* BIOL récessif/-ive.

recharge /ˌriː'tʃɑːdʒ/ *vtr* recharger.

rechargeable /ˌriː'tʃɑːdʒəbl/ *adj* rechargeable.

recidivism /rɪ'sɪdɪvɪzm/ *n* récidive *f*.

recidivist /rɪ'sɪdɪvɪst/ *n* récidiviste *mf*.

recipe /'resəpɪ/ *n* CULIN recette *f* (**for** de); **~ book** livre *m* de recettes; FIG **a ~ for business success** une recette pour réussir dans les affaires; **it's a ~ for disaster** ça mène tout droit à la catastrophe.

recipient /rɪ'sɪpɪənt/ *n* (receiver) (of mail) destinataire *mf*; (of benefits, aid, cheque) bénéficiaire *mf*; (of prize, award) lauréat/-e *m/f*.

reciprocal /rɪ'sɪprəkl/ *adj* réciproque.

reciprocally /rɪ'sɪprəklɪ/ *adv* réciproquement.

reciprocate /rɪ'sɪprəkeɪt/ **I** *vtr* retourner [*compliment*]; payer [qch] de retour [*love, kindness*]; rendre [*affection, invitation*].
II *vi* rendre la pareille.

reciprocity /ˌresɪ'prɒsətɪ/ *n* réciprocité *f*.

recital /rɪ'saɪtl/ *n* (of music, poetry) récital *m*; (narration) récit *m*.

recitation /ˌresɪ'teɪʃn/ *n* récitation *f*.

recite /rɪ'saɪt/ *vtr, vi* réciter.

reckless /'reklɪs/ *adj* [*person, driving*] imprudent.

recklessly /'reklɪslɪ/ *adv* [*act*] avec imprudence; [*promise, spend*] de manière inconsciente.

recklessness /'reklɪsnɪs/ *n* imprudence *f*.

reckon /'rekən/ **I** *vtr* **1** (judge) considérer (**that** que); **she is ~ed (to be) the cleverest** elle est considérée comme la plus intelligente; **2○** (think) **to ~ (that)** croire que; **I ~ he's about 50** à mon avis il a à peu près 50 ans; **to ~ to do** compter faire; **3** (calculate accurately) calculer [*amount*]; **4○** (believe to be good) **I don't ~ your chances of success** je doute de vos chances de succès; **5○** (like) estimer [*person*].
II *vi* calculer.
▪ **reckon on○**: ¶ **~ on [sb/sth]** compter sur; ¶ **~ on doing** compter faire.
▪ **reckon up** calculer.
▪ **reckon with**: **~ with [sb/sth]** compter avec.

reckoning /'rekənɪŋ/ *n* GEN (estimation) estimation *f*; (accurate calculation) calculs *mpl*.
IDIOMS **day of ~** RELIG jour *m* du Jugement (dernier).

reclaim /rɪ'kleɪm/ *vtr* **1** ECOL reconquérir [*coastal land*]; mettre en valeur [*site*]; assécher [*marsh*]; défricher [*forest*]; assainir [*polluted land*]; irriguer [*desert*];

(recycle) récupérer [*glass, metal*]; **2** (get back) récupérer [*deposit, money*].

reclaimable /rɪˈkleɪməbl/ *adj* [*waste product*] récupérable; [*expenses*] remboursable.

reclamation /ˌrekləˈmeɪʃn/ *n* **1** (recycling) récupération *f*; **2** (of land) mise *f* en valeur; (of marsh) assèchement *m*; (of polluted land) assainissement *m*; (of forest) défrichement *m*.

recline /rɪˈklaɪn/ *vi* [*person*] s'allonger; [*seat*] s'incliner.

reclining /rɪˈklaɪnɪŋ/ *adj* **1** ART [*figure*] allongé; **2** [*seat*] inclinable.

recluse /rɪˈkluːs/ *n* reclus/-e *m/f*.

reclusive /rɪˈkluːsɪv/ *adj* solitaire.

recognition /ˌrekəɡˈnɪʃn/ *n* **1** (identification) reconnaissance *f*; **they've changed the town beyond ~** ils ont rendu la ville méconnaissable; **2** (realization) reconnaissance *f* (**of** de); **3** GEN, POL (acknowledgement) reconnaissance *f*; **to receive ou win ~ for** être reconnu pour [*talent, work*]; **in ~ of** en reconnaissance de; **4** COMPUT (of data) reconnaissance *f*; **5** AVIAT (identification) identification *f*.

recognizable /ˌrekəɡˈnaɪzəbl, ˈrekəɡnaɪzəbl/ *adj* reconnaissable.

recognizably /ˌrekəɡˈnaɪzəblɪ, ˈrekəɡnaɪzəblɪ/ *adv* manifestement.

recognize /ˈrekəɡnaɪz/ **I** *vtr* **1** (identify) reconnaître [*person, voice, sound, place*] (**by** à; **as** comme étant); identifier [*sign, symptom*] (**as** comme étant); **2** (acknowledge) reconnaître [*problem, fact, government, claim*]; **3** US (in debate) donner la parole à [*speaker*].
II recognized *pp adj* **1** (acknowledged) [*expert, organization*] reconnu; **2** COMM (accredited) [*firm, supplier*] accrédité; **~d dealer** concessionnaire *m* attitré.

recoil I /ˈriːkɔɪl/ *n* (of gun) recul *m*; (of spring) détente *f*.
II /rɪˈkɔɪl/ *vi* **1** [*person*] (physically) avoir un mouvement de recul (**from, at** devant); (mentally) reculer (**from** devant); **to ~ in horror** reculer d'horreur; **2** [*gun*] reculer en tirant; [*spring*] se détendre.

recollect /ˌrekəˈlekt/ **I** *vtr* se souvenir de, se rappeler.
II *vi* se souvenir; **as far as I ~** autant que je m'en souvienne.

recollection /ˌrekəˈlekʃn/ *n* souvenir *m*; **to have some ~ of** se souvenir vaguement de; **to the best of my ~** autant que je m'en souvienne.

recommence /ˌriːkəˈmens/ *vtr, vi* recommencer (**doing** à faire).

recommend /ˌrekəˈmend/ *vtr* **1** (commend) recommander [*person, company, film*] (**as** comme étant); **2** (advise) conseiller, recommander; **3** (favour) **the strategy has much to ~ it** la stratégie présente de nombreux avantages; **the hotel has little to ~ it** on ne peut pas dire grand-chose en faveur de cet hôtel.

recommendation /ˌrekəmenˈdeɪʃn/ *n* recommandation *f* (**to** à; **on** sur); **on the ~ of** sur la recommandation de; **to give sb a ~** recommander qn; **to write sb a ~** donner une lettre de recommandation à qn.

recommend: **~ed daily amount, RDA** *n* apports *mpl* quotidiens recommandés, AQR; **~ed reading** *n* livres *mpl* conseillés *or* recommandés; **~ed retail price** *n* prix *m* de vente conseillé.

recompense /ˈrekəmpens/ **I** *n* **1** (reward) récompense *f* (**for** de); **2** JUR dédommagement *m* (**for** pour).
II *vtr* **1** SOUT (reward) récompenser (**for** de); **2** JUR dédommager (**for** de).

reconcilable /ˈrekənsaɪləbl/ *adj* [*differences*] conciliable; [*views*] compatible (**with** avec).

reconcile /ˈrekənsaɪl/ *vtr* **1** (after quarrel) réconcilier [*people*]; **to be** ou **become ~d** se réconcilier (**with** avec); **2** (see as compatible) concilier [*attitudes, views*] (**with** avec); **3** (persuade to accept) **to ~ sb to sth/to doing** réconcilier qn avec qch/avec l'idée de faire; **to become ~d to sth** se résigner à qch.

reconciliation /ˌrekənˌsɪlɪˈeɪʃn/ *n* réconciliation *f*.

recondition /ˌriːkənˈdɪʃn/ *vtr* remettre [qch] à neuf.

reconnaissance /rɪˈkɒnɪsns/ *n* reconnaissance *f*.

reconnoitre GB, **reconnoiter** US /ˌrekəˈnɔɪtə(r)/ MIL **I** *vtr* reconnaître.
II *vi* faire une reconnaissance.

reconsider /ˌriːkənˈsɪdə(r)/ **I** *vtr* réexaminer.
II *vi* (think further) y repenser.

reconstitute /ˌriːˈkɒnstɪtjuːt, US -tuːt/ *vtr* **1** ADMIN, POL reconstituer; **2** CULIN réhydrater.

reconstruct /ˌriːkənˈstrʌkt/ *vtr* **1** (rebuild) reconstruire [*building*]; réédifier [*system*]; reconstituer [*text*]; MED reconstituer; **2** [*police*] faire une reconstitution de [*crime*].

reconstruction /ˌriːkənˈstrʌkʃn/ *n* **1** (of building) reconstruction *f*; (of system) réédification *f*; **2** (of object, event, crime) reconstitution *f*; **3** MED reconstitution *f*.

reconvene /ˌriːkənˈviːn/ *vi* se réunir à nouveau.

record I /ˈrekɔːd, US ˈrekərd/ *n* **1** (written account) (of events) compte-rendu *m*; (of official proceedings) procès-verbal *m*; **to keep a ~ of sth** noter qch; **I have no ~ of your application** je n'ai aucune trace de votre demande; **the hottest summer on ~** l'été le plus chaud qu'on ait jamais enregistré; **to be on ~ as saying that...** avoir déclaré officiellement que...; **to say sth off the ~** dire qch en privé; **I'd like to set the ~ straight** je voudrais mettre les choses au clair; **2** (data) (also **~s**) (historical, public) archives *fpl*; (personal, administrative) dossier *m*; **3** (history) (of individual) passé *m*; (of organization, group) réputation *f*; **to have a good ~ on sth** avoir une bonne réputation en ce qui concerne; **4** AUDIO disque *m* (**by, of** de); **5** (best performance) record *m* (**for, in** de); **6** JUR (also **criminal ~**) casier *m* judiciaire.
II /ˈrekɔːd, US ˈrekərd/ *noun modifier* **1** AUDIO [*company, label, shop*] de disques; [*industry*] du disque; **2** (best) [*result, sales, time*] record (*inv, after n*); **to be at a ~ high/low** être à son niveau le plus haut/bas.
III /rɪˈkɔːd/ *vtr* **1** (note) noter; **2** (on disc, tape) enregistrer; **3** (register) [*equipment*] enregistrer [*temperature*]; [*dial*] indiquer [*pressure, speed*]; **4** (provide an account of) rapporter [*event*].
IV /rɪˈkɔːd/ *vi* [*video, tape recorder*] enregistrer.

record book *n* livre *m* des records.

record-breaker /ˈrekɔːdbreɪkə(r), US ˈrekərd-/ *n* **to be a ~** avoir battu un record.

record: **~-breaking** *adj* record (*inv, after n*); **~ card** *n* fiche *f*; **~ deck** *n* AUDIO platine *f* disques.

recorded /rɪˈkɔːdɪd/ *adj* **1** (on tape, record) enregistré; **2** (documented) [*case, sighting*] connu; [*fact*] reconnu; **~ delivery** GB POST recommandé *m*.

recorder /rɪˈkɔːdə(r)/ *n* MUS flûte *f* à bec.

record-holder /ˈrekɔːdhəʊldə(r), US ˈrekərd-/ *n* recordman/recordwoman *m/f*.

recording /rɪˈkɔːdɪŋ/ *n* enregistrement *m*; **to make a ~ of sth** enregistrer qch.

record: **~ library** *n* discothèque *f* de prêt; **~ player** *n* tourne-disque *m*; **~s office** *n* (of births, deaths) bureau *m* des archives; JUR (of court records) greffe *m*; **~ token** *n* chèque-cadeau *m* pour disques.

recount /rɪˈkaʊnt/ *vtr* raconter, conter.

re-count I /ˈriːkaʊnt/ *n* POL deuxième compte *m* des suffrages.
II /ˌriːˈkaʊnt/ *vtr* recompter.

recoup /rɪˈkuːp/ *vtr* compenser [*losses*]; **to ~ one's costs** rentrer dans ses frais.

recourse /rɪˈkɔːs/ *n* recours *m* (**to** à).

recover /rɪˈkʌvə(r)/ **I** *vtr* **1** (get back) retrouver, récupérer [*money, vehicle*]; récupérer [*territory*]; (from water) repêcher, retrouver [*body, wreck*]; **to ~ one's sight/health** recouvrer la vue/santé; **to ~ one's confidence/one's strength** reprendre confiance/des forces; **2** (recoup) recouvrer [*loan, taxes, costs*] (**from** auprès de); réparer, compenser [*losses*].
II *vi* (from illness) se remettre, se rétablir (**from** de); (from defeat, mistake) se ressaisir (**from** après); [*economy*] se redresser; [*shares, currency*] remonter.

recoverable /rɪˈkʌvərəbl/ *adj* **1** FIN recouvrable; **2** ECOL, IND récupérable.

recovery /rɪˈkʌvərɪ/ *n* **1** (getting better) rétablissement *m*, guérison *f*; FIG (of team, player) ressaisissement *m*; **to be on the road to ~** être sur la voie de la guérison; **to make a ~** (from illness) se rétablir, guérir; (from mistake, defeat) se ressaisir; **2** ECON, FIN (of economy, country, company, market) relance *f*, reprise *f*; (of shares, prices) remontée *f*; **3** (getting back) (of vehicle) rapatriement *m*; (of money) récupération *f*; (of costs, debts) recouvrement *m*; (of losses) réparation *f*.

recovery: **~ room** *n* MED salle *f* de réveil; **~ vehicle** *n* AUT (car) voiture *f* de dépannage; (truck) camion *m* de dépannage.

recreate /'rekriett, ,ri:kri'eit/ *vtr* recréer.

recreation /,rekri'eiʃn/ **I** *n* **1** (leisure) loisirs *mpl*; **what do you do for ~?** que faites-vous pour vous détendre?; **2** (pastime) récréation *f*; **3** SCH (break) récréation *f*.

II *noun modifier* [*facilities, centre*] de loisirs; **~ area** (indoor) salle *f* de récréation; (outdoor) terrain *m* de jeux; **~ ground** terrain *m* de jeux; **~ room** US salle *f* de jeux.

recreational /,rekri'eiʃənl/ *adj* [*facilities*] de loisirs.

recreational: **~ drug** *n*: *drogue que l'on prend de façon occasionnelle*; **~ vehicle, RV** *n* US camping-car *m*.

recrimination /ri,krimi'neiʃn/ *n* récrimination *f*.

rec room○ /'rek rʊm/ *n* US salle *f* de jeux.

recruit /ri'kru:t/ **I** *n* recrue *f*.
II *vtr* MIL, POL recruter [*soldier, member, agent*] (**from** dans); GEN recruter, embaucher [*staff*].
III *vi* recruter.

recruiting officer *n* officier *m* recruteur.

recruitment /ri'kru:tmənt/ *n* recrutement *m*.

rectangle /'rektæŋgl/ *n* rectangle *m*.

rectangular /rek'tæŋgjʊlə(r)/ *adj* rectangulaire.

rectify /'rektifai/ *vtr* GEN, MATH, CHEM rectifier.

rectitude /'rektitju:d, US -tu:d/ *n* droiture *f*.

rector /'rektə(r)/ *n* RELIG pasteur *m*.

rectory /'rektəri/ *n* presbytère *m* (anglican).

rectum /'rektəm/ *n* rectum *m*.

recumbent /ri'kʌmbənt/ *adj* LITTÉR allongé.

recuperate /ri'ku:pəreit/ **I** *vtr* réparer [*loss*].
II *vi* MED se rétablir (**from** de), récupérer.

recuperation /ri,ku:pə'reiʃn/ *n* **1** (of losses) réparation *f*; **2** MED rétablissement *m* (**from** de), récupération *f*.

recur /ri'kɜ:(r)/ *vi* (*p prés etc* **-rr-**) [*event, error, dream*] se reproduire; [*problem, illness*] réapparaître; [*theme, phrase*] revenir; MATH [*number*] se répéter à l'infini.

recurrence /ri'kʌrəns/ *n* (of illness) récurrence *f*; (of symptom) réapparition *f*.

recurrent /ri'kʌrənt/ *adj* récurrent.

recurring /ri'kɜ:rɪŋ/ *adj* [*thought, pain*] récurrent; MATH **~ decimal** suite *f* décimale illimitée.

recyclable /,ri:'saikləbl/ *adj* recyclable.

recycle /,ri:'saikl/ *vtr* ECOL recycler [*paper, waste*].

recycling /,ri:'saikliŋ/ *n* ECOL recyclage *m*.

red /red/ ▶**818**| **I** *n* **1** (colour) rouge *m*; **in ~** en rouge; **2**○ PEJ (also **Red**) (communist) rouge *mf*; **3** (deficit) **to be in the ~** [*person, account*] être à découvert; [*company*] être en déficit; **4** (wine) rouge *m*; **5** (red ball) bille *f* rouge (*de billard/snooker*).

II *adj* (in colour) GEN rouge (**with** de); [*hair*] roux/rousse; **to go** ou **turn ~** rougir; **~ in the face** tout rouge; **there'll be ~ faces when**... certains vont être bien gênés quand...

IDIOMS **to be caught ~-handed** être pris/-e la main dans le sac○; **to see ~** voir rouge; **not to have a ~ cent** US ne pas avoir un sou○.

red: **~ admiral** *n* ZOOL vulcain *m*; **~ blood cell** *n* globule *m* rouge; **~-blooded** *adj* [*male*] ardent; **~ cabbage** *n* chou *m* rouge; **~ card** *n* SPORT carton *m* rouge; **~ carpet** *n* tapis *m* rouge.

redcoat /'redkəʊt/ *n* **1** GB (at camp) animateur/-trice *m/f*; **2** MIL soldat *m* anglais (*du XVIIIᵉ siècle*).

red: **Red Cross** *n* Croix-Rouge *f*; **~ currant** *n* groseille *f*; **~ deer** *n* cerf *m* commun.

redden /'redn/ *vtr, vi* rougir.

reddish /'rediʃ/ *adj* rougeâtre; **~ hair** cheveux tirant sur le roux.

redecorate /,ri:'dekəreit/ *vtr* repeindre et retapisser, refaire.

redeem /ri'di:m/ **I** *vtr* **1** (exchange) échanger [*voucher*] (**for** contre); (for cash) convertir [qch] en espèces [*bond, security*]; **2** (pay off) racheter [*pawned goods*]; **her one ~ing feature** ou **quality is**... ce qui la rachète, c'est...; **3** (salvage) rattraper [*occasion*]; sauver [*situation*]; racheter [*fault*]; **4** (satisfy) s'acquitter de [*obligation*]; tenir [*pledge*]; **5** RELIG racheter.
II *v refl* **to ~ oneself** se racheter.

redeemable /ri'di:məbl/ *adj* **1** FIN [*bond, security*] convertible; [*loan, mortgage*] remboursable; **2** COMM [*voucher*] échangeable; [*pawned goods*] rachetable.

Redeemer /ri'di:mə(r)/ *n* RELIG Rédempteur *m*.

redefine /,ri:di'fain/ *vtr* redéfinir.

redemption /ri'dempʃn/ *n* **1** FIN (of loan, debt, bill) remboursement *m*; **2** RELIG rédemption *f*; **beyond** ou **past ~** [*situation*] irrémédiable; [*machine*] irréparable; [*person*] HUM irrécupérable.

redesign /,ri:di'zain/ *vtr* transformer [*area, building*]; **to ~ a logo** créer un nouveau logo.

redevelop /,ri:di'veləp/ *vtr* réaménager [*site, town*].

redevelopment /,ri:di'veləpmənt/ *n* réaménagement *m*.

red: **~-eyed** *adj* aux yeux rouges; **~-faced** *adj* (temporarily) rouge; FIG (embarrassed) penaud; (permanently) rougeaud; **~ grouse** *n* grouse *f*; **~-haired** *adj* roux/rousse; **~head** *n* roux/rousse *m/f*; **~headed** *adj* roux/rousse; **~ herring** *n* (distraction) faux problème *m*.

red-hot /,red'hɒt/ **I**○ *n* US hot-dog *m*.
II *adj* LIT [*metal, coal*] chauffé au rouge; FIG [*passion, lover*] ardent; [*news*] tout frais/toute fraîche.

redial /,ri:'daɪəl/ TELECOM **I** *vtr* refaire [*number*].
II *vi* recomposer le numéro.

redial: **~ button** *n* touche *f* bis; **~ facility** *n* rappel *m* du dernier numéro composé.

redid /,ri:'dɪd/ *prét* ▶ **redo**.

Red Indian *n* INJUR Peau-Rouge *mf*.

redirect /,ri:di'rekt/ *vtr* canaliser [*resources*]; dévier [*traffic*]; faire suivre, réexpédier [*mail*].

rediscover /,ri:di'skʌvə(r)/ *vtr* redécouvrir.

red: **~-letter day** *n* jour *m* mémorable; **~ light** *n* feu *m* rouge; **~ light area** *n* quartier *m* chaud; **~ meat** *n* viande *f* rouge; **~ mullet** *n* rouget *m*.

redneck /'rednek/ **I** *n* INJUR péquenaud/-e○ *m/f*
OFFENSIVE.
II *adj* ultraréactionnaire.

redness /'rednis/ *n* rougeur *f*.

redo /,ri:'du:/ *vtr* (*3ᵉ pers sg prés* **redoes**; *prét* **redid**; *pp* **redone**) refaire.

redolent /'redələnt/ *adj* LITTÉR **to be ~ of sth** LIT sentir qch; FIG évoquer qch.

redone /,ri:'dʌn/ *pp* ▶ **redo**.

redouble /,ri:'dʌbl/ *vtr, vi* redoubler; **to ~ one's efforts** redoubler d'efforts.

redoubtable /ri'daʊtəbl/ *adj* redoutable.

red pepper *n* poivron *m* rouge.

redraft /,ri:'drɑ:ft/ *vtr* rédiger [qch] à nouveau.

redress /ri'dres/ **I** *n* GEN, JUR réparation *f*; **they have no (means of) ~** ils n'ont aucun recours.
II *vtr* réparer [*error, wrong*]; redresser [*situation*]; **to ~ the balance** rétablir l'équilibre.

red: **Red Sea** *pr n* mer *f* Rouge; **~skin** *n* INJUR Peau-Rouge *mf*; **~ snapper** *n* vivaneau *m*; **Red Square** *pr n* place *f* Rouge; **~ squirrel** *n* écureuil *m* roux; **~ tape** *n* paperasserie *f*.

reduce /ri'dju:s, US -'du:s/ **I** *vtr* **1** (make smaller) réduire [*inflation, number, pressure, impact*] (**by** de); baisser [*prices, temperature*]; MED résorber [*swelling*]; faire baisser [*fever*]; **the jackets have been ~d by 50%** COMM le prix des vestes a été réduit de 50%; **'~ speed now'** AUT 'ralentir'; **2** (in scale) réduire [*map, article*]; **3** (alter the state of) **to ~ sth to shreds** réduire qch en pièces; **to ~ sb to tears** faire pleurer qn; **to be ~d to begging** en être réduit à la mendicité; **4** (simplify) réduire [*argument, equation, existence*]; **5** JUR réduire [*sentence*]; **6** CULIN faire réduire [*sauce, stock*].

II *vi* CULIN [*sauce*] réduire.

III reduced *pp adj* réduit; **~d goods** marchandises en solde; **in ~d circumstances** SOUT dans la gêne.

reductio ad absurdum /rɪˌdʌktɪəʊ æd əbˈsɜːdəm/ *n* raisonnement *m* par l'absurde.

reduction /rɪˈdʌkʃn/ *n* **1** (decrease) (of volume, speed) réduction *f* (**in** de); (of weight, size, cost) diminution *f* (**in** de); **2** COMM réduction *f*, rabais *m*; **3** (simplification) réduction *f*; **4** CHEM réduction *f*.

reductive /rɪˈdʌktɪv/ *adj* réducteur/-trice.

redundancy /rɪˈdʌndənsɪ/ *n* IND licenciement *m*.

redundant /rɪˈdʌndənt/ *adj* **1** GB IND [*worker*] licencié; **to be made ~** être licencié; **2** (not needed) [*information, device*] superflu; [*land, machinery*] inutilisé; **to feel ~** se sentir de trop; **3** GB (outdated) [*technique, practice*] inutile; [*craft*] dépassé; **4** COMPUT, LING redondant.

red: **~ wine** *n* vin *m* rouge; **~ wine vinegar** *n* vinaigre *m* de vin rouge; **~wood** *n* séquoia *m*.

reed /riːd/ **I** *n* **1** BOT roseau *m*; **2** MUS anche *f*.

II *noun modifier* **1** [*basket, hut*] en roseau; **2** MUS [*instrument*] à anche.

IDIOMS **to be a broken ~** être quelqu'un sur qui on ne peut plus compter.

re-educate /ˌriːˈedʒʊkeɪt/ *vtr* rééduquer.

reedy /ˈriːdɪ/ *adj* [*voice, tone*] aigu/-uë.

reef /riːf/ *n* (in sea) récif *m*, écueil *m*.

reefer /ˈriːfə(r)/ *n* **1** (also **~ jacket**) caban *m*; **2**° (to smoke) joint *m*, cigarette *f* de marijuana.

reef knot *n* nœud *m* plat.

reek /riːk/ **I** *n* LIT, FIG relent *m*.

II *vi* (stink) **to ~ of sth** LIT puer qch; FIG avoir des relents de qch.

reel /riːl/ **I** *n* **1** GEN bobine *f*; (for fishing) moulinet *m*; **~-to-~** [*tape recorder*] à bobines; **2** (dance) quadrille *m* écossais.

II *vi* (sway) [*person*] tituber; **he ~ed across the room** il a traversé la pièce en titubant; **the blow sent him ~ing** le coup l'a projeté en arrière; **the government is still ~ing after its defeat** le gouvernement ne s'est pas encore remis de sa défaite.

IDIOMS **off the ~** US sans hésiter.

■ **reel in** ramener [*fish*].

■ **reel off**: **~ off** [sth] débiter [*list, names*].

re-elect /ˌriːɪˈlekt/ *vtr* réélire.

re-election /ˌriːɪˈlekʃn/ *n* réélection *f*; **to stand for** GB ou **run for** US se représenter (aux élections).

re-emerge /ˌriːɪˈmɜːdʒ/ *vi* [*person, sun*] réapparaître; [*problem*] resurgir.

re-enact /ˌriːɪˈnækt/ *vtr* **1** reconstituer [*crime*]; rejouer [*role*]; **2** JUR remettre en vigueur.

re-enlist /ˌriːɪnˈlɪst/ *vi* se rengager.

re-enter /ˌriːˈentə(r)/ **I** *vtr* entrer à nouveau dans.

II *vi* (come back in) [*person, vehicle etc*] revenir.

re-entry /ˌriːˈentrɪ/ *n* GEN, AEROSP rentrée *f*; FIG (into politics etc) retour *m* (**into** dans).

re-entry visa *n* visa *m* aller-retour.

re-examine /ˌriːɪgˈzæmɪn/ *vtr* réexaminer [*issue, problem*]; interroger à nouveau [*witness*].

ref /ref/ *n* **1** COMM *abrév écrite* = **reference I 3**; **2**° SPORT (*abrév* = **referee**) arbitre *m*.

refectory /rɪˈfektrɪ, ˈrefiktrɪ/ *n* réfectoire *m*.

refer /rɪˈfɜː(r)/ (*p prés etc* **-rr-**) **I** *vtr* **1** (pass on) renvoyer [*task, problem, enquiry*] (**to** à); **to ~ sb to** [*person*] envoyer qn à [*department*]; [*critic, text*] renvoyer qn à [*article, footnote*]; **2** JUR déférer [*case*] (**to** à); **3** MED **to be ~red to a specialist** être envoyé en consultation chez un spécialiste.

II *vi* **1** (allude to, talk about) **to ~ to** parler de, faire allusion à [*person, topic, event*]; **2** (as name, label) **she**

~s to him as Bob elle l'appelle Bob; **3** (signify) **to ~ to** [*number, date, term*] se rapporter à; **4** (consult) **to ~ to** consulter [*notes, article*].

referee /ˌrefəˈriː/ **I** *n* **1** SPORT arbitre *m*; **2** GB (giving job reference) personne *f* pouvant fournir des références.

II *vtr, vi* arbitrer.

reference /ˈrefrəns/ **I** *n* **1** (allusion) référence *f* (**to** à), allusion *f* (**to** à); **to make ~ to sb/sth** faire allusion à qn/qch; **there are three ~s to his son in the article** son fils est mentionné trois fois dans l'article; **2** (consultation) **to do sth without ~ to sb/sth** faire qch sans consulter qn/qch; **'for ~ only'** (on library book) 'consultation sur place'; **for future ~** pour information; **without ~ to** sans tenir compte de [*statistics, needs*]; **3** (in book, letter, memo) référence *f*; **please quote this ~** prière de rappeler cette référence; **4** (also **~ mark**) renvoi *m*; **5** (testimonial) références *fpl*; **6** (referee) personne *f* pouvant fournir des références; **7** LING référence *f*; **8** GEOG **map ~s** coordonnées *fpl*.

II with reference to *prep phr* en ce qui concerne, quant à; **with ~ to your letter/request** suite à votre lettre/demande.

III *vtr* fournir les sources de [*book, article*].

reference: **~ book** *n* ouvrage *m* de référence; **~ library** *n* bibliothèque *f* d'ouvrages de référence; **~ number** *n* numéro *m* de référence; **~ point** *n* FIG point *m* de repère.

referendum /ˌrefəˈrendəm/ *n* (*pl* **-da**) référendum *m*.

referral /rɪˈfɜːrəl/ *n* **1** MED ADMIN (person) patient/-e *m/f* envoyé/-e à un confrère; (system) *fait d'envoyer un malade chez un spécialiste*; **2** GEN (of matter, problem) renvoi *m* (**to** à).

refill I /ˈriːfɪl/ *n* (for fountain pen) cartouche *f*; (for ballpoint, lighter, perfume) recharge *f*.

II /ˌriːˈfɪl/ *vtr* recharger [*pen, lighter*]; remplir [qch] à nouveau [*glass, bottle*].

refine /rɪˈfaɪn/ *vtr* **1** IND raffiner [*oil, sugar etc*]; **2** (improve) peaufiner [*theory*]; raffiner [*manners*]; affiner [*method, taste, language*].

refined /rɪˈfaɪnd/ *adj* **1** IND [*oil, sugar etc*] raffiné; [*metal*] affiné; **2** (cultured) raffiné; **3** (improved) [*method, model*] très au point; [*theory, concept*] peaufiné.

refinement /rɪˈfaɪnmənt/ *n* (elegance) raffinement *m*.

refinery /rɪˈfaɪnərɪ/ *n* raffinerie *f*.

refit I /ˈriːfɪt/ *n* (of shop, factory etc) rééquipement *m*; NAUT réarmement *m*.

II /ˌriːˈfɪt/ *vtr* (*p prés etc* **-tt-**) réarmer [*ship*]; rééquiper [*shop, factory*].

reflate /ˌriːˈfleɪt/ *vtr* ECON relancer.

reflation /ˌriːˈfleɪʃn/ *n* ECON relance *f*.

reflect /rɪˈflekt/ **I** *vtr* **1** LIT, FIG refléter; **to be ~ed in sth** LIT, FIG se refléter dans qch; **he saw himself/her face ~ed in the mirror** il a vu son reflet/le reflet de son visage dans le miroir; **2** (throw back) renvoyer, réfléchir [*light, heat*]; **3** (think) se dire, penser.

II *vi* **1** (think) réfléchir (**on, upon** à); **2** **to ~ well/badly on sb** faire honneur/du tort à qn; **how is this going to ~ on the school?** quelles vont être les conséquences pour l'école?

reflection /rɪˈflekʃn/ *n* **1** (image) LIT, FIG reflet *m* (of de), image *f* (**of** de); **2** (thought) réflexion *f*; **on ~** à la réflexion; **3** (idea) réflexion *f*, pensée *f*; (remark) remarque *f*; **4** (criticism) **it is a sad ~ on our society that** ce n'est pas à la gloire de notre société que.

reflective /rɪˈflektɪv/ *adj* **1** [*mood*] pensif/-ive; [*person*] réfléchi; **2** [*material, surface*] réfléchissant.

reflector /rɪˈflektə(r)/ *n* **1** (on vehicle) catadioptre *m*; **2** (of light, heat) réflecteur *m*.

reflex /ˈriːfleks/ **I** *n* réflexe *m*.

II *adj* GEN, ANAT réflexe; **a ~ action** un réflexe.

reflexive /rɪˈfleksɪv/ LING **I** *n* (also **~ verb**) verbe *m* pronominal réfléchi.

II *adj* réfléchi.

refloat /ˌriːˈfləʊt/ *vtr* NAUT, ECON renflouer.

reforestation /ˌriːˌfɒrəˈsteɪʃn/ *n* reboisement *m*.

reform /rɪˈfɔːm/ **I** *n* réforme *f*.

British regions and counties

The names of British regions and counties usually have the definite article in French, except when used with the preposition en.

In, to and from somewhere

Most counties and regions are masculine; with these, in and to are translated by dans le, *and from by* du:

to live in Sussex	= vivre dans le Sussex
to go to Sussex	= aller dans le Sussex
to come from Sussex	= venir du Sussex

Note however:

Cornwall	= la Cournouailles
to live in Cornwall	= vivre en Cornouailles
to go to Cornwall	= aller en Cornouailles
to come from Cornwall	= venir de la Cornouailles

Uses with nouns

There are rarely French equivalents for English forms like Cornishmen, *and it is always safe to use* de *with the definite article:*

Cornishmen	= les habitants *mpl* de la Cornouailles
Lancastrians	= les habitants du Lancashire

In other cases, du *is often possible:*

a Somerset accent	= l'accent du Somerset
the Yorkshire countryside	= les paysages du Yorkshire

but it is usually safe to use du comté de:

the towns of Fife	= les villes du comté de Fife
the rivers of Merioneth	= les rivières du comté de Merioneth
Grampian cattle	= le bétail de la région des Grampians

II *vtr* réformer.

III *vi* se réformer.

IV reformed *pp adj* [*state, system*] réformé; [*criminal*] repenti; RELIG [*church*] réformé; **he's a ~ed character** il s'est assagi.

reformat /ˌriːˈfɔːmæt/ *vtr* COMPUT reformater.

reformation /ˌrefəˈmeɪʃn/ *n* GEN réforme *f*; **the Reformation** RELIG la Réforme.

reformer /rɪˈfɔːmə(r)/ *n* réformateur/-trice *m/f*.

refrain /rɪˈfreɪn/ **I** *n* MUS, LITERAT, FIG refrain *m*.
II *vi* se retenir; **to ~ from doing** s'abstenir de faire; **he could not ~ from saying** il n'a pas pu s'empêcher de dire; **please ~ from smoking** SOUT ayez l'obligeance de ne pas fumer FML.

refresh /rɪˈfreʃ/ *vtr* [*bath, drink*] rafraîchir; [*rest*] reposer; **to ~ oneself** se rafraîchir; **to ~ sb's memory** rafraîchir la mémoire à qn.

refresher course /rɪˈfreʃə kɔːs/ *n* cours *m* de recyclage.

refreshing /rɪˈfreʃɪŋ/ *adj* [*drink, shower*] rafraîchissant; [*rest*] réparateur/-trice; [*insight*] original.

refreshment /rɪˈfreʃmənt/ *n* (rest) repos *m*; (food, drink) restauration *f*; **~s** (drinks) rafraîchissements *mpl*; **light ~s** repas *m* léger.

refreshment bar, **refreshment stall** *n* buvette *f*.

refrigerate /rɪˈfrɪdʒəreɪt/ **I** *vtr* frigorifier; **'keep ~d'** 'conserver au réfrigérateur'.
II refrigerated *pp adj* [*product*] frigorifié; [*transport*] frigorifique.

refrigeration /rɪˌfrɪdʒəˈreɪʃn/ *n* réfrigération *f*.

refrigerator /rɪˈfrɪdʒəreɪtə(r)/ **I** *n* (appliance) réfrigérateur *m*, frigidaire® *m*; (room) chambre *f* frigorifique.
II *noun modifier* [*truck, wagon*] frigorifique.

refuel /ˌriːˈfjuːəl/ (*p prés etc* **-ll-** GB, **-l-** US) **I** *vtr* LIT ravitailler [*qch*] en carburant; FIG ranimer.
II *vi* se ravitailler en carburant.

refuge /ˈrefjuːdʒ/ *n* **1** refuge *m* (**from** contre); **to take ~ from** se mettre à l'abri de [*danger, people*]; s'abriter de [*weather*]; **to take ~ in** se réfugier dans [*place, drink, drugs*]; **2** (hostel) foyer *m*.

refugee /ˌrefjʊˈdʒiː, US ˈrefjʊdʒiː/ **I** *n* réfugié/-e *m/f*.
II *noun modifier* [*camp*] de réfugiés; [*status*] de réfugié.

refund /ˈriːfʌnd/ *n* remboursement *m*.
II /rɪˈfʌnd/ *vtr* rembourser.

refurbish /ˌriːˈfɜːbɪʃ/ *vtr* rénover.

refurbishment /ˌriːˈfɜːbɪʃmənt/ *n* rénovation *f*.

refusal /rɪˈfjuːzl/ *n* **1** GEN refus *m* (**to do** de faire); (to application, invitation) réponse *f* négative; **2 to give sb first ~** COMM donner la priorité à qn.

refuse¹ /rɪˈfjuːz/ **I** *vtr* refuser (**to do** de faire).
II *vi* refuser.

refuse² /ˈrefjuːs/ *n* GB (household) ordures *fpl*; (industrial) déchets *mpl*; (garden) déchets *mpl* de jardinage.

refuse /ˈrefjuːs/: **~ bin** *n* GB poubelle *f*; **~ chute** *n* GB vide-ordures *m inv*; **~ collector** ▶ **1251**] *n* GB éboueur *m*; **~ disposal** GB *n* traitement *m* des ordu-

res; **~ disposal unit** *n* broyeur *m* d'ordures; **~ dump** *n* GB décharge *f* publique; **~ lorry** *n* GB camion *m* des éboueurs.

refute /rɪˈfjuːt/ *vtr* réfuter.

regain /rɪˈgeɪn/ *vtr* retrouver [*health, sight, freedom*]; reconquérir [*power, seat*]; retrouver [*balance, composure*]; reprendre [*lead, control*]; rattraper [*time*]; **to ~ possession of** rentrer en possession de; **to ~ consciousness** reprendre connaissance.

regal /ˈriːgl/ *adj* royal.

regale /rɪˈgeɪl/ *vtr* régaler (**with** de).

regalia /rɪˈgeɪlɪə/ *npl* insignes *mpl*; **in full ~** LIT, HUM en grande tenue.

regally /ˈriːgəlɪ/ *adv* majestueusement.

regard /rɪˈgɑːd/ **I** *n* **1** (consideration) égard *m* FML; **out of ~ for** par égard pour; **2** (esteem) estime *f* (**for** pour); **to hold sb/sth in high ~** avoir beaucoup d'estime pour qn/qch; **to have little ~ for money** faire peu de cas de l'argent; **3** (connection) **with ou in ~ to** en ce qui concerne; **in this ~** à cet égard.
II regards *npl* (good wishes) amitiés *fpl*; **kindest ~s** avec toutes mes (or nos) amitiés; **give them my ~s** transmettez-leur mes amitiés.
III *vtr* **1** (consider) considérer; **to ~ sb with suspicion** se montrer soupçonneux à l'égard de qn; **highly ~ed** très apprécié; **2** (concern) SOUT concerner.

regarding /rɪˈgɑːdɪŋ/ *prep* concernant.

regardless /rɪˈgɑːdlɪs/ **I** *prep* **~ of cost/age** sans tenir compte du prix/de l'âge; **~ of the weather** quel que soit le temps.
II *adv* malgré tout.

regatta /rɪˈgætə/ *n* régate *f*.

regency /ˈriːdʒənsɪ/ *n* régence *f*.

regenerate /rɪˈdʒenəreɪt/ **I** *vtr* régénérer.
II *vi* se régénérer.

regeneration /rɪˌdʒenəˈreɪʃn/ *n* GEN régénération *f*; (urban) restauration *f*.

regent /ˈriːdʒənt/ *n* POL HIST régent/-e *m/f*.

reggae /ˈregeɪ/ *n* reggae *m*.

regime, **régime** /reɪˈʒiːm, ˈreʒiːm/ *n* POL régime *m*.

regiment /ˈredʒɪmənt/ *n* MIL, FIG régiment *m*.

regimental /ˌredʒɪˈmentl/ *adj* du régiment.

regimented /ˈredʒɪmentɪd/ *adj* soumis à une discipline toute militaire.

Regina /rəˈdʒaɪnə/ *n* GB JUR **~ v Jones** la Couronne contre Jones.

region /ˈriːdʒən/ *n* région *f*; (**somewhere**) **in the ~ of £300** environ 300 livres sterling.

regional /ˈriːdʒənl/ *adj* régional; **~ development** IND aménagement *m* du territoire.

regionalism /ˈriːdʒənəlɪzəm/ *n* régionalisme *m*.

register /ˈredʒɪstə(r)/ **I** *n* **1** GEN, ADMIN, COMM registre *m*; SCH cahier *m* des absences; **~ of births, marriages and deaths** registre public de l'état civil; **2** MUS, LING, COMPUT registre *m*; **3** US (till) caisse *f* enregistreuse.
II *vtr* **1** [*member of the public*] déclarer [*birth, death, marriage*]; faire immatriculer [*vehicle*]; faire enregis-

trer [*luggage, company*]; déposer [*trademark, patent, complaint*]; [*official*] inscrire [*student*]; enregistrer [*name, birth, death, company*]; immatriculer [*vehicle*]; **to be ~ed (as) disabled** être officiellement reconnu handicapé; **2** [*instrument*] indiquer [*speed, temperature*]; [*person*] exprimer [*anger, disapproval*]; **to ~ six on the Richter scale** [*earthquake*] atteindre la magnitude six sur l'échelle de Richter; **3** (mentally) (notice) remarquer; (realize) se rendre compte; **4** (record) enregistrer [*loss, gain*]; **5** POST envoyer [qch] en recommandé [*letter*]; enregistrer [*luggage*].

III vi **1** [*person*] (to vote, for course, school) s'inscrire; (at hotel) se présenter; (with police, for taxes) se faire recenser (**for** pour); (for shares) souscrire (**for** à); **to ~ for a course** s'inscrire à un cours; **to ~ with a doctor** s'inscrire sur la liste des patients d'un médecin; **2** [*speed, temperature, earthquake*] être enregistré; **his name didn't ~ with me** FIG son nom ne me disait rien.

registered /'redʒɪstəd/ adj **1** [*voter*] inscrit; [*vehicle, student*] immatriculé; [*charity*] ~ agréé; [*firearm*] déclaré; [*company*] inscrit au registre du commerce; [*nurse*] diplômé d'État; COMM [*shares*] nominatif/-ive; **2** POST [*letter*] recommandé; **~ post** envoi m recommandé; **by ~ post** en recommandé.

registered trademark n nom m déposé.

registrar /ˌredʒɪ'strɑ:(r), 'redʒ-/ ▶ **1251** | n GB ADMIN officier m d'état civil; UNIV responsable mf du bureau de la scolarité; GB MED adjoint m; GB JUR greffier/ -ière m/f en chef.

registration /ˌredʒɪ'streɪʃn/ n (of person) (for course) inscription f; (for taxes) ~ déclaration f; (for national service) recensement m militaire; (of trademark, patent) dépôt m; (of birth, death, marriage) déclaration f; (of company, luggage) enregistrement m; AUT année f de première immatriculation.

registration: **~ number** n numéro m d'immatriculation or minéralogique; **~ plate** n plaque f d'immatriculation or minéralogique.

registry /'redʒɪstrɪ/ n GB salle f des registres.

registry office n GB bureau m de l'état civil; **to get married in a ~** se marier civilement.

regress /rɪ'gres/ vi BIOL, PSYCH régresser (**to** au stade de); FIG régresser; **to ~ to childhood** retomber en enfance.

regression /rɪ'greʃn/ n régression f.

regressive /rɪ'gresɪv/ adj BIOL, PSYCH régressif/-ive.

regret /rɪ'gret/ **I** n regret m (**about** à propos de; **that** que + subj); **to have no ~s about doing** ne pas regretter d'avoir fait; **to my great ~** à mon grand regret.
II vtr (p prés etc -**tt**-) regretter (**that** que + subj); **to ~ doing** regretter d'avoir fait; **I ~ to say that...** je suis au regret de dire que...; **I ~ to inform you that** j'ai le regret de vous informer que; **it is to be ~ted that** il est regrettable que (+ subj).

regretful /rɪ'gretfl/ adj plein de regrets.

regretfully /rɪ'gretfəlɪ/ adv (reluctantly) à regret.

regrettable /rɪ'gretəbl/ adj regrettable (**that** que + subj).

regrettably /rɪ'gretəblɪ/ adv **1** (sadly) malheureusement; **2** (very) [*slow, weak*] fâcheusement.

regroup /ˌri:'gru:p/ vi se regrouper.

regular /'regjʊlə(r)/ **I** n **1** (habitual client, visitor) habitué/-e m/f; **2** GB MIL soldat m de métier; **3** US (petrol) ordinaire m.
II adj **1** [*habit, job, income, interval etc*] ALSO MED, LING régulier/-ière; **on a ~ basis** de façon régulière; **~ features** traits réguliers; **to take ~ exercise** prendre de l'exercice régulièrement; **to be in ~ employment** avoir un emploi permanent; **he's a ~ guy**° US c'est un chic type°; **2** (usual) [*activity, customer, visitor*] habituel/-elle; COMM [*price, size*] normal; RADIO, TV [*listener*] fidèle; **3** GB ADMIN, MIL [*army, soldier*] de métier; [*officer, policeman*] de carrière; [*staff*] permanent; **4** (honest) régulier/-ière; **5**° (thorough) véritable (*before n*); **a ~ crook** un véritable escroc.

regularity /ˌregjʊ'lærətɪ/ n régularité f.

regularize /'regjʊləraɪz/ vtr régulariser.

regularly /'regjʊlɪ/ adv régulièrement.

regulate /'regjʊleɪt/ vtr **1** réguler [*behaviour, activity*]; réglementer [*use*]; **well-~d** bien réglé; **state-~d** sous le contrôle de l'état; **2** (adjust) régler [*mechanism*].

regulation /ˌregjʊ'leɪʃn/ **I** n **1** (rule) (for safety, fire) consigne f; (for discipline) règlement m; (legal) disposition f réglementaire; **EC ~s** réglementation f communautaire; **fire ~s** (laws) normes fpl anti-incendie; **under the (new) ~s** selon la (nouvelle) réglementation; **against the ~s** contraire au règlement or aux normes; **2** (process) réglementation f.
II noun modifier [*width, length etc*] réglementaire; HUM [*garment*] de rigueur.

regulator /'regjʊleɪtə(r)/ n **1** (device) régulateur m; **2** (person) régulateur/-trice m/f; **3** ECON organisme m de contrôle.

regulatory /'regjʊleɪtrɪ, US -tɔ:rɪ/ adj de contrôle.

regurgitate /rɪ'gɜ:dʒɪteɪt/ vtr régurgiter; FIG PÉJ ressortir.

rehabilitate /ˌri:ə'bɪlɪteɪt/ vtr **1** (medically) rééduquer; (to society) réinsérer [*handicapped person, ex-prisoner*]; réhabiliter [*addict*]; **2** GEN, POL réhabiliter.

rehabilitation /ˌri:əbɪlɪ'teɪʃn/ n **1** (of person) (medical) rééducation f; (social) réinsertion f; **2** GEN, POL réhabilitation f.

rehabilitation centre GB, **rehabilitation center** US n (for the handicapped) centre m de rééducation; (for addicts etc) centre m de réinsertion.

rehash PÉJ **I** /'ri:hæʃ/ n resucée° f.
II /ˌri:'hæʃ/ vtr remanier, piller PÉJ.

rehearsal /rɪ'hɜ:sl/ n THEAT répétition f (**of** de); FIG préparation f (**of** de); **in ~** en répétition.

rehearse /rɪ'hɜ:s/ **I** vtr THEAT répéter [*scene*]; faire répéter [*performer*]; FIG préparer [*speech, excuse*].
II vi répéter (**for** pour).

reheat /ˌri:'hi:t/ vtr réchauffer.

rehouse /ˌri:'haʊz/ vtr reloger.

reign /reɪn/ **I** n LIT, FIG règne m; **in the ~ of** sous le règne de; **~ of terror** FIG règne de la terreur; **the Reign of Terror** HIST la Terreur.
II vi LIT, FIG régner (**over** sur).

reigning /'reɪnɪŋ/ adj [*monarch*] régnant; [*champion*] en titre.

reimburse /ˌri:ɪm'bɜ:s/ vtr rembourser.

reimbursement /ˌri:ɪm'bɜ:smənt/ n remboursement m (**of** de; **for** pour).

rein /reɪn/ n rêne f; **to hold the ~s** LIT, FIG tenir les rênes; **to keep sb on a tight ~** FIG tenir qn de près; **to give full** ou **free ~ to** donner libre cours à.
■ **rein in**: **~ in** [sth] freiner [qch] (avec les rênes) [*horse*]; FIG contenir.

reincarnate /ˌri:ɪn'kɑ:neɪt/ vtr **to be ~d** se réincarner (**as** en).

reincarnation /ˌri:ɪnkɑ:'neɪʃn/ n réincarnation f.

reindeer /'reɪndɪə(r)/ n (pl ~) renne m.

reinforce /ˌri:ɪn'fɔ:s/ vtr GEN, MIL renforcer; FIG renforcer [*feeling, trend*]; **~d concrete** béton m armé.

reinforcement /ˌri:ɪn'fɔ:smənt/ n **1** (action) renforcement m (**of** de); **2** (support) renfort m; **~s** MIL, FIG renforts.

reinstate /ˌri:ɪn'steɪt/ vtr réintégrer [*employee*]; rétablir [*legislation*].

reintegrate /ˌri:'ɪntɪgreɪt/ vtr réintégrer (**into** dans).

reinvigorate /ˌri:ɪn'vɪgəreɪt/ vtr revigorer.

reissue /ˌri:'ɪʃu:/ **I** n (book, record) réédition f; CIN reprise f.
II vtr rééditer [*book, record*]; ressortir [*film*]; COMM émettre [qch] à nouveau [*shares*].

reiterate /ri:'ɪtəreɪt/ vtr réitérer.

reiteration /ri:ˌɪtə'reɪʃn/ n réitération f.

reject I /'ri:dʒekt/ n COMM marchandise f de deuxième choix.
II /rɪ'dʒekt/ vtr GEN, MED, PSYCH rejeter; refuser

[*candidate, manuscript*]; démentir [*claim, suggestion*]; repousser [*suitor*].

rejection /rɪ'dʒekʃn/ *n* GEN, MED, PSYCH rejet *m*; (of. candidate, manuscript) refus *m*; **to meet with ~** se heurter à un refus.

rejection: **~ letter** *n* lettre *f* de refus; **~ slip** *n* avis *m* de refus.

rejig /ˌriː'dʒɪg/ GB, **rejigger** /ˌriː'dʒɪgə(r)/ US *vtr* réviser.

rejoice /rɪ'dʒɔɪs/ I *vtr* réjouir; **to ~ that** se réjouir du fait que.

II *vi* se réjouir (**at, over** de); **to ~ in** se réjouir de.

rejoicing /rɪ'dʒɔɪsɪŋ/ *n* (jubilation) allégresse *f*; **~s** (celebrations) réjouissances *fpl*.

rejoin /riː'dʒɔɪn/ *vtr* GÉN rejoindre; réintégrer [*team, organization*]; [*road*] rejoindre [*coast, route*]; **to ~ ship** NAUT rallier le bord.

rejoinder /rɪ'dʒɔɪndə(r)/ *n* GEN, JUR réplique *f*.

rejuvenate /rɪ'dʒuːvɪneɪt/ *vtr* LIT, FIG rajeunir.

rejuvenation /rɪˌdʒuːvɪ'neɪʃn/ *n* LIT, FIG rajeunissement *m*.

rekindle /ˌriː'kɪndl/ *vtr* LIT, FIG ranimer.

relapse I /'riːlæps/ *n* MED, FIG rechute *f*.

II /rɪ'læps/ *vi* GEN retomber; MED rechuter.

relate /rɪ'leɪt/ I *vtr* 1 (connect) **to ~ sth and sth** établir un rapport entre qch et qch; **to ~ sth to sth** associer qch à qch; 2 raconter [*story*] (**to** à).

II *vi* 1 (have connection) **to ~ to** se rapporter à; **everything relating to him** tout ce qui a un rapport avec lui; 2 (communicate) **to ~ to** s'entendre avec; **I can't ~ to the character** le personnage ne me touche pas; **I can ~ to that!** ça, je comprends!

related /rɪ'leɪtɪd/ *adj* 1 [*person, language*] apparenté (**by, through** par; **to** à); **to be ~ by marriage** être parents par alliance; 2 (connected) [*subject*] connexe (**to** à); [*area, idea, incident*] lié (**to** à); [*species*] similaire (**to** à); **the murders are ~** les crimes sont liés; **drug/work-~** lié à la drogue/au travail.

relation /rɪ'leɪʃn/ I *n* 1 (relative) parent/-e *m/f*; **my ~s** ma famille; 2 (connection) rapport *m*; **to bear no ~ to** n'avoir aucun rapport avec; **in ~ to** par rapport à; **with ~ to** en ce qui concerne.

II **relations** *npl* GEN (dealings) relations *fpl*; EUPH (intercourse) relations *fpl* sexuelles.

relationship /rɪ'leɪʃnʃɪp/ *n* 1 (between people) relations *fpl*; **to form ~s** se lier; **to have a good ~ with** avoir de bonnes relations avec; **a working ~** des relations professionnelles; **sexual ~** relation sexuelle; **we have a good ~** nous nous entendons bien; 2 (connection) rapport *m* (**to, with** avec); 3 (family bond) lien *m* de parenté (**to** avec).

relative /'relətɪv/ I *n* 1 (relation) parent/-e *m/f*; **my ~s** ma famille; 2 LING relatif *m*.

II *adj* relatif/-ive; **the ~ merits of X and Y** les mérites respectifs de X et Y; **~ to** (compared to) par rapport à; **supply is ~ to demand** l'offre varie en fonction de la demande.

relatively /'relətɪvlɪ/ *adv* relativement; **~ speaking** toutes proportions gardées.

relativism /'relətɪvɪzəm/ *n* relativisme *m*.

relativity /ˌrelə'tɪvətɪ/ *n* relativité *f* (**of** de).

relax /rɪ'læks/ I *vtr* relâcher [*grip, concentration*]; décontracter [*jaw, muscle*]; assouplir [*restrictions, discipline*]; détendre [*body*].

II *vi* 1 [*person*] se détendre; **~!** ne t'en fais pas!; 2 [*grip*] se relâcher; [*jaw, muscle*] se décontracter; [*discipline, restrictions*] s'assouplir.

relaxation /ˌriːlæk'seɪʃn/ *n* 1 (recreation) détente *f*; **what do you do for ~?** qu'est-ce que vous faites pour vous détendre?; 2 (of grip, concentration) relâchement *m*; (of restrictions, discipline) assouplissement *m* (**in** de); (of body) détente *f*.

relaxed /rɪ'lækst/ *adj* GEN détendu, décontracté; [*muscle*] décontracté.

relaxing /rɪ'læksɪŋ/ *adj* [*atmosphere, activity*] délassant; [*period, vacation*] reposant.

relay I /'riːleɪ/ *n* 1 (of workers) équipe *f* (*de relais*); (of

horses) attelage *m*; 2 RADIO, TV émission retransmise; 3 (also **~ race**) course *f* de relais.

II *vtr* /'riːleɪ, riː'leɪ/ (*prét, pp* **relayed**) RADIO, T relayer (**to** à); FIG transmettre [*message*] (**to** à).

relay station *n* RADIO, TV relais *m*.

release /rɪ'liːs/ I *n* 1 (liberation) libération *f*; **on his ~ from prison** à sa sortie de prison; 2 FIG soulagemen *m*; **death came as a merciful ~** la mort est venue comme une délivrance; 3 MIL (of missile) lancement *m* (of bomb) largage *m*; 4 (for press) communiqué *m*; 5 CIN sortie *f*; **the film is now on general ~** le film passe maintenant dans toutes les grandes salles de cinéma; 6 (film, video, record) nouveauté *f*; 7 (discharge form) décharge *f*.

II *vtr* 1 libérer [*prisoner*]; dégager [*accident victim*] relâcher [*animal*]; **to ~ sb from** FIG dégager qn de [*promise, obligation*]; 2 faire jouer [*catch, clasp*]; PHOT déclencher [*shutter*]; AUT desserrer [*hand brake*]; 3 décocher [*arrow*]; larguer [*bomb*]; lancer [*missile*]; 4 lâcher [*object, arm, hand*]; **to ~ one's grip** lâcher prise; **to ~ one's grip of sth** lâcher qch; 5 (to public) communiquer [*statement*]; publier [*photo*]; faire sortir [*film, video, record*].

relegate /'relɪgeɪt/ *vtr* 1 reléguer [*person, object, issue*] (**to** à); 2 GB SPORT reléguer (**to** en); **to be ~d** descendre dans la division inférieure.

relegation /ˌrelɪ'geɪʃn/ *n* GEN relégation *f* (**to** à); GB SPORT relégation *f* (**to** en).

relent /rɪ'lent/ *vi* [*person, government*] céder.

relentless /rɪ'lentlɪs/ *adj* [*ambition*] implacable; [*noise, activity*] incessant; [*attack*] acharné.

relentlessly /rɪ'lentlɪslɪ/ *adv* (incessantly) sans arrêt; (mercilessly) inexorablement.

relevance /'reləvəns/ *n* pertinence *f* (**to** pour), intérêt *m* (**to** pour); **the ~ of politics to daily life** le rapport entre la politique et la vie quotidienne; **to be of ~ to** être lié à.

relevant /'reləvənt/ *adj* 1 [*issue, facts, remark, point*] pertinent; [*information, resource*] utile; **to be ~ to** avoir rapport à; 2 (appropriate) [*chapter*] correspondant; [*period*] en question; **~ document** JUR pièce *f* justificative; **the ~ authorities** les autorités compétentes.

reliability /rɪˌlaɪə'bɪlətɪ/ *n* (of friend, witness) honnêteté *f*; (of employee, firm) sérieux *m*; (of car, machine) fiabilité *f*; (of information, memory) exactitude *f*.

reliable /rɪ'laɪəbl/ *adj* [*friend, witness*] digne de confiance, fiable; [*employee, firm*] sérieux/-ieuse; [*car, memory, account*] fiable; [*information, source*] sûr.

reliably /rɪ'laɪəblɪ/ *adv* [*work*] correctement; **to be ~ informed that** tenir de source sûre que.

reliance /rɪ'laɪəns/ *n* dépendance *f* (**on** vis-à-vis de).

reliant /rɪ'laɪənt/ *adj* **to be ~ on** être dépendant de.

relic /'relɪk/ *n* 1 FIG (custom, building) vestige *m* (**of** de); (object) relique *f* (**of** de); 2 RELIG relique *f*.

relief /rɪ'liːf/ I *n* 1 (from pain, distress) soulagement *m*; **to my ~** à mon grand soulagement; **it was a ~ to them that** ils ont été soulagés que (+ *subj*); 2 (help) aide *f*, secours *m*; **famine ~** aide aux victimes de la famine; **to come to the ~ of sb** venir à l'aide ou au secours de qn; **tax ~** allégement fiscal; **to be on ~** US bénéficier des aides sociales; 3 (diversion) divertissement *m*; **to provide light ~** apporter un peu de divertissement; 4 (of garrison, troops) délivrance *f*; 5 ART, ARCHIT, GEOG relief *m*; **in ~** en relief; **to throw sth into ~** mettre qch en relief.

II *noun modifier* [*operation*] de secours; [*programme, project, effort*] d'aide; [*guard, shift*] de relève; [*bus, train*] supplémentaire.

relief: **~ agency** *n* organisation *f* humanitaire; **~ fund** *n* GEN fonds *m* d'aide; (in emergency) fonds *m* de secours; **~ map** *n* carte *f* en relief; **~ road** *n* route *f* de délestage; **~ supplies** *npl* secours *mpl*; **~ work** *n* travail *m* humanitaire; **~ worker** *n* secouriste *mf*.

relieve /rɪ'liːv/ I *vtr* 1 soulager [*pain, suffering, tension*]; dissiper [*boredom*]; remédier à [*poverty, famine*]; alléger [*debt*]; rompre [*monotony*]; **to be ~d that** être soulagé que (+ *subj*); **to be ~d at** être soulagé par [*news, results*]; **to ~ congestion** MED, AUT décongestionner; **2 to ~ sb of** débarrasser qn de [*plate, coat*]; soulager qn de [*burden*]; **to ~ sb of a post** relever qn de son poste; **3** (help) venir en aide à, secourir [*troops, population*]; **4** relever [*worker, sentry*]; **to ~ the guard** relever la garde; **5** MIL délivrer [*town*].

II *v refl* **to ~ oneself** EUPH se soulager EUPH.

religion /rɪˈlɪdʒən/ *n* religion *f*; **what ~ is he?** de quelle religion est-il?; **it's against my ~ to…** c'est contraire à ma religion de… ALSO HUM; **to get ~**○ PÉJ devenir bigot; **to lose one's ~** perdre la foi.

religious /rɪˈlɪdʒəs/ I *n* religieux/-ieuse *m/f*.

II *adj* GEN religieux/-ieuse; [*war*] de religion; [*person*] croyant; **Religious Education** ou **Instruction** instruction *f* religieuse.

religiously /rɪˈlɪdʒəslɪ/ *adv* LIT religieusement; FIG rituellement.

relinquish /rɪˈlɪŋkwɪʃ/ *vtr* SOUT renoncer à [*claim, right, privilege*] (**to** en faveur de); céder [*task, power*] (**to** à); abandonner [*responsibility*]; **to ~ one's hold** ou **grip on sth** lâcher qch.

relish /ˈrelɪʃ/ I *n* **1** **with ~** [*eat, drink, perform*] avec un plaisir évident; [*say*] avec délectation or (gloatingly) en jubilant; **2** (flavour) saveur *f*; FIG (appeal) attrait *m*; **3** CULIN condiment *m*.

II *vtr* savourer [*food*]; FIG se réjouir de [*prospect*]; **I don't ~ the thought of telling her the news** je me passerais bien de lui annoncer la nouvelle.

relocate /ˌriːləʊˈkeɪt, US riːˈləʊkeɪt/ I *vtr* muter.

II *vi* [*company*] déménager; [*employee*] être muté.

relocation /ˌriːləʊˈkeɪʃn/ *n* (of company) relocalisation *f*, déménagement *m*; (of employee) mutation *f* (**to** à, en); (of refugees) transfert *m* (**to** vers).

relocation: **~ allowance** *n* prime *f* de relogement; **~ package** *n* indemnités *fpl* de déménagement.

reluctance /rɪˈlʌktəns/ *n* GEN réticence *f* (**to do** à faire); **to do sth with ~** faire qch à contrecœur.

reluctant /rɪˈlʌktənt/ *adj* [*person*] peu enthousiaste; [*consent, promise*] accordé à contrecœur; **to be ~ to do** être peu disposé à faire; **she is a rather ~ celebrity** elle est devenue une célébrité malgré elle.

reluctantly /rɪˈlʌktəntlɪ/ *adv* à contrecœur.

rely /rɪˈlaɪ/ *vi* **1** (be dependent) **to ~ on** GEN dépendre de; reposer sur [*method, technology, exports*]; **he relies on her for everything** il s'en remet à elle pour tout; **2** (count) **to ~ on sb/sth** compter sur qn/qch (**to do** pour faire); **she cannot be relied (up)on to help** on ne peut pas compter sur elle pour aider.

remain /rɪˈmeɪn/ I *vi* **1** (be left) rester; **the fact ~s that** il reste que, toujours est-il que; **it ~s to be seen whether** il reste à voir si; **2** (stay) [*person, memory*] rester, demeurer; [*problem, doubt*] subsister; **to ~ standing** rester debout; **to ~ silent** garder le silence; **to ~ hopeful** continuer à espérer; **if the weather ~s fine** si le temps se maintient au beau.

II **remaining** *pres p adj* restant; **for the ~ months of my life** pendant les mois qu'il me reste à vivre.

remainder /rɪˈmeɪndə(r)/ I *n* **1** (remaining things, money) ALSO MATH reste *m*; (people) autres *mfpl*; (time) reste *m*, restant *m*.

II **remainders** *npl* COMM invendus *mpl* soldés.

remains /rɪˈmeɪnz/ *npl* **1** (of meal, fortune) restes *mpl*; (of building) vestiges *mpl*, restes; **2** (corpse) restes *mpl*.

remake I /ˈriːmeɪk/ *n* nouvelle version *f*, remake *m*.

II /ˌriːˈmeɪk/ *vtr* (*prét, pp* **remade**) refaire.

remand /rɪˈmɑːnd, US rɪˈmænd/ I *n* **to be on ~** (in custody) être en détention provisoire; (on bail) être en liberté sous caution.

II *vtr* renvoyer [*case, accused*]; **to be ~ed in custody** être placé en détention provisoire; **to be ~ed on bail** être mis en liberté sous caution.

remand: **~ centre** *n* GB centre *m* de détention (provisoire); **~ home** *n* GB centre *m* de détention (*pour mineurs*); **~ prisoner** *n* GB prisonnier/-ière *m/f* en détention provisoire.

remark /rɪˈmɑːk/ I *n* remarque *f* (**about** à propos de, sur), réflexion *f* (**about** à propos de, sur).

II *vtr* **1** (comment) faire remarquer (**that** que; **to** à); **2** (notice) SOUT remarquer (**that** que).

■ **remark on**, **remark upon**: **~ on** ou **upon** [sth] faire des remarques sur or à propos de (**to** à).

remarkable /rɪˈmɑːkəbl/ *adj* remarquable (**that** que + *subj*).

remarkably /rɪˈmɑːkəblɪ/ *adv* remarquablement.

remarry /ˌriːˈmærɪ/ *vi* se remarier.

remaster /riːˈmɑːstə(r)/ *vtr* AUDIO remasteriser.

rematch /ˈriːmætʃ/ *n* SPORT GEN match *m* de retour; (in boxing) deuxième combat *m*.

remedial /rɪˈmiːdɪəl/ *adj* GEN [*measures*] de redressement; MED curatif/-ive; SCH [*class*] de rattrapage.

remedy /ˈremədɪ/ I *n* MED, FIG remède *m* (**for** à, contre).

II *vtr* remédier à; **the situation cannot be remedied** la situation est sans remède.

remember /rɪˈmembə(r)/ I *vtr* **1** (recall) se souvenir de, se rappeler [*fact, name, place, event*]; se souvenir de [*person*]; **to ~ that** se rappeler que, se souvenir que; **to ~ doing** se rappeler avoir fait, se souvenir d'avoir fait; **I don't ~ anything about it** je n'en ai aucun souvenir; **that's worth ~ing** c'est bon à savoir; **a night to ~** une soirée mémorable; **2** (not forget) **to ~ to do** penser à faire, ne pas oublier de faire; **did you ~ to feed the cat?** tu as pensé à donner à manger au chat?; **~ that it's fragile** n'oublie pas que c'est fragile; **~ where you are!** un peu de tenue!; **she ~ed me in her will** EUPH elle ne m'a pas oublié dans son testament; **3** (commemorate) commémorer [*battle, war dead*]; **4** (convey greetings) **she asks to be ~ed to you** elle m'a prié de vous transmettre son bon souvenir.

II *vi* se souvenir; **if I ~ rightly** si je me souviens bien; **not as far as I ~** pas que je sache; **as far as I can ~** pour autant que je me souvienne.

remembrance /rɪˈmembrəns/ *n* souvenir *m*.

Remembrance Day, **Remembrance Sunday** GB *n*: *jour consacré à la mémoire des soldats tués au cours des deux guerres mondiales.*

remind /rɪˈmaɪnd/ I *vtr* rappeler; **to ~ sb of sth/sb** rappeler qch/qn à qn; **to ~ sb to do/that** rappeler à qn de faire/que; **you are ~ed that** nous vous rappelons que; **I forgot to ~ her about the meeting** j'ai oublié de lui reparler de la réunion; **that ~s me** à propos.

II *v refl* **to ~ oneself** se dire (**that** que).

reminder /rɪˈmaɪndə(r)/ *n* rappel *m* (**of** de; **that** du fait que); **a ~ to sb to do** un rappel à qn lui demandant de faire; **(letter of) ~** ADMIN (lettre *f* de) rappel *m*; **to be a ~ of sth** rappeler qch; **~s of the past** souvenirs *mpl* du passé.

reminisce /ˌremɪˈnɪs/ *vi* évoquer ses souvenirs (**about** de).

reminiscence /ˌremɪˈnɪsns/ *n* (recalling) réminiscence *f*; (memory) souvenir *m*.

reminiscent /ˌremɪˈnɪsnt/ *adj* **to be ~ of sb/sth** faire penser à qn/qch.

remiss /rɪˈmɪs/ *adj* négligent; **it was ~ of him not to reply** c'était négligent de sa part de ne pas répondre.

remission /rɪˈmɪʃn/ *n* (of sentence, debt) remise *f*; MED, RELIG rémission *f*.

remit /ˈriːmɪt/ *n* attributions *fpl* (**to do** pour faire; **for** pour); **it's outside my ~** ce n'est pas dans mes attributions.

remittance /rɪˈmɪtns/ *n* (payment) versement *m*; (allowance) rente *f*.

remix MUS I /ˈriːmɪks/ *n* (version *f*) remix *m*.

II /ˌriːˈmɪks/ *vtr* remixer.

remnant /ˈremnənt/ *n* GEN reste *m*; (of building, past) vestige *m*; COMM (of fabric) coupon *m*.

remonstrate /ˈremənstreɪt/ *vi* protester; **to ~ with sb** faire des remontrances à qn.

remorse /rɪˈmɔːs/ *n* remords *m* (**for** de); **a feeling of**

~ un remords; **she felt no ~ for her crime** elle n'éprouvait aucun remords d'avoir commis ce crime.

remorseful /rɪ'mɔ:sfl/ *adj* plein de remords.

remorseless /rɪ'mɔ:slɪs/ *adj* **1** (brutal) impitoyable; **2** [*ambition*] implacable; [*optimism*] perpétuel/-elle.

remorselessly /rɪ'mɔ:slɪslɪ/ *adv* implacablement.

remote /rɪ'məʊt/ *adj* **1** (distant) [*era*] lointain; [*antiquity*] haut; [*ancestor, country, planet*] éloigné; **in the ~ future/past** dans un avenir/passé lointain; **in the ~st corner of Asia** au fin fond de l'Asie; **2** [*area, village*] isolé; **~ from society** à l'écart de la société; **3** FIG (aloof) [*person*] distant; **4** (slight) [*chance, connection*] vague, infime; **I haven't (got) the ~st idea** je n'en ai pas la moindre idée; **there is only a ~ possibility that** il est très peu probable que (+ *subj*).

remote access *n* COMPUT téléconsultation *f*, accès *m* à distance.

remote control *n* télécommande *f*; **to operate sth by ~** télécommander qch.

remote-controlled *adj* télécommandé.

remotely /rɪ'məʊtlɪ/ *adv* **1** [*situated*] à l'écart de tout; **2** (slightly) [*resemble*] vaguement; **he's not ~ interested** ça ne l'intéresse pas du tout.

remoteness /rɪ'məʊtnɪs/ *n* isolement *m* (**from** par rapport à); (in time) éloignement *m* (dans le temps) (**from** par rapport à); FIG (of person) attitude *f* distante (**from** envers).

remould GB, **remold** US /'ri:məʊld/ *n* GB pneu *m* rechapé.

remount /ˌri:'maʊnt/ *vtr* enfourcher [qch] de nouveau [*bicycle*]; **to ~ a horse** se remettre en selle.

removable /rɪ'mu:vəbl/ *adj* amovible.

removal /rɪ'mu:vl/ **I** *n* **1** (of tax, barrier, threat) suppression *f*; (of doubt, worry) disparition *f*; (of demonstrators) expulsion *f*; (of troops) retrait *m*; MED ablation *f*; **stain ~** détachage *m*; **2** (change of home, location) déménagement *m* (**from** de; **to** à); **3** (of employee, official) renvoi *m*; (of leader) déposition *f*, révocation *f*. **II** *noun modifier* [*costs, firm, van*] de déménagement; **~ man** déménageur *m*.

remove /rɪ'mu:v/ **I** *n* SOUT **to be at one ~ from/at many ~s from** être tout proche de/très loin de. **II** *vtr* **1** GEN, MED enlever (**from** de); enlever, ôter [*clothes, shoes*]; enlever, faire partir [*stain*]; enlever, supprimer [*paragraph, word*]; supprimer [*tax, subsidy*]; **to ~ goods from the market** retirer des marchandises de la vente; **to ~ sb's name from a list** rayer qn d'une liste; **to be ~d to hospital** GB être emmené à l'hôpital; **to ~ one's make-up** se démaquiller; **to be far ~d from** être très éloigné de [*reality, truth*]; **cousin once/twice ~d** cousin au deuxième/troisième degré; **2** (oust) renvoyer [*employee*]; **to ~ sb from office** démettre qn de ses fonctions; **3** (dissiper) [*suspicion, fears*]; chasser [*doubt*]; écarter [*obstacle*]; supprimer [*threat*]; **4** EUPH (kill) supprimer; **5** COMPUT effacer.

remover /rɪ'mu:və(r)/ *n* (person) déménageur *m*; ▶ **stain remover etc.**

remunerate /rɪ'mju:nəreɪt/ *vtr* rémunérer (**for** pour).

remuneration /rɪˌmju:nə'reɪʃn/ *n* SOUT rémunération *f*.

renal /'ri:nl/ *adj* rénal.

rename /ˌri:'neɪm/ *vtr* rebaptiser.

rend /rend/ *vtr* (*prét, pp* **rent**) LIT, FIG déchirer.

render /'rendə(r)/ *vtr* **1** (make) **to ~ sth impossible** rendre qch impossible; **2** (give) rendre [*allegiance*] (**to** à); apporter [*assistance*] (**to** à); **'for services ~ed'** 'pour services rendus'; **3** LITERAT, MUS rendre [*style, nuance*]; traduire [*text*] (**into** en); **4** enduire [*wall*].

rendering /'rendərɪŋ/ *n* **1** ART, LITERAT, MUS interprétation *f* (**of** de); (translation) traduction *f* (**of** de); **2** (in building) enduit *m*.

rendezvous /'rɒndɪvu:/ **I** *n* (*pl* **~**) rendez-vous *m* *inv*; **to have a ~ with sb** avoir rendez-vous avec qn. **II** *vi* **to ~ with sb** rejoindre qn.

rendition /ren'dɪʃn/ *n* interprétation *f*.

renegade /'renɪgeɪd/ **I** *n* (abandoning beliefs) renégat/-e *m/f*; (rebel) rebelle *mf*. **II** *adj* (abandoning beliefs) renégat; (rebel) rebelle.

renege /rɪ'ni:g, -'neɪg/ *vi* se rétracter; **to ~ on an agreement** revenir sur sa parole.

renew /rɪ'nju:, US -'nu:/ **I** *vtr* GEN renouveler; renouer [*acquaintance*]; reprendre [*negotiations*]. **II renewed** *pp adj* [*interest, optimism*] accru; [*attack, call*] renouvelé.

renewable /rɪ'nju:əbl, US -'nu:əbl/ *adj* renouvelable.

renewal /rɪ'nju:əl, US -'nu:əl/ *n* GEN renouvellement *m*; (of hostilities) reprise *f*; (of interest) regain *m*; **to come up for ~** arriver à expiration.

renounce /rɪ'naʊns/ *vtr* GEN renoncer à; renier [*faith, friend*]; dénoncer [*agreement, treaty*].

renovate /'renəveɪt/ *vtr* rénover [*building*].

renovation /ˌrenə'veɪʃn/ *n* rénovation *f*; **~s** travaux *mpl* de rénovation; **property in need of ~** maison à rénover.

renown /rɪ'naʊn/ *n* renommée *f*.

renowned /rɪ'naʊnd/ *adj* célèbre (**for** pour).

rent /rent/ **I** *prét, pp* ▶ **rend**. **II** *n* **1** (for accommodation) loyer *m*; **for ~** à louer; **2** (rip) LIT, FIG déchirure *f*. **III** *vtr* **1** (hire) louer [*car, house*]; **2** (let) = **rent out**. **IV** *vi* [*tenant*] être locataire; **he ~s to students** [*landlord*] il loue des logements à des étudiants. ■ **rent out: ~ [sth] out, ~ out [sth]** louer (**to** à).

rental *n* (of car, premises, equipment) location *f*; (of phone line) abonnement *m*; **car ~** location de voitures.

rent-free /ˌrent'fri:/ **I** *adj* [*house*] prêté. **II** *adv* [*live, use*] sans payer de loyer.

renunciation /rɪˌnʌnsɪ'eɪʃn/ *n* GEN renonciation *f* (**to** à); (of faith, friend) reniement *m* (**of** de).

reopen /ˌri:'əʊpən/ *vtr, vi* rouvrir.

reopening /ˌri:'əʊpənɪŋ/ *n* réouverture *f*.

reorganization /ˌri:ˌɔ:gənaɪ'zeɪʃn/ *n* réorganisation *f*.

reorganize /ˌri:'ɔ:gənaɪz/ **I** *vtr* réorganiser. **II** *vi* se réorganiser.

rep /rep/ ▶ **1251** *n* **1** COMM, IND (*abrév* = **representative**) représentant *m* (de commerce); **2** THEAT *abrév* ▶ **repertory**; **3** (fabric) reps *m*.

repackage /ˌri:'pækɪdʒ/ *vtr* **1** COMM reconditionner [*product*]; **2** FIG reconditionner [*pay offer*]; modifier l'image publique de [*politician, media personality*].

repaid /ˌri:'peɪd/ *prét, pp* ▶ **repay**.

repaint /ˌri:'peɪnt/ *vtr* repeindre.

repair /rɪ'peə(r)/ **I** *n* **1** GEN réparation *f*; NAUT (of hull) radoub *m*; **under ~** [*building*] en réparation; [*ship*] au radoub; **the ~s to the roof** la réparation du toit; **to be (damaged) beyond ~** ne pas être réparable; **'road under ~'** 'travaux'; **2** SOUT (condition) **to be in good/bad ~** être en bon/mauvais état; **to keep sth in good ~** (bien) entretenir qch. **II** *vtr* GEN réparer; NAUT radouber [*hull*]. **III** *vi* (go) SOUT se retirer.

repair: **~ kit** *n* trousse *f* de réparation; **~man** *n* réparateur *m*.

reparation /ˌrepə'reɪʃn/ *n* SOUT réparation *f*; **~s** POL indemnités *fpl* de guerre.

repartee /ˌrepa:'ti:/ *n* (conversation) échange *m* de bons mots; (wit) repartie *f*; (reply) réplique *f*, repartie *f*.

repatriate /ˌri:'pætrɪeɪt, US -'peɪt-/ *vtr* rapatrier.

repatriation /ˌri:pætrɪ'eɪʃn, US -peɪt-/ *n* rapatriement *m*.

repay /rɪ'peɪ/ *vtr* (*prét, pp* **repaid**) rembourser [*person, sum*]; rendre [*hospitality, favour*]; **how can I ever ~ you (for your kindness)?** comment pourrai-je jamais vous remercier (de votre gentillesse)?

repayment /rɪ'peɪmənt/ *n* remboursement *m* (**on de**; **to** à); **to fall behind with one's ~s** accumuler des arriérés de remboursement; **~ mortgage** emprunt *m* hypothécaire à remboursements.

repeal /rɪ'pi:l/ **I** *n* JUR abrogation *f* (**of** de). **II** *vtr* abroger.

repeat /rɪ'piːt/ **I** _n_ GEN répétition _f_; RADIO, TV rediffusion _f_; MUS reprise _f_.
II _vtr_ GEN répéter; SCH redoubler [_year_]; recommencer [_course_]; RADIO, TV rediffuser [_programme_]; MUS reprendre; **to be ~ed** GEN se répéter; RADIO, TV être rediffusé; COMM [_offer_] être renouvelé; **to ~ oneself** se répéter.

repeated /rɪ'piːtɪd/ _adj_ [_warnings, requests, attempts_] répété; [_defeats, setbacks_] successif/-ive; MUS repris.

repeatedly /rɪ'piːtɪdlɪ/ _adv_ plusieurs fois, à plusieurs reprises.

repel /rɪ'pel/ _vtr_ (_p prés etc_ **-ll-**) GEN, PHYS repousser; FIG (disgust) dégoûter; **to be ~led by sb** trouver qn repoussant.

repellent /rɪ'pelənt/ _adj_ repoussant; ▶**insect repellent**.

repent /rɪ'pent/ **I** _vtr_ se repentir de.
II _vi_ se repentir.

repentance /rɪ'pentəns/ _n_ repentir _m_.

repentant /rɪ'pentənt/ _adj_ repentant FML.

repercussion /ˌriːpə'kʌʃn/ _n_ répercussion _f_.

repertoire /'repətwɑː(r)/ _n_ répertoire _m_.

repertory /'repətrɪ, US -tɔːrɪ/ _n_ **1 to work in ~** THEAT jouer avec une troupe de province; **2** = **repertoire**.

repetition /ˌrepɪ'tɪʃn/ _n_ répétition _f_.

repetitious /ˌrepɪ'tɪʃəs/ _adj_ répétitif/-ive.

repetitive /rɪ'petɪtɪv/ _adj_ répétitif/-ive.

repetitiveness /rɪ'petɪtɪvnɪs/ _n_ répétitivité _f_.

replace /rɪ'pleɪs/ _vtr_ **1** (put back) remettre [_lid, cork_]; remettre [qch] à sa place [_book, ornament_]; **to ~ the receiver** raccrocher; **2** remplacer [_goods_] (**with** par); (in job) remplacer [_person_]; **3** COMPUT remplacer.

replacement /rɪ'pleɪsmənt/ **I** _n_ **1** (person) remplaçant/-e _m/f_ (**for** de); **we will give you a ~** COMM (article) on vous le/la remplacera; **2** (act) remplacement _m_; **3** (spare part) pièce _f_ de rechange.
II _noun modifier_ [_staff_] intérimaire; [_engine, part_] de rechange.

replay I /'riːpleɪ/ _n_ SPORT match _m_ rejoué; FIG répétition _f_.
II /ˌriː'pleɪ/ _vtr_ MUS rejouer [_piece_]; AUDIO écouter [qch] à nouveau [_record_]; SPORT rejouer.

replenish /rɪ'plenɪʃ/ _vtr_ GEN remplir de nouveau (**with** de); reconstituer [_stocks_].

replete /rɪ'pliːt/ _adj_ (after eating) rassasié (**with** de).

replica /'replɪkə/ _n_ réplique _f_, copie _f_ (**of** de).

replicate /'replɪkeɪt/ **I** _vtr_ reproduire.
II _vi_ MED se reproduire (par réplication).

reply /rɪ'plaɪ/ **I** _n_ GEN, JUR réponse _f_.
II _vtr, vi_ répondre.

report /rɪ'pɔːt/ **I** _n_ **1** (written account) GEN, ADMIN rapport _m_ (**on** sur); (of commission, enquiry) rapport _m_ d'enquête; (verbal account, minutes) compte-rendu _m_; GB SCH bulletin _m_ scolaire; US SCH (review) critique _f_; **have you had any ~s of lost dogs?** est-ce qu'on a signalé des chiens perdus?; **2** (in media) communiqué _m_; (longer) reportage _m_; **3** (noise) détonation _f_.
II reports _npl_ (unsubstantiated news) **we are getting ~s of heavy fighting** des combats intensifs auraient lieu; **according to ~s** selon certaines sources; **I've heard ~s that** j'ai entendu dire que.
III _vtr_ **1** GEN, ADMIN signaler [_fact, event_]; (in media) faire le compte rendu de [_debate_]; **to ~ sth to sb** transmettre qch à qn [_result, decision, news_]; **five people are ~ed dead** on signale cinq morts; **he is ~ed to have said that...** il aurait dit que...; **did she have anything of interest to ~?** avait-elle quelque chose d'intéressant à raconter?; **he ~ed that my parents are well** il m'a dit que mes parents vont bien; **2** (make complaint about) signaler; PÉJ dénoncer [_person_].
IV _vi_ **1** (give account) **to ~ on** faire un compte-rendu sur [_talks, progress_]; JOURN faire un reportage sur [_events_]; **he will ~ to Parliament on the negotiations** il fera un compte-rendu des négociations au parlement; **2** (present findings) [_committee, group_] faire

son rapport (**on** sur); **3** (present oneself) se présenter; **~ to reception** présentez-vous à la réception; **to ~ for duty** prendre son service; **to ~ sick** se faire porter malade; **to ~ to one's unit** MIL rejoindre son unité; **4** ADMIN **to ~ to** être sous les ordres (directs) de [_manager, superior_].
■ **report back 1** [_employee_] se présenter; **2** (present findings) présenter un rapport.

report card _n_ US bulletin _m_ scolaire.

reportedly /rɪ'pɔːtɪdlɪ/ _adv_ **he is ~ unharmed** il serait indemne.

reporter /rɪ'pɔːtə(r)/ ▶**1251** _n_ journaliste _mf_, reporter _mf_.

reporting /rɪ'pɔːtɪŋ/ _n_ JOURN reportages _mpl_.

repose /rɪ'pəʊz/ SOUT **I** _n_ repos _m_; **in ~** au repos.
II _vi_ (lie buried) reposer.

repository /rɪ'pɒzɪtrɪ, US -tɔːrɪ/ _n_ **1** (of secret, authority) dépositaire _mf_; **2** (place) dépôt _m_ (**of, for** de).

repossess /ˌriːpə'zes/ _vtr_ [_bank_] saisir [_house_]; [_creditor_] reprendre possession de [_property, goods_].

repossession /ˌriːpə'zeʃn/ _n_ saisie _f_ immobilière.

reprehensible /ˌreprɪ'hensɪbl/ _adj_ répréhensible.

represent /ˌreprɪ'zent/ _vtr_ **1** (act on behalf of) GEN, JUR, POL représenter [_person_]; **under-~ed** insuffisamment représenté; **well ~ed** (numerous) bien représenté; **2** (present) présenter [_person, event_] (**as** comme); **3** (convey) exposer [_facts, reasons_]; **4** [_painting etc_] représenter; (be symbol of) (on map etc) représenter; **5** (constitute) représenter.

representation /ˌreprɪzen'teɪʃn/ _n_ **1** GEN, POL représentation _f_ (**of** de; **by** par); **2 to make ~s to sb** (requests) faire des démarches _fpl_ auprès de qn; (complain) se plaindre officiellement auprès de qn.

representational /ˌreprɪzen'teɪʃənl/ _adj_ ART figuratif/-ive.

representative /ˌreprɪ'zentətɪv/ **I** ▶**1251** _n_ GEN représentant/-e _m/f_; COMM représentant/-e _m/f_, agent _m_ (commercial); US POL député _m_.
II _adj_ représentatif/-ive (**of** de), typique (**of** de).

repress /rɪ'pres/ _vtr_ GEN réprimer; PSYCH refouler.

repression /rɪ'preʃn/ _n_ GEN répression _f_; PSYCH refoulement _m_.

repressive /rɪ'presɪv/ _adj_ répressif/-ive.

reprieve /rɪ'priːv/ **I** _n_ **1** JUR remise _f_ de peine; **2** (delay) sursis _m_; **3** (respite) répit _m_.
II _vtr_ **1** JUR accorder une remise de peine à [_prisoner_]; **2 the school was ~d** (temporarily) l'école a bénéficié d'un sursis.

reprimand /'reprɪmɑːnd, US -mænd/ **I** _n_ ADMIN, GEN réprimande _f_.
II _vtr_ ADMIN, GEN réprimander.

reprint I /'riːprɪnt/ _n_ réimpression _f_.
II /ˌriː'prɪnt/ _vtr_ réimprimer; **the book is being ~ed** le livre est en réimpression.

reprisal /rɪ'praɪzl/ _n_ représailles _fpl_; **in ~ for** ou **against** en représailles contre; **to take ~s** exercer des représailles.

reproach /rɪ'prəʊtʃ/ **I** _n_ reproche _m_; **above** ou **beyond ~** irréprochable.
II _vtr_ reprocher à [_person_]; **to ~ sb with** ou **for sth** reprocher qch à qn; **to ~ oneself for** ou **with sth** se reprocher qch.

reproachful /rɪ'prəʊtʃfl/ _adj_ [_person, remark, look_] réprobateur/-trice; [_letter, word_] de reproche.

reproachfully /rɪ'prəʊtʃfəlɪ/ _adv_ [_look at_] d'un air réprobateur; [_say_] d'un ton réprobateur.

reprocess /ˌriː'prəʊses/ _vtr_ retraiter.

reprocessing plant /ˌriː'prəʊsesɪŋ/ _n_ (also **nuclear ~**) usine _f_ de retraitement (des déchets nucléaires).

reproduce /ˌriːprə'djuːs, US -'duːs/ **I** _vtr_ reproduire.
II _vi_ BIOL (also **~ oneself**) se reproduire.

reproduction /ˌriːprə'dʌkʃn/ _n_ reproduction _f_.

reproduction furniture _n_ meubles _mpl_ de style.

reproductive /ˌriːprə'dʌktɪv/ _adj_ reproducteur/-trice.

reproof /rɪ'pruːf/ _n_ réprimande _f_.

reprove /rɪ'pruːv/ *vtr* réprimander (**for doing** de faire).

reproving /rɪ'pruːvɪŋ/ *adj* réprobateur/-trice.

reptile /'reptaɪl, US -tl/ *n* ZOOL reptile *m* ALSO FIG.

republic /rɪ'pʌblɪk/ *n* républiquef.

republican /rɪ'pʌblɪkən/ **I** *n* républicain/-e *m/f*.
II *adj* républicain.

Republican /rɪ'pʌblɪkən/ **I** *n* POL Républicain/-e *m/f*.
II *adj* républicain.

republicanism /rɪ'pʌblɪkənɪzəm/ *n* GEN républicanisme *m*; **Republicanism** POL US tendance *f* républicaine; (in Northern Ireland) Républicanisme *m*.

republish /ˌriː'pʌblɪʃ/ *vtr* rééditer.

repudiate /rɪ'pjuːdɪeɪt/ *vtr* GEN rejeter; abandonner [*violence, aim*]; JUR refuser d'honorer [*contract*].

repudiation /rɪˌpjuːdɪ'eɪʃn/ *n* (of charge, claim, violence) rejet *m*; (of treaty) refus *m* d'honorer.

repugnance /rɪ'pʌgnəns/ *n* aversion *f* (**for sth** pour qch; **for sb** contre qn).

repugnant /rɪ'pʌgnənt/ *adj* répugnant; **to be ~ to sb** répugner à qn.

repulse /rɪ'pʌls/ *vtr* GEN, MIL repousser.

repulsion /rɪ'pʌlʃn/ *n* répulsion*f*.

repulsive /rɪ'pʌlsɪv/ *adj* repoussant.

reputable /'repjʊtəbl/ *adj* de bonne réputation.

reputation /ˌrepjʊ'teɪʃn/ *n* réputation *f* (**as** de); **to have a good/bad ~** avoir bonne/mauvaise réputation; **he has a ~ for honesty** il a la réputation d'être honnête.

repute /rɪ'pjuːt/ *n* **of ~** réputé; **a house of ill ~** EUPH une maison close.

reputed /rɪ'pjuːtɪd/ *adj* réputé; JUR putatif/-ive; **he is ~ to be very rich** à ce que l'on dit il serait très riche.

reputedly /rɪ'pjuːtɪdlɪ/ *adv* à ce que l'on dit.

request /rɪ'kwest/ **I** *n* **1** demande *f* (**for** de; **to** à), requête *f* (**for** de; **to** à); **on ~** sur demande; **at the ~ of** sur la demande de; **by popular ~** à la demande générale; **2** RADIO dédicace *f*; **to play a ~ for sb** passer un disque à la demande de qn.
II *vtr* demander (**from** à); **to ~ sb to do** demander à qn de faire; **to ~ sb's help** demander de l'aide à qn; **to ~ that** demander que (+ *subj*); **you are ~ed not to smoke** prière de ne pas fumer; **as ~ed** (in correspondance) conformément à votre demande.

request stop *n* GB arrêt *m* facultatif.

requiem /'rekwɪem/ *n* requiem *m*; **~ mass** messe *f* de requiem.

require /rɪ'kwaɪə(r)/ **I** *vtr* **1** (need) avoir besoin de [*help, money, staff*]; **as ~d** en cas de besoin; **2** (necessitate) [*job, situation*] exiger [*funds, qualifications*]; **to ~ that** exiger que (+ *subj*); **to ~ sth of** ou **from** exiger qch de; **to be ~d to do** être tenu de faire.
II required *pp adj* [*amount, size, qualification*] exigé; **by the ~d date** en temps voulu.

requirement /rɪ'kwaɪəmənt/ *n* **1** (need) besoin *m*; **to meet sb's ~s** satisfaire les besoins de qn; **2** (condition) condition *f*; **university entrance ~s** conditions d'entrée à l'université; **to fulfil** ou **meet the ~s** remplir les conditions; **3** (obligation) obligation *f* (**to do** de faire); **4** US UNIV matière *f* obligatoire.

requisite /'rekwɪzɪt/ **I** *n* condition *f* (**for** pour).
II requisites *npl* (for artist, office) fournitures *fpl*; **toilet ~s** articles *mpl* de toilette.
III *adj* exigé, requis.

requisition /ˌrekwɪ'zɪʃn/ **I** *n* MIL réquisition*f*.
II *vtr* MIL réquisitionner.

reroof /ˌriː'ruːf/ *vtr* refaire la toiture de [*building*].

reroute /ˌriː'ruːt/ *vtr* changer l'itinéraire de [*flight*]; dévier [*traffic*].

rerun /'riːrʌn/ *n* (also **re-run**) CIN, THEAT reprise *f*; TV rediffusion*f*; FIG répétition*f*.

resat /ˌriː'sæt/ *prét, pp* ▶ **resit** *vtr*.

reschedule /ˌriː'ʃedjuːl, US -'skedʒʊl/ *vtr* GEN (change time) changer l'heure de; (change date) changer la date de [*performance*]; COMM rééchelonner [*debt*].

rescind /rɪ'sɪnd/ *vtr* abroger [*law*]; annuler [*decision, treaty*]; résilier [*contract*]; casser [*judgment*].

rescue /'reskjuː/ **I** *n* **1** (aid) secours *m*; **to come/go to sb's ~** venir/aller au secours de qn; **to come/go to the ~** venir/aller à la rescousse de; **2** (operation) sauvetage *m* (**of** de); **air-sea ~** service aéro-naval de sauvetage.
II *noun modifier* [*bid, mission, operation*] de sauvetage.
III *vtr* (save) sauver [*person*]; (salvage) récupérer [*object*]; (aid) porter secours à [*person, company*]; venir à l'aide de [*industry*]; (release) libérer.

rescue party *n* équipe*f* de secours.

rescuer /'reskjuːə(r)/ *n* sauveteur *m*.

rescue worker *n* secouriste *mf*.

research /rɪ'sɜːtʃ, 'riːsɜːtʃ/ **I** *n* GEN, UNIV, MED recherche *f* (**into, on** sur); (for media) documentation *f* (**into** sur); **animal ~** expériences *fpl* sur les animaux; **a piece of ~** une recherche.
II *noun modifier* [*grant, project*] de recherche; [*student*] qui fait de la recherche; [*funding*] pour la recherche; **~ work** recherche *f*; **~ scientist** chercheur/-euse *m/f*.
III *vtr* GEN, UNIV faire des recherches sur [*topic*]; préparer [*book, article*]; (in media) se documenter sur [*issue*]; **well ~ed** bien documenté; **to ~ the market** COMM faire une étude de marché.

research: ~ and development, R&D *n* recherche-développement *f*, recherche *f* et développement *m*; **~ assistant** ▶ 1251 *n* GB UNIV assistant/-e *m/f* d'un chercheur.

researcher /rɪ'sɜːtʃə(r), 'riːsɜːtʃə(r)/ ▶ 1251 *n* GEN chercheur/-euse *m/f*; TV documentaliste *mf*.

research: ~ establishment *n* centre *m* de recherches; **~ fellow** *n* GB UNIV chercheur/-euse *m/f* universitaire.

resell /ˌriː'sel/ *vtr* (*prét, pp* **resold**) revendre.

resemblance /rɪ'zembləns/ *n* ressemblance *f* (**between** entre; **to** avec); **to bear a close ~ to** ressembler fort à; **family ~** air *m* de famille.

resemble /rɪ'zembl/ *vtr* ressembler à; **to ~ each other** se ressembler.

resent /rɪ'zent/ *vtr* en vouloir à [*person*] (**for doing** d'avoir fait); mal supporter [*change, system*]; ne pas aimer [*tone, term*]; **to ~ having to do** ne pas supporter de faire; **I ~ that remark** cette réflexion ne me plaît pas du tout; **to ~ the fact that** ne pas supporter le fait que (+ *subj*).

resentful /rɪ'zentfl/ *adj* plein de ressentiment (**at** à; **of** à l'égard de).

resentment /rɪ'zentmənt/ *n* ressentiment *m* (**about** au sujet de; **against** envers; **at** à l'égard de).

reservation /ˌrezə'veɪʃn/ *n* **1** (doubt) réserve *f*; **without ~** sans réserve; **with some ~s** avec certaines réserves; **to have ~s about sth** avoir des doutes sur qch; **2** (booking) réservation *f*; **do you have a ~?** avez-vous réservé?; **3** US (Indian land) réserve*f*.

reservation desk *n* bureau *m* des réservations.

reserve /rɪ'zɜːv/ **I** *n* **1** (resource, stock) réserve *f*; **oil ~s** réserves de pétrole; **to keep sth in ~** tenir qch en réserve; **2** (reticence) réserve *f*; **to lose one's ~** sortir de sa réserve; **3** (doubt) réserve *f*; **4** MIL **the ~, the ~s** la réserve; **5** SPORT remplaçant/-e *m/f*; **6** (area of land) réserve*f*; **wildlife ~** réserve naturelle.
II *noun modifier* [*fund, supplies, steam, forces*] de réserve; [*player*] remplaçant.
III *vtr* **1** (set aside) réserver; **she ~s her fiercest criticism for...** elle réserve ses critiques les plus féroces pour...; **to ~ one's strength** ménager ses forces; **to ~ the right to do sth** se réserver le droit de faire qch; **to ~ judgment** réserver son jugement; **2** (book) réserver [*room, seat*].

reserved /rɪ'zɜːvd/ *adj* **1** [*person*] réservé; **to be ~ about sth** rester réservé sur qch; **2** [*table, room*] réservé; **3** COMM **all rights ~** tous droits réservés.

reserve price *n* GB prix *m* minimum.

reservist /rɪ'zɜːvɪst/ *n* réserviste *m*.

reservoir /'rezəvwɑː(r)/ *n* réservoir *m*.

reset /ˌriːˈset/ vtr (p prés **-tt-**; prét, pp **reset**) GEN régler [machine]; remettre [qch] à l'heure [clock].

resettle /ˌriːˈsetl/ I vtr réinstaller [person]; repeupler [area].
II vi se réinstaller.

reshuffle /ˌriːˈʃʌfl/ I n POL remaniement m; **cabinet ~** remaniement ministériel.
II vtr **1** POL remanier; **2** rebattre [cards].

reside /rɪˈzaɪd/ vi SOUT (live) résider, habiter (**with** avec); FIG résider (**in** dans).

residence /ˈrezɪdəns/ n **1** SOUT (dwelling) maison f, demeure f; (in property ad) maison f; **2** ADMIN, JUR (in area, country) résidence f; **place of ~** lieu m de résidence; **to take up ~** élire domicile; **~ permit** permis m de séjour; **to be in ~** SOUT [monarch] être au château; ▶ **hall of residence**; **3** US UNIV (also **~ hall**) résidence f universitaire.

resident /ˈrezɪdənt/ I n (of city, region) résident/-e m/f; (of street) riverain/-e m/f; (of hostel) résident/-e m/f; (of guest house) pensionnaire mf; **the local ~s** les habitants du quartier; **~s association** association f de quartier.
II adj [population] local; [staff, tutor] à demeure; [band] permanent; **to be ~ in** résider dans.

residential /ˌrezɪˈdenʃl/ adj [area] résidentiel/-ielle; [staff] à demeure; [course] en internat; **~ home** GB (for elderly) maison f de retraite; (for disabled) institution f pour handicapés; (for youth) foyer m d'accueil; **to be in ~ care** être pris en charge par une institution.

residual /rɪˈzɪdjʊəl, US -dʒʊ-/ adj **1** [prejudice, need] persistant; [income] résiduel/-elle; **2** CHEM résiduel/-elle.

residue /ˈrezɪdjuː, US -duː/ n GEN, CHEM résidu m (**of** de); FIG reste m (**of** de).

resign /rɪˈzaɪn/ I vtr démissionner de [post, job].
II vi démissionner (**as** du poste de; **from** de; **over** à cause de).
III v refl **to ~ oneself** se résigner (**to** à).

resignation /ˌrezɪɡˈneɪʃn/ n **1** (from post) démission f (**from** de; **as** du poste de); **to hand in one's ~** donner sa démission; **2** (patience) résignation f.

resigned /rɪˈzaɪnd/ adj résigné (**to** à).

resilience /rɪˈzɪlɪəns/ n (of person) (mental) détermination f; (physical) résistance f physique; (of industry, economy) faculté f de reprise; (of material) élasticité f.

resilient /rɪˈzɪlɪənt/ adj **1** (morally) déterminé; (physically) résistant; **2** [material] élastique.

resin /ˈrezɪn, US ˈrezn/ n résine f.

resist /rɪˈzɪst/ I vtr **1** s'opposer à [attempt, reform]; résister à [attack]; **2** résister à [temptation, suggestion]; **to ~ doing** s'empêcher de faire; **3** résister à [rust, heat].
II vi résister.

resistance /rɪˈzɪstəns/ n résistance f (**to** à); **to meet with ~** se heurter à une résistance; **to put up ~** résister; **his ~ is low** sa résistance est amoindrie; **to build up a ~ to sth** devenir plus résistant à qch.
IDIOMS **to take the line** ou **path of least ~** choisir la voie de la facilité.

Resistance /rɪˈzɪstəns/ n POL HIST **the ~** la Résistance.

resistance: **~ fighter** n résistant/-e m/f; **~ movement** n mouvement m de résistance.

resistant /rɪˈzɪstənt/ adj **1** [virus] rebelle (**to** à); **heat-/ rust-~** résistant à la chaleur/à la rouille; **water-~** imperméable; **2** (opposed) **~ to** réfractaire à.

resit GB I /ˈriːsɪt/ n session f de rattrapage.
II /ˌriːˈsɪt/ vtr (prét, pp **resat**) repasser [exam, test].

resolute /ˈrezəluːt/ adj [person] résolu.

resolutely /ˈrezəluːtlɪ/ adv résolument.

resolution /ˌrezəˈluːʃn/ n **1** (determination) résolution f; **2** (decree) résolution f (**against** contre; **that** selon laquelle); **to pass a ~** voter une résolution; **3** (promise) résolution f (**to do** de faire); **to make a ~ to do** prendre la résolution de faire; **4** (solving of problem) résolution f (**of** de); **5** COMPUT résolution f.

resolve /rɪˈzɒlv/ I n (determination) détermination f;

to strengthen/weaken sb's ~ rendre qn plus/ moins décidé; **2** (decision) résolution f.
II vtr **1** (solve) résoudre [dispute]; dissiper [doubts]; **2** (decide) **to ~ that** décider que; **to ~ to do** résoudre de faire.
III vi (decide) [person, government] résoudre; **to ~ on doing** résoudre de faire.
IV v refl **to ~ itself** se résoudre.

resonant /ˈrezənənt/ adj [voice] sonore.

resonate /ˈrezəneɪt/ vi résonner (**with** de).

resort /rɪˈzɔːt/ I n **1** (resource) recours m; **as a last ~** en dernier recours; **2** (holiday centre) lieu m de villégiature; **seaside ~** station f balnéaire; **ski ~** station f de ski.
II vi **to ~ to** recourir à.

resound /rɪˈzaʊnd/ vi **1** [noise] retentir (**through** partout dans); **2** [place] retentir (**with** de).

resounding /rɪˈzaʊndɪŋ/ adj [cheers] retentissant; [success] éclatant; **a ~ 'no'** un 'non' retentissant.

resource /rɪˈsɔːs, -ˈzɔːs, US ˈriːsɔːrs/ I n GEN, COMPUT, ECON, IND, ADMIN ressource f; **natural/ energy ~s** ressources naturelles/énergétiques; **the world's ~s of coal** les ressources mondiales en charbon.
II vtr accorder les ressources nécessaires à [institution]; **to be under-~d** ne pas disposer de ressources suffisantes.

resource centre GB, **resource center** US n centre m de documentation.

resourceful /rɪˈsɔːsfl, -ˈzɔːsfl, US ˈriːsɔːrsfl/ adj [person] plein de ressources, débrouillard○.

resource(s) room n salle f de documentation.

respect /rɪˈspekt/ I n **1** (admiration) respect m, estime f; **to win the ~ of sb** gagner l'estime de qn; **to command ~** imposer le respect; **2** (politeness) respect m; **out of ~** par respect (**for** pour); **you've got no ~!** tu ne respectes rien!; **with (all due) ~** sauf votre respect; **in ~ of** (as regards) pour ce qui est de; **with ~ to** par rapport à; **3** (regard) (for human rights, privacy) respect m (**for** de); **4** (aspect) égard m; **in this ~** à cet égard; **in many ~s** à bien des égards; **in what ~?** à quel égard?
II **respects** npl respects mpl; **to offer** ou **pay one's ~s to sb** présenter ses respects à qn; **to pay one's last ~s to sb** rendre un dernier hommage à qn.
III vtr (honour) respecter; **as ~s sth** quant à qch.

respectability /rɪˌspektəˈbɪlətɪ/ n respectabilité f.

respectable /rɪˈspektəbl/ adj **1** (reputable) [person] respectable; [upbringing] bon/bonne; **in ~ society** entre gens convenables; **2** (adequate) [crowd] respectable; [performance] honorable; **to finish a ~ fourth** terminer honorablement quatrième.

respectably /rɪˈspektəblɪ/ adv (reputably) convenablement, correctement; (creditably) honorablement.

respectful /rɪˈspektfl/ adj respectueux/-euse (**to, towards** envers).

respectfully /rɪˈspektfəlɪ/ adv respectueusement.

respecting /rɪˈspektɪŋ/ prep concernant.

respective /rɪˈspektɪv/ adj respectif/-ive.

respiration /ˌrespɪˈreɪʃn/ n respiration f.

respirator /ˈrespɪreɪtə(r)/ n (apparatus) respirateur m; **to be on a ~** être sous respirateur.

respiratory /rɪˈspɪrətrɪ, US -tɔːrɪ/ adj respiratoire.

respite /ˈrespaɪt, ˈrespɪt/ n **1** SOUT (relief) répit m (**from** dans); **a brief ~** un court répit; **2** COMM, JUR (delay) sursis m.

resplendent /rɪˈsplendənt/ adj SOUT resplendissant; **to look ~** être resplendissant.

respond /rɪˈspɒnd/ vi **1** (answer) répondre (**to** à; **with** par); **2** (react) réagir (**to** à); [car] répondre; **to ~ to pressure** POL, ADMIN céder aux pressions; **3** (listen, adapt) s'adapter; **4** RELIG (by speaking) répondre.

respondent /rɪˈspɒndənt/ n **1** (to questionnaire) personne f interrogée; **2** JUR défendeur/-eresse m/f.

response /rɪˈspɒns/ n **1** (answer) réponse f (**to** à); **in ~ to** en réponse à; **2** (reaction) réaction f (**to** à; **from**

de); **to meet with a favourable ~** être bien reçu; **3** RELIG **the ~s** les répons *mpl*.

responsibility /rɪˌspɒnsəˈbɪlətɪ/ *n* responsabilité *f* (**for** de); **to take a ~ for sth** prendre la responsabilité de qch; **a sense of ~** le sens des responsabilités; **to take no ~** décliner toute responsabilité; **it's not my ~ to do** ce n'est pas à moi de faire; **it's your ~** c'est à vous de vous en occuper; **to claim ~ for an attack** revendiquer une attaque.

responsible /rɪˈspɒnsəbl/ *adj* **1** (to blame) **~ for killing ten people** responsable de la mort de dix personnes; **2** (in charge) **~ for producing the leaflets** chargé de produire les brochures; **3** (accountable) **to be ~ to sb** être responsable devant qn; **I won't be ~ for my actions** je ne réponds plus de moi; **4** (trustworthy) responsable; **5** [*job*] à responsabilités.

responsive /rɪˈspɒnsɪv/ *adj* **1** (alert) [*audience, class, pupil*] réceptif/-ive; **2** AUT [*car*] nerveux/-euse.

respray I /ˈriːspreɪ/ *n* **the car had been given a ~** on avait repeint la voiture.
II /ˌriːˈspreɪ/ *vtr* repeindre [*vehicle*].

rest /rest/ **I** *n* **1** (what remains) **the ~** (of food, day, story) le reste (**of** de); **for the ~ of my life** pour le restant de mes jours; **for the ~**... pour ce qui est du reste...; **and all the ~ of it**○ et tout et tout○; **2** (other people) **he is no different from the ~** (of them) il n'est pas différent des autres; **why can't you behave like the ~ of us?** pourquoi ne peux-tu pas faire comme nous?; **3** (repose, inactivity) repos *m*; **to have a ~** se reposer; **4** (break) pause *f*; **let's have a little ~** et si on faisait une petite pause?; **5** (lie-down) sieste *f*; **to have a ~** faire la sieste; **6** (support) support *m*; **7** MUS pause *f*; **8** (immobility) **to come to ~** s'arrêter.
II *vtr* **1** (lean) **to ~ sth on** appuyer qch sur [*surface*]; **2** (allow to rest) reposer [*legs*]; ne pas utiliser [*injured limb*]; laisser [qch] au repos [*horse*]; **3** AGRIC laisser [qch] en jachère [*land*]; **4** JUR **to ~ one's case** conclure; **I ~ my case** FIG il n'y a rien à ajouter.
III *vi* **1** se reposer; **I won't ~ until I know** je n'aurai de cesse de savoir; **to ~ easy** être tranquille; **2** (be supported) **to ~ on** reposer sur; **3** [*actor*] **to be ~ing** être sans engagement; **4** **to ~ in peace** reposer en paix; **God ~ his soul** Dieu ait son âme; **5** FIG **to let the matter ~** en rester là; **you can't just let it ~ there!** tu ne peux pas laisser les choses en l'état!
IDIOMS **a change is as good as a ~** PROV le changement a les mêmes vertus que le repos; **and there the matter ~s** voilà la situation actuelle.
■ **rest on**: **~ on** [sb/sth] **1** [*eyes*] s'arrêter sur; **2** [*decision*] reposer sur [*assumption*].
■ **rest up** se reposer.
■ **rest with**: **~ with** [sb/sth] être entre les mains de.

restart /ˌriːˈstɑːt/ *vtr* **1** reprendre [*talks*]; **2** remettre [qch] en marche [*engine*].

restate /ˌriːˈsteɪt/ *vtr* réaffirmer.

restaurant /ˈrestrɒnt, US -ərənt/ *n* restaurant *m*.

restaurant car *n* GB wagon-restaurant *m*.

rest cure *n* LIT cure *f* de repos; HUM sinécure *f*.

restful /ˈrestfl/ *adj* [*holiday*] reposant; [*place*] paisible.

rest home *n* maison *f* de retraite.

resting place /ˈrestɪŋ/ *n* **his last ~** sa dernière demeure.

restitution /ˌrestɪˈtjuːʃn, US -ˈtuː-/ *n* GEN, JUR restitution *f*.

restive /ˈrestɪv/ *adj* [*crowd*] énervé; [*animal*] rétif/-ive.

restless /ˈrestlɪs/ *adj* [*person*] agité; **to get up some ~** [*audience*] commencer à donner des signes d'impatience; [*populace*] commencer à s'agiter; **to feel ~** (in job) avoir envie de changer.

restlessly /ˈrestlɪslɪ/ *adv* nerveusement.

restlessness /ˈrestlɪsnɪs/ *n* **1** (physical) agitation *f*; **2** (of character) instabilité *f*.

restock /ˌriːˈstɒk/ **I** *vtr* regarnir [*shelf*] (**with** en); réapprovisionner [*shop*] (**with** en); repeupler [*river*] (**with** de).
II *vi* se réapprovisionner.

restoration /ˌrestəˈreɪʃn/ *n* **1** (of territory) restitution *f* (**to** à); **2** (of monarchy, painting) restauration *f*; (of democracy) rétablissement *m*.

restore /rɪˈstɔː(r)/ *vtr* **1** (return) restituer, rendre [*property*] (**to** à); **2** (bring back) rétablir [*health*]; rendre [*faculty*]; redonner [*good humour*] (**to** à); rétablir [*peace, monarchy, rights*]; **to be ~d to health** être rétabli; **to ~ sb to power** ramener qn au pouvoir; **you ~ my faith in humanity** tu me redonnes confiance dans le genre humain; **3** (repair) restaurer; **4** COMPUT redimensionner [*window*].

restorer /rɪˈstɔːrə(r)/ *n* (person) restaurateur/-trice *m/f*.

restrain /rɪˈstreɪn/ **I** *vtr* **1** (hold back) retenir [*person*]; contenir [*crowd*]; maîtriser [*animal*]; **to ~ sb from doing sth** empêcher qn de faire qch; **2** (curb) limiter [*spending*]; maîtriser [*inflation*].
II *v refl* **to ~ oneself** se retenir.

restrained /rɪˈstreɪnd/ *adj* [*style*] sobre; [*manner*] calme; [*reaction*] modéré; [*person*] posé.

restraining order /rɪˈstreɪnɪŋ/ *n* injonction *f*.

restraint /rɪˈstreɪnt/ *n* **1** (moderation) modération *f*; **2** (restriction) restriction *f*; **wage ~** contrôle *m* des salaires; **3** (constraint) contrainte *f*.

restrict /rɪˈstrɪkt/ **I** *vtr* limiter [*activity, growth*] (**to** à); restreindre [*freedom*]; réserver [*access, membership*] (**to** à); **visibility was ~ed** la visibilité était limitée.
II *v refl* **to ~ oneself to sth** se limiter à qch.

restricted /rɪˈstrɪktɪd/ *adj* [*growth, movement*] limité; [*document*] confidentiel/-ielle; [*film*] US interdit aux moins de 17 ans; [*parking*] réglementé.

restriction /rɪˈstrɪkʃn/ *n* **1** (rule) règlement *m*; **~s** règlements *mpl* contrôlant [*advertising, activities*]; **~s on arms sales** limitations *fpl* de ventes d'armes; **credit ~s** encadrement *m* (*sg*) du crédit; **currency ~s** contrôle *m* (*sg*) des devises; **parking ~s** règles *fpl* de stationnement; **price ~s** contrôle *m* (*sg*) des prix; **speed ~s** limitations *fpl* de vitesse; **travel ~s** restrictions *fpl* à la libre circulation (des citoyens); **weight ~s** (for vehicles) limitations *fpl* de poids; **2** (limiting) (of amount) limitation *f* (**on** de); (of freedom) restrictions *fpl* (**of** à).

restrictive /rɪˈstrɪktɪv/ *adj* restrictif/-ive.

re-string /ˌriːˈstrɪŋ/ *vtr* (*prét, pp* **re-strung**) changer les cordes de [*instrument*]; recorder [*racket*]; renfiler [*necklace, beads*].

rest room *n* US toilettes *fpl*.

restyle I /ˈriːstaɪl/ *n* nouvelle coiffure *f*.
II /ˌriːˈstaɪl/ *vtr* changer la ligne de [*car*]; transformer [*shop*]; **to ~ sb's hair** faire une nouvelle coupe (de cheveux) à qn.

result /rɪˈzʌlt/ **I** *n* **1** (consequence) résultat *m* (**of** de), conséquence *f* (**of** de); **as a ~ of** à la or par suite de; **as a ~** en conséquence; **2** (outcome) résultat *m*; **exam(ination) ~s** résultats aux examens.
II results *npl* COMM, FIN résultats *mpl*.
III *vi* résulter; **to ~ in** avoir pour résultat.

resume /rɪˈzjuːm, US -ˈzuːm/ **I** *vtr* reprendre [*talks*]; regagner [*seat*]; renouer [*relations*].
II *vi* reprendre.

résumé /ˈrezjuːmeɪ, US ˌrezʊˈmeɪ/ *n* **1** (summary) résumé *m*; **2** US (cv) curriculum vitae *m inv*.

resumption /rɪˈzʌmpʃn/ *n* reprise *f* (**of** de).

resurface /ˌriːˈsɜːfɪs/ **I** *vtr* refaire (la surface de).
II *vi* [*submarine*] faire surface; [*rumour*] réapparaître; [*person*] refaire surface.

resurgence /rɪˈsɜːdʒəns/ *n* GEN résurgence *f*; (of interest) regain *m*; (of economy) reprise *f*.

resurrect /ˌrezəˈrekt/ *vtr* ressusciter.

resurrection /ˌrezəˈrekʃn/ *n* résurrection *f*; RELIG **the Resurrection** la Résurrection.

resuscitate /rɪˈsʌsɪteɪt/ *vtr* MED réanimer.

resuscitation /rɪˌsʌsɪˈteɪʃn/ *n* réanimation *f*.

retail /ˈriːteɪl/ **I** *n* vente *f* au détail.
II *noun modifier* [*business, sector*] de détail.
III *adv* au détail.
IV *vtr* vendre [qch] au détail.
V *vi* **to ~ at** se vendre au détail à.

retailer /'ri:teɪlə(r)/ *n* détaillant *m*.

retailing /'ri:teɪlɪŋ/ I *n* distribution *f*.
II *noun modifier* [*giant, sector*] de la distribution; [*group, operations*] de distribution.

retail: ~ **price** *n* prix *m* de détail; ~ **price index**, **RPI** *n* indice *m* des prix à la consommation; ~ **sales** *npl* ventes *fpl* au détail; ~ **trade** *n* (companies) détaillants *mpl*; (industry) commerce *m* de détail.

retain /rɪ'teɪn/ *vtr* garder [*control, identity*]; conserver [*heat, title*]; retenir [*water, fact*]; engager [*lawyer*].

retainer /rɪ'teɪnə(r)/ *n* **1** (fee) somme *f* versée à l'avance (*pour s'assurer des services de quelqu'un*); **2**‡ (servant) domestique *mf*.

retaining wall *n* mur *m* de soutènement.

retake I /'ri:teɪk/ *n* CIN nouvelle prise *f*.
II /ˌri:'teɪk/ *vtr* (*prét* **retook**; *pp* **retaken**) **1** CIN faire une nouvelle prise de [*scene*]; **2** SCH, UNIV repasser [*exam*]; **3** MIL reprendre [*town*].

retaliate /rɪ'tælɪeɪt/ *vi* réagir.

retaliation /rɪˌtælɪ'eɪʃn/ *n* **in** ~ **for** en représailles de.

retarded /rɪ'tɑ:dɪd/ *adj* **1** PSYCH retardé; **2**◦ (stupid) débile◦.

retch /retʃ/ *vi* avoir des haut-le-cœur.

retd *abrév écrite* = **retired**.

retention /rɪ'tenʃn/ *n* MED rétention *f*.

retentive /rɪ'tentɪv/ *adj* [*memory*] fidèle, bon.

rethink I /'ri:θɪŋk/ *n* **to have a** ~ **y** repenser.
II /ˌri:'θɪŋk/ *vtr* (*prét, pp* **rethought**) repenser.

reticence /'retɪsns/ *n* réticence *f* (**on, about** à propos de).

reticent /'retɪsnt/ *adj* réticent; **to be** ~ **about sth** être discret sur qch.

retina /'retɪnə, US 'retənə/ *n* rétine *f*.

retinue /'retɪnju:, US 'retənu:/ *n* escorte *f*.

retire /rɪ'taɪə(r)/ I *vi* **1** (from work) prendre sa retraite; **2** (withdraw) se retirer (**from** de); **3**† **to** ~ (**to bed**) aller se coucher; **4** SPORT abandonner; **to** ~ **from sth** se retirer de qch.
II **retired** *pp adj* retraité.
III **retiring** *pres p adj* (leaving job) qui prend sa retraite; (shy) réservé.

retirement /rɪ'taɪəmənt/ *n* retraite *f*; **to take early** ~ partir en retraite anticipée; **to come out of** ~ reprendre ses activités (après avoir pris sa retraite).

retirement: ~ **age** *n* âge *m* de la retraite; ~ **bonus** *n* prime *f* de départ à la retraite.

retirement home *n* **1** (individual) maison *f* pour la retraite; **2** (communal) maison *f* de retraite.

retirement pension *n* (pension *f* de) retraite *f*.

retort /rɪ'tɔ:t/ I *n* (reply) riposte *f*.
II *vtr* rétorquer (**that** que).

retrace /ri:'treɪs/ *vtr* **to** ~ **one's steps** revenir sur ses pas.

retract /rɪ'trækt/ I *vtr* rétracter [*statement, claws*]; escamoter [*landing gear*].
II *vi* [*landing gear*] s'escamoter.

retractable /rɪ'træktəbl/ *adj* [*landing gear*] escamotable; [*pen*] à pointe rétractable.

retrain /ˌri:'treɪn/ I *vtr* recycler.
II *vi* se recycler.

retraining /ˌri:'treɪnɪŋ/ *n* recyclage *m*.

retread /'ri:tred/ *n* pneu *m* rechapé.

retreat /rɪ'tri:t/ I *n* **1** (withdrawal) retraite *f*; **to beat a hasty** ~ battre en retraite précipitamment; **to sound the** ~ MIL sonner la retraite; **2** (house) retraite *f*; **3** RELIG retraite *f*; **to go on a** ~ faire une retraite.
II *vi* **1** GEN [*person*] se retirer (**into** dans; **from** de); **2** MIL [*army*] se replier (**to** sur); **3** FIG **to** ~ **into a dream world** se réfugier dans un monde imaginaire; **4** [*flood water*] reculer.

retrench /rɪ'trentʃ/ *vi* SOUT se restreindre dans ses dépenses.

retrenchment /rɪ'trentʃmənt/ *n* SOUT (economizing) restriction *f* (des dépenses).

retrial /ˌri:'traɪəl/ *n* JUR nouveau procès *m*.

retribution /ˌretrɪ'bju:ʃn/ *n* SOUT châtiment *m*.

retrievable /rɪ'tri:vəbl/ *adj* **1** GEN recouvrable; **2** COMPUT accessible.

retrieval /rɪ'tri:vl/ *n* COMPUT extraction *f*.

retrieve /rɪ'tri:v/ *vtr* récupérer [*object*]; redresser [*situation*]; rapporter [*pheasant*]; extraire [*data*].

retro /'retrəʊ/ *n, adj* rétro (*m*).

retrograde /'retrəgreɪd/ *adj* rétrograde.

retrospect /'retrəʊspekt/: **in retrospect** *adv phr* rétrospectivement.

retrospective /ˌretrə'spektɪv/ I *n* (also ~ **exhibition** ou ~ **show**) ART, CIN rétrospective *f*.
II *adj* **1** GEN rétrospectif/-ive; **2** JUR, ADMIN rétroactif/-ive.

retrospectively /ˌretrə'spektɪvlɪ/ *adv* **1** JUR, ADMIN rétroactivement; **2** GEN rétrospectivement.

retrovirus /'retrəʊvaɪərəs/ *n* rétrovirus *m*.

retry /ˌri:'traɪ/ *vtr* **1** JUR juger à nouveau [*case*]; **2** COMPUT essayer de relancer [*operation*].

retune /ˌri:'tju:n, US -'tu:n/ *vtr* MUS accorder; RADIO, TELECOM, AUT régler.

return /rɪ'tɜ:n/ I *n* **1** LIT, FIG (getting back, going back) retour *m* (**to** à; **from** de); **on your** ~ **to work** dès que vous aurez repris votre travail; **2** (recurrence) retour *m* (**of** de); **3** (restitution, bringing back) (of law, practice) retour *m* (**of** de); (of object) restitution *f* (**of** de); **4** (sending back) renvoi *m* (**of** de); **5** FIN (yield on investment) rendement *m* (**on** de); (on capital) rémunération *f*; **the law of diminishing** ~**s** la loi des rendements décroissants; **6** (travel ticket) aller-retour *m inv*; **7** THEAT billet *m* rendu à la dernière minute; **8** (unsold book) invendu *m*.
II **returns** *npl* POL résultats *mpl*.
III **in return** *adv phr* en échange (**for** de).
IV *vtr* **1** (give back) rendre; (pay back) rembourser; **2** (bring back, take back) rapporter (**to** à); **3** (put back) remettre; **4** (send back) renvoyer; '~ **to sender**' 'retour à l'expéditeur'; **5** (give, issue in return) rendre [*greeting*]; **to** ~ **the favour** en faire autant; **6** (reciprocate) répondre à [*love*]; **7** MIL riposter à [*fire*]; **8** SPORT renvoyer [*ball*]; **9** (rejoin) répliquer; **10** JUR prononcer [*verdict*]; **11** FIN rapporter [*profit*]; **12** POL élire [*candidate*]; **13** TELECOM **to** ~ **sb's call** rappeler qn.
V *vi* **1** (come back) revenir (**from** de); **2** (go back) retourner (**to** à); **3** (get back from abroad) rentrer (**from** de); **4** (get back home) rentrer chez soi; **5** (resume) **to** ~ **to** reprendre [*activity*]; **to** ~ **to power** revenir au pouvoir; **6** (recur) [*symptom, doubt*] réapparaître; [*days, times*] revenir.
IDIOMS **by** ~ **of post** par retour du courrier; **many happy** ~**s!** bon anniversaire!

returner /rɪ'tɜ:nə(r)/ *n* femme *f* qui reprend le travail.

return: ~ **fare** *n* prix *m* d'un billet aller-retour; ~**ing officer** *n* GB président/-e *m/f* d'un bureau d'élections; ~ **ticket** *n* billet *m* aller-retour; ~ **trip** *n* retour *m*; ~ **visit** *n* retour *m*.

reunification /ˌri:ju:nɪfɪ'keɪʃn/ *n* réunification *f*.

reunion /ˌri:'ju:nɪən/ *n* réunion *f*.

reunite /ˌri:ju:'naɪt/ *vtr* (*gén au passif*) réunir [*family*]; réunifier [*party*]; **he was** ~**d with his family** il a retrouvé sa famille.

reusable /ˌri:'ju:zəbl/ *adj* réutilisable.

reuse /ˌri:'ju:z/ *vtr* réutiliser.

rev◦ /rev/ I *n* AUT (*abrév* = **revolution** (per minute)) tour *m* (par minute).
II *vtr* (*p prés etc* -**vv**-) (also ~ **up**) monter le régime de [*engine*].

Rev(d) *n*: *abrév écrite* = **Reverend**.

revaluation /ˌri:vælju:'eɪʃn/ *n* réévaluation *f*.

revalue /ˌri:'vælju:/ *vtr* COMM, FIN réévaluer.

revamp /ˌri:'væmp/ *vtr* rajeunir [*image*]; réorganiser [*company*]; retaper◦ [*building, clothing*].

rev counter° n GB compte-tours m inv.

reveal /rɪ'viːl/ I vtr **1** (make public) dévoiler [truth]; révéler [secret]; **to ~ that** révéler que; **to ~ sth to sb** révéler qch à qn; **to ~ all** (divulge) tout dire; **2** (make visible) découvrir [view, picture]; **~ed religion** religion f révélée.
II v refl **to ~ oneself** [person] se montrer; [God] se révéler.

revealing /rɪ'viːlɪŋ/ adj **1** [remark] révélateur/-trice; **2** [blouse] décolleté.

revel /'revl/ I npl **~s** festivités fpl.
II vi (p prés etc **-ll-, -l-** US) **to ~ in sth** se délecter de qch.

revelation /ˌrevə'leɪʃn/ n révélation f.

revelatory /ˌrevə'leɪtri, US -tɔːri/ adj révélateur/-trice.

reveller, US **reveler** /'revələ(r)/ n fêtard/-e° m/f.

revelry /'revlri/ n (also **revelries**) réjouissances fpl.

revenge /rɪ'vendʒ/ I n **1** (punitive act) vengeance f; **to take** ou **get one's ~** se venger (**for** de; **on** sur); **2** (getting even) revanche f.
IDIOMS **~ is sweet** la vengeance est un plat qui se mange froid.

revenue /'revənjuː, US -ənuː/ I n revenus mpl.
II **revenues** npl oil **~s** revenus mpl pétroliers.

reverberate /rɪ'vɜːbəreɪt/ vi [hills, sound] résonner (**with** de; **through** dans, par); [shock] se propager.

revere /rɪ'vɪə(r)/ vtr révérer.

reverence /'revərəns/ n profond respect m.

Reverend /'revərənd/ ▶ 937 | n **1** (Protestant) pasteur m; **2** (as title) **the ~ Jones** (Anglican) le révérend Jones; **~ Mother** Révérende Mère; **~ Father** Révérend Père.

reverent /'revərənt/ adj [hush] religieux/-ieuse; [expression] de respect.

reverently /'revərəntli/ adv avec vénération.

revers /rɪ'vɪə(r)/ npl (lapels) revers mpl.

reversal /rɪ'vɜːsl/ n GEN (of policy, roles) renversement m; (of order, trend) inversion f; (of fortune) revers m.

reverse /rɪ'vɜːs/ I n **1** (opposite) **the ~** le contraire; **2** (back) **the ~** (of coin) le revers; (of banknote) le verso; (of fabric) l'envers m; **3** (setback) revers m; **4** AUT (also **~ gear**) marche f arrière.
II adj **1** (opposite) [effect] contraire; **2** (other) **the ~ side** (of coin) le revers; (of fabric) l'envers m; **3** [somersault] en arrière; **to answer the questions in ~ order** répondre aux questions en commençant par la dernière; **4** AUT **~ gear** marche f arrière.
III **in reverse** adv phr [do, function] en sens inverse.
IV vtr inverser [trend, process]; renverser [roles]; faire rouler [qch] en marche arrière [car]; **to ~ a car out of a garage** sortir une voiture d'un garage en marche arrière; **to ~ the charges** appeler en PCV.
V vi [driver] faire marche arrière; **to ~ down the lane/into a parking space** descendre l'allée/se garer en marche arrière.

reverse charge call n appel m en PCV.

reversible /rɪ'vɜːsəbl/ adj (all contexts) réversible.

reversing light /rɪ'vɜːsɪŋ/ n feu m de recul.

reversion /rɪ'vɜːʃn, US -ʒn/ n retour m (**to** à).

revert /rɪ'vɜːt/ vi **to ~ to** reprendre [habit, name]; redevenir [wilderness]; **to ~ to normal** redevenir normal; **to ~ to type** LIT retourner au type primitif; **he ~ed to type** FIG le naturel a repris le dessus.

review /rɪ'vjuː/ I n **1** GEN, ADMIN, JUR, POL (reconsideration) révision f (**of** de); (report) rapport m (**of** sur); **under ~** [policy] en train d'être réexaminé; [salaries] en train d'être révisé; **to come under ~** être réexaminé; **to be subject to ~** pouvoir être reconsidéré; **2** (critical assessment) critique f (**of** de); **rave ~**° revue f excellente; **to write a ~** faire une critique; **3** JOURN (magazine) revue f; **4** MIL revue f; **5** US SCH, UNIV (of lesson) révision f.
II vtr **1** (re-examine) reconsidérer [situation]; réviser [attitude, policy]; passer [qch] en revue [troops]; **2** LITERAT faire la critique de [book, film etc]; **to be well/badly ~ed** se faire bien/mal accueillir par la critique; **3** US SCH, UNIV réviser [subject, lesson].

review: **~ board** n ADMIN comité m de révision; **~ copy** n exemplaire m de service de presse.

reviewer /rɪ'vjuːə(r)/ n critique m.

revise /rɪ'vaɪz/ I n (in printing) seconde f (épreuve f).
II vtr **1** (alter) réviser [estimate, figures]; changer [attitude]; **to ~ one's position** revenir sur sa position; **to ~ one's opinion of sb/sth** réviser son jugement sur qn/qch; **~d upwards/downwards** [figures, profits etc] révisé à la hausse/à la baisse; **2** GB (for exam) réviser [subject]; **3** (correct) réviser [text].
III vi GB réviser.

revision /rɪ'vɪʒn/ n révision f.

revisit /ˌriː'vɪzɪt/ vtr revisiter [museum etc]; retourner voir [person, childhood home]; FIG revoir.

revitalization /ˌriːvaɪtəlaɪ'zeɪʃn, US -lɪ'z-/ n **1** (of economy) relance f; **2** (of depressed area) renaissance f.

revitalize /riː'vaɪtəlaɪz/ vtr **1** relancer [economy]; faire démarrer [company]; **2** revitaliser [complexion].

revival /rɪ'vaɪvl/ n (of economy) reprise f; (of interest) regain m; (of custom, language) renouveau m; (of law) remise f en vigueur; THEAT reprise f.

revivalist /rɪ'vaɪvəlɪst/ adj **1** RELIG revivaliste; **2** ARCHIT, MUS etc **Greek/Gothic ~** néo-grec/-gothique.

revive /rɪ'vaɪv/ I vtr **1** GEN remonter; (from coma, faint etc) faire reprendre connaissance à [person]; **2** FIG raviver [custom]; ranimer [interest, hopes]; remettre en vigueur [law]; relancer [debate, career, movement]; remettre [qch] à la mode [style, fashion]; revigorer [economy]; **to ~ sb's (flagging) spirits** remonter le moral à qn; **3** THEAT reprendre [play].
II vi [person] (from coma, faint) reprendre connaissance; [interest] renaître; [economy] reprendre.

revocation /ˌrevə'keɪʃn/ n (of will, edict) révocation f; (of decision, order) annulation f.

revoke /rɪ'vəʊk/ vtr révoquer [will, edict]; annuler [decision, order].

revolt /rɪ'vəʊlt/ I n (physical) révolte f (**against** contre); (verbal) rébellion f (**over** contre); **to be in ~** être en révolte ou en rébellion; **to rise in ~** se soulever.
II vtr dégoûter, révolter.
III vi (physically) se révolter (**against** contre); (verbally) se rebeller (**against, over** contre).

revolting /rɪ'vəʊltɪŋ/ adj **1** (physically) répugnant; (morally) révoltant; **2**° [food] infect; [person] affreux/-euse.

revolution /ˌrevə'luːʃn/ n **1** POL, FIG révolution f (**in** dans); **2** AUT, TECH tour m; **3** (of planet) révolution f.

revolutionary /ˌrevə'luːʃənəri, US -neri/ n, adj révolutionnaire (mf).

revolutionize /ˌrevə'luːʃənaɪz/ vtr révolutionner.

revolve /rɪ'vɒlv/ vi **1** LIT tourner; **2** FIG **to ~ around** (be focused on) être axé sur.

revolving /rɪ'vɒlvɪŋ/ adj [chair] pivotant; [stage] tournant; **~ door** porte f à tambour.

revue /rɪ'vjuː/ n THEAT revue f.

revulsion /rɪ'vʌlʃn/ n dégoût m (**against** pour); **to feel ~ at sth** être dégoûté par qch.

reward /rɪ'wɔːd/ I n (recompense) récompense f; **a £50 ~** 50 livres sterling de récompense.
II vtr récompenser (**for** de, pour).
IDIOMS virtue is its own **~** PROV la vertu est sa propre récompense.

rewarding /rɪ'wɔːdɪŋ/ adj [experience] enrichissant; [job] gratifiant; **financially ~** rémunérateur/-trice.

rewind /ˌriː'waɪnd/ vtr (prét, pp **rewound**) rembobiner [tape, film].

rewind button n bouton m de retour en arrière.

rewire /ˌriː'waɪə(r)/ vtr refaire l'installation électrique de.

reword /ˌriː'wɜːd/ vtr reformuler.

rework /ˌriː'wɜːk/ vtr retravailler [theme, metal].

reworking /ˌriː'wɜːkɪŋ/ n nouvelle version f.

rewrite /ˌriː'raɪt/ vtr (prét **rewrote**; pp **rewritten**) ré(é)crire [story, history].

RFC n SPORT (abrév = **rugby football club**) club m de rugby.

rhapsodize /'ræpsədaɪz/ *vi* **to ~ about** ou **over sth** s'extasier sur qch.

rhapsody /'ræpsədɪ/ *n* MUS rhapsodie *f.*

rhd *n: abrév* ▶ **right-hand drive**.

rhesus /'ri:səs/ *n* rhésus *m.*

rhesus: **~ baby** *n* enfant *m* rhésus; **~ factor** *n* facteur *m* rhésus; **~ negative** *adj* rhésus négatif *inv*; **~ positive** *adj* rhésus positif *inv.*

rhetoric /'retərɪk/ *n* LITERAT rhétorique *f*; **the ~ of terrorism** le discours terroriste; **empty ~** mots *mpl* creux.

rhetorical /rɪ'tɒrɪkl, US -'tɔːr-/ *adj* rhétorique.

rhetorically /rɪ'tɒrɪklɪ, US -'tɔːr-/ *adv* [*ask*] sans s'attendre à une réponse; **~ (speaking)** d'un point de vue tout à fait théorique.

rheumatic /ruː'mætɪk/ *adj* [*joint*] rhumatisant; [*pain*] rhumatismal.

rheumatic fever ▶ **1002** *n* rhumatisme *m* articulaire aigu.

rheumatism /'ruːmətɪzəm/ ▶ **1002** *n* rhumatisme *m.*

rheumatoid arthritis ▶ **1002** *n* polyarthrite *f* rhumatoïde.

rheumatologist /ˌruːmə'tɒlədʒɪst/ ▶ **1251** *n* rhumatologue *mf.*

rheumatology /ˌruːmə'tɒlədʒɪ/ *n* rhumatologie *f.*

rheumy /'ruːmɪ/ *adj* LITTÉR [*eyes*] chassieux/-ieuse.

Rhine /raɪn/ ▶ **1214** *pr n* Rhin *m.*

rhinestone /'raɪnstəʊn/ **I** *n* diamant *m* fantaisie.

II *adj* en strass.

rhino /'raɪnəʊ/ *n* (*pl* **~s** ou **~**) rhinocéros *m.*

rhinoceros /raɪ'nɒsərəs/ *n* (*pl* **-eroses**, **-eri** ou **~**) rhinocéros *m.*

rhombus /'rɒmbəs/ *n* (*pl* **-buses** ou **-bi**) losange *m.*

Rhone /rəʊn/ ▶ **1214** *pr n* Rhône *m.*

rhubarb /'ruːbɑːb/ **I** *n* **1** CULIN rhubarbe *f*; **2** GB '**~, ~**' *simulation du bruit d'une foule.*

II *noun modifier* [*pie*] à la rhubarbe; [*jam*] de rhubarbe; [*leaf*] de rhubarbe.

rhyme /raɪm/ **I** *n* **1** (poem) vers *mpl*; (children's) comptine *f*; **2** (fact of rhyming) rime *f*; **to find a ~ for sth** trouver un mot qui rime avec qch.

II *vi* rimer (**with** avec).

IDIOMS **without ~ or reason** sans rime ni raison.

rhyming: **~ couplet** *n* distique *m* rimé; **~ slang** *n*: *argot consistant à remplacer un mot par une locution qui rime avec ce mot.*

rhythm /'rɪðəm/ *n* GEN MUS, LITERAT rythme *m.*

rhythm and blues *n* rhythm and blues *m.*

rhythmic(al) /'rɪðmɪk(l)/ *adj* [*beat*] rythmé; [*movement*] rythmique; [*breathing*] régulier/-ière.

rhythm section *n* MUS section *f* rythmique.

RI *n* **1** SCH (*abrév* = **religious instruction**) ~ catéchisme *m*; **2** US POST *abrév écrite* = **Rhode Island**.

rib /rɪb/ **I** *n* **1** ANAT, CULIN côte *f*; **2** (in umbrella) baleine *f*; (in plane, building) nervure *f*; **3** (stitch) côte *f.*

II *vtr*° (*p prés etc* **-bb-**) (tease) taquiner.

ribald /'rɪbld/ *adj* paillard.

ribbed /rɪbd/ *adj* [*garment*] à côtes; [*ceiling, vault*] à nervures; [*seashell*] strié.

ribbing /'rɪbɪŋ/ *n* **1** (in knitting) côtes *fpl*; **2** (teasing) **to give sb a ~** taquiner qn.

ribbon /'rɪbən/ *n* **1** ruban *m*; **2** FIG **a ~ of smoke** un filet de fumée; **in ~s** en lambeaux *mpl.*

ribbon development *n: concentration d'habitations le long d'un axe routier.*

rib: **~ cage** *n* cage *f* thoracique; **~ roast** *n* côte *f* de bœuf; **~ tickler**° *n* histoire *f* drôle or tordante°.

rice /raɪs/ *n* riz *m.*

rice: **~field** *n* rizière *f*; **~ paper** *n* CULIN galette *f* de pain azyme; ART papier *m* de riz; **~ pudding** *n* riz *m* au lait.

rich /rɪtʃ/ **I** *n* (+ *v pl*) **the ~** les riches *mpl.*

II riches *npl* richesses *fpl.*

III *adj* [*person, soil, furnishings*] riche; **to grow** ou

get ~ s'enrichir; **to make sb ~** enrichir qn; **~ in** riche en [*vitamins*].

IV -rich *combining form* oil-/protein-**~** riche en pétrole/protéines.

IDIOMS **that's a bit ~**°! GB ça, c'est un peu fort°! IRON; **to strike it ~** faire fortune.

richly /'rɪtʃlɪ/ *adv* [*ornamented, coloured*] richement; **~ deserved** amplement mérité.

richness /'rɪtʃnɪs/ *n* richesse *f.*

Richter scale /'rɪktə/ *n* échelle *f* de Richter; **on the ~** sur l'échelle de Richter.

rick /rɪk/ **I** *n* (of hay) meule *f.*

II *vtr* **to ~ one's ankle** GB se faire une entorse à la cheville.

rickets /'rɪkɪts/ ▶ **1002** *n* (+ *v sg*) rachitisme *m.*

rickety /'rɪkətɪ/ *adj* **1** (shaky) [*chair, coalition*] branlant; [*house*] délabré; **2** MED rachitique.

rickshaw /'rɪkʃɔː/ *n* pousse-pousse *m inv.*

rid /rɪd/ **I** *vtr* (*p prés* **-dd-**; *prét, pp* **rid**) **to ~ the house of mice** débarrasser la maison des souris; **to ~ the world of famine** venir à bout de la famine.

II *pp adj* **to get ~ of** se débarrasser de [*old car, guests*]; faire cesser [*poverty*]; se défaire de [*prejudice*].

riddance /'rɪdns/ *n*: IDIOMS **good ~ (to bad rubbish)**! bon débarras°!

ridden /'rɪdn/ **I** *pp* ▶ **ride**.

II -ridden *combining form* guilt-**~** rongé par un sentiment de culpabilité; flea-**~** infesté de puces; cliché-**~** bourré d'idées reçues.

riddle /'rɪdl/ **I** *n* **1** (puzzle) devinette *f*; **2** (mystery) énigme *f*; **he's a ~** c'est une énigme.

II *vtr* **1** (perforate) **to ~ sth with** cribler qch de [*bullets*]; **2** (undermine) **to be ~d with** être rongé par [*disease, guilt*]; fourmiller de [*errors, ambiguities*]; **it's ~d with corruption** la corruption règne.

ride /raɪd/ **I** *n* **1** (from A to B) trajet *m* (**in, on** en, à); (for pleasure) tour *m*, promenade *f*, balade° *f*; **it's a five-minute ~ by taxi** c'est à cinq minutes en taxi; **to go for a ~** aller faire un tour; **to give sb a ~** US emmener qn (en voiture); **2** (in horse race) course *f*; (for pleasure) promenade *f* à cheval; **3** FIG (path) parcours *m*; **an easy ~** un parcours facile; **4** AUT **smooth ~** confort *m*; **5** (bridlepath) allée *f* cavalière.

II *vtr* (*prét* **rode**; *pp* **ridden**) **1** (as rider) monter [*animal*]; rouler à [*bike*]; **can you ~ a bike?** sais-tu faire du vélo?; **to ~ a good race** [*jockey*] courir une belle course; **do you want to ~ my bike/horse?** est-ce que tu veux prendre mon vélo/monter mon cheval?; **to ~ one's bike up/down the road** monter/descendre la rue à vélo; **2** US (travel on) prendre [*subway*]; parcourir [*range*]; **3** (float on) chevaucher [*wave*].

III *vi* (*prét* **rode**; *pp* **ridden**) **1** (sitting) **to ~ astride** être à califourchon; **to ~ behind** être en croupe; (journeying) **she rode to London on her bike** elle est allée à Londres à vélo; **to ~ across** traverser; **to ~ along sth** longer qch; (being carried) **to ~ in** ou **on** prendre [*bus*]; **riding on a wave of popularity** FIG porté par une vague de popularité; **2** (horse-riding) faire du cheval; (as jockey) courir; **he ~s well** [*person*] c'est un bon cavalier; FIG (of tricky situation) **there's a lot riding on this project** beaucoup de choses sont en jeu dans ce projet.

IDIOMS **to be in for a rough** or **bumpy ~** avoir à affronter des temps difficiles; **to be riding for a fall** courir à sa perte; **to be riding high** (person) baigner dans l'euphorie; **to give sb a rough ~** donner du fil à retordre à qn; **to go along for the ~** y aller pour le plaisir; **to let sth** ou **things ~** laisser courir; **to take sb for a ~**° (swindle) rouler qn°.

■ **ride about, ride around** se déplacer.

■ **ride off** partir; **to ~ off to** se diriger vers.

■ **ride out**: ¶ **~ out** aller (**to** jusqu'à); ¶ **~ [sth] out, ~ out [sth]** surmonter [*crisis*]; survivre à [*recession*]; **to ~ out the storm** FIG surmonter la crise.

■ **ride up 1** (approach) [*rider*] s'approcher (**to** de); **2** (rise) [*skirt*] remonter.

rider /'raɪdə(r)/ *n* **1** (person) (on horse) cavalier/-ière *m/f*; (on motorbike) motocycliste *mf*; (on bike) cycliste *mf*;

(in bike race) coureur/-euse *m*/*f*; (in horse race) jockey *m*; **2** (as proviso) correctif *m*; (to document) annexe *f*.

ridge /rɪdʒ/ I *n* **1** GEOG (along mountain top) arête *f*, crête *f*; (on hillside) corniche *f*; **2** (raised strip) (on rock, metal surface) strie *f*; (in ploughed land) crête *f*, billon *m*; **3** (on roof) faîte *m*, faîtage *m*; **4** METEOROL ~ **of high pressure** ligne *f* de hautes pressions.

ridge tent *n* (tente *f*) canadienne *f*.

ridicule /'rɪdɪkjuːl/ I *n* ridicule *m*; **to hold sb up to** ~ tourner qn en ridicule.

II *vtr* tourner [qch] en ridicule.

ridiculous /rɪ'dɪkjʊləs/ *adj* ridicule.

ridiculously /rɪ'dɪkjʊləslɪ/ *adv* ridiculement.

riding /'raɪdɪŋ/ ▶ 949 I *n* équitation *f*; **to go** ~ faire de l'équitation.

II *noun modifier* [*clothes, boots, lesson*] d'équitation.

riding: ~ **breeches** *npl* culotte *f* d'équitation; ~ **crop** *n* cravache *f*; ~ **habit** *n* tenue *f* d'amazone; ~ **school** *n* centre *m* équestre; ~ **stables** *n* manège *m*.

rife /raɪf/ *adj* (*après v*) **to be** ~ [*crime*] régner; **speculation was** ~ les conjectures allaient bon train.

riff /rɪf/ *n* riff *m*; **guitar** ~ un riff à la guitare.

riffle /'rɪfl/ *vtr* (also ~ **through**) feuilleter [*pages*].

riffraff /'rɪfræf/ *n* PÉJ populace *f* PEJ.

rifle /'raɪfl/ I *n* MIL fusil *m*; (at fairground) carabine *f*.

II *vtr* vider [*wallet, safe*].

■ **rifle through**: ~ **through** [sth] fouiller dans.

rifle range *n* MIL champ *m* de tir; (at fairground) stand *m* de tir.

rift /rɪft/ *n* **1** (disagreement) désaccord *m*; (permanent) rupture *f*; **2** (split) (in rock) fissure *f*; (in clouds) trouée *f*.

rift valley *n* rift *m*.

rig /rɪg/ I *n* (for drilling oil) (on land) tour *f* de forage; (off-shore) plate-forme *f* pétrolière; (piece of equipment) appareil *m*; **lighting** ~ système *m* d'éclairage.

II *vtr* (*p prés etc* -**gg**-) (control fraudulently) truquer [*election, result*].

■ **rig out** (dress) **he was** ~**ged out in his best clothes** il portait ses plus beaux habits.

■ **rig up**: ~ **up** [sth] installer [*equipment*]; improviser [*clothesline, shelter*].

rigging /'rɪgɪŋ/ *n* **1** NAUT gréement *m*; **2** (fraudulent control) (of election, competition, result) truquage *m*.

right /raɪt/ ▶ 870 I I *n* **1** (side, direction) droite *f*; **keep to the** ~ AUT tenez votre droite; **on** ou **to your** ~ à votre droite; **take the second** ~ prenez la deuxième à droite; **2** POL (also **Right**) **the** ~ la droite; **3** (morally) bien *m*; **to be in the** ~ avoir raison; **4** (just claim) droit *m*; **to have a** ~ **to sth** avoir droit à qch; **the** ~ **to work/to strike** le droit au travail/de grève; **she has no** ~ **to do it** elle n'a pas le droit de le faire; **what** ~ **have you to criticize me?** de quel droit est-ce que vous me critiquez?; **I've got every** ~ **to be annoyed** j'ai toutes les raisons d'être agacé; **human** ~**s** droits de l'homme; **civil** ~**s** droits civils; **to be within one's** ~**s** être dans son droit; **her husband is a celebrity in his own** ~ son mari est une célébrité à part entière; **the gardens are worth a visit in their own** ~ à eux seuls, les jardins méritent la visite; **5** (in boxing) droite *f*.

II **rights** *npl* **1** COMM, JUR droits *mpl*; **film** ~**s** droits d'adaptation cinématographique; **sole** ~**s** l'exclusivité *f* des droits; **2** (moral) **the** ~**s and wrongs of a matter** les aspects *mpl* moraux d'une question.

III *adj* **1** (as opposed to left) droit, de droite; **on my** ~ **hand** (position) sur ma droite; **2** (morally correct) bien; (fair) juste; **it's not** ~ **to steal** ce n'est pas bien de voler; **it's only** ~ c'est normal; **I thought it** ~ **to tell him** j'ai jugé bon de le lui dire; **it is only** ~ **and proper** ce n'est que justice; **to do the** ~ **thing** faire ce qu'il faut; **I hope we're doing the** ~ **thing** j'espère que nous ne faisons pas une erreur; **to do the** ~ **thing by sb** faire son devoir envers qn; **3** (correct, true) [*choice, direction, size*] bon/bonne; [*word*] juste; (accurate) [*time*] exact; **to be** ~ [*person*] avoir raison; [*answer*] être juste; **you're quite** ~! tu as tout à fait raison!; **that's the** ~ **answer** c'est la bonne réponse;

that's ~ c'est ça; **that can't be** ~ ça ne peut pas être ça; **what's the** ~ **time?** quelle est l'heure exacte?; **it's not the** ~ **time** ce n'est pas le bon moment; **is that** ~? (asking) est-ce que c'est vrai?; (double-checking) c'est ça?; **am I** ~ **in thinking that...?** ai-je raison de penser que...?; **is this the** ~ **train for Dublin?** c'est bien le train pour Dublin?; **is this the** ~ **way to the station?** est-ce que c'est la bonne direction pour aller à la gare?; **the** ~ **side of a piece of material** l'endroit *m* d'un tissu; **to get one's facts** ~ être sûr de ce qu'on avance; **you've got the spelling** ~ l'orthographe est bonne; **let's hope he gets it** ~ **this time** espérons qu'il y arrivera cette fois-ci; **it wouldn't look** ~ **if we didn't attend** ça serait mal vu si on n'y assistait pas; **how** ~ **you are!** comme vous avez raison!; **time proved him** ~ le temps lui a donné raison; **4** (most suitable) qui convient; **the** ~ **clothes for gardening** des vêtements qui conviennent au jardinage; **the model that's** ~ **for you** le modèle qui vous convient; **the** ~ **person for the job** la personne qu'il faut pour le poste; **you need to have the** ~ **equipment** il te faut le matériel approprié; **when the time is** ~ quand le moment sera venu; **to be in the** ~ **place at the** ~ **time** être là où il faut au bon moment; **to know the** ~ **people** connaître des gens bien placés; **he was careful to say all the** ~ **things** il a pris grand soin de dire tout ce qu'il faut dire dans ce genre de situation; **5** (in good order) [*machine, vehicle*] en bon état, qui fonctionne bien; (healthy) [*person*] bien portant; **I don't feel quite** ~ **these days** je ne me sens pas très bien ces jours-ci; **the engine isn't quite** ~ le moteur ne fonctionne pas très bien; **there's something not quite** ~ **about him** il a quelque chose de bizarre; **I sensed that things were not quite** ~ j'ai senti qu'il y avait quelque chose qui n'allait pas; **6** (in order) **to put** ou **set** ~ corriger [*mistake*]; réparer [*injustice*]; arranger [*situation*]; réparer [*machine*]; **to put** ou **set one's watch** ~ remettre sa montre à l'heure; **they gave him a month to put** ou **set things** ~ ils lui ont donné un mois pour tout arranger; **to put** ou **set sb** ~ détromper qn; **7** MATH [*angle*] droit; **at** ~ **angles to** à angle droit avec, perpendiculaire à; **8** GB (emphatic) **he's a** ~ **idiot!** c'est un idiot fini!; **it's a** ~ **mess** c'est un vrai gâchis; **9** GB (ready) prêt.

IV *adv* **1** (of direction) à droite; **to turn/look** ~ tourner/regarder à droite; **they looked for him** ~, **left and centre** ils l'ont cherché partout; **they are arresting people** ~, **left and centre** ils arrêtent les gens en masse; **2** (directly) droit, directement; **it's** ~ **in front of you** c'est droit or juste devant toi; **I'll be** ~ **back** je reviens tout de suite; **the path goes** ~ **down to the river** le chemin conduit tout droit à la rivière; ~ **before/after** juste avant/après; **to walk** ~ **up to sb** marcher droit vers qn; **3** (exactly) ~ **in the middle of the room** en plein milieu or au beau milieu de la pièce; ~ **now** (immediately) tout de suite; US (at this point in time) en ce moment; **I'm staying** ~ **here** je ne bougerai pas d'ici; ~ **there** juste là; ~ **on the river** juste au bord de la rivière; **4** (correctly) juste, comme il faut; **you're not doing it** ~ tu ne fais pas ça comme il faut; **to guess** ~ deviner juste; **if I remember** ~ si je me souviens bien; **5** (completely) tout; ~ **around the garden** tout autour du jardin; **go** ~ **back to the beginning** revenez tout au début; ~ **at the bottom** tout au fond; ~ **at the top of the house** tout en haut de la maison; **to read a book** ~ **through** lire un livre jusqu'au bout; **she looked** ~ **through me** FIG elle a fait semblant de ne pas me voir; **to turn the central heating** ~ **up** mettre le chauffage central à fond; ~ **up until the 1950s** jusque dans les années 50; **we're** ~ **behind you!** nous vous soutenons totalement!; **6** ▶ 937 GB (in titles) **the Right Honourable** le très honorable; **the Right Honourable Gentleman** (form of address in parliament) ≈ notre distingué collègue; **7** (very well) bon; ~, **let's have a look** bon, voyons ça.

V *vtr* **1** (restore to upright position) redresser; **2** (correct) réparer; **to** ~ **a wrong** redresser un tort.

VI *v refl* **to ~ oneself** [*person*] se redresser; **to ~ itself** [*ship, situation*] se rétablir.

IDIOMS **to see sb**○ ~ (financially) dépanner○ qn; (in other ways) sortir qn d'affaire; **~ you are**○!, **~-oh**○! GB d'accord!; **~ enough**○ effectivement; **by ~s** normalement, en principe; **to put sth to ~s** arranger qch.

right: **~ angle** *n* angle *m* droit; **~-angled triangle** *n* triangle *m* rectangle; **~ away** *adv* tout de suite.

righteous /ˈraɪtʃəs/ *adj* vertueux/-euse.

righteously /ˈraɪtʃəslɪ/ *adv* de façon vertueuse.

rightful /ˈraɪtfl/ *adj* légitime.

rightfully /ˈraɪtfəlɪ/ *adv* [*mine*] légitimement; [*belong*] en droit.

right-hand /ˈraɪthænd/ *adj* du côté droit; **on the ~ side** sur la droite.

right: **~-hand drive, rhd** *n* conduite *f* à droite; **~-handed** *adv* [*person*] droitier/-ière; [*blow*] du droit; **~-hand man** *n* bras *m* droit.

rightly /ˈraɪtlɪ/ *adv* **1** (accurately) correctement; **2** (justifiably) à juste titre; **and ~ so** et pour cause; **~ or wrongly** à tort ou à raison; **3** (with certainty) au juste; **I can't ~ say** je ne peux pas dire; **I don't ~ know** je ne sais pas au juste.

right: **~-minded** *adj* bien-pensant; **~-of-centre** *adj* POL centre-droite *inv*; **~ off** *adv* tout de suite.

right of way *n* **1** AUT priorité *f*; **2** (over land) droit *m* de passage; **'no ~'** 'entrée *f* interdite'.

right-on○ /ˌraɪtˈɒn/ **I** *adj* PÉJ **they're very ~**○ ils s'appliquent à être idéologiquement corrects sur tout. **II right on!** *excl* ça marche!

right: **~s issue** *n* émission *f* de droits de souscription; **~-thinking** *adj* bien-pensant.

right wing I *n* POL **the ~** la droite. **II right-wing** *adj* POL [*attitude*] de droite; **they are very ~** ils sont très à droite.

rigid /ˈrɪdʒɪd/ *adj* [*rules, person, material*] rigide; [*controls, timetable*] strict; **to stand ~** se tenir très raide. IDIOMS **to bore sb ~**○ ennuyer qn à mourir.

rigidity /rɪˈdʒɪdətɪ/ *n* rigidité *f*.

rigidly /ˈrɪdʒɪdlɪ/ *adv* [*oppose*] fermement; [*obey, control*] rigoureusement; [*stick to, apply*] strictement.

rigmarole /ˈrɪgmərəʊl/ *n* (fuss) cirque○ *m*.

rigorous /ˈrɪgərəs/ *adj* **1** (strict) [*discipline*] rigoureux/-euse; [*regime*] sévère; [*adherence*] strict; **2** (scrupulous) rigoureux/-euse.

rigorously /ˈrɪgərəslɪ/ *adv* rigoureusement.

rigour GB, **rigor** US /ˈrɪgə(r)/ *n* rigueur *f*.

rig-out○ /ˈrɪgaʊt/ *n* tenue *f*.

rile /raɪl/ *vtr* énerver.

rim /rɪm/ **I** *n* bord *m*; (in basketball) anneau *m*; **with a gold ~** cerclé d'or. **II -rimmed** *combining form* **gold-~med spectacles** lunettes *fpl* à monture d'or.

rimless glasses /ˈrɪmlɪs/ *n* lunettes *fpl* non cerclées.

rind /raɪnd/ *n* **1** (on cheese) croûte *f*; (on bacon) couenne *f*; **2** (on fruit) peau *f*; **lemon ~** CULIN zeste *m* de citron.

ring /rɪŋ/ **I** *n* **1** (hoop) (for gymnast, attaching rope) anneau *m*; **a diamond/wedding ~** une bague de diamants/ une alliance; **2** (circle) (of people, on page) cercle *m*; **to put a ~ round** entourer [qch] d'un cercle [*ad*]; **to have ~s under one's eyes** avoir les yeux cernés; **3** (sound) (at door) coup *m* de sonnette; (of phone) sonnerie *f*; **to have a nice ~ to it** sonner bien; **that has a familiar ~ (to it)** j'ai déjà entendu ça quelque part; **4** GB (phone call) coup *m* de téléphone or fil○; **5** SPORT (for horses, circus) piste *f*; (for boxing) ring *m*; **6** (of smugglers) réseau *m*; (of dealers, speculators) syndicat *m*; **7** (to mark bird) bague *f*; **8** (round planet) anneau *m*; **9** (on cooker) (electric) plaque *f*; (gas) brûleur *m*.
II *vtr* **1** (cause to sound) (*prét* **rang**; *pp* **rung**) faire sonner [*bell*]; **to ~ the doorbell** ou **bell** sonner; **2** GB TELECOM (*prét* **rang**; *pp* **rung**) appeler; **3** (en-

circle) (*prét, pp* **ringed**) [*trees*] entourer; [*police*] encercler; **4** ZOOL, ECOL (*prét, pp* **ringed**) baguer.
III *vi* (*prét* **rang**; *pp* **rung**) **1** (sound) [*bell, telephone*] sonner; **the doorbell rang** on a sonné à la porte; **2** (sound bell) [*person*] sonner; **to ~ at the door** sonner à la porte; **'please ~ for service'** 'prière de sonner'; **3** (resonate) [*footsteps, laughter, words*] résonner; **that noise makes my ears ~** ce bruit fait bourdonner mes oreilles; **to ~ true/false** sonner vrai/creux; **4** GB TELECOM téléphoner; **to ~ for** appeler [*taxi*].
IDIOMS **to ~ down/up the curtain** baisser/lever le rideau; FIG **to ~ down the curtain on an era** marquer la fin d'une ère; **to ~ in the New Year** fêter le Nouvel An; **to run ~s round** éclipser.
■ **ring back** GB rappeler.
■ **ring in** GB (to work) téléphoner au bureau.
■ **ring off** GB raccrocher.
■ **ring out**: **~ out** [*voice, cry*] retentir; [*bells*] sonner.
■ **ring up** GB: ¶ **~ up** téléphoner; ¶ **~ up** [*sth*] **1** (phone) téléphoner à [*station*]; **2** (on till) enregistrer; ¶ **~ up** [*sb*], **~** [*sb*] **up** téléphoner à [*friend*].

ring: **~-a-ring-a-roses** ▶ 949 *n*: ronde et jeu enfantins; **~ binder** *n* classeur *m* à anneaux; **~-fence** *vtr* GB réserver; **~ finger** *n* annulaire *m*.

ringing /ˈrɪŋɪŋ/ *n* **1** (noise of bell, alarm) sonnerie *f*; **2** (in ears) bourdonnement *m*.

ring: **~leader** *n* meneur/-euse *m/f*; **~let** *n* anglaise *f*; **~master** *n* Monsieur Loyal; **~-pull** *n* anneau *m*.

ringroad /ˈrɪŋrəʊd/*n* GB périphérique *m*; **inner ~** ceinture *f*.

ringside /ˈrɪŋsaɪd/ *n* **at the ~** près du ring.
IDIOMS **to have a ~ seat** FIG être aux premières loges.

rink /rɪŋk/ *n* patinoire *f*.

rinse /rɪns/ **I** *n* rinçage *m*; **to give sth a ~** rincer qch.
II *vtr* (to remove soap) rincer; (wash) laver.
■ **rinse out**: ¶ **~ out** [*colour*] partir au lavage; ¶ **~** [*sth*] **out**, **~ out** [*sth*] rincer [*glass*].

rinse cycle *n* cycle *m* de rinçage.

riot /ˈraɪət/ **I** *n* **1** GEN (disturbance) émeute *f*, révolte *f*; **football ~** affrontement *m* de supporters; **prison ~** mutinerie *f*; **2 a ~ of** une profusion de [*colours*]; **3**○ **to be a ~** (hilarious) être tordant○.
II *vi* GEN se soulever; [*prisoner*] se mutiner.
IDIOMS **to run ~** (behave wildly) LIT se déchaîner; FIG [*imagination*] se débrider; [*plant*] proliférer.

Riot Act *n* JUR, HIST loi *f* britannique antiémeutes.
IDIOMS **to read sb the riot act** chapitrer qn.

rioter /ˈraɪətə(r)/ *n* GEN émeutier/-ière *m/f*; (in prison) mutin *m*.

riot gear *n* tenue *f* antiémeutes.

rioting /ˈraɪətɪŋ/ *n* ₵ émeutes *fpl*, bagarres *fpl*.

riotous /ˈraɪətəs/ *adj* [*laughter*] exubérant; [*welcome*] délirant; [*living, evening*] débridé.

riotously /ˈraɪətəslɪ/ *adv* **~ funny** à se tordre or mourir de rire.

riot: **~ police** *n* forces *fpl* d'ordre; **~ shield** *n* bouclier *m* antiémeutes; **~ squad** *n* brigade *f* antiémeutes.

rip /rɪp/ **I** *n* (tear) accroc *m* (**in** dans).
II *vtr* (*p prés etc* **-pp-**) **1** (tear) déchirer; **to ~ a hole in sth** faire un trou dans qch; **to ~ sth to pieces** ou **shreds** réduire qch en pièces; **2** (snatch, pull) **to ~ sth down** ou **out** arracher qch.
III *vi* (*p prés etc* **-pp-**) [*fabric*] se déchirer.
IDIOMS **to let ~**○ tempêter○; **to let ~ at sb** engueuler○ qn.
■ **rip apart**: **~** [*sth*] **apart 1** LIT [*bomb blast*] déchiqueter; **2**○ FIG défoncer [*team, team's defences*].
■ **rip off**: ¶ **~ off** [*sth*], **~** [*sth*] **off 1** LIT arracher [*garment, roof*]; **2**○ (steal) rafler○ [*idea, design*]; ¶ **~** [*sb*] **off**○ arnaquer○.
■ **rip open**: **~ open** [*sth*], **~** [*sth*] **open** déchirer.

Rivers

The English word river *can be either* fleuve *or* rivière *in French. Major rivers, all of which flow into the sea, are* fleuves: *the rest are* rivières. *Here are some examples of* fleuves *in France:* la Garonne, la Loire, la Seine, le Rhin, le Rhône *and* la Somme: *other* fleuves *include:* le Nil, le Danube, le Gange, le Tage, l'Indus, l'Amazone, le Congo, le Mississippi, le Niger *and* le Saint-Laurent.

The following French rivers are rivières: la Marne, l'Oise, l'Allier, la Dordogne, la Saône.

As in English, French uses the definite article with names of rivers:

the Thames	= la Tamise
to go down the Rhine	= descendre le Rhin
to live near the Seine	= habiter près de la Seine
the course of the Danube	= le cours du Danube

In English you can say the X, the X river *or* the river *X. In French it is always* le X (*or* la X):

the river Thames	= la Tamise
the Potomac river	= le Potomac

When the name of the river is used as an adjective, French has de + *definite article:*

Seine barges	= les péniches de la Seine
a Rhine castle	= un château des bords du Rhin
the Rhine estuary	= l'estuaire du Rhin

■ **rip through**: ~ **through** [sth] [*bomb, blast*] défoncer [*building*].

■ **rip up**: ~ **up** [sth], ~ [sth] **up** déchirer [*paper, contract*]; arracher [*floorboards*].

RIP (*abrév* = **requiescat** ou **requiescant in pace**) qu'il/elle repose en paix or qu'ils/elles reposent en paix.

ripcord /'rɪpkɔːd/ *n* poignée *f* d'ouverture.

ripe /raɪp/ *adj* **1** [*fruit*] mûr; [*cheese*] fait; **2 the time is** ~ c'est le moment; ~ **for development** (site) bon pour la construction; **3** [*language*] grossier/-ière; **to smell** ~ sentir mauvais.
IDIOMS **to live to a** ~ **old age** vivre jusqu'à un âge très avancé.

ripen /'raɪpən/ **I** *vtr* mûrir [*fruit*]; affiner [*cheese*].
II *vi* [*fruit*] mûrir; [*cheese*] se faire.

ripeness /'raɪpnɪs/ *n* LIT, FIG maturité *f*.

rip: ~-**off**○ *n* arnaque◗ *f*; ~-**off artist**○, ~-**off merchant**○ *n* arnaqueur/-euse◗ *m/f*.

ripping†○ /'rɪpɪŋ/ *adj* épatant, sensationnel/-elle.

ripple /'rɪpl/ **I** *n* **1** (in water, corn, hair) ondulation *f*; **2** (sound) **a** ~ **of applause** une cascade d'applaudissements; **3** (repercussion) répercussion *f*; **4** (ice cream) glace *f* panachée.
II *vtr* faire des vaguelettes à la surface de [*water*]; **to** ~ **one's muscles** faire saillir ses muscles.
III *vi* **1** [*water*] se rider; (making noise) clapoter; **2** [*corn*] ondoyer; [*hair*] onduler; [*muscles*] saillir.

ripple effect *n* effet *m* secondaire.

rip-roaring○ /'rɪprɔːrɪŋ/ *adj* [*success*] dingue○.

rise /raɪz/ **I** *n* **1** (increase) (in amount, number, inflation, rates) augmentation *f* (**in** de); (in prices, pressure) hausse *f* (**in** de); (in temperature) élévation *f* (**in** de); (in standards) amélioration *f* (**in** de); **2** GB (also **pay** ~, **wage** ~) augmentation *f* (of salaire); **3** (progress) (of person) ascension *f*; (of empire) essor *m*; (of ideology) montée *f*; **her** ~ **to fame** son accession à la gloire; **4** (slope) montée *f*; **5** (hill) butte *f*; **6 to give** ~ **to** FIG donner lieu à [*rumours, speculation*]; susciter [*resentment, frustration*]; causer [*problem, unemployment*].
II *vi* (*prét* **rose**, *pp* **risen**) **1** (become higher) [*water*] monter; [*price, temperature*] augmenter; [*voice*] devenir plus fort; **to** ~ **above** [*temperature, amount*] dépasser; **2** FIG (intensify) [*pressure*] augmenter; [*tension*] monter; [*frustration, hopes*] grandir; **3** (get up) [*person*] se lever; (after falling) se relever; **to** ~ **from the dead** ressusciter; '~ **and shine!**' 'debout!'; **4** (meet successfully) **to** ~ **to** se montrer à la hauteur de

[*occasion, challenge*]; **5** (progress) [*person*] réussir; **to** ~ **to** devenir [*director, manager*]; s'élever à [*rank*]; **to** ~ **to fame** atteindre la célébrité; **to** ~ **through the ranks** gravir tous les échelons; **6** (slope upwards) [*road*] monter; [*cliff*] s'élever; **7** (appear over horizon) [*sun, moon*] se lever; **8** GEOG (have source) **to** ~ **in** [*river*] prendre sa source dans [*area*]; **9** CULIN [*cake*] lever; **10** [*committee, parliament*] lever la séance.
IDIOMS **to get a** ~ **out of sb**○ faire enrager qn.
■ **rise above**: ~ **above** [sth] (overcome) surmonter.
■ **rise up** (ascend) [*bird, plane*] s'élever; [*smoke*] monter; [*building*] se dresser; (rebel) se soulever.

risen /'rɪzn/ **I** *pp* ▶ **rise**.
II *adj* RELIG ressuscité.

riser /'raɪzə(r)/ *n* (person) **to be an early** ~ être un/une lève-tôt.

rising /'raɪzɪŋ/ **I** *n* (rebellion) soulèvement *m*.
II *adj* [*costs, unemployment, temperature*] en hausse; [*demand*] en augmentation; [*tension*] grandissant; [*sun, moon*] levant; [*politician, singer*] en pleine ascension; [*talent*] prometteur/-euse.
III *adv* **to be** ~ **twelve** aller sur ses douze ans.

risk /rɪsk/ **I** *n* **1** GEN risque *m*; **is there any** ~ **of him catching the illness?** est-ce qu'il risque d'attraper la maladie?; **there is no** ~ **to consumers** il n'y a aucun danger pour le consommateur; **to run a** ~ courir un risque; **to take** ~**s** prendre des risques; **it's not worth the** ~ le risque est trop grand; **at** ~ menacé; **to put one's health at** ~ compromettre sa santé; **at one's own** ~ à ses risques et périls; **at the** ~ **of seeming ungrateful** au risque de paraître ingrat; **'at owner's** ~**'** 'aux risques et périls du propriétaire'; **2** (in banking, insurance) **to be a good/bad** ~ être un bon/mauvais risque.
II *vtr* **1** (endanger) **to** ~ **one's life/neck** risquer sa vie/peau; **2** (venture) **to** ~ **doing** courir le risque de faire; **to** ~ **death** risquer la mort; **to** ~ **one's all** risquer le tout pour le tout; **we decided to** ~ **it** nous avons décidé de prendre le risque; **let's** ~ **it anyway** c'est un risque à prendre.

risk-taker /'rɪsksteɪkə(r)/ *n* fonceur/-euse○ *m/f*; **to be a** ~ aimer prendre des risques.

risky /'rɪskɪ/ *adj* [*decision, undertaking*] risqué; [*share, investment*] à risques.

risotto /rɪ'zɒtəʊ/ *n* (*pl* ~**s**) risotto *m*.

risqué /'riːskeɪ, US rɪ'skeɪ/ *adj* osé.

rite /raɪt/ *n* rite *m*; **to perform a** ~ accomplir un rite; ~ **of passage** rite de passage.

ritual /'rɪtʃʊəl/ **I** *n* rituel *m*, rites *mpl*; **the courtship** ~ ZOOL le cérémonial d'approche.
II *adj* [*dance, murder*] rituel/-elle; [*visit*] traditionnel/-elle.

ritualistic /ˌrɪtʃʊə'lɪstɪk/ *adj* [*activity*] rituel/-elle; (religious) ritualiste.

ritually /'rɪtʃʊəlɪ/ *adv* (ceremonially) selon le rituel; FIG (routinely) rituellement.

ritzy○ /'rɪtsɪ/ *adj* chic *inv*.

rival /'raɪvl/ **I** *n* (person) rival/-e *m/f*; (company) concurrent/-e *m/f*.
II *adj* [*team, business*] rival; [*claim*] opposé.
III *vtr* (*p prés etc* -**ll**-, -**l**- US) (equal) égaler (**in** en); (compete favourably) rivaliser avec (**in** de); **to** ~ **sb/sth in popularity** rivaliser de popularité avec qn/qch.

rivalry /'raɪvlrɪ/ *n* rivalité *f* (**between** entre).

river /'rɪvə(r)/ *n* **1** (flowing into sea) fleuve *m*; (tributary) rivière *f*; **up** ~/**down** ~ en amont/en aval; **2** FIG (of lava, blood) fleuve *m*.
IDIOMS **to sell sb down the** ~ trahir qn.

riverbank /'rɪvəbæŋk/ *n* berge *f*; **along the** ~ le long de la rivière.

river: ~ **basin** *n* bassin *m* fluvial; ~**boat** *n* navire *m* à aubes; ~ **police** *n* police *f* fluviale.

riverside /'rɪvəsaɪd/ **I** *n* berges *fpl*.
II *adj* [*pub*] au bord de la rivière.

river traffic *n* navigation *f* fluviale.

rivet /'rɪvɪt/ **I** *n* rivet *m*.

II *vtr* **1** (captivate) **to be ~ed** être captivé; **2** (fix) **to be ~ed to the spot** [*person*] être cloué sur place.

riveting /ˈrɪvɪtɪŋ/ *adj* fascinant.

Riviera /ˌrɪvɪˈeərə/ *n* **the Italian ~** la Riviera; **the French ~** la Côte d'Azur.

rivulet /ˈrɪvjʊlɪt/ *n* (stream) ruisselet *m*.

RN *n* GB *abrév* ▶ **Royal Navy**.

roach /rəʊtʃ/ *n* **1** (fish) (*pl* ~) gardon *m*; **2**° US (insect) cafard *m*.

road /rəʊd/ **I** *n* **1** (between places) route *f*; **the ~ to Leeds** la route de Leeds; **the ~ north** la route du nord; **the ~ home** la route qui mène à la maison; **the ~ back to** la route du retour à; **are we on the right ~ for Oxford?** c'est bien la route pour Oxford?; **follow the ~ ahead** allez tout droit; **three hours on the ~** trois heures de route; **across the ~** de l'autre côté de la route, en face; **it's just along the ~** c'est juste un peu plus loin; **down the ~** plus bas, plus loin; **by ~** par la route; **transported by ~** transporté par ou sur route; **to take (to) the ~** prendre la route, se mettre en route; **to be on the ~** [*car*] être en état de rouler; [*driver*] être sur la route; [*band, performers*] être en tournée; **I've been on the ~ all night** j'ai roulé toute la nuit; **to be off the ~** [*vehicle*] être hors d'usage; [*driver*] être sur la route; **3** FIG (way) voie *f* (**to** de); **to be on the ~ to success** être sur la voie du succès; **to be on the right ~** être sur la bonne voie; **we don't want to go down that ~** nous ne voulons pas suivre cette voie; **somewhere along the ~ she learned** en cours de route elle a appris; **to reach the end of the ~** déboucher sur une impasse.

II *noun modifier* [*condition, network, map, safety*] routier/-ière; [*repair*] des routes; [*accident*] de la route.

IDIOMS **let's get this show on the ~!** c'est parti!

roadblock /ˈrəʊdblɒk/ *n* barrage *m* routier; **police ~** barrage de police.

road: **~ haulage** *n* transports *mpl* routiers; **~ hog**° *n* chauffard° *m*; **~holding** *n* tenue *f* de route; **~house** *n* (inn) relais *m* (routier); **~ hump** *n* ralentisseur *m*; **~ manager** ▶ 1251 *n* organisateur/ -trice *m/f* de tournée; **~-mender** ▶ 1251 *n* cantonnier *m*; **~ movie** *n* road-movie *m*; **~ racing** ▶ 949 *n* compétition *f* sur route; **~roller** *n* rouleau *m* compresseur; **~ sense** *n* conscience *f* des dangers de la route.

roadshow /ˈrəʊdʃəʊ/ *n* **1** (play, show) spectacle *m* de tournée; **2** (publicity tour) tour *m* promotionnel.

roadside /ˈrəʊdsaɪd/ **I** *n* bord *m* de la route; **at** ou **by** ou **on the ~** au bord de la route.

II *noun modifier* au bord de la route; **~ repairs** réparations *fpl* de fortune.

road: **~sign** *n* panneau *m* de signalisation; **~sweeper** ▶ 1251 *n* (person) balayeur/-euse *m/f*; (machine) balayeuse *f*; **~ tax** *n* taxe *f* routière; **~ test** *n* essai *m* sur route; **~ transport** *n* transports *mpl* routiers; **~ user** *n* usager *m* de la route; **~works** *npl* travaux *mpl* (routiers); **~worthy** *adj* en état de rouler.

roam /rəʊm/ **I** *vtr* parcourir [*countryside*]; faire le tour de [*shops*]; **to ~ the streets** traîner dans les rues.

II *vi* **to ~ through** parcourir [*countryside*]; faire le tour de [*building*].

■ **roam around** [*person*] vadrouiller°.

roar /rɔː(r)/ **I** *n* (of lion) rugissement *m*; (of person) hurlement *m*; (of crowd) clameur *f*; (of engine) vrombissement *m*; (of traffic, waterfall) grondement *m*; (of sea) mugissement *m*; **to give a ~** [*lion*] rugir; [*person*] hurler; **~ of laughter** un éclat de rire; **a ~ of applause** un tonnerre d'applaudissements.

II *vi* rugir; [*person*] vociférer (**at sb** devant qn); [*sea, wind*] mugir; [*fire*] ronfler; [*crowd*] hurler; [*engine*] vrombir; **to ~ with pain** rugir de douleur.

roaring /ˈrɔːrɪŋ/ **I** *n* (of lion, person) rugissement *m*; (of crowd) clameur *f*; (of storm, wind, sea) mugissement *m*; (of thunder, waterfall) grondement *m*; (of engine) vrombissement *m*.

II *adj* **1** (loud) [*engine, traffic*] grondant; **a ~ fire** une belle flambée; **2** (success) fou/folle; **to do a ~ trade** faire des affaires en or (**in** dans la vente de).

roast /rəʊst/ **I** *n* CULIN rôti *m*; US barbecue *m*.

II *adj* [*meat, potatoes*] rôti; **~ beef** rôti *m* de bœuf, rosbif *m*; **~ chestnuts** châtaignes *fpl* grillées.

III *vtr* rôtir [*meat, potatoes*]; (faire) griller [*chestnuts*]; torréfier [*coffee beans*]; **to be ~ed alive** FIG être grillé vif.

IV *vi* [*meat*] rôtir; **I'm ~ing**°! je crève de chaud°!

roaster /ˈrəʊstə(r)/ *n* CULIN (chicken) poulet *m* à rôtir; (oven pan) plat *m* à rôtir.

roasting /ˈrəʊstɪŋ/ **I**° *n* **to give sb a ~** passer un bon savon à qn°.

II *adj* CULIN [*chicken, pan*] à rôtir.

rob /rɒb/ *vtr* (*p prés etc* **-bb-**) **1** [*thief*] voler [*person*]; dévaliser [*bank, train*]; **to be ~bed of sth** se faire voler qch; **2** (deprive) **to ~ sb of** priver qn de.

IDIOMS **to ~ sb blind** escroquer qn.

robber /ˈrɒbə(r)/ *n* voleur/-euse *m/f*; **train ~** bandit *m*.

robbery /ˈrɒbərɪ/ *n* vol *m*; **it's sheer ~!** FIG c'est du vol!

robe /rəʊb/ **I** *n* robe *f*; **christening ~** robe de baptême; **ceremonial ~s** vêtements *mpl* de cérémonie.

II *vtr* vêtir; **~d in white** vêtu de blanc.

robin /ˈrɒbɪn/ *n* **1** rouge-gorge *m*; **2** US merle *m* migrateur.

Robin Hood *pr n* HIST Robin des bois.

robot /ˈrəʊbɒt/ *n* (in sci-fi, industry) robot *m* ALSO PEJ.

robotic /rəʊˈbɒtɪk/ *adj* [*movement, voice*] de robot; [*tool, device, machine*] robotisé.

robotics /rəʊˈbɒtɪks/ *n* (+ *v sg*) robotique *f*.

robotization /ˌrəʊbətaɪˈzeɪʃn, US -tɪˈz-/ *n* robotisation *f*.

robust /rəʊˈbʌst/ *adj* [*health, person, toy*] robuste; [*economy*] solide; [*humour*] fruste; [*reply, attitude, tackle*] énergique; [*wine, flavour*] corsé.

robustly /rəʊˈbʌstlɪ/ *adv* **1** [*made*] solidement; **2** FIG [*answer, defend*] avec force; [*confident*] foncièrement.

robustness /rəʊˈbʌstnɪs/ *n* (of object) robustesse *f*; (of answer, defence) fermeté *f*; (of economy) solidité *f*.

rock /rɒk/ **I** *n* **1** ¢ (substance) roche *f*; **solid ~** roche dure; **hewn out of solid ~** taillé dans le roc; **2** ¢ (boulder) rocher *m*; **on the ~s** [*ship*] sur les récifs; [*drink*] avec des glaçons; FIG [*marriage*] aller à vau-l'eau; **3** (stone) pierre *f*; **'falling ~s'** 'chute de pierres'; **4** (also **~ music**) rock *m*; **5** GB (sweet) sucre *m* d'orge.

II *noun modifier* [*band, concert, musician*] rock; [*industry*] du rock.

III *vtr* **1** (move gently) balancer [*cradle*]; bercer [*baby, boat*]; **2** (shake) [*tremor*] secouer; [*scandal*] ébranler.

IV *vi* **1** (sway) se balancer; **to ~ back and forth** se balancer d'avant en arrière; **to ~ with laughter** être secoué de rire; **2** (shake) trembler; **3** (dance) danser le rock.

IDIOMS **solid/hard as a ~** solide/dur comme le roc.

rock and roll /ˌrɒk ən ˈrəʊl/ *n* (also **rock'n'roll**) rock and roll *m*.

rock bottom /ˌrɒk ˈbɒtəm/ *n* **to be at ~** être au plus bas; **to hit ~** toucher le fond.

rock: **~ bun** *n* GB petit gâteau aux raisins secs; **~ candy** *n* US friandise à base de sucre candi; **~ climber** *n* varappeur/-euse *m/f*.

rock climbing ▶ 949 *n* varappe *f*; **to go ~** faire de la varappe.

rock crystal *n* cristal *m* de roche.

rocker /ˈrɒkə(r)/ *n* **1** US (chair) fauteuil *m* à bascule; **2** (on cradle, chair) bascule *f*; **3** (also **~ switch**) interrupteur *m* à bascule.

IDIOMS **to be/go off one's ~**° débloquer°.

rockery /ˈrɒkərɪ/ *n* GB rocaille *f*.

rocket /ˈrɒkɪt/ **I** *n* **1** GEN, MIL fusée *f*; **2** BOT, CULIN roquette *f*.

II *noun modifier* [*base*] de lancement de fusées; [*research*] spatiale.

III *vi* **1** [*price, profit*] monter en flèche; **to ~ from 10 to 100** grimper de 10 à 100; **2** [*person, car*] **to ~ past sb** passer en trombe devant qn.

rocket: **~ engine** *n* moteur-fusée *m*; **~ launcher** *n* lance-fusées *m inv*; **~-propelled** *adj* autopropulsé; **~ ship** *n* vaisseau *m* spatial.

rock: **~ face** *n* paroi *f* rocheuse; **~fall** *n* chute *f* de pierres; **~ formation** *n* formation *f* rocheuse.

Rockies /'rɒkiːz/ *pr npl* (montagnes *fpl*) Rocheuses *fpl*.

rocking /'rɒkɪŋ/ *n* (gentle) balancement *m*; (vigorous) ballottement *m*.

rocking: **~ chair** *n* fauteuil *m* à bascule; **~ horse** *n* cheval *m* à bascule.

rock: **~ lobster** *n* langouste *f*; **~ painting** *n* peinture *f* rupestre; **~ salmon** *n* GB CULIN roussette *f*; **~ salt** *n* sel *m* gemme; **~ star** *n* rock-star *f*; **~-steady** *adj* extrêmement stable.

rocky /'rɒkɪ/ *adj* **1** [*beach, path, road*] rocailleux/-euse; [*coast*] rocheux/-euse; **a ~ road** FIG un chemin difficile; **2** [*relationship, period*] difficile; [*business*] précaire.

Rocky Mountains *pr npl* montagnes *fpl* Rocheuses.

rod /rɒd/ *n* **1** GEN, TECH (stick) tige *f*; (curtain/stair ~ tringle à rideaux/de marche; **2** (for punishment) baguette *f*; **3** (for fishing) canne *f* à pêche; **4** (staff of office) bâton *m* de commandement.

IDIOMS **to make a ~ for one's own back** s'attirer des ennuis; **spare the ~ and spoil the child** PROV qui aime bien châtie bien PROV.

rode /rəʊd/ *prét* ▶ **ride**.

rodent /'rəʊdnt/ *n* rongeur *m*.

rodeo /'rəʊdɪəʊ/ *n* (*pl* **~s**) rodéo *m*.

roe /rəʊ/ *n* **1** ¢ (eggs) œufs *mpl* (de poisson); **2** (milt) laitance *f*.

roe: **~buck** *n* (*pl* **~**) chevreuil *m*; **~ deer** *n* (*pl* **~**) GEN chevreuil *m*; (female) chevrette *f*.

roger /'rɒdʒə(r)/ *excl* **1** TELECOM reçu; **2**° (OK) d'accord!

rogue /rəʊg/ **I** *n* **1** HUM coquin *m*; **2** PÉJ fripouille *f*; **~s' gallery** (file) fichier *m* de police.
II *noun modifier* **1** (maverick) solitaire; **2** PÉJ (dishonest) véreux/-euse.

roguish /'rəʊgɪʃ/ *adj* espiègle, coquin.

role /rəʊl/ *n* THEAT, FIG rôle *m* (**of** de); **to take a ~** interpréter un rôle; **title ~** rôle-titre *m*.

role: **~ model** *n* GEN, PSYCH modèle *m*; **~-play** *n* PSYCH psychodrame *m*; SCH jeu *m* de rôle; **~ reversal**, **~ swapping** *n* permutation *f* de rôles.

roll /rəʊl/ **I** *n* **1** (of paper, cloth) rouleau *m*; (of banknotes) liasse *f*; (of flesh) bourrelet *m*; **a ~ of film** une pellicule; **2** (bread) petit pain *m*; **cheese ~** sandwich *m* au fromage; **3** (of ship, train) roulis *m*; **4** (in gymnastics) roulade *f*; **5** AVIAT tonneau *m*; **6** GAMES (of dice) lancer *m*; **7** (of drums) roulement *m*; (of thunder) grondement *m*; **8** (register) liste *f*; **electoral ~** listes électorales; **to call the ~** faire l'appel.
II *vtr* **1** (push) rouler [*ball, log*]; **to ~ sth away** rouler qch pour l'éloigner (**from** de); **2** (make) **to ~ sth into a ball** faire une boulette de [*paper*]; faire une boule de [*clay, dough*]; faire une pelote de [*wool*]; **3** (flatten) étendre [*dough*]; rouler [*lawn*]; laminer [*metal*]; **4** (turn) **to ~ one's eyes** rouler des yeux; **5** faire tourner [*camera, presses*]; **6** GAMES faire rouler [*dice*]; **7** LING **to ~ one's 'r's** rouler les 'r's.
III *vi* **1** (move) rouler (**onto** sur); **to ~ backwards** reculer; **to ~ down** [*car, rock*] dévaler [*hill*]; **to ~ into** entrer en [*station*]; entrer dans [*city*]; **to ~ off** tomber de; **2** (rotate) [*car, plane*] faire un tonneau; [*eyes*] rouler dans leurs orbites; **3** (sway) [*ship*] tanguer; **4** (reverberate) [*thunder*] gronder; [*drum*] rouler; **5** (function) [*camera, press*] tourner.

IDIOMS **heads will ~!** des têtes vont tomber!; **~ on the holidays!** vivement les vacances!; **to be ~ing in**

it° rouler sur l'or; **to be X and Y ~ed into one** être à la fois X et Y.

■ **roll about** GB, **roll around** [*animal, person*] se rouler; [*marbles, tins*] rouler.

■ **roll back**: **~** [*sth*] **back**, **~ back** [*sth*] **1** (push back) rouler [*carpet*]; **2** FIG faire reculer [*years*]; repousser [*frontiers*].

■ **roll down**: **~** [*sth*] **down**, **~ down** [*sth*] baisser [*blind, sleeve*].

■ **roll in 1** [*tourists, money*] affluer; [*clouds*] s'assembler; [*tanks, trucks*] avancer; **2** (stroll in) s'amener°.

■ **roll off**: **~ off** [*sth*] sortir de [*production line*].

■ **roll on** [*time*] passer.

■ **roll out**: **~** [*sth*] **out**, **~ out** [*sth*] étirer [*pastry*]; dérouler [*rug*].

■ **roll over**: **¶ ~** se retourner; **to ~ over on one's stomach** rouler sur le ventre; **¶ ~** [*sb*] **over** tourner [*patient*] (**onto** sur).

■ **roll up**: **¶ ~ up** °(arrive) s'amener°, arriver; **~ up!** approchez!; **¶ ~ up** [*sth*], **~** [*sth*] **up** enrouler [*rug, poster*]; **to ~ up one's sleeves** retrousser ses manches; **to ~ sth/sb up in** enrouler qch/qn dans.

roll-call *n* MIL appel *m*.

rolled gold *n* or *m* plaqué; **~ watch** montre *f* plaquée or.

roll: **~ed oats** *npl* flocons *mpl* d'avoine; **~ed-up** *adj* roulé.

roller /'rəʊlə(r)/ *n* **1** IND, TECH rouleau *m*; **paint ~** rouleau de peintre; **2** (curler) bigoudi *m*; **3** (wave) rouleau *m*.

roller: **~ball** *n* stylo *m* à bille; **~ blind** *n* store *m*; **~ coaster** *n* montagnes *fpl* russes; **~drome** *n* piste *f* de patin à roulettes.

roller-skate /'rəʊləskeɪt/ **I** *n* patin *m* à roulettes.
II *vi* faire du patin à roulettes.

roller-skating /'rəʊləskeɪtɪŋ/ ▶ **949** *n* patinage *m* à roulettes; **to go ~** faire du patin à roulettes.

roller: **~-skating rink** *n* patinoire *f*; **~ towel** *n* essuie-main *m* à enrouleur.

rollicking /'rɒlɪkɪŋ/ *adj* [*comedy*] bouffon/-onne.

rolling: **~ pin** *n* rouleau *m* à pâtisserie; **~ stock** *n* RAIL matériel *m* roulant; **~ stone** *n* FIG vagabond/-e *m/f*; **~ strike** *n* IND grève *f* tournante.

roll: **~mop** *n* rollmops *m*; **~neck** *n* col *m* roulé; **~ of honour** GB, **~ of honor** US *n* SCH, SPORT tableau *m* d'honneur; MIL liste *f* des soldats tombés au champ d'honneur; **~-on** *n* déodorant *m* à bille.

roll-on roll-off I *n* roulage *m*.
II *adj* **~ ferry** navire *m* roulier.

roll-top desk *n* bureau *m* cylindre.

ROM /rɒm/ *n: abrév* ▶ **read-only memory**.

roman /'rəʊmən/ *n, adj* (print) romain (*m*).

Roman /'rəʊmən/ **I** *n* Romain/-e *m/f*.
II *adj* [*empire, calendar, alphabet, law, road*] romain.

Roman: **~ candle** *n* chandelle *f* romaine; **~ Catholic**, **RC** *n, adj* catholique (*mf*); **~ Catholicism** *n* catholicisme *m*.

romance /rəʊ'mæns/ *n* **1** (of era, place) charme *m*; (of travel) côté *m* romantique; **2** (love affair) histoire *f* d'amour; (love) amour *m*; (passing affair) aventure *f*; **3** (novel) roman *m* d'amour; (film) film *m* d'amour; **4** LITERAT (medieval) roman *m* du moyen âge.

Romance /rəʊ'mæns/ *n, adj* LING romane (*m*).

Romanesque /ˌrəʊmə'nesk/ *adj* roman.

Romania /rəʊ'meɪnɪə/ ▶ **840** *pr n* Roumanie *f*.

Romanian /rəʊ'meɪnɪən/ ▶ **1100**, **1038** **I** *n* **1** (person) Roumain/-e *m/f*; **2** (language) roumain *m*.
II *adj* roumain.

Roman: **~ nose** *n* nez *m* aquilin; **~ numerals** *npl* chiffres *mpl* romains.

romantic /rəʊ'mæntɪk/ **I** *n* romantique *mf*.
II *adj* **1** [*setting, story, person*] romantique; **2** (involving affair) sentimental; **3** [*novel, film*] d'amour.

Romantic /rəʊ'mæntɪk/ *n, adj* romantique (*mf*).

romantically /rəʊ'mæntɪklɪ/ *adv* [*behave, sing, play*] de façon romantique.

romantic: ~ **comedy** *n* comédie *f* sentimentale; ~ **fiction** *n* (genre) romans *mpl* d'amour; (in bookshop) 'sentiment' *m*.

romanticism /rəʊ'mæntɪsɪzəm/ *n* romantisme *m*.

romanticize /rəʊ'mæntɪsaɪz/ *vtr* idéaliser [*person*]; présenter [qch] sous un jour romantique [*period*].

Romany /'rɒmənɪ/ *n* Tzigane *mf*, Romani *mf*.

Rome /rəʊm/ *pr n* Rome.
IDIOMS ~ **wasn't** built in a day PROV Rome ne s'est pas faite en un jour PROV; **when in** ~ **do as the Romans do** PROV il faut faire comme les gens du pays.

Romeo /'rəʊmɪəʊ/ *pr n* **1** (character) Roméo *m*; **2** FIG don Juan *m*.

romp /rɒmp/ I *n* **1** (frolic) ébats *mpl*; **2** (easy victory) victoire *f* facile.
II *vi* s'ébattre; **to** ~ **home** l'emporter facilement.

rompers /'rɒmpəz/ *npl* (also **romper suit**) barboteuse *f*.

roof /ruːf/ I *n* **1** (of building, car etc) toit *m*; **under one** ~ sous le même toit; **a room under the** ~ une chambre sous les toits ou combles; **to have a** ~ **over one's head** avoir un toit sur la tête; **2** ANAT **the** ~ **of the mouth** la voûte du palais.
II *vtr* faire la couverture de [*building*].
IDIOMS **to go through** ou **hit the** ~○ [*person*] sauter au plafond○; [*prices*] battre tous les records○; **to raise the** ~ (be angry) sauter au plafond○; (make noise) faire un boucan de tous les diables○.
■ **roof in, roof over**: ~ **in** [sth], ~ **over** [sth], ~ [sth] **over** couvrir.

roofer /'ruːfə(r)/ ▶ **1251** *n* couvreur *m*.

roofing /'ruːfɪŋ/ *n* **1** (material) toiture *f*, couverture *f*; **2** (process) pose *f* de la toiture.

roofing felt *n* carton *m* bitumé.

roof: ~ **light** *n* ARCHIT, CONSTR fenêtre *f* de toit; ~ **rack** *n* galerie *f*.

rooftop /'ruːftɒp/ *n* toit *m*; **to shout sth from the** ~**s** crier qch sur tous les toits.

rook /rʊk/ *n* **1** ZOOL (corbeau) freux *m*; **2** GAMES tour *f*.

rookery /'rʊkərɪ/ *n* colonie *f* de freux.

rookie○ /'rʊkɪ/ *n* US bleu○ *m*.

room /ruːm, rʊm/ I *n* **1** (for living) pièce *f*; (for sleeping) chambre *f*; (for working) bureau *m*; (for meetings, teaching, operating) salle *f*; **in the next** ~ dans la pièce d'à côté; '~**s to let**' 'chambres à louer'; ~ **159** la chambre 159; ~ **and board** chambre avec repas; **to get** ~ **and board** être logé (et) nourri; **2** ¢ (space) place *f*; **to make** ~ faire de la place; **3** (opportunity) ~ **for improvement** possibilité *f* d'amélioration; ~ **for manoeuvre** marge *f* de manœuvre.
II *vi* US loger (**with** chez).
III **-roomed** *combining form* **4-**~**ed** de 4 pièces.

rooming house /'ruːmɪŋ/ *n* immeuble *m* locatif.

roommate /'ruːmmeɪt/ *n* **1** (in same room) camarade *mf* de chambre; **2** US (flatmate) compagnon/compagne *m/f* d'appartement.

room service *n* service *m* de chambre.

room temperature *n* température *f* ambiante; **at** ~ [*wine*] chambré.

roomy /'ruːmɪ/ *adj* [*car, house*] spacieux/-ieuse; [*garment*] large; [*bag, cupboard*] grand.

roost /ruːst/ I *n* (perch, tree) perchoir *m*.
II *vi* (in trees) percher (pour la nuit); (in attic) se nicher.
IDIOMS **to rule the** ~ faire la loi.

rooster /'ruːstə(r)/ *n* coq *m*.

root /ruːt/ I *n* **1** BOT, LING, MATH, FIG racine *f*; **to take** ~ [*plant*] prendre racine; [*idea, value*] s'établir; [*industry*] s'implanter; **to pull sth up by the** ~**s** déraciner qch; **she has no** ~**s** elle n'a aucune racine; **to destroy sth** ~ **and branch** détruire complètement qch; **2** (of problem) fond *m*; (of evil) origine *f*; **at the** ~

of à l'origine de; **to get to the** ~ **of the problem** prendre le problème à la racine.
II *noun modifier* **1** FIG [*cause, issue*] fondamental; **2** BOT [*growth*] des racines; [*system*] radiculaire.
III *vtr* **to be** ~**ed in** être ancré dans; **deeply-**~**ed** LIT, FIG bien enraciné; ~**ed to the spot** figé sur place.
IV *vi* **1** BOT prendre racine; **2** (search) fouiller.
■ **root around, root about** fouiller (**in** dans).
■ **root for**○: ~ **for** [sb] encourager.
■ **root out**: ¶ ~ **out** [sth], ~ [sth] **out** traquer [*corruption*]; ¶ ~ **out** [sb], ~ [sb] **out** déloger [*person*].

root: ~ **beer** *n* US boisson *pétillante nonalcoolisée aux extraits de plantes*; ~ **canal work** *n* MED dévitalisation *f*; ~ **ginger** *n* gingembre *m* frais; ~**less** *adj* sans racines; ~ **sign** *n* MATH radical *m*; ~ **word** *n* mot *m* racine.

rope /rəʊp/ I *n* GEN, SPORT corde *f*; FIG (of pearls) rang *m*; **the** ~ (hanging) la corde; **to be on the** ~**s** (in boxing) être dans les cordes; FIG avoir le dos au mur.
II *vtr* **1** attacher [*victim, animal*] (**to** à); encorder [*climber*]; **2** US (lasso) prendre au lasso.
IDIOMS **to give sb plenty of** ~ laisser à qn toute la liberté qu'il/elle veut; **to know the** ~**s** connaître les ficelles○.
■ **rope in**○: ~ [sb] **in**, ~ **in** [sb] **1** GB (to help with task) embaucher○; **2** US (trick) **to get** ~**d in** se faire embringuer○.
■ **rope off**: ~ **off** [sth], ~ [sth] **off** barrer [qch] avec une corde.

rope ladder *n* échelle *f* de corde.

rop(e)y○ /'rəʊpɪ/ *adj* GB **to feel** ~ se sentir patraque○.

rosary /'rəʊzərɪ/ *n* (prayer) rosaire *m*; (beads) chapelet *m*.

rose /rəʊz/ I *prét* ▶ **rise**.
II *n* **1** BOT (flower) rose *f*; (shrub) rosier *m*; **an English** ~ une Anglaise au teint de porcelaine; **the Wars of the Roses** GB HIST la guerre des Deux-Roses; **2** (colour) rose *m*; **3** (nozzle) (on watering can) pomme *f* d'arrosoir; (on shower) pomme *f* de douche.
IDIOMS **life is not a bed of** ~**s** ce n'est pas tous les jours la fête; **everything is coming up** ~**s** tout se passe merveilleusement bien; **to come up smelling of** ~**s** s'en tirer sans tache.

rose: ~**bed** *n* parterre *m* de roses; ~**bowl** *n* vase *m* (spécialement conçu pour les roses); ~**bud** *n* bouton *m* de rose; ~ **bush** *n* rosier *m*.

rose-coloured GB, **rose-colored** US /'rəʊzkʌləd/ ▶ **818** *adj* **1** (red) vermeil/-eille; **2** (optimistic) à l'eau de rose.
IDIOMS **to see the world through** ~ **spectacles** voir la vie en rose.

rose: ~**garden** *n* roseraie *f*; ~**hip** *n* gratte-cul *m*, cynorhodon *m*; ~**hip syrup** *n* sirop *m* d'églantine.

rosemary /'rəʊzmərɪ, US -merɪ/ *n* romarin *m*.

rose: ~ **petal** *n* pétale *m* de rose; ~ **pink** ▶ **818** *adj* rose; ~**-red** ▶ **818** *adj* vermeil/-eille; ~**-tinted** ▶ **818** *adj* = **rose-coloured**.

rosette /rəʊ'zet/ *n* **1** (for winner) cocarde *f*; (on horse) flot *m*; (on gift) nœud *m*; **2** BOT rosette *f*.

rose: ~**water** *n* eau *f* de rose; ~ **window** *n* rosace *f*; ~**wood** *n* bois *m* de rose.

rosin /'rɒzɪn, US 'rɒzn/ *n* colophane *f*.

roster /'rɒstə(r)/ *n* (also **duty** ~) tableau *m* de service.

rostrum /'rɒstrəm/ *n* (pl **-trums** ou **-tra**) estrade *f*.

rosy /'rəʊzɪ/ *adj* (pink) rose; [*dawn*] rosé; **things are looking** ~ FIG les choses s'annoncent bien; **to paint a** ~ **picture** FIG peindre un tableau favorable.
IDIOMS **everything in the garden is** ~ tout va très bien.

rot /rɒt/ I *n* **1** LIT pourriture *f*; FIG mal *m*; **the** ~ **set in when...** les choses ont commencé à se gâter quand...
II *vtr* (*p prés etc* **-tt-**) pourrir.

III *vi* (*p prés etc* **-tt-**) (also ~ **away**) LIT pourrir; FIG [*person*] moisir○.

rota /ˈrəʊtə/ *n* GB tableau *m* de service; **on a ~ basis** à tour de rôle.

rotary /ˈrəʊtərɪ/ **I** *n* US AUT rond-point *m*. **II** *adj* rotatif/-ive.

rotary clothes line *n* séchoir *m* parapluie.

rotate /rəʊˈteɪt, US ˈrəʊteɪt/ **I** *vtr* **1** faire tourner [*blade*]; faire pivoter [*mirror*]; **2** (alternate) faire [*qch*] à tour de rôle [*job*]; alterner [*roles*]. **II** *vi* [*blade, handle, wings*] tourner.

rotating /rəʊˈteɪtɪŋ, US ˈrəʊteɪtɪŋ/ *adj* **1** [*blade, globe*] tournant; **2** [*post, presidency*] tournant.

rotation /rəʊˈteɪʃn/ *n* **1** (of blade etc) rotation *f*; **2** (taking turns) **to work in ~** travailler par roulement or à tour de rôle.

rote /rəʊt/ *n* **by ~** par cœur.

rote learning *n* par cœur○ *m*.

rotisserie /rəʊˈtiːsərɪ/ *n* rôtissoire *f*.

rotor /ˈrəʊtə(r)/: ~ **arm** *n* AUT toucheau *m*; ~ **blade** *n* pale *f* de rotor.

rotproof /ˈrɒtpruːf/ *adj* imputrescible.

rotten /ˈrɒtn/ **I** *adj* **1** [*produce*] pourri; [*teeth*] gâté; [*smell*] de pourriture; **2** (corrupt) pourri○; **3**○ (bad) [*weather*] pourri; [*food*] infect; [*cook, driver*] exécrable; **I feel ~ about it** j'en suis malade; **that was a ~ thing to do!** c'était vraiment un sale coup○! **II** *adv* **to spoil sb ~**○ pourrir qn○.

rotten apple *n* FIG brebis *f* galeuse.

rotund /rəʊˈtʌnd/ *adj* [*person*] grassouillet/-ette; [*stomach*] rebondi; [*object, building*] aux formes arrondies.

rotunda /rəʊˈtʌndə/ *n* rotonde *f*.

rouble /ˈruːbl/ **▶ 849** *n* rouble *m*.

rouge† /ruːʒ/ *n* rouge *m* à joues.

rough /rʌf/ **I** *n* **1** (in golf) rough *m*; **2** (draft) brouillon *m*; (sketch) ébauche *f*; **in ~** au brouillon. **II** *adj* **1** [*hand, skin, material*] rêche; [*surface, rock*] rugueux/-euse; [*terrain*] cahoteux/-euse; [*landscape*] sauvage; **to smooth** (**off**) **the ~ edges** (of stone, glass) polir; **2** (brutal) [*person, behaviour, sport*] brutal, violent; [*area*] dur; **to be ~ with** être brutal avec; **to get ~** devenir violent; **3** (approximate) [*description, map*] sommaire [*figure, idea, estimate*] approximatif/-ive; ~ **justice** justice *f* sommaire or expéditive; **4** (difficult) dur, difficile; **to be ~ on sb** [*person*] être dur avec qn; **it's ~ on you** c'est dur pour toi; **a ~ time** une période difficile; **to give sb a ~ ride** rendre la vie dure à qn; **5** (crude) grossier/-ière; **6** (harsh) [*voice, taste, wine*] âpre; **7** (stormy) [*sea, crossing*] agité; [*weather*] gros/grosse; [*landing*] mouvementé; **8**○ **to feel ~** se sentir patraque○. **III** *adv* (outdoors) **to sleep ~** dormir à la dure. IDIOMS **to ~ it** vivre à la dure.

■ **rough out**: ~ **out** [*sth*] esquisser, ébaucher.

■ **rough up**○: ~ [**sb**] **up**, ~ **up** [**sb**] (manhandle) malmener; (beat up) tabasser○.

roughage /ˈrʌfɪdʒ/ *n* ¢ fibres *fpl*.

rough: ~**-and-ready** *adj* [*person, manner*] fruste; [*conditions*] rudimentaire; [*method, system*] sommaire; ~**-and-tumble** *n* LIT chahut *m*; FIG mêlée *f* (of de); ~**cast** *n* CONSTR crépi *m*; ~ **diamond** *n* (gem) diamant *m* brut; GB (man) brave homme *m*.

roughen /ˈrʌfn/ *vtr* rendre [*qch*] rêche or rugueux.

rough-hewn /ˈrʌfhjuːn/ *adj* [*wood*] équarri.

roughly /ˈrʌflɪ/ *adv* **1** [*calculate, describe, indicate*] grossièrement, rapidement; ~ **speaking** en gros, approximativement; ~ **10%** à peu près 10%; **2** [*treat, hit*] brutalement; **3** [*make, grate*] grossièrement.

roughness /ˈrʌfnɪs/ *n* **1** (of skin, surface, material) rugosité *f*; (of terrain) inégalité *f*; **2** (violence) brutalité *f*; **3** (lack of sophistication) (of person) rudesse *f*.

rough paper *n* feuille *f* de brouillon.

roughrider *n* dresseur/-euse *m/f* de chevaux.

roughshod /ˈrʌfʃɒd/ *adj*: IDIOMS **to ride ~ over** se moquer (totalement) de.

rough work *n* SCH brouillon *m*.

roulette /ruːˈlet/ *n* roulette *f*.

Roumania *pr n* = **Romania**.

round /raʊnd/

■ **Note** *round* often appears after verbs in English (*change round, gather round, pass round*). For translations, consult the appropriate verb entry (**change, gather, pass**).
– For *go round, get round* see the entries **go, get**.

I *adv* **1** GB (on all sides) **all ~** tout autour; **whisky all ~!** du whisky pour tout le monde!; **to go all the way ~** faire tout le tour; **2** GB (in circles) **to go ~ and ~** [*carousel*] tourner (en rond); [*person*] FIG tourner en rond; LIT aller et venir; **3** GB (to specific place, home) **to go ~** to passer à; **to ask sb ~** dire à qn de passer à la maison; **to invite sb ~ for lunch** inviter qn à déjeuner (chez soi); **I'll be ~ in a minute** j'arrive (dans un instant); **4** GB **three metres ~** de trois mètres de circonférence; **5** GB (as part of cycle) **all year ~** toute l'année; **this time ~** cette fois-ci.

II *prep* GB **1** (expressing location) autour de [*table etc*]; **to sit ~ the fire** s'asseoir au coin du feu; **the wall goes right ~ the house** le mur fait le tour de la maison; **what do you measure ~ the waist?** combien fais-tu de tour de taille?; **2** (expressing direction) **to go ~ the corner** tourner au coin de la rue; **just ~ the corner** tout près; **to go ~ a bend** (in road) prendre un virage; **to go ~ an obstacle** contourner un obstacle; **3** (on visit) **her sister took us ~ Oxford** sa sœur nous a fait visiter Oxford; **to go ~ the shops** faire les magasins.

III round about *adv phr* **1** (approximately) à peu près, environ; **it happened ~ about here** ça s'est passé par ici; **2** (vicinity) **the people ~ about** les gens des environs.

IV *n* **1** (set, series) série *f* (**of** de); **the daily ~ of activities** le train-train quotidien; **2** (in competition) rencontre *f*; **qualifying ~** match *m* de qualification; **3** (in golf, cards) partie *f*; (in boxing, wrestling) round *m*; **4** (in showjumping) parcours *m*; **5** (in election) tour *m*; **6** (of drinks) tournée *f*; **7** MIL (unit of ammunition) balle *f*; ~ **of ammunition** cartouche *f*; **8** MIL (shot fired) salve *f*; **9** (burst) ~ **of applause** salve *f* d'applaudissements; **to get a ~ of applause** être applaudi; **10** (of bread) **a ~ of toast** une tournée *f*; **11** (route) tournée *f*; **to do one's ~s** [*doctor*] visiter ses malades; [*postman*] faire sa tournée; [*guard*] faire sa ronde; **to do** ou **go the ~s** [*rumour, flu*] circuler; **to go** ou **do the ~s of** faire le tour de; **12** (circular shape) rondelle *f* (**of** de); **13** MUS (canon) canon *m*.

V *adj* **1** (circular, spherical, curved) rond; ~**-faced** au visage rond; **her eyes grew ~** elle a ouvert des yeux ronds; **to have ~ shoulders** avoir le dos voûté; **2** (complete) [*figure*] rond; **in ~ figures, that's £100** ça fait 100 livres sterling en arrondissant; **a ~ dozen** une douzaine exactement; **a nice ~ sum** une somme rondelette○.

VI *vtr* contourner [*headland*]; **to ~ the corner** tourner au coin; **to ~ a bend** prendre un virage.

■ **round down**: ~ [*sth*] **down**, ~ **down** [*sth*] arrondir [*qch*] au chiffre inférieur.

■ **round off**: ~ **off** [*sth*], ~ [*sth*] **off 1** (finish off) finir [*meal, evening*] (**with** par); conclure [*speech*]; parfaire [*education*]; **2** (alter) arrondir [*corner, edge, figure*].

■ **round on** GB: ~ **on** [*sb*] attaquer violemment; **she ~ed on me** elle m'est tombée dessus○.

■ **round up**: ~ **up** [*sb/sth*], ~ [*sb/sth*] **up 1** regrouper [*people*]; rassembler [*livestock*]; **to be ~ed up** être pris dans une rafle; **2** arrondir [*qch*] au chiffre supérieur [*figure*].

roundabout /ˈraʊndəbaʊt/ **I** *n* GB (in fairground etc) manège *m*; GB (in playpark) tourniquet *m*; (for traffic) rond-point *m*. **II** *adj* **to come by a ~ way** faire un détour; **by ~ means** par des moyens détournés; **a ~ way of saying** une façon détournée or alambiquée○ de dire. IDIOMS **it's swings and ~s** ce que tu gagnes d'un côté, tu le perds de l'autre.

round brackets *npl* GB parenthèses *fpl*.

:ounded /'raʊndɪd/ adj **1** [shape, edge] arrondi; **2** [phrase] bien tourné; [account] détaillé.

:ounders /'raʊndəz/ n GB SPORT (+ v sg) ≈ baseball m.

:oundly /'raʊndlɪ/ adv [condemn] sans ambages; [defeat] joliment.

:ound-neck(ed) sweater n pull-over m ras-de-cou inv.

:oundness /'raʊndnɪs/ n rondeur f.

:ound robin n SPORT tournoi m.

:ound-shouldered /ˌraʊndˈʃəʊldəd/ adj **to be ~** avoir le dos voûté.

round-the-clock adj GB [care, surveillance] 24 heures sur 24; **~ shifts** les trois-huit m inv.

:ound: ~-the-world adj autour du monde; **~ trip** n aller-retour m.

roundup /'raʊndʌp/ n **1** (swoop) rafle f; **2** (herding) rassemblement m (**of** de); **3** (summary) résumé m.

roundworm n ascaris m.

rouse /raʊz/ vtr **1** SOUT **to ~ sb from a deep sleep** tirer qn d'un sommeil profond; **2** (stir) réveiller [person]; susciter [anger, interest]; soulever [public opinion]; **to ~ sb to action** pousser qn à l'action.

rousing /'raʊzɪŋ/ adj [reception] enthousiaste; [speech] galvanisant; [music] exaltant.

rout /raʊt/ **I** n déroute f, défaite f.
II vtr MIL mettre en déroute; FIG battre à plates coutures.
■ **rout out 1** (find) dénicher; **2** (force out) déloger.

route /ruːt/ **I** n **1** GEN (way) chemin m; (to work) trajet m (**to** pour aller à); **on the ~ to Oxford** sur le chemin d'Oxford; **to plan a ~** décider d'un itinéraire; **2** (for transport) route f; **shipping ~** route maritime; **domestic ~s** les lignes intérieures; **bus ~** ligne d'autobus; **Route 86** US l'autoroute f 86; **3** (official itinerary) parcours m; **4** FIG (to power etc) voie f (**to** de); **5** US /raʊt/ (**newspaper**) **~** tournée f de livraison.
II vtr expédier, acheminer [goods]; **this flight is ~d to Athens via Rome** ce vol va à Athènes via Rome.

route march n marche f d'entraînement.

routine /ruːˈtiːn/ **I** n **1** (procedure) routine f; **office ~** travail m de routine; **to establish a ~** (at work) s'organiser; (for spare time) se faire un emploi du temps; **2** (drudgery) routine f (**of** de); **3** MUS, THEAT (act) numéro m; **4°** PÉJ (obvious act) numéro° m; **5** COMPUT sous-programme m; **6** SPORT enchaînement m.
II adj **1** (normal) [enquiry, matter] de routine; **it's fairly ~** c'est la routine; **~ maintenance** entretien m courant; **2** (uninspiring) routinier/-ière.

routinely /ruːˈtiːnlɪ/ adv **1** [check, review] systématiquement; **2** [tortured, abused] régulièrement.

roving /'rəʊvɪŋ/ adj [ambassador] itinérant; **to have a ~ eye** être toujours à l'affût d'une aventure.

row¹ /rəʊ/ ▶949| **I** n **1** (line) (of people, plants, stitches) rang m (**of** de); (of houses, seats, books) rangée f (**of** de); **seated in a ~** assis en rang; **a ~ of cars** une file de voitures; **~ after ~ of** rang après rang de; **in the front ~** au premier rang; **2** (succession) **six times in a ~** six fois de suite; **the third week in a ~** la troisième semaine d'affilée; **3** (in boat) **to go for a ~** faire de la barque.
II vtr **to ~ a boat up the river** remonter la rivière à la rame; **to ~ a race** faire une course d'aviron.
III vi ramer; **to ~ across** traverser [qch] à la rame [river, lake].

row² /raʊ/ **I** n **1** (dispute) (public) querelle f; (private) dispute f (**about, over** à propos de); **a family ~** une dispute (familiale); **to have a ~ with** se disputer avec; **2** (noise) tapage m; **to make a ~** faire du tapage.
II vi se disputer (**with** avec; **about, over** à propos de).

rowan /'rəʊən, 'raʊ-/ n **1** (tree) sorbier m; **2** (berry) sorbe f.

rowboat /'rəʊbəʊt/ n US bateau m à rames.

rowdiness /'raʊdɪnɪs/ n (noise) tapage m; (violence) bagarre° f; (in class) chahut m.

rowdy /'raʊdɪ/ adj (noisy) tapageur/-euse; (violent) bagarreur/-euse; (in class) chahuteur/-euse.

rower /'rəʊə(r)/ n rameur/-euse m/f, nageur/-euse m/f.

rowing /'rəʊɪŋ/ ▶949| n aviron m; **~ boat** GB bateau m à rames; **~ machine** rameur m.

rowlock /'rəʊlɒk/ n GB dame f de nage, tolet m.

royal /'rɔɪəl/ **I°** n (person) membre m de la famille royale.
II adj royal; **the ~ 'we'** le pluriel de majesté; **to give sb a ~ welcome** faire un accueil royal à qn.

royal: Royal Air Force, RAF n GB armée f de l'air britannique; **~ blue** ▶818| n, adj bleu (m) roi inv; **~ flush** n quinte f royale.

Royal Highness ▶937| n His **~** Son Altesse f royale; Your **~** Votre Altesse f.

royal: ~ icing n GB glaçage m aux blancs d'œufs; **~ jelly** n gelée f royale; **Royal Mail** n GB service m postal britannique; **Royal Marines** npl GB fusiliers-marins mpl britanniques; **Royal Navy** n GB marine f britannique; **Royal Society** n GB Académie f des Sciences.

royalty /'rɔɪəltɪ/ n **1** ¢ (person) membre m d'une famille royale; (persons) membres mpl d'une famille royale; **2** (state of royal person) royauté f; **3** (money) (to author, musician) droits mpl d'auteur; (on patent, coal deposits) royalties fpl.

Royal Ulster Constabulary, RUC n GB police f d'Irlande du Nord.

RP n GB (abrév = **Received Pronunciation**) RP f (prononciation de l'anglais considérée comme standard).

RPI abrév ▶ retail price index.

rpm (abrév = **revolutions per minute**) tr/min.

RRP GB (abrév écrite = **recommended retail price**) prix m de détail conseillé.

RSPCA n GB (abrév = **Royal Society for the Prevention of Cruelty to Animals**) société f protectrice des animaux.

Rt Hon GB abrév écrite = **Right Honourable**.

rub /rʌb/ **I** n **1** (massage) friction f; **to give [sth] a ~** frictionner [back]; bouchonner [horse]; **2** (polish) coup m de chiffon; **to give [sth] a ~** donner un coup de chiffon à [table]; frotter [stain].
II vtr (p prés etc **-bb-**) **1** (touch) se frotter [chin, eyes]; **2** (polish) frotter [stain, surface]; **to ~ sth away** faire disparaître qch; **3** (massage) frictionner; **4** (apply) **to ~ sth on to the skin** appliquer qch sur la peau; **to ~ sth into the skin** faire pénétrer qch dans la peau; **5** (incorporate) **~ the cream into your skin** faire pénétrer la pommade en massant; **6** (chafe) blesser [heel]; frotter contre [mudguard].
III vi (p prés etc **-bb-**) **1** (scrub) frotter; **2** (chafe) **these shoes ~** ces chaussures me blessent.
IDIOMS: **to ~ salt into sb's wounds** remuer le couteau dans la plaie; **to ~ sb up the wrong way** prendre qn à rebrousse-poil°; **to ~ shoulders with sb** côtoyer or fréquenter qn.
■ **rub along**: **to ~ along with** s'entendre assez bien avec [person].
■ **rub down**: ¶ **~ [sb] down**, **~ down [sb]** frictionner [athlete]; ¶ **~ [sth] down**, **~ down [sth] 1** (massage) bouchonner [horse]; **2** (smooth) poncer [plaster, wood].
■ **rub in**: **~ [sth] in**, **~ in [sth]** faire pénétrer [lotion]; **there's no need to ~ it in°!** FIG inutile d'en rajouter°!
■ **rub off**: ¶ **~ off** [dye, ink] déteindre; **the chalk ~s off easily** la craie s'efface facilement; ¶ **~ [sth] off**, **~ off [sth]** faire disparaître [stain].
■ **rub out**: ¶ **~ out** s'effacer; ¶ **~ [sth] out**, **~ out [sth]** effacer.

rubber /'rʌbə(r)/ **I** n **1** (substance) caoutchouc m; **made of ~** en caoutchouc; **2** GB (eraser) gomme f; **3** (for cleaning) chiffon m; **4°** US (condom) préservatif m, capote° f; **5** (in games) partie f.

II *noun modifier* [*ball, sole*] de ou en caoutchouc.

rubber: **~ band** *n* élastique *m*; **~ bullet** *n* balle *f* de caoutchouc; **~ check**○ US chèque *m* en bois○; **~ dinghy** *n* canot *m* pneumatique; **~ glove** *n* gant *m* en or de caoutchouc.

rubberneck○ /ˈrʌbənek/ *n* **1** (onlooker) curieux/-ieuse *m/f*; **2** (tourist) touriste *mf*.

rubber: **~ plant** *n* caoutchouc *m*; **~ plantation** *n* plantation *f* d'hévéas; **~ sheet** *n* alaise *f*; **~-soled** *adj* à semelles de caoutchouc.

rubber stamp *n* **1** LIT tampon *m*; **2** FIG PÉJ **to be a ~ for sb's decisions** [*body, group*] entériner sans discuter les décisions de qn.

rubber: **~ tapping** *n* récolte *f* du latex par saignée; **~ tree** *n* hévéa *m*.

rubbery /ˈrʌbərɪ/ *adj* caoutchouteux/-euse.

rubbing /ˈrʌbɪŋ/ *n* **1** (friction) frottement *m*; **2** (picture) reproduction *f* par frottement.

rubbish /ˈrʌbɪʃ/ **I** *n* **1** (refuse) déchets *mpl*; (domestic) ordures *fpl*; (from garden) détritus *mpl*; (on site) gravats *mpl*; **2** (inferior goods) camelote○ *f*; (discarded objects) saletés○ *fpl*; **3** (nonsense) **to talk ~** raconter n'importe quoi; **this book is ~**○! ce livre est nul○!
II *vtr* GB descendre [qn/qch] en flammes.

rubbish: **~ bin** *n* GB poubelle *f*; **~ chute** *n* GB vide-ordures *m inv*; **~ collection** *n* GB ramassage *m* des ordures; **~ dump** GB décharge *f* (publique); **~ heap** *n* tas *m* d'ordures.

rubble /ˈrʌbl/ *n* ¢ (after explosion) décombres *mpl*; (on site) gravats *mpl*.

rub-down /ˈrʌbdaʊn/ *n* **to give sb a ~** frictionner qn; **to give [sth] a ~** bouchonner [*horse*]; poncer [*woodwork, plaster*].

rubella /ruːˈbelə/ ▶ 1002 *n* rubéole *f*.

rubric /ˈruːbrɪk/ *n* SOUT rubrique *f*.

ruby /ˈruːbɪ/ ▶ 818 **I** *n* **1** (gem) rubis *m*; **2** (also **~ red**) rouge *m* rubis.
II *noun modifier* [*bracelet, necklace*] de rubis; **a ~ ring** une bague rubis.
III *adj* [*liquid, lips*] vermeil/-eille; **~ port** porto *m* (ruby); **~ wedding** noces *fpl* de vermeil.

RUC *n*: *abrév* ▶ **Royal Ulster Constabulary**.

ruck /rʌk/ *n* **1** (in rugby) mêlée *f* ouverte; **2** (crease) faux pli *m*.

rucksack /ˈrʌksæk/ *n* sac *m* à dos.

rudder /ˈrʌdə(r)/ *n* (on boat) gouvernail *m*; (on plane) gouverne *f*.

ruddy /ˈrʌdɪ/ *adj* [*cheeks*] coloré; [*sky*] rougeâtre.

rude /ruːd/ *adj* **1** (impolite) [*comment*] impoli; [*person*] mal élevé; **to be ~ to sb** être impoli envers qn; **it is ~ to do** il est impoli or c'est mal élevé de faire; **I don't mean to be ~ but**... je ne veux pas vous vexer mais...; **2** (indecent) [*joke*] grossier/-ière; [*book*] osé; **a ~ word** un gros mot; **3** (abrupt) brutal.
IDIOMS **to be in ~ health** LITTÉR avoir une santé de fer.

rudely /ˈruːdlɪ/ *adv* (impolitely) de façon impolie; (abruptly) brutalement.

rudeness /ˈruːdnɪs/ *n* manque *m* de correction.

rudimentary /ˌruːdɪˈmentrɪ/ *adj* rudimentaire.

rudiments /ˈruːdɪmənts/ *npl* rudiments *mpl* (**of** de).

rue /ruː/ **I** *n* BOT rue *f*.
II *vtr* LITTÉR se repentir de [*decision*].

rueful /ˈruːfl/ *adj* [*smile*] attristé; [*thought*] triste.

ruefully /ˈruːfəlɪ/ *adv* tristement.

ruff /rʌf/ *n* (of lace) fraise *f*; (of fur, feathers) collier *m*.

ruffian† /ˈrʌfɪən/ *n* voyou *m*.

ruffle /ˈrʌfl/ **I** *n* (at sleeve) manchette *f*; (at neck) ruche *f*; (on shirt front) jabot *m*; (on curtain) volant *m*.
II *vtr* **1** ébouriffer [*hair, fur*]; hérisser [*feathers*]; rider [*water*]; **2** (disconcert) énerver; (upset) froisser.

ruffled /ˈrʌfld/ *adj*: IDIOMS **to smooth ~ feathers** calmer le jeu.

rug /rʌg/ *n* **1** (mat, carpet) tapis *m*; (by bed) descente *f* de lit; **2** GB (blanket) plaid *m*, couverture *f*.

IDIOMS **to be as snug as a bug in a ~**○ être bien au chaud.

rugby /ˈrʌgbɪ/ ▶ 949 *n* rugby *m*.

rugby: **~ league** *n* rugby *m* à 13; **~ tackle** *n* plaquage *m*; **~ union** *n* rugby *m* à 15.

rugged /ˈrʌgɪd/ *adj* **1** [*landscape*] accidenté; [*coastline*] déchiqueté; **2** [*man, features*] rude; **3** (tough) [*character*] coriace; [*defence*] acharné; **4** (durable) solide.

ruin /ˈruːɪn/ **I** *n* **1** ¢ (collapse) (physical, financial) ruine *f*; (moral) perte *f*; **in a state of ~**, **in ~s** en ruines; **to fall into ~** tomber en ruines; **2** (building) ruine *f*; **~s** LIT, FIG ruines *fpl* (**of** de).
II *vtr* **1** (destroy) ruiner [*economy, career*]; **to ~ one's health** se ruiner la santé; **to ~ one's eyesight** s'abîmer la vue; **2** (spoil) gâcher [*holiday, meal*]; abîmer [*clothes*]; gâter [*child, pet*]; **it's ~ing our lives** ça nous gâche la vie.
IDIOMS **to go to rack and ~** se délabrer.

ruined /ˈruːɪnd/ *adj* **1** (derelict) en ruines; **2** (spoilt) [*holiday, meal*] gâché; [*clothes, furniture*] abîmé; [*reputation*] ruiné; (financially) ruiné.

ruinous /ˈruːɪnəs/ *adj* [*costs*] ruineux/-euse; [*prices*] exorbitant; [*course of action*] désastreux/-euse.

rule /ruːl/ **I** *n* **1** (regulation) (of game, language) règle *f*; (of school, organization) règlement *m*; **the ~s of the game** les règles or la règle du jeu; **to bend the ~s** contourner les règles or le règlement; **against the ~s** contraire aux règles or au règlement (**to do** de faire); **it is a ~ that** il est de règle que (+ *subj*); **~s and regulations** réglementation *f*; **I make it a ~ always to do** j'ai pour règle de toujours faire; **2** (usual occurrence) règle *f*; **as a ~** généralement; **3** ¢ (authority) domination *f*, gouvernement *m*; **under the ~ of a tyrant** sous la domination d'un tyran; **majority ~** gouvernement majoritaire; **4** (for measuring) règle *f*.
II *vtr* **1** POL [*ruler, law*] gouverner; [*monarch*] régner sur; [*party*] diriger; [*army*] commander; **2** (control) [*person, money, consideration*] diriger [*behaviour, life*]; [*factor*] dicter [*strategy*]; **to be ~d by sb** se laisser diriger par qn; **to let one's heart ~ one's head** laisser son cœur dominer sa raison; **3** (draw) faire, tirer [*line*]; **~d paper** papier réglé; **4** [*court, umpire*] **to ~ that** décréter que.
III *vi* **1** [*monarch, anarchy*] régner; **2** [*court, umpire*] statuer.
■ **rule out**: **~ out** [*sth*], **~** [*sth*] **out 1** (eliminate) exclure [*possibility, candidate*] (**of** de); **to ~ out doing** exclure de faire; **2** (prevent) interdire [*activity*].

rule: **~book** *n* règlement *m*; **~ of law** *n* POL séparation *f* constitutionnelle de la justice et du pouvoir; **~ of thumb** *n* principe *m* de base.

ruler /ˈruːlə(r)/ *n* **1** (leader) dirigeant/-e *m/f*; **2** (measure) règle *f*.

ruling /ˈruːlɪŋ/ **I** *n* décision *f* (**against** à l'encontre de; **by** de; **on** sur); **to give a ~** rendre une décision.
II *adj* **1** (in power) dirigeant; **2** (dominant) dominant.

rum /rʌm/ *n* rhum *m*; **white ~** rhum blanc.

rumble /ˈrʌmbl/ **I** *n* (of thunder, artillery, trucks) grondement *m*; (of stomach) gargouillement *m*.
II *vtr* ○GB **we've been ~d!** on nous a démasqués!
III *vi* **1** [*thunder, artillery*] gronder; [*stomach*] gargouiller; **2** (trundle) **to ~ by** passer bruyamment.

rumble: **~ seat** *n* US AUT spider *m*; **~ strip** *n* bande *f* sonore (*sur l'autoroute*).

rumbling /ˈrʌmblɪŋ/ *n* (of thunder, vehicles) grondement *m*; (of stomach, pipes) gargouillement *m*; **~s** FIG murmures *mpl*.

rumbustious /rʌmˈbʌstɪəs/ *adj* bruyant.

ruminant /ˈruːmɪnənt/ *n, adj* ruminant (*m*).

ruminate /ˈruːmɪneɪt/ *vi* **1** FIG **to ~ on** ou **about** ruminer sur; **2** ZOOL ruminer.

rummage /ˈrʌmɪdʒ/ **I** *n* **1** (look) **to have a ~ in** fouiller dans; **2** US (jumble) vieilleries *fpl*.
II *vi* fouiller (**through** dans; **for** à la recherche de).

rummy /ˈrʌmɪ/ ▶ 949 *n* rami *m*.

rumored US = **rumoured**.

rumour GB, **rumor** US /ˈruːmə(r)/ *n* rumeur *f*, bruit *m* (about sur); **to start a ~** faire courir une rumeur or un bruit; **~s are circulating that, ~ has it that** le bruit court que; **there is no truth in any of the ~s** les rumeurs sont dénuées de tout fondement.

rumoured GB, **rumored** US /'ruːməd/ *adj* **it is ~ that** il paraît que, on dit que.

rumourmonger GB, **rumormonger** US /'ruːməmʌŋgə(r)/ *n* personne *f* qui fait courir une rumeur.

rump /rʌmp/ *n* **1** (also **~ steak**) rumsteck *m*; **2** (of animal) croupe *f*; (of bird) croupion *m*; **3** HUM (of person) postérieur *m*; **4** (of party) vestiges *mpl*.

rumple /'rʌmpl/ *vtr* ébouriffer [*hair*]; froisser [*clothes, sheets, papers*].

rumpus○ /'rʌmpəs/ *n* (noise) boucan○ *m*; (protest) esclandre *m* (**over** au sujet de).

rumpus room *n* US salle *f* de jeux.

rum toddy *n* grog *m*.

run /rʌn/ **I** *n* **1** (act of running) course *f*; **a two-mile ~** une course de deux miles; **to go for a ~** aller courir; **to take the dog for a ~** aller faire courir le chien; **to break into a ~** se mettre à courir; **to take a ~ at** prendre son élan pour franchir [*hedge*]; **to give sb a clear ~** FIG laisser le champ libre à qn (**at doing** pour faire); **2** (flight) **on the ~** en fuite; **to be on the ~ from** fuir; **to have sb on the ~** LIT mettre qn en fuite; FIG réussir à effrayer qn; **to make a ~ for it** fuir, s'enfuir; **3** (series) série *f*; **to have a ~ of luck** être en veine; **to have a ~ of bad luck** jouer de malchance; **4** THEAT série *f* de représentations; **to have a six-month ~** tenir l'affiche pendant six mois; **5** (trend) (of events, market) tendance *f*; **the ~ of the cards/dice was against me** le jeu était contre moi; **in the normal ~ of things** dans l'ordre normal des choses; **6** (series of thing produced) (in printing) tirage *m*; (in industry) série *f*; **7** FIN (on Stock Exchange) ruée *f* (**on** sur); **8** (trip, route) trajet *m*; **the ~ up to York** le trajet jusqu'à York; **9** (in cricket, baseball) point *m*; **10** (for rabbit, chickens) enclos *m*; **11** (in tights, material) échelle *f*; **12** (for skiing etc) piste *f*; **13** (in cards) suite *f*.

II *vtr* (*p prés* **-nn-**; *prét* **ran**; *pp* **run**) **1** (cover by running) courir [*distance, marathon*]; **to ~ a race** faire une course; **she ran a very fast time** elle a fait un très bon temps; **2** (drive) **to ~ sb to the station** conduire qn à la gare; **to ~ sb home** reconduire qn; **to ~ sth over to sb's house** apporter qch chez qn en voiture; **to ~ the car into a tree** jeter la voiture contre un arbre; **3** (pass, move) **to ~ one's hand over** passer la main sur; **to ~ one's eye(s) over** parcourir rapidement; **to ~ a duster over** passer un coup de chiffon sur; **to ~ one's pen through** rayer; **4** (manage) diriger; **a well-/badly-run organization** une organisation bien/mal dirigée; **stop trying to ~ my life!** arrête de vouloir diriger ma vie!; **who is ~ning things here?** qui est-ce qui commande ici?; **5** (operate) faire fonctionner [*machine*]; faire tourner [*motor*]; exécuter [*program*]; entretenir [*car*]; **to ~ tests on** effectuer des tests sur; **to ~ a check on sb** prendre des renseignements sur qn; **6** (organize, offer) organiser [*competition, course*]; mettre [qch] en place [*bus service*]; **7** (pass) passer [*cable*]; **8** (cause to flow) faire couler [*bath*]; ouvrir [*tap*]; **9** (publish) publier [*article*]; **10** (pass through) franchir [*rapids*]; forcer [*blockade*]; brûler [*red light*]; **11** (smuggle) faire passer [qch] en fraude; **12** (enter) faire courir [*horse*]; présenter [*candidate*].

III *vi* (*p prés* **-nn-**; *prét* **ran**; *pp* **run**) **1** (move quickly) [*person, animal*] courir; **to ~ across/down sth** traverser/descendre qch en courant; **to ~ around the house** courir dans toute la maison; **to ~ for ou to catch the bus** courir pour attraper le bus; **to ~ for the exit** courir vers la sortie; **to ~ in the 100 metres** courir le 100 mètres; **to come ~ning** courir (**towards** vers); **2** (flee) fuir, s'enfuir; **to ~ for one's life** s'enfuir pour sauver sa peau○; **~ for your life!**, **~ for it**○! sauve qui peut!, déguerpissons○!; **there's nowhere to ~ (to)** il n'y a nulle part où aller; **to go ~ning to one's parents** se réfugier chez ses parents; **3**○ (rush off) filer○; **4** (function) [*machine*]

marcher; **to leave the engine ~ning** laisser tourner le moteur; **to ~ off** fonctionner sur [*mains, battery*]; **to ~ on** marcher à [*diesel, unleaded*]; **to ~ fast/slow** [*clock*] prendre de l'avance/du retard; **the organization ~s very smoothly** l'organisation fonctionne parfaitement; **5** (continue, last) [*contract, lease*] courir; **to ~ from... to...** [*school year, season*] aller de... à...; **6** THEAT [*play, musical*] tenir l'affiche (**for** pendant); **this show will ~ and ~!** ce spectacle tiendra l'affiche pendant des mois!; **7** (pass) **to ~ past/through** [*frontier, path*] passer/traverser; **to ~ (from) east to west** aller d'est en ouest; **the road ~s north for about ten kilometres** la route va vers le nord sur une dizaine de kilomètres; **to ~ parallel to** être parallèle à; **a scar ~s down her arm** une cicatrice court le long de son bras; **8** (move) [*sledge, vehicle*] glisser; [*curtain*] coulisser; **to ~ through sb's hands** [*rope*] filer entre les mains de qn; **a pain ran up my leg** une douleur m'est remontée le long de la jambe; **a wave of excitement ran through the crowd** un frisson d'excitation a parcouru la foule; **his eyes ran over the page** il a parcouru la page des yeux; **9** (operate regularly) circuler; **a ferry ~s between X and Y** il existe un ferry entre X et Y; **10** (flow) **my nose is ~ning** j'ai le nez qui coule; **tears ran down his face** les larmes coulaient sur son visage; **the streets will be ~ning with blood** FIG le sang coulera à flots dans les rues; **11** (flow when wet or melted) [*dye, garment*] déteindre; [*makeup, butter*] couler; **12** (as candidate) se présenter; **to ~ for** être candidat/-e au poste de [*mayor, governor*]; **to ~ for president** être candidat/-e à la présidence; **13** (be worded) **the telex ~s...** le télex se présente or est libellé comme suit...; **so the argument ~s** selon l'argument habituellement avancé; **14** (snag) filer.
IDIOMS **to give sb the ~ of sth** mettre qch à la disposition de qn; **in the long ~** à long terme; **in the short ~** à brève échéance.

■ **run about**, **run around**: **~ around** courir; **to ~ around**○ **with** voir○.

■ **run across**○: **~ across** [*sth/sb*] tomber sur○.

■ **run along** se sauver○, filer○.

■ **run at**: **~ at** [sth] **1** (charge towards) se précipiter sur; **2** (be at) atteindre, être de l'ordre de.

■ **run away**: ¶ **~ away 1** (flee) s'enfuir (**from sb** devant qn; **to do** pour faire); **to ~ away from home** s'enfuir de chez soi; **2** (run off) [*liquid*] couler; ¶ **~ away with** [sth/sb] **1** (flee) partir avec; **2** (carry off easily) rafler○; **3** (get into one's head) **to ~ away with the idea that** s'imaginer que.

■ **run down**: ¶ **~ down** [*battery*] se décharger; [*watch*] retarder; [*machine, company*] s'essouffler; ¶ **~ down** [sth/sb], **~** [sth/sb] **down 1** (in vehicle) renverser; **2** (allow to decline) réduire [*production, defences*]; user [*battery*]; **3** (disparage) dénigrer; **4** (track down) retrouver [*person*]; dénicher○ [*thing*].

■ **run in**: **~ in** [sth], **~** [sth] **in** roder [*car*]; **'~ning in'** 'en rodage'.

■ **run into**: **~ into** [sth/sb] **1** (collide with) heurter, rentrer dans○ [*car, wall*]; **2** (encounter) rencontrer [*person, difficulty*]; **to ~ into debt** s'endetter; **3** (amount to) se compter en [*hundreds, millions*].

■ **run off 1** (leave) partir en courant; **to ~ off with** partir avec; **2** [*liquid*] couler.

■ **run on**: ¶ **~ on** [*meeting*] se prolonger; ¶ **~ on** [sth] (be concerned with) [*mind*] être préoccupé par; [*conversation*] porter sur; ¶ **~ on** [sth], **~** [sth] **on 1** (in printing) faire suivre [qch] sans alinéa; **2** LITERAT faire enjamber [*line*].

■ **run out** ¶ **1** (become exhausted) [*supplies, oil*] s'épuiser; **time is ~ning out** le temps manque; **my patience is ~ning out** je suis en train de perdre patience; **2** (have no more) [*pen, machine*] être vide; **sorry, I've run out** désolé, je n'en ai plus; **3** (expire) expirer; ¶ **~ out of** ne plus avoir de [*petrol, time, money, ideas*]; **to be ~ning out of** n'avoir presque plus de [*petrol etc*].

■ **run out on**: **~ out on** [sb] abandonner.

■ **run over**: ¶ **~ over 1** [*meeting, programme*] se prolonger; **to ~ over by an hour** dépasser l'horaire prévu d'une heure; **2** (overflow) déborder; ¶ **~ over [sth]** (run through) passer [qch] en revue [*arrangements*]; ¶ **~ over [sth/sb]**, **~ [sth/sb] over 1** (injure) renverser; (kill) écraser; **2** (drive over) passer sur [*bump*]. ■ **run through**: ¶ **~ through [sth] 1** (be present in) se retrouver dans [*work*]; **2** (look through) parcourir [*list, article*]; (discuss) passer [qch] en revue; ¶ **~ through [sth]**, **~ [sth] through** répéter [*scene, speech*]; **to ~ sth through the computer** passer qch dans l'ordinateur. ■ **run to** FIG (extend to) **her tastes don't ~ to jazz** elle n'est pas très portée sur le jazz. ■ **run up**: **~ up [sth] 1** (accumulate) accumuler [*debt*]; **2** (make) fabriquer [*dress*]; **3** (raise) hisser [*flag*]. ■ **run up against**: **~ up against [sth]** se heurter à [*difficulty*].

runaround /ˈrʌnəraʊnd/ n **he's giving me/her the ~**○ il se défile○.

runaway /ˈrʌnəweɪ/ adj **1** (having left) [*teenager*] fugueur/-euse; [*slave*] fugitif/-ive; [*father*] en fuite; **2** (out of control) [*vehicle*] incontrôlé; [*horse*] emballé; [*inflation*] galopant; **3** (great) [*success, victory*] éclatant.

rundown /ˈrʌndaʊn/ n **1** (report) récapitulatif m (on de); **2** (of industry, factory) réduction f de l'activité.

run-down /ˌrʌnˈdaʊn/ adj **1** (exhausted) fatigué, à plat○; **2** (shabby) décrépit.

rung /rʌŋ/ I pp ▶ **ring**.
II n **1** (of ladder) barreau m; **2** (in hierarchy) échelon m.

run-in○ /ˈrʌnɪn/ n prise f de bec○.

runner /ˈrʌnə(r)/ n **1** (person, animal) coureur m; **2** (horse) partant/-e m/f; **3** (messenger) estafette f; **4** (for door, seat) glissière f; (for drawer) coulisseau m; (for curtain) chariot m; (on sled) patin m; **5** (in hall/on stairs) chemin m de couloir/d'escalier.
IDIOMS **to do a ~**○ (not pay) s'esquiver sans payer; (from home) déménager à la cloche de bois.

runner: **~ bean** n GB haricot m d'Espagne; **~ up** n (pl **~s up**) second/-e m/f (to après).

running /ˈrʌnɪŋ/ I n **1** (sport, exercise) course f à pied; **2** (management) direction f (of de).
II adj **1** (flowing) [*water*] courant; [*tap*] ouvert; [*knot*] coulant; **~ sore** LIT plaie f suppurante; FIG abcès m; **2 five days ~** cinq jours de suite.
IDIOMS **to be in/out of the ~** être/ne plus être dans la course (**for** pour); **to make the ~** LIT, FIG mener la course.

running: **~ battle** n éternel conflit m (**with** avec, **contre**); **~ board** n marchepied m; **~ commentary** n commentaire m ininterrompu; **~ costs** n (of scheme) dépenses fpl courantes; (of car) frais mpl d'entretien; **~ mate** n GEN co-candidat/-e m/f; (vice-presidential) candidat/-e m/f à la vice-présidence; **~ time** n durée f; **~ total** n total m cumulé; **~ track** n piste f.

runny /ˈrʌnɪ/ adj [*jam, sauce*] liquide; [*butter*] fondu; [*omelette*] baveux/-euse; [*boiled egg*] mollet; **to have a ~ nose** avoir le nez qui coule.

run: **~-of-the-mill** adj ordinaire, banal; **~proof** adj [*fabric*] indémaillable; [*makeup*] résistant à l'eau.

runt /rʌnt/ n **1** (of litter) le plus faible d'une portée; **2** PÉJ (weakling) avorton m PÉJ.

run-through /ˈrʌnθruː/ n (practice) répétition f; (summary) aperçu m.

run-up /ˈrʌnʌp/ n **1** SPORT course f d'élan; **to take a ~** prendre son élan pour sauter; **2** (preceding period) **the ~ to** la dernière ligne droite avant.

runway /ˈrʌnweɪ/ n AVIAT piste f d'aviation.

rupee /ruːˈpiː/ ▶ **849** n roupie f.

rupture /ˈrʌptʃə(r)/ I n **1** MED (hernia) hernie f; (of blood vessel, kidney) rupture f; **2** TECH (in tank, container) rupture f; **3** (in relations) rupture f (**between** entre).
II vtr **1** MED **to ~ oneself** se faire une hernie; **~d** éclaté; **2** rompre [*relations, unity*].
III vi **1** [*appendix*] se rompre; **2** [*container*] éclater.

rural /ˈrʊərəl/ adj (country) rural; (pastoral) champêtre.

ruse /ruːz/ n stratagème m.

rush /rʌʃ/ I n **1** (of crowd) ruée f (**to do** pour faire); **a ~ for the door** une ruée vers la porte; **to make a ~ for sth** [*crowd*] se ruer vers qch; [*individual*] se précipiter vers qch; **2** (hurry) **to be in a ~** être pressé (**to do** de faire); **there's no ~** ce n'est pas pressant; **in a ~** en vitesse; **it all happened in such a ~** tout s'est passé si vite; **what's the ~?** pourquoi faire vite?; **is there any ~?** y a-t-il urgence?; **3** (peak time) (during day) heure f de pointe; (during year) période f de pointe; **the morning ~** l'heure de pointe du matin; **beat the ~!** évitez la foule!; **4** (surge) (of liquid, adrenalin) montée f; (of air) bouffée f; (of emotion) vague f; (of complaints) flot m; **a ~ of blood to the head** FIG un coup de tête; **5** (plant) jonc m.
II **rushes** npl CIN rushes mpl, épreuves fpl de tournage.
III vtr **1** (transport urgently) **to ~ sth to** envoyer qch d'urgence à; **to be ~ed to the hospital** être emmené d'urgence à l'hôpital; **2** (do hastily) expédier [*task, speech*]; **don't try to ~ things** ne va pas trop vite; **3** (pressurize, hurry) presser, bousculer [*person*]; **4** (charge at) sauter sur [*person*]; prendre d'assaut [*building*]; **5** US UNIV essayer de devenir membre de [*sorority, fraternity*].
IV vi **1** [*person*] (make haste) se dépêcher (**to do** de faire); (rush forward) se précipiter (**to do** pour faire); **don't ~** ne te précipite pas; **to ~ out of the room** se précipiter hors de la pièce; **to ~ at** se précipiter sur; **to ~ down the stairs/past** descendre l'escalier/passer à toute vitesse; **to ~ along** marcher à toute vitesse; **2** (travel) **to ~ past** passer à toute vitesse; **to ~ along at 120 km/h** filer à 120 km/h; **the sound of ~ing water** le bruit de l'eau jaillissante.
■ **rush into**: ¶ **~ into [sth]** se lancer dans [*commitment, purchase, sale*]; **to ~ into marriage** se marier précipitamment; ¶ **~ [sb] into doing** pousser [qn] à faire; **don't be ~ed into it** ne te laisse pas bousculer.
■ **rush out**: ¶ **~ out** sortir en vitesse; ¶ **~ out [sth]**, **~ [sth] out** sortir or publier [qch] en vitesse.
■ **rush through**: ¶ **~ through [sth]** expédier [*task*]; parcourir [qch] en vitesse [*book*]; ¶ **~ [sth] through**, **~ through [sth]** adopter en vitesse [*legislation*]; traiter en priorité [*order, application*]; ¶ **~ [sth] through to** envoyer [qch] d'urgence à.

rushed /rʌʃt/ adj [*attempt, letter*] expédié.

rush: **~ hour** n heures fpl de pointe; **~ job**○ n travail m urgent, urgence f.

rusk /rʌsk/ n biscuit m pour bébés.

russet /ˈrʌsɪt/ I n **1** (colour) brun m roux; **2** (apple) canada f inv.
II adj roussâtre.

Russia /ˈrʌʃə/ ▶ **840** pr n Russie f.

Russian /ˈrʌʃn/ ▶ **1100**, **1038** I n **1** (person) Russe mf; **2** (language) russe m.
II adj russe; **~ class** cours m de russe.

Russian: **~ Federation** n Fédération f de Russie; **~ roulette** n roulette f russe; **~-speaking** adj russophone.

rust /rʌst/ I n AGRIC, CHEM rouille f.
II vtr LIT rouiller; **~ed** rouillé; **to become ~ed** se rouiller.
III vi LIT se rouiller; FIG [*skill*] s'altérer.

rustic /ˈrʌstɪk/ I n campagnard/-e m/f; PÉJ rustaud/-e m/f.
II adj [*furniture*] rustique; [*charm*] champêtre; [*accent*] rustique.

rustle /ˈrʌsl/ I n (of paper, dry leaves) froissement m; (of leaves, silk) bruissement m.
II vtr froisser [*papers etc*]; **stop rustling your newspaper!** arrête de faire du bruit avec ton journal!
■ **rustle up**: **~ up [sth]** préparer [qch] en vitesse.

rustler /ˈrʌslə(r)/ n US voleur/-euse m/f de bétail ou de chevaux.

rustling /ˈrʌslɪŋ/ n ▶ **rustle** I.

rust-proof /ˈrʌstpruːf/ adj [*material*] inoxydable; [*paint, coating*] antirouille.

rusty /'rʌstɪ/ *adj* LIT, FIG rouillé.

rut /rʌt/ *n* **1** (in ground) ornière *f*; **2** (routine) **to get into/be in a ~** s'enliser/être enlisé dans la routine; **3** ZOOL (mating) **the ~** le rut.

ruthless /'ru:θlɪs/ *adj* impitoyable (**in** dans).

ruthlessly /'ru:θlɪslɪ/ *adv* impitoyablement.

rutting /'rʌtɪŋ/ *n* rut *m*; **~ season** saison du rut.

RV *n* US AUT (*abrév* = **recreational vehicle**) camping-car *m*, auto-caravane *f*.

Rwanda /rʊ'ændə/ ▶ **840**| *pr n* Rwanda *m*.

Rx US *n* MED *symbole signifiant 'ordonnance'*.

rye /raɪ/ *n* **1** (cereal) seigle *m*; **2** US (also **~ whiskey**) whisky *m* à base de seigle.

rye: **~ bread** *n* pain *m* de seigle; **~ grass** *n* ivraie *f* vivace.

Ss

s, S /es/ n **1** (letter) s, S m; **2** S abrév écrite = **South**; **3** S (abrév écrite = **Saint**) St/Ste; **4** abrév écrite = **small**.

SA n **1** abrév écrite = **South Africa**; **2** abrév écrite = **South America**.

sabbath /'sæbəθ/ n (also **Sabbath**) (Jewish) sabbat m; (Christian) jour m du seigneur.

sabbatical /sə'bætɪkl/ **I** n congé m sabbatique; **on ~** en congé sabbatique.
II adj [leave, year] sabbatique.

saber n US = **sabre**.

sable /'seɪbl/ **I** n (fur, animal) zibeline f.
II noun modifier [hat, garment] en zibeline; **~ coat/ stole** zibeline f.

sabotage /'sæbətɑːʒ/ **I** n sabotage m.
II vtr saboter [equipment, campaign, discussion].

saboteur /ˌsæbə'tɜː(r)/ n saboteur/-euse m/f.

sabre, saber US /'seɪbə(r)/ n sabre m; **~ rattling** rodomontade f.

sac /sæk/ n **1** ANAT, BOT sac m; **2** ZOOL poche f.

saccharin /'sækərɪn/ n saccharine f.

saccharine /'sækəriːn/ adj PÉJ **1** [sentimentality, novel] à l'eau de rose; [smile] mielleux/-euse f; **2** [drink, food] trop sucré.

sachet /'sæʃeɪ, US sæ'ʃeɪ/ n sachet m.

sack /sæk/ **I** n **1** (bag) sac m; **potato ~** sac à pommes de terre; **mail ~** sac postal; **2**° (dismissal) **to get the ~** se faire mettre à la porte°; **to give sb the ~** mettre qn à la porte°; **to be threatened with the ~** être menacé de renvoi; **3**° (bed) **to hit the ~**° se coucher; **4** (pillage) sac m.
II vtr **1**° (dismiss) mettre [qn] à la porte°; **2** (pillage) mettre [qch] à sac.

sackcloth /'sækklɒθ/ n toile f à sac.
IDIOMS **to wear ~ and ashes** faire son mea culpa.

sackful /'sækfʊl/, **sackload** /'sækləʊd/ n sac m.

sacking /'sækɪŋ/ n **1** (canvas) toile f à sac; **2**° (dismissal) licenciement m.

sacrament /'sækrəmənt/ n (religious ceremony) sacrement m.

Sacrament /'sækrəmənt/ n (Communion bread) Saint sacrement m; **to receive the ~(s)** communier.

sacred /'seɪkrɪd/ **I** the **~** le sacré.
II adj **1** (holy) sacré (**to** pour); **to hold sth ~** tenir qch pour sacré; **2** (revered) [name] sacré; [tradition] sacro-saint; **is nothing ~?** HUM il n'y a rien de sacré?; **3** (binding) [duty] sacré; [trust] inviolable.

sacred cow n FIG vache f sacrée.

sacrifice /'sækrɪfaɪs/ **I** n sacrifice m (**to** à; **of** de).
II vtr **1** FIG sacrifier (**to** à); **principles ~d on the altar of profit** les principes immolés sur l'autel du profit; **2** RELIG offrir [qch] en sacrifice (**to** à).
III v refl **to ~ oneself** se sacrifier (**for** pour).

sacrificial /ˌsækrɪ'fɪʃl/ adj [victim] offert en sacrifice; FIG **to be the ~ lamb** être sacrifié.

sacrilege /'sækrɪlɪdʒ/ n RELIG, FIG, HUM sacrilège m.

sacrilegious /ˌsækrɪ'lɪdʒəs/ adj sacrilège.

sacristy /'sækrɪstɪ/ n sacristie f.

sacrosanct /'sækrəʊsæŋkt/ adj sacro-saint.

sad /sæd/ adj **1** (unhappy) triste; **to be ~ to do** [person] être triste de faire; **it makes me ~ cela me rend triste; **to be ~ that** [person] être triste que (+ subj); **we are ~ about** ou **at the accident** l'accident nous attriste; **it's ~ that** c'est triste que (+ subj);

was a **~ sight** c'était triste à voir; **2** (unfortunate) [fact, duty, truth] triste (before n); **~ to say,...** c'est malheureux à dire, mais...; **3** (deplorable) [attitude, situation] navrant; **it's a ~ state of affairs when one can't/one has to**... c'est lamentable de ne pas pouvoir/d'avoir à...; **it's a ~ day for democracy** c'est un sombre jour pour la démocratie.
IDIOMS **to be a ~der but wiser person** avoir reçu une leçon dure mais profitable.

sadden /'sædn/ **I** vtr attrister; **it ~s me that** cela m'attriste que (+ subj).
II saddened pp adj attristé; (stronger) affligé.

saddle /'sædl/ **I** n **1** (on horse, bike) selle f; **to climb into the ~** se mettre en selle; **2** GB CULIN **~ of lamb/venison** selle f d'agneau/de chevreuil; **~ of hare** râble m de lièvre; **3** GEOG (ridge) col m.
II vtr **1** seller [horse]; **2** (impose) **to ~ sb with sth** mettre qch sur les bras de qn [responsibility, task].
III v refl **to ~ oneself with sth** se mettre qch sur les bras.
▪ **saddle up: ~ up** seller son cheval.

saddle bag n sacoche f.

saddler /'sædlə(r)/ **▶ 1251** | n sellier m, bourrelier m.

saddlery /'sædlərɪ/ n sellerie f.

sadism /'seɪdɪzəm/ n sadisme m.

sadist /'seɪdɪst/ n sadique mf.

sadistic /sə'dɪstɪk/ adj sadique.

sadly /'sædlɪ/ adv **1** (with sadness) tristement; **he will be ~ missed** il nous manquera beaucoup; **2** (unfortunately) malheureusement; **3** (emphatic) **he is ~ lacking in sense** le bon sens lui fait cruellement défaut; **you are ~ mistaken** vous vous trompez fortement.

sadness /'sædnɪs/ n tristesse f.

sae n: abrév ▶ **stamped addressed envelope**.

safari /sə'fɑːrɪ/ n safari m; **to go on ~** aller faire un safari.

safari: **~ hat** n casque m colonial; **~ jacket** n saharienne f; **~ park** n parc m (zoologique) (où les animaux vivent en semi-liberté).

safe /seɪf/ **I** n coffre-fort m.
II adj **1** (after ordeal, risk) [person] sain et sauf; [object] intact; **we know they are ~** nous les savons hors de danger; **to hope for sb's ~ return** espérer que qn reviendra sans encombre; **~ and sound** sain et sauf; **2** (free from threat, harm) **to be ~** [person] être en sécurité; [document, valuables] être en lieu sûr; [company, job, reputation] ne pas être menacé; **to feel ~** se sentir en sécurité; **is the bike ~ here?** est-ce qu'on peut laisser le vélo ici sans risque?; **he's ~ in bed** il dort tranquillement dans son lit; **have a ~ journey!** bon voyage!; **to keep sb ~** protéger qn (**from** contre, de); **to keep sth ~** (protect) mettre qch à l'abri (**from** de); (store) garder qch en lieu sûr; **to be ~ from** être à l'abri de [attack, curiosity]; **to be ~ with sb** ne rien risquer avec qn; **3** (risk-free) [product, toy, level, method] sans danger; [place, environment, vehicle, route] sûr; [structure, building] solide; [animal] inoffensif/-ive; [speed] raisonnable; **the ~st way to do is** façon la plus sûre de faire; **to watch from a ~ distance** observer à distance respectueuse; **let's go—it's ~** allons-y—il n'y a plus de danger; **it's not ~** c'est dangereux; **to be ~ for sb** être sans danger pour qn; **the toy/park is not ~ for children** le jouet/ parc est dangereux pour les enfants; **it is ~ to swim there** on peut s'y baigner sans danger; **it is not ~ to do** il est dangereux de faire; **that car is not ~ to**

drive cette voiture est dangereuse; **to make sth ~** rendre [qch] (plus) sûr [*premises, beach*]; rendre [qch] inoffensif-ive [*bomb*]; **4** (prudent) [*investment*] sûr; [*estimate, choice*] prudent; [*topic*] anodin; **the ~st thing to do would be to leave** le plus sûr serait de partir; **it would be ~r not to do** il vaudrait mieux ne pas faire; **it is ~ to say that** on peut dire à coup sûr que; **it's ~ to assume that** on peut raisonnablement penser que; **5** (reliable) [*driver*] prudent; **to be in ~ hands** être en bonnes mains.
IDIOMS **as ~ as houses** GB (secure) [*person*] en sécurité; [*place*] sûr; (risk-free) sans risque; **better ~ than sorry!** mieux vaut prévenir que guérir!; **just to be on the ~ side** simplement par précaution; **to play (it) ~** être prudent.

safe bet *n* **it's a ~** c'est quelque chose de sûr; **it's a ~ that** il est certain que.

safe-breaker *n* perceur *m* de coffres-forts.

safe-conduct /ˌseɪfˈkɒndʌkt/ *n* **1** (guarantee) laissez-passer *m inv* (**to** pour); **2** (document) sauf-conduit *m*.

safe-deposit box *n* coffre *m* (à la banque).

safeguard /'seɪfɡɑːd/ I *n* garantie *f*.
II *vtr* protéger (**against, from** contre).

safe house *n* refuge *m*.

safekeeping /ˌseɪfˈkiːpɪŋ/ *n* **to give sth to sb for ~** confier qch à la garde de qn.

safely /'seɪflɪ/ *adv* **1** (unharmed) [*come back*] (of person) sans encombre; (of parcel, goods) sans dommage; (of plane) [*land, take off*] sans problème; **I arrived ~** je suis bien arrivé; **you can walk around quite ~** vous pouvez vous promener en toute sécurité; **2** (without worry or risk) [*leave, do, go*] en toute tranquillité; [*assume, say*] avec certitude; **3** (causing no concern) [*locked, hidden*] bien; **to be ~ tucked up in bed** être bien bordé dans son lit; **he's ~ behind bars** heureusement il est sous les verrous; **4** (carefully) prudemment.

safeness /'seɪfnɪs/ *n* (of structure) solidité *f*; (of method, product) sécurité *f*; (of investment) sûreté *f*.

safe: ~ passage *n* laissez-passer *m inv* (**to** pour; **for sb** pour qn); **~ seat** *n* POL siège *m* assuré; **~ sex** *n* rapports *mpl* sexuels sans risque.

safety /'seɪftɪ/ I *n* sécurité *f*; **there are fears for her ~** on est inquiet sur son sort; **in ~** en (toute) sécurité; **to help sb to ~** aider qn à se mettre à l'abri; **to flee to ~** (in building, place) courir se mettre à l'abri; (abroad) se réfugier à l'étranger; **to reach ~** parvenir en lieu sûr; **in the ~ of one's home** chez soi en sécurité; **road ~** sécurité routière; **~ in the home** la sécurité domestique.
II *noun modifier* [*check, code, level, limit, measure, regulations, test*] de sécurité; [*bolt, blade, strap*] de sûreté.
IDIOMS **there's ~ in numbers** plus on est nombreux, moins on court de risques.

safety: ~ belt *n* ceinture *f* de sécurité; **~ catch** *n* cran *m* de sûreté; **~ curtain** *n* rideau *m* de fer; **~ glass** *n* verre *m* de sécurité; **~ helmet** *n* casque *m* de protection; **~ match** *n* allumette *f* de sûreté; **~ net** *n* LIT filet *m* (de protection); FIG filet *m* de sécurité; **~ pin** *n* épingle *f* de sûreté.

saffron /'sæfrən/ I *n* safran *m*; **~ rice** riz au safran.
II ▶818 *adj* (also **~ yellow**) safran *inv*.

sag /sæɡ/ *vi* (*p prés etc* **-gg-**) **1** [*beam, mattress*] s'affaisser; [*tent, rope*] ne pas être bien tendu; **2** [*flesh*] être flasque; **3** (weaken) **her spirits ~ged** elle a perdu courage; **4** (fall) [*currency*] baisser.

saga /'sɑːɡə/ *n* **1**○ (lengthy story) histoire *f*; **2** LITERAT saga *f*.

sagacious /səˈɡeɪʃəs/ *adj* SOUT [*person*] sagace.

sagacity /səˈɡæsətɪ/, **sagaciousness** /səˈɡeɪʃəsnɪs/ *n* sagacité *f*.

sage /seɪdʒ/ I *n* **1** BOT sauge *f*; **2** (wise person) sage *m*.
II *adj* (wise) avisé; **to give ~ advice** donner de sages conseils.

sage green ▶818 *n, adj* vert (*m*) cendré *inv*.

sagely /'seɪdʒlɪ/ *adv* [*reply, nod*] avec sagesse.

sagging /'sæɡɪŋ/ *adj* **1** [*beam*] affaissé; [*cable*] mal tendu; [*flesh*] flasque; **2** [*spirits*] défaillant.

Sagittarius /ˌsædʒɪˈteərɪəs/ ▶1418 *n* Sagittaire *m*.

sago /'seɪɡəʊ/ *n* sagou *m*; **~ pudding** bouillie *f* de sagou au lait.

Sahara /səˈhɑːrə/ *pr n* Sahara *m*; **the ~ desert** le désert du Sahara.

said /sed/ I *prét, pp* ▶ **say**.
II *pp adj* dit; **the ~ Mr X** le dit M. X; **on the ~ day** le jour dit.

sail /seɪl/ I *n* **1** (on boat) voile *f*; **2** (navigation) **to set ~** prendre la mer; **to set ~ from/for** partir en bateau de/pour; **to be under ~** être en mer; **a ship in full ~** un navire toutes voiles dehors; **3** (on windmill) aile *f*; **4** (journey) **to go for a ~** faire un tour en bateau.
II *vtr* **1** (be in charge of) piloter [*ship*]; (steer) manœuvrer [*ship*]; **2** (travel across) traverser [qch] en bateau [*ocean, channel*]; **3** (own) avoir [*yacht*].
III *vi* **1** (travel) voyager en bateau; **to ~ around the world** faire le tour du monde en bateau; **2** (move across water) [*ship*] **to ~ across** traverser [*ocean*]; **to ~ into** entrer dans [*port*]; **3** (set sail) prendre la mer; **the boat ~s at 10 am** le bateau part à 10 h; **4** (as hobby) faire de la voile; **to go ~ing** faire de la voile; **5** (move smoothly) **to ~ past sb** [*person*] passer près de qn sans même le/la remarquer; **the ball ~ed over the fence** la balle est passée par-dessus la barrière.
IDIOMS **to ~ close to the wind** jouer avec le feu; **to take the wind out of sb's ~s** rabattre le caquet à qn.
■ **sail through**: **~ through** [sth] gagner [qch] facilement [*match*]; **to ~ through an exam** réussir un examen les doigts dans le nez○.

sail: ~board *n* planche *f* à voile; **~boarder** *n* véliplanchiste *mf*; **~boarding** *n* planche *f* à voile; **~boat** *n* voilier *m*.

sailing /'seɪlɪŋ/ ▶949 I *n* **1** (sport) voile *f*; **2** (departure) **the next ~** le prochain bateau; **three ~s a day** trois bateaux par jour.
II *noun modifier* [*club, holiday, instructor*] de voile; [*boat*] à voiles; [*time, date*] de départ du bateau.

sailing ship /'seɪlɪŋ/ *n* voilier *m*.

sailor /'seɪlə(r)/ *n* ▶1192 (seaman) marin *m*; **to be a good/bad ~** avoir/ne pas avoir le pied marin.

sailor suit *n* costume *m* marin.

sailplane /'seɪlpleɪn/ *n* planeur *m*.

saint /seɪnt, snt/ *n* RELIG, FIG saint-e *m/f*.

sainthood /'seɪnthʊd/ *n* sainteté *f*.

saintly /'seɪntlɪ/ *adj* [*person*] plein de bonté.

saint's day *n* fête *f*.

sake /seɪk/ *n* **1** (purpose) **for the ~ of principle** pour le principe; **for the ~ of clarity, for clarity's ~** pour la clarté; **for the ~ of argument** à titre d'exemple; **to kill for the ~ of killing** tuer pour le plaisir de tuer; **to do sth for its own ~** faire qch pour le plaisir; **for old times' ~** en souvenir du bon vieux temps; **2** (benefit) **for the ~ of sb, for sb's ~** par égard pour qn; **for all our ~s** dans notre intérêt à tous; **I'm telling you this for your own ~** c'est pour ton bien que je te dis cela; **3** (in anger, in plea) **for God's/heaven's ~!** pour l'amour de Dieu/du ciel!

salacious /səˈleɪʃəs/ *adj* salace.

salad /'sæləd/ *n* salade *f*; **bean/ham ~** salade de haricots/au jambon; **mixed ~** salade composée.

salad: ~ bar *n* buffet *m* de crudités; **~ bowl** *n* saladier *m*; **~ cream** *n* GB ≈ sauce *f* mayonnaise; **~ days** *npl* LITTÉR années *fpl* de jeunesse; **~ dressing** *n* sauce *f* pour salade; **~ oil** *n* huile *f* de table; **~ servers** *npl* couverts *mpl* à salade; **~ spinner** *n* essoreuse *f* à salade.

salami /səˈlɑːmɪ/ *n* saucisson *m* sec.

salaried /'sælərɪd/ *adj* salarié.

salary /'sælərɪ/ *n* salaire *m*.

sale /seɪl/ I *n* **1** (selling) vente *f*; **for ~** à vendre; **to put sth up for ~** mettre qch en vente; **on ~** GB en vente; US en solde; **to go on ~** GB être mis en vente; US être mis en solde; **I'll take them on a ~ or**

return basis je les prends sous condition de reprise des invendus; **2** (event) (in shop) solde *f*; (auction) vente *f*; **book** ~ vente de livres; **in the** ~(**s**) GB, on ~ US en solde; **to have a** ~ solder; **3** (by salesman) vente *f*; **to make a** ~ réaliser une vente.
  II sales *npl* **1** (amount sold) ventes *fpl*; **2** (career) commerce *m*; **3** (department) service *m* des ventes; **4** (event) **the** ~**s** les soldes *fpl*; **the** ~**s are on** c'est la saison des soldes; **the summer** ~**s** les soldes estivales.

saleable /'seɪləbl/ *adj* vendable, demandé.

sale: ~ **item** *n* article *m* soldé; ~ **of work** *n* vente *f* de charité; ~ **price** *n* prix *m* soldé; ~**room** *n* hôtel *m* des ventes; ~**s assistant** ▶1251 *n* GB vendeur/-euse *m/f*; ~**sclerk** ▶1251 *n* US vendeur/ -euse *m/f*; ~**s director** ▶1251 *n* directeur/-trice *m/ f* commercial/-e; ~**s executive** ▶1251 *n* cadre *m* commercial; ~**s figures** *npl* chiffre *m* de ventes, chiffre *m* d'affaires; ~**s force** *n* force *f* de vente; ~**sgirl** ▶1251 *n* vendeuse *f*.

salesman /'seɪlzmən/ ▶1251 *n* (*pl* -**men**) **1** (representative) représentant *m*; **insurance** ~ représentant d'assurances; **2** (in shop, showroom) vendeur *m*; **used car** ~ revendeur *m* de voitures d'occasion.

sale: ~**s manager** *n* = **sales director**; ~**s office** *n* bureau *m* des ventes; ~**sperson** ▶1251 *n* vendeur/-euse *m/f*; ~**s pitch** *n* baratin○ *m* publicitaire; ~**s rep, sales representative** ▶1251 *n* représentant/-e *m/f*; ~**s staff** *n* commerciaux *mpl*, équipe *f* commerciale; ~**s tax** *n* US taxe *f* à l'achat; ~**swoman** ▶1251 *n* (representative) représentante *f*; (in shop) vendeuse *f*.

salient /'seɪlɪənt/ *adj* saillant; (principal) essentiel/-ielle.

saline /'seɪlaɪn/ **I** *n* MED (also ~ **solution**) sérum *m* physiologique; ~ **drip** perfusion *f* de sérum physiologique.
  II *adj* [*liquid, spring*] salé; [*deposit*] salin.

saliva /sə'laɪvə/ *n* salive *f*.

salivate /'sælɪveɪt/ *vi* saliver.

sallow /'sæləʊ/ *adj* (pale) cireux/-euse.

sally /'sælɪ/ *n* **1**† MIL sortie *f*; **2** (witty remark) trait *m* d'esprit, saillie *f*.
  ■ **sally forth** se mettre en route avec entrain.

salmon /'sæmən/ **I** *n* saumon *m*.
  II *noun modifier* [*fillet, pâté*] de saumon; [*fishing, sandwich*] au saumon.

salmonella /,sælmə'nelə/ ▶1002 *n* (*pl* -**æ** ou -**as**) BIOL salmonelle *f*.

salmon: ~ **pink** ▶818 *n, adj* rose (*m*) saumon *inv*; ~ **steak** *n* darne *f* de saumon; ~ **trout** *n* truite *f* saumonée.

salon /'sælɒn, US sə'lɒn/ *n* salon *m*; **hairdressing/ beauty** ~ salon de coiffure/de beauté.

saloon /sə'lu:n/ **I** *n* **1** (also ~ **car**) GB AUT berline *f*; **2** GB (also ~ **bar**) salle *f* confortable (*d'un pub*); US (in Wild West) saloon *m*, bar *m* (*du Far West américain*); **3** (on boat) salon *m*.

salsify /'sælsɪfɪ/ *n* salsifis *m*.

salt /sɒlt/ **I** *n* **1** CHEM, CULIN sel *m*; **there's too much** ~ **in the rice** le riz est trop salé; **to put** ~ **on** saler; **2**○ †(sailor) **an old** ~ un vieux loup de mer.
  II *noun modifier* [*crystal, solution*] de sel; [*industry, refining*] du sel; [*water, lake*] salé; [*beef, pork*] salé.
  III *vtr* saler [*meat, fish, road, path*].
  IDIOMS **to be the** ~ **of the earth** être le sel de la terre; **you should take his remarks with a grain** ou **a pinch of** ~ il ne faut pas prendre ses remarques pour argent comptant; **any teacher worth his** ~ **knows that** tout enseignant digne de ce nom sait cela.
  ■ **salt away:** ~ **away** [**sth**], ~ [**sth**] **away** mettre [qch] de côté.

salt: ~**cellar** *n* salière *f*; ~ **flat** *n* marais *m* salant.

saltiness /'sɔːltɪnɪs/ *n* **1** (taste) (of food) goût *m* salé; **2** (salt content) (of solution, water) teneur *f* en sel.

salt: ~ **marsh** *n* salin *m*; ~**mine** *n* mine *f* de sel;

~**pan** *n* puits *m* de sel; ~**shaker** *n* salière *f*; ~**water** *adj* [*fish*] de mer; [*mammal*] marin.

salty /'sɔːltɪ/ *adj* [*water, food, flavour*] salé.

salubrious /sə'lu:brɪəs/ *adj* LIT salubre; FIG [*neighbourhood*] tout à fait respectable.

salutary /'sæljʊtrɪ, US -terɪ/ *adj* salutaire.

salutation /,sælju:'teɪʃn/ *n* (greeting) salutation *f*; (in letter) forme *f* d'adresse.

salute /sə'lu:t/ **I** *n* **1** MIL, GEN (greeting) salut *m*; **to give a** ~ faire un salut; **to take the** ~ assister au défilé des troupes; **victory** ~ V *m* de la victoire; **2** (firing of guns) salve *f*; **a 21-gun** ~ une salve de 21 coups de canon; **3** (tribute) hommage *m* (**to** à).
  II *vtr, vi* (all contexts) saluer.

salvage /'sælvɪdʒ/ **I** *n* **1** (rescue) sauvetage *m* (**of** de); **2** (reward) prime *f* de sauvetage.
  II *noun modifier* [*operation, team*] de sauvetage.
  III *vtr* **1** (rescue) sauver [*cargo, belongings*] (**from** de); effectuer le sauvetage de [*ship*]; **2** FIG sauver [*plan, marriage, reputation*]; sauver [*game*]; préserver [*pride*]; **3** (save for recycling) récupérer.

salvation /sæl'veɪʃn/ *n* salut *m*.

Salvation Army *n* Armée *f* du Salut.

salve /sælv, US sæv/ **I** *n* LIT, FIG (balm) baume *m*.
  II *vtr* **to** ~ **one's conscience** soulager sa conscience.

salver /'sælvə(r)/ *n* plateau *m* (à boissons).

salvo /'sælvəʊ/ *n* (*pl* -**os** ou -**oes**) MIL FIG salve *f*.

same /seɪm/ **I** *adj* **1** (identical) même; **to be the** ~ être le or la même; **the result was the** ~ le résultat était le même; **people are the** ~ **everywhere** les gens sont partout les mêmes; **it's the** ~ **everywhere** c'est partout la même chose; **it is the** ~ **with** il en est de même pour; **to look the** ~ être pareil; **to be the** ~ **as sth** être comme qch; **it's as riding a bike** c'est comme de faire du vélo; **one wine is the** ~ **as another to him** pour lui un vin en vaut un autre; **the** ~ **time last week** la semaine dernière à la même heure; **the** ~ **time last year** l'année dernière à la même époque; ~ **time** ~ **place** même heure même endroit; **in the** ~ **way** (in a similar manner) de la même manière (**as** que); (likewise) de même; **to feel the** ~ **way about** avoir les mêmes sentiments à l'égard de; **to think the** ~ **way on** ou **about sth** être du même avis sur qch; **to go the** ~ **way as** LIT aller dans la même direction que; FIG connaître le même sort que; **the** ~ **thing** la même chose; **it's the** ~ **thing** c'est pareil; **it amounts** ou **comes to the** ~ **thing** cela revient au même; **it's all the** ~ **to me** ça m'est complètement égal; **if it's all the** ~ **to you** si ça ne te fait rien; **2** (for emphasis) (very) même (**as** que); **the** ~ **one** le/la même; '**ready the** ~ **day**' 'prêt dans la journée'; **that** ~ **week** la même semaine; **later that** ~ **day** plus tard dans la journée; **at the** ~ **time** en même temps; **they are one and the** ~ (**person**) il s'agit d'une seule et même personne; **the very** ~ exactement le or la même; **the very** ~ **day that** le jour même où; **3** (unchanged) même; **she's not the** ~ **woman** ce n'est plus la même femme; **to be still the** ~ être toujours le/la même; **things are just the** ~ **as ever** rien n'a changé; **it's/he's the** ~ **as ever** c'est/il est toujours pareil; **my views are the** ~ **as they always were** mes opinions n'ont pas changé; **she's much the** ~ elle n'a pas beaucoup changé; **to remain** ou **stay the** ~ ne pas changer; **things were never the** ~ **again** rien n'était plus comme avant; **it's not the** ~ **without you** ce n'est pas pareil sans toi; **the** ~ **old excuse** toujours la vieille excuse.
  II the same *adv phr* de la même façon; **to feel the** ~ **as sb** penser comme qn; **to feel the** ~ **about** avoir les mêmes sentiments à l'égard de; **life goes on just the** ~ la vie continue (comme d'habitude).
  III the same *pron* **1** (the identical thing) la même chose (**as** que); **I'll have the** ~ je prendrai la même chose; **the** ~ **applies to** ou **goes for** il en va de même pour; **to say the** ~ **about** en dire autant de; **to do the** ~ **as sb** faire comme qn; **we're hoping to do the** ~ **on**

espère en faire autant; **I would do the ~ for you** j'en ferais autant pour toi; **I 'd do the ~ again** je recommencerais; **the ~ to you!** (in greeting) à toi aussi, à toi de même!; (of insult) et toi-même⚬!; **(the) ~ again please!** la même chose s'il vous plaît!; **it'll be more of the ~!** PÉJ c'est reparti pour un tour!; **2** JUR celui-ci/celle-ci *m*/*f*.

IDIOMS **all the ~..., just the ~,...** tout de même,...; **thanks all the ~** merci quand même.

same-day /ˌseɪm'deɪ/ *adj* [*processing, service*] effectué dans la journée.

sameness /'seɪmnɪs/ *n* PÉJ monotonie *f*.

Samoa /sə'məʊə/ ▸ **840** *pr n* Samoa *m*.

sample /'sɑ:mpl, US 'sæmpl/ **I** *n* **1** (of product, fabric, rock etc) échantillon *m*; **to take a soil ~** prélever un échantillon de sol; **2** MED, BIOL (of individual for analysis) prélèvement *m*; (one of many kept in lab) échantillon *m*; **to take a blood ~** faire une prise de sang; **3** ECOL, BIOL (of water etc) prélèvement *m*; **4** (of public, population) panel *m*, échantillon *m*.
II *noun modifier* **1** COMM [*cassette, video*] de promotion; **~ bottle/packet** échantillon *m*; **2** (representative) [*question*] type; **~ prices** prix *mpl* donnés à titre d'exemple.
III *vtr* **1** goûter (à) [*food, wine*]; **to ~ the delights of Paris** goûter aux plaisirs de Paris; **2** (test) essayer [*products*]; sonder [*opinion, market*].

sampling /'sɑ:mplɪŋ, US 'sæmpl-/ *n* **1** (taking of specimens) prélèvement *m*, échantillonnage *m*; **2** (of population group) échantillonnage *m*.

sanatorium /ˌsænə'tɔ:rɪəm/ *n* (*pl* **~ s** ou **-ria**) GB (clinic) sanatorium *m*; (in school) infirmerie *f*.

sanctify /'sæŋktɪfaɪ/ *vtr* sanctifier.

sanctimonious /ˌsæŋktɪ'məʊnɪəs/ *adj* PÉJ supérieur.

sanction /'sæŋkʃn/ **I** *n* **1** (authorization) autorisation *f*; (approval) sanction *f*; **2** (deterrent) **legal ~, criminal ~** sanction *f* pénale; **3** POL, ECON sanction *f*.
II **sanctions** *npl* sanctions *fpl*; **trade ~s** sanctions économiques/commerciales; **to impose ~s** prendre des sanctions; **to break ~s against a country** violer l'embargo contre un pays.
III *vtr* (permit) autoriser; (approve) sanctionner.

sanctity /'sæŋktətɪ/ *n* **1** (of life, law) inviolabilité *f*; **2** RELIG sainteté *f*.

sanctuary /'sæŋktʃʊərɪ, US -erɪ/ *n* **1** (safe place) refuge *m*; **a place of ~** un refuge; **to seek ~** chercher asile; **2** (holy place) sanctuaire *m*; **3** (for wildlife) réserve *f*; (for mistreated pets) refuge *m*.

sanctum /'sæŋktəm/ *n* (*pl* **-tums** ou **-ta**) **1** (private place) refuge *m*; **2** RELIG **the (inner) ~** (in temple) le Saint des Saints; (holy place) le sanctuaire.

sand /sænd/ **I** *n* sable *m*.
II **sands** *npl* **1** (beach) plage *f*; **2** (desert) sables *mpl*.
III *vtr* **1** (also **~ down**) (smooth) poncer [*floor*]; frotter ou passer [qch] au papier de verre [*woodwork*]; **2** (put sand on) sabler [*icy road*].
IDIOMS **to stick** ou **bury one's head in the ~** pratiquer la politique de l'autruche.

sandal /'sændl/ *n* sandale *f*.

sandalwood /'sændlwʊd/ *n* santal *m*.

sandbag /'sændbæg/ **I** *n* sac *m* de sable.
II *vtr* (*p prés etc* **-gg-**) (against gunfire) renforcer [qch] avec des sacs de sable [*position*].

sand: ~bank *n* banc *m* de sable; **~blast** *vtr* décaper [qch] à la sableuse.

sandboy /'sænd,bɔɪ/ *n*: IDIOMS **as happy as a ~** gai comme un pinson.

sand: ~ castle *n* château *m* de sable; **~ dune** *n* dune *f*.

sander /'sændə(r)/ *n* ponceuse *f*.

sand: ~lot *n* US terrain *m* vague (*où les enfants jouent*); **~man** *n* marchand *m* de sable.

sandpaper /'sændpeɪpə(r)/ **I** *n* papier *m* de verre.
II *vtr* poncer [*plaster, wood*]; polir [*glass, metal*].

sandpit /'sændpɪt/ *n* (for children) bac *m* à sable.

sandstone /'sændstəʊn/ *n* grès *m*; **white/red ~** grès blanc/rose.

sandstorm *n* tempête *f* de sable.

sandwich /'sænwɪdʒ, US -wɪtʃ/ **I** *n* **1** sandwich *m*; **cucumber ~** sandwich au concombre; **2** GB (cake) génoise *f* (*fourrée*).
II *vtr* **to be ~ed between** [*car, building, person*] être pris en sandwich entre, être coincé entre.

sandwich: ~ bar *n* sandwich bar *m*; **~ course** *n* GB cours *m* avec stage pratique; **~ loaf** *n* pain *m* en tranches; **~ man** ▸ **1251** *n* homme-sandwich *m*.

sandy /'sændɪ/ *adj* **1** [*beach*] de sable; [*path, soil*] sablonneux/-euse; [*sediment*] sableux/-euse; **2** (yellow) [*hair*] blond roux *inv*; [*colour*] sable *inv* (*after n*).

sane /seɪn/ *adj* **1** (not mad) [*person*] sain d'esprit; **it's the only thing that keeps me ~** c'est la seule chose qui m'empêche de devenir fou; **2** (reasonable) [*policy, judgment*] sensé.

sang /sæŋ/ *prét* ▸ **sing**.

sanguine /'sæŋgwɪn/ *adj* optimiste; **to take a ~ view** voir les choses avec optimisme.

sanitarium US = **sanatorium**.

sanitary /'sænɪtrɪ, US -terɪ/ *adj* **1** [*engineer, facilities*] sanitaire; **2** (hygienic) hygiénique; (clean) propre.

sanitary: ~ protection *n* garniture *f* périodique; **~ towel** GB, **~ napkin** US *n* serviette *f* hygiénique or périodique.

sanitation /ˌsænɪ'teɪʃn/ *n* ▸ **1251** (toilets) ₵ installations *fpl* sanitaires; **~ worker** US éboueur *m*.

sanitize /'sænɪtaɪz/ *vtr* **1** PÉJ (tone down) aseptiser [*art, politics*]; expurger [*document*]; rendre [qch] plus acceptable [*violence*]; **2** (sterilize) désinfecter.

sanity /'sænɪtɪ/ *n* **1** (mental health) équilibre *m* mental; **to preserve one's ~** rester sain d'esprit; **2** (sense) bon sens *m*; **~ prevailed** le bon sens l'emporta.

sank /sæŋk/ *prét* ▸ **sink** III.

San Marino /ˌsæn mə'ri:nəʊ/ ▸ **840** *pr n* Saint-Marin *m*.

Sanskrit /'sænskrɪt/ ▸ **1038** *n* sanscrit *m*.

Santa (Claus) /'sæntə (klɔ:z)/ *pr n* le père Noël.

Santiago /ˌsæntɪ'ɑ:gəʊ/ ▸ **1343** *pr n* **1** (also **~ de Compostela**) (in Spain) Saint Jacques de Compostelle; **2** (in Chile) Santiago.

sap /sæp/ **I** *n* sève *f*; **the ~ rises** la sève monte.
II *vtr* (weaken) saper [*strength, courage, confidence*].

sapling /'sæplɪŋ/ *n* jeune arbre *m*.

sapper /'sæpə(r)/ ▸ **1192** *n* GB MIL soldat *m* du génie.

sapphire /'sæfaɪə(r)/ ▸ **818** **I** *n* **1** (stone) saphir *m*; **2** (colour) bleu *m* saphir.
II *adj* (colour) bleu saphir *inv*.

Saracen /'særəsn/ *n* Sarrasin/-e *m*/*f*.

saranwrap® /sə'rænræp/ *n* US = scellofrais® *m*.

sarcasm /'sɑ:kæzəm/ *n* sarcasme *m*.

sarcastic /sɑ:'kæstɪk/ *adj* sarcastique.

sarcastically /sɑ:'kæstɪklɪ/ *adv* d'un ton sarcastique.

sarcophagus /sɑ:'kɒfəgəs/ *n* (*pl* **-gi** ou **-guses**) sarcophage *m*.

sardine /sɑ:'di:n/ *n* ZOOL, CULIN sardine *f*.

Sardinia /sɑ:'dɪnɪə/ ▸ **1022** *pr n* Sardaigne *f*.

Sardinian /sɑ:'dɪnɪən/ ▸ **1100**, **1038** **I** *n* **1** (person) Sarde *mf*; **2** (language) sarde *m*.
II *adj* sarde.

sardonic /sɑ:'dɒnɪk/ *adj* [*laugh, look*] sardonique; [*person, remark*] acerbe.

sardonically /sɑ:'dɒnɪklɪ/ *adv* [*laugh*] sardoniquement; [*comment, say*] de façon acerbe.

Sargasso Sea ▸ **1117** *pr n* mer *f* des Sargasses.

sartorial /sɑ:'tɔ:rɪəl/ *adj* vestimentaire.

SAS *n* GB (*abrév* = **Special Air Service**) commandos *mpl* britanniques aéroportés.

sash /sæʃ/ *n* **1** (round waist) large ceinture *f* (*en tissu*); (ceremonial) écharpe *f* (*servant d'insigne*); **2** (window frame) châssis *m* d'une fenêtre à guillotine.

sashay⚬ /'sæʃeɪ/ *vi* (casually) marcher d'un air dégagé; (seductively) marcher de manière aguichante.

sash window *n* fenêtre *f* à guillotine.

sassy⚬ /'sæsɪ/ *adj* US (cheeky) culotté⚬; (smart) chic.

sat /sæt/ *prét, pp* ▶ **sit**.

Sat ▶ **1390** *abrév écrite* = **Saturday**.

SAT /sæt/ *n* **1** GB SCH *abrév* = **Standard Assessment Task**; **2** US SCH *abrév* ▶ **Scholastic Aptitude Test**.

Satan /'seɪtn/ *pr n* Satan.

satanic /sə'tænɪk/ *adj* [*rites*] satanique.

satanist, Satanist /'seɪtənɪst/ *n*: personne qui voue un culte à Satan.

satchel /'sætʃəl/ *n* cartable *m* (*à bandoulière*).

sated /'seɪtɪd/ *adj* SOUT (*jamais épith*) [*desire*] assouvi; [*person*] rassasié; [*appetite*] satisfait; **to be ~ with** être repu de.

satellite /'sætəlaɪt/ **I** *n* satellite *m*.
II *noun modifier* [*broadcasting, transmission*] par satellite; [*town, country, photograph*] satellite.

satellite: **~ dish** *n* antenne *f* parabolique; **~ television, ~ TV** *n* télévision *f* par satellite.

satiate /'seɪʃɪeɪt/ *vtr* rassasier [*person*]; satisfaire [*appetite*]; assouvir [*desire*]; **~d with** FIG repu de.

satiety /sə'taɪətɪ/ *n* satiété *f*.

satin /'sætɪn, US 'sætn/ **I** *n* satin *m*.
II *noun modifier* [*garment, shoe*] de satin; **with a ~ finish** satiné.

satinwood /'sætɪnwʊd, US 'sætn-/ *n* **1** (tree) chloroxylon *m*; **2** (wood) bois *m* satiné de l'Inde.

satire /'sætaɪə(r)/ *n* satire *f* (**on** sur).

satiric(al) /sə'tɪrɪk/ *adj* satirique.

satirically /sə'tɪrɪklɪ/ *adv* d'une manière satirique.

satirist /'sætərɪst/ *n* satiriste *mf*.

satirize /'sætəraɪz/ *vtr* faire la satire de; **~d by** qui a été l'objet de la satire de.

satisfaction /ˌsætɪs'fækʃn/ *n* ∉ **1** (pleasure) satisfaction *f*; **to express ~ with sth** se déclarer satisfait de qch; **to get** ou **derive ~ from sth** retirer des satisfactions de qch; **to get** ou **derive ~ from doing sth** éprouver du plaisir à faire qch; **he felt he had done the work to his own ~** il était satisfait de son travail; **the conclusions were to everybody's ~** les conclusions ont satisfait tout le monde; **2** (fulfilment) satisfaction *f*; **3** (compensation) dédommagement *m*; (apology) réparation *f*; **to obtain ~ (for sth)** obtenir satisfaction (pour qch).

satisfactorily /ˌsætɪs'fæktərəlɪ/ *adv* de manière satisfaisante.

satisfactory /ˌsætɪs'fæktərɪ/ *adj* satisfaisant; **to be ~ to sb** convenir à qn; **the solution is less than ~** la solution est loin d'être satisfaisante; **his work is far from ~** son travail laisse fort à désirer; **her condition was said to be ~** son état a été déclaré satisfaisant; **to bring a matter to a ~ conclusion** mener une affaire à bien.

satisfied /'sætɪsfaɪd/ *adj* **1** (pleased) satisfait (**with, about, de**); **not ~ with winning the match, they...** non contents de gagner le match, ils...; **now are you ~?** tu es content maintenant?; **2** (convinced) convaincu (**by** par; **that** que).

satisfy /'sætɪsfaɪ/ **I** *vtr* **1** (fulfil) satisfaire [*person, need, desires, curiosity*]; assouvir [*hunger, desire*]; **2** (persuade, convince) convaincre; **3** (meet) satisfaire à [*criteria, demand, requirements, conditions*].
II *v refl* **to ~ oneself** s'assurer (**that** que).

satisfying /'sætɪsfaɪɪŋ/ *adj* **1** (filling) [*meal*] substantiel/-ielle; **2** (rewarding) [*job*] qui apporte de la satisfaction; [*life*] bien rempli; [*relationship*] heureux/-euse; **3** (pleasing) [*result, progress*] satisfaisant.

saturate /'sætʃəreɪt/ *vtr* **1** (soak) tremper [*clothes, ground*] (**with** de); FIG saturer [*market*] (**with** de); **2** CHEM saturer.

saturation /ˌsætʃə'reɪʃn/ **I** *n* saturation *f*.
II *noun modifier* [*campaign, coverage*] de saturation; [*bombing*] intensif/-ive.

saturation point *n* point *m* de saturation; **to reach ~** arriver à saturation.

Saturday /'sætədeɪ, -dɪ/ ▶ **1390** *n* samedi *m*; **he has a ~ job** GB il a un petit boulot○ le samedi.

Saturn /'sætən/ *pr n* **1** MYTHOL Saturne *m*; **2** (planet) Saturne *f*.

sauce /sɔːs/ *n* **1** CULIN sauce *f*; **orange ~** sauce à l'orange; **tomato ~** sauce tomate; **2**○ †(impudence) toupet○ *m*.
IDIOMS **what's ~ for the goose is ~ for the gander** ce qui vaut pour l'un vaut pour l'autre.

sauce: **~boat** *n* saucière *f*; **~pan** *n* casserole *f*.

saucer /'sɔːsə(r)/ *n* soucoupe *f*.

saucily /'sɔːsɪlɪ/ *adv* avec impertinence.

saucy† /'sɔːsɪ/ *adj* **1** [*person*] (impudent) impertinent; (suggestive) égrillard; **2** [*hat, dress etc*] aguichant.

Saudi /'saʊdɪ/ ▶ **1100** (also **~ Arabian**) **I** *n* Saoudien/-ienne *m/f*.
II *adj* saoudien/-ienne.

Saudi Arabia /ˌsaʊdɪ ə'reɪbɪə/ ▶ **840** *pr n* Arabie *f* saoudite.

sauerkraut /'saʊəkraʊt/ *n* choucroute *f*.

sauna /'sɔːnə, 'saʊnə/ *n* sauna *m*.

saunter /'sɔːntə(r)/ **I** *n* **to go for a ~** faire une petite balade○.
II *vi* (also **~ along**) marcher d'un pas nonchalant; **to ~ off** s'éloigner d'un pas nonchalant.

sausage /'sɒsɪdʒ, US 'sɔːs-/ *n* (for cooking) saucisse *f*; (ready to eat) saucisson *m*.

sausage: **~ dog**○ *n* teckel *m*; **~ meat** *n* chair *f* à saucisse; **~ roll** *n* feuilleté *m* à la chair à saucisse.

sauté /'səʊteɪ, US səʊ'teɪ/ CULIN **I** *adj* (also **sauté(e)d**) sauté.
II *vtr* (*p prés* **-ing** ou **-eeing**; *prét, pp* **-éd** ou **-éed**) faire sauter.

savage /'sævɪdʒ/ **I** *n* sauvage *mf* ALSO PEJ.
II *adj* **1** LIT [*blow, beating*] violent; [*attack*] sauvage; **2** FIG [*temper*] violent; [*mood, satire*] féroce; [*criticism*] virulent; [*price increases*] violent.
III *vtr* **1** (maul) [*dog*] attaquer [qn/qch] sauvagement; [*lion*] déchiqueter; **2** FIG descendre [qch/qn] en flammes.

savagely /'sævɪdʒlɪ/ *adv* **1** LIT [*beat, attack*] sauvagement; **2** FIG [*criticize, satirize*] férocement.

savagery /'sævɪdʒrɪ/ *n* (of war, primitive people) barbarie *f*; (of attack) (physical) sauvagerie *f*; (verbal) férocité *f*.

save /seɪv/ **I** *n* **1** SPORT arrêt *m* de but; **2** COMPUT sauvegarde *f*.
II *vtr* **1** (rescue) sauver; **she ~d him from falling** elle l'a empêché de tomber; **she ~d the country from civil war** elle a évité au pays de sombrer dans la guerre civile; **to ~ sb from himself** protéger qn contre lui-même; **to ~ sb's life** LIT, FIG sauver la vie à qn; **he can't speak German to ~ his life**○! il ne parle pas un mot d'allemand!; **to ~ the day** ou **the situation** sauver la situation; **2** (put by, keep) mettre [qch] de côté [*money, food*]; garder [*goods, documents*]; **to have money ~d** avoir de l'argent de côté; **to ~ sth for sb, to ~ sb sth** garder qch pour qn; **3** (economize on) économiser [*money, energy*]; gagner [*time, space*]; **to ~ one's energy/voice** ménager ses forces/sa voix; **you'll ~ money/£20** vous ferez des économies/une économie de 20 livres; **to ~ sb sth** faire économiser qch à qn [*money*]; éviter qch à qn [*trouble, expense, journey*]; faire gagner qch à qn [*time*]; **to ~ sb/sth (from) having to do** éviter à qn/qch de faire; **to ~ doing** éviter de faire; **4** SPORT arrêter [*penalty*]; **5** RELIG sauver; **6** COMPUT sauvegarder, enregistrer (**on, to** sur); **7** (also **~ up**) (collect) collectionner.
III *vi* **1** (put by funds) = **save up**; **2** (economize) économiser, faire des économies; **to ~ on** faire des économies de [*energy, paper*].
IV *v refl* **to ~ oneself 1** (rescue oneself) LIT, FIG s'en tirer; **to ~ oneself (from) having to do** éviter de faire; **2** (keep energy) se réserver (**for** pour); **3** (avoid waste) **to ~ oneself money** économiser; **to ~ oneself time** gagner du temps; **to ~ oneself a journey** s'éviter un déplacement.

■ **save up** faire des économies; **to ~ up for** mettre de l'argent de côté pour s'acheter [*car, house*]; mettre de l'argent de côté pour s'offrir [*holiday*].

saver /'seɪvə(r)/ *n* épargnant/-e *m/f*.

saving /'seɪvɪŋ/ **I** *n* **1** (reduction) économie *f* (**in** de; **on** sur); **2** ¢ FIN (activity) épargne *f*; **3** (conservation) économie *f*; **energy** ~ économies *fpl* d'énergie.
II savings *npl* économies *fpl*; **to live off one's** ~**s** vivre de ses économies.
III -saving (*combining form*) **energy-/fuel-**~ qui réduit la consommation d'énergie/de carburant.

saving grace *n* bon côté *m*; **it's his** ~ c'est ce qui le sauve.

saving: ~**s account** *n* GB compte *m* d'épargne; US compte *m* rémunéré; ~**s and loan (association)**, **S & L** *n* US société *f* d'investissement et de crédit immobilier; ~**s bank** *n* caisse *f* d'épargne; ~**s certificate** *n* bon *m* de caisse.

saviour GB, **savior** US /'seɪvɪə(r)/ *n* sauveur *m*.

savoir-faire /ˌsævwɑː'feə(r)/ *n* **1** (social) savoir-vivre *m inv*; **2** (practical) savoir-faire *m inv*.

savor /'seɪvə(r)/ *n* US = **savour**.

savory /'seɪvərɪ/ *n, adj* US = **savoury**.

savour GB, **savor** US /'seɪvə(r)/ **I** *n* **1** LIT saveur *f*; **2** FIG goût *m*; **life has lost its** ~ **for her** elle a perdu goût à la vie; **3** (trace, hint) pointe *f*.
II *vtr* LIT, FIG savourer.
III *vi* **to** ~ **of** sentir.

savoury GB /'seɪvərɪ/ **I** *n* (pie, flan, stew) plat *m* salé; (after dessert) GB canapé *m* (*servi après le dessert*).
II *adj* **1** CULIN (not sweet) salé; (appetizing) appétissant; ~ **biscuits** biscuits *mpl* apéritif; **2** FIG **not a very individual/area** un individu/quartier peu recommandable; **the less** ~ **aspects of the matter** le côté plutôt louche de l'affaire.

Savoy /sə'vɔɪ/ ▶ 1177 **I** *pr n* Savoie *f*.
II *noun modifier* [*cuisine, wines*] de Savoie; **the** ~ **Alps** les Alpes *fpl* savoyardes.

savoy cabbage *n* chou *m* de Milan.

saw /sɔː/ **I** *prét* ▶ **see**.
II *n* scie *f*; **electric/power** ~ scie électrique/mécanique.
III *vtr* (*prét* **sawed**; *pp* **sawn** GB, **sawed** US) scier; **to** ~ **through/down/off** scier.
■ **saw up**: ~ **up [sth]**, ~ **[sth] up** débiter qch à la scie.

sawdust *n* sciure *f* (de bois).

sawed /sɔːd/ *pp* US ▶ **saw** III.

saw: ~**fish** *n* poisson-scie *m*; ~**mill** *n* scierie *f*.

sawn /sɔːn/ *pp* GB ▶ **saw** III.

sawn-off /'sɔːnɒf/ *adj* GB [*shotgun*] à canon scié.

sax° /sæks/ ▶ 1097 *n* (*pl* ~**es**) (*abrév* = **saxophone**) saxo° *m*.

Saxon /'sæksn/ **I** *pr n* (person) Saxon/-onne *m/f*; (language) saxon *m*.
II *adj* saxon/-onne.

saxophone /'sæksəfəʊn/ ▶ 1097 *n* saxophone *m*.

saxophonist /sæk'sɒfənɪst/ ▶ 1251, 1097 *n* saxophoniste *mf*.

say /seɪ/ **I** *n* **to have one's** ~ dire ce qu'on a à dire (**on** sur); **to have a** ~/**no** ~ **in sth** avoir/ne pas avoir son mot à dire sur qch; **to have no** ~ **in the matter** ne pas avoir voix au chapitre; **to have a** ~ **in appointing sb** avoir son mot à dire sur la nomination de qn; **they want more** ou **a bigger** ~ ils veulent avoir davantage leur mot à dire; **to have the most** ou **biggest** ~ avoir le plus de poids.
II *vtr* (*prét, pp* **said**) **1** [*person*] dire [*words, prayer, hello, no*] (**to** à); **'hello,' he said** 'bonjour,' dit-il; ~ **after me...** répète après moi...; **to** ~ **one's piece** dire ce qu'on a à dire; **to** ~ **(that)** dire que; **she** ~**s he's ill** elle dit qu'il est malade; **how nice of you to** ~ **so** merci, c'est gentil; **didn't I** ~ **so?** je l'avais bien dit!; **if ou though I do** ~ **so myself!** je ne devrais pas le dire, mais...!; **so they** ~ (agreeing) il paraît; **or so they** ~ (doubtful) du moins c'est ce qu'on dit; **or so he** ~**s** du moins c'est ce qu'il prétend; **so to** ~ pour ainsi dire; **as you** ~... comme tu le dis...; **as they** ~ comme on dit; **I don't care what anyone** ~**s** je me moque du qu'en-dira-t-on;

people ou **they** ~ **she's very rich, she is said to be very rich** on dit qu'elle est très riche; **to** ~ **sth on a subject** parler d'un sujet; **she'll have something to** ~ **about that!** elle aura certainement quelque chose à dire là-dessus!; **to** ~ **sth to oneself** se dire qch; **what do you** ~ **to that?** qu'est-ce que tu en dis? **what do you** ~ **to the argument that...?** que répondez-vous à l'argument selon lequel...?; **what would you** ~ **to a little walk?** qu'est-ce que tu dirais d'une petite promenade?; **what (do you)** ~ **we eat now**°? et si on mangeait maintenant?; **that's for the committee to** ~ c'est au comité de décider; **it's not for me to** ~ ce n'est pas à moi de le dire; **you said it**°! tu l'as dit!; **you can** ~ **that again!** ça, tu peux le dire°!; **I should** ~ **it is/they were!** et comment°!; **well said!** bien dit!; ~ **no more**° ça va, j'ai compris!°; **let's** ~ **no more about it** n'en parlons plus; **enough said**° ça va, j'ai compris°; **there's no more to be said** il n'y a rien à ajouter; **it goes without** ~**ing that** il va sans dire que; **don't** ~ **I didn't warn you!** tu ne pourras pas dire que je ne t'avais pas prévenu!; **don't** ~ **it's raining again!** ne me dis pas qu'il recommence à pleuvoir!; **you might just as well** ~ **education is useless** autant dire que l'instruction est inutile; **that is to** ~ c'est-à-dire; **that's not to** ~ **that** cela ne veut pas dire que; **he was displeased, not to** ~ **furious** il était mécontent, pour ne pas dire furieux; **I'll** ~ **this for her...** je dois dire à sa décharge que...; **I must** ~ **(that)** je dois dire que; **to have a lot to** ~ **for oneself** être bavard; **what have you got to** ~ **for yourself?** (reprimand) qu'est-ce que tu as comme excuse?; (jocular greeting) qu'est-ce que tu deviens?; **that's** ~**ing a lot**° ce n'est pas peu dire; **2** [*writer, book, letter, report, map*] dire; [*painting, music, gift*] exprimer; [*sign, clock, poster, dial, gauge*] indiquer; [*gesture, signal*] signifier; **it** ~**s on the radio/in the rules that** la radio/le règlement dit que; **it** ~**s here that** il est dit ici que; **3** (guess) dire; **how high would you** ~ **it is?** à ton avis, quelle en est la hauteur?; **I'd** ~ **it was a bargain** à mon avis c'est une bonne affaire; **I'd** ~ **she was about 25** je lui donnerais environ 25 ans; **4** (assume) to ~ **(that)** supposer que (+ *subj*), mettre que (+ *indic or subj*); **let's** ~ **there are 20** mettons ou supposons qu'il y en ait 20.
III *vi* (*prét, pp* **said**) **1** stop when I ~ arrête quand je te le dis; **he wouldn't** ~ il n'a pas voulu le dire; **you don't** ~! IRON sans blague!, pas possible!; ~**s you**°! (taunting) que tu dis°!; ~**s who**°?, **who** ~**s**°? (sceptical) ah oui°?; (on whose authority?) et sur les ordres de qui?; **2†** GB **I** ~! (listen) écoute, dis donc;
IV *adv* disons, mettons; ~, **£50 for petrol** disons ou mettons, 50 livres sterling pour l'essence.
V *excl* US dis-donc!
IDIOMS **it doesn't** ~ **much for their marriage** cela en dit long sur leur mariage; **it** ~**s a lot for sb/sth** c'est tout à l'honneur de qn/qch; **that** ~**s it all** c'est tout dire, cela se passe de commentaires; **there's a lot to be said for that method** cette méthode est très intéressante à bien des égards; **there's a lot to be said for keeping quiet** il y a intérêt à se taire; **when all is said and done** tout compte fait, en fin de compte.

saying /'seɪɪŋ/ *n* dicton *m*; **as the** ~ **goes** comme on dit.

s/c *adj* (*abrév écrite* = **self-contained**) indépendant.

SC *n* US POST *abrév écrite* = **South Carolina**.

scab /skæb/ *n* **1** MED croûte *f*; **2** (on plant, animal) gale *f*; **3**° PÉJ (strikebreaker) jaune° *m* PÉJ, briseur *m* de grève.

scabby /'skæbɪ/ *adj* **1** [*skin*] couvert de croûtes *fpl*; **2** [*animal, plant*] attaqué par la gale; **3**° (nasty) moche°.

scab labour° *n* PÉJ personnel qui remplace des travailleurs en grève.

scaffold /'skæfəʊld/ *n* (gallows) échafaud *m*; TECH échafaudage *m*.

scaffolding /'skæfəʊldɪŋ/ *n* échafaudage *m*.

scald /skɔːld/ **I** *n* brûlure *f* (*causée par un liquide bouillant*).

II *vtr* **1** (burn) ébouillanter [*person*]; **2** CULIN ébouillanter; (nearly boil) faire chauffer [qch] sans bouillir.

III *v refl* **to ~ oneself** s'ébouillanter.

IDIOMS **to run off like a ~ed cat** prendre ses jambes à son cou.

scalding /'skɔːldɪŋ/ *adj* brûlant; **~ hot** brûlant.

scale /skeɪl/ **I** *n* **1** (extent) (of crisis, disaster, success, violence) étendue *f*; (of reform, development, defeat, recession, task) ampleur *f*; (of activity, operation) envergure *f*; (of support, change) degré *m*; **on a large/small ~** [*map*] à grande/petite échelle; **on a modest ~** [*building*] d'une ampleur modeste; **to do sth on a large ~** FIG faire qch sur une grande échelle; **2** (grading system) échelle *f*; **pay ~, salary ~** échelle des salaires; **on a ~ of 1 to 10** sur une échelle allant de 1 à 10; **3** (for maps, models) échelle *f*; **on a ~ of 2 km to 1 cm** à une échelle de 1 cm pour 2 km; **4** (on gauge etc) graduation *f*; **5** (for weighing) balance *f*; **6** MUS gamme *f*; **7** (on fish, insect) écaille *f*; **8** (deposit) (in kettle) (dépôt *m*) calcaire *m*; (on teeth) tartre *m*.

II scales *npl* balance *f*.

III *vtr* **1** (climb) escalader; **2** (take scales off) écailler.

IDIOMS **the ~s fell from my eyes** tout d'un coup j'ai compris.

■ **scale down**: **~ [sth] down, ~ down [sth]** réduire l'échelle de [*drawing, map*]; FIG réduire.

■ **scale up**: **~ [sth] up, ~ up [sth] 1** augmenter l'échelle de [*drawing, map*]; **2** FIG augmenter [*activity, work*].

scale: **~d-down** *adj* réduit; **~ drawing** *n* dessin *m* à l'échelle; **~ pan** *n* plateau *m* de balance.

scallop, scollop /'skɒləp/ **I** *n* **1** ZOOL pecten *m*; **2** CULIN coquille *f* Saint-Jacques; **3** (in sewing) feston *m*.

II *vtr* **1** (in sewing) festonner; **2** CULIN **~ed potatoes ~** gratin *m* de pommes de terre.

scalp /skælp/ **I** *n* **1** ANAT cuir *m* chevelu; **2** FIG (trophy) scalp *m*; **he's after my ~**○ il veut ma peau○.

II *vtr* **1** (remove scalp) scalper; **2**○ US FIG (defeat) écraser; **3**○ US (sell illegally) revendre [qch] au marché noir.

scaly /'skeɪlɪ/ *adj* [*wing, fish*] écailleux/-euse; [*skin, fruit, bark*] squameux/-euse; [*plaster, wall*] écaillé.

scam○ /skæm/ *n* escroquerie *f*.

scamper /'skæmpə(r)/ *vi* (also **~ about, ~ around**) [*child, dog*] gambader; [*mouse*] trottiner; **to ~ away** ou **off** détaler.

scampi /'skæmpɪ/ *npl* (fresh) langoustines *fpl*; (breaded) scampi *mpl*.

scan /skæn/ **I** *n* **1** MED (CAT) scanner *m*; (ultrasound) échographie *f*; **2** (radar, TV) balayage *m*; (picture) analyse *f*.

II *vtr* (*p prés etc* **-nn-**) **1** (cast eyes over) lire rapidement [*page, newspaper*]; **2** (examine) scruter [*faces, crowd, horizon*]; **3** [*light, radar*] balayer; **4** MED faire un scanner de [*organ*].

III *vi* (*p prés etc* **-nn-**) LITERAT pouvoir se scander.

scandal /'skændl/ *n* **1** (incident, outcry) scandale *m*; **the Grunard ~** l'affaire *f* Grunard; **2** (gossip) potins○ *mpl*; (shocking stories) histoires *fpl* scandaleuses.

scandalize /'skændəlaɪz/ *vtr* (shock) scandaliser.

scandalmonger /'skændlmʌŋɡə(r)/ *n* mauvaise langue *f*.

scandalmongering /'skændlmʌŋɡə(r)ɪŋ/ *n* commérage *m*.

scandalous /'skændələs/ *adj* scandaleux/-euse.

scandal sheet *n* journal *m* à scandales.

Scandinavia /ˌskændɪ'neɪvɪə/ *pr n* Scandinavie *f*.

scanner /'skænə(r)/ *n* **1** MED (CAT) scanner *m*; **2** (for bar codes etc) lecteur *m* optique; **3** (radar) scanner *m*.

scant /skænt/ *adj* [*concern, coverage*] maigre; **a ~ five metres** à peine cinq mètres; **to show ~ regard for sth** avoir peu de respect pour qch.

scantily /'skæntɪlɪ/ *adv* insuffisamment; **~ clad, ~ dressed** très légèrement vêtu; **~ cut** très échancré.

scanty /'skæntɪ/ *adj* [*meal, report, supply*] maigre; [*information*] sommaire; [*knowledge*] rudimentaire; [*swimsuit*] minuscule.

scapegoat /'skeɪpɡəʊt/ *n* bouc *m* émissaire (**for** de).

scar /skɑː(r)/ **I** *n* LIT, FIG cicatrice *f*; (from knife on face) balafre *f*; **acne ~s** traces *fpl* d'acné.

II *vtr* (*p prés etc* **-rr-**) LIT, FIG marquer; (with knife on face) balafrer; FIG défigurer [*landscape*]; **to ~ sb for life** LIT laisser à qn une cicatrice permanente; FIG marquer qn pour la vie.

III *vi* (*p prés etc* **-rr-**) se cicatriser.

scarce /skeəs/ *adj* (rare) rare; (insufficient) limité; **to become ~** se faire rare.

IDIOMS **to make oneself ~**○ s'éclipser○.

scarcely /'skeəslɪ/ *adv* **1** (hardly) à peine; **it ~ matters** il n'importe guère; **~ a week passes without someone telephoning me** presque chaque semaine quelqu'un me téléphone; **~ anybody** presque personne; **we have ~ any money** nous n'avons pratiquement pas d'argent; **~ ever** presque jamais; **2** (not really) IRON difficilement; **I can ~ accuse him** je peux difficilement l'accuser.

scarcity /'skeəsɪtɪ/ *n* **1** (dearth) pénurie *f* (**of** de); **2** (rarity) rareté *f* (**of** de); **~ value** valeur *f* de rareté.

scare /skeə(r)/ **I** *n* **1** (fright) peur *f*; **to give sb a ~** faire peur à qn; **2** (alert) alerte *f*; **bomb ~** alerte à la bombe; **3** (rumour) bruits *mpl* alarmistes; **food ~** alerte *f* à l'intoxication *f* alimentaire.

II *vtr* faire peur à; **to ~ sb into doing sth** forcer à faire qch par intimidation; **to ~ sb stiff**○ paralyser qn de peur.

III *vi* **to ~ easily** s'effrayer facilement.

■ **scare away, scare off**: **~ away [sth/sb], ~ [sth/sb] away** LIT faire fuir; FIG dissuader.

scarecrow /'skeəkrəʊ/ *n* épouvantail *m*.

scared /skeəd/ *adj* [*animal, person*] effrayé; [*look*] apeuré; **to be** ou **feel ~** avoir peur; **to be ~ about sth** craindre qch; **to be ~ stiff**○ **of/of doing** avoir une peur bleue de/de faire○.

scare: **~mongering** *n* alarmisme *m*; **~ tactic** *n* tactique *f* alarmiste.

scarf /skɑːf/ *n* (*pl* **scarves**) (long) écharpe *f*; (square) foulard *m*.

scarlet /'skɑːlət/ **▶818** *n, adj* (colour) écarlate (*f*).

scarlet: **~ fever ▶1002** *n* scarlatine *f*; **~ woman** *n* femme *f* de mauvaise vie.

scarper○ /'skɑːpə(r)/ *vi* GB déguerpir.

scarves /skɑːvz/ *pl* ▶ **scarf**.

scary○ /'skeərɪ/ *adj* (inspiring fear) qui fait peur.

scathing /'skeɪðɪŋ/ *adj* [*remark, report, tone, wit*] cinglant; [*criticism*] virulent; [*look*] noir.

scatter /'skætə(r)/ **I** *n* **1** (of houses, stars, papers) éparpillement *m* (**of** de); **2** (statistics) dispersion *f*.

II *vtr* (also **~ around, ~ about**) (throw around) répandre [*seeds, earth*]; éparpiller [*books, papers, clothes*]; disperser [*debris*]; **to be ~ed around** être éparpillé; **to be ~ed with sth** être jonché de qch.

III *vi* [*people, animals, birds*] se disperser.

scatter-brained *adj* [*person*] étourdi; [*idea*] farfelu○.

scattered /'skætəd/ *adj* [*houses, population, clouds*] épars; [*books, litter*] éparpillé; [*support*] clairsemé; **~ showers** averses *fpl* intermittentes.

scattering /'skætərɪŋ/ *n* (of leaves, papers, people) éparpillement *m*; (of shops etc) constellation *f*.

scatty○ /'skætɪ/ *adj* GB étourdi.

scavenge /'skævɪndʒ/ **I** *vtr* LIT récupérer (**from** dans).

II *vi* **to ~ for food** [*bird, animal*] chercher de la nourriture; **to ~ in** ou **through the dustbins for sth** [*person*] faire les poubelles à la recherche de qch; [*dog*] fouiller les poubelles à la recherche de qch.

scavenger /'skævɪndʒə(r)/ *n* **1** (animal) charognard *m*; **2** (for food) faiseur *m* de poubelles; **3** (for objects) récupérateur *m*.

scenario /sɪ'nɑːrɪəʊ, US -'nær-/ *n* (*pl* **~s**) CIN scénario *m*; FIG (hypothetical situation) cas *m* de figure.

scene /siːn/ *n* **1** (in play, film, novel) scène *f*; **first, let's set the ~: a villa in Mexico** situons le décor d'abord: une villa au Mexique; **the ~ was set for a major tragedy** FIG tous les éléments étaient réunis pour qu'une grande tragédie se produise; **2** THEAT décor *m*; **behind the ~s** LIT, FIG dans les coulisses *fpl*; **3** (location) lieu *m*; **these streets have been the ~ of violent fighting** ces rues ont été le théâtre de violents affrontements; **to come on the ~** [*police, ambulance*] arriver sur les lieux; FIG arriver; **you need a change of ~** tu as besoin de changer de décor; **4** (sphere, field) scène *f*; **the jazz/fashion ~** le monde du jazz/de la mode; **it's not my ~°** ce n'est pas mon genre; **5** (emotional incident) scène *f*; **there were ~s of violence** il y a eu des incidents violents; **6** (image, sight) image *f*; **7** (view) vue *f*, tableau *m*; ART scène *f*.

scene designer, **scene painter** ▶ 1251 | *n* THEAT décorateur/-trice *m/f*.

scenery /'si:nǝrı/ *n* ¢ **1** (landscape) paysage *m*; FIG décor *m*; **2** THEAT décors *mpl*; **a piece of ~** un élément de décor.

scene shifter ▶ 1251 | *n* machiniste *mf*.

scenic /'si:nɪk/ *adj* [*drive, route, walk*] panoramique; [*location, countryside*] pittoresque.

scent /sent/ **I** *n* **1** (smell) odeur *f*; (perfume) parfum *m*; **2** (body smell) (of animal) fumet *m*; (in hunting) piste *f*; FIG relents *mpl*; **to pick up the ~** LIT, FIG trouver la piste; **to throw the dogs off the ~** brouiller la piste aux chiens; **to be (hot) on the ~ of sth/sb** suivre qch/qn à la trace.
II *vtr* (smell) flairer; FIG pressentir [*danger*].
■ **scent out**: **~** [sth] **out**, **~ out** [sth] flairer.

scented /'sentɪd/ **I** *adj* GEN parfumé (**with** de); [*air*] odorant.
II -scented *combining form* (with scent added) parfumé à; (natural) à l'odeur de.

sceptic GB, **skeptic** US /'skeptɪk/ *n* sceptique *mf*.

sceptical GB, **skeptical** US /'skeptɪkl/ *adj* sceptique (**about, of** en ce qui concerne).

sceptically GB, **skeptically** US /'skeptɪklɪ/ *adv* avec scepticisme *m*.

scepticism GB, **skepticism** US /'skeptɪsɪzǝm/ *n* scepticisme *m* (**about** à propos de).

schedule /'ʃedju:l, US 'skedʒʊl/ **I** *n* **1** ADMIN, COMM, TECH programme *m*; (projected plan) prévisions *fpl*; **to be ahead of/behind ~** être en avance/en retard sur les prévisions; **to work to a tight ~** travailler selon un programme serré; **to draw up** ou **make out a ~** établir un programme; **to be on ~** progresser comme prévu; **finished on ~** fini à temps; **according to ~** comme prévu; **a ~ of events** un calendrier; **2** (of appointments) programme *m* ALSO TV; **to fit sb/sth into one's ~** intégrer qn/qch dans son programme; **3** (timetable) horaire *m*; **to arrive on/ahead of/behind ~** arriver à l'heure/en avance/en retard; **4** COMM, JUR (list) (of charges) barème *m*; (of repayments) taux *m*; (of contents) inventaire *m*; (to a contract) annexe *f*.
II *vtr* prévoir; (arrange) programmer; **the plane is ~d to arrive at 2.00** l'avion est attendu à 2 h; **the station is ~d for completion in 1997** la gare doit être terminée en 1997.

schedule: **~d building** *n* GB immeuble *m* classé; **~d flight** *n* vol *m* régulier; **~d territories** *npl* GB zone *f* sterling.

scheduling /'ʃedju:lɪŋ, US 'skedʒʊl-/ *n* (of project, work) programmation *f*; (of monument) GB classification *f*.

scheme /ski:m/ **I** *n* **1** (plan) projet *m*, plan *m*; **a ~ for sth/for doing** un plan pour qch/pour faire; **2** GB ADMIN (system) système *m*, projet *m*; **road ~** projet de développement routier; **insurance/pension ~** régime *m* d'assurances/de retraite; **3** PÉJ (impractical idea) plan *m*; **4** (plot) combine *f*; **5** (for house, garden etc) plan *m*.
II *vi* PÉJ comploter (**to do** pour faire).
IDIOMS **in the overall** ou **whole ~ of things** si on considère la situation dans son ensemble; **she was unsure how she fitted into the ~ of things** elle ne savait pas où elle se situait.

scheming /'ski:mɪŋ/ PÉJ **I** *n* ¢ machinations *fpl*.
II *adj* [*person*] intrigant.

schizophrenic /ˌskɪtsǝʊ'frenɪk/ **I** *n* schizophrène *mf*.
II *adj* GEN schizophrénique; [*patient*] schizophrène.

schmal(t)zy° /'ʃmɔ:ltsı/ *adj* GEN larmoyant; [*music*] sirupeux/-euse.

scholar /'skɒlǝ(r)/ *n* **1** (learned person) érudit/-e *m/f*; **Hebrew ~** spécialiste *mf* de l'hébreu; **2** (student with scholarship) lauréat/-e *m/f* détenteur/-trice d'une bourse.

scholarly /'skɒlǝlı/ *adj* **1** (erudite) érudit; **2** [*journal, periodical, circles*] (academic) universitaire; (serious) intellectuel/-elle; **3** [*appearance*] d'intellectuel.

scholarship /'skɒlǝʃɪp/ *n* **1** (award) bourse *f* (**to** pour); **2** (meticulous study) érudition *f*; **3** (body of learning) savoir *m*; (of individual, work) érudition *f*.

scholastic /skǝ'læstɪk/ *adj* **1** (philosopher) scolastique; **2** (of school) scolaire.

Scholastic Aptitude Test, **SAT** *n* US examen *m* d'admission à l'université.

school /sku:l/ **I** *n* **1** SCH, UNIV école *f*; **broadcasts for ~s** émissions *fpl* scolaires; **~ starts/finishes** les cours commencent/finissent; **no ~ today** pas de classe aujourd'hui; **to go to medical ~** faire des études de médecine; **2** US (university) université *f*; **3** (of painting, literature, thought) école *f*; **4** (of whales etc) banc *m*.
II *noun modifier* GEN [*holiday, outing, life, uniform, year*] scolaire; (of particular school) [*facilities*] de l'école.
III *vtr* dresser [*horse*]; **to ~ sb in sth** enseigner qch à qn.

schoolbag *n* sac *m* de classe; (traditional) cartable *m*.

schoolboy /'sku:lbɔı/ **I** *n* GEN élève *m*; (of primary age) écolier *m*; (secondary) collégien *m*; (sixth former) GB lycéen *m*.
II *noun modifier* **1** [*attitude, behaviour*] de collégien; [*slang, word*] d'élève; **2** [*champion, player*] junior.

school: **~ bus** *n* car *m* scolaire; **~ captain** *n* GB SCH élève choisi pour représenter l'école; **~child** *n* écolier/-ière *m/f*; **~ council** *n*: conseil d'enseignants et de représentants des élèves; **~days** *npl* années *fpl* d'école; **~ dinner** *n* = **school lunch**; **~ fees** *n* frais *mpl* de scolarité; **~friend** *n* camarade *mf* de classe; **~girl** *n* GEN élève *f*; (of primary age) écolière *f*; (secondary) collégienne *f*; (sixth former) GB lycéenne *f*; **~ graduation age** *n* US SCH = **school leaving age**; **~house** *n* école *f*.

schooling /'sku:lɪŋ/ *n* (of child) scolarité *f*; (of horse) dressage *m*.

school: **~ inspector** ▶ 1251 | *n* inspecteur/-trice *m/ f*; **~-leaver** *n* GB jeune *mf* ayant fini sa scolarité; **~ leaving age** *n* âge *m* de fin de scolarité; **~ lunch** *n* repas *m* de la cantine scolaire; **~master** ▶ 1251 | *n* enseignant *m*; **~mate** *n* camarade *mf* d'école; **~mistress** ▶ 1251 | *n* enseignante *f*; **~ prefect** *n* GB SCH élève de terminale chargé de la discipline; **~ record** *n* ~ dossier *m* scolaire; **~ report** GB, **~ report card** US *n* bulletin *m* scolaire; **~room** *n* salle *f* de classe; **~teacher** ▶ 1251 | *n* GEN enseignant/-e *m/f*; (secondary) professeur *m*; (primary) GEN instituteur/-trice *m/f*; ADMIN professeur *m* des écoles; **~work** *n* travail *m* de classe.

schooner /'sku:nǝ(r)/ *n* (boat) goélette *f*; (glass) US grande chope *f* (à bière); GB grand verre *m* à Xérès.

sciatica /saı'ætɪkǝ/ ▶ 1002 | *n* MED sciatique *f*.

science /'saɪǝns/ **I** *n* science *f*; **to teach ~** enseigner les sciences.
II *noun modifier* [*exam, subject*] scientifique; [*faculty*] des sciences; [*teacher, textbook*] de sciences.
IDIOMS **to blind sb with ~** épater qn avec sa science.

scientific /ˌsaɪǝn'tıfɪk/ *adj* scientifique; **it's a very ~ game** c'est un jeu qui exige de l'analyse intellectuelle.

scientifically /ˌsaɪǝn'tıfɪklı/ *adv* [*investigate, show*] scientifiquement.

scientist /'saɪǝntɪst/ ▶ 1251 | *n* GEN scientifique *mf*; (eminent) savant *m*.

Scillies /'sılız/, **Scilly Isles** /'sılı aılz/ ▶ 1022 | *pr n* (îles *fpl*) Sorlingues *fpl*.

scintillate /'sɪntɪleɪt, US -təleɪt/ *vi* LIT scintiller; FIG briller.

scintillating /'sɪntɪleɪtɪŋ, US -təleɪtɪŋ/ *adj* LIT scintillant; FIG [*person, conversation*] brillant; [*wit*] vif/vive.

scissors /'sɪzəz/ *npl* ciseaux *mpl*; **a ~-and-paste job** FIG PÉJ un tissu d'idées glanées à droite à gauche.

scoff /skɒf, US skɔːf/ I *vtr* **1** (mock) **'love!' she ~ed** 'l'amour!' dit-elle avec dédain; **2**° GB (eat) engloutir°, bouffer°.
II *vi* se moquer (**at** de).

scold /skəʊld/ I *vtr* gronder (**for doing** pour avoir fait).
II *vi* râler°.

scolding /'skəʊldɪŋ/ *n* ¢ gronderie *f*; **to give sb a ~** gronder qn.

scone /skɒn, skəʊn, US skəʊn/ *n* GB scone *m* (*petit pain rond*).

scoop /skuːp/ I *n* **1** (implement) (for shovelling) pelle *f*; (for measuring) mesure *f*; (for ice cream) cuillère *f* à glace; **2** (scoopful) (of coffee, flour) mesure *f*; (of earth) pelletée *f*; (of ice cream) boule *f*; **3** (in journalism) exclusivité *f*; **to get a ~** obtenir un scoop°.
II° *vtr* décrocher° [*prize, sum, story*].
■ **scoop out**: **~ out** [sth], **~** [sth] **out** creuser; **to ~ the flesh out of a tomato** évider une tomate.
■ **scoop up**: **~** [sth] **up**, **~ up** [sth] pelleter [*earth, snow*]; recueillir [*water*]; soulever [*child*].

scooter /'skuːtə(r)/ *n* **1** (child's) trottinette *f*; **2** (motorized) scooter *m*; **3** US (boat) yacht *m* à glace.

scope /skəʊp/ *n* **1** (opportunity) possibilité *f*; **there is ~ for sb to do** il y a des possibilités pour qn de faire; **to give sb ~ to do** laisser toute latitude à qn de faire; **2** (range) (of plan) envergure *f*; (of inquiry, report, study, book) portée *f*; (of changes, disaster, knowledge, power) étendue *f*; **to be within/outside the ~ of the study** faire partie du/sortir du champ de l'étude; **3** (capacity) compétences *fpl*; **to be within/beyond the ~ of sb** entrer dans/dépasser les compétences de qn.

scorch /skɔːtʃ/ I *n* (also **~ mark**) légère brûlure *f*.
II *vtr* [*fire*] brûler; [*sun*] dessécher [*grass, trees*]; griller [*lawn*]; [*iron etc*] roussir [*fabric*]; **~ed earth policy** MIL tactique *f* de la terre brûlée.

scorcher° /'skɔːtʃə(r)/ *n* journée *f* de canicule.

scorching° /'skɔːtʃɪŋ/ *adj* (also **~ hot**) [*heat, day*] torride; [*sun*] brûlant; [*weather, summer*] caniculaire.

score /skɔː(r)/ I *n* **1** (points gained) SPORT score *m*; (in cards) marque *f*; **there is still no ~** le score est toujours zéro à zéro; **the final ~ was 3–1** le score final était de 3 à 1; **to keep (the) ~** GEN marquer les points; (in cards) tenir la marque; **what's the ~?** (in game, match) où en est le jeu ou le match?; **to know the ~** FIG savoir où on est; **2** (in exam, test) note *f*, résultat *m*; **3** MUS (written music) partition *f*; (for ballet) musique *f* (du ballet); (for film) musique *f* (du film); **4** (twenty) **a ~** vingt *m*, une vingtaine *f*; **three ~ years and ten** soixante-dix ans; **by the ~** à la pelle; **~s of requests** des tas de demandes; **5** (account) sujet *m*; **on this** ou **that ~** à ce sujet.
II *vtr* **1** SPORT marquer [*goal, point*]; remporter [*victory, success*]; **to ~ 9 out of 10** avoir 9 sur 10; **to ~ a hit** (in swordsmanship) toucher; (in shooting) mettre dans le mille; FIG remporter un grand succès; **2** MUS (arrange) adapter; (orchestrate) orchestrer; CIN composer la musique de [*film*]; **3** (mark) (with chalk, ink) marquer; (cut) entailler; inciser [*meat, fish*].
III *vi* **1** SPORT (gain point) marquer un point (obtain goal) marquer un but; **to ~ well** ou **highly** obtenir un bon résultat; **to ~ over** ou **against sb** (in argument, debate) prendre le dessus sur qn; **2** (keep score) marquer les points; **3**° (be successful) avoir du succès.
IDIOMS **to settle a ~** régler ses comptes.
■ **score off**: ¶ **~ off** [sth], **~** [sth] **off** rayer; ¶ **~ off** [sb] (in argument) marquer des points sur.
score: **~board** *n* GEN tableau *m* d'affichage; **~card** *n* GEN, SPORT carte *f* de score; (in cards) feuille *f* de marque; **~line** *n* score *m*.
scorer /'skɔːrə(r)/ *n* marqueur/-euse *m*/*f*.
scoresheet /'skɔːʃiːt/ *n* feuille *f* de match.

scoring /'skɔːrɪŋ/ *n* **1** SPORT **to open the ~** ouvrir la marque; **2** MUS arrangement *m*.

scorn /skɔːn/ I *n* mépris *m*; **to pour** ou **heap ~ on** accabler [qn] de mépris [*person*]; dénigrer [*attempt, argument, organization*].
II *vtr* **1** (despise) mépriser [*person, action*]; dédaigner [*fashion, make-up*]; **2** (reject) GEN rejeter; accueillir avec mépris [*claim, suggestion*]; **3** SOUT **to ~ to do** ne pas daigner faire.

scornful /'skɔːnfl/ *adj* méprisant; **to be ~ of** manifester du mépris pour.

scornfully /'skɔːnfəli/ *adv* avec mépris, dédaigneusement.

Scorpio /'skɔːpɪəʊ/ ▶ **1418** *n* Scorpion *m*.

Scot /skɒt/ ▶ **1100** *n* Écossais/-e *m*/*f*.

scotch /skɒtʃ/ *vtr* étouffer [*rumour, revolt*]; contrecarrer [*plans*]; anéantir [*hopes*].

Scotch /skɒtʃ/ *n* (also **~ whisky**) whisky *m*, scotch *m*.

Scotch: **~ egg** *n* GB œuf dur enrobé de chair à saucisse; **~ mist** *n* bruine *f*, crachin *m*; **~ pine** *n* = **Scots pine**; **~ tape**® *n* US scotch® *m*.

scot-free /ˌskɒt'friː/ *adj* **to get off** ou **go ~** (unpunished) s'en tirer sans être inquiété; (unharmed) s'en sortir indemne.

Scotland /'skɒtlənd/ ▶ **840** *pr n* Écosse *f*.

Scotland Yard *n* Scotland Yard (*police judiciaire britannique*).

Scots: **~man** *n* Écossais *m*; **~ pine** *n* pin *m* sylvestre; **~woman** *n* Écossaise *f*.

Scottish /'skɒtɪʃ/ ▶ **1100** *adj* écossais.

Scottish: **~ National Party, SNP** *n* Parti *m* national écossais; **~ Office** *n* POL ministère *m* des Affaires écossaises.

scoundrel /'skaʊndrəl/ *n* PÉJ gredin *m*; HUM chenapan *m*.

scour /'skaʊə(r)/ *vtr* **1** (scrub) récurer; **2** (search) parcourir (**for** à la recherche de); **to ~ the shops for sth** faire le tour des magasins à la recherche de qch.

scourer /'skaʊərə(r)/ *n* (pad) tampon *m* à récurer.

scourge /skɜːdʒ/ I *n* LIT, FIG fléau *m*.
II *vtr* **1** LIT fouetter; **2** FIG [*ruler*] opprimer; [*famine, disease, war*] frapper.

scouring powder *n* poudre *f* à récurer.

scout /skaʊt/ I *n* **1** (boy) (Catholic) scout *m*; (non-Catholic) éclaireur *m*; **2** MIL éclaireur *m*; **to have a ~ around** MIL aller en reconnaissance; FIG explorer; **3** (also **talent ~**) découvreur/-euse *m*/*f* de nouveaux talents.
II *noun modifier* [*camp, leader, movement*] scout; [*uniform*] de scout; [*troop*] de scouts.
■ **scout around** MIL aller en reconnaissance; GEN explorer; **to ~ around for sth** rechercher qch.

scouting /'skaʊtɪŋ/ *n* scoutisme *m*.

scowl /skaʊl/ I *n* air *m* renfrogné; **with a ~** d'un air renfrogné.
II *vi* prendre un air renfrogné.

scrabble /'skræbl/ *vi* **1** (also **~ around**) (search) fouiller; **2** (scrape) gratter; **he ~d desperately for a hold** il a cherché désespérément à s'accrocher quelque part.

scrag /skræg/ *n* CULIN (also **~ end**) collet *m* de mouton.

scraggy /'skrægɪ/ *adj* [*person*] maigrichon/-onne; [*part of body*] décharné; [*animal*] famélique.

scram° /skræm/ *vi* (*p prés etc* **-mm-**) filer°.

scramble /'skræmbl/ I *n* **1** (rush) course *f*; **2** (climb) escalade *f*; **3** AVIAT, MIL décollage *m* d'urgence.
II *vtr* **1** CULIN **to ~ eggs** faire des œufs brouillés; **2** RADIO, TELECOM brouiller; TV coder; **3** MIL faire décoller [qch] d'urgence.
III *vi* **1** (clamber) grimper; **to ~ up/down** escalader; **to ~ over** escalader; **to ~ through** se frayer un passage à travers; **to ~ to one's feet** se lever en sursaut; **2** (compete) **to ~ for** se disputer; **to ~ to**

do se dépêcher de faire; **3** (rush) **to ~ for** se précipiter sur; **to ~ to do** se démener pour faire.

scrambler /'skræmblə(r)/ *n* **1** RADIO, TELECOM brouilleur *m*; **2** GB (motorcyclist) trialiste *mf*.

scrambling /'skræmblɪŋ/ ▶ 949 | *n* **1** SPORT motocross *m*; **2** RADIO, TELECOM brouillage *m*; TV cryptage *m*.

scrap /skræp/ **I** *n* **1** (fragment) (of paper, cloth) petit morceau *m*; (of news, information, verse) fragment *m*; (of conversation) bribe *f*; (cutting) coupure *f*; (of land) parcelle *f*; **there wasn't a ~ of evidence** FIG il n'y avait pas la moindre preuve; **she never does a ~ of work** elle ne fiche○ jamais rien; **2**○ (fight) bagarre○ *f*; **3** (old iron) ferraille *f*; **to sell sth for ~** mettre qch à la casse.
II scraps *npl* (of food) restes *mpl*.
III *noun modifier* [*price, value*] à la casse.
IV *vtr* (*p prés etc* **-pp-**) **1**○ FIG (do away with) abandonner; **2** LIT détruire [*aircraft etc*].
V○ *vi* (*p prés etc* **-pp-**) (fight) se bagarrer○ (**with** avec).

scrap: **~book** *n* album *m* (de coupures de journaux etc); **~** (**metal**) **dealer** ▶ 1251 | *n* marchand *m* de ferraille.

scrape /skreɪp/ **I** *n* **1**○ (awkward situation) **to get into a ~** s'attirer des ennuis; **to get sb into a ~** mettre qn dans le pétrin○; **2** (sound) raclement *m*.
II *vtr* **1** gratter [*vegetables, shoes*]; **2** (damage) érafler; **3** (injure) écorcher; **4** (making noise) racler; **5**○ **to ~ a living** s'en sortir à peine (**doing** en faisant); **she ~d a ten in biology** elle a laborieusement décroché un dix en biologie.
III *vi* **1 to ~ against sth** [*car part*] érafler qch; **2** (economize) économiser le moindre sou.
IDIOMS **to ~ the bottom of the barrel** être à court d'idées (or d'imagination or de personnes qualifiées etc).
■ **scrape by** (financially) s'en sortir à peine; (in situation) s'en tirer de justesse.
■ **scrape home** SPORT gagner de justesse.
■ **scrape in** (to university, class) entrer de justesse.
■ **scrape off**: **~ off** [sth], **~** [sth] **off** enlever [qch] en grattant.
■ **scrape out**: **~ out** [sth], **~** [sth] **out** nettoyer [qch] en grattant [*saucepan*].
■ **scrape through**: ¶ **~ through** s'en tirer de justesse; ¶ **~ through** [sth] réussir [qch] de justesse [*exam, test*].
■ **scrape together**: **~** [sth] **together**, **~ together** [sth] arriver à amasser [*sum of money*].
■ **scrape up** = **scrape together**.

scraper /'skreɪpə(r)/ *n* (for decorating) couteau *m* de peintre; (for shoes) grattoir *m*.

scrap heap /'skræp hi:p/ *n* **to be thrown on** ou **consigned to the ~** être mis au rebut.

scrap: **~ iron** *n* ferraille *f*; **~ merchant** ▶ 1251 | *n* marchand *m* de ferraille; **~ metal** *n* ferraille *f*; **~ paper** *n* papier *m* brouillon.

scrappy /'skræpɪ/ *adj* **1** (disorganized) [*report*] décousu; [*game*] désordonné; [*meal*] de bric et de broc; **2**○ US PÉJ (pugnacious) bagarreur/-euse○.

scrap yard /'skræp jɑ:d/ *n* chantier *m* de ferraille, casse *f*.

scratch /skrætʃ/ **I** *n* **1** (wound) GEN égratignure *f*; (from a claw, fingernail) griffure *f*; **2** (on metal, furniture) éraflure *f*; (on record, disc, glass) rayure *f*; **3** (to relieve an itch) **to have a ~** se gratter; **4** (sound) grattement *m*; **5**○ **he/his work is not up to ~** il/son travail n'est pas à la hauteur; **6** (zero) **to start from ~** partir de zéro; **7** SPORT **to play off ~** jouer scratch.
II *adj* [*team*] de fortune; [*meal*] improvisé; **he's a ~ golfer** il joue scratch.
III *vtr* **1** (cancel) supprimer; effacer [*file*]; **2** (trace) **to ~ one's initials on sth** graver ses initiales sur qch; **3** [*cat, person*] griffer; [*thorns, rosebush*] égratigner; **to ~ sb's eyes out** arracher les yeux à quelqu'un; **4** (react to itch) gratter; **to ~ an itch** se gratter; **to ~ one's head** LIT se gratter la tête; FIG être perplexe; **5** (damage) GEN érafler; rayer [*record*]; [*cat*] se faire les griffes sur [*furniture*]; **6** SPORT retirer, scratcher.
IV *vi* **1** (relieve itch) se gratter; **2** (inflict injury) griffer.
V *v refl* **to ~ oneself** se gratter.

IDIOMS **you ~ my back and I'll ~ yours** un service en vaut un autre; **~ a translator and you'll find a writer underneath!** dans tout traducteur il y a un écrivain qui sommeille!
■ **scratch around** gratter (**in** dans).

scratch: **~ mark** *n* éraflure *f*; **~ pad** *n* bloc-notes *m*; **~ tape** *n* bande *f* de travail; **~ test** *n* MED test *m* cutané; **~ video** *n* cassette *f* de montage.

scratchy /'skrætʃɪ/ *adj* [*fabric, wool*] rêche.

scrawl /skrɔ:l/ **I** *n* gribouillage *m*.
II *vtr, vi* gribouiller.

scrawny /'skrɔ:nɪ/ *adj* décharné, maigre.

scream /skri:m/ **I** *n* **1** (of person, animal) cri *m* (perçant); (stronger) hurlement *m*; (of brakes) grincement *m*; (of tyres) crissement *m*; **~s of laughter** éclats *mpl* de rire; **2**○ **to be a ~** être tordant○.
II *vtr* LIT crier; FIG [*headline*] annoncer (en titre).
III *vi* [*person, animal, bird*] crier; (stronger) hurler; [*brakes*] grincer; [*tyres*] crisser; FIG [*colour*] crier; **to ~ at sb** crier après qn○; **to ~ with** hurler de [*fear, pain, rage*]; pousser des cris de [*excitement, pleasure*]; **to ~ with laughter** rire aux éclats.
IDIOMS **to ~ the place down** pousser des hurlements; **to drag sb kicking and ~ing to the dentist** traîner qn de force chez le dentiste.

screaming /'skri:mɪŋ/ *n* cris *mpl*; (stronger) hurlements *mpl*.

scree /skri:/ *n* éboulis *m*.

screech /skri:tʃ/ **I** *n* GEN cri *m* strident; (of tyres) crissement *m*.
II *vtr* hurler.
III *vi* [*person, animal*] pousser un cri strident; [*tyres*] crisser.

screen /skri:n/ **I** *n* **1** CIN, COMPUT, TV écran *m*; **on ~** COMPUT sur l'écran; CIN, TV à l'écran; **he writes for the ~** CIN il écrit pour le cinéma; **2** (folding panel) paravent *m*; (partition) cloison *f* mobile; (to protect) écran *m*; **a ~ of trees** un rideau d'arbres; **3** FIG couverture *f*; **4** MED visite *f* de dépistage.
II *noun modifier* CIN [*actor, star*] de cinéma; [*appearance, debut*] cinématographique, au cinéma.
III *vtr* **1** (show on screen) TV projeter; TV diffuser; **2** (conceal) cacher; (protect) protéger; **3** (test) examiner le cas de [*applicants*]; contrôler le statut de [*refugees*]; contrôler [*baggage*]; MED faire passer des tests de dépistage à [*patient*]; **to be ~ed** [*staff*] faire l'objet d'une enquête de sécurité; **to ~ sb for cancer** faire passer à qn des tests de dépistage du cancer.
■ **screen off**: **~ off** [sth], **~** [sth] **off** isoler.

screen: **~ door** *n* porte *f* munie d'une moustiquaire; **~ dump** *n* COMPUT recopie *f* d'écran.

screening /'skri:nɪŋ/ *n* **1** (showing) CIN projection *f*; TV diffusion *f*; **2** (testing) sélection *f*; MED (of patients) examens *mpl* de dépistage; **cancer ~** dépistage *m* du cancer; **3** (vetting) filtrage *m*.

screening: **~ room** *n* CIN salle *f* de projection; **~ service** *n* MED service *m* de dépistage.

screen: **~play** *n* CIN scénario *m*; **~ printing** *n* sérigraphie *f*; **~ rights** *npl* droits *mpl* d'adaptation à l'écran; **~ test** *n* CIN bout *m* d'essai; **~ wash** *n* (device) lave-glace *m*; (liquid) liquide *m* lave-glace; **~writer** ▶ 1251 | *n* CIN, TV scénariste *mf*.

screw /skru:/ **I** *n* **1** TECH vis *f*; **2** AVIAT, NAUT hélice *f*; **3**○ GB (prison guard) maton/-onne○ *m/f*.
II *vtr* **1** TECH visser (**into** dans); **2**○ (extort) **to ~ sth out of sb** extorquer qch à qn.
III *vi* TECH **to ~ onto/into se visser sur/dans.
IDIOMS **to have one's head ~ed on** avoir la tête sur les épaules; **to put the ~s on sb**○ forcer la main à qn.
■ **screw down**: ¶ **~ down** se visser; ¶ **~** [sth] **down**, **~ down** [sth] visser (à fond).
■ **screw in**: ¶ **~ in** se visser; ¶ **~** [sth] **in**, **~ in** [sth] visser.
■ **screw on**: ¶ **~ on** se visser; ¶ **~** [sth] **on**, **~ on** [sth] visser.
■ **screw round**: **to ~ one's head round** tourner la tête.

■ **screw together**: ¶ ~ **together** se visser l'un à l'autre; ¶ ~ **[sth] together**, ~ **together [sth]** assembler [qch] avec des vis.

■ **screw up**: ¶ ~ **up**° (mess up) cafouiller°; ¶ ~ **[sth] up**, ~ **up [sth] 1** (crumple) froisser; **to** ~ **up one's eyes** plisser les yeux; **to** ~ **up one's face** faire la grimace; **2**° (make a mess of) faire foirer° [*plan, task*]; **3** (summon) **to** ~ **up the courage to do** trouver le courage de faire; ¶ ~ **[sb] up**° perturber [*person*]; **~ed up**° perturbé.

screw-cap *n* bouchon *m* à vis.

screwdriver /'skruːdraɪvə(r)/ *n* **1** (tool) tournevis *m*; **2** (cocktail) vodka-orange *f*.

screw-in *adj* [*lightbulb*] à vis.

screw top I *n* bouchon *m* à vis.
II **screw-top** *noun modifier* [*jar*] avec un couvercle à vis; [*bottle*] avec un bouchon à vis.

screwy° /'skruːɪ/ *adj* cinglé°.

scribble /'skrɪbl/ **I** *n* gribouillage *m*.
II *vtr, vi* LIT, FIG griffonner, gribouiller.

■ **scribble down**: ~ **[sth] down**, ~ **down [sth]** griffonner.

■ **scribble out**: ~ **[sth] out**, ~ **out [sth]** raturer.

scrimmage /'skrɪmɪdʒ/ *n* **1** US (in football) mêlée *f*; **2** (struggle) bousculade *f*.

scrimp /skrɪmp/ *vi* économiser; **to** ~ **on sth** lésiner sur qch PÉJ; **to** ~ **and save** se priver de tout.

script /skrɪpt/ **I** *n* **1** (text) CIN, RADIO, TV script *m*; THEAT texte *m*; **2** (handwriting) écriture *f*; **3** GB SCH, UNIV copie *f* (d'examen).
II *vtr* écrire le scénario de [*film etc*].

scripture /'skrɪptʃə(r)/ *n* RELIG (also **Holy Scripture, Holy Scriptures**) (Christian) Saintes Écritures *fpl*; (other) textes *mpl* sacrés.

scriptwriter /'skrɪptraɪtə(r)/ ▶ 1251 *n* CIN, RADIO, TV scénariste *mf*.

scroll /skrəʊl/ **I** *n* **1** (manuscript, painting) rouleau *m*; **2** ARCHIT, ART volute *f*.
II *vtr* COMPUT **to** ~ **sth up/down** faire défiler qch vers le haut/vers le bas.
III *vi* COMPUT défiler.

Scrooge° /skruːdʒ/ *n* grippe-sou *m*.

scrounge° /skraʊndʒ/ **I** *n* **to be on the** ~ être toujours en train de mendier.
II *vtr* quémander [*favour*]; **to** ~ **sth off sb** piquer° qch à qn [*cigarette*]; taper° qn de qch [*money*].
III *vi* **1** ~ **off sb** vivre sur le dos de qn; **2 to** ~ **(around) for sth** chercher qch.

scrounger° /'skraʊndʒə(r)/ *n* parasite *m*.

scrub /skrʌb/ **I** *n* **1** (clean) **to give sth a (good)** ~ (bien) nettoyer qch; **2** BOT broussailles *fpl*; **3** (beauty product) gommage *m*.
II *v* (*p prés etc* **-bb-**) **1** (clean) GEN frotter; nettoyer [*vegetable*]; **to** ~ **one's nails** se brosser les ongles; **2**° (scrap) laisser tomber°.
III *vi* (*p prés etc* **-bb-**) nettoyer, frotter.
IV *v refl* (*p prés etc* **-bb-**) **to** ~ **oneself** se frotter.

■ **scrub down**: ~ **down [sth/sb]**, ~ **[sth/sb] down** nettoyer [qch/qn] à fond.

■ **scrub off**: ~ **off [sth]**, ~ **[sth] off** nettoyer, enlever [*stain, graffiti*].

■ **scrub out**: ~ **out [sth]**, ~ **[sth] out** (clean inside) récurer; (rub out) effacer.

■ **scrub up** se stériliser les mains (*avant une opération*).

scrubbing brush, scrub brush US *n* brosse *f* de ménage.

scruff /skrʌf/ *n* **1** (nape) **by the** ~ **of the neck** par la peau du cou; **2**° GB (untidy person) **he's a bit of a** ~° il est peu soigné.

scruffy /'skrʌfɪ/ *adj* [*clothes, person*] dépenaillé; [*flat, town*] délabré.

scrum /skrʌm/ *n* **1** (rugby) mêlée *f*; **2**° GB bousculade *f*.

scrum half *n* SPORT demi *m* de mêlée.

scrummage /'skrʌmɪdʒ/ *n* (in rugby) mêlée *f*.

scrunch /skrʌntʃ/ **I** *n* crissement *m*.
II *vi* [*footsteps, tyres*] crisser.

■ **scrunch up**: ¶ ~ **up** US se tasser; ¶ ~ **[sth] up**, ~ **up [sth]** faire une boule de.

scruple /'skruːpl/ **I** *n* scrupule *m* (**about** vis-à-vis de).
II *vi* **not to** ~ **to do** n'avoir aucun scrupule à faire.

scrupulous /'skruːpjʊləs/ *adj* scrupuleux/-euse.

scrutinize /'skruːtɪnaɪz, US -tənaɪz/ *vtr* scruter [*face, motives*]; examiner [qch] minutieusement [*document*]; vérifier [*accounts, votes*]; surveiller [*election*].

scrutiny /'skruːtɪnɪ, US -skruːtənɪ/ *n* **1** (investigation) examen *m*; **close** ~ examen approfondi; **to come under** ~ être examiné; **to avoid** ~ échapper au contrôle; **2** (surveillance) surveillance *f*; **3** (look) regard *m* scrutateur.

scuba diving ▶ 949 *n* plongée *f* sous-marine.

scud /skʌd/ *vi* (*p prés etc* **-dd-**) [*ship*] fuir; **to** ~ **across the sky** [*cloud*] filer dans le ciel.

scuff /skʌf/ **I** *n* (also ~ **mark**) GEN rayure *f*; (on leather) éraflure *f*.
II *vtr* érafler [*shoes*]; rayer [*floor, furniture*]; **to** ~ **one's feet** traîner les pieds.

scuffle /'skʌfl/ **I** *n* bagarre *f*.
II *vi* se bagarrer.

scull /skʌl/ **I** *n* (in boat) outrigger *m*; (single oar) godille *f*; (one of a pair) aviron *m*.
II *vi* (with one oar) godiller; (with two oars) ramer en couple.

scullery /'skʌlərɪ/ *n* GB arrière-cuisine *f*.

sculpt /skʌlpt/ *vtr, vi* sculpter.

sculptor /'skʌlptə(r)/ ▶ 1251 *n* sculpteur *m*.

sculpture /'skʌlptʃə(r)/ **I** *n* sculpture *f*.
II *noun modifier* [*class, gallery*] de sculpture.

scum /skʌm/ *n* **1** (on pond) couche *f* d'algues, de mousse etc; **2** (on liquid) mousse *f*; **3** (on bath) crasse *f*; **they're the** ~ **of the earth** ce sont des moins que rien.

scurf /skɜːf/ *n* (dandruff) pellicules *fpl*; (dead skin) peau *f* morte.

scurrilous /'skʌrɪləs/ *adj* calomnieux/-ieuse.

scurry /'skʌrɪ/ **I** *n* (*tjrs sg*) **the** ~ **of feet** le bruit de pas rapides.
II *vi* (*prét, pp* **-ried**) se précipiter; **to** ~ **to and fro** courir dans tous les sens; **to** ~ **away, to** ~ **off** se sauver.

scuttle /'skʌtl/ **I** *n* **1** (hatch) écoutille *f*; **2** ▶ **coal scuttle**.
II *vtr* LIT saborder [*ship*]; FIG faire échouer.
III *vi* **to** ~ **away** ou **off** filer; **to** ~ **across sth** traverser qch à toute vitesse.

scythe /saɪð/ **I** *n* faux *f inv*.
II *vtr* faucher [*grass*].

SD *n* US POST *abrév* ▶ **South Dakota**.

SDLP *n* POL (in Ireland) (*abrév* = **Social Democratic and Labour Party**) SDLP *m*.

SE ▶ 1157 *n* (*abrév* = **southeast**) SE *m*.

sea /siː/ ▶ 1117 **I** *n* **1** GEN mer *f*; **beside** ou **by the** ~ au bord de la mer; **the open** ~ le large; **at** ~ être en mer; **once out to** ~ une fois en pleine mer; **to put (out) to** ~, **to go to** ~ prendre la mer; **a long way out to** ~ très loin de la côte; **by** ~ [*travel*] en bateau; [*send*] par bateau; **to bury sb at** ~ immerger le corps de qn; **2** (as career) **to go to** ~ (join Navy) s'engager dans la marine; (join ship) se faire engager comme marin; **3** (sailor's life) **the** ~ la vie de marin; **4** FIG **a** ~ **of** une nuée de [*faces*].
II **seas** *npl* **the heavy** ~s la tempête; **to sink in heavy** ~s couler par gros temps.
III *noun modifier* [*air, breeze*] marin; [*bird, water*] de mer; [*crossing, voyage*] par mer; [*battle*] naval; [*creature*] de la mer; [*power*] maritime.
IDIOMS **to be all at** ~ être complètement perdu; **to get one's** ~ **legs** s'habituer au roulis.

sea: ~ **anemone** *n* anémone *f* de mer; ~ **bass** *n* loup *m* de mer; **~bed** *n* fonds *mpl* marins; **~board** *n* côte *f*; ~ **bream** *n* dorade *f*; ~ **captain** ▶ 1192 *n* capitaine *m* de la marine marchande; ~ **change** *n* transformation *f* radicale; ~ **defences** GB, ~ **defenses** US *npl* digues *fpl*;

Seasons

*French never uses capital letters for names of seasons
as English sometimes does.*

spring	=	le printemps
summer	=	l'été *m*
autumn *or* fall	=	l'automne *m*
winter	=	l'hiver *m*
in spring	=	au printemps
in summer	=	en été
in autumn *or* fall	=	en automne
in winter	=	en hiver

In the following examples, summer *and* été *are used as
models for all the season names.*
*French normally uses the definite article, whether or not
English does*

I like summer *ou* I like the summer	=	j'aime l'été
during the summer	=	pendant l'été
		or au cours de l'été
in early summer	=	au début de l'été
in late summer	=	à la fin de l'été
for the whole summer	=	pendant tout l'été

throughout the summer	=	tout au long de l'été
next summer	=	l'été prochain
last summer	=	l'été dernier
the summer before last	=	il y a deux ans en été
the summer after next	=	dans deux ans en été

However, ce *may replace the definite article*

this summer	=	cet été

There is never any article when en *is used*

in summer	=	en été
until summer	=	jusqu'en été

Seasons used as adjectives with other nouns

De *alone, without article, is the usual form, e.g.*

summer clothes	=	des vêtements d'été
the summer collection	=	la collection d'été
the summer sales	=	les soldes d'été
a summer day	=	une journée d'été
a summer evening	=	un soir d'été
a summer landscape	=	un paysage d'été
summer weather	=	un temps d'été

~ dog *n* (vieux) loup *m* de mer; **~ dumping** *n* déversement *m* de déchets en mer.

seafaring /'si:feərɪŋ/ *adj* [*nation*] de marins; **my ~
days** ma vie de marin; **a ~ man** un marin.

seafood /'si:fu:d/ **I** *n* fruits *mpl* de mer.
II *noun modifier* [*dish*] de fruits de mer; [*sauce*] aux
fruits de mer.

sea: ~front *n* front *m* de mer; **~green** ▶ 818 *n*,
adj vert (*m*) d'eau *inv*; **~gull** *n* mouette *f*; **~ horse**
n hippocampe *m*; **~kale** *n* chou *m* marin.

seal /si:l/ **I** *n* **1** ZOOL phoque *m*; **2** JUR, GEN (*insignia*)
sceau *m*; **to set one's ~ on** LIT apposer son cachet
sur; FIG conclure; **to set the ~ on** sceller [*friendship*]; confirmer [*trend, regime*]; **to give sth one's ~
of approval** approuver qch; **look for our ~ of quality** exigez le label de qualité; **3** (to keep intact) joint
m (*on container*) plomb *m*; (*on package, letter*) cachet *m*; (*on
door*) scellés *mpl*; **4** (*closure*) fermeture *f*.
II *vtr* **1** cacheter [*letter*]; **2** (*close*) sceller [*oil well,
pipe*]; boucher [*gap*]; **3** (make airtight, watertight) fermer
[*qch*] hermétiquement [*jar, tin*]; **4** FIG sceller [*alliance*] (**with** par); conclure [*deal*] (**with** par); **to ~
sb's fate** décider du sort de qn.
III sealed *pp adj* [*envelope*] cacheté; [*door*] scellé;
[*orders*] sous pli cacheté; [*jar*] fermé hermétiquement.
■ **seal in** conserver [*flavour*].
■ **seal off**: **~** [*sth*] **off**, **~ off** [*sth*] **1** (isolate) isoler;
2 (cordon off) GEN boucler; barrer [*street*].
■ **seal up**: **~** [*sth*] **up**, **~ up** [*sth*] fermer [*qch*]
hermétiquement [*jar*]; boucher [*gap*].

sea lane *n* couloir *m* de navigation.

sealant /'si:lənt/ *n* (coating) enduit *m* d'étanchéité;
(filler) mastic *m*.

seal cull, seal culling *n* massacre *m* des phoques.

sea level *n* niveau *m* de la mer.

sealing wax *n* cire *f* à cacheter.

sea lion *n* lion *m* de mer.

sealskin /'si:lskɪn/ **I** *n* peau *f* de phoque.
II *noun modifier* [*coat, gloves*] en peau de phoque.

seam /si:m/ **I** *n* **1** (in garment) couture *f*; **to be bursting at the ~s** [*building*] être bondé; [*suitcase*] être
plein à craquer; **to come apart at the ~** LIT
craquer; FIG s'écrouler; **2** (of coal) veine *f*.
II *vtr* (in sewing) coudre.

seaman /'si:mən/ ▶ 1192 *n* (*pl* **-men**) MIL, NAUT
matelot *m*; (amateur) marin *m*.

seamed /si:md/ *adj* [*stockings, tights*] à coutures.

sea: ~ mile *n* mille *m* marin; **~ mist** *n* brume *f*.

seamless /'si:mlɪs/ *adj* [*garment, cloth*] sans coutures;
[*transition*] sans heurts; [*process, whole*] continu.

seamy /'si:mɪ/ *adj* [*scandal*] sordide; [*area*] malfamé.

seance /'seɪɑ:ns/ *n* séance *f* de spiritisme.

seaplane *n* hydravion *m*.

sear /sɪə(r)/ *vtr* (scorch) calciner; (seal) cautériser
[*wound*]; saisir [*meat*]; (wither) flétrir.

search /sɜ:tʃ/ **I** *n* **1** (seeking) recherches *fpl* (**for sb/sth**)
pour retrouver qn/qch); **in ~ of** à la recherche de; **2**
(examination) fouille *f* (**of** de); **to carry out a ~ of sth**
fouiller qch; **3** COMPUT recherche *f*.
II *vtr* **1** (examine) GEN fouiller; fouiller dans [*cupboard, drawer, memory*]; **2** (scrutinize) examiner (attentivement) [*page, map, records*]; **~ me**○! aucune idée!,
j'en sais rien○!; **3** COMPUT rechercher dans [*file*].
III *vi* **1** (seek) chercher; **to ~ for** *ou* **after sb/sth**
chercher qn/qch; **2** (examine) **to ~ through** fouiller
dans [*cupboard, bag*]; examiner [*records, file*]; **3**
COMPUT **to ~ for** rechercher [*data, item, file*].
■ **search about, search around** chercher.
■ **search out**: **~** [*sb/sth*] **out**, **~ out** [*sb/sth*] découvrir.

searcher /'sɜ:tʃə(r)/ *n* sauveteur/-euse *m/f*.

searching /'sɜ:tʃɪŋ/ *adj* [*look, question*] pénétrant.

search: ~light *n* projecteur *m*; **~ party** *n* équipe
f de secours; **~ warrant** *n* JUR mandat *m* de perquisition.

searing /'sɪərɪŋ/ *adj* [*heat*] incandescent; [*pace, pain*]
fulgurant; [*criticism, indictment*] virulent.

sea: ~ route *n* voie *f* maritime; **~ salt** *n* CULIN
sel *m* de mer; IND sel *m* marin; **~shell** *n* coquillage
m; **~shore** *n* (part of coast) littoral *m*; (beach) plage *f*.

seasick /'si:sɪk/ *adj* **to be** *ou* **get** *ou* **feel ~** avoir le
mal de mer.

seasickness /'si:sɪknɪs/ *n* mal *m* de mer.

seaside /'si:saɪd/ **I** *n* **the ~** le bord de la mer.
II *noun modifier* [*holiday*] à la mer; [*hotel*] en bord de
mer; [*town*] maritime; **~ resort** station *f* balnéaire.

season /'si:zn/ **I** *n* **1** (time of year) saison *f*; **strawberries are in/out of ~** c'est/ce n'est pas la saison des
fraises; **out of ~** hors saison; **late in the ~** dans
l'arrière-saison; **the holiday ~** la période des
vacances; **a ~ of French films** un cycle du cinéma
français; **2** (festive period) **the Christmas ~** la période
de Noël; **Season's greetings!** (on Christmas cards)
Joyeuses fêtes!
II *vtr* **1** CULIN (with spices) relever; (with condiments)
assaisonner; **~ with salt and pepper** salez et
poivrez; **2** TECH sécher [*timber*]; abreuver [*cask*].

seasonal /'si:zənl/ *adj* GEN saisonnier/-ière; [*fruit,
produce*] de saison.

seasonally /'si:zənəlɪ/ *adv* selon la saison; **~
adjusted figures** FIN chiffres *mpl* corrigés en fonction
des variations saisonnières.

seasoned /'si:znd/ *adj* **1** [*timber*] bien séché; **2** FIG
[*soldier*] aguerri; [*traveller*] grand (*before n*); [*politician, leader*] chevronné; [*campaigner, performer*] expérimenté; **3** CULIN [*dish*] assaisonné; **highly ~**
relevé, épicé; **4** [*wine*] vieilli en fût.

seasoning /'si:znɪŋ/ n CULIN assaisonnement m.

season: **~ ticket** n (for travel) carte f d'abonnement; SPORT, THEAT abonnement m; **~ ticket holder** n (for travel) détenteur/-trice m/f de carte d'abonnement; SPORT, THEAT abonné/-e m/f.

seat /si:t/ I n **1** (allocated place) place f; **has everybody got a ~?** est-ce que tout le monde est assis?; **take** ou **have a ~** asseyez-vous; **2** POL siège m; **safe/marginal ~** siège sûr/menacé; **to have a ~ on the council** siéger au conseil; **3** (type, object) GEN, AUT siège m; (bench-type) banquette f; **the back ~** la banquette arrière; **sit in the front ~** assieds-toi à l'avant; **4** (location, centre) siège m; **~ of government/learning** siège du gouvernement/savoir; **5** (residence) résidence f familiale; **6** (on horse) **to have a good ~** avoir une bonne assiette; **7** EUPH postérieur m; **8** (of trousers) fond m.

II **-seat** combining form a 150-**~ plane/cinema** un avion/cinéma de 150 places.

III vtr **1** (assign place to) placer [person]; **2 the car ~s five** c'est une voiture à cinq places; **the table ~s six** c'est une table de six couverts; **the room ~s 30 people** la salle peut accueillir 30 personnes.

IV v refl **to ~ oneself** prendre place (**at** à).

V **seated** pp adj assis.

IDIOMS **to take/occupy a back ~** FIG se mettre/se tenir en retrait.

seatbelt n ceinture f (de sécurité).

-seater /'si:tə(r)/ combining form a **two~** (plane) un avion m à deux places; (car) un coupé; (sofa) un (canapé) deux places; **all~ stadium** GB stade m sans places debout.

seating /'si:tɪŋ/ I n (chairs) sièges mpl; (places) places fpl assises; **to introduce extra ~** ajouter plus de sièges; **I'll organize the ~** je placerai les gens. II noun modifier **~ capacity** nombre m de places assises; **~ plan** plan m de table.

sea: **~ trout** n truite f de mer; **~ urchin** n oursin m; **~ view** n vue f sur la mer; **~wall** n digue f.

seaward /'si:wəd/ I adj [side of building] qui donne sur la mer; [side of cape] qui fait face au large. II adv (also **~s**) [fly, move] vers la mer; [gaze] vers le large.

sea: **~weed** n algue f marine; **~worthy** adj [ship, vessel] en état de naviguer.

sec /sek/ n **1** (abrév écrite **= second**) s; **2**○ (short instant) instant m.

secateurs /ˌsekə'tɜ:z, 'sekətɜ:z/ npl GB sécateur m.

secede /sɪ'si:d/ vi faire sécession (**from** de).

secession /sɪ'seʃn/ n sécession f (**from** de).

secluded /sɪ'klu:dɪd/ adj retiré.

seclusion /sɪ'klu:ʒn/ n isolement m (**from** à l'écart de).

second ▶812|, 1112|, 854| I /'sekənd/ n **1** (unit of time) ALSO MUS, MATH, PHYS seconde f; (instant) instant m; **they should arrive any ~ now** ils devraient arriver d'un instant à l'autre; **at six o'clock to the ~** à six heures pile; **2** (ordinal number) deuxième m/f, second/-e m/f; **X was the most popular in the survey, but Y came a close ~** dans le sondage X était le plus populaire mais Y suivait de près; **he came a poor ~** il est arrivé deuxième, mais loin derrière le premier; **the problem of crime was seen as ~ only to unemployment** le problème du crime venait juste derrière le chômage; **3** (date) **the ~ of May** le deux mai; **4** GB UNIV **upper/lower ~** licence f avec mention bien/assez bien; **5** (also **~ gear**) AUT deuxième f, seconde f; **6** (defective article) article m qui a un défaut; **7** (in boxing) soigneur m; (in duel) témoin m.

II○ **seconds** /'sekəndz/ npl rab○ m.

III /'sekənd/ adj deuxième, second; **the ~ teeth** dents définitives; **every ~ Monday** un lundi sur deux; **to have** ou **take a ~ helping (of sth)** reprendre (de qch); **to have a ~ chance to do sth** avoir une nouvelle chance de faire; **to ask for a ~ opinion** (from doctor) demander l'opinion d'un autre médecin.

IV /'sekənd/ adv **1** (in second place) deuxième ou **finish ~** (in race, competition) arriver deuxième; **I agreed to speak ~** j'ai accepté de parler le deuxième; **the ~ biggest building** le deuxième bâtiment de par sa grandeur; **the fact that he's my father comes ~** le fait qu'il soit mon père est secondaire; **2** (also **secondly**) deuxièmement.

V vtr **1** /'sekənd/ appuyer [motion, proposal]; **2** /sɪ'kɒnd/ MIL, COMM détacher (**from** de; **to** à).

IDIOMS **to be ~ nature** être automatique; **to be ~ to none** être sans pareil; **to do sth without (giving it) a ~ thought** faire qch sans réfléchir; **on ~ thoughts** à la réflexion; **to have ~ thoughts** avoir quelques hésitations ou doutes; **to have ~ thoughts about doing** avoir moins envie de faire.

secondary /'sekəndrɪ, US -derɪ/ I n MED métastase f. II adj GEN, LING, PSYCH, SCH secondaire; [sense, meaning] dérivé; **~ to sth** moins important que qch.

secondary: **~ health care** n ~ soins mpl hospitaliers; **~ infection** n surinfection f; **~ modern (school)** n GB ~ collège m d'enseignement général; **~ school** n ~ école f secondaire.

second ballot n second tour m, deuxième tour m (du scrutin).

second best I n pis-aller m; **as a ~, I suppose it will do** je suppose que faute de mieux, cela fera l'affaire. II adv **he came off** GB ou **out** US **~** il a été largement battu.

second chamber n chambre f haute.

second class I n **1** (for post) ~ acheminement m lent; **2** RAIL deuxième classe f. II **second-class** adj **1** (for post) au tarif lent; **2** RAIL de deuxième classe; **3** GB UNIV **~ degree** ~ licence f obtenue avec mention assez bien; **4** (second rate) de qualité inférieure; **~ citizen** citoyen/-enne m/f de seconde zone. III adv [travel] en deuxième classe; [send] au tarif lent.

second: **~ cousin** n cousin/-e m/f issu/-e de germains; **~ degree** n UNIV ~ diplôme m de troisième cycle.

seconder /'sekəndə(r)/ n personne f qui appuie une motion.

second-guess○ /ˌsekənd'ges/ vtr anticiper.

second hand I /'sekəndhænd/ n (on watch, clock) trotteuse f.
II **second-hand** /ˌsekənd'hænd/ adj [clothes, car, goods] d'occasion; [market] de l'occasion; [news, information, report] de seconde main; [opinion] d'emprunt; **~ dealer** vendeur/-euse m/f d'objets d'occasion; **~ car dealer** ou **salesman** vendeur/-euse m/f de voitures d'occasion; **~ value** valeur f à la revente. III adv [buy] d'occasion; [hear] indirectement.

second in command ▶1192| n MIL commandant m en second; the second m, adjoint m.

secondly /'sekəndlɪ/ adv deuxièmement.

secondment /sɪ'kɒndmənt/ n **on ~** en détachement.

second name n **1** (surname) nom m de famille; **2** (second forename) deuxième prénom m.

second: **~-rate** adj GEN de second ordre; [product] de qualité inférieure; **~ sight** n double vue f.

secrecy /'si:krəsɪ/ n secret m; **why all the ~?** pourquoi tous ces secrets?; **she's been sworn to ~** on lui a fait jurer le secret; **an air of ~** un air de mystère.

secret /'si:krɪt/ I n **1** (unknown thing) secret m; **to tell sb a ~** confier un secret à qn; **to let sb in on a ~** mettre qn dans le secret; **I make no ~ of my membership of the party** je ne fais pas mystère de mon appartenance au parti; **it's an open ~ that** tout le monde sait que; **there's no ~ about who** tout le monde sait qui; **2** (ideal method) secret m (**of** de).
II adj GEN secret/-ète; [contributor] anonyme; **to keep sth ~ from sb** cacher qch à qn; **to be a ~ drinker** boire en cachette.
III **in secret** adv phr GEN en secret.

secretarial /ˌsekrəˈteərɪəl/ *adj* [*course, skills, work*] de secrétaire; [*college, staff*] de secrétariat.

secretariat /ˌsekrəˈteərɪət/ *n* secrétariat *m*.

secretary /ˈsekrətrɪ, US -rəterɪ/ ▶1251 *n* **1** ADMIN secrétaire *mf* (**to sb** de qn); **2** GB POL **Foreign/Home Secretary** ministre *m* des Affaires étrangères/de l'Intérieur; **Secretary of State for the Environment** ministre *m* de l'Environnement; **3** US POL **Defense Secretary** ministre *m* de la Défense; **Secretary of State** ministre *m* des Affaires étrangères.

secrete /sɪˈkriːt/ *vtr* **1** BIOL, MED sécréter [*fluid*]; **2** (hide) cacher.

secretion /sɪˈkriːʃn/ *n* BIOL, MED sécrétion *f*.

secretive /ˈsiːkrətɪv/ *adj* GEN secret/-ète; [*expression, conduct*] mystérieux/-ieuse; **to be ~ about sth** faire un mystère de qch.

secretively /ˈsiːkrətɪvlɪ/ *adv* (mysteriously) énigmatiquement; (furtively) furtivement.

secretly /ˈsiːkrɪtlɪ/ *adv* secrètement.

secret: **~ police** *n* police *f* secrète; **~ service** *n* services *mpl* secrets; **Secret Service** *n* US services *mpl* chargés de la protection du président; **~ society** *n* société *f* secrète; **~ weapon** *n* LIT, FIG arme *f* secrète.

sect /sekt/ *n* secte *f*.

sectarian /sekˈteərɪən/ *n, adj* sectaire (*mf*).

section /ˈsekʃn/ **I** *n* **1** (part) (of train, aircraft, town, forest, area) partie *f*; (of pipe, tunnel, road, river) tronçon *m*; (of object, kit) élément *m*; (of fruit) quartier *m*; (of population, group) tranche *f*; **2** (department) GEN service *m*; (of library, shop) rayon *m*; **3** (of act, bill, report) article *m*; (of newspaper) rubrique *f*; **under ~ 24** aux termes de l'article 24; **4** (of book) passage *m* (**on** sur); (larger) partie *f* (**on** qui traite de); **5** MIL groupe *m*; **6** BIOL lamelle *f*; **7** MATH section *f*; **8** US (sleeping car) compartiment-couchettes *m*.
II *vtr* sectionner [*document, text*]; segmenter [*computer screen*].
■ **section off**: **~ off** [sth], **~** [sth] **off** séparer [*part, area*].

sector /ˈsektə(r)/ *n* (all contexts) secteur *m*.

secular /ˈsekjʊlə(r)/ *adj* [*politics, law, society, education*] laïque; [*belief, music*] profane; [*priest, power*] séculier/-ière.

secularize /ˈsekjʊləraɪz/ *vtr* séculariser, laïciser [*society, education*]; séculariser [*church property*].

secure /sɪˈkjʊə(r)/ **I** *adj* **1** (not threatened) [*job, marriage, income*] stable; [*base, foundation*] solide; [*investment*] sûr; **2** [*hiding place, route*] sûr; **to be ~ against sth** être à l'abri de qch; **3** [*padlock, knot*] solide; [*structure, ladder*] stable; [*foothold*] sûr; [*rope*] bien attaché; [*door*] bien fermé; **4** PSYCH [*feeling*] de sécurité; [*background*] sécurisant; **to feel ~** se sentir en sécurité; **to be ~ in the knowledge that** avoir la certitude que.
II *vtr* **1** (procure, obtain) GEN obtenir; atteindre [*objective*]; **2** (make firm, safe) bien attacher [*rope*]; bien fermer [*door*]; fixer [*wheel*]; stabiliser [*ladder*]; **3** (make safe) protéger [*house, camp*]; assurer [*position, future, job*]; **4** FIN garantir [*loan*].

securely /sɪˈkjʊəlɪ/ *adv* **1** (carefully) [*fasten, fix, tie*] solidement; [*wrap, tuck, pin*] soigneusement; **2** (safely) en sûreté; **3** FIG (well and truly) bel et bien.

secure unit *n* (in children's home) *section surveillée dans une maison de rééducation*; (in psychiatric hospital) quartier *m* de haute sécurité.

securities /sɪˈkjʊərətɪz/ FIN **I** *npl* titres *mpl*.
II *noun modifier* [*company, market*] des titres.

security /sɪˈkjʊərətɪ/ **I** *n* **1** (of person, child, financial position, investment) sécurité *f*; **~ of employment**, **job ~** sécurité de l'emploi; **2** (for site, prison, nation, VIP) sécurité *f*; **state** ou **national ~** sûreté *f* de l'État; **3** (department) service *m* de sécurité; **4** (guarantee) garantie *f* (**on** sur); **to stand ~ for sb** se porter garant de qn; **5** FIN titre *m*.
II *noun modifier* [*badge, camera, check, forces, measures*] de sécurité; [*firm, staff*] de surveillance.

security: **~ guard** ▶1251 *n* garde *m* sécurité, vigile *m*; **~ leak** *n* fuite *f* (*d'information*); **~ officer** ▶1251 *n* responsable *mf* de la sécurité; **~ risk** *n* (person) danger *m* pour la sécurité; **~ van** *n* GB fourgon *m* blindé.

sedate /sɪˈdeɪt/ **I** *adj* [*person*] posé; [*lifestyle, pace*] tranquille.
II *vtr* mettre [qn] sous calmants [*patient*].

sedative /ˈsedətɪv/ **I** *n* sédatif *m*, calmant *m*.
II *adj* [*effect, drug*] sédatif/-ive.

sedentary /ˈsedntrɪ, US -terɪ/ *adj* sédentaire.

sediment /ˈsedɪmənt/ *n* GEN dépôt *m*; (in wine) lie *f*.

seduce /sɪˈdjuːs, US -ˈduːs/ *vtr* **1** (sexually) [*person*] séduire; **2** FIG [*idea, project etc*] tenter; **to be ~d into doing** se laisser convaincre de faire.

seduction /sɪˈdʌkʃn/ *n* **1** (act of seducing) séduction *f*; **2** (attractive quality) attrait *m* (**of** de).

seductive /sɪˈdʌktɪv/ *adj* [*person*] séduisant; [*argument, proposal*] alléchant; [*smile*] aguicheur/-euse.

see /siː/ **I** *n* (of bishop) évêché *m*; (of archbishop) archevêché *m*.
II *vtr* (*prét* **saw**; *pp* **seen**) **1** (perceive, look at) voir; **there's nobody to be seen** il n'y a personne en vue; **there was going to be trouble: I could ~ it coming** ou **I could ~ it a mile off** il allait y avoir des problèmes: je le sentais venir; **I don't know what you ~ in him**○ je ne sais pas ce que tu lui trouves○; **I must be ~ing things!** j'ai des visions!; **to ~ one's way (clear) to doing sth** trouver le moyen de faire qch; **2** (visit) voir [*expert, country, building*]; **I'm ~ing a psychiatrist** je vais chez un psychiatre; **to ~ the sights** faire du tourisme; **they ~ a lot of each other** ils se voient souvent; **~ you!**○ salut!○; **~ you next week**○! à la semaine prochaine!; **he's ~ing a married woman** il fréquente une femme mariée; **3** (receive) recevoir; **4** (understand) voir [*advantage, problem*]; comprendre [*joke*]; **do you ~ what I mean?** tu vois ce que je veux dire?; **5** (consider) voir; **to ~ sb as** considérer qn comme [*leader, hero*]; **I ~ it as an opportunity** je pense que c'est une occasion à saisir; **I ~ it as an insult** je prends ça pour une insulte; **it can be seen from this example that** cet exemple nous montre que; **it remains to be seen whether** ou **if** reste à voir si; **6** (envisage) **I can't ~ sb/sth doing** je ne pense pas que qn/qch puisse faire; **I can ~ a time when this country will be independent** je peux imaginer qu'un jour ce pays sera indépendant; **7** (make sure) **to ~ (to it) that** veiller à ce que (+ *subj*); **8** (witness) voir; (experience) connaître [*poverty, war*]; **next year will ~ the completion of the road** la route sera terminée l'année prochaine; **9** (accompany) **to ~ sb to the station** accompagner qn à la gare; **to ~ sb home** raccompagner qn chez lui/elle.
III *vi* (*prét* **saw**; *pp* **seen**) **1** (with eyes) voir; **I can't ~** je ne vois rien; **~ for yourself** voyez vous-même; **so I ~** c'est ce que je vois; **you can ~ for miles** on y voit à des kilomètres; **2** (understand) voir; **now I ~** maintenant, je comprends; **as far as I can ~** autant que je puisse en juger; **3** (check , find out) **I'll go and ~** je vais voir; **we'll just have to wait and ~** il ne nous reste plus qu'à attendre; **4** (think, consider) **I'll have to ~** il faut que je réfléchisse; **let's ~**, **let me ~** voyons (un peu).
IV *v refl* (*prét* **saw**; *pp* **seen**) **to ~ oneself** LIT, FIG se voir; **I can't ~ myself as** ou **being...** je ne pense pas que je vais être...
IDIOMS I'll ~ you right○ je ne te laisserai pas tomber○; **now I've seen it all!** j'aurai tout vu!
■ **see about**: **~ about** [sth] s'occuper de; **we'll soon ~ about that**○! IRON c'est ce qu'on va voir!; **to ~ about doing** penser à faire.
■ **see off**: **~** [sb] **off**, **~** [off] **sb 1** (say goodbye to) dire au revoir à qn; **2** (throw out) **the drunk was seen off the premises** on a mis l'ivrogne à la porte.
■ **see out**: ¶ **~** [sth] **out**, **~ out** [sth] **we have enough coal to ~ the winter out** nous avons assez de charbon pour passer l'hiver; ¶ **~** [sb] **out** raccompagner [qn] à la porte; **I'll ~ myself out** GEN

je m'en vais mais ne vous dérangez pas; (in big building) je trouverai la sortie, ne vous dérangez pas. ■ **see through**: ¶ **~ through** [sth] déceler [*deception, lie*]; **it was easy enough to ~ through the excuse** il était évident que c'était une fausse excuse; ¶ **~ through** [sb] percer [qn] à jour; ¶ **~** [sth] **through** mener [qch] à bonne fin; ¶ **~** [sb] **through**: **there's enough food to ~ us through the week** il y a assez à manger pour tenir toute la semaine; **this money will ~ you through** cet argent te dépannera. ■ **see to**: **~ to** [sth] s'occuper de.

seed /siːd/ **I** *n* **1** BOT (of plant) graine *f*; (fruit pip) pépin *m*; **2** ⊄ (for sowing) semences *fpl*; CULIN graines *fpl*; **to go** ou **run to ~** LIT [*plant*] monter en graine; FIG [*person*] se ramollir; [*organization, country*] être en déclin; **3** FIG (beginning) germes *mpl*; **4** SPORT tête *f* de série; **the top ~** la tête de série numéro un. **II** *vtr* **1** (sow) ensemencer [*field, lawn*] (**with** de); **2** CULIN (also **deseed**) épépiner; **3** SPORT classer [qn] tête de série; **to be ~ed sixth** ou (**number**) **six** être classé tête de série numéro six; **a ~ed player** une tête de série.

seed: **~bed** *n* LIT semis *m*; FIG pépinière *f*; **~ box** *n* = **seed tray**; **~cake** *n* gâteau *m* au carvi.

seedless /ˈsiːdlɪs/ *adj* sans pépins.

seedling /ˈsiːdlɪŋ/ *n* plant *m*.

seed: **~ merchant** ▶ 1251 *n* (person) grainetier/ -ière *m/f*; **~ tray** *n* germoir *m*.

seedy /ˈsiːdɪ/ *adj* **1** (shabby) [*hotel, street*] miteux/-euse; [*person*] minable; **2** (disreputable) [*activity, person*] louche; [*area, club*] mal famé; **3**○ (ill) patraque○.

seeing /ˈsiːɪŋ/ *conj* **~ that**, **~ as** étant donné que, vu que.

seek /siːk/ (*prét, pp* **sought**) **I** *vtr* **1** (try to obtain) chercher [*agreement, means, refuge, solution*]; demander [*advice, help, backing, redress*]; **to ~ revenge** chercher à se venger; **to ~ one's fortune** chercher fortune; **2** (look for) [*police, employer, person*] rechercher. **II** **-seeking** *combining form* en quête de; **pleasure-~ing** en quête de plaisir. **III** *vi* **to ~ for** ou **after sth** rechercher qch. ■ **seek out**: **~ out** [sth/sb], **~** [sth/sb] **out** aller chercher, dénicher.

seeker /ˈsiːkə(r)/ *n* **~ after** ou **for sth** personne *f* en quête de qch.

seem /siːm/ *vi* **1** (give impression) sembler; (less formal) avoir l'air; **he ~s to be looking for**... on dirait qu'il cherche...; **it would ~ so/not** on dirait que oui/non; **the whole house ~ed to shake** on aurait dit que toute la maison tremblait; **things are not always what they ~** les apparences sont souvent trompeuses; **how does she ~ today?** comment va-t-elle aujourd'hui?; **2** (have impression) **it ~s to me that** il me semble que (+ *indic*); **it ~s as if** ou **as though** il semble que (+ *subj*); **I ~ to have offended him** j'ai l'impression que je l'ai vexé; **I ~ to have forgotten my money** je crois que j'ai oublié mon argent; **it ~s hours since we left** on dirait qu'il y a des heures que nous sommes partis; **it ~ed like a good idea at the time** cela avait l'air d'une bonne idée; **3** (expressing criticism) **he ~s to think that**... il a l'air de croire que...; **they don't ~ to realize that**... ils n'ont pas l'air de se rendre compte que...; **what ~s to be the problem?** quel est le problème?; **4** (despite trying) **he can't ~ to do** on dirait qu'il n'arrive pas à faire; **I just can't ~ to do** je n'arrive pas à faire.

seeming /ˈsiːmɪŋ/ *adj* [*ease, lack*] apparent.

seemingly /ˈsiːmɪŋlɪ/ *adv* apparemment.

seen /siːn/ *pp* ▶ **see**.

seep /siːp/ *vi* suinter; **to ~ away** s'écouler; **to ~ through sth** [*water, gas*] s'infiltrer à travers qch; [*light*] filtrer à travers qch.

seepage /ˈsiːpɪdʒ/ *n* (trickle) suintement *m*; (leak) (from container) fuite *f*; (into structure, soil) infiltration *f*.

seesaw /ˈsiːsɔː/ **I** *n* LIT tapecul *m*; FIG (motion) va-et-vient *m inv*. **II** *vi* LIT faire du tapecul; FIG [*price, rate*] osciller.

seethe /siːð/ *vi* **1** [*water*] bouillonner; **2 to ~ with rage** bouillir de colère; **3** (teem) grouiller; **seething with unrest** en proie à l'agitation.

see-through /ˈsiːθruː/ *adj* transparent.

segment I /ˈsegmənt/ *n* **1** ANAT, COMPUT, LING, ZOOL segment *m*; (of orange) quartier *m*; **2** (of economy, market) secteur *m*; (of population, vote) part *f*. **II** /segˈment/ *vtr* segmenter [*market, surface*]; couper [qch] en quartiers [*orange*].

segregate /ˈsegrɪgeɪt/ *vtr* **1** (separate) séparer (**from** de); **2** (isolate) isoler (**from** de).

segregated /ˈsegrəgeɪtɪd/ *adj* [*education, parliament, society*] ségrégationniste; [*area, school*] où la ségrégation raciale (or religieuse) est en vigueur; [*facilities*] séparé.

segregation /ˌsegrɪˈgeɪʃn/ *n* (of races, religions, social groups) ségrégation *f* (**from** de); (of rivals) séparation *f*; (of prisoners) isolement *m*.

seismic /ˈsaɪzmɪk/ *adj* sismique.

seismograph /ˈsaɪzməgrɑːf, US -græf/ *n* sismographe *m*.

seismology /saɪzˈmɒlədʒɪ/ *n* sismologie *f*.

seize /siːz/ **I** *vtr* **1** LIT (take hold of) saisir; **to ~ hold of** se saisir de [*person*]; s'emparer de [*object*]; saisir sur [*idea*]; **2** FIG (grasp) saisir [*opportunity, moment*]; prendre [*initiative*]; **to be ~d by** être pris de [*emotion*]; **3** MIL, POL (capture) s'emparer de [*territory, prisoner, power*]; prendre [*control*]; **4** JUR saisir [*arms, drugs*]; appréhender [*person*]. **II** *vi* [*engine, mechanism*] se gripper. ■ **seize on**, **seize upon**: **~ on** [sth] sauter sur. ■ **seize up** [*engine*] se gripper; [*limb etc*] se bloquer.

seizure /ˈsiːʒə(r)/ *n* **1** (taking) (of territory, installation, power) prise *f*; (of arms, drugs, property) saisie *f*; (of person) (legal) arrestation *f*; (illegal) capture *f*; (of hostage) prise *f*; **2** MED, FIG attaque *f*.

seldom /ˈseldəm/ *adv* rarement; **~ if ever** rarement, pour ne pas dire jamais.

select /sɪˈlekt/ **I** *adj* [*group, audience*] privilégié; [*hotel, restaurant*] chic *inv*, sélect; [*area*] chic *inv*, cossu; **a ~ few** seulement quelques privilégiés. **II** *vtr* sélectionner (**from, from among** parmi). **III** **selected** *pp adj* [*poems, letters*] choisi; [*candidate, country, question, materials*] sélectionné; [*ingredients*] de premier choix; **in ~ed stores** dans certains magasins; **pilot programmes in ~ed areas** des programmes pilotes dans des zones-test.

select committee *n* commission *f* d'enquête.

selection /sɪˈlekʃn/ **I** *n* GEN, SPORT sélection *f*; **to make a ~** (for purchase) faire un choix; **~s from Mozart** morceaux *mpl* choisis de Mozart. **II** *noun modifier* [*panel, process*] de sélection.

selective /sɪˈlektɪv/ *adj* **1** (positively biased) [*memory, recruitment*] sélectif/-ive; [*admission, education*] basé sur la sélection; **she should be more ~ about the friends she makes** elle devrait mieux choisir ses amis; **2** (negatively biased) [*account, perspective*] tendancieux/-ieuse; **3** AGRIC [*weedkiller*] sélectif/-ive; **~ breeding** sélection *f* artificielle (*en élevage*).

selector /sɪˈlektə(r)/ *n* **1** GB SPORT (person) sélectionneur/-euse *m/f*; **2** TECH (device) sélecteur *m*.

self /self/ *n* (*pl* **selves**) **1** GEN, PSYCH moi *m*; **he's back to his old ~ again** il est redevenu lui-même; **one's better ~** le meilleur de soi/de lui/d'elle etc; **2** FIN (on cheque) moi-même.

self: **~-acting** *adj* automatique; **~-addressed envelope**, **SAE** *n* enveloppe *f* à mon/votre etc adresse; **~-adhesive** *adj* autocollant; **~-analysis** *n* auto-analyse *f*; **~-apparent** *adj* évident; **~-appointed** *adj* autonommé; **~-appraisal** *n* auto-évaluation *f*; **~-assembly** *adj* en kit; **~-assessment** *n* auto-évaluation *f*; **~-assurance** *n* assurance *f*.

self-assured /ˌselfəˈʃɔːd, US -ˈʃʊərd/ *adj* plein d'assurance; **to be very ~** avoir beaucoup d'assurance.

self: **~-awareness** *n* conscience *f* de soi/de lui-même etc; **~-belief** *n* confiance *f* en soi/en elle etc.

self-catering /ˌselfˈkeɪtərɪŋ/ adj GB [flat, accommodation] meublé; ~ **holiday** vacances fpl en location.

self: ~-**centred** GB, ~-**centered** US adj égocentrique; ~-**coloured** GB, ~-**colored** US adj uni; ~-**confessed** adj avoué; ~-**confidence** n assurance f; ~-**confident** adj sûr de soi/de lui etc.

self-conscious /ˌselfˈkɒnʃəs/ adj 1 (shy) timide; **to be** ~ **about sth/about doing** être gêné par qch/de faire; 2 [style, artistry] conscient; 3 (aware) conscient de ma/sa etc personne.

self-consciously /ˌselfˈkɒnʃəslɪ/ adv 1 (shyly) timidement; 2 (deliberately) consciemment.

self-contained /ˌselfkənˈteɪnd/ adj 1 [flat] indépendant; [project, unit] autonome; 2 [person] réservé.

self: ~-**control** n sang-froid m; ~-**controlled** adj [person] maître/maîtresse de soi/de lui-même/d'elle-même etc; [behaviour, manner] contrôlé; ~-**correcting** adj à système autocorrecteur; ~-**critical** adj critique à l'égard de soi/de lui-même/d'elle-même etc; ~-**deception** n aveuglement m à son/votre etc propre égard.

self-defeating /ˌselfdɪˈtiːtɪŋ/ adj autodestructeur/-trice; **that would be** ~ cela irait à l'encontre du but recherché.

self-defence GB, **self-defense** US /ˌselfdɪˈfens/ I n GEN autodéfense f; JUR légitime défense f.
II noun modifier [class, instructor] d'autodéfense.

self: ~-**denial** n abnégation f; ~-**deprecating** adj [person] qui se dénigre; [joke, manner, remark] d'autodénigrement.

self-destruct /ˌselfdɪˈstrʌkt/ I adj d'autodestruction.
II vi s'autodétruire.

self: ~-**destructive** adj autodestructeur/-trice; ~-**determination** n GEN, POL autodétermination f; ~-**determining** adj [country] autonome; [action, move] d'autodétermination; ~-**drive** adj GB [car, van] de location sans chauffeur; [holiday] en voiture; ~-**educated** adj autodidacte; ~-**effacing** adj effacé; ~-**elected** adj LIT [committee] autoélu; [leader] autoproclamé.

self-employed /ˌselfɪmˈplɔɪd/ I n **the** ~ (+ v pl) les travailleurs mpl indépendants.
II adj indépendant; **to be** ~ travailler à son compte.

self: ~-**employment** n travail m indépendant; ~-**esteem** n amour-propre m; ~-**evident** adj évident; ~-**evidently** adv de toute évidence.

self-examination /ˌselfɪɡˌzæmɪˈneɪʃn/ n 1 (of conscience, motives) examen m de conscience; 2 MED auto-examen m.

self-explanatory /ˌselfɪkˈsplænətrɪ, US -tɔːrɪ/ adj explicite.

self-expression /ˌselfɪkˈspreʃn/ n expression f de soi/de lui-même etc; **a means of** ~ un moyen de s'exprimer.

self-financing /ˌselfˈfaɪnænsɪŋ/ I n autofinancement m.
II adj autofinancé.

self: ~-**fulfilment** n accomplissement m de soi; ~-**governing** adj autonome; ~-**governing trust** n GB organisme médical qui gère son budget de manière autonome; ~-**government** n autonomie f.

self-help /ˌselfˈhelp/ I n **to learn** ~ apprendre à se débrouiller seul.
II noun modifier [group, scheme, meeting] d'entraide; ~ **book** manuel m d'aide.

self: ~-**image** n image f de soi-même/de lui-même etc; ~-**important** adj PÉJ suffisant; ~-**imposed** adj auto-imposé; ~-**improvement** n Ø progrès mpl personnels; ~-**induced** adj auto-infligé; ~-**indulgence** n complaisance f; ~-**indulgent** adj complaisant; ~-**inflicted** adj auto-infligé; ~-**interest** n intérêt m personnel; ~-**interested** adj intéressé.

selfish /ˈselfɪʃ/ adj égoïste (**to do** de faire).

selfishly /ˈselfɪʃlɪ/ adv égoïstement.

selfishness /ˈselfɪʃnɪs/ n égoïsme m.

self-knowledge n connaissance f de soi/de lui-même etc.

selfless /ˈselflɪs/ adj [person] dévoué; [action, devotion] désintéressé.

selflessly /ˈselflɪslɪ/ adv [give, donate] sans penser à soi/à lui etc.

selflessness /ˈselflɪsnɪs/ n (of person) dévouement m; (of action, devotion) désintéressement m.

self: ~-**loading** adj [gun, rifle] automatique; ~-**locking** adj à verrouillage automatique.

self-made /ˌselfˈmeɪd/ adj [star, millionaire] qui s'est fait tout seul (after n); ~ **man** self-made man m.

self: ~-**management** n COMM autogestion f; ~-**motivated** adj très motivé; ~-**obsessed** adj obsédé par sa/ma etc personne; ~-**perpetuating** adj qui se perpétue (after n); ~-**pitying** adj [person] qui s'apitoie sur son sort; ~-**portrait** n autoportrait m; ~-**possessed** adj [person] maître/maîtresse de soi; ~-**possession** n maîtrise f de soi/de lui-même etc; ~-**preservation** n autoconservation f; ~-**proclaimed** adj autoproclamé; ~-**raising flour** GB, ~-**rising flour** US n farine f à gâteau; ~-**regard** n (concern for oneself) égard m pour soi-même/lui-même etc; ~-**regulating** adj, ~-**regulatory** adj autorégulateur/-trice; ~-**regulation** n autorégulation f; ~-**reliant** adj autosuffisant; ~-**representation** n (before tribunal) possibilité f de se représenter; ~-**respect** n respect m de soi/de lui-même etc; ~-**respecting** adj [teacher, journalist, comedian] (worthy of that name) qui se respecte (after n); [person] respectueux/-euse de ma/sa etc personne; ~-**restraint** n retenue f; ~-**righteous** adj PÉJ satisfait de soi/de lui-même etc; ~-**righteously** adv PÉJ [say, behave] en se donnant raison; ~-**rising flour** n US= **self-raising flour**; ~-**rule** n autonomie f; ~-**ruling** adj autonome; ~-**sacrifice** n abnégation f; ~-**satisfied** adj PÉJ satisfait de soi/de lui-même etc; ~-**sealing** adj autocollant.

self-seeking /ˌselfˈsiːkɪŋ/ I n égoïsme m.
II adj égoïste.

self-service /ˌselfˈsɜːvɪs/ I n libre-service m.
II adj [cafeteria] en libre-service.

self: ~-**styled** adj autoproclamé; ~-**sufficiency** n (all contexts) autosuffisance f; ~-**sufficient** adj autosuffisant (**in** en matière de); ~-**supporting** adj (all contexts) indépendant; ~-**taught** adj autodidacte; ~-**willed** adj entêté.

sell /sel/ I◦ n (deception, disappointment) déception f; **it was a real** ~! qu'est-ce qu'on s'est fait avoir◦!
II vtr (prét, pp **sold**) 1 GEN, COMM vendre; **to** ~ **sth at** ou **for £5 each** vendre qch 5 livres sterling pièce; '**stamps sold here**' 'ici on vend des timbres'; **the novel has sold millions (of copies)** le roman s'est vendu à des millions d'exemplaires; **to** ~ **sth back** revendre qch; 2 (promote sale of) faire vendre; **her name will help to** ~ **the film** son nom aidera à promouvoir le film; 3 (put across) faire accepter, vendre PÉJ [idea, image, policy, party]; 4◦ (cause to appear true) **to** ~ **sb sth, to** ~ **sth to sb** faire avaler◦ qch à qn [lie, story, excuse]; 5 (betray) trahir.
III vi (prét, pp **sold**) 1 [person, shop, dealer] vendre; '~ **by June 27**' 'date limite de vente: 27 juin'; 2 [goods, product, house, book] se vendre; **the new model is/isn't** ~**ing (well)** le nouveau modèle se vend bien/mal.
IV v refl (prét, pp **sold**) 1 (prostitute oneself) **to** ~ **oneself** LIT, FIG se vendre (**to** à; **for** pour); 2 (put oneself across) **to** ~ **oneself** se vendre◦.
IDIOMS **to be sold on** être emballé◦ par [idea, person].
■ **sell off**: ~ [sth] **off**, ~ **off** [sth] GEN liquider; (in sale) solder.
■ **sell out**: ¶ ~ **out** 1 GEN, COMM [merchandise] se vendre; **we've sold out of tickets** tous les billets ont été vendus; **sorry, we've sold out** désolé, mais nous avons tout vendu; 2 THEAT **the play has sold out** la pièce affiche complet; 3 FIN vendre ses parts (**to** à); 4◦ (betray one's principles) retourner sa veste; ¶ ~

[sth] **out**, **~ out** [sth] **1** GEN, COMM **the concert is sold out** le concert affiche complet; **2** FIN vendre. ■ **sell up: ~ up** vendre (tout).

sell-by date n date f limite de vente.

seller /'selə(r)/ n **1** (person) vendeur/-euse m/f; **2 it's a good/poor ~** cela se vend bien/mal.

seller's market n FIN marché m à la hausse; COMM marché m où la demande est forte.

selling /'selɪŋ/ I n ∉ vente f; **telephone ~** vente par téléphone.
II noun modifier [cost, price, rate] de vente.

selling: ~-off n (of company, assets) liquidation f; (of stock) écoulement m; **~ point** n (all contexts) argument m de vente.

Sellotape® /'seləʊteɪp/ I n scotch® m.
II sellotape vtr scotcher.

sellout /'selaʊt/ I n **1 the show was a ~** le spectacle affichait complet; **the product has been a ~** le produit s'est très bien vendu; **2** ○ (betrayal) revirement m.
II noun modifier [concert, performance, production] à guichets fermés.

selvage, selvedge /'selvɪdʒ/ n lisière f.

selves /selvz/ pl ▶ self.

semantic /sɪ'mæntɪk/ adj sémantique.

semantics /sɪ'mæntɪks/ I n (subject) (+ v sg) sémantique f.
II npl (meaning) (+ v pl) sémantique f.

semblance /'sembləns/ n semblant m; **to maintain a ~ of composure** garder un air dégagé.

semi /'semɪ/ I○ n **1** GB (house) maison f jumelée; **2** US AUT semi-remorque f.
II semi+ combining form **1** (half) semi-, demi-; **2** (partly) plus ou moins.

semi: ~automatic n, adj semi-automatique (m); **~autonomous** adj semi-autonome; **~basement** n GB ~ rez-de-jardin m inv; **~circle** n demi-cercle m; **~circular** adj semi-circulaire; **~colon** n point-virgule m; **~conscious** adj à peine conscient; **~darkness** n pénombre f, demi-jour m; **~detached** (**house**) n maison f jumelée; **~final** n demi-finale f; **~finalist** n demi-finaliste mf.

seminal /'semɪnl/ adj (major) déterminant.

seminar /'semɪnɑ:(r)/ n séminaire m (on sur).

semiotics /ˌsemɪ'ɒtɪks/ n (+ v sg) sémiotique f.

semi: ~precious adj semi-précieux/-ieuse; **~skilled** adj [work] d'ouvrier spécialisé; [worker] spécialisé; **~skimmed** adj demi-écrémé.

Semitic /sɪ'mɪtɪk/ adj **1** GEN sémite; **2** LING sémitique.

semitone n MUS demi-ton m.

semolina /ˌseməˈliːnə/ n semoule f.

Sen 1 abrév écrite = **senator**; **2** abrév écrite = **senior**.

senate /'senɪt/ n **1** POL, HIST sénat m; **2** UNIV conseil m (d'université).

senator /'senətə(r)/ **▶ 937** n sénateur m (**for** de).

send /send/ vtr (prét, pp **sent**) **1** (dispatch) envoyer; **to ~ sth to sb, to ~ sb sth** envoyer qch à qn; **they'll ~ a car for you** ils enverront une voiture vous chercher; **to ~ sb home** (from school, work) renvoyer qn chez lui/elle; **~ her my love!** embrasse-la de ma part; **~ them my regards** transmettez-leur mes amitiés; **to ~ word that** faire dire que; **2** (cause to move) **the noise sent people running** le bruit a fait courir les gens; **to ~ share prices soaring** faire monter le cours des actions; **to ~ shivers down sb's spine** donner froid dans le dos à qn; **3** (cause to become) rendre; **to ~ sb mad** rendre qn fou; **to ~ sb into a rage** mettre qn dans une rage folle; **to ~ sb to sleep** endormir qn. IDIOMS **to ~ sb packing**○, **to ~ sb about her/his business**○ envoyer balader qn○.
■ **send around** US = **send round**.
■ **send away: ¶ ~ away for** [sth] commander [qch] par correspondance; **¶ ~** [sb/sth] **away** faire

partir; **¶ to ~ a child away to boarding school** envoyer un enfant en pension.
■ **send down: ¶ ~** [sb/sth] **down, ~ down** [sb/sth] envoyer; **~ him down to the second floor** dites-lui de descendre au deuxième étage; **¶ ~** [sb] **down 1** GB UNIV renvoyer [qn] de l'université; **2**○ GB envoyer qn en prison.
■ **send for: ~ for** [sb/sth] appeler [doctor, taxi, plumber]; demander [reinforcements].
■ **send in: ~** [sb/sth] **in, ~ in** [sb/sth] envoyer [letter, form, troops]; faire entrer [visitor]; **to ~ in one's application** poser sa candidature.
■ **send off: ¶ ~** [sth] **off for** [sth] commander [qch] par correspondance; **¶ ~** [sth] **off, ~ off** [sth] (post) expédier; **¶ ~** [sb] **off, ~ off** [sb] SPORT expulser; **¶ ~** [sb] **off to** envoyer [qn] à.
■ **send on: ~** [sb] **on (ahead)** (as scout) envoyer [qn] en éclaireur; **~ him on ahead to open up the shop** dites-lui de partir devant ouvrir le magasin; **¶ ~** [sth] **on, ~ on** [sth] (send in advance) expédier [qch] à l'avance; (forward) faire suivre.
■ **send out: ¶ ~ out for** [sth] envoyer quelqu'un chercher; **¶ ~** [sth] **out, ~ out** [sth] **1** (post) envoyer; **2** émettre [light]; **¶ ~** [sb] **out** faire sortir [pupil]; **to ~ sb out for** envoyer qn chercher.
■ **send round** GB: **~** [sb/sth] **round, ~ round** [sb/sth] **1** (circulate) faire circuler; **2** (cause to go) envoyer.
■ **send up: ~** [sth] **up** (post) envoyer; **¶ ~** [sb] **up**○ **1** GB (parody) parodier; **2** US (put in prison) mettre or envoyer [qn] en prison; **¶ ~** [sb/sth] **up, ~ up** [sb/sth] **1** (into space) envoyer; **2** (to upper floor) **you can ~ him up now** vous pouvez lui dire de monter maintenant.

sender /'sendə(r)/ n expéditeur/-trice m/f.

send: ~-off n adieux mpl; **~-up**○ n GB parodie f.

senile /'siːnaɪl/ adj sénile ALSO PEJ.

senile dementia n démence f sénile.

senior /'siːnɪə(r)/ I n **1** (older person) aîné/-e m/f; **to be sb's ~ by ten years** avoir dix ans de plus que qn; **to be sb's ~** être plus âgé que qn; **2** (superior) supérieur/-e m/f; **3** GB SCH élève mf dans les grandes classes; **4** US SCH élève mf de terminale; **5** US UNIV étudiant/-e mf de licence; **6** SPORT senior m.
II noun modifier **1** SPORT [league, player] senior; **2** US UNIV [year, prom] de fin d'études.
III adj **1** (older) [person] plus âgé; **Mr Becket ~** M. Becket père; **2** (superior) [person] plus haut placé; [civil servant, diplomat] haut (before n); [aide, employee, minister] haut placé; [colleague] plus ancien/-ienne; [figure] prédominant; [job, post] supérieur; **to be ~ to sb** être le supérieur de qn.

senior: ~ citizen n personne f du troisième âge; **~ editor ▶ 1251** n rédacteur/-trice m/f en chef; **~ executive** n cadre m supérieur; **~ high school** n US SCH ~ lycée m.

seniority /ˌsiːnɪ'ɒrətɪ, US -'ɔːr-/ n **1** (in years) âge m; (in rank) statut m supérieur; **in order of ~** par ordre hiérarchique; **2** (in years of service) ancienneté f.

senior: ~ management n ADMIN direction f; **~ manager** n cadre m supérieur; **~ officer** n (police) officier m de police supérieur; ADMIN haut/-e fonctionnaire m/f; **~ partner** n associé/-e m/f principal/-e; **~ school** n GB (secondary school) lycée m; (older pupils) grandes classes fpl; **~ staff** n ADMIN cadres mpl supérieurs.

sensation /sen'seɪʃn/ n **1** (feeling, impression, stir) sensation f; **to cause** OU **create a ~** faire sensation. **2**○ (person) **to be a ~** être formidable.

sensational /sen'seɪʃənl/ adj **1** GEN, PÉJ sensationnel/-elle; **~ story/article** histoire f/article m à sensation PÉJ; **2**○ (emphatic) sensationnel/-elle.

sensationalism /sen'seɪʃənəlɪzəm/ n GEN PÉJ recherche f du sensationnel.

sensationalist /sen'seɪʃənəlɪst/ adj PÉJ [headline, story, writer] à sensation PÉJ.

sensationalize /sen'seɪʃənəlaɪz/ vtr PÉJ faire un reportage à sensation sur [event, story].

sensationally /sen'seɪʃənəlɪ/ adv (luridly) [write, describe] en dramatisant PEJ.

sense /sens/ I n 1 (faculty, ability) sens m; ~ of hearing ouïe f; ~ of sight vue f; ~ of smell odorat m; ~ of taste goût m; ~ of touch toucher m; to dull/sharpen the ~s émousser/aiguiser les sens; a ~ of direction le sens de l'orientation; to lose all ~ of time perdre toute notion du temps; 2 (feeling) a ~ of un sentiment de; a ~ of purpose le sentiment d'avoir un but; the town has a great ~ of community la ville a un grand sens de la communauté; 3 (practical quality) bon sens m; to have more ~ than to do avoir suffisamment de bon sens pour ne pas faire; 4 (reason) there's no ~ in doing cela ne sert à rien de faire; what's the ~ in getting angry? à quoi sert-il de se fâcher?; to make ~ of sth comprendre qch; I can't make ~ of this article je ne comprends rien à cet article; it makes ~ to do c'est une bonne idée de faire; to make ~ [sentence, film, theory] avoir un sens; what he said didn't make much ~ to me ce qu'il a dit ne m'a pas semblé très logique; 5 (meaning) GEN, LING sens m; in the ~ that en ce sens que; he is in a ou one ou some ~ right to complain, but... dans un certain sens il a raison de se plaindre, mais... II **senses** npl (sanity) raison f; to bring sb to his ~s ramener qn à la raison; to take leave of one's ~s perdre la raison ou l'esprit m. III vtr 1 (be aware of) deviner (that que); to ~ danger sentir un danger; 2 [machine] détecter. IDIOMS to knock ou pound US some ~ into sb ramener qn à la raison; to see ~ entendre raison; to talk ~ dire des choses sensées.

senseless /'senslɪs/ adj 1 (pointless) [violence] gratuit; [idea, discussion] absurde; [act, waste] insensé; 2 (unconscious) sans connaissance; to knock sb ~ faire perdre connaissance à qn.

senselessly /'senslɪslɪ/ adv de manière insensée.

sensible /'sensəbl/ adj 1 (showing common sense) [person, attitude] raisonnable; [policy, solution, investment] judicieux/-ieuse; 2 (practical) [garment] pratique; [diet] intelligent; 3 (perceptible) sensible.

sensibly /'sensəblɪ/ adv [eat, act, talk] de façon raisonnable; [dressed] de façon pratique; [chosen] de façon judicieuse; ~ priced à un prix raisonnable.

sensitive /'sensətɪv/ adj 1 (easily affected, aware) sensible; 2 (delicate) [situation] délicat; [discussions, issue, job] difficile; [information] confidentiel/-ielle.

sensitively /'sensətɪvlɪ/ adv [speak, treat, react] avec délicatesse; [chosen, portrayed] avec sensibilité.

sensitivity /ˌsensə'tɪvətɪ/ n sensibilité f (to à).

sensitize /'sensətaɪz/ vtr (all contexts) sensibiliser.

sensor /'sensə(r)/ n détecteur m.

sensory /'sensərɪ/ adj sensoriel/-ielle; ~ deprivation perte f sensorielle.

sensual /'senʃʊəl/ adj sensuel/-elle.

sensuality /ˌsenʃʊ'ælətɪ/ n sensualité f.

sensuous /'senʃʊəs/ adj sensuel/-elle.

sent /sent/ prét, pp ▶ **send**.

sentence /'sentəns/ I n 1 JUR peine f; to be under ~ of death être condamné à mort; to serve a ~ purger une peine; to pass ~ on sb prononcer une peine contre qn; 2 LING phrase f. II vtr condamner (to à; to do à faire; for pour).

sentiment /'sentɪmənt/ n 1 (feeling) sentiment m; public ~ le sentiment général; 2 (opinion) opinion f; 3 (sentimentality) GEN sentimentalité f; PEJ sensiblerie f.

sentimental /ˌsentɪ'mentl/ adj sentimental ALSO PEJ; to be ~ about faire du sentiment pour [children, animals]; évoquer [qch] avec émotion [past].

sentimentality /ˌsentɪmen'tælətɪ/ n sentimentalité f; PEJ sensiblerie f.

sentimentally /ˌsentɪ'mentəlɪ/ adv sentimentalement.

sentinel /'sentɪnl/ n factionnaire m.

sentry /'sentrɪ/ n sentinelle f.

sentry: ~ box n guérite f; ~ duty n faction f.

separable /'sepərəbl/ adj séparable (from de).

separate I **separates** /'sepərəts/ npl (garments) coordonnés mpl.
II /'sepərət/ adj 1 (with singular noun) [piece, organization] à part; [discussion, issue, occasion] autre; the flat is ~ from the rest of the house l'appartement est indépendant du reste de la maison; a ~ appointment for each child un rendez-vous pour chaque enfant; under ~ cover POST sous pli séparé; 2 (with plural noun) [sections, discussions, problems] différent; [organizations, agreements, treaties] distinct; they have ~ rooms ils ont chacun leur chambre; they asked for ~ bills (in restaurant) ils ont demandé chacun leur addition.
III /'sepərət/ adv keep the knives ~ rangez les couteaux séparément; keep the knives ~ from the forks séparez les couteaux des fourchettes.
IV /'sepəreɪt/ vtr 1 (divide) LIT séparer; FIG diviser; the child became ~d from his mother l'enfant s'est retrouvé séparé de sa mère; to ~ the issue of pay from that of working hours dissocier la question des salaires de celle des heures de travail; 2 (also ~ out) (sort out) répartir [people]; trier [objects].
V /'sepəreɪt/ vi (all contexts) se séparer (from de).
VI **separated** /'sepəreɪtɪd/ pp adj séparé.

separately /'sepərətlɪ/ adv (all contexts) séparément.

separation /ˌsepə'reɪʃn/ n GEN séparation f.

separatist /'sepərətɪst/ n, adj séparatiste (mf).

sepia /'siːpɪə/ n 1 ▶818 (colour) sépia f; 2 ZOOL seiche f.

Sept abrév écrite = **September**.

September /sep'tembə(r)/ ▶1090 n septembre m.

septic /'septɪk/ adj infecté; to go ~ s'infecter.

septicaemia /ˌseptɪ'siːmɪə/ ▶1002 n septicémie f.

septic tank n fosse f septique.

sequel /'siːkwəl/ n (all contexts) suite f (to à).

sequence /'siːkwəns/ n 1 (of problems) succession f; (of photos) série f; the ~ of events la suite des événements; 2 (order) ordre m; 3 (in film) séquence f; the dream ~ la scène de rêve; 4 (dance) numéro m de danse; 5 LING ~ of tenses concordance f des temps; 6 MUS séquence f; 7 COMPUT, MATH séquence f.

sequential /sɪ'kwenʃl/ adj séquentiel/-ielle.

sequin /'siːkwɪn/ n paillette f.

Serbia /'sɜːbɪə/ ▶840 pr n Serbie f.

Serbo-Croat(ian) /ˌsɜːbəʊ'krəʊæt, -krəʊ'eɪʃn/ ▶1038 n, adj (language) serbo-croate (m).

serene /sɪ'riːn/ adj serein.

serenity /sɪ'renətɪ/ n sérénité f.

sergeant /'sɑːdʒənt/ ▶1192 n 1 GB MIL sergent m; 2 US MIL caporal-chef m; 3 (in police) ~ brigadier m.

serial /'sɪərɪəl/ I n 1 (story) feuilleton m; TV ~ feuilleton télévisé; 2 (publication) périodique m.
II adj COMPUT [input, printer, transfer] série inv.

serialization /ˌsɪərɪəlaɪ'zeɪʃn, US -lɪ'z-/ n adaptation f en feuilleton.

serialize /'sɪərɪəlaɪz/ vtr adapter [qch] en feuilleton.

serial killer n meurtrier m en série.

serial number n (of machine, car etc) numéro m de série; US (of soldier) numéro m matricule.

series /'sɪəriːz/ n (pl ~) 1 GEN série f; a ~ of books une collection de livres; 2 RADIO, TV, LITERAT série f; this is the last in the present ~ voici la dernière partie de ce programme; 3 SPORT championnat m (à plusieurs épreuves); 4 ELEC série f.

serious /'sɪərɪəs/ adj 1 (not frivolous or light) [person, expression, discussion, issue, offer, purpose] sérieux/-ieuse; [work, literature, actor, survey] de qualité; [attempt, concern] réel/réelle; to be ~ about sth prendre qch au sérieux; to be ~ about doing avoir vraiment l'intention de faire; is he ~ about her? est-ce qu'il tient vraiment à elle?; to give ~ thought to sth penser sérieusement à qch; you can't be ~ tu veux rire°; being a parent is a ~ business être parent est une grande responsabilité; to make ~ money° gagner beaucoup d'argent; if you want to do some ~ shopping° si tu veux vraiment faire des courses; 2 (grave) [accident, crime, problem] grave; [concern, doubt, misgiving] sérieux/-ieuse]; **this is a very ~ matter** l'affaire est très grave.

seriously /ˈsɪərɪəslɪ/ adv **1** (not frivolously) sérieusement; **are you ~ suggesting that...?** tu veux vraiment dire que...?; **but ~,...** blague à part,...○; **to take sb/sth ~** prendre qn/qch au sérieux; **he takes himself too ~** il se prend trop au sérieux; **2** (gravely) [ill, injured, at risk, flawed] gravement; [mislead, underestimate] vraiment; **3**○ (extremely) vraiment.

seriousness /ˈsɪərɪəsnɪs/ n **1** (of person, film, study, approach) sérieux m; (of tone, occasion, reply) gravité f; (of intention) sincérité f; **in all ~** sérieusement; **2** (of illness, damage, allegation, problem, situation) gravité f.

sermon /ˈsɜːmən/ n sermon m.

seropositive /ˌsɪərəʊˈpɒzɪtɪv/ adj séropositif/-ive.

serpent /ˈsɜːpənt/ n (all contexts) serpent m.

serrated /sɪˈreɪtɪd, US ˈsereɪtɪd/ adj dentelé; **~ knife** couteau-scie m.

serum /ˈsɪərəm/ n sérum m; **snake-bite ~** sérum antivenimeux.

servant /ˈsɜːvənt/ n **1** ▶1251 (in household) domestique mf; **to keep a ~** avoir un domestique; **~ girl** bonne f; **~'s hall** office m; **2** FIG serviteur m.

serve /sɜːv/ I n SPORT service m; **it's my ~** à moi de servir; **to have a big ~** avoir un très bon service. II vtr **1** (work for) servir [country, cause, public]; travailler au service de [employer, family]; **to ~ sb/sth well** rendre de grands services à qn/qch; **2** (attend to customers) servir; **are you being ~d?** on vous sert?; **3** CULIN servir; **to ~ sb with sth** servir qch à qn; **~s four** (in recipe) pour quatre personnes; **4** (provide facility) [public utility, power station, reservoir] alimenter; [public transport, library, hospital] desservir; **5** (satisfy) servir [interests]; satisfaire [needs]; **6** (function) être utile à; **this old pen has ~d me well** ce vieux stylo m'a été très utile; **if my memory ~s me well** si j'ai bonne mémoire; **to ~ sb as sth** servir de qch à qn; **to ~ a purpose** ou **function** être utile; **to ~ no useful purpose** ne servir à rien; **to ~ the** ou **sb's purpose** faire l'affaire; **7** (spend time) **to ~ a term** POL remplir un mandat; **to ~ one's time** (in prison) purger sa peine; **to ~ a sentence** purger une peine (de prison); **to ~ five years** faire cinq ans de prison; **8** JUR **to ~ a writ on sb** assigner qn en justice; **to ~ a summons on sb** citer qn à comparaître; **to ~ notice of sth on sb** JUR, FIG signifier qch à qn; **9** SPORT servir. III vi **1** (in shop, church) servir; (at table) faire le service; **2** (on committee, in government) exercer ses fonctions (**as** de); **to ~ on** être membre de [committee, jury]; **3** MIL servir; **4** (meet a need) faire l'affaire; **to ~ as sth** servir de qch; **this should ~ as a warning** cela devrait nous servir d'avertissement; **the photo ~d as a reminder to me of the holidays** la photo me rappelait les vacances; **5** SPORT servir; **Bruno to ~** au service, Bruno.

IDIOMS **it ~s you right!** ça t'apprendra!

■ **serve out**: **~ out** [sth], **~** [sth] **out** finir [term of duty]; purger [prison sentence].

■ **serve up**: ¶ **~ up** CULIN servir; ¶ **~ up** [sth], **~** [sth] **up 1** CULIN servir; **to ~ sth up again** resservir qch; **2**○ FIG, PEJ resservir [idea, policy]; donner [excuse].

serve-and-volley adj [player] service-volée inv.

server /ˈsɜːvə(r)/ n **1** SPORT, COMPUT serveur m; **2** CULIN couvert m de service; **3** RELIG servant m.

server-managed adj COMPUT géré par serveur.

service /ˈsɜːvɪs/ I n **1** (department, facility) service m; **(accident and) emergency ~** service des urgences; **for ~s rendered** COMM pour services rendus; **it's all part of the ~** (don't mention it) c'est tout naturel; (it's all included) tout est compris; **'normal ~ will be resumed as soon as possible'** 'dans quelques instants la suite de votre programme'; **my ~s don't come cheap!** je me fais payer cher!; **2** (work, period of work done) GEN, ADMIN, MIL service m; **I'm at your**

~ je suis à votre service; **to put** ou **place sth at sb's ~** mettre qch à la disposition de qn; **he gave his life in the ~ of his country** il a donné sa vie pour servir son pays; **to be in ~** HIST travailler comme domestique; **3** COMM (customer care) service m (**to** à); **to get good/bad ~** être bien/mal servi; **15% for ~** 15% pour le service; **4** (from machine, vehicle, product) usage m; **to give good** ou **long ~** [machine] fonctionner longtemps; [vehicle, product, garment] faire de l'usage; **it went out of ~ years ago** il n'est plus en service depuis des années; **'out of ~'** (on bus) 'hors service'; (on machine) 'en panne'; **5** (transport facility) service m (**to** pour); **to run a regular ~** assurer un service régulier; **an hourly bus/train ~** un autobus/train toutes les heures; **the number 28 bus ~** la ligne du 28; **6** AUT, TECH (overhaul) révision f; **7** RELIG office m; **Sunday ~** office du dimanche; **marriage ~** cérémonie f nuptiale; **8** (crockery) service m; **9** SPORT service m; **your ~!** à toi de servir!; **10** (good turn) service m; **to do sb a ~** rendre service à qn; **to be of ~ to sb** [person] aider qn; [thing] être utile à qn. II **services** npl **1 the ~s** MIL, NAUT les armées; **2** (on motorway) aire m de services. III noun modifier MIL [pay, pension] militaire; [personnel] de l'armée; [life] dans l'armée. IV vtr **1** (overhaul) faire la révision de [vehicle]; entretenir [machine]; **to have one's car ~d** faire réviser sa voiture; **2** FIN payer les intérêts de [debt].

serviceable /ˈsɜːvɪsəbl/ adj (usable) utilisable.

service area n aire f de services.

service break n SPORT **to have a ~** avoir fait le break.

service centre GB, **service center** US n centre m de service après-vente.

service charge n **1** (in restaurant) service m; **there is a ~** le service n'est pas compris; **what is the ~?** le service est de combien?; **2** (in banking) frais mpl de gestion de compte; **3** (for property maintenance) charges fpl locatives.

service: ~ company n société f de service; **~ contract** n COMM contrat m d'entretien; **~ department** n (office) service m entretien; (workshop) atelier m d'entretien; **~ elevator** n US = **service lift**; **~ engineer** ▶1251 n technicien m de maintenance; **~ entrance** n entrée f des fournisseurs; **~ flat** n GB appartement m (dont le ménage est assuré par l'agence de location); **~ game** n service m; **~ hatch** n passe-plats m inv; **~ industry** n (company) industrie f de service; (sector) secteur m tertiaire; **~ lift** n GB (in hotel, building) ascenseur m de service; (for heavy goods) monte-charge m; **~man** n militaire m; **~ road** n GB, GEN voie f d'accès; CONSTR voie f de service; **~ sector** n secteur m tertiaire; **~ station** n station-service f; **~woman** n femme f soldat.

servicing /ˈsɜːvɪsɪŋ/ n AUT, TECH révision f.

serving /ˈsɜːvɪŋ/ I n (helping) portion f; **enough for four ~s** pour quatre personnes. II adj [officer] MIL en activité; ADMIN en exercice.

serving: ~ dish n plat m (de service); **~ hatch** n passe-plats m inv; **~ spoon** n cuillère f de service.

session /ˈseʃn/ n **1** POL (term) session f; **2** ADMIN, JUR, POL, GEN (sitting) séance f; **emergency ~** séance exceptionnelle; **the court is in ~** JUR le tribunal tient séance; **to go into closed** ou **private ~** siéger à huis clos; **3** (meeting) réunion f; (informal discussion) discussion f; **drinking ~**○ beuverie f; **4** GB (year) année f scolaire; US (term) trimestre m; (period of lessons) cours mpl; **5** MUS, SPORT séance f; **training ~** SPORT séance d'entraînement; **6** FIN séance f; **trading ~** séance de Bourse.

set /set/ I n **1** (collection) (of keys, spanners, screwdrivers) jeu m; (of golf clubs, stamps, coins, chairs) série f; (of cutlery) service m; (of encyclopedias) collection f; FIG (of data, rules, instructions, tests) série f; **a new ~ of clothes** des vêtements neufs; **they're sold in ~s of 10** ils sont vendus par lots mpl de 10; **a ~ of fingerprints** des empreintes fpl digitales; **a ~ of traffic lights** des feux mpl (de signalisation); **2** (kit, game) **a**

chess ~ un jeu d'échecs; **a magic ~** une mallette de magie; **3** (pair) **a ~ of sheets** une paire de draps; **a ~ of footprints** l'empreinte des deux pieds; **a ~ of false teeth** un dentier; **my top/bottom ~** (of false teeth) la partie supérieure/inférieure de mon dentier; **one ~ of grandparents lives in Canada** deux de mes grands-parents habitent au Canada; **both ~s of parents agreed with us** ses parents comme les miens étaient d'accord avec nous; **4** SPORT (in tennis) set *m*; **5** (television) poste *m*; **6** (group) (social) monde *m*; (sporting) milieu *m*; **the smart** ou **fashionable ~** les gens *mpl* à la mode; **7** (scenery) THEAT décor *m*; CIN, TV plateau *m*; **8** MATH ensemble *m*; **9** GB SCH (class, group) groupe *m*; **10** (hair-do) mise *f* en plis; **to have a shampoo and ~** se faire faire un shampooing et une mise en plis.

II *adj* **1** (fixed) (*épith*) [*procedure, rule, task*] bien déterminé; [*time, price*] fixe; [*menu*] à prix fixe; [*formula*] toute faite; [*idea*] arrêté; **I had no ~ purpose** je n'avais pas d'objectif précis; **~ phrase** expression *f* consacrée; **~ expression** locution *f* figée; **to be ~ in one's ideas** ou **opinions** avoir des idées bien arrêtées; **to be ~ in one's ways** avoir ses habitudes; **the weather is ~ fair** le temps est au beau fixe; **2** (stiff) [*expression, smile*] figé; **3** SCH, UNIV (prescribed) **there are five ~ topics on the history syllabus** il y a cinq sujets au programme d'histoire; **4** (ready) prêt (**for** pour); **to be** (all) **~ to leave** être prêt à partir; **5** (determined) **to be** (**dead**) **~ against sth/doing** être tout à fait contre qch/l'idée de faire; **he's really ~ against my resigning** il est tout à fait contre ma démission; **to be ~ on sth/on doing** tenir absolument à qch/à faire; **6** (firm) [*jam, honey*] épais/épaisse; [*cement*] dur; [*yoghurt*] ferme.

III *vtr* (*p prés* **-tt-**; *prét, pp* **set**) **1** (place, position) placer [*object*]; monter [*gem*]; **to ~ sth before sb** LIT placer qch devant qn; **to ~ sth in the ground** enfoncer qch dans le sol; **to ~ sth into sth** encastrer qch dans qch; **to ~ sth straight** LIT (align) remettre qch droit [*painting*]; FIG (tidy) remettre de l'ordre dans qch; **to ~ sth upright** redresser qch; **a house set among the trees** une maison située au milieu des arbres; **to ~ matters** ou **the record straight** FIG mettre les choses au point; **his eyes are set very close together** ses yeux sont très rapprochés; **2** (prepare) mettre [*table*]; tendre [*trap*]; **~ three places** mets trois couverts; **to ~ the stage** ou **scene for sth** FIG préparer le lieu de qch; **the stage is set for the final** tout est prêt pour la finale; **to ~ one's mark** ou **stamp on sth** laisser sa marque sur qch; **3** (affix, establish) fixer [*date, deadline, place, price, target*]; lancer [*fashion, trend*]; donner [*tone*]; établir [*precedent, record*]; **to ~ a good/bad example to sb** montrer le bon/mauvais exemple à qn; **to ~ one's sights on** viser; **4** (adjust) mettre [qch] à l'heure [*clock*]; mettre [*alarm clock, burglar alarm, timer*]; programmer [*magnétoscope*]; **to ~ the oven to 180°** mettre le four sur 180°; **to ~ the video to record the film** programmer le magnétoscope pour enregistrer le film; **~ your watch by mine** règle ta montre sur la mienne; **I set the heating to come on at 6 am** j'ai réglé le chauffage pour qu'il se mette en route à six heures; **5** (start) **to ~ sth going** mettre qch en marche [*machine*]; **to ~ sb laughing/thinking** faire rire/réfléchir qn; **to ~ sb to work doing** charger qn de faire; **6** (impose, prescribe) [*teacher*] donner [*homework, essay*]; poser [*problem*]; créer [*crossword puzzle*]; **to ~ an exam** préparer les sujets d'examen; **to ~ a book for study** mettre un texte au programme; **to ~ sb the task of doing** charger qn de faire; **7** CIN, LITERAT, THEAT, TV situer; **to ~ a book in 1960/New York** situer un roman en 1960/à New York; **the film is set in Munich** le film se passe à Munich; **8** MUS **to ~ sth to music** mettre qch en musique; **9** (in printing) composer [*text, type*] (**in** en); **10** MED immobiliser [*broken bone*]; **11** (style) **to ~ sb's hair** faire une mise en plis à qn; **to have one's hair set** se faire faire une mise en plis; **12** (cause to harden) faire prendre [*jam, concrete*].

IV *vi* (*p prés* **-tt-**; *prét, pp* **set**) **1** [*sun*] se coucher; **2**

[*jam, concrete*] prendre; [*glue*] sécher; **3** MED [*fracture*] se ressouder.

IDIOMS to be well set-up○ (financially) avoir les moyens○; **to make a** (**dead**) **~ at sb**○ GB se lancer à la tête de qn○.

■ **set about**: ¶ **~ about** [*sth*] se mettre à [*work, duties*]; **to ~ about doing** commencer à faire; **to ~ about the job** ou **task** ou **business of doing** commencer à faire; **I don't know how to ~ about it** je ne sais pas comment m'y prendre; ¶ **~ about** [*sb*]○ attaquer qn (**with** avec).

■ **set against**: ¶ **~** [*sb*] **against** monter qn contre; **to ~ oneself against sth** s'opposer à qch; ¶ **~ sth against sth** confronter qch à qch; **the benefits seem small, set against the risks** par rapport aux risques les bénéfices semblent maigres.

■ **set apart**: **~** [*sb/sth*] **apart** distinguer (**from** de).

■ **set aside**: **~** [*sth*] **aside**, **~ aside** [*sth*] **1** (put down) poser [qch] de côté; **2** (reserve) réserver [*area, room, time*] (**for** pour); mettre [qch] de côté [*money, stock*]; **3** (disregard) mettre [qch] de côté [*differences*]; **4** ADMIN, JUR (reject) rejeter [*decision, verdict*]; casser [*judgment, ruling*].

■ **set back**: **~** [*sth*] **back 1** (position towards the rear) reculer; **the house is set back from the road** la maison est située un peu en retrait de la route; **2** retarder [*clock, watch*]; ¶ **~ back** [*sth*], **~** [*sth*] **back** (delay) retarder; ¶ **~** [*sb*] **back**○ coûter les yeux de la tête à○.

■ **set by**: **~** [*sth*] **by**, **~ by** [*sth*] mettre [qch] de côté.

■ **set down**: ¶ **~** [*sb/sth*] **down** déposer [*passenger*]; poser [*object*]; ¶ **~ down** [*sth*], **~** [*sth*] **down 1** (establish) fixer [*conditions*]; **2** (record) enregistrer [*event, fact*]; **to ~ down one's thoughts** consigner ses pensées par écrit; **3** poser [*helicopter*].

■ **set forth**: ¶ **~ forth** se mettre en route; ¶ **~ forth** [*sth*] exposer [*facts*]; présenter [*argument*].

■ **set in**: ¶ **~ in** [*infection*] se déclarer; [*complications*] survenir; [*winter*] arriver; [*depression*] s'installer; **the rain has set in for the afternoon** la pluie va durer toute l'après-midi; ¶ **~** [*sth*] **in** rapporter [*sleeve*].

■ **set off**: ¶ **~ off** partir (**for** pour); **to ~ off on a journey** partir en voyage; **to ~ off to do** partir faire; **he set off on a long description** il s'est lancé dans une longue description; ¶ **~** [*off*] **sth**, **~** [*sth*] **off 1** (trigger) faire partir [*firework*]; faire exploser [*bomb*]; déclencher [*riot, row, panic, alarm*]; **2** (enhance) mettre [qch] en valeur; ¶ **~** [*sb*] **off** faire pleurer [*baby*]; **she laughed and that set me off** elle a ri et ça m'a fait rire à mon tour; **don't mention politics, you know it always ~s him off** ne parle pas de politique, tu sais bien que quand il est parti on ne peut plus l'arrêter.

■ **set on**: ¶ **~ on** [*sb*] attaquer qn; ¶ **~** [*sth*] **on sb** lâcher [qch] contre qn [*dog*]; **to ~ sb onto sb** ou **sb's track** mettre qn sur la piste de qn.

■ **set out**: ¶ **~ out** (leave) se mettre en route (**for** pour); **we set out from Paris at 9 am** nous avons quitté Paris à 9 heures; **to ~ out on a journey** partir en voyage; **to ~ out to do** (intend) [*book, report, speech*] avoir pour but de faire; [*person*] chercher à faire; ¶ **~** [*sth*] **out**, **~ out** [*sth*] **1** (spread out) disposer [*goods, chairs, chessmen*]; disposer [*food*]; étaler [*books, papers*]; organiser [*information*]; **2** (state, explain) présenter [*ideas*]; formuler [*objections, terms*].

■ **set to** s'y mettre.

■ **set up**: ¶ **~ up** (establish oneself) [*business person, trader*] s'établir; **to ~ up on one's own** s'établir à son compte; **to ~ up** (**shop**) **as a decorator** s'établir en tant que décorateur; **to ~ up in business** monter une affaire; ¶ **~** [*sth*] **up**, **~ up** [*sth*] **1** (erect) monter [*stand, stall*]; assembler [*equipment, easel*]; déplier [*deckchair*]; ériger [*roadblock*]; dresser [*statue*]; **to ~ up home** ou **house** s'installer; **to ~ up camp** installer un campement; **2** (prepare) préparer [*experiment*]; **3** (found, establish) créer [*business, company*]; implanter [*factory*]; former [*group, charity*]; constituer

committee]; ouvrir [*fund*]; lancer [*scheme*]; **4** (start) provoquer [*vibration*]; susciter [*reaction*]; **5** (organize) organiser [*conference, meeting*]; mettre [qch] en place [*procedures*]; **6** (in printing) composer [*page*]; ¶ **~** [sb] **up 1** (establish in business) **she set her son up (in business) as a gardener** elle a aidé son fils à s'installer comme jardinier; **2** (improve one's health, fortune) remettre [qn] sur pied; **that deal has set her up for life** grâce à ce contrat elle n'aura plus à se soucier de rien; **3**° GB (trap) [*police*] tendre un piège à [*criminal*]; [*colleague, friend*] monter un coup contre [*person*]; **4** COMPUT installer, configurer; ¶ **~** [oneself] **up 1** COMM **she set herself up as a financial adviser** elle s'est mise à son compte comme conseiller financier; **to ~ oneself up in business** se mettre à son compte; **2** (claim) **I don't ~ myself up to be an expert** je ne prétends pas être expert; **she ~s herself up as an authority on French art** elle prétend faire autorité en matière d'art français.
■ **set upon**: **~ upon** [sb] attaquer qn.

setback /'setbæk/ *n* **1** GEN, MIL revers *m* (**for** pour); **to suffer a ~** essuyer un revers; **this would be a ~ to our plans** cela compromettrait nos projets; **a temporary ~** un recul passager; **2** FIN recul *m*.

set: **~ designer** ▶1251 *n* THEAT décorateur/-trice *m/f*; **~ piece** *n* SPORT coup *m* préparé; MUS morceau *m* célèbre; THEAT ferme *f*; **~ play** *n* SPORT, GEN coup *m* préparé; **~ point** *n* balle *f* de set; **~ square** *n* GB TECH équerre *f*.

settee /se'ti:/ *n* canapé *m*.

setter /'setə(r)/ *n* (dog) setter *m*.

setting /'setɪŋ/ *n* **1** (for building, event, film, novel) cadre *m*; **a house in a riverside ~** une maison au bord d'une rivière; **Milan will be the ~ for the film** le film va se passer à Milan; **Dublin is the ~ for her latest novel** l'action de son dernier roman se passe à Dublin; **2** (in jewellery) monture *f*; **3** (position on dial) position *f* (de réglage); **speed ~** vitesse *f*; **put the iron on the highest ~** mets le fer à repasser au maximum; **4** MUS arrangement *m*; **5 the ~ of the sun** le coucher du soleil.

setting lotion *n* fixateur *m*.

setting-up /ˌsetɪŋ'ʌp/ *n* (of committee, programme, scheme, business) création *f*; (of inquiry) ouverture *f*; (of factory) implantation *f*.

settle /'setl/ **I** *n* banquette *f* coffre.
II *vtr* **1** (position comfortably) installer [*person, animal*]; **to get the children ~d for the night** mettre les enfants au lit; **2** (calm) calmer [*stomach, nerves*]; **3** (resolve) régler [*matter, business, dispute*]; mettre fin à [*conflict*]; régler, résoudre [*problem*]; **~ it among yourselves** réglez ça entre vous; **that's ~d** voilà qui est réglé; **that ~s it! I'm leaving tomorrow!** (making decision) c'est décidé! je pars demain!; (in exasperation) c'en est trop! je pars demain!; **to ~ an argument** (as referee) trancher; **4** (agree on) fixer; **nothing is ~d yet** rien n'est encore fixé; **5** (put in order) **to ~ one's affairs** mettre de l'ordre dans ses affaires; **6** COMM régler [*bill, debt*]; **7** (colonize) coloniser.
III *vi* **1** (come to rest) [*bird, insect, wreck*] se poser; [*dust, dregs*] se déposer; **to let the dust ~** LIT laisser retomber la poussière; FIG attendre que les choses se calment; **to ~ over** [*clouds*] descendre sur; [*silence, grief*] s'étendre sur; **2** (become resident) GEN s'installer; (more permanently) se fixer; **3** (become compacted) se tasser; **4** (calm down) GEN se calmer; (go to sleep) s'endormir; [*weather*] se mettre au beau fixe; **5** (take hold) **to be settling** [*snow*] tenir; [*mist*] persister; **6** JUR régler; **to ~ out of court** parvenir à un règlement à l'amiable.
IV *v refl* **to ~ oneself in** s'installer dans [*chair, bed*].
IDIOMS **to ~ a score with sb** régler ses comptes avec qn.
■ **settle back** s'installer confortablement; **to ~ back in** se caler dans [*chair*].
■ **settle down 1** (get comfortable) s'installer (**on** sur; **in** dans); **2** (calm down) [*person*] se calmer; [*situation*] s'arranger; **~ down!** du calme!; **to ~ down to**

work se concentrer sur son travail; **to ~ down to doing** se résoudre à faire; **3** (marry) se ranger.
■ **settle for**: **~ for** [sth] se contenter de; **why ~ for less?** pourquoi se contenter de moins?
■ **settle in 1** (move in) s'installer; **2** (become acclimatized) s'adapter.
■ **settle on**: **~ on** [sth] choisir [*name, colour*].
■ **settle up 1** (pay) payer; **to ~ up with** régler [*waiter, tradesman*]; **2** (sort out who owes what) faire les comptes.

settled /setld/ *adj* stable; **I feel ~ here** (in home) je me sens chez moi.

settlement /'setlmənt/ *n* **1** (agreement) accord *m*; **2** (resolving) règlement *m* ALSO JUR; **3** FIN constitution *f* (**on** en faveur de); **4** (social work centre) centre *m* social; **5** (dwellings) village *m*; **6** (colonization) implantation *f*.

settler /'setlə(r)/ *n* colon *m*.

set-to° /'settu:/ *n* prise *f* de bec°, dispute *f*.

set-up° /'setʌp/ **I** *n* **1** (system) organisation *f*; (trap) traquenard° *m*.
II *noun modifier* [*costs*] initial; [*time*] de préparation.

seven /'sevn/ ▶1112|, 713| *n, adj* sept (*m*) *inv*.

seventeen /ˌsevn'ti:n/ ▶1112|, 713| *n, adj* dix-sept (*m*) *inv*.

seventeenth /ˌsevn'ti:nθ/ ▶1112|, 854| **I** *n* **1** (in order) dix-septième *mf*; **2** (of month) dix-sept *m inv*; **3** (fraction) dix-septième *m*.
II *adj, adv* dix-septième.

seventh /'sevnθ/ ▶1112|, 854| **I** *n* **1** (in order) septième *mf*; **2** (of month) sept *m inv*; **3** (fraction) septième *m*; **4** MUS septième *f*.
II *adj, adv* septième.

seventies /'sevntɪz/ ▶854|, 713| *npl* **1 the ~** les années *fpl* soixante-dix; **2 to be in one's ~** avoir plus de soixante-dix ans; **a man in his ~** un septuagénaire.

seventieth /'sevntɪəθ/ ▶1112| **I** *n* **1** (in order) soixante-dixième *mf*; **2** (fraction) soixante-dixième *m*.
II *adj, adv* soixante-dixième.

seventy /'sevntɪ/ ▶1112|, 713| *n, adj* soixante-dix (*m*) *inv*.

seventy-eight /ˌsevntɪ'eɪt/ *n* AUDIO **a ~** (**record ou disc**) un soixante-dix-huit tours *m inv*.

seven-year itch *n* démon *m* de l'infidélité (après sept ans de mariage).

sever /'sevə(r)/ *vtr* **1** LIT sectionner [*wire, limb, artery*]; couper [*rope, branch*]; **to ~ sth from** séparer qch de; **2** FIG rompre [*relations*]; couper [*contact*].

several /'sevrəl/ **I** *pron* **~ of you/us** plusieurs d'entre vous/d'entre nous; **~ of our group** plusieurs membres de notre groupe.
II *quantif* **1** (a few) plusieurs; **~ books** plusieurs livres; **2** SOUT (respective) respectif/-ive.

severally /'sevrəlɪ/ *adv* séparément.

severance /'sevərəns/ *n* **1** (separation) rupture *f*; **2** (redundancy) licenciement *m*; **~ pay** indemnités *fpl* de licenciement.

severe /sɪ'vɪə(r)/ *adj* **1** (extreme) [*problem, damage, shortage, injury, depression, shock*] grave; [*weather, cold, winter*] rigoureux/-euse; [*headache*] violent; [*loss*] lourd; **2** (harsh) sévère; **3** (austere) austère.

severely /sɪ'vɪəlɪ/ *adv* **1** (seriously) [*restrict, damage*] sévèrement; [*affect, shock*] durement; [*disabled*] gravement; [*injured*] grièvement; **2** (harshly) [*treat, speak*] sévèrement; [*beat*] violemment; **3** (austerely) de façon austère.

severity /sɪ'verətɪ/ *n* **1** (seriousness) (of problem, situation, illness) gravité *f*; (of shock, pain) violence *f*; **2** (harshness) (of sentence, treatment) sévérité *f*; (of climate) rigueur *f*.

Seville orange /səˌvɪl'ɒrəndʒ/ *n* orange *f* amère.

sew /səʊ/ (*prét* **sewed**; *pp* **sewn**, **sewed**) **I** *vtr* coudre; **to ~ sth on to sth** coudre qch sur; **he ~ed the button back on** il a recousu le bouton.
II *vi* coudre, faire de la couture.
■ **sew up**: **~** [sth] **up**, **~ up** [sth] **1** (reseam) [*hole, tear*]; faire [*seam*]; (re)coudre [*wound*]; **2**° (settle) conclure [*deal*]; conclure [qch] victorieusement [*game*];

(control) dominer [*market*]; **they've got the match sewn up** ils sont sûrs de gagner le match; **the deal is all sewn up!** l'affaire est dans le sac○!

sewage /'suːɪdʒ, 'sjuː-/ n ₵ eaux *fpl* usées.

sewage: ~ **disposal** n évacuation *f* des eaux usées; ~ **farm** n = **sewage works**; ~ **works** n champ m d'épandage.

sewer /'suːə(r), 'sjuː-/ n égout m.

sewing /'səʊɪŋ/ **I** n (activity) couture *f*; (piece of work) ouvrage m.
II noun modifier [*scissors, thread*] à coudre.

sewing: ~ **basket** n corbeille *f* à ouvrage; ~ **machine** n machine *f* à coudre.

sewn /səʊn/ pp ▶ **sew**.

sex /seks/ **I** n **1** (gender) sexe m; **2** (intercourse) (one act) rapport m sexuel; (repeated) rapports *mpl* sexuels.
II noun modifier [*organ*] sexuel/-elle.
III vtr déterminer le sexe de [*animal*].

sex: ~ **abuse** n violence *f* sexuelle; ~ **act** n acte m sexuel; ~ **appeal** n sex-appeal m; ~ **attack** n agression *f* sexuelle.

sex change n **to have a** ~ changer de sexe.

sex: ~ **discrimination** n discrimination *f* sexuelle; ~ **drive** n libido *f*; ~ **education** n éducation *f* sexuelle.

sexism /'seksɪzəm/ n sexisme m.

sexist /'seksɪst/ n, adj sexiste (*mf*).

sex: ~ **life** n vie *f* sexuelle; ~ **offender** n délinquant/-e *m/f* sexuel/-elle.

sexual /'sekʃʊəl/ adj sexuel/-elle.

sexual: ~ **abuse** n violence *f* sexuelle; ~ **harassment** n harcèlement m sexuel; ~ **intercourse** n rapports *mpl* sexuels.

sexuality /ˌsekʃʊ'ælətɪ/ n **1** (sexual orientation) sexualité *f*; **2** (eroticism) érotisme m.

sexually /'sekʃʊəlɪ/ adv [*dominant, explicit, mature*] sexuellement; [*transmit, infect*] par voie sexuelle; ~ **abused** victime de violence sexuelle.

sexually transmitted disease, **STD** n maladie *f* sexuellement transmissible, MST.

sexy○ /'seksɪ/ adj **1** (erotic) [*book, film, show*] érotique; [*person, clothing*] sexy○ inv; **2** [*image, product*] accrocheur○/-euse.

S Glam n GB POST abrév écrite = **South Glamorgan**.

sh /ʃ/ excl chut!

shabbily /'ʃæbɪlɪ/ adv [*dressed*] pauvrement, de façon miteuse; [*behave, treat*] de manière peu élégante.

shabby /'ʃæbɪ/ adj [*person*] habillé de façon miteuse; [*room, furnishings, clothing*] miteux/-euse; [*treatment*] mesquin.

shack /ʃæk/ n cabane *f*.
■ **shack up**○: **to** ~ **up with sb** se maquer● avec qn.

shackle /'ʃækl/ **I** n LIT fer m; FIG chaîne *f*.
II vtr mettre [qn] aux fers.

shade /ʃeɪd/ **I** n **1** (shadow) ombre *f*; **2** (of colour) ton m; FIG (of opinion, meaning) nuance *f*; **an attractive** ~ **of blue** un beau bleu; **a solution that should appeal to all** ~**s of opinion** une solution qui devrait plaire à toutes les tendances; **3** (small amount, degree) **a** ~ **too loud** un tout petit peu trop fort; **a** ~ **of resentment** un soupçon de ressentiment; **4** (also **lamp** ~) abat-jour m inv; **5** US (also **window** ~) store m.
II shades npl **1**○ (sunglasses) lunettes *fpl* de soleil; **2** (undertones) ~**s of Mozart** ça fait penser à Mozart.
III vtr **1** (screen) donner de l'ombre à; **the hat** ~**d her face** le chapeau projetait une ombre sur son visage; **the garden was** ~**d by trees** le jardin était ombragé par des arbres; **to** ~ **one's eyes (with one's hand)** s'abriter les yeux de la main; **2** = **shade in**.
IV vi (blend) [*colour, tone*] se fondre (**into** en).
V shaded pp adj **1** (shady) ombragé; **2** [*lamp*] avec un abat-jour; **3** ART (also ~**-in**) GEN sombre; (produced by hatching) hachuré.

IDIOMS **to put sb in the** ~ éclipser qn; **to put sth in the** ~ surpasser or surclasser qch.
■ **shade in**: ~ **in** [sth], ~ [sth] **in** ombrer [*drawing*]; (by hatching) hachurer; [*child*] colorier.

shading /'ʃeɪdɪŋ/ n ₵ (in painting) ombres *fpl*; (hatching) hachures *fpl*.

shadow /'ʃædəʊ/ **I** n **1** (shade) LIT, FIG ombre *f*; **to live in the** ~ **of** (near) vivre à proximité de [*mine, power station*]; (in fear of) vivre dans la crainte de [*Aids, unemployment, war*]; **to stand in the** ~**s** se tenir dans l'ombre; **she's a** ~ **of her former self** elle n'est plus que l'ombre d'elle-même; **the war casts a long** ~ les effets de la guerre se font toujours sentir; **to have** ~**s under one's eyes** avoir les yeux cernés; **2** (person who follows another) GEN ombre *f*; (detective) détective m qui file qn; **to put a** ~ **on sb** faire filer or suivre qn; **3** (hint) **not a** ~ **of suspicion** pas le moindre soupçon; **without** ~ **or beyond the** ~ **of a doubt** sans l'ombre d'un doute.
II shadows npl LITTÉR (darkness) ténèbres *fpl*.
III vtr **1** LIT projeter une ombre sur; **2** (follow) filer.

shadow: ~ **box** vtr boxer à vide; ~ **boxing** n LIT entraînement de boxe sans adversaire; FIG attaque *f* purement formelle; ~ **cabinet** n GB POL cabinet m fantôme; ~ **minister** n GB POL = **shadow secretary**; ~ **play** n théâtre m d'ombres.

shadow secretary n GB POL **the** ~ **for employment/foreign affairs** le porte-parole de l'opposition dans le domaine de l'emploi/des affaires étrangères.

shadowy /'ʃædəʊɪ/ adj **1** (dark) sombre; **2** (indistinct) [*image, outline*] flou; [*form*] indistinct; **3** (mysterious) mystérieux/-ieuse.

shady /'ʃeɪdɪ/ adj **1** [*place*] ombragé; **2** (dubious) véreux/-euse.

shaft /ʃɑːft, US ʃæft/ n **1** (rod) (of tool) manche m; (of arrow) tige *f*; (of spear, sword) hampe *f*; (in machine) axe m; (on a cart) brancard m; **2** (passage, vent) puits m; **3** FIG (of wit) trait m; ~ **of light** rai m; ~ **of lightning** éclair m.

shaggy /'ʃægɪ/ adj [*hair, beard, eyebrows*] en broussailles; [*animal*] poilu; [*carpet*] à longues mèches.

shaggy dog story n histoire *f* drôle sans queue ni tête.

shake /ʃeɪk/ **I** n **1 to give sb/sth a** ~ GEN secouer qn/qch; **with a** ~ **of the head** avec un hochement de tête; **2** (also **milk-**~) milk-shake m.
II vtr (prét **shook**; pp **shaken**) **1** secouer; '~ **before use**' 'agiter avant emploi'; **he shook the seeds out of the packet** il a fait tomber les graines du paquet; **to** ~ **powder over the carpet** répandre de la poudre sur le tapis; **to** ~ **salt over the dish** saupoudrer le plat de sel; **to** ~ **one's fist at sb** menacer qn du poing; **I shook him by the shoulders** je l'ai pris par les épaules et je l'ai secoué; **to** ~ **one's head** hocher la tête; **to** ~ **hands with sb, to** ~ **sb's hand** serrer la main de qn, donner une poignée de main à qn; **to** ~ **hands on the deal** se serrer la main pour conclure l'affaire; **to** ~ **hands on it** (after argument) se serrer la main en signe de réconciliation; **2** FIG ébranler [*belief, confidence, faith, person*]; [*event, disaster*] secouer; **it really shook me to find out that...** cela m'a vraiment donné un choc de découvrir que...; **3** US (get rid of) = **shake off**.
III vi (prét **shook**; pp **shaken**) **1** (tremble) trembler; **to** ~ **with** trembler de [*fear, cold, emotion*]; se tordre de [*laughter*]; **2** (shake hands) **they shook on it** (on deal, agreement) ils se sont serré la main en signe d'accord; (after argument) ils se sont serré la main en signe de réconciliation; '~!' 'serrons-nous la main!'
IV v refl (prét **shook**; pp **shaken**) **to** ~ **oneself** [*person, animal*] se secouer.
IDIOMS **in a** ~○ ou **two** ~**s**○ en un clin d'œil; **to be no great** ~**s**○ ne pas valoir grand-chose; **to have the** ~**s**○ (from fear, cold, infirmity) avoir la tremblote○; (from alcohol, fever) trembler.
■ **shake about** GB, **shake around**: ¶ ~ **about** ou **around** être secoué; ¶ ~ [sth] **about** ou **around** secouer [qch] dans tous les sens.
■ **shake off**: ~ [sb/sth] **off**, ~ **off** [sb/sth] se dé-

barrasser de [*cold, depression, habit, person*]; se défaire de [*feeling*].

■ **shake out**: ¶ ~ [sth] **out**, ~ **out** [sth] secouer; **to** ~ **some tablets out of a bottle** secouer un flacon pour en faire tomber quelques comprimés; ¶ ~ [sb] **out of** secouer [qn] pour le faire sortir de [*mood*].

■ **shake up**: ¶ ~ **up** [sth], ~ [sth] **up** agiter [*bottle, mixture*]; ¶ ~ [sb/sth] **up**, ~ **up** [sb/sth] **1** LIT, FIG secouer; **2** (reorganize) COMM réorganiser (radicalement); POL remanier [*cabinet*].

shaken /'ʃeɪkən/ ▶ **shake**.
II *adj* (shocked) choqué; (upset) bouleversé.

shaker /'ʃeɪkə(r)/ *n* (for cocktails) shaker *m*; (for dice) gobelet *m* à dés; (for salt) salière *f*; (for pepper) poivrière *f*; (for salad) saladier *m*.

shake-up /'ʃeɪkʌp/ *n* COMM réorganisation *f* (importante); POL remaniement *m*.

shakily /'ʃeɪkɪlɪ/ *adv* [*say, speak*] d'une voix tremblante; [*walk*] d'un pas chancelant; **he writes** ~ il écrit en tremblant; **they started rather** ~ leur début était chancelant or mal assuré.

shaky /'ʃeɪkɪ/ *adj* **1** [*chair, ladder*] branlant; **my hands are rather** ~ j'ai les mains qui tremblent; **I feel a bit** ~ je me sens un peu flageolant; **2** FIG [*relationship, position*] instable; [*argument*] peu solide; [*knowledge, memory*] peu sûr; [*regime*] chancelant; **3** FIG (uncertain) [*start*] chancelant; **we got off to a rather** ~ **start** (in relationship, business) au début cela a été difficile pour nous; (in performance) nous étions très peu sûrs de nous au début; **my French is a bit** ~ mon français est un peu hésitant.

shall /ʃæl, ʃəl/

■ **Note** When *shall* is used to form the future tense in English, the same rules apply as for *will*. You will find a note on this and on question tags and short answers near the entry *will*.

modal aux **1** (in future tense) **I** ~ ou **I'll see you tomorrow** je vous verrai demain; **we** ~ **not** ou **shan't have a reply before Friday** nous n'aurons pas de réponse avant vendredi; **2** (in suggestions) ~ **I set the table?** est-ce que je mets la table?; ~ **we go to the cinema tonight?** et si on allait au cinéma ce soir?; **let's buy some peaches,** ~ **we?** et si on achetait des pêches?; **3** SOUT (in commands, contracts etc) **you** ~ **do as I say** tu dois faire ce que je te dis; **the sum** ~ **be paid on signature of the contract** le montant devra être versé à la signature du contrat; **thou shalt not steal** BIBLE tu ne voleras point.

shallot /ʃə'lɒt/ *n* **1** GB échalote *f*; **2** US cive *f*.

shallow /'ʃæləʊ/ ▶ 1045 **I shallows** *npl* bas-fonds *mpl*.
II *adj* [*container, hollow, water, grave*] peu profond; [*stairs*] aux marches basses; [*breathing, character, response*] superficiel/-ielle; [*writing, conversation*] plat; [*wit*] creux/creuse; **the** ~ **end of the pool** l'extrémité la moins profonde de la piscine.

shallowness /'ʃæləʊnɪs/ *n* (of water) peu *m* de profondeur; (of person) manque *m* de profondeur; (of conversation) caractère *m* superficiel.

sham /ʃæm/ **I** *n* (person) imposteur *m*; (organization) imposture *f*; (democracy, election) parodie *f*; (ideas, views) mystification *f*; (activity) supercherie *f*.
II *adj* (épith) [*election, democracy*] prétendu (*before n*); [*object, building*] factice; [*organization*] fantoche.
III *vtr* (*p prés etc* -mm-) **to** ~ **sleep/death** faire semblant de dormir/d'être mort.
IV *vi* (*p prés etc* -mm-) faire semblant.

shamble /'ʃæmbl/ *vi* aller d'un pas traînant.

shambles○ /'ʃæmblz/ *n* (of administration, room) pagaille○ *f*; (of meeting etc) désastre *m*.

shame /ʃeɪm/ **I** *n* **1** (embarrassment, disgrace) honte *f*; **he has no (sense of)** ~ il n'a honte de rien; **to feel** ~ **at** être honteux/-euse de; **to my eternal** ~ à ma très grande honte; **the** ~ **of it!** quelle honte!; **to bring** ~ **on** être or faire la honte de; ~ **on you!** tu devrais avoir honte!; **there were cries of '**~**!'** les gens criaient au scandale; **2** (pity) **it is a** ~ **that** c'est

dommage que (+ *subj*); **it was a great** ou **such a** ~ **(that) she lost** c'est tellement dommage qu'elle ait perdu; **it's a** ~ **about the factory closing** c'est dommage que l'usine ait fermé or ferme; **it's a** ~ **about your father** (if not very serious matter) c'est dommage pour ton père; (if serious) je suis désolé pour ton père; **nice costumes**—~ **about the play**○! les costumes étaient réussis—mais la pièce○!; **isn't it a** ~**?** c'est vraiment dommage.
II *vtr* **1** (embarrass) faire honte à; **I was** ~**d by her words** ses paroles m'ont fait honte; **to** ~ **sb into doing** obliger qn à faire en lui faisant honte; **2** (disgrace) déshonorer (**by doing** en faisant); **they** ~**d the nation** ils ont fait la honte de la nation.
IDIOMS **to put sb to** ~ faire honte à qn; **your garden puts the others to** ~ tous les jardins semblent minables comparés au tien.

shamefaced /ˌʃeɪm'feɪst/ *adj* [*person, look*] penaud.

shameful /'ʃeɪmfl/ *adj* [*conduct, waste*] honteux/-euse; **it is** ~ **that** c'est une honte que (+ *subj*).

shamefully /'ʃeɪmfəlɪ/ *adv* [*behave*] honteusement; [*mistreated*] abominablement; ~ **ignorant** d'une ignorance crasse.

shameless /'ʃeɪmlɪs/ *adj* [*person*] éhonté; [*attitude, negligence*] effronté; **a** ~ **display** of un étalage impudique de [*emotion, wealth*]; **to be quite** ~ **about** n'avoir pas du tout honte de.

shamelessly /'ʃeɪmlɪslɪ/ *adv* [*behave*] sans vergogne.

shaming /'ʃeɪmɪŋ/ *adj* [*defeat, behaviour*] humiliant.

shampoo /ʃæm'puː/ **I** *n* (all contexts) shampooing *m*.
II *vtr* (3ᵉ *pers sg prés* -**poos**; *prét, pp* -**pooed**) faire un shampooing à [*customer, pet*]; **to** ~ **one's hair** se faire un shampooing.

shamrock /'ʃæmrɒk/ *n* trèfle *m*.

shandy /'ʃændɪ/, **shandygaff** /'ʃændɪgæf/ US *n* panaché *m*.

Shangri-La /ˌʃæŋgrɪ'lɑː/ *n* paradis *m* terrestre.

shank /ʃæŋk/ *n* **1** ZOOL jambe *f*; CULIN jarret *m*; **2** (of knife) soie *f*; (of golf-club) manche *m*; (of drill-bit) queue *f*; (of screw) tige *f*; (of shoe) cambrure *f*.

shan't /ʃɑːnt/ = **shall not**.

shanty /'ʃæntɪ/ *n* **1** (hut) baraque *f*; **2** (song) chanson *f* de marins.

shantytown /'ʃæntɪtaʊn/ *n* bidonville *m*.

shape /ʃeɪp/ **I** *n* **1** (of object, building etc) forme *f*; (of person) silhouette *f*; **a square** ~ une forme carrée; **what** ~ **is it?** de quelle forme est-ce?; **to be an odd** ~ avoir une drôle de forme; **to be the right** ~ [*object*] avoir la forme qu'il faut; [*person*] avoir la silhouette qu'il faut; **to be round in** ~ avoir la forme d'un rond; **it's like a leaf in** ~ de forme cela ressemble à une feuille; **in the** ~ **of** en forme de [*star, cat*]; **to mould sth into** ~ donner forme à qch en le modelant; **to keep one's** ~ [*person*] garder sa ligne; **to take** ~ [*sculpture, building*] prendre forme; **to lose its** ~ [*garment*] se déformer; **to bend sth out of** ~ gauchir qch; **in all** ~**s and sizes** de toutes les formes et de toutes les tailles; **2** (optimum condition) forme *f*; **to be out of** ~ ne pas être en forme; **to get in** ~ se mettre en forme; **to knock sth into** ~ mettre qch au point or en état [*project, idea, essay*]; **3** FIG (character, structure) GEN forme *f*; (of organization) structure *f*; **to take** ~ [*plan, project, idea*] prendre forme; [*events*] prendre tournure; **the likely** ~ **of currency union** la forme que prendra probablement l'union monétaire; **my contribution took the** ~ **of helping...** j'ai contribué en aidant...; **developments which have changed the** ~ **of our lives** des développements qui ont changé notre mode de vie; **the** ~ **of things to come** ce que sera l'avenir; **tips in any** ~ **or form are forbidden** les pourboires de toutes sortes sont interdits; **I don't condone violence in any** ~ **or form** je n'approuve pas la violence, sous quelque forme que ce soit; **4** (guise) **in the** ~ **of** sous (la) forme de [*money etc*]; en la personne de [*policeman etc*]; **5** (vague form) forme *f*, silhouette *f*; **6** CULIN (mould) moule *m*.
II *vtr* **1** (fashion, mould) [*person*] modeler [*clay*];

sculpter [*wood*]; [*wind*] façonner, sculpter [*rock*]; [*hair-dresser*] couper [*hair*]; **~ the dough into balls** faites des boules avec la pâte; **to ~ the cardboard into a triangle** faire un triangle dans le carton; **2** FIG [*person, event*] influencer; (stronger) déterminer [*future, idea*]; modeler [*character*]; [*person*] formuler [*policy, project*]; **to play a part in shaping the country's future** avoir un rôle dans la détermination de l'avenir du pays; **3** (in sewing) (fit closely) ajuster [*garment*].

■ **shape up 1** (develop) [*person*] s'en sortir; **how are things shaping up at (the) head office?** quelle tournure prennent les choses au siège?; **2** (meet expectations) être à la hauteur; **if he doesn't ~ up, fire him** s'il n'est pas à la hauteur, renvoie-le; **3** (improve one's figure) se mettre en forme.

shaped /ʃeɪpt/ **I** *adj* **to be ~ like sth** avoir la forme de qch; **a teapot ~ like a house** une théière en forme de maison.
II -shaped *combining form* **star-/V-~** en forme d'étoile/de V; **oddly-~** de forme étrange.

shapeless /ˈʃeɪplɪs/ *adj* sans forme, informe.

shapely /ˈʃeɪplɪ/ *adj* [*leg*] bien galbé; [*woman*] bien fait.

shard /ʃɑːd/ *n* tesson *m*.

share /ʃeə(r)/ **I** *n* **1** (of money, food, profits, blame) part *f* (**of** de); **to have a ~ in** être pour quelque chose dans, contribuer à [*success etc*]; **to have more than one's fair ~ of** avoir plus que sa part de [*bad luck*]; **to do one's ~ of sth** faire sa part de qch; **to pay one's (fair) ~** payer sa part; **to have a ~ in a company** avoir une participation dans une société; **to own a half-~** posséder la moitié; **2** FIN action *f*; **3** AGRIC soc *m* (de charrue).
II *noun modifier* FIN [*capital, issue*] d'actions; [*price*] des actions.
III *vtr* partager [*money, house, opinion*] (**with** avec); partager [*chore*]; **we ~ a birthday** nous avons notre anniversaire le même jour; **we ~ an interest in animals** nous aimons tous les deux les animaux.
IV *vi* **to ~ in** prendre part à [*success, happiness, benefits*].
IDIOMS **~ and ~ alike** il faut partager.
■ **share out**: **~** [*sth*] **out**, **~ out** [*sth*] (amongst selves) partager [*food etc*]; (amongst others) répartir [*food etc*]; **we ~d the cakes out between us** nous nous sommes partagé les gâteaux.

shared /ʃeəd/ *adj* [*house, interest, grief*] partagé; [*space, facilities etc*] commun.

shareholder /ˈʃeəhəʊldə(r)/ *n* actionnaire *mf*; **the ~s** l'actionnariat *m*.

share: **~ option scheme** *n* plan *m* de participation par achat d'actions; **~-out** *n* partage *m*, répartition *f*.

shark /ʃɑːk/ *n* requin *m* ALSO FIG.

sharp /ʃɑːp/ **I** *n* MUS dièse *m*.
II *adj* **1** [*razor*] tranchant; [*edge*] coupant; [*blade, scissors, knife*] bien aiguisé; [*saw*] bien affûté; **2** (pointed) [*tooth, fingernail, end, needle*] pointu; [*pencil*] bien taillé; [*features*] anguleux/-euse; [*nose*] pointu; **3** (abrupt) [*angle*] aigu/-uë; [*bend, reflex*] brusque; [*drop, incline*] fort; [*fall, rise*] brusque, brutal; **4** (acidic) [*taste, smell*] âcre; [*fruit*] acide; **5** (piercing) [*pain, cold*] vif/vive; [*cry*] aigu/-uë; [*blow*] sévère; [*frost*] fort, intense; **6** FIG (aggressive) [*tongue*] acéré; [*tone*] acerbe; **7** (alert) [*person, mind*] vif/vive; [*eyesight*] perçant; [*hearing*] fin; **to have a ~ wit** avoir de la repartie; **to keep a ~ lookout** rester sur le qui-vive (**for** pour); **to have a ~ eye for sth** FIG avoir l'œil pour qch; **8** PÉJ (clever) [*businessman, person*] malin/-igne; **~ operator** filou *m*; **9** (clearly defined) [*image, sound, distinction*] net/nette; [*contrast*] prononcé; **to bring sth into ~ focus** LIT cadrer qch avec netteté; FIG faire passer qch au premier plan; **10**○ GB [*suit*] tape-à-l'œil *inv* PÉJ; **11**○ US (stylish) chic *inv*; **12** MUS dièse (too high) aigu/-uë.
III *adv* **1** (abruptly) [*stop*] net; **to turn ~ left** tourner brusquement vers la gauche; **2**○ (promptly) **at 9 o'clock ~** à neuf heures pile○; **3** MUS [*sing, play*] trop haut.

IDIOMS **to be at the ~ end** être en première ligne; **to look ~**○ se dépêcher.

sharpen /ˈʃɑːpən/ **I** *vtr* **1** LIT aiguiser, affûter [*blade*]; tailler [*pencil*]; **to ~ its claws** [*cat*] se faire les griffes; **2** (accentuate) rendre [qch] plus net [*contrast*]; affiner [*focus*]; régler [*image*]; **3** (make stronger) aviver [*anger, desire*]; aiguiser [*appetite*]; affiner [*reflexes*]; **to ~ sb's wits** dégourdir l'esprit de qn.
II *vi* [*tone, voice, look*] se durcir; [*pain*] s'aviver.

sharpener /ˈʃɑːpənə(r)/ *n* (for pencil) taille-crayon *m*; (for knife) fusil *m*, aiguisoir *m*.

sharp-eyed /ˌʃɑːpˈaɪd/ *adj* à la vue perçante; FIG vigilant.

sharpish○ /ˈʃɑːpɪʃ/ *adv* GB illico○, vite.

sharply /ˈʃɑːplɪ/ *adv* **1** (abruptly) [*turn, change, rise, fall*] brusquement, brutalement; [*stop*] net; **2** (harshly) [*speak*] d'un ton brusque; [*criticize*] vivement, sévèrement; [*look*] durement; **3** (distinctly) [*differ, define*] nettement; **to bring sth ~ into focus** LIT cadrer qch avec netteté; FIG faire passer qch au premier plan; **4** (perceptively) [*drawn*] avec acuité; [*aware*] vivement.

sharpness /ˈʃɑːpnɪs/ *n* **1** (of blade, scissors) tranchant *m* (**of** de); **2** (of turn, bend) angle *m* brusque (**of** de); **3** (of image, sound) netteté *f* (**of** de); **4** (of voice, tone) brusquerie *f* (**of** de); **5** (acidity) (of taste) piquant *m*; (of smell) âcreté *f*; (of fruit, drink) acidité *f*.

sharp: **~ practice** *n* filouterie *f*; **~shooter** *n* tireur/-euse *m/f* d'élite.

shatter /ˈʃætə(r)/ **I** *vtr* LIT fracasser [*glass*]; FIG rompre [*silence*]; briser [*life, hope*]; démolir [*nerves*].
II *vi* [*window, glass*] voler en éclats.

shattered /ˈʃætəd/ *adj* **1** [*dream*] brisé; [*life, confidence*] anéanti; **2** (devastated) effondré; ○(tired) crevé○.

shattering /ˈʃætərɪŋ/ *adj* [*blow, effect*] accablant; [*news*] bouleversant.

shave /ʃeɪv/ **I** *n* **to have a ~** se raser; **to give sb a ~** raser qn.
II *vtr* (*pp* **~d** ou **shaven**) **1** LIT [*barber*] raser [*person*]; **to ~ sb's beard off** raser la barbe de qn; **to ~ one's legs** se raser les jambes; **2** (plane) raboter [*wood*]; **3** FIG réduire [*prices, profits*].
III *vi* (*pp* **~d** ou **shaven**) [*person*] se raser.
IDIOMS **that was a close ~**! je l'ai/il l'a etc échappé belle!

shaver /ˈʃeɪvə(r)/ *n* (also **electric ~**) rasoir *m* électrique.

shaving /ˈʃeɪvɪŋ/ **I** *n* **1** (process) rasage *m*; **2** (of wood, metal) copeau *m*.
II *noun modifier* [*cream, foam*] à raser; [*kit*] de rasage.

shaving: **~ brush** *n* blaireau *m*; **~ mirror** *n* petit miroir *m*; **~ soap** *n* savon *m* à barbe.

shawl /ʃɔːl/ *n* châle *m*.

she /ʃiː/

■ **Note** *she* is translated by elle: *she closed the door* = elle a fermé la porte. For particular usages, see the entry below.

I *pron* elle; **~'s not at home** elle n'est pas chez elle; **here ~ is** la voici; **there ~ is** la voilà; SHE **didn't take it** ce n'est pas elle qui l'a pris; **he lives in Dublin but ~ doesn't** il habite Dublin mais elle non; **~'s a genius** c'est un génie; **~ who** celle qui; **~ who must be obeyed** HUM la patronne HUM; **~ and I** elle et moi; **~'s a lovely boat** c'est un beau bateau.
II *n* **it's a ~**○ (of baby) c'est une fille; (of animal) c'est une femelle.

sheaf /ʃiːf/ *n* (*pl* **sheaves**) (of corn, flowers) gerbe *f*; (of papers) liasse *f*.

shear /ʃɪə(r)/ **I** *vtr* (*prét* **sheared**; *pp* **shorn**) tondre.
II *vi* **shorn** *pp adj* FIG dépouillé (**of** de).
■ **shear off**: **¶ ~ off** [*metal component*] céder; **¶ ~ off** [*sth*], **~** [*sth*] **off** tondre [*hair, fleece*]; [*accident, storm*] emporter [*branch*].

shears /ʃɪəz/ *npl* **1** (for garden) cisaille *f*; **2** (for sheep) tondeuse *f*.

sheath /ʃiːθ/ *n* **1** (case) (of sword) fourreau *m*; (of knife, cable) gaine *f*; **2** BOT gaine *f*.

sheathe /ʃiːð/ *vtr* rengainer [*sword, dagger*]; rentrer [*claws*]; gainer [*cable*]; **~d in** gainé de [*silk etc*].

sheaves /ʃiːvz/ *npl* ▶ **sheaf**.

shebang⁰ /ʃɪˈbæŋ/ *n* US **the whole ~**⁰ tout le tremblement⁰.

shed /ʃed/ **I** *n* GEN remise *f*, abri *m*; (lean-to) appentis *m*; (bigger) (at factory site, port etc) hangar *m*.
II *vtr* (*prét, pp* **shed**) **1** verser [*tears*]; perdre [*leaves, weight*]; [*lorry*] déverser [*load*]; enlever [*clothes*]; se débarrasser de [*inhibitions, image*]; **to ~ skin** [*snake*] muer; **to ~ blood** (one's own) perdre du sang; **too much blood has been shed** trop de sang a coulé; **to ~ jobs** ou **staff** EUPH supprimer des emplois; **2** (transmit) répandre [*light, happiness*].

she'd /ʃiːd, ʃɪd/ = **she had**, **she would**.

sheen /ʃiːn/ *n* (of hair) éclat *m*; (of silk) lustre *m*.

sheep /ʃiːp/ *n* (*pl* **~**) mouton *m*; (ewe) brebis *f*; **black ~** brebis *f* galeuse; **lost ~** brebis *f* égarée.
IDIOMS **to count ~** FIG compter les moutons; **to make ~'s eyes at sb** faire les yeux doux à qn; **may as well be hung for a ~ as for a lamb** tant qu'à être condamné pour un crime, autant qu'il en vaille la peine.

sheep: **~ dog** *n* chien *m* de berger; **~ farm** *n* ferme *f* d'élevage de moutons; **~ farmer** ▶ **1251** *n* éleveur *m* de moutons.

sheepish /ʃiːpɪʃ/ *adj* penaud.

sheepshearing *n* tonte *f*.

sheepskin /ʃiːpskɪn/ *n* **1** peau *f* de mouton; **2**⁰ US UNIV diplôme *m*.

sheep station *n* élevage *m* de moutons (*en Australie*).

sheer /ʃɪə(r)/ **I** *adj* **1** (pure) [*boredom, hypocrisy, stupidity*] pur; **out of ~ malice/stupidity** par pure méchanceté/bêtise; **by ~ hard work** uniquement grâce à son acharnement au travail; **by ~ accident** tout à fait par accident; **2** (utter) **the ~ immensity of it** son immensité même; **3** (steep) [*cliff*] à pic; **4** (fine) [*fabric*] léger/-ère, fin; [*stockings*] extra-fin.
II *adv* [*rise, fall*] à pic.
■ **sheer away**, **sheer off** faire une embardée.

sheet /ʃiːt/ *n* **1** (of paper, stamps) feuille *f*; **2** (for bed) drap *m*; (shroud) linceul *m*; **waterproof ~** alaise *f*; **3** (printed) (periodical) périodique *m*; (newspaper) journal *m*; **fact** ou **information ~** bulletin *m* d'informations; **4** (of plastic, rubber) feuille *f*; (of canvas, tarpaulin) bâche *f*; (of metal) plaque *f*; (thinner) feuille *f*; (of glass) plaque *f*; (thinner) vitre *f*; **5** (of ice etc) couche *f*; (thicker) plaque *f*; (of mist, fog) nappe *f*; (of flame) rideau *m*; **in ~s** [*rain*] à torrents; **6** NAUT écoute *f*; **7**⁰ US JUR casier *m*.
IDIOMS **to be as white as a ~** être blanc comme un linge.

sheeting /ʃiːtɪŋ/ *n* (fabric) toile *f* à draps; (iron) tôle *f*; **plastic ~** bâche *f* en plastique.

sheet: **~ iron** *n* tôle *f*; **~ lightning** *n* ¢ éclairs *mpl* de chaleur; **~ metal** *n* AUT tôle *f*; **~ music** *n* ¢ partitions *fpl*.

sheik /ʃeɪk, US ʃiːk/ *n* cheik *m*.

shekel /ʃekl/ **I** ▶ **849** *n* (currency) shekel *m*.
II shekels⁰ *npl* (money) fric⁰ *m*, argent *m*.

shelf /ʃelf/ *n* (*pl* **shelves**) **1** (at home) GEN étagère *f*; (in oven) plaque *f*; (in shop, fridge) rayon *m*; **a set of shelves** une étagère; **2** GEOG (of rock, ice) corniche *f*.
IDIOMS **to be left on the ~** (remain single) rester vieille fille.

shelf-life /ʃelflaɪf/ *n* **1** LIT (of product) durée *f* de conservation; **2** FIG (of technology, pop music) durée *f* de vie; (of politician, star) période *f* de gloire.

shelf mark *n* cote *f*.

shell /ʃel/ **I** *n* **1** BOT, ZOOL (of egg, nut, snail) coquille *f*; (of crab, tortoise, shrimp) carapace *f*; **sea ~** coquillage *m*; **to develop a hard ~** FIG [*person*] se forger une carapace; **to come out of one's ~** FIG sortir de sa coquille; **2** MIL (bomb) obus *m*; (cartridge) cartouche *f*; **3** TECH (of vehicle) carcasse *f*; (of building) cage *f*; (of machine) enveloppe *f*; (of nuclear plant) enceinte *f* de confinement; **4** (remains) (of building) carcasse *f*.

II *vtr* **1** MIL pilonner [*town, installation*]; **2** CULIN écosser [*peas*]; décortiquer [*prawn, nut*]; écailler [*oyster*].
■ **shell out**⁰: ¶ **~ out** casquer⁰ (for pour); ¶ **~ out [sth]** débourser [*sum*] (for pour).

she'll /ʃiːl/ = **she will**.

shellac /ʃəˈlæk, ˈʃelæk/ US **I** *n* gomme-laque *f*.
II *vtr* (*prét etc* **-ck-**) (varnish) lacquer.

shellfish /ʃelfɪʃ/ *npl* **1** ZOOL crustacés *mpl*; (mussels, oysters) coquillages *mpl*; **2** CULIN fruits *mpl* de mer.

shelling /ʃelɪŋ/ *n* pilonnage *m*.

shell: **~ pink** ▶ **818** *adj* nacré; **~-proof** *adj* blindé; **~-shocked** *adj* LIT [*soldier*] traumatisé (*par un bombardement*); FIG en état de choc.

shell suit *n* survêtement *m* en nylon®.

shelter /ʃeltə(r)/ **I** *n* **1** ¢ (protection) abri *m*; **in the ~ of** à l'abri de; **to take ~ from** se mettre à l'abri de [*danger*]; s'abriter de [*weather*]; **to give sb ~** [*person*] donner un abri à qn; [*hut, tree*] offrir un abri à qn; [*country*] donner asile à qn; **2** (covered place) abri *m* (**from** contre); **3** (for homeless) refuge *m*; (for refugee) asile *m*.
II *vtr* **1** (protect) (against weather) abriter (**from, against** de); (from truth) protéger (**from** de); **2** (give refuge, succour to) accueillir [*refugee, criminal*]; **to ~ sb from sb/sth** accueillir qn pour qu'il échappe à qn/qch.
III *vi* **1** se mettre à l'abri; **to ~ from the storm** s'abriter de l'orage; **2** [*refugee, fugitive*] se réfugier.

sheltered accommodation *n* GB foyer-résidence *m*.

shelve /ʃelv/ **I** *vtr* **1** (postpone) mettre [qch] en suspens [*plan*]; **2** (store on shelf) mettre [qch] sur les rayons; **3** (provide with shelves) garnir [qch] d'étagères.
II *vi* [*beach, sea bottom etc*] descendre en pente.

shelves /ʃelvz/ *pl* ▶ **shelf**.

shelving /ʃelvɪŋ/ *n* ¢ (at home) étagères *fpl*; (in shop) rayons *mpl*.

shepherd /ʃepəd/ ▶ **1251** **I** *n* berger *m*.
II *vtr* **1** (host) escorter [*person*] (**into** jusque dans); **2** (herdsman) guider [*animals*].

shepherdess /ˌʃepəˈdes, US ˈʃepərdɪs/ ▶ **1251** *n* bergère *f*.

shepherd: **~'s crook** *n* houlette *f*; **~'s pie** *n* hachis *m* Parmentier.

sherbet /ˈʃɜːbət/ *n* **1** GB (powder) confiserie *f* en poudre *f* acidulée; **2** US (sorbet) sorbet *m*.

sheriff /ˈʃerɪf/ ▶ **1251** *n* shérif *m*.

sherry /ˈʃerɪ/ *n* xérès *m*, sherry *m*.

she's /ʃiːz/ = **she is**, **she has**.

Shetland /ˈʃetlənd/ ▶ **1022** **I** *pr n* (also **~ Islands**) îles *fpl* Shetland; **in ~**, **in the ~s** dans les îles Shetland.
II *noun modifier* [*scarf, sweater*] en shetland.
III *adj* [*crofter, family*] shetlandais.

shhh /ʃ/ *excl* chut!

Shia(h) /ˈʃiːə/ **I** *n* chiisme *m*.
II *adj* chiite.

shied /ʃaɪd/ *prét, pp* ▶ **shy** II.

shield /ʃiːld/ **I** *n* **1** MIL bouclier *m*; (in heraldry) écusson *m*; FIG protection *f* (**against** contre); **2** SPORT ~ trophée *m*; **3** TECH (on machine) écran *m* de protection; **4** US (policeman's badge) insigne *m*.
II *vtr* (from weather, danger) protéger; (from authorities) (by lying) couvrir; (by harbouring) donner asile à [*suspect, criminal*]; **to ~ one's eyes** se protéger les yeux.

shift /ʃɪft/ **I** *n* **1** (alteration) changement *m* (**in** de), modification *f* (**in** de); **a sudden ~ in public opinion** un retournement de l'opinion publique; **a ~ to the left** POL un glissement vers la gauche; **the ~ from agriculture to industry** le passage de l'agriculture à l'industrie; **2** IND (period of time) période *f* de travail; (group of workers) équipe *f*; **to be on night ~s** être d'équipe de nuit; **to work an eight-hour ~** faire les trois-huit; **3** (dress) robe *f* droite; †(undergarment) chemise *f*; **4** LING mutation *f*; **5** US AUT = **gear-shift**; **6** (on keyboard) = **shift key**.
II *vtr* **1** (move) déplacer [*furniture, vehicle*]; bouger,

remuer [*arm*]; THEAT changer [*scenery*]; **to ~ sth away from** éloigner qch de [*wall, window*]; **to ~ one's position** FIG changer de position or d'avis; **2** (get rid of) faire partir, enlever [*stain, dirt*]; **I can't ~ this cold**○! GB je n'arrive pas à me débarrasser de mon rhume!; **3** (transfer) (to another department) affecter; (to another town, country) muter [*employee*]; FIG rejeter [*blame*] (**onto** sur); **to ~ attention away from a problem** détourner l'attention d'un problème; **4** US AUT **to ~ gear** changer de vitesse.

III *vi* **1** (also **~ about**) [*load*] bouger; **to ~ uneasily in one's chair** remuer dans son fauteuil l'air mal à l'aise; **to ~ from one foot to the other** se dandiner d'un pied sur l'autre; **2** (move) **the scene ~s to Ireland** CIN, THEAT la scène se situe maintenant en Irlande; **this stain won't ~!** cette tache ne veut pas partir; **~**○! GB pousse-toi○!; **3** (change) [*attitude*] se modifier; [*wind*] tourner; **opinion has ~ed to the right** l'opinion a glissé vers la droite; **4**○ GB (go quickly) [*person*] se grouiller○; [*vehicle*] foncer○; **5** US AUT **to ~ into second gear** passer en seconde.

IV *v refl* **to ~ oneself** se pousser.

shifting /'ʃɪftɪŋ/ *adj* [*belief*] changeant; [*population*] toujours renouvelé.

shift key *n* touche *f* de majuscule.

shiftless /'ʃɪftlɪs/ *adj* **1** (lazy) paresseux/-euse, apathique; **2** (lacking initiative) qui manque d'ambition.

shift: **~ lock** *n* touche *f* de verrouillage des majuscules; **~ system** *n* IND travail *m* par équipes.

shift work *n* travail *m* posté; **to be on ~** faire un travail posté.

shifty /'ʃɪftɪ/ *adj* [*person, manner*] louche.

Shiite /'ʃiːaɪt/ **I** *n* Chiite *mf*.

II *adj* chiite.

shilling /'ʃɪlɪŋ/ ▶ 849 *n* shilling *m*.

IDIOMS **to take the King's** OU **Queen's ~** GB partir sous les drapeaux.

shillyshally○ /'ʃɪlɪʃælɪ/ *vi* tergiverser.

shimmer /'ʃɪmə(r)/ *vi* **1** [*jewels, water*] scintiller; [*silk*] chatoyer; **2** (in heat) [*landscape*] vibrer.

shin /ʃɪn/ *n* tibia *m*.

■ **shin up**: **~ up** [*sth*] grimper à [*tree*].

■ **shin down**: **~ down** [*sth*] descendre [qch] en s'agrippant [*tree*].

shinbone /'ʃɪnbəʊn/ *n* tibia *m*.

shindig○ /'ʃɪndɪɡ/, **shindy**○ /'ʃɪndɪ/ *n* **1** (disturbance) ramdam○ *m*; **to kick up a ~** faire du ramdam○; **2** (party) nouba○ *f*.

shine /ʃaɪn/ **I** *n* GEN lustre *m*; (of parquet) brillant *m*.

II *vtr* **1** (*prét, pp* **shone**) braquer [*light, torch*] (**on** sur); **2** (*prét, pp* **shined**) faire reluire [*brass*]; cirer [*shoes*].

III *vi* (*prét, pp* **shone**) **1** [*hair, light, sun*] briller; [*brass, floor*] reluire; **to ~ through** percer [*mist, gloom*]; **the light is shining in my eyes** j'ai la lumière dans les yeux; **2** FIG (be radiant) [*eyes*] briller (**with** de); [*face*] rayonner (**with** de); **3** (excel) briller; **to ~ at** être brillant en [*science, languages etc*].

IDIOMS **to ~ up to sb**○ US passer de la pommade○ à qn; **to take a ~ to sb**○ s'enticher○ de qn; FIG **to take the ~ off sth** gâcher qch.

■ **shine in** pénétrer (**through** par).

■ **shine through** [*talent*] éclater au grand jour.

■ **shine out** [*light*] briller, apparaître.

shingle /'ʃɪŋɡl/ *n* **1** ¢ (pebbles) galets *mpl*; **2** CONSTR (tile) bardeau *m*; **3**○ US (nameplate) plaque *f*.

shingles /'ʃɪŋɡlz/ ▶ 1002 *npl* MED zona *m*.

shinguard, shinpad /'ʃɪnɡɑːd, 'ʃɪnpæd/ *n* jambière *f*.

shining /'ʃaɪnɪŋ/ *adj* **1** (shiny) [*car*] étincelant; [*hair*] brillant; [*bald spot, metal*] luisant; [*floor*] reluisant; **2** (glowing) [*eyes*] brillant; [*face*] radieux/-ieuse; **3** FIG [*achievement*] brillant; [*example*] parfait.

shinty /'ʃɪntɪ/ *n* GB SPORT hockey *m* (simplifié).

shiny /'ʃaɪnɪ/ *adj* **1** [*metal, surface, hair*] brillant; **2** [*shoes, wood*] bien ciré; **3** [*seat of trousers*] lustré.

ship /ʃɪp/ **I** *n* navire *m*; (smaller) bateau *m*; **passenger ~** paquebot *m*.

II *vtr* (*p prés etc* **-pp-**) **1** (send) (by sea) transporter [qch] par mer; (by air) transporter [qch] par avion; (overland) acheminer; **2** (take on board) charger [*cargo*]; rentrer [*oars*]; **to ~ water** embarquer de l'eau.

IDIOMS **we are like ~s that pass in the night** nous ne faisons que nous croiser; **the ~ of state** le char de l'État; **the ~ of the desert** (camel) le vaisseau du désert; **to run a tight ~** mener tout le monde à la baguette; **when my ~ comes in** quand j'aurai fait fortune.

■ **ship off**: **~** [*sth/sb*] **off**, **~ off** [*sth/sb*] expédier ALSO HUM.

ship: **~building** *n* construction *f* navale; **~load** *n* cargaison *f*.

shipment /'ʃɪpmənt/ *n* **1** (cargo) (by sea) cargaison *f*; (by air, land) chargement *m*; **2** (sending) expédition *f*.

ship owner *n* armateur *m*.

shipper /'ʃɪpə(r)/ *n* expéditeur/-trice *m/f*.

shipping /'ʃɪpɪŋ/ **I** *n* **1** (boats) navigation *f*, trafic *m* maritime; **attention all ~!** avis à toutes les embarcations!; **2** (sending) acheminement *m*.

II *noun modifier* [*agent, office*] maritime; [*charges*] de transport.

shipping: **~ clerk** ▶ 1251 *n* expéditionnaire *mf*; **~ company** *n* (sea) compagnie *f* maritime; (road) entreprise *f* de transport routier; **~ forecast** *n* météo *f* marine; **~ lane** *n* couloir *m* de navigation; **~ line** *n* compagnie *f* de navigation.

ship: **~'s company** *n* équipage *m*; **~'s doctor** ▶ 1251 *n* médecin *m* de bord; **~shape** *adj* GB bien en ordre; **~-to-shore radio** *n* liaison *f* radio avec la côte.

shipwreck /'ʃɪprek/ **I** *n* (event) naufrage *m*; (ship) épave *f*.

II *vtr* **to be ~ed** faire naufrage; **a ~ed sailor** un marin naufragé.

shipyard *n* chantier *m* naval.

shire /'ʃaɪə(r)/ *n* GB **1**† comté *m* (du centre de l'Angleterre); **2** POL **the ~s** les provinces.

shirk /ʃɜːk/ **I** *vtr* esquiver [*task, duty*]; fuir [*responsibility*]; éluder [*problem*]; **to ~ doing sth** éviter de faire qch.

II *vi* se défiler.

shirker /'ʃɜːkə(r)/ *n* tire-au-flanc○ *m inv*.

shirt /ʃɜːt/ ▶ 1260 *n* (man's) chemise *f*; (woman's) chemisier *m*; (for sport) maillot *m*.

IDIOMS **keep your ~ on**○! du calme!; **to lose one's ~**○ laisser jusqu'à sa dernière chemise○; **to sell the ~ off one's back** vendre père et mère○.

shirtfront *n* plastron *m*.

shirt-sleeve /'ʃɜːtsliːv/ *n* manche *f* de chemise; **in one's ~s** en manches de chemise; **to roll up one's ~s** remonter ses manches (de chemise) ALSO FIG.

shirttail /'ʃɜːteɪl/ *n* **1** (of shirt) pan *m* de chemise; **2**○ US (in newspaper) *commentaire en bas d'un article*.

shirttail cousin *n* US cousin/-e *m/f* à la mode de Bretagne.

shirty○ /'ʃɜːtɪ/ *adj* GB [*person*] de mauvais poil○; **to get ~** prendre la mouche○.

shish-kebab /'ʃiːʃkəbæb/ *n* chiche-kebab *m*.

shit❶ /ʃɪt/ **I** *n* **1** (excrement) merde❶ *f*, crotte○ *f*; **2** (also **bull~**) conneries❶ *fpl*.

II *excl* merde❶!; **tough ~**! tant pis!

shiver /'ʃɪvə(r)/ **I** *n* LIT, FIG frisson *m*; **to give a ~** avoir un frisson; **to send a ~ down sb's spine** faire courir un frisson dans le dos à qn.

II shivers *npl* frissons *mpl*; **an attack of the ~s** un accès de frissons; **to give sb the ~s** LIT donner des frissons à qn; FIG donner froid dans le dos à qn.

III *vi* (with cold) grelotter (**with** de); (with fear) frémir (**with** de); (with disgust) frissonner (**with** de).

shivery /'ʃɪvərɪ/ *adj* (feverish) fébrile.

shoal /ʃəʊl/ *n* **1** (of fish) banc *m*; **2** GEOG (of sand) banc *m* de sable; (shallows) bas-fond *m*.

shock /ʃɒk/ **I** *n* **1** (psychological) choc *m*; **to get** OU **have a ~** avoir un choc; **to give sb a ~** faire un choc à qn; **the ~ of seeing** le choc de voir; **it came**

as a bit of a ~ cela m'a fait comme un choc; **her death came as a ~ to us** sa mort a été un choc pour nous; **it's a ~ to the system when**... c'est un vrai choc quand...; **to recover from** ou **get over the ~** surmonter le choc; **he's in for a nasty° ~** il va avoir un sacré° choc; **to express one's ~** (indignation) exprimer son indignation; (amazement) exprimer sa surprise; **~!** **horror!** JOURN ou HUM scandale épouvantable!; **2** MED état *m* de choc; **to be in (a state of) ~** être en état de choc; **to treat sb for ~** soigner qn en état de choc; **in deep ~** en grave état de choc; **to be suffering from ~** souffrir d'un choc; **3** ELEC décharge *f*; **to get a ~** prendre une décharge; **to give sb a ~** donner une décharge à qn; **4** (impact) (of collision) choc *m*; (of earthquake) secousse *f*; (of explosion) souffle *m*; **5** (of corn) gerbe *f*; FIG (of hair) tignasse *f*; **6°** (also **~ absorber**) amortisseur *m*.
II° *noun modifier* [*effect*] de choc; [*result*] sidérant.
III *vtr* (distress) consterner; (scandalize) choquer; **she's not easily ~ed** on ne la choque pas facilement.
shock absorber *n* amortisseur *m*.
shocking /'ʃɒkɪŋ/ *adj* **1** (upsetting) [*sight*] consternant; (scandalous) [*news*] choquant; **2°** (appalling) désastreux/ -euse°.
shocking pink ▶ 818 *n, adj* rose (*m*) vif *inv*.
shock: **~proof**, **~ resistant** *adj* antichoc *inv*; **~ troops** *npl* troupes *fpl* de choc.
shock wave *n* **1** LIT onde *f* de choc; **2** FIG remous *mpl*; **to send ~s through the stock market** provoquer des remous à la Bourse.
shod /ʃɒd/ I *prét, pp* ▶ **shoe** II.
II *pp adj* chaussé; **well/poorly ~** bien/mal chaussé.
shoddily /'ʃɒdɪlɪ/ *adv* **1 to be ~ made/built** être de fabrication/de construction sommaire; **2** [*behave*] avec bassesse.
shoddy /'ʃɒdɪ/ *adj* **1** [*product*] de mauvaise qualité; [*work*] mal fait; **2** [*behaviour*] mesquin; **a ~ trick** un sale tour.
shoe /ʃuː/ ▶ 1260 I *n* **1** (footwear) chaussure *f*; **2** (for horse) fer *m*; **3** (also **brake ~**) AUT sabot *m* de frein.
II *vtr* (*p prés* **shoeing**; *prét, pp* **shod**) ferrer [*horse*].
IDIOMS **it's a question of dead men's ~s** il s'agit d'attendre la mort de quelqu'un pour prendre sa place; **in my/your etc ~s** à ma/ta etc place; **to save ~ leather** ménager ses semelles; **to shake** ou **shiver in one's ~s** avoir peur; **to step into sb's ~s** prendre la place de qn.
shoe: **~horn** *n* chausse-pied *m*; **~lace** *n* lacet *m* de chaussure; **~maker** ▶ 1251 *n* cordonnier/-ière *m/f*; **~ polish** *n* cirage *m*; **~ rack** *n* porte-chaussures *m inv*; **~ repairer** ▶ 1251 *n* cordonnier *m*; **~shine (boy)** *n* cireur *m* de chaussures; **~ shop** ▶ 1251 *n* magasin *m* de chaussures; **~ size** ▶ 1260 *n* pointure *f*.
shoestring /'ʃuːstrɪŋ/ *n* US lacet *m* de chaussure.
IDIOMS **on a ~°** avec peu de moyens.
shoe tree *n* embauchoir *m*.
shone /ʃɒn/ *prét, pp* ▶ **shine**.
shoo /ʃuː/ I *excl* ouste!
II *vtr* (also **~ away**) chasser.
shook /ʃʊk/ *prét* ▶ **shake**.
shoot /ʃuːt/ I *n* **1** BOT (young growth) pousse *f*; (offshoot) rejeton *m*; **2** GB (hunt meeting) partie *f* de chasse; **3** CIN tournage *m*.
II *vtr* (*prét, pp* **shot**) **1** (fire) tirer [*bullet, arrow*] (**at** sur); lancer [*missile*] (**at** sur); **2** (hit with gun) tirer sur [*person, animal*]; (kill) abattre [*person, animal*]; **she shot him in the leg** elle lui a tiré dans la jambe; **to be shot in the back** recevoir une balle dans le dos; **to ~ sb for desertion** fusiller qn pour désertion; **to ~ sb dead** abattre qn; **shot to pieces** LIT criblé de balles; FIG réduit à néant; **3** (direct) **to ~ questions at sb** bombarder qn de questions; **4** CIN, PHOT (film) tourner [*film, scene*]; prendre [*qch*] (en photo) [*subject*]; **5** (push) mettre [*bolt*]; **6** (in canoeing) **to ~ the rapids** franchir les rapides; **7** (in golf) **to ~ 75** faire un score de 75; **8** US GAMES jouer à [*pool, craps*]; **9** (in hunting) chasser [*game*]; **10°** (inject) ▶ **shoot up°**.

III *vi* (*prét, pp* **shot**) **1** (fire a gun) tirer (**at** sur); **2** (move suddenly) **to ~ forward** s'élancer à toute vitesse; **the car shot past** la voiture est passée en trombe; **to ~ to fame** FIG percer, devenir célèbre subitement; **3** CIN tourner; **4** SPORT (in football etc) tirer, shooter; **5** (in hunting) [*person*] chasser.
IV *v refl* (*prét, pp* **shot**) **to ~ oneself** se tirer une balle.
IDIOMS **~°!** US vas-y, parle!; **to ~ a line** frimer°; **to ~ oneself in the foot°** agir contre son propre intérêt.
■ **shoot down**: **~ down** [*sb/sth*], **~** [*sb/sth*] **down** AVIAT, MIL abattre, descendre° [*plane, pilot*]; **to ~** [*sb/sth*] **down in flames** LIT, FIG descendre [*qn/qch*] en flammes [*person, plane, argument*].
■ **shoot out**: **~ out** [*flame, water*] jaillir; [*car*] sortir en trombe.
■ **shoot up**: **¶ ~ up 1** [*flames, spray*] jaillir; FIG [*prices, profits*] monter en flèche; **2** (grow rapidly) [*plant*] pousser vite; **that boy has really shot up!** FIG qu'est-ce que ce garçon a poussé!; **¶ ~ up** [*sth*], **~** [*sth*] **up** (inject)° se shooter à° [*heroin*].
shooting /'ʃuːtɪŋ/ I *n* **1** (act) (killing) meurtre *m* (par arme à feu); **2** (firing) coups *mpl* de feu, fusillade *f*; **3** (by hunters) chasse *f*; **4** ▶ 949 SPORT (at target etc) tir *m*; **5** CIN tournage *m*.
II *adj* [*pain*] lancinant.
shooting: **~ gallery** *n* stand *m* de tir; **~ range** *n* stand *m* de tir; **~ star** *n* étoile *f* filante; **~ stick** *n* canne-siège *f*.
shoot-out° /'ʃuːtaʊt/ *n* fusillade *f*.
shop /ʃɒp/ I *n* **1** (store) magasin *m*; (small, fashionable) boutique *f*; **to go to the ~s** aller faire les courses *fpl*; **to set up ~** LIT, FIG s'installer; **to shut up ~°** LIT, FIG fermer boutique; **2** US (in department store) rayon *m*; **3** (workshop) atelier *m*; **4** US SCH atelier *m*; **5°** GB (shopping) **the weekly ~** les courses pour la semaine; **to do a big ~** faire le plein°.
II° *vtr* (*p prés etc* **-pp-**) GB donner°, vendre.
III *vi* (*p prés etc* **-pp-**) faire ses courses; **to go ~ping** GEN aller faire des courses; (as browser) aller faire les magasins.
IDIOMS **all over the ~°** GB FIG partout; **to talk ~** parler boutique.
■ **shop around** (compare prices) faire le tour des magasins (**for** pour trouver); FIG (compare courses, services etc) bien chercher.
shop: **~ assistant** ▶ 1251 *n* GB vendeur/-euse *m/f*; **~ fitter** ▶ 1251 *n* GB installateur/-trice *m/f* de magasins.
shopfloor /ˌʃɒp'flɔː(r)/ *n* **problems on the ~** des problèmes parmi les ouvriers.
shop: **~ front** *n* devanture *f*; **~keeper** ▶ 1251 *n* commerçant/-e *m/f*; **~lifter** *n* voleur/-euse *m/f* à l'étalage.
shopping /'ʃɒpɪŋ/ *n* (activity, purchases) courses *fpl*.
shopping: **~ bag** *n* sac *m* à provisions; **~ basket** *n* panier *m*; **~ centre** GB, **~ center** US, **~ mall** US *n* centre *m* commercial; **~ precinct** *n* zone *f* commerçante.
shopping trip *n* **to go on a ~** aller faire les magasins.
shopping trolley *n* caddie® *m*.
shop: **~-soiled** *adj* [*garment*] sali; **~ steward** *n* représentant/-e *m/f* syndical/-e; **~ window** *n* vitrine *f* ALSO FIG; **~worn** *adj* US ▶ **shop-soiled**.
shore /ʃɔː(r)/ *n* **1** (edge) (of sea) côte *f*, rivage *m*; (of lake) rive *f*; (of island) côte *f*; **off the ~ of** NAUT au large de; **2** (dry land) terre *f*; **on ~** à terre; **from ship to ~** en liaison avec la côte; **3** (beach) grève *f*, plage *f*.
■ **shore up**: **~ up** [*sth*], **~** [*sth*] **up** LIT étayer; FIG soutenir.
shore leave *n* permission *f* de descendre à terre.
shorn /ʃɔːn/ *pp* ▶ **shear**.
short /ʃɔːt/ ▶ 1045 I *n* **1** (drink) alcool *m* fort; **2** ELEC = **short circuit**; **3** CIN court métrage *m*; **4** FIN (deficit) manque *m*, déficit *m*.
II shorts *npl* short *m*; (underwear) caleçon *m*.

Shops, trades and professions

Shops

In English you can say at the baker's *or at* the baker's shop; *in French the construction with* chez (*at the house or premises of …*) *is common but you can also use the name of the particular shop:*

at the baker's	= chez le boulanger *or* à la boulangerie
I'm going to the grocer's	= je vais chez l'épicier *or* à l'épicerie
I bought it at the fishmonger's	= je l'ai acheté chez le poissonnier *or* à la poissonnerie
go to the chemist's	= va à la pharmacie *or* chez le pharmacien
at *or* to the hairdresser's	= chez le coiffeur/la coiffeuse
to work in a butcher's	= travailler dans une boucherie

Chez is also used with the names of professions:

at *or* to the doctor's	= chez le médecin
at *or* to the lawyer's	= chez le notaire
at *or* to the dentist's	= chez le dentiste

Note that there are specific names for the place of work of some professions:

the lawyer's office	= l'étude *f* du notaire
the doctor's surgery (GB) *or* office (US)	= le cabinet du médecin

Cabinet is also used for architects and dentists. If in doubt, check in the dictionary.

People

Talking of someone's profession, we could say he is a dentist. *In French this would be either* il est dentiste *or* c'est un dentiste. *Only when the sentence begins with* c'est *can the indefinite article (*un *or* une*) be used.*

Paul is a dentist	= Paul est dentiste
she is a dentist	= elle est dentiste *or* c'est une dentiste
she's a geography teacher	= elle est professeur de géographie *or* c'est un professeur de géographie

With adjectives, only the c'est *construction is possible:*

she is a good dentist	= c'est une bonne dentiste

In the plural, if the construction begins with ce sont *then you need to use* des (*or* de *before an adjective):*

they are mechanics	= ils sont mécaniciens *or* ce sont des mécaniciens
they are good mechanics	= ce sont de bons mécaniciens

Trades and professions

what does he do?	= qu'est-ce qu'il fait?
what's your job?	= qu'est-ce que vous faites dans la vie?
I'm a teacher	= je suis professeur
to work as a dentist	= travailler comme dentiste
to work for an electrician	= travailler pour un électricien
to be paid as a mechanic	= être payé comme mécanicien
he wants to be a baker	= il veut devenir boulanger

III *adj* **1** (not long-lasting) [*stay, memory, period*] court (*before n*); [*course*] de courte durée; [*conversation, speech, chapter*] bref/brève; [*walk*] petit (*before n*); **a ~ time ago** il y a peu de temps; **in four ~ years** en quatre brèves années; **to work ~er hours** travailler moins d'heures; **the days are getting ~er** les jours diminuent *or* raccourcissent; **the ~ answer is that** la réponse est tout simplement que; **2** (not of great length) court (*before n*); **the suit is too ~ in the sleeves** les manches du costume sont trop courtes; **to have one's hair cut ~** se faire couper les cheveux court; **3** (not tall) [*person*] petit; **4** (scarce) **to be in ~ supply** être difficile à trouver; **time is getting ~** le temps presse; **5** (inadequate) [*rations*] insuffisant; **he gave me a ~ measure** (in shop) il a triché sur le poids; **6** (lacking) **he is ~ of sth** il lui manque qch; **to be ~ on** [*person*] manquer de [*talent, tact*]; **to go ~ of, to run ~ of** manquer de [*clothes, money, food*]; **my wages are £30 ~** il me manque 30 livres sterling sur mon salaire; **7** (in abbreviation) **Tom is ~ for Thomas** Tom est le diminutif de Thomas; **this is Nicholas, Nick for ~!** je te présente Nicholas, mais on l'appelle Nick; **8** (abrupt) **to be ~ with sb** être brusque avec qn; **9** LING [*vowel*] bref/brève; **10** FIN [*loan, credit*] à court terme; **11** CULIN [*pastry*] brisé.
IV *adv* (abruptly) [*stop*] net; **to stop ~ of doing** se retenir pour ne pas faire.
V in short *adv phr* bref.
VI short of *prep phr* **1** (just before) un peu avant; **2** (just less than) pas loin de; **that's nothing ~ of blackmail!** c'est du chantage, ni plus ni moins!; **3** (except) **~ of doing** à moins de faire.
VII *vtr, vi* ELEC = **short-circuit**.
IDIOMS **~ and sweet** bref/brève; **to bring up *or* pull sb up ~** couper qn dans son élan; **to sell oneself ~** se sous-estimer; **to make ~ work of sth/sb** expédier qch/qn; **to be caught ~** être pris d'un besoin pressant; **the long and ~ of it is that they…** en un mot (comme cent), ils…

shortage /'ʃɔːtɪdʒ/ *n* pénurie *f*, manque *m* (**of** de); **housing ~** crise *f* du logement; **there is no ~ of applicants** les candidats ne manquent pas.

short: **~ back and sides** *n* coupe *f* de cheveux masculine (*dégageant la nuque et les oreilles*); **~bread**, **~cake** *n* sablé *m*; **~-change** *vtr* LIT ne pas rendre toute sa monnaie à; FIG rouler⁰.

short circuit /ˌʃɔːt'sɜːkɪt/ **I** *n* court-circuit *m*.
II short-circuit *vtr* LIT, FIG court-circuiter.
III short-circuit *vi* faire court-circuit.

short: **~comings** *npl* points *mpl* faibles; **~crust pastry** *n* pâte *f* brisée.

shortcut *n* **1** LIT raccourci *m*; **2** FIG **to take ~s** bâcler⁰; **there are no ~s to becoming a musician** on ne s'improvise pas musicien.

shorten /'ʃɔːtn/ **I** *vtr* abréger [*visit, life*]; raccourcir [*garment, talk*]; réduire [*time, list*]; alléger [*syllabus*]; **to ~ sail** NAUT réduire la voilure.
II *vi* [*days, odds*] diminuer.

shortening /'ʃɔːtnɪŋ/ *n* **1** CULIN matière *f* grasse; **2** (reduction) réduction *f*; **3** (abridging) abrégement *m*.

shortfall /'ʃɔːtfɔːl/ *n* (in budget, accounts) déficit *m*; (in earnings, exports etc) manque *m*; **there is a ~ of £10,000 in our budget** il manque 10 000 livres sterling dans notre budget; **to make up the ~** FIG combler le déficit.

shorthand /'ʃɔːthænd/ **I** *n* **1** COMM sténographie *f*, sténo⁰ *f*; **in ~** en sténo⁰; **2** FIG (verbal shortcut) formule *f* consacrée.
II *noun modifier* [*notebook, qualification*] de sténo⁰.

short-handed /ˌʃɔːt'hændɪd/ *adj* (in company) à court de personnel; (on site) à court de main-d'œuvre.

shorthand-typist ▶ 1251 *n* sténo-dactylo *f*.

shortlist /'ʃɔːtlɪst/ **I** *n* liste *f* des candidats sélectionnés.
II *vtr* sélectionner [*applicant*] (**for** pour).

short-lived /ˌʃɔːt'lɪvd, US -'laɪvd/ *adj* [*triumph, happiness*] de courte durée; [*effect*] passager/-ère; **to be ~** ne pas durer longtemps.

shortly /'ʃɔːtlɪ/ *adv* **1** (very soon) [*return*] bientôt; [*be published*] prochainement; **2** (a short time) **~ after(-wards)/before** peu (de temps) après/avant.

short: **~-range** *adj* [*weather forecast*] à court terme; **~ sight** *n* myopie *f*.

shortsighted /ˌʃɔːt'saɪtɪd/ *adj* **1** LIT myope; **2** FIG (lacking foresight) [*person*] peu clairvoyant; [*policy, decision*] à courte vue.

shortsightedness /ˌʃɔːt'saɪtɪdnɪs/ *n* **1** LIT myopie *f*; **2** FIG manque *m* de perspicacité (**about** à propos de).

short-sleeved /ˌʃɔːt'sliːvd/ *adj* à manches courtes.

short-staffed /ˌʃɔːt'stɑːft, US -stæft/ *adj* **to be ~** manquer de personnel.

---

should

Meaning *ought to*

When *should* is used to mean *ought to*, it is translated by the conditional tense of *devoir*:

we should leave at seven = nous devrions partir à
sept heures

The past *should have* meaning *ought to have* is translated by the past conditional of *devoir*:

she should have told him the truth = elle aurait dû lui
dire la vérité

The same verb is used in negative sentences:

you shouldn't do that = vous ne devriez pas
faire ça

he shouldn't have resigned = il n'aurait pas dû
démissionner

For the conjugation of *devoir*, see the French verb tables.

In conditional sentences

When *should* is used as an auxiliary verb to form the conditional, *should* + verb is translated by the conditional of the appropriate verb in French:

I should like to go to Paris = j'aimerais aller à
Paris

I should have liked to go to Paris = j'aurais aimé aller à
Paris

As a subjunctive in purpose clauses

When *should* is used as an auxiliary verb in *that* clauses, *should* + verb is translated by the subjunctive of the appropriate verb in French:

in order that they should understand = pour qu'ils
comprennent

For particular usages see the entry **should**.

---

short: **~-stay** *adj* [*car park*] de courte durée; [*hostel, housing*] à court terme; **~ story** *n* LITERAT nouvelle *f*; **~-tempered** *adj* coléreux/-euse.

short term **I** *n* **in the ~** (looking to future) dans l'immédiat; (looking to past) pendant un temps, pour commencer.
II short-term *adj* GEN, FIN à court terme.

short: **~ time** *n* (in industry) chômage *m* partiel; **~wave** *n* ondes *fpl* courtes.

shot /ʃɒt/ **I** *prét, pp* ▶ **shoot**.
II *n* **1** (from gun etc) coup *m* (de feu); **to fire** ou **take a ~ at sb/sth** tirer sur qn/qch; **to fire the opening ~** FIG ouvrir le feu; **2** SPORT (in tennis, golf, cricket) coup *m*; (in football) tir *m*; **to have** ou **take a ~ at goal** (in football) tirer au but; **'good ~!'** 'bien joué!'; **3** PHOT photo *f* (**of** de); **4** CIN plan *m* (**of** de); **action ~** scène *f* d'action; **out of ~** CIN hors champ; **5** (injection) piqûre *f*; **to give sb a ~** faire une piqûre à qn; **6** (attempt) **to have a ~ at doing** essayer de faire qch; **to give it one's best ~** faire de son mieux; **7** (in shotputting) poids *m*; **8** (pellet) **C** balle *f*, plomb *m*; (pellets collectively) **¢** plomb *m*; **9** (person who shoots) **a good ~** un bon tireur; **10°** (dose) **a ~ of** une lampée° de [*whisky*].
III *adj* **1** (also **~ through**) [*silk*] changeant; **~ (through) with** [*material*] strié de [*gold etc*]; **2°** (also **~ away**) **he is ~** (away) il n'a plus toute sa tête; **his nerves were ~** il était à bout de nerfs.
IDIOMS to call the ~s dicter la loi; **to be ~ of** être débarrassé de; **to give sth a ~ in the arm** revigorer qch; **he'd go like a ~** il partirait sans hésiter; **it was a ~ in the dark** ça a été dit au hasard.

shotgun /'ʃɒtɡʌn/ *n* fusil *m*.

shot: **~gun wedding** *n* mariage *m* forcé; **~ put** *n* SPORT lancer *m* de poids.

should /ʃʊd, ʃəd/ *modal aux* (*conditional of* **shall**) **1** (ought to) **you ~ have told me before** tu aurais dû me le dire avant; **why shouldn't I do it?** pourquoi est-ce que je ne le ferais pas?; **that ~ be them arriving now!** ça doit être eux qui arrivent!; **how ~ I know?** comment veux-tu que je le sache?; **as it ~ be** (in order) en ordre; ...**which is only as it ~ be** ...ce qui

est parfaitement normal; **flowers! you shouldn't have!** des fleurs! il ne fallait pas!; **2** (in conditional sentences) **had he asked me, I ~ have accepted** s'il me l'avait demandé, j'aurais accepté; **I don't think it will happen, but if it ~...** je ne pense pas que cela arrive, mais si toutefois cela arrivait...; **if you ~ change your mind,...** si vous changez d'avis,...; **~ the opportunity arise** si l'occasion se présente; **3** (expressing purpose) **in order that they ~ understand** pour qu'ils comprennent; **we are anxious that he ~ succeed** nous souhaitons vivement qu'il réussisse; **4** (in polite formulas) **I ~ like a drink** je prendrais volontiers un verre; **I ~ like to go there** j'aimerais bien y aller; **5** (expressing opinion) **I ~ think so!** je l'espère!; **I ~ think not!** j'espère bien que non!; **'how long?'—'an hour, I ~ think'** 'combien de temps?'—'une heure, je suppose'; **I ~ think she must be about 40** à mon avis, elle doit avoir 40 ans environ; **I ~ say so!** et comment!; **who ~ walk in but John!** devine qui est arrivé—John!; **and then what ~ happen, but it began to rain!** et devine quoi—il s'est mis à pleuvoir!

shoulder /'ʃəʊldə(r)/ **I** *n* ▶ **765** **1** ANAT épaule *f*; **on** ou **over one's ~** à l'épaule; **on** ou **over one's ~s** sur les épaules; **too tight across the ~s** trop étroit d'épaules; **to put one's ~s back** rejeter les épaules en arrière; **if you need a ~ to cry on** si tu as besoin d'une épaule pour pleurer; **to have round ~s** avoir le dos rond; **to look over one's ~** LIT, FIG regarder derrière soi; **the burden is ou falls on my ~s** la charge m'incombe; **~ to ~** [*stand*] côte à côte; [*work*] coude à coude ou côte à côte; **2** (on mountain) replat *m*; **3** (on road) bas-côté *m*; **4** CULIN épaule *f*.
II *vtr* **1** LIT mettre [qch] sur l'épaule [*bag, implement*]; **to ~ arms** MIL se mettre au port d'armes; **~ arms!** MIL mettez l'épaule!; **2** FIG se charger de [*burden, expense, task*]; endosser [*responsibility*]; **3** (push) **to ~ sb aside** écarter qn d'un coup d'épaule.
IDIOMS to stand head and ~s above sb LIT dépasser qn d'une bonne tête; FIG laisser qn loin derrière; **to have a good head on one's ~s** avoir la tête sur les épaules; **to have an old head on young ~s** être mûr avant l'âge; **to put one's ~ to the wheel** s'atteler à la tâche; **to rub ~s with sb** côtoyer qn; **straight from the ~°** [*comment, criticism*] franc/franche.

shoulder: **~ bag** *n* sac *m* à bandoulière; **~ blade** *n* omoplate *f*; **~-length** *adj* [*hair*] mi-long; **~ pad** *n* épaulette *f*; **~ strap** *n* (of garment) bretelle *f*; (of bag) bandoulière *f*.

shouldn't /'ʃʊdnt/ = **should not**.

shout /ʃaʊt/ **I** *n* **1** (cry) cri *m* (**of** de); **2°** GB (round of drinks) tournée *f*.
II *vtr* **1** (cry out) crier; (stronger) hurler; **2°** GB (buy) **to ~ a round (of drinks)** payer une tournée.
III *vi* crier; **to ~ at sb** crier après qn; **to ~ at ou to sb to do** crier à qn de faire; **to ~ for help** crier pour demander de l'aide.
IDIOMS I'll give you a ~ je te ferai signe; **it's nothing to ~ about** ça n'a rien d'extraordinaire.
■ shout down: **~ [sb] down** faire taire [qn] (en criant plus fort que lui).
■ shout out: **¶ ~ out** pousser un cri; **¶ ~ out [sth]** lancer [qch] à haute voix [*names, answers*].

shouting /'ʃaʊtɪŋ/ *n* **¢** cris *mpl*.
IDIOMS it's all over bar the ~ c'est pratiquement terminé.

shove /ʃʌv/ **I** *n* **to give sb/sth a ~** pousser qn/qch.
II *vtr* **1** (push) pousser; **to ~ sth through** pousser qch dans [*letterbox*]; pousser qch par [*gap*]; **to ~ sb/sth aside** écarter qn/qch en le poussant; **to ~ sth in sb's face** fourrer° qch sous le nez de qn; **to ~ sth down sb's throat** FIG imposer qch à qn; **2** (stuff hurriedly) fourrer°; **3** (jostle) bousculer [*person*]; **he ~d his way to the front of the crowd** il s'est frayé un chemin à travers la foule.
III *vi* pousser; **people were pushing and shoving** les gens poussaient et se bousculaient.

IDIOMS **if push comes to** ~ au pire; ~ **off**○! tire-toi○!

■ **shove over**○: ~ **over** se pousser.

■ **shove up**○ se pousser.

shove halfpenny /ˌʃʌv 'heɪpnɪ/ ▶ 949⏐ n GB ≈ jeu m de palet (sur table).

shovel /ˈʃʌvl/ I n (spade) pelle f; (digger) pelleteuse f.

II vtr enlever [qch] à la pelle [dirt, leaves, snow] (off de); **to ~ sth into sth** verser qch dans qch à l'aide d'une pelle; **to ~ food into one's mouth**○ s'enfourner○ la nourriture dans la bouche.

■ **shovel up**: ~ **up** [sth], ~ [sth] **up** ramasser [qch] à la pelle.

shovelful /ˈʃʌvlfʊl/ n pelletée f (of de).

show /ʃəʊ/ I n 1 (as entertainment) THEAT, GEN spectacle m; (particular performance) représentation f; CIN séance f; RADIO, TV émission f; (of slides) projection f; **family ~** spectacle pour tous; **on with the ~!** (introduction) place au spectacle!; 2 COMM (of cars, boats etc) salon m; (of fashion) défilé m; (of flowers, crafts) exposition f; **to be on ~** être exposé; 3 (of feelings) semblant m; (of strength) démonstration f; (of wealth) étalage m; **to make** ou **put on a (great) ~ of doing** s'évertuer pour la galerie à faire; **he made a ~ of concern** il a affiché sa sollicitude; **to be all for** ou **just for ~** être de l'esbroufe○; 4 (performance) **the team put up a good ~** l'équipe s'est bien défendue; **it was a poor ~ not to thank them** ce n'était pas très adroit de ne pas les remercier; **good ~!** bravo!; 5○ (business, undertaking) affaire f; **she runs the whole ~** c'est elle qui fait marcher l'affaire.

II vtr (prét **showed**; pp **shown**) 1 (present for viewing) montrer [person, object, photo] (**to** à); présenter [ticket, fashion collection] (**to** à); [TV channel, cinema] passer [film]; **to ~ sb sth** montrer qch à qn; 2 (display competitively) présenter [animal]; exposer [flower, vegetables]; 3 (reveal) montrer [feeling, principle, fact]; [garment] laisser voir [underclothes, dirt]; [patient] présenter [symptoms]; **to ~ interest in** montrer de l'intérêt pour; **it ~s that** cela montre bien que; 4 (indicate) montrer [object, trend, loss, difficulty]; indiquer [time, direction, area]; 5 (demonstrate) [reply] témoigner de [wit, intelligence]; [gesture, gift] témoigner de [respect, gratitude]; **to ~ favouritism towards sb, to ~ sb favouritism** favoriser qn; **to ~ one's age** accuser son âge; **as shown in diagram 12** comme on le voit figure 12; 6 (prove) démontrer [truth, guilt]; **to ~ that** [document] prouver que; [findings] démontrer que; [expression] montrer que; 7 (conduct) **to ~ sb to their seat** [host, usher] placer qn; **to ~ sb to their room** accompagner qn à sa chambre; **to ~ sb to the door** reconduire qn; 8○ (teach a lesson to) **I'll ~ him!** (as revenge) je vais lui apprendre○!; (when challenged) je lui ferai voir○!

III vi (prét **showed**; pp **shown**) 1 (be noticeable) [stain, label] se voir; [emotion] GEN se voir; (in eyes) se lire; 2 (be exhibited) [artist] exposer; [film] passer.

IDIOMS **it just goes to ~** c'est ça la vie; ~ **a leg**○! debout!; **to have nothing to ~ for sth** ne rien avoir tiré de qch; **to ~ one's face**○ montrer son nez○; **to ~ one's hand** abattre son jeu; **to ~ the way forward** ouvrir la voie; **to steal the ~** être l'attraction.

■ **show in**: ~ [sb] **in** faire entrer.

■ **show off**: ¶ ~ **off**○ faire le fier/la fière; ¶ ~ [sb/sth] **off**, ~ **off** [sb/sth] mettre [qch] en valeur [special feature]; faire admirer [skill]; exhiber [baby, car].

■ **show out**: ~ [sb] **out** accompagner [qn] à la porte.

■ **show round**: ~ [sb] **round** faire visiter.

■ **show up**: ¶ ~ **up** 1 (be visible) [mark] se voir; [details, colour] ressortir; 2○ (arrive) se montrer○; ¶ ~ **up** [sth] révéler [fault, mark]; ¶ ~ [sb] **up** 1 (let down) faire honte à [person]; 2 (reveal truth about) **to ~ sb up for what he/she is** montrer la vraie nature de qn.

show biz○, **show business** n industrie f du spectacle.

showboat n US bateau-théâtre m.

showcase /ˈʃəʊkeɪs/ I n 1 LIT vitrine f; 2 FIG (for paintings, ideas) vitrine f; (for new artist etc) tremplin m.

II noun modifier [village, prison] modèle.

showdown /ˈʃəʊdaʊn/ n confrontation f.

shower /ˈʃaʊə(r)/ I n 1 (for washing) douche f; **in the ~** sous la douche; 2 METEOROL averse f; **light/heavy ~** petite/grosse averse; 3 (of confetti, sparks) pluie f; (of praise, gifts) avalanche f; 4 US fête f; 5○ GB PÉJ bande f.

II vtr 1 (wash) doucher [dog, child]; 2 **to ~ sth on ou over sb/sth, to ~ sb/sth with sth** [fire, volcano] faire pleuvoir qch sur qn/qch; [person] asperger qn/qch de qch [water etc]; 3 FIG **to ~ sb with sth, to ~ sth on sb** couvrir qn de [gifts, compliments].

III vi 1 [person] prendre une douche; 2 (rain) **ash ~ed down** une pluie de cendres est retombée.

shower: ~ **attachment** n douchette f de lavabo; ~ **cap** n bonnet m de douche; **~proof** adj imperméabilisé.

showery /ˈʃaʊərɪ/ adj [day, weather] pluvieux/-ieuse.

show: **~girl** n girl f; **~-ground** n GEN champ m de foire; (for horses) terrain m de concours; ~ **house** n maison-témoin f.

showing /ˈʃəʊɪŋ/ n 1 CIN (screening) séance f; 2 (performance) GEN prestation f; SPORT performance f.

showjumper /ˈʃəʊdʒʌmpə(r)/ n 1 (person) cavalier/-ière m/f de saut; 2 (horse) cheval m de saut.

showman /ˈʃəʊmən/ n **to be a ~** FIG avoir le sens du spectacle.

shown /ʃəʊn/ pp ▶ **show** II, III.

show: **~-off**○ n m'as-tu-vu○ mf inv; ~ **of hands** n vote m à mains levées.

showpiece /ˈʃəʊpiːs/ n (exhibit) œuvre f exposée; (in trade fair) objet m exposé; **this hospital is a ~** FIG cet hôpital est un modèle du genre.

showroom /ˈʃəʊruːm, -rʊm/ n exposition f; **to look at cars in a ~** regarder les voitures exposées; **in ~ condition** dans un état impeccable.

show: **~stopper**○ n clou○ m d'un spectacle; ~ **trial** n procès m pour l'exemple.

shrank /ʃræŋk/ prét ▶ **shrink** II, III.

shrapnel /ˈʃræpnl/ n ⊄ éclats mpl d'obus.

shred /ʃred/ I n 1 FIG (of evidence, emotion, sense, truth) parcelle f; 2 (of paper, fabric) lambeau m.

II vtr (p prés etc **-dd-**) déchiqueter [paper]; râper [vegetables]; **~ded newspaper** déchirures fpl de journaux.

shredder /ˈʃredə(r)/ n (for paper) déchiqueteuse f.

shrew /ʃruː/ n 1 ZOOL musaraigne f; 2† (woman) PÉJ mégère f.

shrewd /ʃruːd/ adj [person] habile; [face] plein d'astuce; [move, assessment, investment] astucieux/-ieuse; **to have a ~ idea that** être porté à croire que; **to make a ~ guess** deviner juste.

shrewdly /ˈʃruːdlɪ/ adv [act] habilement; [assess] avec perspicacité.

shriek /ʃriːk/ I n 1 (of pain, fear) cri m perçant, hurlement m; (of delight) cri m; **~s of laughter** éclats mpl de rire; 2 (of bird) cri m.

II vi crier, hurler (**in, with** de).

shrift /ʃrɪft/ n **to give sb/sth short ~** expédier qn/qch sans ménagements.

shrill /ʃrɪl/ I adj 1 [voice, cry, laugh] perçant; [whistle, tone] strident; 2 PÉJ [criticism] vigoureux/-euse.

II vi [bird] pousser un cri aigu; [telephone] retentir.

shrimp /ʃrɪmp/ n ZOOL, CULIN crevette f grise.

shrimping /ˈʃrɪmpɪŋ/ n pêche f à la crevette.

shrine /ʃraɪn/ n 1 (place) lieu m de pèlerinage (**to** consacré à); 2 (alcove) autel m; (building) chapelle f.

shrink /ʃrɪŋk/ I○ n HUM psy○ mf, psychiatre mf.

II vtr (prét **shrank**; pp **shrunk** ou **shrunken**) faire rétrécir [fabric]; [tribesman] réduire [head].

III vi (prét **shrank**; pp **shrunk** ou **shrunken**) 1 [fabric] rétrécir; [forest, area] reculer; [boundaries] se rapprocher; [economy, sales] être en recul; [resources, *funds*] s'amenuiser; [*old person, body*] se tasser; **to ~ from 200 to 50** tomber de 200 à 50; **to have shrunk to nothing** [*team, household*] être quasiment réduit à néant; [*person*] n'avoir plus que la peau sur les os; **2** (recoil) **to ~ from** se dérober devant [*conflict, responsibility*]; **to ~ from doing** hésiter à faire.

shrinkage /'ʃrɪŋkɪdʒ/ *n* (of fabric) rétrécissement *m*; (of economy) recul *m*; (of resources, area) diminution *f*.

shrinking /'ʃrɪŋkɪŋ/ *adj* [*population, market*] en baisse; [*asset*] qui se raréfie; [*audience*] qui s'amenuise.

shrinking violet *n* HUM personne *f* timorée.

shrink-wrap /'ʃrɪŋkræp/ **I** *n* film *m* plastique.
II *vtr* (*p prés etc* **-pp-**) emballer [qch] sous film plastique.

shrivel /'ʃrɪvl/ **I** *vtr* (*p prés etc* **-ll-, -l-** US) [*sun, heat*] flétrir [*skin*]; dessécher [*plant, leaf*].
II *vi* (*p prés etc* **-ll-, -l-** US) (also **~ up**) [*fruit, vegetable*] se ratatiner; [*skin*] se flétrir; [*plant, leaf, meat*] se dessécher.

shroud /ʃraʊd/ **I** *n* **1** (cloth) linceul *m*, suaire *m*; **2** FIG voile *m* (**of** de); **3** NAUT hauban *m*.
II *vtr* envelopper [*body, person*] (**in** dans).

Shrove Tuesday *n* RELIG mardi *m* gras.

shrub /ʃrʌb/ *n* arbuste *m*.

shrubbery /'ʃrʌbərɪ/ *n* (in garden) massif *m* d'arbustes; (collectively) arbustes *mpl*.

shrug /ʃrʌg/ **I** *n* (also **~ of the shoulders**) haussement *m* d'épaules.
II *vtr* (*p prés etc* **-gg-**) hausser les épaules *fpl*.
■ **shrug off**: **~ off** [sth], **~** [sth] **off** ignorer [*problem, rumour*].

shrunk /ʃrʌŋk/ *pp* ▶ **shrink** II, III.

shrunken /'ʃrʌŋkən/ *adj* [*person, body*] rabougri; [*budget*] réduit; **~ head** tête *f* réduite.

shucks /ʃʌks/ *excl* US (in irritation) zut○, mince○; (in embarrassment) allons donc.

shudder /'ʃʌdə(r)/ **I** *n* **1** (of person) frisson *m* (**of** de); **the news sent a ~ of terror through them** à l'annonce de la nouvelle, un frisson de terreur les parcourut; **with a ~** en frissonnant; **2** (of vehicle) secousse *f*; **to give a ~** avoir une secousse.
II *vi* **1** [*person*] frissonner; **to ~ with** frissonner de [*fear etc*]; **I ~ to think!** j'en ai des frissons rien que d'y penser!; **2** [*vehicle*] (once) avoir un soubresaut; **to ~ to a halt** avoir quelques soubresauts et s'arrêter.

shuffle /'ʃʌfl/ **I** *n* **1** (way of walking) pas *mpl* traînants; **2** (sound of walk) bruit *m* de pas traînants.
II *vtr* **1** (also **~ about**) déplacer [*objects, people*]; **2 to ~ one's feet** (**in embarrassment**) agiter ses pieds (par embarras); **3** (mix together) mélanger [*papers*]; **4** GAMES battre [*cards*].
III *vi* traîner les pieds; **to ~ along** marcher en traînant les pieds.
■ **shuffle off**: **¶ ~ off** partir en traînant les pieds; **¶ ~ off** [sth] se décharger de [*responsibility, blame, guilt*] (**on(to)** sb sur qn).

shufty○ /'ʃʊftɪ/ *n* GB **to have a ~ at sth** jeter un coup d'œil sur qch.

shun /ʃʌn/ *vtr* (*p prés etc* **-nn-**) **1** (avoid) fuir [*people, publicity*]; dédaigner [*work*]; **2** (reject) rejeter.

shunt /ʃʌnt/ **I** *n* MED, ELEC shunt *m*.
II *vtr* **1**○ (send) expédier○; **to be ~ed from place to place** être expédié d'un endroit à l'autre; **to ~ sb back and forth** ballotter qn d'un côté à l'autre; **2** RAIL (move) aiguiller [*wagon, engine*] (**into** sur).
III *vi* **to ~ back and forth** manœuvrer.

shush /ʃʊʃ/ **I** *excl* chut!
II○ *vtr* faire taire [*person*].

shut /ʃʌt/ **I** *adj* (closed) [*door, book, box, mouth, shop*] fermé; **to slam the door ~** claquer la porte (pour bien la fermer); **to slam ~** se refermer en claquant; **to keep one's mouth**○ **~** se taire.
II *vtr* (*p prés* **-tt-**; *prét, pp* **shut**) **1** (close) fermer; **~ your mouth** ou **trap**○ ou **face**○! ferme-la○!; **2** (confine) = **shut up 2**.
III *vi* (*p prés* **-tt-**; *prét, pp* **shut**) **1** [*door, book, box, mouth*] se fermer; **2** [*office, factory*] fermer.

■ **shut away**: **~** [sb/sth] **away**, **~ away** [sb/sth] (lock up) enfermer [*person*]; mettre [qch] sous clé [*valuables, medicine*].
■ **shut down**: **¶ ~ down** [*business*] fermer; [*machinery*] s'arrêter; **¶ ~** [sth] **down**, **~ down** [sth] fermer [*business*]; arrêter [*machinery*].
■ **shut in**: **~** [sb/sth] **in** enfermer [*person, animal*]; **to feel shut in** FIG se sentir étouffé.
■ **shut off**: **~** [sth] **off**, **~ off** [sth] couper [*supply, motor*]; arrêter [*oven, fan*]; fermer [*valve*].
■ **shut out**: **~ out** [sth/sb], **~** [sth/sb] **out 1** (keep out) laisser [qch] dehors [*animal, person*]; éliminer [*noise*]; **to be shut out** être à la porte; **2** (keep at bay) chasser [*thought*]; **3** (reject) repousser [*world*]; **to feel shut out** se sentir exclu; **4** (block) empêcher [qch] d'entrer [*light*]; bloquer [*view*].
■ **shut up**: **¶ ~ up**○ se taire (**about** au sujet de); **¶ ~** [sb] **up**, **~ up** [sb] **1**○ (silence) faire taire; **2** (confine) enfermer (**in** dans); **3** (close) fermer [*house*]; **to ~ up shop**○ LIT, FIG fermer boutique○.

shutdown /'ʃʌtdaʊn/ *n* GEN fermeture *f*; (of nuclear reactor) arrêt *m* (du réacteur).

shut-eye○ /'ʃʌtaɪ/ *n* **to get some ~** (short sleep) piquer un roupillon○.

shutout *n* US victoire *f* écrasante (*l'équipe perdante ne marquant aucun point*).

shutter /'ʃʌtə(r)/ *n* **1** (on window) (wooden, metal) volet *m*; (on shopfront) store *m*; **to put up the ~s** LIT fermer le magasin; FIG fermer boutique○; **2** PHOT obturateur *m*; **~ speed** vitesse *f* d'obturation.

shuttle /'ʃʌtl/ **I** *n* **1** (transport service) navette *f* ALSO AEROSP; **2** SPORT (also **~cock**) volant *m*.
II *vtr* transporter [*passengers*].
III *vi* **to ~ between** faire la navette entre.

shuttle: **~ bus** *n* navette *f*; **~ diplomacy** *n* POL démarches *fpl* diplomatiques; **~ service** *n* service *m* de navette.

shy /ʃaɪ/ **I** *adj* **1** (timid) [*person*] timide (**with, of** avec); [*animal*] farouche (**with, of** avec); **2** (afraid) **to be ~ of** avoir peur de; **3** (avoid) **to fight ~ of** fuir devant.
II *vi* [*horse*] faire un écart (**at** devant).
■ **shy away** se tenir à l'écart (**from** de); **to ~ away from doing** répugner à faire.

shyness /'ʃaɪnɪs/ *n* timidité *f*.

Siamese /ˌsaɪə'miːz/ ▶ **1100**, **1038** **I** *n* **1** (person) Siamois/-e *m/f*; **2** (language) siamois *m*; **3** (cat) siamois/-e *m/f*.
II *adj* siamois.

Siberia /saɪ'bɪərɪə/ ▶ **840** *pr n* Sibérie *f*.

sibling /'sɪblɪŋ/ *n* frère/sœur *m/f*.

Sicily /'sɪsɪlɪ/ ▶ **1022** *pr n* Sicile *f*.

sick /sɪk/ **I** *n* **1 the ~** (+ *v pl*) les malades *mpl*; **2**○ GB (vomit) vomi *m*.
II *adj* **1** (ill) malade; **to feel ~** ne pas se sentir bien; **to take ~** GB tomber malade; **off ~** GB absent pour cause de maladie; **to go ~**○ se faire porter malade; **2** (nauseous) **to be ~** vomir; **to feel ~** avoir mal au cœur; **you'll make yourself ~** tu vas te rendre malade; **to have a ~ feeling in one's stomach** (from nerves) avoir l'estomac noué; **worried ~** malade d'inquiétude; **3** (tasteless) [*joke, story*] malsain, de mauvais goût; **4** (disturbed) [*mind, imagination*] malsain; **5** (disgusted) écœuré, dégoûté; **you make me ~!** tu m'écœures!; **it's enough to make you ~!** il y a de quoi vous rendre malade!; **6**○ (fed-up) **to be ~ of sth/sb**○ en avoir assez or marre de qn/qch; **to be ~ and tired of sth/sb**○ en avoir ras le bol○ de qch/qn; **to be ~ of the sight of sth/sb**○ ne plus supporter qch/qn.
■ **sick up**○ GB: **~ up** [sth], **~** [sth] **up**○ vomir.

sick: **~ bay** *n* infirmerie *f*; **~bed** *n* lit *m* de malade.

sicken /'sɪkən/ **I** *vtr* rendre [qn] malade; FIG écœurer.
II *vi* **1** [*person, animal*] LITTÉR tomber malade, dépérir; **to be ~ing for something** couver quelque chose; **2** FIG (grow weary) **to ~ of** se lasser de.

sickening /'sɪkənɪŋ/ *adj* **1** [*sight*] qui soulève le cœur;

[*smell, cruelty*] écœurant; **2**○ (annoying) [*person, behaviour*] insupportable.

sickle /'sɪkl/ n faucille f.

sick leave n congé m de maladie.

sickly /'sɪklɪ/ adj **1** [*person*] maladif/-ive; [*plant*] mal en point; [*complexion*] blafard; **2** [*smell, taste*] écœurant; [*colour*] fadasse; **~ sweet** douceâtre.

sickness /'sɪknɪs/ n **1** (illness) maladie f; **in ~ and in health** ~ pour le meilleur et pour le pire; **2** (nausea) **bouts of ~** vomissements mpl.

sickness: **~ benefit** n ₵ GB prestations fpl de l'assurance-maladie; **~ insurance** n assurance f maladie.

sick: **~ note**○ n (for school) mot m d'excuse; (for work) certificat m médical; **~pay** n indemnité f de maladie; **~room** n (in school, institution) infirmerie f; (at home) chambre f de malade.

side /saɪd/ **I** n **1** (part) (of person's body, object, table) côté m; (of animal's body, hill, boat) flanc m; (of ravine, cave) paroi f; (of box) (outer) côté m; (inner) paroi f; **on my left/right** ~ à ma gauche/droite; **on one's/its ~** sur le côté; **~ by ~** côte à côte; **don't leave my ~** reste près de moi; **the north ~ of town** le nord de la ville; **'this ~ up'** (on box) 'haut'; **2** (surface of flat object) (of paper, cloth) côté m; (of record) face f; **the right ~** (of cloth) l'endroit m; (of paper) le recto; **the wrong ~** (of cloth) l'envers m; (of coin) le revers; (of paper) le verso; **3** (edge) (of lake, road) bord m; (of building) côté m; **at ou by the ~ of** au bord de [*lake, road*]; **4** (aspect) (of person, argument) côté m; (of problem, question) aspect m; (of story) version f; **she's on the arts ~** (academically) elle a opté pour les lettres; **he's on the marketing ~** (in company) il fait partie du service de marketing; **5** (opposing group) côté m, camp m; **to take ~s** prendre position; **6** (team) équipe f; **you've really let the ~ down** FIG tu nous as laissé tomber; **7** (page) page f; **8** (line of descent) **on his mother's ~** du côté de sa mère; **9**○ (TV channel) chaîne f.

II noun modifier [*door, window, entrance, view*] latéral.

III -sided combining form **six-~d figure** figure f à six côtés; **many-~d problem** problème m complexe.

IV on the side adv phr **with salad on the ~** avec de la salade; **to do sth on the ~** (in addition) faire qch à côté; (illegally) faire qch au noir.

IDIOMS like the ~ of a house énorme; **time is on our ~** le temps travaille pour nous; **to be on the safe ~** (allowing enough time) pour calculer large; (to be certain) pour être sûr; **(a bit) on the big ~** plutôt grand; **to get on the wrong ~ of sb** prendre qn à rebrousse-poil; **to get on the right ~ of sb** se mettre bien avec qn; **to have right on one's ~** être dans son droit; **to put sth to one ~** mettre [qch] de côté [*object, task*]; **to take sb to one ~** prendre qn à part.
■ **side with** se mettre du côté de [*person*].

side: **~ arm** n arme f de protection; **~board** n buffet m; **~boards** GB, **sideburns** npl (on face) pattes fpl; **~ dish** n CULIN plat m d'accompagnement; **~ effect** n LIT (of drug) effet m secondaire; FIG (of action) répercussion f; **~ issue** n question f annexe; **~kick**○ n acolyte m.

sidelight /'saɪdlaɪt/ n **1** AUT feu m de position; **2** (window) (in house) lucarne f; (in car) déflecteur m.

sideline /'saɪdlaɪn/ n **1** (extra) à-côté m; **as a ~** comme à-côté; **2** SPORT ligne f de touche; **over the ~** en touche; **on the ~s** LIT, FIG sur la touche.

side: **~long** adj [*look*] oblique; **~ order** n CULIN portion f; **~ plate** n petite assiette f; **~ road** n petite route f; **~ saddle** n selle f d'amazone; **~ show** n (at fair) attraction f; **~splitting**○ adj très drôle; **~step** vtr (p prés etc **-pp-**) LIT éviter [*opponent*]; FIG éluder [*issue*]; **~ street** n petite rue f; **~swipe** vtr emboutir [qch] sur le côté.

sidetrack vtr FIG fourvoyer [*person*]; **to get ~ed** se fourvoyer.

sidewalk n US trottoir m.

sideways /'saɪdweɪz/ **I** adj [*look, glance*] de travers; **a**

~ move in his career une bifurcation dans sa carrière.

II adv [*move*] latéralement; [*carry*] sur le côté; [*park*] de biais; [*look at*] de travers; **~ on** [*person*] de profil.

IDIOMS to knock sb ~ FIG sidérer qn.

side-whiskers /said/ npl favoris mpl.

siding /'saɪdɪŋ/ n **1** RAIL voie f de garage; **2** US (weatherproof coating) revêtement m extérieur.

sidle /'saɪdl/ vi **to ~ into/out/of** se faufiler dans/hors de; **to ~ up to** s'avancer furtivement vers qn.

SIDS /sɪdz/ n MED abrév ▶ **sudden infant death syndrome**.

siege /siːdʒ/ n siège m; **to lay ~ to sth** LIT, FIG assiéger qch.

Sierra Leone /sɪˌerəlɪˈəʊn/ **▶ 840** pr n Sierra Leone f.

siesta /sɪˈestə/ n sieste f; **to have a ~** faire la sieste.

sieve /sɪv/ **I** n (for draining) passoire f; (for sifting) tamis m; (for coal, stones) crible m; (for wheat) van m.

II vtr tamiser [*earth, flour*]; passer [qch] au crible [*coal*]; vanner [*wheat*].

sift /sɪft/ **I** vtr **1** (sieve) tamiser, passer [qch] au tamis [*flour, soil*]; passer [qch] au crible [*coal*]; vanner [*wheat*]; **2** FIG (sort) passer [qch] au crible [*data, evidence, information*].
■ **sift out**: ¶ **~ out** [sb] (dispose of) éliminer [*troublemakers*]; ¶ **~ out** [sth] extraire [*gold etc*].
■ **sift through**: **~ through** [sth] trier.

sifter /'sɪftə(r)/ n saupoudreuse f.

sigh /saɪ/ **I** n soupir m; **to breathe** ou **heave a ~** pousser un soupir.

II vi **1** (exhale) soupirer, pousser un soupir; **to ~ with relief** pousser un soupir de soulagement; **2** (complain) **to ~ over sth** se lamenter sur qch; **3** (whisper) [*wind*] gémir; [*trees*] bruisser.

sight /saɪt/ **I** n **1** (faculty) vue f; **to have good/poor ~** avoir une bonne/mauvaise vue; **2** (act of seeing) vue f; **at first ~** à première vue; **at the ~ of** à la vue [*of blood*]; **at the ~ of her** en la voyant; **this was my first ~ of** c'était la première fois que je voyais; **to catch ~ of sb/sth** apercevoir qn/qch; **to lose ~ of sb/sth** LIT, FIG perdre qn/qch de vue; **we mustn't lose ~ of the fact that** FIG nous ne devons pas perdre de vue que; **to know sb by ~** connaître qn de vue; **I can't stand the ~ of him!** je ne peux pas le voir (en peinture)!; **3** (range of vision) **to be in ~** [*land, border*] être en vue; [*peace, freedom*] être proche; **the end is in ~!** on approche de la fin!; **there wasn't a soldier in ~** il n'y avait pas un soldat en vue; **to come into ~** apparaître; **to be out of ~** (hidden) être caché; (having moved) ne plus être visible; **to do sth out of ~ of sb** faire qch sans être vu par qn; **to stay out of ~** rester caché; **to keep sb/sth out of ~** cacher qn/qch; **don't let her out of your ~!** ne la quitte pas des yeux!; **4** (thing seen) spectacle m; **a ~ to behold** un spectacle à voir; **it was not a pretty ~!** IRON ce n'était pas beau à voir!; **5** (a shock to see) (place) porcherie f; (person) **you're a ~!** tu n'es pas présentable!

II sights npl **1** (places worth seeing) attractions fpl touristiques (**of** de); **to see the ~s** visiter; **to show sb the ~s** (in town) faire visiter la ville à qn; **2** (on rifle, telescope) viseur m; **3** FIG **to have sth in one's ~s** avoir qch dans sa ligne de mire; **to have sb in one's ~s** avoir qn dans le collimateur○; **to set one's ~s on sth** viser qch; **to raise/lower one's ~s** viser plus haut/plus bas.

IDIOMS a damned ou **jolly** GB **~ better** beaucoup mieux; **out of ~, out of mind** PROV loin des yeux, loin du cœur PROV; **out of ~!**○ fantastique○!

sighted /'saɪtɪd/ adj [*person*] doué de la vue.

sight: **~-read** vtr, vi déchiffrer; **~-reading** n déchiffrage m.

sightseeing /'saɪtsiːɪŋ/ n tourisme m; **to go ~** faire du tourisme.

sight: **~seer** n GEN touriste mf; PÉJ badaud/-e m/f; **~ unseen** adv COMM [*buy*] sur description.

sign /saɪn/ **I** n **1** (symbolic mark) signe m, symbole m;

the pound ~ le symbole de la livre sterling; **2** (object) (roadsign, billboard) panneau *m*; (smaller, indicating opening hours) pancarte *f*; (outside inn, shop) enseigne *f*; **3** (gesture) geste *m*; **the ~ of the cross** le signe de la croix; **4** (signal) signal *m*; **the ~ for us to leave** le signal du départ; **5** (visible evidence) signe *m*; **there was no ~ of life** il n'y avait aucun signe de vie; **there was no ~ of any troops** il n'y avait pas l'ombre d'un soldat; **6** (indication, pointer) signe *m*; **this is a ~ that** c'est que signe que, ça indique que; **the ~s are that** tout indique que; **there is no ~ ou there are no ~s of** il n'y a rien qui annonce [*change, solution*]; **to show ~s of** montrer des signes de [*stress, talent*]; **to show ~s of doing** sembler faire; **7** ▶1418 (of zodiac) signe *m*; **what ~ are you?** tu es de quel signe?

II *vtr* **1** (put signature to) signer; **~ed, sealed and delivered** LIT dûment signé et remis à qui de droit; FIG terminé; **2** (on contract) engager [*footballer, band*].

III *vi* **1** GEN signer; **~ for** signer un reçu pour; **2** SPORT signer son contrat; **3** (signal) **to ~ to sb to do** faire signe à qn de faire; **4** (communicate) communiquer en langage des sourds-muets.

▪ **sign away**: **~ away** [sth], **~** [sth] **away** renoncer à [qch] par écrit [*rights, inheritance*].

▪ **sign in**: ¶ **~ in** signer le registre (à l'arrivée); ¶ **~ in** [sb], **~** [sb] **in** inscrire [*guest*].

▪ **sign off** (all contexts) terminer.

▪ **sign on**: **~ on 1** GB (for benefit) pointer au chômage; **2** (to course of study) s'inscrire (**for** à, dans).

▪ **sign out** signer le registre (au départ).

▪ **sign up**: ¶ **~ up 1** (in forces, by contract) s'engager; **2** (for course) s'inscrire (**for** à, dans); ¶ **~ up** [sb] engager [*player, filmstar*].

signal /'sɪɡnl/ **I** *n* **1** (cue) signal *m* (**for** de); **to give the ~ to attack** donner le signal de l'attaque; **this is a ~ to do** cela indique qu'il faut faire; **2** (sign, indication) signe *m* (**of** de); **to be a ~ that** être signe que, indiquer que; **to send a ~ to sb that** indiquer (clairement) à qn que; **3** RAIL signal *m*; **4** RADIO, TV, ELEC signal *m*; **to read the ~s** FIG comprendre.

II *adj* [*honour*] véritable (*before n*); [*failure*] notoire.

III *vtr* (*p prés etc* **-ll-** GB, **-l-** US) **1** (gesture) **to ~ (to sb) that** faire signe (à qn) que; **to ~ sb to do** faire signe à qn de faire; **2** (indicate) indiquer [*shift, determination, support*]; annoncer [*release*]; **to ~ one's intention to do** annoncer son intention de faire; **to ~ that** indiquer que; **3** (mark) marquer [*end, beginning, decline*].

IV *vi* (*p prés etc* **- ll-** GB, **-l-** US) faire des signes.

signal: **~ box** *n* RAIL poste *m* d'aiguillage *m*; **~man** ▶1251 *n* RAIL aiguilleur *m*.

signatory /'sɪɡnǝtrɪ, US -tɔ:rɪ/ *n, adj* signataire (*mf*).

signature /'sɪɡnǝtʃǝ(r)/ *n* signature *f*; **to put** ou **set one's ~ to** apposer sa signature à [*letter, document*].

signature tune *n* indicatif *m*.

signboard /'saɪnbɔ:d/ *n* panneau *m* d'affichage.

signet ring /'sɪɡnɪtrɪŋ/ *n* chevalière *f*.

significance /sɪɡ'nɪfɪkǝns/ *n* **1** (importance) importance *f*; **not of any ~, of no ~** sans aucune importance; **2** (meaning) signification *f*.

significant /sɪɡ'nɪfɪkǝnt/ *adj* **1** (substantial) considérable; **2** (important) important; **3** (meaningful) [*gesture*] éloquent; [*name, figure*] significatif/-ive; [*phrase*] lourd de sens; **it is ~ that** il est significatif que (+ *subj*).

significantly /sɪɡ'nɪfɪkǝntlɪ/ *adv* **1** (considerably) sensiblement; **2** (meaningfully) [*named*] de façon significative.

signify /'sɪɡnɪfaɪ/ *vtr* **1** (denote) [*symbol, gesture, statement*] indiquer; [*dream*] signifier; **2** (display) exprimer [*disapproval, joy*]; **to ~ that** indiquer que.

signing /'saɪnɪŋ/ *n* **1** (of treaty) signature *f*; **2** (of footballer) signature *f*; **3** = **sign language**.

sign language *n* code *m* or langage *m* gestuel.

signpost /'saɪnpǝʊst/ **I** *n* **1** GEN panneau *m* indicateur; **2** (old free-standing type) poteau *m* indicateur; **3** FIG (pointer) indice *m*, indication *f*.

II *vtr* indiquer; **to be ~ed** être indiqué.

signposting *n* signalisation *f* routière.

Sikh /siːk/ *n, adj* sikh (*mf*).

silage /'saɪlɪdʒ/ *n* fourrage *m* ensilé, ensilage *m*.

silence /'saɪlǝns/ **I** *n* **1** (quietness) silence *m*; **in ~** en silence; **~ fell** le silence se fit; **2** (pause) silence *m*; **3** (absence of communication) silence *m* (**about, on, over** sur); **to break one's ~** sortir de son silence; **right of ~** JUR droit pour un accusé de se taire avant ou pendant son procès; **4** (discretion) silence *m*.

II *vtr* **1** (quieten) faire taire [*person, enemy guns*]; **2** (gag) faire taire [*critic, press*].

silencer /'saɪlǝnsǝ(r)/ *n* MIL, GB AUT silencieux *m*.

silent /'saɪlǝnt/ *adj* **1** (quiet) silencieux/-ieuse; **to be ~** se taire; **to remain** ou **stay ~** rester silencieux; **to fall ~** se taire; **2** (taciturn) taciturne; **3** (unexpressed) [*disapproval, prayer*] muet/muette; **4** CIN muet/muette; **the ~ screen** le cinéma muet; **5** LING muet/muette.

IDIOMS **as ~ as the grave** muet comme une tombe.

silently /'saɪlǝntlɪ/ *adv* [*appear, leave, move*] silencieusement; [*listen, pray, stare, work*] en silence.

silent: **~ majority** *n* majorité *f* silencieuse; **~ partner** *n* COMM, JUR commanditaire *m*.

Silesia /saɪ'liːzɪǝ/ ▶840 *pr n* Silésie *f*.

silhouette /ˌsɪluː'et/ **I** *n* silhouette *f*.

II *vtr* **to be ~d against sth** se détacher sur qch.

silicon /'sɪlɪkǝn/ *n* silicium *m*.

silicon chip *n* COMPUT puce *f* électronique.

silicone /'sɪlɪkǝʊn/ *n* CHEM silicone *f*; (in pharmacy) silicone *m*; **~ rubber** silicone *m* élastomère.

Silicon Valley *pr n* Silicon Valley *f*, zone *f* d'industries électroniques.

silk /sɪlk/ **I** *n* **1** (fabric) soie *f*; **2** (thread) fil *m* de soie; **3** (clothing) soierie *f*; **4** (of spider) soie *f*; **5** GB, JUR avocat *m* de la couronne.

II *noun modifier* [*garment*] de soie.

IDIOMS **as soft** ou **smooth as ~** doux comme de la soie.

silken /'sɪlkǝn/ *adj* **1** (shiny) soyeux/-euse; **2** (made of silk) de soie; **3** (soft) [*voice*] doux/douce; PÉJ douce-reux/-euse PÉJ.

silk: **~ factory** *n* soierie *f*; **~ farming** *n* sériciculture *f*; **~ finish** *adj* [*fabric*] soyeux/-euse; [*paint*] satiné; **~ hat** *n* haut-de-forme *m*; **~ route** *n* route *f* de la soie; **~-screen printing** *n* sérigraphie *f*; **~ square** *n* carré *m* de soie; **~worm** *n* ver *m* à soie.

silky /'sɪlkɪ/ *adj* **1** [*fabric, hair, skin*] soyeux/-euse; **2** (soft) [*voice*] doux/douce; PÉJ doucereux/-euse PÉJ.

sill /sɪl/ *n* (of window) (interior) rebord *m*; (exterior) appui *m*.

silliness /'sɪlɪnɪs/ *n* sottise *f*, stupidité *f*.

silly /'sɪlɪ/ **I** *adj* [*person*] idiot; [*question, game*] stupide; [*behaviour, clothes*] ridicule; **don't be ~** ne dis pas de bêtises; **what a ~ thing to do!** quelle bêtise!; **to make sb look ~** faire passer qn pour un/-e idiot/-e.

II *adv* **to drink oneself ~** s'abrutir d'alcool; **to bore sb ~** assommer qn.

silly season /'sɪlɪ/ *n* GB période *f* creuse (*où la presse se contente de frivolités*).

silo /'saɪlǝʊ/ *n* (*pl* ~**s**) AGRIC, MIL silo *m*.

silt /sɪlt/ **I** *n* limon *m*, vase *f*.

II *vi* (also **~ up**) [*river*] (with mud) s'envaser; (with sand) s'ensabler.

silver /'sɪlvǝ(r)/ ▶818 **I** *n* **1** (metal, colour) argent *m*; **2** (silverware) argenterie *f*; (cutlery) couverts *mpl* en argent; (coins) monnaie *f*; **3** (medal) médaille *f* d'argent.

II *adj* [*ring, coin*] en argent; [*hair, moon*] argenté; [*paint*] gris métallisé *inv*.

silver: **~ birch** *n* bouleau *m* argenté; **~ foil** *n* GB papier *m* d'aluminium; **~-gilt** *n* vermeil *m*; **~-grey** ▶818 *adj* [*hair, silk*] gris-argent *inv*; [*paint*] gris métallisé *inv*; **~-haired** *adj* aux cheveux argentés; **~ jubilee** *n* (date) vingt-cinquième anniversaire *m*; **~ paper** *n* papier *m* d'argent; **~ plated** *adj* plaqué argent; **~ screen** *n* CIN écran *m*; **~ service** *n* service *m* stylé; **~side** *n* CULIN gîte *m*; **~smith** ▶1251 *n* orfèvre *mf*;

since

as a preposition
In time expressions
since is used in English after a verb in the present perfect or progressive present perfect tense to indicate when something that is still going on started. To express this French uses a verb in the present tense + *depuis*:

I've been waiting since Saturday = j'attends depuis samedi

I've lived in Rome since 1988 = j'habite à Rome depuis 1988

When *since* is used after a verb in the past perfect tense, French uses the imperfect + *depuis*:

*I had been waiting
since nine o'clock* = j'attendais depuis neuf heures

In negative time expressions
Again *since* is translated by *depuis*, but in negative sentences the verb tenses used in French are the same as those used in English:

I haven't seen him since Saturday = je ne l'ai pas vu depuis samedi

I hadn't seen him since 1978 = je ne l'avais pas vu depuis 1978

As a conjunction
In time expressions
When *since* is used as a conjunction, it is translated by *depuis que* and the tenses used in French parallel exactly those used with the preposition *depuis* (see above):

since she's been living in Oxford = depuis qu'elle habite à Oxford

since he'd been in Paris = depuis qu'il était à Paris

Note that in time expressions with *since* French native speakers will generally prefer to use a noun where possible when English uses a verb:

I haven't seen him since he left = je ne l'ai pas vu depuis son départ

*she's been living in Nice since
she got married* = elle habite à Nice depuis son mariage

For particular usages see the entry *since*.

Meaning because
When *since* is used to mean *because* it is translated by *comme* or *étant donné que*:

*since she was ill,
she couldn't go* = comme elle était malade *or* étant donné qu'elle était malade, elle ne pouvait pas y aller

As an adverb
When *since* is used as an adverb it is translated by *depuis*:

he hasn't been seen since = on ne l'a pas vu depuis

For particular usages see III in the entry *since*.

~ware *n* (solid) argenterie *f* massive; (plate) métal *m* argenté; **~ wedding** *n* noces *fpl* d'argent.

silvery /'sılvərı/ *adj* **1** [*hair*] argenté; **2** [*sound*] argentin.

similar /'sımılə(r)/ *adj* similaire, analogue; **something** ~ quelque chose de similaire; ~ **to** analogue à, comparable à; **it's** ~ **to riding a bike** c'est comme faire du vélo; ~ **in price** comparable pour ce qui est du prix; **it is** ~ **in appearance to...** ça ressemble à...; ~ **in colour** dans les mêmes tons.

similarity /ˌsımı'lærətı/ *n* (fact of resembling) ressemblance *f*, similarité *f* (**to, with** avec; **in** dans).

similarly /'sımıləlı/ *adv* [*behave, dressed*] de la même façon; [*elaborate, hostile*] aussi (*before adj*); **and ~,...** et de même,...

simile /'sımılı/ *n* comparaison *f*.

simmer /'sımə(r)/ **I** *vtr* faire cuire [qch] à feu doux [*soup*]; laisser frémir [*water*].
II *vi* **1** [*soup*] cuire à feu doux, mijoter; [*water*] frémir; **2** FIG [*person*] (with discontent) bouillonner (**with** de); (with passion, excitement) frémir (**with** de); [*revolt, violence*] couver.
■ **simmer down**○ [*person*] se calmer.

simper /'sımpə(r)/ *vi* PÉJ minauder.

simpering /'sımpərıŋ/ *adj* PÉJ [*person*] minaudier/-ière; [*smile*] affecté.

simple /'sımpl/ *adj* **1** (not complicated) simple; **it's a ~ matter to change a wheel** c'est très simple de changer une roue; **the ~ truth** la vérité pure et simple; **I can't make it any ~r** je ne peux pas simplifier davantage; **what could be ~r?** rien de plus facile!; **computing made ~** l'informatique à la portée de tous; **2** (not elaborate) [*dress, furniture, style*] sobre; [*food, tastes*] simple; **3** (unsophisticated) simple; **4** (dimwitted) simplet/-ette○, simple d'esprit; **5** (basic) [*structure*] simple; [*sentence, tense*] simple.

simple: ~ **fraction** *n* fraction *f*; **~-minded** *adj* PÉJ [*person*] simple d'esprit; [*attitude*] naïf/naïve.

simpleton /'sımpltən/ *n* simple *mf* d'esprit.

simplicity /sım'plısətı/ *n* (all contexts) simplicité *f*.

simplification /ˌsımplıfı'keıʃn/ *n* simplification *f*.

simplify /'sımplıfaı/ *vtr* simplifier.

simplistic /sım'plıstık/ *adj* simpliste.

simply /'sımplı/ *adv* **1** [*write, dress, live*] simplement, avec simplicité; **to put it ~...** en deux mots...; **2** (merely) simplement; **it's ~ a question of explaining** il suffit d'expliquer; **3** (absolutely) absolument.

simulate /'sımjʊleıt/ *vtr* **1** (feign) simuler [*anger, illness, grief*]; affecter [*interest*]; **2** (reproduce) simuler [*behaviour, conditions*]; imiter [*blood, sound*].

simulated /'sımjʊleıtıd/ *adj* **1** (fake) [*fur, pearls*] artificiel/-ielle; **2** (feigned) [*anger, grief*] simulé, feint.

simulation /ˌsımjʊ'leıʃn/ *n* simulation *f*.

simulator /'sımjʊleıtə(r)/ *n* simulateur *m*.

simulcast /'sıməlkɑːst, US -kæst/ *vtr* diffuser [qch] simultanément à la radio et à la télévision.

simultaneity /ˌsımltə'niːətı, US ˌsaım-/ *n* simultanéité *f*.

simultaneous /ˌsıml'teınıəs, US ˌsaım-/ *adj* simultané; **to be ~** avoir lieu en même temps (**with** que).

simultaneously /ˌsıml'teınıəslı, US ˌsaım-/ *adv* simultanément.

sin /sın/ **I** *n* péché *m*, crime *m*; **to live in ~** vivre dans le péché; **it's a ~ to steal** voler est un péché.
II *vi* (*p prés etc* **-nn-**) pécher (**against** contre).
IDIOMS **for my ~s** HUM malheureusement pour moi.

since /sıns/ **I** *prep* depuis; **she'd been a teacher ~ 1965** elle était professeur depuis 1965; **she's been waiting ~ 10 am** elle attend depuis 10 heures; **I haven't seen him ~ then** je ne l'ai pas vu depuis; **~ arriving** ou **~ his arrival he...** depuis son arrivée ou depuis qu'il est arrivé, il...
II *conj* **1** (from the time when) depuis que; **~ he's been away** depuis qu'il est absent; **ever ~ I married him** depuis que nous nous sommes mariés, depuis notre mariage; **it's 10 years ~ we last met** cela fait 10 ans que nous ne nous sommes pas revus; **2** (because) comme, étant donné que; **~ you're so clever, why don't you do it yourself?** puisque tu es tellement malin, pourquoi ne le fais-tu pas toi-même?
III *adv* depuis.

sincere /sın'sıə(r)/ *adj* [*person, apology, thanks, belief*] sincère; [*attempt*] réel/réelle.

sincerely /sın'sıəlı/ *adv* sincèrement; **Yours ~, Sincerely yours** US (end of letter) Veuillez agréer, Monsieur/Madame, l'expression de mes sentiments les meilleurs; (less formally) Cordialement (vôtre).

sincerity /sın'serətı/ *n* sincérité *f*; **with ~** sincèrement.

sine /saın/ *n* MATH sinus *m*.

sinew /'sɪnjuː/ *n* ANAT tendon *m*.

sinewy /'sɪnjuːɪ/ *adj* **1** [*person, animal*] (mince et) musclé; **2** [*meat*] tendineux/-euse.

sinful /'sɪnfl/ *adj* [*pleasure, thought, waste*] immoral; [*world*] impie; **a ~ man** un pécheur.

sing /sɪŋ/ **I** *vtr* (*prét* **sang**; *pp* **sung**) chanter; **to ~ a role** chanter dans un rôle; **to ~ the part of** chanter dans le rôle de; **to ~ sth for sb** chanter qch pour qn; **to ~ sb to sleep** chanter pour endormir qn; **to ~ sb's praises** chanter les louanges de qn.

II *vi* (*prét* **sang**; *pp* **sung**) **1** [*person*] chanter; **to ~ in/out of tune** chanter juste/faux; **to ~ to an accompaniment** chanter avec un accompagnement; **2** [*bird, cricket, kettle*] chanter; [*wind*] siffler; **to make sb's ears ~** faire siffler les oreilles de qn; **3**○ (confess) se mettre à table○.

IDIOMS **to ~ a different** OU **another song** changer d'avis.

■ **sing out**: ¶ **~ out** (sing loud) entonner; (call out) appeler; ¶ **~ out** [*sth*] (shout) crier.

■ **sing up** chanter plus fort.

sing. *abrév écrite* = **singular**.

sing-along /'sɪŋəlɒŋ/ *n* US **to have a ~** chanter ensemble.

Singapore /ˌsɪŋə'pɔː(r)/ ▶ 1343|, 1022|, 840| *pr n* Singapour *f*; **in/to ~** à Singapour.

singe /sɪndʒ/ **I** *n* (also **~ mark**) GEN légère brûlure *f*; (from iron) roussissure *f*.

II *vtr* (*p prés* **singeing**) brûler [qch] légèrement [*hair, clothing*]; (when ironing) roussir [*clothes*].

singer /'sɪŋə(r)/ *n* chanteur/-euse *m/f*; **he's a good ~** il chante bien.

singing /'sɪŋɪŋ/ **I** *n* **1** MUS chant *m*; **to teach ~** enseigner le chant; **opera ~** chant d'opéra; **to hear ~** entendre chanter; **2** (of kettle, wind) sifflement *m*.

II *noun modifier* [*lesson*] de chant; [*career*] dans la chanson; **~ voice** voix *f*.

single /'sɪŋgl/ **I** *n* **1** (also **~ ticket**) aller *m* simple; **2** TOURISM (also **~ room**) chambre *f* à une personne; **3** MUS (record) 45 tours *m*.

II *adj* **1** (sole) seul; **a ~ rose** une seule rose; **in a ~ day** en une seule journée; **2** (not double) [*sink*] à un bac; [*unit*] simple; [*door*] à un battant; [*wardrobe*] à une porte; [*sheet, duvet*] pour une personne; **inflation is in ~ figures** ECON l'inflation est inférieure à 10%; **3** (for one) [*bed, tariff, portion*] pour une personne; **4** (unmarried) célibataire; **5** (used emphatically) **every ~ day** tous les jours sans exception; **every ~ one of those people** chacune de ces personnes; **there wasn't a ~ person there** il n'y avait absolument personne; **not a ~ thing was left** il ne restait pas la moindre chose; **6** (describing main cause, aspect) **the ~ most important factor** le facteur principal.

■ **single out**: **~** [*sb/sth*] **out**, **~ out** [*sb/sth*] [*person*] choisir; **to be ~d out for** faire l'objet de [*special treatment, praise*]; être l'objet de [*attention*]; être la proie de [*criticism*].

single: **~-breasted** *adj* [*jacket*] droit; **~ combat** *n* combat *m* singulier; **~ cream** *n* ~ crème *f* fraîche liquide; **~ currency** *n* monnaie *f* unique; **~ decker** *n* autobus *m* sans impériale; **~ file** *adv* en file indienne; **~-handedly** *adv* tout seul; **~ market** *n* marché *m* unique.

single-minded /ˌsɪŋgl'maɪndɪd/ *adj* [*determination*] farouche; [*person*] tenace, résolu; **to be ~ about doing** être résolu à faire.

single mother *n* mère *f* qui élève ses enfants seule.

single parent *n* parent *m* isolé; **~ family** famille monoparentale.

single-party /ˌsɪŋgl'pɑːtɪ/ *adj* [*government, rule*] parti unique.

singles /'sɪŋglz/ *n* **1** SPORT (event) **the women's ~** le simple dames; **2** (people) célibataires *mpl*.

singles: **~ bar** *n* bar *m* de rencontres pour célibataires; **~ charts** *npl* palmarès *m* des 45 tours.

single: **~ seater** *n* avion *m* monoplace; **~-sex** *adj* non mixte; **~-sided disk** *n* disquette *f* simple face; **~-storey** *adj* [*house*] de plain-pied.

singlet /'sɪŋglɪt/ *n* GB **1** SPORT maillot *m*; **2** (vest) maillot *m* de corps.

single-track *adj* [*line, road*] à une voie; FIG [*commitment*] entier/-ière.

singly /'sɪŋglɪ/ *adv* **1** (one by one) un à un; **2** (alone) individuellement.

singsong /'sɪŋsɒŋ/ GB **I** *n* **to have a ~** chanter ensemble.

II *adj* [*voice, dialect*] chantant.

singular /'sɪŋgjʊlə(r)/ **I** *n* LING singulier *m*; **in the ~** au singulier.

II *adj* **1** LING [*noun, verb*] au singulier; **2** (strange) singulier/-ière.

sinister /'sɪnɪstə(r)/ *adj* sinistre.

sink /sɪŋk/ **I** *n* **1** (basin) (in kitchen) évier *m*; (in bathroom) lavabo *m*; **double ~** évier à deux bacs; **2** (cesspit) LIT fosse *f* d'aisance; FIG cloaque *m*; **3** (also **~hole**) doline *f*.

II *vtr* (*prét* **sank**; *pp* **sunk**) **1** NAUT (by scuttling) couler; (by torpedo) torpiller; **2** (bore) forer [*oil well*]; creuser [*foundations*]; **3** (embed) enfoncer [*post, pillar*]; **to ~ one's teeth into** mordre à pleines dents dans [*sandwich*]; **the dog sank its teeth into my arm** le chien a planté ses crocs dans mon bras; **4**○ GB (drink) descendre○ [*drink*]; **5** SPORT mettre [qch] dans le trou [*billiard ball*]; rentrer [*putt*]; **6** (destroy) [*scandal*] faire couler [*party*]; **without capital we're sunk** sans capital nous sommes perdus; **7** (invest) **to ~ money into sth** engloutir de l'argent dans qch.

III *vi* (*prét* **sank**; *pp* **sunk**) **1** (fail to float) couler; **to ~ without a trace** FIG tomber dans les oubliettes; **2** (drop to lower level) [*sun, water level, pressure*] baisser; [*cake*] redescendre; **the sun ~s in the West** le soleil disparaît à l'ouest; **to ~ to the floor** s'effondrer; **to ~ to one's knees** tomber à genoux; **to ~ into a chair** s'affaler dans un fauteuil; **to ~ into a deep sleep** sombrer dans un profond sommeil; **3** FIG (fall) baisser; **he has sunk in my estimation** il a baissé dans mon estime; **4** (subside) [*building, wall*] s'effondrer; **to ~ into** s'enfoncer dans [*mud*]; sombrer dans [*anarchy, obscurity*]; **to ~ under the weight of** [*shelf*] plier sous le poids de [*boxes etc*]; [*person, company*] crouler sous le poids de [*debt*].

■ **sink in 1** [*lotion, water*] pénétrer; **2** FIG [*news, announcement*] faire son chemin; **it took several minutes for the truth to ~ in** il m'a fallu plusieurs minutes pour accepter la vérité.

sinker /'sɪŋkə(r)/ *n* **1** (in fishing) plomb *m*; **2** US CULIN ~ beignet *m*.

IDIOMS **he fell for the story hook, line and ~** il a gobé○ toute cette histoire.

sinking /'sɪŋkɪŋ/ **I** *n* **1** NAUT (accidental) naufrage *m*; (by torpedo) torpillage *m*; **2** (of well, shaft) forage *m*.

II *adj* [*feeling*] angoissant.

sink unit *n* évier *m* encastré.

sinner /'sɪnə(r)/ *n* pécheur/-eresse *m/f*.

sinuous /'sɪnjʊəs/ *adj* sinueux/-euse.

sinus /'saɪnəs/ *n* (*pl* **~es**) sinus *m inv*.

sinusitis /ˌsaɪnə'saɪtɪs/ ▶ 1002| *n* sinusite *f*.

sip /sɪp/ **I** *n* petite gorgée *f*.

II *vtr* (*p prés etc* **-pp-**) boire [qch] à petites gorgées.

siphon /'saɪfn/ **I** *n* siphon *m*.

II *vtr* (also **~ off**) **1** siphonner [*petrol, water*]; **2** détourner [*money*] (**out of** from de; **into** au profit de).

sir /sɜː(r)/ ▶ 937| *n* **1** (form of address) Monsieur *m*; **yes ~** GEN oui, Monsieur; (to president) oui, Monsieur le président; (to headmaster) oui, Monsieur le directeur; MIL oui, mon commandant or mon lieutenant etc; **Dear Sir** Monsieur; **2** GB **Sir James** Sir James; **3**○ US (emphatic) **yes/no ~** ça oui/non○!

sire /'saɪə(r)/ *vtr* engendrer.

siren /'saɪərən/ *n* **1** (alarm) sirène *f*; **2** MYTHOL sirène *f* ALSO FIG.

sirloin /'sɜːlɔɪn/ *n* aloyau *m*.

sirloin steak *n* biftek *m* dans l'aloyau.

sissy○ /'sɪsɪ/ **I** *n* PÉJ (coward) poule *f* mouillée○; **he's a real ~!** (effeminate) c'est une vraie fille!

II *adj* **that's a ~ game!** c'est un jeu de fille!.

sister /'sɪstə(r)/ I *n* **1** (sibling) sœur *f*; **2** GB MED infirmière *f* chef; **3** RELIG (also **Sister**) sœur *f*; **4** (fellow woman) sœur *f*.
II *noun modifier* [*company*] sœur; [*publication*] apparenté; **~ country**, **~ state** pays frère; **~ nation** nation sœur.

sisterhood /'sɪstəhʊd/ *n* **1** RELIG communauté *f* religieuse; **2** (in feminism) solidarité *f* féminine.

sister-in-law *n* (*pl* **sisters-in-law**) belle-sœur *f*.

sisterly /'sɪstəlɪ/ *adj* **1** [*feeling*] fraternel/-elle; [*rivalry*] entre sœurs; **2** [*solidarity*] féminin.

sit /sɪt/ I *vtr* (*p prés* **-tt-**; *prét*, *pp* **sat**) **1** (put) **to ~ sb in/near** asseoir qn dans/près de; **to ~ sth on/near** placer qch sur/près de; **2** GB SCH, UNIV se présenter à, passer [*exam*].
II *vi* (*p prés* **-tt-**; *prét*, *pp* **sat**) **1** (take a seat) s'asseoir; **to ~ on the floor** s'asseoir par terre; **2** (be seated) être assis; [*bird*] être perché (**on** sur); **to be ~ting reading** être assis à lire; **to ~ over** être penché sur; **to ~ for two hours** rester assis pendant deux heures; **to ~ quietly** être tranquillement assis; **to ~ still** se tenir tranquille; **to ~ at home** rester à la maison; **don't just ~ there!** ne reste pas là à ne rien faire!; **3** [*committee, court*] siéger; **4** (hold office) **to ~ as** être [*judge, magistrate*]; **to ~ on** faire partie de [*committee, jury*]; **5** (fit) **to ~ well/badly (on sb)** [*suit, jacket*] bien/mal tomber (sur qn); **power ~s lightly on her** FIG le pouvoir ne lui pèse guère; **6** (remain untouched) **the books were still ~ting on the desk** les livres étaient toujours sur le bureau; **7** AGRIC, ZOOL **to ~ on** couver [*eggs*].
IDIOMS **to make sb ~ up and take notice** faire réagir qn.
■ **sit about**, **sit around** rester assis à ne rien faire.
■ **sit back 1** (lean back) se caler dans son fauteuil; **2** (relax) se détendre; **to ~ back on one's heels** s'asseoir sur les talons.
■ **sit down**: **¶ ~ down** s'asseoir (**at** à; **in** dans; **on** sur); **to ~ down to dinner** se mettre à table; **¶ ~ [sb]** down asseoir qn; **to ~ oneself down** s'asseoir.
■ **sit in** [*observer*] assister (**on** à).
■ **sit on**○: **~ on [sth/sb]** (not deal with) garder [qch] sous le coude○.
■ **sit out**: **¶ ~ out** s'asseoir dehors; **¶ ~ [sth] out** (stay to the end) rester jusqu'à la fin de; (not take part in) ne pas jouer [*game*]; attendre la fin de [*war*].
■ **sit through**: **~ through [sth]** assister à.
■ **sit up**: **¶ ~ up 1** (raise oneself upright) se redresser; **to be ~ing up** être assis; **~ up straight!** tiens-toi droit!; **2** (stay up late) rester debout (**doing** pour faire); **to ~ up with sb** veiller qn; **¶ ~ [sb/ sth] up** redresser.

sitcom○ /'sɪtkɒm/ *n* (*abrév* = **situation comedy**) sitcom *m*.

sit-down /'sɪtdaʊn/ *n* GB **to have a ~** s'asseoir.

sit-down strike *n* grève *f* sur le tas.

site /saɪt/ I *n* **1** (also **building ~**) (before building) terrain *m*; (during building) chantier *m*; **2** (land for specific activity) terrain *m*; **caravan ~** terrain de caravaning; **3** (of building, town) emplacement *m*, site *m*; **4** (of recent event, accident) lieux *mpl*.
II *vtr* construire [*building*]; **to be ~d** être situé.

sit-in /'sɪtɪn/ *n* sit-in *m inv*, manifestation *f* avec occupation des locaux.

sitter /'sɪtə(r)/ *n* **1** ART, PHOT modèle *m*; **2** (babysitter) babysitter *mf*.

sitting /'sɪtɪŋ/ I *n* **1** (session) séance *f*; **I read it at one ~** je l'ai lu d'un seul trait; **2** (period in which food is served) service *m*; **3** (incubation period) couvaison *f*.
II *adj* **1** (seated) **in a ~ position** assis; **2** AGRIC [*hen*] couveuse *f*.

sitting: **~ duck** *n* cible *f* or victime *f* facile; **~ room** *n* salon *m*; **~ target** *n* LIT, FIG cible *f* facile; **~ tenant** *n* JUR locataire *mf* dans les lieux.

situate /'sɪtjʊeɪt, US 'sɪtʃʊeɪt/ *vtr* **1** Lit situer; **to be ~d** être situé, se trouver; FIG **to be well ~d to do** être bien placé pour faire; **2** (put in context) situer.

situation /ˌsɪtjʊ'eɪʃn, US ˌsɪtʃʊ-/ *n* **1** (set of circumstances) situation *f*; **in the present economic ~** dans la conjoncture économique or la situation économique actuelle; **in an interview ~** lors d'un entretien; **the housing ~ is worsening** la crise du logement s'aggrave; **he doesn't know how to behave in social ~s** il ne sait pas comment se conduire en société; **2** (of house, town etc) situation *f*; **3** † ou SOUT (job) situation *f*, emploi *m*; **'~s vacant'** 'offres *fpl* d'emploi'.

situation comedy *n* comédie *f* de situation.

sit-ups /'sɪtʌps/ *npl* abdominaux *mpl*.

six /sɪks/ **▶ 1112**, **713** I *n* six *m inv*.
II *adj* six *inv*.
IDIOMS **to be (all) at ~es and sevens** [*person*] ne pas savoir ou donner de la tête; [*affairs*] être sens dessus dessous; **it's ~ of one and half a dozen of the other** c'est bonnet blanc et blanc bonnet, c'est du pareil au même; **to be ~ foot under** être enterré; **knock sb for ~**○ GB laisser qn KO○.

six: **Six Counties** *pr npl* six comtés *mpl* de l'Irlande du Nord; **~-pack** *n* pack *m* de six; **~pence** *n* GB (ancienne) pièce *f* de six pence.

sixteen /ˌsɪk'stiːn/ *n*, *adj* **▶ 1112**, **713** seize (*m*) *inv*.

sixteenth /sɪk'stiːnθ/ **▶ 1112**, **854** I *n* **1** (in order) seizième *mf*; **2** (of month) seize *m inv*; **3** (fraction) seizième *m*.
II *adj*, *adv* seizième.

sixth /sɪksθ/ **▶ 1112**, **854** I *n* **1** (in order) sixième *mf*; **2** (of month) six *m inv*; **3** (fraction) sixième *m*; **4** MUS sixième *f*; **5** GB SCH **▶ sixth form**.
II *adj*, *adv* sixième.

sixth form GB SCH *n* (lower) ~ classes *fpl* de première; (upper) ~ classes *fpl* de terminale; **in the ~** en première or en terminale.

sixth: **~ form college** *n* GB SCH lycée *m* (*n'ayant que des classes de première et terminale*); **~ former** *n* ~ élève *mf* de terminale; **~ sense** *n* sixième sens *m*.

sixties /'sɪkstɪz/ **▶ 713**, **854** *npl* **1** (decade) **the ~** les années *fpl* soixante; **2** (age) **to be in one's ~** avoir entre soixante et soixante-dix ans.

sixtieth /'sɪkstɪəθ/ **▶ 1112** I *n* **1** (in order) soixantième *mf*; **2** (fraction) soixantième *m*.
II *adj*, *adv* soixantième.

sixty /'sɪkstɪ/ **▶ 1112**, **713** *n*, *adj* soixante (*m*) *inv*.

size /saɪz/ **▶ 1260** I *n* **1** (dimensions) (of person, head, tree, envelope, picture) taille *f*; (of container, room, building, region) grandeur *f*; (of apple, egg, book, parcel) grosseur *f*; (of carpet, bed, machine) dimensions *fpl*; **it's about the ~ of an egg/of this room** c'est à peu près de la grosseur d'un œuf/de la grandeur de cette pièce; **he's about your ~** il est à peu près de ta taille; **to increase in ~** [*tree*] pousser; [*company, town*] s'agrandir; **to cut sth to ~** découper qch à la dimension voulue; **to be of a ~** [*people, boxes*] être de la même taille; **2** (number) (of population, audience) importance *f*; (of class, school, company) effectif *m*; **3** (of garment) taille *f*; (of collar) encolure *f*; (of shoes, gloves) pointure *f*; **what ~ do you take?** (in clothes) quelle taille faites-vous?; (in shoes) quelle pointure faites-vous?, vous chaussez du combien?; **to take ~ X** (in clothes) faire du X; (in shoes) chausser or faire du X; **'one ~'** 'taille unique'; **try this for ~** LIT essayez ceci pour voir si c'est votre taille; FIG essayez ceci pour voir si cela vous convient; **4** (substance) (for paper, textiles) apprêt *m*; (for plaster) colle *f*.
II *vtr* **1** classer [qch] selon la grosseur [*eggs, fruit*]; **2** TECH apprêter [*textile, paper*]; encoller [*plaster*]; **3** COMPUT dimensionner [*window*].
IDIOMS **that's about the ~ of it!** c'est à peu près ça!; **to cut sb down to ~** remettre qn à sa place.
■ **size up**: **~ up [sb/sth]**, **~ [sb/sth] up** se faire une opinion de [*person*]; évaluer [qch] du regard [*surroundings*]; évaluer [*situation*]; mesurer [*problem*].

sizeable /'saɪzəbl/ *adj* [*proportion*] non négligeable; [*amount, fortune*] assez important; [*house, field, town*] assez grand; **to have a ~ majority** être largement majoritaire.

sizzle /'sɪzl/ *vi* grésiller.

Sizes

In the following tables of equivalent sizes, French sizes have been rounded up, where necessary. (It is always better to have clothes a little too big than a little too tight.)

Men's shoe sizes

in UK & US	in France
6½	39
7	40
7½	41
8½	42
9	43
10	44
11	45
12	46

Women's shoe sizes

In UK	in US	in France
3	6	35
3½	6½	36
4	7	37
5	7½	38
6	8	39
7	8½	40
8	9	41

Men's clothing sizes

in UK & US	in France
28	38
30	40
32	42
34	44
36	46
38	48
40	50
42	52
44	54
46	56

Women's clothing sizes

In UK	in US	in France
8	4	34
10	6	36
12	8	38–40
14	10	42
16	12	44–46
18	14	48
20	16	50

Note that for shoe and sock sizes French uses pointure, *so a size 37 is* une pointure 37. *For all other types of garment (even stockings and tights) the word* taille *is used, so a size 16 shirt is* une chemise taille 40, *etc.*

Men's shirt collar sizes

in UK & US	in France	in UK & US	in France
14	36	16½	41
14½	37	17	42
15	38	17½	43
15½	39	18	44
16	40		

what size are you?	= quelle taille faites-vous? *or* quelle pointure faites-vous?
I take size 40 (*in clothes*)	= je prends du 40 *or* je fais du 40
I take size 7 (*in shoes*)	= je chausse du 40 *or* je fais du 40
my collar size is 15	= je porte un 38 *or* je porte du 38
I'm looking for collar size 16	= je cherche un 40
his shoe size is 39	= il chausse du 39
a pair of shoes size 39	= une paire de chaussures pointure 39
have you got the same thing in a 16?	= avez-vous ce modèle en 40?
have you got this in a smaller size?	= avez-vous ce modèle dans une plus petite taille (*or* pointure)? *or* avez-vous ce modèle en plus petit?
have you got this in a larger size?	= avez-vous ce modèle dans une plus grande taille (*or* pointure)? *or* avez-vous ce modèle en plus grand?
they haven't got my size	= ils n'ont pas ma taille (*or* ma pointure)

sizzling /'sızlıŋ/ *adj* [*fat, sausage*] qui grésille; **a ~ sound** un grésillement.

skate /skeıt/ **I** *n* **1** (ice) patin *m* à glace; (roller) patin *m* à roulettes; **2** (fish) raie *f*.
II *vi* patiner (**on, along** sur); **to ~ across** ou **over** traverser [qch] en patins [*pond, lake*].
IDIOMS **get your ~s on**○! grouille-toi○!; **to be skating on thin ice** s'aventurer sur un terrain glissant.

skate: **~board** *n* skateboard *m*, planche *f* à roulettes; **~boarder** *n* skateur/-euse *m/f*; **~boarding ▶ 949** *n* skateboard *m*, planche *f* à roulettes.

skater /'skeıtə(r)/ *n* patineur/-euse *m/f*.

skating /'skeıtıŋ/ ▶ 949 *n* patinage *m*; **to go ice ~** faire du patin à glace.

skating: **~ boots** *npl* GB patins *mpl* à glace; **~ rink** *n* (ice) patinoire *f*; (roller-skating) piste *f* de patins à roulettes.

skein /skeın/ *n* (of wool) écheveau *m*.

skeletal /'skelıtl/ *adj* ANAT, FIG squelettique.

skeletal code *n* COMPUT séquence *f* paramétrable.

skeleton /'skelıtn/ **I** *n* ANAT, CONSTR squelette *m*; (of plan, novel) grandes lignes *fpl*.
II *noun modifier* FIG [*staff*] réduit au strict minimum.
IDIOMS **to have a ~ in the cupboard** GB ou **closet** US avoir un cadavre dans le placard○.

skeleton key *n* passe-partout *m inv*.

skeptic *n*, *adj* US = **sceptic**.

skeptical *adj* US = **sceptical**.

skeptically *adv* US = **sceptically**.

skepticism *n* US = **scepticism**.

sketch /sketʃ/ **I** *n* **1** (drawing, draft) esquisse *f*; (hasty outline) croquis *m*; **rough ~** ébauche *f*; **2** (comic scene) sketch *m*; **3** (brief account) aperçu *m*; **a character ~ of sb** une ébauche du personnage de qn.
II *vtr* **1** (make drawing of) faire une esquisse de; (hastily) faire un croquis de; **2** (describe briefly) ébaucher.
III *vi* (as art, hobby) faire des esquisses.
■ **sketch in**: **~ in** [sth], **~** [sth] **in** (by drawing) ajouter l'esquisse de; FIG (by describing) donner un aperçu de.

sketch: **~book** *n* (for sketching) carnet *m* à croquis; (book of sketches) carnet *m* de croquis; **~pad** *n* bloc *m* à dessin.

sketchy /'sketʃı/ *adj* [*information, details*] insuffisant; [*memory*] vague; [*work*] rapide.

skew /skju:/ **I** *n* **on the ~** de travers.
II *vtr* **1** (distort) fausser [*result, survey*]; (deliberately) déformer [*result*]; **2** (angle) incliner [*object*].
III *vi* (also **~ round**) [*vehicle, ship*] obliquer.

skewer /'skju:ə(r)/ **I** *n* (for kebab) brochette *f*; (for joint) broche *f*.
II *vtr* embrocher [*joint*]; mettre [qch] en brochette [*chicken pieces*].

ski /ski:/ **I** *n* **1** SPORT (for snow) ski *m*; (for water) ski *m* (nautique); **cross-country ~s** skis *mpl* de fond; **downhill ~s** skis *mpl* alpins; **on ~s** à ski; **2** AVIAT patin *m*.
II *vi* (*prét, pp* **ski'd** ou **skied**) (as hobby) faire du ski; (move on skis) skier; **to ~ down a slope** descendre une pente à skis.

ski binding *n* fixation *f* (de ski).

ski boot /ski:/ *n* chaussure *f* de ski.

skid /skıd/ **I** *n* **1** (of car etc) dérapage *m*; **to correct a ~** redresser or contrôler un dérapage; **2** FIG (of prices) dérapage *m*; **3** (to help move sth) traîneau *m*.
II *vi* (*p prés etc* **-dd-**) déraper (**on** sur); **to ~ off the road** déraper et sortir de la route; **to ~ across the floor** glisser sur le sol; **to ~ to a halt** [*vehicle*] s'arrêter dans un dérapage.
IDIOMS **to put the ~s under sb** (undermine) faire échouer qn; (pressurize) obliger qn à faire vite.

skid mark /skıd/ *n* trace *f* de pneus.

skier /'ski:ə(r)/ *n* skieur/-euse *m/f*.

skies /skaız/ *pl* ▶ **sky**.

skiff /skıf/ *n* GEN petite embarcation *f* légère; (working boat) youyou *m*.

skiing /'ski:ıŋ/ ▶ 949 *n* ski *m*; **to go ~** faire du ski; **cross country ~** ski *m* de fond; **downhill ~** ski *m* alpin.

skiing: **~ holiday** *n* vacances *fpl* de neige; **~ instructor ▶ 1251** *n* moniteur/-trice *m/f* de ski.

ski jump I *n* **1** (jump) saut *m* à skis; **2** (ramp) tremplin *m* (de ski).
II *vi* faire du saut à skis.

ski jumping ▶ 949 *n* saut *m* à skis.

skilful GB, **skillful** US /'skılfl/ *adj* **1** (clever) [*person*] habile, adroit; [*portrayal*] excellent; **~ at sth** habile en qch; ~ **at doing** habile à faire; ~ **with his hands** adroit de ses mains; **2** (requiring talent) [*operation*] délicat.

skilfully GB, **skillfully** US /ˈskɪlfəlɪ/ *adv* **1** (with ability) [*play, write*] habilement; [*written*] de façon habile; **2** (with agility) adroitement.

skilfulness GB, **skillfulness** US /ˈskɪlflnɪs/ *n* (mental) habileté *f* (**at doing** à faire); (physical) adresse *f*.

ski lift *n* remontée *f* mécanique.

skill /skɪl/ I *n* **1** ¢ (flair) (intellectual) habileté *f*, adresse *f*; (physical) dextérité *f*; ~ **at** habileté or adresse à; ~ **at doing** habileté à faire; **to have** ~ être doué; **with** ~ avec talent; **2** C (special ability) (acquired) compétence *f*, capacités *fpl*; (innate) aptitude *f*; (practical) technique *f*; (gift) talent *m*; **your** ~**(s)** as vos talents de [*linguist, politician, mechanic*]; ~ **at** ou **in doing** talent à faire; ~ **at** ou **in sth** compétence en qch.
II **skills** *npl* (training) connaissances *fpl*.

skilled /skɪld/ *adj* **1** (trained) [*labour, work*] qualifié; **semi-**~ spécialisé; **2** (talented) [*actor, negotiator*] consommé; **to be** ~ **as** avoir des talents de [*writer, diplomat*]; **to be** ~ **at doing** savoir faire.

skillet /ˈskɪlɪt/ *n* poêle *f* (à frire).

skillful *adj* US ▶ **skilful**.

skillfully *adv* US ▶ **skilfully**.

skillfulness *n* US ▶ **skilfulness**.

skim /skɪm/ I *vtr* (*p prés etc* -**mm-**) **1** (remove cream) écrémer; (remove scum) écumer; (remove fat) dégraisser; **2** (touch lightly) [*plane, bird*] raser, frôler [*surface, treetops*]; **it only** ~**s the surface of the problem** ça ne fait qu'effleurer le problème; **3** (read quickly) parcourir; **4**° US FIN ne pas déclarer [*part of income*].
II *vi* (*p prés etc* -**mm-**) **1** [*plane, bird*] **to** ~ **over** ou **across** ou **along sth** raser qch; **2** [*reader*] **to** ~ **through** ou **over sth** parcourir qch; **to** ~ **over** passer rapidement sur [*event, facts*].

ski mask *n* cagoule *f* de ski.

skim milk, **skimmed milk** *n* lait *m* écrémé.

skimp /skɪmp/ *vi* **to** ~ **on** lésiner sur [*expense, food, materials*]; économiser [*effort*].

skimpily /ˈskɪmpɪlɪ/ *adv* [*work, make*] à la va-vite; [*stocked*] maigrement; ~ **dressed** en tenue minimale.

skimpy /ˈskɪmpɪ/ *adj* [*garment*] minuscule; [*portion, allowance, income*] maigre (*before n*); [*work*] maigre.

skin /skɪn/ I *n* **1** (of person) peau *f*; **2** (of animal) peau *f*; **leopard** ~ peau de léopard; **3** CULIN (of fruit, vegetable, sausage) peau *f*; (of onion) pelure *f*; **remove the** ~ éplucher; **4** (on hot milk, cocoa) peau *f*.
II *vtr* (*p prés etc* -**nn-**) **1** CULIN dépecer [*animal*]; **2** (graze) **to** ~ **one's knee** s'écorcher le genou.
IDIOMS **I've got you under my** ~ je t'ai dans la peau°; **to have a thick** ~ être insensible; **to jump out of one's** ~ sauter au plafond°; **to be** ou **get soaked to the** ~ être trempé jusqu'aux os°; **it's no** ~ **off my nose** ou **back**° je m'en balance°; **to keep one's eyes** ~**ned** rester attentif or vigilant; **by the** ~ **of one's teeth** de justesse.

skin: ~ **cancer** ▶ **1002** *n* cancer *m* de la peau; ~ **care** *n* ¢ soins *mpl* pour la peau; ~ **cream** *n* crème *f* pour la peau; ~**-deep** *adj* superficiel/-ielle; ~ **disease** *n* maladie *f* de peau; ~ **diver** *n* plongeur/-euse *m/f*; ~ **diving** ▶ **949** *n* plongée *f* sous-marine; ~**flint** *n* radin/-e° *m/f*.

skin graft *n* **1** (also ~ **grafting**) greffe *f* de la peau; **2** (grafted area) greffon *m* de peau.

skinhead *n* GB (youth) skinhead *m*.

skinny° /ˈskɪnɪ/ *adj* maigre.

skinny-ribbed sweater *n* pull-chaussette *m*.

skint° /skɪnt/ *adj* GB fauché°.

skin: ~ **test** *n* cuti-réaction *f*; ~**tight** *adj* moulant.

skip /skɪp/ I *n* **1** (jump) petit bond *m*; **2** GB (rubbish container) benne *f*.
II *vtr* (*p prés etc* -**pp-**) **1** (not attend) sauter [*meeting, lunch, school*]; **2** (leave out) sauter [*pages, chapter*]; **to** ~ **the formalities** sauter les formalités; ~ **it°!** laisse tomber!; **3**° (leave) **to** ~ **town** filer° de la ville.
III *vi* (*p prés etc* -**pp-**) **1** (jump) (once) bondir; (several

times) sautiller; **2** (with rope) sauter à la corde; **3** (travel, move) **she** ~**ped from Paris to Lyons** elle a fait un saut de Paris à Lyon; **to** ~ **from one chapter to another** sauter d'un chapitre à l'autre.

ski: ~ **pants** *n* fuseau *m* (de ski); ~ **pass** *n* forfait-skieur *m*.

skipjack /ˈskɪpdʒæk/ *n* (also ~ **tuna**) (canned) ≈ thon *m* blanc.

ski: ~ **plane** *n* avion *m* à skis; ~ **pole** *n* = **ski stick**.

skipper /ˈskɪpə(r)/ *n* **1** NAUT (of merchant ship) capitaine *m*; (of fishing boat) patron *m*; (of yacht) skipper *m*; **2** GEN (leader) chef *m*.

skipping /ˈskɪpɪŋ/ ▶ **949** *n* saut *m* à la corde.

skipping rope *n* corde *f* à sauter.

ski: ~ **racer** *n* skieur/-euse *m/f* alpin/-e; ~ **racing** ▶ **949** *n* ski *m* alpin; ~ **rack** *n* porte-skis *m inv*; ~ **resort** *n* station *f* de ski.

skirl /skɜːl/ *n* son *m* aigu (de la cornemuse).

skirmish /ˈskɜːmɪʃ/ *n* **1** (fight) GEN accrochage *m*; MIL escarmouche *f*; **2** (argument) prise *f* de bec°.

skirt /skɜːt/ ▶ **949** I *n* **1** (garment, of dress) jupe *f*; (of frock coat) basques *fpl*; **2** (of vehicle, machine) jupe *f*; **3**° (woman) minette° *f*.
II *vtr* contourner [*wood, city*]; esquiver [*problem*].
IDIOMS **to cling to one's mother's** ~**s** s'accrocher aux jupes de sa mère.

■ **skirt round**, **skirt around:** ~ **round** [sth] contourner.

skirting board *n* plinthe *f*.

skirt length *n* (piece of fabric) hauteur *f* de jupe; ~**s vary** la longueur des jupes varie.

ski: ~ **run** *n* piste *f* de ski; ~ **slope** *n* piste *f*; ~ **stick** *n* bâton *m* de ski; ~ **suit** *n* combinaison *f* de ski.

skit /skɪt/ *n* (parody) parodie *f* (**on** de); (sketch) sketch *m* (satirique) (**on, about** sur).

ski: ~ **touring** ▶ **949** *n* randonnée *f* à skis; ~ **tow** *n* téléski *m*.

skittish /ˈskɪtɪʃ/ *adj* **1** (difficult to handle) capricieux/-ieuse; **2** (playful) joueur/-euse.

skittle /ˈskɪtl/ ▶ **949** I *n* quille *f*.
II **skittles** *npl* (jeu *m* de) quilles *fpl*.

skive° /skaɪv/ *vtr* GB (also ~ **off**) **1** (shirk) tirer au flanc°; **2** (be absent) (from school) sécher l'école°; (from work) ne pas aller au boulot°; **3** (leave early) se tirer°.

skivvy /ˈskɪvɪ/ *n*° GB LIT, FIG bonne *f* à tout faire.

ski wax *n* fart *m*.

skulduggery /skʌlˈdʌɡərɪ/ *n* ¢ magouille° *f*.

skulk /skʌlk/ *vi* rôder; **to** ~ **out/off** sortir/s'éloigner furtivement.

skull /skʌl/ *n* **1** ANAT crâne *m*; **2**° (brain) crâne *m*.

skull: ~ **and crossbones** *n* (emblem) tête *f* de mort; (flag) pavillon *m* à tête de mort; ~ **cap** *n* (Catholic) calotte *f*; (Jewish) kippa *f*.

skunk /skʌŋk/ I *n* ZOOL moufette *f*; (fur) sconse *m*.
II *vtr* (defeat) battre [qn] à plates coutures° [*team, opponent*].

sky /skaɪ/ I *n* ciel *m*; **clear** ~ ciel dégagé; **open** ~ ciel dégagé; **in(to) the** ~ dans le ciel; **the** ~ **over Paris** le ciel de Paris; **a patch of blue** ~ une trouée de ciel bleu; **there are blue skies ahead** FIG il y a une éclaircie à l'horizon.
II **skies** *npl* METEOROL ciel *m*; FIG, LITTÉR cieux *mpl*; ART ciels *mpl*; **summer skies** ciel d'été; **a day of rain and cloudy skies** un jour pluvieux et couvert; **to take to the skies** [*plane*] décoller.
IDIOMS **the** ~**'s the limit** tout est possible; **reach for the** ~°! haut les mains!

sky: ~**-blue** ▶ **818** *n, adj* bleu (*m*) ciel *inv*; ~**cap** *n* US porteur *m* (*dans un aéroport*); ~**diver** *n* parachutiste *mf* (en chute libre); ~**diving** ▶ **949** *n* parachutisme *m* (en chute libre).

sky-high /ˌskaɪˈhaɪ/ I *adj* [*prices, rates*] exorbitant.
II *adv* **to rise** ~ monter en flèche; **to blow sth** ~ faire voler qch en éclats.

sky: **~jacker**○ *n* pirate *m* de l'air; **~lark** *n* alouette *f* des champs; **~larking**○ *n* chahut *m*; **~light** *n* fenêtre *f* à tabatière; **~line** *n* (in country-side) ligne *f* d'horizon; (in city) ligne *f* des toits.

skyrocket /'skaɪrɒkɪt/ **I** *n* fusée *f*.
II *vi* [*price, inflation*] monter en flèche.

skyscraper *n* gratte-ciel *m inv.*

sky: **~ train** *n* aérotrain *m*; **~ways** *npl* US AVIAT couloirs *mpl* aériens; **~writing** *n* publicité *f* tracée dans le ciel (*par un avion*).

S & L *n* US *abrév* ▶ **savings and loan (association)**.

slab /slæb/ *n* **1** (piece) (of stone, wood, concrete) dalle *f*; (of meat, cheese, cake) pavé *m*; (of ice) plaque *f*; (of chocolate) tablette *f*; **fishmonger's** ~ étal *m* de poissonnier; **2**○ (operating table) billard○ *m*, table *f* d'opération; (mortuary table) table *f* d'autopsie.

slack /slæk/ **I** *n* **1** LIT (in rope, cable) mou *m*; **to take up the ~ in a rope** tendre une corde; **to take up the ~** FIG (take over) prendre le relais; **2** FIG (in schedule etc) marge *f*; **3** (coal) poussier *m*.
II slacks *npl* pantalon *m*; **a pair of ~s** un pantalon.
III *adj* **1** (careless) [*worker*] peu consciencieux/-ieuse; [*management*] négligent; [*student*] peu appliqué; [*work*] peu soigné; **to be ~ about doing** négliger de faire; **to get ~** [*worker, discipline, surveillance*] se relâcher; **2** (not busy) [*period*] creux/creuse (*after n*); [*demand, sales*] faible; **business is ~** les affaires tournent au ralenti; **3** (loose, limp) détendu; **to go ~** se détendre.
IV *vi* [*worker*] se relâcher dans son travail.
■ **slack off** [*business, trade*] diminuer; [*rain*] se calmer.

slacken /'slækən/ **I** *vtr* **1** (release) donner du mou à [*rope, cable*]; lâcher [*reins*]; relâcher [*grip, pressure*]; desserrer [*nut*]; **2** (reduce) réduire [*pace*]; **3** (loosen) assouplir [*control*].
II *vi* **1** (loosen) [*grip, pressure, rope*] se relâcher; [*nut, bolt*] se desserrer; **his grip on the rope ~ed** il a relâ-ché sa prise sur la corde; **2** (ease off) [*activity, pace, speed, business*] ralentir; [*pressure, interest*] diminuer; [*rain, gale*] se calmer.
■ **slacken off** = **slack off.**

slackening /'slækənɪŋ/ *n* (of grip, discipline, skin) relâ-chement *m*; (of pace, business, economy) ralentissement *m*; (of tension) diminution *f*.

slacker /'slækə(r)/ *n* GEN fainéant/-e *m/f*, tire-au-flanc○ *m inv.*

slackness /'slæknɪs/ *n* (of worker) laisser-aller *m inv*; (in trade, economy) stagnation *f*; (in discipline, security) relâ-chement *m*.

slag /slæg/ *n* ¢ (from coal) GB stériles *mpl*; (from metal) scories *fpl*; **~ heap** terril *m*.

slain /sleɪn/ *pp* ▶ **slay**.

slake /sleɪk/ *vtr* LIT étancher [*thirst*]; FIG assouvir.

slalom /'slɑːləm/ ▶ **949**] *n* slalom *m*.

slam /slæm/ **I** *n* **1** (of door) claquement *m*; **2** GAMES chelem *m*.
II *vtr* (*p prés etc* **-mm-**) **1** (shut loudly) [*person*] claquer [*door*]; [*wind*] faire claquer [*door*]; **to ~ sth shut** fermer brutalement qch; **to ~ the door behind one** sortir en claquant la porte derrière soi; **to ~ the door in sb's face** LIT, FIG claquer la porte au nez de qn; **2** (with violence) **to ~ one's fist on the table** taper du poing sur la table; **to ~ sb into a wall** jeter qn contre le mur; **to ~ on the brakes**○ freiner à mort○; **3**○ (criticize) critiquer [qn] violemment; **4**○ (defeat) écraser.
III *vi* (*p prés etc* **-mm-**) **1** [*door*] claquer (**against** contre); **to ~ shut** se refermer en claquant; **2 to ~ into sth** [*vehicle*] s'écraser contre qch; [*boxer, body*] heurter violemment qch.
■ **slam down**: ¶ **~ down** [*heavy object*] s'écraser (**onto** sur); ¶ **~ down** [sth], **~** [sth] **down** raccro-cher violemment [*phone*]; refermer violemment [*lid, car bonnet*]; jeter brutalement [*object*] (**on, onto** sur).

slammer○ /'slæmə(r)/ *n* **the ~** la taule○.

slander /'slɑːndə(r), US 'slæn-/ **I** *n* **1** (statement) calomnie *f*; **2 ¢** JUR diffamation *f* orale; **to sue sb for ~** intenter un procès en diffamation contre qn.
II *vtr* GEN calomnier; JUR diffamer.

slanderous /'slɑːndərəs, US 'slæn-/ *adj* GEN calomnieux/-ieuse; JUR diffamatoire.

slang /slæŋ/ *n* argot *m*; **army ~** argot militaire.

slanging match *n* GB prise *f* de bec.

slangy○ /'slæŋɪ/ *adj* [*style*] argotique.

slant /slɑːnt, US slænt/ **I** *n* **1** (perspective) point *m* de vue (**on** sur); **with a European ~** d'un point de vue européen; **to give a new ~ on sth** offrir un angle nouveau sur qch; **2** PÉJ (bias) tendance *f*; **3** (slope) pente *f*; **4** (in printing) barre *f* oblique.
II *vtr* **1** (twist) présenter [qch] avec parti pris [*story, facts*]; **2** (lean) incliner [*object*].
III *vi* **1** [*floor, ground*] être en pente; [*handwriting*] pencher (**to** vers); [*painting*] être de travers.
IV slanting *pres p adj* [*roof*] en pente; **~ing eyes** yeux *mpl* bridés.

slanted /'slɑːntɪd, US 'slæn-/ *adj* **1** (biased) orienté (**to, towards** vers); **2** (sloping) en pente.

slantwise /'slɑːntwaɪz, US 'slæn-/ *adv* (also **slant-ways**) en biais.

slap /slæp/ **I** *n* **1** (blow) tape *f* (**on** sur); (stronger) claque *f* (**on** sur); **a ~ on the face** une gifle; **it was a real ~ in the face for him** FIG il a reçu une claque; **to give sb a ~ on the back** FIG (in congratulation) félici-ter qn; **2** (sound of blow) (bruit *m* d'une) claque *f*.
II *adv* = **slap bang.**
III *vtr* (*p prés etc* **-pp-**) **1** (hit) donner une tape à [*person, animal*]; **to ~ sb for/for doing** gifler qn pour/pour avoir fait; **to ~ sb on the leg, to ~ sb's leg** donner une tape à qn sur la jambe; **to ~ sb on the back** (in friendly way) donner une (grande) claque or tape dans le dos de qn; FIG (congratulate) féliciter qn; **to ~ sb in the face** LIT gifler qn; **to ~ sb on the wrist** FIG taper sur les doigts de qn; **2** (put) **he ~ped the money (down) on the table** il a flanqué○ l'argent sur la table; **she ~ped some make-up on her face** elle s'est maquillée en vitesse; **they ~ped○ 50p on the price** ils ont gonflé○ le prix de 50 pence.
■ **slap down**: ¶ **to ~ sth down on** flanquer○ qch sur [*table, counter*]; ¶ **~** [sb] **down** rembarrer.

slap bang○ /,slæp'bæŋ/ *adv* **he ran ~ into the wall** il s'est cogné en plein dans le mur en courant; **~ in the middle (of)** au beau milieu (de).

slapdash /'slæpdæʃ/ *adj* [*person*] brouillon/-onne○; [*work*] bâclé○, fait à la va-vite; **in a ~ way** à la va-vite.

slapstick /'slæpstɪk/ *n* comique *m* tarte à la crème, slapstick *m.*

slap-up○ /'slæpʌp/ *adj* GB **a ~ meal** un bon gueule-ton○.

slash /slæʃ/ **I** *n* **1** (wound) balafre *f* (**on** à); **2** (cut) (in fabric, seat, tyre) lacération *f*; (in painting, wood) entaille *f*; **3** (in printing) barre *f* oblique; **4** COMM, FIN réduction *f*; **a 10% ~ in prices** une réduction de 10% sur les prix; **5** (in skirt) fente *f*; (in sleeve) crevé *m.*
II *vtr* **1** (wound) balafrer [*cheek*]; faire une balafre à [*person*]; couper [*throat*]; entailler [*face*]; **to ~ one's wrists** se tailler les veines; **2** (cut) taillader [*painting, fabric, tyres*]; trancher [*cord*]; **to ~ one's way through** se tailler un chemin à travers [*under-growth*]; **3** (reduce) réduire [qch] (considérablement), sacrifier [*price*]; réduire [qch] (considérablement) [*amount, spending, size*]; **to ~ 40% off the price** ré-duire le prix de 40%; **4** (in dressmaking) fendre [*skirt*].
III *vi* **to ~ at** cingler [*grass*]; frapper [qch] d'un grand coup [*ball*]; **to ~ through** trancher [*cord*]; tail-lader [*fabric*].

slasher film○, **slasher movie**○ US *n* film *m* d'horreur sanglant.

slat /slæt/ *n* **1** (of shutter, blind) lamelle *f*; (of table, bench, bed) lame *f*; **2** AVIAT bec *m* de sécurité.

slate /sleɪt/ **I** *n* **1** (rock) ardoise *f*; **made of ~** en ardoise; **2** (piece, tablet) ardoise *f*; **a roof ~** une ardoise; **3** US POL liste *f* de candidature.
II *vtr* **1** LIT couvrir [qch] d'ardoises [*roof*]; **2**○ GB (criti-

cize) [*press, critic*] taper sur○ [*film, politician, policy*] (**for** pour); **3** US POL mettre [qn] sur la liste [*candidate*].
IDIOMS **to put sth on the ~**○ mettre qch sur l'ardoise○; **to wipe the ~ clean** faire table rase.

slate: **~ blue ▶ 818 |** *n, adj* bleu (*m*) ardoise *inv*; **~ grey** GB, **~ gray** US **▶ 818 |** *n, adj* gris (*m*) ardoise *inv*.

slater /'sleɪtə(r)/ **▶ 1251 |** *n* **1** (roofer) couvreur-ardoisier *m*; **2** (quarrier) ardoisier *m*; **3** ZOOL cloporte *m*.

slating /'sleɪtɪŋ/ *n* **1** (laying slates) pose *f* des ardoises; **2**○ GB (criticism) **to get a ~ from sb** se faire démolir par qn○.

slatted /'slætɪd/ *adj* [*table*] en lames; [*shutter*] à lamelles.

slaughter /'slɔːtə(r)/ **I** *n* **1** (in butchery) abattage *m*; **to go to ~** aller à l'abattoir; **2** (massacre) massacre *m*, boucherie *f*; (road deaths) carnage *m*.
II *vtr* **1** (in butchery) abattre; **2** (massacre) massacrer; **3**○ FIG (defeat) écraser.
IDIOMS **like a lamb to the ~** comme un agneau à l'abattoir.

slaughterhouse /'slɔːtəhaʊs/ *n* abattoir *m*.

Slav /slɑːv, US slæv/ **I** *n* Slave *mf*.
II *adj* slave.

slave /sleɪv/ **I** *n* **1** (servant) esclave *mf*; **2** FIG **to be a ~ to** ou **of** être l'esclave de [*fashion*]; **a ~ to convention** l'esclave des conventions.
II *noun modifier* **1** [*colony*] d'esclaves; [*market*] aux esclaves; **2** COMPUT asservi.
III *vi* (also **~ away**) travailler comme un forçat, trimer○; **to ~ (away) at housework** s'escrimer à faire le ménage.

slave: **~ driver** *n* LIT HIST surveillant *m* d'esclaves; FIG négrier/-ière *m*/*f* FIG; **~ labour** *n* (activity) travail *m* de forçat; (manpower) main-d'œuvre *f* esclave.

slaver /'slævə(r)/ **I** *n* salive *f*.
II *vi* (drool) baver; **to ~ over** [*animal*] saliver devant; PÉJ ou HUM [*person*] baver devant.

slavery /'sleɪvərɪ/ *n* **1** (practice, condition) esclavage *m*; **to be sold into ~** être vendu comme esclave; **2** FIG **~ to** asservissement à [*fashion*].

slave ship *n* (vaisseau *m*) négrier *m*.

slave trade *n* commerce *m* des esclaves; **the African ~** la traite des Noirs.

slave-trader *n* marchand *m* d'esclaves, PÉJ négrier *m*.

slavish /'sleɪvɪʃ/ *adj* (all contexts) servile.

slavishly /'sleɪvɪʃlɪ/ *adv* servilement.

slaw /slɔː/ *n* US = **coleslaw**.

slay /sleɪ/ *vtr* (*prét* **slew**; *pp* **slain**) LITTÉR (kill) faire périr [*enemy*]; pourfendre [*dragon*].

SLD GB POL *n* (*abrév* = **Social and Liberal Democrat**) parti *m* Démocrate Socio-Libéral.

sleaze○ /sliːz/ *n* PÉJ (pornography) pornographie *f*; (corruption) corruption *f*.

sleazy○ /'sliːzɪ/ *adj* PÉJ [*club, area, character*] louche; [*story, aspect*] scabreux/-euse; [*café, hotel*] borgne.

sled /sled/ **I** *n* luge *f*; (pulled) traîneau *m*.
II *vi* (*p prés etc* **-dd-**) faire de la luge; **to go ~ding** faire de la luge.

sledge /sledʒ/ **I** *n* **1** GB luge *f*; **2** (pulled) traîneau *m*.
II *vi* GB faire de la luge; **to go sledging** faire de la luge.

sledgehammer /'sledʒhæmə(r)/ *n* masse *f*.

sleek /sliːk/ *adj* **1** (glossy) [*hair*] lisse et brillant; [*animal*] au poil lisse et brillant; **2** (smooth) [*elegance*] raffiné; [*shape*] élégant; [*figure*] mince et harmonieux/-ieuse; **3** (prosperous-looking) à l'air cossu.

sleep /sliːp/ **I** *n* sommeil *m*; **to go** ou **get to ~** s'endormir; **to go back to ~** se rendormir; **to send** ou **put sb to ~** endormir qn; **to get some ~** ou **to have a ~** GEN dormir; (have a nap) faire un petit somme; **my leg has gone to ~**○ j'ai la jambe engourdie; **I didn't get any ~** ou **a wink of ~ last night** j'ai passé une nuit blanche, je n'ai pas fermé

l'œil de la nuit; **I need my ~** il me faut beaucoup de sommeil; **to have a good night's ~** passer une bonne nuit, bien dormir; **to rock a baby to ~** bercer un bébé jusqu'à ce qu'il s'endorme; **to walk in one's ~** marcher en dormant; **I could do it in my ~**! je pourrais le faire les yeux fermés!; **she's losing ~ over it** ça l'empêche de dormir; **don't lose any ~ over it!** ne t'en fais pas pour ça!; **to put an animal to ~** EUPH faire piquer un animal.
II *vtr* (*prét, pp* **slept**) **the house ~s six (people)** on peut loger ou coucher six personnes dans la maison.
III *vi* (*prét, pp* **slept**) **1** dormir; **to ~ soundly** (deeply) dormir profondément, dormir à poings fermés; (without worry) dormir tranquille, dormir sur ses deux oreilles; **to ~ on one's feet** dormir debout; **~ tight!** dors bien!; **2** (stay night) **to ~ at a friend's house** coucher chez un ami; **to ~ with sb** EUPH (have sex) coucher avec qn.
IDIOMS **the big ~** le sommeil des morts; **to cry oneself to ~** pleurer jusqu'à épuisement; **to ~ like a log** ou **top** dormir comme une souche ou un loir; **to ~ it off**○ cuver son vin○.
■ **sleep around**○ coucher à droite et à gauche○.
■ **sleep in** (stay in bed late) faire la grasse matinée; (oversleep) dormir trop tard.
■ **sleep on** continuer à dormir; **to ~ on a decision** attendre le lendemain pour prendre une décision; **I'd like to ~ on it** je préférerais dormir dessus.
■ **sleep out** dormir ou coucher à la belle étoile.
■ **sleep over**: **to ~ over at sb's house** passer la nuit ou coucher chez qn.

sleeper /'sliːpə(r)/ **I** *n* **1** dormeur/-euse *m*/*f*; **to be a sound ~** avoir le sommeil profond; **2** RAIL (berth) couchette *f*; (sleeping car) wagon-lit *m*, voiture-lit *f*; (train) train-couchettes *m*; **3** GB (on railway track) traverse *f*; **4** GB (earring) dormeuse *f*; **5**○ US (successful book, film etc) succès *m* à retardement; **6** (spy) espion/-ionne *m*/*f* en sommeil.
II sleepers *npl* US grenouillère *f*.

sleepily /'sliːpɪlɪ/ *adv* d'un ton or d'un air endormi.

sleeping /'sliːpɪŋ/ *adj* qui dort, endormi.
IDIOMS **let ~ dogs lie** il ne faut pas réveiller le chat qui dort.

sleeping: **~ bag** *n* sac *m* de couchage; **~ car** *n* voiture-lit *f*, wagon-lit *m*; **~ partner** *n* GB COMM commanditaire *mf*; **~ pill** *n* somnifère *m*; **~ policeman**○ *n* GB ralentisseur *m*; **~ quarters** *npl* (in barracks) chambrée *f*; (dormitory) dortoir *m*; **~ sickness ▶ 1002 |** *n* maladie *f* du sommeil; **~ tablet** *n* somnifère *m*.

sleepless /'sliːplɪs/ *adj* [*vigil, hours*] sans sommeil; **to pass a ~ night** passer une nuit blanche.

sleeplessness /'sliːplɪsnɪs/ *n* insomnie *f*.

sleep: **~walk** *vi* marcher en dormant, être somnambule; **~walking** *n* somnambulisme *m*.

sleepy /'sliːpɪ/ *adj* [*voice, village*] endormi, somnolent; **to feel** ou **be ~** avoir envie de dormir, avoir sommeil; **to make sb ~** [*fresh air*] donner envie de dormir à qn; [*wine*] endormir qn, assoupir qn.

sleepyhead○ /'sliːpɪhed/ *n* endormi/-e *m*/*f*; '**get up, ~!**' 'debout, paresseux/-euse!'

sleet /sliːt/ *n* neige *f* fondue.

sleeve /sliːv/ *n* **1** (of garment) manche *f*; **to pull** ou **tug at sb's ~** tirer qn par la manche; **to roll up one's ~s** LIT, FIG retrousser ses manches; **2** (of record) pochette *f*; (of CD) boîtier *m*; **3** TECH (inner) chemise *f*; (outer) gaine *f*; (short outer) manchon *m*.
IDIOMS **to laugh up one's ~** rire sous cape; **to wear one's heart on one's ~** laisser voir ses sentiments; **to have something up one's ~** avoir quelque chose en réserve; **to have a few tricks up one's ~** FIG avoir plus d'un tour dans son sac.

sleeveless /'sliːvlɪs/ *adj* sans manches.

sleigh /sleɪ/ *n* traîneau *m*.

sleight of hand /ˌslaɪtəv'hænd/ *n* **1** (dexterity) dextérité *f*; **2** (trick) tour *m* de passe-passe.

slender /'slendə(r)/ *adj* **1** (thin) [*person*] mince; [*waist*] fin; [*finger*] effilé; [*neck*] gracile; [*stem, arch*] élancé; **2**

(slight) [*majority*] faible (*before n*); **to win by a ~ margin** gagner de justesse; **3** (meagre) [*income, means*] modeste, maigre [*income*].

slenderness /'slendənɪs/ *n* **1** (of person) sveltesse *f*; (of part of body) minceur *f*; **2** (of margin) étroitesse *f*.

slept /slept/ *prét, pp* ▶ **sleep**.

sleuth /slu:θ/ *n* limier *m*, détective *m*.

S-level *n* GB SCH (*abrév* = **Special Level**) *épreuve optionnelle d'un niveau supérieur que l'on passe à l'âge de dix-huit ans.*

slew /slu:/ *pp* ▶ **slay**.

slice /slaɪs/ **I** *n* **1** (portion) (of bread, meat, fish) tranche *f*; (of cheese) morceau *m*; (of pie, tart) part *m*; (of lemon, cucumber, sausage) rondelle *f*; **2** (proportion) (of income, profits) part *f*; (of territory, population) partie *f*; **3** CULIN (utensil) spatule *f*; **4** SPORT slice *m*.

II *vtr* **1** (section) couper [qch] (en tranches) [*loaf, roast*]; couper [qch] en rondelles [*lemon, cucumber*]; **2** (cleave) fendre [*water, air*]; **to ~ sb's throat** trancher la gorge à qn; **3** SPORT slicer, couper [*ball*].

III *vi* **to ~ through** fendre [*water, air*]; trancher [*timber, rope, meat*].

sliced bread *n* pain *m* en tranches.

IDIOMS **it's the best** OU **greatest thing since ~**○! HUM on n'a pas fait mieux depuis l'invention du fil à couper le beurre.

slice: **~d loaf** *n* pain *m* en tranches; **~ of life** *n* CIN, THEAT tranche *f* de vie.

slick /slɪk/ **I** *n* **1** (on water) nappe *f* de pétrole; (on shore) marée *f* noire; **2** (tyre) slick *m*.

II *adj* **1** (adept) [*production, campaign*] habile; [*operation, deal*] mené rondement; **2** PÉJ (superficial) qui a un éclat plutôt superficiel; **3** PÉJ (insincere) [*person*] roublard○; [*answer*] astucieux/-ieuse; [*excuse*] facile; **~ salesman** vendeur qui a du bagou○; **4** US (slippery) [*road*] glissant; [*hair*] lissé.

slicker /'slɪkə(r)/ *n* US (raincoat) ciré *m*.

slickly /'slɪklɪ/ *adv* **1** (cleverly) [*presented*] de manière habile; [*worded*] habilement; **2** (smoothly) [*carried out*] efficacement; **3** (stylishly) [*dressed*] de manière branchée○.

slickness /'slɪknɪs/ *n* (of film, style) brillant *m*; (of answer, person) habileté *f*; (of salesman) bagou○ *m*; (of magician) dextérité *f*; (of operation) efficacité *f*.

slide /slaɪd/ **I** *n* **1** (chute) (in playground, factory) toboggan *m*; (for logs) glissoir *m*; (on ice) glissoire *f*; **2** PHOT diapositive *f*; **lecture with ~s** conférence avec projections; **3** (microscope plate) lame *f* porte-objet; **4** GB (hair clip) barrette *f*; **5** MUS (slur) coulé *m*; **6** MUS (on trombone) coulisse *f*; **7** FIG (decline) baisse *f* (**in** de).

II *vtr* (*prét, pp* **slid**) (move) faire glisser [*bolt, component*]; **to ~ sth forward** faire glisser quelque chose vers l'avant.

III *vi* (*prét, pp* **slid**) **1** (also **~ about** GB, **~ around**) (slip) [*car, person*] glisser, partir en glissade (**into** dans; **on** sur); **to ~ off** glisser de [*roof, table, deck*]; sortir de [*road*]; **2** (move) **to ~ down** dévaler [*slope*]; glisser le long de [*bannister*]; **to ~ in and out** [*drawer, component*] coulisser; **to ~ up and down** [*window*] coulisser de bas en haut; **to ~ out of** se glisser hors de [*seat, room*]; **3** (decline) [*prices, shares*] baisser; **the economy is sliding into recession** l'économie est sur la pente de la récession; **to let sth ~** laisser qch aller à la dérive.

■ **slide back:** **~ [sth] back, ~ back [sth]** reculer [*car seat*]; tirer [*bolt*]; refermer [*hatch, sunroof*].

slide: **~ projector** *n* projecteur *m* de diapositives; **~ rule** GB, **~ ruler** US *n* règle *f* à calcul; **~ show** *n* (at exhibition) diaporama *m*; (at lecture, at home) séance *f* de projection; **~ trombone** ▶ **1097** *n* trombone *m* à coulisse.

sliding /'slaɪdɪŋ/ *adj* [*door*] coulissant; [*roof*] ouvrant.

sliding: **~ scale** *n* échelle *f* mobile; **~ seat** *n* (in car) siège *m* réglable; (in boat) banc *m* à glissière.

slight /slaɪt/ **I** *n* affront *m* (**on** à; **from** de la part de).

II *adj* **1** [*change, delay, movement, rise*] léger/-ère (*before n*); [*risk, danger*] faible (*before n*); [*pause, hesitation*] petit (*before n*); **the chances of it happening are**

~ il y a de faibles chances pour que cela arrive; **not to have the ~est difficulty** ne pas avoir la moindre difficulté; **not in the ~est** pas le moins du monde; **2** (in build) mince; **to be ~ of build** être mince.

III *vtr* **1** (offend) humilier [*person*]; **2** US (underestimate) sous-estimer.

slighting /'slaɪtɪŋ/ *adj* [*remark, reference*] offensant.

slightly /'slaɪtlɪ/ *adv* GEN légèrement; [*embarrassed, uneasy, unfair*] un peu; **~ built** mince.

slim /slɪm/ **I** *adj* **1** (shapely) [*person, figure*] mince; **~ build** mince; **to get ~** devenir mince, s'amincir; **2** (thin) [*book, volume*] mince; [*watch, calculator*] plat; **3** (slight) [*chance, margin*] mince.

II *vtr* (*p prés etc* **-mm-**) = **slim down**.

III *vi* (*p prés etc* **-mm-**) GB (lose weight) maigrir; **I'm ~ming** je fais un régime pour maigrir.

■ **slim down:** ¶ **~ down 1** [*person*] maigrir, perdre du poids; **2** [*organization*] réduire ses effectifs; ¶ **~ [sth] down, ~ down [sth]** réduire les effectifs de, dégraisser○ [*industry*]; réduire [*workforce*].

slime /slaɪm/ *n* GEN dépôt *m* gluant or visqueux; (on river-bed) vase *f*; (on beach) algues *fpl*; (of slug, snail) bave *f*.

slimline /'slɪmlaɪn/ *adj* [*garment*] amincissant; [*drink*] diététique.

slimmer /'slɪmə(r)/ *n* GB personne *f* suivant un régime amaigrissant; **~s' disease**○ anorexie *f* mentale.

slimy /'slaɪmɪ/ *adj* **1** [*weed, mould*] visqueux/-euse; [*plate*] gluant; [*wall*] suintant; **2** GB PÉJ (obsequious) servile; **3** US PÉJ (sleazy) louche.

sling /slɪŋ/ **I** *n* **1** (weapon) fronde *f*; (smaller) lance-pierres *m inv*; **2** (for support) MED écharpe *f*; (for carrying baby) porte-bébé *m*; (for carrying load) élingue *f*; **3** SPORT (in climbing) boucle *f* d'assurance.

II *vtr* (*prét, pp* **slung**) **1**○ (throw) LIT, FIG lancer [*object, insult*] (**at** à); **to ~ a bag over one's shoulder** mettre un sac sur son épaule; **2** (carry or hang loosely) **to ~ sth from** suspendre qch à [*beam, branch, hook*]; **to be slung over/across/round sth** être jeté par dessus/en travers de/autour de qch; **to ~ sth over one's shoulder** porter [qch] en bandoulière [*bag, rifle*].

■ **sling out**○: ¶ **~ [sth] out, ~ out [sth]** jeter; ¶ **~ [sb] out** flanquer○ [qn] à la porte.

sling: **~back** *n* escarpin *m* à bride; **~shot** *n* lance-pierres *m inv*.

slink /slɪŋk/ *vi* (*prét, pp* **slunk**) **to ~ in** entrer furtivement; **to ~ off** [*person*] s'éloigner furtivement; [*dog*] s'en aller la queue basse.

slinky /'slɪŋkɪ/ *adj* [*dress*] moulant, sexy○.

slip /slɪp/ **I** *n* **1** (error) GEN erreur *f*; (by schoolchild) faute *f* d'étourderie; (faux pas) gaffe○ *f*; **to make a ~** faire une erreur ou une faute d'étourderie; **a ~ of the tongue** un lapsus; **2** (piece of paper) bout *m* de papier; (receipt) reçu *m*; **a ~ of paper** un bout de papier; **3** (slipping) glissade *f* involontaire; (stumble) faux pas *m*; **4**○ †(slender person) **a ~ of a girl** une fille frêle; **5** (petticoat) (full) combinaison *f*; (half) jupon *m*.

II *vtr* (*p prés etc* **-pp-**) **1** (slide) **to ~ [sth] into sth** glisser [qch] dans qch [*note, coin, joke*]; **to ~ one's feet into one's shoes** enfiler ses chaussures; **to ~ [sth] out of sth** sortir [qch] de qch [*object, foot, hand*]; **she ~ped the shirt over her head** (put on) elle a enfilé la chemise; (take off) elle a retiré la chemise; **to ~ sth into place** mettre qch en place; **to ~ a car into gear** embrayer; **2**○ (give surreptitiously) **to ~ sb sth, to ~ sth to sb** glisser qch à qn; **3** (escape from) [*dog*] se dégager de [*leash*]; [*boat*] filer [*moorings*]; **it ~ped my notice** ou **attention that** je ne me suis pas aperçu que; **it had ~ped my mind (that)** j'avais complètement oublié (que); **to let ~ an opportunity** ou **a chance (to do)** laisser échapper une occasion (de faire); **to let ~ a remark** laisser échapper une remarque; **4** (in knitting) **to ~ a stitch** glisser une maille; **5** MED **to ~ a disc** avoir une hernie discale; **6** AUT **to ~ the clutch** faire patiner l'embrayage.

III *vi* (*p prés etc* **-pp-**) **1** (slide) **~ into** passer [*dress*];

s'adapter à [*rôle*]; tomber dans [*coma*]; sombrer douce-ment dans [*madness*]; **to ~ out of** enlever [*dress, coat*]; **2** (slide quietly) **to ~ into/ out of** se glisser dans/hors de [*room, building*]; **to ~ across the border** passer la frontière en cachette; **3** (slide accidentally) [*person, vehicle*] glisser (**on** sur; **off** de); [*knife, pen*] glisser, déraper; [*load*] tomber; **the glass ~ped out of his hand** le verre lui a échappé des mains; **to ~ through sb's fingers** FIG filer entre les doigts de qn; **4**° (lose one's grip) **I must be ~ping!** je baisse°!.
IDIOMS **to give sb the ~** semer° qn.
■ **slip away** (leave unnoticed) partir discrètement.
■ **slip back: ¶ ~ back** [*person*] revenir discrète-ment (**to** à); **¶ ~ [sth] back** glisser, remettre.
■ **slip by** [*life, weeks, months*] s'écouler; [*time*] passer.
■ **slip in: ¶ ~ in** (enter quietly) [*person*] entrer dis-crètement; [*animal*] entrer furtivement; **a few errors have ~ped in** il y a quelques erreurs; **¶ ~ [sth] in, ~in [sth]** glisser [*remark*].
■ **slip off: ¶ ~ off** partir discrètement; **¶ ~ [sth] off, ~ off [sth]** enlever.
■ **slip on: ~ [sth] on, ~ on [sth]** passer, enfiler.
■ **slip out 1** (leave quietly) [*person*] sortir discrète-ment; **to ~ out to** faire un saut° à [*shop*]; **2 it just ~ped out!** ça m'a échappé!
■ **slip up**° faire une gaffe° (**on** à propos de).
slip: ~knot *n* nœud *m* coulant; **~-on (shoe)** *n* mocassin *m*.
slippage /'slɪpɪdʒ/ *n* **1** (delay) retard *m*; **2** (discrepancy) décalage *m*.
slipped disc *n* MED hernie *f* discale.
slipper /'slɪpə(r)/ *n* (houseshoe) pantoufle *f*.
slippery /'slɪpərɪ/ *adj* **1** (difficult to grip) [*road, fish*] glissant; **2** (difficult to deal with) [*subject*] délicat; **a ~ customer**° un personnage suspect.
IDIOMS **to be on the ~ slope** être sur une pente savonneuse.
slippy° /'slɪpɪ/ *adj* (slippery) [*path, surface*] glissant.
slip: ~ road *n* bretelle *f* d'accès à l'autoroute; **~shod** *adj* [*person*] négligent (**about, in** dans); [*appearance, work*] négligé, peu soigné; **~stream** *n* sillage *m*; **~-up**° *n* bourde° *f*.
slit /slɪt/ **I** *n* fente *f* (**in** dans); **to make a ~ in sth** faire une fente dans qch; **his eyes narrowed to ~s** il plissa les yeux.
II *adj* [*eyes*] bridé; [*skirt*] fendu.
III *vtr* (*prét, pp* **slit**) (on purpose) faire une fente dans; (by accident) déchirer; **to ~ a letter open** ouvrir une lettre; **to ~ sb's throat** égorger qn; **to ~ one's wrists** s'ouvrir les veines.
slither /'slɪðə(r)/ *vi* glisser; **to ~ about on sth** avoir du mal à garder son équilibre sur qch.
sliver /'slɪvə(r)/ *n* (of glass) éclat *m*; (of soap) reste *m*; (of food) mince tranche *f*.
Sloane /sləʊn/ *n* GB PÉJ (also **~ Ranger**) *femme* BCBG°.
slob° /slɒb/ *n* (lazy) flemmard/-e° *m/f*; (messy) cochon/-onne° *m/f*; **fat ~!** gros lard°!
slobber° /'slɒbə(r)/ *vi* baver; **to ~ over [sb/sth]**° baver d'attendrissement devant.
sloe /sləʊ/ *n* **1** (fruit) prunelle *f*; **2** (bush) prunellier *m*.
slog° /slɒg/ **I** *n* **1** (hard work) **a hard ~** un travail dur; **it was a real ~** c'était vraiment dur; **2** (hard stroke) coup *m* violent.
II *vtr* (*p prés etc* **-gg-**) **1** (hit hard) frapper [qn] violem-ment [*opponent*]; taper de toutes ses forces dans [*ball*]; **to ~ it out** LIT, FIG se battre; **2** (progress with diffi-culty) **to ~ one's way through** se frayer un chemin à travers.
III *vi* (*p prés etc* **-gg-**) **1** (work hard) travailler dur, bosser°; **2** (progress with difficulty) **we ~ged up the hill** nous avons escaladé la colline avec effort.
■ **slog away** travailler dur (**at** sur).
slop /slɒp/ **I** *n* **1** AGRIC (pigswill) pâtée *f*; **2**° PÉJ (food) bouillie *f*; **3**° PÉJ (sentimentality) sentimentalité *f*.
II slops *npl* (food) aliment *m* liquide; (dirty water) eaux *fpl* sales.
III *vtr* (*p prés etc* **-pp-**) renverser.

IV *vi* (*p prés etc* **-pp-**) (also **~ over**) déborder.
■ **slop around, slop about** [*person*] traînasser.
■ **slop out** vider sa tinette (*en prison*).
slope /sləʊp/ **I** *n* (incline) GEN pente *f*; (of writing) incli-naison *f*; (hillside) flanc *m*; **north/south ~** versant *m* nord/sud; **uphill ~** montée *f*; **downhill ~** descente *f*; **upper ~s** sommet *m* de la montagne.
II *vi* GEN être en pente; [*writing*] pencher (**to** vers).
sloping /'sləʊpɪŋ/ *adj* [*ground, roof*] en pente; [*ceiling*] incliné; [*shoulders*] tombant; [*writing*] penché.
sloppily /'slɒpɪlɪ/ *adv* n'importe comment; **~ run** mal administré.
sloppiness /'slɒpɪnɪs/ *n* (of thinking, discipline) manque *m* de rigueur; (of work) manque *m* de soin; (of dress) dé-braillé *m*.
sloppy /'slɒpɪ/ *adj* **1**° (careless) [*personal appearance*] débraillé; [*language, workmanship*] peu soigné; [*management, administration*] laxiste; [*discipline, pro-cedure*] relâché; [*method, thinking*] qui manque de rigueur; **to be a ~ eater** manger salement; **2**° (over-emotional) sentimental; **3** GB (baggy) ample.
slosh /slɒʃ/ **I** *vtr* **1**° (spill) répandre (en éclaboussant) [*liquid*]; **2**⁹ GB (hit) flanquer un coup° à.
II° *vi* (also **~ about**) clapoter.
III° **sloshed** *pp adj* bourré°; **to get ~ed** prendre une cuite°.
slot /slɒt/ **I** *n* **1** (for coin, ticket) fente *f*; (for letters) ouverture *f*; (groove) rainure *f*; **2** (in schedule) créneau *m*; **a prime-time ~** une tranche horaire de grande écoute; **3** (job) place *f*.
II *vtr* (*p prés etc* **-tt-**) **to ~ sth into a machine** insé-rer qch dans une machine; **to ~ a film into the time-table** trouver un créneau pour un film dans le programme.
III *vi* (*p prés etc* **-tt-**) **to ~ into sth** [*coin, piece*] s'insérer dans; **to ~ into place** ou **position** s'encas-trer.
■ **slot in: ¶ ~ in** se mettre en place; **¶ ~ [sth] in, ~ in [sth]** insérer [*coin, piece*]; trouver un créneau pour [*film, programme*]; placer [*person*].
■ **slot together: ¶ ~ together** s'emboîter; **¶ ~ [sth] together** emboîter.
sloth /sləʊθ/ *n* **1** ZOOL paresseux *m*; **2** SOUT (idleness) paresse *f*.
slot: ~ machine *n* GAMES machine *f* à sous; (for vending) distributeur *m* automatique; **~ meter** *n* (for gas, electricity) compteur *m* à pièces; (parking meter) parcmètre *m*; **~ted spoon** *n* ≈ écumoire *f*.
slouch /slaʊtʃ/ **I** *n* **1 to walk with a ~** marcher le dos voûté; **2**° (lazy person) traîne-savates *m inv*.
II *vi* **1** (sit or stand badly) être avachi; **2** (also **~ around**) traînasser.
Slovakia /slə'vækɪə/ **▶ 840** *pr n* Slovaquie *f*.
Slovenia /slə'viːnɪə/ **▶ 840** *pr n* Slovénie *f*.
slovenliness /'slʌvnlɪnɪs/ *n* laisser-aller *m inv*.
slovenly /'slʌvnlɪ/ *adj* [*person, dress, appearance, speech, style*] négligé; [*habits*] malpropre; [*work*] bâclé.
slow /sləʊ/ **I** *adj* **1** (not quick, dull) lent; **to be ~ to do** tarder à faire; **to be ~ in doing** être lent à faire; **2** (slack) GEN stagnant; [*economic growth*] lent; **3** (dim) lent (d'esprit); **4** [*clock, watch*] **to be ~** retarder; **to be 10 minutes ~** retarder de 10 minutes; **5** [*oven*] doux/douce; **6** [*pitch, court*] lourd.
II *adv* GEN lentement; **to go ~** [*workers*] freiner la production; **~-acting** à action lente.
III *vtr, vi* ▶ **slow down**.
■ **slow down: ¶ ~ down** ralentir; **to ~ (down) to a crawl** rouler au pas; **to ~ (down) to 2%** tomber à 2%; **¶ ~ down [sth/sb], ~ [sth/sb] down** ralentir.
■ **slow up** = **slow down**.
slow: ~coach° *n* GB traînard/-e° *m/f*; **~ cooker** *n* mijoteuse *f* électrique; **~down** *n* ralentissement *m*; **~ handclapping** *n*: applaudissements expri-mant l'impatience ou le mécontentement; **~ lane** *n* (in UK) voie *f* de gauche; (elsewhere) voie *f* de droite.
slowly /'sləʊlɪ/ *adv* lentement.
slow motion *n* ralenti *m*; **in ~** au ralenti.

slow-moving /ˌsləʊˈmuːvɪŋ/ adj lent.

slowness /ˈsləʊnɪs/ n LIT lenteur f; (of pitch, court, mind, intelligence) lourdeur f.

slow: ~poke○ n US = **slowcoach**; **~ train** n omnibus m; **~-witted** adj à l'esprit lent.

sludge /slʌdʒ/ n (mud) vase f.

slug /slʌg/ I n **1** ZOOL limace f; **2**○ (bullet) balle f; **3** (of alcohol) lampée○ f; **4**○ (blow) coup m.
II○ vtr (p prés etc **-gg-**) **1**○ (hit) cogner [person]; **to ~ sb one**○ en envoyer une à qn○; **2**○ US SPORT taper○ dans [ball].
IDIOMS **to ~ it out**○ se tabasser○.

slug bait n granulés mpl antilimaces.

sluggish /ˈslʌgɪʃ/ adj **1** [person, animal] léthargique; [circulation, reaction] lent; [traffic] engorgé; [river] stagnant; **2** FIN qui stagne; **after a ~ start** après un démarrage difficile.

slug pellets npl = **slug bait**.

sluice /sluːs/ n (also **~way**) canal m.
■ **sluice down**: **~ down** [sth], **~** [sth] **down** laver [qch] à grande eau.

sluice gate n vanne f.

slum /slʌm/ I n **1** (poor area) quartier m pauvre; **the ~s** les bas-quartiers mpl; **2** (dwelling) taudis m.
II vi○ (p prés etc **-mm-**) (also **~ it**) s'encanailler.

slumber /ˈslʌmbə(r)/ LITTÉR I n sommeil m.
II vi LIT, FIG sommeiller.

slum clearance n démolition f de taudis.

slump /slʌmp/ I n **1** FIN, ECON effondrement m (**in** de); **to experience a ~** s'effondrer; **2** (in popularity) chute f (**in** de); (in support) baisse f (**in** de).
II vi [demand, trade, value, price] chuter (**from** de; **to** à; **by** de); [economy, market] s'effondrer; [support, popularity] être en forte baisse; [person, body] s'affaler○.

slung /slʌŋ/ prét, pp ▶ **sling**.

slunk /slʌŋk/ prét, pp ▶ **slink**.

slur /slɜː(r)/ I n **1** (aspersion) calomnie f; **to cast a ~ on sb/sth** répandre des calomnies sur qn/qch; **to be a ~ on sb/sth** porter atteinte à qn/qch; **a racial ~** une diffamation raciale; **2** MUS liaison f.
II vtr (p prés etc **-rr-**) **1** to **~ one's speech** ou **words** manger ses mots; **2** MUS lier.
III slurred pp adj [voice, words, speech] inarticulé.

slurp /slɜːp/ vtr aspirer [qch] bruyamment.

slurry /ˈslʌrɪ/ n **1** (of cement) gâchis m; **2** (waste) (from animals) purin m; (from factory) déchets mpl.

slush /slʌʃ/ n **1** (melted snow) neige f fondue; **2**○ PÉJ (sentimentality) sensiblerie f; **3** US CULIN granité m.

slush fund n caisse f noire.

slushy /ˈslʌʃɪ/ n **1** LIT [snow] fondu; [street] couvert de neige fondue; **2**○ FIG [novel, film] à l'eau de rose, sentimental.

slut○ /slʌt/ n INJUR traînée○ f OFFENSIVE.

sly /slaɪ/ adj (cunning) rusé; (secretive) entendu.
IDIOMS **on the ~** en douce○, en cachette.

slyly /ˈslaɪlɪ/ adv (with cunning) malicieusement; (secretively) [say] d'un ton entendu; [smile, look] d'un air entendu.

smack /smæk/ I n **1** (blow) (with hand) claque f; (on face) gifle f; (with bat) coup m; **2** (sound) (of object) bruit m sec; (by hand or person) coup m; **3** (loud kiss) gros baiser m.
II adv○ (also **~ bang**, **~ dab** US) en plein○; **~ in the middle of** en plein milieu de.
III vtr (on face) gifler [person]; taper [object] (**on** sur; **against** contre); **she ~ed him (on the bottom)** ou **she ~ed his bottom** elle lui a donné une claque sur les fesses.
IV vi **1** (hit) **to ~ into** ou **against sth** taper contre qch; **2** (have suggestion of) **to ~ of** sentir.
IDIOMS **to ~ one's lips** se lécher les babines (**at sth** à l'idée de qch); **a ~ in the eye** une gifle.

small /smɔːl/ ▶ **1260** I n **the ~ of the back** le creux du dos.
II○ **smalls** npl GB EUPH petit linge m.

III adj **1** (not big) GEN petit; [increase, majority, proportion, quantity, amount, stake] faible; **his influence was ~** son influence était négligeable; **the ~ matter of the £1,000 you owe me** IRON la bagatelle de 1 000 livres sterling que tu me dois IRON; **it is written with a ~ letter** ça s'écrit avec un minuscule; **in his** ou **her own ~ way** GEN à sa façon; **to cut sth up ~** couper qch en petits morceaux; **the ~est room** EUPH le petit coin○ EUPH; **2** (petty) [person, act] mesquin; **3** (not much) **to have ~ cause for worrying** ou **to worry** n'avoir guère de raisons de s'inquiéter; **it is ~ comfort** ou **consolation to sb** c'est une piètre consolation pour qn; **~ wonder he left!** pas étonnant qu'il soit parti!; **4** (quiet) [voice, noise] petit; [sound] faible; **5** (humiliated) **to feel** ou **look ~** être dans ses petits souliers○; **to make sb feel** ou **look ~** humilier qn.
IV adv [write] petit.

small: ~ ad n GB petite annonce f; **~ change** n petite monnaie f; **~ claims court** n GB, JUR tribunal m d'instance; **~holding** n GB AGRIC petite exploitation f; **~ hours** npl petit matin m; **~ intestine** n intestin m grêle; **~-minded** adj mesquin; **~pox** ▶ **1002** n variole f.

small print n **1** LIT petits caractères mpl; **2** FIG **to read the ~** lire tout jusque dans les moindres détails; **to read the ~ of a contract** éplucher un contrat.

small-scale /ˌsmɔːlˈskeɪl/ adj [model] réduit; [map, plan] à petite échelle; [industry] petit (before n).

small talk n banalités fpl; **to make ~** faire la conversation.

small-town adj PÉJ provincial.

smart /smɑːt/ I adj **1** (elegant) élégant; **2**○ (intelligent) [child, decision] malin; [politician, journalist] habile; **it was definitely the ~ choice** c'est certainement ce qu'il fallait choisir; **3** [restaurant, hotel, street] chic inv; **the ~ set** le beau monde; **4** (stinging) [blow] vif/vive; [rebuke] cinglant; **5** (brisk) **to walk at a ~ pace** marcher à vive allure; **that was ~ work!** ça a été vite fait!; **6** COMPUT intelligent.
II vi **1** (sting) brûler; **2** FIG (emotionally) être piqué au vif; **they are ~ing over** ou **from their defeat** ils sont sous le coup de leur défaite.

smart: ~ alec(k)○ n gros malin○/grosse maligne○ m/f; **~ bomb** n bombe f intelligente; **~ card** n COMPUT, FIN carte f à puce.

smarten /ˈsmɑːtn/: ■ **smarten up**: **~** [sth/sb] **up**, **~ up** [sth/sb] embellir; **he's really ~ed himself up** il s'est beaucoup arrangé.

smartly /ˈsmɑːtlɪ/ adv **1** [dressed] (neatly) soigneusement; (elegantly) élégamment; **2** (quickly) sèchement; **3** (briskly) vivement; **4** (cleverly) avec malice.

smart money○ n **the ~ was on Desert Orchid** Desert Orchid était une mise sûre; **the ~ is on our shares** nos actions sont un investissement.

smash /smæʃ/ I n **1** (crash) (of glass, china) bruit m fracassant; (of vehicles) fracas m; **~! there goes another plate!** crac! encore une assiette cassée!; **2**○ (also **~-up**) (accident) collision f; **3**○ (also **~ hit**) MUS tube○; CIN film m à grand succès; **to be a ~** faire un tabac○; **4** FIN (collapse) débâcle f; (on stock exchange) krach m; **5** SPORT (tennis) smash m.
II vtr **1** briser (**with** avec); (more violently) fracasser; **thieves ~ed their way into the shop** les voleurs sont entrés dans la boutique en cassant tout; **she ~ed the car into a tree** elle est rentrée dans un arbre; **2** (destroy) écraser [demonstration, opponent]; démanteler [drugs ring]; **3** SPORT pulvériser○ [record]; **to ~ the ball** faire un smash.
III vi **1** (disintegrate) se briser, se fracasser (**on** sur, **against** contre); **2** (crash) **to ~ into** [vehicle] aller s'écraser contre; **the raiders ~ed through the door** les cambrioleurs ont enfoncé la porte; **3** FIN faire faillite.
■ **smash down**: **~** [sth] **down**, **~ down** [sth] enfoncer.
■ **smash in**: **~** [sth] **in** défoncer [door, skull].

■ **smash open**: ~ [sth] **open**, ~**open** [sth] défoncer.

■ **smash up**: ~ [sth] **up**, ~ **up** [sth] démolir; **they'll ~ the place up!** ils vont tout casser!

smash-and-grab⁰ GB *n* (also ~ **raid**) cambriolage *m* (*avec destruction de vitrine*).

mashed /smæʃt/ *adj* **1**⁰ (on alcohol) bourré⁰; (on drugs) défoncé⁰ (**on** à); **2** [*limb, vehicle*] écrasé; [*window*] fracassé.

mashing⁰ /'mæʃɪŋ/ *adj* GB épatant⁰.

mattering /'mætərɪŋ/ *n* notions *fpl*; **to have a ~ of Russian** avoir quelques connaissances en russe; **a ~ of culture** quelques bribes de culture.

smear /smɪə(r)/ I *n* **1** (mark) (spot) tache *f*; (streak) traînée *f*; **2** (defamation) propos *m* diffamatoire; **a ~ on sb's character** une tache sur la réputation de qn; **3** MED = **smear test**.

II *vtr* **1** (dirty) faire des taches sur; **her face was ~ed with jam** elle avait le visage barbouillé de confiture; **2** (slander) diffamer [*person*]; salir [*reputation*]; **3** (spread) étaler [*butter, paint*]; appliquer [*lotion*].

III *vi* [*ink, paint*] s'étaler; [*lipstick, make-up*] couler.

smear: ~ **campaign** *n* campagne *f* de diffamation (**against** contre); ~ **tactics** *npl* manœuvres *fpl* diffamatoires; ~ **test** *n* MED frottis *m*.

smell /smel/ I *n* **1** (odour) odeur *f*; **what a ~!** comme ça sent mauvais!; **2** (sense) odorat *m*; **sense of ~** odorat *m*; **3** (action) **to have a ~ of** sentir un peu; **4** FIG relents *mpl*.

II *vtr* (*prét, pp* **smelled**, **smelt** GB) **1** LIT sentir; **I can ~ burning** ça sent le brûlé; **2** FIG (detect) GEN flairer; repérer [*liar, cheat*].

III *vi* (*prét, pp* **smelled**, **smelt** GB) **1** (have odour) sentir; **this flower doesn't ~** cette fleur ne sent rien; **to ~ of roses** sentir la rose; **that ~s like curry** ça sent le curry; FIG **to ~ of** sentir [*corruption*]; **2** (have sense of smell) avoir de l'odorat.

■ **smell out**: ~ [sth] **out**, ~ **out** [sth] **1** LIT [*dog*] flairer; **2** FIG GEN découvrir; démasquer [*spy, traitor*]; **3** (cause to stink) empester.

smelling salts *npl* MED sels *mpl*.

smelly /'smelɪ/ *adj* LIT GEN qui sent mauvais.

smelt /smelt/ I *prét, pp* ▶ **smell**.

II *vtr* extraire [qch] par fusion [*metal*]; fondre [*ore*].

smile /smaɪl/ I *n* sourire *m*; **to give a ~** sourire; **to give sb a ~** adresser un sourire à qn; **with a ~** en souriant.

II *vtr* **'Of course,' he ~d** 'bien sûr,' dit-il en souriant; **to ~ a sad smile** avoir un sourire triste.

III *vi* sourire (**at sb** à qn; **with** de); **we ~d at the idea** cette idée nous a fait sourire; **to ~ to oneself** sourire intérieurement; **keep smiling!** garde le sourire!

■ **smile on**: ~ **on** [sb/sth] [*luck, fortune, weather*] sourire à; [*person, police, authority*] être favorable à.

smiling /'smaɪlɪŋ/ *adj* souriant.

smirk /smɜːk/ I *n* (self-satisfied) petit sourire *m* satisfait; (knowing) sourire *m* en coin.

II *vi* (in a self-satisfied way) avoir un petit sourire satisfait; (knowingly) avoir un sourire en coin.

smith /smɪθ/ ▶ **1251** *n* maréchal-ferrant *m*.

smithereens /ˌsmɪðə'riːnz/ *npl* **in ~** en mille morceaux.

smithy /'smɪðɪ/ *n* forge *f*.

smitten /'smɪtn/ *adj* **1** (afflicted) ~ **by** rongé par [*guilt, regret*]; terrassé par [*illness*]; **2** (in love) fou/folle d'amour.

smock /smɒk/ I *n* blouse *f*, sarrau *m*.

II *vtr* faire des smocks à.

smog /smɒg/ *n* smog *m*.

smog mask *n* masque *m* antipollution.

smoke /sməʊk/ I *n* **1** (fumes) fumée *f*; **to go up in ~**⁰ LIT brûler, partir en fumée; FIG tomber à l'eau⁰; **2**⁰ (cigarette) clope⁰ *f*; **to have a ~** fumer.

II *vtr* **1** fumer [*cigarette etc*]; **2** CULIN fumer.

III *vi* (all contexts) fumer.

IV **smoked** *pp adj* fumé.

IDIOMS **to ~ like a chimney**⁰ fumer comme un pompier⁰.

■ **smoke out**: ¶ ~ [sth] **out**, ~ **out** [sth] enfumer [*animal*]; ¶ ~ [sb] **out**, ~ **out** [sb] LIT déloger qn en l'enfumant; FIG débusquer.

smoke: ~ **alarm** *n* détecteur *m* de fumée; ~ **bomb** *n* grenade *f* fumigène; ~**-dried** *adj* fumé; ~**-filled** *adj* enfumé.

smokeless /'sməʊklɪs/ *adj* [*fuel*] non polluant.

smoker /'sməʊkə(r)/ *n* **1** (person) fumeur/-euse *m/f*; **a light ~** une personne qui fume peu; **2** (on train) compartiment *m* fumeurs.

smoke screen *n* **1** MIL écran *m* de fumée; **2** FIG diversion *f*; **to create** OU **throw up a ~** faire diversion.

smokey = **smoky**.

smoking /'sməʊkɪŋ/ I *n* ~ **and drinking** le tabac et l'alcool; **to give up ~** arrêter de fumer; **'no ~'** 'défense de fumer'.

II *adj* **1** (emitting smoke) qui fume; [*cigarette*] allumé; **2** (for smokers) [*compartment, section*] fumeurs (*after n*).

smoking: ~ **ban** *n* interdiction *f* de fumer; ~ **compartment** GB, ~ **car** US *n* compartiment *m* fumeurs; ~**-related** *adj* [*disease*] associé au tabac; ~ **room** *n* fumoir *m*.

smoky /'sməʊkɪ/ I⁰ *n* US motard⁰ *m* (*de la police*).

II *adj* [*atmosphere, room*] enfumé; [*fire*] qui fume; [*cheese, ham, bacon, glass*] fumé.

smolder *vi* US = **smoulder**.

smooth /smuːð/ I *adj* **1** LIT (even, without bumps) [*stone, sea, surface, skin, fabric*] lisse; [*road*] plan; [*curve, line, breathing*] régulier/-ière; [*sauce, paste*] homogène; [*crossing, flight*] sans heurts; [*movement*] aisé; [*music, playing*] fluide; **the tyres are worn ~** les pneus sont lisses; **the engine is very ~** le moteur tourne parfaitement rond; **2** (problem-free) paisible; **the bill had a ~ passage through Parliament** la loi a été adoptée sans difficultés par le Parlement; **3** [*taste, wine, whisky*] moelleux/-euse; **4** (suave) GEN, PEJ [*person*] mielleux/-euse; [*manners, appearance*] onctueux/-euse; **to be a ~ talker** être enjôleur/-euse.

II *vtr* **1** (flatten out) lisser; (get creases out) défroisser; **to ~ the creases from sth** défroisser qch; **~ the cream into your skin** étalez la crème sur votre peau; **2** FIG (ease) faciliter [*process, path*].

IDIOMS **to take the rough with the ~** prendre les choses comme elles viennent; **the course of true love never did run ~** l'amour vrai n'a jamais été facile à vivre.

■ **smooth away**: ~ **away** [sth], ~ [sth] **away** LIT, FIG faire disparaître.

■ **smooth down**: ~ [sth] **down**, ~ **down** [sth] GEN lisser; polir [*wood, rough surface*].

■ **smooth out**: ~ [sth] **out**, ~ **out** [sth] **1** LIT (lay out) étendre; (remove creases) défroisser; **2** FIG aplanir [*difficulties*]; faire disparaître [*imperfections*].

■ **smooth over**: ~ **over** [sth] FIG atténuer [*differences, awkwardness*]; aplanir [*difficulties, problems*]; **to ~ things over** arranger les choses.

smoothly /'smuːðlɪ/ *adv* **1** (easily) LIT [*move, flow, glide*] doucement; [*start, stop, brake, land*] en douceur; [*write, spread*] de façon unie; FIG (without difficulties) sans heurts; **the key turned ~ in the lock** la clé a tourné facilement dans la serrure; **to run ~** LIT tourner rond; FIG marcher bien; [*holiday*] se dérouler sans problèmes; **things are going very ~ for me** tout va bien pour moi; **2** (suavely) GEN en douceur; PEJ mielleusement.

smoothness /'smuːðnɪs/ *n* **1** LIT (of surface, skin) aspect *m* lisse; (of crossing, flight) tranquillité *f*; (of car, machine) régularité *f*; (of music) fluidité *f*; (of movement) aisance *f*; **2** FIG (absence of problems) harmonie *f*; **3** (of wine, taste) douceur *f*; **4** (suaveness) onctuosité *f*.

smooth running I *n* (of machinery) bon fonctionnement *m*; (of organization, event) bonne marche *f*.

II **smooth-running** *adj* [*machinery*] qui tourne bien; [*organization, event*] qui marche bien.

smooth-tongued *adj* PEJ enjôleur/-euse.

smorgasbord /'smɔːgəsbɔːd/ n CULIN buffet m (à la scandinave).

smother /'smʌðə(r)/ vtr **1** (stifle) étouffer; **2** (cover) couvrir (**with** de); **to be ~ed in blankets** être tout emmitouflé dans des couvertures.

smoulder GB, **smolder** US /'sməʊldə(r)/ vi LIT se consumer; FIG couver; **to ~ with** se consumer de [resentment, jealousy].

smouldering GB, **smoldering** US /'sməʊldərɪŋ/ adj **1** LIT [fire, cigarette] qui se consume; [ashes, ruins] fumant; **2** FIG (intense) sourd; (sexy) ardent.

smudge /smʌdʒ/ **I** n (mark) trace f.
II vtr étaler [make-up, print, ink, wet paint]; faire des traces sur [paper, paintwork].
III vi [paint, ink, print, make-up] s'étaler.
IV smudged pp adj [paint, make-up] qui a coulé (after n); [writing, letter] maculé; [paper, cloth] taché.

smudgy /'smʌdʒɪ/ adj **1** (marked) [paper, face] taché; [writing, letter] à moitié effacé; **2** (indistinct) [photograph, image] voilé; [outline] estompé.

smug /smʌg/ adj suffisant; **to be ~ about winning** être fier d'avoir gagné.

smuggle /'smʌgl/ **I** vtr GEN faire passer [qch] clandestinement [message, food] (**into** dans); faire du trafic de [arms, drugs]; (to evade customs) faire passer [qch] en contrebande; **to ~ sth/sb in** faire entrer qch/qn clandestinement; **to ~ sth through** ou **past customs** faire passer qch en fraude.
II vi faire de la contrebande.
III smuggled pp adj de contrebande.

smuggler /'smʌglə(r)/ n contrebandier/-ière m/f; **drug/arms ~** passeur/-euse m/f de drogue/d'armes.

smuggling /'smʌglɪŋ/ n GEN contrebande f; **drug/arms ~** trafic m de drogue/d'armes.

smut /smʌt/ n (vulgarity) grivoiseries fpl; (stain) tache f.

smutty /'smʌtɪ/ adj (crude) grivois; (dirty) noir.

snack /snæk/ **I** n **1** (small meal) repas m léger; (instead of meal) casse-croûte m inv; **to have** ou **eat a ~** manger quelque chose; **2** (crisps, peanuts etc) amuse-gueule m inv.
II vi grignoter, manger légèrement.

snag /snæg/ **I** n **1** (hitch) inconvénient m (**in** de); **there's just one ~** il y a un problème; **2** (tear) accroc m (**in** à); **3** (projection) aspérité f (**in** sur).
II vtr (p prés etc **-gg-**) (tear) filer [tights, stocking] (**on** contre); accrocher [sleeve, garment, fabric] (**on** à); se casser [fingernail]; s'égratigner [hand, finger].
III vi (p prés etc **-gg-**) (catch) **to ~ on** [rope, fabric] s'accrocher à; [propeller, part] frotter contre.

snail /sneɪl/ n escargot m.

snake /sneɪk/ **I** n ZOOL serpent m; PÉJ (person) traître/traîtresse m/f.
II vi [road] serpenter (**through** à travers).
IDIOMS **a ~ in the grass** PÉJ un traître/une traîtresse.

snake: **~bite** n morsure f de serpent; **~ charmer** n charmeur/-euse m/f de serpent; **~s and ladders** ▶ 949 | n GB GAMES ≈ jeu m de l'oie.

snap /snæp/ ▶ 949 | **I** n **1** (of branch) craquement m; (of fingers, lid, elastic) claquement m; **2** (bite) claquement m; **3**○ PHOT photo f; **4** GAMES ≈ bataille f.
II adj [decision, judgment, vote] rapide.
III○ excl **~! we're wearing the same tie!** coïncidence! nous portons la même cravate!
IV vtr (p prés etc **-pp-**) **1** (click) faire claquer [fingers, jaws, elastic]; **to ~ sth shut** fermer qch avec un bruit sec; **2** (break) (faire) casser net; **3** (say crossly) dire [qch] hargneusement; **4**○ PHOT prendre une photo de.
V vi (p prés etc **-pp-**) **1** LIT (break) se casser; **2** FIG (lose control) [person] craquer○; **my patience finally ~ped** ma patience était arrivée à bout; **3** (click) **to ~ open/shut** s'ouvrir/se fermer d'un coup sec; **4** (speak sharply) parler hargneusement.
IDIOMS **~ out of it**○! cesse de faire la tête!; **~ to it**○! et plus vite que ça○!; **to ~ to attention** MIL se figer au garde-à-vous.

■ **snap at**: **~ at** [sth/sb] **1** (speak sharply) parle hargneusement à; **2** (bite) essayer de mordre.

■ **snap off**: **¶ ~ off** casser net; **¶ ~ off** [sth], [sth] off casser net.

■ **snap up**: **~ up** [sth] sauter sur [bargain, chance].

snap: **~ fastener** n bouton-pression m; **~-on** a [lid, attachment] à pression.

snappy /'snæpɪ/ adj **1** (bad-tempered) hargneux/-euse **2** (lively) [rhythm, reply] rapide; (punchy) [advertisemen accrocheur/-euse; **3**○ (smart) [clothing] chic inv.
IDIOMS **make it ~**○! grouille-toi○!

snapshot /'snæpʃɒt/ n photo f.

snare /sneə(r)/ **I** n piège m ALSO FIG.
II vtr prendre [qn/qch] au piège [animal, person].

snarl /snɑːl/ **I** n **1** (growl) grondement m; **'you' better watch out!' he said with a ~** 'tu ferai mieux de faire attention!' dit-il d'un ton hargneux; **2** (grimace) mine f hargneuse; **3** (tangle) (in single rope, flex nœud m; (of several ropes, flexes) enchevêtrement m.
II vtr rugir; **'don't be so stupid,' he ~ed** 'ne sois pas si stupide,' dit-il d'un ton hargneux.
III vi [animal] gronder férocement; [person] grogner **the dog ~ed at me** le chien m'a montré les dents.
■ **snarl up**: **¶ ~ up** [rope] s'emmêler; **¶ ~ up** [sth] bloquer; **to be ~ed up** être bloqué; [economy, system] être paralysé; **I got ~ed up in the traffic** j'ai été pris dans les embouteillages; **the hook got ~ed up in the net** l'hameçon s'est pris dans le filet.

snarl-up /'snɑːlʌp/ n (in traffic) embouteillage m; (in distribution network) blocage m.

snatch /snætʃ/ **I** n (pl **~es**) **1** (fragment) (of conversation) bribe f; (of poem, poet) quelques vers mpl; (of concerto, composer) quelques mesures fpl; (of tune) quelques notes fpl; **2** (grab) **to make a ~ at sth** essayer d'attraper qch; **3** (theft) vol m; **bag ~** vol à l'arraché; **4** SPORT (in weightlifting) arraché m.
II vtr **1** (grab) attraper [book, key]; saisir [opportunity]; arracher [victory]; prendre [lead]; **to ~ sth from sb** arracher qch à qn; **2**○ (steal) voler [handbag, jewellery, kiss] (**from** à); kidnapper [baby]; **3** (take hurriedly) **try to ~ a few hours' sleep** essaie de dormir quelques heures; **have we got time to ~ a meal?** avons-nous le temps de manger quelque chose en vitesse?
III vi **to ~ at sth** tendre vivement la main vers [rope, letter].
■ **snatch away**: **~** [sth] **away** arracher qch (**from** sb à qn).
■ **snatch up**: **~ up** [sth] ramasser [qch] en vitesse [clothes, papers]; saisir [child]; **to ~ up a bargain** faire une affaire.

snazzy○ /'snæzɪ/ adj tape-à-l'œil○ inv.

sneak /sniːk/ **I**○ n PÉJ **1** GB (tell-tale) rapporteur/-euse m/f; **2** (devious person) sournois/-e m/f.
II noun modifier [raid] en traître; [visit] furtif/-ive.
III vtr **1**○ (have secretly) manger [qch] en cachette [chocolate etc]; fumer [qch] en cachette [cigarette]; **2**○ (steal) voler (**out of, from** dans); **they ~ed him out by the back door** ils l'ont fait sortir discrètement par la porte de derrière; **to ~ a look at sth** jeter un coup d'œil furtif à qch.
IV vi **1** (move furtively) **to ~ away** s'éclipser discrètement; **to ~ around** rôder; **to ~ in/out** entrer/ sortir furtivement; **to ~ into** se faufiler dans [room, bed]; **to ~ up on sb/sth** s'approcher sans bruit de qn/qch; **she ~ed out of the room** elle s'est glissée hors de la pièce; **2**○ GB (tell tales) rapporter; **to ~ on sb** dénoncer qn.

sneaker /'sniːkə(r)/ n US basket f, tennis f.

sneaking /'sniːkɪŋ/ adj [suspicion] vague; **she has a ~ suspicion that he's lying** elle a le vague sentiment qu'il ment; **I have a ~ admiration for her** je ne peux m'empêcher de l'admirer.

sneak preview n avant-première f; **to give sb a ~ of sth** montrer qch à qn en avant-première.

sneaky /'sniːkɪ/ adj **1** PÉJ (cunning) GEN sournois; [method, plan] rusé; **2** (furtive) **to have a ~ look at sth** regarder qch en cachette.

sneer /snɪə(r)/ **I** n (expression) sourire m méprisant.

II *vi* (smile) sourire avec mépris; (speak) railler.

sneering /'snɪərɪŋ/ **I** *n* railleries *fpl.*
II *adj* [*remark*] railleur/-euse; [*smile*] méprisant.

sneeze /sniːz/ **I** *n* éternuement *m.*
II *vi* éternuer.
IDIOMS **it is not to be ~d at** ce n'est pas à dédaigner.

snide /snaɪd/ *adj* sournois.

sniff /snɪf/ **I** *n* **1** (of person with cold or crying) reniflement *m*; (of disgust, disdain) grimace *f*; **2** (inhalation) inhalation *f*; **to take a ~ of** sentir.
II *vtr* [*dog*] flairer; [*person*] humer [*air*]; sentir [*perfume, food*]; inhaler [*glue, cocaine*].
III *vi* LIT renifler; FIG faire une moue; **to ~ at sth** LIT renifler; FIG faire la grimace à [*idea*]; faire la fine bouche devant [*food*]; **a free car is not to be ~ed at** une voiture gratuite, ça ne se refuse pas.
■ **sniff out**: ~ **out** [*sth*] GEN LIT, FIG flairer.

sniffer dog *n*: *chien policier entraîné pour détecter la drogue ou les explosifs.*

sniffle○ /'snɪfl/ **I** *n* (sniff) reniflement *m*; (slight cold) petit rhume *m.*
II *vi* renifler.

sniffy○ /'snɪfɪ/ *adj* dédaigneux/-euse; **to be ~ about sth** faire la fine bouche au sujet de qch.

snigger /'snɪɡə(r)/ **I** *n* ricanement *m.*
II *vi* ricaner; **to ~ at** [*sb/sth*] se moquer de [*person*]; ricaner en entendant [*remark*]; ricaner en voyant [*appearance, action*].

snip /snɪp/ **I** *n* **1** (action) petit coup *m* (de ciseaux etc); **2** (onomat) cliquetis *m*; **3** (piece of fabric) échantillon *m*; **4**○ (bargain) (bonne) affaire *f*; **5** (horse) gagnant *m* sûr.
II *vtr* (*p prés etc* -**pp**-) découper (à petits coups de ciseaux etc) [*fabric, paper*]; tailler [*hedge*].
■ **snip off**: ~ [*sth*] **off**, ~ **off** [*sth*] couper.

snipe /snaɪp/ **I** *n* ZOOL bécassine *f.*
II *vi* **to ~ at** (shoot) tirer sur; (criticize) envoyer des piques à.

sniper /'snaɪpə(r)/ *n* MIL tireur *m* embusqué.

sniping /'snaɪpɪŋ/ *n* ⊄ piques *fpl.*

snippet /'snɪpɪt/ *n* (*gén pl*) (of conversation, information) bribes *pl*; (of text, fabric, music) fragment *m.*

snivel /'snɪvl/ *vi* (*p prés etc* -**ll**-) pleurnicher.

snob /snɒb/ **I** *n* snob *mf.*
II *noun modifier* [*value, appeal*] pour les snobs.

snobbery /'snɒbərɪ/ *n* snobisme *m.*

snobbish /'snɒbɪʃ/ *adj* snob *inv.*

snook /snuːk/ *n*: IDIOMS **to cock a ~ at sb** faire la nique à qn.

snooker /'snuːkə(r)/ ▶ 949 **I** *n* **1** (game) snooker *m* (*variante du billard*); **2** (shot) coup *m* fumant.
II *vtr* SPORT, FIG coincer [*player, person*].

snoop○ /snuːp/ **I** *n* fouineur/-euse *m/f.*
II *vi* espionner; **to ~ into** mettre son nez○ dans.
■ **snoop around**○ fouiner, fureter.

snoop around○ *n* **to have a ~** jeter un coup d'œil.

snooping○ /'snuːpɪŋ/ *n* espionnage *m.*
II *adj* fouineur/-euse○.

snooty○ /'snuːtɪ/ *adj* [*restaurant, club, college*] huppé; [*tone, person*] prétentieux/-ieuse.

snooze○ /snuːz/ **I** *n* petit somme *m.*
II *vi* sommeiller.

snore /snɔː(r)/ **I** *n* ronflement *m.*
II *vi* ronfler.

snoring /'snɔːrɪŋ/ *n* ⊄ ronflements *mpl.*

snorkel /'snɔːkl/ **I** *n* (US **schnorkel**) **1** (for swimmer) tuba *m*; **2** (on submarine) schnorchel *m.*
II *vi* (*p prés etc* -**ll**-) faire de la plongée avec tuba.

snorkelling /'snɔːklɪŋ/ ▶ 949 *n* SPORT plongée *f* avec tuba.

snort /snɔːt/ **I** *n* (of horse, bull) ébrouement *m*; (of person, pig) grognement *m.*
II *vtr* ARGOT DES DROGUÉS sniffer.
III *vi* [*person, pig*] grogner; [*horse, bull*] s'ébrouer; **to ~ with laughter** rire comme un cheval.

snot○ /snɒt/ *n* (mucus) morve *f.*

snotty○ /'snɒtɪ/ *adj* **1** [*nose*] plein de morve; **2** [*person*] prétentieux/-ieuse.

snout /snaʊt/ *n* museau *m*; (of pig) groin *m.*

snow /snəʊ/ **I** *n* (all contexts) neige *f.*
II *v impers* neiger; **it's ~ing** il neige.
■ **snow in** (also ~ **up**): **to be ~ed in** être bloqué par la neige.
■ **snow under**: **to be ~ed under** LIT être couvert de neige; FIG être submergé (**with** de).

snowball /'snəʊbɔːl/ **I** *n* LIT boule *f* de neige.
II *vi* FIG [*profits, problem*] faire boule de neige.
IDIOMS **it hasn't got a ~'s chance in hell**○ c'est perdu d'avance.

snow: ~**bank** US *n* congère *f*; ~ **blindness** *n* cécité *f* des neiges.

snowboard /'snəʊbɔːd/ SPORT **I** *n* surf *m* des neiges.
II *vi* faire du surf des neiges.

snow: ~**boot** *n* après-ski *m inv*; ~**bound** *adj* GEN bloqué par la neige; [*region*] paralysé par la neige; ~ **chains** *npl* AUT chaînes *fpl*; ~**drift** *n* congère *f*; ~**drop** *n* BOT perce-neige *m inv*; ~**fall** *n* chute *f* de neige; ~**flake** *n* flocon *m* de neige; ~**man** *n* bonhomme *m* de neige; ~ **mobile** *n* AUT motoneige *f*; ~ **plough** GB, ~ **plow** US *n* AUT, SPORT chasse-neige *m inv*; ~ **report** *n* METEOROL bulletin *m* d'enneigement; ~ **shoe** *n* raquette *f*; ~**storm** *n* tempête *f* de neige; ~ **suit** *n* combinaison *f* de ski; ~ **tyre** GB, ~ **tire** US *n* pneu *m* clouté.

snowy /'snəʊɪ/ *adj* **1** LIT (after a snowfall) enneigé; (usually under snow) neigeux/-euse; **it will be ~ tomorrow** il neigera demain; **2** FIG (white) blanc/blanche (comme neige).

Snr. *abrév écrite* = **Senior**.

snub /snʌb/ **I** *n* rebuffade *f.*
II *vtr* (*p prés etc* -**bb**-) rembarrer; **to be ~bed** essuyer une rebuffade (**by** de la part de).

snub: ~ **nose** *n* nez *m* retroussé; ~-**nosed** *adj* au nez retroussé.

snuff /snʌf/ **I** *n* tabac *m* à priser.
II *vtr* (put out) moucher [*candle*].
IDIOMS **to ~ it**○ casser sa pipe○.
■ **snuff out**: ~ **out** [*sth*] **1** moucher [*candle*]; **2** FIG éteindre [*hope, interest*]; étouffer [*rebellion, enthusiasm*]; **3**○ (kill) descendre○ [*person*].

snuffle /'snʌfl/ **I** *n* (of animal, person) reniflement *m*; **to have the ~s** renifler parce qu'on est enrhumé.
II *vi* renifler.
■ **snuffle around** renifler.

snug /snʌɡ/ **I** *n* GB petite arrière-salle *d'un bar.*
II *adj* [*bed, room*] douillet; [*coat*] chaud.

snuggle /'snʌɡl/ *vi* se blottir (**into** dans).
■ **snuggle up** se blottir (**against, beside** contre).

snugly /'snʌɡlɪ/ *adv* **the coat fits** ~ le manteau est parfaitement ajusté; **the lid should fit** ~ le couvercle devrait s'adapter parfaitement; **he's ~ tucked up in bed** il est bien au chaud dans son lit.

so /səʊ/ **I** *adv* **1** (so very) si, tellement; **not ~**○ **thin as** pas aussi maigre que; **I'm not feeling ~ good**○ je ne me sens pas très bien; **2** (to limited extent) **we can only work ~ fast and no faster** nous ne pouvons vraiment pas travailler plus vite; **you can only do ~ much (and no more)** tu ne peux rien faire de plus; **3** (in such a way) **~ arranged that** organisé d'une telle façon que; **walk ~** marchez comme ça; **and ~ on and ~ forth** et ainsi de suite; **just as in the 19th century, ~ today** tout comme au XIXᵉ siècle, aujourd'hui; **~ be it!** soit!; **she likes everything to be just ~** elle aime que les choses soient parfaitement en ordre; **4** (for that reason) **~ it was that** c'est ainsi que; **she was young and ~ lacked experience** elle était jeune et donc sans expérience; **5** (true) **is that ~?** c'est vrai?; **if (that's)** ~ si c'est vrai; **6** (also) aussi; **~ is she** elle aussi; **if they accept ~ do I** s'ils acceptent, j'accepte aussi; **7**○ (thereabouts) environ; **20 or ~** environ 20; **8** (as introductory remark) **~ there you are** te voilà donc; **~ that's the reason** voilà donc pourquoi; **~ you're going are you?** alors tu y vas?; **9** (avoiding repetition) **he's conscientious, perhaps too much ~** il est consciencieux, peut-être même trop; **he's the owner or ~ he claims** c'est le propriétaire du moins c'est ce qu'il prétend ; **he dived and as he did ~**... il a plongé et en le faisant...; **perhaps ~** c'est possible; **I believe ~** je crois; **I believe** c'est ce que je crois; **I'm afraid ~** j'ai bien peur que oui or si; **~ it would appear** c'est ce qu'il semble; **~ to speak** si je puis dire; **I told you ~** je te l'avais bien dit; **~ I see** je le vois bien; **who says ~?** qui dit ça?; **only more ~** mais encore plus; **the question is unsettled and will remain ~** la question n'est pas résolue et ne le sera pas; **10** SOUT (referring forward or back) **if you ~ wish you may**... si vous le souhaitez, vous pouvez...; **11** (reinforcing a statement) **'I thought you liked it?'—'~ I do'** 'je croyais que ça te plaisait'—'mais ça me plaît'; **'it's broken'—'~ it is'** 'c'est cassé'—'je le vois bien!'; **'I'm sorry'—'~ you should be'** 'je suis désolé'—'j'espère bien'; **it just ~ happens that** il se trouve justement que; **12**° (refuting a statement) **'he didn't hit you'—'he did ~!'** 'il ne t'a pas frappé?'—'si, il m'a frappé'; **I can ~ make waffles** si, je sais faire les gaufres; **13**° (as casual response) et alors; **'I'm leaving'—'~?'** 'je m'en vais'—'et alors?'; **~ why worry!** et alors, il n'y a pas de quoi t'en faire!

II so (**that**) *conj phr* **1** (in such a way that) de façon à ce que; **she wrote the instructions ~ that they'd be easily understood** elle a rédigé les instructions de façon à ce qu'elles soient faciles à comprendre; **2** (in order that) pour que.

III so as *conj phr* pour.

IV so much *adv phr, pron phr* **1** (also **~ many**) (such large quantity) tant de; **~ much of her life** une si grande partie de sa vie; **~ many of her friends** un si grand nombre de ses amis; **2** (also **~ many**) (limited amount) **I can only make ~ much bread** je ne peux pas faire plus de pain; **there's only ~ much you can take** il y a des limites à ce qu'on peut supporter; **3** (to such an extent) tellement; **~ much worse** tellement pire; **~ much ~ that** à un tel point que; **thank you ~ much** merci beaucoup; **4** (in contrasts) **not ~ much X as Y** moins X que Y.

V so much as *adv phr* (even) même; **he never ~ much as apologized** il ne s'est même pas excusé.

VI so much for *prep phr* **1** (having finished with) **~ much for that problem, now for**... assez parlé de ce problème, parlons maintenant de...; **2**° (used disparagingly) **~ much for equality** bonjour l'égalité; **~ much for saying you'd help** c'était bien la peine de dire que tu aiderais.

VII so long as° *conj phr* ▶ **long**.

IDIOMS **~ long**°! à bientôt!; **~ much the better** tant mieux; **~ is ~** comme ci comme ça; **~ there!** d'abord!

soak /səʊk/ I *n* **1** **to give sth a ~** GB faire tremper qch; **to have a ~** prendre un long bain; **2**° (drunk) poivrot/-ote° *m/f*.
II *vtr* **1** (wet) tremper; **to get ~ed** se faire tremper; **2** (immerse) faire tremper.
III *vi* **1** (be immersed) tremper; **to leave sth to ~** mettre qch à tremper; **2** (be absorbed) **to ~ into** être absorbé par; **to ~ through** traverser.
IV *v refl* **to ~ oneself** se tremper.
V **soaked** *pp adj* tremper; **to be ~ed through** ou **~ed to the skin** être trempé jusqu'aux os.
VI **-soaked** *combining form* **blood-~ed** imbibé de sang; **sweat-~ed** trempé de sueur; **sun-~ed** ensoleillé.
■ **soak away** [*water*] être absorbé.
■ **soak in** pénétrer.
■ **soak off**: ¶ **~ off** se décoller; ¶ **~ [sth] off, ~ off [sth]** décoller [qch] en le mouillant.
■ **soak up**: ¶ **~ [sth] up, ~ up [sth]** absorber; ¶ **~ up [sth]** s'imprégner de [*atmosphere*]; **to ~ up the sun** faire le plein° de soleil.

soaking /ˈsəʊkɪŋ/ I *n* GB douche° *f*.
II *adj* trempé; **I'm ~ wet** je suis trempé jusqu'aux os.

soap /səʊp/ I *n* **1** (for washing) savon *m*; **a bar of ~**

un savon; **2**° (flattery) (also **soft ~**) pommade° *f*; **3**° = **soap opera**.
II *vtr* savonner.

soapbox /ˈsəʊpbɒks/ *n* tribune *f* improvisée; **to get on one's ~** enfourcher son cheval de bataille; **~ orator** harangueur/-euse *m/f*.

soap: **~dish** *n* porte-savon *m inv*; **~flakes** *npl* savon *m* en paillettes; **~ opera** *n* RADIO, TV PÉJ feuilleton *m*; **~ powder** *n* lessive *f* (en poudre); **~suds** *npl* (foam) mousse *f* de savon.

soapy /ˈsəʊpi/ *adj* **1** LIT [*water*] savonneux/-euse; [*hands, face*] plein de savon; **2** (cajoling) GEN mielleux/-euse; [*manner*] onctueux/-euse.

soar /sɔː(r)/ *vi* **1** (rise sharply) GEN monter en flèche; [*hopes, spirits*] s'accroître considérablement; **2** GEN, FIN (rise) **to ~ beyond/above/through** dépasser; **to ~ to** atteindre; **3** (rise up) = **soar up**; **4** (glide) planer; **5** LITTÉR [*sound*] s'élever; [*tower, cliffs*] se dresser.
■ **soar up** [*bird, plane*] prendre son essor; [*ball*] filer.

soaring /ˈsɔːrɪŋ/ *adj* [*inflation, demand, profits*] en forte progression; [*prices, temperatures*] en forte hausse; [*hopes, popularity*] croissant; [*spire*] élancé.

sob /sɒb/ I *n* sanglot *m*.
II *vtr* (*p prés etc* **-bb-**) **to ~ oneself to sleep** s'endormir à force de sangloter.
III *vi* (*p prés etc* **-bb-**) sangloter.
IDIOMS **to ~ one's heart out** pleurer toutes les larmes de son corps.

sobbing /ˈsɒbɪŋ/ I *n* ₵ sanglots *mpl*.
II *adj* [*child*] sanglotant.

sober /ˈsəʊbə(r)/ I *adj* **1** (not drunk) **I'm ~** je n'ai pas bu d'alcool; (in protest) je ne suis pas ivre; **2** (no longer drunk) dessoûlé; **3** (serious) [*person*] sérieux/-ieuse; [*mood*] grave; **4** (realistic) GEN modéré; [*reminder*] réaliste; **5** (discreet) [*colour, style*] sobre.
II *vtr* (make serious) [*news, reprimand*] calmer.
■ **sober up**: **~ up** dessoûler.

sobering /ˈsəʊbərɪŋ/ *adj* **it was a ~ thought** cette pensée donnait à réfléchir.

soberly /ˈsəʊbəli/ *adv* **1** (seriously) [*speak*] avec modération; [*describe*] avec sobriété; **2** (discreetly) [*dressed*] discrètement; [*decorated*] sobrement.

sobriety /səˈbraɪəti/ *n* **1** (moderation) sobriété *f*; **2** (seriousness) sérieux *m*.

sob story /sɒb/° *n* mélo° *m*.

soccer /ˈsɒkə(r)/ ▶ **949**] I *n* football *m*.
II *noun modifier* [*player, team, club*] de football; [*star*] du football; **~ violence** violence *f* dans les tribunes.

sociable /ˈsəʊʃəbl/ *adj* [*person*] sociable; [*village*] accueillant.

social /ˈsəʊʃl/ I *n* (party) soirée *f*; (gathering) réunion *f*.
II *adj* **1** (relating to human society) social; **2** (recreational) [*activity*] de groupes; [*call, visit*] amical; **he's a ~ drinker** il boit de l'alcool en société; **he's got no ~ skills** il ne sait pas se comporter en société; **3** [*animal*] social.

social: **~ climber** *n* (still rising) arriviste *mf*; (at his/her peak) parvenu/-e *mf*; **~ club** *n* club *m*; **~ column** *n* carnet *m* mondain.

social conscience *n* **to have a ~** être conscient des injustices sociales.

social: **~ democrat** *n* social-démocrate *mf*; **~ engagement** *n* obligation *f* sociale; **~ evening** *n* soirée *f*; **~ event** *n* événement *m* mondain; **~ gathering** *n* réunion *f* entre amis; **~ insurance** *n* US **~** sécurité *f* sociale.

socialism /ˈsəʊʃəlɪzəm/ *n* socialisme *m*.

socialist /ˈsəʊʃəlɪst/ *n, adj* (also **Socialist**) socialiste (*mf*).

socialite /ˈsəʊʃəlaɪt/ *n* mondain/-e *m/f*.

socialize /ˈsəʊʃəlaɪz/ *vi* (mix socially) rencontrer des gens; **to ~ with sb** fréquenter qn.

social life *n* (of person) vie *f* sociale; (of town) vie *f* culturelle.

socially /ˈsəʊʃəli/ *adv* [*meet, mix*] en société; [*acceptable*] en société; [*inferior, superior*] du point de vue social; [*oriented*] vers le social; **I know him ~**, **not professionally** je le connais personnellement, mais pas sur le plan professionnel.

social: **~ misfit** *n* inadapté/-e *m/f*; **~ outcast** *n* paria *m*; **~ register** *n* US carnet *m* mondain.

social scene *n* **she's well known on the London ~** elle est très connue dans la société londonienne.

social: **~ science** *n* science *f* sociale; **~ secretary** *n* (of club) secrétaire *mf* (du club).

social security *n* (benefit) aide *f* sociale; **to be on ~** recevoir l'aide sociale.

social: Social Security Administration, SSA *n* US *service de gestion de la retraite et des pensions;* **~ service** *n* US ▶ **social work**; **Social Services** *npl* GB services *mpl* sociaux; **~ studies** *n* (+ *v sg*) sciences *fpl* humaines; **~ welfare** *n* protection *f* sociale; **~ work** *n* travail *m* social; **~ worker** ▶ **1251**] *n* travailleur/-euse *m/f* social/-e.

society /sə'saɪətɪ/ **I** *n* **1** (community) société *f*; **2** (club) (for social) association *f*; (for mutual hobbies) club *m*; (for intellectual, business, contact) société *f*; **drama ~** société de théâtre; **3** (upper classes) (also **high ~**) haute société *f*; **fashionable ~** le beau monde.
II *noun modifier* [*artist, columnist, photographer, wedding*] mondain; [*hostess*] des soirées mondaines; **~ gossip** échos *mpl* mondains.

sociological /ˌsəʊsɪə'lɒdʒɪkl/ *adj* [*study, research, issue*] sociologique; [*studies*] de sociologie.

sociologist /ˌsəʊsɪ'ɒlədʒɪst/ ▶ **1251**] *n* sociologue *mf*.

sociology /ˌsəʊsɪ'ɒlədʒɪ/ *n* sociologie *f*.

sock /sɒk/ ▶ **1260**] **I** *n* (US *pl* **~s** OU **sox**) **1** (footwear) chaussette *f*; **2** AVIAT (also **wind ~**) manche *f* à air; **3**○ (punch) beigne○ *f*.
II○ *vtr* flanquer une beigne○ à.
IDIOMS **to put a ~ in it**○ la boucler○; **to ~ it to them**○ donner le maximum; **to pull one's ~s up**○ se remuer.

socket /'sɒkɪt/ *n* **1** ELEC (for plug) prise *f* (de courant); (for bulb) douille *f*; **2** ANAT (of joint) cavité *f* articulaire; (of eye) orbite *f*; **he nearly pulled my arm out of its ~** il a failli me déboîter le bras.

soda /'səʊdə/ **I** *n* **1** CHEM soude *f*; **2** (also **washing ~**) soude *f* ménagère; **3** (also **~ water**) eau *f* de seltz; **whisky and ~** whisky *m* soda; **4** (also **~ pop**) US soda *m*.
II *noun modifier* [*bottle*] de soda; [*crystals*] de soude.

soda: **~ fountain** *n* US distributeur *m* de soda; **~ siphon** *n* siphon *m* d'eau de seltz.

sodden /'sɒdn/ *adj* **1** (wet through) [*towel, clothing*] trempé; [*ground*] détrempé; **2** FIG **~ with drink** abruti d'alcool.

Sod's Law○ /ˌsɒdz'lɔ:/ *n* HUM loi *f* de l'emmerdement⁹ maximum.

sofa /'səʊfə/ *n* canapé *m*.

sofa bed *n* canapé-lit *m*.

soft /sɒft, US so:ft/ *adj* **1** (not rigid or firm) [*ground*] meuble; SPORT lourd; [*rock, metal*] tendre; [*snow*] léger/-ère; [*bed, cushion*] moelleux/-euse; [*fabric, fur, skin, hand*] doux/douce; [*brush, hair, leather*] souple; [*muscle*] flasque; [*dough, butter*] mou/molle; **to get ~** [*ground, butter, mixture*] s'amollir; **to make sth ~** amollir [*ground*]; ramollir [*butter, mixture*]; adoucir [*hard water, skin*]; **~ to the touch** doux au toucher; **~ ice cream** glace *f* italienne; **2** (muted) [*colour, sound*] doux/douce; [*step, knock*] feutré; **~ lighting** éclairage *m* tamisé; **3** (gentle, mild) [*air, climate, rain, water, breeze, look, words*] doux/douce; [*pressure, touch*] léger/-ère; [*landing*] AVIAT en douceur; [*eyes, heart*] tendre; [*approach*] GEN diplomatique; POL modéré; **the ~ left** la gauche modérée; **to take a ~ line with sb** adopter une ligne modérée avec qn; **4** (not sharp) [*outline*] flou; [*fold*] souple; **5** ECON [*market*] instable à la baisse; **6** (lenient) [*parent, teacher*] (trop) indulgent; **7**○ (in love) **to be ~ on sb** en pincer○ pour qn; **8** (idle) [*life, job*] peinard○; **9**○ (stupid) stupide; **to be ~ in the head** être ramolli du cerveau.

soft: **~back** *n* livre *m* à couverture plastifiée; **~ball** *n* US *variante du baseball;* **~-boiled** *adj* [*egg*] à la coque; **~-centred** *adj* [*chocolate*] fourré; **~ cheese** *n* fromage *m* à pâte molle; **~ copy** *n* COMPUT visualisation *f* sur écran; **~ drink** *n* boisson *f* non alcoolisée; **~ drug** *n* drogue *f* douce.

soften /'sɒfn, US 'so:fn/ **I** *vtr* **1** LIT (make less firm or rough) amollir [*ground, metal*]; adoucir [*skin, hard water*]; ramollir [*butter*]; **2** FIG atténuer [*blow, impact, shock, pain, resistance*]; adoucir [*refusal*]; assouplir [*attitude, position, rule*]; minimiser [*fact*]; **3** (make quieter) adoucir [*sound, voice*]; **4** (make less sharp) adoucir [*form, outline, light*].
II *vi* **1** LIT [*light, outline, music, colour*] s'adoucir; [*skin*] devenir plus doux; [*substance, ground*] se ramollir; **2** FIG [*person, approach*] s'assouplir (**towards sb** vis-à-vis de qn); **3** ECON fléchir.
■ **soften up**: ¶ **~ up** amollir; ¶ **~ up** [*sb*], **~ [sb] up** affaiblir [*opponent*]; attendrir [*customer*].

softener /'sɒfnə(r), US 'so:f-/ *n* **1** (also **fabric ~**) (produit *m*) assouplissant *m*; **2** (also **water ~**) adoucisseur *m*.

softening /'sɒfnɪŋ, US 'so:f-/ *n* **1** (becoming soft) LIT (of substance, surface) ramollissement *m*; FIG (of light, colour, outline, water) adoucissement *m*; (of character, attitude) assouplissement *m* (**towards sb/sth** vis-à-vis de qn/qch); (of sound) atténuation *f*; **2** FIN fléchissement *m*.

soft focus *n* flou *m* artistique.

soft: **~ fruit** *n* ¢ fruits *mpl* charnus; **~ furnishings** *npl* tapis et tissus *mpl* d'ameublement; **~-hearted** *adj* qui se laisse facilement apitoyer or attendrir.

softly /'sɒftlɪ, US 'so:ft-/ *adv* GEN doucement.

softly-softly /'sɒftlɪ'sɒftlɪ, US ˌso:ftlɪ'so:ftlɪ/ *adj* [*approach*] ultraprudent; **to take a ~ approach** prendre des gants.

softness /'sɒftnɪs, US 'so:ft-/ *n* (of texture, surface, skin, colour, light, outline, character, sound) douceur *f*; (of substance) consistance *f* molle; FIG (of attitude, approach, view) modération *f*; (in economy) fléchissement *m*.

soft option *n* **to take the ~** choisir la facilité.

soft-pedal /ˌsɒft'pedl, US ˌso:ft-/ **I soft pedal** *n* MUS pédale *f* douce.
II *vi* (*p prés etc* **-ll-** GB, **-l-** US) **1** MUS mettre la pédale douce; **2** FIG mettre un bémol FIG (**on** à).

soft: **~ porn** *n* soft○ *m*; **~ sell** *n* (méthode *f* de) vente *f* persuasive.

soft soap I *n* **1** LIT savon *m* semi-liquide; **2**○ FIG flagornerie○ *f*.
II soft-soap *vtr* FIG passer de la pommade○ à.

soft-spoken /ˌsɒft'spəʊkn, US ˌso:ft-/ *adj* à la voix douce; **to be ~** avoir une voix douce.

soft spot○ *n* **to have a ~ for sb** avoir un faible○ pour qn.

soft: **~ target** *n* MIL, FIG cible *f* vulnérable; **~ tissue** *n* MED parties *fpl* charnues; **~-top** *n* AUT décapotable *f*; **~ touch**○ *n* poire○ *f*; **~ toy** *n* peluche *f*.

software /'sɒftweə(r), US 'so:ft-/ **I** *n* logiciel *m*.
II *noun modifier* [*development, engineering, protection*] informatique; [*company, designer*] de logiciels; [*industry, market*] du logiciel; **~ product** logiciel *m*.

software: **~ house** *n* fabricant *m* de logiciels; **~ package** *n* COMPUT progiciel *m*.

softwood /'sɒftwʊd, US 'so:ft-/ *n* **1** (timber) bois *m* tendre; **2** (tree) conifère *m*.

softy○ /'sɒftɪ, US 'so:ftɪ/ *n* **1** PÉJ (weak person) mauviette○ *f*; **2** (indulgent person) bonne pâte○ *f*.

soggy /'sɒgɪ/ *adj* [*ground*] détrempé; [*food*] ramolli.

soh /səʊ/ *n* MUS sol *m*.

soil /sɔɪl/ **I** *n* sol *m*, terre *f*; **on British ~** en territoire britannique.
II *vtr* LIT, FIG salir.

solace /'sɒləs/ **I** *n* (feeling of comfort) consolation *f*; (source of comfort) réconfort *m*.
II *vtr* consoler (**for** de).

solar /'səʊlə(r)/ *adj* GEN solaire; [*warmth*] du soleil.

solar: ~ **eclipse** n éclipse f de soleil; ~ **heating** n chauffage m solaire; ~ **panel** n panneau m solaire; ~ **power** n énergie f solaire.

sold /səʊld/ prét, pp ▶ **sell**.

solder /'səʊldə(r), 'sɒ-, US 'sɒdər/ **I** n soudure f.
II vtr, vi souder (**onto, to** à).

soldering iron n fer m à souder.

soldier /'səʊldʒə(r)/ ▶ **1251** **I** n soldat m; **old** ~ ancien combattant m; **regular** ~ militaire m de carrière.
II vi être militaire ou dans l'armée.
■ **soldier on** persévérer malgré tout.

soldierly /'səʊldʒəlɪ/ adj [person] à l'allure militaire; [appearance, bearing] militaire.

sole /səʊl/ **I** n **1** (fish) sole f; **2** (of shoe, sock, iron) semelle f; (of foot) plante f.
II adj **1** (single) seul, unique; **for the** ~ **purpose of doing** uniquement pour faire; **2** (exclusive) GEN exclusif/-ive; [trader] indépendant; **to be in** ~ **charge of sth** être seul responsable de qch.
III vtr ressemeler [shoe].
IV -**soled** combining form **rubber/leather**-~**d shoes** chaussures à semelle de caoutchouc/cuir.

sole beneficiary n JUR légataire m universel.

solecism /'sɒlɪsɪzəm/ n **1** LING solécisme m; **2** (social) bévue f.

solely /'səʊlɪ/ adv (wholly) entièrement; (exclusively) uniquement.

solemn /'sɒləm/ adj **1** (serious) GEN solennel/-elle; [duty, warning] formel/-elle; **2** (reverent) solennel/-elle.

solemnity /sə'lemnətɪ/ **I** n solennité f.
II solemnities npl cérémonial m ¢.

solemnize /'sɒləmnaɪz/ vtr célébrer [marriage]; ratifier [treaty].

sol-fa /ˌsɒl'fɑː, US ˌsəʊl-/ n solfège m.

solicit /sə'lɪsɪt/ **I** vtr **1** (request) GEN solliciter; rechercher [business, orders]; **2** [prostitute] racoler.
II vi **1** [prostitute] racoler; **2** (request) **to** ~ **for** GEN solliciter; rechercher [orders].

soliciting /sə'lɪsɪtɪŋ/ n JUR racolage m.

solicitor /sə'lɪsɪtə(r)/ ▶ **1251** n **1** GB JUR (for documents, oaths) ≈ notaire m; (for court and police work) ≈ avocat/-e m/f; **a firm of** ~**s** ≈ un cabinet d'avocats; **2** US COMM démarcheur/-euse m/f.

solicitous /sə'lɪsɪtəs/ adj SOUT [expression, person] plein de sollicitude; [enquiry, letter, response] attentionné (**about** sur).

solid /'sɒlɪd/ **I** n CHEM, MATH solide m.
II solids npl (food) aliments mpl solides.
III adj **1** (not liquid or gaseous) solide; **to go** ou **become** ~ se solidifier; **2** (of one substance) GEN massif/-ive; **the gate was made of** ~ **steel** le portail était tout en acier; **a tunnel cut through** ~ **rock** un tunnel taillé dans la masse rocheuse; **3** (dense) compact; **4** (unbroken) [line, expanse] continu; **a** ~ **area of red** une surface rouge unie; **5** (uninterrupted) **five** ~ **days, five days** ~ cinq jours entiers; **6** (strong) GEN solide; [building] massif/-ive; **to be on** ~ **ground** FIG être en terrain sûr; **7** (reliable) [information] solide; [advice, worker, work] sérieux/-ieuse; [investment] sûr; **8** (firm) [grip] ferme; **the strike has remained** ~ la grève n'a pas fléchi; **9** (respectable) modèle.
IV adv [freeze] complètement; FIG [vote] massivement; **the play is booked** ~ la pièce affiche complet.

solidarity /ˌsɒlɪ'dærətɪ/ n solidarité f; **to feel** ~ **with sb** se sentir solidaire de qn.

solid fuel n combustible m solide.

solidify /sə'lɪdɪfaɪ/ **I** vtr solidifier.
II vi [liquid] se solidifier; [honey, oil] se figer.

solidity /sə'lɪdətɪ/ n (of construction, relationship, currency) solidité f; (of research, arguments) sérieux m.

solidly /'sɒlɪdlɪ/ adv **1** [built] solidement; **2** ~ **packed** [crowd] compact; [earth] très tassé; **3** (continuously) sans interruption; **4** (staunchly) [conservative, socialist] à cent pour cent; **they are** ~ **behind him** ils le soutiennent massivement.

solid-state /ˌsɒlɪd'steɪt/ adj [microelectronics] à semi conducteur(s); ~ **physics** physique f des solides.

solitaire /ˌsɒlɪ'teə(r), US 'sɒlɪteər/ ▶ **949** n **1** (ring, board game) solitaire m; **2** US (with cards) réussite f.

solitary /'sɒlɪtrɪ, US -terɪ/ **I** n (loner) solitaire mf.
II adj **1** (unaccompanied) [occupation, walker] solitaire; **2** (lonely) [person] très seul; [farm, village] isolé; **3** (single) seul; **a** ~ **case of** un cas unique de.

solitary confinement n JUR, MIL isolement m cellulaire.

solo /'səʊləʊ/ **I** n GEN, MUS solo m.
II adj **1** MUS **for** ~ **piano** pour piano solo; **for** ~ **voice** pour voix seule; **2** [album, flight, pilot] en solo.
III adv [dance, fly, perform, play] en solo.

soloist /'səʊləʊɪst/ n soliste mf.

solstice /'sɒlstɪs/ n solstice m.

soluble /'sɒljʊbl/ adj (all contexts) soluble; **water-**~ soluble dans l'eau.

solution /sə'luːʃn/ n **1** (answer) solution f (**to** de); **2** CHEM (dissolving) dissolution f; (mixture) solution f.

solve /sɒlv/ vtr résoudre [equation, problem]; élucider [crime]; trouver la solution de [mystery]; trouver la solution à [clue, crossword]; trouver une solution à [crisis, poverty].

solvency /'sɒlvənsɪ/ n FIN solvabilité f.

solvent /'sɒlvənt/ **I** n CHEM solvant m.
II adj **1** CHEM dissolvant; **2** FIN solvable.

solvent abuse n usage m de solvants hallucinogènes.

sombre GB, **somber** US /'sɒmbə(r)/ adj sombre.

some /sʌm/

■ **Note** When some is used as a quantifier to mean an unspecified amount of something, it is translated by du, de l' before vowel or mute h, de la or des according to the gender and number of the noun that follows: I'd like some bread = je voudrais du pain; have some water = prenez de l'eau; we've bought some beer = nous avons acheté de la bière; they've bought some peaches = ils ont acheté des pêches.
– But note that where some is followed by an adjective preceding a plural noun, de alone is used in all cases: some pretty dresses = de jolies robes.
– For particular usages see I below.
– When some is used as a pronoun it is translated by en which is placed before the verb in French: would you like some? = est-ce que vous en voulez?; I've got some = j'en ai.
– For particular usages see II below.

I det, quantif **1** (an unspecified amount or number) ~ **cheese** du fromage; ~ **old socks** de vieilles chaussettes; **2** (certain: in contrast to others) certains; ~ **children like it** certains enfants aiment ça; **in** ~ **ways, I agree** d'une certaine façon, je suis d'accord; ~ **people say that** certaines personnes disent que; **in** ~ **parts of Europe** dans certaines parties de l'Europe; **3** (a considerable amount or number) **he has** ~ **cause for complaint** il a des raisons de se plaindre; **it will take** ~ **doing** ça ne va pas être facile à faire; **we stayed there for** ~ **time** nous sommes restés là assez longtemps; **we waited for** ~ **years** nous avons attendu plusieurs années; **he hadn't seen her for** ~ **years** ça faisait plusieurs années qu'il ne l'avait pas vue; **a** (little, a slight) **the meeting did have** ~ **effect** la réunion a eu un certain effet; **the candidate needs to have** ~ **knowledge of computers** le candidat doit avoir certaines ou un minimum de connaissances en informatique; **you must have** ~ **idea where the house is** tu dois avoir une idée de l'endroit où la maison se trouve; **this money will go** ~ **way towards compensating her for her injuries** cet argent compensera un peu ses blessures; **to** ~ **extent** dans une certaine mesure; **well that's** ~ **consolation anyway!** c'est toujours ça^O!; **5** PÉJ (unspecified, unknown) ~ **man came to the house** un homme est venu à la maison; **a car of** ~ **sort,** ~ **sort of car** une sorte de voiture; **6**^O (a remarkable) **that was** ~ **film!** ça c'était un film!; **that's** ~ **woman**

ou **man!** c'est quelqu'un!; **7**○ (not much) ~ **help you are!** IRON c'est ça que tu appelles aider!; ~ **mechanic he is!** tu parles d'un mécanicien!; **'I'd like the work to be finished by Monday'—'~ hope!** 'j'aimerais que le travail soit fini avant lundi'—'tu rêves○!'
II pron **1** (an unspecified amount or number) **I'd like ~ of those** j'en voudrais quelques-uns comme ça; **(do) have ~!** servez-vous!; **(do) have ~ more!** reprenezen!; **2** (certain ones: in contrast to others) ~ **(of them) are blue** certains sont bleus; ~ **say that** certaines personnes disent que; **I agree with ~ of what you say** je suis d'accord avec une partie de ce que tu dis; ~ **(of them) arrived early** certains d'entre eux sont arrivés tôt.
III adv **1** (approximately) environ; ~ **20 people** environ 20 personnes; ~ **£50** autour de 50 livres sterling; **2**○ US (a lot) un peu; **from here to the town center in 5 minutes, that's going ~**○ aller d'ici au centre ville en 5 minutes, il faut le faire.
IDIOMS ~ **people!** ah vraiment, il y a des gens!

somebody /'sʌmbədɪ/ pron **1** (unspecified person) quelqu'un; ~ **famous** quelqu'un de célèbre; **Mr Somebody(-or-other)** M. Machin; **ask John or Henry or ~** demande à John, à Henry ou à n'importe qui d'autre; **2** (important person) **he (really) thinks he's ~** il ne se prend pas pour n'importe qui; **they think they're ~** ils se prennent pour des gens importants.
IDIOMS ~ **up there likes me** il y a quelqu'un là-haut qui veille sur moi.

somehow /'sʌmhaʊ/ adv **1** (by some means) (also ~ **or other**) (of future action) d'une manière ou d'une autre; (of past action) je ne sais comment; **2** (for some reason) ~ **it doesn't seem very important** en fait, ça ne semble pas très important; ~ **he never seems to get it right** il semble que rien ne lui réussisse jamais.

someone /'sʌmwʌn/ pron = **somebody**.

someplace /'sʌmpleɪs/ adv = **somewhere**.

somersault /'sʌməsɔːlt/ **I** n **1** (of gymnast) roulade f; (of child) galipette f; (of diver) saut m périlleux; (accidental) culbute f; **2** (of vehicle) tonneau m.
II vi [gymnast] faire une roulade; [diver] faire un saut périlleux; [vehicle] faire un tonneau.

something /'sʌmθɪŋ/ **I** pron **1** (unspecified thing) quelque chose; ~ **new/interesting** quelque chose de nouveau/d'intéressant; **he's always trying to get ~ for nothing** il est radin○; **there's ~ wrong** il y a un problème; ~ **or other** quelque chose; **she's ~ (or other) in the army** elle est je ne sais quoi dans l'armée; **2** (thing of importance, value etc) **it proves ~** ça prouve quelque chose; **to make ~ of oneself** ou **one's life** réussir sa vie; **he got ~ out of it** il en a tiré quelque chose; **he is quite** ou **really ~!** c'est vraiment un numéro!; **do you want to make ~ out of it?** tu veux te battre?; **that house is quite** ou **really ~!** cette maison c'est quelque chose!; **there's ~ in what he says** il y a du vrai dans ce qu'il dit; **you've got ~ there!** là, tu n'as pas tort!; **he has a certain ~** il a un petit quelque chose; **'I've found the key'—'well that's ~ anyway'** 'j'ai trouvé la clé'—'c'est déjà ça'; **we gave him ~ for his trouble** nous lui avons donné un petit quelque chose pour le dérangement; **3** (forgotten, unknown name, amount etc) **his name's Andy ~** il s'appelle Andy quelque chose; **in nineteen-sixty-~** en mille neuf cent soixante et quelques; **she's gone shopping or ~** elle est allée faire les courses ou quelque chose comme ça; **are you stupid or ~?** tu es bête ou quoi○?
II adv **1** (a bit) un peu; ~ **over/under £20** un peu plus de/en dessous de 20 livres sterling; ~ **around 100 kilos** environ 100 kilos; **2**○ **he was howling ~ awful** ou **shocking** il n'arrêtait pas de hurler.
III something of adv phr (rather, quite) **he is** (also) ~ **of an actor** il est aussi un assez bon acteur; **she is** ~ **of an expert on…** elle est assez experte en…; **it was ~ of a surprise** c'était assez étonnant; **it was ~ of a disaster** c'était plutôt désastreux.

sometime /'sʌmtaɪm/ **I** adv **we'll have to do it ~** il va falloir qu'on le fasse un jour ou l'autre; **all holidays have to end ~** toutes les vacances ont une fin;

I'll tell you about it ~ je te raconterai ça un de ces jours; **I'll phone you ~ tomorrow/next week** je te téléphonerai demain dans la journée/dans le courant de la semaine prochaine.
II adj **1** (former) ancien/-ienne; **2** US occasionnel/-elle.

sometimes /'sʌmtaɪmz/ adv parfois, quelquefois; (in contrast) ~ **angry,** ~ **depressed** tantôt en colère, tantôt déprimé.

somewhat /'sʌmwɒt/ adv (with adj) plutôt; (with verb, adverb) un peu; ~ **differently** un peu différemment; ~ **surprisingly** de façon quelque peu surprenante; ~ **to her surprise** à sa grande surprise.

somewhere /'sʌmweə(r)/ adv **1** (some place) quelque part; **she's ~ about** ou **around** elle est quelque part par là; ~ **hot** un endroit chaud; **he needs ~ to sleep** il a besoin d'un endroit pour dormir; ~ **or other** je ne sais où; ~ **(or other) in Asia** quelque part en Asie; **they live in Manchester or ~**○ ils habitent à Manchester ou quelque chose comme ça; **2** (at an unspecified point in range) ~ **between 50 and 100 people** entre 50 et 100 personnes; ~ **around 10 o'clock** autour de 10 heures.
IDIOMS **now we're getting ~!** (in questioning) voilà enfin des informations utiles!; (making progress) on arrive enfin à quelque chose!

son /sʌn/ n **1** (male child) fils m (**of** de); **an only ~** fils unique; **my ~ and heir** mon héritier; **2**○ (as form of address) (kindly) fiston○ m; (patronizingly) mon gars m.
IDIOMS **every mother's ~ (of them)** tous autant qu'ils sont.

sonata /sə'nɑːtə/ n sonate f; **violin ~** sonate pour violon.

song /sɒŋ/ n **1** MUS chanson f; **give us a ~** chantenous quelque chose; **to burst into ~** se mettre à chanter; **2** (of bird) chant m (**of** de).
IDIOMS **for a ~**○ pour rien.

song and dance n THEAT chanson f dansée.
IDIOMS **to make a ~ about sth**○ GB faire toute une histoire de qch.

song: ~**bird** n oiseau m chanteur; ~**writer** ▶ **1251** n (of words) parolier/-ière m/f; (of words and music) auteur-compositeur m de chansons.

sonic /'sɒnɪk/ adj [vibration] sonore; ~ **interference** parasites mpl.

sonic boom n bang m.

son-in-law /'sɒnɪnlɔː/ n gendre m.

sonnet /'sɒnɪt/ n sonnet m.

sonorous /'sɒnərəs, sə'nɔːrəs/ adj GEN sonore; [name] ronflant.

soon /suːn/ adv **1** (in a short time) bientôt; **it will ~ be three years since we met** voici bientôt trois ans que nous nous sommes rencontrés; **see you ~!** à bientôt!; **2** (quickly) vite; **it ~ became clear that** il est vite devenu évident que; **3** (early) tôt; ~ **enough** assez tôt; **the ~er the better** le plus tôt sera le mieux; **the ~er we leave, the ~er we'll get there** plus nous partirons tôt et plus nous y serons vite; **as ~ as possible** dès que possible; **I spoke too ~** j'ai parlé trop vite!; **as ~ as he arrives** dès qu'il arrivera; **~er or later** tôt ou tard; **all too ~ the summer was over** l'été est passé bien trop vite; **tomorrow at the ~est** demain au plus tôt; **and not a moment too ~!** il était temps!; **4** (not long) **they left ~ after us** ils sont partis peu après nous; ~ **afterwards** peu après; **no ~er had I done sth than…** j'avais à peine fait qch que…; **5** (rather) **I would just as ~ do X as do Y** j'aime autant faire X que faire Y; **I would ~er not do** j'aime autant ne pas faire; ~**er him than me!** plutôt lui que moi!; **he would ~er die than do** il préférerait mourir que de faire.
IDIOMS **least said ~est mended** PROV moins on en dit, mieux ça vaut; **no ~er said than done** aussitôt dit aussitôt fait.

soot /sʊt/ n suie f.

soothe /suːð/ **I** vtr GEN calmer; apaiser [sunburn].
II vi [voice] rassurer; [lotion, massage] faire du bien.
■ **soothe away**: ~ **away** [sth], ~ [sth] **away** calmer.

soothing /'suːðɪŋ/ adj [cream, music, person, presence, voice] apaisant; [effect] calmant; [word] rassurant.

soothingly /'suːðɪŋlɪ/ adv [stroke] de façon apaisante; [speak] de façon rassurante.

sooty /'sʊtɪ/ adj (covered in soot) [object] couvert de suie; [air] chargé de suie; (black) tout noir.

sop /sɒp/ I n **1** (of bread) morceau m de pain trempé; **2** (concession) concession f; **as a ~ to her pride** pour flatter son orgueil; **to offer sth as a ~ to sb** offrir qch pour amadouer qn.
II vtr (p prés etc -**pp**-) tremper [bread, cake] (**in** dans).
■ **sop up**: ~ **up** [sth], ~ [sth] **up** éponger.

sophisticated /sə'fɪstɪkeɪtɪd/ adj **1** (smart) [person] (cultured) raffiné, sophistiqué PÉJ; (elegant) chic inv; [clothes, fashion] recherché PÉJ; [restaurant, resort] chic inv; [magazine] sophistiqué; **2** (discriminating) [mind, taste] raffiné; [audience, public] averti; [civilization] évolué; **3** (elaborate, complex) [equipment, technology] sophistiqué; [argument, joke] subtil; [style] recherché.

sophistication /sə,fɪstɪ'keɪʃn/ n **1** (smartness) (of person) (in lifestyle) raffinement m, sophistication f PÉJ; (in judgment) finesse f; (in appearance) chic m; (of restaurant, resort, magazine) chic m; (of mind, tastes) raffinement m; **lack of ~** simplicité f; **2** (of audience, public) caractère m averti; **3** (complexity) (of equipment) sophistication f; (of discussion, joke) subtilité f.

sophomore /'sɒfəmɔː(r)/ n US UNIV étudiant/-e en deuxième année d'université; SCH étudiant/-e en deuxième année de lycée.

soporific /,sɒpə'rɪfɪk/ adj (sleep-inducing) soporifique.

sopping /'sɒpɪŋ/ adj (also ~ **wet**) trempé.

soppy◦ /'sɒpɪ/ adj PÉJ sentimental.

soprano /sə'prɑːnəʊ, US -'præn-/ ▶ 1380 I n (pl ~**s**) **1** (person) soprano mf; **2** (voice, instrument) soprano m.
II adj GEN de soprano; [part, aria] pour soprano.

sorcerer /'sɔːsərə(r)/ n sorcier m.

sorcery /'sɔːsərɪ/ n (witchcraft) sorcellerie f.

sordid /'sɔːdɪd/ adj sordide; **to go into all the ~ details of sth** HUM raconter qch dans tous ses détails.

sore /sɔː(r)/ I n plaie f.
II adj **1** (sensitive) [eyes, throat, nose, gums] irrité; [muscle, tendon, arm, foot] endolori; **to have a ~ throat** avoir mal à la gorge; **to be** ou **feel ~ (all over)** avoir mal (partout); **my leg is still a bit ~** ma jambe me fait encore un peu mal; **you'll only make it ~ by scratching** tu vas t'irriter encore plus si tu te grattes; **2**◦ SURTOUT US (peeved) vexé; **to be ~ about** ou **over sth** être vexé par qch; **to be ~ at sb** en vouloir à qn; **to get ~** se vexer; **3** LITTÉR **to be in ~ need of sth** avoir grand besoin de qch; **4** (delicate) [subject, point] délicat.
IDIOMS **to be like a bear with a ~ head** être d'une humeur massacrante◦; **it is a sight for ~ eyes** ça réjouit le cœur de voir cela.

sorely /'sɔːlɪ/ adv [tempted] fortement; **~ tried, ~ tested** mis à rude épreuve; **medical aid is ~ needed** on a grandement besoin d'aide médicale.

sorority /sə'rɒrətɪ, US -'rɔːr-/ n US UNIV association f d'étudiantes; (sisterhood) confrérie f féminine.

sorrel /'sɒrəl, US 'sɔːrəl/ n **1** CULIN (edible) oseille f; **2** BOT (also **wood ~**) oxalis m.

sorrow /'sɒrəʊ/ n (grief) chagrin m; **to my ~** à mon grand chagrin.

sorrowful /'sɒrəʊfl/ adj GEN douloureux/-euse; [voice] triste.

sorry /'sɒrɪ/ I adj **1** (apologetic) désolé; (for emphasis) navré; **I'm terribly ~** je suis vraiment désolé, je suis navré; **I'm ~ I'm late** je suis désolé d'être en retard; **I'm ~ for the delay** je suis désolé du retard; **I'm ~ to be a nuisance but...** excusez-moi de vous embêter, mais...; **to be ~ about** s'excuser de [behaviour, mistake, change]; **~ about that!** (je suis) désolé!; **to say ~** s'excuser; **2** (sympathetic) **to be ~ to hear of sth/to hear that** être désolé d'apprendre qch/d'apprendre que; **I'm very ~ about your uncle** je suis désolé à propos de ton oncle; **3** (regretful) **to be ~ to do** regretter de faire; **will you be ~ to go**

back? est-ce que tu auras des regrets en rentrant?; **no-one will be ~ to see him go!** personne ne regrettera son départ!; **and, I'm ~ to say** et malheureusement; **I felt ~ about it afterwards** j'ai eu des remords par la suite; **do it now or you'll be ~!** fais-le maintenant ou tu t'en repentiras!; **4** (pitying) **to be** ou **feel ~ for sb** plaindre qn ALSO IRON; **to feel ~ for oneself** s'apitoyer sur soi-même; **5** (pathetic) [state, sight, business] triste; [person] minable; **this is a ~ state of affairs!** c'est vraiment lamentable!
II excl **1** (apologizing) désolé!; **2** (failing to hear, understand) **~?** pardon?; **3** (interrupting) **~, time is running out** je suis désolé, mais nous n'avons plus beaucoup de temps; **so we have two, ~, three options** nous avons donc deux, pardon, trois options; **4** (adding a comment) **~, may I just say that** excusez-moi, je voudrais simplement ajouter que.

sort /sɔːt/ I n **1** (kind, type) sorte f, genre m; **books, records—that ~ of thing** des livres, des disques, ce genre de choses; **that's my ~ of holiday** GB ou **vacation** US c'est le genre de vacances que j'aime; **I'm not that ~ of person** ce n'est pas mon genre; **it's some ~ of computer** c'est une sorte d'ordinateur; **this must be some ~ of joke** ça doit être une plaisanterie; **I need a bag of some ~** j'ai besoin d'un sac quelconque; **you must have some ~ of idea** tu dois avoir une idée; **an odd** ou **strange ~ of chap** un drôle de type; **radiation of any ~ is harmful** toutes les sortes de radiation sont dangereuses; **any ~ of knife will do** n'importe quel couteau fera l'affaire; **what ~ of person would do such a thing?** qui pourrait faire une chose pareille?; **what ~ of person does she think I am?** pour qui me prend-elle?; **you know the ~ of thing (I mean)** tu vois ce que je veux dire; **the same ~ of thing** la même chose; **something of that** ou **the ~** quelque chose comme ça; **I didn't say anything of the ~!** je n'ai jamais dit une chose pareille!; **nothing of the ~** (not in the least) pas du tout; **'I'll pay'—'you'll do nothing of the ~!'** 'je vais payer'—'il n'en est pas question!'; **2** (in vague description) espèce f, sorte f; **some ~ of bird** une sorte ou espèce d'oiseau; **3** (type of person) **I know his ~** je connais les gens de son espèce; **we see all ~s here** on voit toutes sortes de gens ici; **he's a good ~** c'est un brave type; **4** COMPUT tri m.
II **of sorts, of a sort** adv phr **a duck of ~s** ou **of a ~** une sorte de canard; **progress of ~s** un semblant de progrès.
III **sort of** adv phr **1** (a bit) **~ of cute** plutôt mignon/-onne; **to ~ of understand** comprendre plus ou moins; **'is it hard?'—'~ of'** 'est-ce que c'est difficile?'—'plutôt, oui'; **2** (approximately) **~ of blue-green** dans les bleu-vert; **it just ~ of happened** c'est arrivé comme ça; **he was just ~ of lying there** il était étendu par terre comme ça.
IV vtr **1** (classify, arrange) classer [data, files, stamps]; trier [letters, apples, potatoes]; **to ~ books into piles** ranger des livres en piles; **2** (separate) séparer.
IDIOMS **to be** ou **feel out of ~s** (ill) ne pas être dans son assiette; (grumpy) être de mauvais poil◦; **it takes all ~s (to make a world)** PROV il faut de tout pour faire un monde PROV.
■ **sort out**: ¶ ~ [sth] **out**, ~ **out** [sth] **1** (resolve) régler [problem, matter]; **to ~ out the confusion** dissiper un malentendu; **it will take me hours to ~ this mess out** il va me falloir des heures pour remettre de l'ordre dans tout ça; **I'll ~ it out** je m'en occuperai; **it's time to ~ this thing out** il est temps de tirer cette affaire au clair; **2** (organize) s'occuper de [details, arrangements]; clarifier [ideas]; trouver [replacement]; **I'll ~ something out with Tim** j'arrangerai quelque chose avec Tim; **3** (tidy up, put in order) ranger [desk]; classer [files]; mettre de l'ordre dans [finances, affairs]; **4** (select) trier; **5** (mend) réparer; ¶ ~ **out** [sth] **1** (separate) **to ~ out the clean socks from the dirty** séparer les chaussettes propres des chaussettes sales; **2** (establish) **to ~ out who is responsible** établir qui est responsable; **we're still trying to ~ out what happened** nous essayons toujours de comprendre ce qui s'est passé; ¶ ~ [sb] **out**◦ **1**

(punish) régler son compte à qn○; **2** (help) aider; ¶ **~ [oneself] out** (get organized) s'organiser; (in one's personal life) résoudre ses problèmes; **things will ~ themselves out** les choses vont s'arranger d'elles-mêmes; **the problem ~ed itself out** le problème s'est résolu de lui-même.
■ **sort through**: **~ through** [sth] regarder.

sort code n FIN code m d'agence.

sorter /'sɔːtə(r)/ ▶ **1251** | n **1** (person) trieur/-euse m/f; **2** (machine) GEN trieuse f; AGRIC trieur m.

sorting /'sɔːtɪŋ/ n **1** GEN triage m, tri m; **2** (post) tri m postal.

sorting office n (post) centre m de tri.

SOS n LIT SOS m; FIG appel m (au secours).

so-so○ /ˌsəʊ'səʊ/ **I** adj moyen/-enne.
II adv comme ci comme ça○.

sotto voce /ˌsɒtəʊ 'vəʊtʃɪ/ adv [say, add] à mi-voix.

sought /sɔːt/ pp ▶ **seek**.

sought-after /'sɔːtɑːftə(r), US -æf-/ adj [person, skill] demandé, recherché; [job, brand, area] prisé.

soul /səʊl/ n **1** (immortal, essential) âme f; **to sell one's ~** FIG donner n'importe quoi; **bless my ~†**!, **upon my ~†**! grand Dieu!; **to be the ~ of discretion** être la discrétion même; **2** (emotional appeal) **to lack ~** [performance] être plat; [city] ne pas avoir d'âme; **he has no ~**! HUM il est trop terre-à-terre!; **3** (person) **a sensitive ~** une âme sensible; **she's a motherly ~** elle est très maternelle; **you mustn't tell a ~**! ne le dis à personne!; **'many people there?'—'not a ~'** 'il y avait du monde?'—'personne', 'pas un chat○'; **4** ₵ MUS (also **~ music**) soul m.

IDIOMS **it's good for the ~** HUM ça forme le caractère; **to be the life and ~ of the party** être un or une boute-en-train; **to throw oneself into sth heart and ~** se donner corps et âme à qch.

soul: **~-destroying** adj abrutissant; **~ food** n US cuisine traditionnelle des Afro-Américains.

soulful /'səʊlfl/ adj (all contexts) mélancolique.

soulless /'səʊllɪs/ adj [building, office block] sans âme; [job] abrutissant; [interpretation] plat.

soul: **~ mate** n âme f sœur; **~-searching** n débat m intérieur; **~-stirring** adj très émouvant.

sound /saʊnd/ **I** n **1** PHYS, TV, RADIO son m; **2** (noise) GEN bruit m; (of bell, instrument, voice) son m; **a grating ~** un grincement; **without a ~** sans bruit; **3** FIG (impression from hearsay) **a 24 hour flight? I don't like the ~ of that!** un vol de 24 heures? cela ne me tente pas!; (when situation is threatening) **a reorganization? I don't like the ~ of that** une restructuration? ça m'inquiète; **by the ~ of it** d'après ce qu'on a dit; **he was in a bad temper that day, by the ~ of it** il semble que ce jour-là il ait été de mauvaise humeur; **4** MED sonde f; **5** GEOG détroit m; **6** MUS **the Motown ~** le style de Motown.
II noun modifier TV, RADIO [engineer] du son.
III adj **1** (in good condition) [building, heart, constitution] solide; [lungs] sain; [health] bon/bonne; **of ~ mind** sain d'esprit; **2** (well-founded) GEN solide; [judgment] sain; [sleep] profond; **some ~ advice** un bon conseil; **he has a ~ grasp of the basic grammar** il a une bonne compréhension des bases grammaticales; **a ~ move** une décision or démarche avisée; **3** (of good character) **he's very ~** on peut avoir confiance en lui; **4** FIN, COMM [investment] bon/bonne, sûr; [management] sain; **5** (correct, acceptable) **that is ~ economics** du point de vue économique, c'est très sensé; **our products are ecologically ~** nos produits ne nuisent pas à l'environnement; **she's politically ~** elle a des idées politiques de bon ton.
IV vtr **1** faire retentir [siren]; **to ~ one's horn** klaxonner; LIT, FIG **to ~ the alarm** sonner l'alarme; **2** MUS, MIL GEN sonner; **3** LING prononcer [letter]; (in de); **4** (express) donner [warning]; **to ~ a note of caution** lancer un appel à la prudence.
V vi **1** (seem) sembler; **it ~s as if he's really in trouble** il semble qu'il ait vraiment des ennuis; **it ~s dangerous** ça a l'air dangereux; **it doesn't ~ to me**

as if she's interested je ne pense pas qu'elle soit intéressée; **2** (give impression by voice or tone) **to ~ banal/boring** paraître banal/ennuyeux; **you make it ~ interesting** à t'écouter ça a l'air intéressant; **you ~ as if you've got a cold** on dirait que tu es enrhumé; **you ~ like my mother!** on dirait ma mère qui parle!; **I don't want to ~ pessimistic** je ne voudrais pas avoir l'air pessimiste; **spell it as it ~s** écris-le comme ça se prononce; **3** (convey impression) faire; **she calls herself Geraldine—it ~s more sophisticated** elle se fait appeler Géraldine—ça fait plus sophistiqué; **it may ~ silly, but...** ça a peut-être l'air idiot, mais...; **4** (make a noise) GEN sonner; [siren] hurler.
VI adv **to be ~ asleep** dormir à poings fermés.
■ **sound off**○ rebattre les oreilles aux gens○.
■ **sound out**: **~ out** [sb], **~** [sb] **out** sonder, interroger.

sound: **~ archives** npl archives fpl sonores; **~ barrier** n mur m du son; **~ bite** n: bref extrait d'une interview enregistrée; **~ effect** n effet m sonore; **~ head** n CIN lecteur m de son; (on tape recorder) tête f de lecture du son.

sounding /'saʊndɪŋ/ **I** n LIT, FIG sondage m; **to take ~s** faire des sondages.
II -sounding combining form **a grand-~/English-~ name** un nom qui fait bien/qui fait anglais.

sounding-board /'saʊndɪŋbɔːd/ n FIG personne f sur qui on peut tester ses idées.

sound insulation n isolation f acoustique.

soundless /'saʊndlɪs/ adj silencieux/-ieuse.

soundlessly /'saʊndlɪslɪ/ adv sans bruit.

sound: **~ level** n niveau m sonore; **~ library** n sonothèque f.

soundly /'saʊndlɪ/ adv [sleep] à poings fermés; **we can sleep ~ in our beds, now that...** nous pouvons dormir tranquilles, maintenant que...; [beat, defeat] à plates coutures; [built, based] solidement.

soundness /'saʊndnɪs/ n (correctness) sûreté f.

sound-proof /'saʊndpruːf/ **I** adj [wall, room] insonorisé; [material] insonorisant.
II vtr insonoriser [room].

sound: **~-proofing** n insonorisation f; **~ system** n (hi-fi) stéréo○ f; (for disco etc) sono○ f; **~-track** n MUS, TV, CIN (of film) bande f sonore; (on record etc) bande f originale.

sound wave n onde f sonore.

soup /suːp/ n CULIN soupe f, potage m.
IDIOMS **to be in the ~** être dans le pétrin○.
■ **soup up**: **~ up** [sth], **~** [sth] **up** gonfler.

soup: **~ kitchen** n soupe f populaire; **~ plate** n assiette f creuse; **~spoon** n cuillère f à soupe; **~ tureen** n soupière f.

sour /'saʊə(r)/ **I** adj **1** (bitter) aigre; **to go ~** LIT tourner; FIG se dégrader; **2** (bad-tempered) revêche.
II vtr gâter [relations, atmosphere].
III vi [attitude] s'aigrir; [relationship] se dégrader.

source /sɔːs/ **I** n **1** (origin, informant) source f (**of** de) also Geog, LITERAT; **energy/food ~s** ressources fpl énergétiques/alimentaires; **at ~** à la source; **2** (cause) **~ of** source f de [anxiety, resentment, satisfaction]; cause f de [problem, error, infection, pollution]; origine f de [rumour].
II noun modifier [book, code, language, program] source; **~ material** sources fpl.
III vtr se procurer [products, energy].

sourdough n US levain m.

sour-faced adj [person] à la mine revêche.

sour grapes npl dépit m; **it's (a touch of) ~**! c'est du dépit!

south /saʊθ/ ▶ **1157** | **I** n sud m.
II adj GEN sud inv; [wind] GEN du sud; METEOROL de sud.
III adv [move] vers le sud; [lie, live] au sud (**of** de).

south: **South Africa** ▶ **840** | pr n Afrique f du Sud; **South America** ▶ **840** | pr n Amérique f du Sud; **~bound** adj en direction du sud; **~east** ▶ **1157** | n sud-est m; **~eastern** ▶ **1157** | adj sud-est inv.

southern /'sʌðən/ ► 1157┃ *adj* [*coast, boundary*] sud *inv*; [*state, region, town, accent*] du sud.

Southern Alps *pr npl* Alpes *fpl* néo-zélandaises.

southerner /'sʌðənə(r)/ *n* ~**s** les gens *mpl* du Sud.

southernmost *adj* à l'extrême sud.

south: ~**-facing** *adj* exposé au sud; **South Pole** *pr n* pôle *m* Sud; **South Sea Islands** ► 1022┃ *pr npl* Océanie *f*.

southward /'saʊθwəd/ ► 1157┃ **I** *adj* [*side*] sud *inv*; [*wall, slope*] du côté sud; [*journey*] vers le sud.
II *adv* (also ~**s**) vers le sud.

southwest /ˌsaʊθ'west/ ► 1157┃ *n* sud-ouest *m*.

southwestern /ˌsaʊθ'westən/ ► 1157┃ *adj* sud-ouest *inv*.

souvenir /ˌsuːvə'nɪə(r)/, US 'suːvənɪər/ *n* souvenir *m*.

sovereign /'sɒvrɪn/ **I** *n* (monarch) souverain/-e *m*/*f*; (coin) souverain *m*.
II *adj* [*power, state, contempt*] souverain (*after n*).

sovereignty /'sɒvrəntɪ/ *n* souveraineté *f*.

Soviet Union /ˌsəʊvɪət 'juːnɪən/ ► 840┃ *pr n* HIST Union *f* soviétique.

sow[1] /saʊ/ *n* (pig) truie *f*.

sow[2] /səʊ/ *vtr* (*prét* **sowed**, *pp* **sowed, sown**) **1** semer [*seeds, corn*]; **2** ensemencer [*field*].

sowing /'səʊɪŋ/ *n* ¢ semailles *fpl*.

sown /səʊn/ *pp* ► **sow**[2].

soya /'sɔɪə/ **I** *n* soja *m*.
II *noun modifier* [*bean, burger, flour, milk*] de soja.

soya sauce, soy sauce *n* sauce *f* soja.

sozzled○ /'sɒzld/ *adj* pinté○, cuité○.

spa /spaː/ *n* (town) station *f* thermale; (health club) club *m* de remise en forme.

space /speɪs/ **I** *n* **1** ¢ (room) place *f*, espace *m*; **to sell** (advertising) ~ **in a newspaper** vendre des espaces publicitaires dans un journal; **to give sb** ~ FIG laisser de la liberté à qn; **to invade sb's (personal)** ~ empiéter sur l'espace vital de qn; **2** C (gap, area of land) GEN espace *m*; MUS interligne *m*; **in the** ~ **provided** dans la case prévue à cet effet; **'watch this** ~**!'** 'à suivre'; **open** ~**s** espaces *mpl* libres; **3** (interval of time) intervalle *m*; **in the** ~ **of five minutes** en l'espace de cinq minutes; **in a short** ~ **of time** en très peu de temps; **4** ¢ (also **outer** ~) espace *m*.
II *noun modifier* AEROSP, PHYS [*research, programme, lab, vehicle, rocket*] spatial.
III *vtr* espacer.
▪ **space out**: **to** ~ **out** [sth], ~ [sth] **out** GEN espacer; échelonner [*payments*].

space: ~ **age** *n* ère *f* spatiale; ~**-bar** *n* barre *f* d'espacement; ~**craft** *n* (*pl* ~) vaisseau *m* spatial.

spaced out○ *adj* **he's completely** ~○ il plane○ complètement.

space flight *n* AEROSP **1** (activity) voyages *mpl* inter-planétaires; **2** (single journey) vol *m* spatial.

space: ~ **helmet** *n* AEROSP casque *m* de cosmonaute; **Space Invaders**® *n* (+ *v sg*) jeu électronique *de combats dans l'espace*; ~**man** *n* cosmonaute *m*; ~ **race** *n* course *f* pour la conquête de l'espace; ~**-saving** *adj* qui gagne de la place; ~**ship** *n* vaisseau *m* spatial; ~ **station** *n* station *f* orbitale; ~**suit** *n* combinaison *f* spatiale; ~**woman** *n* cosmonaute *f*.

spacing /'speɪsɪŋ/ *n* GEN espacement *m*; (of payments) échelonnement *m*; **in single/double** ~ en simple/double interligne.

spacious /'speɪʃəs/ *adj* spacieux/-ieuse.

spaciousness /'speɪʃəsnɪs/ *n* ¢ grandeur *f*.

spade /speɪd/ ► 949┃ *n* (tool) bêche *f*, pelle *f*; (in cards) pique *m*.
IDIOMS **to call a** ~ **a** ~ appeler un chat un chat.

spade: ~**ful** *n* pelletée *f*; ~**work** *n* FIG travail *m* de base.

Spain /speɪn/ ► 840┃ *pr n* Espagne *f*.

span /spæn/ **I** *n* **1** (period of time) durée *f*; **time** ~ espace *m* de temps; **over a** ~ **of several years** sur

une période de plusieurs années; **2** (width) (across hand, arms, wings) envergure *f*; (of bridge) travée *f*; (of arch) portée *f*; **the bridge crosses the river in a single** ~ le pont enjambe la rivière d'une seule travée; **the whole** ~ **of human history** FIG la totalité ou l'ensemble de l'histoire de l'humanité.
II *vtr* (*p prés etc* **-nn-**) **1** [*bridge, arch*] enjamber; **2** FIG (encompass) s'étendre sur; **a group** ~**ning the age range 10 to 14** un groupe comprenant les enfants âgés de 10 à 14 ans.

Spaniard /'spænjəd/ ► 1100┃ *n* Espagnol/-e *m*/*f*.

spaniel /'spænjəl/ *n* épagneul *m*.

Spanish /'spænɪʃ/ ► 1100┃, 1038┃ **I** *n* **1** (people) **the** ~ les Espagnols *mpl*; **2** (language) espagnol *m*.
II *adj* espagnol.

Spanish Armada /ˌspænɪʃ aː'maːdə/ *n* **the** ~ l'Invincible Armada *f*.

spank /spæŋk/ **I** *n* fessée *f*.
II *vtr* donner une fessée à.

spanking /'spæŋkɪŋ/ **I** *n* fessée *f*.
II○ *adj* **at a** ~ **pace** à une belle allure.
III○ *adv* **a** ~ **new car** une voiture flambant neuve.

spanner /'spænə(r)/ *n* GB clé *f* (*de serrage*); **adjustable** ~ clé à molette.
IDIOMS **to put** ou **throw a** ~ **in the works** mettre du sable dans l'engrenage.

spar /spaː(r)/ *vi* (*p prés etc* **-rr-**) [*boxers*] échanger des coups; [*debaters*] se livrer à des joutes oratoires; **to** ~ **with** s'entraîner à la boxe avec [*partner*]; FIG s'affronter à [*opponent*].

spare /speə(r)/ **I** *n* TECH, GEN (part) pièce *f* de rechange; (wheel) roue *f* de secours; **use my pen, I've got a** ~ prends mon stylo, j'en ai un autre.
II *adj* **1** (surplus) [*cash, capacity*] restant; [*capital, land, chair, seat*] disponible; [*copy*] en plus; **I've got a** ~ **ticket** j'ai un ticket en trop; **a** ~ **moment** un moment de libre; **2** (in reserve) GEN de rechange; [*wheel*] de secours; **3** [*person, build*] élancé; [*design, building, style*] simple; **4**○ GB (mad) dingue○.
III *vtr* **1** **to have sth to** ~ avoir qch de disponible; **have my pen, I've got one to** ~ prends mon stylo, j'en ai un autre; **to catch the train with five minutes to** ~ prendre le train avec cinq minutes d'avance; **I have no time to** ~ **for doing** je n'ai pas de temps à perdre à faire; **the project was finished with only days to** ~ le projet a été terminé seulement quelques jours avant la date limite; **2** (treat leniently) épargner; **to** ~ **sb sth** épargner qch à qn; **3 can you** ~ **a minute/a pound?** as-tu un moment/une livre?; **to** ~ **a thought for** penser à; **4** (manage without) se passer de [*person*]; **to** ~ **sb for** se passer de qn pour [*task*].
IV *v refl* **to** ~ **oneself sth** s'épargner qch; **to** ~ **oneself the trouble of doing** s'épargner l'ennui de faire; **to** ~ **oneself the expense of** faire l'économie de.
IDIOMS **to** ~ **no effort** faire tout son possible; **to** ~ **no pains** se donner du mal.

spare: ~ **part** *n* AUT, TECH pièce *f* de rechange; ~ **part surgery** *n* chirurgie *f* de remplacement; ~ **rib** *n* CULIN travers *m* de porc; ~ **room** *n* chambre *f* d'amis; ~ **time** *n* ¢ loisirs *mpl*.

spare tyre GB, **spare tire** US *n* **1** AUT pneu *m* de rechange; **2**○ (fat) bourrelet *m*.

spare wheel *n* AUT roue *f* de secours.

sparing /'speərɪŋ/ *adj* [*person, use*] parcimonieux/-ieuse; **to be** ~ **with** (economical) économiser; (mean) être avare de; (careful) utiliser [qch] avec parsimonie.

sparingly /'speərɪŋlɪ/ *adv* [*use, add*] en petite quantité.

spark /spaːk/ **I** *n* **1** GEN, ELEC étincelle *f*; **2** FIG (hint) (of originality) éclair *m*; (of enthusiasm) étincelle *f*; (of intelligence) lueur *f*; **the** ~ **has gone out of their relationship** leur relation a perdu tout son piment.
II *vtr* = **spark off**.
III *vi* [*fire*] jeter des étincelles; [*wire, switch*] faire des étincelles.
▪ **spark off**: ~ **off** [sth] susciter [*interest, anger, fear*]; provoquer [*controversy, speculation, reaction,*

panic]; être à l'origine de [*friendship, affair*]; déclencher [*war, riot*]; entraîner [*growth, change*].

sparkle /'spɑːkl/ **I** *n* **1** (of light, star, tinsel) scintillement *m*; (in eye) éclair *m*; FIG (of performance) éclat *m*; **she's lost her ~** elle a perdu sa joie de vivre; **to add ~ to sth** donner du brillant à [*glasses etc*].
II *vi* **1** (flash) [*flame, light*] étinceler; [*jewel, frost, metal, water*] scintiller; [*eyes*] briller (**with** de); FIG [*conversation*] être émaillé de; **2** [*drink*] pétiller.

sparkler /'spɑːklə(r)/ *n* (firework) cierge *m* magique.

sparkling /'spɑːklɪŋ/ **I** *adj* **1** [*light*] étincelant; [*jewel, water*] scintillant; [*eyes*] brillant (**with** de); **2** [*conversation, wit*] plein de brio; **3** [*drink*] pétillant.
II *adv* (for emphasis) **~ clean** étincelant de propreté; **~ white** d'un blanc étincelant.

spark plug *n* ELEC, AUT bougie *f*.

spar: **~ring match** *n* (in boxing) combat *m* d'entraînement; FIG prise *f* de becᵒ; **~ring partner** *n* (in boxing) sparring-partner *m*; FIG adversaire *m/f*.

sparrow /'spærəʊ/ *n* moineau *m*.

sparse /spɑːs/ *adj* [*population, vegetation, hair*] clairsemé; [*furnishings*] rare (*before n*); [*resources*] maigre; [*information*] épars; [*use*] modéré; **trading was ~** la Bourse était calme.

sparsely /'spɑːslɪ/ *adv* peu; **~ wooded/attended** peu boisé/fréquenté; **~ populated** à faible population.

Spartan /'spɑːtən/ *adj* LIT, FIG spartiate.

spasm /'spæzəm/ *n* (of pain) spasme *m* (**of** de); (of anxiety, panic, rage, coughing) accès *m* (**of** de).

spasmodic /spæz'mɒdɪk/ *adj* [*activity*] intermittent; [*coughing, cramp*] spasmodique.

spasmodically /spæz'mɒdɪklɪ/ *adv* par à-coups.

spastic /'spæstɪk/ *n, adj* MED handicapé/-e (*m/f*) moteur.

spat /spæt/ **I** *prét, pp* ▶ **spit**.
IIᵒ *n* (quarrel) prise *f* de becᵒ (**with** avec).

spate /speɪt/ *n* **1 in full ~** GB [*river*] en pleine crue; [*person*] en plein discours; **2 a ~ of** une série de [*incidents*].

spatial /'speɪʃl/ *adj* spatial.

spatter /'spætə(r)/ **I** *n* **1** (of liquid) éclaboussure *f*; **a ~ of rain** une petite pluie; **2** (sound) crépitement *m*.
II *vtr* (splash) éclabousser (**with** de).
III *vi* crépiter (**on** sur; **against** contre).

spatula /'spætjʊlə/ *n* GEN spatule *f*; MED abaisse-langue *m inv*.

spawn /spɔːn/ **I** *n* (of frog, fish) frai *m*.
II *vtr* engendrer [*product, imitation etc*].
III *vi* **1** ZOOL frayer; **2** (multiply) se multiplier.

spay /speɪ/ *vtr* enlever les ovaires de [*animal*].

speak /spiːk/ **I** **-speak** *combining form* jargon *m*; **computer-~** jargon informatique.
II *vtr* (*prét* **spoke**; *pp* **spoken**) **1** parler [*language*]; **can you ~ English?** parlez-vous (l')anglais?; **'French spoken'** 'on parle français'; **English as it is spoken** l'anglais tel qu'on le parle; **2** (tell, utter) dire [*truth, poetry*]; prononcer [*word, name*]; **to ~ one's mind** dire ce qu'on pense.
III *vi* (*prét* **spoke**; *pp* **spoken**) **1** (talk) parler (**to** à; **about, of** de); **to ~ in a whisper** parler tout bas; **to ~ ill/well of sb** dire du mal/du bien de qn; **to ~ through** parler par l'intermédiaire de [*medium, interpreter*]; **who's ~ing please?** (on phone) qui est à l'appareil s'il vous plaît?; **(this is) Camilla ~ing** c'est Camilla; **'is that Miss Durham?'—'~ing!'** 'Mademoiselle Durham?'—'c'est moi!'; **this is your captain ~ing** AVIAT ici le commandant de bord; **~ing of which, have you booked a table?** tiens, à propos, as-tu réservé une table?; **~ing of lunch, Nancy...** à propos du déjeuner, Nancy...; **she is well spoken of in academic circles** elle est bien considérée dans le milieu universitaire; **he spoke very highly of her** il a parlé d'elle en termes très élogieux; **~ing as a layman...** en tant que non-spécialiste...; **generally ~ing** en règle générale; **roughly ~ing** en gros; **strictly ~ing** à proprement parler; **relatively**

~ing relativement parlant; **we've had no trouble to ~ of** nous n'avons pas eu de problème spécial; **they've got no money to ~ of** ils n'ont pour ainsi dire pas d'argent; **not to ~ of the expense** sans parler du coût; **so to ~** pour ainsi dire; **2** (converse) parler (**about, of** de; **to, with** à); **they're not ~ing (to each other)** ils ne se parlent pas; **I know her by sight but not to ~ to** je la connais de vue mais je ne lui ai jamais parlé; **3** (make a speech) parler; (more formal) prendre la parole; **to ~ from the floor** POL parler de sa place; **to ~ about** OU **on** parler de; **to ~ for** parler en faveur de; **4** LITTÉR **to ~ of** témoigner de [*suffering, emotion*].
■ **speak for:** **~ for** [**sth/sb**] **1** (on behalf of) parler pour LIT; parler de FIG; **to ~ for oneself** s'exprimer; **~ing for myself...** pour ma part...; **~ for yourself!** parle pour toi!; **the facts ~ for themselves** les faits parlent d'eux-mêmes; **2** (reserve) **to be spoken for** [*object*] être réservé or retenu; [*person*] ne pas être libre.
■ **speak out:** **~ out** se prononcer; **don't be afraid! ~ out!** n'aie pas peur! exprime-toi!
■ **speak to:** **~ to** [**sth**] commenter [*motion*].
■ **speak up:** **~ up** (louder) parler plus fort; **2** (dare to speak) intervenir; **to ~ up for sb/sth** intervenir en faveur de qn/qch.

speakeasy /'spiːkiːzɪ/ *n* US HIST bar *m* clandestin.

speaker /'spiːkə(r)/ *n* **1** (person talking) personne *f* qui parle; (orator, public speaker) orateur/-trice *m/f*; (invited lecturer) conférencier/-ière *m/f*; (one of several conference lecturers) intervenant/-e *m/f*; **2** (of foreign language) **an Italian/a French ~** un/-e italophone/francophone *m/f*; **a Russian ~** quelqu'un qui parle le russe; **3** (also **Speaker**) GB POL président/-e *m/f* des Communes; **4** ELEC, MUS haut-parleur *m*.

speaking /'spiːkɪŋ/ **I** *n* (elocution) élocution *f*; (pronunciation) prononciation *f*.
II **-speaking** *combining form* **English-/French-~** anglophone/francophone; **Welsh-~** [*person*] qui parle le gallois; [*area*] de langue galloise.

speaking engagement *n* **to have a ~** devoir prononcer un discours.

speaking part, speaking role *n* rôle *m*.

speaking terms *npl* **we're not on ~** nous ne nous adressons pas la parole.

speaking tour *n* tournée *f* de conférences.

spear /spɪə(r)/ **I** *n* **1** (weapon) lance *f*; **2** (of plant) tige *f*; (of asparagus) pointe *f*; (of broccoli) branche *f*.
II *vtr* harponner [*fish*]; transpercer (d'un coup de lance) [*person*]; **2** (with fork etc) piquer.

spear carrier *n* figurant/-e *m/f*.

spearhead /'spɪəhed/ **I** *n* LIT, FIG fer *m* de lance.
II *vtr* mener [*campaign, offensive, revolt, reform*].

spearmint /'spɪəmɪnt/ *n* menthe *f* verte.

specᵒ /spek/ **I** *n* **1** (*abrév* = **specification**) spécification *f*; **to ~** selon les spécifications fournies; **2** (*abrév* = **speculation**) **on ~** à tout hasard.
II **specs**ᵒ *npl* (*abrév* = **spectacles**) binocles ᵒ *mpl*.

special /'speʃl/ **I** *n* **1** CULIN plat *m* du jour; **the chef's ~** la spécialité du chef; **2** (broadcast) émission *f* spéciale; **3** (bus) car *m* spécial; (train) train *m* spécial.
II *adj* **1** (official, for a specific purpose) spécial; **2** (marked) [*affection, interest*] tout/-e particulier/-ière; **3** (particular) [*reason, motive, significance, treatment*] particulier/-ière; **to make a ~ effort** faire un effort; **4** (unique) [*offer, deal, package, skill*] spécial; [*case, quality*] particulier/-ière; **what is so ~ about this computer?** qu'est-ce que cet ordinateur a de particulier?; **I want to make this Christmas really ~** je voudrais que ce Noël sorte de l'ordinaire; **5** (out of the ordinary) [*announcement, guest*] spécial; **as a ~ treat** à titre de faveur spéciale; **going anywhere ~?** est-ce que tu sors quelque part?; **you're ~ to me** tu m'es très cher/chère; **the wine is something ~** le vin est exceptionnel; **what's so ~ about him?** qu'est-ce qu'il a de si extraordinaire?; **6** (personal) [*chair, recipe*] personnel/-elle; [*friend*] très cher/chère.

special: **~ agent** *n* agent *m* secret; **Special**

Speed

Speed of road, rail, air etc. travel

In French, speed is measured in kilometres per hour:

100 kph = *approximately 63 mph*
100 mph = *approximately 160 kph*
 50 mph = *approximately 80 kph*

X miles per hour	= X miles à l'heure
X kilometres per hour	= X kilomètres à l'heure *or* X kilomètres-heure
100 kph	= 100 km/h
what speed was the car going at?	= à quelle vitesse la voiture roulait-elle?
it was going at 150 kph	= elle roulait à 150 km/h (*cent cinquante kilomètres-heure*)
it was going at fifty (*mph*)	= elle roulait à quatre-vingts à l'heure (*i.e. at 80 kph*)
the speed of the car was 200 kph	= la vitesse de la voiture était de 200 km/h (*the de must not be omitted here*)
what was the car doing?	= la voiture faisait du combien?
it was doing ninety (*mph*)	= elle faisait du 150 (*du cent cinquante: i.e. 150 kph*)
it was going at more than 200 kph	= elle roulait à plus de 200 km/h
it was going at less than 40 kph	= elle roulait à moins de 40 km/h
A was going at the same speed as B	= A roulait à la même vitesse que B
A was going faster than B	= A roulait plus vite que B
B was going slower than A	= B roulait moins vite que A *or* B roulait plus lentement que A

Speed of light and sound

sound travels at 330 metres per second	= le son se déplace à 330 m/s (*trois cent trente mètres-seconde or mètres à la seconde*)
the speed of light is 186,300 miles per second	= la vitesse de la lumière est de 300 000 km/s (*trois cent mille kilomètres-seconde or kilomètres à la seconde*) (*note that the de must not be omitted here*)

Branch *n* GB service *m* de contre-espionnage et de lutte contre la subversion interne; **~ delivery** *n* POST service *m* exprès.

special effect I *n* CIN, TV effet *m* spécial.
II **special effects** *noun modifier* [*specialist, team*] des effets spéciaux; [*department*] effets spéciaux.

special interest group *n* POL groupe *m* défendant des intérêts particuliers.

specialism /'speʃəlɪzəm/ *n* spécialité *f*.

specialist /'speʃəlɪst/ I ► **1251** *n* GEN, MED spécialiste *mf* (**in** de); **heart ~** cardiologue *m*.
II *adj* [*shop, knowledge, care, equipment*] spécialisé; [*help*] d'un spécialiste; [*work*] de spécialiste.

speciality GB /ˌspeʃɪ'ælətɪ/, **specialty** US /'speʃəltɪ/ *n* spécialité *f*.

specialize /'speʃəlaɪz/ *vi* se spécialiser; **to ~ in** se spécialiser en; **we ~ in repairing computers** notre spécialité consiste à réparer les ordinateurs; **a company specializing in machinery** une entreprise spécialisée dans les machines.

special licence *n* GB JUR dispense *f* de bans.

specially /'speʃəlɪ/ *adv* **1** (specifically) spécialement; **I made it ~ for you** je l'ai fait exprès pour toi; **2** (particularly) GEN particulièrement; [*like, enjoy*] surtout.

special needs *npl* **1** SOCIOL problèmes *mpl*; **2** SCH difficultés *fpl* d'apprentissage scolaire.

special: ~ relationship *n* POL lien *m* privilégié; **~ school** *n* GB établissement *m* médico-éducatif pour enfants handicapés.

specialty /'speʃəltɪ/ *n* US = **speciality**.

species /'spiːʃiːz/ *n* (*pl* **~**) (all contexts) espèce *f*.

specific /spə'sɪfɪk/ I **specifics** *npl* éléments *mpl* spécifiques; **to get down to (the) ~s** entrer dans les détails.
II *adj* précis; **~ to** spécifique de.

specifically /spə'sɪfɪklɪ/ *adv* **1** (specially) spécialement (**for** pour); **2** (explicitly) explicitement; **3** (in particular) en particulier; **more ~** plus particulièrement.

specification /ˌspesɪfɪ'keɪʃn/ I *n* **1** (also **specifications**) (of design, building) spécification *f* (**for, of** de); **built to sb's ~s** fabriqué selon les spécifications de qn; **2** GEN, JUR (stipulation) stipulation *f* (**that** que).
II **specifications** *npl* caractéristiques *fpl*.

specification sheet *n* fiche *f* technique.

specify /'spesɪfaɪ/ I *vtr* stipuler; [*person*] préciser (**that** que; **where** où; **who** qui); **as specified above** comme stipulé ci-dessus; **unless otherwise specified** sauf indication contraire.
II **specified** *pp adj* [*amount, date, day, value, way*] spécifié.

specimen /'spesɪmən/ I *n* (of rock, urine, handwriting) échantillon *m* (**of** de); (of blood, tissue) prélèvement (**of** de); (of species, plant) spécimen *m* (**of** de).
II *noun modifier* [*page, copy, signature*] spécimen *inv*.

specious /'spiːʃəs/ *adj* SOUT [*argument, reasoning*] spécieux/-ieuse; [*glamour, appearance*] trompeur/-euse.

speck /spek/ *n* (small piece) (of dust, soot) grain *m*; (of dirt, mud) petite tache *f* (**of** de); (of blood, ink, light) point *m*; **a ~ on the horizon** un petit point à l'horizon.

speckle /'spekl/ I *n* (on person's skin, egg) petite tache *f*; (on bird, animal, fabric) moucheture *f*.
II *vtr* [*rain*] tacheter; [*sun*] marquer [qch] de petites taches; [*flecks*] moucheter.

spec sheet /'spekʃiːt/ *n* fiche *f* technique.

spectacle /'spektəkl/ I *n* spectacle *m*.
II *noun modifier* [*case*] à lunettes; [*frame, lens*] de lunettes.
III **spectacles** *npl* lunettes *fpl*.

spectacular /spek'tækjʊlə(r)/ I *n* superproduction *f*.
II *adj* spectaculaire.

spectacularly /spek'tækjʊləlɪ/ *adv* de façon spectaculaire; **it was ~ successful** cela a été une réussite spectaculaire.

spectator /spek'teɪtə(r)/ *n* spectateur/-trice *m/f*.

spectator sport *n* sport *m* qui attire beaucoup de spectateurs.

specter *n* US = **spectre**.

spectre GB, **specter** US /'spektə(r)/ *n* spectre *m*.

spectrum /'spektrəm/ *n* (*pl* **-tra, -trums**) **1** PHYS spectre *m*; **2** (range) gamme *f*; **people across the political ~** des gens de toutes les tendances politiques.

speculate /'spekjʊleɪt/ I *vtr* **to ~ that** supposer que; **it has been widely ~d that** on a beaucoup spéculé sur le fait que.
II *vi* GEN, FIN spéculer (**about** à propos de); **to ~ as to why** spéculer sur les raisons pour lesquelles.

speculation /ˌspekjʊ'leɪʃn/ *n* **1** ¢ GEN spéculations *fpl*; **~ about** ou **over who will win** spéculations sur le gagnant probable; **2** FIN spéculation *f* (**in** sur).

speculative /'spekjʊlətɪv, US also 'spekjələtɪv/ *adj* (all contexts) spéculatif/-ive.

speculator /'spekjʊleɪtə(r)/ *n* spéculateur/-trice *m/f*.

sped /sped/ *prét, pp* ► **speed** II, III.

speech /spiːtʃ/ *n* **1** (oration) discours *m* (**on** sur; **about** à propos de); THEAT tirade *f*; **to give/deliver a ~** tenir/prononcer un discours; **2** (faculty) parole *f*; (spoken form) langage *m*; **direct/indirect ~** LING discours *m* direct/indirect; **in ~** par le langage; **3** (language) langage *m*; **4** US SCH, UNIV expression *f* orale.

speech: ~ and drama *n* SCH, UNIV art *m* dramatique; **~ clinic** *n* centre *m* d'orthophonie; **~ day** *n*

GB SCH (jour *m* de la) distribution *f* des prix; ~ **defect** *n* = **speech impediment**.

speechifying /'spi:tʃɪfaɪŋ/ *n* PÉJ belles paroles *fpl*.

speech: **~-impaired** *adj* (not having speech) muet/-ette; (having a speech impediment) qui a un défaut d'élocution; **~ impediment** *n* défaut *m* d'élocution.

speechless /'spi:tʃlɪs/ *adj* muet/-ette; **to be ~ with** rester muet de; **I was ~ at the news** la nouvelle m'a laissé sans voix; **I'm ~**○! je suis soufflé○!

speech: **~ recognition** *n* COMPUT reconnaissance *f* de la parole; **~ synthesis** *n* COMPUT synthèse *f* de la parole; **~ therapist** ▶1251 *n* orthophoniste *mf*; **~ training** *n* cours *m* de diction; **~writer** ▶1251 *n* personne *f* qui écrit des discours.

speed /spi:d/ **I** *n* **1** (velocity of vehicle, wind, record) vitesse *f*; (rapidity of response, reaction) rapidité *f*; **at (a) great ~** à toute vitesse; **at ~** [*go, run*] à toute vitesse; [*work, read*] en quatrième vitesse; **to pick up ~** prendre de la vitesse; **'full ~ ahead!'** 'en avant toute!'; **what ~ were you doing?** à quelle vitesse est-ce que tu roulais?; **2** (gear) vitesse *f*; **3** PHOT (of film) sensibilité *f*; (of shutter) vitesse *f* d'obturation; **4**○ (drug) amphétamines *fpl*.
II *vtr* (*prét, pp* **sped** ou **speeded**) hâter [*process, recovery*]; rendre [qch] plus fluide [*traffic*]; **to ~ sb on his/her way** souhaiter bon voyage à qn.
III *vi* **1** (*prét, pp* **sped**) (move swiftly) **to ~ along** aller à toute allure; **to ~ away** partir à toute vitesse; **the train sped past** le train est passé à toute vitesse; **2** (*prét, pp* **speeded**) (drive too fast) conduire trop vite; **he was caught ~ing** il a eu une contravention (pour excès de vitesse).
■ **speed up**: ¶ ~ **up** [*walker, train*] aller plus vite; [*athlete, car*] accélérer l'allure; [*worker*] accélérer; ¶ ~ **up** [*sth*], ~ [*sth*] **up** GEN accélérer.

speed: **~boat** *n* hors-bord *m*; **~ camera** *n* ~ cinémomètre *m*.

speed hump *n* ralentisseur *m*.

speedily /'spi:dɪli/ *adv* rapidement.

speeding /'spi:dɪŋ/ *n* AUT excès *m* de vitesse.

speed limit *n* limitation *f* de vitesse; **to drive within the ~** conduire en respectant la limitation de vitesse.

speedometer /spɪ'dɒmɪtə(r)/ *n* compteur *m* (de vitesse).

speed: **~ reading** *n* lecture *f* rapide; **~ restriction** *n* limitation *f* de vitesse; **~ skating** ▶949 *n* patinage *m* de vitesse; **~ trap** *n* AUT contrôle *m* de vitesse; **~-up** *n* accélération *f*; **~way racing** ▶949 *n* course *f* de vitesse à moto.

speedy /'spi:dɪ/ *adj* rapide.

speed zone *n* US zone *f* à vitesse limitée.

speleology /ˌspi:lɪ'ɒlədʒɪ/ ▶949 *n* spéléologie *f*.

spell /spel/ **I** *n* **1** (period) moment *m*, période *f*; **for a ~** pendant un certain temps; **a ~ in hospital** un séjour à l'hôpital; **a warm ~** une période de beau temps; **rainy ~** ondée *f*; **sunny ~** éclaircie *f*; **to go through a bad ~** traverser une mauvaise passe; **2** (magic words) formule *f* magique; **evil ~** maléfice *m*; **to be under a ~** être envoûté; **to cast** ou **put a ~ on sb** LIT, FIG jeter un sort à qn; **to break a ~** rompre un sortilège; **to break the ~** FIG rompre le charme; **to be under sb's ~** FIG être sous le charme de qn.
II *vtr* (*pp, prét* **spelled** ou **spelt**) **1** (aloud) épeler; (on paper) écrire; **she ~s her name with an e** son nom s'écrit avec e; **to ~ sth properly** orthographier qch correctement; **C-A-T ~s cat** les lettres C-A-T forment le mot cat; **2** (imply) signifier [*danger, disaster, ruin*]; sonner [*end*].
III *vi* (*pp, prét* **spelled** ou **spelt**) connaître l'orthographe; **he ~s badly/well** il a une mauvaise/bonne orthographe.
■ **spell out**: ~ **out** [*sth*], ~ [*sth*] **out** LIT épeler [*word*]; FIG expliquer [qch] clairement; **do I have to ~ it out?** est-ce qu'il faut que je te fasse un dessin?

spellbinding *adj* envoûtant.

spellbound *adj* envoûté (**by** par); **to hold sb ~** tenir qn sous le charme.

spellcheck(er) *n* COMPUT correcteur *m* orthographique.

speller /'spelə(r)/ *n* **a good/bad ~** une personne bonne/mauvaise en orthographe.

spelling /'spelɪŋ/ ▶1280 **I** *n* orthographe *f*.
II *noun modifier* [*mistake, test*] d'orthographe.

spelt /spelt/ *prét, pp* ▶ **spell** II, III.

spend /spend/ **I** *n* FIN frais *mpl*.
II *vtr* (*prét, pp* **spent**) **1** dépenser [*money, salary*] (**on** en); **2** passer [*time*]; **3** épuiser [*ammunition, energy, resources*].
III *vi* (*prét, pp* **spent**) dépenser.

spender /'spendə(r)/ *n* **to be a big ~** être dépensier/-ière.

spending /'spendɪŋ/ *n* dépenses *fpl*; **~ on education** dépenses d'éducation; **credit-card ~** achats *mpl* sur carte de crédit; **defence ~** dépense *f* en matière de défense; **government ~**, **public ~** dépense *f* publique.

spending: **~ cut** *n* GEN réduction *f* des dépenses; POL restriction *f* budgétaire; **~ money** *n* argent *m* de poche; **~ power** *n* FIN pouvoir *m* d'achat; **~ spree** *n* folie○ *f* (de dépense).

spendthrift /'spendθrɪft/ **I** *n* **to be a ~** être dépensier/-ière.
II *adj* [*person*] dépensier/-ière; [*habit, policy*] dispendieux/-ieuse.

spent /spent/ **I** *prét, pp* ▶ **spend**.
II *adj* **1** (used) [*bullet*] perdu; [*battery*] déchargé; [*match*] utilisé; **2** (exhausted) [*person*] fourbu; [*passion*] éteint; **to be a ~ force** FIG avoir perdu toute force.

sperm /spɜ:m/ *n* **1** (cell) spermatozoïde *m*; **2** (semen) sperme *m*.

sperm bank *n* banque *f* de sperme.

sperm donor *n* donneur *m* de sperme.

spermicidal /ˌspɜ:mɪ'saɪdl/ *adj* spermicide.

spew /spju:/ **I** *vtr* **1** (also ~ **out**) vomir [*smoke, lava, propaganda*]; cracher [*insults, coins, paper*]; **2**○ (also ~ **up**) dégobiller○.
II *vi* (also ~ **out**) [*smoke, insults*] jaillir.

sphere /sfɪə(r)/ *n* **1** (shape) sphère *f*; **2** (planet) sphère *f* céleste; **3** (field) domaine *m* (**of** de); **~ of influence** sphère *f* d'influence; **4** (social circle) milieu *m*.

spherical /'sferɪkl/ *adj* sphérique.

spice /spaɪs/ **I** *n* **1** CULIN épice *f*; **mixed ~** épices mélangées; **2** FIG piment *m*.
II *noun modifier* [*jar, rack*] à épices; [*trade, route*] des épices.
III *vtr* **1** CULIN épicer [*food*]; **2** (also ~ **up**) pimenter [*life, story*].
IDIOMS variety is the ~ of life la diversité est le sel de la vie.

spick-and-span *adj* impeccable.

spicy /'spaɪsɪ/ *adj* **1** [*food*] épicé; **2** [*story*] croustillant.

spider /'spaɪdə(r)/ *n* **1** ZOOL araignée *f*; **2** GB (straps) fixe-bagages *m inv*; **3** US poêle *f* (munie de pieds).

spiderweb *n* US toile *f* d'araignée.

spidery /'spaɪdərɪ/ *adj* [*writing*] en pattes de mouche.

spiel○ /ʃpi:l, us spi:l/ *n* baratin○ *m*.

spike /spaɪk/ **I** *n* (point) pointe *f* ALSO SPORT.
II spikes *npl* SPORT chaussures *fpl* à pointes.
III *vtr* **1** (pierce) embrocher; **2**○ corser [*drink*] (**with** de); **3** (reject) mettre [qch] au panier [*story*]; **4** SPORT (in volleyball) **to ~ the ball** faire un smash; **5** (thwart) contrecarrer [*scheme*]; étouffer [*rumour*].
IDIOMS to ~ sb's guns déjouer les plans de qn.

spiky /'spaɪkɪ/ *adj* **1** (having spikes) [*hair*] en brosse *inv*; [*branch*] piquant; [*object*] acéré; **2**○ GB (short-tempered) revêche.

spill /spɪl/ **I** *n* **1** (of oil, etc) déversement *m* accidentel; **2** (fall) accrochage *m*; (from horse) chute *f*; **3** (for lighting candles) allume-feu *m inv*.
II *vtr* (*prét, pp* **spilt** ou **~ed**) **1** (pour) (overturn) renverser (**onto, over** sur); (drip) laisser tomber; **2** (disgorge) déverser [*oil, rubbish, chemical*].
III *vi* (*prét, pp* **spilt** ou **~ed**) (empty out) se répandre;

Spelling and punctuation

The alphabet and accents

The names of the letters are given below with their pronunciation in French and, in the right-hand column, a useful way of clarifying difficulties when you are spelling names etc.
A comme Anatole means A for Anatole, and so on.

		When spelling aloud
A	[ɑ]	A comme Anatole
B	[be]	B comme Berthe
C	[se]	C comme Célestin
ç	[sesedij]	c cédille
D	[de]	D comme Désiré
E	[ə]	E comme Eugène
é	[eaksategy] or [aaksategy]	e accent aigu
è	[eaksagrav] or [aaksagrav]	e accent grave
ê	[ɛaksasir kɵflɛks] or [ɵaksasir kɵflɛks]	e accent circonflexe
ë	[ɵtrema]	e tréma
F	[ɛf]	F comme François
G*	[ʒe]	G comme Gaston
H	[aʃ]	H comme Henri
I	[i]	I comme Irma
J*	[ʒi]	J comme Joseph
K	[ka]	K comme Kléber
L	[ɛl]	L comme Louis
M	[ɛm]	M comme Marcel
N	[ɛn]	N comme Nicolas
O	[o]	O comme Oscar
P	[pe]	P comme Pierre
Q	[ky]	Q comme Quintal
R	[er]	R comme Raoul
S	[ɛs]	S comme Suzanne
T	[te]	T comme Thérèse
U	[y]	U comme Ursule
V	[ve]	V comme Victor
W	[dubləve]	W comme William
X	[iks]	X comme Xavier
Y	[igrɛk]	Y comme Yvonne
Z	[zɛd]	Z comme Zoé

Spelling

capital B	= B majuscule
small b	= b minuscule
it has got a capital B	= cela s'écrit avec un B majuscule
in small letters	= en minuscules
double t	= deux t [døte]
double n	= deux n [døzɛn] (note the liaison which would also be used in deux l, deux r etc.)
apostrophe	= apostrophe [apɔstrɔf]
d apostrophe	= d apostrophe [deapɔstrɔf]
hyphen	= trait d'union
rase-mottes has got a hyphen	= rase-mottes s'écrit avec un trait d'union

Dictating punctuation

.	point *or* un point (*full stop*)
,	virgule (*comma*)
:	deux points (*colon*)
;	point-virgule (*semicolon*)
!	point d'exclamation† (*exclamation mark*)
?	point d'interrogation† (*question mark*)
	à la ligne (*new paragraph*)
(	ouvrez la parenthèse (*open brackets*)
)	fermez la parenthèse (*close brackets*)
()	entre parenthèses (*in brackets*)
[]	entre crochets (*in square brackets*)
—	tiret (*dash*)
...	points de suspension (*three dots*)
« *ou* "	ouvrez les guillemets (*open inverted commas*)
» *ou* "	fermez les guillemets (*close inverted commas*)
«» *ou* ""	entre guillemets (*in inverted commas*)

The use of inverted commas in French

In novels and short stories, direct speech is punctuated differently from English:

The inverted commas lie on the line, e.g. «Tiens, dit-elle, en ouvrant les rideaux, les voilà !»

This example also shows that the inverted commas are not closed after each stretch of direct speech. In modern texts they are often omitted altogether (though this is still sometimes frowned on):

Il l'interrogea :
– Vous êtes arrivé quand ?
– Pourquoi cette question ? Je n'ai rien fait de mal.
– C'est ce que nous allons voir.

Note the short dash in this case that introduces each new speaker. Even if inverted commas had been used in the above dialogue, they would have been opened before vous and closed after voir, and not used at other points.

English-style inverted commas are used in French to highlight words in a text:

Le ministre a voulu "tout savoir" sur la question.

---

* *Note the difference between English and French pronunciation of g and j.*
† *Note that, unlike English, French has a space before ! and ? and : and ;, e.g. Jamais !, Pourquoi ? etc. This is not usual, however, in dictionaries, where it would take up too much room.*
‡ *Single inverted commas are not much used in French.*

---

to ~ **from** ou out of couler de; to ~ **(out) into** ou **onto the street** [*crowds, people*] se répandre dans la rue.

IDIOMS (**it's**) **no use crying over spilt milk** ça ne sert à rien de pleurer sur ce qui est fait; **to ~ the beans**○ vendre la mèche○; **to ~ blood** verser le sang. ■ **spill out**: ¶ ~ **out** LIT se répandre; ¶ ~ **out** [*sth*], ~ [*sth*] **out** LIT laisser échapper; FIG révéler [*secrets*]; débiter [*story*]. ■ **spill over** LIT déborder; **to ~ over into** FIG GEN s'étendre à; dégénérer en [*looting, hostility*].

spillage /'spɪlɪdʒ/ n **1** (of oil, chemical, effluent) déversement m accidentel; **oil ~** déversement m accidentel d'hydrocarbures; **2** (spilling) ¢ déversement m.

spillover /'spɪləʊvə(r)/ n US (overflow) (of traffic) excédent m; (of liquid) débordement m.

spilt /spɪlt/ *prét, pp* ▸ **spill** II, III.

spin /spɪn/ **I** n **1** (of wheel) tour m; (of dancer, skate) pirouette f; **to give sth a ~** faire tourner qch; **2** SPORT effet m; **to put ~ on a ball** donner de l'effet à une balle; **3** AVIAT **to go into a ~** descendre en vrille; **4** (pleasure trip) tour m; **to go for a ~** aller faire un tour; **5** US (interpretation) **to put a new ~ on sth** aborder qch sous un nouvel angle. **II** *vtr* (*p prés* -**nn**-; *prét, pp* **spun**) **1** lancer [*top*]; faire tourner [*globe, wheel*]; **2** (flip) **to ~ a coin** tirer à pile ou face; **3** filer [*wool, thread*]; **4** [*spider*] tisser; **5** (wring out) essorer qch à la machine [*clothes*]; **6**

raconter [*tale*]; **he spun me some tale about missing his train** il a prétendu qu'il avait raté son train. **III** *vi* (*p prés* -**nn**-; *prét, pp* **spun**) **1** (rotate) [*wheel*] tourner; [*weathercock, top*] tournoyer; [*dancer*] pirouetter; **to go ~ning through the air** [*ball, plate*] aller valser○; **the car spun off the road** la voiture est allée valser○ dans la nature; **2** FIG tourner; **my head is ~ning** j'ai la tête qui tourne; **the room was ~ning** les murs de la pièce tournaient; **3** (turn wildly) [*wheels*] patiner; [*plane*] descendre en vrille. IDIOMS **to be in a ~** être dans tous ses états; **to ~ one's wheels** US FIG ne pas avancer FIG. ■ **spin along** [*car*] filer. ■ **spin out**: ~ [*sth*] **out**, ~ **out** [*sth*] prolonger [*visit*]; faire traîner [qch] en longueur [*speech*]; ménager [*money*]. ■ **spin round**: ¶ ~ **round** [*person*] se retourner rapidement; [*dancer, skater*] pirouetter; **she spun round in her chair** elle a pivoté sur sa chaise; [*car*] faire un tête-à-queue; ¶ ~ [*sb/sth*] **round** faire tourner [*wheel*]; faire tournoyer [*dancer, top*].

spinach /'spɪnɪdʒ, US -ɪtʃ/ n **1** (plant) épinard m; **2** ¢ (vegetable) épinards mpl.

spinal /'spaɪnl/ adj [*injury, damage*] de la colonne vertébrale; [*nerve, muscle*] spinal; [*disc, ligament*] vertébral.

spinal: ~ **column** n colonne f vertébrale; ~ **cord** n moelle f épinière.

spindle /'spɪndl/ n broche f.

spindly /'spɪndlɪ/ *adj* [*tree, plant*] haut et dégarni; [*legs*] grêle.

spin: **~-drier**, **~ dryer** *n* essoreuse *f*; **~-dry** *vtr* essorer [qch] (à la machine).

spine /spaɪn/ *n* **1** (spinal column) colonne *f* vertébrale; **it sent shivers up and down my ~** (of fear) cela m'a donné des frissons dans le dos; (of pleasure) cela m'a fait frissonner; **2** FIG (backbone) nerf *m*; **3** (prickle) (of plant) épine *f*; (of animal) piquant *m*; **4** (of book) dos *m*.

spine-chilling *adj* qui donne la chair de poule.

spineless /'spaɪnlɪs/ *adj* **1** ZOOL invertébré; **2** PÉJ (weak) mou/molle.

spinning /'spɪnɪŋ/ **I** *n* (for cloth) filage *m*. **II** *noun modifier* [*thread, wool*] à filer.

spinning: **~ machine** *n* métier *m* à filer; **~ mill** *n* filature *f*; **~ top** *n* toupie *f*; **~ wheel** *n* rouet *m*.

spin-off /'spɪnɒf/ **I** *n* **1** (incidental benefit) retombée *f* favorable; **2** (by-product) sous-produit *m* (**of, from** de); **3** TV, CIN adaptation *f*; **TV ~ from the film** adaptation télévisée du film.
II *noun modifier* [*effect, profit*] secondaire; [*technology, product*] dérivé; **~ series** TV feuilleton télévisé adapté d'un film.

spinster /'spɪnstə(r)/ *n* JUR célibataire *f*; PÉJ vieille fille *f*.

spiny /'spaɪnɪ/ *adj* [*plant*] épineux; [*animal*] couvert de piquants.

spiral /'spaɪərəl/ **I** *n* **1** (shape) GEN, MATH, AVIAT spirale *f*; **in a ~** [*object, spring, curl*] en forme de spirale; **2** (trend) spirale *f*; **a ~ of violence** une escalade de violence; **a downward/upward ~** une descente/montée en spirale.
II *noun modifier* [*motif, spring, structure*] en spirale.
III *vi* (*p prés etc* **-ll-** GB, **-l-** US) **1** ECON monter en flèche; **to ~ downwards** tomber en flèche; **2** (of movement) **to ~ up(wards)/down(wards)** (gently) monter/descendre en spirale or en tournoyant; (rapidly) monter/descendre en vrille.
IV spiralling GB, **spiraling** US *pres p adj* qui monte en flèche.

spiral: **~ binding** *n* (reliure *f* à) spirales *fpl*; **~ notebook** *n* cahier *m* à spirales; **~ staircase** *n* escalier *m* en colimaçon.

spire /'spaɪə(r)/ *n* ARCHIT flèche *f*.

spirit /'spɪrɪt/ **I** *n* **1** (essential nature) (of law, game, era) esprit *m*; **it's not in the ~ of the agreement** ce n'est pas conforme à l'esprit de l'accord; **2** (mood, attitude) esprit *m* (**of** de); **in a ~ of friendship** dans un esprit amical; **a ~ of forgiveness** une intention d'indulgence; **a ~ of optimism** une tendance à l'optimisme; **to do sth in the right/wrong ~** faire qch de façon positive/négative; **to take a remark in the right/wrong ~** bien/mal prendre une remarque; **to enter into the ~ of sth** se conformer à l'esprit de qch; **that's the ~oʃ** c'est ça!; **3** (courage, determination) courage *m*; **to show ~** se montrer courageux/-euse; **to break sb's ~** briser la résistance de qn; **a performance full of ~** une interprétation pleine de brio; **with ~** [*play, defend*] avec détermination; **4** (soul) GEN, MYTHOL, RELIG esprit *m*; **the life of the ~** la vie spirituelle; **the Holy Spirit** le Saint-Esprit; **5** (person) esprit *m*; **6** (drink) alcool *m* fort; **wines and ~s** COMM vins et spiritueux *mpl*; **7** CHEM alcool *m*.
II spirits *npl* **to be in good/poor ~s** être de bonne/mauvaise humeur; **to be in high ~s** être d'excellente humeur; **to keep one's ~s up** garder le moral; **to raise sb's ~s** remonter le moral de qn; **my ~s rose/sank** j'ai repris/perdu courage.
III *noun modifier* [*lamp, stove*] à alcool.
IV *vtr* **to ~ sth/sb away** faire disparaître qch/qn; **to ~ sth in/out** introduire/sortir discrètement qch.

spirited /'spɪrɪtɪd/ *adj* [*horse, debate, reply*] fougueux/ -euse; [*music, performance*] plein d'entrain; [*attack, defence*] vif/vive.

spiritless /'spɪrɪtləs/ *adj* [*person*] qui manque d'entrain.

spirit level *n* niveau *m* à bulle.

spiritual /'spɪrɪtʃʊəl/ **I** *n* MUS spiritual *m*.

II *adj* (all contexts) spirituel/-elle; **~ adviser** ou **director** directeur *m* de conscience.

spiritualism /'spɪrɪtʃʊəlɪzəm/ *n* (occult) spiritisme *m*.

spiritualist /'spɪrɪtʃʊəlɪst/ *n, adj* spiritiste (*mf*).

spirituality /,spɪrɪtʃʊ'ælətɪ/ *n* spiritualité *f*.

spiritually /'spɪrɪtʃʊəlɪ/ *adv* sur le plan spirituel.

spit /spɪt/ **I** *n* **1** (saliva) (in mouth) salive *f*; (on ground) crachat *m*; **to give a ~** cracher; **2** CULIN broche *f*; **rotating ~** tournebroche *m*; **3** (of land) pointe *f*.
II *vtr* (*p prés* **-tt-**; *prét, pp* **spat**) **1** LIT [*person, volcano*] cracher; [*pan*] projeter [*oil*]; **2** FIG proférer [*oath, venom*].
III *vi* (*p prés* **-tt-**; *prét, pp* **spat**) **1** LIT [*cat, person*] cracher (**at, on** sur; **into** dans; **out of** de); **to ~ in sb's face** LIT, FIG cracher à la figure de qn; **2** (be angry) **to ~ with** écumer de [*rage, anger*]; **3** (crackle) [*oil, sausage*] grésiller; [*logs, fire*] crépiter.
IV *v impers* (*p prés* **-tt-**; *prét, pp* **spat**) **it's ~ting** (with rain) il bruine.
IDIOMS **~ and polish** huile *f* de coude; **to be the (dead) ~ of sb** être le portrait tout craché de qn.
■ **spit out**: **~** [*sth*] **out**, **~ out** [*sth*] LIT cracher [*blood, drink*]; FIG proférer [*phrase, word*].
■ **spit up**: **~** [*sth*] **up**, **~ up** [*sth*] cracher [*blood*].

spite /spaɪt/ **I** *n* (malice) méchanceté *f*; (vindictiveness) rancune *f*.
II in spite of *prep phr* malgré; **in ~ of the fact that** bien que.
III *vtr* faire du mal à; (less strong) ennuyer.
IDIOMS **to cut off one's nose to ~ one's face** se punir soi-même.

spiteful /'spaɪtfl/ *adj* [*person*] (malicious) méchant; (vindictive) rancunier/-ière; [*remark*] méchant; [*article*] fielleux/-euse; **~ gossip** commérages *mpl*.

spitefully /'spaɪtfəlɪ/ *adv* méchamment.

spitting /'spɪtɪŋ/ *n* **~ is a dirty habit** cracher est une habitude dégoûtante.
IDIOMS **to be the ~ image of sb** être le portrait (tout) craché de qn; **to be within ~ distance of** être à deux pas de.

spittle /'spɪtl/ *n* **1** (of person) (in mouth) salive *f*; (on surface) crachat *m*; **2** (of animal) bave *f*.

splash /splæʃ/ **I** *n* **1** (sound) plouf *m*; **to make a big ~** LIT faire un grand plouf; FIG faire sensation; **2** (patch) (of mud) tache *f*; (of water, oil) éclaboussure *f*; (of colour) touche *f*; (of tonic, soda) goutte *f*.
II *vtr* **1** (spatter) éclabousser; **to ~ sth over sb/sth** éclabousser qn/qch de qch; **2** (sprinkle) **to ~ water on to one's face** s'asperger le visage d'eau; **3** (maliciously) **to ~ water onto** envoyer de l'eau sur; **4** (in newspaper) mettre [qch] à la une; **the news was ~ed across the front page** la nouvelle s'étalait à la une des journaux.
III *vi* **1** (spatter) faire des éclaboussures (**onto, over** sur); **water was ~ing from the tap** l'eau giclait du robinet; **2** (move) **to ~ through sth** [*person*] traverser qch en pataugeant; [*car*] traverser qch en faisant des éclaboussures; **3** (in sea, pool) faire des éclaboussures (**in** dans).
■ **splash around**: ¶ **~ around** barboter (**in** dans); ¶ **~** [*sth*] **around** envoyer [qch] partout.
■ **splash down** amerrir.
■ **splash out**⁰ (spend money) faire des folies; **to ~ out on sth** faire la folie de s'offrir qch.

splash: **~-back** *n* revêtement *m* (autour d'un évier, d'une baignoire); **~board** *n* AUT garde-boue *m* *inv*; **~down** *n* amerrissage *m*; **~guard** *n* = **splash-board**.

splatter /'splætə(r)/ **I** *n* (of rain, bullets) crépitement *m*.
II *vtr* **to ~ sb/sth with sth**, **to ~ sth over sb/sth** éclabousser qn/qch de qch; **the car ~ed mud everywhere** la voiture a fait gicler de la boue partout.
III *vi* **1** [*ink, paint, mud*] **to ~ onto** ou **over sth** gicler sur qch; **2** [*body, fruit etc*] s'écraser.
IV splattered *pp adj* **1** **~ed with** éclaboussé de; **blood-/mud-~ed** éclaboussé de sang/de boue; **2** (squashed) écrasé.

splay /spleɪ/ **I** *vtr* évaser [*end of pipe etc*]; ébraser [*side of window, door*]; écarter [*legs, feet, fingers*].
II *vi* (also ~ **out**) [*end of pipe*] être évasé.
III splayed *pp adj* [*feet, fingers, legs*] écarté.

spleen /spliːn/ *n* **1** ANAT rate *f*; **2** FIG (bad temper) mauvaise humeur *f*.

splendid /'splendɪd/ *adj* [*building, scenery, collection, ceremony*] splendide; [*idea, achievement, holiday, performance, victory*] formidable○, merveilleux/-euse; [*opportunity*] fantastique○; **we had a ~ time!** on s'est vraiment bien amusé!; **she did a ~ job** elle a fait un travail remarquable; **~!** (c'est) formidable○!

splendidly /'splendɪdlɪ/ *adv* magnifiquement, merveilleusement.

splendour GB, **splendor** US /'splendə(r)/ *n* splendeur *f*; **to live in ~** vivre fastueusement.

splice /splaɪs/ **I** *n* (in rope) épissure *f*; (in tape, film) raccord *m*.
II *vtr* GEN coller [*tape, film*]; épisser [*ends of rope*]; FIG amalgamer.

splint /splɪnt/ *n* **1** MED attelle *f*; **to put sb's leg in a ~** éclisser la jambe de qn; **2** (sliver of wood) allume-feu *m inv*.

splinter /'splɪntə(r)/ **I** *n* (of glass, metal, wood) éclat *m*; (of bone) esquille *f*; **to get a ~ in one's finger** s'enfoncer une écharde dans le doigt.
II *vtr* LIT faire voler [qch] en éclats [*glass, windscreen etc*]; fendre [*wood*]; FIG scinder [*party, group*].
III *vi* LIT [*glass, windscreen*] se briser; [*wood*] se fendre; FIG [*party, alliance etc*] se scinder.

splinter group *n* groupe *m* dissident.

split /splɪt/ **I** *n* **1** LIT (in fabric, garment) déchirure *f*; (in rock, wood) fissure *f*; (in skin) crevasse *f*; **2** (in party, movement, alliance) scission *f* (**in** de); (stronger) rupture *f* (**between** entre; **in, into** dans); **a three-way ~** une scission en trois groupes; **3** (share-out) partage *m*; **4** US (small bottle) (of soft drink) petite bouteille *f*; (of wine) demi-bouteille *f*; **5** CULIN (dessert) ≈ coupe *f* glacée.
II splits *npl* grand écart *m*.
III *adj* [*garment*] déchiré; [*seam*] défait; [*lip*] fendu.
IV *vtr* (*p prés* **-tt-**; *prét, pp* **split**) **1** (cut, slit) fendre [*wood, log, rock, lip, slate, seam*] (**in, into** en); déchirer [*fabric, garment*]; **2** (cause dissent) diviser [*party, movement, alliance*]; **the committee was (deeply) split on** or **over this issue** la commission était (extrêmement) divisée sur cette question; **3** (divide) ▶ **split up**; **4** (share) partager; **to ~ sth three ways** partager qch en trois.
V *vi* (*p prés* **-tt-**; *prét, pp* **split**) **1** [*wood, log, rock, slate*] se fendre (**in, into** en); [*garment*] se déchirer; [*seam*] se défaire ; **to ~ in(to) two** [*stream, road*] se diviser en deux; **my head's ~ting** FIG j'ai horriblement mal à la tête; **2** GEN, POL [*party, movement, alliance*] se diviser; (stronger) se scinder; **3** (divide) ▶ **split up**; **4**○ GB (tell tales) cafarder○; **5**○ (leave) filer○.
IDIOMS **to ~ the difference** couper la poire en deux; **to ~ one's sides○** (laughing) se tordre de rire.
■ **split off**: ¶ ~ **off** [*branch, piece*] se détacher (**from** de); [*path*] bifurquer; [*political group*] faire scission; [*company*] se séparer (**from** de); ¶ ~ [*sth*] **off** détacher [*piece*]; **to ~ sth off from** détacher qch de [*piece*]; séparer qch de [*company, section*].
■ **split open**: ¶ ~ **open** [*bag, fabric*] se déchirer; [*seam*] se défaire; ¶ ~ [*sth*] **open** fendre [*box, coconut*]; **to ~ one's head open** se fendre le crâne.
■ **split up**: ¶ ~ **up** [*band, couple, members, parents*] se séparer; [*crowd, demonstrators*] se disperser; [*alliance, consortium*] éclater; [*federation*] se scinder (**into** en); **to ~ up with** quitter [*husband etc*]; **to ~ up into groups of five** se mettre en groupes de cinq; ¶ ~ [*sb*] **up** séparer [*friends, partners, group members*] (**from** de); **everyone tried to ~ the couple up** tout le monde a essayé de les écarter l'un de l'autre; **to ~ the children up into groups** répartir les enfants en petits groupes; ¶ ~ [*sth*] **up**, ~ **up** [*sth*] partager [*area, group*] (**into** en); diviser [*area, group*] (**into** en).

split: ~ **decision** *n* SPORT décision *f* partagée; ~ **ends** *npl* cheveux *mpl* fourchus; ~ **infinitive** *n*:

erreur de grammaire consistant à introduire un adverbe au milieu d'un infinitif, entre 'to' et le verbe.

split level I *n* **the flat is on ~s** l'appartement a des demi-étages.
II split-level *adj* [*cooker*] à plaques de cuisson et four indépendants; [*apartment*] sur deux niveaux.

split: ~ **peas** *npl* pois *mpl* cassés; ~ **personality** *n* double personnalité *f*; ~ **pin** *n* goupille *f* fendue; ~ **screen** *n* écran *m* divisé, split screen *m*.

split second I *n* fraction *f* de seconde.
II split-second *noun modifier* [*decision*] éclair *inv*; **the success of the mission depends on ~ timing** pour réussir il faut que la mission suive un programme fixé à la seconde près.

split: ~ **shift** *n* poste *m* fractionné; **~-site** *adj* [*factory, school*] dont les locaux sont dispersés; ~ **ticket** *n* US POL vote *m* pour une liste panachée.

splitting /'splɪtɪŋ/ **I** *n* (division) (of wood, stone) fendage *m*; (of group, profits, proceeds) répartition *f*.
II *adj* **to have a ~ headache** avoir horriblement mal à la tête.

splurge○ /splɜːdʒ/ **I** *n* folie○ *f*.
II *vtr* claquer○ [*money*] (**on** pour).
III *vi* (also ~ **out**) claquer○ (**on** pour).

splutter /'splʌtə(r)/ **I** *n* (of person) (spitting) crachotement *m*; (stutter) bafouillement *m*; (of engine) crachotement *m*; (of fire, sparks) grésillement *m*.
II *vtr* (also ~ **out**) bafouiller [*excuse, apology, words*].
III *vi* [*person*] (stutter) bafouiller; (spit) crachoter; [*fire, fat, candle, match, sparks*] grésiller; **the engine ~ed to a stop** le moteur s'est arrêté dans un crachotement.

spoil /spɔɪl/ **I spoils** *npl* (of war) butin *m*; (political, commercial) profits *mpl*; (sporting) gains *mpl*.
II *vtr* (*prét, pp* **~ed** ou **~t** GB) **1** (mar) GEN gâcher (**by doing** en faisant); gâter [*place, taste, effect*]; **it will ~ your appetite** ça va te couper l'appétit; **to ~ sth for sb** gâcher qch à qn; **they ~ it** ou **things for other people** ils gâchent le plaisir des autres; **to ~ sb's enjoyment of sth** empêcher qn de profiter de qch; **why did you go and ~ everything?** pourquoi as-tu tout gâché?; **to ~ sb's fun** (thwart) contrarier qn; **2** (ruin) abîmer; **to ~ one's chances of doing** gâcher ses chances de faire (**by doing** en faisant); **3** (pamper) gâter [*person, pet*] (**by doing** en faisant); **to ~ sb rotten○** pourrir qn; **to ~ sb with** gâter qn en lui offrant [*gift, trip*]; **4** POL rendre [qch] nul/nulle [*ballot paper*].
III *vi* (*prét, pp* **~ed** ou **~t** GB) [*product, foodstuff*] s'abîmer; [*meat*] se gâter; **your dinner will ~!** ça ne va plus être bon!
IV *v refl* (*prét, pp* **~ed** ou **~t** GB) **to ~ oneself** se faire un petit plaisir; **let's ~ ourselves and eat out!** faisons-nous plaisir en allant au restaurant!
IDIOMS **to be ~ing for a fight** chercher la bagarre○.

spoiled, spoilt GB /spɔɪld, spɔɪlt/ **I** *prét, pp* ▶ **spoil** II, III, IV.
II *adj* **1** PÉJ [*child, dog*] gâté; **a ~ brat○** un gamin pourri○; **2** POL [*ballot paper*] nul/nulle.
IDIOMS **to be ~ for choice** avoir l'embarras du choix.

spoiler /'spɔɪlə(r)/ *n* **1** AUT becquet *m*; **2** AVIAT aérofrein *m*.

spoilsport○ /'spɔɪlspɔːt/ *n* **to be a ~** faire son rabat-joie.

spoilt /spɔɪlt/ GB *prét, pp, adj* ▶ **spoiled**.

spoke /spəʊk/ **I** *prét* ▶ **speak** II, III.
II *n* (in wheel) rayon *m*; (on ladder) barreau *m*.
IDIOMS **to put a ~ in sb's wheel** mettre des bâtons dans les roues à qn.

spoken /'spəʊkən/ **I** *pp* ▶ **speak** II, III.
II *adj* [*word, dialogue, language*] parlé.

spokesman, spokesperson, spokeswoman *n* porte-parole *m inv*.

sponge /spʌndʒ/ **I** *n* **1** (for cleaning) éponge *f*; **a child's mind is like a ~** le cerveau d'un enfant assimile tout; **2** ¢ (material) éponge *f*; **3** ZOOL éponge *f*; **4** (also ~ **cake**) génoise *f*; **5** MED (pad) compresse *f*.
II *vtr* frotter [qch] avec une éponge [*material, stain*];

éponger [*wound, excess liquid*]; laver [qch] avec une éponge [*surface*].
III° *vi* PÉJ **to ~ off** ou **on** vivre sur le dos de [*family, state*].
■ **sponge down**: **~** [sth] **down, ~ down** [sth] laver [qch] avec une éponge [*car, surface*].

sponge: **~ bag** *n* GB trousse *f* de toilette; **~ finger** *n* GB biscuit *m* à la cuiller; **~ mop** *n* balai-éponge *m*; **~ pudding** *n* GB *gâteau cuit au bain-marie et servi chaud*.

sponger° /'spʌndʒə(r)/ *n* PÉJ parasite *m* PÉJ.

sponge: **~ roll** *n* GB biscuit *m* roulé; **~ rubber** *n* caoutchouc *m* mousse.

spongy /'spʌndʒɪ/ *adj* [*ground, wood*] spongieux/-ieuse; [*texture*] moelleux/-euse; [*flesh*] mou/molle.

sponsor /'spɒnsə(r)/ **I** *n* **1** COMM, FIN (advertiser, backer) sponsor *m*; **2** (patron) mécène *m*; **3** (guarantor) garant/-e *m/f*; **4** RELIG (godparent) parrain/marraine *m/f*; **5** (for charity) *personne qui parraine un participant à une épreuve sportive organisée dans un but caritatif*; **6** POL (of bill, motion, law) initiateur/-trice *m/f*.
II *vtr* **1** COMM, FIN (fund) sponsoriser [*event, team*]; financer [*student, course, enterprise*]; **2** (support) soutenir [*violence, invasion*]; **3** POL (advocate) présenter [*bill*]; **4** (for charity) parrainer [*person*]; **~ed swim** épreuve *f* de natation parrainée.

sponsorship /'spɒnsəʃɪp/ *n* **1** COMM, FIN (corporate funding) parrainage *m*, sponsorat *m* (**from** de); **to seek/raise ~ for sth** chercher/trouver des sponsors pour qch; **2** (backing) (financial) sponsorat *m*; (cultural) patronage *m*; (moral, political) parrainage *m*; **3 C** (also **~ deal**) contrat *m* de parrainage; **4** POL (of bill, motion) soutien *m*.

spontaneity /ˌspɒntə'neɪətɪ/ *n* spontanéité *f*.

spontaneous /spɒn'teɪnɪəs/ *adj* spontané.

spontaneously /spɒn'teɪnɪəslɪ/ *adv* spontanément.

spoof° /spuːf/ **I** *n* (parody) parodie *f* (**on** de).
II *noun modifier* (parody) **a ~ horror film** une parodie de film d'horreur.
III *vtr* (parody) parodier [*book, film*].

spook° /spuːk/ **I** *n* **1** (ghost) fantôme *m*; **2** US (spy) espion/-ionne *m/f*.
II *vtr* (frighten) effrayer [*person*]; (haunt) hanter.

spooky° /'spuːkɪ/ *adj* [*house, atmosphere*] sinistre; [*story*] qui fait froid dans le dos.

spool /spuːl/ *n* bobine *f*.

spoon /spuːn/ **I** *n* cuillère *f*; (for tea, coffee) petite cuillère *f*.
II *vtr* (in cooking, serving) **to ~ sth into a dish/bowl** mettre qch dans un plat/bol avec une cuillère.
IDIOMS **to be born with a silver ~ in one's mouth** naître dans la soie.

spoonerism /'spuːnərɪzəm/ *n* contrepèterie *f* (involontaire).

spoon-feed /'spuːnfiːd/ *vtr* **1** nourrir [qn] à la petite cuillère [*baby, invalid*]; **2** FIG PÉJ [*teacher*] mâcher le travail à [*students*].

spoonful /'spuːnfʊl/ *n* (*pl* **-fuls** ou **-sful**) cuillerée *f*, cuillère *f*.

sporadic /spə'rædɪk/ *adj* sporadique.

sporadically /spə'rædɪklɪ/ *adv* sporadiquement.

sporran /'spɒrən/ *n* sporran *m* (*bourse en cuir ou en fourrure portée sur le devant du kilt*).

sport /spɔːt/ **▶ 949** **I** *n* **1** (physical activity) sport *m*; **2** SCH (subject) activités *fpl* sportives; **3** SOUT (fun) **to have great ~** s'amuser beaucoup; **4**° (person) **to be a good/bad ~** (in games) être beau/mauvais joueur; (when teased) bien/mal prendre la plaisanterie.
II *vtr* arborer [*hat, rose, moustache*].

sport coat *n* US = **sports jacket**.

sporting /'spɔːtɪŋ/ *adj* **1** [*event*] sportif/-ive; **2** (generous) [*offer*] généreux/-euse; **it's very ~ of you** c'est très généreux de votre part; **to have a ~ chance of winning** avoir de bonnes chances de gagner.

sportingly /'spɔːtɪŋlɪ/ *adv* sportivement, généreusement.

sport: **~s car** *n* voiture *f* de sport; **~scast** *n* US

émission *f* sportive; **~s centre** GB, **~s center** US *n* centre *m* sportif; **~s club** *n* club *m* sportif; **~s day** *n* GB fête *f* des sports; (in school, club etc) terrain *m* de sports; **~s hall** *n* salle *f* omnisports; **~s jacket** *n* GB veste *f* en tweed; **~sman** *n* sportif *m*; **~s shirt** *n* maillot *m* de sport; **~swear** *n* sportswear *m*; **~swoman** *n* sportive *f*.

sporty° /'spɔːtɪ/ *adj* (fond of sport) sportif/-ive.

spot° /spɒt/ **I** *n* **1** (dot) (on animal) tache *f*; (on fabric) pois *m*; (on dice, domino) point *m*; **to see ~s before one's eyes** voir trouble; **2** (stain) tache *f*; **3** (pimple) bouton *m*; **to come out in ~s** être couvert de boutons; **4** (place) endroit *m*; **to be on the ~** GEN être sur place; **to decide on the ~** décider sur-le-champ; **this record has been on the top** ou **number one ~ for two weeks** ce disque a été numéro un pendant deux semaines; **5**° (small amount) **a ~ of cream/sightseeing** un peu de crème/de tourisme; **to have** ou **be in a ~ of bother (with)** avoir quelques petits ennuis (avec); **6**° (difficulty) situation *f* embêtante; **to be in a ~ (tight)** être dans une situation embêtante; **7** COMM spot *m* publicitaire; **8** TV, RADIO (regular slot) temps *m* d'antenne; **9** (moral blemish) tache *f*; **10** (light) CIN, THEAT projecteur *m*; (in home, display) spot *m*; **11** SPORT (for penalty kick) point *m* de pénalty; (for snooker ball) mouche *f*.
II *vtr* (*p prés etc* **-tt-**) **1** (see) apercevoir [*person*]; voir [*car, roadsign, book*]; **to ~ that…** s'apercevoir que…; **well ~ted!** bien vu!; **2** (recognize) reconnaître [*car, person, symptoms, opportunity*]; repérer [*defect, difference, bargain*]; observer [*birds, trains*]; **3** (stain) tacher.
III *v impers* (*p prés etc* **-tt-**) (rain) **it's ~ting** il tombe quelques gouttes.
IDIOMS **to change one's ~s** changer son caractère; **to knock ~s off sth/sb** être bien meilleur que qch/qn.

spot check I *n* (unannounced) contrôle *m* surprise (**on** sur); (random) contrôle *m* fait au hasard (**on** sur).
II spot-check *vtr* effectuer un contrôle surprise sur [*passengers*].

spot fine *n* amende *f* à régler sur le lieu de l'infraction.

spotless /'spɒtlɪs/ *adj* impeccable.

spotlessly /'spɒtlɪslɪ/ *adv* **~ clean** d'une propreté impeccable.

spotlight /'spɒtlaɪt/ **I** *n* **1** (light) CIN, THEAT projecteur *m*; (in home) spot *m*; **2** FIG (focus of attention) **to be in** ou **under the ~** [*person*] être sur la sellette; **the ~ is on Aids** le sida fait la une; **to turn** ou **put the ~ on sb/sth** attirer l'attention sur qn/qch.
II *vtr* (*prét, pp* **-lit** ou **-lighted**) **1** CIN, THEAT diriger les projecteurs sur [*actor, area*]; **2** FIG (highlight) mettre [qch] en lumière [*problem*].

spot-on /ˌspɒt'ɒn/ *adj* GB exact; **he was absolutely ~** il a mis dans le mille.

spot price *n* FIN prix *m* sur place.

spotted /'spɒtɪd/ *adj* [*fabric*] à pois (*after n*); [*fur, dog*] tacheté.

spotted dick *n* GB CULIN pudding *m* aux raisins secs.

spotter /'spɒtə(r)/ *n* **▶ train spotter**.

spotting /'spɒtɪŋ/ *n* MED pertes *fpl* de sang.

spotty /'spɒtɪ/ *adj* **1** (pimply) [*adolescent, skin*] boutonneux/-euse; **he's very ~** il est plein de boutons; **2** (patterned) [*dress, fabric*] à pois (*after n*); [*dog*] tacheté.

spot-weld *vtr* souder [qch] par points.

spouse /spaʊz, US spaʊs/ *n* époux/épouse *m/f*.

spout /spaʊt/ **I** *n* (of kettle, teapot) bec *m* verseur; (of tap) brise-jet *m*; (of hose) orifice *m*; (of fountain) jet *m*; (of gutter) gargouille *f*.
II *vtr* **1** (spurt) [*pipe, fountain*] faire jaillir; **2** PÉJ (recite) débiter [*poetry, statistics, theories*] (**at** à).
III *vi* **1** (spurt) jaillir; **2**° GB PÉJ (also **~ forth**) (talk) discourir (**about** sur); **3** [*whale*] souffler.
IDIOMS **to be up the ~**° GB être fichu°.

sprain /spreɪn/ **I** *n* entorse *f*; (less severe) foulure *f*.

II *vtr* **to ~ one's ankle/wrist** se faire une entorse à la cheville/au poignet; (less severely) se fouler la cheville/le poignet.

sprang /spræŋ/ *prét* ▶ **spring III, IV**.

sprat /spræt/ *n* sprat *m*.

sprawl /sprɔːl/ **I** *n* (of suburbs, buildings etc) étendue *f*; **the ~ of Paris** l'agglomération parisienne.

II *vi* [*person*] s'étaler; [*town, forest*] s'étaler; **to lay ~ed across the sofa** être étalé sur le canapé.

sprawling /ˈsprɔːlɪŋ/ *adj* [*suburb, city*] tentaculaire; [*handwriting*] qui s'étale dans tous les sens.

spray /spreɪ/ **I** *n* **1 ¢** (seawater) embruns *mpl*; (other) nuages *mpl* de (fines) gouttelettes; **2** (container) (for perfume) vaporisateur *m*; (for antifreeze, deodorant, paint etc) bombe *f*; (for inhalant, throat, nose) pulvérisateur *m*; **3** (shower) (of sparks) gerbe *f*; (of bullets) pluie *f*; **4** (of flowers) (bunch) gerbe *f*; (single branch) rameau *m*; (single flowering stem) branche *f*.

II *noun modifier* [*deodorant*] en spray; [*paint, starch*] en atomiseur.

III *vtr* vaporiser [*liquid*]; asperger [*person*] (**with** de); arroser [*demonstrator, oilslick*] (**with** de); **to ~ sth onto sth** (onto fire) projeter qch sur qch [*foam, water*]; **to ~ sth over sb/sth** asperger qn/qch de qch [*water*]; FIG **to ~ sb/sth with** arroser qn/qch de [*bullets*].

IV *vi* gicler; (more violently) jaillir; **to ~ over/out of** gicler sur/de.

spray: **~ can** *n* bombe *f*, aérosol *m*; **~ gun** *n* pistolet *m* à peinture; (for inhalant, throat, nose) vaporisateur. ~**-on** *adj* [*conditioner, glitter*] en vaporisateur.

spread /spred/ **I** *n* **1** (dissemination) (of disease, drugs) propagation *f*; (of news, information) diffusion *f*; (of democracy, infection, weapons) progression *f*; **the ~ of sth to** l'extension *f* de qch à [*group, area*]; **2** (extent, range) (of wings, branches) envergure *f*; (of arch) portée *f*; (of products, services) éventail *m*; **3** (in newspaper) **double-page ~** page *f* double; **4** CULIN pâte *f* à tartiner; **5** (assortment of dishes) festin *m*; **6** US AGRIC grand ranch *m*.

II *vtr* (*prét, pp* **spread**) **1** (unfold) étendre [*cloth, map, rug*]; (lay out) étaler [*cloth, newspaper, map*]; (put) mettre [*cloth, newspaper*]; [*bird*] déployer [*wings*]; **to ~ a cloth on the table** mettre une nappe sur la table; ▶ **wing**; **2** (apply in layer) étaler [*butter, jam, glue*]; **~ the butter thinly on the bread** étaler une mince couche de beurre sur le pain; **3** (distribute over area) disperser [*forces, troops*]; étaler [*cards, documents*]; épandre [*fertilizer*]; répartir [*workload, responsibility*]; **to ~ grit** ou **sand** sabler; **we have to ~ our resources very thin(ly)** nous devons ménager nos ressources; **4** (also **~ out**) (space out) étaler, échelonner [*payments, meetings, cost*] (**over** sur); **5** (diffuse, cause to proliferate) propager [*disease, fire*]; semer [*confusion, panic*]; faire circuler [*rumour, story, lie*]; **to ~ sth to sb** transmettre [qch] à qn [*infection, news*]; **to ~ the word that** dire à tout le monde que.

III *vi* (*prét, pp* **spread**) **1** [*butter, glue*] s'étaler; **2** (cover area or time, extend) [*forest, drought, network*] s'étendre (**over** sur); [*experience, training*] s'étendre (**over** sur); **3** (proliferate) [*disease, fear, fire*] se propager; [*rumour, story*] circuler; [*stain*] s'étaler; **the rumour was ~ing that** le bruit courait que; **to ~ to** [*fire, disease, strike*] s'étendre à, gagner [*building, region*]; **the disease spread from the liver to the kidney** la maladie s'est propagée du foie aux reins; **rain will ~ to most regions** la pluie va s'étendre à la plupart des régions.

IDIOMS **to ~ oneself too thin** FIG faire trop de choses à la fois.

■ **spread around**, **spread about**: **~ [sth] around** faire circuler [*rumour*]; **to ~ it around that** faire courir le bruit que.

■ **spread out**: ¶ **~ out** [*group*] se disperser (**over** sur); [*wings, tail*] se déployer; [*landscape, town, woods*] s'étendre; ¶ **~ [sth] out**, **~ out [sth] 1** (open out, unfold) étendre [*cloth, map, rug, newspaper*] (**on, over** sur); (lay, flatten out) étaler [*cloth, newspaper, map*] (**on,**

over sur); **2** (distribute over area) étaler [*cards, trinkets*]; disperser [*forces*].

spread-eagled *adj* bras et jambes écartés.

spreadsheet *n* COMPUT tableur *m*.

spree /spriː/ *n* **to go on a ~** (drinking) faire la bringue○; **to go on a shopping ~** aller faire des folies dans les magasins; **to go on a killing ~** être pris d'une folie meurtrière.

sprig /sprɪg/ *n* (of herb) brin *m*; (of holly, mistletoe) petite branche *f*.

sprightly /ˈspraɪtlɪ/ *adj* alerte, gaillard.

spring /sprɪŋ/ **I** *n* ▶ **1235** | **1** (season) printemps *m*; **2** TECH (coil) ressort *m*; **to be like a coiled ~** FIG (tense) être tendu; **3** (leap) bond *m*; **4** (elasticity) élasticité *f*; **to have a ~ in one's step** marcher d'un pas allègre; **5** (water source) source *f*.

II *noun modifier* [*weather, flowers*] printanier/-ière; [*day, equinox*] de printemps.

III *vtr* (*prét* **sprang**; *pp* **sprung**) **1** (set off) déclencher [*trap, lock*]; **2** (develop) **to ~ a leak** [*tank*] commencer à fuir; **3** (cause unexpectedly) **to ~ sth on sb** annoncer qch de but en blanc à qn [*news*]; **to ~ a surprise** faire une surprise (**on** à); **4**○ (liberate) libérer.

IV *vi* (*prét* **sprang**; *pp* **sprung**) **1** (jump) bondir (**onto** sur); **to ~ at sb** se jeter sur qn; **to ~ from/over sth** sauter d'un bond de/par-dessus de qch; **to ~ to one's feet** se lever d'un bond; **2** (move suddenly) **to ~ open/shut** [*door, panel*] s'ouvrir/se fermer brusquement; **to ~ into action** passer à l'action; **to ~ to sb's defence** se précipiter pour défendre qn; **tears sprang to his eyes** les larmes lui sont montées aux yeux; **the first name that sprang to mind was Egbert** le premier prénom qui m'est venu à l'esprit a été (celui d') Egbert; **to ~ into** ou **to life** [*machine, motor*] se mettre en marche or route; **3** (originate) **to ~ from** [*jealousy, fear*]; **where did these people ~ from?** d'où sortent ces gens?

■ **spring back 1** (step back) reculer d'un bond; **2** (return to its position) [*lever*] reprendre sa place.

■ **spring up 1** (get up) [*person*] se lever d'un bond; **2** (appear) [*problem*] surgir; [*weeds, flowers*] sortir de terre; [*building*] apparaître; [*trend*] apparaître.

spring: **~ balance** *n* balance *f* à ressort; ~**board** *n* SPORT, FIG tremplin *m* (**to, for** vers).

spring chicken *n* CULIN jeune poulet *m*, poulette *f*. IDIOMS **he's no ~** il n'est plus tout jeune.

spring: ~**-clean** *vtr* nettoyer [qch] de fond en comble [*house*]; ~**-cleaning** *n* grand nettoyage *m* de printemps; **~ onion** *n* GB CULIN ciboule *f*; **~ roll** *n* CULIN rouleau *m* de printemps.

springtime /ˈsprɪŋtaɪm/ *n* LIT, FIG printemps *m*; **in the ~** au printemps.

spring: **~ vegetable** *n* légume *m* de primeur; **~ water** *n* eau *f* de source.

springy /ˈsprɪŋɪ/ *adj* [*mattress, seat*] élastique; [*floorboards, ground, curls*] souple.

sprinkle /ˈsprɪŋkl/ **I** *n* (of salt, flour etc) pincée *f*. **II** *vtr* **1** (scatter) **to ~ sth with sth** saupoudrer qch de [*salt, sugar*]; parsemer qch de [*herbs*]; **~ with water** humecter qch; **2** (water) arroser [*lawn*].

sprinkler /ˈsprɪŋklə(r)/ *n* (for lawn) arroseur *m*; (for field) canon *m* arroseur; (for fires) diffuseur *m*.

sprinkler system *n* (of building) système *m* d'extinction automatique.

sprinkling /ˈsprɪŋklɪŋ/ *n* (of salt, sugar) petite pincée *f*; (of snow) fine couche *f*.

sprint /sprɪnt/ **I** *n* (race) sprint *m*, course *f* de vitesse; **the final ~** LIT, FIG la dernière ligne droite (avant l'arrivée).

II *vi* SPORT sprinter; GEN courir (à toute vitesse).

sprite /spraɪt/ *n* lutin *m*, elfe *m*.

spritzer /ˈsprɪtsə(r)/ *n*: vin blanc additionné d'eau gazeuse.

sprout /spraʊt/ **I** *n* **1** (on plant, tree) pousse *f*; (on potato) germe *m*; **2** CULIN (also **Brussels ~**) chou *m* de Bruxelles.

II *vtr* se laisser pousser [*beard*]; **to ~ shoots** germer.
III *vi* **1** [*bulb, seed, shoot*] germer; [*grass, weeds*] pousser; **buds are ~ing on the trees** les arbres bourgeonnent; **2** (develop) [*antlers, horns*] pousser; FIG [*child*] pousser vite; **3** FIG (appear) = **sprout up**.
■ **sprout up** [*plants*] surgir de terre; FIG [*buildings, suburbs*] pousser comme des champignons.

spruce /spruːs/ **I** *n* **1** (also **~ tree**) épicéa *m*; **2** (wood) bois *m* d'épicéa.
II *adj* [*person*] soigné; [*house, garden*] bien tenu.
■ **spruce up**: **~ up** [*sth/sb*], **~** [*sth/sb*] **up** faire beau/belle [*person*]; astiquer [*house*].

sprung /sprʌŋ/ **I** *pp* ▶ **spring** III, IV.
II *adj* [*mattress*] à ressorts; **well-~** souple.

spry /spraɪ/ *adj* alerte, gaillard.

spud○ /spʌd/ *n* patate○ *f*, pomme *f* de terre.

spun /spʌn/ **I** *prét, pp* ▶ **spin** II, III.
II *adj* [*glass, gold, sugar*] filé; **~ silk** schappe *f*.

spur /spɜː(r)/ **I** *n* **1** FIG (stimulus) motif *m*; **to be the ~ for** ou **of sth** être la raison de qch; **to act as a ~ to** être une incitation à [*crime, action*]; **2** (for horse) éperon *m*; **3** ZOOL, ANAT éperon *m*; **4** (of rock) contrefort *m*; **5** RAIL (also **~ track**) embranchement *m*.
II *vtr* (*p prés etc* **-rr-**) **1** (stimulate) encourager [*growth, increase*]; inciter [*action, reaction*]; **to ~ sb to sth/to do** inciter qn à qch/à faire; **2** [*rider*] éperonner [*horse*].
IDIOMS **on the ~ of the moment** sur l'impulsion du moment; **to win one's ~s** faire ses preuves.
■ **spur on**: **~** [*sth/sb*] **on**, **~ on** [*sth/sb*] **1** LIT lancer [qch] d'un coup d'éperon [*horse*]; **2** FIG (encourage) [*success, good sign, government*] encourager; [*fear, threat, example*] stimuler; **to ~ sb on to greater efforts** inciter qn à redoubler d'efforts.

spurious /ˈspjʊərɪəs/ *adj* [*argument, notion, allegation*] fallacieux/-ieuse; [*excuse*] inventé; [*evidence, credentials*] faux/fausse; [*sentiment*] feint.

spurn /spɜːn/ *vtr* refuser [qch] (avec mépris) [*advice, offer, help, gift*]; éconduire [*suitor*].

spur road *n* GB embranchement *m*.

spurt /spɜːt/ **I** *n* **1** (gush) (of water, oil, blood) giclée *f*; (of flame) jaillissement *m*; (of steam) jet *m*; **2** (burst) (of energy) sursaut *m*; (of activity, enthusiasm) regain *m*; (in growth) poussée *f*; **to put on a ~** [*runner, cyclist*] pousser une pointe de vitesse; **to do sth in ~s** faire qch par à-coups.
II *vtr* **the wound was ~ing blood** le sang giclait de la blessure; **the pipes are ~ing water** l'eau jaillit des tuyaux.
III *vi* (gush) jaillir (**from, out of** de).
■ **spurt out**: **~ out** [*flames, liquid*] jaillir.

sputter /ˈspʌtə(r)/ *n, vtr, vi* = **splutter**.

sputum /ˈspjuːtəm/ *n* ₵ crachat *m*, expectorations *fpl*.

spy /spaɪ/ **I** *n* **1** (political, industrial) espion/-ionne *m/f*; (for police) indicateur/-trice *m/f*.
II *noun modifier* [*film, network*] d'espionnage.
III *vtr* remarquer, discerner [*figure, object*].
IV *vi* **to ~ on sth/sb** espionner qch/qn; **to ~ for sb** faire de l'espionnage pour le compte de qn.

spy: ~ glass *n* longue-vue *f*; **~hole** *n* judas *m*.

spying /ˈspaɪɪŋ/ *n* espionnage *m*.

spy ring *n* réseau *m* d'espionnage.

sq. (*abrév écrite* = **square**) MATH carré; **10 ~ m** 10 m².

Sq *abrév écrite* = **Square**.

squab /skwɒb/ *n* ZOOL pigeonneau *m*.

squabble /ˈskwɒbl/ **I** *n* dispute *f*, prise *f* de bec○.
II *vi* se disputer, se chamailler○ (**over** à propos de).

squabbling /ˈskwɒblɪŋ/ *n* ₵ chamailleries○ *fpl*, disputes *fpl*.

squad /skwɒd/ *n* GEN, MIL escouade *f*; SPORT sélection *f*.

squad car *n* voiture *f* de police.

squaddie /ˈskwɒdɪ/ *n* GB bidasse○ *m*, soldat *m*.

squadron /ˈskwɒdrən/ *n* **1** GB MIL escadron *m*; **2** AVIAT, NAUT escadrille *f*.

squadron leader ▶ 1192| *n* GB AVIAT, MIL commandant *m* (de l'armée de l'air).

squalid /ˈskwɒlɪd/ *adj* [*house, street*] sordide; [*furnishings, clothes*] crasseux/-euse; [*affair, story*] sordide.

squall /skwɔːl/ **I** *n* **1** METEOROL bourrasque *f*, rafale *f* (**of** de); (at sea) grain *m*; **2** (cry) hurlement *m*.
II *vi* [*baby*] hurler, brailler.

squalor /ˈskwɒlə(r)/ *n* (of house, street, conditions, life) caractère *m* sordide, misère *f* (noire).

squander /ˈskwɒndə(r)/ *vtr* gaspiller [*money, opportunities, talents, resources, time*]; gâcher [*youth, health*].

square /skweə(r)/ **I** *n* **1** (in town) place *f*; (in barracks) cour *f*; **main ~** grand-place *f*; **2** (four-sided shape) carré *m*; (in board game, crossword) case *f*; (of glass, linoleum) carreau *m*; **to divide a page up into ~s** quadriller une feuille; **3** MATH (self-multiplied) carré *m*; **4** MATH, TECH (instrument) équerre *f*; **5**○ (old-fashioned person) ringard/-e○ *m/f*.
II *adj* **1** (right-angled) [*shape, box, jaw, shoulders*] carré; (correctly aligned) bien droit; **2** ▶ 1309| MATH [*metre, mile*] carré; **four ~ metres** quatre mètres carrés; **an area four metres ~** une surface de quatre mètres sur quatre; **3** FIG (level, quits) **to be (all) ~** [*accounts*] être équilibré; [*people*] être quitte; [*teams*] être à égalité; **it's all ~ at two all** il y a égalité à deux partout; **4** (honest) honnête; **to give sb a ~ deal** traiter qn de façon honnête; **5**○ (boring) ringard○.
III *adv* (directly) **he hit me ~ on the jaw** il m'a frappé en plein dans la mâchoire; **she looked me ~ in the eye** elle m'a regardé droit dans les yeux.
IV *vtr* **1** LIT équarrir [*stone, timber*]; couper [qch] au carré ou à angle droit [*corner, end, section*]; **to ~ one's shoulders** redresser les épaules; **2** (settle) régler [*account, debt*]; **3** SPORT égaliser [*score, series*]; **4** (win over) (persuade) s'occuper de; (bribe) graisser la patte à○ [*person*]; **go home early, I'll ~ it with the boss** pars avant l'heure, j'arrangerai ça avec le patron; **I have problems squaring this with my conscience** j'ai du mal à concilier cela avec ma conscience.
V squared *pp adj* **1** [*paper*] quadrillé; **2** MATH [*number*] au carré.
IDIOMS **to go back to ~ one** retourner à la case départ.
■ **square up**: ¶ **~ up 1** (prepare to fight) LIT se mettre en garde (**to** face à); FIG faire face (**to** à); **2** (settle accounts) régler ses comptes; ¶ **~ up** [*sth*], **~** [*sth*] **up 1** (cut straight) couper [qch] au carré [*paper, wood, corner*]; **2** (align correctly) mettre [qch] bien droit.
■ **square with**: **~ with** [*sth*] (be consistent with) correspondre à, cadrer avec [*evidence, fact*].

square bracket *n* crochet *m*; **in ~s** entre crochets.

square: ~ dance *n* quadrille *m*; **~ dancing** *n* ₵ quadrille *m* américain.

squarely /ˈskweəlɪ/ *adv* **1** (directly) [*strike, hit, land*] LIT en plein milieu; **to look ~ at** regarder [qch] bien en face [*problem, situation*]; **~ behind sth** directement derrière qch; **2** (honestly) honnêtement; **3** (fully) **the blame rests ~ on his shoulders** la responsabilité repose entièrement sur lui.

square: ~ meal *n* vrai repas *m*; **~ measure** *n* mesure *f* de superficie; **~ root** *n* racine *f* carrée.

squash /skwɒʃ/ **I** *n* **1** SPORT ▶ 949| squash *m*; **2** (drink) sirop *m*; **3** (vegetable) courge *f*; **4** (crush) **it will be a bit of a ~** on va être un peu serrés.
II *vtr* **1** (crush) écraser [*fruit, insect*]; aplatir [*hat*]; **2** (force) **to ~ sth/sb into sth** caser qch/qn dans qch; **3** (put down) rabattre le caquet à○ [*person*]; écraser [*revolt*]; stopper [*rumour*]; rejeter [*idea*].
III *vi* **1** (become crushed) s'écraser; **2** (pack tightly) [*people*] s'entasser (**into** dans).
■ **squash in**○: ¶ **~ in** se faire de la place; ¶ **~ in** [*sth/sb*], **~** [*sth/sb*] **in** trouver de la place pour.
■ **squash up**○: **~ up** se serrer (**against** contre); **to ~ oneself up against** s'aplatir contre.

squashy○ /ˈskwɒʃɪ/ *adj* mou/molle.

squat /skwɒt/ **I** *n* **1** (position) position *f* accroupie; **2**○ (home) squat○ *m*.
II *adj* [*person, structure, object*] trapu.

III *vi* (*p prés etc* **-tt-**) **1** (crouch) être accroupi; **2** (also **~ down**) s'accroupir; **3** (inhabit) **to ~ in** squattériser○, squatter○ [*building*].

squatter /'skwɒtə(r)/ *n* squatter○ *m*.

squaw /skwɔ:/ *n* INJUR squaw *f*.

squawk /skwɔ:k/ **I** *n* (of hen) gloussement *m*; (of duck, parrot etc) cri *m* rauque; (of person) cri *m* aigu.
II *vi* [*hen*] pousser des gloussements; [*duck, parrot, crow etc*] pousser des cris rauques; [*baby*] brailler; [*person*] crier d'une voix hystérique.

squeak /skwi:k/ **I** *n* (noise) (of door, wheel, mechanism, chalk) grincement *m*; (of mouse, soft toy) couinement *m*; (of furniture, shoes) craquement *m*; (of infant) vagissement *m*; **without a ~**○ sans broncher; **there wasn't a ~ from her**○ elle n'a pas émis le moindre mot.
II *vi* [*door, wheel, chalk*] grincer; [*mouse, toy*] couiner; [*shoes, furniture*] craquer; [*child*] glapir.

squeaky /'skwi:kɪ/ *adj* [*voice*] aigu/-uë; [*gate, hinge, wheel*] grinçant; **~ shoes** des chaussures qui craquent.

squeaky-clean○ *adj* **1** LIT propre et net; **2** FIG PÉJ [*person*] trop parfait; [*company*] à l'image trop soignée.

squeal /skwi:l/ **I** *n* (of animal, person) cri *m* aigu; (of brakes) grincement *m*; (of tyres) crissement *m*; **~s of laughter** des rires perçants.
II *vi* **1** (squeak) pousser des cris aigus (**in, with** de); **to ~ with laughter** rire d'une voix aiguë; **2**○ (inform) vendre la mèche○; **to ~ on sb** balancer○ qn.

squeamish /'skwi:mɪʃ/ *adj* **1** (easily sickened) impressionnable, sensible; **2** (prudish) prude.

squeegee /'skwi:dʒi:/ *n* GEN, PHOT raclette *f*; (for floor) balai-éponge *m*.

squeeze /skwi:z/ **I** *n* **1** (application of pressure) **to give sth a ~** presser qch [*hand, tube*]; **to give sb a ~** serrer qn dans ses bras; **2** (small amount) **a ~ of glue/lemon** un peu de colle/citron; **3** ECON, FIN resserrement *m* (**on** de); **to feel the ~** se sentir coincé financièrement; **to put the ~ on**○ faire pression sur [*debtors*]; **4**○ (crush) **I can get past, but it will be a tight ~** je peux passer mais ce sera un peu juste.
II *vtr* **1** (press) presser [*lemon, bottle, tube*]; serrer [*arm, hand*]; appuyer sur [*bag, parcel, trigger*]; percer [*spot*]; **to ~ glue/toothpaste onto sth** mettre de la colle/du dentifrice sur qch; **2** FIG (get) **I ~d £10 out of dad** j'ai réussi à obtenir 10 livres sterling de papa; **to ~ the truth/a confession out of sb** arracher la vérité/un aveu à qn; **3** (fit) **we can ~ a few more people into the room** on a encore de la place pour quelques personnes dans la salle; **I can just ~ into that dress** je rentre tout juste dans cette robe; **to ~ behind/between/under sth** se glisser derrière/entre/sous qch; **4** ECON, FIN resserrer [*profit, margins*]; asphyxier [*small businesses*].
■ **squeeze in**: ¶ **~ in** [*person*] se glisser; ¶ **~ [sb] in** [*doctor etc*] faire passer [qn] entre deux rendez-vous.
■ **squeeze out**: ¶ **~ out** [*person*] arriver à sortir; ¶ **~ [sth] out** extraire [*juice, water*]; **to ~ water out of** essorer [*cloth, sponge*].
■ **squeeze past**: ¶ **~** [*car, person*] passer.

squelch /skweltʃ/ **I** *n* **the ~ of water in their boots** le flic flac de l'eau dans leurs bottes.
II *vi* [*water, mud*] glouglouter; **to ~ along/in/out** avancer/entrer/sortir en pataugeant.

squelchy /'skweltʃɪ/ *adj* [*ground, mud*] boueux/-euse.

squib /skwɪb/ *n* pétard *m*.
IDIOMS **to be a damp ~**○ GB [*event*] être décevant; [*venture, revelation*] être un pétard mouillé○.

squid /skwɪd/ *n* calmar *m*, encornet *m*.

squidgy○ /'skwɪdʒɪ/ *adj* GB moelleux/-euse.

squiggle /'skwɪgl/ *n* gribouillis *m*.

squint /skwɪnt/ **I** *n* MED (strabismus) strabisme *m*; **to have a ~** loucher.
II *vi* **1** (look) plisser les yeux; **2** MED loucher.

squire /'skwaɪə(r)/ *n* **1** (gentleman) ~ châtelain *m*; **2** (retainer) écuyer *m*; **3**○ GB cheerio○! salut, chef○ *m*!; **4** US (judge) juge *m* (de paix); (lawyer) avocat *m*.

squirm /skwɜ:m/ *vi* (wriggle) [*person, snake, worm etc*]

se tortiller; [*fish*] frétiller; [*person*] (in pain, agony) se tordre; FIG (with embarrassment) être très mal à l'aise.

squirrel /'skwɪrəl, US 'skwɜ:rəl/ *n* écureuil *m*.

squirt /skwɜ:t/ **I** *n* **1** (jet) jet *m*; **2** (small amount) goutte *f*; **3**○ PEJ (person) **a little ~** un petit morveux○.
II *vtr* faire gicler; **he ~ed some soda water into the glass** il a versé une giclée d'eau de Seltz dans le verre; **to ~ water at sb, to ~ sb with water** asperger qn d'eau.
III *vi* [*liquid*] jaillir (**from, out of** de).
■ **squirt out**: ¶ **~ out** [*water, oil*] jaillir (**of , from** de); ¶ **~ [sth] out, ~ out [sth]** faire gicler [*liquid*].

Sr 1 *abrév écrite* = **Senior**; **2** *abrév écrite* = **Sister**.

SRN *n* GB *abrév* ▶ **State Registered Nurse**.

SS 1 NAUT (*abrév* = **steamship**) **the ~** Titanic le Titanic; **2** MIL HIST **the ~** les SS *mpl*.

SSA *n* US *abrév* ▶ **Social Security Administration**.

st *n* GB *abrév écrite* = **stone**.

St *n* **1** *abrév écrite* = **Saint**; **2** *abrév écrite* = **Street**.

stab /stæb/ **I** *n* **1** (act) coup *m* de couteau; **a ~ in the back** FIG un coup en traître; **2** FIG (of pain) élancement *m*; (of anger, jealousy) accès *m*; **a ~ of fear** une peur soudaine; **3**○ (attempt) essai *m*, tentative *f*; **to make a ~ at sth/at doing** s'essayer à qch/à faire.
II *vtr* (*p prés etc* **-bb-**) **1** (pierce) poignarder [*person*]; piquer dans [*meat, food*]; **to ~ sb to death** tuer qn à coups de couteau; **to ~ sb in the back** LIT, FIG poignarder qn dans le dos; **2** (poke) frapper.
III *v refl* (*p prés etc* **-bb-**) **to ~ oneself** se blesser avec un couteau.

stabbing /'stæbɪŋ/ **I** *n* agression *f* au couteau.
II *adj* [*pain*] lancinant.

stability /stə'bɪlətɪ/ *n* GEN, CHEM stabilité *f*.

stabilize /'steɪbəlaɪz/ **I** *vtr* GEN stabiliser; MED rendre [qch] plus stable [*medical condition*].
II *vi* se stabiliser.
III stabilizing *pres p adj* [*effect, influence*] stabilisateur/-trice.

stabilizer /'steɪbəlaɪzə(r)/ *n* **1** AVIAT, NAUT, TECH (device) stabilisateur *m*; **2** (substance) stabilisant *m*.

stable /'steɪbl/ **I** *n* **1** (building) écurie *f*; **2** (string of racehorses) écurie *f* (de courses); **3** FIG (of companies, publications) empire *m*; (of people) équipe *f*.
II stables *npl* riding **~s** manège *m*.
III *adj* **1** (steady) stable; **2** (psychologically) équilibré; **3** CHEM, PHYS stable.
IV *vtr* mettre [qch] à l'écurie [*horse*].

stable boy ▶ **1251** | *n* garçon *m* d'écurie.

stable door *n* porte *f* d'écurie.
IDIOMS **to close the ~ after the horse has bolted** fermer la cage quand les oiseaux se sont envolés.

stab wound *n* coup *m* de couteau (*blessure*).

staccato /stə'kɑ:təʊ/ **I** *adj* **1** MUS [*notes, vocals*] staccato *inv*; **2** GEN [*gasps, shots*] saccadé.
II *adv* [*play*] staccato.

stack /stæk/ **I** *n* **1** (pile) (of books, chairs, papers, plates, wood) pile *f*; (of hay, straw) meule *f*; **2** (chimney) cheminée *f*; **3** COMPUT pile *f*.
II stacks *npl* **1** (in library) rayons *mpl*; **2**○ **~s of** plein de○ [*food, work*]; **we've got ~s**○ **of time** nous avons tout notre temps.
III *vtr* **1** AGRIC mettre [qch] en meule [*hay, straw*]; **2** (also **~ up**) (pile) empiler [*boxes, books, plates, chairs*]; **3** (fill) remplir [*shelves*]; **4** AVIAT, TELECOM mettre [qch] en attente [*planes, calls*].
IDIOMS **to blow one's ~**○ se mettre en boule○; **to have the odds** ou **cards ~ed against one** avoir tout contre soi.
■ **stack up**: **~ up** [sth], **~** [sth] **up** empiler.

stadium /'steɪdɪəm/ *n* (*pl* **-iums** ou **-ia**) stade *m*.

staff /stɑ:f, US stæf/ **I** *n* **1** (*pl* **staves** /steɪvz/ ou **~s**) (stick) (for walking) canne *f*; (of crozier) crosse *f*; (as weapon) bâton *m*; **2** (*pl* **~s**) (employees) personnel *m*; **to be on the ~ of a company** faire partie du personnel d'une entreprise; **a small business with a ~ of ten** une petite entreprise de dix employés; **3** ¢ (also **teaching**

~) SCH, UNIV personnel *m* enseignant; **member of ~** enseignant/-e *m/f*; **a ~ of 50** un effectif de 50 enseignants; **4 ¢** MIL état-major *m*; **5** (*pl* **staves** /steɪvz/ ou **~s**) MUS portée *f*.
II *vtr* [*owner*] trouver du personnel pour [*company*]; **the restaurant is entirely ~ed by Italians** tout le personnel du restaurant est italien.

staff: **~ college** *n* MIL ~ école *f* supérieure de guerre; **~ discount** *n* rabais *m* accordé au personnel.

staffing /'stɑːfɪŋ, US 'stæf-/ *n* **to have ~ problems** avoir des problèmes de recrutement.

staffing levels *npl* nombre *m* d'employés.

staff: **~ meeting** *n* SCH réunion *f* du personnel enseignant; **~ nurse** *n* infirmier/-ière *m/f*; **~ officer ▶1192** *n* officier *m* d'état-major; **~ of office** *n* bâton *m* de commandement; **~ room** *n* SCH salle *f* des professeurs.

Staffs *n* GB POST abrév écrite = **Staffordshire**.

stag /stæg/ *n* **1** ZOOL cerf *m*; **2** GB FIN loup *m* de la finance.

stage /steɪdʒ/ **I** *n* **1** (phase) (of illness, career, life, development, match) stade *m* (**of, in** de); (of project, process, plan) phase *f* (**of, in** de); (of journey, negotiations) étape *f* (**of, in** de); **the baby has reached the walking ~** le bébé commence à marcher; **at this ~** (at this point) à ce stade; (yet, for the time being) pour l'instant; **at this ~ in** ou **of your career** à ce stade de votre carrière; **at an earlier/later ~** à un stade antérieur/ultérieur; **at every ~** à chaque étape; **she ought to know that by this ~** ça fait longtemps qu'elle devrait le savoir; **by ~s** par étapes; **~ by ~** étape par étape; **in ~s** en plusieurs étapes; **the project is still in its early ~s** le projet en est encore à ses débuts; **she's going through a difficult ~** elle traverse une période difficile; **2** (raised platform) GEN estrade *f*; THEAT scène *f*; **to go on ~** monter sur or entrer en scène; **to hold the ~** LIT, FIG être le point de mire; **to set the ~** THEAT monter le décor; **to set the ~ for sth** FIG préparer qch; **3** THEAT **the ~** le théâtre; **to go on the ~** faire du théâtre; **4** FIG (setting) (actual place) théâtre *m*; (backdrop) scène *f*.
II *noun modifier* THEAT [*play, equipment*] de théâtre; [*production*] théâtral; [*career, performance*] au théâtre.
III *vtr* **1** (organize) organiser [*event, rebellion, strike*]; fomenter [*coup*]; **2** (fake) simuler [*quarrel, scene*]; **the whole thing was ~d** ce n'était qu'une mise en scène; **3** THEAT monter [*play, performance*].

stage: **~coach** *n* diligence *f*; **~craft** *n* technique *f* scénique; **~ designer ▶1251** *n* décorateur/-trice *m/f* de théâtre; **~ direction** *n* indication *f* scénique; **~ door** *n* entrée *f* des artistes; **~ fright** *n* trac *m*; **~hand ▶1251** *n* machiniste *m*; **~ left** *adv* côté *m* cour; **~-manage** *vtr* FIG orchestrer; **~-manager ▶1251** *n* régisseur/-euse *m/f*; **~ name** *n* nom *m* de théâtre; **~ right** *adv* côté *m* jardin; **~-struck** *adj* passionné de théâtre; **~ whisper** *n* THEAT, FIG aparté *m*.

stagey *adj* = **stagy**.

stagger /'stægə(r)/ **I** *n* (movement) **with a ~** (weakly) d'un pas chancelant; (drunkenly) en titubant.
II *vtr* **1** (astonish) stupéfier, abasourdir; **2** (spread out) échelonner [*holidays, journeys, payments*].
III *vi* [*person*] (from weakness, illness) chanceler; (drunkenly) tituber; [*animal*] vaciller; **to ~ in/out/off** entrer/sortir/s'en aller en chancelant.
IV staggered *pp adj* (astonished) abasourdi.

staggering /'stægərɪŋ/ *adj* [*amount, increase*] prodigieux/-ieuse; [*news*] renversant; [*event*] bouleversant; [*achievement, contrast*] stupéfiant; [*success*] étourdissant.

staggeringly /'stægərɪŋli/ *adv* incroyablement.

stag hunting *n* chasse *f* au cerf.

staging /'steɪdʒɪŋ/ *n* **1** THEAT mise *f* en scène; **2** (for spectators) gradins *mpl* provisoires.

staging post *n* MIL poste *m* de ravitaillement; FIG point *m* de transition.

stagnant /'stægnənt/ *adj* stagnant.

stagnate /stæg'neɪt, US 'stægneɪt/ *vi* FIG [*person, economy, sales*] stagner; LIT [*water*] stagner, croupir.

stagnation /stæg'neɪʃn/ *n* stagnation *f*.

stag night, **stag party** *n* soirée *f* pour enterrer une vie de garçon.

stagy /'steɪdʒɪ/ *adj* PÉJ théâtral.

staid /steɪd/ *adj* guindé PÉJ.

stain /steɪn/ **I** *n* **1** (mark) LIT, FIG tache *f*; **it will leave a ~** ça fera une tache; **without a ~ on one's character** avec une réputation sans tache; **2** (dye) (for wood, fabric etc) teinture *f*.
II *vtr* **1** (soil) tacher [*clothes, carpet, table etc*]; **2** BIOL, TECH teindre [*wood, fabric, specimen*].
III *vi* [*fabric*] se tacher.
IV -stained *combining form* **oil/ink-~ed** taché d'huile/d'encre.

stain: **~ed glass** *n* (glass) verre *m* coloré; **~ed glass window** *n* vitrail *m*.

stainless /'steɪnlɪs/ *adj* [*reputation etc*] sans tache.

stainless steel *n* acier *m* inoxydable.

stain: **~ remover** *n* détachant *m*; **~-resistant** *adj* antitaches *inv*.

stair /steə(r)/ **I** *n* **1** (step) marche *f* (d'escalier); **2** (staircase) SOUT escaliers *mpl*.
II stairs *npl* (staircase) **the ~s** les escaliers *mpl*; **a flight of ~s** un escalier; **to fall down the ~s** tomber dans l'escalier.

stair: **~case** *n* escalier *m*; **~ rod** *n* tringle *f* d'escalier; **~way** *n* escalier *m*; **~well** *n* cage *f* d'escalier.

stake /steɪk/ **I** *n* **1** GAMES, FIG (amount risked) enjeu *m*; **to play for high ~s** LIT, FIG jouer gros; **to raise the ~s** LIT augmenter l'enjeu; FIG monter la mise; **to be at ~** FIG être en jeu; **there is a lot at ~** FIG ce n'est pas à prendre à la légère; **to put sth at ~** LIT, FIG mettre qch en jeu; **2** (investment) participation *f* (**in** dans); **3** (pole) (support) pieu *m*; (thicker) poteau *m*; (marker) piquet *m*; **4** HIST (for execution) bûcher *m*; **to be burnt at the ~** être brûlé sur le bûcher.
II *vtr* **1** (gamble) miser [*money, property*]; risquer [*reputation*]; **I would ~ my life on it** j'en mettrais ma tête à couper°; **2** (support) mettre un tuteur à [*plant, tree*]; **3** US (back) financer [*person*].
■ **stake out**: **~ out** [**sth**], **~** [**sth**] **out** [*police*] surveiller [*place*].

stakeout° *n* planque° *f*.

stalactite /'stæləktaɪt, US stə'læk-/ *n* stalactite *f*.

stalagmite /'stæləgmaɪt, US stə'læg-/ *n* stalagmite *f*.

stale /steɪl/ **I** *adj* **1** (old) [*bread, cake*] rassis; [*beer*] éventé; [*air*] vicié; **to go ~** [*bread*] se rassir; FIG [*relationship*] perdre de son charme; **to smell ~** [*room, house*] sentir le renfermé; **2** (hackneyed) [*jokes, ideas*] éculé; [*style, convention*] usé; **3** (tired) [*player*] usé.
II *vi* [*pleasure*] s'affaiblir; [*pastime*] perdre son charme.

stalemate /'steɪlmeɪt/ *n* **1** (in chess) pat *m*; **2** (deadlock) impasse *f*.

staleness /'steɪlnɪs/ *n* (of food) manque *m* de fraîcheur; (of air) caractère *m* vicié; (of ideas) banalité *f*.

stalk /stɔːk/ **I** *n* **1** BOT, CULIN (of grass, rose, broccoli) tige *f*; (of leaf, apple, pepper) queue *f*; (of mushroom) pied *m*; (of cabbage) trognon *m*; **2** ZOOL (organ) pédicule *m*.
II *vtr* **1** (hunt) [*hunter*] chasser [*qch*] à l'approche; [*animal*] chasser; [*murderer*] suivre; **2** FIG [*fear, danger*] régner sur; [*disease*] sévir; [*killer*] rôder dans [*place*].
III *vi* **1** (walk) **to ~ out of the room** (angry) quitter la pièce d'un air furieux; **2** (prowl) **to ~ through** rôder dans [*countryside, streets*].
IDIOMS **my eyes were out on ~s**° j'avais les yeux qui me sortaient des orbites.

stalking horse *n* POL homme *m* de paille.

stall /stɔːl/ **I** *n* **1** (at market, fair) stand *m*; (kiosk) kiosque *m*; **2** (in stable) stalle *f*; **3** (in horse-race) barrière *f* de départ; **4** (in church) stalle *f*; **5** (cubicle) (for shower) compartiment *m*; US (for lavatory) cabinet *m*; **6** US (parking space) place *f* de parking.
II stalls *npl* GB THEAT orchestre *m*; **in the ~s** à l'orchestre.

III *vtr* **1** AUT caler [*engine, car*]; **2** (hold up) bloquer [*talks, action, process*]; faire patienter [*person*].
IV *vi* **1** AUT caler; AVIAT décrocher; **2** (buy time) temporiser; **3** (stagnate) [*market*] stagner; [*talks*] se bloquer.

stallholder *n* marchand/-e *m/f*.

stallion /'stæliən/ *n* étalon *m*.

stalwart /'stɔːlwət/ **I** *n* fidèle *mf*.
II *adj* (loyal) [*defender, member, supporter*] loyal; [*support*] inconditionnel/-elle; [*defence, resistance*] vaillant.

stamina /'stæminə/ *n* résistance *f*, endurance *f*.

stammer /'stæmə(r)/ **I** *n* bégaiement *m*.
II *vtr, vi* bégayer.

stamp /stæmp/ **I** *n* **1** POST timbre *m*; **a three franc** ~ un timbre à trois francs; **'no** ~ **needed'** 'ne pas affranchir'; **2** (token) (for free gift) timbre *m*; (towards bill) bon *m*; **3** (marking device) (rubber) tampon *m*; (metal) cachet *m*; (for metals) étampe *f*; (for gold) poinçon *m*; **date** ~ timbre *m* dateur; **to give sth one's** ~ **of approval** FIG donner son accord à qch; **4** FIG (hallmark) marque *f*; **to set one's** ~ **on sth** imprimer sa marque sur qch; **5** (calibre) trempe *f*; **6** (of feet) piétinement *m*; **with a** ~ **of her foot** en tapant du pied.
II *vtr* **1** (mark) apposer [qch] au tampon [*date, name*] (on sur); tamponner [*ticket, book*]; marquer [*goods, boxes*]; viser [*document, ledger, passport*]; **to** ~ **one's authority on sth** imprimer son autorité sur qch; **2** (with foot) **to** ~ **one's foot** (in anger) taper du pied; **to** ~ **one's feet** (rhythmically) taper des pieds; (for warmth) battre la semelle; **to** ~ **sth into the ground** enfoncer qch dans le sol du pied; **3** POST affranchir [*envelope*].
III *vi* **1** (thump foot) [*person*] taper du pied; [*horse*] piaffer; **to** ~ **on** écraser (du pied) [*toy, foot*]; **2** (walk heavily) **to** ~ **into/out of sth** entrer dans/sortir de qch en tapant des pieds; **3** (crush) **to** ~ **on** LIT piétiner [*soil, ground*]; FIG écarter [*idea, suggestion*].
■ **stamp out**: ~ **out** [sth], ~ [sth] **out 1** (put out) éteindre [qch] en piétinant [*fire*]; **2** (crush) éradiquer [*disease*]; réprimer [*fraud*]; supprimer [*crime*].

stamp: ~**-collecting** *n* philatélie *f*; ~**-collector** *n* philatéliste *mf*; ~ **duty** *n* JUR droit *m* de timbre; ~**ed addressed envelope, sae** *n* enveloppe *f* timbrée à votre/son etc adresse.

stampede /stæm'piːd/ **I** *n* **1** (rush) (of animals) débandade *f*; (of humans) ruée *f*; **2** (rodeo) rodéo *m*.
II *vtr* **1** LIT jeter la panique parmi [*animals, spectators*]; semer la panique dans [*crowd*]; **2** FIG (force sb's hand) **to** ~ **sb into doing** forcer qn à faire.
III *vi* [*animals*] courir en troupeau; [*people, crowd*] se précipiter.

stamping ground° *n* GB LIT, FIG domaine *m*.

stance /staːns, stæns/ *n* LIT, FIG position *f*.

stanch *vtr* US = **staunch**.

stand /stænd/ **I** *n* **1** (furniture) (for coats) portemanteau *m*; (for hats) porte-chapeau *m*; (for plant, trophy) guéridon *m*; (for music) pupitre *m* à musique; **2** (stall) (on market) éventaire *m*; (kiosk) kiosque *m*; (at exhibition, trade fair) stand *m*; **3** (in stadium) tribunes *fpl*; **4** (witness box) barre *f*; **to take the** ~ aller à la barre; **5** (stance) position *f*; **to take** ou **make a** ~ **on sth** prendre position sur qch; **6** (resistance to attack) résistance *f*; (to make) **a last** ~ (livrer) une dernière bataille; **7** (standstill) **to come to a** ~ s'arrêter.
II *vtr* (*prét, pp* **stood**) **1** (place) mettre [*person, object*]; ~ **it over there** mets-le là-bas; **2** (bear) supporter; **he can't** ~ **doing** il ne supporte pas de faire; **she won't** ~ **any nonsense** elle ne tolère pas qu'on fasse des bêtises; **3**° (pay for) **to** ~ **sb sth** payer qch à qn; **4** JUR **to** ~ **trial** passer en jugement; **5** (be liable) **to** ~ **to lose sth** risquer de perdre qch; **she** ~**s to gain a million pounds** elle peut gagner un million de livres sterling.
III *vi* (*prét, pp* **stood**) **1** (also ~ **up**) se lever; **2** (be upright) [*person*] se tenir debout; [*object*] tenir debout; **to remain** ~**ing** rester debout; **there's not much of the cathedral still** ~**ing** il ne reste que des ruines de la cathédrale; **don't just** ~ **there, do something!** ne reste pas planté° là! fais quelque chose!; **3** (be posi-

tioned) [*building etc*] être; (clearly delineated) se dresser; **the train was** ~**ing at the platform for half an hour** le train est resté une demi-heure à quai; **4** (step) **to** ~ **on** marcher sur; **5** (be) **to** ~ **empty** [*house*] rester vide; **to** ~ **accused of sth** être accusé de qch; **to** ~ **ready** être prêt; **as things** ~... étant donné l'état actuel des choses...; **I want to know where I** ~ FIG je voudrais savoir où j'en suis; **where do you** ~ **on capital punishment?** quelle est votre position sur la peine de mort?; **nothing** ~**s between me and the job** rien ne s'oppose à ce que j'obtienne ce poste; **to** ~ **in sb's way** LIT bloquer le passage à qn; FIG faire obstacle à qn; **6** (remain valid) [*offer, agreement*] rester valable; **7** (measure) **the hill** ~**s 500 metres high** la colline fait 500 mètres de haut; **8** (be at certain level) **the total** ~**s at 300** le total est de 300; **9** (be a candidate) se présenter; **to** ~ **for parliament** se présenter aux élections législatives; **10** (not move) [*water, mixture*] reposer.
IDIOMS **to leave sb** ~**ing** devancer qn; **to** ~ **up and be counted** se faire entendre.
■ **stand about, stand around** rester là (**doing** à faire).
■ **stand aside** s'écarter (**to do** pour faire).
■ **stand back: 1** (move back) [*person*] reculer (**from** de); FIG prendre du recul (**from** par rapport à); **2** (be situated) [*house*] être en retrait (**from** par rapport à).
■ **stand by**: ¶ ~ **by 1** [*army, emergency services*] être prêt à intervenir; **to be** ~**ing by to do** [*services*] être prêt à faire; **2** (refuse to act) rester là; **he stood by and did nothing** il est resté là sans intervenir; ¶ ~ **by** [sb/sth] (be loyal to) soutenir [*person*]; s'en tenir à [*principles, decision*]; assumer [*actions*].
■ **stand down** (resign) démissionner.
■ **stand for**: ~ **for** [sth] **1** (represent) [*party, person*] représenter [*ideal*]; **2** (denote) [*initials*] vouloir dire; [*company, name*] être un gage de [*quality etc*]; **3** (tolerate) [*person*] tolérer [*reduction, insubordination*].
■ **stand in**: **to** ~ **in for sb** remplacer qn.
■ **stand off** (reach a stalemate) aboutir à une impasse.
■ **stand out 1** (be noticeable) [*person*] sortir de l'ordinaire; [*building, design*] se détacher (**against** sur) ; [*work, ability, person*] être remarquable; **to** ~ **out from** [*person*] se distinguer de [*group*]; **2** (protrude) [*veins*] saillir.
■ **stand over**: ~ **over** [sb] être sur le dos de° [*employee etc*].
■ **stand to** MIL être en état d'alerte.
■ **stand up**: ¶ ~ **up 1** (rise) se lever (**to do** pour faire); **2** (stay upright) se tenir debout; **3** (withstand investigation) [*theory, story*] tenir debout; **to** ~ **up to** résister à [*investigation*]; **4** (resist) **to** ~ **up to** tenir tête à [*person*]; **5** (defend) **to** ~ **up for** défendre; ¶ ~ [sth] **up** redresser [*object*]; **to** ~ **sth up against/on** mettre qch contre/sur; ¶ ~ [sb] **up**° (fail to meet) poser un lapin à°.

standard /'stændəd/ **I** *n* **1** (level of quality) niveau *m*; ~**s of service** la qualité du service; **this wine is excellent by any** ~**s** ce vin est incontestablement excellent **to have high/low** ~**s** [*worker*] être très/peu consciencieux; [*school, institution*] être d'un bon/mauvais niveau; **to have double** ~**s** faire deux poids deux mesures; **2** (official specification) norme *f* (**for** de); **3** (requirement) (of student, work) niveau *m* requis; (of hygiene, safety) critères *mpl*; **not to be up to** ~ ne pas avoir le niveau requis; **to set the** ~ **for others to follow** imposer un modèle à suivre; **by today's** ~**s** selon les critères actuels; **4** (banner) étendard *m*; **5** (song) standard *m*.
II *adj* **1** (normal) [*size, equipment, rate*] standard; [*procedure*] habituel/-uelle; [*image*] traditionnel/-elle; **it's** ~ **practice to do** il est d'usage de faire; **this model includes a car radio as** ~ ce modèle est équipé en série d'une autoradio; **2** (authoritative) [*work*] de référence; **3** (also ~ **class**) GB RAIL [*ticket*] de seconde classe.

standard: Standard Assessment Task *n* GB SCH test *m* d'aptitude scolaire (*par tranches d'âge*); ~**-bearer** *n* MIL, FIG porte-drapeau *m*; ~ **deviation**

n (in statistics) écart-type *m*; **~-issue** *adj* réglementaire.

standardization /ˌstændədaɪˈzeɪʃn/, US -dɪˈz-/ *n* normalisation *f*.

standardize /ˈstændədaɪz/ *vtr* normaliser, standardiser.

standard: **~ lamp** *n* GB lampadaire *m*; **~ of living** *n* niveau *m* de vie; **~ time** *n* heure *f* légale.

standby /ˈstændbaɪ/ I *n* 1 (person) remplaçant/-e *m/f*; (food, ingredient) remplacement *m*; **to be on ~** [*army, emergency services*] être prêt à intervenir; (for airline ticket) être en stand-by.
II *noun modifier* 1 (emergency) [*circuit, battery*] de secours; 2 TOURISM [*passenger, ticket*] en stand-by.

standee /stænˈdiː/ *n* (spectator) spectateur/-trice *m/f* debout; (passenger) voyageur/-euse *m/f* debout.

stand-in /ˈstændɪn/ *n* GEN remplaçant/-e *m/f*; CIN, THEAT doublure *f*.

standing /ˈstændɪŋ/ I *n* 1 (reputation) réputation *f*, rang *m* (with chez); **of high** ou **considerable ~** très réputé; 2 (time) **of long ~** de longue date.
II *adj* 1 (permanent) [*army, committee*] actif/-ive; 2 (continuing) [*rule, invitation*] permanent; **his absent-mindedness is a ~ joke among his friends** sa distraction est un constant sujet de plaisanterie pour ses amis; 3 SPORT [*jump*] sans élan.

standing: **~ charge** *n* frais *mpl* d'abonnement *m*; **~ order** *n* FIN virement *m* automatique; **~ ovation** *n* ovation *f* debout; **~ room** *n* ₵ places *fpl* debout; **~ stone** *n* pierre *f* levée.

stand-off /ˈstændɒf/ *n* 1 (stalemate) impasse *f*; 2 SPORT = **stand-off half**.

stand: **~-off half** *n* SPORT demi *m* d'ouverture; **~-offish** *adj* [*person, manner*] distant; **~pipe** *n* colonne *f* d'alimentation; **~point** *n* point *m* de vue.

standstill /ˈstændstɪl/ *n* 1 (stop) (of traffic) arrêt *m*; (of economy, growth) point *m* mort; **to be at a ~** [*traffic*] être à l'arrêt; [*factory, services*] être au point mort; [*talks*] être arrivé à une impasse; **to bring sth to a ~** paralyser qch [*traffic, factory*]; 2 ECON gel *m*.

stand-up /ˈstændʌp/ *n* (also **~ comedy**) one man show *m* comique.
II *adj* 1 THEAT, TV **~ comedian** comique *mf*; 2 [*buffet*] debout *inv*; 3 (aggressive) [*argument*] en règle.

stank /stæŋk/ *prét* ▶ **stink** II.

Stanley knife® /ˈstænlɪˌnaɪf/ *n* cutter *m*.

stanza /ˈstænzə/ *n* strophe *f*.

staple /ˈsteɪpl/ I *n* 1 (for paper) agrafe *f*; 2 CONSTR (U-shaped) clou *m* cavalier; 3 (basic food) aliment *m* de base; 4 ECON (crop) culture *f* principale; (product) principale fabrication *f*; (industry) industrie *f* de base; 5 FIG (topic, theme) sujet *m* principal; 6 (fibre) fibre *f*.
II *adj* (épith) [*product, food, diet*] de base; [*crop, meal*] principal.
III *vtr* (attach) agrafer (**to** à; **onto** sur).

staple gun *n* agrafeuse *f*.

stapler /ˈsteɪplə(r)/ *n* agrafeuse *f*.

star /stɑː(r)/ I *n* 1 (in sky) étoile *f*; **the ~s are out** les étoiles brillent; 2 (celebrity) vedette *f*, star *f*; 3 (asterisk) astérisque *m*; 4 (award) (to hotel, restaurant) étoile *f*; (to pupil) bon point *m*; 5 MIL (mark of rank) étoile *f*.
II **stars** *npl* horoscope *m*; **it's written in the ~s** c'est écout.
III **-star** *combining form* TOURISM **three-/four-~** hotel hôtel (à) trois/quatre étoiles.
IV *vtr* (*p prés etc* **-rr-**) 1 [*film, play*] avoir [qn] pour vedette [*actor*]; **a comedy ~ring Lenny Henry** une comédie avec Lenny Henry en vedette; 2 (mark with star) (*gén* ou *passif*) marquer [qch] d'un astérisque; 3 (decorate) parsemer (**with** de).
V *vi* (*p prés etc* **-rr-**) [*actor*] jouer le rôle principal (**in** dans); **to ~ as Dracula** jouer (le rôle de) Dracula; **Meryl Streep also ~s** Meryl Streep est également à l'affiche.
IDIOMS **to reach for the ~s** vouloir décrocher la lune; **to see ~s** voir trente-six chandelles.

star anise /ˌstɑːrəˈniːz/ *n* anis *m* étoilé.

starboard /ˈstɑːbəd/ I *n* NAUT tribord *m*; **to turn to ~** virer sur la droite; 2 AVIAT droite *f*.
II *noun modifier* tribord *m*; **on the ~ side** à tribord.

starch /stɑːtʃ/ I *n* 1 ₵ (carbohydrate) féculents *mpl*; **wheat ~** amidon *m* de blé; **potato ~** fécule *f* de pomme de terre; 2 (for clothes) amidon *m*.
II *vtr* amidonner, empeser.

star chart *n* carte *f* du ciel.

starchy /ˈstɑːtʃɪ/ *adj* 1 [*food, diet*] riche en féculents; 2 [*substance*] amylacé; 3○ PÉJ [*person, tone*] guindé.

stardom /ˈstɑːdəm/ *n* vedettariat *m*; **to rise to ~** devenir une vedette.

stare /steə(r)/ I *n* regard *m* fixe; **she gave me a ~** son regard s'est posé sur moi.
II *vi* regarder fixement; **to ~ at sb/sth** regarder fixement qn/qch; **to ~ at sb in disbelief** regarder qn d'un air incrédule; **to ~ up at sb/sth** lever les yeux pour regarder qn/qch; **to ~ back at sb** rendre son regard à qn.
IDIOMS **to be staring sb in the face** crever les yeux à qn○; **disaster was staring me in the face** j'étais au bord de la catastrophe.
■ **stare down = stare out.**
■ **stare out**: **~ [sb] out**, **~ out [sb]** faire baisser les yeux à.

star: **~fish** *n* étoile *f* de mer; **~ fruit** *n* carambole *f*; **~gazer** *n* (astrologer) astrologue *mf*; (astronomer) astronome *mf*.

staring /ˈsteərɪŋ/ *adj* [*eyes*] fixe; [*people, crowd*] curieux/-ieuse.

stark /stɑːk/ *adj* 1 (bare) [*landscape, building, appearance*] désolé; [*room, decor*] nu; [*lighting*] cru; [*beauty*] âpre; 2 (unadorned) [*statement, fact*] brut; [*warning, reminder*] sévère; 3 (total) [*contrast*] saisissant; **in ~ contrast to** en opposition totale avec.
IDIOMS **to be ~ naked** être complètement nu; **~ raving mad**○, **~ staring mad**○ GB complètement dingue○ or cinglé○.

starkly /ˈstɑːklɪ/ *adv* (bluntly) carrément.

starless /ˈstɑːlɪs/ *adj* sans étoiles.

starlet /ˈstɑːlɪt/ *n* starlette *f*.

starlight *n* lumière *f* des étoiles.

starling /ˈstɑːlɪŋ/ *n* étourneau *m*.

starry /ˈstɑːrɪ/ *adj* [*night, sky*] étoilé; [*eyes*] brillant.

starry-eyed *adj* ébloui (**about** par).

star: **Stars and Stripes** *n* (+ *v sg*) bannière *f* étoilée; **~ sign** *n* signe *m* astrologique; **Star-spangled Banner** *n* bannière *f* étoilée; **~struck** *adj* impressionné par la célébrité; **~-studded** *adj* [*cast, line-up*] avec de nombreuses vedettes.

star system *n* 1 (in sky) système *m* stellaire; 2 CIN star-system *m*.

start /stɑːt/ I *n* 1 (beginning) début *m*; **at the ~** au début; (right) **from the start** dès le début; **to make a ~ on doing** se mettre à faire; **to make an early ~** (on journey) partir tôt; **that's a good ~** LIT c'est un bon début; IRON ça commence bien; **to make a fresh** ou **new ~** prendre un nouveau départ; **from ~ to finish** d'un bout à l'autre; **for a ~** pour commencer; 2 (advantage) avantage *m*; (in time, distance) avance *f*; **to give sb a ~ in business** aider qn à démarrer dans les affaires; 3 SPORT ligne *f* de départ; 4 (movement) **with a ~** en sursaut.
II *vtr* 1 (begin) commencer [*day, activity*]; entamer [*bottle, packet*]; **to ~ doing** ou **to do** commencer à faire, se mettre à faire; **don't ~ that again!** ne recommence pas!; 2 (cause, initiate) déclencher [*quarrel, war*]; instaurer [*custom*]; mettre [*fire*]; être à l'origine de [*trouble, rumour*]; lancer [*fashion, enterprise*]; **to ~ a family** avoir des enfants; 3 (activate) faire démarrer [*car*]; mettre [qch] en marche [*machine*].
III **to start with** *adv phr* 1 (firstly) d'abord, premièrement; 2 (at first) au début; 3 (at all) **I should never have told her to ~ with** pour commencer, je n'aurais jamais dû lui en parler.
IV *vi* 1 (begin) GEN commencer (**by doing** par faire); (in job) débuter (**as** comme); **to ~ again** ou **afresh** recommencer; **to ~ on** commencer [*memoirs,*

US states

In some cases, there is a French form of the name, but not always. Each state has a gender in French and is used with the definite article, except after the preposition en:

Arkansas = l'Arkansas *m*
California = la Californie
Texas = le Texas

So:

Arkansas is beautiful = l'Arkansas est beau
I like California = j'aime la Californie
do you know Texas? = connaissez-vous le Texas?

In, to and from somewhere

For in *and* to *use* en *for feminine states and for masculine ones beginning with a vowel:*

in Alaska = en Alaska
to Alaska = en Alaska
in California = en Californie
to California = en Californie

For in *and* to *use* au *for masculine states beginning with a consonant:*

in Texas = au Texas
to Texas = au Texas

For from *use* de *for feminine states and for masculine ones beginning with a vowel:*

from California = de Californie
from Alaska = d'Alaska

For from *use* du *for masculine states beginning with a consonant:*

from Texas = du Texas

Coming from somewhere: uses with another noun

There are a few words e.g. californien, new-yorkais, texan *used as adjectives and as nouns (with a capital letter) referring to the inhabitants. In other cases it is usually safe to use* de *for feminine states, and to use* de l' *or* du *for masculine states:*

the Florida countryside = les paysages de Floride
Illinois representatives = les représentants de l'Illinois

but

a Louisiana accent = l'accent de la Louisiane
New-Mexico roads = les routes du Nouveau-Mexique

---

journey]; **let's get ~ed on the washing-up** allez! on fait la vaisselle; **don't ~ on me** (in argument) ne recommence pas avec moi; **the day will ~ cloudy** il fera nuageux en début de journée; **~ing Wednesday**... à compter de mercredi...; **2** (depart) partir; **3** (jump nervously) sursauter (**in** de); **4** AUT, TECH [*car, engine, machine*] démarrer.
IDIOMS **~ as you mean to go on** prenez tout de suite les choses en main; **the ~ of something big** un début prometteur.
■ **start back 1** (begin to return) prendre le chemin du retour; **2** (step back) faire un bond en arrière.
■ **start off:** ¶ **~ off 1** (set off) [*train, bus*] démarrer; [*person*] partir; **2** (begin) [*person*] commencer (**by doing** par faire; **with** par); [*employee*] débuter; ¶ **~ [sb/sth] off, ~ off [sb/sth] 1** (begin) commencer [*visit, talk*] (**with** par); mettre [qch] en route [*programme*]; **2**○ GB (cause to do) **don't ~ her off laughing** ne la fais pas rire; **don't ~ him off** ne le provoque pas; **3** (put to work) mettre [qch] en marche [*machine*]; **4** SPORT faire partir [*competitors*].
■ **start out 1** (set off) (on journey) partir; **he ~ed out with the aim of**... FIG il avait d'abord pour but de...; **2** (begin) [*matter, business, employee*] débuter.
■ **start over** US recommencer (à zéro).
■ **start up:** ¶ **~ up** [*engine*] démarrer; [*noise*] retentir; [*person*] débuter; ¶ **~ [sth] up, ~ up [sth]** faire démarrer [*car*]; ouvrir [*shop*]; créer [*business*].

starter /'stɑːtə(r)/ *n* **1** SPORT (participant) partant/-e *m/f*; **to be a fast ~** être rapide au départ; **2** SPORT (official) starter *m*; **3** AUT, TECH démarreur *m*; **4** CULIN hors d'œuvre *m inv*.
IDIOMS **for ~s**○ pour commencer.

start: **~ing line** *n* SPORT ligne *f* de départ; **~ing pistol** *n* SPORT pistolet *m* de starter; **~ing point** *n* point *m* de départ; **~ing price** *n* cote *f* au départ; **~ing salary** *n* salaire *m* de départ.

startle /'stɑːtl/ *vtr* **1** (take aback) surprendre; **2** (alarm) [*sight, sound, person*] effrayer.

startled /'stɑːtld/ *adj* **1** (taken aback) surpris (**at** de); **2** (alarmed) effrayé; **a ~ cry** un cri d'effroi.

startling /'stɑːtlɪŋ/ *adj* saisissant.

startlingly /'stɑːtlɪŋlɪ/ *adv* [*different*] étonnamment; **~ beautiful** d'une beauté saisissante.

start-up costs *npl* COMM frais *mpl* de mise en route.

star turn *n* **1** (act) clou *m* FIG; **2** (person) vedette *f*.

starvation /stɑː'veɪʃn/ **I** *n* famine *f*; **to die of ~** mourir de faim.
II *noun modifier* [*rations*] de survie; [*wages*] de misère.

starvation diet *n* **to go on a ~** suivre un régime draconien.

starve /stɑːv/ **I** *vtr* **1** (deliberately) priver [qn] de nourriture, affamer; **to ~ oneself** se sous-alimenter; **to ~ sb to death** laisser qn mourir de faim; **2** (deprive) **to ~ sb/sth of** priver qn/qch de [*cash, oxygen, affection*]; **to be ~d of** être en mal de [*company, conversation*].
II *vi* mourir de faim.
■ **starve out:** **~ [sb] out, ~ out [sb]** affamer.

starving /'stɑːvɪŋ/ *adj* **1**○ (hungry) **to be ~** mourir or crever○ de faim; **2** (hunger-stricken) affamé.

stash○ /stæʃ/ **I** *n* **1** (hiding place) cachette *f*; **2** (hidden supply) provision *f*.
II *vtr* cacher [*money, drugs*] (**in** dans; **under** sous).
■ **stash away**○: **~ [sth] away, ~ away [sth]** mettre [qch] de côté.

stasis /'steɪsɪs, 'stæsɪs/ *n* (stagnation) stagnation *f*.

state /steɪt/ **I** *n* **1** (condition) état *m*; **what ~ is the car in?** dans quel état est la voiture?; **the present ~ of affairs** l'état actuel des choses; **a shocking/an odd ~ of affairs** une situation scandaleuse/très étrange; **to be in a good/bad ~** être en bon/mauvais état; **in a good/bad ~ of repair** bien/mal entretenu; **he's in a confused ~** (of mind) il ne sait plus où il en est; **to be in no ~ to do** ne pas être en état de faire; **he's not in a fit ~ to drive** il n'est pas en état de conduire; **in a liquid ~** à l'état liquide; **a ~ of emergency/shock** un état d'urgence/de choc; **what's the ~ of play?** GEN où en êtes-vous?; **2** POL (nation) (also **State**) État *m*; **a ~ within a ~** un État dans l'État; **3** (region, area) État *m*; **4** POL (government) État *m*; **5** (ceremonial) pompe *f*; **in ~** en grande pompe; **she will lie in ~** sa dépouille sera exposée; **robes of ~** tenue *f* d'apparat.
II States *npl* **the States** les États-Unis *mpl*.
III *noun modifier* **1** (government) [*school, sector*] public/-ique; [*enterprise, pension, TV, railways, secret*] d'État; [*budget, subsidy*] de l'État; **~ election** (at a national level) élection *f* nationale; US élection *f* au niveau d'un État; **2** (ceremonial) [*coach, occasion*] d'apparat; [*banquet*] de gala; [*funeral*] national; [*visit*] officiel/-ielle.
IV *vtr* **1** (express, say) exposer [*fact, opinion, truth*]; (provide information) indiquer [*age, income, whereabouts*]; **to ~ that** [*person*] déclarer que; **to ~ one's case** GEN exposer son cas; JUR présenter son dossier; **as ~d above/below** comme mentionné ci-dessus/ci-dessous; **2** (specify) spécifier [*amount, place, terms*]; exprimer [*preference*]; **at ~d times** à des dates fixes.
IDIOMS **to be in a ~** être dans tous ses états.

state: **State capital** *n* US capitale *f* d'État; **State Capitol** *n* US POL assemblée *f* législative d'État; **~-controlled** *adj* contrôlé par l'État; **State Department** *n* US, POL ministère *m* américain des affaires étrangères; **~-funded** adj subventionné par l'État.

State house n US (for legislature) siège m du Parlement; (for public events) édifice m public.

stateless /'steɪtlɪs/ adj apatride; **~ persons** les apatrides.

Stateline n US frontière f (entre États).

stately /'steɪtlɪ/ adj imposant.

stately home n GB château m.

statement /'steɪtmənt/ n **1** (expression of view) déclaration f (**by** de; **on, about** à propos de); (official) communiqué m; **~ of belief** profession f de foi; **~ of fact** exposé m des faits; **2** FIN (of bank account) relevé m de compte; **a financial ~** un état de la situation financière; **3** JUR déclaration f.

state: **~ of the art** adj [equipment] ultramoderne; [technology] de pointe; **~-owned** adj [company] étatique; **State Registered Nurse, SRN ▶ 1251** n GB MED ~ infirmier/-ière m/f diplômé/-e d'État; **~room** n NAUT cabine f particulière; **~-run** adj [newspaper, radio, television] contrôlé par l'État; [company] géré par l'État; **State's attorney** n US JUR avocat/-e m/f représentant l'État.

State's evidence n US JUR **to turn ~** dénoncer ses complices.

state: **~side** adj des États-Unis; **~sman** n (pl -men) homme m d'État; **~smanlike** adj digne d'un homme d'État; **~ trooper** n US policier m d'État; **~wide** adj, adv US dans tout l'État.

static /'stætɪk/ **I** n **1** (also **~ electricity**) électricité f statique; **2** RADIO, TV (interference) parasites mpl.
II adj **1** (stationary) [scene, actor, display] statique; [image] fixe; [traffic] bloqué; **2** (unchanging) [society, values] immuable; [style, ideas] statique; **3** (stable) [population, prices, demand] stationnaire; **4** PHYS statique; **5** COMPUT [memory] statique; [data] fixe.

station /'steɪʃn/ **I** n **1** RAIL gare f; **2** RADIO, TV station f; TV chaîne f; **3** MIL, NAUT (base) base f; **4** MIL, NAUT, GEN (post) poste m; **at one's ~** à son poste; **5** (also **police ~**) commissariat m; (small) poste m de police; **6** AGRIC élevage m; **7**† (rank) condition f; **to get ideas above one's ~** ne pas avoir les moyens de ses ambitions.
II vtr poster [guard]; stationner [troops]; **to be ~ed in Germany** être en garnison en Allemagne.
III v refl **to ~ oneself** se poster.

stationary /'steɪʃənrɪ, US -nerɪ/ adj [queue, vehicle] à l'arrêt; [traffic] bloqué; [prices] stable.

station break n US RADIO, TV page f de publicité.

stationer /'steɪʃnə(r)/ **▶ 1251** n (also **~'s**) (shop) papeterie f.

stationery /'steɪʃnərɪ, US -nerɪ/ **I** n **1** (writing materials) papeterie f; (for office) fournitures fpl (de bureau); **2** (writing paper) papier m à lettres.
II noun modifier [cupboard] à fournitures; **~ department** papeterie f.

stationery shop GB **▶ 1251** n papeterie f.

station: **~master ▶ 1251** n chef m de gare; **~ wagon** n US break m.

statistic /stə'tɪstɪk/ n statistique f (**on** de); **~s show that...** d'après les statistiques...

statistical /stə'tɪstɪkl/ adj statistique.

statistically /stə'tɪstɪklɪ/ adv statistiquement.

statistician /ˌstætɪ'stɪʃn/ **▶ 1251** n statisticien/-ienne m/f.

statistics /stə'tɪstɪks/ n (subject) (+ v sg) statistique f.

statue /'stætʃuː/ n statue f.

statuesque /ˌstætʃʊ'esk/ adj sculptural.

stature /'stætʃə(r)/ n **1** (height) taille f; **small/tall of** ou **in ~** de petite/grande taille; **2** (status) envergure f; **intellectual ~** stature f intellectuelle.

status /'steɪtəs/ n (pl **-uses**) **1** (position) position f; **2** ¢ (prestige) prestige m; **3** (official categorization) statut m (**as** de); **legal/charitable ~** statut légal/d'œuvre charitable; **financial ~** situation f financière; **refugee ~** statut de réfugié.

status: **~ bar** n COMPUT barre f d'état; **~ quo** n statu quo m; **~ symbol** n signe m de prestige.

statute /'stætʃuːt/ n JUR, POL texte m de loi; **by ~** par la loi.

statute book n **to be on the ~** être en vigueur.

statutory /'statʃʊtərɪ, US -tɔːrɪ/ adj [powers, requirements, sick pay] légal; [body] officiel/-ielle.

staunch /stɔːntʃ/ **I** adj [supporter, defence] loyal; [defender] ardent.
II vtr **staunch, stanch** US /stɔːntʃ, stɑːntʃ/ **1** LIT étancher [wound]; **2** FIG arrêter [decline].

staunchly /'stɔːntʃlɪ/ adv [defend, oppose] fermement; [Catholic, Communist] résolument.

stave /steɪv/ n MUS portée f.
■ **stave off** (prét, pp **staved**): **~ off** [sth] tromper [hunger, fatigue]; empêcher [bankruptcy, crisis]; écarter [threat].

stay /steɪ/ **I** n **1** (visit, period) séjour m; **to have an overnight ~ in Athens** passer la nuit à Athènes; **'enjoy your ~!'** 'bon séjour!'; **2** JUR **~ of execution** sursis m (à l'exécution de la peine capitale).
II stays npl corset m.
III vi **1** (remain) rester; **to ~ for lunch** rester (à) déjeuner; **to ~ in teaching** rester dans l'enseignement; **to ~ in nursing** continuer comme infirmier/-ière; **to ~ in business** (not go under) rester à flot; **to ~ put** ne pas bouger; **'~ tuned!'** (on radio) 'restez avec nous!'; **computers are here to ~** les ordinateurs ne sont pas près de disparaître; **2** (have accommodation) loger; **to ~ in a hotel/at a friend's house** loger à l'hôtel/chez un ami; **3** (spend the night) passer la nuit; **why don't you ~?** tu pourrais passer la nuit ici; **to ~ overnight** passer la nuit; **4** (visit for unspecified time) **to come to ~** (for a few days) venir passer quelques jours (**with** chez); (for a few weeks) venir passer quelques semaines (**with** chez); **do you often have people to ~?** tu as souvent des gens chez toi?
■ **stay away 1** (not come) ne plus venir; **go away and ~ away!** va-t-en et ne reviens plus!; **to ~ away from** éviter [town centre]; ne pas s'approcher de [window, strangers]; **2** (not attend) **to ~ away from work** s'absenter de son travail.
■ **stay in 1** (not go out) rester à la maison; **2** [hook, nail] tenir.
■ **stay out 1** (remain away) **to ~ out late/all night** rentrer tard/ne pas rentrer de la nuit; **to ~ out of trouble** éviter les ennuis; **to ~ out of sb's way** éviter qn; **~ out of this!** ne t'en mêle pas!; **2** (continue strike) continuer la grève.
■ **stay up 1** (as treat, waiting for sb) veiller; **2** (as habit) se coucher tard; **3** (not fall down) tenir.

stay-at-home n, adj GB casanier/-ière (m/f).

stayer /'steɪə(r)/ n (person) **to be a ~** être tenace.

staying-power n endurance f; SPORT **to have ~** avoir du fond.

STD n: abrév ▶ **sexually transmitted disease**.

STD (area) code n GB indicatif m.

stead /sted/ n **in sb's ~** à la place de qn.
IDIOMS **to stand sb in good ~** s'avérer utile pour qn.

steadfast /'stedfɑːst, US -fæst/ adj [determination, belief, refusal] tenace; [gaze] franc/franche; **to be ~ in one's belief** être ferme dans sa croyance.

steadfastly /'stedfɑːstlɪ, US -fæstlɪ/ adv [attached, loyal] indéfectiblement; **to cling ~ to one's beliefs** s'accrocher à ses convictions.

steadily /'stedɪlɪ/ adv **1** (gradually) progressivement; **2** (without interruption) sans interruption; **3** [gaze] sans détourner le regard.

steady /'stedɪ/ **I** adj **1** (continual) [stream, increase, decline] constant; [rain] incessant; [breathing, drip, speed, progress] régulier/-ière; **2** (unwavering) [hand] ferme; FIG [faith] immuable; **3** (stable) stable; **to keep** ou **hold sth ~** bien tenir qch; **he isn't very ~ on his feet** (from age) il n'est plus très ferme sur ses jambes; (from drunkenness) il titube; **to hold ~** [interest rates] se maintenir; **4** (calm) [voice] ferme; [gaze] calme; **5** (reliable) [job] fixe; [relationship] durable;

[*wórker*] fiable; **do you have a ~ boyfriend?** tu sors avec quelqu'un?
II° *excl* GB **~!** ou **~ on!** (reprovingly) doucement!
III *vtr* **1** (stop moving) tenir [*camera*]; **2** (control) **to ~ one's nerves** se calmer les nerfs.
IV *vi* LIT, FIG se stabiliser.
V *v refl* **to ~ oneself** (physically) rétablir son équilibre; (mentally) se calmer.
IDIOMS **to go ~ with sb**° sortir avec qn.

steak /steɪk/ *n* (of beef) steak *m*; **~ and chips** steak frites; **salmon/tuna ~** darne *f* de saumon/thon.

steak: **~ and kidney pie**, **~ and kidney pudding** *n* GB tourte *f* au bœuf et aux rognons; **~house** *n* (restaurant *m*) grill *m*; **~ sandwich** *n* sandwich *m* au biftek.

steal /stiːl/ I° *n* (bargain) **it's a ~!** c'est donné!
II *vtr* (*prét* **stole**; *pp* **stolen**) (thieve) voler (**from sb à** qn); FIG **to ~ a few minutes' sleep** s'offrir un douce quelques minutes de sommeil; **to ~ a glance at** jeter un coup d'œil à; **to ~ a kiss** voler un baiser.
III *vi* (*prét* **stole**; *pp* **stolen**) **1** (thieve) voler; **to ~ from sb** voler qn; **to ~ from a house** cambrioler une maison; **our luggage was stolen from the car** on nous a volé nos bagages dans la voiture; **2** (creep) LIT **to ~ out of the room** quitter la pièce subrepticement; **to ~ up on sb** s'approcher de qn subrepticement.
IDIOMS **to ~ a march on sb** prendre qn de vitesse; **to ~ the show** éclipser tout le monde.

stealing /'stiːlɪŋ/ *n* vol *m*.

stealth /stelθ/ *n* **with ~** furtivement.

stealthily /'stelθɪlɪ/ *adv* furtivement.

stealthy /'stelθɪ/ *adj* [*step, glance*] furtif/-ive.

steam /stiːm/ I *n* **1** (vapour) vapeur *f*; (in room, on window) buée *f*; **powered by ~** à vapeur; **2** (from pressure) pression *f*; **full ~ ahead!** FIG en avant toute!
II *noun modifier* [*bath, cloud*] de vapeur; [*iron, railway*] à vapeur.
III *vtr* faire cuire [qch] à la vapeur [*vegetables*]; **to ~ open a letter** décacheter une lettre à la vapeur; **~ed pudding** GB pudding cuit à la vapeur.
IV *vi* (give off vapour) fumer, dégager de la vapeur; **to ~ through the countryside** traverser la campagne en crachant des nuages de fumée.
IDIOMS **to get up** ou **pick up ~** [*machine*] prendre de la vitesse; [*campaign*] prendre de l'importance; **to run out of ~** s'essouffler; [*worker*] peiner; **to let off ~** se défouler; **under one's own ~** par ses propres moyens.
■ **steam up**: ¶ **~ up** [*window, glasses*] s'embuer; ¶ **~** [**sth**] **up** embuer [*window*]; **to get ~ed up** FIG se mettre dans tous ses états (**over** à propos de).

steam: **~boat** *n* bateau *m* à vapeur; **~ engine** *n* locomotive *f* à vapeur.

steamer /'stiːmə(r)/ *n* (boat) vapeur *m*.

steaming /'stiːmɪŋ/ *adj* [*bath*] très chaud; [*tea*] brûlant.

steam: **~ locomotive** *n* = **steam engine**; **~ power** *n* vapeur *f*.

steamroller /'stiːmrəʊlə(r)/ I *n* rouleau *m* compresseur.
II *vtr* briser [*opposition, rival*]; **to ~ a bill through** imposer un projet de loi à [*parliament*].

steamship *n* GEN navire *m* à vapeur; (for passengers) paquebot *m*.

steamy /'stiːmɪ/ *adj* **1** [*room, window*] embué; [*climate*] chaud et humide; **2**° (erotic) torride.

steel /stiːl/ I *n* **1** (metal) acier *m*; **made of ~** en acier; **2** (knife sharpener) aiguisoir *m*.
II *noun modifier* [*bodywork*] en acier; [*plate, production, manufacturer*] d'acier.
III *v refl* **to ~ oneself** s'armer de courage.

steel: **~ band** *n* steel band *m* (*ensemble musical dont les instruments sont des bidons etc*); **~ guitar** ▶ 1097 | *n* guitare *f* hawaïenne; **~ industry** *n* sidérurgie *f*; **~worker** ▶ 1251 | *n* sidérurgiste *mf*; **~works**, **~yard** *n* installations *fpl* sidérurgiques.

steely /'stiːlɪ/ *adj* **1** [*nerves*] inébranlable; **~-eyed** au regard d'acier; **2** [*sky*] gris plombé *inv*.

steep /stiːp/ I *adj* **1** (sloping) [*descent, stairs*] raide; [*street*] escarpé; [*roof*] en pente raide; [*ascent*] abrupt; **a ~ drop** un à-pic; **2** (sharp) [*rise, fall*] fort (*before n*); **3**° (excessive) [*price*] exorbitant; [*bill*] salé°.
II *vtr* (soak) **to ~ sth in** faire tremper qch dans.
III *vi* tremper (in dans).
IDIOMS **that's a bit ~**°! c'est un peu fort°!

steeped /stiːpt/ *adj* **to be ~ in** être imprégné de.

steeple /'stiːpl/ *n* (tower) clocher *m*; (spire) flèche *f*.

steeple: **~chase** *n* (for horses) steeple-chase *m*; (in athletics) 3000m steeple *m*; **~jack** ▶ 1251 | *n* réparateur/-trice *m/f* de clochers (et de hautes cheminées).

steeply /'stiːplɪ/ *adv* **1** [*rise, drop*] à pic; **2** FIN [*rise*] en flèche.

steer /stɪə(r)/ I *n* **1** (animal) bouvillon *m*; **2**° US (tip) **a bum ~** un mauvais tuyau°.
II *vtr* **1** (control direction of) piloter; **2** (guide) LIT diriger, guider [*person*]; FIG orienter [*conversation*]; **to ~ a course through** FIG manœuvrer délicatement à travers; **to ~ a bill through parliament** faire aboutir un projet de loi.
III *vi* **1** GEN piloter; **the car ~s well** la direction (de la voiture) répond bien; **2** NAUT gouverner; **to ~ towards** ou **for** mettre le cap sur.
IDIOMS **to ~ clear of sth/sb** se tenir à l'écart de qch/qn; **to ~ a middle course** adopter une position médiane.

steering /'stɪərɪŋ/ *n* (mechanism) direction *f*.

steering: **~ column** *n* AUT colonne *f* de direction; **~ committee** *n* ADMIN comité *m* directeur; **~ lock** *n* AUT blocage *m* de direction; **~ wheel** *n* AUT volant *m*.

stem /stem/ I *n* **1** (of flower, leaf) tige *f*; (of fruit) queue *f*; **2** (of glass) pied *m*; (of pipe) tuyau *m*.
II *vtr* (*p prés etc* **-mm-**) arrêter [*flow*]; FIG enrayer [*advance, tide, increase, inflation*]; contenir [*protest*].
III *vi* (*p prés etc* **-mm-**) **to ~ from** provenir de.

stem ginger *n* gingembre *m* confit.

stench /stentʃ/ *n* puanteur *f*; FIG odeur *f* nauséabonde.

stencil /'stensɪl/ I *n* **1** (card) pochoir *m*; **2** (pattern) dessin *m* au pochoir.
II *vtr* décorer [qch] au pochoir [*fabric, surface*].

stencilling, **stenciling** US /'stensɪlɪŋ/ *n* (technique) technique *f* du pochoir.

stenography /ste'nɒgrəfɪ/ *n* US sténographie *f*.

step /step/ I *n* **1** (pace) pas *m*; **to take a ~** faire un pas; **to walk** ou **keep in ~** marcher au pas; **I was a few ~s behind her** je la suivais de près; **to fall into ~ with sb** se mettre au même pas que qn; **one ~ out of line** un pas de travers; **to be out of ~ with the times** ne plus être dans le coup; **to watch one's ~** LIT faire attention où l'on met les pieds; **you'd better watch your ~**°! FIG tu ferais mieux de faire attention!; **to be one ~ ahead of the competition** FIG avoir une longueur d'avance sur ses concurrents; **I'm with you every ~ of the way** FIG tu peux compter sur moi; **2** (footsteps) pas *m*; **3** FIG (move) pas *m*; **a ~ forwards/backwards** un pas en avant/en arrière; **it's a ~ in the right direction** c'est un pas dans la bonne voie; **to be one ~ closer to victory** approcher de la victoire; **the first ~ is to...** la première chose à faire est de...; **it's a ~ up for him** il a gravi un échelon; **4** FIG (measure) mesure *f*; (course of action) démarche *f*; **to take ~s to do** prendre des mesures pour faire; **5** FIG (stage) étape *f* (in dans); **to go one ~ further** aller plus loin; **6** (way of walking) pas *m*; **7** (dance step) pas *m*; **8** (stair) marche *f*; **a flight of ~s** (to upper floor) un escalier *m*; (outside building) des marches *fpl*.
II **steps** *npl* **1** (small ladder) escabeau *m*; **2** (outdoor) marches *fpl*.
III *vi* (*p prés etc* **-pp-**) marcher (**in** dans; **on** sur); **to ~ into** entrer dans [*lift*]; monter dans [*dinghy*]; **to ~ into sb's office** entrer dans le bureau de qn; **just ~ this way** si vous voulez bien me suivre; **to ~ off**

descendre de [*pavement*]; **to ~ onto** monter sur [*scales, pavement*]; **to ~ over** enjamber; **to ~ through** passer derrière [*curtains*]; **to ~ out of line** FIG faire un pas de travers; **to ~ up to** s'approcher de [*microphone*].

IDIOMS **to ~ on it**○ se grouiller❶; **to ~ on the gas**○ appuyer sur le champignon○; **one ~ at a time** chaque chose en son temps.

■ **step aside 1** (physically) s'écarter (**in order to** pour); **2** (in job transfer) céder sa place (**in favour of** à).

■ **step back** FIG prendre du recul (**from** par rapport à).

■ **step down**: **~ down** GEN se retirer; (as electoral candidate) se désister.

■ **step in** intervenir (**and do** pour faire).

■ **step up**: **~ up** [*sth*] accroître [*production*]; intensifier [*campaign*]; renforcer [*surveillance*].

stepbrother *n* demi-frère *m*.

step-by-step **I** *adj* [*guide*] complet/-ète; [*reduction*] progressif/-ive.
II step by step *adv* [*analyse*] point par point; [*explain*] étape par étape.

step: **~child** *n* beau-fils/belle-fille *m/f*; **~ladder** *n* escabeau *m*; **~parent** *n* beau-père/belle-mère *m/f*; **~ping stone** *n* LIT pierre *f* de gué; FIG tremplin *m*; **~sister** *n* demi-sœur *f*.

stereo /'steriəʊ/ **I** *n* **1** (technique) stéréo *f*; **2** (also **~ system**) chaîne *f* stéréo; **car ~** autoradio *m* stéréo; **personal ~** baladeur *m*.
II *noun modifier* [*cassette, cassette-player*] stéréo *inv*; [*recording, broadcast*] en stéréo.

stereophonic /ˌsteriə'fɒnɪk/ *adj* stéréophonique.

stereoscopic /ˌsteriə'skɒpɪk/ *adj* stéréoscopique.

stereotype /'steriətaɪp/ **I** *n* (person, idea) stéréotype *m*.
II *vtr* GEN stéréotyper [*person*].

sterile /'sterail, US 'sterəl/ *adj* (all contexts) stérile.

sterilize /'sterəlaɪz/ *vtr* stériliser.

sterling /'stɜːlɪŋ/ **I** *n* ▶849 FIN livre *f* sterling *inv*; **~ was up/down** la livre sterling était en hausse/en baisse; **£100 ~** 100 livres sterling.
II *noun modifier* FIN [*payment*] en livres sterling.
III *adj* (*épith*) (excellent) remarquable.

sterling silver *n* argent *m* fin.

stern /stɜːn/ **I** *n* NAUT poupe *f*.
II *adj* GEN sévère; [*message*] grave.

sternly /'stɜːnlɪ/ *adv* [*say, speak*] sévèrement; [*look*] d'un air sévère.

steroid /'stɪərɔɪd, 'ste-/ *n* stéroïde *m*; **to be on ~s** prendre des stéroïdes; **anabolic ~** anabolisant *m*.

stet /stet/ (in proofreading) bon.

stetson /'stetsn/ *n* chapeau *m* de cow-boy.

stew /stjuː, US stuː/ **I** *n* ragoût *m*; (with game) civet *m*; (with veal, chicken) blanquette *f*.
II *vtr* cuire [*qch*] en ragoût; cuire [*qch*] en civet [*game*]; faire cuire [*fruit, vegetables*]; **~ed apples** compote *f* de pommes.
III *vi* **1** [*meat*] cuire à l'étouffée; [*fruit*] cuire (dans son jus); **2**○ FIG [*person*] (in heat) crever de chaud❶.
IDIOMS **to be/get in a ~**○ (worry) être/se mettre dans tous ses états; **to ~ in one's own juice**○ mijoter dans son jus○.

steward /stjʊəd, US 'stuːərd/ *n* (on plane, ship) steward *m*; (of club) intendant/-e *m/f*; (at races) organisateur *m*.

stewardess /'stjʊədes, US 'stuːərdəs/ *n* (on plane) hôtesse *f* (de l'air).

stg *n*: *abrév écrite* = **sterling** I.

stick /stɪk/ **I** *n* **1** (piece of wood) bâton *m*; (for kindling) bout *m* de bois; (for lollipop) bâton *m*; **2** (also **walking ~**) canne *f*; **3** (rod-shaped piece) **a ~ of chalk/dynamite** un bâton de craie/dynamite; **a ~ of celery** une branche de céléri; **a ~ of rhubarb** une tige de rhubarbe; **a ~ of (French) bread** une baguette; **4** SPORT (in hockey) crosse *f*; **5** (conductor's baton) baguette *f*; **6**○ (piece of furniture) **a few ~s of furniture** quelques meubles; **7**○ GB (person) **a funny old ~** un drôle de bonhomme/une drôle de bonne femme *m/f*; **he's a dry old ~** il manque d'humour;

8○ (criticism) **to get** ou **take (some) ~** se faire critiquer; **to give sb (some) ~** critiquer qn violemment.
II○ **sticks** *npl* **in the ~s** en pleine cambrousse❶, dans la campagne.
III *vtr* (*prét, pp* **stuck**) **1 to ~ sth into sth** planter qch dans qch; **he stuck a knife in her** il l'a poignardée; **2** (put) **he stuck his head round the door** il a passé la tête dans l'entrebâillement de la porte; **she stuck her hands in her pockets** elle a enfoncé ses mains dans ses poches; **~ your coat on the chair**○ mets ton manteau sur la chaise; **to ~ an advert in the paper**○ mettre une annonce dans le journal; **to ~ sb in a home**○ mettre qn dans une maison de retraite; **3** (fix) coller [*poster, stamp*] (**to** à); **'~ no bills'** 'défense d'afficher'; **4**○ GB (bear) supporter [*person*]; **I can't ~ it any longer** je n'en peux plus; **5**○ (impose) **to ~ an extra £10 on the price** augmenter le prix de 10 livres; **I was stuck with Frank** je me suis retrouvé avec Frank.
IV *vi* (*prét, pp* **stuck**) **1** [*stamp, glue*] coller; **to ~ to the pan** [*sauce, rice*] coller au fond de la casserole, attacher○; **2** (jam) [*drawer, door, lift*] se coincer; **3** (remain) rester; **to ~ in sb's memory** ou **mind** rester gravé dans la mémoire de qn; **to make the charges ~ around**○! reste là!.
IDIOMS **to have** ou **get hold of the wrong end of the ~** mal comprendre; **to up ~s**○ plier bagages.

■ **stick at**: **~ at** [*sth*] persévérer dans [*task*]; **~ at it!** persévère!

■ **stick by**: **~ by** [*sb*] rester fidèle à [*friend*].

■ **stick out**: ¶ **~ out** [*nail, sharp object*] dépasser (**of** de); **his ears ~ out** il a les oreilles décollées; **his stomach ~s out** il a un gros ventre; **her teeth ~ out** elle a les dents qui avancent; ¶ **~ [sth] out, ~ out [sth] 1** (cause to protrude) **to ~ out one's hand/foot** tendre la main/le pied; **to ~ out one's chest** bomber le torse; **to ~ one's tongue out** tirer la langue; **2** (cope with) **to ~ it out**○ tenir le coup○.

■ **stick to**: **~ to [sth/sb] 1** (keep to) s'en tenir à [*facts, point, plan, diet*]; maintenir [*story, version*]; **2** (follow) suivre; **3** (stay faithful to) rester fidèle à.

■ **stick together**: ¶ **~ together 1** (become fixed to each other) [*pages*] se coller; **2**○ (be loyal) se serrer les coudes○, être solidaire; **3**○ (not separate) rester ensemble; ¶ **~ [sth] together** coller [*pieces*].

■ **stick up**: ¶ **~ up** (project) se dresser; **to ~ up for sb** (defend) défendre qn; (side with) prendre le parti de qn; **to ~ up for oneself** défendre ses intérêts; ¶ **~ [sth] up, ~ up [sth]** (put up) mettre [*poster, notice*]; **~ 'em up**○! haut les mains!

sticker /'stɪkə(r)/ *n* autocollant *m*.

sticker price *n* prix *m* affiché.

stick: **~ing plaster** *n* sparadrap *m*; **~ing point** *n* point *m* de désaccord; **~ insect** *n* phasme *m*; **~-in-the-mud**○ *n* routinier/-ière○ *m/f*.

stickler /'stɪklə(r)/ *n* (person) **to be a ~ for sth** être à cheval sur qch.

stick: **~-on** *adj* [*label*] adhésif/-ive; **~-up**○ *n* braquage○ *m*, hold-up *m*.

sticky /'stɪkɪ/ *n* **1** (tending to adhere) [*hand, floor, substance*] collant; [*label*] adhésif/-ive; **2** (hot and humid) lourd; **3** (sweaty) moite; **to feel** ou **be hot and ~** transpirer; **4** (difficult) [*situation, problem*] difficile.
IDIOMS **to come to a ~ end** mal finir.

sticky: **~ bun**○ *n* GB *petit pain enrobé de sucre*; **~ tape**○ *n* GB Scotch® *m*, ruban *m* adhésif.

stiff /stɪf/ **I**○ *n* **1** (corpse) macchabée❶ *m*; **2** US (humourless person) rabat-joie *mf inv*.
II *adj* **1** (restricted in movement) GEN raide; (after sport, sleeping badly) courbaturé; **to have a ~ neck** avoir un torticolis; **to have ~ legs** (after sport) avoir des courbatures dans les jambes; **2** (hard to move) [*drawer*] dur à ouvrir; [*lever*] dur à manier; **3** (rigid) [*cardboard*] raide; **4** CULIN **beat the egg whites until ~** battre les blancs en une neige ferme; **5** (not relaxed) [*manner, style*] compassé; **6** (harsh) [*warning, sentence*] sévère; **7** (difficult) [*exam, climb*] difficile; [*competition*] rude;

[*opposition*] fort; **8** (high) [*charge, fine*] élevé; **9** (strong) [*breeze*] fort; **a ~ drink** un remontant.

III *adv*° **to be bored ~** s'ennuyer à mourir; **to be frozen ~** être frigorifié°; **to be scared ~** avoir une peur bleue; **to scare sb ~** faire une peur bleue à qn.

IDIOMS **to keep a ~ upper lip** encaisser° sans broncher.

stiffen /'stɪfn/ **I** *vtr* renforcer [*card*]; raidir [*structure*]; empeser [*fabric*].

II *vi* **1** (grow tense) [*person*] se raidir; **2** CULIN [*egg whites*] devenir ferme; [*mixture*] prendre de la consistance; **3** [*joint*] s'ankyloser; [*limbs*] se raidir.

stiffly /'stɪflɪ/ *adv* **1** [*say*] avec froideur; **~ polite** d'une politesse rigide; **2** [*move*] avec raideur.

stiffness /'stɪfnɪs/ *n* (physical) raideur *f*; (of manner) froideur *f*.

stifle /'staɪfl/ *vtr* étouffer; **it's stifling!** on étouffe!

stigma /'stɪgmə/ *n* (*pl* **-mas** ou **-mata**) stigmate *m*.

stigmatize /'stɪgmətaɪz/ *vtr* stigmatiser.

stile /staɪl/ *n* (in wall, hedge) échalier *m*.

stiletto /stɪ'letəʊ/ *n* (*pl* **-tos**) **1** (also **~ heel**) (shoe, heel) talon *m* aiguille; **2** (dagger) stylet *m*.

still[1] /stɪl/ *adv* **1** (up to and including a point in time) encore; (when nothing has changed) toujours; **eat this bread while it's ~ fresh** mange ce pain pendant qu'il est (encore) frais; **you're ~ too young** (not old enough yet) tu es encore trop jeune; (you were and still are too young) tu es toujours trop jeune; **I ~ have some money left** il me reste encore de l'argent; **2** (expressing surprise) toujours, encore; **I ~ can't believe it!** je n'arrive toujours pas à le croire!; **3** (yet to happen) encore; **it has ~ to be decided** c'est encore à décider; **there is ~ a chance that** il est encore possible que (+ *subj*); **if I'm ~ alive** si je suis encore en vie; **4** (nevertheless) quand même; **it ~ doesn't explain why** cela n'explique toujours pas pourquoi; **~, it's the thought that counts** enfin, c'est l'intention qui compte; **5** (with comparatives: even) encore; **better/ worse ~** encore mieux/pire.

still[2] **I** *n* **1** (distillery) distillerie *f*; **2** (photo) photographie *f* or photo *f* de plateau; **3** (quiet) **the ~ of the night** LITTÉR le silence de la nuit.

II *adj* **1** (motionless) calme; **2** (peaceful) tranquille; **3** [*drink*] non gazeux/-euse; [*water*] plat.

III *adv* **1** (immobile) [*lie, stay*] immobile; **to hold [sth] ~** bien tenir [*camera, mirror*]; **2** (calmly) **to sit ~** se tenir tranquille; **to keep** ou **stand ~** ne pas bouger.

IV *vtr* faire taire [*critic*]; calmer [*doubt*].

IDIOMS **~ waters run deep** il faut se méfier de l'eau qui dort.

stillbirth /stɪl/ *n* mort *f* à la naissance.

still /stɪl/: **~born** *adj* LIT, FIG mort-né/-e; **~ life** *n* (*pl* **-lifes**) nature *f* morte.

stillness /'stɪlnɪs/ *n* (of lake, evening) calme *m*.

stilt /stɪlt/ *n* (pole) échasse *f*; **on ~s** monté sur des échasses.

stilted /'stɪltɪd/ *adj* guindé.

stimulant /'stɪmjʊlənt/ *n* stimulant *m* (**to** de).

stimulate /'stɪmjʊleɪt/ *vtr* stimuler [*appetite, creativity, person*]; encourager [*demand*].

stimulating /'stɪmjʊleɪtɪŋ/ *adj* (all contexts) stimulant.

stimulation /ˌstɪmjʊ'leɪʃn/ *n* stimulation *f* (**of** de).

stimulus /'stɪmjʊləs/ (*pl* **-li**) *n* **1** (physical) stimulus *m*; **2** (boost) impulsion *f*; **3** (incentive) stimulant *m*.

sting /stɪŋ/ **I** *n* **1** (of insect) aiguillon *m*; **2** (result of being stung) piqûre *f*; **bee ~** piqûre d'abeille; **3** (pain) sensation *f* de brûlure; **4**° US (rip-off) arnaque *f*.

II *vtr* (*prét, pp* **stung**) **1** [*insect*] piquer; **2** [*wind*] cingler; **3** FIG [*criticism*] blesser, piquer [qn] au vif.

III *vi* (*prét, pp* **stung**) [*eyes, antiseptic*] piquer; [*cut*] cuire; **my knee ~s** mon genou me cuit.

IDIOMS **a ~ in the tail** une mauvaise surprise; **to take the ~ out of** rendre [qch] moins blessant [*remark*]; atténuer l'effet de [*action*].

stingily /'stɪndʒɪlɪ/ *adv* chichement.

stinginess /'stɪndʒɪnɪs/ *n* radinerie° *f*.

stinging /'stɪŋɪŋ/ *adj* **1** [*remark*] blessant; **2** [*sensation*] de brûlure; [*pain*] cuisant.

stinging nettle *n* ortie *f*.

stingy /'stɪndʒɪ/ *adj* PÉJ [*person*] radin°; [*firm*] près de ses sous°; [*amount*] mesquin.

stink /stɪŋk/ **I** *n* **1** (stench) (mauvaise) odeur *f*; **there's an awful ~!** ça pue!; **2**° (row) esclandre *m*; **to kick up** ou **cause a ~** causer un esclandre.

II *vi* (*prét* **stank**; *pp* **stunk**) puer; **to ~ of petrol/ death** puer l'essence/la mort; **it ~s** ça pue; **to ~ of corruption** sentir la corruption à plein nez.

stink-bomb *n* boule *f* puante.

stinker° /'stɪŋkə(r)/ *n* casse-tête *m*; **the test was a real ~** l'interrogation était vachement° dure.

stinking /'stɪŋkɪŋ/ *adj* **1** (foul-smelling) puant; **2**° (horrible) (*épith*) infect; **a ~ cold** un rhume carabiné.

IDIOMS **to be ~ rich**° être bourré de fric°.

stint /stɪnt/ **I** *n* **to do a three-year ~ with a company** travailler trois ans pour une entreprise; **I've done my ~ for today** j'en ai assez fait pour aujourd'hui.

II *v refl* **to ~ oneself** se priver (**of** de).

stipend /'staɪpend/ *n* traitement *m* (*salaire*).

stipple /'stɪpl/ *vtr* TECH pointiller; **a ~d effect** un effet granité.

stipulate /'stɪpjʊleɪt/ *vtr* stipuler (**that** que).

stipulation /ˌstɪpjʊ'leɪʃn/ *n* condition *f*.

stir /stɜː(r)/ **I** *n* **1 to give the sauce a ~** remuer la sauce; **2 to cause (quite) a ~** faire sensation.

II *vtr* (*p prés etc* **-rr-**) **1** (mix) remuer [*liquid, sauce*]; mélanger [*paint, powder*]; **to ~ sth into sth** incorporer qch à qch; **2** (move slightly) [*breeze*] agiter [*leaves, papers*]; **3** (move, arouse) émouvoir [*person*]; exciter [*curiosity*]; stimuler [*imagination*]; évoquer [*memories*]; **to ~ sb to pity** inspirer de la pitié à qn.

III *vi* (*p prés etc* **-rr-**) **1** (move gently) [*leaves, papers*] trembler; [*curtains*] remuer; [*person*] **to ~ in one's sleep** bouger en dormant; **2** (awaken) bouger.

IV *v refl* (*p prés etc* **-rr-**) **to ~ oneself** se secouer°.

■ **stir in**: **~ [sth] in**, **~ in [sth]** incorporer [*flour, powder*]; ajouter [*eggs, milk*].

■ **stir up**: ¶ **~ [sth] up**, **~ up [sth] 1** (whip up) [*wind*] faire voler [*dust, leaves*]; **2** FIG provoquer [*trouble*]; attiser [*hatred, unrest*]; remuer [*past*]; **to ~ things up**° envenimer les choses; ¶ **~ [sb] up**, **~ up [sb]** exciter [*crowd*].

stir-crazy° US *adj* rendu fou/folle par la réclusion.

stir-fry /'stɜːfraɪ/ **I** *n* CULIN sauté *m*.

II *vtr* (*prét, pp* **-fried**) faire sauter [*beef, vegetable*].

stirring /'stɜːrɪŋ/ **I** *n* **to feel a ~ of desire** avoir une bouffée de désir; **the first ~s of nationalism** les premières manifestations du nationalisme.

II *adj* [*story*] passionnant; [*music, performance, speech*] enthousiasmant; **to be ~ stuff**° être passionnant.

stirrup /'stɪrəp/ *n* (all contexts) étrier *m*.

stitch /stɪtʃ/ **I** *n* **1** (in sewing, embroidery) point *m*; (single loop in knitting, crochet) maille *f*; (style of knitting, crochet) point *m*; **2** MED point *m* de suture; **to have ~es** se faire recoudre; **she had 10 ~es** on lui a fait 10 points de suture (**in, to** à); **to have one's ~es out** se faire retirer les fils; **3** (pain) point *m* de côté; **to have/ get** (a) **~** avoir/attraper un point de côté.

II *vtr* **1** coudre (**to, onto** à); **2** MED recoudre.

IDIOMS **a ~ in time saves nine** un point à temps en épargne cent; **to be in ~es**° rire aux larmes; **to have sb in ~es**° faire rire qn aux larmes.

■ **stitch together**: **~ [sth] together** LIT assembler [*garment*]; FIG concocter rapidement [*agreement*].

■ **stitch up**: **~ up [sth]**, **~ [sth] up** recoudre.

stitching /'stɪtʃɪŋ/ *n* couture *f*.

St John's Ambulance Brigade *n* GB *organisation bénévole qui assure les premiers soins*.

stoat /stəʊt/ *n* hermine *f*.

stock /stɒk/ **I** *n* **1 ¢** (in shop, warehouse) stock *m*; **to have sth in ~** (in shop) avoir qch en magasin; (in warehouse) avoir qch en stock; **to be out of ~** [*product, model*] être épuisé; **we're out of ~** nous n'en avons plus; **the smaller size is out of** ~ il n'y a plus de petites tailles; **2** (supply, store) (on large scale) stock *m* (**of** de); (on domestic scale) provisions *fpl*; **~s are running low** les stocks sont presque épuisés; **to get in** *ou* **lay in** ~**s of provisions** faire des stocks; **while** ~**s last** jusqu'à épuisement des stocks; **3** FIN (capital) ensemble *m* du capital *or* des actions d'une sociét é; **4** (descent) souche *f*, origine *f*; **to be of peasant** ~ être de souche paysanne; **to come from farming** ~ venir d'une famille d'agriculteurs; **5** (standing) cote *f*; **his** ~ **has risen** sa cote a monté; **6** CULIN bouillon *m*; **beef** ~ bouillon *m* de bœuf; **7** (flower) giroflée *f* d'hiver; **8** (cravat) lavallière *f*; **9** (+ *v pl*) (cattle) bétail *m*, cheptel *m* bovin; (bloodstock) chevaux *mpl* de race.

II stocks *npl* **1** HIST, JUR **the** ~**s** le pilori; **2** GB FIN valeurs *fpl*, titres *mpl*; **government** ~ fonds *mpl* d'État; ~**s closed higher/lower** la Bourse a clôturé en hausse/en baisse; ~**s and shares** valeurs *fpl* mobilières; **3** US actions *fpl*.

III *adj* [*size*] courant; [*answer*] classique; [*character*] stéréotypé.

IV *vtr* **1** COMM (sell) avoir, vendre; **we don't** ~ **it** nous n'en faisons pas; **2** (with supplies) remplir [*larder, fridge*]; garnir [*shelves*]; approvisionner [*shop*]; peupler [*lake*]; **well-~ed** [*garden, library*] bien fourni.

IDIOMS FIG **to take** ~ faire le point (**of** sur).

■ **stock up** s'approvisionner (**with, on** en).

stockade /stɒˈkeɪd/ *n* (fence) palissade *f*.

stock: **~broker** ▶ 1251 | *n* agent *m* de change; **~broker belt** *n* GB banlieue *f* cossue.

stockbroking /ˈstɒkbrəʊkɪŋ/ **I** *n* commerce *m* de titres en Bourse.

II *noun modifier* [*firm*] de courtage en Bourse.

stock: ~ **car** *n* (for racing) stock-car *m*; **~-car racing** ▶ 949 | *n* course *f* de stock-cars; **~-cube** *n* bouillon-cube® *m*.

stock exchange *n* (also **Stock Exchange**) **the** ~ la Bourse; **to be listed on the** ~ être coté en Bourse.

stockholder /ˈstɒkhəʊldə(r)/ *n* actionnaire *mf*.

stocking /ˈstɒkɪŋ/ ▶ 1260 | *n* bas *m*; **silk** ~ bas de soie; **in one's ~(ed) feet** en chaussettes; **Christmas** ~ ≈ soulier *m* de Noël.

stock-in-trade *n* spécialité *f*; **irony is part of the** ~ **of any teacher** l'ironie fait partie de la panoplie de tout professeur.

stockist /ˈstɒkɪst/ *n* COMM dépositaire *mf*.

stock market I *n* **1** (stock exchange) Bourse *f* des valeurs; **2** (prices, trading activity) marché *m* des valeurs. **II** *noun modifier* [*crash, trading*] boursier/-ière; [*quotation, flotation*] en Bourse; ~ **price** *ou* **value** cote *f*.

stockpile /ˈstɒkpaɪl/ **I** *n* réserves *fpl*. **II** *vtr* stocker [*weapons*]; faire des stocks *or* des réserves de [*food, goods*].

stock: **~piling** *n* stockage *m*; **~pot** *n* marmite *f*; ~ **room** *n* magasin *m*.

stock-still *adv* **to stand** ~ rester cloué sur place.

stocktaking /ˈstɒkteɪkɪŋ/ *n* inventaire *m*.

stocky /ˈstɒkɪ/ *adj* [*person*] trapu; [*animal*] râblé.

stodge /stɒdʒ/ *n* ℂ GB (food) aliments *mpl* bourratifs.

stodgy /ˈstɒdʒɪ/ *adj* [*food*] bourratif/-ive.

stoical /ˈstəʊɪkl/ *adj* stoïque.

stoicism /ˈstəʊɪsɪzəm/ *n* stoïcisme *m*.

stoke /stəʊk/ *vtr* (also ~ **up**) alimenter [*fire, furnace*]; FIG entretenir [*fires, flames*].

stole /stəʊl/ **I** *prét* ▶ **steal** II, III. **II** *n* étole *f*.

stolen /ˈstəʊlən/ *pp* ▶ **steal** II, III.

stolid /ˈstɒlɪd/ *adj* [*person, character*] flegmatique.

stolidly /ˈstɒlɪdlɪ/ *adv* imperturbablement.

stomach /ˈstʌmək/ **I** *n* estomac *m*; (belly) ventre *m*; **to have a pain in one's** ~ avoir mal au ventre *or* à l'estomac; **to lie on one's** ~ être à plat ventre; **to do sth on an empty** ~ faire qch à jeun; **to be sick to one's** ~ être profondément dégoûté; **to have a strong** ~ LIT, FIG avoir l'estomac bien accroché°; **to turn sb's** ~ écœurer qn. **II** *noun modifier* [*ulcer, operation*] à l'estomac; [*cancer*]

de l'estomac; **to have** ~ **ache** avoir mal au ventre; **to have** ~ **trouble** souffrir de troubles gastriques.

III *vtr* supporter [*person, attitude*]; **I can't** ~ **that guy**°! je ne peux pas encaisser° ce type°!

IDIOMS **your eyes are bigger than your** ~ tu as les yeux plus grands que le ventre.

stomp /stɒmp/ *vi* (walk heavily) **to** ~ **in/out** entrer/ sortir d'un pas lourd; **he ~ed off in a rage** il est parti à grands pas furieux.

stomping ground *n* endroit *m* préféré.

stone /stəʊn/ ▶ 1392 | **I** *n* **1** ℂ (material) pierre *f*; (**made**) **of** ~ en pierre; **2** pierre *f*; (slightly smaller) caillou *m*; (standing stone) menhir *m*; (engraved headstone) stèle *f*; **to lay a** ~ poser une pierre; **not a** ~ **was left standing** tout était dévasté; **3** (also **precious** ~) (gem) pierre *f*; **4** (in fruit) noyau *m*; **5** MED calcul *m*; **kidney** ~ calcul *m* rénal; **6** GB (weight) = 6,35 kg.

II *noun modifier* [*wall, floor*] en pierre; [*jar*] en grès.

III *vtr* **1 to** ~ **sb to death** lapider qn; **2** (remove stone from) dénoyauter [*peach, cherry*].

IDIOMS **to leave no** ~ **unturned** ne négliger aucun détail; **it's a** ~**'s throw from here** c'est à deux pas d'ici; **to sink like a** ~ couler à pic.

Stone Age *n* Âge *m* de pierre.

stone circle *n* enceinte *f* de monolithes, cromlech *m*.

stone-cold I *adj* glacé.

II *adv* ~ **sober** parfaitement sobre.

stoned° /stəʊnd/ *adj* défoncé°; **to get** ~ se défoncer° (**on** à).

stone: **~-deaf** *adj* sourd comme un pot°; ~ **mason** ▶ 1251 | *n* tailleur/-euse *m/f* de pierre.

stonewall /ˌstəʊnˈwɔːl/ *vi* **1** SPORT jouer un jeu défensif; **2** (filibuster) faire de l'obstruction.

stone: **~walling** *n* obstructionnisme *m*; **~ware** *n* poterie *f* en grès; **~washed** *adj* délavé.

stonily /ˈstəʊnɪlɪ/ *adv* d'un air *ou* d'un ton glacial.

stony /ˈstəʊnɪ/ *adj* **1** (rocky) pierreux/-euse; **2** FIG (cold) [*look, silence*] glacial.

IDIOMS **to fall on** ~ **ground** tomber dans le vide.

stony-broke° *adj* GB fauché°, à sec°.

stood /stʊd/ *prét, pp* ▶ **stand** II, III.

stooge /stuːdʒ/ *n* **1**° (dogsbody) larbin *m*; **2** (partner in comedy act) faire-valoir *m inv*.

stool /stuːl/ *n* (furniture) tabouret *m*.

IDIOMS **to fall between two ~s** n'être ni chair ni poisson.

stool pigeon° *n* mouchard/-e *m/f*.

stoop /stuːp/ **I** *n* **1** (curvature) **to have a** ~ avoir le dos voûté; **to walk with a** ~ marcher courbé; **2** US (veranda) perron *m*.

II *vi* **1** (be bent over) être voûté; **2** (lean forward) se pencher; **to** ~ **down** se baisser; **3** (debase oneself) **to** ~ **so low as to do sth** s'abaisser jusqu'à faire qch; **to** ~ **to lying** s'abaisser jusqu'à mentir.

stop /stɒp/ **I** *n* **1** (halt, pause) arrêt *m*; (short stay) GEN halte *f*; (stopover) escale *f*; **the train makes three ~s** le train fait trois arrêts *or* s'arrête trois fois; **our next** ~ **will be** (**in**) **Paris** (on tour, trip) notre prochaine halte sera Paris; **next** ~ **Dover** le prochain arrêt à Douvres; **all these ~s and starts!** tous ces arrêts et redémarrages!; **to bring sth to a** ~ arrêter qch; **to come to a** ~ s'arrêter; **to put a** ~ **to** mettre fin à; **2** (stopping place) arrêt *m*; **3** (in telegram) stop *m*; **4** (on organ) (pipes) jeu *m* d'orgues; (knob) registre *m* d'orgues.

II *noun modifier* [*button, lever, signal*] d'arrêt.

III *vtr* (*p prés etc* **-pp-**) **1** (cease) arrêter, cesser [*work, noise, activity*]; ~ **it!** arrête!; (that's enough) ça suffit!; **to** ~ **doing** arrêter *or* cesser de faire; **to** ~ **smoking** arrêter *or* cesser de fumer; **2** (bring to a halt) (completely) GEN arrêter; [*strike, power cut*] entraîner l'arrêt de [*activity, production*]; (temporarily) GEN interrompre; [*strike, power cut*] provoquer une interruption de [*activity, production*]; **rain ~ped play** la pluie a interrompu la partie; **to** ~ **a bullet** recevoir une balle; **3** (prevent) empêcher [*war, publication*]; empêcher [qch] d'avoir lieu [*event*]; arrêter [*person*]; **what's ~ping you?** qu'est-ce qui te retient?, qu'est-ce qui t'en empêche?; **to ~ sb (from) doing** empêcher qn de faire; **there's nothing to ~ you** faites donc!; **4** (refuse to provide) (definitively) supprimer [*allowance*]; arrêter [*payments, deliveries, subscription*]; couper [*gas, electricity, water*]; (suspend) suspendre [*grant, payment, leave*]; **to ~ a cheque** faire opposition à un chèque; **to ~ £50 out of sb's pay** GB retenir 50 livres sur le salaire de qn; **5** (plug) boucher [*gap, hole*]; [*leak*] arrêter.

IV *vi* (*p prés etc* **-pp-**) **1** (halt) s'arrêter; **2** (cease) GEN s'arrêter; [*pain, worry*] cesser; **not to know when to ~** ne pas savoir s'arrêter; **this is going to have to ~** il va falloir que cela cesse; **without ~ping** sans arrêt; **you didn't ~ to think** tu n'as pas pris le temps de réfléchir; **3°** GB (stay) rester; **to ~ for dinner** rester dîner; **I can't ~** je n'ai vraiment pas le temps.

V *v refl* (*p prés etc* **-pp-**) **I can't ~ myself** je ne peux pas m'en empêcher; **I nearly fell but I ~ped myself** j' ai failli tomber mais je me suis rattrapé.

IDIOMS **to pull out all the ~s** frapper un grand coup (**to do** pour faire).

■ **stop by**°: ¶ **~ by** passer; **to ~ by Brad's** passer chez Brad; ¶ **~ by** [*sth*] passer à [*shop, café*].

■ **stop off** faire un arrêt; **to ~ off in Bristol** faire un arrêt à Bristol; **to ~ off at Paul's house** passer chez Paul.

■ **stop over** (breaking journey) faire escale.

■ **stop up**: **~** [*sth*] **up**, **~ up** [*sth*] boucher [*hole*].

stopcock *n* robinet *m* d'arrêt.

stopgap /'stɒpgæp/ **I** *n* bouche-trou *m*. **II** *noun modifier* [*measure*] provisoire.

stop: **~-go** *adj* [*policy*] d'oscillation; **~-off** *n* (quick break) arrêt *m*; (longer) halte *f*; **~over** *n* escale *f*.

stoppage /'stɒpɪdʒ/ *n* **1** (strike) interruption *f* (de travail); **2** GB (deduction from wages) retenue *f* (sur salaire).

stopper /'stɒpə(r)/ *n* (for bottle, jar) bouchon *m*.

stopping /'stɒpɪŋ/ **I** *n* '**no ~**' 'arrêt *m* interdit'. **II** *noun modifier* AUT [*distance, time*] d'arrêt.

stopping train *n* omnibus *m*.

stop-press /ˌstɒp'pres/ *n* dernières nouvelles *fpl*.

stop: **~ sign** *n* (panneau *m* de) stop *m*; **~watch** *n* chronomètre *m*.

storage /'stɔːrɪdʒ/ **I** *n* **1** (of food, fuel, goods) stockage *m*; **to be in ~** [*furniture*] être au garde-meuble; **2** (space) espace *m* de rangement; **3** COMPUT (facility) mémoire *f*; (process) mise *f* en mémoire. **II** *noun modifier* [*compartment, space*] de rangement.

storage: **~ device** *n* COMPUT mémoire *f*; **~ heater** *n* ELEC radiateur *m* électrique à accumulation; **~ jar** *n* (glass) bocal *m* (de rangement); **~ tank** *m* réservoir *m*, tank *m*; **~ unit** *n* (cupboard) meuble *m* de rangement.

store /stɔː(r)/ **I** *n* **1 ▶ 1251** (shop) magasin *m*; (smaller) boutique *f*; **the big ~s** les grands magasins; **2** (supply) (of food, fuel, paper) réserve *f*, provision *f*; (of information) fonds *mpl*; **3** (place) (for food, fuel) réserve *f*; (for furniture) garde-meuble *m*; (for military supplies) magasin *m*; **4** (storage) **to put sth in(to) ~** mettre qch au garde-meuble [*furniture*]; mettre qch en magasin, entreposer [*goods*]; FIG **what's in ~ in 1996?** qu'est-ce que 1996 nous réserve? **II** *stores npl* (supplies) provisions *fpl*. **III** *vtr* **1** (keep till needed) conserver [*food, information*]; ranger [*objects, furniture*]; stocker [*nuclear waste, chemicals*]; engranger [*crops, grain*]; **2** COMPUT mettre [qch] en mémoire, mémoriser [*data*]. IDIOMS **to set great ~ by sth** attacher beaucoup d'importance à qch.

■ **store up**: **~ up** [*sth*] accumuler; **you're storing up trouble for yourself** tu ne fais qu'accumuler les ennuis.

store: **~ cupboard** *n* armoire *f* de rangement; **~ detective ▶ 1251** *n* surveillant/-e *m*/*f* (*dans un magasin*); **~house** *n* entrepôt *m*; **~keeper ▶ 1251** *n* US commerçant/-e *m*/*f*; **~room** *n* (in house, school, office) réserve *f*; (in factory, shop) magasin *m*.

storey GB, **story** US /'stɔːrɪ/ *n* (*pl* **-reys** GB, **-ries** US) étage *m*; **on the third ~** GB au troisième étage; US au quatrième étage; **a three-storeyed building** GB, **a three storied building** US un bâtiment de trois étages.

stork /stɔːk/ *n* cigogne *f*.

storm /stɔːm/ **I** *n* **1** (weather) tempête *f*; (thunderstorm) orage *m*; **the ~ broke** la tempête a éclaté; **to weather a ~** FIG surmonter une mauvaise passe; **2** (attack) **to take a town by ~** MIL prendre une ville d'assaut; **she took Broadway by ~** FIG elle a remporté un succès foudroyant à Broadway; **3** (outburst) tempête *f*; **a ~ of criticism** une tempête de critiques.

II *vtr* **1** (invade) prendre [qch] d'assaut [*citadel, prison*]; **2** (roar) **'get out!' he ~ed** 'sortez!' cria-t-il dans un accès de colère.

III *vi* **to ~ off** partir avec fracas; **he ~ed off in a temper** il est parti furibond.

storm: **~cloud** *n* LIT nuage *m* orageux; FIG nuage *m* noir; **~ damage** *n* dégâts *mpl* causés par la tempête; **~ door** *n* double porte *f*; **~ force wind** *n* vent *m* de tempête.

storming /'stɔːmɪŋ/ *n* prise *f*.

storm: **~ lantern** *n* lampe-tempête *f*; **~ trooper** *n* membre *m* de section d'assaut; **~ warning** *n* avis *m* de tempête; **~ window** *n* double fenêtre *f*.

stormy /'stɔːmɪ/ *adj* **1** [*weather, sky, night*] orageux/-euse; [*sea*] houleux/-euse; **2** (turbulent) [*meeting*] houleux/-euse; [*relationship*] orageux/-euse; **~ scenes** éclats *mpl*.

story /'stɔːrɪ/ *n* **1** (account) histoire *f* (**of** de); **it's a true ~** c'est une histoire vécue; **to stick to/change one's ~** maintenir/changer sa version des faits; **what is the real ~?** où est la vérité?; **2** (tale) GEN histoire *f* (**about, of** de); LITERAT conte *m* (**of** de); **read us a (bedtime) ~!** tu nous lis une histoire?; **3** (in newspaper) article *m* (**on, about** sur); **exclusive ~** reportage *m* exclusif; **4** (lie) histoire *f*; **to make up a ~** inventer une histoire (**about** à propos de); **5** (rumour) rumeur *f* (**about** sur); **6** (also **~ line**) histoire *f*; **7** US (floor) étage *m*; **first ~** rez-de-chaussée *m*; **second ~** premier étage *m*.

IDIOMS **but that's another ~** mais ça c'est une autre histoire; **to cut a long ~ short** bref; **that's not the whole ~** ce n'est pas tout; **that's the ~ of my life!** c'est toujours la même chose, avec moi!; **it's always the same ~, it's the same old ~** c'est toujours la même chose; **every picture tells a ~** ça se passe de commentaires; **a likely ~!** elle est bien bonne, celle-là°!; **the ~ goes/has it that** on raconte/dit que; **what's the ~°?** qu'est-ce qui se passe ?

storybook /'stɔːrɪbʊk/ *n* livre *m* de contes.

storyteller /'stɔːrɪtelə(r)/ *n* **1** (writer) conteur/-euse *m*/*f*; **2** (liar) menteur/-euse *m*/*f*.

stout /staʊt/ **I** *n* (drink) stout *f*. **II** *adj* **1** (fat) [*person*] corpulent; [*animal*] gros/grosse; **to grow ~** s'épaissir; **2** (strong) gros/grosse (*before n*); **3** (valiant) acharné.

stoutly /'staʊtlɪ/ *adv* [*deny, resist*] avec acharnement.

stoutness /'staʊtnɪs/ *n* (of person) corpulence *f*.

stove /stəʊv/ *n* **1** (cooker) cuisinière *f*; **electric/gas ~** cuisinière électrique/à gaz; **2** (heater) poêle *m*. IDIOMS **to slave over a hot ~** HUM trimer devant ses fourneaux.

stow /stəʊ/ *vtr* (pack) ranger [*baggage, ropes*].

■ **stow away**: ¶ **~ away** voyager clandestinement; ¶ **~** [*sth*] **away**, **~ away** [*sth*] ranger [*baggage*].

stowaway /'stəʊəweɪ/ *n* passager/-ère *m*/*f* clandestin/-e.

straddle /'strædl/ **I** *n* (also **~ jump**) SPORT rouleau *m* (ventral).

II *vtr* **1** (physically) [*person*] enfourcher [*horse, bike*]; s'asseoir à califourchon sur [*chair*]; **2** (geographically) [*village*] être traversé par [*border*].

strafe /strɑːf, streɪf/ *vtr* mitrailler [qn] en rase-mottes.

straggle /'strægl/ **I** *vi* **1** (spread untidily) **to ~ along**

s'étendre au hasard le long de [*road, beach, railtrack*]; **2** (*dawdle*) traîner.

II straggling *pres p adj* [*village, suburb*] s'étendant au hasard.

straggler /'stræglə(r)/ *n* traînard/-e *m*/*f*.

straggly /'stræglɪ/ *adj* [*hair, beard*] en désordre.

straight /streɪt/ **I** *n* SPORT ligne *f* droite; **back ~** côté *m* opposé de la piste; **home ~** dernière ligne droite.

II *adj* **1** (not bent or curved) GEN droit; [*hair*] raide; **dead ~** GEN tout droit; **in a ~ line** en ligne droite; **2** (level, upright) GEN bien droit; [*bedclothes, tablecloth*] bien mis; **the picture/your tie isn't ~** le tableau/ta cravate est de travers; **3** (tidy, in order) en ordre; **to get** OU **put sth ~** LIT, FIG mettre qch en ordre; **4** (clear) **to get sth ~** comprendre qch; **now let's get one thing ~** que ce soit bien clair; **to put sb ~ about sth** éclairer qn sur qch; **to put** OU **set the record ~** établir la vérité; **5** (honest, direct) [*person*] honnête, droit; [*answer*] clair; **to be ~ with sb** jouer franc-jeu avec qn; **6** (unconditional) [*majority, profit*] net/nette; [*choice*] simple; **to do a ~ swap** faire simplement l'échange; **a ~ fight** GB une élection à deux candidats; **7** (undiluted) [*drink*] sec, sans eau; **8** (consecutive) [*wins, defeats*] consécutif/-ive; **she got ~ 'A's** SCH elle a eu très bien partout; **in ~ sets** SPORT en deux (or trois) sets; **9** THEAT [*actor, role*] sérieux/-ieuse; **10**° (heterosexual) hétéro° *inv*.

III *adv* **1** (not obliquely) GEN droit; [*shoot*] juste; **stand up ~!** tenez-vous droit!; **sit up ~!** asseyez-vous convenablement!; **she held her arm out ~** elle a étendu le bras devant elle; **to go/keep ~ ahead** aller/continuer tout droit; **to look ~ ahead** regarder droit devant soi; **to look sb ~ in the eye** regarder qn droit dans les yeux; **he headed ~ for the bar** il s'est dirigé droit vers le bar; **the car was coming ~ at me** la voiture se dirigeait droit sur moi; **she was looking ~ at me** elle regardait droit dans ma direction; **~ above our heads** juste au-dessus de nos têtes; **~ up in the air** droit en l'air; **the bullet went ~ through his body** la balle lui a traversé le corps de part en part; **they drove ~ past me** ils sont passés droit devant moi; **she drove ~ into a tree** elle est rentrée droit dans un arbre; **2** (without delay) **to go ~ back to Paris** rentrer directement à Paris; **she wrote ~ back** elle a répondu immédiatement; **to come ~ to the point** aller droit au fait; **~ after** tout de suite après; **~ away, ~ off** tout de suite; **he read it ~ off** il l'a lu d'une seule traite; **she told him ~ out that** elle lui a dit carrément or sans ambages que; **it seemed like something ~ out of the Middle Ages** cela semblait sortir tout droit du Moyen Âge; **3** (frankly) tout net; **I'll tell you ~** je vous le dirai tout net; **give it to me ~**° dis-moi la vérité; **~ out** carrément; **to play ~ with sb** FIG jouer franc-jeu avec qn; **4** THEAT [*act, produce*] de manière classique; **5** (neat) [*drink*] sec or sans eau.

IDIOMS **to keep a ~ face** garder son sérieux; **the ~ and narrow** le droit chemin; **to go ~**° [*criminal*] se ranger; **~ up?**° GB sans blague?°

straightaway /'streɪtəweɪ/ *adv* tout de suite.

straighten /'streɪtn/ *vtr* **1** tendre [*arm, leg*]; redresser [*picture, teeth*]; ajuster [*tie, hat*]; refaire (en ligne droite) [*road*]; défriser [*hair*]; **to ~ one's back** OU **shoulders** se redresser; **to have one's nose ~ed** se faire refaire le nez; **to have one's teeth ~ed** se faire redresser les dents; **2** (tidy) mettre [qch] en ordre [*room*]; mettre de l'ordre sur [*desk*].

■ **straighten out**: ¶ **~ out** [*road*] devenir droit; **~ out** [sth], **~** [sth] **out** FIG tirer [qch] au clair [*problem*]; **to ~ things out** arranger les choses.

■ **straighten up**: ¶ **~ up 1** LIT [*person*] se redresser; **2** FIG (tidy up) mettre de l'ordre; ¶ **~ up** [sb/sth], **~** [sb/sth] **up** (tidy) ranger [*objects, room*]; **to ~ oneself up** s'arranger.

straight-faced *adj* à l'air sérieux.

straightforward /ˌstreɪt'fɔːwəd/ *adj* **1** (honest) [*answer, person*] franc/franche; **2** (simple) [*account, explanation, case, question*] simple.

straight: **~-laced** *adj* collet-monté *inv*; **~ man** *n* THEAT faire-valoir *m inv*.

straightness /'streɪtnɪs/ *n* (of hair) raideur *f*.

strain /streɪn/ **I** *n* **1** GEN, PHYS (weight) effort *m*, contrainte *f* (**on** sur); (from pulling) tensions *fpl* (**on** de); **to put a ~ on** fatiguer [*heart, lungs*]; **to take the ~** [*beam, rope*] être soumis à des efforts or des sollicitations; **the rope can't take the ~** la corde ne résistera pas; **2** (pressure) (on person) stress *m*; (in relations) tension *f*; **mental** OU **nervous ~** tension *f* nerveuse; **to put a ~ on** avoir un effet néfaste sur [*relationship*]; créer des tensions au sein de [*alliance*]; grever [*economy, finances*]; mettre [qch] à rude épreuve [*patience , goodwill*]; **to be under ~** [*person*] être stressé; [*relations*] être tendu; **he can't take the ~** il supporte mal la situation; **the ~ was beginning to tell** la fatigue commençait à se faire sentir; **it's getting to be a ~** ça commence à devenir pénible; **3** (injury) muscle *m* froissé; **4** (breed) (of animal) race *f*; (of plant, seed) variété *f*; (of virus, bacteria) souche *f*; **5** (style) veine *f*, ton *m*; **in the same ~** dans la même veine.

II strains *npl* air *m*; **to the ~s of** aux accents de.

III *vtr* **1** **to ~ one's eyes** (to see) plisser les yeux; **to ~ one's ears** tendre l'oreille; **to ~ every muscle** tendre tous ses muscles; **2** FIG grever [*resources, finances*]; compromettre [*relationship*]; mettre [qch] à rude épreuve [*patience*]; **3** (injure) **to ~ a muscle** se froisser un muscle; **to ~ one's shoulder** se froisser un muscle de l'épaule; **to ~ one's eyes** se fatiguer les yeux; **to ~ one's back** se faire un tour de reins; **4** (sieve) passer [*sauce*]; égoutter [*vegetables, pasta*].

IV *vi* **to ~ at** tirer sur [*leash, rope*].

■ **strain off**: **~** [sth] **off, ~ off** [sth] faire égoutter [*water, liquid, fat*].

strained /streɪnd/ *adj* **1** (tense) tendu; **2** (injured) [*muscle*] froissé; **3** (sieved) [*baby food*] en purée.

strainer /'streɪnə(r)/ *n* passoire *f*.

strait /streɪt/ **I** *n* GEOG détroit *m*; **the Straits of Gibraltar** le détroit de Gibraltar.

II straits *npl* **to be in dire ~s** être aux abois.

straitened /'streɪtnd/ *adj* **in ~ circumstances** dans la gêne.

straitjacket /'streɪtdʒækɪt/ *n* **1** LIT camisole *f* de force; **2** FIG carcan *m*.

strait laced /ˌstreɪt 'leɪst/ *adj* collet monté *inv*.

strand /strænd/ **I** *n* **1** (of hair) mèche *f*; (of fibre, wire) fil *m*; (of beads) rangée *f*; **2** FIG (element) élément *m*.

II *vtr* **to be ~ed** être bloqué; **to leave sb ~ed** laisser qn en rade°.

III stranded *pp adj* [*climber, traveller*] bloqué.

strange /streɪndʒ/ *adj* **1** (unfamiliar) inconnu; **a ~ man** un inconnu; **2** (odd) bizarre; **it is ~ (that)** il est bizarre que (+ *subj*); **it feels ~** cela fait une drôle d'impression; **there's something ~ about her** elle a quelque chose de bizarre; **in a ~ way**... curieusement...; **~ as that might seem** aussi bizarre que cela puisse paraître; **~ but true** incroyable mais vrai; **~ to say** c'est curieux à dire; **3** (unwell) bizarre; **4** (unaccustomed) **to be ~ to** être étranger/-ère à.

strangely /'streɪndʒlɪ/ *adj* [*behave, react*] d'une façon étrange; [*quiet, empty*] étrangement; **she looks ~ familiar** c'est curieux, son visage ne m'est pas étranger; **~ enough,**... chose étrange,...

strangeness /'streɪndʒnɪs/ *n* (of place, routine, thought, feeling) étrangeté *f*.

stranger /'streɪndʒə(r)/ *n* étranger/-ère *m*/*f*; **a complete** OU **total ~** un parfait inconnu; **'hello, ~**°!' 'tiens, un revenant°!'; **I'm a ~ here myself!** je ne suis pas d'ici!

strangers' gallery *n* GB tribune *f* réservée au public.

strangle /'stræŋgl/ *vtr* **1** (throttle) [*person*] étrangler; **to ~ sb to death** tuer qn par strangulation; **I could cheerfully have ~d him** HUM je l'aurais étranglé de bon cœur; **2** (stifle) étouffer [*creativity, project*]; entraver [*development, growth*].

stranglehold /'stræŋglhəʊld/ *n* **1** (physical grip) étranglement *m*; **2** FIG (powerful control) mainmise *f*.

strangler /'stræŋglə(r)/ *n* étrangleur/-euse *m/f*.

strangulate /'stræŋgjʊleɪt/ *vtr* étrangler.

strangulation /ˌstræŋgjʊ'leɪʃn/ *n* **1** (of person) strangulation *f*; **2** FIG (of economy) étranglement *m*.

strap /stræp/ **I** *n* **1** (on shoe) bride *f*; (on bag, case, harness) courroie *f*; (on watch) bracelet *m*; (on handbag) bandoulière *f*; (on bus, train) poignée *f*; (on dress, bra, overalls) bretelle *f*; **the ~ has broken** la bretelle a lâché; **2†** (punishment) **the ~** le fouet.
II *vtr* (*p prés etc* **-pp-**) **1** (secure) attacher (**to** à); **to ~ sb into** attacher qn dans [*pram*]; **to ~ sb/sth down** ou **in** ou **on** attacher qn/qch; **2** SPORT (bandage) bander.

straphanger *n* voyageur/-euse *m/f* debout (*inv*).

strapless /'stræplɪs/ *adj* [*bra, dress*] sans bretelles.

strapped○ /stræpt/ *adj* **to be ~ for** être à court de [*cash, staff*].

strapping /'stræpɪŋ/ *adj* costaud.

strata /'strɑːtə, US 'streɪtə/ *pl* ▶ **stratum**.

stratagem /'strætədʒəm/ *n* stratagème *m*.

strategic /strə'tiːdʒɪk/, **strategical** /strə'tiːdʒɪkl/ *adj* stratégique.

strategically /strə'tiːdʒɪklɪ/ *adv* [*plan, develop*] stratégiquement; [*important, placed*] du point de vue stratégique.

strategist /'strætədʒɪst/ *n* stratège *m*.

strategy /'strætədʒɪ/ *n* stratégie *f*; **business ~** stratégie des affaires.

stratosphere /'strætəsfɪə(r)/ *n* stratosphère *f*.

stratum /'strɑːtəm, US 'streɪtəm/ *n* (*pl* **-ta**) (social) couche *f*; (in geology) strate *f*.

straw /strɔː/ **I** *n* paille *f*; (stem) fétu *m* or brin *m* de paille; (for thatch) chaume *m*; (for drinking) paille *f*.
II *noun modifier* [*bag, hat*] de paille.
IDIOMS **to draw the short ~** tirer le mauvais numéro; **to grasp** ou **clutch at ~s** se raccrocher à une chimère; **the last** ou **final ~** la goutte qui fait déborder le vase; **a ~ in the wind** un indice.

strawberry /'strɔːbrɪ, US -berɪ/ **I** *n* fraise *f*; **wild ~** fraise des bois; **strawberries and cream** fraises à la crème; **~ bed** carré *m* de fraises.
II *noun modifier* [*flan, tart*] aux fraises; [*ice cream*] à la fraise; [*jam, field*] de fraises.

strawberry blonde I *n* femme *f* aux cheveux blond vénitien.
II *adj* [*hair*] blond vénitien *inv*.

straw: **~-coloured** *adj* paille *inv*; **~ poll** *n* POL sondage *m* non-officiel.

stray /streɪ/ **I** *n* (animal) animal *m* égaré; (dog) chien *m* errant; (cat) chat *m* vagabond.
II *adj* [*dog*] errant; [*cat*] vagabond; [*sheep*] égaré; [*bullet*] perdu; [*car, tourist*] isolé.
III *vi* **1** LIT (wander) GEN s'égarer; **to ~ from the road** s'écarter de la route; **to ~ from the house** s'éloigner de la maison; **to ~ onto the road** [*animal*] divaguer sur la route; **2** FIG [*eyes, mind*] errer; [*thoughts*] vagabonder; **to ~ from the point** s'écarter du sujet; **3** commit adultery) avoir une aventure.

streak /striːk/ **I** *n* **1** (in character) côté *m*; **2** (period) **to be on a winning/losing ~** être dans une bonne/mauvaise passe; **3** (mark) (of paint, substance, water) traînée *f*; (of light) rai *m*; **~ of lightning** éclair *m*; **4** (in hair) mèche *f*; **to have ~s done** se faire faire des mèches.
II *vtr* **1** (make lines across) strier [*sea, sky*]; **2** (in hairdressing) **to get one's hair ~ed** se faire faire des mèches.
III *vi* (move fast) **to ~ past** passer comme une flèche.
IV **streaked** *pp adj* (with tears) sillonné (**with** de); (with dirt) maculé (**with** de); (with colour, light) strié (**with** de).

streaky /'striːkɪ/ *adj* [*surface*] couvert de traînées.

streaky bacon *n* GB bacon *m* entrelardé.

stream /striːm/ **I** *n* **1** ruisseau *m*; **2** FIG **a ~ of** un flot de [*traffic, customers, questions*]; un jet de [*light*]; une coulée de [*lava*]; un écoulement de [*water*]; **a ~ of abuse** un torrent d'insultes; **3** GB, SCH groupe *m* de niveau; **the top/middle/bottom ~** le groupe des élèves forts/moyens/faibles;

II *vtr* GB, SCH répartir [qch/qn] en groupes de niveau.
III *vi* **1** (flow) ruisseler; **sunlight was ~ing into the room** le soleil entrait à flots dans la pièce; **tears were ~ing down his face** les larmes ruisselaient le long de ses joues; **2** (move) **people ~ed out of the theatre** un flot de gens sortait du théâtre; **they ~ed through the gates** ils ont franchi le portail en foule; **3** [*banners, hair*] **to ~ in the wind** flotter au vent; **4** [*eyes, nose*] couler; **my eyes were ~ing** j'avais les yeux qui coulaient.

streamer /'striːmə(r)/ *n* (of paper) banderole *f*.

streaming /'striːmɪŋ/ *n* GB, SCH répartition *f* par groupes de niveau.
II○ *adj* **a ~ cold** un très gros rhume.

streamline /'striːmlaɪn/ *vtr* **1** (in design) caréner; **2** (make more efficient) rationaliser [*distribution, production*]; EUPH (cut back) dégraisser [*company*].

streamlined /'striːmlaɪnd/ *adj* **1** (in design) [*cooker, furniture*] aux lignes modernes; [*hull, body*] caréné; **2** (more efficient) [*production, system*] simplifié.

stream of consciousness *n* courant *m* de conscience.

street /striːt/ **I** *n* rue *f*; **in** ou **on the ~** dans la rue; **across** ou **over GB the ~** de l'autre côté de la rue; **to take to the ~s** [*rioters*] descendre dans la rue; **the man in the ~** l'homme de la rue.
II *noun modifier* [*plan*] des rues; [*culture*] de la rue.
IDIOMS **it's right up your ~**○ (taste) c'est exactement ce qui te plairait; (ability, dexterity etc) c'est ton rayon; **to be ~s ahead of**○ GB être bien meilleur que.

street: **~car** *n* US tramway *m*; **~ cleaner** *n* (person) balayeur *m*; (machine) balayeuse *f*; **~ clothes** *npl* US habits *mpl* de tous les jours.

street cred○ /ˌstriːt 'kred/ *n* **to have ~** être dans le coup○.

street: **~ door** *n* porte *f* d'entrée; **~ guide** *n* indicateur *m* des rues; **~lamp** *n* (old gas-lamp) réverbère *m*; (modern) lampadaire *m*.

street level *n* rez-de-chaussée *m*; **at ~** au rez-de-chaussée.

street: **~light** *n* réverbère *m*; **~ lighting** *n* éclairage *m* des rues; **~ market** *n* marché *m* en plein air; **~ plan** *n* ▶ **street guide**; **~ theatre** GB, **~ theater** US *n* théâtre *m* de rue; **~ value** *n* valeur *f* à la revente; **~walker** *n* prostituée *f*; **~wise**○ *adj* [*person*] dégourdi○.

strength /streŋθ/ *n* **1** (power) (of person, wind, government) force *f*; (of lens, magnet, voice, army, economy) puissance *f*; **to build up one's ~** (after illness) reprendre des forces; **2** (dynamism, resources) forces *fpl*; **to save one's ~** ménager ses forces; **3** (toughness) (of structure, equipment) solidité *f*; (of material, substance) résistance *f*; **4** (concentration) (of solution) titre *m*; (of dose) concentration *f*; **alcoholic ~** teneur *f* en alcool; **5** (intensity) (of bond) force *f*; (of feeling) intensité *f*; (of bulb) puissance *f*; **6** FIN fermeté *f*; **to gain ~** se raffermir; **7** (resolution) force *f*; **~ of character** force de caractère; **~ of purpose** détermination *f*; **8** (credibility) (of argument) force *f*; (of case, claim) solidité *f*; **convicted on the ~ of the evidence** condamné sur la base des témoignages; **I got the job on the ~ of my research** j'ai obtenu le poste grâce à mes recherches; **9** (asset) qualité *f*; **10** (total size) **at full ~** au complet; **to bring the team up to ~** compléter l'équipe.
IDIOMS **to go from ~ to ~** (person) aller de succès en succès; **give me ~**○! HUM c'est pas possible○!

strengthen /'streŋθn/ **I** *vtr* renforcer [*building, government, argument, love, position*]; consolider [*bond, links*]; affirmer [*power, role*]; fortifier [*muscles*]; raffermir [*dollar, economy*]; **to ~ sb's hand** FIG consolider la position de qn.
II *vi* (of muscles) se fortifier; [*wind*] augmenter (de force); [*economy, yen*] se raffermir (**against** vis-à-vis de).

strengthening /'streŋθnɪŋ/ **I** *n* (of numbers of people) renforcement *m*; (of bond, ties) **a ~ of the ties between us** une coopération plus étroite.

II *adj* [*current, wind*] qui augmente de forces (*after n*); [*currency, pound*] qui se consolide (*after n*).

strenuous /'strenjʊəs/ *adj* **1** (demanding) [*exercise*] énergique; [*day, schedule*] chargé; [*work, activity, job*] ardu; **2** (determined) [*protest, disagreement*] vigoureux/ -euse; [*effort*] acharné.

strenuously /'strenjʊəslɪ/ *adv* [*deny*] vigoureusement.

stress /stres/ **I** *n* **1** (nervous) tension *f*, stress *m*; **emotional/mental** ~ tension émotionnelle/nerveuse; **signs of** ~ signes *mpl* de tension; **to be under** ~ ou **suffer from** ~ être stressé; **in times of** ~ en période de stress; **the ~es and strains of modern life** les agressions *fpl* de la vie moderne; **2** (emphasis) **to lay** ou **put** ~ **on** mettre l'accent *m* sur, insister sur [*fact, problem*]; **3** PHYS effort *m*; **subject to high ~es** soumis à des efforts importants; **4** LING (in particular case) accent *m*; **the** ~ **falls on**... l'accent tombe sur...; **5** (whole system) accentuation *f*.
II *vtr* **1** (emphasize) mettre l'accent *m* or insister sur [*issue, difficulty, advantage*]; **to** ~ **the importance of sth** souligner l'importance *f* de qch; **to** ~ **the need for sth/to do** souligner la nécessité de qch/de faire; **to** ~ **the point that** insister sur le fait que; **to** ~ **(that)** souligner que; **2** LING, MUS accentuer [*note, syllable*].
▪ **stress out**○: ~ **[sb] out** stresser [qn].

stressed /strest/ *adj* **1** GEN (also ~ **out**) (emotionally) stressé; **to feel** ~ se sentir stressé; **2** PHYS (*épith*) [*components, covering, structure*] travaillant; **3** LING accentué.

stress fracture *n* fracture *f* de fatigue.

stressful /'stresfl/ *adj* stressant.

stress mark *n* accent *m*.

stretch /stretʃ/ **I** *n* **1** (in gymnastics) extension *f*; **to have a** ~ s'étirer; **to be at full** ~ [*rope, elastic*] être tendu au maximum; [*factory, office*] être à plein régime; **at a** ~ FIG à la rigueur; **2** (elasticity) élasticité *f*; **3** (section) (of road, track) tronçon *m*; (of coastline, river) partie *f*; **4** (of water, countryside) étendue *f*; **5** (period) période *f*; **I did an 18-month** ~ **in Tokyo** j'ai travaillé 18 mois à Tokyo; **to work for 12 hours at a** ~ travailler 12 heures d'affilée; **6**○ (prison sentence) peine *f*.
II *adj* [*fabric, waist*] extensible; [*limo*] longue.
III *vtr* **1** (extend) tendre [*rope, spring, net*]; **to** ~ **one's arms** s'étirer les bras; **to** ~ **one's legs** FIG se dégourdir les jambes; **to** ~ **one's wings** LIT, FIG déployer ses ailes; **2** (increase the size) LIT étirer [*elastic*]; tirer sur [*fabric*]; élargir [*shoe*]; (distort) déformer [*garment, shoe*]; **3** FIG déformer [*truth*]; contourner [*rules, regulations*]; **to** ~ **a point** (make concession) faire une exception; (exaggerate) aller trop loin; **4** (push to the limit) abuser de [*patience*]; utiliser [qch] au maximum [*budget, resources*]; pousser [qn] au maximum de ses possibilités [*person*]; **the system is** ~**ed to the limit** le système est surchargé; **I need a job that** ~**es me** j'ai besoin d'un travail qui me stimule; **isn't that** ~**ing it a bit**○? vous ne poussez pas un peu○?; **5** (eke out) faire durer [*supplies*].
IV *vi* **1** (extend over limbs) s'étirer; **2** [*road, track, event*] s'étaler (**for, over** sur); [*forest, water, beach, moor*] s'étendre (**for** sur); **to** ~ **to** ou **as far as sth** [*flex, string*] aller jusqu'à qch; **how far does the queue** ~? jusqu'où va la queue?; **the weeks** ~**ed into months** les semaines devenaient des mois; **3** (become larger) [*elastic*] s'étendre; [*shoe*] s'élargir; (undesirably) [*fabric, garment*] se déformer; **4**○ (afford) **I think I can** ~ **to a bottle of wine** je pense que je peux me permettre une bouteille de vin; **the budget won't** ~ **to a new computer** le budget ne peut pas supporter l'achat d'un nouvel ordinateur.
V *v refl* **to** ~ **oneself** s'étirer; FIG faire un effort.
▪ **stretch out**: ¶ ~ **out** s'étendre; ¶ ~ **out** [sth], ~ **[sth] out** tendre [*hand, foot*]; étendre [*arm, leg*]; étaler [*nets, sheet*]; **I** ~**ed my speech out to an hour** j'ai fait durer mon discours pendant une heure.

stretcher /'stretʃə(r)/ *n* MED brancard *m*.

stretcher: ~-**bearer** ▶1251▮ *n* brancardier/-ière *m/*

f; ~ **case** *n* blessé/-e *m/f* grave (*incapable de se déplacer*).

stretch mark *n* vergeture *f*.

stretchy /'stretʃɪ/ *adj* extensible.

strew /struː/ *vtr* (*prét* **strewed**; *pp* **strewed** ou **strewn**) éparpiller [*clothes, litter, paper*]; répandre [*sand, straw, wreckage*]; semer [*flowers*].

stricken /'strɪkən/ *adj* **1** [*face, look, voice*] affligé; [*area*] sinistré; ~ **with**, ~ **by** frappé de [*illness*]; pris de [*fear, guilt*]; atteint de [*chronic illness*]; **2** [*plane, ship*] en détresse.

strict /strɪkt/ *adj* **1** (not lenient) GEN strict (**about** sur); [*view*] rigide; [*silence*] absolu; [*Catholic*] de stricte observance; **in** ~ **confidence** à titre strictement confidentiel; **in** ~ **secrecy** dans le plus grand secret; **on the** ~ **understanding that** à la condition expresse que.

strictly /'strɪktlɪ/ *adv* **1** [*treat*] avec sévérité; **2** (absolutely) [*confidential, functional*] strictement; ~ **speaking** à proprement parler; ~ **between ourselves**... que ceci reste entre nous...; **that is not** ~ **true** ceci n'est pas tout à fait vrai.

strictness /'strɪktnɪs/ *n* GEN sévérité *f*; (of views, principles) rigueur *f*.

stricture /'strɪktʃə(r)/ *n* condamnation *f* (**against** de).

stride /straɪd/ **I** *n* **1** (long step) enjambée *f*; **2** (gait) démarche *f*; **to lengthen one's** ~ allonger le pas.
II *vi* (*prét* **strode**; *pp* **stridden**) **to** ~ **across/out/ in** traverser/sortir/entrer à grands pas; **to** ~ **up and down sth** arpenter qch.
IDIOMS **to get into one's** ~ trouver son rythme; **to make great** ~**s** faire de grands progrès; **to put sb off his/her** ~ faire perdre le rythme à qn; **to take sth in one's** ~ (cope practically) prendre qch calmement; (cope emotionally) accepter qch avec sérénité.

strident /'straɪdnt/ *adj* [*sound, voice*] strident; [*statement, group*] véhément.

strife /straɪf/ *n* (conflict) conflits *mpl* (**among** au sein de; **in** dans); (dissent) querelles *fpl*.

strife-torn, **strife-ridden** *adj* déchiré par les conflits.

strike /straɪk/ **I** *n* **1** IND, COMM grève *f*; **to come out on** ~ se mettre en grève; **2** (attack) attaque *f* (**on, against** contre); **3** (in mining) découverte *f* (d'un gisement); **lucky** ~ FIG coup *m* de chance.
II *noun modifier* IND, COMM [*committee, notice*] de grève; [*leader*] des grévistes.
III *vtr* (*prét, pp* **struck**) **1** (hit) GEN frapper; heurter [*rock, tree, pedestrian*]; **to** ~ **sth with** taper qch avec; **he struck his head on the table** il s'est cogné la tête contre la table; **to be struck by lightning** être touché par la foudre; **to** ~ **sb a blow** LIT, FIG porter un coup à qn; **to** ~ **sb dead** [*lightning*] foudroyer qn; **to be struck dumb with amazement** être frappé d'étonnement; **'earthquake** ~**s San Francisco'** (headline) 'San Francisco secoué par un tremblement de terre'; **to** ~ **terror into sb** ou **sb's heart** frapper qn de terreur; **3** (make impression on) [*idea, thought*] venir à l'esprit de; [*resemblance*] frapper; **it** ~**s me as funny that** je trouve drôle que (+ *subj*); **to** ~ **sb as odd** paraître étrange à qn; **how does the idea** ~ **you?** qu'est-ce que vous pensez de cette idée?; **how did he** ~ **you?** quelle impression vous a-t-il faite?; **it** ~**s me (that)** à mon avis; **I was struck** ~ **with him** il m'a plu; **4**○ (discover) tomber sur○; **5** (achieve) conclure [*bargain*]; **to** ~ **a balance** trouver le juste milieu; **6** (ignite) frotter [*match*]; **7** [*clock*] sonner; **it had just struck two** deux heures venaient de sonner; **8** (delete) supprimer; **9** (dismantle) démonter [*tent*]; **to** ~ **camp** lever le camp; **10** FIN frapper [*coin*].
IV *vi* (*prét, pp* **struck**) **1** (deliver blow) [*person*] frapper; [*bomb*] tomber; **my head struck against a beam** ma tête a heurté une poutre; **to** ~ **at** attaquer; **2** (attack) [*killer, disease, storm*] frapper; [*army, animal*] attaquer; **disaster struck** la catastrophe s'est produite; **Henry** ~**s again**○! HUM Henry nous en a fait encore une○; **3** IND, COMM faire (la) grève; **to**

strikebreaker

~ for/against faire (la) grève pour obtenir/pour protester contre; **4** [*match*] s'allumer; **5** [*clock*] sonner; **6** (proceed) **to ~ north** prendre au nord des terres; **to ~ across** prendre à travers [*field, country*]. ■ **strike back** (retaliate) riposter (**at** à). ■ **strike down**: **~** [*sb*] **down**, **~ down** [*sb*] terrasser; **to be struck down by** (by illness) (affected) être frappé par; (incapacitated) être terrassé par; (by bullet) être abattu de.
■ **strike off**: ¶ **~ off** prendre (**across** à travers); ¶ **~** [*sb*] **off**, **~ off** [*sb*] (delete) rayer; ¶ **~** [*sb*] **off** radier [*doctor*]; **~ off** [*sb/sth*] **off sth** rayer [*qn/qch*] de qch [*list*].
■ **strike out**: ¶ **~ out 1** (hit out) frapper; s'en prendre à [*critics*]; **2** (proceed) **to ~ out towards** s'élancer vers; FIG **to ~ out in new directions** adopter de nouvelles orientations ; **to ~ out on one's own** GEN voler de ses propres ailes; (in business) s'établir à son compte; ¶ **~** [*sth*] **out**, **~ out** [*sth*] (delete) rayer.
■ **strike up**: ¶ **~ up** [*orchestra*] commencer à jouer; ¶ **~ up** [*sth*] (start) [*orchestra*] attaquer; **to ~ up an acquaintance with** faire connaissance avec; **to ~ up a conversation with** engager la conversation avec; **to ~ up a friendship with** se lier d'amitié avec; **to ~ up a relationship with** établir des rapports avec.
strike: **~breaker** *n* briseur/-euse *m/f* de grève; **~ force** *n* MIL force *m* d'intervention; **~ fund** *n* caisse *f* de grève; **~ pay** *n* indemnité *f* de grève.
striker /'straɪkə(r)/ *n* **1** gréviste *mf*; **2** (in football) attaquant/-e *m/f*.
striking /'straɪkɪŋ/ I *adj* **1** (of clock) sonnerie *f*; **2** (of coin) frappe *f*.
II *adj* **1** [*person, clothes, pictures*] que l'on remarque; [*design*] qui se remarque; [*similarity, contrast*] frappant; **2** IND, COMM [*worker*] gréviste.
striking distance *n* **1** MIL **to be within ~** [*army, troops*] être à portée de canon (**of** de); **2** FIG **to be within ~ of London** être près de Londres.
strikingly /'straɪkɪŋlɪ/ *adv* GEN remarquablement; [*stand out, differ*] de manière frappante.
string /strɪŋ/ I *n* **1** ₵ (twine) ficelle *f*; **a piece of ~** un bout de ficelle; **tied up with ~** ficelé; **2** (on garment) cordon *m*; (on bow, racket) corde *f* MUS, (on puppet) fil *m*; **to pull the ~s** LIT, FIG tirer les ficelles; **3** (series) **a ~ of** un défilé de [*visitors, boyfriends*]; une série de [*crimes, novels*]; une succession de [*successes, awards*]; une chaîne de [*shops*]; une kyrielle de [*insults*]; **4** (set) **~ of** onions chapelet *m* d'oignons; **~ of pearls** collier *m* de perles; **~ of islands** chapelet *m* d'îles; **a ~ of racehorses** une écurie (de courses); **5** CULIN (in bean) fil *m*.
II **strings** *npl* MUS **the ~s** les cordes *fpl*.
III *vtr* (*prét, pp* **strung**) **1** MUS, SPORT corder [*racket*]; monter [*guitar, violin*]; **to ~** [*sth*] **tightly** faire un cordage tendu à [*racket*]; **2** (thread) enfiler (**on** sur); **3** (hang) **to ~ sth up** above/across suspendre qch au-dessus de/en travers de; **to ~ sth up on** accrocher qch à; **to ~ sth between** suspendre qch entre.
IDIOMS **to have sb on a ~** mener qn à la baguette; **to pull ~s** faire jouer le piston; **without ~s** ou **with no ~s attached** sans conditions.
■ **string along**: GB: ¶ **~ along** suivre; **to ~ along with sb** accompagner qn; ¶ **~** [*sb*] **along** PÉJ mener qn en bateau PÉJ.
■ **string out**: ¶ **~ out** s'échelonner; ¶ **~** [*sth*] **out**, **~ out** [*sth*] échelonner les; **to be strung out along** [*vehicles*] s'échelonner le long de [*road*]; **to be strung out across** [*people*] se déployer dans [*field*].
■ **string together**: **~** [*sth*] **together**, **~ together** [*sth*] aligner [*sentences, words*]; enchaîner [*songs*].
■ **string up**: **~** [*sb*] **up** pendre [qn] haut et court.
string: **~ bag** *n* filet *m* à provisions; **~ bean** *n* haricot *m* à écosser.
stringency /'strɪndʒənsɪ/ *n* **1** (of criticism, law, measure) sévérité *f*; **2** (of control, regulation, test) rigueur *f*.
stringent /'strɪndʒənt/ *adj* [*measure, standard*] rigoureux/-euse; [*ban, order*] formel/-elle.

stringently /'strɪndʒəntlɪ/ *adv* [*observe, respect*] scrupuleusement; [*apply, treat*] avec rigueur; [*examine, test*] rigoureusement.
string: **~ instrument**, **~ed instrument** ▶ 1097| *n* instrument *m* à cordes; **~-pulling**○ *n* piston○ *m*.
stringy /'strɪŋɪ/ *adj* **1** PÉJ CULIN filandreux/-euse; **2** PÉJ [*hair*] plat et sec; **3** (wiry) [*person, build*] filiforme.
strip /strɪp/ I *n* **1** (narrow piece) bande *f* (**of** de); **a ~ of garden/beach** un jardin/une plage tout/-e en longueur; **centre** GB OU **median** US **~** terre-plein *m* central; **2** (striptease) strip-tease *m*; **3** SPORT tenue *f*.
II *vtr* (*p prés etc* **-pp-**) **1** (also **~ off**) (remove) enlever [*clothes, paint*]; **to ~ sth from ou off sth** enlever ou arracher qch de qch; **2** (remove everything from) déshabiller [*person*]; vider [*house, room*]; dépouiller [*tree, plant*]; défaire [*bed*]; (remove paint from) décaper; (dismantle) démonter; **to ~ sb of** dépouiller qn de [*belongings, rights*]; **to ~ sb of his/her rank** dégrader qn; **he was ~ped of his title** on lui a retiré son titre; **3** (damage) écraser le filet de [*screw*].
III *vi* (*p prés etc* **-pp-**) se déshabiller.
IV **stripped** *pp adj* [*pine, wood*] décapé.
IDIOMS **to tear sb off a ~**, **to tear a ~ off sb**○ enguirlander○ qn.
■ **strip down**: ¶ **~ down** se déshabiller; ¶ **~** [*sth*] **down**, **~ down** [*sth*] démonter [*gun, engine*]; défaire [*bed*]; décaper [*woodwork*].
■ **strip off**: ¶ **~ off** [*person*] se déshabiller; ¶ **~** [*sth*] **off**, **~ off** [*sth*] enlever [*paint, wallpaper, clothes*]; arracher [*leaves*].
strip: **~ cartoon** *n* bande *f* dessinée; **~ club** *n* boîte○ *f* de strip-tease.
stripe /straɪp/ *n* **1** (on fabric, wallpaper) rayure *f*; (on crockery) filet *m*; **2** (on animal) (isolated) rayure *f*; (one of many) zébrure *f*; **3** MIL galon *m*.
striped /straɪpt/ *adj* rayé; **blue ~** rayé de bleu, à rayures bleues.
strip: **~ light** *n* lampe *f* au néon; **~ lighting** *n* éclairage *m* au néon *m*.
stripper /'strɪpə(r)/ ▶ 1251| *n* strip-teaseur/-euse *m/f*.
strip-search /'strɪpsɜːtʃ/ I *n* fouille *f* corporelle.
II *vtr* faire subir une fouille corporelle à [*person*].
strip show *n* strip-tease *m*.
stripy /'straɪpɪ/ *adj* rayé, à rayures.
strive /straɪv/ *vi* (*prét* **strove**; *pp* **striven**) (try) s'efforcer; **to ~ for sth** rechercher qch.
strobe /strəʊb/ *n* (also **~ light**) lumière *f* stroboscopique; **~ lighting** éclairage *m* stroboscopique.
strode /strəʊd/ *prét* ▶ **stride** II.
stroke /strəʊk/ I *n* **1** (blow) GEN, SPORT coup *m*; **on the ~ of four** à quatre heures sonnantes; **2** FIG (touch) coup *m*; **at one** ou **at a single ~** d'un seul coup; **a ~ of luck** un coup de chance; **a ~ of genius** un trait de génie; **3** (single movement in swimming) mouvement *m* des bras; (particular style) nage *f*; **4** ART (mark of pen) trait *m*; (mark of brush) touche *f*; **5** (in punctuation) barre *f* oblique; **6** MED congestion *f* cérébrale; **7** (caress) caresse *f*; **to give sb/sth a ~** caresser qn/qch.
II *noun modifier* MED **~ victim**, **~ patient** personne *f* victime d'une congestion cérébrale.
III *vtr* **1** (caress) caresser; **2** SPORT (in rowing) **to ~ an eight** être le chef de nage d'un huit.
IDIOMS **not to do a ~ of work** ne rien faire; **to put sb off their ~** (upset timing) faire perdre le rythme à qn; (disconcert) faire perdre les pédales○ à qn.
stroll /strəʊl/ I *n* promenade *f*, tour *m*.
II *vi* **1** (also **~ about**, **~ around**) (walk) se promener; (aimlessly) flâner; **to ~ in** entrer sans se presser; **2**○ (also **~ home**) (win) gagner facilement.
stroller /'strəʊlə(r)/ *n* **1** (walker) promeneur/-euse *m/f*; (more aimless) flâneur/-euse *m/f*; **2** US (pushchair) poussette *f*.
strong /strɒŋ, US strɔːŋ/ *adj* **1** (powerful) [*arm, person, current, wind*] fort; [*army, swimmer, country, state*] puissant; **the workforce is 500 ~** la main-d'œuvre est forte de 500 personnes; **2** (sturdy) LIT solide; FIG [*bond*] profond; [*cast, candidate, team, alibi*]

bon/bonne; [*currency, market*] ferme; **to have a ~ stomach**○ FIG avoir l'estomac bien accroché○; **3** (concentrated) GEN fort; [*coffee*] serré; **4** (alcoholic) alcoolisé; **5** (noticeable) GEN fort; [*colour*] soutenu; [*rhythm*] cadencé; **6** (heartfelt) [*conviction*] intime; [*desire, feeling*] profond; [*believer, supporter*] acharné; [*opinion*] arrêté; [*criticism, opposition, reaction*] vif/vive; **I have a ~ feeling that she won't come** je suis pratiquement sûr qu'elle ne viendra pas; **in the ~est possible terms** sans détours; **~ language** mots *mpl* grossiers; **7** (resolute) [*ruler, leadership*] à poigne; [*action, measure, sanction*] sévère; **8** [*chance, possibility*] fort; **9** (good) **to be ~ on physics** être fort en physique; **he finished the race a ~ second** il a fini la course juste derrière le premier; **spelling is not my ~ point** l'orthographe n'est pas mon fort; **10** LING [*verb*] fort; [*syllable*] accentué.
IDIOMS **to be still going ~** se porter toujours très bien.

strong-arm /'strɒŋɑːm, US 'strɔːŋ-/ **I** *adj* brutal; **~ tactics** la manière forte.
II *vtr* **to ~ sb into doing** forcer qn à faire.

strong: **~box** *n* coffre-fort *m*; **~hold** *n* LIT forteresse *f*; FIG fief *m*.

strongly /'strɒŋlɪ, US 'strɔːŋlɪ/ *adv* **1** (with force) LIT [*blow*] fort; [*defend oneself*] vigoureusement; FIG [*criticize, attack, object, oppose, advise*] vivement; [*protest, deny*] énergiquement; [*suggest, support, defend, suspect*] fortement; [*believe*] fermement; **to feel ~ about sth** avoir des idées arrêtées sur qch; **~ held beliefs** des croyances fortement ancrées; **to be ~ in favour of/ against sth** être absolument pour/contre qch; **2** (solidly) solidement; **3 to smell ~** dégager une forte odeur; **~ flavoured** très relevé.

strongly-worded *adj* exprimé en termes très vifs.

strong: **~-minded** *adj* obstiné; **~room** *n* chambre *f* forte; **~-willed** *adj* obstiné.

stroppy○ /'strɒpɪ/ *adj* GB ronchon/-onne○.

strove /strəʊv/ *prét* ▶ **strive**.

struck /strʌk/ *prét, pp* ▶ **strike** III, IV.

structural /'strʌktʃərəl/ *adj* **1** [*problem, reform*] structurel/-elle; **2** PHYS, LING structural; **3** TECH [*defect*] de construction; **~ alterations** transformations *fpl*; **~ damage** dégâts *mpl* matériels.

structural: **~ engineer** ▶ **1251**] *n* ingénieur *m* des ponts et chaussées; **~ engineering** *n* génie *m* civil.

structurally /'strʌktʃərəlɪ/ *adv* GEN, BOT, PHYS structurellement; TECH du point de vue de la construction; **~ sound** de construction solide.

structure /'strʌktʃə(r)/ **I** *n* **1** (organization) structure *f*; **wage ~** échelle *f* des salaires; **career ~** plan *m* de carrière; **2** (building) construction *f*; (manner of construction) construction *f*.
II *vtr* structurer [*ideas, essay*]; organiser [*day*].

struggle /'strʌgl/ **I** *n* **1** (battle, fight) LIT, FIG lutte *f* (**over** au sujet de; **to do** pour faire); **to put up a** (**fierce**) **~** se défendre (avec acharnement); **2** (scuffle) rixe *f*; **3** (difficult task) **it was a ~** cela a été dur; **I find it a real ~ to do** ou **doing** il m'est très difficile de faire; **they had a ~ to do** ou **doing** ils ont eu du mal à faire.
II *vi* **1** LIT (put up a fight) se débattre; (tussle, scuffle) se battre; **to ~ free** se dégager; **2** FIG (try hard) lutter; (stronger) se démener; **to ~ with a problem/one's conscience** être aux prises avec un problème/sa conscience; **3** (have difficulty) éprouver des difficultés; **to ~ to keep up** avoir du mal à suivre; **4** (move with difficulty) **he ~d into/out of his jeans** a enfilé/ enlevé son jean avec difficulté; **to ~ to one's feet** se lever avec peine.
■ **struggle along, struggle on** LIT avancer à grand-peine; FIG persévérer.
■ **struggle back** revenir à grand-peine ou avec peine.
■ **struggle through**: ¶ **~ through** se sortir tant bien que mal; ¶ **~ through** [*sth*] se frayer péniblement un chemin dans [*snow, jungle, crowd*].

struggling /'strʌglɪŋ/ *adj* [*writer, artist*] qui essaie de percer.

strum /strʌm/ (*p prés etc* **-mm-**) **I** *vtr* (carelessly) gratter [*guitar, tune*]; (gently) jouer doucement (de) [*guitar*]; **to ~ a tune** jouer doucement un air.
II *vi* gratter (**on** sur); jouer doucement (**on** de).

strung /strʌŋ/ *prét, pp* ▶ **string** III.

strung out○ /ˌstrʌŋ 'aʊt/ *adj* (addicted) **to be ~ on** être accro○ à [*drug*]; **to be ~** (from drugs) être en état de manque; GEN être au bout du rouleau○.

strung up○ /ˌstrʌŋ 'ʌp/ *adj* nerveux/-euse.

strut /strʌt/ **I** *n* (support) montant *m*.
II *vi* (also **~ about**) (*p prés etc* **-tt-**) se pavaner.

stub /stʌb/ **I** *n* GEN bout *m*; (of cheque, ticket) talon *m*.
II *vtr* (*p prés etc* **-bb-**) **to ~ one's toe** se cogner l'orteil.
■ **stub out**: **~ [sth] out, ~ out [sth]** écraser.

stubble /'stʌbl/ *n* (straw) chaume *m*; (beard) barbe *f* de plusieurs jours.

stubbly /'stʌblɪ/ *adj* [*chin*] non rasé.

stubborn /'stʌbən/ *adj* [*person, animal, government*] entêté; [*behaviour*] obstiné; [*independence*] tenace; [*resistance, refusal*] opiniâtre; [*stain, illness*] rebelle.

stubbornly /'stʌbənlɪ/ *adv* [*refuse, deny, resist*] obstinément; [*behave, act*] de manière têtue.

stubby /'stʌbɪ/ *adj* [*finger, tail*] court; [*person*] trapu.

stucco /'stʌkəʊ/ *n* (*pl* **~s** ou **~es**) (outside plaster-work) enduit *m*; (decorative work) stuc *m*.

stuck /stʌk/ **I** *prét, pp* ▶ **stick** III, IV.
II *adj* **1** (caught) coincé; **to get ~ in mud** s'enliser dans la boue; **to be ~ with**○ se farcir [*task*]; ne pas pouvoir se débarrasser de [*object, person*]; **2**○ (stumped) **to be ~** sécher○; **3** (in a fix) **to be ~** être coincé; **to be ~ for cash** ne pas avoir d'argent; **to be ~ for something to say** ne pas savoir quoi dire.
IDIOMS **to be ~ on sb**○ avoir qn dans la peau○.

stuck-up○ /ˌstʌk'ʌp/ *adj* bêcheur/-euse○.

stud /stʌd/ *n* **1** (on jacket, tyre) clou *m*; (on door) clou *m* à grosse tête; (earring) clou *m* d'oreilles; (on shoe) clou *m*; (on boot) crampon *m*; (in road) clou *m* à catadioptre; (wheel bolt) goujon *m* de roue; **2** (horse farm) haras *m*; **he's at ~** il est à la reproduction.

studded /'stʌdɪd/ *adj* **1** LIT [*jacket, tyre*] garni de clous; [*door, beam*] clouté; **~ boots, ~ shoes** SPORT chaussures *fpl* à crampons; **2 ~ with** GEN parsemé de; constellé de [*diamonds, jewels*].

student /'stjuːdnt, US 'stuː-/ **I** *n* élève *mf*; UNIV étudiant/-e *mf*; **a ~ of history** une personne qui s'intéresse à l'histoire.
II *noun modifier* UNIV [*life, unrest*] étudiant.

student: **~ driver** *n* US *personne qui apprend à conduire*; **~ grant** *n* UNIV bourse *f* d'études; **~ ID card** *n* US UNIV carte *f* d'étudiant; **~ nurse** *n* élève *mf* infirmier/-ière; **~ teacher** *n* enseignant/-e *m/f* stagiaire; **~ union** *n* (union) syndicat *m* étudiant; (building) maison *f* des étudiants.

studhorse *n* étalon *m*.

studied /'stʌdɪd/ *adj* étudié.

studio /'stjuːdɪəʊ, US 'stuː-/ *n* (*pl* **~s**) **1** GEN studio *m*; (of painter) atelier *m*; **2** CIN société *f* de production.

studio: **~ audience** *n* public *m* de studio; **~ portrait** *n* PHOT portrait *m* d'art; **~ theatre** GB, **~ theater** US *n* théâtre *m* de poche.

studious /'stjuːdɪəs, US 'stuː-/ *adj* (hardworking) studieux/-ieuse; (deliberate) étudié.

stud mare *n* (jument *f*) poulinière *f*.

study /'stʌdɪ/ **I** *n* GEN, ART, MUS étude *f*; (room) bureau *m*; **a ~ in bigotry** un modèle de bigoterie.
II studies *npl* études *fpl*; **computer studies** informatique *f*; **social studies** sciences *fpl* humaines.
III *noun modifier* [*leave, period, group, visit*] d'étude; **~ tour** ou **trip** voyage *m* d'études.
IV *vtr* (all contexts) étudier; **to ~ to be a teacher** faire des études pour être enseignant.
V *vi* (revise) réviser; (be educated) faire ses études (**under sb** avec qn).
IDIOMS **his face was a ~!** il fallait voir sa tête!

study aid *n* outil *m* pédagogique (destiné à l'élève).

study hall n US **1** (room) salle f d'étude; **2** (period) heure f d'étude.

stuff /stʌf/ I n ¢ **1** (unnamed substance) truc○ m; **what's that ~ in the bottle?** qu'est-ce que c'est dans la bouteille?; **that cement ~** cette espèce de ciment; **she loves the ~** elle adore ça; **expensive ~, caviar** ça coûte cher, le caviar; **we've sold lots of the ~** nous en avons vendu beaucoup; **it's strong ~** c'est costaud○; **2**○ (unnamed objects) trucs○ mpl; (implying disorder) bazar○ m; (belongings) affaires fpl; **3**○ (content of speech, book, film etc) **who wrote this ~?** GEN qui a écrit ça?; PÉJ qui a écrit cette chose?; **there's some good ~ in this article** il y a de bonnes choses dans cet article; **have you read much of her ~?** as-tu lu beaucoup de ce qu'elle a écrit?; **it's romantic ~** c'est romantique; **do you believe all that ~ about his private life?** tu crois à tout ce qu'on dit sur sa vie privée?; **4** (fabric) LIT étoffe f; FIG essence f; **to be made of somewhat coarser ~** être plus grossier de nature.
II vtr **1** (fill, pack) garnir, rembourrer (**with** de); (implying haste) bourrer (**with** de); (block up) boucher (**with** avec); **2** (pack in) fourrer○; **to ~ sth up one's jumper** cacher qch sous son pull; **to ~ food into one's mouth** se bâfrer○; **3** CULIN farcir; **4** [taxidermist] empailler.
III **stuffed** pp adj CULIN farci; [toy animal] en peluche; [bird, fox] empaillé.
IDIOMS **a bit of ~**○ PÉJ une gonzesse○ PÉJ; **to do one's ~**○ faire ce qu'on a à faire; **to know one's ~**○ connaître son affaire○; **that's the ~**○! c'est bon!
■ **stuff up**; **~ [sth] up, ~ up [sth]** boucher.

stuffed shirt○ n PÉJ **to be a ~** être pompeux et suffisant.

stuffiness /'stʌfɪnɪs/ n **1** (airlessness) atmosphère f étouffante; **2** (staidness) raideur f.

stuffing /'stʌfɪŋ/ n **1** CULIN farce f; **2** (of furniture, pillow) rembourrage m; (of stuffed animal) paille f.
IDIOMS **to knock the ~ out of sb**○ [illness] mettre qn à plat○; [defeat, loss, event] démoraliser qn.

stuffy /'stʌfɪ/ adj **1** (airless) étouffant; **2** (staid) guindé; **3** [nose] bouché.

stultifying /'stʌltɪfaɪŋ/ adj abrutissant.

stumble /'stʌmbl/ I n faux pas m.
II vi **1** (trip) trébucher (**on**, **on** sur); **2** (stagger) **to ~ in/out/off** entrer/sortir/s'en aller en chancelant; **3** (in speech) hésiter; **to ~ over** buter sur.
■ **stumble across**: **~ across [sth]** FIG tomber par hasard sur.
■ **stumble on**: **~ on [sth], ~ upon [sth]** FIG tomber par hasard sur.

stumbling block /'stʌmblɪŋ blɒk/ n obstacle m.

stump /stʌmp/ I n (of tree) souche f; (of candle, pencil, tooth) bout m; (limb) moignon m; (in cricket) piquet m.
II vtr **1**○ (perplex) déconcerter; **to be ~ed by sth** être en peine d'expliquer qch; **to be ~ed for an answer** ne pas trouver de réponse; **I'm ~ed** (in quiz) je sèche○; (nonplussed) aucune idée; **2** US POL faire une tournée électorale dans [state].
III vi **1** (stamp) **to ~ in/out** entrer/sortir d'un air mécontent; **2** US POL faire une tournée électorale.
■ **stump up** GB débourser (**for** pour).

stumpy /'stʌmpɪ/ adj [person, legs] courtaud.

stun /stʌn/ vtr (p prés etc **-nn-**) LIT assommer; FIG stupéfier.

stung /stʌŋ/ prét, pp ▶ **sting** II, III.

stunned /stʌnd/ adj **1** (dazed) assommé; **2** (amazed) [person] stupéfait; [silence] figé.

stunning /'stʌnɪŋ/ adj **1** (beautiful) sensationnel/-elle; **2** (amazing) stupéfiant; **3** [blow] étourdissant.

stunt /stʌnt/ I n **1** (for attention) coup m organisé, truc○ m; **2** CIN, TV (with risk) cascade f; **aerial ~s** acrobaties fpl aériennes; **3**○ US numéro○ m.
II vtr empêcher [development]; BOT étioler [plant].

stunted /'stʌntɪd/ adj LIT [tree, plant] rabougri; [body] chétif/-ive; FIG retardé.

stunt: **~man** ▶ 1251| n cascadeur m; **~ pilot** ▶ 1251| n pilote m de voltige.

stupefaction /ˌstjuːpɪˈfækʃn/ n (all contexts) stupeur f.

stupefy /'stjuːpɪfaɪ, US 'stuː-/ vtr **1** (astonish) stupéfier; **2** (make torpid) abrutir.

stupefying /'stjuːpɪfaɪɪŋ, US 'stuː-/ adj stupéfiant.

stupendous /stjuːˈpendəs, US stuː-/ adj [achievement, idea, film, size] prodigieux/-ieuse; [building, view] fantastique; [loss, folly] incroyable.

stupid /'stjuːpɪd, US 'stuː-/ adj **1** (unintelligent) stupide; **it is ~ of you to do** c'est idiot de ta part de faire; **I've done something ~** j'ai fait une bêtise; **the ~ car won't start!** cette idiote de voiture ne veut pas démarrer!; **2** (in a stupor) abruti (**with** de).

stupidity /stjuːˈpɪdəti, US stuː-/ n (foolishness) bêtise f; (lack of intelligence) stupidité f.

stupidly /'stjuːpɪdlɪ, US stuː-/ adv bêtement.

stupor /'stjuːpə(r), US 'stuː-/ n stupeur f; **to be in a ~** être à moitié hébété; **in a drunken ~** hébété par l'alcool.

sturdy /'stɜːdɪ/ adj robuste.

stutter /'stʌtə(r)/ I n bégaiement m; **to have a ~** bégayer.
II vtr, vi bégayer.

St Valentine's Day n la Saint-Valentin.

sty /staɪ/ n **1** (for pigs) porcherie f; **2** (also **stye**) MED orgelet m.

style /staɪl/ I n **1** (manner) style m ALSO LITERAT; **2** (elegance) classe f; **to bring a touch of ~ to** ajouter de la classe à; **to marry in ~** se marier en grande pompe; **to live in ~** mener grand train; **to travel in ~** voyager princièrement; **she likes to do things in ~** elle aime faire les choses en grand; **3** (design) (of car, clothing) modèle m; (of house) type m; **4** (fashion) mode f; (hairstyle) coupe f; **5** (approach) genre m; **I don't like your ~** je n'aime pas ton genre.
II **-style** combining form **Californian-~** de style californien; **Italian-~** à l'italienne.
III vtr **1** (design) concevoir [car, kitchen, building]; créer [collection, dress]; **2** couper [hair].
IV v refl **to ~ oneself sth** se donner le titre de qch.

styling /'staɪlɪŋ/ I n **1** (design) conception f; **2** (contours) ligne f; **3** (in hairdressing) coupe f.
II noun modifier [gel, mousse, product] fixant; [equipment] de coiffure; **~ brush** brosse f ronde.

stylish /'staɪlɪʃ/ adj **1** (smart) [car, coat, flat] beau/belle; [person] élégant; [resort, restaurant] chic inv; **2** (accomplished) [director, performance, player] de grande classe; [thriller, writer] sophistiqué.

stylist /'staɪlɪst/ ▶ 1251| n **1** (hairdresser) coiffeur/-euse m/f; **2** (writer) styliste m/f; **3** (fashion designer) styliste m/f; **4** COMM, IND concepteur/-trice m/f.

stylistic /staɪˈlɪstɪk/ adj COMM stylistique; **~ device** LITERAT procédé m stylistique.

stylized○ /'staɪlaɪzd/ adj (non-realist) stylisé.

stylus /'staɪləs/ n (pl **-li** ou **-luses**) AUDIO pointe f de lecture.

stymied○ /'staɪmɪd/ adj (thwarted) coincé.

suave /swɑːv/ adj GEN onctueux/-euse; [person] mielleux/-euse.

sub /sʌb/ n **1** SPORT abrév = **substitute**; **2** NAUT abrév = **submarine**; **3** abrév = **subscription**; **4** US abrév = **substitute teacher**.

subaqua /ˌsʌbˈækwə/ adj [club] de plongée.

subcommittee /'sʌbkəmɪtɪ/ n sous-comité m.

subconscious /ˌsʌbˈkɒnʃəs/ I n **the ~** le subconscient.
II adj GEN inconscient; PSYCH subconscient.

subconsciously /ˌsʌbˈkɒnʃəslɪ/ adv GEN inconsciemment; PSYCH de façon subconsciente.

subcontinent /ˌsʌbˈkɒntɪnənt/ n sous-continent m.

subcontract /ˌsʌbkənˈtrækt/ vtr sous-traiter (**to**, **out to** à).

subcontracting /ˌsʌbkənˈtræktɪŋ/ n sous-traitance f.

subcontractor /ˌsʌbkənˈtræktə(r)/ ▶ 1251| n sous-traitant m.

subdivide /ˌsʌbdɪ'vaɪd/ **I** *vtr* subdiviser [*house, site*]. **II** *vi* se subdiviser.

subdue /səb'dju:, US -'du:/ *vtr* soumettre [*people, nation*]; mater [*rebellion*]; contenir [*emotion*].

subdued /səb'dju:d, US -'du:d/ *adj* [*person, mood*] silencieux/-ieuse; [*voice*] terne; [*excitement, reaction*] contenu; [*lighting*] tamisé; [*colour*] atténué.

subedit /ˌsʌb'edɪt/ *vtr* GB corriger [*text*].

subheading /'sʌbhedɪŋ/ *n* (in text) sous-titre *m*.

subhuman /ˌsʌb'hju:mən/ *adj* [*behaviour*] monstrueux/-euse.

subject I /'sʌbdʒɪkt/ *n* **1** (topic) sujet *m* also Art, PHOT, LING; **to change** ou **drop the ~** parler d'autre chose; **to raise a ~** soulever une question; **while we're on the ~ of bonuses**... pendant que nous en sommes aux primes...; **2** (at school, college) matière *f*; (for research, study) sujet *m*; **her ~ is genetics** elle est spécialisée en génétique; **3** (focus) objet *m*; **to be the ~ of an inquiry** faire l'objet d'une enquête; **4** (citizen) sujet/-ette *m/f*. **II** /'sʌbdʒɪkt/ *adj* **1** (subservient) asservi; **to be ~ to** être soumis à [*law, rule*]; **2** (liable) **to be ~ to** être sujet/-ette à [*flooding, fits*]; être passible de [*tax*]; **prices are ~ to increases** les prix peuvent subir des augmentations; **flights are ~ to delay** les vols sont susceptibles d'être en retard; **3** (dependent) **to be ~ to** dépendre de [*approval*]; **'~ to alteration** 'sous réserve de modification'; **'~ to availability'** (of flights, tickets) 'dans la limite des places disponibles'; (of goods) 'dans la limite des stocks disponibles'. **III** /səb'dʒekt/ *vtr* (expose) **to ~ sb to sth** faire subir qch à qn; **to be ~ed** devoir supporter [*noise*]; faire l'objet de [*attacks*]; être soumis à [*torture*]; **to ~ sth to heat** exposer qch à la chaleur.

subject: **~ heading** *n* sujet *m*; **~ index** *n* (in book) index *m* des sujets traités; (in library) fichier *m* par sujets.

subjection /səb'dʒekʃn/ *n* sujétion *f* (**to** à).

subjective /səb'dʒektɪv/ *adj* subjectif/-ive.

subject matter *n* sujet *m*.

sub judice /ˌsʌb 'dʒu:dɪsɪ, sʊb 'ju:dɪkeɪ/ *adj* devant les tribunaux.

subjugate /'sʌbdʒʊɡeɪt/ *vtr* subjuguer [*country, people*]; dompter [*desire*]; soumettre [*will*].

subjunctive /səb'dʒʌŋktɪv/ **I** *n* subjonctif *m*. **II** *adj* [*form, tense*] du subjonctif; [*mood*] subjonctif/-ive.

sublet /'sʌblet, ˌsʌb'let/ *vtr, vi* (*p prés* **-tt-**; *prét, pp -let*) sous-louer.

sublime /sə'blaɪm/ **I** *n* **the ~** le sublime. **II** *adj* **1** (great) sublime; **2** [*indifference*] suprême.

sublimely /sə'blaɪmlɪ/ *adv* **1** [*play, perform, sing*] d'une façon sublime; **2** [*indifferent*] suprêmement.

subliminal /səb'lɪmɪnl/ *adj* subliminal.

submachine gun /ˌsʌbmə'ʃi:n/ *n* mitraillette *f*.

submarine /ˌsʌbmə'ri:n, US 'sʌb-/ **I** *n* NAUT sous-marin *m*. **II** *adj* [*plant, life, cable*] sous-marin.

submerge /səb'mɜ:dʒ/ **I** *vtr* [*sea, flood*] submerger; [*person*] immerger (**in** dans); **to remain ~d** [*submarine*] rester en plongée. **II submerged** *pp adj* LIT, FIG submergé. **III** *v refl* **to ~ oneself in** se plonger dans [*work*].

submission /səb'mɪʃn/ *n* **1** (obedience, subjection) soumission *f* (**to** à) ALSO SPORT; **to frighten sb into ~** réduire qn par la peur; **2** (of application etc) soumission *f* (**to** à); **3** (report) rapport *m*; **4** JUR conclusions *fpl*; **to make a ~ that** suggérer que.

submissive /səb'mɪsɪv/ *adj* GEN soumis; [*behaviour*] docile.

submit /səb'mɪt/ (*p prés etc* **-tt-**) **I** *vtr* **1** soumettre [*report, accounts, plan, script*] (**to** à); présenter [*bill, application, resignation*] (**to** à); déposer [*claim, estimate*] (**to** à); **2** (propose) **to ~ that** suggérer que. **II** *vi* se soumettre; **to ~ to** subir [*indignity, injustice*]; céder à [*will, demand, discipline*]; JUR se soumettre à [*decision*].

subnormal /ˌsʌb'nɔ:ml/ *adj* **1** PEJ [*person*] arriéré; **2** [*temperature*] au-dessous de la normale.

subordinate I /sə'bɔ:dɪnət, US -dənət/ *n* subalterne *mf*. **II** /sə'bɔ:dɪnət/ *adj* [*officer, rank, position*] subalterne; [*issue, matter, question*] secondaire (**to** par rapport à). **III** /sə'bɔ:dɪneɪt/ *vtr* GEN, LING subordonner (**to** à).

subordinate clause *n* LING proposition *f* subordonnée.

subpoena /sə'pi:nə/ **I** *n* assignation *f* à comparaître. **II** *vtr* assigner [qn] à comparaître.

subroutine /'sʌbru:ti:n/ *n* sous-programme *m*.

subscribe /səb'skraɪb/ *vi* **1 to ~ to** (agree with) partager [*view, values*]; **2** (be subscriber) s'abonner; **to ~ to** être abonné à [*magazine etc*]; **3 to ~ to** donner (de l'argent) à [*charity, fund*].

subscriber /səb'skraɪbə(r)/ *n* **1** COMM (to periodical etc) abonné/-e *m/f* (**to** de); **2** TELECOM abonné/-e *m/f* (du téléphone); **3** FIN souscripteur *m*.

subscription /səb'skrɪpʃn/ *n* **1** (magazine) abonnement *m* (**to** à); **2** GB (to association, scheme) cotisation *f* (**to** à); **3** (to fund) don *m* (**to** à).

subscription rate *n* tarif *m* d'abonnement.

subsection /'sʌbsekʃn/ *n* JUR alinéa *m*; GEN paragraphe *m*.

subsequent /'sʌbsɪkwənt/ *adj* (in past) ultérieur; (in future) à venir.

subsequently /'sʌbsɪkwəntlɪ/ *adv* par la suite.

subservient /səb'sɜ:vɪənt/ *adj* **1** PEJ servile PEJ (**to** envers); **2** (less important) subordonné (**to** à).

subset /'sʌbset/ *n* MATH sous-ensemble *m*.

subside /səb'saɪd/ *vi* **1** (die down) [*storm, wind, applause, noise*] s'apaiser; [*emotion*] se calmer; [*laughter, fever, excitement*] retomber; [*threat*] diminuer; [*flames*] reculer; **2** (sink) [*water*] se retirer; [*building, land*] s'affaisser; **3** (sink down) [*person*] s'effondrer.

subsidence /səb'saɪdns, 'sʌbsɪdns/ *n* affaissement *m*.

subsidiary /səb'sɪdɪərɪ, US -dɪerɪ/ **I** *n* (also **~ company**) filiale *f*. **II** *adj* (secondary) secondaire (**to** par rapport à).

subsidize /'sʌbsɪdaɪz/ *vtr* subventionner.

subsidy /'sʌbsɪdɪ/ *n* subvention *f* (**to, for** à).

subsist /səb'sɪst/ *vi* subsister.

subsistence /səb'sɪstəns/ *n* subsistance *f*.

subsistence: **~ farming** *n* agriculture *f* de subsistance; **~ level** *n* niveau *m* minimum pour vivre; **~ wage** *n* minimum *m* vital de misère.

substance /'sʌbstəns/ *n* **1** (matter) substance *f*; **2** (of argument, talks) essentiel *m*; (of book) substance *f*; **3** (of argument) poids *m*; (of claim) fondement *m*; (of play, book) fond *m*; **there is no ~ to the allegations** les allégations sont dénuées de fondement; **to lend ~ to** donner du crédit à [*rumour*]; **something of ~** quelque chose d'important.

substance abuse *n* abus *m* de substances toxiques.

substandard /ˌsʌb'stændəd/ *adj* [*goods, housing*] de qualité inférieure; [*essay, performance*] insuffisant; [*workmanship*] défectueux/-euse.

substantial /səb'stænʃl/ *adj* **1** (in amount) [*sum, quantity*] important; [*imports, loss*] considérable; [*majority, number*] appréciable; [*meal*] substantiel/-ielle; **2** (in degree) [*change, difference, fall, impact, risk, damage*] considérable; [*role*] important; **3** (solid) LIT, FIG solide; **4** (wealthy) [*business*] financièrement solide.

substantially /səb'stænʃəlɪ/ *adv* **1** (considerably) GEN considérablement; [*higher, lower, better, less*] nettement; **2** (mainly) en grande partie.

substantiate /səb'stænʃɪeɪt/ *vtr* justifier [*allegation*]; appuyer [qch] par des preuves [*statement*].

substitute /'sʌbstɪtju:t, US -tu:t/ **I** *n* **1** (person) GEN, SPORT remplaçant/-e *m/f*; **2** (product, substance) produit *m* de substitution; **coffee ~** succédané *m* de café; **sugar ~** édulcorant *m* de synthèse; **there is no ~ for a good education** rien ne remplace une bonne éducation; **there is no ~ for real leather** rien ne vaut le cuir véritable.

II *noun modifier* [*machine, device*] de remplacement; [*family, parent*] adoptif/-ive; SPORT [*player*] de remplacement.
III *vtr* substituer (**for** à).
IV *vi* **to ~ for sb/sth** remplacer qn/qch.
substitute: **~'s bench** *n* SPORT banc *m* de touche; **~ teacher** *n* SCH remplaçant/-e *m/f*.
substitution /ˌsʌbstɪˈtjuːʃn, US -ˈtuː-/ *n* substitution *f* (**for** à).
substratum /ˌsʌbˈstrɑːtəm, US ˈsʌbstreɪtəm/ *n* (*pl* **-strata**) GEN (basis) fond *m*; (subsoil) sous-sol *m*; (bedrock) substratum *m*; SOCIOL couche *f*.
subterranean /ˌsʌbtəˈreɪnɪən/ *adj* souterrain.
subtext /ˈsʌbtekst/ *n* LITERAT thème *m* sous-jacent; FIG message *m* sous-jacent.
subtitle /ˈsʌbtaɪtl/ I *n* sous-titre *m*.
II *vtr* sous-titrer.
subtitling /ˈsʌbtaɪtlɪŋ/ *n* sous-titrage *m*.
subtle /ˈsʌtl/ *adj* **1** (barely perceptible) GEN subtil; [*change*] imperceptible; **2** (finely tuned) [*argument, analysis, allusion*] subtil; [*humour*] très fin; [*performance, idea, strategy*] habile; [*hint*] voilé; **3** (perceptive) [*analyst*] perspicace; [*person, mind*] subtil; **4** (delicate) GEN subtil; [*lighting*] tamisé.
subtlety /ˈsʌtltɪ/ *n* **1** GEN subtilité *f*; **2** (of film, book, music, style) complexité *f*; (of flavour) délicatesse *f*.
subtly /ˈsʌtlɪ/ *adv* [*change*] imperceptiblement; [*different*] légèrement; [*argue*] avec subtilité; [*analyse, act*] avec finesse; [*flavoured, coloured*] délicatement.
subtotal /ˈsʌbtəʊtl/ *n* sous-total *m*.
subtract /səbˈtrækt/ I *vtr* MATH soustraire (**from** de).
II *vi* faire des soustractions.
subtraction /səbˈtrækʃn/ *n* soustraction *f*.
suburb /ˈsʌbɜːb/ I *n* GEN banlieue *f*; **inner ~** faubourg *m*.
II **suburbs** *npl* **the ~s** la banlieue; **the outer ~s** la grande banlieue.
suburban /səˈbɜːbən/ *adj* **1** [*street, shop, train*] de banlieue; [*development*] suburbain; US [*shopping mall*] à l'extérieur de la ville; **~ sprawl** (phenomenon) développement *m* des banlieues; **2** PÉJ [*outlook*] étroit; [*values*] de petit-bourgeois.
suburbanite /səˈbɜːbənaɪt/ *n* PÉJ banlieusard/-e *m/f*.
suburbia /səˈbɜːbɪə/ *n* ¢ banlieue *f*.
subvention /səbˈvenʃn/ *n* **1** C (subsidy) subvention *f*; **2** ¢ (financing) subventions *fpl*.
subversion /səˈbɜːʃn, US -ˈbɜːrʒn/ *n* subversion *f*.
subversive /səbˈvɜːsɪv/ I *n* (person) élément *m* subversif.
II *adj* (all contexts) subversif/-ive.
subvert /səbˈvɜːt/ *vtr* déstabiliser [*government*]; corrompre [*agent*]; faire échouer [*negotiations*].
subway /ˈsʌbweɪ/ I *n* **1** GB (for pedestrians) passage *m* souterrain; **2** US (underground railway) métro *m*.
II *noun modifier* US [*station*] de métro; [*train*] souterrain.
sub-zero /ˌsʌbˈzɪərəʊ/ *adj* inférieur à zéro.
succeed /səkˈsiːd/ I *vtr* succéder à; **she ~ed him as president** elle lui a succédé à la présidence.
II *vi* **1** (achieve success) réussir; **to ~ in doing** réussir à faire; **2** (accede) succéder; **to ~ to** succéder à.
succeeding /səkˈsiːdɪŋ/ *adj* (in past) suivant; (in future) à venir; **with each ~ year** d'année en année.
success /səkˈses/ *n* **1** succès *m*, réussite *f*; **to meet with ~** avoir du succès; **to make a ~ of** GEN réussir; faire un succès de [*business, venture*]; **sb's ~ in** le succès de qn à [*exam, election*]; **his ~ in overcoming his problems** la façon dont il a surmonté ses difficultés; **~ with women** succès auprès des femmes; **2** (person, thing that succeeds) succès *m*; **to be a ~ with** avoir du succès auprès de.
successful /səkˈsesfl/ *adj* **1** (effective) [*attempt, operation, partnership*] réussi; [*plan, campaign*] couronné de succès; [*treatment, policy*] efficace; **to be ~ in** ou **at doing** réussir à faire; **2** [*film, writer*] (profitable) à succès; (well regarded) apprécié; [*businessman, company*]

prospère; [*career*] brillant; **to be ~** réussir; **3** [*candidate, outcome*] heureux/-euse; [*applicant*] retenu; [*team, contestant*] victorieux/-ieuse; **her application was not ~** sa candidature n'a pas été retenue.
successfully /səkˈsesfəlɪ/ *adv* avec succès.
succession /səkˈseʃn/ *n* **1** (sequence) série *f*; **in ~** de suite; **in close** ou **quick ~** coup sur coup; **2** (inheriting) succession *f* (**to** à); (descent) héritiers *mpl*.
successive /səkˈsesɪv/ *adj* GEN successif/-ive; [*day, week, year*] consécutif/-ive; **with each ~ disaster…** à chaque nouvelle catastrophe…
successor /səkˈsesə(r)/ *n* **1** (person) successeur *m* (**of** ou **to sb** de qn; **to sth** à qch); **to be sb's ~ as** succéder à qn en tant que; **2** (invention, concept) remplaçant/-e *m/f*.
success: **~ rate** *n* taux *m* de réussite; **~ story** *n* réussite *f*.
succinct /səkˈsɪŋkt/ *adj* GEN succinct; [*person*] concis.
succour GB, **succor** US /ˈsʌkə(r)/ *n* secours *m*.
succulent /ˈsʌkjʊlənt/ I *n* plante *f* grasse.
II *adj* GEN, BOT succulent.
succumb /səˈkʌm/ *vi* (all contexts) succomber (**to** à).
such /sʌtʃ/ I *pron* (this) **~ is life** c'est la vie; **she's a good singer and recognized as ~** c'est une bonne chanteuse et elle est reconnue comme telle.
II *det* **1** (of kind previously mentioned) (replicated) tel/telle; (similar) pareil/-eille; (of similar sort) de ce type (*after n*); **~ a situation** une telle situation; **in ~ a situation** dans une situation pareille; **and other ~ arguments** et autres arguments de ce type; **a mouse or some ~ animal** une souris ou un animal semblable; **there was some ~ case last year** il s'est produit la même chose l'année dernière; **there's no ~ person** il/elle n'existe pas; **you'll do no ~ thing!** il n'en est pas question!; **2** (of specific kind) **to be ~ that** être tel/telle que; **his movements were ~ as to arouse suspicion** il se conduisait de telle façon qu'il éveillait les soupçons; **in ~ a way that** d'une telle façon que; **3** (any possible) **~ money as I have** le peu d'argent ou tout l'argent que j'ai; **until ~ time as** jusqu'à ce que; **4** (so great) tel/telle; **~ was his admiration that** son admiration était telle que; **5** IRON (of such small worth, quantity) **we picked up the apples, ~ as there were** nous avons ramassé les rares pommes qu'il y avait par terre.
III *adv* **1** (to a great degree) (with adjectives) si, tellement; (with nouns) tel/telle; **~ a nice boy!** un garçon si gentil!; **~ good quality as this** une telle qualité; **it was ~ (a lot of) fun** on s'est tellement amusé; **~ a lot of problems** tant de problèmes; **there were (ever°) ~ a lot of people** il y avait beaucoup de monde.
IV **such as** *det phr, conj phr* comme, tel/telle que; **~ a house as this, a house ~ as this** une maison comme celle-ci; **a person ~ as her** une personne comme elle; **~ as?** (as response) comme quoi par exemple?; **there are no ~ things as giants** les géants n'existent pas; **have you ~ a thing as a screwdriver?** auriez-vous un tournevis par hasard?
such and such *det* tel/telle; **on ~ a topic** sur tel ou tel sujet.
suchlike /ˈsʌtʃlaɪk/ I *pron* **and ~** (of people) et autres; **lions, tigers and ~** les lions, les tigres et autres fauves.
II *adj* de ce type.
suck /sʌk/ I *n* **to give sth a ~** sucer qch; **to have a ~ of sth** goûter à qch (en suçant).
II *vtr* **1** (drink in) aspirer [*liquid, air*] (**through** avec); (extract) sucer (**from** de); **to ~ sb dry** FIG (of affection) vampiriser qn; (of money) pomper° qn jusqu'au dernier sou; **2** (have in mouth) GEN sucer; [*baby*] téter; **3** [*current, wind, mud*] entraîner; **to be ~ed down** ou **under** être entraîné au fond; **to get ~ed into** FIG être entraîné dans.
III *vi* [*baby*] téter; **to ~ on** tirer sur [*pipe*].
IV **sucking** *pres p adj* [*noise*] de succion.
■ **suck in**: **~ in** [*sth*], **~** [*sth*] **in** [*machine*] aspirer;

to ~ **in one's cheeks** creuser les joues; **to ~ in one's stomach** rentrer l'estomac.
■ **suck out**: ~ [sth] out, ~ out [sth] aspirer [*air, liquid, dirt*] (**from** de); sucer [*poison, blood*] (**from** de).
■ **suck up**: ¶ ~ up○ faire de la lèche○; **to ~ up to sb** cirer les pompes à qn○; ¶ ~ [sth] up, ~ up [sth] pomper [*liquid*]; aspirer [*dirt*].

sucker /'sʌkə(r)/ n **1**○ (dupe) bonne poire○ f; **he's a ~ for compliments** les compliments le font craquer○; **2** BOT surgeon m; **3** (pad) ventouse f.

sucking pig /'sʌkɪŋ/ n cochon m de lait.

sucrose /'suːkrəʊz, -rəʊs/ n saccharose f.

suction /'sʌkʃn/ n succion f; **by ~** par succion.

suction: ~ **pad** n ventouse f; ~ **pump** n pompe f aspirante.

Sudan /suːˈdɑːn/ ▶ 840⟩ pr n (also **the ~**) Soudan m.

sudden /'sʌdn/ adj [*impulse, death*] soudain; [*movement*] brusque; **all of a ~** tout à coup; **it was all very ~** ça s'est passé très vite.

sudden: ~ **death play-off** n GB SPORT *penalties pour départager deux équipes*; ~ **infant death syndrome**, **SIDS** n MED mort f subite du nourrisson.

suddenly /'sʌdnlɪ/ adv [*die, grow pale*] subitement; [*happen*] tout à coup.

suddenness /'sʌdnnɪs/ n GEN soudaineté f; (of death, illness) caractère m subit.

suds /sʌdz/ npl (also **soap ~**) (foam) mousse f (de savon); (soapy water) eau f savonneuse.

sue /suː, sjuː/ I vtr JUR intenter un procès à; **to ~ sb for divorce** demander le divorce à qn; **to ~ sb for damages** réclamer à qn des dommages-intérêts.
II vi JUR intenter un procès.

suede /sweɪd/ I n daim m; imitation ~ suédine f.
II noun modifier [*shoe, glove*] en daim.

suet /'suːɪt, 'sjuːɪt/ n graisse f de rognon de bœuf.

suffer /'sʌfə(r)/ I vtr **1** (undergo) GEN subir; souffrir de [*hunger*]; **she ~ed a great deal of pain** elle a beaucoup souffert; **he ~ed a severe neck injury** il a été gravement blessé au cou; **to ~ a heart attack** avoir une crise cardiaque; **the region has ~ed severe job losses** la région a enregistré d'importantes pertes d'emplois; **2** (tolerate) supporter.
II vi **1** (with illness) **to ~ from** GEN souffrir de; avoir [*headache, cold*]; **to ~ from depression** être dépressif/-ive; **2** (experience pain) souffrir; **you'll ~ for it later** vous le regretterez plus tard; **3** (do badly) [*company, profits, popularity*] souffrir; [*health, quality, work*] s'en ressentir; **the project ~s from a lack of funds** le problème du projet, c'est qu'il est insuffisamment financé.

sufferance /'sʌfərəns/ n **I'm only here on ~** je suis tout juste toléré ici.

sufferer /'sʌfərə(r)/ n victime f; **leukemia ~s** les leucémiques mpl.

suffering /'sʌfərɪŋ/ I n ₵ souffrances fpl (**of** de).
II adj souffrant.

suffice /səˈfaɪs/ SOUT I vtr suffire à.
II vi suffire.

sufficient /səˈfɪʃnt/ adj suffisamment, assez de; **a ~ amount** une quantité suffisante; **to be ~** suffire; **to be quite ~** suffire largement; **to be ~ for sb to do** suffire à qn pour faire.

sufficiently /səˈfɪʃntlɪ/ adv suffisamment, assez.

suffix /'sʌfɪks/ n suffixe m.

suffocate /'sʌfəkeɪt/ I vtr [*smoke, fumes*] asphyxier; [*person, pillow, rage, anger*] étouffer.
II vi **1** LIT (by smoke, fumes) [*crowd*] être asphyxié; (by pillow) être étouffé; **2** FIG suffoquer (**with** de).

suffocating /'sʌfəkeɪtɪŋ/ adj [*smoke, fumes*] asphyxiant; [*atmosphere*] étouffant; [*heat*] suffocant.

suffocation /ˌsʌfəˈkeɪʃn/ n (by smoke, fumes, enclosed space, crowd) asphyxie f; (by pillow) étouffement m.

suffrage /'sʌfrɪdʒ/ n (right) droit m de vote; (system) suffrage m.

suffragette /ˌsʌfrəˈdʒet/ n suffragette f.

suffuse /səˈfjuːz/ SOUT I vtr se répandre sur.
II **suffused** pp adj ~**d with** [*style*] imprégné de; [*person*] envahi de [*melancholy*]; [*landscape*] inondé de [*light*].

sugar /'ʃʊɡə(r)/ I n **1** CULIN sucre m; **brown ~** sucre m roux; **2**○ (endearment) chéri/-e m/f.
II noun modifier [*industry, prices*] du sucre; [*production, refinery*] de sucre; [*spoon, canister*] à sucre.
III vtr sucrer [*tea, coffee*].
IDIOMS **to ~ the pill** dorer la pilule○.

sugar: ~ **beet** n betterave f à sucre; ~ **bowl** n sucrier m; ~ **cane** n canne f à sucre; ~ **cube** n morceau m de sucre; ~ **daddy** n vieux protecteur m (d'une jeune fille); ~**ed almond** n dragée f; ~**free** n sans sucre; ~ **lump** n morceau m de sucre; ~ **pea** n mange-tout m inv; ~ **plantation** n plantation f de canne à sucre.

sugary /'ʃʊɡərɪ/ adj LIT sucré; FIG, GEN mielleux/-euse; [*sentimentality*] mièvre.

suggest /səˈdʒest, US səɡˈdʒ-/ vtr **1** (put forward for consideration) suggérer; **can you ~ how/where...?** selon vous, comment/où...?; **it would be wrong to ~ that...** il serait faux de prétendre que...; **what are you ~ing?** qu'est-ce que vous insinuez?; **I venture to ~ that...** je me risque à dire que...; **2** (recommend) suggérer; **the committee ~s that steps be taken** le comité suggère que des mesures soient prises; **I ~ waiting** je suggère d'attendre; **an idea ~ed itself** (to me) une idée m'est venue à l'esprit; **3** (indicate) sembler indiquer (**that** que); **it was more difficult than the result might ~** ce fut plus difficile que le résultat ne semble l'indiquer; **4** (evoke) évoquer.

suggestible /səˈdʒestəbl, US səɡˈdʒ-/ adj influençable.

suggestion /səˈdʒestʃn, US səɡˈdʒ-/ n **1** (proposal) suggestion f (**about** à propos de; **as to** en ce qui concerne); **any ~s?** vous avez des idées?; **there is no ~ that** on n'a jamais dit que; **there is no ~ of fraud** rien ne laisse supposer qu'il y a eu fraude; **at ou on sb's ~** sur ou suivant le conseil de qn; **there was some ~ that** il a été suggéré que; **2** (hint) GEN soupçon m; (of smile) pointe f; **3** PSYCH suggestion f; **the power of ~** la puissance de suggestion.

suggestions box n boîte f à idées.

suggestive /səˈdʒestɪv, US səɡˈdʒ-/ adj (all contexts) suggestif/-ive; **to be ~ of sth** évoquer qch.

suicidal /ˌsuːɪˈsaɪdl, ˌsjuː-/ adj LIT, FIG suicidaire.

suicidally /ˌsuːɪˈsaɪdəlɪ, sjuː-/ adv [*depressed*] jusqu'au suicide; [*behave, decide, drive*] de manière suicidaire.

suicide /'suːɪsaɪd, 'sjuː-/ I n (action) LIT, FIG suicide m; (person) suicidé/-e m/f; **to commit ~** se suicider.
II noun modifier [*attempt, bid, rate, note*] de suicide.

suit /suːt, sjuːt/ I n **1** (man's) costume m; (woman's) tailleur m; **to be wearing a ~ and tie** être en costume cravate; **a ~ of clothes** une tenue; **a ~ of armour** une armure (complète); **2** JUR (lawsuit) procès m; **3** (in cards) couleur f; **to be sb's strong ~** FIG être le point fort de qn; **to follow ~** FIG faire de même.
II vtr **1** [*colour, outfit*] aller à; **to ~ sb down to the ground**○ aller à qn comme un gant; **2** [*date, climate, arrangement*] convenir à; ~**s me**○! ça me va!; **she's liberal when it ~s her** elle est libérale quand ça l'arrange; **it ~s him to live alone** ça lui plaît de vivre seul; **3** [*part, job*] convenir à; **a loan that ~s your needs** un prêt qui répond parfaitement à vos besoins; **4** (adapt) **to ~ sth to** adapter qch à.
III vi convenir
IV v refl **to ~ oneself** faire comme on veut.

suitability /ˌsuːtəˈbɪlətɪ, ˌsjuːt-/ n (of person) aptitude f (**for** pour); (of site, location) commodité f.

suitable /'suːtəbl, 'sjuː-/ adj [*clothing, employment, qualification, venue*] adéquat; [*candidate*] apte; [*treatment, gift*] approprié; **did you see anything ~?** as-tu vu quelque chose qui (te) convienne? **to be ~ for** convenir à [*person*]; bien se prêter à [*climate, activity, occasion*]; être fait pour [*role*]; être apte à [*job*]; **to be a ~ model for sb** être un exemple convenable pour qn; **to be ~ to** convenir à; **now seems a ~ time** il semble que ce soit le moment opportun.

suitably /'suːtəblɪ, 'sjuː-/ adv **1** [dressed, qualified] convenablement; **2** (to the right degree) [austere] suffisamment; [chastened, impressed] dûment.

suitcase /'suːtkeɪs, 'sjuː-/ n valise f; **to be living out of a ~** passer sa vie à se déplacer.

suite /swiːt/ n **1** (furniture) mobilier m; **2** (rooms) suite f; **a ~ of rooms** une suite f; **3** LITTÉR (retinue) suite f; **4** MUS suite f.

suited /'suːtɪd, 'sjuː-/ adj **to be ~ to** [place, vehicle, clothes] être commode pour; [class, game, format, style] convenir à; [person] être fait pour; **they are ideally ~ (to each other)** ils sont faits l'un pour l'autre.

sulfur n US ▶ **sulphur**.

sulk /sʌlk/ **I** n **to be in a ~** bouder.
II sulks npl **to have (a fit of) the ~s** bouder.
III vi bouder (**about, over** à cause de).

sulkiness /'sʌlkɪnɪs/ n **1** (characteristic) caractère m maussade; **2** (behaviour) bouderies fpl.

sulky /'sʌlkɪ/ adj (all contexts) boudeur/-euse; **to look ~** faire la tête.

sullen /'sʌlən/ adj [person, expression] renfrogné; [day, sky, mood] maussade; [silence] obstiné.

sulphur GB, **sulfur** US /'sʌlfə(r)/ n soufre m.

sulphuric acid n acide m sulfurique.

sultana /sʌl'tɑːnə, US -'tænə/ n CULIN raisin m de Smyrne.

sultry /'sʌltrɪ/ adj **1** [day, place] étouffant; [weather] lourd; **2** [voice] voluptueux/-euse; [woman, look] sensuel/-elle.

sum /sʌm/ n **1** (amount of money) somme f; **a large/small ~ of money** une grosse/petite somme; **2** (calculation) calcul m; **to be good at ~s** être bon en calcul; **to do one's ~s** FIG faire ses comptes; **3** (total) LIT somme f; **the ~ of** FIG la somme de [experience, happiness]; l'ensemble m de [achievements].
■ **sum up**: ¶ **~ up 1** GEN récapituler; **to ~ up, I'd like to say...** pour récapituler, je voudrais dire...; **2** JUR résumer; ¶ **~ up [sth] 1** (summarize) résumer; **2** (judge accurately) apprécier [situation]; se faire une idée de [person].

summa cum laude /ˌsʊmə kʊm 'laʊdeɪ/ n US UNIV ~ mention f très bien.

summarily /'sʌmərəlɪ, US sə'merəlɪ/ adj sommairement.

summarize /'sʌməraɪz/ vtr GEN résumer; récapituler [argument, speech].

summary /'sʌmərɪ/ **I** n résumé m.
II adj GEN, JUR sommaire.

summer /'sʌmə(r)/ **I** ▶ **1235** n été m; **in the ~ of 1991** pendant l'été 1991.
II noun modifier [weather, evening, resort, clothes, vacation] d'été; **~ tourist** ou **visitor** estivant/-e m/f.

summer: **~ camp** n US colonie f de vacances; **~ holiday** GB, **~ vacation** US GEN vacances fpl (d'été); SCH, UNIV grandes vacances fpl; **~house** n: abri rustique dans un jardin; **~ resort** n station f estivale; **~ school** n université f d'été; **~ term** n SCH, UNIV troisième trimestre m.

summertime /'sʌmətaɪm/ n **1** (period) été m; **2** GB **summer time** (by clock) heure f d'été.

summery /'sʌmərɪ/ adj estival; **it's quite ~** on se croirait en été.

summing-up /ˌsʌmɪŋ'ʌp/ n GEN récapitulation f; JUR résumé m.

summit /'sʌmɪt/ **I** n sommet m; **Nato ~** sommet de l'OTAN; **peace ~** sommet m pour la paix.
II noun modifier [meeting, talks] au sommet.

summon /'sʌmən/ vtr **1** (call for) GEN faire venir; convoquer [ambassador]; **to ~ sb to a meeting** convoquer qn à une réunion; **to ~ sb in** faire entrer qn; **to ~ sb to do sth** sommer qn de faire qch; **to ~ help** appeler à l'aide; **to ~ reinforcements/a taxi** appeler des renforts/un taxi; **2** JUR citer; **3** (convene) convoquer.
■ **summon up**: **~ up [sth]** (gather) rassembler

[energy]; (evoke) évoquer [image]; **to ~ up spirits** appeler les esprits.

summons /'sʌmənz/ **I** n **1** JUR citation f (**to do** à faire; **for** pour); **to serve a ~** signifier une citation; **to serve sb with a ~** citer qn à comparaître; **2** GEN (order) injonction f (**from** de; **to** à).
II vtr citer (**to** à; **to do** à faire; **for** pour).

sump /sʌmp/ n **1** (for draining water) puisard m; **2** AUT carter m; **~ oil** huile f de carter.

sumptuous /'sʌmptʃʊəs/ adj somptueux/-euse.

sum total n (of money) montant m total; (of achievements) ensemble m; **is that the ~ of your achievements?** IRON c'est tout ce que tu as fait?

sun /sʌn/ **I** n soleil m; **in the ~** au soleil; **don't lie right in the ~** ne vous allongez pas en plein soleil; **you should come out of the ~** vous devriez vous mettre à l'ombre; **a place in the ~** (position) un endroit ensoleillé; (house) une maison dans le sud; **it's the most beautiful place under the ~** c'est l'endroit le plus beau du monde; **they sell everything under the ~** ils vendent de tout; **to be up before the ~** être levé avant l'aube.
II v refl (p prés etc **-nn-**) **to ~ oneself** [person] prendre le soleil; [animal] se chauffer au soleil.

Sun abrév écrite = **Sunday**.

sunbaked /'sʌnbeɪkt/ adj brûlé par le soleil.

sunbathe /'sʌnbeɪð/ **I** GB n bain m de soleil.
II vi se faire bronzer.

sun: **~bather** n personne f qui prend un or des bain(s) de soleil; **~bathing** n bains mpl de soleil; **~beam** n LIT, FIG rayon m de soleil; **~bed** n (lounger) chaise f longue ; (with sunlamp) lit m solaire; **~ blind** n GB store m; **~ block** n crème f écran total; **~burn** n coup m de soleil.

sunburned, sunburnt /'sʌnbɜːnt/ adj (burnt) brûlé par le soleil; (tanned) GB bronzé; **to get ~** (burn) attraper un coup de soleil; (tan) GB bronzer.

Sunday /'sʌndeɪ, -dɪ/ ▶ **1390** **I** pr n dimanche m.
II Sundays pr n/pl **the ~s** les journaux mpl du dimanche.
III noun modifier [newspaper, lunch] du dimanche.
IDIOMS **he'll never do it, not in a month of ~s** il ne fera la semaine des quatre jeudis.

Sunday best n (dressed) **in one's ~** endimanché.

Sunday: **~ observance** n observance f du repos dominical; **~ opening** n ouverture f dominicale (des commerces et des bars); **~ trading** n commerce m dominical.

sun: **~deck** n (on ship) pont m supérieur; (in house) terrasse f; **~dial** n cadran m solaire; **~down** n = **sunset**; **~drenched** adj inondé de soleil; **~dress** n robe f bain de soleil; **~-dried** adj séché au soleil.

sundry /'sʌndrɪ/ **I sundries** npl articles mpl divers.
II adj [items, objects, occasions] divers; (to) **all and ~** GEN (à) tout le monde; (critical) (à) n'importe qui.

sunflower /'sʌnflaʊə(r)/ **I** n tournesol m.
II noun modifier [oil, seed] de tournesol; [margarine] au tournesol.

sung /sʌŋ/ pp ▶ **sing**.

sun: **~glasses** npl lunettes fpl de soleil; **~ hat** n chapeau m de soleil.

sunk /sʌŋk/ pp ▶ **sink** II, III.

sunken /'sʌŋkən/ adj **1** (under water) [treasure, wreck] immergé; [vessel] englouti; **2** (recessed) [cheek] creux/ creuse; [eye] cave; **3** (low) [bath] encastré; [garden, living area] en contrebas.

sunlamp /'sʌnlæmp/ n (for tanning) lampe f à bronzer; MED lampe f à rayons ultraviolets.

sunlight /'sʌnlaɪt/ n lumière f du soleil; **in the ~** au soleil; **in direct ~** en plein soleil.

sun: **~lit** adj ensoleillé; **~ lotion** n = **suntan lotion**; **~lounger** n chaise f longue.

sunny /'sʌnɪ/ adj **1** [weather, day] ensoleillé; [room] (facing the sun) exposé au soleil; (sunlit) ensoleillé; **~ interval** période f ensoleillée; **it's going to be ~** il va faire (du) soleil; **2** [*child, temperament*] enjoué; **~ side up** [*egg*] sur le plat.

sun: **~ oil** n = **suntan oil**; **~ porch** n petite véranda f; **~rise** n lever m du soleil; **~rise industry** n US industrie f en pleine expansion; **~roof** n toit m ouvrant; **~screen** n filtre m solaire.

sunset /ˈsʌnset/ **I** n LIT coucher m du soleil; FIG crépuscule m.
II adj US ADMIN, JUR de durée d'application limitée.

sunset industry n US industrie f en déclin.

sun: **~shade** n (parasol) parasol m; (awning) auvent m; (in car) pare-soleil m inv; **~shield** n pare-soleil m inv.

sunshine /ˈsʌnʃaɪn/ **I** n **1** LIT soleil m; **12 hours of ~** 12 heures d'ensoleillement; **2**° (term of address) coco/cocotte° m/f.
II adj US ADMIN, JUR [*law, bill, clause*] sur la transparence.

sunshine roof n = **sunroof**.

sunstroke n insolation f.

suntan /ˈsʌntæn/ n bronzage m; **to get a ~** bronzer.

sun: **~tan cream** n crème f solaire; **~tan lotion** n lotion f solaire; **~tanned** adj bronzé; **~tan oil** n huile f solaire; **~trap** n coin m ensoleillé; **~ umbrella** n parasol m; **~up**° n US = **sunrise**; **~ visor** n (in car) pare-soleil m inv; (for eyes) visière f; **~ worshipper** n GEN fanatique m/f du soleil.

super /ˈsuːpə(r), ˈsjuː-/ **I** n **1** US (petrol) super (carburant) m; **2**° abrév = **superintendent**.
II° adj, excl formidable.
III super+ combining form super-.

superannuated /ˌsuːpərˌænjʊˈeɪtɪd, ˌsjuː-/ adj LIT mis à la retraite; FIG suranné.

superannuation /ˌsuːpərˌænjʊˈeɪʃn, ˌsjuː-/ **I** n retraite f complémentaire; **~ scheme** régime m de retraite.

superb /suːˈpɜːb, sjuː-/ adj superbe.

Super Bowl n US SPORT championnat de football américain.

supercilious /ˌsuːpəˈsɪliəs, ˌsjuː-/ adj dédaigneux/-euse.

superficial /ˌsuːpəˈfɪʃl, ˌsjuː-/ adj superficiel/-ielle.

superficiality /ˌsuːpəˌfɪʃɪˈæləti, ˌsjuː-/ n GEN caractère m superficiel; PÉJ manque m de profondeur.

superfine /ˈsuːpəfaɪn, ˈsjuː-/ adj [*flour, chocolate, needle*] extra-fin; [*quality*] surfin; **~ sugar** US sucre m en poudre.

superfluity /ˌsuːpəˈfluːəti, ˌsjuː-/ n (overabundance) surabondance f.

superfluous /suːˈpɜːfluəs, sjuː-/ adj superflu (**to** sth pour qch); **to feel (rather) ~** se sentir de trop.

superhuman /ˌsuːpəˈhjuːmən, ˌsjuː-/ adj surhumain.

superimpose /ˌsuːpərɪmˈpəʊz, ˌsjuː-/ vtr superposer [*picture, soundtrack*] (**on** à); **~d images** images en surimpression.

superintend /ˌsuːpərɪnˈtend, ˌsjuː-/ vtr surveiller [*person, work*]; diriger [*organization, research*].

superintendent /ˌsuːpərɪnˈtendənt, ˌsjuː-/ n **1** (supervisor) responsable m/f; **2** (in police) cf commissaire m de police; **3** US (for apartments) concierge m/f; **4** US (also **school ~**) inspecteur/-trice m/f.

superior /suːˈpɪərɪə(r), sjuː-, sʊ-/ **I** n GEN, RELIG supérieur/-e m/f.
II adj **1** GEN supérieur (**to** à; **in** en); [*product*] de qualité supérieure; (better than another) meilleur; **in ~ numbers** en plus grand nombre; **2** (condescending) condescendant.

superior court n US cour d'appel inférieure à la cour d'appel suprême.

superiority /suːˌpɪərɪˈɒrəti, sjuː-, US -ˈɔːr-/ n (all contexts) supériorité f (**over, to** sur; **in** en).

superlative /suːˈpɜːlətɪv, sjuː-/ **I** n LING superlatif m.
II adj **1** [*performance, service*] superbe; [*physical condition*] exceptionnel/-elle; [*match, player*] de toute première classe; **2** LING superlatif.

superlatively /suːˈpɜːlətɪvlɪ, sjuː-/ adv parfaitement.

superman /ˈsuːpəmæn, ˈsjuː-/ n (pl **-men**) surhomme m.

supermarket /ˈsuːpəmɑːkɪt, ˈsjuː-/ n supermarché m.

supernatural /ˌsuːpəˈnætʃrəl, ˌsjuː-/ **I** n surnaturel m.
II adj surnaturel/-elle.

supernumerary /ˌsuːpəˈnjuːmərəri, ˌsjuː-, US -ˈnuːmreri/ **I** n **1** ADMIN surnuméraire m/f; **2** CIN, THEAT (extra) figurant/-e m/f.
II adj (all contexts) surnuméraire.

superpower /ˈsuːpəpaʊə(r), ˈsjuː-/ n superpuissance f; **~ summit** sommet des superpuissances.

superscript /ˈsuːpəskrɪpt, ˈsjuː-/ adj [*number, letter*] en exposant.

supersede /ˌsuːpəˈsiːd, ˌsjuː-/ vtr GEN remplacer; supplanter [*belief, theory*].

supersonic /ˌsuːpəˈsɒnɪk, ˌsjuː-/ adj supersonique.

superstition /ˌsuːpəˈstɪʃn, ˌsjuː-/ n superstition f.

superstitious /ˌsuːpəˈstɪʃəs, ˌsjuː-/ adj superstitieux/-ieuse.

superstore /ˈsuːpəstɔː(r), ˈsjuː-/ n (large supermarket) hypermarché m; (specialist shop) grande surface f.

superstructure /ˈsuːpəstrʌktʃə(r), ˈsjuː-/ n superstructure f.

supertax /ˈsuːpətæks, ˈsjuː-/ n FIN impôt supplémentaire sur les très hauts revenus.

supervise /ˈsuːpəvaɪz, ˈsjuː-/ **I** vtr **1** (watch over) superviser [*activity, staff, student, work*]; surveiller [*child, patient*]; diriger [*thesis*]; **2** (control) diriger.
II vi [*supervisor*] superviser; [*doctor, parent*] surveiller; [*manager*] diriger.

supervision /ˌsuːpəˈvɪʒn, ˌsjuː-/ n **1** (of staff, work) supervision f; **she is responsible for the ~ of two students** UNIV elle dirige les recherches de deux étudiants; **2** (of child, patient, prisoner) surveillance f.

supervisor /ˈsuːpəvaɪzə(r), ˈsjuː-/ ▶1251 | n **1** ADMIN, COMM responsable m; **factory ~** ≈ contremaître m; **shop ~** chef m de rayon; **2** CONSTR contremaître m; **site ~** chef m de chantier; **3** GB UNIV (for thesis) directeur/-trice m/f de thèse; **4** US SCH directeur/-trice m/f d'études.

supervisory /ˈsuːpəvaɪzəri, ˈsjuː-, US ˌsuːpəˈvaɪzəri/ adj de supervision; **she's a ~ officer** elle fait partie du personnel d'encadrement; **in a ~ capacity** en qualité de superviseur.

supine /ˈsuːpaɪn, ˈsjuː-/ **I** n LING supin m.
II adj **1** [*person*] étendu sur le dos; **to be ~** être allongé sur le dos; **2** [*complacency*] mou/molle.

supper /ˈsʌpə(r)/ n **1** (evening meal) dîner m; **what's for ~?** qu'est-ce qu'on mange ce soir?; **to have** ou **eat ~** dîner; **2** (late snack) collation f (du soir); **3** (after a show) souper m; **4** RELIG **the Last Supper** la Cène.

supper: **~ club** n US restaurant m; **~ licence** n GB JUR autorisation de vendre de l'alcool après l'heure légale aux repas; **~ time** n heure f du dîner.

supplant /səˈplɑːnt/ vtr GEN supplanter; évincer [*lover, rival*].

supple /ˈsʌpl/ adj GEN souple; [*mind*] délié.

supplement **I** /ˈsʌplɪmənt/ n **1** (to diet, income) complément m (**to** à); **2** TOURISM supplément m (**of** de); **a single room ~** un supplément pour chambre à un lit; **flight ~** supplément m de vol; **3** (newspaper section) supplément m.
II vtr GEN compléter (**with** de); augmenter [*income, staff*] (**with** de).

supplementary /ˌsʌplɪˈmentri, US -teri/ adj GEN supplémentaire; [*heating, income, pension*] d'appoint; [*charge, payment*] additionnel/-elle.

supplementary benefit n GB autrefois allocation versée aux personnes n'ayant pas droit au chômage.

suppleness /ˈsʌplnɪs/ n (all contexts) souplesse f.

supplier /səˈplaɪə(r)/ n fournisseur m (**of, to** de).

supply /səˈplaɪ/ **I** n **1** (stock) réserves fpl; **a plentiful ~ of money** des réserves abondantes d'argent; **in short/plentiful ~** difficile/facile à obtenir; **to get in**

a ~ of sth s'approvisionner en qch; **2** (of fuel, gas) alimentation *f* (**of** en); (of food) approvisionner *m*; **the blood ~ to the heart** le sang qui alimente le cœur; **3** (action of providing) fourniture *f* (**to** à).
II supplies *npl* **1** (food, equipment) réserves *fpl*; **food supplies** ravitaillement *m*; **to cut off sb's supplies** couper les vivres à qn; **2** (for office, household) (machines, electrical goods) matériel *m*; (stationery, small items) fournitures *fpl*; **3** GB POL, ADMIN crédits *mpl*.
III *noun modifier* [*ship, train*] ravitailleur/-euse; [*route*] (for industry) d'approvisionnement; (for population) de ravitaillement; **~ company** fournisseur *m*.
IV *vtr* **1** (provide) GEN fournir (**to, for** à); apporter [*companionship*] (**to** à); **to ~ arms to sb, to ~ sb with arms** fournir des armes à qn; **to keep sb supplied with** approvisionner régulièrement qn en; **to keep a machine supplied with fuel** assurer l'alimentation d'un appareil en combustible; **to keep sb supplied with information** tenir qn au courant de ce qui se passe; **2** (provide food, fuel for) ravitailler (**with** en); **3** (provide raw materials for) approvisionner (**with** en); **4** (fulfil) subvenir à [*needs, wants*]; répondre à [*demand, need*].

supply: **~ and demand** *n* l'offre *f* et la demande; **~ teacher** *n* GB suppléant/-e *m/f*.

support /sə'pɔːt/ **I** *n* **1** (moral, financial, political) soutien *m*, appui *m*; **there is considerable public ~ for the strikers** les grévistes bénéficient du soutien d'une grande partie de la population; **there is little public ~ for this measure** il y a peu de gens favorables à cette mesure; **~ for the party is increasing** le parti a de plus en plus de partisans; **air/land/sea ~** MIL appui *m* aérien/terrestre/maritime; **to give sb/sth (one's) ~** apporter son soutien à qn/qch; **in ~ of sb/sth** en faveur de qn/qch; **in ~ of this theory** pour appuyer cette théorie; **a collection in ~ of war victims** une collecte au profit des victimes de guerre; **means of ~** (financial) moyens *mpl* de subsistance; **2** (physical, for weight) GEN support *m*; (for limb) appareil *m* de maintien; **athletic ~** coquille *f*; **he used his stick as a ~** il s'appuyait sur sa canne; **3** (person) soutien *m*; **to be a ~ to sb** aider qn; **Paul was a great ~** Paul a été (d')un soutien précieux; **4** (at concert) (band) groupe *m* de la première partie.
II *vtr* **1** (provide moral, financial backing) GEN soutenir; donner à [*charity*]; **the museum is ~ed by public funds** le musée est subventionné par l'État; **2** (physically) supporter [*weight*]; soutenir [*person*]; **3** (validate) confirmer; **4** (maintain) [*breadwinner, land, farm*] faire vivre, subvenir aux besoins de; [*charity*] aider; **he has a wife and children to ~** il a une femme et des enfants à charge; **she ~ed her son through college** elle a payé les études de son fils; **5** (put up with) endurer; **6** COMPUT prendre en charge.
III *v refl* **to ~ oneself** subvenir à ses propres besoins.

supporter /sə'pɔːtə(r)/ *n* GEN partisan *m*; POL sympathisant/-e *m/f*; SPORT supporter *m*.

support group *n* groupe *m* de soutien.

supporting /sə'pɔːtɪŋ/ *adj* **1** CIN, THEAT **'best ~ actor/actress'** 'meilleur second rôle masculin/féminin'; **~ cast** les seconds rôles; **2** [*wall*] de soutènement; **3** **~ evidence** preuves *fpl* à l'appui.

supportive /sə'pɔːtɪv/ *adj* [*person, organization*] d'un grand secours; [*role, network*] de soutien.

support: **~ services** *n* services *mpl* d'assistance technique; **~ stockings** *npl* bas *mpl* de maintien; **~ system** *n* GEN réseau *m* de soutien; **~ tights** *npl* collant *m* anti-fatigue.

suppose /sə'pəʊz/ **I** *vtr* **1** (think) **to ~ (that)** penser or croire que; **to ~ sb to be sth** croire qn qch; **who do you ~ I saw yesterday?** devine un peu qui j'ai vu hier; **2** (admit, assume) supposer (**that** que); **it is generally ~d that** tout le monde croit que; **I ~ so/ not** je suppose que oui/non; **even supposing he's there** même en supposant qu'il soit là; **~ (that) it's true, what will you do?** imagine que ça soit vrai, qu'est-ce que tu feras?; **~ (that) he doesn't come?**

et s'il ne vient pas?; **3** (making a suggestion) **~ we go to a restaurant?** et si on allait au restaurant?
II supposed *pp adj* **1** (putative) [*father, owner*] présumé (*before n*), putatif/-ive; [*advantage, benefit*] prétendu (*before n*); **2** (expected) **to be ~d to** être censé faire; **there was ~d to be a room for us** nous étions censés avoir une chambre; **3** (alleged) **it's ~d to be a good hotel** il paraît que c'est un bon hôtel.

supposedly /sə'pəʊzɪdlɪ/ *adv* **to be ~ rich** être censé être riche; **the ~ developed nations** les pays soi-disant développés; **~ she's very shy** il paraît qu'elle est très timide.

supposing /sə'pəʊzɪŋ/ *conj* **~ (that) he says no?** et s'il dit non?; **~ your income is X, you pay Y** supposons que ton revenu soit de X, tu paieras Y.

supposition /ˌsʌpə'zɪʃn/ *n* (guess) supposition *f*; (assumption) hypothèse *f*.

suppository /sə'pɒzɪtrɪ, US -tɔːrɪ/ *n* suppositoire *m*.

suppress /sə'pres/ *vtr* contenir [*anger, excitement*]; refouler [*sexuality*]; supprimer [*evidence, information*]; interdire [*newspaper*]; abolir [*party, group*]; réprimer [*smile, urge, opposition, rebellion*]; étouffer [*criticism, scandal, yawn*]; dissimuler [*truth*]; mettre fin à [*activity*]; retenir [*tears*]; empêcher [*growth*]; affaiblir [*immune system*]; inhiber [*symptom, reaction*]; **to ~ a sneeze** se retenir d'éternuer.

suppressant /sə'presnt/ *n* (drug etc) inhibiteur *m*.

suppression /sə'preʃn/ *n* **1** (of party) abolition *f*; (of truth) dissimulation *f*; (of newspaper) interdiction *f*; (of activity, demonstration, information, report, facts) suppression *f*; (of revolt) répression *f*; (of scandal) étouffement *m*; PSYCH (of feeling) (deliberate) répression *f*; (involuntary) refoulement *m*; **2** (of growth, development) retard *m*.

suppurate /'sʌpjʊreɪt/ *vi* suppurer.

supremacy /su:'preməsɪ, sju:-/ *n* **1** (power) suprématie *f*; **2** (greater ability) supériorité *f*.

supreme /su:'priːm, sju:-/ *adj* [*ruler, power, achievement, courage*] suprême; [*importance*] capital; [*stupidity, arrogance*] extrême; **to reign ~** FIG régner; **to make the ~ sacrifice** mourir pour la patrie.

Supreme Commander *n* MIL Commandant *m* en chef.

supremely /su:'priːmlɪ, sju:-/ *adv* [*difficult*] extrêmement; [*happy, important*] suprêmement.

supremo /su:'priːməʊ, sju:-/ *n* (*pl* **-mos**) leader *m*.

surcharge /'sɜː:tʃɑːdʒ/ **I** *n* **1** GEN supplément *m*; **2** ELEC, POST surcharge *f*.
II *vtr* faire payer un supplément à [*person*].

sure /ʃɔː(r), US ʃʊər/ **I** *adj* **1** (certain) sûr (**about, of** de); **I feel ~ that** je suis sûr que; **I'm not ~ when he's coming** je ne sais pas trop quand il viendra; **to be ~ of one's facts** être sûr de son fait; **one thing you can be ~ of**... une chose est sûre...; **I'm ~ I don't know, I don't know I'm ~** je n'en ai pas la moindre idée; **we can never be ~** on n'est jamais sûr de rien; **I wouldn't be so ~ about that!** ce n'est pas si sûr que ça!; **I won't invite them again, and that's for ~○!** une chose est sûre, je ne les inviterai plus!; **we'll be there next week for ~!** on y sera la semaine prochaine sans faute!; **nobody knows for ~** personne ne (le) sait au juste; **there's only one way of finding out for ~** il n'y a qu'une seule façon de s'en assurer or d'en avoir la certitude; **he is, to be ~, a very charming man** c'est certes un homme très charmant; **to make ~ that** (ascertain) s'assurer que; (ensure) faire en sorte que; **make ~ all goes well** fais en sorte que tout se passe bien; **make ~ you phone me** n'oublie pas de m'appeler; **she made ~ to lock the door behind her** elle a fait bien attention de fermer la porte derrière elle; **he's a ~ favourite** c'est le grand favori; **2** (bound) **he's ~ to fail** il va sûrement échouer; **3** (confident) **sure ~ of oneself** sûr de soi; **4** (reliable) [*friend*] sûr; [*method, remedy*] infaillible; **the ~st way to do** le moyen le plus efficace de faire; **she was chain-smoking, a ~ sign of agitation** elle fumait sans arrêt, ce qui montrait bien

qu'elle était agitée; **5** (steady) [*hand, footing*] sûr; **to have a ~ aim** bien viser.
II *adv* **1**○ (yes) bien sûr; **'you're coming?'—'~!'** 'tu viens?'—'bien sûr!'; **2**○ (certainly) **it ~ is cold** ça oui, il fait froid; **that ~ smells good**○! qu'est-ce que ça sent bon○!; **3 ~ enough** effectivement.
IDIOMS **as ~ as eggs is eggs**○, **as ~ as I'm standing here** aussi sûr que deux et deux font quatre; **~ thing**○! US d'accord!

sure: **~-fire**○ *adj* garanti; **~-footed** *adj* agile.

surely /'ʃɔːlɪ, US 'ʃʊərlɪ/ *adv* **1** (expressing certainty) sûrement, certainement; **~ we've met before?** nous nous sommes déjà rencontrés, n'est-ce pas?; **you noted his phone number, ~?** tu as noté son numéro de téléphone, j'imagine?; **~ you can understand that?** c'est quelque chose que tu peux comprendre, n'est-ce pas?; **2** (expressing surprise) tout de même; **~ you don't think that's true!** tu ne penses quand même pas que c'est vrai!; **~ not!** pas possible!; **~ to God** ou **goodness you've written that letter by now!** ne me dis pas que tu n'as pas encore écrit cette lettre!; **3** (expressing disagreement) **'it was in 1991'—'1992, ~'** 'c'était en 1991'—'1992, tu veux dire'; **4** (yes) bien sûr.

sureness /'ʃɔːnɪs, US 'ʃʊərnɪs/ *n* (of technique) précision *f*; (of intent) certitude *f*; **~ of touch** précision.

surety /'ʃɔːrətɪ, US 'ʃʊərtɪ/ *n* FIN JUR (money) dépôt *m* de garantie; (guarantor) garant/-e *m/f*; **to stand ~ for sb** se porter garant de qn.

surf /sɜːf/ **I** *n* vagues *fpl* (déferlantes).
II *vi* faire du surf.

surface /'sɜːfɪs/ **I** *n* **1** LIT surface *f*; **on the ~** (of liquid) à la surface; (of solid) sur la surface; **2** FIG apparence *f*; **to skim the ~ of** effleurer [*problem, issue*]; **beneath the ~ he's shy** au fond il est timide; **to come** ou **rise to the ~** se manifester; **3** (of solid, cube) côté *m*; **4** (worktop) plan *m* de travail.
II *noun modifier* LIT [*transport*] de surface; [*worker*] en surface; [*wound*] superficiel/-ielle; **~ measurements** superficie *f*, FIG superficiel/-ielle.
III *vtr* faire le revêtement de; **to ~ sth with** revêtir qch de.
IV *vi* **1** LIT [*person, object*] remonter à la surface; [*submarine*] faire surface; **2** FIG [*tension, anxiety, racism*] se manifester; [*problem, evidence, scandal*] apparaître; **3** (reappear) [*person*] (after absence) refaire surface○; (from bed) se lever; [*object*] réapparaître.

surface: **~ area** *n* superficie *f*; **~ mail** *n* courrier *m* par voie de surface; **~ noise** *n* bruit *m* de surface; **~ tension** *n* tension *f* superficielle; **~-to-air** *adj* sol-air; **~-to-surface** *adj* sol-sol.

surf: **~board** *n* planche *f* de surf; **~boarding** ▶ 949 *n* surf *m*; **~boat** *n* surf-boat *m*.

surfeit /'sɜːfɪt/ *n* excès *m* (**of** de).

surfer /'sɜːfə(r)/ *n* surfeur/-euse *m/f*.

surfing /'sɜːfɪŋ/ ▶ 949 *n* surf *m*; **to go ~** aller faire du surf.

surge /sɜːdʒ/ **I** *n* **1** (of water) brusque montée *f*; (of blood, energy, adrenalin) montée *f*; (of anger, desire) accès *m*; (of optimism, enthusiasm) élan *m*; **he felt a ~ of anger** il sentit la colère monter en lui; **2** (rise) (in prices, unemployment, inflation) hausse *f* (**in** de); (in demand, imports) accroissement *m* (**in** de); **3** (also **power ~**) surtension *f*; **4** (increase in speed) remontée *f*.
II *vi* **1** [*water, waves*] déferler; [*blood, energy, emotion*] monter; **the crowd ~d into the stadium** la foule s'est engouffrée dans le stade; **the crowd ~d (out) onto the streets** la foule a déferlé dans les rues; **to ~ forward** [*crowd*] avancer en masse; [*car*] démarrer en trombe○; **2** [*runner*] s'élancer.
III surging *pres p adj* [*prices*] en hausse.

surgeon /'sɜːdʒən/ ▶ 1251 *n* chirurgien *m*.

surgery /'sɜːdʒərɪ/ *n* **1** MED (operation) chirurgie *f*; **to have ~**, **to undergo ~** se faire opérer; **to need ~** avoir besoin d'une opération; **2** GB MED (building) cabinet *m*; **doctor's ~** cabinet médical; **3** GB (consultation time) (of doctor) (heures *fpl* de) consultation *f*; (of MP)

Surface area measurements

Note that French has a comma where English has a decimal point.

1 sq in	=	6,45 cm² (*centimètres carrés*)*
1 sq ft	=	929,03 cm²
1 sq yd	=	0,84 m² (*mètres carrés*)
1 acre	=	40,47 ares
		0,4 ha (*hectares*)
1 sq ml	=	2,59 km² (*kilomètres carrés*)

* *There are three ways of saying 6,45 cm², and other measurements like it:* six virgule quarante-cinq centimètres carrés, *or* (less formally) six centimètres carrés virgule quarante-cinq, *or* six centimètres carrés quarante-cinq.
For more details on how to say numbers, ▶ 1112 .

how big is your garden?	= quelle est la superficie de votre jardin?
what's its area?	= il a quelle superficie?
it's 200 square metres	= il mesure 200 mètres carrés
its surface area is 200 square metres	= il mesure 200 mètres carrés de superficie
it's 20 metres by 10 metres	= il mesure 20 mètres sur 10 mètres *or* il fait 20 mètres sur 10 mètres
sold by the square metre	= vendu au mètre carré
there are 10,000 square centimetres in a square metre	= il y a 10 000 centimètres carrés dans un mètre carré
10,000 square centimetres make one square metre	= 10 000 centimètres carrés font un mètre carré
A is the same area as B	= A a la même superficie que B
A and B are the same area	= A et B ont la même superficie

Note the French construction with de, *coming after the noun it describes:*

a 200-square-metre plot	= un terrain de 200 mètres carrés

---

permanence *f*; **to take ~** assurer la consultation; **4** US (operating room) salle *f* d'opération.

surgical /'sɜːdʒɪkl/ *adj* GEN chirurgical; [*boot, stocking*] orthopédique; [*precision*] FIG scientifique.

surgical: **~ appliance** *n* appareil *m* orthopédique; **~ dressing** *n* pansement *m*.

surgically /'sɜːdʒɪklɪ/ *adv* [*treat*] par opération; **to remove sth ~** opérer qch.

surgical: **~ shock** *n* choc *m* opératoire; **~ spirit** *n* alcool *m* (à 90 degrés).

surly /'sɜːlɪ/ *adj* revêche.

surmise /sə'maɪz/ *vtr* conjecturer (**that** que).

surmount /sə'maʊnt/ *vtr* GEN surmonter; résoudre [*problem*].

surname /'sɜːneɪm/ *n* nom *m* de famille.

surpass /sə'pɑːs, US -pæs/ **I** *vtr* GEN surpasser (**in** en); dépasser [*expectations*]; **to ~ sth in size/height** être plus grand/haut que qch.
II *v refl* **to ~ oneself** se surpasser.

surplus /'sɜːpləs/ **I** *n* (*pl* **-es**) GEN surplus *m*; ECON, COMM excédent *m*; **to be in ~** être excédentaire; **trade ~** excédent commercial.
II *adj* (*tjrs épith*) GEN [*milk, clothes*] en trop; ECON, COMM [*money, food, labour*] excédentaire.

surprise /sə'praɪz/ **I** *n* **1** (unexpected event, gift) surprise *f*; **the result came as** ou **was no ~** le résultat n'a surpris personne; **that's a bit of a ~** c'est surprenant; **it comes as** ou **is no ~ that** il n'est pas surprenant que (+ *subj*); **it comes as** ou **is a ~ to hear that** c'est une surprise d'apprendre que; **it came as no ~ to us to hear that** nous n'avons pas été surpris d'apprendre que; **it came as** ou **was a complete ~ to me** je ne m'y attendais pas du tout; **to spring a ~ on sb** faire une surprise à qn; **~, ~!** ô surprise!; **is**

he in for a ~! ça va être la surprise!; **2** (astonishment) surprise *f*, étonnement *m*; **to express ~ at sth** se déclarer surpris par qch; **much to my ~** à ma grande surprise; **to take sb by ~** GEN prendre qn au dépourvu; MIL surprendre qn.
II *noun modifier* (unexpected) GEN surprise; [*announcement, closure, result*] inattendu; **~ tactics** LIT, FIG tactique *f* fondée sur l'effet de la surprise; **to pay sb a ~ visit** aller voir qn sans le prévenir.
III *vtr* **1** (astonish) surprendre; **it ~d them that** ils ont été surpris que (+ *subj*); **it might ~ you to know that**... tu seras peut-être surpris d'apprendre que...; **nothing ~s me any more!** je ne m'étonne plus de rien!; **you (do) ~ me!** IRON tu m'étonnes! **go on, ~ me** allez, dis toujours!; **2** (come upon) surprendre [*intruder*]; attaquer [qch] par surprise [*garrison*].

surprised /sə'praɪzd/ *adj* étonné; **I'm not ~** ça ne m'étonne pas; **don't look so ~** ne prends pas cet air surpris; **I would be ~ if** cela m'étonnerait que (+ *subj*); **oh, you'd be ~** détrompe-toi; **I'm ~ at him!** je ne m'attendais pas à cela de sa part!

surprising /sə'praɪzɪŋ/ *adj* étonnant, surprenant; **what is even more ~ is that he**... plus surprenant encore, il...

surprisingly /sə'praɪzɪŋlɪ/ *adv* [*calm, cheap, strong*] incroyablement; [*bad*] très; [*well*] étonnamment; **~ frank** d'une franchise étonnante; **they didn't know her, ~ enough** chose étonnante, ils ne la connaissaient pas; **not ~, ...** (ce n'est) pas étonnant que... (+ *subj*).

surreal /sə'rɪəl/ *adj* surréaliste.

surrealist /sə'rɪəlɪst/ *n, adj* surréaliste (*mf*).

surrender /sə'rendə(r)/ **I** *n* **1** MIL (of army) capitulation *f* (**to** devant); (of soldier, town) reddition *f* (**to** à); **2** (of territory, power) abandon *m* (**to** à); (of policy) rachat *m*; **3** (of weapons, ticket, document) remise *f* (**to** à); **4** FIG (to joy, despair) abandon *m* (**to** à).
II *vtr* **1** MIL livrer [*town*] (**to** à); **2** (give up) GEN céder (**to** à); racheter [*policy*]; **3** (hand over) GEN remettre (**to** à); rendre [*passport*] (**to** à).
III *vi* **1** MIL GEN se rendre (**to** à); [*country*] capituler (**to** devant); **I ~** je me rends; FIG je cède; **2 to ~ to** se livrer à [*passion, despair*].
IV *v refl* **to ~ oneself to** se livrer à [*emotion*].

surreptitious /ˌsʌrəp'tɪʃəs/ *adj* [*glance, gesture*] furtif/-ive; [*search, exit*] discret/-ète.

surrogate /'sʌrəgeɪt/ **I** *n* **1** (substitute) substitut *m* (**for** de); **2** (also **~ mother**) mère *f* porteuse.
II *adj* [*sibling, father, religion*] de substitution, de remplacement.

surround /sə'raʊnd/ **I** *n* GB **1** (for fireplace) encadrement *m*; **2** (border) bordure *f*.
II *vtr* LIT, FIG entourer; [*police*] encercler [*building*]; cerner [*person*].
III *v refl* **to ~ oneself with** s'entourer de.

surrounding /sə'raʊndɪŋ/ *adj* environnant; **the ~ area** ou **region** les environs *mpl*.

surroundings /sə'raʊndɪŋz/ *npl* GEN cadre *m*; (of town) environs *mpl*; **in their natural ~** dans leur milieu naturel.

surtax /'sɜːtæks/ *n* (on income) impôt *m* supplémentaire; (additional tax) surtaxe *f*.

surveillance /sɜː'veɪləns/ **I** *n* surveillance *f*.
II *noun modifier* [*equipment*] de surveillance; [*camera*] de surveillance vidéo.

survey I /'sɜːveɪ/ *n* **1** GEN enquête *f* (**of** sur); (by questioning people) sondage *m*; (study, overview of work) étude *f* (**of** de); **a ~ of 500 young people** un sondage effectué parmi 500 jeunes gens; **2** GB (in housebuying) (inspection) expertise *f* (**on** de); (report) rapport *m* d'expertise; **3** GEOG (action) (of land) étude *f* topographique; **4** GEOG (map) (of land) levé *m* topographique; **5** (rapid examination) rapide examen *m*.
II /sə'veɪ/ *vtr* **1** (investigate) GEN faire une étude de [*market, trends*]; (by questioning people) faire un sondage parmi [*people*]; faire un sondage sur [*opinions, intentions*]; **2** GB (in housebuying) faire une expertise de; **3** GEOG faire l'étude topographique de [*area*]; **4** GEN (look at) contempler.

surveying /sə'veɪɪŋ/ *n* **1** GB (in housebuying) expertise *f* (immobilière); **2** GEOG topographie *f*.

surveyor /sə'veɪə(r)/ **▶ 1251** *n* **1** GB (in housebuying) expert *m* (en immobilier); **2** (for map-making) topographe *mf*; (for industry, oil) ingénieur *m* topographique.

survival /sə'vaɪvl/ **I** *n* GEN survie *f* (**of** de); (of custom, belief) survivance *f* (**of** de); **the ~ of the fittest** la survie des plus forts.
II *noun modifier* [*kit, equipment, course*] de survie.

survive /sə'vaɪv/ **I** *vtr* **1** (live through) LIT survivre à [*winter, operation*]; réchapper de [*accident*]; FIG surmonter [*crisis*]; **2** (live longer than) survivre à [*person*].
II *vi* **1** FIG survivre; **to ~ on sth** vivre de qch; **I'll ~** je m'en tirerai.

surviving /sə'vaɪvɪŋ/ *adj* survivant; **the longest ~ patient** le patient qui a vécu le plus longtemps.

survivor /sə'vaɪvə(r)/ *n* (of accident, attack) rescapé/-e *m/f*; **to be a ~** FIG (resilient) avoir de la ressource.

susceptibility /səˌseptə'bɪlɪtɪ/ *n* **1** GEN sensibilité *f* (**to** à); (to disease) prédisposition *f* (**to** à); **2** (impressionability) impressionnabilité *f*.

susceptible /sə'septəbl/ *adj* **1** GEN sensible (**to** à); (to disease) prédisposé (**to** à); **2** (impressionable) impressionnable.

suspect I /'sʌspekt/ *n* suspect/-e *m/f*.
II /'sʌspekt/ *adj* [*claim, person, vehicle*] suspect; [*item*] d'authenticité douteuse; [*water*] douteux/-euse.
III /sə'spekt/ *vtr* **1** (believe) soupçonner [*murder, plot*]; **to ~ that** penser que; **we strongly ~ that**... nous avons de bonnes raisons de croire que...; **it isn't, I ~, a very difficult task** ce n'est pas, à mon avis, une tâche très difficile; **2** (doubt) douter de [*truth, motives*]; **3** (be aware of) **she ~s nothing** elle ne se doute de rien; **4** (have under suspicion) soupçonner [*person*].
IV suspected *pp adj* présumé; **a ~ed war criminal** une personne soupçonnée de crimes de guerre.

suspend /sə'spend/ *vtr* **1** (hang) suspendre (**from** à); **2** (float) **to be ~ed in** [*balloon, feather*] flotter dans; **3** (call off) GEN suspendre; interrompre [*services, match*]; **4** réserver [*comment, judgment*]; **to ~ disbelief** accepter les invraisemblances; **5** suspendre [*employee, official, sportsman*]; exclure [qn] temporairement [*pupil*]; **6** JUR **her sentence was ~ed** elle a été condamnée avec sursis.

suspended animation *n* LIT engourdissement *m*; **to be in a state of ~** FIG [*service, business*] végéter.

suspended sentence *n* condamnation *f* avec sursis.

suspender belt *n* GB porte-jarretelles *m inv*.

suspenders /sə'spendəz/ *npl* **1** GB (for stockings) jarretelles *fpl*; (for socks) fixe-chaussettes *mpl*; **2** US bretelles *fpl*.

suspense /sə'spens/ *n* (tension) suspense *m*; **to keep sb in ~** laisser qn dans l'expectative; **I'd prefer to keep them in ~** je préfère ménager mes effets; **the ~ is killing me!** je n'en peux plus d'attendre!

suspension /sə'spenʃn/ *n* **1** (postponement) (of meeting, trial, services, match) interruption *f*; (of talks, hostilities, payments, quotas) suspension *f*; **2** (temporary dismissal) GEN suspension *f*; (of pupil) exclusion *f* temporaire.

suspension: ~ bridge *n* pont *m* suspendu; **~ points** *npl* points *mpl* de suspension.

suspicion /sə'spɪʃn/ *n* **1** (mistrust) méfiance *f* (**of** de); **to view sb/sth with ~** se méfier de qn/qch; **to arouse ~** éveiller des soupçons; **2** (of guilt) **to be arrested on ~ of murder** être arrêté sur présomption de meurtre; **he is under ~** il est considéré comme suspect; **to be above ~** être à l'abri de tout soupçon; **3** (idea, feeling) **to have a ~ that** soupçonner que; **I have a strong ~ that she is lying** je suis presque sûr qu'elle ment; **to have ~s about sb/sth** avoir des doutes *mpl* quant à qn/qch; **I have my ~s** j'ai ma petite idée là-dessus.

suspicious /sə'spɪʃəs/ *adj* **1** (wary) méfiant; **to be ~**

of se méfier de [*person, motive, scheme*]; **to be ~ that** soupçonner que; **we became ~** on a commencé à se douter que quelque chose n'allait pas; **2** (suspect) GEN suspect; [*behaviour, activity*] louche.

suspiciously /sə'spɪʃəslɪ/ *adv* **1** (warily) d'un air soupçonneux; **2** (oddly) [*behave, act*] de façon suspecte; [*quiet, heavy, keen*] étrangement; [*clean, tidy*] IRON étonnamment; **it sounded ~ like a heart attack to me** cela m'avait tout l'air d'être une crise cardiaque.

suss○ /sʌs/ *vtr* GB résoudre [*problem*]; **to have it ~ed** (understand) avoir tout compris; **she's got it ~ed** (she's successful) elle s'est bien débrouillée.
■ **suss out**○: **~ [sth/sb] out, ~ out [sth/sb]** (understand) comprendre; **to go and ~ things** ou **the situation out** aller voir ce qui se passe.

sustain /sə'steɪn/ **I** *vtr* **1** (maintain) GEN maintenir; poursuivre [*war, policy*]; **2** MUS soutenir; **3** (provide strength) (physically) donner des forces à; (morally) soutenir; **4** (support) soutenir; **to ~ life** rendre la vie possible; **5** (suffer) recevoir [*injury*]; éprouver [*loss*]; subir, essuyer [*defeat, damage*]; **6** JUR faire droit à [*claim*]; admettre [*objection*]; **objection ~ed!** objection accordée!
II sustained *pp adj* GEN soutenu; [*applause, period*] prolongé; MUS tenu.

sustainable /sə'steɪnəbl/ *adj* **1** ECOL [*development, forestry*] durable; [*resource*] renouvelable; **2** ECON [*growth*] viable.

sustenance /'sʌstɪnəns/ *n* (nourishment) valeur *f* nutritive; (food) nourriture *f*.

SW *n* **1** ▶ **1157** GEOG (*abrév* = **southwest**) SO *m*; **2** RADIO (*abrév* = **short wave**) OC *fpl*.

swab /swɒb/ **I** *n* MED (for cleaning) tampon *m*; (specimen) prélèvement *m*.
II *vtr* (*p prés etc* **-bb-**) MED nettoyer [qch] avec un tampon; GEN (also **~ down**) laver.

swagger /'swægə(r)/ **I** *n* démarche *f* arrogante; **with a ~** en se pavanant.
II *vi* **1** (walk) se pavaner; **2** (boast) fanfaronner.

swallow /'swɒləʊ/ **I** *n* **1** ZOOL hirondelle *f*; **2** (gulp) gorgée *f*.
II *vtr* **1** (eat) avaler; **2** encaisser○ [*insult, sarcasm*]; ravaler [*pride, anger*]; **3**○ (believe) avaler○.
III *vi* avaler; (nervously) avaler sa salive.
■ **swallow back**: **~ back [sth], ~ [sth] back** LIT, FIG ravaler.
■ **swallow up**: **~ up [sth], ~ [sth] up** LIT, FIG engloutir [qch]; **I wanted the ground to ~ me up** j'avais envie de disparaître sous terre.

swam /swæm/ *prét* ▶ **swim** II, III.

swamp /swɒmp/ **I** *n* marais *m*, marécage *m*.
II *vtr* inonder; **to be ~ed with** ou **by** être inondé de [*applications, mail*]; être débordé de [*work*]; être envahi par [*tourists*].

swan /swɒn/ **I** *n* cygne *m*.
II○ *vi* (*p prés etc* **-nn-**) GB **to ~ around** ou **about** se pavaner; **to ~ in** arriver comme une fleur○.

swanky○ /'swæŋkɪ/ *adj* (posh) rupin○.

swan: **~sdown** *n* (feathers) duvet *m* de cygne; (fabric) molleton *m*; **~song** FIG *n* chant *m* du cygne.

swap○ /swɒp/ **I** *n* échange *m*.
II *vtr* (*p prés etc* **-pp-**) échanger.
■ **swap around**: **~ [sth] around, ~ around [sth]** permuter.
■ **swap over** GB: ¶ **~ over** échanger; ¶ **~ [sth] over, ~ over [sth]** permuter.

swarm /swɔːm/ **I** *n* (of bees) essaim *m*; (of flies, locusts) nuée *f*; **~s of people** une masse de personnes.
II *vi* **1** (move in swarm) [*bees*] essaimer; **2** [*people*] **to ~ into/out of** entrer/sortir en masse; **to ~ around** se presser autour de; [*place*] **to be ~ing with** grouiller de [*people*].

swarthy /'swɔːðɪ/ *adj* basané.

swashbuckling /'swɒʃbʌklɪŋ/ *adj* [*adventure, tale*] de cape et d'épée; [*hero, appearance*] bravache.

swat /swɒt/ **I** *n* **1** (object) tapette *f* à mouches; **2** (action) tape *f*.

II *vtr* (*p prés etc* **-tt-**) écraser [*fly, wasp*] (**with** avec).

swath(e) /swɔːθ, sweɪð/ *n* **1** (band) (of grass, corn) andain *m*; (of land) bande *f*; **2** (cloth) drapé *m*.
IDIOMS **to cut a ~ through** se frayer un chemin au milieu de.

swathe /sweɪð/ *vtr* envelopper (**in** dans).

sway /sweɪ/ **I** *n* **to hold ~** avoir une grande influence; **to hold ~ over** dominer.
II *vtr* **1** (influence) influencer; **to ~ sb in favour of doing** déterminer qn à faire; **to ~ the outcome in sb's favour** faire pencher la balance en faveur de qn; **2** (rock) osciller; **to ~ one's hips** se déhancher; **to ~ one's body** se balancer.
III *vi* [*tree, building, bridge*] osciller; [*vessel, carriage*] tanguer; [*person, body*] (from weakness, inebriation) chanceler; (to music) se balancer.

swear /sweə(r)/ (*prét* **swore**; *pp* **sworn**) **I** *vtr* **1** GEN, JUR (promise) jurer; **to ~ (an oath of) allegiance to** faire serment d'allégeance à; **to ~ sb to secrecy** faire jurer le secret à qn; **to be sworn into office** prêter serment; **2** (curse) '**damn!**' **he swore** 'bon Dieu!' jura-t-il; **to ~ at** pester contre; **to be** ou **get sworn at** se faire injurier.
II *vi* **1** (curse) jurer; **he never ~s** il ne dit jamais de gros mots; **2** (attest) **I wouldn't** ou **couldn't ~ to it** je n'en jurerais pas.
■ **swear by**○: **~ by [sth/sb]** ne jurer que par [*remedy, expert*].
■ **swear in**: **~ in [sb], ~ [sb] in** faire prêter serment à; **to be sworn in** prêter serment.

swearing /'sweərɪŋ/ *n* ¢ jurons *mpl*.

swearing-in ceremony *n* cérémonie *f* d'investiture.

swearword /'sweəwɜːd/ *n* juron *m*, gros mot *m*.

sweat /swet/ **I** *n* (perspiration) sueur *f*; **to be in a ~** être en sueur; **to be dripping with ~** être en nage; **to break out into a ~** se mettre à suer; **to work up a (good) ~** se prendre une bonne suée; **in a cold ~** LIT dans une sueur froide; **to be in a cold ~ about sth** FIG avoir des sueurs froides à l'idée de qch.
II sweats *npl* US survêtement *m*.
III *vtr* CULIN faire suer [*vegetables*].
IV *vi* **1** LIT [*person, animal*] suer; [*hands, feet, cheese*] transpirer; **2**○ FIG (wait anxiously) **to let** ou **make sb ~** laisser mariner○ qn.
IDIOMS **no ~**○! pas de problème!; **to be in a ~**○ être dans tous ses états; **to ~ blood over sth** suer sang et eau sur qch.
■ **sweat off**: **~ [sth] off, ~ off [sth]** perdre [qch] à force de transpirer.
■ **sweat out**: **to ~ it out**○ s'armer de patience.
■ **sweat over**○: **to ~ over [sth]** en suer○ pour faire ou écrire.

sweat: **~band** *n* SPORT bandeau *m*; (on hat) cuir *m* intérieur; **~ed labour** *n* main-d'œuvre *f* exploitée.

sweater /'swetə(r)/ ▶ **1260** *n* pull *m*.

sweat: **~ pants** *npl* US pantalon *m* de survêtement; **~shirt** *n* sweatshirt *m*; **~shop** *n* atelier *m* où on exploite le personnel; **~suit** *n* survêtement *m*.

sweaty /'swetɪ/ *adj* **1** [*person*] en sueur; [*palm*] moite; [*foot, cheese*] qui transpire; [*clothing*] couvert de sueur; **2** (hot) [*atmosphere*] étouffant; [*work*] laborieux/-ieuse.

swede /swiːd/ *n* GB rutabaga *m*.

Swede /swiːd/ ▶ **1100** *n* Suédois/-e *m/f*.

Sweden /'swiːdn/ ▶ **840** *pr n* Suède *f*.

Swedish /'swiːdɪʃ/ **I** *n* (language) suédois *m*.
II *adj* suédois.

sweep /swiːp/ **I** *n* **1** (also **~ out**) coup *m* de balai; **to give sth a ~** donner un coup de balai à qch; **2** (movement) **with a ~ of his arm** d'un grand geste du bras; **to make a wide ~ south** faire un grand crochet vers le sud; **3** (of land, woods, hills, cliffs) étendue *f*; (of lawn) surface *f*; (of fabric) drapé *m*; **4** (of events, history, novel, country) ampleur *f*; (of opinion) éventail *m*; (of telescope, gun) champ *m*; **5** (search) (on land) exploration *f*; (by air) survol *m*; (attack) sortie *f*; (to capture) ratissage *m*; **to make a ~ of** (search) (on land) explorer; (by air) survoler; (to capture) ratisser; **6** (also **chimney ~**) ramoneur *m*.

II *vtr* (*prét*, *pp* **swept**) **1** (clean) balayer [*floor*, *path*]; ramoner [*chimney*]; **2** (remove with brush) to **~ the crumbs off a table** ramasser les miettes d'une table; **3** (push) **to ~ sth off the table** faire tomber qch de la table (d'un grand geste de la main); **to ~ sb off his/her feet** [*sea*, *wave*] emporter qn; FIG (romantically) faire perdre la tête à qn; **to ~ sb overboard** entraîner qn par-dessus bord; **to be swept into power** être porté au pouvoir avec une majorité écrasante; **4** (spread through) [*disease*, *crime*, *panic*, *craze*] déferler sur; [*storm*, *fire*] ravager; [*rumour*] se répandre dans; **5** (search, survey) [*beam*, *searchlight*] balayer; [*person*] parcourir [qch] des yeux; MIL [*vessel*, *submarine*] sillonner; [*police*] ratisser (**for** à la recherche de); **to ~ sth for mines** déminer qch.

III *vi* (*prét*, *pp* **swept**) **1** (clean) = **sweep up**; **2** LIT, FIG (move) **to ~ in/out** (quickly) entrer/sortir rapidement; (majestically) entrer/sortir majestueusement; **the wind swept in from the east** le vent soufflait de l'est; **to ~ into** [*invaders*] envahir; **to ~ (in)to power** être porté au pouvoir (avec une majorité écrasante); **to ~ to victory** remporter une victoire écrasante; **to ~ through** [*disease*, *crime*, *panic*, *craze*, *change*] déferler sur; [*fire*, *storm*] ravager; [*rumour*] se répandre dans; **to ~ over** [*searchlight*] balayer; [*gaze*] parcourir; **3** (extend) **the road ~s north** la route décrit une large courbe vers le nord; **the mountains ~ down to the sea** les montagnes descendent majestueusement jusqu'à la mer.

IDIOMS **to ~ sth under the carpet** GB OU **rug** US escamoter qch.

■ **sweep along**: **~ [sb/sth] along** entraîner; **to be swept along by** être emporté par [*crowd*]; être entraîné par [*public opinion*].

■ **sweep aside**: **~ [sb/sth] aside**, **~ aside [sb/sth]** écarter [*person*, *objection*]; repousser [*offer*].

■ **sweep away**: **~ [sb/sth] away**, **~ away [sb/sth] 1** LIT emporter; **2** FIG balayer [*obstacle*, *difficulty*]; **to be swept away by** se laisser entraîner par [*enthusiasm*, *optimism*]; être emporté par [*passion*].

■ **sweep out**: **~ [sth] out**, **~ out [sth]** balayer.

■ **sweep up**: **¶ ~ up** balayer; **¶ ~ up [sth]**, **~ [sth] up 1** (with broom) balayer; **2** (with arms) ramasser [qch] d'un geste large; **3** FIG **to be swept up in** être entraîné par [*wave of nationalism*, *of enthusiasm*].

sweeper /'swiːpə(r)/ *n* **1** (cleaner) (person) balayeur/-euse *m/f*; (machine) balayeuse *f*; **2** SPORT libero *m*.

sweeping /'swiːpɪŋ/ **I sweepings** *npl* balayures *fpl*.
II *adj* **1** (far-reaching) [*change*] radical; [*legislation*, *power*] d'une portée considérable; [*cuts*, *gains*, *losses*] considérable; **2** (too general) [*assertion*] péremptoire; [*statement*] trop général; **~ generalization** généralisation *f* à l'emporte-pièce; **3** [*movement*, *curve*] large.

sweet /swiːt/ **I** *n* **1** GB (candy) bonbon *m*; (dessert) dessert *m*; **2**° (term of endearment) ange *m*.
II *adj* **1** LIT [*food*, *tea*] sucré; [*fruit*] (not bitter) doux/douce; (sugary) sucré; [*wine*, *cider*] (not dry) doux/douce; (sugary) sucré; [*taste*] sucré; [*perfume*] (pleasant) doux/douce; (sickly) écœurant; **to have a ~ tooth** aimer les sucreries; **2** (kind) [*person*] gentil/-ille; [*face*, *voice*] doux/douce; **3** (pure) [*water*, *smell*] bon/bonne; [*sound*] mélodieux/-ieuse; **4** (cute) GEN mignon/-onne; [*old person*] adorable; **5** [*certainty*, *solace*] doux/douce; **6** IRON **to go one's own ~ way** agir comme ça lui/leur etc plaît.
III *adv* **to taste ~** avoir un goût sucré; **to smell ~** sentir bon.
IDIOMS **to keep sb ~** amadouer qn; **to whisper ~ nothings into sb's ear** susurrer des douceurs à l'oreille de qn.

sweet: **~-and-sour** *adj* aigre-doux/-douce; **~bread** *n* (veal) ris *m* de veau; (lamb) ris *m* d'agneau.

sweet chestnut *n* **1** (nut) châtaigne *m*; **2** (tree) châtaignier *m*.

sweetcorn /'swiːtkɔːn/ *n* maïs *m*.

sweeten /'swiːtn/ *vtr* **1** sucrer [*food*, *drink*]; parfumer [*air*]; **2** rendre [qch] plus tentant [*offer*].
■ **sweeten up**: **~ [sb] up**, **~ up [sb]** amadouer.

sweetener /'swiːtnə(r)/ *n* **1** (in food) édulcorant *m*; **2**° (bribe) incitation *f*; (illegal) pot-de-vin° *m*.

sweetheart /'swiːthɑːt/ *n* (boyfriend) petit ami *m*; (girlfriend) petite amie *f*.

sweetly /'swiːtlɪ/ *adv* [*say*, *smile*] gentiment; [*sing*] d'une voix mélodieuse; [*dressed*, *decorated*] joliment.

sweet: **~meal** *adj* GB **~** à la farine non blutée; **~-natured** *adj* ▶ **sweet-tempered**.

sweetness /'swiːtnɪs/ *n* **1** (of food, drink) goût *m* sucré; **2** (of perfume, smile) douceur *f*; (of sound) harmonie *f*; (of music) son *m* mélodieux; (of person) gentillesse *f*.
IDIOMS **to be all ~ and light** être tout conciliant.

sweet: **~ pea** *n* pois *m* de senteur; **~ potato** *n* patate *f* douce; **~-talk**° *vtr* baratiner°; **~-tempered** *adj* [*person*] doux/douce; **~ trolley** *n* GB chariot *m* des desserts; **~ william** *n* œillet *m* de poète.

swell /swel/ **I** *n* **1** (of waves) houle *f*; **2** MUS crescendo *m* et diminuendo *m*; **3** (of belly) rondeur *f*.
II° *adj* US **1** (smart) [*car*, *outfit*] classe° *inv*; [*restaurant*] chic *inv*; **2** (great) formidable.
III *vtr* (*prét* **swelled**; *pp* **swollen** OU **swelled**) **1** (increase) GEN gonfler; augmenter [*membership*, *number*]; **2** (fill) [*wind*] gonfler; [*floodwater*] grossir.
IV *vi* (*prét* **swelled**; *pp* **swollen** OU **swelled**) **1** (expand) [*fruit*, *sail*, *stomach*] se gonfler; [*dried fruit*, *wood*] gonfler; [*ankle*, *gland*] enfler; [*river*] grossir; **2** (increase) GEN s'accroître; **to ~ to 20,000** [*total*] atteindre 20000; **3** (grow louder) [*music*] devenir plus fort; [*note*, *sound*] monter; **4** (ooze) s'écouler.
IDIOMS **to have a swollen head**° avoir la grosse tête°.

■ **swell up** [*ankle*, *finger*] enfler.

swelling /'swelɪŋ/ **I** *n* (on limb, skin) enflure *f*; (on head) bosse *f*; (of crowd, population) accroissement *m*.
II *adj* croissant; **a ~ tide** FIG une poussée.

sweltering° /'sweltərɪŋ/ *adj* [*conditions*] accablant; [*day*, *heat*] torride; **it's ~ in here** on étouffe ici.

swept /swept/ *prét*, *pp* ▶ **sweep** II, III.

swept-back *adj* [*hair*] coiffé en arrière.

swerve /swɜːv/ **I** *n* écart *m*.
II *vtr* [*driver*] faire faire un écart à [*vehicle*].
III *vi* **1** LIT [*person*, *vehicle*] faire un écart; **to ~ into sth** aller s'écraser contre qch; **to ~ off the road** sortir de la route; **2** FIG **to ~ from** s'écarter de.

swift /swɪft/ **I** *n* ZOOL martinet *m*.
II *adj* rapide, prompt; **~ to do** prompt à faire.

swiftly /'swɪftlɪ/ *adv* rapidement, vite.

swig° /swɪg/ **I** *n* gorgée *f* (**of** de).
II *vtr* (*p prés etc* **-gg-**) descendre°, boire à grands traits.

swill /swɪl/ **I** *n* (food) pâtée *f* (des porcs).
II° *vtr* (drink) écluser°, boire.
■ **swill around**, **swill about** se répandre.
■ **swill down**: **~ [sth] down**, **~ down [sth] 1**° (drink) descendre°, avaler; **2** (wash) laver [qch] à grande eau.

swim /swɪm/ **I** *n* baignade *f*; **to go for a ~** (in sea, river) aller se baigner; (in pool) aller à la piscine.
II *vtr* (*p prés* **-mm-**; *prét* **swam**; *pp* **swum**) nager [*distance*, *stroke*]; traverser [qch] à la nage [*river*]; faire [qch] à la nage [*race*].
III *vi* (*p prés* **-mm-**; *prét* **swam**; *pp* **swum**) **1** [*person*, *animal*] nager (**in** dans; **out to** vers, jusqu'à); **to ~ across sth** traverser qch à la nage; **2** (be bathed) **to be ~ming in** baigner dans [*sauce*]; **the kitchen was ~ming in water** la cuisine était inondée; **3** (wobble) [*scene*, *room*] tourner.
IDIOMS **to be in the ~** être dans le coup°; **sink or ~** marche ou crève°.

swimmer /'swɪmə(r)/ *n* nageur/-euse *m/f*.

swimming /'swɪmɪŋ/ ▶ 949 **I** *n* natation *f*; **to go ~** (in sea, river) aller se baigner; (in pool) aller à la piscine.

II *noun modifier* [*contest, lessons, course*] de natation.

swimming: **~ baths** *npl* piscine *f*; **~ cap** *n* GB bonnet *m* de bain; **~ costume** *n* GB maillot *m* de bain; **~ instructor** ▶ 1251⌋ *n* maître-nageur *m*; **~ pool** *n* piscine *f*.

swimming trunks *npl* slip *m* de bain; **a pair of ~** un slip de bain.

swimsuit /ˈswɪmsuːt, -sjuːt/ *n* maillot *m* de bain.

swindle /ˈswɪndl/ I *n* escroquerie *f*; **a tax ~** une fraude fiscale.

II *vtr* escroquer; **to ~ sb out of sth** soutirer or escroquer qch à qn.

swindler /ˈswɪndlə(r)/ *n* escroc *m*.

swine /swaɪn/ *n* (pig) (*pl* **~**) porc *m*.

IDIOMS **to cast pearls before ~** jeter des perles aux pourceaux.

swing /swɪŋ/ I *n* **1** (movement) (of pendulum, needle) oscillation *f*; (of body) balancement *m*; SPORT swing *m*; **to aim** ou **take a ~ at** essayer de donner un coup de poing à; **2** (in voting, public opinion) revirement *m* (in de); (in prices, values, economy) fluctuation *f* (in de); (in business activity) variation *f* (in de); (in mood) saute *f* (in de); **a ~ away from** (in opinions) un mouvement contre; (in behaviour, buying habits) un rejet de; **3** (in playground) balançoire *f*; **4** (rhythm) rythme *m*.

II *vtr* (*prét, pp* **swung**) **1** (to and fro) balancer; **2** (move around, up, away) **to ~ a child round and round** faire tournoyer un enfant; **she swung the telescope through 180°** elle a fait pivoter le télescope de 180°; **3** (cause to change) **to ~ a trial sb's way** faire basculer un procès en faveur de qn; **to ~ the voters** faire changer les électeurs d'opinion; **4** (cause to succeed) remporter [*election, match*]; **to ~ a deal** emporter une affaire; **can you ~ it for me?** tu peux arranger ça pour moi?

III *vi* (*prét, pp* **swung**) **1** (to and fro) GEN se balancer; [*pendulum*] osciller; **to ~ on the gate** se balancer sur le portillon; **2** (move along, around) **to ~ onto the ground** (with rope) s'élancer sur le sol; **to ~ up into the saddle** se mettre en selle d'un geste vif; **to ~ open** s'ouvrir; **the car swung into the drive** la voiture s'est engagée dans l'allée; **to ~ around** [*person*] se retourner (brusquement); **to ~ around in one's chair** pivoter sur sa chaise; **3 to ~ at** (with fist) lancer un coup de poing à; **4** FIG (change) **to ~ from optimism to despair** passer de l'optimisme au désespoir ; **the party swung towards the left** le parti basculait vers la gauche; **5** [*music, musician*] avoir du rythme; **6**○ (be lively) **a club which really ~s** une boîte qui est vraiment branchée○.

IDIOMS **to go with a ~**○ [*party*] marcher du tonnerre○; **to get into the ~ of things**○ se mettre dans le bain○; **to be in full ~** battre son plein○.

swing: **~bin** *n* poubelle *f* à couvercle basculant; **~bridge** *n* pont *m* tournant; **~ door** GB, **~ing door** US *n* porte *f* battante.

swingeing /ˈswɪndʒɪŋ/ *adj* GEN drastique; [*attack*] violent.

swinging /ˈswɪŋɪŋ/ *adj* [*band*] qui swingue (*after n*); [*place, nightlife*] branché○.

swingometer /ˌswɪŋˈɒmɪtə(r)/ *n* indicateur *m* de tendances.

swipe /swaɪp/ I *n* **to take a ~ at** LIT essayer de frapper; FIG attaquer.

II○ *vtr* (steal) piquer○, voler.

III *vi* **to ~ at** LIT essayer de frapper; FIG attaquer.

swirl /swɜːl/ I *n* (shape) tourbillon *m* (of de).

II *vi* tourbillonner.

III **swirling** *pres p adj* tourbillonnant.

swish /swɪʃ/ I *n* (of water, skirt) bruissement *m*.

II○ *adj* chic.

III *vi* [*fabric*] bruire; [*whip*] siffler.

Swiss /swɪs/ ▶ 1100⌋ I *n* Suisse *mf*.

II *adj* suisse.

Swiss: **~ chard** *n* bette *f*; **~ cheese** *n* gruyère *m*, emmenthal *m*.

switch /swɪtʃ/ I *n* **1** (change) changement *m* (in de); **the ~ (away) from gas to electricity** le passage du

gaz à l'électricité; **a ~ to the Conservatives** un glissement en faveur des conservateurs; **2** (for light) interrupteur *m*; (on radio, appliance) bouton *m*; **on/off ~** interrupteur *m* marche-arrêt; **the ~ is on/off** c'est allumé/éteint; **3** (whip) badine *f*.

II *vtr* **1** (change) reporter [*support, attention*] (to sur); **to ~ brands/flights** changer de marque/vol; **she ~ed from the violin to the viola** elle est passée du violon à l'alto; **could you ~ the TV over?** est-ce que tu pourrais changer de chaîne?; **2** (also **~ round**) (change position of) intervertir; **I've ~ed the furniture round** j'ai changé la disposition des meubles.

III *vi* **1** (change) LIT, FIG changer; **to ~ between two languages** alterner entre deux langues; **we have ~ed (over) from oil to gas** nous sommes passés du mazout au gaz; **in the end she ~ed back to teaching** finalement elle est revenue à l'enseignement; **2** (also **~ over** ou **round**) [*people*] (change positions) changer; (change scheduling) permuter.

■ **switch off**: ¶ **~ off 1** (turn off) s'éteindre; **2**○ (stop listening) décrocher○; ¶ **~ off** [sth], **~** [sth] **off** éteindre [*appliance, light, engine*]; couper [*supply*].

■ **switch on**: ¶ **~ on** s'allumer; ¶ **~ on** [sth], **~** [sth] **on** allumer.

■ **switch over** TV, RADIO changer de programme.

switch: **~back** *n* GB (rollercoaster) montagnes *fpl* russes; (road) route *f* en lacet; **~blade** *n* US (couteau *m* à) cran *m* d'arrêt; **~board** *n* (installation) standard *m*; (staff) standardistes *mfpl*; **~board operator** ▶ 1251⌋ *n* standardiste *mf*; **~over** *n* passage *m* (from de; to à).

Switzerland /ˈswɪtsələnd/ ▶ 840⌋ *pr n* Suisse *f*.

swivel /ˈswɪvl/ I *adj* [*lamp*] pivotant, orientable.

II *vtr* (*p prés etc* **-ll-** GB, **-l-** US) GEN faire pivoter; tourner [*eyes, head, body*].

III *vi* (*p prés etc* **-ll-** GB, **-l-** US) pivoter.

■ **swivel round**: ¶ **~ round** pivoter; ¶ **~** [sth] **round**, **~ round** [sth] faire pivoter [qch].

swivel chair, **swivel seat** *n* fauteuil *m* tournant, chaise *f* tournante.

swollen /ˈswəʊlən/ I *pp* ▶ **swell** III, IV.

II *adj* [*ankle, gland*] enflé; [*eyes*] gonflé; [*river*] en crue.

IDIOMS **to have a ~ head**○, **to be ~headed**○ avoir la grosse tête○.

swoon /swuːn/ I *n* LITTÉR pâmoison *f*.

II *vi* LIT défaillir (**with** de); FIG se pâmer (**with** de).

swoop /swuːp/ I *n* **1** (of bird, plane) descente *f* en piqué; **2** (police raid) rafle *f*.

II *vi* **1** [*bird, bat, plane*] plonger; **to ~ down** descendre en piqué; **to ~ down on** fondre sur; **2** [*police, raider*] faire une descente.

swoosh /swʊʃ/ *vi* onomat [*tall grass, leaves*] bruire.

swop /swɒp/ *n*, *vtr* = **swap**.

sword /sɔːd/ *n* épée *f*.

IDIOMS **to be a double-edged** ou **two-edged ~** être une arme à double tranchant; **to cross ~s with sb** croiser le fer avec qn.

swordfish /ˈsɔːdfɪʃ/ *n* espadon *m*.

swore /swɔː(r)/ *prét* ▶ **swear**.

sworn /swɔːn/ I *pp* ▶ **swear**.

II *adj* **1** JUR [*statement*] fait sous serment; **2** (avowed) [*enemy*] juré; [*ally*] pour la vie.

swot○ /swɒt/ I *n* bûcheur-euse○ *m/f*.

II *vi* (*p prés etc* **-tt-**) bûcher○.

swum /swʌm/ *pp* ▶ **swim** II, III.

swung /swʌŋ/ *prét, pp* ▶ **swing** II, III.

swung dash *n* tilde *m*.

sycamore /ˈsɪkəmɔː(r)/ *n* sycomore *m*.

sycophant /ˈsɪkəfænt/ *n* flagorneur-euse *m/f*.

sycophantic /ˌsɪkəˈfæntɪk/ *adj* flagorneur-euse.

syllable /ˈsɪləbl/ *n* syllabe *f*; **in words of one ~** en termes simples; **not one ~** pas un seul mot.

syllabus /ˈsɪləbəs/ *n* (*pl* **-buses** ou **-bi**) programme *m*.

syllogism /ˈsɪlədʒɪzəm/ *n* syllogisme *m*.

sylph /sɪlf/ *n* (fairy, slender girl) sylphide *f*.

symbol /ˈsɪmbl/ *n* (all contexts) symbole *m* (**of, for** de).

symbolic(al) /sɪm'bɒlɪk(l)/ *adj* symbolique (**of** de).
symbolism /'sɪmbəlɪzəm/ *n* symbolisme *m*.
symbolize/'sɪmbəlaɪz/ *vtr* symboliser (**by** par).
symmetric(al) /sɪ'metrɪk(l)/ *adj* symétrique.
symmetry /'sɪmətrɪ/ *n* symétrie *f*.
sympathetic /ˌsɪmpə'θetɪk/ *adj* **1** (compassionate) compatissant; (understanding) compréhensif/-ive; (kindly) gentil/-ille; (disposed) bien disposé (**to, towards** à l'égard de); **he is ~ to their cause** il est solidaire de leur cause; **2** (friendly) sympathique; **3** [*development*] qui s'harmonise bien avec l'environnement; **4** MED (ortho)sympathique.
sympathetically /ˌsɪmpə'θetɪklɪ/ *adv* (compassionately) avec compassion; (kindly) avec bienveillance; (favourably) favorablement.
sympathize /'sɪmpəθaɪz/ *vi* **1** (feel compassion) témoigner de la sympathie (**with** à); **I ~ with you in your grief** je compatis à votre douleur; **I ~, I used to be a teacher** je comprends, moi aussi j'ai été professeur; **2** (support) **to ~ with** être solidaire de [*cause, organization*]; souscrire à [*aims, views*].
sympathizer /'sɪmpəθaɪzə(r)/ *n* (supporter) sympathisant/-e *m/f* (**of** de); (at funeral etc) personne *f* qui témoigne de la compassion.
sympathy /'sɪmpəθɪ/ **I** *n* **1** (compassion) compassion *f*; **2** (solidarity) solidarité *f*; **to be in ~ with sb** être d'accord avec qn; **I have little ~ for their cause** j'ai peu de sympathie pour leur cause; **3** (affinity) affinité *f*. **II sympathies** *npl* **what are her political ~s?** quelles sont ses tendances *fpl* politiques?; **to have left-wing ~s** être de gauche; **my ~s lie with the workers** je suis du côté des ouvriers.
symphony /'sɪmfənɪ/ *n* LIT, FIG symphonie *f*.
symphony orchestra *n* orchestre *m* symphonique.
symptom /'sɪmptəm/ *n* (all contexts) symptôme *m*.
sync(h) /sɪŋk/ *n* (*abrév* = **synchronization**) synchronisation *f*; **in/out of ~** LIT bien/mal synchronisé; **to be in/out of ~ with** FIG être en phase/déphasé par rapport à.
synchronization /ˌsɪŋkrənaɪ'zeɪʃn/ *n* synchronisation *f*; **in/out of ~** bien/mal synchronisé.
synchronize /'sɪŋkrənaɪz/ **I** *vtr* synchroniser. **II** *vi* être synchrone.
syndicate I /'sɪndɪkət/ *n* **1** (of people) syndicat *m*; (of companies) consortium *m*; **to be a member of a ~** [*industrialist*] être syndicataire; [*banker*] faire partie d'un consortium; **3** (news agency) syndicat *m* de distribution; **3** (association) (of criminals) association *f* de malfaiteurs; (for lottery) association *f* de joueurs; **drug(s) ~** cartel *m* de la drogue. **II** /'sɪndɪkeɪt/ *vtr* **1** vendre [qch] par l'intermédiaire d'un syndicat de distribution [*column*]; **~d in over 50 newspapers** publié simultanément dans plus de 50

journaux; **2** US RADIO, TV (sell) distribuer [qch] sous licence; **3** (assemble) syndiquer [*workers*].
III syndicated *pp adj* [*columnist*] d'agence; [*loan*] participatif; [*shares*] syndiqué.
syndrome /'sɪndrəʊm/ *n* (all contexts) syndrome *m*.
synonym /'sɪnənɪm/ *n* synonyme *m* (**of, for** de).
synonymous /sɪ'nɒnɪməs/ *adj* synonyme (**with** de).
synopsis /sɪ'nɒpsɪs/ *n* (*pl* **-ses**) GEN synopsis *m*; (of book) résumé *m*.
syntactic(al) /sɪn'tæktɪk(l)/ *adj* GEN syntaxique; **~ errors** erreurs de syntaxe.
syntax /'sɪntæks/ *n* syntaxe *f*.
synthesis /'sɪnθəsɪs/ *n* (*pl* **-ses**) synthèse *f*.
synthesize /'sɪnθəsaɪz/ *vtr* GEN synthétiser; CHEM, IND produire [qch] par synthèse.
synthesizer /'sɪnθəsaɪzə(r)/ *n* synthétiseur *m*.
synthetic /sɪn'θetɪk/ **I** *n* (textile) (fibre *f*) synthétique *m*; (substance) produit *m* synthétique. **II** *adj* synthétique.
syphon *n* = **siphon**.
Syria /'sɪrɪə/ ▶ 840 | *pr n* Syrie *f*.
syringe /sɪ'rɪndʒ/ **I** *n* seringue *f*. **II** *vtr* GEN, MED seringuer; **to have one's ears ~d** se faire déboucher les oreilles (avec une seringue).
syrup /'sɪrəp/ *n* sirop *m*; **cough ~** sirop contre la toux.
system /'sɪstəm/ *n* GEN système *m* (**for doing, to do** pour faire); **filing ~** système de classement; **gambling ~** système de probabilités; **public address ~** système de sonorisation; **road/river ~** réseau *m* routier/fluvial; **reproductive ~** appareil *m* reproducteur; **to lack ~** manquer d'organisation; **to store sth in the ~** COMPUT mettre qch en mémoire; **stereo ~** chaîne *f* stéréo; **braking ~** dispositif *m* de freinage; **to work within the ~** agir de l'intérieur du système; **to beat the ~** contourner le système; **to get sth out of one's ~** LIT rendre qch; FIG⊙ oublier qch.
systematic /ˌsɪstə'mætɪk/ *adj* [*person, approach*] méthodique; [*method, way*] rationnel/-elle; [*attempts, abuse, destruction*] systématique.
systematically /ˌsɪstə'mætɪklɪ/ *adv* [*work, list*] méthodiquement; [*arrange, destroy*] systématiquement.
systematize /'sɪstəmətaɪz/ *vtr* systématiser.
system: **~s analysis** *n* analyse *f* de systèmes; **~s analyst** ▶ 1251 | *n* analyste *mf* de systèmes; **~s design** *n* conception *f* de systèmes; **~s disk** *n* disque *m* système; **~s engineer** ▶ 1251 | *n* ingénieur *m* système; **~s engineering** *n* architecture *f* des systèmes; **~(s) software** *n* logiciel *m* de base; **~s programmer** ▶ 1251 | *n* programmeur *m* d'étude; **~s theory** *n* théorie *f* des systèmes.

t, T /tiː/ n (letter) t, T m.
IDIOMS **that's Robert to a T** c'est signé Robert.

tab /tæb/ n **1** (on garment) (decorative) patte f; **2** (on can) languette f; (on files) onglet m; (for identification) étiquette f; **3** US (bill) note f; **to pick up the ~** LIT, FIG payer la note; **4** COMPUT (tabulator) tabulatrice f; (of word processor, typewriter) (device) tabulateur m; (setting) marque f de tabulation; **to set ~s** placer des marques de tabulation.
IDIOMS **to keep ~s on sb**○ tenir qn à l'œil○.

tabby(cat) /'tæbɪ/ n chat/chatte m/f tigré/-e.

table /'teɪbl/ **I** n **1** (furniture) table f; **to lay** ou **set the ~** mettre le couvert; **to put sth on the ~** GB FIG (propose) avancer qch; US (postpone) ajourner qch; **the offer is still on the ~** l'offre tient toujours; **2** (list) table f, tableau m; **3** MATH table f; **the six-times ~** la table de six; **4** SPORT (also **league ~**) classement m.
II vtr **1** GB présenter [bill, amendment]; **to ~ sth for discussion** soumettre qch au débat; **2** US (postpone) ajourner.
IDIOMS **she drank everyone under the ~** quand tous les autres étaient soûls, elle se tenait toujours debout; **to turn the ~s on sb** renverser les rôles aux dépens de qn; **to lay** ou **put one's cards on the ~** jouer cartes sur table.

table: **~cloth** n nappe f; **~ d'hôte** adj à prix fixe; **~ football** ▶ 949 | n baby-foot m.

table manners npl **to have good/bad ~** savoir/ne pas savoir se tenir à table.

table: **~ mat** n (under plate) set m de table; (under serving-dish) dessous-de-plat m inv; **~ napkin** n serviette f (de table); **~spoon** n (object) cuillère f de service; CULIN (also **~ful**) cuillerée f à soupe (GB = 18 ml, US = 15 ml).

tablet /'tæblɪt/ n **1** (pill) comprimé m (**for** pour); **2** (commemorative) plaque f (commémorative); **3** (of chocolate) tablette f; **4** COMPUT tablette f; **5** US (writing pad) bloc-notes m.

table: **~ tennis** n tennis m de table, ping-pong® m; **~ware** n vaisselle f.

tabloid /'tæblɔɪd/ **I** n (also **~ newspaper**) tabloïde m PEJ; **the ~s** la presse populaire.
II noun modifier **1** PEJ [journalism, journalist, press] populaire; **2** [format, size] tabloïd(e).

taboo /təˈbuː/ n, adj tabou (m).

tabulate /'tæbjʊleɪt/ vtr (set out) présenter [qch] sous forme de tableau; (in typing) tabuler.

tabulation /ˌtæbjʊˈleɪʃn/ n (of data, results) disposition f en tableaux; (in typing) tabulation f.

tabulator /'tæbjʊleɪtə(r)/ n (on typewriter) tabulateur m; (on computer) tabulateur m.

tachograph /'tækəɡrɑːf, US -ɡræf/ n tachygraphe m.

tacit /'tæsɪt/ adj tacite.

tack /tæk/ **I** n **1** (nail) clou m; **2** US (drawing pin) punaise f; **3** (approach) tactique f; **4** NAUT bordée f; **5** (for horse) sellerie f; **6** (stitch) point m de bâti.
II vtr **1** (nail) **to ~ sth to** clouer qch à; **2** (in sewing) bâtir.
III vi [sailor] faire une bordée; [yacht] louvoyer.
■ **tack on**: **~ [sth] on**, **~ on [sth]** (stitch) fixer [qch] à points de bâti; FIG ajouter [qch] après coup [clause, ending, building] (**to** à).
■ **tack up**: **~ [sth] up**, **~ up [sth]** fixer.

tacking /'tækɪŋ/ n (stitching) bâti m.

tackle /'tækl/ **I** n **1** SPORT (in soccer, hockey) tacle m; (in rugby, American football) plaquage m; **2** (equipment) équipement m; (for fishing) articles mpl de pêche; **3** NAUT, TECH (on ship) gréement m; (for lifting) palan m.
II vtr **1** (handle) GEN s'attaquer à; **2** (confront) **to ~ sb** prendre qn de front; **to ~ sb about** parler à qn de; **3** SPORT (intercept) (in soccer, hockey) tacler; (in rugby, American football) plaquer; **4** (take on) maîtriser [intruder].
III vi (in soccer, hockey) tacler; (in rugby, American football) plaquer.

tacky /'tækɪ/ adj **1** (sticky) collant; **the paint is still ~** la peinture n'est pas encore tout à fait sèche; **2**○ PEJ [place, garment, object] tocard○ PEJ.

tact /tækt/ n tact m.

tactful /'tæktfl/ adj [person, suggestion, reply, letter, intervention] plein de tact; [enquiry] discret/-ète; [attitude, approach] diplomatique; **to be ~ with sb** user de tact avec qn.

tactfully /'tæktfəlɪ/ adv [say, behave, reply, refuse] avec tact; [ask, enquire, phrased] avec diplomatie; [decide, refuse, refrain] par tact.

tactic /'tæktɪk/ n **1** GEN tactique f; **a delaying ~** une tactique dilatoire; **2** (military science) **~s** (+ v sg) tactique f.

tactical /'tæktɪkl/ adj tactique.

tactical voting n vote m utile.

tactician /tæk'tɪʃn/ n tacticien/-ienne m/f.

tactless /'tæktlɪs/ adj GEN indélicat; **to be ~** [person, remark] manquer de tact.

tactlessly /'tæktlɪslɪ/ adv indélicatement.

tadpole /'tædpəʊl/ n têtard m.

taffeta /'tæfɪtə/ n taffetas m.

tag /tæɡ/ **I** n **1** (label) GEN étiquette f; (on cat, dog) plaque f; (on file) onglet m; (for hanging) bride f; (nickname) étiquette f; **2** (game) (jeu m de) chat m; **3** LING tag m; **4** (quotation) GEN citation f; (hackneyed) lieu m commun; **5** (for criminal) marqueur m.
II vtr (p prés etc **-gg-**) (label) étiqueter [goods]; marquer [clothing, criminal]; apposer un onglet sur [file].
■ **tag along** suivre; **to ~ along behind** ou **after sb** suivre qn.
■ **tag on**: **~ [sth] on**, **~ on [sth]** rajouter [paragraph, phrase]; **to ~ sth onto sth** attacher qch à qch [label, note].

tagging /'tæɡɪŋ/ n (for criminal) marquage m.

tag: **~ question** n LING queue f de phrase interrogative; **~ wrestling** ▶ 949 | n catch m à quatre.

tail /teɪl/ **I** n GEN, ZOOL queue f.
II tails npl **1** (tailcoat) habit m; **white tie and ~s** queue-de-pie f; **2** (of coin) pile f; **heads or ~s?** pile ou face?
III○ vtr suivre [suspect, car] (**to** jusqu'à); **we're being ~ed** on est pris en filature.
IDIOMS **I can't make head (n)or ~ of this** je ne comprends rien du tout à cela; **to be on sb's ~** suivre qn de près; **to go off with one's ~ between one's legs** partir la queue basse; **to turn ~** tourner les talons.
■ **tail off 1** (reduce) [figures, demand] diminuer; **2** (fade) [remarks] cesser; [voice] s'éteindre.

tail: **~back** n GB bouchon m; **~board** n hayon m; **~ end** n (last piece) (of joint) dernier morceau m; (of film, conversation) fin *f*; **~gate** *n* hayon *m*; **~light** *n* feu *m* arrière; **~-off** *n* diminution *f*.

tailor /ˈteɪlə(r)/ ▶ 1251 ⌋ **I** *n* tailleur *m*.
II *vtr* **1** (adapt) **to ~ sth to** adapter qch à [*needs, person*]; **to ~ sth for** concevoir qch pour [*user, market*]; **2** (make) confectionner.
III tailored *pp adj* [*garment*] ajusté.

tailor-made /ˌteɪləˈmeɪd/ *adj* fait sur mesure; **to be ~ for sth/sb** [*system, course*] être conçu spécialement pour qch/qn.

tailspin /ˈteɪlspɪn/ *n* **1** AVIAT vrille *f*; **to go into a ~** descendre en vrille; **2** FIG dégringolade° *f*.

taint /teɪnt/ **I** *n* **1** (mark) (of crime, corruption, cowardice) souillure *f*; (of insanity, heresy) tare *f*; **2** (trace) trace *f*.
II *vtr* souiller [*public figure, reputation*]; polluer [*air, water*]; gâter [*meat, food*].

tainted /ˈteɪntɪd/ *adj* **1** (contaminated) [*food*] avarié; [*water, air*] pollué (**with** par); **2** (sullied) [*reputation, organization*] entaché (**with** de); [*money*] mal acquis.

take /teɪk/ ▶ 1260 ⌋ **I** *n* **1** CIN prise *f* (de vues); MUS enregistrement *m*; **2** (catch) (of fish) prise *f*; (of game) tableau *m* de chasse.
II *vtr* (*prét* **took**; *pp* **taken**) **1** (take hold of) prendre [*object, money*]; **to ~ sth from** prendre qch sur [*shelf, table*]; prendre qch dans [*drawer, box*]; **to ~ sth out of** sortir qch de [*pocket*]; **to ~ sb by the hand/throat** prendre qn par la main/à la gorge; **to ~ a knife to sb** attaquer qn avec un couteau; **2** (carry with one) emporter, prendre [*object*]; (carry to a place) emporter, porter [*object*]; **to ~ sth sb, to ~ sth to sb** apporter qch à qn; **did he ~ an umbrella (with him)?** est-ce qu'il a emporté un parapluie?; **to ~ a letter to the post office** porter une lettre à la poste; **to ~ sth upstairs/downstairs** monter/descendre qch; **to ~ the car to the garage** emmener la voiture au garage; **he took her some flowers** il lui a apporté des fleurs; **3** (accompany, lead) emmener [*person*]; **to ~ sb to** [*bus, road*] conduire qn à [*place*]; **to ~ sb to school/work** emmener qn à l'école/au travail; **I'll ~ you up to your room** je vais vous conduire à votre chambre; **you can't ~ him anywhere!** HUM il n'est pas sortable!; **I'll ~ you through the procedure** je vous montrerai comment on procède; **his work ~s him to many different countries** son travail l'appelle à se déplacer dans beaucoup de pays différents; **what took you to Brussels?** qu'est-ce que vous êtes allé faire à Bruxelles?; **4** (go by) prendre [*bus, taxi, plane, road, path*]; **5** (negotiate) [*driver, car*] prendre [*corner, bend*]; [*horse*] sauter [*fence*]; **6** (capture, win) [*army*] prendre [*fortress, city, chess piece*]; (in cards) faire [*trick*]; [*person*] remporter [*prize*]; **7** (have) prendre [*bath, shower, holiday*]; prendre [*milk, sugar, pills*]; **we ~ the Gazette** nous recevons la Gazette; **I'll ~ a pound of apples, please** donnez-moi une livre de pommes, s'il vous plaît; **~ a seat** asseyez-vous; **8** (accept) accepter [*job, cheque, credit card, bribe*]; prendre [*patients, pupils, phone call*]; [*machine*] accepter [*coins*]; supporter [*pain, criticism*]; accepter [*punishment*]; **will you ~ £10 for the radio?** je vous offre 10 livres sterling en échange de votre radio; **that's my last offer, ~ it or leave it!** c'est ma dernière proposition, c'est à prendre ou à laisser!; **whisky? I can ~ it or leave it!** le whisky? je peux très bien m'en passer; **I find their attitude hard to ~** je trouve leur attitude difficile à accepter; **he can't ~ being criticized** il ne supporte pas qu'on le critique; **she just sat there and took it** elle est restée là et ne s'est pas défendue; **he can't ~ a joke** il ne comprend pas la plaisanterie; **I can't ~ any more!** je n'en peux plus!; **9** (require) [*activity, course of action*] demander, exiger [*patience, skill, courage*]; LING [*verb*] prendre [*object*]; [*preposition*] être suivi de [*case*]; **it ~s patience to do** il faut de la patience pour faire; **it ~s three hours to get there** il faut trois heures pour y aller; **it won't ~ long** ça ne prendra pas longtemps; **it took her ten minutes to repair it** elle a mis dix minutes pour le réparer; **the wall won't ~ long to build** le mur sera vite construit; **to have what it ~s** avoir tout ce qu'il faut (**to do pour**

faire); **that'll ~ some doing!** ce ne sera pas facile!; **she'll ~ some persuading** ce sera difficile de la convaincre; **10** (react to) prendre [*news, matter, comments*]; **to ~ things one step at a time** prendre les choses une par une; **11** (adopt) adopter [*view, attitude*]; prendre [*measures, steps*]; **to ~ the view ou attitude that** être d'avis que, considérer que; **12** (assume) **I ~ it that** je suppose que; **to ~ sb for ou to be sth** prendre qn pour qch; **what do you ~ me for?** pour qui est-ce que tu me prends?; **what do you ~ this poem to mean?** comment est-ce que vous interprétez ce poème?; **13** (consider) prendre [*person, example, case*]; **~ Jack (for example), he has brought a family up by himself** prends Jack, il a élevé une famille tout seul; **14** (record) prendre [*notes, statement, letter*]; prendre [*pulse, temperature, blood pressure*]; PHOT prendre [*photograph*]; **to ~ sb's measurements** (for clothes) prendre les mesures de qn; **to ~ a reading** lire les indications; **15** (hold) [*hall, bus*] pouvoir contenir [*50 people, 50 passengers*]; [*tank, container*] avoir une capacité de [*quantity*]; **the suitcase won't ~ any more clothes** il est impossible de mettre plus de vêtements dans cette valise; **16** SCH, UNIV (study) prendre, faire [*subject*]; suivre [*course*]; prendre [*lessons*] (**in** de); (sit) passer [*exam, test*]; (teach) [*teacher, lecturer*] faire cours à [*students*]; **to ~ sb for Geography** faire cours de géographie à qn; **17** (wear) (in clothes) faire [*size*]; (in shoes) quelle taille faîtes-vous?; (in shoes) quelle est votre pointure?, quelle pointure faites-vous?; **I ~ a size 5** (in shoes) je chausse du 38; **18** MATH (subtract) soustraire [*number, quantity*]; **ten ~ three is seven** dix moins trois égalent sept; **19** (officiate at) [*priest*] célébrer [*service*].
III *vi* (*prét* **took**; *pp* **taken**) (have desired effect) [*drug*] faire effet; [*dye*] prendre; (grow successfully) [*plant*] prendre.

IDIOMS to be on the ~° toucher des pots-de-vin; **to ~ it ou a lot out of sb** fatiguer beaucoup qn; **to ~ it upon oneself to do** prendre sur soi de faire; **to ~ sb out of themselves** changer les idées à qn; **you can ~ it from me** croyez-moi.

■ **take aback**: **~ [sb] aback** interloquer [*person*].
■ **take after**: **~ after [sb]** tenir de [*parent*].
■ **take against**: **~ against [sb]** prendre [qn] en grippe.
■ **take along**: **~ [sb/sth] along, ~ along [sb/sth]** emporter [*object*]; emmener [*person*].
■ **take apart**: ¶ **~ apart** se démonter; ¶ **~ [sth] apart 1** (separate into parts) démonter [*car, machine*]; **2°** (criticize) descendre [qch] en flammes° [*essay, film, book*]; ¶ **~ [sb /sth] apart°** (defeat) massacrer°.
■ **take aside**: **~ [sb] aside** prendre [qn] à part.
■ **take away**: **~ [sb/sth] away, ~ away [sb/sth] 1** (remove) enlever [*object*]; emmener [*person*]; supprimer [*pain, grief*]; **to ~ away sb's appetite** faire perdre l'appétit à qn; **2** (subtract) soustraire [*number*]; **ten ~ away seven is three** dix moins sept égalent trois; **that doesn't ~ anything away from his achievement** FIG ça n'enlève rien à ce qu'il a accompli.
■ **take back**: ¶ **~ [sth] back, ~ back [sth] 1** (return to shop) rapporter [*goods*]; **2** (retract) retirer [*statement, words*]; ¶ **~ [sb] back** (cause to remember) rappeler des souvenirs à [*person*]; ¶ **~ [sb/sth] back, ~ back [sb/sth]** (accept again) reprendre.
■ **take down**: **~ [sth] down, ~ down [sth] 1** enlever [*picture, curtains*]; démonter [*tent, scaffolding*]; **2** (write down) noter [*name, statement, details*].
■ **take hold**: **~ hold** [*disease, epidemic*] s'installer; [*idea, ideology*] se répandre; [*influence*] s'accroître; **to ~ hold of** (grasp) prendre [*object, hand*]; FIG (overwhelm) [*feeling, anger*] envahir [*idea*] prendre.
■ **take in**: ¶ **~ [sb] in, ~ in [sb] 1** (deceive) tromper; **don't be taken in by appearances** ne te fie pas aux apparences; **I wasn't taken in by him** je ne me suis pas laissé prendre à son jeu; **2** (allow to stay) recueillir [*person, refugee*]; prendre [*lodger*]; ¶ **~ in [sth] 1** (understand) saisir, comprendre [*situation*]; **2** (observe) noter [*detail*]; embrasser [*scene*]; **3** (encompass)

inclure [*developments*]; **4** (absorb) absorber [*nutrients, oxygen*]; FIG s'imprégner de [*atmosphere*]; **5** [*boat*] prendre [*water*]; **6** (in sewing) reprendre [*garment*]; **7** (accept for payment) faire [qch] à domicile [*washing, mending*]; **8**○ (visit) aller à [*play, exhibition*].

■ **take off**: ¶ ~ **off 1** (leave the ground) [*plane*] décoller; **2** (be successful) [*idea, fashion*] prendre; [*product*] marcher; [*sales*] décoller; **3**○ (leave hurriedly) filer○; ¶ ~ **[sth] off 1** (deduct) **to ~ £10 off (the price)** réduire le prix de 10 livres sterling; **2** (have as holiday) **to ~ two days off** prendre deux jours de congé; **I'm taking next week off** je suis en congé la semaine prochaine; ¶ ~ **[sth] off, ~ off [sth] 1** (remove) enlever [*clothing, shoes*]; enlever [*lid, feet, hands*] (**from** de); supprimer [*dish, train*]; amputer [*limb*]; **to ~ sth off the market** retirer qch du marché; **2** (withdraw) annuler [*show, play*]; ¶ ~ **[sb] off, ~ off [sb] 1**○ (imitate) imiter [*person*]; **2** (remove) **to ~ sb off the case** [*police*] retirer l'affaire à qn; **to ~ oneself off** partir.

■ **take on**: ¶ ~ **on** (get upset) **don't ~ on so** (stay calm) ne t'énerve pas; (don't worry) ne t'en fais pas; ¶ ~ **[sb/sth] on, ~ on [sb/sth] 1** (employ) embaucher [*staff, worker*]; (compete against) jouer contre [*team, player*]; (fight) se battre contre [*person, opponent*]; **to ~ sb on at chess** jouer aux échecs contre qn; **3** (accept) prendre [*responsibilities, work, task*]; **4** (acquire) prendre [*look, colour, meaning*].

■ **take out**: ¶ ~ **out** s'enlever; ¶ ~ **[sth] out, ~ out [sth] 1** (remove) sortir [*object*] (**from, of** de); extraire [*tooth*]; enlever [*appendix*]; (from bank) retirer [*money*]; ~ **your hands out of your pockets!** enlève tes mains de tes poches!; **2** **to ~ sth out on sb** passer qch sur qn [*anger, frustration*]; **to ~ it out on sb** s'en prendre à qn; ¶ ~ **[sb] out** (go out with) sortir avec [*person*]; **to ~ sb out to dinner** emmener qn dîner.

■ **take over**: ¶ ~ **over 1** (take control) [*army, faction*] prendre le pouvoir; **2** (be successor) [*person*] prendre la suite; **to ~ over from** remplacer [*predecessor*]; ¶ ~ **over [sth]** (take control of) prendre le contrôle de [*town, country*]; reprendre [*business*]; FIN racheter, prendre le contrôle de [*company*].

■ **take part** prendre part; **to ~ part in** participer à [*production, activity*].

■ **take place** avoir lieu.

■ **take to**: ~ **to [sb/sth] 1** (develop liking for) se prendre de sympathie pour [*person*]; **he has really taken to his new job** son nouvel emploi lui plaît vraiment beaucoup; **2** (begin) **to ~ to doing** se mettre à faire; **he's taken to smoking** il s'est mis à fumer; **3** (go) se réfugier dans [*forest, hills*]; **to ~ to one's bed** se mettre au lit; **to ~ to the streets** descendre dans la rue.

■ **take up**: ¶ ~ **up** (continue story etc) reprendre; **to ~ up with** s'attacher à [*person, group*]; ¶ ~ **up [sth] 1** (lift up) enlever [*carpet, pavement, track*]; prendre [*pen*]; **2** (start) se mettre à [*golf, guitar*]; prendre [*job*]; **to ~ up a career as an actor** se lancer dans le métier d'acteur; **to ~ up one's duties** OU **responsibilities** entrer dans ses fonctions; **3** (continue) reprendre [*story, discussion, cry, refrain*]; **4** (accept) accepter [*offer, invitation*]; relever [*challenge*]; **to ~ up sb's case** JUR accepter de défendre qn; **5** **to ~ sth up with sb** soulever [qch] avec qn [*matter*]; **6** (occupy) prendre [*space, time, energy*]; **7** (adopt) prendre [*position, stance*]; **8** (in sewing) (shorten) raccourcir [*skirt, curtains etc*]; **9** (absorb) absorber [*liquid*]; ¶ ~ **[sb] up 1** (adopt) adopter; **2 to ~ sb up on** (challenge) reprendre qn sur [*point, assertion*]; (accept) **to ~ sb up on an invitation/an offer** accepter l'invitation/l'offre de qn.

take-away /'teɪkəweɪ/ *n* GB **1** (meal) repas *m* à emporter; **2** (restaurant) restaurant *m* qui fait des plats à emporter.

take-home pay *n* salaire *m* net.

taken /'teɪkən/ I *pp* ▶ **take II, III**.
II *adj* **1** (occupied) **to be ~** [*seat, room*] être occupé; **2** (impressed) **to be ~ with** être emballé○ par [*idea,*

---

person]; **she's quite/very ~ with him** il lui plaît assez/beaucoup.

take-off /'teɪkɒf/ *n* **1** AVIAT décollage *m*; **2**○ (imitation) imitation *f* (**of** de).

take-out /'teɪkaʊt/ *adj* US [*food*] à emporter.

takeover /'teɪkəʊvə(r)/ *n* FIN rachat *m*; POL prise *f* de pouvoir.

takeover bid *n* FIN offre *f* publique d'achat, OPA *f*.

taker /'teɪkə(r)/ *n* preneur/-euse *m/f*.

take-up /'teɪkʌp/ *n* (of benefit, rebate, shares) demande *f*.

taking /'teɪkɪŋ/ I *n* prise *f*; **it was his for the ~** il n'avait qu'à se donner la peine de le prendre.
II **takings** *npl* recette *f*.

talc /tælk/, **talcum (powder)** /'tælkəm (ˌpaʊdə(r))/ *n* talc *m*.

tale /teɪl/ *n* (story) histoire *f*; (fantasy story) conte *m*; (narrative, account) récit *m*; (legend) légende *f*; **the figures tell the same/another ~** les chiffres disent la même chose/tout autre chose; **the recent events tell their own ~** les récents événements parlent d'eux-mêmes; **to spread** ou **tell ~s** raconter des histoires.

IDIOMS **a likely ~!** et puis quoi encore!; **dead men tell no ~s** les morts ne parlent pas; **to live to tell the ~** être encore là pour en parler; **to tell ~s out of school** révéler des choses indiscrètes.

talent /'tælənt/ *n* talent *m*; **to have a ~ for** être doué pour; **there's a lot of ~ in that team** il y a beaucoup de gens de talent dans cette équipe.

talent contest *n* concours *m* de jeunes talents or d'amateurs (*pour découvrir de futures vedettes*).

talented /'tæləntɪd/ *adj* doué, talentueux/-euse.

talent: ~ **scout** *n* découvreur/-euse *m/f* de nouveaux talents; ~ **show** *n* = **talent contest**.

talisman /'tælɪzmən, 'tælɪs-/ *n* talisman *m*.

talk /tɔːk/ I *n* **1** (talking, gossip) propos *mpl*; **there is ~ of sth/of doing** il est question de qch/de faire; **there is ~ that** on dit que; **he's all ~** il parle beaucoup mais agit peu; **it's just ~** ce ne sont que des paroles en l'air; **they are the ~ of the town** on ne parle que d'eux; **2** (conversation) conversation *f*, discussion *f*; **to have a ~ with sb** parler à qn; **3** (speech) exposé *m* (**about, on** sur); (more informal) causerie *f*; **to give a ~** faire un exposé.
II **talks** *npl* GEN négociations *fpl*; POL pourparlers *mpl*; **arms ~s** conférence sur le désarmement; **pay ~s** négociations salariales.
III *vtr* parler; **to ~ business** parler affaires; **to ~ nonsense** raconter n'importe quoi; **we're ~ing three years**○ il faut compter trois ans; **we're ~ing big money**○ **here** il s'agit ici de sommes importantes; **to ~ sb into/out of doing** persuader/dissuader qn de faire; **you've ~ed me into it!** vous m'avez convaincu!; **he ~ed his way out of it** il s'en est tiré grâce à son bagout○.
IV *vi* GEN parler; (gossip) bavarder; **to ~ to oneself** parler tout seul; **to ~ at sb** parler à qn sans l'écouter; **to keep sb ~ing** faire parler qn aussi longtemps que possible; **~ing of tennis…** à propos de tennis…; **look who's ~ing!**, **you're a fine one to ~, you can ~!** tu peux parler!; **now you're ~ing!** eh bien voilà!; **~ about stupid**○! comme idiotie, ça se pose un peu là○!

■ **talk back** répondre (insolemment) (**to** à).

■ **talk down**: **to ~ down to sb** parler à qn avec condescendance.

■ **talk over**: ¶ ~ **[sth] over** discuter de [*matter, issue*]; ¶ ~ **[sb] over** faire changer [qn] d'avis.

■ **talk round**: ¶ ~ **round [sth]** tourner autour de [*subject*]; ¶ ~ **[sb] round** faire changer [qn] d'avis.

■ **talk through**: ~ **[sth] through** discuter de [qch] tranquillement.

talkative /'tɔːkətɪv/ *adj* bavard.

talked-about /'tɔːktəbaʊt/ *adj* **the much ~ group** le groupe dont on a beaucoup parlé.

talker /'tɔːkə(r)/ *n* **to be a good ~** avoir de la conversation; **he's not a great ~** il n'est pas bavard;

to be a slow/fluent ~ parler lentement/avec aisance.

talking /'tɔːkɪŋ/ **I** n **there's been enough ~** assez de paroles!; **I'll do the ~** c'est moi qui parlerai; **'no ~!'** 'silence!'
II adj [bird, doll] qui parle.

talking: **~ book** n livre m enregistré (à l'usage des non-voyants); **~ heads** npl interlocuteurs/-trices mpl/ fpl; **~ point** n sujet m de conversation.

talking-to /'tɔːkɪntuː/ n réprimande f.

tall /tɔːl/ ▶1045 adj [person] grand; [building, tree, grass, chimney, mast] haut; **he's six feet ~** ~ il mesure un mètre quatre-vingts; **to get** ou **grow ~er** grandir.
IDIOMS **that's (a bit of) a ~ order!** c'est beaucoup demander!; **a ~ story** ou **tale** une histoire à dormir debout; **to walk** ou **sb's hide** flanquer une raclée à qn○; **to feel (about) ten feet ~** se sentir tout fier.

tallness /'tɔːlnɪs/ n (of person) grande taille f; (of building, tree, chimney, mast) hauteur f.

tally /'tælɪ/ **I** n compte m.
II vi concorder.

talon /'tælən/ n ZOOL serre f.

tambourine /ˌtæmbəˈriːn/ ▶1097 n tambourin m.

tame /teɪm/ **I** adj **1** [animal] apprivoisé; **to become** ou **grow ~** [animal] s'apprivoiser; **2** (unadventurous) [story, party] sans relief; [reform] timide; [reply, ending of book, film] plat.
II vtr GEN apprivoiser; dompter [lion, tiger]; FIG soumettre [person]; contenir [opposition].

tamely /'teɪmlɪ/ adv (meekly) docilement; (flatly) platement.

tamper /'tæmpə(r)/ vi **to ~ with** tripoter [machinery, lock]; trafiquer [accounts, evidence, product].

tan /tæn/ **I** n **1** (also **sun~**) bronzage m; (weather-beaten) hâle m; **to get a ~** bronzer; **2** (colour) fauve m.
II adj fauve.
III vtr (p prés etc **-nn-**) **1** bronzer; **2** tanner [animal hide]; **to ~ sb's hide** flanquer une raclée à qn○.
IV vi (p prés etc **-nn-**) bronzer.

tandem /'tændəm/ n tandem m; **in ~** en tandem.

tang /tæŋ/ n (taste) goût m acidulé; (smell) odeur f piquante.

tangent /'tændʒənt/ n (all contexts) tangente f; **to fly off at a ~** [object, ball] dévier; **to go off at** ou **on a ~** (in speech) partir dans une digression.

tangerine /ˈtændʒəriːn/ **I** n (fruit, colour) mandarine f.
II adj mandarine inv.

tangible /'tændʒəbl/ adj tangible.

tangibly /'tændʒəblɪ/ adv (clearly) manifestement.

tangle /'tæŋgl/ **I** n (of hair, string, wires) enchevêtrement m; (of clothes, sheets) fouillis m; **in a ~** tout embrouillé; **to get in** ou **into a ~** s'embrouiller; **to get in** ou **into a ~** FIG [person] s'empêtrer.
II vtr= **tangle up.**
III vi **1** [hair, string, cable] s'emmêler; **2** = **tangle up.**
■ **tangle up:** ¶ **~ up** s'embrouiller; ¶ **~ up** [sth], **~** [sth] **up** embrouiller; **to get ~d up** [hair, string, wires] s'emmêler; [clothes] s'entortiller; [person] FIG s'empêtrer.
■ **tangle with:** **~ with** [sb/sth] se frotter à.

tangled /'tæŋgld/ adj **1** [hair, wool, wire] emmêlé; [brambles, wires, wreckage] enchevêtré; **2** [situation] embrouillé.

tango /'tæŋgəʊ/ **I** n tango m.
II vi danser le tango.
IDIOMS **it takes two to ~** tous les torts ne peuvent pas être du même côté.

tangy /'tæŋɪ/ adj acidulé.

tank /tæŋk/ n **1** (container) (for storage) réservoir m; (for heating oil) cuve f; (for water) citerne f; (for processing) cuve f; (small) bac m; (for fish) aquarium m; AUT réservoir m; **2** MIL char m (de combat).

tankard /'tæŋkəd/ n chope f (souvent en métal).

tanker /'tæŋkə(r)/ n **1** NAUT navire-citerne m; **oil ~, petrol ~** pétrolier m; **2** (lorry) camion-citerne m.

tankful /'tæŋkfʊl/ n (of petrol) réservoir m plein (of de); (of water) citerne f pleine (of de).

tanned /tænd/ adj (also **sun~**) bronzé.

tannin /'tænɪn/ n tanin m.

tanning /'tænɪŋ/ n **1** (by sun) bronzage m; **2** (of hides) tannage m.

Tannoy® /'tænɔɪ/ n GB **the ~** le système de haut-parleurs; **over the ~** par les haut-parleurs.

tantalize /'tæntəlaɪz/ vtr allécher.

tantalizing /'tæntəlaɪzɪŋ/ adj [suggestion] tentant; [possibility] séduisant; [glimpse] excitant, qui fait envie; [smell] alléchant.

tantalizingly /'tæntəlaɪzɪŋlɪ/ adv **to be ~ close to victory** être à deux doigts de la victoire; **the truth was ~ elusive** la vérité était cruellement insaisissable.

tantamount /'tæntəmaʊnt/ adj **to be ~ to** équivaloir à, être équivalent à.

tantrum /'tæntrəm/ n crise f (de colère); **to throw** ou **have a ~** piquer une crise○.

tap /tæp/ **I** n **1** (for water, gas) robinet m; **the cold/hot ~** le robinet d'eau froide/chaude; **to turn the ~ on/off** ouvrir/fermer le robinet; **on ~** [beer] pression inv; [wine] en fût; FIG disponible; **2** (blow) petit coup m; **he felt a ~ on his shoulder** il a senti une tape sur son épaule; **she heard a ~ at the door** elle a entendu frapper à la porte; **to give sth a ~** donner un petit coup à qch; **3** (listening device) **to put a ~ on a phone** mettre un téléphone sur écoute.
II vtr (p prés etc **-pp-**) **1** (knock) [person] taper (douce-ment); (repeatedly) tapoter; **to ~ a rhythm** battre la mesure; **2** (install listening device) mettre [qch] sur écoute [telephone]; **3** (extract contents) mettre en perce [barrel]; inciser [rubber tree]; exploiter [resources, energy]; **to ~ sb for money○** taper○ qn.
III vi (p prés etc **- pp-**) [person, finger, foot] taper.
■ **tap in:** **~** [sth] **in, ~ in** [sth] enfoncer [nail, peg]; COMPUT taper [information, number].

tap dance n (also **~ dancing**) claquettes fpl.

tape /teɪp/ **I** n **1** GEN bande f (magnétique); (cassette) cassette f; (video) cassette f vidéo; (recording) enregistre-ment m; **to play a ~** mettre une cassette; **on ~** en cassette; **to make a ~ of** faire un enregistrement de; **2** (strip of fabric) ruban m; **3** (also **adhesive ~, sticky ~**) scotch® m; **4** SPORT (in race) fil m d'arri-vée; **5** (for measuring) mètre m ruban.
II vtr **1** (record) enregistrer; **to ~ sth from** enregis-trer qch transmis à [radio, TV]; **2** (stick) **to ~ sb's hands together** attacher les mains de qn avec du scotch®; **to ~ sth to** coller qch à [surface, door].
IDIOMS **to have sb ~d○** savoir ce que vaut qn; **to have sth ~d○** connaître qch comme sa poche.
■ **tape up:** **~** [sth] **up, ~ up** [sth] recoller [qch] avec du scotch® [parcel, box].

tape: **~ deck** n platine f cassette; **~ head** n tête f de lecture; **~ measure** n GEN mètre m ruban; (re-tractable) mètre m enrouleur.

taper /'teɪpə(r)/ **I** n (spill) bougie f filée; (candle) cierge m.
II vtr tailler [qch] en pointe [stick, fabric].
III vi [sleeve, trouser leg] se resserrer; [column, spire] s'effiler; **to ~ to a point** se terminer en pointe.
■ **taper off:** ¶ **~ off** diminuer; ¶ **~ off** [sth], **~** [sth] **off** diminuer [qch] progressivement.

tape: **~ recorder** n magnétophone m; **~ record-ing** n enregistrement m.

tapered /'teɪpəd/, **tapering** /'teɪpərɪŋ/ adj [trousers] en forme de fuseau; [sleeves] aux poignets étroits; [column, wing] fuselé; [finger, flame] effilé.

tapestry /'tæpəstrɪ/ n tapisserie f.

tapeworm /'teɪpwɜːm/ n ver m solitaire, ténia m.

tap water n eau f du robinet.

tar /tɑː(r)/ **I** n GEN goudron m; (on roads) bitume m.
II noun modifier [road, paper] goudronné; **~ content** (of cigarette) taux m de goudron.

III *vtr* (*p prés etc* **-rr-**) goudronner [*road, roof*].
IDIOMS **to ~ everyone with the same brush** mettre tout le monde dans le même sac.

target /'tɑːgɪt/ I *n* **1** GEN cible *f*; MIL objectif *m*; **to be right on ~** LIT être en plein dans la cible; FIG mettre en plein dans le mille; **2** (goal, objective) objectif *m*; **to meet one's ~** atteindre son but; **the figures are way below ~** les chiffres sont très insuffisants; **3** (butt) cible *f*; **to be the ~ of** être objet de [*abuse, ridicule*].
II *noun modifier* [*date, figure*] prévu; [*audience, group*] visé, ciblé.
III *vtr* **1** MIL (aim) diriger [*weapon, missile*]; (choose as objective) prendre [qch] pour cible [*city, site, factory*]; **2** FIG (in marketing) viser [*group, sector*]; **to be ~ed at** [*product, publication*] viser [*group*].

targeting /'tɑːgɪtɪŋ/ *n* **1** COMM ciblage *m* (**of** de); **2** MIL **the ~ of enemy bases** la prise de bases ennemies comme objectif.

target: **~ language** *n* langue *f* cible; **~ practice** *n* ȼ exercices *mpl* de tir sur cible; **~ price** *n* prix *m* indicatif.

tariff /'tærɪf/ I *n* (price list) tarif *m*; (customs duty) droit *m* de douane.
II *noun modifier* [*agreement, barrier, cut*] tarifaire; [*reform*] des tarifs douaniers.

tarmac /'tɑːmæk/ I *n* **1** (also **Tarmac**®) macadam *m*; **2** GB (of airfield) piste *f*.
II *noun modifier* [*road, footpath*] goudronné.
III *vtr* (*p prés etc* **-ck-**) goudronner.

tarnish /'tɑːnɪʃ/ I *vtr* ternir ALSO FIG.
II *vi* se ternir ALSO FIG.

tarpaulin /tɑː'pɔːlɪn/ *n* (material) toile *f* de bâche; (sheet) bâche *f*.

tarragon /'tærəgən/ *n* estragon *m*.

tart /tɑːt/ I *n* **1** CULIN (individual) tartelette *f*; GB (large) tarte *f*; **2** INJUR pute *f*.
II *adj* [*flavour*] aigrelet/-ette; [*remark*] acerbe.
■ **tart up**○ GB: **¶ ~ [sth] up, ~ up [sth]** retaper○ [*house, room*]; **¶ ~ oneself up** se pomponner○.

tartan /'tɑːtn/ *n, adj* écossais (*m*).

tartar /'tɑːtə(r)/ *n* **1** (deposit) tartre *m*; **2** (formidable person) (woman) virago *f*; (man) croque-mitaine *m*.

tartly /'tɑːtlɪ/ *adv* [*say*] d'un ton acerbe.

task /tɑːsk, US tæsk/ *n* tâche *f*; **a hard ~** une lourde tâche; **to have the ~ of doing** avoir pour tâche de faire.
IDIOMS **to take sb to ~** réprimander qn.

task force *n* MIL corps *m* expéditionnaire; (of police) détachement *m* spécial; (committee) groupe *m* de travail.

taskmaster /'tɑːskmɑːstə(r), US 'tæsk-/ *n* tyran *m*; **to be a hard ~** être très exigeant.

tassel /'tæsl/ *n* (ornamental) gland *m*; (on corn etc) barbe *f*.

taste /teɪst/ I *n* **1** (sensation, sense) goût *m*; **to leave a bad** ou **nasty ~ in the mouth** LIT, FIG laisser un arrière-goût; **have a ~ of this** goûtes-en un peu; **add just a ~ of brandy** ajoutez une goutte de cognac; **2** (brief experience) GEN expérience *f*; (foretaste) avant-goût *m*; **a ~ of life in a big city** un aperçu de la vie dans une grande ville; **3** (liking, preference) goût *m*; **to acquire** ou **develop a ~ for sth** prendre goût à qch; **is this to your ~?** est-ce que ceci vous convient?; **there's no accounting for ~s** chacun ses goûts; **add salt to ~** saler à volonté; **4** (sense of beauty, appropriateness) goût *m*; **she has exquisite ~ in clothes** elle s'habille avec un goût exquis; **that's a matter of ~** ça dépend des goûts; **it would be in bad** ou **poor ~ to do** ce serait de mauvais goût de faire.
II *vtr* **1** (perceive flavour) sentir (le goût de); **2** (try) goûter; **3** FIG (experience) goûter à [*freedom, success, power*]; connaître [*failure, hardship*].
III *vi* (have flavour) **to ~ sweet** avoir un goût sucré; **to ~ horrible** avoir mauvais goût; **the milk ~s off to me** je crois que ce lait est tourné; **to ~ like sth** avoir le goût de qch; **it ~s of pineapple** cela a un goût d'ananas.

taste bud *n* papille *f* gustative.

tasteful /'teɪstfl/ *adj* de bon goût.

tastefully /'teɪstfəlɪ/ *adv* avec goût.

tasteless /'teɪstlɪs/ *adj* **1** [*remark, joke*] de mauvais goût; **2** (without flavour) [*food, drink*] insipide; [*medicine, powder*] qui n'a aucun goût.

taster /'teɪstə(r)/ *n* **1** (person) (to check quality) dégustateur/-trice *m/f*; (to check for poison) goûteur/-euse *m/f*; **2** (foretaste) avant-goût *m* (**of, for** de).

tasting /'teɪstɪŋ/ I *n* dégustation *f*.
II -tasting *combining form* **pleasant-~** (au goût) agréable; **sweet-~** (au goût) sucré.

tasty /'teɪstɪ/ *adj* [*food*] succulent.

tattered /'tætəd/ *adj* [*clothing*] dépenaillé; [*book, document*] en lambeaux; [*person*] déguenillé.

tatters /'tætəz/ *npl* lambeaux *mpl*; **to be in ~** [*clothing*] être en lambeaux; [*career, reputation*] être en ruines; [*hopes*] réduit à néant.

tattle /'tætl/ I *n* (also **tittle-tattle**) commérages *mpl*.
II *vi* jaser (**about** sur).

tattoo /tə'tuː, US tæ'tuː/ I *n* **1** (on skin) tatouage *m*; **2** MIL (parade) parade *f* militaire.
II *vtr* tatouer (**on** sur).

tatty○ /'tætɪ/ *adj* GB [*appearance*] négligé; [*carpet, garment*] miteux/-euse; [*book, shoes*] en mauvais état; [*building, furniture*] délabré.

taught /tɔːt/ *prét, pp* ▶ **teach**.

taunt /tɔːnt/ I *n* raillerie *f*.
II *vtr* railler [*person*] (**about, over** à propos de).

taunting /'tɔːntɪŋ/ I *n* ȼ railleries *fpl*.
II *adj* railleur/-euse, moqueur/-euse.

Taurus /'tɔːrəs/ ▶ **1418** *n* Taureau *m*.

taut /tɔːt/ *adj* tendu.

tauten /'tɔːtn/ I *vtr* tendre.
II *vi* se tendre.

tautology /tɔː'tɒlədʒɪ/ *n* tautologie *f*.

tawdry /'tɔːdrɪ/ *adj* [*clothes*] voyant; [*jewellery*] clinquant; [*furnishings, house*] de mauvais goût; FIG [*motives, methods*] bas/basse; [*affair*] minable.

tawny /'tɔːnɪ/ *adj* ▶ **818** fauve.

tawny owl *n* ZOOL chouette *f* hulotte.

tax /tæks/ I *n* (on goods, services, property) taxe *f*; (on income, profits) impôt *m*; **sales ~** taxe à l'achat; **~ is deducted at source** les impôts sont retenus à la source; **to be liable for ~** être imposable.
II *vtr* **1** imposer [*earnings, person*]; taxer [*luxury goods*]; **2** AUT **to ~ a vehicle** payer la vignette; **the car is ~ed till November** la vignette est valable jusqu'en novembre; **3** (strain) mettre [qch] à l'épreuve [*patience*].

taxable /'tæksəbl/ *adj* imposable.

tax: **~ allowance** *n* abattement *m*; **~ arrears** *npl* arriérés *mpl* fiscaux.

taxation /tæk'seɪʃn/ *n* **1** (imposition of taxes) imposition *f*; **2** (revenue from taxes) impôts *mpl*.

tax: **~ bracket** *n* tranche *f* d'imposition du revenu; **~ break** *n* réduction *f* d'impôt; **~ burden** *n* charge *f* fiscale; **~ code** *n* code *m* d'imposition; **~ collector** *n* percepteur *m*; **~-deductible** *adj* déductible des impôts; **~ disc** *n* vignette *f* (automobile); **~ evasion** *n* fraude *f* fiscale; **~-exempt** *adj* exonéré d'impôt; **~ exile** *n*: personne qui s'est expatriée pour raisons fiscales; **~ form** *n* feuille *f* d'impôts; **~-free** *adj* [*income*] exempt d'impôt; **~ haven** *n* paradis *m* fiscal.

taxi /'tæksɪ/ I *n* taxi *m*; **by ~** en taxi.
II *vi* [*plane*] rouler doucement.

tax incentive *n* incitation *f* fiscale.

taxing /'tæksɪŋ/ *adj* épuisant.

taxi rank GB, **taxi stand** *n* station *f* de taxis.

taxman○ /'tæksmæn/ *n* **the ~** le fisc.

tax office *n* perception *f*.

taxpayer /'tækspeɪə(r)/ *n* contribuable *mf*.

tax return *n* **1** (form) feuille *f* d'impôts; **2** (declaration) déclaration *f* de revenus; **to file a ~** faire sa déclaration d'impôts.

TB *n*: *abrév* ▶ **tuberculosis**.

tbsp *n*: *abrév écrite* = **tablespoon**.

te /tiː/ *n* MUS (also **ti**) si *m*.

tea /tiː/ *n* **1** thé *m*; **2** GB (light afternoon meal) thé *m*; (for children) goûter *m*; (evening meal) dîner *m*.
IDIOMS **it's not my cup of ~** ce n'est pas mon truc○; **to give sb ~ and sympathy** réconforter qn.

tea: **~ bag** *n* sachet *m* de thé; **~ break** *n* GB ~ pause-café *f*; **~ caddy** *n* boîte *f* à thé; **~ cake** *n* GB brioche *f* aux raisins.

teach /tiːtʃ/ (*prét, pp* **taught**) **I** *vtr* **1** (instruct) enseigner à [*children, adults*]; (impart) enseigner [*foreign language, biology*]; **to ~ sb about sth** GEN enseigner qch à qn; (practical skill) apprendre qch à qn; **he taught me (how) to drive** il m'a appris à conduire; **she ~es swimming** elle est professeur de natation; **to ~ school** US être instituteur/-trice; **to ~ sb a lesson** FIG [*person*] donner une bonne leçon à qn; [*experience*] servir de leçon à qn; **2** (advocate) enseigner [*creed, virtue*].
II *vi* enseigner.
III *v refl* **to ~ oneself to do** s'apprendre à faire; **to ~ oneself Spanish** apprendre l'espagnol tout seul.
IDIOMS **you can't ~ an old dog new tricks** il est difficile de déranger les vieilles habitudes.

teacher /ˈtiːtʃə(r)/ **▶ 1251** *n* (in general) enseignant/-e *m/f*; (secondary) professeur *m*; (primary) instituteur/-trice *m/f*; (special needs) éducateur/-trice *m/f*.

teacher training *n* formation *f* pédagogique.

teaching /ˈtiːtʃɪŋ/ **I** *n* enseignement *m*; **to go into** ou **enter ~** entrer dans l'enseignement; **to do some ~ in the evenings** donner quelques cours le soir.
II *noun modifier* [*career, post*] d'enseignant; [*method, qualification*] pédagogique; [*staff*] enseignant.

teaching aid *n* support *m* pédagogique.

teaching assistant, TA **▶ 1251** *n* **1** US UNIV chargé/-e *m/f* d'enseignement; **2** GB SCH *personne sans diplôme d'enseignement qui aide l'instituteur*.

teaching hospital *n* centre *m* hospitalo-universitaire, CHU.

teaching practice *n* GB stage *m* de formation pédagogique; **to be on** ou **be doing ~** être en stage.

tea: **~ cloth** *n* GB (for drying) torchon *m* (à vaisselle); **~ cosy** GB, **~ cozy** US *n* couvre-théière *m inv*.

teacup /ˈtiːkʌp/ *n* tasse *f* à thé.
IDIOMS **a storm in a ~** une tempête dans un verre d'eau.

teak /tiːk/ *n* teck *m*.

tea lady **▶ 1251** *n* GB *employée qui distribue du thé dans les bureaux*.

tea leaf *n* feuille *f* de thé; **to read the tea-leaves ~** lire dans le marc de café.

team /tiːm/ **I** *n* **1** (of people) équipe *f*; **to work well as a ~** faire un bon travail d'équipe; **2** (of animals) attelage *m*.
II *vtr* (coordinate) associer [*garment*] (**with** à).
■ **team up**: ¶ **~ up** [*people*] faire équipe; [*organizations*] s'associer; ¶ **~ [sb] up** associer.

team: **~ member** *n* équipier/-ière *m/f*; **~ spirit** *n* esprit *m* d'équipe.

teamster /ˈtiːmstə(r)/ *n* US routier *m*.

teamwork *n* collaboration *f*.

tea: **~ party** *n* thé *m*; (for children) goûter *m*; **~ plate** *n* petite assiette *f*.

teapot /ˈtiːpɒt/ *n* théière *f*.

tear¹ /teə(r)/ **I** *n* GEN accroc *m*; MED déchirure *f*.
II *vtr* (*prét* **tore**; *pp* **torn**) **1** (rip) déchirer [*garment, paper*]; mettre [qch] en pièces [*flesh, prey*]; **to ~ sth from** ou **out of** arracher qch de [*book, notepad*]; **I've torn a hole in my coat** j'ai fait un accroc à mon manteau; **to ~ sth to pieces** ou **bits** ou **shreds** LIT mettre qch en morceaux; FIG démolir○ [*proposal, book, film*]; **to ~ sb to pieces** FIG descendre qn en flammes; **to ~ one's hair (out)** LIT, FIG s'arracher les cheveux; **to ~ a muscle** se déchirer un muscle;

to be torn between FIG être tiraillé entre [*options, persons*]; **2** (remove by force) arracher.
III *vi* (*prét* **tore**; *pp* **torn**) **1** (rip) se déchirer; **2** (rush) **to ~ out/off/past** sortir/partir/passer en trombe; **to ~ up/down the stairs** monter/descendre les escaliers quatre à quatre; **3** (pull forcefully) **to ~ at** [*animal*] déchiqueter [*flesh, prey*]; [*person*] s'attaquer à [*rubble*]; **4**○ (criticize) **to ~ into** enguirlander○ [*person*]; démolir○ [*play, film, book*].
IV tearing *pres p adj* **1 a ~ing sound** un bruit de déchirement; **2**○ **to be in a ~ing hurry** GB être terriblement pressé (**to do** de faire).
IDIOMS **that's torn it**○! GB il ne manquait plus que ça!
■ **tear apart**: ¶ **~ [sth] apart, ~ apart [sth] 1** (destroy) LIT mettre [qch] en pièces [*prey*]; démolir [*building*]; FIG déchirer [*couple, organization, country*]; démolir○ [*film, novel, essay*]; **2** (separate) séparer [*connected items*]; ¶ **~ [sb] apart 1**○ (criticize) descendre [qn] en flammes; **2** (dismember) mettre [qn] en pièces; (separate) séparer [*two people*].
■ **tear away**: ¶ **~ away [sth]** se déchirer; ¶ **~ away [sth]** arracher [*wrapping, bandage*]; ¶ **~ [sb] away** arracher [*person*]; **to ~ one's gaze away** détacher ses yeux.
■ **tear down**: **~ [sth] down, ~ down [sth]** démolir [*building, wall*].
■ **tear off**: **~ [sth] off, ~ off [sth]** (remove) (carefully) détacher; (violently) arracher.
■ **tear open**: **~ [sth] open, ~ open [sth]**, **~ [sth] open** ouvrir [qch] en le/la déchirant.
■ **tear out**: **~ [sth] out, ~ out [sth]** détacher [*coupon, cheque*]; arracher [*page, picture*].
■ **tear up**: **~ [sth] up, ~ up [sth] 1** (destroy) déchirer [*letter, document*]; **2** (remove) déraciner [*tree*]; arracher [*tracks*]; défoncer [*pavement*].

tear² /tɪə(r)/ *n* larme *f*; **close to ~s** au bord des larmes; **to burst into ~s** fondre en larmes; **to shed ~s** pleurer; **it brought ~s to her eyes, it moved her to ~s** elle en avait les larmes aux yeux.
IDIOMS **to end in ~s** [*game, party*] finir par des pleurs; [*campaign, experiment*] mal se terminer.

tearaway /ˈteərəweɪ/ *n* casse-cou *m inv*.

tear /tɪə(r)/: **~drop** *n* larme *f*; **~ duct** *n* conduit *m* lacrymal.

tearful /ˈtɪəfl/ *adj* [*person, face*] en larmes; [*voice*] larmoyant; **to feel ~** avoir envie de pleurer; **a ~ reunion** des retrouvailles émues.

tearfully /ˈtɪəfəlɪ/ *adv* (*say, tell*) les larmes aux yeux.

tear gas /tɪə(r)/ *n* gaz *m* lacrymogène.

tear-jerker /ˈtɪədʒɜːkə(r)/ *n* HUM, PÉJ **this film is a real ~** ce film est un vrai mélo○.

tear-off /ˈteərɒf/ *adj* [*coupon, slip*] détachable.

tear-stained /ˈtɪəsteɪnd/ *adj* [*face*] barbouillé de larmes; [*pillow, letter*] mouillé de larmes.

tease /tiːz/ **I** *n* **1** (joker) taquin/-e *m/f*; **2** (woman) PÉJ allumeuse *f* PÉJ.
II *vtr* **1** (provoke) taquiner [*person*] (**about** à propos de); tourmenter [*animal*]; **2** (backcomb) crêper [*hair*].
III *vi* taquiner.

teasel /ˈtiːzl/ *n* BOT cardère *f*.

teaser /ˈtiːzə(r)/ *n* **1**○ (puzzle) colle○ *f*; **2** (person) taquin/-e *m/f*.

tea: **~ service, ~ set** *n* service *m* à thé; **~ shop** *n* GB salon *m* de thé.

teasing /ˈtiːzɪŋ/ **I** *n* GEN taquineries *fpl*.
II *adj* taquin, moqueur/-euse.

tea: **~spoon** *n* petite cuillère *f*, cuillère *f* à café; **~spoonful** *n* cuillerée *f* à café; **~ strainer** *n* passe-thé *m inv*, passoire *f* (à thé).

teat /tiːt/ *n* **1** (of cow, goat, ewe) trayon *m*; **2** GB (on baby's bottle) tétine *f*.

tea: **~time** *n* (in the afternoon) l'heure *f* du thé; (in the evening) l'heure *f* du dîner; **~ towel** *n* GB torchon *m* (à vaisselle).

tech /tek/ *n* ○GB *abrév* ▶ **technical college**.

technical /ˈteknɪkl/ *adj* **1** GEN, SPORT technique; **a**

~ **hitch** un incident technique; **the ~ staff** les techniciens; **2** JUR [*point, detail*] de procédure; ~ **offence** quasi-délit *m*.

technical: ~ **college** *n* institut *m* d'enseignement technique; ~ **drawing** *n* dessin *m* industriel.

technicality /ˌteknɪ'kælətɪ/ *n* **1** GEN (technical detail) détail *m* technique (**of** de); **2** (minor detail) point *m* de détail; **the case was dismissed on a ~** JUR l'affaire a été renvoyée pour vice de forme; **3** (technical nature) technicité *f*.

technically /'teknɪklɪ/ *adv* **1** (strictly speaking) théoriquement; **2** (technologically) [*advanced, backward, difficult, possible*] techniquement; **3** (in technique) [*good, bad*] sur le plan technique.

technician /tek'nɪʃn/ ▶ 1251 *n* (all contexts) technicien/-ienne *m/f*.

technique /tek'niːk/ *n* **1** (method) technique *f*; **2** (skill) technique *f*.

technocrat /'teknəkræt/ *n* technocrate *mf*.

technological /ˌteknə'lɒdʒɪkl/ *adj* technologique.

technologically /ˌteknə'lɒdʒɪklɪ/ *adv* sur le plan technologique.

technology /tek'nɒlədʒɪ/ *n* (all contexts) technologie *f*; **information ~** informatique *f*.

teddy /'tedɪ/ *n* (also ~ **bear**) ours *m* en peluche.

tedious /'tiːdɪəs/ *adj* ennuyeux/-euse.

tedium /'tiːdɪəm/ *n* **1** (boredom) ennui *m*; **2** (tediousness) manque *m* d'intérêt.

teem /tiːm/ **I** *vi* **to ~ with, to be ~ing with** regorger de [*people*]; abonder en [*wildlife*]; fourmiller de [*ideas*].
II *v impers* **it was ~ing (with rain)** il pleuvait des cordes.
III teeming *pres p adj* [*city, continent, ocean*] grouillant (**with** de); [*masses, crowds*] grouillant.

teen○ /tiːn/ *adj* [*fashion*] pour les jeunes; [*idol*] des jeunes.

teenage /'tiːneɪdʒ/ *adj* [*daughter, son*] qui est adolescent/-e; [*singer, player*] jeune; [*illiteracy, drugtaking*] chez les adolescents; [*pregnancy*] précoce; [*fashion, problem*] des adolescents.

teenager /'tiːneɪdʒə(r)/ *n* jeune *mf*, adolescent/-e *m/f*.

teens /tiːnz/ *npl* adolescence *f*; **to be in one's ~** être adolescent/-e; **to be in one's early/late ~** être au début/à la fin de l'adolescence.

tee-shirt /'tiːʃɜːt/ *n* tee-shirt, T-shirt *m*.

teeter /'tiːtə(r)/ *vi* vaciller; **to ~ on the edge** ou **brink of sth** FIG être au bord de qch.

teeter-totter /'tiːtətɒtə(r)/ *n* US bascule *f*.

teeth /tiːθ/ *npl* ▶ **tooth**.

teethe /tiːð/ *vi* faire ses dents.

teething /'tiːðɪŋ/ *n* poussée *f* des dents.

teething troubles *npl* FIG difficultés *fpl* initiales.

teetotal /tiː'təʊtl, US 'tiː'təʊtl/ *adj* **I'm ~** je ne bois jamais d'alcool.

teetotaller GB, **teetotaler** US /tiː'təʊtələ(r)/ *n* personne *f* qui ne boit jamais d'alcool.

TEFL /'tefl/ *n* (*abrév* = **Teaching of English as a Foreign Language**) enseignement *m* de l'anglais langue étrangère.

tel *n* (*abrév écrite* = **telephone**) tél.

tele+ /'telɪ-/ *combining form* télé+.

telecast /'telɪkɑːst, US -kæst/ **I** *n* émission *f* de télévision.
II *vtr* (*prét, pp* **telecast(ed)**) diffuser [qch] à la télévision.

telecommunications /ˌtelɪkəˌmjuːnɪ'keɪʃnz/ **I** *n* (+ *v sg ou pl*) télécommunications *fpl*.
II *noun modifier* [*expert*] en télécommunications; [*firm, satellite*] de télécommunications; [*industry*] des télécommunications.

telecommuting /ˌtelɪkə'mjuːtɪŋ/ *n* télétravail *m*.

teleconference /'telɪkɒnfərəns/ *n* téléconférence *f*.

telegram /'telɪgræm/ *n* télégramme *m*.

telegraph /'telɪgrɑːf, US -græf/ **I** *n* **1** TELECOM télégraphe *m*; **2** NAUT transmetteur *m* d'ordres.
II *noun modifier* [*pole, post, wire*] télégraphique.
III *vtr* télégraphier.

telegraphy /tɪ'legrəfɪ/ *n* télégraphie *f*.

telemarketer /telɪ'mɑːkɪtə(r)/ *n* téléprospecteur/-trice *m/f*.

telemarketing /'telɪmɑːkɪtɪŋ/ *n* télémarketing *m*.

telemessage /'telɪmesɪdʒ/ *n* GB télégramme *m*.

telepathic /ˌtelɪ'pæθɪk/ *adj* [*communication*] télépathique; [*person*] télépathe.

telepathy /tɪ'lepəθɪ/ *n* télépathie *f*.

telephone /'telɪfəʊn/ **I** *n* téléphone *m*; **on** ou **over the ~** au téléphone; **to be on the ~** (connected) avoir le téléphone; (talking) être au téléphone.
II *noun modifier* [*conversation, equipment, message*] téléphonique; [*engineer*] du téléphone.
III *vtr* téléphoner à, appeler [*person, organization*]; téléphoner [*instructions, message*]; **to ~ France** téléphoner en France, appeler la France.
IV *vi* appeler, téléphoner.

telephone: ~ **answering machine** *n* répondeur *m* téléphonique; ~ **banking** *n* FIN transactions *fpl* bancaires télématiques; ~ **book** *n* = **telephone directory**; ~ **booth**, ~ **box** GB *n* cabine *f* téléphonique; ~ **call** *n* appel *m* téléphonique; ~ **directory** *n* annuaire *m* (du téléphone); ~ **exchange** *n* centrale *f* téléphonique; ~ **number** *n* numéro *m* de téléphone; ~ **operator** ▶ 1251 *n* standardiste *mf*; ~ **subscriber** *n* abonné/-e *m/f* au téléphone.

telephonist /tɪ'lefənɪst/ ▶ 1251 *n* GB standardiste *mf*.

telephoto lens /'telɪfəʊtəʊ lenz/ *n* téléobjectif *m*.

Telepoint /'telɪpɔɪnt/ *n* TELECOM Pointel *m*.

teleprinter /'telɪprɪntə(r)/ *n* téléscripteur *m*.

telesales /'telɪseɪlz/ *n* (+ *v sg*) télévente *f*.

telescope /'telɪskəʊp/ **I** *n* télescope *m*, lunette *f* SPEC.
II *vtr* LIT replier [*stand, umbrella*]; FIG condenser [*content, series*] (**into** en).
III *vi* [*stand, umbrella*] être télescopique; [*car, train*] se télescoper.

telescopic /ˌtelɪ'skɒpɪk/ *adj* [*aerial, stand, umbrella*] télescopique; ~ **lens** PHOT téléobjectif *m*; ~ **sight** (on gun) lunette *f* de visée.

teleshopping /'telɪʃɒpɪŋ/ *n* téléachat *m*.

televise /'telɪvaɪz/ **I** *vtr* téléviser.
II televised *pp adj* télévisé.

television /'telɪvɪʒn, -'vɪʒn/ **I** *n* **1** (medium) télévision *f*; **on/for ~** à la/pour la télévision; **live on ~** en direct à la télévision; **it makes good ~** ça marche à la télévision; **2** (set) téléviseur *m*.
II *noun modifier* [*broadcast, camera, channel, producer, studio*] de télévision; [*documentary, news, play*] télévisé; [*film, script*] pour la télévision; [*interview*] à la télévision.

television: ~ **dinner** *n* plateau-télévision *m*; ~ **licence** *n* redevance *f* télévision; ~ **lounge** *n* salle *f* de télévision; ~ **programme** *n* émission *f* de télévision; ~ **screen** *n* écran *m* de télévision; ~ **set** *n* téléviseur *m*, poste *m* de télévision.

televisual /ˌtelɪ'vɪʒʊəl/ *adj* télévisuel/-elle.

telex /'teleks/ ▶ 1251 **I** *n* télex *m*.
II *noun modifier* [*number*] de télex; ~ **machine** = télex *m*; ~ **operator** télexiste *mf*.
III *vtr* télexer.

tell /tel/ (*prét, pp* **told**) **I** *vtr* **1** GEN [*person*] dire [*lie, truth*]; raconter [*joke, story*]; prédire [*future*]; [*manual, gauge*] indiquer; **to ~ sb about** ou **of sth** parler de qch à qn; **to ~ sb to do** dire à qn de faire; **to ~ sb not to do** GEN dire à qn de ne pas faire; (forbid) défendre à qn de faire; **to ~ sb how to do/what to do** expliquer à qn comment faire/ce qu'il faut faire; **to ~ the time** [*clock*] indiquer or marquer l'heure; [*person*] lire l'heure; **can you ~ me the time please?** peux-tu me dire l'heure (qu'il est), s'il te plaît?; **I was told that** on m'a dit que; **his behaviour ~s us a lot about his character** son comportement nous en dit long sur sa personnalité; **I told you so!**,

what did I ~ you! je te l'avais bien dit!; **you're ~ing me!** à qui le dis-tu!; **it's true, I ~ you!** puisque je te dis que c'est vrai!; **do as you are told!** fais ce qu'on te dit!; **she just won't be told!** elle ne veut pas écouter ce qu'on lui dit; **~ me all about it!** racontez-moi tout!; **I could ~ you a thing or two about her!** je pourrais vous en dire long sur elle!; **2** (deduce) **you can ~ (that) he's lying** on voit bien qu'il ment; **I can ~ (that) he's disappointed** je sais qu'il est déçu; **you can ~ a lot from the clothes people wear** la façon dont les gens s'habillent est très révélatrice; **3** (distinguish) distinguer; **he can't ~ right from wrong** il ne sait pas distinguer le bien du mal; **can you ~ the difference?** est-ce que vous voyez la différence?; **how can you ~ which is which?, how can you ~ them apart?** comment peut-on les distinguer l'un de l'autre?

II vi **1** (reveal secret) **promise me you won't ~!** promets-moi de ne pas le répéter!; **that would be ~ing!** je ne peux pas le dire!; **2** (be evidence of) **to ~ of** témoigner de; **3** (know for certain) savoir; **as ou so far as I can ~** pour autant que je sache; **how can you ~?** comment le sais-tu?; **you never can ~** on ne sait jamais; **4** (produce an effect) **her age is beginning to ~** elle commence à faire son âge; **her inexperience told against her at the interview** son inexpérience a joué contre elle lors de son entretien.

III v refl **to ~ oneself** se dire (**that** que).

IDIOMS **to ~ all** tout raconter; **~ me another○!** à d'autres○!; **to ~ sb where to get off○** envoyer promener qn; **you ~ me!** je n'en sais rien!, à ton avis?; **to ~ it like it is** parler net; **time (alone) will ~** (seul) l'avenir le dira.

■ **tell off**: **~ [sb] off** (scold) réprimander [person]; **she got told off for arriving late** elle s'est fait disputer○ parce qu'elle était arrivée en retard.

■ **tell on**: **~ on [sb] 1** (reveal information about) dénoncer [person] (**to** à); **2** (have visible effect on) **the strain is beginning to ~ on him** on commence à voir sur lui les effets de la fatigue; **her age is beginning to ~ on her** elle commence à faire son âge.

teller /'telə(r)/ **▶ 1251** I n **1** (in bank) caissier/-ière m/f; **2** (in election) scrutateur/-trice m/f.

telling /'telɪŋ/ I n récit m; **a funny story that lost nothing in the ~** une histoire drôle qui ne perdait rien à être racontée; **her adventures grew more and more fantastic in the ~** ses aventures devenaient de plus en plus fantastiques à mesure qu'elle les racontait.

II adj **1** (effective) [blow] bien porté; [argument] efficace; **2** (revealing) [remark, omission] révélateur/-trice.

IDIOMS **there's no ~ what will happen next** personne ne peut dire ce qui va se passer maintenant.

tellingly /'telɪŋlɪ/ adv **1** (effectively) efficacement; **2** (revealingly) **~, he did not allude to this** fait révélateur, il n'y a pas fait allusion.

telling-off /ˌtelɪŋ'ɒf/ n réprimande f.

tell-tale /'telteɪl/ I n rapporteur/-euse m/f.

II adj [sign] révélateur/-trice.

telly○ /'telɪ/ n GB télé○ f.

temerity /tɪ'merətɪ/ n audace f.

temp /temp/ GB I n intérimaire mf.

II vi travailler comme intérimaire.

temper /'tempə(r)/ I n **1** (mood) humeur f; **to be in a good/bad ~** être de bonne/mauvaise humeur; **to be in a ~** être en colère; **to keep ou control one's ~** se contrôler; **to lose one's ~** se mettre en colère (**with** contre); **to fly into a ~** exploser; **~s flared ou frayed** les esprits se sont emportés; **2** (nature) caractère m; **to have a sweet ~** être d'un caractère doux; **to have a hot ou quick ~** être irascible; **to have a nasty ~** avoir un sale caractère.

II vtr **1** (moderate) tempérer; **2** IND tremper [steel].

temperament /'temprəmənt/ n **1** (nature) tempérament m; **2** (excitability) humeur f.

temperamental /ˌtemprə'mentl/ adj **1** (volatile) capricieux/-ieuse; **2** (natural) [affinity] naturel/-elle; [differences] de tempérament.

temperamentally /ˌtemprə'mentəlɪ/ adv **1** (by nature) psychologiquement; **they were ~ unsuited** il y avait entre eux incompatibilité de caractère; **2** (in volatile manner) de façon capricieuse.

temperance /'tempərəns/ n **1** (moderation) modération f; **2** (being teetotal) sobriété f, tempérance f.

temperate /'tempərət/ adj [climate, zone] tempéré; [person, habit] modéré.

temperature /'temprətʃə(r)/, US 'tempərtʃʊər/ n **1** METEOROL, PHYS température f; **at room ~** à température ambiante; **2** MED température f; **to be running ou to have a ~** avoir de la température or de la fièvre; **to have a ~ of 39°** avoir 39° de fièvre.

temper tantrum n caprice m.

tempest /'tempɪst/ n LITTÉR LIT, FIG tempête f.

tempestuous /tem'pestʃʊəs/ adj [relationship, sea, wind] tempétueux/-euse; [music] impétueux/-euse.

temping /'tempɪŋ/ n **to do ~** faire des intérims mpl.

temping job n intérim m.

template /'templeɪt/ n GEN gabarit m; COMPUT modèle m.

temple /'templ/ n **1** (building) temple m; **2** (on face) tempe f.

tempo /'tempəʊ/ n (pl **~s** ou **tempi**) MUS tempo m; FIG rythme m; **at a fast ~** sur un tempo rapide.

temporal /'tempərəl/ adj temporel/-elle.

temporarily /'tempərəlɪ, US -'perərɪlɪ/ adv (for a limited time) temporairement; (provisionally) provisoirement.

temporary /'temprərɪ, US -'perərɪ/ adj [job, contract] temporaire; [manager, secretary] intérimaire; [arrangement, accommodation] provisoire; **on a ~ basis** à titre provisoire.

temporize /'tempəraɪz/ vi atermoyer.

tempt /tempt/ vtr tenter; **to be ~ed** être tenté; **to ~ sb with** attirer qn avec qch; **to ~ sb into doing sth** inciter qn à faire qch; **can I ~ you to a whisky?** puis-je vous offrir un whisky?

IDIOMS **to ~ fate** ou **providence** tenter le destin or sort.

temptation /temp'teɪʃn/ n tentation f; **to give in to ~** céder à la tentation; **to put ~ in sb's way** exposer qn à la tentation.

tempting /'temptɪŋ/ adj [offer, discount, suggestion] alléchant; [food, smell] appétissant; [idea] tentant.

temptress /'temptrɪs/ n tentatrice f.

ten /ten/ **▶ 1112|, 713|, 812|** I n **1** (number) dix m inv; **in ~s** [sell] par dizaines; [count] de dix en dix; **~s of thousands** des dizaines de milliers; **2○** US (also **~-dollar bill**) billet m de dix dollars.

II adj dix inv.

IDIOMS **~ to one (it'll rain)** dix contre un○ (qu'il va pleuvoir).

tenable /'tenəbl/ adj **1** (valid) [theory, suggestion] défendable; **2** (available) **the job is ~ for a year** le poste est accordé pour un an.

tenacious /tɪ'neɪʃəs/ adj tenace.

tenacity /tɪ'næsətɪ/ n ténacité f.

tenancy /'tenənsɪ/ n location f; **six-month ~** bail m de six mois; **terms of ~** conditions de bail.

tenancy agreement n bail m.

tenant /'tenənt/ n locataire mf.

ten-cent store /ˌtensent 'stɔː(r)/ n US bazar m.

tend /tend/ I vtr soigner [patient]; entretenir [garden]; s'occuper de [stall, store].

II vi **1** (incline) **to ~ to do** avoir tendance à faire; **to ~ towards sth** pencher vers qch; **I ~ to think that** j'inclinerais à penser que; **it ~s to be the case** c'est en général le cas; **2** (look after) **to ~ to** soigner [patient]; s'occuper de [guests]; **to ~ to sb's needs** veiller aux besoins de qn.

tendency /'tendənsɪ/ n tendance f (**to, towards** à; **to do** à faire); **there is a ~ for people to arrive late** les gens ont tendance à arriver en retard.

tendentious /ten'denʃəs/ adj tendancieux/-ieuse.

tender /'tendə(r)/ I n **1** (offer) soumission; **to put work out to ~** mettre un ouvrage en adjudication;

Temperature

Temperatures in French are written as in the tables below.
Note the space in French between the figure and the
degree sign and letter indicating the scale. When the scale
letter is omitted, temperatures are written thus: 20°; 98,4°
etc. (French has a comma, where English has a decimal
point).

For how to say numbers in French, ▶ **1112 |**.

Celsius or centigrade (C)	Fahrenheit (F)	
100 °C	212 °F	température d'ébullition de l'eau (boiling point)
90 °C	194 °F	
80 °C	176 °F	
70 °C	158 °F	
60 °C	140 °F	
50 °C	122 °F	
40 °C	104 °F	
37 °C	98,4 °F	
30 °C	86 °F	
20 °C	68 °F	
10 °C	50 °F	
0 °C	32 °F	température de congélation de l'eau (freezing point)
−10 °C	14 °F	
−17,8 °C	0 °F	
−273,15 °C	−459,67 °F	le zéro absolu (absolute zero)

−15°C   = −15 °C (moins quinze degrés Celsius)
the thermometer
says 40°   = le thermomètre indique quarante degrés
above 30°C   = plus de trente degrés Celsius
over 30° Celsius = plus de trente degrés Celsius
below 30°   = en dessous de trente degrés

People

body temperature is 37°C = la température du corps est de* 37 °C (trente-sept degrés Celsius)
what is his temperature? = quelle est sa température?
his temperature is 38° = il a trente-huit (de* fièvre)
* *The* de *is obligatory here.*

Things

how hot is the milk? *ou* what
temperature is the milk? = à quelle température est le lait?
it's 40°C   = il est à 40 °C
what temperature does
water boil at?   = à quelle température l'eau bout-elle?
it boils at 100°C = elle bout à 100 °C
at a temperature of 200° = à une température de deux cents degrés
A is hotter than B = A est plus chaud que B
B is cooler than A = B est moins chaud que A
B is colder than A = B est plus froid que A
A is the same
temperature as B = A est à la même température que B
A and B are the
same temperature = A et B sont à la même température

Weather

what's the
temperature today? = quelle température fait-il aujourd'hui? (*this French phrase is also the equivalent of both* how hot is it? *and* how cold is it?)
it's 65°F   = il fait 65 °F (*soixante-cinq degrés Fahrenheit*)
it's 40 degrees = il fait 40 degrés
Nice is warmer (*or*
hotter) than London = il fait plus chaud à Nice qu'à Londres
it's the same temperature in
Paris as in London = il fait la même température à Paris qu'à Londres

---

to invite **~s** faire un appel d'offres; **2** (currency) ▶ **legal tender**.
II *adj* **1** (soft) [*food*] tendre; [*bud, shoot*] fragile; **2** (loving) [*kiss, love, smile*] tendre; **~ care** sollicitude *f*; **3** (sensitive) [*bruise, skin*] sensible; **4** (young) **at the ~ age of two** à l'âge tendre de deux ans.
III *vtr* offrir [*money*]; présenter [*apology, fare*]; donner [*resignation*].
IV *vi* soumissionner, faire une soumission.
tenderhearted /ˌtendəˈhɑːtɪd/ *adj* sensible.
tenderize /ˈtendəraɪz/ *vtr* attendrir.
tender: **~loin** *n* CULIN milieu *m* de filet de porc; **~loin district** *n* US quartier *m* malfamé.
tenderly /ˈtendəlɪ/ *adv* tendrement.
tenderness /ˈtendənɪs/ *n* **1** (gentleness) tendresse *f*; **2** (soreness) sensibilité *f*; **3** (texture) (of shoot) fragilité *f*; (of meat) tendreté *f*.
tendon /ˈtendən/ *n* tendon *m*.
tendril /ˈtendrəl/ *n* (of plant) vrille *f*; (of hair) mèche *f* folle.
tenement /ˈtenəmənt/ *n* (also **~ block** ou **~ building** GB, **~ house** US) immeuble *m* ancien (*souvent délabré et insalubre*).
tenet /ˈtenɪt/ *n* GEN principe *m*; PHILOS, POL, RELIG dogme *m*.
tenfold /ˈtenfəʊld/ **I** *adj* décuple.
II *adv* **to increase** ou **multiply ~** décupler.
ten four /ˌten ˈfɔː(r)/ US **I** *n* **that's a ~** c'est exact.
II *excl* message reçu!
tenner○ /ˈtenə(r)/ *n* GB (note) billet *m* de dix livres.
tennis /ˈtenɪs/ ▶ **949 |** *n* tennis *m*; **a game of ~** une partie de tennis; **men's ~** tennis masculin.
tennis: **~ court** *n* court *m* de tennis, tennis *m inv*; **~ whites** *npl* tenue *f* de tennis blanche.
tenor /ˈtenə(r)/ ▶ **1380 |** *n* **1** MUS (singer, voice) ténor *m*; **2** (of speech, reply) (tone) ton *m*; (drift, meaning) sens *m*; **3**

(quality) **the even ~ of his life** le cours régulier de sa vie.
tenpin bowling /ˌtenpɪn ˈbəʊlɪŋ/ GB, **tenpins** US ▶ **949 |** *n* bowling *m* (à dix quilles).
tense /tens/ **I** *n* LING temps *m*; **the present ~** le présent (**of** de); **in the past ~** au passé.
II *adj* (strained) GEN tendu; [*moment*] de tension; **to make sb ~** rendre qn nerveux.
III *vtr* tendre [*muscle*]; raidir [*body*]; **to ~ oneself** se raidir.
■ **tense up**: **1** (stiffen) [*muscle*] se tendre; [*body*] se raidir; **2** (become nervous) [*person*] se crisper.
tensely /ˈtenslɪ/ *adv* (avec) les nerfs tendus; **to smile ~** avoir un sourire crispé.
tension /ˈtenʃn/ *n* GEN tension *f* (**within** au sein de; **over** au sujet de); (suspense) suspense *m*.
tent /tent/ *n* tente *f*.
tentacle /ˈtentəkl/ *n* tentacule *m*.
tentative /ˈtentətɪv/ *adj* [*inquiry, smile, suggestion*] timide; [*movement*] hésitant; [*conclusion, offer*] provisoire.
tentatively /ˈtentətɪvlɪ/ *adv* [*agree, conclude*] provisoirement; [*smile, speak*] timidement; [*suggest*] prudemment.
tenterhooks /ˈtentəhʊks/ *npl* IDIOMS **to be on ~** être sur des charbons ardents; **to keep sb on ~** faire languir qn.
tenth /tenθ/ ▶ **1112 |**, **854 |** **I** *n* **1** (in order) dixième *mf*; **2** (of month) dix *m inv*; **3** (fraction) dixième *m*.
II *adj* dixième.
III *adv* [*come, finish*] dixième, en dixième position.
tent: **~ peg** *n* piquet *m* de tente; **~ pole** GB, **~ stake** US *n* mât *m* de tente.
tenuous /ˈtenjʊəs/ *adj* [*link*] ténu; [*distinction, theory*] mince.
tenure /ˈtenjʊə(r), US tenjər/ *n* **1** (right of occupancy) **~**

of land/property jouissance *f* d'un droit à un terrain/ une propriété; **tenants do not have security of ~** les locataires n'ont pas de bail assuré; **2** UNIV (job security) titularisation *f* d'emploi; **to have ~** être titulaire; **3** (period of office) fonction *f*.

tenured /'tenjʊə(r)d, US tenjərd/ *adj* [*professor*] titulaire; [*job*] de titulaire.

tepid /'tepɪd/ *adj* tiède.

tercentenary /,tɜ:sen'ti:nərɪ, tɜ:'sentənerɪ/ *n* tricentenaire *m*.

term /tɜ:m/ **I** *n* **1** (period of time) GEN période *f*, terme *m*; SCH, UNIV trimestre *m*; JUR (duration of lease) durée *f* (de bail); **the president's first ~ of office** le premier mandat du président; **~ of imprisonment** peine *f* de prison; **to have reached (full) ~** (of pregnancy) être à terme; **autumn/spring/summer ~** SCH, UNIV premier/deuxième/troisième trimestre *m*; **2** (word, phrase) terme *m*; **~ of abuse** injure *f*; **she condemned their action in the strongest possible ~s** elle a condamné leur action très fermement; **3** (limit) terme *m* ALSO MATH. **II terms** *npl* **1** (conditions) GEN termes *mpl*; (of will) dispositions *fpl*; COMM conditions *fpl* de paiement; **name your own ~s** fixez vos conditions; **~s and conditions** JUR modalités *fpl*; **~s of trade** COMM, ECON termes de l'échange international; **on easy ~s** COMM avec facilités *fpl* de paiement; **~s of surrender** POL conditions de la reddition; **~s of reference** attributions *fpl*; **2 to come to ~s with** assumer [*identity, past, condition, disability*]; accepter [*death, defeat, failure*]; affronter [*issue*]; **3** (relations) termes *mpl*; **they are on first-name ~s** ils s'appellent par leurs prénoms; **4** (point of view) **in his/their** etc **~s** selon ses/leurs etc critères. **III in terms of** *prep phr* **1** GEN, MATH (as expressed by) en fonction de; **2** (from the point of view of) du point de vue de, sur le plan de; **they own very little in ~s of real property** ils ne possèdent pas grand-chose en fait de biens immobiliers; **I was thinking in ~s of how much it would cost** j'essayais de calculer combien cela coûterait. **IV** *vtr* appeler, nommer.

terminal /'tɜ:mɪnl/ **I** *n* **1** (at station) terminus *m*; AVIAT aérogare *f*; **rail ~** terminus *m*; **oil ~** terminal *m* pétrolier; **ferry ~** gare *f* maritime; **2** COMPUT terminal *m*; **3** ELEC borne *f*. **II** *adj* **1** [*stage, point*] terminal; MED [*illness, patient*] (incurable) incurable; (at final stage) en phase terminale; FIG [*boredom*] mortel/-elle○; **2** COMM, SCH trimestriel/-ielle.

terminally /'tɜ:mɪnəlɪ/ *adv* **the ~ ill** les mourants *mpl*.

terminal: **~ point, ~ station** *n* RAIL terminus *m*; **~ ward** *n* MED = unité *f* de soins palliatifs.

terminate /'tɜ:mɪneɪt/ **I** *vtr* **1** mettre fin à [*arrangement, discussion, meeting, phase, relationship*]; résilier [*contract*]; interrompre [*pregnancy*]; annuler [*agreement*]; arrêter [*treatment*]; **2** US renvoyer [*employee*]; **3**○ (kill) liquider○. **II** *vi* **1** (end) [*agreement, meeting, commercial contract*] se terminer; [*employment, offer, work contract*] prendre fin; [*speaker, programme*] terminer; [*road*] s'arrêter; **2** (end route) s'arrêter; **'this train ~s at Oxford'** 'Oxford, terminus du train'.

termination /,tɜ:mɪ'neɪʃn/ *n* **1** (ending) (of contract) résiliation *f*; (of service) interruption *f*; (of discussion, relations, scheme) fin *f*; **2** MED interruption *f* de grossesse; **3** LING terminaison *f*.

terminology /,tɜ:mɪ'nɒlədʒɪ/ *n* terminologie *f*.

terminus /'tɜ:mɪnəs/ *n* (*pl* **-ni** ou **-nuses**) GB terminus *m*.

terrace /'terəs/ **I** *n* **1** (veranda) terrasse *f*; **2** ARCHIT alignement *m* de maisons (*identiques et contiguës*). **II terraces** *npl* (in stadium) gradins *mpl*. **III** *vtr* arranger [*qch*] en terrasses [*garden, hillside*].

terrace(d) house *n* maison *f* (*située dans un alignement de maisons identiques et contiguës*).

terracotta /,terə'kɒtə/ *n* **1** (earthenware) terre *f* cuite; **2** (colour) ocre brun *m*.

terrain /'tereɪn/ *n* GEN, MIL terrain *m*; **all-~ vehicle** véhicule *m* tout terrain.

terrestrial /tə'restrɪəl/ *adj* terrestre.

terrible /'terəbl/ *adj* **1** [*pain, noise, sight, temper*] épouvantable; [*accident, fight*] terrible; [*mistake*] grave; **2**○ [*food, weather*] affreux/-euse; **to be ~ at** être nul en [*rugby, maths*]; **he's a ~ liar** c'est un menteur invétéré; **I feel ~** (guilty) je me sens coupable; (ill) je ne me sens pas bien du tout; **you look ~ in that hat** ce chapeau ne te va absolument pas; **it was a ~ shame** c'était vraiment dommage.

terribly /'terəblɪ/ *adv* **1** (very) [*flattered, pleased, obvious*] très; [*clever, easy, hot, polite*] extrêmement; **~ well/badly** fort bien/mal; **I'm ~ sorry** je suis navré; **2** (badly) [*limp, suffer, injured*] horriblement; [*worry*] terriblement; [*sing, drive, write*] affreusement mal.

terrific /tə'rɪfɪk/ *adj* **1** (huge) [*amount, incentive, pleasure, size*] énorme; [*pain, heat, noise*] épouvantable; [*argument*] violent; [*speed*] fou/folle; [*accident, problem, shock, worry*] terrible; [*struggle*] acharné; **2**○ (wonderful) formidable; **to look ~** (healthy) avoir l'air en pleine forme○; (attractive) être superbe; **we had a ~ time** on s'est vraiment bien amusé.

terrifically /tə'rɪfɪklɪ/ *adv* (extremely) [*difficult, gifted, kind, large*] extrêmement; [*expensive, hot, noisy*] épouvantablement.

terrified /'terɪfaɪd/ *adj* [*animal, face, person*] terrifié; [*scream*] de terreur; **to be ~ of** avoir une terreur folle de.

terrify /'terɪfaɪ/ *vtr* terrifier.
  IDIOMS **to ~ the life out of sb**○ donner une peur bleue à qn○.

terrifying /'terɪfaɪɪŋ/ *adj* (frightening) terrifiant; (alarming) effroyable.

terrifyingly /'terɪfaɪɪŋlɪ/ *adv* GEN terriblement; [*fast, normal, real*] effroyablement; [*shake, tilt*] de façon terrifiante.

territorial /,terə'tɔ:rɪəl/ *adj* (all contexts) territorial.

Territorial Army *pr n* GB armée *f* de réservistes volontaires.

territory /'terətrɪ, US 'terɪtɔ:rɪ/ *n* **1** (land) territoire *m* ALSO POL; **her home ~** son territoire; **2** (of salesperson) secteur *m*; **3** (area of influence, knowledge) domaine *m*; **I'm on familiar ~** je suis sur mon terrain; **4** US SPORT camp *m*.

terror /'terə(r)/ **I** *n* **1** (fear) terreur *f*; **to have a ~ of** être terrifié par; **to strike ~ into (the heart of) sb** semer la terreur chez qn; **2** (unruly person) terreur *f*. **II** *noun modifier* [*tactic*] d'intimidation; **a ~ campaign** une vague terroriste.

terrorism /'terərɪzəm/ *n* terrorisme *m*.

terrorist /'terərɪst/ **I** *n* terroriste *mf*. **II** *noun modifier* [*attack, bomb, group, plot*] terroriste; **a ~ bombing** un attentat à la bombe.

terrorize /'terəraɪz/ *vtr* terroriser; **to ~ sb into doing** terroriser qn jusqu'à ce qu'il/qu'elle fasse.

terror-stricken /'terəstrɪkən/ *adj* frappé de terreur.

terry /'terɪ/ *n* (also **~ towelling** GB, **~ cloth** US) tissu *m* éponge.

terse /tɜ:s/ *adj* [*style*] succinct; [*person, statement*] laconique.

tertiary /'tɜ:ʃərɪ, US -ʃɪerɪ/ *adj* [*era, industry, sector*] tertiaire; [*education, college*] supérieur; [*burn*] au troisième degré; [*syphilis*] au stade tertiaire.

Terylene® /'terəli:n/ *n* tergal® *m*.

TESL /'tesl/ *n* (*abrév* = **Teaching English as a Second Language**) enseignement *m* de l'anglais langue étrangère.

test /test/ **I** *n* **1** (of person, ability, resources) GEN épreuve *f*, PSYCH test *m*; SCH, UNIV (written) contrôle *m*; (oral) épreuve *f* orale; **a method that has stood the ~ of time** une méthode éprouvée; **tomorrow's match should be a good ~ of the team's capabilities** le match de demain devrait permettre de savoir de quoi

l'équipe est capable; **the best ~ of a good novel is**... le meilleur critère pour juger de la valeur d'un roman est...; **2** COMM, IND, TECH essai *m*; **3** MED (of blood, urine) analyse *f*; (of organ) examen *m*; (to detect virus, cancer) test *m* de dépistage; CHEM analyse *f*; **4** AUT (also **driving ~**) examen *m* du permis de conduire.
II *vtr* **1** GEN évaluer [*intelligence, efficiency*]; SCH (in classroom) interroger (**on** en); (at exam time) contrôler; PSYCH tester; **2** COMM, TECH essayer; MED, CHEM analyser [*blood, urine, sample*]; expérimenter [*new drug*]; **to have one's eyes ~ed** se faire faire un examen des yeux; **he was ~ed for Aids** on lui a fait subir un test de dépistage du sida; **all the new equipment has been ~ed for faults** le nouveau matériel a été entièrement testé et essayé; **to ~ the water** [*swimmer*] prendre la température de l'eau; FIG tâter le terrain; **3** (strain) mettre [qch] à l'épreuve [*strength, patience*].
III *vi* **to ~ for starch/for alcohol** (in laboratory) faire une recherche d'amidon/d'alcool; **to ~ for an infection/allergy** faire des analyses pour trouver la cause d'une infection/allergie; **his blood ~ed negative** son analyse de sang a été négative.

testament /'testəmənt/ *n* **1** JUR **the last will and ~ of** les dernières volontés de; **2** (proof) témoignage *m*; **to be a ~ to sth** témoigner de qch; **3 the Old/the New Testament** l'Ancien/le Nouveau Testament.

test: **~ ban** *n* interdiction *f* d'essais nucléaires; **~ card** *n* GB TV mire *f*; **~ case** *n* JUR procès *m* qui fait jurisprudence.

test-drive /'testdraɪv/ **I** *n* essai *m* de route.
II *vtr* faire faire un essai de route à, essayer.

tester /'testə(r)/ *n* **1** (person) contrôleur/-euse *m/f*; (device) testeur *m*; **2** (sample) (of make-up, perfume) échantillon *m*.

test: **~ flight** *n* vol *m* d'essai; **~-fly** *vtr* essayer.

testicle /'testɪkl/ *n* testicule *m*.

testify /'testɪfaɪ/ **I** *vtr* témoigner (**that** que).
II *vi* témoigner; **to ~ to** FIG attester, témoigner de.

testily /'testɪlɪ/ *adv* [*say, reply*] avec irritation.

testimonial /ˌtestɪ'məʊnɪəl/ *n* **1**† (reference) lettre *f* de recommandation; **2** (tribute) témoignage *m*.

testimony /'testɪmənɪ, US -məʊnɪ/ *n* GEN témoignage *m*; JUR déposition *f*; **to give ~** faire une déposition.

testing /'testɪŋ/ **I** *n* TECH, IND essai *m*; (of drug, cosmetic) expérimentation *f*; (of blood, water etc) analyse *f*; (of person) GEN mise *f* à l'épreuve; MED examen *m*; PSYCH tests *mpl*; SCH contrôles *mpl* (des connaissances).
II *adj* éprouvant.

testing ground *n* MIL site *m* d'essais (nucléaires); IND, TECH banc *m* d'essai; FIG terrain *m* d'essai.

test market /test'mɑːkɪt/ **I** *n* marché *m* test.
II *vtr* commercialiser [qch] à titre expérimental.

test: **~ marketing** *n* test *m* de marché; **~ match** *n* match *m* international (*de cricket*).

test paper *n* **1** CHEM (papier *m*) réactif *m*; **2** GB SCH, UNIV interrogation *f* écrite.

test: **~ pattern** *n* US TV mire *f*; **~ piece** *n* MUS morceau *m* de concours; **~ pilot** *n* pilote *m* d'essai; **~ run** *n* essai *m*; **~ tube** *n* éprouvette *f*; **~-tube baby** *n* bébé-éprouvette *m*.

testy /'testɪ/ *adj* [*person*] irritable; [*comment, reply*] irrité.

tetanus /'tetənəs/ ▶1002 **I** *n* tétanos *m*.
II *noun modifier* [*injection, vaccine*] antitétanique.

tetchy /'tetʃɪ/ *adj* GEN grincheux/-euse; [*behaviour*] emporté.

tether /'teðə(r)/ *vtr* attacher (**to** à).
IDIOMS **to be at the end of one's ~** être au bout du rouleau○.

Teutonic /tjuː'tɒnɪk, US tuː-/ *adj* germanique.

text /tekst/ *n* texte *m* (**by** de).

textbook /'tekstbʊk/ **I** *n* manuel *m* (**about, on** sur).
II *adj* [*case, landing, pregnancy*] exemplaire; [*example*] parfait.

textile /'tekstaɪl/ **I** *n* textile *m*.
II textiles *npl* textile *m*.

text processing *n* COMPUT traitement *m* de texte.

textual /'tekstʃʊəl/ *adj* de texte.

texture /'tekstʃə(r)/ *n* LIT, FIG texture *f*; (of music) caractère *m*.

textured /'tekstʃəd/ *adj* texturé; **rough-~** de texture grossière.

TGWU *n* GB (*abrév* = **Transport and General Workers' Union**) *un des principaux syndicats britanniques.*

Thames /temz/ ▶1214 *pr n* **the** (**river**) **~** la Tamise.
IDIOMS **he'll never set the ~ on fire** GB il ne fera jamais d'étincelles.

than /ðæn, ðən/

■ **Note** When *than* is used as a preposition in expressions of comparison, it is translated by *que* (or *qu'* before a vowel or mute 'h'): *he's taller than me* = il est plus grand que moi; *London is bigger than Oxford* = Londres est plus grand qu'Oxford.
– For expressions with numbers, temperatures etc see the entry below.
– See also the entries *more, less, hardly, soon, rather, other.*
– When *than* is used as a conjunction, it is translated by *que* and the verb following it is preceded by *ne*: *it was farther than I thought* = c'était plus loin que je ne pensais. However, French speakers often try to phrase the comparison differently: *it was more difficult than we expected* = c'était plus difficile que prévu. For other uses see the entry below.
– See also the entries *hardly, rather, soon.*

I *prep* **1** (in comparisons) que; **thinner ~ him** plus mince que lui; **he has more ~ me** il en a plus que moi; **I was more surprised ~ annoyed** j'étais plus étonné qu'ennuyé; **2** (expressing quantity, degree, value) de; **more/less ~ 100** plus/moins de 100; **more ~ half** plus de la moitié; **temperatures lower ~ 30 degrees** des températures de moins de 30 degrés.
II *conj* **1** (in comparisons) que; **he's older ~ I am** il est plus âgé que moi; **it took us longer ~ we thought it would** ça nous a pris plus de temps que prévu; **it was further away ~ I remembered** c'était plus loin que dans mon souvenir; **2** (expressing preferences) **I'd sooner** ou **rather do X ~ do Y** je préférerais faire X que (de) faire Y; **3** (when) **hardly** ou **no sooner had he left ~ the phone rang** à peine était-il parti que le téléphone a sonné; **4** US (from) **to be different ~ sth** être différent de qch.

thank /θæŋk/ *vtr* remercier [*person*]; **we've got Sue to ~ for that** c'est à Sue que nous devons cela ALSO IRON; **you've only got yourself to ~ for that** tu ne peux t'en prendre qu'à toi-même!; **I'll ~ you to do** je te serais reconnaissant de faire; **he won't ~ you for doing** il ne va pas apprécier que tu fasses; **~ God!, ~ goodness** ou **heavens!** Dieu merci!

thankful /'θæŋkfl/ *adj* (grateful) reconnaissant; (relieved) soulagé; **that's something to be ~ for!** c'est déjà un soulagement!

thankfully /'θæŋkfəlɪ/ *adv* **1** (luckily) heureusement; **2** (with relief) avec soulagement; (with gratitude) avec gratitude.

thankless /'θæŋklɪs/ *adj* [*task, person*] ingrat.

thanks /θæŋks/ **I** *npl* remerciements *mpl*; **'received with ~'** COMM 'avec nos remerciements'
II thanks to *prep phr* grâce à; **we did it, no ~ to you!** on a réussi, mais tu n'y es pour rien○!
III○ *excl* merci!; **~ a lot** merci beaucoup ALSO IRON; **no ~** non merci.

Thanksgiving (**Day**) *n* US jour *m* d'Action de Grâces.

thank you /'θæŋkjuː/ **I** *n* (also **thank-you, thankyou**) merci *m*; **to say ~ to sb, to say one's ~s to sb** dire merci à qn.
II *noun modifier* [*letter, gift*] de remerciement.
III *adv* merci; **~ very much** AUSSI IRON merci beaucoup ALSO IRON; **no ~** non merci.

that

As a determiner

In French, determiners agree in gender and number with the noun they precede; *that* is translated by *ce* + masculine singular noun (*ce monsieur*), *cet* + masculine singular noun beginning with a vowel or mute 'h' (*cet homme*) and *cette* + feminine singular noun (*cette femme*); *those* is translated by *ces*.

Note, however, that the above translations are also used for the English *this* (plural *these*). So when it is necessary to insist on *that* as opposed to another or others of the same sort, the adverbial tag *-là* is added to the noun:

> *I prefer THAT version* = je préfère cette version-là

For particular usages, see the entry *that*.

As a pronoun meaning *that one, those ones*

In French, pronouns reflect the gender and number of the noun they are referring to. So *that* is translated by *celui-là* for a masculine noun, *celle-là* for a feminine noun and *those* is translated by *ceux-là* for a masculine noun and *celles-là* for a feminine noun:

> *I think I like that one (dress) best* = je crois que je préfère celle-là

For other uses of *that, those* as pronouns (e.g. *who's that?*) and for adverbial use (e.g. *that much, that far*) there is no straightforward translation, so see the entry *that* for examples of usage.

When used as a relative pronoun, *that* is translated by *qui* when it is the subject of the verb and by *que* when it is the object:

> *the man that stole the car* = l'homme qui a volé la voiture
> *the film that I saw* = le film que j'ai vu

Remember that in the present perfect and past perfect tenses, the past participle will agree with the noun to which *que* as object refers:

> *the apples that I bought* = les pommes que j'ai achetées

When *that* is used as a relative pronoun with a preposition it is translated by *lequel* when standing for a masculine singular noun, by *laquelle* when standing for a feminine singular noun, by *lesquels* when standing for a masculine plural noun and by *lesquelles* when standing for a feminine plural noun:

> *the chair that I was sitting on* = la chaise sur laquelle j'étais assise
> *the children that I bought*
> *the books for* = les enfants pour lesquels j'ai acheté les livres

Remember that in cases where the English preposition used would normally be translated by *à* in French (e.g. *to, at*), the translation of the whole (prep + rel pron) will be *auquel, à laquelle, auxquels, auxquelles*:

> *the girls that I was talking to* = les filles auxquelles je parlais

Similarly, where the English preposition used would normally be translated by *de* in French (e.g. *of, from*), the translation of the whole (prep + rel pron) will be *dont* in all cases:

> *the Frenchman that*
> *I received a letter from* = le Français dont j'ai reçu une lettre

When used as a conjunction, *that* can almost always be translated by *que* (*qu'* before a vowel or mute 'h'):

> *she said that she would do it* = elle a dit qu'elle le ferait

In certain verbal constructions, *que* is followed by a subjunctive in French. If you are in doubt about the construction to use, consult the appropriate verb entry. For particular usages see the entry *that*.

---

that I /ðæt, ðət/ *det* (*pl* **those**) ce/cet/cette/ces; ~ **chair/~ man over there** cette chaise/cet homme là-bas; **I said THAT dress!** j'ai dit cette robe-là!; **you can't do it ~ way** tu ne peux pas le faire comme ça; **he went ~ way** il est allé par là; **those patients (who are) able to walk** les patients qui sont capables de marcher; ~ **train crash last year** la collision ferroviaire qui a eu lieu l'an dernier; ~ **lazy son of yours** ton paresseux de fils.
II /ðæt/ *dem pron* (*pl* **those**) **1** (that one) celui-/celle-/ceux-/celles-là; **we prefer this to** ~ nous préférons celui-ci à celui-là; **2** (the thing or person observed or mentioned) cela, ça, ce; **what's** ~? qu'est-ce que c'est que ça?; **who's** ~? GEN qui est-ce?; (on phone) qui est à l'appareil?; **is** ~ **John?** c'est John?; **who told you** ~? qui t'a dit ça?; ~**'s how he did it** c'est comme ça qu'il l'a fait; **what did he mean by** ~? qu'est-ce qu'il entendait par là?; ~**'s bureaucrats for you!** c'est ça les bureaucrates!; **before** ~, **he had always lived in London** avant cela, il avait toujours vécu à Londres; **3** (before relative pronoun) **those who...** ceux qui...
III /ðət/ *rel pron* (subject) qui; (object) que; (with preposition) lequel/laquelle/lesquels/lesquelles; **the woman** ~ **won** la femme qui a gagné; **the book** ~ **I bought** le livre que j'ai acheté; **the house** ~ **they live in** la maison dans laquelle ils vivent; **the man** ~ **I received the letter from** l'homme dont j'ai reçu la lettre; **the day** ~ **she arrived** le jour où elle est arrivée.
IV /ðət/ *conj* **1** GEN que; **he said** ~ **he had finished** il a dit qu'il avait fini; **it's likely** ~ **they are out** il est probable qu'ils sont sortis; **2** (expressing wish) **oh** ~ **he would come** s'il pouvait venir; (expressing surprise) ~ **she should treat me so badly!** comment peut-elle me traiter comme ça!; ~ **it should come to this!** comment peut-on en arriver là!
V /ðæt/ *adv* (to the extent shown) **it's about** ~ **thick** c'est à peu près épais comme ça; **she's** ~ **much smaller than me** elle est plus petite que moi de ça; **I**

can't do ~ **much work in one day** je ne peux pas faire autant de travail dans une journée; **he can't swim** ~ **far** il ne peut pas nager aussi loin.
IDIOMS ...**and (all)** ~ ...et tout ça; ...**and he's very nice at** ~! ...et en plus il est très gentil!; **I might well go at** ~! en fait, je pourrais bien y aller!; **at** ~, **he got up and left** en entendant cela, il s'est levé et est parti; **with** ~ **he got up and left** sur ce il s'est levé et est parti; ~**'s to say...;** c'est-à-dire...; ~**'s it!** (that's right) c'est ça!; (that's enough) ça suffit!; **I don't want to see you again and** ~**'s** ~! je ne veux pas te revoir point final!; **well,** ~**'s it then!** il n'y a rien de plus à faire!

thatch /θætʃ/ **I** *n* (roof) chaume *m*.
II *vtr* couvrir [qch] de chaume.

thatch: ~**ed cottage** *n* chaumière *f*; ~**ed roof** *n* toit *m* de chaume.

thaw /θɔː/ **I** *n* **1** METEOROL dégel *m*; **2** (political) détente *f*; **a** ~ **in her attitude towards me** (social) une amélioration *f* dans son attitude envers moi.
II *vtr* faire fondre [*ice, snow*]; décongeler [*frozen food*].
III *vi* **1** LIT [*snow*] fondre; [*ground, frozen food*] dégeler; **2** FIG se détendre.
IV *v impers* dégeler.
■ **thaw out:** ¶ ~ **out** [*frozen food, ground*] dégeler; [*person, fingers*] se réchauffer; ¶ ~ [*sth*] **out,** ~ **out** [*sth*] [*person*] décongeler [*frozen food*]; dégeler [*ground*].

the /ði, ðə, devant une voyelle ou emphatique ðiː/ *det* **1** (specifying, identifying etc) le/la/l'/les; **two chapters of** ~ **book** deux chapitres du livre; **I met them at** ~ **supermarket** je les ai rencontrés au supermarché; **2** (best etc) THE **French restaurant** le meilleur restaurant français; THE **way of losing weight** la façon la plus efficace de perdre des kilos; **3** (with era) ~ **fifties** les années cinquante; **4** (with adj) ~ **impossible** l'impossible; **she buys only** ~ **best** elle n'achète que ce qu'il y a de mieux; **5** (with comparative adj) **the news made her all** ~ **sadder** la nouvelle n'a fait que la

the

In French, determiners agree in gender and number with the noun they precede; *the* is translated by *le* + masculine singular noun (*le chien*), by *la* + feminine singular noun (*la chaise*), by *l'* + masculine or feminine singular noun beginning with a vowel or mute 'h' (*l'auteur, l'homme, l'absence, l'histoire*) and by *les* + plural noun (*les hommes, les femmes*).

When *the* is used after a preposition in English, the two words (prep + *the*) are often translated by one word in French. If the preposition would normally be translated by *de* in French (*of, about, from* etc.) the prep + *the* is translated by *du* + masculine noun (*du chien*), by *de la* + feminine noun (*de la femme*), by *de l'* + singular noun beginning with a vowel or mute 'h' (*de l'auteur, de l'histoire*) and by *des* + plural noun (*des hommes, des femmes*). If the preposition would usually be translated by *à* (*at, to* etc.) the prep + *the* is translated according to the number and gender of the noun, by *au* (*au chien*), *à la* (*à la femme*), *à l'* (*à l'enfant*), *aux* (*aux hommes, aux femmes*).

Other than this, there are few problems in translating *the* into French. The following cases are, however, worth remembering as not following exactly the pattern of the English:

the good, the poor etc.	= les bons, les pauvres *etc.*
Charles the First,	= Charles Premier,
Elizabeth the Second etc.	Elizabeth Deux *etc.*
she's THE violinist of the century	
	= c'est LA violoniste du siècle *or* c'est la plus grande violoniste du siècle
the Tudors,	= les Tudor
the Batemans etc.	les Bateman *etc.*

For expressions such as *the more, the better*, see the entry *the*.

This dictionary contains usage notes on such topics as *weight measurement, days of the week, rivers, illnesses, aches and pains, the human body,* and *musical instruments,* many of which use *the*; for the index to these notes ▶ **1419**.

For other particular usages of *the* see the entry **the**.

rendre encore plus triste; **6** (in double comparatives) ~ **more I learn** ~ **less I understand** plus j'apprends moins je comprends; ~ **sooner** ~ **better** le plus tôt sera le mieux; ~ **longer he waits** ~ **harder it will be** plus il attendra plus ce sera difficile; **7** (with superlatives) ~ **fastest train** le train le plus rapide; ~ **prettiest house in the village** la maison la plus jolie du village.

theatre, theater US /ˈθɪətə(r)/ **I** **n** **1** (place, art form) théâtre *m* ALSO MIL; **2** US (cinema) cinéma *m*; **3** (also **lecture** ~) amphithéâtre *m*; **4** GB (also **operating** ~) salle *f* d'opération.
II *noun modifier* **1** THEAT [*audience, lover, owner, seat, ticket*] de théâtre; [*company, production, programme, stage, workshop*] théâtral; [*manager, staff*] du théâtre; [*visit*] au théâtre; **2** GB MED [*nurse*] au bloc *m* opératoire; [*equipment*] du bloc *m* opératoire; **3** US (cinema) [*owner, seat*] de cinéma; [*manager*] du cinéma.
theatre: ~**goer** *n* amateur *mf* de théâtre; ~**land** *n* quartier *m* des théâtres.
theatrical /θɪˈætrɪkl/ *adj* [*star*] du théâtre; [*group, photographer*] de théâtre; [*agency, family, gesture, production, technique*] théâtral.
theatrically /θɪˈætrɪklɪ/ *adv* [*gifted*] pour le théâtre; [*effective, striking*] du point de vue théâtral; [*behave*] de façon théâtrale.
theatricals /θɪˈætrɪklz/ *npl* théâtre *m*.
theft /θeft/ *n* vol *m* (**of** de).
their /ðeə(r)/

■ **Note** In French, determiners agree in gender and number with the noun they precede. So *their* is translated by *leur* + masculine or feminine singular noun (*leur chien, leur maison*) and by *leurs* + plural noun (*leurs enfants*).
– When *their* is stressed, *à eux* (masculine, mixed) or *à elles* (feminine) is added after the noun: THEIR house = leur maison à eux/à elles.
– For *their* used with parts of the body ▶ **765**.

det leur/leurs.
theirs /ðeəz/

■ **Note** In French, possessive pronouns reflect the gender and number of the noun they are standing for; *theirs* is translated by *le leur, la leur, les leurs,* according to what is being referred to.
– For examples and particular usages see below.

pron **my car is red but** ~ **is blue** ma voiture est rouge mais la leur est bleue; **the green hats are** ~ les chapeaux verts sont à eux or elles; **which house is** ~**?** c'est laquelle leur maison?; **the money wasn't** ~ **to give away** ils or elles n'avaient pas à donner cet argent; **I saw them with that dog of** ~ PÉJ je les ai vus avec leur sale chien○.
them /ðem, ðəm/ **▶ 1328**] *pron* **both of** ~ tous/ toutes les deux; **both of** ~ **work in London** ils/elles travaillent à Londres tous/toutes les deux; **some of** ~

quelques-uns d'entre eux or quelques-unes d'entre elles; **take** ~ **all** prenez-les tous/toutes; **none of** ~ **wants it** aucun/-e d'entre eux/elles ne le veut; **every single one of** ~ chacun/-e d'entre eux/elles.
theme /θiːm/ *n* **1** (topic, motif) thème *m* ALSO MUS, LING; **2** US (essay) rédaction *f*.
theme: ~ **park** *n* parc *m* de loisirs (à thème); ~ **song,** ~ **tune** *n* CIN musique *f*; RADIO, TV indicatif *m*; FIG rengaine *f*.
themselves /ðəmˈselvz/

■ **Note** When used as a reflexive pronoun, direct and indirect, *themselves* is translated by *se* (or *s'* before a vowel or mute h).
– When used as an emphatic the translation is *eux-mêmes* in the masculine and *elles-mêmes* in the feminine: they did it themselves = ils l'ont fait eux-mêmes or elles l'ont fait elles-mêmes.
– After a preposition the translation is *eux* or *elles* or *eux-mêmes* or *elles-mêmes: they bought the painting for themselves* = (masculine or mixed gender) ils ont acheté le tableau pour eux or pour eux-mêmes; (feminine gender) elles ont acheté le tableau pour elles or pour elles-mêmes.

pron **1** (reflexive) se/s'; **they washed** ~ ils se sont lavés; **2** (emphatic) eux-mêmes/elles-mêmes; **3** (after preposition) eux/elles, eux-mêmes/elles-mêmes; **(all) by** ~ tous seuls/toutes seules.
then /ðen/

■ **Note** When *then* is used to mean *at that time*, it is translated by *alors* or *à ce moment-là*: I was working in Oxford then = je travaillais alors à Oxford or je travaillais à Oxford à ce moment-là. Note that *alors* always comes immediately after the verb in French.
– For particular usages see I1 in the entry below.
– For translations of *since then, until then* see the entries *since, until*.
– When *then* is used to mean *next* it can be translated by either *puis* or *ensuite*: a man, a horse and then a dog = un homme, un cheval puis or et ensuite un chien.
– For particular usages see I2 in the entry below.
– When *then* is used to mean *in that case* it is translated by *alors*: then why worry? = alors pourquoi s'inquiéter?
– For all other uses see the entry below.

I *adv* **1** (at that point in time) alors, à ce moment-là; (implying more distant past) en ce temps-là; **we were living in Dublin** ~ nous habitions alors à Dublin; **just** ~ **she heard a noise** à ce moment-là elle a entendu un bruit; **a large sum of money even** ~ une grosse somme d'argent même à cette époque; **people were idealistic** ~ en ce temps-là les gens étaient idéalistes; **from** ~ **on, life became easier** à partir de ce moment-là la vie est devenue plus facile; **since** ~ **there has been little news** depuis on a eu peu de nouvelles; **by** ~ **the damage had been done** le mal

them

When used as a direct object pronoun, referring to people, animals or things, *them* is translated by *les*:

I know them = je les connais

Note that the object pronoun normally comes before the verb in French and that in compound tenses like the present perfect and past perfect, the past participle agrees in gender and number with the direct object pronoun:

he's seen them (them being
masculine or of mixed gender) = il les a vus
(them being all feminine gender) = il les a vues

In imperatives, the direct object pronoun is translated by *les* and comes after the verb:

catch them! = attrape-les! (*note the hyphen*)

When used as an indirect object pronoun, *them* is translated by *leur*:

I gave them it or I gave it to them = je le leur ai donné

In imperatives, the indirect object pronoun is translated by *leur* and comes after the verb:

phone them! = téléphone-leur! (*note the hyphen*)

After prepositions and the verb to be, the translation is *eux* for masculine or mixed gender and *elles* for feminine gender:

he did it for them = il l'a fait pour eux or pour elles
it's them = ce sont eux or ce sont elles

For particular usages see the entry **them**.

était déjà fait; **they will let us know by ~** nous aurons la réponse à ce moment-là; **if things haven't changed by ~** si d'ici là les choses n'ont pas changé; **we won't be in contact until ~** nous ne serons pas en contact avant (ce moment-là); ▶**there**; **2** (in sequences: afterwards, next) puis, ensuite; **~ came the big news** puis or ensuite on nous a annoncé la grande nouvelle; **~ after that...** ensuite...; **and ~ what?** (with bated breath) et ensuite?; **3** (in that case) alors; **I saw them if not yesterday ~ the day before** je les ai vus hier ou avant-hier; **if it's a problem for you ~ say so** si ça te pose un problème dis-le; **if they're so nice ~ why not stay with them?** s'ils sont si agréables pourquoi ne pas rester avec eux?; **~ why did you tell her?** mais alors pourquoi est-ce que tu le lui as dit?; **how about tomorrow ~?** et demain ça irait?; **well try this ~** et bien alors essaie ça; **~ what DO they want?** mais alors qu'est-ce qu'ils veulent?; **4** (summarizing statement: therefore) donc; **these ~ are the results of the policy** voici donc les résultats de cette politique; **overall ~ it would seem that** en résumé il semble donc que; **5** (in addition, besides) puis...aussi; **and ~ there's the fare to consider** et puis il faut aussi tenir compte du prix de billet; **6** (modifying previous statement: on the other hand) d'un autre côté; **she's good but ~ so is he** elle est bonne mais lui aussi; **they said it would rain but ~ they're often wrong** ils ont prévu de la pluie mais ils se trompent souvent; **he looks anxious but ~ he always does** il a l'air inquiet mais de toute façon il a toujours cet air-là; **7** (rounding off a topic: so) alors; **it's all arranged ~?** tout est arrangé alors?; **that's all right ~** ça va alors; **8** (focusing on topic) bon; **now ~ what's all this?** bon, qu'est-ce qui se passe?; **what's the problem ~?** alors quel est le problème?
II *adj* (*épith*) **the ~ prime minister** le premier ministre de l'époque; **the ~ mayor of New York, Mr X** M. X, qui était alors maire de New York.

thence /ðens/ *adv* **1** (from there) de là; **2** (therefore) de cela.

theologian /ˌθɪəˈləʊdʒən/ *n* théologien/-ienne *m/f*.

theological /ˌθɪəˈlɒdʒɪkl/ *adj* [*debate, issue, thought, writing*] théologique; [*book, college, faculty, study*] de théologie; [*student*] en théologie.

theology /θɪˈɒlədʒɪ/ *n* théologie *f*.

theorem /ˈθɪərəm/ *n* théorème *m*.

theoretical /ˌθɪəˈretɪkl/ *adj* théorique.

theoretically /ˌθɪəˈretɪklɪ/ *adv* théoriquement; **~ speaking** en théorie.

theorize /ˈθɪəraɪz/ *vi* théoriser.

theory /ˈθɪərɪ/ *n* théorie *f*.

therapeutic /ˌθerəˈpjuːtɪk/ *adj* thérapeutique.

therapist /ˈθerəpɪst/ *n* thérapeute *mf*.

therapy /ˈθerəpɪ/ **I** *n* MED, PSYCH thérapie *f*; **to have** ou **be in ~** suivre une thérapie.
II *noun modifier* [*group, session*] de thérapie.

there /ðeə(r)/

■ **Note** *there* is generally translated by *là* after prepositions: *near there* = près de là etc and when emphasizing the location of an object/a point etc visible to the speaker: *put them there* = mettez-les là.
– Remember that *voilà* is used to draw attention to a visible place/object/person: *there's my watch* = voilà ma montre, whereas *il y a* is used for generalizations: *there's a village nearby* = il y a un village tout près.
– *there* when unstressed with verbs such as *aller* and *être* is translated by *y*: *we went there last year* = nous y sommes allés l'année dernière, but not where emphasis is made: *it was there that we went last year* = c'est là que nous sommes allés l'année dernière.
– For examples of the above and further uses of *there* see the entry below.

I *pron* (as impersonal subject) il; **~ seems** ou **appears to be** il semble y avoir; **~ is/are** il y a; **~ are many reasons** il y a beaucoup de raisons; **~ is some left** il en reste; **once upon a time ~ was** il était une fois; **~'ll be a singsong later** on va chanter plus tard; **~'s no denying that** personne ne peut nier que.
II *adv* **1** (that place or point) là; **up to ~, down to ~** jusque là; **put it in ~** mettez-le là-dedans; **in ~ please** (ushering sb) par là s'il vous plaît; **2** (at or to that place) là; **stand ~** mettez-vous là; **go over ~** va là-bas; **since we were last ~** depuis la dernière fois que nous y sommes allés; **it's ~ that** GEN c'est là que; (when indicating) c'est là où; **to go ~ and back in an hour** faire l'aller et retour en une heure; **take the offer while it's ~** FIG profite de l'occasion pendant que c'est possible; **3** (to draw attention) (to person, activity etc) voilà; (to place) là; **what have you got ~?** qu'est-ce que tu as là?; **~ goes the coach** voilà le car qui s'en va; **~ you go again** FIG ça y est, c'est reparti; **~ you are** (seeing somebody arrive) vous voilà; (giving object) tenez, voilà; (that's done) et voilà; **~'s a bus coming** voilà un bus; **that paragraph ~** ce paragraphe; **my colleague ~ will show you** mon collègue va vous montrer; **which one? this one or that one ~?** lequel? celui-ci ou celui-là?; **~'s why!** ça explique tout!; **4** (indicating arrival) là; **will she be ~ now?** est-ce qu'elle y est maintenant?; **when do they get ~?** quand est-ce qu'ils arrivent là-bas?; **~ I was at last** j'étais enfin là-bas; **the train won't be ~ yet** le train ne sera pas encore là; **we get off ~** c'est là qu'on descend; **5** (indicating juncture) là; **~ we must finish** nous devons nous arrêter là; **~ was our chance** c'était notre chance; **so ~ we were in the same cell** et comme ça on s'est retrouvé dans la même cellule; **6** (emphatic) **hello ~!** salut!; **hey you ~!** eh toi là-bas!
III there and then *adv phr* directement.
IV there again *adv phr* (on the other hand) d'un autre côté.
V *excl* **~ ~!** (soothingly) allez! allez!; **~!** (triumphantly) voilà! ; **~, I told you!** voilà, je te l'avais bien dit!; **~, you've woken the baby!** c'est malin, tu as réveillé le bébé!

thereabouts /ˈðeərəbaʊts/ GB, **thereabout** /ˈðeərəbaʊt/ US *adv* **1** (in the vicinity) par là; **2** (roughly) **100 dollars or ~** 100 dollars environ.

thereafter /ðeərˈɑːftə(r)/ *adv* par la suite.

thereby /ðeəˈbaɪ, ˈðeə-/ *adv* ainsi.
IDIOMS **~ hangs a tale** c'est toute une histoire.

there'd /ðeəd/ = **there had**, **there would**.

therefore /ˈðeəfɔː(r)/ *adv* donc, par conséquent.

therein /ðeərˈɪn/ *adv* **1** (in that) **~ lies...** c'est en cela

que réside...; **the aircraft and the persons** ~ l'avion
et les personnes qui sont/étaient à l'intérieur; **2** JUR
(in contract) **contained** = ci-inclus.

here'll /ðeəl/ = **there will**.

here's /ðeəz/ = **there is, there has**.

hereupon /ˌðeərəˈpɒn/ adv SOUT sur ce.

herm /θɜːm/ n thermie f.

hermal /ˈθɜːml/ **I** n courant m ascendant.
II adj GEN thermique; [spring, treatment] thermal.

hermal baths npl thermes mpl.

hermal imaging n thermographie f.

hermic /ˈθɜːmɪk/ adj thermique.

hermometer /θəˈmɒmɪtə(r)/ n thermomètre m.

hermos flask n bouteille f thermos®.

hermostat /ˈθɜːməstæt/ n thermostat m.

hermostatic /ˌθɜːməˈstætɪk/ adj thermostatique.

hesaurus /θɪˈsɔːrəs/ n (pl **-ri** ou **-ruses**) **1** (of syno-
nyms etc) dictionnaire m analogique; **2** (of particular
ield) lexique m.

hese /ðiːz/ pl ▶ **this**.

hesis /ˈθiːsɪs/ n (pl **theses**) **1** UNIV (doctoral) thèse f;
(master's) mémoire m; **2** (theory) thèse f.

hey /ðeɪ/

■ **Note** they is translated by ils (masculine) or elles (feminine). For a group of people or things of mixed gender ils
is always used. The emphatic form is eux (masculine) or
elles (feminine). For examples and exceptions, see below.

pron ~ **have already gone** (masculine or mixed) ils
sont déjà partis; (feminine) elles sont déjà parties; **here
~ are! les voici!; **there ** ~ are!** les voilà!; THEY
won't **be there** (masculine or mixed) ils ne seront pas là,
eux; (feminine) elles ne seront pas là, elles; **she bought
one but ~ didn't** elle en a acheté un mais eux pas.

hey'd /ðeɪd/ = **they had, they would**.

hey'll /ðeɪl/ = **they will**.

hey're /ðeə(r)/ = **they are**.

hey've /ðeɪv/ = **they have**.

hick /θɪk/ **I** adj **1** [object, substance, feature] épais/
épaisse; [forest, vegetation, fog] dense, épais/épaisse;
[accent] fort (before n); **to be 6 cm** ~ faire 6 cm
l'épaisseur m; **how** ~ **is the wall?** quelle est
l'épaisseur du mur?; **to make sth ~er** épaissir qch;
to be ~ **with** être plein de [smoke, noise]; être chargé
de [emotion]; **fields** ~ **with poppies** des champs
couverts de coquelicots; **the ground was** ~ **with
ants** le sol grouillait de fourmis; **2**° (stupid) bête; **I
can't get it into his** ~ **head that** je n'arrive pas à
lui enfoncer dans le crâne° que; **3**° (friendly) **they're
very** ~ (with each other) ils sont très liés; **4**° (unreasonable) **it's a bit** ~ **expecting me to do that!** c'est
un peu raide° d'espérer que je ferai ça!
II adv **don't spread the butter on too** ~ ne mets
pas trop de beurre; **the bread was sliced** ~ le pain
était coupé en tranches épaisses; **the snow lay** ~ **on
the ground** il y avait une épaisse couche de neige sur
le sol.
IDIOMS **to lay it on** ~° forcer la dose°; **offers of
help are coming in** ~ **and fast** des propositions
d'aide affluent de toutes parts; **through** ~ **and thin**
contre vents et marées; **to be in the** ~ **of** être au
beau milieu de.

hicken /ˈθɪkən/ **I** vtr (all contexts) épaissir.
II vi [sauce, soup, fog, snow, cloud, waistline]
s'épaissir; [accent] devenir plus fort; [voice] s'enrouer;
[traffic] devenir plus dense.
IDIOMS **the plot** ~**s!** l'affaire se corse!

hickening /ˈθɪkənɪŋ/ n GEN, CULIN épaississant m.

hicket /ˈθɪkɪt/ n fourré m.

hickly /ˈθɪklɪ/ adv [spread] en une couche épaisse;
[cut] en morceaux épais; [say, speak] d'une voix
enrouée; **the grass grew** ~ l'herbe poussait dru; **a
~-wooded landscape** un paysage très boisé.

hickness /ˈθɪknɪs/ n GEN épaisseur f.

hick: ~**set** adj trapu; [hedge] touffu; **~-skinned**
adj insensible.

thief /θiːf/ n (pl **thieves**) voleur/-euse m/f; **stop** ~!
au voleur!
IDIOMS **set a** ~ **to catch a** ~ seul un voleur peut
en attraper un autre; **to be as thick as thieves**
s'entendre comme larrons en foire.

thieve /θiːv/ vtr, vi voler.

thieves /θiːvz/ pl ▶ **thief**.

thieving /ˈθiːvɪŋ/ **I** n vol m.
II adj ~ **children** enfants qui volent.

thigh /θaɪ/ n cuisse f.

thigh: ~**bone** n fémur m; ~**boot** n cuissarde f.

thimble /ˈθɪmbl/ n dé m à coudre.

thin /θɪn/ **I** adj **1** (in width) [nose, lips, stick, wall]
mince; [line, stripe, string, wire] fin; [strip] étroit; **2** (in
depth) [slice, layer] fin, mince; **the ice is** ~ la couche
de glace n'est pas très épaisse; **3** (in consistency) [mud,
mixture] liquide; [soup, liquid, sauce] clair; [oil] fluide;
4 (lean) maigre; **to get** ~ maigrir; **5** (fine) [card,
paper] fin; [fabric, mist] léger/-ère; **6** (in tone) (high-
pitched) aigre; (weak) fluet/fluette; **7** [population, crowd,
hair] clairsemé; **8** FIG [excuse] peu convaincant; [evid-
ence] insuffisant; [plot] squelettique; **to wear** ~
[joke, excuse] être usé; **my patience is wearing** ~ je
commence à perdre patience; **the plot is wearing** ~.
II° adv [slice] en tranches fpl fines; [spread] en couche
mince.
III vtr (p prés etc **-nn-**) **1** (also ~ **down**) diluer
[paint]; allonger [sauce, soup]; **2** (disperse) = **thin out**.
IV vi (p prés etc **-nn-**) (also ~ **out**) [fog, mist] se
disperser; [crowd] se disperser; [hair] se raréfier.
V **thinning** pres p adj [hair, crowd] clairsemé.
IDIOMS **to be** ~ **on the ground** être rare; **to get** ~
on top se dégarnir; **to have a** ~ **time of it** traverser
une période difficile.
■ **thin down** US maigrir.
■ **thin out**: ~ [sth] **out**, ~ **out** [sth] éclaircir [seed-
lings, hedge]; réduire [population].

thing /θɪŋ/ **I** n **1** (object) chose f, truc° m; **what's this
** ~ **for?** à quoi sert ce truc°?; **there isn't a** ~ **to eat
in the house!** il n'y a rien à manger dans cette
maison!; **the one** ~ **he wants for his birthday is a
bike** tout ce qu'il veut pour son anniversaire, c'est un
vélo; **it was a big box** ~ c'était une espèce de grosse
boîte; **2** (action, task, event) chose f; **she'll do great ~s
in life** elle ira loin dans la vie; **that's the worst** ~
you could have said c'est (vraiment) LA chose à ne
pas dire; **the best** ~ **(to do) would be to go and
see her** le mieux serait d'aller la voir; **that was
a silly** ~ **to do** c'était stupide de faire cela; **there
wasn't a** ~ **I could do** je ne pouvais rien y faire; **it's
a good** ~ **you came** heureusement que tu es venu;
the ~ **to do is to listen carefully to him** ce qu'il
faut faire c'est l'écouter attentivement; **I'm sorry, but
I haven't done a** ~ **about it yet** je suis désolé, mais
je ne m'en suis pas encore occupé; **the heat does
funny ~s to people** la chaleur a de drôles d'effets
sur les gens; **it's all right if you like that sort of** ~
ce n'est pas mal pour ceux qui aiment ça; **3** (matter,
fact) chose f; **the** ~ **to remember is...** ce dont il faut
se souvenir c'est...; **I couldn't hear a** ~ **(that) he
said** je n'ai rien entendu de ce qu'il a dit; **I said/did
no such** ~! je n'ai rien dit/fait de tel!; **the whole
** ~ **is crazy!** c'est idiot tout cela!; **the** ~ **is, (that)...**
ce qu'il y a, c'est que...; **the only** ~ **is,...** la seule
chose, c'est que...; **the funny** ~ **is...** le plus drôle
c'est que ...; **the good** ~ **(about it) is...** ce qu'il y a
de bien, c'est que...; **the** ~ **about him is that he's
very honest** ce qu'il faut lui reconnaître, c'est qu'il
est très honnête; **the** ~ **about him is that he can't
be trusted** le problème avec lui c'est qu'on ne peut
pas lui faire confiance; **4** (person, animal) **she's a pretty
little** ~ c'est une jolie petite fille; **you lucky** ~°!
veinard/-e°!; **you stupid** ~°! espèce d'idiot°!; **(the)
stupid** ~° (of object) sale truc°!
II **things** npl **1** (personal belongings, equipment) affaires
fpl; **to wash up the breakfast ~s** faire la vaisselle
du petit déjeuner; **2** (situation, circumstances, matters) les
choses fpl; **to see ~s as they really are** voir les
choses en face; **~s are getting better/worse** cela

s'améliore/empire; **how are ~s with you?, how are ~s going?** comment ça va?; **why do you want to change ~s?** pourquoi est-ce que tu veux tout changer?; **to worry about ~s** se faire du souci; **as ~s are** ou **stand** dans l'état actuel des choses; **as ~s turned out** en fin de compte; **all ~s considered** tout compte fait.

IDIOMS **it's not the done ~ (to do)** ça ne se fait pas (de faire); **it's the in ~**° c'est à la mode; **she was wearing the latest ~ in hats** elle portait un chapeau dernier cri; **that's just the ~** ou **the very ~!** c'est tout à fait ce qu'il me/te/lui etc faut!; **it's become quite the ~ (to do)** c'est devenu à la mode (de faire); **it was a close** ou **near ~** c'était juste; **he's on to a good ~**° il a trouvé le bon filon°; **he likes to do his own ~**° il aime faire ce qui lui plaît; **for one ~...(and) for another ~...** premièrement... et deuxièmement...; **to have a ~ about**° (like) craquer pour° [*blondes, bearded men*]; adorer [*emeralds, old cars*]; (hate) ne pas aimer; **to make a big ~ (out) of it**° en faire toute une histoire; **to know a ~ or two about sth**° s'y connaître en qch; **I could tell you a ~ or two about him**°! je pourrais vous en raconter sur son compte!; **and then, of all ~s, she...** et alors, allez savoir pourquoi°, elle...; **I must be seeing/hearing ~s!** je dois avoir des visions/ entendre des voix!; **it's** ou **it was (just) one of those ~s** c'est la vie; **it's one (damned) ~ after another**°! les embêtements° n'en finissent plus!; **one ~ led to another and...** et, de fil en aiguille...; **taking one ~ with another** tout bien considéré; **what with one ~ and another, I haven't had time to read it** avec tout ce que j'ai eu à faire je n'ai pas eu le temps de le lire; **to (try to) be all ~s to all men** (essayer de) faire plaisir à tout le monde.

thingumabob° /ˈθɪŋəməbɒb/, **thingumajig**° /ˈθɪŋəmədʒɪg/ *n* truc° *m*, machin° *m*.

think /θɪŋk/ **I** *n* **to have a ~ about sth** GB réfléchir à qch.
II *vtr* (*prét, pp* **thought**) **1** (hold view, believe) croire; **I ~ so** je crois; **I don't ~ so, I ~ not** je ne crois pas; **'is he reliable?'—'I'd like to ~ so but...'** 'peut-on lui faire confiance?'—'j'espère bien mais...'; **to ~ it best to do/that** penser qu'il serait préférable de faire/que; **I ~ it's going to rain** j'ai l'impression qu'il va pleuvoir; **what do you ~ it will cost?** combien ça va coûter à ton avis?; **him, a millionaire? I don't ~!** IRON lui un millionnaire? sans blague!; **2** (imagine) imaginer, croire; **who'd have thought it!** qui l'aurait cru?; **I never thought you meant it!** je ne t'ai jamais pris au sérieux!; **I can't ~ how/why etc** je n'ai aucune idée comment/pourquoi etc; **I can't ~ where I've put my keys** je ne sais pas du tout où j'ai mis mes clés; **who do you ~ you are?** (indignantly) pour qui vous prenez-vous?; **what on earth do you ~ you're doing?** mais qu'est-ce que tu fais?; **I thought as much!** je m'en doutais!; **six weeks' holiday! that's what you ~!** six semaines de vacances! tu te fais des idées!; **and to ~ that I believed him!** GB et dire que je le croyais!; **3** (have thought, idea) penser; **I didn't ~ to check** je n'ai pas pensé à vérifier; **I was just ~ing: suppose we sold the car?** je me posais la question: si nous vendions la voiture?; **we're ~ing sex here**° c'est de sexe qu'il s'agit; **let's ~ Green**°! pensons écolo°!; **4** (rate, assess) **to ~ a lot/not much of** penser/ne pas penser beaucoup de bien de; **5** (remember) penser; **to ~ where/how** se rappeler où/comment.
III *vi* (*prét, pp* **thought**) **1** GEN penser; (before acting or speaking) réfléchir; **I'll have to ~ about it** il faudra que j'y réfléchisse; **to ~ hard** bien réfléchir; **to ~ clearly** ou **straight** avoir les idées claires; **to ~ for oneself** avoir des opinions personnelles; **I'm sorry, I wasn't ~ing** je m'excuse, je ne sais pas où j'avais la tête; **we are ~ing in terms of economics** nous voyons les choses du point de vue économique; **let's ~: three people at £170 each** voyons: trois personnes à 170 livres sterling chacune...; **come to ~ of it...** maintenant que j'y pense...; **he thought better of it** il est revenu sur sa décision; **2** (take into

account) **to ~ about** ou **of sb/sth** penser à qn/qch; **can't ~ of everything!** je ne peux pas penser à tout; **3** (consider) **to ~ of sb as** considérer qn comme; **h ~s of himself as an expert** il se prend pour un spé cialiste; **4** (have in mind) **to ~ of doing** envisager d faire; **to ~ about doing** penser à faire; **whateve were you ~ing of?** qu'est-ce qui t'a pris?; **5** (imagin **to ~ of** penser à; **a million pounds, ~ of that!** u million de livres, t'imagines°!; **6** (tolerate idea) (*tjrs né* **not to ~ of doing** ne pas penser à faire; **I couldn ~ of letting you pay** il n'est pas question que je t laisse payer; **7** (remember) **to ~ of** se rappeler; **if yo ~ of anything else** si autre chose vous vient à l'e prit.

IDIOMS **to have another ~ coming**° GB se trompe lourdement; **to ~ on one's feet** réfléchir vite e bien.

■ **think again** (reflect more) se repencher sur la que tion; (change mind) changer d'avis; **if that's what yo ~, you can ~ again** si c'est ça que tu penses, tu t trompes.

■ **think ahead** bien réfléchir (à l'avance); **~in ahead to our retirement,...** quand nous serons à l retraite,...

■ **think back** se reporter en arrière (**to** à).

■ **think out:** **~ out** [sth], **~** [sth] **out** bien réfl chir à; **well/badly thought out** bien/mal conçu.

■ **think over:** **~ over** [sth], **~** [sth] **over** réfléchir à.

■ **think through:** **~ through** [sth], **~** [sth through** bien réfléchir à [*proposal, action*]; faire l tour de [*problem, question*].

■ **think up:** **~ up** [sth] inventer.

thinker /ˈθɪŋkə(r)/ *n* penseur/-euse *m/f*.

thinking /ˈθɪŋkɪŋ/ **I** *n* **1** (reflection) réflexion *f*; **to d some (hard) ~** (beaucoup) réfléchir; **2** (way o thinks) pensée *f*; **current ~ is that** GB la tendanc actuelle de l'opinion est que; **to my way of ~** à mo avis.
II *adj* [*person*] réfléchi; **the ~ person's pin-up** sex symbol des intellectuels.

think-tank /ˈθɪŋktæŋk/ *n* groupe *m* de réflexion.

thin-lipped /ˌθɪnˈlɪpt/ *adj* [*person*] aux lèvres mince [*smile*] pincé.

thinly /ˈθɪnlɪ/ *adv* **1** (sparingly) [*slice*] en tranches fines [*spread*] en couche mince; [*butter*] légèrement; **2** F **~ disguised** à peine déguisé.

thinner /ˈθɪnə(r)/ **I** *comparative adj* ▶ **thin**.
II *n* (also **thinners** + *v sg*) diluant *m*.

thin-skinned /ˌθɪnˈskɪnd/ *adj* susceptible.

third /θɜːd/ **▶ 1112**, **854** **I** *n* **1** (in order) troisièn *mf*; **2** (of month) trois *m inv*; **3** (fraction) tiers *m*; **4** (als **~-class degree**) GB UNIV = *licence avec mentio passable*; **5** MUS tierce *f*; **6** (also **~ gear**) AUT tro sième *f*.
II *adj* troisième.
III *adv* [*come, finish*] troisième; (in list) troisièmement
IDIOMS **~ time lucky!** la troisième fois sera bonne!

third-class /ˌθɜːdˈklɑːs/ **I** *adj* **1** **~ mail** US POST plis *mpl* non urgents; **2** GB UNIV **~ degree** = **thir I 4**.
II **third class** *adv* **to send sth ~** envoyer qch e pli non urgent.

third degree° /ˌθɜːd dəˈgriː/ *n* **to give sb the ~** LIT soumettre qn à un interrogatoire musclé; ~ [*parent, teacher*] soumettre qn à une interrogation.

thirdhand /ˌθɜːdˈhænd/ **I** *adj* [*vehicle, garment*] d'occa sion; [*report, evidence*] indirect.
II *adv* [*hear, learn*] de manière indirecte.

thirdly /ˈθɜːdlɪ/ *adv* troisièmement.

third party /ˌθɜːdˈpɑːtɪ/ **I** *n* (in insurance, law) tiers *m*.
II **third-party** *noun modifier* **~ insurance** ass rance *f* au tiers; **~ liability** responsabilité *f* civile.

third: **~ person** *n* troisième personne *f*; **~-rat** *adj* PÉJ GEN de troisième ordre PÉJ; [*work*] m diocre; **Third World** *n* tiers-monde *m*.

thirst /θɜːst/ *n* LIT, FIG soif *f* (**for** de).

hirstily /'θɜːstɪlɪ/ *adv* [*drink*] à grands traits.
hirsty /'θɜːstɪ/ *adj* LIT, FIG assoiffé; **to be ~** LIT, FIG avoir soif; **to make sb ~** donner soif à qn.
hirteen /,θɜː'tiːn/ ▶**1112**], **854**], **713**] I *n* treize *m inv*.
II *adj* treize *inv*.
hirteenth /,θɜː'tiːnθ/ ▶**1112**], **854**] I *n* **1** (in order) treizième *mf*; **2** (of month) treize *m inv*; **3** (fraction) treizième *m*.
II *adj, adv* treizième.
hirtieth /'θɜːtɪəθ/ ▶**1112**], **854**] I *n* **1** (in order) trentième *mf*; **2** (of month) trente *m inv*; **3** (fraction) trentième *m*.
II *adj, adv* trentième.
hirty /'θɜːtɪ/ ▶**1112**], **713**], **812**] I *n* trente *m inv*; **at seven-thirty** à sept heures trente.
II *adj* trente *inv*.
hirty something *n* jeune cadre de plus de trente ans qui s'installe, fonde une famille, etc.
his /ðɪs/ I *det* (*pl* **these**) ce/cet/cette/ces; **~ paper is too thin** ce papier est trop mince; **~ man is dangerous** cet homme est dangereux; **~ lamp doesn't work** cette lampe ne marche pas; **do it ~ way not that way** fais-le comme ça et pas comme ça; **~ woman came up to me**○ une femme est venue vers moi○.
II *pron* **what's ~?** qu'est-ce que c'est?; **who's ~?** GEN qui est-ce?; (on telephone) qui est à l'appareil?; **whose is ~?** à qui appartient ceci?; **~ is the dining room** voici la salle à manger; **where's ~?** (on photo) c'est où?; **~ is my sister Pauline** (introduction) voici ma sœur Pauline; (on photo) c'est ma sœur, Pauline; **~ is not the right one** ce n'est pas le bon; **what did you mean by ~?** qu'est-ce que tu voulais dire par là?; **who did ~?** qui a fait ça?; **what's all ~ about?** qu'est-ce que c'est que cette histoire?; **~ is what happens when** voilà ce qui se passe quand.
III *adv* **it's ~ big** c'est grand comme ça; **having got ~ far it would be a pity to stop now** LIT, FIG maintenant qu'on est arrivé jusque-là ce serait dommage de s'arrêter; **I can't eat ~ much** je ne peux pas manger tout ça ; **I didn't realize it was ~ serious** je ne m'étais pas rendu compte que c'était sérieux à ce point-là.
IDIOMS **we sat around talking about ~ and that** nous avons parlé de tout et de rien; **to run ~ way and that** courir dans tous les sens.
thistle /'θɪsl/ *n* chardon *m*.
tho' *abrév écrite* = **though.**
thong /θɒŋ/ I *n* **1** (on whip) lanière *f*; **2** (on shoe, garment) lacet *m*; **3** (underwear) string *m* ficelle.
II **thongs** *npl* US (sandals) tongs *fpl*.
thorn /θɔːn/ *n* **1** (on plant) épine *f*; **2** (bush) buisson *m* épineux.
IDIOMS **to be a ~ in sb's side** être une source d'irritation pour qn.
thorny /'θɔːnɪ/ *adj* LIT, FIG épineux/-euse.
thorough /'θʌrə, US 'θʌrəʊ/ *adj* **1** (detailed) GEN approfondi; [*preparation, search, work*] minutieux/-ieuse; **to give sth a ~ cleaning** nettoyer qch à fond; **he did a ~ job on the repair work** il a fait toutes les réparations nécessaires; **to have a ~ grasp of sth** maîtriser parfaitement qch; **2** (meticulous) minutieux/-ieuse; **3 to make a ~ nuisance of oneself** se rendre totalement insupportable.
thoroughbred /'θʌrəbred/ I *n* pur-sang *m*.
II *adj* de pure race.
thoroughfare /'θʌrəfeə(r)/ *n* rue *f*; **'no ~'** 'passage interdit'.
thoroughgoing /'θʌrəgəʊɪŋ/ *adj* [*analysis, education*] en profondeur; [*commitment*] absolu; [*preparation*] minutieux/-ieuse.
thoroughly /'θʌrəlɪ, US 'θʌrəʊlɪ/ *adv* **1** (meticulously) GEN à fond; [*check, prepare, search, test*] minutieusement; **2** (completely) [*convincing, dangerous, clean, reliable, deserved*] tout à fait; [*depressing, confusing, unpleasant*] profondément; [*beaten*] complètement; **to ~ enjoy sth/doing** être tout à fait ravi de qch/de

---

this

As a determiner

In French, determiners agree in gender and number with the noun they precede; *this* (plural *these*) is translated by *ce* + masculine singular noun (*ce monsieur*) BUT by *cet* + masculine singular noun beginning with a vowel or mute 'h' (*cet arbre, cet homme*), by *cette* + feminine singular noun (*cette femme*) and by *ces* + plural noun (*ces livres, ces histoires*).

Note, however, that the above translations are also used for the English *that* (plural *those*). So when it is necessary to insist on *this* as opposed to another or others of the same sort, the adverbial tag *-ci*, giving the idea of *this one* here, is added to the noun:

I prefer THIS version = je préfère cette version-ci

For particular usages see the entry *this*.

This dictionary contains usage notes on such topics as *time units*, *days of the week* and *months of the year*. For the index to these notes ▶**1419**].

As a pronoun meaning *this one*

In French, pronouns reflect the gender and number of the noun they are referring to. So *this* is translated by *celui-ci* for a masculine noun, *celle-ci* for a feminine noun; *those* is translated by *ceux-ci* for a masculine plural noun, *celles-ci* for a feminine plural noun:

of all the dresses this is the prettiest one
= de toutes les robes celle-ci est la plus jolie

For other uses of *this* used as a pronoun (*who's this?*, *this is my brother*, etc.) and for *this* used as an adverb (*it was this big* etc.), see the entry *this*.

---

faire; **3** (without reservation) [*agree, approve*] parfaitement; [*recommend*] chaleureusement.
thoroughness /'θʌrənɪs, US 'θʌrəʊnɪs/ *n* (all contexts) minutie *f*.
those /ðəʊs/ *pl* ▶ **that.**
though /ðəʊ/ I *conj* **1** (emphasizing contrast: although) bien que; **strange ~ it may seem** si bizarre que ça puisse paraître; **talented ~ he is, I don't like him** il a beau être doué, je ne l'aime pas; **2** (modifying information: but) bien que, mais; **a foolish ~ courageous act** un acte stupide quoique courageux; **that was delicious ~ I say so myself!** sans me vanter, c'était délicieux!
II *adv* quand même, pourtant.
thought /θɔːt/ I *prét, pp* ▶ **think** II, III.
II *n* **1** (idea) idée *f*, pensée *f*; **that's a ~!** ça c'est une idée!; **it was just a ~** ce n'était qu'une idée comme ça; **what a kind ~!** comme c'est gentil!; **2** ¢ (reflection) pensée *f*; **deep in ~** plongé dans ses pensées; **after much ~** après mûre réflexion; **3** (consideration) considération *f*; **to give ~ to sth** considérer qch; **we never gave it much ~** nous n'y avons pas beaucoup réfléchi; **don't give it another ~** n'y pense plus; **to put a lot of ~ into a gift** choisir un cadeau avec beaucoup de soin; **4** (intention) **to have no ~ of doing** n'avoir aucune intention de faire; **I've given up all ~s of moving** j'ai abandonné toute idée de déménagement.
III **thoughts** *npl* **1** (mind) pensées *fpl* (**about** au sujet de); **to collect** ou **gather one's ~s** rassembler ses esprits; **my ~s were elsewhere** je pensais à autre chose; **2** (opinions) opinion *f*.
thoughtful /'θɔːtfl/ *adj* **1** (reflective) GEN pensif/-ive; [*silence*] profond; **2** (considerate) [*person, gesture*] prévenant; [*letter, gift*] gentil/-ille; **3** (well thought-out) riche en réflexion.
thoughtfully /'θɔːtfəlɪ/ *adv* **1** (considerately) [*behave, treat*] avec prévenance; [*chosen, worded*] avec attention; **2** [*stare, smile*] d'un air pensif; **3** [*write, describe*] de façon réfléchie.
thoughtfulness /'θɔːtflnɪs/ *n* **1** (kindness) prévenance *f*; **2** (of expression, character) sérieux *m*.
thoughtless /'θɔːtlɪs/ *adj* irréfléchi; **to be ~ towards** manquer de considération pour.

thoughtlessly /'θɔːtlɪslɪ/ *adv* (insensitively) sans considération; (unthinkingly) sans réfléchir.

thought-out /ˌθɔːt'aʊt/ *adj* **well/badly ~** bien/mal conçu.

thought: **~ process** *n* mécanismes *mpl* de la pensée; **~-provoking** *adj* qui fait réfléchir.

thousand /'θaʊznd/ ▶1112 I *n* (figure) mille *m inv*; **a ~ and two** mille deux; **about a ~** un millier.
II thousands *npl* milliers *mpl* (**of** de); **in their ~s** par milliers; **to lose ~s** perdre une fortune.
III *adj* mille *inv*; **four ~ pounds** quatre mille livres; **about a ~ people** un millier de personnes.

thousandth /'θaʊzndθ/ ▶1112 I *n* **1** (fraction) millième *m*; **2** (in order) millième *mf*.
II *adj*, *adv* millième.

thrash /θræʃ/ I *n* **1**○ GB (party) grande fête *f*; **2** MUS thrash *m*.
II *vtr* **1** (whip) rouer [qn] de coups; **2**○ MIL, SPORT écraser.
■ **thrash about**, **thrash around**: ¶ **~ about**, **~ around** se débattre; ¶ **~ [sth] around** agiter.
■ **thrash out**: **~ out [sth]** venir à bout de [*difficulties*, *problem*]; réussir à élaborer [*plan*, *compromise*].

thrashing /'θræʃɪŋ/ *n* LIT, FIG raclée *f*.

thread /θred/ I *n* **1** LIT fil *m*; **to be hanging by a ~** LIT, FIG ne tenir qu'à un fil; **2** FIG fil *m*; **common ~** point *m* commun; **to pull all the ~s together** faire la synthèse; **to pick up the ~s of** reprendre le cours de [*career*, *life*]; **3** (of screw) filetage *m*.
II *vtr* **1** LIT enfiler [*bead*, *needle*]; introduire [*film*, *tape*]; **2** FIG **to ~ one's way through** se faufiler entre.
III *vi* [*beads*, *needle*] s'enfiler; [*film*, *tape*] passer.
■ **thread up**: **~ up [sth]** enfiler le fil de [*sewing machine*].

threadbare /'θred.beə/ *adj* LIT, FIG usé jusqu'à la corde.

threat /θret/ *n* (all contexts) menace *f* (**to** pour); **to make ~s against sb** lancer des menaces contre qn; **to pose a ~ to** être une menace pour; **to be under ~** être menacé (**from** par).

threaten /'θretn/ I *vtr* menacer; **to be ~ed with extinction** risquer de disparaître.
II *vi* [*danger*, *bad weather*] menacer; **to ~ to do** risquer de faire.

threatening /'θretnɪŋ/ *adj* GEN menaçant; [*letter*] de menaces; **to receive ~ phone calls** recevoir des menaces par téléphone.

three /θriː/ ▶1112, 713, 812 I *n* trois *m inv*; **to play the best of ~** SPORT jouer la revanche et la belle.
II *adj* trois *inv*.

three-cornered /ˌθriː'kɔːnəd/ *adj* [*object*] triangulaire; [*discussion*] tripartite; **~ hat** tricorne *m*.

three: **~-day event** *n* concours *m* complet; **~-dimensional** *adj* en trois dimensions.

three: **~-legged** *adj* [*object*] à trois pieds; **~-piece suit** *n* (costume *m*) trois-pièces *m inv*; **~-piece suite** *n* salon *m* trois pièces; **~-ply wool** *n* laine *f* triple.

three-quarter /ˌθriː'kwɔːtə(r)/ I *n* SPORT trois-quarts *m*.
II *adj* [*portrait*] de trois-quarts; [*sleeve*] trois-quarts.

three-quarters /ˌθriː'kwɔːtəz/ ▶1336, 812 I *n* trois-quarts *mpl*; **~ of an hour** trois-quarts d'heure.
II *adv* [*empty*, *full*, *done*] aux trois-quarts.

three: **~ R's** *n* SCH les trois disciplines *fpl* fondamentales; **~some** *n* groupe *m* de trois; **~-way** *adj* [*junction*] à trois voies; [*split*] en trois; [*discussion*, *battle*] tripartite; **~-wheeler** *n* (car) voiture *f* à trois roues.

thresh /θreʃ/ I *vtr* battre.
II *vi* battre le blé.

threshold /'θreʃəʊld, -həʊld/ *n* (all contexts) seuil *m*; **to cross the ~** franchir le seuil.

threw /θruː/ *prét* ▶ **throw** II, III, IV.

thrift /θrɪft/ *n* **1** (frugality) économie *f*; **2** BOT armeri *f*.

thrift shop *n* boutique *f* d'articles d'occasion.

thrifty /'θrɪftɪ/ *adj* [*person*] économe (**in** dans); [*life*, *meal*] économique.

thrill /θrɪl/ I *n* **1** (sensation) frisson *m*; **2** (pleasure) plaisir *m*; **to get a ~** ou **one's ~s** se donner des sensations fortes; **what a ~!** quelle émotion!
II *vtr* (with joy) transporter [qn] de joie; (with admiration) GEN transporter [qn] d'admiration; passionner [*readers*, *viewers*].
III *vi* frissonner (**at**, **to** à).
IV thrilled *pp adj* ravi; **~ed with** enchanté de.
IDIOMS **the ~s and spills of sth** les sensations fortes que procure qch.

thriller /'θrɪlə(r)/ *n* CIN, LITERAT, TV thriller *m*.

thrilling /'θrɪlɪŋ/ *adj* GEN palpitant; [*concert*, *moment*, *sensation*] exaltant.

thrive /θraɪv/ *vi* (*prét* **throve** ou **thrived**; *pp* **thrived**) **1** LIT GEN se développer; [*plant*] pousser bien; **2** FIG [*business*, *community*] prospérer; **she ~s on hard work** le travail lui réussit; **children ~ on affection** les enfants ont besoin d'affection pour s'épanouir.

thriving /'θraɪvɪŋ/ *adj* [*business*, *community*] florissant; [*person*] prospère; [*plant*, *animal*] en pleine santé.

throat /θrəʊt/ *n* gorge *f*; **sore ~** mal *m* de gorge; **to have a lump in one's ~** avoir la gorge nouée; **to stick in sb's ~** LIT se coincer dans la gorge de qn.
IDIOMS **to be at each other's ~s**○ se disputer; **to cut one's own ~** travailler à sa propre ruine; **to jump down sb's ~**○ s'en prendre à qn.

throaty /'θrəʊtɪ/ *adj* **1** (husky) guttural; **2**○ (with sore throat) enroué.

throb /θrɒb/ I *n* **1** (of engine, machine) vibration *f*; (of music) rythme *m*; **2** (of heart, pulse) battement *m*; (of pain) élancement *m*.
II *vi* (*p prés etc* **-bb-**) **1** [*heart*, *pulse*] battre; **my head is ~bing** ça me lance dans la tête; **2** [*motor*] vibrer; [*music*, *building*] résonner; **~bing with life** fourmillant d'activité.

throbbing /'θrɒbɪŋ/ I *n* **1** (of heart, pulse, blood) battement *m*; (of pain) élancement *m*; **2** (of motor) vibration *f*; (of music, drum) rythme *m*.
II *adj* **1** [*pain*, *ache*, *sound*, *music*] lancinant; [*head*, *finger*] souffrant de douleurs lancinantes; **2** [*engine*, *motor*] qui vibre.

throes /θrəʊz/ *npl* **1** death **~** agonie *f* ALSO FIG; **2 to be in the ~ of sth/of doing** être au beau milieu de qch/de faire.

throne /θrəʊn/ *n* trône *m*; **on the ~** sur le trône.
IDIOMS **the power behind the ~** l'éminence grise.

throng /θrɒŋ, US θrɔːŋ/ I *n* foule *f* (**of** de).
II *vtr* envahir [*street*, *square*, *town*].
III *vi* **to ~ to** ou **towards** converger vers; **to ~ around** se masser autour de.

throttle /'θrɒtl/ I *n* **1** (also **~ valve**) pointeau *m*; **2** (accelerator) accélérateur *m*; **at full ~** à toute vitesse.
II *vtr* LIT étrangler (**with** avec); FIG asphyxier [*growth*, *project*].

through /θruː/ I *prep* **1** (from one side to the other) à travers; **the nail went right ~ the wall** le clou a traversé le mur; **to stick one's finger ~ the slit** passer son doigt dans la fente; **to poke sth ~ a hole** enfoncer qch dans un trou; **to drill ~ a cable** toucher un fil électrique avec une perceuse; **he was shot ~ the head** on lui a tiré une balle dans la tête; **it has a crack running ~ it** il est fêlé; **2** (via, by way of) **to go ~ the town centre** passer par le centreville; **go straight ~ that door** passez cette porte; **to look ~** regarder avec [*binoculars*, *telescope*]; regarder par [*hole*, *window*]; **3** (past) **to go ~ a red light**; **to get** ou **go ~** passer à travers [*barricade*]; passer [*customs*]; **4** (among) **to fly ~ the clouds** voler au milieu des nuages; **to leap ~ the trees** sauter de branche en branche; **5** (expressing source or agency) it was ~ her that I got this job c'est par son intermédiaire que j'ai eu ce travail; **to book sth ~ a travel agent** réserver qch dans une agence de voyage; **I only know her ~ her writings** je ne la connais qu'à travers ses écrits; **6** (because of) ~ **carelessness** par négligence; ~ **illness** pour cause de maladie; **7** (until the end of) **all** ou **right ~ the day** toute la journée; **8** (up to and including) jusqu'à; **from Friday ~ to Sunday** de vendredi jusqu'à dimanche; **open April ~ September** US ouvert d'avril à fin septembre.

II adj **1**○ (finished) fini; **are you ~ with the paper?** as-tu fini de lire le journal?; **we're ~** (of a couple) c'est fini entre nous; **2** (direct) [train, ticket, route] direct; [freight] à forfait; **'no ~ road'** 'voie sans issue'; **'~ traffic'** (on roadsign) 'autres directions'; ~ **traffic uses the bypass** pour contourner la ville on prend la rocade; **3** (successful) **to be ~ to the next round** être sélectionné pour le deuxième tour; **4** GB **your trousers are ~ at the knee** ton pantalon est troué au genou.

III adv **1** (from one side to the other) **the water went right ~** l'eau est passée à travers; **to let sb ~** laisser passer qn; **cooked right ~** bien cuit; **2** (from beginning to end) **to read/play sth right ~** lire/jouer qch jusqu'au bout; **I'm halfway ~ the article** j'ai lu la moitié de l'article; **3** TELECOM **you're ~** je vous passe votre correspondant.

IV through and through adv phr **to know sth ~ and ~** connaître qch comme sa poche; **English ~ and ~** anglais jusqu'au bout des ongles.

IDIOMS **to have been ~ a lot** en avoir vu des vertes et des pas mûres○; **you really put her ~ it** tu lui en as vraiment fait voir de toutes les couleurs○.

hroughout /θru:'aʊt/ **I** prep **1** (all over) ~ **France** dans toute la France, ~ **the world** dans le monde entier; **2** (for the duration of) tout au long de; ~ **his life** ta vie; ~ **history** à travers l'histoire.
II adv **1** (in every part) partout; **2** (the whole time) tout le temps.

hrough: **~put** n COMPUT, IND débit m; **~way** n US voie f rapide ou express.

hrove /θrəʊv/ prét ▶ **thrive**.

hrow /θrəʊ/ **I** n **1** SPORT, GAMES (in football) touche f; (of javelin, discus etc) lancer m; (in judo, wrestling etc) jeté m; (of dice) coup m; **2**○ (each) **CDs £5 a ~!** les compacts à cinq livres (la) pièce!; **3** US (blanket) jeté m (de lit); (rug) carpette f.

II vtr (prét **threw**; pp **thrown**) **1** GEN, GAMES, SPORT (project) (with careful aim) lancer; (downwards) jeter; (with violence) projeter; ~ **the ball up high** lance la balle en hauteur; **she threw her apron over her head** elle s'est couvert la tête avec son tablier; **she threw her arms around my neck** elle s'est jetée à mon cou; **he was thrown clear and survived** il a été éjecté et a survécu; **two jockeys were thrown** deux jockeys ont été désarçonnés; **to ~ a six** (in dice) faire un six; **2** FIG (direct) lancer [punch, question]; jeter [glance, look]; envoyer [kiss]; projeter [image, light, shadow] (on sur); faire [shadow] (on sur); **we are ready for all the problems that Europe can ~ at us** FIG nous somme prêts à affronter tous les problèmes que l'Europe nous pose; **to ~ money at a project** dépenser sans compter pour un projet; **to ~ suspicion on sb/sth** faire naître des soupçons sur qn/qch; **3** FIG (disconcert) désarçonner; **to ~ [sth/sb] into confusion** ou **disarray** semer la confusion dans [meeting, group]; semer la confusion parmi [people]; **4** TECH actionner [switch, lever]; **the operator threw the machine into gear/reverse** l'opérateur a embrayé l'engin/passé la marche arrière; **5**○ (indulge in) **to ~ a fit** FIG piquer une crise○; **6**○ (organize) **to ~ a party** faire une fête○; **7** (in pottery) **to ~ a pot** tourner un pot.

III vi (prét **threw**; pp **thrown**) lancer.

IV v refl (prét **threw**; pp **thrown**) **to ~ oneself** se jeter (on**to** sur); **to ~ oneself to the ground** se jeter par terre; **to ~ oneself into** LIT se jeter dans; FIG se plonger dans.

IDIOMS **it's ~ing it down**○! GB ça dégringole○!; **to ~ in one's lot with sb** rejoindre qn.

■ **throw around, throw about**: ¶ ~ **[sth] around 1 to ~ a ball around** s'envoyer un ballon; **2** FIG lancer au hasard [ideas etc]; **to ~ money around** jeter l'argent par les fenêtres; ¶ ~ **oneself around** se débattre.

■ **throw aside**: ~ **aside [sth]**, ~ **[sth] aside** LIT lancer [qch] sur le côté; FIG rejeter.

■ **throw away**: ¶ GAMES jeter une carte; ¶ ~ **[sth] away**, ~ **away [sth] 1** LIT jeter; FIG gâcher [chance, life]; gaspiller [money]; **he threw away any advantage he might have had** il n'a pas su profiter de son avantage; **2** (utter casually) lancer [qch] négligemment [remark, information].

■ **throw back**: ~ **back [sth]**, ~ **[sth] back back** [fish]; relancer [ball]; **she threw it back at him** elle le lui a rendu en lui jetant à la figure; **we have been thrown back on our own resources** FIG nous avons dû recourir à nos propres ressources.

■ **throw in**: ~ **in [sth]**, ~ **[sth] in 1** COMM (give free) faire cadeau de; **2** (add) ajouter [ingredient]; **3** faire [remark].

■ **throw off**: ¶ ~ **off [sth]**, ~ **[sth] off 1** (take off) ôter [qch] en vitesse [clothes]; écarter [bedclothes]; **2** FIG (cast aside) se débarrasser de [cold, handicap, pursuers]; se soulager de [burden]; se libérer de [tradition]; sortir de [depression]; **3** FIG (compose quickly) faire [qch] en cinq minutes [poem, music]; ¶ ~ **off [sb]**, ~ **[sb] off** (eject) (from bus, train, plane) expulser.

■ **throw on**: ~ **on [sth]**, ~ **[sth] on** (put on) enfiler [qch] en vitesse.

■ **throw open**: ~ **open [sth]**, ~ **[sth] open 1** ouvrir grand [door, window]; **2** FIG (to public) ouvrir.

■ **throw out**: ¶ ~ **out [sb/sth]**, ~ **[sb/sth] out** jeter [rubbish]; expulser [person] (**of** de); (from membership) renvoyer (**of** de); **to be thrown out of work** être licencié; ¶ ~ **out [sth]**, ~ **[sth] out 1** (extend) ~ **your chest out** sortez la poitrine; **2** (reject) GEN JUR rejeter [application, decision]; POL repousser [bill]; **3** (utter) lancer [comment]; (casually) **he just threw out some comment about wanting...** il a juste dit qu'il voulait...; ¶ ~ **[sb] out** (mislead) déconcerter; **that's what threw me out** c'est ce qui m'a fait me tromper.

■ **throw over**: GB: ~ **over [sb]**, ~ **[sb] over** laisser tomber○.

■ **throw together**: ¶ ~ **[sb] together** réunir [people]; ¶ ~ **[sth] together** GEN improviser; mélanger [ingredients].

■ **throw up**: ¶ ~ **up**○ vomir; ¶ ~ **up [sth]**, ~ **[sth] up 1**○ (abandon) laisser tomber [job]; **2** (reveal) faire apparaître [fact]; créer [idea, problem, obstacle]; engendrer [findings, question, statistic]; **3** cracher [smoke]; émettre [spray]; vomir [lava]; **4** (toss into air) projeter [stone]; lever [arms, hands]; lancer [ball]; **5** (open) ouvrir grand [window]; **6** (vomit) vomir.

throwaway /'θrəʊəweɪ/ adj **1** (discardable) jetable; **2** (wasteful) [society] de consommation; **3** [remark] désinvolte; [entertainment, style] à l'emporte-pièce.

throwback /'θrəʊbæk/ n LIT survivant/-e m/f; FIG survivance f (**to** de).

thrower /'θrəʊə(r)/ n SPORT, GEN lanceur/-euse m/f.

throw-in /'θrəʊɪn/ n SPORT touche f.

thrown /θrəʊn/ pp ▶ **throw** II, III, IV.

thru prep US = **through**.

thrush /θrʌʃ/ n **1** ZOOL grive f; **2 ▶ 1002**] MED (oral) muguet m (buccal); (vaginal) mycose f vaginale.

thrust /θrʌst/ **I** n **1** LIT, GEN, MIL, TECH, ARCHIT poussée f; **sword** ~ coup m d'épée; **2** (of argument, essay) portée f; **3** FIG (attack) **that was a ~ at you** ça c'était une pointe dirigée contre toi.

II vtr (prét, pp **thrust**) **to ~ sth towards** ou **at sb** mettre brusquement qch sous le nez de qn; **to ~ sth into sth** enfoncer qch dans qch; **to ~ sb/sth away** ou **out of the way** pousser violemment qn/qch.

III v refl (prét, pp **thrust**) **to ~ oneself to the front of the crowd** il s'est frayé un passage jusqu'au premier rang de la foule; **to ~ oneself forward** LIT se lancer en avant; FIG se mettre en avant; **to ~ oneself on** ou **onto sb** imposer sa présence à qn.

■ **thrust aside**: ~ [sth/sb] aside, ~ aside [sth/sb] LIT repousser; FIG rejeter.

■ **thrust back**: ~ [sth] back, ~ back [sth] repousser.

■ **thrust forward**: ¶ ~ **forward** se précipiter en avant; ¶ ~ [sth] **forward**, ~ **forward** [sth] pousser [qch] en avant.

■ **thrust on**, **thrust onto** = **thrust upon**.

■ **thrust out**: ~ [sth] out, ~ out [sth] tendre brusquement [hand]; lancer [leg]; projeter [qch] en avant [jaw, chin]; sortir [qch] (d'un geste brusque) [implement].

■ **thrust upon**: ~ [sth] upon sb imposer [qch] sur qn; some have greatness thrust upon them parfois ce sont les circonstances qui font les grands hommes.

thrusting /'θrʌstɪŋ/ adj GEN agressif/-ive; [ambition] puissant.

thud /θʌd/ I n bruit m sourd.

II vi (p prés etc **-dd-**) faire un bruit sourd; they **~ded up the stairs** ils ont monté l'escalier à pas lourds; her heart was **~ding** son cœur battait à tout rompre.

thug /θʌg/ n (hooligan) voyou m; (hired heavy) casseur m.

thumb /θʌm/ I n pouce m.

II vtr 1 feuilleter [book, magazine]; a well-~ed book un livre qui a beaucoup servi; 2○ (hitchhiking) to ~ a lift ou a ride faire du stop○.

IDIOMS to be all ~s être très maladroit; to be under sb's ~ être sous la domination de qn; to ~ one's nose at sb LIT faire un pied de nez à qn; FIG faire la nique○ à qn; to stick out like a sore ~ faire tache PEJ.

■ **thumb through**: ~ through [sth] feuilleter [book, magazine].

thumb: ~ index n répertoire m à onglets; ~nail sketch n FIG (of person) esquisse f (de caractère); (of event) aperçu m.

thumbs down○ /ˌθʌmz'daʊn/ n (signal) to give sb/sth the ~ FIG rejeter qn/qch; to get the ~ [candidate, proposal, idea] être rejeté; [new product, experiment] être mal accueilli.

thumbs up○ /ˌθʌmz'ʌp/ n to give sb/sth the ~ (approve) approuver qn/qch; start the car when I give you the ~ démarre quand je te fais signe; she gave me the ~ as she came out of the interview elle m'a fait signe que l'entretien s'était bien passé.

thumbtack /'θʌmtæk/ I n punaise f.

II vtr fixer [qch] avec des punaises.

thump /θʌmp/ I n 1 (blow) (grand) coup m; 2 (sound) bruit m sourd.

II vtr donner un coup de poing à [person]; donner un coup de poing sur [table].

III vi 1 (pound) [heart] battre violemment; [music, rhythm] résonner; my head is ~ing j'ai la tête qui m'élance; to ~ on marteler [table]; 2 (clump) to ~ upstairs monter l'escalier à pas lourds.

thumping /'θʌmpɪŋ/ I n 1 (of drums) battement m; 2○ (beating) raclée○ f.

II adj 1○ (emphatic) ~ big, ~ great énorme; 2 (loud) [noise] sourd; [rhythm, sound] lancinant; [headache] lancinant.

thunder /'θʌndə(r)/ I n 1 METEOROL tonnerre m; a clap ou peal of ~ un coup de tonnerre; 2 (noise) (of hooves) fracas m; (of traffic) grondement m; (of cannons, applause) tonnerre m.

II vtr (shout) (also ~ out) hurler.

III vi 1 (roar) [person, cannon] tonner; [hooves] faire un bruit de tonnerre (on sur); 2 (rush) to ~ along ou past passer dans un vacarme assourdissant.

IV v impers tonner.

IDIOMS to steal sb's ~ couper l'herbe sous le pied de qn; with a face like ~ ou as black as ~ l'air furieux.

thunder: ~bolt n METEOROL foudre f; FIG coup m de tonnerre; ~clap n coup m de tonnerre; ~cloud n nuage m porteur d'orage.

thundering /'θʌndərɪŋ/ I adj 1 (angry) [rage] noir; 2

(huge) [success] énorme; [nuisance] véritable; [noise] assourdissant.

II○ adv GB (intensifier) a ~ great skyscraper un gratte-ciel gigantesque.

thunderous /'θʌndərəs/ adj 1 (loud) [welcome] tonitruant; [music, noise] assourdissant; ~ applause un tonnerre d'applaudissements; 2 (angry) [face, expression] orageux/-euse; [look] furieux/-ieuse.

thunder: ~storm n orage m; ~struck adj abasourdi.

thundery /'θʌndərɪ/ adj orageux/-euse.

Thur, **Thurs** abrév écrite = **Thursday**.

Thursday /'θɜːzdeɪ, -dɪ/ ▶ 1390| pr n jeudi m.

thus /ðʌs/ adv ainsi; ~ **far** jusqu'à présent.

thwack /θwæk/ I n (blow) coup m; (with hand) claque f (sound) coup m sec.

II vtr frapper (vigoureusement).

thwart /θwɔːt/ I vtr contrecarrer, contrarier [plan] contrecarrer les desseins de [person].

II **thwarted** pp adj contrarié (in dans).

thy‡ /ðaɪ/ det = **your**.

thyme /taɪm/ n thym m.

thyroid /'θaɪrɔɪd/ n (also ~ **gland**) thyroïde f.

ti /tiː/ n MUS si m.

tiara /tɪ'ɑːrə/ n (woman's) diadème m; (Pope's) tiare f.

Tibet /tɪ'bet/ pr n Tibet m.

tick /tɪk/ I n 1 (of clock) tic-tac m; 2 (mark on paper) coche f; to put a ~ against sth cocher qch; 3 ZOO tique f; 4○ GB (short time) seconde f; I won't be a ~ j'en ai (juste) pour une seconde; 5○ GB (credit) on ~ à crédit.

II vtr (make mark) cocher [box, name, answer].

III vi [bomb, clock, watch] faire tic-tac; I know what makes him ~ FIG je sais ce qui le motive.

■ **tick away** [time] passer; [clock, meter] tourner.

■ **tick by** [hours, minutes] passer.

■ **tick off**: ¶ ~ [sth] off, ~ off [sth] (mark) coche [name, item]; ¶ ~ [sb] off 1○ GB (reprimand) réprimander [person]; 2○ (annoy) embêter [person].

■ **tick over** GB LIT, FIG tourner.

ticker tape /'tɪkəteɪp/ n bande f de téléscripteur; to give sb a ~ welcome ou reception accueillir qn par une pluie de serpentins.

ticket /'tɪkɪt/ I n 1 GEN billet m (for pour); (for bus underground, cloakroom, left-luggage) ticket m; (for library carte f; (label) étiquette f; admission by ~ only entrée sur présentation d'un billet; 2○ AUT (for fine PV○ m; 3 US POL (of political party) liste f (électorale) (platform) programme m; to run on the Republican ~ se présenter sur la liste des Républicains.

II vtr étiqueter [goods, baggage].

IDIOMS that's (just) the ~○! voilà (exactement) ce qu'il nous faut!

ticket: ~ agency n agence f de spectacles; ~ inspector ▶ 1251| n contrôleur m; ~ office (office) bureau m de vente (des billets); (booth) guichet m; ~ tout n GB revendeur/-euse m/f de billets au marché noir.

ticking /'tɪkɪŋ/ n 1 (of clock) tic-tac m; 2 (material) toile f à matelas; (cover) housse f.

tickle /'tɪkl/ I n chatouillement m.

II vtr 1 [person, feather] chatouiller; [wool, garment] gratter; 2○ FIG (gratify) chatouiller [palate, vanity] exciter [senses]; (amuse) amuser [person]; to ~ sb' fancy amuser qn.

III vi [blanket, garment] gratter; [feather] chatouiller.

IDIOMS ~d pink ou to death ravi.

tickling /'tɪklɪŋ/ n chatouillement m.

ticklish /'tɪklɪʃ/ adj 1 [person] chatouilleux/-euse; 2 (tricky) [situation, problem] épineux/-euse.

tick-tack-toe ▶ 949| n US (jeu m de) morpion m.

tidal /'taɪdl/ adj [river] à marée; [current, flow, waters] de marée; [energy, power] marémoteur/-trice.

tidal wave n LIT, FIG raz-de-marée m inv.

tidbit /'tɪdbɪt/ n US (of food) gâterie f; (of gossip) cancan○ m.

tiddly○ /'tɪdlɪ/ *adj* GB (drunk) pompette○.

tiddlywinks /'tɪdlɪwɪŋks/ ▶ 949 *n* jeu *m* de puce.

tide /taɪd/ *n* marée *f*; FIG (of emotion) vague *f*; (of events) cours *m*; **the ~ is in/out** c'est la marée haute/basse; **the ~ is turning** la marée change; **to go/swim against the ~** LIT, FIG aller/nager à contre-courant; **the ~ has turned** FIG la chance a tourné (du bon côté).
IDIOMS **time and ~ wait for no man** on ne peut pas arrêter le temps.
■ **tide over**: **~** [sb] **over** dépanner.

tidemark *n* LIT ligne *f* de marée haute; GB FIG (line of dirt) marque *f* de saleté.

tidily /'taɪdɪlɪ/ *adv* GEN soigneusement; [*dress*] de façon soignée.

tidiness /'taɪdɪnɪs/ *n* (of place) ordre *m*; (of appearance) aspect *m* soigné; (of person) sens *m* de l'ordre.

tidings /'taɪdɪŋz/ *npl* LITTÉR nouvelles *fpl*.

tidy /'taɪdɪ/ **I** *n* GB = **tidy-out**.
II *adj* **1** [*house, room, desk*] bien rangé; [*garden, work, person, appearance*] soigné; [*habits*] ordonné; [*hair*] bien coiffé; **to make oneself ~** s'arranger; **2**○ [*amount*] beau/belle.
III *vtr* = **tidy up**.
IV *vi* = **tidy up**.
■ **tidy away**: **~** [sth] **away**, **~ away** [sth] ranger.
■ **tidy out**: **~** [sth] **out**, **~ out** [sth] ranger.
■ **tidy up**: ¶ **~ up** faire du rangement; **to ~ up after** ranger derrière [*person*]; ¶ **~ up** [sth], **~** [sth] **up** ranger [*house, room, objects*]; mettre de l'ordre dans [*garden, town, finances*]; arranger [*appearance, hair*]; ¶ **~ oneself up** s'arranger.

tidy-out /'taɪdɪaʊt/, **tidy-up** /'taɪdɪʌp/ *n* GB rangement *m*; **to have a ~** faire du rangement.

tie /taɪ/ **I** *n* **1** (piece of clothing) cravate *f*; **2** (fastener) attache *f*; **3** (bond) (*gén pl*) lien *m*; **family ~s** liens *mpl* familiaux; **4** (constraint) contrainte *f*; **5** GEN, SPORT (draw) match *m* nul; **the match ended in a ~** les deux équipes ont fait match nul; **there was a ~ for second place** il y a eu ex-aequo pour la deuxième place; **there was a ~ between the candidates** les candidats ont obtenu le même nombre de voix.
II *vtr* (*p prés* **tying**) **1** (attach) attacher [*label, animal*] (**to** à); ligoter [*hands*]; ficeler [*parcel, chicken*] (**with** avec); (join in knot) nouer [*scarf, cravate*]; attacher [*laces*]; **~ a knot in the string** fais un nœud à la ficelle; **2** (link) associer (**to** à); **to be ~d to** être lié à [*growth, activity*]; FIN être indexé sur [*inflation, interest*]; **3** **to be ~d to** (constrained by) être rivé à [*job*]; être cloué○ à [*house*].
III *vi* (*p prés* **tying**) **1** (fasten) s'attacher; **2** GEN, SPORT (draw) (in match) faire match nul; (in race) être ex aequo; (in vote) [*candidates*] obtenir le même nombre de voix.
■ **tie back**: **~** [sth] **back**, **~ back** [sth] nouer [qch] derrière [*hair*]; attacher [qch] sur le côté [*curtain*].
■ **tie down**: **~** [sb/sth] **down**, **~ down** [sb/sth] (hold fast) attacher [*person*]; **she feels ~d down** FIG elle se sent coincée○; **he doesn't want to be ~d down** il ne veut pas perdre sa liberté; **to ~ sb down to sth** (limit) imposer qch à qn; **to ~ sb down to an exact date** arriver à soutirer une date exacte à qn; **to ~ oneself down** s'astreindre (**to** à).
■ **tie in with**: ¶ **~ in with** [sth] **1** (tally) concorder avec [*fact, event*]; **2** (have link) être en rapport avec; ¶ **~** [sth] **in with sth**, **~ in** [sth] **with sth** (combine) combiner [qch] avec qch.
■ **tie on**: **~** [sth] **on**, **~ on** [sth] attacher.
■ **tie together**: **~** [sth] **together**, **~ together** [sth] attacher [*bundles, objects*].
■ **tie up**: **~** [sb/sth] **up**, **~ up** [sb/sth] **1** (secure) ligoter [*prisoner*]; ficeler [*parcel*]; attacher [*animal*]; **2** FIN (freeze) immobiliser [*capital*]; bloquer [*shares*]; **3** (finalize) régler [*details, matters*]; conclure [*deal*]; **to ~ up the loose ends** régler les derniers détails; **4** (hinder) bloquer [*procedure*]; US bloquer [*traffic, route*]; US suspendre [*production*]; **5** **to be ~d up** (be busy) être pris.

tie break(er) *n* (in tennis) tie-break *m*; (in quiz) question *f* subsidiaire.

tie-dye /'taɪdaɪ/ *vtr* chiner par teinture.

tier /tɪə(r)/ **I** *n* (of cake, sandwich) étage *m*; (of organization, system) niveau *m*; (of seating) gradin *m*; ▶ **two-tier**.
II *vtr* constituer [qch] en niveaux [*organization, system*]; disposer [qch] en gradins [*seating*].
III **tiered** *pp adj* [*seating*] en gradins; [*system*] à plusieurs niveaux; **~ed cake** pièce *f* montée.

tiff /tɪf/ *n* (petite) querelle *f*.

tiger /'taɪgə(r)/ *n* tigre *m*.

tight /taɪt/ ▶ 1260 | **I tights** *npl* GB collant *m*.
II *adj* **1** (firm) [*grip*] ferme; [*knot*] serré; (taut) [*rope, voice*] tendu; **to hold sb in a ~ embrace** tenir qn serré dans ses bras; **2** (constrictive) [*space*] étroit; [*clothing*] serré; (closefitting) [*jacket, shirt*] ajusté; **my shoes are too ~** mes chaussures sont trop étroites; **a pair of ~ jeans** un jean moulant; **there were six of us in the car, it was a ~ squeeze** on était six dans la voiture, on était très serré; **3** (strict) [*security, deadline*] strict; [*discipline*] rigoureux/-euse; [*budget, credit*] serré; **to exercise ~ control over sth/sb** contrôler strictement qch/qn; **to be ~ (with one's money)**○ être près de ses sous; **money is a bit ~ these days** je suis/on est un peu juste ces temps-ci; **4** (packed, compact) serré; **5** (sharp) [*angle, turn*] aigu/-uë.
III *adv* [*hold, grip*] fermement; **to fasten/close sth ~** bien attacher/fermer qch; **hold ~!** cramponne-toi!; **sit ~!** ne bouge pas!; **I just sat ~ and waited for the scandal to pass** FIG je suis resté tranquillement dans mon coin en attendant que le scandale passe.
IDIOMS **to be in a ~ spot** OU **situation** OU **corner** être dans une situation difficile; **to run a ~ ship** tout avoir à l'œil.

tighten /'taɪtn/ **I** *vtr* serrer [*lid, screw*]; resserrer [*grip*]; tendre [*spring, bicycle chain*]; renforcer [*security, restrictions*]; durcir [*legislation, policy*].
II *vi* **1** (contract) [*lips*] se serrer; [*muscle*] se contracter; **2** [*screw, nut*] se resserrer; [*laws, credit controls*] se durcir.
IDIOMS **to ~ one's belt** se serrer la ceinture.
■ **tighten up**: **~ up** [sth], **~** [sth] **up** resserrer [*screw, hinge*]; renforcer [*security*]; durcir [*legislation*]; **to ~ up on** durcir la réglementation en matière de [*immigration, fiscal policy*].

tight: **~-fisted**○ *adj* PÉJ radin○; **~-fitting** *adj* ajusté; **~-knit** *adj* FIG uni.

tight-lipped /ˌtaɪt'lɪpt/ *adj* **they are remaining ~ about the events** ils se refusent à tout commentaire sur les événements; **he watched, ~** il a regardé d'un air pincé ou d'un air réprobateur.

tightly /'taɪtlɪ/ *adv* [*grasp, hold*] fermement; [*embrace*] bien fort; [*tied, fastened*] bien; [*controlled*] strictement; **the ~ packed crowd** la foule dense et serrée; **a ~ stretched rope** une corde très tendue.

tightness /'taɪtnɪs/ *n* (of space, garment) étroitesse *f*; (of restrictions, security) rigueur *f* (**of** de); **to feel a ~ in one's chest** se sentir oppressé.

tight: **~rope** *n* corde *f* raide; **~rope walker** *n* funambule *mf*.

tile /taɪl/ **I** *n* (for roof) tuile *f*; (for floor, wall) carreau *m*.
II *vtr* poser des tuiles sur [*roof*]; carreler [*floor, wall*].
IDIOMS **to have a night** OU **go out on the ~s**○ GB faire la noce○.

tiling /'taɪlɪŋ/ *n* ¢ (tiles) (of roof) tuiles *fpl*; (of floor, wall) carrelage *m*.

till[1] /tɪl/ ▶ **until**.

till[2] /tɪl/ *n* caisse *f*; **to have one's hand in the ~** piocher dans la caisse.

tiller /'tɪlə(r)/ *n* NAUT barre *f*.

till receipt *n* ticket *m* (de caisse).

tilt /tɪlt/ **I** *n* **1** (incline) inclinaison *f*; **to be on** OU **at a ~** être incliné; **2** **to have** OU **take a ~ at** FIG s'en prendre à [*person, organization*]; s'essayer à [*championship*]; **at full ~** à toute vitesse.
II *vtr* (slant) pencher [*table, sunshade*]; incliner [*head*]; rabattre [*hat, cap*].

Time units

Lengths of time

a second = une seconde
a minute = une minute
an hour = une heure
a day = un jour
a week = une semaine
a month = un mois
a year = un an/une année
a century = un siècle

For time by the clock, ▶ 812 ; for days of the week,
▶ 1390 ; for months, ▶ 1090 ; for dates, ▶ 854 .

How long?

Note the various ways of translating take *into French.*

how long does it take? = combien de temps faut-il?
it took me a week = cela m'a pris une semaine
     or il m'a fallu une semaine
I took an hour to finish it = j'ai mis une heure pour le
     terminer
the letter took a month
to arrive = la lettre a mis un mois pour
     arriver
it'll take at least a year = il faudra une bonne année
     or il faudra au moins un an
it'll only take a moment = c'est l'affaire de quelques
     instants

Translate both spend *and* have *as* passer:

to have a wonderful evening = passer une soirée
     merveilleuse
to spend two days in Paris = passer deux jours à Paris

Use dans *for* in *when something is seen as happening in*
the future:

I'll be there in an hour = je serai là dans une heure
she said she'd be there in an hour = elle a dit qu'elle serait
     là dans une heure
in three weeks' time = dans trois semaines

Use en *for* in *when expressing the time something took or*
will take:

he did it in an hour = il l'a fait en une heure

The commonest translation of for *in the 'how long' sense is*
pendant:

I worked in the factory for a year = j'ai travaillé à l'usine
     pendant un an

But use pour *for* for *when the length of time is seen as*
being still to come:

we're here for a month = nous sommes là pour
     un mois
they'll take the room for a week = ils vont prendre la
     chambre pour huit jours

And use depuis *for* for *when the action began in the past*
and is or was still going on:

she has been here for a week = elle est ici depuis huit jours
she had been there for a year = elle était là depuis un an
I haven't seen her for years = je ne l'ai pas vue depuis
     des années

Note the use of de *when expressing how long something*
lasted or will last:

a two-minute delay = un retard de deux minutes
a six-week wait = une attente de six semaines
an eight-hour day = une journée de huit heures
six weeks' sick leave = un congé de maladie de six
     semaines
five weeks' pay = cinq semaines de salaire

When?

In the past

when did it happen? = quand est-ce que c'est arrivé?
two minutes ago = il y a deux minutes
a month ago = il y a un mois
years ago = il y a des années
it'll be a month ago on Tuesday = ça fera un mois mardi
it's years since he died = il y a des années qu'il est mort
a month earlier = un mois plus tôt
a month before = un mois avant
     or un mois auparavant

the year before = l'année d'avant
     or l'année précédente
the year after = l'année d'après
     or l'année suivante
a few years later = quelques années plus tard
after four days = au bout de quatre jours
last week = la semaine dernière
last month = le mois dernier
last year = l'année dernière
a week ago yesterday = il y a eu huit jours hier
a week ago tomorrow = il y aura huit jours demain
the week before last = il y a quinze jours
over the past few months = au cours des derniers mois

In the future

when will you see him? = quand est-ce que tu le verras?
in a few days = dans quelques jours
     (*see also above, the phrases*
     with in *translated by* dans)
any day now = d'un jour à l'autre
next week = la semaine prochaine
next month = le mois prochain
next year = l'année prochaine
this coming week = (dans) la semaine qui vient
     or (*more formally*) (au cours
     de) la semaine à venir
over the coming months = au cours des mois à venir
a month from tomorrow = dans un mois demain

How often?

how often does it happen? = cela arrive tous les
     combien?
every Thursday = tous les jeudis
every week = toutes les semaines
every year = tous les ans
every second day = tous les deux jours
every third month = tous les trois mois
day after day = jour après jour
year after year = année après année
the last Thursday of the month = le dernier jeudi du mois
five times a day = cinq fois par jour
twice a month = deux fois par mois
three times a year = trois fois par an
once every three months = une fois tous les trois
     mois

How much an hour (etc)?

how much do you get
an hour? = combien gagnez-vous de l'heure?
I get $20 = je gagne 20 dollars de l'heure
to be paid $20 an hour = être payé 20 dollars de l'heure

but note:

to be paid by the hour = être payé à l'heure
how much do you get a week? = combien gagnez-vous
     par semaine?
how much do you earn a month? = combien gagnez-vous
     par mois?
$3,000 a month = 3 000 dollars par mois
$40,000 a year = 40 000 dollars par an

Forms in *-ée: an/année, matin/matinée* etc.

The -ée forms are often used to express a rather vague
amount of time passing or spent in something, and so tend
to give a subjective slant to what is being said, as in:

a long day/evening/year = une longue
     journée/soirée/année
a whole day = toute une journée *or* une
     journée entière
we spent a lovely day there = nous y avons passé une
     journée merveilleuse
a painful evening = une soirée pénible

When an exact number is specified, the shorter forms are
generally used, as in:

it lasted six days = cela a duré six jours
two years' military service = deux ans de service
     militaire
she spent ten days in England = elle a passé dix jours en
     Angleterre

However there is no strict rule that applies to all of these
words. If in doubt, check in the dictionary.

III *vi* **1** (slant) pencher; **2 to ~ at** FIG s'en prendre à [*person, organization*].

timber /'tɪmbə(r)/ *n* (for building) bois *m* (de construction); (trees) arbres *mpl*; (beam) poutre *f*.

timbered /'tɪmbə(r)d/ *adj* [*house*] en bois; **half-~ house** maison *f* à colombages.

timber: **~land** *n* US terrain *m* forestier exploitable; **~ yard** *n* scierie *f*.

timbre /'tɪmbə(r), 'tæmbrə/ *n* timbre *m*.

time /taɪm/ ▶ 812 **I** *n* **1** (continuum) temps *m*; **in ou with ~, in the course of ~** avec le temps; **as ~ goes/went by** avec le temps; **at this point in ~** à l'heure qu'il est; **for all ~** à jamais; **2** (specific duration) temps *m*; **flight/journey ~** durée *f* du vol/voyage; **I was waiting for you here all the ~** je t'attendais ici et je n'ai pas bougé; **she was lying all the ~** elle mentait depuis le début; **you've got all the ~ in the world, you've got plenty of ~** tu as tout ton temps; **it'll be a long ~ before I go back there!** je n'y retournerai pas de sitôt!; **you took a long ~!**, **what a (long) ~ you've been!** tu en as mis du temps!; **we had to wait for a long ~** nous avons dû attendre longtemps; **a long ~ ago** il y a longtemps; **we haven't heard from her for some ~** ça fait un moment qu'on n'a pas eu de ses nouvelles; **in no ~ at all**, **in next to no ~** en moins de deux; **in five days'/weeks'~** dans cinq jours/semaines; **within the agreed ~** dans les délais convenus; **in your own ~** (at your own pace) à ton rythme; (outside working hours) en dehors des heures de travail; **on company ~** pendant les heures de bureau; **my ~ is my own** je suis maître de mon temps; **3** (hour of the day, night) heure *f*; **what ~ is it?**, **what's the ~?** quelle heure est-il?; **the ~ is 11 o'clock** il est 11 heures; **10 am French ~** 10 heures, heure française; **this ~ last week/year** il y a exactement huit jours/un an; **by this ~ next year** d'ici un an; **on ~** à l'heure; **the train ~s** les horaires *mpl* des trains; **it's ~ for bed** c'est l'heure d'aller au lit; **it's ~ we started** il est temps de commencer; **to lose ~** [*clock*] retarder; **that clock keeps good ~** cette horloge est toujours à l'heure; **about ~ too!** ce n'est pas trop tôt!; **not before ~!** il était (or il est) grand temps!; **to arrive in good ~** arriver en avance; **in ~ for Christmas** à temps pour Noël; **to be behind ~** avoir du retard; **twenty minutes ahead of ~** vingt minutes avant l'heure prévue; **4** (era, epoch) époque *f*; **in Dickens' ~s** du temps de Dickens; **at the ~** à l'époque; **~ was ou there was a ~ when one could...** à une certaine époque on pouvait...; **to be behind the ~s** être en retard sur son époque; **to keep up ou move with the ~s** être à la page; **in ~s past, in former ~s** autrefois; **it's just like old ~s** c'est comme au bon vieux temps; **peace in our ~** la paix de notre vivant; **at my ~ of life** à mon âge; **she was a beautiful woman in her ~** c'était une très belle femme dans son temps; **it was before my ~** (before my birth) je n'étais pas encore né; (before I came here) je n'étais pas encore ici; **if I had my ~ over again** si je pouvais recommencer ma vie; **to die before one's ~** mourir prématurément; **5** (moment) moment *m*; **at ~s** par moments; **at the right ~** au bon moment; **this is no ~ for jokes** ce n'est pas le moment de plaisanter; **at all ~s** à tout moment; **any ~ now** d'un moment à l'autre; **the ~ has come for action** l'heure est venue d'agir; **by the ~ I finished the letter the post had gone** le temps de finir ma lettre et le courrier était parti; **by the ~ she had got downstairs he had gone** avant qu'elle n'arrive en bas il était déjà parti; **by this ~ most of them were dead** la plupart d'entre eux étaient déjà morts; **some ~ this week** dans la semaine; **some ~ next month** dans le courant du mois prochain; **for the ~ being** pour l'instant; **from that ou this ~ on** à partir de ce moment; **when the ~ comes** le moment venu; **in ~s of crisis** dans les périodes de crise; **until such ~ as** jusqu'à ce que; **I can't be in two places at the same ~** je ne peux pas être partout à la fois; **6** (occasion) fois *f*; **nine ~s out of ten** neuf fois sur dix;

three ~s a month trois fois par mois; **~ after ~**, **~ and ~ again** maintes fois; **three at a ~** trois à la fois; **she passed her driving test first ~ round** elle a eu son permis du premier coup; **from ~ to ~** de temps en temps; **for months at a ~** pendant des mois entiers; **(in) between ~s** entre-temps, **7** (experience) **to have a tough ou hard ~ doing** avoir du mal à faire; **he's having a rough ou hard ou tough ~** il traverse une période difficile; **we had a good ~** on s'est bien amusé; **to have an easy ~ (of it)** se la couler douce°; **the good/bad ~s** les moments heureux/difficiles; **she enjoyed her ~ in Canada** elle a beaucoup aimé son séjour au Canada; **8** ADMIN (hourly rate) **to work/be paid ~** travailler/être payé à l'heure; **to be paid ~ and a half** être payé une fois et demie le tarif normal; **9** MUS mesure *f*; **to beat ou mark ~** battre la mesure; **in waltz ~** sur un rythme de valse; **10** SPORT temps *m*; **a fast ~** un bon temps; **to keep ~** chronométrer; **11** MATH, FIG **three ~s four** trois fois quatre; **ten ~s longer/ stronger** dix fois plus long/plus fort; **eight ~s as much** huit fois autant.
II *vtr* **1** (schedule) GEN prévoir; fixer [*appointment, meeting*]; **we ~ our trips to fit in with school holidays** nous faisons coïncider nos voyages avec les vacances scolaires; **to be well-/badly-timed** être opportun/inopportun; **the announcement was perfectly ~d** la déclaration est tombée à point nommé; **2** (judge) calculer [*blow, shot*]; **to ~ a joke** choisir le moment pour faire une plaisanterie; **3** (measure speed, duration) chronométrer [*athlete, cyclist*]; mesurer la durée de [*journey, speech*].
III *v refl* **to ~ oneself** se chronométrer.
IDIOMS **from ~ out of mind** depuis la nuit des temps; **there is a ~ and place for everything** il y a un temps pour tout; **there's always a first ~** il y a un début à tout; **he'll tell you in his own good ~** il te le dira quand il en aura envie; **all in good ~** chaque chose en son temps; **only ~ will tell** l'avenir nous le dira; **to pass the ~ of day with sb** échanger quelques mots avec qn; **to have ~ on one's hands** (for brief period) avoir du temps devant soi; (longer) avoir beaucoup de temps libre; **to have a lot of ~ for sb** apprécier beaucoup qn; **I've got no ~ for that sort of attitude** je ne supporte pas ce genre d'attitude; **to do ~°** (prison) faire de la taule°; **give me Lauren Bacall every ~!** rien ne vaut Lauren Bacall!; **long ~ no see°!** ça fait un bail° (qu'on ne s'est pas vu)!

time: **~ bomb** *n* LIT, FIG bombe *f* à retardement; **~ check** *n* annonce *f* de l'heure; **~-consuming** *adj* qui prend du temps (*after n*); **~ delay** *n* délai *m*; **~ difference** *n* décalage *m* horaire; **~-frame** *n* (period envisaged) calendrier *m*; (period allocated) délai *m*; **~-honoured** *adj* consacré par l'usage.

timekeeper /'taɪmkiːpə(r)/ *n* SPORT chronométreur *m*; GEN **to be a good ~** être toujours à l'heure.

time-lag *n* décalage *m*.

timeless /'taɪmlɪs/ *adj* éternel/-elle.

time-limit /'taɪmlɪmɪt/ *n* **1** (deadline) date *f* limite; **within the ~** dans les délais; **2** (maximum duration) durée *f* maximum; **there's a 20-minute ~ on speeches** les discours ne doivent pas dépasser 20 minutes.

timely /'taɪmlɪ/ *adj* opportun.

time machine *n* machine *f* à explorer le temps.

time off /ˌtaɪm 'ɒf/ *n* (leave) congé *m*; (free time) temps *m* libre; **to take ~ from work to go to the dentist's** prendre du temps sur son travail pour aller chez le dentiste.

time-out *n* SPORT temps *m* mort; (break) temps *m* de repos.

timer /'taɪmə(r)/ *n* GEN minuterie *f*; (for cooking) minuteur *m*.

timesaver /'taɪmseɪvə(r)/ *n* **a dishwasher is a real ~** un lave-vaisselle fait vraiment gagner du temps.

time: **~-scale** *n* période *f* (de temps); **~share** *n* (house) maison *f* en multipropriété; (apartment) appartement *m* en multipropriété; **~-sheet** *n* feuille *f* de présence; **~-signal** *n* signal *m* horaire; **~span** *n* durée *f*; **~-switch** *n* minuterie *f*.

timetable /'taɪmteɪbl/ **I** *n* (schedule) GEN emploi *m* du temps; (for plans, negotiations) calendrier *m*; (for buses, trains etc) horaire *m*; **a ~ for reform** un calendrier de réformes; **to work to a strict ~** suivre un programme de travail très stricte.
II *vtr* fixer l'heure de [*class, lecture*]; fixer la date de [*meeting, negotiations*]; **the bus is ~d to leave at 11.30 am** le bus doit partir à 11 h 30.

time: **~ trial** *n* (in cycling) épreuve de sélection contre la montre; (in athletics) épreuve *f* de sélection; **~-wasting** *n* perte *f* de temps; **~-worn** *adj* consacré par l'usage; **~ zone** *n* fuseau *m* horaire.

timid /'tɪmɪd/ *adj* GEN timide; [*animal*] craintif/-ive.

timidity /tɪ'mɪdətɪ/ *n* timidité *f*.

timing /'taɪmɪŋ/ *n* **1** (scheduling) **the ~ of the announcement was unfortunate** le moment choisi pour la déclaration était inopportun; **there is speculation about the ~ of the election** la date choisie pour l'élection donne lieu à bien des conjectures; **to get one's ~ right/wrong** bien/mal choisir son moment; **2** (coordination) (of operation) minutage *m*; **3** AUT réglage *m* de l'allumage; **4** MUS sens *m* du rythme; THEAT **to have a good sense of ~** savoir rythmer son débit.

timorous /'tɪmərəs/ *adj* timoré.

timpani /'tɪmpənɪ/ **▶ 1097** *npl* timbales *fpl*.

tin /tɪn/ **I** *n* **1** (metal) étain *m*; **2** GB (can) boîte *f* (de conserve); **to eat out of ~s** se nourrir de conserves; **to come out of a ~** être de la conserve; **3** (container) (for biscuits, cake) boîte *f*; (for paint) pot *m*; (for baking) moule *m*; (for roasting) plat *m* (à rôtir).
II *noun modifier* [*mug, bath*] en étain.
III *vtr* GB (*p prés etc* **-nn-**) mettre [qch] en boîte.
IV tinned *pp adj* GB [*meat, fruit*] en boîte.

tin can *n* boîte *f* en fer-blanc.

tin foil /'tɪnfɔɪl/ *n* papier *m* (d')aluminium.

tinge /tɪndʒ/ **I** *n* (all contexts) nuance *f*.
II *vtr* teinter (**with** de).

tingle /'tɪŋgl/ **I** *n* (physical) picotement *m*; (psychological) frisson *m*.
II *vi* (physically) picoter; (psychologically) frissonner.

tingling /'tɪŋglɪŋ/ *n* picotements *mpl*.

tingly /'tɪŋglɪ/ *adj* **my fingers have gone all ~** j'ai des picotements dans les doigts.

tin: **~ god** *n* PÉJ petit chef *m*; **~ hat** *n* casque *m*.

tinker /'tɪŋkə(r)/ *vi* (also **to ~ about** ou **around**) bricoler; **to ~ with** bricoler [*car, machine*]; faire des retouches à [*wording, document*].

tinkle /'tɪŋkl/ **I** *n* tintement *m*; **to give sb a ~** GB passer un coup de fil à qn○.
II *vtr* faire tinter.
III *vi* tinter.

tinkling /'tɪŋklɪŋ/ *n* tintement *m*.

tinny /'tɪnɪ/ *adj* **1** [*sound, music*] grêle; **2** (badly made) [*radio, car*] de camelote.

tin: **~ opener** *n* GB ouvre-boîte *m*; **~pot** *adj* GB PÉJ [*dictatorship, organization*] de pacotille.

tinsel /'tɪnsl/ *n* ¢ (decoration) guirlandes *fpl*; FIG, PÉJ clinquant *m*.

tint /tɪnt/ **I** *n* (trace) nuance *f*; (pale colour) teinte *f*; (hair colour) shampooing *m* colorant.
II *vtr* teinter; **to get one's hair ~ed** se faire faire un shampooing colorant.
III tinted *pp adj* [*colour*] teinté; [*glass, window, spectacles*] fumé; [*hair*] teint.

tiny /'taɪnɪ/ *adj* [*person, object, house*] tout petit; [*improvement*] très faible.

tip /tɪp/ **I** *n* **1** (end) (of stick, sword, pen, shoe, cue, ski, spire, landmass) pointe *f*; (of branch, leaf, shoot, tail, feather) extrémité *f*; (of finger, nose, tongue, wing) bout *m*; (protective cover) (on umbrella) pointe *f*; (on shoe heel) bout *m* ferré; **to stand on the ~s of one's toes** être sur la pointe des pieds; **2** GB (waste dump) décharge *f*; **3**○ GB (mess) fouillis *m*; **4** (gratuity) pourboire *m*; **a £5 ~** 5

livres de pourboire; **5** (practical hint) truc○ *m*, conseil *m*; (in betting, speculation) tuyau○ *m*.
II -tipped *combining form* **silver-/pink-/spiky-~ed** à bout argenté/rose/pointu.
III *vtr* (*p prés etc* **-pp-**) **1** (tilt) incliner; (pour) verser; (dump) déverser [*waste, rubbish*]; **to ~ sth to one side** incliner qch sur le côté; **to ~ sth on its side** mettre qch sur le côté; **to ~ one's chair back** se balancer sur sa chaise; **to ~ sth upside down** retourner qch; **to ~ sth down the sink** verser qch dans l'évier; **to ~ sth away** jeter qch; **to ~ the scales at 60 kg** peser 60 kilos; **to ~ the balance** ou **scales** FIG faire pencher la balance; **to ~ sb over the edge** FIG faire basculer qn; **2** (predict) **to ~ sb/sth to win** prédire que qn/qch va gagner; **to be ~ped as a future champion** être donné comme futur champion; **3** (give money to) donner un pourboire à [*waiter, driver*]; **to ~ sb £5** donner 5 livres de pourboire à qn; **4** (put something on the end of) recouvrir le bout de [*sword, cane, heel*]; **5** (gently push) **to ~ the ball over the net/past the goalkeeper** frapper la balle délicatement pour l'envoyer de l'autre côté du filet/dans le but.
IV *vi* (*p prés etc* **-pp-**) **1** (tilt) s'incliner; **to ~ forward/back** pencher vers l'avant/vers l'arrière; **2** FIG faire pencher [*balance, scales*] pencher.
■ **tip down**○ GB DIAL: **it is tipping** (**it**) **down** il tombe des cordes○.
■ **tip off**: **~ off [sb]**, **~ [sb] off** avertir.
■ **tip out**: **~ out [sth]**, **~ [sth] out** vider.
■ **tip over**: ¶ **~ over** [*chair, cupboard*] basculer; [*bucket, pile*] se renverser; ¶ **~ over [sth]**, **~ [sth] over** faire basculer [*chair, cupboard*]; renverser [*bucket, pile*].
■ **tip up**: ¶ **~ up** s'incliner, se pencher; ¶ **~ up [sth]**, **~ [sth] up** incliner [*cup, bottle*]; pencher [*chair, wardrobe*].

tip-off *n* dénonciation *f*.

tipper lorry GB, **tipper truck** *n* camion *m* à benne basculante.

tipple○ /'tɪpl/ **I** *n* (drink) boisson *f* alcoolisée.
II *vi* siroter.

tipster /'tɪpstə(r)/ *n* pronostiqueur/-euse *m/f*.

tipsy /'tɪpsɪ/ *adj* pompette○.

tiptoe /'tɪptəʊ/ **I** *n* **on ~** sur la pointe des pieds.
II *vi* marcher sur la pointe des pieds.

tip-top○ /,tɪp'tɒp/ *adj* excellent.

tire /'taɪə(r)/ **I** *n* US pneu *m*.
II *vtr* (make tired) fatiguer.
III *vi* **1** (get tired) se fatiguer; **2** (get bored) **to ~ of** se lasser de.
■ **tire out**: **~ [sb] out** épuiser; **to be ~d out** être éreinté; **to ~ oneself out** se fatiguer (**doing** à faire).

tired /'taɪəd/ *adj* **1** (weary) GEN fatigué; [*voice*] las/lasse; **it makes me ~** ça me fatigue; **2** (bored) **to be ~ of sth/of doing** en avoir assez de qch/de faire; **to grow** ou **get ~ of sth/of doing** se lasser de qch/de faire; **3** (hackneyed) rebattu; **4** (worn out) [*machine*] usé; [*clothes, curtains*] défraîchi; **5** (wilted) [*lettuce*] fané.

tiredness /'taɪədnɪs/ *n* fatigue *f*.

tireless /'taɪəlɪs/ *adj* [*person*] inlassable, infatigable; [*efforts*] constant.

tirelessly /'taɪəlɪslɪ/ *adv* sans relâche.

tiresome /'taɪəsəm/ *adj* [*person, habit*] agaçant; [*problem, duty*] fastidieux/-ieuse.

tiring /'taɪərɪŋ/ *adj* fatigant (**to do** de faire).

tissue /'tɪʃuː/ *n* **1** ANAT, BOT tissu *m*; **2** (handkerchief) mouchoir *m* en papier; **3** (also **~ paper**) papier *m* de soie; **4** FIG tissu *m*; **a ~ of lies** un tissu de mensonges.

tit /tɪt/ *n* ZOOL mésange *f*.
IDIOMS **~ for tat** un prêté pour un rendu.

titbit /'tɪtbɪt/ *n* GB (of food) gâterie *f*; (of gossip) cancan○ *m*.

titillating /'tɪtɪleɪtɪŋ/ *adj* émoustillant.

titivate /'tɪtɪveɪt/ *vtr* bichonner; **to ~ oneself** se pomponner.

title /'taɪtl/ **I** n GEN, JUR, SPORT titre m.
II titles npl CIN générique m.
III vtr intituler [book, play].

titled /'taɪtld/ adj titré.

title: ~ **fight** n combat m pour le titre; **~holder** n tenant/-e m/f du titre; ~ **role** n rôle m titre.

titter /'tɪtə(r)/ **I** n ricanement m.
II vi ricaner.

tittle-tattle /'tɪtltætl/ n potins mpl (**about** sur).

titular /'tɪtjʊlə(r)/, US -tʃʊ-/ adj [president, head] nominal; [professor, status] titulaire.

tizzy◦ /'tɪzɪ/ n **to be in/get into a ~** être dans/se mettre dans tous ses états.

T-junction /'ti:dʒʌŋkʃn/ n intersection f en T.

TM n (abrév = **trademark**) marque f de fabrique.

TN US POST abrév écrite = **Tennessee**.

to /tə, devant une voyelle tʊ, tu:, emphatique tu:/ ▶ 812| **I** infinitive particle **1** (expressing purpose) pour; **to do sth ~ impress one's friends** faire qch pour impressionner ses amis; **2** (linking consecutive acts) **he looked up ~ see**... en levant les yeux, il a vu...; **3** (after superlatives) à; **the youngest ~ do** le or la plus jeune à faire; **4** (avoiding repetition of verb) **'did you go?'—'no I promised not ~'** tu y es allé?'—'non j'avais promis de ne pas le faire'; **'are you staying?' '—I want ~ but...'** 'tu restes?'—j'aimerais bien mais...'; **5** (following impersonal verb) **it is difficult ~ do sth** il est difficile de faire qch; (expressing wish) **oh ~ be able to stay in bed!** HUM ô pouvoir rester au lit!
II prep **1** (in direction of) à [shops, school]; (with purpose of visiting) chez [doctor's, dentist's]; (towards) vers; **she's gone ~ Mary's** elle est partie chez Mary; **to Paris** à Paris; **to Spain** en Espagne; ~ **town** en ville; **the road ~ the village** la route qui mène au village; **trains ~ and from** les trains à destination et en provenance de [place]; **turned ~ the wall** tourné vers le mur; **with his back ~ them** en leur tournant le dos; **holding the letter ~ his chest** tenant la lettre contre sa poitrine; **2** (up to) jusqu'à; ~ **the end/this day** jusqu'à la fin/ce jour; **50 ~ 60 people** entre 50 et 60 personnes; **in five ~ ten minutes** d'ici cinq à dix minutes; **3** (in telling time) **ten (minutes) ~ three** trois heures moins dix; **it's five ~** il est moins cinq; **4** (introducing direct or indirect object) [give, offer] à; **give the book ~ Sophie** donne le livre à Sophie; **be nice ~ your brother** sois gentil avec ton frère; ~ **me/my daughter it's just a minor problem** pour moi/ma fille ce n'est qu'un problème mineur; **5** (in toasts, dedications) à; ~ **prosperity** à la prospérité; (on tombstone) ~ **our dear son** à notre cher fils; **6** (in accordance with) **is it ~ your taste?** c'est à ton goût?; **to dance ~ the music** danser sur la musique; **7** (in relationships, comparisons) **to win by three goals ~ two** gagner par trois buts à deux; **perpendicular ~ the ground** perpendiculaire au sol; **next door ~ the school** à côté de l'école; **8** (showing accuracy) **three weeks ~ the day** trois semaines jour pour jour; ~ **scale** à l'échelle; ~ **time** à l'heure; **9** (showing reason) **to invite sb ~ dinner** inviter qn à dîner; ~ **this end** à cette fin; **10** (belonging to) de; **the key ~ the safe** la clé du coffre; **a room ~ myself** une chambre pour moi tout seul; **personal assistant ~ the director** assistant/-e m/f du directeur; **there's no sense ~ it** ça n'a aucun sens; **11** (on to) [tied] à; [pinned] à [noticeboard etc]; sur [lapel, dress]; **12** (showing reaction) à; ~ **his surprise/dismay** à sa grande surprise/ consternation.
III /tu:/ adv **1**◦ (closed) fermé; **to push the door ~** fermer la porte.
IDIOMS **that's all there is ~ it** (it's easy) c'est aussi simple que ça; (not for further discussion) un point c'est tout; **there's nothing ~ it** ce n'est pas compliqué; **what a ~-do**◦! quelle histoire◦!; **what's it ~ you**◦? qu'est-ce que ça peut te faire?

toad /təʊd/ n crapaud m.

toadstool n champignon m vénéneux.

toady /'təʊdɪ/ **I** n flagorneur/-euse m/f.

to
This dictionary contains usage notes on such topics as *the clock, weight measurement, games and sports* etc. Many of these use the preposition *to*. For the index to these notes ▶ 1419|.

When *to* is used as a preposition with movement verbs (*go, travel* etc.) it is often translated by *à* but remember to use *en* with feminine countries (*en France*) and *au* with masculine countries (*au Portugal*); ▶ 840|.

Remember when using *à* in French that *à + le* always becomes *au* and *à + les* always becomes *aux*.

When *to* forms the infinitive of a verb taken alone (by a teacher, for example) it needs no translation:
to go = aller
to find = trouver etc.

However, when *to* is used as part of an infinitive giving the meaning *in order to*, it is translated by *pour*:
he's gone into town to buy a shirt
= il est parti en ville pour acheter une chemise

to is also used as part of an infinitive after certain adjectives: *difficult to understand, easy to read* etc. Here *to* is usually translated by *à*: *difficile à comprendre, facile à lire*:
it's easy to read = c'est facile à lire

However, when the infinitive has an object *to* is usually translated by *de*:
it's easy to lose one's way = il est facile de perdre son chemin

To check translations, consult the appropriate adjective entry: **difficult, easy** etc.

to is also used as part of an infinitive after certain verbs: *she told me to wash my hands, I'll help him to tidy the room* etc. Here the translation, usually either *à* or *de*, depends on the verb used in French. To find the correct translation, consult the appropriate verb entry: **tell, help** etc. For all other uses see the entry **to**.

II vi **to ~ to** flagorner [patron, boss].

to and fro /tu: ən 'frəʊ/ adv [swing] d'avant en arrière; **to go ~** [person] ne pas arrêter d'aller et venir.

toast /təʊst/ **I** n **1** (grilled bread) toast m; **a piece** ou **slice of ~** un toast; **2** (tribute) toast m; **to drink a ~** lever son verre; **3** (popular person) **the ~ of** l'idole de [group]; **she's the ~ of the town** on ne parle que d'elle.
II vtr **1** CULIN faire griller; **2** (propose a toast to) porter un toast à.
III toasted pp adj grillé.
IDIOMS **to be as warm as ~** [person] être bien au chaud; [bed, room] être bien chaud.

toaster /'təʊstə(r)/ n grille-pain m inv.

toast rack n porte-toasts m inv.

tobacco /tə'bækəʊ/ **I** n (pl ~**s**) tabac m.
II noun modifier [company, leaf] de tabac; [industry] du tabac; ~ **tin** GB, ~ **can** US boîte f à tabac; ~ **plant** tabac m.

tobacconist /tə'bækənɪst/ ▶ 1251|, 1251| n GB (person) buraliste mf; ~**'s (shop)** bureau m de tabac.

toboggan /tə'bɒgən/ **I** n luge f, toboggan m.
II vi **to ~ down a hill** descendre une pente en luge.

tobogganning /tə'bɒgənɪŋ/ ▶ 949| n luge f.

today /tə'deɪ/ ▶ 854|, 1390| **I** n LIT, FIG aujourd'hui m; **what's ~'s date?** on est le combien aujourd'hui◦?, quel jour sommes-nous aujourd'hui?; ~ **is Monday** (aujourd'hui) nous sommes lundi.
II adv GEN aujourd'hui; (nowadays) de nos jours; ~ **week, a week from ~** dans une semaine aujourd'hui; **a month ago ~** il y a un mois aujourd'hui; **all day ~** toute la journée d'aujourd'hui; **later ~** plus tard dans la journée.
IDIOMS **he's here ~, gone tomorrow** il va et il vient.

toddle /'tɒdl/ vi **1** (walk) [child] faire ses premiers pas;

to ~ to the door aller d'un pas chancelant vers la porte; **2**○ (go) **to ~ into town** faire un tour en ville.
■ **toddle about**, **toddle around** [*child*] trottiner.
■ **toddle off**○ s'en aller, partir.

toddler /'tɒdlə(r)/ *n* bébé *m* (*qui fait ses premiers pas*).

toddy /'tɒdɪ/ *n* grog *m*.

toe /təʊ/ ▶765 *n* **1** ANAT orteil *m*; **big/little ~** gros/petit orteil; **to stand on one's ~s** être sur la pointe des pieds; **to tread** ou **step on sb's ~s** LIT, FIG marcher sur les pieds de qn; **2** (of sock, shoe) bout *m*.
IDIOMS **to keep sb on their ~s** obliger qn à ne pas relâcher ses efforts; **to ~ the line** marcher droit; **to ~ the party line** suivre la ligne du parti; **from top to ~** de la tête aux pieds.

toehold /'təʊhəʊld/ *n* (in climbing) prise *f*; FIG (access) **to get** ou **gain a ~ in** s'introduire dans [*market, organization*].

toffee /'tɒfɪ, US 'tɔːfɪ/ *n* caramel *m* (au beurre).
IDIOMS **he can't sing/write for ~**○ GB il est incapable de chanter/d'écrire.

toffee: **~ apple** *n* pomme *f* d'amour (*caramélisée*); **~-nosed**○ *adj* GB PÉJ snobinard○ PÉJ.

together /tə'geðə(r)/

■ **Note** *together* in its main adverbial senses is almost always translated by *ensemble*.
– *together* frequently occurs as the second element in certain verb combinations (*get together, pull together, put together, tie together* etc). For translations for these, see the appropriate verb entry (**get, pull, tie** etc).
– For examples and further uses, see the entry below.

I *adv* **1** GEN ensemble; **they're always ~** ils sont toujours ensemble; **to get back ~ again** se remettre ensemble; **to be close ~** être rapprochés; **she's cleverer than all the rest of them put ~** elle est plus intelligente que tous les autres réunis; **we're all in this ~** nous sommes tous impliqués dans cette affaire; **they belong ~** (objects) ils vont ensemble; (people) ils sont faits l'un pour l'autre; **the talks brought the two sides closer ~** les négociations ont rapproché les deux parties; **2** (at the same time) à la fois; **they were all talking ~** ils parlaient tous à la fois; **all my troubles seem to come ~** tous mes ennuis semblent arriver en même temps; **3** (without interruption) d'affilée; **for four days ~** pendant quatre jours d'affilée.
II○ *adj* équilibré.
III together with *prep phr* (as well as) ainsi que; (in the company of) avec.
IDIOMS **to get one's act ~**, **to get it ~**○ s'organiser.

togetherness /tə'geðənɪs/ *n* (in team, friendship) camaraderie *f*; (in family, couple) intimité *f*.

toggle /'tɒgl/ *n* (fastening) bouton *m* de duffel-coat.

Togo /'təʊgəʊ/ ▶840 *pr n* Togo *m*.

toil /tɔɪl/ **I** *n* labeur *m*.
II *vi* **1** (also **toil away**) (work) peiner; **2** (struggle) **to ~ up the hill** monter péniblement la côte.

toilet /'tɔɪlɪt/ *n* toilettes *fpl*; **public ~(s)** toilettes publiques.

toilet: **~ bag** *n* trousse *f* de toilette; **~ paper**, **~ tissue** *n* papier *m* toilette.

toiletries /'tɔɪlɪtrɪz/ *npl* articles *mpl* de toilette.

toilet: **~ roll** *n* (roll) rouleau *m* de papier toilette; (tissue) papier *m* toilette; **~ seat** *n* lunette *f* de WC; **~ soap** *n* savon *m* de toilette.

toilet-train /'tɔɪlɪttreɪn/ *vtr* **to ~ a child** apprendre à un enfant la propreté.

toing and froing /ˌtuːɪŋ ən 'frəʊɪŋ/ *n* **all this ~** toutes ces allées et venues.

token /'təʊkən/ **I** *n* **1** (for machine, phone) jeton *m*; **2** (voucher) bon *m*; **book/record ~** chèque-cadeau *m* pour livre/pour disque; **3** (symbol) témoignage *m*; **a ~ of** un signe de [*esteem, gratitude, affection*]; **but by the same ~**... mais de la même façon...
II *adj* GEN symbolique; **to make a ~ effort/**

gesture PÉJ faire un effort/geste pour la forme; **she's the ~ woman** PÉJ c'est la femme de service.

told /təʊld/ *prét, pp* ▶**tell**.

tolerable /'tɒlərəbl/ *adj* (bearable) tolérable; (adequate) acceptable.

tolerably /'tɒlərəblɪ/ *adv* assez.

tolerance /'tɒlərəns/ *n* GEN, MED tolérance *f*.

tolerant /'tɒlərənt/ *adj* tolérant.

tolerantly /'tɒlərəntlɪ/ *adv* avec tolérance.

tolerate /'tɒləreɪt/ *vtr* (permit) tolérer [*attitude, difference*]; (put up with) supporter [*isolation, treatment*].

toll /təʊl/ **I** *n* **1** (number) **the ~ of** le nombre de [*victims*]; **death ~** nombre *m* de victimes (**from** de); **2** (levy) (on road, bridge) péage *m*; **3** (of bell) GEN son *m*; (for funeral) glas *m*.
II *vtr* sonner [*bell*].
III *vi* sonner.
IDIOMS **to take a heavy ~** (on lives) faire beaucoup de victimes; (on industry, environment) causer beaucoup de dégâts; **to take its** ou **their ~** faire des ravages.

toll: **~booth** *n* poste *m* de péage; **~ bridge** *n* pont *m* à péage; **~ call** *n* US communication *f* interurbaine; **~-free** *adj* US [*call, number*] gratuit.

Tom /tɒm/ *pr n*: IDIOMS **every ~, Dick and Harry**○ n'importe qui.

tomato /tə'mɑːtəʊ, US tə'meɪtəʊ/ **I** *n* (*pl* **~es**) tomate *f*.
II *noun modifier* [*puree*] de tomate; [*juice, salad*] de tomates; [*soup*] à la tomate; **~ sauce** sauce *f* tomate.

tomb /tuːm/ *n* tombeau *m*.

tomboy /'tɒmbɔɪ/ *n* garçon *m* manqué.

tombstone /'tuːmstəʊn/ *n* pierre *f* tombale.

tomcat /'tɒmkæt/ *n* matou *m*.

tome /təʊm/ *n* gros volume *m*.

tomfoolery /tɒm'fuːlərɪ/ *n* pitreries *fpl*, âneries *fpl*.

tomorrow /tə'mɒrəʊ/ ▶854, 1390 **I** *n* LIT, FIG demain *m*; **~ will be a difficult day** la journée de demain sera difficile; **who knows what ~ may bring?** de quoi demain sera-t-il fait?; **I'll do it by ~** je le ferai d'ici demain.
II *adv* LIT, FIG demain; **see you ~!** à demain!; **~ week, a week ~** demain en huit; **early ~** tôt dans la journée de demain; **as from ~** à partir de demain; **first thing ~** dès demain.
IDIOMS **~ is another day** demain il fera jour; **never put off till ~ what can be done today** PROV il ne faut jamais remettre au lendemain ce qu'on peut faire le jour même PROV; **to live like there was no ~** vivre chaque jour comme si c'était le dernier.

tomorrow: **~ afternoon** *n, adv* demain après-midi; **~ evening** *n, adv* demain soir; **~ morning** *n, adv* demain matin.

tom-tom /'tɒmtɒm/ *n* tam-tam *m*.

ton /tʌn/ ▶1392, 789 *n* **1** (in weight) GB (also **gross ~** ou **long ~**) ~ 1016 kg; US (also **net ~** ou **short ~**) ~ 907 kg; **metric ~** tonne *f*; **2**○ (a lot) **~s of** des tas de○ [*food, paper, bands*]; **her new car is ~s better than the other one** sa nouvelle voiture est mille fois mieux que l'autre.
IDIOMS **they'll come down on us like a ~ of bricks** ils vont nous tomber dessus○.

tonal /'təʊnl/ *adj* tonal.

tonality /tə'nælətɪ/ *n* tonalité *f*.

tone /təʊn/ **I** *n* **1** GEN, MUS (quality of sound) timbre *m*; TELECOM tonalité *f*; **2** (character of voice) ton *m*; **his ~ of voice** son ton; **in angry/serious ~s** avec colère/avec sérieux; **3** (character) (of letter, speech, meeting) ton *m*; **to set the ~** donner le ton à (**for** à); **to lower the ~ of** rabaisser le niveau de [*conversation*]; dégrader l'image de [*area*]; **4** (colour) ton *m*; **5** (firmness of muscle) tonus *m*.
II *vtr* (also **~ up**) tonifier.
III *vi* (also **~in**) (blend) [*colours*] s'harmoniser.
■ **tone down**: **~ down** [*sth*], **~** [*sth*] **down** LIT atténuer [*colours, criticism*]; adoucir le ton de [*letter, statement*].

tone-deaf /ˌtəʊnˈdef/ adj MUS **to be ~** ne pas avoir l'oreille musicale.

toneless /ˈtəʊnlɪs/ adj atone.

Tonga /ˈtɒŋgə/ ▶ 840│, 1022│ pr n Tonga fpl; **the ~ islands** les îles fpl Tonga.

tongs /tɒŋz/ npl (for coal) pincettes fpl; (in laboratory, for sugar) pince f.
IDIOMS **to go at it hammer and ~** (quarrel) se disputer violemment; (work) travailler avec acharnement.

tongue /tʌŋ/ I n **1** GEN, ANAT, CULIN langue f; (flap on shoe) languette f; **to stick one's ~ out at sb** tirer la langue à qn; **to lose/find one's ~** FIG avaler/retrouver sa langue; **2** (language) langue f; **native ~** langue d'origine.
II vtr MUS détacher [note, passage].
IDIOMS **has the cat got your ~**⁰? tu as avalé ta langue?; **to get the rough side ou edge of sb's ~** subir les paroles désobligeantes de qn; **I have his name on the tip of my ~** j'ai son nom sur le bout de la langue; **to loosen sb's ~** délier la langue de qn; **I can't get my ~ round it** je n'arrive pas à le prononcer; **a slip of the ~** un lapsus; **watch your ~!** surveille tes paroles!

tongue: **~-in-cheek** adj, adv au deuxième degré; **~-tied** adj muet/-ette; **~-twister** n: phrase amusante pour exercice de diction.

tonic /ˈtɒnɪk/ I n **1** (drink) (also **~ water**) eau f tonique; **a gin and ~** un gin tonic; **2** MED remontant m; **to be a ~ for sb** FIG remonter le moral de qn; **3** MUS tonique f.
II adj tonique; **~ wine** vin m tonique.

tonight /təˈnaɪt/ I n **~ will be overcast** le temps sera couvert ce soir.
II adv (this evening) ce soir; (after bedtime) cette nuit.

toning /ˈtəʊnɪŋ/ adj **1** [colours] harmonisé; **2** [gel, cream] tonifiant.

tonnage /ˈtʌnɪdʒ/ n GEN tonnage m (**of** de); (total weight) volume m.

tonne /tʌn/ ▶ 1392│ n tonne f.

tonsil /ˈtɒnsl/ n amygdale f; **to have one's ~s out** se faire opérer des amygdales.

tonsillitis /ˌtɒnsɪˈlaɪtɪs/ ▶ 1002│ n amygdalite f.

too /tuː/ adv

■ **Note** When too means also it is generally translated by aussi: me too = moi aussi; can I have some too? = est-ce que je peux en avoir aussi?
– When too means to an excessive degree it is translated by trop: too high, too dangerous trop haut, trop dangereux.
– For examples of the above and further usages, see the entry below.

1 (also) aussi; **'I love you'—'I love you ~'** 'je t'aime'—'moi aussi, je t'aime'; **have you been to India ~?** (like me) est-ce que toi aussi tu es allé en Inde?; (as well as others) est-ce que tu es allé en Inde aussi?; **she's kind but she's strict ~** elle est gentille mais elle est stricte; **she was very annoyed and quite right ~!** elle était vraiment agacée et il y avait de quoi!; **about time ~!** il est bien temps!; **'I'm sorry'—'I should think so ~!'** 'je m'excuse'—'j'espère bien!'; **...and in front of your mother ~!** ...et devant ta mère en plus!; **2** (excessively) trop; **the coat is ~ big for him** le manteau est trop grand pour lui; **it's ~ early to leave** il est trop tôt pour partir; **~ many/~ few people** trop de/trop peu de gens; **I ate ~ much** j'ai trop mangé; **he was in ~ much of a hurry to talk** il était trop pressé pour parler; **it was ~ silly for words** d'une bêtise sans nom; **it was ~ little ~ late** c'était trop peu trop tard; **you're ~ kind!** vous êtes trop aimable!; **they'll be only ~ pleased to help** ils seront ravis de rendre service; **he's only ~ ready to criticize** il ne rate pas une occasion de critiquer; **she hasn't been ~ well recently** elle n'est pas vraiment en forme ces temps-ci; **that's ~ bad!** (a pity) c'est tellement dommage!; (hard luck) tant pis!; **~ right!** et comment!; **we're not ~ thrilled** on ne peut pas dire que nous

soyons ravis; **I'm not ~ sure about that** je n'en suis pas si sûr; **'they've arrived'—'none ~ soon!'** 'ils sont arrivés'—'ce n'est pas trop tôt!'; ▶ **all**, **only**.

took /tʊk/ prét ▶ **take** II, III.

tool /tuːl/ I n GEN, COMPUT outil m; **a set of ~s** un jeu d'outils; **management ~s** instruments mpl de gestion; **to down ~s** GB (go on strike) se mettre en grève; (take break from work) arrêter de travailler.
II vtr travailler, repousser [leather].

tool: **~box** n boîte f à outils; **~ house** n US = **tool shed**; **~ kit** n trousse f à outils; **~ shed** n cabane f à outils.

toot /tuːt/ I n (sound) (of car-horn) coup m de klaxon®; (of train whistle) coup m de sifflet.
II vtr **to ~ one's horn** donner un coup de klaxon®.
III vi [car horn] klaxonner; [train] donner un coup de sifflet.

tooth /tuːθ/ I n (pl **teeth**) dent f; **set of teeth** (false) dentier m; **to cut one's teeth** LIT faire ses dents; **to cut one's teeth on** FIG se faire les dents sur.
II **-toothed** combining form **fine-/wide-~ed comb** peigne m fin/à dents larges.
IDIOMS **to be a bit long in the ~**⁰ n'être plus tout jeune; **to be fed up to the back teeth** en avoir par-dessus la tête; **to do sth in the teeth of** faire qch malgré or en dépit de; **to get one's teeth into sth** s'investir (à fond) dans qch; **to lie through one's teeth** mentir effrontément; **to set sb's teeth on edge** agacer qn.

toothache /ˈtuːθeɪk/ n mal m de dents; **to have ~** GB ou **a ~** avoir mal aux dents.

tooth: **~brush** n brosse f à dents; **~ decay** n carie f dentaire; **~less** adj [grin, person] édenté; FIG [law, organization] inefficace; **~paste** n dentifrice m; **~pick** n cure-dents m inv.

toothy /ˈtuːθɪ/ adj **to give a ~ grin** sourire de toutes ses dents.

top /tɒp/ I n **1** (highest or furthest part) (of page, ladder, stairs, wall) haut m; (of list) tête f; (of mountain, hill) sommet m; (of garden, field) (autre) bout m; (of vegetable) fane f; (of box, cake) dessus m; (surface) surface f; **at the ~ of** en haut de [page, stairs, street, scale]; au sommet de [hill]; en tête de [list]; **at the ~ of the building** au dernier étage de l'immeuble; **at the ~ of the table** à la place d'honneur; **the ~ of the milk** la crème du lait; **to be at the ~ of one's list** FIG venir en tête de sa liste; **to be at the ~ of the agenda** FIG être une priorité; MIL **to go over the ~** monter à l'assaut; **2** (highest position) haut m; **to aim for the ~** viser haut; **to get to ou make it to the ~** réussir; **to be ~ of the class** être le premier/la première de la classe; **to be ~ of the bill** THEAT être la tête d'affiche; **3** (cap, lid) (of pen) capuchon m; (of bottle) GEN bouchon m; (with serrated edge) capsule f; (of paint-tin, saucepan) couvercle m; **4** (item of clothing) haut m; **a sleeveless summer ~** un haut sans manches pour l'été; **5** (toy) toupie f.
II adj **1** (highest) [step, storey] dernier/-ière; [bunk] de haut; [button, shelf, layer, lip] supérieur; [speed] maximum; [concern, priority] FIG majeur; **in the ~ left-hand corner** en haut à gauche; **the ~ notes** MUS les notes les plus hautes; **the ~ tax band** la catégorie des plus imposables; **to pay the ~ price for sth** [buyer] acheter qch au prix fort; **to get ~ marks** SCH avoir dix sur dix or vingt sur vingt; **2** (furthest away) [field, house] du bout; **3** (leading) [adviser, authority, agency] plus grand; [job] élevé; [wine, restaurant] meilleur; **one of their ~ chefs** l'un de leurs plus grands chefs; **to be in the ~ three** être dans les trois premiers.
III **on top of** prep phr **1** sur [cupboard, fridge, layer]; **to live on ~ of each other** FIG vivre les uns sur les autres; **to be on ~ of a situation** FIG contrôler la situation; **things are getting on ~ of her** FIG (she's depressed) elle est déprimée; (she can't cope) elle ne s'en sort plus; **2** (in addition to) en plus de [salary, workload].
IV vtr (p prés etc **-pp-**) **1** (head) être en tête de [charts, polls]; **2** (exceed) dépasser [sum, figure]; **3** (finish off)

GEN compléter (**with** par); CULIN recouvrir [*cake*]; **a mosque ~ped with three domes** une mosquée surmontée de trois coupoles.

V° *v refl* (*p prés etc* **-pp-**) **to ~ oneself** se suicider.

IDIOMS **on ~ of all this, to ~ it all** par-dessus le marché°; **from ~ to bottom** de fond en comble; **to be over the ~, to be OTT**° [*behaviour, reaction*] être exagéré; **to be/stay on ~** avoir/garder le dessus; **to be ~ dog** être le chef; **to come out on ~** (win) l'emporter; (survive) s'en sortir; **to feel on ~ of the world** être aux anges; **to say things off the ~ of one's head** (without thinking) dire n'importe quoi; **I'd say 30, but that's just off the ~ of my head** (without checking) moi, je dirais 30, mais c'est approximatif; **to shout at the ~ of one's voice** crier à tue-tête.

■ **top off**: **~ off** [**sth**], **~** [**sth**] **off** compléter.

■ **top up**: **¶ to ~ up with petrol** faire le plein; **~ up** [**sth**], **~** [**sth**] **up** remplir (à nouveau) [*tank, glass*].

top-and-tail /ˌtɒpən'teɪl/ *vtr* équeuter [*fruit*]; effiler [*beans*].

topaz /'təʊpæz/ *n, adj* topaze (*f*) (*inv*).

top: **~ banana**° *n* US gros bonnet *m*; **~ brass**° *n* huiles *fpl*; **~ class** *adj* de premier ordre; **~-flight** *adj* de premier ordre; **~ hat** *n* haut-de-forme *m*; **~-heavy** *adj* [*structure, object*] lourd du haut; FIG [*firm, bureaucracy*] mal équilibré (*ayant trop de cadres par rapport aux employés subalternes*).

topic /'tɒpɪk/ *n* (subject) (of conversation, conference) sujet *m*; (of essay, research) thème *m*.

topical /'tɒpɪkl/ *adj* d'actualité.

topicality /ˌtɒpɪ'kælətɪ/ *n* actualité *f*.

topless /'tɒplɪs/ *adj* [*model*] aux seins nus; [*bar*] où les serveuses ont les seins nus; **~ swimsuit** monokini *m*.

top: **~-level** *adj* [*talks, negotiations*] au plus haut niveau; **~ management** *n* (haute) direction *f*; **~most** *adj* [*branch, fruit*] le/la plus haut/-e; **~-notch** *adj* [*business, executive*] de premier ordre; **~-of-the-range** *adj* [*model*] haut de gamme *inv*.

topping /'tɒpɪŋ/ *n* (of jam, cream) nappage *m*; **with a ~ of bread crumbs** recouvert d'une couche de chapelure.

topple /'tɒpl/ **I** *vtr* LIT, FIG renverser.
II *vi* (sway) [*vase, pile of books*] vaciller; (fall) (also **~ over**) [*vase, person*] basculer; [*pile of books*] s'effondrer; **to ~ over the edge of** tomber de [*cliff, table*].

top: **~-ranking** *adj* important; **~ secret** *adj* ultra-secret; **~ security** *adj* de haute sécurité; **~soil** *n* couche *f* arable; **~ spin** *n* lift *m*.

topsy-turvy° /ˌtɒpsɪ'tɜːvɪ/ *adj, adv* sens dessus dessous.

torch /tɔːtʃ/ **I** *n* (burning) torche *f*; GB (flashlight) lampe *f* de poche.
II *vtr* mettre le feu à [*building*].
IDIOMS **to carry the ~ for democracy** porter le flambeau de la démocratie.

torchlight /'tɔːtʃlaɪt/ **I** *n* **by ~** (burning torches) à la lueur des flambeaux; GB (electric) à la lueur d'une lampe électrique ou de poche.
II *noun modifier* (also **torchlit**) aux flambeaux.

tore /tɔː(r)/ *prét* ▶ **tear**[1] II, III.

torment **I** /'tɔːment/ *n* supplice *m*.
II /tɔː'ment/ *vtr* tourmenter.

tormentor /tɔː'mentə(r)/ *n* persécuteur/-trice *m/f*.

torn /tɔːn/ **I** *pp* ▶ **tear**[1] II, III.
II *adj* (all contexts) déchiré.

tornado /tɔː'neɪdəʊ/ *n* (*pl* **~es** ou **~s**) tornade *f*.

torpedo /tɔː'piːdəʊ/ **I** *n* MIL torpille *f*.
II *vtr* LIT, FIG torpiller.

torpid /'tɔːpɪd/ *adj* torpide.

torrent /'tɒrənt, US 'tɔːr-/ *n* torrent *m*; FIG flot *m*.

torrential /tə'renʃl/ *adj* torrentiel/-ielle.

torrid /'tɒrɪd, US 'tɔːr-/ *adj* torride.

torso /'tɔːsəʊ/ *n* (*pl* **~s**) torse *m*.

tortoise /'tɔːtəs/ *n* tortue *f*.

tortoiseshell /'tɔːtəsʃel/ *n* **1** (shell) écaille *f*; **2** ZOOL (butterfly) vanesse *f*; (cat) chatte *f* écaille de tortue.

tortuous /'tɔːtʃʊəs/ *adj* LIT, FIG tortueux/-euse.

torture /'tɔːtʃə(r)/ **I** *n* LIT torture *f*; FIG supplice *m*.
II *vtr* LIT torturer; FIG tourmenter.

Tory /'tɔːrɪ/ *n* GB Tory *mf*, conservateur/-trice *m/f*.

toss /tɒs/ **I** *n* (*pl* **~es**) **1** (throw) jet *m*; **a ~ of the head** un mouvement brusque de la tête; **2** (of coin) **to decide sth on the ~ of a coin** décider qch à pile ou face.
II *vtr* **1** (throw) lancer [*ball, stick, dice*]; faire sauter [*pancake*]; tourner [*salad*]; **~ me the newspaper** balance-moi° le journal; **to ~ a coin** tirer à pile ou face; **2** (throw back) [*animal*] secouer [*head, mane*]; **to ~ one's head** [*person*] rejeter la tête en arrière; **3** (unseat) [*horse*] désarçonner [*rider*]; **4** (move violently) [*wind*] agiter [*branches, leaves*]; [*waves*] ballotter [*boat*].
III *vi* **1** (turn restlessly) [*person*] se retourner; **I ~ed and turned all night** je me suis tourné et retourné toute la nuit; **2** (flip a coin) tirer à pile ou face; **to ~ for first turn** tirer le premier tour à pile ou face.
IDIOMS **I don't** ou **couldn't give a ~**° je m'en fiche pas mal°.

■ **toss about, toss around**: **¶ ~ about** [*boat, person*] être ballotté; **¶ ~** [**sth**] **around** LIT [*people*] se faire des passes avec [*ball*]; FIG machouiller [*ideas*].

■ **toss away**: **~** [**sth**] **away, ~ away** [**sth**] jeter.

■ **toss back**: **~** [**sth**] **back, ~ back** [**sth**] renvoyer.

■ **toss off**°: **~** [**sth**] **off, ~ off** [**sth**] expédier.

■ **toss out**: **¶ ~** [**sth**] **out, ~ out** [**sth**] jeter [*newspaper, empty bottles*]; **¶ ~** [**sb**] **out** éjecter (**from** de).

■ **toss up** (flip a coin) tirer à pile ou face.

toss-up° /'tɒsʌp/ *n* **let's have a ~ to decide** décidons à pile ou face; **it's a ~ between a pizza and a sandwich** il faut choisir entre une pizza et un sandwich.

tot /tɒt/ *n* **1**° (toddler) tout/-e petit/-e enfant *m/f*; **2** (of whisky, rum) petite dose *f*, doigt *m*.

■ **tot up** GB: **¶ ~ up** [*person*] additionner; **¶ ~ up** [**sth**], **~** [**sth**] **up** faire le total de [qch].

total /'təʊtl/ **I** *n* total *m*; **in ~** au total; **it comes to a ~ of £200** cela fait 200 livres sterling en tout.
II *adj* **1** (added together) [*cost, amount, profit*] total; **2** (complete) [*effect*] global; [*disaster, eclipse*] total; [*ignorance*] complet/-ète.
III *vtr* (*p prés etc* **-ll-** GB, **-l-** US) **1** (add up) additionner [*figures*]; **2** (reach) se monter à [*sum*].

totalitarian /ˌtəʊtælɪ'teərɪən/ *n, adj* totalitaire (*mf*).

totalize /'təʊtəlaɪz/ *vtr* totaliser.

totally /'təʊtəlɪ/ *adv* [*blind, deaf*] complètement; [*unacceptable, convinced*] totalement; [*agree, change, new, different*] entièrement.

totem /'təʊtəm/ *n* (pole) totem *m*; (symbol) symbole *m*.

totter /'tɒtə(r)/ *vi* [*person, regime, government*] chanceler; (drunkenly) tituber; [*baby*] trébucher; [*pile of books, building*] chanceler.

tottering /'tɒtərɪŋ/ *adj* GEN LIT, FIG chancelant; [*step*] mal assuré.

touch /tʌtʃ/ **I** *n* **1** (physical contact) contact *m* (physique); **the ~ of her hand** le contact de sa main; **at the slightest ~** (of button) à la moindre pression; **I felt a ~ on my shoulder** j'ai senti qu'on me touchait l'épaule; **2** (sense) toucher *m*; **by ~** au simple toucher; **3** (style, skill) (of artist, writer) touche *f*; (of musician) toucher *m*; **to lose one's ~** perdre la main; **a fine ~ at the net** (in tennis) un toucher délicat au filet; **the Spielberg ~** le style Spielberg; **this house lacks the feminine ~** on voit qu'il n'y a pas de femme dans cette maison; **he lacks the human ~** il manque de chaleur humaine; **a clever ~** un trait spirituel; **her gift was a nice ~** son cadeau était un geste délicat; **4** (little) **a ~** un petit peu; **just a ~** (more) un tout petit peu (plus); **there's a ~ of class/of genius about her** elle a quelque chose d'élégant/de génial; **he's got a ~ of flu** il est un peu grippé; **with a ~ of sadness in her voice** avec une

Towns and cities

Occasionally the gender of a town is clear because the name includes the definite article, e.g. Le Havre or La Rochelle. In most other cases, there is some hesitation, and it is always safer to avoid the problem by using la ville de:

Toulouse is beautiful = la ville de Toulouse est belle

In, to and from somewhere

For in *and* to *with the name of a town, use* à *in French; if the French name includes the definite article,* à *will become* au, à la, à l' *or* aux:

to live in Toulouse	=	vivre à Toulouse
to go to Toulouse	=	aller à Toulouse
to live in Le Havre	=	vivre au Havre
to go to Le Havre	=	aller au Havre
to live in La Rochelle	=	vivre à La Rochelle
to go to La Rochelle	=	aller à La Rochelle
to live in Les Arcs	=	vivre aux Arcs
to go to Les Arcs	=	aller aux Arcs

Similarly, from *is* de, *becoming* du, de la, de l' *or* des *when it combines with the definite article in town names:*

to come from Toulouse	=	venir de Toulouse
to come from Le Havre	=	venir du Havre
to come from La Rochelle	=	venir de La Rochelle
to come from Les Arcs	=	venir des Arcs

Belonging to a town or city

English sometimes has specific words for people of a certain city or town, such as Londoners, New Yorkers or Parisians, but mostly we talk of the people of Leeds or the inhabitants of San Francisco. On the other hand, most towns in French-speaking countries have a corresponding adjective and noun, and a list of the best-known of these is given at the end of this note.

The noun forms, spelt with a capital letter, mean a person from X:

| the inhabitants of Bordeaux | = | les Bordelais *mpl* |
| the people of Strasbourg | = | les Strasbourgeois *mpl* |

The adjective forms, spelt with a small letter, are often used where in English the town name is used as an adjective:

| Paris shops | = | les magasins parisiens |

However, some of these French words are fairly rare, and it is always safe to say les habitants de X, *or, for the adjective, simply* de X. *Here are examples of this, using some of the nouns that commonly combine with the names of towns:*

a Bordeaux accent	=	un accent de Bordeaux
Toulouse airport	=	l'aéroport de Toulouse
the La Rochelle area	=	la région de La Rochelle
Limoges buses	=	les autobus de Limoges
the Le Havre City Council	=	le conseil municipal du Havre
Lille representatives	=	les représentants de Lille
Les Arcs restaurants	=	les restaurants des Arcs
the Geneva road	=	la route de Genève
Brussels streets	=	les rues de Bruxelles
the Angers team	=	l'équipe d'Angers
the Avignon train	=	le train d'Avignon

but note

| Orleans traffic | = | la circulation à Orléans |

Names of cities and towns in French-speaking countries and their adjectives

Remember that when these adjectives are used as nouns, meaning a person from X or the people of X, they are spelt with capital letters.

Aix-en-Provence	=	aixois(e)
Alger	=	algérois(e)
Angers	=	angevin(e)
Arles	=	arlésien(ne)
Auxerre	=	auxerrois(e)
Avignon	=	avignonnais(e)
Bastia	=	bastiais(e)

Bayonne	=	bayonnais(e)
Belfort	=	belfortain(e)
Berne	=	bernois(e)
Besançon	=	bisontin(e)
Béziers	=	biterrois(e)
Biarritz	=	biarrot(e)
Bordeaux	=	bordelais(e)
Boulogne-sur-Mer	=	boulonnais(e)
Bourges	=	berruyer(-ère)
Brest	=	brestois(e)
Bruges	=	brugeois(e)
Bruxelles	=	bruxellois(e)
Calais	=	calaisien(ne)
Cannes	=	cannais(e)
Carcassonne	=	carcassonnais(e)
Chambéry	=	chambérien(ne)
Chamonix	=	chamoniard(e)
Clermont-Ferrand	=	clermontois(e)
Die	=	diois(e)
Dieppe	=	dieppois(e)
Dijon	=	dijonnais(e)
Dunkerque	=	dunkerquois(e)
Fontainebleau	=	bellifontain(e)
Gap	=	gapençais(e)
Genève	=	genevois(e)
Grenoble	=	grenoblois(e)
Havre, Le	=	havrais(e)
Lens	=	lensois(e)
Liège	=	liégeois(e)
Lille	=	lillois(e)
Lourdes	=	lourdais(e)
Luxembourg	=	luxembourgeois(e)
Lyon	=	lyonnais(e)
Mâcon	=	mâconnais(e)
Marseille	=	marseillais(e) *or* phocéen(ne)
Metz	=	messin(e)
Modane	=	modanais(e)
Montpellier	=	montpelliérain(e)
Montréal	=	montréalais(e)
Moulins	=	moulinois(e)
Mulhouse	=	mulhousien(ne)
Nancy	=	nancéien(ne)
Nantes	=	nantais(e)
Narbonne	=	narbonnais(e)
Nevers	=	nivernais(e)
Nice	=	niçois(e)
Nîmes	=	nîmois(e)
Orléans	=	orléanais(e)
Paris	=	parisien(ne)
Pau	=	palois(e)
Périgueux	=	périgourdin(e)
Perpignan	=	perpignanais(e)
Poitiers	=	poitevin(e)
Pont-à-Mousson	=	mussipontain(e)
Québec	=	québécois(e)
Reims	=	rémois(e)
Rennes	=	rennais(e)
Roanne	=	roannais(e)
Rouen	=	rouennais(e)
Saint-Étienne	=	stéphanois(e)
Saint-Malo	=	malouin(e)
Saint-Tropez	=	tropézien(ne)
Sancerre	=	sancerrois(e)
Sète	=	sétois(e)
Sochaux	=	sochalien(ne)
Strasbourg	=	strasbourgeois(e)
Tarascon	=	tarasconnais(e)
Tarbes	=	tarbais(e)
Toulon	=	toulonnais(e)
Toulouse	=	toulousain(e)
Tours	=	tourangeau(-elle)
Tunis	=	tunisois(e)
Valence	=	valentinois(e)
Valenciennes	=	valenciennois(e)
Versailles	=	versaillais(e)
Vichy	=	vichyssois(e)

note de tristesse dans sa voix; **a ~ of sarcasm/of garlic** une pointe de raillerie/d'ail; **5** (communication) contact *m*; **to get/stay in ~ with** se mettre/rester en contact avec; **he's out of ~ with reality** il est déconnecté de la réalité; **6** SPORT touche *f*.
II *vtr* **1** (come into contact with) toucher; (interfere with) toucher à; **to ~ sb on the shoulder** toucher l'épaule de qn; **to ~ ground** atterrir; **he ~ed his hat politely** il a porté poliment la main à son chapeau; **the police can't ~ me** la police ne peut rien contre moi; **I never ~ alcohol** je ne prends jamais d'alcool; **2** (affect) GEN toucher; (adversely) affecter; (as matter of concern) concerner; **we were most ~ed** nous avons été très touchés; **3** (reach) [*price, temperature*] atteindre [*level*]; **when it comes to cooking, no-one can ~ him** pour la cuisine, personne ne peut l'égaler.
III *vi* (come together) [*wires, hands*] se toucher; **'do not ~'** 'ne pas toucher'.
IDIOMS **to be an easy** ou **a soft ~**○ être un pigeon○; **it's ~ and go whether he'll make it through the night** il risque fort de ne pas passer la nuit.
■ **touch down**: **~ down 1** AVIAT atterrir; **2** SPORT (in rugby) marquer un essai.
■ **touch off**: **~** [*sth*] **off, ~ off** [*sth*] faire partir [*firework*]; déclencher [*riot, debate*].
■ **touch (up)on**: **~ (up)on** [*sth*] effleurer.
■ **touch up**: **~** [*sth*] **up, ~ up** [*sth*] retoucher.

touchdown /'tʌtʃdaʊn/ *n* **1** AVIAT atterrissage *m*; **2** SPORT essai *m*.

touché /tu:'ʃeɪ, 'tu:ʃeɪ, US tu:'ʃeɪ/ *excl* FIG bien dit!

touched /tʌtʃt/ *adj* **1** (emotionally) touché; **2**○ (mad) dérangé○.

touching /'tʌtʃɪŋ/ *adj* touchant.

touch: **~ line** *n* SPORT ligne *f* de touche; **~paper** *n* papier *m* nitraté; **~stone** *n* LIT, FIG pierre *f* de touche; **~-tone** *adj* [*telephone*] à touches; **~-type** *vi* taper au toucher; **~-typing** *n* dactylographie *f* au toucher; **~wood** *n* amadou *m*.

touchy /'tʌtʃɪ/ *adj* [*person*] susceptible (**about** sur la question de); [*subject, issue*] délicat.

tough /tʌf/ **I** *n* (person) dur *m*.
II *adj* **1** [*businessman*] coriace; [*criminal*] endurci; [*policy, measure, law*] sévère; [*opposition, competition, criticism*] rude; **a ~ guy** un dur○; **to get ~ with sb** se montrer dur avec qn; **~ talk** propos *mpl* inflexibles; **that's ~ luck!** manque de pot○!; (unsympathetically) tant pis pour toi!; **2** (difficult) difficile; **to have a ~ time** avoir des difficultés; **she's having a ~ time** elle traverse une période difficile; **3** (robust) [*person, animal*] robuste; [*plant, material*] résistant; PÉJ [*meat*] coriace PÉJ; **4** (rough) [*area, school*] dur.
III○ *excl* tant pis pour toi!
IDIOMS **to be as ~ as old boots** être coriace.
■ **tough out**○: **~** [*sth*] **out** faire face à [*situation*]; **to ~ it out** tenir le coup○.

toughen /'tʌfn/ *vtr* renforcer [*leather, plastic*]; tremper [*glass, steel*]; durcir [*skin*]; (also **~ up**) endurcir [*person*]; renforcer [*law*].
■ **toughen up**: ¶ **~ up** [*person*] s'endurcir; ¶ **~** [*sb*] **up, ~ up** [*sb*] endurcir [*person*].

tough-minded *adj* ferme et résolu.

toughness /'tʌfnɪs/ *n* **1** (of businessman, criminal) dureté *f*; (of law, measure) sévérité *f*; (of way of life) dureté *f*; **2** (robustness) (of person, plant) résistance *f*; (of material, leather) robustesse *f*; PÉJ (of meat) dureté *f*; **3** (difficulty) (of work, question) difficulté *f*.

toupee /'tu:peɪ, US tu:'peɪ/ *n* postiche *m*.

tour /tʊə(r), tɔ:(r)/ **I** *n* **1** TOURISM (of country) circuit *m*; (of city) tour *m*; (of building) visite *f*; (trip in bus) excursion *f*; **cycling/walking ~** randonnée *f* cycliste/pédestre; **to go on a ~ of** visiter [*one thing*]; faire le circuit de [*several things*]; **he took me on a ~ of his house** il m'a fait visiter sa maison; **a ~ of inspection** une tournée d'inspection; **2** MUS, SPORT, THEAT, UNIV tournée *f*; **a ~ of duty** MIL une période de service.
II *vtr* **1** TOURISM visiter [*building, country, gallery*];

2 MUS, SPORT être en tournée en [*country*]; THEAT [*production*] tourner en [*country*].
III *vi* **1** TOURISM **to go ~ing** faire du tourisme; **2** [*orchestra, play, team*] être en tournée.

tourer /'tʊərə(r), tɔ:rə(r)/ *n* (sports car) cabriolet *m* décapotable; GB (caravan) camping-car *m*; (bicycle) vélo *m* de randonnée.

touring /'tʊərɪŋ, 'tɔ:r-/ **I** *n* **1** TOURISM tourisme *m*; **2** MUS, SPORT, THEAT tournée *f*.
II *adj* [*exhibition, holiday*] itinérant; [*company, show*] en tournée; [*production*] de tournée.

tourism /'tʊərɪzəm, 'tɔ:r-/ *n* tourisme *m*.

tourist /'tʊərɪst, 'tɔ:r-/ **I** *n* touriste *mf*.
II *noun modifier* [*centre, guide, resort, season*] touristique; **the ~ trade** le tourisme.

tourist: **~ class** *n* AVIAT classe *f* touriste; **~ (information) office** *n* (in town) syndicat *m* d'initiative; (national organization) office *m* du tourisme; **~ trap** *n* piège *m* à touristes.

touristy○ /'tʊərɪstɪ, 'tɔ:r-/ *adj* PÉJ envahi par les touristes.

tournament /'tɔ:nəmənt, US 'tɜ:rn-/ *n* tournoi *m*.

tousle /'taʊzl/ **I** *vtr* ébouriffer [*hair*].
II **tousled** *pp adj* [*hair*] ébouriffé; [*person, appearance*] débraillé.

tout /taʊt/ **I** *n* **1** GB (selling tickets) revendeur *m* de billets au marché noir; **2** COMM (soliciting custom) racoleur/-euse○ *m/f* PÉJ; **3** (racing) vendeur *m* de tuyaux.
II *vtr* **1** [*street seller*] vendre (en faisant du boniment); **2** GB (illegally) revendre [qch] au marché noir [*tickets*]; **3** (publicize) vanter les mérites de [*product, invention*].
III *vi* **to ~ for business** racoler○ la clientèle.

tow /təʊ/ **I** *n* AUT **to be on ~** être en remorque; **to give sb a ~** remorquer qn; (following) **a father with two children in ~** FIG un père accompagné de deux enfants.
II *vtr* remorquer, tracter [*trailer, caravan*].
■ **tow away**: **~ away** [*sth*], **~** [*sth*] **away** [*police*] emmener [qch] à la fourrière; [*recovery service*] remorquer.

toward(s) /tə'wɔ:d(z), tɔ:d(z)/

■ **Note** When *towards* is used to talk about direction or position, it is almost always translated by *vers*: *she ran toward(s) him* = elle a couru vers lui. For particular usages see the entry below.
– When *toward(s)* is used to mean *in relation to*, it is translated by *envers*: *his attitude toward(s) his parents* = son attitude envers ses parents. For particular usages see the entry below.

prep **1** (in the direction of) vers; **~ the east** vers l'est; **he was standing with his back ~ me** il était dos à moi; **2** (near) vers; **~ the end of** vers la fin de [*day, month, life*]; **3** (in relation to) envers; **their attitude ~ Europe** leur attitude envers l'Europe; **to be friendly/hostile ~ sb** se montrer cordial/hostile envers qn; **4** (as contribution) **the money will go ~ a new car** l'argent servira à payer une nouvelle voiture; **to save ~ a holiday** faire des économies pour partir en vacances.

towel /'taʊəl/ **I** *n* serviette *f* (de toilette); ▶ **bath towel, tea towel**.
II *vtr* (*p prés etc* **-ll-**, US **-l-**) essuyer (avec une serviette).
IDIOMS **to throw** ou **chuck**○ **in the ~** jeter l'éponge.

towelling /'taʊəlɪŋ/ *n* (cloth) tissu *m* éponge.

towel rail *n* porte-serviettes *m inv*.

tower /'taʊə(r)/ **I** *n* tour *f*.
II *vi* **to ~ above** ou **over** dominer [*village, street*].
IDIOMS **to be a ~ of strength** être solide comme un roc.

tower block *n* GB tour *f* (d'habitation).

towering /'taʊərɪŋ/ *adj* (*épith*) GEN imposant; FIG [*performance*] excellent.

town /taʊn/ [▶ **1343**] *n* ville *f*; **to go into ~** aller en ville; **she's out of ~ at the moment** elle n'est pas là en ce moment; **look me up next time you're in ~** viens me voir la prochaine fois que tu passeras par ici.

IDIOMS **to go out on the ~**, **to have a night on the ~** faire la noce; **to go to ~ on** ne pas lésiner sur [*decor, catering*]; exploiter [qch] à fond [*story, scandal*]; **he's the talk of the ~** on ne parle que de lui.

town: **~-and-country planning** *n* aménagement *m* du territoire; **~ centre** *n* centre-ville *m*; **~ clerk** *n* GB secrétaire *mf* de mairie; **~ council** *n* GB conseil *m* municipal; **~ hall** *n* mairie *f*; **~ house** *n* petite maison *f* en centre ville; (mansion) hôtel *m* particulier; **~ meeting** *n* US assemblée *f* générale des habitants d'une commune; **~ planning** *n* GB urbanisme *m*; **~sfolk** *npl* = **townspeople**; **~ship** *n* GEN commune *f*; (in South Africa) township *m*; **~speople** *npl* citadins *mpl*.

tow: **~path** *n* chemin *m* de halage; **~ truck** *n* dépanneuse *f*.

toxic /'tɒksɪk/ *adj* toxique.

toxic waste *n* déchets *mpl* toxiques.

toxin /'tɒksɪn/ *n* toxine *f*.

toy /tɔɪ/ **I** *n* jouet *m*.
II *noun modifier* [*plane, train, railway*] miniature; [*car, boat*] petit; [*gun, telephone*] d'enfant.
III *vi* **to ~ with** jouer avec [*object, feelings*]; caresser [*idea*]; **to ~ with one's food** chipoter.

toy: **~ boy**○ *n* GB PÉJ gigolo *m*; **~ dog** *n* chien *m* d'appartement; **~ poodle** *n* caniche *m* nain; **~shop** *n* magasin *m* de jouets.

trace /treɪs/ **I** *n* **1** (evidence) trace *f*; **there is no ~ of** il ne reste aucune trace de; **without ~** [*disappear, sink*] sans laisser de traces; **2** (hint) (of irony, flavour, garlic) soupçon *m*; (of accent) pointe *f*; (of chemical, drug) trace *f*; **3** (of harness) trait *m*.
II *vtr* **1** (locate) retrouver [*person, weapon, car*]; dépister [*fault*]; déterminer [*cause*]; **to ~ sb to** retrouver la trace de qn dans [*hideout*]; **the call was ~d to a London number** on a pu établir que le coup de téléphone venait d'un numéro à Londres; **2** faire l'historique de [*development, growth*]; retracer [*life, progress*]; faire remonter [*origins, ancestry*]; **3** (also **~ out**) (draw) GEN tracer; (copy) décalquer [*map, outline*].
IDIOMS **to kick over the ~s** ruer dans les brancards.
■ **trace back**: **~ [sth] back**, **~ back [sth]** faire remonter (**to** à).

tracer /'treɪsə(r)/ *n* **1** MIL (bullet) balle *f* traçante; (shell) obus *m* traçant; **2** CHEM, MED traceur *m*; **3** (instrument) traceur *m*.

tracery /'treɪsərɪ/ *n* GEN (of pattern, frost) fin réseau *m*; ARCHIT remplage *m*.

tracing /'treɪsɪŋ/ *n* **1** (of map, motif, diagram) calque *m*; **2** (procedure) calquage *m*.

tracing paper *n* papier-calque *m*.

track /træk/ **I** *n* **1** (print) (of animal, person) expreintes *fpl*, traces *fpl*; (of vehicle) traces *fpl*; **2** LIT, FIG (course, trajectory) (of person) trace *f*; (of missile, aircraft, storm) trajectoire *f*; **to cover one's ~s** brouiller les pistes; **to be on ~** [*talks, negotiations*] se dérouler comme prévu; **to be on the wrong ~** faire fausse route; **to keep ~ of** [*person*] se tenir au courant de [*developments, events*]; suivre le fil de [*conversation*]; [*police*] suivre les mouvements de [*criminal*]; [*computer*] tenir à jour [*bank account, figures*]; **to lose ~ of** perdre de vue [*friend*]; perdre la trace de [*document, aircraft, suspect*]; perdre le fil de [*conversation*]; **to lose ~ of (the) time** perdre la notion du temps; **to make ~s for sth** se diriger vers qch; **we'd better be making ~s** il est temps de partir; **to stop dead in one's ~s** s'arrêter net; **3** (path, road) sentier *m*, chemin *m*; SPORT piste *f*; (**motor-**)**racing ~** (open-air) circuit *m*; (enclosed) autodrome *m*; **cycling ~** vélodrome *m*; **dog-racing ~** *n* **4** RAIL voie *f* ferrée; US (platform) quai *m*; **to leave the ~(s)** [*train*] dérailler; **5** (song on record, tape, CD) morceau *m*; (recording channel on tape) piste *f*; **6** (of tank, tractor) chenille *f*; **7** US SCH (stream) groupe *m* de niveau.
II *noun modifier* SPORT [*event, race*] de vitesse.

III *vtr* suivre la trace de [*person, animal*]; suivre la trajectoire de [*rocket, plane, comet*].
IDIOMS **to come from the wrong side of the ~s** venir des quartiers pauvres.
■ **track down**: **~ [sb/sth] down**, **~ down [sb/sth]** retrouver [*person, object*].

tracked /trækt/ *adj* [*vehicle*] chenillé, à chenilles.

tracker /'trækə(r)/ *n* (of animal) traqueur *m*; (of person) poursuivant/-e *m/f*.

tracker dog *n* chien *m* policier.

track lighting *n* rampe *f* de spots d'éclairage.

track record *n* **to have a good ~** GEN avoir de bons antécédents; [*professional person*] avoir de bons antécédents professionnels; **a candidate with a proven ~ in sales** un candidat ayant une bonne expérience commerciale.

track: **~ shoe** *n* chaussure *f* de course à pointes; **~suit** *n* survêtement *m*.

tract /trækt/ *n* **1** (of land, forest) étendue *f*; **2** ANAT **digestive/respiratory ~** appareil *m* digestif/respiratoire; **3** (pamphlet) traité *m*; **4** US (housing development) lotissement *m*.

tractable /'træktəbl/ *adj* [*person*] docile; [*problem*] soluble.

traction /'trækʃn/ *n* GEN traction *f*; (of wheel) adhérence *f*.

traction engine *n* locomobile *f*.

tractor /'træktə(r)/ *n* tracteur *m*.

trade /treɪd/ **I** *n* **1** (activity) commerce *m*; **to do a good ~** faire de bonnes affaires; **2** (sector of industry) industrie *f*; **she's in the furniture ~** elle travaille dans l'ameublement; **3** (profession) (manual) métier *m*; (intellectual) profession *f*; **by ~** de métier.
II *noun modifier* [*route, agreement, balance, deficit*] commercial; [*sanctions, embargo*] économique; [*association, journal*] professionnel/-elle; [*barrier*] douanier/-ière.
III *vtr* échanger.
IV *vi* COMM faire du commerce; **to ~ in sth with sb** vendre qch à qn; **to ~ at $10** FIN s'échanger à $10; **to ~ on** FIG exploiter [*name, reputation, image*].
■ **trade in**: **~ [sth] in**, **~ in [sth]** COMM he **~d in his old car for a new one** on lui a repris sa vieille voiture et il en a acheté une nouvelle.
■ **trade off**: **~ [sth] off**, **~ off [sth]** échanger.
■ **trade up** US = **trade in**.

trade: **Trade Descriptions Act** *n* GB COMM JUR *loi qui protège le consommateur des désignations mensongères de marchandise*; **~ discount** *n* remise *f* professionnelle; **~ fair** *n* salon *m*; **~ figures** *npl* résultats *mpl* financiers.

trade-in /'treɪdɪn/ **I** *n* reprise *f* (*d'un article usagé à l'achat d'un article neuf*).
II *adj* [*price*] avec reprise; [*value*] de reprise.

trademark /'treɪdmɑːk/ *n* **1** COMM marque *f* (de fabrique); **2** (also **Trademark, Registered Trademark**) marque *f* déposée; **3** **the professionalism which is his ~** FIG le professionnalisme qui le caractérise.

trade name *n* nom *m* (de marque).

trade-off /'treɪdɒf/ *n* **1** (balance) compromis *m*; **2** (exchange) échange *m*.

trader /'treɪdə(r)/ *n* **1** COMM commerçant/-e *m/f*; **2** FIN (at Stock Exchange) opérateur/-trice *m/f* (en Bourse).

trade: **~ secret** *n* secret *m* de fabrication; HUM secret *m* d'État; **~sman** *n* (delivery man) livreur *m*; (shopkeeper) commerçant *m*; **~sman's entrance** *n* entrée *f* de service; **~s union** *n* GB ▶ **trade union**; **Trades Union Congress**, **TUC** *n* GB Confédération *f* des syndicats (britanniques).

trade union I *n* syndicat *m*.
II *noun modifier* [*activist, leader, movement*] syndical.

trade: **~ union member** *n* syndiqué/-e *m/f*; **~ war** *n* guerre *f* commerciale; **~ wind** *n* alizé *m*.

trading /'treɪdɪŋ/ **I** *n* **1** COMM commerce *m*; **2** FIN (at Stock Exchange) transactions *fpl* (boursières); **at the end of ~** à la fermeture du marché.

II *adj* [*nation*] commerçant; [*partner*] commercial.

trading: ~ **estate** *n* GB zone *f* industrielle; ~ **post** *n* poste *m* d'approvisionnement (*dans une région isolée*); **Trading Standards Department** *n*: *direction régionale de la protection des consommateurs*.

tradition /trə'dɪʃn/ *n* tradition *f*.

traditional /trə'dɪʃənl/ *adj* traditionnel/-elle.

traditionalist /trə'dɪʃənəlɪst/ *n*, *adj* traditionaliste (*mf*).

traditionally /trə'dɪʃənəlɪ/ *adv* traditionnellement.

traffic /'træfɪk/ I *n* 1 AUT circulation *f*; AVIAT, NAUT, RAIL trafic *m*; ~ **into/out of London** la circulation vers/en sortant de Londres; **to hold up the** ~ provoquer un bouchon; **air/passenger** ~ trafic aérien/de voyageurs; 2 (dealing) (in drugs, arms, slaves, goods) trafic *m* (**in** de); (in ideas) mouvement *m* (**in** de).
II *noun modifier* [*accident, problem, regulations*] de la circulation; ~ **flow** circulation *f*.
III *vi* (*p prés etc* **-ck-**) **to** ~ **in** faire du trafic de [*drugs, cocaine, arms, stolen goods*].

traffic duty *n* **to be on** ~ faire la circulation.

traffic: ~ **island** *n* refuge *m*; ~ **jam** *n* embouteillage *m*.

trafficker /'træfɪkə(r)/ *n* trafiquant/-e *m/f* (**in** de).

traffic: ~ **lights** *npl* feux *mpl* (de signalisation or tricolores); ~ **policeman** *n* agent *m* de la circulation; ~ **signal** *n* = **traffic lights**; ~ **warden**
▶ 1251 *n* GB contractuel/-elle *m/f*.

tragedy /'trædʒədɪ/ *n* GEN, THEAT tragédie *f*.

tragic /'trædʒɪk/ *adj* GEN, THEAT tragique.

tragically /'trædʒɪklɪ/ *adv* tragiquement.

trail /treɪl/ I *n* 1 (path) chemin *m*, piste *f*; 2 (of blood, dust, slime) traînée *f*, trace *f*; **to leave a** ~ **of destruction behind one** tout détruire sur son passage; 3 (trace) trace *f*, piste *f*.
II *vtr* 1 (follow) [*animal, person*] suivre la piste de; [*car*] suivre; 2 (drag) traîner; **to** ~ **one's hand in the water** laisser traîner sa main dans l'eau.
III *vi* 1 [*skirt, scarf*] traîner; [*plant*] pendre; 2 **to** ~ **in/out** entrer/sortir en traînant les pieds; 3 (lag) traîner; **our team were** ~**ing by 3 goals to 1** notre équipe avait un retard de 2 buts; **to** ~ **badly** [*racehorse, team*] être à la traîne.
■ **trail away**, **trail off** s'arrêter (peu à peu).

trail: ~ **bike** *n* moto *f* tout-terrain; ~ **blazer** *n* pionnier/-ière *m/f*; ~**-blazing** *adj* innovateur/-trice.

trailer /'treɪlə(r)/ *n* 1 (vehicle, boat) remorque *f*; 2 US (caravan) caravane *f*; 3 CIN bande-annonce *f*.

trailing /'treɪlɪŋ/ *adj* [*plant*] rampant.

train /treɪn/ I *n* 1 RAIL train *m*; (underground) rame *f*; **on** OU **in the** ~ dans le train; **slow** ~ omnibus *m*; **a** ~ **to Paris** un train pour Paris; **to go to Paris by** ~ aller à Paris en train; 2 (succession) (of events) série *f*; **the bell interrupted my** ~ **of thought** la sonnette a interrompu le fil de mes pensées; 3 (procession) (of animals, vehicles, people) file *f*; (of mourners) cortège *m*; MIL train *m*; 4 (motion) **to set** ou **put sth in** ~ mettre qch en train; 5† (retinue) suite *f*; **the war brought famine in its** ~ FIG la guerre a entraîné la famine dans son sillage; 6 (on dress) traîne *f*.
II *noun modifier* [*crash, station*] ferroviaire; [*timetable*] des trains; [*driver, ticket*] de train; [*strike*] des chemins de fer.
III *vtr* 1 GEN, MIL, SPORT former [*staff, worker, musician*] (**to do** à faire); entraîner [*athlete, player*] (**to do** à faire); dresser [*circus animal, dog*]; **to be** ~**ed on the job** être formé sur le tas; **to** ~ **sb as a pilot/engineer** donner à qn une formation de pilote/d'ingénieur; 2 (aim) braquer [*gun, binoculars*] (**on** sur); 3 palisser [*plant, tree*].
IV *vi* 1 GEN (for profession) être formé, étudier; **he's** ~**ing to be a doctor** il suit une formation de docteur; 2 SPORT s'entraîner.

trained /treɪnd/ *adj* [*staff, worker*] qualifié; [*professional*] diplômé; [*voice, eye, ear*] exercé; [*singer, actor*] professionnel/-elle; [*animal*] dressé; **well** ~ bien

formé; [*animal*] bien dressé; **when will you be fully** ~? quand est-ce que tu auras fini ta formation?

trainee /treɪ'niː/ *n* stagiaire *mf*.

trainer /'treɪnə(r)/ *n* 1 (of athlete, horse) entraîneur/-euse *m/f*; (of circus animal, dogs) dresseur/-euse *m/f*; 2 GB (shoe) (high) basket *f*; (low) tennis *m*.

training /'treɪnɪŋ/ I *n* 1 GEN formation *f*; (less specialized) apprentissage *m*; ~ **in medicine** formation à la médecine; 2 MIL, SPORT entraînement *m*; **to be in** ~ GEN s'entraîner; (following specific programme) suivre un entraînement; **to be out of** ~ manquer d'entraînement.
II *noun modifier* GEN [*course, period, scheme, agency*] de formation; [*manual*] d'instruction; MIL, SPORT d'entraînement.

training: ~ **college** *n* GB GEN école *f* professionnelle; (for teachers) centre *m* de formation pédagogique; ~ **ship** *n* navire-école *m*.

train: ~ **set** *n* petit train *m*; ~ **spotter** *n* passionné/-e *m/f* de trains.

traipse /treɪps/ *vi* traîner; **to** ~ **around town** traîner partout dans la ville.

trait /treɪ, treɪt/ *n* trait *m*.

traitor /'treɪtə(r)/ *n* traître/traîtresse *m/f* (**to** à); **to turn** ~ trahir.

trajectory /trə'dʒektərɪ/ *n* trajectoire *f*.

tram /træm/ *n* GB (also **tramcar**†) tramway *m*.

tramp /træmp/ I *n* 1 (vagrant) (rural) vagabond *m*; (urban) clochard/-e *m/f*; 2 (sound) bruit *m*; **I heard the** ~ **of feet** j'ai entendu un bruit de pas; 3 (hike) marche *f*.
II *vi* 1 (hike) marcher; 2 (walk heavily) marcher à pas lourds.

trample /'træmpl/ I *vtr* piétiner; **to** ~ **sth underfoot** piétiner qch.
II *vi* **to** ~ **on** LIT piétiner; FIG fouler [qn/qch] aux pieds.

trampoline /'træmpəliːn/ *n* trampoline *m*.

trance /trɑːns, US træns/ *n* transe *f*; FIG état *m* second; **to go into a** ~ LIT entrer en transe.

tranquil /'træŋkwɪl/ *adj* tranquille.

tranquillity, **tranquility** US /ˌtræŋ'kwɪlətɪ/ *n* tranquillité *f*.

tranquillize, **tranquilize** US /'træŋkwɪlaɪz/ *vtr* mettre [qn] sous tranquillisants.

tranquillizer, **tranquilizer** US /'træŋkwɪlaɪzə(r)/ *n* tranquillisant *m*.

transact /træn'zækt/ *vtr* négocier [*business, rights*].

transaction /træn'zækʃn/ I *n* 1 GEN, COMM, FIN transaction *f*; (on stock exchange) opération *f*; **cash/credit card** ~ transaction en liquide/effectuée avec une carte de crédit; 2 (negotiating) **the** ~ **of business** les relations *fpl* d'affaires.
II **transactions** *npl* (of society etc) actes *mpl*.

transatlantic /ˌtrænzət'læntɪk/ *adj* [*crossing, flight*] transatlantique; [*attitude, accent*] d'outre-atlantique *inv*.

transcend /træn'send/ *vtr* GEN, PHILOS transcender; (surpass) surpasser.

transcendental /ˌtrænsen'dentl/ *adj* transcendantal.

transcribe /træn'skraɪb/ *vtr* GEN, MUS transcrire.

transcript /'trænskrɪpt/ *n* 1 (copy) transcription *f*; 2 US SCH duplicata *m* de livret scolaire.

transcription /ˌtræn'skrɪpʃn/ *n* transcription *f*.

transfer I /'trænsfɜː(r)/ *n* 1 GEN transfert *m*; (of property, debt) cession *f*; (of funds) virement *m*; 2 (relocation) (of player, patient, prisoner) transfert *m*; (of employee) mutation *f*; 3 GB (on skin, china, paper) décalcomanie *f*; (on T-shirt) transfert *m*.
II /træns'fɜː(r)/ *vtr* (*p prés etc* **-rr-**) 1 GEN transférer, virer [*money*]; céder [*property, power*]; reporter [*allegiance, support*]; **I'm** ~**ring you to reception** je vous passe la réception; 2 (relocate) transférer [*office, prison er, player*]; muter [*employee*].
III /træns'fɜː(r)/ *vi* (*p prés etc* **-rr-**) 1 [*player, passenger*] être transféré; [*employee*] être muté; 2

AVIAT [*traveller*] changer d'avion; **3** UNIV [*student*] (change university) changer d'université; (change course) changer de cours.

transferable /træns'fɜːrəbl/ *adj* GEN, JUR transmissible; FIN négociable.

transference /'trænsfərəns, US træns'fɜːrəns/ *n* GEN, PSYCH transfert *m*.

transfer: **~ lounge** *n* salle *f* de transit; **~ passenger** *n* passager/-ère *m*/*f* en transit; **~red charge call** *n* appel *m* en PCV.

transfigure /træns'fɪgə(r), US -gjər/ *vtr* SOUT transfigurer.

transfix /træns'fɪks/ *vtr* LIT transpercer; **~ed** FIG (fascinated) fasciné; (horrified) paralysé d'horreur.

transform /træns'fɔːm/ *vtr* transformer.

transformation /ˌtrænsfə'meɪʃn/ *n* transformation *f*.

transformer /træns'fɔːmə(r)/ *n* transformateur *m*.

transfusion /træns'fjuːʒn/ *n* transfusion *f*.

transgression /trænz'greʃn/ *n* **1** JUR transgression *f* (against de); **2** RELIG péché *m*.

transient /'trænziənt, US 'trænʃnt/ *adj* [*phase*] transitoire; [*emotion, beauty*] éphémère; [*population*] de passage.

transistor /træn'zɪstə(r), -'sɪstə(r)/ *n* transistor *m*.

transit /'trænzɪt, -sɪt/ **I** *n* transit *m*; **in ~** en transit.
II *noun modifier* [*camp, lounge*] de transit; [*passenger*] en transit.

transition /træn'zɪʃn, -'sɪʃn/ **I** *n* transition *f*.
II *noun modifier* [*period, point*] de transition.

transitional /træn'zɪʃənl, -'sɪʃənl/ *adj* [*arrangement, measure*] transitoire; [*period*] de transition.

transitive /'trænzətɪv/ *adj* transitif/-ive.

transitory /'trænzɪtrɪ, US -tɔːrɪ/ *adj* [*stage*] transitoire; [*hope, pain*] passager/-ère.

translate /trænz'leɪt/ **I** *vtr* traduire; **to ~ theory into practice** traduire la théorie en pratique.
II *vi* [*person*] traduire; [*word, phrase, text*] se traduire; **this word does not ~** ce mot est intraduisible.

translation /trænz'leɪʃn/ *n* traduction *f*.

translator /trænz'leɪtə(r)/ *n* traducteur/-trice *m*/*f*.

translucent /trænz'luːsnt/ *adj* translucide.

transmissible /trænz'mɪsəbl/ *adj* transmissible.

transmission /trænz'mɪʃn/ *n* (all contexts) transmission *f*.

transmit /trænz'mɪt/ (*p prés etc* **-tt-**) **I** *vtr* transmettre.
II *vi* émettre.

transmitter /trænz'mɪtə(r)/ *n* RADIO, TV émetteur *m*; TELECOM capsule *f* microphonique; **radio ~** émetteur *m* radio.

transmute /trænz'mjuːt/ *vtr* CHEM, FIG transmuer.

transparency /træns'pærənsɪ/ *n* **1** GEN, FIG transparence *f*; **2** PHOT GEN diapositive *f*; (for overhead projector) transparent *m*.

transparent /træns'pærənt/ *adj* LIT, FIG transparent.

transparently /træns'pærəntlɪ/ *adv* (obviously) manifestement.

transpire /træn'spaɪə(r), trɑ-/ *vi* **1** (become known) apparaître; **it ~d that** il est apparu par la suite que; **2** (give off) [*plant*] transpirer.

transplant /træns'plɑːnt, US -'plænt/ **I** *n* (operation) transplantation *f*, greffe *f*; (organ, tissue transplanted) transplant *m*; **to have a heart ~** subir une transplantation cardiaque.
II *vtr* transplanter [*plant, tree*]; repiquer [*seedlings*]; MED transplanter, greffer.

transport /træns'pɔːt/ **I** *n* **1** transport *m*; **air/road ~** transport aérien/par route; **to travel by public ~** utiliser les transports en commun; **I haven't got any ~ at the moment** je n'ai pas de moyen de locomotion en ce moment; **2** MIL (ship) (navire *m* de) transport *m* de troupes; (aircraft) (avion *m* de) transport *m* de troupes; **3** (rapture) **to go into ~s of delight** tomber dans des transports de joie.
II *noun modifier* [*costs, facilities, ship*] de transport; [*industry, strike, system*] des transports.

III *vtr* transporter [*passengers, goods*] (**from** de; **to** à).

transportation /ˌtrænspɔː'teɪʃn/ *n* **1** US = **transport I 1, II**; **2** (of passengers, goods) transport *m*; **3** HIST (of criminals) transport *m*.

transport café *n* GB café *m* de routiers.

transporter /træns'pɔːtə(r)/ *n* MIL transport *m*.

transpose /træn'spəʊz/ *vtr* GEN, MATH, MUS transposer.

transposition /ˌtrænspə'zɪʃn/ *n* GEN, MATH, MUS transposition *f*.

transsexual /trænz'sekʃʊəl/ *n*, *adj* transsexuel/-elle (*m*/*f*).

transverse /'trænzvɜːs/ **I** *n* partie *f* transversale.
II *adj* transversal.

transvestite /trænz'vestaɪt/ *n* travesti/-e *m*/*f*.

trap /træp/ **I** *n* **1** (snare) piège *m*; **to set a ~ for** poser un piège pour [*animal*]; tendre un piège à [*person*]; **to fall into the ~ of doing** FIG commettre l'erreur de faire; **2** (vehicle) cabriolet *m*; **3**⁰ (mouth) **shut your ~!** ta gueule⁰!
II *vtr* (*p prés etc* **-pp-**) **1** LIT, FIG (snare) prendre [qn/qch] au piège [*animal, person*]; **2** (catch, immobilize) coincer [*person, finger*]; retenir [*heat*].

trapdoor /'træpdɔː(r)/ *n* trappe *f*.

trapeze /trə'piːz, US træ-/ *n* trapèze *m*.

trapper /'træpə(r)/ *n* trappeur *m*.

trappings /'træpɪŋz/ *npl* (dress) apparat *m*; **the ~ of** les signes *mpl* extérieurs de [*wealth, success*].

trash /træʃ/ *n* ¢ **1** US (refuse) (in streets) déchets *mpl*; (household) ordures *fpl*; **2**⁰ PÉJ (goods) camelote⁰ *f*; (nonsense) âneries *fpl*; **the film is (absolute) ~** le film est (complètement) nul⁰.

trash: **~can** *n* US poubelle *f*; **~ heap** *n* tas *m* d'ordures.

trashy⁰ /'træʃɪ/ *adj* PÉJ [*novel, film*] nul/nulle⁰; [*goods*] de pacotille PÉJ.

trauma /'trɔːmə, US 'trɑʊ-/ *n* (*pl* **-as**, **-ata**) MED, PSYCH, FIG traumatisme *m*.

traumatic /trɔː'mætɪk, US trɑʊ-/ *adj* PSYCH, FIG traumatisant; MED traumatique.

traumatize /'trɔːmətaɪz, US 'trɑʊ-/ *vtr* traumatiser.

travel /'trævl/ **I** *n* voyages *mpl*; **foreign ~** voyages à l'étranger.
II travels *npl* voyages *mpl*; **he's off on his ~s again** il repart en voyage.
III *noun modifier* [*plans*] de voyage; [*brochure, company*] de voyages; [*expenses*] de déplacement; [*business*] de tourisme; [*writer*] de récits de voyage.
IV *vtr* (*p prés etc* **-ll-**, US **-l-**) parcourir [*country, road, distance*].
V *vi* (*p prés etc* **-ll-**, US **-l-**) **1** (journey) [*person*] voyager; **he ~s widely** il voyage beaucoup; **to ~ abroad/to Brazil** aller à l'étranger/au Brésil; **2** (move) [*person, object, plane, boat*] aller; [*car, train*] aller, rouler; PHYS [*light, sound*] se propager; **bad news ~s fast** les mauvaises nouvelles vont vite; **to ~ at 50 km/h** rouler à 50 km/h; **the train was ~ling through a tunnel** le train traversait un tunnel; **to ~ faster than the speed of sound** dépasser la vitesse du son; **to ~ a long way** [*person*] faire beaucoup de chemin; **his eye ~led along the line of men** il a promené son regard sur la rangée d'hommes; **3** COMM (as sales rep) **to ~ in** être représentant en [*product*]; **4 to ~ well** [*cheese, wine*] supporter le transport.
VI -travelled GB, **-traveled** US *combining form* **much-** ou **well-~led** [*road, route*] fréquenté; **widely-~led** [*person*] qui a beaucoup voyagé.

travel: **~ agency** *n* agence *f* de voyages; **~ agent** ▸1251], 1251] *n* agent *m* de voyages; **~ bureau** *n* = **travel agency**; **~ card** *n* GB carte *f* de transport; **~ insurance** *n* assurance *f* voyage.

traveller GB, **traveler** US /'trævlə(r)/ *n* **1** (voyager) voyageur/-euse *m*/*f*; **2** (commercial) représentant *m* de commerce; **3** GB (gypsy) nomade *mf*.

traveller's cheque GB, **traveler's check** US *n* chèque-voyage *m*.

travelling GB, **traveling** US /'trævlɪŋ/ **I** *n* GEN voyages *mpl*; (on single occasion) voyage *m*; **to go ~** partir en voyage; **the job involves ~** le poste exige des déplacements.
II *adj* **1** [*actor, company, circus*] itinérant; [*bank*] mobile; **the ~ public** les usagers des transports en commun; **2** [*companion, rug*] de voyage; [*conditions*] (on road) de route; **3** [*scholarship*] de voyage; [*allowance, expenses*] de déplacement.

travelling: **~ library** *n* bibliobus *m*; **~ salesman** ▶ 1251 *n* voyageur *m* de commerce.

travelogue /'trævəlɒg/ GB, **travelog** US /'trævəlɔːg/ *n* (film) film *m* de voyage; (talk) conférence *f* sur son voyage or ses voyages.

travel-sick /'trævlsɪk/ *adj* **to be** OU **get ~** souffrir du mal des transports.

travel-sickness **I** *n* mal *m* des transports.
II *noun modifier* [*pills*] contre le mal des transports.

traverse /trə'vɜːs/ *vtr* SOUT franchir [*ocean, desert*]; [*comet, route*] traverser.

travesty /'trævəstɪ/ *n* ART, LITERAT, FIG farce *f*.

trawl /trɔːl/ **I** *m* (net) filet *nm*.
II *vtr* pêcher dans [*water, bay*], FIG écumer [*place*].
III *vi* pêcher au chalut.

trawler /'trɔːlə(r)/ *n* chalutier *m*.

tray /treɪ/ *n* GEN plateau *m*; **baking ~** plaque *f* à pâtisserie; **ice ~** bac *m* à glaçons; **in-/out-~** corbeille *f* arrivée/départ.

treacherous /'tretʃərəs/ *adj* traître.

treacherously /'tretʃərəslɪ/ *adv* traîtreusement.

treachery /'tretʃərɪ/ *n* traîtrise *f*.

treacle /'triːkl/ *n* GB (black) mélasse *f*; (golden syrup) mélasse *f* raffinée.

tread /tred/ **I** *n* **1** (footstep) pas *m*; **2** (of stair) dessus *m* (d'une marche); **3** (of tyre) (pattern) sculptures *fpl*; (outer surface) chape *f*.
II *vtr* (*prét* **trod**; *pp* **trodden**) fouler [*street, path, area*]; **to ~ water** nager sur place; **to ~ sth underfoot** piétiner qch; **a well-trodden path** LIT, FIG une voie très empruntée.
III *vi* (*prét* **trod**; *pp* **trodden**) (walk) marcher; **to ~ on** (walk) marcher sur; (squash) piétiner; **to ~ carefully** ou **warily** FIG être prudent.

treadmill /'tredmɪl/ *n* FIG (dull routine) train-train *m*.

treason /'triːzn/ *n* trahison *f*; **high ~** haute trahison.

treasonable /'triːzənəbl/ *adj* qui constitue une trahison.

treasure /'treʒə(r)/ **I** *n* trésor *m*; FIG (prized person) (woman) perle *f*; (man) homme *m* en or.
II *vtr* **1** (cherish) chérir [*person, memory, gift*]; **2** (prize) tenir beaucoup à [*friendship, possession*].
III **treasured** *pp adj* précieux/-ieuse.

treasure house *n* **a ~ of information** FIG une mine d'informations.

treasurer /'treʒərə(r)/ *n* **1** (on committee) trésorier/-ière *m/f*; **2** US (in company) directeur *m* financier.

treasure trove *n* (all contexts) trésor *m*.

treasury /'treʒərɪ/ *n* **1** FIN trésorerie *f*; **2** FIG (anthology) trésor *m*; **3** (in cathedral) trésor *m*; (in palace) chambre *f* forte.

Treasury /'treʒərɪ/ *n* (also **~ Department**) FIN, POL ministère *m* des finances.

treat /triːt/ **I** *n* (pleasure) (petit) plaisir *m*; (food) gâterie *f*; **I took them to the museum as a ~** je les ai emmenés au musée pour leur faire plaisir; **oysters! what a ~!** des huîtres! vous nous gâtez!; **as a special ~ I was allowed to stay up late** exceptionnellement on m'a permis de me coucher plus tard; **a ~ in store** une bonne surprise; **it's my ~** c'est moi qui paie; **to stand sb a ~** offrir qch à qn.
II⁰ **a treat** *adv phr* GB **the plan worked a ~** le projet a marché comme sur des roulettes⁰; **the show went down a ~ with the children** les enfants ont adoré le spectacle.
III *vtr* **1** GEN traiter [*person, animal, object, topic*]; **to ~ sb well/badly** bien traiter/maltraiter qn; **to ~ sb/sth with care** prendre soin de qn/qch; **to ~ sb**

with suspicion se montrer méfiant à l'égard de qn; **to ~ sth as** considérer qch comme [*idol, shrine*]; **they ~ the house like a hotel** ils prennent la maison pour un hôtel; **to ~ the whole thing as a joke** prendre toute l'affaire à la plaisanterie; **2** MED traiter [*patient, disease*]; **3** (process) traiter [*chemical, fabric, water*]; **4** (pay for) **to ~ sb to sth** payer or offrir qch à qn.
IV *v refl* **to ~ oneself to** s'offrir [*holiday, hairdo*].

treatise /'triːtɪs, -ɪz/ *n* traité *m* (**on** sur).

treatment /'triːtmənt/ *n* **1** GEN (of person) traitement *m*; **special ~** (preferential) traitement de faveur; (unusual) traitement spécial; **it won't stand up to rough ~** ça ne résistera pas aux mauvais traitements; **2** MED (by specific drug, method) traitement *m*; (general care) soins *mpl*; **a course of ~** un traitement; **to receive ~ for sth** être sous traitement pour qch, recevoir des soins pour qch; **to undergo ~** être en traitement; **3** (processing) traitement *m*.

treaty /'triːtɪ/ *n* **1** POL traité *m*; **peace ~** traité de paix; **2** COMM JUR contrat *m*; **for sale by private ~** à vendre de gré à gré.

treble /'trebl/ **I** *n* **1** AUDIO aigus *mpl*; **2** MUS (voice) soprano *m* (*de garçon avant la mue*); (boy) soprano *m*.
II *adj* **1** triple; **to reach ~ figures** atteindre la centaine; **2** MUS [*voice*] de soprano (*avant la mue*).
III *det* trois fois; **~ the amount** trois fois la quantité.
IV *vtr, vi* tripler.

tree /triː/ *n* arbre *m*; **an apple ~/a cherry ~** un pommier/un cerisier; **the ~ of life** l'arbre de vie.
IDIOMS **he can't see the wood** GB OU **forest** US **for the ~s** il se perd dans les détails; **money doesn't grow on ~s** l'argent ne se trouve pas sous les sabots d'un cheval; **to be at the top of the ~** être arrivé au sommet.

tree: **~-covered** *adj* boisé; **~house** *n* cabane *f* dans un arbre.

treeless /'triːlɪs/ *adj* dénué d'arbres.

tree: **~-lined** *adj* bordé d'arbres; **~ ring** *n* cerne *m*; **~ stump** *n* souche *f*; **~top** *n* cime *f* (d'un arbre); **~ trunk** *n* tronc *m* d'arbre.

trefoil /'trefɔɪl/ *n* BOT, ARCHIT trèfle *m*.

trek /trek/ **I** *n* (long journey) randonnée *f*; (laborious) randonnée *f* pénible.
II *vi* (*p prés etc* **-kk-**) **to ~ across/through** traverser péniblement [*desert, jungle*]; **I had to ~ into town** je me suis tapé⁰ le trajet à pied jusqu'à la ville.

trekking /'trekɪŋ/ ▶ 949 *n* **to go ~** faire de la randonnée pédestre.

trellis /'trelɪs/ *n* GEN treillis *m*; (sturdier) treillage *m*.

tremble /'trembl/ *vi* trembler.

trembling /'tremblɪŋ/ **I** *n* tremblement *m*.
II *adj* tremblant.

tremendous /trɪ'mendəs/ *adj* **1** (great) [*effort, improvement, amount*] énorme; [*pleasure*] immense; [*storm, explosion*] violent; [*success*] fou/folle⁰; **2**⁰ (marvellous) formidable⁰.

tremendously /trɪ'mendəslɪ/ *adv* extrêmement.

tremor /'tremə(r)/ *n* GEN tremblement *m*; (of delight, fear) frisson *m*; (in earthquake) secousse *f*.

tremulous /'tremjʊləs/ *adj* [*voice*] (with emotion) tremblant; (from weakness) tremblotant; (with excitement) frémissant; [*smile*] timide.

trench /trentʃ/ *n* GEN, MIL tranchée *f*.

trenchant /'trentʃənt/ *adj* incisif/-ive.

trench coat *n* imperméable *m*, trench-coat *m*.

trend /trend/ *n* **1** (tendency) tendance *f*; **a ~ in** tendance dans le domaine de [*medicine, education*]; **a ~ away from** un désintérêt pour [*arts, studies*]; **2** (fashion) mode *f*; **to set a new ~** lancer une nouvelle mode.

trendsetter /'trendsetə(r)/ *n* innovateur/-trice *m/f*; **to be a ~** lancer des modes.

trendy⁰ /'trendɪ/ **I** *n* branché/-e⁰ *m/f*.
II *adj* branché⁰.

trepidation /ˌtrepɪˈdeɪʃn/ n appréhension f.

trespass /ˈtrespəs/ vi (enter unlawfully) GEN s'introduire illégalement; **to ~ on** GEN pénétrer illégalement dans; JUR violer [property]; **'no ~ing'** 'défense d'entrer'; **to ~ on** FIG abuser de [time, generosity].

trespasser /ˈtrespəsə(r)/ n intrus/-e m/f; **'~s will be prosecuted'** 'défense d'entrer sous peine de poursuites'.

trestle /ˈtresl/ n tréteau m.

trial /ˈtraɪəl/ I n 1 JUR procès m; **to be on ~** être jugé; **to go to ~** [case] être jugé; **to go on ~**, **to stand ~** passer en jugement; **to come up for ~** [person] comparaître en justice; [case] être jugé; **to put sb on ~** LIT juger qn; FIG [press, public] condamner qn; 2 (test) (of machine, recruit, vehicle) essai m; (of drug, new product) test m; **to put sth through ~s** soumettre qch à des essais or tests; **take it on ~** prenez-la à l'essai; **by ~ and error** par expérience; 3 MUS, SPORT épreuve f; 4 (trouble) épreuve f; (less strong) difficulté f; **the ~s of being a mother** les épreuves de la maternité; **to be a ~** [person] être pénible à supporter.
II noun modifier [period, separation] d'essai; **on a ~ basis** à titre expérimental.

trial run n essai m; **to take a car for a ~** essayer une voiture.

triangle /ˈtraɪæŋgl/ n triangle m.

tribal /ˈtraɪbl/ adj tribal.

tribe /traɪb/ n tribu f.

tribulation /ˌtrɪbjʊˈleɪʃn/ n **trials and ~s** tribulations fpl.

tribunal /traɪˈbjuːnl/ n tribunal m.

tribune /ˈtrɪbjuːn/ n (platform) tribune f.

tributary /ˈtrɪbjʊtərɪ, US -terɪ/ n affluent m.

tribute /ˈtrɪbjuːt/ n hommage m; **to pay ~ to** rendre hommage à; **as a ~ to** en hommage à; **floral ~** GEN fleurs fpl; (spray) gerbe f; (wreath) couronne f; **this is a ~ to her genius** FIG cela témoigne de son génie.

trice /traɪs/ n **in a ~** en un rien de temps.

tricentenary /ˌtraɪsenˈtiːnərɪ/ n, adj tricentenaire (m).

trick /trɪk/ I n 1 GEN tour m; (dishonest) combine f, truc° m; **a clever ~** un tour habile; **a ~ of the light** un effet de lumière; 2 (by magician, conjurer, dog) tour m; **he is up to his ~s again** il continue à faire des siennes; 3 (knack, secret) astuce f; **to have a ~ of doing sth** avoir le chic pour faire qch; **to know a ~ or two** ou **a few ~s** s'y connaître (**about** en); 4 (habit, mannerism) manie f; **to have a ~ of doing** avoir la manie de faire; 5 (in cards) pli m; **to take** ou **win a ~** faire un pli.
II noun modifier [photo, shot] truqué.
III vtr duper, rouler°; **to ~ sb into doing sth** amener qn à faire qch par la ruse; **to ~ sb out of their inheritance** escroquer qn de son héritage.
IDIOMS **the ~s of the trade** les ficelles du métier; **that will do the ~** ça fera l'affaire; **he never misses a ~** il ne rate jamais un détail.

trickery /ˈtrɪkərɪ/ n tromperie f.

trickle /ˈtrɪkl/ I n (of liquid) filet m; (of powder, sand) écoulement m; (of investment, orders) petite quantité f; (of people) petit nombre m.
II vi **to ~ down** dégouliner le long de [pane, wall]; **to ~ from** couler de [tap, spout]; **to ~ into** [liquid] s'écouler dans [container]; [people] s'infiltrer dans [country, organization]; [ball] rouler dans [net]; **to ~ out of** [liquid] suinter de [crack, wound].
■ **trickle away** [water] s'écouler lentement; [people] s'éloigner lentement.
■ **trickle in** arriver au compte-gouttes.

trick question n question f piège.

trickster /ˈtrɪkstə(r)/ n escroc m.

tricky /ˈtrɪkɪ/ adj 1 [decision, business, task] difficile; [problem, question] épineux/-euse; [situation] délicat; 2 (sly, wily) malin/-igne.

tricolour GB, **tricolor** US /ˈtrɪkələ(r), US ˈtraɪkʌlə(r)/ n drapeau m tricolore.

tricycle /ˈtraɪsɪkl/ n (cycle) tricycle m.

tried /traɪd/ I prét, pp ▶ **try** II, III.
II pp adj **a ~ and tested remedy** un médicament infaillible.

trifle /ˈtraɪfl/ I n 1 **a ~** (slightly) un peu; 2 (triviality) (gift, money) bagatelle f; (matter, problem) détail m; **to waste time on ~s** perdre son temps à des broutilles; 3 GB CULIN ≈ diplomate m.
II vi **to ~ with** jouer avec [feelings, affections]; **to ~ with sb** traiter qn à la légère.

trifling /ˈtraɪflɪŋ/ adj [sum, cost, detail] insignifiant.

trigger /ˈtrɪgə(r)/ I n 1 (on gun) gâchette f; **to pull the ~** appuyer sur la gâchette; 2 (on machine) manette f; 3 FIG **to be the ~ for sth** déclencher qch.
II vtr = **trigger off**.
■ **trigger off: ~ off [sth]** déclencher.

trigger-happy° /ˈtrɪgəhæpɪ/ adj 1 LIT à la gâchette facile; 2 FIG impulsif/-ive.

trigonometry /ˌtrɪgəˈnɒmətrɪ/ n trigonométrie f.

trilby /ˈtrɪlbɪ/ n GB chapeau m en feutre, feutre m.

trill /trɪl/ I n 1 MUS trille m; 2 LING r roulé m.
II vtr 1 MUS triller; 2 LING rouler.
III vi triller.

trilogy /ˈtrɪlədʒɪ/ n trilogie f.

trim /trɪm/ I n 1 (cut) (of hair) coupe f d'entretien; (of hedge) taille f; 2 (good condition) **to keep oneself in ~** se maintenir en bonne forme physique; 3 (border) (on clothing) bordure f; (of braid) galon m; (on woodwork) moulure f; 4 AUT **exterior ~** finition f extérieure; **interior ~** garniture f intérieure.
II adj [garden, person] soigné; [boat, house] bien tenu; [figure] svelte; [waist] fin.
III vtr (p prés etc **-mm-**) 1 (cut) couper [hair, grass, material]; tailler [beard, hedge]; ébouter [wood]; 2 (reduce) réduire [budget, expenditure, workforce] (**by** de); raccourcir [article, speech] (**by** de); 3 CULIN dégraisser [meat]; 4 (decorate) décorer [tree, furniture]; border [dress, handkerchief].

trimming /ˈtrɪmɪŋ/ n (on clothing) garniture f; (on soft furnishings) passementerie f; **~s** CULIN (with dish) accompagnements mpl traditionnels; (of pastry) rognures fpl; **with all the ~s** FIG avec tout le tralala°.

Trinidad /ˈtrɪnɪdæd/ ▶ **1022** pr n (l'île f de) la Trinité f.

Trinity /ˈtrɪnətɪ/ n **the ~** la Trinité f.

Trinity term n GB UNIV troisième trimestre m.

trinket /ˈtrɪŋkɪt/ n babiole f.

trio /ˈtriːəʊ/ n trio m (**of** de).

trip /trɪp/ I n 1 (journey) (abroad) voyage m; (excursion) excursion f; **business ~** voyage d'affaires; **to be away on a ~** être en voyage; **we did the ~ in five hours** nous avons fait le trajet en cinq heures; **it's only a short ~ into London** c'est juste un petit tour à Londres; 2° ARGOT DES DROGUÉS trip° m.
II vtr (p prés etc **-pp-**) GEN faire trébucher; (with foot) faire un croche-pied à [person].
III vi (p prés etc **-pp-**) 1 (also **~ over**, **~ up**) (stumble) trébucher, faire un faux pas; **to ~ on** ou **over** trébucher sur [step, rock]; se prendre les pieds dans [scarf, rope]; 2 **to ~ along** [child] gambader; [adult] marcher d'un pas léger.
■ **trip up:** ¶ **~ up** trébucher; FIG (make an error) se tromper; ¶ **~ [sb] up**, **~ up [sb]** GEN faire trébucher; (with foot) faire un croche-pied à.

tripe /traɪp/ n ¢ CULIN tripes fpl; FIG °(nonsense) foutaises° fpl.

triple /ˈtrɪpl/ adj GEN triple; MUS **in ~ time** à trois temps.

triplet /ˈtrɪplɪt/ n (child) triplé/-e m/f.

triplicate /ˈtrɪplɪkət/ n **in ~** adv phr en trois exemplaires.

tripod /ˈtraɪpɒd/ n trépied m.

tripper /ˈtrɪpə(r)/ n excursionniste mf, touriste mf.

trite /traɪt/ adj banal; **~ comments** banalités fpl.

triumph /ˈtraɪʌmf/ I n triomphe m.
II vi triompher (**over** de).

triumphant /traɪˈʌmfnt/ adj [*person, team*] triomphant; [*return, success*] triomphal.

triumphantly /traɪˈʌmfntlɪ/ adv [*march, return*] triomphalement; [*say*] d'une voix triomphante.

triumvirate /traɪˈʌmvɪrət/ n triumvirat m.

trivia /ˈtrɪvɪə/ npl (+ v sg ou pl) futilités fpl.

trivial /ˈtrɪvɪəl/ adj [*matter, scale, film*] insignifiant; [*error, offence*] léger/-ère; [*conversation, argument, person*] futile.

triviality /ˌtrɪvɪˈælɪtɪ/ n banalité f.

trivialize /ˈtrɪvɪəlaɪz/ vtr GEN banaliser; minimiser [*rôle, art*].

trod /trɒd/ prét ▶ **tread** II, III.

trodden /ˈtrɒdn/ pp ▶ **tread** II, III.

Trojan /ˈtrəʊdʒən/ I n HIST Troyen/-enne m/f.
II adj troyen/-enne; the ~ **War** la guerre de Troie.
IDIOMS **to work like a** ~ GB travailler comme un forçat.

troll /trəʊl/ n troll m.

trolley /ˈtrɒlɪ/ n **1** GB (on wheels) chariot m; **drinks** ~ chariot à boissons; **2** US tramway m.

trolley: ~ **bus** n trolleybus m; ~ **car** n tramway m, tram m.

troop /truːp/ I n troupe f.
II noun modifier [*movements, carrier*] de troupes; [*train, plane*] de transport de troupes.
III vi **to** ~ **in/out** entrer/sortir en masse.

trooper /ˈtruːpə(r)/ n **1** MIL homme m de troupe; **2** US (policeman) policier m.
IDIOMS **to swear like a** ~ jurer comme un charretier ou troupier.

trooping /ˈtruːpɪŋ/ n the **Trooping of the Colour** GB parade f militaire.

trophy /ˈtrəʊfɪ/ n trophée m.

tropic /ˈtrɒpɪk/ n tropique m; the ~ **of Cancer** le tropique du Cancer; **in the** ~**s** sous les tropiques.

tropical /ˈtrɒpɪkl/ adj tropical.

trot /trɒt/ I n trot m; **at a** ~ au trot; **to break into a** ~ [*animal*] se mettre au trot; [*person*] se mettre à trotter.
II vi (p prés etc **-tt-**) [*animal, rider*] trotter; [*person*] courir, trotter○; [*child*] trottiner.
IDIOMS **on the** ~○ (one after the other) coup sur coup; (continuously) d'affilée.
■ **trot out**○: ~ **out** [sth] débiter [*excuse, explanation, argument*].

trotter /ˈtrɒtə(r)/ n **pigs'** ~**s** CULIN pieds mpl de cochon.

trouble /ˈtrʌbl/ I n ₵ **1** (problems) GEN problèmes mpl; (personal) ennuis mpl; **engine** ~ problèmes de moteur; **this car has been nothing but** ~ cette voiture ne m'a apporté que des ennuis; **to get sb into** ~ créer des ennuis à qn; **to make** ~ **for oneself** s'attirer des ennuis; **to be asking for** ~ chercher des ennuis; **the** ~ **with you is that** l'ennui avec toi c'est que; **back** ~ mal m de dos; **what's the** ~? qu'est-ce qui ne va pas?; **2** (difficulties) GEN difficultés fpl; **to be in** ou **get into** ~ GEN [*person*] avoir des ennuis; [*company*] avoir des difficultés; **to have** ~ **doing** avoir du mal à faire; **to get sb out of** ~ tirer qn d'affaire; **to stay out of** ~ éviter des ennuis; **3** (effort, inconvenience) peine f; **it's not worth the** ~ cela n'en vaut pas la peine; **to take the** ~ **to do**, **to go to the** ~ **of doing** se donner la peine de faire; **to save sb the** ~ **of doing** épargner à qn la peine de faire; **to go to a lot of** ~ se donner beaucoup de mal; **I don't want to put you to any** ~ je ne veux pas te déranger; **it's no** ~ cela ne me dérange pas; **to be more** ~ **than it's worth** donner plus de mal qu'il n'en vaut la peine; **not to be any** ~ [*child*] être sage; [*task*] ne poser aucun problème; **all that** ~ **for nothing** tout ce mal pour rien; **nothing is too much** ~ **for him** il est très serviable; **if it's too much** ~, **say so** si ça t'ennuie, dis-le-moi; **all the** ~ **and expense** tous les dérangements et toutes les dépenses; **4** (discord) GEN problèmes mpl; (with personal involvement) ennuis mpl; **I don't want any** ~ je ne veux pas

d'ennuis; **there'll be** ~ il y aura du remous; **expect** ~ [*police*] s'attendre à des incidents; **to be looking for** ~ chercher les ennuis; **to get into** ~ s'attirer des ennuis; **to make** ~ faire des histoires○; **it will lead to** ~ ça va mal finir; **at the first sign of** ~ au moindre signe d'agitation; **there's** ~ **brewing** il y a de l'orage dans l'air FIG.
II **troubles** npl soucis mpl; **money** ~**s** problèmes mpl d'argent.
III vtr **1** (disturb, inconvenience) [*person*] déranger [*person*]; **to** ~ **sb for sth** déranger qn pour lui demander qch; **may** ou **could I** ~ **you to do?** puis-je vous demander de faire?; **I won't** ~ **you with the details** je te fais grâce des détails; **2** (bother) **to be** ~**d by** être incommodé par [*cough, pain*]; **3** (worry) tracasser [*person*]; tourmenter [*mind*]; **don't let that** ~ **you** ne te tracasse pas pour cela.
IV vi **to** ~ **to do** se donner la peine de faire.
V v refl **to** ~ **oneself to do** se donner la peine de faire.

troubled /ˈtrʌbld/ adj [*person, expression*] soucieux/-ieuse; [*mind*] inquiet/-iète; [*sleep, times, area*] agité; LITTÉR [*waters*] troublé.

trouble: ~**free** adj [*period, operation*] sans problèmes; ~**maker** n fauteur/-trice m/f de troubles; ~**shooter** n GEN conciliateur/-trice m/f; TECH expert m; IND consultant/-e m/f en gestion des entreprises; ~**some** adj [*person*] ennuyeux/-euse; [*problem*] gênant; [*cough, pain*] désagréable; ~ **spot** n point m chaud.

trough /trɒf, US trɔːf/ n **1** (for drinking) abreuvoir m; (for animal feed) auge f; **2** (depression) (between waves, hills, on graph) ALSO ECON creux m; **to have peaks and** ~**s** avoir des hauts et des bas; **3** METEOROL zone f dépressionnaire.

trouser /ˈtraʊzə(r)/ **▶ 1260**] I noun modifier [*belt, leg*] de pantalon.
II **trousers** npl pantalon m; **short** ~**s** short m.
IDIOMS **to wear the** ~**s** GB porter la culotte○.

trouser suit n GB ensemble-pantalon m.

trousseau /ˈtruːsəʊ/ n trousseau m (de mariage).

trout /traʊt/ I n truite f.
II noun modifier [*fishing*] à la truite; [*stream*] à truites.

trowel /ˈtraʊəl/ n **1** (for cement) truelle f; **2** (for gardening) déplantoir m.
IDIOMS **to lay it on with a** ~○ mettre le paquet○.

truancy /ˈtruːənsɪ/ n absentéisme m.

truant /ˈtruːənt/ n **to play** ~ faire l'école buissonnière.

truce /truːs/ n trêve f.

truck /trʌk/ I n **1** (lorry) camion m; **2** (rail wagon) wagon m de marchandises.
II vtr camionner.
III vi US conduire un camion.
IDIOMS **to have no** ~ **with sb/sth** GB ne rien avoir à faire avec qn/qch.

truck driver ▶ 1251] n routier m.

trucker○ /ˈtrʌkə(r)/ **▶ 1251**] n (lorry driver) routier m.

trucking /ˈtrʌkɪŋ/ n (transporting) transport m routier.

truckload /ˈtrʌkləʊd/ n (of goods, produce) chargement m (**of** de); (of soldiers, refugees) camion m (**of** de).

truck stop n (restaurant m) routier m.

truculent /ˈtrʌkjʊlənt/ adj agressif/-ive.

trudge /trʌdʒ/ vi (also ~ **along**) marcher d'un pas lourd; **to** ~ **through the snow** marcher péniblement dans la neige; **to** ~ **round the shops** se traîner de magasin en magasin.

true /truː/ I adj **1** (based on fact) [*news, fact, story*] vrai; (from real life) [*story*] vécu; **it is** ~ **to say that** on peut dire que; **the same is** ou **holds** ~ **of the new party** il en va de même pour le nouveau parti; **to prove** ~ se révéler exact; **it can't be** ~! ce n'est pas possible!; **that's** ~ (when agreeing) c'est juste; **too** ~○! je ne vous/te le fais pas dire!; **2** (real, genuine) [*god, cost, meaning, democracy, American*] vrai; [*identity, age*] véritable; **to come** ~ se réaliser; **it is hard to get the** ~ **picture** il est difficile de savoir ce qui se passe vraiment or en réalité; **an artist in the ~ sense of the word** un artiste dans toute l'acception du terme; **3** (heartfelt, sincere) [*feeling, repentance, understanding*] sincère; **~ love** le véritable amour; **4** (accurate) [*copy*] conforme; [*assessment*] correct, juste; **to be ~ to life** [*film, book*] être vrai; **5** (faithful, loyal) [*servant, knight*] fidèle; **to be ~ to sth** être fidèle à qch; **6** CONSTR **to be out of ~** [*window, post, frame*] ne pas être d'aplomb; **7** MUS [*note, instrument*] juste.

II *adj* (straight) [*aim, fire*] juste.

IDIOMS **to be too good to be ~** être trop beau pour être vrai; **~ to form, he...** égal à lui-même, il...; **to be/remain ~ to type** [*person*] être/rester semblable à lui-même/elle-même etc.

true: **~-blue** *adj* [*conservative, loyalist*] bon teint *inv*; **~-life** *adj* [*adventure, story*] vécu; **~love** *n* LITTÉR bien-aimé/-e *m/f*.

truffle /ˈtrʌfl/ *n* truffe *f*.

truism /ˈtruːɪzəm/ *n* truisme *m*.

truly /ˈtruːlɪ/ *adv* **1** (extremely) [*amazing, delighted, sorry, horrendous*] vraiment; **2** (really, in truth) [*be, belong, think*] vraiment; **really and ~?** vraiment?; **well and ~** carrément; **3** (in letter) **yours ~** je vous prie d'agréer l'expression de mes sentiments distingués FML; ...**and who got it all wrong? yours ~!** (referring to oneself) ...et qui s'est trompé? mézigue○!

trump /trʌmp/ **I** *n* GAMES atout *m*.

II trumps *npl* GAMES atout *m*; **spades are ~s** atout pique.

III *vtr* **1** GAMES couper; **2** (beat) battre [*person, rival*].

IDIOMS **to come up** ou **turn up ~s** sauver la situation.

trump card *n* atout *m*.

trumped-up /ˌtrʌmptˈʌp/ *adj* [*charge*] forgé de toutes pièces.

trumpet /ˈtrʌmpɪt/ ▶ **1097** **I** *n* **1** MUS (instrument, player) trompette *f*; **2** (elephant call) barrissement *m*.

II *noun modifier* [*solo*] de trompette; **~ call** FIG vibrant appel *m*.

III *vtr* [*group, party*] vanter les mérites de [*lifestyle, success*]; [*newspaper*] claironner.

IV *vi* [*elephant*] barrir.

IDIOMS **to blow one's own ~** vanter ses propres mérites.

trumpeter /ˈtrʌmpɪtə(r)/ ▶ **1251**, **1097** *n* trompettiste *mf*.

truncate /trʌŋˈkeɪt, US ˈtrʌŋ-/ *vtr* **1** tronquer [*text*]; écourter [*process, journey, event*]; **2** COMPUT, MATH tronquer.

truncheon /ˈtrʌntʃən/ *n* matraque *f*.

trundle /ˈtrʌndl/ **I** *vtr* **to ~ sth out** sortir qch; **to ~ sth in** entrer en poussant qch.

II *vi* [*vehicle*] avancer lourdement; **the lorries were trundling up and down the street** les camions montaient et descendaient lourdement la rue.

trunk /trʌŋk/ **I** *n* **1** (of tree, body) tronc *m*; **2** (of elephant) trompe *f*; **3** (for travel) malle *f*; **4** US (car boot) coffre *m*; **5** (duct) conduite *f*.

II trunks *npl* maillot *m* de bain (*pour hommes*).

truss /trʌs/ **I** *n* **1** (of hay) botte *f*; **2** MED bandage *m* herniaire; **3** CONSTR armature *f*, ferme *f*.

II *vtr* **1** (bind) = **truss up**; **2** CONSTR armer.

■ **truss up**: **~ up** [*sth*], **~** [*sth*] **up** brider, trousser [*chicken*]; ligoter [*person*]; botteler [*hay*].

trust /trʌst/ **I** *n* **1** (faith) confiance *f*; **to put one's ~ in** se fier à; **to take sth on ~** croire qch sur parole; **2** JUR (arrangement) fidéicommis *m*; (property involved) propriété *f* fiduciaire; **3** FIN (large group of companies) trust *m*; **4** FIN ▶ **investment trust**.

II *vtr* **1** (believe) se fier à [*person, judgment*]; **2** (rely on) faire confiance à; **~ her!** (amused or annoyed) tu peux compter sur elle pour ça!; **3** (entrust) **to ~ sb with sth** confier qch à qn; **4** (hope) espérer.

III *vi* **to ~ in** faire confiance à [*person*]; croire en [*God, fortune*]; **to ~ to luck** se fier au hasard.

IV trusted *pp adj* [*friend*] fidèle.

V *v refl* **to ~ oneself to do** être sûr de pouvoir faire; **I couldn't ~ myself to speak** j'ai préféré me taire.

trust company *n* société *f* fiduciaire.

trustee /trʌsˈtiː/ *n* **1** (who administers property in trust) fiduciaire *m*; **2** (who administers a company) administrateur/-trice *m/f* (**of** de).

trust fund *n* fonds *m* en fidéicommis.

trusting /ˈtrʌstɪŋ/ *adj* [*person*] qui fait facilement confiance aux gens; **you're too ~** tu es trop naïf/naïve.

trustworthy /ˈtrʌstwɜːðɪ/ *adj* [*staff, firm*] sérieux/-ieuse; [*source*] fiable; [*confidante, lover*] digne de confiance.

trusty /ˈtrʌstɪ/ *adj* †HUM fidèle.

truth /truːθ/ *n* **1** (real facts) **the ~** la vérité; **the whole ~** toute la vérité; **the ~ (of the matter) is that** la vérité, c'est que; **whatever the ~ of the matter** quoi qu'il en soit; **to tell you the ~**○ à vrai dire; **nothing could be further from the ~** c'est absolument faux; **2** (accuracy) **to confirm/deny the ~ of sth** confirmer/nier l'exactitude de qch; **3** PHILOS, RELIG vérité *f*; **4** (foundation) **there is no ~ in that** c'est absolument faux; **there is some ~ in it** il y a du vrai dans cela.

IDIOMS **~ will out** la vérité se fera jour; **~ is stranger than fiction** la réalité dépasse la fiction; **to tell sb a few home ~s** dire à qn ses quatre vérités.

truth drug *n* sérum *m* de vérité.

truthful /ˈtruːθfl/ *adj* [*person*] honnête; [*account, version*] vrai; **to be absolutely** ou **perfectly ~** en toute franchise.

truthfully /ˈtruːθfəlɪ/ *adv* sans mentir.

truthfulness /ˈtruːθflnɪs/ *n* véracité *f*.

try /traɪ/ (*pl* **tries**) **I** *n* **1** (attempt) essai *m*; **to have a ~ at doing** essayer de faire; **nice ~!** bel essai!; IRON bel effort!; **to have a good ~** faire tout ce qu'on peut; **2** SPORT (in rugby) essai *m*.

II *vtr* (*prét, pp* **tried**) **1** (attempt) essayer de répondre à [*exam question*]; **to ~ doing** ou **to do** essayer de faire; **to ~ hard to do** faire de gros efforts pour faire; **to ~ one's hardest** ou **best to do** faire tout son possible pour faire; **let's ~ and phone them** essayons de leur téléphoner; **it's ~ing to rain/snow** il a l'air de vouloir pleuvoir/neiger; **2** (test out) essayer [*tool, product, method, activity*]; prendre [qn] à l'essai [*person*]; [*thief*] essayer d'ouvrir [*door, window*]; tourner [*door knob*]; **to ~ one's hand at pottery/weaving** s'essayer à la poterie/au tissage; **~ that for size** ou **length** essaie pour voir si ça te va; **I'll ~ anything once** je suis toujours prêt à faire de nouvelles expériences; **3** (taste) goûter [*food*]; **4** (consult) demander à [*person*]; consulter [*book*]; **~ the library** demandez à la bibliothèque; **5** (subject to stress) mettre [qch] à rude épreuve [*tolerance, faith*]; **to ~ sb's patience** pousser qn à bout; **6** JUR juger [*case, criminal*].

III *vi* (*prét, pp* **tried**) (make attempt) essayer; **to ~ again** (to perform task) recommencer; (to see somebody) repasser; (to phone) rappeler; **~ and relax** essaie de rester calme; **to ~ for** essayer d'obtenir [*loan, university place*]; essayer de battre [*world record*]; essayer d'avoir [*baby*]; **just you ~!** (as threat) essaie un peu○!; **keep ~ing!** essaie encore!; **I'd like to see you ~!** j'aimerais bien t'y voir!; **she did it without even ~ing** elle l'a fait sans le moindre effort; **at least you tried** au moins tu as fait tout ce que tu as pu.

IDIOMS **these things are sent to ~ us** HUM tout ça c'est pour notre bien.

■ **try on**: **~** [*sth*] **on**, **~ on** [*sth*] essayer [*hat, dress*]; **to ~ it on**○ FIG bluffer.

■ **try out**: ¶ **~ out** [*sportsman*] faire un essai; [*actor*] auditionner; ¶ **~** [*sth*] **out**, **~ out** [*sth*] essayer [*machine, theory, language, recipe*]; ¶ **~** [*sb*] **out**, **~ out** [*sb*] prendre [qn] à l'essai.

trying /ˈtraɪɪŋ/ *adj* [*person*] pénible; [*experience*] éprouvant.

tsar /zɑː(r)/ *n* tsar *m*.

T-shaped *adj* en (forme de) T.

T-shirt *n* T-shirt *m*.

tsp *abrév écrite* = **teaspoonful**.

tub /tʌb/ *n* **1** (large) (for flowers, water) bac *m*; (small) (for ice cream, pâté) pot *m*; **2** (contents) pot *m*; **3** US (bath) baignoire *f*.

tubby° /'tʌbɪ/ *adj* grassouillet/-ette°.

tube /tjuːb, US 'tuːb/ *n* **1** (cylinder, container) tube *m*; **2**° GB **the** ~ le métro (londonien); **3**° US (TV) télé° *f*; **4** (in TV set) tube *m* cathodique.

IDIOMS **to go down the** ~**s** [*plans*] tomber à l'eau; [*economy*] tomber en ruines.

tuberculosis /tjuː‚bɜːkjʊ'ləʊsɪs, US 'tuː-/ ▶1002 *n* tuberculose *f*.

tubing /'tjuːbɪŋ, US 'tuː-/ *n* tuyauterie *f*.

tub-thumping /'tʌbθʌmpɪŋ/ *n* éloquence *f* de bas étage.

tubular /'tjuːbjʊlə(r), US 'tuː-/ *adj* tubulaire.

TUC *n*: *abrév* ▶ **Trades Union Congress**.

tuck /tʌk/ **I** *n* GEN pli *m*; (to shorten) pli *m* horizontal.

II *vtr* glisser; **to** ~ **one's shirt into one's trousers** rentrer sa chemise dans son pantalon; **to** ~ **one's trousers into one's boots** enfiler son pantalon dans ses bottes; **to** ~ **a blanket under sb** plier une couverture sous qn; **she** ~**ed her feet up under her** elle a ramené ses pieds sous elle; **it** ~**ed its head under its wing** il a enfoui la tête sous son aile.

▪ **tuck away**: ~ [*sth*] **away**, ~ **away** [*sth*] **1** (safely, in reserve) enfouir [*object*]; mettre en sécurité [*money, valuable*]; **2** (hard to find) **to be** ~**ed away** [*village, document, object*] se nicher (**in** dans; **behind** derrière).

▪ **tuck in**: ¶ ~ **in** (start eating) attaquer; ¶ ~ **in** [*sth*], ~ [*sth*] **in** rentrer [*garment, shirt*]; border [*bedclothes*]; ¶ ~ [*sb*] **in**, ~ **in** [*sb*] border.

▪ **tuck up**: ~ **up** [*sb*], ~ [*sb*] **up** border.

Tue(s) *abrév écrite* = **Tuesday**.

Tuesday /'tjuːzdeɪ, -dɪ, US 'tuː-/ ▶1390 *pr n* mardi *m*.

tuft /tʌft/ *n* touffe *f*.

tufted /'tʌftɪd/ *adj* [*grass*] en touffes; [*bird*] huppé; [*carpet*] touffeté.

tug /tʌɡ/ **I** *n* **1** (pull) (on rope, in sails) résistance *f*; (on fishing line) secousse *f*; **to give sth a** ~ tirer sur qch; **to feel a** ~ **of loyalties** se sentir partagé; **2** NAUT (also **tug boat**) remorqueur *m*.

II *vtr* (*p prés etc* **-gg-**) (pull) tirer.

III *vi* (*p prés etc* **-gg-**) **to** ~ **at** ou **on** tirer sur [*rope, hair*].

tug-of-love /‚tʌɡəv'lʌv/ *n* GB *lutte entre les parents pour la garde de l'enfant*.

tug-of-war /‚tʌɡəv'wɔː(r)/ *n* SPORT gagne-terrain *m*; FIG lutte *f*.

tuition /tjuː'ɪʃn, US tuː-/ *n* cours *mpl*.

tuition fees *npl* frais *mpl* pédagogiques.

tulip /'tjuːlɪp, US 'tuː-/ *n* tulipe *f*.

tumble /'tʌmbl/ **I** *n* **1** (fall) chute *f*; **to take a** ~ [*person*] faire une chute; [*price, share*] chuter; **2** (of clown, acrobat) culbute *f*; **3** (jumble) tas *m*.

II *vi* **1** (fall) [*person, object*] tomber (**off, out of** de); **to** ~ **down sth** [*water*] dévaler qch en cascade; **2** [*price, share, currency*] chuter; **3** SPORT [*clown, acrobat, child*] faire des culbutes; **4**° **to** ~ **to sth** (understand) comprendre [*fact, plan*].

▪ **tumble down** [*wall, building*] s'écrouler.

▪ **tumble out** [*contents*] se renverser; [*words, feelings*] jaillir en désordre.

tumble: ~**down** *adj* délabré; ~**-drier**, ~**-dryer** *n* sèche-linge *m inv*; ~**-dry** *vtr* sécher (en machine).

tumbler /'tʌmblə(r)/ *n* (glass) verre *m* droit.

tummy° /'tʌmɪ/ *n* LANG ENFANTIN ventre *m*.

tumour GB, **tumor** US /'tjuːmə(r), US 'tuː-/ *n* tumeur *f*.

tumult /'tjuːmʌlt, US 'tuː-/ *n* **1** (noise) tumulte *m*; **to be in** ~ [*feelings*] être en émoi; **2** (disorder) agitation *f*.

tumultuous /tjuː'mʌltjʊəs, US 'tuː-/ *adj* tumultueux/-euse.

tuna /'tjuːnə, US 'tuː-/ *n* (also ~ **fish**) thon *m*.

tune /tjuːn, US tuːn/ **I** *n* **1** MUS air *m*; **2** MUS (accurate pitch) **to be in/out of** ~ LIT, FIG être/ne pas être en accord; **to sing in/out of** ~ chanter juste/faux; **3**° (amount) **to the** ~ **of** pour un montant de.

II *vtr* accorder [*musical instrument*]; régler [*engine, radio, TV*]; **stay** ~**d!** restez à l'écoute!

IDIOMS **to call the** ~ mener la danse; **to change one's** ~, **to sing a different** ~ changer d'avis; **to dance to sb's** ~ se plier aux exigences de qn.

▪ **tune in** ¶ mettre la radio; **to** ~ **in to** se mettre à l'écoute de [*programme*]; régler sur [*channel*]; ¶ ~ [*sth*] **in** régler (**to** sur).

▪ **tune up** ¶ [*musician*] s'accorder; ¶ ~ **up** [*sth*], ~ [*sth*] **up** accorder [*musical instrument*].

tuneful /'tjuːnfl, US 'tuː-/ *adj* mélodieux/-ieuse.

tuner /'tjuːnə(r), US 'tuː-/ *n* **1** ▶1251 MUS (person) accordeur *m*; **organ/piano** ~ accordeur *m* d'orgues/de piano; **2** AUDIO (unit) tuner *m*; (knob) (bouton *m* de) réglage.

tunic /'tjuːnɪk, US 'tuː-/ *n* GEN tunique *f*; (uniform) (for nurse, schoolgirl) blouse *f*; (for soldier) vareuse *f*.

tuning /'tjuːnɪŋ, US 'tuː-/ *n* (of musical instrument, choir) accord *m*; (of radio, TV, engine) réglage *m*.

tuning fork *n* MUS diapason *m*.

Tunisia /tjuː'nɪzɪə, US tuː-/ ▶840 *pr n* Tunisie *f*.

tunnel /'tʌnl/ **I** *n* tunnel *m*; **to use a** ~ emprunter un tunnel.

II *vtr, vi* (*p prés etc* **-ll-** GB, **-l-** US) creuser.

IDIOMS **to see (the) light at the end of the** ~ voir le bout du tunnel.

tunnel vision *n* MED rétrécissement *m* (tubulaire) du champ visuel; FIG **to have** ~ avoir des œillères.

tuppence /'tʌpəns/ *n* deux pence.

turbine /'tɜːbaɪn/ *n* turbine *f*.

turbo /'tɜːbəʊ/ *n* (engine) turbo *m*; (car) turbo *f*.

turbocharged /‚tɜːbəʊ'tʃɑːdʒd/ *adj* turbo *inv*.

turbot /'tɜːbət/ *n* turbot *m*.

turbulence /'tɜːbjʊləns/ *n* ∉ **1** (of air) turbulences *fpl*; (of waves) turbulence *f*; **2** (turmoil) agitation *f*; (unrest) perturbations *fpl*.

turbulent /'tɜːbjʊlənt/ *adj* **1** [*water*] agité; **2** [*times, situation*] agité; [*career, history*] mouvementé; [*passions, character, faction*] turbulent.

tureen /tə'riːn/ *n* soupière *f*.

turf /tɜːf/ **I** *n* (*pl* ~**s**, **turves**) **1** (grass) gazon *m*; (peat) tourbe *f*; **2** (horse racing) **the** ~ le turf *m*.

II *vtr* **1** gazonner [*lawn, patch, pitch*]; **2**° (throw) balancer°.

▪ **turf out**: ~ **out** [*sb/sth*], ~ [*sb/sth*] **out** virer°.

turf accountant ▶1251 *n* bookmaker *m*.

turgid /'tɜːdʒɪd/ *adj* [*style*] boursouflé; [*water*] gonflé.

Turk /tɜːk/ ▶1100 *n* (person) Turc/Turque *m/f*.

turkey /'tɜːkɪ/ *n* **1** (bird) dinde *f*; **2**° US PÉJ THEAT, CIN (flop) bide° *m*; (bad film) navet° *m*; **3**° US (person) cloche° *f*.

IDIOMS **to talk** ~° dire les choses toutes crues°.

Turkey /'tɜːkɪ/ ▶840 *pr n* Turquie *f*.

Turkish /'tɜːkɪʃ/ ▶1100, 1038 **I** *n* (language) turc *m*.

II *adj* turc/turque.

Turkish: ~ **bath** *n* bain *m* turc; ~ **coffee** *n* café *m* turc; ~ **delight** *n* loukoum *m*; ~ **towel** *n* serviette *f* éponge.

turmeric /'tɜːmərɪk/ *n* (plant) curcuma *m*; (spice) safran *m* des Indes.

turmoil /'tɜːmɔɪl/ *n* (political, emotional) désarroi *m*.

turn /tɜːn/ ▶870 **I** *n* **1** (in games, sequence) tour *m*; **whose** ~ **is it?** c'est à qui le tour?; '**miss a** ~' 'passez votre tour'; **to be sb's** ~ **to do** être au tour de qn de faire; **it was his** ~ **to feel rejected** il se sentait rejeté à son tour; **to have a** ~ **on** ou **at** ou **with the computer** utiliser l'ordinateur à son tour; **to take** ~**s at doing**, **to take it in** ~**s to do** faire qch à tour de rôle; **take it in** ~**s!** chacun son tour!;

by ~s tour à tour; **to speak out of ~** FIG commettre un impair; **2** (circular movement) tour *m*; **to give sth a ~** tourner qch; **to do a ~** [*dancer*] faire un tour; **to take a ~ in the park** faire un tour dans le parc; **3** (in vehicle) virage *m*; **to make** OU **do a left/right ~** tourner à gauche/à droite; **to do a ~ in the road** faire un demi-tour; **'no left ~'** 'défense de tourner à gauche'; **4** (bend, side road) tournant *m*, virage *m*; **take the next right ~, take the next ~ on the right** prenez la prochaine (rue) à droite; **5** (change, development) tournure *f*; **to take a ~ for the better** [*person, situation*] s'améliorer; [*things, events*] prendre une meilleure tournure; **to take a ~ for the worse** [*situation*] se dégrader; [*health*] s'aggraver; **to be on the ~** [*luck, milk*] commencer à tourner; [*tide*] commencer à changer; ▶**century**; **6**° GB (attack) crise *f*; **a giddy** OU **dizzy ~** avoir le vertige; **to have a funny ~** se sentir tout/-e chose°; **it gave me quite a ~, it gave me a nasty ~** ça m'a fait un coup°; **7** (act) numéro *m*.

II in turn *adv phr* **1** (in rotation) [*answer, speak*] à tour de rôle; **she spoke to each of us in ~** elle nous a parlé chacun à notre tour; **2** (linking sequence) à son tour.

III *vtr* **1** (rotate) [*person*] tourner [*wheel, handle*]; serrer [*screw*]; [*mechanism*] faire tourner [*cog, wheel*]; **to ~ the key in the door** OU **lock** (lock up) fermer la porte à clé; (unlock) tourner la clé dans la serrure; **2** (turn over, reverse) retourner [*mattress, soil, steak, collar*]; tourner [*page*]; **to ~ one's ankle** se tordre la cheville; **it ~s my stomach** cela me soulève le cœur; **3** (change direction of) tourner [*chair, head, face, car*]; **to ~ one's back on** LIT tourner le dos à [*group, place*]; FIG laisser tomber [*friend, ally*]; abandonner [*homeless, needy*]; **4** (focus direction of) **to ~ sth on sb** braquer qch sur qn [*gun, hose, torch*]; FIG diriger qch sur qn [*anger, scorn*]; **5** (transform) **to ~ sth white/black** blanchir/noircir qch; **to ~ sth milky/opaque** rendre qch laiteux/opaque; **to ~ sth into** transformer qch en [*office, car park, desert*]; **to ~ water into ice/wine** changer de l'eau en glace/vin; **to ~ a book into a film** adapter un livre pour l'écran; **to ~ sb into** [*magician*] changer qn en [*frog*]; [*experience*] faire de qn [*extrovert, maniac*]; **6** (deflect) détourner [*person, conversation*] (**towards** vers; **from** de); **7**° (pass the age of) **he has ~ed 50** il a 50 ans passés; **she has just ~ed 20/30** elle vient d'avoir 20/30 ans; **8** (on lathe) tourner [*wood, piece, spindle*].

IV *vi* **1** (change direction) [*person, car, plane, road*] tourner; [*ship*] virer; **to ~ down** OU **into** tourner dans [*street, alley*]; **to ~ towards** tourner en direction de [*village, mountains*]; **the conversation ~ed to Ellie** on en est venu/ils en sont venus à parler d'Ellie; **2** (reverse direction) [*person, vehicle*] faire demi-tour; [*tide*] changer; [*luck*] tourner; ▶**turn around**; **3** (revolve) [*key, wheel, planet*] tourner; [*person*] se tourner; **to ~ in one's chair** se retourner dans son fauteuil; **to ~ and walk out of the room** faire demi-tour et sortir de la pièce; **I ~ed once again to my book** j'ai repris encore une fois ma lecture; **4** FIG (hinge) **to ~ on** [*argument*] tourner autour de [*point, issue*]; [*outcome*] dépendre de [*factor*]; **5** (spin round angrily) **to ~ on sb** [*dog*] attaquer qn; [*person*] se retourner contre qn; **6** FIG (resort to) **to ~ to** se tourner vers [*person, religion*]; **to ~ to drink/drugs** se mettre à boire/se droguer; **I don't know where** OU **which way to ~** je ne sais plus où donner de la tête°; **7** (change) **to ~ into** [*person, tadpole*] se transformer en [*frog*]; [*sofa*] se transformer en [*bed*]; [*situation, evening*] tourner à [*farce, disaster*]; **to ~ to** [*substance*] se changer en [*ice, gold*]; [*fear, surprise*] faire place à [*horror, relief*]; **8** (become by transformation) devenir [*pale, cloudy, green*]; **to ~ white/black/red** blanchir/noircir/rougir; **the weather is ~ing cold/warm** le temps se rafraîchit/se réchauffe; **9**° (become) devenir [*Conservative, Communist*]; **businesswoman ~ed politician** ancienne femme d'affaires devenue politicienne; **10** (go sour) [*milk*] tourner; **11** [*trees, leaves*] jaunir.

IDIOMS **at every ~** (all the time) à tout moment; (everywhere) partout; **one good ~ deserves another**

PROV c'est un prêté pour un rendu; **to be done to a ~** être cuit à point; **to do sb a good ~** rendre un service à qn.

■ **turn about** faire demi-tour.

■ **turn against**: ¶ **~ against [sb/sth]** se retourner contre; ¶ **~ [sb] against** retourner [qn] contre.

■ **turn around**: ¶ **~ around 1** (to face other way) [*person*] se retourner; [*bus, vehicle*] faire demi-tour; **you can't just ~ around and say you've changed your mind** tu ne peux pas tout simplement dire que tu as changé d'avis; **2** (revolve, rotate) [*object, windmill, dancer*] tourner; **3** (change trend) **the market has ~ed around** il y a eu un renversement de situation sur le marché; ¶ **~ [sth] around, ~ around [sth] 1** (to face other way) tourner [qch] dans l'autre sens [*object*]; **2** (reverse decline in) redresser [*situation, economy, company*]; **3** (rephrase) reformuler [*question, sentence*].

■ **turn aside** se détourner (**from** de).

■ **turn away**: ¶ **~ away** se détourner; ¶ **~ [sth] away, ~ away [sth]** détourner [*head, torch*]; ¶ **~ [sb] away, ~ away [sb]** refuser [*spectator, applicant*]; ne pas laisser entrer [*salesman, caller*].

■ **turn back**: ¶ **~ back 1** (turn around) (on foot) rebrousser chemin; (in vehicle) faire demi-tour; **there's no ~ing back** FIG il n'est pas question de revenir en arrière; **2** (in book) revenir; ¶ **~ [sth] back, ~ back [sth] 1** (rotate backwards) reculer [*dial, clock*]; **2** (fold back) rabattre [*sheet, lapel*]; replier [*corner, page*]; ¶ **~ [sb] back, ~ back [sb]** refouler [*people, vehicles*].

■ **turn down**: ¶ **~ down: his mouth ~s down at the corners** il a une bouche aux commissures tombantes; ¶ **~ [sth] down, ~ down [sth] 1** (reduce) baisser [*volume, radio, gas*]; **2** (fold over) rabattre [*sheet, collar*]; retourner [*corner of page*]; ¶ **~ [sb/sth] down, ~ down [sb/sth]** refuser [*person, request*]; rejeter [*offer, suggestion*].

■ **turn in**: ¶ **~ in 1**° (go to bed) aller se coucher; **2** (point inwards) **to ~ in on itself** [*leaf, page*] se recroqueviller; **to ~ in on oneself** FIG se replier sur soimême; ¶ **~ in [sth], ~ [sth] in**° **1** (hand in) rendre [*badge, homework*]; **2** (produce) **to ~ in a profit** rapporter un bénéfice; **to ~ in a good performance** [*player*] bien jouer; [*company*] avoir de bons résultats; **3** (give up) laisser tomber° [*job, activity*]; ¶ **~ [sb] in, ~ in [sb]** livrer [*suspect*]; ¶ **~ oneself in** se livrer.

■ **turn off**: ¶ **~ off 1** (leave road) tourner; **~ off at the next exit** prends la prochaine sortie; **2** [*motor, fan*] s'arrêter; ¶ **~ off [sth], ~ [sth] off 1** (stop) éteindre [*light, oven, TV, radio*]; fermer [*tap*]; couper [*water, gas, engine*]; **2** (leave) quitter [*road*]; ¶ **~ [sb] off**° rebuter.

■ **turn on**: ¶ **~ on [sth], ~ [sth] on** allumer [*light, oven, TV, radio, gas*]; ouvrir [*tap*]; ▶**charm**; ¶ **~ [sb] on, ~ on [sb]**° exciter.

■ **turn out**: ¶ **~ out 1** (be eventually) **to ~ out well/badly** bien/mal se terminer; **to ~ out differently** prendre une tournure différente; **to ~ out all right** s'arranger; **it depends how things ~ out** cela dépend de la façon dont les choses vont tourner; **to ~ out to be wrong/easy** (prove to be) se révéler faux/facile; **it ~s out that** il se trouve que; **as it ~ed out** en fin de compte; **2** (come out) [*crowd, people*] venir; **3** (point outwards) **his toes** OU **feet ~ out** il a les pieds tournés en dehors; ¶ **~ [sth] out, ~ out [sth] 1** (turn off) éteindre [*light*]; **2** (empty) vider [*pocket, bag*]; CULIN démouler [*mousse*]; **3** (produce) fabriquer [*goods*]; former [*scientists, graduates*]; ¶ **~ [sb] out, ~ out [sb]** (evict) mettre [qn] à la porte.

■ **turn over**: ¶ **~ over 1** (roll over) [*person, vehicle*] se retourner; **2** (turn page) tourner la page; **3** [*engine*] se mettre en marche; ¶ **~ [sth/sb] over, ~ over [sth/sb] 1** (turn) tourner [*page, paper*]; retourner [*card, object, mattress, soil, patient*]; **2** (hand over) remettre [*object, money, find, papers*]; livrer [*person*] (**to** à); remettre la succession de [*company*]; transmettre [*control, power*]; **3** (reflect) **I've been ~ing it over in my mind** j'y ai bien réfléchi; **4**° GB (rob) cambrioler [*shop, place*]; **5** FIN (have turnover of) faire un chiffre d'affaires de [*amount*].

■ **turn round** GB = **turn around**.

■ **turn up**: ¶ **~ up 1** (arrive, show up) arriver, se pointer○; **don't worry—it will ~ up** ne t'inquiète pas—tu finiras par le retrouver; **2** (present itself) [*opportunity, job*] se présenter; **3** (point up) [*corner, edge*] être relevé; ¶ **~ up** [sth], **~** [sth] **up 1** (increase, intensify) augmenter [*heating, volume, gas*]; mettre [qch] plus fort [*TV, radio, music*]; **2** (point up) relever [*collar*]; **3** (discover) déterrer [*buried object*]; [*person*] découvrir [*information*].

turnaround /'tɜːnəraʊnd/ *n* **1** (in attitude) revirement *m*; **2** (of fortune) revirement *m* (**in** de); (for the better) redressement *m* (**in** de).

turn: **~coat** *n* traître/traîtresse *m/f*, personne *f* qui retourne sa veste○; **~down** *n* baisse *f*.

turned-out /ˌtɜːnd'aʊt/ *adj* **to be well ~** être élégant.

turned-up /ˌtɜːnd'ʌp/ *adj* [*nose*] retroussé.

turning /'tɜːnɪŋ/ **▶870** *n* **1** GB (in road) virage *m*; **to take a wrong ~** tourner au mauvais endroit; **the next ~ on the right** la prochaine (rue) à droite; **I've missed my ~** j'aurais dû tourner plus tôt; **2** (work on lathe) tournage *m*.

turning: **~ circle** *n* rayon *m* de braquage; **~ point** *n* tournant *m* (**in, of** de).

turnip /'tɜːnɪp/ *n* navet *m*.

turnoff /'tɜːnɒf/ *n* **1** (in road) embranchement *m*; **2**○ (person) **to be a real ~** être vraiment repoussant.

turn: **~ of mind** *n* tournure *f* d'esprit; **~ of phrase** *n* (expression) expression *f*; (way of expressing oneself) façon *f* de parler.

turn-on○ /'tɜːnɒn/ *n* **to be a real ~** être vachement○ excitant.

turnout /'tɜːnaʊt/ *n* **1** (to vote, strike, demonstrate) taux *m* de participation; **there was a magnificent ~ for the parade** beaucoup de gens sont venus voir le défilé; **2** (clearout) nettoyage *m*; **3**○ (appearance) tenue *f*.

turnover /'tɜːnəʊvə(r)/ *n* **1** (of company) chiffre *m* d'affaires; **2** (rate of replacement) (of stock) rotation *f*; (of staff) taux *m* de renouvellement; **3** CULIN chausson *m*.

turn: **~pike** *n* (tollgate) barrière *f* de péage; US (toll expressway) autoroute *f* à péage; **~stile** *n* GEN tourniquet *m*; (to count number of visitors) compteur *m* pour entrées.

turntable /'tɜːnteɪbl/ *n* **1** (on record player) platine *f*; **2** RAIL, AUT plaque *f* tournante.

turnup /'tɜːnʌp/ *n* GB (of trousers) revers *m*.

IDIOMS **a ~ for the books** GB une grande surprise.

turpentine /'tɜːpəntaɪn/ *n* térébenthine *f*.

turret /'tʌrɪt/ *n* (all contexts) tourelle *f*.

turtle /'tɜːtl/ *n* GB tortue *f* marine; US tortue *f*.

IDIOMS **to turn ~** se retourner.

turtle: **~ dove** *n* tourterelle *f*; **~neck** *n* (neckline) col *m* montant.

Tuscany /'tʌskənɪ/ *pr n* Toscane *f*.

tusk /tʌsk/ *n* (of elephant, walrus) défense *f*.

tussle /'tʌsl/ **I** *n* empoignade *f* (**for** pour).

II *vi* être aux prises.

tussock /'tʌsək/ *n* touffe *f* d'herbe.

tut /tʌt/ **I** *excl* tss-tss!

II *vi* (*p prés etc* **-tt-**) produire un tss-tss de désapprobation.

tutee /tjuː'tiː, US tuː-/ *n* GEN étudiant/-e *m/f*; (individual) élève *mf* particulier/-ière.

tutor /'tjuːtə(r), US tuː-/ **▶1251** **I** *n* **1** (private teacher) professeur *m* particulier; **2** GB UNIV (teacher) chargé/ -e *m/f* de travaux dirigés; (for general welfare) conseiller/ -ère *m/f* d'éducation; **3** US UNIV assistant/-e *m/f*; **4** GB SCH (of class) professeur *m* principal; (of year group) responsable *mf* pédagogique d'année; **5** MUS (instruction book) méthode *f*.

II *vtr* donner des leçons particulières à (**in** de).

III *vi* donner des cours (**in** de).

tutorial /tjuː'tɔːrɪəl, US tuː-/ *n* UNIV (group) classe *f* de travaux dirigés; (private) cours *m* privé.

tuxedo /tʌk'siːdəʊ/ *n* US smoking *m*.

TV○ *n* (*abrév* = **television**) télé○ *f*.

TV: **~ dinner** *n* plateau *m* télé; **~ screen** *n* écran *m* télé.

twaddle○ /'twɒdl/ *n* balivernes *fpl*.

twain‡ /tweɪn/ *npl* **the ~** les deux; **never the ~ shall meet** les deux sont inconciliables.

twang /twæŋ/ **I** *n* (of string, wire) vibration *f*; (of tone) ton *m* nasillard.

II *vtr* pincer [*instrument*].

III *vi* [*string, wire*] produire une vibration; [*instrument*] vibrer.

tweak /twiːk/ **I** *n* **1** (tug) coup *m* sec; **2** COMPUT amélioration *f*.

II *vtr* tordre [*ear, nose*]; tirer [*hair, moustache*].

twee○ /twiː/ *adj* GB PÉJ [*house, décor*] mièvre; [*manner*] emprunté.

tweezers /'twiːzəz/ *npl* GEN pincettes *fpl*; (for eyebrows) pince *f* à épiler.

twelfth /twelfθ/ **▶1112**, **854** **I** *n* **1** (in order) douzième *mf*; **2** (of month) douze *m inv*; **3** (fraction) douzième *m*; **4** MUS douzième *f*.

II *adj, adv* douzième.

twelve /twelv/ **▶1112**, **713**, **812** **I** *n* douze *m inv*.

II *adj* douze *inv*; **the Twelve** BIBLE les douze apôtres.

twentieth /'twentɪəθ/ **▶1112**, **854** **I** *n* **1** (in order) vingtième *mf*; **2** (of month) vingt *m*; **3** (fraction) vingtième *m*.

II *adj, adv* vingtième.

twenty /'twentɪ/ **▶1112**, **713**, **812** *n, adj* vingt (*m*) *inv*.

twenty: **~-one** **▶949** *n* GAMES vingt-et-un *m*; **~-twenty** *adj* [*vision*] de dix à chaque œil.

twerp○ /twɜːp/ *n* PÉJ crétin/-e○ *m/f*.

twice /twaɪs/ *adv* deux fois; **~ a day** ou **daily** deux fois par jour; **she's ~ his age** elle a le double de son âge; **~ as much, ~ as many** deux fois plus; **~ over** deux fois; **you need to be ~ as careful** il faut redoubler de prudence.

IDIOMS **once bitten ~ shy** PROV chat échaudé craint l'eau froide PROV.

twiddle /'twɪdl/ *vtr* tripoter; **to ~ one's thumbs** LIT, FIG se tourner les pouces.

twig /twɪg/ **I** *n* brindille *f*.

II○ *vtr, vi* (*p prés etc* **-gg-**) piger○.

twilight /'twaɪlaɪt/ **I** *n* LIT, FIG crépuscule *m*.

II *noun modifier* [*hours*] du crépuscule; [*world*] énigmatique; **~ years** dernières années.

twilight zone *n* zone *f* d'ombre.

twill /twɪl/ *n* sergé *m*.

twin /twɪn/ **I** *n* **1** (one of two children) jumeau/-elle *m/f*; **2** (one of two objects) **this vase is the ~ to yours** ce vase est celui qui va avec le tien.

II *noun modifier* **1** [*brother, sister*] jumeau/-elle; **2** (two) [*masts, propellers*] jumeaux/-elles (*after n*); [*speakers*] jumelés; **the ~ aims of** le double but de.

III *vtr* (*p prés etc* **-nn-**) jumeler [*town*] (**with** avec).

twine /twaɪn/ **I** *n* ficelle *f*.

II *vtr* enrouler [*rope*] (**around** autour de).

III *v refl* **to ~ itself** [*snake, vine*] s'enrouler.

twinge /twɪndʒ/ *n* (of pain) élancement *m*; (of conscience, doubt) accès *m*; (of jealousy) pointe *f*.

twinkle /'twɪŋkl/ **I** *n* (of light, jewel) scintillement *m*; (of eyes) pétillement *m*.

II *vi* [*light, star, jewel*] scintiller; [*eyes*] pétiller.

twinkling /'twɪŋklɪŋ/ **I** *n* scintillement *m*.

II *adj* [*light, star, eyes*] scintillant.

IDIOMS **in the ~ of an eye** en un clin d'œil.

twinning /'twɪnɪŋ/ *n* jumelage *m*.

twin town *n* ville *f* jumelle.

twirl /twɜːl/ **I** *n* **1** (spin) tournoiement *m*; **to do a ~** [*person*] tournoyer; **2** (spiral) volute *f*.

II *vtr* faire tournoyer [*baton, lasso, partner*]; tortiller [*hair, moustache*]; entortiller [*ribbon, vine*].

III vi [dancer] tournoyer; **to ~ round** (turn round) se retourner brusquement.

twist /twɪst/ **I** n **1** (action) **he gave the cap a ~** (to open) il a dévissé le bouchon; (to close) il a vissé le bouchon; **with a couple of ~s she unscrewed the lid** en deux tours de poignet elle a dévissé le couvercle; **2** (in rope, cord, wool) tortillon m; (in road) zigzag m; (in river) coude m; **3** FIG (in play, story) coup m de théâtre; (episode in crisis, events) rebondissement m; **the ~s and turns of the plot** le fil tortueux de l'intrigue; **4** (small amount) (of yarn, thread, hair) torsade f; **a ~ of lemon** une tranche de citron; **5** (dance) **the ~** le twist.
II vtr **1** (turn) tourner [knob, handle]; (open) dévisser [cap, lid]; (close) visser [cap, lid]; **to ~ sth off** dévisser qch [cap, lid]; **he ~ed around in his chair** il s'est retourné dans son fauteuil; **to ~ sb's arm** LIT tordre le bras à qn; FIG forcer la main à qn; **2** (wind, twine) **to ~ threads together** torsader des fils; **to ~ X round Y** enrouler X autour de Y; **she ~ed the scarf (round) in her hands** elle tortillait l'écharpe entre ses doigts; **3** (bend, distort) tordre [metal, rod, branch]; FIG déformer [words, facts, meaning]; **his face was ~ed with pain** son visage était tordu de douleur; **4** (injure) **to ~ one's ankle/wrist** se tordre le bras/le poignet; **to ~ one's neck** attraper un torticolis.
III vi **1** [person] **he lay ~ing and writhing on the ground** il se tordait et se contorsionnait sur le sol; **to ~ round** (turn round) se retourner; **2** [rope, flex, coil] s'entortiller; [river, road] serpenter; **to ~ and turn** [road, path] serpenter.
IDIOMS **(to have a) ~ in the tail** (avoir un) dénouement inattendu; **to go round the ~**○ devenir fou/folle; **to drive sb round the ~**○ rendre qn fou/folle.

twisted /'twɪstɪd/ adj [wire, metal, rod] tordu; [rope, cord] entortillé; [ankle, wrist] tordu; PÉJ [logic] faux/fausse; [sense of humour] malsain.

twisting /'twɪstɪŋ/ adj sinueux/-euse.

twit○ /twɪt/ n idiot/-e m/f.

twitch /twɪtʃ/ **I** n **1** (tic) tic m; **to have a ~ in one's eye** avoir un tic à l'œil; **2** (spasm) soubresaut m; **to give a ~** avoir un soubresaut; **3** (jerk) **to give the curtain a ~** réajuster le rideau d'un coup sec.
II vtr tirer sur [qch] d'un coup sec [fabric, curtain]; **the dog ~ed its ears** le chien remuait les oreilles.
III vi **1** (quiver) [person, animal] trembloter; [mouth] trembler; [eye] cligner nerveusement; [limb, muscle] tressauter; [fishing line] vibrer; **2** (tug) **to ~ at** [person] tirer d'un coup sec sur [curtain].

twitchy /'twɪtʃɪ/ adj agité.

twitter /'twɪtə(r)/ **I** n gazouillement m; **to be all of a ~** HUM être tout excité/tout excitée.
II vi [bird] gazouiller; [person] babiller.

two /tu:/ ► 1112|, 812|, 713| **I** n deux m inv; **in ~s** par deux; **in ~s and threes** par deux ou trois, deux ou trois à la fois.
II det deux inv.
III pron deux inv; **I bought ~ of them** j'en ai acheté deux; **to break sth in ~** casser qch en deux.
IDIOMS **that makes ~ of us** nous sommes tous les deux dans le même cas; **to be in ~ minds about doing** hésiter à faire; **to put ~ and ~ together** faire le rapprochement; **there are ~ sides to every story** ~ autant d'hommes, autant d'avis.

two: **~-bit**○ adj PÉJ US [show, comedian] médiocre, à la gomme○; **~-edged** adj FIG à double tranchant; **~-faced** adj PÉJ hypocrite, fourbe.

twofold /'tu:fəʊld/ **I** adj double.
II adv doublement.

two: **~-party system** n POL système m bipartite; **~penny-halfpenny**○ adj GB PÉJ de rien du tout; **~-phase** adj ELEC diphasé; **~-piece** n (also **~-piece suit**) (woman's) tailleur m; (man's) costume m (deux-pièces); **~-pin** adj [plug, socket] à deux fiches; **~-ply** adj [wool] à deux fils; [wood] contreplaqué à double épaisseur; **~-seater** n AUT voiture f à deux places; AVIAT avion m à deux places; **~some** n (two people) couple m; **~-storey** adj à

deux étages; **~-tier** adj [bureaucracy] à deux niveaux or étages; PÉJ [society, health service etc] à deux vitesses.

two-time○ /'tu:taɪm/ **I** vtr être infidèle envers, tromper [partner].
II vi être infidèle.

two-tone adj (in hue) de deux tons; (in sound) à deux tons ou timbres.

two-way /,tu:'weɪ/ adj **1** [street] à double sens; [traffic] dans les deux sens; FIG [communication, exchange] bilatéral; **2** ELEC [switch] va-et-vient inv.

two: **~-way mirror** n glace f sans tain; **~-way radio** n émetteur-récepteur m; **~-wheeler**○ n (vehicle, bicycle) deux-roues m inv.

TX US POST abrév écrite = **Texas**.

tycoon /taɪ'ku:n/ n magnat m; **publishing ~** magnat de l'édition.

type /taɪp/ **I** n **1** (variety, kind) type m, genre m; **he's an army ~** il a le genre militaire; **you're not my ~** tu n'es pas mon genre; **they're our ~ of people** c'est le genre de personnes que nous aimons bien; **I'm not that ~**, **I don't go in for that ~ of thing** ce n'est pas mon genre; **he's one of those pretentious university ~s** c'est un de ces individus prétentieux de l'université; **I know his ~** PÉJ je connais les gens de son espèce; **you know the ~ of thing I mean** vous voyez à peu près ce que je veux dire; **he's reverted to ~** il est le naturel a repris le dessus; **to play ou be cast against ~** CIN, THEAT jouer à contre-emploi; **2** (in printing) caractères mpl; **printed in small/large ~** imprimé en petits/ gros caractères.
II vtr **1** taper (à la machine) [word, letter]; **a ~d letter** une lettre dactylographiée; **2** (classify) classifier [blood sample]; cataloguer [person] (**as** comme).
III vi taper (à la machine).

■ **type in**: **~ in** [sth], **~** [sth] **in** taper [word, character].

■ **type out**: **~ out** [sth], **~** [sth] **out** taper (à la machine) [letter].

■ **type over**: **~ over** [sth] (erase) effacer.

■ **type up**: taper, dactylographier FML.

type: **~cast** vtr (prét, pp **-cast**) THEAT, FIG cataloguer [person]; **~face** n police f (de caractères); **~script** n texte m dactylographié; **~set** vtr composer; **~setter** n typographe mf; **~setting** n composition f; **~writer** n machine f à écrire; **~written** adj tapé (à la machine), dactylographié FML.

typhoid /'taɪfɔɪd/ ► 1002| n (also **~ fever**) (fièvre f) typhoïde f.

typhoon /taɪ'fu:n/ n typhon m.

typical /'tɪpɪkl/ adj [case, example, day, village] typique; [generosity, compassion] caractéristique; **~ feature** caractéristique f; **it's ~ of him to be late** cela ne m'étonne pas de lui qu'il soit en retard; **~!** ça ne m'étonne pas!

typically /'tɪpɪklɪ/ adv [behave] (of person) comme à mon/ton etc habitude; **~ English** [place, behaviour] typiquement anglais; **she's ~ English** c'est l'Anglaise type.

typify /'tɪpɪfaɪ/ vtr [feature, behaviour] caractériser; [person, institution] être le type même de; **as typified by the EC** comme le représente la CE.

typing /'taɪpɪŋ/ **I** n **1** (skill) dactylographie f; **my ~ is slow** ma frappe est lente; **2** (typed material) **two pages of ~** deux pages dactylographiées.
II noun modifier [course] de dactylo; [error] de frappe; [paper] pour machine à écrire.

typing pool n **to work in the ~** travailler au service dactylo○.

typing speed n vitesse f de frappe.

typist /'taɪpɪst/ n dactylo mf.

typographic(al) /,taɪpə'ɡræfɪk(l)/ adj typographique.

typography /taɪ'pɒɡrəfɪ/ n typographie f.

tyrannic(al) /tɪ'rænɪk(l)/ adj tyrannique.

tyrannize /'tɪrənaɪz/ **I** vtr tyranniser.
II vi tyranniser; **to ~ over sb** tyranniser qn.

tyranny /'tɪrənɪ/ *n* tyrannie *f* (**over** sur).

tyrant /'taɪərənt/ *n* tyran *m*.

tyre GB, **tire** US /'taɪə(r)/ *n* pneu *m*; **spare ~** LIT pneu *m* de rechange; FIG (fat) bourrelet *m*.

tyre: **~ lever** *n* démonte-pneu *m*; **~ pressure** *n* pression *f* des pneus; **~ pressure gauge** *n* manomètre *m* (pour pneus).

tzar *n* = **tsar**.

Uu

u, U /juː/ *n* **1** (letter) u, U *m*; **2** GB CIN (*abrév* = **universal**) ~ tous publics.

U-bend *n* (in pipe) courbure *f* en U; (in road) virage *m* en épingle à cheveux.

ubiquitous /juːˈbɪkwɪtəs/ *adj* omniprésent.

udder /ˈʌdə(r)/ *n* pis *m*.

UFO *n* (*abrév* = **unidentified flying object**) ovni *m* *inv*.

Uganda /juːˈgændə/ **▶ 840** *pr n* Ouganda *m*.

Ugandan /juːˈgændən/ **▶ 1100** **I** *n* Ougandais/-e *m/f*. **II** *adj* ougandais/-e.

ugliness /ˈʌglɪnɪs/ *n* laideur *f*.

ugly /ˈʌglɪ/ *adj* **1** (hideous) [*person, appearance, furniture, building*] laid; [*sound*] désagréable; [*wound*] vilain (*before n*); **to be an ~ sight** être hideux/-euse à voir; **2** (vicious) [*situation, conflict*] dangereux/-euse; [*tactics, campaign*] bas/basse; **to be in an ~ mood** [*group, mob*] gronder; [*individual*] être d'une humeur massacrante○.

IDIOMS **an ~ customer**○ un sale type○; **as ~ as sin** laid comme un pou; **racism rears its ~ head** on voit surgir le spectre du racisme.

UK ▶ 840 **I** *pr n* (*abrév* = **United Kingdom**) Royaume-Uni *m*. **II** *noun modifier* [*citizen, passport*] britannique.

Ukraine /juːˈkreɪn/ **▶ 840** *pr n* **the ~** l'Ukraine *f*.

Ukrainian /juːˈkreɪnɪən/ **▶ 1100, 1038** **I** *n* **1** (person) Ukrainien/-ienne *m/f*; **2** (language) ukrainien *m*. **II** *adj* ukrainien/-ienne.

ulcer /ˈʌlsə(r)/ *n* ulcère *m*.

Ulster /ˈʌlstə(r)/ **I** *pr n* Ulster *m*, Irlande *f* du Nord. **II** *noun modifier* [*people, accent*] d'Irlande du Nord.

ulterior /ʌlˈtɪərɪə(r)/ *adj* **1** (hidden) [*motive, purpose*] inavoué; **without any ~ motive** sans arrière-pensée; **2** (subsequent) ultérieur.

ultimate /ˈʌltɪmət/ **I** *n* **the ~ in** le nec plus ultra de [*comfort, luxury*]. **II** *adj* **1** (result, destination] final; [*sacrifice*] ultime (*before n*); **~ power lies with the president** en dernier ressort c'est le président qui a le pouvoir de décision; **the ~ weapon** l'arme absolue; **2** (fundamental) [*question, truth*] fondamental.

ultimately /ˈʌltɪmətlɪ/ *adv* en fin de compte, au bout du compte.

ultimatum /ˌʌltɪˈmeɪtəm/ *n* (*pl* **~s** ou **-mata**) ultimatum *m*; **to issue an ~** adresser un ultimatum (**to** à); **cease-fire ~** ultimatum de cessez-le-feu.

ultraconservative /ˌʌltrəkənˈsɜːvətɪv/ *adj* ultra-conservateur/-trice.

ultramarine /ˌʌltrəməˈriːn/ *n, adj* outremer (*m*) (*inv*).

ultrasound /ˈʌltrəsaʊnd/ *n* ultrasons *mpl*.

ultrasound: **~ scan** *n* échographie *f*; **~ scanner** *n* échographe *m*.

ultraviolet /ˌʌltrəˈvaɪələt/ *adj* ultraviolet/-ette.

umber /ˈʌmbə(r)/ *n* ART terre *f* d'ombre.

umbilical /ʌmˈbɪlɪkl, ˌʌmbɪˈlaɪkl/ *adj* ombilical; **~ cord** cordon *m* ombilical.

umbrage /ˈʌmbrɪdʒ/ *n* **to take ~** prendre ombrage (**at** de).

umbrella /ʌmˈbrelə/ *n* parapluie *m*; **under the ~ of** FIG (protection) sous la protection de; (authority) sous l'égide de.

umbrella: **~ stand** *n* porte-parapluies *m* *inv*; **~**

term *n* terme *m* générique; **~ tree** *n* magnolia *m* parasol.

umpire /ˈʌmpaɪə(r)/ **I** *n* SPORT, FIG arbitre *m*. **II** *vtr* SPORT arbitrer. **III** *vi* SPORT être l'arbitre; **to ~ at a match** arbitrer un match.

umpteen○ /ˌʌmpˈtiːn/ *adj* des tas de○; **~ times** trente-six fois.

umpteenth○ /ˌʌmpˈtiːnθ/ *adj* énième.

UN *pr n* (*abrév* = **United Nations**) **the ~** l'ONU *f*.

unabashed /ˌʌnəˈbæʃt/ *adj* **he seemed quite ~** il ne semblait aucunement décontenancé.

unabated /ˌʌnəˈbeɪtɪd/ *adj* **to continue ~** [*fighting, storm*] continuer avec la même violence.

unable /ʌnˈeɪbl/ *adj* **to be ~ to do** (lacking means or opportunity) ne pas pouvoir faire; (lacking knowledge or skill) ne pas savoir faire; (incapable, not qualified) être incapable de faire.

unabridged /ˌʌnəˈbrɪdʒd/ *adj* intégral.

unacceptable /ˌʌnəkˈseptəbl/ *adj* [*proposal, suggestion*] inacceptable; [*behaviour, situation*] inadmissible.

unaccompanied /ˌʌnəˈkʌmpənɪd/ *adj* [*child, baggage*] non accompagné; [*man, woman*] seul; MUS sans accompagnement.

unaccountable /ˌʌnəˈkaʊntəbl/ *adj* [*phenomenon, feeling*] inexplicable.

unaccounted /ˌʌnəˈkaʊntɪd/ *adj* **to be ~ for** GEN être introuvable; **two of the crew are still ~ for** deux membres de l'équipage sont toujours portés disparus.

unaccustomed /ˌʌnəˈkʌstəmd/ *adj* [*luxury, speed, position*] inhabituel/-elle; **to be ~ to sth/to doing** ne pas avoir l'habitude de qch/de faire.

unacknowledged /ˌʌnəkˈnɒlɪdʒd/ *adj* [*genius, contribution*] non reconnu; **her letter remained ~** on n'a pas accusé réception de sa lettre.

unacquainted /ˌʌnəˈkweɪntɪd/ *adj* **to be ~ with sth/sb** ne pas connaître qch/qn; **to be ~ with the facts** ne pas être au courant des faits.

unadorned /ˌʌnəˈdɔːnd/ *adj* [*walls*] sans ornement; **the plain ~ facts** les faits tout simples.

unadulterated /ˌʌnəˈdʌltəreɪtɪd/ *adj* [*water*] pur; [*wine*] non frelaté; FIG [*pleasure, misery*] pur (*before n*); **~ nonsense** des bêtises pures et simples.

unadventurous /ˌʌnədˈventʃərəs/ *adj* [*meal*] pas très original; [*person, production, style*] qui manque d'audace.

unaffected /ˌʌnəˈfektɪd/ *adj* **1** (untouched) **to be ~** ne pas être affecté (**by** par); **2** (natural, spontaneous) tout simple.

unaffectedly /ˌʌnəˈfektɪdlɪ/ *adv* sans affectation.

unafraid /ˌʌnəˈfreɪd/ *adj* [*person*] sans peur.

unaided /ʌnˈeɪdɪd/ **I** *adj* **~ by sth** sans l'aide de qch. **II** *adv* [*stand, sit, walk*] sans aide extérieure.

unaltered /ʌnˈɔːltəd/ *adj* inchangé.

unambiguous /ˌʌnæmˈbɪgjʊəs/ *adj* sans équivoque.

unambiguously /ˌʌnæmˈbɪgjʊəslɪ/ *adv* [*define, deny*] sans équivoque; [*interpret*] sans ambiguïté.

unambitious /ˌʌnæmˈbɪʃəs/ *adj* [*person*] sans ambition; [*reform*] modeste; [*novel*] sans prétention.

unanimity /ˌjuːnəˈnɪmətɪ/ *n* unanimité *f* (**between, among** entre).

unanimous /juːˈnænɪməs/ *adj* unanime.

unanimously /juːˈnænɪməslɪ/ *adv* [*agree, condemn, approve*] unanimement; [*vote, acquit*] à l'unanimité.

unannounced /ˌʌnəˈnaʊnst/ *adv* [*arrive, call*] sans prévenir.

unanswerable /ʌnˈɑːnsərəbl, US ˌʌnˈæn-/ *adj* [*question*] à laquelle il n'y a pas de réponse possible; [*remark, case*] irréfutable.

unanswered /ʌnˈɑːnsəd, US ʌnˈæn-/ *adj* [*letter, question*] resté sans réponse.

unappealing /ˌʌnəˈpiːlɪŋ/ *adj* peu attrayant.

unappetizing /ʌnˈæpɪtaɪzɪŋ/ *adj* peu appétissant.

unappreciated /ˌʌnəˈpriːʃɪeɪtɪd/ *adj* [*work of art*] non reconnu; **to feel ~** se sentir sous-estimé.

unappreciative /ˌʌnəˈpriːʃətɪv/ *adj* [*person, audience*] ingrat.

unapproachable /ˌʌnəˈprəʊtʃəbl/ *adj* inaccessible.

unarmed /ʌnˈɑːmd/ *adj* [*person*] non armé; [*combat*] sans armes.

unashamedly /ˌʌnəˈʃeɪmɪdlɪ/ *adv* ouvertement.

unasked /ʌnˈɑːskt, US ʌnˈæskt/ *adv* [*come, attend*] sans être invité; **to do sth ~** faire qch spontanément.

unassailable /ˌʌnəˈseɪləbl/ *adj* GEN inattaquable; [*optimism, case*] à toute épreuve.

unassisted /ˌʌnəˈsɪstɪd/ *adv* sans assistance.

unassuming /ˌʌnəˈsjuːmɪŋ, US ˌʌnəˈsuː-/ *adj* modeste.

unattached /ˌʌnəˈtætʃt/ *adj* **1** [*part, element*] détaché, FIG [*organization*] indépendant; **2** (single) [*person*] célibataire.

unattainable /ˌʌnəˈteɪnəbl/ *adj* inaccessible.

unattended /ˌʌnəˈtendɪd/ *adj* [*vehicle, dog, child*] laissé sans surveillance.

unattractive /ˌʌnəˈtræktɪv/ *adj* [*furniture, characteristic, idea*] peu attrayant; [*person*] peu attirant; [*proposition*] peu intéressant (**to** pour).

unauthorized /ʌnˈɔːθəraɪzd/ *adj* GEN fait sans autorisation; [*visit*] interdit.

unavailable /ˌʌnəˈveɪləbl/ *adj* [*person*] qui n'est pas disponible; [*information*] qu'on ne peut pas obtenir; **to be ~ for comment** se refuser à tout commentaire.

unavailing /ˌʌnəˈveɪlɪŋ/ *adj* SOUT [*efforts*] vain.

unavoidable /ˌʌnəˈvɔɪdəbl/ *adj* inévitable.

unavoidably /ˌʌnəˈvɔɪdəblɪ/ *adv* **he was ~ detained** il n'a absolument pas pu se libérer.

unaware /ˌʌnəˈweə(r)/ *adj* **1** (not informed) **to be ~ of sth/that** ignorer qch/que; **2** (not conscious) **to be ~ of sth** ne pas être conscient de qch; **she was ~ of his presence** ne savait pas qu'il était là; **to be politically ~** ne pas être politisé.

unawares /ˌʌnəˈweəz/ *adv* **to catch** ou **take sb ~** prendre qn au dépourvu.

unbalanced /ʌnˈbælənst/ *adj* **1** [*person, mind*] instable; **2** (biased) [*reporting*] partial; **3** (uneven) [*diet, economy, load*] pas équilibré.

unbearable /ʌnˈbeərəbl/ *adj* insupportable.

unbearably /ʌnˈbeərəblɪ/ *adv* **1** [*hurt, tingle*] de manière insupportable; **2** (emphatic) [*hot, cynical, tedious*] incroyablement.

unbeatable /ʌnˈbiːtəbl/ *adj* imbattable; **it's ~ value** c'est un prix imbattable.

unbeaten /ʌnˈbiːtn/ *adj* [*player, team*] invaincu; [*score, record*] qui n'a pas été battu.

unbecoming /ˌʌnbɪˈkʌmɪŋ/ *adj* SOUT [*garment*] peu seyant; [*behaviour*] inconvenant.

unbeknown /ˌʌnbɪˈnəʊn/, **unbeknownst** /ˌʌnbɪˈnəʊnst/ *adv* **~ to sb** à l'insu de qn.

unbelievable /ˌʌnbɪˈliːvəbl/ *adj* incroyable.

unbeliever /ˌʌnbɪˈliːvə(r)/ *n* incroyant/-e *m/f*.

unbend /ʌnˈbend/ (*prét, pp* **-bent**) **I** *vtr* (straighten) détordre.
II *vi* devenir moins inflexible.

unbending /ʌnˈbendɪŋ/ *adj* inflexible.

unbias(s)ed /ʌnˈbaɪəst/ *adj* impartial.

unbidden /ʌnˈbɪdn/ *adv* LITTÉR **to do sth ~** faire qch sans en être prié.

unbind /ʌnˈbaɪnd/ *vtr* (*prét, pp* **-bound**) délier.

unbleached /ʌnˈbliːtʃt/ *adj* [*cloth*] écru; [*flour*] non blanchi.

unblock /ʌnˈblɒk/ *vtr* déboucher [*pipe, sink*].

unbolt /ʌnˈbəʊlt/ **I** *vtr* déverrouiller [*door*].
II unbolted *pp adj* **to be ~ed** ne pas être verrouillé.

unborn /ʌnˈbɔːn/ *adj* [*child*] à naître; FIG [*generation*] à venir; **her ~ child** l'enfant qu'elle porte/portait etc.

unbounded /ʌnˈbaʊndɪd/ *adj* [*joy*] sans bornes; [*love*] démesuré.

unbowed /ʌnˈbaʊd/ *adj* LITTÉR invaincu.

unbreakable /ʌnˈbreɪkəbl/ *adj* incassable.

unbridled /ʌnˈbraɪdld/ *adj* [*imagination*] débridé; [*optimism*] effréné.

unbroken /ʌnˈbrəʊkən/ *adj* **1** (uninterrupted) [*sequence, silence, view*] ininterrompu; [*curve*] parfait; **to descend in an ~ line from** descendre en ligne directe de; **2** (intact) [*pottery*] intact; **it's an ~ record** le record n'a pas été battu.

unbuckle /ʌnˈbʌkl/ *vtr* déboucler [*belt*]; défaire la boucle de [*shoe*].

unburden /ʌnˈbɜːdn/ *v refl* SOUT **to ~ oneself** confier (**to sb** à qn).

unbusinesslike /ʌnˈbɪznɪslaɪk/ *adj* [*person*] qui n'a pas le sens des affaires; [*method, conduct*] peu professionnel/-elle.

unbutton /ʌnˈbʌtn/ *vtr* déboutonner.

uncalled-for /ʌnˈkɔːldfɔː(r)/ *adj* [*remark*] déplacé.

uncannily /ʌnˈkænɪlɪ/ *adv* (very much) incroyablement; (surprisingly) étrangement.

uncanny /ʌnˈkænɪ/ *adj* **1** (strange) [*resemblance*] étrange; [*accuracy*] étonnant; **2** (frightening) troublant.

uncared-for /ʌnˈkeədfɔː(r)/ *adj* [*house*] mal entretenu; [*pet*] mal soigné; **an ~ child** un enfant dont on s'occupe mal.

uncaring /ʌnˈkeərɪŋ/ *adj* [*world*] indifférent.

unceasingly /ʌnˈsiːsɪŋlɪ/ *adv* sans cesse.

uncensored /ʌnˈsensəd/ *adj* [*film, book*] non censuré; FIG [*version*] intégral.

unceremonious /ˌʌnˌserɪˈməʊnɪəs/ *adj* [*departure, end*] précipité.

unceremoniously /ˌʌnˌserɪˈməʊnɪəslɪ/ *adv* [*dismiss*] sans cérémonie.

uncertain /ʌnˈsɜːtn/ **I** *adj* **1** (unsure) incertain; **to be ~ about** ne pas être certain de; **to be ~ whether to stay** ne pas savoir si l'on doit rester; **it is ~ whether** il n'est pas certain que (+ *subj*); **2** (changeable) [*temper*] instable; [*weather*] variable.
II in no ~ terms *adv phr* [*state*] en termes on ne peut plus clairs.

uncertainty /ʌnˈsɜːtntɪ/ *n* incertitude *f* (**about** en ce qui concerne).

uncertified /ʌnˈsɜːtɪfaɪd/ *adj* ADMIN [*document*] non certifié.

unchallenged /ˌʌnˈtʃælɪndʒd/ *adj* incontesté; **to go ~** [*statement, decision*] ne pas être récusé.

unchangeable /ʌnˈtʃeɪndʒəbl/ *adj* immuable.

unchanged /ʌnˈtʃeɪndʒd/ *adj* inchangé.

unchanging /ʌnˈtʃeɪndʒɪŋ/ *adj* immuable.

uncharacteristic /ˌʌnkærɪktəˈrɪstɪk/ *adj* [*generosity*] peu habituel/-elle; **it was ~ of him to...** ce n'est pas son genre de...

uncharitable /ʌnˈtʃærɪtəbl/ *adj* peu charitable (**to** de faire).

unchecked /ʌnˈtʃekt/ **I** *adj* **1** (uncontrolled) [*development, proliferation*] incontrôlé; **2** (unverified) non vérifié.
II *adv* [*develop, grow, spread*] de manière incontrôlée.

uncivil /ʌnˈsɪvɪl/ *adj* discourtois (**to** envers).

uncivilized /ʌnˈsɪvɪlaɪzd/ *adj* **1** (inhumane) [*treatment, conditions*] inhumain; **2** (uncouth, rude) grossier/-ière; **3** (barbarous) [*people, nation*] non civilisé.

unclaimed /ʌnˈkleɪmd/ *adj* [*lost property, reward*] non réclamé.

unclassified /ʌn'klæsɪfaɪd/ adj [document, information] non classifié; [road] non classé.

uncle /'ʌŋkl/ n oncle m.
IDIOMS Bob's your ~! GB c'est simple comme bonjour!; **to cry** ~ US demander grâce.

unclean /ʌn'kli:n/ adj 1 [water, beaches] sale; 2 RELIG impur.

unclear /ʌn'klɪə(r)/ adj 1 (après v) [motive, reason, circumstances] peu clair; [future] incertain; **it is** ~ **how/whether**... on ne sait pas très bien comment/ si...; **to be** ~ **about sth** [person] ne pas être sûr de qch; 2 (not comprehensible) [instructions, voice] pas clair; [answer] peu clair; [handwriting] difficile à lire.

uncleared /ʌn'klɪəd/ adj [cheque] non compensé; [goods] non dédouané.

unclench /ʌn'klentʃ/ vtr desserrer [fist, jaw].

unclog /ʌn'klɒg/ vtr (p prés etc **-gg-**) déboucher [pipe].

uncoil /ʌn'kɔɪl/ **I** vtr dérouler.
II vi [spring] se détendre; [rope, snake] se dérouler.

uncollected /ʌnkə'lektɪd/ adj [mail, luggage] non réclamé; [taxes] non perçu; [refuse] non ramassé.

uncomfortable /ʌn'kʌmftəbl, US -fərt-/ adj 1 [shoes, seat] inconfortable; [journey, heat] pénible; **you look** ~ **in that chair** tu n'as pas l'air à l'aise dans ce fauteuil; **the jacket feels** ~ la veste n'est pas confortable; 2 (emotionally) [feeling, silence, situation, reminder] pénible; **to be/to feel** ~ être/se sentir gêné; **to make sb (feel)** ~ mettre qn mal à l'aise; **to be** ~ **about** se sentir gêné par [rôle, decision, fact]; **I feel** ~ **talking about it** ça me gêne d'en parler; **to make life** ou **things** ~ **for sb** rendre la vie difficile à qn.

uncomfortably /ʌn'kʌmftəblɪ, US -fərt-/ adv 1 [seated] inconfortablement; [loud, bright] désagréablement; **it's** ~ **hot** il fait une chaleur pénible; 2 (awkwardly) [say, laugh] d'un air gêné; **to be** ~ **aware of sth** se rendre compte avec gêne de qch.

uncommon /ʌn'kɒmən/ adj rare; **it is not** ~ **to do** il n'est pas rare de faire.

uncommonly /ʌn'kɒmənlɪ/ adv (very) exceptionnellement; **not** ~ (often) assez souvent.

uncommunicative /ʌnkə'mju:nɪkətɪv/ adj peu communicatif/-ive; **to be** ~ **about sth** se montrer réservé sur qch.

uncomplaining /ʌnkəm'pleɪnɪŋ/ adj [patience, acceptance] résigné; [person] qui ne se plaint pas.

uncomplainingly /ʌnkəm'pleɪnɪŋlɪ/ adv sans se plaindre.

uncomplicated /ʌn'kɒmplɪkeɪtɪd/ adj [plot] pas compliqué; [meal] simple.

uncomplimentary /ʌnkɒmplɪ'mentrɪ, US -terɪ/ adj peu flatteur/-euse.

uncompromising /ʌn'kɒmprəmaɪzɪŋ/ adj [person, attitude] intransigeant; [standards] sans concession.

uncompromisingly /ʌn'kɒmprəmaɪzɪŋlɪ/ adv [reply, state] catégoriquement; [harsh] implacablement.

unconcealed /ʌnkən'si:ld/ adj non déguisé.

unconcerned /ʌnkən'sɜ:nd/ adj (uninterested) indifférent (**with** à); (not caring) insouciant; (untroubled) imperturbable.

unconditional /ʌnkən'dɪʃənl/ adj [obedience] inconditionnel/-elle; [offer, surrender] sans condition.

unconditionally /ʌnkən'dɪʃənlɪ/ adv [support, surrender] inconditionnellement; [promise, lend] sans condition.

unconfirmed /ʌnkən'fɜ:md/ adj non confirmé.

uncongenial /ʌnkən'dʒi:nɪəl/ adj [atmosphere, job] peu agréable; [person] peu sympathique.

unconnected /ʌnkə'nektɪd/ adj 1 GEN [incidents, facts] sans lien entre eux/elles; **to be** ~ **with** [event, fact] n'avoir aucun rapport avec; [person] n'avoir aucun lien avec; 2 ELEC, TELECOM pas branché.

unconscious /ʌn'kɒnʃəs/ **I** n the ~ l'inconscient m.
II adj 1 (insensible) sans connaissance; **to be** ~ faire perdre connaissance à qn; **to fall** ~ perdre connaissance; 2 (unaware) **to be** ~ **of sth/of doing**

ne pas être conscient de qch/de faire; 3 (unintentional) [bias, impulse, hostility] inconscient.

unconsciously /ʌn'kɒnʃəslɪ/ adv inconsciemment.

unconsciousness /ʌn'kɒnʃəsnɪs/ n 1 (comatose state) inconscience f; 2 (unawareness) inconscience f.

unconstitutional /ʌnkɒnstɪ'tju:ʃənl/ adj inconstitutionnel/-elle.

uncontested /ʌnkən'testɪd/ adj GEN incontesté; POL [seat] non disputé.

uncontrollable /ʌnkən'trəʊləbl/ adj GEN incontrôlable; [tears] qu'on ne peut retenir.

uncontrollably /ʌnkən'trəʊləblɪ/ adv [laugh, sob] sans pouvoir se contrôler; [increase, decline] irrésistiblement; **his hand shook** ~ sa main tremblait de manière incontrôlable.

uncontroversial /ʌnkɒntrə'vɜ:ʃl/ adj anodin.

unconventional /ʌnkən'venʃənl/ adj peu conventionnel/-elle.

unconvinced /ʌnkən'vɪnst/ adj pas convaincu; **to be** ~ **of sth** ne pas être convaincu de qch; **to be** ~ **that** ne pas être convaincu que.

unconvincing /ʌnkən'vɪnsɪŋ/ adj peu convaincant.

uncooked /ʌn'kʊkt/ adj non cuit.

uncooperative /ʌnkəʊ'ɒpərətɪv/ adj peu coopératif/-ive.

uncoordinated /ʌnkəʊ'ɔ:dɪneɪtɪd/ adj [effort, performance, service] désordonné; **to be** ~ [person] manquer de coordination.

uncork /ʌn'kɔ:k/ vtr déboucher [bottle, wine].

uncorroborated /ʌnkə'rɒbəreɪtɪd/ adj non corroboré; ~ **evidence** JUR preuve f par présomption.

uncountable /ʌn'kaʊntəbl/ adj LING indénombrable.

uncouple /ʌn'kʌpl/ vtr détacher [wagon]; découpler [locomotive].

uncouth /ʌn'ku:θ/ adj [person] grossier/-ière; [accent] peu raffiné.

uncover /ʌn'kʌvə(r)/ vtr 1 (expose) dévoiler [scandal]; 2 (discover) découvrir [evidence, treasure]; 3 (remove covering from) découvrir [body].

uncritical /ʌn'krɪtɪkl/ adj peu critique; **to be** ~ **of sb/sth** ne pas être critique envers qn/qch.

uncritically /ʌn'krɪtɪklɪ/ adv [accept, endorse] sans se poser de questions; [regard] sans faire preuve d'esprit critique.

uncross /ʌn'krɒs, US -'krɔ:s/ vtr décroiser [legs, arms].

unctuous /'ʌŋktjʊəs/ adj onctueux/-euse, mielleux/-euse.

uncultivated /ʌn'kʌltɪveɪtɪd/ adj (all contexts) inculte.

uncut /ʌn'kʌt/ adj 1 [branch, crops] non coupé; 2 [film, version] intégral; 3 [book] aux pages non coupées; [page] non coupé; 4 [gem] non taillé.

undamaged /ʌn'dæmɪdʒd/ adj [crops] non endommagé; [building, reputation] intact; **psychologically** ~ psychologiquement indemne.

undated /ʌn'deɪtɪd/ adj [letter, painting] non daté.

undaunted /ʌn'dɔ:ntɪd/ adj imperturbable; ~ **by criticism** nullement ébranlé par les critiques.

undecided /ʌndɪ'saɪdɪd/ adj [person] indécis; [outcome] incertain; **the jury is** ~ le jury n'a pas encore décidé.

undeclared /ʌndɪ'kleəd/ adj 1 (illegal) non déclaré; 2 (unspoken) inavoué.

undefended /ʌndɪ'fendɪd/ adj 1 [frontier, citizens] non défendu; [chess piece] non protégé; 2 JUR [case] non contesté.

undefined /ʌndɪ'faɪnd/ adj 1 [objective] non défini; [nature] indéterminé; [space] vague; 2 COMPUT indéfini.

undelivered /ʌndɪ'lɪvəd/ adj [mail] non distribué.

undemanding /ʌndɪ'mɑ:ndɪŋ, US -'mænd-/ adj [task] peu fatigant; [person] peu exigeant.

undemocratic /ʌndemə'krætɪk/ adj antidémocratique.

undemonstrative /ʌndɪ'mɒnstrətɪv/ adj peu démonstratif/-ive.

undeniable /ˌʌndɪˈnaɪəbl/ *adj* (irrefutable) indéniable; (clear) incontestable.

undeniably /ˌʌndɪˈnaɪəblɪ/ *adv* GEN incontestablement; [*superb, powerful, beautiful*] indiscutablement.

under /ˈʌndə(r)/

■ **Note** When *under* is used as a straightforward preposition in English it can almost always be translated by *sous* in French: *under the table* = sous la table; *under a sheet* = sous un drap; *under a heading* = sous un titre.
– *under* is often used before a noun in English to mean *subject to* or *affected by* (under control, under fire, under oath, under review etc). For translations, consult the appropriate noun entry (**control, fire, oath, review** etc).
– *under* is also often used as a prefix in combinations such as *undercook, underfunded, underprivileged* and *undergrowth, underpass*. These combinations are treated as headwords in the dictionary.
– For particular usages, see the entry below.

I *prep* **1** (physically beneath or below) sous; ~ **the bed** sous le lit; ~ **it** en dessous; **it's** ~ **there** c'est là-dessous; **to come out from** ~ **sth** sortir de dessous qch; **2** (less than) ~ **£10** moins de 10 livres sterling; **children** ~ **five** les enfants de moins de cinq ans or en dessous de cinq ans; **a number** ~ **ten** un nombre inférieur à dix; **temperatures** ~ **10°C** des températures inférieures à 10°C; **3** (according to) ~ **the law** selon la loi; **fined** ~ **a rule** condamné à une amende en vertu d'une règle; **4** (subordinate to) sous; **I have 50 people** ~ **me** j'ai 50 employés sous mes ordres; **5** (in classification) sous; **do I look for Le Corbusier** ~ **'le' or 'Corbusier'?** est-ce que je dois chercher Le Corbusier sous 'le' ou 'Corbusier'?
II *adv* **1** (physically beneath or below something) [*crawl, sit, hide*] en dessous; **to go** ~ [*diver, swimmer*] disparaître sous l'eau; **2** (less) moins; **£10 and** ~ 10 livres sterling et moins; **children of six and** ~ des enfants de six ans et moins; **to run five minutes** ~ [*event, programme*] durer cinq minutes de moins que prévu; **3** (anaesthetized) **to put sb** ~ endormir qn; **4** (subjugated) **to keep sb** ~ opprimer qn; **5** (below, later in text) **see** ~ voir ci-dessous.

underachieve /ˌʌndərəˈtʃiːv/ *vi* SCH ne pas obtenir les résultats dont on est capable.

underage /ˌʌndərˈeɪdʒ/ *adj* ~ **drinker** personne qui consomme de l'alcool sans avoir atteint l'âge légal; **to be** ~ être mineur/-e.

underarm /ˈʌndərɑːm/ *adj* [*deodorant*] pour les aisselles; [*hair*] des aisselles; [*service, throw*] à la cuillère.

undercarriage /ˈʌndəkærɪdʒ/ *n* AVIAT train *m* d'atterrissage.

undercharge /ˌʌndəˈtʃɑːdʒ/ **I** *vtr* faire porter un débit moindre à [*account*]; **he** ~**d me for the wine** il m'a fait payer le vin moins cher qu'il n'aurait dû.
II *vi* **he** ~**d for the wine** il a fait payer le vin moins cher qu'il n'aurait dû.

underclassman /ˌʌndəˈklæsmən/ *n* US SCH, UNIV étudiant m de première année.

underclothes /ˈʌndəkləʊðz/ *npl* sous-vêtements *mpl*.

undercoat /ˈʌndəkəʊt/ *n* **1** (of paint, varnish) couche *f* de fond; **2** US AUT peinture *f* antirouille pour châssis.

undercook /ˌʌndəˈkʊk/ *vtr* ne pas faire assez cuire; **the meat is** ~**ed** la viande n'est pas assez cuite.

undercover /ˌʌndəˈkʌvə(r)/ *adj* GEN clandestin; ~ **agent** agent *m* secret.

undercurrent /ˈʌndəkʌrənt/ *n* **1** (in water) GEN courant *m* profond; (in sea) courant *m* sous-marin; **2** FIG courant *m* sous-jacent.

undercut I /ˈʌndəkʌt/ *n* **1** GB CULIN filet *m*; **2** SPORT balle *f* coupée.
II /ˌʌndəˈkʌt/ *vtr* (*p prés* -**tt**-; *prét, pp* -**cut**) **1** COMM concurrencer [qn] en offrant des prix plus intéressants; concurrencer [*prices*]; **2** (cut away) miner [*cliff, bank*]; **3** FIG saper [*position, efforts*]; couler° [*person*]; **4** ECON réduire [*inflation*]; **5** SPORT couper.

underdeveloped /ˌʌndədɪˈveləpt/ *adj* [*country*] sous-développé; [*person, physique*] peu développé; PHOT pas assez développé.

underdog /ˈʌndədɒg, US -dɔːg/ *n* **1** (in society) opprimé/-e *m*/*f*; **2** (in game, contest) perdant/-e *m*/*f*.

underdone /ˌʌndəˈdʌn/ *adj* [*food*] pas assez cuit; [*steak*] GB saignant.

underemployed /ˌʌndərɪmˈplɔɪd/ *adj* [*person*] sous-employé; [*resources, equipment etc*] sous-exploité.

underequipped /ˌʌndərɪˈkwɪpt/ *adj* sous-équipé.

underestimate /ˌʌndərˈestɪmeɪt/ *vtr* sous-estimer.

underexpose /ˌʌndərɪkˈspəʊz/ *vtr* PHOT sous-exposer.

underfed /ˌʌndəˈfed/ *adj* sous-alimenté.

underfeed /ˌʌndəˈfiːd/ *vtr* (*prét, pp* -**fed**) sous-alimenter.

underfeeding /ˌʌndəˈfiːdɪŋ/ *n* sous-alimentation *f*.

underfloor /ˈʌndəflɔː(r)/ *adj* [*pipes, wiring*] (wooden floor) situé sous le plancher; (concrete floor) situé sous le sol; ~ **heating** chauffage par le sol.

underfoot /ˌʌndəˈfʊt/ *adv* sous les pieds; **the ground was wet** ~ le sol était humide; **to trample sb/sth** ~ LIT, FIG fouler qn/qch aux pieds.

underfunded /ˌʌndəˈfʌndɪd/ *adj* insuffisamment financé.

underfunding /ˌʌndəˈfʌndɪŋ/ *n* manque *m* de fonds.

undergo /ˌʌndəˈgəʊ/ *vtr* (*prét* -**went**; *pp* -**gone**) subir [*change, test, operation*]; suivre [*treatment, training*]; endurer [*hardship*]; **to** ~ **surgery** subir une intervention chirurgicale; **to be** ~**ing renovations** être en rénovation.

undergraduate /ˌʌndəˈgrædʒʊət/ *n* ~ étudiant/-e *m*/*f* (*de première, deuxième ou troisième année*).

underground I /ˈʌndəgraʊnd/ *n* **1** GB (subway) métro *m*; **on the** ~ dans le métro; **2** (secret movement) mouvement *m* clandestin; **3** ART, MUS, THEAT underground *m*.
II /ˈʌndəgraʊnd/ *noun modifier* GB [*network*] de métro; [*map, strike*] du métro.
III /ˈʌndəgraʊnd/ *adj* **1** (below ground) souterrain; **2** (secret) clandestin; **3** ART, MUS, THEAT [*art, film, movement*] underground *inv*.
IV /ˌʌndəˈgraʊnd/ *adv* **1** (below ground) sous terre; **2** (secretly) **to go** ~ passer dans la clandestinité.

undergrowth /ˈʌndəgrəʊθ/ *n* sous-bois *m*.

underhand /ˌʌndəˈhænd/ *adj* **1** (also US **underhanded**) PÉJ [*person, method*] sournois; **an** ~ **trick** un sale coup°; ~ **dealings** magouilles° *fpl*; **2** SPORT **to have an** ~ **serve** servir à la cuillère.

underlay /ˌʌndəˈleɪ/ **I** *prét* ▶ **underlie**.
II *vtr* (*prét, pp* -**laid**) **to be underlaid by** avoir une sous-couche de [*gravel, rock*].

underlie /ˌʌndəˈlaɪ/ *vtr* (*p prés* -**lying**; *prét* -**lay**; *pp* -**lain**) **1** [*rock*] être sous [*topsoil*]; **2** [*theory*] sous-tendre [*principle, work*].

underline /ˌʌndəˈlaɪn/ *vtr* LIT, FIG souligner.

underling /ˈʌndəlɪŋ/ *n* PÉJ subordonné/-e *m*/*f*.

underlying /ˌʌndəˈlaɪɪŋ/ **I** *p prés* ▶ **underlie**.
II *adj* [*claim*] prioritaire; [*problem*] sous-jacent.

undermanned /ˌʌndəˈmænd/ *adj* [*factory*] en sous-effectif *inv*.

undermentioned /ˌʌndəˈmenʃnd/ *adj* [*item, list*] ci-dessous; [*person*] nommé ci-dessous; [*name*] cité ci-dessous.

undermine /ˌʌndəˈmaɪn/ *vtr* **1** LIT saper [*cliff, foundations, road*]; **2** FIG (shake, subvert) saper [*authority, efforts*]; ébranler [*confidence, position, value*].

underneath /ˌʌndəˈniːθ/ **I** *n* dessous *m*.
II *adj* d'en dessous.
III *adv* LIT, FIG dessous, en dessous.
IV *prep* LIT, FIG sous, au-dessous de; **from** ~ **a pile of books** de dessous une pile de livres.

undernourished /ˌʌndəˈnʌrɪʃt/ *adj* sous-alimenté.

underpaid /ˌʌndəˈpeɪd/ *prét, pp* ▶ **underpay**.

underpants /ˈʌndəpænts/ *npl* slip *m*; **a pair of** ~ un slip.

underpass /ˈʌndəpɑːs, US -pæs/ *n* **1** (for traffic) voie *f* inférieure (*dans un échangeur*); **2** (for pedestrians) passage *m* souterrain.

underpay /ˌʌndə'peɪ/ *vtr* (*prét, pp* **-paid**) **1** (pay badly) sous-payer [*employee*]; **2** (pay too little) **I was underpaid this month** je n'ai pas eu mon salaire intégral ce mois-ci.

underpin /ˌʌndə'pɪn/ *vtr* (*p prés etc* **-nn-**) **1** CONSTR étayer [*wall*]; reprendre [qch] en sous-œuvre, étayer [*building*]; FIG (strengthen) être à la base de [*religion, society*]; étayer [*currency, power, theory*].

underplay /ˌʌndə'pleɪ/ *vtr* **1** GEN minimiser [*aspect, impact*]; **2** THEAT jouer [qch] de façon plate [*role*].

underpopulated /ˌʌndə'pɒpjʊleɪtɪd/ *adj* sous-peuplé.

underprivileged /ˌʌndə'prɪvəlɪdʒd/ *adj* [*area, background, person*] défavorisé.

underproduction /ˌʌndəprə'dʌkʃn/ *n* sous-production *f*.

underrate /ˌʌndə'reɪt/ *vtr* sous-estimer.

underripe /ˌʌndə'raɪp/ *adj* (fruit) pas mûr; (cheese) pas fait.

undersea /ˌʌndəsiː/ *adj* sous-marin.

underseal /ˈʌndəsiːl/ *n* AUT (peinture *f*) antirouille *m*.

under-secretary /ˌʌndə'sekrətrɪ, US -terɪ/ *n* (also **~ of state**) GB POL sous-secrétaire *mf* d'État.

undersell /ˌʌndə'sel/ (*prét, pp* **-sold**) **I** *vtr* **1** (undercut) vendre moins cher que [*competitor*]; **2** (sell discreetly) pratiquer une publicité trop discrète pour [*product*].
II *vi* vendre à bas prix.
III *v refl* **to ~ oneself** se dévaloriser.

undersexed /ˌʌndə'sekst/ *adj* **to be ~** avoir un faible appétit sexuel.

undershirt /ˈʌndəʃɜːt/ *n* US maillot *m* de corps.

undershoot /ˌʌndə'ʃuːt/ (*prét, pp* **-shot**) **I** *vtr* se poser avant [*runway*].
II *vi* [*aircraft*] atterrir trop court; [*pilot*] se présenter trop court.

undersigned /ˌʌndə'saɪnd/ *n* soussigné/-e *m/f*; **we, the ~** nous, soussignés.

undersized /ˌʌndə'saɪzd/ *adj* [*person*] chétif/-ive; [*portion, ration*] maigre (*before n*); [*animal, plant*] rachitique.

understaffed /ˌʌndə'stɑːft, US -'stæft/ *adj* **to be ~** manquer de personnel.

understand /ˌʌndə'stænd/ (*prét, pp* **-stood**) **I** *vtr* **1** (intellectually) comprendre; **is that understood?** c'est compris?; **to ~ that/how** comprendre que/comment; **I can't ~ why** je n'arrive pas à comprendre pourquoi; **to make oneself understood** se faire comprendre; **2** (emotionally) comprendre; **I don't ~ you** je ne te comprends pas; **to ~ sb doing** comprendre que qn fasse; **3** (interpret) comprendre; **as I ~ it** si je comprends bien; **I understood him to say** OU **as saying that...** j'ai compris qu'il disait que...; **4** (believe) **to ~ that** croire que; **it was understood that** on pensait que; **he was given to ~ that** on lui a donné à entendre que; **you won I ~** vous avez gagné si je comprends bien; **5** (accept mutually) **to be understood** être entendu; **I thought that was understood** je pensais que c'était entendu; **6** LING (imply) **to be understood** [*subject*] être sous-entendu.
II *vi* **1** (comprehend) comprendre (**about** à propos de); **2** (sympathize) comprendre; **I quite ~** je comprends tout à fait.

understandable /ˌʌndə'stændəbl/ *adj* compréhensible; **it's ~** ça se comprend, c'est compréhensible.

understandably /ˌʌndə'stændəblɪ/ *adv* naturellement.

understanding /ˌʌndə'stændɪŋ/ **I** *n* **1** (grasp of subject, issue) compréhension *f*; **to show an ~ of** faire preuve d'une bonne compréhension de; **2** (perception, interpretation) interprétation *f*; **our ~ was that** nous avions compris que; **3** (arrangement) entente *f* (**about** sur; **between** entre); **there is an ~ that** il est entendu que; **on that ~** sur cette base; **4** (sympathy) compréhension *f*; **5** (powers of reason) entendement *m*.
II *adj* [*tone*] bienveillant; [*person*] compréhensif/-ive.

understandingly /ˌʌndə'stændɪŋlɪ/ *adv* avec bienveillance.

understatement /ˈʌndəsteɪtmənt/ *n* **1** (remark) litote *f*, euphémisme *m*; **that's an ~!** c'est le moins qu'on puisse dire!; **2** ¢ (style) (of person) réserve *f*, sens *m* de la litote; **3** (subtlety) (of dress, decor) discrétion *f*.

understood /ˌʌndə'stʊd/ *prét, pp* ▶ **understand**.

understudy /ˈʌndəstʌdɪ/ *n* THEAT doublure *f* (**to** de).

undertake /ˌʌndə'teɪk/ *vtr* (*prét* **-took**; *pp* **-taken**) **1** (carry out) entreprendre [*search, study, trip*]; occuper [*function*]; se charger de [*mission, offensive*]; **2** (guarantee) **to ~ to do** s'engager à faire.

undertaker /ˈʌndəteɪkə(r)/ *n* **1** (person) entrepreneur *m* de pompes funèbres; **2** (company) entreprise *f* de pompes funèbres; **at the ~'s** aux pompes funèbres.

undertaking /ˌʌndə'teɪkɪŋ/ *n* **1** (venture) entreprise *f*; **2** (promise) garantie *f*; **to give sb an ~ that** promettre à qn que; **to give a written ~ to do** s'engager par écrit à faire; **3** (company) entreprise *f*; **4** ¢ (funeral business) pompes *fpl* funèbres.

under-the-counter *adj* [*goods, supply, trade*] illicite; [*payment*] sous le manteau.

undertone /ˈʌndətəʊn/ *n* **1** (low voice) voix *f* basse; **in an ~** à voix basse; **2** (undercurrent) **an ~ of jealousy** un relent de jalousie; **comic ~s** un côté comique; **3** (hint) nuance *f*.

undertow /ˈʌndətəʊ/ *n* **1** (of wave) reflux *m*; **2** (at sea) contre-courant *m*; **3** (influence) influence *f* sous-jacente.

undervalue /ˌʌndə'væljuː/ *vtr* **1** FIN sous-évaluer; **2** (not appreciate) sous-estimer [*person, quality*]; ne pas apprécier [qch] à sa juste valeur [*opinion, theory*].

undervoltage /ˈʌndəvəʊltɪdʒ/ *n* ELEC sous-tension *f*.

underwater /ˌʌndə'wɔːtə(r)/ **I** *adj* [*cable, exploration, test, world*] sous-marin; [*lighting*] sous l'eau; [*birth*] dans l'eau.
II *adv* sous l'eau.

underway /ˌʌndə'weɪ/ *adj* **to be ~** [*vehicle*] être en route; [*filming, talks*] être en cours; **to get ~** [*vehicle*] se mettre en route; [*preparation, season*] commencer; **to get sth ~** mettre qch en route.

underwear /ˈʌndəweə(r)/ *n* ¢ sous-vêtements *mpl*.

underweight /ˌʌndə'weɪt/ *adj* maigre; **this child is four kilos ~** il manque quatre kilos à cet enfant.

underwent /ˌʌndə'went/ *prét* ▶ **undergo**.

underwired /ˌʌndə'waɪəd/ *adj* [*bodice, bra*] à armature.

underworld /ˈʌndəwɜːld/ *n* **1** (criminal world) milieu *m*, pègre *f*; **the criminal ~** le milieu; **2** MYTHOL **the ~** les enfers *mpl*.

underwrite /ˌʌndə'raɪt/ *vtr* (*prét* **-wrote**; *pp* **-written**) **1** (in insurance) garantir, souscrire [*policy*]; souscrire [*risk*]; assurer [*property*]; **2** FIN financer [*project*]; prendre en charge [*expense, loss*]; **3** (approve) donner son accord à [*decision*]; soutenir [*proposal, theory*].

underwriter /ˈʌndəraɪtə(r)/ *n* **1** FIN (of share issue) soumissionnaire *m*; **2** (in insurance) assureur *m*, souscripteur *m*.

undeservedly /ˌʌndɪ'zɜːvɪdlɪ/ *adv* [*blame, punish*] injustement; [*praise, reward, win*] de façon imméritée.

undeserving /ˌʌndɪ'zɜːvɪŋ/ *adj* **~ of praise** indigne de louanges.

undesirable /ˌʌndɪ'zaɪərəbl/ **I** *n* indésirable *mf*.
II *adj* [*aspect, habit, result*] indésirable; [*influence*] néfaste; [*friend*] peu recommandable; **it is ~ to do it** n'est pas souhaitable de faire; **~ alien** JUR étranger/ -ère *m/f* indésirable.

undetected /ˌʌndɪ'tektɪd/ **I** *adj* [*intruder*] inaperçu; [*cancer*] non décelé; [*flaw, movement*] non détecté; [*crime*] non découvert.
II *adv* [*break in, listen*] sans être aperçu; **to go ~** [*person*] rester inaperçu; [*cancer*] rester non décelé; [*crime*] rester non découvert.

undetermined /ˌʌndɪ'tɜːmɪnd/ *adj* **1** (unknown) indéterminé; **2** (unresolved) [*problem*] indéterminé; [*outcome*] inconnu.

undeterred /ˌʌndɪˈtɜːd/ adj **to be ~ by sth/sb** ne pas se laisser démonter par qch/qn.

undeveloped /ˌʌndɪˈveləpt/ adj [person, fruit] chétif/-ive; [limb, organ] atrophié; [land] inexploité; [idea, theory] en état de germe; [country] sous-développé.

undid /ʌnˈdɪd/ prét ▶ undo.

undignified /ʌnˈdɪɡnɪfaɪd/ adj [behaviour, fate, person] indigne; [haste, language] choquant; [position] inélégant.

undiluted /ˌʌndaɪˈljuːtɪd/ adj [liquid, version] non dilué; [admiration] sans retenue; [hostility, passion] sans mélange; [Christianity, Marxism] à l'état pur.

undiminished /ˌʌndɪˈmɪnɪʃt/ adj GEN intact; [appeal] toujours aussi fort.

undimmed /ʌnˈdɪmd/ adj [beauty, memory] intact; [eyesight] parfait.

undiplomatic /ˌʌndɪpləˈmætɪk/ adj **he is ~** il manque de diplomatie; **it was ~ of you to say that** ce n'était pas diplomatique de votre part de dire cela.

undipped /ʌnˈdɪpt/ adj AUT **with ~ headlights** en pleins phares.

undisciplined /ʌnˈdɪsɪplɪnd/ adj indiscipliné.

undiscovered /ˌʌndɪsˈkʌvəd/ adj [secret] non révélé; [land] inexploré; [species] inconnu; [crime, document] non découvert; [talent] méconnu.

undiscriminating /ˌʌndɪˈskrɪmɪneɪtɪŋ/ adj sans discernement.

undisguised /ˌʌndɪsˈɡaɪzd/ adj [anger, curiosity] non déguisé (after n).

undisputed /ˌʌndɪˈspjuːtɪd/ adj [capital, champion, leader] incontesté; [fact, right] incontestable.

undistinguished /ˌʌndɪˈstɪŋɡwɪʃt/ adj [career, building] médiocre; [appearance, person] insignifiant.

undisturbed /ˌʌndɪˈstɜːbd/ adj [peaceful] [sleep, night] paisible, tranquille; **to work ~ by the noise** travailler sans être dérangé par le bruit.

undivided /ˌʌndɪˈvaɪdɪd/ adj [loyalty] entier/-ière; **to give sb one's ~ attention** accorder à qn toute son attention.

undo /ʌnˈduː/ vtr (3ᵉ pers sg prés **-does**; prét **-did**; pp **-done**) **1** (unfasten) défaire [fastening, lock]; ouvrir [zip, parcel]; **2** (cancel out) détruire [good, effort]; réparer [harm]; **3** COMPUT annuler.
IDIOMS **what's done cannot be undone** ce qui est fait est fait.

undone /ʌnˈdʌn/ **I** pp ▶ undo.
II adj **1** (not fastened) [parcel, button] défait; **to come ~** se défaire; **2** (not done) **to leave sth ~** ne pas faire qch.

undoubtedly /ʌnˈdaʊtɪdlɪ/ adv indubitablement.

undress /ʌnˈdres/ **I** vtr déshabiller; **to ~ oneself** se déshabiller.
II vi se déshabiller.

undressed /ʌnˈdrest/ adj **1** GEN déshabillé; **to get ~** se déshabiller; **2** CULIN sans assaisonnement; **3** CONSTR [metal, stone] à nu.

undrinkable /ʌnˈdrɪŋkəbl/ adj **1** (unpleasant) imbuvable; **2** (dangerous) non potable.

undue /ʌnˈdjuː, US -ˈduː/ adj excessif/-ive.

undulate /ˈʌndjʊleɪt, US -dʒʊ-/ **I** vi onduler.
II undulating pres p adj [movement] sinueux/-euse; [surface, landscape] onduleux/-euse; [plants] ondoyant.

unduly /ʌnˈdjuːlɪ, US -ˈduːlɪ/ adv [concerned, optimistic, surprised] excessivement; [flatter, worry] outre mesure.

undying /ʌnˈdaɪɪŋ/ adj [love] éternel/-elle.

unearned /ʌnˈɜːnd/ adj **1** GEN immérité; **2** FIN **~ income** rentes fpl.

unearthly /ʌnˈɜːθlɪ/ adj **1** [apparition, light, sight] surnaturel/-elle; [cry, silence] étrange; [beauty] immatériel/-ielle; **2** (unreasonable) **at an ~ hour** à une heure indue.

uneasily /ʌnˈiːzɪlɪ/ adv **1** (anxiously) avec inquiétude; **2** (uncomfortably) avec gêne; **3** (with difficulty) avec difficulté.

uneasiness /ʌnˈiːzɪnɪs/ n **1** (worry) appréhension f (about au sujet de); **2** (dissatisfaction) malaise m.

uneasy /ʌnˈiːzɪ/ adj **1** (worried) [person] inquiet/-iète (about, at au sujet de); [conscience] pas tranquille; **I had an ~ feeling that** j'avais le sentiment désagréable que; **2** (precarious) [compromise] difficile; [alliance, peace] boiteux/-euse; [silence] gêné; **3** (agitated) [sleep] agité; **4** (ill at ease) mal à l'aise.

uneconomical /ˌʌniːkəˈnɒmɪkl, -ˌekə-/ adj **1** (wasteful) pas économique; **2** (not profitable) pas rentable.

uneducated /ʌnˈedʒʊkeɪtɪd/ adj **1** [person] sans instruction; **2** PÉJ [person, speech] inculte; [accent, tastes] commun.

unemotional /ˌʌnɪˈməʊʃnl/ adj [person, approach] impassible; [reunion] froid; [account] qui n'appelle pas aux sentiments.

unemployed /ˌʌnɪmˈplɔɪd/ **I** n the ~ (+ v pl) les chômeurs mpl.
II adj **1** (out of work) au chômage, sans emploi; **~ people** chômeurs mpl; **2** FIN [capital] inutilisé.

unemployment /ˌʌnɪmˈplɔɪmənt/ n chômage m; **with ~ at 20%** avec un chômage de 20%.

unemployment **~ benefit** GB, **~ compensation** US allocations fpl de chômage; **~ figures** npl chiffres mpl du chômage.

unending /ʌnˈendɪŋ/ adj sans fin.

unenterprising /ʌnˈentəpraɪzɪŋ/ adj [person, organization, behaviour] sans initiative; [decision, policy] timide.

unenthusiastic /ˌʌnɪnˌθjuːzɪˈæstɪk, US -ˌθuːz-/ adj peu enthousiaste (about au sujet de).

unenviable /ʌnˈenvɪəbl/ adj peu enviable.

unequal /ʌnˈiːkwəl/ adj **1** (not equal) [amounts, contest, pay] inégal; **2** (inadequate) **to be ~ to** ne pas être à la hauteur de [task].

unequalled, **unequaled** US /ʌnˈiːkwəld/ adj [achievement, quality, record] inégalé; [person] incomparable (as en tant que).

unequivocal /ˌʌnɪˈkwɪvəkl/ adj [person, declaration] explicite; [attitude, answer, pleasure, support] sans équivoque.

unerring /ʌnˈɜːrɪŋ/ adj infaillible.

Unesco, **UNESCO** /juːˈneskəʊ/ pr n (abrév = **United Nations Educational, Scientific and Cultural Organization**) UNESCO f.

unethical /ʌnˈeθɪkl/ adj **1** GEN, COMM contraire à la morale (to do de faire); **2** MED contraire à la déontologie (to do de faire).

uneven /ʌnˈiːvn/ adj **1** (variable) [colouring, hem, results, rhythm, teeth] irrégulier/-ière; [contest, performance, surface] inégal; [voice] tremblant; **2** SPORT **~ bars** barres fpl asymétriques.

uneventful /ˌʌnɪˈventfl/ adj [day, occasion, life, career] ordinaire; [journey, period] sans histoires; [place] où il ne se passe rien.

unexciting /ˌʌnɪkˈsaɪtɪŋ/ adj sans intérêt.

unexpected /ˌʌnɪkˈspektɪd/ **I** n the ~ l'imprévu m.
II adj [arrival, danger, event, success] imprévu; [ally, gift, outcome, announcement] inattendu; [death, illness] inopiné.

unexpectedly /ˌʌnɪkˈspektɪdlɪ/ adv [happen] à l'improviste; [large, small, fast] étonnamment.

unexplored /ˌʌnɪkˈsplɔːd/ adj inexploré.

unexposed /ˌʌnɪkˈspəʊzd/ adj PHOT vierge.

unfailing /ʌnˈfeɪlɪŋ/ adj [support] fidèle; [kindness, optimism] à toute épreuve; [efforts] constant; [source] intarissable.

unfair /ʌnˈfeə(r)/ adj [person, action, decision, advantage] injuste (to, on envers; to do de faire); [play, tactics] irrégulier/-ière; [trading] frauduleux/-euse; [competition] déloyal.

unfair dismissal n JUR licenciement m abusif.

unfairly /ʌnˈfeəlɪ/ adv [treat] injustement; [play] irrégulièrement; [critical] injustement; **to be ~ dismissed** JUR faire l'objet d'un licenciement abusif.

unfairness /ʌnˈfeənɪs/ n injustice f.

unfaithful /ʌnˈfeɪθfl/ adj [*partner*] infidèle (**to** à).

unfaithfulness /ʌnˈfeɪθflnɪs/ n infidélité f.

unfaltering /ʌnˈfɔːltərɪŋ/ adj [*step, voice*] assuré; [*devotion, loyalty*] à toute épreuve.

unfamiliar /ˌʌnfəˈmɪlɪə(r)/ adj **1** (strange) [*face, name, place*] pas familier/-ière (**to** à); [*appearance, concept, feeling, situation*] inhabituel/-elle (**to** à); [*artist, subject*] mal connu; **2 to be ~ with sth** mal connaître qch.

unfamiliarity /ˌʌnfəmɪlɪˈærətɪ/ n **1** (strangeness) caractère m insolite; **2 his ~ with sth** sa mauvaise connaissance de qch.

unfashionable /ʌnˈfæʃənəbl/ adj qui n'est pas à la mode.

unfasten /ʌnˈfɑːsn/ vtr défaire [*clothing, button*]; ouvrir [*bag, zip*].

unfathomable /ʌnˈfæðəməbl/ adj LITTÉR insondable LITER.

unfavourable /ʌnˈfeɪvərəbl/ adj défavorable (**for sth** à qch; **to** à).

unfeeling /ʌnˈfiːlɪŋ/ adj [*person*] insensible (**towards** envers); [*remark*] dépourvu de tact; [*attitude, behaviour*] froid.

unfettered /ʌnˈfetəd/ adj [*liberty, right, competition, market*] sans entraves; [*emotion, expression, power*] sans retenue.

unfinished /ʌnˈfɪnɪʃt/ adj [*work, product*] inachevé; [*matter*] en cours; **we have some ~ business** nous avons des choses à régler.

unfit /ʌnˈfɪt/ adj **1** (unhealthy) (ill) malade; (out of condition) **I'm ~** physiquement, je ne suis pas en forme; **2** (sub-standard) [*housing*] inadéquat; [*pitch, road*] impraticable (**for** à); **~ for human habitation/consumption** impropre à l'habitation/la consommation humaine; **3** (unsuitable) [*parent*] inapte; **~ for work** inapte au travail; **~ to run the country** inapte à gouverner le pays; **4** JUR incapable; **to be ~ to give evidence** être inapte à témoigner.

unflagging /ʌnˈflægɪŋ/ adj [*energy*] infatigable; [*interest*] inlassable.

unflappable○ /ʌnˈflæpəbl/ adj imperturbable.

unflattering /ʌnˈflætərɪŋ/ adj [*clothes, portrait*] peu flatteur/-euse; **to be ~ to sb** [*clothes, hairstyle*] ne pas avantager qn; [*portrait, description*] ne pas flatter qn.

unflatteringly /ʌnˈflætərɪŋlɪ/ adv d'une manière peu flatteuse.

unflinching /ʌnˈflɪntʃɪŋ/ adj **1** [*stare*] impassible; [*courage*] à toute épreuve; [*commitment*] inébranlable; **2** [*account*] impitoyable.

unflinchingly /ʌnˈflɪntʃɪŋlɪ/ adv inébranlablement.

unfold /ʌnˈfəʊld/ I vtr **1** (open) déplier [*paper*]; déployer [*wings*]; décroiser [*arms*]; **2** FIG dévoiler [*plan*].
II vi **1** [*deckchair, map*] se déplier; [*flower, leaf*] s'ouvrir; **2** FIG [*scene*] se dérouler; [*mystery*] se dévoiler.

unforeseeable /ˌʌnfɔːˈsiːəbl/ adj imprévisible.

unforeseen /ˌʌnfɔːˈsiːn/ adj imprévu.

unforgettable /ˌʌnfəˈgetəbl/ adj inoubliable.

unforgivable /ˌʌnfəˈgɪvəbl/ adj impardonnable.

unforgivably /ˌʌnfəˈgɪvəblɪ/ adv **rude/biased** d'une grossièreté/d'un parti pris impardonnable.

unforgiving /ˌʌnfəˈgɪvɪŋ/ adj impitoyable.

unformed /ʌnˈfɔːmd/ adj [*idea, belief*] informe; [*personality*] pas encore formé.

unforthcoming /ˌʌnfɔːˈθkʌmɪŋ/ adj réservé (**about** au sujet de).

unfortunate /ʌnˈfɔːtʃənət/ adj **1** (pitiable) malheureux/-euse; **2** (regrettable) [*incident, choice*] malencontreux/-euse; [*remark*] fâcheux/-euse; **3** (unlucky) malchanceux/-euse; **to be ~ enough to do** avoir la malchance de faire.

unfortunately /ʌnˈfɔːtʃənətlɪ/ adv [*end*] fâcheusement; [*worded*] malencontreusement; **~, she...** malheureusement, elle...

unfounded /ʌnˈfaʊndɪd/ adj sans fondement.

unfreeze /ʌnˈfriːz/ (prét **-froze**; pp **-frozen**) vtr **1**

faire dégeler [*pipe*]; **2** FIN libérer [*prices*]; débloquer [*assets*]; **3** COMPUT libérer.

unfriendly /ʌnˈfrendlɪ/ adj [*person, attitude*] peu amical, inamical; [*reception*] hostile; [*place, climate*] inhospitalier/-ière; [*remark*] malveillant; [*product*] nocif/-ive.

unfroze /ʌnˈfrəʊz/ prét ▶ **unfreeze**.

unfrozen /ʌnˈfrəʊzn/ pp ▶ **unfreeze**.

unfulfilled /ˌʌnfʊlˈfɪld/ adj [*ambition*] non réalisé; [*desire, need*] inassouvi; [*promise*] non tenu; [*condition*] non rempli; [*prophecy*] inaccompli; **to feel ~** se sentir insatisfait.

unfurnished /ʌnˈfɜːnɪʃt/ adj [*accommodation*] non meublé.

ungainly /ʌnˈgeɪnlɪ/ adj gauche, maladroit.

ungenerous /ʌnˈdʒenərəs/ adj **1** (mean) peu généreux/-euse (**to** envers); **2** (unsympathetic) dur (**towards** envers); **that was ~ of you** ce n'était pas très charitable de ta part.

ungentlemanly /ʌnˈdʒentlmənlɪ/ adj discourtois (**of** de la part de).

ungodly /ʌnˈgɒdlɪ/ adj GEN impie; **at some ~ hour** à une heure indue.

ungovernable /ʌnˈgʌvənəbl/ adj **1** [*country, people*] ingouvernable; **2** [*desire, anger*] indomptable.

ungracious /ʌnˈgreɪʃəs/ adj désobligeant (**of** de la part de).

ungrammatical /ˌʌngrəˈmætɪkl/ adj incorrect.

ungrateful /ʌnˈgreɪtfl/ adj ingrat (**of** de la part de; **towards** envers).

ungrudging /ʌnˈgrʌdʒɪŋ/ adj [*support*] inconditionnel/-elle; [*praise*] sincère.

unguarded /ʌnˈgɑːdɪd/ adj **1** (unprotected) sans surveillance; **2** (careless) [*remark, criticism*] irréfléchi.

unhampered /ʌnˈhæmpəd/ adj **~ by** sans être encombré par [*luggage*]; sans être entravé par [*red tape*].

unhappily /ʌnˈhæpɪlɪ/ adv **1** (miserably) d'un air malheureux; **~ married** malheureux en mariage; **2** (unfortunately) malheureusement; **3** (inappropriately) malencontreusement.

unhappiness /ʌnˈhæpɪnɪs/ n **1** (misery) tristesse f; **2** (dissatisfaction) mécontentement m (**about, with** au sujet de).

unhappy /ʌnˈhæpɪ/ adj **1** (miserable) [*person, childhood*] malheureux/-euse; [*face, occasion*] triste; **2** (dissatisfied) mécontent; **to be ~ about** ou **with sth** ne pas être satisfait de qch; **3** (concerned) inquiet/-iète (**about** à propos de); **to be ~ about doing** ne pas aimer faire; **to be ~ at the idea that** être contrarié par l'idée que; **4** (unfortunate) [*situation, choice*] malheureux/-euse.

unharmed /ʌnˈhɑːmd/ adj [*person*] indemne; [*object*] intact.

unhealthy /ʌnˈhelθɪ/ adj **1** MED, FIG [*person, cough*] maladif/-ive; [*economy, diet*] malsain; [*conditions*] insalubre; **2** (unwholesome) malsain.

unheard-of /ʌnˈhɜːdɒv/ adj **1** (shocking) inouï; **2** (previously unknown) [*levels, price*] record inv; [*actor, brand*] inconnu; **previously ~** inconnu jusqu'alors.

unheated /ʌnˈhiːtɪd/ adj non chauffé.

unheeded /ʌnˈhiːdɪd/ adj **to go ~** [*warning, plea*] rester vain.

unhelpful /ʌnˈhelpfl/ adj [*employee*] peu serviable; [*witness*] peu coopératif/-ive; [*remark*] qui n'apporte rien d'utile; [*attitude*] peu obligeante.

unhesitating /ʌnˈhezɪteɪtɪŋ/ adj spontané.

unhide /ʌnˈhaɪd/ vtr (prét **-hid**; pp **-hidden**) COMPUT afficher.

unhindered /ʌnˈhɪndəd/ adj [*access*] libre; [*freedom*] total; **~ by** sans être entravé par [*rules*]; sans être encombré par [*luggage*].

unhinge /ʌnˈhɪndʒ/ vtr (p prés **-hingeing**) **1** LIT enlever [*qch*] de ses gonds [*door*]; **2**○ FIG déstabiliser [*person, mind*].

unholy /ʌnˈhəʊlɪ/ adj **1** (shocking) [*alliance, pact*] contre nature; **2** (horrendous) épouvantable; **3** (profane) impie.

unhook /ʌnˈhʊk/ *vtr* dégrafer [*skirt*]; décrocher [*picture*] (**from** de).

unhopeful /ʌnˈhəʊpfl/ *adj* [*person*] pessimiste; [*situation*] guère encourageant; [*outlook, start*] guère prometteur/-euse.

unhurried /ʌnˈhʌrɪd/ *adj* [*person*] posé; [*pace, meal*] tranquille.

unhurt /ʌnˈhɜːt/ *adj* indemne.

unhygienic /ˌʌnhaɪˈdʒiːnɪk/ *adj* [*conditions*] insalubre; [*way, method*] peu hygiénique.

UNICEF /ˈjuːnɪsef/ *n* (*abrév* = **United Nations Children's Fund**) UNICEF *m*, FISE *m*.

unicorn /ˈjuːnɪkɔːn/ *n* licorne *f*.

unidentified /ˌʌnaɪˈdentɪfaɪd/ *adj* non identifié.

unification /ˌjuːnɪfɪˈkeɪʃn/ *n* unification *f* (**of** de).

uniform /ˈjuːnɪfɔːm/ **I** *n* uniforme *m*; **out of** ~ MIL en civil.
II *adj* [*temperature*] constant; [*shape, size, colour*] identique.

uniformity /juːnɪˈfɔːmɪtɪ/ *n* uniformité *f*.

unify /ˈjuːnɪfaɪ/ *vtr* unifier.

unilateral /juːnɪˈlætrəl/ *adj* unilatéral.

unimaginable /ˌʌnɪˈmædʒɪnəbl/ *adj* inimaginable.

unimaginably /ˌʌnɪˈmædʒɪnəblɪ/ *adv* incroyablement.

unimaginative /ˌʌnɪˈmædʒɪnətɪv/ *adj* [*person*] sans imagination; [*style, production*] sans originalité; **to be** ~ manquer d'imagination.

unimaginatively /ˌʌnɪˈmædʒɪnətɪvlɪ/ *adv* [*talk, write, describe*] platement; [*captain, manage*] sans brio.

unimpaired /ˌʌnɪmˈpeəd/ *adj* intact.

unimpeachable /ˌʌnɪmˈpiːtʃəbl/ *adj* irréprochable; JUR non récusable.

unimpeded /ˌʌnɪmˈpiːdɪd/ *adj* [*access, influx*] libre; **to be** ~ **by sth** ne pas être entravé par qch.

unimportant /ˌʌnɪmˈpɔːtnt/ *adj* sans importance (**for, to** pour).

unimpressed /ˌʌnɪmˈprest/ *adj* (by person, performance) peu enthousiaste; **to be** ~ **by** être peu impressionné par [*person, performance*]; n'être guère convaincu par [*argument*].

uninformative /ˌʌnɪnˈfɔːmətɪv/ *adj* **to be** ~ ne rien apporter.

uninformed /ˌʌnɪnˈfɔːmd/ *adj* [*person*] sous-informé (**about** quant à); **the** ~ **reader** le non-spécialiste.

uninhabitable /ˌʌnɪnˈhæbɪtəbl/ *adj* inhabitable.

uninhibited /ˌʌnɪnˈhɪbɪtɪd/ *adj* [*attitude*] direct; [*person*] sans complexes (**about** en ce qui concerne); [*performance, remarks*] sans retenue; **to be** ~ **about doing** n'avoir aucun complexe à faire.

uninitiated /ˌʌnɪˈnɪʃɪeɪtɪd/ **I** *n* **the** ~ (+ *v pl*) le profane (+ *v sg*).
II *adj* [*person*] non initié (**into** dans).

uninjured /ʌnˈɪndʒəd/ *adj* indemne; **to escape** ~ sortir indemne.

uninspired /ˌʌnɪnˈspaɪəd/ *adj* [*approach, team, times*] terne; [*performance*] honnête; [*budget, syllabus*] sans imagination; **to be** ~ [*person*] manquer d'inspiration; [*strategy*] manquer d'imagination.

uninsured /ˌʌnɪnˈʃɔːd, US ˌʌnɪnˈʃʊəd/ *adj* non assuré.

unintelligible /ˌʌnɪnˈtelɪdʒəbl/ *adj* incompréhensible (**to** pour).

unintended /ˌʌnɪnˈtendɪd/ *adj* [*slur, irony*] involontaire; [*consequence*] non voulu; **to be** ~ ne pas être voulu.

unintentional /ˌʌnɪnˈtenʃənl/ *adj* involontaire.

uninterested /ʌnˈɪntrəstɪd/ *adj* indifférent (**in** à).

uninteresting /ʌnˈɪntrəstɪŋ/ *adj* sans intérêt.

uninvited /ˌʌnɪnˈvaɪtɪd/ *adj* **1** (unsolicited) [*attentions*] non sollicité; [*remark*] gratuit; **2** (without invitation) ~ **guest** intrus/-e *m/f*.

uninviting /ˌʌnɪnˈvaɪtɪŋ/ *adj* [*place, prospect*] rébarbatif/-ive; [*food*] peu appétissant.

union /ˈjuːnɪən/ **I** *n* **1** (also **trade** ~) IND syndicat *m*; **to join a** ~ se syndiquer; **2** POL union *f*; **3** (uniting) union *f*; (marriage) union *f*, mariage *m*; **4** (also **student** ~) GB UNIV (building) maison *f* des étudiants; (organization) syndicat *m* d'étudiants.
II Union *pr n* US POL États-Unis *mpl*; US HIST Union *f*.
III *noun modifier* IND [*card, movement*] syndical.

union: ~ **bashing** *n* IND attaques *fpl* contre le pouvoir des syndicats; ~ **dues** *npl* cotisation *f* syndicale.

Unionist /ˈjuːnɪənɪst/ *n, adj* POL unioniste (*mf*).

unionize /ˈjuːnɪənaɪz/ *vtr* IND syndicaliser.

union: **Union Jack** *n* drapeau *m* du Royaume-Uni; ~ **member** *n* IND syndiqué/-e *m/f*; **Union of Soviet Socialist Republics, USSR** *pr n* HIST Union *f* des Républiques Socialistes Soviétiques, URSS *f*; ~ **shop** *n* US IND *établissement dont tous les employés doivent être ou devenir membres d'un même syndicat*.

unique /juːˈniːk/ *adj* **1** (sole) unique (**in that** en ce que); **to be** ~ **in doing** être seul à faire; **to be** ~ **to** être particulier à; **2** (remarkable) [*individual, skill*] unique, exceptionnel/-elle.

unisex /ˈjuːnɪseks/ *adj* unisexe.

unison /ˈjuːnɪsn, ˈjuːnɪzn/ *n* **in** ~ [*say, recite, sing*] à l'unisson.

unit /ˈjuːnɪt/ *n* **1** (whole) unité *f*; **2** (group with specific function) GEN groupe *m*; (in army, police) unité *f*; **3** (building, department) GEN, MED service *m*; IND unité *f*; **casualty** ~ service des urgences; **production** ~ unité de production; **4** (in measurements) ALSO MATH unité *f*; **monetary** ~ unité monétaire; **5** (part of machine) unité *f*; **6** (piece of furniture) élément *m*; **7** UNIV unité *f* de valeur; **8** SCH (in textbook) unité *f*; **9** US (apartment) appartement *m*.

unitary /ˈjuːnɪtrɪ, US -terɪ/ *adj* unitaire.

unite /juːˈnaɪt/ **I** *vtr* unir (**with** à).
II *vi* s'unir (**with** à).

united /juːˈnaɪtɪd/ *adj* [*group, front*] uni (**in** dans); [*effort*] conjoint.
IDIOMS ~ **we stand, divided we fall** PROV l'union fait la force PROV.

united: **United Arab Emirates** ▶ 840] *pr npl* Émirats *mpl* arabes unis; **United Kingdom** (**of Great Britain and Northern Ireland**) ▶ 840] *pr n* Royaume-Uni *m* (de Grande-Bretagne et d'Irlande du Nord); **United Nations** (**Organization**) *n* (Organisation *f* des) Nations *fpl* unies; **United States** (**of America**) ▶ 840] *pr n* États-Unis *mpl* (d'Amérique).

unit: ~ **furniture** *n* mobilier *m* en éléments; ~ **trust** *n* GB FIN société *f* d'investissement à capital variable, SICAV *f*.

unity /ˈjuːnɪtɪ/ *n* unité *f*.

Univ *abrév écrite* = **University**.

universal /juːnɪˈvɜːsl/ **I** *n* PHILOS universel *m*.
II universals *npl* PHILOS universaux *mpl*.
III *adj* **1** (general) [*acclaim, reaction*] général; [*education, health care*] pour tous; [*principle, truth, message*] universel/-elle; [*use*] généralisé; **the suggestion gained** ~ **acceptance** la suggestion a été acceptée par tout le monde; **2** LING universel/-elle.

universally /juːnɪˈvɜːsəlɪ/ *adv* [*believed, criticized*] par tous, universellement; [*known, loved*] de tous.

universal time *n* temps *m* universel.

universe /ˈjuːnɪvɜːs/ *n* univers *m*.

university /juːnɪˈvɜːsətɪ/ **I** *n* université *f*.
II *noun modifier* [*degree, town*] universitaire; [*place*] à l'université; ~ **entrance** entrée *f* à l'université.

unjust /ʌnˈdʒʌst/ *adj* injuste (**to** envers).

unjustifiably /ʌnˈdʒʌstɪfaɪəblɪ/ *adv* [*claim, condemn*] sans justification; [*act*] d'une manière injustifiable.

unjustified /ʌnˈdʒʌstɪfaɪd/ *adj* injustifié.

unkempt /ʌnˈkempt/ *adj* [*person, appearance*] négligé; [*hair*] ébouriffé; [*beard*] peu soigné.

unkind /ʌnˈkaɪnd/ *adj* [*person, thought, act*] pas très gentil/-ille; [*remark*] hostile; [*climate, environment*] rude; [*fate*] LITTÉR cruel/-elle; **it was a bit ~** ce n'était pas très gentil; **it was ~ of her to do** ce n'était pas très gentil de sa part de faire; **to be ~ to sb** (by deed) ne pas être gentil avec qn; (verbally) être méchant avec qn.

unkindness /ʌn'kaɪndnɪs/ n (of person) dureté f; LITTÉR (of fate) cruauté f.

unknown /ʌn'nəʊn/ **I** n **1** (unfamiliar place or thing) inconnu m; **2** (person not famous) inconnu/-e m/f; **3** MATH inconnue f.
II adj inconnu; **the place was ~ to me** l'endroit m'était inconnu; **~ to me, they had already left** à mon insu, ils étaient déjà partis; **it is not ~ for sb to do** il arrive à qn de faire; **~ quantity** MATH inconnue f; **she is an ~ quantity** FIG (her abilities are untested) on ne sait pas ce qu'elle vaut; (not much is known about her) on sait peu de choses sur elle; **Mr X, address ~** M. X, adresse inconnue.

Unknown Soldier, Unknown Warrior n Soldat m inconnu.

unladylike /ʌn'leɪdɪlaɪk/ adj inélégant.

unlatch /ʌn'lætʃ/ vtr soulever le loquet de; **to leave the door ~ed** laisser la porte sans (mettre le) loquet.

unlawful /ʌn'lɔːfl/ adj [*activity, possession*] illégal; [*killing*] indiscriminé; [*detention*] arbitraire; [*arrest*] (without cause) arbitraire; (with incorrect procedure) sommaire; **~ assembly** JUR rassemblement m de nature à troubler l'ordre public.

unlawfully /ʌn'lɔːfəlɪ/ adv **1** JUR de façon criminelle; **~ detained** détenu arbitrairement; **2** GEN illégalement.

unleaded /ʌn'ledɪd/ adj [*petrol*] sans plomb.

unleash /ʌn'liːʃ/ vtr **1** (release) lâcher [*animal*]; libérer [*aggression*]; déchaîner [*violence, passion*]; déverser [*torrent*]; **2** (trigger) déclencher [*wave, war*]; **3** (launch) lancer [*force, attack*] (**against** contre).

unless /ən'les/ conj **1** (except if) à moins que (+ subj), à moins de (+ infinitive), sauf si (+ indic); **he won't come ~ you invite him** il ne viendra pas à moins que tu (ne) l'invites ou sauf si tu l'invites; **she can't take the job ~ she finds a nanny** elle ne peut pas accepter le poste à moins de trouver une nourrice; **~ I get my passport back, I can't leave the country** si je ne récupère pas mon passeport je ne pourrai pas quitter le pays; **it won't work ~ you plug it in!** ça ne marchera pas si tu ne le branches pas!; **~ I'm very much mistaken** si je ne m'abuse FML ou à moins que je (ne) me trompe; **~ otherwise agreed** sauf accord contraire; **2** (except when) sauf quand.

unlicensed /ʌn'laɪsnst/ adj [*activity*] non autorisé; [*vehicle*] non immatriculé; [*transmitter*] sans licence.

unlike /ʌn'laɪk/ **I** prep **1** (in contrast to) contrairement à, à la différence de; **2** (different from) différent de; **they are quite ~ each other** ils ne se ressemblent pas du tout; **3** (uncharacteristic of) **it's ~ her (to be so rude)** ça ne lui ressemble pas ou ce n'est pas du tout son genre (d'être aussi impolie).
II adj (jamais épith) **the two brothers are ~ in every way** les deux frères ne se ressemblent pas du tout.

unlikely /ʌn'laɪklɪ/ adj **1** (unexpected) improbable, peu probable; **it is ~ that** il est peu probable que (+ subj); **they are ~ to succeed** il est peu probable qu'ils réussissent; **2** (strange) [*partner, choice, situation*] inattendu; **3** (probably untrue) [*story*] invraisemblable; [*excuse*] peu probable.

unlimited /ʌn'lɪmɪtɪd/ adj illimité.

unlined /ʌn'laɪnd/ adj **1** [*garment, curtain*] sans doublure; **2** [*paper*] non réglé; **3** [*face*] sans rides.

unlisted /ʌn'lɪstɪd/ adj **1** GEN [*campsite, hotel*] non homologué; **2** FIN [*account*] ne figurant pas sur les registres; [*company, share*] non coté; **3** TELECOM **her number is ~** elle n'est pas dans l'annuaire; **4** CONSTR, JUR [*building*] non classé.

unlit /ʌn'lɪt/ adj **1** [*room, street*] non éclairé; **to be ~** ne pas être éclairé; **2** [*cigarette, fire*] non allumé.

unload /ʌn'ləʊd/ **I** vtr **1** décharger [*goods, vessel*]; **2** TECH décharger [*gun, camera*]; **3** COMM déverser

[*stockpile, goods*] (**on**(**to**) sur); **4** FIG **to ~ one's problems** s'épancher (**on**(**to**) auprès de).
II vi [*truck, ship*] décharger.

unloading /ʌn'ləʊdɪŋ/ n déchargement m.

unlock /ʌn'lɒk/ vtr (with key) ouvrir; **to be ~ed** ne pas être fermé à clé.

unlovable /ʌn'lʌvəbl/ adj rebutant.

unloved /ʌn'lʌvd/ adj **to feel ~** [*person*] se sentir délaissé.

unloving /ʌn'lʌvɪŋ/ adj [*person, behaviour*] peu affectueux/-euse.

unluckily /ʌn'lʌkɪlɪ/ adv malheureusement (**for** pour).

unlucky /ʌn'lʌkɪ/ adj **1** (unfortunate) [*person*] malchanceux/-euse; [*coincidence, event*] malencontreux/-euse; [*day*] de malchance; **to be ~ enough to do** avoir la malchance de faire; **you were ~ not to get the job** c'est pure malchance que tu n'aies pas obtenu le poste; **he is ~ in love** il n'a jamais de chance en amour; **2** (causing bad luck) néfaste, maléfique; **it's ~ to walk under a ladder** ça porte malheur de marcher sous une échelle.

unmade /ʌn'meɪd/ adj [*bed*] défait; [*road*] non goudronné.

unmanageable /ʌn'mænɪdʒəbl/ adj [*child, animal*] farouche; [*prison, system*] ingérable; [*hair*] rebelle; [*size, number*] démesuré.

unmanly /ʌn'mænlɪ/ adj pusillanime.

unmanned /ʌn'mænd/ adj [*flight, rocket*] non habité; [*train*] automatique; **to leave the desk ~** laisser le bureau sans personne.

unmarked /ʌn'mɑːkt/ adj **1** (not labelled) [*container*] sans étiquette; [*police car*] banalisé; **2** (unblemished) [*skin*] sans marques; **3** LING non marqué; **4** SPORT démarqué.

unmarketable /ʌn'mɑːkɪtəbl/ adj non commercialisable.

unmarried /ʌn'mærɪd/ adj célibataire.

unmask /ʌn'mɑːsk, US -'mæsk/ vtr LIT, FIG démasquer.

unmentionable /ʌn'menʃənəbl/ adj **1** (improper to mention) [*activity*] inracontable; [*subject*] tabou; **2** (unspeakable) [*suffering*] indescriptible.

unmistakable /ˌʌnmɪ'steɪkəbl/ adj **1** (recognizable) caractéristique (**of** de); **2** (unambiguous) sans ambiguïté; **3** (marked) net/nette.

unmistakably /ˌʌnmɪ'steɪkəblɪ/ adv [*smell, hear*] distinctement; [*his, hers*] indubitablement.

unmitigated /ʌn'mɪtɪgeɪtɪd/ adj [*disaster*] complet/-ète; [*cruelty*] non tempéré; [*terror, nonsense*] absolu; [*liar*] fini.

unmotivated /ʌn'məʊtɪveɪtɪd/ adj **1** (lacking motive) [*crime, act*] gratuit; **2** (lacking motivation) [*person*] non motivé.

unmoved /ʌn'muːvd/ adj **1** (unperturbed) indifférent (**by** à); **2** (not moved emotionally) insensible (**by** à).

unmusical /ʌn'mjuːzɪkl/ adj [*sound*] discordant; [*person*] peu musicien/-ienne.

unnamed /ʌn'neɪmd/ adj **1** (name not divulged) [*company, source*] dont le nom n'a pas été divulgué; **2** (without name) [*club, virus*] **as yet ~** encore à la recherche d'un nom.

unnatural /ʌn'nætʃrəl/ adj **1** (odd) anormal; **it is ~ that** ce n'est pas normal que (+ subj); **2** (affected) [*style, laugh*] affecté; **3** (unusual) [*silence, colour*] insolite; **4** (unhealthy) [*interest*] malsain.

unnecessary /ʌn'nesəsrɪ, US -serɪ/ adj **1** (not needed) inutile; **it is ~ to do** il est inutile de faire; **it is ~ for you to do** il est inutile que tu fasses; **2** (uncalled for) déplacé.

unnerving /ʌn'nɜːvɪŋ/ adj déroutant.

unnoticed /ʌn'nəʊtɪst/ adj inaperçu.

UNO /'juːnəʊ/ n (abrév = **United Nations Organization**) ONU f.

unobjectionable /ˌʌnəb'dʒekʃənəbl/ adj inoffensif/-ive.

unobservant /ˌʌnəb'zɜːvənt/ adj peu perspicace.

unobserved /ˌʌnəb'zɜːvd/ adj inaperçu.

unobstructed /ˌʌnəb'strʌktɪd/ adj [view, exit] dégagé.

unobtainable /ˌʌnəb'teɪnəbl/ adj 1 COMM [supplies] impossible à se procurer; 2 TELECOM [number] impossible à obtenir.

unobtrusive /ˌʌnəb'truːsɪv/ adj [person] effacé/-ète; [site, object, noise] discret/-ète.

unoccupied /ʌn'ɒkjʊpaɪd/ adj 1 [house, block, shop] inoccupé; [seat] libre; 2 MIL [territory] libre.

unofficial /ˌʌnə'fɪʃl/ adj [figure] officieux/-ieuse; [candidate] indépendant; [biography] non autorisé; [strike] sauvage.

unofficially /ˌʌnə'fɪʃəlɪ/ adv [tell, estimate] officieusement.

unopened /ʌn'əʊpənd/ adj [bottle, packet] non entamé; [package] non ouvert.

unorganized /ʌn'ɔːɡənaɪzd/ adj 1 [labour, worker] non syndiqué; 2 [event] mal organisé; [group] qui ne sait pas s'organiser.

unoriginal /ˌʌnə'rɪdʒənl/ adj [idea, plot, style] sans originalité; **to be ~** manquer d'originalité.

unorthodox /ʌn'ɔːθədɒks/ adj (unconventional) peu orthodoxe.

unpack /ʌn'pæk/ vtr défaire [suitcase]; déballer [belongings].

unpacking /ʌn'pækɪŋ/ n déballage m.

unpaid /ʌn'peɪd/ adj [bill, tax] impayé; [debt] non acquitté; [work, volunteer] non rémunéré; **~ leave** congé m sans solde.

unpalatable /ʌn'pælətəbl/ adj 1 FIG [truth, statistic] inconfortable; [advice] dur à avaler; 2 [food] qui n'a pas bon goût.

unparalleled /ʌn'pærəleld/ adj 1 (unequalled) [strength, luxury] sans égal; [success] hors pair; 2 (unprecedented) sans précédent.

unpardonable /ʌn'pɑːdənəbl/ adj impardonnable.

unpasteurized /ʌn'pɑːstʃəraɪzd/ adj [milk] cru; [cheese] au lait cru.

unperturbed /ˌʌnpə'tɜːbd/ adj imperturbable.

unpick /ʌn'pɪk/ vtr 1 LIT (undo) défaire; 2 démêler [truth] (from de).

unplaced /ʌn'pleɪst/ adj [competitor] non classé; [horse] non placé.

unplanned /ʌn'plænd/ adj [stoppage, increase] imprévu; [pregnancy, baby] non prévu.

unpleasant /ʌn'pleznt/ adj désagréable.

unpleasantness /ʌn'plezntnɪs/ n 1 (of odour, experience, remark) caractère m désagréable; 2 (bad feeling) dissensions fpl (between entre).

unplug /ʌn'plʌɡ/ vtr (p prés etc **-gg-**) débrancher [appliance]; déboucher [sink].

unpolished /ʌn'pɒlɪʃt/ adj 1 LIT [floor] non ciré; [silver] non astiqué; [gem] non poli; 2 FIG [person] gauche; [manners] fruste; [form] ébauché.

unpolluted /ˌʌnpə'luːtɪd/ adj [water] non pollué; [mind] non contaminé.

unpopular /ʌn'pɒpjʊlə(r)/ adj impopulaire (**with** auprès de); **to be ~ with sb** être mal en cours auprès de qn.

unprecedented /ʌn'presɪdentɪd/ adj sans précédent.

unpredictable /ˌʌnprɪ'dɪktəbl/ adj [event] imprévisible; [weather] incertain; **he's ~** on ne sait jamais à quoi s'attendre avec lui.

unprejudiced /ʌn'predʒʊdɪst/ adj [person] sans préjugés; [opinion, judgment] impartial.

unpremeditated /ˌʌnpriː'medɪteɪtɪd/ adj non prémédité.

unprepared /ˌʌnprɪ'peəd/ adj 1 (not ready) [person] pas préparé (**for** pour); **to be ~ to do** ne pas être disposé à faire; **to catch sb ~** prendre qn au dépourvu; 2 [speech] improvisé; [translation] non préparé.

unprepossessing /ˌʌnˌpriːpə'zesɪŋ/ adj peu avenant.

unpretentious /ˌʌnprɪ'tenʃəs/ adj sans prétention.

unprincipled /ʌn'prɪnsəpld/ adj peu scrupuleux/-euse.

unprivileged /ʌn'prɪvɪlɪdʒd/ adj défavorisé.

unprofessional /ˌʌnprə'feʃənəl/ adj peu professionnel/-elle.

unprofitable /ʌn'prɒfɪtəbl/ adj 1 FIN [company, venture] non rentable; 2 FIG [investigation, discussion] improductif/-ive.

unprompted /ʌn'prɒmptɪd/ adj non sollicité.

unpronounceable /ˌʌnprə'naʊnsəbl/ adj imprononçable.

unprotected /ˌʌnprə'tektɪd/ adj 1 (unsafe) [person, area] sans protection (**from** contre); 2 (bare) [wood, metal] sans revêtement.

unprovoked /ˌʌnprə'vəʊkt/ adj [attack, aggression] délibéré; **the attack was ~** l'attaque n'avait pas été provoquée.

unpublished /ʌn'pʌblɪʃt/ adj non publié.

unpunished /ʌn'pʌnɪʃt/ adj [crime, person] impuni; **to go ~** [crime] rester impuni.

unqualified /ʌn'kwɒlɪfaɪd/ adj 1 (without qualifications) non qualifié; **to be ~** ne pas être qualifié (**for** pour; **to do** pour faire); 2 (total) [support, respect] inconditionnel/-elle; [ceasefire] sans condition; [success] grand.

unquenchable /ʌn'kwentʃəbl/ adj [thirst, fire] inextinguible.

unquestionable /ʌn'kwestʃənəbl/ adj incontestable.

unquestioning /ʌn'kwestʃənɪŋ/ adj inconditionnel/-elle.

unquote /ʌn'kwəʊt/ adv fin de citation.

unravel /ʌn'rævl/ **I** vtr (p prés etc **-ll-** GB, **-l-** US) défaire [knitting]; démêler [thread, mystery]; dénouer [intrigue].
II vi (p prés etc **-ll-** GB, **-l-** US) [knitting] se défaire; [mystery, thread] se démêler; [plot] se dénouer.

unreadable /ʌn'riːdəbl/ adj [book, writing] illisible.

unreal /ʌn'rɪəl/ adj 1 (not real) [situation, conversation] irréel/-éelle; **it seemed a bit ~ to me** j'avais un peu l'impression de rêver; 2° PÉJ (unbelievable) incroyable; 3° (amazingly good) incroyable.

unrealistic /ˌʌnrɪə'lɪstɪk/ adj [expectation, aim] irréaliste; [character, presentation] peu réaliste; [person] qui manque de réalisme.

unrealizable /ʌn'rɪəlaɪzəbl/ adj irréalisable.

unrealized /ʌn'rɪəlaɪzd/ adj [ambition, potential] non réalisé; **to be** ou **remain ~** ne pas être réalisé.

unreasonable /ʌn'riːznəbl/ adj 1 (not rational) [views, behaviour, expectation] irréaliste; **it's not ~** ce n'est pas déraisonnable; 2 (excessive) [price] excessif/-ive; [demand] irréaliste; **at an ~ hour** à une heure indue.

unreasonably /ʌn'riːznəblɪ/ adv [behave] de façon peu raisonnable; **~ high rents** des loyers excessifs; **not ~** à juste titre.

unreasoning /ʌn'riːzənɪŋ/ adj [person, response] irrationnel/-elle.

unreceptive /ˌʌnrɪ'septɪv/ adj peu réceptif/-ive (**to** à).

unrecognizable /ʌn'rekəɡnaɪzəbl/ adj méconnaissable.

unrecognized /ʌn'rekəɡnaɪzd/ adj 1 (unacknowledged) méconnu (**by** de); **to go ~** rester méconnu; 2 POL [regime, government] non reconnu; 3 **he crossed the city ~** il a traversé la ville sans être reconnu.

unreconstructed /ˌʌnriːkən'strʌktɪd/ adj (all contexts) irréductible.

unrecorded /ˌʌnrɪ'kɔːdɪd/ adj **to go ~** ne pas être répertorié.

unrefined /ˌʌnrɪ'faɪnd/ adj 1 [flour, sugar] non raffiné; [oil] brut, non raffiné; 2 [person, manners, style] peu raffiné.

unreflecting /ˌʌnrɪ'flektɪŋ/ adj irréfléchi.

unregistered /ʌn'redʒɪstəd/ adj [claim, firm, animal] non enregistré; [birth] non déclaré; [letter] non recommandé; [vehicle] non immatriculé; **to go ~** passer inaperçu.

unrehearsed /ˌʌnrɪ'hɜːst/ adj [response, action, speech] impromptu; [play] sans répétitions.

unrelated /ˌʌnrɪˈleɪtɪd/ *adj* **1** (not logically connected) sans rapport (**to** avec); **his success is not ~ to the fact that he has money** son succès n'est pas sans rapport avec sa fortune; **2** (as family) **to be ~** ne pas avoir de lien de parenté.

unrelenting /ˌʌnrɪˈlentɪŋ/ *adj* [*heat, stare, person*] implacable; [*pursuit, zeal, position*] acharné.

unreliability /ˌʌnrɪˌlaɪəˈbɪlətɪ/ *n* (of person) manque *m* de sérieux; (of machine, method, technique) manque *m* de fiabilité.

unreliable /ˌʌnrɪˈlaɪəbl/ *adj* [*evidence*] douteux/-euse; [*method, employee*] peu sûr; [*equipment*] peu fiable; **she's very ~** on ne peut pas compter sur elle.

unrelieved /ˌʌnrɪˈliːvd/ *adj* [*substance, colour*] uniforme; [*darkness, gloom, anxiety*] permanent; [*boredom*] mortel/-elle.

unremarkable /ˌʌnrɪˈmɑːkəbl/ *adj* quelconque.

unremarked /ˌʌnrɪˈmɑːkt/ *adj* **to go** ou **pass ~** passer inaperçu.

unremitting /ˌʌnrɪˈmɪtɪŋ/ *adj* [*boredom, flow*] incessant; [*hostility*] implacable; [*pressure, effort*] continu; [*struggle*] sans relâche.

unremittingly /ˌʌnrɪˈmɪtɪŋlɪ/ *adv* inlassablement.

unrepeatable /ˌʌnrɪˈpiːtəbl/ *adj* **1** (unique) [*bargain, sight*] unique en son genre; [*offer*] exceptionnel/-elle; **2** (vulgar) **his comment was ~** son commentaire était du genre à ne pas répéter.

unrepentant /ˌʌnrɪˈpentənt/ *adj* impénitent.

unreported /ˌʌnrɪˈpɔːtɪd/ *adj* [*incident, attack*] non déclaré.

unrepresentative /ˌʌnreprɪˈzentətɪv/ *adj* non représentatif/-ive.

unrequited /ˌʌnrɪˈkwaɪtɪd/ *adj* [*love*] sans retour.

unreserved /ˌʌnrɪˈzɜːvd/ *adj* **1** (free) [*seat*] non réservé; **2** (wholehearted) [*support, welcome*] sans réserve.

unresisting /ˌʌnrɪˈzɪstɪŋ/ *adj* sans résistance.

unresolved /ˌʌnrɪˈzɒlvd/ *adj* irrésolu.

unresponsive /ˌʌnrɪˈspɒnsɪv/ *adj* peu réceptif/-ive.

unrest /ʌnˈrest/ *n* ¢ **1** (dissatisfaction) malaise *m*; **2** (agitation) troubles *mpl*.

unrestrained /ˌʌnrɪˈstreɪnd/ *adj* [*growth*] effréné; [*emotion*] non contenu; [*freedom*] sans limites.

unrestricted /ˌʌnrɪˈstrɪktɪd/ *adj* [*access*] libre (*before n*); [*power*] illimité; [*testing, disposal*] incontrôlé; [*warfare*] à outrance; [*roadway*] dégagé.

unrewarding /ˌʌnrɪˈwɔːdɪŋ/ *adj* (unfulfilling) peu gratifiant; (thankless) ingrat.

unripe /ʌnˈraɪp/ *adj* [*fruit*] pas mûr; [*wheat*] en herbe.

unrivalled /ʌnˈraɪvld/ *adj* sans égal.

unroll /ʌnˈrəʊl/ *vtr* dérouler.

unromantic /ˌʌnrəˈmæntɪk/ *adj* peu romantique; **to be ~** manquer de romantisme.

unruffled /ʌnˈrʌfld/ *adj* **1** (calm) imperturbable; **to be ~** ne pas être perturbé (**by** par); **2** (smooth) [*water, hair*] lisse.

unruly /ʌnˈruːlɪ/ *adj* [*behaviour, hair*] indiscipliné.

unsafe /ʌnˈseɪf/ *adj* **1** [*environment*] malsain; [*drinking water*] non potable; [*goods*] dangereux/-euse; [*working conditions*] risqué; **the car is ~ to drive** il est dangereux de conduire cette voiture; **the building was declared ~** l'édifice a été déclaré dangereux; **2** (threatened) **to feel ~** ne pas se sentir en sécurité; **3** JUR [*conviction, verdict*] douteux/-euse.

unsaid /ʌnˈsed/ *adj* **to leave sth ~** passer qch sous silence.

unsalaried /ʌnˈsælərɪd/ *adj* non rémunéré.

unsalted /ʌnˈsɔːltɪd/ *adj* non salé.

unsatisfactory /ˌʌnsætɪsˈfæktərɪ/ *adj* insatisfaisant.

unsatisfied /ʌnˈsætɪsfaɪd/ *adj* [*person*] insatisfait; [*need*] inassouvi; **she remains ~** elle n'est pas toujours pas satisfaite (**with** de).

unsatisfying /ʌnˈsætɪsfaɪŋ/ *adj* peu satisfaisant.

unsavoury GB, **unsavory** US /ʌnˈseɪvərɪ/ *adj* [*business, individual*] louche, répugnant; [*object, smell*] peu appétissant.

unscathed /ʌnˈskeɪðd/ *adj* (all contexts) indemne.

unscented /ʌnˈsentɪd/ *adj* non parfumé.

unscheduled /ʌnˈʃedjuːld, US ʌnˈskedʒʊld/ *adj* [*appearance, speech*] surprise (*after n*); [*flight*] supplémentaire; [*stop*] qui n'a pas été prévu.

unscientific /ˌʌnsaɪənˈtɪfɪk/ *adj* [*approach*] non scientifique; **to be ~** [*method, theory*] ne pas être scientifique; [*person*] ne pas avoir l'esprit scientifique.

unscramble /ʌnˈskræmbl/ *vtr* déchiffrer [*code, words*]; remettre de l'ordre dans [*ideas, thoughts*].

unscrew /ʌnˈskruː/ *vtr* dévisser.

unscrupulous /ʌnˈskruːpjʊləs/ *adj* [*person*] sans scrupules; [*tactic*] peu scrupuleux/-euse; **she is completely ~** elle n'a aucun scrupule.

unsealed /ʌnˈsiːld/ *adj* [*envelope*] décacheté.

unseasonable /ʌnˈsiːznəbl/ *adj* [*food, clothing*] hors de saison.

unseasoned /ʌnˈsiːznd/ *adj* **1** [*food*] non assaisonné; **2** [*wood*] vert.

unseat /ʌnˈsiːt/ *vtr* **1** (unsaddle) désarçonner [*rider*]; **2** POL **the MP was ~ed** le député a perdu son siège.

unseeded /ʌnˈsiːdɪd/ *adj* SPORT non classé.

unseemly /ʌnˈsiːmlɪ/ *adj* SOUT inconvenant FML.

unseen /ʌnˈsiːn/ **I** *n* GB SCH **a French ~** une version française non préparée.
II *adj* **1** (invisible) [*figure, hands*] invisible; **2** SCH non préparé.
III *adv* [*escape, slip away*] sans être vu.

unselfconscious /ˌʌnselfˈkɒnʃəs/ *adj* (natural, spontaneous) naturel/-elle; (uninhibited) sans complexes.

unselfish /ʌnˈselfɪʃ/ *adj* [*person*] qui pense aux autres; [*act*] désintéressé.

unselfishness /ʌnˈselfɪʃnɪs/ *n* désintéressement *m*.

unsentimental /ˌʌnsentɪˈmentl/ *adj* [*speech, account, film, novel*] qui ne donne pas dans la sensiblerie; [*person*] qui ne fait pas de sentiment.

unsettled /ʌnˈsetld/ *adj* **1** [*weather, economic climate*] instable; **2** (not paid) [*account*] impayé; **3** (disrupted) [*schedule*] perturbé.

unsettling /ʌnˈsetlɪŋ/ *adj* [*question, experience*] troublant; [*work of art*] dérangeant; **psychologically ~** traumatisant.

unshak(e)able /ʌnˈʃeɪkəbl/ *adj* inébranlable.

unshaken /ʌnˈʃeɪkən/ *adj* [*person*] imperturbable (**by** devant); [*belief, spirit*] inébranlable.

unshaven /ʌnˈʃeɪvn/ *adj* pas rasé.

unshockable /ʌnˈʃɒkəbl/ *adj* **she's ~** rien ne peut la choquer.

unshrinkable /ʌnˈʃrɪŋkəbl/ *adj* irrétrécissable.

unsightliness /ʌnˈsaɪtlɪnɪs/ *n* laideur *f*.

unsightly /ʌnˈsaɪtlɪ/ *adj* [*blemish*] disgracieux/-ieuse; [*building*] laid.

unsigned /ʌnˈsaɪnd/ *adj* [*document, letter*] non signé.

unsinkable /ʌnˈsɪŋkəbl/ *adj* **1** [*ship, object*] insubmersible; **2** FIG, HUM [*personality*] que rien ne peut atteindre.

unskilled /ʌnˈskɪld/ *adj* [*worker, labour*] non qualifié; [*job, work*] qui n'exige pas de qualification professionnelle.

unskimmed /ʌnˈskɪmd/ *adj* [*milk*] non écrémé.

unsmiling /ʌnˈsmaɪlɪŋ/ *adj* [*person*] qui ne sourit pas; [*face*] grave.

unsociable /ʌnˈsəʊʃəbl/ *adj* peu sociable.

unsocial /ʌnˈsəʊʃl/ *adj* **~ hours** heures *fpl* indues.

unsold /ʌnˈsəʊld/ *adj* invendu.

unsolicited /ˌʌnsəˈlɪsɪtɪd/ *adj* non sollicité.

unsolved /ʌnˈsɒlvd/ *adj* [*problem*] non résolu; [*murder*] non éclairci.

unsophisticated /ˌʌnsəˈfɪstɪkeɪtɪd/ *adj* [*person*] sans façons; [*mind*] simple; [*analysis*] simpliste.

unsound /ʌnˈsaʊnd/ *adj* [*roof, ship*] en mauvais état; [*argument*] peu valable; [*credits, investment*] FIN douteux/-euse; **he is politically ~, his views are politically ~** il a des idées politiques suspectes; **to**

be of ~ mind JUR ne pas jouir de toutes ses facultés mentales.

unsparing /ʌnˈspeərɪŋ/ adj **1 to be ~ in one's efforts to do ne** pas ménager ses efforts pour faire; **2** (merciless) impitoyable.

unsparingly /ʌnˈspeərɪŋlɪ/ adv **1** [give] sans compter; [strive] de tout son être; **2** [critical] implacablement.

unspeakable /ʌnˈspiːkəbl/ adj **1** (dreadful) [pain, sorrow] inexprimable; [noise] épouvantable; [act] innommable; **2** (inexpressible) indescriptible.

unspeakably /ʌnˈspiːkəblɪ/ adv **1** (dreadfully) épouvantablement; **2** (inexpressibly) **~ beautiful** d'une beauté indescriptible.

unspent /ʌnˈspent/ adj **1** LIT [money] non dépensé; **2** FIG [rage] toujours vivace.

unspoiled /ʌnˈspɔɪld/ adj [landscape, town] préservé intact; **she was ~ by fame** la célébrité ne l'avait pas changée.

unspoilt /ʌnˈspɔɪlt/ adj [island, area] préservé.

unspoken /ʌnˈspəʊkən/ adj **1** (secret) inexprimé; **2** (implicit) tacite.

unsportsmanlike /ʌnˈspɔːtsmənlaɪk/ adj SPORT **~ conduct** conduite indigne d'un sportif.

unstable /ʌnˈsteɪbl/ adj (all contexts) instable.

unstated /ʌnˈsteɪtɪd/ adj [violence, assumption] tacite; [policy, conviction] inexprimé.

unstatesmanlike /ʌnˈsteɪtsmənlaɪk/ adj indigne d'un homme d'État.

unsteadily /ʌnˈstedɪlɪ/ adv [walk, rise] en chancelant.

unsteady /ʌnˈstedɪ/ adj **1** (wobbly) [steps, legs, voice] chancelant; [ladder] instable; [hand] tremblant; **to be ~ on one's feet** marcher de façon mal assurée; **2** (irregular) [rhythm, speed] irrégulier/-ière.

unstinting /ʌnˈstɪntɪŋ/ adj [effort] soutenu; [support] généreux/-euse; **to be ~ in one's praise of sb** se répandre en louanges sur qn.

unstitch /ʌnˈstɪtʃ/ vtr **to come ~ed** se découdre.

unstoppable /ʌnˈstɒpəbl/ adj [force, momentum] irrésistible; [athlete, leader] imbattable.

unstrap /ʌnˈstræp/ (p prés etc **-pp-**) vtr **1** (undo) défaire les sangles de [suitcase]; **2** (detach) détacher [case, bike] (**from** de).

unstressed /ʌnˈstrest/ adj LING [vowel, word] non accentué.

unstrung /ʌnˈstrʌŋ/ adj **to come ~** [racket, instrument] se détendre; [beads] se désenfiler.

unstuck /ʌnˈstʌk/ adj **1** LIT **to come ~** se décoller; **2°** FIG [person, organization] connaître un échec, aller à vau l'eau; [plans] tomber à l'eau; **to come ~ in one's exams** échouer à ses examens.

unsubsidized /ʌnˈsʌbsɪdaɪzd/ adj non subventionné.

unsubstantiated /ˌʌnsəbˈstænʃɪeɪtɪd/ adj non corroboré.

unsuccessful /ˌʌnsəkˈsesfl/ adj **1** [campaign] infructueux/-euse; [production, film] sans succès; [lawsuit] perdu; [love affair] malheureux/-euse; [search] vain; **to be ~** [attempt] échouer; **2** [candidate] (for job) malchanceux/-euse; (in election) malheureux/-euse; [businessperson] malchanceux/-euse; [artist] inconnu; **to be ~ in doing** ne pas réussir à faire.

unsuccessfully /ˌʌnsəkˈsesfəlɪ/ adv [try] en vain; [challenge, bid] sans succès.

unsuitable /ʌnˈsuːtəbl/ adj [location, clothing, accommodation, time] inapproprié; [moment] inopportun; [friend] peu convenable; **to be ~** ne pas convenir (**for sb** à qn); **to be ~ for a job** ne pas être fait pour un travail.

unsuitably /ˈʌnˈsuːtəblɪ/ adv **he was ~ dressed** sa tenue était inappropriée; **to be ~ matched** ne pas être faits l'un pour l'autre.

unsuited /ʌnˈsuːtɪd/ adj [place, person] inadapté (**to** à); **posts ~ to their talents** des postes qui ne conviennent pas à leurs aptitudes; **she was ~ to country life** elle n'était pas faite pour la vie à la campagne; **they're ~ (as a couple)** ils sont mal assortis.

unsupervised /ʌnˈsuːpəvaɪzd/ adj [activity] non encadré; [child] laissé sans surveillance.

unsupported /ˌʌnsəˈpɔːtɪd/ adj **1** [allegation, hypothesis] non confirmé; **2** MIL [troops] sans renfort; **3** [family, mother] sans soutien de famille.

unsure /ʌnˈʃɔː(r), US -ˈʃʊər/ adj peu sûr (**of** de); **to be ~ about how/about going** ne pas savoir très bien comment/si on doit partir; **to be ~ of oneself** manquer de confiance en soi.

unsurpassed /ˌʌnsəˈpɑːst, US -ˈpæs-/ adj [beauty] sans égal; **to be ~** être inégalé (**in** dans; **as** comme).

unsuspected /ˌʌnsəˈspektɪd/ adj insoupçonné.

unsuspecting /ˌʌnsəˈspektɪŋ/ adj [person] naïf/-ïve, sans méfiance; [public] non averti; **completely ~** sans aucune méfiance.

unsweetened /ʌnˈswiːtnd/ adj sans sucre, non sucré.

unswerving /ʌnˈswɜːvɪŋ/ adj inébranlable.

unsympathetic /ˌʌnsɪmpəˈθetɪk/ adj **1** (uncaring) [person, attitude, manner, tone] peu compatissant; **to be ~ to sb** se montrer peu compatissant envers qn; **2** (unattractive) [person, character] antipathique; [environment, building] peu attirant; **3** (unsupportive) **to be ~ to** ne pas soutenir [cause, movement, policy]; **she is ~ to the cause** elle ne sympathise pas avec la cause.

unsystematic /ˌʌnsɪstəˈmætɪk/ adj peu méthodique.

untainted /ʌnˈteɪntɪd/ adj [food] non avarié; [reputation] non entaché; [mind] non corrompu.

untamed /ʌnˈteɪmd/ adj [passion, person, lion] indompté; [garden, beauty] (à l'état) sauvage; [bird, fox] non dressé.

untangle /ʌnˈtæŋgl/ vtr démêler [threads] ALSO FIG; élucider [difficulties, mystery]; **to ~ oneself** (from net, situation) se dégager (**from** de).

untapped /ʌnˈtæpt/ adj inexploité.

untaxed /ʌnˈtækst/ adj **1** [income] non imposable; [goods] non taxé; **2** GB AUT [car] sans vignette.

untenable /ʌnˈtenəbl/ adj [position, standpoint] intenable; [claim, argument] indéfendable.

untested /ʌnˈtestɪd/ adj **1** [theory] non vérifié; [method, drug] non testé; **2** PSYCH [person] non testé.

unthinkable /ʌnˈθɪŋkəbl/ adj [prospect, action] impensable.

unthinking /ʌnˈθɪŋkɪŋ/ adj [person] irréfléchi; [remark, criticism] inconsidéré.

unthinkingly /ʌnˈθɪŋkɪŋlɪ/ adv [behave, react] sans réfléchir.

unthought-of /ʌnˈθɔːtɒv/ adj original, inédit; **hitherto ~** encore inédit.

untidily /ʌnˈtaɪdɪlɪ/ adv [kept, scattered, strewn] en désordre; **~ dressed** habillé de façon débraillée.

untidiness /ʌnˈtaɪdɪnɪs/ n désordre m.

untidy /ʌnˈtaɪdɪ/ adj [person] (in habits) désordonné; (in appearance) peu soigné; [habits, clothes] négligé; [room] en désordre.

untie /ʌnˈtaɪ/ vtr (p prés **-tying**) défaire, dénouer [knot, rope, laces]; défaire [parcel]; délier [hands, hostage]; **to come ~d** [laces, parcel] se défaire; [hands] se délier.

until /ənˈtɪl/

■ **Note** When used as a preposition in positive sentences until is translated by jusqu'à: they're staying until Monday = ils restent jusqu'à lundi.
– Remember that jusqu'à + le becomes jusqu'au and jusqu'à + les becomes jusqu'aux: until the right moment = jusqu'au bon moment; until the exams = jusqu'aux examens.
– In negative sentences not until is translated by ne...pas avant: I can't see you until Friday = je ne peux pas vous voir avant vendredi.
– When used as a conjunction in positive sentences until is translated by jusqu'à ce que + subjunctive: we'll stay here until Maya comes back = nous resterons ici jusqu'à ce que Maya revienne.
– In negative sentences where the two verbs have different subjects not until is translated by ne...pas avant

que + *subjunctive*: *we won't leave until Maya comes back* = nous ne partirons pas avant que Maya revienne.
– In negative sentences where the two verbs have the same subject *not until* is translated by *ne…pas avant de* + *infinitive*: *we won't leave until we've seen Claire* = nous ne partirons pas avant d'avoir vu Claire.
– For more examples and particular usages see the entry below.

I *prep* **1** (also **till**) (up to a specific time) jusqu'à; (after negative verb) avant; **~ Tuesday** jusqu'à mardi; **~ the sixties** jusqu'aux années soixante; **~ very recently** il n'y a encore pas si longtemps; **~ a year ago** jusqu'à il y a un an; **~ now** jusqu'à présent; **~ then** jusqu'à ce moment-là, jusque-là; **(up) ~ 1901** jusqu'en or jusqu'à 1901; **valid (up) ~ April 1993** valable jusqu'en avril 1993 ; **~ the day he died** jusqu'à sa mort; **~ well after midnight** bien au-delà de minuit; **to wait ~ after Easter** attendre après Pâques; **from Monday ~ Saturday** du lundi au samedi; **put it off ~ tomorrow** remets-le à demain; **~ such time as you find work** jusqu'à ce que tu trouves (*subj*) du travail, en attendant que tu trouves (*subj*) du travail; **I won't know ~ Tuesday** je n'aurai pas la réponse avant mardi; **they didn't ring ~ the following day** ils n'ont pas appelé avant le lendemain; **it wasn't ~ the 50's that**… ce n'est qu'à partir des années cinquante que…; **2** (as far as) jusqu'à.
II *conj* (also **till**) jusqu'à ce que (+ *subj*); (in negative constructions) avant que (+ *subj*), avant de (+ *infinitive*); **we'll stay ~ a solution is reached** nous resterons jusqu'à ce que nous trouvions une solution; **let's watch TV ~ they arrive** regardons la télévision en attendant qu'ils arrivent (*subj*); **things won't improve ~ we have democracy** la situation ne s'améliorera pas tant que nous ne serons pas en démocratie; **stir mixture ~ (it is) smooth** CULIN mélangez bien jusqu'à obtenir une pâte lisse; **~ you are dead** JUR jusqu'à ce que mort s'ensuive; **wait ~ I get back** attends que je revienne (*subj*); **I'll wait ~ I get back** j'attendrai d'être rentré (**before doing** pour faire); **she waited ~ she was alone/they were alone** elle a attendu d'être seule/qu'ils soient seuls; **don't look ~ I tell you to** ne regarde pas avant que je te le dise; **you can't leave ~ you've completed the course** tu ne peux pas partir avant d'avoir fini le stage.

untimely /ʌnˈtaɪmlɪ/ *adj* LITTÉR [*arrival, intervention*] inopportun; [*death*] prématuré; **to come to an ~ end** [*person, project*] connaître une fin prématurée.

untiring /ʌnˈtaɪərɪŋ/ *adj* [*person, enthusiasm*] infatigable (**in** dans).

untold /ʌnˈtəʊld/ *adj* **1** (not quantifiable) **~ millions** des millions et des millions; **~ damage** d'énormes dégâts; **2** (endless) [*misery, damage, joy*] indicible.

untouched /ʌnˈtʌtʃt/ *adj* **1** (unchanged, undisturbed) intact; **2** (unscathed) indemne; **3** (unaffected) non affecté (**by** par); **4** (uneaten) intact; **to leave a meal ~** laisser un repas sans y toucher.

untoward /ˌʌntəˈwɔːd, US ʌnˈtɔːrd/ *adj* fâcheux/-euse.

untraceable /ʌnˈtreɪsəbl/ *adj* introuvable.

untrained /ʌnˈtreɪnd/ *adj* **1** [*worker*] sans formation; **2** [*voice*] non travaillé; [*eye*] inexercé; [*artist, actor*] non formé; **to be ~** n'avoir aucune formation (**in** en); **3** [*animal*] non dressé.

untranslatable /ˌʌntrænzˈleɪtəbl/ *adj* intraduisible (**into** en).

untreated /ʌnˈtriːtɪd/ *adj* [*sewage, water*] non traité; [*illness*] non soigné; [*road*] non sablé.

untried /ʌnˈtraɪd/ *adj* **1** [*recruit*] inexpérimenté; [*method*] non essayé; [*product*] non testé; **2** JUR [*prisoner*] non jugé.

untroubled /ʌnˈtrʌbld/ *adj* [*face, life*] paisible; [*person*] serein; **to be ~** (by news) ne pas être troublé (**by** par).

untrue /ʌnˈtruː/ *adj* **1** (false) faux/fausse; **2 it is ~ to say that** il est faux or inexact de dire que.

untrustworthy /ʌnˈtrʌstwɜːðɪ/ *adj* [*source, information*] douteux/-euse; [*person*] indigne de confiance; [*witness*] non digne de foi.

untruthful /ʌnˈtruːθfl/ *adj* [*person*] menteur/-euse; [*account*] mensonger/-ère.

untypical /ʌnˈtɪpɪkl/ *adj* [*person, behaviour*] hors du commun; **to be ~ of sb** ne pas ressembler à qn (**to do** de faire).

unused[1] /ʌnˈjuːst/ *adj* (unaccustomed) **to be ~ to sth/to doing** ne pas être habitué à qch/à faire.

unused[2] /ʌnˈjuːzd/ *adj* (not used) [*machine, building*] inutilisé; [*stamp*] neuf/neuve; **'computer, ~'** (in ad) 'ordinateur, état neuf'.

unusual /ʌnˈjuːʒl/ *adj* [*colour, flower*] peu commun; [*feature, occurrence*] peu commun, inhabituel/-elle; [*dish, person*] original; **of ~ intelligence** d'une intelligence hors du commun; **to have an ~ way of doing** avoir une manière originale de faire; **it is ~ to find/see** il est rare de trouver/voir; **it's ~ for sb to do** il est rare que qn fasse; **there's nothing ~ about it** cela n'a rien d'extraordinaire.

unusually /ʌnˈjuːʒlɪ/ *adv* **1** (exceptionally) [*large, difficult, talented*] exceptionnellement; **2** (surprisingly) exceptionnellement; **~ for her, she**… chose rare, elle…

unutterable /ʌnˈʌtərəbl/ *adj* indicible.

unvarying /ʌnˈveərɪŋ/ *adj* [*routine*] invariable.

unveil /ʌnˈveɪl/ *vtr* dévoiler [*statue, details*].

unveiling /ʌnˈveɪlɪŋ/ *n* **1** (of statue) dévoilement *m*; **2** (official ceremony) inauguration *f*; **3** (of latest model, details) annonce *f*.

unvoiced /ʌnˈvɔɪst/ *adj* **1** (private) inexprimé; **2** LING non voisé.

unwaged /ʌnˈweɪdʒd/ *adj* [*work, worker*] non salarié.

unwanted /ʌnˈwɒntɪd/ *adj* [*goods, produce*] superflu; [*pet*] abandonné; [*visitor*] indésirable; [*child*] non souhaité; **to feel ~** se sentir de trop.

unwarranted /ʌnˈwɒrəntɪd, US -ˈwɔːr-/ *adj* injustifié.

unwary /ʌnˈweərɪ/ **I** *n* **the ~** (+ *v pl*) les imprudents. **II** *adj* [*person*] sans méfiance.

unwashed /ʌnˈwɒʃt/ *adj* [*clothes, dishes*] sale, pas lavé.

unwavering /ʌnˈweɪvərɪŋ/ *adj* [*devotion*] inébranlable; [*gaze*] résolu.

unwearable /ʌnˈweərəbl/ *adj* immettable.

unwearying /ʌnˈwɪərɪɪŋ/ *adj* [*patience*] inlassable.

unwelcome /ʌnˈwelkəm/ *adj* **1** [*visitor, interruption*] importun; **she felt most ~** elle ne se sentait pas la bienvenue; **to make sb feel ~** faire sentir à qn qu'il n'est pas le bienvenu; **2** [*news*] fâcheux/-euse; [*truth*] gênant; [*proposition*] inopportun.

unwelcoming /ʌnˈwelkəmɪŋ/ *adj* [*atmosphere*] peu accueillant.

unwell /ʌnˈwel/ *adj* souffrant; **he is feeling ~** il ne se sent pas très bien; **are you ~?** vous êtes souffrant?

unwholesome /ʌnˈhəʊlsəm/ *adj* malsain.

unwieldy /ʌnˈwiːldɪ/ *adj* [*tool*] peu maniable; [*parcel*] encombrant; [*bureaucracy, organization*] lourd.

unwilling /ʌnˈwɪlɪŋ/ *adj* [*attention, departure*] forcé; **he is ~ to do it** il n'est pas disposé à le faire; (stronger) il ne veut pas le faire; **~ accomplice** complice malgré moi/lui etc.

unwillingly /ʌnˈwɪlɪŋlɪ/ *adv* à contrecœur.

unwillingness /ʌnˈwɪlɪŋnɪs/ *n* réticence *f* (**to do** à faire).

unwind /ʌnˈwaɪnd/ (*prét, pp* **-wound**) **I** *vtr* dérouler. **II** *vi* **1** [*tape, cable, scarf*] se dérouler; **2** (relax) se relaxer.

unwise /ʌnˈwaɪz/ *adj* [*choice, loan, decision*] peu judicieux/-ieuse; [*person*] imprudent; **it is ~ to do** il est imprudent de faire.

unwittingly /ʌnˈwɪtɪŋlɪ/ *adv* **1** (innocently) innocemment; **2** (without wanting to) involontairement; **3** (accidentally) accidentellement.

unworldly /ʌnˈwɜːldlɪ/ *adj* **1** (not materialistic) détaché de ce monde; **2** (naive) naïf/naïve; **3** (spiritual) surnaturel/-elle.

unworthy /ʌn'wɜːðɪ/ adj indigne (**of** de).

unwrap /ʌn'ræp/ (p prés etc **-pp-**) vtr déballer.

unwritten /ʌn'rɪtn/ adj **1** (tacit) [rule, agreement] tacite; **2** (not written) [story, song] non écrit; [tradition] oral.

unyielding /ʌn'jiːldɪŋ/ adj **1** LIT rigide; **2** FIG inflexible.

unzip /ʌn'zɪp/ (p prés etc **-pp-**) **I** vtr défaire la fermeture à glissière de [garment, bag].
II vi s'ouvrir.

up /ʌp/

■ **Note** up appears frequently in English as the second element of phrasal verbs (get up, pick up etc). For translations, consult the appropriate verb entry (get, pick etc).

I adj **1** (out of bed) **she's ~** elle est levée; **they're often ~ early** ils se lèvent souvent tôt; **we were ~ very late last night** nous nous sommes couchés très tard hier soir; **they were ~ all night** ils ont veillé toute la nuit; **I was still ~ at 2 am** j'étais toujours debout à 2 heures du matin; **2** (higher in amount, level) **sales/prices are ~ (by 10%)** les ventes/les prix ont augmenté (de 10%); **shares/numbers are ~** les actions sont/le nombre est en hausse; **production is ~ (by) 5%** la production a augmenté de 5%; **his temperature is ~ 2 degrees** sa température a augmenté de 2°; **sales are 10% ~ on last year** les ventes ont augmenté de 10% par rapport à l'an dernier; **3**○ (wrong) **what's ~?** qu'est-ce qui se passe?; **what's ~ with him?** qu'est-ce qu'il lui arrive?; **there's something ~** il y a quelque chose qui ne va pas; **what's ~ with the TV?** qu'est-ce qu'elle a à la télé?; **there's something ~ with the brakes** il y a un problème avec les freins; **4** (erected, affixed) **the notice is ~ on the board** l'annonce est affichée sur le panneau; **is the tent ~?** est-ce que la tente est déjà montée?; **the building will soon be ~** le bâtiment sera bientôt terminé; **he had his hand ~ for five minutes** il a gardé la main levée pendant cinq minutes; **5** (open) **she had her umbrella ~** elle avait son parapluie ouvert; **the hood of the car was ~** la capote de la voiture était fermée; **the blinds were ~** les stores étaient levés; **when the lever is ~ the machine is off** si le levier est vers le haut la machine est arrêtée; **when the barrier is ~ you can go through** quand la barrière est levée vous pouvez passer; **6** (finished) **'time's ~!'** 'le temps est épuisé!'; **his leave is almost ~** son congé est presque terminé; **it's all ~**○ **with him** il est fini○; **7** (facing upwards) **'this side ~'** (on parcel, box) 'haut'; **she was floating face ~** elle flottait sur le dos; **the bread landed with the buttered side ~** la tartine est tombée côté beurré vers le haut; **8** (rising) **the river is ~** la rivière est en crue; **the wind is ~** le vent est fort; **his colour's ~** il est tout rouge; **her blood's ~** FIG la moutarde lui monte au nez; **9** (pinned up) **her hair was ~** elle avait les cheveux relevés; **10** (cheerful) **to be ~** être en forme; **11** (being repaired) **the road is ~** la route est en travaux; **12** (in upward direction) **the escalator** l'escalier mécanique qui monte; **13** (on trial) **to be ~ before a judge** passer devant le tribunal; **he's ~ for murder** il est accusé de meurtre.
II adv **1** (high) **~ here/there** là-haut; **~ on the wardrobe** sur l'armoire; **~ in the tree/the clouds** dans l'arbre/les nuages; **~ on top of the mountain** au sommet de la montagne; **~ to/in London** à Londres; **~ to/in Scotland** en Écosse; **~ North** au Nord; **four floors ~ from here** quatre étages au-dessus; **I live two floors ~** j'habite au deuxième étage; **the second shelf ~** la deuxième étagère en partant du bas; **I'm on my way ~** je monte; **I'll be right ~** je monte tout de suite; **all the way ~** jusqu'en haut, jusqu'au sommet; **2** (ahead) d'avance; **to be four points ~ (on sb)** avoir quatre points d'avance (sur qn); **they were two goals ~** ils menaient avec deux buts d'avance; **she's 40–15 ~** (in

tennis) elle mène 40–15; **3** (upwards) **t-shirts from £2 ~** des t-shirts à partir de deux livres; **from (the age of) 14 ~** à partir de 14 ans; **4** (to high status) **~ the workers!** vive les travailleurs!
III prep **1** (at, to higher level) **~ the tree** dans l'arbre; **~ a ladder** sur une échelle; **the library is ~ the stairs** la bibliothèque se trouve en haut de l'escalier; **he ran ~ the stairs** il a monté l'escalier en courant; **the road ~ the mountain** la route qui gravit la montagne; **2** (in direction) **it's ~ the road** c'est plus loin dans la rue; **she lives ~ that road there** elle habite dans cette rue; **he lives just ~ the road** il habite juste à côté; **his office is ~ the corridor from mine** son bureau est dans le même couloir que le mien; **he walked ~ the road** il a remonté la rue; **she's got water ~ her nose** elle a de l'eau dans le nez; **he put it ~ his sleeve** il l'a mis dans sa manche.
IV up above adv phr, prep phr GEN au-dessus; RELIG au ciel; **~ above sth** au-dessus de qch.
V up against prep phr **~ against the wall** contre le mur; **to be** ou **come ~ against opposition** rencontrer de l'opposition; **they're ~ against a very strong team** ils sont confrontés à une équipe très forte; **it helps to know what you are ~ against** il faut savoir ce contre quoi on se bat; **we're really ~ against it** on a vraiment des problèmes.
VI up and about adv phr (out of bed) debout, réveillé; (after illness) **to be ~ and about again** être de nouveau sur pied.
VII up and down adv phr, prep phr **1** (to and fro) **to walk** ou **pace ~ and down** aller et venir, faire les cent pas; **he was walking ~ and down the garden** il faisait les cent pas dans le jardin; **2** (throughout) **~ and down the country** dans tout le pays.
VIII up and running adv phr, adv phr **to be ~ and running** [company, project] bien marcher; [system] bien fonctionner; **to get sth ~ and running** faire marcher or fonctionner qch.
IX up for prep phr **he's ~ for election** il se présente aux élections; **the subject ~ for discussion is...** le sujet qu'on aborde est...
X up to prep phr **1** (to particular level) jusqu'à; **~ to here** jusqu'ici; **~ to there** jusque là; **I was ~ to my knees in water** j'étais dans l'eau jusqu'aux genoux; **2** (as many as) jusqu'à, près de; **~ to 50 dollars** jusqu'à 50 dollars; **~ to 500 people** près de 500 personnes; **reductions of ~ to 50%** des réductions qui peuvent atteindre 50%; **tax on profits of ~ to £150,000** les impôts sur les bénéfices de moins de 150 000 livres sterling; **to work for ~ to 12 hours a day** travailler jusqu'à 12 heures par jour; **3** (until) jusqu'à; **~ to 1964** jusqu'en 1964; **~ to 10.30 pm** jusqu'à 22 h 30; **~ to now** jusqu'à maintenant; **4** (good enough for) **I'm not ~ to it** (not capable) je n'en suis pas capable; (not well enough) je n'en ai pas la force; **I'm not ~ to going to London** je n'ai pas le courage d'aller à Londres; **I'm not ~ to writing a book** je ne suis pas capable d'écrire un livre; **the play wasn't ~ to much** la pièce n'était pas formidable; **this work wasn't ~ to your usual standard** ce travail n'est pas au niveau de ce que vous faites d'habitude; **5** (expressing responsibility) **it's ~ to him to do** c'est à lui de faire; **it's ~ to you!** c'est à toi de décider!; **if it were ~ to me** si ça dépendait de moi; **6** (doing) **what is he ~ to?** qu'est-ce qu'il fait?; **what are those children ~ to?** qu'est-ce qu'ils fabriquent○ ces enfants?; **they're ~ to something** ils mijotent○ quelque chose.
XI vtr (p prés etc **-pp-**) (increase) augmenter.
XII vi (p prés etc **-pp-**) **he ~ped and left** tout d'un coup il s'est levé et est parti.

IDIOMS **the company is on the ~ and ~** ça marche très bien pour l'entreprise; **to be one ~ on sb** faire mieux que qn; **to be (well) ~ on** s'y connaître en [art, history etc]; être au courant de [news, developments]; **the ~s and downs** les hauts et les bas (**of** de).

up and coming adj prometteur/-euse.

upbeat /'ʌpbiːt/ adj FIG optimiste.

upbringing /'ʌpbrɪŋɪŋ/ *n* éducation *f*.

update I /'ʌpdeɪt/ *n* mise *f* à jour (**on** de); **news ~** dernières nouvelles *fpl*.
II /ʌp'deɪt/ *vtr* **1** (revise) mettre [qch] à jour [*database, figure*]; actualiser [*price*]; **2** (modernize) moderniser [*machinery*]; remettre [qch] au goût du jour [*image*]; **3** mettre [qn] au courant [*person*] (**on** de).

upfront○ /ʌp'frʌnt/ I *adj* **1** (frank) franc/franche; **2** (conspicuous) en vue; **3** [*money*] payé d'avance.
II *adv* [*pay*] d'avance.

upgrade /ʌp'greɪd/ *vtr* **1** (modernize) moderniser; (improve) améliorer; **2** COMPUT améliorer [*software, hardware*]; **3** (raise) promouvoir [*person*]; revaloriser [*job*].

upheaval /ʌp'hi:vl/ *n* **1** C (disturbance) (political, emotional) bouleversement *m*; (physical) (in house etc) remue-ménage *m inv*; **2** ¢ (instability) (political, emotional) bouleversements *mpl*; (physical) remue-ménage *m inv*; **emotional ~** un bouleversement affectif.

uphill /ʌp'hɪl/ I *adj* **1** LIT [*road, slope*] qui monte; **2** FIG (difficult) [*task*] difficile; **it will be an ~ struggle** OU **battle** cela va être difficile.
II *adv* [*go, walk*] en montée; **the path led ~** le sentier montait; **it's ~ all the way** LIT ça monte tout le temps; FIG ce n'est pas une tâche facile.

uphold /ʌp'həʊld/ *vtr* (*prét, pp* **-held**) soutenir [*principle*]; faire respecter [*law*]; confirmer [*decision*].

upholster /ʌp'həʊlstə(r)/ *vtr* rembourrer [*chair, sofa*].

upholsterer /ʌp'həʊlstərə(r)/ ▶ 1251 | *n* tapissier/-ière *m/f*.

upholstery /ʌp'həʊlstərɪ/ *n* **1** (covering) revêtement *m*; **2** (stuffing) rembourrage *m*; **3** (technique) tapisserie *f*.

upkeep /'ʌpki:p/ *n* **1** (care) (of house, garden) entretien *m* (**of** de); (of animal) garde *f* (**of** de); **2** (cost of care) frais *mpl* d'entretien.

uplifting /ʌp'lɪftɪŋ/ *adj* tonique.

upmarket /ʌp'mɑ:kɪt/ *adj* [*car, hotel*] haut de gamme; [*area*] riche.

upmost /'ʌpməʊst/ *adj* ▶ **uppermost**.

upon /ə'pɒn/ *prep* **1** FML ▶ **on** | **1**, 3, 7, 10; **2** (linking two nouns) **thousands ~ thousands of people** des milliers et des milliers de personnes; **disaster ~ disaster** un désastre après l'autre; **3** (imminent) **spring is almost ~ us** le printemps approche.

upper /'ʌpə(r)/ I *n* **1** (of shoe) empeigne *f*; '**leather ~**' 'dessus en cuir'; **2** ARGOT DES DROGUÉS stimulant *m*.
II *adj* **1** (in location) [*shelf*] supérieur; [*deck*] supérieur; [*jaw, lip*] supérieur; [*teeth*] du haut; **the ~ body** la partie supérieure du corps; **2** (in rank) supérieur; **3** (on scale) [*register, scale*] supérieur; **the ~ limit** la limite maximale (**on** de); **temperatures are in the ~ twenties** les températures dépassent 25°.
IDIOMS **to be on one's ~s**○ être dans la dèche○; **to have/get the ~ hand** avoir/prendre le dessus. ▶ **stiff**.

upper case *adj* **~ letters** (lettres *fpl*) majuscules *fpl*.

upper circle *n* THEAT deuxième balcon *m*.

upper class I *n* (*pl* **~es**) **the ~**, **the ~es** l'aristocratie *f* et la haute bourgeoisie.
II **upper-class** *adj* [*accent, background, person*] distingué; **in ~ circles** dans la haute société.

upper crust○ HUM I *n* **the ~** le gratin○ *m*.
II **upper-crust** *adj* [*accent, family*] de la haute○.

upper: **Upper House** *n* Chambre *f* haute; **~-income bracket** *n* tranche *f* des revenus élevés.

upper middle class *n* **the ~**, **the ~es** la haute bourgeoisie *f*.

uppermost /'ʌpəməʊst/ *adj* **1** (highest) [*deck, branch*] le plus haut; (in rank) [*echelon*] le plus élevé; **2** (to the fore) prédominant; **to be ~ in sb's mind** être au premier plan des pensées de qn.

upper sixth *n* GB SCH cf (classe *f*) terminale *f*.

upright /'ʌpraɪt/ I *n* **1** CONSTR montant *m*; **2** (in football) montant *m* de but.
II *adj* LIT, FIG droit; **to stay ~** [*person*] rester debout.

III *adv* **to stand ~** se tenir droit; **to sit ~** (action) se redresser.

upright: **~ freezer** *n* congélateur *m* armoire; **~ piano** ▶ 1097 | *n* piano *m* droit.

uprising /'ʌpraɪzɪŋ/ *n* soulèvement *m*.

upriver /ʌp'rɪvə(r)/ *adv* vers l'amont.

uproar /'ʌprɔ:(r)/ *n* **1** (violent indignation) indignation *f*; **to cause an international ~** soulever une indignation internationale; **2** (noisy reaction) tumulte *m*; **to cause (an) ~** déclencher un tumulte de protestations; **3** (chaos) **to be in ~** être dans la plus vive agitation.

uproarious /ʌp'rɔ:rɪəs/ *adj* **1** (funny) désopilant; **2** (rowdy) [*behaviour*] tapageur/-euse; [*laughter*] toni-truant.

uproot /ʌp'ru:t/ *vtr* LIT, FIG déraciner.

upset I /'ʌpset/ *n* **1** (surprise, setback) POL, SPORT revers *m*; **to suffer an ~** subir un revers; **to cause an ~** causer la surprise; **2** (upheaval) bouleversement *m*; **3** (distress) peine *f*; **4** MED **to have a stomach ~** avoir un problème d'estomac.
II /ʌp'set/ *vtr* (*p prés* **-tt-**; *prét, pp* **-set**) **1** (distress) [*sight, news*] retourner, bouleverser; [*person*] faire de la peine à; **2** (annoy) contrarier; **3** FIG (throw into disarray) bouleverser [*plan*]; déjouer [*calculations*]; affecter [*pattern, situation*]; **4** (destabilize) rompre [*balance*]; (knock over) renverser; **5** POL, SPORT (topple) déloger [*leader, party*]; **6** MED rendre [qn] malade [*person*]; perturber [*digestion*].
III /ʌp'set/ *pp adj* **to be** ou **feel ~** (distressed) être très affecté (**at, about** par); (annoyed) être contrarié (**at, about** par); **to get ~** (angry) se fâcher (**about** pour); (distressed) se tracasser (**about** pour).

upsetting /ʌp'setɪŋ/ *adj* (distressing) navrant, affligeant; (annoying) contrariant.

upshot /'ʌpʃɒt/ *n* résultat *m*.

upside down /ʌpsaɪd 'daʊn/ I *adj* LIT à l'envers; FIG sens dessus dessous; **~ cake** CULIN gâteau *m* renversé.
II *adv* **1** LIT à l'envers; **2** FIG **to turn the house ~** mettre la maison sens dessus dessous; **to turn sb's life ~** bouleverser la vie de qn.

upstage /ʌp'steɪdʒ/ I *adv* THEAT [*stand*] au fond de la scène; [*move*] vers le fond de la scène.
II *vtr* THEAT, FIG éclipser.

upstairs /ʌp'steəz/ I *n* haut *m*; **the ~ is much nicer** le haut est beaucoup plus joli; **there is no ~** il n'y a pas d'étage.
II *noun modifier* [*room*] du haut; [*neighbours*] du dessus; **an ~ bedroom** une chambre à l'étage; **the ~ bedroom** la chambre du haut; **the ~ flat** GB l'appartement du haut or d'en haut; **with ~ bathroom** avec salle de bains à l'étage.
III *adv* en haut; **to go ~** monter (l'escalier).
IDIOMS **he hasn't got much ~**○ il n'a pas grand-chose dans le ciboulot○ or dans la tête; **to be kicked ~**○ recevoir une promotion placard.

upstart /'ʌpstɑ:t/ *n, adj* arriviste (*mf*).

upstate /'ʌpsteɪt/ I *adj* **~ New York** la partie nord de l'État de New York.
II *adv* **to go/come from ~** aller vers le/venir du nord (*d'un État*).

upstream /ʌp'stri:m/ *adv* [*travel*] vers l'amont; **~ from here** en amont d'ici.

upsurge /'ʌpsɜ:dʒ/ *n* (of violence) montée *f* (**of** de); (in debt, demand, industrial activity) augmentation *f* (**in** de).

uptake /'ʌpteɪk/ *n*: IDIOMS **to be quick/slow on the ~**○ comprendre/ne pas comprendre vite.

uptight○ /ʌp'taɪt/ *adj* (tense) tendu; PÉJ (reserved) coincé○.

up-to-date /ʌptə'deɪt/ *adj* **1** (modern, fashionable) [*music, clothes*] à la mode; [*equipment*] moderne; **2** (containing latest information) [*records, timetable*] à jour; [*information*] récent; **to keep sth up to date** tenir qch à jour; **3** (informed) [*person*] au courant; **to keep up to date with** se tenir au courant de [*developments*]; être au courant de [*gossip*]; **to bring/to keep sb up to date** mettre/tenir qn au courant (**about** de).

up-to-the-minute *adj* [*information*] dernier/-ière.

uptown /ˌʌpˈtaʊn/ US I *adj* (smart) chic.
II *adv* **1** (upmarket) **to move ~** aller habiter dans un quartier résidentiel chic; FIG réussir socialement; **2** (central) **to go ~** aller dans le centre.

upturned /ˌʌpˈtɜːnd/ *adj* [*box*] posé à l'envers; [*brim*] remonté; [*soil*] retourné; [*nose*] retroussé.

upward /ˈʌpwəd/ I *adj* [*push, movement*] vers le haut; [*path, road*] qui monte; [*trend*] à la hausse; **an ~ slope** une montée.
II *adv* ▶ **upwards**.

upwardly mobile *adj* en pleine ascension sociale.

upwards /ˈʌpwədz/ I *adv* **1** LIT [*look, point*] vers le haut; **to go ~ move ~** monter; **2** FIG **to push prices ~** faire monter les prix; **from five years/£10 ~** à partir de cinq ans/10 livres sterling.
II **upwards of** *prep phr* plus de.

uranium /jʊˈreɪnɪəm/ *n* uranium *m*.

urban /ˈɜːbən/ *adj* [*environment, life, transport*] urbain; [*school*] en ville; **~ dweller** citadin/-e *m/f*.

urban blight, **urban decay** *n* dégradation *f* urbaine.

urbane /ɜːˈbeɪn/ *adj* [*person*] plein de savoir-faire; [*grace, style*] raffiné.

urbanization /ˌɜːbənaɪˈzeɪʃn/, US -nɪˈz-/ *n* urbanisation *f*.

urbanize /ˈɜːbənaɪz/ *vtr* **to become ~d** s'urbaniser.

urban: **~ planner** ▶ 1251 *n* urbaniste *mf*; **~ planning** *n* urbanisme *m*.

urchin /ˈɜːtʃɪn/ *n* gamin *m*; **street ~** gamin des rues.

urge /ɜːdʒ/ I *n* forte envie *f*, désir *m* (**to do** de faire).
II *vtr* (encourage) préconiser [*caution, restraint, resistance*]; **to ~ sb to do** conseiller vivement à qn de faire; (stronger) pousser or exhorter qn à faire; **I ~d them not to go** je leur ai vivement déconseillé d'y aller; **to ~ patience on sb** exhorter qn à la patience.
■ **urge on**: **~ on** [sb], **~** [sb] **on 1** (encourage) encourager; **to ~ sb on to do** inciter or pousser qn à faire; **2** (make go faster) talonner [*horse*].

urgency /ˈɜːdʒənsɪ/ *n* (of situation, appeal, request) urgence *f*; (of voice, tone) insistance *f*; **a matter of ~** une affaire urgente; **to do sth as a matter of ~** faire qch d'urgence; **there's no ~** ce n'est pas urgent.

urgent /ˈɜːdʒənt/ *adj* **1** (pressing) [*case, need*] urgent, pressant; [*message, demand*] urgent; [*investigation, measures*] d'urgence; **to be in ~ need of** avoir un besoin urgent de; **it is ~ that we (should) find a solution** il est urgent que nous trouvions une solution; **it's ~!** c'est urgent!; **it requires your ~ attention** il faut que vous vous en occupiez d'urgence; **2** (desperate) [*plea, tone*] insistant, pressant.

urgently /ˈɜːdʒəntlɪ/ *adv* [*request*] d'urgence; [*plead*] instamment; **books are ~ needed** il y a un besoin urgent de livres.

urinal /jʊəˈraɪnl, ˈjʊərɪnl/ *n* (place) urinoir *m*; (fixture) urinal *m*.

urinary /ˈjʊərɪnərɪ, US -nerɪ/ *adj* urinaire.

urinate /ˈjʊərɪneɪt/ *vi* uriner.

urine /ˈjʊərɪn/ *n* urine *f*.

urn /ɜːn/ *n* urne *f*.

urologist /jʊəˈrɒlədʒɪst/ ▶ 1251 *n* urologue *mf*.

Uruguay /ˈjʊərəgwaɪ/ ▶ 840 *pr n* Uruguay *m*.

us /ʌs, əs/

■ **Note** The direct or indirect object pronoun *us* is always translated by *nous*: *she knows us* = elle nous connaît. Note that both the direct and the indirect object pronouns come before the verb in French and that in compound tenses like the present perfect and past perfect, the past participle agrees in gender and number with the direct object pronoun: *he's seen us* (masculine or mixed gender object) il nous a vus; (*feminine object*) il nous a vues.
– In imperatives *nous* comes after the verb: *tell us!* = dis-nous!; *give it to us or give us it* = donne-le-nous (note the hyphens).

– After the verb *to be* and after prepositions the translation is also *nous*: *it's us* = c'est nous.
– For expressions with *let us* or *let's* see the entry **let**.
– For particular usages see the entry below .

pron nous; **both of ~** tous/toutes les deux; **every single one of ~** chacun/-e d'entre nous; **people like ~** des gens comme nous; **some of ~** quelques uns/ unes d'entre nous; **she's one of ~** elle est des nôtres; **give ~ a hand, will you**○? tu peux me donner un coup de main s'il te plaît?; **give ~ a look**○! fais voir!

US I *n* (*abrév* = **United States**) USA *mpl*.
II *adj* américain.

USA *n* (*abrév* = **United States of America**) USA *mpl*.

USAF (*abrév* = **United States Air Force**) *n* armée *f* de l'air des États-Unis.

usage /ˈjuːsɪdʒ, ˈjuːzɪdʒ/ *n* **1** (custom) usage *m*, coutume *f*; **2** LING usage *m*; **in ~** en usage; **3** (way sth is used) utilisation *f*; **4** (amount used) consommation *f*.

use I /juːs/ *n* **1** ¢ (act of using) (of substance, object, machine) emploi *m*, utilisation *f* (**of** de); (of word, expression, language) emploi *m*, usage *m* (**of** de); **the ~ of force** le recours à la force, l'usage de la force; **the ~ of sth as/for sth** l'emploi or l'utilisation de qch comme/pour qch; **for the ~ of sb**, **for ~ by sb** (customer, staff) à l'usage de qn; **for my own ~** pour mon usage personnel; **to make ~ of sth** utiliser qch; **to put sth to good ~**, **to make good ~ of sth** tirer bon parti de qch; **while the machine is in ~** lorsque la machine est en service or en fonctionnement; **external ~ only** usage externe; **a word in common** ou **general ~** un mot d'usage courant; **out of** ou **no longer in ~** [*machine*] (broken) hors service; (because obsolete) plus utilisé; [*word, expression*] plus en usage; **worn with ~** râpé par l'usage; **this machine came into ~ in the 1950s** cette machine a fait son apparition pendant les années cinquante; **the new system comes into ~ next year** le nouveau système entrera en service l'année prochaine; **2** ¢ (way of using) (of resource, object, material) utilisation *f*; (of term) emploi *m*; **she has her ~s** elle a son utilité; **to have no further ~ for sth/sb** ne plus avoir besoin de qch/qn; **3** (right to use) **to have the ~ of** avoir l'usage de [*house, car, kitchen*]; avoir la jouissance de [*garden*]; **to let sb have the ~ of sth** permettre à qn de se servir de qch; **to lose/still have the ~ of one's legs** perdre/ conserver l'usage de ses jambes; **with ~ of** avec usage de [*kitchen*]; **4** (usefulness) **to be of ~** être utile (**to** à); **to be (of) no ~** [*object*] ne servir à rien; [*person*] n'être bon à rien; **to be (of) no ~ to sb** [*object*] ne pas servir à qn; [*person*] n'être d'aucune utilité à qn; **what ~ is a wheel without a tyre?** à quoi sert une roue sans pneu?; **what's the ~ of crying?** à quoi bon pleurer?; **oh, what's the ~?** oh, et puis à quoi bon?; **it's no ~ asking me** inutile de me demander.
II /juːz/ *vtr* **1** (employ) se servir de, utiliser [*object, car, room, money, tool*]; employer, utiliser [*method*]; employer [*word, expression*]; profiter de, saisir [*opportunity*]; faire jouer [*influence*]; avoir recours à [*blackmail, force, power*]; utiliser [*knowledge, talent*]; **to ~ sth/sb as sth** se servir de qch/qn comme qch; **to ~ sth for sth/to do** se servir de or utiliser qch pour qch/ pour faire; **to be ~d for sth/to do** servir à qch/à faire, être utilisé pour qch/pour faire; **~ your head** ou **loaf**○! fais marcher un peu ta cervelle○!; **I could ~**○ **a drink!** j'aurais bien besoin d'un verre!; **2** (also **~ up**) (consume) consommer [*fuel, food*]; utiliser [*water, leftovers*]; **3** (exploit) PÉJ se servir de [*person*]; **4** (take habitually) prendre [*drugs*].
III **used** *pp adj* [*car*] d'occasion; [*crockery*] sale.
■ **use up**: **~** [sth] **up**, **~ up** [sth] finir, utiliser [*remainder, food*]; dépenser [*money, savings*]; épuiser [*supplies, fuel, energy*].

used¹

■ **Note** To translate *used to do*, use the imperfect tense in French: *he used to live in York* = il habitait York. To stress

that something was done repeatedly, you can use *avoir l'habitude de faire*: *she used to go out for a walk in the afternoon* = elle avait l'habitude de sortir se promener l'après-midi.
– To emphasize a contrast between past and present, you can use *avant*: *I used to love sport* = j'adorais le sport avant.
– For more examples and particular usages, see the entry below.

I /juːst/ *modal aux* **I** ~ **to do** je faisais; **he didn't** ~ **to** ou **he** ~ **not to smoke** il ne fumait pas avant; **didn't she** ~ **to smoke?** est-ce qu'elle ne fumait pas, avant?; **she** ~ **to smoke, didn't she?** elle fumait avant, non?; **it** ~ **to be thought that** avant on pensait que; **there** ~ **to be a pub here** il y avait un pub ici (dans le temps).
II /juːzt/ *adj* (accustomed) **to be** ~ **to sth** avoir l'habitude de qch, être habitué à qch; **I'm not** ~ **to this sort of treatment** je n'ai pas l'habitude qu'on me traite (*subj*) ainsi; **to be** ~ **to sb** être habitué à qn; **to get** ~ **to s'habituer à**; **to be** ~ **to doing** avoir l'habitude de faire; **to get** ~ **to doing** s'habituer à faire; **to be** ~ **to sb doing** être habitué à ce que qn fasse; **I'm not** ~ **to it** je n'ai pas l'habitude; **it takes a bit of getting** ~ **to** ça prend du temps pour s'y habituer.
used² /juːzd/ *prét, pp, pp adj* ► **use** II, III.

useful /ˈjuːsfl/ *adj* **1** (helpful) utile; ~ **for doing** utile pour faire; **to be** ~ **to sb** être utile à qn; **it is** ~ **to do** il est utile de faire; **to make oneself** ~ se rendre utile; **2**° (competent) [*footballer, cook etc*] bon/bonne (*before n*); **to be** ~ **with a gun** savoir se servir d'un fusil, savoir manier un fusil; **to be** ~ **at cooking** savoir cuisiner.

usefulness /ˈjuːsflnɪs/ *n* utilité *f*.

useless /ˈjuːslɪs/ *adj* **1** (not helpful) inutile; **it's** ~ **to do** ou **doing** il est inutile de faire; **2** (not able to be used) inutilisable; **3**° (incompetent) incapable, nul/nulle°; **to be** ~ **at sth/doing** être nul en qch/pour (ce qui est de) faire.

uselessly /ˈjuːslɪslɪ/ *adv* inutilement.

uselessness /ˈjuːslɪsnɪs/ *n* **1** (of object, machine, effort, information) inutilité *f*; **2** (of person) incompétence *f*.

user /ˈjuːzə(r)/ *n* **1** (of road, public transport, service) usager *m*; (of product, machine, credit card) utilisateur/-trice *m/f*; **2** (also **drug** ~) toxicomane *mf*; **cocaine** ~ cocaïnomane *mf*; **heroin** ~ heroïnomane *mf*; **3** PÉJ (exploiter) homme/femme *m/f* intéressé/-e.

user: ~ **friendliness** *n* COMPUT convivialité *f*; GEN facilité *f* d'emploi; ~**-friendly** *adj* COMPUT convivial; GEN facile à utiliser.

usher /ˈʌʃə(r)/ ► 1251 | **I** *n* (at function, lawcourt) huissier *m*; (in theatre, church) placeur *m*.
II *vtr* conduire, escorter; **to** ~ **sb in/out** faire entrer/sortir qn; **to** ~ **sb to the door** conduire qn à la porte.
■ **usher in**: ~ **in** [sth] ouvrir la voie à [*era, negotiations*]; introduire [*scheme, reforms*].

usherette /ˌʌʃəˈret/ ► 1251 | *n* ouvreuse *f*.

USMC *n* US (*abrév* = **United States Marine Corps**) corps *m* des marines américains.

USN *n* US (*abrév* = **United States Navy**) marine *f* des États-Unis.

USSR ► 840 | *n* HIST (*abrév* = **Union of Soviet Socialist Republics**) URSS *f*.

usual /ˈjuːʒl/ **I**° *n* **the** ~ la même chose que d'habi-

tude; **'what did he say?'—'oh, the** ~**'** 'qu'est-ce qu'il a dit?'—'oh, toujours la même chose'; **your** ~, **sir?** (in bar) comme d'habitude, monsieur?
II *adj* [*behaviour, form, procedure, problem, route, place, time*] habituel/-elle; [*word, term*] usuel/-elle; **earlier than** ~ plus tôt que d'habitude; **it is** ~ **to do, the** ~ **practice is to do** il est d'usage de faire; **they did all the** ~ **things** ils ont fait tout ce qu'il est d'usage de faire; **she was her** ~ **cheerful self** elle était gaie, comme d'habitude; **as** ~ comme d'habitude; **'business as** ~**'** 'la vente continue'; **as is** ~ **at this time of year** comme il est d'usage à cette époque de l'année; **more/less than** ~ plus/moins que d'habitude.

usually /ˈjuːʒəlɪ/ *adv* d'habitude, normalement; **more than** ~ **friendly** plus aimable que d'habitude.

usurp /juːˈzɜːp/ *vtr* usurper.

usurper /juːˈzɜːpə(r)/ *n* usurpateur/-trice *m/f*.

UT US POST *abrév écrite* = **Utah**.

utensil /juːˈtensl/ *n* ustensile *m*.

uterus /ˈjuːtərəs/ *n* utérus *m*.

utilitarian /ˌjuːtɪlɪˈteərɪən/ **I** *n* PHILOS utilitariste *mf*.
II *adj* **1** [*doctrine, ideal*] utilitariste; **2** (practical) [*object, vehicle*] utilitaire; [*building*] fonctionnel/-elle; [*clothing*] pratique.

utility /juːˈtɪlətɪ/ **I** *n* **1** (usefulness) utilité *f*; **2** (also **public** ~) (service) service *m* public, commodité *f*.
II utilities *npl* US factures *fpl*.
III *noun modifier* (functional) [*vehicle*] tous usages *inv*; [*object*] utilitaire.

utility: ~ **company** *n* société *f* chargée d'assurer un service public; ~ **room** *n* buanderie *f*.

utilization /ˌjuːtəlaɪˈzeɪʃn/ *n* utilisation *f*.

utilize /ˈjuːtəlaɪz/ *vtr* utiliser [*object, idea*]; exploiter [*resource*].

utmost /ˈʌtməʊst/ **I** *n* **to do** ou **try one's** ~ **to come** faire tout son possible pour venir; **to do sth to the** ~ **of one's abilities** faire qch au maximum de ses capacités; **at the** ~ au maximum, au plus.
II *adj* **1** (greatest) [*caution, ease, secrecy*] le plus grand/la plus grande (*before n*); [*limit*] extrême; **of the** ~ **importance** extrêmement important; **with the** ~ **haste** aussi vite que possible; **2** (furthest) **the** ~ **ends of the earth** les confins *mpl* de la terre.

Utopia /juːˈtəʊpɪə/ *n* utopie *f*.

Utopian /juːˈtəʊpɪən/ **I** *n* utopiste *mf*.
II *adj* utopique.

utter /ˈʌtə(r)/ **I** *adj* [*disaster, amazement, despair*] total; [*sincerity*] absolu; [*fool, scoundrel*] fieffé (*before n*); [*stranger*] parfait (*before n*); ~ **rubbish!** pure sottise!
II *vtr* **1** prononcer [*word, curse*]; pousser [*cry*]; émettre [*sound*]; **2** JUR répandre [*libel*]; mettre en circulation [*forged banknotes*].

utterance /ˈʌtərəns/ *n* **1** (statement) parole *f*; **to give** ~ **to** exprimer, formuler; **2** LING énoncé *m*.

utterly /ˈʌtəlɪ/ *adv* complètement; **we** ~ **condemn this action** nous condamnons cette action jusqu'au bout.

U-turn *n* demi-tour *m*; FIG volte-face *f inv*; **to do a** ~ FIG faire volte-face.

UV *adj* (*abrév* = **ultraviolet**) ultraviolet/-ette.

Uzbekistan /ˌʌzbekɪˈstɑːn, ˌuz-/ ► 840 | *pr n* Ouzbékistan *m*.

Vv

v, V /viː/ *n* **1** (letter) v, V *m*; **2 v** (*abrév écrite =* **versus**) contre; **3 v** (*abrév écrite =* **vide**) voir; **4 V** ELEC (*abrév écrite =* **volt**) V, volt *m*.

vac○ /væk/ *n* GB (*abrév =* **vacation**) vacances *fpl*.

vacancy /ˈveɪkənsɪ/ *n* **1** (free room) chambre *f* libre; **'vacancies'** 'chambres libres'; **'no vacancies'** 'complet'; **2** (unfilled job) poste *m* à pourvoir, poste *m* vacant; **a ~ for an accountant** un poste de comptable à pourvoir; **to fill a ~** pourvoir un poste (**for** de); **to advertise a ~** faire paraître une offre d'emploi; **'no vacancies'** 'pas d'embauche'.

vacant /ˈveɪkənt/ *adj* **1** (unoccupied) [*flat, room, seat*] libre, disponible; [*office, land*] inoccupé; **2** (available) [*job, post*] vacant, à pourvoir; **to become** ou **fall ~** se libérer; **'Situations ~'** 'offres d'emploi'; **3** (dreamy) [*look, stare*] absent; [*expression*] vide.

vacant lot *n* US terrain *m* vague.

vacantly /ˈveɪkəntlɪ/ *adv* [*answer, stare*] d'un air absent.

vacant possession *n* GB JUR jouissance *f* immédiate.

vacate /vəˈkeɪt, US ˈveɪkeɪt/ *vtr* quitter [*house, premises, job*]; libérer [*room, seat*].

vacation /vəˈkeɪʃn, US veɪ-/ I *n* GEN, UNIV vacances *fpl*; JUR vacances *fpl* judiciaires; **on ~** en vacances; **to take a ~** prendre des vacances.
II *vi* US **he's ~ing in Miami** il est en vacances à Miami.

vacationer /vəˈkeɪʃənə(r), US veɪ-/ *n* US vacancier/-ière *m/f*.

vaccinate /ˈvæksɪneɪt/ *vtr* vacciner (**against** contre).

vaccination /ˌvæksɪˈneɪʃn/ *n* vaccination *f* (**against** contre); **to have a ~** se faire vacciner.

vaccine /ˈvæksiːn, US vækˈsiːn/ *n* vaccin *m* (**against** contre); **tetanus ~** vaccin contre le tétanos.

vacillate /ˈvæsəleɪt/ *vi* hésiter (**over** au sujet de).

vacuous /ˈvækjʊəs/ *adj* SOUT [*person, look, expression*] niais; [*optimism, escapism*] béat PÉJ.

vacuum /ˈvækjʊəm/ I *n* **1** PHYS vide *m*; **to create a ~** faire le vide; **2** (lonely space) vide *m*; **emotional ~** vide affectif; **it left a ~ in our lives** ça a fait un grand vide dans notre vie; **3** (*also* **~ cleaner**) aspirateur *m*; **4** (*also* **~ clean**) **to give [sth] a ~** passer un coup d'aspirateur sur [*carpet*]; passer l'aspirateur dans [*room*].
II *vtr* passer [qch] à l'aspirateur [*carpet*]; passer l'aspirateur dans [*room*].

vacuum: **~ bottle** *n* US = **vacuum flask**; **~ cleaner** *n* aspirateur *m*; **~ flask** *n* bouteille *f* thermos®; **~ pack** *vtr* emballer [qch] sous vide.

vagabond /ˈvægəbɒnd/ *n, adj* vagabond/-e (*m/f*).

vagary /ˈveɪgərɪ/ *n* SOUT caprice *m*.

vagina /vəˈdʒaɪnə/ *n* (*pl* **-nas** ou **-nae**) vagin *m*.

vagrancy /ˈveɪgrənsɪ/ *n* GEN, JUR vagabondage *m*.

vagrant /ˈveɪgrənt/ *n, adj* GEN, JUR vagabond/-e (*m/f*).

vague /veɪg/ *adj* **1** (imprecise) [*person, account, idea, memory, rumour, term*] vague; **2** (evasive) **to be ~ about** rester vague sur ou évasif/-ive au sujet de [*plans, past*]; **3** (distracted) [*person, expression*] distrait; [*gesture*] vague; **to look ~** avoir l'air distrait; **4** (faint, slight) [*sound, smell, taste*] vague, imprécis; [*fear, embarrassment*] vague (*before n*); [*doubt*] léger/-ère (*before n*); **5** (unsure) **I am (still) a bit ~ about**

events je ne sais (toujours) pas très bien ce qui s'est passé.

vaguely /ˈveɪglɪ/ *adv* **1** (faintly, slightly) vaguement; **it seems ~ familiar** cela me dit vaguement quelque chose; **it feels ~ like a bee sting** cela fait un peu comme une piqûre d'abeille; **2** (distractedly) [*smile, gaze, say*] d'un air distrait or vague; [*wander, move about*] distraitement; **3** (imprecisely) [*remember, understand, reply*] vaguement; [*describe*] de manière vague or imprécise; [*defined, formulated*] vaguement.

vagueness /ˈveɪgnɪs/ *n* **1** (imprecision) (of wording, proposals) flou *m*; (of thinking) imprécision *f*; (of image) manque *m* de netteté; **2** (absent-mindedness) distraction *f*.

vain /veɪn/ I *adj* **1** (conceited) vaniteux/-euse, vain (*after n*); **to be ~ about sth** tirer vanité de qch; **2** (futile) [*attempt, hope*] vain (*before n*); [*show*] futile.
II **in vain** *adv* en vain.
IDIOMS **to take sb's name in ~** HUM parler de qn (derrière son dos).

vainly /ˈveɪnlɪ/ *adv* **1** (futilely) [*try, wait, struggle*] vainement, en vain; **2** (conceitedly) [*look, stare*] avec vanité.

valance /ˈvæləns/ *n* (on bed base) tour *m* de lit; (round canopy) lambrequin *m*; (above curtains) cantonnière *f*.

valency /ˈveɪlənsɪ/ *n* CHEM, LING valence *f*.

valentine /ˈvæləntaɪn/ *n* (*also* **~ card**) carte *f* de la Saint-Valentin.

Valentine('s) Day *n* la Saint-Valentin.

valet /ˈvælɪt, -leɪ/ ▶ **1251** I *n* **1** (employee) valet *m* de chambre; **2** (rack) valet *m* de nuit.
II *vtr* nettoyer [*clothes, car interior*].

valiant /ˈvæliənt/ *adj* [*soldier*] vaillant; [*attempt*] courageux/-euse; **to make a ~ attempt to do** tenter courageusement de faire; **to make a ~ effort to smile** s'efforcer bravement de sourire.

valiantly /ˈvæliəntlɪ/ *adv* [*fight*] vaillamment; [*try*] courageusement.

valid /ˈvælɪd/ *adj* **1** (still usable) [*passport, licence*] valide; [*ticket, offer*] valable; **2** (well-founded) [*argument, excuse*] valable; [*complaint*] fondé; [*point, comment*] pertinent; [*comparison*] légitime; **3** (in law) valide, valable.

validate /ˈvælɪdeɪt/ *vtr* **1** prouver le bien-fondé de [*claim, theory*]; **2** valider [*document, passport*].

validity /vəˈlɪdətɪ/ *n* JUR (of ticket, document, consent) validité *f*; **2** (of argument, excuse, method) validité *f*; (of complaint, objection) bien-fondé *m*.

valley /ˈvælɪ/ *n* (*pl* **~s**) vallée *f*; (small) vallon *m*.

valour GB, **valor** US /ˈvælə(r)/ *n* LITTÉR valeur *f* LITER, bravoure *f*.
IDIOMS **discretion is the better part of ~** PROV prudence est mère de sûreté PROV.

valuable /ˈvæljʊəbl/ *adj* **1** [*commodity, asset*] de valeur; **to be ~** avoir de la valeur; **very ~** de grande valeur; **2** [*advice, information, lesson*] précieux/-ieuse.

valuables /ˈvæljʊəblz/ *npl* objets *mpl* de valeur.

valuation /ˌvæljʊˈeɪʃn/ *n* (of house, land, company) évaluation *f*; (of antique, art) expertise *f*; **to have a ~ done on sth** faire évaluer qch; **a ~ of £50** une valeur estimée de 50 livres sterling.

value /ˈvæljuː/ I *n* **1** (monetary worth) valeur *f*; **of little ~** de peu de valeur; **of no ~** sans valeur; **to have a ~ of £5** valoir 5 livres sterling; **to the ~ of** pour une valeur de; **2** (usefulness, general worth) valeur *f*; **to**

have ou **be of educational** ~ avoir une valeur éducative; **the ~ of sb as** la valeur de qn en tant que; **the ~ of doing** l'importance de faire; **novelty ~** caractère nouveau; **3** (worth relative to cost) **to be good ~** avoir un bon rapport qualité-prix; **to be good ~ at £5** ne pas être cher/chère à 5 livres sterling; **you get good ~ at Buymore** on en a pour son argent à Buymore; **to get ~ for money** en avoir pour son argent; **a ~-for-money product** un produit qui vous en donne pour votre argent; **4** (standards, ideals) valeur *f*; **family ~s** valeurs familiales.
II *vtr* **1** (assess worth of) évaluer [*house, asset, company*] (at à); expertiser [*antique, jewel, painting*]; **to have sth ~d** faire évaluer ou expertiser qch; **2** (appreciate) apprécier [*person, friendship, opinion, help*]; tenir à [*reputation, independence, life*]; **to ~ sb as a friend** apprécier qn en tant qu'ami.

value-added tax, **VAT** *n* taxe *f* à la valeur ajoutée, TVA *f*.

valued /'vælju:d/ *adj* [*person*] apprécié; [*contribution, opinion*] précieux/-ieuse.

valueless /'væljulis/ *adj* sans valeur (*after n*).

valuer /'væljuə(r)/ ▶ 1251 *n* expert *m*.

valve /vælv/ *n* **1** (in machine, engine) soupape *f*; (on tyre, football) valve *f*; **2** ANAT (of organ) valvule *f*; **3** (of mollusc, fruit) valve *f*; **4** (on brass instrument) piston *m*; **5** GB lampe *f*.

vamp /væmp/ *n* **1**† PÉJ (woman) vamp *f*; **2** (on shoe) empeigne *f*.

vampire /'væmpaɪə(r)/ *n* vampire *m*; ~ **bat** vampire *m*.

van /væn/ *n* **1** AUT (small, for deliveries etc) fourgonnette *f*, camionnette *f*; (larger, for removals etc) fourgon *m*; **2** US (camper) auto-caravane *f*, camping-car *m*; **3** (vanguard) avant-garde *f*.

vandal /'vændl/ *n* vandale *mf*.

vandalism /'vændəlɪzəm/ *n* vandalisme *m*.

vandalize /'vændəlaɪz/ *vtr* vandaliser.

van driver ▶ 1251 *n* chauffeur *m* de camionnette.

vane /veɪn/ *n* **1** (also **weather ~**) girouette *f*; **2** (of windmill) aile *f*.

vanguard /'væŋgɑ:d/ *n* MIL, FIG avant-garde *f*; **in the ~** à l'avant-garde.

vanilla /və'nɪlə/ **I** *n* CULIN, BOT vanille *f*.
II *noun modifier* [*sauce, icecream*] à la vanille; [*pod, plant*] de vanille; ~ **essence** extrait *m* de vanille.

vanish /'vænɪʃ/ *vi* disparaître (**from** de); **to ~ into the distance** disparaître au loin; **to ~ into thin air** FIG se volatiliser.

vanishing /'vænɪʃɪŋ/ **I** *n* disparition *f*.
II *adj* [*species, environment*] en voie de disparition.
IDIOMS **to do a ~ act** se volatiliser.

vanishing: ~ **cream** *n* crème *f* de jour; ~ **point** *n* point *m* de fuite; ~ **trick** *n* tour *m* de passe-passe.

vanity /'vænəti/ *n* vanité *f*.

vanity: ~ **case** *n* vanity-case *m*; ~ **mirror** *n* AUT miroir *m* de courtoisie; ~ **unit** *n* meuble *m* sous-vasque.

vanquish /'væŋkwɪʃ/ *vtr* LITTÉR défaire LITER, vaincre [*enemy*].

vantage point *n* **1** GEN, MIL point *m* de vue, position *f* élevée; **from the ~ of** du haut de; **2** FIG (point of view) perspective *f*.

vapid /'væpɪd/ *adj* [*person, expression, remark, debate*] mièvre, fade; [*style, novel*] insipide, fade.

vaporize /'veɪpəraɪz/ **I** *vtr* vaporiser [*liquid*].
II *vi* se vaporiser.

vaporizer /'veɪpəraɪzə(r)/ *n* vaporisateur *m*.

vapour GB, **vapor** US /'veɪpə(r)/ *n* vapeur *f*.

vapour trail *n* traînée *f* de condensation, traînée *f* d'un avion.

variable /'veərɪəbl/ **I** *n* GEN, COMPUT, MATH variable *f*.
II *adj* GEN, COMPUT variable.

variance /'veərɪəns/ *n* **1** GEN désaccord *m* (**between** entre); **to be at ~ with** être en désaccord avec [*evi-*

dence, facts]; **my views are at ~ with his** mes opinions divergent des siennes; **that is at ~ with what you said yesterday** cela ne concorde pas avec ce que vous avez dit hier; **2** MATH variance *f*.

variant /'veərɪənt/ **I** *n* variante *f* (**of** de; **on** par rapport à).
II *adj* [*colour, species, strain*] différent; ~ **reading** ou **text** ou **version** variante *f*; ~ **form** BOT variante *f*.

variation /ˌveərɪ'eɪʃn/ *n* **1** (change) variation *f*, différence *f* (**in, of** de); **regional ~s** variations régionales; ~ **between A and B** différence *f* entre A et B; **subject to considerable ~** sujet à des variations importantes; **2** (version) version *f* (**of** de); (new version) variante *f* (**of** de); MUS variation *f* (**on** sur).

varicose /'værɪkəʊs/ *adj* variqueux/-euse; ~ **veins** varices *fpl*.

varied /'veərɪd/ *adj* varié.

variegated /'veərɪgeɪtɪd/ *adj* **1** GEN varié; **2** BOT, ZOOL panaché.

variety /və'raɪətɪ/ **I** *n* **1** (diversity, range) variété *f* (**in, of** de); **wide ~** grande variété; **for a ~ of reasons** pour diverses raisons; **the dresses come in a ~ of sizes** ces robes existent dans un grand choix de tailles; **2** (type) GEN type *m*; BOT variété *f*; **3** ¢ THEAT, TV variétés *fpl*.
II *noun modifier* [*artist, act*] de variétés.

various /'veərɪəs/ *adj* **1** (different) différents (*before n*); **at their ~ addresses** à leurs différentes adresses; **2** (several) divers; **at ~ times** à diverses reprises; **in ~ ways** de diverses manières.

variously /'veərɪəslɪ/ *adv* (in different ways) [*arranged, decorated*] de différentes manières; (by different people) [*called, described, estimated*] à tour de rôle.

varnish /'vɑ:nɪʃ/ **I** *n* vernis *m*.
II *vtr* vernir [*woodwork*]; **to ~ one's nails** se vernir les ongles.

varnishing /'vɑ:nɪʃɪŋ/ *n* vernissage *m*.

vary /'veərɪ/ **I** *vtr* varier [*menu, programme*]; faire varier [*flow, temperature*]; changer de [*pace, route*].
II *vi* [*objects, people, tastes*] varier (**with, according to** selon); **to ~ from sth** différer de qch; **to ~ from X to Y** varier de X à Y; **they ~ in cost/in size** ils varient quant au coût/à la taille.

varying /'veərɪɪŋ/ *adj* [*amounts, degrees, opinions*] variable; [*circumstances*] varié; **with ~ (degrees of) success** avec plus ou moins de succès.

vascular /'væskjʊlə(r)/ *adj* ANAT, BOT vasculaire.

vase /vɑ:z, US veɪs, veɪz/ *n* vase *m*.

vasectomy /və'sektəmɪ/ *n* vasectomie *f*.

vast /vɑ:st, US væst/ *adj* **1** (quantitatively) [*amount, sum, improvement, difference*] énorme; [*number*] très grand; [*knowledge*] extrêmement étendu; **the ~ majority** la très grande majorité; **2** (spatially) [*room, area, plain*] vaste (*before n*), immense.

vastly /'vɑ:stlɪ, US væstlɪ/ *adv* [*improved, overrated, superior*] considérablement, infiniment; [*complex, popular*] terriblement; [*different*] complètement.

vastness /'vɑ:stnɪs, US væstnɪs/ *n* immensité *f*.

vat /væt/ *n* cuve *f*; **beer/wine ~** cuve à bière/vin.

VAT *n* (*abrév* = **value-added tax**) GB TVA *f*.

vaudeville /'vɔ:dəvɪl/ *n* THEAT variétés *fpl*.

vault /vɔ:lt/ **I** *n* **1** (roof) voûte *f*; **the ~ of heaven** la voûte céleste; **2** (cellar) (of house, for wine) cave *f*; (tomb) caveau *m*; (of bank) chambre *f* forte; (for safe-deposit boxes) salle *f* des coffres; **3** (jump) saut *m*.
II *vtr* GEN, SPORT sauter par-dessus [*fence, bar*].
III *vi* GEN, SPORT sauter (**over** par-dessus).

vaulted /'vɔ:ltɪd/ *adj* ARCHIT voûté.

vaulting /'vɔ:ltɪŋ/ **I** *n* **1** ARCHIT voûtes *fpl*; **2** ▶ 949 (in gym) saut *m*.
II *adj* [*ambition, arrogance*] démesuré.

VC *n* **1** (*abrév* = **vice chairman**) vice-président/-e *m/ f*; **2** GB UNIV (*abrév* = **vice chancellor**) ~ président/ -e *m/f* d'université.

VCR *n* (*abrév* = **video cassette recorder**) magnétoscope *m*.

VD ▶ 1002 ┃ (*abrév* = **venereal disease**) **I** *n* MST *f*.
II *noun modifier* [*clinic*] de vénérologie.
VDU *n* (*abrév* = **visual display unit**) écran *m* de
visualisation; **~ operator** opérateur/-trice *m/f* de
terminal de visualisation.
veal /viːl/ **I** *n* veau *m*.
II *noun modifier* [*stew, cutlet*] de veau.
vector /'vektə(r)/ *n* **1** BIOL, MATH vecteur *m*; **2**
AVIAT trajectoire *f*.
veer /vɪə(r)/ *vi* **1** LIT (change direction) [*ship*] virer;
[*person, road*] tourner; **to ~ away from/towards**
sth se détourner de/vers qch; **to ~ away** ou **off** s'éloigner; **to ~ off course** dévier de sa route; **to ~**
across the road traverser la route; **2** FIG [*person,*
opinion] changer; **to ~ (away) from sth** se détourner de qch; **to ~ towards sth** se tourner vers
qch.
vegan /'viːgən/ *n, adj* végétalien/-ienne (*m/f*).
veganism /'viːgənɪzəm/ *n* végétalisme *m*.
vegetable /'vedʒtəbl/ **I** *n* **1** (edible plant) légume *m*
(as opposed to mineral, animal) végétal *m*; **3**° FIG **to**
become a ~ être réduit à l'état de légume.
II *noun modifier* [*knife, dish*] à légumes; [*soup, patch*]
de légumes; [*fat, oil, matter*] végétal; **~ garden** potager *m*; **~ peeler** épluche-légumes *m*.
vegetarian /,vedʒɪ'teərɪən/ *n, adj* végétarien/-ienne
(*m/f*).
vegetarianism /,vedʒɪ'teərɪənɪzəm/ *n* végétarisme *m*.
vegetate /'vedʒɪteɪt/ *vi* végéter.
vegetation /,vedʒɪ'teɪʃn/ *n* végétation *f*.
vehemence /'viːəməns/ *n* (of speech, action) véhémence *f*; (of feelings) intensité *f*.
vehement /'viːəmənt/ *adj* [*tirade, gesture, attack*] véhément; [*dislike, disapproval*] violent.
vehemently /'viːəməntlɪ/ *adv* [*speak, react*] avec véhémence.
vehicle /'vɪəkl/, US 'viːhɪkl/ *n* **1** AUT véhicule *m*;
'closed to ~s' 'interdit à la circulation'; **2** (medium)
véhicule *m* (**for** de).
vehicular /vɪ'hɪkjʊlə(r)/, US vi:-/ *adj* **'no ~ access'**,
'no ~ traffic' 'circulation interdite'.
veil /veɪl/ **I** *n* **1** (on face) voile *m* ALSO RELIG; (on hat) voilette
f; **to take the ~** prendre le voile; **2** FIG voile *m*; **a**
~ of secrecy le voile du secret; **let's draw a ~**
over that episode oublions cet épisode.
II *vtr* **1** [*mist, cloud*] voiler; **2** FIG (hide) dissimuler
[*emotion*].
III veiled *pp adj* **1** [*person*] voilé; **2** (indirect) [*hint,*
threat] voilé; **thinly ~ed** [*allusion*] à peine voilé.
vein /veɪn/ *n* **1** (blood vessel) veine *f*; **2** (on insect wing,
leaf) nervure *f*; **3** (thread of colour) (in marble) veine *f*; (in
cheese) veinure *f*; **4** (of ore) veine *f*; **5** (theme) veine *f*;
to continue in a similar ~ continuer dans la même
veine; **a ~ of nostalgia** un élément de nostalgie; **in**
the same ~ dans la même esprit.
veined /veɪnd/ *adj* [*hand, rock, cheese*] veiné; [*leaf*]
nervuré.
Velcro® /'velkrəʊ/ *n* velcro® *m*.
vellum /'veləm/ *n* vélin *m*; **in/on ~** en/sur vélin.
velocity /vɪ'lɒsətɪ/ *n* **1** TECH vitesse *f*; **2** FML vélocité *f*.
velvet /'velvɪt/ **I** *n* velours *m*; **crushed ~** velours
frappé.
II *noun modifier* [*garment, curtain*] en velours.
III *adj* [*skin, eyes*] de velours; [*tones, softness*] velouté;
FIG [*glove, revolution*] de velours.
velvety /'velvətɪ/ *adj* velouté.
venal /'viːnl/ *adj* vénal.
vending machine *n* distributeur *m* automatique.
vendor /'vendə(r)/ *n* **1** (in street, kiosk) marchand/-e *m/*
f; **2** (as opposed to buyer) vendeur/-euse *m/f*; **3** US
(machine) distributeur *m* automatique.
veneer /vɪ'nɪə(r)/ *n* **1** (on wood) placage *m*; **2** FIG (surface show) vernis *m*.
venerable /'venərəbl/ *adj* vénérable.
venerate /'venəreɪt/ *vtr* vénérer.

veneration /,venə'reɪʃn/ *n* vénération *f* (**for** pour).
venereal /və'nɪərɪəl/ ▶ 1002 ┃ *adj* vénérien/-ienne; **~**
disease maladie *f* vénérienne.
Venetian blind *n* store *m* vénitien.
Venezuela /,venɪ'zweɪlə/ ▶ 840 ┃ *pr n* Venezuela *m*.
vengeance /'vendʒəns/ *n* vengeance *f*; **to take ~**
(up)on sb se venger de qn; **with a ~** de plus belle.
venial /'viːnɪəl/ *adj* SOUT véniel/-ielle.
Venice /'venɪs/ ▶ 1343 ┃ *pr n* Venise.
venison /'venɪsn, -zn/ *n* (viande *f* de) chevreuil *m*.
venom /'venəm/ *n* ZOOL, FIG venin *m*.
venomous /'venəməs/ *adj* ZOOL, FIG venimeux/-
-euse.
venous /'viːnəs/ *adj* veineux/-euse.
vent /vent/ **I** *n* **1** (outlet for gas, pressure) bouche *f*,
conduit *m*; **air ~** bouche d'aération; **to give ~ to**
FIG décharger [*anger, feelings*]; **2** (of volcano) cheminée
f; **3** (slit) fente *f*; **4** US (window) déflecteur *m*.
II *vtr* **1** FIG (release) décharger [*anger, spite, frustra-*
tion] (**on** sur); **2** (let out) évacuer [*gas, smoke*].
III *vi* [*gas, chimney, volcano*] s'évacuer.
ventilate /'ventɪleɪt/ *vtr* **1** (provide with air) aérer
[*room*]; **2** MED ventiler.
ventilation /,ventɪ'leɪʃn/ *n* **1** aération *f*, ventilation *f*;
~ shaft puits *m* d'aérage; **2** MED (of patient) ventilation *f* artificielle.
ventilator /'ventɪleɪtə(r)/ *n* **1** MED respirateur *m* artificiel; **2** CONSTR (opening) aérateur *m*; (fan) ventilateur *m*.
ventriloquist /ven'trɪləkwɪst/ ▶ 1251 ┃ *n* ventriloque
mf; **~'s dummy** pantin *m* de ventriloque.
venture /'ventʃə(r)/ **I** *n* **1** COMM, FIN (undertaking)
aventure *f*, entreprise *f*; **a publishing/media ~** une
aventure éditoriale/médiatique; **her first ~ into**
marketing sa première expérience dans le marketing;
2 (experiment) essai *m*; **his first ~ into fiction** sa
première tentative dans le domaine de la fiction.
II *vtr* **1** (offer) hasarder [*opinion, suggestion*]; **to ~**
the opinion that hasarder l'opinion selon laquelle;
might I ~ a suggestion? puis-je me permettre une
suggestion?; **to ~ to do** se risquer à faire; **2** (gamble)
risquer [*bet, money*] (**on** sur).
III *vi* **1** (go) **to ~ into** s'aventurer dans [*place, street,*
city]; **to ~ out(doors)** s'aventurer dehors; **to ~**
forth LITTÉR se risquer à sortir; **2** COMM (make foray)
to ~ into se lancer dans [*retail market, publishing*].
IDIOMS **nothing ~d nothing gained** qui ne risque
rien n'a rien.
venture capital *n* capital-risque *m*.
venue /'venjuː/ *n* lieu *m*; **the ~ for the match will**
be le match aura lieu à.
veracity /və'ræsətɪ/ *n* SOUT véracité *f*.
veranda(h) /və'rændə/ *n* véranda *f*; **on the ~** sous
la véranda.
verb /vɜːb/ *n* verbe *m*.
verbal /'vɜːbl/ *adj* GEN, LING verbal.
verbally /'vɜːbəlɪ/ *adv* verbalement.
verbatim /vɜː'beɪtɪm/ **I** *adj* [*report, account*] textuel/
-elle.
II *adv* [*describe, record*] mot pour mot.
verbena /vɜː'biːnə/ *n* verveine *f*.
verbose /vɜː'bəʊs/ *adj* verbeux/-euse.
verdict /'vɜːdɪkt/ *n* **1** JUR verdict *m*; **to return a ~**
rendre un verdict; **to reach a ~** arriver au verdict; **a**
~ of guilty un verdict positif; **the ~ was suicide**
l'enquête a conclu au suicide; **2** FIG (opinion) verdict
m; **well, what's the ~?** eh bien, qu'est-ce que tu en
penses?; **to give one's ~ on sth** se prononcer sur
qch.
verdigris /'vɜːdɪgrɪs, -griːs/ *n* vert-de-gris *m inv*.
verge /vɜːdʒ/ *n* **1** GB (by road) accotement *m*, bas-côté
m; **soft ~** accotement non stabilisé; **2** (brink) **on the**
~ of au bord de [*tears*]; au seuil de [*adolescence,*
death]; **on the ~ of success** sur le point de réussir;
on the ~ of doing sur le point de faire; **to bring** ou
drive sb to the ~ of amener qn au bord de [*bank-*

ruptcy, despair, suicide]; **to bring** ou **drive sb to the
~ of doing** amener qn au point de faire.
■ **verge on**: **~ on** [**sth**] friser [*panic, stupidity*].

verger /'vɜːdʒə(r)/ **▶1251** *n* RELIG bedeau *m*.

verifiable /'verɪfaɪəbl/ *adj* vérifiable.

verification /ˌverɪfɪ'keɪʃn/ *n* vérification *f*.

verify /'verɪfaɪ/ *vtr* vérifier.

veritable /'verɪtəbl/ *adj* SOUT véritable.

vermicelli /ˌvɜːmɪ'selɪ, -'tʃelɪ/ *n* ¢ (pasta, chocolate)
vermicelle *m*.

vermilion /və'mɪlɪən/ **▶818** *n, adj* vermillon (*m*)
inv.

vermin /'vɜːmɪn/ *n* **1** ¢ (rats etc) animaux *mpl* nuisi-
bles; **2** (lice, insects) vermine *f*; **3** PÉJ (person) canaille
f.

vermouth /'vɜːməθ, US vər'muːθ/ *n* vermouth *m*.

vernacular /və'nækjʊlə(r)/ **I** *n* **1** (language) **the ~** la
langue vulgaire; **in the ~** (in local dialect) en dialecte;
2 (jargon) jargon *m*.
II *adj* [*architecture*] en style local; [*writing*] dans la
langue vulgaire.

verruca /və'ruːkə/ *n* (*pl* **-cae** ou **-cas**) verrue *f*
plantaire.

versatile /'vɜːsətaɪl/ *adj* **1** (flexible) [*person*] plein de
ressources, aux talents divers (*after n*); [*mind*] souple;
2 (with many uses) [*vehicle*] polyvalent; [*equipment*] à
usages multiples.

versatility /ˌvɜːsə'tɪlətɪ/ *n* **1** (flexibility) (of person)
adaptabilité *f*; (of mind) souplesse *f*; **2** (of equipment)
polyvalence *f*.

verse /vɜːs/ *n* **1** (poems) poésie *f*; **to write ~** écrire
des poèmes; **2** (form) vers *mpl*; **in ~** en vers; **3** (part of
poem) strophe *f*; (of song) couplet *m*; **4** BIBLE verset *m*;
5 (single line) vers *m*.

versed /vɜːst/ *adj* (also **well-versed**) versé (**in** dans).

versifier /'vɜːsɪfaɪə(r)/ *n* rimailleur/-euse *m/f*.

version /'vɜːʃn, US -ʒn/ *n* version *f* (**of** de).

versus /'vɜːsəs/ *prep* (all contexts) contre.

vertebra /'vɜːtɪbrə/ *n* (*pl* **-brae**) vertèbre *f*.

vertebral /'vɜːtɪbrəl/ *adj* vertébral.

vertebrate /'vɜːtɪbreɪt/ *n, adj* vertébré (*m*).

vertex /'vɜːteks/ *n* (*pl* **-tices**) **1** MATH sommet *m*; **2**
ANAT vertex *m*.

vertical /'vɜːtɪkl/ **I** *n* verticale *f*; **out of the ~** pas
d'aplomb.
II *adj* [*line, take-off*] vertical; [*cliff*] à pic.

vertically /'vɜːtɪklɪ/ *adv* verticalement.

vertigo /'vɜːtɪɡəʊ/ *n* vertige *m*; **to get ~** avoir le
vertige.

verve /vɜːv/ *n* brio *m*, verve *f*.

very /'verɪ/ **I** *adj* **1** (actual) même (*after n*); **this ~
second** à la seconde même; **2** (ideal) **the ~ person I
need** exactement la personne qu'il me faut; **the ~
thing I need** exactement ce qu'il me faut; **3** (ultimate)
tout; **from the ~ beginning** depuis le tout début; **at
the ~ front** tout devant; **to the ~ end** jusqu'au
bout; **on the ~ edge** à l'extrême bord; **4** (mere) [*mention, thought*] seul (*before n*); **the ~ idea!** quelle idée!
II *adv* **1** (extremely) très; **I'm ~ sorry** je suis vraiment
désolé; **~ well** très bien; **she couldn't ~ well do
that** elle ne pouvait pas vraiment faire cela; **that's all
~ well but** c'est fort bien mais; **~ much** beaucoup;
I didn't eat/find ~ much je n'ai pas mangé/trouvé
grand-chose; **to be ~ much a city dweller** être un
vrai citadin; **2** (absolutely) **the ~ best thing** de loin la
meilleure chose; **in the ~ best of health** en pleine
santé; **at the ~ latest** au plus tard; **at the ~ least**
tout au moins; **the ~ first** le tout premier; **the ~
same words** exactement les mêmes mots; **the ~
next day** le lendemain même; **the ~ next person I
met** la toute première personne que j'ai rencontrée
ensuite; **a car of your ~ own** ta propre voiture.

vespers /'vespəz/ *n* (+ *v sg ou pl*) vêpres *fpl*.

vessel /'vesl/ *n* **1** NAUT vaisseau *m*; **2** ANAT
vaisseau *m*; **3** (container) vase *m*; (for liquids only) coupe
f; **4** FIG (person) instrument *m* (**for** de).

vest /vest/ **▶1260** **I** *n* **1** (underwear) maillot *m* de corps;
2 (for sport) débardeur *m*; **3** US (waistcoat) gilet *m*.
II *vtr* conférer [*authority, power*] (**in** à).

vested interest *n* **1** GEN intérêt *m* personnel; **to
have a ~** être personnellement intéressé (**in** dans);
2 JUR droit *m* acquis.

vestige /'vestɪdʒ/ *n* **1** (trace) (*gén pl*) (of civilization, faith,
system) vestige *m*; (of emotion, truth, stammer) trace *f*;
2 ANAT, ZOOL vestige *m*.

vestment /'vestmənt/ *n* habit *m* sacerdotal.

vest pocket US **I** *n* poche *f* de gilet.
II **vest-pocket** *adj* [*dictionary, calculator*] de poche.

vestry /'vestrɪ/ *n* RELIG sacristie *f*.

vet /vet/ **I** *n* **▶1251** **1** (*abrév* = **veterinary
surgeon**) vétérinaire *mf*; **2**○ US MIL ancien
combattant *m*, vétéran *m*.
II *vtr* (*p prés etc* **-tt-**) mener une enquête approfondie
sur [*person*]; passer [qch] en revue [*plan*]; approuver
[*publication*].

veteran /'vetərən/ **I** *n* GEN vétéran *m*; MIL ancien
combattant *m*, vétéran *m*.
II *noun modifier* [*sportsman, politician*] chevronné;
[*marathon*] vétéran; **a ~ campaigner** un vieux
routier.

veteran: **~ car** *n* GB voiture *f* ancienne (*construite
avant 1905*); **Veterans Day** *n* US jour *m* des anciens
combattants.

veterinary /'vetrɪnrɪ, US 'vetərɪnərɪ/ **▶1251** *n, adj* vétérinaire (*mf*).

veterinary: **~ surgeon** **▶1251** *n* vétérinaire *mf*;
~ surgery *n* clinique *f* vétérinaire.

veto /'viːtəʊ/ **I** *n* (*pl* **-toes**) **1** (practice) veto *m*; **2** (right)
droit *m* de veto (**over, on** sur).
II *vtr* (*3ᵉ pers sg prés* **-toes**; *prét, pp* **-toed**) mettre or
opposer son veto à.

vetting /'vetɪŋ/ *n* contrôle *m*; **security ~** enquête *f*
de sécurité.

vex /veks/ *vtr* (annoy) contrarier; (worry) tracasser.

vexation /vek'seɪʃn/ *n* (annoyance) contrariété *f*; (worry)
tracas *m*.

vexatious /vek'seɪʃəs/ *adj* [*situation*] contrariant;
[*person*] agaçant.

vexed /vekst/ *adj* **1** (annoyed) mécontent (**with** de);
2 (problematic) [*question, issue, situation*] épineux/-euse.

vexing /'veksɪŋ/ *adj* = **vexatious**.

VHF *n* (*abrév* = **very high frequency**) VHF.

via /'vaɪə/ *prep* **1** (by way of) (on ticket, timetable) via;
GEN en passant par; **2** (by means of) par.

viability /vaɪə'bɪlətɪ/ *n* **1** (feasibility) (of company, government, farm) viabilité *f*; (of project, idea, plan) validité *f*;
2 BIOL, ZOOL, MED viabilité *f*.

viable /'vaɪəbl/ *adj* **1** (feasible) [*company, government,
farm*] viable; [*project, idea, plan*] réalisable, valable;
2 BIOL, ZOOL, MED viable.

viaduct /'vaɪədʌkt/ *n* viaduc *m*.

vibes○ /vaɪbz/ *npl* **to have good/bad ~** dégager de
bonnes/mauvaises vibrations○.

vibrant /'vaɪbrənt/ *adj* **1** (lively) [*person, place, personality*] plein de vie; [*colour*] éclatant; **2** (resonant)
sonore; **a voice ~ with emotion** une voix vibrante
d'émotions.

vibrate /vaɪ'breɪt, US 'vaɪbreɪt/ **I** *vtr* faire vibrer.
II *vi* vibrer (**with** de).

vibration /vaɪ'breɪʃn/ *n* vibration *f*.

vicar /'vɪkə(r)/ *n* pasteur *m* (*anglican ou de l'Église
épiscopale*).

vicarage /'vɪkərɪdʒ/ *n* presbytère *m*.

vicarious /vɪ'keərɪəs, US vaɪ'k-/ *adj* (indirect) indirect;
(delegated) [*power*] délégué.

vice /vaɪs/ **I** *n* **1** vice *m*; HUM faiblesse *f*; **2** (also **vise**
US) TECH étau *m*.
II *noun modifier* [*laws*] sur les mœurs; [*scandal*] de
mœurs.

vice: **~-captain** *n* SPORT capitaine *m* en second;
~-chair *n* vice-président/-e *m/f*; **~-chancellor**
▶1251 *n* GB UNIV président/-e *m/f* d'Université; US

JUR *juge assistant(e)*; **~-president**, **VP** *n* vice-président/-e *m/f*; **~-presidential** *adj* [*candidate, race*] à la vice-présidence; [*residence*] vice-présidentiel/-ielle; **~-principal** *n* SCH (of senior school) proviseur *m* adjoint; (of junior school, college) directeur/-trice *m/f* adjoint/-e; **~ squad** *n* brigade *f* des mœurs.

vicinity /vɪˈsɪnətɪ/ *n* voisinage *m*; **in the (immediate) ~ of** Oxford à proximité (immédiate) d'Oxford.

vicious /ˈvɪʃəs/ *adj* [*person, animal, power*] malfaisant; [*speech, attack, price cut, revenge*] brutal; [*rumour, sarcasm, lie*] malveillant.

vicious circle *n* cercle *m* vicieux.

viciously /ˈvɪʃəslɪ/ *adv* **1** (savagely) brutalement; **2** (perversely) méchamment.

victim /ˈvɪktɪm/ *n* LIT, FIG victime *f*; **to fall ~ to** être victime de [*disease, disaster*]; succomber à [*charm*].

victimization /ˌvɪktɪmaɪˈzeɪʃn/ *n* persécution *f*.

victimize /ˈvɪktɪmaɪz/ *vtr* persécuter.

victor /ˈvɪktə(r)/ *n* vainqueur *m*.

Victorian /vɪkˈtɔːrɪən/ **I** *n* homme/femme *m/f* de l'époque victorienne.
II *adj* GEN victorien/-ienne; [*writer, poverty*] de l'époque victorienne.

victorious /vɪkˈtɔːrɪəs/ *adj* victorieux/-ieuse.

victory /ˈvɪktərɪ/ *n* victoire *f*; **to win a ~** remporter une victoire.

video **I** *n* (*pl* **~s**) **1** (also **~ recorder**) magnétoscope *m*; **2** (also **~ cassette**) cassette *f* vidéo; **on ~** en vidéo; **3** (also **~ film**) vidéo *f*; **4** US (television) télévision *f*.
II *noun modifier* [*company, footage*] de vidéo; [*market*] de la vidéo; [*channel, evidence, link, game, recording*] vidéo; [*interview*] en vidéo; [*distributor*] de vidéos.
III *vtr* (*3ᵉ pers sg prés* **~s**; *prét, pp* **~ed**) **1** (from TV) enregistrer [qch]; **2** (on camcorder) filmer [qch] en vidéo.

video: **~ camera** *n* caméra *f* vidéo; **~ clip** *n* CIN, TV extrait *m*; **~ library** *n* vidéothèque *f*; **~ shop** GB, **~ store** US ▶ **1251** *n* magasin *m* (de) vidéo.

videotape /ˈvɪdɪəʊteɪp/ **I** *n* bande *f* vidéo.
II *vtr* enregistrer [qch] en vidéo.

videotaping /ˈvɪdɪəʊteɪpɪŋ/ *n* enregistrement *m* en vidéo.

vie /vaɪ/ *vi* (*p prés* **vying**) rivaliser (**with** avec).

Vietnam /ˌvjetˈnæm/ ▶ **840** *pr n* Viêt Nam *m*.

view /vjuː/ **I** *n* **1** LIT, FIG vue *f*; **the trees cut off the ~** la vue est cachée par les arbres; **you're blocking my ~!** tu me bouches la vue!; **we moved forward to get a better ~** nous nous sommes avancés pour mieux voir; **to have a front ~ of sth** voir qch de face; **an overall ~ of** une vue d'ensemble de; **an inside ~ of the situation** une idée de la situation vue de l'intérieur; **to take the long(-term) ~ of sth** avoir une vision à long terme de qch; **the lake was within ~ of the house** on pouvait voir le lac de la maison; **to do sth in (full) ~ of sb** faire qch devant qn or sous les yeux de qn; **to have sth in ~** FIG penser faire qch; **to keep sth in ~** LIT, FIG ne pas perdre qch de vue; **to disappear from ~** LIT disparaître; **to hide sth from ~** cacher qch; **to be on ~** [*exhibition*] être présenté; [*new range*] être exposé; **2** (personal opinion, attitude) avis *m*, opinion *f*; **point of ~** point *m* de vue; **in his ~** à son avis; **in the ~ of Mr Jones** selon M. Jones; **3** (of exhibition, house) visite *f*; (of film) projection *f*; (of new range) présentation *f*.
II in view of *prep phr* (considering) vu, étant donné.
III with a view to *prep phr* **with a ~ to sth** en vue de qch; **with a ~ to sb** ou **sb's doing** afin que qn fasse.
IV *vtr* **1** (consider) considérer; (envisage) envisager; **to ~ sb with suspicion** être méfiant à l'égard de qn; **2** (look at) GEN voir [*scene, building, exhibition*]; visiter [*house, castle*]; visionner [*slide, microfiche*]; examiner [*documents*]; regarder [*television, programme*].
V *vi* TV regarder la télévision.

viewer /ˈvjuːə(r)/ *n* **1** (of TV) téléspectateur/-trice *m/f*;

2 (of exhibition, property) visiteur/-euse *m/f*; **3** PHOT visionneuse *f*.

viewfinder /ˈvjuːˌfaɪndə(r)/ *n* viseur *m*.

viewing /ˈvjuːɪŋ/ **I** *n* **1** TV **we plan our ~ ahead** nous choisissons à l'avance ce que nous allons regarder (à la télévision); **'and that concludes Saturday night's ~'** 'et avec ceci se termine votre programme du samedi soir'; **essential ~ for teachers** à voir impérativement par les enseignants; **the film makes compulsive ~** le film est captivant; **2** (of exhibition, house) visite *f*; (of film) projection *f*; (of new range) présentation *f*; **'~ by appointment only'** 'visite sur rendez-vous uniquement'.
II *noun modifier* TV [*trends, patterns*] d'écoute; [*habits, preferences*] des téléspectateurs; **~ figures** taux *m* d'écoute; **the ~ public** les téléspectateurs *mpl*.

view: **~phone** *n* vidéophone *m*; **~point** *n* (all contexts) point *m* de vue.

vigil /ˈvɪdʒɪl/ *n* GEN veille *f*; (by sickbed) veillée *f*; RELIG vigile *f*; POL manifestation *f* silencieuse.

vigilance /ˈvɪdʒɪləns/ *n* vigilance *f*.

vigilant /ˈvɪdʒɪlənt/ *adj* vigilant.

vigilante /ˌvɪdʒɪˈlæntɪ/ **I** *n* membre *m* d'un groupe d'autodéfense.
II *noun modifier* [*group, attack, role*] d'autodéfense.

vigor *n* US = **vigour**.

vigorous /ˈvɪɡərəs/ *adj* [*person, plant, attempt, exercise*] vigoureux/-euse; [*campaign*] énergique; [*denial*] catégorique; [*defender, supporter*] ardent.

vigorously /ˈvɪɡərəslɪ/ *adv* GEN vigoureusement; [*defend, campaign, deny*] énergiquement.

vigour GB, **vigor** US /ˈvɪɡə(r)/ *n* GEN vigueur *f*; (of campaign, efforts) énergie *f*.

vile /vaɪl/ *adj* **1** (unpleasant) [*smell, taste*] infect; [*weather*] abominable; [*place, experience, colour*] horrible; [*mood, behaviour*] exécrable; **2** (wicked) vil, ignoble.

vilification /ˌvɪlɪfɪˈkeɪʃn/ *n* diffamation *f* (**of** de).

villa /ˈvɪlə/ *n* (in town) pavillon *m*; (for holiday) villa *f*.

village /ˈvɪlɪdʒ/ **I** *n* (place, community) village *m*.
II *noun modifier* [*shop, fête, school*] du village.

village: **~ green** *n* terrain *m* communal; **~ hall** *n* salle *f* des fêtes.

villager /ˈvɪlɪdʒə(r)/ *n* villageois/-e *m/f*.

villain /ˈvɪlən/ *n* (scoundrel) canaille *f*; (criminal) bandit *m*; (in book, film) méchant *m*; (child) coquin/-e *m/f*.

villainous /ˈvɪlənəs/ *adj* GEN infâme; [*plot, expression*] diabolique.

vindicate /ˈvɪndɪkeɪt/ *vtr* GEN donner raison à; JUR innocenter [*person*]; justifier [*action, claim, judgment*].

vindication /ˌvɪndɪˈkeɪʃn/ *n* GEN justification *f*; JUR (of person) disculpation *f*.

vindictive /vɪnˈdɪktɪv/ *adj* [*person, behaviour*] vindicatif/-ive; [*decision, action*] revanchard.

vine /vaɪn/ *n* **1** (producing grapes) vigne *f*; **2** (climbing plant) plante *f* grimpante.

vinegar /ˈvɪnɪɡə(r)/ *n* vinaigre *m*.

vinegary /ˈvɪnɪɡərɪ/ *adj* LIT de vinaigre; FIG acide.

vineyard /ˈvɪnjəd/ *n* vignoble *m*.

vintage /ˈvɪntɪdʒ/ **I** *n* **1** (wine) millésime *m*; **2** (era) époque *f*.
II *adj* **1** [*wine, champagne*] millésimé; [*port*] vieux/vieille; **2** [*performance, comedy*] classique; **it's ~ Armstrong** c'est du Armstrong du meilleur cru.

vintage: **~ car** *n* voiture *f* d'époque; **~ year** *n* LIT, FIG grande année *f*.

vinyl /ˈvaɪnl/ **I** *n* **1** vinyle *m*; **2** (record) disque *m* noir.
II *noun modifier* GEN en vinyle; [*paint*] vinylique.

viola[1] /vɪˈəʊlə/ ▶ **1097** *n* (violon *m*) alto *m*.

viola[2] /ˈvaɪələ/ *n* BOT (genus) violacée *f*; (flower) pensée *f*.

violate /ˈvaɪəleɪt/ *vtr* **1** (infringe) GEN violer; transgresser [*criteria, duty, taboo*]; JUR enfreindre [*rule, regulation*]; **2** profaner [*sacred place*]; troubler [*peace*].

violation /ˌvaɪəˈleɪʃn/ *n* **1** GEN violation *f*; (of criteria, duty, taboo) transgression *f*; **2** (of sacred place) profanation *f*; **3** JUR infraction *f*.

violence /'vaɪələns/ *n* LIT, FIG violence *f*; **two days of ~** deux jours d'incidents violents.

violent /'vaɪələnt/ *adj* **1** violent; **a ~ attack** (physical) une attaque violente; (verbal) une attaque virulente; **2** (sudden) [*acceleration, braking*] soudain; [*change, contrast*] brutal; **3** [*colour*] criard.

violently /'vaɪələntlɪ/ *adv* **1** [*push, attack, blush, cough, shake*] violemment; [*struggle*] furieusement; [*assault*] sauvagement; **to die ~** mourir de mort violente; **to be ~ ill** ou **sick** GB avoir de violentes nausées; **2** [*brake, swerve, alter, swing*] brusquement; **3** [*react, object*] violemment.

violet /'vaɪələt/ ▶ 818 I *n* **1** BOT violette *f*; **2** (colour) violet *m*.
II *adj* violet/-ette.

violin /ˌvaɪə'lɪn/ ▶ 1097 *n* violon *m*.

VIP (*abrév* = **very important person**) I *n* personnalité *f* (en vue).
II *adj* réservé aux personnalités; **to give sb (the) ~ treatment** recevoir qn en hôte de marque.

viper /'vaɪpə(r)/ *n* ZOOL, FIG vipère *f*.

virgin /'vɜːdʒɪn/ I *n* (woman) (femme) vierge *f*; (man) homme *m* vierge.
II *adj* (all contexts) vierge.

virginal /'vɜːdʒɪnl/ I *n* MUS virginal *m*.
II *adj* GEN innocent; [*white, innocence*] virginal.

Virginia creeper /vɜː'dʒɪnjəˌkriːpə(r)/ *n* vigne *f* vierge.

virginity /və'dʒɪnətɪ/ *n* virginité *f*.

Virgo /'vɜːgəʊ/ ▶ 1418 I *n* Vierge *f*.

virile /'vɪraɪl, US 'vɪrəl/ *adj* LIT, FIG viril.

virologist /vaɪə'rɒlədʒɪst/ ▶ 1251 *n* virologue *mf*, virologiste *mf*.

virtual /'vɜːtʃʊəl/ *adj* **1** (almost complete) quasi-total; **to be a ~ prisoner** être pratiquement prisonnier/ière; **she is the ~ ruler of the country** de fait c'est elle qui dirige le pays; **2** COMPUT, PHYS virtuel/-elle.

virtually /'vɜːtʃʊəlɪ/ *adv* pratiquement, presque; **it's ~ impossible** c'est quasiment° impossible; **~ every household** chaque ménage ou presque.

virtual reality *n* réalité *f* virtuelle.

virtue /'vɜːtʃuː/ I *n* **1** (goodness) vertu *f*; **a woman of easy ~** une femme de petite vertu; **2** (advantage) avantage *m*; **to extol the ~s of sth** vanter les mérites de qch.
II **by virtue of** *prep phr* en raison de.

virtuoso /ˌvɜːtjʊ'əʊsəʊ, -zəʊ/ I *n* (*pl* **-sos** ou **-si**) virtuose *mf* (**of** de).
II *adj* de virtuose.

virtuous /'vɜːtʃʊəs/ *adj* vertueux/-euse.

virtuously /'vɜːtʃʊəslɪ/ *adv* **1** (morally) [*behave, live*] de façon vertueuse; [*help, act*] vertueusement; **2** (self-righteously) avec satisfaction.

virulent /'vɪrʊlənt/ *adj* MED, FIG virulent.

virus /'vaɪərəs/ ▶ 1002 *n* MED, COMPUT virus *m*.

visa /'viːzə/ *n* visa *m*.

vis-à-vis /ˌviːzɑː'viː/ I *n* (person) homologue *m*.
II *prep* (in relation to) par rapport à; (concerning) en ce qui concerne.

visceral /'vɪsərəl/ *adj* LIT, FIG viscéral; [*power, performance*] qui vous prend aux tripes°.

viscose /'vɪskəʊz, -kəʊs/ *n* viscose *f*.

viscount /'vaɪkaʊnt/ ▶ 937 *n* vicomte *m*.

viscous /'vɪskəs/ *adj* visqueux/-euse, gluant.

vise /vaɪs/ *n* US étau *m*.

visibility /ˌvɪzə'bɪlətɪ/ *n* **1** (ability to see) visibilité *f*; **to have restricted ~** avoir une visibilité limitée; **2** (ability to be seen) visibilité *f*.

visible /'vɪzəbl/ *adj* **1** (able to be seen) visible; **clearly ~** bien visible; **2** (concrete) [*improvement, sign*] évident; [*evidence*] flagrant; **with no ~ means of support** sans ressources apparentes.

visibly /'vɪzəblɪ/ *adv* (to the eye) visiblement; (clearly) manifestement.

vision /'vɪʒn/ I *n* **1** (idea, mental picture, hallucination) vision *f*; **to appear to sb in a ~** apparaître à qn; **Rousseau's ~ of the ideal society** l'idée de la société idéale selon Rousseau; **2** (imaginative foresight) sagacité *f*; **a man of ~** un visionnaire; **3** (ability to see) vue *f*; **to have blurred ~** voir trouble; **to come into ~** devenir visible; **4** (visual image) image *f*.
II *vtr* US imaginer.

visionary /'vɪʒənrɪ, US 'vɪʒənerɪ/ *n*, *adj* visionnaire (*mf*).

vision mixer *n* (person) réalisateur *m* de direct; (equipment) mélangeur *m* d'images.

visit /'vɪzɪt/ I *n* **1** (call) visite *f*; **a state ~** une visite officielle; **a flying ~** une visite éclair; **on her first/last ~ to China, she...** la première/dernière fois qu'elle est allée en Chine, elle...; **to pay a ~ to sb, to pay sb a ~** aller voir qn; **to have a ~ from** recevoir la visite de; **to make a ~ to** visiter; **2** (stay) séjour *m*; **to go on a ~** faire un séjour.
II *vtr* **1** (call on, see) aller voir; **2** (inspect) inspecter; **3** (on holiday etc) **to ~ sb** venir chez qn; **to ~ a country** faire un séjour dans un pays; **come and ~ us for a few days** venez passer quelques jours avec nous; **4** US (socially) **to ~ with** aller voir; **5**† **to ~ sth (up)on sb** infliger qch à qn.

visiting /'vɪzɪtɪŋ/ *adj* [*statesman*] en visite; [*athlete*] visiteur/-euse; [*orchestra*] invité.

visiting: **~ card** *n* US carte *f* de visite; **~ hours** *npl* heures *fpl* de visite; **~ lecturer** *n* (short term) maître *m* de conférence invité; (long term) maître *m* de conférence associé; **~ nurse** ▶ 1251 *n* US infirmier/-ière *m/f* à domicile; **~ team** *n* visiteurs/-euses *mpl/fpl*; **~ time** *n* heures *fpl* de visite.

visitor /'vɪzɪtə(r)/ *n* **1** (caller) invité/-e *m/f*; **we have ~s** nous avons de la visite; **2** (tourist) visiteur/-euse *m/f*; **I've been a regular ~ to France** je vais souvent en France; **3** (animal, bird) migrateur *m*.

visitor: **~ centre** *n* centre *m* d'accueil et d'information des visiteurs; **~s' book** *n* (in exhibition) livre *m* d'or; (in hotel) registre *m*.

visor /'vaɪzə(r)/ *n* (eyeshade) visière *f*; AUT pare-soleil *m inv*.

vista /'vɪstə/ *n* LIT panorama *m*; FIG perspective *f*.

visual /'vɪʒʊəl/ I **visuals** *npl* (photographs, pictures) images *fpl*; CIN effets *mpl* visuels.
II *adj* (all contexts) visuel/-elle.

visual: **~ aid** *n* support *m* visuel; **~ arts** *npl* arts *mpl* plastiques; **~ display terminal**, **VDT**, **~ display unit**, **VDU** *n* COMPUT écran *m* de visualisation.

visualize /'vɪʒʊəlaɪz/ *vtr* **1** (picture) s'imaginer; **2** (envisage) envisager.

visually /'vɪʒʊəlɪ/ *adv* visuellement.

visually handicapped *adj* (partially-sighted) malvoyant; (non-sighted) nonvoyant.

visually impaired *n* the **~** (+ *v pl*) les malvoyants *mpl*.

vital /'vaɪtl/ *adj* **1** (essential) [*asset, document, information, research, supplies, interest*] primordial; [*match, support, factor*] décisif/-ive; [*service, help*] indispensable; [*treatment, organ*] vital; **of ~ importance** d'une importance capitale; **2** (lively) [*person*] plein de vie ou de vitalité; [*culture, music*] vivant.

vitality /vaɪ'tælətɪ/ *n* vitalité *f*.

vitally /'vaɪtəlɪ/ *adv* [*important*] extrêmement; [*needed*] absolument.

vital statistics *n* COMM, ADMIN données *fpl* démographiques; HUM GEN informations *fpl* essentielles; (of woman) mensurations *fpl*.

vitamin /'vɪtəmɪn, US 'vaɪt-/ I *n* vitamine *f*; **with added ~s**, **~ enriched** vitaminé.
II *noun modifier* [*requirements*] en vitamines; **to have a high ~ content** être riche en vitamines.

vitreous /'vɪtrɪəs/ *adj* [*enamel*] vitrifié; [*rock, china*] vitreux/-euse.

The human voice

Voices and singers

		voice	singer
soprano	=	soprano *m*	soprano *m* or *f* (depending on whether a boy soprano or a woman)
mezzo-soprano	=	mezzo-soprano *m*	mezzo-soprano *f*
contralto	=	contralto *m*	contralto *f*
alto (female)	=	contralto *m*	contralto *f*
alto (male)	=	haute-contre *f*	haute-contre *m*
counter-tenor	=	haute-contre *f*	haute-contre *m*
tenor	=	ténor *m*	ténor *m*
baritone	=	baryton *m*	baryton *m*
bass-baritone	=	baryton-basse *m*	baryton-basse *m*
bass	=	basse *f*	basse *f*

In the following examples tenor *and* ténor *stand for any of the above voices:*

he's a tenor	=	il est ténor *or* c'est un ténor
he sings tenor	=	il chante ténor
a tenor voice	=	une voix de ténor
the tenor part	=	la partie ténor
a tenor solo	=	un solo de ténor

vitriolic /ˌvɪtrɪˈɒlɪk/ *adj* CHEM de vitriol; FIG au vitriol.

vituperative /vɪˈtjuːpərətɪv, US vaɪˈtuːpəreɪtɪv/ *adj* injurieux/-ieuse.

viva I /ˈvaɪvə/ *n* GB UNIV oral *m*.
II /viːˈvɑː/ *excl* vive!; **~ freedom!** vive la liberté!

vivacious /vɪˈveɪʃəs/ *adj* plein de vivacité.

vivacity /vɪˈvæsətɪ/ *n* vivacité *f*.

vivid /ˈvɪvɪd/ *adj* **1** (bright) [*colour, light*] vif/vive; [*garment*] aux couleurs vives; **2** (graphic) [*imagination*] vif/vive; [*memory, picture*] (très) net/nette; [*dream, impression, description, example, language, imagery*] frappant.

vividly /ˈvɪvɪdlɪ/ *adv* [*shine*] d'une lumière éclatante; [*picture, dream*] de façon très nette; [*describe*] de façon très vivante; **~ coloured** aux couleurs vives; **I remember it ~!** je m'en souviens très bien!

vividness /ˈvɪvɪdnɪs/ *n* (of colour, light, sunset, garment) éclat *m*; (of memory, dream, description) netteté *f*; (of language, imagery) richesse *f*; (of style) vigueur *f*.

vivisect /ˈvɪvɪsekt/ *vtr* pratiquer une vivisection sur.

vivisection /ˌvɪvɪˈsekʃn/ *n* vivisection *f*.

vixen /ˈvɪksn/ *n* **1** ZOOL renarde *f*; **2** PÉJ (woman) mégère *f*.

viz /vɪz/ *adv* SOUT (*abrév* = **videlicet**) à savoir.

vocabulary /vəˈkæbjʊlərɪ, US -lerɪ/ *n* GEN vocabulaire *m*; (glossary) lexique *m*.

vocal /ˈvəʊkl/ **I vocals** *npl* chant *m*; **who did the ~s?** qui a assuré la partie vocale?; **to do the backing ~s** faire les chœurs.
II *adj* **1** LIT vocal; **2** (vociferous) qui se fait entendre.

vocalist /ˈvəʊkəlɪst/ *n* chanteur/-euse *m/f* (*dans un groupe pop*).

vocalize /ˈvəʊkəlaɪz/ **I** *vtr* **1** LIT vocaliser; **2** FIG exprimer.
II *vi* MUS vocaliser, faire des vocalises.

vocally /ˈvəʊkəlɪ/ *adv* **1** MUS vocalement; **2** (vociferously) haut et fort.

vocation /vəʊˈkeɪʃn/ *n* vocation *f*.

vocational /vəʊˈkeɪʃənl/ *adj* GEN professionnel/-elle; [*syllabus, approach*] à orientation professionnelle; **~ course** stage *m* de formation professionnelle.

vociferous /vəˈsɪfərəs, US vəʊ-/ *adj* [*person, protest*] véhément.

vogue /vəʊg/ **I** *n* vogue *f* (**for** de); **to go out of ~** se démoder; **to be out of ~** être démodé.
II *noun modifier* [*word*] en vogue, à la mode.

voice /vɔɪs/ **I** *n* **1** (speaking) voix *f*; **in a loud ~** à haute voix; **in a low ~** à voix basse; **in a cross ~**

d'une voix irritée; **keep your ~ down!** baisse la voix!; **his ~ is breaking** sa voix mue; **to lose one's ~** (when ill) perdre la voix; **to give ~ to sth** exprimer qch; **at the top of one's ~** à tue-tête; **2** (for singing) voix *f*; **to have a good ~** avoir une belle voix; **to be in fine ~** être en voix; **3** (opinion, expression) voix *f*; **to have a ~** avoir voix au chapitre (**in sth** en matière de qch; **in doing** pour ce qui est de faire); **to add one's ~ to sth** unir sa voix à qch; **to demand sth with one ~** exiger unanimement qch; **4** (representative organization) porte-parole *m*; **5** LITERAT (of writer) style *m*; **narrative ~** voix *f* du narrateur; **6** LING voix *f*.
II **-voiced** *combining form* **hoarse-/deep-~d** à la voix rauque/grave.
III *vtr* exprimer [*concern, grievance*]; sonoriser [*consonant*].
IDIOMS **to like the sound of one's own ~** s'écouter parler.

voice: ~ box *n* larynx *m*; **~d consonant** *n* consonne *f* sonore.

voiceless /ˈvɔɪslɪs/ *adj* [*minority, group*] privé de la parole.

voice: ~-over *n* voix-off *f*; **~ print** *n* empreinte *f* vocale; **~ vote** *n* US vote *m* par acclamation.

void /vɔɪd/ **I** *n* LIT, FIG vide *m*; **to fill the ~** combler le vide.
II *adj* **1** JUR [*contract, agreement*] nul/nulle; [*cheque*] annulé; **to make** *ou* **render ~** annuler; **2** (empty) vide; **~ of** dépourvu de.
III *vtr* JUR annuler.

vol /vɒl/ *n* (*pl* **-s**) *abrév* = **volume**.

volatile /ˈvɒlətaɪl, US -tl/ *adj* **1** CHEM volatil; **2** FIG [*situation*] explosif/-ive; [*person*] lunatique; [*mood*] changeant; **3** ECON instable.

volcanic /vɒlˈkænɪk/ *adj* volcanique.

volcano /vɒlˈkeɪnəʊ/ *n* (*pl* **-noes** *ou* **-nos**) volcan *m*.

volition /vəˈlɪʃn, US vəʊ-/ *n* volonté *f*; **of one's own ~** de son propre gré.

volley /ˈvɒlɪ/ **I** *n* **1** SPORT (in tennis) volée *f*; (in soccer) reprise *f* de volée; **2** (of gunfire) salve *f*; (of missiles) volée *f*; **3** FIG (series) **a ~ of** un feu roulant de [*questions, words*]; une bordée de [*insults, oaths*].
II *vtr* (in tennis) prendre [*qch*] de volée; (in soccer) reprendre [*qch*] de volée.
III *vi* (in tennis) jouer à la volée.

volleyball /ˈvɒlɪˌbɔːl/ ▶ **949**] **I** *n* volley(-ball) *m*.
II *noun modifier* [*match, court*] de volley(-ball).

volt /vəʊlt/ *n* volt *m*; **nine-~ battery** pile *f* de neuf volts.

voltage /ˈvəʊltɪdʒ/ *n* tension *f*.

volume /ˈvɒljuːm, US -jəm/ **I** *n* **1** GEN, AUDIO, PHYS volume *m*; (of container) capacité *f*; **by ~** au volume; **2** (book) volume *m*; (part of set) tome *m*.
II *noun modifier* COMM (bulk) [*production, purchasing, sales*] en nombre.
IDIOMS **to speak ~s (about)** en dire long (sur).

volume: ~ control *n* AUDIO (bouton *m* de) réglage *m* du volume; **~ discount** *n* COMM remise *f*, ristourne *f* (sur quantité).

voluntarily /ˈvɒləntrəlɪ, US ˌvɒlənˈterɪlɪ/ *adv* de plein gré, volontairement.

voluntary /ˈvɒlntrɪ, US -terɪ/ **I** *n* MUS voluntary *m*.
II *adj* **1** (not imposed) [*consent, euthanasia*] volontaire; [*statement*] spontané; [*agreement, ban*] librement consenti; [*participation*] facultatif/-ive; [*sanction*] non obligatoire; **on a ~ basis** sur une base volontaire; **2** (unpaid) bénévole; **to work on a ~ basis** travailler bénévolement; **3** [*movement*] volontaire.

voluntary: ~ hospital *n* US ≈ hôpital *m* privé; **~ redundancy** *n* GB départ *m* volontaire.

volunteer /ˌvɒlənˈtɪə(r)/ **I** *n* **1** GEN, MIL volontaire *mf*; **2** (unpaid worker) bénévole *mf*.
II *noun modifier* **1** (unpaid) [*driver, fire brigade, helper, work*] bénévole; **2** MIL [*force, division*] de volontaires.
III *vtr* **1** (offer) offrir; **to ~ to do** offrir de faire, se porter volontaire pour faire; **2** (divulge) fournir [*qch*]

spontanément; **'it was me,'** he **~ed** 'c'était moi,' dit-il lui-même.
IV *vi* **1** GEN se porter volontaire (**for** pour); **2** MIL s'engager comme volontaire.
voluptuous /vəˈlʌptʃʊəs/ *adj* voluptueux/-euse.
vomit /ˈvɒmɪt/ **I** *n* vomi *m*.
II *vtr*, *vi* vomir.
vomiting /ˈvɒmɪtɪŋ/ *n* vomissement *m*.
voodoo /ˈvuːduː/ *n*, *noun modifier* vaudou (*m*).
voracious /vəˈreɪʃəs/ *adj* vorace.
vortex /ˈvɔːteks/ *n* (*pl* **~es** ou **-tices**) LIT, FIG tourbillon *m*.
vote /vəʊt/ **I** *n* **1** (choice) vote *m*; **to cast one's ~** voter; **one man one ~ ~** suffrage universel; **that gets my ~!** FIG moi je suis pour!; **2** (franchise) **the ~** le droit de vote; **3** (ballot) vote *m*; **to have a ~** voter; **to take a ~ on** voter sur; **to put sth to the ~** mettre qch aux voix; **4** (body of voters) voix *fpl*; **by a majority ~** à la majorité des voix; **to increase one's ~ by 10%** recevoir 10% de voix en plus.
II *vtr* **1** (affirm choice of) voter; **what** ou **how do you ~?** pour qui voter?; **to ~ sb into/out of office** élire/ne pas réélire qn; **2** (authorize) **to ~ sb sth** accorder qch à qn; **3**° (propose) proposer.
III *vi* voter; **to ~ for reform** voter en faveur de la réforme; **to ~ on whether** voter pour décider si; **let's ~ on it** mettons-le aux voix.
IDIOMS **to ~ with one's feet** (by leaving) quitter le navire°.
■ **vote down**: **~** [sb/sth] **down**, **~ down** [sb/sth] battre [qn] aux voix [*person*]; rejeter [*motion*].
■ **vote in**: **~** [sb] **in**, **~ in** [sb] élire.
■ **vote out**: **~** [sb/sth] **out**, **~ out** [sb/sth] ne pas réélire [*person*]; rejeter [*motion*].
■ **vote through**: **~** [sth] **through**, **~ through** [sth] faire adopter.
vote: **~ of censure** *n* POL vote *m* sur une motion de censure; **~ of confidence** *n* POL, FIG vote *m* de confiance (**in** en); **~ of thanks** *n* discours *m* de remerciement.
voter /ˈvəʊtə(r)/ *n* POL électeur/-trice *m/f*.
voter: **~ registration** *n* US inscription *f* sur les listes électorales; **~ registration card** *n* US carte *f* d'électeur.
voting /ˈvəʊtɪŋ/ **I** *n* scrutin *m*.
II *noun modifier* [*patterns, intentions, rights*] de vote.
voting: **~ age** *n* majorité *f* électorale; **~ booth** *n* isoloir *m*.
vouch /vaʊtʃ/ *vtr* **to ~ that** garantir que.
■ **vouch for**: **~ for** [sb/sth] **1** (informally) répondre de [*person*]; témoigner de [*fact*]; **2** (officially) se porter garant de.
voucher /ˈvaʊtʃə(r)/ *n* **1** (for gift, concession) bon *m*; **2** (receipt) reçu *m*.
vow /vaʊ/ **I** *n* (religious) vœu *m*; (of honour) serment *m*; **to be under a ~ of silence** avoir fait le serment de garder le secret.
II *vows* *npl* **1** RELIG vœux *mpl*; **2 marriage** ou **wedding ~s** serments *mpl* du mariage.
III *vtr* faire vœu de; **to ~ to do** jurer de faire; (privately) se jurer de faire.
vowel /ˈvaʊəl/ **I** *n* voyelle *f*.
II *noun modifier* [*sound*] vocalique; **~ shift** mutation *f* vocalique.
vox pop° /ˌvɒks ˈpɒp/ *n* **1** (also **vox populi**) opinion *f* publique; **2** TV, RADIO interviews *mpl* pris dans la rue.
voyage /ˈvɔɪdʒ/ **I** *n* LIT, FIG voyage *m*; **on the ~**

pendant le voyage; **to go on a ~** partir en voyage; **the outward ~** le voyage aller.
II *vi* LITTÉR voyager; **to ~ across** traverser.
V-sign /ˈviːsaɪn/ *n* (victory sign) V *m* de la victoire; (offensive gesture) GB geste *m* obscène.
VSO *n* GB (*abrév* = **Voluntary Service Overseas**) coopération *f* civile.
vulgar /ˈvʌlgə(r)/ *adj* **1** [*furniture, clothes*] de mauvais goût; [*behaviour, curiosity*] déplacé; [*taste*] douteux/-euse; [*person*] vulgaire; **2** (rude) grossier/-ière.
vulgar fraction *n* MATH fraction *f* ordinaire.
vulgarity /vʌlˈgærətɪ/ *n* **1** (of furniture, clothes) mauvais goût *m*; (of person, behaviour) vulgarité *f*; **2** (rudeness) grossièreté *f*.
vulgarize /ˈvʌlgəraɪz/ *vtr* **1** populariser [*place, activity*]; vulgariser [*study, theory, art*]; **2** (make rude) rendre [qch] vulgaire.
vulgarly /ˈvʌlgəlɪ/ *adv* **1** [*dressed, furnished*] avec mauvais goût; [*behave*] avec vulgarité; **2** (rudely) avec grossièreté.
vulnerable /ˈvʌlnərəbl/ *adj* vulnérable (**to** à).
vulture /ˈvʌltʃə(r)/ *n* LIT, FIG vautour *m*.
vying /ˈvaɪɪŋ/ *p prés* ▶ **vie**.

Volume measurement

For pints, gallons, litres etc. ▶ **789** .
Note that French has a comma where English has a decimal point.

1 cu in	=	$16{,}38 \text{ cm}^3$
1 cu ft	=	$0{,}03 \text{ m}^3$
1 cu yd	=	$0{,}76 \text{ m}^3$

There are three ways of saying $16{,}38 \text{ cm}^3$, *and other measurements like it:* seize virgule trente-huit centimètres cubes *or* (*less formally*) seize centimètres cubes virgule trente-huit *or* seize centimètres cubes trente-huit. *For more details on how to say numbers,* ▶ **1112** .

what is its volume?	= quel est son volume?
its volume is 200 cubic metres	= ça fait 200 mètres cubes
it's 200 cubic metres	= ça fait 200 mètres cubes
it's one metre by two metres by three metres	= ça mesure un mètre sur deux mètres sur trois mètres
sold by the cubic metre	= vendu au mètre cube
A has a greater volume than B	= le volume de A est supérieur à celui de B
B has a smaller volume than A	= le volume de B est inférieur à celui de A

Note the use of de *in this construction.*

there are a million cubic centimetres in a cubic metre	= il y a un million de centimètres cubes dans un mètre cube
a million cubic centimetres make one cubic metre	= un million de centimètres cubes font un mètre cube

Note the French construction with de, *coming after the noun it describes:*

a 200-cubic-metre tank	= un réservoir de 200 mètres cubes

Ww

w, W /'dʌblju:/ *n* **1** (letter) w, W *m*; **2 W** ELEC *abrév écrite* = **watt**; **3 W** GEOG *abrév écrite* = **West**.

WA *n*: *abrév écrite* = **Washington**.

wad /wɒd/ I *n* **1** (bundle) liasse *f*; **2** (lump) balle *f*.
II **wads** *npl* US **~s of**○ des tas○ de.

wadding /'wɒdɪŋ/ *n* **1** (padding) ouatage *m*; **2** (for gun) bourre *f*.

waddle /'wɒdl/ I *n* dandinement *m*.
II *vi* [*duck, person*] se dandiner.

wade /weɪd/ *vi* **1** (in water) **to ~ into the water** entrer dans l'eau; **to ~ ashore** regagner la rive à pied; **2** (proceed with difficulty) **to ~ through sth** LIT se frayer un chemin pour traverser qch; **I managed to ~ through the work** j'ai réussi péniblement à terminer le travail.
■ **wade in**○ **1** (start with determination) se mettre au travail; **2** (attack) passer à l'attaque.
■ **wade into**○: ¶ **~ into [sth]** se mettre à [*task*]; ¶ **~ into [sb]** (attack) se jeter sur.

wader /'weɪdə(r)/ *n* **1** ZOOL échassier *m*; **2** US personne *f* en train de barboter.

waders /'weɪdəz/ *npl* cuissardes *fpl*.

wafer /'weɪfə(r)/ *n* CULIN gaufrette *f*; RELIG hostie *f*; (of silicon) tranche *f* (de silicium); (on letter) cachet *m*.

wafer-thin /ˌweɪfə'θɪn/ *adj* ultrafin.

waffle /'wɒfl/ I *n* **1** CULIN gaufre *f*; **2**○ PÉJ (empty words) verbiage *m*; (in essay) remplissage *m*.
II○ *vi* (also **~ on**) (speaking) bavasser○; (writing) faire du remplissage.

waffle iron *n* CULIN gaufrier *m*.

waft /wɒft, US wæft/ I *vtr* **to ~ sth through/towards** [*wind*] apporter qch dans/vers.
II *vi* **to ~ towards** flotter dans la direction de; **to ~ up** monter.

wag /wæg/ I *vtr* (*p prés etc* **-gg-**) remuer [*tail*]; hocher [*head*]; **to ~ one's finger at sb** agiter son doigt dans la direction de qn.
II *vi* (*p prés etc* **-gg-**) [*tail*] remuer, frétiller; [*head*] s'agiter; **tongues will ~** FIG ça va faire jaser.
IDIOMS **it's the tail ~ging the dog** c'est le monde à l'envers.

wage /weɪdʒ/ I *n* (also **~s**) salaire *m*.
II *noun modifier* [*agreement, claim, inflation, negotiations, rate, settlement, talks*] salarial; [*increase, rise*] de salaire; [*policy, restraint, freeze*] des salaires.
III *vtr* mener [*campaign*]; **to ~ (a) war against sth/sb** LIT, FIG faire la guerre contre qch/qn.

waged /weɪdʒd/ *adj* salarié.

wage earner *n* **1** (person earning a wage) salarié/-e *m/f* (hebdomadaire); **2** (breadwinner) soutien *m* de famille.

wage packet *n* **1** LIT (envelope) enveloppe *f* de paie; **2** (money) paie *f*.

wager /'weɪdʒə(r)/ I *n* pari *m*; **to make** ou **lay a ~** parier.
II *vtr* parier (**on** sur; **that** que).

wage: **~ round** *n* réajustement *m* des salaires; **~s council** *n* ~ commission *f* des salaires; **~ sheet, ~ slip** *n* feuille *f* de paie.

waggle /'wægl/ I *vtr* remuer [*tail*]; faire bouger [*tooth, ear, object*]; (shake) agiter [*object*]; **to ~ one's hips** rouler des hanches.
II *vi* (also **~ around, ~ about**) remuer.

waggon GB, **wagon** /'wægən/ *n* **1** (horse-drawn) chariot *m*; **2** GB RAIL wagon *m* (de marchandises); **3** US = **station wagon**; **4** US (petit) chariot *m* (jouet).

IDIOMS **to be on the ~**○ être au régime sec HUM.

wagon train *n* US HIST convoi *m* de chariots.

waif /weɪf/ *n* enfant *m* abandonné.

wail /weɪl/ I *n* (of person, wind) gémissement *m*; (of siren) hurlement *m*; (of musical instrument) son *m* plaintif.
II *vtr* **'oh no!' he ~ed** 'oh non!' gémit-il.
III *vi* [*person, wind*] gémir; [*siren*] hurler; [*music*] pleurer.

wailing /'weɪlɪŋ/ I *n* (of person) gémissements *mpl*; (of wind) gémissement *m*; (of siren) hurlement *m*; (of music) son *m* plaintif.
II *adj* GEN plaintif/-ive; [*siren*] strident.

Wailing Wall *pr n* Mur *m* des Lamentations.

waist /weɪst/ I **▶ 1260** *n* taille *f*; **to have a 70 cm ~** avoir un tour de taille de 70 cm.

waist: **~band** *n* ceinture *f*; **~coat** *n* GB gilet *m*.

waisted /'weɪstɪd/ *adj* cintré; **a high-~ dress** une robe à taille haute.

waist: **~line** *n* ligne *f*; **~ measurement ▶ 1260** *n* tour *m* de taille.

wait /weɪt/ I *n* attente *f*; **an hour's ~** une heure d'attente; **to have a long ~** devoir attendre longtemps; **it will only be a short ~** ce ne sera pas long.
II *vtr* **1** (await) attendre; **don't ~ dinner for me**○ US ne m'attendez pas pour dîner; **2** US **to ~ table** servir à table.
III *vi* **1** (remain patiently) attendre; **to keep sb ~ing** faire attendre qn; **to ~ for sb/sth** attendre qn/qch; **to ~ for sb/sth to do** attendre que qn/qch fasse; **to ~ to do** attendre de faire; **she can't ~ to start** elle a hâte de commencer; **I can hardly ~ to do** je meurs d'impatience de faire; **you'll just have to ~ and see** attends et tu verras; **(just you) ~ and see** tu verras bien○; **just you ~!** (as threat) tu vas voir○!; **~ for it!** tiens-toi bien○!; MIL pas encore!; **2** (be left until later) attendre; **3** (serve) **to ~ at** ou **on table** être serveur/-euse *m/f*.
IDIOMS **to lie in ~** être à l'affût; **to lie in ~ for sb** [*ambushers*] guetter qn; [*reporter, attacker*] tendre une embuscade à qn.
■ **wait around, wait about** GB attendre.
■ **wait behind** attendre un peu; **to ~ behind for sb** attendre qn.
■ **wait on**: **~ on [sb]** (serve) servir; **to be ~ed on** être servi; **to ~ on sb hand and foot** être aux petits soins pour qn.
■ **wait up 1** (stay awake) veiller; **to ~ up for sb** veiller jusqu'au retour de qn; **2** US (stay patiently) **~ up!** attends!

waiter /'weɪtə(r)/ **▶ 1251** *n* serveur *m*; '**~!**' 'monsieur!'; **~ service** service *m* à table.

waiter service *n* service *m* à table.

waiting /'weɪtɪŋ/ I *n* attente *f*; '**no ~**' 'arrêt et stationnement interdits'.
II *adj* (épith) [*taxi, crowd*] qui attend/attendait etc; [*reporter*] à l'affût; **sb's ~ arms** les bras ouverts de qn.

waiting game *n* attentisme *m*; **to play a ~** faire de l'attentisme.

waiting: **~ list** *n* liste *f* d'attente; **~ room** *n* salle *f* d'attente.

waitress /'weɪtrɪs/ **▶ 1251** *n* serveuse *f*; '**~!**' 'madame!', 'mademoiselle!'

waive /weɪv/ *vtr* déroger à [*rule*]; renoncer à [*claim, demand, right*]; supprimer [*fee, condition*].

waiver /ˈweɪvə(r)/ *n* JUR renonciation *f*.

wake /weɪk/ **I** *n* **1** LIT, FIG sillage *m*; **2** (over dead person) veillée *f* funèbre (*accompagnée de célébrations*).
II *vtr* (also **~ up**) (*prét* **woke**, **waked**†; *pp* **woken**, **waked**†) LIT, FIG réveiller (**from** de); **to ~ sb from a dream** tirer qn d'un rêve.
III *vi* (also **~ up**) (*prét* **woke**, **waked**†; *pp* **woken**, **waked**†) se réveiller; **I woke (up) to find him gone** à mon réveil, il était parti; **to ~ (up) from a deep sleep** sortir d'un profond sommeil; **she finally woke (up) to her responsibilities** elle est finalement revenue à ses responsabilités.
■ **wake up**: ¶ **~ up** se réveiller; **~ up!** LIT réveille-toi!; FIG ouvre les yeux! ; **to ~ up to sth** FIG prendre conscience de qch; ¶ **~ up [sb]**, **~ [sb] up = wake** II.

wakeful /ˈweɪkfl/ *adj* éveillé; **to have a ~ night** passer une nuit blanche.

waken /ˈweɪkən/ *vtr*, *vi* = **wake** II, III.

waker /ˈweɪkə(r)/ *n* **to be an early/late ~** se réveiller tôt/tard.

wake-up call *n* réveil *m* téléphoné.

waking /ˈweɪkɪŋ/ **I** *n* (état *m* de) veille *f*; **between sleeping and ~** dans un demi-sommeil.
II *adj* **in** ou **during one's ~ hours** pendant la journée.

Wales /weɪlz/ ▶ 840 *pr n* pays *m* de Galles.

walk /wɔːk/ **I** *n* **1** promenade *f*; (shorter) tour *m*; (hike) randonnée *f*; **it's about ten minutes' ~** c'est environ à dix minutes à pied; **on the ~ home** en rentrant à pied à la maison; **to go for** ou **on a ~** (aller) faire une promenade; **to have** ou **take a ~** faire une promenade; (shorter) faire un tour○; **to take sb for a ~** emmener qn faire une promenade or (shorter) un tour○; **to take the dog for a ~** promener le chien; **it's a long ~ back to the hotel** il y a une longue marche d'ici à l'hôtel; **2** (gait) démarche *f*; **3** (pace) pas *m*; **to slow down to a ~** se mettre à marcher (*après avoir couru*); **4** (path) allée *f*; **people from all ~s of life** des gens de tous les milieux; **5** SPORT épreuve *f* de marche.
II *vtr* **1** (cover on foot) faire [qch] à pied [*path*, *road*]; parcourir [qch] à pied [*countryside*]; (patrol) parcourir; **I can't ~ another step** je ne peux pas faire un pas de plus; **to ~ it**○ SPORT gagner haut la main; **2** (lead, escort) conduire [*horse etc*]; promener [*dog*]; **to ~ sb home** raccompagner qn chez lui/elle.
III *vi* **1** (in general) marcher; (for pleasure) se promener; (not run) aller au pas; (not ride or drive) aller à pied; **to ~ with a limp** boiter; **'~'** US (at traffic lights) 'traversez'; **it's not very far, let's ~** ce n'est pas très loin, allons-y à pied; **to ~ across** ou **through sth** traverser qch (à pied) (*see note*); **a policeman ~ed by** un policier est passé; **he ~ed up/down the road** il a remonté/descendu la rue (à pied) (*see note*); **we've been ~ing round in circles for hours** nous tournons en rond depuis des heures; **someone was ~ing around** ou **about upstairs** quelqu'un allait et venait à l'étage supérieur; **I'd just ~ed in at the door when...** je venais à peine de passer la porte, quand...; **suddenly in ~ed my father** soudain voilà que mon père est entré; **to ~ in one's sleep** être somnambule; **to ~ up and down** faire les cent pas; **to ~ up and down a room** arpenter une pièce; **shall I ~ with you to the bus?** veux-tu que je t'accompagne au bus?; **2**○ HUM (disappear) se faire la malle○.
IDIOMS **take a ~!**○! US dégage○!; **you must ~ before you can run** il ne faut pas brûler les étapes.

■ Note *à pied* is often omitted with movement verbs if we already know that the person is on foot. If it is surprising or ambiguous, *à pied* should be included.

■ **walk across** ¶ traverser; **to ~ across to sth/sb** s'approcher de qch/qn; ¶ **~ across [sth]** traverser.
■ **walk around**: ¶ **~ around** LIT se promener; (aimlessly) traîner; ¶ **~ around [sth]** (to and fro) faire un tour dans; (make circuit of) faire le tour de; **we ~ed**

around Paris for hours nous nous sommes promenés dans Paris pendant des heures.
■ **walk away 1** LIT s'éloigner (**from** de); **2** FIG **to ~ away from a problem** fuir un problème; **3** FIG (survive unscathed) sortir indemne (**from** de); **4 to ~ away with** gagner [qch] haut la main [*game*, *tournament*]; remporter [qch] haut la main [*election*]; décrocher [*prize*, *honour*]; **5** SPORT **to ~ away from sb/sth** laisser qn/qch loin derrière.
■ **walk back** revenir sur ses pas (**to** jusqu'à); **we ~ed back (home)** nous sommes rentrés à pied.
■ **walk in** entrer; **who should ~ in but my husband!** devine qui est arrivé?—mon mari!; **'please ~ in'** (sign) 'entrez sans frapper'.
■ **walk into**: **~ into [sth] 1** (enter) entrer dans; **she ~ed into that job** FIG elle a eu ce poste sans lever le petit doigt; **2** tomber dans [*trap*, *ambush*]; **you ~ed right into that one**○! tu es tombé dans le panneau○!; **3** (bump into) rentrer dans.
■ **walk off**: ¶ **~ off 1** LIT partir brusquement; **2**○ FIG **to ~ off with sth** (innocently) partir avec qch; (as theft) filer○ avec qch; ¶ **~ off [sth]**, **~ [sth] off** se promener pour faire passer [*hangover*, *large meal*].
■ **walk on 1** (continue) continuer à marcher; **2** THEAT être figurant.
■ **walk out 1** LIT sortir (**of** de); **2** FIG (desert) partir; **to ~ out on** laisser tomber○ [*lover*]; rompre [*contract*, *undertaking*]; **3** (as protest) partir en signe de protestation; (on strike) se mettre en grève.
■ **walk over**: **~ over** (a few steps) s'approcher (**to** de); (a short walk) faire un saut○ (**to** à); ¶ **~ over [sb]** (humiliate) marcher sur les pieds de; **he lets her ~ all over him** elle le mène au bout du nez.
■ **walk round**: ¶ **~ round** faire le tour; ¶ **~ round [sth]** (round edge of) faire le tour de; (visit) visiter.
■ **walk through**: ¶ **~ through** LIT traverser; ¶ **~ through [sth] 1** (traverse) traverser [*house*, *forest*]; passer [*door*]; par courir [*streets*]; marcher dans [*snow*, *mud*, *grass*]; **2** THEAT répéter les déplacements de.
■ **walk up to ~ up to** s'approcher de.

walkabout /ˈwɔːkəbaʊt/ *n* bain *m* de foule.

walker /ˈwɔːkə(r)/ *n* **1** (for pleasure) promeneur/-euse *m/f*; (for exercise) marcheur/-euse *m/f*; **she's a fast ~!** elle marche vite!; **2** (for baby) trotteur *m*.

walkie-talkie /ˌwɔːkɪˈtɔːkɪ/ *n* talkie-walkie *m*.

walk-in /ˈwɔːkɪn/ *adj* **1** [*closet*] où l'on peut tenir debout; **2** US [*apartment*] de plain-pied sur la rue; [*clinic*] qui reçoit les clients sans rendez-vous.

walking /ˈwɔːkɪŋ/ **I** *n* (for pleasure) promenades *fpl* à pied; (for exercise, sport) marche *f* à pied.
II *adj* HUM **she's a ~ dictionary** c'est un dictionnaire ambulant.

walking boots *npl* chaussures *fpl* de marche.

walking distance *n* **to be within ~** être à quelques minutes de marche (**of** de).

walking: **~ frame** *n* MED déambulateur *m*; **~ holiday** *n* vacances *fpl* de randonnée.

walking pace *n* pas *m*; **at a ~** au pas.

walking: **~ race** *n* épreuve *f* de marche; **~ shoes** *npl* chaussures *fpl* de marche; **~ stick** *n* canne *f*; **~ tour** *n* randonnée *f* à pied; **~ wounded** *npl* blessés *mpl* capables de marcher.

walkman® /ˈwɔːkmən/ *n* (*pl* **-mans**) walkman® *m*, baladeur *m*.

walk-on /ˌwɔːkˈɒn/ **I** *n* THEAT figurant/-e *m/f*.
II *adj* [*role*] de figurant.

walk: **~out** *n* (from conference) départ *m* en signe de protestation; (strike) grève *f* surprise; **~over** *n* victoire *f* facile (**for** pour); **~-up** *n* US immeuble *m* sans ascenseur; **~way** *n* allée *f*.

wall /wɔːl/ *n* **1** GEN, LIT, FIG mur *m*; **2** (of cave, tunnel) paroi *f*; **3** ANAT paroi *f*; **the stomach ~** la paroi stomacale; **4** (of tyre) flanc *m*.
IDIOMS **to be a fly on the ~** être une mouche; **to be off the ~**○ [*person*] être dingue○; [*comments*] être incohérent; **to drive sb up the ~**○ exaspérer qn; **to**

go to the ~ faire faillite; **to have sb up against the** ~ mettre qn au pied du mur.
■ **wall in**: ~ **in** [sth], ~ [sth] **in** entourer.
■ **wall off**: ~ **off** [sth], ~ [sth] **off** (block off) condamner; (separate by wall) séparer [qch] par un mur.
■ **wall up**: ~ **up** [sb/sth], ~ [sb/sth] **up** emmurer.

wall: ~**bars** npl espalier m; ~ **chart** n affiche f; ~ **covering** n revêtement m mural; ~ **cupboard** n élément m (mural).

walled /wɔːld/ adj [city] fortifié; [garden] clos.

wallet /ˈwɒlɪt/ n (for notes) portefeuille m; (for documents) porte-documents m inv; **kind to your** ~ bon marché.

walleyed° /ˈwɔːlaɪd/ adj **to be** ~ loucher.

wallflower /ˈwɔːlflaʊə(r)/ n BOT giroflée f jaune.
IDIOMS **to be a** ~ faire tapisserie.

wall: ~ **hanging** n tapisserie f; ~ **heater** n radiateur m mural; ~ **light** n applique f murale; ~-**mounted** adj fixé au mur.

wallop° /ˈwɒləp/ **I** n **1** (punch) beigne° f; **2** (loud noise) vlan!
II vtr **1** (hit) flanquer une raclée à° [person]; taper dans [ball]; **2** (defeat) battre [qn] à plates coutures.

walloping° /ˈwɒləpɪŋ/ **I** n raclée f.
II adj, adv super.

wallow /ˈwɒləʊ/ **I** n **to have a** ~ se vautrer.
II vi **1 to** ~ **in** se vautrer dans [mud, luxury]; se complaire dans [self-pity, nostalgia]; **2** [ship] ballotter.

wallpaper /ˈwɔːlpeɪpə(r)/ **I** n papier m peint.
II vtr tapisser [room].

wall-to-wall /ˌwɔːltəˈwɔːl/ adj **1** ~ **carpet** moquette f; **2** FIG **the** ~ **silence of large art galleries** le silence complet des grandes galeries d'art.

walnut /ˈwɔːlnʌt/ **I** n **1** (nut) noix f; **2** (tree, wood) noyer m.
II noun modifier [cake, yoghurt] aux noix; [oil, shell] de noix; [furniture] en noyer.

walrus /ˈwɔːlrəs/ n morse m; ~ **moustache** moustache f à la gauloise.

waltz /wɔːls, US wɔːlts/ **I** n valse f.
II vi **1** (dance) danser la valse; **2 to** ~ **out of sth** sortir de qch d'un pas désinvolte; **3 to** ~ **off with sth** gagner qch haut la main°; **to** ~ **through an exam** réussir un examen facilement.

wan /wɒn/ adj blême.

wand /wɒnd/ n (all contexts) baguette f.

wander /ˈwɒndə(r)/ **I** n promenade f; **to have ou take a** ~ faire une balade°; **to have a** ~ **round the shops** faire un tour dans les magasins.
II vtr parcourir; **to** ~ **the streets** traîner dans la rue.
III vi **1** (walk, stroll) se promener; **the chickens are free to** ~ les poulets sont libres d'aller et de venir; **to** ~ **around town** se balader en ville; **to** ~ **in and out of the shops** flâner dans les magasins; **2** (stray) errer; **to** ~ **into the next field** s'égarer dans le champ voisin; **to** ~ **away** s'éloigner (from de); **3 to** ~ **in** arriver tranquillement; **to** ~ **over to ou up to sb** s'approcher tranquillement de qn; **4** [mind, attention] (through boredom, inattention) s'égarer ; (through age, illness) divaguer; [eyes, hands] errer (**over** sur); **her mind** ~**ed back to** son esprit revenait sur; **to** ~ **off the point ou subject** s'éloigner du sujet.
■ **wander about, wander around** (stroll) se balader; (when lost) errer.
■ **wander off** [child, animal] s'éloigner.

wanderer /ˈwɒndərə(r)/ n voyageur/-euse m/f.

wandering /ˈwɒndərɪŋ/ adj [person] itinérant; [animal] voyageur/-euse [gaze, eye] qui s'égare; [attention, mind] vagabond.

wanderings /ˈwɒndərɪŋz/ npl **1** (journeys) vagabondages mpl; **2** (confusion) divagations fpl.

wanderlust /ˈwɒndəlʌst/ n envie f de voyager.

wane /weɪn/ **I** n **to be on the** ~ être sur le déclin.
II vi [moon] décroître; FIG diminuer.

wangle° /ˈwæŋgl/ **I** n (trick) combine° f.

II vtr carotter° [gift]; réussir à obtenir [leave, meeting]; **to** ~ **sth out of sb** soutirer qch à qn [job, money, promise]; **to** ~ **sth for sb** arranger qch à qn°; **to** ~ **one's way into** réussir à s'introduire dans.

waning /ˈweɪnɪŋ/ **I** n (of moon) déclin m; FIG (lowering) baisse f (**of** de); (weakening) déclin m (**of** de).
II adj [moon] décroissant; [popularity] en baisse.

wanly /ˈwɒnlɪ/ adv [smile] d'un air las; [shine] d'une lueur blême.

wanna /ˈwɒnə/ = **want to, want a**.

wannabe(e)° /ˈwɒnəbiː/ n: personne qui rêve d'être célèbre.

want /wɒnt/ **I** n **1** (need) besoin m; **to be in** ~ **of** avoir besoin de; **2** (deprivation) LITTÉR indigence f; **3** (lack) défaut m; **for** ~ **of** à défaut ou faute de; **it's not for** ~ **of trying** ce n'est pas faute d'avoir essayé.
II vtr **1** (desire) vouloir; **I** ~ (as general statement) je veux; (would like) je voudrais; (am seeking) je souhaite; **what ou how much do you** ~ **for this chair?** combien voulez-vous pour ce fauteuil?; **I** ~ **the job finished** je voudrais que ce travail soit fini; **I don't** ~ **to** je n'ai pas envie; **to** ~ **sb to do** vouloir que qn fasse; **where do you** ~ **me?** où voulez-vous que je me mette?; **he doesn't** ~ **much does he?** IRON il est toujours aussi peu exigeant! IRON; **they just don't** ~ **to know** ils préfèrent ne rien savoir; **2**° (need) avoir besoin de; **you won't be** ~**ed at the meeting** on n'aura pas besoin de vous à la réunion; **to** ~ **to do**° devoir faire; **you** ~ **to watch out** tu devrais faire attention; **what do they** ~ **with all those machines?** pourquoi est-ce qu'ils ont besoin de toutes ces machines?; **what do you** ~ **with me?** qu'est-ce que vous me voulez?; **all that's** ~**ed is your signature** il ne manque plus que votre signature; **several jobs** ~ **doing** GB il y a plusieurs tâches à faire; **3** (require presence of) demander; **you're** ~**ed on the phone** on vous demande au téléphone; **the boss** ~**s you** le patron veut te voir; **to be** ~**ed by the police** être recherché par la police; **I know when I'm not** ~**ed** je sens bien que je suis de trop.
III vi **to** ~ **for** manquer de.
■ **want in**° **1** (asking to enter) vouloir entrer; **2** (asking to participate) vouloir participer; **I** ~ **in on the deal** je veux être dans le coup°.
■ **want out**° **1** (asking to exit) vouloir sortir; **2** (discontinuing participation) vouloir laisser tomber°; **to** ~ **out of** vouloir se retirer de.

want ad n US petite annonce f.

wanted /ˈwɒntɪd/ adj **1** (by police) recherché par la police; **2** (loved) **to be (very much)** ~ (before birth) être (très) désiré; (after birth) être (très) aimé.

wanted list n liste f des suspects.

wanting /ˈwɒntɪŋ/ adj **to be** ~ faire défaut; **to be** ~ **in** manquer de; **to be found** ~ être réprouvé.

wanton /ˈwɒntən, US ˈwɔːn-/ adj **1** [cruelty, damage, waste] gratuit; [disregard] délibéré; **2** LITTÉR [mood] joueur/-euse; **3**† (immoral) dévergondé.

wantonly /ˈwɒntənlɪ, US ˈwɔːn-/ adv **1** (gratuitously) sans raison; **2** LITTÉR (playfully) de façon capricieuse; **3**† (provocatively) de façon dévergondée.

war /wɔː(r)/ **I** n **1** (armed conflict) guerre f; ~ **broke out** la guerre a éclaté; **in the** ~ à la guerre; **to go off to the** ~ partir à la guerre; **to go to** ~ **against** entrer en guerre contre; **to wage** ~ **on** faire la guerre contre; **to be at** ~ **with a country** être en guerre avec un pays; **a** ~ **over ou about** une guerre pour [land, independence]; une guerre sur [issue]; **2** FIG (competition) guerre f; **price/trade** ~ guerre des prix/commerciale; **a** ~ **of words** un conflit verbal; **3** FIG (to eradicate sth) lutte f; **to wage** ~ **on ou against** mener une lutte contre.
II noun modifier [correspondent, crime, dance, effort, film, historian, medal, widow, wound] de guerre; [cemetery, leader, grave, zone] militaire; [hero] de la guerre; ~ **deaths** victimes fpl de la guerre; **he has a good** ~ **record** il a de bons états de service.
III vi (p prés etc -**rr**-) **to** ~ **with a country** être en guerre contre un pays (**over** à cause de).

warble /'wɔːbl/ *vi* **1** [*bird*] gazouiller; **2** PÉJ [*singer*] roucouler.

war: ~ **cabinet** *n* conseil *m* de guerre; ~ **cry** *n* cri *m* de guerre ALSO FIG.

ward /wɔːd/ *n* **1** (in hospital) (unit) service *m*; (room) unité *f*; (building) pavillon *m*; **he's in** ~ **3** il est à l'unité 3; **maternity** ~ service de maternité; **hospital** ~ salle *f* d'hôpital; **2** POL circonscription *f* électorale; **3** (also ~ **of court**) pupille *m*; **to be made a** ~ **of court** être placé sous tutelle judiciaire.
■ **ward off**: ~ **off** [*sth*] chasser [*evil, predator*]; faire taire [*criticism*]; écarter [*threat*]; éviter [*bankruptcy, disaster*].

warden /'wɔːdn/ ▶ 1251 *n* GEN directeur/-trice *m*/*f*; (of park, estate) gardien/-ienne *m*/*f*.

warder /'wɔːdə(r)/ *n* GB gardien/-ienne *m*/*f*.

wardrobe /'wɔːdrəʊb/ *n* (furniture) armoire *f*; (set of clothes) garde-robe *f*; THEAT costumes *mpl*.

wardrobe: ~ **assistant** ▶ 1251 *n* assistant/-e *m*/*f* costumier/-ière; ~ **director** *n* costumier/-ière *m*/*f*.

ward: ~**room** *n* MIL NAUT carré *m* (des officiers); ~ **round** *n* MED visite *f* (*du médecin hospitalier*); ~ **sister** *n* GB MED infirmière *f* en chef.

ware /weə(r)/ **I** *n* ¢ articles *mpl*.
II wares *npl* marchandises *fpl*.

warehouse /'weəhaʊs/ **I** *n* entrepôt *m*.
II *vtr* entreposer.

warfare /'wɔːfeə(r)/ *n* **modern** ~ conflits *mpl* modernes; **chemical** ~ guerre *f* chimique.

war: ~ **game** *n* MIL manœuvre *f* militaire; GAMES jeu *m* de stratégie (militaire); ~ **games** *npl* GAMES (with nonmilitary participants) guerre *f* simulée; ~**head** *n* ogive *f*; ~ **horse** *n* LIT cheval *m* de bataille; FIG (campaigner) vétéran *m*.

warily /'weərɪlɪ/ *adv* **1** (cautiously) avec prudence; **2** (mistrustfully) avec méfiance.

warlike /'wɔːlaɪk/ *adj* [*people*] guerrier/-ière; [*mood, words*] belliqueux/-euse.

warm /wɔːm/ **I**° *n* **1** GB **the** ~ le chaud; **2 to give sth a** ~ GEN chauffer; réchauffer [*part of body*].
II *adj* **1** (not cold) GEN chaud; [*trail*] (encore) frais/fraîche; **in** ~ **weather** quand il fait chaud; **to be** ~ [*person*] avoir chaud; [*weather*] faire chaud; **it's nice and** ~ **in here** on est bien au chaud ici; **in a** ~ **oven** CULIN à four très doux; **'serve** ~' CULIN 'servir tiède'; **to get (oneself)** ~ se réchauffer; **you're getting** ~**er!** (in guessing game) tu chauffes!; **to get sb/sth** ~ réchauffer qn/qch; **to keep (oneself)** ~ (wrap up) ne pas prendre froid; (take exercise) se réchauffer; (stay indoors) rester au chaud; **to keep sb** ~ tenir chaud à qn; **to keep sth** ~ tenir [qch] au chaud [*food*]; chauffer [qch] (en permanence) [*room*]; **2** (enthusiastic) GEN chaleureux/-euse; [*admiration, support*] enthousiaste; **to have a** ~ **heart** être chaleureux/-euse; ~(**est**) **regards** meilleures amitiés; **3** (mellow) [*colour*] chaud; [*sound*] chaleureux/-euse.
III *vtr* chauffer [*plate, food, water*]; réchauffer [*implement, bed*]; se réchauffer [*part of body*].
IV *vi* [*food, liquid, object*] chauffer.
V *v refl* **to** ~ **oneself** se réchauffer.
■ **warm to, warm towards**: ~ **to** [*sb/sth*] se prendre de sympathie pour [*acquaintance*]; s'enthousiasmer pour [*artist, idea*]; s'attaquer avec enthousiasme à [*task*]; **'and then,'** he said, ~**ing to his theme** 'ensuite,' dit-il, de plus en plus enthousiaste.
■ **warm up**: ¶ ~ **up 1** [*person, room, house*] se réchauffer; [*food, liquid, car, engine, radio*] chauffer; **2** FIG (become lively) s'animer; **3** [*athlete*] s'échauffer; [*singer*] s'échauffer la voix; [*orchestra, musician*] se préparer; ¶ ~ **up** [*sth*], ~ [*sth*] **up 1** (heat) réchauffer [*room, bed, person*]; faire réchauffer [*food*]; **2** (prepare) chauffer° [*audience*]; échauffer [*player, athlete*]; [*singer*] s'échauffer [*voice*]; [*musician*] chauffer [*instrument*].

warm-blooded /,wɔːm'blʌdɪd/ *adj* ZOOL à sang chaud; FIG ardent.

war memorial *n* monument *m* aux morts.

warm-hearted *adj* chaleureux/-euse.

warming /'wɔːmɪŋ/ **I** *n* réchauffement *m*.
II *adj* LIT qui réchauffe; FIG de plus en plus chaleureux/-euse.

warmly /'wɔːmlɪ/ *adv* **1** LIT chaudement; **the sun shone** ~ le soleil était chaud; **2** FIG, GEN chaleureusement; [*speak, praise*] avec enthousiasme.

warmongering /'wɔːmʌŋgərɪŋ/ **I** *n* propagande *f* belliciste.
II *adj* [*person, article*] belliciste.

warmth /wɔːmθ/ *n* LIT, FIG chaleur *f*; **he replied with some** ~ **that** il a répondu vivement que.

warm-up /'wɔːmʌp/ *n* MUS, SPORT, THEAT échauffement *m*.

warn /wɔːn/ *vtr* avertir (**that** que); **to** ~ **that** dire or annoncer que; **to** ~ **sb about** ou **against sth** mettre qn en garde contre qch; **to** ~ **sb about** ou **against doing** déconseiller à qn de faire; **to** ~ **sb to do** conseiller or dire à qn de faire; **you have been** ~**ed!** tu es prévenu!; **I shan't** ~ **you again** c'est la dernière fois que je te le dis.
II *vi* **to** ~ **of sth** annoncer qch.
■ **warn off**: ~ [*sb*] **off**, ~ **off** [*sb*] décourager; **to** ~ **sb off doing** déconseiller à qn de faire; **to** ~ **sb off one's land** demander à qn de quitter ses terres.

warning /'wɔːnɪŋ/ **I** *n* GEN avertissement *m*; (by an authority) avis *m*; (by light, siren) signal *m*; **a** ~ **against sth** une mise en garde contre qch; **a** ~ **about** ou **on sth** une mise en garde à propos de qch; **to give sb a** ~ **not to do** déconseiller à qn de faire; **to give sb** ~ avertir qn (**of** de); **advance** ~ préavis *m*; **health** ~ mise en garde; **flood** ~ avis de crue; **an official** ~ un avis officiel.
II *noun modifier* **1** (giving notice of danger) [*siren, bell, light*] d'alarme; [*notice*] d'avertissement; ~ **shot** LIT, FIG coup *m* de semonce; ~ **sign** LIT panneau *m* d'avertissement; FIG signe *m* annonciateur; **2** (threatening) [*gesture, tone*] de mise en garde; (stronger) menaçant.

warp /wɔːp/ **I** *n* **1** (deformity) déformation *f* (**in** de); **2** (in weave) chaîne *f*; **3** FIG **the** ~ (**and woof**) **of sth** l'étoffe *f* dont qch est fait.
II *vtr* LIT déformer; FIG pervertir [*mind, personality*]; fausser [*judgment, thinking*].
III *vi* se déformer.

warpaint /'wɔːpeɪnt/ *n* MIL peinture *f* de guerre.

warpath /'wɔːpɑːθ/ *n*:
IDIOMS **to be on the** ~ être sur le sentier de la guerre.

warped /wɔːpt/ *adj* **1** LIT déformé; **to become** ~ se déformer; **2** FIG [*mind, humour*] tordu; [*personality, sexuality*] perverti; [*account, judgment, view*] faussé.

warplane /'wɔːpleɪn/ *n* avion *m* militaire.

warrant /'wɒrənt, US 'wɔːr-/ **I** *n* **1** JUR mandat *m*; **to issue a** ~ établir un mandat; **a** ~ **for sb's arrest** un mandat d'arrêt contre qn; **a** ~ **is out for his arrest** un mandat a été lancé contre lui; **2** FIN bon *m* de souscription; **dividend** ~ coupon *m* de dividende.
II *vtr* (justify) justifier; (guarantee) garantir; (bet) parier.
III *vi* parier.
IV warranted *pp adj* (justified) justifié; (guaranteed) garanti.

warrant card *n* plaque *f* (de police).

warranty /'wɒrəntɪ, US 'wɔːr-/ *n* COMM garantie *f*; (insurance) condition *f* d'application.

warren /'wɒrən, US 'wɔːrən/ *n* **1** (rabbits') garenne *f*; **2** (building, maze of streets) labyrinthe *m*.

warring /'wɔːrɪŋ/ *adj* [*parties, nations*] en conflit.

warrior /'wɒrɪə(r), US 'wɔːr-/ *n, adj* guerrier/-ière (*m*/*f*).

Warsaw /'wɔːsɔː/ ▶ 1343 *pr n* Varsovie.

warship /'wɔːʃɪp/ *n* navire *m* de guerre.

wart /wɔːt/ *n* (on skin) verrue *f*.
IDIOMS **to describe sb** ~**s and all** décrire qn avec tous ses défauts.

wartime /'wɔːtaɪm/ **I** *n* **in** ~ en temps de guerre.
II *noun modifier* [*economy, memories, rationing*] de

guerre; **a story set in ~ Berlin** une histoire qui se passe à Berlin pendant la guerre.

war-torn *adj* déchiré par la guerre.

wary /ˈweərɪ/ *adj* **1** (cautious) prudent; **to be ~** montrer de la circonspection (**of** vis-à-vis de); **2** (distrustful) méfiant; **to be ~** se méfier (**of** de).

was /wɒz, wəz/ *prét* ▶ **be**.

wash /wɒʃ/ **I** *n* **1** Ȼ (by person) **to give [sth] a ~** laver [*window, floor*]; nettoyer [*object*]; lessiver [*paintwork*]; se laver [*hands, face*]; **to give sb a ~** débarbouiller [*child*]; **to have a quick ~** faire un brin de toilette°; **2** (laundry process) lavage *m*; **weekly ~** lessive *f* hebdomadaire; **in the ~** (about to be cleaned) au sale; (being cleaned) au lavage; **3** (from boat) remous *m*; **4** (coating) GEN couche *f* (de peinture); ART lavis *m*; **5** (for face) lotion *f*.

II *noun modifier* **frequent ~ shampoo** shampooing *m* pour lavages fréquents; **pen and ~ drawing** dessin *m* à la plume et au lavis.

III /wɒʃ, US wɔːʃ/ *vtr* **1** (clean) laver [*person, clothes, floor*]; nettoyer [*object, wound*]; lessiver [*surface*]; **to get ~ed** se laver; **to ~ one's hands/face** se laver les mains/le visage; **to ~ the dishes** faire la vaisselle; **2** (carry along) entraîner [*silt, debris*]; **to ~ sb/sth overboard** emporter qn/qch par-dessus bord; **3** LITTÉR (lap against) lécher; **4** (coat) ART laver; GEN, TECH passer une légère couche de peinture sur [*wall*].

IV *vi* (clean oneself) [*person*] se laver, faire sa toilette; [*animal*] faire sa toilette; (clean clothes) faire la lessive; (become clean) se laver; **that excuse won't ~ with me**° FIG cette excuse ne me satisfait pas.

V *v refl* **to ~ oneself** [*person*] se laver; [*animal*] faire sa toilette.

IDIOMS **it will all come out in the ~** (be revealed) tout finira bien par se savoir; (be resolved) tout finira par s'arranger; **to ~ one's hands of** se laver les mains de [*matter*]; se désintéresser de [*person*].

■ **wash away**: ¶ **~ [sth] away, ~ away [sth] 1** (clean) faire partir; **2** (carry off) emporter [*structure, debris*]; (by erosion) éroder; ¶ **~ [sb] away** emporter.

■ **wash down**: **~ [sth] down, ~ down [sth] 1** (clean) laver [qch] à grande eau [*surface, vehicle*]; lessiver [*paintwork*]; **2**° faire descendre [*pill*]; faire passer [*unpleasant food*]; arroser [*food*].

■ **wash off**: ¶ **~ off** partir au lavage; ¶ **~ [sth] off, ~ off [sth]** faire partir [qch] à l'eau; **to ~ the mud off the car** laver la voiture pour faire partir la boue.

■ **wash out**: ¶ **~ out 1** (disappear by cleaning) [*stain*] partir au lavage; [*colour*] passer; **2**° US **she ~ed out of college** elle s'est fait recaler aux examens d'entrée en fac°; ¶ **~ [sth] out, ~ out [sth] 1** (remove by cleaning) faire partir [qch] au lavage [*stain*]; faire passer [*colour*]; **2** (rinse inside) rincer; **3** (clean quickly) passer [qch] à l'eau.

■ **wash over**: LIT balayer; **everything I say just ~es over him** tout ce que je dis glisse sur lui; **a great feeling of relief ~ed over me** un immense soulagement m'a envahi.

■ **wash through**: **~ [sth] through** passer [qch] à l'eau.

■ **wash up**: ¶ **~ up 1** GB (do dishes) faire la vaisselle; **2** US (clean oneself) faire un brin de toilette°; ¶ **~ [sth] up, ~ up [sth] 1** (clean) laver [*plate*]; nettoyer [*pan*]; **2** (bring to shore) rejeter.

washable /ˈwɒʃəbl, US ˈwɒːʃ-/ *adj* lavable.

wash: **~-and-wear** *adj* d'entretien facile; **~basin** *n* lavabo *m*; **~bowl** *n* US lavabo *m*; **~cloth** *n* US lavette *f*.

washed-out /ˌwɒʃtˈaʊt, US ˌwɒːʃ-/ *adj* **1** (faded) délavé; **2** (tired) épuisé.

washed-up° /ˌwɒʃtˈʌp, US ˌwɔːʃ-/ *adj* (finished) fichu°; US (tired) épuisé.

washer /ˈwɒʃə(r), US ˈwɒːʃər/ *n* **1** TECH rondelle *f*; (as seal) joint *m*; **2**° machine *f* à laver.

washer-dryer /ˌwɒʃəˈdraɪə(r), US ˌwɔːʃ-/ *n* lave-linge/sèche-linge *m inv*.

wash: **~-hand basin** *n* lavabo *m*; **~house** *n* buanderie *f*.

washing /ˈwɒʃɪŋ, US ˈwɔːʃɪŋ/ *n* **1** (act) (of oneself) toilette *f*; (of clothes) lessive *f*; **2** (laundry) (to be cleaned) linge *m* sale; (when clean) linge *m*; **to do the ~** faire la lessive.

washing: **~ facilities** *npl* douches-lavabos *fpl*; **~ line** *n* corde *f* à linge; **~ machine** *n* machine *f* à laver; **~ powder** *n* GB lessive *f* (en poudre); **~ soda** *n* soude *f* ménagère; **~-up** *n* GB vaisselle *f*; **~-up bowl** *n* GB cuvette *f* (pour la vaisselle); **~-up liquid** *n* GB liquide *m* à vaisselle; **~-up water** *n* GB eau *f* de vaisselle.

wash: **~ leather** *n* peau *f* de chamois; **~ load** *n* capacité *f* de lavage.

washout /ˈwɒʃaʊt/ *n* **1**° (project, system) fiasco *m*; **2**° (person) nullité° *f*; **3** (game, camp) fiasco *m* dû à la pluie.

wash: **~room** *n* toilettes *fpl*; **~stand** *n* US lavabo *m*.

wasn't /ˈwɒznt/ = **was not**.

wasp /wɒsp/ *n* guêpe *f*.

WASP /wɒsp/ *n* US (*abrév* = **White Anglo-Saxon Protestant**) membre de l'élite des blancs protestants d'origine anglo-saxonne.

waspish /ˈwɒspɪʃ/ *adj* acerbe.

wastage /ˈweɪstɪdʒ/ *n* **1** (of money, resources, talent) gaspillage *m*; (of heat, energy) déperdition *f*; **through ~** par gaspillage; **2** (also **natural ~**) ECON élimination *f* naturelle.

waste /weɪst/ **I** *n* **1** (squandering) GEN gaspillage *m* (**of** de); (of time) perte *f* (**of** de); **that was a complete ~ of an afternoon** l'après-midi a été perdu pour rien; **a ~ of effort** un effort inutile; **taking taxis is a ~ of money** prendre des taxis c'est jeter l'argent par les fenêtres; **it's a ~ of time trying to explain it** on perd son temps à essayer de l'expliquer; **to go to ~** être gaspillé; **that's another good opportunity gone to ~** et voilà encore une bonne occasion de perdue; **to let sth go to ~** gaspiller qch; **there is no ~, every part is used** il n'y a pas de déchets, chaque élément est utilisé; **2** Ȼ (detritus) GEN, IND déchets *mpl* (**from** de); **3** (wasteland) désert *m*.

II wastes *npl* **1** (wilderness) étendues *fpl* sauvages; **2** US = **waste I 2**.

III *adj* **1** [*food*] inutilisé; [*heat, energy*] gaspillé; [*water*] usé; **~ materials** OU **matter** déchets *mpl*; **~ products** IND déchets *mpl* de fabrication; BIOL, MED déchets *mpl*; **~ plastics** plastiques *mpl* de rebut; **2** [*land*] inculte; **3 to lay ~ (to)** dévaster.

IV *vtr* **1** (squander) gaspiller [*food, energy, money, talents*]; perdre [*time, opportunity*]; user [*strength*]; gâcher [*youth*]; **all our efforts were ~d** tous nos efforts ont été vains; **he didn't ~ words** il a été franc et direct; **she ~d no time in contacting the police** elle a appelé la police sans perdre un instant; **subtlety is ~d on her** la subtilité lui passe au-dessus de la tête; **good wine is ~d on him** il n'est pas capable d'apprécier un bon vin; **2** (make weaker) atrophier; **3**° US (kill) supprimer°.

V *vi* se perdre.

IDIOMS **~ not want not** PROV l'économie protège du besoin.

■ **waste away** dépérir.

waste: **~basket** *n* corbeille *f* à papier; **~bin** *n* GB (for paper) corbeille *f* à papier; (for rubbish) poubelle *f*.

wasted /ˈweɪstɪd/ *adj* **1** [*care, effort, expense, life, vote*] inutile; [*commodity, energy, years*] gaspillé; **another ~ opportunity** encore une occasion de perdue; **2** (fleshless) [*body, limb*] décharné; [*face*] émacié; (weak) [*body, limb*] atrophié.

waste disposal I *n* traitement *m* des déchets.

II *noun modifier* [*company, industry, system*] de traitement des déchets.

waste: **~ disposal unit** *n* GB broyeur *m* d'ordures; **~ dump** *n* dépotoir *m*.

wasteful /ˈweɪstfl/ *adj* [*product, machine*] qui consomme beaucoup; [*method, process*] peu économique; [*person*] gaspilleur/-euse; **to be ~ of** gaspiller [*resources, energy*]; perdre beaucoup de [*space, time*].

wastefully /'weɪstfəlɪ/ adv inutilement.

wastefulness /'weɪstflnɪs/ n (extravagance) gaspillage m; (inefficiency) manque m de rentabilité.

waste: ~**land** n (urban) terrain m vague; (rural) terre f à l'abandon; FIG désert m; ~**paper** n ₵ vieux papiers mpl; ~**paper basket**, ~**paper bin** GB n corbeille f à papier; ~ **pipe** n tuyau m de vidange; ~ **service** n service m de voirie.

wasting /'weɪstɪŋ/ adj [disease] débilitant.

watch /wɒtʃ/ **I** n **1** (timepiece) montre f; **my ~ is slow/fast** ma montre retarde/avance; **to set one's ~** mettre sa montre à l'heure; **you can set your ~ by him** vous pouvez vous régler sur lui; **2** (surveillance) GEN, MIL surveillance f (**on** sur); **to keep ~** monter la garde; **to keep** (a) **~ on sb/sth** LIT, FIG surveiller qn/qch; **to be on the ~** être sur ses gardes; **to be on the ~ for sb/sth** LIT guetter qn/qch; FIG être à l'affût de qn/qch; **to set a ~ on sb/sth** tenir qn/qch à l'œil; **tornado ~** METEOROL surveillance f des cyclones; **3** NAUT (time on duty) quart m.
II noun modifier [chain, spring, strap] de montre.
III vtr **1** LIT (look at) regarder; (observe) observer; **is there anything worth ~ing on television?** y a-t-il quelque chose à voir à la télévision?; **the match, ~ed by a huge crowd**... le match, suivi par une foule immense...; **2** FIG suivre [career, development]; surveiller [situation]; **we had to sit by and ~ the collapse of all our hopes** nous avons dû assister impuissants à l'effondrement de tous nos espoirs; **3** LIT (keep under surveillance) surveiller; **~ this notice-board for further details** lire ce panneau d'affichage pour plus de détails; **4** (pay attention to) faire attention à [obstacle, dangerous object etc]; surveiller [language, manners, time, money, weight]; **you don't spill it** fais attention à ne pas le renverser; **~ that she doesn't go out alone** veille à ce qu'elle ne sorte pas seule; **~ where you put that paint-brush!** ne mets pas ce pinceau n'importe où!; **~ it**○! fais gaffe○!; **to ~ one's step** LIT, FIG regarder où on met les pieds; **~ your back**○! LIT attention devant!; FIG surveille tes arrières!; **5** (look after) garder.
IV vi **1** (look) regarder; **they are ~ing to see what will happen next** ils attendent pour voir ce qui va se passer maintenant; **2†** (keep vigil) veiller.
V v refl **to ~ oneself** LIT se regarder; FIG faire attention.
■ **watch for**: **~ for** [sb/sth] guetter [person, event]; surveiller l'apparition de [symptom, phenomenon].
■ **watch out** (be careful) faire attention (**for** à); (keep watch) guetter; **~ out!** attention!; **I'll ~ out for her when I'm in town** je guetterai si je la vois quand je serai en ville; **~ out for trouble!** gare aux ennuis!
■ **watch over**: **~ over** [sb/sth] veiller sur [person]; veiller à [interests, rights, welfare].

watchable /'wɒtʃəbl/ adj qui se laisse regarder.

watchband /'wɒtʃbænd/ n US bracelet m de montre.

watchdog /'wɒtʃdɒg/ n **1** (dog) chien m de garde; **2** ADMIN, ECON (person) observateur m; (organization) organisme m de surveillance; **consumer ~** service m de protection du consommateur.

watcher /'wɒtʃə(r)/ n (at event) spectateur/-trice m/f; (hidden) guetteur/-euse m/f; (monitoring) observateur/-trice m/f; **television ~** téléspectateur/-trice m/f.

watchful /'wɒtʃfl/ adj vigilant.

watchmaker /'wɒtʃˌmeɪkə(r)/ **▶ 1251** n horloger/-ère m/f.

watchman /'wɒtʃmən/ **▶ 1251** n **1** HIST (night) ~ veilleur m (de nuit); **2** (guard) gardien m.

watchword /'wɒtʃwɜːd/ n GEN (slogan) slogan m.

water /'wɔːtə(r)/ **I** n eau f; **drinking ~** eau potable; **by ~** par bateau; **under ~** (submerged) sous l'eau; (flooded) inondé; **at high/low ~** à marée haute/basse; **to let in ~** prendre l'eau; **to pass ~** uriner; **to turn the ~ on/off** ouvrir/fermer le robinet; **he lives across the ~** il habite sur le continent; **the wine was flowing like ~** le vin coulait à flots; **to keep one's head above ~** LIT garder la tête hors de l'eau; FIG (financially) faire face à ses engagements.

II waters npl **1** MED, NAUT eaux fpl; **2** (spa water) **to take the ~s** faire une cure thermale.
III noun modifier [glass, jug, tank] à eau; [filter, pump] à eau; [pipe, shortage] d'eau; [industry] de l'eau.
IV vtr arroser [lawn, plant]; irriguer [crop, field]; abreuver [livestock].
V vi **the smell of cooking makes my mouth ~** l'odeur de cuisine me fait venir l'eau à la bouche; **the smoke made her eyes ~** la fumée l'a fait pleurer.
IDIOMS **to spend money like ~** jeter l'argent par les fenêtres; **not to hold ~** [theory] ne pas tenir debout.
■ **water down**: **~ down** [sth] LIT couper [qch] d'eau; FIG GEN atténuer; édulcorer [description].

water: **~ authority** n compagnie f des eaux; **~ bird** n oiseau m aquatique; **~ board** n compagnie f des eaux; **~ bottle** n (for cyclist) bidon m; **~ butt** n citerne f; **~colour** GB, **~color** US n (paint) peinture f pour aquarelle; (painting) aquarelle f; **~-cooled** adj à refroidissement à eau; **~cress** n cresson m (de fontaine); **~ divining** n radiesthésie f.

watered-down /ˌwɔːtəd'daʊn/ adj **1** LIT coupé d'eau; **2** FIG GEN atténué; [version] édulcoré.

water: **~ed silk** n soie f moirée; **~fall** n cascade f; **~ filter** n filtre m à eau; **~front** n (in harbour) front m de mer; (by lakeside, riverside) bord m de l'eau; **~-heater** n chauffe-eau m (inv); **~ hole** n point m d'eau; **~ ice** n sorbet m.

watering /'wɔːtərɪŋ/ n arrosage m; AGRIC irrigation f.

watering can n arrosoir m.

water: **~ lily** n nénuphar m; **~ line** n ligne f de flottaison; **~logged** adj [pitch] détrempé; [carpet] plein d'eau; **~ main** n canalisation f d'eau.

watermark /'wɔːtəmɑːk/ n **1** (of sea) laisse f; (of river) ligne f des hautes eaux; **2** (on paper) filigrane m.

water: **~ meadow** n prairie f inondable; **~melon** n pastèque f; **~ mill** n moulin m à eau; **~ power** n énergie f hydraulique.

waterproof /'wɔːtəpruːf/ **I** n (coat) imperméable m.
II waterproofs npl vêtements mpl imperméables.
III adj [coat] imperméable; [make-up] résistant à l'eau.

water: **~ rates** npl GB taxe f sur l'eau; **~-resistant** adj qui resiste à l'eau; **~shed** n GEOG ligne f de partage des eaux; FIG tournant m.

waterside /'wɔːtəsaɪd/ **I** n bord m de l'eau.
II noun modifier [cafe, hotel, house] au bord de l'eau; [plant, wildlife] du bord de l'eau.

water-ski /'wɔːtəskiː/ SPORT **I** n ski m nautique.
II vi faire du ski nautique.

water: **~-skiing** **▶ 949** n ski m nautique; **~ slide** n toboggan m de piscine; **~ softener** n (equipment) adoucisseur m (d'eau); (substance) adoucissant m; **~-soluble** adj soluble dans l'eau; **~ sport** n sport m nautique; **~ supply** n (in an area) approvisionnement m en eau; (to a building) alimentation f en eau.

water system n (network) (for town) système m d'approvisionnement en eau; (for building) système m d'alimentation en eau.

water table n GEOG niveau m hydrostatique.

watertight /'wɔːtətaɪt/ adj **1** LIT étanche; **2** FIG (perfect) infaillible; **3** FIG (irrefutable) [argument, case] incontestable; [alibi] irréfutable.

water: **~ tower** n château m d'eau; **~ trough** n abreuvoir m; **~way** n voie f navigable; **~ wheel** n roue f hydraulique; **~ wings** npl bracelets mpl de natation; **~works** n TECH station f de pompage.

watery /'wɔːtərɪ/ adj **1** LIT GEN trop liquide; [coffee] trop léger/-ère; **2** FIG pâle; **3** (secreting liquid) [eye] qui pleure; [vegetables] mal égoutté.

watt /wɒt/ n watt m; **100-~ bulb** ampoule de 100 watts.

wattage /'wɒtɪdʒ/ n puissance f en watts.

wave /weɪv/ **I** n **1** (hand gesture) signe m (de la main); **she gave him a ~ from the bus** elle lui a fait signe du bus; **with a ~ of his wand** d'un coup de baguette magique; **2** (of water) vague f; **to make ~s** [wind]

faire des vagues; FIG (cause a stir) faire du bruit; (cause trouble) créer des histoires; **3** (outbreak, surge) vague *f*; **4** (in hair) cran *m*; **5** PHYS onde *f*.
II *vtr* **1** (move from side to side) GEN agiter; brandir [*stick, gun*]; **2 to ~ goodbye to** LIT faire au revoir de la main à; FIG **you can ~ goodbye to your chances of winning** tu peux dire adieu à tes chances de gagner; **3** (direct) **they ~d us on/away** ils nous ont fait signe d'avancer/de nous éloigner; **4 to have one's hair ~d** se faire faire une mise en plis.
III *vi* **1** (with hand) **to ~ to** ou **at sb** saluer qn de la main; **to ~ to sb to do** faire signe à qn de faire; **2** [*branches*] onduler; [*corn*] ondoyer; [*flag*] flotter au vent.
■ **wave around**, **wave about**: ¶ **~ around** [*flag, washing*] flotter; ¶ **~** [*sth*] **around** brandir; **to ~ one's arms around** agiter les bras dans tous les sens.
■ **wave aside**: ¶ **~** [*sth*] **aside**, **~ aside** [*sth*] repousser [qch] d'un geste; ¶ **~** [*sb*] **aside** écarter qn.
■ **wave off**: **~** [*sb*] **off**, **~ off** [*sb*] faire au revoir de la main à qn.
wave: **~ band** *n* bande *f* de fréquence; **~ energy** *n* = **wave power**; **~length** *n* PHYS, RADIO longueur *f* d'onde; **~ power** *n* énergie *f* des vagues.
waver /ˈweɪvə(r)/ *vi* **1** (weaken) [*person, look*] vaciller; [*courage, faith, love*] faiblir; [*voice*] trembler; **2** (flicker) [*flame, light*] vaciller; [*needle*] osciller; **3** (hesitate) hésiter (**between** entre; **over** sur).
wavering /ˈweɪvərɪŋ/ **I** *n* **1** (hesitation) hésitation *f*; **2** (of flame) vacillement *m*.
II *adj* [*person, politician, voice*] hésitant; [*voter*] indécis; [*confidence, courage, faith, flame*] vacillant.
wavy /ˈweɪvɪ/ *adj* [*hair, line*] ondulé.
wax /wæks/ **I** *n* GEN cire *f*; (for skis) fart *m*; (mineral wax) paraffine *f*; (in ear) cérumen *m*.
II *noun modifier* [*candle, figure, polish, seal*] en cire.
III *vtr* **1** cirer [*floor, table*]; lustrer [*car*]; farter [*ski*]; **2** (depilate) épiler [qch] à la cire.
IV *vi* **1** [*moon*] croître; **2 to ~ lyrical** disserter avec lyrisme.
V waxed *pp adj* [*fabric, wood*] ciré; [*paper*] paraffiné; [*thread*] poissé; **~ed jacket** GB ciré *m*.
waxy /ˈwæksɪ/ *adj* [*skin, texture*] cireux/-euse; [*potato*] ferme.
way /weɪ/ **I** *n* **1** (route, road) chemin *m* (**from** de; **to** à); **to live over the ~**° habiter en face; **the quickest ~ to town** le chemin le plus court pour aller en ville; **if we go this ~** si nous prenons cette route; **to ask the ~ to** demander le chemin pour aller à; **how did that find its ~ in here?** comment est-ce que c'est arrivé ici?; **the ~ ahead** LIT le chemin devant moi/eux etc; **the ~ ahead looks difficult** FIG l'avenir s'annonce difficile; **there is no ~ around the problem** il n'y a pas moyen de contourner le problème; **on the ~ back** sur le chemin du retour; **on the ~ back from the meeting** en revenant de la réunion; **the ~ forward** FIG la clé de l'avenir; **the ~ in** l'entrée (**to** de); **'~ in'** 'entrée'; **the ~ out** la sortie (**of** de); **the quickest ~ out is through here** c'est par ici que l'on sort le plus vite; **there's no ~ out** FIG il n'y a pas d'échappatoire; **a ~ out of our difficulties** un moyen de nous sortir de nos difficultés; **the ~ up** la montée; **on the ~** en route; **we're on the ~ to Mary's** nous allons chez Mary; **on the ~ past** en passant; **I'm on my ~** j'arrive; **on your ~ through town** en traversant la ville; **his house is on your ~ to town** tu passes devant chez lui en allant au centre-ville; **I must be on my ~** il faut que je parte; **to go on one's ~** se remettre en route; **to send sb on his ~** (tell to go away) envoyer promener qn°; **to be well on the** ou **one's ~ to doing** être bien parti pour faire; **to be on the ~ out** FIG passer de mode; **she's got four kids and another one on the ~**° elle a quatre gosses et un autre en route°; **to be out of sb's ~** ne pas être sur le chemin de qn; **don't go out of your ~ to do** ne t'embête pas à faire; **to go out of one's ~ to make sb feel uncomfortable** tout faire pour que qn se sente mal à

l'aise; **out of the ~** (isolated) isolé; (unusual) extraordinaire; **along the ~** LIT en chemin; FIG en cours de route; **by ~ of** (via) en passant par; **to go the ~ of sb/sth** finir comme qn/qch; **to make one's ~ towards** se diriger vers; **to make one's ~ along** avancer le long de; **to make one's own ~ there** se débrouiller seul pour y arriver; **to lie one's ~ out of trouble** se sortir d'affaire en mentant; **2** (direction) direction *f*, sens *m*; **which ~ did he go?** dans quelle direction est-il parti?; **he went that ~** il est parti par là; **come** ou **step this ~** suivez-moi, venez par ici; **'this ~ for the zoo'** 'vers le zoo'; **'this ~ up'** 'haut'; **to look this ~ and that** regarder dans toutes les directions; **to look the other ~** (to see) regarder de l'autre côté; (to avoid unpleasant thing) détourner les yeux; FIG (to ignore) fermer les yeux; **to go every which ~** partir dans tous les sens; **the other ~ up** dans l'autre sens; **the right ~ up** dans le bon sens; **the wrong ~ up** à l'envers; **to turn sth the other ~ around** retourner qch; **I didn't ask her, it was the other ~ around** ce n'est pas moi qui lui ai demandé, c'est l'inverse; **the wrong/right ~ around** dans le mauvais/bon sens; **you're Ben and you're Tom, is that the right ~ around?** tu es Ben, et toi tu es Tom, c'est bien ça?; **if you're ever down our ~** si jamais tu passes près de chez nous; **she's coming our ~** elle vient vers nous; **an opportunity came my ~** une occasion s'est présentée; **to put sth sb's ~**° filer qch à qn°; **everything's going my ~** tout me sourit; **3** (space in front, projected route) passage *m*; **to be in sb's ~** empêcher qn de passer; **to be in the ~** gêner le passage; **she won't let anything get in the ~ of her ambition** elle ne laissera rien entraver son ambition; **to get out of the ~** s'écarter (du chemin); **to get out of sb's ~** laisser passer qn; **put that somewhere out of the ~** mets ça quelque part où ça ne gêne pas; **out of my ~!** pousse-toi!; **get him out of the ~ before the boss gets here!** fais-le disparaître d'ici avant que le patron arrive!; **once the election is out of the ~** une fois les élections passées; **to keep out of the ~** rester à l'écart; **to keep out of sb's ~** éviter qn; **to keep sb out of sb's ~** (to avoid annoyance) tenir qn à l'écart de qn; **to keep sth out of sb's ~** (to avoid injury, harm) garder qch hors de portée de qn; **to make ~** s'écarter; **to make ~ for sb/sth** faire place à qn/qch; **4** (distance) distance *f*; **it's a long ~** c'est loin (**to** jusqu'à) ; **to be a short ~ off** LIT être près; **my birthday is still some ~ off** mon anniversaire est encore loin; **we still have some ~ to go before doing** LIT, FIG nous avons encore du chemin à faire avant de faire; **to go all the ~ to China** faire tout le voyage jusqu'en Chine; **I'm with you** ou **behind you all the ~** je suis de tout cœur avec toi; **5** (manner) façon *f*, manière *f*; **do it this/that ~** fais-le comme ceci/cela; **let me explain it another ~** laisse-moi t'expliquer autrement; **to do sth the French ~** faire qch comme les Français; **to do sth the right/wrong ~** faire bien/mal qch; **you're going about it the wrong ~** tu t'y prends très mal; **try to see it my ~** mets-toi à ma place; **in his/her/its own ~** à sa façon; **to have a ~ with sth** s'y connaître en qch; **to have a ~ with children** savoir s'y prendre avec les enfants; **she certainly has a ~ with her**° GB elle sait décidément s'y prendre avec les gens; **a ~ of doing** (method) une façon ou manière de faire; (means) un moyen de faire; **to my ~ of thinking** à mon avis; **that's the ~ to do it!** voilà comment il faut s'y prendre!; **that's the ~!** voilà, c'est bien!; **what a ~ to run a company!** en voilà une façon de gérer une entreprise!; **I like the ~ he dresses** j'aime la façon dont il s'habille; **whichever ~ you look at it** de quelque façon que tu envisages les choses; **either ~, she's wrong** de toute façon, elle a tort; **one ~ or another** d'une façon ou d'une autre; **one ~ and another it's been rather eventful** tout compte fait ça a été assez mouvementé; **I don't care one ~ or the other** ça m'est égal; **no two ~s about it** cela ne fait aucun doute; **you can't have it both ~s** on ne peut pas avoir le beurre et l'argent du beurre; **no ~!**° pas question!°; **6** (respect, aspect) sens

m; **in a ~ it's sad** en un sens c'est triste; **in a ~ that's true** dans une certaine mesure c'est vrai; **can I help you in any ~?** puis-je faire quoi que ce soit?; **in every ~ possible** dans la mesure du possible; **in many ~s** à bien des égards; **in some ~s** à certains égards; **in no ~, not in any ~** aucunement; **this is in no ~ a criticism** cela n'est en aucune façon une critique; **not much in the ~ of news** il n'y a pas beaucoup de nouvelles; **what have you got in the ~ of drinks?** qu'est-ce que vous avez comme boissons?; **by ~ of light relief** en guise de divertissement; **7** (custom, manner) coutume *f*, manière *f*; **that's the modern ~** c'est la coutume d'aujourd'hui; **I know all her little ~s** je connais toutes ses petites habitudes; **that's just his ~** il est comme ça; **it's the ~ of the world** c'est la vie; **8** (will, desire) **to get one's ~, to have one's own ~** faire à son idée; **she likes (to have) her own ~** elle aime n'en faire qu'à sa tête; **if I had my ~...** si cela ne tenait qu'à moi...; **have it your (own) ~** comme tu voudras.
II *adv* **we went ~ over budget** le budget a été largement dépassé; **to be ~ out** (in guess, estimate) être loin du compte; **to go ~ beyond what is necessary** aller bien au-delà de ce qui est nécessaire; **that's ~ out of order** je trouve ça un peu fort.
III *by the way adv phr* en passant; **by the ~,...** à propos,...; **what time is it, by the ~?** quelle heure est-il, au fait?; **but that's just by the ~** mais ce n'est qu'une parenthèse.

waylay /ˌweɪˈleɪ/ *vtr* (*prét*, *pp* **-laid**) [*bandit, attacker*] attaquer; [*beggar, friend*] arrêter, harponner⁰ HUM.

way-out⁰ /ˌweɪˈaʊt/ *adj* **1** (unconventional) excentrique; **2**† (great) super⁰, formidable.

way: **~s and means** *npl* moyens *mpl*; **Ways and Means (Committee)** *n* POL Commission *f* des Finances.

wayside /ˈweɪsaɪd/ *n* LITTÉR bord *m* de la route.
IDIOMS **to fall by the ~** (morally) quitter le droit chemin; (fail) être éliminé; (fall through) tomber à l'eau.

wayward /ˈweɪwəd/ *adj* [*person, nature*] difficile; [*horse*] incontrôlable; [*husband, wife*] volage.

we /wiː, wɪ/

■ **Note** In standard French, *we* is translated by *nous* but in informal French *on* is frequently used: *we're going to the cinema* = nous allons au cinéma or (*more informally*) on va au cinéma.
– *on* is also used in correct French to refer to a large, vaguely defined group: *we shouldn't lie to our children* = on ne devrait pas mentir à ses enfants. For particular usages see the entry below.

pron nous; **~ left at six** GEN nous sommes partis à six heures; (informal) on est parti⁰ à six heures; **~ Scots like the sun** nous autres Écossais, nous aimons le soleil; **WE didn't say that** GEN nous, nous n'avons pas dit cela; (informal) nous, on n'a pas dit ça⁰; **~ four are agreed that** nous quatre sommes convenus que; **~ all make mistakes** tout le monde peut se tromper.

weak /wiːk/ *adj* **1** (in bodily functions) [*person, animal, muscle, limb*] faible; [*health, ankle, heart, eyes, chest, nerves*] fragile; [*digestion*] difficile; [*stomach*] délicat; [*intellect*] médiocre; [*memory*] défaillant; [*chin*] fuyant; [*mouth*] tombant; **to be ~ with** ou **from** être affaibli par; **to grow** ou **become ~(er)** [*person*] s'affaiblir; [*pulse, heartbeat*] faiblir; **2** TECH GEN peu solide; [*structure*] fragile; **3** (lacking authority, strength) [*government, team, pupil, performance*] faible; [*parent, teacher*] qui manque de fermeté; [*script, novel*] inconsistant; [*plot*] mince; [*actor, protest, excuse, argument*] peu convaincant; [*evidence*] peu concluant; **~ link** ou **point** ou **spot** LIT, FIG point *m* faible; **to grow** ou **become ~er** [*government, team*] s'affaiblir; [*position*] devenir de plus en plus précaire; **in a ~ moment** dans un moment de faiblesse; **4** (faint) [*light, current, sound, laugh*] faible; [*tea, coffee*] léger/-ère; [*solution*] dilué; **5** ECON, FIN GEN faible (**against** par rapport à); [*share*] à bas prix; **6** LING (regular) faible; (unaccented) inaccentué.

weaken /ˈwiːkən/ **I** *vtr* **1** LIT affaiblir [*person, heart, structure*]; diminuer [*resistance*]; rendre [qch] moins solide [*joint, wall*]; **2** FIG nuire à l'autorité de [*government*]; affaiblir [*company, authority, resolve, cause, defence*]; diminuer [*support, influence*]; amoindrir [*argument, power*]; nuire à [*morale*]; ébranler [*will*]; **3** (dilute) diluer; **4** ECON, FIN affaiblir [*economy, currency*]; faire baisser [*prices, demand, shares*].
II *vi* **1** (physically) GEN s'affaiblir; [*grip*] se relâcher; **2** (lose power) [*government, country, resistance*] fléchir; [*support, alliance*] se relâcher; **3** ECON être en baisse.

weakening /ˈwiːkənɪŋ/ *n* **1** (physical) GEN affaiblissement *m*; (of structure) dégradation *f*; **2** (loss of power) GEN, FIN affaiblissement *m*; (of ties, alliance, friendship) relâchement *m*.

weak-kneed /ˌwiːkˈniːd/ *adj* faible.

weakling /ˈwiːklɪŋ/ *n* (physically) gringalet *m*.

weakly /ˈwiːklɪ/ *adv* [*move, struggle*] faiblement; (ineffectually) mollement.

weak-minded /ˌwiːkˈmaɪndɪd/ *adj* **1** (indecisive) irrésolu; **2** EUPH (simple) faible d'esprit.

weakness /ˈwiːknɪs/ *n* **1** (weak point) point *m* faible; **2** (liking) faible *m*; **3** (physical) (of person, limb, eyesight, heart, memory) faiblesse *f*; (of digestion) délicatesse *f*; (of structure) fragilité *f*; **4** (lack of authority) GEN faiblesse *f*; (of evidence, position) fragilité *f*; **5** (faintness) GEN faiblesse *f*; (of tea, solution) légèreté *f*; **6** FIN faiblesse *f*.

weak-willed /ˌwiːkˈwɪld/ *adj* **to be ~** manquer de fermeté.

weal /wiːl/ *n* (mark) marque *f* (de coup).

wealth /welθ/ *n* **1** (possessions) fortune *f*; **2** (state) richesse *f*; **3** (resources) richesses *fpl*; **4** (large amount) **a ~ of** une mine de [*information, opportunity*]; une profusion de [*detail, ideas*]; énormément de [*experience, talent*]; un grand nombre de [*books, documents*].

wealthy /ˈwelθɪ/ *adj* riche.

wean /wiːn/ *vtr* LIT sevrer [*baby*]; FIG **to ~ sb away from** ou **off sth** détourner qn de qch; **to ~ sb from/onto sth** faire passer qn de/à qch.

weapon /ˈwepən/ **I** *n* LIT, FIG arme *f*.
II *noun modifier* (also **weapons**) [*capability, factory, manufacturer, system*] d'armes.

wear /weə(r)/ **I** *n* ⊄ **1** (clothing) vêtements *mpl*; **sports ~** tenue *f* de sport; **2** (use) **for everyday ~** de tous les jours; **for summer ~** pour l'été; **to stretch with ~** s'assouplir à l'usage; **I've had three years' ~ out of these boots** ces bottes m'ont duré trois ans; **there's some ~ left in these tyres** ces pneus ne sont pas encore usés; **3** (damage) usure *f* (**on** de); **~ and tear** usure *f*; **normal ~ and tear** usure normale; **to get heavy ~** servir beaucoup; **to look the worse for ~** (damaged) être abîmé; **to be somewhat the worse for ~** (drunk) être ivre; (tired) être épuisé.
II *vtr* (*prét* **wore**; *pp* **worn**) **1** (be dressed in) porter; **to ~ blue** s'habiller en bleu; **to ~ one's hair short** avoir les cheveux courts; **to ~ one's skirts long** s'habiller long; **to ~ one's clothes loose** aimer les vêtements lâches; **2** (put on, use) mettre; **I haven't got a thing to ~** je n'ai rien à me mettre; **to ~ make-up** se maquiller; **3** (display) **his face** ou **he wore a puzzled frown** il fronçait les sourcils d'un air perplexe; **4** (damage by use) user; **to ~ a hole in** trouer; **to ~ a track in** creuser un sentier dans; **5**⁰ (accept) tolérer [*behaviour*]; accepter [*excuse*].
III *vi* (*prét* **wore**; *pp* **worn**) **1** (become damaged) s'user; **my patience is ~ing thin** je commence à être à bout de patience; **2** (withstand use) **a fabric that will ~ well** un tissu solide; **he's worn very well** FIG il est encore bien pour son âge.
■ **wear away**: ¶ **~ away** [*inscription*] s'effacer; [*tread, cliff, façade*] s'user; ¶ **~ away [sth]**, **~ [sth] away** [*rubbing, footsteps*] user; [*water*] ronger.
■ **wear down**: ¶ **~ down** s'user; **to be worn down** être usé; ¶ **~ down [sth]**, **~ [sth] down** LIT user; FIG saper; ¶ **~ [sb] down** épuiser.
■ **wear off**: ¶ **~ off 1** [*drug, effect*] se dissiper;

The days of the week

Note that the French uses lower-case letters for the names of days; also, French speakers normally count the week as starting on Monday.

Write the names of days in full; do not abbreviate as in English (Tues, Sat and so on). The French only abbreviate in printed calendars, diaries etc.

Monday	= lundi	Friday	= vendredi
Tuesday	= mardi	Saturday	= samedi
Wednesday	= mercredi	Sunday	= dimanche
Thursday	= jeudi		

What day is it?

(Lundi in this note stands for any day; they all work the same way; for more information on dates in French ▶ 854 |.)

what day is it? = quel jour sommes-nous?
  or (very informally) on est quel jour?
it is Monday = nous sommes lundi
today is Monday = c'est lundi aujourd'hui

Note the use of French le for regular occurrences, and no article for single ones. (Remember: do not translate on.)

on Monday = lundi
on Monday, we're going to the zoo = lundi, on va au zoo
I'll see you on Monday morning = je te verrai lundi matin

but

on Mondays = le lundi
on Mondays, we go to the zoo = le lundi, on va au zoo
I see her on Monday mornings = je la vois le lundi matin

Specific days

Monday afternoon = lundi après-midi
one Monday evening = un lundi soir
that Monday morning = ce lundi matin-là
last Monday night = la nuit de lundi dernier or (if evening) lundi dernier dans la soirée

early on Monday = lundi matin de bonne heure
late on Monday = lundi soir tard
this Monday = ce lundi
that Monday = ce lundi-là
that very Monday = précisément ce lundi-là
last Monday = lundi dernier
next Monday = lundi prochain
the Monday before last = l'autre lundi
a month from Monday = dans un mois lundi
in a month from last Monday = dans un mois à dater de lundi dernier
finish it by Monday = termine-le avant lundi
from Monday on = à partir de lundi

Regular events

every Monday = tous les lundis
each Monday = chaque lundi
every other Monday = un lundi sur deux
every third Monday = un lundi sur trois

Sometimes

most Mondays = presque tous les lundis
some Mondays = certains lundis
on the second Monday in the month = le deuxième lundi de chaque mois
the odd Monday or the occasional Monday = le lundi de temps en temps

Happening etc. on that day

Monday's paper = le journal de lundi or de ce lundi
the Monday papers = les journaux du lundi
Monday flights = les vols du lundi
the Monday flight = le vol du lundi
Monday closing (of shops) = la fermeture du lundi
Monday's classes = les cours de lundi or de ce lundi
Monday classes = les cours du lundi
Monday trains = les trains du lundi

[sensation] passer; **2** (come off) s'effacer; **¶** ~ [sth] **off**, ~ **off** [sth] effacer [inscription]. ■ **wear on** [day, evening] s'avancer. ■ **wear out**: **¶** ~ **out** s'user; **my patience is beginning to** ~ **out** je commence à perdre patience; **¶** ~ **out** [sth], ~ [sth] **out** user; **to** ~ **out one's welcome** lasser l'amabilité de ses hôtes; **¶** ~ [sb] **out** épuiser. ■ **wear through** [elbow, trousers] se trouer; [sole, metal, fabric] se percer.

wearable /'weərəbl/ adj mettable.

wearily /'wɪərɪlɪ/ adv [sigh, smile, gesture] d'un air las; [say, ask] d'un ton las; [get up] péniblement.

weariness /'wɪərɪnɪs/ n lassitude f.

wearing /'weərɪŋ/ adj (exhausting) fatigant; (irritating) pénible.

weary /'wɪərɪ/ **I** adj [person, smile, sigh, voice, gesture] las/lasse; [eyes, limbs, mind] fatigué; [journey, task, day] fatigant; [routine] lassant; **to grow** ~ se lasser. **II** vtr lasser, fatiguer. **III** vi se lasser (**of** de; **of doing** de faire).

weasel /'wi:zl/ n **1** ZOOL belette f; **2** PÉJ (sly person) sournois/-e m/f; ~ **words** mots mpl équivoques.

weather /'weðə(r)/ **I** n temps m; **what's the** ~ **like?** quel temps fait-il?; **the** ~ **here is hot** il fait chaud ici; **in hot/cold** ~ quand il fait chaud/froid; **you can't go out in this** ~! tu ne peux pas sortir par un temps pareil!; **when the good** ~ **comes** quand il fera beau; **if the** ~ **breaks** si le temps change; **if the** ~ **clears up** si le temps s'arrange; ~ **permitting** si le temps le permet; **in all** ~**s** par tous les temps; **whatever the** ~ LIT par tous les temps; FIG qu'il pleuve ou qu'il vente. **II** noun modifier [chart, check, conditions, map, satellite, station] météorologique; [centre] de météorologie. **III** vtr **1** (withstand) LIT essuyer; FIG se tirer de; **to** ~ **the storm** FIG surmonter la crise; **2** éroder [rocks, stone]; battre [landscape, hills]; hâler [face].

IV vi [rocks, landscape] s'éroder; **he has not** ~**ed well** FIG il n'a pas bien vieilli. **V weathered** pp adj [stone] patiné; [face] hâlé. IDIOMS **to be under the** ~ ne pas se sentir bien; **to keep a** ~ **eye on sb/sth** avoir qn/qch à l'œil; **to make heavy** ~ **of sth** avoir du mal à faire qch; **he made heavy** ~ **of it** il en a fait tout un plat○.

weather: ~ **balloon** n ballon-sonde m météorologique; ~**beaten** adj [face] hâlé; [stone, brick] érodé; ~ **forecast** n bulletin m météorologique; ~ **forecaster** ▶ 1251 | n (on TV) présentateur/-trice m/f de la météo; (in weather centre) météorologue mf, météorologiste mf; ~**man**○ n (on TV) = **weather forecaster**.

weatherproof /'weðəpru:f/ **I** adj [garment, shoe] imperméable; [shelter, door] étanche. **II** vtr imperméabiliser [fabric, garment].

weather: ~ **report** n = **weather forecast**; ~ **vane** n girouette f.

weave /wi:v/ **I** n tissage m. **II** vtr (prét **wove** ou **weaved**; pp **woven** ou **weaved**) **1** tisser; **2** (interlace) GEN tresser; [spider] tisser; **3** FIG inventer [story]; **4** (move) **to** ~ **one's way through sth** se faufiler entre qch. **III** vi (prét **wove** ou **weaved**) **to** ~ **in and out** se faufiler (**of** entre); **to** ~ **towards sth** (drunk) s'approcher en titubant de qch; (avoiding obstacles) se frayer un chemin vers qch. **IV woven** pp adj [fabric, cloth, jacket] tissé.

weaving /'wi:vɪŋ/ **I** n tissage m. **II** noun modifier [frame, machine, machinery] à tisser; [factory, mill] de tissage; [industry] du tissage.

web /web/ n **1** (also **spider's** ~) toile f (d'araignée); **2** FIG **a** ~ **of** un réseau de [ropes, lines]; **a** ~ **of lies** ou **deceit** un tissu de mensonges; **3** ZOOL palmure f.

webbing /'webɪŋ/ n ¢ (material) sangles fpl.

web foot n (pl **web feet**) patte f palmée.

wed /wed/ **I** n the newly ~**s** les jeunes mariés mpl. **II** vtr (p prés etc **-dd-**; prét, pp **wedded** ou **wed**) **1**

LIT épouser; **to get wed** se marier; **2** FIG allier; **to be ~ded to** être attaché à.

III vi (p prés etc **-dd-**; prét, pp **wedded** ou **wed**) se marier.

IV wedded pp adj marié; **~ded bliss** HUM bonheur m conjugal; **my lawful ~ded wife** mon épouse légitime.

we'd /wiːd/ = **we had, we would**.

Wed abrév écrite = **Wednesday**.

wedding /ˈwedɪŋ/ **I** n **1** mariage m; **a church ~** un mariage religieux; **2** (also **~ anniversary**) noces fpl.

II noun modifier [cake, ceremony, present] de mariage.

wedding bells npl LIT cloches fpl; **I can hear ~** FIG je crois qu'il y a un mariage dans l'air.

wedding: ~ breakfast n repas m de mariage; **~ day** n jour m des noces; **~ dress, ~ gown** n robe f de mariée; **~ march** n marche f nuptiale; **~ night** n nuit f de noces; **~ reception** n repas m de mariage; **~ ring** n alliance f; **~ vows** n vœux mpl.

wedge /wedʒ/ **I** n **1** (to insert in rock, wood etc) coin m; (to hold sth in position) cale f; (of cake, pie, cheese) morceau m; **a ~ of lemon** une tranche de citron; **2** (in golf) cocheur m de sable; **3** (heel) semelle f compensée; (shoe) chaussure f à semelle compensée.

II noun modifier **~-shaped** en forme de coin.

III vtr **1** (make firm) **to ~ sth in** ou **into place** caler qch; **to ~ a door open** caler une porte pour la tenir ouverte; **the door is ~d shut** (stuck) la porte est coincée; **2** (jam) **to ~ sth into** enfoncer qch dans; **to be ~d against/between** être coincé contre/entre.

IV v refl **to ~ oneself** se coincer.

IDIOMS **to drive a ~ between X and Y** monter X contre Y; **it's (only) the thin end of the ~** ce n'est qu'un début.

■ **wedge in**: **~ [sb/sth] in, ~ in [sb/sth]** coincer.

Wednesday /ˈwenzdeɪ, -dɪ/ ► **1390** n mercredi m.

wee /wiː/ **I** n° GB pipi° m.

II adj (tout) petit.

III vi° GB faire pipi.

weed /wiːd/ **I** n **1** (wild plant) mauvaise herbe f; (in water) herbes fpl aquatiques; **2**° GB PÉJ mauviette° f PÉJ; **3**° marijuana f.

II vtr, vi désherber.

■ **weed out**: ¶ **~ [sb] out, ~ out [sb]** GEN éliminer; se débarrasser de [employee]; ¶ **~ [sth] out, ~ out [sth]** se débarrasser de [stock, items]; arracher [dead plants].

weeding /ˈwiːdɪŋ/ n désherbage m; **to do some ~** désherber.

weedkiller /ˈwiːdkɪlə(r)/ n désherbant m, herbicide m.

weedy /ˈwiːdɪ/ adj **1**° PÉJ [person, build] malingre; [character, personality] faible; **2** (full of weeds) [garden] envahi de mauvaises herbes; [pond] envahi d'herbes aquatiques.

week /wiːk/ ► **1336** n semaine f; **what day of the ~ is it?** quel jour de la semaine sommes-nous?; **the ~ before last** il y a deux semaines; **the ~ after next** dans deux semaines; **every other ~** tous les quinze jours; **I'll do it some time this ~** je le ferai dans le courant de la semaine; **~ in ~ out** toutes les semaines; **a ~ today** GB, **today ~** aujourd'hui en huit; **a ~ yesterday** GB, **a ~ from yesterday** US il y a eu huit jours ou une semaine hier; **a ~'s wages** une semaine de salaire; **to pay by the ~** payer à la semaine; **during the ~** GEN pendant la semaine; (Monday to Friday) en semaine; **the working** ou **work** US **~** la semaine de travail; **the ~ ending June 10** la semaine du 3 au 10 juin.

weekday /ˈwiːkdeɪ/ **I** n jour m de (la) semaine; **on ~s** en semaine.

II noun modifier [evening, morning, programme] de la semaine; [train] circulant du lundi au vendredi; [flight] assuré du lundi au vendredi.

weekend /ˌwiːkˈend, US ˈwiːk-/ **I** n week-end m; **the ~ after (that)** le week-end suivant; **at the ~** GB,

on the ~ US pendant le week-end; **at ~s** GB, **on ~s** US le week-end.

II noun modifier [break] de week-end; [performance] du samedi et du dimanche; **~ bag** petit sac m de voyage; **~ cottage** résidence f secondaire; **~ ticket** ticket m valable (uniquement) le week-end.

III vi passer le week-end.

weekly /ˈwiːklɪ/ **I** n (newspaper) journal m hebdomadaire; (magazine) (revue f) hebdomadaire m.

II adj hebdomadaire; **on a ~ basis** à la semaine.

III adv [pay] à la semaine; [check] chaque semaine; [meet, leave] une fois par semaine.

weep /wiːp/ **I** n **to have a little ~** verser quelques larmes.

II vtr (prét, pp **wept**) **to ~ tears of joy** verser des larmes de joie.

III vi (prét, pp **wept**) **1** (cry) pleurer (over sur); **to ~ for sb** pleurer sur le sort de qn; **2** (ooze) suinter.

weeping /ˈwiːpɪŋ/ n ¢ pleurs mpl.

weeping willow n saule m pleureur.

weepy /ˈwiːpɪ/ adj [film] larmoyant; **to feel ~** avoir envie de pleurer.

weigh /weɪ/ **I** vtr **1** LIT peser; **to ~ sth in one's hand** soupeser qch; **2** FIG GEN évaluer; peser [consequences, risk, words]; **to ~ sth against sth** mettre en balance qch et qch; **to ~ sth in the balance** évaluer soigneusement qch; **3** NAUT **to ~ anchor** lever l'ancre.

II vi **1** (have influence) **to ~ with sb** compter pour qn; **to ~ against sb** faire du tort à qn; **to ~ in sb's favour** jouer en faveur de qn; **2** (be a burden) **to ~ on sb** peser sur qn; **to ~ on sb's mind** préoccuper qn.

III v refl **to ~ oneself** se peser.

■ **weigh down**: ¶ **~ down on [sb/sth]** peser sur; ¶ **~ down [sth/sb], ~ [sth/sb] down** LIT surcharger [vehicle]; bloquer [papers]; FIG accabler; **to be ~ed down with** crouler sous le poids de [luggage]; être comblé de [gifts, prizes]; être accablé de [worry].

■ **weigh in 1** [boxer, wrestler] se faire peser; [jockey] aller au pesage; **2** (contribute) contribuer; **to ~ in with sth** donner qch; **3** (intervene in debate) intervenir.

■ **weigh out** peser [ingredients, quantity].

■ **weigh up**: **~ up [sth/sb], ~ [sth/sb] up 1** FIG évaluer [situation]; juger [person]; mettre [qch] en balance [options, risks]; **after ~ing things up, I decided...** tout bien pesé, j'ai décidé...; **2** LIT peser [goods].

weighing machine /ˈweɪɪŋ məˌʃiːn/ n **1** (for people) balance f; **2** (for luggage, freight) bascule f.

weight /weɪt/ ► **1392** **I** n LIT, FIG poids m; **to put on ~** prendre du poids; **to be under/over 1 kilo in ~** avoir un poids inférieur/supérieur à 1 kilo; **by ~** au poids; **what is your ~?** combien pesez-vous?; **not to carry much ~** FIG ne pas peser lourd (with pour); **to add one's ~ to sth** faire jouer son influence en faveur de qch; **to throw one's ~ behind sth** soutenir qch à fond; **to give due ~ to a proposal** accorder à une proposition l'importance qu'elle mérite.

II vtr **1** LIT lester; **2** (bias) **to ~ sth against sb/sth** faire jouer qch contre qn/qch; **to ~ sth in favour of sb/sth** faire jouer qch en faveur de qn/qch; **3** (in statistics) pondérer.

IDIOMS **by (sheer) ~ of numbers** par la force du nombre; **to be a ~ off one's mind** être un grand soulagement; **to pull one's ~** faire sa part de travail; **to take the ~ off one's feet** s'asseoir; **to throw one's ~ about** ou **around** faire l'important/-e m/f.

■ **weight down**: **~ down [sth], ~ [sth] down** retenir [qch] avec un poids [paper]; lester [body].

weighting /ˈweɪtɪŋ/ n (of index, variable) pondération f; **London ~** indemnité f pour résidence à Londres.

weightlessness /ˈweɪtlɪsnɪs/ n **1** (in space) apesanteur f; **2** (of dancer) légèreté f aérienne.

weight: ~-lifter n haltérophile m; **~ training** ► **949** n musculation f (en salle); **~watcher** n (in group) personne f qui suit un régime amaigrissant.

Weight measurement

Note that French has a comma where English has a decimal point.

1 oz	= 28,35 g* (*grammes*)	1 cwt	= 50,73 kg
1 lb†	= 453,60 g	1 ton	= 1014,60 kg
1 st	= 6,35 kg (*kilos*)		

* *There are three ways of saying 28,35 g and other measurements like it:* vingt-huit virgule trente-cinq grammes, *or* (*less formally*) vingt-huit grammes virgule trente-cinq, *or* vingt-huit grammes trente-cinq.
For more details on how to say numbers, ▶ **1112** |.

† *English a pound is translated by* une livre *in French, but note that the French* livre *is actually 500 grams (half a kilo).*

People

what's his weight?	=	combien pèse-t-il?
how much does he weigh?	=	combien pèse-t-il?
he weighs 10 st (*or* 140 lbs)	=	il pèse 63 kg 500 (soixante-trois kilos et demi)
he weighs more than 20 st	=	il pèse plus de 127 kilos

Things

what does the parcel weigh?	=	combien pèse le colis?
how heavy is it?	=	quel poids fait-il?

it weighs ten kilos	=	il pèse dix kilos
about ten kilos	=	environ dix kilos
it was 2 kilos over weight	=	il pesait deux kilos de trop
A weighs more than B	=	A pèse plus lourd que B
A is heavier than B	=	A est plus lourd que B
B is lighter than A	=	B est plus léger que A
A is as heavy as B	=	A est aussi lourd que B
A is the same weight as B	=	A a le même poids que B
A and B are the same weight	=	A et B ont le même poids
6 lbs of carrots	=	six livres de carottes
2 kilos of butter	=	deux kilos de beurre
1½ kilos of tomatoes	=	un kilo cinq cents de tomates
sold by the kilo	=	vendu au kilo
there are about two pounds to a kilo	=	il y a à peu près deux livres anglaises dans un kilo

Note the French construction with de, *coming after the noun it describes:*

a 3-lb potato	=	une pomme de terre de trois livres
a parcel 3 kilos in weight	=	un colis de trois kilos

weighty /'weɪtɪ/ *adj* **1** (serious) de grand poids; **2** [*book*] monumental; [*object, responsibility*] lourd.

weir /wɪə(r)/ *n* (dam) barrage *m*.

weird /wɪəd/ *adj* (odd) bizarre; (eerie) mystérieux/-ieuse.

welcome /'welkəm/ **I** *n* accueil *m*.
II *noun modifier* [*speech*] de bienvenue.
III *adj* **1** (gratefully received) bienvenu; **that's a ~ sight!** ça fait plaisir à voir!; **nothing could be more ~!** rien ne pourrait tomber plus à propos!; **2** (warmly greeted) **to be ~** être le bienvenu/la bienvenue *m*/*f*; **to make sb ~** (on arrival) réserver un bon accueil à qn; (over period of time) accueillir qn à bras ouverts; **3** (warmly invited) **if you want to finish my fries you're ~ to them** (politely) si tu veux finir mes frites, ne te gêne pas; **if you want to watch such rubbish you're ~ to it!** (rudely) si tu veux regarder ces idioties, libre à toi!; **you're ~** (acknowledging thanks) de rien.
IV *excl* (to respected guest) soyez le bienvenu/la bienvenue *m*/*f* chez nous!; (greeting friend) entre donc!; **~ back, ~ home!** je suis content que tu sois de retour!
V *vtr* accueillir [*person*]; se réjouir de [*news, decision, change*]; être heureux/-euse de recevoir [*contribution*]; accueillir favorablement [*initiative, move*]; **we would ~ your view on this matter** nous aimerions savoir ce que vous pensez de cette affaire; **'please ~ our guest tonight, Willie Mays'** 'applaudissons notre invité d'honneur, Willie Mays'.
IDIOMS **to wear out one's ~** abuser de l'hospitalité de qn.
■ **welcome back**: **~ back** [*sb*], **~** [*sb*] **back** accueillir [qn] à son retour; (more demonstratively) faire fête à [qn] à son retour.
■ **welcome in**: **~ in** [*sb*], **~** [*sb*] **in** faire entrer [qn] chez soi.

welcoming /'welkəmɪŋ/ *adj* GEN accueillant; [*ceremony, committee*] d'accueil.

weld /weld/ **I** *vtr* LIT, FIG souder (**on, to** à).
II *vi* [*metal, joint*] être soudé ensemble.

welding /'weldɪŋ/ *n* **1** LIT soudage *m*; **2** FIG union *f*.

welfare /'welfeə(r)/ **I** *n* **1** GEN (well-being) bien-être *m inv*; (interest) intérêt *m*; **to be concerned about sb's ~** se faire du souci pour le sort de qn; **to be responsible for sb's ~** avoir la responsabilité de qn; **2** (state assistance) assistance *f* sociale; (money) aide *f* sociale; **to go on ~** US demander l'aide sociale.
II *noun modifier* [*system*] de protection sociale; **~ cuts** réductions *fpl* dans les dépenses sociales.

welfare: **~ benefit** *n* prestation *f* sociale; **~ department** *n* service *m* d'aide sociale; **~ services** *n* services *mpl* sociaux; **~ state** *n* (as

concept) État-providence *m*; (stressing state assistance) protection *f* sociale; **~ work** *n* assistance *f* sociale.

well¹ /wel/ **I** *adj* (*comparative* **better**, *superlative* **best**) **1** (in good health) **to feel ~** se sentir bien; **are you ~?** vous allez bien?, tu vas bien?; **she's not ~ enough to travel** elle n'est pas en état de voyager; **he's not a ~ man** il a des problèmes de santé; **she doesn't look at all ~** elle n'a pas l'air en forme du tout; **to get ~** se rétablir; **'how is he?'—'as ~ as can be expected'** 'comment va-t-il?'—'pas trop mal étant donné les circonstances'; **2** (in satisfactory state) bien; **all is not ~ in their marriage** il y a des problèmes dans leur mariage; **that's all very ~, but** tout ça c'est bien beau, mais; **it's all very ~ for you to laugh, but** tu peux rire, mais; **~ and good** c'est très bien; **3** (prudent) **it would be just as ~ to check** il vaudrait mieux vérifier; **it would be as ~ for you not to get involved** tu ferais mieux de ne pas t'en mêler; **4** (fortunate) **it was just as ~ for him that the shops were still open** il a eu de la chance que les magasins aient été encore ouverts; **the flight was delayed, which was just as ~** le vol a été retardé, ce qui n'était pas plus mal.
II *adv* (*comparative* **better**, *superlative* **best**) **1** (satisfactorily) bien; **he isn't eating very ~** il ne mange pas beaucoup; **that boy will do ~** ce garçon ira loin; **he hasn't done as ~ as he might** il n'a pas réussi aussi bien qu'il aurait pu; **I did ~ in the general knowledge questions** je me suis bien débrouillé pour les questions de culture générale; **to do ~ at school** être bon/bonne élève; **mother and baby are both doing ~** la mère et l'enfant se portent bien; **the operation went ~** l'opération s'est bien passée; **you did ~ to tell me** tu as bien fait de me le dire; **we'll be doing ~ if we get there on time** on aura de la chance si on arrive à l'heure; **~ done!** bravo!; **he has done very ~ for himself** il s'en tire très bien; **to do oneself ~** bien se soigner; **to do ~ by sb** se montrer généreux/-euse avec qn; **some businessmen did quite ~ out of the war** certains hommes d'affaires se sont enrichis pendant la guerre; **she didn't come out of it very ~** (of situation) elle ne s'en est pas très bien sortie; (of article, programme etc) ce n'était pas très flatteur pour elle; **2** (used with modal verbs) **you may ~ be right** il se pourrait bien que tu aies raison; **I can ~ believe it** je veux bien le croire, je n'ai pas de mal à le croire; **it may ~ be that** il se pourrait bien que; **I couldn't very ~ say no** je ne pouvais difficilement dire non; **you may ~ ask!** je me le demande bien!; **we may as ~ go home** on ferait aussi bien de rentrer; **'shall I shut the door?'—'you might as ~'** 'est-ce que je ferme la porte?'—'pourquoi pas'; **she looked shocked, as ~**

she might elle a eu l'air choquée, ce qui n'avait rien d'étonnant; **3** (intensifier) bien, largement; **it was ~ worth waiting for** ça valait vraiment la peine d'attendre; **the weather remained fine ~ into September** le temps est resté au beau fixe pendant une bonne partie du mois de septembre; **she was active ~ into her eighties** elle était toujours active même au-delà de ses quatre-vingts ans; **profits are ~ above average** les bénéfices sont nettement supérieurs à la moyenne; **4** (approvingly) **to speak ~ of sb** dire du bien de qn; **5 to wish sb ~** souhaiter beaucoup de chance à qn.

III *excl* **1** (expressing astonishment) eh bien!; (expressing indignation, disgust) ça alors!; (expressing disappointment) tant pis!; (after pause in conversation, account) bon; (qualifying statement) enfin; **~, you may be right** après tout, tu as peut-être raison; **~, that's too bad** c'est vraiment dommage; **~, then, what's the problem?** alors, quel est le problème?; **oh ~, there's nothing I can do about it** ma foi, je n'y peux rien; **~, ~, ~, so you're off to America?** alors comme ça, tu pars aux États-Unis!; **very ~ then** très bien.

IV as well *adv phr* aussi.

V as well as *prep phr* aussi bien que; **they have a house in the country as ~ as an apartment in Paris** ils ont à la fois une maison à la campagne et un appartement à Paris; **by day as ~ as by night** de jour comme de nuit.

IDIOMS **to be ~ in with sb**○ être bien avec qn○; **to be ~ up in sth** s'y connaître en qch; **to leave ~ alone** GB OU **~ enough alone** US ne pas s'en mêler; **you're ~ out of it**○! heureusement que tu n'as plus rien à voir avec ça!; **~ and truly** bel et bien.

well² /wel/ **I** *n* (in ground) puits *m*; (pool) source *f*.
II *vi* = **well up**.
■ **well up** monter.

we'll /wi:l/ = **we shall**; **we will**.

well-attended *adj* **the meeting was ~** il y avait beaucoup de monde à la réunion.

well ~-behaved *adj* [*child*] sage; [*animal*] bien dressé; **~-being** *n* bien-être *m inv*.

well-bred /ˌwel'bred/ *adj* **1** [*person*] (of good birth) bien né; (having good manners) bien élevé; **2** [*animal*] GEN de pure race; [*horse*] pur sang.

well-defined *adj* [*outline*] net/nette; [*role, boundary*] bien défini.

well-disposed /ˌweldɪ'spəʊzd/ *adj* **to be ~ towards** être bien disposé envers [*person*]; être favorable à [*regime, idea, policy*].

well ~ done *adj* CULIN bien cuit; [*task*] bien fait; **~-educated** *adj* (having a good education) instruit; (cultured) cultivé; **~-founded** *adj* fondé; **~-heeled**○ *adj* riche.

well-informed /ˌwelɪn'fɔːmd/ *adj* bien informé (**about** sur); **he's very ~** il est très au courant de l'actualité; **~ source** JOURN source *f* sérieuse.

wellington (boot) /ˈwelɪŋtən/ *n* GB botte *f* de caoutchouc.

well ~-judged *adj* [*statement, phrase*] bien senti; [*performance*] intelligent; **~-kept** *adj* bien entretenu.

well-known /ˌwel'nəʊn/ *adj* **1** (famous) célèbre; **to be ~ to sb** être connu de qn; **2 it is ~ that, it is a ~ fact that** il est bien connu que.

well ~-liked *adj* très apprécié; **~-made** *adj* bien fait; **~-mannered** *adj* bien élevé; **~-meaning** *adj* bien intentionné; [*advice, suggestion, gesture*] qui part d'une bonne intention.

well-meant /ˌwel'ment/ *adj* **his offer was ~, but** sa proposition partait d'une bonne intention, mais; **my remarks were ~** je ne voulais pas être désagréable dans ce que je disais.

well-nigh /ˌwel'naɪ/ *adv* SOUT pratiquement, presque.

well-off /ˌwel'ɒf/ **I** *n* (+ *v pl*) **the ~** les gens *mpl* aisés; **the less ~** les plus défavorisés *mpl*.
II *adj* (wealthy) aisé; **you don't know when you're**

~ tu ne connais pas ton bonheur; **to be ~ for** avoir beaucoup de [*space, provisions etc*].

well ~-read *adj* cultivé; **~-respected** *adj* très respecté; **~-spoken** *adj* [*person*] qui parle bien.

well-spoken-of *adj* **he's very ~** on dit beaucoup de bien de lui.

well ~-thought-of *adj* apprécié; **~-thought-out** *adj* bien élaboré.

well-timed *adj* qui tombe/tombait à point; **that was well timed!** (of entrance, phonecall etc) c'est bien tombé!

well-to-do I *n* **the ~** (+ *v pl*) les gens *mpl* aisés.
II *adj* aisé.

well-trodden /ˌwel'trɒdn/ *adj* **a ~ path** LIT, FIG une voie très empruntée.

well ~-wisher *n* GEN personne *f* qui veut témoigner sa sympathie; POL sympathisant/-e *m/f*; **~-worn** *adj* [*carpet, garment*] élimé; [*steps, floorboards*] usé; FIG rebattu.

welsh /welʃ/ *vi* **to ~ on** manquer à [*promise, deal*].

Welsh /welʃ/ ▶ 1100 , 1038 , **I** *n* **1** (language) gallois *m*; **2** (people) **the ~** les Gallois *mpl*.
II *adj* gallois.

Welsh rarebit, Welsh rabbit *n* toast *m* au fromage.

welt /welt/ *n* (on shoe) trépointe *f*; (on garment) bordure *f* en côtes; (on skin) marque *f* (de coup).

wend /wend/ *vtr* **to ~ one's way** cheminer (**to, towards** vers).

went /went/ *prét* ▶ **go**.

wept /wept/ *prét, pp* ▶ **weep**.

were /wɜː(r), wə(r)/ *prét* ▶ **be**.

we're /wɪə(r)/ = **we are**.

weren't /wɜːnt/ = **were not**.

west /west/ ▶ 1157 , **I** *n* ouest *m*.
II West *n* POL, GEOG **the West** l'Ouest *m*, l'Occident *m*.
III *adj* GEN ouest *inv*; [*wind*] d'ouest.
IV *adv* [*move*] vers l'ouest; [*lie, live*] à l'ouest (**of** de).
IDIOMS **to go ~** (die) EUPH passer l'arme à gauche.

west: **West Bank** *pr n* Cisjordanie *f*; **West Bengal** *pr n* Bengale-Occidental *m*; **~bound** *adj* en direction de l'ouest.

West Country *pr n* GB **the ~** le Sud-Ouest (de l'Angleterre).

West End *pr n* GB **the ~** le West End *m* (*quartier de théâtres et de boutiques chic au centre ouest de Londres*).

westerly /ˈwestəlɪ/ **I** *n* vent *m* d'ouest.
II *adj* [*wind*] d'ouest; [*point*] à l'ouest; [*area*] de l'ouest; [*breeze*] venant de l'ouest.

western /ˈwestən/ ▶ 1157 , **I** *n* CIN western *m*.
II *adj* (*épith*) **1** GEOG [*coast, boundary*] ouest *inv*; [*town, region, custom, accent*] de l'ouest; **2** POL occidental.

westerner /ˈwestənə(r)/ *n* Occidental/-e *m/f*.

Western Isles ▶ 1022 , *pr npl* îles *fpl* Hébrides occidentales.

westernize /ˈwestənaɪz/ *vtr* occidentaliser.

west-facing /ˈwestfeɪsɪŋ/ *adj* exposé à l'ouest.

West Indian /ˌwest 'ɪndɪən/ ▶ 1100 , **I** *n* Antillais/-e *m/f*.
II *adj* antillais.

West Indies /ˌwest 'ɪndiːz/ ▶ 840 , 1022 , *pr npl* Antilles *fpl*.

West Point *n* US West Point *m* (*académie militaire américaine*).

westward /ˈwestwəd/ ▶ 1157 , **I** *adj* [*side*] ouest; [*wall, slope*] du côté ouest; [*journey, route*] vers l'ouest.
II *adv* (also **~s**) vers l'ouest.

wet /wet/ **I** *n* **1** (dampness) humidité *f*; **the car won't start in the ~** la voiture ne veut pas démarrer par temps humide; **the tyre performs well in the ~** le pneu a de bons résultats sur terrain mouillé; **2**○ GB PÉJ chiffe *f* molle○ PÉJ; **3** GB POL conservateur/-trice *m/f* modéré/-e.
II *adj* **1** (damp) mouillé; **~ with rain** mouillé par la

---

what

As a pronoun
In questions
When used in questions as an object pronoun, *what* is translated by *que* or *qu'est-ce que*. After *que* the verb and subject are inverted and a hyphen is placed between them:
> *what is he doing?* = que fait-il? *or* qu'est-ce qu'il fait?

When used in questions as a subject pronoun, *what* is translated by *qu'est-ce qui*:
> *what happened?* = qu'est-ce qui s'est passé?

Used with preposition
After a preposition the translation is *quoi*. Unlike in English, the preposition must always be placed immediately before *quoi*:
> *with what did she cut it?* = avec quoi l'a-t-elle coupé?
> *or what did she cut it with?*

To introduce a clause
When used to introduce a clause as the object of the verb, *what* is translated by *ce que* (*ce qu'* before a vowel):
> *I don't know what he wants* = je ne sais pas ce qu'il veut

When *what* is the subject of the verb it is translated by *ce qui*:
> *tell me what happened* = raconte-moi ce qui s'est passé

For particular usages see **I** in the entry **what**.

As a determiner
what used as a determiner is translated by *quel, quelle, quels* or *quelles* according to the gender and number of the noun that follows:
> *what train did you catch?* = quel train as-tu pris?
> *what books do you like?* = quels livres aimes-tu?
> *what colours do you like?* = quelles couleurs aimes-tu?

For particular usages see **II** in the entry **what**.

---

pluie; **~ with blood** mouillé de sang; **her face was ~ with tears** son visage était baigné de larmes; **to get ~** se faire mouiller; **to get one's feet ~** se mouiller les pieds; **to get the floor ~** tremper le sol; **~ through** trempé; **2** (freshly applied) GEN humide; '**~ paint**' 'peinture fraîche'; **the ink is still ~** l'encre n'est pas encore sèche; **to keep sth ~** empêcher qch de sécher; **3** (rainy) [*weather, season, day*] humide; [*conditions*] d'humidité; [*spell*] de pluie; **tomorrow, the North will be ~** demain, il pleuvra dans le nord; **when it's ~** quand il pleut; **4** GB PÉJ [*person*] qui manque de caractère; [*remark*] sans intérêt; **don't be so ~!** du nerf!; **5** GB POL modéré. **III** *vtr* **1** (*p prés* **-tt-**; *prét, pp* **wet**) mouiller [*floor, object, clothes*]; **2** (urinate in or on) **to ~ one's pants/the bed** [*child*] faire pipi dans sa culotte/dans son lit. **IV** *v refl* **to ~ oneself** GEN mouiller sa culotte; [*child*] faire pipi dans sa culotte.

wet: **~ blanket**○ *n* rabat-joie *mf inv*; **~ fish** *n* GB poisson *m* frais; **~land** *n* terres *fpl* marécageuses; **~-look** *adj* [*plastic, leather*] luisant.

wetness /'wetnɪs/ *n* humidité *f*.

wetnurse /'wetnɜːs/ **I** *n* nourrice *f*.
II wet-nurse *vtr* LIT allaiter [*baby*].

wet suit *n* combinaison *f* de plongée.

we've /wiːv/ *abrév* = **we have**.

W Glam *n*: *abrév écrite* = **West Glamorgan**.

whack /wæk, US hwæk/ **I** *n* **1** (blow) (grand) coup *m*; **2**○ (share) part *f*; **to do one's ~** faire ce qu'on doit; **3** GB○ (wage) **to pay/earn top ~** payer/recevoir un très gros salaire; **4**○ (try) essai *m*; **to get first ~ at sth** avoir la primeur de qch. **II** *excl* paf! **III** *vtr* **1** (hit) battre [*person, animal*]; frapper [*ball*]; **2**○ GB (defeat) piler○; **3** FIG **to ~ £10 off the price** réduire le prix de dix livres.

whacked○ /wækt, US hwækt/ *adj* (tired) vanné○; US défoncé○.

---

whacking○ /'wækɪŋ, US 'hwæk-/ **I** *n* raclée○ *f*.
II *adj* GB énorme.

whacky○ /'wækɪ, US 'hwækɪ/ *adj* [*person*] dingue○; [*joke*] farfelu○; [*party, clothes*] délirant○.

whale /weɪl, US hweɪl/ **I** *n* **1** ZOOL baleine *f*; **2**○ **a ~ of a difference/story** une super○ différence/histoire; **to have a ~ of a time** s'amuser comme un fou. **II** *vtr* US (thrash) LIT, FIG donner une raclée○ à.

whaler /'weɪlə(r), US 'hweɪlər/ **▶ 1251** *n* **1** (ship) baleinier *m*; **2** (person) pêcheur *m* de baleines.

whaling /'weɪlɪŋ, US 'hweɪlɪŋ/ *n* **1** (whale fishing) pêche *f* à la baleine; **to go ~** aller pêcher la baleine; **2**○ US (thrashing) LIT, FIG raclée○ *f*.

wham /wæm, US hwæm/ **I** *n* grand coup *m*.
II *excl* vlan!

whammy /'wæmɪ, US 'hwæmɪ/ *n* US poisse *f*.

wharf /wɔːf, US hwɔːf/ **I** *n* (*pl* **wharves**) quai *m*.
II *vi* [*boat*] se mettre à quai.

what /wɒt, US hwɒt/ **I** *pron* **1** (what exactly) (as subject) qu'est-ce qui; (as object) que, qu'est-ce que; (with prepositions) quoi; **~ is happening?** qu'est-ce qui se passe?; **~ are you doing?** qu'est-ce que tu fais?; **with ~?** avec quoi?; **and ~ else?** et quoi d'autre?; **~ is to be done?** que faire?; **~ does it matter?** qu'est-ce que ça peut faire?; **~'s her telephone number?** quel est son numéro de téléphone?; **~'s that button for?** à quoi sert ce bouton?; **~ for?** (why) pourquoi?; (concerning what) à propos de quoi?; **~'s it like?** comment c'est?; **~'s this called in Flemish?, ~'s the Flemish for this?** comment dit-on cela en flamand?; **~ did it cost?** combien est-ce que ça a coûté?; **2** (in rhetorical questions) **~'s life without love?** que serait la vie sans l'amour?; **~'s the use?** (enquiringly) à quoi bon?; (exasperatedly) à quoi ça sert?; **~ does he care?** qu'est-ce que ça peut bien lui faire?; **3** (whatever) **do ~ you want** fais ce que tu veux; **4** (in clauses) (as subject) ce qui; (as object) ce que, (*before vowel*) ce qu'; **this is ~ is called a 'monocle'** c'est ce qu'on appelle un 'monocle'; **do you know ~ that device is?** sais-tu ce que c'est que cet appareil?; **~ I need is** ce dont j'ai besoin c'est; **drinking ~ looked like whisky** buvant quelque chose qui ressemblait à du whisky; **and ~'s more** et en plus; **and ~'s worse** ou **better** et en plus; **5**○ (when guessing) **it'll cost, ~, £50** ça coutera, quoi, dans les 50 livres?; **6** (inviting repetition) **~'s that?, ~ did you say?** qu'est-ce que tu as dit?; **he earns ~?** il gagne combien?; **he did ~?** il a fait quoi?; **George ~?** George comment? **II** *det* **1** (which) quel/quelle/quels/quelles; **~ time is it?** quelle heure est-il?; **2** (in exclamations) quel/quelle; **~ a nice car!** quelle belle voiture!; **~ a strange thing to do!** quelle drôle d'idée!; **~ use is that?** LIT, FIG à quoi ça sert?; **3** (the amount of) **~ money he earns he spends** tout ce qu'il gagne, il le dépense; **~ little she has** le peu qu'elle a, tout ce qu'elle a; **~ few friends she had** les quelques amis qu'elle avait. **III what about** *prep phr* **1** (when drawing attention) **~ about the letter they sent?** et la lettre qu'ils ont envoyée, alors?; **~ about the children?** et les enfants (alors)?; **2** (when making suggestion) **~ about a meal out?** et si on dînait au restaurant?; **~ about Tuesday?** qu'est-ce que tu dirais de mardi?; **3** (in reply) '**~ about your sister?**'—'**~ about her?**' 'et ta sœur?'—'quoi ma sœur?' **IV what if** *prep phr* et si. **V what with** *prep phr* **~ with her shopping bags and her bike** avec ses sacs à provisions et son vélo en plus; **~ with the depression and unemployment** entre la dépression et le chômage; **~ with one thing and another** avec ceci et cela. **VI** *excl* quoi!, comment! IDIOMS **I'll tell you ~** tu sais quoi; **to give sb ~ for**○ GB passer un savon○ à qn; **to know ~'s ~** s'y connaître; **well, ~ do you know** IRON tout arrive; **~ do you think I am**○! tu me prends pour quoi!; **~'s it to you**○? en quoi ça vous regarde?

what: **~-d'yer-call-him**○, **~'s-his-name**○ *n* Machin○ *m*; **~-d'yer-call-it**○, **~'s-its-name**○ *n* machin○ *m*.

whatever /wɒt'evə(r), US hwɒt-/ **I** *pron* **1** (that which) (as subject) ce qui; (as object) ce que; **to do ~ is required** faire ce qui est exigé; **2** (anything that) (as subject) tout ce qui; (as object) tout ce que; **do ~ you like** fais tout ce que tu veux; **~ he says goes** c'est lui qui décide; **~ you say** (as you like) tout ce qui vous plaira; **3** (no matter what) quoi que (+ *subj*); **~ happens** quoi qu'il arrive; **~ it costs it doesn't matter** quel que soit le prix, ça n'a pas d'importance; **4** (what on earth) (as subject) qu'est-ce qui; (as object) qu'est-ce que; **~'s the matter?** qu'est-ce qui ne va pas?; **~ do you mean?** qu'est-ce que tu veux dire par là? ; **'let's go'—'~ for?'** 'allons-y'—'pour quoi faire?'; **~ next!** qu'est-ce que ça sera la prochaine fois?; **5**° (the like) **curtains, cushions and ~** des rideaux, des coussins et toutes sortes de choses.
II *det* **1** (any) **~ hope he once had** tous les espoirs qu'il avait; **they eat ~ food they can get** ils mangent tout ce qu'ils trouvent à manger; **2** (no matter what) **~ the reason** quelle que soit la raison; **for ~ reason** pour je ne sais quelle raison; **any race of ~ creed** toutes les races quelles que soient leurs croyances; **3** (expressing surprise) **~ idiot forgot the key?** quel est l'imbécile qui a oublié la clé?
III *adv* (at all) **to have no idea ~** ne pas avoir la moindre idée; **'any chance?'—'none ~'** 'il y a une chance?'—'pas la moindre'; **'any petrol?'—'none ~'** 'il y a de l'essence?'—'pas du tout'; **anything ~** n'importe quoi.

whatnot /'wɒtnɒt, US 'hwɒt-/ *n* **1** (furniture) étagère *f*; **2**° (unspecified person or thing) machin° *m*; **3**° (and so on) ...**and ~**... et ainsi de suite.

whatsit /'wɒtsɪt, US 'hwɒt-/ *n* machin° *m*, truc° *m*.

whatsoever /ˌwɒtsəʊ'evə(r), US 'hwɒt-/ *adv* = **whatever III**.

wheat /wiːt, US hwiːt/ *n* blé *m*.

wheat: **~ germ** *n* germe *m* de blé; **~meal** *n* farine *f* complète.

wheedle /'wiːdl, US 'hwiːdl/ *vtr* **to ~ sth out of sb** soutirer qch à qn par la cajolerie.

wheel /wiːl, US hwiːl/ **I** *n* **1** (on vehicle) roue *f*; (on furniture) roulette *f*; **2** (for steering) volant *m*; NAUT roue *f* (de gouvernail); **to be at** ou **behind the ~** être au volant; **3** (in mechanism) rouage *m* ALSO FIG.
II° **wheels** *npl* bagnole° *f*; **have you got ~s**°? tu es motorisé°?
III *vtr* pousser; **they ~ed me into the operating theatre** ils m'ont emmené dans la salle d'opération sur un chariot.
IV *vi* **1** (also **~ round**) (circle) [*bird*] tournoyer; **2** (turn sharply) [*person, regiment*] faire demi-tour; [*car, motorbike*] braquer fortement; [*ship*] virer de bord.
V **-wheeled** *combining form* **a three-/four-~ed vehicle** un véhicule à trois/quatre roues.
IDIOMS **to ~ and deal** magouiller°; **it's ~s within ~s** l'affaire est plus compliquée qu'elle n'en a l'air.
■ **wheel in** = **wheel out**.
■ **wheel out**: **~ [sth] out, ~ out [sth]** remettre [qch] sur le tapis [*argument, story*]; ressortir [*excuse, statistics*].

wheel: **~barrow** *n* brouette *f*; **~chair** *n* fauteuil *m* roulant.

wheelclamp /'wiːlklæmp, US 'hwiːl-/ **I** *n* AUT sabot *m* de Denver.
II *vtr* mettre un sabot de Denver à [*car*].

wheeler /'wiːlə(r), US 'hwiːlər/ *combining form* **it's a two/three-~** (vehicle) il/elle a deux/trois roues.

wheeler dealer° *n* PÉJ magouilleur/-euse° *m/f*.

wheeling and dealing *n* (+ *v sg*) PÉJ GEN manigances *fpl*; (during negotiations) tractations *fpl*.

wheeze /wiːz, US hwiːz/ **I** *vtr* dire d'une voix rauque.
II *vi* [*person, animal*] ahaner; [*engine*] crachoter.

wheezy /'wiːzɪ, US 'hwiːzɪ/ *adj* [*voice, cough*] rauque; **to have a ~ chest** avoir la respiration sifflante.

when /wen, US hwen/ **I** *pron* **1** (with prepositions) quand; **since ~?** depuis quand? ALSO IRON; **2** (the time when) **that was ~ it all started to go wrong** c'est à ce moment-là que tout a commencé à mal aller; **that's**

---

when

when can very often be translated by *quand* in time expressions:

when did she leave? = quand est-ce qu'elle est partie?
or elle est partie quand?
or quand est-elle partie?

Note that in questions *quand* on its own requires inversion of the verb and subject:

when are they arriving? = quand arrivent-ils?

but when followed by *est-ce que* needs no inversion:
quand est-ce qu'ils arrivent?

Occasionally a more precise time expression is used in French:

when's your birthday? = quelle est la date de ton anniversaire?
when did he set off? = à quelle heure est-il parti?

Remember that the future tense is used after *quand* if future time is implied:

tell him when you see him = dis-le-lui quand tu le verras

It is often possible to give a short neat translation for a *when* clause if there is no change of subject in the sentence:

when I was very young,
I lived in Normandy = tout jeune, j'habitais en Normandie
when he was leaving,
he asked for my address = en partant, il m'a demandé mon adresse

In expressions such as *the day when, the year when*, *où* is used:

the day when we got married = le jour où nous nous sommes mariés

For examples of the above and further uses of *when*, see the entry **when**.

~ I was born (day) c'est le jour où je suis né; (year) c'est l'année où je suis né; **he spoke of ~ he was a child** il a parlé de l'époque où il était enfant.
II *adv* **1** (as interrogative) quand (est-ce que); **~ are we leaving?** quand est-ce qu'on part?; **I wonder ~ the film starts** je me demande à quelle heure commence le film; **I forget exactly ~** (time) j'ai oublié l'heure exacte; (date) j'ai oublié la date exacte; **tell me** ou **say ~** (pouring drink) dis-moi stop; **2** (as relative) **in 1993 ~** en 1993 quand; **at the time ~** (precise moment) au moment où; (during same period) à l'époque où; **the week ~ it all happened** la semaine où tout s'est passé; **on those rare occasions ~** les rares fois où; **it's times like that ~** c'est dans ces moments-là que; **one morning ~ he was getting up, he...** un matin où se levant, il...; **3** (then) **she resigned in May, since ~ we've had no applicants** elle a démissionné en mai, et depuis (lors) nous n'avons reçu aucune candidature; **until ~ we must stay calm** d'ici là nous devons rester calmes; **by ~ we will have received the information** d'ici là nous aurons reçu toutes les informations; **4** (whenever) quand; **he's only happy ~ he's moaning** il n'est content que quand il rouspète; **~ I sunbathe, I get freckles** chaque fois que je prends un bain de soleil, j'ai des taches de rousseur; **~ possible** dans la mesure du possible.
III *conj* **1** (at the precise time when) quand, lorsque; **~ she reaches 18** quand elle aura 18 ans; **2** (during the period when) quand, lorsque; **~ he was at school** quand il était à l'école; **3** (as soon as) quand, dès que; **I was strolling along ~ all of a sudden...** je marchais tranquillement quand tout d'un coup...; **4** (when it is the case that) alors que; **why buy their products ~ ours are cheaper?** pourquoi acheter leurs produits alors que les nôtres sont moins chers?; **5** (whereas) alors que; **he refused ~ I would have gladly accepted** il a refusé alors que j'aurais été ravi d'accepter.

whenever /wen'evə(r), US hwen-/ *adv* **1** (as interrogative) **~ will he arrive?** quand est-ce qu'il va finir par arriver?; **~ did she find the time?** comment est-ce qu'elle a bien pu trouver le temps?; **2** (no matter when) **~ you want** quand tu veux; **till ~ you like** aussi longtemps que tu veux; **~ he does it, it won't matter** il peut le faire quand il veut, ça n'a pas d'importance; **I'll come ~ it is convenient** je viendrai quand cela vous arrangera; **3**° (some time) **or ~** ou n'importe quand; **4** (every time that) chaque fois que; **~ I see a black cat, I make a wish** chaque fois que je vois un chat noir, je fais un vœu; **5** (expressing doubt) **she promised to return them soon, ~ that might be!** elle a promis de les rendre bientôt, mais je ne sais pas quand.

where /weə(r), US hweər/

■ **Note** *where* is generally translated by *où*: *where are the plates?* = où sont les assiettes?; *do you know where he's going?* = est-ce que tu sais où il va?; *I don't know where the knives are* = je ne sais pas où sont les couteaux.
– Note that in questions *où* on its own requires inversion of the verb: *where are you going?* = où allez-vous? but *où* followed by *est-ce que* needs no inversion: où est-ce que vous allez?

I *pron* **1** (with prepositions) où; **from ~?** d'où?; **near ~?** près d'où?; **to go up to ~ sb is standing** s'approcher de qn; **not from ~ I'm standing** LIT pas de là où je suis, FIG ce n'est pas mon avis; **2** (the place or point where) là que; **this is ~ it happened** c'est là que c'est arrivé; **that is ~ he's mistaken** c'est là qu'il se trompe; **France is ~ you'll find good wine** c'est en France que vous trouverez du bon vin.
II *adv* **1** (as interrogative) où (est-ce que); **~ is my coat?** où est mon manteau?; **~ does Martin figure in all this?** qu'est-ce que Martin vient faire dans tout ça?; **~'s the harm?** quel mal y a-t-il à ça?; **~'s the problem?** je ne vois pas le problème; **~ have you got to in your book?** où est-ce que vous en êtes dans votre lecture?; **2** (as indirect interrogative) où; **I wonder ~ he's going** je me demande où il va; **to know ~ one is going** savoir où on va; FIG savoir ce qu'on veut; **you don't know ~ it's been!** tu ne sais pas où ça a traîné!; **3** (as relative) où; **the village ~ we live** le village où nous habitons; **in several cases ~** dans plusieurs cas où; **4** (here where, there where) **stay ~ it's dry** reste à l'abri; **it's cold ~ we live** il fait froid là où nous habitons; **it's not ~ you said** (not there) ça n'y est pas; (found elsewhere) ce n'est pas là où tu crois; **5** (wherever) où; **put them/go ~ you want** mets-les/va où tu veux; **6** (whenever) quand; **~ necessary** si nécessaire; **she's stupid ~ he's concerned** elle se conduit toujours de façon stupide quand il s'agit de lui; **~ possible** dans la mesure du possible.
III *conj* = **whereas**.

whereabouts **I** /'weərəbauts, US 'hweər-/ *n* **do you know his ~?** savez-vous où il est?
II /ˌweərə'bauts/ *adv* GEN où; **'I've put them in the living room'—'~?'** 'je les ai mis dans le salon'—'où ça?'

whereas /ˌweər'æz, US ˌhweər-/ *conj* **she likes dogs ~ I prefer cats** elle aime les chiens mais moi je préfère les chats; **he chose to stay quiet ~ I would have complained** il a choisi de ne rien dire alors que moi je me serais sûrement plaint.

whereby /weə'bai, US hweər-/ *conj* **a system ~ all staff will carry identification** un système qui prévoit que tous les membres du personnel auront une carte; **the criteria ~ allowances are allocated** les critères selon lesquels les allocations sont attribuées.

whereupon /ˌweərə'pon, US ˌhweər-/ *conj* SOUT sur quoi.

wherever /weər'evə(r), US hweər-/ *adv* **1** (as interrogative) **~ did you put them?** où est-ce que tu as bien pu les mettre?; **~ has he got to?** où est-ce qu'il a bien pu passer?; **2** (anywhere) **~ she goes I'll go** où qu'elle aille, j'irai; **~ you want** où tu veux; **we'll meet ~'s convenient for you** nous nous retrouverons là où ça t'arrange; **3**° (somewhere) **or ~** ou n'importe où ailleurs; **4** (whenever) **~ there's an**

oasis, there's a settlement dès qu'il y a une oasis, il y a une implantation; **~ necessary** quand c'est nécessaire ; **~ possible** dans la mesure du possible; **5** (expressing doubt) **she's from Vernoux ~ that is!** elle vient de Vernoux mais ne me demande pas où c'est!

wherewithal /'weəwɪˌðɔːl/ *n* **the ~** les moyens *mpl*.

whet /wet, US hwet/ *vtr* (*p prés etc* **-tt-**) **1** (stimulate) **to ~ the appetite** stimuler l'appétit; **the book ~ted his appetite for travel** les livres lui donnèrent envie de voyager; **2**‡ aiguiser.

whether /'weðə(r), US 'hweðər/

■ **Note** When *whether* is used to mean *if*, it is translated by *si*: *I wonder whether she got my letter* = je me demande si elle a reçu ma lettre. See 1 in the entry below.
– *whether* often occurs after verbs such as *ask*, *doubt*, *decide*, *know*, *say*, *see* and *wonder*, with adjectives such as *doubtful*, *sure*, and with nouns like *doubt*, *question*. You can find further examples at these entries.
– In *whether...or not* sentences *whether* is translated by *que* and the verb that follows is in the subjunctive: *whether you agree or not* = que vous soyez d'accord ou non. See 2 in the entry below.

conj **1** (when outcome is uncertain: if) si; **I wasn't sure ~ to answer or not** ou **~ or not to answer** je ne savais pas s'il fallait répondre, je n'étais pas sûr qu'il faille répondre; **I wonder ~ it's true** je me demande si c'est vrai; **the question is ~ anyone is interested** le problème est de savoir si quelqu'un est intéressé; **she was worried about ~ to invite them** elle se demandait si elle devait les inviter; **2** (when outcome is fixed: no matter if) **you're going to school ~ you like it or not!** tu iras à l'école que cela te plaise ou non!; **~ you have children or not, this book should interest you** que vous ayez des enfants ou non, ce livre devrait vous intéresser; **~ or not people are happy is of little importance** que les gens soient heureux ou non ce n'est pas très important; **everyone, ~ students or townspeople, celebrates** tout le monde, que ce soient les étudiants ou les habitants de la ville, fait la fête.

which /wɪtʃ, US hwɪtʃ/ **I** *pron* **1** (also **~ one**) lequel *m*, laquelle *f*; **~ do you want, the red skirt or the blue one?** laquelle est-ce que tu veux, la jupe rouge ou la bleue?; **~ of the groups...?** (referring to one) lequel des groupes...?; (referring to several) lesquels des groupes...?; **show her ~ you mean** montre-lui celui/celle etc que tu veux dire; **decide ~ you ~ you have?** est-ce que tu as une préférence?; **I don't mind ~** ça m'est égal; **can you tell ~ is ~?** peux-tu les distinguer?; **2** (relative to preceding noun) (as subject) qui; (as object) que; (after prepositions) lequel/laquelle/ lesquels/lesquelles; **the contract ~ he's spoken about** ou about ~ he's spoken le contrat dont il a parlé; **3** (relative to preceding clause or concept) (as subject) ce qui; (as object) ce que; **~ reminds me...** ce qui me fait penser que...; **we'll be moving, before ~ we need to...** nous allons déménager mais avant il faut que nous...; **he's resigned, from ~ we must assume that** il a démissionné, d'où on peut déduire que.
II *det* **1** (interrogative) quel/quelle/quels/quelles (*before n*); **~ books?** quels livres?; **~ one of the children?** lequel ou laquelle des enfants?; **2** (relative) **he left the room, during ~ time...** il a quitté la pièce et pendant ce temps-là...; **you may wish to join, in ~ case...** vous voulez peut-être vous inscrire, auquel cas...

whichever /wɪtʃ'evə(r), US hwɪtʃ-/ **I** *pron* **1** (the one that) (as subject) celui *m* qui, celle *f* qui; (as object) celui *m* que, celle *f* que; **'which restaurant?'—'~ is nearest'** 'quel restaurant?'—'celui qui est le plus proche'; **come at 2 or 2.30, ~ suits you best** viens à 14 h ou 14 h 30, comme cela te convient le mieux; **choose either alternative, ~ is the cheaper** choisis la moins chère des deux solutions; **2** (no matter which one) (as subject) quel *m* que soit celui qui, quelle *f* que soit celle qui; (as object) quel *m* que soit celui que, quelle *f* que soit celle que; **'do you want the big**

which

As a pronoun

In questions

When *which* is used as a pronoun in questions it is translated by *lequel, laquelle, lesquels* or *lesquelles* according to the gender and number of the noun it is referring to:

> there are three peaches,
> which do you want? = il y a trois pêches, laquelle veux-tu?

> 'Lucy's borrowed three of your books'
> 'which did she take?' = 'Lucy t'a emprunté trois livres'
> 'lesquels a-t-elle pris?'

The exception to this is when *which* is followed by a superlative adjective, when the translation is *quel, quelle, quels* or *quelles*:

> which is the biggest
> (apple)? = quelle est la plus grande?
> which are the least
> expensive (books)? = quels sont les moins chers?

In relative clauses as subject or object

When *which* is used as a relative pronoun as the subject of a verb, it is translated by *qui*:

> the book which is on the table = le livre qui est sur la table
> the books which are on the table = les livres qui sont sur la table

When *which* is the object of a verb it is translated by *que* (*qu'* before a vowel or mute 'h'):

> the book which Tina is reading = le livre que lit Tina

Note the inversion of subject and verb; this is the case where the subject is a noun but not where the subject is a pronoun:

> the book which I am reading = le livre que je lis

In compound tenses such as the present perfect and past perfect, the past participle agrees in gender and number with the noun *que* is referring to:

> the books which I gave you = les livres que je t'ai donnés
> the dresses which she
> bought yesterday = les robes qu'elle a achetées hier

In relative clauses after a preposition

Here the translation is *lequel, laquelle, lesquels* or *lesquelles* according to the gender and number of the noun referred to:

> the road by which we came = la route par laquelle
> or the road which we came by nous sommes venus

> the expressions for which we have translations
> = les expressions pour lesquelles nous avons une traduction

Remember that if the preposition would normally be translated by *à* in French (*to, at* etc.), the preposition + *which* is translated by *auquel, à laquelle, auxquels* or *auxquelles*:

> the addresses to which we sent letters
> = les adresses auxquelles nous avons envoyé des lettres

With prepositions normally translated by *de* (*of, from* etc.) the translation of the preposition *which* becomes *dont*:

> a blue book, the title of which I've forgotten
> = un livre bleu dont j'ai oublié le titre

However, if *de* is part of a prepositional group, as for example in the case of *près de* meaning *near,* the translation becomes *duquel, de laquelle, desquels* or *desquelles*:

> the village near which they live = le village près duquel ils habitent
> the houses near which she was waiting
> = les maisons près desquelles elle attendait

The translation *duquel* etc. is also used where a preposition + noun precedes *of which*:

> a hill at the top of which there is a house
> = une colline au sommet de laquelle il y a une maison

As a determiner

In questions

When *which* is used as a determiner in questions it is translated by *quel, quelle, quels* or *quelles* according to the gender and number of the noun that follows:

> which car is yours? = quelle voiture est la vôtre?
> which books did he borrow? = quels livres a-t-il empruntés?

Note that in the second example the object precedes the verb so that the past participle agrees in gender and number with the object.

For translations of *which* as a determiner in relative clauses see **II 2** in the entry **which**.

---

piece or the small piece?'—'~' 'est-ce que tu veux le gros ou le petit morceau?'—'n'importe'.
II *det* **1** (the one that) **let's go to ~ station is nearest** allons à la gare la plus proche; **you may have ~ dress you prefer** tu peux avoir la robe que tu préfères; **2** (no matter which) **it won't matter ~ hotel we go to** peu importe l'hôtel où nous irons; **I'll be happy ~ horse wins** quel que soit le cheval qui gagne je serai content; **3** (which on earth) **~ one do you mean?** mais duquel/de laquelle est-ce que tu peux bien parler?

whiff /wɪf, US hwɪf/ *n* (of perfume, food, dung) odeur *f* **(of** de); (of smoke, garlic) bouffée *f* **(of** de); FIG relent *m* **(of** de).

while /waɪl, US hwaɪl/ **I** *conj* **1** (although) bien que, quoique; **2** (as long as) tant que; **3** (during the time that) pendant que; **he made a sandwich ~ I phoned** il s'est fait un sandwich pendant que je téléphonais; **he collapsed ~ mowing the lawn** il a eu un malaise alors qu'il tondait le gazon; **4** (at the same time as) (+*gerund*); **I fell asleep ~ watching TV** je me suis endormi en regardant la télé; **close the door ~ you're about** ou **at it** ferme la porte pendant que tu y es; **'MOT ~ you wait'** 'contrôle technique express'; **5** (whereas) tandis que.

II *n* **a ~ ago** ou **back** il y a quelque temps; **a ~ later** quelque temps plus tard; **for a good ~** pendant longtemps; **a short** ou **little ~ ago** il y a peu de temps; **it will be** ou **take a ~** cela va prendre un certain temps; **to stop for a ~** s'arrêter un peu; **after a ~ he fell asleep** au bout d'un moment il s'est endormi; **he worked, humming all the ~** il travaillait tout en chantonnant; **and all the ~** ou **the whole ~, he was cheating on her** et depuis le début, il la trompait; **once in a ~** de temps en temps; **in between ~s** entre-temps.
■ **while away**: **~ away [sth]** tuer [*time*].

whilst /waɪlst, US hwaɪlst/ *conj* = **while I**.

whim /wɪm, US hwɪm/ *n* caprice *m*; **on a ~** sur un coup de tête.

whimper /'wɪmpə(r), US 'hwɪm-/ **I** *n* gémissement *m*.
II *vtr* **'I'm cold,' she ~ed** 'j'ai froid,' dit-elle en gémissant.
III *vi* **1** [*person, animal*] gémir; **2** PÉJ (whinge) [*person*] pleurnicher.

whimsical /'wɪmzɪkl, US 'hwɪm-/ *adj* [*person*] fantasque; [*play, tale, manner, idea*] saugrenu.

whine /waɪn, US hwaɪn/ **I** *n* (of person, animal) geignement *m*; (of engine) plainte *f*; (of bullet) sifflement *m*.
II *vtr* **'I'm hungry,' he ~d** 'j'ai faim,' dit-il d'une voix geignarde.

III *vi* (complain) se plaindre (**about** de); (snivel) pleurnicher; [*dog*] gémir.

whining /'waɪnɪŋ, US 'hwaɪn-/ **I** *n* (complaints) jérémiades *fpl*; (of engine) gémissements *mpl* aigus; (of dog) gémissements *mpl*.
II *adj* [*voice*] (complaining, high-pitched) geignard; [*child*] pleurnicheur/-euse; [*letter*] de réclamation.

whinny /'wɪnɪ, US 'hwɪnɪ/ **I** *n* faible hennissement *m*.
II *vi* [*horse*] hennir doucement.

whip /wɪp, US hwɪp/ **I** *n* **1** (for punishment) fouet *m*; (for horse) cravache *f*; **2** GB POL (official) *député chargé d'assurer la discipline de vote des membres de son parti*; (summons) convocation *f* (*envoyée aux membres d'un parti lors d'une séance de Parlement importante*); **three-line ~** convocation *f* urgente; **3** CULIN mousse *f*.
II *vtr* (*p prés etc* **-pp-**) **1** (beat) fouetter; **2** CULIN fouetter [*cream*]; battre [*qch*] en neige [*egg whites*]; **3**○ (remove quickly) **I ~ped the key out of his hand** je lui ai arraché la clé des mains; **4** GB (steal) piquer○ (**from sb** à qn).
III○ *vi* (*p prés etc* **-pp-**) **to ~ round** se retourner brusquement.
■ **whip away**: **~ away** [*sth*], **~** [*sth*] **away** [*person*] retirer prestement; [*wind*] faire voler.
■ **whip back**: **¶ ~ back** revenir brusquement en arrière; **¶ ~ back** [*sth*], **~** [*sth*] **back** récupérer [*qch*] brusquement.
■ **whip in**: **¶ ~ in** [*sth*], **~** [*sth*] **in 1** rassembler [*hounds*]; **2** CULIN incorporer [*qch*] (*avec un fouet*); **¶ ~ in** [*sb*], **~** [*sb*] **in** US POL rallier.
■ **whip off**: **~ off** [*sth*], **~** [*sth*] **off** enlever [*qch*] à toute vitesse.
■ **whip on**: **~ on** [*sth*], **~** [*sth*] **on 1** enfiler [*qch*] à toute vitesse; **2** cravacher [*horse*].
■ **whip out**: **~ out** [*sth*] sortir [*qch*] brusquement.
■ **whip through** expédier [*task, book*].
■ **whip up**: **~ up** [*sth*] **1** (incite) attiser [*hatred*]; ranimer [*indignation, hostility*]; éveiller [*interest*]; rallier [*support*]; inciter [*unrest*]; **2** CULIN battre [*qch*] au fouet; **3** (produce) préparer [*qch*] en vitesse.

whip hand *n* **to have the ~** avoir le dessus; **to have the ~ over sb** l'emporter sur qn.

whiplash injury *n* MED coup *m* du lapin.

whipping /'wɪpɪŋ, US 'hwɪp-/ *n* correction *f* (*au fouet*).

whipping boy *n* souffre-douleur *m inv*.

whip-round○ *n* GB collecte *f*.

whirl /wɜːl, US hwɜːl/ **I** *n* LIT, FIG GEN tourbillon *m* (**of** de); (spiral motif) spirale *f*.
II *vtr* (swirl) faire tournoyer; **to ~ sb along/away** entraîner/emmener qn à toute vitesse.
III *vi* **1** [*dancer*] tournoyer; [*blade, propeller*] tourner; [*snowflakes, dust, mind, thoughts*] tourbillonner; **2** [*person, vehicle*] **to ~ past** filer à toute vitesse.
IDIOMS **to give sth a ~**○ essayer qch.
■ **whirl round**: **¶ ~ round** [*person*] se retourner brusquement; **¶ ~** [*sth*] **round** faire tournoyer.

whirl: **~pool** *n* tourbillon *m*; **~pool bath** *n* bain *m* bouillonnant; **~wind** *n* tourbillon *m*.

whirr /wɜː(r), US hwɜːr/ **I** *n* (of motor) vrombissement *m*; (of toy, camera, insect) bourdonnement *m*; (of wings) bruissement *m*.
II *vi* [*motor*] vrombir; [*camera, fan*] tourner; [*insect*] bourdonner; [*wings*] bruire.

whisk /wɪsk, US hwɪsk/ **I** *n* CULIN (also **egg ~**) (manual) fouet *m*; (electric) batteur *m*.
II *vtr* **1** CULIN battre; **2** (transport quickly) **he was ~ed off to meet the president** on l'a emmené sur le champ rencontrer le président; **she was ~ed off to hospital** elle a été emmenée d'urgence à l'hôpital; **3** (flick) **she ~ed the fly away** elle a chassé la mouche d'un geste.
III *vi* **he ~ed off** il est parti rapidement; **he ~ed around the room with a duster** il a donné un rapide coup de chiffon dans la pièce.

whisker /'wɪskə(r), US 'hwɪ-/ **I** *n* **1** LIT poil *m* de moustache; **2** FIG **to lose/win by a ~** perdre/gagner d'un poil○.
II whiskers *npl* (of animal) moustaches *fpl*; (of man)

(side-whiskers) favoris *mpl*; (beard) barbe *f*; (moustache) moustache *f*.

whisper /'wɪspə(r), US 'hwɪs-/ **I** *n* LIT GEN chuchotement *m*; FIG rumeur *f*; **to speak in a ~ ou in ~s** parler à voix basse; **his voice dropped to a ~** il a baissé la voix et s'est mis à chuchoter.
II *vtr* chuchoter (**to** à); **to ~ sth to sb** chuchoter qch à qn; **it is ~ed that** FIG on dit que.
III *vi* GEN chuchoter; [*water*] murmurer; **to ~ to sb** parler à voix basse à qn.

whispering /'wɪspərɪŋ, US 'hwɪ-/ **I** *n* GEN chuchotement *m*; FIG rumeurs *fpl* insidieuses.
II *adj* [*person*] qui chuchote; [*leaves, trees, wind, water*] murmurant.

whispering: **~ campaign** *n* campagne *f* de diffamation; **~ gallery** *n* galerie *f* à écho.

whistle /'wɪsl, US 'hwɪ-/ **I** *n* **1** (small pipe) sifflet *m*; (siren) sirène *f*; **to blow the** ou **one's ~** donner un coup de sifflet; **2** (sound) GEN sifflement *m*; (with small pipe) coup *m* de sifflet.
II *vtr* GEN siffler; (casually) siffloter [*melody*].
III *vi* **1** (make noise) siffler; **to ~ at sb/sth** siffler qn/qch; **to ~ for** siffler [*dog*]; **2** (move fast) **to ~ past** ou **by** [*bullet*] passer en sifflant; [*train*] passer à toute vitesse.
IDIOMS **to blow the ~ on sb** dénoncer qn; **to blow the ~ on sth** révéler qch; **you can ~ for it**○! tu peux toujours courir○!; **to ~ in the dark** essayer de se donner du courage.
■ **whistle up**○: **~ up** [*sth*] dégoter○.

whistle-stop tour *n* (by diplomat, president) tournée *f* éclair *inv* (**of** de); (by candidate on campaign) tournée *f* électorale (**of** de).

Whit /wɪt, US hwɪt/ *n*: *abrév* ▶ **Whitsun**.

white /waɪt, US hwaɪt/ ▶818| **I** *n* **1** (colour, part of egg, eye) blanc *m*; **2** (also **White**) (Caucasian) Blanc/Blanche *m/f*; **3** (wine) blanc *m*; **4** (in chess, draughts) blancs *mpl*.
II whites *npl* **tennis/chef's ~s** tenue *f* de tennis/de chef-cuisinier.
III *adj* **1** blanc/blanche; **2** [*race, child, skin*] blanc/blanche; [*area*] habité par des Blancs; [*culture, prejudice, fears*] des Blancs; **a ~ man/woman** un Blanc/une Blanche; **3** (pale) pâle (**with** de); **to go** ou **turn ~** pâlir (**with** de).
IDIOMS **he would swear black was ~** il a l'esprit de contradiction; **the men in ~ coats** HUM les infirmiers psychiatriques; **whiter than ~** plus blanc/blanche que neige.

whitebait /'waɪtbeɪt, US 'hwaɪt-/ *n* (raw) blanchaille *f*; (fried) petite friture *f*.

white: **~board** *n* tableau *m* blanc; **~ coffee** *n* (at home) café *m* au lait; (in café) café *m* crème; **~-collar** *adj* [*job, work*] d'employé de bureau; [*staff*] de bureau; [*vote*] des cols blancs; [*neighbourhood*] US résidentiel/-ielle.

white elephant *n* PÉJ **1** (item, knicknack) bibelot *m*; **2** (public project) réalisation *f* coûteuse et peu rentable.

white goods *n* **1** (appliances) gros électro-ménager *m*; **2** (linens) blanc *m* ∅.

white-haired /ˌwaɪt'heəd, US ˌhwaɪt-/ *adj* aux cheveux blancs.

Whitehall /'waɪthɔːl, US 'hwaɪt-/ *pr n* GB POL *avenue à Londres où sont concentrés les principaux ministères et administrations publiques*.

white: **~ hope** *n* espoir *m*; **~ horses** *n* (waves) moutons *mpl*; **~ hot** *adj* LIT, FIG incandescent.

White knight *n* **1** GEN sauveur *m*; **2** FIN chevalier *m* blanc.

white: **~ lead** *n* blanc *m* de céruse; **~ lie** *n* pieux mensonge *m*.

whiten /'waɪtn, US 'hwaɪtn/ **I** *vtr* blanchir.
II *vi* [*sky, face, cheeks*] pâlir; [*knuckles*] blanchir.

whitener /'waɪtnə(r), US 'hwaɪt-/ *n* **1** (for clothes) agent *m* blanchissant; **2** (for shoes) produit *m* pour blanchir; **3** (for coffee, tea) succédané *m* de lait en poudre.

whiteness /'waɪtnɪs, US 'hwaɪt-/ *n* blancheur *f*.

whiteout /'waɪtaʊt, US 'hwaɪt-/ n METEOROL voile m blanc.

White Russian n **1** (Tsarist) Russe mf blanc/blanche; **2** (Byelorussian) Biélorusse mf.

white spirit n white-spirit m.

white tie I n **1** (tie) nœud m papillon blanc; **2** (formal dress) habit m; **~ and tails** queue f de pie.

II white-tie noun modifier [dinner, occasion] habillé.

white: **~ trash** n ¢ US PÉJ pauvre Blanc/Blanche; **~wall (tyre)** GB, **~wall (tire)** US n pneu m à flanc blanc.

whitewash /'waɪtwɒʃ, US 'hwaɪt-/ **I** n **1** (for walls) lait m de chaux; **2** FIG (cover-up) mise f en scène; **3**° SPORT déculottée° f.

II vtr **1** LIT blanchir [qch] à la chaux; **2** (also **~ over**) FIG blanchir; **3**° SPORT flanquer une déculottée à°; **4** FIN réhabiliter.

white: **~ water** n eau f vive; **~ wedding** n mariage m en blanc.

whitey /'waɪtɪ, US 'hwaɪtɪ/ adj [blue] laiteux/-euse.

whither /'wɪðə(r), US 'hwɪðər/ adv LITTÉR où.

whiting /'waɪtɪŋ, US 'hwaɪt-/ n (pl **~**) ZOOL merlan m.

whitish /'waɪtɪʃ, US 'hwaɪt-/ ▶818 adj tirant sur le blanc, blanchâtre PÉJ.

Whit Monday n lundi m de Pentecôte.

Whitsun /'wɪtsn, US hwɪ-/ n (also **Whitsuntide**) Pentecôte f.

Whit Sunday n Pentecôte f.

whittle /'wɪtl, US 'hwɪt-/ vtr tailler [qch] au couteau.

■ **whittle away**: ¶ **~ away** [sth] FIG réduire [advantage, lead]; ¶ **~ away at** [sth] LIT tailler [stick]; FIG réduire [advantage, lead, profits].

■ **whittle down**: **~ down** [sth], **~** [sth] **down** réduire (**to** à).

whizz /wɪz, US hwɪz/ **I** n **1**° (expert) as° m (**at** en); **2** (whirr) sifflement m; **3**° (quick trip) tour m rapide (**around** de); **4**° CULIN **give the mixture a ~ in the blender** faites passer rapidement le mélange au mixer. **II**° vtr (deliver quickly) filer°.

III vi **to ~ by** ou **past** [arrow, bullet] passer en sifflant; [car] passer à toute allure; [person] passer rapidement; **to ~ up sth** réduire qch en purée.

whizz-kid° /'wɪzkɪd, US 'hwɪz-/ n jeune prodige m.

who /huː/

■ **Note** who is translated by qui.

– In questions qui on its own as the object of a verb requires inversion of the verb: who did he call? = qui a-t-il appelé? but qui followed by est-ce que or est-ce qui needs no inversion: qui est-ce qu'il a appelé? Note, however, that the form il a appelé qui? is also used in spoken French.

– For particular usages see the entry below.

---

pron **1** (interrogative) (as subject) qui (est-ce qui); (as object) qui (est-ce que); (after prepositions) qui; **~ knows the answer?** qui connaît la réponse?; **~ did you invite?** qui est-ce que tu as invité?, qui as-tu invité?; **~'s going to be there?** qui sera là?; **~ was she with?** avec qui était-elle?; **~ did you get it from?** qui te l'a donné?; **do you know ~'s ~?** est-ce que tu sais qui est qui?; **I was strolling along when ~ should I see but Diane** je me promenais et devine qui j'ai rencontré...Diane; **~ shall I say is calling?** (on phone) c'est de la part de qui?; **2** (relative) (as subject) qui; (as object) que; (after prepositions) qui; **his friend, ~ lives in Paris** son ami qui habite Paris; **his friend ~ he sees once a week** l'ami qu'il voit une fois par semaine; **he/she ~** celui/celle qui; **they** ou **those ~** ceux/celles qui; **those ~ have something to say should speak up now** quiconque a quelque chose à dire doit le dire or ceux qui ont quelque chose à dire doivent le dire maintenant; **3** (whoever) **bring ~ you like** tu peux amener qui tu veux; **~ do you think you are?** tu te prends pour qui?; **~'s he to tell you what to do?** de quel droit est-ce qu'il te donne des ordres?

WHO n (abrév = **World Health Organization**) OMS f.

who'd /huːd/ = **who had**, **who would**.

whodun(n)it /ˌhuːˈdʌnɪt/ n polar° m, roman m policier.

whoever /huːˈevə(r)/ pron **1** (the one that) **~ wins the election will have to deal with the problem** celui ou celle qui gagnera les élections devra faire face au problème; **2** (anyone that) qui; **invite ~ you like** invite qui tu veux; **~ saw the accident should contact the police** quiconque a assisté à l'accident devrait contacter la police; **3** (all who) tous ceux qui; **4** (no matter who) **come out ~ you are** qui que vous soyez, sortez de là; **write to the minister or ~** écris au ministre ou à n'importe qui d'autre; **5** (who on earth) qui; **~ did that to you?** (mais) qui a bien pu te faire ça?

whole /həʊl/ **I** n **1** (total unit) tout m; **as a ~** (not in separate parts) en entier; (overall) dans l'ensemble; **taken as a ~** pris dans l'ensemble; **2** (all) **the ~ of** tout/-e; **the ~ of London is talking about it** tout Londres en parle; **nearly the ~ of Berlin was destroyed** Berlin a été presque entièrement détruit.

II adj **1** (entire) tout, entier/-ière; (more emphatic) tout entier/-ière; **the most beautiful city in the ~ world** la plus belle ville du monde; **a ~ hour** une heure entière; **a ~ day** toute une journée; **the ~ truth** toute la vérité; **this doesn't give the ~ picture** ceci ne dit pas tout; **let's forget the ~ thing!** oublions tout ça!; **she made the ~ thing up** elle a tout inventé; **2** (emphatic use) **he looks a ~ lot better** il a vraiment bien meilleure mine; **there were a ~ lot of them** [objects] il y en avait tout un tas°; [people] il y en avait toute une bande°; **a ~ lot of money** un tas° d'argent; **that goes for the ~ lot of you!** ça s'applique à vous tous!; **a ~ new way of life** un mode de vie complètement différent; **that's the ~ point of the exercise** c'est tout l'intérêt de l'exercice; **3** (intact) intact; **to make sb ~** guérir qn.

III adv [swallow, cook] tout entier.

IV on the whole adv phr dans l'ensemble.

whole: **~food** n GB produits mpl biologiques; **~food shop** ▶1251 n GB magasin m de produits diététiques; **~grain** adj complet/-ète.

wholehearted /ˌhəʊlˈhɑːtɪd/ adj sans réserve; **to be in ~ agreement with** être en accord total avec.

whole: **~heartedly** adv sans réserve; **~meal** adj complet/-ète; **~ milk** n lait m entier; **~ number** n (nombre m) entier m.

wholesale /'həʊlseɪl/ **I** n vente f en gros.

II adj **1** COMM de gros; **2** (large-scale) [destruction, alteration, commitment] total; [acceptance, rejection] en bloc; [attack] sur tous les fronts.

III adv **1** COMM en gros; **I can get it for you ~** je peux vous l'avoir au prix de gros; **2** FIG en bloc.

wholesaler /'həʊlseɪlə(r)/ n grossiste mf, marchand/-e m/f en gros; **wine ~** marchand de vin en gros.

wholesome /'həʊlsəm/ adj **1** (healthy) sain; **2** (decent) [person] bien propre; [entertainment] innocent.

wholewheat adj = **wholemeal**.

who'll /huːl/ = **who will**, **who shall**.

wholly /'həʊllɪ/ adv entièrement, tout à fait.

whom /huːm/

■ **Note** In questions, qui on its own requires inversion of the verb: whom do you wish to see? = qui voulez-vous voir? but qui followed by est-ce que needs no inversion: qui est-ce que vous voulez voir?

---

pron **1** (interrogative) qui (est-ce que); (after prepositions) qui; **~ did she meet?** qui a-t-elle rencontré?, qui est-ce qu'elle a rencontré?; **to ~ are you referring?** à qui est-ce que vous faites allusion?; **the article is by ~?** de qui est l'article?; **2** (relative) que; (after prepositions) qui; **the minister ~ he'd seen** le ministre qu'il avait vu; **the person to ~/of ~ I spoke** la personne à qui/de qui or dont j'ai parlé; **those ~ he baptized** ceux qu'il a baptisés; ...**four of ~ are young and all of ~ are single** ...dont quatre sont jeunes et qui sont tous célibataires; **Kirsten and Matthew, both of** ~ **had ridden before** Kirsten et Matthew, qui avaient déjà fait du cheval tous les deux; **she pointed to the boys, one of** ~ **was laughing** elle a indiqué le groupe de garçons dont un riait; **he was particular about** ~ **he chose** il était exigeant quant à ceux qu'il choisissait; **3** (whoever) qui.

whoop /huːp, wuːp, US hwuːp/ **I** *n* (shout) cri *m*.
II *vi* **1** (shout) pousser des cris (**with** de); **2** MED avoir une quinte de toux (*due à la coqueluche*).
■ **whoop it up**○ s'éclater○.

whoopee○ /'wʊpiː, US 'hwʊ-/ **I** *n* **to make** ~ HUM (make love) faire l'amour; (have fun) faire la foire○.
II *excl* youpi!

whooping cough ▶ **1002**| *n* coqueluche *f*.

whoosh○ /wʊʃ, US hwʊʃ/ **I** *excl* zoum!
II *vi* **to** ~ **in/past** entrer/passer à toute allure.

whopper○ /'wɒpə(r), US 'hwɒpər/ *n* (large thing) monstre *m*; (lie) bobard○ *m*.

whopping○ /'wɒpɪŋ, US 'hwɒpɪŋ/ *adj* (also ~ **great**) monstre○.

whore /hɔː(r)/ *n* INJUR prostituée *f*.

who're /'huːə(r)/ = **who are**.

whorl /wɜːl, US hwɜːl/ *n* (of cream, chocolate etc) spirale *f*; (on fingerprint) volute *f*; (shell pattern) spire *f*.

who's /huːz/ = **who is**, **who has**.

whose /huːz/ **I** *pron* à qui; ~ **is this?** à qui est ceci?; ~ **did you take?** tu as pris celui/celle etc de qui?
II *adj* **1** (interrogative) ~ **pen is that?** à qui est ce stylo?; **do you know** ~ **car was stolen?** est-ce que tu sais à qui appartenait la voiture volée?; ~ **coat did you take?** tu as pris le manteau de qui?; **with** ~ **permission?** avec la permission de qui?; **2** (relative) **the boy** ~ **dog was killed** le garçon dont le chien a été tué.

Who's Who *pr n* ~ bottin® *m* mondain.

who've /huːv/ = **who have**.

why /waɪ, US hwaɪ/

■ **Note** *why* translates as *pourquoi* in French, but see **II**, **III** below for exceptions.
– As with other words such as *où, quand, comment etc*, questions are formed by inserting *est-ce que* after the question word: *why did you go?* = pourquoi est-ce que tu y es allé? or by inverting the subject and verb after the question word, which is slightly more formal: pourquoi y es-tu allé? In spoken French the question word can be put at the end: *tu y es allé pourquoi?*
– *why* occurs with certain reporting verbs such as *ask, explain, know, think* and *wonder*. For translations, see these entries.

I *adv* **1** (in questions) pourquoi; ~ **do you ask?** pourquoi est-ce que tu me poses la question?, pourquoi me poses-tu la question?; **'I'm annoyed'—'~ is that?'** 'je suis vexé'—'pourquoi?'; **oh no,** ~ **me?** oh non, pourquoi est-ce que ça me tombe dessus○?; **'it's not possible'—'~ not?'** 'ce n'est pas possible'—'pourquoi pas?'; **'can I apply?'—'I don't see** ~ **not'** 'est-ce que je peux m'inscrire?'—'je ne vois pas pourquoi tu ne pourrais pas'; **2** (when making suggestions) pourquoi; ~ **don't we go away for the weekend?** pourquoi ne pas partir quelque part pour le week-end?; ~ **don't I invite them for dinner?** et si je les invitais à manger?; ~ **not send off now for our brochure?** pourquoi ne pas demander dès maintenant notre brochure?; **3** (expressing irritation, defiance) pourquoi; ~ **can't you be quiet?** tu ne peux pas te taire?; ~ **do I bother?** à quoi ça sert que je me donne du mal?; ~ **should they get all the praise?** pourquoi est-ce que c'est eux qui auraient tous les compliments?; **'tell them'—'~ should I?'** 'dis-leur'—'et pourquoi (est-ce que je devrais le faire)?'; **4** (also ~**ever**) (expressing surprise) ~**ever not?** GB pourquoi pas?
II *conj* pour ça; **that is** ~ **they came** c'est pour ça qu'ils sont venus; **that's not** ~ **I asked** ce n'est pas pour ça que j'avais posé la question; **so that's** ~! (finally understanding) ah, c'est pour ça!; **'~?'—'because you're stubborn, that's** ~!**'** 'pourquoi?'—'parce que tu es têtu, c'est tout!'; **the reason** ~ la raison

pour laquelle; **I need to know the reason** ~ j'ai besoin de savoir pourquoi; ▶ **reason I** 1.
III† *excl* mais.

WI *n* **1** GB *abrév* ▶ **Women's Institute**; **2** US POST *abrév écrite* = **Wisconsin**; **3** *abrév écrite* = **West Indies**.

wick /wɪk/ *n* (of candle, lamp etc) mèche *f*.

wicked /'wɪkɪd/ *adj* **1** (evil) [*person*] méchant; [*heart, deed*] cruel/-elle; [*plot*] pernicieux/-ieuse; [*intention*] mauvais; **2** (mischievous) malicieux/-ieuse; **3** (naughty) pervers; **4** (vicious) [*wind*] méchant; [*weapon*] redoutable; [*sarcasm*] cinglant; **a** ~ **tongue** une mauvaise langue; **5**○ (terrible) **a** ~ **waste** un vrai gâchis; **it was a** ~ **shame** c'était vraiment une honte.
IDIOMS **no peace** OU **rest for the** ~ pas de repos pour les braves○.

wickedly /'wɪkɪdlɪ/ *adv* **1** (maliciously) avec malice; **2** (evilly) avec méchanceté.

wickedness /'wɪkɪdnɪs/ *n* **1** (evil) (of person, deed, regime, heart) cruauté *f*; **the** ~ **of all that waste** le scandale de tout ce gâchis; **2** (of grin, joke) malice *f*.

wicker /'wɪkə(r)/ **I** *n* (also **wickerwork**) osier *m*.
II *noun modifier* [*basket, furniture*] en osier.

wicket /'wɪkɪt/ *n* **1** (field gate) portillon *m*; (sluice gate) petite porte *f* d'écluse; **2** US (transaction window) guichet *m*; **3** SPORT guichet *m*.
IDIOMS **to be on a sticky** ~○ être dans le pétrin○.

wide /waɪd/ **I** *adj* **1** (broad) GEN large; [*margin*] grand; **how** ~ **is your garden?** quelle est la largeur de votre jardin?; **it's 30 cm** ~ il a 30 cm de large; **they're making the street** ~r ils élargissent la rue; **her eyes were** ~ **with fear** ses yeux étaient agrandis par la peur; **2** (immense) vaste; **3** (extensive) [*variety, choice*] grand; **a woman of** ~ **interests** une femme qui s'intéresse à beaucoup de choses; **a** ~ **range of products** une vaste gamme de produits; **a** ~ **range of opinions** une grande variété d'opinions; **in the** ~**st sense of the word** au sens le plus large du mot; **4** SPORT [*ball, shot*] perdu.
II *adv* **to open one's eyes** ~ ouvrir grand les yeux; **his eyes are** ~ **apart** il a les yeux très écartés; **open** ~! ouvrez grand (la bouche)!; **to be** ~ **of the mark** [*ball*] être à côté; FIG [*guess*] être loin de la vérité.

wide: ~**-angle lens** *n* objectif *m* à grand angle; ~ **awake** *adj* complètement éveillé.

wide-eyed /ˌwaɪd'aɪd/ *adj* **1** (with fear, surprise) **he was** ~ il ouvrait de grands yeux; ~ **with fear** les yeux écarquillés de peur; **2** (naïve) [*person, innocence*] ingénu.

widely /'waɪdlɪ/ *adv* **1** (commonly) largement; **it is** ~ **believed that** beaucoup de gens pensent que; **a country** ~ **admired for its technology** un pays qui fait l'admiration générale pour sa technologie; **to be** ~ **available** [*product*] être en vente libre; **to be** ~ **known** être bien connu (**for** pour); **these are not** ~ **held views** ce ne sont pas des opinions très répandues; **2** [*spaced*] à de grands intervalles; [*travel, differ*] beaucoup.

widely-read /ˌwaɪdlɪ'red/ *adj* [*student*] qui lit beaucoup; [*author*] beaucoup lu.

widen /'waɪdn/ **I** *vtr* GEN élargir; étendre [*powers*]; **this has** ~**ed their lead in the opinion polls** ceci a renforcé leur position dominante dans les sondages.
II *vi* **1** [*river, road*] s'élargir; **his eyes** ~**ed** il a ouvert grand les yeux; **2** (increase) **the gap is** ~**ing between rich and poor** le fossé entre riches et pauvres s'élargit.
III *widening pres p adj* [*division*] de plus en plus grand; [*gap*] qui s'élargit de plus en plus.

wide open *adj* **1** [*door, window, eyes*] grand ouvert; **2 the race is** ~ l'issue de la course est indécise; **3 to lay oneself** ~ **to criticism** prêter le flanc à la critique.

wide-ranging /ˌwaɪd'reɪndʒɪŋ/ *adj* GEN de grande envergure; **a** ~ **discussion** une discussion couvrant un grand nombre de sujets.

wide screen *n* CIN grand écran *m*.

will¹

The future tense

When *will* is used to express the future in English, the future tense of the French verb is generally used:

he'll come = il viendra

In spoken and more informal French or when the very near future is implied, the present tense of *aller* + *infinitive* can be used:

I'll do it now = je vais le faire tout de suite

If the subject of the modal auxiliary *will* is *I* or *we*, *shall* is sometimes used instead of *will* to talk about the future. For further information, consult the entry *shall* in the dictionary.

Note that *would* and *should* are treated as separate entries in the dictionary.

Tag questions

French has no direct equivalent of tag questions like *won't he?* or *will they?* There is a general tag question *n'est-ce pas?* which will work in many cases:

you'll do it tomorrow, won't you? = tu le feras demain, n'est-ce pas?

In cases where an opinion is being sought, *non?* meaning *is that not so?* can be useful:

that will be easier, won't it? = ce sera plus facile, non?

In many other cases the tag question is simply not translated at all and the speaker's intonation will convey the implied question.

Short answers

Again, there is no direct equivalent for short answers like *no she won't, yes they will* etc. Where the answer *yes* is given to contradict a negative question or statement, the most useful translation is *si*:

'they won't forget' 'yes they will' = 'ils n'oublieront pas' 'si' *or* (for more emphasis) 'bien sûr que si'

Where the answer *no* is given to contradict a positive question or statement the most useful translation is *bien sûr que non*:

'she'll post the letter, won't she?' 'no she won't' = 'elle va poster la lettre?' 'bien sûr que non'

In reply to a standard enquiry the tag will not be translated:

'you'll be ready at midday then?' 'yes I will' = 'tu seras prêt à midi?' 'oui'

For more examples and other uses, see the entry *will*.

---

widespread /ˈwaɪdspred/ *adj* [*epidemic*] généralisé; [*devastation*] étendu; [*belief*] très répandu.

widow /ˈwɪdəʊ/ **I** *n* GEN veuve *f*; **golf ~** HUM femme *f* délaissée par son mari golfeur; **war ~** veuve de guerre.
II *vtr* **to be ~ed** devenir veuf/veuve *m/f*; **she has been ~ed for two years** elle est veuve depuis deux ans.

widower /ˈwɪdəʊə(r)/ *n* veuf *m*.

width /wɪdθ, wɪtθ/ ▶1045 *n* **1** largeur *f*; **it is 30 metres in ~** il fait or mesure 30 mètres de large; **2** (of fabric) lé *m*.

widthways, **widthwise** /ˈwɪdθweɪz, ˈwɪtθ-, ˈwɪdθwaɪz, ˈwɪtθ-/ *adv* dans la largeur.

wield /wiːld/ *vtr* LIT brandir; FIG exercer (**over** sur).

wife /waɪf/ *n* (*pl* **wives**) (spouse) GEN femme *f*; ADMIN, JUR épouse *f*; **the baker's/farmer's ~** la boulangère/la fermière.

wife battering *n* violence *f* corporelle contre les femmes.

wig /wɪg/ *n* (whole head) perruque *f*; (partial) postiche *m*.

wiggle° /ˈwɪgl/ **I** *n* **a ~ of the hips** un roulement des hanches; **to give sth a ~** faire bouger qch.
II *vtr* faire bouger [*tooth, object*]; **to ~ one's hips** rouler des hanches; **to ~ one's toes** agiter les orteils.
III *vi* [*snake, worm*] se tortiller.

wild /waɪld/ **I** *n* **in the ~** [*conditions, life*] en liberté; **to grow in the ~** pousser à l'état sauvage; **the call of the ~** l'appel de la nature.
II wilds *npl* **to live in the ~s of Arizona** habiter au fin fond de l'Arizona.
III *adj* **1** (in natural state, desolate) sauvage; **~ beast** bête fauve; **the pony is still quite ~** le poney est encore assez farouche; **2** (turbulent) [*wind*] violent; [*sea*] agité; **it was a ~ night** c'était une nuit de tempête; **3** (unrestrained) [*party, laughter, person*] fou/folle; [*imagination*] délirant; [*applause*] déchaîné; **to go ~** se déchaîner; **she led a ~ life in her youth** elle a fait les quatre cents coups dans sa jeunesse; **his hair was ~ and unkempt** il avait les cheveux en bataille; **~ mood swings** changements d'humeur brutaux; **4°** (furious) furieux/-ieuse; **he'll go ou be ~!** ça va le mettre hors de lui!; **5°** (enthusiastic) **to be ~ about** être un fana° de; **I'm not ~ about him/it** il/ça ne m'emballe° pas; **6** (outlandish) [*idea*] fou/folle; [*claim, accusation*] extravagant; [*story*] farfelu°.
IV *adv* **1** [*grow*] à l'état sauvage; **those children are allowed to run ~!** on permet à ces enfants de faire

n'importe quoi!; **to let one's imagination run ~** laisser libre cours à son imagination.

wild boar *n* sanglier *m*.

wild card *n* **1** GAMES, COMPUT joker *m*; **2** FIG (unpredictable element) élément *m* imprévisible; **3** SPORT wild-card *f*.

wildcat /ˈwaɪldkæt/ **I** *n* ZOOL chat *m* sauvage.
II *adj* US [*scheme, venture*] risqué.

wildcat strike *n* grève *f* sauvage.

wild dog *n* dingo *m*.

wilderness /ˈwɪldənɪs/ *n* **1** (wasteland) étendue *f* sauvage et désolée; **2** (uncultivated area) étendue *f* sauvage; **the garden has become a ~** le jardin est devenu une vraie jungle.
IDIOMS **to be a voice crying in the ~** prêcher dans le désert.

wild-eyed /ˌwaɪldˈaɪd/ *adj* au regard égaré.

wildfire /ˈwaɪldfaɪə(r)/ *n* **to spread like ~** se répandre comme une traînée de poudre.

wild: **~ flower** *n* fleur *f* des champs, fleur *f* sauvage; **~fowl** *n* (wild bird) oiseau *m* sauvage; (birds collectively) oiseaux *mpl* sauvages; (game) gibier *m* à plume.

wild-goose chase /ˌwaɪldˈguːs tʃeɪs/ *n* **it turned out to be a ~** ça n'a abouti à rien; **to lead sb on a ~** mettre qn sur une mauvaise piste.

wild: **~life** *n* (animals) faune *f*; (animals and plants) faune *f* et flore *f*; **~life park**, **~life reserve**, **~life sanctuary** *n* réserve *f* naturelle.

wildly /ˈwaɪldlɪ/ *adv* **1** (recklessly) [*spend, talk*] de façon insensée; [*fire*] au hasard; **to hit out/run ~** envoyer des coups/courir dans tous les sens; **2** [*wave, gesture*] de manière très agitée; [*applaud*] à tout rompre; **to fluctuate ~** subir des fluctuations violentes; **his heart was beating ~** son cœur battait à tout rompre; **3** [*enthusiastic, optimistic*] extrêmement.

wildness /ˈwaɪldnɪs/ *n* **1** (of landscape) aspect *m* sauvage; (of weather) violence *f*; **2** (disorderliness) (of person) caractère *m* débridé; (of appearance) désordre *m*; (of party) folie *f*; **3** (extravagance) (of idea) extravagance *f*.

wild: **~ rose** *n* rosier *m* sauvage; **~ water rafting** ▶949 *n* rafting *m*; **Wild West** *n* Far West *m*.

wiles /waɪlz/ *npl* ruses *fpl*.

wilful GB, **willful** US /ˈwɪlfl/ *adj* [*person, behaviour*] volontaire ALSO JUR; [*damage, disobedience*] délibéré.

wilfully GB, **willfully** US /ˈwɪlfəlɪ/ *adv* **1** (in headstrong way) obstinément; **2** (deliberately) délibérément.

will¹ /wɪl, əl/ **I** *modal aux* **1** (to express the future) **she'll help you** elle t'aidera; (in the near future) elle va t'aider; **must I phone him or ~ you?** est-ce que je dois lui téléphoner ou est-ce que tu vas le faire?; **I've said I'll repay you and I ~** j'ai dit que je te rembourserai et je le ferai; **2** (expressing consent, willingness) **'~ you help me?'—'yes, I ~'** 'est-ce que tu m'aideras?'—'oui, bien sûr'; **he won't cooperate** il ne veut pas coopérer; **'have a chocolate'—'thank you, I ~'** 'prends un chocolat'—'volontiers, merci'; **I ~ not be talked to like that** je n'accepte pas qu'on me parle sur ce ton; **I won't have it said of me that I'm mean** il ne sera pas dit que je suis mesquin; **~ you or won't you?** c'est oui ou c'est non?; **do what** ou **as you ~** fais ce que tu veux; **~ do**○! d'accord!; **3** (in commands, requests) **~ you pass the salt, please?** est-ce que tu peux me passer le sel, s'il te plaît?; **'I can give the speech'—'you ~ not!'** 'je peux faire le discours'—'pas question!'; **'I'll do it'—'no you won't'** 'je vais le faire'—'il n'en est pas question'; **~ you please listen to me!** est-ce que tu vas m'écouter!; **wait a minute ~ you!** attends un peu!; **4** (in offers, invitations) **~ you marry me?** est-ce que tu veux m'épouser?; **you'll have another cake, won't you?** vous prendrez bien un autre gâteau?; **5** (expressing custom or habit) **they ~ usually ask for a deposit** ils demandent généralement une caution; **any teacher ~ tell you that...** n'importe quel professeur te dira que...; **these things ~ happen** ce sont des choses qui arrivent; (in exasperation) **she ~ keep repeating the same old jokes** elle n'arrête pas de répéter les mêmes blagues; **6** (expressing conjecture or assumption) **that ~ be my sister** ça doit être ma sœur; **they won't be aware of what has happened** ils ne doivent pas savoir ce qui s'est passé; **that ~ have been last month** ça devait être le mois dernier; **you'll have gathered that** vous aurez compris que; **7** (expressing ability or capacity to do) **the lift ~ hold 12** l'ascenseur peut transporter 12 personnes; **that jug won't hold a litre** ce pichet ne contient pas un litre; **this chicken won't feed six** ce poulet n'est pas assez gros pour six personnes; **the car won't start** la voiture ne veut pas démarrer.

II vtr **1** (urge) **to ~ sb's death** souhaiter ardemment la mort de qn; **to ~ sb to do** supplier mentalement qn de faire; **to ~ sb to live** prier pour que qn vive; **2** (wish, desire) vouloir; **3** JUR léguer.

III v refl **he ~ed himself to stand up** au prix d'un effort surhumain il a réussi à se lever.

will² /wɪl/ **I** n **1** volonté f (**to do** de faire); **to have a strong/weak ~** avoir beaucoup/peu de volonté; **to have a ~ of one's own** faire ce qu'on a envie de faire; **strength of ~** force de caractère; **against my ~** contre mon gré; **to do sth with a ~** faire qch de bon cœur; **to lose the ~ to live** ne plus avoir envie de vivre; **2** JUR testament m; **the last ~ and testament of** les dernières volontés de; **to leave sb sth in one's ~** léguer qch à qn.

II at will adv phr [select, take] à volonté; **you can change it at ~** tu peux le changer quand tu veux.

IDIOMS **where there's a ~ there's a way** PROV quand on veut on peut PROV.

willful adj US = **wilful**.

William /'wɪljəm/ pr n Guillaume; **~ the Conqueror** Guillaume le Conquérant.

willing /'wɪlɪŋ/ adj **1** (prepared) **to be ~ to do** être prêt à faire; **I'm quite ~** je veux bien; **I'm more than ~ to help you** j'accepte volontiers de vous aider; **2** (eager) [pupil, helper] de bonne volonté; [slave] consentant; [recruit, victim] volontaire; **to show ~** faire preuve de bonne volonté; **we need some ~ hands to clean up** nous avons besoin de volontaires pour nettoyer; **3** [sacrifice] volontaire.

IDIOMS **the spirit is ~ but the flesh is weak** l'esprit est ardent mais la chair est faible.

willingly /'wɪlɪŋlɪ/ adv [accept, help] volontiers; [work] avec bonne volonté; **did she go ~?** est-elle partie de son propre gré?

willingness /'wɪlɪŋnɪs/ n **1** (readiness) volonté f (**to do** de faire); **2** (helpfulness) bonne volonté f.

willow /'wɪləʊ/ n **1** (also **~ tree**) saule m; **2** (wood) (bois m de) saule m; **3** (for weaving) osier m.

willow pattern n motif m chinois (bleu sur fond blanc).

willowy /'wɪləʊɪ/ adj [person, figure] élancé.

will power n volonté f (**to do** de faire).

willy-nilly /ˌwɪlɪ'nɪlɪ/ adv (regardless of choice) bon gré mal gré.

wilt /wɪlt/ **I** vtr faire dépérir [plant].

II vi LIT [plant, flower] se faner; FIG [person] (from heat, fatigue) se sentir faible; (at daunting prospect) perdre courage.

III wilted pp adj fané.

Wilts n GB POST abrév écrite = **Wiltshire**.

wily /'waɪlɪ/ adj rusé.

wimp○ /wɪmp/ n PÉJ (ineffectual) lavette○ f; (fearful) poule f mouillée.

■ **wimp out** se défiler○.

wimpish○ /'wɪmpɪʃ/, **wimpy**○ /'wɪmpɪ/ adj PÉJ [person] mollasson/-onne○; [behaviour] mou/molle○.

win /wɪn/ **I** n **1** (victory) victoire f (**over** sur); **to have a ~ over sb in sth** remporter une victoire sur qn dans qch; **2** (successful bet) pari m gagnant.

II vtr (p prés **-nn-**; prét, pp **won**) **1** GAMES, MIL, SPORT gagner; POL gagner [election, votes] (**from sb** aux dépens de qn); gagner les élections dans [region, city] (**from sb** aux dépens de qn); **to ~ a (parliamentary) seat** être élu député (**from sb** aux dépens de qn); **2** (acquire) obtenir [reprieve] (**from** de); gagner [friendship, heart] s'attirer [sympathy]; s'acquérir [support] (**of** de); **it won him the admiration of his colleagues** cela lui a valu l'admiration de ses collègues; **to ~ sb's love/respect** se faire aimer/respecter de qn.

III vi (p prés **-nn-**; prét, pp **won**) gagner; **to ~ against sb** l'emporter sur qn; **to ~ by two goals** gagner de deux buts; **you ~!** (in argument) je m'incline!; **I've done my best to please her, but you just can't ~** j'ai tout fait pour lui plaire, mais rien à faire; **~ or lose, the discussions have been valuable** quoi qu'il arrive, les discussions ont été profitables; **it's a ~ or lose situation** tout se joue là-dessus.

IDIOMS **~ some, lose some** on ne peut pas gagner à tous les coups.

■ **win back**: **~ [sth] back, ~ back [sth]** récupérer [support, votes] (**from sb** sur qn); regagner [affection, respect]; reprendre [prize, territory] (**from** à).

■ **win out** l'emporter; **to ~ out over sth** vaincre qch.

■ **win over, win round**: **~ over [sb]**, **~ [sb] over** convaincre.

■ **win through** finir par gagner; **to ~ through to** SPORT se qualifier pour [semifinal etc].

wince /wɪns/ **I** n grimace f.

II vi grimacer, faire une grimace.

winch /wɪntʃ/ **I** n treuil m.

II vtr **to ~ sth down/up** descendre/hisser qch au treuil.

wind¹ /wɪnd/ **I** n **1** METEOROL vent m; **North ~** vent du nord; **the ~ is blowing** il y a du vent; **which way is the ~ blowing?** d'où vient le vent?; **a high ~** un vent fort; **2** (breath) souffle m; **to knock the ~ out of** couper le souffle à; **to get one's ~** reprendre souffle; **to get one's second ~** FIG reprendre ses forces; **3** FIG vent m; **the ~ of change** le vent du changement; **there is something in the ~** il y a quelque chose dans l'air; **4** (flatulence) vents mpl; **to break ~** lâcher un vent; **to bring up ~** avoir des renvois; **5** MUS **the ~s** les instruments mpl à vent.

II vtr **1** (make breathless) [blow] couper la respiration à; [exertion] essouffler; **2** faire son rot à [baby].

IDIOMS **to get ~ of** avoir vent de; **to get the ~ up**○ avoir la trouille○; **to put the ~ up sb**○ flanquer la trouille○ à qn; **to see which way the ~ blows** voir de quel côté souffle le vent.

wind² /waɪnd/ **I** n **1** (of road) tournant m; **2** (movement) (of handle) tour m.

II vtr (prét, pp **wound**) **1** (coil up) enrouler; **she wound her arms around him** elle l'a enlacé; **2** (also **~ up**) remonter [clock, toy]; **3** donner un tour de [handle]; **4 to ~ one's** ou **its way** serpenter.

III *vi* (*prét*, *pp* **wound**) GEN serpenter (**along** le long de); [*stairs*] tourner.
■ **wind down**: ¶ ~ **down 1** [*organization*] réduire ses activités; [*activity, production*] toucher à sa fin; [*person*] se détendre; **2** [*clockwork*] être sur le point de s'arrêter; ¶ ~ **down** [sth], ~ [sth] **down 1** baisser [*car window*]; **2** mettre fin à [*activity, organization*].
■ **wind in**: ~ **in** [sth], ~ [sth] **in** remonter [*cable, line, fish*].
■ **wind on**: ¶ ~ **on** [*film*] s'enrouler; ¶ ~ **on** [sth], ~ [sth] **on** enrouler.
■ **wind up**: ¶ ~ **up 1** (finish) [*event*] se terminer (**with** par); [*speaker*] conclure; **2**○ (end up) finir, se retrouver; ¶ ~ **up** [sth], ~ [sth] **up 1** liquider [*business*]; fermer [*account*]; mettre fin à [*campaign, meeting, project*]; JUR régler [*estate*]; **2** remonter [*clock, car window*]; ~ [sb] **up**, ~ **up** [sb] **1** (tease) faire marcher [*person*]; **2** (make tense) énerver.

wind /wɪnd/: **~blown** *adj* ébouriffé par le vent; **~borne** *adj* apporté par le vent; **~break** *n* (natural) brise-vent *m inv*; (on beach) pare-vent *m inv*; **~cheater** *n* GB coupe-vent *m inv*; **~chill factor** *n* facteur *m* de refroidissement de la température dû au vent; **~ chimes** *npl* carillon *m* éolien; **~ energy** *n* énergie *f* éolienne.

winder /'waɪndə(r)/ *n* (for watch) remontoir *m*; (for wool, thread) dévidoir *m*; (for window) lève-glace *m inv*.

windfall /'wɪndfɔːl/ *n* LIT fruit *m* tombé par terre; FIG aubaine *f*.

wind /wɪnd/: **~fall profit** *n* profit *m* inattendu; **~ gauge** *n* anémomètre *m*.

winding /'waɪndɪŋ/ *adj* GEN sinueux/-euse; [*stairs*] en spirale.

winding-up *n* (of business, affairs) clôture *f*.

wind instrument ▶ 1097 | *n* instrument *m* à vent.

windless /'wɪndləs/ *adj* sans vent.

windmill /'wɪndmɪl/ *n* **1** moulin *m* à vent; **2** (toy) moulinet *m*.

window /'wɪndəʊ/ *n* **1** (of house, room, vehicle, envelope) fenêtre *f* ALSO COMPUT; (of shop, public building) vitrine *f*; (of plane) hublot *m*; (stained glass) vitrail *m*; **I'd like a seat by a ~** AVIAT j'aimerais une place côté fenêtre; **to look out of** ou **through the ~** regarder par la fenêtre; **2** (for service at bank or post office) guichet *m*; **3** (space in diary, time) créneau *m*.
IDIOMS **to go** ou **fly out the ~**○ [*plans*] tomber à l'eau; [*hopes*] s'écrouler.

window: **~ blind** *n* store *m*; **~ box** *n* jardinière *f*; **~ cleaner** *n* (person) laveur/-euse *m/f* de carreaux; (product) produit *m* pour nettoyer les vitres; **~ display** *n* COMM vitrine *f*; **~ dresser** ▶ 1251 | *n* étalagiste *mf*.

window dressing *n* **1** LIT composition *f* de vitrines; **2** FIG **it's all ~** PÉJ c'est de la poudre aux yeux○; **3** FIN habillage *m* de bilan.

window: **~ frame** *n* châssis *m* de fenêtre; **~ ledge** *n* appui *m* de fenêtre; **~pane** *n* carreau *m*.

window-shopping *n* **to go ~** faire du lèche-vitrines○ *m inv*.

windowsill *n* rebord *m* de fenêtre.

wind /wɪnd/: **~pipe** *n* trachée-artère *f*; **~power** *n* énergie *f* éolienne; **~screen** *n* GB AUT pare-brise *m inv*; **~screen washer** *n* GB AUT lave-glace *m*; **~screen wiper** *n* GB AUT essuie-glace *m inv*; **~shield** *n* US AUT = **windscreen**; **~sleeve**, **~sock** *n* manche *f* à air; **~surf** *vi* faire de la planche à voile; **~surfer** *n* (person) véliplanchiste *mf*; (board) planche *f* à voile; **~swept** *adj* venteux/-euse.

windward /'wɪndwəd/ **I** *n* côté *m* du vent.
II *adj, adv* contre le vent.

windy /'wɪndɪ/ *adj* **1** [*place*] venteux/-euse; [*day*] de vent; **it** ou **the weather was very ~** il faisait beaucoup de vent; **2** PÉJ (verbose) verbeux/-euse.

wine /waɪn/ ▶ 818 | **I** *n* **1** (drink) vin *m*; **2** (colour) lie-de-vin *m*.

II *noun modifier* [*production*] de vin; [*cellar, glass, cask*] à vin.
III *adj* (also **~-coloured**) lie-de-vin *inv*.
IDIOMS **to ~ and dine** manger dans les bons restaurants.

wine: **~ bar** *n* bar *m* à vin; **~ box** *n* = cubitainer® *m*; **~ cellar** *n* cave *f*.

wine cooler *n* **1** (ice bucket) seau *m* à rafraîchir; **2** US (drink) boisson légèrement alcoolisée.

wine growing I *n* viticulture *f*.
II *noun modifier* [*region*] vinicole.

wine: **~ list** *n* carte *f* des vins; **~ merchant** ▶ 1251 | *n* négociant *m* en vins; **~ producer** ▶ 1251 | *n* viticulteur/-trice *m/f*.; **~ rack** *n* cellier *m*; **~ shop** ▶ 1251 | *n* marchand *m* de vin; **~ taster** ▶ 1251 | *n* dégustateur/-trice *m/f* de vins; **~ tasting** *n* dégustation *f* de vins; **~ vinegar** *n* vinaigre *m* de vin; **~ waiter** ▶ 1251 | *n* sommelier/-ière *m/f*.

wing /wɪŋ/ **I** *n* **1** (of bird, insect) aile *f*; **to be on the ~** être en vol; **2** (of building, plane, car) aile *f*; (of armchair) oreille *f*; **3** MIL, POL aile *f*; (unit in air force) escadre *f*; **4** SPORT (player) ailier *m*; (side of pitch) aile *f*; **to play on the right ~** être ailier droit.
II wings *npl* **1** THEAT **the ~s** les coulisses *fpl*; **to be waiting in the ~s** FIG attendre son heure; **2** AVIAT **to get one's ~s** obtenir l'insigne de pilote.
III *vtr* **1** **to ~ one's way** voler vers; **2** [*bullet*] érafler.
IDIOMS **to clip sb's ~s** rogner les ailes à qn; **to spread one's ~s** (entering adult life) voler de ses propres ailes; (entering wider career) voir autre chose.

wing: **~ chair** *n* fauteuil *m* à oreilles; **~ collar** *n* col *m* cassé; **~ commander** ▶ 1192 | *n* lieutenant-colonel *m* de l'armée de l'air.

winged /wɪŋd/ *adj* GEN ailé; [*insect*] volant.

winger○ /'wɪŋə(r)/ *n* GB ailier *m*.

wing: **~ forward** *n* (in rugby) avant *m* troisième ligne; **~ half** *n* (in soccer) demi-droit *m*; **~ mirror** *n* GB rétroviseur *m* extérieur; **~ nut** *n* écrou *m* à oreilles; **~span** *n* envergure *f*; **~ three-quarter** *n* (in rugby) trois-quarts aile *m*.

wink /wɪŋk/ **I** *n* clin *m* d'œil; **to give sb a ~** faire un clin d'œil à qn; **we didn't get a ~ of sleep all night** nous n'avons pas fermé l'œil de la nuit.
II *vtr* **to ~ one's eye** cligner de l'œil.
III *vi* **1** cligner de l'œil; **to ~ at sb** faire un clin d'œil à qn; **2** [*light*] clignoter; [*jewellery*] briller.
IDIOMS **a nod is as good as a ~ to a blind horse** ou **man** c'est bien, on a compris; **to tip sb the ~**○ avertir qn.

winner /'wɪnə(r)/ *n* **1** (victor) gagnant/-e *m/f*; **to be the ~(s)** SPORT finir gagnant; **to be on to a ~** jouer gagnant; **to back the ~** parier sur le gagnant; **~ takes all** GAMES le gagnant rafle tout; **2** (success) **to be a ~** avoir un gros succès.

winning /'wɪnɪŋ/ **I** *n* réussite *f*.
II winnings *npl* gains *mpl*.
III *adj* **1** (victorious) gagnant; **2** [*smile*] engageant; **to have ~ ways** avoir du charme.

winning post *n* poteau *m* d'arrivée.

winning streak *n* **to be on a ~** être dans une bonne période.

winsome /'wɪnsəm/ *adj* [*person*] charmant.

winter /'wɪntə(r)/ ▶ 1235 | **I** *n* hiver *m*.
II *noun modifier* [*activity, clothes, weather*] d'hiver.
III *vi* passer l'hiver.

winter: **~ sleep** *n* hibernation *f*; **~ sports** *npl* sports *mpl* d'hiver; **~time** *n* hiver *m*.

wintry /'wɪntrɪ/ *adj* LIT hivernal; FIG glacé.

wipe /waɪp/ **I** *n* **1** (act of wiping) **to give sth a ~** (with dry cloth) donner un coup de torchon à qch; (with wet cloth) donner un coup d'éponge sur qch; **2** (for face, baby) lingette *f*; MED tampon *m*; **3** CIN effaçage *m*.
II *vtr* **1** (mop) essuyer (**on** sur; **with** avec); **to ~ one's nose** se moucher; **to ~ one's bottom** se torcher; **to ~ sth clean** essuyer qch; **~ that smile**

off **your face!** arrête de sourire!; **2** CIN, COMPUT, RADIO, TV effacer.

■ **wipe away**: ~ **away** [sth], ~ [sth] **away** essuyer [*tears, sweat*]; faire partir [*dirt, mark*].

■ **wipe down**: ~ **down** [sth], ~ [sth] **down** nettoyer [*wall, floor*].

■ **wipe off**: ~ **off** [sth], ~ [sth] **off 1** faire partir [*dirt, mark*]; **2** AUDIO, CIN, COMPUT, VIDEO effacer.

■ **wipe out**: ~ **out** [sth], ~ [sth] **out 1** (clean) nettoyer; **2** (erase) effacer; **3** FIG effacer [*memory, past*]; liquider [*debt*]; annuler [*chances, gains, losses*]; anéantir [*enemy, population*]; **4**○ (defeat) lessiver○.

■ **wipe up**: ¶ ~ **up** essuyer la vaisselle; ¶ ~ **up** [sth], ~ [sth] **up** essuyer.

wipe-clean *adj* facile à nettoyer.

wiper /'waɪpə(r)/ *n* **1** AUT (also **windscreen** ~ GB, **windshield** ~ US) essuie-glace *m inv*; **2** (cloth) torchon *m*.

wiper: ~ **arm** *n* AUT bras *m* d'essuie-glace; ~ **blade** *n* AUT balai *m* d'essuie-glace.

wire /'waɪə(r)/ **I** *n* **1** (length of metal) fil *m*; **2** US (telegram) télégramme *m*.
II *vtr* **1** ELEC **to** ~ **a house** installer l'électricité dans une maison; **to** ~ **a plug/a lamp** connecter une prise/une lampe; **2** (send telegram to) télégraphier à.
IDIOMS **down to the** ~ US jusqu'au tout dernier moment; **to pull** ~ US se faire pistonner○; **to get one's** ~**s** ou **lines crossed** se comprendre de travers.
■ **wire up**: ~ [sth] **up to sth** relier [qch] à qch.

wire: ~ **brush** *n* brosse *f* métallique; ~ **cutters** *npl* cisailles *fpl*; ~ **glass** *n* verre *m* armé.

wireless /'waɪəlɪs/ *n* (transmitter, receiver) radio *f*.

wireless: ~ **message** *n* message *m* radio(phonique); ~ **operator** ▶ 1251| *n* radiotélégraphiste *mf*; ~ **room** *n* cabine *f* radio; ~ **set**† *n* poste *m* de radio; ~ **telegraphy** *n* télégraphie *f* sans fil.

wire: ~ **mesh** *n* treillis *m* métallique; ~ **netting** *n* grillage *m*; ~ **service** *n* (agency) agence *f* de presse; (facility) lignes *fpl* d'une agence de presse; ~ **tapping** *n* espionnage *m* électronique; ~ **wool** *n* paille *f* de fer.

wiring /'waɪərɪŋ/ *n* (in house) installation *f* électrique; (in appliance) circuit *m* (électrique); **the** ~ **in the oven is faulty** le four est mal connecté.

wiry /'waɪərɪ/ *adj* **1** [*person*] maigre; **2** [*hair*] raide; **to have a** ~ **coat** [*animal*] avoir le poil raide.

wisdom /'wɪzdəm/ *n* sagesse *f*; **to doubt** ou **question the** ~ **of doing** douter qu'il soit sage de faire; **in his** ~ IRON dans son infinie sagesse.

wisdom tooth *n* dent *f* de sagesse.

wise /waɪz/ **I** SOUT† *n* façon *f*.
II *adj* **1** (prudent) GEN sage; [*choice*] judicieux/-ieuse; **it is** ~ **of sb to do** il est prudent de la part de qn de faire; **you would be** ~ **to do** tu ferais bien de faire; **to be** ~ **enough to do** avoir le bon sens de faire; **was that** ~? était-ce bien raisonnable?; **to be** ~ **after the event** être sage après coup; **2** (learned) pertinent; **to be none the** ~**r** (understand no better) ne pas être plus avancé; (not realize) ne s'apercevoir de rien; **to be sadder and** ~**r** tirer une leçon d'une triste expérience; **3**○ (aware) **to be** ~ **to** être au courant de; **to get** ~ **to** prendre le coup de [*situation*]; **to get** ~ **to sb** saisir○ à qui on a affaire.
III -**wise** *combining form* **1** (direction) dans le sens de; **length-**~ dans le sens de la longueur; **2** (with regard to) **work-**~ pour ce qui est du travail.
IDIOMS **a word to the** ~:... en tout cas un conseil:...

wise: ~**crack** *n* vanne○ *f*; ~ **guy**○ *n* gros malin○ *m*.

wisely /'waɪzlɪ/ *adv* judicieusement.

Wise Men *npl* **the three** ~ les Rois *mpl* Mages.

wish /wɪʃ/ **I** *n* (desire) désir *m* (**for** de; **to do** de faire); (in story) souhait *m* (**for** de); **to make a** ~ faire un vœu; **to grant sb's** ~ GEN accéder au désir de qn; [*fairy*] exaucer le souhait de qn; **I have no** ~ **to disturb you** je n'ai pas l'intention de vous déranger.
II wishes *npl* vœux *mpl*; **good** ou **best** ~**es** meilleurs vœux; (ending letter) bien amicalement; **please**

give him my best ~**es** je vous prie de lui faire toutes mes amitiés.
III *vtr* **1** (expressing longing) **I** ~ **he were here** si seulement il était ici; **I just** ~ **we lived closer** si seulement nous habitions plus près; **he** ~**ed he had written** il regrettait de ne pas avoir écrit; **he wishes his mother would write** il voudrait que sa mère écrive; **he bought it and then** ~**ed he hadn't** il l'a acheté et puis a regretté de l'avoir fait; **I** ~**ed myself single again** j'aurais voulu être à nouveau célibataire; **2** (express congratulations, greetings) souhaiter; **to** ~ **sb joy** ou **happiness** souhaiter à qn d'être heureux; **to** ~ **sb joy of sth/sb** IRON souhaiter bien du plaisir à qn avec qch/qn; **we** ~**ed each other goodbye and good luck** nous nous sommes dit au revoir et bonne chance; **I** ~**ed him well** j'espérais que tout irait bien pour lui; **3** (want) souhaiter; (weaker) désirer.
IV *vi* **1** (desire, want) vouloir; **just as you** ~ comme vous voudrez; **to** ~ **for** souhaiter, espérer; **what more could one** ~ **for?** qu'est-ce qu'on pourrait espérer ou souhaiter de plus?; **2** (in fairy story) faire un vœu.
■ **wish on**: ~ [sth] **on sb** fourguer○ [qch] à qn.

wish: ~**bone** *n* bréchet *m*; ~ **fulfilment** *n* PSYCH accomplissement *m* du désir.

wishful thinking /,wɪʃfl 'θɪŋkɪŋ/ *n* **that's** ~ c'est prendre ses désirs pour des réalités.

wishy-washy○ /'wɪʃɪwɒʃɪ/ *adj* **1** [*colour*] délavé; **2** PÉJ [*person, approach*] incolore et inodore○.

wisp /wɪsp/ *n* (of hair) mèche *f*; (of straw) brin *m*; (of smoke, cloud) volute *f*; **a** ~ **of a girl** un petit bout de fille.

wispy /'wɪspɪ/ *adj* [*hair, beard*] fin; [*cloud, smoke*] léger/-ère; [*piece, straw*] menu.

wistful /'wɪstfl/ *adj* (sad) mélancolique; (nostalgic) nostalgique.

wit /wɪt/ **I** *n* **1** (sense of humour) esprit *m*; **to have a quick/ready** ~ avoir la repartie facile/l'esprit d'à-propos; **to have a dry** ~ être pince-sans-rire; **2** (witty person) personne *f* spirituelle.
II wits *npl* (intelligence) intelligence *f*; (presence of mind) présence *f* d'esprit; **to have** ou **keep (all) one's** ~**s about one** (vigilant) rester attentif/-ive; (level-headed) conserver sa présence d'esprit; **to collect** ou **gather one's** ~**s** rassembler ses esprits; **to sharpen one's** ~**s** se dégourdir l'esprit; **to frighten sb out of their** ~**s** faire une peur épouvantable à qn; **to pit one's** ~**s against sb** se mesurer (intellectuellement) à qn; **to live by one's** ~**s** vivre d'expédients; **to lose one's** ~**s** ne plus savoir où on est; **a battle of** ~**s** une joute verbale.
III *to wit adv phr* SOUT à savoir.
IDIOMS **to be at one's** ~**s'** **end** ne plus savoir quoi faire.

witch /wɪtʃ/ *n* sorcière *f*.

witch: ~**craft** *n* sorcellerie *f*; ~ **doctor** *n* shaman *m*; ~**-hunt** *n* LIT, FIG chasse *f* aux sorcières.

with /wɪð, wɪθ/

■ **Note** If you have any doubts about how to translate a phrase or expression beginning with *with* (with a vengeance, with all my heart, with a bit of luck, with my blessing etc) you should consult the appropriate noun entry (*vengeance, heart, luck, blessing* etc).
– *with* is often used after verbs in English (dispense with, part with, get on with etc). For translations, consult the appropriate verb entry (*dispense, part, get* etc).
– This dictionary contains Usage Notes on such topics as the human body and illnesses, aches and pains which use the preposition *with*. For the index to these Notes ▶ 1419|.
– For further uses of *with*, see the entry below.

---

1 (in descriptions) **a girl** ~ **black hair** une fille aux cheveux noirs; **the boy** ~ **the broken leg** le garçon à la jambe cassée; **a boy** ~ **a broken leg** un garçon avec une jambe cassée; **a dress** ~ **a large collar** une robe avec un large col; **a TV** ~ **remote control** une télévision avec télécommande; **furnished** ~ **antiques** décoré avec des meubles anciens; **covered** ~ **mud** couvert de boue; **wet** ~ **dew** couvert de rosée; **to lie** ~ **one's eyes closed** être allongé les

yeux fermés; **filled** ~ rempli de; **2** (involving, concerning) avec; **a treaty/a discussion** ~ **sb** un traité/une discussion avec qn; **3** (indicating an agent) avec; **to hit sb** ~ **sth** frapper qn avec qch; **to walk** ~ **a stick** marcher avec une canne; **to cut sth** ~ **a penknife** couper qch avec un canif; **4** (indicating manner, attitude) ~ **difficulty/pleasure** avec difficulté/plaisir; **to be patient** ~ **sb** être patient avec qn; **'OK,' he said** ~ **a smile/sigh** 'd'accord,' a-t-il dit en souriant/soupirant; **delighted** ~ **sth** ravi de qch; **5** (according to) **to increase** ~ **time** augmenter avec le temps; **to expand** ~ **heat** se dilater sous l'action de la chaleur; **to vary** ~ **the temperature** varier selon la température; **6** (accompanied by, in the presence of) avec; **to travel** ~ **sb** voyager avec qn; **bring a friend** ~ **you** viens avec un ami; **she's got her brother** ~ **her** (on one occasion) elle est avec or accompagnée de son frère; (staying with her) son frère est chez elle; **to live** ~ **sb** (in one's own house) vivre avec qn; (in their house) vivre chez qn; **I'll be** ~ **you in a second** je suis à vous dans un instant; **take your umbrella** ~ **you** emporte ton parapluie; **7** (owning, bringing) **passengers** ~ **tickets** les passagers munis de billets; **people** ~ **qualifications** les gens qualifiés; **somebody** ~ **your experience** quelqu'un qui a ton expérience; **have you got the report** ~ **you?** est-ce que tu as (amené) le rapport?; **8** (in relation to, as regards) **the frontier** ~ **Belgium** la frontière avec la Belgique; **how are things** ~ **you?** comment ça va?; **what's up** ~ **Amy?**, **what's** ~ **Amy?** US qu'est-ce qui ne va pas avec Amy?; **what do you want** ~ **another car?** qu'est-ce que tu veux faire d'une deuxième voiture?; **it's a habit** ~ **her** c'est une habitude chez elle; **9** (showing consent, support) **I'm** ~ **you on this matter** je suis tout à fait d'accord avec toi là-dessus; **I'm** ~ **you 100%** ou **all the way** je suis tout à fait d'accord avec toi; **10** (because of) **sick** ~ **worry** malade or mort d'inquiétude; **to blush** ~ **embarrassment** rougir d'embarras; **I can't do it** ~ **you watching** je ne peux pas le faire si tu me regardes; ~ **summer coming** avec l'été qui approche; **11** (remaining) ~ **only two days to go before the election** alors qu'il ne reste plus que deux jours avant les élections; **12** (suffering from) **people** ~ **Aids/leukemia** les personnes atteintes du sida/de la leucémie; **to be ill** ~ **flu** avoir la grippe; **to be in bed** ~ **chickenpox** être au lit avec la varicelle; **13** (in the care or charge of) **you're safe** ~ **us** tu es en sécurité avec nous; **the blame lies** ~ **him** c'est de sa faute; **14** (against) avec; **the war** ~ **Germany** la guerre avec l'Allemagne; **to be in competition** ~ **sb** être en concurrence avec qn; **15** (showing simultaneity) ~ **the approach of spring** à l'approche du printemps; ~ **the introduction of the reforms** avec l'introduction des nouvelles réformes; ~ **that, he left** sur ce, il est parti; **16** (employed by, customer of) **a reporter** ~ **the Gazette** un journaliste de la Gazette; **he's** ~ **the UN** il travaille pour l'ONU; **we're** ~ **the National Bank** nous sommes à la National Bank; **17** (in the same direction as) **to sail** ~ **the wind** naviguer dans le sens du vent; **to drift** ~ **the tide** dériver avec le courant.
IDIOMS **to be** ~ **it**° (on the ball) être dégourdi; (trendy) être dans le vent; **I'm not really** ~ **it today**° j'ai l'esprit ailleurs aujourd'hui; **get** ~ **it**°! (wake up) réveille-toi!; (face the facts) redescends sur terre!; **I'm not** ~ **you, can you repeat?** je ne te suis pas, tu peux répéter?

withdraw /wɪð'drɔː, wɪθ'd-/ (*prét* **-drew**, *pp* **-drawn**) **I** *vtr* retirer [*hand, money, support, application, offer*] (**from** de); retirer [*aid, permission*] (**from** à); renoncer à, retirer [*claim*]; rétracter [*accusation, statement*]; MIL retirer [*troops*] (**from** de); POL rappeler [*diplomat*]; **to** ~ **a product from sale** COMM retirer un produit de la vente; **to** ~ **one's labour** GB IND faire un arrêt de travail.
II *vi* **1** [*person, troops*] se retirer (**from** de); [*applicant, candidate*] se retirer; **to** ~ **from a game** se retirer d'un jeu; **to** ~ **to one's room** se retirer dans sa chambre; **to** ~ **from one's position** MIL abandonner sa position; **2** PSYCH se replier.

withdrawal /wɪð'drɔːəl, wɪθ'd-/ *n* **1** GEN, FIN, MIL retrait *m* (**of**, **from** de); POL (of ambassador) rappel *m*; **he has made several** ~**s from his account** il a effectué plusieurs retraits de son compte; ~ **of labour** GB arrêt *m* de travail; **2** PSYCH repli *m* sur soi; **3** (of drug addict) état *m* de manque.

withdrawal slip *n* bordereau *m* de retrait.

withdrawal symptoms *npl* symptômes *mpl* de manque; **to be suffering from** ~ être en état de manque.

withdrawn /wɪð'drɔːn, wɪθ'd-/ **I** *pp* ▶ **withdraw**.
II *adj* [*person*] renfermé, replié sur soi-même.

wither /'wɪðə(r)/ **I** *vtr* flétrir.
II *vi* se flétrir.
■ **wither away** [*hope, interest*] s'évanouir.

withered /'wɪðəd/ *adj* [*plant, skin, cheek*] flétri; [*arm*] atrophié.

withering /'wɪðərɪŋ/ *adj* [*look*] plein de mépris; [*contempt, comment*] cinglant.

withhold /wɪð'həʊld/ *vtr* (*prét, pp* **-held**) différer [*payment*]; retenir [*tax, grant, rent*]; refuser [*consent, permission*]; ne pas divulguer [*information*].

within /wɪ'ðɪn/ **I** *prep* **1** (enclosed in) ~ **the city walls** dans l'enceinte de la ville; ~ **the boundaries of the estate** dans l'enceinte de la propriété; **to lie** ~ **Italy's borders** être en Italie; **2** (inside) ~ **the party** au sein du parti; **conditions** ~ **the camp** les conditions de vie dans le camp; **candidates from** ~ **the company** les candidats internes; **it appeals to something deep** ~ **us all** cela touche quelque chose de profond en nous; **it's a play** ~ **a play** c'est une pièce dans la pièce; **3** (in expressions of time) **I'll do it** ~ **the hour** je le ferai en moins d'une heure; **15 burglaries** ~ **a month** 15 cambriolages en moins d'un mois; **'please reply** ~ **the week'** 'prière de répondre dans la semaine'; **'use** ~ **24 hours of purchase'** 'à consommer dans les 24 heures'; ~ **minutes he was back** quelques minutes plus tard il était de retour; **they died** ~ **a week of each other** ils sont morts à une semaine d'intervalle; **4** (not more than) **to be** ~ **several metres of sth** être à quelques mètres seulement de qch; **it's accurate to** ~ **a millimetre** c'est exact au millimètre près; ▶ **inch**; **5** (not beyond the range of) **to be** ~ **sight** LIT [*coast, town*] être en vue; FIG [*end*] être proche; **stay** ~ **sight of the car** ne vous éloignez pas de la voiture; **to be** ~ **range of** être à portée de [*enemy guns*]; **6** (not beyond a permitted limit) **to stay** ~ **budget** ne pas dépasser le budget; **to live** ~ **one's income** vivre selon ses moyens.
II *adv* à l'intérieur; **seen from** ~ vu de l'intérieur.

without /wɪ'ðaʊt/ **I** *prep* **1** (lacking, not having) sans; ~ **a key** sans clé; **to be** ~ **friends** ne pas avoir d'amis; **to be** ~ **shame** n'avoir aucune honte; **she left** ~ **it** elle est partie sans; **2** (not) sans; ~ **doing** sans faire; **do it** ~ **him noticing** fais-le sans qu'il s'en aperçoive; ~ **saying a word** sans mot dire.
II *adv* à l'extérieur; **from** ~ de l'extérieur.

withstand /wɪð'stænd/ *vtr* (*prét, pp* **-stood**) résister à.

witness /'wɪtnɪs/ **I** *n* **1** GEN, JUR (person) témoin *m*; **she was a** ~ **to the accident** elle a été témoin de l'accident; ~ **for the prosecution/the defence** témoin à charge/à décharge; **to call sb as a** ~ citer qn comme témoin; **2** (testimony) témoignage *m*; **to be** ou **bear** ~ **to sth** témoigner de qch.
II *vtr* **1** (see) être témoin de, assister à; **2** (at official occasion) servir de témoin lors de la signature de [*document, treaty*]; être témoin à [*marriage*]; **3** FIG **we are about to** ~ **a transformation of the economy** nous sommes sur le point d'assister à une transformation de l'économie; **his hard work has paid off, (as)** ~ **his exam results** son travail acharné a payé, comme en témoignent ses résultats d'examen.

witness box GB, **witness stand** US *n* barre *f* des témoins.

witticism /'wɪtɪsɪzəm/ *n* bon mot *m*.

wittily /'wɪtɪlɪ/ *adv* avec esprit.

witty /'wɪtɪ/ *adj* spirituel/-elle.

wives /waɪvz/ pl ▶ **wife**.

wizard /'wɪzəd/ n **1** (magician) magicien m; **2** FIG (expert) **to be a ~ at** avoir le génie de [chess, computing etc]; **to be a ~ at doing** être très fort pour faire.

wizened /'wɪznd/ adj ratatiné.

wk abrév écrite = **week**.

wobble /'wɒbl/ **I** n (in voice) tremblement m; (in movement) oscillation f; FIG vacillation f.
II vtr faire bouger [table, tooth].
III vi [table, chair] branler; [pile of books, plates etc] osciller; [voice] trembler; [person] (on bicycle) osciller; (on ladder, tightrope) chanceler; **his legs were wobbling under him** ses jambes flageolaient.

wobbly /'wɒblɪ/ adj [table, chair] bancal; [tooth] branlant; [chin, voice, jelly] tremblotant; [handwriting, line] tremblant; FIG [theory, plot] boiteux/-euse; **he is still a bit ~ on his legs** il est encore un peu faible sur ses jambes.
IDIOMS **to throw a ~**○ GB piquer une crise○.

woe /wəʊ/ **I** n malheur m.
II excl‡ OU HUM **~ betide him if he's late** gare à lui s'il est en retard.

woeful /'wəʊfl/ adj **1** (mournful) [look] affligé; [story, sight] affligeant; **2** (deplorable) [lack] déplorable.

woke /wəʊk/ prét ▶ **wake** II, III.

woken /'wəʊkən/ pp ▶ **wake** II, III.

wolf /wʊlf/ **I** n (pl **wolves**) loup m; **she-~** louve f.
II vtr (also **~ down**) engloutir.
IDIOMS **to cry ~** crier au loup; **to keep the ~ from the door** mettre qn à l'abri du besoin; **a lone ~** un/une solitaire m/f.

wolf: **~ cub** n louveteau m; **~ dog** US, **~hound** GB n chien-loup m.

wolfish /'wʊlfɪʃ/ adj féroce.

wolf-whistle /'wʊlfwɪsl, US -hwɪ-/ **I** n sifflement m (au passage d'une femme).
II vi siffler (au passage d'une femme).

wolves /wʊlvz/ pl ▶ **wolf**.

woman /'wʊmən/ **I** n (pl **women**) femme f; **the working ~** la femme active; **a ~ comes in to clean twice a week** une femme de ménage vient deux fois par semaine; **she's her own ~** elle est maîtresse de sa vie; **to talk about sth ~ to ~** parler de qch entre femmes; **for heaven's sake, ~!** mais enfin tu es idiote ou quoi?; **the other ~** PÉJ l'autre.
II noun modifier **a ~ Prime Minister** une femme premier ministre; **women drivers** les femmes au volant; **he has lots of women friends** il a beaucoup d'amies; **women voters** électrices fpl; **women writers** femmes fpl écrivains.
IDIOMS **a ~'s place is in the home** la place d'une femme est au foyer.

womanizer /'wʊmənaɪzə(r)/ n coureur m (de jupons○).

womanly /'wʊmənlɪ/ adj féminin.

woman police constable, **WPC** n GB femme f agent de police.

womb /wuːm/ n ventre m, utérus m.

women /'wɪmɪn/ pl ▶ **woman**.

women: **~'s group** n groupe m féministe; **Women's Institute**, **WI** n GB association de femmes qui s'intéresse aux problèmes du foyer et qui organise des œuvres de bienfaisance; **Women's Liberation Movement**, **Women's Lib**○, **WLM** n mouvement m de libération de la femme, MLF m; **~'s magazine** n magazine m féminin; **~'s movement** n mouvement m des femmes; **~'s page** n JOURN page f des lectrices; **~'s refuge** n foyer m pour femmes battues; **~'s studies** npl études fpl féministes; **~'s suffrage** n droit m de vote pour les femmes.

won /wʌn/ prét, pp ▶ **win** II, III.

wonder /'wʌndə(r)/ **I** n **1** (miracle) merveille f; **it's a ~ that** c'est extraordinaire que; **(it's) no ~ that** (ce n'est) pas étonnant que; **small** OU **little ~ that** ce n'est guère étonnant que; **she's a ~** elle est merveilleuse!; **the ~s of modern medicine** les prodiges de la médecine moderne; **2** (amazement) émerveillement m; **in ~** avec émerveillement; **lost in ~** émerveillé.
II noun modifier [cure, drug] miracle (after n).
III vtr **1** (ask oneself) se demander; **I ~ how/why** je me demande comment/pourquoi; **I ~ if you could help me?** peut-être pourriez-vous m'aider?; **it makes you ~** on peut se poser des questions; **it makes you ~ why/if/how** c'est à se demander pourquoi/si/comment; **2** (be surprised) **I ~ that** cela m'étonne que (+ subj).
IV vi **1** (think) **to ~ about sth** penser à qch; **2** (be surprised) **to ~ at sth** s'étonner de qch; (admiringly) s'émerveiller de qch; **they'll be late again, I shouldn't ~** cela ne m'étonnerait pas qu'ils soient encore en retard.

wonderful /'wʌndəfl/ adj [book, film, meal, experience, holiday] merveilleux/-euse; [musician, teacher] excellent; [achievement] beau/belle (before n); **to be ~ with** savoir comment s'y prendre avec [children, animals]; **to be ~ with computers** s'y connaître en informatique; **I feel ~** je suis en pleine forme; **you look ~!** (healthy) tu as l'air en pleine forme!; (attractive) tu es superbe!

wonderfully /'wʌndəfəlɪ/ adv (very) très; (splendidly) admirablement.

wondering /'wʌndərɪŋ/ adj (full of wonder) émerveillé; (puzzled) étonné.

wonderland /'wʌndəlænd/ n pays m enchanté.

wonky○ /'wʌŋkɪ/ adj GB **1** (crooked) de traviole○; **2** (wobbly) [furniture] bancal; [legs] flageolant; **3** (faulty) **the television is ~** la télé est détraquée○.

wont /wəʊnt, US wɔːnt/ adj **to be ~ to do** avoir coutume de faire; **as is his/their ~** comme à son/leur habitude.

won't /wəʊnt/ = **will not**.

woo /wuː/ vtr courtiser.

wood /wʊd/ **I** n **1** (fuel, timber) bois m; **2** (barrel) fût m; **3** (forest) bois m; **4** SPORT (in bowls) boule f (en bois); (in golf) bois m.
II woods npl bois mpl.
III noun modifier [fire, smoke] de bois.
IDIOMS **touch ~!** GB, **knock on ~!** US touchons du bois!; **we are not out of the ~ yet** on n'est pas encore sorti de l'auberge.

wood: **~block** n (for flooring) latte f; US ART planche f; **~-block floor** n parquet m; **~-burning stove** n = **wood stove**; **~carving** n sculpture f sur bois; **~craft** n connaissance f des bois; **~cut** n (block) planche f; (print) xylographie f; **~cutting** n abattage m des arbres.

wooded /'wʊdɪd/ adj boisé; **thickly ~** très boisé.

wooden /'wʊdn/ adj **1** GEN en bois; [leg] de bois; **2** FIG figé.

wooden: **~ horse** n cheval m de Troie ALSO FIG; **~ nickel** n US objet m sans valeur; **~ spoon** n cuillère f de bois; FIG prix m de consolation.

woodland /'wʊdlənd/ **I** n bois m.
II noun modifier [animal, plant] des bois; [scenery] boisé; [walk] dans les bois; **~ management** exploitation f forestière.

wood: **~louse** n cloporte m; **~pecker** n pic m; **~ pigeon** n pigeon m ramier; **~pile** n tas m de bois; **~ shavings** npl copeaux mpl; **~shed** n remise f à bois; **~ stove** n poêle m à bois.

woodwind /'wʊdwɪnd/ **I** npl bois mpl.
II noun modifier [instrument] à bois; [player] d'instrument à bois; [section] des bois.

woodwork /'wʊdwɜːk/ **I** n (carpentry) menuiserie f; (doors, windows etc) boiseries fpl.
II noun modifier [teacher, class] de menuiserie; [student] en menuiserie.
IDIOMS **to come out of the ~**○ HUM surgir d'un peu partout○.

woodworm /'wʊdwɜːm/ n (disease) maladie f du ver à bois; **to have ~** être vermoulu.

woody /'wʊdɪ/ adj [hill, landscape] boisé; [plant, stem] ligneux/-euse; [smell] de bois.

wool /wʊl/ **I** *n* laine *f*; **pure (new)** ~ pure laine (vierge).
II *noun modifier* [*carpet, coat, shop*] de laine; [*trade*] lainier/-ière.
IDIOMS **to pull the** ~ **over sb's eyes** duper qn.

woollen GB, **woolen** US /'wʊlən/ **I** *n* **1** (garment) lainage *m*; **2** (piece of cloth) tissu *m* en laine.
II *adj* [*garment*] de laine; ~ **mill** lainerie *f*.

woolly GB, **wooly** US /'wʊlɪ/ **I** *n*○ lainage *m*.
II *adj* [*garment*] de laine; [*animal coat*] laineux/-euse; [*cloud*] cotonneux/-euse; FIG [*thinking*] flou.

woozy○ /'wuːzɪ/ *adj* **to feel** ~ avoir la tête qui tourne.

Worcs *n* GB POST *abrév écrite* = **Worcestershire**.

word /wɜːd/ **I** *n* **1** (verbal expression) mot *m*; **those were his very** ~**s** ce sont ses propres mots; **to have no** ~**s to express sth** ne pas trouver les mots pour exprimer qch; **long** ~**s** mots savants; **with these** ~**s he left** sur ces mots il est parti; **in your own** ~**s** avec tes propres mots; **I don't think 'aunt' is quite the right** ~ je ne suis pas sûr que 'tante' soit le mot qui convienne; **the last** ~ FIG le dernier cri (in en); **to get a** ~ **in** placer un mot; **not in so many** ~**s** pas exactement; **in other** ~**s** en d'autres termes; **the spoken** ~ la langue parlée; **to put one's feelings** ou **thoughts into** ~**s** exprimer ce qu'on ressent; **there's no such** ~ **as 'can't'** 'impossible' n'est pas français; **what's the Greek** ~ **for 'table'?** comment dit-on 'table' en grec?; **a** ~ **of warning** un avertissement; **a** ~ **of advice** un conseil; **I've said my last** ~ **on the subject** j'ai dit tout ce que j'avais à dire sur le sujet; **too sad for** ~**s** trop triste; **in the** ~**s of Washington** pour reprendre l'expression de Washington; **I believed every** ~ **he said** je croyais tout ce qu'il me disait; **I mean every** ~ **of it** je pense ce que je dis; **a** ~ **to all those who...** quelques conseils pour tous ceux qui...; **a man of few** ~**s** un homme peu loquace; **2** (anything, something) mot *m*; **not a** ~ **to anybody** pas un mot à qui que ce soit; **I don't believe a** ~ **of it** je n'en crois pas un mot; **not to have a good** ~ **to say about sb** n'avoir rien de bon à dire de qn; **I want to say a** ~ **about honesty** je voudrais dire quelque chose au sujet de l'honnêteté; **I didn't say a** ~! je n'ai pas ouvert la bouche!; **he won't hear a** ~ **against her** il ne supporte pas qu'on dise quoi que ce soit contre elle; **3 ¢** (information) nouvelles *fpl* (**about** concernant); **there is no** ~ **of the missing climbers** on est sans nouvelles des alpinistes disparus; **we are hoping for** ~ **that all is well** nous espérons de bonnes nouvelles; ~ **got out that...** la nouvelle a transpiré que...; **to bring/send** ~ **that** annoncer/faire savoir que; **he left** ~ **at the desk that...** il a laissé un message à la réception disant que...; **4** (promise, affirmation) parole *f*; **he gave me his** ~ il m'a donné sa parole; **to break one's** ~ ne pas tenir parole; **to hold sb to his/her** ~ obliger qn à tenir parole; **a woman of her** ~ une femme de parole; **to take sb's** ~ **for it** croire qn sur parole; **to doubt sb's** ~ douter des paroles de qn; **take my** ~ **for it!** crois-moi!; **to go back on one's** ~ revenir sur sa promesse; **to be as good as one's** ~ tenir parole; **5** (rumour) ~ **has it that he's a millionaire** on dit qu'il est millionnaire; ~ **got round** ou **around that...** le bruit a couru que...; **6** (command) ordre *m*; **if you need anything just say the** ~ si tu as besoin de quoi que ce soit, dis-le; **just say the** ~ **and I'll come** tu n'as qu'un mot à dire et je viendrai; **their** ~ **is law** ils font la loi.
II words *npl* **1** (oratory) paroles *fpl*; **empty** ~**s** paroles vides de sens; **2** THEAT, MUS (of play) texte *m*; (of song) paroles *fpl*.
III -worded *combining form* **a carefully-**~**ed letter** une lettre soigneusement formulée; **a strongly-**~**ed statement** un communiqué ferme.
IV *vtr* formuler [*reply, letter, statement*].
IDIOMS **my** ~! (in surprise) ma parole!; (in reproof) tu vas voir!; **right from the** ~ **go** dès le départ; **to have a** ~ **with sb about sth** parler (un peu) à qn à propos de qch; **to have** ~**s with sb** s'accrocher avec

qn; **to put in a good** ~ **for sb** glisser un mot en faveur de qn.

word: ~ **blindness** *n* dyslexie *f*; ~**break** *n* coupure *f* (du mot); ~**count** *n* COMPUT nombre *m* de mots; ~**-for-word** *adj, adv* mot à mot *inv*; ~ **game** *n* jeu *m* de lettres.
wording /'wɜːdɪŋ/ *n* formulation *f*.
wordlist /'wɜːdlɪst/ *n* GEN liste *f* de mots; (in dictionary) nomenclature *f*.
word-of-mouth I *adj* [*promise*] verbal.
II by word of mouth *adv phr* verbalement.
word-perfect /ˌwɜːd'pɜːfɪkt/ *adj* parfait; **to be** ~ [*person*] connaître son texte sur le bout des doigts.
word: ~ **processing, WP** *n* COMPUT traitement *m* de texte; ~ **processor** *n* COMPUT machine *f* à traitement de texte.
wordy /'wɜːdɪ/ *adj* verbeux/-euse.
wore /wɔː(r)/ *prét* ▶ **wear II, III**.

work /wɜːk/ **I** *n* **1** (physical or mental activity) travail *m* (**on** sur); **to be at** ~ **on sth** être en train de travailler à qch; **to go** ou **set** ou **get to** ~ se mettre au travail; **to set to** ~ **doing** se mettre à faire; **to put a lot of** ~ **into** travailler [*essay, speech*]; passer beaucoup de temps sur [*meal, preparations*]; **to put** ou **set sb to** ~ faire travailler qn; **we put him to** ~ **doing** nous lui avons donné pour tâche de faire; **it was hard** ~ **doing** ça a été dur de faire; **to be hard at** ~ travailler consciencieusement; **your essay needs more** ~ tu dois travailler davantage ta rédaction; **to make short** ou **light** ~ **of sth** expédier qch; **to make short** ~ **of sb** envoyer promener qn; **it's all in a day's** ~ c'est une question d'habitude; **it's hot/thirsty** ~ ça donne chaud/soif; **2** (occupation) travail *m*; **to be in** ~ avoir du travail ou un emploi; **place of** ~ lieu *m* de travail; **to be off** ~ (on vacation) être en congé; **to be off** ~ **with flu** être en arrêt de travail parce qu'on a la grippe; **to be out of** ~ être au chômage; **3** (place of employment) (office) bureau *m*; (factory) usine *f*; **to go to** ~ aller au travail; **don't phone me at** ~ ne me téléphone pas à mon travail; **4** (building, construction) travaux *mpl* (**on** sur); **5** (papers) **take one's** ~ **home** LIT emporter du travail chez soi; FIG ramener ses soucis professionnels à la maison; **6** (achievement, product) (essay, report) travail *m*; (artwork, novel, sculpture) œuvre *f* (**by** de); (study) ouvrage *m* (**by** de; **on** sur); **is this all your own** ~? est-ce que vous l'avez fait tout seul?; **to mark students'** ~ noter les devoirs des étudiants; **a** ~ **of genius** une œuvre de génie; **a** ~ **of reference** un ouvrage de référence; **this attack is the** ~ **of professionals** l'attaque est l'œuvre de professionnels; **7** (research) recherches *fpl* (**on** sur); **8** (effect) **to go to** ~ [*drug, detergent*] agir.
II works *npl* **1** (factory) usine *f*; ~**s canteen** cantine *f* de l'usine; **2** (building work) travaux *mpl*; **3**○ (everything) (**full** ou **whole**) ~**s** toute la panoplie○.
III *noun modifier* [*clothes, shoes*] de travail; [*phone number*] au travail.
IV *vtr* **1** (drive) **to** ~ **sb hard** surmener qn; **2** (labour) **to** ~ **shifts** travailler en équipes (de travail posté); **to** ~ **days/nights** travailler de jour/de nuit; **to** ~ **one's way through university** travailler pour payer ses études; **to** ~ **one's way through a book** lire péniblement un livre, venir à bout○ d'un livre; **to** ~ **a 40 hour week** faire la semaine de 40 heures; **3** (operate) se servir de; **4** (exploit commercially) exploiter; **5** (have as one's territory) couvrir [*region*]; **6** (consume) **to** ~ **one's way through** (use) utiliser [*amount, quantity*]; **7** (bring about) **to** ~ **wonders** LIT, FIG faire des merveilles; **8** (use to one's advantage) **to** ~ **the system** profiter du système; **how did you manage to** ~ **it?** comment as-tu pu arranger ça?; **I've** ~**ed things so that...** j'ai arrangé les choses de sorte que...; **9** (fashion) travailler [*clay, metal*]; **10** (embroider) broder; **11** (manoeuvre) **to** ~ **sth into** introduire qch dans [*slot, hole*]; **to** ~ **a lever up and down** actionner un levier; **12** (exercise) faire travailler [*muscles*]; **13** (move) **to** ~ **one's way through** se frayer un passage à travers [*crowd*]; **to** ~ **one's way along** avancer le long de [*ledge*]; **to** ~ **one's hands free** se libérer les

mains; **it ~ed its way** ou **itself loose** cela s'est desserré peu à peu; **to ~ its way into** passer dans; **start at the top and ~ your way down** commencez par le haut et continuez jusqu'en bas.

V *vi* **1** (engage in activity) travailler (**doing** à faire); **to ~ at home** travailler à domicile; **to ~ for a living** gagner sa vie; **to ~ in oils** [*painter*] travailler à l'huile; **2** (strive) lutter (**against** contre; **for** pour; **to do** pour faire); **to ~ towards** se diriger vers [*solution*]; s'acheminer vers [*compromise*]; négocier [*agreement*]; **3** (function) fonctionner; **to ~ on electricity** marcher ou fonctionner à l'électricité; **to ~ off the mains** marcher sur secteur; **the washing machine isn't ~ing** la machine à laver est en panne; **4** (act, operate) **it doesn't** ou **things don't ~ like that** ça ne marche pas comme ça; **to ~ on the assumption that** présumer que; **to ~ in sb's favour**, **to ~ to sb's advantage** tourner à l'avantage de qn; **to ~ against sb**, **to ~ to sb's disadvantage** jouer en la défaveur de qn; **5** (be successful) [*treatment*] avoir de l'effet; [*detergent, drug*] agir; [*plan*] réussir; [*argument*] tenir debout; **flattery won't ~ with me** la flatterie ne marche pas avec moi; **the adaptation really ~s** l'adaptation est vraiment réussie; **6** [*face, features*] se contracter.

VI *v refl* **1** (labour) **to ~ oneself too hard** se surmener; **to ~ oneself to death** se tuer à la tâche; **2 to ~ oneself into a rage** se mettre en colère.

IDIOMS **to ~ one's way up** gravir tous les échelons; **to ~ one's way up the company** faire son chemin dans l'entreprise.

■ **work around**: **~ around to** [sth] aborder; **it took him ages to ~ around to what he wanted to say** il lui a fallu un temps fou pour exprimer ce qu'il avait à dire; **to ~ the conversation around to sth** faire tourner la conversation autour de qch.

■ **work in**: **~ in** [sth], **~** [sth] **in 1** glisser [*joke*]; mentionner [*fact, name*]; **2** CULIN incorporer.

■ **work off**: **~** [sth] **off**, **~ off** [sth] **1** (remove) retirer [*lid*]; **2** (repay) travailler pour rembourser [*loan, debt*]; **3** (get rid of) se débarrasser de [*excess weight*]; dépenser [*excess energy*]; passer [*anger, frustration*].

■ **work on**: ¶ **~ on** continuer à travailler; ¶ **~ on** [sb] travailler○ [*person*]; ¶ **~ on** [sth] travailler à [*book, report*]; travailler sur [*project*]; s'occuper de [*case, problem*]; chercher [*cure, solution*]; examiner [*idea*]; **'have you found a solution?'—'I'm ~ing on it'** 'as-tu trouvé une solution?'—'j'y réfléchis'.

■ **work out**: ¶ **~ out 1** (exercise) s'entraîner; **2** (go according to plan) marcher; **3** (add up) **to ~ out at** GB ou **to ~ out** US s'élever à; ¶ **~ out** [sth], **~** [sth] **out 1** (calculate) calculer [*amount*]; **2** (solve) trouver [*answer, reason, culprit*]; résoudre [*problem*]; comprendre [*clue*]; **3** (devise) concevoir [*plan, scheme*]; trouver [*route*]; ¶ **~** [sb] **out** comprendre [*person*]; **I can't ~ her out** je n'arrive pas à la comprendre.

■ **work over**: **~** [sb] **over** passer [qn] à tabac○.

■ **work to**: **~ to** [sth] s'astreindre à [*budget*]; **to ~ to deadlines** travailler en respectant des délais.

■ **work up**: ¶ **~ up** [sth] développer [*interest*]; accroître [*support*]; **to ~ up the courage to do** trouver le courage de faire; **to ~ up some enthusiasm for** s'enthousiasmer pour; **to ~ up an appetite** s'ouvrir l'appétit; ¶ **~ up to** [sth] se préparer à; ¶ **~ up** [sb], **~** [sb] **up 1** (excite) exciter [*child, crowd*]; **he ~ed the crowd up into a frenzy** il a mis la foule en délire; **2** (annoy) énerver; **to get ~ed up, to ~ oneself up** s'énerver; **to ~ oneself up into a state** ou **frenzy** se mettre dans tous ses états.

workable /'wɜːkəbl/ *adj* **1** (feasible) [*idea, plan*] réalisable; [*system*] pratique; [*arrangement*] possible; **2** AGRIC, IND exploitable; [*cement*] maniable.

workaday /'wɜːkədeɪ/ *adj* [*clothes, life*] ordinaire.

workaholic○ /ˌwɜːkə'hɒlɪk/ *n* bourreau *m* de travail.

work: **~ basket** *n* corbeille *f* à ouvrage; **~bench** *n* établi *m*; **~book** *n* (blank) cahier *m*; (with exercises) livre *m* d'exercices; **~day** *n* GEN jour *m* de travail; COMM jour *m* ouvrable.

worker /'wɜːkə(r)/ **I** *n* **1** (employee) (in manual job)

ouvrier/-ière *m/f*; (in white-collar job) employé/-e *m/f*; **she's a good/slow ~** elle travaille bien/lentement; **2** (proletarian) prolétaire *mf*.

II *noun modifier* [*ant, bee*] ouvrier/-ière.

worker: **~ participation** *n* participation *f* des travailleurs à la gestion; **~s' control** *n* autogestion *f*.

work: **~ ethic** *n* culte *m* puritain du travail; **~ experience** *n* stage *m*; **~-force** *n* (+ *v sg ou pl*) (in industry) main-d'œuvre *f*; (in service sector) effectifs *mpl*; **~horse** *n* FIG bête *f* de travail; **~-in** *n* occupation *f* du lieu de travail (sans arrêt de la production).

working /'wɜːkɪŋ/ **I** *n* **1** (functioning) fonctionnement *m*; **2** (shaping, preparation) travail *m* (**of** de); **3** (draft solution) calculs *mpl*; **4** IND (mine) chantier *m* de mine; (quarry) chantier *m* de carrière.

II workings *npl* LIT, FIG rouages *mpl*.

III *adj* **1** [*parent, woman*] qui travaille; [*conditions, environment, methods*] de travail; [*population, life*] actif/-ive; [*lunch, day, week*] de travail; **during ~ hours** (in office) pendant les heures de bureau; (in shop) pendant les heures de travail; **we have a good ~ relationship** nous avons de bons rapports professionnels; **2** (provisional) [*document, hypothesis*] de travail; [*definition, title*] provisoire; **3** (functional) [*model*] qui fonctionne; [*mine*] en exploitation; **to have a ~ knowledge of** connaître les éléments de base de; **in full ~ order** en parfait état de marche; **4** ECON [*expenses, stock*] d'exploitation.

working class I *n* classe *f* ouvrière; **the ~es** les classes *fpl* laborieuses.

II working-class *adj* [*area, background, childhood, family, life*] ouvrier/-ière; [*culture, London*] prolétarien/-ienne; [*person*] de la classe ouvrière.

working: **~ dog** *n* chien *m* d'utilité; **~ majority** *n* majorité *f* suffisante; **~-over**○ *n* passage *m* à tabac○; **~ party** *n* ADMIN groupe *m* de travail; MIL escouade *f*; **~ week** *n* semaine *f* (de travail).

workload /'wɜːkləʊd/ *n* charge *f* de travail; **to have a light/heavy ~** avoir peu/beaucoup de travail.

work: **~man** *n* ouvrier *m*; **~manlike** *adj* (effective) soigné; PÉJ (uninspired) honnête.

workmanship /'wɜːkmənʃɪp/ *n* **a carpenter famous for sound ~** un menuisier connu pour la qualité de son travail; **furniture of the finest ~** des meubles d'une belle facture; **a piece of poor** ou **shoddy ~** du travail mal fait or bâclé.

work: **~mate** *n* collègue *mf* de travail; **~ of art** *n* œuvre *f* d'art; **~out** *n* séance *f* de mise en forme; **~pack** *n* fiches *fpl* de travail; **~ permit** *n* permis *m* de travail.

workplace /'wɜːkpleɪs/ **I** *n* lieu *m* de travail.

II *noun modifier* [*creche, nursery*] d'entreprise.

work: **~room** *n* atelier *m*; **~s committee**, **~ council** *n* GB IND comité *m* d'entreprise; **~-sharing** *n* partage *m* du travail; **~sheet** *n* IND feuille *f* d'opérations; SCH feuille *f* de questions; **~shop** *n* atelier *m*; **~shy** *adj* PÉJ paresseux/-euse; **~s manager** ▶ 1251 │ *n* directeur *m* d'usine; **~space** *n* COMPUT espace *m* de travail; **~station** *n* poste *m* de travail; **~ study** *n* étude *f* ergonomique; **~ surface** *n* plan *m* de travail; **~table** *n* table *f* de travail; **~top** *n* plan *m* de travail; **~-to-rule** *n* grève *f* du zèle.

world /wɜːld/ **I** *n* **1** (planet) monde *m*; **throughout the ~** dans le monde entier; **to go round the ~** faire le tour du monde; **this ~ and the next** le monde d'ici-bas et l'au-delà; **the next ~** l'autre monde; **to lead the ~ in electronics** être à la pointe de l'électronique; **to come into the ~** voir le jour; **2** (group of people) monde *m*; **the ~ of politics** le monde de la politique; **to go up in the ~** faire son chemin; **to go down in the ~** déchoir; **for all the ~ to see** devant tout le monde; **the outside ~** le reste du monde; **3** (section of the earth) pays *mpl*; **the Eastern/Western ~** les pays de l'Est/occidentaux; **4** (environment) monde *m*, univers *m*; **he lives in a ~ of his own** ou **a private ~** il vit dans un monde à part.

II *noun modifier* [*events, leader, politics*] mondial; [*record, tour, championship*] du monde; [*cruise*] autour du monde.

IDIOMS (all) the ~ and his wife HUM tout le monde; a ~ away from sth très éloigné de qch; to be on top of the ~ être aux anges; for all the ~ like/as if exactement comme/comme si; he's one of the Don Juans of this ~ c'est un véritable Don Juan; how in the ~ did you know? comment diable l'as-tu su?; to get the best of both ~s gagner sur les deux tableaux; I'd give the ~ to do je donnerais n'importe quoi pour faire; a man of the ~ un homme d'expérience; not for (all) the ~ pas pour tout l'or du monde; out of this ~ extraordinaire; that's the way of the ~ c'est la vie; there's a ~ of difference il y a une différence énorme; it did him the ou a ~ of good ça lui a fait énormément de bien; he'll never set the ~ on fire il ne fera jamais d'étincelles; to think the ~ of sb penser le plus grand bien de qn; to watch the ~ go by regarder le monde s'agiter; what/where/who etc in the ~? que/où/qui etc diable?; ~s apart diamétralement opposé.

world: **~-beater** *n* (person) personne *f* qui surpasse les autres; (product) produit *m* qui se vend le mieux; **~-beating** *adj* qui surpasse les autres; **~-class** *adj* de niveau mondial; **World Cup** *n* (in football) Coupe *f* du Monde; **World Fair** *n* Exposition *f* universelle; **~-famous** *adj* mondialement connu; **World Health Organization, WHO** *n* Organisation *f* mondiale de la santé.

world leader *n* **1** POL chef *m* d'État; **2** (best in the world) SPORT meilleur/-e *m/f* du monde; COMM (company) leader *m* mondial.

worldly /'wɜːldlɪ/ *adj* **1** (not spiritual) matériel/-ielle; **~ goods** les biens matériels; **~ wisdom** la sagesse des nations; **2** (materialistic) PÉJ matérialiste.

worldly-wise /ˌwɜːldlɪ'waɪz/ *adj* avisé, qui a de l'expérience.

world: **~ power** *n* puissance *f* mondiale; **World Service** *n* GB service *m* international de la BBC; **~view** *n* vision *f* du monde.

world war *n* guerre *f* mondiale; **World War One/ Two** la Première/Seconde Guerre mondiale.

world-weary *adj* fatigué de la vie.

world(-)wide /ˌwɜːld'waɪd/ **I** *adj* mondial. **II** *adv* dans le monde entier.

worm /wɜːm/ **I** *n* **1** ver *m*; **a dog with ~s** un chien infesté de vers; **2**° (wretch) vermine° *f*; **3** COMPUT (disk) (*abrév* = **write-once read many times**) disque *m* inscriptible une seule fois; (virus) virus *m*.
II *vtr* **1** [*vet*] vermifuger; **2** (wriggle) **to ~ one's way** LIT se faufiler (**along** le long de); FIG s'insinuer (**into** dans); **to ~ one's way into sb's affections** gagner les bonnes grâces de qn.
IDIOMS **the ~ has turned** la situation s'est renversée; **a can of ~s** un sac de nœuds.
■ **worm out**: **~** [sth] **out** arracher (**of sb** à qn).

worm: **~-eaten** *adj* [*fruit*] véreux/-euse; [*wood*] vermoulu; **~hole** *n* (in fruit, plant) trou *m* de ver; (in wood) vermoulure *f*.

wormy /'wɜːmɪ/ *adj* **1** [*wood*] vermoulu; [*fruit*] véreux/-euse; **2** US (grovelling) [*person*] servile.

worn /wɔːn/ **I** *pp* ▶ **wear** II, III.
II *adj* [*carpet, clothing, shoe, tyre*] usé; [*façade, stone*] abîmé; [*tread*] lisse.

worn-out /ˌwɔːn'aʊt/ *adj* **1** [*carpet, brake*] complètement usé; **2** (exhausted) [*person*] épuisé.

worried /'wʌrɪd/ *adj* soucieux/-ieuse; **to be ~ about sb/sth** se faire du souci or s'inquiéter pour qn/qch; **to be ~ about doing** avoir peur de faire; **to be ~ that** avoir peur que; **there's no need to be ~** il n'y a pas de souci à se faire.

worrier /'wʌrɪə(r)/ *n* anxieux/-ieuse *m/f*.

worry /'wʌrɪ/ **I** *n* **1** ₵ (anxiety) soucis *mpl* (**about, over** à propos de); **2** (problem) souci *m* (**about, over** au sujet de); **that's the least of my worries** c'est le dernier de

mes soucis; **he's a ~ to his parents** il cause des soucis à ses parents.
II *vtr* **1** (concern) inquiéter; **I ~ that** j'ai peur que; **it worried him that he couldn't find the keys** ça l'a inquiété de ne pas trouver les clés; **2** (alarm) tracasser; **3** (bother) ennuyer; **would it ~ you if I opened the window?** est-ce que ça vous ennuierait que j'ouvre la fenêtre?; **4** (chase) harceler [*sheep*]; (toss about) secouer [qch] entre les dents.
III *vi* (be anxious) s'inquiéter; **to ~ about** ou **over sth/sb** s'inquiéter pour qch/qn; **to ~ about doing** avoir peur de faire; **I ~ for his sanity sometimes** je me fais parfois du souci pour sa santé mentale; **there's nothing to ~ about** il n'y a pas lieu de s'inquiéter; **not to ~** ne t'inquiète pas; **he'll be punished, don't you ~!** il sera puni, tu peux en être sûr!; **he said it's nothing to ~ about** il a dit qu'il n'y avait là rien d'inquiétant.
IV *v refl* **to ~ oneself** s'inquiéter, se faire du souci (**about sb** au sujet de qn; **about sth** à propos de qch); **to ~ oneself sick over sth** se ronger les sangs au sujet de qch.
■ **worry at**: **~ at** [sth] LIT secouer [qch] entre les dents; FIG retourner [qch] dans tous les sens [*problem*].

worry beads *npl* chapelet *m* antistress.

worrying /'wʌrɪɪŋ/ **I** *n* all this **~ is making you ill** tout ce souci que tu te fais te rend malade.
II *adj* inquiétant; **the ~ thing is that** ce qu'il y a d'inquiétant c'est que.

worse /wɜːs/ **I** *adj* (*comparative of* **bad**) **1** (more unsatisfactory, unpleasant) pire; **there's only one thing ~ than** il n'y a qu'une chose qui soit pire que; **the noise is ~** il y a plus de bruit; **to get ~** [*pressure, noise*] augmenter; [*conditions, weather*] empirer; **'you missed the bus'—'yes luck!'** 'tu as raté le bus'—'oui pas de veine°!'; **2** (more serious, severe) pire (**than** que); **it looks ~ than it is!** ça a l'air pire que ça ne l'est en vérité!; **it couldn't be ~!** ça ne pourrait pas être pire!; **and what is ~, she doesn't care** et le pire, c'est que ça lui est égal; **to go from bad to ~** aller de pire en pire; **to get ~ (and ~)** [*illness, conflict*] s'aggraver; [*patient*] aller de plus en plus mal; **to be made ~** être aggravé (**by** par); **you'll only make things ou it ~!** tu ne feras qu'empirer les choses!; **and to make matters ~, he lied** et pour ne rien arranger, il a menti; **3** (of lower standard) pire (**than** que); **to be even ~ at languages** être encore plus mauvais en langues; **4** (more unwell, unhappy) **he's getting ~** il va plus mal; **the cough is getting ~** la toux empire; **to feel ~** (more ill) se sentir plus malade; (more unhappy) aller moins bien; **his death made me feel ~** sa mort m'a démoralisé encore plus; **he is none the ~ for the experience** il ne se porte pas plus mal après cette expérience; **so much the ~ for them!** tant pis pour eux!; **5** (more inappropriate) **he couldn't have chosen a ~ place to meet** il n'aurait pas pu choisir un lieu de rendez-vous moins approprié; **the decision couldn't have come at a ~ time** la décision n'aurait pas pu arriver à un moment plus inopportun.
II *n* **there is ~ to come** ce n'est pas encore le pire; **to change for the ~** empirer; **things took a turn for the ~** les choses ont empiré.
III *adv* (*comparative of* **badly**) **1** (more unsatisfactorily, incompetently) moins bien (**than** que); **to behave ~** se conduire plus mal; **she could do ~ than follow his example** ce ne serait pas si mal si elle suivait son exemple; **2** (more seriously, severely) [*cough, bleed, vomit*] plus; **~ still** pire encore.

worsen /'wɜːsn/ **I** *vtr* aggraver [*situation, problem*].
II *vi* [*condition, health, weather, situation*] se détériorer; [*problem, crisis, shortage, flooding*] s'aggraver.

worsening /'wɜːsnɪŋ/ **I** *n* aggravation *f* (**of** de).
II *adj* [*situation*] en voie de détérioration; [*problem, shortage*] en voie d'aggravation.

worse off *adj* **1** (less wealthy) **to be ~** avoir moins d'argent (**than** que); **to end up ~** finir avec moins d'argent; **I'm £10 a week ~** j'ai dix livres de moins par semaine; **2** (in a worse situation) **to be ~** être dans une situation pire; **to be no ~ without sth** pouvoir parfaitement se passer de qch.

worship /'wɜːʃɪp/ **I** *n* **1** (veneration) GEN vénération *f*; RELIG culte *m*; **2** (religious practice) pratique *f* religieuse; **freedom of ~** liberté *f* de culte; **place of ~** lieu *m* de culte; **an act of ~** un acte de dévotion. **II Worship** *pr n* GB ▶937| (for man) monsieur *m*; (for woman) madame *f*; **his Worship the mayor** Monsieur le maire. **III** *vtr* (*p prés etc* **-pp-**) **1** RELIG (venerate) adorer; (give praise) rendre hommage à; **2** (idolize) LIT vénérer; FIG être en adoration devant. **IV** *vi* (*p prés etc* **-pp-**) pratiquer sa religion.

worshipper /'wɜːʃɪpə(r)/ *n* (in established religion) fidèle *mf*; (in nonestablished religion) adorateur/-trice *m/f*.

worst /wɜːst/ **I** *n* **1** (most difficult, unpleasant) **the ~** le/la pire *m/f*; **the storm was one of the ~ in recent years** la tempête était parmi les pires qu'il y ait eu ces dernières années; **last year was the ~ for strikes** du point de vue des grèves l'année dernière a été la pire; **they're the ~ of all** (people) ce sont eux les pires; (things, problems, ideas) c'est ce qu'il y a de pire; **he's not the ~** il y a pire que lui; **we're over the ~ now** nous avons passé le pire; **the ~ was yet to come** le plus dur était encore à venir; **the ~ of it is there's no solution** le pire c'est qu'il n'y a pas de solution; **during the ~ of the recession** au plus fort de la crise; **the ~ of the heat is over** les plus fortes chaleurs sont passées; **do your ~!** essaie un peu pour voir!; **2** (expressing the most pessimistic outlook) **the ~** le pire *m*; **to think the ~ of sb** avoir une mauvaise opinion de qn; **if the ~ were to happen, if the ~ came to the ~** (in serious circumstances) dans le pire des cas; (involving fatality, death) si le pire devait arriver; **3** (most unbearable) **to be at its ~** aller au plus mal; **at its ~, the noise could be heard everywhere** quand le bruit était à sa puissance maximum, on l'entendait partout; **when the heat is at its ~** au plus fort de la chaleur; **these are fanatics at their ~** ce sont des fanatiques dans ce qu'ils ont de pire; **when you see people at their ~** quand on voit les gens sous leur plus mauvais jour; **I'm at my ~ in the morning** (in temper) c'est le matin que je suis de plus mauvaise humeur; **4** (most negative trait) **to bring out the ~ in sb** mettre à jour ce qu'il y a de plus mauvais chez qn; **5** (of the lowest standard, quality) **the ~** le plus mauvais/la plus mauvaise *m/f*; **to be the ~ at French** être le plus mauvais en français. **II** *adj* (*superlative of* **bad**) **1** (most unsatisfactory, unpleasant) plus mauvais; **the ~ book I've ever read** le plus mauvais livre que j'aie jamais lu; **hypocrites of the ~ kind** des hypocrites de la pire espèce; **the ~ thing about the film is** ce qu'il y a de pire dans le film c'est; **and the ~ thing about it is (that)** et le pire c'est que; **2** (most serious) plus grave; **one of the ~ recessions** une des crises les plus graves; **the ~ mistake you could have made** la pire erreur possible; **3** (most inappropriate) pire; **the ~ possible place to do** le pire endroit pour faire; **she rang at the ~ possible time** elle a téléphoné au plus mauvais moment; **it's the ~ thing you could have said!** c'était vraiment la chose à ne pas dire!; **4** (of the poorest standard) pire, plus mauvais. **III** *adv* **the children suffer (the) ~** ce sont les enfants qui souffrent le plus; **they were (the) ~ affected** ou **hit by the strike** ce sont eux qui ont été les plus touchés par la grève; **to smell the ~** sentir le plus mauvais; **to come off ~** perdre le plus; **the ~-off groups in society** les groupes les plus démunis de la société; **the ~-behaved child he'd ever met** l'enfant le plus mal élevé qu'il ait jamais rencontré; **~ of all,...** le pire de tout, c'est que...; **they did (the) ~ of all the group in the exam** ce sont eux qui ont le moins bien réussi l'examen.

worsted /'wʊstɪd/ *n* tissu *m* en laine peignée.

worth /wɜːθ/ **I** *n* **¢ 1** FIN (measure, quantity) **five pounds' ~ of sth** pour cinq livres de qch; **thousands of pounds' ~ of damage** des milliers de

livres de dégâts; **a day's ~ of fuel** un jour de combustible; **a week's ~ of supplies** une semaine de provisions; **to get one's money's ~** en avoir pour son argent; **2** (value, usefulness) valeur *f*; **of no ~** sans valeur; **what is its ~ in pounds?** combien cela fait-il en livres sterling? **II** *adj* **1** (of financial value) **to be ~ sth** valoir qch; **the pound is ~ 10 francs** la livre vaut 10 francs; **it's not ~ much** ça ne vaut pas grand-chose; **he is ~ £50,000** sa fortune s'élève à 50 000 livres; **2** (of abstract value) **to be ~ sth** valoir qch; **an experienced worker is ~ three novices** un travailleur expérimenté vaut trois débutants; **unsubstantiated reports are not ~ much** les rapports sans fondement concret ne valent pas grand-chose; **it's as much as my job's ~ to give you the keys** je risque mon emploi si je te donne les clés; **the house is only ~ what you can get for it** la maison ne vaut que ce qu'elle vaut; **to be ~ a mention** mériter une mention; **to be ~ a try** valoir la peine d'essayer; **to be ~ it** valoir la peine; **don't get upset, he's not ~ it** ne te fâche pas, il n'en vaut pas la peine; **the book isn't ~ reading** le livre ne vaut pas la peine d'être lu; **that suggestion is ~ considering** la suggestion mérite réflexion; **that's ~ knowing** cela est utile à savoir; **everyone ~ knowing had left town** tous ceux qui comptaient avaient quitté la ville; **what he doesn't know about farming isn't ~ knowing** il sait tout ce qu'on peut savoir sur le travail à la ferme; **those little pleasures that make life ~ living** ces petits plaisirs qui rendent la vie agréable. IDIOMS **for all one is ~** de toutes ses forces; **for what it's ~** pour ce que cela vaut; **to be ~ sb's while** valoir le coup; **if you come I'll make it ~ your while** si tu viens, tu ne le regretteras pas.

worthily /'wɜːðɪlɪ/ *adv* dignement.

worthless /'wɜːθlɪs/ *adj* sans valeur; **he's ~** c'est un bon à rien.

worthwhile /wɜːθ'waɪl/ *adj* [*discussion, undertaking, visit*] qui en vaut la peine; [*career, project*] intéressant; **to be ~ doing** valoir la peine de faire; **it's been well ~** cela en valait vraiment la peine.

worthy /'wɜːðɪ/ **I** *n* notable *m*. **II** *adj* **1** (deserving) **to be ~ of sth** mériter qch, être digne de qch; **~ of note** digne d'intérêt; **to be ~ of doing** mériter d'être fait; **2** (admirable) [*cause*] noble; [*citizen, friend*] digne; **3** (appropriate) **~ of sth/sb** digne de qn/qch; **a speech ~ of the occasion** un discours digne des circonstances.

would /wʊd, wəd/

■ **Note** When *would* is used with a verb in English to form the conditional tense, *would + verb* is translated by the present conditional of the appropriate verb in French and *would have + verb* by the past conditional of the appropriate verb: *I would do it if I had time* = je le ferais si j'avais le temps; *I would have done it if I had had time* = je l'aurais fait si j'avais eu le temps; *he said he would fetch the car* = il a dit qu'il irait chercher la voiture. – For more examples, particular usages and all other uses of *would* see the entry below.

modal aux (aussi *'d*; *nég* **wouldn't**) **1** (in sequence of past tenses, in reported speech) **she said she wouldn't come** elle a dit qu'elle ne viendrait pas; **we thought we ~ be late** nous avons pensé que nous serions en retard; **I was sure you'd like it** j'étais sûr que ça te plairait; **they promised that they'd come back** ils ont promis de revenir; **he thought she ~ have forgotten** il pensait qu'elle aurait oublié; **I wish he ~ shut the door!** il pourrait fermer la porte!; **I wish you'd be quiet!** tu ne pourrais pas te taire!; **2** (in conditional statements) **it ~ be wonderful if they came** ce serait merveilleux s'ils venaient; **if we'd left later we ~ have missed the train** si nous étions partis plus tard nous aurions raté le train; **we wouldn't be happy anywhere else** nous ne serions heureux nulle part ailleurs; **who ~ ever have believed it?** qui l'aurait cru?; **you wouldn't have thought it possible!** on n'aurait jamais cru que c'était possible!; **wouldn't it be nice if...** ce serait bien si...; **it cost far less than**

I ~ **have expected** ça a coûté beaucoup moins cher que je n'aurais pensé; **3** (expressing willingness to act) **do you know anyone who ~ do it?** est-ce que tu connais quelqu'un qui le ferait?; **they couldn't find anyone who ~ take the job** ils n'arrivaient pas à trouver quelqu'un qui accepte le poste; **she just wouldn't listen** elle ne voulait rien entendre; **after that I wouldn't eat any canned food** après cela je ne voulais plus manger de conserves; **he wouldn't do a thing to help** il n'a rien voulu faire pour aider; **the police wouldn't give any further details** la police a refusé de donner plus de détails; **they asked me to leave but I wouldn't** ils m'ont demandé de partir mais j'ai refusé; **4** (expressing inability to function) **the door wouldn't close** la porte ne voulait pas se fermer; **5** (expressing desire, preference) **we ~ like to stay another night** nous aimerions rester une nuit de plus; **we'd really love to see you** nous aimerions vraiment te voir; **I ~ much rather travel alone** je préférerais nettement voyager seul; **she ~ have preferred a puppy** elle aurait préféré un chiot; **I wouldn't mind another slice of cake** je prendrais bien un autre morceau de gâteau; **it's what he ~ have wanted** c'est ce qu'il aurait voulu; **6** (in polite requests or proposals) **~ you like something to eat?** voudriez-vous quelque chose à manger?; **~ you like some more tea?** voulez-vous encore du thé?; **~ you help me set the table?** est-ce que tu pourrais m'aider à mettre la table?; **switch off the radio, ~ you?** éteins la radio, tu veux?; **~ you like to go to a concert?** est-ce que tu aimerais aller à un concert?; **~ you give her the message?** est-ce que vous voulez bien lui transmettre le message?; **~ you mind not smoking please?** est-ce que ça vous ennuierait de ne pas fumer s'il vous plaît?; **7** (used to attenuate statements) **it ~ seem that he was right** il semblerait qu'il avait raison; **so it ~ seem** c'est ce qu'il semble; **you ~ think they'd be satisfied!** on aurait pu penser qu'ils seraient satisfaits!; **I wouldn't say that** je ne dirais pas ça; **I ~ have thought it was obvious** j'aurais pensé que c'était évident; **I wouldn't know** je ne pourrais pas vous le dire; **8** (when giving advice) **I wouldn't do that if I were you** je ne ferais pas ça à ta place; **I ~ check the timetable first** tu ferais bien de vérifier l'horaire d'abord; **I'd give her a ring now** tu devrais lui téléphoner maintenant; **wouldn't it be better to write?** est-ce que ce ne serait pas mieux d'écrire?; **9** (expressing exasperation) **'he denies it'—'well he ~, wouldn't he?'** 'il le nie'—'évidemment, tu ne le contredis pas'; **of course you ~ contradict him!** bien sûr il a fallu que tu le contredises!; **'she put her foot in it**°—**'she ~!'** 'elle a mis les pieds dans le plat'°—'tu m'étonnes!'; **10** (expressing an assumption) **what time ~ that be?** c'était vers quelle heure?; **I suppose it ~ have been about 3 pm** je pense qu'il était à peu près 15 h 00; **let's see, that ~ be his youngest son** voyons, ça doit être son plus jeune fils; **it ~ have been about five years ago** ça devait être il y a environ cinq ans; **you'd never have guessed she was German** on n'aurait jamais cru qu'elle était allemande; **11** (indicating habitual event or behaviour in past: used to) **she ~ sit for hours at the window** elle passait des heures assise à la fenêtre.

would-be /ˈwʊdbiː/ adj (desirous of being) **~ investors** des investisseurs en puissance; **~ intellectuals** PÉJ des soi-disant intellectuels PÉJ; (having intended to be) **the ~ thieves were arrested** les voleurs ont été arrêtés avant qu'ils aient pu passer à l'acte.

wouldn't /ˈwʊd(ə)nt/ = **would not**.

would've /ˈwʊdəv/ = **would have**.

wound¹ /wuːnd/ I n **1** (injury) blessure f; **a ~ to** ou **in the head** une blessure à la tête; **to die from** ou **of one's ~s** succomber à ses blessures; **2** (cut, sore) plaie f; **3** FIG blessure f; **it takes time for the ~s to heal** il faut longtemps pour que les plaies se cicatrisent.
II vtr (all contexts) blesser.
IDIOMS FIG **to lick one's ~s** panser ses blessures; **to rub salt into the ~** remuer le couteau dans la plaie.

wound² /waʊnd/ prét, pp ▶ **wind²** II, III.

wounded /ˈwuːndɪd/ I n **the ~** (+ v pl) les blessés/-es m/f.
II adj blessé; **~ in the arm** blessé au bras.

wounding /ˈwuːndɪŋ/ adj blessant.

wove /wəʊv/ prét ▶ **weave** II, III.

woven /ˈwəʊvn/ pp, pp adj ▶ **weave** II, III.

wow° /waʊ/ I n **1** (success) succès m; **2** AUDIO (distortion) pleurage m.
II excl hou là!
III vtr (enthuse) emballer° [person].

WP abrév = **word processing**.

WPC n: abrév ▶ **woman police constable**.

wpm (abrév = **words per minute**) mots/min.

WRAC n MIL (abrév = **Women's Royal Army Corps**) services féminins de l'armée britannique.

WRAF n (abrév = **Women's Royal Air Force**) services féminins de l'armée de l'air britannique.

wrangle /ˈræŋgl/ I n querelle f.
II vi se quereller (**over, about** sur, à propos de).

wrangling /ˈræŋglɪŋ/ n tractations fpl (**over** à propos de).

wrap /ræp/ I n **1** (shawl) châle m; (stole) étole f; (dressing-gown) peignoir m; **2** (packaging) emballage m; **3** CIN **it's a ~** c'est dans la boîte.
II vtr (p prés etc **-pp-**) LIT (in paper) emballer (**in** dans); (in blanket, garment) envelopper (**in** dans); **to ~ a book in paper** envelopper un livre dans du papier; **I ~ped a handkerchief around my finger** je me suis noué un mouchoir autour du doigt; **to ~ tape around a join** enrouler du ruban adhésif autour d'une jointure; **to be ~ped in** LIT (for warmth, protection) être emmitouflé dans; (for disposal) être enveloppé dans; FIG être enveloppé de [mystery]; **would you like it ~ped?** je vous fais un paquet?
III v refl (p prés etc **-pp-**) **to ~ oneself in sth** s'envelopper dans qch.
IV **-wrapped** combining form **foil-/plastic-~ped** emballé dans du papier d'aluminium/du plastique.
IDIOMS **to keep sth/to be under ~s** garder qch/être secret; **to take the ~s off sth** dévoiler qch.
■ **wrap up**: ¶ **~ up 1** (dress warmly) s'emmitoufler; **~ up well** ou **warm!** couvre-toi bien!; **2**° GB (shut up) la fermer°; **~ up!** ferme-la!°; ¶ **~ up [sth], [sth] up 1** LIT faire [parcel]; envelopper [gift, purchase]; emballer [rubbish]; **it's cold, ~ the children up warm!** il fait froid, couvre bien les enfants!; **2** FIG (terminate) conclure; **3** (settle) régler [project, event]; conclure [deal, negotiations]; s'assurer [title, victory]; **4** (involve) **to be ~ped up in** ne s'occuper que de [person, child]; être absorbé dans [activity, work]; être absorbé par [problem]; **they are completely ~ped up in each other** ils ne vivent que l'un pour l'autre; **he is ~ped up in himself** il est replié sur lui-même; **there is £50,000 ~ped up in the project** il y a 50 000 livres sterling d'investies dans le projet; **5** FIG dissimuler [ideas] (**in** derrière).

wrap-around adj [window, windscreen] panoramique; [skirt] portefeuille.

wrapper /ˈræpə(r)/ n (of sweet, chocolate etc) papier m; (of package) emballage m; (of newspaper) bande f; **sweet ~** papier m de bonbon.

wrapping /ˈræpɪŋ/ n emballage m.

wrapping paper n (brown) papier m d'emballage; (decorative) papier m cadeau.

wreak /riːk/ vtr assouvir [revenge] (**on** sur); **to ~ havoc** ou **damage** infliger des dégâts; **to ~ havoc** ou **damage on sth** dévaster qch.

wreath /riːθ/ n **1** (of flowers, leaves) couronne f; **to lay a ~** déposer une gerbe; **2** (of smoke) ruban m.

wreathe /riːð/ I vtr (weave, fashion) lisser.
II **wreathed** pp adj **~d in** enveloppé de [mist, smoke]; **to be ~d in smiles** être tout sourire.

wreck /rek/ I n **1** (car, plane) (crashed) épave f; (burnt out) carcasse f; **2**° (old car) tas m de ferraille°; **3** (sunken ship) épave f; **4** (sinking, destruction) (of ship)

naufrage *m*; FIG **the ~ of sb's hopes/dreams** le naufrage des espoirs/rêves de qn; **5** (person) épave *f*.
II *vtr* **1** LIT [*explosion, fire, vandals, looters*] dévaster; [*person, driver, crash, impact*] détruire; **2** FIG ruiner [*career, chances, future, health, life, marriage*]; gâcher [*holiday, weekend*]; faire échouer [*negotiations*].

wreckage /'rekɪdʒ/ *n* **1** LIT (of plane, car) épave *f*; (of building) décombres *mpl*; **2** FIG naufrage *m*.

wrecked /rekt/ *adj* **1** LIT [*car, plane*] accidenté; [*ship*] naufragé; [*building*] démoli; **2** FIG ruiné; **3**○ (exhausted) claqué○.

wren /ren/ *n* ZOOL roitelet *m*.

wrench /rentʃ/ **I** *n* **1** (tool) tourne-à-gauche *m inv*; **2** (movement) (of handle, lid) mouvement *m* brusque (tournant); **3** FIG déchirement *m*.
II *vtr* tourner [qch] brusquement [*handle*]; **to ~ one's ankle/knee** se tordre la cheville/le genou; **to ~ sth from sb** arracher qch à qn; **to ~ sth away from** ou **off sth** arracher qch de qch; **to ~ a door open** ouvrir une porte d'un mouvement brusque.
III *vi* **to ~ at sth** tirer sur qch.
IV *v refl* **to ~ oneself free** se dégager d'un mouvement brusque.
IDIOMS **to throw a ~ in the works** US créer des difficultés.

wrest /rest/ *vtr* (all contexts) arracher (**from sb** à qn).

wrestle /'resl/ **I** *vtr* **to ~ sb for sth** lutter contre qn pour qch; **to ~ sb to the ground** terrasser qn.
II *vi* **1** SPORT faire du catch; **2** (struggle) **to ~ with** se débattre avec [*person, problem, homework, conscience*]; se battre avec [*controls, zip, suitcase*]; lutter contre [*temptation*].

wrestler /'reslə(r)/ *n* **1** SPORT catcheur/-euse *m/f*; **2** HIST lutteur *m*.

wrestling /'reslɪŋ/ **▶ 949** *n* **1** SPORT catch *m*; **2** HIST lutte *f*.

wretch /retʃ/ *n* **1** (unlucky) miséreux/-euse *m/f*; **2** (evil) misérable *mf* ALSO HUM; (child) HUM coquin/-e *m/f*.

wretched /'retʃɪd/ *adj* **1** (miserable) [*person*] infortuné; [*appearance, conditions*] misérable; [*weather*] affreux/-euse; [*accommodation*] minable; **to feel ~** (ill) être à plat; (due to hangover) se sentir abruti; **to feel ~ about sth** être honteux/-euse de; **what ~ luck!** quelle malchance!; **2**○ (damned) fichu○.

wretchedly /'retʃɪdlɪ/ *adv* **1** (badly, pitifully) [*treat*] très mal; [*clothed, furnished*] misérablement; [*paid, small*] dérisoirement; **2** (unhappily) piteusement.

wretchedness /'retʃɪdnɪs/ *n* **1** (unhappiness) détresse *f*; **2** (poverty) misère *f*.

wriggle /'rɪgl/ **I** *vtr* **to ~ one's toes/fingers** remuer les orteils/doigts; **to ~ one's way out of sth** LIT, FIG se sortir de qch.
II *vi* [*person*] s'agiter, gigoter; [*snake, worm*] se tortiller; **to ~ along the ground** ramper en se tortillant; **to ~ under sth** se glisser sous qch; **to ~ free** arriver à se dégager.
■ **wriggle about**, **wriggle around** GEN se tortiller; [*fish*] frétiller.
■ **wriggle out** se dégager or se sortir en se tortillant; **to ~ out of sth** FIG se défiler devant [*task, duty*].

wriggly /'rɪglɪ/ *adj* [*snake, worm*] frétillant; [*person*] remuant.

wring /rɪŋ/ **I** *n* **to give sth a ~** essorer qch.
II *vtr* (*prét, pp* **wrung**) **1** (also **~ out**) (squeeze) (by twisting) tordre; (by pressure, centrifugal force) essorer; **2** FIG (extract) arracher (**from, out of** à); **3** (twist) **to ~ sb's/sth's neck** LIT, FIG tordre le cou à qn/qch; **to ~ one's hands** se tordre les mains; FIG se lamenter.
III **wringing** *adv* **~ing wet** trempé.
■ **wring out: ~ [sth] out**, **~ out [sth**] tordre [*cloth, clothes*]; **to ~ the water out from one's clothes** essorer ses vêtements.

wrinkle /'rɪŋkl/ **I** *n* **1** (on skin) ride *f*; (in fabric) pli *m*; **to iron out the ~s** LIT enlever les plis au fer à repasser; FIG aplanir les difficultés.
IDIOMS **he knows a ~ or two** il est loin d'être bête.
II *vtr* **1** rider [*skin*]; **to ~ one's nose** faire la

grimace (**at** a); **to ~ one's forehead** plisser le front; **2** froisser [*fabric*].
III *vi* [*skin*] se rider; [*fabric*] se froisser; [*wallpaper*] se gondoler; [*rug, mat*] faire des plis.

wrinkled /'rɪŋkld/ *adj* **1** [*face, skin*] ridé; [*brow*] froncé; [*apple*] fripé; **2** [*fabric, clothing*] froissé; [*stockings*] qui font des plis.

wrinkly○ /'rɪŋklɪ/ *adj* = **wrinkled**.

wrist /rɪst/ **▶ 765** *n* poignet *m*.
IDIOMS **to get a slap on the ~** se faire taper sur les doigts.

wrist: ~band *n* (for tennis, on sleeve) poignet *m*; (on watch) bracelet *m* (de montre); **~watch** *n* montre-bracelet *f*.

writ /rɪt/ **I** *n* JUR assignation *f* (**for** pour); **to issue** ou **serve a ~** assigner qn en justice.
II *vtr* (*prét, pp* désuets du verbe **write**) FIG **disappointment was ~ large across his face** la déception se lisait sur son visage.

write /raɪt/ (*prét* **wrote**; *pp* **written**) **I** *vtr* **1** (put down on paper) écrire [*letter, novel*]; composer [*song, symphony*]; rédiger [*business letter, article, essay*]; faire [*cheque, prescription*]; écrire [*software, program*]; **I wrote home** j'ai écrit à ma famille; **to ~ sth into a contract** inclure qch dans un contrat; **guilt was written all over her face** FIG la culpabilité se lisait sur son visage; **he had 'policeman' written all over him** FIG ça crevait les yeux qu'il était policier; **2** US (compose a letter to) écrire à [*person*].
II *vi* **1** (form words, correspond) écrire; **to ~ in pencil** écrire au crayon; **this pen doesn't ~** ce stylo n'écrit pas; **I have nothing to ~ with** je n'ai rien pour écrire; **2** (compose professionally) écrire (**for** pour); **I ~ for a living** je suis écrivain de métier; **to ~ about** ou **on** traiter de.
■ **write away** écrire (**to** à); **to ~ away for sth** demander qch par écrit [*catalogue, details*].
■ **write back:** ¶ **~ back** répondre (**to** à); ¶ **~ back [sth]** écrire [*letter*].
■ **write down: ~ [sth] down**, **~ down [sth]** **1** (note) noter [*details, name*]; mettre [qch] par écrit [*ideas, suggestions*]; **2** (record) consigner [qch] par écrit [*information*]; **3** FIN dévaluer [*stocks*].
■ **write in:** ¶ **~ in** écrire (**to sb** à qn; **to do** pour faire); **please ~ in with your suggestions** vous êtes invités à nous envoyer vos suggestions; **to ~ in to** écrire une lettre à; ¶ **~ [sb] in** US POL inscrire le nom de [*candidate*].
■ **write off:** ¶ **~ off** écrire une lettre (**to** à); **to ~ off for** écrire pour demander; ¶ **~ [sth/sb] off** **1** (wreck) GEN bousiller○ complètement [*car*]; **2** (in bookkeeping) passer [qch] par pertes et profits [*bad debt, loss*]; amortir [*capital*]; **3** (end) annuler [*debt, project*]; **4** (dismiss) [*critic*] enterrer○.
■ **write out:** ¶ **~ [sth] out**, **~ out [sth]** **1** (put down on paper) écrire; **2** (copy) copier; ¶ **~ [sb] out** supprimer [*character*] (**of** de).
■ **write up: ~ [sth] up**, **~ up [sth]** **1** (produce in report form) rédiger; **2** FIN réévaluer [*asset*].

write-in *n* US POL vote *m* par correspondance.

write-off /'raɪtɒf/ *n* **1** US (in taxation) somme *f* déductible de la déclaration des revenus; **2** (wreck) épave *f*.

write once read many disk *n* COMPUT disque *m* inscriptible une seule fois.

writer /'raɪtə(r)/ **▶ 1251** *n* (professional) écrivain *m*; (amateur) auteur *m*; **sports ~** journaliste *mf* spécialisé/-e en sport; **he's a neat ~** il écrit avec soin.

writer's block *n* angoisse *f* de la page blanche.

write-up /'raɪtʌp/ *n* **1** (review) critique *f*; **2** (account) rapport *m* (**of** sur); **3** US (in bookkeeping) fausse déclaration *f* (dans un bilan).

writhe /raɪð/ *vi* (also **~ about**, **~ around**) se tortiller; **to ~ in agony** se tordre de douleur.

writing /'raɪtɪŋ/ *n* **1** ¢ (activity) **~ is her life** écrire, c'est sa vie; **2** (handwriting) écriture *f*; **his ~ is poor/good** il écrit mal/bien; **3** (words and letters) écriture *f*; **to put sth in ~** mettre qch par écrit; **4** (literature)

littérature *f*; **American ~** littérature américaine; **the ~s of Colette** l'œuvre *m* de Colette; **it was an excellent piece of ~** c'était très bien écrit.
IDIOMS **the ~ is on the wall** la catastrophe est imminente.

writing: **~ case** *n* nécessaire *m* de correspondance; **~ desk** *n* secrétaire *m*; **~ pad** *n* bloc *m* de papier à lettres; **~ paper** *n* papier *m* à lettres.

written /'rɪtn/ **I** *pp* ▶ **write.**
II *adj* écrit; **he failed the ~ paper** il a échoué à l'écrit; **~ evidence/proof** ADMIN pièces *fpl* justificatives; JUR preuves *fpl* écrites; **the ~ word** l'écriture *f*.

wrong /rɒŋ, US rɔːŋ/ **I** *n* **1** ₡ (evil) mal *m*; **in their eyes, she could do no ~** pour eux, tout ce qu'elle faisait était parfait; **2** (injustice) tort *m*; **to right a ~** réparer un tort; **the rights and ~s of the matter** les aspects moraux de la question; **3** JUR délit *m*.
II *adj* **1** (incorrect) (ill-chosen) mauvais; (containing errors) erroné; **it's the ~ glue for the purpose** ce n'est pas la colle qu'il faut; **to prove to be ~** se révéler faux; **to go the ~ way** se tromper de chemin; **to take the ~ road** se tromper de route; **to take the ~ turning** GB ou **turn** ne pas tourner au bon endroit; **to give the ~ answer** ne pas donner la bonne réponse; **everything I do is ~** je ne fais jamais rien de bien; **it was the ~ thing to say** c'était la chose à ne pas dire; **to say the ~ thing** faire une gaffe; **don't get the ~ idea** ne te méprends pas; **don't get me ~, I'm not saying that he's stupid but...** ne te méprends pas, je ne dis pas qu'il est idiot mais...; **don't get me ~, I'm not criticizing you** ne le prends pas mal, je ne te critique pas; **you've got the ~ number** vous faites erreur; **2** (reprehensible) **it is ~ to do** c'est mal de faire; **she hasn't done anything ~** elle n'a rien fait de mal; **it was ~ of me to do** je n'aurais pas dû faire; **it is ~ for sb to do** ce n'est pas juste que qn fasse; **it is ~ that** c'est injuste que; **there's nothing ~ with** ou **in sth** il n'y a pas de mal à qch; **what's ~ with trying?** quel mal y a-t-il à essayer?; **(so) what's ~ with that?** où est le mal?; **3** (mistaken) **to be ~** [*person*] avoir tort, se tromper; **that's where you're ~** c'est là que tu te trompes; **how ~ can you be!** comme on peut se tromper!; **I might be ~** il se peut que je me trompe; **to be ~ about** se tromper sur; **she was ~ about him** elle s'est trompée sur son compte; **am I ~ in thinking that...?** ai-je tort de penser que...?; **to prove sb ~** donner tort à qn; **4** (not as it should be) **there is something (badly) ~** il y a quelque chose qui ne va pas (du tout); **there's something ~ with this computer** il y a un problème avec cet ordinateur; **what's ~ with your arm?** qu'est-ce que tu as au bras?; **what's ~ with you?** (to person suffering) qu'est-ce que tu as?; (to person behaving oddly)

qu'est-ce qui t'arrive?; **nothing ~ is there?** tout va bien?
III *adv* **to get sth ~** se tromper de qch [*date, time, details*]; se tromper dans qch [*calculations*]; **I think you've got it ~** je pense que tu te trompes; **to go ~** [*person*] se tromper; [*machine*] ne plus marcher; [*plan*] ne pas marcher; **you won't go far ~ if...** vous ne risquez pas de faire fausse route si...; **you can't go ~** (in choice of route) tu ne peux pas te tromper; (are bound to succeed) tu peux être tranquille.
IV *vtr* (treat unjustly) faire du tort à [*person, family*].
IDIOMS **to be in the ~** être dans mon/ton etc tort; **to be ~ in the head**○ être dérangé○; **to get into the ~ hands** tomber dans de mauvaises mains; **to get on the ~ side of sb** se faire mal voir de qn; **to go down the ~ way** [*food, drink*] passer de travers; **two ~s don't make a right** on ne répare pas une injustice avec une autre; **you've got me all ~** vous ne m'avez pas du tout compris.

wrong: **~doer** *n* malfaiteur *m*; **~doing** *n* méfait *m*; **~foot** *vtr* SPORT prendre [qn] à contre-pied; FIG prendre [qn] au dépourvu.

wrongful /'rɒŋfl, US 'rɔːŋ-/ *adj* JUR arbitraire.

wrongfully /'rɒŋfəlɪ, US 'rɔːŋ-/ *adv* JUR injustement.

wrong-headed /,rɒŋ'hedɪd, US ,rɔːŋ-/ *adj* **1** (stubborn) buté; **2** (perverse) [*policy, decision*] aveugle.

wrongly /'rɒŋlɪ, US 'rɔː-/ *adv* mal; **he concluded, ~, that...** il a conclu, à tort, que...; **rightly or ~** à tort ou à raison.

wrote /rəʊt/ *prét* ▶ **write.**

wrought /rɔːt/ **I** *prét, pp* **it ~ havoc** ou **destruction** cela a fait des ravages; **the changes ~ by sth** les changements apportés par qch.
II *adj* **1** [*silver, gold*] travaillé; **2 finely/carefully ~** [*plot, essay*] finement/soigneusement travaillé.

wrought: **~ iron** *n* fer *m* forgé; **~ iron work** *n* ferronnerie *f*.

wrung /rʌŋ/ *prét, pp* ▶ **wring II.**

wry /raɪ/ *adj* **1** (ironic) narquois; **to have a ~ sense of humour** être pince-sans-rire; **2** (disgusted) **to make a ~ face** faire une drôle de tête.

wt *n*: *abrév écrite* = **weight.**

WV US POST *abrév écrite* = **West Virginia.**

WWI *n*: *abrév écrite* = **World War One.**

WWII *n*: *abrév écrite* = **World War Two.**

WY US POST *abrév écrite* = **Wyoming.**

WYSIWYG /'wɪzɪwɪg/ COMPUT (*abrév* = **what you see is what you get**) *affichage sur l'écran conforme à l'impression finale.*

Xx

x, X /eks/ *n* **1** (letter) x, X *m*; **2 x** MATH x *m*; **for x people** pour x personnes; **3 X** (anonymous person, place) X *m*; **Ms X** Mme X; **X marks the spot** l'endroit est marqué d'une croix; **4 x** (at end of letter) **x x x** grosses bises; **5 X** (as signature) croix *f*.

X certificate *n* GB **the film was given an ~** le film a été interdit aux moins de 18 ans.

xenophobia /ˌzenəˈfəʊbɪə/ *n* xénophobie *f*.

xerox, Xerox® /ˈzɪərɒks/ **I** *n* **1** (machine) photocopieuse *f*; **2** (process) (procédé de) photocopie *f*; **3** (copy) (photo)copie *f*. **II** *vtr* photocopier.

Xmas *n*: *abrév écrite* = **Christmas**.

X rated *adj* [*film, video*] interdit aux moins de 18 ans.

X-ray /ˈeksreɪ/ **I** *n* **1** (ray) rayon *m* X; **2** (photo) radiographie *f*, radio○ *f*; **3** (process) radiographie *f*, radioscopie *f*; **to have an ~** se faire radiographier; **to give sb an ~** faire une radiographie à qn.
II *vtr* radiographier.

X-ray: **~ machine** *n* générateur *m* à rayons X; **~ unit** *n* service *m* de radiologie.

y, Y /waɪ/ *n* **1** (lettre) y, Y *m*; **2 y** MATH y *m*.

yacht /jɒt/ **I** *n* yacht *m*.
II *noun modifier* [*crew*] de yacht; [*race*] de yachts; ~ **club** yacht-club *m*.
III *vi* faire du yachting.

yachting /ˈjɒtɪŋ/ ▶949 **I** *n* yachting *m*.
II *noun modifier* [*clothes*] de yachtman; [*enthusiast*] du yachting; [*course*] de yachting; [*holiday*] en yacht.

yahoo /jəˈhuː/ **I** *n* abruti-e° *m/f*.
II *excl* hourra!

yak /jæk/ *n* ZOOL yack *m*.

Yale® /jeɪl/ *n* (also **Yale lock**) serrure *f* de sûreté.

yam /jæm/ *n* **1** (tropical) igname *f*; **2** US (sweet potato) patate *f* douce.

yank /jæŋk/ **I** *n* coup *m* sec.
II *vtr* tirer [*person, rope*].
■ **yank off**: ~ [sth] off, ~ off [sth] arracher.

Yank° /jæŋk/ *n* INJUR Yankee *mf* OFFENSIVE.

Yankee /ˈjæŋkɪ/ *n* **1** US (inhabitant of New England) habitant-e *m/f* de la Nouvelle Angleterre; (of North) habitant/-e *m/f* du Nord (des États-Unis); **2** (soldier) Nordiste *m*; **3** (American) INJUR yankee *m* OFFENSIVE.

yap /jæp/ *vi* [*dog*] japper (**at** après).

yapping /ˈjæpɪŋ/ **I** *n* ¢ jappements *mpl*.
II *adj* [*dog*] jappeur/-euse.

yard /jɑːd/ *n* **1** ▶1045 **1** yard *m* (= *0.9144 m*); **2** FIG **she writes poetry by the** ~ elle écrit des pages et des pages de poésie; **3** (of house, farm, prison, hospital) cour *f*; **4** US (garden) jardin *m*; **5** (for storage) dépôt *m*; (for construction) chantier *m*.
II Yard *pr n* GB **the** ~ *police judiciaire britannique*.

yardstick /ˈjɑːdstɪk/ *n* FIG point *m* de référence.

yarn /jɑːn/ *n* (wool) fil *m* (à tricoter); (tale) histoire *f*.

yashmak /ˈjæʃmæk/ *n* voile *m* islamique.

yawn /jɔːn/ **I** *n* LIT bâillement *m*; **to give a** ~ bâiller; FIG (bore) **what a** ~°! que c'est barbant°!
II *vi* **1** [*person*] bâiller; **2** FIG [*abyss, chasm*] béer.

yawning /ˈjɔːnɪŋ/ **I** *n* bâillements *mpl*.
II *adj* [*abyss*] béant; FIG **the** ~ **gap between the two countries** l'abîme qui sépare les deux pays.

yd *abrév écrite* = **yard** 1.

yea /jeɪ/ *n‡ particle* oui *m*.
II *n* POL **the** ~**s and the nays** les oui et les non.

yeah /jeə/ *particle* ouais°, oui; **oh** ~? vraiment?

year /jɪə(r), jɜː(r)/ ▶1336 **I** *n* **1** (period of time) an *m*, année *f*; **two** ~**s ago** il y a deux ans; **all (the) year round** toute l'année; **over the** ~**s** au cours des ans ou des années; **the** ~ **before last** il y a deux ans; ~ **by** ~ d'année en année; ~ **in** ~ **out** tous les ans; **for the first time in** ~**s** pour la première fois depuis des années; **it was a** ~ **ago last October that I heard the news** il y a eu un an en octobre que j'ai appris la nouvelle; **it will be four** ~**s in July since he died** cela fera quatre ans en juillet qu'il est mort; **it's a** ~ **since I heard from him** je n'ai plus de ses nouvelles depuis un an; **in all my** ~**s as a journalist** dans toute ma carrière de journaliste; **to earn £30,000 a** ~ gagner 30 000 livres sterling par an; **2** (indicating age) **to be 19** ~**s old** ou **19** ~**s of age** avoir 19 ans; **a two-**~**-old child** un enfant de deux ans; **3** SCH, UNIV année *f*; **4** GB SCH (pupil) **first/second-**~ ~ élève *mf* de sixième/cinquième.
II years *npl* **1** (age) âge *m*; **from her earliest** ~**s** dès son plus jeune âge; **2**° (a long time) **but that would take** ~**s!** ça prendrait une éternité!; **it's** ~**s**

since we last met! ça fait un siècle qu'on ne s'est pas vus!; **this job has put** ~**s on me!** ce travail m'a vieilli de 10 ans!

yearbook /ˈjɪəbʊk, ˈjɜː-/ *n* **1** (directory) annuaire *m*; **2** US SCH, UNIV album *m* de promotion.

yearly /ˈjɪəlɪ, ˈjɜː-/ **I** *adj* [*visit, income*] annuel/-elle.
II *adv* annuellement.

yearn /jɜːn/ *vi* **1** (desire) **to** ~ **for** désirer (avoir) [*child, food*]; aspirer à [*freedom*]; attendre [*era, event*]; **to** ~ **to do** avoir très envie de faire; **2** (miss) **she** ~**s for her son** son fils lui manque terriblement.

yearning /ˈjɜːnɪŋ/ **I** *n* désir *m* ardent (**for** de).
II yearnings *npl* aspirations *fpl*.

year-round *adj* [*supply, source*] permanent; **for** ~ **use** pour être utilisé toute l'année.

yeast /jiːst/ *n* levure *f*.

yell /jel/ **I** *n* (shout) cri *m*; (of rage, pain) hurlement *m*.
II *vtr* crier [*warning*]; (louder) hurler [*insults*].
III *vi* (shout) crier; **to** ~ **at sb** crier après qn.

yelling /ˈjelɪŋ/ **I** *n* cris *mpl*.
II *adj* [*mob, crowd*] vociférant.

yellow /ˈjeləʊ/ ▶818 **I** *n* jaune *m*.
II *adj* **1** (in colour) jaune; **to go** ou **turn** ~ jaunir; **the lights are on** ~ les feux sont à l'orange; **2**° (cowardly) trouillard°.
III *vtr, vi* jaunir.

yellow: ~**-belly**° *n* trouillard/-e° *m/f*; ~ **card** *n* SPORT carton *m* jaune.

yellowish /ˈjeləʊɪʃ/ ▶818 *adj* tirant sur le jaune, jaunâtre PÉJ.

yellow: ~ **metal** *n* (brass) cuivre *m* jaune; (gold) métal *m* jaune; ~ **pages** *npl* pages *fpl* jaunes.

yellowy /ˈjeləʊɪ/ ▶818 *adj* tirant sur le jaune, jaunâtre PÉJ.

yelp /jelp/ **I** *n* (of person) glapissement *m*; (of animal) (of pain, fear) glapissement *m*; (of happiness) jappement *m*.
II *vi* [*person*] glapir (**with** de); [*animal*] (with pain, fear) glapir; (with happiness) japper.

Yemen /ˈjemən/ ▶840 *pr n* Yémen *m*; **North/South** ~ HIST Yémen *m* du Nord/du Sud.

yen /jen/ ▶849 **I** *n* **1** FIN yen *m*; **2**° (craving) **to have a** ~ **for sth/to do** avoir grande envie de qch/de faire.

yeoman /ˈjəʊmən/ *n* (*pl* **-men**) **1** (also ~ **farmer**) GB HIST franc tenancier *m*; **2** GB MIL HIST cavalier *m* (volontaire); ~ **of the guard** membre *m* de la garde royale.

yep° /jep/, **yup**° /jʌp/ *particle* US ouais°, oui.

yes /jes/

■ *Note* **yes** is translated by **oui**, except when used in reply to a negative question when the translation is **si** or, more emphatically, **si, si** or **mais si**: *'did you see him?'*—*'yes (I did)'* = *'est-ce que tu l'as vu?'*—*'oui (je l'ai vu)'*; *'you're not hungry, are you?'*—*'yes I am'* = *'tu n'as pas faim?'*—*'si (j'ai faim)'*
– Note that there are no direct equivalents in French for tag questions and short replies such as *yes I did, yes I am*.
– For some suggestions on how to translate these, see the notes at **do** and **be**.

particle, n oui; (in reply to negative question) si; **to say** ~ dire oui; **the** ~**es and the nos** les oui et les non.

yes-man° *n* (*pl* **-men**) PÉJ lèche-bottes *m inv*.

yesterday /ˈjestədeɪ, -dɪ/ ▶854, 1390 **I** *n* **1** LIT hier *m*; ~ **was a sad day for all of us** la journée

you

In English *you* is used to address everybody, whereas French has two forms: *tu* and *vous*. The usual word to use when you are speaking to anyone you do not know very well is *vous*. This is sometimes called the *polite form* and is used for the subject, object, indirect object and emphatic pronoun:

would you like some coffee? = voulez-vous du café?
can I help you? = est-ce que je peux vous aider?
what can I do for you? = qu'est-ce que je peux faire pour vous?

The more informal pronoun *tu* is used between close friends and family members, within groups of children and young people, by adults when talking to children and always when talking to animals; *tu* is the subject form, the direct and indirect object form is *te* (*t'* before a vowel) and the form for emphatic use or use after a preposition is *toi*:

would you like some coffee? = veux-tu du café?
can I help you? = est-ce que je peux t'aider?
there's a letter for you = il y a une lettre pour toi

As a general rule, when talking to a French person use *vous*, wait to see how they address you and follow suit. It is safer to wait for the French person to suggest using *tu*. The suggestion will usually be phrased as *on se tutoie?* or *on peut se tutoyer?*

Note that *tu* is only a singular pronoun and *vous* is the plural form of *tu*.

Remember that in French the object and indirect object pronouns are always placed before the verb:

she knows you = elle vous connaît *or* elle te connaît

In compound tenses like the present perfect and the past perfect, the past participle agrees in number and gender with the direct object:

I saw you on Saturday
(to one male: polite form) = je vous ai vu samedi
(to one female: polite form) = je vous ai vue samedi
(to one male: informal form) = je t'ai vu samedi
(to one female: informal form) = je t'ai vue samedi
(to two or more people, male or mixed) = je vous ai vus samedi
(to two or more females) = je vous ai vues samedi

When *you* is used impersonally as the more informal form of *one* it is translated by *on* for the subject form and by *vous* or *te* for the object form, depending on whether the comment is being made amongst friends or in a more formal context:

you can do as you like here = on peut faire ce qu'on veut ici
these mushrooms can make you ill = ces champignons peuvent vous rendre malade *or* ces champignons peuvent te rendre malade
you could easily lose your bag here = on pourrait facilement perdre son sac ici

Note that *your* used with *on* is translated by *son/sa/ses* according to the gender and number of the noun that follows.

For verb forms with *vous*, *tu* and *on* see the French verb tables. For particular usages see the entry **you**.

---

d'hier a été triste pour nous tous; **~ was the fifth of April** hier nous étions le cinq avril; **the day before ~** avant-hier; **2** FIG (the past) **~'s fashions** la mode d'hier; **~'s men** PÉJ hommes *mpl* du passé; **all our ~s** tout notre passé.
II *adv* **1** LIT hier; **I saw her only ~** je l'ai vue pas plus tard qu'hier; **all day ~** toute la journée d'hier; **it was ~ week** OU **a week** cela fait une semaine hier; **early/late ~** tôt/tard dans la journée d'hier; **only ~ he was saying to me...** hier encore il me disait...; **2** FIG (in the past) hier, autrefois.

yesterday: **~ afternoon** *n, adv* hier après-midi; **~ evening** *n, adv* hier soir; **~ morning** *n, adv* hier matin.

yet /jet/ **I** *conj* (nevertheless) pourtant.
II *adv* **1** (up till now, so far: with negatives) encore, jusqu'à présent; (in questions) déjà; (with superlatives) jusqu'ici; **it's not ready ~**, **it's not ~ ready** ce n'est pas encore prêt; **has he arrived ~?** est-il (déjà) arrivé?; **not ~** pas encore, pas pour l'instant; **this is his best/worst ~** c'est ce qu'il a fait de mieux/de pire jusqu'ici; **it's the best ~** jusqu'ici, c'est le mieux; **2** (also **just ~**) (now) tout de suite, encore; **don't start (just) ~** ne commence pas tout de suite; **3** (still) encore; **they may ~ come** ils pourraient encore arriver; **he'll finish it ~** il va le finir; **the news has ~ to reach them** il faut encore que la nouvelle leur parvienne; **the as ~ unfinished building** le bâtiment encore inachevé; **there is a year to go ~ before he retires** il reste encore un an avant qu'il parte en retraite; **he won't come for hours ~** il ne viendra pas avant quelques heures; **4** (even, still: with comparatives etc) encore; **~ more cars** encore plus de voitures; **~ louder** encore plus fort; **~ another attack** encore une autre attaque; **~ again** encore une fois.

yew /juː/ *n* **1** (also **~ tree**) if *m*; **2** (wood) bois *m* d'if.

Y-fronts *npl* GB slip *m* ouvert.

YHA GB (*abrév* = **Youth Hostels Association**) association *f* des auberges de jeunesse.

yield /jiːld/ **I** *n* GEN, FIN rendement *m*; **the annual milk ~** la production laitière annuelle.
II *vtr* **1** GEN, AGRIC produire; **2** FIN rapporter; **3** (provide) donner, fournir [*information, result, meaning*];

produire [*clue*]; livrer [*secret*]; **4** (surrender) céder (**to** à); **to ~ ground to** MIL, FIG céder du terrain à.
III *vi* **1** (give in) (to person, temptation, pressure, threats) céder (**to** à); (to army, arguments) se rendre (**to** à); **~ to force** céder devant la force; **to ~ to persuasion** se laisser persuader; **2** (under weight, pressure) céder; **3** (be superseded) **to ~ to** [*technology*] céder le pas à; [*land, countryside*] céder la place à; **4** (be productive) **to ~ well/poorly** avoir un bon/mauvais rendement; **5** US AUT céder le passage (**to** à).
■ **yield up** livrer [*secret, treasure*].

yielding /'jiːldɪŋ/ *adj* [*person*] (accommodating) accommodant; (submissive) soumis.

YMCA (*abrév* = **Young Men's Christian Association**) ~ Union *f* Chrétienne des Jeunes Gens.

yodel /'jəʊdl/ *vi* (*p prés etc* **-ll-**) jodler, iodler.

yoghurt /'jɒgət, US 'jəʊgərt/ *n* yaourt *m*, yoghourt *m*.

yoke /jəʊk/ **I** *n* **1** LIT (for oxen) joug *m*; (for person) palanche *f*; FIG joug *m*; **to throw off the ~** briser le joug; **2** (of garment) empiècement *m*.
II *vtr* LIT (also **~ up**) atteler; FIG joindre.

yokel /'jəʊkl/ *n* PEJ péquenaud/-e° *m/f*, plouc° *mf*.

yolk /jəʊk/ *n* jaune *m* (d'œuf).

yonks° /jɒŋks/ *npl* GB **I haven't seen him for ~** ça fait une éternité que je ne l'ai pas vu.

yore /jɔː(r)/ *n* LITTÉR **in days of ~** jadis.

you /juː, jə/ *pron* **1** (addressing sb) **I saw ~ on Saturday** (one person) (polite) je vous ai vu samedi; (informal) je t'ai vu samedi; (more than one person) je vous ai vus samedi; **YOU would never do that** (polite) vous, vous ne feriez jamais cela; (informal) toi, tu ne ferais jamais ça; **there's a manager for ~°!** IRON ça c'est un patron!; **~ English** vous autres Anglais; **~ idiot°!** espèce d'imbécile°!; **~ two can stay** vous deux vous pouvez rester; **do ~ people smoke?** vous fumez?; **2** (as indefinite pronoun) (subject) on; (object, indirect object) vous, te; **~ never know!** on ne sait jamais!; **they say sweets give ~ spots** on dit que les bonbons donnent des boutons.

you'd /juːd/ = **you had**, **you would**.

you: **~-know-what°** *pron* vous-savez-quoi, tu-sais-quoi; **~-know-who°** *pron* qui-vous-savez, qui-tu-sais.

you'll /juːl/ = **you will**.

young /jʌŋ/ **I** *n* **1** (young people) **the ~** les jeunes *mpl*, la jeunesse *f*; **for ~ and old** (**alike**) pour les jeunes comme pour les vieux; **2** (animal's offspring) petits *mpl*. **II** *adj* jeune; **to be ~ at heart** avoir l'esprit jeune; **she is ten years ~er than him** elle a dix ans de moins que lui; **I feel ten years ~er** j'ai l'impression d'avoir rajeuni de dix ans; **in my ~er days** quand j'étais jeune; **you're only ~ once!** on n'est jeune qu'une fois; **children as ~ as five years old worked** des enfants dont certains n'avaient que cinq ans travaillaient; **the night is ~** la nuit ne fait que commencer; **Mr Brown the ~er** M. Brown le jeune; (Mr Brown's son) M. Brown fils; **~ lady** jeune femme *f*; **~ people** jeunes gens *mpl*; **~ person** jeune *m*; **the ~er generation** la jeune génération; **her ~er brother** son frère cadet; **the two ~er children** les deux cadets; **I'm not as ~ as I used to be** je n'ai plus 20 ans; **we're not getting any ~er** nous ne rajeunissons pas.

young blood *n* sang *m* neuf.

youngish /ˈjʌŋɪʃ/ *adj* assez jeune.

young-looking *adj* **to be ~** faire (très) jeune.

young offender *n* délinquant/-e *m/f*.

youngster /ˈjʌŋstə(r)/ *n* **1** (young person) jeune *m*; **2** (child) enfant *mf*.

your /jɔː(r), jʊə(r)/ *det* votre/vos; (more informally) ton/ta/tes; **you should always look after ~ skin** il faut prendre soin de sa peau.

you're /jʊə(r), jɔː(r)/ = **you are**.

yours /jɔːz, US jʊərz/

■ **Note** For a full note on the use of the *vous* and *tu* forms in French, see the entry **you**.
– In French, possessive pronouns reflect the gender and number of the noun they are standing for. When *yours* is referring to only one person it is translated by *le vôtre, la vôtre, les vôtres* or, more familiarly, *le tien, la tienne, les tiens, les tiennes*. When *yours* is referring to more than one person it is translated by *le vôtre, la vôtre, les vôtres*.
– For examples and particular usages see the entry below.

pron **my car is red but ~ is blue** ma voiture est rouge mais la vôtre or la tienne est bleue; **which house is ~?** votre or ta maison c'est laquelle?; **he's a colleague of ~** c'est un de vos or tes collègues; **it's not ~** ce n'est pas à vous or à toi; **the money wasn't ~ to give away** vous n'aviez pas à donner cet argent; **~ was not an easy task** votre tâche n'était pas facile; **I'm fed up○ with that dog of ~!** j'en ai marre de ton sale chien○!

yourself /jɔːˈself, US jʊərˈself/

■ **Note** For a full note on the use of the *vous* and *tu* forms in French, see the entry **you**.
– When used as a reflexive pronoun, direct and indirect, *yourself* is translated by *vous* or familiarly *te* or *t'* before a vowel: **you've hurt yourself** = vous vous êtes fait mal or tu t'es fait mal.
– In imperatives, the translation is *vous* or *toi*: **help yourself** = servez-vous or sers-toi.
– When used in emphasis the translation is *vous-même* or *toi-même*: **you yourself don't know** = vous ne savez pas vous-même or tu ne sais pas toi-même.
– After a preposition the translation is *vous* or *vous-même* or *toi* or *toi-même*: **you can be proud of yourself** = vous pouvez être fier de vous or vous-même, tu peux être fier de toi or toi-même.

pron **1** (reflexive) vous, te, (*before vowel*) t'; **have you hurt ~?** est-ce que tu t'es fait mal?; **2** (in imperatives) vous, toi; **3** (emphatic) vous-même, toi-même; **4** (after prep) vous, vous-même, toi, toi-même; **5** (expressions) (**all**) **by ~** tout seul/toute seule; **you're not ~ today** tu n'as pas l'air dans ton assiette aujourd'hui.

your

For a full note on the use of the *vous* and *tu* forms in French, see the entry **you**.

In French, determiners agree in gender and number with the noun they qualify. So *your*, when addressing one person, is translated by *votre*, or more familiarly *ton*, + masculine singular noun (*votre chien* or *ton chien*), by *votre* or *ta* + feminine singular noun (*votre maison* or *ta maison*) and by *vos* or *tes* + plural noun (*vos enfants* or *tes enfants*). Note that *ton* is used with a feminine noun beginnning with a vowel or mute 'h' (*ton adresse*).

When addressing more than one person, the translation is *votre* + singular noun and *vos* + plural noun. When *your* is stressed, *à vous* or *à toi* is added after the noun:
  your house = votre maison à vous

When used impersonally to mean *one's*, *your* is translated by *son*, *sa* or *ses* when *you* is translated by *on*:
  you buy your tickets at the door = on prend ses billets à l'entrée

The translation after an impersonal verb in French is *son*, *sa*, *ses*:
  you have to buy your tickets at the door = il faut prendre ses billets à l'entrée

Note, however the following:
  sweets are bad for your teeth = les bonbons sont mauvais pour les dents
  your average student = l'étudiant moyen

For *your* used with parts of the body ▶ **765**.

yourselves /jəˈselvz/

■ **Note** When used as a reflexive pronoun, direct and indirect, *yourselves* is translated by *vous*: **help yourselves** = servez-vous.
– When used as an emphatic, the translation is *vous-mêmes*: **do it yourselves** = faites-le vous-mêmes.
– After a preposition the translation is *vous* or *vous-mêmes*: **did you buy it for yourselves?** = est-ce que vous l'avez acheté pour vous or pour vous-mêmes?

pron **1** (reflexive) vous; **2** (emphatic) vous-mêmes; **3** (after prep) vous, vous-mêmes; **all by ~** tous seuls/toutes seules.

youth /juːθ/ **I** *n* (*pl* **~s** /juːðz/) **1** (young man) jeune homme *m*; **a gang of ~s** PÉJ une bande de jeunes gens; **2** (being young) jeunesse *f*; **despite his ~** malgré son jeune âge; **3** (young people) jeunes *mpl*. **II** *noun modifier* [*club*] de jeunes; [*TV, magazine*] pour les jeunes or la jeunesse; [*culture*] des jeunes.

youthful /ˈjuːθfl/ *adj* **1** (young) jeune; **2** (typical of youth) de la jeunesse; **his ~ looks** ou **appearance** son air jeune; **she's very ~ for 65, she's a very ~ 65** elle fait très jeune pour ses 65 ans.

youth: **~ hostel** *n* auberge *f* de jeunesse; **~ hostelling** *n* randonnée *f* avec logement en auberges de jeunesse; **~ leader** ▶ **1251** *n* animateur/-trice *m/f* de groupe de jeunes; **~ work** *n* travail *m* social auprès des jeunes; **~ worker** ▶ **1251** *n* éducateur/ -trice *m/f*.

you've /juːv/ = **you have**.

yo-yo® /ˈjəʊjəʊ/ **I** *n* **1** GEN yo-yo® *m*; **2**○ US PÉJ (fool) abruti/-e○ *m/f*. **II**○ *vi* [*prices, inflation*] fluctuer.

yr *abrév écrite* = **year**.

Yugoslavia /ˌjuːɡəʊˈslɑːvɪə/ ▶ **840** *pr n* Yougoslavie *f*.

Yule log /ˈjuːl lɒɡ/ *n* bûche *f* de Noël.

yuppie /ˈjʌpɪ/ *n* PÉJ jeune cadre *m* dynamique, yuppie *m* PEJ.

yuppie flu ▶ **1002** *n* PÉJ syndrome *m* de la fatigue chronique.

YWCA (*abrév* = **Young Women's Christian Association**) ≈ Union *f* Chrétienne des Jeunes Femmes.

Zz

The signs of the Zodiac

Aries	= le Bélier	21 mars–20 avril
Taurus	= le Taureau	21 avril–20 mai
Gemini	= les Gémeaux	21 mai–21 juin
Cancer	= le Cancer	22 juin–22 juillet
Leo	= le Lion	23 juillet–22 août
Virgo	= la Vierge	23 août–22 septembre
Libra	= la Balance	23 septembre–23 octobre
Scorpio	= le Scorpion	24 octobre–21 novembre
Sagittarius	= le Sagittaire	22 novembre–21 décembre
Capricorn	= le Capricorne	22 décembre–19 janvier
Aquarius	= le Verseau	20 janvier–18 février
Pisces	= les Poissons	19 février–20 mars

I'm Leo	= je suis Lion
I'm Gemini	= je suis Gémeaux
born in Leo *or* under the sign of Leo	= né sous le signe du Lion
born in Gemini	= né sous le signe des Gémeaux
Leos/Arians are very generous	= les Lions/les Béliers sont très généreux
what's the horoscope for Leos?	= que dit l'horoscope pour les Lions?
the sun is in Leo	= le soleil est au Lion

All the signs work in the same way in French.

---

z, Z /zed, US zi:/ *n* z, Z *m*.

zany /'zeɪnɪ/ *adj* loufoque○.

zap○ /zæp/ **I** *n* (energy) tonus *m*.
II *vtr* (*p prés etc* **-pp-**) **1** (destroy) détruire [*town*]; tuer [*person, animal*]; **2** (fire at) tirer sur [*person*]; **3** COMPUT (delete) supprimer.
III *vi* (*p prés etc* **-pp-**) **to ~ into town** faire un saut○ en ville; **to ~ from channel to channel** zapper○.

zapper○ /'zæpə(r)/ *n* télécommande *f*.

zeal /zi:l/ *n* **1** (fanaticism) GEN zèle *m*; (religious) ferveur *f*; **2** (enthusiasm) ardeur *f*, zèle *m*.

zealot /'zelət/ *n* GEN, PEJ fanatique *mf*.

zealous /'zeləs/ *adj* [*supporter*] zélé; [*determination*] acharné; **to be ~ to do** avoir très envie de faire.

zebra /'zebrə, 'zi:-/ *n* zèbre *m*.

zebra crossing *n* GB passage *m* pour piétons.

zero /'zɪərəʊ/ ▶ 1112 **I** *n* GEN, MATH, METEOROL zéro *m*.
II *noun modifier* [*altitude, growth, inflation*] zéro *inv*; [*confidence, interest, development*] nul/nulle.
■ **zero in** MIL viser; **to ~ in on sth** MIL viser [*target*], FIG (pinpoint) cerner [*problem*]; se rabattre sur [*option*]; foncer droit sur [*person*]; repérer [*place*].

zero: **~ gravity** *n* apesanteur *f*; **~ hour** *n* MIL, FIG heure *f* H; **~-rated** *adj* GB exempté de TVA.

zest /zest/ *n* **1** (enthusiasm) entrain *m*; **2** (piquancy) piquant *m*; **3** (of fruit) zeste *m*.

zigzag /'zɪgzæg/ **I** *n* zigzag *m*.
II *vi* (*p prés etc* **-gg-**) [*person, road*] zigzaguer; [*river*] serpenter; **to ~ up** monter en zigzag.

zilch○ /zɪltʃ/ *n* que dalle○.

Zimbabwe /zɪm'bɑ:bwɪ, -weɪ/ ▶ 840 *pr n* Zimbabwe *m*.

zimmer® /'zɪmə(r)/ *n* GB déambulateur *m*.

zinc /zɪŋk/ *n* zinc *m*.

zinc: **~ ointment** *n* pommade *f* à l'oxyde de zinc; **~ oxide** *n* oxyde *m* de zinc.

zing○ /zɪŋ/ **I** *n* **1** (sound) sifflement *m*; **2** (energy) entrain *m*.
II *vtr* US FIG (criticize) démolir○ [*person*].
III *vi* siffler.
■ **zing along**○ US [*car*] filer○ à toute allure.

Zionism /'zaɪənɪzəm/ *n* sionisme *m*.

zip /zɪp/ **I** *n* **1** fermeture *f* à glissière, fermeture *f* éclair®; **to do up/undo a ~** fermer/ouvrir une fermeture à glissière; **2**○ (energy) tonus *m*; **3** (sound) sifflement *m*; **4** US POST = **zip code**; **5**○ US (zero) zéro *m*.
II *vtr* (*p prés etc* **-pp-**) **to ~ sth open/shut** ouvrir/fermer la fermeture à glissière de qch.
III○ *vi* (*p prés etc* **-pp-**) **to ~ along, to ~ past** filer à toute allure.
■ **zip on** ¶ s'attacher par une fermeture à glissière; ¶ **~ [sth] on, ~ on [sth]** remonter la fermeture à glissière de qch.
■ **zip through**○: **to ~ through a book** lire un livre en diagonale○.
■ **zip up** ¶ [*garment, bag*] se fermer par une fermeture à glissière; ¶ **~ [sb/sth] up, ~ up [sb/sth]** remonter la fermeture à glissière de qn/qch.

zip: **~ code** *n* US POST code *m* postal; **~ fastener** *n* = **zip I 1**.

zipper /'zɪpə(r)/ *n* US = **zip I 1**.

zippy○ /'zɪpɪ/ *adj* [*vehicle*] qui pète le feu○.

zither /'zɪðə(r)/ ▶ 1097 *n* cithare *f*.

zodiac /'zəʊdɪæk/ *n* zodiaque *m*.

zombie /'zɒmbɪ/ *n* RELIG zombi(e) *m*; FIG abruti/-e *m/f*.

zonal /'zəʊnl/ *adj* [*administration*] par zone; [*boundary, organizer*] de zone; [*soil, climate*] zonal.

zone /zəʊn/ **I** *n* (all contexts) zone *f*.
II *vtr* **1** (divide) diviser [*qch*] en zones; **2** (assign) réserver; **~d for housing** réservé au logement.

zoning /'zəʊnɪŋ/ *n* découpage *m* par zones.

zonked /zɒŋkt/ *adj* (also **zonked out**) (tired) crevé○; (drunk) bourré○; (on drugs) défoncé○.

zoo /zu:/ *n* zoo *m*.

zoological /ˌzəʊə'lɒdʒɪkl/ *adj* zoologique.

zoologist /zəʊ'ɒlədʒɪst/ ▶ 1251 *n* zoologue *mf*, zoologiste *mf*.

zoology /zəʊ'ɒlədʒɪ/ *n* zoologie *f*.

zoom /zu:m/ **I** *n* **1** (of traffic, aircraft) vrombissement *m*, vacarme *m*; **2** PHOT (also **~ lens**) zoom *m*.
II *vi* **1**○ (move quickly) **to ~ past** passer en trombe; **to ~ around** passer à toute vitesse dans; **he's ~ed off to Paris** il a foncé○ à Paris; **2**○ [*prices*] monter en flèche; **3** AVIAT monter en chandelle.
■ **zoom in** CIN, PHOT faire un zoom avant (**on** sur).
■ **zoom out** CIN, PHOT faire un zoom arrière.

zucchini /zu:'ki:nɪ/ *n* (*pl* **~** ou **~s**) US courgette *f*.

zwieback /'zwi:bæk, 'tsvi:bɑ:k/ *n* US ~ biscotte *f*.

Index of English lexical usage notes

Liste des notes d'usage lexicales françaises

French verbs

Standard verb endings

	-er	-ir	-r, -re			-er	-ir	-r, -re
	INDICATIVE Present					**SUBJUNCTIVE Present**		
Singular 1	-e	-is	-s *or* -e	Singular 1		-e	-(iss)e	-e
2	-es	-is	-s *or* -es	2		-es	-(iss)es	-es
3	-e	-it	-t *or* -e	3		-e	-(iss)e	-e
Plural 1	-ons	-(iss)ons	-ons	Plural 1		-ions	-(iss)ions	-ions
2	-ez	-(iss)ez	-ez	2		-iez	-(iss)iez	-iez
3	-ent	-(iss)ent	-ent	3		-ent	-(iss)ent	-ent
	INDICATIVE Imperfect					**SUBJUNCTIVE Imperfect**		
Singular 1	-ais	-(iss)ais	-ais	Singular 1		-asse	-sse	-sse
2	-ais	-(iss)ais	-ais	2		-asses	-sses	-sses
3	-ait	-(iss)ait	-ait	3		-ât	-ît	-ît *or* -ût
Plural 1	-ions	-(iss)ions	-ions	Plural 1		-assions	-ssions	-ssions
2	-iez	-(iss)iez	-iez	2		-assiez	-ssiez	-ssiez
3	-aient	-(iss)aient	-aient	3		-assent	-issent	-ssent
	INDICATIVE Past historic					**IMPERATIVE Present**		
Singular 1	-ai	-is	-s	Singular				
2	-as	-is	-s					
3	-a	-it	-t	3		-e	-s	-s
Plural 1	-âmes	-îmes	-mes	Plural 1		-ons	-(iss)ons	-ons
2	-âtes	-îtes	-tes	2		-ez	-(iss)ez	-ez
3	-èrent	-irent	-rent					
	INDICATIVE Future					**CONDITIONAL Present**		
Singular 1	-erai	-rai	-rai	Singular 1		-erais	-rais	-rais
2	-eras	-ras	-ras	2		-erais	-rais	-rais
3	-era	-ra	-ra	3		-erait	-rait	-rait
Plural 1	-erons	-rons	-rons	Plural 1		-erions	-rions	-rions
2	-erez	-rez	-rez	2		-eriez	-riez	-riez
3	-eront	-ront	-ront	3		-eraient	-raient	-raient
	INFINITIVE					**PARTICIPLE**		
Present	-er	-ir	-r *or* -re	Present		-ant	-(iss)ant	-ant
				Past		-é	-i	-i *or* -u

1 aimer

INDICATIVE

Present

j'	aime
tu	aimes
il	aime
nous	aimons
vous	aimez
ils	aiment

Imperfect

j'	aimais
tu	aimais
il	aimait
nous	aimions
vous	aimiez
ils	aimaient

Past historic

j'	aimai
tu	aimas
il	aima
nous	aimâmes
vous	aimâtes
ils	aimèrent

Future

j'	aimerai
tu	aimeras
il	aimera
nous	aimerons
vous	aimerez
ils	aimeront

Perfect

j'	ai	aimé
tu	as	aimé
il	a	aimé
nous	avons	aimé
vous	avez	aimé
ils	ont	aimé

Pluperfect

j'	avais	aimé
tu	avais	aimé
il	avait	aimé
nous	avions	aimé
vous	aviez	aimé
ils	avaient	aimé

Past anterior

j'	eus	aimé
tu	eus	aimé
il	eut	aimé
nous	eûmes	aimé
vous	eûtes	aimé
ils	eurent	aimé

Future perfect

j'	aurai	aimé
tu	auras	aimé
il	aura	aimé
nous	aurons	aimé
vous	aurez	aimé
ils	auront	aimé

IMPERATIVE

Present

aime	
aimons	
aimez	

Past

aie	aimé
ayons	aimé
ayez	aimé

SUBJUNCTIVE

Present

(que) j'	aime
(que) tu	aimes
(qu')il	aime
(que) nous	aimions
(que) vous	aimiez
(qu')ils	aiment

Imperfect

(que) j'	aimasse
(que) tu	aimasses
(qu')il	aimât
(que) nous	aimassions
(que) vous	aimassiez
(qu')ils	aimassent

Perfect

(que) j'	aie	aimé
(que) tu	aies	aimé
(qu')il	ait	aimé
(que) nous	ayons	aimé
(que) vous	ayez	aimé
(qu')ils	aient	aimé

Pluperfect

(que) j'	eusse	aimé
(que) tu	eusses	aimé
(qu')il	eût	aimé
(que) nous	eussions	aimé
(que) vous	eussiez	aimé
(qu')ils	eussent	aimé

CONDITIONAL

Present

j'	aimerais
tu	aimerais
il	aimerait
nous	aimerions
vous	aimeriez
ils	aimeraient

Past I

j'	aurais	aimé
tu	aurais	aimé
il	aurait	aimé
nous	aurions	aimé
vous	auriez	aimé
ils	auraient	aimé

Past II

j'	eusse	aimé
tu	eusses	aimé
il	eût	aimé
nous	eussions	aimé
vous	eussiez	aimé
ils	eussent	aimé

PARTICIPLE

Present aimant

Past aimé, -e
ayant aimé

INFINITIVE

Present aimer

Past avoir aimé

2 plier

INDICATIVE

Present

je	plie
tu	plies
il	plie
nous	plions
vous	pliez
ils	plient

Imperfect

je	pliais
tu	pliais
il	pliait
nous	pliions
vous	pliiez
ils	pliaient

Past historic

je	pliai
tu	plias
il	plia
nous	pliâmes
vous	pliâtes
ils	plièrent

Future

je	plierai
tu	plieras
il	pliera
nous	plierons
vous	plierez
ils	plieront

Perfect

j'	ai	plié
tu	as	plié
il	a	plié
nous	avons	plié
vous	avez	plié
ils	ont	plié

Pluperfect

j'	avais	plié
tu	avais	plié
il	avait	plié
nous	avions	plié
vous	aviez	plié
ils	avaient	plié

Past anterior

j'	eus	plié
tu	eus	plié
il	eut	plié
nous	eûmes	plié
vous	eûtes	plié
ils	eurent	plié

Future perfect

j'	aurai	plié
tu	auras	plié
il	aura	plié
nous	aurons	plié
vous	aurez	plié
ils	auront	plié

IMPERATIVE

Present

plie	
plions	
pliez	

Past

aie	plié
ayons	plié
ayez	plié

SUBJUNCTIVE

Present

(que) je	plie
(que) tu	plies
(qu')il	plie
(que) nous	pliions
(que) vous	pliiez
(qu')ils	plient

Imperfect

(que) je	pliasse
(que) tu	pliasses
(qu')il	pliât
(que) nous	pliassions
(que) vous	pliassiez
(qu')ils	pliassent

Perfect

(que) j'	aie	plié
(que) tu	aies	plié
(qu')il	ait	plié
(que) nous	ayons	plié
(que) vous	ayez	plié
(qu')ils	aient	plié

Pluperfect

(que) j'	eusse	plié
(que) tu	eusses	plié
(qu')il	eût	plié
(que) nous	eussions	plié
(que) vous	eussiez	plié
(qu')ils	eussent	plié

CONDITIONAL

Present

je	plierais
tu	plierais
il	plierait
nous	plierions
vous	plieriez
ils	plieraient

Past I

j'	aurais	plié
tu	aurais	plié
il	aurait	plié
nous	aurions	plié
vous	auriez	plié
ils	auraient	plié

Past II

j'	eusse	plié
tu	eusses	plié
il	eût	plié
nous	eussions	plié
vous	eussiez	plié
ils	eussent	plié

PARTICIPLE

Present pliant

Past plié, -e
ayant plié

INFINITIVE

Present plier

Past avoir plié

3 finir

INDICATIVE

Present
je	finis
tu	finis
il	finit
nous	finissons
vous	finissez
ils	finissent

Imperfect
je	finissais
tu	finissais
il	finissait
nous	finissions
vous	finissiez
ils	finissaient

Past historic
je	finis
tu	finis
il	finit
nous	finîmes
vous	finîtes
ils	finirent

Future
je	finirai
tu	finiras
il	finira
nous	finirons
vous	finirez
ils	finiront

Perfect
j'	ai	fini
tu	as	fini
il	a	fini
nous	avons	fini
vous	avez	fini
ils	ont	fini

Pluperfect
j'	avais	fini
tu	avais	fini
il	avait	fini
nous	avions	fini
vous	aviez	fini
ils	avaient	fini

Past anterior
j'	eus	fini
tu	eus	fini
il	eut	fini
nous	eûmes	fini
vous	eûtes	fini
ils	eurent	fini

Future perfect
j'	aurai	fini
tu	auras	fini
il	aura	fini
nous	aurons	fini
vous	aurez	fini
ils	auront	fini

IMPERATIVE

Present
	finis
	finissons
	finissez

Past
	aie fini
	ayons fini
	ayez fini

SUBJUNCTIVE

Present
(que) je	finisse
(que) tu	finisses
(qu')il	finisse
(que) nous	finissions
(que) vous	finissiez
(qu')ils	finissent

Imperfect
(que) je	finisse
(que) tu	finisses
(qu')il	finît
(que) nous	finissions
(que) vous	finissiez
(qu')ils	finissent

Perfect
(que) j'	aie	fini
(que) tu	aies	fini
(qu')il	ait	fini
(que) nous	ayons	fini
(que) vous	ayez	fini
(qu')ils	aient	fini

Pluperfect
(que) j'	eusse	fini
(que) tu	eusses	fini
(qu')il	eût	fini
(que) nous	eussions	fini
(que) vous	eussiez	fini
(qu')ils	eussent	fini

CONDITIONAL

Present
je	finirais
tu	finirais
il	finirait
nous	finirions
vous	finiriez
ils	finiraient

Past I
j'	aurais	fini
tu	aurais	fini
il	aurait	fini
nous	aurions	fini
vous	auriez	fini
ils	auraient	fini

Past II
j'	eusse	fini
tu	eusses	fini
il	eût	fini
nous	eussions	fini
vous	eussiez	fini
ils	eussent	fini

PARTICIPLE

Present finissant

Past fini, -e
ayant fini

INFINITIVE

Present finir

Past avoir fini

4 offrir

INDICATIVE

Present
j'	offre
tu	offres
il	offre
nous	offrons
vous	offrez
ils	offrent

Imperfect
j'	offrais
tu	offrais
il	offrait
nous	offrions
vous	offriez
ils	offraient

Past historic
j'	offris
tu	offris
il	offrit
nous	offrîmes
vous	offrîtes
ils	offrirent

Future
j'	offrirai
tu	offriras
il	offrira
nous	offrirons
vous	offrirez
ils	offriront

Perfect
j'	ai	offert
tu	as	offert
il	a	offert
nous	avons	offert
vous	avez	offert
ils	ont	offert

Pluperfect
j'	avais	offert
tu	avais	offert
il	avait	offert
nous	avions	offert
vous	aviez	offert
ils	avaient	offert

Past anterior
j'	eus	offert
tu	eus	offert
il	eut	offert
nous	eûmes	offert
vous	eûtes	offert
ils	eurent	offert

Future perfect
j'	aurai	offert
tu	auras	offert
il	aura	offert
nous	aurons	offert
vous	aurez	offert
ils	auront	offert

IMPERATIVE

Present
	offre
	offrons
	offrez

Past
	aie offert
	ayons offert
	ayez offert

SUBJUNCTIVE

Present
(que) j'	offre
(que) tu	offres
(qu')il	offre
(que) nous	offrions
(que) vous	offriez
(qu')ils	offrent

Imperfect
(que) j'	offrisse
(que) tu	offrisses
(qu')il	offrît
(que) nous	offrissions
(que) vous	offrissiez
(qu')ils	offrissent

Perfect
(que) j'	aie	offert
(que) tu	aies	offert
(qu')il	ait	offert
(que) nous	ayons	offert
(que) vous	ayez	offert
(qu')ils	aient	offert

Pluperfect
(que) j'	eusse	offert
(que) tu	eusses	offert
(qu')il	eût	offert
(que) nous	eussions	offert
(que) vous	eussiez	offert
(qu')ils	eussent	offert

CONDITIONAL

Present
j'	offrirais
tu	offrirais
il	offrirait
nous	offririons
vous	offririez
ils	offriraient

Past I
j'	aurais	offert
tu	aurais	offert
il	aurait	offert
nous	aurions	offert
vous	auriez	offert
ils	auraient	offert

Past II
j'	eusse	offert
tu	eusses	offert
il	eût	offert
nous	eussions	offert
vous	eussiez	offert
ils	eussent	offert

PARTICIPLE

Present offrant

Past offert, -e
ayant offert

INFINITIVE

Present offrir

Past avoir offert

5 recevoir

INDICATIVE

Present

je	reçois
tu	reçois
il	reçoit
nous	recevons
vous	recevez
ils	reçoivent

Imperfect

je	recevais
tu	recevais
il	recevait
nous	recevions
vous	receviez
ils	recevaient

Past historic

je	reçus
tu	reçus
il	reçut
nous	reçûmes
vous	reçûtes
ils	reçurent

Future

je	recevrai
tu	recevras
il	recevra
nous	recevrons
vous	recevrez
ils	recevront

Perfect

j'	ai	reçu
tu	as	reçu
il	a	reçu
nous	avons	reçu
vous	avez	reçu
ils	ont	reçu

Pluperfect

j'	avais	reçu
tu	avais	reçu
il	avait	reçu
nous	avions	reçu
vous	aviez	reçu
ils	avaient	reçu

Past anterior

j'	eus	reçu
tu	eus	reçu
il	eut	reçu
nous	eûmes	reçu
vous	eûtes	reçu
ils	eurent	reçu

Future perfect

j'	aurai	reçu
tu	auras	reçu
il	aura	reçu
nous	aurons	reçu
vous	aurez	reçu
ils	auront	reçu

IMPERATIVE

Present

	reçois
	recevons
	recevez

Past

	aie	reçu
	ayons	reçu
	ayez	reçu

SUBJUNCTIVE

Present

(que) je	reçoive
(que) tu	reçoives
(qu')il	reçoive
(que) nous	recevions
(que) vous	receviez
(qu')ils	reçoivent

Imperfect

(que) je	reçusse
(que) tu	reçusses
(qu')il	reçût
(que) nous	reçussions
(que) vous	reçussiez
(qu')ils	reçussent

Perfect

(que) j'	aie	reçu
(que) tu	aies	reçu
(qu')il	ait	reçu
(que) nous	ayons	reçu
(que) vous	ayez	reçu
(qu')ils	aient	reçu

Pluperfect

(que) j'	eusse	reçu
(que) tu	eusses	reçu
(qu')il	eût	reçu
(que) nous	eussions	reçu
(que) vous	eussiez	reçu
(qu')ils	eussent	reçu

CONDITIONAL

Present

je	recevrais
tu	recevrais
il	recevrait
nous	recevrions
vous	recevriez
ils	recevraient

Past I

j'	aurais	reçu
tu	aurais	reçu
il	aurait	reçu
nous	aurions	reçu
vous	auriez	reçu
ils	auraient	reçu

Past II

j'	eusse	reçu
tu	eusses	reçu
il	eût	reçu
nous	eussions	reçu
vous	eussiez	reçu
ils	eussent	reçu

PARTICIPLE

Present recevant

Past reçu, -e
ayant reçu

INFINITIVE

Present recevoir

Past avoir reçu

6 rendre

INDICATIVE

Present

je	rends
tu	rends
il	rend
nous	rendons
vous	rendez
ils	rendent

Imperfect

je	rendais
tu	rendais
il	rendait
nous	rendions
vous	rendiez
ils	rendaient

Past historic

je	rendis
tu	rendis
il	rendit
nous	rendîmes
vous	rendîtes
ils	rendirent

Future

je	rendrai
tu	rendras
il	rendra
nous	rendrons
vous	rendrez
ils	rendront

Perfect

j'	ai	rendu
tu	as	rendu
il	a	rendu
nous	avons	rendu
vous	avez	rendu
ils	ont	rendu

Pluperfect

j'	avais	rendu
tu	avais	rendu
il	avait	rendu
nous	avions	rendu
vous	aviez	rendu
ils	avaient	rendu

Past anterior

j'	eus	rendu
tu	eus	rendu
il	eut	rendu
nous	eûmes	rendu
vous	eûtes	rendu
ils	eurent	rendu

Future perfect

j'	aurai	rendu
tu	auras	rendu
il	aura	rendu
nous	aurons	rendu
vous	aurez	rendu
ils	auront	rendu

IMPERATIVE

Present

	rends
	rendons
	rendez

Past

	aie	rendu
	ayons	rendu
	ayez	rendu

SUBJUNCTIVE

Present

(que) je	rende
(que) tu	rendes
(qu')il	rende
(que) nous	rendions
(que) vous	rendiez
(qu')ils	rendent

Imperfect

(que) je	rendisse
(que) tu	rendisses
(qu')il	rendît
(que) nous	rendissions
(que) vous	rendissiez
(qu')ils	rendissent

Perfect

(que) j'	aie	rendu
(que) tu	aies	rendu
(qu')il	ait	rendu
(que) nous	ayons	rendu
(que) vous	ayez	rendu
(qu')ils	aient	rendu

Pluperfect

(que) j'	eusse	rendu
(que) tu	eusses	rendu
(qu')il	eût	rendu
(que) nous	eussions	rendu
(que) vous	eussiez	rendu
(qu')ils	eussent	rendu

CONDITIONAL

Present

je	rendrais
tu	rendrais
il	rendrait
nous	rendrions
vous	rendriez
ils	rendraient

Past I

j'	aurais	rendu
tu	aurais	rendu
il	aurait	rendu
nous	aurions	rendu
vous	auriez	rendu
ils	auraient	rendu

Past II

j'	eusse	rendu
tu	eusses	rendu
il	eût	rendu
nous	eussions	rendu
vous	eussiez	rendu
ils	eussent	rendu

PARTICIPLE

Present rendant

Past rendu, -e
ayant rendu

INFINITIVE

Present rendre

Past avoir rendu

7 être

INDICATIVE

Present

je	suis
tu	es
il	est
nous	sommes
vous	êtes
ils	sont

Imperfect

j'	étais
tu	étais
il	était
nous	étions
vous	étiez
ils	étaient

Past historic

je	fus
tu	fus
il	fut
nous	fûmes
vous	fûtes
ils	furent

Future

je	serai
tu	seras
il	sera
nous	serons
vous	serez
ils	seront

Perfect

j'	ai	été
tu	as	été
il	a	été
nous	avons	été
vous	avez	été
ils	ont	été

Pluperfect

j'	avais	été
tu	avais	été
il	avait	été
nous	avions	été
vous	aviez	été
ils	avaient	été

Past anterior

j'	eus	été
tu	eus	été
il	eut	été
nous	eûmes	été
vous	eûtes	été
ils	eurent	été

Future perfect

j'	aurai	été
tu	auras	été
il	aura	été
nous	aurons	été
vous	aurez	été
ils	auront	été

IMPERATIVE

Present

sois
soyons
soyez

Past

aie	été
ayons	été
ayez	été

SUBJUNCTIVE

Present

(que) je	sois
(que) tu	sois
(qu')il	soit
(que) nous	soyons
(que) vous	soyez
(qu')ils	soient

Imperfect

(que) je	fusse
(que) tu	fusses
(qu')il	fût
(que) nous	fussions
(que) vous	fussiez
(qu')ils	fussent

Perfect

(que) j'	aie	été
(que) tu	aies	été
(qu')il	ait	été
(que) nous	ayons	été
(que) vous	ayez	été
(qu')ils	aient	été

Pluperfect

(que) j'	eusse	été
(que) tu	eusses	été
(qu')il	eût	été
(que) nous	eussions	été
(que) vous	eussiez	été
(qu')ils	eussent	été

CONDITIONAL

Present

je	serais
tu	serais
il	serait
nous	serions
vous	seriez
ils	seraient

Past I

j'	aurais	été
tu	aurais	été
il	aurait	été
nous	aurions	été
vous	auriez	été
ils	auraient	été

Past II

j'	eusse	été
tu	eusses	été
il	eût	été
nous	eussions	été
vous	eussiez	été
ils	eussent	été

PARTICIPLE

Present étant

Past été (invariable)
ayant été

INFINITIVE

Present être

Past avoir été

8 avoir

INDICATIVE

Present

j'	ai
tu	as
il	a
nous	avons
vous	avez
ils	ont

Imperfect

j'	avais
tu	avais
il	avait
nous	avions
vous	aviez
ils	avaient

Past historic

j'	eus
tu	eus
il	eut
nous	eûmes
vous	eûtes
ils	eurent

Future

j'	aurai
tu	auras
il	aura
nous	aurons
vous	aurez
ils	auront

Perfect

j'	ai	eu
tu	as	eu
il	a	eu
nous	avons	eu
vous	avez	eu
ils	ont	eu

Pluperfect

j'	avais	eu
tu	avais	eu
il	avait	eu
nous	avions	eu
vous	aviez	eu
ils	avaient	eu

Past anterior

j'	eus	eu
tu	eus	eu
il	eut	eu
nous	eûmes	eu
vous	eûtes	eu
ils	eurent	eu

Future perfect

j'	aurai	eu
tu	auras	eu
il	aura	eu
nous	aurons	eu
vous	aurez	eu
ils	auront	eu

IMPERATIVE

Present aie
ayons
ayez

Past aie eu
ayons eu
ayez eu

SUBJUNCTIVE

Present

(que) j'	aie
(que) tu	aies
(qu')il	ait
(que) nous	ayons
(que) vous	ayez
(qu')ils	aient

Imperfect

(que) j'	eusse
(que) tu	eusses
(qu')il	eût
(que) nous	eussions
(que) vous	eussiez
(qu')ils	eussent

Perfect

(que) j'	aie	eu
(que) tu	aies	eu
(qu')il	ait	eu
(que) nous	ayons	eu
(que) vous	ayez	eu
(qu')ils	aient	eu

Pluperfect

(que) j'	eusse	eu
(que) tu	eusses	eu
(qu')il	eût	eu
(que) nous	eussions	eu
(que) vous	eussiez	eu
(qu')ils	eussent	eu

CONDITIONAL

Present

j'	aurais
tu	aurais
il	aurait
nous	aurions
vous	auriez
ils	auraient

Past I

j'	aurais	eu
tu	aurais	eu
il	aurait	eu
nous	aurions	eu
vous	auriez	eu
ils	auraient	eu

Past II

j'	eusse	eu
tu	eusses	eu
il	eût	eu
nous	eussions	eu
vous	eussiez	eu
ils	eussent	eu

PARTICIPLE

Present ayant

Past eu, -e
ayant eu

INFINITIVE

Present avoir

Past avoir eu

9 aller

INDICATIVE

Present
je	vais
tu	vas
il	va
nous	allons
vous	allez
ils	vont

Imperfect
j'	allais
tu	allais
il	allait
nous	allions
vous	alliez
ils	allaient

Past historic
j'	allai
tu	allas
il	alla
nous	allâmes
vous	allâtes
ils	allèrent

Future
j'	irai
tu	iras
il	ira
nous	irons
vous	irez
ils	iront

Perfect
je	suis	allé
tu	es	allé
il	est	allé
nous	sommes	allés
vous	êtes	allés
ils	sont	allés

Pluperfect
j'	étais	allé
tu	étais	allé
il	était	allé
nous	étions	allés
vous	étiez	allés
ils	étaient	allés

Past anterior
je	fus	allé
tu	fus	allé
il	fut	allé
nous	fûmes	allés
vous	fûtes	allés
ils	furent	allés

Future perfect
je	serai	allé
tu	seras	allé
il	sera	allé
nous	serons	allés
vous	serez	allés
ils	seront	allés

IMPERATIVE

Present
va	
allons	
allez	

Past
sois	allé
soyons	allés
soyez	allés

SUBJUNCTIVE

Present
(que) j'	aille	
(que) tu	ailles	
(qu')il	aille	
(que) nous	allions	
(que) vous	alliez	
(qu')ils	aillent	

Imperfect
(que) j'	allasse	
(que) tu	allasses	
(qu')il	allât	
(que) nous	allassions	
(que) vous	allassiez	
(qu')ils	allassent	

Perfect
(que) je	sois	allé
(que) tu	sois	allé
(qu')il	soit	allé
(que) nous	soyons	allés
(que) vous	soyez	allés
(qu')ils	soient	allés

Pluperfect
(que) je	fusse	allé
(que) tu	fusses	allé
(qu')il	fût	allé
(que) nous	fussions	allés
(que) vous	fussiez	allés
(qu')ils	fussent	allés

CONDITIONAL

Present
j'	irais
tu	irais
il	irait
nous	irions
vous	iriez
ils	iraient

Past I
je	serais	allé
tu	serais	allé
il	serait	allé
nous	serions	allés
vous	seriez	allés
ils	seraient	allés

Past II
je	fusse	allé
tu	fusses	allé
il	fût	allé
nous	fussions	allés
vous	fussiez	allés
ils	fussent	allés

PARTICIPLE

Present allant

Past
allé, -e	
étant allé	

INFINITIVE

Present aller

Past être allé

10 faire

INDICATIVE

Present
je	fais
tu	fais
il	fait
nous	faisons
vous	faites
ils	font

Imperfect
je	faisais
tu	faisais
il	faisait
nous	faisions
vous	faisiez
ils	faisaient

Past historic
je	fis
tu	fis
il	fit
nous	fîmes
vous	fîtes
ils	firent

Future
je	ferai
tu	feras
il	fera
nous	ferons
vous	ferez
ils	feront

Perfect
j'	ai	fait
tu	as	fait
il	a	fait
nous	avons	fait
vous	avez	fait
ils	ont	fait

Pluperfect
j'	avais	fait
tu	avais	fait
il	avait	fait
nous	avions	fait
vous	aviez	fait
ils	avaient	fait

Past anterior
j'	eus	fait
tu	eus	fait
il	eut	fait
nous	eûmes	fait
vous	eûtes	fait
ils	eurent	fait

Future perfect
j'	aurai	fait
tu	auras	fait
il	aura	fait
nous	aurons	fait
vous	aurez	fait
ils	auront	fait

IMPERATIVE

Present
fais	
faisons	
faites	

Past
aie	fait
ayons	fait
ayez	fait

SUBJUNCTIVE

Present
(que) je	fasse	
(que) tu	fasses	
(qu')il	fasse	
(que) nous	fassions	
(que) vous	fassiez	
(qu')ils	fassent	

Imperfect
(que) je	fisse	
(que) tu	fisses	
(qu')il	fît	
(que) nous	fissions	
(que) vous	fissiez	
(qu')ils	fissent	

Perfect
(que) j'	aie	fait
(que) tu	aies	fait
(qu')il	ait	fait
(que) nous	ayons	fait
(que) vous	ayez	fait
(qu')ils	aient	fait

Pluperfect
(que) j'	eusse	fait
(que) tu	eusses	fait
(qu')il	eût	fait
(que) nous	eussions	fait
(que) vous	eussiez	fait
(qu')ils	eussent	fait

CONDITIONAL

Present
je	ferais
tu	ferais
il	ferait
nous	ferions
vous	feriez
ils	feraient

Past I
j'	aurais	fait
tu	aurais	fait
il	aurait	fait
nous	aurions	fait
vous	auriez	fait
ils	auraient	fait

Past II
j'	eusse	fait
tu	eusses	fait
il	eût	fait
nous	eussions	fait
vous	eussiez	fait
ils	eussent	fait

PARTICIPLE

Present faisant

Past
fait, -e	
ayant fait	

INFINITIVE

Present faire

Past avoir fait

PASSIVE être aimé

INDICATIVE

Present

je	suis	aimé
tu	es	aimé
il	est	aimé
nous	sommes	aimés
vous	êtes	aimés
ils	sont	aimés

Imperfect

j'	étais	aimé
tu	étais	aimé
il	était	aimé
nous	étions	aimés
vous	étiez	aimés
ils	étaient	aimés

Past historic

je	fus	aimé
tu	fus	aimé
il	fut	aimé
nous	fûmes	aimés
vous	fûtes	aimés
ils	furent	aimés

Future

je	serai	aimé
tu	seras	aimé
il	sera	aimé
nous	serons	aimés
vous	serez	aimés
ils	seront	aimés

Perfect

j'	ai	été	aimé
tu	as	été	aimé
il	a	été	aimé
nous	avons	été	aimés
vous	avez	été	aimés
ils	ont	été	aimés

Pluperfect

j'	avais	été	aimé
tu	avais	été	aimé
il	avait	été	aimé
nous	avions	été	aimés
vous	aviez	été	aimés
ils	avaient	été	aimés

Past anterior

j'	eus	été	aimé
tu	eus	été	aimé
il	eut	été	aimé
nous	eûmes	été	aimés
vous	eûtes	été	aimés
ils	eurent	été	aimés

Future perfect

j'	aurai	été	aimé
tu	auras	été	aimé
il	aura	été	aimé
nous	aurons	été	aimés
vous	aurez	été	aimés
ils	auront	été	aimés

IMPERATIVE

Present

sois	aimé
soyons	aimés
soyez	aimés

Past (*obsolete*)

SUBJUNCTIVE

Present

(que)	je	sois	aimé
(que)	tu	sois	aimé
(qu')	il	soit	aimé
(que)	nous	soyons	aimés
(que)	vous	soyez	aimés
(qu')	ils	soient	aimés

Imperfect

(que)	je	fusse	aimé
(que)	tu	fusses	aimé
(qu')	il	fût	aimé
(que)	ns	fussions	aimés
(que)	vs	fussiez	aimés
(qu')	ils	fussent	aimés

Perfect

(que)	j'	aie	été	aimé
(que)	tu	aies	été	aimé
(qu')	il	ait	été	aimé
(que)	ns	ayons	été	aimés
(que)	vs	ayez	été	aimés
(qu')	ils	aient	été	aimés

Pluperfect

(que)	j'	eusse	été	aimé
(que)	tu	eusses	été	aimé
(qu')	il	eût	été	aimé
(que)	ns	eussions	été	aimés
(que)	vs	eussiez	été	aimés
(qu')	ils	eussent	été	aimés

CONDITIONAL

Present

je	serais	aimé
tu	serais	aimé
il	serait	aimé
nous	serions	aimés
vous	seriez	aimés
ils	seraient	aimés

Past I

j'	aurais	été	aimé
tu	aurais	été	aimé
il	aurait	été	aimé
ns	aurions	été	aimés
vs	auriez	été	aimés
ils	auraient	été	aimés

Past II

j'	eusse	été	aimé
tu	eusses	été	aimé
il	eût	été	aimé
ns	eussions	été	aimés
vs	eussiez	été	aimés
ils	eussent	été	aimés

PARTICIPLE

Present étant aimé

Past été aimé
ayant été aimé

INFINITIVE

Present être aimé

Past avoir été aimé

REFLEXIVE s'adonner

INDICATIVE

Present

je	m'	adonne
tu	t'	adonnes
il	s'	adonne
nous	nous	adonnons
vous	vous	adonnez
ils	s'	adonnent

Imperfect

je	m'	adonnais
tu	t'	adonnais
il	s'	adonnait
nous	nous	adonnions
vous	vous	adonniez
ils	s'	adonnaient

Past historic

je	m'	adonnai
tu	t'	adonnas
il	s'	adonna
nous	nous	adonnâmes
vous	vous	adonnâtes
ils	s'	adonnèrent

Future

je	m'	adonnerai
tu	t'	adonneras
il	s'	adonnera
nous	nous	adonnerons
vous	vous	adonnerez
ils	s'	adonneront

Perfect

je	me	suis	adonné
tu	t'	es	adonné
il	s'	est	adonné
ns	ns	sommes	adonnés
vs	vs	êtes	adonnés
ils	se	sont	adonnés

Pluperfect

je	m'	étais	adonné
tu	t'	étais	adonné
il	s'	était	adonné
ns	ns	étions	adonnés
vs	vs	étiez	adonnés
ils	s'	étaient	adonnés

Past anterior

je	me	fus	adonné
tu	te	fus	adonné
il	se	fut	adonné
ns	ns	fûmes	adonnés
vs	vs	fûtes	adonnés
ils	se	furent	adonnés

Future perfect

je	me	serai	adonné
tu	te	seras	adonné
il	se	sera	adonné
ns	ns	serons	adonnés
vs	vs	serez	adonnés
ils	se	seront	adonnés

IMPERATIVE

Present adonne - toi
adonnons - nous
adonnez - vous

Past (*obsolete*)

SUBJUNCTIVE

Present

(que) je	m'	adonne
(que) tu	t'	adonnes
(qu') il	s'	adonne
(que) ns	ns	adonnions
(que) vs	vs	adonniez
(qu') ils	s'	adonnent

Imperfect

(que) je	m'	adonnasse
(que) tu	t'	adonnasses
(qu') il	s'	adonnât
(que) ns	ns	adonnassions
(que) vs	vs	adonnassiez
(qu') ils	s'	adonnassent

Perfect

(que) je	me	sois	adonné
(que) tu	te	sois	adonné
(qu') il	se	soit	adonné
(que) ns	ns	soyons	adonnés
(que) vs	vs	soyez	adonnés
(qu') ils	se	soient	adonnés

Pluperfect

(que) je	me	fusse	adonné
(que) tu	te	fusses	adonné
(qu') il	se	fût	adonné
(que) ns	ns	fussions	adonnés
(que) vs	vs	fussiez	adonnés
(qu') ils	se	fussent	adonnés

CONDITIONAL

Present

je	m'	adonnerais
tu	t'	adonnerais
il	s'	adonnerait
nous	nous	adonnerions
vous	vous	adonneriez
ils	s'	adonneraient

Past I

je	me	serais	adonné
tu	te	serais	adonné
il	se	serait	adonné
ns	ns	serions	adonnés
vs	vs	seriez	adonnés
ils	se	seraient	adonnés

Past II

je	me	fusse	adonné
tu	te	fusses	adonné
il	se	fût	adonné
ns	ns	fussions	adonnés
vs	vs	fussiez	adonnés
ils	se	fussent	adonnés

PARTICIPLE

Present s'adonnant

Past s'étant adonné

INFINITIVE Present

Present s'adonner

Past s'être adonné

INFINITIVE	Rules	INDICATIVE			
		Present	**Imperfect**	**Past Historic**	**Future**
11 créer	*always* é	je crée, -es, -e, -ent nous créons, -ez	je créais …	je créai …	je créerai …
12 placer	c	je place, -es, -e, -ez, -ent	nous placions, -iez	ils placèrent	je placerai …
	ç *before* a *and* o	nous plaçons	je plaçais, -ais, -ait, -aient	je plaçai, -as, -a, -âmes, -âtes	
13 manger	g	je mange, -es, -e, -ez, -ent	nous mangions, -iez	ils mangèrent	je mangerai …
	ge *before* a *and* o	nous mangeons	je mangeais, -eais, -eait, -eaient	je mangeai, -as, -a, -âmes, -âtes	
14 céder	è *before silent final syllable*	je cède, -es, -e, -ent			
	é	nous cédons, -ez	je cédais …	je cédai …	je céderai …
15 assiéger	è *before silent final syllable*	j'assiège, -es, -e, -ent			
	ge *before* a *and* o	nous assiégeons	j'assiégeais, -eais, -eait, -eaient	j'assiégeai	
	é *before silent syllable*				j'assiégerai …
16 lever	è *before silent syllable*	je lève, -es, -e, -ent			je lèverai …
	e	nous levons, -ez	je levais …	je levai …	
17 geler	è *before silent syllable*	je gèle, -es, -e, -ent			je gèlerai …
	e	nous gelons, -ez	je gelais …	je gelai …	
18 acheter	è *before silent syllable*	j'achète, -es, -e, -ent			j'achèterai …
	e	nous achetons, -ez	j'achetais …	j'achetai …	
19 appeler	ll *before mute* e	j'appelle, -es, -e, -ent			j'appellerai …
	l	nous appelons, -ez	j'appelais …	j'appelai …	
20 jeter	tt *before mute* e	je jette, -es, -e, -ent			je jetterai …
	t	nous jetons, -ez	je jetais …	je jetai …	
21 payer	i *before mute* e	je paie, -es, -e, -ent			je paierai …
	or y	je paye, -es, -e, -ent nous payons, -ez	je payais …	je payai …	je payerai …

CONDITIONAL	SUBJUNCTIVE		IMPERATIVE	PARTICIPLE		
Present	**Present**	**Imperfect**		**Present**	**Past**	
je créerais …	que je crée …	que je créasse …	crée créons, -ez	créant	créé, -e	**11**
je placerais …	que je place …	que je plaçasse …	place, -ez plaçons	plaçant	placé, -e	**12**
je mangerais …	que je mange …	que je mangeasse …	mange, -ez mangeons	mangeant	mangé, -e	**13**
je céderais …	que je cède, -es, -e, -ent que nous cédions, -iez	que je cédasse …	cède cédons, -ez	cédant	cédé, -e	**14**
j'assiégerais …	que j'assiège … que nous assiégions, -iez	que j'assiégeasse …	assiège assiégeons	assiégeant	assiégé, -e	**15**
je lèverais …	que je lève, -es, -e, -ent que nous levions, -iez	que je levasse …	lève levons, -ez	levant	levé, -e	**16**
je gèlerais …	que je gèle, -es, -e, -ent que nous gelions, -iez	que je gelasse …	gèle gelons, -ez	gelant	gelé, -e	**17**
j'achèterais …	que j'achète, -es, -e, -ent que nous achetions, -iez	que j'achetasse …	achète achetons, -ez	achetant	acheté, -e	**18**
j'appellerais …	que j'appelle, -es, -e, -ent que nous appelions, -iez	que j'appelasse …	appelle appelons, -ez	appelant	appelé, -e	**19**
je jetterais …	que je jette, -es, -e, -ent que nous jetions, -iez	que je jetasse …	jette jetons, -ez	jetant	jeté, -e	**20**
je paierais … je payerais …	que je paie, -es, -e, -ent que je paye, -es, -e, -ent que nous payions, -iez	que je payasse …	paie paye payons, -ez	payant	payé, -e	**21**

INFINITIVE	Rules	INDICATIVE			
		Present	**Imperfect**	**Past Historic**	**Future**
22 essuyer	i *before mute* e	j'essuie, -es, -e, -ent			j'essuierai ...
	y	nous essuyons, -ez	j'essuyais ...	j'essuyai ...	
23 employer	i *before mute* e	j'emploie, -es, -e, -ent			j'emploierai ..
	y	nous employons, -ez	j'employais ...	j'employai ...	
24 envoyer	i *before mute* e	j'envoie, -es, -e, -ent			
	y	nous envoyons, -ez	j'envoyais ...	j'envoyai ...	
	err				j'enverrai ...
25 haïr	i	je hais, -s, -t			
	ï	ns haïssons, -ez, -ent	je haïssais ...	je haïs ... (haïmes, haïtes)	je haïrai ...
26 courir		je cours ...	je courais ...	je courus ...	je courrai ...
27 cueillir		je cueille, -es, -e, nous cueillons ...	je cueillais ...	je cueillis ...	je cueillerai ...
28 assaillir		j'assaille, -es, -e, nous assaillons, -ez, -ent	j'assaillais ...	j'assaillis ...	j'assaillirai ...
29 fuir	i *before consonants and* e	je fuis, -s, -t, -ent		je fuis ...	je fuirai ...
	y *before* a, ez, i, o	nous fuyons, -ez	je fuyais ...		
30 partir	*without* t	je pars ...			
	with t	il part ...	je partais ...	je partis ...	je partirai ...
31 bouillir	ou	je bous, s, t			
	ouill	nous bouillons ...	je bouillais ...	je bouillis ...	je bouillirai ...
32 couvrir		je couvre, -es, -e, nous couvrons ...	je couvrais ...	je couvris ...	je couvrirai ...
33 vêtir		je vêts ...	je vêtais ...	je vêtis ...	je vêtirai ...
34 mourir	eur	je meurs, -s, -t, -ent			
	our	nous mourons, -ez	je mourais ...	je mourus ...	je mourrai ...
35 acquérir	quier	j'acquiers, -s, -t, -ièrent			
	quer	nous acquérons -ez	j'acquérais ...		j'acquerrai ...
	qu			j'acquis ...	

CONDITIONAL	SUBJUNCTIVE		IMPERATIVE	PARTICIPLE	
Present	Present	Imperfect		Present	Past
j'essuierais ...	que j'essuie, -es, -e, -ent		essuie		**22**
	que nous essuyions, -iez	que j'essuyasse ...	essuyons, -ez	essuyant	essuyé, e
j'emploierais ...	que j'emploie, -es, -e, -ent		emploie		**23**
	que nous employions, -iez	que j'employasse ...	employons, -ez	employant	employé, -e
	que j'envoie, -es, -e, -ent		envoie		**24**
	que nous envoyions, -iez	que j'envoyasse ...	envoyons, -ez	envoyant	envoyé, -e
j'enverrais ...					
			hais		**25**
je haïrais ...	que je haïsse, qu'il haïsse	que je haïsse, qu'il haït	haïssons, haïssez	haïssant	haï, -e
je courrais ...	que je coure ...	que je courusse ...	cours, courons, -ez	courant	couru, -e **26**
je cueillerais ...	que je cueille ...	que je cueillisse ...	cueille cuillons, -ez	cueillant	cueilli, -e **27**
j'assaillirais ...	que j'assaille ...	que j'assaillisse	assaille assaillons, -ez	assaillant	assailli, -e **28**
je fuirais ...	que je fuie, -es, -e, -ent	que je fuisse ...	fuis		fui, -e **29**
	que nous fuyions, -iez		fuyons, -ez	fuyant	
			pars		**30**
je partirais ...	que je parte ...	que je partisse ...	partons, -ez	partant	parti, -e
			bous		**31**
je bouillirais ...	que je bouille ...	que je bouillisse ...	bouillons, -ez	bouillant	bouilli, -e
je couvrirais ...	que je couvre, -es, -e, que nous couvrions ...	que je couvrisse ...	couvre couvrons, -ez	couvrant	couvert, -e **32**
je vêtirais ...	que je vête ...	que je vêtisse ...	vêts vêtons, vêtez	vêtant	vêtu, -e **33**
	que je meure ...		meurs		mort, -e **34**
je mourrais ...		que je mourusse ...	mourons, -ez	mourant	
	que j'acquière, -es, -e, -ent		acquiers		**35**
j'acquerrais ...	que nous acquérions, -iez		acquérons, -ez	acquérant	
		que j'acquisse ...			acquis, -e

INFINITIVE	Rules	INDICATIVE			
		Present	**Imperfect**	**Past Historic**	**Future**
36 venir	i	je viens, -s, -t, -nent		je vins ... ils vinrent	je viendrai ...
	e	nous venons, -ez	je venais ...		
37 gésir	*Defective*	je gis, tu gis, il gît, nous gisons, -ez, -ent	je gisais ...		
38 ouïr	*Archaic*	j'ois ... nous oyons ...	j'oyais ...	j'ouïs ...	j'ouïrai ...
39 pleuvoir		il pleut ils pleuvent	il pleuvait ils pleuvaient	il plut ils plurent	il pleuvra ils pleuvront
40 pourvoir	i	je pourvois, -s, -t, -ent			je pourvoirai ...
	y	nous pourvoyons, -ez	je pourvoyais ...		
	u			je pourvus ...	
41 asseoir	ie	j'assieds, -ds, -d			j'assiérai ...
	ey	nous asseyons, -ez, -ent	j'asseyais ...		
	i			j'assis ...	
asseoir (oi/oy *replace* ie/ey)	oi	j'assois, -s, -t, -ent			j'assoirai ...
	oy	nous assoyons, -ez	j'assoyais ...		
42 prévoir	oi	je prévois, -s, -t, -ent			je prévoirai ...
	oy	nous prévoyons, -ez	je prévoyais ...		
	i/u			je prévis ...	
43 mouvoir	eu	je meus, -s, -t, -vent			
	ou	nous mouvons, -ez	je mouvais ...		je mouvrai ...
	u			je mus, -s, -t, -(û)mes, -(û)tes, -rent	
44 devoir	û *in the past participle masc. sing.*	je dois, -s, -t -vent nous devons, -ez	je devais ...	je dus ...	je devrai ...
45 valoir	au, aille	je vaux, -x, -t			je vaudrai ...
	al	nous valons, -ez, -ent	je valais ...	je valus ...	
prévaloir					

CONDITIONAL	SUBJUNCTIVE		IMPERATIVE	PARTICIPLE	
Present	Present	Imperfect		Present	Past

36

| je viendrais … | que je vienne, -es, -e, -ent | que je vinsse … | viens | | |
| | que nous venions, -iez | | venons, -ez | venant | venu, -e |

37

| | | | | gisant | |

38

| j'ouïrais … | que j'oie … | que j'ouïsse … | ois | | ouï, -e |
| | que nous oyions … | | oyons, -ez | oyant | |

39

| il pleuvrait | qu'il pleuve | qu'il plût | | pleuvant | plu |
| ils pleuvraient | qu'ils pleuvent | qu'ils plussent | | | |

40

je pourvoirais …	que je pourvoie, -es, -e, -ent		pourvois		
	que nous pourvoyions, -iez		pourvoyons, -ez	pourvoyant	
		que je pourvusse …			pourvu, -e

41

j'assiérais …			assieds		
	que j' asseye …		asseyons, -ez	asséyant	
	que nous asseyions …				
		que j'assisse …			assis, -e
j'assoirais …	que j'assoie, -es, -e, -ent		assois		
	que nous assoyions, -iez		assoyons, -ez	assoyant	

42

je prévoirais …	que je prévoie, -es, -e, -ent		prévois		
	que ns prévoyions, -iez		prévoyons, -ez	prévoyant	
		que je prévisse …			prévu, -e

43

	que je meuve, -es, -e, -ent		meus		
je mouvrais …	que nous mouvions, -iez		mouvons, -ez	mouvant	
		que je musse …			mû, mue

44

| | que je doive, -es, -e, -ent | que je dusse … | dois | | dû, due |
| je devrais … | que nous devions, -iez | | devons, -ez | devant | |

45

je vaudrais …	que je vaille, -es, -e, -ent		vaux		
	que nous valions, -iez	que je valusse …	valons, -ez	valant	valu, -e
	que je prévale, -es, -e				

INFINITIVE	Rules	INDICATIVE			
		Present	Imperfect	Past Historic	Future
46 voir	oi	je vois, -s, -t, -ent			
	oy	nous voyons, -ez	je voyais ...		
	i/e/u			je vis ...	je verrai ...
47 savoir	5 forms	je sais, -s, -t, nous savons, -ez, -ent	je savais ...	je sus ...	je saurai ...
48 vouloir	veu/veuil	je veux, -x, -t, veulent			
	voul/voudr	nous voulons, -ez	je voulais ...	je voulus ...	je voudrai ...
49 pouvoir	eu/u(i)	je peux, -x, -t, peuvent		je pus ...	
	ouv/our	nous pouvons, -ez	je pouvais ...		je pourrai ...
50 falloir	*Impersonal*	il faut	il fallait	il fallut	il faudra
51 déchoir	choir *and* échoir *are defective*	je déchois, -s, -t, -ent			
		nous déchoyons, -ez	je déchoyais ...	je déchus ...	je décherrai ...
52 prendre	prend	je prends, -ds, -d			je prendrai ...
	pren	nous prenons, -ez ils prennent	je prenais ...		
	pri(s)			je pris ...	
53 rompre		je romps, -ps, -pt, nous rompons ...	je rompais ...	je rompis ...	je romprai ...
54 craindre	ain/aind	je crains, -s, -t			je craindrai ...
	aign	nous craignons, -ez, -ent	je craignais ...	je craignis ...	
55 peindre	ein	je peins, -s, -t			je peindrai ...
	eign	nous peignons, -ez, -ent	je peignais ...	je peignis ...	
56 joindre	oin/oind	je joins, -s, -t			je joindrai ...
	oign	nous joignons, -ez, -ent	je joignais ...	je joignis ...	
57 vaincre	ainc	je vaincs, -cs, -c			je vaincrai ...
	ainqu	nous vainquons, -ez, -ent	je vainquais ...	je vainquis ...	
58 traire	i	je trais, -s, -t, -ent		*(obsolete)*	je trairai ...
	y	nous trayons, -ez	je trayais ...		

CONDITIONAL	SUBJUNCTIVE		IMPERATIVE	PARTICIPLE	
Present	Present	Imperfect		Present	Past
	que je voie, -es, -e, -ent		vois			**46**
	que nous voyions, -iez		voyons, -ez	voyant	
je verrais ...		que je visse ...			vu, -e
je saurais ...	que je sache ...	que je susse ...	sache, -ons, -ez	sachant	su, -e	**47**
	que je veuille, -es, -e, -ent		veux (veuille)			**48**
je voudrais ...	que nous voulions, -iez	que je voulusse ...	voulons, -ez (veuillez)	voulant	voulu, -e
	que je puisse ...	que je pusse ...	(obsolete)		pu	**49**
je pourrais ...				pouvant	
il faudrait	qu'il faille	qu'il fallût	(no form)	(obsolete)	fallu	**50**
	que je déchoie, -es, -e, -ent		déchois	(no form but échéant)		**51**
je décherrais ...	que nous déchoyions, -iez	que je déchusse ...	déchoyons, -ez		déchu, -e
je prendrais ...			prends			**52**
	que je prenne ...		prenons, -ez	prenant	
		que je prisse ...			pris, -e
je romprais ...	que je rompe ...	que je rompisse ...	romps -pons, -pez	rompant	rompu, -e	**53**
je craindrais ...			crains		craint, -e	**54**
	que je craigne ...	que je craignisse ...	craignons, -ez	craignant	
je peindrais ...			peins		peint, -e	**55**
	que je peigne ...	que je peignisse ...	peignons, -ez	peignant	
je joindrais ...			joins		joint, -e	**56**
	que je joigne ...	que je joignisse ...	joignons, -ez	joignant	
je vaincrais ...			vaincs		vaincu, -e	**57**
	que je vainque ...	que je vainquisse ...	vainquons, -ez	vainquant	
je trairais ...	que je traie, -es, -e, -ent	(obsolete)	trais		trait, -e	**58**
	que nous trayions, -yiez		trayons, -ez	trayant	

INFINITIVE	Rules	INDICATIVE			
		Present	**Imperfect**	**Past Historic**	**Future**
59 plaire	ai	je plais, tu plais, il plaît (*but* il tait) nous plaisons ...	je plaisais ...		je plairai ...
	u			je plus ...	
60 mettre	met	je mets, nous mettons	je mettais ...		je mettrai ...
	mis			je mis ...	
61 battre	t	je bats, -ts, -t			
	tt	nous battons ...	je battais ...	je battis ...	je battrai ...
62 suivre	ui	je suis, -s, -t			
	uiv	nous suivons ...	je suivais ...	je suivis ...	je suivrai ...
63 vivre	vi/viv	je vis, -s, -t, nous vivons ...	je vivais ...		je vivrai ...
	véc			je vécus ...	
64 suffire		je suffis, -s, -t, nous suffisons ...	je suffisais ...	je suffis ...	je suffirai ...
65 médire		je médis, -s, -t, nous médisons, vous médisez (*but* vous dites, redites)	je médisais ...	je médis ...	je médirai ...
66 lire	i	je lis, -s, -t			je lirai ...
	is	nous lisons, -ez, -ent	je lisais ...		
	u			je lus ...	
67 écrire	i	j'écris, -s, -t			j'écrirai ...
	iv	nous écrivons, -ez, -ent	j'écrivais ...	j'écrivis ...	
68 rire		je ris, -s, -t, nous rions ...	je riais ... nous riions, -iez	je ris ... nous rîmes ...	je rirai ...
69 conduire		je conduis ...	je conduisais ...	je conduisis...	je conduirai ..
70 boire	oi	je bois, -s, -t, -vent			je boirai ...
	u(v)	nous buvons, -ez	je buvais ...	je bus ...	
71 croire	oi	je crois, -s, -t, ils croient			je croirai ...
	oy	nous croyons, -ez	je croyais ...		
	u			je crus ...	

CONDITIONAL	SUBJUNCTIVE		IMPERATIVE	PARTICIPLE		
Present	**Present**	**Imperfect**		**Present**	**Past**	
je plairais ...	que je plaise ...		plais plaisons, -ez	plaisant		**59**
		que je plusse ...			plu	
je mettrais ...	que je mette ...		mets mettons, -ez	mettant		**60**
		que je misse ...			mis, -e	
			bats			**61**
je battrais ...	que je batte ...	que je battisse ...	battons, -ez	battant	battu, -e	
			suis			**62**
je suivrais ...	que je suive ...	que je suivisse ...	suivons, -ez	suivant	suivi, -e	
			vis			**63**
je vivrais ...	que je vive ...		vivons, -ez	vivant		
		que je vécusse ...			vécu, -e	
je suffirais ...	que je suffise ...	que je suffisse ...	suffis suffisons, -ez	suffisant	suffi (*but* confit, déconfit, frit, circoncis)	**64**
je médirais ...	que je médise ... que nous médisions, -iez	que je médisse ...	médis médisons médisez (*but* dites, redites)	médisant	médit	**65**
			lis			**66**
je lirais ...	que je lise ...		lisons, -ez	lisant		
		que je lusse ...			lu, -e	
			écris		écrit, -e	**67**
j'écrirais ...	que j'écrive ...	que j'écrivisse ...	écrivons, -ez ·	écrivant		
			ris, rions,	riant	ri	**68**
je rirais ...	que je rie ...	que je risse ...	riez			
	que nous riions, -iez	que nous rissions ...				
je conduirais ...	que je conduise ...	que je conduisisse ...	conduis conduisons, -ez	conduisant	conduit, -e (*but* lui, nui)	**69**
			bois			**70**
je boirais ...	que je boive, -es, -e, -ent					
	que nous buvions, -iez	que je busse ...	buvons, -ez	buvant	bu, -e	
je croirais ...	que je croie ...		crois			**71**
			croyons, -ez	croyant		
		que je crusse ...			cru, -e	

INFINITIVE	Rules	INDICATIVE			
		Present	**Imperfect**	**Past Historic**	**Future**
72 croître	oî	je croîs, -s, -t			je croîtrai ...
	oiss	nous croissons, -ez, -ent	je croissais ...		
	û			je crûs ...	
73 connaître		je connais, -s, -ssons, -ssez, -ssent	je connaissais ...	je connus ...	
	î *before* t	il connaît			je connaîtrai ...
74 naître	î *before* t	je nais, nais, naît			je naîtrai ...
	naisse	nous naissons, -ez, -ent	je naissais ...		
	naqu			je naquis ...	
75 résoudre	ou/oudr	je résous, -s, -t		(absoudre	je résoudrai...
	ol/olv	nous résolvons, -ez, -ent	je résolvais ...	*and* dissoudre *have no past historic*)	
	olu			je résolus ...	
76 coudre	oud	je couds, -ds, -d			je coudrai ...
	ous	nous cousons, -ez, -ent	je cousais ...	je cousis ...	
77 moudre	moud	je mouds, -ds, -d			je moudrai ...
	moul	nous moulons, -ez, -ent	je moulais ...	je moulus ...	
78 conclure		je conclus, -s, -t, nous concluons, -ez, -ent	je concluais ...	je conclus ...	je conclurai ...
79 clore	*Defective*	je clos, -os, -ôt ils closent	(*obsolete*)	(*obsolete*)	je clorai ...
80 maudire		je maudis, -s, -t nous maudissons, -ez, -ent	je maudissais ...	je maudis ...	je maudirai ...

CONDITIONAL	SUBJUNCTIVE		IMPERATIVE	PARTICIPLE	
Present	**Present**	**Imperfect**		**Present**	**Past**
je croîtrais...	que je croisse ...	que je crûsse ...	croîs croissons, -ez	croissant	crû, crue (*but* accru, -e) **72**
je connaîtrais ...	que je connaisse ...	que je connusse ...	connais, -ssons, -ssez	connaissant	connu, -e **73**
je naîtrais ...	que je naisse ...	que je naquisse ...	nais naissons, -ez	naissant	né, -e **74**
je résoudrais ...	que je résolve ...	que je résolusse ...	résous résolvons, -ez	résolvant	(absous, -oute; **75** dissous, -oute) résolu, -e
je coudrais ...	que je couse ...	que je cousisse ...	couds cousons, -ez	cousant	cousu, -e **76**
je moudrais ...	que je moule ...	que je moulusse ...	mouds moulons, -ez	moulant	moulu, -e **77**
je conclurais ...	que je conclue ...	que je conclusse ...	conclus concluons, -ez	concluant	conclu, -e **78** (*but* inclus, -e)
je clorais ...	que je close ...	(*obsolete*)	clos	closant	clos, -e **79**
je maudirais ...	que je maudisse qu'il maudisse	que je maudisse qu'il maudît	maudis -ssons, -ssez	maudissant	maudit, -e **80**

Verbes irréguliers anglais

Vous trouverez ci-après la liste des formes irrégulières des verbes qui figurent dans le dictionnaire, à l'exception :

- des verbes composés s'écrivant avec un trait d'union et dont l'un des éléments est un verbe irrégulier (ex. *baby-sit*) ;
- des verbes dont on double la dernière consonne au prétérit et au participe passé (ex. *spot*) (la conjugaison est indiquée dans le dictionnaire pour cette catégorie) ;
- des verbes dont le *y* final devient *-ie* dès que l'on ajoute la désinence *-d* ou *-s* (ex. *try*).

Les verbes dont les formes irrégulières ne s'appliquent qu'à certains sens sont signalés par un astérisque (*) (ex. *costed*).

Infinitif	Prétérit	Participe Passé
abide	abode, abided	abode, abided
arise	arose	arisen
awake	awoke	awoken
be	was/were	been
bear	bore	borne
beat	beat	beaten
become	became	become
befall	befell	befallen
begin	began	begun
behold	beheld	beheld
bend	bent	bent
beseech	beseeched, besought	beseeched, besought
beset	beset	beset
bet	bet, betted	bet, betted
bid	bade, bid	bidden, bid
bind	bound	bound
bite	bit	bitten
bleed	bled	bled
blow	blew	blown
break	broke	broken
breed	bred	bred
bring	brought	brought
broadcast	broadcast	broadcast
browbeat	browbeat	browbeaten
build	built	built
burn	burned, burnt *GB*	burned, burnt *GB*
bust	bust, busted *GB*	bust, busted *GB*
buy	bought	bought
cast	cast	cast
catch	caught	caught
choose	chose	chosen

Infinitif	Prétérit	Participe Passé
cleave	clove, cleaved	cleft, cleaved, cloven
cling	clung	clung
come	came	come
cost	cost, *costed	cost, *costed
creep	crept	crept
crow	crowed, crew‡	crowed
cut	cut	cut
deal	dealt	dealt
dig	dug	dug
dive	dived *GB*, dove *US*	dived
do	did	done
draw	drew	drawn
dream	dreamed, dreamt *GB*	dreamed, dreamt *GB*
drink	drank	drunk
drive	drove	driven
dwell	dwelt	dwelt
eat	ate	eaten
fall	fell	fallen
feed	fed	fed
feel	felt	felt
fight	fought	fought
find	found	found
flee	fled	fled
fling	flung	flung
floodlight	floodlit	floodlit
fly	flew	flown
forbear	forbore	forborne
forbid	forbade, forbad	forbidden
forecast	forecast	forecast
foresee	foresaw	foreseen
foretell	foretold	foretold
forget	forgot	forgotten
forgive	forgave	forgiven
forsake	forsook	forsaken
forswear	forswore	forsworn
freeze	froze	frozen
gainsay	gainsaid	gainsaid
get	got	got, gotten *US*
give	gave	given
go	went	gone
grind	ground	ground
grow	grew	grown
hamstring	hamstrung	hamstrung
hang	hung, *hanged	hung, *hanged
have	had	had

Infinitif	Prétérit	Participe Passé	Infinitif	Prétérit	Participe Passé
hear	heard	heard	overrun	overran	overrun
heave	heaved, *hove	heaved, *hove	oversee	oversaw	overseen
hew	hewed	hewn, hewed	overshoot	overshot	overshot
hide	hid	hidden	oversleep	overslept	overslept
hit	hit	hit	overtake	overtook	overtaken
hold	held	held	overthrow	overthrew	overthrown
hurt	hurt	hurt	partake	partook	partaken
inlay	inlaid	inlaid	pay	paid	paid
inset	inset	inset	plead	pleaded, pled US	pleaded, pled US
interweave	interwove	interwoven	prove	proved	proved, proven
			put	put	put
keep	kept	kept			
kneel	kneeled, knelt	kneeled, knelt	quit	quit, quitted	quit, quitted
knit	knitted, knit	knitted, knit			
know	knew	known	read /ri:d/	read /red/	read /red/
			rebuild	rebuilt	rebuilt
lay	laid	laid	recast	recast	recast
lead	led	led	redo	redid	redone
lean	leaned, leant GB	leaned, leant GB	remake	remade	remade
leap	leaped, leapt GB	leaped, leapt GB	rend	rent	rent
learn	learned,	learned,	repay	repaid	repaid
	learnt GB	learnt GB	resell	resold	resold
leave	left	left	reset	reset	reset
lend	lent	lent	resit	resat	resat
let	let	let	retake	retook	retaken
lie	lay	lain	rewrite	rewrote	rewritten
light	lit, *lighted	lit, *lighted	rid	rid	rid
lose	lost	lost	ride	rode	ridden
			ring	rang	rung
make	made	made	rise	rose	risen
mean	meant	meant	run	ran	run
meet	met	met			
mishear	misheard	misheard	saw	sawed	sawed, sawn GB
mislay	mislaid	mislaid	say	said	said
mislead	misled	misled	see	saw	seen
misread	misread	misread	seek	sought	sought
/ˌmɪs'riːd/	/ˌmɪs'red/	/ˌmɪs'red/	sell	sold	sold
mistake	mistook	mistaken	send	sent	sent
misunder-	misunderstood	misunderstood	set	set	set
stand			sew	sewed	sewn, sewed
mow	mowed	mowed, mown	shake	shook	shaken
			shear	sheared	shorn, *sheared
outbid	outbid	outbid,	shed	shed	shed
		outbidden US	shine	shone, *shined	shone, *shined
outdo	outdid	outdone	shoe	shod	shod
outgrow	outgrew	outgrown	shoot	shot	shot
output	output,	output,	show	showed	shown
	outputted	outputted	shrink	shrank	shrunk,
outrun	outran	outrun	shrunken		
outsell	outsold	outsold	shut	shut	shut
overcome	overcame	overcome	sing	sang	sung
overdo	overdid	overdone	sink	sank	sunk
overdraw	overdrew	overdrawn	sit	sat	sat
overeat	overate	overeaten	slay	slew	slain
overhang	overhung	overhung	sleep	slept	slept
overhear	overheard	overheard	slide	slid	slid
overlay	overlaid	overlaid	sling	slung	slung
overpay	overpaid	overpaid	slink	slunk	slunk
override	overrode	overridden	slit	slit	slit

Infinitif	Prétérit	Participe Passé	Infinitif	Prétérit	Participe Passé
smell	smelled, smelt *GB*	smelled, smelt *GB*	tell	told	told
sow	sowed	sowed, sown	think	thought	thought
speak	spoke	spoken	thrive	thrived, throve	thrived, thriven‡
speed	sped, *speeded	sped, *speeded	throw	threw	thrown
spell	spelled, spelt *GB*	spelled, spelt *GB*	thrust	thrust	thrust
spend	spent	spent	tread	trod	trodden
spill	spilled, spilt *GB*	spilled, spilt *GB*	undercut	undercut	undercut
spin	spun, span‡	spun	undergo	underwent	undergone
spit	spat	spat	underlie	underlay	underlain
split	split	split	underpay	underpaid	underpaid
spoil	spoiled, spoilt *GB*	spoiled, spoilt *GB*	undersell	undersold	undersold
spotlight	spotlit, spotlighted	spotlit, spotlighted	understand	understood	understood
			undertake	undertook	undertaken
spread	spread	spread	underwrite	underwrote	underwritten
spring	sprang	sprung	undo	undid	undone
stand	stood	stood	unfreeze	unfroze	unfrozen
stave	staved, stove	staved, stove	unwind	unwound	unwound
steal	stole	stolen	uphold	upheld	upheld
stick	stuck	stuck	upset	upset	upset
sting	stung	stung	wake	woke	woken
stink	stank	stunk	waylay	waylaid	waylaid
strew	strewed	strewed, strewn	wear	wore	worn
stride	strode	stridden	weave	wove, weaved	woven, weaved
strike	struck	struck	wed	wedded, wed	wedded, wed
string	strung	strung	weep	wept	wept
strive	strove	striven	wet	wet, wetted	wet, wetted
sublet	sublet	sublet	win	won	won
swear	swore	sworn	wind /waɪnd/	wound /waʊnd/	wound /waʊnd/
sweep	swept	swept	withdraw	withdrew	withdrawn
swell	swelled	swollen, swelled	withhold	withheld	withheld
swim	swam	swum	withstand	withstood	withstood
swing	swung	swung	wring	wrung	wrung
take	took	taken	write	wrote	written
teach	taught	taught			
tear	tore	torn			

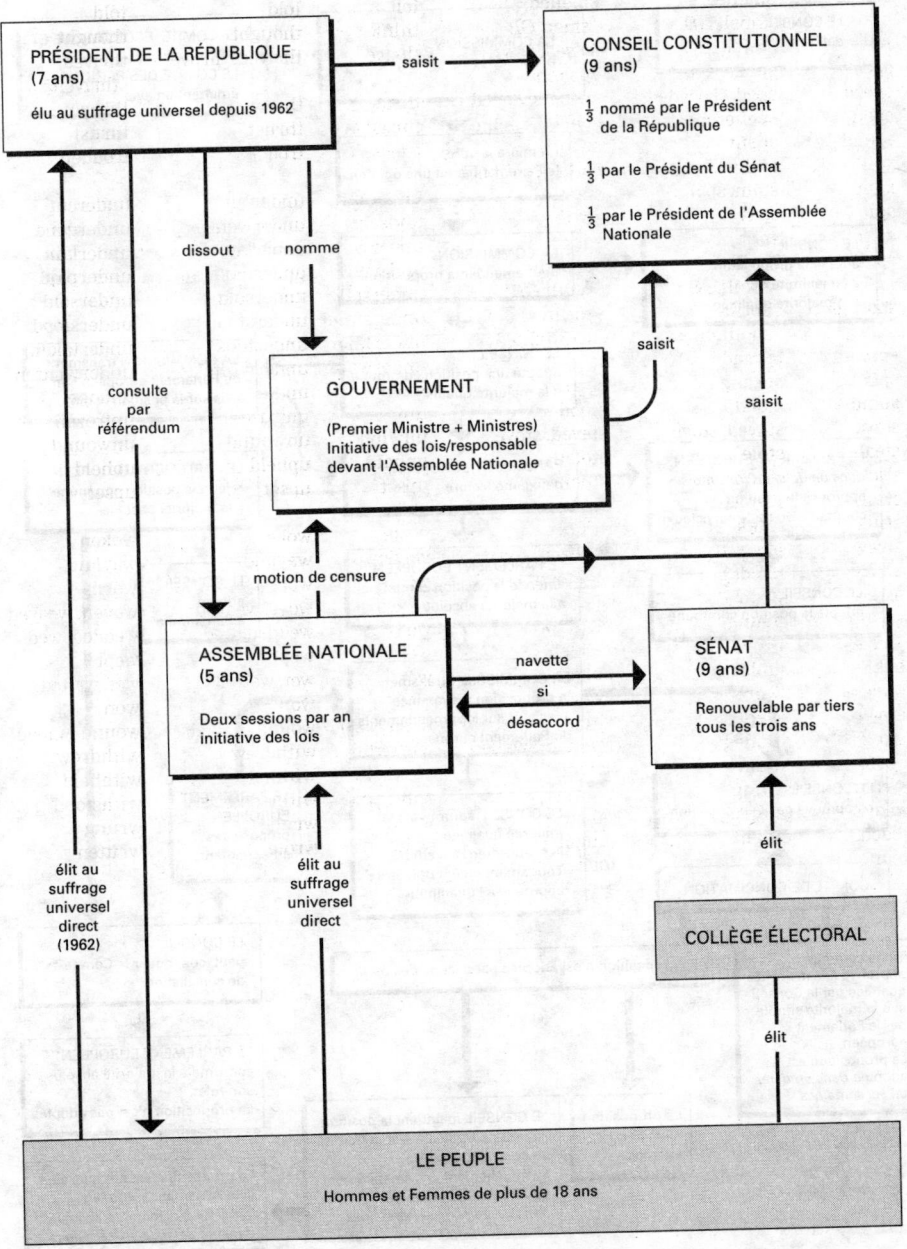

PRÉSIDENT DE LA RÉPUBLIQUE
(7 ans)

élu au suffrage universel depuis 1962

saisit →

CONSEIL CONSTITUTIONNEL
(9 ans)

$\frac{1}{3}$ nommé par le Président de la République

$\frac{1}{3}$ par le Président du Sénat

$\frac{1}{3}$ par le Président de l'Assemblée Nationale

dissout   nomme

consulte
par
référendum

saisit

saisit

GOUVERNEMENT

(Premier Ministre + Ministres)
Initiative des lois/responsable
devant l'Assemblée Nationale

motion de censure

ASSEMBLÉE NATIONALE
(5 ans)

Deux sessions par an
initiative des lois

navette

si

désaccord

SÉNAT
(9 ans)

Renouvelable par tiers
tous les trois ans

élit au
suffrage
universel
direct
(1962)

élit au
suffrage
universel
direct

élit

COLLÈGE ÉLECTORAL

élit

LE PEUPLE

Hommes et Femmes de plus de 18 ans

Le droit de vote (antérieurement à 21 ans) est fixé à 18 ans depuis 1974

Circuit des décisions communautaires

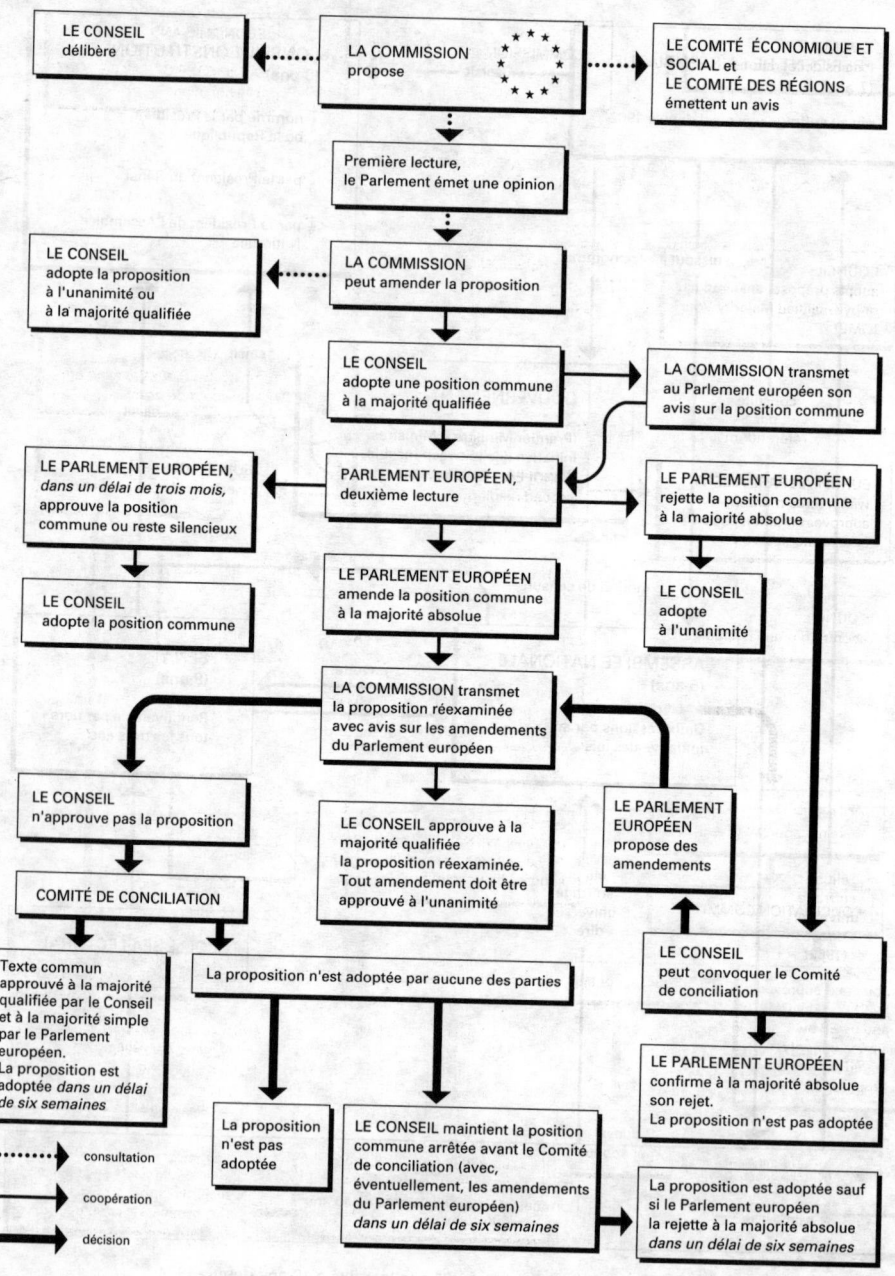

Procedure for legislation

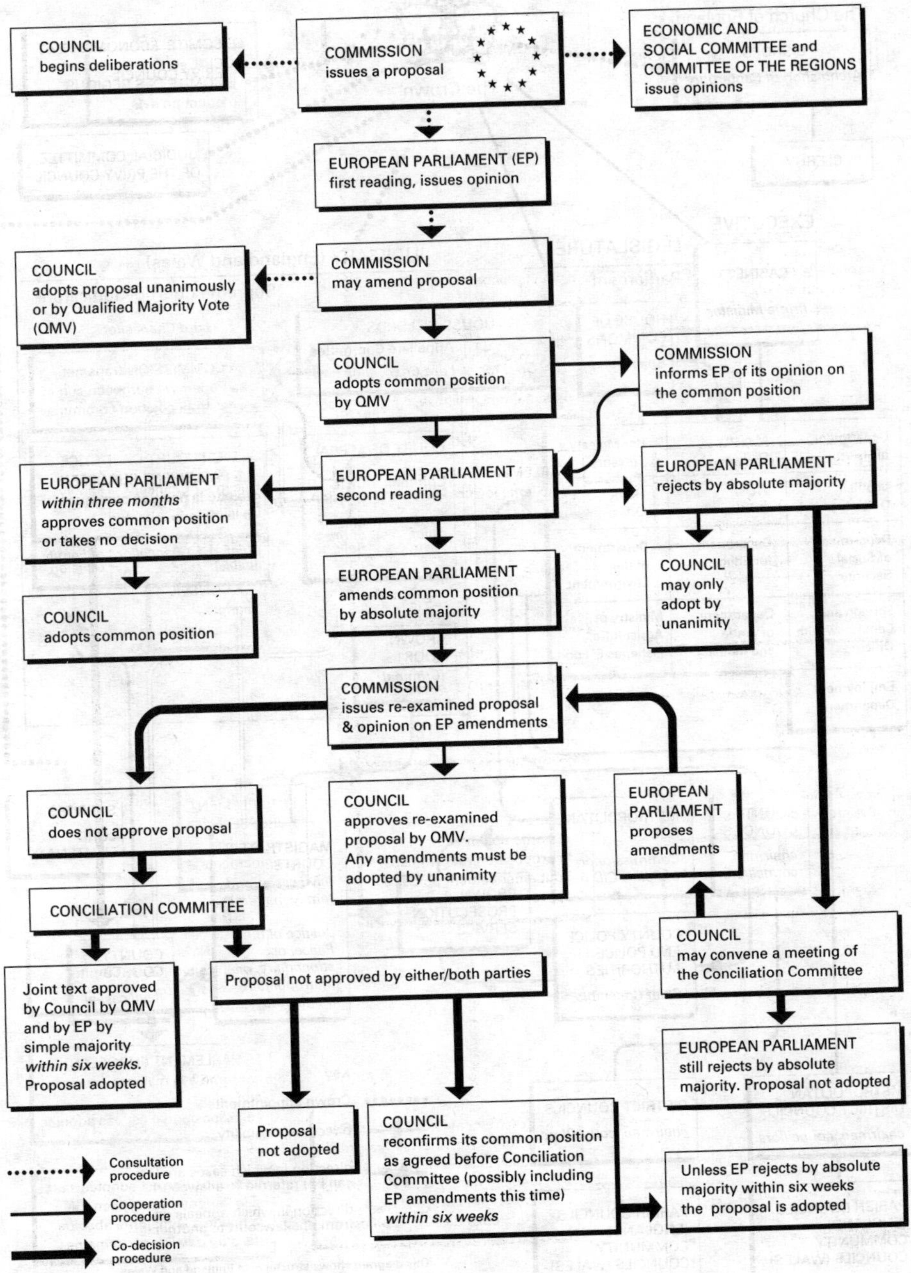

```
COUNCIL                    COMMISSION          ★ ★ ★          ECONOMIC AND
begins deliberations  ◄····  issues a proposal  ★     ★  ····► SOCIAL COMMITTEE and
                                              ★       ★        COMMITTEE OF THE REGIONS
                                               ★ ★ ★           issue opinions
```

```
EUROPEAN PARLIAMENT (EP)
first reading, issues opinion
```

```
COUNCIL                        COMMISSION
adopts proposal unanimously  ◄····  may amend proposal
or by Qualified Majority Vote
(QMV)
```

```
COUNCIL                        COMMISSION
adopts common position         informs EP of its opinion on
by QMV                         the common position
```

```
EUROPEAN PARLIAMENT            EUROPEAN PARLIAMENT       EUROPEAN PARLIAMENT
within three months            second reading           rejects by absolute majority
approves common position
or takes no decision
```

```
COUNCIL                        EUROPEAN PARLIAMENT       COUNCIL
adopts common position         amends common position    may only
                               by absolute majority       adopt by
                                                          unanimity
```

```
COMMISSION
issues re-examined proposal
& opinion on EP amendments
```

```
COUNCIL            COUNCIL                    EUROPEAN
does not approve   approves re-examined       PARLIAMENT
proposal           proposal by QMV.           proposes
                   Any amendments must be     amendments
                   adopted by unanimity
```

```
CONCILIATION COMMITTEE                                   COUNCIL
                                                         may convene a meeting of
                                                         the Conciliation Committee
```

```
Joint text approved    Proposal not approved by either/both parties    EUROPEAN PARLIAMENT
by Council by QMV                                                       still rejects by absolute
and by EP by                                                           majority. Proposal not adopted
simple majority
within six weeks.
Proposal adopted
```

```
                       Proposal       COUNCIL
                       not adopted    reconfirms its common position     Unless EP rejects by absolute
                                      as agreed before Conciliation      majority within six weeks
                                      Committee (possibly including      the proposal is adopted
                                      EP amendments this time)
                                      within six weeks
```

```
········►   Consultation
            procedure

─────►      Cooperation
            procedure

━━━━►       Co-decision
            procedure
```

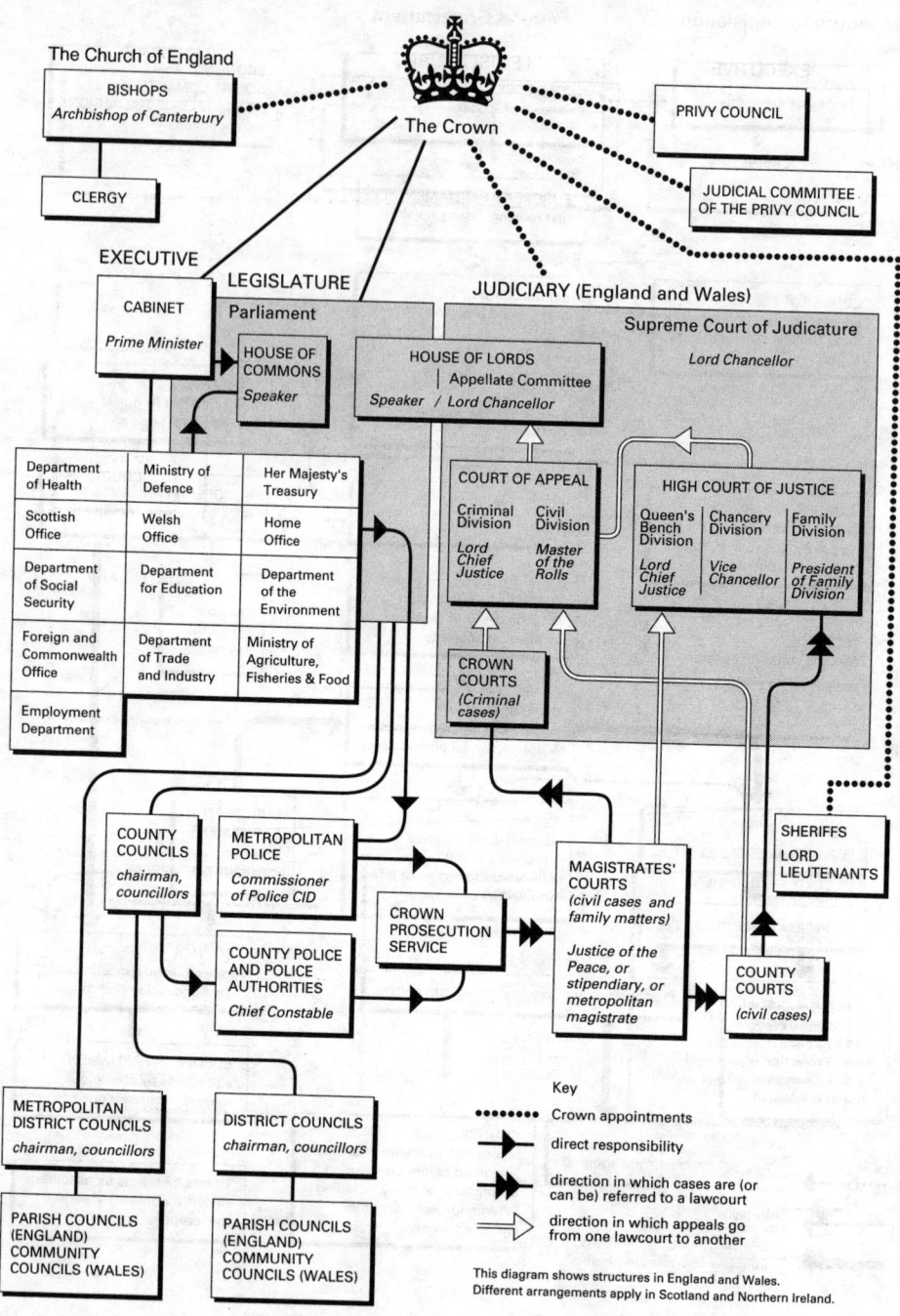

The Church of England

BISHOPS
Archbishop of Canterbury

CLERGY

The Crown

PRIVY COUNCIL

JUDICIAL COMMITTEE
OF THE PRIVY COUNCIL

EXECUTIVE

CABINET
Prime Minister

LEGISLATURE

Parliament

HOUSE OF
COMMONS
Speaker

HOUSE OF LORDS
| Appellate Committee
Speaker / Lord Chancellor

JUDICIARY (England and Wales)

Supreme Court of Judicature
Lord Chancellor

Department of Health	Ministry of Defence	Her Majesty's Treasury
Scottish Office	Welsh Office	Home Office
Department of Social Security	Department for Education	Department of the Environment
Foreign and Commonwealth Office	Department of Trade and Industry	Ministry of Agriculture, Fisheries & Food
Employment Department		

COURT OF APPEAL

| Criminal Division | Civil Division |
| *Lord Chief Justice* | *Master of the Rolls* |

HIGH COURT OF JUSTICE

| Queen's Bench Division | Chancery Division | Family Division |
| *Lord Chief Justice* | *Vice Chancellor* | *President of Family Division* |

CROWN
COURTS
(Criminal cases)

COUNTY
COUNCILS
*chairman,
councillors*

METROPOLITAN
POLICE
*Commissioner
of Police CID*

COUNTY POLICE
AND POLICE
AUTHORITIES
Chief Constable

CROWN
PROSECUTION
SERVICE

MAGISTRATES'
COURTS
*(civil cases and
family matters)*

*Justice of the
Peace, or
stipendiary, or
metropolitan
magistrate*

SHERIFFS

LORD
LIEUTENANTS

COUNTY
COURTS
(civil cases)

METROPOLITAN
DISTRICT COUNCILS
chairman, councillors

DISTRICT COUNCILS
chairman, councillors

PARISH COUNCILS
(ENGLAND)
COMMUNITY
COUNCILS (WALES)

PARISH COUNCILS
(ENGLAND)
COMMUNITY
COUNCILS (WALES)

Key

•••••••• Crown appointments

→ direct responsibility

⇒ direction in which cases are (or can be) referred to a lawcourt

⇨ direction in which appeals go from one lawcourt to another

This diagram shows structures in England and Wales.
Different arrangements apply in Scotland and Northern Ireland.

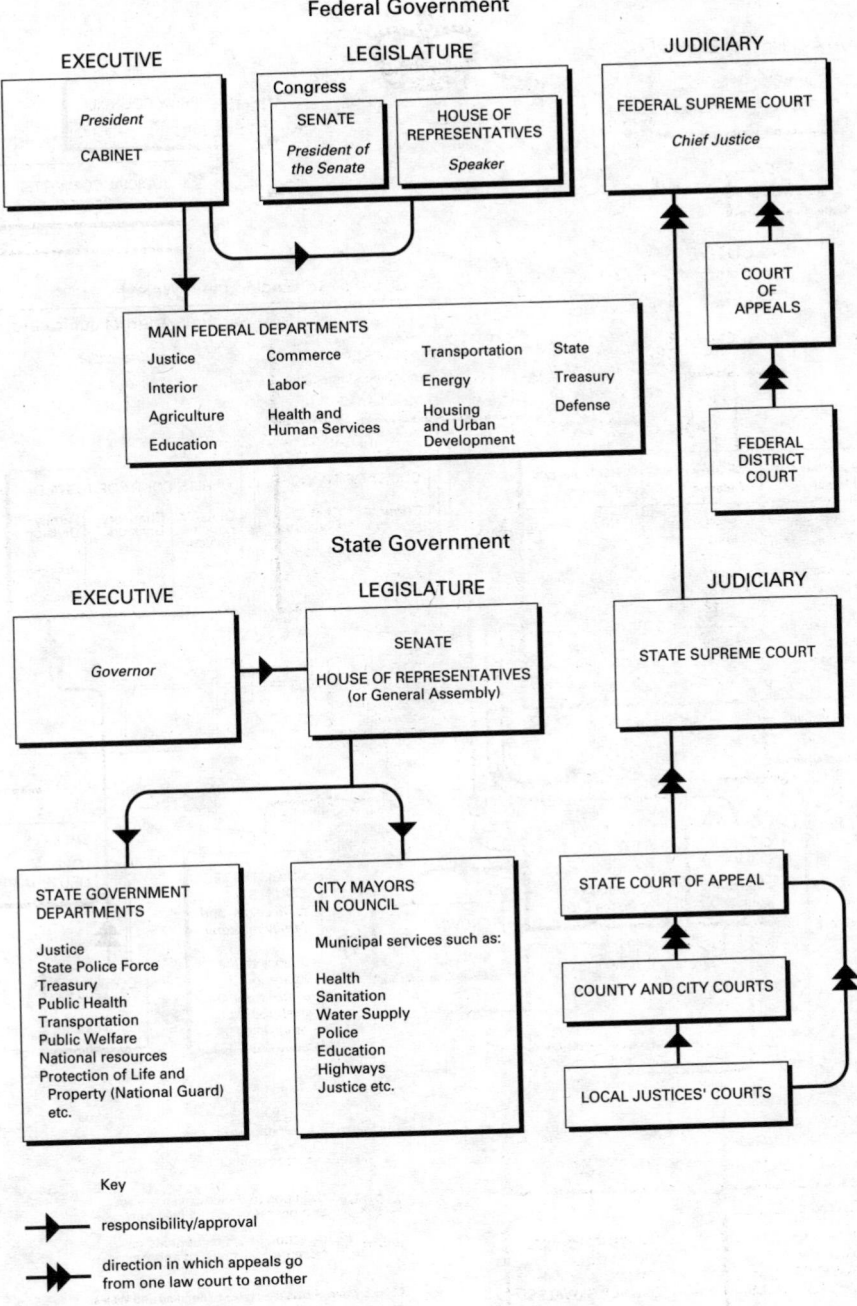

Federal Government

EXECUTIVE

President

CABINET

LEGISLATURE

Congress

SENATE

President of the Senate

HOUSE OF REPRESENTATIVES

Speaker

JUDICIARY

FEDERAL SUPREME COURT

Chief Justice

COURT OF APPEALS

MAIN FEDERAL DEPARTMENTS

Justice	Commerce	Transportation	State
Interior	Labor	Energy	Treasury
Agriculture	Health and Human Services	Housing and Urban Development	Defense
Education			

FEDERAL DISTRICT COURT

State Government

EXECUTIVE

Governor

LEGISLATURE

SENATE

HOUSE OF REPRESENTATIVES (or General Assembly)

JUDICIARY

STATE SUPREME COURT

STATE GOVERNMENT DEPARTMENTS

Justice
State Police Force
Treasury
Public Health
Transportation
Public Welfare
National resources
Protection of Life and Property (National Guard) etc.

CITY MAYORS IN COUNCIL

Municipal services such as:

Health
Sanitation
Water Supply
Police
Education
Highways
Justice etc.

STATE COURT OF APPEAL

COUNTY AND CITY COURTS

LOCAL JUSTICES' COURTS

Key

→ responsibility/approval

⇒ direction in which appeals go from one law court to another